The New Partridge Dictionary of Slang and Unconventional English

First published in 1937, Eric Partridge's brilliant magnum opus, *The Dictionary of Slang and Unconventional English*, set new standards in the spirited and intelligent appraisal of slang.

This two-volume *The New Partridge Dictionary of Slang and Unconventional English* takes on the mantle to present a definitive record of the slang of the last sixty years. Containing over 65,000 entries, the slang and unconventional English of the English-speaking world since 1945 is detailed with the same thorough, intense and lively scholarship that characterised Partridge's own work.

Editors **Tom Dalzell** and **Terry Victor** have worked to continue the Partridge tradition in an evolutionary and accessible way. American and British English slang are given equal prominence and the dictionary also boasts entries from Australia, New Zealand, Canada, India, South Africa, Ireland, the Caribbean and other countries where English is spoken. Entries are given a published source and, where possible, an early or significant example of the term's use in print.

Like its forebear, *The New Partridge Dictionary of Slang and Unconventional English* is a monumental piece of work infused with humour and learning – a prize for anyone with a love of, and a fascination with, language.

The New Partridge Dictionary of Slang and Unconventional English

Volume II: J – Z

Tom Dalzell (Senior Editor)
and
Terry Victor (Editor)

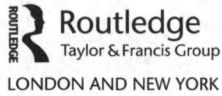

Routledge
Taylor & Francis Group
LONDON AND NEW YORK

First published 2006
by Routledge
2 Park Square, Milton Park, Abingdon, Oxon OX14 4RN

Simultaneously published in the USA and Canada
by Routledge
270 Madison Ave, New York, NY 10016

Routledge is an imprint of the Taylor & Francis Group

Typeset in Parisine-Regular by the Alden Group, Oxford
Printed in the UK by Bell and Bain Ltd, Glasgow

British Library Cataloguing in Publication Data
A catalogue record for this book is available from the British Library

Library of Congress Cataloging in Publication Data
A catalog record has been requested

ISBN10: 0-415-21258-8	ISBN13: 978-0-415-21258-8	(2 volume set)
ISBN10: 0-415-25937-1	ISBN13: 978-0-415-25937-8	(volume I)
ISBN10: 0-415-25938-X	ISBN13: 978-0-415-25938-5	(volume II)

CONTENTS

Jj

J *noun*

1 a marijuana cigarette *US, 1967*
'J' is for **JOINT**.
- Sorry old bus, he said to Urge as he felt his shirt pocket for a J. — Gurney Norman, *Divine Right's Trip (Last Whole Earth Catalog)*, p. 13, 1971
- Disgusted with the ignorance of the local population, we ducked into a toilet to smoke up another j, find the right direction. — Odie Hawkins, *Men Friends*, p. 51, 1989
- And a fat ass J, of some bubonic chronic that made me choke — Snoop Doggy Dogg, *Gin and Juice*, 1993
- I nod and light up the jay. — Kevin Williamson, *Heart of the Bass (Disco Biscuits)*, p. 113, 1996
- Mind if I smoke a jay? — *The Big Lebowski*, 1998
- Livin' it is smoking a J in a dope café in Amsterdam. — Martha Cinadar, *Living It*, 1998
- Now Vita was lighting a jay, needing to get baked before she could turn herself into an International Chick. — Elmore Leonard, *Be Cool*, p. 48, 1999
- — Mike Haskins, *Drugs*, p. 291, 2003

2 in a deck of playing cards, a jack *US*
- — George Percy, *The Language of Poker*, p. 49, 1988
- — Michael Dalton, *Blackjack*, p. 58, 1991

3 money *US*
An abbreviation of **JACK**.
- — Ralph de Sola, *Crime Dictionary*, p. 74, 1982

JA *noun*

1 Jamaica *JAMAICA*
- I only jus' reach back from J.A after almost a year, y'know. — Donald Gorgon, *Cop Killer*, p. 15, 1994

2 a Jamaican *JAMAICA*
- [W]e've paid the JA outside, six and a half foot of Jamaican Aggro[.] — John King, *Human Punk*, p. 25, 2000

jaapie *noun*
▷ see: **JAPIE**

jab *noun*
an intravenous drug injection *US, 1914*
- — David Maurer and Victor Vogel, *Narcotics and Narcotic Addiction*, p. 419, 1973

jab *verb*
to inject a drug intravenously *US, 1908*
- — Richard A. Spears, *The Slang and Jargon of Drugs and Drink*, p. 283, 1986
- — Mike Haskins, *Drugs*, p. 290, 2003

jabba; fat jabba *noun*
an overweight or unattractive person, especially a school fellow; especially used as a playground insult *UK*
After the character of Jabba the Hutt, introduced to cinema goers in *Return of the Jedi*, 1983.
- — Chris Lewis, *The Dictionary of Playground Slang*, p. 121, 2003

jabber *noun*

1 a syringe *US*
- — Ralph de Sola, *Crime Dictionary*, p. 74, 1982

2 a drug user who injects drugs *US*
- — David Maurer and Victor Vogel, *Narcotics and Narcotic Addiction*, p. 419, 1973

3 a boxer *US, 1904*
- Big-time Mex jabber – incomprehensible. — James Ellroy, *White Jazz*, p. 258, 1992

jabbing jabba *noun*
the act of anal sex *UK*
A nicely alliterative turn of phrase. Jabba the Hutt, created by George Lucas, is an excrementally ugly character from the *Star Wars* films; hence 'jabbing' (thrusting) into **SHIT**.
- — *Sky Magazine*, July 2001

jab-off *noun*
the flooding sensations of exhilaration and euphoria following a heroin injection *US*
- — David Maurer and Victor Vogel, *Narcotics and Narcotic Addiction*, p. 419, 1973

jabroney; jabroni *noun*
▷ see: **JIBONEY**

jack *noun*

1 anything at all; nothing at all *US, 1973*
- Junior Stebbens, I recently realized, don't know jack about brakes. — Joe Bob Briggs, *Joe Bob Goes to the Drive-In*, p. 48, 1987
- Then the firin pin hit a empty spot an you end up with jack. — Jess Mowry, *Way Past Cool*, p. 7, 1992
- It's been, what, nearly a week and you haven't given me jack. — Christopher Brookmyre, *The Sacred Art of Stealing*, p. 17, 2002

2 the anus *UK, 1984*
Notably in 'up your jack!'.

3 an act of masturbation *US*
- After surviving their first ambush at Al Gharraf, a couple of Marines even admitted to an almost frenzied need to get off combat jacks. — *Rolling Stone*, 24th July 2003

4 semen *US*
Possibly by back-formation from **JACK OFF** (to masturbate).
- Any moke can shoot jack into a woman make a kid. — Joel Rose, *Kill Kill Faster Faster*, p. 47, 1997

5 a sexually transmitted infection *AUSTRALIA, 1944*
Short for 'jack in the box', rhyming slang for **POX**.
- 'He give me a stifficate sayin' I got no jack, no crabs, no nothin',' she said proudly[.] — Lance Peters, *The Dirty Half-Mile*, p. 92, 1979
- Hope you get the jack, lady. — Robert English, *Toxic Kisses*, p. 46, 1979
- — Thommo, *The Dictionary of Australian Swearing and Sex Sayings*, p. 129, 1985

6 methylated spirits as an alcoholic drink *UK*
Probably a variation of **JAKE**.
- — *Sunday Times*, 13th August 1961: 'Prison saves the jack drinkers'

7 a homemade alcoholic beverage, usually applejack or raisinjack *US, 1894*
- Since that time they had been into a jug of Jack together a few times. — Odie Hawkins, *The Busting Out of an Ordinary Man*, p. 56, 1985

8 tobacco *US*
- — Vincent J. Monteleone, *Criminal Slang*, p. 130, 1949

9 a small heroin pill *UK*
- — *Bournemouth Evening Echo*, 19th August 1967
- — Home Office, *Glossary of Terms and Slang Common in Penal Establishments*, July 1978
- Dr. Feelgood's cure had apparently intensified my problem, and the little white "jacks," tiny pills of pure heroin, made some contribution as well. — Peter Coyote, *Sleeping Where I Fall*, p. 166, 1998

10 in bowls, the small white ball that serves as a target for the bowls *UK*
- The little white ball is variously known as the jack, the kitty, the kate, the cot, the pot and the white, according to where you live. — David Bryant, *The Game of Bowls*, p. 39, 1990

11 money *US, 1890*
- Dope crabbed Phil's effect by saying that Garrity had cleaned up some jack playing the market. — James T. Farrell, *Saturday Night*, p. 32, 1947
- What you need is a vacation. A decent one – with jack to spend – maybe at the seashore or up at Lake George. — Philip Wylie, *Opus 21*, p. 335, 1949
- The same guy what gets the pay-off jack, I guess. — Mickey Spillane, *My Gun is Quick*, p. 135, 1950
- From time to time, socialites and even foreign noblemen who need the jack obby for it. — Jack Lait and Lee Mortimer, *Washington Confidential*, p. 167, 1951
- All the jack he'd made in the rackets was gone. — Jim Thompson, *Savage Night*, p. 5, 1953
- He dress like he got the jack fer tippin. — Robert Gover, *One Hundred Dollar Misunderstanding*, p. 20, 1961

- And then He said, "Let there be a bunch of sleazy guys hanging around Camden, New Jersey, trying to hustle up enough jack so they can move to Atlantic City." —Joe Bob Briggs, *Joe Bob Goes to the Drive-In*, p. 5, 1987

12 a counterfeit double-headed coin *AUSTRALIA, 1936*
Origin unknown.
- —Ryan Aven-Bray, *Ridgey Didge Oz Jack Lang*, p. 32, 1983

13 a robbery *US, 1988*
- The Cadillac is rolling up to the intersection where the "jack" is taking place. —*Menace II Society*, 1993
- Parker told the investigators she and friends stopped to buy a bottle of soda, then decided to "do a jack," street slang for a robbery. —*Tampa (Florida) Tribune*, p. 1, 19th August 1997

14 a police officer or detective *UK, 1889*
- We've only got the military Jacks to worry about. —Vince Kelly, *The Bogeyman*, p. 109, 1956
- Remember the robbery in Bondi, you know the one where Bluey give it to those jacks, six of them there were? —Kevin Mackey, *The Cure*, p. 100, 1970
- A barman in a [Leeds] shebeen [says], "I don't care what the jacks say [...] He [the Yorkshire Ripper] may not be a blackie but we've had the lot round here." —*New Society*, 14th June 1979
- —Ryan Aven-Bray, *Ridgey Didge Oz Jack Lang*, p. 32, 1983
- —Shane Maloney, *Nice Try*, p. 192, 1998

15 a friend *BAHAMAS*
- —Patricia Clinton-Meicholas, *More Talkin' Bahamian*, p. 60, 1995

16 a kookaburra *AUSTRALIA, 1898*
Shortening of 'laughing jackass'.

17 a peek or a look *NEW ZEALAND*
- You should have a jack at her diary. —H. Beaton, *Outside In*, p. 74, 1984

Jack *noun*
an all-purpose male name; any man; used as a male-to-male form of address *UK, 1706*
Predominantly black use.
- So bye now Jacks, Jims and Jeffs. —Lavada Durst, *The Jives of Dr. Hepcat*, 1953

▷ **see:** JACK JONES

jack *verb*

1 to steal, to take by force – especially of street crime *US, 1930*
Adopted from 'jack' (to hijack).
- I knew that Bobo had snuck in again, and now he was trying to jack me for a dollar. —Joe Bob Briggs, *Joe Bob Goes to the Drive-In*, p. 14, 1987
- Who was it nigga? Who jacked you? —*Menace II Society*, 1993
- Even Al Gore can't muster enough balls to admit the fact that he got jacked. —Suroosh Alvi et al., *The Vice Guide*, p. 196, 2002
- Someone tries to jack me probably every week. —*The Guardian*, p. 9, 27th February 2002
- If you're wearing a hundred grand round your neck, you've gotta think about other things. Like you might get jacked. —*Mixmag*, p. 75, April 2003

2 to lift or raise or move something, as with a carjack *AUSTRALIA*
- 'Nisbet,' he snapped, 'if you c'n hear me, then jack that bloody aircraft round!' —W.R. Bennett, *Wingman*, p. 13, 1961
- [T]he least you can do, dear boy, is jack yourself off your fat bronze and see what it's all about. —W.R. Bennett, *Wingman*, p. 72, 1961
- Hoisting myself up as it peaked, I was jacked heavily and took a verticle drop. —Kathy Lette, *Girls' Night Out*, p. 190, 1987
- [T]here was always the possibility that an armed accomplice could burst into the courtroom and try to jack her out. —William Dodson, *The Sharp End*, p. 110, 2001

3 (of a male) to masturbate *US*
- I wanted to take my dick out and start jacking right there. —*Kids*, 1995

4 to convey a cartridge into the chamber of a firearm *AUSTRALIA*
- Ivana jacked another round into the chamber. —Harrison Biscuit, *The Search for Savage Henry*, p. 86, 1995

5 to abandon, to dismiss *UK, 1961*
- Jacked me for a civvy. —Alexander Baron, *From the City, from the Plough*, 1948
- 5 or 7 miles in boots, followed by sit-ups and press-ups, then 100 metre piggyback races and fireman's carries up hills. More people jacked. —Andy McNab, *Immediate Action*, p. 59, 1995

6 to serve (a prison sentence) *US*
- Said, "Gee, judge, that's no time / I got a brother on Levenworth jackin' ninety-nine." —Bruce Jackson, *Get Your Ass in the Water and Swim Like Me*, p. 52, 1966

7 to move the plunger of a hypodermic syringe back and forth *AUSTRALIA*
- Having ingeniously dealt with this crisis Rick had a long soothing shot jacking the plunger to extend the flash[.] —Kevin Mackey, *The Cure*, p. 107, 1970

8 to flush blood in and out of a hypodermic syringe *AUSTRALIA*
- SUTTON: (ritual injection nervously verbalizing, jacking the blood) It give you something to live for. —Kevin Mackey, *The Cure*, p. 2, 1970

9 to cease; to shirk *UK*
- —*The Felstedian*, December 1947

▸ **jack your jaw**
to talk incessantly *US*
- "My problem is that I'd rather put people in jail than sit around the Field Office all day jacking my jaws about how much the federal cost-of-living pay raise is going to be," Chance said. —Gerald Petievich, *To Live and Die in L.A.*, p. 27, 1983

▸ **jack your joint**
to manoeuvre your penis during sex *US*
- [H]e'd be working, jacking his joint, lost, working at it, and he could feel the come building[.] —Joel Rose, *Kill Kill Faster Faster*, p. 163, 1997

▸ **jack your root**
to frustrate *US*
- —Connie Eble (Editor), *UNC-CH Campus Slang*, p. 4, Fall 1980

jack *adjective*

1 used for describing any medium used for inspiration while masturbating *US*
Followed by the medium – 'jack pictures', 'jack flick', 'jack book', etc.
- —Charles Shafer, *Folk Speech in Texas Prisons*, p. 208, 1990

2 had enough of; fed up with *AUSTRALIA, 1889*
- —John Wynnum, *Tar Dust*, p. 24, 1962
- —Frank Hardy, *The Yarns of Billy Borker*, p. 139, 1965
- I could do with a break to tell the truth. I'm fair jack of Earl's Court. —Barry Humphries, *The Wonderful World of Barry McKenzie*, p. 6, 1968
- —Frank Hardy, *Hardy's People*, p. 154, 1986

Jack; Jack's *nickname*
Jack Daniels™ whisky *US*
- I listened at first, sipping my Jack's and water[.] —Lester Bangs, *Psychotic Reactions and Carburetor Dung*, p. 109, 1972
- Pull me down a bottle of Jack. I'm gettin' tanked tonight. —Quentin Tarantino, *From Dusk Till Dawn*, p. 2, 1995

jackabaun *noun*
in Newfoundland, a mischievous person not to be trusted *CANADA*
This word may have descended from the British 'jacobin' (a political reformer).
- A saucy, deceitful person. My aunt caught a young man picking her berries. Next time she saw him she called him an ugly jackabaun. —*oral informant in Dictionary of Newfoundland English*, p. 271, 1982

jackal's wedding *noun*
a time when the sun shines and it rains; a sunshower *INDIA*
Glossed as a 'village expression' by Nigel Hankin, *Hanklyn-Janklyn*, 2003.

Jack and Danny *noun*

1 the buttocks, the anus *UK*
Rhyming slang for **FANNY**, formed from characters played by Jack Nicholson and Danny Lloyd in the Stanley Kubrick film, *The Shining*, 1980.
- —Ray Puxley, *Cockney Rabbit*, 1992

2 the vagina *UK*
Rhyming slang for **FANNY** (the vagina).
- I'm goin' to put my rocket up the cunt's jack an' danny. —Bernard Dempsey and Kevin McNally, *Lock, Stock ... & Two Hundred Smoking Kalashnikovs*, p. 129, 2000

3 a story, lies *UK*
Rhyming slang for **FANNY**.
- A straight question needs a straight answer, no Jack and Danny, are you willing to come on board as a partner? —J.J. Connolly, *Layer Cake*, p. 18, 2000

Jack and Jill; Jack-and-Jill; jack *noun*

1 a bill *UK, 1960*
Rhyming slang.
- "Bet you the jack-an-jill," I snapped. "Ow, do belt up and leave off[.]" —Derek Raymond (Robin Cook), *The Crust on its Uppers*, p. 60, 1962
- He'll note down what jack-and-jills they want paying[.] —Andrew Nickolds, *Back to Basics*, p. 55, 1994

2 a till, a cash register *UK, 1932*
Rhyming slang.
- "Thank you kindly." He nodded at the till. Don't get cold. you get back to the old Jack and Jill."—Anthony Masters, *Minder*, p. 80, 1984

3 a hill *UK, 1934*
Rhyming slang, formed on the nursery rhyme couple who went up the hill.

4 a fool *AUSTRALIA*
Rhyming slang for **DILL** (a fool).
- —Jim McNeil, *The Chocolate Frog and The Old Familiar Juice*, 1973

5 the (contraceptive) pill *UK*
Rhyming slang.
- She's wantin tae come aff the jack.—Michael Munro, *The Patter, Another Blast*, 1988
- I couldn't believe it. She told me she was on the Jack and then she got pregnant.—Bodmin Dark, *Dirty Cockney Rhyming Slang*, 2003

6 a pill *UK, 1992*
Rhyming slang.
- —Angela Devlin, *Prison Patter*, p. 65, 1996
- —Chris Baker and Andrew Day, *Lock, Stock ... & a Fist Full of Jack and Jills*, p. 149, 2000

Jackanory *noun*
a story *UK*
Either deriving from, or the inspiration for, BBC television storytelling programme *Jackanory*, 1965–96.
- —*Daily Telegraph*, 17th December 1972: 'Slang it to Me in Rhyme'
- I thought my public transport days were well and truly behind me, but there I am, roysh [right], upstairs on the 46a, texting JP and Christian to find out what the Jackanory is about tonight, when all of a sudden my mobile rings and it's, like, the old ma—Paul Howard, *Ross O'Carroll-Kelly*, p. 72, 2003

jackaroo *noun*
▷ see: **JACKEROO**

jack around *verb*
1 to engage in horseplay *US*
- —*American Speech*, p. 276, December 1963: 'American Indian student slang'

2 to fool around *US, 1962*
- Fone one thing, he likes to jack around in the stock market with our money.—Dan Jenkins, *Semi-Tough*, p. 63, 1972

jackass *noun*
a fool *UK, 1823*
A male ass and thus an elaboration of **ASS** (a fool).
- Graham Greene, one of the greatest novelists never to be honoured by the jackasses who award the Nobel Prize[.]—*The Guardian*, 30th November 2002

jackatar *noun*
a Newfoundlander of mixed French and Micmac ancestry *CANADA*
- Here, the Scots remained resistant to intermarriage with the French for many years, labelling the French 'Jack-o-tars', a synonym for half-breeds.—John Szwed, *Private Cultures and Public Imagery*, p. 31, 1966

jack benny *noun*
in hold 'em poker, a three and a nine as the first two cards dealt to a player *US, 1981*
Comedian Benny perpetually claimed that he was 39 years old.
- —Thomas L. Clark, *The Dictionary of Gambling and Gaming*, p. 109, 1987

jack boat; jack schooner *noun*
a two-spar gaff-rigged fishing boat in Cape Breton and Newfoundland *CANADA*
- The "jack schooners" or "jack boats" so-called in Cape Breton, or "two-spar boats" as they are known in Newfoundland, were 40 or 50 feet from stemhead to taffrail. They were gaff-rigged on both masts and they usually carried a longish bowsprit.—*National Fisherman*, p. 36, 24th March 1982

jack boy *noun*
a street criminal who relies almost exclusively upon force and terror *US, 1989*
- He liked jackboys because they were crazy. They made their living ripping off street dealers for their blow and change and busting into crackhouses with assault weapons.—Elmore Leonard, *Rum Punch*, p. 27, 1992

Jack Canuck *noun*
a Canadian *CANADA*
- What is the origin of the nickname Jack Canuck? It probably comes from the name Connaught, the nickname given more than 100 years ago by French Canadians to Canadians of Irish origin.—*Ottawa Citizen*, p. 12/5, 30th May 1963

Jack Dash *noun*
an act of urination *UK: SCOTLAND*
Glasgow rhyming slang for **SLASH**.
- Ah'll just have a quick Jack Dash then we're off.—Michael Munro, *The Patter, Another Blast*, 1988

jackdaw and rook *noun*
a book; specifically, in the theatre, the text of a play ('the book') *UK*
Originally theatrical.
- —Julian Franklyn, *A Dictionary of Rhyming Slang*, 1960

Jack Dee *noun*
urine; an act of urination *UK*
Rhyming slang for **WEE** or **PEE**, formed from the name of a UK comedian-actor (b.1962). Also used as a verb.
- —Ray Puxley, *Fresh Rabbit*, 1998

Jack Doyle *noun*
a boil *UK*
Rhyming slang, formed from the name of an Irish boxer, 1913–78.
- —Ray Puxley, *Cockney Rabbit*, 1992
- —Ray Puxley, *Fresh Rabbit*, 1998

jacked *adjective*
1 stolen, especially if taken in a mugging (a violent street crime) *US*
Alas, in ever wider-use since the early 1980s.
- Over the past year or so, I've had two phones stolen, or "jacked" and I've been threatened with a knife countless times.—*The Guardian*, p. 9, 27th February 2002

2 caffeinated *US*
Borrowing from the language of car fuel for application to the world of coffee drinks and, to a lesser extent, soft drinks.
- —Connie Eble (Editor), *UNC-CH Campus Slang*, p. 4, Fall 1996

3 very muscular *US*
- —Connie Eble (Editor), *UNC-CH Campus Slang*, p. 5, November 2003

jacked up; jacked *adjective*
1 drunk, drug-intoxicated, exhilarated *US, 1935*
- [T]his whole show and all its floodlit drug-jacked realer-than-life trappings[.]—Lester Bangs, *Psychotic Reactions and Carburetor Dung*, p. 36, 1970
- Yeah we'll show her what it's all about / We'll get her jacked up on some cheap champagne.]—Scissor Sisters, *Take Your Mama*, 2004

2 infected with a sexually transmitted infection *AUSTRALIA, 1950*

jackeen *noun*
a Dubliner *IRELAND*
A derivative of Jack, an abbreviation of John (Bull), the national nickname for an English man originating from the character named John Bull who features as a stereotypical Englishman in 'The History of John Bull', a collection of pamphlets written by John Arbuthnot (1667–1735), issued in 1712.
- The tramps scarpered, the street-traders pushing prams scarpered, half of Dublin scarpered as if they all had something to hide. And you can be sure most of them did too, the ignorant fuckin' Jackeen cunts.—Ardal O'Hanlon, *The Talk of the Town*, p. 7, 1998
- Siobhan dips her toe into the age-old "Jackeens" versus "Culchies" debate to great effect. Michelle is from Dublin and proud of it – "Dublin is the capital of Ireland, and it's the best and everyone else is a Culchie," she baldly states.—*Irish Times*, 19th May 2001

jacker *noun*
1 a robber, a hijacker *US*
- You're certain this bale of cotton was carried by the meat delivery truck used by the jackers?—Chester Himes, *Cotton Comes to Harlem*, p. 108, 1965
- That was three days after those jigaboo dope jackers muscled Mack and Bone while they were delivering the eight kilos to Soutside wholesalers.—Iceberg Slim (Robert Beck), *Death Wish*, p. 38, 1977

2 a camouflage expert *US*
- —*American Speech*, p. 97, May 1956: 'Smugglers' argot in the Southwest'

jackeroo; jackaroo *noun*
an apprentice station hand working on, and learning how to manage, a cattle or sheep station *AUSTRALIA, 1845*
Origin unknown. Suggestions have been legion, such as: the male name Jack blended with 'kangaroo'; a corruption of Johnny Raw; and borrowings from various Australian Aboriginal languages. Originally it was a Queensland word referring to a man living away from settled areas, and so may be referable to a native Queensland language.
- —Nino Culotta (John O'Grady), *They're A Weird Mob*, p. 133, 1957
- If all this sounds confusing, mixed up among the cowboys, drovers, station hands and stockmen were the jackaroos – privileged upper-class pastoral apprentices being trained, not really as stockmen but as future bosses. —Herb Wharton, *Cattle Camp*, p. 77, 1994

jackeroo; jackaroo *verb*
to work as a jackeroo *AUSTRALIA, 1875*

jacket *noun*
1 a personnel file, especially in prison or the military *US, 1944*
- The jacket said she was 38 years old, and her number was J-019–20 and she lived in KB-2 of the women's unit. —Clarence Cooper Jr, *The Farm*, p. 42, 1967
- If you ever get the chance, see what reason they have in my jacket for the 1962 transfer to San Quentin from Tracy. —George Jackson, *Soledad Brother*, p. 220, 24th March 1970
- The general's going to put a letter of reprimand in your jacket, but hell, all that'll do is hurt your chances for promotion to captain. —Philip Caputo, *A Rumor of War*, p. 319, 1977
- Two-time loser with a Quentin jacket. —James Ellroy, *Blood on the Moon*, p. 83, 1984

2 an executive not involved with actual production *US*
- —Anna Scotti and Paul Young, *Buzzwords*, p. 6, 1997

3 a capsule of Nembutal™, a central nervous system depressant *US*
- —*American Speech*, p. 27, February 1952: 'Teen-age hophead jargon'

▸ **get a jacket; wear a jacket**
(used of a man) to accept, unknowingly, another man's child as your own *JAMAICA*
- However, for the fear of getting a 'jacket', that is supporting and housing another man's child, in this harsh economic climate, has led to a reluctance to accept responsibility. —*Xnews*, p. 8, 2nd July 1997

▸ **give (someone) a jacket**
(used of a woman) to name someone as the father of her child who is not actually the father *JAMAICA*
- —Peter Patrick, *Some Recent Jamaican Creole Words*, 2003

▸ **put the jacket on someone**
to frame someone, setting them up to take the blame *US*
- —Bill Reilly, *Big Al's Official Guide to Chicagoese*, p. 38, 1982

jacket *verb*
(used of a school boy) to give a girl your school jacket, signifying a steady dating relationship *US*
- —*Look*, p. 88, 10th August 1954

jack flaps *noun*
fancy clothes worn by a man in pursuit of female companionship *US*
- —Elementary Electronics, *Dictionary of CB Lingo*, p. 79, 1976

Jack Flash *noun*
a crash, a smash *UK*
Rhyming slang, probably formed from the title of the Rolling Stones' song, 'Jumping Jack Flash', 1968.
- —Ray Puxley, *Cockney Rabbit*, 1992

jack hat *noun*
a condom *UK*
Combines **JACK** (semen) with a cover; possibly a reference to Jack 'The Hat' McVitie, a murder victim of the Kray twins.
- —David Rowan, *A Glossary for the 90s*, 1998

Jack Herer *noun*
an extremely potent strain of marijuana, a hybrid of three of the strongest varieties *UK*
Named in honour of Jack Herer, also known as 'The Emperor of Hemp', a high-profile campaigner for the legalisation of cannabis. Glossed as 'only for the intrepid' by Nick Jones, *Spliffs*, 2003.

Jack Horner; little Jack Horner *noun*
a corner *UK, 1931*
Rhyming slang; its various uses glossed as 'may be stood in, turned around or cut' by Ray Puxley, *Cockney Rabbit*, 1992.

jackie *noun*
in the circus or carnival, a story of past deeds or escapades *US*
- —Joe McKennon, *Circus Lingo*, p. 51, 1980

Jackie Dash; jackie *noun*
an act of urination *UK*
Rhyming slang, formed, apparently, from the name of a union official in London's dockland. **JACK DASH**, however, is recorded in Glasgow in 1988.
- —Ray Puxley, *Fresh Rabbit*, 1998

Jackie Howe; Jacky Howe; jacky-howe *noun*
a dark blue or black sleeveless singlet worn by rural labourers *AUSTRALIA, 1930*
Named after Jackie (John Robert) Howe (d.1920), a champion shearer.
- Scotty was a little chap in a 'Jackie Howe' singlet with a shock of loose hair[.] —Ion L. Idriess, *Over the Range*, p. 190, 1947
- —Jim Ramsay, *Cop It Sweet!*, p. 49, 1977
- The publican was a short, fat fulla in a blue jacky-howe and football shorts[.] —Sam Weller, *Old Bastards I Have Met*, p. 22, 1979

Jackie Trent *adjective*
dishonest, corrupt *UK*
Rhyming slang for **BENT**, formed from the name of a popular singer (b.1940).
- —John Ayto, *The Oxford Dictionary of Rhyming Slang*, 2002

jack in; jack it in *verb*
1 to abandon, to quit *UK, 1961*
- —Tom Hibbert, *Rockspeak!*, p. 90, 1983
- The old me would 'ave gone storming out, but I'm not going to jack it in. I wouldn't like to lose this relationship. —Sally Cline, *Couples*, p. 199, 1998
- I decided to jack the job in[.] —Niall Griffiths, *Kelly + Victor*, p. 77, 2002
- Brad was thinking of jacking the job in because of Alison's constant sniping. —Colin Butts, *Is Harry Still on the Boat?*, p. 19, 2003

2 to log onto the Internet *US*
- —Christian Crumlish, *The Internet Dictionary*, p. 103, 1995

jackin' the beanstalk *verb*
(of a male) masturbating *US*
Cleverly punning **JACK OFF** (to masturbate) and **STALK** (the erect penis) with the famous fairytale.

Jack-in-the-black *noun*
black-labelled Jack Daniels™ whisky *US*
- —Gregory Clark, *Words of the Vietnam War*, p. 252, 1990

jack in the box *noun*
1 the penis *UK*
Like the toy, it pops up at the least touch.

2 syphilis *UK, 1954*
Rhyming slang for **POX**. The shortened form 'jack' is first recorded in Australia, 1944.
- —Ray Puxley, *Cockney Rabbit*, 1992

jack it up
to have sexual intercourse with (someone) *AUSTRALIA*
- [S]ome of the other kids made jokes about her, and suggested that Mr. Horwood was probably jacking it up her three or four times a night. —*Alvin Purple*, p. 19, 1974

jack-jawed *adjective*
dim-witted *US*
- They're dope dealers, a bunch of jack-jawed no-good hophead motherfuckers. —Gerald Petievich, *The Quality of the Informant*, p. 18, 1985

Jack Johnson *noun*
an axe with the blade sticking up *CANADA*
Jack Johnson was a heavyweight champion boxer, the first black to win the title; his victory spurred the search for a 'Great White Hope'.
- —Lewis Poteet, *Country Talk*, p. 46, 1992

Jack Jones; Jack; Jack Malone *noun*

a state of isolation, alone *UK, World War 1, first recorded 1925*
Imperfect rhyming slang for 'alone', yet in practice the rhyme often seems to be with 'own': 'on your jack' (on your own); a feeling of abandonment is often implied.

- It is a strange feeling being locked up on your jack for a few days. — Frank Norman, *Bang To Rights*, p. 25, 1958
- You'd have a job to get through them on your Jack Jones, without a lot of silly so and so's shooting at you. — Derek Bickerton, *Payroll*, p. 32, 1959
- [T]hose who are on their Jack Jones; a man without a tit willow [a pillow] to lay his head on[.] — Ronnie Barker, *Fletcher's Book of Rhyming Slang*, p. 39, 1979
- But if Roy's in the shit he can fuckin' get himself out of it on his fuckin' jack, or he can fuckin' stew in it if he wants. — J.J. Connolly, *Know Your Enemy [britpulp]*, p. 151, 1999

Jack Ketch *noun*

a term of imprisonment *UK*
Rhyming slang for **STRETCH**.

- — Ray Puxley, *Fresh Rabbit*, 1998

jack-knife *verb*

to double up at the waist *US*

- I lay between the Waldorf's excellent sheets jack-knifed with panic. — Max Shulman, *The Many Loves of Dobie Gillis*, p. 29, 1951

▸**jack-knife your legs**

(used of a man) to straighten your legs so that the crease of the trousers stands out and the turn-ups fall over the shoes *US*

- This is fight night. Shoot cuffs, boy, jack-knife yo' legs. Get down. — *Buzz*, p. 76, May 1994

Jack Lang *noun*

slang; rhyming slang; Australian slang *AUSTRALIA, 1977*
Rhyming slang, formed from the name of Australian state politician Jack (John Thomas) Lang (1876–1975).

- — Jim Ramsay, *Cop It Sweet!*, p. 49, 1977
- — Ryan Aven-Bray, *Ridgey Didge Oz Jack Lang*, p. 32, 1983
- [The poem] provides numerous gems of slang from the shearing sheds and the city pushes, yet again, not one example of what is known in the argot as 'Old Jack Lang'. — John Meredith, *Learn to talk Old Jack Lang*, p. 7–8, 1984

jackleg *noun*

a gambler who cheats *US*

- — Vincent J. Monteleone, *Criminal Slang*, p. 130, 1949

jackleg *adjective*

unschooled, untrained *US, 1837*

- Mrs. Rogers – who was also a jackleg preacher (she did not have a church) called everybody "child," "brother," or "sister." — Claude Brown, *Manchild in the Promised Land*, p. 24, 1965
- But as far as taking a jackleg lawyer, you don't uses them for anything but errand boys. — Bruce Jackson, *Outside the Law*, p. 134, 1972

jacko *noun*

an oppossum *NEW ZEALAND*

- Possum hunters have many more euphemistic names for Trichosurus vulpecular, eg. coon, jacko or monkey. — Graeme Marshall, *Possum Hunting in New Zealand*, p. 1, 1984

jack-off *noun*

1 an act of masturbation *US, 1952*

- Whenever I can slip into my office and log on, I'm doing a quick jack-off session. — Howard Stern, *Miss America*, p. 27, 1995

2 a despised person *US, 1938*

- And never mind those jack-offs who keep saying you'll never make it as a sportswriter. — Hunter S. Thompson, *Songs of the Doomed*, p. 235, 1981

jack off *verb*

1 (used of a male) to masturbate *US, 1916*
Derives from 'jack' (an erection) now obsolete, combined with **JERK OFF** (to masturbate).

- Everybody is getting their kicks but me! I'm almost ready to pull up and start jacking off, when I remember I've got her phone number[.] — John Clellon Holmes, *Go*, p. 137, 1952
- [H]e push home the heroin and the boy who jacked off fifty years ago shine immaculate through the ravaged flesh, fill the outhouse with the sweet nutty smell of young male lust. — William Burroughs, *Naked Lunch*, p. b, 1957
- "Krankeit, the great rebel, the man who had the guys to jack off in the face of a Supreme Court decision, is shocked," he said. — Terry Southern, *Candy*, p. 96, 1958
- Still, having jacked off in the toilet, feeling rested & tonite's sleep (not to spoil it) being a long one, will write anyhow. — Neal Cassady, *The First Third*, 30th August 1965
- The one alternative amusement was watching the Melly brothers, George and Ed, who ordinarily spent their lunch hour jacking off in the boy's rest room. — Larry McMurtry, *The Last Picture Show*, p. 35, 1966
- And pretty soon you'll find yourself jackin off in the toilet in the middle of the night when everybody else is sleeping. — Clarence Cooper Jr, *The Farm*, p. 196, 1967
- "Shit, you mean you don't know how to jack off?" "You mean pull it?" I asked my guide. — Oscar Zeta Acosta, *The Autobiography of a Brown Buffalo*, p. 82, 1972
- John found Dom jacking off lotus-posture on a prayer rug looking at a wall of East St. Louis. — Ed Sanders, *Tales of Beatnik Glory*, p. 126, 1975
- VINCENT: So you're gonna go out there, drink your drink, say "Goodnight, I've had a very lovely evening," go home, and jack off. And that's all you're gonna do. — *Pulp Fiction*, 1994
- Did this mean we were expected to jack-off in the bracken? And more to the point, jill-off? — Kitty Churchill, *Thinking of England*, p. 199, 1995
- If you wanna watch me jack off, it's ten bucks. — *Boogie Nights*, 1997

2 to manipulate the injection of a drug such that the drug enters the blood stream slowly *US, 1967*

- When the blood reached the top of the dropper, she backed it up into her veins, working the blood in the dropper slowly as she jacked the works off. — Donald Goines, *Dopefiend*, p. 10, 1971
- Once it was in that was that to me. A lotta fellows liked jacking it off once they struck red. They would play with it 'til the point would plug up on 'em[.] — A.S. Jackson, *Gentleman Pimp*, p. 99, 1973
- — David Maurer and Victor Vogel, *Narcotics and Narcotic Addiction*, p. 419, 1973

jack-off artist *noun*

a masturbater *US*

- "Any creeps call in?" Of course creeps had called – who else would bother. "The usual jack-off artists," Nina reported. — Carl Hiaasen, *Native Tongue*, p. 30, 1991

jack-off bar *noun*

a truck's emergency brake *US*

- — Montie Tak, *Truck Talk*, p. 91, 1971

jack-off flare *noun*

a small, hand-launched aerial flare *US, 1987*
The term is based on comparing images.

- — Linda Reinberg, *In the Field*, p. 116, 1991

jack-off party *noun*

a male gathering for mutual masturbation *UK*

- The BBC had sent us to film a jack-off party [...] I had to direct these gays and get them to take their clothes off and form a circle... and I'll leave the rest to your imagination. — *Attitude*, p. 11, October 2003

jack of spades *noun*

sunglasses *UK*
Rhyming slang for **SHADES**.

- — Ray Puxley, *Cockney Rabbit*, 1992

jack of the dust *noun*

aboard ship, a storekeeper of cleaning supplies *US*

- — Hans Halberstadt, *USCG: Always Ready*, p. 128, 1986: 'Glossary'

jack-pack *noun*

a contraption used by a masturbating male to simulate the sensation of penetration *US*

- — *Maledicta*, p. 218, 1979: 'Kinks and queens: linguistic and cultural aspects of the terminology for gays'

jack picture *noun*

a photograph used while masturbating *US*

- Cause all the punks, every punk that's in our tank has a jack picture, every one of them. A jack picture / Some picture of a woman. Some of them have just the head of a woman but they jack off with it anyway. — Bruce Jackson, *In the Life*, p. 403, 1972

jackpot *noun*

1 serious trouble *US, 1887*

- Sooner or later Jessie's going to cook up something with you and you're going to wind up in a jackpot. — Vincent Patrick, *Family Business*, p. 40, 1985

2 a lot of logs crossed in every direction *US, 1905*

- Also, undesirable trouble of any kind. — Tom Parkin, *WetCoast Words*, p. 76, 1989

3 in the circus or carnival, a story of past deeds *US*

- — Joe McKennon, *Circus Lingo*, p. 51, 1980

jackrabbit *noun*

a driver who starts through an intersection at the first hint of a green light *US*

- — *American Speech*, p. 269, December 1962: 'The language of traffic policemen'

jackrabbit parole *noun*

escape from prison *US*

- — William K. Bentley and James M. Corbett, *Prison Slang*, p. 108, 1992

jack ready *adjective*

sexually aroused *US*

- — Charles Shafer, *Folk Speech in Texas Prisons*, p. 208, 1990

Jack Rice *noun*

used as a notional figure in descriptions of large objects *AUSTRALIA, 1945*

From the name of a famous racehorse.

- He may even be fortunate enough to have a roll Jack Rice couldn't jump over. — Sidney J. Baker, *The Austrialian Language*, 1966
- [T]he name was probably a tribute to that prince of hurdlers whose exploits gave rise to the expression, 'so big that Jack Rice couldn't jump over it'. — Joe Andersen, *Winners Can Laugh*, 1982

Jack Robinson *noun*

▸ **before you can say Jack Robinson; quicker than you can say Jack Robinson**

instantly; almost instantly; very quickly *UK, 1700*

- [B]e hauled in front of the shrink before you can say Jack Robinson. — Jack Dann (Editor), *Dreaming Down-Under*, p. 258, 2002
- One word and you'll be back up here before you can say Jack fucking Robinson. — Danny King, *The Bank Robber Diaries*, p. 179, 2002

jack-roll *verb*

1 to rob or pick a pocket, especially to rob a drunk *US, 1916*

- — Lou Shelly, *Hepcats Jive Talk Dictionary*, p. 26, 1945
- After a few days or weeks the girls are told some big spenders wouldn't miss a few dollars if a girl picked up his change or even his wallet. This "jackrolling" works well on drunks. — Lee Mortimer, *Women Confidential*, p. 144, 1960

2 to abduct a woman *SOUTH AFRICA*

As a crime, this was especially commonplace in the late 1980s; after 'the Jackrollers', a gang of kidnappers from the Diepkloof area of Soweto.

- [W]hite South Africans in particular seem to take a perverse pleasure from their stories of how a friend of a friend was jackrolled or murdered in their beds or shot for their mobile phone. — Patrick Neate, *Where You're At*, p. 84, 2003

jack-roller *noun*

a person who robs drunks *US, 1922*

- Jackrollers and pimps walked wise-eyed. — Willard Motley, *Let No Man Write My Epitaph*, p. 59, 1958
- According to Attorney General Lynch's own figures, California's overall crime picture makes the Angels look like a gang of petty jack-rollers. — Hunter S. Thompson, *Hell's Angels*, p. 35, 1966

jacks *noun*

a toilet *IRELAND*

- There's a big jacks under the stand. — Roddy Doyle, *The Van*, p. 92, 1991

Jack's *nickname*

▷ see: **JACK**

jack's alive *noun*

five, especially as five pounds sterling *UK, 1931*

Rhyming slang for 'five', sometimes abbreviated to 'jack's'.

- Alright I'll bet you a jacks that I nick you down to larking within one moon from now. — Frank Norman, *Bang To Rights*, p. 123, 1958
- A jacks is £5; a cockun (cock & hen) £10[.] — *The Guardian*, 30th October 2002

jack schooner *noun*

▷ see: **JACK BOAT**

jack shit *noun*

nothing, a pittance *US, 1969*

- I'm strictly a club caddy, and proud of it. Those tour baggies ain't nothin'. Carrying single bags for a good player ain't jack shit. — James Ellroy, *Brown's Requiem*, p. 43, 1981
- MR. WHITE: Without medical attention, this man won't live through the night. That bullet in his belly is my fault. Now while that might not mean jack shit to you, it means a helluva lot to me. — *Reservoir Dogs*, 1992
- We didn't know jack shit about any riot. It just happened. — *Natural Born Killers*, 1994
- It meant jack shit really. — Andy McNab, *Immediate Action*, p. 14, 1995
- What did you learn at school today? / Jack shit — Ian Dury, *Jack Shit George*, 1998
- [L]et's stick to what we do have, which I believe at the last count was jack-shit, am I right? — Christopher Brookmyre, *Not the End of the World*, p. 222, 1998
- I've given all I got I got jack shit back — Lupine Howl *125*, 2001

jack-slap *verb*

to slap (someone) forcefully *US*

- — Connie Eble (Editor), *UNC-CH Campus Slang*, p. 4, Fall 1981

Jackson *noun*

1 a twenty-dollar note *US*

From the portrait of US President Andrew Jackson on the note.

- He said, "A Jackson frogskin! Whr'd yu git it, Mama?" — Iceberg Slim (Robert Beck), *Mama Black Widow*, p. 114, 1969
- "I see you again," Slick had told her, "it better be behind a pile of dead Presidents. Take a load of Jacksons and Grants get you off my shit list, girl." — John Sayles, *Union Dues*, p. 181, 1977
- For a jackson Belly scored an eight milligram jug, half her normal dose[.] — Seth Morgan, *Homeboy*, p. 188, 1990

2 used as a male-to-male term of address *US, 1941*

- Cook with gas and go to town! Solid Jackson! Ride on down! — Haenigsen, *Jive's Like That*, 1947
- — Lavada Durst, *The Jives of Dr. Hepcat*, p. 1, 1953

Jackson five *noun*

one hundred dollars in twenty-dollar notes *US, 1983*

A portrait of US President Andrew Jackson is found on the face of a $20 note, enabling this pun on the 1970s Motown recording group.

- — Thomas L. Clark, *The Dictionary of Gambling and Gaming*, p. 109, 1987

Jackson Pollocks; jacksons *noun*

the testicles; hence, nonsense, rubbish *UK*

Rhyming slang for **BOLLOCKS**, based on artist Jackson Pollock (1912–56).

- He needs a good kick in the Jacksons. — *www.LondonSlang.com*, June 2002
- Modern art is a load of Jacksons. — *Antiquarian Book Review*, p. 18, June 2002

Jack Sprat *noun*

1 the fat (of meat) *UK*

Rhyming slang.

- — Julian Franklyn, *A Dictionary of Rhyming Slang*, 1960

2 an annoying or troublesome child *UK*

Rhyming slang for **BRAT**.

- — Ray Puxley, *Cockney Rabbit*, 1992

Jack Straw *noun*

marijuana *UK, 1998*

Jack Straw MP, UK Home Secretary 1997–2001, responsible for strengthening anti-drug legislation, was embarrassed when his son was arrested for possession of marijuana. Within days the rhyming slang 'Jack Straw' for **DRAW** (marijuana) had been added to the lexicon.

- SOMETHING POSITIVE MUST COME OUT OF THE SAGA OF JACK STRAW AND HIS SON WILLIAM'S INVOLVEMENT WITH DRUGS — *The People Newspaper*, 4th January 1998

jacksy; jacksie; jaxie *noun*

the buttocks; the anus *UK, 1943*

- Alas the motorist drove into his jacksy, causing serious pelvic and hip injuries. — *Loaded*, p. 30, June 2003
- [As an introduction to a list of famous homosexuals] Fact: pounding in the jacksie could make you as important as this lot! — *The FHM Little Book of Bloke*, p. 144, June 2003: 'Gayness explained'

Jack Tar; jolly Jack Tar *noun*

1 a sailor *UK, 1781*

An elaboration of **TAR**.

- The ghostly pirates of the Black Pearl [...] all talk with the absurd Jolly Jack Tar accents that one associates with press gangs[.] — *The Guardian*, 7th August 2003

2 a bar *UK*

Rhyming slang.

- — Julian Franklyn, *A Dictionary of Rhyming Slang*, 1960

Jack the Bear *noun*

in motor racing, a driver who performs very well *US*

- — John Edwards, *Auto Dictionary*, p. 87, 1993

Jack the biscuit *noun*

a show-off; someone who is important or self-important enough to be ostentatious *UK*

JACK (a man) 'takes the biscuit' (defeats all rivals).

- Dont think me pie and mash (flash) for giving it [behaving in the manner of] Jack the biscuit (chap, top cat). —private correspondence with a prison inmate, *HMP Blunden, Suffolk*, January 2002
- I feel like Jack the biscuit in my new trainers. —Chris Lewis, *The Dictionary of Playground Slang*, p. 122, 2003

Jack the Dripper *noun*

the penis *UK*

A pun on the name of legendary serial killer Jack the Ripper.

- Knob, dick, John Thomas, Jack the Dripper ... Stand-up comedian Richard Herring may not have been called all of these. —*Bang*, p. 112, November 2003

Jack the Lad *noun*

1 someone noticeably sharper, smarter or smugger than the rest; a rogue *UK*

In *Prison Patter*, 1996, Angela Devlin notes that this term is used to excuse dubious – possibly criminal – behaviour by young males.

- Even if I had / I'm a bit of a Jack the Lad[.] —Ian Dury, *Clever Trevor*, 1977
- —*New Society*, 4th June 1981
- [S]he was watching a cocky young Jack-the-lad sailor swagger along a Shanghai street[.] —John King, *White Trash*, p. 123, 2001
- At best a rather immature jack the lad and at worst an insensitve bullying moron. —Ben Elton, *High Society*, p. 251–252, 2002

2 in criminal circles, an exemplary criminal *UK*

- Jimmy'd never shop us. He's Jack the Lad. Jesus, Jimmy and me are like bleeding cousins. —Ted Lewis, *Jack Carter's Law*, p. 16, 1974

Jack the Lad *adjective*

bad *UK*

Rhyming slang.

- —Ray Puxley, *Cockney Rabbit*, 1992

Jack the Ripper *noun*

1 a kipper (a smoked fish) *UK*

- —Ray Puxley, *Cockney Rabbit*, 1992

2 a striptease artist *UK*

Rhyming slang for **STRIPPER**.

- —Bodmin Dark, *Dirty Cockney Rhyming Slang*, 2003

3 a slipper *UK*

Rhyming slang, based on the name of the legendary late C19 Whitechapel murderer. In *Cockney Rabbit* (1992), Ray Puxley notes the use amongst schoolboys of 'Jack the Ripper' as the instrument of corporal punishment (which has not been permitted in UK schools since 1986). In 2002 'Jack the Rippers' is current for 'prison-issue slippers'.

jack-up *noun*

1 a tablet of sodium amobarbital (trade name Amytal™), a central nervous system depressant *US*

- —David Maurer and Victor Vogel, *Narcotics and Narcotic Addiction*, p. 419, 1973

2 an injection of drugs *UK*

From the verb.

- [A] jack up of smack [heroin]. —Angela Devlin, *Prison Patter*, p. 65, 1996

jack up *verb*

1 to inject drugs *US, 1975*

- A sensitive and gentle guy. If he could not get junk he would jack up aspirin, he even jacked up in the fingers which had once made music. —Paul E Willis, *Profane Culture*, p. 184, 1978
- —Angela Devlin, *Prison Patter*, p. 65, 1996
- Which is why I came here to jack up. —Ben Elton, *High Society*, p. 164, 2002
- —Mike Haskins, *Drugs*, p. 290, 2003

2 to raise *US, 1904*

- Viceroy Wilson adjusted his Carrera sunglasses, lit up a joint, jacked up the a/c, and mellowed out behind the Caddy's blue-tinted windows. —Carl Hiaasen, *Tourist Season*, p. 58, 1986
- And this is preferable to you because Music-Town jacks up their prices, and some of this money goes in your pocket. —*Empire Records*, 1995

3 (of the surf) to increase in swell *AUSTRALIA*

- The lines were jacking up with the tide and pounding the reef. —Kathy Lette, *Girls' Night Out*, p. 188, 1987

4 to rob with force *US, 1965*

- By Thursday they'll jack somebody up to get money for the weekend. —Edwin Torres, *After Hours*, p. 332, 1979

5 to arrest or detain for questioning by police *US, 1967*

- On each fall he had been "jacked up" for either strong-arm robbery or "till tapping" [stealing money from a cash register drawer]. —Iceberg Slim (Robert Beck), *Pimp*, p. 33, 1969

6 to be uncooperative; to object, to refuse to comply *AUSTRALIA, 1898*

- When we made trouble, Tuttle wouldn't be in it; when the company jacked-up, Tuttle scabbed. —Eric Lambert, *The Veterans*, p. 107, 1954

jack-up fence *noun*

a large wire fence with barbed wire across the top *US*

Criminals lift victims and hang them on the top of the fence as they rob them. Noted in 1994.

- —Fiona Pitt-Kethley, *Red Light Districts of the World*, p. 85, 2000

Jacky *noun*

a kookaburra *AUSTRALIA, 1898*

▸ **sit up like Jacky**

to sit up straight in a perky or self-important manner *AUSTRALIA, 1941*

Baker (1945) suggests that this refers to sitting up straight 'as an aboriginal is supposed to do in company with whites', though it should be noted that the kookaburra habitually sits up on an exposed branch or fencetop surveying an area of ground for insect and reptile food, and impertinently ignores the frequent attacks of other birds.

- As we were rattling along north to Darwin I happened to look back out of the guard's can and there they were – sitting up like Jacky in the commissioner's car behind us. —Patsy Adam-Smith, *Folklore of the Australian Railwaymen*, p. 180, 1969
- —Frank Hardy, *The Outcasts of Foolgarah*, p. 57, 1971
- He's very fussy, your producer, sitting up there like Jacky the third day running and writing out his cues like he never saw lights before. —*Janie Stagestruck*, p. 87, 1972

Jacky Howe; jacky-howe *noun*

▷ **see: JACKIE HOWE**

Jacky Jacky; Jacky *noun*

an Australian Aboriginal man *AUSTRALIA, 1845*

- You see if you call a Maori Hori it's just like calling an American negro Sambo, or an Australian aborginal Jacky. —Frank Hardy, *The Yarns of Billy Borker*, p. 113, 1965
- Jacky Jacky was tied to a tree. One soldier fired and wounded him in the neck, a second fired and broke his jaw. —Al Grassby and Marji Hill, *Six Australian Battlefields*, p. 39, 1988

Jacob's crackers *noun*

the testicles *UK*

Also shortened form 'jacobs'. Rhyming slang for **KNACKERS**; from the branded savoury biscuits. Usage popularised by comedian Joe Pasquale in the television programme *I'm A Celebrity, Get Me Out of Here*, December 2004.

- [W]hen enjoying a bath with Three Degrees star Sheila Ferguson he [Joe Pasquale] told her: "I'm comfortable with anything, love, but you don't want to see my Jacobs hanging out". —*The Scotsman*, 6th December 2004

Jacob's crackers *adjective*

tired, exhausted *UK*

Rhyming slang leading to **KNACKERED**; a variant of **CREAM CRACKERED** formed on a premier brand of cream crackers.

- —Bodmin Dark, *Dirty Cockney Rhyming Slang*, 2003

Jacob's ladder *noun*

a sturdy rope ladder dropped from a hovering helicopter for descent to and ascent from the ground *US*

- Early the next morning engineers and medical personnel reached the unit, descending through the jungle canopy on "Jacob's ladders" dropped from the rear of the hovering CH-47 Chinook helicopter. —Shely L. Stanton, *The Rise and Fall of an American Army*, p. 94, 1985

jade gate *noun*

▷ **see: GATE TO HEAVEN**

jader *noun*

in Newfoundland, a person not liked, a nuisance *CANADA*

- Tom Murphy is a soaker, oh / Ned Jackman is a jader, / and John Scott a mailbag trader. —*Daily News*, p. 2, 2nd September 1944

jafa *noun*

1 a resident of Auckland *NEW ZEALAND*

From '*j*ust *a*nother *f*ucking *A*uklander'.

- —David McGill, *David McGill's Complete Kiwi Slang Dictionary*, p. 72, 1998

2 a scientist *ANTARCTICA, 1987*
An abbreviation of '*j*ust *a*nother *f*ucking *a*cademic'. 'Jafo' is a variant where the scientist is an '*o*bserver'.
- — Bernadette Hince, *The Antarctic Dictionary*, p. 195, 2000
- — *Cool Antarctica*, 2003: 'Antarctic slang'

jaffa *noun*
an infertile man *UK*
Probably an allusion to a seedless Jaffa orange.
- Somebody been saying I'm a jaffa? Those kids are mine. And the wife hasn't got no complaints. — Liz Evans, *Barking!*, p. 194, 2001

jag *noun*
1 a period of time spent entirely focused on a single activity, often with the defining term prefixed *US, 1913*
- I is on a health jag now I due for release[.] — Jeremy Cameron, *Brown Bread in Wengen*, p. 109, 1999
- [V]ague feelings of paranoia and weirdness, irritability, loss of appetite, crying jags, a sudden compulsive desire to go to Yosemite National Park[.] — Carl Franz, *The People's Guide to Mexico*, p. 254, 2002

2 a drinking or drug binge *US, 1892*
- It was like waiting for the accentuated heat of your heart when you're on a reefer jag[.] — Mezz Mezzrow, *Really the Blues*, p. 181, 1946
- It was past midnight, and Frank was coming out of the marijuana jag and feeling lousy. — Irving Shulman, *The Amboy Dukes*, p. 44, 1947
- They stood at the bar like two cats having a sip of something cold to dampen their dry jag, and ordered beer. — Chester Himes, *Cotton Comes to Harlem*, p. 129, 1965

3 a state of alcohol or drug intoxication *UK, 1678*
- [T]aken two or three at one time with coffee, they gave a wonderful jag. The capsules were blue so we called them blue boys. After we got jagged we found no one would know what we were talking about when we said blue boys. — Chester Himes, *Cast the First Stone*, p. 247, 1952
- 300 jags seems kinda fantastic. — Clarence Cooper Jr, *The Farm*, p. 192, 1967

4 an act of solvent abuse *UK*
- The child becomes dependent on a regular "jag". — *New Society*, 20th June 1963

5 a social engagement; a date *IRELAND*
- He has a jag with that girl tonight. — Seáen Beecher, *A Dictionary of Cork Slang*, p. 12, 1983
- "I'll have to flake away", says Tizzy. "I've a jag tonight." — Gaye Shortland, *Mind that 'tis my Brother*, p. 20, 1995

6 a loner lacking social skills *US*
- — *Washington Post*, 14th October 1993

7 a small load on a truck *US*
- — Montie Tak, *Truck Talk*, p. 91, 1971

Jag *noun*
a Jaguar car *US, 1953*
- You're maybe out on the turnpike, just cruising along about 85 miles an hour, and here comes some joker in a Jag or something foreign like that. — Robert Gover, *One Hundred Dollar Misunderstanding*, p. 143, 1961
- My car always stood out like a bloody sore thumb in that parking lot filled with gleaming new models, Lincolns, Jags, even a Mercedes, none of them ever over two years old. — Clancy Sigal, *Going Away*, p. 9, 1961
- One morning we got a flat tyre (we were using my Jag)[.] — Derek Raymond (Robin Cook), *The Crust on its Uppers*, p. 23, 1962
- Two of Spino's terrible Bomato assassins from Sicily watched for the highway approach just outside Chicago of Cocio's Jag. — Iceberg Slim (Robert Beck), *Death Wish*, p. 246, 1977
- My boss got a Caddy like this. And a Jag. Jag XK426. Got the Jag after he forced his partner to sell out. — *Saturday Night Fever*, 1977
- Terry sat beside Arthur as he drove his Jag slowly through the crowded streets. — Anthony Masters, *Minder*, p. 58, 1984
- "He ain't gonna be in the Jag no more," Letch said. — Joseph Wambaugh, *Floaters*, p. 213, 1996
- There was me, Jen, Terry Turo, Daniella, Seymour and Johnny Jacket all squashed in my Jag. — Dave Courtney, *Raving Lunacy*, p. 227, 2000

jag *verb*
to work as a male prostitute *US*
- — Helen Dahlskog (Editor), *A Dictionary of Contemporary and Colloquial Usage*, p. 34, 1972

jagabat *noun*
a promiscuous woman; a prostitute *TRINIDAD AND TOBAGO, 1992*
- — Lise Winer, *Dictionary of the English/Creole of Trinidad & Tobago*, 2003

jagged *adjective*
drunk or drug-intoxicated *US, 1737*
First recorded by Benjamin Franklin.
- [T]aken two or three at one time with coffee, they gave a wonderful jag. The capsules were blue so we called them blue boys. After we got jagged we found no one would know what we were talking about when we said blue boys. — Chester Himes, *Cast the First Stone*, p. 247, 1952
- "Jagged to the gills," the sergeant said, looking minutely about the room. — Chester Himes, *The Real Cool Killers*, p. 69, 1959

jagger *noun*
a tattoo artist *US, 1947*
- — Don Wilmeth, *The Language of American Popular Entertainment*, p. 143, 1981

Jagger's lip; jagger's *noun*
a chip *UK*
Rhyming slang, formed from a prominent characteristic of Rolling Stones' singer Mick Jagger (b.1943).
- If brains were made of dripping you wouldn't have enough to fry a Jagger's. — Ray Puxley, *Fresh Rabbit*, 1998

jaggy nettle; jaggy *noun*
a kettle *UK: SCOTLAND*
Glasgow rhyming slang; 'jaggy' means 'prickly'.
- Stick the jaggy on for a coffee. — Michael Munro, *The Patter, Another Blast*, 1988

jag house *noun*
a brothel that caters to male homosexuals *US*
- — Helen Dahlskog (Editor), *A Dictionary of Contemporary and Colloquial Usage*, p. 34, 1972

jag-off *noun*
a despicable, offensive or dim-witted person *US, 1938*
- Great idea jag-off! — *The Breakfast Club*, 1985
- Past the jag-off guard who gets an extra C-note a week just to watch the door. — *Casino*, 1995
- I didnt deserve to exist. Child fucker. Fat jagoff. — Peter Sotos, *Index*, p. 90, 1996
- Shut up, jagoff! — *Austin Powers*, 1999

jag off *verb*
to manipulate the injection of a drug such that the drug enters the blood stream slowly *US*
- Extra Black Johnson, like so many of them, likes to jag off. — Willard Motley, *Let No Man Write My Epitaph*, p. 158, 1958

jags *adjective*
sexually aroused *SOUTH AFRICA*
- Checking Pamela Anderson and Tommy Lee on the Internet made me so jags. — *Surfrikan Slang*, 2004

jag up *verb*
to inject drugs *UK: SCOTLAND*
In Glasgow slang, presumably a variation of **JACK UP**.
- — Michael Munro, *The Complete Patter*, p. 83, 1996

jahalered *adjective*
drunk *UK*
- — *e-cyclopaedia*, 20th March 2002

jail *noun*
in horse racing, the first month after a claimed horse is in a new stable *US*
Racing rules limit the conditions under which the horse may be raced during the first month.
- — Tom Ainslie, *Ainslie's Complete Guide to Thoroughbred Racing*, p. 333, 1976

▸ **in jail**
in pool, said of a cue ball that is touching another ball or the rail, leaving the player with no good opportunity to make a shot *US*
- — Steve Rushin, *Pool Cool*, p. 16, 1990

jail *verb*
to serve a prison sentence, especially without losing hope or sanity *US*
- But you like jailing, Red. Nunn didn't. — Malcolm Braly, *On the Yard*, p. 325, 1967
- Then he stepped out on the gallery, slamming the door behind him with the experience of a convcit who has been jailing for a long time. — Donald Goines, *Black Gangster*, p. 8, 1977
- I told him, he wouldn't listen. He never learned how to jail. You know, live in a place like that. So he died. — Elmore Leonard, *Stick*, p. 173, 1983
- Jailin' was an art form and lifestyle both. The style was walkin' slow, drinkin' plenty of water, and doin' your own time; the art was lightin' cigarets from wall sockets, playin' the dozens, cuttin' up dream jackpots, and slow'in your metabolism[.] — Seth Morgan, *Homeboy*, p. 122, 1990
- Elvin, eating pizza, said he'd give him some pointers on how to jail. — Elmore Leonard, *Maximum Bob*, p. 47, 1991

▸ **be jailing**
to wear your trousers or shorts very low, below the buttocks, with your boxer shorts visible above the trouser line *US*
From the image of prisoners who are not allowed to have belts and whose trousers thus sag.
- —Connie Eble (Editor), *UNC-CH Campus Slang*, p. 1, Fall 1993

jail arithmetic *noun*
in prison, any method used to keep track of your time served and the time remaining on your sentence *US*
- —Vincent J. Monteleone, *Criminal Slang*, p. 131, 1949

jailbait; gaol-bait *noun*
a sexually alluring girl under the legal age of consent *US, 1930*
- —Lou Shelly, *Hepcats Jive Talk Dictionary*, p. 26, 1945
- "Now they start in grammar school, and the streets are full of jail bait," Jack said. —James T. Farrell, *Saturday Night*, p. 36, 1947
- But he didn't want Alice fooling around with a kid who was definitely jail bait and on the make. —Irving Shulman, *The Amboy Dukes*, p. 34, 1947
- You're wasting your time, Gran'pa. I'm jailbait. —George Mandel, *Flee the Angry Strangers*, p. 5, 1948
- I want both you little jailbaits to stay right here in this room and don't move. —Chester Himes, *The Real Cool Killers*, p. 49, 1959
- The girls are mostly jailbait chicks, radically underage and looking it in their baby fat, pedal pushers, unskillful mascara, and ponytails. —Herbert Gold, *The Age of Happy Problems*, p. 211, 1962
- Morty, that fucking chick is jail bait if I ever seen it! I mean, she's a fucking child, for Christ fucking sake! —Terry Southern, *Blue Movie*, p. 149, 1970
- Another guy in Corpus Christi was on his nineteenth year when he made it with his girlfriend's jailbait daughter, who wanted to get at the old lady. —Darryl Ponicsan, *The Last Detail*, p. 13, 1970
- Then I heard a forty-seven-year-old guy named Herman searching for jailbait. —Anka Radakovich, *The Wild Girls Club*, p. 67, 1994
- But who's gonna believe me when I'm front-paged for shagging jailbait? So it's trousers up an' head for the door. —Ben Elton, *High Society*, p. 227, 2002

jailbird; gaol-bird *noun*
a prisoner or ex-convict *UK, 1661*
- [T]hey made me lay around there for six weeks, doing the kind of easy bit a jailbird always dreams about. —Mezz Mezzrow, *Really the Blues*, p. 310, 1946
- Jail birds, cons, and other unfortunate victims of bad laws call this ingenious invention a Fifi Bag. —*Screw*, p. 23, 27th October 1969
- I'll pop another tiny bottle of champers on the ice for our delicious jailbird. —Barry Humphries, *Bazza Pulls It Off!*, 1971
- Since those jailbirds took little Nathan I been doin' some thinking, and I ain't too proud of myself. —*Raising Arizona*, 1987
- —Angela Devlin, *Prison Patter*, p. 66, 1996

jail bollocks *noun*
difficulties presented by fellow-prisoners and officers *UK*
- —Angela Devlin, *Prison Patter*, p. 66, 1996

jailcraft *noun*
a prison-officer's knowledge of the day-to-day running of a prison *UK*
- —Angela Devlin, *Prison Patter*, p. 66, 1996

jailee *noun*
a prison officer *UK*
A deliberate role-reversal for the jailer.
- —Angela Devlin, *Prison Patter*, p. 66, 1996

jail gay *noun*
a prisoner who, while generally heterosexual, adopts homosexuality as a temporary practice while in prison *UK*
- [N]ot all who locate themselves within this community are full-time homosexuals; some are "jail gays" only and may well have wives and girlfriends who visit regularly, unaware of their imprisoned partner's complex coping strategy. —*The Guardian*, 25th February 2000: 'A life inside'

jailhouse *noun*
a type of bet in an illegal numbers game lottery *US*
- Then to be on the safe side he also played jail house, death row, lady come back, two-timing woman, pile of rocks, dark days and trouble. —Chester Himes, *A Rage in Harlem*, p. 23, 1957

jailhouse flowers *noun*
the solicitation of sexual relations by non-lexical verbalisation *US*
- I heard someone making squeaky sounds from between compressed lips. A sound that was a universal expression in prison, it meant getting hit on. I went on working, vaguely wondering who was getting the jailhouse flowers. —Piri Thomas, *Seven Long Times*, p. 168, 1974

jailhouse lawyer *noun*
a prisoner with some expertise, real and/or perceived, in the criminal justice system *US, 1926*
- [A]ll the cons went ape, everybody writing papers, and the jailhouse lawyers were ridin' high talking all that jive about searching and seizing illegal evidence. —Edwin Torres, *Carlito's Way*, p. 50, 1975
- The guy I shot's got a brother was in Jackson, was in Marquette, and learned a few things there talking to the jailhouse lawyer. —Elmore Leonard, *Split Images*, p. 28, 1981
- Chester, after 15 years of incessant legal activity on his behalf by the eminent jailhouse lawyer, Victor Huge Feldman, was being released. —Odie Hawkins, *Great Lawd Buddha*, p. 57, 1990

jailhouse punk *noun*
a man who becomes a passive homosexual while in prison *US*
- —Ralph de Sola, *Crime Dictionary*, p. 74, 1982

jailhouse turnout *noun*
a previously heterosexual man who becomes homosexual in prison *US, 1965*
- Your jailhouse turnouts are treated like a machine; when someone wants sex and they haven't got a free-world queen of their own then they go to the jailhouse turnouts. —Bruce Jackson, *In the Life*, p. 365, 1972
- — *Male Swinger Number 3*, p. 47, 1981: 'The complete gay dictionary'

jail politician *noun*
a prisoner who stirs up disaffection and unrest, or one who manipulates prison officers *UK*
- —Angela Devlin, *Prison Patter*, p. 66, 1996

jail-wise *adjective*
sophisticated with respect to survival in prison *US*
- I was jail-wise in picking my friends. —Piri Thomas, *Down These Mean Streets*, p. 257, 1967

jake *noun*
1 Jamaica ginger, a potent and dangerous illegally manufactured alcohol *US, 1923*
- —Jerry Robertson, *Oil Slanguage*, p. 72, 1954

2 methylated spirits as an alcoholic drink *UK, 1932*
- Jake is meths, in the language of the Row. —Geoffrey Fletcher, *Down Among the Meths Men*, p. 38, 1966
- They [vagrant alcoholics] subsist on a diet of methylated spirits (jake or the blue), surgical spirit (surge or the white) and other forms of crude alcohol. —Peter Ackroyd, *London The Biography*, p. 359, 2000

3 a vagrant alcoholic addicted to methylated spirits *UK*
- I came up with a Jake in Charing Cross, and gave him five bob to go and get a meal. —Geoffrey Fletcher, *Down Among the Meths Men*, p. 39, 1966

4 a social outcast *US*
- —Connie Eble (Editor), *UNC-CH Campus Slang*, p. 4, Fall 1989

5 a person identified as a potential crime victim *US*
- Prosecutors allege that Everybodytalksabout and Lopez were drinking in Pioneer Square with several other people that morning when someone said they'd spooted a "Jake." —*Seattle Times*, p. B3, 13th February 1997

6 a uniformed police officer *US*
- —Carsten Stroud, *Close Pursuit*, p. 273, 1987

jake *adjective*
honest, upright, equitable, correct *US, 1914*
- —James T. Farrell, *Saturday Night*, p. , 1947
- He had enough money to marry one, and with her teaching too, they could get on jake, save, have a little apartment, and they ought to be happy. —James T. Farrell, *Saturday Night*, p. 26, 1947
- Everything's jake here. —Jim Thompson, *Savage Night*, p. 38, 1953
- I was jake with Bobo all the time, but now that it's happened[.] —Jim Thompson, *The Grifters*, p. 183, 1963
- "He's quite a nice person." "You can say that shit again," I spoke, pulling her giggling body in to me. "He's jake with me". —Jim Carroll, *Forced Entries*, p. 98, 1987
- When he was finished, he took a machine gun as evidence, promising to return it in a few days if everything was jake. —Kim Rich, *Johnny's Girl*, p. 165, 1993

jaked *adjective*
drunk *UK: SCOTLAND*
- This is the most jaked I've felt in years[.] —Ian Pattison, *Rab C. Nesbitt*, 1988

jaked out *adjective*
in a drunken stupor *UK: SCOTLAND*
- Ye'll maybe see wan or two guys jaked oot at a table. —Michael Munro, *The Patter, Another Blast*, 1988

jaked up *adjective*

drunk *UK: SCOTLAND*

Derives from **JAKE** (methylated spirits as an alcoholic drink).

- —Michael Munro, *The Patter, Another Blast*, 1988
- — *e-cyclopaedia*, 20th March 2002

jake (it) *verb*

to give something less than a full effort; to feign an injury *US*

- —Zander Hollander and Paul Zimmerman, *Football Lingo*, p. 69, 1967

Jake man *noun*

a vagrant alcoholic addicted to methylated spirits *UK*

From **JAKE** (methylated spirits).

- The Jake men all know me[.]—Geoffrey Fletcher, *Down Among the Meths Men*, p. 38, 1966

jaker *noun*

in sports, a player who chronically claims injuries *US*

From basketball.

- —Zander Hollander, *Baseball Lingo*, p. 72, 1967
- According to Steinbrenner, Piniella called Mark Salas "a bum" and said Rickey Henderson should be traded because he's "a jaker" who fakes injuries.— *Washington Post*, p. B1, 12th August 1987
- Feeling he was portrayed as a jaker, Grant blasted the competence of team medics.— *Orlando (Florida) Sentinel Tribune*, p. C1, 13th March 1998

jakerloo; jakealoo; jakeaboo *adjective*

all right; fine *AUSTRALIA, 1919*

An elaboration of **JAKE**. The obsolete faux Latin term 'jakalorum' was recorded as early as 1905.

- In that case I'll be getting along to prepare the revolution by seeing everything's jakeaboo at the shed.—Dymphna Cusack, *Picnic Races*, p. 97, 1962

jakes *noun*

the police *US*

- —Kenn "Naz" Young, *Naz's Dictionary of Teen Slang*, p. 65, 1993

jakey *noun*

1 Jamaica ginger, a fruit flavoured alcoholic drink *CANADA*

- "Jakey," or Jamaica ginger, fruit-flavoured and alcoholic, is intended for food preparation but consumed as a crude cocktail along the South Shore.—Lewis Poteet, *The South Shore Phrase Book*, p. 63, 1999

2 a meths drinker, thus an alcoholic in desperate straits *UK*

From **JAKE** (methylated spirits as an alcoholoc drink).

- What, do I look like a bleedin jakey, do I?—Niall Griffiths, *Sheepshagger*, p. 184, 2001
- Her hand's tremblin like a jakey's reachin for his first pint of the day.—Niall Griffiths, *Kelly + Victor*, p. 66, 2002

jakey *adjective*

1 alcoholic *UK*

- [J]akey lowlife bludgeons fellow jakey lowlife after three-day drinking binge.—Christopher Brookmyre, *The Sacred Art of Stealing*, p. 196, 2002

2 socially inept, unaware of current fashions and trends *US*

- —Connie Eble (Editor), *UNC-CH Campus Slang*, p. 4, Fall 1989

3 odd looking *US*

- — *American Speech*, p. 235, October 1964: 'Student slang in Hays, Kansas'

4 said of a light jail sentence *UK*

From **JAKE** (methylated spirits as an alcoholic drink).

- He wasn't being locked away forever, just a few months [...] "A Jakey sentence," someone called it, referring to the comparable stretches winos and down-and-outs tended to get.—Christopher Brookmyre, *Boiling a Frog*, p. 40, 2000

jall *verb*

▷ **see: JOL**

jallopy; jalopy; jaloppie; jollopy; gillopy *noun*

a cheap, dilapidated or old motor vehicle, especially a car *US, 1926*

- Of a weekend, there is nothing my companion and I like more [...] than to jump in the jalopy, put on some Penguin Cafe Orchestra and tootle along the coast road in search of the sleeping small towns of East Sussex[.]— *The Guardian*, 25th November 2000

jam *noun*

1 a difficult position, an awkward situation; a difficulty; trouble *US, 1914*

- The Committee on Standards in Public Life [...] was set up in a rush by a prime minister in a jam who couldn't cope with the clouds of murk engulfing his government.— *The Guardian*, 14th January 2000
- Golliwog stunt leaves Tory in a jam .— *The Guardian*, 6th September 2001

2 a recorded song *US, 1937*

- Fuck dat honky shit. Got to get me some motown jams, dig it? — *Platoon*, 1986
- I push it the way it is, the record'll get some nods, yeah, it's pretty good stuff, slightly different, but you won't get the buzz you need – hey shit, this jam reaches out and moves you.—Elmore Leonard, *Be Cool*, p. 280, 1999
- Radio won't even play my jam / 'Cause I am whatever you say I am[.]—Eminem (Marshall Mathers), *The Way I Am*, 2000

3 a record album *US*

Usually in the plural.

- —Connie Eble (Editor), *UNC-CH Campus Slang*, p. 4, March 1981

4 blues, jazz or rock music simultaneously improvised by an informal gathering of musicians; a period spent making such music *UK, 1929*

- Lined up across the stage during the final blues jam was a most unlikely combination of musicians[.]— *The Guardian*, 12th November 2003

5 a party with loud music *US*

- This is an all-the-way-live ghetto jam.— *Menace II Society*, 1993
- There was park jams going on.— *A2Z [quoting KRS-One, 1994]*, p. 56, 1995
- The high point at the jam [was] where everyone starts battling each other, trying to do the dopest moves and get the most props.—Alex Ogg, *The Hip Hop Years [quoting 'Crazy Legs' Richie Colon]*, p. 16, 1999

6 cocaine *US*

- If that man goes out and does a hundred dollars jam a night, that is her fault.—Christina and Richard Milner, *Black Players*, p. 85, 1972
- —Richard A. Spears, *The Slang and Jargon of Drugs and Drink*, p. 286, 1986

7 amphetamines *US, 1953*

- —Richard A. Spears, *The Slang and Jargon of Drugs and Drink*, p. 286, 1986
- —Mike Haskins, *Drugs*, p. 279, 2003

8 sex *US*

- Everybody plays jam in that park, gets their trim.—Hal Ellson, *Duke*, p. 61, 1949

9 the vagina *US*

- —Edith A. Folb, *runnin' down some lines*, p. 243, 1980

10 in homosexual usage, any heterosexual man *US*

An abbreviation of '*j*ust *a m*an'.

- — *Male Swinger Number 3*, p. 47, 1981: 'The complete gay dictionary'

11 the corpse of a person who has died with massive injuries *US*

- — *Maledicta*, p. 180, Summer/Winter 1986–1987: 'Sexual slang: prostitutes, pedophiles, flagellators, transvestites, and necrophiles'

12 a fight, especially a gang fight *US*

- —William K. Bentley and James M. Corbett, *Prison Slang*, p. 90, 1992

13 a gathering of skateboarders *US*

- —Albert Cassorla, *The Skateboarder's Bible*, p. 201, 1976

14 petty smuggling *US*

- — *American Speech*, p. 96, May 1956: 'Smugglers' argot in the Southwest'

▷ **see: CULTURE JAM**

jam *verb*

1 to play music with others, improvising *US, 1935*

- We hung out on the beach all day long, jamming our heads off, while the people gathered around us like sandflies.—Mezz Mezzrow, *Really the Blues*, p. 87, 1946
- We have a combo going at the school and I sometimes jam in Springfield and Worcester.—Nat Hentoff, *Jazz Country*, p. 139, 1965
- Jamming the next day we got totally shitfaced[.]—Lester Bangs, *Psychotic Reactions and Carburetor Dung*, p. 219, 1977
- Pat Martino, the Philadelphia musician who once jammed with the late guitar legend Wes Montgomery[.]— *The Guardian*, 7th November 2003

2 to dance *TRINIDAD AND TOBAGO, 1986*

- —Lise Winer, *Dictionary of the English/Creole of Trinidad & Tobago*, 2003

3 to excel *US*

- —Connie Eble (Editor), *UNC-CH Campus Slang*, p. 5, Fall 1984

4 to have sex *US*

- —Robert A. Wilson, *Playboy's Book of Forbidden Words*, p. 149, 1972
- —John A. Holm, *Dictionary of Bahamian English*, p. 13, 1982
- —Lise Winer, *Dictionary of the English/Creole of Trinidad & Tobago*, 2003

5 to coerce, to threaten, to pressure *US, 1971*

- Meanwhile, the Puerto Ricans been gettin' jammed since the forties and ain't nobody said nothin'.—Edwin Torres, *Carlito's Way*, p. 5, 1975
- The big problem was the big "If" involved with trying to jam fifteen or twenty dudes who did a lot of jamming themselves.—Odie Hawkins, *Chicago Hustle*, p. 39, 1977
- Cameron, I'm sorry. I didn't mean to jam you.— *Ferris Buehler's Day Off*, 1986

6 to leave quickly; to travel at high speeds *US, 1965*
- There is nothing on the road – with the exception of a few sports or racing cars – that can catch an artfully hopped-up outlaw 74 as long as there's room to "jam it" or "screw it on." — Hunter S. Thompson, *Hell's Angels*, p. 97, 1966
- As soon as the last shot was fired, he threw himself back into the car. "C'mon man, jam it!!!" he screamed to Buddy. — Donald Goines, *Inner City Hoodlum*, p. 153, 1975
- Heather, I feel awful, like I'm going to throw up. Can we jam, please? — *Heathers*, 1988
- [H]e can keep up with me on my skates and I'm jamming through the crowds of people like a hell bat. — Francesca Lia Block, *Missing Angel Juan*, p. 299, 1993

7 in gambling, to cheat (another player) *US*
- Poor Soapy got caught jammin' some players at the Purple Tiger, which was a little card club down on the wharf, by the pier. — Stephen Cannell, *King Con*, p. 3–4, 1997

8 to subvert advertising matter *US*
- On the prowl with "adbusters" out to "jam" the meaning of those billboards with their own messages. — Naomi Klein, *No Logo*, 2001

9 in surfing, to obstruct or block another surfer's ride *US*
- — Midget Farrelly and Craig McGregor, *The Surfing Life*, p. 191, 1967

10 to surf with speed and intensity *US*
- — Michael V. Anderson, *The Bad, Rad, Not to Forget Way Cool Beach and Surf Discriptionary*, p. 9, 1988

jam *adjective*
heterosexual *US, 1935*
Eventually supplanted by **STRAIGHT**.
- — Donald Webster Cory and John P. LeRoy, *The Homosexual and His Society*, p. 265, 1963: 'A lexicon of homosexual slang'
- — *Fact*, p. 26, January-February 1965

JAM
used as Internet shorthand to mean '*j*ust *a m*inute' *US*
- — Andy Ihnatko, *Cyberspeak*, p. 106, 1997

Jamaican *noun*
marijuana cultivated in Jamaica *US, 1974*
- — Richard A. Spears, *The Slang and Jargon of Drugs and Drink*, p. 286, 1986

Jamaican assault vehicle *noun*
any sports utility vehicle *US*
New York police slang; SUV's are favoured by Jamaican criminals.
- — Samuel M. Katz, *Anytime Anywhere*, p. 388, 1997: 'The extremely unofficial and completely off-the-record NYPD/ESU truck-two glossary'

Jamaican blue mountain *noun*
a type of marijuana cultivated in Jamaica *US*
- [W]e lit up a couple Jamaican Blue Mountain joints and started talking about what the deal should be. — Odie Hawkins, *Los Angeles*, p. 168–169, 1994

Jamaican bomber *noun*
a large marijuana cigarette, made with what is claimed to be Jamaican marijuana *US*
- — Vann Wesson, *Generation X Field Guide and Lexicon*, p. 98, 1997

Jamaican gold *noun*
a variety of marijuana cultivated in Jamaica *US*
- — Richard A. Spears, *The Slang and Jargon of Drugs and Drink*, p. 286, 1986
- — Mike Haskins, *Drugs*, p. 288, 2003

Jamaican switch *noun*
a type of confidence swindle *US*
There are many variations of the swindle, but the common element is the swindler pretending to be a foreigner with a lot of money in need of help.
- He used to hang around downtown and work with a Gypsy dame on pigeon drops and once in a while a Jamaican switch. — Joseph Wambaugh, *The Blue Knight*, p. 158, 1973
- Police warned residents of South Los Angeles to beware of an elaborate fraud scheme involving suspects who feign a Jamaican or other foreign accent and pretend to be worried about holding money in a big city. The so-called "Jamaican Switch" is usually aimed at elderly people[.] — *Los Angeles Times*, p. 2, 23rd May 1985
- 'Jamaican switch' is a con played by a person who fakes a foreign accent and tells a trusting individual he has a sum of money saved from his country but doesn't trust U.S. banks[.] — *Daily Oklahoman*, p. 25, 15th December 1996
- Roy and Frank plan to spring the old "Jamaican switch" on a wealth mark ("you're the rope, I'm inside") even as Roy experiments with his new parental role. — *The Village Voice*, p. 79, 16th September 2003

jam and bread *noun*
the bleed period of the menstrual cycle *US*
Red on white imagery.
- — Karen Houppert, *The Curse*, 1999

jam and butter!
used as a mild oath *NEW ZEALAND*
- — David McGill, *David McGill's Complete Kiwi Slang Dictionary*, p. 62, 1998

jam band *noun*
a musical band known for long improvisations *US*
- It will include the well-known pianists Marian McPartland and Dorothy Donegan, a quintet of women led by the saxophonist Willene Barton, Melba Liston and Company, an ensemble of four women and three men, and a women's jam band. — *New York Times*, p. C14, 3rd July 1981
- First came the announcement that the mightiest jam band of them all, Phish, will end a 21-year run at the end of their summer tour[.] — *Guitar Player*, p. 30, 1st September 2004

jam box *noun*
a portable radio and cassette player with large speakers *US*
- — Connie Eble (Editor), *UNC-CH Campus Slang*, p. 3, Fall 1982

jam-buster *noun*
1 an assistant yardmaster in a railroad yard *US, 1938*
- — Norman Carlisle, *The Modern Wonder Book of Trains and Railroading*, p. 265, 1946

2 in Winnipeg, a jam doughnut *CANADA*
- One might consume a jambuster at the Peg's famous windy crossroads of Portage and "Pain." — Bill Casselman, *Canadian Food Words*, p. 193, 1998

jam butty *noun*
a police car *UK*
A combination of **JAM-JAR** (a car) and **BUTTY** (a sandwich), describing a white car with a red stripe.
- [H]alf a dozen jam butties[.] — Max Marquis, *Vengeance*, 1990

jam Cecil *noun*
1 cocaine *US, 1975*
- — Richard A. Spears, *The Slang and Jargon of Drugs and Drink*, p. 286, 1986

2 amphetamines *UK, 1977*
- — Richard A. Spears, *The Slang and Jargon of Drugs and Drink*, p. 286, 1986
- — Mike Haskins, *Drugs*, p. 279, 2003

Jam Down *adjective*
Jamaican *JAMAICA*
- [Y]ou can't beat a good draw of Jam Down sensi [marijuana], no way. — Donald Gorgon, *Cop Killer*, p. 66, 1994

James Earl dog *noun*
a marijuana cigarette *US*
- — Connie Eble (Editor), *UNC-CH Campus Slang*, p. 4, October 1986

James Hunt *noun*
a cunt (in all senses, but especially as a term of abuse) *UK*
Rhyming slang, formed from the name of the UK racing driver, 1947–93.
- — Tom Nind, *Rude Rhyming Slang*, p. 13, 2003

Jamie *noun*
any General Motors truck *US*
- — Montie Tak, *Truck Talk*, p. 92, 1971

jam-jams *noun*
▷ **see:** JAMMY-JAMS

jam-jar *noun*
a motor car *UK*
Rhyming slang, originally (late C19) applied to a tram, and probably almost as old as the car.
- — Julian Franklyn, *A Dictionary of Rhyming Slang*, p. 82, 1960
- [W]e squeezed into my jam-jar / And drove back to my gaff. — Ronnie Barker, *Fletchers Book of Rhyming Slang*, p. 21, 1979

jammed *adjective*
1 describes the altered state of a public image, usually a billboard, once it has been subverted by cultural activists *US*
- I woke up and every billboard on my street had been "jammed" with anticorporate slogans by midnight bandits. — Naomi Klein, *No Logo*, 2001
- [A]s yellow cabs got stuck in gridlock, the jammed ads jostled with the real ones[.] — Naomi Klein, *No Logo*, 2001

2 experiencing a drug overdose *US*
- —Vincent J. Monteleone, *Criminal Slang*, p. 132, 1949

3 (used of the collective bets in a hand of a poker game) formed by many bets and raised bets *US*
- —Peter O. Steiner, *Thursday Night Poker*, p. 413, 1996

4 (used of prison sentences) concurrent *US*
- —Ralph de Sola, *Crime Dictionary*, p. 151, 1982

jammed up *adjective*

1 under great pressure *US*
- Phillips' wife didn't know how jammed up he was.—Leonard Shecter and William Phillips, *On the Pad*, p. 48, 1973

2 experiencing a drug overdose *US*
- —Eugene Landy, *The Underground Dictionary*, p. 111, 1971

jammer *noun*

1 in American casinos, a skilled and adaptable dealer *US*
- —Steve Kuriscak, *Casino Talk*, p. 33, 1985

2 a popular, trend-setting, respected person *US*
Hawaiian youth usage.
- —Douglas Simonson, *Pidgin to da Max Hana Hou*, 1982

▷ **see:** CULTURAL JAMMER

jammered *verb*

of a place, packed with people *IRELAND*
- He looked over at the bar. He'd never get near it; it was jammered. —Roddy Doyle, *The Van*, p. 153, 1991

jammers *adjective*

very-crowded, jam-packed *IRELAND*
- —Colin Murphy and Donal O'Dea, *The Book of Feckin' Irish Slang*, p. 40, 2004

jammie *noun*

a party with loud music *US*
A variation of 'jam'.
- —Lois Stavsky et al., *A2Z*, p. 56, 1995

jammies *noun*

pyjamas *US, 1967*
- I'll bet it takes you longer to get into your jammies at night than it does to throw on that blue suit[.]—Joseph Wambaugh, *The New Centurions*, p. 52, 1970
- A dinner jacket! Wuddya think, he was wearing his damn jammies! — *Raising Arizona*, 1987
- And I in my jammies with the holes in the toes / had just sipped my latte and started to doze.— *Seattle Times*, p. A14, 25th December 1992
- It might be a matter of waiting until you hear that familiar rumble coming down the street, then running out in your puka shirt jammies with 10 bucks in an envelope to give to the driver.— *Honolulu Advertiser*, p. 1B, 30th December 2003

jamming; jammin' *adjective*

excellent *US*
- —Douglas Simonson, *Pidgin to da Max Hana Hou*, 1982
- —Connie Eble (Editor), *UNC-CH Campus Slang*, p. 5, Spring 1982
- [R]ock concerts have long past stopped being groovy or rockin' and have now officially reached the realm of jammin' good.— *The Times of India*, 30th September 2002

jammy *noun*

the penis *US*
- —Anna Scotti and Paul Young, *Buzzwords*, p. 23, 1997

▷ **see:** JEMMY

jammy *adjective*

exceedingly lucky, fortunate; profitable *UK, 1915*
Jam has long been seen as a luxury, hence phrases like **JAM ON IT** (something pleasant) and a general sense that possession of jam is a definition of luck or prosperity.
- BEN: [shouting from cell] You lucky bastards! You lucky, jammy bastards!—Monty Python, *Life of Brian*, 1979
- [H]ow jammy and fake and clueless they are.—Kevin Sampson, *Powder*, p. 127, 1999
- Your kids would have an easier life than you, jammy sods[.]—Mark Steel, *Reasons to be Cheerful*, p. 3, 2001

jammy dodger *verb*

from the male perspective, to have sex *UK*
Rhyming slang for **ROGER** (to have sex), formed from the brand name of a popular biscuit. The noun is 'a jammy dodgering'.
- —Ray Puxley, *Fresh Rabbit*, 1998

jammy-jams; jam-jams *noun*

pyjamas *US*
- If you got her kitty outfit off, you might as well've put her jammy-jams on, she was through for the evening.—Elmore Leonard, *Swag*, p. 137, 1976
- Now you caught me in my jam-jams.—Joseph Wambaugh, *The Secrets of Harry Bright*, p. 247, 1985

jamoke *noun*

1 a despicable or ignorant person *US, 1946*
- I don't rate your chances none too good if that jamoke's going to defend you at trial in a court of law and all that stuff.—George V. Higgins, *The Rat on Fire*, p. 18, 1981
- When he had calmed down, Mazilli nodded in the direction that Touhey had gone. "Fuckin' jamoke," he said.—Richard Price, *Clockers*, p. 104, 1992
- And the poor jamoke's T-shirt keeps threatening to soak up this nasty fluid.—Anthony Petkovich, *The X Factory*, p. 195, 1997

2 coffee *US, 1895*
- —Jerry Robertson, *Oil Slanguage*, p. 72, 1954
- [L]ike Dixon, who is able to sip the most degradedly awful pos's-end poison and yet beam like an Idiot, "Mm-m m! Best Jamoke west o' the Alleghenies!"—Thomas Pynchon, *Mason & Dixon*, p. 467, 1997

jam on it *noun*

an agreeable surplus or an enhancement; a cause of extra satisfaction *UK, 1919*
- So secure are these voters in Labour's continuing power that they think they can afford fun and jam on it too.— *The Guardian*, 3rd May 2000

jam pail curling *noun*

in the Canadian prairies, curling with cement poured into old jam pails as curling stones *CANADA*
- On river ice, flooded back yards, or just the naturally icy roads, what jam pail curling lacks in finesse it makes up for in enthusiasm and fun.—Chris Thain, *Cold as a Bay Street Banker's Heart*, p. 92, 1987

jampot *noun*

in homosexual usage, the anus and rectum *US, 1941*
- — *Male Swinger Number 3*, p. 47, 1981: 'The complete gay dictionary'

jam rag *noun*

a sanitary towel *UK, 1966*
Plays on conventional 'jam' (to block) and the conventional colour of jam, red, for the menstrual blood, with 'rag' for the materials involved.
- It was worse than that scene in Carrie where Sissy Spacek gets bombarded with jam rags, thought Anna.—Jenny Eclair, *Camberwell Beauty*, p. 197–198, 2000
- [A]dverts on the telly for jam rags and tammys and fings like dat[.] —Sacha Baron-Cohen *Da Gospel According to Ali G*, 2001

jam roll *noun*

1 unemployment benefit; any government office from which it is administrated *UK, 1992*
Rhyming slang for **THE DOLE**.
- I just go'a sort my jam roll. Nood signin'?—Nick Barlay, *Curvy Lovebox*, p. 83, 1997

2 a fool; a despised person *UK*
Rhyming slang for **ARSEHOLE**.
- Anyone with any sense knows that all jazz musicians are jam rolls. —Bodmin Dark, *Dirty Cockney Rhyming Slang*, 2003

3 parole *UK, 1995*
Rhyming slang. Shortened to 'jam'.
- —Angela Devlin, *Prison Patter*, p. 66, 1996
- Getting a five, and with a drop of jam-roll getting out in three, is as much as I can get my head round[.]—J.J. Connolly, *Layer Cake*, p. 241, 2000
- "I saved the guy's life," he insists, brandishing the card under uninterested noses. "Surely that makes jam worth hoping for?"— *The Guardian*, 2nd March 2000: 'A life inside'

jams *noun*

1 pyjamas *US, 1973*
- "Oh, hi, Nick," said Dwayne, exhibiting everything except embarrassment. "Whatcha got those 'jams on for?"—C.D. Payne, *Youth in Revolt*, p. 272, 1993

2 trousers *US*
- —Collin Baker et al., *College Undergraduate Slang Study Conducted at Brown University*, p. 144, 1968

3 bright, long, multi-coloured swimming trunks *AUSTRALIA, 1966*
- —Jim Allen, *Locked in Surfing for Life*, p. 194, 1970

jam sandwich *noun*
a police car *UK*
JAM-JAR (a car), plus visual metaphor.
- [J]am sandwich[...] white police car with red stripe—Peter Chippindale, *The British CB Book*, p. 156, 1981
- —Angela Devlin, *Prison Patter*, p. 66, 1996
- We were just heading for some bright lights in the distance, with all the money in our pockets, when a jam sandwich pulled up beside us[.]—Lenny McLean, *The Guv'nor*, p. 22, 1998

jam session *noun*
1 a gathering of musicians who play in a collective, improvised fashion *US, 1933*
- —Lou Shelly, *Hepcats Jive Talk Dictionary*, p. 26, 1945
- I think the term "jam session" originated right in that cellar. Long before that, of course, the colored boys used to get together and play for kicks, but those were mostly private sessions, strictly for professional musicians[.]—Mezz Mezzrow, *Really the Blues*, p. 148, 1946
- I'm arranging a jam session to make an album for Jerry Newman's record company, with Allen Eager on tenor[.]—Jack Kerouac, *Letter to Neal Cassady*, p. 471, April 1955
- It is probable that the elongated Mexico was the father of what today is known as the jam session.—Robert Sylvester, *No Cover Charge*, p. 48, 1956
- [M]usicians would come to some prearranged Harlem after-hours spot and have thirty- and forty-piece jam sessions that would last into the next day.—Malcolm X and Alex Haley, *The Autobiography of Malcolm X*, p. 83, 1964

2 an informal, unstructured group discussion *US*
- Would you want your mother hanging around one of your jam sessions?—Dick Clark, *To Goof or Not to Goof*, p. 113, 1963

jam tart *noun*
1 heart *UK*
Rhyming slang.
- I wish you a happy New Year. My jam tart goes with you all.—Ronnie Barker, *Fletcher's Book of Rhyming Slang*, p. 39, 1979
- [W]e English take considerable jam tart from the repose of our gaffs.—Andrew Nickolds, *Back to Basics*, p. 25, 1994

2 a girlfriend; hence (patronisingly) a young woman *UK, 1960*
Often simplified to 'jam'. Simple rhyming slang for 'sweetheart'; however when used more generally it may also be an elaboration of **TART** (a young woman, especially of easy morals).
- By cripes, I'll feature with this jam tart or I'll bust me flamin' boiler. —Barry Humphries, *The Wonderful World of Barry McKenzie*, 1968
- [W]henever I see a decent jam tart with a good set of top bollocks I'm in like Flynn, NO PROBS!—Barry Humphries, *Bazz Pulls It Off!*, 1971
- In the upstairs corridor of Racecourse Annie's number one bawdy house, jam tart Joylene led farmer Joe past a tattooed, muscular looking man[.]—Lance Peters, *The Dirty Half-Mile*, p. 198, 1979
- [U]nwilling to tolerate the public insults to his sister, unwilling to endure taunts of "Bloater", of "Fat Jam"[.]—Mark Powell, *Snap*, p. 99, 2001

jam up *verb*
1 to cause trouble; to place in a troubling situation *US, 1836*
- He took a job. And he fumbled it. Now he's jammed up. Jammed up bad.—*Gone in 60 Seconds*, 2000

2 to confront *US*
- —William K. Bentley and James M. Corbett, *Prison Slang*, p. 93, 1992

jam-up *adjective*
1 excellent, pleasing *US, 1823*
- It made my smeller tingle, got me scared and excited me too, put me on edge – it promised a rare jam-up kick, some once-in-a-lifetime thrill.—Mezz Mezzrow, *Really the Blues*, p. 97, 1946
- It was jam-up. Jelly-tight. It was, it was a really a kick joint.—Bruce Jackson, *In the Life*, p. 122, 1972

2 in pool, playing well and luckily *US*
- —Steve Rushin, *Pool Cool*, p. 17, 1990

jam week *noun*
the bleed period of the menstrual cycle *UK*
- —*The FHM Little Book of Bloke*, p. 69, June 2003: 'JAM WEEK ESSENTIALS'

jandals *noun*
rubber sandals *NEW ZEALAND*
- —Louis S. Leland, *A Personal Kiwi-Yankee Dictionary*, p. 55, 1984

Jane; jane *noun*
1 a public toilet for women *US*
Playing on **JOHN** (a toilet).
- —Connie Eble (Editor), *UNC-CH Campus Slang*, p. 5, April 1997

2 marijuana *UK*
- My sweet Lady Jane/When I see you again/Your servant am I/And will humbly remain[.]—The Rolling Stones, *Lady Jane*, 1966
- Sweet Jane, Sweet[.]—Lou Reed (performed by the Velvet Underground), *Sweet Jane*, 1970
- —Mike Haskins, *Drugs*, p. 288, 2003

3 a woman, a girlfriend *US, 1865*
Generic use of popular name. Also 'Janie'.
- In the old days when Nolan's dance hall was here on the corner, every decent-looking jane who came to the Sunday-afternoon dances was gone on him.—James T. Farrell, *Saturday Night*, p. 30, 1947
- One of the sights of Washington is the outpouring of the janes at five o'clock.—Jack Lait and Lee Mortimer, *Washington Confidential*, p. 78, 1951
- Come here little Queenie... or ah / Has the cat got your tongue? My best shot for a C note baby she said / That's why this Janie's got a gun—Aerosmith *Black Cherry*, 1973

Jane, please, not in front of the men!
used for expressing disapproval of a public display of affection *US*
A signature line of Captain Wilton Parmenter to Jane Angelic Thrift on the television comedy *F Troop* (ABC, 1965–67). Repeated with referential humour.

Janet Street-Porter; Janet *noun*
a quarter (¼ oz measure of marijuana) *UK*
Rhyming slang, formed from the name of a well-known broadcaster and journalist.
- —Ray Puxley, *Fresh Rabbit*, 1998

Jane Wayne Day *noun*
a day on which wives of US Marines go through a series of exercises designed to give them a sense of what their husbands go through *US*
- Shanna Reed got a major workout for tonight's Major Dad when her character, Polly, joins other Marine wives in Jane Wayne Day.—*USA Today*, 23rd October 1989

jang *noun*
the penis *US*
- —Helen Dahlskog (Editor), *A Dictionary of Contemporary and Colloquial Usage*, p. 34, 1972

janglers *noun*
▸ **take the janglers**
to become upset *IRELAND*
- She took the janglers when she got the smell of drink off him. —Terence Dolan, *A Dictionary of Hiberno-English*, p. 283, 1999

janglies *noun*
in caving and pot-holing, assorted pieces of single-rope-technique (SRT) metallic equipment *UK*
Echoic.
- —David Morrison of Wessex Cave Club, 29th February 2004

Jan Hammered; Jan'd *adjective*
drunk *UK*
An elaboration of **HAMMERED** (drunk), playing on the name of Czech born jazz keyboardist Jan Hammer (b.1948).
- —*e-cyclopaedia*, 20th March 2002

janitor *noun*
an ordinary infantry soldier *US*
Gulf war usage.
- —*American Speech*, p. 392, Winter 1991: 'Among the new words'

jank *verb*
to steal *US*
- —Rick Ayers (Editor), *Slang Dictionary*, p. 11, 2001

jankers *noun*
confinement to barracks (as a military punishment) *UK, 1916*
- He was always getting into trouble, finding himself consigned to jankers or even on occasion the glass-house.—Ian Rankin, *Black and Blue*, p. 361, 1997

jankity *adjective*
old, broken down *US*
- — Rick Ayers (Editor), *Berkeley High Slang Dictionary*, p. 28, 2004

janky *adjective*
broken, dysfunctional, inoperative *US*
- Janky (adj.) – Cheap, raggedy or just improper in some sort of way. — *Corpus Christi (Texas) Caller-Times*, p. H1, 24th October 1999
- — *Ebony Magazine*, p. 156, August 2000: 'How to Talk to the New Generation'
- — Chris Lewis, *The Dictionary of Playground Slang*, p. 123, 2003

janner *noun*
1 a West Countryman *UK, 1984*
Originally restricted to someone with a Devon burr.
2 a member of a southwest England subcultural urban adolescent grouping defined by a hip-hop dress and jewellery sense (and an urge to act older than their years) *UK, 2004*
By extension of the previous sense.

janny talk *noun*
the speech of a mummer, distorted to conceal identity *CANADA*
'Janny' is a variant of 'John,' as in 'John Jacks', listed by the *English Dialect Dictionary* as a common name in England for mummers.
- When the janneys come to a house they wish to visit, they open, without knocking, the storm-door, stick their heads inside and sing out 'Any janneys in tonight?' in the high-pitched, squeaky voice that janneys always use–janney-talk. — *Christmas Mumming in Newfoundland*, p. 211, 1969

Jap *noun*
1 a Japanese person *US, 1854*
Derogatory.
- Jack, the guy who said he'd give his right arm for a friend and did when he stopped a bastard of a Jap from slitting me in two. — Mickey Spillane, *I, The Jury*, p. 5, 1947
- But then came the influx of Japs from the West Coast states. — Jack Lait and Lee Mortimer, *New York Confidential*, p. 77–78, 1948
- I wished I were a Denver Mexican, or even a poor overworked Jap, anything but what I was[.] — Jack Kerouac, *On the Road*, p. 180, 1957
- Do not use to describe a Japanese person or Japanese-American. — Multicultural Management Program Fellows, *Dictionary of Cautionary Words and Phrases*, 1989
- And I even liked the Japs. Whenever you waved to them they'd bow a little bit. — Joseph Wambaugh, *Floaters*, p. 98, 1996
- Japs, Yanks, Krauts, Aussies – you name it, we robbed them. — Kevin Sampson, *Outlaws*, p. 7, 2001

2 someone who attacks from behind and/or without warning *US*
- But if you're a Jap or a turkey or you're going to punk out it's going to be bad stuff for you. — Hal Ellson, *Duke*, p. 31, 1949

3 an unannounced test *US, 1967*
- — Collin Baker et al., *College Undergraduate Slang Study Conducted at Brown University*, p. 144, 1968

JAP *noun*
a spoiled Jewish girl or woman; a *J*ewish-*A*merican *p*rincess *US, 1972*
The term was wildly popular in the early 1980s, with the expected onslaught of joke books, J.A.P. handbooks, etc.
- The resident chaplain is a shy rabbi, one of the sexually active girls describes herself smugly as a Jewish American Princess and remnants of excruciating ethnic humor litter the comic junkheap. THe parents of the J.A.P. are exploited for kneejerk ridicule [.] — *Washington Post*, p. D4, 26th May 1980
- — *Maledicta*, p. 99–100, Summer/Winter 1981: 'Acrimonious acroynyms for ethnic groups'
- Trent stops by and tells me about how "a couple of hystserial J.a.p.'s" in Bel Air have seen what they called some kind of monster, talk of a werewolf. — Bret Easton Ellis, *Less Than Zero*, p. 77, 1985
- Q:What do J.A.P.'s most often make for dinner? A: Reservations. — Leo Rosten, *The Joys of Yinglish*, p. 250, 1989
- I was raised in the good life, destined for JAPhood – the coddled existence of a Jewish American Princess. — Cleo Odzer, *Goa Freaks*, p. 10, 1995
- "As long as you actually know what it's like to be offended by terms like J.A.P.," reasons Traig, "I think it's okay to say them." — *East Bay Express (California)*, 27th March 2002

jap *verb*
to attack without warning *US, 1942*
An allusion to the Japanese attack at Pearl Habor.
- They going to Jap us if they get the chance, only we ain't going to let them. — Hal Ellson, *Duke*, p. 76, 1949
- [O]ne side or another may at any sudden moment "jap" an unwary alien. — Harrison E. Salisbury, *The Shook-up Generation*, p. 23, 1958
- "Look out, ya gonna get japped," she shouted. — Piri Thomas, *Down These Mean Streets*, p. 53, 1967

Jap *adjective*
Japanese *US, 1869*
Unkind.
- It was that crazy, wild-eyed, unleashed hatred that the first Jap bomb on Pearl Harbour let loose in a flood. — Chester Himes, *If He Hollers Let Him Go*, p. 4, 1945

Japanese beetle *noun*
any small, Japanese-made car *US*
Punning on the insect and the Volkswagen.
- — Wayne Floyd, *Jason's Authentic Dictionary of CB Slang*, p. 19, 1976

Japanese safety boots *noun*
rubber flip-flops (footwear) *AUSTRALIA*
- I see you wear Japanese safety boots. — *Wordmap (www.abc.net.au/wordmap)*, 2003

Japanglish *noun*
a blend of Japanese and English spoken in Japan *UK*
A variation of conventional 'Japlish'.
- Could 'Japanglish' be a legitimate language? — *The Guardian*, 1st May 2001

Jap crap *noun*
imports from Japan, especially motorcycles *US*
- His shop, Kicked Back Motor Works, is a mama-and-pop operation, where he and Sandy repair and rebuild Harleys and only Harleys. "No Jap Crap," reads his business card. — *People*, p. 82, 4th August 1986
- Epithets such as "rice burner," and "Jap crap" are frequent. — *Orlando Sentinel Tribune*, p. A1, 28th February 1993
- — James Lambert, *The Macquarie Book of Slang*, p. 129, 1996
- — David McGill, *David McGill's Complete Kiwi Slang Dictionary*, p. 72, 1998

Jap cunt *adjective*
Japanese; a Japanese *UK*
Deliberately offensive combination of **JAP** (Japanese) and **CUNT** (someone or something unpleasant).
- [T]ried working for one of those japcunt factories cos there's nowt else to do[.] — Patrick Jones, *Everything Must Go*, p. 145, 2000

Jap hash *noun*
chop suey or chow mein *US*
- — *Maledicta*, p. 164, 1979: 'A glossary of ethnic slurs in American English'

japie; jaapie; jarpie; yarpie *noun*
1 an Afrikaner *SOUTH AFRICA, 1949*
Contemptuous; derived from Jaap a diminutive of the Afrikaans name Jakob.
- — Jean Branford, *A Dictionary of South African English*, 1978

2 a South African *SOUTH AFRICA, 1956*
May be jocular, contemptuous or affectionate.
- — Penny Silva, *A Dictionary of South African English*, 1996

3 an unsophisticated person, especially one from a rural area *SOUTH AFRICA, 1964*
Patronising if not offensive.
- — Penny Silva, *A Dictionary of South African English*, 1996

Jap on Anzac Day *noun*
a person to whom you would wish ill luck *AUSTRALIA*
Australians fought against the Japanese in World War 2, and Anzac Day is a national holiday commemorating Australian service men and women.
- 'Hey, love. You wouldn't give this to a Jap on Anzac Day.' 'Well, you can't bring it back, you already bit it.' — *Starstruck*, 1982
- Bloody Wollongong. Fair dinkum – you wouldn't send a Jap there on Anzac Day. — Robert G. Barrett, *Davo's Little Something*, p. 37, 1992

Japper *noun*
a motorcycle manufactured in Japan *AUSTRALIA*
- — James Lambert, *The Macquarie Book of Slang*, 1996

jap scrap *noun*
a motorcyle manufactured in Japan *US*
- — Connie Eble (Editor), *UNC-CH Campus Slang*, p. 6, Spring 1988
- — Paladin Press, *Inside Look at Outlaw Motorcyle Gangs*, p. 36, 1992

Jap's eye; japper *noun*
the opening in the glans of the penis *UK*
From the resemblance in shape to the racial stereotype.
- Make sure u has not bought salty popcorn coz dey will sting your japseye. — Sacha Baron-Cohen, *Da Gospel According to Ali G*, p. 103, 2001
- [S]he was surprised that me japper wasn't sideways. — Niall Griffiths, *Kelly + Victor*, p. 58, 2002
- I went through the whole spatula up the jap's eye treatment etc. — Richard Herring, *Talking Cock*, p. 202, 2003
- The Japanese refer to the Jap's Eye as "The German's Mouth", because it never smiles. — *Popbitch*, 30th September 2004

Jap-slapper *noun*
a martial artist *UK*
A reference to the Japanese who invented or developed so many of the recognised disciplines.
- [H]e was a fellow jap-slapper of Mick's. — Andy McNab (writing of the late 1970s/early 80s), *Immediate Action*, p. 161, 1995

Jap-slapping *noun*
the martial arts of unarmed combat *UK*
- In conjunction with the pistol, we learned unarmed combat – or, as some called it, jap-slapping. — Andy McNab (writing of the late 1970s/early 80s), *Immediate Action*, p. 151, 1995

Jap-slaps *noun*
a sandal that is not bound to the foot, usually worn around swimming pools or at the beach *US*
Hawaiian youth usage.
- — Douglas Simonson, *Pidgin to da Max Hana Hou*, 1982

jar *noun*
1 a glass of beer *UK, 1925*
Originally Lincolnshire dialect.
- I know you think he's stopped off for a jar, but it's just as likely he's been kept at a job. — Troy Kennedy Martin, *Z Cars*, p. 61, 1962
- 'A couple of jars of the old nut brown,' he ordered. — John Wynnum, *Jiggin' in the Riggin*, p. 37, 1965
- Cripes, I've had a real cow of a day, as regards the odd ice cold jar. — Barry Humphries, *The Wonderful World of Barry McKenzie*, p. 7, 1968
- I had me a jar in Flanagan's bar[.] — Niall Griffiths, *Kelly + Victor*, p. 42, 2002

2 any dark-skinned person *NEW ZEALAND, 1997*
Prison usage.
- — Harry Orsman, *A Dictionary of Modern New Zealand Slang*, p. 71, 1999

jar *verb*
▸ **jar the deck**
to wake up and get up *US*
- — *American Speech*, p. 288, December 1962: 'Marine Corps slang'

jar *adjective*
(of jewellery) fake *UK*
Abbreviated from **JARGOON**.
- The tom [jewellery] was all jar. The pussies [fur] had the moth. — Charles Raven, *Underworld Nights*, p. 56, 1956

jar dealer *noun*
a drug dealer who sells pills in large quantities *US*
- — Edward R. Bloomquist, *Marijuana*, p. 343, 1971

jarg *adjective*
fake *UK*
From **JARGOON** (fake jewellery).
- Drought's usually good for any jarg gear like that that's knocking around. — Kevin Sampson, *Outlaws*, p. 82, 2001

jargon *noun*
confusion *US*
- — Rick Ayers (Editor), *Slang Dictionary*, p. 11, 2001

jargoon; jar *noun*
an item of replica jewellery with less value than the original; counterfeit or paste-jewellery used in confidence tricks *UK*
From conventional 'jargoon' (a type of zircon).
- [A] white sapphire or zircon in place of a diamond. This is known as a jargoon. [...] A really first-rate jargoon is indistinguishable at a glance from a genuine groin [a ring][.] — Charles Raven, *Underworld Nights*, p. 64, 1956

jarhead *noun*
1 a US Marine *US, 1943*
Originally an army mule, then a member of the US Army, especially a member of the football team (1931).
- — *American Speech*, p. 288, December 1962: 'Marine Corps slang'
- The jar-heads were there for three days playing war. — Darryl Ponicsan, *The Last Detail*, p. 15, 1970
- "I hear there're so many fruit marines being busted, the jarheads at Camp Pendleton are afraid to be seen eating a banana," said Ranatti. — Joseph Wambaugh, *The New Centurions*, p. 178, 1970

2 a habitual user of crack cocaine *US*
- — Peter Johnson, *Dictionary of Street Alcohol and Drug Terms*, p. 101, 1993

jark *verb*
to 'neutralise' a weapon by planting a transmitter *UK*
Military; probably from the obsolete sense as 'a pass guaranteeing safe conduct'.
- [T]he weapon would have been dug up by an SAS team, bugged for tracing purposes and rendered harmless – "jarked" in special forces parlance[.] — Chris Ryan, *The Watchman*, p. 134, 2001

jarking *noun*
the act of 'neutralising' a weapon by planting transmitters *UK*
Military.
- "Jarking", the planting of miniature transmitters inside weapons, more correctly known as "technical attack", had started in the late seventies[.] — Andy McNab, *Immediate Action*, p. 277, 1995

jarmies *noun*
pyjamas *NEW ZEALAND*
- Twenty years of marriage suggests things most people just dream of comfortably enjoying in middle age: winceyette nighties and matching jarmies, hot water bottles and watching telly in bed. — *Sunday Star-Times*, p. A9, 11th November 2001

jarms *noun*
pyjamas *AUSTRALIA*
- You'll be pleased to hear I'm wearing a clean change of jarms. — Barry Humphries, *A Nice Night's Entertainment*, p. 132, 1971
- — Barry Humphries, *A Nice Night's Entertainment*, p. 207, 1981

jar of jam *noun*
a pram *UK*
Rhyming slang. The earlier sense as 'tram' is now obsolete.
- — Ray Puxley, *Cockney Rabbit*, 1992

jarpie *noun*
▷ see: **JAPIE**

jar pot *noun*
marijuana that is so potent that it must be stored in a pot or airtight jar to contain the smell *US*
- — Connie Eble (Editor), *UNC-CH Campus Slang*, p. 5, Spring 1992

jarrah-jerker *noun*
in Western Australia, a bush worker, especially a logger *AUSTRALIA, 1965*
Jarrah is a type of Australian native tree.
- — Jim Ramsay, *Cop It Sweet!*, p. 49, 1977

jarred up *adjective*
drunk *UK: SCOTLAND*
After **JAR** (a glass of beer).
- It's a waste a time gettin jarred up before the gemme. — Michael Munro, *The Patter, Another Blast*, p. 37, 1988

J. Arthur Rank; J. Arthur *noun*
1 an act of masturbation; a masturbator *UK, 1980*
Rhyming slang for **WANK**, based on the name of UK cinema tycoon Lord Rank (1888–1972).
- You turned up, signed a few forms. Then, a quick indulgence in a bit of a J. Arthur Rank, and hey presto, there you were fresh, relaxed, glowing with satisfaction, ten quid richer, sharing a post-coital cigarette with yourself. — Joseph O'Connor, *The the Irish Male at Home and Abroad*, p. 99, 1996
- Danny was reduced to having a J Arthur in the marital bed[.] — Jenny Eclair, *Camberwell Beauty*, p. 223, 2000

2 a bank *UK, 1977*
Rhyming slang, based on the name of film millionaire Joseph Arthur Rank (1888–1972). Sometimes shortened to the simple 'Arthur'.

jasper *noun*
1 a lesbian or a bisexual woman *US, 1954*
Robert Wilson hypothesises that the Reverend John Jasper, a pious man of God, lent his name in this good-is-bad etymology.
- 2 got seriously hurt and a jasper cut 1 on the arm with a bottle. — Clarence Cooper Jr, *The Farm*, p. 139, 1967

- Eventually, the craftier of the two jaspers wore the doll down and turned her out. They had to keep the secret of their romance from the other jasper because she was tough and built like a football player. —Iceberg Slim (Robert Beck), *Pimp*, p. 44, 1969
- —Robert A. Wilson, *Playboy's Book of Forbidden Words*, p. 149, 1972
- She was a three-way wench, played Jasper in a pinch / And took 'em around the horn. —Dennis Wepman et al., *The Life*, p. 81, 1976
- One jasper even cut another one over me! —Clarence Major, *All-Night Visitors*, p. 212, 1998

2 **a person of no consequence** *UK, 1896*
From a stereotypical rural name.
- A week later I received a letter from some fuck head called "Lon" of Research and man, like this jasper really poured the shit out thick. —*Screw*, p. 13, 27th June 1969
- Dot is just as cold, or colder, than any jasper we could put on the case. —Donald Goines, *Black Gangster*, p. 124, 1977

jasper broad *noun*
a lesbian or bisexual woman *US*
- You ever hear of what they call a "jasper broad?" That iss one who is bisexual, she likes both men and women. —Bruce Jackson, *In the Life*, p. 178, 1972

Jasper Carrot *noun*
a parrot *UK*
Rhyming slang, formed from the name of a popular Birmingham-born comedian.
- —Ray Puxley, *Fresh Rabbit*, 1998

Jatz crackers *noun*
the testicles *AUSTRALIA*
Rhyming slang for **KNACKERS**. From the name of a brand of savoury cracker.
- Some fans might remember it as the match in which Sri Lankan opener Mahanama collected two vicious blows to the 'Jatz Crackers'. —Rod Marsh, *Two For The Road*, p. 57, 1992

jaul *noun*
▷ see: **JOL**

jaunt *noun*
in horse racing, a race, especially an unimportant one *US*
- —David W. Maurer, *Argot of the Racetrack*, p. 38, 1951

java *noun*
coffee *US, 1850*
- They duck out for smokes at the same time and have their crullers and java in the same lunchroom or greasy spoon. —Jack Lait and Lee Mortimer, *New York Confidential*, p. 142, 1948
- Right up the street under the el was an all-night hash joint, and what I needed was a couple mugs of good black java to bring me around. —Mickey Spillane, *My Gun is Quick*, p. 6, 1950
- Foxes young and old sitting on front porches and in back yards along with dogs, cats, chickens and ducks, eating boiled shrimp, chittterlings and drinking java[.] —Steve Cannon, *Groove, Bang, and Jive Around*, p. 154, 1969

java patrol *noun*
in trucking, a stop for coffee *US*
- —Mary Elting, *Trucks at Work*, 1946

jaw *verb*
1 **to talk, especially in an argumentative or scolding fashion** *UK, 1748*
- The boys were jawing in the office by the stove and the cash register[.] —Jack Kerouac, *Letter to Neal Cassady*, p. 296, 10th January 1951
- I figured you'd done all the jawing you had to do when I talked to you an hour or so ago. —Jim Thompson, *The Killer Inside*, p. 66, 1952
- It was a slow morning for my friend and we jawed around. —Clancy Sigal, *Going Away*, p. 165, 1961
- She kept jawing at me to go back, and her putting me down all the time was worse than the silence. —Nat Hentoff, *Jazz Country*, p. 37, 1965
- Several months passed before I drove by the Conqueror's favorite bar and decided to drop in and jaw a bit with him. —Iceberg Slim (Robert Beck), *The Naked Soul of Iceberg Slim*, p. 126, 1971
- He stared at the man's back as he took his place on the fringe of a circle of dudes arguing, jawing at each other, as usual. What else was there to do in the county jail, after the watery oatmeal, crusty toast, and slimy coffee? —Odie Hawkins, *Chicago Hustle*, p. 103, 1977

2 **in pool, to hit a ball that bounces off the sides of a pocket without dropping** *US*
- —Steve Rushin, *Pool Cool*, p. 17, 1990

jaw artist *noun*
a person skilled at the giving of oral sex *US*
- —Robert A. Wilson, *Playboy's Book of Forbidden Words*, p. 150, 1972

jawblock *verb*
to chat, to talk *US*
- I used to see Scarface around there and jawblock with him sometimes. —Mezz Mezzrow, *Really the Blues*, p. 24, 1946
- Leo was in no mood for jawblocking but he sat down anyhow. —Bernard Wolfe, *The Late Risers*, p. 242, 1954

jawbone *noun*
credit obtained by arguing for it *US, 1862*
- The mower parts would have been charged, or, in the language of the country, put on his jawbone. —Paul St. Pierre, *Breaking Smith's Quarter Horse*, p. 98, 1966

jawbone shack *noun*
on the railways, a small office in a switching yard *US*
- —Ramon Adams, *The Language of the Railroader*, p. 86, 1977

jaw dropper *noun*
a great surprise *CANADA*
- —Jack Chambers (Editor), *Slang Bag 93 (University of Toronto)*, p. 4, Winter 1993

jawfest *noun*
1 **a long, aimless conversation** *US, 1915*
- —Joseph E. Ragen and Charles Finston, *Inside the World's Toughest Prison*, p. 805, 1962: 'Penitentiary and underworld glossary'

2 **a prolonged session of oral sex** *US*
- —Dale Gordon, *The Dominion Sex Dictionary*, p. 93, 1967

jawflap *noun*
a gossip *US*
- First thing you know, that Steerman be back gettin us busy with one of those Village jawflaps make you feel like you sat through a bad double feature eatin sourballs. —George Mandel, *Flee the Angry Strangers*, p. 78, 1952

jaw-jack *verb*
to chatter loudly and with no purpose; hence, to talk on citizens' band radio *US, 1962*
- [J]aw jacking [...] talking on CB[.] —Peter Chippindale, *The British CB Book*, p. 156, 1981

jawl *verb*
▷ see: **JOL**

jaws *noun*
1 **the buttocks** *US*
- —Gary K. Farlow, *Prison-ese*, p. 34, 2002

2 **in dominoes, the 6–6 piece** *US*
- —Dominic Armanino, *Dominoes*, p. 17, 1959

▶ **case of the jaws**
a harsh reprimand *US*
- —Carl Fleischhauer, *A Glossary of Army Slang*, p. 27, 1968

jaws of Jewry *noun*
in Newfoundland, great risk or danger *CANADA*
- The schooner began to settle in the water and sink so the man went and got his Bible and began to read. The schooner settled back to normal and returned from the Jaws of Jewry. —G.M. Story, *oral citation in Dictionary of Newfoundland English*, p. 275, 1982

Jax *nickname*
Jacksonville, Florida *US, 1936*
Also known as 'The Cesspool of the South'.
- —Jim Crotty, *How to Talk American*, p. 113, 1997

jaxie *noun*
▷ see: **JACKSY**

jaxied *adjective*
drunk *UK*
Probably from **JACKSY** (the anus), thus a form of **ARSEHOLED** (drunk).
- —*e-cyclopaedia*, 20th March 2002

jay *noun*
1 **a bank** *US*
An abbreviation of **JUG** (a bank).
- —Hyman E. Goldin et al., *Dictionary of American Underworld Lingo*, p. 110, 1950

2 **a jungle** *NEW ZEALAND*
Vietnam war usage.
- —Harry Orsman, *A Dictionary of Modern New Zealand Slang*, p. 71, 1999

3 coffee *US*
Probably an abbreviation of **JAVA**.
- —Joseph E. Ragen and Charles Finston, *Inside the World's Toughest Prison*, p. 805, 1962: 'Penitentiary and underworld glossary'

Jay Kay *noun*
a take-away meal *UK, 2001*
Popney rhyming slang, based on singer Jay Kay (b.1969) of popular group Jamiroquai. Popney was contrived for *www.music365.co.uk*, an Internet music site.

jay-naked *adjective*
completely naked *US*
- I been taken for spook, wop, and one faggot (used to come to the door jay-naked when I was delivering clothes for a cleaner) said I was Armenian. —Edwin Torres, *Carlito's Way*, p. 19, 1975

jay neg *noun*
an older black person *TRINIDAD AND TOBAGO*
- —Lise Winer, *Dictionary of the English/Creole of Trinidad & Tobago*, 2003

Jayzus!; Jaysus!
a Hiberno-English pronunciation of 'Jesus', used as a blasphemous expletive *IRELAND*
- The guard assumed a gruff voice, said, 'Listen here to me, boy, for Jazus' sake,' and lectured me for ten minutes on the fine art of relieving oneself in public without giving scandal. —Hugh Leonard, *Out After Dark*, p. 95, 1989
- The man who spawned a litter-load of feline headlines and purr-fect puns is without doubt a consummate professional and gentleman, but jayzus, put in front of a microphone he's up there with Fine Gael in the sleep-inducing stakes; albeit, no doubt, with a better line in jokes. — *Munster Express*, 27th September 2002

jazz *noun*
1 nonsense *US, 1951*
- "Don't hand me that jazz," said the wolf impatiently. —Steve Allen, *Bop Fables*, p. 22, 1955
- No time, ain't got no time for all this jazz with Opal. —Sara Harris, *The Lords of Hell*, p. 51, 1967
- The lawyers stepped forward to cop pleas for another chance, mercy and all that jazz. —Piri Thomas, *Down These Mean Streets*, p. 246, 1967
- You hear a lot of jazz about Soul Food. —Eldridge Cleaver, *Soul on Ice*, p. 29, 1968

2 stuff *US*
- They want him to make the radio and the video and all that jazz – eh can't make all that jazz. —William "Lord" Buckley, *The Nazz*, 1951
- I could walk out this fuckin' store with half a shelf fulla this jazz if I wanted to. —Odie Hawkins, *Ghetto Sketches*, p. 125, 1972

3 semen *US, 1932*
- Momo wipes the jazz off Jasmin. —Anthony Petkovich, *The X Factory*, p. 190, 1997

4 heroin *CANADA*
- —Richard A. Spears, *The Slang and Jargon of Drugs and Drink*, p. 287, 1986

▸ **the jazz**
the general details (of something) *UK*
- [W]iggling their bodies in front of the DJ console... You know the jazz: fantastic! —Wayne Anthony, *Spanish Highs*, p. 156, 1999

jazz *verb*
1 to have sex with someone *US, 1918*
- I dont jazz cops. —Jim Thompson, *The Killer Inside*, p. 10, 1952
- Hey, Austin boy-ee-ee, let's jazz her. —John Clellon Holmes, *The Horn*, p. 110, 1958
- I say, Baby this daddy was not drinkin, he was on top a me, jazzin! —Robert Gover, *Here Goes Kitten*, p. 117, 1964
- So many girls will chase you, by appointment only, you'll be jazzing. —Iceberg Slim (Robert Beck), *Trick Baby*, p. 219, 1969
- De Boya does that to a spray-painter, what's he gonna do to a guy he finds out's been jazzing his wife, room one sixty-seven the Holiday Inn. —Elmore Leonard, *Cat Chaser*, p. 206, 1982

2 of a male, to orgasm *UK*
After **JAZZ** (semen).
- [S]o good I jazzed. So if you're listening, boys, you owe me a pair of boxers. — *Kerrang!*, p. 4, 28th August 2004

jazz about; jazz around *verb*
to cause trouble, to annoy *US, 1917*
- We don't want no jazzing around with them. —Hal Ellson, *Duke*, p. 81, 1949
- Don't you dare come jazzing about on our manor, or we'll have you good and proper. —John Peter Jones, *Feather Pluckers*, p. 60, 1964

jazzbo *noun*
a fervent jazz enthusiast *US, 1921*
- Though powerless to dispense club dates, the dopers has the power of youth, looks, exuberance, suicidal tendencies, and the PR edge of being hotshot jazzbos. —Larry Rivers, *What Did I Do?*, p. 22, 1992

jazz cigarette *noun*
a marijuana cigarette *UK*
- The "jazz cigarette" prevails on the very scene after which it's named[.] — *Drugs An Adult Guide*, p. 38, December 2001

jazzed *adjective*
excited, enthusiastic *US, 1918*
- I'm so fuckin' jazzed! — *Jerry Maguire*, 1996

jazzed-up *adjective*
revised and augmented, improved *US, C20*
- He won't be a distorted idol for all those teenagers ... filling their nights with jazzed-up sex dreams. —William Bast, *The Myth Makers [Six Granada Plays]*, p. 174, 1958

jazz joint *noun*
a brothel *US, 1927*
- — *Maledicta*, p. 148, Summer/Winter 1986–1987: 'Sexual slang: prostitutes, pedophiles, flagellators, transvestites, and necrophiles'

jazz nazi *noun*
a purist jazz fan *CANADA*
- "If you want to be what I call a jazz nazi, it's true we can be criticized. And what is jazz anyway? We wind up with all these hybrid styles of music that may not be jazz per se but are related and yet hold their own." Pure-bred or mongrel? He cares not. — *Montreal Gazette*, p. A4, 5th July 2002

jazz up *verb*
to modernise; to enliven; in a specialised sense, to convert classical music into pop *UK, 1984*
- Schlorship is vital and without their collections, museums would just be 'jazzed-up theme parks'. — *The Observer*, 21st July 2002

jazz Woodbine *noun*
a marijuana cigarette *UK*
A variation of **JAZZ CIGARETTE**; **WOODBINE** is a slang generic for 'a cheap cigarette'.
- —Tom Hibbert, *Rockspeak!*, p. 91, 1983
- They would sit in his music room having a few drinks and "jazz woodbines", and listening to records. —Jim Drury, *Ian Dury and the Blockheads – Song by Song*, p. 85, 2003

jazzy *adjective*
showy; ostentatious *US, 1923*
- We've got to go and get our hair done. Get henna'd up real jazzy for Connie boy. —Bernard Wolfe, *The Late Risers*, p. 132, 1954
- I could buy the jazziest board this side of the great divide. —Frederick Kohner, *Gidget*, p. 23, 1957
- [A] car park full of jazzy motors. —John Peter Jones, *Feather Pluckers*, p. 42, 1964
- I'm not wearing this outfit, it's a bit too jazzy for a funeral. —Caroline Aherne and Craig Cash, *The Royle Family*, 1999

JB *noun*
a person with 'jet black' skin *US, 1946*
- —Kenn "Naz" Young, *Naz's Underground Dictionary*, p. 40, 1973

J Bay *nickname*
Jeffrey's Bay, west of Port Elizabeth, South Africa *SOUTH AFRICA*
- —Trevor Cralle, *The Surfin'ary*, p. 60, 1991

J-bird *noun*
1 a person in or recently released from jail *US*
An abbreviation of **JAILBIRD**.
- —Eugene Landy, *The Underground Dictionary*, p. 112, 1971

2 in a deck of playing cards, a jack or knave *US*
An elaboration of **J**.
- — *American Speech*, p. 99, May 1951: 'The vocabulary of poker'
- —Albert H. Morehead, *The Complete Guide to Winning Poker*, p. 266, 1967

JBM *adjective*
in horse racing, said of a horse that has only won one race *US*
An abbreviation of '*j*ust *b*eaten *m*aiden'.
- —Tom Ainslie, *Ainslie's Complete Guide to Thoroughbred Racing*, p. 333, 1976

JB's *noun*
sandals, flip-flops *US*
An abbreviation of '*J*esus *b*oots'.

J Carroll Naish *noun*
an act of urination *UK*
Rhyming slang for **SLASH**, formed from the name of the US film actor, 1887–1973.
- —Ronnie Barker, *Fletcher's Book of Rhyming Slang*, 1979

J-cat *noun*
a person who is more crazy than eccentric *US*
- —Jim Crotty, *How to Talk American*, p. 353, 1997

J City *nickname*
Juarez, Mexico *US*
- — *Current Slang*, p. 20, Spring 1970

J C water-walkers *noun*
sandals *US*
An allusion to Jesus Christ (JC) walking on water, presumably in sandals.
- — *Current Slang*, p. 20, Spring 1970

JD *noun*
1 a juvenile delinquent *US, 1956*
- None of us wanted to be lawbreakers and we would have been shocked silly had anyone called us j.d.'s. —Dick Clark, *To Goof or Not to Goof*, p. 181, 1963
- Greasers. You know, like hoods. JD's. —S.E. Hinton, *The Outsiders*, p. 85, 1967
- Johnny Havilland has heard from the J.D.'s at school that an auto graveyard on the edge of Ossining niggertown is a chrome treasure trove. —James Ellroy, *Because the Night*, p. 514, 1984

2 Jack Daniels™, a brand name Tennessee sourmash whisky *US, 1981*
Initialism.
- [A] JD and Coke[.] — *GQ*, p. 68, July 2001
- Thanks. I'll have a JD and coke if you're buying. —Colin Butts, *Is Harry Still on the Boat?*, p. 227, 2003

JD card *noun*
a police citation issued to a transgressing juvenile, requiring participation in a Police Athletic League team to avoid incarceration *US*
- Cool Breeze lived somewhere in Harlem, and had gotten his JD card at about the same time as Kenny. —Emmett Grogan, *Ringolevio*, p. 13, 1972

Jean *noun*
a female customer of a prostitute *US*
An extrapolation of **JOHN**.
- No Jean or John this whore couldn't con / 'Cause that trick was never born. —Dennis Wepman et al., *The Life*, p. 81, 1976

Jean and Dinah *noun*
prostitutes *TRINIDAD AND TOBAGO, 1993*
- —Lise Winer, *Dictionary of the English/Creole of Trinidad & Tobago*, 2003

Jean-Claude Van Damme; Jean-Claude *noun*
ham *UK*
Rhyming slang, formed with cruel wit – **HAM** (to be a poor actor) – from the name of the Belgian film actor, also known as 'the muscles from Brussels' (b.1960).
- —Ray Puxley, *Fresh Rabbit*, 1998

jeans at half mast *noun*
engaged in the passive role in anal sex *US*
- —Hyman E. Goldin et al., *Dictionary of American Underworld Lingo*, p. 110, 1950

Jedi *noun*
a member of an exclusive and influential group *UK*
Based on a cast of characters created by George Lucas and introduced in the film *Star Wars*, 1977.
- But undoubtedly, behind all of these conspicuously undamaging responses were the subtle mind-tricks of Elspeth Doyle and the art of the New Labour Spin-Jedi. —Christopher Brookmyre, *Boiling a Frog*, p. 105, 2000

Jedi master *noun*
in the language of hang gliding, an experienced, expert flier *US*
- —Erik Fair, *California Thrill Sports*, p. 328, 1992

jee!
▷ see: **GEE!**

jeegee; jee gee *noun*
heroin *US, 1971*
Possibly plays on 'gee gee' (a horse) and **HORSE** (heroin).
- —Richard A. Spears, *The Slang and Jargon of Drugs and Drink*, p. 287, 1986
- —Robert Ashton, *This is Heroin*, 2002
- —Mike Haskins, *Drugs*, p. 284, 2003

jeely jar *noun*
a car *UK: SCOTLAND*
Glasgow rhyming slang.
- Is this the new jeely jar, eh? —Michael Munro, *The Patter, Another Blast*, 1988

jeep *noun*
an inexperienced enlisted man *US*
Air Force usage during the Vietnam war.
- — *Current Slang*, p. 16, Summer 1970

jeepers creepers!; jeepers!; creepers!
used as a mild oath *US, 1928*
A euphemism for 'Jesus Christ!'.
- "Wayne! Get down here." Oh creepers! I thought I was done for[.] —Wayne Anthony, *Spanish Highs*, p. 33, 1999
- —United Artists *Jeepers Creepers*, 2001
- "Jeepers," blurted Tanya, slightly more awake now. —Andrew Holmes, *Sleb*, p. 41, 2002

Jeep girl *noun*
a Chinese prostitute attached to US armed forces *US*
- — *American Speech*, p. 74, February 1946: 'Some words of war and peace from 1945'

jeer, jeercase *nouns*
▷ see: **JERE, JERECASE**

jeeter *noun*
a lieutenant *US, 1941*
- —Lou Shelly, *Hepcats Jive Talk Dictionary*, p. 46, 1945

jeez!; jeese!; geez!
used as a mild oath *US, 1830*
A euphemised 'Jesus'.
- Jeez! I could be up that like a rat up a drain! —Barry Humphries, *Bazza Pulls It Off!*, 1971
- Jeez, that's a nice name. —Edwin Torres, *Q & A*, p. 63, 1977
- Geez, on my prom night I went around this park five, six times. — *Manhattan*, 1979
- The nuns got off easy. Jeez. Cigarette burns. — *The Bad Lieutenant*, 1992
- VELMA: Oh man, I love this song. LUCY: Jeez, you love every song. — *Smoke Signals*, 1998
- Jeez, Warren, you know you're not supposed to leave the yard by yourself. — *Something About Mary*, 1998
- Bad enough I'd announced my wedding date, now I had it all planned out. A barbecue! Jeez! It was like I had no control over my mouth. —Janet Evanovich, *Seven Up*, p. 63–64, 2001
- – Let it go, Easty. – I can't fucking let it go! – Jeez, you've lost none of the blaze. —Mark Powell, *Snap*, p. 40, 2001

jeezan ages!; jeezan peas!; jeezan rice!
used for expressing shock and surprise *TRINIDAD AND TOBAGO, 1992*
Euphemisms for 'Jesus Christ!'.
- —Lise Winer, *Dictionary of the English/Creole of Trinidad & Tobago*, 2003

jeezer *noun*
a fellow *US, 1972*
- —John Gould, *Maine Lingo*, p. 146, 1975

Jeez Louise!
used as a mild oath *US*
- [J]eeze Louise, what a crazy notion. —Frederick Kohner, *Gidget*, p. 141, 1957

jeezly *adverb*
used as an all-purpose intensifier *US, 1885*
This variation on 'Jesus' is a staple of language in maritime Canada.
- I never saw such jeezly poor fishing! —John Gould, *Maine Lingo*, p. 146, 1975
- On one trip, we couldn't even drive 20 miles to the Halifax airport without the whole jeezly car filling up with putrid smoke. —Harry Bruce, *Movin' East*, Methuen 1985

Jeezo-groveler *noun*
a Christian *US*
Based on an unconventional diminutive of Jesus this is literally, if offensively, someone who kneels before Jesus.
- The revolutionaries who got this country [US] started were not [...] a bunch of wig-headed Jeezo-Grovelers, whimpering for guidance from The Unseen Hand. —Frank Zappa, *The Real Frank Zappa Book*, p. 313, 1989

Jeezuz!
used for expressing exasperation *UK*
An exaggeratedly stressed 'Jesus!'.
- How the fuck are people gonna take us seriously while our postal address is L fucken 60? The tenderloin or what, la? Jeezuz! —Kevin Sampson, *Powder*, p. 14, 1999

Jeff *noun*
1 an all-purpose name for a man *US*
- Don't be a bear and act like a square get with the jeffs that are going somewhere —Lavada Durst, *The Jives of Dr. Hepcat*, 1953

2 a white person, especially one who is hostile towards black people *US*
- Chalk the walking Jeffs. —Chester Himes, *The Real Cool Killers*, p. 120, 1959
- "The agent's a goddam guinea, just like the owner," Red charged. "Them Jeffs is workin' together." —Ross Russell, *The Sound*, p. 144, 1961

3 a dull individual, a pest *US, 1938*
Originally a shortened form of Jefferson Davis, the president of the Confederate States of America throughout its existence during the US Civil War, 1861–65. Afro-American slang remembered him as a southern white racist, and reduced him to the status of pest.

jeff *verb*
to behave obsequiously in the hope of winning approval *US*
- "Naturally," the saleslady said, doing what Masha Lee called "jeffing." —Clarence Cooper Jr, *The Scene*, p. 34, 1960
- Then he said, "Well kiss my dead mammy's ass, if it ain't Macking Youngblood. The whore's pet and the pimp's fret." The junkie bastard was jeffing on me[.] —Iceberg Slim (Robert Beck), *Pimp*, p. 63, 1969

Jeff *verb*
to lie or at least to exaggerate *US*
- —William K. Bentley and James M. Corbett, *Prison Slang*, p. 46, 1992

Jefferson airplane *noun*
a used match split to hold the butt of a partially smoked marijuana joint *US*
Many musicians take names from drugs slang, but the reverse happened here. Jefferson Airplane was a successful San Franciscan rock band associated with 1960s drugs culture and psychedelic culture. The name, a humorous coinage for an imaginary blues musician, Blind Thomas Jefferson Airplane, was first given to a dog; only later to an improvised **DOG END** holder.

jejo *noun*
▷ see: **YEYO**

Jekyll and Hyde; jekyll *noun*
a forgery, a fake *UK*
Rhyming slang, extended from the adjective sense of **SNIDE** (false, counterfeit, sham, bogus, etc.).
- A copied painting, a moody Rolex, a dodgy bank note. They're all "Jekylls". —Ray Puxley, *Cockney Rabbit*, 1992

Jekyll and Hyde; jekyll *adjective*
false, counterfeit, sham, bogus, two-faced *UK*
Rhyming slang for **SNIDE**; a neat pun formed from, and referring to the dual personality of the eponymous character in *The Strange Case of Dr Jekyll and Mr Hyde*, by Robert Louis Stevenson, 1886.
- —John Gosling, *The Ghost Squad*, 1959
- Cody's game was deception and he'd worked his way up from kiting, lying down Jekyll paper with a cheque card, through credit cards, and into something a whole lot more sophisticated. —J.J. Connolly, *Layer Cake*, p. 96, 2000

Jekyll and Hydes; jekylls *noun*
trousers *UK*
Rhyming slang for **STRIDES**.
- —Ray Puxley, *Cockney Rabbit*, 1992

jell *noun*
a person with few thoughts and no sense of fashion *US*
- —Sue Black, *The Totally Awesome Val guide*, p. 21, 1982

jell *verb*
to leave hastily, to escape *UK*
English gypsy use.
- Let's jell, bruv, before the gavvers [the police] come and we get loud [arrested]. —Jimmy Stockin, *On The Cobbles*, p. 67, 2000

jellied eel *noun*
a wheel *UK*
Rhyming slang.
- —Ray Puxley, *Cockney Rabbit*, 1992

jellied eel *verb*
to transport *UK*
Rhyming slang for 'wheel'.
- —Ray Puxley, *Cockney Rabbit*, 1992

jellied eels *noun*
a private vehicle *UK*
Rhyming slang for 'wheels'.
- "Have you got jellied eels?" means, have you got means of transport? —Ray Puxley, *Cockney Rabbit*, 1992

jellies *noun*
soft, plastic, apparently edible sandals *US*
- By employing another '90s tactic of loading a single item with as many styles as possible, the jelly evolved beyond the simple flat heel into a chunky high heel that was sometimes flecked with glitter. —Steven Daly and Nalthaniel Wice, *alt.culture*, p. 119, 1995

jello arms *noun*
in surfing, exhausted, rubbery arms from paddling *US*
- —Mitch McKissick, *Surf Lingo*, 1987

jelly *noun*
1 the vagina *US, 1926*
- The damage had already been done, and what was left just to be pure jelly. —Donald Goines, *The Busting Out of an Ordinary Man*, p. 19, 1985

2 sexual intercourse *US, 1926*
- "Nothin', ain't nothin' wrong" ... he answered her lamely, revving himself back up to a slow jelly, trying to come again. —Odie Hawkins, *Chicago Hustle*, p. 110, 1977

3 a sexually permissive female *UK, 1989*
- —Vincent J. Monteleone, *Criminal Slang*, p. 132, 1949

4 a capsule of Temazepam™, a branded tranquillizer; any central nervous system depressant; in the plural it refers to the drug in general *UK*
A term embraced by US youth after seeing the film *Trainspotting*.
- Its street name is JELLIES because in one of its forms it looks like gelatine jelly babies. —Macfarlane, Macfarlane and Robson, *The User*, p. 100, 1996
- —Connie Eble (Editor), *UNC-CH Campus Slang*, p. 4, Fall 1996
- I can do a trip [on LSD] or some jellies and it's just a quick trip to Disneyland y'know? —Shaun Ryder, *Shaun Ryder... in His Own Words*, 1997
- The jellies and the coke and the hash? I don't know if it's a great combination[.] —Stella Duffy, *Jail Bait [britpulp]*, p. 118, 1999
- Her dad [...] sleeps all day, lives on strong cider and pills; jellies to calm him down. —Cath Staincliffe, *Trainers*, p. 57, 1999

5 cocaine *UK, 1998*
- —Nick Constable, *This is Cocaine*, p. 181, 2002

▷ see: **GELLY**

jelly *verb*
to explode, especially with gelignite *UK*
- [I]t were fucking boss when they jellied the place. —Kevin Sampson, *Clubland*, p. 234, 2002

jelly *adjective*
excellent *UK*
From a song performed by Destiny's Child.

jelly baby *noun*
1 an expert in the use of gelignite *UK*
From the name of a popular sweet manufactured in the shape of a 'baby', extending 'jelly' (gelignite).
- —Angus Hall, *On the Run*, 1974

2 a tablet of Temazepam™, a branded tranquillizer *UK*
- Temazepam are called "green or yellow eggs", "jellies" and "jelly babies", "rugby balls" or "temazzies". —James Kay and Julian Cohen, *The Parents' Complete Guide to Young People and Drugs*, p. 150, 1998

3 an amphetamine tablet *US*
- —Eugene Landy, *The Underground Dictionary*, p. 112, 1971
- —Carl Chambers and Richard Heckman, *Employee Drug Abuse*, p. 206, 1972

jellybag *noun*

1 a condescending Englishman in the Canadian West *CANADA*

- The type of Englishman who looked down his nose at the strange beings in the colonies was considered to be worth no more than the contents of the jellybag after the jelly has been made – mushy garbage. — Chris Thain, *Cold as a Bay Street Banker's Heart*, p. 92 – 93, 1987

2 a large fuel cell made of rubber or plastic *US*
Vietnam war usage.

- — *Army Information Digest*, January 1965
- — Carl Fleischhauer, *A Glossary of Army Slang*, p. 27, 1968

3 a 1936 Chevrolet lowered in the rear *US, 1955*

- — *Maledicta*, p. 166, 1979: 'A glossary of ethnic slurs in American English'

jellybeans *noun*
crack cocaine *UK, 1998*

- — Mike Haskins, *Drugs*, p. 282, 2003

jelly belly *noun*
a fat person *UK, 1896*

- What a Jelly Belly I am! Why can't I get rid of this paunch? — Leil Lowndes, *How to be a People Magnet*, p. 55, 2001

jelly blubber *noun*
a jellyfish *AUSTRALIA, 1943*

- The only thing I ran over all day was a school of jelly blubbers. — Bob Staines, *Wot a Whopper*, p. 23, 1982

jellybone *noun*
a telephone *UK*
Rhyming slang, used by courier controllers.

- — Ray Puxley, *Cockney Rabbit*, 1992

jelly box *noun*
the vagina *AUSTRALIA*

- — James McDonald, *A Dictionary of Obscenity, Taboo and Euphemism*, p. 16, 1988

jelly doughnut; jelly donut *noun*
an overweight female Red Cross volunteer in Vietnam *US*

- — Linda Reinberg, *In the Field*, p. 116, 1991

jellyhash *noun*
an extremely potent variety of hashish produced in Holland *UK*

- — Nick Jones, *Spliffs*, p. 93, 2003

jellyhead *noun*
a habitual user of crack cocaine *UK*
Combines 'jelly', as in **JELLYBEANS** (crack cocaine) with **HEAD** (a user).

- [T]he lowest of the low. Skag-hags [heroin-users] and jellyheads, emaciated young girls[.] — Kevin Sampson, *Powder*, p. 55, 1999

jelly on the belly *noun*
semen ejaculated on a woman's stomach *AUSTRALIA*

- — Thommo, *The Dictionary of Australian Swearing and Sex Sayings*, p. 73, 1985

jelly roll *noun*

1 the vagina *US, 1914*

- Say now, if you don't believe my jellyroll is fine / ask Good-Cock Lulu, that's a bitch a mine. — Bruce Jackson, *Get Your Ass in the Water and Swim Like Me*, p. 139, 1964

2 a used tampon or sanitary towel *US*

- — Helen Dahlskog (Editor), *A Dictionary of Contemporary and Colloquial Usage*, p. 34, 1972

jelly sandwich *noun*
a sanitary towel *US*

- — Edith A. Folb, *runnin' down some lines*, p. 243, 1980

jelly tight *adjective*
excellent *US*

- It was jam-up. Jelly-tight. It was, it was a really a kick joint. — Bruce Jackson, *In the Life*, p. 122, 1972

jelly tot *noun*
a young boy who tries to act older than he is *US*
Teen slang.

- — *Newsweek*, p. 28, 8th October 1951

jemmy; jammy *noun*
a short crowbar used by burglars *UK, 1811*
Known in the US as a 'jimmy'.

- — Angela Devlin, *Prison Patter*, p. 66, 1996

jemmy *verb*
to force open with a short crowbar *UK, 1893*

- [T]wo days later he's jemmying open their French doors[.] — Danny King, *The Burglar Diaries*, p. 79, 2001

Jennifer Justice; Jennifer *noun*
a police officer; the police *UK*
An example of **CAMP** trans-gender assignment.

- — Paul Baker, *Polari*, p. 178, 2002

jenny *noun*

1 a fence-wire spinner *NEW ZEALAND*

- This well presented design for a jenny to handle either plain or barb wire on one-man fencing jobs comes from Wayne McDrury. — *New Zealand Farmer*, p. 73, 23rd February 1978

2 a merry-go-round *US*

- Terminology — Gene Sorrows, *All About Carnivals*, p. 20, 1985

3 in the television and film industries, a mobile source of direct current *UK*

- — Oswald Skilbeck, *ABC of Film and TV Working Terms*, p. 62, 1960

▷ **see: GENNY**

Jenny barn *noun*
the ward for women in a narcotic treatment hospital *US*

- — *American Speech*, p. 87, May 1955: 'Narcotic argot along the Mexican Border'

Jenny Hill; jenny *noun*
a pill *UK, 1937*
Rhyming slang, formed from the name of a music hall performer, 1851 – 96.

- — Ray Puxley, *Cockney Rabbit*, 1992

Jenny Lea; Jenny Lee *noun*

1 a key *UK, 1961*
Rhyming slang.

- — Ray Puxley, *Cockney Rabbit*, 1992

2 tea *UK*
Rhyming slang.

- Mum's making me Jenny Lee! — *The Sweeney*, p. 9, 1976

Jenny Lind *noun*
wind *UK*
Rhyming slang, used in reference both to the weather and bodily functions; formed from the name of a mid-C19 singer and cultural icon, popularly known as 'The Swedish Nightingale', 1820 – 87.

- — Ray Puxley, *Cockney Rabbit*, 1992

Jenny Riddle *noun*
an act of urination *UK*
Rhyming slang for **PIDDLE**; a variation/feminisation of the better known **JIMMY RIDDLE**.

- — Ray Puxley, *Fresh Rabbit*, 1998

Jenny Wren; jenny *noun*
Ben Truman™ beer *UK*
Rhyming slang.

- A pint of Jenny. — Ray Puxley, *Cockney Rabbit*, 1992

jere; jeer *noun*

1 the buttocks, the backside *UK, 1936*
Rhyming slang for 'rear'; informed by the earlier sense as 'turd'.

2 a turd *UK*

- — Patrick O'Shaughnessy, *Market Trader's Slang*, 1979

3 a male homosexual *UK*
Rhyming slang for **QUEER**, playing on the word's sense as 'buttocks'.

- — Julian Franklyn, *A Dictionary of Rhyming Slang*, 1961

jerecase; jeercase *noun*
the buttocks *UK*
An elaboration of **JERE; JEER**.

- I'm not going to lick his jeercase. — Patrick O'Shaughnessy, *Market Trader's Slang*, 1979

Jeremiah *noun*
a fire *UK, 1934*
Rhyming slang, especially among urban labourers; occasionally 'Obadiah'.

- [H]is daughter was sitting by the Jeremiah, on her favourite Lionel Blair [chair]. — Ronnie Barker, *Fletcher's Book of Rhyming Slang*, p. 27, 1979

Jeremied *adjective*
drunk *UK*
Probably in celebration of a man called Jeremy who may not even remember the reason why.
• — *e-cyclopaedia*, 20th March 2002

Jeremy Beadle *verb*
to irritate, to annoy, to provoke *UK*
Rhyming slang for **NEEDLE**, formed from the name of a television prankster (b.1949).
• — Ray Puxley, *Fresh Rabbit*, 1998

jerk *noun*
1 an idiot, a fool *US, 1919*
• VERONICA: Just give me a cup, jerk. — *Heathers*, 1988
2 in a gambling establishment, a hanger-on who runs errands for gamblers *US*
• — John Scarne, *Scarne's Guide to Modern Poker*, p. 282, 1979

jerk *verb*
to tow a disabled car home with the help of a neighbour *CANADA*
• A "jerk" is the horse-era version of a tow. The term may still be heard in rural areas, applied to the rescue of broken-down cars. — Chris Thain, *Cold as a Bay Street Banker's Heart*, p. 93, 1987

▸ **jerk the chicken**
of a male, to masturbate *UK*
• [A] final dash to my bedroom and it's a trawl through the pages as I jerk the chicken. Nearly four minutes later, it's all over! — *The FHM Little Book of Bloke*, p. 61, June 2003

▸ **jerk the gherkin**
of a male, to masturbate *UK*
• Perkins was furkin' jerkin' his gherkin — George Forwood, 1962
• [A] last tomato...a slice of ham...some sugar for the ants...couldn't make it to the goats...a last jerk of the gherkin...just in case...you never know...I'd like to die erect[.] — Jack Hibberd, *A Stretch of the Imagination*, p. 35, 1971
• [W]hile the other bastards are busy getting the dirty waters off their chests [having sex] a bloke like me runs the risk of goin' blind jerkin' the gerkin [sic]!!! — Barry Humphries, *Bazza Pulls It Off!*, 1971
• Spanking the monkey. Flogging the bishop. Choking the chicken. Jerking the gherkin. — *American Beauty*, 1999
• "The boy is masturbating" [...] Jerking the gerkin[.] — Erica Orloff and JoAnn Baker, *Dirty Little Secrets*, p. 65, 2001

▸ **jerk the turk; jerk your turkey**
of a male, to masturbate *UK*
It is said of a man's genitalia that when shaved it resembles 'a plucked turkey hanging in a shop' yet this appears to be a lone instance of a 'turkey' used as a 'penis'; 'turk', an abbreviation of 'turkey', is a convenient rhyme for 'jerk' which describes the physical action.

▸ **jerk your mutton**
to masturbate *UK*
'Mutton' (penis) dates from the C16 and is now obsolete except in uses such as this and 'mutton bayonet', 'mutton dagger'; 'mutton' (vagina) dates from the same period: subsequent usages are as 'a woman or women', 'a promiscuous woman', 'a prostitute' and the surviving 'mutton dressed as lamb'.

jerk around; jerk about *verb*
to tease someone, sometimes maliciously *US, 1972*
• [S]he was doing her best to jerk him about. — John Williams, *Cardiff Dead*, p. 61, 2000

jerker *noun*
in the car sales business, a car manufactured before World War 2 *US*
• — *Cars*, p. 40, December 1953

jerk fitting *noun*
(on a car, truck or tractor) a grease nipple *CANADA*
• A jerk (the same one dating your daughter) may be operating the grease gun but the term "jerk nipple" really refers to pulling the grease gun off the fitting. — Chris Thain, *Cold as a Bay Street Banker's Heart*, p. 93, 1987

jerk-off *noun*
1 a single act of masturbation, especially by a male *US, 1928*
• The Jerk-off! If you don't know how, let me explain it. — Angelo d'Arcangelo, *The Homosexual Handbook*, p. 88, 1968
2 a contemptible fool *US, 1932*
• The sneaky son-of-a-bitch Mickey-Finned the jerkoff on duty one night, slipping something into his beer. — Christopher Brookmyre, *The Sacred Art of Stealing*, p. 386, 2002

jerk off *verb*
1 to masturbate *UK, 1896*
A reasonably accurate description of the physical activity involved.
• The climax of this conversation was in a question he posed to me. "Do you know how to 'jerk off'?" — Phyllis and Eberhard Kronhausen, *Sex Histories of American College Men*, p. 79, 1960
• I began to wonder if any of them was jerking off while we was sentenced, they all seemed to relish it so much. — John Peter Jones, *Feather Pluckers*, p. 156, 1964
• Suddenly Johnny realizes the man is jerking off looking at him. — John Rechy, *Numbers*, p. 154, 1967
• You see, grown up men like to get laid and they like to get Frenched, but they don't like to get jerked off. — Delle Brehan, *Kicks is Kicks*, p. 59, 1970
• He thought she meant for him to jerk her off or otherwise affect her. — William T. Vollman, *Whores for Gloria*, p. 14, 1991
• I caught Spiderman jerkin' off in a booth to a Wonder Woman comic — Funkdoobiest *Superheroes*, 1995
• Howard, why do you always say you jerk off and stuff? — Howard Stern, *Miss America*, p. 7, 1995
• Standing nearby the stage, we see a black guy jerking off near Jasmin's tits. — Anthony Petkovich, *The X Factory*, p. 196, 1997
• You jerk off before all big dates, right? — *Something About Mary*, 1998
• I'll jerk off if I feel the need and I guess she does[.] — Sally Cline, *Couples*, p. 28, 1998
• But she knew boys had her picture up over their beds to look at when they jerked off. — Francesca Lia Block, *I Was a Teenage Fairy*, p. 78, 1998
2 to tease; to mislead *US, 1968*
• I think Coyle was jerking you off. — George Higgins, *The Friends of Eddie Coyle*, p. 97, 1971
3 to cause the withdrawal (of a criminal charge, a witness scheduled to testifiy, etc) *US*
• — Hyman E. Goldin et al., *Dictionary of American Underworld Lingo*, p. 110, 1950

jerk-silly *adjective*
obsessed with masturbation *US*
• — Joseph E. Ragen and Charles Finston, *Inside the World's Toughest Prison*, p. 805, 1962: 'Penitentiary and underworld glossary'

jerkwater *noun*
a dull-minded person *US, 1958*
• — William K. Bentley and James M. Corbett, *Prison Slang*, p. 35, 1992

Jerkwater *noun*
a contemptuous name for a location *US*
• Killed for vagrancy in Jerkwater, USA. — *Rambo, First Blood*, 1982

jerkwater *adjective*
provincial *US, 1897*
• He'd killed half a dozen people before he picked up a jerkwater Ph.D., and edged into psychiatry. — Jim Thompson, *The Killer Inside*, p. 167, 1952
• "What," he asked, "are we going to do for broads in a jerkwater town like Putnam's Landing?" — Max Shulman, *Rally Round the Flag, Boys!*, p. 157, 1957
• — J. Herbert Lund, *Herb's Hot Box of Railraod Slang*, p. 108, 1975
• Here I come to your jerkwater little country and spend my good American dollars[.] — William Burroughs, *Queer*, p. 59, 1985

jerky *noun*
used as a male-to-male, peer-to-peer term of address *US*
Jocular, from 'The Jerky Boys' (two young men who elevated prank telephone calls to comedic art).
• — Connie Eble (Editor), *UNC-CH Campus Slang*, p. 5, March 1996

jerky *adjective*
foolish, stupid *US, 1932*
From **JERK** (an idiot).
• [O]ne of those jerky radio pundits[.] — Howard Stern, *Miss America*, p. 291, 1995

jerry *noun*
something that is not as well made as it appears *TRINIDAD AND TOBAGO, 1987*
• — Lise Winer, *Dictionary of the English/Creole of Trinidad & Tobago*, 2003

Jerry *verb*
to realise; to comprehend; to 'tumble' to an idea *AUSTRALIA, 1894*
• — Jim Ramsay, *Cop It Sweet!*, p. 49, 1977
• — Ryan Aven-Bray, *Ridgey Didge Oz Jack Lang*, p. 32, 1983
• I should have jerried when from 20 metres away I heard him laugh as Rabs handed the money. — Paul Vautin, *Turn It Up!*, p. 204, 1995

Jerry; Gerry *nickname*

1 a German; the Germans *US, 1915*

Derogatory, often as an abstract reference to Germans as the enemy whether at war or football. Possibly derived from 'Jerry' (a chamber pot) in reference to the shape of German military helmets; more likely, as 'Gerry', an elaborated abbreviation of 'German'.

- There was one right on our flank, full of Jerries. — Derek Bickerton, *Payroll*, p. 32, 1959
- The two best wars this country has fought were against the Jerries. — *Harold and Maude*, 1971
- Jerry's annoyed. He's sent up a couple of Stukkas. — Johnny Speight, *It Stands to Reason*, p. 60, 1973
- "Listen, any more of that and I'm going to nick you under the Race Relations Act -" "That's for Lucozades [black people] – not for Jerries." — Anthony Masters, *Minder*, p. 158, 1984
- When I go to see my mother she says yes, she was terrified, thought it was the Jerries again. — Kevin Sampson, *Outlaws*, p. 148, 2001

2 a foreman on a railway track crew *US, 1867*

- — Norman Carlisle, *The Modern Wonder Book of Trains and Railroading*, p. 265, 1946

Jerry Lee *noun*

urination; an act of urination *UK*

Rhyming slang for **WEE** or **PEE**, formed from the name of rock 'n' roll singer and piano player, Jerry Lee Lewis (b.1935).

- — Ray Puxley, *Cockney Rabbit*, 1992

Jerry Springer *noun*

1 an ugly person *UK*

Rhyming slang for **MINGER**, formed from the name of the UK-born US television personality (b.1944).

- — Susie Dent, *The Language Report*, p. 98, 2003

2 heroin *UK*

Named after a US chat-show host.

- — Robert Ashton, *This Is Heroin*, p. 206, 2002
- — Mike Haskins, *Drugs*, p. 284, 2003

Jersey *noun*

the state of New Jersey *US*

- I was even over in Jersey for a while. — Philip Wylie, *Opus 21*, p. 111, 1949
- They was supposed to go someplace in Jersey. — Mickey Spillane, *Return of the Hood*, p. 87, 1964
- What do people from Jersey drink? — *King of Comedy*, 1976

Jersey bean *noun*

a resident of Jersey (in the Channel Islands) *UK*

- The locals call themselves Jersey beans. Residents of Guernsey call residents of Jersey crappos. — John Lahr, *Dame Edna Everage and the Rise of Western Civilisation*, p. 198, 1991

jersey chaser *noun*

a female college student who is attracted to athletes *US*

- — Connie Eble (Editor), *UNC-CH Campus Slang*, p. 6, October 2002

Jersey girls *nickname*

a small group of women living in New Jersey whose husbands were killed in the World Trade Center on 11th September 2001, and who pressured a reluctant Bush administration into appointing a commission to investigate the attack *US*

Evocative of an unrelated song by Bruce Springsteen.

- The commission grew largely out of pressure from families of victims, including four New Jersey widows who call themselves "the Jersey girls." — *New York Times*, p. 43, 22nd December 2002
- Kristen Breitweiser, one of the three widows known as "the Jersey girls," who helped pressure Congress into creating the commission, said the White House's actions are often at odds with its assurances it is providing the commission with "unprecedent cooperation." — *Chicago Tribune*, p. C1, 8th April 2004

Jersey highball *noun*

a glass of milk *US*

- — Marcus Hanna Boulware, *Jive and Slang of Students in Negro Colleges*, 1947

Jersey lightning *noun*

inexpensive, inferior whisky *US, 1848*

- — Vincent J. Monteleone, *Criminal Slang*, p. 132, 1949

Jersey side of the snatch play *noun*

middle age *US*

Borrowed from the slang of bowlers, where the 'Jersey side' is to the left of the head pin.

- They were introduced to an insignificant, graying man – "on the Jersey side of the snatch lay," in hipster language, meaning that Narco was over forty and wondering if life would ever begin again. — Ross Russell, *The Sound*, p. 113, 1961
- — Clarence Major, *Dictionary of Afro-American Slang*, p. 71, 1970
- "I'm on the Jersey side of snatch." Likely it had been years since his swinging lingam had nudged itself into the sweet enclosing lips of the yoni. — Brian Preston, *Pot Planet*, p. 26, 2002

Jesse James *noun*

1 in craps, a nine rolled with a four and a five *US*

Jesse James was shot with a 45 calibre handgun.

- — Steve Kuriscak, *Casino Talk*, p. 69, 1985

2 in hold 'em poker, a four and a five as the first two cards dealt to a player *US, 1981*

- — Thomas L. Clark, *The Dictionary of Gambling and Gaming*, p. 110, 1987

Jesse Owens *noun*

▸ **on the Jesse Owens**

fast *US, 1948*

- — Harold Wentworth and Stuart Berg Flexner, *Dictionary of American Slang*, p. 9, 1960

jessie *noun*

1 an effeminate man; a male homosexual *UK, 1958*

A female name used as a generic.

- Why do you have to look like a poof with that style of hair, you look a right jessy[.] — John McCririck, *John McCririck's World of Betting*, p. 8, 1991
- [A]nything less than a triple marks me out as a soft shandy-drinking, southern jessie. — *GQ*, p. 67, July 2001

2 a pretty red-headed girl *US*

- — Marcus Hanna Boulware, *Jive and Slang of Students in Negro Colleges*, 1947

jesum crow!

used for expressing surprise, dismay or disgust *US*

- — *Current Slang*, p. 15, Spring 1971

Jesus *adjective*

used as an adjectival intensifier *BAHAMAS*

- Every Jesus t'ing root up. — John A. Holm, *Dictionary of Bahamian English*, p. 114, 1982

Jesus and his brothers *noun*

J & B™ whisky *SOUTH AFRICA*

Scamto youth street slang (South African townships).

- Fancy some Jesus and his brothers[?] — Rebecca Harrison, *Reuters*, 8th February 2005

Jesus boots; Jesus shoes; Jesus slippers *noun*

sandals *US, 1942*

- — *American Speech*, p. 235, October 1964: 'Student slang in Hays, Kansas'
- — Helen Dahlskog (Editor), *A Dictionary of Contemporary and Colloquial Usage*, p. 34, 1972
- He was wearing a bright aloha shirt, khaki shorts, Jesus boots and mirrored sky-shooters[.] — Kinky Friedman, *Steppin' on a Rainbow*, p. 103, 2001

Jesus Christ almighty!; Jesus Christ!; Jesus!

used as a register of anger, frustration, wonder, etc *US*

Blasphemous by derivation, probably blasphemous in use.

- [T]he car is completely covered in blood. It's all over everything, including Jules and Vincent. JULES: Jesus Christ Almighty! — *Pulp Fiction*, 1994

Jesus Christing *adjective*

used as an intensifier *UK*

- Fuckin Jesus Christin twattin cuntin fuckin hell! — Niall Griffiths, *Grits*, p. 42, 2000

Jesus Christ on a bike!

▹ see: **CHRIST ON A BIKE!**

Jesus clip *noun*

any small clip that is destined to be dropped, leading to an outburst of 'Oh Jesus!' because it will not be found *US*

Biker (motorcyle) and bicyclist usage.

- — Lennard Zinn, *Zinn and the Art of Mountain Bike Maintenance*, p. 331, 2001

Jesus freak *noun*

a fervent Christian, especially a recent convert *US, 1966*

- Jesus freaks out in the street / Handing ticket out for God. — Bernie Taupin (performed by Elton John), *Tiny Dancer*, 1971
- These goddman Jesus freaks! They're multiplying like rats! — Hunter S. Thompson, *Fear and Loathing in Las Vegas*, p. 134, 1971
- "Jesus Freaks" harassed the third annual Christopher Street West Parade in Los Angeles — *The Advocate*, p. 5, 19th July 1972

• And who then had their sordid squabble taken out of their hands by vengeful cops and Jesus freaks[.] — Hunter S. Thompson, *Songs of the Doomed*, p. 298, 1990

Jesus freakery *noun*
fervent Christianity *UK*
• It is the era of the Big Search – a quest for the eternal high, through meditation, brown rice, alpha readings, guruism, primal screaming, Jesus freakery, LSD or a munchy, crunchy granola of them all. — Richard Neville writing in 'Oz', 1972, *Out Of My Mind*, p. 4, 1996

Jesus fuck!
used for registering an intense reaction *UK*
This combination of two individually powerful words serves when neither 'Jesus!' nor **FUCK!** has strength enough.
• But the shite [rubbish] they all sing along to in here, by the way – Jesus fuck! It's all fucking Kenny Rogers and fucking Neil Diamond and that. — Kevin Sampson, *Outlaws*, p. 205, 2001
• Jesus fuck, Ianto. Lef it, mun! — Niall Griffiths, *Sheepshagger*, p. 19, 2001

Jesus fucking Christ!
used as an all-purpose oath of surprise, approval, disapproval, anger, etc *US*
The most common use of the intensifying infix in the US.
• "Jesus fucking Christ. I'm sorry I said it." — Cecil Brown, *The Life & Loves of Mr. Jiveass Nigger*, p. 132, 1969

Jesus gliders *noun*
sandals *US*
• — Connie Eble (Editor), *UNC-CH Campus Slang*, p. 3, Fall 1990

Jesus H. Christ!
used in oaths *US, 1892*
Occasional substitutions of the middle initial, which is nothing more than a humorous, intensifying embellishment.
• [H]is Angst was suddenly interrupted by a voice in the seat beside him saying explosively, "Jesus H. Christ!" — Max Shulman, *Rally Round the Flag, Boys!*, p. 133, 1957
• I wouldn't be able to go out to Malibu for at least ten days! Jesus H. Christ! — Frederick Kohner, *Gidget*, p. 58, 1957
• I mean, Jesus A. Christ, you're not the only who's got a stake in this. — Clarence Cooper Jr, *Black*, p. 66, 1963
• Mr. "Jesus H. Christ"? — *Los Angeles Free Press*, p. 7, 25 June 1965
• Jesus H. Christ! And to think he actually gets twenty-five bucks an hour – or rather, forty-five minutes – for that nonsense. — Oscar Zeta Acosta, *The Autobiography of a Brown Buffalo*, p. 15, 1972
• I mean, Jesus H. Christ. Day after day, night after night, it just doesn't stop. — George V. Higgins, *The Rat on Fire*, p. 105, 1981
• Jesus H. Christ, get him for me. — George V. Higgins, *Penance for Jerry Kennedy*, p. 117, 1985
• What in the name of Jesus H. Christ are you animals doing in my bed? — *Full Metal Jacket*, 1987
• "Matter of fact it was over the golf course now you come to mention it. Know how it is when you're both members. Get chatting." "Jesus H. fucking Christ and his rabbit." — Jeremy Cameron, *Brown Bread in Wengen*, p. 20, 1999

Jesus juice *noun*
white wine *US*
Allegedly coined by singer Michael Jackson. It was also claimed, in a *Vanity Fair* article that Jackson called red wine 'Jesus blood'. Within months the term was widespread.
• Michael Jackson plied young boys with wine he called "Jesus Juice", a former business adviser claimed this week. — *Sunday Times (South Africa)*, 1st February 2004

Jesus nut *noun*
the main nut and bolt holding a helicopter's rotor blade to the body of the aircraft *US*
Presumably one prayed to Jesus that the nut and bolt did not fail.
• A lot of people thought it opened you to some kind of extra danger, like ground fire spilling in on you instead of just severing the hydraulic system or cutting off the Jesus nut that held the rotor on. — Michael Herr, *Dispaches*, p. 255–256, 1977
• — Linda Reinberg, *In the Field*, p. 116, 1991

Jesus shoes; Jesus slippers
▷ **see: JESUS BOOTS**

Jesus stiff *noun*
a person who feigns religion to obtain food, lodging, or better privileges in prison *US*
• — Hyman E. Goldin et al., *Dictionary of American Underworld Lingo*, p. 110, 1950

Jesus to Jesus and eight hands around!
used as a cry of disbelief *US*
• — John Gould, *Maine Lingo*, p. 146, 1975

Jesus weejuns *noun*
sandals *US*
• — *Current Slang*, p. 7, Spring 1969

Jesus wept!
used as an expression of annoyance, despair, disgust, impatience, etc *UK, 1937*
The shortest verse in the Bible (John 11: 35) used as a catchphrase.

jet *noun*
the recreational drug ketamine *US*
• — US Department of Justice, *Street Terms*, October 1994

jet *verb*
to leave in a hurry *US*
• — Collin Baker et al., *College Undergraduate Slang Study Conducted at Brown University*, p. 145, 1968
• Disgusted, the knock [narcotics officer] grabbed Rodney's arm. "C'mon, motherfucker. Let's jet, let's jet." — Richard Price, *Clockers*, p. 258, 1992
• [S]ay you're going to take a piss and jet up out that bitch through the emergency exit. — *Hip-Hop Connection*, p. 22, July 2002

jet bumper *noun*
in pinball, a bumper that upon impact with the ball scores and then propels the ball back into play *US*
• — Bobbye Claire Natkin and Steve Kirk, *All About Pinball*, p. 113, 1977

jet fuel *noun*
phencyclidine, the recreational drug known as PCP or angel dust *US*
• — US Department of Justice, *Street Terms*, October 1994

jethro *noun*
a coat *UK*
English gypsy use.
• — Jimmy Stockin, *On The Cobbles*, p. 10, 2000

jet jockey *noun*
a jet pilot *US, 1950*
• — *American Speech*, p. 158–159, May 1960: 'The burgeoning of 'jockey''
• — Linda Reinberg, *In the Field*, p. 116, 1991
• Also, Dan "Chicken Hawk" Quayle is the official poster boy of Vietnam War draft dodgers and "Spoon Fed Boy" George W. "Jet Jockey" Bush is the personification of that same lack of courage and guts. — *Augusta (Georgia) Chronicle*, p. A5, 10th June 2000
• "I'd love to be here when those jet jockeys from Apocalypse Now get up to Chu Lai." — Nelson DeMille, *Up Country*, p. 387, 2002

jew *noun*
a jewfish or jewfish collectively *AUSTRALIA, 1902*
• What he couldn't do with jew or bream and a few spuds is not worth talking about[.] — Sam Weller, *Old Bastards I Have Met*, p. 38, 1979
• That fish was no 'Jew', but a bloody Murray cod! — Bob Staines, *Wot a Whopper*, p. 55, 1982

Jew; Jew down *verb*
to bargain aggressively about a price *US, 1818*
'An offensive and stereotypical phrase.' (Multicultural Management Program Fellows, *Dictionary of Cautionary Words and Phrases*, 1989)
• The damned niggers wanted to jew the price down and then stay on all night too. — Nathan Heard, *Howard Street*, p. 44, 1968
• Being Jewish, I didn't want to pay list price for myself and Einar, and so haggled (or "Jewed down" as they say in the Arab press). — *Screw*, p. 21, 13th April 1970
• This ain't Delancy Street, and you ain't gonna jew me down, homeding. — *New Jack City*, 1990
• He jewed me up to twenty-five – I agreed. — James Ellroy, *White Jazz*, p. 32, 1992
• Through some "Jewing down" I bought it for $10,500, studio possibilities and all, about a stone's throw from Toylsome Lane. — Larry Rivers, *What Did I Do?*, p. 329, 1992
• Don't ever try to out-Jew me, little man. I'm twice the Jew you'll ever be. — Kenneth Lonergan, *This is Our Youth*, p. 38, 2000
• I don't dodge guilt. And I don't Jew outta payin' my comeuppance. — *Kill Bill*, 2003

Jewboy *noun*
a Jewish man *UK, 1796*
Not said kindly.
• Proper little jewboy was Henry. — John Peter Jones, *Feather Pluckers*, p. 118, 1964

- [H]e could picture the guy now: little Jew-boy with a cowboy hat, string tie and high-heeled boots, and horn-rimmed glasses and a big fucking cigar. — Elmore Leonard, *Mr. Majestyk*, p. 104, 1974
- We always had a stray wop or Jew-boy and plenty of spades with our gangs. — Edwin Torres, *Carlito's Way*, p. 9, 1975

Jew canoe *noun*

1 a Cadillac *US, 1973*

- "I said Dad let me have the big Jew canoe tonight," Sammy said, cackling his high-pitched laugh. "Why do you call it that, Sammy?" "So I can beat the Christians to the punch." — Pat Conroy, *The Great Santini*, p. 369, 1976
- The haberdashery lot was packed with Jew canoes and guinea gunboats[.] — James Ellroy, *The Big Nowhere*, p. 401, 1988
- — Lewis Poteet, *Car & Motorcyle Slang*, p. 114, 1992

2 a Jaguar car *UK*

Upper-class society usage.

- — Ann Barr and Peter York, *The Official Sloane Ranger Handbook*, p. 158, 1982

jeweller's shop *noun*

in mining, a rich deposit of opal or gold *AUSTRALIA, 1853*

- Old Joe Parsnip stumbled into a jeweller's shop not far from where our shaft had been. — Frank Hardy, *The Yarns of Billy Borker*, p. 142, 1965

jewelry *noun*

1 handcuffs *US, 1845*

- — Vincent J. Monteleone, *Criminal Slang*, p. 132, 1949

2 highly polished brass fittings on any firefighting equipment *US*

- — *American Speech*, p. 274, December 1954: 'Fire terms: additional words and definitions'

3 ornamental lights on a long-haul truck *US*

- — Bill Davis, *Jawjacking*, p. 56, 1977

Jew flag *noun*

paper money *US, 1915*

- — Joseph E. Ragen and Charles Finston, *Inside the World's Toughest Prison*, p. 805, 1962: 'Penitentiary and underworld glossary'

Jew gear *noun*

neutral gear, used while coasting downhill *US*

- — *American Speech*, p. 44, February 1963: 'Trucker's language in Rhode Island'

jewie *noun*

a jewfish or jewfish collectively *AUSTRALIA, 1917*

- — Jim Ramsay, *Cop It Sweet!*, p. 50, 1977
- [T]he regulations say you can only keep fish that are pan size, and those jewies are too big! — Bob Staines, *Wot a Whopper*, p. 14, 1982

jewish *noun*

clothes; fabrics and materials *SOUTH AFRICA*

Scamto youth street slang (South African townships).

- — *The Times*, 12th February 2005

Jewish by hospitalization *noun*

in homosexual usage, circumcised but not Jewish *US*

- — *Maledicta*, p. 58, 1986 – 1987: 'A continuation of a glossary of ethnic slurs in American English'

Jewish corned beef *noun*

in homosexual usage, a circumcised penis *US*

- — *Maledicta*, p. 58, 1986 – 1987: 'A continuation of a glossary of ethnic slurs in American English'

Jewish foreplay *noun*

pleading without results *US*

- — *Maledicta*, p. 58, 1986 – 1987: 'A continuation of a glossary of ethnic slurs in American English'

Jewish joanna *noun*

a cash register *UK*

A variation of **JEWISH PIANO**; formed from a racial stereotype and rhyming slang **JOANNA** (a piano).

- — David Powis, *The Signs of Crime*, 1977

Jewish lightning *noun*

an act of arson as a part of a fraudulent insurance claim *US*

- — *Maledicta*, p. 58, 1986 – 1987: 'A continuation of a glossary of ethnic slurs in American English'
- [A]n incident of Jewish lightning took out his ailing plant-hire business. — Greg Williams, *Diamond Geezers*, p. 46, 1997

Jewish overdrive *noun*

coasting down a hill with the car or truck in neutral *US*

- — *American Speech*, p. 205, Fall 1969: 'Truck driver's jargon'
- — Montie Tak, *Truck Talk*, p. 92, 1971
- — *Maledicta*, p. 165, 1979: 'A glossary of ethnic slurs in American English'

Jewish penicillin *noun*

chicken soup *US*

- I had made lunch for him .. feeling poorly as he was ... you know, a little Jewish penicillin (chicken soup). — Angelo d'Arcangelo, *The Homosexual Handbook*, p. 94, 1968
- — *Maledicta*, p. 165, 1979: 'A glossary of ethnic slurs in American English'

Jewish people's time *noun*

used for denoting a lack of punctuality *US*

- Like Mexican Time and the onetime JPT, Jewish People's time, C.P.T. is a phrase that draws the lines of the ghetto. — Paul Jacobs, *Prelude to a Riot*, p. 12, 1967

Jewish piano *noun*

a cash register *US, 1935*

A racial stereotype is at the root of this allusion to another instrument with keys that makes 'music'. 'Jewish pianola' is an Australian variant.

- — David Powis, *The Signs of Crime*, 1977

Jewish sidewall *noun*

white rubber sidewalls affixed to blackwall tyres *US*

- — *Maledicta*, p. 165, 1979: 'A glossary of ethnic slurs in American English'

Jewish typewriter *noun*

a cash register *UK*

Racial stereotyping.

Jew sheet *noun*

an accounting, literal or figurative, of money owed by friends *US*

- — *Maledicta*, p. 57, 1986 – 1987: 'A continuation of a glossary of ethnic slurs in American English'

Jewtown *noun*

a neighbourhood inhabited predominantly by Jewish people *US*

- But I'm scouting some promising territory over in Jew Town when I see a janitor wheel a bike into the basement of a tenement house. — Rocky Garciano (with Rowland Barber), *Somebody Up There Likes Me*, p. 32, 1955
- I'd always go in Jew town and pick pockets on Sundays. — Henry Williamson, *Hustler!*, p. 89, 1965
- Jewtown. That's exactly what it was, the place where the Jews lived and worked. — Odie Hawkins, *Scars and Memories*, p. 27, 1987

Jewy Louis *noun*

vulgar ostentation masquerading as tasteful interior decor *UK*

Upper-class society usage, damning the fake-furniture of the *nouveau riche* by comparing it with the genuine exuberance and style of Louis XV or Louis XVI period furniture and design.

- — Ann Barr and Peter York, *The Official Sloane Ranger Handbook*, p. 158, 1982

jhaat *noun*

pubic hair *TRINIDAD AND TOBAGO*

Hindi used by English speakers.

- — Lise Winer, *Dictionary of the English/Creole of Trinidad & Tobago*, 2003

jhatoor *noun*

the penis *TRINIDAD AND TOBAGO*

Hindi, used in English conversation.

- — Lise Winer, *Dictionary of the English/Creole of Trinidad & Tobago*, 2003

jheri curl *noun*

a relaxed, wet-look styling for naturally kinky black hair *UK*

Created by and named after Jheri (Robert) Redding (1907 – 98).

- [T]he other one was short and fat, had jheri curls and wore several earrings in one ear. — Karline Smith, *Moss Side Massive*, p. 121, 1994

J-hole *noun*

someone who makes despising easy *US*

From a Will Farell skit on *Saturday Night Live*.

- — Connie Eble (Editor), *UNC-CH Campus Slang*, p. 6, Fall 2001

jhoosh *noun*

▷ see: **ZHOOSH**

jib *noun*

1 the mouth *UK, 1860*

- Don't let the word pimp come outta your 'jib' in my presence. — Iceberg Slim (Robert Beck), *Pimp*, p. 122, 1969

- If a bitch ever made love to a nigger's dick, by hugging, kissing, and placing it in her jib, this one did. —A.S. Jackson, *Gentleman Pimp*, p. 72, 1973

2 on the coast of Nova Scotia, a small piece of land, especially triangular in shape *CANADA*
- Other than its [nautical] use to describe a triangular stay-sail, 'jib' is sometimes used to describe a small irregular piece of land, especially a triangular piece such as one that might be cut diagonally out of a squared field by a road or a stream. — *Nova Scotia Historical Quarterly*, p. 24, December 1980

jib *verb*
to tease *UK*
From 'jibe' (to taunt or insult).
- I feel like jibbing him but he's almost crying anyway. — Martin King and Martin Knight, *The Naughty Nineties*, p. 54, 1999

jibberjabber; jibber-jabber *noun*
meaningless chatter *UK, 1922*
- —Lou Shelly, *Hepcats Jive Talk Dictionary*, p. 26, 1945
- She forgot her curiosity quickly enough and turned to a jitterbugging jibberjabber about life behind the counter in the department store. —Robert Gover, *The Maniac Responsible*, p. 93, 1963
- [I]ncompetent Jacks-in-office who hide the whole thing under their cautiously cretinous jibber-jabber. —G. Legman, *The Fake Revolt*, p. 14, 1967

jiboney; jabroni; jabroney *noun*
1 a low-level gangster, a tough *US, 1921*
- You, you fucking jabroney. One more word out of you and I'm bringing you in. —Edwin Torres, *Q & A*, p. 122, 1977
- "I doubt that," the tall jaboney says, and he looks me up and down like he's ready to step on me and squash me like a bug. —Robert Campbell, *Nibbled to Death by Ducks*, p. 97, 1989
- You mean we're not taking any crap from that roody-poo jabroni Ronald DeChooch. —Janet Evanovich, *Seven Up*, p. 211, 2001

2 a newly immigrated foreigner; hence someone inexperienced or unsophisticated *US, 1960*
- — *San Jose Mercury News*, 11th May 1999

jibs *noun*
the teeth *US*
- —Roger D. Abrahams, *Deep Down in the Jungle*, p. 261, 1970

jiffy *noun*
1 a moment, a short space of time *UK, 1785*
Also shortened to 'jiff'.
- Hang on a jiff though, will you? —Barry Humphries, *Bazza Pulls It Off!*, 1971
- [W]e go'a pick up her mum from Harlesden [...] -When? – In a jiffy. —Nick Barlay, *Curvy Lovebox*, p. 54, 1997

2 in computing, a tick of the computer clock, usually one millisecond *US*
- "The swapper runs every six jiffies" means that the virtual memory management routine is executed once for every six ticks of the computer's clock, or ten times a second. —Guy L. Steele et al., *The Hacker's Dictionary*, p. 85, 1983

jiffy *adjective*
instant *US*
- The jiffy coffee lay in my stomach like a solid and the heat of it ran from my pores. —Philip Wylie, *Opus 21*, p. 226, 1949

jig *noun*
1 a black person *US, 1922*
Offensive.
- Anyway, since you beat up the two jigs nobody will talk to me. —Mickey Spillane, *I, The Jury*, p. 90, 1947
- Want I should lock the jib in the drunk tank? —Thurston Scott, *Cure it with Honey*, p. 187, 1951
- A lot of crazy jigs in the desert throwing spears at Italian planes. —Gilbert Sorrentino, *Steelwork*, p. 15, 1970
- Then after that if a guy was a Spic or a Jig it was his business. I mean it was his business, if he wanted to cling with his own kind. —Eugene Boe (Compiler), *The Wit & Wisdom of Archie Bunker*, p. 183, 1971
- And the jig says, no, he's going to load it right there. —George V. Higgins, *The Friends of Eddie Doyle*, p. 22, 1971
- And this is sportree in the Zulu outfit, in case anybody doesn't know he's a jig. —Elmore Leonard, *Swag*, p. 25, 1976
- That fuckin' jig's gonna wish he never came outa the jungle. —*Raging Bull*, 1980
- Word's going around that in addition to losing Ganz for the second time, and in addition to Haden busting you back to Patrolman, some jig beat the crap out of you. — *48 Hours*, 1982
- "Goddamn jib," Dale Junior said. Two of them, young black guys coming from the pickup now as Raylan got out and walked back toward them... —Elmore Leonard, *Riding the Rap*, p. 10–11, 1995

2 sexual intercourse *AUSTRALIA*
- —James McDonald, *A Dictionary of Obscenity, Taboo and Euphemism*, p. 75, 1988

3 a deception; trickery; mischief *US, 1777*
- God knows what kind of jig he was dreaming up for himself. —Clancy Sigal, *Going Away*, p. 215, 1961

4 in Newfoundland, a thread from a garment used to predict a date with a person of the opposite sex *CANADA*
- If you happened to pick a ravel or thread, locally called a 'jig,' off your clothes, it could be used to determine the initial of your next date or boyfriend. —G.M. Story, *oral citation from Dictionary of Newfoundland English*, p. 277, 1982

jig *verb*
1 to stab (someone) *US*
- —Anna Scotti and Paul Young, *Buzzwords*, p. 136, 1997

2 to play truant from school *AUSTRALIA*
- —Jim Ramsay, *Cop It Sweet!*, p. 50, 1977

jigaboo *noun*
a black person *US, 1926*
Offensive.
- You know those "dancing jigaboo" toys that you wind up? —Malcolm X and Alex Haley, *The Autobiography of Malcolm X*, p. 57, 1964
- No, you and that big jigaboo sat there laughing with each other – oh boy, are we having fun, taking Mr. Magic to jail. —Elmore Leonard, *Glitz*, p. 317, 1985

jigaboo joy shop *noun*
a car supply shop specialising in chrome and other tawdry car accessories *US, 1950*
- — *Maledicta*, p. 168, 1979: 'A glossary of ethnic slurs in American English'

jig act *verb*
to act foolishly or disruptively *IRELAND*
- Missus Callaghan was out from behind the counter in a shot. Out now. None of that jig-acting. —Eamonn Sweeney, *Waiting for the Healer*, p. 97, 1997

jig-a-jig; jig-jig *noun*
sexual intercourse *US, 1896*
- I tell 'em how Cholly give me that jig-jig or jail jive[.] —Robert Gover, *JC Saves*, p. 55, 1968

jigger *noun*
1 a bank robber *US*
- We had a pretty good bunch of O'Sullivans, a torch man, a mechanic, a jigger and a hard-shell biscuit who'd been with a gopher mob. We crashed with a get-in betty. — *The New American Mercury*, p. 709, 1950

2 a lookout during a crime *US, 1925*
- —Bruce Jackson, *Outside the Law*, p. 58, 1972: 'Glossary'
- —Charles Shafer, *Folk Speech in Texas Prisons*, p. 208, 1990
- —Mark S. Fleisher, *Beggars & Thieves*, p. 290, 1995: 'Glossary'

3 an illegally constructed radio receiver *AUSTRALIA, 1944*
Prison usage.

4 a concealed device for giving an electric shock to a horse in a race *AUSTRALIA, 1953*
- Once just when a trainer was asking Huck to hit a horse with a battery on the track a DC3 aeroplane flew over. 'No use hitting him the j-j-jigger,' the old Huck said. 'He couldn't w-win a race with the engine of that b-b-b-bloody aeroplane in him.' —Frank Hardy and Athol George Mulley, *The Needy and the Greedy*, p. 97, 1975
- —Ned Wallish, *The Truth Dictionary of Racing Slang*, p. 42, 1989

5 a woman who will dance with a man for a fee *US*
- The dance floor was jammed. The dime jiggers were of every age and every type and a lot of them wore cheap formals and the smiles on their faces were hard and false. —Thurston Scott, *Cure it with Honey*, p. 151, 1951

6 a door *UK, 1567*
An early cant word that survives in English gypsy use.
- —Jimmy Stockin, *On The Cobbles*, p. 10, 2000

7 a slow freight train *US, 1927*
- —Ramon Adams, *The Language of the Railroader*, p. 87, 1977

8 a small railway line hand-car or trolley used in line maintenance *NEW ZEALAND*
- A surfaceman was killed when a train overtook him as he was traveling between Wiri and Homai on a jigger. — *Evening Post*, p. 14, 25th March 1953

jigger *verb*

1 to adjust, especially of numbers or statistics *US*

- If the annuity also covers your spouse, payments can be jiggered to reflect your changing joint life expectancy. — Jane Bryant Quinn, *Making the Most of Your Money*, p. 927, 1997
- President Clinton had cunningly jiggered with the tax code to squeeze enormous sums of money out of comparatively tiny numbers of people. — David Frum, *The Right Man*, p. 50, 2003

2 to serve as a lookout during a crime *US*

- — Mark S. Fleisher, *Beggars & Thieves*, p. 290, 1995: 'Glossary'

▸ **I'll be jiggered!; I'm jiggered!**

used for registering surprise *UK, 1886*

- I'll be jiggered, said Commodore Guff in genuine amazement. — J. Robert King, *Planeshift*, p. 143, 2000

jiggered *adjective*

1 damned, in great trouble *UK, 1837*

Euphemistic replacement for **BUGGERED**.

- We are jiggered," Shelley said. "Jiggered beyond salvation.["] — Christopher Brookmyre, *Boiling a Frog*, p. 291, 2000

2 useless, broken *NEW ZEALAND*

- — Sonya Plowman, *Great Kiwi Slang*, p. 102, 2002

jiggered up; jiggered *adjective*

exhausted *UK*

As 'jiggered up', a nautical coinage first recorded in 1867; possibly a fusing of 'Jesus' and 'buggered', intended as a euphemism for **BUGGERED UP** (exhausted).

- Absolutely jiggered from the flight and the non-stop partying[.] — Kevin Sampson, *Powder*, p. 404, 1999

jigger man *noun*

a lookout during a crime *US, 1924*

- — Vincent J. Monteleone, *Criminal Slang*, p. 132, 1949

jigger moll *noun*

a female lookout for a criminal operation who can also serve as a diversion or distraction *US*

- — *American Speech*, p. 97, May 1956: 'Smugglers' argot in the Southwest'

jiggers!

used as a warning to confederates that a prison guard is approaching *US, 1911*

- If the matron came long the hall someone yelled jiggers! and they ditched the butt. — Willard Motley, *Let No Man Write My Epitaph*, p. 21, 1958
- — Inez Cardozo-Freeman, *The Joint*, p. 509, 1984

jiggin; jigging *noun*

an organised dance *UK: SCOTLAND*

Glasgow slang.

- Are you goin tae the jiggin the night? — Michael Munro, *The Original Patter*, p. 39, 1985

jigging veil *noun*

in Newfoundland, a widow's veil *CANADA*

As with **JIG**, these uses of the word seem to be akin to 'jigging' as a type of fishing.

- A widow's veil was known as a jiggin' veil because it is considered an obvious method of showing men you are now available for marriage. — G. M. Story, *oral citation from Dictionary of Newfoundland English*, p. 278, 1982

jiggle *verb*

(of a woman) to walk so as to accentuate the movement of the breasts *US, 1965*

- — *American Speech*, Fall 1981

jiggle and jog *noun*

a French person *UK*

Rhyming slang for **FROG**.

- — Ronnie Barker, *Fletcher's Book of Rhyming Slang*, 1979
- — Ray Puxley, *Cockney Rabbit*, 1992

jiggle bars *noun*

the raised bars dividing motorway lanes *US*

- — *American Speech*, p. 270, December 1962: 'The language of traffic policemen'

jiggler *noun*

1 a skeleton key for a pin tumbler lock *UK*

- — David Powis, *The Signs of Crime*, 1977

2 a wire used to manipulate a pay phone to make a call without charge *US*

- — Jim Crotty, *How to Talk American*, p. 54, 1997

3 in electric line work, a secondary voltage tester with a glow light indicator *US*

- — A.B. Chance Co., *Lineman's Slang Dictionary*, p. 10, 1980

jiggles and wires *noun*

excitement *US*

- "I'm all jggles and wires!" Ken Kelly whispered to Joe Castillo. — Joseph Wambaugh, *Lines and Shadows*, p. 160, 1984

jiggy *adjective*

rich; hence fashionable, stylish; attractive *US*

- DKNY / Oh my I'm jiggy — Junior MAFIA *Player's Anthem*, 1995
- — *Newsday*, p. B2, 11th October 1997
- A woman or a record both "got me open" but at the moment I write this they both better be "jiggy" if I'm supposed to pay attention. — Nelson George, *Hip Hop America*, p. 209, 1998

▸ **get jiggy; get jiggy with it**

1 to dance, or feel the need to dance to the music *US*

- [W]ish you nig was dancin' the jig / here with this handsome kid / [...] illway to 'ami [Miami] on the interstate floorway / give it up jiggy make it feel like foreplay — Will Smith, *Gettin' Jiggy wit' it*, 1997

2 to have sex; to become sexually intimate *US*

- [W]hen we first got jiggy it was great to go in the shower but when you do it day in day out the novelty wears off. — *Attitude*, p. 146, October 2003

jiggy swiggy *noun*

the current drink of popular choice *UK, 2000*

JIGGY (fashionable), plus a play on **SWIG** (to drink).

- [I]t's the jiggy swiggy at garage clubs[.] — *Sky Magazine*, p. 88, May 2001

jig-jig *noun*

▷ see: **JIG-A-JIG**

jig lover *noun*

a white person who, in the eyes of the racist using the term, treats black people as equals *US*

- — Hyman E. Goldin et al., *Dictionary of American Underworld Lingo*, p. 110, 1950

jig rig *noun*

a car that has been given cheap, showy, useless modifications with no effect on its performance *US*

From a racist stereotype of black values.

- The cars either abandoned jig rigs or welfare wagons in mint condition, but nothing exceptional. — James Ellroy, *Suicide Hill*, p. 610, 1986
- — Lewis Poteet, *Car & Motorcyle Slang*, p. 114, 1992

jigs *noun*

a key *US*

- — Vincent J. Monteleone, *Criminal Slang*, p. 132, 1949

jigtown *noun*

a neighbourhood populated largely by black people *US*

- — *Maledicta*, p. 52, 1986–1987: 'A continuation of a glossary of ethnic slurs in American English'
- Lorna gigged the Katydid Klub, Bido Lito's, Malloy's Next, and a host of dives on the edge of jigtown. — James Ellroy, *Hollywood Nocturnes*, p. 271, 1994
- If you want to grill a jig outside his backyard you don't use a hotel room in jugtown. — Loren D. Estleman, *Jitterbug*, p. 20, 1998

jig up *verb*

to dance in an animated fashion *BAHAMAS*

- — John A. Holm, *Dictionary of Bahamian English*, p. 114, 1982

jihad *noun*

enforcement of school discipline *US*

The Islamic term for 'holy war' adopted as teenspeak, post 11th September 2002.

- It was total jihad. — *The Washington Post*, 19th March 2002

jildi!

quick!, hurry! *INDIA, 1948*

Military slang, from Hindustani *jaldi*.

- — John W. Mussell, *The Token Book of Militarisms*, 1995

jill *noun*

the female form of the jock strap, worn to protect the genitals *CANADA*

The term derives from the 'Jack and Jill' nursery rhyme, as the male version, the 'jockstrap', is also known as the 'jackstrap'.

- It's a latex rubber-coated triangle worn the same way as a jock except it doesn't travel underneath so far. Also used in girls' lacrosse. — Doug Beardsley, *Country on Ice*, p. 116–117, 1988

jilleroo *noun*
a female hand working on a cattle or sheep station *AUSTRALIA, 1943*
Modelled on **JACKEROO**.
- I'm employing a bunch of jillaroos. — Sandra Jobson, *Blokes*, p. 118, 1984
- We had a white girl, a jilleroo, working with us. — Herb Wharton, *Cattle Camp*, p. 165, 1994

jilleroo *verb*
to work as a jilleroo *AUSTRALIA, 1970*
- How was jillerooing today? — Gerald Sweeney, *The Plunge*, p. 122, 1981

jillick *verb*
to throw a stone across water, underhand, to see how many times it skips *CANADA*
- To skim flat stones over water, saying 'A duck and a drake / And a salt-water cake / And a bottle of brandy'. — P.K. Devine, *Folklore of Newfoundland*, p. 99–69, 1937

jillion *noun*
a large, imagined number *US, 1939*
- — Lou Shelly, *Hepcats Jive Talk Dictionary*, p. 13, 1945
- We've got about ninety jillion sea gulls in our neighborhood[.] — Max Shulman, *I was a Teen-Age Dwarf*, p. 22, 1959
- Goddamnit, Shapian. I'm paying you a jillion dollars for a show about food poisons. — Max Shulman, *Anyone Got a Match?*, p. 226, 1964

jillo!
quick!, hurry! *INDIA, 1984*
Military slang, from Hindustani *chalo*. Influenced by **JILDI!**.
- — John W. Mussell, *The Token Book of Militarisms*, 1995

jill off *verb*
(of a woman) to masturbate *US, 1989*
Derivative of the male **JACK OFF**, and used far less frequently.
- All proceeds from this jack- and jill-off fest and the finish-line party went to From Our Streets With Dignity[.]. — *The Village Voice*, 13th June 2000

jillpots *noun*
▸ **his jillpots; her jillpots**
that person, him, her *UK, about 1937*
Circus, itinerant entertainers; probably an elaboration of **JILLS**.
- Anyone not mentioned by name is called "his jills", or "her jills". His or her "jillpots" is also used but there is a hint of derision in this. — Butch Reynolds, *Broken Hearted Clown*, p. 31, 1953

jills *noun*
self, when combined with an appropriate pronoun – thus 'I jills' for me or myself, 'her jills' for her or herself, 'his jills' for him or himself, etc *UK, 1906*
Part of the Shelta vocabulary that is often used by sections of gypsy and Romany society as a means of discreet communication.
- His jills told him to take it out of the horse tent. — Butch Reynolds, *Broken Hearted Clown*, p. 28, 1953

Jim *noun*
1 the name given to a friend or offered as a gesture of friendliness *US, 1899*
Black/jazz slang subverting the racism of **JIM CROW**.
- Jim, this jive you got is gassed. — Mezz Mezzrow, 1946, *quoted in Waiting For The Man by Harry Shapiro*, 1999

2 in film making, an all-purpose forename that is prefixed to a worker's informal job title *UK*
- Sparks is the universal word for a working electrician – though in the film studios usually preceded by Jim: Jim Chippy [carpenter], Jim Rigger, Jim Sparks ... never Jim Producer, though. — Red Daniells, 1980

3 an interested loiterer and observer in an area where sexual trade is conducted *UK*
- Wherever prostitutes congregate with their clients [...] there will be other loiterers – the "jims", the "men in raincoats", who watch the transactions and purchased intimacies in a morbid and unhealthy silence. — David Powis, *The Signs of Crime*, 1977

Jim and Jack *noun*
the back *UK*
Rhyming slang.
- Well, I see Samson as huge and all butch, with great bulging thews and whopping great lallies [legs], with long blond riah [hair] hanging down his Jim and Jack[.] — Barry Took and Marty Feldman, *Round The Horne*, 16th April 1967
- — Paul Baker, *Polari*, p. 178, 2002

Jimbroni *noun*
in American casinos, a dealer with neither great skills nor great reactions to situations *US*
- — Steve Kuriscak, *Casino Talk*, p. 33, 1985

jim cap; jim hat *noun*
a condom *US*
- [N]ow that I wanna flap some skins Brandi ain't down for it even if I wear a jim hat. — *Boyz N The Hood*, 1990
- — Pamela Munro, *U.C.L.A. Slang*, p. 82, 1997

Jim Crow *noun*
1 racial segregation; a racially segregated facility *US, 1921*
- You riding back here in the Jim Crow just like me. — Ralph Ellison, *Invisible Man*, p. 155, 1947
- Bop was so weird, and so apart from any attraction in night club history, that the breaking of the Jim Crow line went unnoticed. — Robert Sylvester, *No Cover Charge*, p. 284, 1956
- I am not like these pseudo-hip characters who immolate themselves in the Negro race which, if you ask me, really is Jim Crow in reverse. — Clancy Sigal, *Going Away*, p. 60, 1961
- [P]erhaps there are fewer breadlines in America, but is Jim Crow gone? — Students for a Democratic Society, *Port Huron Statement*, 15th June 1962

2 in British Columbia logging, a single log load; in Vancouver Island coal mining, a bar for bending track or changing an underground rail switch *CANADA*
- In the US, Jim Crow cars were railroad cars for the exclusive use of negroes. In Canada, only BC had timber big enough to make a "Jim Crow" a one-log load on a rail car or logging truck. — Tom Parkin, *WetCoast Words*, p. 77, 1989

3 on the railways, a tool used to straighten rails *US, 1952*
- — Ramon Adams, *The Language of the Railroader*, p. 87, 1977

Jim-Crow *verb*
to segregate racially *US, 1918*
- He too good to come in? Tell him we don't Jimcrow nobody. — Ralph Ellison, *Invisible Man*, p. 76, 1947

Jim Crow *adjective*
1 racially segregated, reserved for black people *US, 1842*
- "[T]o hell with you and this lousy Jim Crow union too!" I said. — Chester Himes, *If He Hollers Let Him Go*, p. 114, 1945
- And it was in Pontiac that I dug that Jim Crow man in person, a motherferyer that would cut your throat for looking. — Mezz Mezzrow, *Really the Blues*, p. 4, 1946
- — Jack Lait and Lee Mortimer, *Washington Confidential*, p. , 1951
- The District has a single Jim Crow law, segregating Negros and whites – in schools. — Jack Lait and Lee Mortimer, *Washington Confidential*, p. 35, 1951
- He laughs at me and says it was Jim Crow and it's a Jim Crow world, and what's the use. — James T. Farrell, *Kilroy was Here*, p. 67, 1954
- The accommodations are block blooked, with a no Jim Crow clause. — Ross Russell, *The Sound*, p. 60, 1961
- I been light enough to sit in the front of a Jim Crow bus but dark enough to be worried about it. — Edwin Torres, *Carlito's Way*, p. 19, 1975

2 worthless *CANADA*
- "Bad medicine," "chaffy," "snide," "jim-crow," and "pizen" are applied to anything worthless on the Eastern slope of the Rockies. — *Alberta Historical Review*, p. 14/2, Autumn 1962

Jim Dandy *noun*
an excellent example or instance of something *US, 1887*
- Folks, I sure hope these goddamn things work. To make sure, I'll put on both of them, one at the back and one on the end of my Jim Dandy. — Iceberg Silm (Robert Beck), *Trick Baby*, p. 219, 1969
- I went on about how my cousin was a jim-dandy hunter, a heap better than Roscoe's Nelly. — Guy Owen, *The Flim-Flam Man and the Apprentice Grifter*, p. 55, 1972

Jim Fish *noun*
a black person *SOUTH AFRICA, 1930*
Offensive and derogatory.
- — Jean Branford, *A Dictionary of South African English*, 1978

Jiminy Cricket!
used as a mild expletive *US, 1848*
Extended from obsolete 'jiminy!'; 'gemini!', etc., which may derive from *Jesu domine*; modern use is probably intended to be a euphemism for **JESUS CHRIST!**.

jim-jams *noun*

pyjamas *AUSTRALIA*

- [S]he sent me into the lounge room to warm their jim-jams. —Barry Humphries, *A Nice Night's Entertainment*, p. 51, 1961
- Lift your hips. Let's get you out of your jim-jams, you have been a naughty girl, haven't you? —Henry Sloane, *Sloane's Inside Guide to Sex & Drugs & Rock 'n' Roll*, p. 50, 1985
- I'm hoppin about the bedroom with both legs down one jim-jam. —Andrew Nickolds, *Back to Basics*, p. 92, 1994

jimjams *noun*

a heightened sense of anxiety *US, 1896*

- Made me so jimjam jittery, I near nutty already. —Robert Gover, *One Hundred Dollar Misunderstanding*, p. 121, 1961
- Arthur Skidmore was wildly awake with the jimjams[.] —Emmett Grogan, *Final Score*, p. 36, 1976

Jim Johnson *noun*

the equipment needed to inject heroin or another narcotic *US*

- —Richard A. Spears, *The Slang and Jargon of Drugs and Drink*, p. 288, 1986

Jim Jones *noun*

marijuana adulterated with cocaine and phencyclidine, the recreational drug known as PCP or angel dust *UK, 1998*

An eponym from the self-proclaimed messiah of the People's Temple, James (Jim) Warren Jones, 1931–78, who promised followers utopia. In 1977 the sect established Jonestown, an agricultural commune in Guyana, South America. On the 18th November 1978, Jones commanded cultists to drink a punch adulterated with cyanide. The majority obeyed: the mass suicide ('the Jonestown Massacre') took 913 lives, including 276 children. This marijuana cocktail is a metaphor for a dream, represented here as marijuana, that is poisoned.

- —Mike Haskins, *Drugs*, p. 288, 2003

jimmies *noun*

1 gym shoes *NEW ZEALAND, 1995*

- —Harry Orsman, *A Dictionary of Modern New Zealand Slang*, p. 72, 1999

2 tiny pieces of candy sprinkled on ice-cream, biscuits or cake *US, 1947*

- He chops peyote buds into the froth with chocolate jimmies. —Richard Farina, *Been Down So Long*, p. 62, 1966

jimmy *noun*

1 the penis *US, 1988*

- "Gimme gimme gimme" / Jumped on my jimmy and rode me like the wild west —Ice-T, *The Girl Tried To Kill Me*, 1989
- Never sleep alone because my Jimmy is a magnet —Beastie Boys *3 Minute Rule*, 1989
- —Vann Wesson, *Generation X Field Guide and Lexicon*, p. 98, 1997
- —Pamela Munro, *U.C.L.A. Slang*, p. 87, 2001

2 a condom *US, 1990*

- —Judi Sanders, *Faced and Faded, Hanging to Hurl*, p. 23, 1993
- Bitch, stop lyin'! Besides, I had the jimmy on extra tight. —*Menace II Society*, 1993
- He rolled on a jimmy and I sat on top of him. —Amy Sohn, *Run Catch Kiss*, p. 111, 1999
- —Pamela Munro, *U.C.L.A. Slang*, p. 87, 2001

3 an injection of an illegal drug into the skin, not a vein *US*

- —*American Speech*, p. 27, February 1952: 'Teen-age hophead jargon'

4 a short crowbar used by burglars *UK, 1811*

This variation of **JEMMY** is mainly used in the US.

- On a patent lock, we'd use a jimmy, as it's called, or a lockpick. —Malcolm X and Alex Haley, *The Autobiography of Malcolm X*, p. 142, 1964
- [I]'ve got a short jimmy [small crowbar with a bent bill] up each sleeve and I put one over the lock and one under the lock and across, then open the glass door or anything else. —Bruce Jackson, *In the Life*, p. 97, 1972

5 a glass of beer *AUSTRALIA*

Homage to James Boag, a brewer.

- —Maureen Brooks and Joan Ritchie, *Tassie Terms*, p. 76, 1995

6 a railway coal truck *US*

- —Norman Carlisle, *The Modern Wonder Book of Trains and Railroading*, p. 265, 1946

Jimmy *noun*

1 in Glasgow, used as a term of address to any male stranger *UK: SCOTLAND*

- —Michael Munro, *The Original Patter*, p. 39, 1985

2 anything produced by the truck division of General Motors *US, 1953*

- Jimmy superchargers, originally designed for GMC diesel truck engines, are extremely popular in drag racing. —John Lawlor, *How to Talk Car*, p. 65, 1965
- Cab-over Pete with a reefer on / And a Jimmy haulin' hogs[.] —C.W. McCall, *Convoy*, 1976

jimmy *verb*

1 to pry open *US, 1854*

- So I jimmied open the lock and there's like rows and rows of cash just staring at me. —Kenneth Lonergan, *This is Our Youth*, p. 14, 2000

2 to obtain free entry into a cinema, or a theatre, or an enclosure at a race meeting, by underhand means *UK*

- —David Powis, *The Signs of Crime*, 1977

jimmy bottle *noun*

a gallon bottle *TRINIDAD AND TOBAGO*

- —Lise Winer, *Dictionary of the English/Creole of Trinidad & Tobago*, 2003

Jimmy Boyle; jimmy *noun*

foil (used in the preparation of heroin) *UK*

Rhyming slang, based on the name of Jimmy Boyle (b.1944), a convicted murderer turned sculptor and novelist.

- —Angela Devlin, *Prison Patter*, p. 66, 1996
- [P]ipes made from water bottles, burnt Jimmy Boyle, lemons, squeezed, hairy and grey[.] —J.J. Connolly, *Layer Cake*, p. 172, 2000

Jimmy Britt *noun*

shit *AUSTRALIA*

Rhyming slang based on the name of a boxing champion who toured Australia during World War I.

- —Jim Ramsay, *Cop It Sweet!*, p. 50, 1977

Jimmy Britts *noun*

1 diarrhoea *AUSTRALIA, 1950*

Always used with 'the'; rhyming slang for **THE SHITS**, possibly based on the name of a US baseball player in the first decade of C20. Sometimes shortened to 'jimmys'.

- Either the kids radio was on the blink, he decided, or the little punk was packing a dose of the Jimmy Britts. —W.R. Bennett, *Wingman*, p. 13, 1961
- You can still hear Jimmy (Britts=shits) who boxed before the First World War. —*Antiquarian Book Review*, p. 18, June 2002

2 a state of extreme annoyance *AUSTRALIA, 1959*

Rhyming slang for **SHIT!**.

- It seemed basically that oaths beginning with 'B' were acceptable to Father when used by an adult in serious conversation. This naturally cleared bugger, bum, and bastard for his own personal use, while also sparing 'the Jimmy Britts' for special occasions. —Kerry Cue, *Crooks, Chooks and Bloody Ratbags*, p. 154, 1983

jimmy cap; jimmy hat *noun*

a condom *US, 1988*

Worn on a **JIMMY** (penis).

- It's "Jimmy Hats" by BDP —Boogie Down Productions *Jimmy*, 1988
- Jimmy hat is street slang for condom and is also the title of a rap music hit. —*Boston Globe*, p. 27, 15th April 1989

Jimmy dog *noun*

a marijuana cigarette *US*

- —Connie Eble (Editor), *UNC-CH Campus Slang*, p. 4, October 1986

Jimmy Hicks; Jimmy Hix *noun*

1 an injection of drugs *UK, 1950*

Rhyming slang for **FIX**, based on either an unknown Mr Hicks/Hix or guitarist Jimi Hendrix (1942–70), another variation, along with 'jimmy' and 'jimi'.

- —Home Office, *Glossary of Terms and Slang Common in Penal Establishments*, July 1978
- —Ray Puxley, *Cockney Rabbit*, 1992
- —Angela Devlin, *Prison Patter*, p. 66, 1996
- —Ray Puxley, *Fresh Rabbit*, 1998

2 in craps, a roll of six *US, 1919*

From the rhyme.

- —*The Annals of the American Academy of Political and Social Sciences*, p. 126, May 1950

3 in a deck of playing cards, a six *US, 1951*

- —*American Speech*, p. 99, May 1951: 'The vocabulary of poker'

Jimmy Hill; jimmy *noun*

1 a bill *UK*

Rhyming slang, based on the name of former footballer now television sports presenter Jimmy Hill (b.1928).

- Have we paid the Jimmy? —*Antiquarian Book Review*, p. 18, June 2002

2 a pill *UK*
Rhyming slang, formed from the name of former footballer now television sports presenter Jimmy Hill (b.1928).
• —Ray Puxley, *Cockney Rabbit*, 1992

jimmy jacket *noun*
a condom *US*
Collected in an interview with Jim Holliday, 12th June 1997.

jimmy jar *noun*
a demijohn, or container of alcohol *CANADA*
• We samples the jimmie-jar [of rum] and the sampling steadied our nerves.—W.J. Bursey, *Undaunted Pioneer*, p. 87, 1977

Jimmy joint *noun*
the penis *US*
• —John R. Armore and Joseph D. Wolfe, *Dictionary of Desperation*, p. 36, 1976

Jimmy Logie *noun*
a small lump of dried nasal mucus *UK*
Rhyming slang for 'bogie'; formed from the name of an Arsenal footballer of the mid-1950s.
• —Ray Puxley, *Cockney Rabbit*, 1992

Jimmy Mason *noun*
a basin, generally in the sense 'to have had a basinful' (as much as you can tolerate) *UK*
Rhyming slang.
• —Ray Puxley, *Cockney Rabbit*, 1992

Jimmy Nail *adjective*
stale *UK*
Rhyming slang, formed from the name of the actor and singer (b.1954).
• —Ray Puxley, *Fresh Rabbit*, 1998

Jimmy Riddle; jimmy *noun*
an act of urination; urine *UK, 1931*
Rhyming slang for **PIDDLE**.
• Take phone boxes – they've gone from being the old red eyesores, full of jimmy riddle and chip papers, to state-of-the-art open-plan business centres.—Andrew Nickolds, *Back to Basics*, p. 79, 1994

Jimmy Riddle; jimmy *verb*
to urinate *UK*
Rhyming slang for **PIDDLE**.

Jimmy Rollocks *noun*
the testicles *UK*
Rhyming slang for **BOLLOCKS**.
• —Julian Franklyn, *A Dictionary of Rhyming Slang*, 1961

Jimmy Savile *verb*
to travel *UK*
• [F]rom the appalling and patronizing advertising campaign of the early 1980s which featured the irksome UK DJ and media personality Jimmy Savile OBE discussing the supposed benefits of traveling by British Rail.—Tom Hibbert, *Rockspeak!*, p. 92, 1983

Jimmy the sleek *noun*
a condom *US, 1990s*
A play on the nickname Jimmy the Greek (Demetrios Synodinos, later James George Snyder) (1919–96), a well-known gambler. The sleek finish is provided by latex which also takes the gamble out of the situation.

Jimmy Valentine *noun*
a criminal who specialises in breaking into safes *US*
• —Vincent J. Monteleone, *Criminal Slang*, p. 133, 1949

Jimmy White *noun*
shite (in all senses) *UK*
Rhyming slang, formed from the name of UK snooker player Jimmy 'Whirlwind' White (b.1962).
• —Tom Nind, *Rude Rhyming Slang*, p. 13, 2003

Jimmy Woodser *noun*
a person drinking alone at a public bar; a drink taken alone *AUSTRALIA*
From Jimmy Wood, the name of the protagonist in the eponymous song by Australian poet Barcroft Boake (1892). The song originally appeared with a footnote explaining the term, perhaps indicating that it was otherwise unknown and therefore a coinage of Boake's. Some believe that the name refers to a real person, but this has not been substantiated.
• Bluey, never drink another Jimmy Woodser as long as you live. —Harold Lewis, *Crow On A Barbed Wire Fence*, p. 13, 1973

Jimmy Young; jimmy *noun*
1 a tongue *UK*
Rhyming slang.
• "Stop flapping your Jimmy" means keep quiet.—Ray Puxley, *Cockney Rabbit*, 1992
2 a bribe *UK*
Rhyming slang for **BUNG**; formed from the name of a singer-turned-radio disc jockey (b.1923).
• I gave the gatekeeper a Jimmy so we'll be alright.—Ray Puxley, *Cockney Rabbit*, 1992

Jim Pike *noun*
someone who is financing an illegal betting operation *AUSTRALIA*
Rhyming slang for **MIKE**.
• —Ned Wallish, *The Truth Dictionary of Racing Slang*, p. 42, 1989

Jim Skinner; Jimmy Skinner *noun*
▷ **see:** JOE SKINNER

Jimson *noun*
used as a male-to-male term of address *US*
• Jimson, you can believe that cat's wings are not clipped because he is naturally buzzing cuzin.—Lavada Durst, *The Jives of Dr. Hepcat*, p. 1, 1953

jing *noun*
money *US, 1973*
A shortened 'jingle'.
• Got any jing? I told you. They fucked up my pay record in Nam. —Charles Anderson, *The Grunts*, p. 17, 1976

jing-bang *noun*
an uneducated, dirty, noisy person *JAMAICA, 1952*
• —Peter Patrick, *Some Recent Jamaican Creole Words*, 2003

jing-jang *noun*
the penis *US, 1960*
• —*Fact*, p. 26, January-February 1965

jingle *noun*
a telephone call *US, late 1949*
• Well, I mean, I was going to give you a jingle. I was going to let you know I was back in town.—Robert Campbell, *Boneyards*, p. 129, 1992

jingle *verb*
to place a telephone call *US*
• —Edd Byrnes, *Way Out with Kookie*, 1959
• I'm angling to fix Rochester for us, so jingle me at the Sherry Netherlands at least once a week.—Iceberg Slim (Robert Beck), *Long White Con*, p. 205, 1977

jingle bell crew *noun*
a team of pickpockets *US*
• Now mostly applied to the professionals from Colombia, South America, the city's most adroit. The term comes from the way they practice their craft: attaching bells to clothes dummies, which jingle when they "clumsy up" the lift.—Bill Reilly, *Big Al's Official Guide to Chicagoese*, p. 38, 1982

jingles *noun*
pocket change *US*
• —James Harris, *A Convict's Dictionary*, p. 34, 1989

jingly-jangly *adjective*
of music, characterised by the use of acoustic guitars, bright tonal quality and (generally) happy songs *UK*
• Howie from the jingly-jangly Stands is wearing a brilliant green velvet hat.—*The Guardian*, p. 2, 28th June 2004

jink *verb*
1 in aerial combat, to make sudden, evasive movements *UK, 1917*
• —*Time*, p. 34, 10th December 1965
• —Carl Fleischhauer, *A Glossary of Army Slang*, p. 27, 1968

- The separation gave them the room to "jink," to move around up and down, left and right. The rule was never to stay straight and level for long and give the enemy a chance to hit you. —Gerry Carroll, *North S*A*R*, p. 202, 1991

2 to swindle *NEW ZEALAND*
Originally a term from a card game that evolved into wider usage.

- —David McGill, *David McGill's Complete Kiwi Slang Dictionary*, p. 63, 1998

jinker *noun*
in Newfoundland, on a boat, a bringer of bad luck *CANADA*

- Two jinkers in our harbour dwell, / Adventuresome and plucky. / The plans they make all promise well, / But always turn unlucky. —Omar Blondahl, *Newfoundland, Sing!*, p. 34, 1964

jinkers *noun*
harness racing *AUSTRALIA*

- —Ned Wallish, *The Truth Dictionary of Racing Slang*, p. 42, 1989

jinkies *noun*
▸ **the jinkies; the wee jinkies**
applied to anything that is considered excellent *UK: SCOTLAND*

- Aye, yer granny's trifle's the wee jinkies, init son? —Michael Munro, *The Patter, Another Blast*, p. 38, 1988

jinky *adjective*
unlucky *US*
From 'jinx'.

- Don't catch any crippled or cross-eyed marks. They're jinky. —Iceberg Slim (Robert Beck), *Trick Baby*, p. 146, 1969

jinx note *noun*
a two-dollar note *US, 1970*

- —Claudio R. Salvucci, *The Philadelphia Dialect Dictionary*, p. 46, 1996

jippo *noun*
▷ see: GYPO

jipsy *adjective*
anxious, energetic, flighty *TRINIDAD AND TOBAGO, 1984*

- —Lise Winer, *Dictionary of the English/Creole of Trinidad & Tobago*, 2003

jislaaik!; jis!; jiss!
used as an exclamation of such negative feelings as anger, frustration, distress, regret, etc; and of positive feelings such as admiration, approval, wonder, etc *SOUTH AFRICA, 1960*
Possibly a euphemism for 'Jesus!' (by intention, not etymology).

- As the motor builds to a wild howl, slip it into the next gear, each time exclaiming "Jislaaik" or "Good Golly" as you feel the bike accelerate and leap into the distance[.] —*Sunday Times (South Africa)*, 20th June 2002
- Writer Dennis Beckett said of [Obie] Oberholzer: "Jis, but this ou can graft." —*Sunday Times (South Africa)*, 22nd June 2003

jism *noun*
▷ see: JIZZ

jism trail *noun*
semen on a partner's body after ejaculation *US*
A pun on the Chisholm Trail, the major route for cattle drives from Texas to Abilene.

jiss *noun*
excitement, character *IRELAND*

- It's the bold boys yeh'd want to get your hands on. They're more fun. It's someone with a bit of jiss in him yeh'd want. —Billy Roche, *The Wexford Trilogy (Poor Beast in the Rain)*, p. 82, 1992

jisses!; jissus! *noun*
▷ see: JUSSUS!

jit *noun*
1 a nickel; five cents *US, 1913*

- —Lou Shelly, *Hepcats Jive Talk Dictionary*, p. 13, 1945
- "Got a jit? I need a couple more jits to get a bottle," he said. —James T. Farrell, *Saturday Night*, p. 27, 1947
- —John Scarne, *Scarne on Dice*, p. 471, 1974

2 semen *US*

- —Connie Eble (Editor), *UNC-CH Campus Slang*, March 1974

jitney *noun*
1 a sexually available girl *BAHAMAS*
Like the bus, anyone can get on if they have the fare.

- —John A. Holm, *Dictionary of Bahamian English*, p. 114, 1982

2 in poker, a $5 chip *US*

- —George Percy, *The Language of Poker*, p. 49, 1988

jits *adjective*
excellent, nice *SOUTH AFRICA*

jitterbug *noun*
a swing jazz enthusiast *US, 1938*

- Dance floors are crowded with jitterbugs. —Jack Lait and Lee Mortimer, *Washington Confidential*, p. 133, 1951

jitterbug *verb*
1 to fool around *US, 1942*

- Walk calm. No jitterbugging. Wear your cap straight. —Hal Ellson, *Duke*, p. 71, 1949
- You're just jitter-buggin' down there with them three bricks. —Henry Williamson, *Hustler!*, p. 146, 1965

2 to cause a car to bounce up and down suddenly through the use of hydraulic lifts operated by the driver *US*

- —Edith A. Folb, *runnin' down some lines*, p. 243, 1980

3 to fight, especially between gangs *US, 1958*

- —H. Craig Collins, *Street Gangs*, p. 223, 1979

jitters *noun*
uncontrolled shaking; extreme nervousness *US, 1929*

- "Hope you can clear this up quick, Mr. Tracy," he said. "I'm getting the jitters." —Chester Gould, *Dick Tracy Meets the Night Crawler*, p. 24, 1945
- The place was a bad spot to be in at night if you had the jitters. —Mickey Spillane, *I, The Jury*, p. 75, 1947
- Now, Folks, our play together is going to be ragged as hell for a while. But don't let it give you the jitters. —Iceberg Silm (Robert Beck), *Trick Baby*, p. 145, 1969
- Madrid gets the jitters over the changing face of crime. —*The Guardian*, 1st February 2003

jittery *adjective*
nervous, jumpy, on-edge *UK, 1931*

- [T]he fiasco last year has left jittery parents far less ready to accept that disappointing grades may be their child's fault. —*The Observer*, 10th August 2003

jive *noun*
1 swing jazz *US, 1937*

- Hero-worship of Americans and the flashier aspects of American life seem to be the most immediate reason for the popularity of jive[.] —William Sansom, *A Public for Jive [The Public's Progress]*, 1947
- The Blue Mirror, around the corner, specializes in hot jive. —Jack Lait and Lee Mortimer, *Washington Confidential*, p. 132, 1951

2 a highly stylised vernacular that originated with black jazz musicians *US, 1928*
Spoken by **HEP CAT(S)**, incorporating a mix of new coinages or meanings with older adoptions; few original words remain in circulation.

- The night wound up with them accusing me of trying to pass for white, because they couldn't believe that any white man could be as hip to the jive as I was. —Mezz Mezzrow, *Really the Blues*, p. 204, 1946
- That old street jive just comes flooding right back, doesn't it, eh? —Ian Pattison, *Rab C. Nesbitt*, 1988
- Did the stuffed shirts at the BBC think that we didn't get the jive, daddio[?] —Stuart Jeffries, *Mrs Slocombe's Pussy*, p. 24, 2000

3 insincere talk; nonsense *US, 1928*

- [I]f they got mad about it he gave them a line of his soft Southern jive. —Chester Himes, *If He Hollers Let Him Go*, p. 24, 1945
- There were a lot of doctors and druggists in my family, and I used to hear a lot of medical jive when I apprenticed in my uncle's drugstore, so I knew which symptoms went with what sickness. —Mezz Mezzrow, *Really the Blues*, p. 36–37, 1946
- Show me where the kitty lives and I'll believe that jive. —Hal Ellson, *The Golden Spike*, p. 40, 1952
- [F]or God's sake don't listen to that drool how the stuff [drugs] eat you up ... that kind of jive is for squares. —Harry J. Anslinger (US Commissioner of Narcotics), *The Murderers*, p. 174, 1961
- And also how much I would esteem myself once I got rid of them somewhere in the Loop, how I had put myself out for my fellow man and all that jive. —Clancy Sigal, *Going Away*, p. 162, 1961
- But back he came, more dead than alive / And the monkey came up with more of his jive. —Dennis Wepman et al., *The Life*, p. 24, 1976

4 marijuana or a marijuana cigarette *US, 1963*

- It's oney gauge he's on, a little jive. Marijuana ain't no habit like heroin. —George Mandel, *Flee the Angry Strangers*, p. 20, 1948
- I mean, the main studs could have called a conference and set down and worked the whole thing out over a few sticks of this mellow jive. —Ross Russell, *The Sound*, p. 22, 1961
- We can cop some jive anyplace. —Donald Goines, *Cry Revenge*, p. 41, 1974

5 heroin or, less often, opium *US*

- Boy, leave me tell you one thing, if you knew like we know, you'd leave this jive alone[.] —Mezz Mezzrow, *Really the Blues*, p. 248, 1946
- You've been taking dope, horse, jive, anything you want to call it. —Hal Ellson, *The Golden Spike*, p. 22, 1952
- He was a dope fiend, and he told me he had just beat a rap, and needed some jive. —Henry Williamson, *Hustler!*, p. 149, 1965
- You can get right funky, Jo-Jo, when the last of the junk is in sight. You're real cool when there's a lot of the jive, but you get doggish as a motherfucker when it ain't but a little bit left. —Donald Goines, *Crime Partners*, p. 11, 1978
- —Robert Ashton, *This Is Heroin*, p. 206, 2002

jive *verb*

1 to speak with a lack of sincerity *US, 1928*

- Monkey wasn't jiving about that bartender. He wasn't exactly a rabbi[.] —Mezz Mezzrow, *Really the Blues*, p. 74, 1946
- Baby ... doll, baby, you ... you jivin me. You playin aron; right, doll? —George Mandel, *Flee the Angry Strangers*, p. 250, 1952
- Let's hold class for the squares on how to properly jive a chick. —Dan Burley, *Diggeth Thou?*, p. 5, 1959
- The cops put me in the back room. I'm jiving with the spades. —Abbie Hoffman, *Revolution for the Hell of It*, p. 19, 1968
- I jive people if I dont' trust them, see. I jive that motherfucker because I don't feel right with him, you dig my meaning. —Cecil Brown, *The Life & Loves of Mr. Jiveass Nigger*, p. 31, 1969
- "I ain't jiving," says the messenger. "He really wants you right away." —Darryl Ponicsan, *The Last Detail*, p. 12, 1970
- Sapphire puts her hands on her hips to indicate that she ain't jivin' and does mean to be taken seriously. —Carolyn Greene, *70 Soul Secrets of Sapphire*, 1973
- Then Earl said I was jiving[.] —Bobby Seale, *A Lonely Rage*, p. 68, 1978

2 to dance *US, 1938*

- When a band plays one [a rumba], flabbergasted hoofers try to jive to it. —Jack Lait and Lee Mortimer, *Washington Confidential*, p. 133, 1951
- It was Danny and the Juniors singing "At the Hop," which gave Esme and me a chance to do some cool jiving all the way down the corridor to the history class[.] —Max Shulman, *I was a Teen-Age Dwarf*, p. 10, 1959

jive *adjective*

insincere, phony, pretentious *US, 1946*

- This was my first thing on my own since going up there with that jive shit with the Rev. —Babs Gonzales, *Movin' On Down De Line*, p. 32, 1975
- Rack 'em up, house man, and check my gun / I don't want to kill the jive motherfucker; I want to shoot him one. —Dennis Wepman et al., *The Life*, p. 31, 1976
- I felt, no man cared if I were alive/I felt the whole world was so jive. —Village People, *Y.M.C.A.*, 1978
- I would just be cool, I planned, carry my knife, stop running around with that jive Village Gang, and stayout of the way of other fools who would want to jump on me for nothing. —Bobby Seale, *A Lonely Rage*, p. 64, 1978

jive-ass *noun*

an insincere, unreliable person *US, 1967*

- No, he became a hustler, a jiveass, a jazz player who could never quite get the versatility to match the humming in his head[.] —Cecil Brown, *The Life & Loves of Mr. Jiveass Nigger*, p. 8, 1969

jive-ass; jive-arse *adjective*

worthless, unreliable *US, 1959*

- I wasn't weighted down and barred from vicarious ecstasy by no jiveass junior logarithm trash[.] —Lester Bangs, *Psychotic Reactions and Carburetor Dung*, p. 59, 1971
- We goin' take this whole fuckin' jiveass town by the fuckin' throat and make it ours! —Donald Goines, *Inner City Hoodlum*, p. 8, 1975
- That we were never busted at 212 was nothing short of a miracle. And we discovered that Jamie had settled for some jive-arse discount return air tickets that had expired before we'd even finished sleeping off the gig and the party. —Mick Farren, *Give the Anarchist a Cigarette*, p. 229, 2001

jive bomber *noun*

a skilled dancer *US*

- —*Yank*, p. 18, 24th March 1945

jive doo jee *noun*

heroin *UK, 1998*

- —Mike Haskins, *Drugs*, p. 284, 2003

jiver *noun*

an inveterate flatterer *US*

- —Marcus Hanna Boulware, *Jive and Slang of Students in Negro Colleges*, 1947

jive stick *noun*

a marijuana cigarette *US, 1945*

- —*American Speech*, p. 87, May 1955: 'Narcotic argot along the Mexican Border'
- —Richard A. Spears, *The Slang and Jargon of Drugs and Drink*, p. 287, 1986
- —Mike Haskins, *Drugs*, p. 288, 2003

jizz; jizzum; jism; jiz; jizm; gism; gizzum *noun*

semen *US, 1941*

Links to an earlier use as 'life-force, energy, spirit'; a meaning that, occasionally, may still be intended.

- The world network of junkies, tuned on a cord of rancid jissom, tying up in furnished rooms, shivering in the junk-sick morning. —William Burroughs, *Naked Lunch*, p. 6, 1957
- Swallowing gism is rather like getting used to raw clams: you have to give it a chance and before you know it, you're addicted. —*Screw*, p. 9, 1st March 1970
- I didn't much like the sounds of romance the first time I saw jizz. —Oscar Zeta Acosta, *The Autobiography of a Brown Buffalo*, p. 83, 1972
- What you see now is the "cum shot," and it has become a big item in sexflicks. You can watch his jism jettison, and this removes all doubt that there is anything simulated about this sex scene. —*Adam Film World*, p. 58, 1977
- Down in cunt valley where guizzum does flow, / The cocksuckers work for a nickel a blow. —Ed Cray, *Charlotte the Harlot*, *Bawdy Ballads*, p. 96, 1978
- There ain't much to country living / Sweat, piss, jizz and blood. —Warren Zevon, *Play It All Night Long*, 1980
- When he finally spurts his thick jiz, she looks at you, the viewer, with a naughty smile. —*Adult Video*, p. 13, August/September 1986
- Ike had used the word "spoo" – roughly the equivalent of jizz – in a conversation. —Frank Zappa, *The Real Frank Zappa Book*, p. 170, 1989
- She's into it: "Fuck me, you asshole! Come on my tits! Come all over my tits!" And Wallice gets up and turns around, and she's covered with jizz. —Robert Stoller and I.S. Levine, *Coming Attractions*, p. 192, 1991
- [T]he humiliation of parading a jism-stained frock in front of my friend's grandparents[.] —Kitty Churchill, *Thinking of England*, p. 126, 1995
- Candy now makes a big black bastard spurt jizz seconds before he steps into Jasmin's bang boutique. —Anthony Petkovich, *The X Factory*, p. 192, 1997
- How would you like to gargle rat jiz? —*South Park*, 1999
- "I'm not bloody touching him," Angelique replied. "He's covered in jizz." —Christopher Brookmyre, *The Sacred Art of Stealing*, p. 369, 2002

jizz *verb*

to ejaculate *US, 1983*

- He sort of matter-of-factly removed his dork, pressed the length of it against her, and jizzed on her ass[.] —Josh Alan Friedman, *Tales of Times Square*, p. 107, 1986
- Jump start: Lucille's hip huggers, slashed and jizzed on. —James Ellroy, *White Jazz*, p. 53, 1992
- Then, I want you to flick at my nuts while your friend spanks me into the same Dixie cup Silent Bob jizzed in. —Kevin Smith, *Jay and Silent Bob Strike Back*, p. 90, 2001

jizzbag *noun*

an offensive and disgusting person *US*

Literally, 'a condom'.

- Who is this jizzbag judge? Bibe quotes – from what, the Book of Dick? —Carl Hiaasen, *Strip Tease*, p. 71, 1993

jizzer *noun*

a scene in a pornographic film or photograph showing a man ejaculating *US*

- —*Adult Video News*, p. 42, August 1995

jizz joint *noun*

a sex club *US*

- Because of the way it positions itself, this particular jizz joint is not a haven for working-class girls in a dead-end town or junkies supporting a habit. —*Village Voice*, 31st October 2000

jizz-mopper *noun*

an employee in a pornographic video arcade or sex show who cleans up after customers who have come have left *US*

- Randal: You know how much money the average jizz-mopper makes per hour? —*Clerks*, 1994

jizz rag *noun*

a rag used for wiping semen *US*

- "I think you oughta start carrying a jizz rag, Hans," Cecil Higgins said. —Joseph Wambaugh, *The Delta Star*, p. 105, 1983

JJ Cale *noun*

a jail *UK*

Rhyming slang, formed from the name of the US musician (b.1938).

- It's into court in front of the old vanilla fudge [judge] and Billy Fury [jury] where he gets a couple of britneys [years] and JJ Cale. —Mervyn Stutter, *Getting Nowhere Fast*, 21st May 2004

JK!

just kidding! *US*

Used after saying something that sounds improbable.

JLD

(in doctors' shorthand) *just like dad* *UK*

Medical slang; glossed as 'in FLKs [funny looking kids] it is the common aetiology [origin of the condition]' by Adam T. Fox, St Mary's Hospital, London, 10th October 2002.

J-load *nickname*

a generously proportioned backside *UK*

After the widely appreciated hindquarters of film actress and singer Jennifer Lopez (b.1970), popularly known and marketed by the nickname 'J Lo'. Recorded in use in contemporary gay society.

- — *Attitude*, p. 60, July 2003: 'New palare lexicon'

JO *noun*

1 an act of male masturbation *US, 1972*

An abbreviation of **JERK-OFF**.

- I went two weeks with j/o so I would be really hot. [Letter] — *Drummer*, p. 73, 1979

2 a job *US*

- — *Washington Post*, 14th October 1993

JO *verb*

(used of a male) to masturbate *US, 1959*

An abbreviation of the oh-so-common **JERK OFF**.

- I tried to "read between the lines" in the famous Nancy Drew books, searching for some deep secret insinuation of erotica so powerful and pervasive as to account for the extraordinary popularity of these books, but alas, was able to garner no mileage ("J.O." wise) from this innocuous, and seemingly endless, series. — Terry Southern, *Now Dig This*, p. 2, 1986
- This venture falls in the middle range of JO tapes – good enough for aficionados of the format, but not likely to impress viewers who prefer heavier action. — *Adult Video News*, p. 95, February 1993
- — Pamela Munro, *U.C.L.A. Slang*, p. 87, 2001

joan; jone *verb*

to insult in a competitive, quasi-friendly spirit *US, 1939*

- — *The Washington Post*, 7th June 1987
- — *American Speech*, p. 86, Spring 1995: 'Among the new words'
- There are many different terms for playing the dozens, including "bagging, capping, cracking, dissing, hiking, joning, ranking, ribbing, serving, signifying, slipping, sounding and snapping". — James Haskins, *The Story of Hip-Hop*, p. 54, 2000

Joanie *adjective*

profoundly out of touch with current fashions and trends *US*

- — Mary Corey and Victoria Westermark, *Fer Shurr! How to be a Valley Girl*, 1982

joanna; joana; joanner; johanna *noun*

a piano *UK, 1846*

Rhyming slang.

- [H]aving a bit of a ding-dong round the old Joanna [piano]. — Ronnie Barker, *Fletcher's Book of Rhyming Slang*, p. 39, 1979

Joan of Arc *noun*

1 a lark, in phrases such as 'fuck this for a lark' *UK*

Rhyming slang.

- Sod this for a Joan of Arc. — Ray Puxley, *Fresh Rabbit*, 1998

2 a park *UK*

Rhyming slang.

- — Ray Puxley, *Fresh Rabbit*, 1998

3 a shark *AUSTRALIA*

Rhyming slang.

- — Ray Puxley, *Fresh Rabbit*, 1998

job *noun*

1 used as a substitute for a noun which is apparent from context, especially of cars *US, 1896*

Sometimes embellished to 'jobby'.

- The car was a smooth-looking job: light blue, red leather seats, white-wall tires, fancy fog lights, and all the other extras that Benny's brother Sam could buy. — Irving Shulman, *The Amboy Dukes*, p. 51, 1947
- He just got a Jaguar. One of those little English jobs that can do around two hundred miles an hour. — J.D. Salinger, *Catcher in the Rye*, p. 1, 1951
- It's stopped raining. I wonder if you'd care for a run in the old car [...] She's an old job, but she's fast. — Alexander Baron, *A Bit of Happiness [Six Granada Plays]*, p. 200, 1959
- Is that the new car out there? The little red Wop job? — *The Graduate*, 1967
- Rico Carty hit two home runs off him. One of them was a two-run job in the last of the eighth[.] — Jim Bouton, *Ball Four*, p. 341, 1970
- You know, I'd be embarrassed if I let my wheels go the way you've done with this job. — *48 Hours*, 1982
- Manchester's Albert Square, the big public jobby outside the Town Hall. — Tony Wilson, *24 Hour Party People*, p. 132, 2002

2 an inanimate or mechanical article, a thing *UK, 1943*

- [A] small garden which let on to a little park with trees and shrubs and the usual convenience, a key-holder's only job. — Martin Waddell, *Otley*, p. 15, 1966

3 a person *US, 1927*

Usually prefixed with a noun or adjective characteristic.

- The Heswall nut job, sitting on the big basket-chair in the corner[.] — Kevin Sampson, *Powder*, p. 151, 1999

4 a criminal venture, usually a robbery *UK, 1690*

- [T]hey stood on the corners and discussed the deadly gossip of rackets: whore, guys who were cut up, and the dough you could make from one sweet job. — Irving Shulman, *The Amboy Dukes*, p. 2–3, 1947
- [W]hen he got home he would find them lounging about his living room, just back from one of these jobs somewhere in the city[.] — John Clellon Holmes, *Go*, p. 213, 1952
- Let's pull a job. It's money we need. — Hal Ellson, *The Golden Spike*, p. 8, 1952
- We pulled the first job that night[.] — Malcolm X and Alex Haley, *The Autobiography of Malcolm X*, p. 143, 1964
- He pulled that job to pay for the band's room service tab from that Chiwanous gig in Pols city. — *The Blues Brothers*, 1980
- He knew everyone on the Street but when not alone – was usually with a couple of fellows – and knew to be hard core 42nd Street hustlers – who were sharp dressers and reputed to go out occasionally on jobs – maybe a stickup or burglary. — Herbert Huncke, *The Evening Sun Turned Crimson*, p. 45, 1980
- She hooked up with Fred McGar, they've done a couple jobs together. Helluva woman. Good little thief. — *Reservoir Dogs*, 1992
- — Angela Devlin, *Prison Patter*, p. 66, 1996

5 a medical procedure *US, 1943*

A variant of 'job' (a variety), usually combined with a body part: 'nose', 'boob', etc.

- I know you and Sicora got plastic jobs. — James Ellroy, *Hollywood Nocturnes*, p. 260, 1994

6 an act of defecation *US*

- — *American Speech*, p. 62, Spring-Summer 1975: 'Razorback slang'

7 in professional wrestling, a planned, voluntary loss *US*

- But even though I'm writing about a sport that some feel is not "real," this is a real story, and the real truth is I did the job that night (lost the match). — Mick Foley, *Mankind*, p. 7, 1999

8 the injection of a drug for non-medicinal purposes *US*

- — William D. Alsever, *Glossary for the Establishment and Other Uptight People*, p. 17, December 1970
- — Eugene Landy, *The Underground Dictionary*, p. 113, 1971

▸ **do a job**

to defecate *AUSTRALIA, 1942*

Sometimes embellished to 'jobbie'.

▸ **just the job; the job**

exactly what is required *UK, 1943*

- When moving out can be just the job[.] — *The Guardian*, 4th January 2004

▸ **on the job**

having sex, engaged in sexual intercourse *UK, 1966*

- On the job, cripes I wish I was. — Barry Humphries, *Bazza Pulls It Off!*, 1971
- He died on the job you know. — David Williamson, *Don's Party*, p. 61, 1973
- It's not music at all, more like her neighbours on the job. — John King, *Human Punk*, p. 241, 2000

▸ **the job**

the police (as a profession) *UK*

Police slang.

- — *The Official Encyclopaedia of New Scotland Yard*, 1999
- I realised I had just had my first encounter with the Job's Compensation Culture[.] — Duncan MacLaughlin, *The Filth*, p. 62–63, 2002

job *verb*

1 to rob, to steal, to cheat *US, 1889*

- "Pinched. Jobbed. Swiped. Stole," he says, happily. "You know, man, like somebody boosted my threads." — Ken Kesey, *One Flew Over the Cuckoo's Nest*, p. 94, 1962
- So, the Red Sox were jobbed out of Game Three and the bubble-gum chewing Big Red Machine took the Series lead. — Bill Cardoso, *The Maltese Sangweech*, p. 178, 1984
- "He says he's sure he's being jobbed," Breda said. — Joseph Wambaugh, *Fugitive Nights*, p. 118, 1992

2 to suffer a planned, voluntary loss in a professional wrestling match *US*

- In any cause, rumours have Hogan facing someone else (who's willing to job?) in place of Gordy. — *Herb's Wrestling Tidbits*, 4th April 1990
- — *Washington Post*, p. 36, 10th March 2000: 'A wrestling glossary'

- When Backlund refused to hand over the belt, he was screwed out of it in a setup with the Iron Sheik, who in turn jobbed it to Hogan. — *Rampage Magazine*, p. 71, September 2000

3 to hit or strike; to punch *AUSTRALIA, 1915*
- JOB, TO – To attack; to strike. — Gilbert H. Lawson, *A Dictionary of Australian Words and Terms*, 1924
- He was a prisoner, trying to escape, but I apprehended him and jobbed him one. — Alexander Buzo, *Norm and Ahmed*, p. 8, 1969

4 to inject a drug *US*
- — John B. Williams, *Narcotics and Hallucinogenics*, p. 113, 1967

jo bag *noun*
a condom *UK, 1961*
- — *Maledicta*, p. 198, Winter 1980: 'A new erotic vocabulary'

job and finish *noun*
a period of employment that is limited by the time it takes to do a specific task *UK, 1984*
Originally in Merchant Navy use.
- Now we have "job and finish", where you've got to get the job finished in the time. — *The Guardian*, 21st March 2001

jobbed *adjective*
incriminated by false evidence *UK*
- — Angela Devlin, *Prison Patter*, p. 66, 1996

jobber *noun*
a professional wrestler who is regularly assigned to lose to advance the careers of others *US*
- Flair pummeled a jobber and then goaded Sting to come to the ringside. — *Herb's Wrestling Tidbits*, 5th July 1990
- Professional jobbers are unique in their trade. In no other sport is one paid to lose and make his opponent look good while doing so. — Jeff Archer, *Theater in a Squared Circle*, p. 113, 1999
- They ran him through a small army of jobbers. — *Rampage Magazine*, September 2000

jobber to the stars *noun*
a moderately talented professional wrestler who is assigned to lose to the most popular wrestlers *US*
- These guys will be given a few wins before becoming jobbers to the stars, unless they do the unlikely and magically get over. — *Herb's Wrestling Tidbits*, 4th July 1996

jobbie *noun*
1 used as a substitute noun which is apparent from its context; an item *US, 1960*
Extension of **JOB**.
- Standing up she were, straight into the what's it, urinal jobby. — *The Full Monty*, 1997
- [S]he opens really good bottles of red – you know, £8 jobbies – and spills most of it on the carpet. — Jenny Eclair, *Camberwell Beauty*, p. 14, 2000

2 a transaction; a situation; a piece of work; an event; a procedure; an occurrence *US*
A variation of conventional and unconventional **JOB**.
- One hundred per cent green-light [approved] jobbie. — Kevin Sampson, *Outlaws*, p. 90, 2001

3 a turd *UK*
From Scottish dialect *jobbie* (a little job); compare with **BIG JOBS** (defecation). Widely popularised in the 1970s by comedian Billy Connolly.
- "I was going to say that I once did this jobbie that –" Whack. "Ouch." "Don't be disgusting." — Christopher Brookmyre, *Boiling a Frog*, p. 103, 2000

4 a racehorse *US*
- — David W. Maurer, *Argot of the Racetrack*, p. 38, 1951

Jobbie *noun*
a Job Centre *UK*
- Just off to pick up me giro like. Waiting for me it is, in-a Jobbie like. — Niall Griffiths, *Sheepshagger*, p. 50, 2001

jobbie-jabber *noun*
a male homosexual *UK*
A reference to anal sex formed on **JOBBIE** (a turd).
- — Chris Lewis, *The Dictionary of Playground Slang*, p. 125, 2003

jobo; joro *noun*
a woman, mistress or prostitute *US*
From the Japanese, used by US military in Korea.
- — Carl Fleischhauer, *A Glossary of Army Slang*, p. 28, 1968

job out *verb*
to assign a wrestler to lose intentionally to advance the career of another *US*
- Perhaps the sub will be Tom Zenk, who they seem to be jobbing out. — *Herb's Wrestling Tidbits*, 25th October 1990

jobroni; jobrone; gibroni *noun*
a professional wrestler who is regularly assigned to lose *US*
Embellishments of the standard **JOBBER**.
- A star simply uses this medium (television) to build his stature and display his style by manhandling a "gibroni" – an unknown or habitual loser. — Larry Nelson and James Jones, *Stranglehold*, p. 45, 1999
- Bounty Hunters have been beating up jobronis for weeks now and they freaked when Fuller announced Gordy. — Georgiann Makropoulos, *Chatterbox*, 8th August 2000

jobsworth *noun*
anyone in a position of authority (no matter how petty) who reinforces the personal power of office by insistence on the finer details of whichever bureaucracy or rulebook is represented, generally to veto or reject a course of action *UK, 1970*
From the expression, 'It's more than my job's worth'.
- Jobsworth, jobsworth / More than me job's worth. — Jeremy Taylor, *Jobsworth*, 1973
- [S]ome jobsworth will accuse you of being a camped-out diddicoi and serve you with a ten quid overnight parking bill. — John Milne, *Alive and Kicking*, p. 23, 1998
- A few of the screws [prison officers] weren't amused, like Mrs Crabtree and this other one who was a real by-the-book jobsworth character. — Dave Courtney, *Stop the Ride I Want to Get Off*, p. 349, 1999
- They've got to look like lazy incompetent jobsworths[.] — Chris Ryan, *The Watchman*, p. 227, 2001

jock *noun*
1 an athlete, especially a student athlete *US, 1958*
Originally referred to a man's genitals, leading to 'jock strap' as an athletic support, leading to a clipped 'jock' for the support, leading to application to the man wearing the support. Usually, but not always, suggestive of a certain mindlessness.
- — *American Speech*, p. 194, October 1965: 'Notes on campus vocabulary, 1964'
- As with the demonstrations against Marine campus recruiting in the spring of '67, threats of violence from the right will bring hundreds of the usually moderate to the SDS ranks just to align themselves against jock violence. — James Simon Kunen, *The Strawberry Statement*, p. 27, 1968
- — Collin Baker et al., *College Undergraduate Slang Study Conducted at Brown University*, p. 145, 1968
- At sudent sit-ins, it is the "jocks" who try to toss the anarchists out. — Richard Neville, *Play Power*, p. 274, 1970
- — Multicultural Management Program Fellows, *Dictionary of Cautionary Words and Phrases*, 1989
- I guess you could call a tennis player a jock. I think they do wear them. At least the guys do. — C.D. Payne, *Youth in Revolt*, p. 210, 1993

2 a jockey *UK, 1826*
- She's hanging around the track every day. I'm interested, professionally. I find out she's some jock's regular, she's living with the shrimp. — Truman Capote, *Breakfast at Tiffany's*, p. 31, 1958
- He was a senior jock who had ridden in all parts on the globe. — Wilda Moxham, *The Apprentice*, p. 48, 1969

3 a disc jockey *US, 1947*
- [H]uge underground support from a wide variety of jocks[.] — *Ministry*, p. 24, October 2002

4 a navy fighter pilot *US, 1959*
- — *American Speech*, p. 123, Summer 1986: 'The language of Naval fighter pilots'

5 the penis; the male genitals *UK, 1790*
- The ugly big-tit broad would stand there [in the dream] buck naked with a jock three times the size of my own. — Iceberg Slim (Robert Beck), *Trick Baby*, p. 114, 1969
- [O]nce club beats and mediocre lyrics become the fashionable norm it seems everyone, your magazine included, is on the rappers' jocks. — *Hip-Hop Connection*, p. 9, July 2002

6 an athletic support *US*
An abbreviation of 'jock strap'.
- Like the baseball players that they're always catching on the on-deck circle, got their hands down in their jocks, moving their balls around. — George V. Higgins, *Penance for Jerry Kennedy*, p. 31, 1985

7 a computer programmer who enumerates all possible combinations to find the one that solves the problem *US*
- — Guy L. Steele et al., *The Hacker's Dictionary*, p. 85, 1983

Jock *noun*

a Scot *UK, 1788*

Originally armed services' use, then widespread; from the Scottish variant of proper name John.

- Bloody nutters. All them Jocks are nutters. —Anthony Masters, *Minder*, p. 166, 1984
- POLICEMAN: On your way, Jock. Before you get into trouble. NESBITT: Oh, it's Jock noo is it? Wee bit of friendly racism, eh? —Ian Pattison, *Rab C. Nesbitt*, 1988
- It was a Jock that was the making of us. —Kevin Sampson, *Outlaws*, p. 7, 2001

jock *verb*

1 to have sex *UK, 1699*

- —Pamela Munro, *U.C.L.A. Slang*, p. 53, 1989

2 to like; to find attractive *US, 1986*

- Watch, I'm 'a roll up, and y'all niggas gon' be jockin'. —*Menace II Society*, 1993
- —Rick Ayers (Editor), *Berkeley High Slang Dictionary*, p. 28, 2004

Jock *adjective*

Scottish *UK, 1984*

Of military origin.

jock collar *noun*

a rubber ring fitted around the base of the penis *US*

Later and better known as a **COCK RING**.

- Pocket was at the back of the poolroom with an old Jewish peddler of French ticklers, Spanish fly, and jock collars. —Iceberg Slim (Robert Beck), *Trick Baby*, p. 218, 1969

jocked off *verb*

of a professional jockey, to have been deprived of an agreed mount *UK*

- I discovered that two of my three prospective mounts were mine no longer. I had been, in the expressive phrase, jocked off. —Dick Francis, *Nerve*, 1964

jocker *noun*

1 an aggressive, predatory male homosexual *US, 1893*

- They are usually long-terms and are familiarly known to inmates by such local cognomens as "wolves," "top men," "jockers" or "daddies." —*Ebony*, p. 82, July 1951
- Jockers and wolves are synonymous terms to describe the active partners in sodomy. —*New York Mattachine Newsletter*, p. 6, June 1961
- "My, my," the Spook murmured, "not a feather on him. Some jocker's due to score." —Malcolm Braly, *On the Yard*, p. 35, 1967
- Roxie hustles the guys who want a queen, and the kid goes after the ones who want a jocker. —Joseph Wambaugh, *The Blue Knight*, p. 44, 1973
- Inmates subject to rape ("punks") face threats and violence perpetrated by stronger inmates ("daddies,' "jockers," or "booty bandits") who initiate unwanted sexual acts. —*Corrections Today*, p. 100, December 1996

2 an older homosexual male living with and by virtue of the earnings of a younger companion *US, 1890s to 1970s*

Originally tramp slang.

- —*Fact*, p. 26, January-February 1965

jockette *noun*

a female student athlete *US*

Spoken for effect, rarely spontaneously.

- —Connie Eble (Editor), *UNC-CH Campus Slang*, p. 3, Spring 1980

jockey *noun*

1 a prostitute's client *UK*

- Wherever prostitutes congregate with their clients, or "jockeys" as they contemptuously call them. —David Powis, *The Signs of Crime*, 1977

2 a rapist *IRELAND*

- He raped auld [old] ones and kids as well. He is hated, even among the other jockeys, which is what I find incredible. —Howard Paul, *The Joy*, p. 89, 1996

3 a driver of any heavy-load vehicle *UK*

- —*British Road Services Magazine*, December 1951

jockey *verb*

to drive, to operate *US, 1948*

- IMPATIENT CUSTOMER: That's why you're jockeying a register in some fucking local convenience store instead of doing an honest day's work. —*Clerks*, 1994

jockey slut *noun*

a girl who trades her sexual availability to disc jockeys in exchange for hanger-on status *UK*

The dance music magazine *Jockey Slut* was first published in 1997.

- That Sandy isn't cool – she's a donut and a Jockey Slut. —Colin Butts, *Is Harry Still on the Boat?*, p. 363, 2003

jockey's whip *noun*

a bed; a sleep *UK*

Rhyming slang for **KIP**.

- —Julian Franklyn, *A Dictionary of Rhyming Slang*, 1960

jockey's whips *noun*

1 chips *UK*

Rhyming slang.

- —W Mitford, *Lovely She Goes*, 1969

2 LSD *UK*

Rhyming slang for **TRIPS** (LSD).

- —*www.LondonSlang.com*, June 2002

jock itch *noun*

a sweat-induced rash in the crotch *US, 1950*

- He'd developed incurable jock itch, and to his astonishment, his leather gear had independent sweat rings. —Joseph Wambaugh, *Fugitive Nights*, p. 33–34, 1992
- [A] man clad in a pair of leather chaps and a studded codpiece came past attending to a bout of Jock itch. —Kitty Churchill, *Thinking of England*, p. 33, 1995

jock jacket *noun*

a condom *UK*

- —David Rowan, *A Glossary for the 90s*, 1998

Jock Mackay *noun*

a pie, especially a 'Scotch pie' *UK: SCOTLAND*

Glasgow rhyming slang, formed on an imagined or generic Scotsman, also heard of in the wistful expression 'Och aye, Jock Mackay'.

- Ah hud a couple a Jock Mackays fur ma tea. —Michael Munro, *The Patter, Another Blast*, 1988

jocko *noun*

an athlete, a jock *US*

- He was just another jocko, but he was an ace because he was always out with Mickey Mantle and the boys[.] —Jim Bouton, *Ball Four*, p. 81, 1970

Jocko land *noun*

Scotland *UK: ENGLAND*

Extended from **JOCK** (a Scot).

- Home Counties, South coast, Jocko land, all over. —Andrew Nickolds, *Back to Basics*, p. 10, 1994

jocks *noun*

male underwear *IRELAND*

- One shower a week is all you're allowed in here. One shower a week and one new pair of jocks. —Howard Paul, *The Joy*, p. 18, 1996
- At an age when you'd live in fear of someone seeing the colour of your jocks. —Eamonn Sweeney, *Waiting for the Healer*, p. 119, 1997

jock-sniffer *noun*

an obsequious sports fan who tries to associate with athletes *US, 1971*

- Or you see him at Lindell's with the jock sniffers. Every couple of years he offers to buy the Tigers and in between he buys 'em drinks. —Elmore Leonard, *Split Images*, p. 50, 1981

jockstrap *noun*

an athlete *US, mid-1940s*

- He's this nine year old jockstrap in the Little League, see, really far-out kid. —Gurney Norman, *Divine Right's Trip (Last Whole Earth Catalog)*, p. 193, 1971

jock strapper *noun*

an athlete *US*

- Franklin was an all-American jock strapper. a high school letterman according to the conversations they had the first few days in the academy. —Joseph Wambaugh, *The New Centurions*, p. 23, 1970

Jodrell Bank; jodrell *noun*

an act of masturbation *UK, 1992*

Rhyming slang for **WANK** formed on the observatory located in Cheshire.

- [H]e was having a Jodrell spying on some couple in the shrubbery[.] —Kitty Churchill, *Thinking of England*, p. 199, 1995

Jody *noun*

1 the anonymous seducer of a soldier's girlfriend back home *US, 1944*

- The servicemen were always hostile towards a Jodie, especially a black Jodie in his fine Jodie clothes. — Chester Himes, *If He Hollers Let Him Go*, p. 79, 1945
- Then old Jody he turned over with his eyes all red / he said, "I beg your pardon, baby," says, "now what is that you said?" — Bruce Jackson, *Get Your Ass in the Water and Swim Like Me*, p. 93, 1964
- Just like I said, Man, a letter for PFC Edward Haskins. Let's see if Jody's been snooping around that stuff. — Charles Anderson, *The Grunts*, p. 91, 1976
- Ain't no use in going home / Jody's got your girl and gone. — Sandee Shaffer Johnson, *Cadences*, p. 15, 1986
- — Linda Reinberg, *In the Field*, p. 117, 1991

2 a male civilian during wartime *US, 1944*

- I tried to go to college but I couldn't stand it. I felt I was the only Jodie there. — Chester Himes, *Cast the First Stone*, p. 256, 1952

3 a black seducer of white women *US*

- "Jody" is a contraction of "Joe-the-Grinder" ("Sweet spot finder"), whose balls weighed fortyfour pounds, whose penis was gigantic. — Robert deCoy, *The Nigger Bible*, p. 32, 1967

joe *noun*

1 coffee *US, 1930*

Originally tramp slang.

- Won't even trust me for a cup of joe until I get a job. — Mickey Spillane, *My Gun is Quick*, p. 7, 1950
- I do enjoy a good cuppa joe. — *Austin Powers*, 1999
- Right at that moment everyone in Editorial suddenly seemed to crave a good strong cup of joe[.] — Rita Ciresi, *Pink Slip*, p. 107, 1999

2 a condom *NEW ZEALAND*

- Saul muttered "Have you got a safe? A rubber, a joe, don't be stupid?" — *Islands*, p. 54, 1976

Joe *noun*

1 a fool *NEW ZEALAND*

Especially in constructions such as 'make a joe of yourself'.

- The bloody joker that bought it was there, didn't want to make joes of us all. — Jean Watson, *Stand in the Rain*, p. 82, 1965

2 a new worker who cannot perform up to expected standards *US*

- "Don't ever get hit on the head with one of these, some Joe happens to drop it." He told her a Joe was an ironworker who couldn't hack it. — Elmore Leonard, *Killshot*, p. 34, 1989

3 a regular fellow *US, 1911*

- I knew him well. A nice Joe that had a heart of gold. — Mickey Spillane, *I, The Jury*, p. 44, 1947
- He was a good old joe, fat, happy, middlewestern. — Jack Kerouac, *The Dharma Bums*, p. 101, 1958
- And others who seem to represent none but themselves, quirky joes, who shouted to the crowds to buy the Militant, or Sparticist, or National Liberation Front buttons. — Sidney Bernard, *This Way to the Apocalypse*, p. 60–61, 1965

4 used to create an imaginary person, first name Joe, last name the quality or characteristic that is personified *US, 1912*

- I meet the star of the show, Bill Leighton, whom I recognize as the typical Joe Moderator of countless afternoon programs. — James Simon Kunen, *The Strawberry Statement*, p. 56, 1968

5 a member of the Navajo Indian tribe *US*

An abbreviation of Nava-Joe.

- — *American Speech*, p. 271, December 1963: 'American Indian student slang'

6 a prison inmate who is easily imposed upon *UK*

- — Home Office, *Glossary of Terms and Slang Common in Penal Establishments*, July 1978

7 a police officer *US*

- Straite, how later stood outside the store, warned of Remington's approach by yelling: "Here comes the Joes!" – street slang for police officers. — *Washington Post*, p. B3, 30th May 1987

8 Schlitz™ beer *US*

From the full name, the Joseph Schlitz Brewing Company.

- — Connie Eble (Editor), *UNC-CH Campus Slang*, p. 4, March 1979

▸ **out the Joe**

completely drunk *NEW ZEALAND*

- He's out the monk. Really out the Joe. He's made a fair dinkum job of himself today. — Ronald Hugh Morrieson, *Come a Hot Friday*, p. 122, 1964

Joe Baksi; Joe Baxi *noun*

a taxi *UK*

Rhyming slang, based on a US heavyweight boxer well known in the UK. In Glasgow use and also noted in UK prison use.

- Never mind the motor. We'll dive inty a Joe Baxi. — Michael Munro, *The Patter, Another Blast*, 1988
- — Angela Devlin, *Prison Patter*, p. 66, 1996

Joe Balls *noun*

used as a derogatory personification of the typical US soldier *US*

- — *American Speech*, p. 238, October 1946: 'World War II slang of maladjustment'

Joe Blake *noun*

1 a snake *AUSTRALIA, 1905*

Rhyming slang.

- Before we got the diesels we used to keep the firebox pricker red hot and we'd lean out of the cab and job it on a Joe Blake as we passed. — Patsy Adam-Smith, *Folklore of the Australian Railwaymen*, p. 259, 1969

2 a gambling stake; a wooden stake *UK*

Rhyming slang.

- — Ray Puxley, *Cockney Rabbit*, 1992

Joe Blakes *noun*

the shaking symptoms of extreme alcoholism *AUSTRALIA, 1944*

Rhyming slang for the **SHAKES**.

- — David McGill, *David McGill's Complete Kiwi Slang Dictionary*, p. 73, 1998

Joe Bloggs *noun*

everyman; a notional average man *UK, 1969*

- — Louis S. Leland, *A Personal Kiwi-Yankee Dictionary*, p. 56, 1984
- — Ned Wallish, *The Truth Dictionary of Racing Slang*, p. 41, 1989
- Who are we to say that Joe Bloggs and his sister Jane Bloggs aren't having a perfectly good relationship and we're all missing out? — *The Guardian*, 9th January 2002

Joe Blow *noun*

1 an average, typical citizen *US, 1924*

- [I]f Joe Blow has promised to come by and run him home in the chuggedy-chug, he may hang around longer than usual[.] — Dick Clark, *To Goof or Not to Goof*, p. 85, 1963
- I can find a better way of spending my life than behind Joe Blow's desk for twenty-five, thirty dollars a day, you know. — Christina and Richard Milner, *Black Players*, p. 258, 1972
- [I]t was easy going through the usual jailhouse bullshit, answering a lotta things, like, who's doing what, how long Joe Blow been dealing, how'd I get cracked, who cracked me. — A.S. Jackson, *Gentleman Pimp*, p. 127, 1973
- [T]he Joe Blows and their housewives who went about life as usual while the grunts had been counting off their hours and days in the paddies and hills. — Charles Anderson, *The Grunts*, p. 177, 1976

2 an excellent musician *US*

- — Lou Shelly, *Hepcats Jive Talk Dictionary*, p. 28, 1945

Joe Blow biography *noun*

a glowing biographical story about a soldier in his hometown newspaper *US*

- — *American Speech*, p. 74, February 1946: 'Some words of war and peace from 1945'

Joe Bucks *noun*

any wealthy man *BAHAMAS*

- — John A. Holm, *Dictionary of Bahamian English*, p. 114, 1982

Joe Chink *noun*

a heroin addiction *US, 1973*

A further personification of the older **CHINAMAN** (a heroin addiction).

- And Stoney, believe me, I'm gonna git Joe Chink off my back. — A.S. Jackson, *Gentleman Pimp*, p. 73, 1973

Joe College *noun*

a stereotypical male college student *US, 1932*

- Why, Phil, you're all togged out like Joe College. — James T. Farrell, *Saturday Night*, p. 20, 1947
- They we'd throw big wine parties and have girls and end up jumping out of windows and playing Joe College pranks up and down town. — Jack Kerouac, *The Dharma Bums*, p. 22, 1958
- He had been in turn a Joe College hero lionized on the college prom circuit, a missionary of the new jazz in the early days of Swing, and now a war hero of sorts. — Ross Russell, *The Sound*, p. 56, 1961
- He is a firm homosexual but is a handsome young man, who to the average citizen would appear to be a charming Joe College. — *The Market Street Proposition (KFRC radio, San Francisco)*, 8th November 1965
- Joe College has finally arrived. — Mart Crowley, *The Boys in the Band*, p. 41, 1968

- More important, he was the real enemy, we thought, since he was out competition for the hearts and minds of Joe and Susie College, who were naively jumping on his clean-cut haywagon. — Raymond Mungo, *Famous Long Ago*, p. 80, 1970
- "Why dontcha start pickin up ashtrays?" the Manager suggested to her, ringing up drinks for the latecoming Joe Colleges. — Seth Morgan, *Homeboy*, p. 136, 1990
- "I was expecting an older man, but he looked like Joe College," she recalled. — Kathryn Leigh Scott, *The Bunny Years*, p. 52, 1998

Joe Cool *noun*

used for expressing the ultimate in fashion and modernity *US, 1971*

- I smiled my best fucking suave Joe Cool look. — Oscar Zeta Acosta, *The Autobiography of a Brown Buffalo*, p. 41, 1972

Joe Daki *noun*

a Pakistani *UK*

Rhyming slang for **PAKI**.

- — Ray Puxley, *Fresh Rabbit*, 1998

Joe Doe; Joe Roe *noun*

used as a name for a male blind date *US*

Teen slang.

- — *Newsweek*, p. 28, 8th October 1951

Joe Erk *noun*

a fool *UK*

Rhyming slang for **BERK** – in turn, rhyming slang for **CUNT** (a fool).

- — Ray Puxley, *Fresh Rabbit*, 1998

Joe Gurr *noun*

prison *UK, 1938*

Rhyming slang for **STIR**.

- — Angela Devlin, *Prison Patter*, p. 66, 1996

Joe Hero *noun*

a typical hero *US*

- What the fuck was I supposed to do? Be Joe Hero? — Edwin Torres, *Q & A*, 1977

Joe Hook *noun*

1 a crook *UK, 1932*

Rhyming slang, probably influenced by **HOOK** (to steal) or **HOOKY** (stolen, counterfeit).

- — Ray Puxley, *Cockney Rabbit*, 1992

2 a book *UK*

Rhyming slang.

- — Julian Franklyn, *A Dictionary of Rhyming Slang*, 1960
- — John Ayto, *The Oxford Dictionary of Rhyming Slang*, 2002

Joe Hunt; joey *noun*

a foolish or unlikeable person *UK*

Rhyming slang for **CUNT**. The shortened form is probably influenced by **JOEY** (a clown).

- — Julian Franklyn, *A Dictionary of Rhyming Slang*, 1960
- — Ray Puxley, *Cockney Rabbit*, 1992
- Wait till you see the new foreman, he's a right Joe Hunt. — David McGill, *David McGill's Complete Kiwi Slang Dictionary*, p. 63, 1998

Joe Loss *noun*

something of little or no value *UK*

Rhyming slang for **TOSS**, formed from the name of the London-born bandleader, 1909–90.

- I couldn't give a Joe Loss. — Ray Puxley, *Cockney Rabbit*, 1992

Joe Loss *verb*

to toss *UK*

Rhyming slang.

- [D]ecide an outcome by Joe Lossing a coin. — Ray Puxley, *Cockney Rabbit*, 1992

Joe PakiPaki from Opunaki *noun*

the notional, typical New Zealander *NEW ZEALAND*

- — Louis S. Leland, *A Personal Kiwi-Yankee Dictionary*, p. 56, 1984

Joe Patriot *noun*

a prototypical patriot *US*

- I froze on Joe Patriot: booze-flushed, Legion cap, Legion armband. — James Ellroy, *Hollywood Nocturnes*, p. 20, 1994

Joe-pot *noun*

a coffee pot *US*

Korean war usage.

- Coffee was Joe; a coffeepot, a Joe-pot. — William Manchester, *Goodbye, Darkness*, p. 146, 1979

Joe Public *noun*

an average citizen; the regular man on the street *US, 1942*

Originally theatrical of an audience member; gently derogatory.

- Their jazz was only a musical version of the hard-cutting broadsides that two foxy studs named Mencken and Nathan were beginning to shoot at Joe Public in the pages of The American Mercury[.] — Mezz Mezzrow, *Really the Blues*, p. 103, 1946
- [T]hey chose us because they're not Joe fucking Public. — Kevin Sampson, *Clubland*, p. 108, 2002
- [Y]our friendly copper would be face-to-face with Joe Public. — Duncan MacLaughlin, *The Filth*, p. 71, 2002

Joe Punter *noun*

an (imagined) average customer *UK*

A variation of **JOE PUBLIC** (the public). Combines **JOE** (a regular fellow) with **PUNTER** (a generic customer).

- Joe Punter had become a lot more media-savvy recently[.] — Christopher Brookmyre, *Boiling a Frog*, p. 107, 2000

Joe Roe *noun*

▷ see: **JOE DOE**

Joe Rook *noun*

1 a crook *UK*

Perhaps a variant of **JOE HOOK**, possibly influenced by 'rook' (to defraud); may also be an adaptation of **JOE ROURKE** (a pickpocket).

- — Julian Franklyn, *A Dictionary of Rhyming Slang*, 1960

2 a book, in particular the book made by an on-course bookmaker; hence, a bookmaker *UK, 1961*

- — Ray Puxley, *Fresh Rabbit*, 1998

Joe Rookie *noun*

a bookmaker *UK*

Rhyming slang for 'bookie', from **JOE ROOK** (a bookmaker's book).

- — Ray Puxley, *Fresh Rabbit*, 1998

Joe Rourke *noun*

a pickpocket *UK, 1938*

Rhyming slang, formed on synonymous but obsolete 'fork'.

- — Ray Puxley, *Cockney Rabbit*, 1992

joes *noun*

a fit of irritation or depression *AUSTRALIA, 1910*

- Boy oh boy, that word 'relationship' gives me the Joes, especially if it is called a 'caring relationship.' — Barry Humphrie, *The Traveller's Tool*, p. 41, 1985

Joe Schmo; Joe Shmo *noun*

an average, if dull and dim, person *US*

- Joe Schmo, who shares an office with six other guys in a Broadway loft, is in the business of publicizing such pillars of the American scene as second-rate movie, radio and flea circus stars and unpopular potmaine parlors. — *Traverse City (Michigan) Record Eagle*, p. 1, 23rd May 1947
- Like I might find old Joe Schmoe today and buy three bags from him and find that one bag straightens me out. — James Mills, *The Panic in Needle Park*, p. 46, 1966
- How come in former lifetimes, everybody was someone famous. How come nobody ever says that were Joe Schmo? — *Bull Durham*, 1988

Joe Sixpack *noun*

a stereotypical working-class male *US*

- In this Dougherty is not all that different, having an idea to sell Joe Sixpack on tax reform and Sen. George McGovern[.] — *Coshocton (Ohio) Tribune*, p. 6, 10th September 1973
- — *American Speech*, p. 188, Summer 1993: 'Among the new words'

Joe Skinner; Jim Skinner; Jimmy Skinner *noun*

a dinner *UK, 1938*

Rhyming slang.

- [H]e has missed his Jim Skinner[.] — Ronnie Barker, *Fletcher's Book of Rhyming Slang*, p. 39, 1979

Joe Soap *noun*

an easily put-upon employee, a fool *UK, 1943*

Rhyming slang for **DOPE**; originally military.

- — Ray Puxley, *Cockney Rabbit*, 1992

Joe Strummer *noun*

a disappointing or depressing event *UK*

Rhyming slang, formed from the name of the celebrated rock musician, 1952–2002.

- — Ray Puxley, *Fresh Rabbit*, 1998

Joe the grinder *noun*

used as a generic term for the man that a prisoner's wife or girlfriend takes up with while the man is in prison *US*

- Jody say, "Don't front me with that shit because it's not anywhere/ and this is Joe the Grinder and damn that square. — Bruce Jackson, *Get Your Ass in the Water and Swim Like Me*, p. 97, 1964
- The inmates hailed him as Joe the Grinder, giving him the same wry name they gave to the man who made it into their wife's bed while they were locked, hopeless and despairing, in jail. — Malcolm Braly, *On the Yard*, p. 73, 1967
- He should have just taken a dollar out of the wallet, given it to Joe the Grinder, and walked out, instead of blowing her away like he did. — Gerald Petievich, *Money Men*, p. 120, 1981

Joe the toff *adverb*

off, away *UK: SCOTLAND*

Glasgow rhyming slang.

- Right, that's me Joe the toff. Cheerybyes! — Michael Munro, *The Patter, Another Blast*, 1988

joey *noun*

1 a clown *UK, 1889*

An abbreviation of the name of legendary clown Joseph Grimaldi (1779–1837).

- There is a tendency today to talk about any circus funny man who does not wear the clown's full white make-up as an auguste, but really he should be called a joey. — Butch Reynolds, *Broken Hearted Clown*, p. 22, 1954

2 an errand-runner in a drug-dealing operation *UK*

Probably from the previous sense as 'clown'.

- You, you are just the fuckin' gofer anyway son. You're only the Joey as they say at your end of the business. — J.J. Connolly, *Know Your Enemy*, p. 158, 1999
- I became Spencer's gofer, his Joey, and worked a twenty-four-hour shift[.] — Lanre Fehintola, *Charlie Says...*, p. 64, 2000

3 a baby *AUSTRALIA*

- An' you can stuff that bloody muck I bought off you [contraceptive pessaries]. Ma's got another joey in th' pouch, that's how good it is. — Walter Gill, *Petermann Journey*, p. 14, 1968
- Other synonyms [for abortion] include 'slip a joey'[.] — Nancy Keesing, *Lily on the Dustbin*, p. 36, 1982

4 a youthful, attractive homosexual male prostitute *AUSTRALIA*

- — *Maledicta*, p. 220, 1979: 'Kinks and queens: linguistic and cultural aspects of the terminology for gays'

5 a young kangaroo or wallaby still living in the pouch; the young of any marsupial *AUSTRALIA, 1839*

Origin unknown; the earliest example (1828) refers to a young possum. Later 'joey' was also applied to the young of various animals, such as parrots, horses and cattle, but is now restricted as defined.

- Her and the dog put up a kanga with a fair-sized joey[.] — Arthur Upfield, *Bony and the Mouse*, p. 13, 1959
- — Jim Ramsay, *Cop It Sweet!*, p. 50, 1977
- — Glyn Parry, *Mosh*, p. 42, 1996

6 an Anglo-Australian person *AUSTRALIA*

Used as a, somewhat mild, derogatory term by Australians of Mediterranean and Middle Eastern background.

- — Kathy Lette, *Girls' Night Out*, p. 187, 1987
- The badly-maligned 'Wogs' (Dapto dogs/Chocolate frogs) are finally wreaking revenge on Anglo-Saxon kids. 'Aussies' are 'Skips' or 'Joeys'. — *Sydney Morning Herald*, p. 7, 3rd January 1987

7 in prison, illicit goods, an illegal parcel *UK, 1950*

- — Angela Devlin, *Prison Patter*, p. 66, 1996
- Yes please one little ten-pound joey sir! — Jeremy Cameron, *Brown Bread in Wengen*, p. 112, 1999
- We went up to see the guy, brought him up a joey of bits and pieces. — J.J. Connolly, *Layer Cake*, p. 240, 2000

8 a condom *NEW ZEALAND*

- 'We don't sell sex,' she tells me, 'but joeys (condoms). We offer the client a joey for say $40 or $50 more.' — *Metro*, p. 40, April 1984

9 the bleed period of the menstrual cycle *UK, 1984*

Joey *noun*

someone of little importance *UK, 1990*

Rhyming slang for **JOE HUNT** (**CUNT**) informed by **JOEY** (a clown).

- They've got Roy booked as Mister Big and me and Tony as just simple, dumb runners, the Joeys as the top lawman had called us. — J.J. Connolly, *Know Your Enemy [britpulp]*, p. 159, 1999

Joey Grey *noun*

a rabbit stew *UK*

English gypsy use.

- Wally put his apron on and started to make us both up some Joey Grey. — Jimmy Stockin, *On The Cobbles*, p. 83, 2000

Joeys; Johies *nickname*

Johannesburg *SOUTH AFRICA, 1974*

- [T]he question everyone in Joeys is asking is: Have you driven over our lovely new bridge yet? — *Sunday Times (South Africa)*, 27th July 2003

jog *verb*

1 to push with one foot while skateboarding *US*

- — *San Francisco Sunday Examiner & Chronicle*, p. 20, 2nd September 1984: 'Say it right'

2 in Newfoundland, of a boat, to stop (heave to) into the wind, or sail slowly *CANADA*

- I would run her in towards Flint Island and give our vessel room to jog all night and be close to our fishing spot in the morning. — J.M. Fudge, *Life Story*, p. 52, 1960

jogger; jogar *verb*

to entertain, to sing, to play *UK*

Polari, from Italian *giocare* (to play).

- — Paul Baker, *Polari*, p. 178, 2002

joggering omee *noun*

an entertainer *UK*

A combination of **JOGGER** (to entertain) and **OMEE** (a man).

- — Paul Baker, *Polari*, p. 178, 2002

joggy *noun*

a hacksaw *US*

- — Vincent J. Monteleone, *Criminal Slang*, p. 134, 1949

johanna *noun*

▷ see: **JOANNA**

joharito *noun*

heroin *UK*

- — Mike Haskins, *Drugs*, p. 284, 2003

john *noun*

1 a prostitute's client *US, 1906*

From the sense as 'generic man', probably via the criminal use as 'dupe' or 'victim'.

- The johns lined up for Marcelle like it was payday. — Mezz Mezzrow, *Really the Blues*, p. 23, 1946
- Always build a John up. If he has any sort of body at all, say, 'Please, don't ever hurt me.' A John is different from a sucker. — William Burroughs, *Junkie*, p. 30, 1953
- Our hustlers sat on their steps and called to the "Johns" as they passed by — Louis Amstrong, *Satchmo: My Life in New Orleans*, p. 95, 1954
- — Louis Armstrong, *Satchmo: My Life in New Orleans*, p. 95, 1954
- If I don't let a white john with money come here, I must have good reasons. — Chester Himes, *The Real Cool Killers*, p. 80, 1959
- Freddie had done less shoeshining and towel-hustling than selling liquor and reefers, and putting white "Johns" in touch with Negro whores. — Malcolm X and Alex Haley, *The Autobiography of Malcolm X*, p. 49, 1964
- I know who you are. You're a John. I don't know why I like you. — *Easy Rider*, 1969
- So you take a call and you go to a hotel room and there's some John you've never seen before, but he wants you. — *Klute*, 1971
- A ponce might say to a prostitute: "Don't you treat me like a john or I'll mark your face." — David Powis, *The Signs of Crime*, 1977
- Russell recognised some of the pavement princesses, whose pitch this normally was [...] livid at missing their regular johns and champagne tricks on their way back from the City. — Greg Williams, *Diamond Geezers*, p. 203, 1997
- Juan aimed his camera at the coupled couple, not recognising the john[.] — Stewart Home, *Sex Kick [britpulp]*, p. 215, 1999

2 a police officer *AUSTRALIA, 1898*

An abbreviation of John Darm, an obsolete pun on French *gendarme* (a police officer) which appears in several variations in the US from 1858, or an abbreviated form of the older John Hop, rhyming with **COP**. First recorded standing alone in Australia, 1898.

- There's Harmon. Ask him. He's the john, not me. — Arthur Upfield, *Bony and the Mouse*, p. 157, 1959
- As I say, we dug until almost morning, in a cold sweat of fear, not before the johns were after us, which had happened before and would happen again, but because of the offense with which we would be charged. — Clancy Sigal, *Going Away*, p. 356, 1961
- [T]he snag is that he's expecting a john any day now[.] — Derek Raymond (Robin Cook), *The Crust on its Uppers*, p. 42, 1962
- — David McGill, *David McGill's Complete Kiwi Slang Dictionary*, p. 73, 1998

3 in a deck of playing cards, a jack or knave *US*

- — Albert H. Morehead, *The Complete Guide to Winning Poker*, p. 266, 1967

4 a toilet *US, 1942*
- And when I went to see Tristano I overheard some of the cats discussing him in the john. —Jack Kerouac, *Letter to Allen Ginsburg*, p. 141, 2nd January 1948
- Several times I went to San Fran with my gun and when a queer approached me in a bar john I took out the gun and said, "Eh? Eh? What's that you say?" —Jack Kerouac, *On the Road*, p. 73, 1957
- Oh, I mean I want to go to the john. —Sue Rhodes, *And when she was bad she was popular*, p. 117, 1968
- [S]he had said, Wait a minute, and got up and went to the john to piss and came back and got in the same position again. —Cecil Brown, *The Life & Loves of Mr. Jiveass Nigger*, p. 79, 1969
- I stop off by my room and while sitting on the john start reading an article in Newsweek[.] —Lester Bangs, *Psychotic Reactions and Carburetor Dung*, p. 239, 1977
- He pulled up his pants, flushed the john, and stretched out on a steel cot. —Carl Hiaasen, *Tourist Season*, p. 14, 2000

5 a condom *UK*
A shortened form of **JOHNNY** used with over-familiar contempt by prostitutes.
- —David Powis, *The Signs of Crime*, 1977

▷ **see:** JOHN THOMAS

John *noun*
a lieutenant *US, 1937*
- —Carl Fleischhauer, *A Glossary of Army Slang*, p. 28, 1968
- This had disabused Mr. Ripley of the notion that, for some inexplicable reason, the Raiders had turned their armory over to a baby-faced candy-ass second john fresh from Quantico. —W.E.B. Griffin, *The Corps Book II*, p. 300, 1987
- —Linda Reinberg, *In the Field*, p. 81, 1991

John Audley; John Orderly
abridge the performance!; quickly *UK, 1864*
Theatrical, from actor-manager John Richardson (d.1837) who would ask 'Is John Audley here?' to cue a speedy conclusion in readiness for his next audience; by legend this was a technique learnt from a John Audley or Orderly.
- His jills told him to take it out of the horse tent and scarper off ther tober [circus ground], John Orderly [quickly]. —Butch Reynolds, *Broken Hearted Clown*, p. 28, 1953

John Bates *noun*
▷ **see:** BATES

John book *noun*
a prostitute's list of customers *US*
- Also in this class are the freelance call girls with "John Books" (address books with the names and telephone numbers of well-to-do clients who come back as regular customers) or their own. —Bernhardt J. Hurwood, *The Sensuous New York*, p. 17, 1973

John Brown!
used as a non-profane oath *BAHAMAS*
- —John A. Holm, *Dictionary of Bahamian English*, p. 115, 1982

John Bull; john *noun*
1 a tug, a pull *UK*
Rhyming slang.
- [H]e darted forward and gave the commissionaire's sleeve a John Bull[.] —Charles Raven, *Underworld Nights*, p. 37, 1956

2 an arrest *UK, 1984*
Rhyming slang for **PULL**.
- —Ray Puxley, *Cockney Rabbit*, 1992

▸ **on the John Bull; go on the John Bull**
engaged in a casual or recreational quest for a sexual partner *UK*
Rhyming slang for 'on the pull'.
- —Ray Puxley, *Cockney Rabbit*, 1992

John Bull *adjective*
full; drunk *AUSTRALIA*
- —Barry Humphries, *Bazza Pulls It Off!*, 1971
- Anything from a stadium to a stomach can be "John Bull" but the main usage is in reference to being full of alcohol. —Ray Puxley, *Cockney Rabbit*, p. 103–104, 1992

John Cleese *noun*
cheese *UK*
Rhyming slang, formed from the name of the comedy actor and writer (b.1939) who, as a member of *Monty Python's Flying Circus* was, in 1972, partly responsible for the 'Cheese Shop' sketch.
- —Ray Puxley, *Fresh Rabbit*, 1998

John D *noun*
kerosene *US*
An allusion to John D. Rockefeller and hence petroleum-based products.
- —John Gould, *Maine Lingo*, p. 147–148, 1975

John Dory *noun*
the story *AUSTRALIA*
- Well, what's the John Dory? —Kathy Lette, *Girls' Night Out*, p. 89, 1987

John Grieg *noun*
the leg *UK: SCOTLAND*
Glasgow rhyming slang, formed from the name of the Glasgow Rangers footballer.
- A fine pair of John Griegs. —Michael Munro, *The Complete Patter*, 1996

John Hancock *noun*
a person's signature *US, 1887*
From the attention-getting manner in which Hancock signed the Declaration of Independence.
- [W]hy is that doctor so nervous and unwilling to put his John Hancock to any sort of document[?] —Gore Vidal, *Myra Breckinridge*, p. 137, 1984
- It could be Westerburg's if we can get everyone's John Hancock. —*Heathers*, 1988

John Henry *noun*
1 a person's signature *US*
A variant of the more common **JOHN HANCOCK**.
- [Y]ou don't have to put up any cash and you don't have to forfeit any cash, all you have to do is write your John Henry. —Bruce Jackson, *Outside the Law*, p. 132, 1972

2 the penis *US, 1888*
- —Bill Naughton, *One Small Boy*, 1966

John Hop *noun*
a police officer *AUSTRALIA, 1907*
Rhyming slang for **COP**.
- —Patsy Adam-Smith, *Folklore of the Australian Railwaymen*, p. 185, 1969
- Anyhow, if you nab the bastard, everyone'll know that I dobbed him in to the John Hops. —Lance Peters, *The Dirty Half-Mile*, p. 151, 1979
- —Lance Peters, *The Dirty Half-Mile*, p. 167, 1979

John Law *noun*
the police *US, 1906*
- I was made the lookout man and told to stick around out front with my eyes peeled for any signs of John Law. —Mezz Mezzrow, *Really the Blues*, p. 20, 1946
- I don't tell them other bitzes this, but being a lone outlaw in this life, with the johnlaws up one side an the pimps down the other, everybody mouth-waterin for a taste – well you catchin too much mojo at once[.] —Robert Gover, *JC Saves*, p. 55, 1968

Johnnie; Johnny *noun*
a man *UK, 1673*
- [T]he most eminent surgeons from both sides of the border – top Johnnies in their respective fields[.] —Duncan MacLaughlin, *The Filth*, p. 32, 2002

johnny *noun*
1 a condom *UK, 1965*
- —Bob Young and Micky Moody, *The Language of Rock 'n' Roll*, p. 81, 1985
- TRISTE: well used the johnny twice didn't you!! GARY: just seemed a bit of a waste really[.] —Patrick Jones, *Unprotected Sex*, p. 211, 1999
- I was going to use a johnny, but she said it was okay. —John King, *Human Punk*, p. 45, 2000
- Johnnies, I manage to croak. – I've got none. —Niall Griffiths, *Kelly + Victor*, p. 21, 2002

2 a police officer *US*
- —Anna Scotti and Paul Young, *Buzzwords*, p. 136, 1997

3 a toilet *UK, 1850*
- He was taking the only way our directors ever take – you know, from the card room to the -er – thing, the johnny. —Horace McCoy, *Kiss Tomorrow Good-bye*, p. 355, 1948
- "Oh my God," Jenny said, pleasurably tititlated. "I hope I don' have to go use the johnny." —Robert Campbell, *Alice in La-La Land*, p. 271, 1987

4 a prison guard *US*
- —Hyman E. Goldin et al., *Dictionary of American Underworld Lingo*, p. 111, 1950

5 a loose-fitting, abbreviated hospital nightshirt with a slit down the back *US*
- —*American Speech*, p. 75–76, February 1958: 'The hospital Johnny'

6 an inexperienced firefighter *US*
- — *American Speech*, p. 273, December 1954: 'Fire terms: additional words and definitions'

johnnybait *noun*
a sexually alluring young woman or young man *UK*
- — *Sunday Times*, 8th September 1963

johnny ball *noun*
in electric line work, a guy strain insulator *US*
- — A.B. Chance Co., *Lineman's Slang Dictionary*, p. 10, 1980

johnny-be-good *noun*
a police officer; the police *US*
Plays on Chuck Berry's 1958 rock 'n' roll classic 'Johnny B. Goode', punning the inherent quality of goodness displayed by the police; possibly ironic. Black usage.

Johnny Black *nickname*
Johnny Walker™ Black Label whisky *US*
- Buster was trying to look jaunty but his hands were shaking. "Gimme a Johnny Blc," he said. "Neat." — Joseph Wambaugh, *The Golden Orange*, p. 49, 1990

Johnny Bliss *noun*
an act of urination *AUSTRALIA*
Rhyming slang for **PISS**.
- I couldn't bear to watch it, so I ducked out for a Johnny Bliss. — Alexander Buzo, *Rooted*, p. 77, 1969

Johnny Canuck *noun*
a Canadian, especially a soldier *CANADA*
- John comes into many nicknames, here are a few of them. John Bull, Johnny Canuck, a Canadian soldier, and Johnny Raw, a new recruit. — *Canadian Red Cross Junior*, p. 17, November 1957
- That's the spirit of USA which Johnny Canuck will never catch up with. — *Canada Month*, p. 38/2, January 1964

Johnny Cash *noun*
an act of urination *UK*
Rhyming slang for **SLASH**, formed from the name of the US singer, 1932–2003.
- — Ray Puxley, *Cockney Rabbit*, 1992

Johnny-come-lately *noun*
a new recruit; a newcomer; hence, someone inexperienced or unsophisticated *US, 1839*
- I am not a Johnny-come-lately to sing the praises of our magical princess. — *News Of The World*, p. 24, 7th September 1997

Johnny Darky *noun*
a black man *UK*
Offensive.
- [T]he old boy was just another crazy and a Johnny Darky into the bargain. — J.J. Connolly, *Layer Cake*, p. 37, 2000

Johnny Foreigner *noun*
anyone who is not British *UK, 1990*
- The British, it is said, are natural, if not happy queuers. Johnny Foreigner, particularly the Southern European genus, finds it quaintly ridiculous — Adrian Furnham, *The Hopeless, Hapless and Helpless Manager*, p. 113, 2000

Johnny Giles *noun*
haemorrhoids *UK*
Rhyming slang for 'piles'; formed from the name of an Irish footballer (b.1940).
- — Ray Puxley, *Fresh Rabbit*, 1998

Johnny-go-fast *noun*
amphetamines *UK*
- — Mike Haskins, *Drugs*, p. 279, 2003

Johnny Gyppo *noun*
an Egyptian; Egypt personified *UK*
- Johnny Gyppo's like a rat, but like a cornered rat he can be dangerous. — Henry Sloane, *Sloane's Inside Guide to Sex & Drugs & Rock 'n' Roll*, p. 11, 1985

Johnny Ham *noun*
a private investigator *US*
- We're hard on private Johnny Hams what come aroun' totin' iron. — Robert Campbell, *In La-La Land We Trust*, p. 173, 1986

Johnny Horner *noun*
a corner *UK, 1909*
Rhyming slang.
- Just round the Johnny Horner! — *The Sweeney*, p. 9, 1976

Johnny letter *noun*
▷ see: **DEAR JOHN**

Johnny Long Shoes *noun*
the man who steals a prisoner's girlfriend or wife after incarceration *US*
- — Lee McNelis, *30 + And a Wake-Up*, p. 15, 1991

Johnny-no-stars *noun*
a person of limited intelligence and/or ambition *UK*
From a system employed by fast-food giant McDonald's™ that is designed to recognise a worker's achievements and acquisition of skills; to have no stars is seen to be a badge of no intelligence.
- — *www.LondonSlang.com*, June 2002
- — Susie Dent, *The Language Report*, p. 77, 2003

Johnny O'Brien *noun*
in railroading, a boxcar *US*
- — Ramon Adams, *The Language of the Railroader*, p. 87, 1977

Johnny-on-the-spot *noun*
a person who is available whenever needed *US, 1896*
- "There's nothing like being johnny-on-the-spot," Dr. Sherwood says. "Being right there so that when a kid is in trouble he can come and ring your bell at eleven o'clock at night and know that you will answer it." — Harrison E. Salisbury, *The Shook-up Generation*, p. 178, 1958
- No telling what might have happened if I hadn't been right here Johnny-on-the spot when the fire broke out. — Jim Thompson, *Pop. 1280*, p. 151, 1964

Johnny Pissoff *noun*
a very annoying person *US*
- [I]f you think I'm a Johnny Pissoff now, you shoulda seen me in 1968[.] — Lester Bangs, *Psychotic Reactions and Carburetor Dung*, p. 71, 1971

Johnny pump *noun*
a fire hydrant *US*
- One day when the pavements are like sausage griddles, me and Romolo have our trunks on, looking to open a johny pump or two and cool off. — Rocky Garciano (with Rowland Barber), *Somebody Up There Likes Me*, p. 77, 1955

Johnny Raper *noun*
a newspaper *AUSTRALIA, 1983*
Rhyming slang based on the name of an Australian Rugby League football player.
- — Ryan Aven-Bray, *Ridgey Didge Oz Jack Lang*, p. 32, 1983
- I've hit the Johnny Rapers in Steak 'n Kidney. — Kathy Lette, *Girls' Night Out*, p. 180, 1987

Johnny Reb *noun*
any rural white male from the southern US *US, 1884*
- — *Maledicta*, p. 162, Summer/Winter 1978: 'How to hate thy neighbor: a guide to racist maledicta'

Johnny Rollocks *noun*
the testicles *UK*
Rhyming slang for **BOLLOCKS**; a member of the **JIMMY ROLLOCKS** and **TOMMY ROLLOCKS** family.

Johnny Rotten *nickname*
Sir William Wratten, commander of all Royal Air Force assets in the Gulf war *UK*
- — *American Speech*, p. 392, Winter 1991: 'Among the new words'

Johnny Skinner *noun*
a dinner *UK*
Rhyming slang; a part of the **JOE SKINNER** family.

Johnny Thunder *noun*
the combination of an M-16 antipersonnel mine and a M-79 grenade launcher *US*
- — Linda Reinberg, *In the Field*, p. 117, 1991

johnny-too-bad *noun*
a hoodlum, a criminal *JAMAICA*
A reversal of **JOHNNY-BE-GOOD** (a police officer). Immortalised by the thus-titled song by the Slickers in the 1973 Jamaican film *The Harder They Come*. UK black usage.
- Rough was in the takeaway when a couple of Johnny-too-bads jumped him and put him in the boot of the car. —Karline Smith, *Moss Side Massive*, p. 55, 1994

Johnny Tourist *noun*
a holiday-maker *UK*
A personification of the average tourist.
- Step this way for famous and infamous, DJs, promoters, villains, drug smugglers, dealers, Johnny Tourists, hippies, holiday reps, sexual psychotics and other unique, unforgettable characters. —Wayne Anthony, *Spanish Highs*, p. xiv, 1999

Johnny Vaughan *noun*
pornography *UK, 2002*
Rhyming slang for **PORN**, based on television presenter Johnny Vaughan.
- — *www.LondonSlang.com*, June 2002
- —Bodmin Dark, *Dirty Cockney Rhyming Slang*, 2003

Johnny Walker *noun*
an overly talkative person; an informer *UK*
Rhyming slang for 'talker'; possibly derived from the brand name whisky (from its tongue-loosening properties) or, perhaps, formed from the name of a BBC radio disc jockey, in tribute to his fluency.
- —Ray Puxley, *Cockney Rabbit*, 1992

Johnny Walker *nickname*
1 Pope John XXIII *ITALY*
A pun on a whisky brand name; Pope John XXIII (born 1881, ascended 1958, died 1963) earned this nickname from his habit of sneaking out of the Vatican and walking the streets of Rome.
- When asked, one of his strong arms said he was in Saint Peter's Square at the Vatican, because "Johnny Walker is dying." —Emmett Grogan, *Ringolevio*, p. 156, 1972

2 Lt General Walton H. Walker (1889–1950) *US*
Walker served with great distinction in World War I, World War 2, and Korea; he was killed in a car accident in Korea.
- They called him "Johnny Walker" and he was a tough little bulldog of a man, a protege of Patton's, and he died in a jeep accident, just as Patton did, because he couldn't stand the dust and always made his driver go too goddamned fast. —Walter J. Sheldon, *Gold Bait*, p. 31, 1973

Johnny Woodser *noun*
a person drinking alone in a pub *NEW ZEALAND, 1941*
- —David McGill, *David McGill's Complete Kiwi Slang Dictionary*, p. 63, 1998

John O'Groats *noun*
sexual satisfaction *UK*
Rhyming slang for **OATS**, as in 'get your oats'.
- —Ray Puxley, *Cockney Rabbit*, 1992

John Orderly *noun*
▷ see: JOHN AUDLEY

John Peel *noun*
a jellied eel *UK*
Rhyming slang, formed from the name of a legendary huntsman (1776–1854) or BBC radio disc jockey (1993–2004). Ray Puxley, *Cockney Rabbit*, 1992, notes that jellied eels are a culinary tradition of working-class Londoners. Usually plural.

John Prescott *noun*
a waistcoat *UK*
Rhyming slang, formed from the name of the Labour politician (b.1938), UK's Deputy Prime Minister from 1997. The latest of many men, real or imagined, named Prescott who have lent a name to this rhyme.
- —Ray Puxley, *Fresh Rabbit*, 1998

John Q. Law *noun*
the personification of law enforcement *US*
- THE WOLF: Now if we cross the path of any John Q. Laws, nobody does a fuckin' thing 'til I do something. — *Pulp Fiction*, 1994

John Selwyn Gummer *noun*
a disappointing or depressing event *UK*
Rhyming slang for **BUMMER**, formed from the name of a Conservative politician and sometime government minister.
- —Ray Puxley, *Fresh Rabbit*, 1998

johnsie *noun*
the room, apartment or house where you live *US*
- —Connie Eble (Editor), *UNC-CH Campus Slang*, p. 6, October 2002

johnson *noun*
1 the penis *UK, 1863*
Despite an 1862 citation, the word was not widely used in this sense until the 1970s.
- He pulled on his johnson, with his right hand, and closed the door with his left. —Steve Cannon, *Groove, Bang, and Jive Around*, p. 7, 1969
- One of the black guys was nearly demanding a warm-up, some contrivance to stiffen his johnson before the main event. —Josh Alan Friedman, *Tales of Times Square*, p. 94, 1986
- I wanna set Heather on my Johnson and just start spinning her like a fucking pinwheel. — *Heathers*, 1988
- Dakota could barely talk because of the pain and he was up there bragging about his Johnson, which he'd named Mr. Buffy. —Stephen Cannell, *Big Con*, p. 267, 1997
- Ready to spout, he yanks his berubbered johnson out of Jasmin's snatch and fumbles nervously with the condom. —Anthony Petkovich, *The X Factory*, p. 193, 1997
- Whereas without batting an eye a man will refer to his "dick" or his "rod" or his "Johnson." — *The Big Lebowski*, 1998
- DUANE: How big is your johnson? RAMU: Johnson? DUANE: Your wand, your pork sword, your baloney pony. — *The Guru*, 2002

2 a pound of marijuana, especially a pound of marijuana cigarettes *US, 1976*
A pound of marijuana cigarettes would be an 'lb. of J's', hence the initials and the leap to President Lyndon 'LBJ' Baines Johnson.

3 a marijuana cigarette *UK*
- Gimme a toke on that johnson, man. —Nick Brownlee, *This Is Cannabis*, p. 152, 2002

4 crack cocaine *UK, 1998*
- —Mike Haskins, *Drugs*, p. 282, 2003

5 coffee *US*
- —Joseph E. Ragen and Charles Finston, *Inside the World's Toughest Prison*, p. 806, 1962: 'Penitentiary and underworld glossary'

Johnson bar *noun*
the emergency brake on a truck *US*
- —Montie Tak, *Truck Talk*, p. 93, 1971

Johnson family *noun*
1 collectively, the underworld *US, 1926*
- —Hyman E. Goldin et al., *Dictionary of American Underworld Lingo*, p. 111, 1950

2 a mythical family, all of whose members believe that everything is legitimate and righteous *US*
- —Bill Reilly, *Big Al's Official Guide to Chicagoese*, p. 39, 1982

Johnson grass *noun*
marijuana *US*
Johnson grass is a ubquitous weed in the US, hence the pun.
- —Eugene Landy, *The Underground Dictionary*, p. 113, 1971

John Thomas; john *noun*
the penis *UK, 1879*
- [S]neakin' around scribblin' John Thomas's on the wall? —Barry Humphries, *Bazza Pulls It Off!*, 1971
- —David McGill, *David McGill's Complete Kiwi Slang Dictionary*, p. 73, 1998

John Wayne *noun*
1 in the television and film industries, an exaggerated punch *US*
- —John Cann, *The Stunt Guide*, p. 60,: 'Terms and definitions'

2 a bulldozer tank *US*
- —Linda Reinberg, *In the Field*, p. 117, 1991

3 a small, collapsible can opener for use in the field *US, 1973*
Officially known as a P-38.
- — *Maledicta*, p. 260, Summer/Winter 1982: 'Viet-speak'
- —Gregory Clark, *Words of the Vietnam War*, p. 387–388, 1990

4 a train *UK*
Rhyming slang, formed from the name of the US film actor, 1907–79. Noted by Ray Puxley, *Fresh Rabbit*, 1998, but no longer in service.

John Wayne *verb*
to act with reckless disregard for life and safety *US*
One of several military slang terms based on John Wayne (1907–1979), the US actor who portrayed a series of tough Western and army heroes.
- Nothing I like better than John Wayne-ing a goddamn door. —Joseph Wambaugh, *The Blue Knight*, p. 137, 1973
- Why, you can even John Wayne it and pull the son of a bitch with your fucken eyetooth. —Larry Heinemann, *Close Quarters*, p. 45, 1977
- — *Maledicta*, p. 260, Summer/Winter 1982: 'Viet-speak'
- —Linda Reinberg, *In the Field*, p. 117, 1991

John Wayne cookie *noun*
a US Army c-ration biscuit or candy bar *US, 1986*
- —Gregory Clark, *Words of the Vietnam War*, p. 254, 1991

John Wayne High School *nickname*
the US Army's Special Warfare Training School, Fort Bragg, North Carolina *US*
- —Linda Reinberg, *In the Field*, p. 117, 1991

John Wayne's hairy saddle bags *noun*
the testicles hanging in the scrotum *UK*
- — *Roger's Profanisaurus*, December 1997
- —Richard Herring, *Talking Cock*, p. 30, 2003

John Woo *noun*
excrement, faeces *UK*
Rhyming slang, formed from the name of the Chinese film director (b.1946).
- —Tom Nind, *Rude Rhyming Slang*, p. 13, 2003

joil *noun*
▷ **see:** JOL

join *verb*
▸ **join the Air Force**
to die *US*
- —Sally Williams, *"Strong" Words*, p. 147, 1994

▸ **join the birds**
to jump from a moving train before an unavoidable collision *US*
- —J. Herbert Lund, *Herb's Hot Box of Railroad Slang*, p. 114, 1975

joined-up thinking *noun*
coherent, considered and well-organised logic *UK, 1989*
- Joined-up thinking brings results[.] — *The Guardian*, 19th May 2003

join out *verb*
to go to work for a circus *US, 1895*
- —Sherman Louis Sergel, *The Language of Show Biz*, p. 118, 1973

joint *noun*
1 a marijuana cigarette. *US, 1942*
For 50 years, the top of the slang pile, easily deposing its predecessors and fending off challengers.
- "You got a couple of joints to take along?" she asked. —George Mandel, *Flee the Angry Strangers*, p. 173, 1952
- From Jocelyn, a 19-year-old senior, Amy learned to play hooky when high school opened; she also learned that "blowing up a joint" means smoking marijuana. — *Time*, p. 50, 9th June 1952
- Enrique rolled enormous Indian joints, laughed at my American sticks I rolled. —Jack Kerouac, *Letter to Allen Ginsberg*, p. 351, 10th May 1952
- Vesta got out some marijuana cigarettes and offered Dave a "joint." He hadn't known what they were, but he wanted to appear grownup so he took one. —Wenzell Brown, *Monkey on My Back*, p. 32, 1953
- The heroin had worn off but I was still pleasantly high from a joint that Tom and I had smoked on the way to Sheridan Square. —Alexander Trocchi, *Cain's Book*, p. 52, 1960
- To obtain marihuana at all, beats have sometimes been forced to buy it in a form (already rolled into "joints," rather than loose) and at a price (75 cents or $1 per joint) that they say are usually reserved for the rich college crowd. — *Dissent*, p. 352, Summer 1961
- I don't get too high, not on a little middlin' joint like that one. —Ken Kesey, *One Flew Over the Cuckoo's Nest*, p. 286, 1962
- Well I was rolling up a joint at Blaze last night[.] —Chris Farlowe, *Buzz with the Fuzz*, 1964
- I was 22 years of age and shacking with a chick named Julie, I gave her one "joint" which she stashed and later turned over to the cops – a joint that netted me one of the 5-to-life sentences. — *The Berkeley Tribe*, p. 5, 5th-12th September 1969
- VINCENT: Yeah, it's legal, but it ain't a hundred percent legal. I mean you can't walk into a restaurant, roll a joint, and start puffin' away. — *Pulp Fiction*, 1994

2 the equipment used to smoke opium *US*
- I called up Mike and pleaded with him to bring me the joint (the layout) and put me out of my misery. —Mezz Mezzrow, *Really the Blues*, p. 253, 1946

3 a syringe *US, 1953*
- She hit the joint [hypodermic syringe] and knocked it out of the vein and by the time she got herself in, I'm already into a thing. —Bruce Jackson, *In the Life*, p. 223, 1972

4 a pistol *US*
- I'm packing no joint. —Hal Ellson, *Duke*, p. 2, 1949
- He said he got the gun, which he called "a sweet joint," because a guy named "Binky" had threatened his life. —Matt Gryta, *Buffalo (New York) News*, p. 5, 19th November 1994

5 the penis *US, 1931*
- Inez called up Camille on the phone repeatedly and even long talks with her; they even talked about his joint, or so Dean claimed. —Jack Kerouac, *On the Road*, p. 250, 1957
- Not that I got anything against anyone swinging on a joint, dig? – if they wanna[.] —John Rechy, *City of Night*, p. 139, 1963
- Mother, I had heard that some of them fags had bigger joints than the guy that was screwing. —Piri Thomas, *Down These Mean Streets*, p. 55, 1967
- [L]eaving my joint like a rocket it makes right for the light bulb overhead, where to my wonderment and horror, it hits and it hangs. —Philip Roth, *Portnoy's Complaint*, p. 20, 1969
- When one lonely night a man came walking down the street / He had about a yard and a half of joint hanging down by his feet. —Anonymous ("Arthur"), *Shine and the Titanic;The Signifying Monkey; Stackolee*, p. 14, 1971
- You'd fuck her and a half hour later she'd be grabbing your joint wanting to get laid again. —Leonard Shecter and William Phillips, *On the Pad*, p. 74, 1973
- This girl said the guy's joint was infantile, but compared to what? —Elmore Leonard, *City Primeval*, p. 191, 1980
- What you want more of is boys with nice long joints. I know what you are – you're a fag. —Herbert Huncke, *The Evening Sun Turned Crimson*, p. 135, 1980

6 a place, anything from a country to a house *AUSTRALIA*
- You ought to see some of the joints. Of course you can go to flash houses in St Kilda and East Melbourne. —Norman Lindsay, *The Cousin from Fiji*, p. 192, 1945
- There's no bastard been near this joint for days. —Eric Lambert, *The Veterans*, p. 126, 1954
- She's challenged the police to search the joint so often I don't think it's going to be too easy. —Vince Kelly, *The Bogeyman*, p. 39, 1956
- Come out here takin' jobs an' think yer own the joint. Bloody dagoes. —Nino Culotta (John O'Grady), *They're A Weird Mob*, p. 52, 1957
- 'Strike!' Splinter murmured admiringly, 'what a joint for a party!' —J.E. MacDonnell, *Don't Gimme the Ships*, p. 139, 1960
- See y'round the joint, Joe. —W.R. Bennett, *Wingman*, p. 100, 1961
- Mig's jumped 'em the moment they hit the joint – Steeger got his and had to hit the silk. —W.R. Bennett, *Wingman*, p. 123, 1961
- Can I meet you when you pack up at this joint? —John Wynnum, *Tar Dust*, p. 34, 1962
- —Paul Lesley, *PT Command*, p. 118, 1963
- —Wal Watkins, *Race the Lazy River*, p. 20, 1963

7 a prison *US, 1933*
- [Y]ou can be charged in State on one and Federal on the other so that when you walk out of the State joint the Federals meet you at the door. —William Burroughs, *Junkie*, p. 95, 1953
- I was arrested in Arizona, the joint absolutely the worst joint I've ever been in. —Jack Kerouac, *On the Road*, p. 231, 1957
- "Why should I go to the joint?" —Clarence Cooper Jr, *The Scene*, p. 14, 1960
- In the Joint I always get in top shape; no coke, no pot, no pussy, so you work out. —Edwin Torres, *Carlito's Way*, p. 41, 1975
- Well, yeah honey, but these boys tell me they just got outta the joint. — *Raising Arizona*, 1987
- He had been death on basing before he went to the joint[.] —Terry Williams, *The Cocaine Kids*, p. 44, 1989
- You like being out of the joint, fucking a beautiful woman. —Joel Rose, *Kill Kill Faster Faster*, p. 11, 1997

8 an establishment that sells alcohol illegally; any disreputable establishment *US, 1877*
- And here comes the openin' night! And the joint is jumping! —William "Lord" Buckley, *Nero*, 1951
- Jesus wouldn't be afraid to walk into this joint or any other speakeasy to preach the gospel. —Richard Brooks, *Elmer Gantry*, 1960
- [T]he old darling who ran the joint[.] —Derek Raymond (Robin Cook), *The Crust on its Uppers*, p. 20, 1962
- Dad knew where most of the joints in the neighborhood were and many times we had to go from one to another for what seemed like hours. —Claude Brown, *Manchild in the Promised Land*, p. 29, 1965

9 an artistic creation (recording, film, etc), also a trainer as a fashion item, especially in black or hip-hop culture *US, 1988*

- CROOKLYN, a Spike Lee Joint! — *publicity poster*, 1994
- I remember when attractive women were simply "fly" and great records were "da joint." — Nelson George, *Hip Hop America*, p. 209, 1998
- For six years they [Def Jam] were putting out joints, and every single one of those records was either going gold or platinum. — Alex Ogg, *The Hip Hop Years [quoting Bobbito 'The Barber']*, p. 91, 1999
- [T]he multi-million-pound, state-of-the-art sportswear facility, showcasing the latest in hi-tech imported "boxfresh" minty joints[.] — Julian Johnson, *Urban Survival*, p. 67, 2003

10 a hip-hop recording that features more than one leading rapper *US*

Clipped from 'joint recording'.

- We both thought that this was the joint for the first single[.] — Eminem (Marshall Mathers), *Angry Blonde*, 2001
- Have they recorded any new joints? — *Hip-hop Connection*, p. 20, March 2001

11 in horse racing, a battery-powered device used illegally by a jockey to shock a horse during a race *US*

- Frank Wolverton of Santa Rosa, Cal., "a track follower," today was suspended by the Lone Oak Racing Track Board of Stewards for manufacturing electrical "coaxers" allegedly used to stimulate horses in two races. The gimmick is a "joint," or an electric battery held in the palm of the jockey's hand. — *San Francisco News*, p. 21, 7th September 1951

joint girl *noun*

a prostitute working in one specific disreputable establishment *US*

- And I've had what I call "joint girls," and I'm one of the kind of pimps that over the years I've felt if a girl will be a good whore she will work in a joint. — Bruce Jackson, *In the Life*, p. 185, 1972

joint of beef *noun*

a boss *UK*

Rhyming slang for 'chief'.

- Who's the joint of beef around here? — Ray Puxley, *Cockney Rabbit*, 1992

joints *noun*

a pair of any popular brand of athletic shoes *US*

- — *Washington Post*, 14th October 1993

joint-wise *adjective*

sophisticated and skilled at the ways and means of serving a prison sentence gracefully *US*

- — Hyman E. Goldin et al., *Dictionary of American Underworld Lingo*, p. 111, 1950

JOJ *adjective*

*j*ust *o*ff the *j*et *US*

Applied to a recent immigrant or, in the usage of Hawaiian youth, to a tourist recently arrived in Hawaii.

- — Douglas Simonson, *Pidgin to da Max*, 1981
- — Judi Sanders, *Kickin' like Chicken with the Couch Commander*, p. 13, 1992

jojee *noun*

heroin *US, 1971*

- — Richard A. Spears, *The Slang and Jargon of Drugs and Drink*, p. 291, 1986
- — Robert Ashton, *This Is Heroin*, p. 206, 2002
- — Mike Haskins, *Drugs*, p. 284, 2003

joke *noun*

1 a person who is not taken seriously *AUSTRALIA*

- In short, Hurst is a joke. Hefernon is a joke. Tycho is a joke. And the freeway is a joke. — Roy Slaven (John Doyle), *Five South Coast Seasons*, p. 135, 1992
- If, as a male stripper, you don't score bigtime on your first engagement, you are a pillow and a hopeless joke and we don't wish to know you. — *People*, p. 13, 5th July 1999

2 an operation that offers the possibility of improper gain *AUSTRALIA*

- — Ned Wallish, *The Truth Dictionary of Racing Slang*, p. 42, 1989

joke and farce *noun*

the posterior, the buttocks, the anus *UK*

Rhyming slang for **ARSE**.

- — Bodmin Dark, *Dirty Cockney Rhyming Slang*, 2003

joke box *noun*

a good teller of jokes *BAHAMAS*

- — John A. Holm, *Dictionary of Bahamian English*, p. 115, 1982

joker *noun*

a person; a bloke or fellow *AUSTRALIA, 1810*

- 'Hey, you jokers!' called Tully. 'Make your noise outside, can't you. Young Billy here's crook.' — Eric Lambert, *The Veterans*, p. 68, 1954
- You promised her that you'd go back, Randy, and you're the kind of joker who always keeps his word[.] — W.R. Bennett, *Target Turin*, p. 65, 1962
- The joker who said hell hath no fury like a woman, knew all there was to know. — John Wynnum, *Jiggin' in the Riggin'*, p. 97, 1965
- From an artillery joker I met in town last night. — Ray Slattery, *Mobbs' Mob*, p. 26, 1966
- 'What about that damned foreign joker?' — Jean Brooks, *The Opal Witch*, p. 40, 1967
- He's a shifty joker. — Jean Brooks, *The Opal Witch*, p. 103, 1967

joker poker *noun*

any game of poker played with 53 cards, including the joker *US*

- — George Percy, *The Language of Poker*, p. 50, 1988

jokers' jailhouse *noun*

a lunatic asylum *US*

- Maybe I was closer to the jokers' jailhouse than I ever imagined! — Lester Bangs, *Psychotic Reactions and Carburetor Dung*, p. 11, 1971

jol; joll; jorl; jaul *noun*

a good time; a party, a dance, or similar social occasion *SOUTH AFRICA, 1957*

The variations 'jorl' and 'jaul' are representative of the word's pronunciation.

- I agreed to go on a jorl with a friend. — *Sunday Times (South Africa)*, 24th May 1998
- All night joll[.] — *Sunday Times (South Africa)*, 11th November 2001
- THE BIG JOL[.] Pretoria is rocking! — *Sunday Times (South Africa)*, 8th September 2002

jol; joll; jall; jawl; joil; jola; jorl *verb*

1 to go somewhere (especially in search of entertainment); to depart *SOUTH AFRICA, 1946*

- — Partridge, *A Dictionary of the Underworld*, 1950

2 to flirt; to have a love-affair *SOUTH AFRICA, 1969*

- — Penny Silva, *A Dictionary of South African English*, 1996

3 to make merry, to party *SOUTH AFRICA, 1970*

From Afrikaans.

- This is where Pretoria plays and Jo'burg jorls, more especially at weekends. — *Sunday Times*, 2nd August 1998
- Joburg jolled again last night as yet another posh people's place [...] pulled in the first night crowd. — *Sunday Times (South Africa)*, 19th November 2002

Joliet Josie *noun*

a sexually attractive girl under the legal age of consent *US*

Joliet is the site of the major prison in Illinois.

- — Jack Lait and Lee Mortimer, *Chicago Confidential*, p. 301, 1950: 'Loop lexicon'

joller; jawler *noun*

a person who frequents (unsavoury) places of entertainment; a hedonist, a party-goer, etc *SOUTH AFRICA, 1963*

'Jawlere' is spelt as 'joller' is pronounced.

- In his early 20s he [Marius Schoon] shared a small flat above a bar in Long Street, Cape Town, with Robert Kirby and Breyten Breytenbach. His true colours as a joller and non-conformist began to show. — *Sunday Times (South Africa)*, 14th February 1999

jollier *noun*

a good time, a party *UK*

An elaboration of 'jolly'.

- We can have a proper jollier here. — Niall Griffiths, *Kelly + Victor*, p. 52, 2002

jollies *noun*

1 pleasure *US, 1956*

- "I'd be scared," McMurphy said, "that just about the time I was getting my jollies she'd reach around behind me with a thermometer and take my temperature." — Ken Kesey, *One Flew Over the Cuckoo's Nest*, p. 289, 1962
- Let's face it, a lot of women can't make it with just one guy at a time, they can't get their jollies. — Hunter S. Thompson, *Hell's Angels*, p. 192, 1966
- Two brats in harnesses slapped palms, got their jollies. — Steve Cannon, *Groove, Bang, and Jive Around*, p. 116, 1969
- He lags his response to bang the pain junkie with suspense jollies as he stares into her face — Iceberg Slim (Robert Beck), *Doom Fox*, p. 155, 1978
- Serena plays a love object in a house of pleasure, where she is used over and over for other people's jollies. — Kent Smith et al., *Adult Movies*, p. 216, 1982

• The Secret Service guys helped [US President] Harding get his jollies (sound familiar?)[.] —Erica Orloff and JoAnn Baker, *Dirty Little Secrets*, p. 154, 2001

2 thrills *AUSTRALIA*

• As long as China got her jollies bristling her Russian border with bayonets, the US was delighted to look the other way whenever filter-tip Maoism pushed south. —Gerald Sweeney, *Invasion*, p. 11, 1982

3 the female breasts *UK*

• Any bird who gets her jollies out for GQ wants to be in the papers so bad it in't funny[.] —Ben Elton, *High Society*, p. 20, 2002

jollo *noun*

a party or celebration *AUSTRALIA, 1907*

From 'jolly', or perhaps, 'jollification'.

jollop *noun*

1 a strong liquor, especially whisky *AUSTRALIA, 1942*

From an earlier medical sense.

• Maltese is wantin' hearts as well as munney. But I hev some jollopy. —Geoffrey Fletcher, *Down Among the Meths Men*, p. 32, 1966

2 liquid drugs, usually methadone or morphine *UK*

An extension of the original sense as 'a medicine'.

3 a large meal of leftovers *CANADA*

• "Jollop" appears to be a compound of "jowl" and "lap," and is any big mess of food made from kitchen leftovers. —Bill Casselman, *Canadian Food Words*, p. 64–65, 1988

jollopy *noun*

▷ see: **JALLOPY**

jollup *noun*

semen *UK*

• —*Roger's Profanisaurus*, p. 116, 2002

jolly *noun*

1 a good time; an pleasant excursion; a party *UK, 1905*

An abbreviation of '*jolli*fication'.

• [S]he had saved up all this time off and she was planning to get out soon and have a jolly. —Diran Abedayo, *My Once Upon A Time*, p. 54, 2000

• —Bernadette Hince, *The Antarctic Dictionary*, p. 196, 2000

• I've been to a few FA cup finals, usually as part of some sort of corporate jolly. —Frank Skinner, *Frank Skinner*, p. 88, 2001

• [I]n the mood for an epic jolly-up[.] —*Uncut*, p. 170, October 2002

• Summer only personnel may sometimes be referred to by winterers as "on a summer jolly." —*Cool Antarctica*, 2003: 'Antarctic slang'

2 a Royal Marine *UK, 1825*

The Royal Marines are known as 'the Jollies'.

3 in horse race betting, the favourite *UK*

• —John McCririck, *John McCririck's World of Betting*, p. 60, 1991

jolly *verb*

to treat a person with such positive cheeriness that a state of a good humour is encouraged or maintained *UK, 1865*

• The crew arrived at two, mutinous at the prospect of double shifts. I jollied them into a semblance of good humour – told them I was sure it would be thirsty work. —*The Guardian*, 5th September 2002

jolly *adjective*

drunk *UK, 1652*

Originally euphemistic, then colloquial.

• —*e-cyclopaedia*, 20th March 2002

jolly *adverb*

very, exceedingly *UK, 1838*

• Britain has no national bean and sausage dish even though we eat beans in their millions and make some jolly fine sausages. —*The Observer*, 13th October 2002

jolly bean *noun*

an amphetamine tablet *US, 1969*

• —Carl Chambers and Richard Heckman, *Employee Drug Abuse*, p. 206, 1972

jolly for polly *adjective*

eager for money *UK*

• —*Maledicta*, p. 144, Summer/Winter 1986–1987: 'Sexual slang: prostitutes, pedophiles, flagellators, transvestites, and necrophiles'

jolly good show!

▷ see: **GOOD SHOW!**

jolly green *noun*

marijuana *UK, 1998*

A suggestion that **GREEN** (marijuana/**GRASS**) might make you **JOLLY** (drunk), especially if taken in giant portions implied by the brand name character the Jolly Green Giant .

• —Mike Haskins, *Drugs*, p. 288, 2003

Jolly Green Giant *noun*

any of several large military helicopters, especially the CH-3C helicopter, used during the Vietnam war for counterinsurgency airlifts *US, 1965*

• 21 Hueys, holding 7–8 people each, are now availabe to lift us off the rooftops & out to the 3 main pickup points where the Jolly Green Giants can land. —Hunter S. Thompson, *Fear and Loathing in America*, p. 617, April 1975

• —Ian Padden, *U.S. Air Commando*, p. 104, 1985

• —Linda Reinberg, *In the Field*, 1991

jolly hockey sticks *adjective*

redolent of the atmosphere or culture of a girls' public school; also used of a feminine 'country' accent *UK*

Used parodically. Coined for the BBC radio comedy of the early 1950s *Educating Archie*, by comedy actress Beryl Reid, 1918–96.

• There's a touch of the Carol Thatcher good-hearted jolly-hockey-sticks about her [Ann Maxwell][.] —Gyles Brandreth, *Breaking the Code*, p. 3, 1999

jolly Jack Tar *noun*

▷ see: **JACK TAR**

jolly joker *noun*

a poker *UK*

Rhyming slang.

• —Ray Puxley, *Cockney Rabbit*, 1992

jolly Juice *noun*

alcoholic drink *UK*

• [O]ut to drown themselves in one huge, gut-bloating cascade of fermented jolly juice. —Garry Bushell, *The Face*, p. 81, 2001

jolly pop; jolly popper *noun*

an occasional, non-addicted user of heroin *US*

• —Robert Ashton, *This Is Heroin*, p. 209, 2002

jolly well *adverb*

used as an intensifier *UK, 1898*

• But the Labour party does know, or at least, it jolly well should, and its opening shots in the advertising battle are mystifying. —*The Guardian*, 16th May 2001

jolt *noun*

1 a shock *US*

• There are very few angels who won't go far out of their way to lay a bad jolt on the squares[.] —Hunter S. Thompson, *Hell's Angels*, p. 118, 1966

2 a strong and bracing alcoholic drink *US, 1904*

• The Juicehead Kid was a' takin' a jolt. —William "Lord" Buckley, *The Ballad of Dan McGroo*, 1960

• He poured a stiff jolt of bourbon and knocked it back. —Max Shulman, *Anyone Got a Match?*, p. 14, 1964

3 an injection or dose of a drug *US, 1907*

• "I need a jolt," one addict might remark. "I gotta see my connection." —William J. Spillard and Pence James, *Needle in a Haystack*, p. 148, 1945

• [W]hite women learned where they could get a "belt," a "jolt," or a "gow." —Jack Lait and Lee Mortimer, *New York Confidential*, p. 103–104, 1948

• Chico looked at Peewee and knew he was sick, in need of a jolt. —Hal Ellson, *The Golden Spike*, p. 18, 1952

• A fix. A cap. A jolt. A pop. What do they call it in your group, dear? —John D. McDonald, *The Neon Jungle*, p. 71, 1953

• I told him I was liable to die right in his kitchen if I didn't get a jolt. —John M. Murtagh and Sara Harris, *Cast the First Stone*, p. 48, 1957

• And Doc Parker in the back room in his drugstore shooting horse heroin, three grains a jolt. —William Burroughs, *Naked Lunch*, p. 85, 1957

• If he wanted a jolt he'd just step into a side street or an alley and blow a good stick. —Willard Motley, *Let No Man Write My Epitaph*, p. 108, 1958

• "Say, man," Crip's voice warned, "that's a big jolt you got heaped in your hand." —Piri Thomas, *Down These Mean Streets*, p. 110, 1967

• It was very weak stuff, he found; he had to take an extra jolt just to get himself straight. —Nathan Heard, *Howard Street*, p. 111, 1968

• He skin pops a load of Dilaudid into a forearm, swoons for a moment under the jolt. —Iceberg Slim (Robert Beck), *Doom Fox*, p. 157, 1978

• What he did find was a great gym near his hotel where he could get illegal steroid shots in the ass for fifty bucks a jolt. —Stephen Cannell, *Big Con*, p. 160, 1997

4 a prison sentence *US, 1912*

- But a bim that won't bolt while you're doin' a little jolt / is just one out of a thousand my friend. —Bruce Jackson, *Get Your Ass in the Water and Swim Like Me*, p. 116, 1964
- That was the jolt when he blew his pickets. —Malcolm Braly, *On the Yard*, p. 7, 1967
- He turned state's evidence on Wild Wallace, drew a reduced three-to-five jolt at Chino as part of the deal, and was paroled to the war effort early in '42. —James Ellroy, *Hollywood Nocturnes*, p. 129, 1994
- You tell me now, or when Amp Heywood is eventually indicted for that grand larceny, I'll see to it he gets the full jolt. —Stephen Cannell, *King Con*, p. 75, 1997
- I got out of jail ninth of September 1996 after serving a jolt of seventeen and a half years of a fifteen-to-life[.] —Joel Rose, *Kill Kill Faster Faster*, p. 14, 1997

jolt *verb*

1 to shock *US*

- "He jolted me to some unpleasant facts," Bernie said. —Ross Russell, *The Sound*, p. 237, 1961

2 to inject a drug *US, 1953*

- —Richard A. Spears, *The Slang and Jargon of Drugs and Drink*, p. 292, 1986
- —Mike Haskins, *Drugs*, p. 290, 2003

Jolting Joe *noun*

Joe DiMaggio *US*

An extraordinarily gifted player for the New York Yankees baseball team from 1936 to 1951.

- After all, would Jolting Joe ever take as a wife someone whom we could not admire? —Lenny Bruce, *How to Talk Dirty and Influence People*, p. 52, 1965
- What's that you say, Mrs. Robinson / Jolting Joe has left and gone away. —Simon and Garfunkle, *Mrs. Robinson*, 1968

Jo Maxi *noun*

a taxi *IRELAND*

Also abbreviated to 'Jo'.

- [G]et a six-pack from the machine in the jacks and the next thing I know, Bob's your auntie's husband, we're in a Jo Maxi on the way to her pad in Leopardstown. —Paul Howard, *Ross O'Carroll-Kelly*, p. 68, 2003

Jonah *noun*

a superstitious gambler; a gambler perceived by other gamblers to bring bad luck *US, 1849*

- —*The Annals of the American Academy of Political and Social Sciences*, p. 126, May 1950

Jonah *verb*

in craps, to try to influence the roll of the dice with body movements, hand gestures or incantations *US*

- —John Scarne, *Scarne on Dice*, p. 471, 1974

Jonathan Ross; jonathan *noun*

something of little or no value *UK*

Rhyming slang for **TOSS** used in the sense 'not give a toss' formed from the name of a television and radio presenter, chat-show host and film critic (b.1960).

- [C]ouldn't give a Jonathan. —Ray Puxley, *Fresh Rabbit*, 1998

jone *verb*

to put a spell on someone *CANADA*

- A woman went around to houses begging for food, clothing, etc. She would tell the householders if they didn't give what she wanted she would jone them, meaning she would put a spell or curse on them. —M. Kelly, *oral citation in Dictionary of Newfoundland English*, p. 280, 1982

▷ see: JOAN

jones *noun*

1 an addiction *US, 1962*

- Carmen explained she had a jones and since she spoke Spanish, could cop all the stuff Ralph needed very easily. —Babs Gonzales, *I Paid My Dues*, p. 106, 1967
- My transition from Skidrow and Shooting gallery took only a few days, 1 reason being that I had no Jones, no habit, on arrival[.] —Clarence Cooper Jr, *The Farm*, p. 16, 1967
- Bam and Baby June shuffle past ... already a half hour away from pain ... trying, with all their dopefiend cunning, to head Jones off at the pass. —Odie Hawkins, *Ghetto Sketches*, p. 39, 1972
- I wanna talk to all you addicts out there that's got yourself a great big Jones / An' you tried all the methadone / An' you just can't leave that heroin alone. —King/The Mighty Hannibal, *The Truth Shall Make You Free*, 1972
- The only time the High One had seen me without a habit was during our school days, but ever since we were adults I had a Jones. —A.S. Jackson, *Gentleman Pimp*, p. 134, 1973
- The next thing that you know / You've got a jones – / Look out! Look out, here comes the pusher. —The Dramatics, *The Devil is Dope*, 1973
- The Barker drilled that into his head; never cop to your jones. —Seth Morgan, *Homeboy*, p. 42, 1990

2 an intense craving or yearning *US, 1970*

- Yes, I am the victim of a basketball Jones. —Cheech Marin and Tommy Chong, *Basketball Jones*, 1973
- This motherfuckin' jones is killin' me, woman. —Donald Goines, *Cry Revenge*, p. 158, 1974
- There was this terrible cigarette called "Bizonte" that I developed a Jones for. —Odie Hawkins, *Lost Angeles*, p. 83, 1994
- When you've got a love jones, you're like Mr. Magoo: legally blind, always bumping into something, and so deep in it that you have no time for the rest of life. —Chris Rock, *Rock This!*, p. 114, 1997
- The situation is, my man Cameron here has a major jones for Bianca Stratford. —*Ten Things I Hate About You*, 1999
- [M]y jones for hip-hop knew no end. —*The Source*, March 2002

3 heroin *US, 1970*

- Then I heard a knock on the door so I placed a New York News over the Jones and got up to answer the door. —A.S. Jackson, *Gentleman Pimp*, p. 145, 1973
- No more jones, see? I just want a portion of the west side dealin' nothin' but coke. —Vernon E. Smith, *The Jones Men*, p. 8, 1974
- —Mike Haskins, *Drugs*, p. 284, 2003

4 the penis *US, 1966*

- The words stuck in Dip's mind like bubble gum on the brain, and slowly worked their way down to his jones. —Steve Cannon, *Groove, Bang, and Jive Around*, p. 25, 1969
- "Bitch," I yelled. "Enough is enough, turn my jones loose." —Donald Goines, *Whoreson*, p. 145, 1972
- He crossed his legs, trying to push his hardening jones down between his thighs. to keep his thang cooled out, like, after all, three months was a pretty good piece of time to remain unfucked. —Odie Hawkins, *Chicago Hustle*, p. 106, 1977
- Your jones, the quality of your erection was low, low Daddy, Dear. —Iceberg Slim (Robert Beck), *Long White Con*, p. 22, 1977

jones *verb*

to crave *US, 1974*

- I guess in a way Angel Juan is my fix and I've been jonesing for him. —Francesca Lia Block, *Missing Angel Juan*, p. 332, 1993
- I'm jonsein' for 'th Dew,' bigtime! —David Shenk and Steve Silberman, *Skeleton Key*, p. 167, 1994

Joneses *noun*

the notional family next door who are the basis for your aspirations for social equality *UK, 1932*

- Hyacinth Bucket, who took the notion of keeping up with the Joneses to comic extremes[.] —*The Guardian*, 25th February 2003

jones man *noun*

a heroin dealer *US, 1972*

- "Everybody wanta be the jones man," he said. —Vernon E. Smith, *The Jones Men*, p. 32, 1974

jong *noun*

1 a black person, especially a black man *SOUTH AFRICA, 1908*

An offensive term, from older senses as 'a black male servant or slave' derived from Afrikaans *jongen* (a boy).

- —Penny Silva, *A Dictionary of South African English*, 1996

2 used as a friendly, informal term of address, regardless of gender; a boyfriend *SOUTH AFRICA, 1911*

- —Jean Branford, *A Dictionary of South African English*, 1978

jong!

used as an expression of anger, frustration, surprise, pleasure, etc *SOUTH AFRICA, 1956*

- —Penny Silva, *A Dictionary of South African English*, 1996

jonnic; jonnick; jonic; jonick *adjective*

1 true *AUSTRALIA, 1874*

From British dialect.

- 'It's jonnic, I tell you!' Sep Seely claimed, blinking through his fogged glasses as usual. 'Jat Manfu is coming here!' —Ray Slattery, *Mobbs' Mob*, p. 25, 1966
- 'You say this is jonnic?' he checked. 'A stage company with girls, coming to Finnschafen?' —Ray Slattery, *Mobbs' Mob*, p. 26, 1966

2 genuine *AUSTRALIA*

- 'She was all right, eh?' 'She's jonnick, for sure!' —J.E. MacDonnell, *Don't Gimme the Ships*, p. 46, 1960

joobs *noun*

▷ see: JUJUBES

joog *noun*

1 in Newfoundland, especially of alcohol, a small amount, a drop *CANADA*

- When he put the bottle back on the table, there wasn't a joog in it. —Virginia Dillon, *Anglo-Irish Element in Speech of Southwest Coast of Newfoundland*, p. 146, 1968

2 the jugular vein *US*

Also spelt 'jug'.

- —Sally Williams, *"Strong" Words*, p. 148, 1994

joog *verb*

1 to have sex *JAMAICA, 1942*

Sometimes spelt 'jewg'.

- Joog her, man. Joog her, she wants to be jooged. —Steve Cannon, *Groove, Bang, and Jive Around*, p. 37, 1969
- Jooged plenty women too. —Edwin Torres, *After Hours*, p. 440, 1979
- She is not a mother-figure or a sister-image, she is a woman staying with three men, two of them are becoming edgy at the possibility that she may ease away, unjewgged. —Odie Hawkins, *Black Casanova*, p. 55, 1984

2 in Newfoundland, to drain or drink completely *CANADA*

- He jooged the bottle right to the last drop. —Virginia Dillon, *Anglo-Irish Element in Speech of Southern Shore of Newfoundland*, p. 146, 1968

3 to tease *US*

- —Gary K. Farlow, *Prison-ese*, p. 35, 2002

jook *noun*

sexual intercourse *TRINIDAD AND TOBAGO, 1993*

- —Lise Winer, *Dictionary of the English/Creole of Trinidad & Tobago*, 2003

jook *verb*

1 to poke with a sharp object *BARBADOS*

- —Frank A. Collymore, *Barbadian Dialect*, p. 62, 1965

2 to stab *TRINIDAD AND TOBAGO, 1827*

- —Lise Winer, *Dictionary of the English/Creole of Trinidad & Tobago*, 2003

jooks *noun*

trousers *UK: SCOTLAND*

- Aw c'moan, tell that stupit dug [dog] a yours no tae jump up oan the good jooks, eh? —Michael Munro, *The Patter, Another Blast*, p. 38, 1988

jorl, joro *nouns*

▷ **see: JOL, JOBO**

josh *verb*

to mock, to tease; to banter *US, 1852*

- Throughout the Indianapolis weekend there was much back-slapping and joshing with [Murray] Walker[.] — *The Guardian*, 1st October 2001
- [Ralph] Steadman's centrifugal preoccupations spin off in all directions, laboriously ranting and joshing along in what reads like a series of bibulous postcards from the last days of Gonzo. — *The Guardian*, 22nd November 2003

joshed up *adjective*

stylishly dressed and well-presented *UK*

From 'zhoosh' (clothes).

- —Paul Baker, *Polari*, p. 178, 2002

josh it *verb*

to die *UK*

- DAD: Uh, I feel weak as a bloody kitten. DENISE: Give us a fag, Dad, before you josh it. —Caroline Aherne and Craig Cash, *The Royle Family*, 1999

joskin *noun*

a country bumpkin *UK, 1811*

- I watched two homies [men] gazumping [swindling] the joskins[.] —Butch Reynolds, *Broken Hearted Clown*, p. 61, 1954

josser *noun*

an outsider *UK, 1933*

Polari.

- I watched two homies [men] gazumping [swindling] the joskins[.] —Butch Reynolds, *Broken Hearted Clown*, p. 61, 1953
- [W]hen I joined the circus as a josser I found that I had to learn not only new schools but a new language as well. —Butch Reynolds, *Broken Hearted Clown*, p. 28, 1953
- This Joe wasn't a showman. He was an outsider. What circus people call a josser. —Jake Arnott, *He Kills Coppers*, p. 202, 2001

jostle *verb*

to engage in petty swindles *US*

- So Mike spent at least half of his time on the Island doing "five-twenty-nine" for jostling. —William Burroughs, *Junkie*, p. 26, 1953
- I had heard about jostling and the Murphy for a long time, but I didn't know what it was all about. —Claude Brown, *Manchild in the Promised Land*, p. 160, 1965

jostler *noun*

the member of a pickpocket crew whose clumsy bumping into the victim distracts him while a confederate picks the pocket *US, 1929*

- —Hyman E. Goldin et al., *Dictionary of American Underworld Lingo*, p. 111, 1950
- —John M. Murtagh and Sara Harris, *Cast the First Stone*, p. 261, 1957: 'Glossary'

jotters *noun*

▸ **get your jotters; be given your jotters**

to be dismissed from employment *UK*

Glasgow slang.

- —Michael Munro, *The Original Patter*, 1985
- [I]f he bided his time, he'd still be around to see her get her jotters. —Christopher Brookmyre, *The Sacred Art of Stealing*, p. 247, 2002

joual *noun*

the working-class dialect of Frenglish, a mixture of languages, used in Quebec *CANADA*

This term, used by English Quebec speakers rather than 'Frenglish', may derive from a corruption of *cheval* French for 'horse', i.e. 'French spoken on horseback'. Famed and favourite playwright Michel Tremblay wrote all his early plays in 'joual' and refused to allow them to be translated until the separatist party won power in 1976.

- A Quebec working-class dialect that's a striking mix of English and French. Varies from region to region. —Emily *An American's Guide to Canada*, p. 1, 10th November 2001

jouk *verb*

to play truant; to dodge, duck, avoid, hide *CANADA*

- Somebody who wanted to avoid someone [i.e. the truant officer] would jouk around. —T.K. Pratt, *oral citation from Dictionary of Prince Edward Island English*, p. 83, 1988

jounts *noun*

clothing *US*

- — *Washington Post Magazine*, p. 11, 29th March 1987: 'Say wha?'

journo *noun*

a journalist *AUSTRALIA, 1965*

- Anyway, d'you know what a freelance journo makes in the first year? Starvation. —Peter Corris, *Pokerface*, p. 29, 1985
- Pseudo-clever tapping of popular culture, letting the journo know that he's not a pleb. —Kevin Sampson, *Powder*, p. 5, 1999

journo *adjective*

being of journalists or journalism *AUSTRALIA*

- For a year [Suede] were the press darlings, ready with the media-friendly quip. [Brett] Anderson was the journo wet dream. —John Robb, *The Nineties*, p. 339, 1999

joust *noun*

a physical encounter with sexual overtones *UK*

From the conventional sense as 'combat on horseback' with, perhaps, the phallic suggestion of thrusting lances.

- I'm all in favour of a joust with an athletic Judy [woman], and that. —Kevin Sampson, *Outlaws*, p. 81, 2001

jowlster *noun*

a useless troublesome male individual *IRELAND*

- 'If he comes in here don't serve him any drink.' 'Why not?' 'Because I don't want any jowlsters hanging around here', he said and headed for the door. —Billy Roche, *Tumbling Down*, p. 11, 1984

joxy *noun*

the vagina *US*

- —Dale Gordon, *The Dominion Sex Dictionary*, p. 95, 1967

joy *noun*

1 luck, satisfation; especially in the question 'any joy?' and the negative response or interrogative 'no joy' *UK, 1945*

Originally Royal Air Force usage.

- I didn't seem to be having any joy blagging it so I went out and bought a copy. — *The Guardian*, 17th October 2003

2 marijuana *US*

- —Edith A. Folb, *runnin' down some lines*, p. 244, 1980

3 heroin *UK*
- —Robert Ashton, *This Is Heroin*, p. 206, 2002

Joy *noun*
▸ the Joy
Mountjoy Prison in Dublin *IRELAND*
- —Desmond O'Neill, *Life Has No Price*, 1959
- The screws should have known that once he had decided to get out of The Joy he'd do it. —Howard Paul, *The Joy*, p. 75, 1996

joy bang; joy *noun*
an injection of a narcotic, especially heroin, without succumbing to the drug's addictive nature *US*
- Nick also scored for some respectable working people in the Village who indulged in an occasional "joy bang." —William Burroughs, *Junkie*, p. 61, 1953
- —Angela Devlin, *Prison Patter*, p. 67, 1996

joy booter *noun*
an infrequent smoker *US*
- —John Fahs, *Cigarette Confidential*, p. 302, 1996: 'Glosssary'

joybox *noun*
a piano *US, 1942*
- At the Pekin they had Tony Jackson, a New Orleans musician, one of the greatest blues piano players that ever pounded a joybox. —Mezz Mezzrow, *Really the Blues*, p. 45, 1946

joyboy *noun*
a young male homosexual, especially a young male homosexual prostitute *UK, 1961*
- —Dale Gordon, *The Dominion Sex Dictionary*, p. 95, 1967
- There were many other ways; masturbation was first but homosexuals or prisonmade "joy-boys" came in second. —Piri Thomas, *Seven Long Times*, p. 137, 1974
- — *Male Swinger Number 3*, p. 47, 1981: 'The complete gay dictionary'

joy flakes *noun*
a powdered drug, especially cocaine or heroin *US, 1942*
- —Vincent J. Monteleone, *Criminal Slang*, p. 134, 1949
- —Robert Ashton, *This Is Heroin*, p. 206, 2002
- —Mike Haskins, *Drugs*, p. 284, 2003

joy girl *noun*
1 a prostitute *US, 1931*
- I knew it had changed a great deal from the days when they had the gatehouse at the entrance and the private police force, and the gambling casino on the lake, and the fifty-dollar joy girls. —Raymond Chandler, *The Long Goodbye*, p. 85, 1953

2 in a deck of playing cards, any queen *US, 1973*
- —Thomas L. Clark, *The Dictionary of Gambling and Gaming*, p. 111, 1987

joy jelly *noun*
in electric line work, a silicone compound used on underground cable terminators *US*
- —A.B. Chance Co., *Lineman's Slang Dictionary*, p. 10, 1980

joy juice *noun*
1 semen *US*
- Suddenly his legs stiffened, his asshole close, and the joy-juice shot. —Steve Cannon, *Groove, Bang, and Jive Around*, p. 24, 1969
- There, bitch, if you get hungry tonight, there's some joy juice for you to lick on. —Donald Goines, *White Man's Justice, Black Man's Grief*, p. 73, 1973
- He wanted her ass to be good and strong and filled to the brim with the joy juice of the men she'd had that day, and the more the merrier. —A.S. Jackson, *Gentleman Pimp*, p. 154, 1973
- The joy-juice flies as these girls suck, frig their clits, and ready their assholes for cock. — *Adult Video*, p. 66, August/September 1986
- Why do you have to talk dirty like that? Joy juice. I mean, for chrissake. —Robert Campbell, *Juice*, p. 214, 1988

2 any alcoholic beverage, especially whisky *US, 1907*
- —Lou Shelly, *Hepcats Jive Talk Dictionary*, p. 28, 1945
- That didn't mean nothing as his son, Rosita's husband upstairs had his own still and made his own joy juice. —Babs Gonzales, *Movin' On Down De Line*, p. 106, 1975

3 a powerful hallucinogenic drink made from seeds of the datura plant *TRINIDAD AND TOBAGO, 1991*
- —Lise Winer, *Dictionary of the English/Creole of Trinidad & Tobago*, 2003

4 a central nervous system depressant *US, 1954*
- —Mike Haskins, *Drugs*, p. 282, 2003

5 chloral hydrate, used to render someone unconscious *US*
- —Eugene Landy, *The Underground Dictionary*, p. 113, 1971

joy knob *noun*
an attachment to a car steering wheel that facilitates steering with one hand, leaving the other hand free *US*
- Glenn took his right hand from the wheel and put it around her shoulders, steering with the death's-head joy knob. —Earl Thompson, *Tattoo*, p. 234, 1974

Joynson-hicks *noun*
six *UK*
Rhyming slang, formed from the name of Sir William Joynson-Hicks, 1865–1932, who is best remembered as the Conservative Home Secretary at the time of the general strike of 1926.
- —Julian Franklyn, *A Dictionary of Rhyming Slang*, 1960

joy of my life *noun*
a wife *UK, 1936*
Rhyming slang, often ironic.
- —Ray Puxley, *Fresh Rabbit*, 1998

joy plant *noun*
opium; heroin *UK, 1998*
- —Mike Haskins, *Drugs*, p. 284, 2003

joy pop *noun*
an injection of a drug into the skin, not a vein *US, 1922*
- The Royal Roost – swinging up to Harlem – eventually picking up a steady with a cat who was a junky – beginning to take an occasional joy-pop herself. —Herbert Huncke, *The Evening Sun Turned Crimson*, p. 53, 1980

joy-pop *verb*
1 to inject a drug under the skin, not into a vein *US, 1936*
- Fran joy-popped. Just hit with the stuff under her skin. —Willard Motley, *Let No Man Write My Epitaph*, p. 159, 1958
- I'm glad I don't do nothin but joy pop. —Clarence Cooper Jr, *The Scene*, p. 77, 1960
- What really tore it was they turned the place into a regular shooting gallery – blowing pot and joy popping all over the place. —Ross Russell, *The Sound*, p. 199, 1961

2 to fly a helicopter at a low elevation and high speed *US*
- —Linda Reinberg, *In the Field*, p. 118, 1991

joy popper *noun*
an intravenous drug user *US, 1936*
- "Just a joy-popper, eh?" "Well, I find it helps when things are rough[.]" —Douglas Rutherford, *The Creeping Flesh*, 1963
- She [an apartment] was sleazed and greasy from the legions of junkie joy poppers who had fouled her rotten with their shooting galleries. —Iceberg Slim (Robert Beck), *Airtight Willie and Me*, p. 61, 1979
- By this definition I was only a weekend joy popper who had no right to so grandiose a title as Junkie. —Larry Rivers, *What Did I Do?*, p. 194, 1992

joy powder *noun*
any powdered drug, especially cocaine, heroin or morphine *US, 1922*
- —Robert Ashton, *This Is Heroin*, p. 206, 2002
- —Mike Haskins, *Drugs*, p. 284, 2003

joy!; rapture!
used for expressing pleasure in what has just been said *US*
Somewhat sarcastic or, at least, melodramatic.
- —Connie Eble (Editor), *UNC-CH Campus Slang*, p. 5, Fall 1986

joy-ride *noun*
an impulsive excursion in a car that is, from the point of view of the riders, borrowed, but from the point of view of the law, stolen *US, 1915*
- In those days, when automobiles were still a novelty, we got a big kick out of joyriding in somebody else's car. —Mezz Mezzrow, *Really the Blues*, 1946
- Seventy-five percent of all car thefts in the United States are by teenagers out for "joy rides." —Tom Wolfe, *The Kandy-Kolored Tangerine-Flake Streamline Baby*, p. 33, 1965
- Eddy? do you know anybody who might wanna borrow a cab for sumpn? A little outing? A joyride? —Gilbert Sorrentino, *Steelwork*, p. 158, 1970
- I saw this bus and half-stoned I decided to go for a joyride – next thing I know these crazy hippies are banging into the car. —Edwin Torres, *Carlito's Way*, p. 137–138, 1975
- Must've been a joyride situation; they abandoned the car once they hit the retaining wall. — *The Big Lebowski*, 1998
- [A] Volkswagen with a yellow crook lock on the steering wheel, presumably to protect it from any joy-riding fishermen or shepherds[.] —Pete McCarthy, *McCarthy's Bar*, p. 137, 2000

joyride *verb*
to steal a car for a joy-ride *US*
- Usually we went for girls, but this time we just went joy riding. — Hal Ellson, *Duke*, p. 113, 1949
- I had had illegally in my possession about 500 cars – whether just for the moment and to be taken back to its owner before he returned (I.E. on Parking lots) or whether taken for the purpose of so altering its appearance as to keep it for several weeks but mostly only for joyriding. — Neal Cassady, *The First Third*, p. 170, 1971
- You have pleaded guilty to"joy-riding" as a lesser charge to Grand Theft Auto. — *Menace II Society*, 1993

joy-rider *noun*
1 a person who takes pleasure in driving another's vehicle without permission *US*
Extended from **JOY-RIDE**.
- [T]he fucking joyriders burning the hillsides – the temazes stuck on tongues[.] — Patrick Jones, *Everything Must Go*, p. 141, 2000

2 an infrequent user of an addictive drug *US*
- — Hyman E. Goldin et al., *Dictionary of American Underworld Lingo*, p. 111, 1950
- — Eugene Landy, *The Underground Dictionary*, p. 113, 1971

joyriding *noun*
the criminal act of taking another's car for the thrilling pleasure of driving it *US, 1910*
- I used to do a bit of joyriding when we were on drugs[.] — Macfarlane, Macfarlane and Robson, *The User*, p. 106, 1996
- [A] proper little hooligan nicking cars and joyriding, getting in fights because I was unhappy, ram-raiding shops so she didn't know what to do with me. — John King, *Human Punk*, p. 300–301, 2000

joy smoke *noun*
marijuana *US, 1938*
'Joy hemp', 'joy root' and 'joy weed' are also recorded in the 1940s; only 'joy' and 'joy smoke' seem to have survived.
- — Richard A. Spears, *The Slang and Jargon of Drugs and Drink*, p. 287, 1986
- — Mike Haskins, *Drugs*, p. 288, 2003

joystick *noun*
1 the penis *US, 1916*
Probably derived from mechanical imagery, but there is a suggestion (Ray Puxley, *Cockney Rabbit*, 1992) that this may be rhyming slang for **PRICK**.
- — *The Guild Dictionary of Homosexual Terms*, p. 25, 1965
- Help me get a hard on, Patricia. Help me get my joystick up so I don't go crazy. — Sara Harris, *The Lords of Hell*, p. 93, 1967
- I ever catch you cheatin' on me and I'll cut you a great big hole where you got that joy stick swinging. — Vance Donovan, *High Rider*, p. 48, 1969
- She may have one arm around him, or have one hand busy squeezing his gonads and the other hand busy rubbing his joystick augmenting the sucking action of her lips — *Screw*, p. 4, 1st December 1969

2 a marijuana cigarette *US, 1962*
- — Richard A. Spears, *The Slang and Jargon of Drugs and Drink*, p. 293, 1986
- — Mike Haskins, *Drugs*, p. 291, 2003

3 the pole used to carry a pair of balanced objects on your shoulders *US*
- — Carl Fleischhauer, *A Glossary of Army Slang*, p. 28, 1968

joy water *noun*
vaginal lubricant produced as a result of sexual arousal *US*
- [W]hen she climaxed she hollered and screamed and her tasty ass became quite sloppy with joy water. — A.S. Jackson, *Gentleman Pimp*, p. 109, 1973

JP *nickname*
Jamaica Plain, Massachusetts *US*
- — Jim Crotty, *How to Talk American*, p. 26, 1997

JPT *noun*
used for denoting a lack of punctuality *US*
An abbreviation of **JEWISH PEOPLE'S TIME**.
- Like Mexican Time and the onetime JPT, Jewish People's time, C.P.T. is a phrase that draws the lines of the ghetto. — Paul Jacobs, *Prelude to a Riot*, p. 12, 1967

J. Random *noun*
used as a humorous first initial and middle name of a mythical person *US*
- Would you let J. Random Loser marry your daughter? — Guy L. Steele et al., *The Hacker's Dictionary*, p. 86, 1983

J-smoke *noun*
a marijuana cigarette; marijuana *US, 1969*
- — Eugene Landy, *The Underground Dictionary*, p. 111, 1971
- — Richard A. Spears, *The Slang and Jargon of Drugs and Drink*, p. 287, 1986
- — Mike Haskins, *Drugs*, p. 288, 2003

JT *noun*
the penis *UK*
An abbreviation of **JOHN THOMAS** (the penis).

J-town *noun*
a neighbourhood populated by a large number of Japanese-Americans *US*
An abbreviation of 'Japan Town'.
- I've been coming to the Geisha Doll and every other restaurant here in J-town for twenty years so it was no wonder. — Joseph Wambaugh, *The Blue Knight*, p. 40, 1973

Juana *noun*
marijuana *US*
A personified abbreviation.

Juan Doe *noun*
an unidentified Hispanic male *US*
- They knew all about trunk jobs, John Does, Juan Does, gun-shots, accidentals and naturals. — Carl Hiaasen, *Strip Tease*, p. 100, 1993

Juanita *noun*
marijuana *US, 1969*
Another of the seemingly endless **MARY JANE** offspring.

Juan Valdez *noun*
marijuana *US, 1984*
Juan is probably taken from 'mari*juana*', but other than its obvious Spanish roots the etymology of Juan Valdez is uncertain.
- — Richard A. Spears, *The Slang and Jargon of Drugs and Drink*, p. 293, 1986
- — Mike Haskins, *Drugs*, p. 288, 2003

jubes *noun*
▷ **see: JUJUBES**

jubilee *noun*
the buttocks *US*
- — Dale Gordon, *The Dominion Sex Dictionary*, p. 95, 1967

juck; juk; juckie *noun*
a dog; hence, used disparagingly of a man *UK*
Directly from Romany *jook* (a dog). In English gypsy use.
- — Patrick O'Shaughnessy, *Market Trader's Slang*, 1979
- — Jimmy Stockin, *On The Cobbles*, p. 10, 2000

Judas goat *noun*
an animal trained to lead other animals into slaughter *US, 1941*
- You're Judas goats, both of you. — Darryl Ponicsan, *The Last Detail*, p. 95, 1970

Judas hole; Judas eye; Judas window; Judas *noun*
a small peep-hole in a door through which one can see who is outside the door without being seen from outside *US, 1865*
- Inside the steel door of the cell block was a basket of steel bars around the Judas window. — Raymond Chandler, *The Long Goodbye*, p. 44, 1953
- She got her copy of the New York Herald-Tribune from the mat outside her door, first peeping through the Judas window to make certain the coast was clear[.] — Chester Himes, *The Primitive*, p. 12, 1955
- "Like a jail," said Kay. 'Judases,' don't they call them?" — Mary McCarthy, *The Group*, p. 310, 1963
- Upstairs, at the end of a long corridor of doors with painted windows on both sides, there's another door all wood with a Judas hole in the middle of it. I knock and the slide clicks back. — Robert Campbell, *Junkyard Dog*, p. 68, 1986
- — Angela Devlin, *Prison Patter*, p. 67, 1996

Judas priest!
used as an expression of surprise or outrage *US, 1914*
Multiple embellishments.
- After an uncomfortable ten minutes passed, a voice called from the top of the stairs. "Judas Priest on a pony!" — Marilyn Manson, *The Long Hard Road Out of Hell*, p. 11, 1998
- "Well shit. Just shit." We all looked at her in amazement. She never cussed. "Judas priest!" — Haywood Smith, *The Red Hat Club*, p. 20, 2003

judder *noun*
in motor racing, a shuddering effect felt during braking because of tyre imbalance *US*
- — Don Alexander, *The Racer's Dictionary*, p. 35, 1980

judder bars *noun*
haemorrhoids *NEW ZEALAND*
- —David McGill, *David McGill's Complete Kiwi Slang Dictionary*, p. 74, 1998

Judge *noun*
a 1968–73 Pontiac GTO *US*
- —Lewis Poteet, *Car & Motorcyle Slang*, p. 116, 1992

Judge Dread; Judge Dredd *noun*
the head *UK*
Rhyming slang, formed from the title of a series of graphic comic-strip adventures and a 1995 film, or, less likely, a reggae entertainer.
- —Ray Puxley, *Fresh Rabbit*, 1998
- Bits oozing out. You reckon inside some geezer's Judge Dread they got to have a load of gravy. Not this geezer's. —Jeremy Cameron, *Brown Bread in Wengen*, p. 4–5, 1999

Judge Duffy; Judge Dean *noun*
in poker, three tens *US*
The suggestion is that the mythical Judge Duffy, Judge Dean, or whoever, commonly handed out sentences of thirty days.
- —Irwin Steig, *Common Sense in Poker*, p. 185, 1963
- —George Percy, *The Language of Poker*, p. 50, 1988

Judi Dench; Judi *noun*
▷ see: DAME JUDI DENCH

Judy *noun*
1 a woman, a girl *UK, 1812*
Possibly adopted from traditional *Punch and Judy* puppet shows, or simply from the proper name. Earlier variations of the definition specified that she looked ridiculous (giving credence to Punch's wife) or that she was promiscuous.
- [H]e was setting out to cut a rug [dance] with a brand-new judy. —Charles Raven, *Underworld Nights*, p. 66, 1956
- "I'm over sixteen," the girl said following them. "Fancy Smith is crazy about me." "You're a right little Judy aren't you," Watt said, stopping to look at her. "Run home to your mum, and take those handkerchiefs out of the front of your jersey." —Troy Kennedy Martin, *Z Cars*, p. 53, 1962
- This judy nearest me says what about us pulling up for a drink some place. —John Peter Jones, *Feather Pluckers*, p. 41, 1964
- [H]e's a bit of a cad with the Judies, bit of a rake and that. —Kevin Simpson, *Outlaws*, p. 12, 2001
- No lyin in with the judy! —Niall Griffiths, *Kelly + Victor*, p. 12, 2002

2 the meal fed to a prisoner in solitary confinement *US*
- Judy is a ground patty 4" x 4" x 3" that is made up of the entire meal's ingredients and is run through a grinder. They are traditionally served burned on the outside and raw on the inside. —William K. Bentley and James M. Corbett, *Prison Slang*, p. 11, 1992

Judy *adjective*
locked in on a target *US*
- "We were both 'Judy,' meaning locked on," recalled J.C. They next activated their missiles. —Robert K. Wilcox, *Scream of Eagles*, p. 26, 1990

jug *noun*
1 a jail or prison *US, 1816*
- And don't forget they threw some musicians in the jug out in California for ten days[.] —Mezz Mezzrow, *Really the Blues*, p. 262, 1946
- Slugs do it, bugs do it, even funny looking mugs in jugs do it. —Chester Himes, *Cast the First Stone*, p. 72, 1952
- Jake's a nice boy so they give him plenty of privileges in the jug, huh? —Jim Thompson, *Savage Night*, p. 127, 1953
- You want to go to the jug, it's your funeral, but I ain't sending any flowers. —Jim Thompson, *A Swell-Looking Babe*, p. 39, 1954
- Conditions on Skid Row were frightful that winter for all the meths drinkers who had failed to get into the jug. —Geoffrey Fletcher, *Down Among the Meths Men*, p. 16, 1966
- [C]aptains of industry only being allowed out of jug because they're suffering from Alzheimer's Disease ... and then forgetting they've got it. —Andrew Nickolds, *Back to Basics*, p. 6, 1994
- —Angela Devlin, *Prison Patter*, p. 67, 1996

2 a bank *US, 1848*
- He could have a million in the jug. —Iceberg Slim (Robert Beck), *Trick Baby*, p. 111, 1969
- —Bill Reilly, *Big Al's Official Guide to Chicagoese*, p. 39, 1982
- "We should do a jug," Jimmy declared. Billy laughed. "A jug?" ""Yeah," Jimmy went on. "You know, a bank." "I know what a fucking jug is." —Jake Arnott, *He Kills Coppers*, p. 87–88, 2001

3 a glass of beer *AUSTRALIA*
No longer common. Only used colloquially and not when ordering beer at a hotel where a 'jug' is precisely that, a jug of beer that you take back to a table and fill glasses from.
- Let's suck a jug. —J.E. MacDonnell, *Don't Gimme the Ships*, p. 52, 1960
- What say we wander up to the mess and hit oursleves with a jew jugs, Pete? —W.R. Bennett, *Night Intruder*, p. 104, 1962
- [O]ther times your spend the whole week with the feet up just swallowing jugs, and you come up trumps with the foot. —Roy Slaven (John Doyle), *Five South Coast Seasons*, p. 120, 1992

4 a large table jug for beer *AUSTRALIA*
- How many middies does a jug hold? —Bazza and Curly, *Betcha Wrong!*, p. 83, 1990

5 a glass ampoule holding liquid drugs *US*
- —Eugene Landy, *The Underground Dictionary*, p. 24, 1971

6 a small container of amphetamine or methamphetamine in liquid form *US*
- National Institute on Drug Abuse, — *What do they call it again?*, 1980

7 a cylinder in an aeroplane engine *US*
- —*American Speech*, p. 119, May 1963: 'Air refueling words'

8 a carburettor *US, 1942*
- —*Hot Rod Magazine*, p. 13, November 1948: 'Racing jargon'

9 in electric line work, a horizontal post insulator *US*
- —A.B. Chance Co., *Lineman's Slang Dictionary*, p. 10, 1980

jug *verb*
1 to arrest or imprison *US, 1841*
- —Vincent J Monteleone, *Criminal Slang*, 1949
- Thanks for the plug, but that wasn't why I got jugged. —Raymond Chandler, *The Long Goodbye*, p. 95, 1953
- She thought I had flapped my jaws and gotten jugged as a material witness hostage. —Iceberg Slim (Robert Beck), *The Naked Soul of Iceberg Slim*, p. 105, 1971
- The law was one of those Catch-22 things that put you in jail. If you complied with the federal law to buy stamps, then the state law got you for being a bookmaker. If you didn't buy the stamps, the feds jugged you. —Mario Puzo, *Inside Las Vegas*, p. 291, 1977
- The judge was perplexed by his behavior because there was no chance whatsoever that he would have jugged the kid if he'd come in[.] —George V. Higgins, *Penance for Jerry Kennedy*, p. 112, 1985

2 to attack someone with a jug of boiling water, especially sugared water *UK*
- —Angela Devlin, *Prison Patter*, p. 67, 1996
- "Jug him!" said one man (meaning to scald him with a jug or two of boiling water from the urn, mixed with sugar so it would stick). "Cut him!" said another. —*The Guardian*, 30th March 2000: 'A life inside'

3 to have sex with *US, 1965*
- There were few women around the neighborhood that Jonny wanted to jugg and didn't juff, even if they were married. —Claude Brown, *Manchild in the Promised Land*, p. 115, 1965
- You ain't been me, Panther, playing possum boo-koo [many] times she's come in way late ... don't take no bath 'cause she's done had one after he finished jugging in her. —Iceberg Slim (Robert Beck), *Doom Fox*, p. 183, 1978

4 to stab *US*
- —William D. Alsever, *Glossary for the Establishment and Other Uptight People*, p. 17, December 1970

▷ see: JUKE

jug and pail *noun*
a prison or jail *UK, 1992*
A rhyming slang elaboration of JUG (a prison).
- —Angela Devlin, *Prison Patter*, p. 67, 1996

juge *verb*
1 to have sex *US*
- Ask him did he want to juge a colored girl. —Malcolm Braly, *On the Yard*, p. 24, 1967

2 to stab *US*
- Juge said Cooper told him during questioning that was not recorded that he "juged" labi, which is street slang for stabbed. —*Times-Picayune (New Orleans)*, p. C1, 31st March 2000

jugged *adjective*
1 drunk *US, 1923*
Noted as being used by office- and shop-girls.
- —*Fugitives from Fowler*, 22nd May 1958

2 imprisoned *UK*
- —Angela Devlin, *Prison Patter*, p. 67, 1996

jugging *noun*

in prison, an attack with a jug of boiling sugared water *UK*

- [T]he jugging victim had fled the room in agony and terror[.] — *The Guardian*, 13th April 2000: 'A life inside'

juggins *noun*

a dolt *UK, 1882*

- — Tom Hibbert, *Rockspeak!*, p. 92, 1983

juggle *verb*

1 to sell (drugs) *US, 1969*

- Look, Stonewall, you been juggling dope around the corner for a long time now, and you ain't gave me a hot dime. — A.S. Jackson, *Gentleman Pimp*, p. 182, 1973
- — Angela Devlin, *Prison Patter*, p. 67, 1996

2 to engage in criminal business activities *UK*

- The truth was that his baby daughter had inherited a father who juggled for a living[.] — Karline Smith, *Moss Side Massive*, p. 7, 1994

juggler *noun*

1 a retail-level drug dealer *US, 1969*

- The street dealer sells to pushers (sometimes called jugglers). — Burgess Laughlin, *Job Opportunities in the Black Market*, p. 6–6, 1978
- — *Detroit News*, p. 5D, 20th September 2002

2 a member of a train crew who loads and unloads freight at stops on a run *US*

- — Norman Carlisle, *The Modern Wonder Book of Trains and Railroading*, p. 265, 1946

jughandle *noun*

in caving and pot-holing, a handle-shaped outcrop of rock used as an anchor-point *UK*

- — David Morrison of Wessex Cave Club, 29th February 2004

jughandles; juglugs *noun*

prominent ears *UK*

Noted by Albert Petch, 1969.

jug heavy *noun*

a criminal who specialises in robbing bank vaults and safes *US*

- — Vincent J. Monteleone, *Criminal Slang*, p. 135, 1949

jughustler *noun*

1 in oil drilling, a cable-car crew member with a geophone *CANADA*

- The cable truck is manned by "jug-hustlers," so-called because geophones are nicknames "jugs." — R.E. Watters, *BC Centennial Anthology*, p. 419, 1958

2 in oil drilling, the most inexperienced member of a seismic crew *US*

The recording devices carried by the crew resembled and were called 'jugs'.

- — Jerry Robertson, *Oil Slanguage*, p. 73, 1954

jug it!

save your prattle for someone who cares! *US*

- When the chit-chat's a bit on the dry side, tell them to 'jug it' – or leave holding your ears and muttering, 'my nerves.' — *Philadelphia Evening Bulletin*, 11th November 1951

jugs; milk jugs *noun*

the female breasts *US*

A reference to the source of mother's milk; widely known and used.

- Some jugs! — Frederick Kohner, *Gidget*, p. 49, 1957
- "She doesn't even have a pair of decent jugs!" "Jugs," I haughtily replied, "aren't everything." — John Nichols, *The Sterile Cuckoo*, p. 88, 1965
- But not before mention of a new low on NBC television. Johnny Carson, September 20, 1968, to exploit the Wall Street hardening of the arteries interviewed a collitch professor on the phenomenon: "She has the biggest pair of jugs I've ever seen!" — Peter Tamony, *Cheesecake*, p. 9, September 1968
- In other words, she was a fox with big jugs. — Edwin Torres, *After Hours*, p. 178, 1979
- Daddy says tits. Daddy says knockers and jugs and bazooms and dingleberries and jujubes. And then he laughs and goes "wuff! wuff!". — *Journal of British Photography*, 9th May 1980
- The bitch who managed the apartment house where Lee lived; fair jugs, good ass. — Gerald Petievich, *To Die in Beverly Hills*, p. 136, 1983
- Candy Samples and her legendary jugs were booked on 42nd Street. — Josh Alan Friedman, *Tales of Times Square*, p. 98, 1986
- You think I'm gonna let them eat cow's milk when I got these two jugs on me? — Richard Condon, *Prizzi's Glory*, p. 155, 1988
- It was a CERVEZA TECATE calendar featuring a sexpot Aztec warrior queen with little armored pasties tipping big copper jugs. — Seth Morgan, *Homeboy*, p. 42, 1990
- She had a pair of jugs that was so fine / Then I took a look at that behind — Biz Markie, *Young Girl Bluez*, 1993
- I said to her, "I hope I don't get big jugs like yours, Mom." — Anka Radakovich, *The Wild Girls Club*, p. 136–137, 1994

jug up *verb*

to eat *US*

- — William K Bentley and James M. Corbett, *Prison Slang*, 1992

juice *noun*

1 alcohol *US, 1932*

- At the Bucket of Blood, a cafe on Madison street, we sold the juice for close to $200. — Milton Mezzrow, *Really the Blues*, p. 21, 1946
- I took out the bottle. "It's just juice, I said." We all got high then. — Hal Ellson, *Duke*, p. 67, 1949
- It's moot as hell whether the juice blunts or sharpens the senses. — George Mandel, *Flee the Angry Strangers*, p. 100, 1952
- At any rate, I've fixed up a real wild basket of ribs and a bottle of juice. — Steve Allen, *Bop Fables*, p. 37, 1955
- "Nuthin' at all like juice, either," Hassan said. — Ross Russell, *The Sound*, p. 22, 1961
- But what he was doing the whole time was mixing up this juice he calls Summer Snow. — Richard Farina, *Been Down So Long*, p. 62, 1966
- I'd go over to North Beach, and I remember ... most people, at least publicly, used juice instead of pot. — Leonard Wolfe (Editor), *Voices from the Love Generation*, p. 66, 1968
- Folks, this is it for tonight. I've locked the juice cabinet. I can't let you kill yourself. Call me if you want anything except more juice. — Iceberg Slim (Robert Beck), *Trick Baby*, p. 263, 1969
- I was enthralled by the stories of the impounded juice in the government storage houses. — Red Rudensky, *The Gonif*, p. 95, 1970

2 methadone, used to break an opiate addiction *US, 1981*

In many US clinics, the methadone given to recovering heroin addicts is mixed in orange juice so that it cannot be injected.

- — Geoffrey Froner, *Digging for Diamonds*, p. 39, 1989
- Gino was dispensed juice at clinics in two counties and always had doses to sell. — Seth Morgan, *Homeboy*, p. 188, 1990
- — Angela Devlin, *Prison Patter*, p. 67, 1996

3 a powdered narcotic dissolved for injection *US*

- — Anthony Romeo, *The Language of Gangs*, p. 19, 4th December 1962

4 crack cocaine mixed with marijuana *US*

- [A] fat ass J, of some bubonic chronic that made me choke[.] — Snoop Doggy Dogg, *Gin and Juice*, 1993

5 anabolic steroids *US*

- But if one guy stays on the juice, then ego makes the rest stay on, since they want The Look. — *Herb's Wrestling Tidbits*, 28th May 1992
- The Juice, a slang term for steroids, the use of which will now result in player suspensions. — *The Boston Herald*, 4th January 2004

6 blood *US, 1938*

Among others, professional wrestling usage.

- Great brawl in concession stand, quadruple juice. — *Herb's Wrestling Tidbits*, 23rd May 1992
- [O]ff to casualty with a couple of bags of juice hooked up over the royal bed. — Andrew Nickolds, *Back to Basics*, p. 109, 1994
- — *Los Angeles Times Magazine*, 6th August 1995: 'Palm Latitutdes: L.A. Speak'
- I climbed into the ring and the match continued. "Nice juice, huh?" I said to Vader as he set me up for a monstrous forearm to the head. — Mick Foley, *Mankind*, p. 6, 1999

7 in drag racing and hot rodding, any special blend of racing fuel *US*

- — Olney Ross, *Kings of the Drag Strip*, p. 187, 1968

8 petrol, diesel *UK, 1909*

- — *Complete CB Slang Dictionary*, 1976
- — Peter Chippindale, *The British CB Book*, p. 156, 1981
- — Jimmy Stockin, *On The Cobbles*, p. 10, 2000

9 nitroglycerin, used by thieves to blow open vaults or safes *US, 1924*

- — Joseph E. Ragen and Charles Finston, *Inside the World's Toughest Prison*, p. 806, 1962: 'Penitentiary and underworld glossary'

10 energy *UK*

- Glastonbury is losing its juice, man. Its like a big hippie hangover[.] — *The Guardian*, p. 6, 28th June 2004

11 sex *BAHAMAS*

- — John A. Holm, *Dictionary of Bahamian English*, p. 116, 1982

12 pleasure, satisfaction *UK*

- It is of little interest or juice to them how a record came to be. — Paolo Hewitt, *Heaven's Promise*, p. 121, 1999

13 power, influence, sway *US, 1957*

- The Hoffa juice in Las Vegas came from the Teamsters Central States, Southeast and Southwest Areas Pension Fund[.] — Ed Reid and Ovid Demaris, *The Green Felt Jungle*, p. 83, 1963
- Upstairs at Apple there is this one room where you make it if you got juice enough to get past the receptionist. — *The Last Supplement to the Whole Earth Catalog*, p. 70, March 1971
- The vic [victim's] father has juice with the City Council[.] — Robert Crais, *L.A. Requiem*, p. 44, 1999

14 a bribe *UK, 1698*

- Thousands of dollars were spent on bribes – "juice" – blanketing the police force from top to bottom[.] — Ed Reid and Ovid Demaris, *The Green Jungle*, p. 19, 1963

15 interest paid to a loan shark *US, 1935*

- A hundred a week juice for as long as the loan is out. — Vincent Patrick, *The Pope of Greenwich Village*, p. 69, 1979
- You owe fifteen plus the fifteen hundred juice and another fifteen hundred for expenses, driving here from Miami. — Elmore Leonard, *Riding the Rap*, p. 19, 1995
- You owe me the dry cleaner's fifteen grand plus the juice which is what, another – ahh -— *Get Shorty*, 1995
- You're in above the neck, son. You owe me folding, plus the juice. — Greg Williams, *Diamond Geezers*, p. 10, 1997

16 in sports betting, the bookmaker's commission *US*

- All you are betting is the "juice," the one point to win twenty. — Jimmy Snyder, *Jimmy the Greek*, p. 208, 1975
- — *Bay Sports Review*, p. 8, November 1991

17 in pool, spin imparted to the cue ball to affect the course of the object ball or the course of the cue ball after it strikes the object ball *US*

- — Mike Shamos, *The Illustrated Encyclopedia of Billiards*, p. 127, 1993

18 surging surf with big waves *US*

- — Douglas Simonson, *Pidgin to da Max*, 1981
- — Trevor Cralle, *The Surfin'ary*, 1991

19 in a deck of playing cards, a two *US*

An intentional corruption of **DEUCE**.

- — *American Speech*, p. 99, May 1951: 'The vocabulary of poker'

▸ get some juice on

to achieve a drug intoxication *US*

- Give me another tab so I can get some juice on — Stephen Gaskin, *Amazing Dope Tales*, p. 110, 1980

juice *verb*

1 to drink, especially to the point of intoxication *US, 1893*

- I don't think an orange ever tasted any sweeter to me; it was like some nectar the angels juice up on[.] — Mezz Mezzrow, *Really the Blues*, p. 100 - 101, 1946
- I'd just like to caution you that the old days when a musician could juice on the job, try to make all the dames in the joint, and play when and how he pleased are gone. — Ross Russell, *The Sound*, p. 132, 1961
- Shorty would take me to groovy, frantic scenes in different chicks' and cats' pads, where with the lights and juke down mellow, everybody blew gage and juiced back and jumped. — Malcolm X and Alex Haley, *The Autobiography of Malcolm X*, p. 56, 1964
- I would fool with stuff a little bit and I'd see a Chinaman coming – that is, I'd see a habit coming on – and I would back away and smoke reefers for a while, then I'd juice a while. — Bruce Jackson, *In the Life*, p. 180, 1972

2 to energise *US*

- Check out the methane level fore we get back up there and juice the machinery. — John Sayles, *Union Dues*, p. 17, 1977

3 to bleed *US*

Professional wrestling usage.

- The referee juiced from a nonchaku blow. — *Herb's Wrestling Tidbits*, 21st May 1992

4 to bribe; to pay for influence *US*

- I got to make lots of dough to juice the guys I got to juice in order to make lots of dough to juice the guys I got to juice. — Raymond Chandler, *The Long Goodbye*, p. 65, 1953

5 to obtain something through the influence of another *US*

- He got juiced into the Grand. — Lee Solkey, *Dummy Up and Deal*, p. 115, 1980

6 to have sex *BAHAMAS*

Private UK correspondent, 29th August 2002.

- — John A. Holm, *Dictionary of Bahamian English*, p. 116, 1982

▷ see: JUICE UP

▸ juice the G-spot

to engage in oral sex on a woman *US*

- Another way to say "cunnilingus" [...] Juicing the G-spot[.] — Erica Orloff and JoAnn Baker, *Dirty Little Secrets*, p. 86, 2001

juice bar *noun*

a clinic where recovering heroin addicts are administered methadone *US*

Playful, alluding to **JUICE** (methadone).

- — Geoffrey Froner, *Digging for Diamonds*, p. 39, 1989

juice box *noun*

the vagina *CANADA*

- — Bill Casselman, *Canadian Sayings*, p. 106, 2002

juice brakes *noun*

in hot rodding and drag racing, hydraulic brakes *US*

- — Lyle K. Engel, *The Complete Book of Fuel and Gas Dragsters*, p. 152, 1968

juiced; juiced up *adjective*

1 drunk *US, 1941*

- Just look at the difference between you and them other cats, that come uptown juiced to the gills[.] — Mezz Mezzrow, *Really the Blues*, p. 213, 1946
- I was high or juiced most of the time and staying by myself most of the time again except I'd run for Juan. — Hal Ellson, *Duke*, p. 160, 1949
- One stud got juiced and played the flunky, to a very surprised old Brazilian monkey. — Dan Burley, *Diggeth Thou?*, p. 17, 1959
- I went out and get a little juiced up on beer. — Robert Gover, *The Maniac Responsible*, p. 165, 1963
- He's a slender not-yet middle-aged man – well dressed – although in his juiced-up state, his clothes are slightly disheveled. — John Rechy, *City of Night*, p. 97, 1963
- You've gone to the finest school all right, Miss Lonely / But you know you only used to get juiced in it. — Bob Dylan, *Like a Rolling Stone*, 1965
- This town's got four hundred people that stay juiced out of their minds – cause they're depressed because they're there. — Lenny Bruce, *The Essential Lenny Bruce*, p. 95, 1967
- — Collin Baker et al., *College Undergraduate Slang Study Conducted at Brown University*, p. 146, 1968
- And we'd go up to somebody's place and sit on a mattress and get juiced. — Leonard Wolfe (Editor), *Voices from the Love Generation*, p. 66, 1968
- He got juiced and almost ran into a trailer truck coming back. — Babs Gonzales, *Movin' On Down De Line*, p. 117, 1975

2 energised *US, 1978*

- She walked fast towards Canal Street subway, then changed her mind. She was juiced, she'd walk down Broadway. — Chris Niles, *Revenge is the Best Revenge [Tart Noir]*, p. 12, 2002

3 caffeinated *US*

Borrowing from the language of car fuel for application to the world of coffee drinks and, to a lesser extent, soft drinks.

- — Connie Eble (Editor), *UNC-CH Campus Slang*, p. 4, Fall 1996

juiced in *adjective*

enjoying powerful political connections *US*

- He's juiced in. He's the County Commissioner's cousin. — *Casino*, 1995

juice freak *noun*

an alcoholic *US, 1971*

- — Ralph de Sola, *Crime Dictionary*, p. 76, 1982

juice hand *noun*

an electrician, especially in the theatre *US*

- — Wilfred Granville, *The Theatre Dictionary*, p. 181, 1952

juicehead *noun*

an alcoholic *US, 1954*

- The Juicehead Kid was a' takin' a jolt. — William "Lord" Buckley, *The Ballad of Dan McGroo*, 1960
- Now get your ass in the bathroom and wash your mouth out. I want you to kill that fuckin' odor. Where I'm gettin' ready to take you, I don't want the people to think I brought a juice head along with me. — Donald Goines, *Daddy Cool*, p. 95 – 96, 1974
- A fat-ass juice head who was liable to melt with a little heat and a bad-ass spade gunslinger who blew fifty bucks a week on his highs. — Elmore Leonard, *52 Pick-up*, p. 121, 1974
- I'm a junkie. I know you can understand a little because you're a juicehead. — Herbert Huncke, *Guilty of Everything*, p. 131, 1990

juice jockey *noun*

the driver of a petrol-fuelled truck *US*

- — Montie Tak, *Truck Talk*, p. 94, 1971

juice joint *noun*

1 an establishment where alcohol is served illegally *US, 1932*

- "You know that juice joint up on the second floor?" she said. — Mezz Mezzrow, *Really the Blues*, p. 266, 1946
- Officers Phillips and Droge both testified that they, their fellow patrolmen, and in some cases, their supervisors, had accepted regular payments from bottle clubs and "juice joints." — *The Knapp Commission Report on Police Corruption*, p. 144, 1972
- Shot-house operators run informal (and illegal) taverns in their own homes (shot-house operators are often women). The houses go by other names too; gold mine, good-time house, blind tiger, shine parlor, or juicejoint. — Burgess Laughlin, *Job Opportunities in the Black Market*, p. 10–9, 1978

2 a cigarette made with a mixture of marijuana and crack cocaine *UK, 1998*

- — Mike Haskins, *Drugs*, p. 288, 2003

3 a crooked gambling operation *US, 1950*

- — Frank Garcia, *Marked Cards and Loaded Dice*, p. 262, 1962

juice man *noun*

1 a usurer, loan-shark, illegal lender *US, 1961*

- The juiceman may get his working money from another, bigger wholesaler (a downtown connection). — Burgess Laughlin, *Job Opportunities in the Black Market*, p. 11–1, 1978
- "Tony the juice man has a long memory, doesn't he?" the lawyer asked. — Gerald Petievich, *Money Men*, p. 78, 1981
- — David M. Hayano, *Poker Faces*, p. 186, 1982
- Sometimes the average working stiff can find another juiceman who'll lend him enough dimes to pay off the first juiceman, interest and principal, with maybe a couple of C-notes left over. — Robert Campbell, *Juice*, p. 21, 1988
- Master wanted to borrow some bread to keep the dojang going, but the juice man's rates were too high. — Odie Hawkins, *Lost Angeles*, p. 26, 1994

2 an AM radio disc jockey who broadcasts on a powerful, all-night station heard by truckers *US*

- — Porter Bibb, *CB Bible*, p. 97, 1976

3 an electrician *US, 1923*

- But to a Carny time is money, and during down time the juice man is the star performer. — Gene Sorrows, *All About Carnivals*, p. 20, 1985

juice money *noun*

a bribe *US*

- An office, a secretary, a car, juice money for the real estate people, tee boiler room, bleepety, bleepety bleep. — Gerald Petievich, *Money Men*, p. 78, 1981

juicepot *noun*

a carburettor *US*

- — Montie Tak, *Truck Talk*, p. 94, 1971

juicer *noun*

1 a person who abuses alcohol *US*

- And as he continued to be alone, to be apart from the reefer-smokers and juicers and Happy Others who did nothing but be square, his drive to be needed made him seek out a companion[.] — Clarence Cooper Jr, *The Scene*, p. 64, 1960
- Juicers on the wagon are all big coffee fiends. — James Ellroy, *Brown's Requiem*, p. 43, 1981
- He was a friend of the sergeant's. They were the 'juicers' [alcohol drinkers] and I was the 'head' [pot smoker]. — Myra MacPherson, *Long Time Passing*, p. 398, 1984

2 an electrician, especially in the television and film industries *US, 1928*

- — Tony Miller and Patricia George, *Cut! Print! The Language and Structure of Filmmaking*, p. 92, 1977

3 in television and film making, a lamp operator *US*

- — Ralph S. Singleton, *Filmaker's Dictionary*, p. 89, 1990

4 a persuasive and resourceful woman sent out to acquire crack cocaine for others *US*

- — Terry Williams, *Crackhouse*, p. 149, 1992

5 a collector of repayments for a loan shark *UK*

- — Angela Devlin, *Prison Patter*, p. 67, 1996

6 in hot rodding, hydraulic brakes *US*

- — *American Speech*, p. 99, May 1954

juice racket *noun*

usury, loan-sharking, illegal lending *US*

- But this other mess, the juice racket, is ours. — Robert Campbell, *Juice*, p. 213, 1988

juices *noun*

in poker, a pair of twos *US*

Probably a corruption of **DEUCE(S)**.

- — *American Speech*, p. 99, May 1951

juice up; juice *verb*

1 to make exciting or powerful *US, 1964*

- I had a friend over juicing it up[.] — Lester Bangs, *Psychotic Reactions and Carburetor Dung*, p. 107, 1972
- Markie Mann had scrawled on the top [of a script]: Juice this. [...] He didn't know how to juice it, didn't really even understand what juice it meant. To him it was already juiced. Juice better than he could ever do. — Joel Rose, *Kill Kill Faster Faster*, p. 41, 1997

2 to drink to intoxication *US*

- The kids got a little wild. Some of the boys were juicing it up. — Anonymous, *Go Ask Alice*, p. 19, 1971

juicy *adjective*

1 scandalous, sensational, especially in a sexual way *UK, 1883*

- What's the word from the hallowed halls of justice? Anything juicy? — *Body Heat*, 1980

2 (used of a woman) sexually aroused *US*

- Over in the corner sat Sweet Jaw Lucy, looking all juicy. — Roger Abrahams, *Positively Black*, p. 122, 1970

3 said of a traffic accident involving serious injuries *US*

- — *American Speech*, p. 270, December 1962: 'The language of traffic policemen'

4 a low-skill poker game or poker play *US*

- — David M. Hayano, *Poker Faces*, p. 186, 1982

5 (of a wave) powerful, with a large fringing crest *US*

- — Gary Fairmont R. Filosa II, *The Surfer's Almanac*, p. 188, 1977

juicy fruit *noun*

an act of sexual intercourse *AUSTRALIA, 1950*

Rhyming slang for **ROOT**. From the name of a flavour of chewing gum.

juicy G *noun*

salacious gossip *US*

- — Connie Eble (Editor), *UNC-CH Campus Slang*, p. 4, Fall 1989

juicy Lucy *noun*

the vagina *UK*

JUICY is an adjective with suggestive and sexual uses; Lucy is a convenient rhyming name. It may also be worth noting that Juicy Lucy was a moderately successful UK blues band in the late 1960s and early 70s. A controversial, and hence memorable illustration on their 1969 eponymous debut album depicted a plump, naked lady disported in 'juicy fruit' – grapes, etc., but also a slang term for 'sexual intercourse'.

- — *Sky Magazine*, July 2001

juju; ju-ju *noun*

a marijuana cigarette *US, 1940*

Clipped and reduplicated from 'mari*ju*ana'.

- — Richard A. Spears, *The Slang and Jargon of Drugs and Drink*, p. 293, 1986
- — Mike Haskins, *Drugs*, p. 288, 2003

jujubes; joobs; jubes *noun*

the female breasts; the male pectorals *UK*

- Daddy says tits. Daddy says knockers and jugs and bazooms and dingleberries and jujubes. And then he laughs and goes "wuff! wuff!". — *Journal of British Photography*, 9th May 1980
- — Paul Baker, *Polari*, p. 178, 2002

juk *noun*

▷ see: **JUCK**

juke *noun*

a jukebox *US, 1941*

- "You like the groovy music on the juke?" Barrelhouse said. — Ralph Ellison, *Invisible Man*, p. 425, 1947
- He got up and went over to the juke, dropped a quarter in on "Whispering Grass," and everybody turned to look at him when the lyrics began. — Clarence Cooper Jr, *The Scene*, p. 103, 1960
- Shorty would take me to groovy, frantic scenes in different chicks' and cats' pads, where with the lights and juke down mellow, everybody blew gage and juiced back and jumped. — Malcolm X and Alex Haley, *The Autobiography of Malcolm X*, p. 56, 1964

▸ **up your juke**
under the front of your clothing (as a place of concealment or protection) *UK: SCOTLAND*
• The rain was comin on so I shoved the papers up my juke. — Michael Munro, *The Original Patter*, p. 39, 1985

juke; jug *verb*
1 to dance in a boisterous fashion *US, 1933*
It is theorised that the word, today only recognised in the formation **JUKEBOX**, was derived from the African Wolof, Banut or Bambara languages. The term spread through southern blacks from the Gullah, and then into wider slang usage, although with a distinctly southern flavour.
• Now the big black guy said something, grinning, and the whores laughed and started juking around, feeling something about to happen. — Elmore Leonard, *Switch*, p. 23, 1978

2 to fool, to trick *US, 1873*
• Aw, Franchot, who you think you juggin' by tryin' to be so hard? — Nathan Heard, *Howard Street*, p. 30, 1968
• Call Wilhite and Narco more dangerous; call me a bent cop juking their meal ticket. — James Ellroy, *White Jazz*, p. 57, 1992

3 to hit *US, 1872*
• "I'll jug you," he yelled, "by God, I'll jug you." — Ralph Ellison, *Invisible Man*, p. 274, 1947

4 to avoid a blow *UK, 1513*
Circus and carnival usage.
• — Don Wilmeth, *The Language of American Popular Entertainment*, p. 148, 1981

jukebox *noun*
an coin-operated recorded-music player *US, 1939*

juke house *noun*
a brothel *US*
• — *Maledicta*, p. 148, Summer/Winter 1986 – 1987: 'Sexual slang: prostitutes, pedophiles, flagellators, transvestites, and necrophiles'

juke joint *noun*
a bar or club with a jukebox; usually rowdy and teeming with sin *US, 1937*
• A black-white stick-up gang had been clouting markets and juke joints on West Adams[.] — James Ellroy, *Hollywood Nocturnes*, p. 127, 1994

jukey *noun*
a jukebox *UK: SCOTLAND*
• Pump up the fuckin jukey, Cal[.] — Irvine Welsh, *The State of the Party (Disco Biscuits)*, p. 31, 1996

Julian Clary; clary *noun*
a male homosexual *UK*
Rhyming slang for **FAIRY**, formed from the name of an ostentatiously gay comedian (b.1959).
• — Ray Puxley, *Fresh Rabbit*, 1998
• I knew you were a Clary when I heard you had gone for a manicure. — Bodmin Dark, *Dirty Cockney Rhyming Slang*, 2003

Julian Clary *adjective*
vulgar, flashy, ostentatious; impudent; conceited *UK*
Rhyming slang for **LAIRY**.
• — Ray Puxley, *Fresh Rabbit*, 1998

Julius Caesar *noun*
1 a wedge-shaped cheesecutter flat cap *UK*
Rhyming slang for 'cheeser'.
• — Ray Puxley, *Cockney Rabbit*, 1992

2 a freezer *UK*
Rhyming slang.
• — Ray Puxley, *Cockney Rabbit*, 1992

jumble *noun*
a white person *UK*
Derived from the pronunciation of 'John Bull' (a symbol of Britain) by Nigerian immigrants in London.
• Don't Jumbles never skip their rest as well as Spades? — Colin McInnes, *City of Spades*, 1957

jumblie; jumbly *noun*
a jumble sale *UK*
• — *New Society*, 11th August 1977

jumbo *noun*
1 an elephant *UK*
From the name of a famous elephant sold to circus impresario P.T. Barnum by London Zoo in 1882. The elephant died in collision with a train in Ontario in 1885.

2 a jumbo-jet *UK, 1984*
• Soviet sources admit shooting down jumbo. — *The Guardian*, 6th September 1983

3 a large vial of crack cocaine *US*
• The dealers' pitch, "Yo, man, got them jumbos!" echoed from almost every corner surrounding the park. — *Record (Bergen County, New Jersey)*, p. A21, 28th September 1986
• — Terry Williams, *The Cocaine Kids*, p. 137, 1989

4 a quart bottle of beer *US*
Heard in Michigan's Upper Peninsula.

5 a uniformed police constable, especially a clumsy or stupid police constable *UK*
A derogatory term employed by detectives.
• — G.F. Newman, *Sir, You Bastard*, 1970
• — Angus Hall, *On the Run*, 1974

6 the buttocks *NEW ZEALAND*
• — David McGill, *David McGill's Complete Kiwi Slang Dictionary*, p. 74, 1998

jumbo-size *adjective*
very large; or, in the language of advertising, slightly larger than normal *UK, 1967*

Jumbo's trunk *adjective*
drunk *UK, 1923*
Rhyming slang. Jumbo was a famous elephant in 1880s London. His name became an eponym for elephants and an adjective for great size. He inspired this variation on 'elephant's trunk' (drunk).
• — Ray Puxley, *Cockney Rabbit*, 1992

jumbuck *noun*
a sheep *AUSTRALIA, 1824*
The origin of this word has long been conjectured. 'Jumbuck' arose in Australian Aboriginal pidgin, which also had 'jump up' (to appear, to come, to be reincarnated), which may be related, though it is difficult to see how exactly. In 1896 a Mr Meston surmised the hardly credible theory that it was from an Aboriginal word meaning 'the white mist preceding a shower, to which a flock of sheep bore a strong resemblance'. 'Jumbuck' is now all but forgotten except that it occurs in the lyrics of the national song 'Waltzing Matilda'.
• My favourite song was and remains, a song of protest, about a swagman who stole a jumbuk, a sheep, who was a protester, a dissenter[.] — Frank Hardy, *The Outcasts of Foolgarah*, p. 203, 1971
• — Jim Ramsay, *Cop It Sweet!*, p. 50, 1977

jump *noun*
1 an act of sexual intercourse *US, 1931*
• Everybody cleared out, I left, it wasn't fifteen minutes after you did, Benavides went in a bedroom there with the broad, gave her a jump, that was it. — Elmore Leonard, *Glitz*, p. 139, 1985
• Or, Buddy brought her for Foley and he was so horny he couldn't wait, gave her a jump in the trunk of the car. — Elmore Leonard, *Out of Sight*, p. 55, 1996
• I as just showering your mother's stink off me after I gave her a quick jump and sent her home. — Kevin Smith, *Jay and Silent Bob Strike Back*, p. 17, 2001

2 a thrill *UK*
• So maybe I'm one of these twats that's just given to nostalgia. Maybe I am, but I swear the sight of that pub will always give myself a jump. — Kevin Sampson, *Outlaws*, p. 7, 2001

3 a party, especially a party with music *US, 1954*
• You meet your boys and make it to a jump, where you can break night dancing. — Piri Thomas, *Down These Mean Streets*, p. 58, 1967

4 the start *US, 1848*
• In fact, he sincerely believed that she'd known from the jump what he'd eventually ask her to do. — Nathan Heard, *Howard Street*, p. 166, 1968
• I mounted her and asked her to fit the pipe and as always it was a bit tight from the jump. — A.S. Jackson, *Gentleman Pimp*, p. 109, 1973
• She was fascinating to watch and she and I got along splendidly from the jump, the first night I was up there. — Herbert Huncke, *Guilty of Everything*, p. 127, 1990

5 the beginning of a horse race *AUSTRALIA*
- On the day of the rave the Coletti family led the charge at the bagmen causing the horse's price to tumble from six-to-one to evens, before easing slightly before the jump to five-to-four. — Clive Galea, *Slipper*, p. 42, 1988

6 in prison, an unexpected attack *UK*
- — Home Office, *Glossary of Terms and Slang Common in Penal Establishments*, July 1978

7 in the entertainment industry, a move in between engagements, especially by rail *US, 1916*
- No matter how far the jumps between one-nighters, or how remote the town, she was there, ready for the night's musical adventure. — Ross Russell, *The Sound*, p. 82, 1961
- — Joe McKennon, *Circus Lingo*, p. 52, 1980
- — Gene Sorrows, *All About Carnivals*, p. 20, 1985: 'Terminology'

8 the bar in a public house or other licensed premises *AUSTRALIA, 1978*
Following the notion that you have to jump to get attention; alternatively, it's what you have to jump over to get a free beer.
- He clocked the guy leaving his credit card behind the jump for the duration. That evening Chelsea won and it was all back to the hotel bar [...] "My Diners' Club card is with reception," he said. — Martin King and Martin Knight, *The Naughty Nineties*, p. 108, 1999
- I'll leave the readies behind the jump with Ron. — Garry Bushell, *The Face*, p. 158, 2001

▸ **get the jump on; have the jump on**
to get, or have, an advantage over someone *US, 1912*
- Clint Eastwood's Mystic River got the jump on its Oscar rivals when it was named the best film of 2003 by the National Board of Review. — *The Guardian*, 4th December 2003

jump *verb*

1 to have sex *US*
- On the bright Sunday afternoon we visited West Point, Strauss wore a pair of tortoiseshell prescription sunglasses that made me want to jump him. — Rita Ciresi, *Pink Slip*, p. 109, 1999

2 to be lively, wild, full of activity *US, 1938*
- We got hold of a piano somewheres, put up some tables on the porch, and inside of two weeks we had the joint jumping. — Mezz Mezzrow, *Really the Blues*, p. 86, 1946
- [H]e said she was a marvelous cook and everything would jump. — Jack Kerouac, *On the Road*, p. 11, 1957
- Havana was really jumpin in those days – best town I was ever in. — Edwin Torres, *Carlito's Way*, p. 35, 1975

3 to attack physically, especially by surprise or of a sudden *UK, 1789*
- Not like the Socs, who jump greasers and wreck houses and throw beer blasts for kicks[.] — S.E. Hinton, *The Outsiders*, p. 5, 1967
- Weirdos is no fun to jump though, because they don't fight back, they just curl up while you kick them. — *UK Rolling Stone*, 26th July 1969
- — Angela Devlin, *Prison Patter*, p. 67, 1996

4 (of a horse) to begin a race *AUSTRALIA*
- There were seventeen starters and when the field jumped away this particular horse had settled in third place[.] — Joe Brown, *Just for the Record*, p. 202, 1984
- Button Hole jumped well and was in second sport for the first mile[.] — Clive Galea, *Slipper*, p. 6, 1988

5 to board a moving train in order to catch a free ride *US, 1885*
- Many of them walked along the rail line and didn't attempt to jump us. — Patsy Adam-Smith, *Folklore of the Australian Railwaymen*, p. 183, 1969
- He knew I knew he was jumping a ride but he began to pick them [mushrooms] out too and put them in my hat. — Patsy Adam-Smith, *Folklore of the Australian Railwaymen*, p. 185, 1969
- Just jump him out and he'll do the rest. — Joe Andersen, *Winners Can Laugh*, p. 75, 1982

6 to escape, to abscond *UK, 1865*
Originally, 'to jump ship'.
- Then there was Ralph, just jumped Scrubs [Wormwood Scrubs prison], dripping desperation on Jonesy's settee. — Mark Powell, *Snap*, p. 59, 2001

7 to travel from an engagement in one town to the next town where an engagement is scheduled *US*
- He knows what it means to jump five and six hundred miles a night. — Babs Gonzales, *Movin' On Down De Line*, p. 105, 1975

8 to steal a car by creating a short circuit with the ignition system wires to start the engine *US*
- That was all right, jumping cars with Bud Long. — Elmore Leonard, *The Big Bounce*, p. 98, 1969

9 to use specially designed equipment to cause a car to bounce up and down *US*
- One favorite feature is "jumping," using the electric-hydraulic rams in place of shock absorbers. — Lewis Poteet, *Car & Motorcyle Slang*, p. 27, 1992

10 in drag racing, to cross the starting line too soon *US*
- Drag race drivers are disqualified if their cars jump off the starting line before the green light shows. — Ed Radlauer, *Drag Racing Pix Dix*, p. 31, 1970

▸ **jump a rattler**
to board a train illegally *AUSTRALIA, 1905*
- Hitch-hiked, jumped the rattlers all the way across the Nullabor to Kalgoorlie. — Arthur Upfield, *Bony and the Mouse*, p. 71, 1959
- [B]ut seeing as we hadn't paid a train fare since 1930, we jumped the rattler out of Brisbane by force of habit. — Frank Hardy, *The Yarns of Billy Borker*, p. 49, 1965
- Most men 'jumping the rattler' were not going anywhere in particular. They were just keeping moving as required by law. — Patsy Adam-Smith, *Folklore of the Australian Railwaymen*, p. 179, 1969
- 'But the new stationmaster says no one can jump the rattler out of Benson's Valley,' Sniffy persisted. — Frank Hardy, *Legends from Benson's Valley*, p. 139, 1972
- — Frank Hardy, *Hardy's People*, p. 147, 1986

▸ **jump bail**
to deliberately fail to appear in court after bail has been posted, especially by moving away in order to avoid recognition or the court's jurisdiction *US, 1865*
From **JUMP** (to escape).
- — Angela Devlin, *Prison Patter*, p. 67, 1996

▸ **jump out of your skin**
to be greatly startled *UK, 1937*
- The voice spoke directly behind me, and I almost jumped out of my skin. — Lois Duncan, *Stranger with My Face*, p. 34, 1990

▸ **jump salty**
to become angry *US*
- Broads jumped salty and called attention to their ol' man's ears. — Steve Cannon, *Groove, Bang, and Jive Around*, p. 71, 1969

▸ **jump someone's bones**
to have sex *US, 1965*
- Failing that, he would have thoroughly enjoyed jumping on her elegant bones. — Max Shulman, *Anyone Got a Match?*, p. 38, 1964
- Maybe I do want to come over and jump on your bones. — Gerald Petievich, *To Live and Die in L.A.*, p. 27, 1983
- I wondered why I didn't just go in and jump her bones. — Jim Carroll, *Forced Entries*, p. 173, 1987
- He's just another guy who wants to jump your bones. — *American Beauty*, 1999
- No man is ever going to jump your bones until you get some meat on them. — Rita Ciresi, *Pink Slip*, p. 327, 1999

▸ **jump sore**
to anger *US*
- "Jack," I said, "O Jilly, if I've crossed you, don't jump sore." — William "Lord" Buckley, *The Raven*, 1960

▸ **jump stink**
to become angry *US*
- Everything seemed to be going wrong for me and Bud – the whole town jumped stink on us. — Mezz Mezzrow, *Really the Blues*, p. 130, 1946
- Macho, their president, jumped stink and said, "Time man, we got heart[.]" — Piri Thomas, *Down These Mean Streets*, p. 52, 1967

▸ **jump the broomstick**
to enter into a common-law marriage *UK, 1898*
Probably a figurative use of a traditional custom, hence, also, the many variations: 'to jump (over) the besom', 'broom', 'bucket', 'ditch', 'doorstep', etc. Brewer in his *Phrase and Fable* suggests that 'broomstick' is an elaboration of 'brom' (the bit of a bridle) and is thus symbolic of skipping over the restraint of marriage.
- Well, come a little baby lets jump the broomstick, / Come a let's tie the knot[.] — Charles Robins, *Let's Jump the Broomstick*, 1959
- Mum and Dad went from strength to strength, eventually jumping the broomstick at Epsom Downs[.] — Jimmy Stockin, *On The Cobbles*, p. 89, 2000

▸ **jump the green**
to start quickly just after, or before, a traffic light turns green *CANADA*
- Traditionally in Montreal, drivers both burn the yellow and jump the green. It isn't hard to imagine what this custom does to insurance rates. — Lewis Poteet, *Car & Motorcyle Slang*, p. 42, 1992

▸ **jump the gun**
to act prematurely *US, 1942*
From athletics.
- Maybe we'd jumped the gun on this one, been just a little too eager[.] — Lauren Weisberger, *The Devil Wears Prada*, p. 75, 2003

▸ **jump the shark**
of a television programme, to pass a peak of popularity; may also be applied to other entertainments, entertainers or fashions *US*
Coined after a 1977 episode of long-running US television comedy *Happy Days* in which a central character in need of fresh impetus took to water-skis and attempted to leap over a shark.
- Has "SP" [Southpark] "jumped the shark" with its April Fools' episode? — *Los Angeles Times*, p. F48, 9th April 1998
- Gone are the plaudits that greeted Cold Feet's appearance six years ago; in their place are bad puns and nasty suggestions that the show jumped the shark some time ago. — *The Guardian*, 18th March 2003
- Those in the know call it "jumping the shark" – when a successful brand crosses from aspirational cool into "so over" mediocrity. — *The Independent*, 1st February 2004

▸ **jump through hoops**
to be seen to do everything that is required and more *UK, 1917*
- The teams were becoming more and more fed up so that instead of training they were jumping through hoops for all and sundry[.] — Andy McNab (writing of the late 1970s/early 80s), *Immediate Action*, p. 240, 1995

▸ **jump to it**
to make an energetic start or respond energetically to the bidding to do so *UK, 1929*
Often used as an imperative.
- The reason we are together with them is not because America snaps its fingers and we feel we have to jump to it ... We are with them because it is in our interests. — *The Guardian*, 6th September 2002

▸ **jump wires**
to steal a car and start the engine by creating a short circuit with the ignition system wires *US*
- It was a friend of Ryan's, Bud Long, who had taught him how to jump wires: how to short out the starter and run a wire from the battery to the coil[.] — Elmore Leonard, *The Big Bounce*, p. 98, 1969

▸ **jump yellow**
to act in a cowardly manner *US*
- At least he had heart, he fought it out, but you jumped yellow and dove for the bar. — Piri Thomas, *Seven Long Times*, p. 38, 1974

jump-a-dick *noun*
a cricket *CAYMAN ISLANDS*
- — Aarona Booker Kohlman, *Wotcha Say*, p. 24, 1985

jump back *verb*
1 to initiate a fight *US*
- — Carl J. Banks Jr, *Banks Dictionary of the Black Ghetto Language*, 1975

2 to relent, to ease off *US*
- Jump back, Ferris. Cameron's been a good sport. — *Ferris Buehler's Day Off*, 1986

jump ball *noun*
in pool, a ball that leaves the surface of the table *US, 1850*
- — Mike Shamos, *The Illustrated Encyclopedia of Billiards*, p. 127, 1993

jump collar *noun*
an arrest made for show, which will not produce a conviction *US*
- "Don't worry," I said to them. "This is only a jump collar." "Jump collar!" said the Inspector. "Huh! We've got you cold and you know it." — Polly Adler, *A House is Not a Home*, p. 252, 1953

jump CP *noun*
a hastily created, very temporary command post *US*
- — Linda Reinberg, *In the Field*, p. 118, 1991
- Take your jump CP and a company up there first thing tomorrow. — Edward F. Murphy, *The Hill Fights*, p. 69, 2003

jump down *verb*
to attack physically *US*
- But we had on different colors, and they thought we was Bloods – until we jumped down on 'em. — *Rolling Stone*, p. 82, 12th April 2001

▸ **jump down your throat**
to flare up in anger and snap in criticism of, and at, you *UK, 1806*
- And when he said something that implied faint criticism of the Soviet Union, she "jumped down his throat". — *The Guardian*, 10th May 2003

jumped-up *adjective*
conceited, arrogant *UK, 1870*
Similar imagery to **GET ABOVE YOURSELF**.
- I shuts up and starts to take notice of what this jumped-up little twit is telling me. — John Peter Jones, *Feather Pluckers*, p. 77, 1964
- She had become jumped-up, taken on strange ideas. — Sally Cline, *Couples*, p. 60, 1998
- [E]very fuckin jumped-up twat of a boss yer've ever had[.] — Niall Griffiths, *Kelly + Victor*, p. 213, 2002

jumper *noun*
1 a person who threatens to or has jumped to his death, either from heights or in front of a train *US, 1964*
- — *Maledicta*, p. 180, Summer/Winter 1986–1987: 'Sexual slang: prostitutes, pedophiles, flagellators, transvestites, and necrophiles'
- Had a jumper last night, Sarge. Dixie here was walking by, saw the whole thing. — *Lethal Weapon*, 1987
- Got a stiff on the tracks! Putney station. [...] Ever seen a jumper, son? — Duncan MacLaughlin, *The Filth*, p. 63, 2002

2 a small amount of stimulating liquor *CANADA*
- Not a jumper did we take, / Through the d. / No sir not a single cup, / To conjure the monster up, / Not addicted to the cup / In that way. From a poem by Oscar Dhu, Scotstown, Quebec. — Donald Morrison, *Gold Prospecting and Panning*, p. 56, 1988

jumper church *noun*
any fundamental Christian church *BAHAMAS*
- — John A. Holm, *Dictionary of Bahamian English*, p. 116, 1982

jumper lead; jumper wire *noun*
a wire designed for starting a car engine while bypassing the key and ignition system *UK*
- Thieves [...] steal the car of their choice by shorting the ignition with a "jumper" wire. — David Powis, *The Signs of Crime*, 1977

jumpers *noun*
1 a hat *AUSTRALIA*
Rhyming slang from 'jumpers flat' (a type of horse race).
- — Ned Wallish, *The Truth Dictionary of Racing Slang*, p. 42, 1989

2 sports shoes *US*
- — David Claerbaut, *Black Jargon in White America*, p. 70, 1972

jumper steak *noun*
venison or rabbit meat *CANADA*
- As jumper is either deer or rabbit, free meat, taken from the great outdoors, jumper steak was also called government beef or government meat. — Chris Thain, *Cold as a Bay Street Banker's Heart*, p. 94, 1987

jumpies *noun*
sexual intercourse *UK, 1984*
An elaboration of **JUMP**.

jump-in *noun*
a timed beating used as an initiation into a youth gang *US*
- It's called a "jump-in." That's gang vernacular for a handful of gang members jumping on a prospective member and beating him up for 45 seconds. — *Los Angeles Times*, p. Metro Section 1, 20th November 1987

jump in *verb*
to initiate (someone) into a youth gang through a timed group beating *US*
- When they jump you in three of them start to hit you and you got to hit back for 30 seconds. — *Los Angeles Times*, p. E15A, 20th September 1990
- During one ceremony, more than 50 street taggers from the Kings with Style (KW) were "jumped in." This intitiation ceremony [read: beating] is said to last 18 seconds for each prospect. — Bill Valentine, *Gangs and Their Tattoos*, p. 109, 2000
- Shane knew you didn't usually get a street name unless you'd been "jumped in the set"[.] — Stephen J. Cannell, *The Tin Collectors*, p. 147, 2001

jumping *adjective*
used as an intensifier in mild oaths *US, 1815*
- Scared the shit outa me. Jumpin' Jehosophat. — Edwin Torres, *After Hours*, p. 235, 1979

jumping jack *noun*
a *black* person; a *black* snooker ball *UK*
Rhyming slang.
- — Ray Puxley, *Cockney Rabbit*, 1992

jumping junky *noun*
a paratrooper *US*
• —Gregory Clark, *Words of the Vietnam War*, p. 391, 1991

jump joint *noun*
a brothel *US, 1939*
• 'Son, here's twenty dollars; I want you to go to a good whore and get a piece of ass off her.' So they drive to this plush jump joint, and the father say, 'All right, son. You're on your own.'—William Burroughs, *Naked Lunch*, p. 119, 1957

jump juice *noun*
anabolic steroids *US*
• He alternated between four-hundred-pound dead-lifts, shots of jump-juice, and the great Italian cuisine.—Stephen Cannell, *Big Con*, p. 160, 1997

jump off *verb*
1 to happen; to begin *US, 1946*
• Wham! The fanfare jump off!.—William "Lord" Buckley, *Nero*, 1951
• It's past ten o'clock, and ain't nothing jumped off yet.—Donald Goines, *White Man's Justice, Black Man's Grief*, p. 81, 1973

2 to assault *US*
• "You keep fat mouthin, bitch, I'm going to jump off up in your black ass," he warned.—Charles W. Moore, *A Brick for Mister Jones*, p. 27, 1975

jump-out squad *noun*
a unit of police officers in a cruising, unmarked police vehicle, detailed to jump out of their car and apprehend drug-dealers *US*
• "That was no fun," said Detective Dave Hayes, whose wrist is still sore from a fall he took dodging bullets on a chase through Condon Terrace. Hayes' unit became laughingly known among the youths as "The Jump Out Squad."— *The Washington Post*, 28th January 1980
• Police call them "corner deployment units." Local residents refer to them as "jump-out squads."— *The New York Times*, 15th December 2002

jumpover *noun*
a shop robbery *IRELAND*
• "What are ye doin?" "A jumpover. A newsagent's shop."—Howard Paul, *The Joy*, p. 66, 1996

jump-start *verb*
to light a fresh cigarette with the ember of one being finished *US*
• —Ken Weaver, *Texas Crude*, p. 116, 1984

jump-steady *noun*
1 strong, illegally manufactured whisky *US, 1923*
• It is called corn liquor, white lightning, sugar whiskey, skully cracker, popskull, bush whiskey, stump, stumphole, 'splo, ruckus juice, radiator whiskey, rotgut, sugarhead, block and tackle, wildcat, panther's breath, tiger's sweat, Sweet spsirits of cats a-fighting, alley bouyrbon, city gin, cool water, happy Sally, deep shaft, jump steady, old horsey, stingo, bluye John, red eye, pine top, buckeye bark whiskey and see seven stars.— *Star Tribune (Minneapolis)*, p. 19F, 31st January 1999

2 a drink of gin *US*
• Nine or ten jump-steadies and a couple of muggles and up goes your gage.—Hyman E. Goldin et al., *Dictionary of American Underworld Lingo*, p. 112, 1950

jump street *noun*
the inception; the very beginning *US, 1972*
• —William K. Bentley and James M. Corbett, *Prison Slang*, p. 28, 1992

jump-up *noun*
1 theft from lorries *UK*
The criminal *jumps up* onto the back of the vehicle; usually used with 'the'.
• [T]here was nothing for it but the old jump-up.—Charles Raven, *Underworld Nights*, p. 51, 1956
• "Jump ups" was another good earner.—Lenny McLean, *The Guv'nor*, p. 20, 1998
• We had some information about a team at the jump-up. Lorry hijacking.—Jake Arnott, *He Kills Coppers*, p. 116, 2001

2 a steep section of road, as when going up an escarpment *AUSTRALIA, 1847*
• [T]here's a windmill there, not far from the main highway, near the Jump-up.—Herb Wharton, *Cattle Camp*, p. 138, 1994

jump-up artist; jump-up merchant; jump-up man *noun*
a criminal who steals from the back of goods-vehicles *UK, 1951*
• Jump up on to a tailboard, climb up on the lorry or open the back door to a van, roll off whatever you see and hope to find something profitable in the wreckage [...] some kids formed gangs of "jump up" artists.—Brian McDonald, *Elephant Boys*, p. 37, 2000

jump upon; jump on *verb*
to severely criticise or punish *UK, 1868*
• When the music companies jumped on Napster, they were spoiling the fun for a lot of music fans[.]— *The Guardian*, 8th September 2003

jump wire *noun*
a wire designed for starting a car engine while bypassing the key and ignition system *US, 1970s*
• "I don't do it anymore," Stick said. "That was a long time ago." "You just happen to have the jump-wire in your bag."—Elmore Leonard, *Stick*, p. 78, 1983

junco *noun*
heroin *UK*
A variation of JUNK (heroin).
• —Robert Ashton, *This Is Heroin*, p. 206, 2002
• —Mike Haskins, *Drugs*, p. 284, 2003

Juneau sneakers *noun*
slip-on rubber boots *US, 1982*
• —Russell Tabbert, *Dictionary of Alaskan English*, p. 97, 1991

Junebug *noun*
used as a nickname for a male named after his father *US*
• —Clarence Major, *Dictionary of Afro-American Slang*, p. 72, 1970

jungle *noun*
1 a dangerous, rough part of town, especially one where black people live *US, 1926*
• See, it was in the jungle there and he was looking for somebody that could sit in a car without looking like he didn't belong there, you know?—George V. Higgins, *The Friends of Eddie Doyle*, p. 21–22, 1971
• If he thinks I'm going up into the Jungle this time of night, he can shove it.— *Taxi Driver*, 1976

2 an outdoor area favoured by homosexuals for sexual encounters *US*
• I discovered the jungle of Central Park – between the 60s and 70s on the west side.—John Rechy, *City of Night*, p. 62, 1963

3 the female pubic hair; hence the vagina *US*
• —Erica Orloff and JoAnn Baker, *Dirty Little Secrets*, p. 71, 2001

4 a tramp encampment *US, 1908*
• They had gone about fifteen miles down the railroad tracks and holed-up in a jungle.—Chester Himes, *Cast the First Stone*, p. 275, 1952

5 a prison's recreation yard *US*
• —Marlene Freedman, *Alcatraz*, 1983

6 an extremely fast (130–160 beats per minute) form of popular dance music genre that developed in London in 1990–91 *UK*
• —Mo Bean, *Let's Go Clubbing*, p. 295, 1998
• British and European rave styles like bleep-and-bass, breakbeat house, Belgian hardcore, jungle, gabba, big beat and speed garage.—Simon Reynolds, *Energy Flash*, p. xviii, 1998
• [S]moking a lickle draw [marijuana] instead of tooting powders, listening to jungle and chasing young Richards [women]—J.J. Connolly, *Layer Cake*, p. 118, 2000

jungle bunny *noun*
1 a black person *US, 1959*
Highly offensive.
• The dozen or so jungle bunnies I have trafficked with were perfectly ordinary in that department[.]—Gore Vidal, *Myra Breckinridge*, p. 88, 1968
• "Greaseball," said one of the Dukes. Angry glances. "Jungle Bunny," said Peter Udo.—Richard Price, *The Wanderers*, p. 160, 1974
• You fuckin' little jungle bunny!—Donald Goines, *Kenyatta's Last Hit*, p. 211, 1975
• Listen, you shine, we 'bout carved up one jungle bunny t'night.—Larry Heinemann, *Close Quarters*, p. 164, 1977
• You mean by the jungle-bunnies, dontcha Smallwood?—John Sayles, *Union Dues*, p. 283, 1977
• "Klepper, let's go bag the jungle bunny" Kurt says as he rolls the zip gun inside a magazine[.]—Iceberg Slim (Robert Beck), *Doom Fox*, p. 227, 1978
• One of them's a jungle bunny.— *Scum*, 1979
• Dad used to sit around the dinner table, talkin' about how the jungle bunnies in Harlem were going crazy with the Angel Dust.— *New Jack City*, 1990

- Never ceases to amaze me. Fuckin' jungle bunny goes out there, slits some old woman's throat for twenty-five cents. — *Reservoir Dogs*, 1992
- Jungle bunnies play tom-toms[.] — Benjamin Zephaniah, *The SUN*, p. 58, 1992
- So the dude wants to date a jungle bunny. Who gives a shit? — Odie Hawkins, *Amazing Grace*, p. 54, 1993
- Romanies were a race apart – not in the same way as the jungle bunnies, the Pakis or the Chinks[.] — Jimmy Stockin, *On The Cobbles*, p. 14, 2000

2 an Asian person *UK*
- But it is not applied only to people of African origin; schoolchildren in an East Midlands market town were using it of Asian fellow-pupils in 1971. — Beale, 1984

jungle-bunny outfit *noun*
Royal Air Force-issue camouflaged battledress *UK*
A casually and institutionally racist term used by Royal Air Force officer cadets.
- Camouflaged combat kit, known officially as disruptive-pattern clothing and unofficially as jungle-bunny outfits. — Colin Strong and Duff Hart-Davis, *Fighter Pilot*, 1981

junglee *noun*
a wild, unsophisticated, uncivilised person *FIJI*
- He claims that this is "exactly what people forget when they deal with people from the sugar cane areas, they think that we are all 'Jungles'." — *The Enquirer*, p. 4, September 1995

jungle eater *noun*
a Caterpillar D&E bulldozer modified for military land-clearing work *US*
- — Linda Reinberg, *In the Field*, p. 119, 1991

jungle fever *noun*
used of white people, a strong attraction towards black people *US, 1990*
The prominent title of a Spike Lee film (1991).
- But they definitely didn't have a case of "jungle fever," then or now. — Odie Hawkins, *Black Chicago*, p. 159, 1992
- The week after we returned from Catalina was spent convincing him that I'd slept with him out of affection and respect, not out of Jungle Fever. I howled when we suggested this, since weeks before we'd both agreed that the movie was a crock of shit[.] — Armistead Maupin, *Maybe the Moon*, p. 206, 1992
- A few admit to "jungle fever," circa '60s, plus psychological-standup-traged feelings. — Odie Hawkins, *Los Angeles*, 1994
- One girl reported that she'd slept with Robert De Niro, who made "puppy eyes" in bed, then mentioned his incurable case of Jungle Fever. — Anka Radakovich, *The Wild Girls Club*, 1994

jungle fuck *noun*
energetic, even athletic sex *US*
- — Michael Dalton Johnson, *Talking Trash with Redd Foxx*, p. 72, 1994

jungle-happy *adjective*
deranged from prolonged combat in the jungle *US, 1944*
- — *American Speech*, p. 55, February 1947: 'Pacific War language'

Jungle Jim *noun*
a Roman Catholic *UK: SCOTLAND*
Rhyming slang for **TIM** (a Roman Catholic).
- Ah never knew he wis a Jungle Jim. — Michael Munro, *The Original Patter*, 1985
- If anyone was worth bolstering it was the Jungle Jims. — Christopher Brookmyre, *Boiling a Frog*, p. 128, 2000

Jungle Jim *verb*
to swim *UK*
Rhyming slang, remembered by Ray Puxley, *Fresh Rabbit*, 1998, as being in contemporaneous use with the television series *Jungle Jim*, 1955–56.

jungle job *noun*
sex outdoors *US*
- Studs in New York, particularly those working the Public Library and Bryant Park areas, call a frantic quickie in the bushes a "jungle job" or a "Tarzan." — Johnny Shearer, *The Male Hustler*, p. 17, 1966

jungle juice *noun*
1 alcoholic drink *AUSTRALIA, 1942*
- He was [...] chain-smoking and sipping a tumbler of the cheapest Empire port, the kind that is known as Jungle Juice. — Charles Raven, *Underworld Nights*, p. 91, 1956

2 any improvised alcoholic beverage *US*
- — *American Speech*, p. 55, February 1947: 'Pacific War language'

3 illicit alcoholic liquor brewed by soldiers in the tropics *AUSTRALIA, 1942*
Used by World War 2 military.
- Come on, you big ape – put that bloody jungle juice away. — Sumner Locke Elliott, *Rusty Bugles*, p. 55, 1948
- — Jim Ramsay, *Cop It Sweet!*, p. 51, 1977

4 in prison, serious talk about serious situations *US*
- — Charles Shafer, *Folk Speech in Texas Prisons*, p. 208, 1990

jungle light *noun*
in the pornography industry, a light used to illuminate the genitals of the performers *US*
- — *Adult Video News*, p. 50, October 1995

jungle meat *noun*
in homosexual usage, a black man *US*
- — *Male Swinger Number 3*, p. 47, 1981: 'The complete gay dictionary'
- — *Maledicta*, p. 52, 1986–1987: 'A continuation of a glossary of ethnic slurs in American English'

jungle mouth *noun*
very bad breath *US*
- — *American Speech*, p. 62, Spring-Summer 1975: 'Razorback slang'

jungle pussy *noun*
a black woman's vagina; hence black women objectified sexually *US*
- "Hey," said another sick voice, "cop a look at the fat ass on that one. Hairy as a jungle pussy." — Piri Thomas, *Seven Long Times*, p. 67, 1974
- First she said the black thing, like she understood his urge to check out some jungle pussy. — John Williams, *Cardiff Dead*, p. 61, 2000

jungle rot *noun*
any skin rash suffered in tropical and jungle environments *US, 1945*
- "Jungle rot," "New Guinea crud" or "the creeping crud" are U.S. servicemen's names for any & every kind of tropical skin disease. — *Time*, p. 76, 13th August 1946
- A rehab normally lasted only three days, but this one had stretched to ten; plenty of time for the jungle rot to dry out and heal, even enough time to get a suntan. — Charles Anderson, *The Grunts*, p. 27, 1976
- Cures heartburn, jungle rot, the Gee-fucken-Eyes, all them things. — Larry Heinemann, *Close Quarters*, p. 26, 1977
- All of us had done something really brave and stupid to get this three-day R&R, and all of us had varying degrees of jungle rot, which was helped by the sun and salt water. — Nelson DeMille, *Up Country*, p. 280, 2002

jungle rules *noun*
a code of competition or combat in which all is fair *US*
- Of course, if the next election does descend to the jungle rules and if the true stories could ever be told under Australia's defamation laws ... it will not be just a dirty election, it will be raucously Rabelaisian. — *The Advertiser*, 20th November 1986
- The more active ones participated in roughouse games of volleyball, playing by "jungle rules" – anything goes. — Tom Yarborough, *Da Nang Diary*, p. 230, 1990

jungle telegraph *noun*
the informal and haphazard but effective communication by which rumour spreads *UK, 1966*
- [E]ven the barely audible noises winging back along the jungle telegraph from Washington – all turn out to have a single point of focus. — *The Guardian*, 1st June 2002

jungle up *verb*
in oil drilling, to sleep outside *US*
- — Jerry Robertson, *Oil Slanguage*, p. 74, 1954

junglist *noun*
a purveyor or follower of jungle music, a music genre of the 1990s favoured at raves *UK*
- The junglists were looking extremely edgy by then. — Dean Cavanagh, *Mile High Meltdown (Disco Biscuits)*, p. 213, 1996
- Everyone is a junglist now, and if you go and take an E on jungle stuff, you're going to have a downer, know what I mean? — Macfarlane, Macfarlane and Robson, *The User*, p. 3, 1996

junior *noun*
in television and film making, a 1000 watt or 2000 watt light *US*
- — Ralph S. Singleton, *Filmaker's Dictionary*, p. 89, 1990

junior jumper *noun*
a juvenile male who commits a rape *US, 1992*
- — Angela Devlin, *Prison Patter*, p. 67, 1996

junior wolf *noun*

a younger brother *CANADA*

Teen slang, reported by a Toronto newspaper in 1946, and reported as 'obsolescent or obsolete' by Douglas Leechman, 1959.

junk *noun*

1 heroin; morphine; cocaine *US, 1918*

- You've been using junk for about twenty-five years – morphine, cocaine, and heroin. —William J. Spillard and Pence James, *Needle in a Haystack*, p. 39, 1945
- Undoubtedly there's stuff sitting in post-office boxes right now loaded to the brims with the junk. —Mickey Spillane, *I, The Jury*, p. 23, 1947
- Coming off junk! Isn't that mad? —John Clellon Holmes, *Go*, p. 81, 1952
- My first experience with junk was during the War, about 1944 or 1945. —William Burroughs, *Junkie*, p. 19, 1953
- The poor fellow took so much junk into his system he could only weather the greater proportion of his day in that chair with the lamp burning at noon[.] —Jack Kerouac, *On the Road*, p. 150, 1957
- Those are the ones we want – the same bastards who sold junk to young Rickie Halsted. —Clarence Cooper Jr, *The Scene*, p. 28, 1960
- Sometimes I wondered why I bothered to go to see her, and that was the way it was with most of my friends who didn't use junk. —Alexander Trocchi, *Cain's Book*, p. 18, 1960
- Junk kills the sex drive in most people. —Ross Russell, *The Sound*, p. 205, 1961
- That was the question on a lot of them corners, 'cause the junk was still a new scene in the forties. —Edwin Torres, *Carlito's Way*, p. 10, 1975
- We began using junk together and sometimes I would lie around his place for two or three days. —Herbert Huncke, *The Evening Sun Turned Crimson*, p. 39, 1980
- On junk I was insulated, didn't drink, didn't go out much, just shot up and waited for the next shot. —William Burroughs, *Queer*, p. 10, 1985
- Gribbs got twenty years just because he said hello to some fuck who was sneaking around selling junk behind his back. —*Goodfellas*, 1990
- After 14 years... I decided to come off junk. —Shaun Ryder, *Shaun Ryder... in His Own Words*, 1997

2 any illegal drug *US*

- Some kids call all dope "shit" or "junk," terms that were once synonyms for heroin. —Nicholas Von Hoffman, *We Are The People Our Parents Warned Us Against*, p. 65, 1967

3 a drug addict *AUSTRALIA*

- —*The (Sydney) Bulletin*, 26th April 1975

4 the genitals *US*

- She was all over my junk. —Judi Sanders, *Da Bomb!*, p. 16, 1997
- —Don R. McCreary (Editor), *Dawg Speak*, 2001

5 graffiti *US*

- —Jim Crotty, *How to Talk American*, p. 141, 1997

6 in theatre usage, a monologue *US*

- —Don Wilmeth, *The Language of American Popular Entertainment*, p. 149, 1981

junk *verb*

to throw away, to discard, to treat as rubbish *UK, 1916*

- After a year or so with bosozoku, they junk their black leather gear and get office jobs. Rebellion, Japanese style. —Rhiannon Paine, *Too Late for the Festival*, p. 7, 1999

junk bonds *noun*

in poker, a hand that appears attractive but is in fact a poor hand *US*

- —John Vorhaus, *The Big Book of Poker Slang*, p. 24, 1996

junked; junked up *adjective*

under the influence of heroin *US, 1930*

- When she's not junked up, she's too busy figuring ways to get the stuff she needs to think about sex or anything else. —John M. Murtagh and Sara Harris, *Cast the First Stone*, p. 39, 1957
- The night man was junked to the eyes. —Raymond Chandler, *Playback*, p. 73, 1958
- —Ralph de Sola, *Crime Dictionary*, p. 76, 1982

junker *noun*

1 an old and broken-down vehicle *US, 1948*

- I backed off and made a fast run at it, driving the junker straight into the hill like a cannon ball. —Hunter S. Thompson, *Hell's Angels*, p. 152, 1966
- As the Fury junkers descended into the cresent, the line of customer cars peeled out[.] —Richard Price, *Clockers*, p. 512, 1992
- —John Edwards, *Auto Dictionary*, p. 89, 1993
- For the last two weeks, Beano had been selling dead-sleds and junkers to unsuspecting blue-hairs at Bob's Auto Ranch. —Stephen Cannell, *Big Con*, p. 28, 1997

2 a heroin addict *US, 1922*

- In one small town while we were making a check I found a junker and had him arraigned before a county judge for commitment to take a cure. —William J. Spillard and Pence James, *Needle in a Haystack*, p. 89, 1945

3 in competitive surfing, an extremely low score *US*

- —Trevor Cralle, *The Surfin'ary*, p. 61, 1991

junk food *noun*

food with a high calorific and low nutritional content *US, 1971*

- I haven't had a good TV-and-junk-food pig-out in ages. —Armistead Maupin, *Further Tales of the City*, p. 156, 1982

junk hawk *noun*

a heroin addict whose life is completely controlled by the addiction *US*

- Kenny Wisdom was becoming what is known as a junk hawk, that is to say, all he ever did from then on pertained to junk, as his tolerance for the stuff grew even beyond his greed for it. —Emmett Grogan, *Ringolevio*, p. 42, 1972

junkhead *noun*

a heroin addict *US, 1963*

- —Alice in Chains, *Junkhead*, 1992

junk hog *noun*

an opium addict *US*

- —Jack Lait and Lee Mortimer, *Chicago Confidential*, p. 301, 1950: 'Loop lexicon'

junkie *noun*

1 a drug addict, specifically one addicted to heroin *US, 1922*

A user of JUNK (drugs, opiates, heroin).

- Lukey's no junky. It's oney gauge he's on. —George Mandel, *Flee the Angry Strangers*, p. 20, 1948
- I had instructed them to hold themselves out as "junkies" (narcotic users). I was sure that, as soon as the word got around that they "used the stuff," and that they were well-heeled to pay for it, those doing the smuggling would seek them out. —*The New American Mercury*, p. 710, 1950
- I was cutting up to Harlem to see a junkie that Little Rock used to know in Atlanta. —John Clellon Holmes, *Go*, p. 201, 1952
- There was a time when his pride kept him up, for he was different, he thought, no ordinary junkie. —Hal Ellson, *The Golden Spike*, p. 2, 1952
- There were wild Negro queers, sullen guys with guns, shiv-packing seamen, thin, non-committal junkies, and an occasional well-dressed middle-aged detective[.] —Jack Kerouac, *On the Road*, p. 131, 1957
- He said evenly, "I am not a junkie. Lex is for junkies. I ain't hooked." —Clarence Cooper Jr, *The Scene*, p. 100, 1960
- The motorized patrol was usually made twice a day, cop teams making constant saunters along the border streets to check IDs, roll up sleeve and trouser legs for junkie spot checks[.] —Clancy Sigal, *Going Away*, p. 235, 1961
- All the animals come out at night. Whores, skunk pussies, buggers, queens, fairies, dopers, junkies, sick, venal. —*Taxi Driver*, 1976
- "What?" said the assistant, who must think I'm some kind of junkie freak by now, Barbie thought. —Francesca Lia Block, *I Was a Teenage Fairy*, p. 127, 1998
- It was not just the thugs either, but the junkies, prostitutes, heavy drinkers and smokers. —John King, *White Trash*, p. 152, 2001

2 by extension, a person fiercely devoted to an activity *US, 1962*

- A symbol junkie. People like him – that is, the majority – are strung out on symbols. They're so addicted that they prefer abstract symbols to the concrete things which symbols represent. —Tom Robbins, *Another Roadside Attraction*, p. 227, 1971
- She's a young girl out of Berkeley ... a television junkie. —Dan Jenkins, *Life Its Ownself*, p. 294, 1984
- He wondereed if he qualified as a full-fledged TV junkie, a chronic escapist who needed the tube to fill a void he was no longer capable of filling himself. —Armistead Maupin, *Babycakes*, p. 13, 1984
- [A]pplause-junkies like yours truly. —Dave Courtney, *Stop the Ride I Want to Get Off*, p. 195, 1999

junkmobile *noun*

a dilapidated car *US*

- It was exactly the sort of campy junk-mobile that some dumb Yuppie would love. —Carl Hiaasen, *Native Tongue*, p. 206, 1991

junk mooch *noun*

a heroin addict who trades information for heroin *US*

- He was also a junk mooch, who maintained his habit by trading information to the cops for heroin which they had confiscated from arrested addicts and pushers. —Emmett Grogan, *Ringolevio*, p. 54, 1972

junk-on-the-bunk *noun*

a military inspection of a soldier's gear displayed on his bed *US, 1978*

- —Linda Reinberg, *In the Field*, p. 119, 1991

junks *noun*
expensive, brand name basketball trainers *US*
- —*The Washington Post*, p. 15, 15th March 1987
- —Kenn "Naz" Young, *Naz's Dictionary of Teen Slang*, p. 68, 1993

junk tank *noun*
a jail cell reserved for drug addicts *US, 1966*
A play on the earlier and more common **DRUNK TANK**.
- —Eugene Landy, *The Underground Dictionary*, p. 114, 1971
- —William K. Bentley and James M. Corbett, *Prison Slang*, p. 7, 1992

junkyard dog *noun*
1 a ferocious, territorial person *US, 1983*
- I tell myself I got to learn not to let some vague notion get fixed in my head so there's nothing for it but to run it down like I was some crazy junkyard dog[.]—Robert Campbell, *The Cat's Meow*, p. 93, 1988

2 a junkyard operator with connections to organised crime *US*
- "Junkyard dogs" are connected guys in scrapyards.—Henry Hill and Byron Schreckengost, *A Good Fella's Guide to New York*, p. 189, 2003

junt *noun*
a large marijuana cigarette *US*
- —Jim Emerson-Cobb, *Scratching the Dragon*, April 1997

jurassic *adjective*
very old *US*
- —Jum Sanders, *Da Bomb*, p. 9, 1997

jury-nobbling *noun*
an act of corrupting, or otherwise tampering with, a jury or jury member *UK*
From 'nobble' (to corrupt a jury).
- Diplock had stopped jury-nobbling by terrorist intimidators.—Tony Geraghty, *The Irish War*, p. 96, 2000

jury tax *noun*
the perceived penalty of an increased sentence for an accused criminal who refuses a plea bargain, takes his case to jury trial, and loses *US*
- —Jim Crotty, *How to Talk American*, p. 51, 1997
- Will the defendant who insists on a trial be required to pay a "trial penalty" or a "jury tax?"—Cassia C. Spohn, *How Do Judges Decide?*, p. 94, 2003

jussus!; jussis!; jissus!; jisses!
used for expressing anger, frustration, shock, surprise, etc *SOUTH AFRICA, 1942*
From the Afrikaans pronunciation of 'Jesus', as an oath or exclamation.
- "Jussus," chuckled one neighbor, "just say the black peril got him." —Rian Malan, *My Traitor's Heart*, p. 243, 1990

just as I feared; just as *noun*
a beard *UK*
Rhyming slang.
- —Julian Franklyn, *A Dictionary of Rhyming Slang*, 1960

just for today *adverb*
used in twelve-step recovery programmes such as Alcoholics Anonymous to describe an addict's commitment to refraining from his addiction *US*
- —Christopher Cavanaugh, *AA to Z*, p. 113, 1998

justin *noun*
a half-gallon container *NEW ZEALAND*
Filled with beer, *just in* case you run out.
- —David McGill, *David McGill's Complete Kiwi Slang Dictionary*, p. 74, 1998

just-in-caser *noun*
a getaway driver *UK*
- —Angela Devlin, *Prison Patter*, p. 67, 1996

just kidding!
used for humorously acknowledging an error *US*
- —Connie Eble (Editor), *UNC-CH Campus Slang*, p. 6, October 2002

just now *adverb*
any time soon, in a little while (at the appropriate time, eventually, or never, may be implied) *SOUTH AFRICA, 1900*
Influenced by Afrikaans *netnou*. Universally used in South Africa.
- —Jean Branford, *A Dictionary of South African English*, 1978
- —*Lonely Planet Southern Africa*, 2000

just off the banana boat *adjective*
gullible, used of an innocent abroad *UK*
An allusion to the cultural innocence of a newly arrived immigrant.
- "You were trying to pump Harte," Gardiner said. "I'm not just off the banana boat you know,"—Martin Waddell, *Otley*, p. 133, 1966

just one of those things
a catchphrase philosophy to explain the inexplicable, the impossible or the inevitable *US*
It was used by Cole Porter as the title for a popular song in 1935.
- It wasn't his fault he got taken by the Japs. It was just one of those things.—Neville Shute, *The Chequer Board*, 1947
- My brother's arrest was like that. "It was just one of those things." That's what people said, as if it was some sort of comfort. "It was just one of those things." And they were right, it was.—Danny King, *The Bank Robber Diaries*, p. 47, 2002

just quietly *adverb*
just between you and me *AUSTRALIA, 1938*
- He's a good guy, real fun. A bit of a poet, just quietly.—Barry Dickins, *What the Dickins*, p. 115, 1985

Just the facts, m'am.
used for expressing a wish that the speaker confine their remarks to factual matters *US*
A catchphrase from the 1960s US television series *Dragnet*.
- Just the facts, ma'am. "Member that show? Sergeant Friday?—Elmore Leonard, *Glitz*, p. 104, 1985

jute *noun*
a teasing *NEW ZEALAND*
- —David McGill, *David McGill's Complete Kiwi Slang Dictionary*, p. 50, 1998

juve *noun*
a juvenile part or act *UK*
Theatrical.
- Trev's accustomed to leading child-juves.—Ngaio Marsh, *Death at the Dolphin*, 1967

juvie; juvey *noun*
a juvenile detention hall where young offenders are housed or juvenile court where they are tried *US*
- —Miss Cone, *The Slang Dictionary (Hawthorne High School)*, 1965
- You're my best friend. Because you always fucking came to see me while I was in Juvie.—*Repo Man*, 1984
- A half hour later Rocco walked into the amber gloom of the old Juvie annex behind the Western District station house and found four kids cooling their heels.—Richard Price, *Clockers*, p. 591, 1992
- My father made her stay in Juvey until the dishes were stack so high – hell – someone had to come back home to clean the house.—Ralph "Sonny" Barger, *Hell's Angel*, p. 18, 2000

Kk

K *noun*

1 one thousand dollars; one thousand pounds *US, 1965*
Also spelt 'kay'.
- Just his luck to have them discover he was carrying twenty K and cut his throat. —Joseph Wambaugh, *The Black Marble*, p. 380, 1978
- For a K note and two grams of righteous blow you can call me anything short of Sambo. —James Ellroy, *Because the Night*, p. 355, 1984
- Come on, my brother. God is with you, right? Fourteen kay. —*New Jack City*, 1990
- I think I cleared 15K that night, after expenses. —Val McDermid, *Keeping on the Right Side of the Law*, p. 181, 1999
- I've got in the case two kilos of top quality, very pukka, recently imported, cocaine. It's about forty kay or twelve years' worth, depending how you look at it[.] —J.J. Connolly, *Layer Cake*, p. 1, 2000
- "It's all there," he said. "Fifty K in fives, tens and twenties. All used bills." —Kinky Friedman, *Steppin' on a Rainbow*, p. 103, 2001

2 a kilometre *UK*
- Another k and there's a parking place on the right. —Chris Ryan, *Stand By, Stand By*, p. 84, 1996

3 a kilogram, especially of an illegal drug *US*
- I know people who wanta get rid of some Ks, you dig?. —Vernon E. Smith, *The Jones Men*, p. 167, 1974
- The police opened it and found 4K of Charlie! —Dave Courtney, *Raving Lunacy*, p. 183, 2000

4 the recreational drug ketamine *US*
Ketamine hycrochloride is an anaesthetic used recreationally for its hallucinogenic properties.
- It is widely known that drugs like cocaine, the amphetamine derivative Ecstasy, and ketamine, an anesthetic often called "K," have become an integral part of the Morning Party[.] —*New York Times*, p. 22, 17th August 1996
- Too much K (100g) can send you plummeting into a "K-Hole" where the brain seems to detach itself from the body. —*Sky Magazine*, p. 78, July 2001

5 leaves of *catha edulis*, a stimulant also called 'qat', originating in the Horn of Africa and the Arabian peninsula, legally available in the UK and similar to amphetamine in effect when chewed *UK*
Also known as 'khat' and 'kat'.
- —Angela Devlin, *Prison Patter*, p. 67, 1996

6 in a deck of cards, a king *US*
- —Michael Dalton, *Blackjack*, p. 59, 1991

7 a *k*nighthood *UK, 1961*
Used by civil servants; suggestive of a casual familiarity with the honour.
- I understand that there is a phrase in the upper echelons of Whitehall known as Knight-starvation: used derogatively about lesser beings hungry for their K's. —*The Guardian*, 23rd September 1982

8 oral sex on a woman performed according to the strictures of the 'Kivin Method' *US*
- And while you're giving good K, you'll need to place your fingertips on her perineum[.] —*Drugs An Adult Guide*, p. 108, December 2001

K2 *noun*

1 phencyclidine, the recreational drug known as PCP or angel dust *US*
- —William D. Alsever, *Glossary for the Establishment and Other Uptight People*, p. 28, December 1970

2 a hybrid-marijuana *UK*
Named after the second highest place on earth.
- —Nick Jones, *Spliffs*, p. 70, 2003

KA

a known associate of a criminal *US*
- The K.A.s are being checked out. —James Ellroy, *Suicide Hill*, p. 713, 1986
- [T]hen Stan put on a UA flight attendant's jacket and walked down the passenger ramp and onto the plane with a clipboard to see if she was seated with any K.A.'s. —Stephen Cannell, *Big Con*, p. 317–318, 1997

kaalgat *adjective*

in the nude, naked *SOUTH AFRICA*
From Afrikaans *kaal* (bare) and *gat* (hole; anus).
- —Athol Fugard, *Boesman and Lena*, 1978
- The locals called this Englishman Kaalgat (bare-arsed) Stevens. —Breyton Breytenbach, *Dog Heart*, p. 35, 1999

kabak *noun*

marijuana *UK*
- —Mike Haskins, *Drugs*, p. 288, 2003

kabayo *noun*

heroin *US, 1977*
A phonetic approximation of Spanish *caballo* (horse); **HORSE** (heroin).
- —Robert Ashton, *This Is Heroin*, p. 206, 2002
- —Mike Haskins, *Drugs*, p. 284, 2003

ka-ching

used as a representation of the sound of a sale entered on a cash register *US*
- You win the jackpot. Ka-ching. —*Empire Records*, 1995

kack *noun*

faeces *NEW ZEALAND*
- —Louis S. Leland, *A Personal Kiwi-Yankee Dictionary*, p. 57, 1984

▷ **see: CACK**

kacks *noun*

1 trousers *UK*
A variation of **KECKS**; sometimes spelt 'cacks'. Noted in teenage use by James Williamson, 1983; still current in 2003.

2 underpants, knickers *IRELAND*
Sometimes spelt 'kaks'.
- Forgot me washin' yesterday, he said. -No kaks or nothin'. —Roddy Doyle, *The Van*, p. 28, 1991
- Another woman grabbed him by the kacks and tried to yank them off. —Eamonn Sweeney, *Waiting for the Healer*, p. 100, 1997

▸ **relax the kacks**

take it easy *IRELAND*
- Relax de [the] kax, Trace, we've loads o' time. —Donal Ruane, *Tales in a rear view mirror*, p. 20, 2003

kaff *noun*

a marijuana cigarette *UK*
- —Mike Haskins, *Drugs*, p. 291, 2003

kaffall *noun*

the face *US*
Polari; probably an elaboration of **ECAF**.
- What a coddy kaffall dear. Oh vada [observe] the schnozzle [nose] on it dear. —David McKenna, *Storm in a Teacup*, 1993

kaffies *noun*

trousers *UK*
- —Paul Baker, *Polari*, p. 178, 2002

kaffir *noun*

1 a black person, especially a black African *SOUTH AFRICA, 1607*
Offensive, contemptuous, often abusive; its use is actionable under South African law as a *crimen injuria* (a wilful injury to a person's dignity caused by, for instance, the use of obscene language or racial insults). Also applied in an adjectival sense.
- I smelt worse than a kaffir toilet, worse than the pigs at home. —Bryce Courtenay, *Power of One*, p. 5, 1989
- [T]he [tram-] conductor turned to Ismail and J.N. and said in Afrikaans that their "kaffir friend" was not allowed on. —Nelson Mandela, *Long Walk to Freedom*, p. 92, 1994
- A war instigated by "uppity blacks," "cheeky kaffirs," "bolshy muntus," "restless natives," "the houts." —Alexandra Fuller, *Don't Let's Go to the Dogs Tonight*, p. 26, 2001

2 any person who does not accept Islam *TRINIDAD AND TOBAGO*
From the Hindi for 'infidel'.
- — Lise Winer, *Dictionary of the English/Creole of Trinidad & Tobago*, 2003

Kafflik *noun*
a Catholic *UK: SCOTLAND*
- Where Steff came from, football was about religion and religion was about football. Kaffliks supported Celtic. Proddies supported Rangers. — Christopher Brookmyre, *Not the End of the World*, p. 81, 1998

kag; kaggage *noun*
useless or unwanted equipment *UK*
Royal Marine slang; combining 'baggage' and **KACK**.
- Don't bother with that lot – leave it behind. It all just so much kag. — Rick Jolly, *Jackspeak*, p. 159, 1989

kaggie *noun*
▷ **see: CAGGIE**

kahuna *noun*
1 a great or important person or thing *US, 1987*
From an Hawaiian term for 'priest/wiseman'; in this sense often used with 'big'.
- — *American Speech*, p. 254, Fall 1993: 'Among the new words'
- I decided the only way to really hallucinate was to take LSD. That was the big kahuna. — Howard Stern, *Miss America*, p. 95, 1995

2 in computing, an intelligent and wise practitioner *US*
- — Eric S. Raymond, *The New Hacker's Dictionary*, p. 215, 1991

3 a type of marijuana *UK*
- — Nick Jones, *Spliffs*, p. 70, 2003

kai *noun*
food; also, drink *AUSTRALIA, 1872*
'Kai' is the term for 'food' in many Polynesian languages, but in Australia borrowed either from New Zealand English, where it is taken from Maori, or from various Melanesian pidgins.
- He held a cup of kai in both hands, and over the cup's rim he quietly studied the slack mouth and the pinched face. — J.E. MacDonnell, *Sabotage!*, p. 49, 1964

kaka hole *noun*
1 the anus *TRINIDAD AND TOBAGO, 2001*
- — Lise Winer, *Dictionary of the English/Creole of Trinidad & Tobago*, 2003

2 by extension, a despicable person *TRINIDAD AND TOBAGO, 2001*
- — Lise Winer, *Dictionary of the English/Creole of Trinidad & Tobago*, 2003

kakalaylay *noun*
dancing with clear sexual overtones *TRINIDAD AND TOBAGO, 1998*
- — Lise Winer, *Dictionary of the English/Creole of Trinidad & Tobago*, 2003

kaka pipe *noun*
a sewage discharge pipe *ANTARCTICA*
- — *Cool Antarctica*, 2003: 'Antarctic slang'

kaks *noun*
khaki trousers *US*
- [A]nd in the gloaming there are about 250 boys and girls, in sex kaks, you know[.] — Tom Wolfe, *The Pump House Gang*, p. 78, 1968

kalakit *noun*
marijuana *UK*
- — Mike Haskins, *Drugs*, p. 288, 2003

kale *noun*
money *US, 1902*
- — Marcus Hanna Boulware, *Jive and Slang of Students in Negro Colleges*, 1947
- I say, Ain you got no skins, no kale? No bread? No bones, no berries, no boys? — Robert Gover, *One Hundred Dollar Misunderstanding*, p. 22, 1961
- And some lawyer's come and shook you down for every cent of your cocksucken kale. — Bruce Jackson, *Get Your Ass in the Water and Swim Like Me*, p. 88, 1965

Kalgoorlie cooler *noun*
a hessian-walled cabinet for keeping foodstuffs cool by evaporation *AUSTRALIA*
After the West Australian mining town Kalgoorlie.
- [Dinner] nowadays came in varying degrees of coldness out of the refrigerator or ice-chest or Kalgoorlie cooler, according to the degree of amenity the mistress of the house possessed. — Dymphna Cusack, *Picnic Races*, p. 122, 1962

kali; kali weed *noun*
marijuana from Jamaica *JAMAICA*
Rastafarians consider the smoking of 'kali' to be a religious act. This spirituality is apparent in a number of Hindi words adopted into their lexicon. Conventionally, Kali is the Hindu goddess of time, mother and creator of all things, the personification of cosmic force.
- — Ernest Abel, *A Marijuana Dictionary*, p. 119, 1982
- Small well run farms produce the finest Jamaican Kali Weed — Mike Rock, *This Book*, 1999
- — Mike Haskins, *Drugs*, p. 288, 2003

kalied *adjective*
▷ **see: KAYLIED**

kali mist *noun*
a variety of marijuana *UK*
- Which of the following has no sativa in its genetic make up? A) Warlock Haze B) AK47 C) Top44 D) Kali Mist — Brian Preston, *Pot Planet*, p. 245, 2002
- — Nick Jones, *Spliffs*, p. 71, 2003

kali water *noun*
champagne *UK*
From **KAYLIED; KALIED** (drunk).
- — D Clark, *Roast Eggs*, 1981

kalsominer *noun*
a person who claims mining experience and skills he does not have *CANADA*
The word is derived from 'calcimine', a kind of whitewash.
- Don't Flo me, you dammed kalsominer. Two months ago your rounds weren't breaking. — *Western Miner & Oil Review*, p. 18/2, April 1964

kamikaze *noun*
a fall from a surfboard while standing near the nose of the board *AUSTRALIA*
- — Jack Pollard, *The Australian Surfrider*, p. 20, 1963

kamp *adjective*
a homosexual male *AUSTRALIA*
Rare spelling variant of **CAMP**, based on the incorrect folk etymology that it is a C19 acronym for '*k*nown *as m*ale *p*rostitute'.
- Kamp girl required by a gentle Kamp guy to turn on to visual masturbation and quiet kinky things. Girl can dominate. — *Searchlight*, p. 17, 1974
- — Jim Ramsay, *Cop It Sweet!*, p. 51, 1977

kanga *noun*
1 a kangaroo *AUSTRALIA, 1917*
By shortening.
- Her dog put up a kanga with a fair-sized joey, and the dog chased the kanga over the fence into the mulga[.] — Arthur Upfield, *Bony and the Mouse*, p. 13, 1959

2 money *AUSTRALIA, 1953*
From rhyming slang 'kanga(roo)' for **SCREW**.

kangaroo *noun*
1 a Jewish person *UK, 1943*
Rhyming slang, sometimes corrupted to 'kanker' or 'canker'.
- — Julian Franklyn, *A Dictionary of Rhyming Slang*, 1960
- — Ray Puxley, *Cockney Rabbit*, 1992

2 crack cocaine *US*
- From the image of the beast hopping. — US Department of Justice, *Street Terms*, October 1994

3 a tractor adapted for apple-picking *CANADA*
- Walkmen on tractors (and on "kangaroos," as I learned to my pleasure when we visited Kelowna in 1989 and found that's what apple farmers call the machines they ride). — Nadine Erickson, *in The Latest Morningside Papers*, p. 259, 1989

4 a prison warder *UK*
Prisoners' rhyming slang for **SCREW** (a prison warder), often reduced to 'kanga'.
- — Angela Devlin, *Prison Patter*, p. 68, 1996
- They always made the kangas earn their shillings. — J.J. Connolly, *Layer Cake*, p. 8, 2000

kangaroo *verb*
to use a toilet, especially a public toilet, by squatting on the seat *AUSTRALIA, 1942*
- 'No need to stand on the toilet seat, The crabs here jump fifteen feet' refers to 'kangarooing the seat', an Australian habit in Australian public toilets to avoid dangerous buttock-contact with the toilet. — Robert Brain, *Rites Black and White*, p. 86, 1979
- Not wanting to contract any trendy venereal fauna, I kangaroo-ed it. — Kathy Lette, *Girls' Night Out*, p. 59, 1987

kangaroo court *noun*

a body that passes judgment without attention to due process *US, 1853*

- What, in fact, Mr. Griffith is doing in operating a "kangaroo court". — *Flame*, p. 3, 1972
- Talk about a kangaroo court, Rocco – that's a hell of a legal system you guys got. — Edwin Torres, *Carlito's Way*, p. 105, 1975
- The two psychologists they used for their pyschiatric kangaroo court won't talk to us, which always looks bad. — *Natural Born Killers*, 1994

kangarooer *noun*

a hunter of kangaroos *AUSTRALIA, 1836*

- 'This 'ere dingo-yard is nothing else but rot,' said a hardened kangarooer. — Bill Wannan, *Bullockies, Beauts and Bandicoots*, p. 136, 1960

kangaroo-hop *verb*

(of a motor vehicle) to jerk about because the clutch is not released smoothly, an engine problem or the like *AUSTRALIA, 1943*

- Already Shadbolt had spotted the Triumph Mayflower kangaroo-hopping out of a park. — Murray Bail, *Holden's Performance*, p. 164, 1988

kangaroos *noun*

▸ **have kangaroos loose in the top paddock**

to be slightly crazy *AUSTRALIA, 1908*

- — Kathy Lette, *Girls' Night Out*, p. 165, 1987
- He wondered if George hadn't a kangaroo loose in the top paddock. — Linda Jaivin, *Rock n Roll Babes from Outer Space*, p. 104, 1996
- You'd have to have a few 'roos loose in the top paddock not to want to come and join us, 'cos it's the most fun you can have with your reg grundies on. — *Australian Ultimate*, p. 7, 2003

Kangaroo's Arse *noun*

a notional brand name applied to poor quality or cheap Australian wine *UK*

- [A] crate of Special Brew and six Kangaroo's Arse Method Champenois[.] — Ben Elton, *High Society*, p. 24, 2002

Kangaroo Valley *nickname*

Earls Court, London *AUSTRALIA, 1965*

A favourite haunt of Australian tourists.

- Interested tourists can there be taken on a guided tour of Earls Court (or Kangaroo Valley as it is locally known) to see Australians with their hands firmly hooked onto the bar rail, sinking beer after beer after beer. — Sue Rhodes, *Now you'll think I'm awful*, p. 55, 1967
- Oh well – better get back to Kangaroo Valley via the Norf Circular. — Barry Humphries, *The Wonderful World of Barry McKenzie*, p. 2, 1968
- Then along came Bazza McKenzie, whose picturesque adventures made out that the bloke was alive and well, albeit living temporarily in Kangaroo Valley in London. — Sandra Jobson, *Blokes*, p. 31, 1984

kangkalang; kangkatang *noun*

chaos; arguing *TRINIDAD AND TOBAGO, 1993*

- — Lise Winer, *Dictionary of the English/Creole of Trinidad & Tobago*, 2003

Kansas City roll *noun*

a single large-denomination note wrapped around small-denomination notes, giving the impression of a great deal of money *US*

- He loved to flash his "Kansas City roll," probably fifty one-dollar bills folded with a twenty on the inside and a one-hundred dollar bill on the outside. — Malcolm X and Alex Haley, *The Autobiography of Malcolm X*, p. 89, 1964

Kansas grass *noun*

marijuana originating in Kansas *US*

- — Mike Haskins, *Drugs*, p. 288, 2003

Kansas yummy *noun*

an attractive woman who is not easily seduced *US*

A term that need not, and usually does not, apply to a woman actually from Kansas.

- — *American Speech*, p. 19, Spring 1985: 'The language of singles bars'

Kantwork *noun*

a Kentworth truck *US*

Said with irony of an extremely reliable and respected truck.

- — Elementary Electronics, *Dictionary of CB Lingo*, p. 80, 1976

kanya *noun*

marijuana *US*

- — Lois Stavsky et al., *A2Z*, p. 59, 1995

kappa slapper *noun*

a girl member of a subcultural urban adolescent grouping that dresses in Kappa™ clothing *UK*

Certainly in Cheshire, possibly more widespread. Formed from the Kappa brand name and **SLAPPER** (a sexually promiscuous woman).

- If someone called you an Arndale Rat or a Kappa Slapper you'd hit them for not showing you nuff respec. — *The Observer*, 8th June 2003

kaput; caput *adjective*

used up, useless, destroyed *US, 1919*

From the German.

- His role in the affair might, after all, be to draw me on in conversation into revealing that I had nothing to reveal, then... kaput! — Martin Waddell, *Otley*, p. 78, 1966
- Listen, young lady, I'm almost ten years older than you are. Another bout like that, and I'll be done for, kaput. — Doug Lang, *Freaks*, p. 105, 1973
- We were through, kaput. — Odie Hawkins, *Black Casanova*, p. 125, 1984
- Into the toilet for good! Kaput! Fini! Nada! — Terry Southern, *Now Dig This*, p. 12, 1986
- The scene continued on all that summer and into fall, and then it went kaput. — Herbert Huncke, *Guilty of Everything*, p. 158, 1990

karachi *noun*

a mixture of heroin, phenobarbital and the recreational drug methaqualone, best known as Quaaludes™; heroin *UK, 1998*

Named after Karachi in Pakistan, the source of much heroin.

- — Mike Haskins, *Drugs*, p. 284, 2003

kareem *noun*

a car *UK*

While appearing to be an elaboration of 'car' this is rhyming slang, based on the name of legendary basketball player Kareem Abdul-Jabbar (b.1947).

- — *Antiquarian Book Review*, p. 18, June 2002

Karen Carpenter Airlines *nickname*

Quebecair, a charter airline with service from Canada to Europe *CANADA*

Karen Carpenter, of the music family, died at age 32 in 1983 of acute anorexia nervosa.

- I could handle the fact that we got paid sporadically, or that we nicknamed our employer Karen Carpenter Airlines because there was rarely food on board – [despite} linen table cloths, china plates, crystal wine glasses. But the hole made me quit. — *Montreal Gazette*, p. A6, 17 June 2002

kark, kark it *verbs*

▷ **see: CARK, CARK IT**

karma *noun*

fate, luck, destiny *US*

A Buddhist concept adopted by hippies, vaguely understood, simplified and debased in all-purpose usage. 'Good karma' is recognition or portent of good luck , while 'bad karma' generally ascribes blame.

- If you help us clean up you will be rewarded with karma and extra brain cells. — Nicholas Von Hoffman, *We are the People Our Parents Warned Us Against*, p. 146, 1967
- Why in the world are we here/Surely not to live in pain and fear — John Lennon, *Instant Karma*, 1970
- Fucking karma. I'd give the bastard karma – karmfuckingrama! — Stuart Browne, *Dangerous Parking*, p. 81, 2000
- Bad Karma in the Hare Krishna kitchen — *Metro*, p. 3, 12th July 2001

karsey *noun*

▷ **see: CARSEY**

karzy *noun*

a lavatory; also used in a figurative sense *UK, 1961*

From the Italian *casa* (a house) which is also its original use. Many slang words have alternate spellings but users of the karzy have more choices than most: 'khazi'; 'kharzi'; 'kharzie'; 'kazi';' karsi'; 'carsey'; 'carsie'; 'carzie'; 'cawsey'; 'cawsy'. The variations spelt with a 'k' date from the mid-C20. Brendan Behan, *Borstal Boy*, 1958, uses 'cawsy'.

- If you go through one door you're in a karsi and if you go through the other door you're in a back yard[.] — Ted Lewis, *Jack Carter's Law*, p. 54, 22nd June 1974
- Gawd. This is a carsie. — Anthony Masters, *Minder*, p. 73, 1984
- Prince Charles thinking he's been flushed down the karzy[.] — Andrew Nickolds, *Back to Basics*, p. 13, 1994

- I could be in kharzi taking a leak when someone rings. —Kitty Churchill, *Thinking of England*, p. 162, 1995
- Cos when my mam was young they had an iron bath in the backyard and an outside khazi. —Shaun Ryder, *Shaun Ryder... in His Own Words*, 1996
- —Angela Devlin, *Prison Patter*, p. 34, 1996
- [T]he King's collapse with his trousers round his ankles on the kazi[.] —*Drugs An Adult Guide*, p. 49, December 2001
- I was somewhat in need of the khazi. To this, er, end, I was delighted to discover that the event was a latrine-centric affair[.] —*ES Magazine*, p. 3, 22nd June 2001

kashittery *noun*
(among Nova Scotians of German descent) a verbal fuss *CANADA*
- The Lunenburg County "What a kashittery," to mean "what a fuss!" derives from the German "Geschutterei," "an outpouring of words." —Lewis Poteet, *The South Shore Phrase Book*, p. 65, 1999

Kashmir *noun*
pungent and very powerful hashish originating in Kashmir, northern India *UK*
- Kashmir comes in two forms[.] —Mike Rock, *This Book*, 1999

kate *noun*
▸ **the kate**
the army *UK*
Shortened form of obsolete rhyming slang 'Kate Carney' (or Karney) for 'army'; Kate Carney was a popular music hall entertainer in the late C19.
- I finally gets out of the kate in 46 and I starts this place with me gratuity. —John Peter Jones, *Feather Pluckers*, p. 124, 1964

Kate *noun*
1 an attractive prostitute *US*
- —Vincent J. Monteleone, *Criminal Slang*, p. 136, 1949

2 used as a term of address among male homosexuals *US*
- —*Fact*, p. 26, January-February 1965

kate *verb*
to act as a pimp *US*
- —John R. Armore and Joseph D. Wolfe, *Dictionary of Desperation*, p. 37, 1976

Kate and Sidney *noun*
steak and kidney, especially in a steak and kidney pudding or pie *UK*
Rhyming slang that appears to be a Spoonerism until you look again.
- —John Ayto, *The Oxford Dictionary of Slang*, p. 135, 1998

Kate Bush *noun*
marijuana *UK*
Named after British singer Kate Bush (b.1958), disguising **KB** (**KIND BUD**) and gently punning on **BUSH**.
- —Angela Devlin, *Prison Patter*, p. 32, 1996
- —Mike Haskins, *Drugs*, p. 288, 2003

Kate Moss *verb*
to masturbate *UK*
Rhyming slang for 'toss' shortened from 'toss off' formed from the British model (b.1974).
- —Bodmin Dark, *Dirty Cockney Rhyming Slang*, 2003

Kathleen Mavourneen *noun*
1 a habitual criminal *AUSTRALIA, 1917*

2 an indefinite jail sentence *AUSTRALIA, 1910*

Kathleen Mavourneen *adjective*
lasting for an indefinite time *AUSTRALIA, 1903*
From the refrain of a popular song 'It may be for years, it may be forever'.

katydid *noun*
any Kentworth truck *US*
- —Montie Tak, *Truck Talk*, p. 94, 1971

kaya *noun*
marijuana; a marijuana cigarette *JAMAICA*
- Excuse me while I light my spilff —Bob Marley, *Kaya*, 1978
- —Suroosh Alvi et al., *The Vice Guide*, p. b, 2002
- —Mike Haskins, *Drugs*, p. 288, 2003

- Extracts reproduced in the tabloid show Limbaugh referring to "small blue babies" and "the little blues." —*Broward Business Review*, p. 1, 18th November 2003

Kaybecker *noun*
a French-speaking Canadian *US*
An intentional 'Quebec' corruption.
- —John Gould, *Maine Lingo*, p. 100, 1975

kayfabe *noun*
the protection of the inside secrets of professional wrestling *US*
- Jesse Ventura then said something like "Sid doesn't have the guts to violate a restraining order," which has to be taken as a kay fabe comment about puscho Sid's confrontations with Brian Pillman and Arn Anderson. —*Herb's Wrestling Tidbits*, 11th November 1993
- [K]ayfabe n. – pro wrestling's code of secrecy in never revealing that pro wrestling is scripted. —*Los Angeles Times*, p. 10 (Magazine), 6th August 1995
- McMahon was reportedly livid that "kayfabe" (the insider term for the act of keeping up the illusion of reality that is wrestling) had been so blatantly broken[.] —Scott Edelman, *Warrior Queen*, p. 59–60, 1999
- Dutch Mantel once told me that story about how Jerry Lawler fired him for talking to the press about wrestling out of kayfabe. —*World of Wrestling Magazine*, June 1999

kaylied; kalied *adjective*
drunk *UK*
- —Jonathan Gash, *Gold from Gemini*, p. 53, 1978
- [T]o cop an elephant is the usual parlance for getting kaylied. —Ray Puxley, *Cockney Rabbit*, 1992

kayo *noun*
▹ see: **KO**

kayrop *noun*
pork *UK*
Back slang.
- —Ray Puxley, *Cockney Rabbit*, p. 109, 1992

kazh; kasj; cazh *adjective*
pleasant in a casual sort of way *US*
A word deeply rooted in the Valley Girl ethic.
- —Connie Eble (Editor), *UNC-CH Campus Slang*, p. 2, March 1981
- Short for "casual," but can also mean "bitchen." —Jodie Ann Posserello, *The Totally Awesome Val Guide*, p. 21, 1982
- Attractive or desirable; used (as are most terms of praise in the Valley) of possessions. —Jonathan Roberts, *How to California*, p. 166, 1984
- Nothing kasj about those brown and yellow stains. —Seth Morgan, *Homeboy*, p. 4, 1990

KB *noun*
1 a rejection, a setback *UK*
From **KNOCKBACK**.
- —Angela Devlin, *Prison Patter*, p. 68, 1996

2 high quality marijuana *US*
- Initials for kind bud or killer bud. —Jim Emerson-Cobb, *Scratching the Dragon*, April 1997

KB *verb*
to refuse; to reject *UK*
Abbreviated and adapted from **KNOCK BACK** (to reject).
- [H]ow miffed God would be if you KB-ed His job offer. —Christopher Brookmyre, *Not the End of the World*, p. 375, 1998
- You went to them first, ya bastard, didn't you, an' they KBed you as well. —Christopher Brookmyre, *Boiling a Frog*, p. 121, 2000

k-bar *noun*
a US Marine Corps survival knife *US*
- —Christopher Hawke, *For Campaign Service*, 1979

K-boy *noun*
in a deck of playing cards, a king *US, 1943*
- —Peter O. Steiner, *Thursday Night Poker*, p. 413, 1996

KC; Kay Cee *nickname*
Kansas City, Missouri *US, 1895*
- Somewhat younger than Lester Young, also from KC, that gloomy, saintly goof in whom the history of jazz was wrapped[.] —Jack Kerouac, *On the Road*, p. 239, 1957
- [O]nce again she saw him in some little town outside KayCee[.] —John Clellon Holmes, *The Horn*, p. 95, 1958
- His only friends in K.C., the ones he wrote about, were the pimps, clochards, whores, dope pushers, cattle stunners, pickpockets, and he saw no reasonable motive for changing his style[.] —Clancy Sigal, *Going Away*, p. 206, 1961

- Chicago and St. Louis want to lend us some of their men who might be able to spot any new faces around in case it's a push by some of those wise punks from Miami or Philly, or even K.C. — Mickey Spillane, *Last Cop Out*, p. 9, 1972
- I'd say, "Ah, no good, mine comes in fron KC, just came up from Memphis." — Herbert Huncke, *Guilty of Everything*, p. 1, 1990

K capsule *noun*

a capsule containing a mixture of the recreational drug ketamine and MDMA, the recreational drug best known as ecstasy *UK*
From K (ketamine).

- — Gareth Thomas, *This Is Ecstasy*, p. 54, 2002

keb *noun*

a French-speaking Canadian *CANADA*

- [W]e call them Frogs, kebs, or peppers. — Suroosh Alvi et al., *The Vice Guide*, p. 252, 2002

kebab *noun*

the vagina *UK*

- However, the category edibility glosses over the variability within it, which, for FGTs [female genital terms] included frequent reference to meat (e.g., bacon rashers, kebab, meat curtains); fish/seafood (e.g., tuna waterfall; fish, clam); and "sweet tidbits" (e.g. love muffin, fudge, cake-hole). — *Journal of Sex Research*, p. 146, 2001

kecks; keas *noun*

trousers *UK, 1961*
A northern variation of obsolete 'kicks' (trousers), now well known. Also spelt as 'keks' and ' kex'. In Glasgow, the meaning is specialised to 'men's underpants'.

- These are strangling us. — Michael Munro, The Complete Patter, 1996
- [E]veryone begins to take off their shirts. [...] GAZ: And your kegs. — *The Full Monty*, 1997
- [B]ad-tinted swede [hair], bad tan, bad white kecks[.] — Kevin Sampson, *Outlaws*, p. 107, 2001
- [T]he turd at school who's always got chewie [chewing gum] on the arse of his kecks. — *X-Ray*, p. 20, April 2003

ked *noun*

in India, used generically for a gym shoe or a canvas shoe *INDIA*
From a branded range of shoes.

- I must buy a new pair of keds. — Paroo Nihalini, R.K. Tongue and Priya Hosali, *Indian and British English*, 1979
- While for women, sexy is the catchword, but [Hemant] Trevedi frowns upon slacks, keds and jeans. — *The Times of India*, 28th February 2002

kee *noun*

a kilogram (especially of drugs) *UK*
Alternative spelling for **KEY**.

- Nood bags up two kees of weed[.] — Nick Barlay, *Curvy Lovebox*, p. 26, 1997

keebler *noun*

a white person *US*

- — Terry Williams, *Crackhouse*, p. 149, 1992

keech *noun*

1 excrement, shit *UK: SCOTLAND*
Also applied figuratively. Variants include 'keegh' and 'keek'.

- Yi should've thought about that afore yi pinned that bit of blue keech [a Conservative rosette] to your tit. — Ian Pattison, *Rab C. Nesbitt*, 1988
- [H]e finds a bunch of men up to their necks in shit [...] "Right lads, tea break's over, back on your heids." [...] Just as long as the keech completely insulated his ears. — Christopher Brookmyre, *Boiling a Frog*, p. 15, 2000

2 a contemptible person *UK: SCOTLAND, 1985*
Extends from the previous sense.

- [T]he wee keech is right, and I know it. — Ian Pattison, *Rab C. Nesbitt*, 1988

keech *verb*

to defecate *UK: SCOTLAND*

- I was very near keeching myself. — Ian Pattison, *Rab C. Nesbitt*, 1988

keechy *adjective*

soiled with excrement *UK: SCOTLAND, 1985*
From **KEECH** (excrement, faeces).

- Sumdy's left a keechy nappy in that bin. — Michael Munro, *The Complete Patter*, p. 88, 1996

keef *noun*

▷ see: KIEF

keek *verb*

to peek *UK: SCOTLAND, 1911*
Dialect.

- All keeking out, all hypertense in case I break into their Ford Sierras. — Ian Pattison, *Rab C. Nesbitt*, 1988

keel over *verb*

to collapse *UK, 1897*
From the conventional sense (to capsize).

- [I]t limped into the top 40's lower reaches, then keeled over. — *The Guardian*, 4th April 2003

keen *adjective*

good, fashionable *US, 1915*
Still heard, but by the late 1960s used almost exclusively with irony, especially when intensified with 'peachy'.

- "Yeah," said Wilma Hepp, "they sure got some keen stuff nowadays." — Max Shulman, *The Zebra Derby*, p. 166, 1946
- Tonight I got a date with a Sigma, a keen babe, for a hop at the Shoreland Hotel. — James T. Farrell, *Saturday Night*, p. 35, 1947
- "Tell me some more of this keen stuff," she said eagerly. — Max Shulman, *The Many Loves of Dobie Gillis*, p. 45, 1951
- "Just peachy-keen, Harry baby," said Ira. "Just tickety-boo." — Max Shulman, *Anyone Got a Match?*, p. 19, 1964
- Next thing you know he'll find you keen and peachy, you know? — *Annie Hall*, 1977
- A pair of very keen trousers. I like pants that give you a good butt and long legs. — Misstress Barbara, *Mixmag*, p. 20, April 2003

keener *noun*

1 a sycophant *US*

- — Chris Lewis, *The Dictionary of Playground Slang*, p. 129, 2003

2 a school pupil who is enthusiastic about school work *UK, 1984*
From conventional 'keen' (eager). Shortened to 'keeno'.

- Mash up the keeners in the Main Block if you have to! — Jack Allen, *When the Whistle Blows*, p. 50, 2000
- — Susie Dent, *The Language Report*, 2003

keen on *adjective*

enthusiastic about *UK, 1889*

- So few Britons are keen on Europe. There's a surprise. — *The Guardian*, 26th July 2000

keeps *noun*

▸ **for keeps**

permanently *US, 1861*

- If he put her out for keeps, he'd never have the chance to see her when she became sick, and he had no doubt about her one day having to come to him for help. — Donald Goines, *Dopefiend*, p. 46, 1971

keep *verb*

to be in possession of drugs *US*

- Shooting up the Peanut Shit / Of all we need to keep. — Leonard Cohen, *Beautiful Losers*, p. 238, 1966

▸ **keep Bachelor's Hall**

(of a man) to live alone, even temporarily *CANADA*
The *Historical Dictionary of American Slang* finds this phrase in use in the US as well.

- A man whose wife has gone to Newfoundland for a week, leaving him to cook and clean for himself, says "I'm keeping Bachelor's Hall," an elaborate form of the more familiar North American "batching it." — Lewis Poteet, *The South Shore Phrase Book*, p. 65, 1999

▸ **keep dog**

to act as lookout *UK*

- They told me to keep dog. Then they came running out and I ran with them. — Andy McNab, *Immediate Action*, p. 10, 1995

▸ **keep him honest**

in poker, to call a player who is suspected of bluffing *US*

- — Irwin Steig, *Common Sense in Poker*, p. 185, 1963

▸ **keep in (some commodity)**

to keep satisfactorily supplied with income *AUSTRALIA, 1936*

- As for the money for expenses, there is not sufficient cash in Sydney's underworld to keep Al Capone in petrol for a week. — 'Sweeney-ex-crook', *I Confess*, p. 110, 1936

- Earlier this year the Spence household was kept in cornflakes from the proceeds of the top-rating Ten mini-series *Dirtwater Dynasty*. — *Sunday Telegraph*, p. TV Extra 3, 31st July 1988

▸ keep it dark
to say nothing about something; to keep a secret *UK, 1857*
An imperative.
- Government increases secondments from energy, arms and construction industries, but tries to keep it dark[.] — *The Guardian*, 5th October 2002

▸ keep nix
to keep lookout *IRELAND*
- 'Ah, for God's sake, who's going to see you at this hour?...You have a slash. I'll keep nix,' he said. — Hugh Leonard, *Out After Dark*, p. 94, 1989

▸ keep on keeping on
to persevere in the face of all discouragement or misfortune *US*
- [W]hile the sprinters are taking long breaks she keeps on keeping on. — *Washington Post*, p. C9, 20th January 1977
- Meanwhile, something of a favourite phrase, he will 'keep on keeping on' at the riding. — *The Observer*, 2nd November 2003

▸ keep tabs on; keep a tab on
to keep an account of; to note someone's movements or activity, to follow and record *US, 1889*
The original use was of simple accounting: 'to keep a (financial) table on'.
- I won't be able to keep tabs on all the other shite. — Kevin Sampson, *Clubland*, p. 101, 2002

▸ keep the peek
to serve as a lookout during a criminal act *US*
- — John R. Armore and Joseph D, *Wolfe, 'Dictionary of Desperation*, p. 37, 1976

▸ keep under your hat
to maintain secrecy about something; especially used as an imperative for discretion *UK, 1953*
- The driver of the stars' homes tour also pointed out [...] the current homes of Kim Novak, Helena Rubenstein and Madonna – although no one is supposed to know she has moved here, so keep it under your hat. — *The Guardian*, 25th September 1999

▸ keep your cool
to retain your self-possession *US*
- Scholars may screech as Tony Harrison infiltrates modern lingo ("keep your cool," "buddy," "haute couture") into his rhymed couplets. — *Newsweek*, p. 69, 24th March 1975
- The man the French call "Crazy" kept his cool. — *The Guardian*, 17th February 2003

▸ keep your head down
to stay out of trouble *UK*
Military origins.
- Common phrase often used as the end of letters from prisoners. — Angela Devlin, *Prison Patter*, p. 68, 1996

▸ keep your mouth off
to stop talking about *TRINIDAD AND TOBAGO, 1971*
- — Lise Winer, *Dictionary of the English/Creole of Trinidad & Tobago*, 2003

▸ keep your nose clean
to stay out of trouble, to behave yourself *US, 1887*
- I didn't do too bad. I kept me nose clean. I went through the war alright. — Clive Exton, *No Fixed Abode [Six Granada Plays]*, p. 123, 1959

▸ keep yow
to act as lookout while an illegal activity takes place *AUSTRALIA, 1942*
- 'You keep yow,' she said in a muffled voice, 'and whistle "The Prisoner's Song" if anyone comes along'. — Eve Langley, *The Pea-Pickers*, p. 213, 1958

keeper *noun*

1 something or someone worth keeping *US*
- And occasionally there would even be the unique entry – the keeper – that Barb might adopt as a friend. — Dan Jenkins, *Life Its Ownself*, p. 57, 1984

2 any weapon or instrument that can be used as a weapon *US*
- — William K. Bentley and James M. Corbett, *Prison Slang*, p. 87, 1992

3 an arrest that results in criminal charges being filed *US*
- — Carsten Stroud, *Close Pursuit*, p. 273, 1987

4 in common-law, a spouse *TRINIDAD AND TOBAGO, 1884*
- — Lise Winer, *Dictionary of the English/Creole of Trinidad & Tobago*, 2003

5 the person running a two-up gambling game *AUSTRALIA, 1941*
Shortening of **RING-KEEPER**.
- — Vince Kelly, *The Bogeyman*, p. 166, 1956
- — John O'Grady, *It's Your Shout, Mate!*, p. 25, 1972
- You see you'll need a couple of stooges to take the fall as keeper and croupier so the whole thing looks kosher. — Clive Galea, *Slipper*, p. 99, 1988

keep it real!
stay honest!, tell the difficult truth! *US*
- — Connie Eble (Editor), *UNC-CH Campus Slang*, p. 5, April 1997

keep-miss *noun*
a kept mistress *BARBADOS*
- — Frank A. Collymore, *Barbadian Dialect*, p. 64, 1965

keep on trucking!
persevere!; continue *US, 1972*
- [N]ext time you feel like quitting, remember Luis Ramirez – and keep on trucking. — Kevin Nelson, *The Runner's Book of Daily Inspiration*, p. 10, 2000

keep the greasy side down and the shiny side up
used as an admonition to drive safely *US*
Popularised during the citizens' band radio craze of the later 1970s.
- — Wayne Floyd, *Jason's Authentic Dictionary of CB Slang*, p. 20, 1976

keep up your front to make your game!
don't give up! *US*
- — Hy Lit, *Hy Lit's Unbelievable Dictionary of Hip Words for Groovy People*, p. 25, 1968

keep your hair on!
don't get upset! *NEW ZEALAND*
- — Louis S. Leland, *A Personal Kiwi-Yankee Dictionary*, p. 58, 1984

keep your shirt on!
calm down!, relax!, compose yourself! *UK, 1854*
- "[S]uppose I gave you some dirt on Callahan? – Oh, don't interrupt! Keep your shirt on!" – and he held up his hand. — Robert Penn Warren, *All the King's Men*, p. 46, 1946
- Sheridan said. "Keep your shirt on, kid. I think I saw him in there." — Stephen King, *NIghtmares and Dreamscapes*, p. 132, 1993

keester, kef *nouns*
▷ **see: KEISTER, KIEF**

keg *noun*

1 a barrel of beer *AUSTRALIA, 1895*
- We had a keg in the boot and a few dozen tubes between us so there was much chundering en route. — Barry Humphries, *A Nice Night's Entertainment*, p. 77, 1964
- Heat up the barbie and crack a keg! — Kel Richards, *The Aussie Bible*, p. 51, 2003

2 beer *NEW ZEALAND*
- — David McGill, *David McGill's Complete Kiwi Slang Dictionary*, p. 65, 1998

3 25,000 capsules of an illegal drug such as amphetamine *US*
- — William D. Alsever, *Glossary for the Establishment and Other Uptight People*, p. 17, December 1970

4 in television and film making, a 750 watt spotlight that resembles a beer keg *US*
- — Ralph S. Singleton, *Filmaker's Dictionary*, p. 89, 1990

kegger *noun*
a party with a generous supply of beer *US*
From **KEG** (a beer barrel).
- — *Current Slang*, p. 4, Fall 1966
- — Collin Baker et al., *College Undergraduate Slang Study Conducted at Brown University*, p. 147, 1968
- We'll have to start going to keggers, or getting someone to make the beer-run for us to the junction or maybe get our stuff off the streets. — Beatrice Sparks (writing as 'Anonymous'), *Jay's Journal*, p. 30, 1979
- Blow it tonight girls and it's keggers with kids all next year. — *Heathers*, 1988

kegging *adjective*
good, fun *US*
- — Connie Eble (Editor), *UNC-CH Campus Slang*, p. 6, Spring 1991

keg-legs *noun*
generously oversized thighs or calves *US*
Collected from anecdotal evidence of 1960s UK usage and noted as 'an unkind name shouted at girls with "fat" thighs' by Chris Levis, *The Dictonary of Playground Slang*, 2003.
- Joel, a construction worker, had dropped eighty-five pounds, losing what he called his "keg legs" and slimming his beer-bellied waist from forty inches to thirty. —Tony Horwitz, *Confederates in the Attic*, 1999
- —Chris Lewis, *The Dictionary of Playground Slang*, p. 130, 2003

kegler *noun*
a bowler *US*
From the German.
- —Frank Bryan, *Tackle Tenpin Bowling This Way*, 1962

keg-on-legs *noun*
a prodigious drinker of beer *AUSTRALIA*
- —James Lambert, *The Macquarie Book of Slang*, 1996

keg party *noun*
a party at which a keg of beer is supplied for the guests *AUSTRALIA, 1950*
- [There was] a pink house with a keg party on a verandah. —Wilda Moxham, *The Apprentice*, p. 22, 1969
- Nothing like a keg party to drive away the blues, to stop the clocks from ticking the journey to the grave. —Frank Hardy, *The Outcasts of Foolgarah*, p. 186, 1971

keister; keester; keyster *noun*
1 the buttocks *US, 1931*
From the German.
- "And for all of that a lot of those top dogs are paying through the kiester starting now." —Mickey Spillane, *Kiss Me Deadly*, p. 67, 1952
- Want a goddam branding iron up your goddamn keyster? —Bernard Wolfe, *The Late Risers*, p. 200, 1954
- He said, "I ain't paying you a 'fin' a night to sit on your keister." —Iceberg Slim (Robert Beck), *Pimp*, p. 104, 1969
- I don't want to hear about resurrection or Easter / You can shove that Bible up your kiester. —Dennis Wepman et al., *The Life*, p. 119, 1976

2 a travelling bag or satchel *US, 1881*
- —William Bysshe Stein, *American Speech*, p. 150–151, May 1959: 'Notes on the cant of the telephone confidence man'
- —Ramon Adams, *The Language of the Railroader*, p. 89, 1977
- —Don Wilmeth, *The Language of American Popular Entertainment*, p. 150, 1981

3 a safe *US, 1913*
- —Bruce Jackson, *Outside the Law*, p. 57, 1972: 'Glossary'
- I figured that they had a little floor keyster somewhere. —Bruce Jackson, *Outside the Law*, p. 99, 1972

4 a jail or prison *US, 1949*
- —Joe McKennon, *Circus Lingo*, p. 53, 1980

keister bandit *noun*
an aggressive male homosexual who takes the active role in anal sex *US*
- —Hyman E. Goldin et al., *Dictionary of American Underworld Lingo*, p. 114, 1950

keister stash *noun*
a container of contraband hidden in the rectum *US*
- [H]e smuggled out over two hundred dollars in the barrel of a fountain pen, converted to a keister stash. —Malcolm Braly, *On the Yard*, p. 229, 1967

keister stash *verb*
to hide (contraband) in your rectum *US*
- You think he might have something keister stashed? We can X-ray. —Malcolm Braly, *On the Yard*, p. 35, 1967

Keith Moon *noun*
a crazy person *UK*
Rhyming slang for **LOON** formed from the name and nickname of rock musician 'Moon the Loon', 1946–78.
- —Ray Puxley, *Cockney Rabbit*, 1992

keki *noun*
the vagina *TRINIDAD AND TOBAGO*
From the Hindi.
- —Lise Winer, *Dictionary of the English/Creole of Trinidad & Tobago*, 2003

kelly *noun*
1 the stomach, the abdomen, the belly *UK, 1970*
Rhyming slang, abbreviated from **DERBY KELLY**.

2 a hat *US, 1908*
- —Joseph E. Ragen and Charles Finston, *Inside the World's Toughest Prison*, p. 806, 1962: 'Penitentiary and underworld glossary'

kelly bow *noun*
money *UK: SCOTLAND*
Glasgow rhyming slang, perhaps from the name of a gang in the Govan area of Glasgow.
- Ah'd get ye a pint but Ah'm kinna light on the kelly bow at the moment. —Michael Munro, *The Original Patter*, 1985

kelper *nickname*
a native of the Falkland Islands *FALKLAND ISLANDS (MALVINAS), 1900*
- —Bernadette Hince, *The Antarctic Dictionary*, p. 199, 2000
- Two hundred years later, in the early 1980s, another Royal marine officer described the islanders, or Kelpers as they call themselves, as "a mainly drunken, decadent, immoral and indolent collection of dropouts." —John Hughes-Wilson, *Military Intelligence Blunders*, p. 264, 2000
- With a total area of some 12,000 sq. km (4,633 sq. miles) the islands have a population of around 2,500 kelpers (residents, universally of British origin) with 500,000 sheep, plus penguins, geese, whales and seals for company. —Natalie Minnis, *Insight Guide South America*, p. 350, 2002

kelsey hair *noun*
straight hair *US, 1976*
- She was a stomp-down mud-kicker with kelsey hair / A jive-ass bitch but her face was fair. —Dennis Wepman et al., *The Life*, p. 147, 1976

kelt; keltch *noun*
a white person *US, 1912*
- —Clarence Major, *Dictionary of Afro-American Slang*, p. 73, 1970

Kembla *noun*
change *AUSTRALIA, 1966*
Rhyming slang after Kemba Grange, a racecourse south of Sydney.
- —Ned Wallish, *The Truth Dictionary of Racing Slang*, p. 43, 1989

Kembla Grange *noun*
small change *AUSTRALIA, 1955*
Rhyming slang, after a racecourse just south of Sydney.
- His pockets were bulging with Kembla Grange. —Kathy Lette, *Girls' Night Out*, p. 183, 1987

kemp *noun*
a customised car *US, 1953*
- —*American Speech*, p. 99, May 1954
- —John Edwards, *Auto Dictionary*, p. 91, 1993

Ken Dodd *noun*
a roll of banknotes *UK*
Rhyming slang for 'wad' formed from the name of the British comedian (b.1929) who fell foul of the taxman in 1989.
- —Ray Puxley, *Cockney Rabbit*, 1992

Ken Dodds; kenny's *noun*
the testicles *UK*
Rhyming slang for **CODS** formed from the name of British comedian Ken Dodd (b.1929).
- —Ray Puxley, *Cockney Rabbit*, 1992

kenna; kenner *noun*
a house *UK, 1923*
A variation of 'ken' (a house). English gypsy use.
- It was bad enough all being crushed together side by side in kennas[.] —Jimmy Stockin, *On The Cobbles*, p. 43, 2000

kennec *noun*
a non-gypsy or traveller *UK*
English gypsy use.
- —Jimmy Stockin, *On The Cobbles*, p. 10, 2000

kennel *noun*
1 a house *US*
- Pigeon, hop this over to grandma's kennel in the woods. —Haenigsen, *Jive's Like That*, 1947

2 a prison cell *UK*
- —Angela Devlin, *Prison Patter*, p. 68, 1996

kenner *noun*
a school pupil who is enthusiastic about school work *UK, 1984*
From conventional 'keen' (eager). Shortened to 'keeno'.
- —Susie Dent, *The Language Report*, 2003

Kennie *noun*
any Kentworth truck *US*
- —Montie Tak, *Truck Talk*, p. 95, 1971

Kennington Lane *noun*
pain, a pain *UK*
Rhyming slang, formed from a street name in South London.
- —Julian Franklyn, *A Dictionary of Rhyming Slang*, 1961

Kenny Whopper *noun*
in trucking, a Kentworth truck *US*
- —"Slingo", *The Official CB Slang Dictionary Handbook*, p. 36, 1976

Kenosha Cadillac *noun*
any car manufactured by American Motors *US*
American Motors had its main factory in Kenosha, Wisconsin.
- —Wayne Floyd, *Jason's Authentic Dictionary of CB Slang*, p. 20, 1976

Kentish Town *noun*
a halfpenny or penny *UK*
Rhyming slang for 'brown', from the copper colour of the coin.
- —Julian Franklyn, *A Dictionary of Rhyming Slang*, 1961

Kentucky blue *noun*
marijuana grown in Kentucky, 'the Bluegrass State' *US, 1969*
A play on **GRASS** (marijuana).
- —Richard A. Spears, *The Slang and Jargon of Drugs and Drink*, p. 300, 1986
- —Mike Haskins, *Drugs*, p. 288, 2003

Kentucky chrome *noun*
trim on a truck painted with aluminium *US*
- —Montie Tak, *Truck Talk*, p. 95, 1971

Kentucky right turn *noun*
a move to the left before making a righthand turn while driving *US*
- —Jeffrey McQuain, *Never Enough Words*, p. 55, 1999

Kentucky waterfall *noun*
a hairstyle in which the hair is worn short at the front and long at the back *US*
Best known as a **MULLET**.
- —Don R. McCreary (Editor), *Dawg Speak*, 2001
- —Connie Eble (Editor), *UNC-CH Campus Slang*, p. 4, Spring 2001

Kentucky windage *noun*
the adjustment of the aim of a rifle based on intuition *US, 1945*
- —Linda Reinberg, *In the Field*, p. 120, 1991

Keppler Wessels *noun*
the testicles *AUSTRALIA*
- Not one of these stories lacks a moment in which Biff leads with the back of his head, or damages a pavement with his face, or takes a knee in the Keppler Wessels. — *National Times*, p. 31, 16th March 1984

keptie *noun*
a kept woman supported by a rich benefactor *US*
- The goal of very chorine is to end up here as a keptie. —Jack Lait and Lee Mortimer, *Chicago Confidential*, p. 290, 1950

keptive *noun*
a youthful, sexually inexperienced male who is supported by an older homosexual *US*
- — *Maledicta*, p. 157, Summer/Winter 1986 – 1987: 'Sexual slang: prostitutes, pedophiles, flagellators, transvestites, and necrophiles'

kept man *noun*
a procurer of prostitutes; a man who makes his living off the earnings of prostitutes *US*
- — *Maledicta*, p. 148, Summer/Winter 1986 – 1987: 'Sexual slang: prostitutes, pedophiles, flagellators, transvestites, and necrophiles'

kerb crawling *noun*
soliciting for prostitution from a vehicle *AUSTRALIA*
- But kerb crawling, or soliciting for prostitution, was made an offence in 1985 to prevent the resulting 'nuisance' and carries a maximum penalty of nearly $900. — *The West Australian*, 5th October 1991

kerb-crawling *adjective*
working as a prostitute from a vehicle *AUSTRALIA*
- [F]rom the do-anything masseuses of Germany to London's proliferating street-walkers; from the kerb-crawling car girls of East Sydney to the $1000-a-throw ladies who monopolise the bedrooms of Miami during Presidential convention weeks. — *Kings Cross Venus*, p. 14, 1st November 1972

kerchief code *noun*
a designation of a homosexual man's sexual preferences, signalled by the colour of the handkerchief and the pocket in which it is worn *US*
For example, a black handkerchief worn on the left signifies that the wearer is into 'Heavy S&M, Top', while on the right it means 'Heavy S&M, Bottom'.

kerching!
used in response to a profitable triumph *UK*
Echoic of a cash till. Popularised by BBC television children's programme *Kerching!*, the story of a 14-year-old entrepreneur. A 7-year-old from Cardiff is reported to celebrate his mother's capitulation in negotiations for an ice-cream with the triumphant drawing of a fist down into his body and an accompanying cry of 'Kerching!'.
- "Kerching!" goes the Rings! [Headline announcing The Lord of the Rings victory at the BAFTAs] — *iofilm ezine*, 25th February 2002

kerdoing!; kerdoink!; gerdoying!
used as a representation of a moment of violent impact; crash!; wallop! *UK, 1945*
Echoic. Originally recorded in Royal Air Force use.

kerfuffle *noun*
▷ see: **CURFUFFLE**

kerist *noun*
used for 'Christ' *AUSTRALIA*
- Where are you going for kerist's sake? —Barry Humphries, *Bazza Pulls It Off!*, 1971

ker-lunk!
▷ see: **CLUNK!**

Kermit the Frog *noun*
a lavatory *UK*
Rhyming slang for **BOG** formed from the name of a television puppet character in *The Muppet Show*, from 1976.
- —Ray Puxley, *Cockney Rabbit*, 1992

kernel *noun*
a swollen groin gland *BARBADOS*
- —Frank A. Collymore, *Barbadian Dialect*, p. 64, 1965

kero *noun*
kerosene *AUSTRALIA, 1930*
- —Nino Culotta (John O'Grady), *They're A Weird Mob*, p. 75, 1957
- Well, he clambered back up onto the roof with a box of Federal matches and started lighting the kero, and within seconds the whole perimeter of his house was like a bonfire. —Roy Slaven (John Doyle), *Five South Coast Seasons*, p. 2, 1992
- —David McGill, *David McGill's Complete Kiwi Slang Dictionary*, p. 75, 1998

kerosene cowboy *noun*
an air force jet pilot *NEW ZEALAND, 1996*
- —Harry Orsman, *A Dictionary of Modern New Zealand Slang*, p. 74, 1999

kerplop *noun*
used for imitating the sound of something being dropped *US*
- I heard him stumble down the hall to the bedroom and soon his shoes hit the floor, kerplop. —Iceberg Slim (Robert Beck), *Mama Black Widow*, p. 114, 1969

kerry-fisted *adjective*
said of a left-handed person *CANADA*
- The term "kerry-fisted," applied to left-handed people in the Eastern Townships of Quebec, came from the descendants of a Scots family, the Kerrs, from whom came the actress Deborah Kerr, who had a family tendency to left-handedness. —Lewis Poteet, *Talking Country*, p. 49, 1992

Kerry Packered *adjective*
tired, exhausted *UK*
Rhyming slang, extended from **KERRY PACKERS** for **KNACKERS** (the testicles).
- —Bodmin Dark, *Dirty Cockney Rhyming Slang*, 2003

Kerry Packers; kerry's *noun*
the testicles *UK*
Rhyming slang for **KNACKERS**, formed on the name of Australian media tycoon, Kerry Packer (b.1937).
- —Ray Puxley, *Cockney Rabbit*, 1992

kerterver *adjective*
▷ **see:** CATEVER

ket *noun*
1 the recreational drug ketamine *AUSTRALIA*
• Ketamine – sold under various street names including Vitamin K, K and Ket – allows users to feel no pain. — *Daily Telegraphy (Sydney)*, 23rd February 1996
• There are, however, possibly tens of thousands of young people here who have already unwittingly swallowed "K" or "Ket." — *The Herald (Glasgow)*, p. 16, 4th April 1997
• The drug has several street names, including Special K, K and Ket. — *St. Petersburg (Florida) Times*, p. 1, 31st January 1998

2 a kettle *NEW ZEALAND*
• — David McGill, *David McGill's Complete Kiwi Slang Dictionary*, p. 75, 1998

ketaine *adjective*
used to describe someone or something in bad taste *CANADA*
This term, from Quebec French, is used by both anglophones and francophones.
• Her [Celine Dion] kitschy hymns to John Paul II, during his 1984 Canadian papal visit: "She wasn't simply perceived as ketaine (tacky, hickish)," Mr. Leger says. "She was ketaine." — *National Post*, p. D4, 24th May 1997

Ketama; Ketama crumble *noun*
varieties of hashish from the Ketama region of Morocco *UK*
• Ketama crumble is also a cut above regular ketama in terms of its flavour and high. — Nick Jones, *Spliffs*, p. 87, 2003

kettle *noun*
1 a fob watch; a wristwatch *UK, 1889*
Possibly rhyming slang, 'kettle on the hob' for 'fob'; a red kettle is a gold watch, a white or tin kettle is silver.
• [M]orries never hock their gold kettles and never walk or but it[.] — Derek Raymond (Robin Cook), *The Crust on Its Uppers*, p. 21, 1962
• Arthur glanced at the Inspector's watch. "What a lovely kettle[[.]" — Anthony Masters, *Minder*, p. 123, 1984
• — Angela Devlin, *Prison Patter*, p. 68, 1996

2 a steam locomotive *US, 1934*
From the image of steam rising.
• [E]very historic steam excursion is openly cursed by diesel enthusiasts who pray that the "kettle" will break down[.] — Iain Aitch, *A Fête Worse Than Death*, p. 91, 2003

3 a boiler of a steam engine *US, 1828*
• I went on the footplate to help keep the old kettle boiling on the climb out of Campbelltown. — Patsy Adam-Smith, *Folklore of the Australian Railwaymen*, p. 187, 1969

4 in electric line work, an overhead transformer *US*
• — A.B. Chance Co., *Lineman's Slang Dictionary*, p. 11, 1980

kettled *adjective*
drug-intoxicated *UK*
• I was on a real holiday buzz, had a big, erm, party. Y'know, got totally fuckin' kettled. — Shaun Ryder, *Shaun Ryder... in His Own Words*, 1992

kettle on the hob; kettle *noun*
Bob (the diminutive form of Robert) *UK*
Rhyming slang, originally for 'bob' (a shilling); recorded in use between 1946–52.
• — Julian Franklyn, *A Dictionary of Rhyming Slang*, 1961

Kevin; Kev *noun*
a working-class youth considered to be a vulgar or threatening presence *UK*
This derogatory usage by Kevin's upper- and middle-class contemporaries derives from the commonness of the name. Originally restricted to Cornwall and London.
• I mean, I'm not saying Kevs are thick, because I do have some Kev friends who are pretty good blokes, they're quite intelligent....I think if you live in a poor area you're better off being a Kev, because there's going to be more Kevs around. — P.Watt and K.Stenson, *Cool Places*, p. 260, 1998
• [I]nner London kids talk about townies, too, and also call them Kevs (I tried out this term in the countryside, where it was met with bemusement). — Geraldine Bedell, *The Observer*, 9th December 2001

Kevin Costner; kevin *noun*
a male who pretends to date his female friend(s) *SOUTH AFRICA*
Teen slang, after the 1992 film *The Bodyguard* which starred US actor Kevin Coster (b.1955).
• Bit of a Kevin. — *Sunday Times (South Africa)*, 1st June 2003

kewl *adjective*
good, sophisticated, self-possessed *US*
Variation of COOL.
• Girls are not girls, but grrrls, super kewl (cool) young women who have the tenacity and drive to surf the net[...] ("Friendly Grrrls Guide To The Internet – Introduction"). — Marion Leonard, *Cool Places*, p. 110, 1998
• [H]ip-hop style, artists and attitude were "kewl" in the land of the now defunct Beavis and Butthead[.] — *The Source*, p. 66, March 2002

key *noun*
1 a kilogram *US, 1966*
From the first syllable of '*k*ilogram'; the one unit of the metric system that at least some Americans have grasped.
• Not that it's small in the Hight, where grass is available in five-hundred-kilogram lots (2.2 pounds per kilo, or "key" as they say in the trade). — Nicholas Von Hoffman, *We Are The People Our Parents Warned Us Against*, p. 31, 1967
• It was nothing real heavy though the price of a key in one-thousand-ton lots went from fifty to seventy-five dollars and drove the street price in the U.S. from one hundred to two hundred dollars per single key. — Abbie Hoffman, *Woodstock Nation*, p. 68–69, 1969
• Coming in to Los Angeles / Bringing in a couple of keys / Don't touch my bags if you please / Mister Customs Man — Arlo Guthrie, *Coming in to Los Angeles*, 1969
• At the beginning we bought our keys from Sandra Sandusky, one of the biggest dealers on the Lower East Side. — Ann Fettamen, *Trashing*, p. 34–35, 1970
• What crew brought in fifty keys. — Edwin Torres, *Carlito's Way*, p. 49, 1975
• He [the killer] is a big time dealer now with keys [kilograms[and shit, and he shot my uncle seven times. — Terry Williams, *The Cocaine Kids*, p. 33, 1989
• It's like this: I call him up, tell him I got half a key of quality stuff. — *Boogie Nights*, 1997
• Fifteen years for having a key of charlie in your car. Eight years for selling some wraps. — Dave Courtney, *Raving Lunacy*, 2000
• They're flying in from New York tomorrow, and each is carrying one key (kilo) of coke. — Duncan MacLaughlin, *The Filth*, p. 189, 2002

2 the declaration, under the Habitual Criminals Act, that one is a habitual criminal; an indefinite sentence under this act *AUSTRALIA, 1944*
The joke being that one is given the key to let oneself in and out.
• — Jim Ramsay, *Cop It Sweet!*, p. 52, 1977

3 a prison officer *US, 1934*
Often 'keys', even in the singular.
• — Angela Devlin, *Prison Patter*, p. 68, 1996

key *adjective*
excellent, great *US*
• — Connie Eble (Editor), *UNC-CH Campus Slang*, p. 4, Spring 1980
• — Rick Ayers (Editor), *Berkeley High Slang Dictionary*, p. 29, 2004

keyed *adjective*
1 excited *US*
• — *Current Slang*, p. 7, Spring 1968

2 drug-intoxicated *US, 1972*
From an earlier sense as 'drunk'.
• — Richard A. Spears, *The Slang and Jargon of Drugs and Drink*, p. 301, 1986
• — Mike Haskins, *Drugs*, p. 291, 2003
• — *San Francisco Chronicle*, p. E5, 10 August 2003: 'Decoding the unique dialect of Berkeley High'

key happy *adjective*
used of a prison officer who is keen to keep inmates locked in their cells *UK*
• — Angela Devlin, *Prison Patter*, p. 68, 1996

keyhole *verb*
(used of a bullet) to enter a target sideways *US*
• — *American Speech*, p. 194, October 1957: 'Some colloquialisms of the handgunner'

keyholing *noun*
eavesdropping *UK*
From the notion of spying at a keyhole.
• Hilarity knew no bounds the night we eavesdropped on drugged girlfriends talking about the boys, although keyholing doesn't come without a few unwanted insights. — Mick Farren, *Give the Anarchist a Cigarette*, p. 388, 2001

key man *noun*
a person declared a habitual criminal *AUSTRALIA, 1944*

key picker *noun*

a thief who operates in hotels, stealing keys left at the front desk for safekeeping by guests before they are retrieved by a hotel clerk *US*

- He knew all about key pickers; he'd learned the hotel business through the process as "coming up through the front of the house." — Dev Collans with Stewart Sterling, *I was a House Detective*, p. 31, 1954

keyster *noun*

▷ see: KEISTER

keystone *noun*

in circus and carnival usage, a local prosecutor *US*

- — Don Wilmeth, *The Language of American Popular Entertainment*, p. 150, 1981

keys to St E's *noun*

phencyclidine, the recreational drug known as PCP or angel dust *US*

A phencyclidine user in Washington might well find himself at St Elizabeth's hospital for treatment.

- This summer, one brand of PCP is available as "Hinkcley" (referring to John W. Hinckley Jr, who shot President Reagan) or "The Keys to St. E's" – both references to the "craziness" induced by the drug. — *Washington Post*, p. B1, 29th July 1984
- — Peter Johnson, *Dictionary of Street Alcohol and Drug Terms*, p. 104, 1993

key up *verb*

1 to unlock a door *US*

- — Lee McNelis, *30 + And a Wake-Up*, p. 9, 1991

2 to become drug-intoxicated *US*

- Jumpsteady always keyed himself up high on dope when he worked. — Malcolm X and Alex Haley, *The Autobiography of Malcolm X*, p. 90, 1964

K-factor *noun*

(when on a skiing holiday) the presence and number of Germans *UK*

Upper-class society slang; euphemistic for **KRAUT** (a German).

- — Ann Barr and Peter York, *The Official Sloane Ranger Handbook*, p. 124, 1982

KFC *noun*

a male homosexual who is under the age of consent *UK*

An elaboration of **CHICKEN**, from the branding of Kentucky Fried Chicken™ fast-food outlets; recorded in use in contemporary gay society.

- — *Attitude*, p. 60, July 2003: 'New palare lexicon'

KGB *noun*

1 a potent variety of marijuana *US, 1997*

An abbreviation of ***KILLER GREEN BUD***, playing on the familiar initialism of *Komitet Gosudarstvennoi Bezopasnosti*, the Soviet Union's Comittee of State Security, 1954–91.

- — Anna Scotti and Paul Young, *Buzzwords*, p. 137, 1997
- — Mike Haskins, *Drugs*, p. 288, 2003

2 the police *UK*

- KGB's busy, the bastards. — Trevor Griffiths, *Oi For England*, p. 20, 1982

3 the security office of a prison *US*

- — Lee McNelis, *30 + And a Wake-Up*, p. 2, 1991

K grave *noun*

a state of extreme intoxication with the recreational drug ketamine *US*

- For about forty-five minutes he was doing really bad. He was in K-hole, a K-grave. — Suroosh Alvi et al., *The Vice Guide*, p. 66, 2002

khaki *noun*

a uniformed police officer *US*

- There were blues and county khakis and detectives and DA's men all over. — Robert Campbell, *In La-La Land We Trust*, p. 109, 1986

khaki down *verb*

to dress like other members of a youth gang, including khaki trousers *US*

- — Jennifer Blowdryer, *Modern English*, p. 64, 1985

khaki wacky *adjective*

attracted to men in military uniform *US, 1944*

- — Lou Shelly, *Hepcats Jive Talk Dictionary*, p. 28, 1945
- — *Yank*, p. 18, 24th March 1945

khat *noun*

amphetamine; methcathinone; MDMA, the recreational drug best known as ecstasy *US*

From the common name for the African plant that contains the stimulant cathinone as its main active ingredient.

- — Office of National Drug Control Policy, *Drug Facts*, February 2003

khayf *noun*

a marijuana cigarette *UK*

- — Mike Haskins, *Drugs*, p. 291, 2003

khazi *noun*

a toilet *UK*

- — Tom Hibbert, *Rockspeak!*, p. 94, 1983

khazi *verb*

to be very nervous, scared or afraid *UK*

From **KHAZI** (a toilet) hence 'to shit yourself' – based on the bowel-churning properties of fear.

- I was proper khaziing it, I don't mind saying so. — Kevin Sampson, *Outlaws*, p. 49, 2001

kheef *noun*

▷ see: KIEF

Khe Sanh shuffle *noun*

a method of walking honed by combat, always on the lookout for enemy fire *US*

Referring to the US air base in Vietnam during the war.

- When we got near the runway, we did what everyone called "the Khe Sanh shuffle." You looked the way you were going, and you never went more than fifty meters in one shot. It was a half-slouched combined with the opposite of being cross-eyed: One eye always looked where you were going and the other always looked at an alternate route, where you would go if the rounds came in. — Eric Hammel, *Khe Sanh*, p. 245, 1989

khola *noun*

a potent variety of marijuana *NETHERLANDS, 1990s*

K-hole *noun*

a state of intense confusion induced by use of the recreational drug ketamine *US*

- The club has a 100-foot twisting slide lined with flashing lights. It's called the "K-hole," the slang term for the episodes of numbed confusion that ketamine can induce. — *Newsweek*, p. 62, 6th December 1993
- It reportedly resurfaced as "Special K" last year at Manhattan "rave partiesk," taking users to mental territory called "K Land" and the "K hole." — *The Record [Bergen County, New Jersey]*, p. A1, 5th December 1995
- Everybody needs some time away / Just stuck in the k-hole again / An 18-hour holiday / Just stuck in the k-hole again. — NOFX, *Kids in the K Hole*, 1997
- Ann said she's never experienced anything like this K-hole before and said she could see 360 degrees around her[.] — Wayne Anthony, *Spanish Highs*, p. 13, 1999
- They chop up equal amounts of coke and ketamine and end up in a K-hole[.] — *Sky Magazine*, p. 76, July 2001
- For about forty-five minutes he was doing really bad. He was in K-hole, a K-grave. — Suroosh Alvi et al., *The Vice Guide*, p. 66, 2002

Khyber-diver *noun*

a homosexual male *AUSTRALIA*

- Sure, there are any number of frocked-up fruit-baskets, but these kilted Khyber-divers only gown up to look really girly and entertain other shirt-lifters in shady bum bars. — *Picture*, p. 28, 5th February 1992

Khyber Pass; Khyber *noun*

the buttocks, the posterior, the anus *UK, 1943*

Rhyming slang for **ARSE** based on the geographical feature that links Afghanistan and Pakistan.

- Hey listen Pancho, take your hands off me or I'll stick your sombrero up your Khyber. — Paul Vautin, *Turn It Up*, p. 42, 1955
- [E]verybody thought I was Mozart and Liszt, falling flat on my Khyber Pass like that. — Ronnie Barker, *Fletcher's Book of Rhyming Slang*, p. 43, 1979
- He gave me the quickest kick up the Khyber of all time and my ears nearly popped off with the impact. — Rex Hunt, *Tall Tales – and True*, p. 79, 1994
- I was ready for the "bend and spread" routine once you've been through reception, when a screw [prison warder] checks your khyber in case you've got a gun or a razor tucked up there. — Lenny McLean, *The Guv'nor*, p. 41, 1998

▸ **up the Khyber**
in trouble *UK*
From a pun on KHYBER PASS and UP SHIT CREEK (in trouble); possibly coined by screenwriter Talbot Rothwell for the film *Carry On Up The Khyber*, 1968.
- In other words – if I may use an apt expression – you're up the Khyber. You've got ten seconds. —Anthony Masters, *Minder*, p. 133, 1984

ki *noun*
1 a kilogram *US, 1966*
- The kis cost Champ eight grand each for three, but he sold the stepped-on six for twenty-five grand each to his lieutenants, making a profit of a hundred thousand dollars a week for a few hours' work. —Richard Price, *Clockers*, p. 53, 1992
- But there's a ki under the back seat. —*The Bad Lieutenant*, 1992
- Maybe he'd get lucky and find the product – a ki of top grade cocaine. —Donald Gorgon, *Cop Killer*, p. 38, 1994
- The Yout' Man and the Ki —Courttia Newland, *Society Within*, 2000

2 in prison, cocoa or chocolate *UK*
- —Paul Tempest, *Lag's Lexicon*, 1950

kibbles and bits *noun*
small pieces of crack cocaine *US*
A reference to a popular dog food product, suggesting that the pieces of crack cocaine bear some resemblance to the product.
- —*People Magazine*, p. 72, 19 July 1993
- —US Department of Justice, *Street Terms*, October 1994

kibitz *verb*
to comment while others play a game *US, 1927*
From Yiddish (ultimately German) *kiebitzen* (to look on at cards).
- He came over to our table and kibbitzed at the Klobbiotsch [a card game] for a bit. —Charles Raven, *Underworld Nights*, p. 9, 1956
- The Yiddish word "kibitz" is a valuable import because it has no equivalent in English. —Anthony Lejeune, *Daily Telegraph, Colour Supplement*, 10th March 1967
- —Leo Rosten, *The Joys of Yiddih*, 1968
- Mary and Allerton were playing chess. "Howdy," he said. "Don't mind if I kibitz?". —William Burroughs, *Queer*, p. 69, 1985

kibitzer *noun*
a watcher rather than a participant, especially one who offers unsolicited advice *US, 1922*
From Yiddish *kibitser*. *The Kibitzer*, a play by Jo Swerling (1929), made both the title and Edward G. Robinson, its star, famous in the US.
- We are a race of grandstand managers, Monday morning quarter-backs and chronic, incurable kibitzers. —Robert Sylvester, *No Cover Charge*, p. 192, 1956
- All through voir dire, he had his jury selection experts spread around him like card kibitzers, whispering, pointing, and pushing pieces of paper in front of him. —Stephen Cannell, *King Con*, p. 14, 1997

kibosh; kybosh *noun*
1 an end, a finish *UK, 1836*
Almost always heard in the context of 'put the kibosh on' or 'to'.
- The mob was back at the stockyards again, so that put the kybosh on getting out this morning. —Jon Cleary, *The Long Shadow*, p. 221, 1949
- "You're probably from Denver or New York," she said, as though that put the kibosh on me forever. —Clancy Sigal, *Going Away*, p. 148, 1961
- He was a bit anxious yous was going to put the old proverbial kybosh on his night out. —Barry Humphries, *The Wonderful World of Barry McKenzie*, p. 32, 1968
- Oh, I know the papers call him a 'sewer boss' and claim he runs the department and hands out thousands of patronage jobs – before the courts put the kibosh on most of that – without knowing anything about sewers. —Robert Campbell, *In a Pig's Eye*, p. 30, 1991

2 (of pre-decimalisation currency) one shilling and sixpence *UK, 1845*
- Kybosh, one and a kick[.] —Brian McDonald, *Elephant Boys*, p. 202, 2000

kibosh; kybosh *verb*
to put an end to *UK, 1884*
- Davis kiboshed his stage chuckles; snatch jobs were meat and potatotes to him – the kind of cases he loved to work. —James Ellroy, *Hollywood Nocturnes*, p. 162, 1994
- Only the other day Jack De Lorean tried to kibosh one of the great traditions[.] —Andrew Nickolds, *Back to Basics*, p. 82, 1994

kick *noun*
1 pleasure, fun *US, 1928*
- I got my kicks out of rubbing elbows with all those bigtime gamblers and muscle men, and the easy money didn't run me away. —Milton Mezzrow, *Really the Blues*, p. 21, 1946
- After the drinks we all had a stick and got in a kick. —Hal Ellson, *Duke*, p. 105, 1949
- Heah, go on over and plug that dame in the belly! Get real kicks! —John Clellon Holmes, *Go*, p. 13, 1952
- The kick was nothing she'd known in hemp, wine or Nembutal[.] —George Mandel, *Flee the Angry Strangers*, p. 165, 1952
- We get some frantic kicks out of that wheel when we're high. —William Burroughs, *Junkie*, p. 28, 1953
- It's like the kick I used to get from bein' a Jet. —*West Side Story*, 1957
- Dean was having his kicks; he put on a jazz record, grabbed Marylou, held her tight, and bounced against her with the beat of the music. —Jack Kerouac, *On the Road*, p. 125, 1957
- It gave him kicks to spend all day talking to priests, he said. —Clancy Sigal, *Going Away*, p. 68, 1961
- Yeah, I'll play you a couple. Just for kicks. —*The Hustler*, 1961
- The Angels won't admit it, but one of the main kicks they get on a run comes from spooking and jangling citizens along the way. —Hunter S. Thompson, *Hell's Angels*, p. 117, 1966
- They're not the kind of guys are gonna knock her around or decide they want to get their kicks by beating her up or something. —James Mills, *The Panic in Needle Park*, p. 59, 1966
- [I]t was Crane's kick to blow those sailors he encountered along the squalid waterfronts of that vivid never-to-be-recaptured prewar world[.] —Gore Vidal, *Myra Breckinridge*, p. 97, 1968
- He got a secret kick out of this little victory over his tormentors, —Eldridge Cleaver, *Soul on Ice*, p. 33, 1968

2 a fad, a temporary preference or interest *US, 1946*
- I think he sometimes pushes the boat out a bit far when he's off on this hating kick[.] —Derek Raymon (Robin Cook), *The Crust on its Uppers*, p. 24, 1962
- Were you on this religious kick back home, or did you start to crack up here on the post? —*M*A*S*H*, 1970

3 the sudden onset of the effects of a drug *US, 1912*
- They're reefers. If you're gonna smoke y'might's well get a kick out it. —Max Shulman, *The Amboy Dukes*, p. 3, 1947
- There is nothing quite like a kick on dexedrine. —Clancy Sigal, *Going Away*, p. 297, 1961

4 a trouser pocket *US, 1846*
- Some nights I'd try my luck in the crap game, and wind up with a grand or more in my kick. —Mezz Mezzrow, *Really the Blues*, p. 44, 1946
- [H]er mind couldn't lose sight of the fragile druggist lying where they'd left him, bleeding from the head, or of the bloodied nickel plated pistol Angie had in his kick. —George Mandel, *Flee the Angry Strangers*, p. 400, 1952
- I'm about to stuff my pony [£25] in my kick[.] —Derek Raymond (Robin Cook), *The Crust on its Uppers*, p. 39, 1962
- We had more than four hundred quid each in the kick[.] —Frank Hardy, *The Yarns of Billy Borker*, 1965
- He reached in my kick and came out with my prop, then sent one of the salesgirls to get some water. —A.S. Jackson, *Gentleman Pimp*, p. 54, 1973
- Pat arrived from Ireland with plenty of dough in his kick and, being a gambler, headed for Randwick to try his luck. —Frank Hardy and Athol George Mulley, *The Needy and the Greedy*, p. 118, 1975
- Even if the grass had a bundle he would plead poverty. Not that he ever had much in his kick. —*The Sweeney*, p. 50, 1976

5 (of pre-decimalisation currency) sixpence, 6d *UK, 1700*
Rhyming slang that would be more convincing if the 'kick'was plural; usually as 'and a kick' in denominations such as 'two and a kick' (two shillings and sixpence).
- Kybosh, one and a kick[.] —Brian McDonald, *Elephant Boys*, p. 202, 2000

6 money *US*
- —Marcus Hanna Boulware, *Jive and Slang of Students in Negro Colleges*, 1947

7 a bribe *US*
- All bellboys paid a daily "tax" or "kick" to the captains for the privilege of working. —Jim Thompson, *Bad Boy*, p. 366, 1953

8 anything that is shared with another *US*
- —Mark S. Fleisher, *Beggars & Thieves*, p. 290, 1995: 'Glossary'

9 the start of a horse race *AUSTRALIA*
- The horse missed the kick and then stumbled. —Clive Galea, *Slipper*, p. 190, 1988

▸ **hit the kick**
to pay *AUSTRALIA, 1972*
- —John O'Grady, *It's Your Shout, Mate!*, p. 36, 1972
- You go up the shop these detente days, and, pausing to catch your breath and hit the kick for a crumpled quid, you say without thinking to the downtrodden man who leans his nose on the weighing machine, 'Canna Pal ana packeta Drum and papers, mate.' —Barry Dickins, *What the Dickins*, p. 54, 1985

kick *verb*
1 to stop using; to break an addiction *US, 1927*
- Winnie was "kicking her morphine habit" out in some walk-up in Astoria. —John Clellon Holmes, *Go*, p. 10, 1952
- I'm not hooked. And if I was, I could kick it easy. —George Mandel, *Flee the Angry Strangers*, p. 399, 1952

- I once kicked a junk habit with weed. —William Burroughs, *Junkie*, p. 32, 1953
- I'm bogue, but I ain't gonna indulge. I'm tryin to kick. —Clarence Cooper Jr, *The Scene*, p. 13, 1960
- He says he kicked before, the time he went to Lexington. —Alexander Trocchi, *Cain's Book*, p. 76, 1960
- Heroin had been the thing in Harlem for about five years, and I don't think anybody knew anyone who had kicked it. —Claude Brown, *Manchild in the Promised Land*, p. 187, 1965
- I tell you, if you have ever had the flu real bad, just multiply the misery, the aching torture by a thousand. That's what it's like to kick a habit. —Iceberg Slim (Robert Beck), *Pimp*, p. 289, 1969
- When I came out – I had of course kicked my habit – cold turkey – while in prison – I was very careful[.] —Herbert Huncke, *The Evening Sun Turned Crimson*, p. 57, 1980
- But power's a hard drug to kick. The hardest. —Robert Campbell, *Junkyard Dog*, p. 93, 1986
- Someone once wrote that kicking heroin is easy[.] —Lanre Fehintola, *Charlie Says*, p. 190, 2000

2 to defer the gratification of a drug injection by slowly injecting the drug while drawing blood from the vein to mix with the drug in the syringe *US*

- He was waiting anxiously but she took her time, as if dazed, then began to kick it, mixing her blood with the drug and then watching the syringe with eyes that never blinked. —Hal Ellson, *The Golden Spike*, p. 42, 1952

3 to complain *US, 1857*

- So I kick to the paymaster. He says, "Look, you get three squares a day, don't you?" — Haenigsen, *Jive's Like That*, 1947
- So what had she to kick about? —Clarence Cooper Jr, *The Scene*, p. 86, 1960

4 to release from police custody *US*

- One officer said he planned to "kick" a suspect when he got back to the station. — *Los Angeles Times*, p. B1, 19th December 1994

5 (of a jockey) to urge a horse on in a race *AUSTRALIA*

- Sam watched from the enclosure as Stan Davidson, riding at the owner's request, kicked him home. —Joe Andersen, *Winners Can Laugh*, p. 81, 1982
- Jump him out first, position him in the first three or four, kick him clear at the distance and get him to the winning post first. —Clive Galea, *Slipper*, p. 46, 1988

6 (of a horse) to speed up in a race *AUSTRALIA, 1980*

- Around the turn and Elegancy kicked clear but here comes Vertigo. —Paul Vautin, *Turn It Up!*, p. 146, 1995

7 in surfing, to force the nose of the surfboard up out of the water *US*

- —William Desmond Nelson, *Surfing*, p. 222, 1973

8 in trucking, to shift gears *US*

- —Montie Tak, *Truck Talk*, p. 95, 1971

9 in gambling, to raise a bet *US*

- —Richard Jessup, *The Cincinnati Kid*, p. 4, 1963
- —Albert H. Morehead, *The Complete Guide to Winning Poker*, p. 266, 1967

▸kick ass

1 to be especially energetic and exciting; to succeed by your vigorous efforts *US*

'Kick arse' and 'kick butt' are common variations.

- Every night I cried before I went on stage but I still kicked ass when I got out there. — *Ted Nugent 'Ask'*, p. 47, 5th May 1979
- Surprisingly enough she [Kylie Minogue] kicked arse, and had at least a couple of thousand singing along with her, which was quite some achievement. —Wayne Anthony, *Spanish Highs*, p. 80, 1999

2 to use force, to beat up *US*

- Now the monkey had practiced his game till it was sharp as glass / And keep in his heart he knew he could kick the baboon's ass. —Dennis Wepman et al., *The Life*, p. 31, 1976
- CLARENCE: They take him to the police station. And he starts kickin' all the cops' asses. — *True Romance*, 1993

▸kick ass and take names

to overwhelm someone or something in a methodical and determined fashion *US, 1962*

- Some scumbags, all they respect is force. You just gotta kick ass and collected names. —Joseph Wambaugh, *The Blue Knight*, p. 74, 1973
- BLEEK': We had a great night. The cats were kickin' ass and takin' names; wish you could been there. — *Mo' Better Blues*, 1990

▸kick brass

to complain strongly *TRINIDAD AND TOBAGO, 1986*

- —Lise Winer, *Dictionary of the English/Creole of Trinidad & Tobago*, 2003

▸kick for the other team

to be homosexual *AUSTRALIA*

- 'Jo, I kick for the other team!' 'But, I'm like a boy.' —Kathy Lette, *Girls' Night Out*, p. 78, 1987

▸kick into the long grass

to postpone something *UK*

- — Susie Dent, *The Language Report*, p. 82, 2003

▸kick it; kick

to idle, to relax *US, 1983*

- It was on a Sunday. Rick and I were kicking it upon Crenshaw. — *Boyz N The Hood*, 1990
- Hanging out, shooting craps, playing domino's, bagging on each other, and just plain kickin' it. — *Menace II Society*, 1993
- MARSELLUS: Fight through that shit, cause a year from now when you're kickin' it in the Caribbean you're gonna say, Marsellus Wallace was right. — *Pulp Fiction*, 1994

▸kick mud

to work as a prostitute *US, 1963*

- He had a stable of whores kicking mud for him. —Iceberg Slim (Robert Beck), *Trick Baby*, p. 178, 1969
- Chuck had two girls kicking mud around the city of Detroit. —A.S. Jackson, *Gentleman Pimp*, p. 26, 1973

▸kick out the jams

to remove all obstacles, to fight for freedom *US*

- [T]here is a generation of visionary maniac white motherfucker country dope fiend rock and roll freaks who are ready to get down and kick out the jams – ALL THE JAMS – break everything loose and free everybody from their very real and imaginary prisons —John Sinclair, *White Panther Statement*, 1st November 1968
- Kick out the jams, motherfuckers! —MC5 (Motor City Five), *Kick Out the Jams*, 1969
- I'm gonna rock it up and kick out the jams with Psychotic Reaction forever. —Lester Bangs, *Psychotic Reactions and Carburetor Dung*, p. 14, 1971

▸kick sawdust

in circus and carnival usage, to follow or join a show *US*

- —Don Wilmeth, *The Language of American Popular Entertainment*, p. 150, 1981

▸kick ten bells out of; kick ten bells of shit out of

to physically beat someone very severely *UK*

A variation of KNOCK SEVEN BELLS OUT OF.

- —Angela Devlin, *Prison Patter*, p. 68, 1996

▸kick the bucket

to die *UK, 1785*

- The porter had picked the sickest guy in the ward, some poor guy who had it so bad he kicked the bucket a few days later. —Mezz Mezzrow, *Really the Blues*, p. 41, 1946
- If I haven't kicked the bucket by then, maybe we'll be able to get together on something. —Clarence Cooper Jr, *Black*, p. 170, 1963

▸kick the gong

to fool around *US, 1945*

- She'd come up to my room that night, that Sunday, and we'd kicked the gong around for almost an hour[.] —Jim Thompson, *Savage Night*, p. 123, 1953
- I ain't saying she's yarding but we both know she could very well be kicking the gong around. —A.S. Jackson, *Gentleman Pimp*, p. 90, 1973

▸kick the tin

to contribute money *AUSTRALIA, 1965*

- Your turn to kick the tin, Stripey. —John Wynnum, *Jiggin' in the Riggin'*, p. 40, 1965
- He reckoned the Department would kick the tin on this trip. —Barry Humphries, *A Nice Night's Entertainment*, p. 174, 1978
- —Barry Humphries, *A Nice Night's Entertainment*, p. 189, 1981

▸kick to the curb

to break off a relationship *US, 1991*

- —Connie Eble (Editor), *UNC-CH Campus Slang*, p. 6, April 1995
- Kick her to the curb. — *Chasing Amy*, 1997
- But what happens when you get in the car, and you don't make with the head? Don't they kick your ass to the curb? —Kevin Smith, *Jay and Silent Bob Strike Back*, p. 26, 2001
- —Gary K. Farlow, *Prison-ese*, p. 36, 2002

▸kick up bobsy-die

to make a fuss *NEW ZEALAND*

- Been running around kicking up bobsy-die all morning. Must have a hangover, I reckon. —Robin Muir, *Word for Word*, p. 181, 1960

▸kick with the left foot

to be a Catholic *UK, 1984*

- He had ginger hair, kicked with the left foot and, in the words of the then chair of the Standing Commission on Privy Affars 'had his eyes a bit close together and looked like he'd father about 52 wee fecking Taig rabbits'. — *The Observer*, 13th February 2005

▸ **kick your own arse**
to berate yourself *UK: SCOTLAND*
A Glasgow variation of the more familiar 'kick yourself'.
- [T]ippin us the winner and no backin it hissel – he'll be kickin his own arse the night. —Michael Munro, *The Patter, Another Blast*, 1988

▸ **kick your teeth so far down your throat**
to beat someone up *AUSTRALIA*
- I kicked that bastard's teeth so far down his throat he'll have to put his toothbrush up his freckle to clean 'em. — *The Adventures of Barry McKenzie*, 1972

▸ **kick yourself**
to blame yourself, especially to berate yourself *UK*
- As for Eric Ravilious, the influential painter, graphic designer, wood engraver and war artist – kick yourself for failing to spot his 2003 centenary two years previously. — *The Guardian*, 5th January 2003

kick *adjective*
1 excellent *US*
- It was jam-up. Jelly-tight. It was, it was a really a kick joint. —Bruce Jackson, *In the Life*, p. 122, 1972

2 out of style *US*
- — *San Jose Mercury News*, 11th May 1999

kick about *verb*
to be around *AUSTRALIA, 1933*
- What makes me – makes me so wild is 'cause I see splen – ('scuse me, ol' man!) *splen-d'd* bits character kickin' 'bout. Why can't I go draw character where I see it, eh? —Ernest O'Ferrall, *Stories by 'Kodak'*, p. 67, 1933
- Even then he will probably have experienced the common feeling vicariously, through the many excellent surfing films that are kicking about. —Suzy Jarratt, *Permissive Australia*, p. 100, 1970

kick along *verb*
to serve out a prison sentence without letting it get you down *AUSTRALIA, 1950*

kick around *verb*
1 to discuss something *US, 1939*
- Q. "Who actually said, "How about we call this movie '8 Mile'?" A. Marshall did. We kicked it around and we were very specific that it should not be '8 Mile Road'[.] — *The Detroit News*, 26th October 2002

2 to idle; to pass time doing nothing *US*
- "I was just kickin' around," I say. —Francesca Lia Block, *Missing Angel Juan*, p. 347, 1993

kick-ass *adjective*
1 fantastic, excellent, thrilling *US, 1980*
- —Connie Eble (Editor), *UNC-CH Campus Slang*, p. 4, October 1986
- I got out and looked at the Porsche. It was perfect. It was a totally kick-ass car. —Janet Evanovitch, *High Five*, 1999
- It's like, "Oz, hye's just the kick-ass lacrosse player." — *American Pie*, 1999
- [A] kick-ass red lipstick. —Aubrey Dillon-Malone, *I Was a Fugitive from a Hollywood Trivia Factory [quoting Gwyneth Paltrow]*, p. 20, 1999

2 vigorous, powerful, aggressive, assertive *US, 1970*
- Surely a kick-ass cycnism combined with experience, ambition and a side-order of world-weary cool are what we require in the exciting world of television? —Stephen Fry, *Rescuing the Spectacled Bear*, p. 14, 2002

kickback *noun*
1 a commission on a more or less shady deal *US, 1930*
- There have been rumored cases of Casino Managers actually being in cahoots with gamblers to extend them big credit for kickbacks. —Mario Puzo, *Inside Las Vegas*, p. 209, 1977
- Another reason Hy says the promo guy does so well, the label exec who hires him could be getting a kickback. —Elmore Leonard, *Be Cool*, p. 152, 1999
- Bribery, kickbacks and protection rackets allowed bars to stay open after-hours[.] —Simon Napier-Bell, *Black Vinyl White Powder*, p. 40, 2001

2 the resumption of drug use after a prolonged period of non-use *US*
- —Eugene Landy, *The Underground Dictionary*, p. 115, 1971

kick back *verb*
to relax *US, 1972*
- —Dirk Flinthart, *Brotherly Love*, p. 6, 1995
- You think you can put your feet up now, kick back and celebrate with an ice cold 6-pack'o'suds? — *Sick Puppy*, p. 20, 1998
- I just wanna have me a little drink, kick back, relax —Diran Adebayo, *My Once Upon A Time*, p. 38, 2000
- I imagine that he was longing to get home so he could spend time with his family, kick back with his kids and catch up on the day's news. — *The Warcry*, p. 7, 5th July 2003

kickdown *noun*
1 an object or commodity that has been donated *US*
- Food Not Bombs got a shitload of kickdowns from that health food store last night. —Jim Crotty, *How to Talk American*, p. 145, 1997

2 the automatic shift into the next lower gear that occurs with an automatic transmission when applying full throttle *US*
- —John Edwards, *Auto Dictionary*, p. 91, 1993

kick down *verb*
to give, to provide *US*
- When one inmate buys a "box bag" of marijuana, he may kick his friend down a "joint". —William K. Bentley and James M. Corbett, *Prison Slang*, p. 15, 1992
- —David Shenk and Steve Silberman, *Skeleton Key*, p. 169, 1994

kickdown gear *noun*
in a car, a gear designed for sudden bursts of acceleration *US*
- Some of the others were the 1946 Chrysler, which had a "kickdown " gear for sudden bursts of speed[.] —Tom Wolfe, *The Kandy-Kolored Tangerine-Flake Streamline Baby*, p. 132, 1965

kicker *noun*
1 an unforeseen complication *US, 1941*
- Maybe they were playing real cute and sent her in for the kicker. —Mickey Spillane, *One Lonely Night*, p. 89, 1951
- The real kicker came the following year. —Jim Bouton, *Ball Four*, p. 6, 1970
- "Here it comes," said Binky, nudging DeDe under the tablecloth. "She's always got a kicker." —Armistead Maupin, *Tales of the City*, p. 120, 1978
- If you played out your contract with the team you belonged to – because they drafted you out of college – you couldn't go to another club unless that club "compensated" the club you were with. That was the kicker. —Dan Jenkins, *Life Its Ownself*, p. 74, 1984

2 in poker, an unmatched card held in the hand while drawing *US*
- —Irwin Steig, *Common Sense in Poker*, p. 185, 1963

3 in the illegal production of alcohol, any nitrate added to the mash *US*
- —David W. Maurer, *Kentucky Moonshine*, p. 120, 1974

4 a small, yeast-rich amount of an alcoholic beverage used to start the fermentation process in a homemade alcohol-making venture *US*
- —William K. Bentley and James M. Corbett, *Prison Slang*, p. 70, 1992

5 in television and film making, a small light used to outline objects in the foreground *US*
- —Ralph S. Singleton, *Filmaker's Dictionary*, p. 90, 1990

6 in dominoes, the 6–1 piece or any piece with a 5 *US*
- —Dominic Armanino, *Dominoes*, p. 17, 1959

7 a member of a civilian air crew dropping supplies by parachute to troops in remote areas *US*
The handlers literally kicked the supply crates with parachutes out of the plane doors.
- —Gregory Clark, *Words of the Vietnam War*, p. 264, 1990

8 a member of the Mountjoy prison riot squad *IRELAND*
- I was standing outside, wondering to meself [sic] how much mileage Frank Carson could get out of a Mountjoy "hunger-strike" joke, when the Mountjoy riot squad, or "kickers" as we called them, arrived. —Howard Paul, *The Joy*, p. 38, 1996

9 on the railways, a jammed air brake valve *US*
- —J. Herbert Lund, *Herb's Hot Box of Railraod Slang*, p. 8, 1975

10 a linear amplifier for a citizens' band radio *US*
- —Porter Bibb, *CB Bible*, p. 97, 1976

kick in *verb*
to contribute, to share an expense *US, 1906*
- The high school and the Legion Hall kicked in with a total of eight hundred foldin' chairs. —William Bast, *The Myth Makers [Six Granada Plays]*, p. 157, 1958
- 'Cause you're kicking in for food, don't mean you don't gotta eat. — *Saturday Night Fever*, 1977

kicking; kickin' *adjective*
excellent, wonderful, etc *US, 1988*
- My hair was kickin'. (Quoting Pauly Shore) — *Spin Magazine*, 1999
- —Connie Eble (Editor), *UNC-CH Campus Slang*, p. 7, Fall 1999
- [T]he place [Blackpool] he various refers to as "kickin'" and "pony" [awful]. — *Hip-Hop Connection*, p. 34, July 2002

kick in the ass; kick in the pants *noun*
in horse racing, a horse heavily favoured to win a race *US*
- —David W. Maurer, *Argot of the Racetrack*, p. 39, 1951

kick in the balls; kick in the arse; kick in the ass; kick in the pants; kick in the head *noun*
a grave disappointment; a serious setback *UK*
- And to get a fucking £17 wage after the money I'd been used to was a big kick in the balls for me. —Shaun Ryder, *Shaun Ryder... in His Own Words*, 1989

kick into touch *verb*
to finish an activity, to stop doing something or stop something happening *UK*
A sporting allusion.
- He'll knock the tunnel idea on the head. Kick it into touch. —Jack Allen, *When the Whistle Blows*, p. 227, 2000

kick-off *noun*
1 a start; a beginning; the time something begins *UK, 1875*
A figurative use of a sporting actuality.
- Let's have the duty supply bloke and I'll get the loan clothing off my slop chit for a kick-off. —John Wynnum, *Jiggin' in the Riggin'*, p. 73, 1965
- It was as good a kick-off as any. Mike even gave a faint grin. The tide of friendship flowed between them. —Joan Lindsay, *Picnic At Hanging Rock*, p. 98, 1967

2 a rough-house fight *UK*
- I have, in my time, been in quite a few rucks, rumbles, rows, battles, wars, kick-offs and right proper tear-ups. —Dave Courtney, *Dodgy Dave's Little Black Book*, p. 158, 2001

kick off *verb*
1 to begin; to get going *AUSTRALIA, 1924*
- Global Friday kicks off at 9.30pm, tickets $45 on 252 3000. —*Sydney City Hub*, p. 9, 4th April 1996
- [We] had a bit of a groove [dance] when it starts kicking off. —Ben Malbon, *Cool Places*, p. 272, 1998
- It was Ged that kicked the whole thing off. —Kevin Sampson, *Outlaws*, p. 1, 2001

2 to sleep off the effects of an illegal drug *US, 1951*
- —*American Speech*, p. 27, February 1952: 'Teen-age hophead jargon'

3 to die *US, 1908*
- The officers on the scene first aren't talking so it's my guess again that he talked before he kicked off. —Mickey Spillane, *Me, Hood!*, p. 23, 1963

4 to make a fuss, to raise an objection *UK*
- I was surprised they didn't kick off – they really were quite lenient. —Lanre Fehintola, *Charlie Says...*, p. 19, 2000

kick on *verb*
1 to commence *AUSTRALIA, 1949*
- —Ann Barr and Peter York, *The Official Sloane Ranger Handbook*, p. 82, 1982

2 to keep on; to persevere, to continue, especially against adversity *AUSTRALIA, 1949*
- Knowing what I do now gives me the drive to kick on, mate. —Ward McNally, *Supper at Happy Harry's*, p. 88, 1982
- —Clive Galea, *Slipper*, p. 68, 1988

kick out *verb*
1 while surfing, to step on the rear of the surfboard while raising the lead foot and then to pivot the board to end a ride *US*
- They're kicking out in Dohini too. —Brian Wilson and Mike Love, *Surfin' Safari (performed by the Beach Boys)*, 1962
- —Grant W. Kuhns, *On Surfing*, p. 118, 1963

2 to leave a gang *UK*
- —Angela Devlin, *Prison Patter*, p. 68, 1996

kickout hole *noun*
in pinball, a hole in the playfield that registers a score and then ejects the ball back into play *US*
- —Bobbye Claire Natkin and Steve Kirk, *All About Pinball*, p. 113, 1977

kick pad *noun*
a drug rehabiliation facility *US*
- I went to a kick pad over on the east side and asked them to sign me in. —Joseph Wambaugh, *The Blue Knight*, p. 30, 1973

kick pots *verb*
to work mess hall duty *US*
- —Linda Reinberg, *In the Field*, p. 121, 1991

kick rocks!
go away! *US*
- —Jim Goad, *Jim Goad's Glossary of Northwestern Prison Slang*, December 2001

kicks *noun*
shoes *US, 1897*
- I suddenly remembered that Railroad Cox wore nothing but tan knob-toed "kicks." —Iceberg Slim (Robert Beck), *Mama Black Widow*, p. 118, 1969
- Let's see now, them kicks you're wearing got to go for eighty dollars. —Edwin Torres, *Carlito's Way*, p. 54, 1975
- He was always pressed; nothing but the best / Vines and kicks he had. —Dennis Wepman et al., *The Life*, p. 97, 1976
- "Kicks," for shoes, goes nicely with nicks, or knickerbockers, to make your nicks and kicks. While this actually means your pants and shoes, it refers, more generally, to your clothing. —Chris Thain, *Cold as a Bay Street Banker's Heart*, p. 95, 1987

kicks race *noun*
a drag race with no prize, entered for the fun of competing and winning *US*

kick-start *verb*
to give a good start to something; to get something working well *AUSTRALIA*
- This is called The Prairie Oyster and has the added advantage of kick-starting your digestive juices into some kind of life as well. —Ignatius Jones, *The 1992 True Hip Manual*, p. 10, 1992

kick stick *noun*
a marijuana cigarette *US*
A combination of **KICK** (an intoxicating effect) and **STICK** (a cigarette).
- Joints are pulled out of the brims of hats and soon there's no noise except the music and the steady hiss of cats blasting away on kick-sticks. —Piri Thomas, *Down These Mean Streets*, p. 59, 1967
- —Eugene Landy, *The Underground Dictionary*, p. 115, 1971
- —Mike Haskins, *Drugs*, p. 288, 2003

kick up *verb*
1 to complain vigorously, to respond unfavourably and therefore cause problems or trouble *UK, 1789*
Usually in phrases such as 'kick up a row', 'kick up a fuss', 'kick up trouble', etc.
- They had been told they would not be allowed entry to the bar after the game, which left a bad taste, but still no one kicked up. —Jimmy Stockin, *On The Cobbles*, p. 167, 2000

2 (of a jockey) to urge a horse on to a burst of speed *AUSTRALIA*
- At the distance, jockey Tom Hales kicked Grand Flaneur up, and the champion colt put the issue beyond doubt in a few strides. —Maurice Cavanough and Meurig Davies, *Cup Day*, p. 54, 1960

kick upstairs *verb*
to promote to a higher-sounding but less-important position *UK, 1887*
- There will be a change of Defence Secretary, a few BBC executives will be kicked upstairs, and, if we are unlucky, the new, simpering, Hello!-style Today programme will be here to stay. —*The Observer*, 7th September 2003

kicky *adjective*
amusing, entertaining *US, 1942*
- —*American Weekly*, p. 2, 14th August 1955
- I've heard it's really getting to be a kicky bar. —John Rechy, *City of Night*, p. 183, 1963
- —Matt Bradley, *Queer St. U.S.A.*, p. 17, 1965
- —*Male Swinger Number 3*, p. 47, 1981: 'The complete gay dictionary'

kid *noun*
1 a child *UK, 1618*
- Has the father of your kid scarpered? —Mary Hooper, *(megan)2*, p. 48, 1999

2 used as a form of address, usually affectionate *UK*
- Mellors leaned over the table and said in a low voice, "Right, kid, shoot." —Derek Bickerton, *Payroll*, p. 25, 1959
- I don't want to talk about that if you don't mind, kid. It was a long time ago. —*Uncut*, p. 6, February 2002

3 the passive member of a male homosexual relationship, especially in prison *US, 1893*
- "This is my kid," Blocker would say. "Don't you bother this kid." —Chester Himes, *Cast the First Stone*, p. 169, 1952
- Paradoxically, after the seduction is complete and Sam takes his place as Bud's 'kid,' he may punch Bud in the eye every morning before breakfast. —*New York Mattachine Newsletter*, p. 5, August 1961
- A guy'll get him a kid and he'll go to all extremes to treat this cocksucker just as though he was a wife. —Bruce Jackson, *In the Life*, p. 359, 1972

4 a (young) follower of a stated music style *UK*
A UK rock band called the Heavy Metal Kids was formed in 1973.
- [R]ock kids, hip hop heads and ravers lost it to tunes like "I Feel Love". — *Mixmag*, p. 36, June 2003

▸ **our kid**
the eldest boy in the family *UK, 1984*
A colloquial term from the north of England.

kid *verb*
to fool, to pretend *UK, 1811*
- He was just kidding. Wasn't you governor? — Clive Exton, *No Fixed Abode [Six Granada Plays]*, p. 133, 1959
- "Don't be daft, if it is the bogeys [police] how can they touch us?" "With two hot motors round the back? Who are you kidding?" — Derek Bickerton, *Payroll*, p. 43, 1959

Kid Creole *noun*
unemployment benefit; the local offices from which unemployment benefit is managed *UK*
Rhyming slang for **THE DOLE**.
- [S]igning on the Kid Creole every fortnight. — J.J. Connolly, *Layer Cake*, p. 74, 2000

kidder *noun*
1 a teaser, a mocker *UK, 1888*
- Rupert Murdoch said the other day he hadn't made his mind up yet, but never kid a kidder. — *The Observer*, 11th March 2001

2 used as an affectionate form of address to a friend or child *UK*
An elaboration of **KID**.
- You can come again, kidder. — *Boys From the Blackstuff*, 1982
- Do one, kidder. — Kevin Sampson, *Outlaws*, p. 172, 2001

kiddie *noun*
the boss *UK*
A variation of **THE MAN**; 'kiddy' (late C18) is a mainly obsolete term for 'man', surviving here and as 'Kid' when applied to a boxer.
- Trevor is the top kiddie[.] — J.J. Connolly, *Layer Cake*, p. 123, 2000
- It was completely Ged's thing. He was the Kiddie. I owe him big time. — Kevin Simpson, *Outlaws*, p. 1, 2001

kiddie can; kiddie car *noun*
a school bus *US*
- — *Complete CB Slang Dictionary*, 1976
- — Peter Chippindale, *The British CB Book*, p. 156, 1981

kiddie fiddler *noun*
a paedophile *UK*
- The man who's going to die is a kiddie fiddler. — Danny King, *The Hitman Diaries*, p. 51, 2003
- He was not your typical tabloid kiddie-fiddler. He did not have bad skin or lank, greasy hair. — Mark Billingham, *Lazybones*, p. 91, 2003

kiddie stroll *noun*
a street in Vancouver where under-age prostitutes work *CANADA, 2002*
- Last July, a 15-year-old Vancouver girl was charged with forcing a 13-year-old into prostitution after meeting her at a group home. A few weeks later, the younger teen was walking Vancouver's notorious "kiddie stroll." — *Montreal Gazette*, p. A15, 15th April 2002: 'Some pimps too young to charge '

kiddiwink; kiddywink; kiddiewinkie *noun*
a child *UK, 1957*
An elaboration of **KID**; also recorded as 'kiddywinkle', 'kiddywinky' and 'kiddlywink'.
- Thank goodness we didn't have the kiddywinks and Nanny with us. — Rosamunde Pilcher, p. 286, 1995
- This is a kiddiewinkie-free zone, stranger, — *The Guardian*, 4th March 2000
- [A] diet of Eine Kleine Nachtmusik, plus a spot of drumming and a little (but just a little, now) nursery rap, will increase IQ and boost a kiddiwink's chances of getting into the right private school[.] — *The Times*, 2nd November 2004

kiddles *noun*
a young woman *US*
- I'm glad Paul's finishing his schoolwork for now, and I knew he'd get high marks – seeing as how he's married to a smart "kiddles." — Jack Kerouac, *Letter to Caroline and Paul Blake*, p. 105, 2nd March 1947

kiddo *noun*
1 used as a term of address, often affectionately *US, 1905*
- "Hi, kiddo," he said in a tired, cheerful voice. — Ross Russell, *The Sound*, p. 54, 1961
- Hey, what's up, kiddo? Daddy say's you're wearin' a sad face. — *Paper Moon*, 1973
- You'd better stick with me, kiddo. You're too young to be out on your own in this town. — Blanche d'Alpuget, *Turtle Beach*, p. 51, 1981
- Good work, kiddo. — Carl Hiaasen, *Tourist Season*, p. 326, 1986
- Take a run at 'er, kiddo. — *Natural Born Killers*, 1994

2 a youngster, a teenager *US, 1942*
An elaboration of **KID**.
- [A] group of kiddos coming clicking, cracking prattling by. — Colin MacInnes, *Absolute Beginners*, 1959

kiddology *noun*
deception *UK*
Pseudo-scientific, recorded in a BBC Radio 4 programme on class distinctions, 4th February 1980.

kiddy; kiddie *noun*
a small child *UK, 1858*
- Oh Gracie. Didn't you realise Ted would fight to keep the kiddies? Did you even think about it? — Jean Bedford, *Love Child*, p. 31, 1986
- And who d'you think'll mind your kiddie for you? — Mary Hooper, *(megan)2*, p. 49, 1999

kiddyana *noun*
antique toys *UK*
The conventional suffix '-ana' combined with **KIDDY** (a child).
- "Those things I call mere trinketry, not antiques." "You're going too fast." "And kiddyana. That's dealers' slang for toys, mechanised or otherwise, dolls – I always think them gruesome – tin ships, early cars, miniature fairground carousels, lead soldiers — Jonathan Gash, *The Ten Word Game*, p. 197, 2003

kiddy cop *noun*
a police officer assigned to juvenile crime *US*
- I just hated being a kiddy cop. — Joseph Wambaugh, *The Choirboys*, p. 186, 1975

kiddy kingdom *noun*
bliss *BARBADOS*
- — Frank A. Collymore, *Barbadian Dialect*, p. 64, 1965

kiddy porn *noun*
child pornography *US*
- Violence, magic, kiddy porn, rip-offs of the masters (Maxfield Parrish, Dali, and Rene Magritte), the gross out and the giggle – by the early '70s the boundaries were gone. — *Washington Post*, p. B1, 15t August 1977
- I mean real kiddy porn. The illegal kind. — Joseph Wambaugh, *The Glitter Dome*, p. 240, 1981
- But rumors still run wild: conspiracy buffs int at kiddy porn ring starring Williams as chief procurer for unnamd fat cats. — *Washington Post*, p. H1, 10th February 1985
- Hakuta, a father of three, says she wants marketers who do controversial things just to create a stir to draw the line at kiddy porn. — *St. Louis Post-Dispatch*, p. 8, 11th September 1995
- "Kiddy porn is like a drug to thhe perverts who prey on our kids," he says[.] — *Chicago Daily Herald*, p. 40, 17th October 2003

kid fruit *noun*
a male homosexual who achieves gratification from performing oral sex on young men or boys *US*
- Head-hunters, cannibals and kid-fruits are fellators[.] — Arthur V. Huffman, *New York Mattachine Newsletter*, p. 6, June 1961

kid gloves *noun*
▸ **with kid gloves**
delicately, gently, circumspectly, in such a manner so as to avoid upset *US, 1888*
- This report is a whitewash. It treats China with kid gloves[.] — *The Guardian*, 31st October 2003

kid in the khaki shirt *noun*
in horse racing, an imaginary jockey who wins races on horses not favoured to win *AUSTRALIA*
- — Ned Wallish, *The Truth Dictionary of Racing Slang*, p. 44, 1989

kidney *noun*
the brain; by extension, intelligence *TRINIDAD AND TOBAGO*
- — Lise Winer, *Dictionary of the English/Creole of Trinidad & Tobago*, 2003

kidney-buster *noun*
a truck, especially a military truck, that rides roughly *US, 1938*
- — *American Speech*, December 1948

kidney punch; kidney *noun*
a lunch *UK*
Rhyming slang.
- — Julian Franklyn, *A Dictionary of Rhyming Slang*, 1960

kidney-wiper; kidney-scraper *noun*
the penis *US, 1888*
A ribald celebration of a penis of heroic dimensions. A clue to the derivation of the word may rest in the tune to which 'The Tinker' is sung: 'Rosin the Beau', an English folk song (with a wonderfully punning title).
- — *More Rugby Songs*, 1968
- With his jolly great kidney-wiper / And his balls the size of three — Ed Cray, *'The Tinker (II)', 'Bawdy Ballads'*, p. 11, 1978
- — Richard Herring, *Talking Cock*, p. 30, 2003

kidology *noun*
a notional science of teasing or deceiving; a notional science of dealing with children *UK, 1964*
- My first law of kidology is that it is impossible to have an intelligent conversation with an adult human in the presence of its offspring. — Richard Neville writing of 1973 in 'The Living Daylights', *Out Of My Mind*, p. 42, 1996

kids *noun*
a group of homosexual men friends *US*
- — Bruce Rodgers, *The Queens' Vernacular*, p. 120, 1972

Kids *noun*
▸ **The Kids**
All My Children, a popular television daytime drama *US*
- — Connie Eble (Editor), *UNC-CH Campus Slang*, p. 5, Fall 1987

kid show *noun*
a circus or carnival side show *US*
- — Joe McKennon, *Circus Lingo*, p. 53, 1980

kid-simple *noun*
a male homosexual who is obsessively attracted to young men and boys *US*
- — Joseph E. Ragen and Charles Finston, *Inside the World's Toughest Prison*, p. 806, 1962: 'Penitentiary and underworld glossary'
- — *Maledicta*, p. 221, 1979: 'Kinks and queens: linguistic and cultural aspects of the terminology for gays'
- — *Male Swinger Number 3*, p. 47, 1981: 'The complete gay dictionary'

kidstake *noun*
a fake *UK*
Rhyming slang, from **KIDSTAKES** (a pretence).
- — Ray Puxley, *Cockney Rabbit*, 1992

kidstakes *noun*
childish behaviour, especially childish pretence or kidding around; joking *AUSTRALIA, 1912*
From 'kid' (to trick) and 'stakes' (games, competitive undertaking). This unusual sense for the word 'stakes' is also found in the obsolete Australian World War 1 slang term 'bluff-stakes' (a deceitful attempt to coerce someone by bluffing). (Downing, *Digger Dialects*, 1919)
- Reg was too fast off the mark and all his kidstakes during the afternoon had probably been caused by his jealousy of Peter South. — Gavin Casey, *Downhill is Easier*, p. 138, 1946

kid-stuff; kid's stuff; kids' stuff *noun*
any activity characteristic of, or suitable for, children; hence, something easy to do *US, 1929*
- [T]his is a clever balancing trick of words and visuals that gently encourages the reader to keep going. Makes reading seem like kids' stuff. — *The Guardian*, 4th October 2003

kief; kef; keef; kheef; kif; kiff *noun*
marijuana *ALGERIA*
A term found in Morocco and Algeria and imported in 1960s hippie slang.
- Alf's stiff upper lip quivers under the aroma of kif, and home he eventually comes, in a Moroccan djellaba and Indian sandals[.] — Richard Neville, *Play Power*, p. 208, 1970
- New Orleans fags in Mardi Gras drag ("You, Georgette, are absolutley stunning," they had cooed and teased each other), stoned out of their fucking skulls on bennies and kef. — Larry Heinemann, *Paco's Story*, p. 37, 1986
- — Angela Devlin, *Prison Patter*, p. 68, 1996
- Burroughs's Interzone is spaced-out on hashish as well: 'Fights start, stop people walk around, play cards, smoke Kief, all in a vast, timeless dream.' Yage was far more intense, but hashish took Burroughs to this same untimely multidimensional space. — Sadie Plant, *Writing On Drugs*, 1999
- — Mike Haskins, *Drugs*, p. 288, 2003

kielbasa *noun*
the penis *US, 1978*
From *kielbasa* (a red skinned Polish sausage).
- Believing I could do something for her career, she would be ready to please my kielbasa[.] — Howard Stern, *Miss America*, p. 153, 1995

kife *verb*
in circus and carnival usage, to swindle *US, 1931*
- — Don Wilmeth, *The Language of American Popular Entertainment*, p. 151, 1981

kiff *noun*
a marijuana cigarette *UK*
- — Mike Haskins, *Drugs*, p. 291, 2003

kiff-kiff *noun*
a modest, suppressed laugh *TRINIDAD AND TOBAGO*
- — Lise Winer, *Dictionary of the English/Creole of Trinidad & Tobago*, 2003

kike *noun*
a Jewish person *US, 1904*
Not much room for anything but hate with this word. Leo Rosten believes that the term originated at the Ellis Island immigration facility in New York harbour, where Jewish immigrants who could not write were instructed to make a circle, or *kikel* in Yiddish.
- It took just a whispered "kike" or "Jew bastard" from a member of some rival Polish or Irish gang, and fists were flying between us. — Mezz Mezzrow, *Really the Blues*, p. 6, 1946
- He wouldn't be rimmed no sir, not him, because he wasn't the kind of a chump who allowed himself to be chumped by a cheap kike auctioneer. — James T. Farrell, *Willie Collins*, p. 107, 1946
- Tell me, Dadier, what do you think of kikes and mockies and micks and donkeys and frogs and niggers, Dadier. — Evan Hunter, *The Blackboard Jungle*, p. 209, 1954
- [I]ts attitude toward homosexuals bears correspondence to the pain of the liberal or radical at hearing someone utter a word like "nigger" or "kike"[.] — Norman Mailer, *Advertisements for Myself*, p. 223, 1954
- "Son of a bitch kike!" Bubbles screams. "You got gissum all over the couch!" — Philip Roth, *Portnoy's Complaint*, p. 203, 1969
- The crazy kikes had their own ideas. — Mickey Spillane, *Last Cop Out*, p. 51, 1972
- "I've got that kike by the balls," said Lou [Reed], who is Jewish himself. — Lester Bangs, *Psychotic Reactions and Carburetor Dung*, p. 192, 1976
- BRIAN: I'm not a Roman, Mum, and I never will be! I'm a Kike! A Yid! A Hebe! A Hook-nose! I'm Kosher, Mum! I'm a Red Sea Pedestrian, and proud of it! — Monty Python, *Life of Brian*, 1979

kike; kike it *verb*
to walk *US*
- — *Maledicta*, p. 165, 1979: 'A glossary of ethnic slurs in american english'

kike killer *noun*
a club or bludgeon *US*
- — Ralph de Sola, *Crime Dictionary*, p. 79, 1982

kiki *noun*
a homosexual male *US, 1935*
A derisive, short-lived insider term; sometimes spelt 'kai-kai'.
- — G. Legman, *The Language of Homsexuality*, p. 1169, 1941
- Kai-Kai – As an adjective, anally-minded. — Anon., *The Gay Girl's Guide*, p. 11–12, 1949

kiki *adjective*
1 in a homosexual relationship, comfortable with playing both roles in sex *US, 1941*
- "In bed, the difference between femme and butch disappears," they will say. "There everybody is ki-ki." — Donald Webster Cory, *The Lesbian in America*, p. 107, 1964
- She says she is "ki-ki," a frequently heard expression denoting the ability to change roles from passive to aggressive and back again. — Ruth Allison, *Lesbianism*, p. 54, 1967

2 bisexual *US*
- — *American Speech*, p. 57, Spring-Summer 1970: 'Homosexual slang'

Kilburn priory; Kilburn *noun*
a diary, especially a police diary *UK, 1992*
Rhyming slang.
- — Angela Devlin, *Prison Patter*, p. 68, 1996

kill *noun*
1 in roller derby, an extended attack on the other team's jammer [a skater who is eligible to score] *US*
- — Keith Coppage, *Roller Derby to Rollerjam*, 1999

2 semen *US*

- —Ethan Hilderbrant, *Prison Slang*, p. 78, 1998

▸ **the kill**

the moment when a sale is confirmed *UK*

A hunting image with the salesperson as the hunter and the customer as prey; a variation of the sense 'to win'.

- If you were a top car salesman [...] and you didn't go in for the kill on every sale, then the other salesmen would see that and want to take over. —Dave Courtney, *Stop the Ride I Want to Get Off*, p. 8, 1999

kill *verb*

1 to cause someone to laugh uproariously *UK, 1856*

- Iraq's spin doctor – he kills me I'm rather hoping that if one Saddamite survives the war in Iraq, it will be Comical Saeed, the information minister. His has been an amazing act – Goebbels meets Groucho Marx. —*The Guardian*, 8th April 2003

2 to cause pain to someone *UK, 1800*

- I'm goin' back to the wagon, these shoes are killing me[.] —Peter Guralnick, *Last Train to Memphis*, p. 207, 1994

3 to excite, to please, to thrill *US, 1844*

- Joe "King" Oliver was killing them after hours at the Pekin with the same band that played with him at the Dreamland, the New Orleans Creole Jazz Band. —Mezz Mezzrow, *Really the Blues*, p. 46, 1946
- —*Look*, p. 49, 24 November 1959

4 to excel *US, 1900*

- Work is great. I kill at work. —*Fast Times at Ridgemont High*, 1982
- It was totally Pauly, I did like 20 minutes, killed. (Quoting Pauly Shore) —*Spin Magazine*, October 1999
- These London crowds take no prisoners. You have to kill it out there. And remember – if they boo you, that's good! —Julian Johnson, *Urban Survival*, p. 301, 2003

5 to cover with graffiti *US*

- —Jim Crotty, *How to Talk American*, p. 141, 1997

6 in the sport of clayshooting, to hit the target accurately *UK*

- The referee's decision alone as to whether the shooter has or has not "killed" his target. —Chris Cradock, *A Manual of Clayshooting*, p. 172, 1983

7 in handball, racquetball and squash, to hit the ball so low on the front wall that it cannot be returned *US*

- —Paul Haber, *Inside Handball*, p. 66, 1970: 'Glossary'
- —Steve Strandemo and Bill Bruns, *The Racquetball Book*, p. 206, 1977: 'Glossary'

8 in pool, to strike the cue ball such that it stops immediately upon hitting the object ball *US*

- The cue ball rolled too far; he still had a shot on the nine, but not as easy as what simply killing the cue ball would have given him. —Walter Tevis, *The Color of Money*, p. 143, 1984
- —Steve Rushin, *Pool Cool*, p. 18, 1990

9 in volleyball, to hit the ball downward with great force from the top of a jump *US*

- —Bonnie Robison, *Sports Illustrated Volleyball*, p. 94, 1972

10 in bar dice games, to declare that a formerly wild point is no longer wild *US*

- In Liars, if aces are called at the start of the hand they are no longer wild. —Gil Jacobs, *The World's Best Dice Games*, p. 197, 1976

11 to finish consuming something *US*

- Damn bitch, don't kill it. —*Kids*, 1995

▸ **kill big six**

to play dominoes *US*

- —Charles Shafer, *Folk Speech in Texas Prisons*, p. 208, 1990

▸ **kill brain cells**

to get drunk *US*

- —Connie Eble (Editor), *UNC-CH Campus Slang*, p. 3, November 1983

▸ **kill the clock**

in a game governed by time, to delay the game near the end when winning *US*

- —Howard Liss, *Basketball Talk for Beginners*, p. 32, 1970

▸ **kill the sin**

to relieve all the blame for something *BAHAMAS*

- —John A. Holm, *Dictionary of Bahamian English*, p. 118, 1982

▸ **would kill a brown dog**

to be lethal; (of food) dreadful, disgusting, inedible *AUSTRALIA, 1966*

- I had read all about the little nasties which can kill a brown dog with one touch and I was in no mood to have myself fitted for a pine box. —Rex Hunt, *Tall Tales – and True*, p. 13, 1994
- Mate, what about your breath? It'd kill a brown dog at ten paces. —Paul Vautin, *Turn It Up!*, p. 182, 1995

kill *adjective*

excellent *US*

- —Heidi Steffens, *'National Education Association Today*, April 1985: 'A Glossary for rents and other squids'
- This new store is so hot, like totally rad, like I got these kill Guess jeans with a split at the ankle, you know, the kind Courtney has. —Mary Corey and Victoria Westermark, *Fer Shurr! How to be a Valley Girl*, 1982
- —Jonathan Roberts, *How to California*, p. 169, 1984

Killarney carrot *noun*

a large marijuana cigarette *IRELAND*

A regional variation of the **CAMBERWELL CARROT**.

- He leans forward, proffering the Killarney Carrot. "So do you want to light this, or shall I?" —Pete McCarthy, *McCarthy's Bar*, p. 175, 2000

kill button *noun*

the switch button under a motorcyle hand grip that turns the engine off *US*

- —*American Speech*, p. 270, December 1962: 'The language of traffic policemen'
- —Ed Radlauer, *Motorcylopedia*, p. 35, 1973

Kill City *noun*

a 'branded' variety of heroin *UK*

- [N]ames that are designed to appeal to the target consumer group by drumming home the dangerous outlaw status of the product: Homicide, Poison, Kill City, Last Payday, Body Bag, Lethal Injection, Silver Bullet. —Robert Ashton, *This Is Heroin*, p. 55, 2002

killed end *noun*

in bowls, an end (a stage of play) that has to be replayed when the jack is driven out of bounds *UK*

- —David Bryant, *The Game of Bowls*, p. 38, 1990

kill 'em and count 'em

used as a creed by US troops in Vietnam, referring to the importance attached to body counts of enemy dead *US*

- Added to that "kill 'em and count 'em" policy was a special hype about going in for the kill at My Lai. —Myra MacPherson, *Long Time Passing*, p. 585, 1984

killer *noun*

1 an extraordinary example of something *UK, 1835*

- Also I would like to see this Fall's Texas-Rice game, which is always a killer (among us football characters). —Jack Kerouac, *Letter to William S. Burroughs*, p. 109, 14th July 1947

2 a marijuana cigarette *US, 1943*

- —Ernest Abel, *A Marijuana Dictionary*, p. 60, 1982
- —Mike Haskins, *Drugs*, p. 288, 2003

3 *paramethoxyamphetamine*, PMA *UK*

- —www.urban75.com/Drugs/pma.html, August 2004

4 an animal ready to be killed for meat *AUSTRALIA, 1897*

- If you fellas want meat, get a killer – there's some quiet cattle around the water trough. —Herb Wharton, *Cattle Camp*, p. 57, 1994

5 hair pomade *US*

- —Lou Shelly, *Hepcats Jive Talk Dictionary*, p. 13, 1945

killer *adjective*

1 very good *US, 1951*

- One thing that happened with Rockin' Jody was that he would have some just killer weed, and would stone me[.] —Stephen Gaskin, *Amazing Dope Tales*, p. 64, 1980
- I make killer omelets. —Joseph Wambaugh, *The Golden Orange*, p. 148, 1990
- You may even like it, it's a killer rush. —*Break Point*, 1991
- "He was a killer Malibu surfer," Duck said. "I mean, a fine athlete." —Francesca Lia Block, *Witch Baby*, p. 107, 1991
- Eventually, I want to be headlining my own tour, have the number one record on Billboard, have a killer video directed by some hip young guy who's not afraid to take a chance[.] —*Wayne's World 2*, 1993
- We're a killer band, man. —*Airheads*, 1994
- Back at his yard [home], he built up a killer spliff and enjoyed it. —Donald Gorgon, *Cop Killer*, p. 34, 1994
- It's so killer! —*Clueless*, 1995
- Okay, with this pad, the killer wheels? Looks like you really cleaned up your act. —*Something About Mary*, 1998
- You have killer legs. Killer. —*Cruel Intentions*, 1999

2 extremely difficult *US*

- I added a couple killer questions to the test. —*Diner*, 1982

Killer *nickname*

Jerry Lee Lewis, an early US rocker (b.1935) *US*

- —Arnold Shaw, *Dictionary of American Pop/Rock*, p. 203, 1982

killer B's *nickname*

on a sports team, a group of skilled, spirited second stringers *US*

- "I thought we'd be lucky to get a run, the way Maddux was pitching," Craig said. "Then the Killer B's took over." — *United Press International*, 11th June 1991

killer-diller *noun*

a remarkably attractive or successful thing; a wildly good time or thrill *US, 1938*

- — Jack Lait and Lee Mortimer, *New York Confidential*, p. 235, 1948: 'A glossary of Harlemisms'

killer green bud *noun*

a potent strain of marijuana *US, 1980s*

- — Anna Scotti and Paul Young, *Buzzwords*, p. 137, 1997
- — Mike Haskins, *Drugs*, p. 288, 2003

killer Kane *noun*

used as a generic name for a scouting and assassination specialist in the US armed forces *US*

- — Linda Reinberg, *In the Field*, p. 122, 1991

killer rim *noun*

a gold-plated or chrome-plated spoked car wheel *US, 1994*

- — *American Speech*, p. 92, Spring 1996: 'Among the new words'

killer stick *noun*

a marijuana cigarette *US*

- — Ernest Abel, *A Marijuana Dictionary*, p. 60, 1982

killer weed *noun*

1 marijuana *US, 1967*

- — Ernest Abel, *A Marijuana Dictionary*, p. 60, 1982
- — Mike Haskins, *Drugs*, p. 288, 2003

2 phencyclidine mixed with marijuana or another substance in a cigarette *US, 1978*

- They were in Snake Alley selling homemade killer weed, parsley flakes sprinkled with PCP, telling a gay couple in jogging suits and headbands how the dust would stretch their minds, their bodies, grow actual fucking wings on them, man. — Elmore Leonard, *Glitz*, p. 238, 1985

killer whiffer!

used for acknowledging an especially bad-smelling fart *US*

Hawaiian youth usage.

- — Douglas Simonson, *Pidgin to da Max Hana Hou*, 1982

kill fee *noun*

a fee paid when a creative project is cancelled *US*

- In fact, at twenty-seven everything I did was rejected and I lived on kill fees – one third of their usual three hundred or five hundred dollars[.] — Eve Babitz, *L.A. Woman*, p. 149, 1982

kill-fire *noun*

an aggregation of Claymore land mines *US*

- And we set up a kill-fire, a series of Claymores along a road in what's called a phase Claymore. — James Mills, *Words of the Vietnam War*, p. 302, 1986

kill game!

used as warning to end a conversation *US*

- In a prison setting, when a group of 415s are having a meeting and a correctional officer approaches, the one who first sees him will say, "Kill game." — Bill Valentine, *Gangs and Their Tattoos*, p. 19, 2000

killick *noun*

a leading hand *AUSTRALIA*

- 'It runs one each,' Splinter informed him morosely, 'and the killick of the mess cuts her up each meal.' — J.E. MacDonnell, *Don't Gimme the Ships*, p. 69, 1960

killing *noun*

a great financial success *US, 1888*

- "Nope, I made a killing, and it was strictly on the legit," Phil said emphasizing his words with a slicker gesture. — James T. Farrell, *Saturday Night*, p. 32, 1947
- On his visit to Hollywood, Fifie told me that Schylomo had made one big killing; he had robbed a big fur store in the company of some other thief who had promptly collapsed of a heart attack a day afterwards. — Clancy Sigal, *Going Away*, p. 355, 1961

killing *adjective*

extremely funny *UK, 1874*

From the notion encompassed in the phrase 'to die laughing'.

- We killed ourselves. — Ann Barr and Peter York, *The Official Sloane Ranger Handbook*, p. 158, 1982

killing box *noun*

a strategic situation in which it is relatively easy to kill a group of enemy soldiers *US*

- Anyhow, after that, Underhill surprised their point man out in the bushes, and we got the rest of 'em in a killiing box. — Peter Straub, *Koko*, p. 232, 1988

kill rag *noun*

a cloth used by a male to clean up after masturbating *US*

- From kill (semen). — Ethan Hilderbrant, *Prison Slang*, p. 78, 1998

kills *noun*

in the language surrounding the Grateful Dead, the very best concert tapes *US*

Always with 'the'.

- "They can have my car," he says, "but they can't have my kills." — David Shenk and Steve Silberman, *Skeleton Key*, p. 169, 1994

kill switch *noun*

in a racing car, a switch that deactivates the car's electric system, used in an emergency *US*

- — John Edwards, *Auto Dictionary*, p. 91, 1993

kill team; killer team *noun*

a small unit of highly trained scouts sent on a mission to kill enemy *US*

- Green was part of a "killer team" that searched out the enemy in a roaming, random manner. In intensely hostile areas, they were ordered to "get some." — Myra MacPherson, *Long Time Passing*, p. 593, 1984
- — Linda Reinberg, *In the Field*, p. 106, 1991

kill the change *verb*

keep the change *UK*

- [I] told my man he could kill the change. — Diran Adebayo, *My Once Upon A Time*, p. 16, 2000

kill-time joint *noun*

in circus and carnival usage, a cocktail lounge or bar *US*

- — Don Wilmeth, *The Language of American Popular Entertainment*, p. 151, 1981

kilo man *noun*

a drug dealer who deals at the wholesale level, buying and selling kilograms *US*

- All the kilo men and ounce men around town talked about real estate, about getting out, but Strike knew they were all full of shit. — Richard Price, *Clockers*, p. 57, 1992

kilos *noun*

unwanted body weight *AUSTRALIA, 1989*

- I'm here to dance off the kilos. — Christos Tsiolkas, *Loaded*, p. 56, 1995

kilter *noun*

marijuana; a marijuana cigarette *US, 1969*

- — Richard A. Spears, *The Slang and Jargon of Drugs and Drink*, p. 304, 1986
- — Mike Haskins, *Drugs*, p. 288, 2003

kiltie kiltie cauld bum

a childish chant directed at any male wearing a kilt *UK: SCOTLAND*

An elaboration of 'kilt', repeated, then 'cold' (spelt phonetically in a Glasgow accent) and **BUM** (the buttocks).

- — Michael Munro, *The Complete Patter*, 1996

Kimberley *adjective*

used derogatively or jocularly to denigrate by association something as better than it is *AUSTRALIA, 1945*

From Kimberly, Western Australia; in such uses as 'Kimberley mutton' (goat meat) and 'Kimberley oyster' (a meat fritter).

kimchi *noun*

trouble *US, 1979*

'Kimchi' is used as a euphemism for **SHIT**, with the comparison between excrement and the Korean dish made with salted and fermented cabbage not particularly favourable to the dish.

- "We're in deep kimsche," said Slim. — William H. LaBarge and Robert Lawrence Holt, *Sweetwater Gunslinger 201*, 1983
- Think our crews can hack it? We'll be in deep kimshi with Sundown if we lose another bird. — Richard Herman, *The Warbirds*, p. 220, 1989

'kin; 'king *adjective*

used as an intensifier *UK*

A shortening of **FUCKING**.

- Don't take the 'kin piss Mortimer[.] —J.J. Connolly, *Layer Cake*, p. 44, 2000

'kin' arse'oles

used as an exclamation of surprise, anger, amazement *UK*

Lazily or deliberately abbreviated from **FUCKING ARSEHOLES!**.

kind *noun*

marijuana, especially high quality marijuana *US*

As is the case with many drug slang terms, 'kind' is a bit amorphous, at times referring to a marijuana cigarette, at times to the smoker, at times to the drug itself.

- —Jim Emerson-Cobb, *Scratching the Dragon*, April 1997
- —Mike Haskins, *Drugs*, p. 288, 2003

kinda *adjective*

approximately, sort of *US*

A ubiquitously contracted 'kind of'.

- He's kinda big and he's awful strong. — *My Boyfriend's Back*, 1963
- As Donald Fagan [of Steely Dan] was heard to say, "It is kinda strange, isn't it?" —Jay Saporita, *Pourin' It All Out*, p. 101, 1980
- Well, it's kinda a waste for all of us to write our papers, don't you think? — *The Breakfast Club*, 1985
- I kinda know how you feel. —Karline Smith, *Letters to Andy Cole*, p. 136, 1998

kinda sorta *adjective*

almost *US*

- —Connie Eble (Editor), *UNC-CH Campus Slang*, p. 4, Fall 1995

kind bud *noun*

potent marijuana *UK, 1997*

A combination of **KIND** (marijuana) and **BUD** (marijuana) that suggests twice the normal potency.

- Which is higher in CBD (cannabidiol)? A) Kind Bud B) Imported hashish[.] —Brian Preston, *Pot Planet*, p. 245, 2002
- —Mike Haskins, *Drugs*, p. 288, 2003

kinder *noun*

1 high quality marijuana *US*

- His plan was to peddle one last batch of kinder (street slang for excellent marijuana, pronounced to rhyme with "tinder"), get out of the drug business for good, and be living the surf life in California by Independence Day. — *Denver Westword*, 24th January 2002

2 (especially in New South Wales) kindergarten; a kindergarten *AUSTRALIA, 1955*

- I'll come to the kinder. —Peter Corris, *Pokerface*, p. 154, 1985

3 a child in kindergarten *AUSTRALIA*

- And finish up with the nappies and the kinders and everything. —Lyn Richards, *Having Families*, p. 244, 1985

kindergarten *noun*

a reformatory for juvenile offenders *US*

- —Vincent J. Monteleone, *Criminal Slang*, p. 138, 1949
- —Hyman E. Goldin et al., *Dictionary of American Underworld Lingo*, p. 117, 1950

kinderwhore *noun*

a young woman whose dress suggests both youthful innocence and sexual abandon *US*

- Courtney Love and her late husband, Kurt Cobain, started the craze – the kinderwhore look as she calls it – when they frolicked together in little-girl dresses in the early '90s. — *People*, p. 53, 1st August 1994
- In Toyland and Hole's Courtney Love, who called her own slut-infant fashion combo "kinderwhore." —Steven Daly and Nalthaniel Wice, *alt.culture*, p. 15, 1995

Kindest Cut *noun*

a vasectomy *CANADA*

- The Kindest Cut: the operation that inductees say makes a "vast difference" to your sex life. — *Ottawa Citizen quoted in Montreal Gazette*, p. B10, 15th July 2002

Kindly Call Me God *noun*

a KCMG (Knight Commander of the Order of St Michael and St George) *UK, 1961*

A pun elaborated on the initials; used by civil servants demonstrating a jocular familiarity with the honour.

- BERNARD WOOLEY: "Of course in the service, CMG stands for Call Me God. And KCMG for Kindly Call Me God." Jim Hacker: "What does GCMG stand for?" BERNARD WOOLEY: "God Calls Me God." —Anthony Jay and Jonathan Lynn, *Yes Minister ('Doing the Honours')*, 2nd March 1981

kindy; kindie *noun*

kindergarten; a kindergarten *AUSTRALIA, 1969*

- —Louis S. Leland, *A Personal Kiwi-Yankee Dictionary*, p. 58, 1984
- —Paul Vautin, *Turn It Up!*, p. 79, 1995
- When he'd finished it looked like a kid's scribble from kindy. —Phillip Gwynne, *Deadly Unna?*, p. 101, 1998

kineahora!

God forbid! *US*

From the German (not one) and Hebrew (evil eye).

- "We should only live, kineahora, to see that day." —Leo Rosten, *The Joys of Yiddish*, p. 171, 1968

kinell!; 'kin' 'ell!; kinnel!

used as a register of shock or amazement *UK*

A contraction of **FUCKING HELL!**.

- CHRISSIE: When who started cryin'? SNOWY: Yosser. CHRISSIE: Kinell... —Alan Bleasdale, *Boys From the Blackstuff*, 1982
- 'Kin' 'ell... Fucksat for ya bastard? —Nick Barlay, *Curvy Lovebox*, p. 20, 1997
- "Kinell, Beano – Monty Python!" cried Keva. "Couldn't you come out with anything better than that?" —Kevin Sampson, *Powder*, p. 90, 1999
- "Jimmy Jones has got a villa there. Two I think." "Kinnel!" —Garry Bushell, *The Face*, p. 214, 2001

king *noun*

1 an aggressive, 'mannish' lesbian *US*

- — Florida Legislative Investigation Committee (Johns Committee), *Homosexuality and Citizenship in Florida*, 1964: 'Glossary of homosexual terms and deviate acts'
- —Dale Gordon, *The Dominion Sex Dictionary*, p. 97, 1967
- —Anon., *King Smut's Wet Dreams Interpreted*, 1978
- —*Maledicta*, p. 132, Summer/Winter 1982: 'Dyke diction: the language of lesbians'

2 a male leader of a group of Australian Aboriginals *AUSTRALIA, 1830*

- Old Culwaddy the 'king', squatting by the galley fire, looked up questioningly[.] —Ion L. Idriess, *Over the Range*, p. 56, 1947
- Willie is the 'king' of this crowd and staunch to me. —Ion L. Idriess, *Over the Range*, p. 211, 1947
- After I'd been at Tobermary six years, them old tribal kings gave me my wife, Janie. —Herb Wharton, *Cattle Camp*, p. 98, 1994

3 a skilled person (at a specified thing); an adept *AUSTRALIA, 1919*

- Llew Jones, small and nuggety, once a bookmaker's clerk, and now a two-up king. —Leonard Mann, *Flesh in Armour*, p. 37, 1932
- This fella was a bit of a raffle king, like myself. —Frank Hardy, *The Yarns of Billy Borker*, p. 129, 1965
- It was fatty Keenan, living up to his reputation as 'king of the cockatoos [lookouts]'. —Lance Peters, *The Dirty Half-Mile*, p. 46, 1979

4 in Keno, any single number that a player circles to bet on *US*

- —John Mechigian, *Encycopedia of Keno*, p. 111, 1972

5 an outstanding piece of graffiti art *US*

- —Jim Crotty, *How to Talk American*, p. 141, 1997

6 cocaine *UK*

- —Nick Constable, *This is Cocaine*, p. 181, 2002

king *adjective*

great; excellent *AUSTRALIA*

- [T]here were a few king birds there but they were holding hands with these fairies[.] —Martin Sharp, *Oz*, February 1964
- 'That's king,' Arnie grinned. —Wilda Moxham, *The Apprentice*, p. 87, 1969
- This one...is brutally clear in it's [sic] relation of a period in Gerard's life you could pretty much sum up as one king helluva booze binge[.] — *Sick Puppy*, p. 2, 1998

'king *adjective*

▷ see: 'KIN

king and queen; king *noun*

a bean, a baked bean *UK*

Rhyming slang, usually in the plural.

- [K]ings on holy ghost [toast]. —Ray Puxley, *Cockney Rabbit*, 1992

king brown *noun*

(especially in Western Australia) a 750 ml bottle of beer *AUSTRALIA*

Named after a large venomous Australian snake; such beer bottles are typically of brown glass.

- I grew up in WA and always knew them as king browns, I'd never heard them referred to as tallies until I moved to Sydney. — *Wordmap (www.abc.net.au/wordmap)*, 2003

king bud *noun*

marijuana *UK*

- —Mike Haskins, *Drugs*, p. 288, 2003

king crab *noun*
in hold 'em poker, a king and a three as the first two cards dealt to a particular player *US, 1981*
In the game of craps, a three is sometimes referred to as a 'crab'.
- —Thomas L. Clark, *The Dictionary of Gambling and Gaming*, p. 5, 1987

King Dick *noun*
a brick *UK*
Rhyming slang.
- —Julian Franklyn, *A Dictionary of Rhyming Slang*, 1961

King Dickie; King Dicky *noun*
a bricklayer *UK*
Rhyming slang for 'brickie.'
- —Julian Franklyn, *A Dictionary of Rhyming Slang*, 1961

kingdom-come *noun*
1 the after-life; a notional point in the far-distant future *UK, 1785*
- [T]hem durn critters keep grudges till kingdom come. Don't never forget one smack of the whip[.]—David Baldacci, *Wish You Well*, p. 72, 2001

2 the buttocks *UK*
Rhyming slang for **BUM** punning on 'kingdom come' (the after-life, hence heaven).
- Her scotches [legs], long and slender / Reached to her kingdom come[.]—Ronnie Barker, *Fletcher's Book of Rhyming Slang*, p. 21, 1979

King Farouk *noun*
a book *UK*
Rhyming slang, formed from the name of the Egyptian king, 1920–65.
- —Ray Puxley, *Fresh Rabbit*, 1998

kingfish *noun*
a powerful or political figure *US, 1926*
Predates but influenced by the adoption as a nickname for the governor of Louisiana, Huey P. Long (1893–1935).
- Warring is kingfish of Georgetown. He controls its local police precinct as well as its local crime—Jack Lait and Lee Mortimer, *Washington Confidential*, p. 10, 1951
- I'll do a dead-on Kingfish voice as O.J. [Simpson][.]—Howard Stern, *Miss America*, p. 138, 1995

king george *noun*
a gambler who tips generously *US, 1979*
- —Thomas L. Clark, *The Dictionary of Gambling and Gaming*, p. 114, 1987

king-hit *noun*
a powerful punch; a punch or blow that drops a person; the winning blow in a fight; now, a cowardly and unfair punch given to someone unawares or from behind *AUSTRALIA, 1917*
- He never shows his nose in here unless he's tight, and he always tries to get away with a king hit.—Vince Kelly, *The Bogeyman*, p. 176, 1956

king-hit *verb*
to deliver a powerful punch to someone, especially from behind or when they are unawares *AUSTRALIA, 1949*
- Cripes, I just about done me block that time I nearly king hit that greasy drongo!—Barry Humphries, *The Wonderful World of Barry McKenzie*, p. 39, 1968
- To give Commissar McKakie credit where it's due, he put up a fight in the cells, when the constable king-hit him from behind for openers.—Frank Hardy, *The Outcasts of Foolgarah*, p. 169, 1971

king-hit merchant *noun*
a person who king-hits others; a cowardly thug *AUSTRALIA, 1944*
- 'Do this galah over,' he whispered in my ear. 'He's a king-hit merchant.'—Lawson Glassop, *We Were the Rats*, p. 59, 1944
- You're a real king-hit merchant, aren't you Pearce? He didn't even see that coming.—Derek Maitland, *Breaking Out*, p. 34, 1979

King Hussan *noun*
a variety of hashish from Morocco *UK*
Named to honour the Moroccan King who gave official permission for the cultivation of a marijuana crop.
- —Nick Jones, *Spliffs*, p. 88, 2003

kingie *noun*
a kingfish *AUSTRALIA, 1936*
- Then she had another go and, lo and behold, a big kingie snaffled the lure.—Bob Staines, *Wot a Whopper*, p. 14, 1982

king james version *noun*
the most authorative and best in its class *SINGAPORE*
- —Paik Choo, *The Coxford Singlish Dictionary*, p. 59, 2002

King Kong *noun*
1 cheap and potent alcohol, usually illegally manufactured *US, 1940*
- On the second floor was a King Kong speakeasy, where you could get yourself five-cent and ten-cent shots of homebrewed corn[.]—Mezz Mezzrow, *Really the Blues*, p. 247, 1946
- There was Betty who had a double chin and blamed her homely red complexion on Monkey's King Kong.—John M. Murtagh and Sara Harris, *Cast the First Stone*, p. 15–16, 1957
- "Not even a little taste of King Kong," he whined.—Chester Himes, *The Real Cool Killers*, p. 29, 1959
- It was true that Pap Dan did wallow in King Kong until he fell out from the stuff.—Louise Meriwether, *Daddy Was a Number Runner*, p. 28, 1970

2 the penis *UK, 2001*
A pet name from the legendary (fictional) beast.

3 in motor racing, a Dodge or Plymouth with a cylinder head with hemispherical combustion chambers, built for stock car racing *US*
- —John Lawlor, *How to Talk Car*, p. 66, 1965

4 a powerful drug addiction *US, 1970*
- —Gilda and Melvin Berger, *Drug Abuse A-Z*, p. 81, 1990

King Kong pill *noun*
any barbiturate or central nervous system depressant *US*
- —Donald Wesson and David Smith, *Barbiturates*, p. 122, 1977

King Lear *noun*
the ear *UK, 1932*
Rhyming slang, formed from the name of a Shakespeare character.
- —Julian Franklyn, *A Dictionary of Rhyming Slang*, 1960
- —Ray Puxley, *Cockney Rabbit*, 1992

▸ **on the King Lear**
on the scrounge *UK*
Rhyming slang **KING LEAR** for 'the ear', extended into a variation of **ON THE EARHOLE**.
- —Ray Puxley, *Cockney Rabbit*, 1992

King Lear *adjective*
homosexual *UK*
Rhyming slang for **QUEER**.
- —Julian Franklyn, *A Dictionary of Rhyming Slang*, 1960

King Muhammed *noun*
a variety of hashish from Morocco *UK*
- —Nick Jones, *Spliffs*, p. 88, 2003

king of the hill *noun*
an important man in a limited circumstance *US*
From the adult cartoon series *King of the Hill*, 1997.
- I want to wake up in a city that doesn't sleep / And find I'm king of the hill, top of the heap—Fred Ebb, *New York, New York*, 1977
- [T]he main man, the cock of the walk, the king of this particular little hill[.]—James Hawes, *Dead Long Enough*, p. 105, 2000

king of the ring *noun*
a leading bookmaker *AUSTRALIA*
- Last of Australia's old-time 'kings of the ring' was Andy Kerr, of Sydney, known as the 'Coogee Bunyip', because of his habit of early-morning surfing there all year round.—James Holledge, *The Great Australian Gamble*, p. 88, 1966

king of the trough *noun*
in the Maritime Provinces, used as a nonsense reply to 'how are you?' *CANADA*
- —T. K. Pratt, *oral informants in Prince Edward Island Sayings*, p. 76, 1998

kingpin *noun*
an indispensable leader *US, 1867*
- I'm the boss around here and don't you forget it. I'm your kingpin. —Alexander Buzo, *Rooted*, p. 39, 1969
- So if Gregor had been the Kingpin of Filth in Chicago, or if he at least tried to be the Kingpin, I would have respected him.—Lawrence Block, *No Score [The Affairs of Chip Harrison Omnibus]*, p. 88, 1970
- No one enjoyed giving the tall Black kingpin information that was bad.—Donald Goines, *Inner City Hoodlum*, p. 39, 1975

- Sonny Roberts was the biggest dope kingpin in the Bronx and also parts of Harlem in which Doll Baby was not strong. —Robert Deane Pharr, *Giveadamn Brown*, p. 27, 1978
- [T]heir pal spoke highly of the kingpin's missus, and they knew she was kosher (honest). —Wayne Anthony, *Spanish Highs*, p. 178, 1999

king's elevator *noun*
monumental mistreatment *US, 1969*
A back-formation from 'the royal shaft'.
- —*Esquire*, p. 180, June 1983

king's habit *noun*
cocaine *UK*
Surely not a reference to the British royal family.
- —Richard A. Spears, *The Slang and Jargon of Drugs and Drink*, p. 279, 1986
- —Mike Haskins, *Drugs*, p. 280, 2003

kings head *noun*
a shed *UK*
Rhyming slang, formed ironically from the name of a pub.
- If you want me I'll be down the kings head. —Ray Puxley, *Cockney Rabbit*, 1992

kingshit nigger *noun*
a black person who is in charge of an enterprise or event *US*
- —*Maledicta*, p. 159, Summer/Winter 1978: 'How to hate thy neighbor: a guide to racist maledicta'

king snipe *noun*
a foreman of a railway track crew *US, 1916*
- —Norman Carlisle, *The Modern Wonder Book of Trains and Railroading*, p. 265, 1946

King Spliff *noun*
Bob Marley (Robert Nesta Marley, 1947–81), rastafarian, reggae singer *UK*
- That says something, don't it? Not just about how much his music was loved but also about a certain prison recreation: none of us could let pass quietly the death of King Spliff. —Dave Courtney, *Stop the Ride I Want to Get Off*, p. 73, 1999

king's ransom *noun*
an enormous amount of money; an exorbitant price *AUSTRALIA, 1936*
- —James Holledge, *The Great Australian Gamble*, p. 88, 1966

King Tut *noun*
a book that translates dreams into 'lucky' lottery numbers *BAHAMAS*
- —John A. Holm, *Dictionary of Bahamian English*, p. 118, 1982

'kin hell!
used for registering anger, amazement, despair, surprise, etc *UK*
- It's like, 'kin hell, get some control. —Shaun Ryder, *Shaun Ryder... in His Own Words*, 1993

kink *noun*
1 a criminal *US*
- —Joseph E. Ragen and Charles Finston, *Inside the World's Toughest Prison*, p. 806, 1962: 'Penitentiary and underworld glossary'
- "That kink didn't put you on any of those tables up there, did he?" Shane asked. —Stephen J. Cannell, *The Tin Collectors*, p. 325, 2001

2 a thief *US*
- —Hyman E. Goldin et al., *Dictionary of American Underworld Lingo*, p. 117, 1950

3 non-conventional sexuality, especially when fetishistic or sado-masochistic *UK, 1959*
- I was the United Kingdom's most fervent new convert to kink. —Claire Mansfield and John Mendelssohn, *Dominatrix*, p. 19, 2002

4 in a deck of playing cards, a king *US*
- —*American Speech*, p. 100, May 1951

kinker *noun*
a circus performer, especially an acrobat or contortionist *US, 1909*
Not praise.
- —Sherman Louis Sergel, *The Language of Show Biz*, p. 122, 1973
- —Joe McKennon, *Circus Lingo*, p. 53, 1980

kink pie *noun*
a pizza with sausage and mushroom toppings *US*
From the initials for the toppings: S & M. Limited usage, but clever.
- —*Maledicta*, p. 15, 1996: 'Domino's pizza jargon'

kinky *adjective*
1 used for describing any sexual activity that deviates from the speaker's sense of sexually 'normal'; also of any article, enhancement or manner of dress that may be used in such activity *US, 1942*
- She was dead kinky for sweetbreads. —*A Hard Day's Night*, 1964
- On wash day I have to keep a look out in case some kinky boy comes and steals some of my undies off the line. —Geoff Brown, *I Want What I Want*, p. 2, 1966
- [S]everal double-page features about sex-toys and "kinky love games". —Christopher Brookmyre, *Boiling a Frog*, p. 105, 2000
- Kinky boots: the girl will offer clients the chance to kiss, lick, stroke, caress her boots for the purposes of sexual gratification. —Caroline Archer, *Tart Cards*, 2003

2 eccentric, bizarre *US, 1847*
- I mean, don't be stupid. Don't be kinky. —Tony Parsons, *Limelight Blues*, 1983

3 illegal; dishonest *US, 1903*
In prison, used without a sense of perversion.
- —Inez Cardozo-Freeman, *The Joint*, p. 511, 1984

4 stolen *US*
- —Hyman E. Goldin et al., *Dictionary of American Underworld Lingo*, p. 117, 1950

kinky blaggard *noun*
a persuasive talker who gets the desired result *UK*
There seems to be an element of envy in 'a blagger who gets away with it'. Reported by Neill Bradshaw, 8th May 2001. Probably a variation on 'lucky bastard'.

kinnel!
▷ see: KINELL!

kinnikinik *noun*
tobacco of mixed leaves and bark and some real tobacco *CANADA*
- "Kinnikinik" comes from various Indian languages and means "that which is mixed together." —Chris Thain, *Cold as a Bay Street Banker's Heart*, p. 95, 1987

kip *noun*
1 sleep; a period of sleep *UK, 1893*
Following the sense as 'bed'.
- [H]e'd that moment got up from a feather bed after eight hours' solid kip[.] —Derek Raymond (Robin Cook), *The Crust on its Uppers*, p. 39, 1962
- Have a bit of a kip, now, Tom. —Thea Astley, *A Kindness Cup*, p. 50, 1974

2 a bed *US, 1859*
- No Hinky Dink, no Pendergast caters to him, gives him free beer and rot-gut or a kip in the flop on the joint. —Jack Lait and Lee Mortimer, *Washington Confidential*, p. 30, 1951

3 an undesirable place; a place that is dirty or disordered *IRELAND*
- It was a terrible kip, said Jimmy Sr. —Roddy Doyle, *The Van*, p. 274, 1991

4 a small, narrow bat of wood used to toss the coins in a game of two-up *AUSTRALIA, 1887*
Origin unknown. The *English Dialect Dictionary* records *kep* (to throw up into the air, to throw up a ball and catch it), which may be connected.
- The technique seemed to be to turn the wrist slightly but sharply just as the coins were leaving the 'kip'. —John O'Grady, *It's Your Shout, Mate!*, p. 25, 1972

▸ **on the kip**
asleep *US*
- —Hyman E. Goldin et al., *Dictionary of American Underworld Lingo*, p. 117, 1950

kip *verb*
to sleep *UK, 1889*
- It would have been more restful kipping on a pile of hardtack, unbuttered. —Mezz Mezzrow, *Really the Blues*, p. 34, 1946
- [A] friend in the second-hand car business who let him kip on his sofa, and lent him some clobber. —Charles Raven, *Underworld Nights*, p. 19, 1956

kip bag *noun*
a bedroll or sleeping bag *US*
- —Vincent J. Monteleone, *Criminal Slang*, p. 139, 1949

kip dough *noun*
money to be spent on lodging *US*
- On cold nights, 500 to 600 wrecks, who couldn't even summon a coin for a flop (called "kip dough") slept in the old station house on the floor. —Jack Lait and Lee Mortimer, *Chicago Confidential*, p. 59, 1950

kip down *verb*
to go to bed, to prepare for bed, to sleep *UK*
Mainly services; a variation of **KIP**.
- I'd kipped down – they had to wake me to tell me. — Graeme Kent, *The Queen's Corporal [Six Granada Plays]*, p. 93, 1959

kipe; kype *verb*
to steal *US, 1934*
- — *American Speech*, p. 62, Spring-Summer 1975: 'Razorback slang'
- [S]he had so many clothes that it was then that I learned what the word "kype" meant. It meant going to the Broadway and leaving without paying. — Eve Babitz, *Eve's Hollywood*, p. 47, 1984

kipper *noun*
1 someone with red hair *IRELAND*
- Who's the focking kipper? He goes, 'She happens to be part of an experiment I'm conducting,'...'My theory is, redheads who come from a whole family of redheads are invariably bet-down,' and we all go, 'Agreed.' — Paul Howard, *The Teenage Dirtbag Years*, p. 16, 2001

2 the vagina *UK*
- A cockney fellow-soldier, on reading of the birth of Siamese twins, 1954, exclaimed pityingly of the mother, "Poor cow! I bet that split 'er old kipper". — Beale, 1984

3 a Royal Navy sailor; hence, a English person *AUSTRALIA, 1943*
Derogatory; according to Michael Saclier of the Australian National University in 1973 '[I]t derives from the statistically proven similarity between the Englishman and his favourite breakfast food – both are spineless, two-faced and smell' (quoted in Bill Hornadge, *The Ugly Australian*, p. 96, 1975).
- Wasn't a bad bloke really, even though he was a kipper! — John Wynnum, *Tar Dust*, p. 58, 1962

4 a doss-house; a bed; anywhere to sleep *UK, 1984*
Used by down-and-outs.

▸ **do up like a kipper**
to ruin a person's chances *UK*
A variation of **KIPPER**.
- Arthur winced and his eyes darkened with disappointment and anger. He muttered to himself, "He's done me up like a kipper." — Anthony Masters, *Minder*, p. 102, 1984

kipper *verb*
to ruin a person's chances *UK, 1961*
- I listened to her and I trusted her. Fook me. 'Ad I been kippered or what? I felt sick with it[.] — Ben Elton, *High Society*, p. 263, 2002

kipper and bloater *noun*
1 a *motor* vehicle, a motor *UK*
Rhyming slang.
- — *The British Journal of Photography*, 1st June 1979

2 a photograph *UK*
Rhyming slang on a London pronunciation of 'photo'. Can be shortened to 'kipper'.
- Applies to all types of photograph from the holiday snap to "dirty kippers". — Ray Puxley, *Cockney Rabbit*, 1992

kipper and plaice; kipper *noun*
a face, especially one that is not particularly attractive *UK*
Rhyming slang.
- He's got a kipper like a piece of second hand chewing gum. — Ray Puxley, *Cockney Rabbit*, 1992

kipper feast *noun*
oral sex performed on a woman *UK*
From the tired comparison between the smell of fish and the smell of the vagina.
- — Tom Hibbert, *Rockspeak!*, p. 95, 1983
- — James McDonald, *A Dictionary of Obscenity, Taboo and Euphemism*, p. 34, 1988

kipper's knickers *noun*
the acme of perfection, the best *UK: SCOTLAND*
Always used with 'the'; this is a Glasgow variation on such constructions as **BEE'S KNEES** and **CAT'S PAJAMAS**.
- That yin thinks she's the kipper's knickers since Big Joe got aff wi her. — Michael Munro, *The Patter, Another Blast*, p. 40, 1988

kipps *noun*
a brakevan (caboose) *US*
- — Ramon Adams, *The Language of the Railroader*, p. 90, 1977

kippy *adjective*
(of a woman) attractive, well-dressed *CANADA*
- She's quite the lady, she's quite kippy. It means real dressy. — T. K. Pratt, *Dictionary of Prince Edward Island English*, p. 86, 1988

kipsy *noun*
a house or dwelling *AUSTRALIA, 1905*
From 'kip' (a doss house) and the diminutive suffix '-sy'.
- [W]ith many variegated roses, lilacs, ivies and grape-vines, we concealed from his unkindly eye the fact that our "kipsie", as Mia called it, was falling down. — Eve Langley, *The Pea-Pickers*, p. 2, 1958

kishkes *noun*
the intestines *US, 1902*
Yiddish, from the Russian.
- His kishkes, nothing but water since that terrible hour, started turning solid. — Robert Campbell, *Juice*, p. 163, 1988

kismet *noun*
fate, luck, predestination *US, 1849*
From Turkish, Farsi and/or Arabic.
- Kismet, my friend. Maybe you're lucky. — Mickey Spillane, *Return of the Hood*, p. 99, 1964
- It was like kismet, but not, if you see what I mean. — *Sleepless in Seattle*, 1993
- We didn't know jack shit about any riot. It just happened. It was kismet. — *Natural Born Killers*, 1994

kiss *noun*
1 in games such as pool and marbles, a shot that barely touches another *US*
- But his hell was my heaven / when I sighted the eleven / and sank it on a rail shot kiss. — Lightnin' Rod, *Hustlers Convention*, p. 70, 1973
- On the third rack the young man made the nine-ball but scratched on an unlucky kiss[.] — Walter Tevis, *The Color of Money*, p. 202, 1984

2 a student who curries favour with the teacher *US*
An amelioration of **KISS ASS**.
- What a "Z"! The astonishing private language of Bay Area teenagers — *San Francisco Examiner: People*, p. 8, 27th October 1963

kiss *verb*
1 in games such as pool and marbles, to cause one object to barely touch another *US*
- When Babe lagged, he kissed the closest toy, and Babe got first shot. — Bobby Seale, *A Lonely Rage*, p. 31, 1978

2 in pool, to try to make a shot by bouncing the object ball off another ball *US*
- — Steve Rushin, *Pool Cool*, p. 18, 1990

3 to perform oral sex *US, 1941*
- This euphemism has even been employed by medical and technical writers, who call oragenitalism the genital kiss, or, with even greater periphrastic timidity, the kiss of genital stimulation. — G. Legman, *The Language of Homsexuality*, p. 1170, 1941

▸ **kiss arse; kiss ass**
to behave subserviently *UK*
A figurative use of perhaps the most demeaning act that one human can demand another to perform. Mediaeval engravings show devil-worshippers pledging their utter subservience to Satan by lifting his goat-tail and kissing his backside; at that time both 'kiss' and 'arse' were conventionally available to describe such an activity.
- — Collin Baker et al., *College Undergraduate Slang Study Conducted at Brown University*, p. 148, 1968
- So Sensira did a couple of farting little one-off gigs with the Grams, kissed their arses and humped their gear. — Kevin Sampson, *Powder*, p. 7, 1999

▸ **kiss butt**
to behave subserviently *US*
A variation of **KISS ARSE**.

▸ **kiss goodbye**
to concede defeat; to accept an involuntary loss *US, 1906*
- It's my experience that once a mug's been taken by the corner game [a con trick] he's kissed his dough goodbye. — Charles Raven, *Underworld Nights*, p. 91, 1956

▸ **kiss Mary**
to smoke marijuana *US*
- — *Current Slang*, p. 32, Fall 1968

▸ **kiss the couch**
to die *AUSTRALIA*
- — Ned Wallish, *The Truth Dictionary of Racing Slang*, p. 44, 1989

▸ **kiss the eighth pole**
in horse racing, to finish far behind the leader *US*
- —Tom Ainslie, *Ainslie's Complete Guide to Thoroughbred Racing*, p. 334, 1976

▸ **kiss the fish**
to smoke hashish *US*
- —Eugene Landy, *The Underground Dictionary*, p. 116, 1971

▸ **kiss the porcelain**
to vomit *US*
- Joe Castillo tried it and kissed the porcelain at once. —Joseph Wambaugh, *Lines and Shadows*, p. 150, 1984

▸ **kiss the toe**
to drink a shot of Yukon Jack™ whisky in a single gulp, in a glass containing a pickled human toe *CANADA*
- A pair of premiers have kissed the toe. Manitoba's Doer and BC's Campbell became members of the Sourtoe Cocktail Club in Dawson City. The tradition began in 1973, when a Dawson resident found a rumrunners's frostbitten, mummified toe and made the drink. —*Toronto Globe and Mail*, p. A10, 7th June 2002

▸ **kiss your ass goodbye**
to concede defeat, to lose all hope of success or survival *US*
- But when the government has it in for you, you can kiss your ass goodbye. —Howard Stern, *Miss America*, p. 435, 1995

▸ **kiss your sister**
in poker, to come out even in a game *US*
- —John Vorhaus, *The Big Book of Poker Slang*, p. 25, 1996

▸ **kiss your teeth**
to make a scornful sound *JAMAICA*
- —Peter Patrick, *Some Recent Jamaican Creole Words*, 2003

KISS
simple enough to be easily understood, even by the slowest person *US*
Acronym for 'keep it simple, stupid!'.
- Which brings us full circle back to the basic Claiborne philosophy: KISS – Keep It Simple, Stupid. —*Washington Post*, p. D7, 10th October 1979
- Within thirty minutes we were back at the command post briefing the field supervisor and running the KISS assault plan past him. —William Dodson, *The Sharp End*, p. 197, 2001

kiss and cry *noun*
the part of Canadian figure skating championship rinks where contestants wait for their results *CANADA*
- Little blond-haired girls lining up outside the kiss and cry. —*National Post Online*, 28th January 2002

kiss and cuddle *noun*
a muddle *UK*
Rhyming slang that is never reduced to its first element.
- —Ray Puxley, *Cockney Rabbit*, 1992

kiss-and-ride *adjective*
pertaining to areas at transport interchanges designated for dropping off and picking up motor vehicle passengers without parking *AUSTRALIA, 1974*

kiss and tell *verb*
to reveal personal and confidential information, usually of a sexual nature *US, 1970*
- —*American Speech*, Spring 1989

kiss-ass; kiss-arse *noun*
a sycophant; one who curries favour in a self-demeaning fashion *US, 1973*
- Little kiss-ass with the big horn-rim glasses on to show how smart he is. —Elmore Leonard, *Swag*, p. 4, 1976
- [T]elling himself this was all for the better, that he somehow deserved this for betraying his own integrity and becoming a celebrity kiss-ass. —Richard Price, *Clockers*, p. 275, 1992
- BARBARA WALTERS IS SUCH A KISS-ASS. —Howard Stern, *Miss America*, p. 60, 1995
- I was polite, I played kiss-ass to a degree, I'd stand in the phone line for him; we're out gardening, I'd do the stoop work and let him rake. —Elmore Leonard, *Out of Sight*, p. 60, 1996
- These days she saw instead a careerist kiss-arse on the make and another "one of the boys" in the making.. —Christopher Brookmyre, *The Sacred Art of Stealing*, p. 104, 2002

kisser *noun*
1 the mouth *UK, 1860*
Originally boxing slang.
- "That what my aunt needs, a poke in the kisser," Dopey said. —James T. Farrell, *Saturday Night*, p. 34, 1947
- You may get a smack on the kisser, but if you don't you may be bounced out. —Jack Lait and Lee Mortimer, *New York Confidential*, p. 221, 1948
- There was a sketch of what he might have looked like before the bullet got him smack in the kisser. —Mickey Spillane, *One Lonely Night*, p. 27, 1951
- I could at least get the satisfaction of belting you on the kisser – too many glasses to take off. —Jack Kerouac, *Letter to Allen Ginsberg*, p. 363, 8th October 1952
- If you don't give it to him, he belts you one in the kisser. —William Burroughs, *Junkie*, p. 65, 1953
- [N]obody gets it but gets a Sicilian line down his middle – a German boot in the kisser[.] —Jack Kerouac, *The Subterraneans*, p. 71, 1958
- [A] real parachutist's smack right on the kisser; a great blue and black jaw she'd have[.] —Derek Raymond (Robin Cook), *The Crust on its Uppers*, p. 33, 1962
- Wham! Right in the kisser. —Oscar Zeta Acosta, *The Autobiography of a Brown Buffalo*, p. 149, 1972
- The smirk on his lips is a beauty. I remembered how my old man used to say, "Which one of us is going to wipe that jam off your kisser?" when I thought I was smarter than him. —Robert Campbell, *Junkyard Dog*, p. 15, 1986

2 the face *US, 1904*
- They paraded around in teddies or gingham baby rompers with big bows in the back, high-heel shoes, pretty silk ribbons twice as big as their heads, and rouge an inch thick all over their kissers. —Milton Mezzrow, *Really the Blues*, p. 22, 1946
- It wasn't that my kisser would stop clocks, understand, or anything like that. —Jim Thompson, *Savage Night*, p. 2, 1953
- He is a dark, middle-sized, middle-aged geezer with an ugly, oh but definitely ugly, kisser and a navy blue, chiv-scarred jowl. —Charles Raven, *Underworld Nights*, p. 9, 1956
- —Angela Devlin, *Prison Patter*, p. 68, 1996

3 a sycophant *US, 1951*
Shortened 'ass-kisser'.
- MR. HALL: Janet Huon, no tardies. CLASSMATES: Kisser! —*Clueless*, 1995

kissing Mrs *noun*
the act of rubbing the clitoris with the penis *UK*
A narrowed use of **THE MRS** (the vagina).
- —*Sky*, July 2001

kiss it!
used as contemptuous expression of dismissal *UK*
A shortening of **KISS MY ARSE!**.
- (ANTONY CROSSES WITH MUGS.) DENISE: Hey. (MEANING TEAS) Where's ours? ANTONY: (LEAVING ROOM) Kiss it. —Caroline Aherne and Craig Cash, *The Royle Family*, 1999

kiss kiss
goodbye *US*
- —Connie Eble (Editor), *UNC-CH Campus Slang*, p. 4, Fall 1991

kiss-me-arse *noun*
in British Columbia ocean waters, the marbled murrelet *CANADA*
- The "kiss-me-arse," or Marbled Murrelet, characteristically swims ahead of an approaching boat, then impudently flips its tail as it dives to safety. Occasionally called a sea chick. —Tom Parkin, *WetCoast Words*, p. 81–82, 1989

kiss-me-ass; kiss-me-tail *adjective*
inconsequential; petty *TRINIDAD AND TOBAGO, 1972*
- —Lise Winer, *Dictionary of the English/Creole of Trinidad & Tobago*, 2003

kiss me Hardy; kiss me *noun*
Bacardi™ (a branded white rum) *UK*
Rhyming slang, formed from Lord Nelson's legendary last words.
- —Ray Puxley, *Cockney Rabbit*, 1992

kiss me quick; kiss me *noun*
the penis; a fool *UK*
Rhyming slang for **PRICK**, reflecting, to some degree, the type of person who will wear a 'comical' novelty hat bearing the legend 'kiss me quick' when the opportunity arises.
- —Ray Puxley, *Cockney Rabbit*, 1992

kiss-me-quick; kiss-me-kwik *adjective*
describes a seaside resort given to cheap, dated commercialism *UK*
A kiss-me-quick hat is, in many ways, a cultural touchstone.
- You can buy the Titanic in a bottle for a knockdown £9 on Cleethorpes' prom, and some would call that symbolic of the fate awaiting Britain's kiss-me-kwik seaside towns. —*The Guardian*, 10th May 2003

kiss-me-quick hat *noun*

any novelty hat sold at a funfair or seaside resort, especially one bearing a slogan *UK, 1963*

The predominant legend writ large on such hats was 'kiss me quick'.

- I might go for the Kiss Me Quick novelty hat[.] — *Daily Telegraph*, 3rd October 2002
- [Y]ou could have Ribena, a kiss-me-quick hat and a ride on a real donkey[.] — Iain Aitch, *A Féte Worse Than Death*, p. 8, 2003

kiss my arse!; kiss my ass!

used as a contemptuous expression of dismissal *UK*

- A sop to your conscience as you walk on past / You sad motherfuckers can kiss my arse / I'm begging on the cold cold ground — Tom Robinson, *Cold Cold Ground*, 1996
- (DOORBELL GOES.) DENISE: That'll be Dave... get it, Ant. ANTONY: Kiss my arse. — Caroline Aherne and Craig Cash, *The Royle Family*, 1999

kiss my chuddies!

used as an expression of disdain or rejection *UK*

Formed on CHUDDIES (underpants), possibly coined and certainly popularised as a catchphrase by *Goodness Gracious Me*, a BBC comedy sketch programme scripted and performed by four British Asian comedians, first heard on Radio 4 in 1996 but better known from television, since 1999.

- "Kiss my chaddies [sic] (underpants)" was taken up by kids in playgrounds all over the country. They asked their Asian friends what the phrase meant and received their first Punjabi lesson. — *The Sunday Times*, p. 7, 18th May 2003

kiss my grits!

used for humorously expressing defiance *US*

A signature line of Polly Holiday's character Florence Jean 'Flo' Casteleberry on the television comedies *Alice* (CBS, 1976–85) and *Flo* (CBS, 1980–81). Repeated with referential humour.

kiss my tits!

used for showing disdain or rejection *US*

- [I]f you are not happy in life then you can kiss my tits[.] — Howard Stern, *Miss America*, p. ix, 1995

kiss of death *noun*

a generally innocent or well-meant action or contact that results (often predictably) in disastrous consequences *UK, 1948*

By association with the kiss by which Judas betrayed Jesus.

- Is sex the kiss of death for our TV? — *The Observer*, 25th August 2002

kiss-off *noun*

1 a complete rejection *US, 1926*

- Blue came home from Tanja's kiss-off. He looked drawn and tired. — Iceberg Slim (Robert Beck), *Trick Baby*, p. 189, 1969

2 any form of compensation paid to someone who has been dismissed or rejected *UK*

- I would have thought she might try to blackmail a big kiss-off out of me[.] — Danny King, *The Bank Robber Diaries*, p. 223, 2002

kiss off *verb*

to dismiss, to reject *US, 1904*

- [H]e hasn't got enough time in to retire and take the pension and get another job, but too much time in to retire and kiss off the pension. — George V. Higgins, *The Rat on Fire*, p. 41, 1981
- He'd finally kissed off Bobbie by telling her that for the sake of the children, he had to go back home. — Joseph Wambaugh, *Finnegan's Week*, p. 121, 1993

kiss up *verb*

to curry favour *US, 1965*

- — Collin Baker et al., *College Undergraduate Slang Study Conducted at Brown University*, p. 148, 1968

kissy *noun*

an effeminate male *US*

- — J. R. Friss, *A Dictionary of Teenage Slang (Mt. Diablo High)*, 1964

kissy *adjective*

in homosexual usage, exciting, worthy of enthusiasm (usually of an inanimate object) *US*

- — Anon., *The Gay Girl's Guide*, p. 12, 1949
- The new house is heaven – it 'as the kissiest closets. — Bruce Rodgers, *The Queens' Vernacular*, p. 121, 1949

kissy-face *noun*

prolonged kissing *US, 1958*

Introduces a childish tone.

- — *Time*, p. 57, 1st January 1965: 'Students: the slang bag'
- — *Current Slang*, p. 5, Winter 1966
- Billy hugged her and gave her kissy-face. — George V. Higgins, *The Rat on Fire*, p. 95, 1981
- Playing kissy face with him the way she was doing was a game for someone considerably younger. At her age either you did it or you didn't do it. — Robert Campbell, *Alice in La-La Land*, p. 248, 1987
- Tess's playing kissy face with a guy that wears sneakers a Shanghai longshoreman wouldn't be caught dead in. — Joseph Wambaugh, *The Golden Orange*, p. 222, 1990
- The boat was a single's nightmare, made worse by an overabundance of kissy-face honeymooner couples. — Anka Radakovich, *The Wild Girls Club*, p. 73, 1994

kit *noun*

1 clothes *UK*

Conventionally used for sports clothing.

- I bet you're even more of a doll without your kit on. — Kevin Sampson, *Outlaws*, p. 130, 2001

2 in prison, contraband goods *UK*

- — Angela Devlin, *Prison Patter*, p. 68, 1996

3 the equipment needed to prepare and inject heroin or another drug *US, 1959*

- A packet of smack and a kit! Innocent my ass! — Donald Goines, *Kenyatta's Last Hit*, p. 72, 1975
- — Angela Devlin, *Prison Patter*, p. 68, 1996

4 in prison, a letter *UK*

- — Angela Devlin, *Prison Patter*, p. 68, 1996

kit and caboodle *noun*

all of something *US, 1888*

- I think I've had it, kit and caboodle. — John Nichols, *The Sterile Cuckoo*, p. 177, 1965

Kit Carson *noun*

a former Viet Cong who has become a scout or translator for the US Army *US*

The allusion is to the scouting abilities of Kit Carson (1809–68), a legend of the US West.

- He would never be made into a Kit Carson, one of those former VC who had turned coats and chosen to work for the Americans in exchange for amnesty and money. — Barry Sadler, *Casca: The Phoenix*, p. 147, 1985

kitchema *noun*

a pub, a club or a bar *UK*

English gypsy use, from Romany *kitshima* (a tavern).

- — Patrick O'Shaughnessy, *Market Trader's Slang*, 1979
- — Jimmy Stockin, *On The Cobbles*, p. 11, 2000

kitchen *noun*

1 an illicit methamphetamine laboratory *US*

- — Geoffrey Froner, *Digging for Diamonds*, p. 40, 1989

2 in pool, the end of the table where the cue ball is placed at the start of the game *US*

Technically, it is the area between the head string and the head rail of the table.

- — Steve Rushin, *Pool Cool*, p. 18, 1990

3 the hairs on the back of the neck *US*

- I can close my eyes and see women (my Aunt and other ladies getting their hair done) squirming slightly as the hot combs probed the "kitchens." — Odie Hawkins, *Scars and Memories*, p. 12, 1987
- — Ethan Hilderbrant, *Prison Slang*, p. 78, 1998

4 in shuffleboard, the scoring area of the court *US*

- — Omero C. Catan, *Secrets of Shuffleboard Strategy*, p. 68, 1967: 'Glossary of terms'

5 a brakevan (caboose) *US*

- — Ramon Adams, *The Language of the Railroader*, p. 90, 1977

6 the cab of a railway engine *US*

- — Norman Carlisle, *The Modern Wonder Book of Trains and Railroading*, p. 265, 1946

▸ **down in the kitchen**

in trucking, in the truck's lowest gear *US*

- — Montie Tak, *Truck Talk*, p. 50, 1971

kitchen bait *noun*

in shuffleboard, a shot made to entice the opponent to try to go after the disc *US*

- — Omero C. Catan, *Secrets of Shuffleboard Strategy*, p. 64, 1967: 'Glossary of terms'

kitchen door *noun*
the fly on a pair of trousers *TRINIDAD AND TOBAGO*
• —Lise Winer, *Dictionary of the English/Creole of Trinidad & Tobago*, 2003

kitchen lab *noun*
a laboratory where illegal drugs are manufactured, whether or not it is located in a kitchen *US*
• —William D. Alsever, *Glossary for the Establishment and Other Uptight People*, p. 21, December 1970

kitchen rackets *noun*
in Cape Breton, a *ceilidh* or house dance *CANADA*
• Kitchen rackets, his mother had called them, house dances and ceilidhs, Cape Bretoners loved them. "Be honest," he said, "Where'd you find a racket like this in Boston?"—D. R. MacDonald, *Cape Breton Road*, p. 208, 2000

kitchen range *noun*
1 a change (of scene or costume) *UK*
Theatrical rhyming slang.
• —Julian Franklyn, *A Dictionary of Rhyming Slang*, 1960
2 change (small coins) *UK*
Sometimes abbreviated to 'kitchen'.
• —Ray Puxley, *Cockney Rabbit*, 1992

kitchen sink *noun*
a stink *UK*
Rhyming slang, also used as a verb.
• —Ray Puxley, *Cockney Rabbit*, 1992

kitchen sink *adjective*
of a piece of dramatic fiction, grittily realistic in a domestic setting *UK, 1960*
• Kitchen sink drama as literary couple vie for prize.—*The Guardian*, 14th November 2002

kitchy-koo *noun*
▷ see: **COOTCHY-COO**

kite *noun*
1 a letter, note or message *US, 1859*
Largely prison usage.
• And then a simple-minded convict had to write another simple-minded bastard to tell him to keep his mouth shut and Tommy Tucker, to whom he had given the kite to be delivered, and to take it to the director[.]—Chester Himes, *Cast the First Stone*, p. 181, 1952
• They were sending kites out to contact their pushers. – a kite is an illegal letter generally smuggled out by a guard.—Willard Motley, *Let No Man Write My Epitaph*, p. 188, 1958
• One phenomenon not mentioned, which appears peculiar to correctional institutions, are the "kites" or love letters written by one inmate to another.—*New York Mattachine Newsletter*, p. 5, August 1961
• Well, I sent here a kite by my cellmate / the boy who just finished his hitch and was free.—Bruce Jackson, *Get Your Ass in the Water and Swim Like Me*, p. 116, 1964
• I decide maybe it'd have been better if I'd dropped the whole business after the first kite.—Clarence Cooper Jr, *The Farm*, p. 43, 1967
• Maybe I could fly one a couple of my magnetized coping kites (high voltage letters) when I hit the bricks and steal a 'ho!—Iceberg Slim (Robert Beck), *Airtight Willie and Me*, p. 3, 1979
• He caught Harold at the tank gate. "Here. Fly this kite to Kitty."—Seth Morgan, *Homeboy*, p. 89, 1990
2 a cheque, especially a blank or worthless cheque; a stolen credit card or cards *UK, 1805*
• [F]lying dodgy kites with each other at bent spielers[.]—Derek Raymond (Robin Cook), *The Crust on its Uppers*, 1962
• —Angela Devlin, *Prison Patter*, p. 68, 1996
• [A] new batch of Visas was coming in. Pure kite it were – clean as a whistle, not signed or nothing yet, obviously.—Kevin Sampson, *Outlaws*, p. 23, 2001
3 a criminal who deals in cheque and credit card fraud *US*
Variation of **KITER**.
• [N]o one who's totally legit. There's kites, dippers, dealers, spivs, all kinds.—Kevin Sampson, *Outlaws*, p. 161, 2001
4 a hand-rolled tobacco cigarette *US*
• —Judi Sanders, *Kickin' like Chicken with the Couch Commander*, p. 14, 1992
5 a fool *AUSTRALIA*
• But the big, stupid kite!—Robert S. Close, *With Hooves of Brass*, p. 112, 1961
6 a Christian *NEW ZEALAND, 1997*
Prison usage.
• —Harry Orsman, *A Dictionary of Modern New Zealand Slang*, p. 75, 1999
7 the face *US*
• Kite on the twat, by the way. Big long moody gob on him.—Kevin Sampson, *Outlaws*, p. 11, 2001
• [B]ig friggin grin on her kite.—Niall Griffiths, *Kelly + Victor*, p. 163, 2002
8 an ounce of drugs *US*
• "The Wolf was around today. He was holding a kite." "A ounce!"—Willard Motley, *Let No Man Write My Epitaph*, p. 117, 1958
• —Eugene Landy, *The Underground Dictionary*, p. 116, 1971
9 a bus *UK*
• To the bus conductor your ticket is a "brief" and his vehicle is a "tub", "kite" or "barrow".—*Evening News*, 27th April 1954
10 any type of aircraft *UK, 1917*
Modern use has a mainly ironic tone.
11 a glider used in hang-gliding; a hang-glider *AUSTRALIA*
• —James Lambert, *The Macquarie Book of Slang*, 1996
12 a newspaper *AUSTRALIA, 1919*
• You can pass me up the kite if you like.—Jim McNeil, *The Old Familiar Juice*, p. 6, 1973
• —Ned Wallish, *The Truth Dictionary of Racing Slang*, p. 44, 1989

▸ **fly a kite; lay a kite**
to fraudulently issue or pass a worthless cheque *IRELAND, 1805*
Based on **KITE** (a cheque); probably criminal in intent but possibly issued in hope.
• —Angela Devlin, *Prison Patter*, p. 52, 1996

kite *verb*
1 to obtain money or credit from a cheque that is drawn against uncollected funds in a bank account *US, 1839*
• He kited the receipted bills and took the difference from the register.—John D. McDonald, *The Neon Jungle*, p. 40, 1953
• Hicky Demarra and Butcher-boy Messino bragged about how they kited their betting slips, raising the wagers by a factor of ten, and getting paid off the larger beg...—Robert Campbell, *Juice*, p. 156–157, 1988
• I think you do it all, Roman – girls, protection, fraud, you kite checks, steal cars and you shoot people. I leave anything out?—Elmore Leonard, *Be Cool*, p. 186, 1999
2 to send a note or letter *US, 1924*
• I'll kite you a postcard.—Ross Russell, *The Sound*, p. 95, 1961

kite blue *noun*
a worthless cheque *AUSTRALIA*
An elaboration of **KITE**.
• The poor bastard needs an earn to handle those kite blues[.]—*The Sydney Bulletin*, 26th April 1975

kite-flying *noun*
passing worthless cheques *UK*
• He began with a brief lecture on the graft of kite-flying – i.e., forging and uttering cheques.—Charles Raven, *Underworld Nights*, p. 80, 1956

kite-man *noun*
a criminal specialising in cheques and bills of exchange; an issuer of worthless cheques *UK*
• —Paul Tempest, *Lag's Lexicon*, p. 116, 1950

kiter *noun*
a criminal who issues worthless and fraudulent cheques *UK, 1970*
• —Angela Devlin, *Prison Patter*, p. 68, 1996
• [S]tolen property waiting to be fenced, and kiters waiting for the January sales.—Duncan MacLaughlin, *The Filth*, p. 108, 2002

kiting-book *noun*
a cheque book *UK*
• [O]uts his kiting book and scribbles a straight one.—Derek Raymond (Robin Cook), *The Crust on its Uppers*, p. 21, 1962

kit kat *noun*
1 a fool *UK*
Rhyming slang for **PRATT** formed from a popular branded chocolate confectionary bar.
• Shouldn't be allowed you kit kat? It should be compulsory.—Ray Puxley, *Fresh Rabbit*, 1998
2 the recreational drug ketamine *AUSTRALIA*
• Dr. Refsauge, warned that Ketamine – known by various street names such as Special K, Vitamin K, K, Ket and Kit Kat – was primarily for veterinary use and was potentially fatal if taken with other drugs, such as alcohol.—*The Weekend Australian*, 24th February 1996
• Street names: K, Speical K, Kit-Kat.—*Tampa (Florida) Tribune*, p. 1, 13th August 1997

kitsch *noun*
in any of the arts, a work considered to be inferior or pretentious or in dubious taste *UK, 1926*
From German *kitschen* (to throw together, especially if hastily).

- [I]f the sight of Wales welcoming the brave new world to the sound of "Green, Green Grass [of Home]" didn't make you laugh, your kitsch bullshit detector had to be well out of order. —John Williams, *Cardiff Dead*, p. 56, 2000
- [A] rich sleazy kitsch-fest[.] —Naomi Klein, *No Logo*, p. 79, 2001

kitschy *adjective*

vulgarly sentimental *US, 1967*

- Don't take all that cutesy kitschy fuckin' retro-Sixties bullshit out in my apartment. —Kenneth Lonergan, *This is Our Youth*, p. 32, 2000

kitten *noun*

a young girl *US, 1923*

- — *Mr.*, p. 55, April 1966: 'The hippie's lexicon'

kittens *noun*

▸ **have kittens**

to become overly excited *US, 1900*

- It's a good idea, mate, but the Wingco'd have kittens if we didn't stick to the briefing. —W.R. Bennett, *Night Intruder*, p. 61, 1962
- —Alexander Buzo, *The Roy Murphy Show*, p. 130, 1970

kittle *noun*

the collection of empty beer containers that accumulate on a table during a drinking session *AUSTRALIA*

- After an hour we had an impressive kittle on the table. — *Wordmap (www.abc.net.au/wordmap)*, 2003

kitty *noun*

1 a pool of money *US, 1887*
Originally a poker term.

- —Oswald Jacoby, *Oswald Jacoby on Poker*, p. 142, 1947
- Barger went off to get a beer kitty going. —Hunter S. Thompson, *Hell's Angels*, p. 140, 1966
- Walberto was mad at me because he ain't had a chance to chip into my comin'-home kitty. —Edwin Torres, *After Hours*, p. 209, 1979
- At first I reckoned the lack of food in the fridge was 'cause some cheapskate scabs were not putting into the kitty. —Kathy Lette, *Girls' Night Out*, p. 41, 1987
- By sunrise a lot of the players would have blown off all of the night's street profits, some even losing their re-up kitty too. —Richard Price, *Clockers*, p. 171, 1992

2 the vagina *US*
A diminutive of **PUSSY**.

- When it comes to mowing our lickable lawns, the hairstyle you choose for your kitty can be an expression of your personal taste. — *The Village Voice*, 8th–14th November 2000

3 a woman *US, 1936*

- But many a kitty has gone for me even when I didn't have big bread behind me. —Edwin Torres, *Carlito's Way*, p. 19, 1975

4 a guy, a young man *US, 1952*
An extension of **CAT**.

- "Hey, I don't know that kitty at all," Chico said. —Hal Ellson, *The Golden Spike*, p. 39, 1952

5 a jail or prison *US*

- —Hyman E. Goldin et al., *Dictionary of American Underworld Lingo*, p. 117, 1950

6 a Cadillac car *US*

- —Clarence Major, *Dictionary of Afro-American Slang*, p. 73, 1970

kitty litter *noun*

any mixture of sand and salt or other compounds sprinkled on a snowy road or an oil spill on a road *US*

- — Elementary Electronics, *Dictionary of CB Lingo*, p. 80, 1976

kiwi *noun*

a person who shirks work *US*

- —Linda Reinberg, *In the Field*, p. 123, 1991

Kiwi *noun*

a New Zealander; of New Zealand *NEW ZEALAND, 1918*
Named for the national bird of New Zealand. The kiwi is a flightless bird native to New Zealand.

- Well, there were these two Wellington wharfies, great mates, one a Kiwi and the other a Maori. —Frank Hardy, *The Yarns of Billy Borker*, p. 113, 1965
- She was a Kiwi and one of the best flatmates I ever had at Kippax. —John Birmingham, *He Died With a Felafel in his Hand*, p. 189, 1994
- By now all hell has begun to break loose as the Kiwis suspect their man has been got to. —Bernard Dempsey and Kevin McNally, *Lock, Stock ... & Two Hundred Smoking Kalashnikovs*, p. 107, 2000
- [A] mixed group of mainly British, Aussie and Kiwi pissheads. —John King, *Human Punk*, p. 164, 2000

Kiwi *adjective*

of or relating to New Zealand or New Zealanders *AUSTRALIA, 1935*

- A Kiwi hydrographer will be along, too, and five matelots will be selected. —John Wynnum, *Jiggin' in the Riggin'*, p. 14, 1965
- —Roy Higgins and Tom Prior, *The Jockey Who Laughed*, p. 19, 1982
- We explained our position to the Kiwi CO. —Martin Cameron, *A Look at the Bright Side*, 1988
- [A] mixed group of mainly British, Aussie and Kiwi pissheads. —John King, *Human Punk*, p. 164, 2000

Kiwi Ferns *nickname*

the New Zealand women's international Rugby League team *NEW ZEALAND, 1998*
From the logo of New Zealand Rugby League: a pictogram of a kiwi and a fern.

- Kiwi Ferns squad selected to defend title. — *New Zealand Rugby League official website*, 2003

Kiwi green *noun*

a variety of marijuana grown in New Zealand *NEW ZEALAND*

- Cannabis Sativia is better known to us by its Spanish-Mexican name, Marijuana. Or pot, grass, weed, dope, gear, Kiwi green. —R. Rose, *New Zealand Green*, p. 5, 1976

Kiwi steak *noun*

mutton *US*

- — *American Speech*, p. 55, February 1947: 'Pacific war language'

KJ *noun*

1 high quality marijuana *US*
From 'kind joint'.

- —Jim Emerson-Cobb, *Scratching the Dragon*, April 1997

2 a marijuana cigarette enhanced by phencylidine *US*

- Dalaison later said the male pit bull was named "K.J.," which is street slang for "Krystal Joint," a marijuana cigarette laced with PCPC, an illegal tranquilizer. — *San Francisco Chronicle*, p. A13, 6th February 2001

3 phencyclidine, the recreational drug known as PCP or angel dust *US, 1972*

- —US Department of Justice, *Street Terms*, October 1994

klahowya(h)

used as a greeting *CANADA*
A word from the Chinook jargon.

- Klahowya! My tribe with wisdom of forefathers, has observed lack of unity in native land. — *Maclean's*, p. 47/1, 25th July 1964

K land *noun*

the catatonic intoxication experienced when taking the recreational drug ketamine *US*

- It reportedly resurfaced as "Special K" last year at Manhattan "rave parties," taking users to mental territory called "K Land" and the "K hole." — *The Record [Bergen County, New Jersey]*, p. A1, 5th December 1995

klap *verb*

to slap, to smack *SOUTH AFRICA, 1960*
From Afrikaans *klop*.

- [H]is doctor wife said she was leaving him to marry another man.So he "klapped" her. When she returned the slap and bit his finger, he "lost it". — *Sunday Times (South Africa)*, 10th August 2003

klatawa *noun*

a journey *CANADA*

- To "go klatawa" is to go visiting at some special place – perhaps one of the rancheries – and they [Chilcotin] like to travel straight through, not even stopping for camp unless forced to. —R. D. Symons, *Many Trails*, p. 75, 1963

klebbies *noun*

small denominations in any foreign currency *UK*
Royal Navy slang has **ICKIE** as the generic unit of foreign money, which then subdivides into one hundred 'klebbies'.

kleenex *noun*

1 a youthful, sexually inexperienced male who is temporarily the object of an older homosexual's desire *US*

- — *Maledicta*, p. 157, Summer/Winter 1986 – 1987: 'Sexual slang: prostitutes, pedophiles, flagellators, transvestites, and necrophiles'

2 MDMA, the recreational drug best known as ecstasy *US*

- —US Department of Justice, *Street Terms*, October 1994

klep; klepper *noun*
a kleptomaniac; a thief *UK, 1889*
- —Angela Devlin, *Prison Patter*, p. 68, 1996

klepto *noun*
a kleptomaniac *US, 1953*
- "Christ, you really are a klepto, ain't you?" says Billy.—Darryl Ponicsan, *The Last Detail*, p. 108, 1970

klim *noun*
any powdered milk *TRINIDAD AND TOBAGO*
From the branded product manufactured by Borden.
- —Lise Winer, *Dictionary of the English/Creole of Trinidad & Tobago*, 2003

klingon *noun*
a crack cocaine addict *US*
A play on 'cling on', describing an addict's behaviour; based on the Klingons, creatures from outer space in television science fiction series *Star Trek*, since 1969, which leads punningly to the further, no doubt merely fortuitous, suggestion that crack addicts are **SPACED OUT**.
- —Mike Haskins, *Drugs*, p. 292, 2003

Klondike *noun*
1 a prison cell used for solitary confinement *US*
An allusion to Klondike, Alaska, the epitome of remote.
- —Ralph de Sola, *Crime Dictionary*, p. 79, 1982
- —William K. Bentley and James M. Corbett, *Prison Slang*, p. 11, 1992

2 brass or copper, often stolen, sold for scrap *US*
- —Joe McKennon, *Circus Lingo*, p. 53, 1980

klooch; klootch *noun*
a wife, an Indian woman *CANADA*
The term comes from Chinook jargon for 'female/wife'.
- The good breakfast of fried mowitch and bannock was being cooked by Henry's klootch.—R. D. Symons, *Many Trails*, p. 83, 1963

klotsick *adjective*
(among Nova Scotians of German descent) said of a cake that has fallen, failed to rise, or rose and then fell *CANADA*
- Lunenburg County "klotsick," said of a fallen cake, comes from German "klotzig," "heavy, soggy."—Murray Emeneau, *Canadian English*, p. 34–39, 1975

kluge; kludge *noun*
in computing, a makeshift solution to a hardware or software problem *US, 1962*
- —Guy L. Steele, *Coevolution Quarterly*, p. 31, Spring 1981: 'Computer Slang'
- —Guy L. Steele et al., *The Hacker's Dictionary*, p. 86, 1983

klutz; clutz *noun*
a clumsy, awkward person *US, 1956*
Yiddish, from German.
- —*Current Slang*, p. 2, Summer 1966
- —Collin Baker et al., *College Undergraduate Slang Study Conducted at Brown University*, p. 148, 1968
- Sergio was always charging some foreign clutz 10,000 lire ($16) for two liters of gas.—Emmett Grogan, *Ringolevio*, p. 141, 1972
- You klutz! You stupid, bird-brained, flat-headed-—Monty Python, *Life of Brian*, 1979
- I'm lagging behind;, and she says to me, get this – "Hurry up, klutz."—*Jerry Maguire*, 1996

klutzy; clutzy *adjective*
clumsy, awkward *US, 1965*
- He's a klutzy scientist, she helps him get less klutzy[.]—Nicholson Baker, *Vox*, p. 67, 1992
- [S]he can hear good enough to do that klutzy ballet routine.—Howard Stern, *Miss America*, p. xi, 1995

KMAG *noun*
during the Korean war, the US advisors assigned to Republic of Korea troops – the Korean Military Advisory Group *US*
The Korean troops performed so poorly early in the war that the initials took on a new meaning – *K*iss *M*y *A*ss *G*oodbye.

knacked *adjective*
exhausted *UK*
Used by teenagers too exhausted to manage every syllable of **KNACKERED** (exhausted).
Reported by Joanna Williamson, 1982.

knacker *noun*
an unfit or useless individual, especially if overweight *UK*
Royal Navy slang: any food with a high calorie count may be called 'fat knacker pie'.
- —Nigel Foster, *The Making of a Royal Marine Commando*, 1987

knacker *verb*
1 to ruin; to kill *UK, 1887*
From the conventional sense (to slaughter a horse).
- "I'll knacker him for life," Jock shouted.—Troy Kennedy Martin, *Z Cars*, p. 37, 1962
- Or was there something really going on in those strange moments before JO came back and knackered it?—Christopher Brookmyre, *Not the End of the World*, p. 189, 1998

2 to steal *IRELAND*
- We know who ye are. But we knew that they didn't and that some young fella in Rathbawn who had a name for knackering Opels would be getting a wake-up call in a few hours.—Eamonn Sweeney, *Waiting for the Healer*, p. 145, 1997

knacker drinking *noun*
drinking alcohol outside *IRELAND*
- Anyway, said Kenny, knacker drinkin's better than drinkin' in a pub. Especially if you've a free house. That's not knacker drinkin'! said Anto.—Roddy Doyle, *The Van*, p. 23, 1991

knackered *adjective*
tired, worn-out, exhausted *UK, 1949*
Derives from the obsolete 'knacker' (a worn-out horse).
- —Tom Hibbert, *Rockspeak!*, p. 95, 1983
- I cry when I'm knackered.—Shaun Ryder, *Shaun Ryder... in His Own Words*, 1991
- We suddenly realised how knackered we were[.]—Ben Malbon, *Cool Places*, p. 278, 1998
- She was knackered and, stretching her legs out, could easily sit here for the next ten years.—John King, *White Trash*, p. 92, 2001
- How are you, baby? [...] Yeah, not bad. A bit knackered. I'm sure I'll get used to it.—Mark Powell, *Snap*, p. 112, 2001

knacker out; knacker *verb*
to tire out *UK, 1946*
- It's that charlie [cocaine] keeping me up all night. It's knackered me out.—John King, *Human Punk*, p. 254, 2000

knackers *noun*
1 the testicles *UK, 1866*
From an earlier sense (castanets).
- I turned again, and – yeeeoooowww! – a spade handle leapt up at me as I stepped on the end of it, and gave me a resounding whack in the crutch, right in the knackers, de-balling me.—*Alvin Purple*, p. 25, 1974
- L is for LEACHES that hid in the mud. Attach themselves to my knackers and suck out the blood.—Martin Cameron, *A Look at the Bright Side*, 1988
- Please stop bowing, you keep nutting me in the knackers.—Dave Courtney, *Dodgy Dave's Little Black Book*, p. 136, 2001
- This is high-octane funky meets tribal house that grabs you by the knackers and twists 'em.—*Mixmag*, p. 5, April 2003

2 nonsense *UK, 1984*
Identical in use to all senses of **BALLS** or **BOLLOCKS**.

▸ **off your knackers**
drunk or drug-intoxicated *UK, 2001*
- [G]etting up to no good in the pursuit of getting off their knackers on drugs.—*Ministry*, p. 39, January 2002

knackers!
used for registering anger, frustration, dismissal, etc *UK, 1984*
Identical in use to **BALLS!** or **BOLLOCKS!**.

knead *verb*
▸ **knead the noodle**
(of a male) to masturbate *US*
- "The boy and is masturbating" [...] Kneading the noodle[.]—Erica Orloff and JoAnn Baker, *Dirty Little Secrets*, p. 89, 2001

knee-bangers *noun*
long shorts *US*
- —Trevor Cralle, *The Surfin'ary*, p. 65, 1991

kneecap *verb*
to break someone's kneecap or shoot them in the kneecap, almost always as a planned act of retribution *US, 1974*
- All he had to worry about was that nobody should take the notion to kneecap him and leave him for dead.—Robert Campbell, *Alice in La-La Land*, p. 195, 1987

- Jeff Gillooly would have to kneecap half the field to get Tonya into medal contention. — *Washington Post*, p. D1, 24th February 1994
- He's supposed to have a filthy temper. I don't know how many people he's kneecapped — Chris Ryan, *Stand By, Stand By*, p. 103, 1996

kneehigh to a grasshopper *adjective*
very young *US, 1914*
Many variations on this theme have been recorded since 'knee-high to a toad' in 1814, and continue to be coined: '[T]his ass-mother [...] was shakin' shook in Brooklyn when you was knee high to a culpepper coolshank!' (Patrick McCabe, *Emerald Germs of Ireland*, 2003).
- It had always made me feel better to come here, back from the time I was kneehigh to a grasshopper. — Jim Thompson, *The Killer Inside*, p. 27, 1952
- Been knocking around since I was knee-high to a grasshopper. — Sean Glenn, *The Observer*, 18th November 2001

kneel *verb*
▸ **kneel at the altar**
1 to engage in anal sex *US*
- — Joseph E. Ragen and Charles Finston, *Inside the World's Toughest Prison*, p. 806, 1962: 'Penitentiary and underworld glossary'

2 to kneel while performing oral sex on a man *US*
- — *The Guild Dictionary of Homosexual Terms*, p. 26, 1965

kneelo *noun*
a surfer who rides kneeling *AUSTRALIA*
- — Nat Young, *Surfing Fundamentals*, p. 127, 1985
- — Trevor Cralle, *The Surfin'ary*, p. 65, 1991

knee machine *noun*
a short surfboard, a kneeboard or bellyboard *US*
- — Gary Fairmont R. Filosa II, *The Surfer's Almanac*, p. 189, 1977

kneesies *noun*
knee-to-knee contact, usually out of sight such as under a restaurant table *US*
- Mary started playing kneesy under the table. — Mickey Spillane, *I, The Jury*, p. 123, 1947
- [S]o I let him play kneesie under the table, because frankly I didn't find him at all banal; but then one night he took us to a blue movie, and what do you suppose? — Truman Capote, *Breakfast at Tiffany's*, p. 61, 1958
- Kneesies – The touching of the knees together beneath a table while maintaining an attitude of propriety on the outside. — *The Guild Dictionary of Homosexual Terms*, p. 26, 1965
- A lot of the customers like to play kneesies with the hustlers. Maybe it's love foreplay for them. — Johnny Shearer, *The Male Hustler*, p. 78, 1966
- It is a good place for hand-holding, kneesies, and what have you. — Bernhardt J. Hurwood, *The Sensuous New York*, p. 36, 1973

knee-slapper *noun*
a small, white-water wave *US*
- — Trevor Cralle, *The Surfin'ary*, p. 65, 1991

knees-up *noun*
an energetic dance party, a lively gathering *UK, 1963*
From the song 'Knees up Mother Brown!' by Weston and Lee, 1939.
- — Louis S. Leland, *A Personal Kiwi-Yankee Dictionary*, p. 58, 1984
- Revellers from an all night knees-up stayed on their first floor balcony — John Milne, *Alive and Kicking*, p. 195, 1998
- Our end of season knees-up will be in Birmingham[.] — *The New Untouchables*, September – November 2001

knee-tremble *verb*
performing sexual intercourse while standing *AUSTRALIA*
- [C]leaning the bath can be finished knee-trembling against the wall; and arguments can be consummated in some beautiful 69-ing in the marriage bed. — Bettina Arndt, *The Australian Way of Sex*, p. 65, 1985

knee-trembler *noun*
1 sex while standing *AUSTRALIA, 1896*
- She called me a 'knee trembler'; God knows why women get their slang mixed up. She meant a 'no-hoper.' — Sutton Woodfield, *A for Artemis*, p. 144, 1960
- They disappeared round the corner and Bob gave her a knee-trembler and ten minutes later they were back talking as if they'd never been anywhere. — Bluey *Bush Contractors*, p. 153, 1975
- — *Maledicta*, p. 99, 1986 – 1987: 'The poetry of porking'
- — James McDonald, *A Dictionary of Obscenity, Taboo and Euphemism*, p. 79, 1988
- [N]ever aska one-legged man for a knee-trembler. — John Milne, *Alive and Kicking*, p. 56, 1998
- [T]ry to impress her with some tired old patter in the hope of a knee-trembler in one of the shop doorways[.] — Jake Arnott, *He Kills Coppers*, p. 63, 2001

2 a sexually attractive woman *UK*
- [T]he little Asian bird on the till was a touch of a knee trembler so I just finished chatting her and getting nowhere[.] — Jeremy Cameron, *Brown Bread in Wengen*, p. 48, 1999

knicker-nicker *noun*
a stealer of clothes (especially underwear) from a clothesline *UK, 1984*
- — Jean Ure, *The Phantom Knicker Nicker*, 1993

knickers *noun*
▸ **keep your knickers on!**
stay calm!, don't get excited!; don't lose your temper! *UK*
- Yeh yeh, keep-a fuckin knickers on. Doan worry. — Niall Griffiths, *Grits*, p. 20, 2000

knickers!
used as an expression of dismissal, contempt or annoyance *UK, 1971*
A children's 'naughty' word, now in adult hands.
- A (usually) not unfriendly rebuff. For example: "Jim, lend me a quid"; reply. "Knickers!". — David Powis, *The Signs of Crime*, 1977
- Knickers to the DfES [Department for Education and Skills]. — *The Guardian*, 28th May 2002

knickers in a twist; knickers in a knot *noun*
an agitated or flustered condition; a state of panic *AUSTRALIA*
A figurative sense of an uncomfortable condition.
- Don't get your knickers in a twist. It's just a game. — Nicholas Hasluck, *Quarantine*, p. 127, 1978
- If they did not think that retail shops that opened on Saturday afternoons or Sundays would attract a lot of customers, they would not be getting their knickers in a knot as they are. — *Bulletin*, p. 142, 22nd November 1983
- Don't get your knickers in a knot now. — Royce Hall, *The Devil's Portal*, p. 175, 1984
- Don't getcha knickers ina twist over him, honey. — Kevin Sampson, *Powder*, p. 4, 1999
- Her hair was out of kilter and her knickers were in a twist. — Stuart Jeffries, *Mrs Slocombe's Pussy*, p. 107, 2000

knick-knack *noun*
1 a trinket; a small trivial article pleasing for ornament *UK, 1682*
- I've got all these antique knick-knacks. — *As Good As It Gets*, 1997

2 a small penis *US*
- — *Male Swinger Number 3*, p. 47, 1981: 'The complete gay dictionary'

knife and fork *noun*
1 a meal, especially in a restaurant *UK*
- You fancy a knife and fork tomorrow? I'm taking Lesley out to one of them Yankee-style restautants where the steaks come by the square yard. — Garry Bushell, *The Face*, p. 179, 2001

2 pork *UK*
Rhyming slang.
- — Ray Puxley, *Cockney Rabbit*, 1992

3 the money that a betting pool player leaves in reserve for living expenses *US*
- — Steve Rushin, *Pool Cool*, p. 18, 1990

▸ **do you need a knife and fork?; do you want a knife and fork?**
a catchphrase jibe directed at a driver struggling to find the right gear *UK, 1975*
- — Partridge and Beale, *A Dictionary of Catch Phrases*, 1985

knife and gun club *noun*
a hospital casualty department *US*
- — Sally Williams, *"Strong" Words*, p. 154, 1994

knife-happy *adjective*
(used of a surgeon) over-eager to treat with surgery *US*
- — *American Speech*, p. 145 – 148, May 1961: 'The spoken language of medicine; argot, slang, cant'

Knifepoint *nickname*
HM Prison Highpoint in Suffolk *UK*
- [H]e was serving a four-and-a-half year sentence in Highpoint, which the cons jokingly call Knifepoint. — Jimmy Stockin, *On The Cobbles*, p. 134, 2000

knight *noun*
in homosexual usage, a person with syphilis *US*
- — *Male Swinger Number 3*, p. 47, 1981: 'The complete gay dictionary'

knight of the asphalt *noun*
a long-distance trucker *US*
- — Bill Davis, *Jawjacking*, p. 58, 1977

knit *noun*
a shirt or sweater *US*
- — David Claerbaut, *Black Jargon in White America*, p. 70, 1972

knit *verb*
▸ **like knitting fog**
impossible *UK*
- [E]xactly how many city gents ever serve time? [...] Make no mistake: catching them is like knitting fog. Can't be done. — Jonathan Gash, *The Ten Word Game*, p. 101, 2003

knitting circle *noun*
in homosexual usage, a group of men who are too engaged in conversation to seek sex *US*
- — *Male Swinger Number 3*, p. 47, 1981: 'The complete gay dictionary'

knitting needle *noun*
in oil drilling, a tool used to splice wire cable *US*
- — Jerry Robertson, *Oil Slanguage*, p. 75, 1954

knitting needles *noun*
a rapid movement of blades and series of clicks produced when two fencers are practising *UK*
From the similarity in sound and action to that of knitting needles, not the earlier, obsolete 'knitting needle' (a sword).
- — E.D. Morton, *Martini A-Z of Fencing*, 1988

knives *noun*
▸ **at it like knives**
very sexually active *UK*
- [C]onvent girls are at like knives. — Henry Sloane, *Sloane's Inside Guide to Sex & Drugs & Rock 'n' Roll*, p. 81, 1985

knob *noun*
1 the head *UK, 1673*
- If he isn't a murderer he's liable to be one if you don't use your knob and tell me where I can find the room. — Mickey Spillane, *I, The Jury*, p. 101, 1947

2 the penis *UK, 1660*
- That cheesyprick pays overtime about as often as my old lady does my knob, and that bitch ain't gave me some knobbin' since she told me she wants a firm commitment. — Joseph Wambaugh, *Finnegan's Week*, p. 258, 1993
- Everyone's off their heads and wanting to shag on the beach but little grains of sand ain't really knob friendly, know what I mean? — Dave Courtney, *Raving Lunacy*, p. 158, 2000
- I didn't know they [homosexuals] stuck their knobs up each other. — John King, *Human Punk*, p. 84, 2000

3 a fool; an obnoxious, despised person *UK*
- You cheeky fuckin' knob. — Paul Fraser and Shane Meadows, *TwentyFourSeven*, p. 44, 1997
- See them knobs hauling beak [cocaine] round the city? — Kevin Sampson, *Outlaws*, p. 18, 2001
- Then, like some strange sort of Sting-inspired synchronicity, the billions who saw Phallus unanimously thought, Oh my God, who's that knob? — Gretel Killeen, *Hot Buns and Ophelia get shipwrecked*, p. 85, 2001
- He was good-looking if you like that kind of thing but he was a total knob. — Colin Butts, *Is Harry Still on the Boat?*, p. 77–78, 2003

4 the knee *US*
- — Clarence Major, *Dictionary of Afro-American Slang*, p. 74, 1970

5 a sexually transmitted infection *UK*
- — Leslie Thomas, *The Virgin Soldiers*, 1966

▸ **polish a knob**
to perform oral sex on a man *US, 1947*
- When you finish with them come on back around to me, and I'll let you polish this knob until it spits. — Donald Goines, *Dopefiend*, p. 111, 1971

knob *verb*
to have sex with someone *UK, 1988*
Derives from **KNOB** (the penis) but usage is not gender-specific.
- You should get Mario to knob her[.] — Colin Butts, *Is Harry on the Boat?*, p. 140, 1997
- [W]e'd love to knob every single one of them, except the pigs[.] — John King, *Human Punk*, p. 30, 2000
- What, you're still knobbing old Alison? — Colin Butts, *Is Harry Still on the Boat?*, p. 183, 2003

knobber *noun*
1 oral sex performed on a male *US*
- — Pamela Munro, *U.C.L.A. Slang*, p. 54, 1989

2 a fool, used as a general term of contempt *US, 1990*
An elaboration of **KNOB**.
- Maybe it was the knobbers like me left behind[.] — Andy McNab, *Immediate Action*, p. 107, 1995

knobbing *adjective*
used as an intensifier *UK*
Substitutes for **FUCKING**.
- Dey openin' frickin' mezze shops all over the knobbin' place. — Bernard Dempsey and Kevin McNally, *Lock, Stock ... & Two Hundred Smoking Kalashnikovs*, p. 117–118, 2000

knobbly knee *noun*
a key *UK*
Rhyming slang.
- Asking if anyone has seen your "knobbly knees" usually prompts a rude reply. — Ray Puxley, *Cockney Rabbit*, 1992

knobby *noun*
a motorcyle tyre with large treads, used for riding on dirt and trails *US*
- — Ed Radlauer, *Motorcylopedia*, p. 35, 1973

knob-cheese *noun*
smegma collected under the foreskin *UK*
A variation of **COCK CHEESE**.
- — *Roger's Profanisaurus*, 1997
- I'm not fussed about herpes / Just don't come near me with knob-cheese. — Susan Nickson, *Two Pints of Lager and a Packet of Crisps*, 12th April 2004

knob-end *noun*
a despised person *UK*
- Fuckin knob-end he was, aye. Knew fuck all, mun. — Niall Griffiths, *Sheepshagger*, p. 239, 2001
- Well, he's a knobend anyway. An arsehole. — Niall Griffiths, *Kelly + Victor*, p. 60, 2002

knob gag *noun*
a joke about a penis *UK*
- [W]ould we still be finding the penis funny as grown-ups? Is it the prudes' disapproval of the knob gag that actually perpetuates it? — Richard Herring, *Talking Cock*, p. 81, 2003

knob-gobbling *noun*
oral sex on a man *US*
- — *Maledicta*, p. 198, Winter 1980: 'A new erotic vocabulary'

knobhead; nobhead *noun*
a despised person; a fool *US, 1926*
From **KNOB** (the penis).
- Get off, you fucking knobheads[.] — Martin King and Martin Knight, *The Naughty Nineties*, p. 29, 1999
- What was he in for, nobhead? — Caroline Aherne and Craig Cash, *The Royle Family*, 1999
- "What a nob 'ead," he said. "He's never out of the fuckin' office." — *The Guardian*, 26th October 2000: 'A life inside'
- It was far easier for the boys in blue to nick the odd knobhead for possessing a gram of Chas a few miles down the road. — Garry Bushell, *The Face*, p. 34, 2001
- [T]here was something on the desk from Oxfam and coz I'm a knobhead I said, "What's that?" — Chris Martin, *Glastonbury 2002*, 28th June 2002

knob job *noun*
oral sex performed on a man *US, 1968*
- Woody took off with Carmen. 'Tongolele.' Knob-job. — Edwin Torres, *After Hours*, p. 214, 1979
- Joe dropping his pants in the car for a quick knob job during my "smoke break" at the restaurant. — R.J. March, *Hard*, p. 220, 2002

knob-jockey *noun*
a homosexual male; a promiscuous heterosexual female *UK*
A rider of the **KNOB** (the penis).
- — Chris Donald, *Roger's Profanisaurus*, p. 47, 1998
- — Chris Lewis, *The Dictionary of Playground Slang*, p. 132, 2003

knob off *verb*

go away *UK*

- Knob off Danny. — Niall Griffiths, *Sheepshagger*, p. 9, 2001
- Quockie tells him not to be soft an to knob off which, muttering, he, fatly, does. — Niall Griffiths, *Kelly + Victor*, p. 104, 2002

knobs *noun*

the female breasts, especially the nipples *US*

- — Collin Baker et al., *College Undergraduate Slang Study Conducted at Brown University*, p. 148, 1968

▸ **with knobs on**

with interest, intensified, with embellishments *UK, 1930*

- Caleb gives him wild violence of the eye. A look reciprocated with knobs on. — Jack Allen, *When the Whistle Blows*, p. 93, 2000

knob throb *noun*

(of a male) an intense desire for sex *UK*

- [W]hen he has a knob throb for her and she has a clitwobble for him. — Ray Puxley, *Fresh Rabbit*, p. 79, 1998

knock *noun*

1 a setback, especially a monetary loss *UK, 1889*

- I had to get my knocks, plenty of them, before I could understand that. — Mezz Mezzrow, *Really the Blues*, p. 324, 1946

2 a bite (that moment when a fish takes the bait) *UK*

Used by anglers. Noted by Albert Petch, 1969.

3 a promiscuous woman *AUSTRALIA*

- To tell your best mate that one of his family was a knock was unethical and uncalled for. — William Dick, *A Bunch of Ratbags*, p. 158, 1965

▸ **do a knock**

1 to partake in an amorous outing; to go on a date *AUSTRALIA, 1934*

- Belting a bloke don't prove she's against doing a knock with him. — Norman Lindsay, *Halfway to Anywhere*, p. 162, 1947

2 to have sex *AUSTRALIA, 1933*

From 'knock' (an act of sexual intercourse).

▸ **on the knock**

1 on credit; engaged in hire purchase *UK*

- — *Woman's Own*, 28th February 1968
- [A]ll on the knock of course, because this firm was very credit-worthy. — Lenny McLean, *The Guv'nor*, p. 19, 1998

2 to be working as a prostitute *UK, 1969*

- — John Ayto, *Oxford Dictionary of Slang*, p. 86, 1998

▸ **take a knock**

to suffer a setback or a financial loss *UK, 1649*

- I know doctors have taken a knock after the Shipman and Alder Hey cases but I do feel that on the whole we're still valued. — *The Guardian*, 20th March 2003

▸ **take the knock**

to fail to meet your debts *AUSTRALIA*

- 'Taking the knock' was so common among early bookmakers both in Sydney and in Melbourne that many of them had their bags specially made with several name flaps. — James Holledge, *The Great Australian Gamble*, p. 75, 1966
- — Jim Ramsay, *Cop It Sweet!*, p. 53, 1977

knock *verb*

1 to criticise, to disparage *US, 1865*

- [H]e comes in, in his little button-down collar shirt and striped tie, and starts knocking Turgenev for about half an hour. — J.D. Salinger, *Franny and Zooey*, p. 15, 1961
- It's all very well to knock the men in white, Mike, but you must bear in mind that referees have many difficulties confronting them[.] — Alexander Buzo, *The Roy Murphy Show*, p. 107, 1970
- When I got some readers' letters knocking her [Princess Diana] I was saddened. — *The News of the World*, p. 24, 1997
- I mean, who are you to knock what you've never experienced. — *Cruel Intentions*, 1999
- It's like gay sex, don't knock it 'til you try it. — Andrew Fraser, *Attitude*, 25th October 2003

2 to defraud, to cheat, especially by passing a fraudulent cheque or by obtaining and dishonouring a credit arrangement *UK*

- [F]ind a punter to get you out of trouble. Then you knock him. — Derek Raymond (Robin Cook), *The Crust on its Uppers*, p. 26, 1962
- "They all knock me," says Tony. "knocking" is the same as "flying the kite," meaning spinning the credit line out and out. — Tom Wolfe, *The Pump House Gang*, p. 199, 1968

3 to steal; to rob *UK, 1919*

- Nobody knew how to knock a safe at that time. — Bruce Jackson, *In the Life*, p. 66, 1972
- So it's your bliddy fault I knocked her purse! — Ian Pattison, *Rab C. Nesbitt*, 1988

4 to arrest *US*

- — Carsten Stroud, *Close Pursuit*, p. 273, 1987

5 to kill *AUSTRALIA, 1911*

- — Norman Lindsay, *Halfway to Anywhere*, p. 104, 1947
- [K]nocked: murdered. — Jim Ramsay, *Cop It Sweet!*, p. 53, 1977

6 to wound *AUSTRALIA, 1917*

- — Leonard Mann, *Flesh in Armour*, p. 56, 1932
- A cobber got knocked. Going to see him. — Lawson Glassop, *We were the Rats*, p. 174, 1944
- What with the old man getting knocked, and his woman waiting, things had broken all my way. — Robert S. Close, *Love Me Sailor*, p. 197, 1945

7 to exhaust; to debilitate *AUSTRALIA*

- First day of 'ard yacker [work] knocks yer. — Nino Culotta (John O'Grady), *They're A Weird Mob*, p. 51, 1957
- Jees, bloody potent stuff, this. Fair knocks you. — Alexander Buzo, *Rooted*, p. 36, 1969

8 to have sexual intercourse with someone *UK, 1598*

- It was more important to back up your mates than to knock a sheila. — William Dick, *A Bunch of Ratbags*, p. 220, 1965

9 to make an amorous approach to (a person) *AUSTRALIA, 1934*

- Blokes who skite about being adepts in the art of knocking girls can be put to the test. — Norman Lindsay, *Halfway to Anywhere*, p. 49, 1947

10 to be unable to make a move in a game, such as dominoes *UK, 1984*

Almost certainly derived from the player's action of knocking on the table to signal an inability to move.

11 to disclose that a pool player is a professional *US*

- — Steve Rushin, *Pool Cool*, p. 18, 1990

12 to post (a letter) *US*

- For the last six months listeners had "knocked" 2,500 to 3,000 "hunks of linen" a week to the 1290 Club's M.C., young (28) vacant-faced Fred Robbins. — *Time Magazine*, p. 92, 20th January 1947

▸ **couldn't knock the skin off a rice pudding**

weak, impotent; used contemptuously of an inferior fighter *UK, 1984*

- — Partridge and Beale, *A Dictionary of Catch Phrases*, 1985

▸ **knock a chunk off**

to have sex from the male perspective *US*

- I was alone because my partner, a piss-poor excuse for a cop named Syd Bacon, was laying up in a hotel room knocking a chunk off some bubble-assed taxi dancer he was going with. — Joseph Wambaugh, *The Blue Knight*, p. 203, 1973

▸ **knock a fade**

to leave *US*

- — Kenn "Naz" Young, *Naz's Underground Dictionary*, p. 42, 1973

▸ **knock a scarf**

to eat a meal *US*

- — Marcus Hanna Boulware, *Jive and Slang of Students in Negro Colleges*, 1947

▸ **knock at the door**

in horse racing, to have nearly won several recent races *US*

- — Robert Saunders Dowst and Jay Craig, *Playing the Races*, p. 165, 1960

▸ **knock boots**

to have sex, especially anal sex *US*

- JAY: I tell you what, though, I don't care if she is my cousin, I'm gonna knock those boots again tonight. — *Clerks*, 1994
- And Rex, he just wants to go on tour and knock the boots. — *Airheads*, 1994
- — Gary K. Farlow, *Prison-ese*, p. 37, 2002

▸ **knock dog**

to be for sale at a low price *TRINIDAD AND TOBAGO*

- — Lise Winer, *Dictionary of the English/Creole of Trinidad & Tobago*, 2003

▸ **knock 'em cold; knock 'em dead**

to amaze an audience, to have a sensational success *UK, 1961*

From boxing.

- John – who was shaping up to be a first-class pervert – whistled as the driver held the door open for me. "knock 'em dead. hottie." he called after me with an exaggerated wink. — Lauren Weisberger, *The Devil Wears Prada*, p. 263, 2003

▸ **knock for six**

1 to utterly overcome, to inconvenience gravely *UK, 1902*
Cricketing imagery, where a 'six' or 'sixer' is a shot that clears the boundary.
- He zooms down it, knocks 'em for six, what a man! — Barry Oakley, *A Salute to the Great McCarthy*, p. 141, 1970
- Unwilling to test the law for fear a jury might knock his case for a sixer. — *Flame*, p. 3, 1972
- Sir David Tweedie [...] is charged with sorting out an international accounting industry knocked for six by America's corporate scandals. — *The Guardian*, 29th June 2002

2 to astound *UK, 1949*
- [Y]ou may be knocked for six to learn that for them English poetry is a triangular constellation made up of Charles Tomlinson, Geoffrey Hill and Roy Fisher. — *The Guardian*, 17th April 2004

▸ **knock into a cocked hat**
to damage someone or something very considerably *US, 1833*
By late C20 other violent verbs often replace 'knock'.
- [Graham] Norton said: 'I've always fancied turning on the Christmas lights in Oxford Street but this [a stunt for Comic Relief] beats that into a cocked hat.' — *BBC News*, 8th February 2003
- Japan has the UK whipped into a cocked hat. — *The Guardian*, 6th March 2003

▸ **knock into the middle of next week; knock into next week**
to hit violently, even fatally; especially, to deliver a blow that causes insensibility *UK, 1821*
Originally used of boxers.
- He might just as easy have knocked you into the middle of next week. For all he's not outsize, when he's in the mood he can be a tough one to take. — Dell Shannon, *Mark of Murder*, p. 90, 1967

▸ **knock it off**
to have sexual intercourse *AUSTRALIA*
- A mate of mine said his missus was knockin' it off with the bloke that reads the meters[.] — T.A.G. Hungerford, *Stories From Suburban Road*, p. 192, 1983

▸ **knock it on the head**
to stop talking; to stop doing something *AUSTRALIA, 1965*
Often as an imperative.
- At a meeting that afternoon they'd agreed to knock it on the head[.] — *The Guardian*, 22nd November 2002

▸ **knock it out**
to have sex *US*
- — Edith A. Folb, *runnin' down some lines*, p. 244, 1980

▸ **knock one off**
to have sex, especially in a perfunctory manner *US, 1924*
- The moment was there. I wanted to, but I couldn't just ... knock one off. Okay? — Elmore Leonard, *Be Cool*, p. 332, 1999

▸ **knock one out**
to masturbate to orgasm *UK, 1990*
Possibly related to **KNOCK OUT** (to manufacture or supply cheaply).
- Do you need to knock one out 'cos you've not 'ad a shag for so long? — Colin Butts, *Is Harry on the Boat?*, p. 111, 1997
- I really didn't fancy knocking one out in the bogs[.] — Wayne Anthony, *Spanish Highs*, p. 91, 1999
- I've never had a wank over the picture me'self, you know what I mean? I'm not sure that I've got her picture out and purposefully knocked one out over her. — *Q*, p. 13, May 2001
- In fact, he actually considered pulling out his dick and knocking one out right there. — Andrew Holmes, *Sleb*, p. 185, 2002

▸ **knock on the head**
to finish an activity, to stop doing something or stop something happening *UK, 1871*
Often as the exclamatory injunction (knock it on the head!). Obviously derives from a final blow that renders someone unconscious, or kills a snake, or drives a nail home.
- I went over to have a chat and told him to knock it on the head. He wasn't in the mood to be reasonable[.] — Dave Courtney, *Stop the Ride I Want to Get Off*, p. 213, 1999
- Immediately, I knocked the drink and the fags on the head. — Jimmy Stockin, *On The Cobbles*, p. 31 – 32, 2000
- He'll knock the tunnel idea on the head. Kick it into touch. — Jack Allen, *When the Whistle Blows*, p. 227, 2000

▸ **knock out tongue**
to kiss with open mouths *US*
- Some brother has a girl all pinned up against the side of the house knocking out much tongue. — *Menace II Society*, 1993

▸ **knock rotten**
to punch or strike fiercely; to daze (a person) by hitting them; to stun *AUSTRALIA*
- If you criticised beer like that in Sydney or Melbourne, you'd get knocked rotten. — Frank Hardy, *The Yarns of Billy Borker*, p. 113, 1965
- The Doc had worked up so much momentum that he flattened the kid's mate in the same swing and he did not even notice. Both kids were knocked rotten. — Kerry Cue, *Crooks, Chooks and Bloody Ratbags*, p. 195, 1983

▸ **knock seven bells out of**
to physically beat someone very severely *UK, 1929*

▸ **knock spots off**
to surpass *US, 1856*
- There's this bird I've been seeing around, Rufe. A real little darling. Knocks spots off Wendy. — Wilda Moxham, *The Apprentice*, p. 62, 1969
- For sheer wit, sensuality and technical bravura, it knocked spots off anything I saw on that year's fringe. — *The Guardian*, 25th July 2002

▸ **knock the drawing room out of**
to condition or toughen physically *NEW ZEALAND*
- It was not fit to ride and I was not going to ride it again. Mr. Tripp smacked his thigh, clapped his hands and laughed. 'That will knock the drawing room out of you!' he said. — A.J. Balkiston, *My Yesteryears*, p. 16, 1952

▸ **knock the slack out**
to accelerate (a truck or car) *US*
- — Wayne Floyd, *Jason's Authentic Dictionary of CB Slang*, p. 20, 1976

▸ **knock your eyes out**
to astound *AUSTRALIA, 1940*
- This one knocks my eyes out! I only got one eye. I can't stand it. — Christina Stead, *The Man who Loved Children*, p. 65, 1940
- [N]aturally you'll want a proper office, a really swanky one next time, one that'll knock all their eyes out. — Neville Jackson, *No end to the way*, p. 167, 1965

▸ **knock your wig**
to comb your hair *US*
- — Marcus Hanna Boulware, *Jive and Slang of Students in Negro Colleges*, 1947

knockabout *noun*
an itinerant *AUSTRALIA, 1889*
- You read about mateship in the bush. You find it between navvy gangs and hoboes, and other knockabouts, but not much between sedentary station workers. — Wendy Lowenstein and Morag Loh, *The Immigrants*, p. 28, 1977
- A knockabout can be dated by his use of terminology. — Ryan Aven-Bray, *Ridgey Didge Oz Jack Lang*, p. 4, 1983

knock about *verb*

1 to be around *AUSTRALIA, 1889*
- There were a few clouds knocking about yestiddy, but this wind has cooked their chances. — Miles Franklin, *My Career Goes Bung*, p. 213, 1946
- Hey, darl, is there any of that Golden Syrup knockin' about the cupboards? — Barry Dickins, *What the Dickins*, p. 51, 1985

2 to wander without purpose and without a home *TRINIDAD AND TOBAGO, 1904*
- Listen, you've knocked about. You know there are bad types of men everywhere. — D'Arcy Niland, *The Shiralee*, p. 61, 1955
- — Lise Winer, *Dictionary of the English/Creole of Trinidad & Tobago*, 2003

3 to beat someone *UK, 1926*
- Josephine Brand was a slender, extremely pretty girl with two brothers, one older, one younger, who knocked her about. — *The Guardian*, 8th May 2004

knockabout *adjective*

1 experienced, well-travelled *AUSTRALIA*
- This fella's name was Dooley Franks. A real knockabout man. — Frank Hardy, *The Yarns of Billy Borker*, p. 82, 1965
- 'Here!' he said to Miles, simply throwing Miles the other blanket he'd brought, as if he and Miles were old, knockabout kinsmen. — Thomas Keneally, *Bring Larks and Heroes*, p. 232, 1967
- First of the knockabout, slapstick westerns, with John Wayne and Stewart Granger digging for gold in Alaska, and involved with beautiful Capucine. — *The Advertiser*, p. 90, 1st March 1990
- Davenport, a tenacious journalist and Vietnam war-correspondent, was one of those knockabout newspapermen who had moles, informants and mates everywhere. — Robert G. Barrett, *Davo's Little Something*, p. 230, 1992
- There's you knockabout mates who are all good blokes and know what a good time is all about[.] — Paul Vautin, *Turn It Up!*, p. 21, 1995

2 of theatrical entertainment, noisy and violent, slapstick *UK, 1892*
- Writer Guy Jenkin, who also directed, spurned the rapier of true satire for the blunt instrument of knockabout comedy. — *The Guardian*, 2nd December 2002

knock around *verb*

1 to spend time with no fixed abode; to travel about as an itinerant *AUSTRALIA, 1901*
- Hell, I reckon I could tell you things you never heard of and you're a bloke has knocked around. — Wilda Moxham, *The Apprentice*, p. 120, 1969
- Well, all I can say is that I've knocked around the traps and I've lived in Australia man and boy for donkey's years, and in all that time nobody's every tried to slip their pollywaffle up my doughnut. — Barry Humphries, *The Traveller's Tool*, p. 19, 1985

2 to spend time with; to idle *US, 1846*
- Knocking around with Rapp the the Rhythm Kings put the finishing touches on me and straightened me out. — Mezz Mezzrow, *Really the Blues*, p. 53, 1946
- She's knocking around with a bookmaker or a toff from up on the Hill or something. — Frank Hardy, *The Outcasts of Foolgarah*, p. 15, 1971
- Brothers and sisters, before I joined the Army I was a sinner. I smoked, I drank, I swore and I knocked around with bad wimmen. — Sam Weller, *Old Bastards I Have Met*, p. 137, 1979
- Not long afterwards, Arnie and I were out walking and just sort of knocking around the streets and, being near 16th Street where she lived, we visited her. — Herbert Huncke, *The Evening Sun Turned Crimson*, p. 173, 1980

knockaround *adjective*

experienced in the ways of the world, especially the underworld *US, 1949*
- Whores galores. But I could take a knock-around broad only so long. — Edwin Torres, *Carlito's Way*, p. 11, 1975
- I know the score, Vito, I'm a knockaround girl. — Vincent Patrick, *Family Business*, p. 241, 1985

knockback *noun*

1 a refusal; a rejection *AUSTRALIA, 1918*
- When a bush worker came to Toganmain looking for a job he could be pretty certain he wouldn't get a knockback. — Bill Wannan, *Bullockies, Beauts and Bandicoots*, p. 43, 1960
- I never got a knock back when I used to pose at the East Sydney Technical College in the old days. — Barry Humphries, *Bazza Pulls It Off!*, 1971
- — Angela Devlin, *Prison Patter*, p. 68, 1996
- Those are hard faces. Hard from years of fights and self-defence and looking after number one and scowling and knock-backs and disappointment and smacks and zero expectations from day one. — Kevin Sampson, *Outlaws*, p. 163, 2001
- "Knock-back" is a term a lifer adds to vocabulary early on in his sentence. — Erwin James, *The Guardian*, 15th November 2001: 'A life inside'

2 an 'offer by a bookmaker to accept a wager at lower odds or for a lesser stake, in part at full odds with the balance at reduced odds, or at SP (starting price) terms only' *UK*
- — David Bennet, *Know Your Bets*, p. 56, 2001

knock back *verb*

1 to reject, especially sexual advances *AUSTRALIA, 1918*
- Knocking back a free night at the flea-pit too. — Barry Humphries, *Bazza Pulls It Off!*, 1971
- Only the other day I was offered Defence. I knocked it back. — Murray Bail, *Holden's Performance*, p. 210, 1988
- — Angela Devlin, *Prison Patter*, p. 68, 1996
- — David McGill, *David McGill's Complete Kiwi Slang Dictionary*, p. 66, 1998
- No big deal, being knocked back. Just one of those wanky things that this fuckin life's full of. — Niall Griffiths, *Kelly + Victor*, p. 7, 2002

2 to drink *UK, 1931*
- 'Yer gunna pin one on?' 'What is this pin one on, Joe?' 'Knock one back. Gunna 'ave a drink?' — Nino Culotta (John O'Grady), *They're A Weird Mob*, 1957
- You ain't even finished with me and yer thinkin' of knockin' one back at fuckin' Annie's. — Lance Peters, *The Dirty Half-Mile*, p. 109, 1979
- Glen won't mind, and I'll just duck out with the boys, knock back a couple of uh, Co' Colas. — *Raising Arizona*, 1987
- [T]he foam dribbling down your chin as you knock it back in victory! — *Sydney Morning Herald*, 12th October 2002

3 to cost a person a specified amount *UK, 1961*
For example the phrase 'that knocked him back a fiver'.

▸**knock back with a stick**

to get more than enough casual sex *AUSTRALIA, 1950*
A jocular boast of sexual prowess.
- At one stage there it was almost a riot. I was knockin' the rotten things back with a stick. — Robert G. Barrett, *Davo's Little Something*, p. 47, 1992

knockdown *noun*

an introduction (to someone) *US*
- — Edd Byrnes, *Way Out with Kookie*, 1959
- 'I suppose you want a formal knock-down to the skipper,' he said with fine scorn. — Criena Rohan, *Down by the Dockside*, p. 83, 1963

knock down *verb*

1 to earn *US, 1929*
- A well known model can easily knock down a grand a week. Even dubs make $500. — Lee Mortimer, *Women Confidential*, p. 131, 1960
- Washed dishes, uh, used to wash the tables in the pool halls in the Student Union, used to knock down about five dollars a night up there. — Leonard Wolfe (Editor), *Voices from the Love Generation*, p. z, 1968

2 to make a sale at auction *UK, 1760*
From the significant action of an auctioneer's gavel in marking the conclusion of a sale.
- — John Ayto, *The Oxford Dictionary of Slang*, p. 201, 1998

3 to steal *CANADA*
- Knocking down hubcaps or some other rat caper is about their speed. — Hugh Garner, *The Intruders*, p. 39, 1976

4 to rob *US*
- You ever hear of somebody knocking down a post office? — Elmore Leonard, *Swag*, p. 76, 1976

5 to spend the entire sum of money earned for seasonal work in a drinking spree *AUSTRALIA, 1845*
Once a veritable institution this practice was especially common amongst shearers and sailors.

6 to drink *UK, 1960*
A variation of KNOCK BACK (to drink).
- [I]t was no good [...] knocking down gin-and-tonic when there were no wages[.] — Derek Raymond (Robin Cook), *The Crust on its Uppers*, p. 28, 1962
- This ain't Kentucky sipping whiskey. It's Mexican rot gut. You knock it down in one shot. — Quentin Tarantino, *From Dusk Till Dawn*, p. 96, 1995
- By my reckoning, she should just have knocked down her start-me-up cup of coffee[.] — Diran Abedayo, *My Once Upon A Time*, p. 92, 2000

7 to introduce *US*
- — Lavada Durst, *The Jives of Dr. Hepcat*, p. 13, 1953

knock-down drag-out *adjective*

(of a fight) vicious *US, 1827*
- They were having these knock-down drag-out scream-o-ramas about stuff like whether the tuna chunks went in the cupboard and the fridge. — John Birmingham, *He Died With a Felafel in his Hand*, p. 15, 1994

knocked *adjective*

drunk *US*
- — Stewart L. Tubbs and Sylvia Moss, *Human Communication*, p. 121, 1974

knock 'em down rains *noun*

in tropical Australia, seasonal torrential rain *AUSTRALIA, 1946*
- The term "knockem down rains" has been in use for 55 years to my knowledge. — *Wordmap (www.abc.net.au/wordmap)*, 2003

knocker *noun*

1 an inveterate critic; a person addicted to finding faults and making criticisms *US, 1898*
- I hope both these books will answer the professional knockers and provide the information that many now seek. — Max Lake, *Classic Wines of Australia*, p. xi, 1966
- It came to me suddenly about half-way through the Opera House opening festival that the reason Australia is so well populated with knockers is that there is still so much to knock. — Bill Hornadge, *The Ugly Australian*, p. 256, 1974
- Australians are ironically proud of one of its locally acquired meanings and of our reputation as a land of 'knockers' in which sense the word is a portmanteau term embracing elements of scepticism, rejection, complaint, jeering, carping, unreasonable criticism and a few more. — Nancy Keesing, *Lily on the Dustbin*, p. 137, 1982
- The mumbo jumbo of the knocker keeps a lot of people in a job and football wouldn't be the same without them. — Ivor Limb, *Footy's No Joke!*, p. 47, 1986
- Haven't the knockers ever heard of legal tender? — Andrew Nickolds, *Back to Basics*, p. 63, 1994
- The knockers could say what they liked about the NHS [National Health Service], but it worked. — John King, *White Trash*, p. 53, 2001

2 a person who defaults (deliberately) on a hire-purchase agreement *UK*
A narrowing of an earlier use applied to a person who contracts a debt with no intention of repaying it.
- — *Woman's Own*, 28th February 1968

3 a thief or confidence trickster posing as a door-to-door salesman *UK*
- — Angela Devlin, *Prison Patter*, p. 69, 1996

4 in circus and carnival usage, a member of the audience who warns others that something is a fraud *US*
- — Don Wilmeth, *The Language of American Popular Entertainment*, p. 152, 1981

5 someone who discloses that a pool player is in fact a professional *US*
- — Steve Rushin, *Pool Cool*, p. 18, 1990

6 in pinball, a sound effect when an additional ball is won *US*
- — Bobbye Claire Natkin and Steve Kirk, *All About Pinball*, p. 113, 1977

▸ **on the knocker**

1 exactly, precisely *AUSTRALIA*
- 'Are your names Messrs. Gales and Mann?' 'Right on the knocker,' Splinter assured him. — J.E. MacDonnell, *Don't Gimme the Ships*, p. 137, 1960
- [H]is slitted eyes watched the pointers of the bombsight moving together. 'She's coming up right on the knocker, skip.' — W.R. Bennett, *Target Turin*, p. 19, 1962
- 'My room is at the top of a flight of stairs, right at the back of the building.' 'I'll be there. On the knocker!' — John Wynnum, *Tar Dust*, p. 34, 1962

2 right away; promptly *AUSTRALIA, 1962*
- Murphy was a good bookmaker. Gave a bit of credit during a bad trot and always settled on the knocker. — Frank Hardy, *The Yarns of Billy Borker*, p. 102, 1965

3 used of a door-to-door canvasser or salesman *UK, 1934*
- — *The Financial Times*, 16th November 1973
- I shall be out on the knocker working for Frank [Dobson]. — *The Guardian*, 23rd January 2000

▸ **up to the knocker**

thoroughly, perfectly, entirely *AUSTRALIA, 1911*
- I'm out to get even with them all fair up to the knocker. — Norman Lindsay, *Halfway to Anywhere*, p. 79, 1947

knocker and knob *noun*

a job *UK*

Rhyming slang, probably formed of door furniture (rather than body parts).
- — Ray Puxley, *Cockney Rabbit*, 1992

knockers *noun*

1 the female breasts, especially large ones *US, 1934*
- Gonna grab you by the knockers and never let go, hear? — Mezz Mezzrow, *Really the Blues*, p. 174, 1946
- [A]s a sharp guy had once said, if a fellow were hit across the head with one of Rosie's knockers he'd be driven into the sidewalk up to his ankles. — Irving Shulman, *The Amboy Dukes*, p. 218, 1947
- Her name was Lillian Simmons. My brother D.B. used to go around with her for a while. She had very big knockers. — J.D. Salinger, *Catcher in the Rye*, p. 86, 1951
- He skimmed over the movie ads: dames, dames, cleavages, knockers, knockers. — Bernard Wolfe, *The Late Risers*, p. 50, 1954
- Let's see those knockers ... Memo to casting. Get a new monster. This one's a faggot. — Max Shulman, *Rally Round the Flag, Boys!*, p. 66, 1957
- Give me Sofia Loren. Man, on man! Some knockers. — Frederick Kohner, *Gidget*, p. 50, 1957
- She was slight [...] but with great little knockers – breasts being for mothers. — James Kennaway, *Some Gorgeous Surprise*, 1967
- I shouted at the girl with the huge, red knockers. — Oscar Zeta Acosta, *The Autobiography of a Brown Buffalo*, p. 177, 1972
- Is she pretty or flashy or what? She have big knockers? — Elmore Leonard, *52 Pick-up*, p. 40, 1974
- Daddy says tits. Daddy says knockers and jugs and bazooms and dingleberries and jujubes. And then he laughs and goes "wuff! wuff!" — *Journal of British Photography*, 9th May 1980
- In that picture you sent, looked like she had great knockers. — *Diner*, 1982
- Darling blue saucer-eyes and fabulous knockers with nips in distention! — Terry Southern, *Now Dig This*, p. 2, 1986
- The sleazeball agent screamed for twenty minutes how Rossi's would be sued until it bled fish oil for poaching her knockers. — Seth Morgan, *Homeboy*, p. 292, 1990
- At the party tonight there's going to be a girl with knockers this big. — *Dazed and Confused*, 1993
- You'll see who gets the biggest tips – the girls with the knockers, that's who! — Carl Hiaasen, *Strip Tease*, p. 27, 1993
- "The one big difference," says Waters, "was that Divine was a man and his big set of knockers was nothing but a pile of old washrags." — Anka Radakovich, *The Wild Girls Club*, p. 201, 1994
- [H]e was right. I had knockers, not tits, big fat knockers. — Jenny Eclair, *Camberwell Beauty*, p. 54, 2000
- [T]his way-too-small teddy that makes a fucking poor job of holding in her knockers. — Kevin Sampson, *Clubland*, p. 131, 2002

2 dice that have been loaded with mercury that shifts when the dice are tapped *US*
- — *The Annals of the American Academy of Political and Social Sciences*, p. 127, May 1950

knocker shop *noun*

a brothel *AUSTRALIA*
- — Thommo, *The Dictionary of Australian Swearing and Sex Sayings*, p. 77, 1985

knockin' *adjective*

great *US*
- — Rick Ayers (Editor), *Berkeley High Slang Dictionary*, p. 30, 2004

knocking *noun*

criticism; fault-finding *AUSTRALIA*
- Let's face it, for a while Australia's image as a land of culture copped a terrific lot of rubbish and knocking from the expatriate sector, mainly a bunch of know-alls and shirt-lifters, who in my humble viewpoint are lower than the basic wage. — Barry Humphries, *Les Patterson's Australia*, p. [viii], 1978

knockings *noun*

the facts or details, an explanation *UK*
- Noreen be fair! You ain't even heard the knockings. — Jeremy Cameron, *Brown Bread in Wengen*, p. 8, 1999

knocking shop *noun*

a brothel *UK, 1860*
- On some nights he went as far as Clay Street, past the house which the boys at school said was a knocking shop[.] — Ronald McKie, *The Mango Tree*, p. 62, 1975
- Don't give me all that crap. You run a glorified knocking shop. — Anthony Masters, *Minder*, p. 166, 1984
- [A]ll kinds of knocking shops and bars for benders [homosexuals] and cokeheads and all sorts. — Kevin Sampson, *Clubland*, p. 64, 2002

knock it off!; knock off!

stop it!, shut up! *UK, 1883*
- TICH: Ah – they get on my wick. These old fools. What they done with their lives? End your days in a lousy doss house. CORP: Ah, knock off. — Clive Exton, *No Fixed Abode [Six Granada Plays]*, p. 119, 1959
- Stacey knew it was Bob and said knock it off / But Bob wouldn't knock if off 'cause he's crazy and off his rocker[.] — Eminem (Marshall Mathers), *The Kids*, 2000

knock, knock!

1 used as the verbal equivalent of an actual knock on the door when entering another's room, office, etc *UK, 1984*

2 in a game of dominoes or such, used as a signal (often accompanied by the action of knocking on the games table) that the game-player is unable to make a move *UK, 1984*

knocko *noun*

a narcotics police officer *US*
- Knockos making street buys usually came in colors, or at least Italian trying to be Puerto Rican, but not piney-woods white, and they usually acted cool or sneaky, not jumpy. — Richard Price, *Clockers*, p. 3, 1992

knock-off *noun*

1 a product that is designed to be mistaken for an expensive, brand name product *US, 1963*
- The availability of extensive merchandising displays from manufacturers, coupled with enticing trade deals, have made knock-off fragrances an attractive category for retailers. — *Supermarket News*, p. 22, 10th August 1987
- After Fin followed Orson Ellis into his private office, the fat man removed his size 52, double-breasted Armani knockoff, and plopped his bulk into an executive chair. — Joseph Wambaugh, *Finnegan's Week*, p. 6, 1993
- [C]hances are he wasn't talking about one of the Italian designer's $150-plus originals, but one of the thousands of knock-offs that were appearing on New York streets. — Steven Daly and Nalthaniel Wice, *alt.culture*, p. 27, 1995
- This latest action against "knock-off" businesses adds momentum to Cobra's successful campaign to thwart the importation, distribution and sale of "knock-off" [golf] clubs to the marketplace. — *PR Newswire*, 7th September 1995
- Sadly this gem was overlooked at the time of release, even by me, in the then surfeit of crap Terminator/Predator/Robocop knockoffs (Metal Beast, A.P.E.X, Prototype, Cyborg Cop, T-force, Project Shadowcaster, ad fucking nauseum). — *Sick Puppy*, p. 17, 1998
- The boom box was one of those Taiwanese knock-offs, already falling apart. — Shane Maloney, *Nice Try*, p. 186, 1998
- [T]he recent spate of Lock, Stock knockoffs in Britain[.] — Graham Fuller, *Brute Force*, p. 87, 2000

2 the end of a work shift; quitting time *AUSTRALIA, 1916*
- —Gavin Casey, *It's Harder for Girls*, p. 61, 1941
- I'll give a whistle when it's knock-off for lunch.—Robert S. Close, *With Hooves of Brass*, p. 137, 1961

3 a murder *US, 1928*
- So the outfit uses Nigger gorillas like Butcher Knife Brown for the petty knockoffs in Niggertown.—Iceberg Slim (Robert Beck), *Trick Baby*, p. 183, 1969

4 in hot rodding and drag racing, a wheel lug that is easily removed *US, 1960s*
- — Capitol Records, *Hot Rod Jargon*, 1963

knock off *verb*

1 to cease; to stop *UK, 1649*
- These girls worked hard – some of them didn't knock off for a single night.—Milton Mezzrow, *Really the Blues*, p. 23, 1946
- I can knock off drinking.—Kylie Tennant, *Lost Haven*, p. 24, 1946
- So when he suggested knocking off, I didn't have any reason for staying.—Jim Thompson, *Savage Night*, p. 125, 1953

2 to finish a work shift, job, etc *UK, 1649*
- One of our blokes went over to Sydney once and got a job. Knocks off at lunch time and breasts the nearest bar.—John O'Grady, *It's Your Shout, Mate!*, p. 18, 1972
- What time do we knock off around here?—Petra Christian, *The Sexploiters*, p. 46, 1973

3 to kill *US, 1879*
- "When you going to knock Tracy off?" Ripple asked nervously. —Chester Gould, *Dick Tracy Meets the Night Crawler*, p. 40, 1945
- They both had the chance to knock off Jack.—Mickey Spillane, *I, The Jury*, p. 21, 1947
- "Listen, rat" – Benny's face paled – "one more word like that and I'll plug you too. They can only burn me once, and I'd just as soon knock you off to stay alive as not."—Irving Shulman, *The Amboy Dukes*, p. 85, 1947
- So why should I knock you off?—Marvin Wald and Albert Maltz, *The Naked City*, 1947
- One day rival gangsters caught up with Cunningham in an alley in I Street, and there he was knocked off.—Jack Lait and Lee Mortimer, *Washington Confidential*, p. 145, 1951
- Far as you know The Blade hasn't knocked no one off.—Wilda Moxham, *The Apprentice*, p. 31, 1969

4 to defeat; to despatch *US, 1927*
- They knock Port Stephens and Perth off in a straight one-day competition.—Bob Staines, *Wot a Whopper*, p. 27, 1982

5 (of police) to arrest; to raid *US, 1925*
- We'll knock off this croaker.—William J. Spillard and Pence James, *Needle in a Haystack*, p. 18, 1945
- —Peter Laurie, *Scotland Yard*, p. 323, 1970
- —Angela Devlin, *Prison Patter*, p. 69, 1996

6 to rob, to steal *US, 1917*
- Diamond watched with an air of professional concern. "This stuff could get knocked off too," he warned Bacula.—Harry J. Anslinger, *The Murderers*, p. 72, 1961
- I have a great talent for knocking off things[.]—Jamie Mandelkau, *Buttons*, p. 77, 1971
- For now we got to knock the fuckin' joint off. After that, then we'll worry 'bout spendin' the cash.—Donald Goines, *Daddy Cool*, p. 172, 1974
- Somebody was pissed about that truck getting knocked off and the cops had nothing.— *The Usual Suspects*, 1995
- —Angela Devlin, *Prison Patter*, p. 69, 1996

7 to reproduce a brand name item, less expensively and usually illegally *US*
- "Knocking off" is trade slang for copying a competitor's dress, cutting corners to sell it for a lower price.— *Saturday Evening Post*, p. 30, 21st September 1963
- Everybody knocks off everybody else. There are that many of my knits knocked off around Melbourne. Even in the Vic market there's a sign saying "Just like Feathers!"— *Sydney Morning Herald (Sunday Life)*, p. 7, 10th May 1998

8 to sell or dispose of *NEW ZEALAND*
- They make those trinket affairs for him. Then he takes them out and knocks them off in town.—Vincent O'Sullivan, *Shuriken*, p. 28, 1985

9 of a male, to have sex *AUSTRALIA*
- I took her down to Basin Street and to a movie, then took her to my room and knocked her off. I was ready to go after I'd knocked her off one time. But the chick was really something – she couldn't see anybody just knocking her off one time.—Claude Brown, *Manchild in the Promised Land*, p. 182, 1965
- Terry leered at me through the doorway. "I'd knock you off anytime, darling," he said[.]—Petra Christian, *The Sexploiters*, p. 46, 1973

10 to have sexual intercourse with someone *US, 1943*
- "I told them: don't join in the chorus about Sneed Hearn knocking off young birds and bashing the bottle, 'cause he'll only gain votes at the next elections: half his luck, the mugs will say.—Frank Hardy, *The Outcasts of Foolgarah*, p. 111, 1971
- If a sheilah's unattached, the chances are she'll start crapping on about wanting a 'relationship' just because you've knocked her off a couple of times.— Barry Humphries, *The Traveller's Tool*, p. 41, 1985

11 to seduce *AUSTRALIA, 1950*
- Well, he's not knocking orf my sister-in-law and that's for sure, and he's not staying in this house a day longer.—Frank Hardy, *The Outcasts of Foolgarah*, p. 15, 1971

▸ **knock off a piece**

to have sex *US, 1921*
- Doin' the short change scene with the Geech, the grabbing, back to the pad, knocking off a li'l piece with Leelah...—Odie Hawkins, *Chicago Hustle*, p. 64, 1977

knock-off gear *noun*

an item or items of stolen property *UK*
- While I was at Queen's I'd get gypsies continually offering me knock-off gear.—Dave Courtney, *Raving Lunacy*, p. 13, 2000

knock-off time *noun*

the end of a work shift; quitting time *AUSTRALIA, 1867*
- —Nino Culotta (John O'Grady), *They're A Weird Mob*, p. 41, 1957
- At 6 a.m. he bundies on for his first job as a garage mechanic and toils happily until knock-off time at 8.30 a.m.— *Weekend*, p. 7, 1st June 1957
- —Sam Weller, *Old Bastards I Have Met*, p. 10, 1979
- —Clive Galea, *Slipper*, p. 148, 1988

knockout; knock-out *noun*

1 an outstanding, beautiful or outrageous person *UK, 1892*
- 'Cripes! You look a fair knock-out.' 'Do you really think so, Bill?' 'An absolute peach.'—Norman Lindsay, *Halfway to Anywhere*, p. 218, 1947
- So today she had risen early, knocking herself out to be a knockout. —Jim Thompson, *The Grifters*, p. 76, 1963
- You get cleaned up you're a knockout.—Elmore Leonard, *Glitz*, p. 194, 1985
- You'll be glad to know I'm a fucking knockout, five-nine in heels, a neat ass, light-brown hair.—Elmore Leonard, *Be Cool*, p. 38, 1999

2 an excellent thing *UK, 1892*

Literally, 'a thing so excellent that it will render you insensible'.
- Norman Jewison's life of Rubin Carter should have been a knock-out.— *The Observer*, 26th March 2000

knock out *verb*

1 to have a very powerful effect on, to impress profoundly *US, 1890*
- Tony had a natural musical sense I've hardly ever seen equalled, and he wrote a number called Pretty Little Baby that really knocked me out.—Mezz Mezzrow, *Really the Blues*, p. 45, 1946
- "But Dobie," wailed Clothilde. "It's Montgomery Clift. He knocks me out. Doesn't he knock you out?"—Max Shulman, *The Many Loves of Dobie Gillis*, p. 4, 1951
- Guys and gals, it knocks me out to be able to elucidate—Lavada Durst, *The Jives of Dr. Hepcat*, 1953
- It knocked me out, too, when I first broke in here.—Malcolm X and Alex Haley, *The Autobiography of Malcolm X*, p. 48, 1964
- And the Southern girls with the way they talk / They knock me out when I'm down there—Brian Wilson (performed by the Beach Boys), *California Girls*, 1965
- It really knocked me out to hear him give directions.—Lenny Bruce, *How to Talk Dirty and Influence People*, p. 40, 1965

2 to manufacture or supply cheaply *UK, 1876*

The currency of market-traders and sweat-shops, 'knock it out cheap', 'knock them out', adopted into wider use.
- Jeff from FBT and I were in the studio and we had just knocked out a song, but we were trying to come up with more shit.—Eminem (Marshall Mathers), *Angry Blonde*, p. 27, 2001
- [I]t's just a bit of gear [stolen goods] I knock out to a few reliable fellas.—Danny King, *The Burglar Diaries*, p. 31, 2001

3 to produce *AUSTRALIA*
- Of course a chap might knock out a bit of fun shooting pigeons in the cork-woods, and an occasional satin-bird made a good mark in its steel-blue feathers.—Kylie Tennant, *Lost Haven*, p. 248, 1946
- I should have it knocked out by next week...allow a lag for publication...by the end of April I'd say, at the least.—John A. Scott, *Blair*, p. 56, 1988

4 to go to sleep *US*
- —Connie Eble (Editor), *UNC-CH Campus Slang*, p. 6, Spring 2003

5 to burgle in such a thorough manner that nothing of any value remains *UK*
- —Paul Tempest, *Lag's Lexicon*, 1950

knockout *adjective*
excellent, impressive *US, 1920*
- PETE: [A]s you know, Shakespeare was a wonderful writer. DUD: Knockout. — Peter Cook, *Not Only But Also*, 1966
- [S]everal properties to my name – all in knockout postal codes[.] — Andrew Nickolds, *Back to Basics*, p. 127, 1994

knock out drops *noun*
a sedative added to a drink to cause unconciousness, especially with criminal intent *US, 1876*
- — Angela Devlin, *Prison Patter*, p. 69, 1996

knock over *verb*
1 to rob *US, 1925*
- Buster, what did you do, knock over a bank or something? — George Mandel, *Flee the Angry Strangers*, p. 122, 1952
- Ice,' if we only knock over three of 'em, we split maybe ten to fifteen G's between us. — Iceberg Slim (Robert Beck), *Pimp*, p. 252, 1969
- I'll admit under duress that he fucked my mother ... but shikses? I can no more imagine him knocking over a gas station. — Philip Roth, *Portnoy's Complaint*, p. 94, 1969
- We're going to knock over a bank so stiff it'll never get up. — Red Rudensky, *The Gonif*, p. 76, 1970
- "Sure," Phillips said. "Give me the location and we'll knock him over." — Leonard Shecter and William Phillips, *On the Pad*, p. 150, 1973
- To keep an eye on things, I brought in my kid brother Dominick and some desperados from back home and started knockin' over high rollers, casino bosses, bookmakers[.] — *Casino*, 1995

2 to raid an establishment *US, 1929*
- The trip to the form-up point was full of anticipation, with everyone keen to get a start and knock the place over. — William Dodson, *The Sharp End*, p. 229, 2001

3 to kill; to slaughter *US, 1823*
- Maybe you could knock over a fowl for us, Uncle. — Kylie Tennant, *The Honey Flow*, p. 69, 1956

4 to arrest *US, 1924*
- [T]his is not the first time she gets knocked over so she will be cooling it there for quite a while! — John Rechy, *City of Night*, p. 128, 1963

5 to drink *AUSTRALIA, 1924*
- I reckon I could knock over a schooner. — Nino Culotta (John O'Grady), *They're A Weird Mob*, p. 44, 1957
- — Nino Culotta (John O'Grady), *They're A Weird Mob*, p. 85, 1957
- After a while he nodded off and the boys settled down to knocking over a few cans and getting some fish in the boat. — Bob Staines, *Wot a Whopper*, p. 37, 1982

knockround *noun*
a period spent wandering about idling *AUSTRALIA, 1934*
- Oh, just having a bit of a knock round. — Norman Lindsay, *The Cousin from Fiji*, p. 135, 1945

knock round *verb*
to spend time (with someone); to accompany *AUSTRALIA*
- 'I've took a real shine to you, Mac,' Polka went on. 'You'd be a good mate to knock round with.' — D'Arcy Niland, *The Shiralee*, p. 138, 1955

knock shop *noun*
a brothel *AUSTRALIA*
- Excuse I, butting in yous two! But I'm beginning to feel like the spare prick at a knockshop wedding. — Barry Humphries, *The Wonderful World of Barry McKenzie*, p. 46, 1968
- They entered the first of many 'knock shops' and picked their ladies. — Martin Cameron, *A Look at the Bright Side*, 1988

knock sideways *verb*
to astound *UK, 1925*
- When Mum and Dad saw where he was they were knocked sideways. — Kel Richards, *The Aussie Bible*, p. 19, 2003

knock together *verb*
to prepare a marijuana cigarette *UK*
A specialisation of the conventional sense.
- Dave lit up a little "spliffy" which he'd knocked together earlier. — Ken Lukowiak, *Marijuana Time*, p. 62, 2000

knock-up *noun*
a fraudulent system operated to rig the bidding at an auction *UK*
- — *Evening Echo (Bournemouth)*, 17th April 1966

knock up *verb*
1 to impregnate *US, 1813*
- Taking a quick trip to the grave because she got messed up with a rat who knocked her up, played with her awhile, then took off. — Mickey Spillane, *I, The Jury*, p. 69, 1947
- Yeah, well, she got knocked up. At a grind session. — Evan Hunter, *The Blackboard Jungle*, p. 158, 1954
- "It wasn't too ethereal to keep her from geting knocked up," observed Polly. — Max Shulman, *Anyone Got a Match?*, p. 256, 1964
- I probably knocked up your daugther is all. I wanted you to know. — Richard Farina, *Been Down So Long*, p. 226, 1966
- He was always laying bets about when she'd get knocked up. — Dorothy Hewett, *The Chapel Perilous*, p. 52, 1972
- Pauline, this girl, I think maybe I knocked her up. — *Saturday Night Fever*, 1977
- Now I want you to level with me: did you knock this skirt up? — *Something About Mary*, 1998
- She said it was a serviceman from Fort Bliss knocked her up. — Elmore Leonard, *Be Cool*, p. 221, 1999

2 to hammer on the door of a cell to attract the attention of a warder *AUSTRALIA, 1944*
- In this jail you've got to knock up for about an hour before a screw comes to your cell. — Ray Denning, *Prison Diaries*, p. 63, 1978
- Regrettably it had no toilet. If my bowel or bladder cried out for attention I had to 'knock up'. — Murray Farquhar, *Nine Words from the Grave*, p. 162, 1986

knolly bike *noun*
any low-powered motorcycle used by probationary taxi-drivers in the process of learning the geography of London's streets ('doing the knowledge') *UK*
Formed on a shortening of 'the knowledge'.
- [T]he Honda 90 motorcycle, the most common knolly bike. — Ray Puxley, *Fresh Rabbit*, 1998

knot *noun*
1 the head *US*
- Since I had a not knot by nature, you can understand what this kinda exciting female did to a nigger like me. — A.S. Jackson, *Gentleman Pimp*, p. 109, 1973
- Cause if you come up weak, I'm going for your knot and gut / And throw you in the gutter like an ordinary slut. — Dennis Wepman et al., *The Life*, p. 40, 1976

2 a large sum of money *US*
- — Judi Sanders, *Faced and Faded, Hanging to Hurl*, p. 24, 1993
- — Gary K. Farlow, *Prison-ese*, p. 37, 2002

knot-flashing *noun*
public self-exposure by a male for sexual thrills *UK*
Police slang, formed on an otherwise obsolete use of 'knot' (the (head of the) penis).
- — James Fraser, *The Evergreen Death*, 1968

knotty *adjective*
(of hair) in tight curls *BAHAMAS*
- — John A. Holm, *Dictionary of Bahamian English*, p. 119, 1982

Knotty Ash *noun*
cash *UK*
Rhyming slang, from the name of a Liverpool suburb; probably inspired by comedian Ken Dodd, a famous resident of the area, and in particular by his clash with the taxman.
- — Ray Puxley, *Cockney Rabbit*, 1992

know *noun*
▸ **in the know**
trendy, fashionable *US*
- — Vic Fredericks, *Who's Who in Rock 'n Roll*, p. 96, 1958

know *verb*
▸ **know b from bull foot**
to know anything at all *TRINIDAD AND TOBAGO*
Usually used in the negative.
- — Lise Winer, *Dictionary of the English/Creole of Trinidad & Tobago*, 2003

▸ **know backwards**
to have a thorough knowledge of something *UK, 1904*
- La Bohème is an opera most of us think we know backwards – but it is often misunderstood. — *The Guardian*, 28th January 2002

▸ **know how many beans make five**
to be not easily fooled *UK, 1830*
- Oh, I know how many beans make five, Doctor. You don't have to be a Time Lord to cope with A-level maths. — Peter Grimwade, *Doctor Who*, 1983

▸ **know inside out**
to have a thorough knowledge of something *UK, 1921*
- He had worked strenuously with housing associations and knew inside-out the renting and enforcing hell hole of North Kensington. — *The Guardian*, 31st July 2000

▸ know like the back of your hand
to have a thorough knowledge of something *UK, 1943*
A simile that is easier said than done.
- [H]e knows his and Hemingway's part of the lagoon like the back of his hand. — *The Guardian*, 23rd February 2002

▸ know someone who knows someone
to be able to obtain an article for less than its retail price, referring to either wholesale rates or the acquisition of stolen property *UK, 1984*

▸ know the score
to understand what is going on *US*
Referring to a musical score, not the score of a sports contest.
- Murph was a professional musician now, and he knew the score[.] — Mezz Mezzrow, *Really the Blues*, p. 50, 1946

▸ know your onions
having knowledge that comes from experience *US, 1922*
Also in the variations: 'know your apples' (since 1945); 'oats' (since 1926); 'oil' (since 1925). Lesser variations include: 'groceries' (1928); 'okra' (around 1947); 'sweet potatoes' (1928). The formula is also used to describe a specified field of knowledge, e.g. 'know your hockey' (about 1929).
- I know my onions, I've done jobs before[.] — Danny King, *The Burglar Diaries*, p. 116, 2001

▸ know your shit
to have knowledge that comes from experience *US, 1984*
- [T]he majority of Ibiza's clubbers really know their shit and wouldn't accept a half-hearted performance from anybody[.] — Wayne Anthony, *Spanish Highs*, p. 80, 1999

▸ not know from a bar of soap
to not know at all *AUSTRALIA, 1918*
- I don't know these people from a bar of soap anyway. They're Gillian's friends not mine. — Barry Humphries, *A Nice Night's Entertainment*, p. 103, 1968
- — Rex Hunt, *Tall Tales – and True*, p. 84, 1994

▸ not know from the hole in your arse
to be ignorant of *UK*
- "No you fuckin' listen, you come in here without Roy and with some guy I don't know from the hole in my arse..." I fuckin' hate crude women. "... and try to tell me everything's fuckin' cool." — J.J. Connolly, *Know Your Enemy [britpulp]*, p. 156, 1999

▸ not know whether you are Arthur or Martha
to be in a state of confusion *AUSTRALIA*
- Stone the crows, these Movement blokes don't know whether they're Arthur or Martha! — Ray Slatterly, *Mobb's Mob*, p. 57, 1966
- [T]he boys don't know whether they're Arthur or Martha, what with all the talk about Red plots, there, and the latest telegram from Judge Parshall. — Frank Hardy, *The Outcasts of Foolgarah*, p. 76, 1971

▸ not know whether you are coming or going
to be in a state of confusion, befuddlement or perplexity *UK, 1924*
- Both in and out of the sack, they often don't seem to know whether they are coming or going. — *The Observer*, 17th August 2003

know-all *noun*
a person who displays their knowledge in a conceited manner *AUSTRALIA, 1934*
- — Jon Cleary, *The Long Shadow*, p. 54, 1949
- — Vince Kelly, *The Bogeyman*, p. 174, 1956
- 'Also the golden rule is not to move an accident case until first examined by a medical expert.' 'Ah! Know-all, eh!' — Arthur Upfield, *Bony and the Mouse*, p. 16, 1959
- — Dymphna Cusack, *Picnic Races*, p. 71, 1962
- — Frank Hardy, *The Outcasts of Foolgarah*, p. 23, 1971
- Let's face it, for a while Australia's image as a land of culture copped a terrific lot of rubbish and knocking from the expatriate sector, mainly a bunch of know-alls and shirt-lifters, who in my humble viewpoint are lower than the basic wage. — Barry Humphries, *Les Patterson's Australia*, p. [viii], 1978

know-all *adjective*
conceitedly knowledgeable *AUSTRALIA, 1965*
- — Frank Hardy, *The Outcasts of Foolgarah*, p. 197, 1971
- I just couldn't stand Fox...with his know-all doctor's manner. — Xavier Herbert, *Poor Fellow My Country*, p. 974, 1975

knowed-up *adjective*
lucky, and believing that skill not luck produced success *US*
- — Jerry Robertson, *Oil Slanguage*, p. 21, 1954

know-it-all *noun*
a person who knows less than he thinks *US, 1895*
- Don't turn your back on me and my message because of the know-it-alls and cynics around you. — Kel Richards, *The Aussie Bible*, p. 46, 2003

know-it-all *adjective*
conceitedly knowledgeable *UK, 1935*
- Setting his short legs well apart, he prepared to tell this know-it-all prick exactly... — Gerald Sweeney, *The Plunge*, p. 140, 1981

knowledge *noun*
a skill at performing oral sex; a person who is skilled at performing oral sex *US*
An elaboration and play on **HEAD** (oral sex).
- — Connie Eble (Editor), *UNC-CH Campus Slang*, p. 5, November 2002

▸ do the knowledge
of probationary taxi drivers, to learn the geography of London's streets (especially by driving around on a low-powered motorcycle); to take a written examination that tests the newly acquired knowledge *UK, 1978*
- In order to earn their licence, candidates will have to "do the knowledge," a daunting prospect which ultimately provides an unprecedented understanding of the capital and its complex street system. — Malcolm Bobbit, *Taxi!*, p. 116, 1998

knowledge box *noun*
1 the head; the brain *UK, 1785*
- For a busted smeller, a couple of shiners, and a few creases in the knowledge-box he made himself ten grand. — Mezz Mezzrow, *Really the Blues*, p. 21, 1946

2 in railroading, the yardmaster's office *US, 1926*
- — Norman Carlisle, *The Modern Wonder Book of Trains and Railroading*, p. 265, 1946

knowmean?; na mean?
do you know what I mean? *UK*
Used either as a question or as a stress at the end of a statement.
- This is it. My last chance na mean. — Nick Barlay, *Curvy Lovebox*, p. 48, 1997
- They'll be biting our hands off to be part of the Village, knowmean. — Kevin Sampson, *Outlaws*, p. 32, 2001

knuckle *noun*
physical violence; the act of punching *UK*
From the verb sense.
- It's all planning and timing and stopwatches. There's hardly any knuckle at all. — Kevin Sampson, *Outlaws*, p. 16, 2001

▸ go the knuckle
to attack with the fists; to take part in a fist fight *AUSTRALIA, 1944*
- That's when you discovered us. Stacked on a turn. Went the knuckle. Dorabella shot through, abandoning her white bloomers on a low bough. — Jack Hibberd, *A Stretch of the Imagination*, p. 15, 1971
- — Jim Ramsay, *Cop It Sweet!*, p. 53, 1977

knuckle *verb*
to punch with a bare fist *AUSTRALIA*
- This went on for three months until Mother thought if one more person told her to wait for bloody winter she would knuckle them in the nose[.] — Kerry Cue, *Crooks, Chooks and Bloody Ratbags*, p. 124, 1983

knuckle-buster *noun*
1 in car repair, a nut that is tightly fastened, guaranteeing a difficult and painful removal process *US*
- — Lewis Poteet, *Car & Motorcyle Slang*, p. 118, 1992

2 a crescent wrench *US, 1941*
- — Lou Shelly, *Hepcats Jive Talk Dictionary*, p. 46, 1945

knuckle down *verb*
to make an effort and apply yourself to a task *UK, 1864*
- The two officers knuckled down to inspect 540 boxes, moving the heavy containers themselves[.] — William B. McCloskey, *Their Fathers' Work*, p. 111, 2000

knuckleduster *noun*
a large, heavy or over-gaudy ring which may, or may not, be worn for violent purposes *UK, 1896*
An extension of the sense as 'a weapon'.

knuckledusters *noun*
a pair of brass knuckles *US, 1858*
The derivation is as blunt as the practical usage: where it's worn, on the knuckles; what it does, **DUST** (to thrash). Abbreviates as 'duster'.

- Bang goes another pair of knuckledusters — Ronald Searle, *The St. Trinian's Story*, p. 59, 1959
- Whitey crouched beside him, homemade knuckle dusters coiled in his right fist. — James Ellroy, *Blood on the Moon*, p. 20, 1984
- Marcus already had some gear of his own in the boot. A couple of knuckledusters and a massive Bowie knife. — Dave Courtney, *Raving Lunacy*, p. 119, 2000

knucklehead *noun*
a fool, an idiot *US, 1942*
- Where is it? Where's your stash, knucklehead? — Alexander Trocchi, *Cain's Book*, p. 106, 1960
- PUMPKIN: Knucklehead walks in a bank with a telphone, not a pistol, not a shotgun, but a fuckin' phone, cleans the place out, and they don't lift a fuckin' finger. — *Pulp Fiction*, 1994
- She called me knucklehead. — Joel Rose, *Kill Kill Faster Faster*, p. 10, 1997
- US Lieutenant-General William Wallace blamed continuing resistance on "knuckleheads ... operating and fighting on the last orders they were given". — *The Guardian*, 16th April 2003

knuckle junction *noun*
fisticuffs *US*
- If you use any of these lines you better be joking or willing to take that quick trip to 'knuckle junction'. — Michael Dalton Johnson (quoting Redd Foxx), *Talking Trash with Redd Foxx*, p. 87, 1994

knuckle merchant *noun*
a fist-fighter, a rough and ready brawler *UK*
- Even the men in front, the sort of full-time knuckle merchants who don't usually care who they upset, are nice and polite[.] — John King, *Human Punk*, p. 30, 2000

knuckle sandwich *noun*
a punch in the mouth *US*
- — *American Weekly*, p. 2, 14th August 1955
- I'll give that quack [doctor] a knuckle sandwich!!! — Barry Humphries, *Bazza Pulls It Off!*, 1971
- Look, creep, you want a knuckle sandwich? — *American Graffiti*, 1973
- I'll give you a knuckle sandwich I ever see you around here again. — Elmore Leonard, *Gold Coast*, p. 179, 1980
- — Angela Devlin, *Prison Patter*, p. 69, 1996
- Nurse comes in tomorrow an she got 'er a shiner – or less some teeth, jig's up. So no knuckle sandwiches under no circumstances. — *Kill Bill*, 2003

knuckle shuffle *noun*
an act of male masturbation *US*
- Copperknob doing a five knuckle shuffle in the loo[.] — Jack Allen, *When the Whistle Blows*, p. 105, 2000
- — Chris Lewis, *The Dictionary of Playground Slang*, p. 133, 2003

knuckle-shuffle *verb*
to masturbate *UK*
- Okay, okay, I admit it, I knuckle-shuffled the FSA [Financial Services Advisor]. — Christopher Brookmyre, *The Sacred Art of Stealing*, p. 74, 2002

knuckles on the ground
an illustrative quality ascribed to a person of low intellect and primitive appearance *UK*
- [S]ometimes you get a right thickie with his knuckles on the ground [...] who wants to be a brain surgeon. — *New Society*, 7th August 1975

knuckle under *verb*
to concede to a more powerful authority *UK*
The image suggests submission to the rule of the fist but this application is figurative.
- Best of all though, you hadn't given in or knuckled under. — Dave Courtney, *Raving Lunacy*, p. 92, 2000

knuckle up *verb*
to fight *US, 1968*
- — *People Magazine*, p. 72, 19th July 1993

knucks *noun*
knuckles; brass knuckles *US, 1858*
- Crump's cops shook them down nightly for pistols, Arkansas toothpicks, clubs, brass knucks, razors and ice picks. — *Time*, p. 20, 27 May 1946
- Carrying a knife and knucks is like wearing peg pants and a sharp hat. It's like a part of a uniform. — Irving Shulman, *The Amboy Dukes*, p. 165, 1947
- Don't forget the brass knucks. — Bernard Wolfe, *The Late Risers*, p. 29, 1954
- [T]he powerful swing of this brutal bull's fist was made further effective by shiny new heavy brass "knucks" inserted over the fingers – probably being tested for the first time. — Neal Cassady, *The First Third*, p. 25, 1971
- Dig the contents: brass knucks and a .38 snubnose. — James Ellroy, *Hollywood Nocturnes*, p. 49, 1994

knucks-in *adjective*
doing well *TRINIDAD AND TOBAGO, 1987*
From marbles, where the term is used of a player whose aim is true.
- — Lise Winer, *Dictionary of the English/Creole of Trinidad & Tobago*, 2003

KO; kayo *noun*
in boxing, a knock-out *US, 1911*
- [A] winner's a winner no matter how he gets the kayo! — *The Sweeney*, p. 20, 1976
- The Mexican shook, for a moment, like a cerebral palsy victim before he crashed backward to the canvas and lay motionless in kayo slumber. — Iceberg Slim (Robert Beck), *Long White Con*, p. 199, 1977

KO *verb*
to knock-out; to destroy *US, 1921*
- My first box, a big steel fucker, ko-ed one of those sad anonymous blue Samsonite copies[.] — Charlie Hall, *The Box (Disco Biscuits)*, p. 155, 1996

KO *adjective*
exhausted *UK*
An initialism of '*k*nocked-*o*ut'; used by black urban youths.
- I'm KO, I need to get some Zs. — *Live*, p. 39, Winter 2004

Kodak *noun*
police radar used for measuring vehicle speed *US*
- — Lanie Dills, *The Official CB Slanguage Language Dictionary*, p. 43, 1976

Kodak courage *noun*
a brief burst of fearlessness encountered when being photographed *US*
- — Vann Wesson, *Generation X Field Guide and Lexicon*, p. 104, 1997

Kodak moment *noun*
a clichéd moment or event *US*
From a series of Kodak advertisements, urging consumers to take pictures at 'Kodak moments'.
- — Judi Sanders, *Don't Dog by Do, Dude!*, p. 19, 1991
- Look, I really don't feel like having a Kodak moment here. — *American Beauty*, 1999

Kodak poisoning; Kodak-Fuji poisoning *noun*
an imaginary ailment contracted by the subjects of (over-?) enthusiastic photographers *ANTARCTICA, 1983*
Jocular; based on the names of major film manufacturers Kodak and Fuji.
- — Bernadette Hince, *The Antarctic Dictionary*, p. 206, 2000

'koff!
(jocular) don't be stupid!; (serious) go away! *UK*
Phonetic abbreviation of 'fuck off!'.
- "Room for an ample chappie?" "Koff! Ample ... fit three of you in here![")] — Kevin Sampson, *Powder*, p. 440, 1999

koffiemoffie *noun*
a non-white, non-black homosexual male; an air steward on South African Airways *SOUTH AFRICA*
Elaborations of **MOFFIE** (a homosexual male), rhymed with 'coffee', in the first instance for a colour-tone, in the second as a humorous reference to the steward's duties. Gay slang originating among Cape coloureds.
- — Bart Luirink (translated by Loes Nas), *Moffies*, p. 118, 2000

Kojak *noun*
1 a blue flashing lamp that is temporarily attached (by magnets) to the roof of an unmarked police car *UK*
Named after the US television police drama *Kojak*, first shown in the UK on BBC television in 1974, and by which the UK police and public were first made aware of this new crime-fighting tool.
- — *The Official Encyclopaedia of New Scotland Yard*, 1999

2 in hold 'em poker, a king and a jack as the first two cards dealt to a player *US, 1981*
The sound of 'king-jack' suggests the name of a popular police television programme (1973–78) starring Telly Savalas.
- — Thomas L. Clark, *The Dictionary of Gambling and Gaming*, p. 114, 1987

▸ **the Kojak**
a totally depilated pubic mound *UK*
After the eponymous bald-headed detective.
- The Kojak of Full [Bikini Wax:] All hair is removed from the pubic and bottom area. — *Loaded*, p. 5, June 2002

Kojak's moneybox *noun*
the penis *UK*
Kojak, a television detective of the 1970s, was played by bald-headed actor Telly Savalas, 1924–94; thus this unsettling image of a bald head with a slot for coins.
• —Richard Herring, *Talking Cock*, p. 30, 2003

Kojak with a Kodak *noun*
a police officer operating a radar camera; police radar *US*
Combines television detective series *Kojak* (1973–78) with the corporate identity of a leading camera and film manufacturer.
• —*Complete CB Slang Dictionary*, 1976
• —Peter Chippindale, *The British CB Book*, p. 156, 1981

kokalize *verb*
▷ see: COCKALIZE

kokomo *noun*
crack cocaine *UK, 1998*
Plays phonetically on 'coke' in the same way as the earlier sense as 'cocaine user'.
• —Mike Haskins, *Drugs*, p. 282, 2003
▷ see: KOKOMO JOE

kong *noun*
cheap and potent alcoholic drink *US*
An abbreviation of **KING KONG**.
• —Lou Shelly, *Hepcats Jive Talk Dictionary*, p. 13, 1945

konk *noun*
▷ see: CONK

kooch *noun*
a sexually suggestive dance move by a female dancer *US, 1946*
• In this country the strippers adapted the kooch as an element of the strip and sounded out all the suggestive and provocative possibilities[.]—Jack Lait and Lee Mortimer, *Chicago Confidential*, p. 157, 1950

koochie *noun*
the vagina
• Beautifully Shaved Koochies—*Pornographic website*, 3rd December 2001

kook *noun*
1 a mentally disturbed person *US, 1922*
• [S]omeone reads a request from the Monterey County Board of Supervisors that citizens fly American flags to show that "Kooks, Commies, and Cowards do not represent our County."—Joan Didion, *Slouching Toward Bethlehem*, p. 70, 1968
• So, maybe we're not the kook capital we thought we were.—Joe Bob Briggs, *Joe Bob Goes to the Drive-In*, p. 67, 1987
• Now, Bruce is no kook.—Howard Stern, *Miss America*, p. 118, 1995
• Fergus, I know, does not approve of Higher Consciousness tapes and God Insight Boxes and psychics and angels [...] "Kooks." "That's easy to say," I reply, "but if enough people believe it, you can't just write it off."—Melanie McGrath, *Motel Nirvana*, 1995

2 an unskilled novice surfer or snowboarder *US, 1961*
• Move it, kook!—*Point Break*, 1991

3 in television and film making, a light screen designed to cast shadows *US*
• —Ralph S. Singleton, *Filmaker's Dictionary*, p. 91, 1990

kook box *noun*
a paddle board, used by beginner surfers *US*
• —John Severson, *Modern Surfing Around the World*, p. 172, 1964

kook cord *noun*
a line that attaches a surfer's ankle to his surfboard *US*
• —Trevor Cralle, *The Surfin'ary*, p. 66, 1991

kooky *noun*
in drag racing and hot rodding, a bobtail roadster (with a short rear overhang) *US*
• The term was first used to describe the car used on the TV series "77 Sunset Strip" by Edd "Kookie" Byrnes.—John Lawlor, *How to Talk Car*, p. 67, 1965
• —Lyle K. Engel, *The Complete Book of Fuel and Gas Dragsters*, p. 152, 1968

kooky *adjective*
eccentric, if not crazy *US, 1959*
• Married a kooky sucker fan of the manure-and-bruises circuit. —Iceberg Slim (Robert Beck), *Long White Con*, p. 87, 1977
• [G]et shoved aside by the next style-mag endorsed kooky chick who comes along.—*The Times*, 2nd August 2003: 'Play'

Kool and the Gang *adjective*
unemotional and relaxed, calm, imperturbable; excellent, admirable, wonderful *IRELAND*
• She's there, 'Oh my God, Ali's just, like, texted me this second. Are you going to, like, Annabel's tonight? I'm like, 'I could find myself in that vicinity,' playing it totally Kool and the Gang.—Paul Howard, *Ross O'Carroll-Kelly*, p. 71, 2003

Kools *noun*
cigarettes made with tobacco mixed with marijuana *US*
• Kools were regular cigarettes stuffed with a mixture of regular tobacco and marijuana.—Gregory Clark, *Words of the Vietnam War*, p. 392, 1990

kooratz *noun*
a socially inept person *CANADA*
• —Marcel Danesi, *Cool*, p. 116, 1994

kootchy-koo *noun*
▷ see: COOTCHY-COO

korea *noun*
anal sex *FIJI, 1984*
Recorded by Jan Tent.

Korean forklift *noun*
an A-frame backpack used by Koreans to carry large and heavy objects *US*
Korean war usage.
• —Frank Hailey, *Soldier Talk*, p. 36, 1982

kosh *noun*
▷ see: COSH

kosh *adjective*
acceptable, agreeable *US*
An abbreviation of **KOSHER**.
• —Judi Sanders, *Mashing and Munching in Ames*, p. 12, 1994

kosher *verb*
to give the appearance or effect of being fair, honest or legal *UK*
• It was koshered through London Airport inside the bra of a cosy old Swiss governess—Derek Raymond (Robin Cook), *The Crust on its Uppers*, 1962

kosher *adjective*
1 Jewish *US, 1972*
Offensive, a figurative application of the Jewish diet.
• BRIAN: I'm not a Roman, Mum, and I never will be! I'm a Kike! A Yid! A Hebe! A Hook-nose! I'm Kosher, Mum! I'm a Red Sea Pedestrian, and proud of it!—Monty Python, *Life of Brian*, 1979

2 fair, square, proper, satisfactory *UK, 1896*
Yiddish, technically meaning 'fit to eat' (ritually clean in keeping with religious dietary laws). According to Leo Rosten, 'the most resourceful Yiddish word in the English language'. Brought into English slang originally in the East End of London.
• [I]t's gold kettles [pocket watches], the jam jar [car] and a kosher pad [a place to live]: keep going till the next touch [a profitable crime][.] —Derek Raymond (Robin Cook), *The Crust on its Uppers*, 1962
• Pop was chopping a stud's mop and Mom was in her favorite squat behind the stove, which meant the time was kosher for me to do my famous Jimmy Valentine thing.—A.S. Jackson, *Gentleman Pimp*, p. 11, 1973
• She knew things wasn't kosher between me and this crew.—Edwin Torres, *After Hours*, p. 403, 1979
• Naw, I ain't taking no money from you. That don't look too kosher, me taking cash from you.—Richard Price, *Clockers*, p. 331, 1992
• And I'm gonna pop the ignition and wire it to make it look kosher? —Joseph Wambaugh, *Finnegan's Week*, p. 55, 1993
• [Y]ou're sure this tip is kosher?—Donald Gorgon, *Cop Killer*, p. 3, 1994
• TREVOR: It, er, ain't his real name. MIAMI: You amaze me. So what's 'is kosher 'andle?—Bernard Dempsey and Kevin McNally, *Lock, Stock ... & Two Hundred Smoking Kalashnikovs*, p. 103, 2000

3 in homosexual usage, circumcised *US*
• —*Maledicta*, p. 58, 1986–1987: 'A continuation of a glossary of ethnic slurs in American English'

Kosher Canyon *nickname*
a neighbourhood dominated by Jewish people *US*
The most famous is the Fairfax neighbourhood in Los Angeles.
• I could easier put up with all the Hebes in Kosher Canyon chippin their teeth every time you give them a ticket.—Joseph Wambaugh, *The Choirboys*, p. 98, 1975
• It took Irwin forty minutes to make the run from Kosher Canyon. —James Ellroy, *Brown's Requiem*, p. 12, 1981
• In the heart of "Kosher Canyon," Canter's has long served as a meeting place for rockers.—Art Fein, *The L.A. Musical History Tour*, p. 26, 1998

koutchie; cutchie; kouchie; couchie *noun*
a pipe for the smoking of marijuana *JAMAICA*
Celebrated in song by the Mighty Diamonds 'Pass the Koutchie'. This in turn inspired Musical Youth's UK hit 'Pass the Dutchie': the name was presumably changed so that the BBC censors would miss any reference to drugs.
- —The Reggae Crusaders, *Bring the Couchie Come*, 1975
- —Angela Devlin, *Prison Patter*, p. 42, 1996
- —Harry Shapiro, *Waiting For The Man*, 1999

K-pot *noun*
the standard US Army helmet *US*
- Jamison jumped when his K-Pot, the Army Kevlar helmet, appeared in front of his face. —Richard Herman Jr, *Force of Eagles*, p. 326, 1990

krab *noun*
in caving, pot-holing and mountaineering, a karabiner (a coupling device) *UK, 1963*
A colloquial abbreviation, noted in current use.
- —David Morrison of Wessex Cave Club, 29th February 2004

kraut *noun*
1 a German *US, 1841*
From the German dish *sauerkraut*; not necessarily disparaging.
- Isn't it niggers, Dadier? And spics? And krauts, Dadier? —Evan Hunter, *The Blackboard Jungle*, p. 209, 1954
- The lousy slob ratted on me to the M.P.'s about liberating 10 grand of some kraut's gold hoard back in '45[.] —Mickey Spillane, *Me, Hood!*, p. 15, 1963
- Now I saw, get the Krauts on the other side of the fence where they belong, and let's get back to the kind of enemy worth killing and the kind of war this whole country can support. —*Harold and Maude*, 1971
- Birds, locally. I mean apart from the Krauts, you see, well, there's the odd wife[.] —Mike Stott, *Soldiers Talking, Cleanly*, 1978
- I've read his stuff, Plimpl, he's heavy duty. I think he's a kraut. —Terry Southern, *Now Dig This*, p. 234, 1984
- I know I'm not meant to say Krauts and that. One thing I myself am not is a racialist. —Kevin Sampson, *Outlaws*, p. 7, 2001

2 the German language *US, 1948*
- "You speak kraut?" says Mike. [...] "Frog [French]?" he pursued gamely. —Derek Raymond (Robin Cook), *The Crust on its Uppers*, p. 46, 1962
- Another guy don't speak nothing but Kraut, he comes all the way from West Germany. —Elmore Leonard, *Split Images*, p. 109, 1981

krauthead *noun*
a German-American or German immigrant *US, 1928*
- And Mosca playing the game would say, "They wouldn't even look at your krautheads." —Mario Puzo, *The Dark Arena*, p. 90, 1955
- I doubt if the Krautheads could have handled this bunch of hoods. —Red Rudensky, *The Gonif*, p. 38, 1970
- "That phony krauthead," Francis complained[.] —Joseph Wambaugh, *The Choirboys*, p. 112, 1975
- And those given a name were stuck with it forever: Svade, Svenska, Lugan, Schnapps, Moishe, Stosh, Henie, Mockie, Guinea, Canuck, Bohunk, Pork-dodger, Limey, Greaseball, Krauthead, Dutchie, Squarehead, Grick, Mick, Paddy, Goombah, Polski, Dago, Hunkie, Wop —*San Francisco Examiner*, p. A15, 28th July 1997

krautland *noun*
Germany *US, 1955*
- [H]e's been slipping backwards and forward to krautland a bit often. —Derek Raymond (Robin Cook), *The Crust on its Uppers*, p. 51, 1962
- I need a lift. Unless you two want to go back to Krautland as a pair of sopranos. —Guy Ritchie et al, *Lock, Stock ... & Four Stolen Hooves*, p. 88, 2000

krautrock *noun*
German rock music *UK*
- Everybody has been hearing about kraut-rock[.] —Lester Bangs, *Psychotic Reactions and Carburetor Dung*, p. 154, 1975
- —Tom Hibbert, *Rockspeak!*, p. 95, 1983
- Ten music-related university courses that really exist [...] 9. KRAUTROCK – GERMAN STUDIES, University of Michigan —*Q*, p. 38, December 2001

kreeble *verb*
to ruin, partially or completely *US*
- —Steve Salaets, *Ye Olde Hiptionary*, 1970

Kremlin *noun*
1 Scotland Yard *UK*
- —Angela Devlin, *Prison Patter*, p. 69, 1996

2 the headquarters of British Railways *UK*
- —Harvey Sheppard, *Dictionary of Railway Slang*, 1970

kress *adjective*
cheap, inexpensive *US*
From the name of a chain of dime stores/pound shops.
- —Marcus Hanna Boulware, *Jive and Slang of Students in Negro Colleges*, 1947

krills *noun*
crack cocaine *US*
- When [Detective Anderson] Moran went over to Dorismond, he asked whether Dorismond had any"krills" – street slang for crack cocaine. —*New York Post*, p. 4, 28th July 2000

kris *adjective*
▷ see: CRISS

kronenburg *noun*
a women who looks a lot younger from the front than she does from behind *UK*
Formed from the '1664' branding used by Kronenburg™ lager, punning 16 in front and 64 behind.
- —Michael Rosen, *Word of Mouth (BBC Radio 4)*, 15th April 2005

kru *noun*
a tightly knit group of close friends *UK*
A deliberate respelling of **CREW**.
- [Y]our Kru, or your Massive, your Thugs, or Bredrins[.] —Julian Johnson, *Urban Survival*, p. 264, 2003

krunk
used in place of profanity *US*
Coined by the writers of *Late Nite with Conan O'Brien* in 1994 as 'America's newest swear word'. It enjoyed brief popularity.

kryptonite *noun*
crack cocaine *UK, 1998*
From the fictional mineral that weakens comic book superhero Superman (a native of Planet Krypton).
- —Mike Haskins, *Drugs*, p. 282, 2003

kudos *noun*
glory, fame, prestige *UK, 1831*
From Greek κῦδος (praise); originally university slang, in widespread use by 1890.
- I was grateful for all the kudos he give us and the times when he directly bailed us out[.] —Kevin Sampson, *Outlaws*, p. 104–105, 2001

kuduffle soup *noun*
(among Nova Scotians of German descent) a soup of homemade noodles, potatoes, gravy and browned flour *CANADA*
- "Kuduffle," in the Lunenburg County unconventional name for a soup, comes from the German "kartoffeln," "potatoes." —Lewis Poteet, *The South Shore Phrase Book*, p. 67, 1999

kuf *noun*
cocaine *UK*
- You don't wanna go puttin' kuf in there man. —Nick Barlay, *Curvy Lovebox*, p. 56, 1997
- He pushes a little bag of kuf over the desk an' Kingsley starts rackin' up lines on his mirror. —Nick Barlay, *Curvy Lovebox*, p. 59, 1997

ku klux klan *noun*
in poker, three kings *US*
From the klan's initials: KKK.
- —Albert H. Morehead, *The Complete Guide to Winning Poker*, p. 267, 1967

kumba *noun*
marijuana *UK, 1998*
- —Mike Haskins, *Drugs*, p. 288, 2003

kung-fu fighter *noun*
a lighter *UK*
Rhyming slang, based on the popular song by Jamaican-born Carl Douglas.
- —*www.LondonSlang.com*, June 2002

kunka *noun*
the vagina *BAHAMAS*
- —John A. Holm, *Dictionary of Bahamian English*, p. 120, 1982

kunkun *noun*
the vagina *TRINIDAD AND TOBAGO*
- Make sure an tidy yuh kunkun. —Lise Winer, *Dictionary of the English/Creole of Trinidad & Tobago*, 2003

kush *noun*
in circus and carnival usage, money *US*
• —Don Wilmeth, *The Language of American Popular Entertainment*, p. 153, 1981

kushempeng *noun*
marijuana *UK*
• —Mike Haskins, *Drugs*, p. 288, 2003

kustom *adjective*
custom *US*
• Spelling of "custom" koined by George Barris, a top California Kustomizer.—John Lawlor, *How to Talk Car*, p. 67, 1965

kutchie; kutchi *noun*
marijuana *JAMAICA*
Derived from **KOUTCHIE** (a marijuana pipe).
• —The Upsetters, *Kutchi Skank*, 1972
• Pass the Dutchie was a reggae anthem, based on an old Mighty Diamonds' song Pass the Kutchie. Kutchie was slang for marijuana, and so 'dutchie' was substituted as a different kind of pot, this one for cooking in.—Paul Du Noyer, *Encyclopaedia of Singles*, p. 157, 1998
• —Mike Haskins, *Drugs*, p. 288, 2003

Kuwaiti tanker *noun*
used as an all-purpose form of abuse *UK*
Rhyming slang for **WANKER**.
• —Ray Puxley, *Fresh Rabbit*, 1998

kvell *verb*
to overflow with joyful pride *US, 1967*
Yiddish.
• Despite having done a thousand lunch meetings at Nate, 'n Al's, Orson never got the Yiddish right. He said kvel when he meant kvetch, schmutz when he mean schvitz and schlmeil for schlemazel.—Joseph Wambaugh, *Finnegan's Week*, p. 6, 1993
• CHER: My heart is totally bursting. DIONNE: I know. I'm kvelling! —*Clueless*, 1995

kvetch *verb*
to complain, gripe, whine *US, 1950*
Yiddish, used by those who know only five words of the language.
• —Collin Baker et al., *College Undergraduate Slang Study Conducted at Brown University*, p. 149, 1968
• I don't want to have to listen to him kvetch about how nobody ever does anything for anybody but themselves.—Mart Crowley, *The Boys in the Band*, p. 23, 1968
• Is this truth I'm delivering up, or is it just plain kvetching? Or is kvetching for people like me a form of truth?—Philip Roth, *Portnoy's Complaint*, p. 105, 1969

kwaai *adjective*
1 bad, bad-tempered, aggressive *SOUTH AFRICA, 1955*
From Afrikaans *kwaad* (bad, evil).
• —Athol Fugard, *Boesman and Lena*, 1978
• As high as that river's breakage quotient is, it doesn't even come close to that of the River Kwai. Not the one of the movie, mind you, but this one just as kwaai.—*Sunday Times (South Africa)*, 19th February 2002

2 used as an expression of approval; great, excellent, cool *SOUTH AFRICA, 1974*
A reversal of the existing sense on the good-equals-bad formula.
• —Penny Silva, *A Dictionary of South African English*, 1996

K-wobbler *noun*
a Kentworth truck *US*
• —Ed and Ruth Radlauer, *Truck Tech Talk*, p. 33, 1986

K-word *noun*
kaffir (a black person, especially a black African); also applied in an adjectival sense *SOUTH AFRICA, 1982*
Euphemistic for all South African senses, and offensive in all senses, whether abbreviated or used conventionally.
• 'K-Word' Case: DA Woman Cleared—*Cape Argus*, 24th March 2004

KY *noun*
any sexual lubricant *US*
From the branded name of KY Jelly™.
• —Eugene Landy, *The Underground Dictionary*, p. 117, 1971

KY *nickname*
the federal narcotic treatment hospital in Lexington, Kentucky *US, 1962*
• Roy had kicked at K-Y [Lexington, Kentucky] but he started in again. —Jeremy Larner and Ralph Tefferteller, *The Addict in the Street*, p. 236, 1964

kyaw-kyaw *noun*
sarcastic laughter *US*
Also used as a verb.
• The whole court kyaw-kyawed, and back to the Island I went.—Mezz Mezzrow, *Really the Blues*, p. 319, 1946
• Biff hadn't come down with the immedate kyawkyaws.—Bernard Wolfe, *The Late Risers*, p. 202, 1954

kybo *noun*
an outdoor toilet *US*
From a children's acronym – '*k*eep *y*our *b*owels in *o*rder'.
• —Helen Dahlskog (Editor), *A Dictionary of Contemporary and Colloquial Usage*, p. 36, 1972

kybosh *noun*
▷ **see: KIBOSH**

kype *verb*
▷ **see: KIPE**

Ll

L *noun*

1 LSD *UK, 1969*

- —Angela Devlin, *Prison Patter*, p. 69, 1996
- Street names [...] hawk, L, lightning flash, Lucy[.]—James Kay and Julian Cohen, *The Parents' Complete Guide to Young People and Drugs*, p. 141, 1998
- —Mike Haskins, *Drugs*, p. 285, 2003

2 marijuana *US*

Rap and hip-hop slang.

- If you smoke L, you'll enjoy listening to it more[.]—*The Source*, p. 43, December 1993

3 elevation *US*

A surfer 'gets L' when his surfboard soars high into the air on an aerial move.

- —Trevor Cralle, *The Surfin'ary*, p. 43, 1991

▸ **take an L**

to lose a game *US*

From the designation in newspapers of 'wins and losses' as 'W's and 'L's.

- —Connie Eble (Editor), *UNC-CH Campus Slang*, p. 7, Spring 1999

L-12 *noun*

1 an extremely social outcast *US*

The 'L' is for 'loser', twelve times.

- —*People Magazine*, p. 73, 19th July 1993

2 a social outcast who is profoundly out of touch with trends *US*

The suggestion is 'loser times twelve'.

- —*Evening Sun (Baltimore)*, p. 12A, 19th January 1994

l33t; l33t 5p34k *noun*

▷ **see:** LEET TALK

L7; l-seven *noun*

a staid person who is uninterested in or unsympathetic to the fashionable interests of teenagers *US, 1956*

The shapes of L and 7 can combine to form a **SQUARE** (a conventional person). This slang may be entirely gestural in expression: the forefinger and thumb on each hand extended at right angles, left (L) and right (7) combining to make the shape of a square.

- —David Claerbaut, *Black Jargon in White America*, p. 71, 1972
- —*Esquire*, p. 180, June 1983
- We say it's Lesbian Seven. We say it's a level of consciousness when you get to level seven in meditation. We say it's lubrication, a love jelly called L7. There's actually a guitar amp called L7... There's also a panty size L7 – large seven – very apropos for this band.—*Jabberrock [quoting Suzi Gardner of the band L7]*, p. 187, 1997

L8R *adverb*

used in text messaging, to mean 'later' *UK*

A variant spelling; one of several constructions in which a syllable pronounced 'ate' is replaced by the homophone 'eight'.

- Email and texting are great but my little stand against the future is to always put 'see you later' instead of 'c u l8r' – I don't believe in leaving hanging participles!—*The Guardian*, 19th June 2003

la; la-la *noun*

a toilet *NEW ZEALAND*

An abbreviated 'lavatory'.

- —David McGill, *David McGill's Complete Kiwi Slang Dictionary*, p. 68, 1998

▷ **see:** LAR

LA *noun*

any amphetamine or other central nervous system stimulant *US*

A shortened form of 'long-acting' or **LA TURNABOUT**.

- —Richard A. Spears, *The Slang and Jargon of Drugs and Drink*, p. 307, 1986

LA *nickname*

Los Angeles, California *US, 1901*

- As you say, the novel is more important & promising now, and I'll get to see L.A. if nothing else.—Jack Kerouac, *Letter to Caroline Kerouac Blake*, p. 133, 25th September 1947
- "LA." I loved the way she said "LA"; I love the way everybody says "LA" on the Coast[.]—Jack Kerouac, *On the Road*, p. 81, 1957
- RANCHER: Where you fellas from? WYATT: L.A. RANCHER: L.A.? WYATT: Los Angeles.—Peter Fonda, *Easy Rider*, p. 60, 1969

lab *noun*

1 a *lab*oratory *UK, 1895*

- So come up to the lab / And see what's on the slab[.]—Richard O'Brien, *Rocky Horror Show*, 1973

2 a *Lab*rador dog *UK, 1984*

Also variants 'labbie' and 'labby'.

- A trained Lab can detect marijuana or hashish from yards away[.]—September B. Morn, *Training Your Labrador Retriever*, p. 4, 1999

labbe *noun*

the vagina *US*

Possibly derived from 'labia'.

- There's [a...] "cooter," "labbe," "Gladys Siegelman," "VA," "wee wee[".]—Eve Ensler, *The Vagina Monologues*, p. 6, 1998

label *noun*

the name by which a person is known *US, 1928*

- —Hyman E. Goldin et al., *Dictionary of American Underworld Lingo*, p. 121, 1950

labial contact *noun*

a kiss; kissing *US*

- —Marcus Hanna Boulware, *Jive and Slang of Students in Negro Colleges*, 1947

labor skate *noun*

a trade union official *US, 1930*

- —Hyman E. Goldin et al., *Dictionary of American Underworld Lingo*, p. 121, 1950
- And I'm not very bright or I wouldn't be a labor skate.—Jim Thompson, *The Killer Inside*, p. 25, 1952

Labour *noun*

▸ **the Labour**

the Labour Exchange, later the Job Centre (government offices where unemployed persons must register to search for work as a condition for the receipt of state benefits) *UK*

- I'd been out of work for a couple of months and the Labour wouldn't give me no money[.]—John Peter Jones, *Feather Pluckers*, p. 10, 1964

labour day junkie *noun*

someone who uses heroin only occasionally *IRELAND*

- As well as that, he's always bragging about heroin addiction, even though everyone knows the cunt's nothing more than a labour day junkie who spends a tenner on gear when he gets his dole and always tries to persuade someone else to get stoned with him.—Howard Paul, *The Joy*, p. 35, 1996

labradoodle *noun*

a crossbreed of labrador and poodle *US*

- [C]ockapoos – or terra-poos, peke-a-poos, or labradoodles. Lots of mixes are out there, great pets one and all. But a breed? No.—Gina Spadafori and Marty Becker, *Dogs for Dummies*, p. 28, 2001

la buena *noun*

heroin *UK*

From Spanish *buena* (good).

- —Mike Haskins, *Drugs*, p. 284, 2003

lac *noun*

a Cadillac *US, 1990*

- —Judi Sanders, *Faced and Faded, Hanging to Hurl*, p. 24, 1993

lace *noun*

1 a combination of marijuana and cocaine *UK, 1998*

- —Mike Haskins, *Drugs*, p. 293, 2003

2 money *US*
- —Eugene Landy, *The Underground Dictionary*, p. 118, 1971

lace *verb*
to have sexual intercourse *US*
The female is seen here as a drink to be 'laced' by the male's semen.
- Think that I should lace her "Nah it's much safer orally"—Sadat X, Fat Joe & Diamond D, *Nasty Hoes*, 1996

▸ **lace up your boots**
to prepare for a fight *US*
- —Ethan Hilderbrant, *Prison Slang*, p. 156, 1998

lace card *noun*
1 a computer punch card with all the holes punched out *US*
- —Eric S. Raymond, *The New Hacker's Dictionary*, p. 219, 1991

2 the foreskin of an uncircumcised penis *US, 1941*
- —Donald Webster Cory and John P. LeRoy, *The Homosexual and His Society*, p. 265, 1963: 'A lexicon of homosexual slang'
- — *American Speech*, p. 57, Spring-Summer 1970: 'Homosexual slang'
- — *Maledicta*, p. 218, 1979: 'Kinks and queens: linguistic and cultural aspects of the terminology for gays'

lace curtain *noun*
beer *UK, 1961*
Rhyming slang, formed on the name of Burton, and originally applied only to beers from that brewery.
- —Ray Puxley, *Cockney Rabbit*, p. 109, 1992

lace-curtain Irish *noun*
middle-class Irish-American or Irish immigrants *US, 1934*
- Two guineas, one hunku funky lace-curtain Irish mick.—Lenny Bruce, *The Essential Lenny Bruce*, p. 11, 1967
- Like you said, lace curtains all the way.—Edwin Torres, *Q & A*, p. 140, 1977

lace-curtain lesbian *noun*
a lesbian whose mannerisms and affectations do not suggest her sexual preference *US*
- Your fifth grade school teacher or your favorite aunt could be a lesbian. So could any pretty secretary in your office. So could your wife. "Lace curtain" lesbians pass with no difficulty.—*San Francisco Chronicle*, p. 22, 30th June 1969

laced *adjective*
drug-intoxicated, especially marijuana-intoxicated *US, 1988*
- It is one thing to spark up a dubie and get laced at parties, but it is quite another to be fried all day.—*Clueless*, 1995

lace queen *noun*
a homosexual who prefers men with uncircumcised penises *US, 1980s*
- —H. Max, *Gay (S)language*, p. 25, 1988

lace-up *noun*
a shoe or boot that is laced up (as opposed to sandals, slip-ons, etc) *UK, 1887*
- Not nice shoes, more your corrective, orthopaedic jobs for old ladies with beat-up feet, and lace-ups for nurses.—*The Guardian*, 15th February 2003

lack *adjective*
lacking money, style or both *US*
Hawaiian youth usage.
- Oh, Harold, so lack, you!—Douglas Simonson, *Pidgin to da Max Hana Hou*, 1982

lackery *noun*
▸ **give them lackery**
a beating *IRELAND*
- They don't know what they're messing with when they mess with us. We'll give them lackery.—Hugh Leonard, *Out After Dark*, p. 95, 1989

lad *noun*
▸ **bit of a lad**
a young man who is full of self-confidence with which he pursues sensual ambitions *UK, 1984*
An elaboration of 'lad'.
- His biological father had been 16. Bit of a lad. Had a moped.—*The Observer*, 9th November 2003

▸ **the lad**
1 the penis *UK*
- Get yewer lad out for the people!—Niall Griffiths, *Sheepshagger*, p. 142, 2001
- I stands back and pulls the lad out[.]—Kevin Sampson, *Clubland*, p. 89, 2002

2 cancer or tuberculosis *IRELAND*
- Cancer was never mentioned by name. "The Lad" was the sympathetic form of allusion[.]—Bernard Share, *Slanguage*, p. 163, 1997

lads *noun*
▸ **one of the lads**
a woman, especially a young woman, who is seen to be on equal terms with, or part of a society of, men *UK*
- Wright, 42, with a young family, does not come across as super-woman so much as one of the lads.—*The Guardian*, 6th November 2003

▸ **the lads**
male friends, the men of a regular social group, team, etc *UK, 1896*
- One of the lads joked that I turned back the years today.—*The Guardian*, 28th January 2002

ladder *noun*
the main track in a railway yard *US*
- —Norman Carlisle, *The Modern Wonder Book of Trains and Railroading*, p. 265, 1946

laddie *noun*
in a deck of playing cards, a jack *US*
- —George Percy, *The Language of Poker*, p. 50, 1988

laddish *adjective*
used, often disapprovingly, of the lively behaviour of young men responding to those things (alcohol, sport, sex) that appeal to them *UK, 1841*
- His friends, less good-looking but far more laddish, had always had far greater success with women.—Jane Green, *Babyville*, p. 35, 2003

laddishness *noun*
the lively behaviour of young men responding to those things (alcohol, sport, sex) that appeal to them *UK, 1886*
- The Hofmeister bear became such an icon for young drinkers, encapsulating the unrestrained "laddishness" of their behaviour, that it was eventually banned.—Robert Heath, *The Hidden Power of Advertising*, p. 147, 2001

laddo *noun*
a spirited youth, a bit of a lad *UK*
Slightly patronising.
- [I]f you meet one of these laddos[.]—James Hawes, *Dead Long Enough*, p. 22, 2000

ladeez *noun*
ladies, often as a form of address *UK*
Most often in the phrase 'ladeez and germs' (Ladies and Gentlemen).
- Her attacker roared with laughter. "Forget something, ladeez?" —Rochelle Hollander Schwab, *In a Family Way*, p. 133, 1995

ladette *noun*
a young woman characterised by her behaviour and positive involvement in activites (drinking, swearing, sport, etc) stereotypically enjoyed by males *UK, 1995*
- [T]he flipside is her [Sara Cox] reputation elsewhere as a foul-mouthed ladette who's dragging the nation's youth into the gutter. —*The Times Magazine*, p. 18, 15th June 2002

la di da *noun*
the *Daily Star* newspaper *UK*
Rhyming slang.
- —Ray Puxley, *Fresh Rabbit*, 1998

la-di-da; la-di-dah *verb*
to behave in an affectedly cultured manner, when noted from a lower social station *UK*
- [S]ome middle-aged creeps with toffee-nosed accents; and they begins lah-de-dahing it all over the place.—John Peter Jones, *Feather Pluckers*, p. 102, 1964

la-di-da; la-di-dah *adjective*
pertaining to the affectedly cultured speech and manners of the upper-classes, especially when noted from a lower social station; hence, pretentious *US, 1890*
Jocular or pejorative.
- Too busy with Mr. Romeo Roberts, with his blazers and his knife-edge crease and his la-de-da talk.—Alexander Baron, *A Bit of Happiness [Six Granada Plays]*, p. 218, 1959
- One of the doormen in the foyer overheard him and started mocking Jon's accent, putting on this lah-di-dah voice. I thought, Oh dear, mate – you have made a proper mistake here in thinking that Jon's a wanker.—Dave Courtney, *Raving Lunacy*, p. 141, 2000

- Oooh, the man minced. La-di-da. But I can see through you. The fancy accent doesn't impress me. —John King, *White Trash*, p. 80, 2001
- He [Tony Blair] wasn't one of us, he was a la-di-da type. —Mark Steel, *Reasons to be Cheerful*, p. 234, 2001
- What you look for in a greasy spoon is not cookery. There is nothing la-di-da on the premises. The food is plain; that's the deal. —*The New York Times*, 22nd June 2001

la-di-dah; lardy; la-di-da *noun*

a cigar *UK*

Rhyming slang, cleverly echoing the **LA-DI-DAH** status of a cigar smoker.

- [B]eing too poor to bet or have women apart from the Booby, a "la-di-dah" a day is the one luxury. —John McCririck, *John McCririck's World of Betting*, p. 16, 1991

ladies' aid *noun*

in pool, a device used to support the cue stick for a hard-to-reach shot *US*

As the terminology suggests, the device is scorned by skilled players.

- —Steve Rushin, *Pool Cool*, p. 18, 1990

ladies a plate, gents a crate

used in party invitations to request female guests to bring a dish of food and male guests to bring something to drink *NEW ZEALAND*

- —Louis S. Leland, *A Personal Kiwi-Yankee Dictionary*, p. 59, 1984

ladies' delight *noun*

the penis *UK*

- —Richard Herring, *Talking Cock*, p. 30, 2003

ladies' man *noun*

a man who pays great attention to women; a womaniser *AUSTRALIA, 1901*

- Blond with the most piercing blue eyes, handsome in that rugged central European way, he was very much the ladies' man. —Clive Galea, *Slipper*, p. 150, 1988

lads-mag *noun*

a commercial publication that targets young men with aspirational features on hedonistic lifestyles and, in particular, pictures of semi-naked young women *UK*

- [A] trawl through the growing archive of Paula Reid's lads-mag photo-shoots – all erect nipples and see-thru tops[.] —Christopher Brookmyre, *Boiling a Frog*, p. 105, 2000

lady *noun*

1 a prostitute *US*

- Ladies is the polite form, and carries the connotations of "ladies of the evening" and 'sportin' lady, that is, a kind of gallant euphemism. "This is Sheila, one of my ladies." —Christina and Richard Milner, *Black Players*, p. 37, 1972

2 a homosexual man *UK, 1932*

An example of **CAMP** trans-gender assignment.

- —Paul Baker, *Polari*, p. 178, 2002

3 in a deck of playing cards, a queen *US, 1900*

- If the player (with queens) wins the pot, they are "ladies"; but if he loses the pot, they are "whores." —Albert H. Morehead, *The Complete Guide to Winning Poker*, p. 264, 1967

4 cocaine *US, 1974*

- —Robert Sabbag, *Snowblind*, p. 271, 1976
- Street names [...] gold dust, lady, snow, white. —James Kay and Julian Cohen, *The Parents' Complete Guide to Young People and Drugs*, p. 134, 1998
- —Nick Constable, *This is Cocaine*, p. 181, 2002

lady *adjective*

effeminate *UK*

Recorded in contemporary gay use.

- —*Attitude*, p. 60, July 2003: 'New palare lexicon'

ladybits *noun*

the female genitals *UK*

- Do you have any other piercings? Yes, here (points at her ear), here (points at her belly button) and here (points at her ladybits! But then starts laughing) ha ha! I'm only joking. —*FHM*, p. 182, June 2003

Lady Blamey *noun*

a drinking glass made by cutting the top off a bottle using a kerosene-soaked string *AUSTRALIA, 1945*

Taught to the troops by Lady Blamey, the wife of Sir Thomas Blamey, commander of Allied Land Forces in the south-west Pacific.

ladyboy *noun*

a person with mixed sexual physiology, usually the genitals of a male and surgically augmented breasts; a pre-surgery transexual or a transvestite *UK*

A term used most often in association with the sex industry in Bangok, Thailand, but also used by Queer Dady Funk to describe Eminem. The first widespread use of the term was in associatoin with a television documentary aired in November 1992.

- [Y]our ex-classmates think you're a failed pet-food salesman now hiding out in Ecuador with a ladyboy. —*The Observer*, 30th December 2001
- Thai ladyboys try to be accepted through their love of cheerleading. —*Variety*, p. 37, 3rd November 2003
- —*www.adultquarter.com/blossary.html*, January 2004: 'Glossary of adult Internet terms'

lady caine *noun*

cocaine *UK, 1998*

A compound of **LADY** (cocaine) and **CAINE** (cocaine).

- —Mike Haskins, *Drugs*, p. 280, 2003

lady come back *noun*

a type of bet in an illegal numbers game lottery *US*

- Then to be on the safe side he also played jail house, death row, lady come back, two-timing woman, pile of rocks, dark days and trouble. —Chester Himes, *A Rage in Harlem*, p. 23, 1957

lady five fingers *noun*

a boy's or man's hand in the context of masturbation; masturbation *US*

- I wondered if it were a capital crime in this joint to get caught having an affair with "lady five fingers." —Iceberg Slim (Robert Beck), *Pimp*, p. 50 – 51, 1969

lady from Bristol *noun*

a pistol *UK*

Rhyming slang.

- —*This Week*, 10th March 1968

Lady Godiva; godiva; lady *noun*

a five-pound note or the sum of £5 *UK, 1960*

Rhyming slang for a **FIVER**; an appropriately financial allusion to the C11 English noblewoman who rode naked through Coventry to protest against taxes – according to the legend which arose in the C13.

- [A] rich four-by-twoish [Jewish] merchant [...] put his hand into his sky rocket [pocket] and took out a Lady Godiva[.] —Ronnie Barker, *Fletcher's Book of Rhyming Slang*, p. 27, 1979
- I did call an Emergency Helpline at 44p per minute, and it cost me a Lady Godiva[.] —Andrew Nickolds, *Back to Basics*, p. 40, 1994

lady in the red dress *noun*

the bleed period of the menstrual cycle *US*

An elaboration on red imagery stressing the feminine nature of the term.

- —Karen Houppert, *The Curse*, 1999

lady in waiting *noun*

in male homosexual usage, a man who loiters in or near public toilets in the hope of sexual encounters *US*

- —*Male Swinger Number 3*, p. 47, 1981: 'The complete gay dictionary'

Lady Jane *noun*

a common-law wife or girlfriend *CANADA*

- "Lady Jane" is common around Regina, for a union not sanctified by marriage. —Chris Thain, *Cold as a Bay Street Banker's Heart*, p. 97, 1987

ladykiller *noun*

a man who is sexually fascinating to women *UK, 1811*

- You think you are skinny and that makes you a ladykiller. You think you are skinny and that makes you irresistible. —James Lehrer, *White Widow*, p. 113, 2000

lady luck *noun*

good fortune personified *UK, 1205*

- No doubt about it, really looked like Old Lady Luck had crossed me off her list for good. —Mezz Mezzrow, *Really the Blues*, p. 291, 1946

Lady Muck *noun*
a woman who is, in the speaker's opinion, unjustifiably important or esteemed *UK, 1957*
The counterpart to **LORD MUCK**.
- At this point, Lady Muck returned from her psychology course. Christine called her a right snotty cow. Lady Muck called Christine a lazy bitch and slammed the door on her flying pinny strings.— *The Guardian*, 22nd August 2003

lady of the night *noun*
a prostitute *UK, 1925*
- [S]troll (yes, stroll!) up to Piccadilly Circus, pick up ladies of the night, and take them back to Downing Street[.]— *The Guardian*, 7th June 2001

Lady Snow *noun*
cocaine *US*
- "That's my woman, Lady Snow," he told me once. "I sure wish I could cop some."—Piri Thomas, *Down These Mean Streets*, p. 258, 1967

lady's waist *noun*
a small, waisted glass for serving alcoholic drinks *AUSTRALIA, 1934*
- A Lady's Waist used to be either a 5- or 7-ounce measure of beer once served only in the parlour of a pub in New South Wales.—Richard Beckett, *The Dinkum Aussie Dictionary*, p. 33, 1986

Lafayette *noun*
a bet *AUSTRALIA*
Rhyming slang.
- —Ned Wallish, *The Truth Dictionary of Racing Slang*, p. 45, 1989

laff *noun*
a laugh *UK*
- Come an watch this for a laff, Bert.—Troy Kennedy Martin, *Z Cars*, p. 41, 1962
- —*Scooby's All-Star Laff-A-Lympics*, 1980
- I'm not doing this for a laff, you know.— *The Full Monty*, 1997

laff *verb*
to laugh *UK*
- Gerald? Go get shagged – he'd tell every bugger – we'd be laffed out of Sheffield.— *The Full Monty*, 1997

laffmeister *noun*
a comedian *UK*
A combination of **LAFF** (a laugh) and German *meister* (a master, a champion).
- Bernard Manning [...] the most obnoxious and politically incorrect laffmeister on the planet.—Tony Wilson, *24 Hour Party People*, p. 141, 2002

lag *noun*
1 a convict who has been imprisoned for many years *UK, 1812*
- —Marlene Freedman, *Alcatraz*, 1983
- Use of slang was a major criminal culture to deceive those who would "earwig" onto the lags conversation.—Ryan Aven-Bray, *Ridgey Didge Oz Jack Lang*, p. 3, 1983
- Aren't I Australian? I'm that close to the lags of the First Fleet, I could have come over with them in chains and I wouldn't know the difference.—Rodney Hall, *Kisses of the Enemy*, p. 355, 1987
- —Angela Devlin, *Prison Patter*, p. 69, 1996
- [A]n old lag who'd just got out of the Scrubs after a six-stretch[.]—Greg Williams, *Diamond Geezers*, p. 64, 1997

2 an act of urination *UK*
A survival from the obsolete verb form.
- I'm going for a lag.—Patrick O'Shaughessy, *Market Traders' Slang*, 1979

lag *verb*
1 to inform against a person *AUSTRALIA, 1832*
- He certainly was one to lag was Andy Andrews.—Charles Raven, *Underworld Nights*, p. 166, 1956
- This flip might lag me to the jacks.—Kevin Mackey, *The Cure*, p. 63, 1970
- You don't lag on your mates and it's important to have a prior.— *TV Week*, p. 14, 30th May 1992
- They all talked the talk about not lagging on one another and refusing to give up their mates, but in 99 per cent of cases it was all bullshit. —William Dodson, *The Sharp End*, p. 82, 2001

2 to arrest *UK, 1835*
- —*The Annals of the American Academy of Political and Social Sciences*, p. 127, May 1950
- The case was about to come up. I had been lagged for another jumpover (q.v.) I did. The trial would be a formality.—Howard Paul, *The Joy*, p. 68, 1996

3 to be serving a prison sentence *UK, 1927*
Originally, 'to be transported for a crime'.
- —Angela Devlin, *Prison Patter*, p. 69, 1996

4 to urinate *UK*
From an earlier sense as 'water'. A variant spelling is 'lage'.
- —Paul Baker, *Polari*, p. 178, 2002

lage *noun*
a convict *UK*
A variation of **LAG**.
- —Paul Baker, *Polari*, p. 178, 2002

lager lout *noun*
a hooligan fuelled by alcohol, especially lager *UK, 1987*
- They are also alarmed by the advent of the new phenomenon of rural hooliganism, mobs of affluent youths rampaging through country towns which Mr. John Patten, Minister of State at the Home Office, has dubbed 'the Saturday night lager culture' and its associated 'lager louts'.— *The Times*, 27th September 1987
- —Nicholas Jones, *Hackers, Hotting and Hooray Henrys*, p. 39, 1992
- [German] police should be given an unprecedentedly free hand to deal with "nuisance crime" caused by what frustrated Tory ministers once dubbed lager louts.— *The Guardian*, 1st July 2000

lagged *adjective*
1 exhausted, especially from travelling *UK*
An abbreviation of conventional 'jet lagged' (suffering disrupted body rhythms as a result of flying across time zones), from 'lag' (to fail to keep pace).
- I'm still lagged. I'm just gonna doss for a day or two.—Kevin Sampson, *Powder*, p. 412, 1999

2 drunk *UK*
Also 'lagged up'.
- We got completely lagged and started acting up.—Dave Courtney, *Raving Lunacy*, p. 46, 2000

lagger *noun*
1 a contact man in a smuggling enterprise *US*
- —*American Speech*, p. 97, May 1956: 'Smugglers' argot in the Southwest'

2 an informer to the police or authorities *AUSTRALIA, 1967*

lagging *noun*
a prison sentence *UK, 1812*
- [T]he judge gave them all a lagging, and Harry got his first taste of the Moor [HM Prison Dartmoor].—Charles Raven, *Underworld Nights*, p. 48, 1956
- "Alright I supose [sic], how long are you doing?" "A lagging." "Your [sic] f...ing lucky, I'm doing a bleeding neves."—Frank Norman, *Bang To Rights*, p. 17, 1958
- As he entered the hotel some of the regulars who knew us well commiserated, and some told Joey they thought the magistrate had been unfair, but that they were pleased he hadn't copped a lagging. —Ward McNally, *Supper at Happy Harry's*, p. 138, 1982
- —Angela Devlin, *Prison Patter*, p. 69, 1996
- With so much time on their hands some prisoners turned to religion in the search for answers to their problems. For some, it seemed to help them cope with their laggings.—William Dodson, *The Sharp End*, p. 20, 2001

lagging boat *noun*
a drunk *UK*
- Morty gives him a handful of change and the lagging boat wants to shake Mort's hand but Mort ain't keen.—J.J. Connolly, *Layer Cake*, p. 170, 2000

LA glass *noun*
a smokeable methamphetamine that does not dissolve rapidly *US*
- —Geoffrey Froner, *Digging for Diamonds*, p. 69, 1989: 'Types of speed'

lah *noun*
▷ see: **LAR**

Lah *noun*
Los Angeles, California *US*
Rarely heard, and then in northern California and derisively.
- "God ol' Lah!" "Huh?" "Lah. L.A. ... get it?" "Oh ... yeah." "L.A. is Lah. S.F. is Sif."—Armistead Maupin, *Tales of the City*, p. 310, 1978

lahdee; lahdie *adjective*
smart or fashionable *UK*
From **LA-DI-DA** (pretentious).
- —Tom Barling, *Bergman's Blitz*, 1973

lah-di-dah; lah-di *noun*
a famous entertainer, a star *UK*
Rhyming slang.
- A few lah-di's[.]—Ronnie Barker, *Fletcher's Book of Rhyming Slang*, p. 40, 1979

laid-back *adjective*
relaxed, passive, easy-going *US, 1969*
- "[L]aid back" can mean anything from "uninterested" to "lazy slob", and it is used usually by people who don't want to do anything. — *Sunday Times*, 6th August 1979
- "Somehow, I just wanted to get really laid-back," [Neil] Young recalled... "Okay, let's just get really, really mellow and peaceful ... make music that's just as intense as the electric stuff but which comes from a completely different place, a more loving place. — Barney Hoskyns, *Waiting For The Sun*, p. 201, 1996

laid in the aisle *adjective*
very well dressed *US*
- — Hermese E. Roberts, *The Third Ear*, 1971

laid out *adjective*
drunk to the point of passing out *US, 1928*
- — Collin Baker et al., *College Undergraduate Slang Study Conducted at Brown University*, p. 149, 1968

laid, relayed and parlayed *adjective*
thoroughly taken advantage of *US, 1957*
There are multiple variants of the third element – 'waylaid', 'marmalade', etc.
- We been laid, relayed, and waylaid and nobody wants to hear about it. — Edwin Torres, *Carlito's Way*, p. 5, 1975

lain; laine *noun*
▷ see: LANE

lair *noun*
a person who dresses and behaves in a showy manner *AUSTRALIA, 1923*
Back-formation from **LAIRY**. A term of great contempt.
- Pussyfooting by the Federal and State Governments regarding Communist-inspired, organised and aided louts and lairs among university students must end. — Bill Hornadge, *The Ugly Australian*, p. 236, 1969
- There was nothing more loathsome, in their eyes, than a bush lair on a winning streak. — Lance Peters, *The Dirty Half-Mile*, p. 170, 1979

lair *verb*
to behave in a showy, ostentatious way; to be a lair *AUSTRALIA, 1928*
- I improved myself in the dance halls and in general lairing about. — Wendy Lowenstein and Morag Loh, *The Immigrants*, p. 69, 1977

lairise *verb*
to behave in a showy, ostentatious way; to be a lair *AUSTRALIA, 1945*
- 'I think Lucky's suddenly found out what war really means,' I told him. 'He was too busy lairising before.' — Eric Lambert, *The Veterans*, p. 129, 1954
- 'Yeah. You're a bloody marvel,' muttered Davo, getting a bit pissed off at Eddie's lairising; and also a little jealous of Eddie's getting all the attention. — Robert G. Barrett, *Davo's Little Something*, p. 55, 1992

lairy; lary; larey *adjective*
showy, ostentatious, attention-seeking *AUSTRALIA, 1898*
- And while I'm on the subject, get rid of that white puggaree on your hat like all other blokes have. Also, Mr. Bruce told you to straighten out that lairy bash in it. — Eric Lambert, *The Veterans*, p. 100, 1954
- Queen's had the sort of decor that was already lairy enough to fuck with your brain. — Dave Courtney, *Raving Lunacy*, p. 11, 2000
- Six or seven Chinese come outside, pissed and larey, and I can see it coming[.] — John King, *Human Punk*, p. 141, 2000

lakanuki *noun*
a prolonged period of sexual abstinence *US, 1944*
An imitation pidgin 'lack of **NOOKIE**'.
- — *American Speech*, p. 305, December 1947: 'Imaginary diseases in Army and Navy parlance'
- — Robert A. Wilson, *Playboy's Book of Forbidden Words*, p. 157–158, 1972
- — *Maledicta*, p. 56, 1986–1987: 'A continuation of a glossary of ethnic slurs in American English'

lakbay diva *noun*
a dark leafed marijuana *UK, 1998*
Diva is 'goddess' in Latin; 'lacbay' is pig Latin for **BLACK**; this marijuana is a 'black goddess'.
- — Mike Haskins, *Drugs*, p. 288, 2003

Lake Acid *nickname*
Lake Placid, New York *US*
Coined during a concert stop by the Grateful Dead in 1983.
- — David Shenk and Steve Silberman, *Skeleton Key*, p. 173, 1994

Lake Atlantic *nickname*
the Atlantic Ocean on the Florida coast *US*
A tribute to the flat surf conditions found in summer.
- — Trevor Cralle, *The Surfin'ary*, p. 67, 1991

lake pipes *noun*
in hot rodding, straight exhaust pipes, originally designed for speed runs on dry lake beds *US*
- She's got a competition clutch with four on the floor / And she purrs like a kitten till the lake pipes roar. — The Beach Boys, *Little Deuce Coupe*, 1963

lakes of Killarney; lakes; lakie; lakey *adjective*
1 mad, crazy; stupid *UK, 1934*
Imperfect rhyming slang for **BARMY**, formed on a feature of Irish geography.
- — Patrick O'Shaughessy, *Market Traders' Slang*, 1979
- — Ray Puxley, *Cockney Rabbit*, 1992

2 sly, two-faced *UK*
Rhyming slang, on obsolete slang word 'carney' (sly, two-faced).
- — Ray Puxley, *Cockney Rabbit*, 1992

lakester *noun*
in hot rodding, a car with a streamlined body and exposed wheels, designed for racing on dry lake beds *US*
- — John Edwards, *Auto Dictionary*, p. 93, 1993

lala *noun*
the vagina *BAHAMAS*
- — John A. Holm, *Dictionary of Bahamian English*, p. 120, 1982

la-la *noun*
a toilet *AUSTRALIA, 1963*
- — Connie Eble (Editor), *UNC-CH Campus Slang*, p. 7, Fall 1999

La-La Land *noun*
Los Angeles, California *US*
- (Headline) Earl the Voyeur From La La Land — *Screw*, p. 9, 28th August 1972
- "And you're in El-A?" "Yeah, La-La Land." — Odie Hawkins, *Lost Angeles*, p. 166, 1994

lalapalooze *noun*
in poker, a hand that entitles the player to special payment from all other players *US*
- — George Percy, *The Language of Poker*, p. 51, 1988

laldy *noun*
▸ **give it laldy**
to do something enthusiastically, or with great vigour *UK: SCOTLAND*
Glasgow slang.
- The band's been givin it laldy aw night. — Michael Munro, *The Original Patter*, 1985

▸ **give you laldy**
to beat or thrash you *UK: SCOTLAND*
Glasgow slang.
- — Michael Munro, *The Original Patter*, 1985

lally; lallie; lall; lallette; lyle; lally-peg *noun*
the leg *UK*
Polari; usually in the plural.
- Well, I see Samson as huge and all butch, with great bulging thews and whopping great lallies, with long blond riah [hair] hanging down his Jim and Jack[.] — Barry Took and Marty Feldman, *Round The Horne*, 16th April 1967
- Her eek [face] is cod [not good] but the lalls are fab! — the cast of 'Aspects of Love', Prince of Wales Theatre, *Palare (Boy Dancer Talk) for Beginners*, 1989–92
- I can't make my feet or my lallies behave. — Richard Arnold, *GMTV*, 31st December 2002

lally-covers *noun*
trousers *UK*
Polari, from **LALLY** (the leg).
- — Paul Baker, *Polari*, p. 179, 2002

lally-drags *noun*
trousers *UK*
Polari; a combination of **LALLY** (the leg) and **DRAG** (clothing).
- — Paul Baker, *Polari*, p. 179, 2002

lallygag *verb*
▷ see: LOLLYGAG

lam *noun*

1 in cheating schemes, a victim *UK, 1668*
The victims are like 'lambs to slaughter' (easily duped).
- — Frank Garcia, *Marked Cards and Loaded Dice*, p. 262, 1962

2 a young, innocent-looking male prisoner recently arrived at prison, identified as an easy sexual conquest by the population of sexual predators *US, 1922*
- — *Male Swinger Number 3*, p. 47, 1981: 'The complete gay dictionary'

▸ **on the lam**
running away; trying to escape *US, 1928*
- I will have to sub-lease this house to some sucker, and then take it on the lam to Frisco. — Jack Kerouac, *Letter to John Clellon Holmes*, p. 196, 24th June 1949
- Baltimore is a favorite hide-out for Mafiastas on the lam from other towns[.] — Jack Lait and Lee Mortimer, *Washington Confidential*, p. 259, 1951
- He's on the lam from a pen back east[.] — Jim Thompson, *A Swell-Looking Babe*, p. 77, 1954
- She got ten years. She's still on the lam. — Edwin Torres, *After Hours*, p. 376–377, 1979
- [A]n Australian on the lam from a bad life and taken up with a neurotic kibbutznik with three kids. — Sandra Bernhard, *Confessions of a Pretty Lady*, p. 122, 1988

▸ **take it on the lam**
to escape, to run away *US*
- One morning I woke up and found that Joel had helped himself to a good part of the cash, and had taken it on the lam. — Herbert Huncke, *Guilty of Everything*, p. 167, 1990
- I suppose this is where you, what's the word, Lovejoy... scarper? Take it on the lam. — Jonathan Gash, *The Ten Word Game*, p. 139, 2003

lam *verb*
to escape, especially from prison *US, 1886*
- Why the hell don't you lam out of here, bud? — Raymond Chandler, *The Little Sister*, p. 107, 1949
- The lowlier links lam the 36 miles to Baltimore to cup up. — Jack Lait and Lee Mortimer, *Washington Confidential*, 1951
- I'm not lamming from pitiful pittance but my last week's script pay was 18 bucks and I gotta get a bigger job. — Jack Kerouac, *Letter to Neal Cassady*, p. 326, 1st October 1951
- But – why did Connie lam so fast? — Bernard Wolfe, *The Late Risers*, p. 242, 1954
- [S]he was so made and so down deep vindictive that she reported to the police some false trumped-up hysterical crazy charge, and Dean had to lam from Hoboken. — Jack Kerouac, *On the Road*, p. 5, 1957

lamb-brained *adjective*
foolish *NEW ZEALAND*
- — David McGill, *David McGill's Complete Kiwi Slang Dictionary*, p. 78, 1998

lamb down *verb*
to defraud a worker out of their entire end-of-season pay packet by keeping them drunk until it is all spent *AUSTRALIA, 1850*
Now historical.
- Inns on the tracks to the diggings were the scenes of almost continuous revelry and many of the bad old type of landlords, who had graduated in the art of 'lambing down a shepherd'[.] — Russell Ward, *The Australian Legend*, p. 122, 1966

Lambeth Walk *noun*
chalk *UK*
Rhyming slang, used by snooker and pool players.
- — Ray Puxley, *Cockney Rabbit*, 1992

lambsbread *noun*
marijuana from Jamaica, with especially large buds *JAMAICA*
- [L]arge buds from Jamaica, shaped like a lamb's tail, that can be carved like a loaf of bread. — Nick Brownlee, *This Is Cannabis*, p. 152, 2002

lamb's tongue *noun*
a five-dollar note *US*
- — Hyman E. Goldin et al., *Dictionary of American Underworld Lingo*, p. 121, 1950

lame *noun*
a naive, conventional, law-abiding person *US*
- The bar was filling with the lames and fools of the Saturday-workday, loud and boisterous, living it up and acting like people. — Clarence Cooper Jr, *The Scene*, p. 40, 1960
- Pickin' pockets, why that's a hustle for a lame. — Bruce Jackson, *Get Your Ass in the Water and Swim Like Me*, p. 66, 1964
- She dug this lame, some cat who worked in a grocery store. — Claude Brown, *Manchild in the Promised Land*, p. 180, 1965
- [S]ome good Pump House souls are busted, but that is The Life, the world divided into surfer heads and surfer lames[.] — Tom Wolfe, *The Electric Kool-Aid Acid Test*, p. 321, 1968
- He didn't like it that his cronies and the small-time lames were sniggering behind his back. — Nathan Heard, *Howard Street*, p. 89, 1968
- — Eldridge Cleaver, *Soul on Ice*, p. 4, 1968
- A whole lotta lames'll / fall victim to the game. — Lightnin' Rod, *Hustlers Convention*, p. 24, 1973
- Then some lame was puffing on a joint one night, got next to a kitty and said she had to take a poke. — Edwin Torres, *Carlito's Way*, p. 26, 1975
- If we didn't need the lame, he wouldn't be up there now. — Jack W. Thomas, *Heavy Number*, p. 56, 1976
- I've seen excited suckers in my time, but that lame has remained without peer in my memory. — Iceberg Slim (Robert Beck), *Airtight Willie and Me*, p. 23, 1979
- I don't know. He was a lame, that's all. — *Apocalypse Now*, 1979
- At the bottom of Jump-Offs social ladder are the teens and others who make money through legitimate work – variously described as "lames," "squares" and "punks." — Terry Williams, *The Cocaine Kids*, p. 103, 1989

lame *adjective*

1 unfashionable, weak, unspirited *US, 1935*
- — *American Speech*, p. 302, December 1955: 'Wayne University slang'
- Yeah, it's lame, but I've had this idea. — *Empire Records*, 1995
- Cat, that's the lamest idea I've ever heard. — *Get Shorty*, 1995
- Dude, this is seriously lame. I didn't know we were gonna get all dirty and stuff. — *South Park*, 1999

2 short of money *US*
- — George Percy, *The Language of Poker*, p. 51, 1988

lamebrain *noun*
a fool, an idiot *US, 1919*
- Lame-brains like to point out that only colored people are confined to "slums" in Washington[.] — Jack Lait and Lee Mortimer, *Washington Confidential*, p. 122, 1951
- [H]e said the playoff games had made it clear to him that the players had not packaged their best product, as it would have been clear to anyone but a lamebrain owner. — Dan Jenkins, *Life Its Ownself*, p. 309, 1984

lame-brained *adjective*
stupid *US, 1929*
- [A] variety and totality of ills: prejudice, provincialism, hypocrisy, sexual repression, aesthetic poverty, insularity, self-satisfaction, blind propriety, lame-brained deference and moral aggrandisement. And that's just for starters. — *The Guardian*, 9th February 2002

lame duck *noun*

1 a person or organisation that is handicapped or disadvantaged *UK, 1761*
- [T]he nuclear industry and the other lame ducks of Thatcherism. — *The Observer*, 22nd September 2002

2 an act of sexual intercourse *UK*
Rhyming slang for **FUCK**.
- — Bodmin Dark, *Dirty Cockney Rhyming Slang*, 2003

lamed-vovnik *noun*
in Jewish legend, a hidden saint *CANADA*
- The legend has it that in every generation there are 36 secret saints, through whose piety the world exists. Once his act is completed, the lamed-vovnik vanishes back into anonimity. — David Helwig, *Living Here*, p. 113, 2001

lame-o *noun*
a fool, an idiot *US, 1977*
The suffix '-o' is used here to create a noun from an adjective.
- I wish I had a dime for every job that lame-o Florio gave out to his friends. — Howard Stern, *Miss America*, p. 461, 1995
- What a lame-o. Somebody should put him out of his misery. — *American Beauty*, 1999

lamer *noun*
an uninformed Internet user who passes himself off as an expert *US*
- — Andy Ihnatko, *Cyberspeak*, p. 110, 1997

lame rap *noun*
an unfounded arrest *US*
- I was standing on the corner, wasn't even shooting crap / When a policeman came by, picked me up on a lame rap. — Anonymous ("Arthur"), *Shine and the Titanic;The Signifying Monkey; Stackolee*, p. 16, 1971

lame stain *noun*
a completely inept, despised person *US*
- — Vann Wesson, *Generation X Field Guide and Lexicon*, p. 104, 1997

lamington *noun*
a type of small, oblong sponge cake covered with chocolate and desiccated coconut *AUSTRALIA, 1909*
Probably named after Lord Lamington, governor of Queensland 1895–1901.
• You hadn't been so successful we might be having tea and lamingtons at Orange instead. —Rodney Hall, *Kisses of the Enemy*, p. 253, 1987

lamister *noun*
a fugitive from justice *US*
• I lived like a lamister. —Rocky Garciano (with Rowland Barber), *Somebody Up There Likes Me*, p. 92, 1955

lammie *noun*
a lamington *AUSTRALIA*
• You're not going to eat that lammie are ya? —Phillip Gwynne, *Deadly Unna?*, p. 118, 1998

lammo *noun*
a lamington *AUSTRALIA*
• However, if you said 'Get a lammo up ya' he would gladly take one[.] —Bill Cowham, *Legolingo*, p. 23, 1987

lamo *noun*
a person lacking fashion sense and social skills *US*
• — *Washington Post*, 14th October 1993

lam off *verb*
to escape, to run away *UK*
An elaboration of **LAM**.
• I talked too much, nervy at the idea of lamming off as soon as I found a side street. —Jonathan Gash, *The Ten Word Game*, p. 139, 2003

lamor *noun*
a kiss *UK*
Possibly from French *l'amour* (love).
• —Paul Baker, *Polari*, p. 179, 2002

lamp *noun*
1 the eye *UK, 1811*
Usually used in the plural.
• "But what's the matter with the lamps?" Phil asked. —James T. Farrell, *Saturday Night*, p. 28, 1947

2 a look *US, 1926*
• Now for a quick lamp over the slag. —Derek Raymond (Robin Cook), *The Crust on its Uppers*, p. 21, 1962
• I knew it as soon as that Nancy walked into your office and put the lamps on you. —Edwin Torres, *Q & A*, p. 90, 1977

lamp *verb*
1 to look *US, 1907*
• I gave him the double-o after I lamped the engraved card he handed me. —Mezz Mezzrow, *Really the Blues*, p. 261, 1946
• When Anslinger lamped the boys, he went to the lobby and had Lucky called out. —Jack Lait and Lee Mortimer, *Washington Confidential*, p. 184, 1951
• "Crazy, man, crazy," spieled his pal, one eye lamping a real gone gal. —Dan Burley, *Diggeth Thou?*, p. 18, 1959
• [W]e were dying to have a butcher's [look] and lamp all the new bird [women]. —Derek Raymond (Robin Cook), *The Crust on its Uppers*, p. 34, 1962
• He nipped me by my coatsleeve and lamped me with a wicked eye. —Bruce Jackson, *Get Your Ass in the Water and Swim Like Me*, p. 85, 1965
• [W]hen Joe extended his condolences for Archie, the Chinese gangster just lamped him with a freezedried smile. —Seth Morgan, *Homeboy*, p. 264, 1990

2 to hit, to beat *UK, 1954*
• Whoever said you weren't sexy, Elspeth? Tell me, I'll lamp him one. —Christopher Brookmyre, *Boiling a Frog*, p. 24, 2000
• I will lamp any idiot who says we're not rock'n'roll. —*X-Ray*, April 2003

3 to pass time idly, without purpose *US, 1988*
• —Connie Eble (Editor), *UNC-CH Campus Slang*, p. 6, Spring 1991

lamped *adjective*
drunk *UK*
• — *e-cyclopaedia*, 20th March 2002

lampers *noun*
the eyes *US*
• —Kenn "Naz" Young, *Naz's Underground Dictionary*, p. 43, 1973

lamp habit *noun*
an opium addiction *US*
• —Vincent J. Monteleone, *Criminal Slang*, p. 141, 1949

lamp man *noun*
an electrician, especially in the theatre *US*
• —Wilfred Granville, *The Theatre Dictionary*, p. 181, 1952

lamps *noun*
female breasts *IRELAND*
• The lamps on that. -The one in red. -The one in blue. —Patrick McCabe, *Carn*, p. 39, 1993

lamster *noun*
a fugitive from justice or retribution *US, 1904*
• Tourists, servicemen, merchant seamen, gamblers, perverts, drifters, and lamsters from every State in the Union. —William Burroughs, *Junkie*, p. 70–71, 1953
• I later learned that they put a shadow on Gay and checked her calls, hoping she would lead them to the lamster. —Lee Mortimer, *Women Confidential*, p. 35, 1960
• "You know this is a lamster's hangout up here in these sticks," he said. —Chester Himes, *Come Back Charleston Blue*, p. 64, 1966
• —John Scarne, *Scarne on Dice*, p. 472, 1974
• He's a lamster Jap, he's a youth gang member, he did a deuce for B and E and when last seen he was passing out anti-American leaflets. —James Ellroy, *Hollywood Nocturnes*, p. 275, 1994

lance-comical *noun*
a lance corporal *UK*
• But the team job wasn't going to be knocked back a day just because Lance-comical McNab was going to have a baby. —Andy McNab (writing of the late 1970s/early 80s), *Immediate Action*, p. 268, 1995

lance jack *noun*
a lance corporal *UK, 1912*
Army slang.
• How he ever became a lance-jack is a mystery to me. —Ray Slattery, *Mobbs' Mob*, p. 22, 1966
• Acting Corporal, Section Leader. Lance Jack. Not bad for a conscript. —Jake Arnott, *He Kills Coppers*, p. 3, 2001

Lancy; Lanky *noun*
a Lancashire – hence, loosely, also a Yorkshire – employee on the railways *UK*
• —Harvey Sheppard, *Dictionary of Railway Slang*, 1970

land *noun*
1 a fright *IRELAND*
• He let on he didn't hear me and starts walking real fast in behind the kitchens. But I went around the far side and what a land he got when he seen me in front of him. —Patrick McCabe, *The Butcher Boy*, p. 155, 1992

2 a neighbourhood *US*
• —Ellen C. Bellone (Editor), *Dictionary of Slang*, p. 15, 1989

▸ **on the land**
making a living by farming or other rural occupation *AUSTRALIA, 1902*
• He wanted to retire, buy himself a small farm, and live on the land. —Hyllus Maris and Sonia Borg, *Women of the Sun*, p. 162, 1985

land *verb*
to succeed in getting *UK, 1854*
• [Alan] Milburn landed a job with the county council-backed trade union studies information unit, and masterminded the campaign to save shipbuilding in Sunderland. — *The Guardian*, 12th June 2003

land icing *noun*
manure *CANADA*
In the *Dictionary of American Regional English*, 'land dressing' is the term for the same thing.
• [In Quebec's Eastern Townships] "land icing" is manure applied to the fields. —Lewis Poteet, *Talking Country*, p. 49, 1992

Landie *noun*
a Land Rover vehicle *AUSTRALIA*
• The distinctive hat will still be there, as will the Land Rover. But not a military Landie this time. — *West Australian*, p. 14, 6th June 1992

landing deck *noun*
the top of the head *US*
• Tell comes in on the down beat, draws a bead and bounces the Baldwin off Junior's landing deck! — Haenigsen, *Jive's Like That*, 1947

landing gear *noun*
1 the legs *US, 1941*
• —Lou Shelly, *Hepcats Jive Talk Dictionary*, p. 46, 1945

2 on an articulated lorry, the supports that prop up the trailer when it is unhitched *US*

• —Montie Tak, *Truck Talk*, p. 97, 1971

landing strip *noun*

a woman's pubic hair trimmed into the shape of a narrow vertical bar *US*

A visual comparison.

• Crop your hair into a vertical so-called "landing strip" (obviously named by a jet-setting man).— *The Village Voice*, 8th–14th November 2000

landlady *noun*

a brothel madame *US, 1879*

• LANDLADIES' NIGHT AT THE CLUB ALABAM! – FUN AND FROLIC! – COME ONE AND ALL!—Mezz Mezzrow, *Really the Blues*, p. 91, 1946

land line *noun*

a conventional telephone line, as distinguished from a mobile phone or radio *US*

• —Carsten Stroud, *Close Pursuit*, p. 273, 1987

land of cakes *noun*

(from the perspective of people on Nova Scotia islands) the mainland *CANADA*

• The land of cakes was a name given by the people of Cape Sable Island to Barrington where they made cakes of fine white sugar. They on the Island made their cakes of molasses.—Marion Robertson, *Journal of the Margaret Rait*, p. 59, 1984

land of hope *noun*

soap *UK*

Rhyming slang.

• —Julian Franklyn, *A Dictionary of Rhyming Slang*, 1961

land of the big PX *noun*

the United States *US*

The US seen in its commercial glory as one big PX (supermarket/department store). From Vietnam.

• —Carl Fleischhauer, *A Glossary of Army Slang*, p. 30, 1968
• — *Current Slang*, p. 16, Summer 1970
• The other half, since they had already been there, were certain of their survival; they were headed for the fantasyland of the Bix PX, the World, Man – Stateside!—Charles Anderson, *The Grunts*, p. 13, 1976
• I'm going home, back-in-the-world, the land of the big PX and the twenty-four-hour generator.—Larry Heinemann, *Close Quarters*, p. 262, 1977
• Oh, I'm just waiting to get back to the land of the big PX.— *Full Metal Jacket*, 1987

land shark *noun*

a person made wealthy by speculating in land *AUSTRALIA, 1836*

• Scott called me a land shark in the House the other day.—Frank Hardy, *Power Without Glory*, p. 246, 1950

land with *verb*

to impose an onerous duty or unwelcome burden on someone *UK, 1984*

• Well, he'll have to do it himself, I'm not being landed with it.— *The Guardian*, 20th July 2000

lane; lain; laine *noun*

a sucker, a gullible victim *US, 1933*

• Lemme take a sawbuck, man. I got a lain hooked down here[.] —Chester Himes, *If He Hollers Let Him Go*, p. 43, 1945
• The only time the aldermen ever had a meeting was when enough of the waiters ganged up around the bar to talk about the laines they clipped, and the police chief was too busy mixing drinks to bust himself under the prohibition act.—Mezz Mezzrow, *Really the Blues*, p. 66, 1946
• He knew his fortune was surely made / If he didn't do business lanes.—Dennis Wepman et al., *The Life*, p. 105, 1976

lane louse *noun*

a driver who appears oblivious to traffic lanes *US*

• — *American Speech*, p. 270, December 1962

lang

▸ **on the lang**

playing truant *IRELAND*

• Up to 200 local school-children were present to watch the squad go through their paces for almost two hours. How many, in Cork parlance, were on the lang?— *The Examiner*, 4th November 1998

langar *noun*

the penis, also used figuratively as a fool *IRELAND*

• Someone has to be a langer Someone has to be sound Someone has to have a laugh Someone has to be around—John Spillane, *Are We Brilliant or What?*, 2002

langerated *adjective*

drunk *IRELAND*

A variation of **LANGERED**.

• — *e-cyclopaedia*, 20th March 2002

langered; langers *adjective*

drunk *IRELAND, 1982*

From Scottish *langer* (weariness); ultimately conventional English 'langour'.

• —Bernard Share, *Slanguage*, 1997

language *noun*

bad language, swearing, obscene speech *UK, 1886*

• You wouldn't hear no language out of Margi[.]—Kevin Sampson, *Clubland*, p. 189, 2002

Language of the Garden *noun*

in Cape Breton, Gaelic *CANADA*

• "You can call a man down to the lowest of the low in Gaelic, or praise him to the highest. The Language of the Garden." "What garden?" Dan Rory raised his eyebrows. "Eden, of course."—D. R. MacDonald, *Cape Breton Road*, p. 14, 2000

languid *adjective*

utterly relaxed *US*

• —Connie Eble (Editor), *UNC-CH Campus Slang*, p. 3, Fall 1987

lanie *noun*

▷ **see: LARNEY**

Lanky *noun*

a native of Lancashire *UK*

• The lanky is always looking for summat t'eyt [something to eat]. —Peter Wright, *The Lanky Twang*, p. 16, 1972

▷ **see: LANCY**

Lanky *adjective*

of Lancashire *UK: ENGLAND*

• —Peter Wright, *The Lanky Twang*, 1972

Lao green *noun*

a greenish marijuana grown in Southeast Asia, smoked by US troops in Vietnam *US*

• —Linda Reinberg, *In the Field*, p. 125, 1991

Laotian red *noun*

a reddish marijuana, purported to have been grown in Laos *US*

• A friend of mine whose trippin' around in Southeast Asia can mail me a lil' stick or some Laotian red from time to time.—Odie Hawkins, *Great Lawd Buddha*, p. 69, 1990

lap dance *noun*

an intimate sexual performance, involving some degree of physical contact between a female performer and a sitting male *US*

• Tanya says she immediately discerned that we are extremely nice guys and is therefore prepared to offer us a bargain price (two for 30) on the regular $20 lap dances, a house specialty that need not be described in detail for the purposes of this column.— *St. Petersburg (Florida) Times*, p. 1D, 8th May 1988
• The talk goes beyond where to get the best jiggle and flash, to where to find the best lap dance money can buy[.]—Nancy Tamosaitis, *net.sex*, p. 92, 1995
• Any time you want a lap dance with that broad, say the word.—Quentin Tarantino, *From Dusk Till Dawn*, p. 94, 1995
• But what constitutes a lap dance is open to interpretation.—James Ridgeway, *Red Light*, p. 176, 1996
• There's no constitutional right to a lap-dance. That's the gist of a divided Oregon Court of Appeals ruling[.]— *Associated Press*, 31st October 2002

lap dance *verb*

to engage in a sexual performance in which a woman dancer, scantily clad if at all, grinds her buttocks into a sitting male customer's lap *US*

• I progressed from sitting on his lap to no-charge lap dancing.—Anka Radakovich, *The Wild Girls Club*, p. 96, 1994

- My Best Friend Pays My Girlfriend to Lap Dance (Headline)— *San Francisco Examiner*, p. C2, 7th October 1994
- Lap dancing – where the dancer rubs herself against the customer for a longer time – brings in more money.—James Ridgeway, *Red Light*, p. 176, 1996

lap dancer *noun*
a woman who performs lap dances in a sex club *US*
- Sometime around midnight I stopped in Novato to pay my respects at a bachelor party for a male stripper who was marrying a lap dancer from the O'Farrell Theatre.—Hunter S. Thompson, *Generation of Swine*, p. 20, 1985

La Perouse *noun*
alcoholic drink *AUSTRALIA, 1981*
Rhyming slang for **BOOZE**; from the name of a Sydney suburb.
- Consequently, Gwennie was always a bit of a wowser whenever I'd been out on the La Perouse.—Barry Humphries, *The Traveller's Tool*, p. 26, 1985

lap job *noun*
an act of oral sex on a woman *US*
- Like my second lap job a year later was on a neighborhood chick, a year older than me.—*Screw*, p. 5, 7th March 1969

lapper *noun*
the hand *UK*
- —Paul Baker, *Polari*, p. 179, 2002

lappy *noun*
in Queensland, a circuit of a street block in a vehicle done, especially repeatedly, for entertainment *AUSTRALIA*
- They hang lappies every Friday night.— *Wordmap (www.abc.net.au/wordmap)*, 2003

lap up; lap it up *verb*
1 to enjoy receiving flattery; to enthusiastically enjoy any distraction or entertainment *UK, 1890*
- President Jimmy Carter, his [Dylan Thomas's] most famous fan, is still lapping it up.—*The Guardian*, 27th October 2003

2 to approve of and enjoy *UK, 1890*
- Where'd yi get your gear, by the way? I lap it up!—Ian Pattison, *Rab C. Nesbitt*, 1988

lar; lah; la *noun*
used to address a companion or friend *UK*
Mainly Liverpool use.
- Not me. Must be you lah.—*Boys From the Blackstuff: Moonlighter*, 1982
- Them kiddies' faces, lar – worth all the thingy of putting a do like this together.—Kevin Sampson, *Outlaws*, p. 222, 2001

larceny *verb*
to manipulate through insincere flattery *US*
- You don't have to larceny me – I won't flip on you. I'll never flip on nobody again.—Clarence Cooper Jr, *The Scene*, p. 14, 1960

lard *noun*
money *UK*
- Why not? It's your lard isn't it?—*The Belles of St. Trinian's*, 1954

lard-ass; lard-arse *noun*
an overweight person *US, 1918*
- [F]or some reason the idea of circle jerking [participating in group male masturbation] with a needle-dicked lard-arse didn't appeal.—Kitty Churchill, *Thinking of England*, p. 132, 1995
- Hello, lard arse.—Martin King and Martin Knight, *The Naughty Nineties*, p. 46, 1999
- It wasn't as if they were a pair of lard-arses[.]—Pete McCarthy, *McCarthy's Bar*, p. 217, 2000

lard-assed; lard-arsed *adjective*
fat; in the manner of a fat person *US, 1967*
- [Fred Durst] has managed to rut his lard-arsed way through half the glamour models in America[.]—*Loaded*, p. 63, June 2003

lard-butt *noun*
a fat person *US, 1968*
A variation of **LARD-ASS/ARSE** (a fat person); literally **FAT ASS**.
- "You call me fatso again and I'll rearrange your face." "Fatso, fat ass, lard butt, blimpo -"—Janet Evanovich, *Seven Up*, p. 37, 2001

lard head *noun*
a fool *US, 1936*
Conventional 'lard' is a soft white fat, hence the usage here as **FATHEAD**.

lardy *noun*
▷ **see: LA-DI-DAH**

lardy-arsed *adjective*
being blessed with a fat bottom *UK*
A variation of **LARD-ASSED**; combines conventional 'lard' (a cooking fat) with 'arse' (the bottom).
- [P]eople who would never dream of lifting a finger in a sporting event – lardy-arsed couch potatoes[.]—John Robb, *The Nineties*, p. 201, 1999

larey *adjective*
▷ **see: LAIRY**

larf *noun*
nonsense, rubbish *US*
- —John D. Bell et al., *Loosely Speaking*, p. 12, 1966

Largactil shuffle *noun*
the stumbling walk of a heavily sedated prisoner *UK*
Largactil™ is a brand name for *chlorpromazine*, an anti-psychotic drug.
- —Angela Devlin, *Prison Patter*, p. 69, 1996

large *noun*
in betting, the largest wagering unit *AUSTRALIA*
- —Ned Wallish, *The Truth Dictionary of Racing Slang*, p. 45, 1989

▸ **give it the large**
to boast, to brag *UK*
- [A] lot of blokes who give it the large in pubs [...] turn out to be bullshitters[.]—Danny King, *The Burglar Diaries*, p. 61, 2001

large *verb*
to live an extreme and hedonistic lifestyle to its fullest extent *UK*
- DJ Brandon Block has won awards for his uncontrolled partying; dictionary compilers please note, he was also the person who invented the phrase "largin' it".—Dave Haslam, *Adventures of the Wheels of Steel*, p. 115, 2001

large *adjective*
1 famous, successful *US*
- The pair were friends before [Samuel L.] Jackson "got large" and once that had happened, as friends, they naturally helped each other out.—*The Times Magazine*, p. 43, 13th October 2001

2 enthusiastic *US, 1967*
- —Hy Lit, *Hy Lit's Unbelievable Dictionary of Hip Words for Groovy People*, p. 26, 1968

3 very enjoyable, wonderful *US, 1874*
- —Paul Baker, *Polari*, p. 179, 2002

▸ **have it large; give it large; have it**
to enjoy in a very enthusiastic or excessive fashion *UK, 1990s*
- He'd be having it large before the night was out.—Kevin Sampson, *Powder*, p. 198, 1999
- I knew we was gonna have it large and fucking loud[.]—Dave Courtney, *Raving Lunacy*, p. 23, 2000
- We're monsta ravin' mega mixers, rinsin' love machines who want to help anyone – even old people in their twenties – have it as large as we do.—Richard Topping, *Havin' It Large*, p. 5, 2000
- Old-school, baggy ravers really having it[.]—Dave Courtney, *Raving Lunacy*, p. 92, 2000
- So how do you dance when you're giving it large on a Saturday night?—*www.urban75.com*, 2001

large *adverb*
impressive; (of a lifestyle) in an excessive, successful, comfortable or self-indulgent manner *US, 1883*
- —Connie Eble (Editor), *UNC-CH Campus Slang*, p. 5, Spring 1989
- When you were "in effect" you were truly "large" [doing well].—Nelson George, *Hip Hop America*, p. 209, 1998

large charge *noun*
a big thrill *US*
- —*Newsweek*, p. 28, 8th October 1951
- —Hy Lit, *Hy Lit's Unbelievable Dictionary of Hip Words for Groovy People*, p. 50, 1968

large chest for sale; large chest for sale – no drawers
used by prostitutes as an advertising slogan *UK*
A punning euphemism, certainly familiar from shopwindow postcards in the 1970s.
- Instead of soliciting passing males, the hookers of London remained out of sight, if not out of mind, advertising their services on discreetly euphemistic postcards in the windows of local newsagents. "French Lessons", Large Chest for Sale", "Stocks and Bonds", "Remedial Discipline by Stern Governess" – the oblique side of obvious, with a local phone number.—Mick Farren, *Give the Anarchist a Cigarette*, p. 10, 2001

large one; large *noun*
one thousand US dollars; one thousand pounds sterling *US, 1972*
- The guy worked around the clock for free, plus he threw five large into the war chest. —Richard Price, *Clockers*, p. 269, 1992
- Guy owes me fifteen large and takes off, I go after him. —*Get Shorty*, 1995
- For that he gets 200 large. — *Gone in 60 Seconds*, 2000
- He's gonna have to find twenty large. — *EastEnders, BBC TV*, 13th August 2001

large-type *adjective*
extreme *US*
- That guy cut me off! What a large-type asshole! —Judi Sanders, *Da Bomb*, p. 9, 1997

lark *noun*
1 a light-hearted adventure, a spree *UK, 1802*
- When this bit of a lark happened, I suppose I was about 19. —Jimmy Stockin, *On The Cobbles*, p. 117, 2000

2 a line of work *UK, 1934*
- I couldn't wait to get out the game and get into the media lark. —Dave Courtney, *Dodgy Dave's Little Black Book*, p. 20, 2001

lark *verb*
to be criminally active *UK*
Puns on the senses 'a line of work' and 'behaving mischievously'.
- [T]he conversation got round to nicking geezers down to larking[.] —Frank Norman, *Bang To Rights*, p. 123, 1958

lark about; lark around *verb*
to have fun by behaving foolishly or mischievously *UK, 1813*
- [T]he men chaffed one another and larked about as they worked. —Sharyn McCrumb, *Macpherson's Lament*, p. 24, 1992
- Maltesers did a campaign in the same genre, where people are larking around and trying to nick them from one another. — *The Guardian*, 24th May 2004

Larkin *noun*
▸ **down to Larkin; for Larkin**
free, gratis *UK*
Possibly from **LARKING** (theft).
- "Who's paying for this round?" "Shush! It's down to Larkin". —David Powis, *The Signs of Crime*, 1977
- "What's it come to, H?" "Fuck off. Nix, it's for Larkin." —Garry Bushell, *The Face*, p. 153, 2001

larking *noun*
theft *UK*
- —Frank Norman, *Bang to Rights*, 1958

larmer *noun*
an alarmist *BARBADOS*
- —Frank A. Collymore, *Barbadian Dialect*, p. 66, 1965

larney; lanie *noun*
a white man; a boss (it is possible to be both at once) *SOUTH AFRICA, 1956*
Derogatory.
- —Jean Branford, *A Dictionary of South African English*, 1978

La Roche *noun*
▷ see: **ROCHE**

laroped; larrupt *adjective*
drunk *UK*
Derives from **LARRUP** (to thrash).
- — *e-cyclopaedia*, 20th March 2002

larp; larping *noun*
the adult activity of recreating fantasy, generally quasi-mediaeval, adventures, such as those depicted in Tolkein's *Lord of the Rings* trilogy, usually performed with more enthusiam than skill or accuracy *UK*
An acronym of '*l*ive-*a*ction *r*ole-*p*lay' or '*r*ole-*p*laying' that first appeared in the early 1990s.
- Rather than just passively consume Tolkien's lore, they were moved to pick up a [rubber] sword, pack a knapsack and make not just his, but their own fantasy realm a reality. And they called it Larp[.] — *The Guardian*, 13th December 2003

larper *noun*
a *l*ive-*a*ction *r*ole-*p*layer *UK*
From **LARP**.
- To an outsider, the world of the Larper just isn't right. Superficially, it's a bunch of guys in fancy dress running around hitting each other with rubber swords. — *The Guardian*, 13th December 2003

larrikin *noun*
1 a trouble-making youth, usually a male; a thug or tough *AUSTRALIA, 1868*
From British dialect, recorded in Warwickshire and Worcestershire; originally a term of the greatest contempt and the youths so labelled were the subject of much C19 media hype. Journalist Nat Gould described them (1898) as 'hideous-looking fellows, whose features bear traces of unmistakeable indulgence in every loathsome vice'. The amelioration of the term relies on the difference between a 'healthy' disregard for authority and social convention and an 'unhealthy' one.
- —Harvey E. Ward, *Down Under Without Blunder*, p. 41, 1967
- The real heroes of the bush weren't the young larrikins who became outlaws[.] —Bill Wannan, *Folklore of the Australian Pub*, p. 58, 1972
- So there was Father's case. His brood were larrikins. —Kerry Cue, *Crooks, Chooks and Bloody Ratbags*, p. 4, 1983
- One of the larrikins she was knocking around with decided to burn his initials into her arm and she just let him do it. —Kerry Cue, *Crooks, Chooks and Bloody Ratbags*, p. 168, 1983
- He talked like a Collingwood larrikin and dressed like a Collins Street broker so you would think there was a ventriloquist in the room. —Frank Hardy, *Hardy's People*, p. 94, 1986

2 a fun-loving, good-natured mischief-maker; a scallywag *AUSTRALIA, 1891*
Seen as typically Australian and much romanticised in literature, as C.J. Dennis' character, the Sentimental Bloke. Now the prevailing sense.
- Come and I'll introduce you to the greatest bunch of larrikins in Sydney. —Sam Weller, *Old Bastards I Have Met*, p. 31, 1979
- Almost a year to get through to the big loveable larrikin[.] —Robert G. Barrett, *Davo's Little Something*, p. 271, 1992

larrikin *adjective*
of or befitting a larrikin *AUSTRALIA*
- Drink plenty of piss, bet larrikin odds and really have a ball. —Sam Weller, *Old Bastards I Have Met*, p. 135, 1979
- A larrikin smart-arse gambler, an Itie lair, plus a good mate of that Jazza and Guido, two no-goods who would finish up in the boob or worse. —Clive Galea, *Slipper*, p. 16, 1988
- To pursue a local government 'police', with powers to respond to community concerns of larrikin behavior, speeding, graffiti and lawlessness. — *The Messenger*, p. 14, 1st May 1991

larrikinism *noun*
1 delinquent behaviour *AUSTRALIA, 1870*
- You should think of consequences before you get yourself involved in larrikinism. —D.E. Charlwood, *All the Green Year*, p. 109, 1965

2 good-hearted playfulness *AUSTRALIA*
- Her acid-green eyes had more than a glint of larrikinsim. —Kathy Lette, *Girls' Night Out*, p. 62, 1987

larrup *verb*
to beat, to thrash, to hit vigorously *UK, 1823*
- He's just larruped a shot from distance which beat the keeper but not the post – into the side netting. — *The Guardian*, 26th February 2003

larruping *noun*
a thrashing *UK, 1889*
From **LARRUP** (to beat).
- "It would have done them good if they had had a good 'larruping'," the judge [Lord Chief Justice Goddard] surmised. — *The Guardian*, 22nd May 2002

larry *noun*
in a card game, the player who has the last chance to act in a given situation *US, 1950*
- —Thomas L. Clark, *The Dictionary of Gambling and Gaming*, p. 115, 1987

Larry; Larry Tulare *noun*
in carnival usage, an unprofitable day or engagement *US*
- — *American Speech*, p. 281, December 1966: 'More carnie talk from the West Coast'

▸ **doing a Larry**
working as a *locum tenens*, a (temporary) substitute in a professional medical position *UK*
- —Adam T. Fox, St Mary's Hospital, London, 10th October 2002

Larry *adjective*
in circus and carnival usage, worthless *US, 1939*
- —Don Wilmeth, *The Language of American Popular Entertainment*, p. 155, 1981

Larry Cadota *noun*
a worthless novelty sold in the circus or carnival *US*
• —Joe McKennon, *Circus Lingo*, p. 54, 1980

larry-dooley *noun*
a beating; a hiding *AUSTRALIA, 1946*
Origin unknown. Baker (*The Australian Language*, 1966) suggests a connection with a boxer named Larry Foley (1890s) but this seems hardly creditable.
• They'll give his nibs larry-dooley tonight. —Patsy Adam-Smith, *Folklore of the Australian Railwaymen*, p. 118, 1969

larval stage *noun*
the initial burst of enthusiastic and single-minded focus experienced by computer enthusiasts *US*
• A less protracted and intense version of larval stage (typically lasting about a month) may recur when one is learning a new OS or programming language. —Eric S. Raymond, *The New Hacker's Dictionary*, p. 220, 1991

lary *adjective*
▷ **see:** LAIRY

lase *verb*
to print a document on a laser printer *US*
• —Eric S. Raymond, *The New Hacker's Dictionary*, p. 220, 1991

lash *noun*
1 an attempt; a try-out; a go *AUSTRALIA, 1840*
From the earlier sense (a fight; fighting). Often in such phrases as 'have a lash at', 'give it a lash', etc.
• What do you reckon. We give 'em a lash? —Robert G. Barrett, *Davo's Little Something*, p. 40, 1992
2 an act of urination *UK*
• I've got to have a lash. Me back teeth ate floating. —Garry Bushell, *The Face*, p. 81, 2001

▸ **on the lash**
engaged in a hedonistic, alcohol-inspired quest for pleasure *UK*
• ON THE LASH – BINGE DRINKING —Nick Brownlee, *This Is Alcohol*, p. 120, 2002
• We went out on the lash, as we say, and copper being coppers we celebrated. —Duncan MacLaughlin, *The Filth*, p. 187, 2002
• [A]n ingenious short video clip function: perfect for capturing those priceless moments in the office or out on the lash. —*Rated*, p. 54, June 2002

lash *verb*
to dispose of *UK*
Extends the sense of LASH (a urination).
• I keep the free biro and lash the leaflet. —Kevin Sampson, *Outlaws*, p. 211, 2001

▸ **lash into**
to do something in a vigorous manner *IRELAND*
From Irish dialect.
• While I'm lashing the old wax into the hair, my phone rings[.] —Paul Howard, *Ross O'Carroll-Kelly*, p. 186, 2003

lashed; lashed up *adjective*
drunk *UK*
Possibly from LASH-UP (a party) or directly from LASH (a urination), hence PISSED.
• We agree to meet at the bar afterwards and get lashed up. —Martin King and Martin Knight, *The Naughty Nineties*, p. 27, 1999
• [H]alf lashed an drinkin a beer as if ee'd never been away. —Niall Griffiths, *Sheepshagger*, p. 52, 2001

lasher *noun*
a female whose only appeal is sexual *IRELAND*
• And the thing is, roysh [right], she was actually a really nice bird, as in nice person and not just a lasher. —Paul Howard, *Ross O'Carroll-Kelly*, p. 10, 2003

lashings *noun*
plenty *IRELAND, 1829*
• [S]he put me into a hot bath with lashings of disinfectant in the water for my cuts and bruises. —Lee Dunne, *Goodbye to the Hill*, p. 36, 1966
• It [the movie "Kill Bill"] comes complete with lashings of realistic blood and one scene in which about 100 people die. —*The Guardian*, 17th July 2003

lash-up *noun*
1 a heavy drinking session *UK*
• The only time I have a real lash-up is at weddings and funerals. —Jimmy Stockin, *On The Cobbles*, p. 171, 2000
2 an informal social occasion, especially a party *UK*
• —Desmond Bagley, *The Vivero Letter*, 1968
• Mack had not had more than a brief word with him at bar association lash-ups and that sort of thing. —George V. Higgins, *Penance for Jerry Kennedy*, p. 47, 1985

lason sa daga *noun*
LSD *US, 1977*
From the initials, but of unknown origin.
• —Richard A. Spears, *The Slang and Jargon of Drugs and Drink*, p. 309, 1986
• —Mike Haskins, *Drugs*, p. 285, 2003

last call *noun*
death *US*
• —Ramon Adams, *The Language of the Railroader*, p. 92, 1977
• —John Vorhaus, *The Big Book of Poker Slang*, p. 25, 1996

last card in the pack *noun*
1 a snack *UK*
Theatrical rhyming slang.
• —Julian Franklyn, *A Dictionary of Rhyming Slang*, 1960
• —Ray Puxley, *Cockney Rabbit*, 1992
2 dismissal from employment *UK*
Rhyming slang for 'sack'; sometimes abbreviated to 'last card'.
• —Ray Puxley, *Cockney Rabbit*, 1992

last-card Louie *noun*
in stud poker, a player who stays in a hand until his last card, improbably hoping for the one card that can produce a winning hand *US*
• —*American Speech*, p. 100, May 1951: 'The vocabulary of poker'
• —Albert H. Morehead, *The Complete Guide to Winning Poker*, p. 267, 1967

last chance *noun*
the upper balcony in a cinema favoured by homosexuals *US*
• In Chicago, they're called "Gobble Alley." In Los Angeles, some studs refer to the balconies as the "Last Chance." —Johnny Shearer, *The Male Hustler*, p. 77, 1966

lastish *noun*
the most recently published issue of a single-interest fan magazine *US*
• —*American Speech*, p. 27, Spring 1982: 'The langage of science fiction fan magazines'

last mile *noun*
in prison, the walk from the death cell to the execution chamber *US*
• —Hyman E. Goldin et al., *Dictionary of American Underworld Lingo*, p. 122, 1950
• But those are memories from long before my trial / And now it's time to walk that last mile. —Dennis Wepman et al., *The Life*, p. 118, 1976

last of the big spenders; last of the big-time spenders *noun*
used ironically of a mean person, or ruefully of yourself *AUSTRALIA, 1975*
• Soon we will be nostalgic about council-house dwellers as the last of the big spenders. —*The Guardian*, 20th June 1999

LA stop *noun*
a rolling stop at a traffic signal or stop sign *US*
• —Jeffrey McQuain, *Never Enough Words*, p. 54, 1999

last-out *noun*
a work shift that starts at approximately midnight and ends eight hours later *US*
• "Do you always work last out?" O'Shea asks. —Robert Campbell, *Nibbled to Death by Ducks*, p. 144, 1989

last rose of summer *noun*
a hospital patient with an ever-melodramatic belief that death is near *US*
• —Sally Williams, *"Strong" Words*, p. 149, 1994

last waltz *noun*
the walk taken by a prisoner condemned to death from the death cell to the execution chamber *US*
• —Lou Shelly, *Hepcats Jive Talk Dictionary*, p. 28, 1945
• —William K. Bentley and James M. Corbett, *Prison Slang*, p. 105, 1992

last week's pay *noun*
used in horse racing as the epitome of speed *AUSTRALIA*
• —Ned Wallish, *The Truth Dictionary of Racing Slang*, p. 45, 1989

last year's fun on wheels *noun*
a baby in a pram *US*
- — *Complete CB Slang Dictionary*, 1976
- — Peter Chippindale, *The British CB Book*, p. 156, 1981

lat; lats; lat-house *noun*
a latrine *UK*
Mainly military use.
- I remember a fellow recruit, a man from Birmingham, exclaiming, in a very Brummy accent, 1952, "Ooh! A letter from me tart! I'm off to the lats for a wank!" — Beale, *A Dictionary of Slang and Unconventional English*, 1984

latch *noun*
a railway engine throttle *US*
- — Ramon Adams, *The Language of the Railroader*, p. 119, 1977

latch *verb*
to understand *US, 1938*
- — Lavada Durst, *The Jives of Dr. Hepcat*, p. 13, 1953
- It's hardly surprising that charities have latched on to the potential this group represents[.] — *The Guardian*, 2nd November 2003

latchico *noun*
a ruffian *IRELAND*
- As soon as the car was out of sight they made their way to our house where I was standing at the front gate and we were soon joined by the latchico who had thought it great fun to close the door on us. — *Sligo Weekender*, 12th August 2003

latchkey *adjective*
(of a child) unsupervised at the end of the school day because of working parents *US, 1944*
- — *American Speech*, May 1965

latch low *noun*
in trucking, a very low gear *US*
- — Mary Elting, *Trucks at Work*, 1946

late *adjective*
▸ **late as Ellick**
proverbially late *BARBADOS*
- — *Barbadian Dialect*, p. 45, 1965

Late Late *noun*
▸ **the Late Late Show**
a very popular and long running television chat-show hosted by Gay Byrne *IRELAND*
- Myself and Enda would be stuck in here like Darby and Joan, watching the Late Late or something on a Friday[.] — Joseph O'Connor, *Red Roses and Petrol*, p. 23, 1995

late-late show *noun*
any television show that airs very late at night *US, 1956*
- When he stops in the doorways of the dining room, which looks like the Hall of Mirrors in the Palace of Versailles like I seen in that picture about Wilson on the late-late show, I go right on past him. — Robert Campbell, *Junkyard Dog*, p. 136, 1986

late-night *noun*
1 a bus ticket found on the street that is still valid *US*
Prized by drug addicts desperate to raise funds to buy their next dose.
- A street vendor will call out: "Hey, late-night, late night." — Geoffrey Froner, *Digging for Diamonds*, p. 41, 1989

2 a party after a party *US*
- — Don R. McCreary (Editor), *Dawg Speak*, 2001

late-nighter credit card *noun*
a length of rubber hose for siphoning petrol out of other people's cars *CANADA*
- A late-nighter credit card is a piece of rubber or plastic hose, for siphoning gasoline out of someone's tank without attracting too much attention. — Lewis Poteet, *The South Shore Phrase Book*, p. 70, 1999

late night line; late night *noun*
cocaine *UK*
- — Nick Constable, *This is Cocaine*, p. 181, 2002
- — Mike Haskins, *Drugs*, p. 280, 2003

later; laters; lates; later on; late
goodbye *US, 1954*
- — *American Speech*, p. 303, December 1955: 'Wayne University slang'
- — Robert George Reisner, *The Jazz Titans*, p. 160, 1960
- I dug right away what the kick was, so I said, "later," and he split. — Eldridge Cleaver, *Soul on Ice*, p. 46, 1968
- Why? Because you are more scared to be locked up than we are – later! — Bobby Seale, *A Lonely Rage*, p. 272, 1978
- — Connie Eble (Editor), *UNC-CH Campus Slang*, p. 3, April 1978
- No no babes I go'a keep this line open na mean [know what I mean]... La'er babes... Yeah alright. La'ers. — Nick Barlay, *Curvy Lovebox*, p. 54, 1997
- — *San Jose Mercury News*, 11th May 1999
- "Business calls, Pete. Deals to do over my side. Laters, mate." "Yeah, laters." — Garry Bushell, *The Face*, p. 113, 2001
- — Julian Johnson, *Urban Survival*, p. 258, 2003

later for that!
I don't like that idea at all! *US*
- — Connie Eble (Editor), *UNC-CH Campus Slang*, p. 4, Fall 1987

later for you
goodbye *US*
- — Connie Eble (Editor), *UNC-CH Campus Slang*, p. 4, Spring 1983

later, 'tater
goodbye *US*
An embellished **LATER**, with the 'tater' (potato) used only for the sake of reduplication.
- — Connie Eble (Editor), *UNC-CH Campus Slang*, p. 3, April 1978

latex *noun*
a condom *US*
- — Judi Sanders, *Kickin' like Chicken with the Couch Commander*, p. 15, 1992
- [T]hese guys would grudgingly comply, slap on the latex and wake up in the morning to find that Melissa spends the best part of her daylight hours asleep. — John Birmingham, *He Died With a Felafel in his Hand*, p. 22, 1994

lather *noun*
a condition of excitement; agitation, anxiety *UK, 1839*
- Cult television figure Chris Morris has Daily Mail and News of the World readers everywhere in a lather over the latest subject for his satirical programme, Brass Eye. — *The Guardian*, 20th July 2001

lathered *adjective*
drunk *UK*
- Some nights you want to do drugs, but some nights you want to get lathered, and the Brits is a booze night for sure[.] — Ben Elton, *High Society*, p. 13, 2002

lat-house *noun*
▹ **see: LAT**

Latin *noun*
a Mexican, Latin American or Spanish-speaking person *US*
- She's my pretty little baby / Litte Latin Lupe Lu — The Kingsmen, *Little Latin Lupe Lu*, 1964
- [H]e's going by the name Edward Mallon, but you could tell by looking at him he was a greaser. Excuse me, I mean a Latin. I have to watch that. — Elmore Leonard, *Killshot*, p. 182, 1989

latrine Gene *noun*
a soldier with a pathological need to be clean *US*
- — *American Speech*, p. 238, October 1946: 'World War II slang of maladjustment'

latrine lips *noun*
a citizens' band radio user who employs a vocabulary that is considered foul or obscene *US*
- — *Complete CB Slang Dictionary*, 1976
- — Wayne Floyd, *Jason's Authentic Dictionary of CB Slang*, p. 20, 1976
- — Peter Chippindale, *The British CB Book*, p. 156, 1981

latronic
used as a farewell *US*
A corruption of **LATER ON**.
- — Trevor Cralle, *The Surfin'ary*, p. 68, 1991

lats *noun*
1 the *latissimus dorsi* muscles on the lower back *US, 1939*
- He stands very straight, spreading his "lats" like batwings. — John Rechy, *Numbers*, p. 61, 1967
- His "lats" [...] flare from armpits to mid-torso. — John Rechy, *The Sexual Outlaw*, p. 20, 1977
- "You were great in the hayfork scene." "My lats were great in the hayfork scene." — Armistead Maupin, *Further Tales of the City*, p. 104, 1982
- — *American Speech*, p. 200, Fall 1984: 'The language of bodybuilding'

2 skis *US*
Used in Michigan's Upper Peninsula.

▹ **see: LAT**

latte *adjective*
pale *UK*
Italian *latte* (milk), widely used for a style of milky coffee, from which this derives – although *latteo* (milky) would be more correct. Recorded in contemporary gay use.
- —*Attitude*, p. 60, July 2003: 'New palare lexicon'

lattie; latty *noun*
a house or a flat *UK, 1859*
Polari.
- Then they drag him up the ling's lattie, and chain his lallies [legs] to a pillar[.]—Barry Took and Marty Feldman, *Round The Horne*, 16th April 1967
- [S]o I trolled [walked] back to my lattie[.]—the cast of 'Aspects of Love', Prince of Wales Theatre, *Palare (Boy Dancer Talk) for Beginners*, 1989–92
- [I]f you fancy tipping the velvet [oral/anal sex] we could orderly [go] back to my bijou latty down the street.—James Gardiner, *Who's a Pretty Boy Then?*, p. 123, 1997

LA turnabout; LA turnaround *noun*
a long-lasting amphetamine *US, 1970*
- From the image of driving from the East Coast of the US to Los Angeles and back again without resting.—Montie Tak, *Truck Talk*, p. 97, 1971
- —Peter Johnson, *Dictionary of Street Alcohol and Drug Terms*, p. 107, 1993
- —Mike Haskins, *Drugs*, p. 279, 2003

lau *verb*
to place *UK*
Polari.
- Order lau your luppers [fingers] on the strillers [musical instrument] bona [well].—Barry Took and Marty Feldman, *Round The Horne*, 4th June 1967

laugh *noun*
▸ **a laugh**
something funny, something merely amusing, often used ironically *UK, 1930*
- [H]e has never appeared on stage before. But he said, "I will do it. It will be a laugh."—*The Guardian*, 4th June 2004

laugh *verb*
to be in a favourable position *AUSTRALIA*
- We were down two sets to love, then Gary got his big serve working, I chipped in at the net, and we were laughing.—Alexander Buzo, *Rooted*, p. 42, 1969
- —Roy Slaven (John Doyle), *Five South Coast Seasons*, p. 32, 1992
- All we've got to do is get one bloody bridge contract or one hotel, just one, and we're ahead, we're laughing.—Roy Slaven (John Doyle), *Five South Coast Seasons*, p. 76, 1992

▸ **be away laughing**
to make a good start *NEW ZEALAND*
- Wait till the insurance for the truck comes through. Then we're away laughing.—Jean Watson, *Stand in the Rain*, p. 72, 1964

▸ **laugh all the way to the bank**
to be financially successful, especially in the face of long odds or disapproval *UK, 1984*
- Not, I suspect, that JK Rowling gives two snitches for that: she will be laughing all the way to the bank.—*The Observer*, 16th July 2000

▸ **laugh like a drain**
to laugh noisily; to guffaw *UK, 1948*
Referring to the noisy rushing of water down a drain or plughole.
- But, he assured me, he was marrying a real girl – and all I could do was laugh like a kitchen drain.—Sue Rhodes, *Now you'll think I'm awful*, p. 110, 1967
- What older Sloanes think they laugh like. "I laughed like a drain."—Ann Barr and Peter York, *The Official Sloane Ranger Handbook*, p. 158, 1982
- —Clive Galea, *Slipper*, p. 86, 1988
- —Robert G. Barrett, *Davo's Little Something*, p. 205, 1992
- I told her about the Charade and we laughed like drains.—Shane Maloney, *Nice Try*, p. 158, 1998

▸ **laugh your bollocks off**
to laugh uproariously *UK*
- I read about this in one of the papers and laughed my bollocks off.—Danny King, *The Burglar Diaries*, p. 54, 2001

▸ **laugh your nuts off**
to laugh uproariously *UK*
NUTS (the testicles) punning on **NUT** (the head), hence a dubious pun on the more conventional idiom 'laugh your head off'.
- I just headed for this young fella I could see laughing his nuts off at me and hoped for the best.—Dave Courtney, *Raving Lunacy*, p. 12, 2000

▸ **laugh your tits off**
to laugh a great deal *UK*
- [I]'m laughing my tits off and drinking beers with everyone else[.]—Mike Benson, *Room full of Angels (Disco Biscuits)*, p. 25, 1996

laugh and a joke; laugh *noun*
a smoke: a cigarette, a cigar, a pipe or marijuana prepared for smoking *UK, 1880*
Rhyming slang.
- —Jim Phelan, *Tramp at Anchor*, 1954
- —Ray Puxley, *Cockney Rabbit*, 1992

laugh and scratch *verb*
to inject a drug, especially heroin *UK, 1998*
Derives from physical reactions.
- —Mike Haskins, *Drugs*, p. 290, 2003

laugher *noun*
in sports, an easy and overwhelming victory *US, 1961*
- —Zander Hollander and Sandy Padwe, *Basketball Lingo*, p. 63, 1971

laughing academy *noun*
a mental institution *US, 1947*
- —Lawrence Lipton, *The Holy Barbarians*, p. 316, 1959
- —Francis J. Rigney and L. Douglas Smith, *The Real Bohemia*, p. xv, 1961
- Thoughts of straitjackets, of a Gestapo setup, of ex-Nazi male nurses, of Dr F. smiling sinister when he got me into the laughing academy, oh no, oh no no no.—Kevin Mackey, *The Cure*, p. 43, 1970

laughing boy; laughing girl *noun*
used ironically as the title of a gloomy-looking person *US, 1940*
- MILLIGAN: Hallo! Here comes Laughing Boy himself.—Graeme Kent, *The Queen's Corporal [Six Granada Plays]*, p. 94, 1959
- Has laughing boy still got his cob on?—Niall Griffiths, *Kelly + Victor*, p. 48, 2002

laughing Buddha *noun*
a variety of LSD *UK*
- —Angela Devlin, *Prison Patter*, p. 69, 1996

laughing farm *noun*
a mental institution *US, 1965*
- Hey, Joe said, hey, Ziggy, you better go back to the laughin farm.—Gilbert Sorrentino, *Steelwork*, p. 75, 1970

laughing gear *noun*
the mouth *NEW ZEALAND*
- 'Here, get your laughin' gear round that lot,' rump said, handing me a heaped plateful.—Ron Helmer, *Stag Party*, p. 82, 1964

▸ **wrap your laughing gear around**
to eat *AUSTRALIA*
- Here, wrap your laughing gear round this curry. It's bosker.—John Wynnum, *Tar Dust*, p. 34, 1962
- My company certainly makes the sheilahs hungry that's for sure, but unfortunately the thing that most of them want to wrap their laughing gear around is *above* table-level.—Barry Humphries, *The Traveller's Tool*, p. 78, 1985
- —Kathy Lette, *Girls' Night Out*, p. 179, 1987

laughing grass *noun*
marijuana *US, 1954*
Derives from the tendency to laughter experienced by marijuana smokers.
- —Richard A. Spears, *The Slang and Jargon of Drugs and Drink*, p. 309, 1986
- —Mike Haskins, *Drugs*, p. 288, 2003

laughing jackass *noun*
a kookaburra, *Dalceo novaeguineae*; a well-known Australian bird with a loud laugh-like call *AUSTRALIA, 1798*
Now but a little used term.
- Other lads on look-out duty on other posts would not start out until Kukuburra the laughing jackass woke the camp with his ringing peals[.]—Ion L. Idriess, *The Red Chief*, p. 14, 1953

laughing potato *noun*
a new, dry potato *CANADA*
- Laughin' potatoes burst their skins when cooked. And whether the split taties appear to be exploding with mirth, or whether it is the sound they make when they burst, their nickname is apt.—Bill Casselman, *Canadian Food Words*, p. 169, 1998

laughing-sides *noun*
elastic-sided boots *AUSTRALIA, 1937*
- And then there was Father Cooley, with a honey of an accent, and yet Australian too, as though he wore a buckled shoe on one foot and an Australian "laughin'-side" on the other.—Ruth Park, *The Harp In The South*, p. 126, 1948

laughing tobacco *noun*

marijuana *UK*

- It's been said that laughing tobacco can, in fact, cause insanity, but according to [Eric] Schlosser, the reefer madness is on the part of politicians. — *Bang*, p. 100, May 2003

laughing weed *noun*

marijuana *US, 1925*

Derives from the tendency to laughter experienced by marijuana smokers.

- — Richard A. Spears, *The Slang and Jargon of Drugs and Drink*, p. 304, 1986
- Reefers, the so-called 'laughing weed' were described as a far greater menace than opium. — Redmer YSKA, *New Zealand Green*, p. 51, 1990
- — Mike Haskins, *Drugs*, p. 288, 2003

launch *noun*

in drag racing, a quick and powerful start *US*

- — John Edwards, *Auto Dictionary*, p. 94, 1993

launching pad *noun*

1 a place where LSD is taken *US, 1971*

Punning both on **PAD** (a place) and LSD as 'travel'.

- — Richard A. Spears, *The Slang and Jargon of Drugs and Drink*, p. 309, 1986

2 a lavatory seat in a (moving) train *UK*

Inspired by the image of an evacuation into space.

- — Harvey Sheppard, *Dictionary of Railway Slang*, 1970

launder *verb*

to pass ill-gotten gains through a system of changes designed to legitmise their status *UK*

- Nigeria's former dictator, looted his nation of $110 million, also laundered for him by Citibank. — Chalmers Johnson, *The Sorrows of Empire*, p. 274, 2004

laundromat *noun*

a business used to legitimise money gained in criminal enterprises *UK*

A play on **LAUNDER** (to decriminalise money).

- — Angela Devlin, *Prison Patter*, p. 69, 1996

laundry *noun*

1 a business used by organised crime to give illegally gained money the appearance of legitimacy *US*

- I want to get the front money by hitting their laundry, 'cause they can't squeal to the law afterward for fear they'll give up the operation. — Stephen Cannell, *King Con*, p. 111, 1997

2 in homosexual usage, a bulge in a man's crotch *US*

Humourous, suggesting that the bulge is produced by something other than the man's genitals.

- — Guy Strait, *The Lavendar Lexicon*, 1st June 1964
- — *Male Swinger Number 3*, p. 47, 1981: 'The complete gay dictionary'

laundry queen *noun*

in circus and carnival usage, a female dancer *US*

- — Don Wilmeth, *The Language of American Popular Entertainment*, p. 155, 1981

Laura Norda *noun*

law and order *AUSTRALIA*

- The trouble with Silly Sneed (according to Sir Jasper Storeman that is) was he wouldn't toe the line and go in boots and all on Laura Norda. — Frank Hardy, *The Outcasts of Foolgarah*, p. 191, 1971
- Five days ago another Sunday stunt was rolled out by the Premier, Bob Carr, and his attractive assistant Laura Norda. — *www.smh.com.au*, 21st February 2003

Laurel and Hardy *noun*

1 Bacardi™ (a branded white rum) *UK*

Rhyming slang, formed from the names of film comedians Stan Laurel (1890–1965) and Oliver Hardy (1892–1957).

- — Ray Puxley, *Cockney Rabbit*, 1992

2 a yardie (a Jamaican gangster) *UK, 2001*

Rhyming slang, based on film comedians Stan Laurel (1890–1965) and Oliver Hardy (1892–1957).

lav *noun*

1 a word *UK*

- The phrase bona lavs can be used as a sign-off to a letter, meaning "best wishes". — Paul Baker, *Polari*, p. 179, 2002

2 a *lavatory* *UK, 1913*

Variant 'lavvy'.

- They've got a huge public library there with steps given over to thousands of derelicts, a brick "lav" trade and rather dusty shelves. — Angelo d'Arcangelo, *The Homosexual Handbook*, p. 228, 1968
- [S]he went and locked herself in the lavs and had a private little cry[.] — Ted Lewis, *Jack Carter's Law*, p. 157, 1974
- Well I t'ought I'd be hosin' down the lavvy tonight[.] — Nick Barlay, *Curvy Lovebox*, p. 154, 1997
- I remember carrying big buckets of sheep dip to wash outside lavvies[.] — Livi Michael, *Robinson Street*, p. 23, 1999
- I spent most of the night checking out the amusing lav theatre. Highlight of the evening was Naomi Campbell [...] getting her dress caught up in her knickers[.] — *ES Magazine*, p. 3, 22nd June 2001

lavaliers *noun*

the female breasts *US*

- — John D. Bell et al., *Loosely Speaking*, p. 12, 1969

lavender *adjective*

effeminate, homosexual *US, 1929*

- The lavender boys hang around the far end of the bar[.] — Roger Gordon, *Hollywood's Sexual Underground*, p. 18, 1966
- Ever anxious to parsimoniously pinch pennies, Mickey has cast lavender loverboy Touch Vecchio in a key role[.[— James Ellroy, *White Jazz*, p. 7, 1992

lavender fascist *noun*

an uncompromising, politically motivated homosexual *UK*

- [Outing is the] lavender fascist practice of forcing gay celebrities and public figures out in the open. — Alon Shulman, *The Style Bible*, p. 182, 1999

lavvy-diver *noun*

a plumber *UK: SCOTLAND*

From 'lavvy' (a lavatory).

- — Michael Munro, *The Original Patter*, p. 42, 1985

law *noun*

▸ **have the law on**

to inform the police about someone *UK, 1800*

- — John Ayto, *Oxford Dictionary of Slang*, p. 100, 1998

▸ **the law**

1 the police, the law enforcement authorities *US, 1893*

- All I could think of was the law had nailed Mike and Mackey in The Bunk. — Mezz Mezzrow, *Really the Blues*, p. 266, 1946
- We're liable to get pinched for mashing on Sixty-third. I heard the Law is watching that pretty close. — James T. Farrell, *Saturday Night*, p. 38, 1947
- It's the Law, he thought, and he was stricken with fear. — Hal Ellson, *The Golden Spike*, p. 5, 1952
- The Law's after her and we'd better find her before they do. — George Mandel, *Flee the Angry Strangers*, p. 159, 1952
- Two detectives walked in and leaned on the bar, talking to the bartender. Jack jerked his head in their direction. "The law. Let's take a walk." — William Burroughs, *Junkie*, p. 21, 1953
- The men grumble and reluctantly spread themselves along the wall, prodded by the Law. — Odie Hawkins, *Ghetto Sketches*, p. 31, 1972

2 your parents *US*

Teen slang.

- — *American Weekly*, p. 2, 14th August 1955

law *verb*

1 to arrest *US, 1935*

- "Time was," said Pappy Dan, "young fella left town, he was about to be lawed or about to be a father." — John Sayles, *Union Dues*, p. 65, 1977

2 to impersonate the police for the purposes of extortion *UK*

- They were on their way to the Yard to see if he could pick the grafter [confidence trickster] who'd lawed him out of the rogue's gallery. — Charles Raven, *Underworld Nights*, p. 129, 1956

lawdy!

▷ **see: LORDY!**

lawing *noun*

the act of impersonating a police officer for criminal purposes *UK*

- Now bogies [police], as you can imagine, take a very poor view of lawing. They regard it as an unwarranted liberty. — Charles Raven, *Underworld Nights*, p. 130, 1956

lawn *noun*

a woman's pubic hair *US*

- — Roger Blake, *The American Dictionary of Sexual Terms*, p. 118, 1964
- — *Maledicta*, p. 131, Summer/Winter 1982: 'Dyke diction: the language of lesbians'

- When it comes to mowing our lickable lawns, the hairstyle you choose for your kitty can be an expression of your personal taste. — *The Village Voice*, 8th–14th November 2000

lax up *verb*

to have a laxative effect *UK, 1990s*

- Go'a shit bad man [...] Kuf [cocaines]'s laxed me up. — Nick Barlay, *Curvy Lovebox*, p. 144, 1997

lay *noun*

1 an act of sexual intercourse *US, 1928*

- "Hey, guys," he whispered to the room, "what d'ya say we all give the bum a lay and then we'll take back the money?" — Irving Shulman, *The Amboy Dukes*, p. 38, 1947
- [T]he two of you'll laugh and talk me over and agree that women are good lays and there are a lot of them. — Jack Kerouac, *The Subterraneans*, p. 110, 1958
- Past forty, and with her blue look, Fay finds it difficult to interest a John ... Dracula's idea of a good lay. — Alexander Trocchi, *Cain's Book*, p. 35, 1960
- I was about ten and she was probably less, and at the time a lay seemed like such a big deal[.] — Ken Kesey, *One Flew Over the Cuckoo's Nest*, p. 244, 1962
- I felt one's culo and asked, 'How about a lay?' Imagine, just for that she started yelling for her boys. — Piri Thomas, *Down These Mean Streets*, p. 51, 1967
- He asked her what she charged for a lay. She said – "a dollar – I'se a good lay, mister – I'll show you a good time." — Herbert Huncke, *The Evening Sun Turned Crimson*, p. 35, 1980
- "And you're a lousy writer," he said, "and an even lousier lay." — Rita Ciresi, *Pink Slip*, p. 191, 1999

2 a girl or a woman regarded as a sex-partner, usually with a modifying adjective such as easy, good, great, etc *UK, 1635*

- But all things considered I look good. I like men's bums and penises. At 67 years old, I am what you might call an easy lay. — *The Guardian*, 17th November 2003

lay *verb*

to have sex *UK, 1800*

Most often heard in the passive.

- Ella Mae laying me because I wasn't married and she figured she had enough for me and Henry too[.] — Chester Himes, *If He Hollers Let Him Go*, p. 6, 1945
- There had been Marjorie, broken in by Slicker Morris, and after his pioneering effort she had laid for every guy in the place. — James T. Farrell, *Saturday Night*, p. 30, 1947
- You know, all I really want is to get laid. That's what I'm really complaining about. — John Clellon Holmes, *Go*, p. 8, 1952
- When'd you get laid last? — George Mandel, *Flee the Angry Strangers*, p. 221, 1952
- A minute before she'd been all set to lay, and it probably wouldn't have made any difference if I hadn't had a dime. — Jim Thompson, *The Killer Inside*, p. 11, 1952
- How would you like it if people came in on you, laid your girls and then wanted to put it on the cuff? — William Burroughs, *Junkie*, p. 76–77, 1953
- I found this irksome, as I was beginning again to feel lonely and like laying half Manhattan island (the half that was female). — Clancy Sigal, *Going Away*, p. 420, 1961
- [T]hey discussed how it would be to lay that little nurse with the birthmark who went off at midnight." — Ken Kesey, *One Flew Over the Cuckoo's Nest*, p. 289, 1962
- Thus it was that I got laid for the first time in my life in February of that new year[.[— John Nichols, *The Sterile Cuckoo*, p. 96, 1965
- [A]ccording to informed rumour, [Danny Cohn-Bendit] was to have laid [...] the daughter of a member of de Gaulle's cabinet. — Richard Neville, *Play Power*, p. 44, 1970
- I rarely make love / I mostly get laid — Loudon Wainwright III, *Suicide Song*, 1971
- Jimmy, goddamn it – loosen up and get laid. — *Bull Durham*, 1988
- I think you need to get laid or something. — Francesca Lia Block, *I Was a Teenage Fairy*, p. 109, 1998

▸ **lay a batch**

to accelerate a car quickly and in so doing to leave rubber marks on the road *US, 1969*

- — Capitol Records, *Hot Rod Jargon*, 1963
- — Kenn "Naz" Young, *Naz's Dictionary of Teen Slang*, p. 71, 1993

▸ **lay a cable**

to defecate *AUSTRALIA*

- You can 'Go lay a cable' or 'Do number two' Or 'Sit on the tooty' or 'Do a do-do.' — Sam Weller, *Old Bastards I Have Met*, p. 34, 1979
- Cos the mongrel laid a cable in the sandpit[.] — Ian Dury, *This is What We Find*, 1979
- — Sonya Plowman, *Great Kiwi Slang*, p. 112, 2002

▸ **lay a fart**

to fart *US*

- This guy sitting in the row in front of me, Edgar Marsalla, laid this terrific fart. — J.D. Salinger, *The Catcher in the Rye*, 1951

▸ **lay a log**

to defecate *UK*

Extended from **LOG** (a turd).

- [T]he poor old lady had obviously died of a heart attack whilst laying a log, fallen off the shitter and blocked the door with her head. — *FHM*, p. 250, June 2003

▸ **lay chilly**

to relax *US*

- Finally he decided, "We'll crawl down the streambed. Stay low, find a good spot, lay chilly." — A.D. Horne, *The Wounded Generation*, p. 67, 1981
- Originally Vietnam war usage. — *Washington Post Magazine*, p. 17, 28th June 1987: 'Say wha?'
- "Wait!" I said. "Get the ARVN up here first, and tell these guys to lay chilly." — Michael C. Hodgins, *Reluctant Warrior*, p. 152, 1996

▸ **lay dead**

1 to remain silent *US*

- — John R. Armore and Joseph D. Wolfe, *Dictionary of Desperation*, p. 38, 1976

2 to stay in one place; to stay still *US*

- — Babs Gonzales, *Be-Bop Dictionary and History of its Famous Stars*, p. 9, 1949

3 to idle, to waste time fooling around *US*

Vietnam war usage.

- — Linda Reinberg, *In the Field*, p. 125, 1991

▸ **lay dog**

to lie motionless in the jungle *US*

Vietnam war reconnaissance patrol usage.

- — Linda Reinberg, *In the Field*, p. 125, 1991
- I told everyone to lay dog for thirty minutes to see what the gooks were going to do. — John Burford, *LRRP Team Leader*, p. 97, 1994

▸ **lay down some sparks**

to accelerate a car suddenly from rest, bringing the car frame or body into contact with the road and producing a shower of sparks *US*

- — Edith A. Folb, *runnin' down some lines*, p. 244, 1980

▸ **lay down the law**

to dogmatise, especially in an argument; to insist on a mode of behaviour *UK, 1762*

- The incident occurred only a few hours after the coaches of both sides had laid down the law to their players following a lecture from Lloyd about on-field behaviour at the close of play on Wednesday. — *The Guardian*, 12th December 2003

▸ **lay eggs**

to drop bombs *US*

- Anyway, the air force drivers were laying eggs all over the designated VC installations zone we wuz s'pose to move in on and sop up being grunts which is what you do with shit – that's the way they seed us[.] — Clarence Major, *All-Night Visitors*, p. 36, 1998

▸ **lay heat**

to fart *US*

- — Peter Furze, *Tailwinds*, p. 114, 1998

▸ **lay in the cut**

to wait in hiding *US*

- I laid in the cut on Carmen's big butt / And kept her on her knees all night. — Dennis Wepman et al., *The Life*, p. 49, 1976

▸ **lay it down**

1 in motorcyle racing, to spin out or fall, causing the motorcyle and the earth to meet; to intentionally throw a motorcyle on its side in the face of an impending accident *US*

- — Don Dempsey, *American Speech*, p. 270, December 1962: 'The language of traffic policemen'
- — Ed Radlauer, *Motorcylopedia*, p. 38, 1973
- I laid it down. — Douglas Dunford, *Motorcycle Department, Beaulieu Motor Museum*, 1979

2 to explain the rules of a carnival midway game to a potential customer *US*

- — Gene Sorrows, *All About Carnivals*, p. 21, 1985: 'Terminology'

▸ **lay it on**

to inform, to report or explain fully *US*

- You know what to do with the stiffs, and remember to call Amos' ol' lady and lay it on her. — Donald Goines, *Inner City Hoodlum*, p. 108, 1975
- Well, I'm gonna lay it on you one time, for the record. — Edwin Torres, *Carlito's Way*, p. 5, 1975

▸ **lay it on thick; lay it on with a trowel; lay it on**

to do something in an excessive manner *UK, 1600*

- Blair laid it on with a trowel, quoting from the Koran[.] — *The Observer*, 7th October 2001

- In normal circumstances, you could say the song was laying it on a bit thick, but these are not normal circumstances, and the song works to chilling effect. — *The Guardian*, 12th September 2003

▸ **lay on the iron**
in motor racing, to move inside another car on a turn, forcing it up and out of the fastest part of the track *US*
- — John Edwards, *Auto Dictionary*, p. 94, 1993

▸ **lay paper**
to pass counterfeit money or bad cheques *US*
- [H]e goes over there and starts laying this paper [writing checks]. — Bruce Jackson, *In the Life*, p. 286, 1972

▸ **lay pipe**
(used of a male) to have sex *US, 1939*
- — Collin Baker et al., *College Undergraduate Slang Study Conducted at Brown University*, p. 150, 1968
- Gonna lay some pipe, six inches at a time. — Joseph Wambaugh, *The Choirboys*, p. 313, 1975

▸ **lay the leg**
to seduce or attempt to seduce *US*
- — Don Wilmeth, *The Language of American Popular Entertainment*, p. 155, 1981

▸ **lay the note**
to shortchange someone *US*
- — Robert C. Prus and C.R.D. Sharper, *Road Hustler*, p. 170, 1977: 'Glossary of terms'

▸ **lay the smack down**
to engage in a physical fight *US*
- — Connie Eble (Editor), *UNC-CH Campus Slang*, p. 5, Spring 1999

▸ **lay track**
to lie *US*
- — William K. Bentley and James M. Corbett, *Prison Slang*, p. 33, 1992

layabout *noun*
an unemployed idler *UK, 1932*
- He's a nice one, he is. Very nice. Young layabout. — Clive Exton, *No Fixed Abode [Six Granada Plays]*, p. 119, 1959
- Well... yobboes are... well, layabouts. — John Burke and Stuart Douglass, *The Boys*, p. 48, 1962

lay and pay
in casino blackjack games, the practice of laying hands down, turning them over, and paying or collecting all bets at once *US*
- — Lee Solkey, *Dummy Up and Deal*, p. 115, 1980

layback *noun*
a barbiturate, a central nervous system depressant *US, 1970*
- — Richard A. Spears, *The Slang and Jargon of Drugs and Drink*, p. 310, 1986
- — Mike Haskins, *Drugs*, p. 282, 2003

lay bear *noun*
in the carnival, a stuffed bear given to a girl by a game operator in return for sex *US*
- More times that I care to remember, I've witnessed a thirteen or fourteen year old girl being guided to a screened area behind a game booth by one of these perverts, whispering in her ear the promise of a LAY BEAR. — Gene Sorrows, *All About Carnivals*, p. 21, 1985

lay-by *noun*
on the railways, a passing track *US*
- — Norman Carlisle, *The Modern Wonder Book of Trains and Railroading*, p. 265, 1946

lay dead!
wait just a minute! *US*
Teen slang.
- — *San Francisco News*, p. 6, 25th March 1958

laydeez *noun*
ladies *UK*
Jocular; a phonetic spelling of an overly sincere or quasi-American pronunciation.
- [John] Travolta is gifted with the wittiest lines, the smartest cars and a swimming pool awash with sexy laydeez. — *The Guardian*, 27th July 2001

laydown *noun*
a gullible customer or buyer; an easy victim *US, 1935*
- — Peter Mann, *How to Buy a Used Car Without Getting Gypped*, p. 193, 1975
- — M. Allen Henderson, *How Con Games Work*, p. 221, 1985: 'Glossary'
- Beano said once they got that far in the game, it wouldn't matter. The farmer would already be a laydown. — Stephen Cannell, *Big Con*, p. 168, 1997

lay down *verb*
1 to play in a musical performance *US, 1943*
- They laid down not only some of the heaviest music, but a message that was so then and there that it was incredible and uncanny. — *East Village Other*, 20th August 1969

2 to remand in custody *UK*
- — Angela Devlin, *Prison Patter*, p. 69, 1996

laydown merchant *noun*
a criminal who passes or distributes forged money *UK*
- — Angela Devlin, *Prison Patter*, p. 70, 1996

lay down misère *noun*
a certainty *AUSTRALIA*
A card-game usage brought into wider circulation.
- Tindall, on the other had, made no secret he considered Hustler a 'lay down misere'. — James Holledge, *The Great Australian Gamble*, p. 40, 1966
- If, having awoken in unfamiliar surroundings, you have no loose change or paper money on your person at all, it's a *lay down misère* you've been rolled[.] — Barry Humphries, *The Traveller's Tool*, p. 60, 1985
- — Ignatius Jones, *True Hip*, p. 68, 1990

layer *noun*
a bookmaker *UK, 1937*
- — David W. Maurer, *Argot of the Racetrack*, p. 39, 1951
- Another prominent layer, John Wallace, who also had backed the horse, was only too happy to transfer his bets to Thompson[.] — James Holledge, *The Great Australian Gamble*, p. 70, 1966
- — David Bennet, *Know Your Bets*, p. 58, 2001

layette *noun*
▷ **see: LAY-OUT**

lay-for-pay *noun*
sex with a prostitute *US*
- "Who's behind all the muscle, Mamie?" I was going too fast for her. "In the past two weeks we've hauled at least three of you lay-for-pay dames into Bellevue to get patched up." — *Rogue for Men*, p. 45, June 1956

lay-in *noun*
permission from prison authorities to remain in bed in your cell instead of working *US*
- We had a ole doctor, one guy went up there and asked him for a lay-in [permission to stay in the building during the work day] and he told him, "I'm not gonna lay you in." — Bruce Jackson, *In the Life*, p. 307, 1972
- — Reinhold Aman, *Hillary Clinton's Pen Pal: A Guide to Life and Lingo in Federal Prison*, p. 47, 1996

lay into *verb*
to attack verbally or physically *UK, 1838*
- Ah hello Mrs Nugent come in but Nugent was in no humour for ah hello come in or any of that. She lay into ma about the comics and the whole lot. — Patrick McCabe, *The Butcher Boy*, p. 4, 1992
- He got me outside and laid into me with kicks. — Patrick McCabe, *The Butcher Boy*, p. 138, 1992

lay off *verb*
1 in betting, for one bookmaker to place a bet with another bookmaker to reduce the risk of loss *AUSTRALIA, 1877*
- Off-course bookmaking was illegal in New South Wales at that time and starting-price bookmakers like Tony found that the most accurate method of making a book was through research in the pubs of the city, checking on the odds being offered and laying off if the book became too heavy. — Robin Eakin, *Aunts up the Cross*, p. 38, 1965
- He knew all the dream books by heart, the Chinaman in the Daily News; he knew just when to lay off on certain numbers[.] — Edwin Torres, *Carlito's Way*, p. 28, 1975
- You've got such heavy action on a horse, let's say, you're afraid he comes you'll drown in winning slips, you lay off some of it with another book. — Robert Campbell, *Juice*, p. 192–193, 1988
- [B]ookmakers giving to another firm all or part of a bet they've laid[.] — John McCririck, *John McCririck's World of Betting*, p. 60, 1991

2 to stop aggravating or interfering, to cease *US, 1908*
Often as an imperative.
- Press should lay off TV stars, says GMTV's [Penny] Smith — *The Guardian*, 31st October 2002

lay-off bet *noun*
a hedging bet *AUSTRALIA*
- He did not think Coca could win, so he kept the money and did not place the bookie's lay-off bet. — James Holledge, *The Great Australian Gamble*, p. 75, 1966

lay of the day *noun*
in horse racing, the best wager of the day *AUSTRALIA*
- — Ned Wallish, *The Truth Dictionary of Racing Slang*, p. 45, 1989

lay of the land *noun*

in circus and carnival usage, a lead dancer in a sexually oriented dance show *US*

• —Don Wilmeth, *The Language of American Popular Entertainment*, p. 155, 1981

lay-on *noun*

a gift of drugs *UK*

• DAZ: Fagash give us a lay-on. FAGASH: (putting his scales away) None left now, Daz. —Paul Fraser and Shane Meadows, *TwentyFourSeven*, p. 29, 1997
• "Are you asking me for a lay-on?" I asked, not sure what she was expecting me to say. There was no way she'd get a lay-on, she wasn't regular enough and we didn't know where she lived. —Jason Parkinson, *Skateboards and Methadone [The Howard Marks Book of Dope Stories]*, p. 207, 2001

lay on *verb*

to give *US, 1936*

• I'd like you to fall by grandma's joint this afternoon and lay the stuff on her. —Steve Allen, *Bop Fables*, p. 37, 1955
• How many fixes have I laid on you? —Alexander Trocchi, *Cain's Book*, p. 165, 1960
• You gotta bring the cat down and lay one on him and you don't know if they're gonna pull out a French 75 or a Walther. —William "Lord" Buckley, *His Majesty the Policeman*, 1960
• Yes, but who donated it? Who's laying it on? —*Berkeley Barb*, p. 3, 21st October 1966
• "Nutmeg seeds," said Tarzan, grinning. "Here, I'll lay some on you." —Tom Robbins, *Another Roadside Attraction*, p. 272, 1971
• Or if someone lays something on me, as they say. —Doug Lang, *Freaks*, p. 24, 1973
• It was terrible weed, even by South-Central Los Angeles standards, full of dirt, twigs, rag tips 'n foreign matter, but I rolled a twenty joint bag out of it for her and laid it on her. —Odie Hawkins, *Black Casanova*, p. 165, 1984
• He said, "Be my guest," and he laid a joint on me. —Herbert Huncke, *Guilty of Everything*, p. 25, 1990

layout *noun*

1 an apartment or house *US, 1883*

• I said, "Jim, you sure ain't jiving. Your layout is a sonuvabitch." He said, "I got five bedrooms here." —Iceberg Slim (Robert Beck), *Pimp*, p. 130, 1969

2 collectively, the equipment used to smoke opium *US, 1881*

• Mike and me grabbed our layout and out into the airshaft we climbed[.] —Mezz Mezzrow, *Really the Blues*, p. 249, 1946

3 a soldier who lies hidden in a hole observing enemy movements *US*

Korean war usage.

• These two "lay-outs," as they are called, are relieved by the next squad that night. I am interested in standing this particular watch. I can't determine what their function is, since they must hide in a hole all day. —Martin Russ, *The Last Parallel*, p. 90, 1957

lay-out ; layette *noun*

the equipment necessary to prepare and inject a narcotic drug *US, 1882*

• —Richard A. Spears, *The Slang and Jargon of Drugs and Drink*, p. 310, 1986
• —Mike Haskins, *Drugs*, p. 292, 2003

lay out *verb*

to engage in sexual two-timing *IRELAND*

• Minnie believed for a while that he [Batty] had another woman, (or, as Francey put it, that he was layin' out), but it turned out that the only rival was the horse... —Bernard Share, *Slanguage*, p. 188, 2003

lay up *verb*

1 to relax *US*

• —Anthony Romeo, *The Language of Gangs*, p. 19, 4th December 1962
• —Hermese E. Roberts, *The Third Ear*, 1971

2 to paint graffiti on train carriages while standing in a siding *US*

• —Jim Crotty, *How to Talk American*, p. 142, 1997

Lazarus ball *noun*

in pinball, a ball that passes between the flippers but then miraculously bounces back into play *US*

• —Edward Trapunski, *Special When Lit*, p. 153, 1979

laziosis *noun*

laziness, presented with humour as a disease *BELIZE, 1975*

• —Richard Allsopp, *Dictionary of Caribbean English Usage*, p. 340, 1996

lazy arm *noun*

in the television and film industries, a hand-held microphone boom *UK*

• —Oswald Skilbeck, *ABC of Film and TV Working Terms*, p. 76, 1960

lazy-bones *noun*

a loafer, a lazy person *UK, 1592*

• Here they get worse food: refusers, loafers, lazy-bones. —Anne Applebaum, *Gulag*, p. 67, 2003

lazyitis *noun*

laziness, as a 'medical' condition *UK*

A combination of 'lazy' and the suffix **-ITIS** (used to create an imaginary disease).

• —Johnny Speight, *Till Death Us Do Part*, 12th August 1967
• The elegant Mrs Ryder would regularly tell her son he had lazyitis. —Tony Wilson, *24 Hour Party People*, p. 197, 2002

Lazy K *nickname*

HM prison Long Kesh *UK: NORTHERN IRELAND*

Military.

• —Christopher Hawke, *For Campaign Service*, 1979

lazy lob *noun*

a partial erection of the penis *UK*

• —Chris Donald, *Roger's Profanisaurus*, 1998
• He got a lazy lob on. Kara reached down and stroked his penis. —Garry Bushell, *The Face*, p. 57, 2001

lazy money *noun*

money kept in reserve, especially secretly *AUSTRALIA*

• —Ned Wallish, *The Truth Dictionary of Racing Slang*, p. 45, 1989

lazy wind *noun*

a cold, biting wind *AUSTRALIA*

• It was a lazy wind – wouldn't blow around you, blew straight through you. —Kel Richards, *The Aussie Bible*, p. 34, 2003

LBJ *noun*

1 LSD, especially when combined with some other drug *US, 1982*

Probably a jocular transference of initials with those of former US President Lyndon Baines Johnson, 1908–73.

• —Robert Ashton, *This Is Heroin*, p. 209, 2002
• —Mike Haskins, *Drugs*, p. 285, 2003

2 piperidyl benzilate, a hallucinogen *US*

• —William D. Alsever, *Glossary for the Establishment and Other Uptight People*, p. 17, December 1970

3 heroin *UK, 1998*

• —Robert Ashton, *This Is Heroin*, p. 209, 2002
• —Mike Haskins, *Drugs*, p. 284, 2003

4 phencyclidine, the recreational drug known as PCP or angel dust *UK*

• —Robert Ashton, *This Is Heroin*, p. 209, 2002

LBJ *nickname*

during the Vietnam war, the Long Binh military stockade, South Vietnam *US*

• Yeah, you two chickenshits are gonna do about a thousand years in LBJ. —Larry Heinemann, *Close Quarters*, p. 151, 1977
• He's in the L.B.J. – didn't give him no medals or nothing. —*Apocalypse Now*, 1979
• "I'd rather do hard time at LBJ," the man said, his voice suddenly loud and firm. —Larry Heinemann, *Paco's Story*, p. 29, 1986
• Playing on US President Johnson's initials and nickname. —Linda Reinberg, *In the Field*, p. 125, 1991

LBJ Ranch *nickname*

the Long Binh military stockade, South Vietnam *US*

Playing on US President Lyndon B. Johnson's ranch in Johnson City, Texas, outside Austin.

• —Linda Reinberg, *In the Field*, p. 125, 1991

L-bomb *noun*

an explicit declaration of love *US*

• —Connie Eble (Editor), *UNC-CH Campus Slang*, p. 7, October 2002

LB's *noun*

pounds, extra weight *US*

• Susan really put on some LB's this semester. —Connie Eble (Editor), *UNC-CH Campus Slang*, p. 6, Fall 1986

LD *noun*

▷ **see:** **EL D**

lead *noun*

a pencil *BARBADOS*

- —Frank A. Collymore, *Barbadian Dialect*, p. 66, 1965

▸ **get the lead out**

to stop dawdling, to hurry up *US, 1919*

- Get the lead out, fat boy!—Stephen Sondheim, *West Side Story*, 1957
- This goddamn meal is late! Get the fucking lead out, boy!—Iceberg Slim (Robert Beck), *The Naked Soul of Iceberg Slim*, p. 47, 1971
- Come on you guys! Get the lead out.—*Repo Man*, 1984

lead *verb*

▸ **lead up the garden path**

to lead on, to entice *UK, 1925*

- So how could the gurus be worth their fees, first-class air-tickets and fancy suits? They led us up the garden path and left us there in the dark[.]—*The Guardian*, 21st August 2001

lead balloon *noun*

▸ **go down like a lead balloon; go over like a lead balloon**

of an action, to be poorly received, to be unsuccessful, to fail *US, 1960*

- The Conservatives' last attempt at vouchers, for nursery education, went down like a lead balloon.—*The Guardian*, 6th October 2003

lead cocktail *noun*

bullets *US*

- —Vincent J. Monteleone, *Criminal Slang*, p. 143, 1949

leaded *adjective*

caffeinated *US*

Borrowing from the language of car fuel for application to the world of coffee drinks and, to a lesser extent, soft drinks.

- —Connie Eble (Editor), *UNC-CH Campus Slang*, p. 4, Fall 1996

Leader *noun*

▸ **The Leader**

Frank Sinatra, US singer (1915–98) *US*

- The latest casino owner in Las Vegas to embark on the hearts-and-flowers route is Francis Albert Sinatra, better known as The Leader, The General, The Dago, The Pope, and Frankie Boy.—Ed Reid and Ovid Demaris, *The Green Felt Jungle*, p. 74, 1963

leadfoot *noun*

a driver who consistently drives faster than necessary *US, 1938*

- —*Hot Rod Magazine*, p. 13, November 1948: 'Racing jargon'
- —John Edwards, *Auto Dictionary*, p. 95, 1993

lead-foot *verb*

to drive fast *US*

- He made the trip in thirty-five, lead-footing it code Three all the way[.]—James Ellroy, *Suicide Hill*, p. 683, 1986

lead in the pencil *noun*

the ability of a man to achieve an erection and ejaculate *UK, 1925*

- —Roger Blake, *The American Dictionary of Sexual Terms*, p. 118, 1964
- Drink this, Superman. It'll put some lead in your pencil.—*New Jack City*, 1990
- "Hot tea," he declared. "All natural herbs. Here, it'll put lead in your pencil." Keyes shook his head. "No thanks."—Carl Hiaasen, *Tourist Season*, p. 100, 1995

lead joint *noun*

in circus and carnival usage, a shooting gallery concession on the midway *US*

- —Don Wilmeth, *The Language of American Popular Entertainment*, p. 156, 1981

lead on, McDuff!

let's go!; let's get started! *UK, 1912*

A mis-quotation from Shakespeare's *Macbeth* ('Lay on, McDuff') that became a catchphrase.

lead pants *noun*

a slow-moving, work-averse person *US*

- This Rip is a lead pants, strictly from fatigue, allergic to work, no git up and git.—Haenigsen, *Jive's Like That*, 1947

lead-pipe cinch *noun*

an absolute certainty *US, 1894*

- I got a lead pipe cinch … you game?—Odie Hawkins, *Chicago Hustle*, p. 38, 1977

lead poisoning *noun*

wounds inflicted by a gun *US, 1883*

From the lead in bullets.

- —Vincent J. Monteleone, *Criminal Slang*, p. 143, 1949
- Three days later, when she came to, Sugarfoot was croaked from lead poisoning, like forty SWAT-issue rounds worth[.]—Seth Morgan, *Homeboy*, p. 3, 1990
- [T]here were no armed response units lurking about waiting to administer a swift injection of lead poisoning for your trouble.—Garry Bushell, *The Face*, p. 24, 2001

lead singer *noun*

a leader of a criminal gang *US*

- —Anna Scotti and Paul Young, *Buzzwords*, p. 137, 1997

lead sled *noun*

1 any aircraft that is considered underpowered or unresponsive *US, 1961*

- —John Horton, *The Grub Street Dictionary of International Aircraft Nicknames*, p. 81, 1994

2 a CF-100 Canuck jet fighter aircraft *CANADA*

The aircraft first flew in 1950, and is also known as **ALUMINIUM CROW** and **THE CLUNK**.

3 a Boeing 727 aircraft *US*

Allegedly from its heaviness during take off; the plane was produced from the early 1960s to 1984.

- Pilots, who tend not to gush over their magnificent flying machines publicly, called the Boeing 727 the 'three-holer' and 'lead sled'[.]—*Airways Magazine*, August 2002

4 the US Air Force F-105 fighter-bomber *US, 1968*

So named because it was the heaviest single-seat fighter plane in the world.

- —Linda Reinberg, *In the Field*, p. 126, 1991

5 in hot rodding and drag racing, a slow car *US*

- —Lyle K. Engel, *The Complete Book of Fuel and Gas Dragsters*, p. 152, 1968

leaf *noun*

1 marijuana *US*

- It's a cryin' shame they outlawed the leaf.—Ross Russell, *The Sound*, p. 23, 1961
- Man, this is some golden leaf I brought up from New Orleans.—Leon Rappolo, *quoted in Waiting For The Man by Harry Shapiro*, 1999

2 cocaine *US, 1942*

- —Eugene Landy, *The Underground Dictionary*, p. 119, 1971
- The drug and this name derive from the leaves of the coca bush (Erythroxylon coca).—R.C. Garrett et al., *The Coke Book*, p. 200, 1984
- —Angela Devlin, *Prison Patter*, p. 70, 1996

3 a banknote *US, 1929*

An extension of the imagery of **LETTUCE** (money).

leaf colonel *noun*

a lieutenant colonel *US, 1946*

- —*American Speech*, p. 55, February 1947: 'Pacific War language'

leafer *noun*

a cheque, especially when forged or issued fraudulently *UK*

- —Angela Devlin, *Prison Patter*, p. 70, 1996

leaf pipe *noun*

a credit-card-sized pipe for smoking marijuana *UK*

- —Alon Shulman, *The Style Bible*, p. 143, 1999

league *noun*

▸ **out of your league**

used of anything or anyone of a superior quality; to be out of your league is to be of a lesser condition, out-classed *UK, 1966*

- Everybody out of their league[.]—David Peace, *Nineteen Seventy-Four*, p. 288, 1999

leaguey *noun*

a Rugby League player or follower *AUSTRALIA*

- The coach and the captain thinking, 'Rubbish. What would a dumb old leaguey like Gibbo know?'—*Daily Telegraph*, p. 78, 30th July 2003

leak *noun*

1 an act of urination *US, 1918*

The verb 'leak', found in Shakespeare as a vulgar synonym for 'urinate', has been supplanted by the noun use of the term.

- Can't a man take a leak, Chief?—Evan Hunter, *The Blackboard Jungle*, p. 47, 1954

- [F]inally Wallenstein going to the head for a leak[.] —Jack Kerouac, *The Subterraneans*, p. 77, 1958
- He went into the bushes to take a leak. —Willard Motley, *Let No Man Write My Epitaph*, p. 183, 1958
- Poppa pulled the chain as he took a long, long leak. —Piri Thomas, *Down These Mean Streets*, p. 22, 1967
- He had to take a leak, too. —Nathan Heard, *Howard Street*, p. 16, 1968
- Then me bladder tells me I got to have a leak. —John O'Grady, *It's Your Shout, Mate!*, p. 72, 1972
- In the Navy we are taught to wash our hands after a leak. —Martin Cameron, *A Look at the Bright Side*, 1988
- I needed to take a leak and I started to move around. —Herbert Huncke, *Guilty of Everything*, p. 197, 1990
- Can I go take a leak? —*Airheads*, 1994
- I could be in kharzi taking a leak when someone rings. —Kitty Churchill, *Thinking of England*, p. 162, 1995
- I was taking a leak! —*Something About Mary*, 1998
- Christ, I was only taking a leak! —Terry Southern, *Now Dig This*, p. 139, 2001

2 an unauthorised disclosure of confidential or secret information; the person making such a disclosure *US, 1939*
- Thought there was a leak in the Manhattan District. The only leak was in their heads. —Philip Wylie, *Opus 21*, p. 53, 1949

3 in casino gambling, any dealer error or weakness *US*
- —Michael Dalton, *Blackjack*, p. 61, 1991

leak *verb*

1 to urinate *UK, 1596*
- You goan to watch me leak, man? —Evan Hunter, *The Blackboard Jungle*, p. 47, 1954
- [T]he prowl car came by and the cop got out to leak[.] —Jack Kerouac, *On the Road*, p. 90, 1957

2 to sweat *UK*
- [T]he people who had just come in off a run, leaking and panting, would then do map reading. —Andy McNab, *Immediate Action*, p. 59, 1995

3 to ejaculate *FIJI, 1984*
Also embellished as 'leak out' or 'leak off'. Recorded by Jan Tent.

4 to weep *US, 1883*
- Put her in a taxi still leaking. —Jeremy Cameron, *Brown Bread in Wengen*, p. 127, 1999

5 to reveal secret or confidential information in an underhanded, secret manner *US, 1859*
- Once the cops heard Wiley's name they'd leak like the Haitian navy. —Carl Hiaasen, *Tourist Season*, p. 189, 1986

leakage *noun*
in a casino or gambling operation, the money lost to cheats and thieves *US, 1963*
- —Thomas L. Clark, *The Dictionary of Gambling and Gaming*, p. 117, 1987

leaker *noun*

1 in gambling, a bettor who loses large amounts of money quickly *US*
- He lived indoors and loved to see leakers like Harry Stanton Price show up. He lived for dumb bettors with systems. —Stephen Cannell, *Big Con*, p. 203, 1997

2 in motor racing, an engine that is not well maintained, whether or not it actually leaks lubricants or other fluids *US*
- —John Edwards, *Auto Dictionary*, p. 95, 1993

leak light *noun*
in television and film making, unwanted light *US*
- —Ralph S. Singleton, *Filmaker's Dictionary*, p. 93, 1990

leaky bladder *noun*
a ladder *UK*
Rhyming slang.
- —Ray Puxley, *Cockney Rabbit*, 1992

leaky faucet *noun*
a urinary tract or reproductive system disorder causing a urinary or vaginal discharge *US*
- I go back to bed, to find I have a "leaky faucet," so I return to the kitchen, open the freezer and take out a package of vaginal suppositories. —Sandra Bernhard, *Confessions of a Pretty Lady*, p. 84, 1988

leaky leak *noun*
phencyclidine, the recreational drug known as PCP or angel dust *US*
- —*Q Magazine*, p. 75, February 2001

lean *noun*
a combination of syrup, codeine and alcohol *US*
At best you 'lean' after drinking any.
- —Ethan Hilderbrant, *Prison Slang*, p. 80, 1998

lean and linger *noun*
a finger *US, 1929*
Rhyming slang.
- —Ray Puxley, *Cockney Rabbit*, 1992

lean and lurch *noun*
a church *UK*
Rhyming slang.
- —Ray Puxley, *Cockney Rabbit*, 1992

leaner *noun*
a shelf or high table in a bar provided for standing drinkers *NEW ZEALAND*
- The drinking was done standing up, at long bars and chest-high upright tables known as 'leaners'. —*(Wellington) Evening Post*, p. 14, 25th February 1995

lean on *verb*

1 to threaten with force as a means of persuasion; to bring pressure to bear *US, 1931*
- —NJ Crisp, *The London Deal*, 1978

2 to physically assault *US, 1911*
- —Hermese E. Roberts, *The Third Ear*, 1971

leaper *noun*

1 any central nervous system stimulant, especially amphetamine *US*
- —Francis J. Rigney and L. Douglas Smith, *The Real Bohemia*, p. xv, 1961
- So no pussy, no money (Gypsy had spent it buying a shotgun in Ely, Nev.) no leapers, etc., etc. —Neal Cassady, *The First Third*, p. 215, 30th August 1965
- [O]ne of these nervous kids whose quack fills them up with leapers once a month. —Tony Parsons, *Limelight Blues*, 1983
- [A]mphetamine sulphate, also known as SPEED, UPPERS, SULPHATE, SULPH, WHIZZ, LEAPERS,and BILLY. —Macfarlane, Macfarlane and Robson, *The User*, p. 95, 1996
- He'd wake up in the morning, take leapers, cocaine, some morphine, a few tabs of acid and maybe some mandrax. —Simon Napier-Bell, *Black Vinyl White Powder*, p. 69, 2001

2 a cocaine user after sustained cocaine use *US*
From the nervousness produced by cocaine use.
- —David Maurer and Victor Vogel, *Narcotics and Narcotic Addiction*, p. 423, 1973

3 a person who threatens to or actually does jump to their death *US*
- Now, one of the surest indications of a genuine attempt at self-destruction by jumping is the collection of valuables intended to be left behind in the room after the leaper has gone out the window. —Dev Collans with Stewart Sterling, *I was a House Detective*, p. 113, 1954

leapers *noun*
wads of cotton soaked in Benzedrine™ (amphetamine sulphate, a central nervous system stimulant) extracted from an inhaler *US*
- The wads of charged cotton were known as leapers because of the energy and optimism they released in the men who choked them down[.] —Malcolm Braly, *On the Yard*, p. 85, 1967

leaping *adjective*
drug-intoxicated *US, 1925*
- —Richard A. Spears, *The Slang and Jargon of Drugs and Drink*, p. 311, 1986
- —Mike Haskins, *Drugs*, p. 291, 2003

leaping heap *noun*
a Harrier aircraft *UK*
In Royal Air Force use, 2002.

Leaping Lena *noun*

1 a light truck *US*
- —Montie Tak, *Truck Talk*, p. 98, 1971

2 a train that ran from Darwin to Birdum *AUSTRALIA, 1940*
Also known as the 'abortion express'.

leaps *noun*
anxiety, nervousness *US, 1922*
- —Hyman E. Goldin et al., *Dictionary of American Underworld Lingo*, p. 123, 1950

learn *verb*
to teach *UK*
In conventional use from about 1300; in C19 it came to be considered colloquial and, now, vulgar.

Leary's *noun*
LSD *UK*
Named after 'LSD-guru' Timothy Leary, 1920–1996.
• —Mike Haskins, *Drugs*, p. 285, 2003

lease louse *noun*
a dealer in oil field leases *US*
• With no capital and no credit, Pop became a dealer in leases, or, to use a contemporary and contemptuous term, a lease louse.—Jim Thompson, *Bad Boy*, p. 372, 1953

leash *noun*
a line attached at one end to a surfer and at the other to the surfboard *US*
• —Gary Fairmont R. Filosa II, *The Surfer's Almanac*, p. 189, 1977

leather *noun*
1 a wallet or purse *US*
• —Vincent J. Monteleone, *Criminal Slang*, p. 143, 1949
• What we did, ever so often we'd pull off the pigeon drop for maybe twenty-five dollars, with me planting the leather, or work the twenties for a five.—Guy Owen, *The Flim-Flam Man and the Apprentice Grifter*, p. 151, 1972
2 in circus and carnival usage, a pickpocket *US, 1936*
• —Don Wilmeth, *The Language of American Popular Entertainment*, p. 157, 1981
3 in homosexual usage, the anus *US, 1941*
• —*Male Swinger Number 3*, p. 48, 1981: 'The complete gay dictionary'
4 in horse racing, the small whip carried by jockeys *US*
• —David W. Maurer, *Argot of the Racetrack*, p. 40, 1951

leather *verb*
to thrash *UK*
Originally, from early C17, 'to beat with a leather strap'; during mid- to late C19 usage became more generalised.
• [T]he girl's boyfriend catches him and leathers him.—Nicholas Blincoe, *The Beautiful Beaten-up Irish Boy of the Arndale Centre*, p. 10, 1998
• [I]t would have to wait until he had found and leathered whoever was responsible for the bomb.—Christopher Brookmyre, *Not the End of the World*, p. 205, 1998

leather *adjective*
used for denoting leather fetishistic and sado-masochistic symbolism in sexual relationships *US*
• The hostility of the minority "leather" crowd toward the rest of the "gay" world is exceeded by the bitterness of individual homosexuals toward the "straight" world."—*Life*, p. 70, 26th June 1964
• "Leather" bars for the tough-guy tops with their fondness for chains and belts.—Joe David Brown, *Sex in the '60s*, p. 70, 1968
• "Leather" articles and guidebooks – usually written, significantly, by older, perhaps not terribly attractive homosexuals[.]—John Rechy, *The Sexual Outlaw*, p. 259, 1977

leather ass *noun*
in poker, the bodily manifestation of great patience *US, 1981*
• —Thomas L. Clark, *The Dictionary of Gambling and Gaming*, p. 117, 1987

leather bar *noun*
a bar with a homosexual clientele whose fashion sense is leather-oriented and whose sexual tastes are sado-masochistic *US*
• And there are, too, the "leather bars": black-jacketed mesh inside, moving pictures of young men wrestling realistically, murals of motorcyclists at a race[.]—John Rechy, *City of Night*, p. 192, 1963
• —*Fact*, p. 26, January-February 1965
• If you want to get hurt (or if you like getting hurt) Hollywood's leather bars offer a rare assortment of prospective masters for any slave. —Roger Gordon, *Hollywood's Sexual Underground*, p. 25, 1966
• It's a typical leather bar, one of those supermasculine hangouts for people in armor and in revolt against everything in the world that might be thought of as feminine.—Angelo d'Arcangelo, *The Homosexual Handbook*, p. 137, 1968
• Afterwards, one of the members of our group wanted to be driven across town to be dropped off for the evening at a gay leather bar[.] —Jefferson Poland and Valerie Alison, *The Records of the San Francisco Sexual Freedom League*, p. 149, 1971
• Eugene Levitt remarks the same of "leather bar" or extreme enclosure in leather[.]—Gerald and Caroline Greene, *S-M: The Last Taboo*, p. 205, 1974

leather cesspool *noun*
a bar or club that caters to low-lifes *US*
• Most pimps chump off their money. They blow it on drugs, clothes, jewelry, cars and in chrome and leather cesspools.—Iceberg Slim (Robert Beck), *The Naked Soul of Iceberg Slim*, p. 68, 1971

leathered *adjective*
drunk *UK*
Derives from **LEATHER** (to thrash).
• —*e-cyclopaedia*, 20th March 2002

leathering *noun*
a physical thrashing; a verbal thrashing *UK, 1791*
• George Bush takes a leathering ("He's so stupid, he tried to send troops into Celine Dion").—*The Guardian*, 21st August 2001
• After the holidays, Kate passed Vicky outside a local cafe. "I'm going to give you a fucking leathering," she hissed.—*The Guardian*, 10th September 2003

leatherneck *noun*
a US Marine *US, 1890*
Possibly from an earlier usage as 'Royal Marine' (a **BOOTNECK**); ultimately from a leather collar, part of the historical uniform of both services.

Leatherneck Square *nickname*
four US Marine bases in South Vietnam that formed a quadrilateral *US*
• Patrols were keyed to debris left over from the hot summers of '67 and '68 – days when Leatherneck Square was filled with battles[.] —Charles Anderson, *The Grunts*, p. 161, 1976
• They coined a phrase, "Leatherneck Square," for the area we worked in – Dong Ha, Quang Tri, Hue, Cam Lo – the DMZ – all up north. —Al Santoli, *To Bear Any Burden*, p. 134, 1985

leather up *verb*
to prepare the cracks of a safe for the placement of nitroglycerin which will blast it open *US*
• —Vincent J. Monteleone, *Criminal Slang*, p. 142, 1949

leave *noun*
in pool, the position of the balls after a shot *US*
• —Steve Rushin, *Pool Cool*, p. 19, 1990

leave *verb*
▸ **leave cold**
to fail to arouse any interest or excitement *UK, 1857*
• [F]riends were lining up jobs in robotics and logistics, areas which left him cold.—*The Guardian*, 17th March 2003

▸ **leave holding the baby**
to abandon a responsibility and, instead, leave someone else to deal with any difficulties *UK, 1928*
• Steve Hansen [...] was left holding the baby yesterday after [Graham] Henry's decision to resign as Wales coach 20 months before his contract was due to end.—*The Guardian*, 8th February 2002

▸ **leave it**
to stop talking about, to change the subject *UK*
Often as an imperative.
• "You must have some idea." "Look, just fucking leave it. I'm saying zilch."—Colin Butts, *Is Harry on the Boat?*, p. 127, 1997

▸ **leave seeds**
to impregnate *US*
• —Ethan Hilderbrant, *Prison Slang*, p. 81, 1998

leave it! *verb*
used imperatively, to resist a temptation to get into a fight *UK*
A widely used call for peace that appears to be generally ignored and serves, therefore, as little more than a rhetorical spur in the arsenal of aggression.
• But then there was clearly a brief fracas, prompting surrounding journalists to chant "Fight! Fight! Fight!" as John's wife, Pauline, just off-camera, screamed "Leave it, John – he's not worth it!"—*The Guardian*, 19th May 2001

leave it out!
stop that!, shut up! *UK, 1982*
• I give the label a tug and he wobbles [...] Leave it out, he blinks, trying to set things in their rightful place.—John King, *Human Punk*, p. 232, 2000

leave off *verb*
to cease doing something; often as an imperative *UK, 1400*
- I read in the paper that it's Queen Anne's reign [...] I'm a military man sir; it's my duty as a senior scoundrel to ask her majesty, Queen Anne, to leave off raining. — *The Goons*, 22nd December 1958
- US pressure on India and Pakistan to leave off missile development[.] — *The Guardian*, 16th August 1999

leaver *noun*
in drag racing, a driver who starts before the start signal, thereby forfeiting the race *US*
- — John Edwards, *Auto Dictionary*, p. 96, 1993

leaverite *noun*
a worthless mineral *CANADA*
- Leave 'er right there. — Tom Parkin, *oral citation from WetCoast Words*, p. 86, 1989

leaves *noun*
cigarette papers *UK*
- — Angela Devlin, *Prison Patter*, p. 70, 1996

Leb; Lebanese *noun*
1 hashish from cannabis plants cultivated in the Lebanon *UK*
- There's a sixteenth of personal which is a piece of leb I been savin'[.] — Nick Barlay, *Curvy Lovebox*, p. 89, 1997
- Lebanese is almost exclusively grown these days for hashish export — Mike Rock, *This Book*, 1999

2 a Lebanese person, or any person from an Arabic background *AUSTRALIA*
'Leb', 'Lebo' and 'Lebbo' are commonly used derogatorily by Anglo-Australians, but amongst the Arabic-based ethic community used positively, much the same as **WOG**.
- Like, I'm walking down the street the other day, broad daylight and this ugly Leb in a Monaro starts kerb crawling. — Helen Barnes, *The Crypt Orchid*, p. 15, 1994

lebanese *noun*
a lesbian *UK*
A deliberate malapropism, recorded in contemporary gay use.
- — *Attitude*, p. 60, July 2003: 'New palare lexicon'

Lebanese gold; gold Lebanese; gold leb *noun*
golden-hued cannabis resin from the Middle East *UK*
- [A] small, rounded piece of Lebanese gold with outer sacking still attached. — Tony Wilson, *24 Hour Party People*, p. 20, 2002
- — Nick Jones, *Spliffs*, p. 83, 2003

Lebo; Lebbo *noun*
a Lebanese person, or any person from an Arabic background *AUSTRALIA*
- — June Factor, *Kidspeak*, p. 126, 2000

Lebo; Lebbo *adjective*
Lebanese, from an Arabic background *AUSTRALIA*
- Fucking Lebo men, my sister spits out. — Christos Tsiolkas, *Loaded*, p. 35, 1995

leccy; lecki *noun*
electricity *UK*
- DENISE: Blow it [a candle] out, Dad. DAD: Will I buggery, there's another five minutes on that... save the lecki. — Caroline Aherne and Craig Cash, *The Royle Family*, 1999
- [N]o fifties for the leccy meter. — Paul Pritchard, *Rubble Merchants, Slateheads, and Others [Climber's Choice]*, p. 110, 2002

leccy; lecky *adjective*
electric, as in 'lecky kettle', 'leccy blanket', etc *UK, 1984*
- [L]ooked like the whole fucking estate had welshed on the lecky bill. — Ian Rankin, *Black and Blue*, p. 14, 1997
- [H]as he paid the leccy bill? — Jeremy Smith, *The American-British British-American Dictionary*, p. 165, 2004

lech *noun*
▷ see: **LETCH**

lecker *adjective*
▷ see: **LEKKER**

ledge *noun*
an impressive person *AUSTRALIA, 1988*
Shortening of **LEGEND**.
- — James Lambert, *The Macquarie Slang Dictionary*, 1996

lee-gate *verb*
to peep *US*
- I didn't mind a guy lee-gating (peeping). — Edwin Torres, *Carlito's Way*, p. 12, 1975

leem *noun*
a completely inept person *CANADA*
- Another pointed out that there was a particular kind of 'geek,' known specifically as a 'leem' in her school, who was to be viewed as particularly odious. — Marcel Danesi, *Cool*, p. 58, 1994

Lee Marvin *adjective*
very hungry *UK, 1998*
Rhyming slang for 'starving'; based on the name of film actor Lee Marvin, 1924–87.

leery *adjective*
1 bad-tempered, disagreeable; insolent *UK*
- — David Powis, *The Signs of Crime*, 1977

2 distrustful, cautious *UK, 1718*
Originally underworld usage. Also spelt 'leary'.

leet *noun*
an Internet user who is categorised, often self-categorised, as 'elite' *US*
A reduction of 'elite'; used (especially on bulletin-boards) as an antonym for **LAMER**.
- The "leet" (the elite, or most accomplished hackers) boast about the hundreds of "boxes" (computers) they have successfully broken into. — *San Francisco Chronicle*, p. A19, 27th April 1998
- — Susie Dent, *Larpers and Shroomers*, p. 59, 2004

leet talk; leet; l33t; leet speak; l33t 5p34k *noun*
a written slang used for Internet and text communications in which numerals and non-alphabet characters replace letters *US*
After **LEET** (an 'elite' Internet user).
- Leet Talk/Leet Speak. L33t, d00d. Online vocabulary using shortened versions of words, phonetic and numbers in place of letters [...] In it's [sic] most extreme form "leet speak" would look like this: "133+ 543/-\1 < ". — Chris McCubbin, *Anarchy Online*, p. back matter, 2001
- Leet speak is a very flexible language, meaning that there are several ways to spell the same word. — *Anchorage (Alaska) Daily News*, p. F6, 19th March 2004

Lee Van Cleef; lee van *noun*
beef (meat) *UK*
Rhyming slang, formed from the name of a US film actor, 1925–89.
- — Ray Puxley, *Fresh Rabbit*, 1998

left and right *noun*
a fight *UK*
Rhyming slang.
- — Julian Franklyn, *A Dictionary of Rhyming Slang*, 1961

left field *noun*
▸ **out of left field**
unexpected, unforeseen, from nowhere *US, 1946*
- So, I had this thought and – it may seem like it's way out of left field. — *American Pie*, 1999

left field *adjective*
different, out of the ordinary *US, 1967*
Figurative use of baseball jargon.
- ['Just Don't Give a Fuck'] was so left field of what I was normally doin'. — Eminem (Marshall Mathers), *Angry Blonde*, 2001

left-footer *noun*
1 a Roman Catholic *UK, 1961*
Used by Northern Ireland Protestants. Probably derives from a turf-cutting spade that is pushed into the ground with the left foot, but there is also a suggestion that a left-footer is simply 'out of step' with the 'right-minded' user. Noted in Liverpool use by Jim Ramsay, *Cop It Sweet!*, 1977.
- — Fritz Spiegl, *Lern Yerself Scouse*, 1966
- — Harry Orsman and Des Hurley, *The Beaut Little Book of New Zealand Slang*, 1994

2 a homosexual *NEW ZEALAND*
- — David McGill, *David McGill's Complete Kiwi Slang Dictionary*, p. 79, 1998
- Leonardo Da Vinci. Italian artist, inventor and left footer. Liked them young. Charged with sodomy in 1474. — *The FHM Little Book of Bloke*, p. 144, June 2003: 'Gayness Explained'

left-handed *adjective*
homosexual *US, 1929*
- —Helen Dahlskog (Editor), *A Dictionary of Contemporary and Colloquial Usage*, p. 37, 1972

left-handed bricklayer *noun*
a Freemason *UK*
An army coinage; reported by J.A.G. Bigham, 1975.

left-handed cigarette *noun*
a marijuana cigarette *US*
- When we got in their car, Marvin pulled out one of those 'left-handed cigarettes' and lit it.—Odie Hawkins, *The Life and Times of Chester Simmons*, p. 156, 1991

left-hander *noun*
a criminal *UK*
Superstition holds the dextrous (right-handed) to be righteous and the sinister (left-handed) to be evil.
- "You 'been away' [in prison] or something?" "No, not at all." I was momentarily backfooted by her use of the left-handers' euphemism.—Diran Abedayo, *My Once Upon A Time*, p. 118, 2000

left-sided *adjective*
homosexual *UK*
A variation of 'left-handed' current in UK prisons, August 2002, explained by one inmate as 'they are not on the right side of sexuality'.

lefty; leftie *noun*
a political left-winger *US, 1935*
- But this slum is permitted to remain behind the Capitol only so the lefties will have something to breast-beat over.—Jack Lait and Lee Mortimer, *Washington Confidential*, p. 38–39, 1951

lefty; leftie *adjective*
politically left-wing, liberal *US*
- Our generation of leftie twats.—James Hawes, *Dead Long Enough*, p. 91, 2000
- [I]t was presented as evidence of some kind of lefty integrity[.] —Christopher Brookmyre, *The Sacred Art of Stealing*, p. 51–52, 2002

leg *noun*
1 sex; women as sex objects *US*
The functional equivalent of 'ass'.
- They were loaded and they wanted to get off some leg, but it just got to be too many guys.—Hunter S. Thompson, *Hell's Angels*, p. 16, 1966
- I mean, I really go for the broad. It's not the leg so much, getting laid and all, but she acts kind of funny[.]—Steve Cannon, *Groove, Bang, and Jive Around*, p. 29, 1969
- Them cats wearing themselves out on some broad that couldn't do nuthin' but give up a little leg is crazy.—Joseph Nazel, *Black Cop*, p. 96, 1974
- I mean, shit, let's face it, the naughtiest thing I've done in twenty four years is to give a dude some leg without using a condom.—Odie Hawkins, *Great Lawd Buddha*, p. 88, 1990
- A place like college – all that leg around campus – you should be sowing your wild oats.—*Mallrats*, 1995

2 a straight-leg or infantry soldier *US, 1964*
- —Eric Helm, *Vietnam Ground Zero*, p. 215, 1986
- Wickie Randolph Weinstein turned out to be twenty-three and a former Airborne Ranger who contemptuously referred to ground soldiers as "legs."—Jack Olsen, *Cold Kill*, p. 102, 1987
- Even within the services there are rivalries, such as the distinction between the airborne Army soldiers who jump out of airplanes and the "legs" – soldiers who don't.—*Houston Chronicle*, p. 15, 24th January 1991
- It was OK that I couldn't tell him much about anything he understood, having been just a "leg," hahaha. That's what his buddy, this second lieuty, calls infantrymen.—Clarence Major, *All-Night Visitors*, p. 175, 1998

▷ see: LEG OF MUTTON

▸ **around the leg**
currying favour with prison administration *US*
- —James Harris, *A Convict's Dictionary*, p. 36, 1989

▸ **find another leg; grow another leg**
(used of a racehorse) to perform well in muddy track conditions *AUSTRALIA*
- —Ned Wallish, *The Truth Dictionary of Racing Slang*, p. 2, 1989

▸ **get the leg over; get your leg over; get a leg over**
to have sex, generally from a male perspective *UK, 1975*
- Maybe just once he'd like to get the leg over one of these kind of women[.]—Roddy Doyle, *The Van*, 1991
- He nodded toward Barry. "You and your policeman getting a leg over, are you?" "That's none of your business."—Christopher Hyde, *The Second Assassin*, p. 223, 2002

▸ **give you leg**
to tease *US*
- "Hey," Dillon said, "remember last time I saw you, you're giving me a little leg about there's nothing going on?"—George V. Higgins, *The Friends of Eddie Doyle*, p. 79, 1971

▸ **not have a leg to stand on**
in an argument or dispute, to be in a defenceless position *UK, 1594*
- [John Kerry] doesn't have a leg to stand on, the American public will realise pretty quick that he's a phoney.—*The Observer*, 7th March 2004

leg *verb*
to shoplift by hiding merchandise between your legs under a skirt *US*
- Stuff I legged [boosted by hiding it between her legs under her skirt].—Bruce Jackson, *In the Life*, p. 93, 1972

▸ **leg a hand**
in poker, to reserve the right to make a bet even though the player has a good hand *US*
- —John Scarne, *Scarne's Guide to Modern Poker*, p. 283, 1979

▸ **leg it**
to walk, to walk fast, to run; to hurry; to run away *UK, 1601*
- [H]e could still get the 10.01 if he legged it.—P-P Hartnett, *Sad Cunt*, p. 98, 1999
- That skinny geezer got a proper slap before he legged it out the door.—John King, *White Trash*, p. 149, 2001
- I look at the clock. -Yer'd better leg it. It's nearly quarter to.—Niall Griffiths, *Kelly + Victor*, p. 195, 2002

legal *noun*
a lawyer *UK*
- I'd let the legals look at that.—Angela Devlin, *Prison Patter*, p. 71, 1996

legal aid *noun*
lemonade *UK: SCOTLAND*
Glasgow rhyming slang.
- —Michael Munro, *The Patter, Another Blast*, 1988

legal beagle *noun*
a lawyer, especially one who is sharply intelligent or keen *US, 1949*
- —Jerry Robertson, *Oil Slanguage*, p. 78, 1954
- Even Flo Kennedy, our chief lawyer, copped out – though some of the younger legal-beagels (women, bless'em) were ready to carry the fight to the floor of the Pageant[.]—*Screw*, p. 14, 13th October 1969
- —*Legal Eagles*, 1986

legal eagle *noun*
a lawyer *US, 1939*
- [T]wo sessions in Borstal and a bang to rights which backfired because he had a shrewd legal eagle.—*The Sweeney*, p. 29, 1976
- —Legal Eagles, 1986

legalese *noun*
in computing, inpenetrable language *US*
- Though hackers are not afraid of high information density and complexity in language (indeed, they rather enjoy both), they share a deep and abiding loathing for legalese[.]—Eric S. Raymond, *The New Hacker's Dictionary*, p. 221, 1991

legal high *noun*
any substance that is not restricted by drug control legislation that mimics (or is claimed to mimic) the effect of an illegal drug *UK*
- Some legal highs are quite hallucinogenic[.]—Harry Shapiro, *Recreational Drugs*, p. 330, 2004

legalize it *verb*
in trucking, to slow down to the speed limit *US*
- —*Complete CB Slang Dictionary*, p. 8, 1976

legal needle *noun*
the legal speed limit *US*
- —Wayne Floyd, *Jason's Authentic Dictionary of CB Slang*, p. 20, 1976

leg bail *noun*
escape from jail or prison *UK, 1759*
- —Vincent J. Monteleone, *Criminal Slang*, p. 144, 1949

leg before wicket; LBW *noun*

a ticket, especially in the sense of something pleasing or satisfying *UK*

Rhyming slang, from the cricketing term (and its abbreviation).

- —Julian Franklyn, *A Dictionary of Rhyming Slang*, 1962

leg bus *noun*

the adult leg when walking and carrying/dragging a child along *UK*

- "Leg bus" they were shouting as they clamped themselves round a pin and hung on for the laboured journey into the kitchen. —Danny King, *The Bank Robber Diaries*, p. 38, 2002

legend *noun*

1 an impressive person *AUSTRALIA, 1989*

- —Harrison Biscuit, *The Search for Savage Henry*, p. 25, 1995
- 'Legend' was the word I came up with while talking to myself. —Paul Vautin, *Turn It Up!*, p. 203, 1995

2 a surfer with an old-fashioned, long surfboard *AUSTRALIA*

- —Trevor Cralle, *The Surfin'ary*, p. 68, 1991

legend *adjective*

excellent, admirable *IRELAND*

- He's pure legend at home like, there wouldn't be a young one for miles around that he hasn't had a crack at. —Donal Ruane, *Tales in a rear view mirror*, p. 193, 2003

leger *noun*

a stand at a racecourse some distance from the finishing post *AUSTRALIA, 1907*

After St Leger, a famous English horse race.

- Magger is four lengths in front at the leger. —Frank Hardy, *The Yarns of Billy Borker*, p. 108, 1965
- —James Holledge, *The Great Australian Gamble*, p. 48, 1966
- —Joe Andersen, *Winners Can Laugh*, p. 198, 1982

legger *noun*

▸ **do a legger**

to run away, to escape on foot *IRELAND, 1991*

- —Angela Devlin, *Prison Patter*, p. 71, 1996

leggins *noun*

the rubbing of the penis between the thighs of another man until reaching orgasm *US, 1934*

- [I]n leggins men reach ejaculation from the insertion of the penis between one another's legs in a face-to-face, usually horizontal, position. —*New York Mattachine Newsletter*, p. 6, June 1961

leggner *noun*

a year's prison sentence *UK, 1950*

- —Angela Devlin, *Prison Patter*, p. 71, 1996

leggo!

let go! *US, 1884*

An urgent slovening.

- Leggo... you're choking me! —*The Sweeney*, p. 19, 1976

leggo beas' *adverb*

wild, disorderly *JAMAICA, 1991*

From 'let go beast' (an uncontrolled animal).

leggo beast *noun*

a promiscuous young woman *GRENADA, 1976*

leggy *noun*

a cord attached to a surfer and their surfboard *US*

- —Mitch McKissick, *Surf Lingo*, 1987

leg irons *noun*

climbing irons used in electric and telephone line work *US*

- —A.B. Chance Co., *Lineman's Slang Dictionary*, p. 11, 1980

legit *noun*

▸ **on the legit**

legitimate; legitimately *US, 1930*

- Once Side got a shipment of a hundred cases of booze on the legit, and that's when he showed up as nervous as some jello-pudding. —Milton Mezzrow, *Really the Blues*, p. 21, 1946
- "Nope, I made a killing, and it was strictly on the legit," Phil said emphasizing his words with a slicker gesture. —James T. Farrell, *Saturday Night*, p. 32, 1947

legit *adjective*

1 legitimate *UK, 1909*

- "Nope, I made a killing, and it was strictly on the legit," Phil said emphasizing his words with a slicker gesture. —James T. Farrell, *Saturday Night*, p. 32, 1947
- It was the most magnificent legit house ever built[.] —Jack Lait and Lee Mortimer, *New York Confidential*, p. 35, 1948
- Just before the war he went legit. —Mickey Spillane, *Kiss Me Deadly*, p. 60, 1952
- If she's legit, Lucky Luciano was in the paper-bag business. —Bernard Wolfe, *The Late Risers*, p. 274, 1954
- I don't mean the celebs and the legit high rollers, he's got to take care of them and he loves it. —Elmore Leonard, *Glitz*, p. 119, 1985
- You gotta go legit, at least for minute. —Terry Williams, *The Cocaine Kids*, p. 86, 1989
- It's all legit. Totally legit. We're hitched. —Nick Barlay, *Curvy Lovebox*, p. 127, 1997
- Looking around this carriage and there's hardly no one who's totally legit. There's kites, dippers, dealers, spivs, all kinds. —Kevin Sampson, *Outlaws*, p. 161, 2001

2 used to describe serious theatre (drama, as opposed to variety, revue, etc), the acting or an actor employed therein *UK, 1908*

- Success in variety–unlike its rival, 'legit' theatre – did not depend on education or background. —*The Scotsman*, 22nd March 2002

legit *adverb*

honestly, *legit*imately *UK, 1908*

- I get my maggot [money] legit these days. —JF Straker, *Sin and Johnny Inch*, 1968

legits *noun*

dice that have not been altered *US*

- —Robert C. Prus and C.R.D. Sharper, *Road Hustler*, p. 170, 1977: 'Glossary of terms'

legless *adjective*

1 drunk *UK*

- —Andy Fairweather-Low, *Wide Eyed and Legless*, 1976
- "[P]iss artists" are "boozy", "fluffy", "well-gone", "legless", "crocked"[.] —Peter Ackroyd, *London The Biography*, p. 359, 2000
- He was legless and it was cold enough to freeze your piles off[.] —Duncan MacLaughlin, *The Filth*, p. 92, 2002

2 in horse racing, lacking ability *AUSTRALIA*

- —Ned Wallish, *The Truth Dictionary of Racing Slang*, p. 46, 1989

legman *noun*

an assistant who does the leg work *US, 1923*

- Reisemann, big-time legman to the kraut [German] mob. —Derek Raymond (Robin Cook), *The Crust on its Uppers*, p. 95, 1962

lego *noun*

an infantry soldier, not attached to an airborne division *US*

- —Ronald J. Glasser, *365 Days*, p. 243, 1971
- —Linda Reinberg, *In the Field*, p. 126, 1991

leg of beef *noun*

a thief *UK*

Rhyming slang.

- —Ray Puxley, *Cockney Rabbit*, p. 109, 1992

leg of lamb *noun*

an impressive person *AUSTRALIA*

Jocular alteration of **LEGEND**.

- You're a legend. Fucken *leg of lamb*. —Linda Jaivin, *Rock n Roll Babes from Outer Space*, p. 112, 1996

leg of mutton; leg *noun*

a button *UK*

Rhyming slang.

- Mum, my leg's come off, can you sew it back on for me? —Ray Puxley, *Cockney Rabbit*, 1992

leg of pork *noun*

chalk *UK*

Rhyming slang.

- —Ray Puxley, *Fresh Rabbit*, 1998

leg opener *noun*

something, usually an alcoholic drink, which assists in persuading a woman into having sexual intercourse *AUSTRALIA*

- So de old man he giff her some leg opener, eh? —Robert S. Close, *Love Me Sailor*, p. 21, 1945
- I've pointed old percy [urinated], down a couple [of beers]... and bunged a few leg openers into that sheilah [woman] out there!!! —Barry Humphries, *Bazza Pulls It Off!*, 1971

- A pound of sugar was a good leg opener in Catterick in those days. —Johnny Speight, *It Stands to Reason*, p. 66, 1973
- [T]he bloke that's in here with a doll will buy a rose posie as a leg-opener for after. —Sam Weller, *Old Bastards I Have Met*, p. 20, 1979

legover; leg over *noun*
(from a male perspective) conventional sexual intercourse *UK*
Often in phrases 'a bit of leg over', 'get your leg over', etc.
- —Peter Tinniswood, *A Touch of Daniel*, 1969
- I'm strictly a legover man, myself. —Mike Stott, *Soldiers Talking, Cleanly*, 1978

leg piece *noun*
a dance performance in which the female dancers are scantily dressed or naked *US*
- —Sherman Louis Sergel, *The Language of Show Biz*, p. 15, 1973
- —Don Wilmeth, *The Language of American Popular Entertainment*, p. 158, 1981

leg-pull *noun*
an act of teasing or mockery *US, 1895*
From **PULL YOUR LEG**.
- You could see it was no leg pull. —Charles Raven, *Underworld Nights*, p. 10, 1956

leg-rope *verb*
to marry or tie down in a relationship *NEW ZEALAND*
- 'You don't see much of women, Sim, do you?' 'You want to start picking them over for years before you leg-rope one of them. They're like any other possession.' —Guthrie Wilson, *Sweet White White*, p. 63, 1956

legs *noun*
1 in the entertainment industry, staying power and continuing popularity *US, 1978*
- Yeah, I know we lost the bullet, spins are down slightly, but that record still has legs, man. —Elmore Leonard, *Be Cool*, p. 106, 1999

2 stamina in sport; staying power *AUSTRALIA*
- Football is all about 'legs', whether you've 'got em' or you 'haven't got em'. —Ivor Limb, *Footy's No Joke!*, p. 49, 1986

3 the duration of the intoxication from a central nervous system stimulant *US*
- Either the speed "has good legs" or it "doesn't have legs." —Geoffrey Froner, *Digging for Diamonds*, p. 41, 1989

4 (of a shot in pool) momentum, force *US, 1835*
- —Mike Shamos, *The Illustrated Encyclopedia of Billiards*, p. 135, 1993

5 an ability to continue or last *AUSTRALIA*
- You think these abos have got legs for another story? —Harrison Biscuit, *The Search for Savage Henry*, p. 67, 1995

6 a bicycle messenger *CANADA*
- —Jack Chambers (Editor), *Slang Bag 93 (University of Toronto)*, p. 4, Winter 1993

▸ **do your legs**
in police slang, to severely damage your career prospects *UK*
- — *The Official Encyclopaedia of New Scotland Yard*, 1999

▸ **have legs all the way up to your armpits/bum**
to have long, beautiful legs *AUSTRALIA, 1944*
- 'Cor, what a pair of legs!' Dingo pointed to Debbie. 'Yeah, really beaut,' confirmed Sloppy. 'All the way up to the armpits.' —John Wynnum, *Tar Dust*, p. 80, 1962
- Have a look at the last one. The blonde. She'd have a decent pair of legs. All the way up to her bum. —C. Green, *Picnic at Hanging Rock: A film*, p. 23, 1975

leg show *noun*
a stage performance featuring bare-legged female dancers *UK, 1882*
- Not leg shows, either; Dad's favorite playwright, after Shakespeare, was Bernard Shaw. —Mary McCarthy, *The Group*, p. 58, 1963

Leicester square; leicester *noun*
a chair *UK*
Rhyming slang.
- Pull up a Leicester and take the weight off your feet. —Ray Puxley, *Fresh Rabbit*, 1998

lekker; lecker *adjective*
pleasant, excellent, delicious, etc *SOUTH AFRICA, 1847*
From Afrikaans.
- Sex is only lekker if it is flesh to flesh. —Bart Luirink (translated by Loes Nas), *Moffies*, p. 10, 2000
- [T]he right time for filming, now that the light was lekker (nice). —Rupert Isaacson, *The Healing Land*, p. 67, 2003

lel; lell *verb*
to take *UK, 1889*
Polari; the original Romany sense implied seizure or arrest.
- —Paul Baker, *Polari*, p. 179, 2002

lem *noun*
a person who is on his or her own *UK*
A shortening of 'lemon'. Teen slang.
- — Susie Dent, *The Language Report*, p. 77, 2003

lemac *noun*
a Camel™ cigarette *US*
- Reverse spelling. —James Harris, *A Convict's Dictionary*, p. 33, 1989

lemon *noun*
1 a simple-minded fool *US, 1906*
- Don't I look a lemon in these clothes[?] —Ian Dury, *Pardon*, 1980
- — *Maledicta*, p. 265, Summer/Winter 1981: 'By its slang, ye shall know it: the pessimism of prison life'
- I wouldn't invite Terry Duckers, y'lemon. —Caroline Aherne and Craig Cash, *The Royle Family*, 1999

2 anything or anyone that is undesirable *US, 1906*
Probably from the least valuable symbol on a fruit-machine.
- [S]he was wearing a silky white blouse underneath and showing a lot of neck. Giner gulped. And the other one wasn't a lemon either. —John Burke and Stuart Douglass, *The Boys*, p. 118, 1962

3 in marketing, a woman who lives alone and is unlikely to be interested in financial sector products *UK*
Fruit-machine imagery, informed by the previous sense; the complete opposite is a **PLUM**.
- —David Rowan, *Glossary for the 90s*, p. 106, 1998

4 a lesbian *AUSTRALIA*
Perhaps playing on **FRUIT**.
- 'Eergh, a lemon,' shouts one six foot tall metal tipped booted mod at a diminutive feminist. — *Sydney Morning Herald*, p. 25, 1st January 1983

5 a heavily diluted narcotic *US*
- He handed me a lemon and I went looking for him. There wasn't nothing in the stuff but sugar[.] —Hal Ellson, *The Golden Spike*, p. 150–151, 1952
- You the fourth cat who been in here lookin' for that stud. He sellin' lemons again? —Nathan Heard, *Howard Street*, p. 117, 1968

6 a woman's pubic hair, hence the vagina *UK, 1976*

7 in pool, a person who loses intentionally *US*
- —Steve Rushin, *Pool Cool*, p. 19, 1990

8 a light-skinned black person *US*
- —Clarence Major, *Dictionary of Afro-American Slang*, p. 76, 1970

▸ **up the lemon; up the lemon puff**
pregnant *UK*
Rhyming slang for **UP THE DUFF** (pregnant); a lemon puff is a popular biscuit.
- [W]asn't Mary already married, when God came along and got her up the lemon? —Danny King, *The Burglar Diaries*, p. 13, 2001

lemon *adjective*
ostentatious *UK*
- In this end of town it's all young babes with tit-jobs, messers, chancers and hustlers, double-lemon rag-trade guys, lemon meaning flash[.] —J.J. Connolly, *Layer Cake*, p. 72, 2000

lemon 714 *noun*
a tablet of the recreational drug methaqualone, best known as Quaaludes™ *US*
Quaaludes™ were originally manufactured by Rorer, and were stamped 'Rorer 714'. Lemon eventually bought the patent from Rorer, continuing the '714' stamp. Virtually all pills stamped with '714' today are counterfeit.
- —Peter Johnson, *Dictionary of Street Alcohol and Drug Terms*, p. 109, 1993
- A later brand: Lemon 714. It was like achieving the perfect drunken state without the sick feeling or hangover with the mere pop of a $10 pill. — Editors of Ben is Dead, *Retrohell*, p. 169, 1997

lemonade *noun*
1 a spade, either as a suit of cards or in the offensive slang sense of a black person *UK*
- —Ray Puxley, *Cockney Rabbit*, 1992

2 poor quality heroin *US, 1957*
Often shortened to 'lemon'.

- —Francis J. Rigney and L. Douglas Smith, *The Real Bohemia*, p. xx, 1961
- —Sidney Cohen, *The Drug Dilemma*, p. 129, 1969
- —Richard Lingeman, *Drugs from A to Z*, p. 125, 1969
- —Robert Ashton, *This Is Heroin*, p. 209, 2002

lemonade *verb*

in poolroom betting, to miss a shot or lose a game intentionally *US*

- By "stalling" (deliberately missing some shots, leaving hiself out of position, etc.) and by "lemoning" or "lemonading" an occasional game in the session (winning in a deliberately sloppy and seemingly lucky manner, or deliberately losing the game), the hustler keeps his opponent on the hook. —Ned Polsky, *Hustlers, Beats, and Others*, p. 56–57, 1967

lemonade stand *noun*

the small house-like cabin on a lobster boat *US*

- —Kendall Merriam, *The Illustrated Dictionary of Lobstering*, p. 52, 1978

lemon and dash *noun*

a *wash*-place *UK*

Rhyming slang.

- —Julian Franklyn, *A Dictionary of Rhyming Slang*, 1961

lemon and lime *noun*

time *UK*

Rhyming slang.

- —Ray Puxley, *Cockney Rabbit*, 1992

lemon and limes *noun*

a variety of MDMA, the recreational drug best known as ecstasy *UK*

- —Angela Devlin, *Prison Patter*, p. 71, 1996

lemon barley *noun*

cocaine *UK*

- —Angela Devlin, *Prison Patter*, p. 71, 1996

lemon curd *noun*

1 a young woman *UK*

Rhyming slang for **BIRD**. Sometimes abbreviated to 'lemon'.

- —Michael Munro, *The Patter, Another Blast*, 1988
- [S]ome Essex lemon's voice giving it with "Ilford Breakdown Service, Jump-Leads We Got 'Em, Sandra speaking, how can I help you?" —Andrew Nickolds, *Back to Basics*, p. 39, 1994
- You've got lemon curds in cassocks[.] —Andrew Nickolds, *Back to Basics*, p. 163, 1994

2 a piece of excrement *UK*

Rhyming slang for **TURD**.

- —Ray Puxley, *Fresh Rabbit*, 1998

lemon drop *noun*

1 a police officer *UK*

Rhyming slang for **COP**. Sometimes abbreviated to 'lemon'.

- Watch it. Lemons! —Ray Puxley, *Fresh Rabbit*, 1998

2 a birth control pill *US*

Alluding to a popular hard sweet.

- — *Current Slang*, p. 9, Winter 1970

lemon flavour; lemon *noun*

a favour *UK*

Rhyming slang.

- You're gonna take up exercising? Do me a lemon, you're too out of condition to get fit. —Ray Puxley, *Fresh Rabbit*, 1998

lemon player *noun*

a person who plays lemon pool *US*

- No, I doubt it, although sometimes two lemon players will pretend to be bitter rivals and play each other while a third and maybe a fourth member of the team will lay bets among the onlookers. —Iceberg Slim (Robert Beck), *Mama Black Widow*, p. 157–158, 1969

lemon pool *noun*

a pool swindle in which a skilled player lets an opponent win until high stakes are bet and then wins, making it look like he was extremely lucky *US*

- "Soldier, what is lemon pool?" He said, "Little Brother, it's cue stick con played by a shark who never lets the sucker know his true ability." —Iceberg Slim (Robert Beck), *Mama Black Widow*, p. 157, 1969

lemon pop *noun*

a piece of plastic or thin metal used to slip between the molding and the top of the window on push-button locking cars, from which a loop of dental floss is dropped over the post on the door and yanked to open the door *US*

- He told them he'd spot the car a customer wanted and use a slim jim or lemon pop to get in, a slap hammer to yank the ignition, a side kick to extract steering column locks and usually liquid nitrogen to freeze the alarm system. —Elmore Leonard, *Out of Sight*, p. 56, 1996

lemon squash *noun*

a wash *UK*

Rhyming slang.

- —Ray Puxley, *Cockney Rabbit*, 1992

lemon-squeezer; lemon *noun*

a fellow, a man *UK*

Rhyming slang for **GEEZER**.

- —Ronnie Barker, *Fletcher's Book of Rhyming Slang*, 1979

lemon squeezy *adjective*

easy *UK*

Rhyming slang, taken from an elaboration of **EASY-PEASY**.

- You're making it lemon squeezy for them[.] —Ray Puxley, *Fresh Rabbit*, 1998

lemon tart *noun*

a fart *UK*

Rhyming slang.

- —Bodmin Dark, *Dirty Cockney Rhyming Slang*, 2003

lemon tea *noun*

urination; an act of urination *UK*

Rhyming slang for **WEE** or **PEE**, perhaps inspired by the appearance of the drink.

- —Ray Puxley, *Fresh Rabbit*, 1998

lend *noun*

a loan *UK, 1575*

A colloquial or dialect term, also recorded in Australia and New Zealand.

- TRUE GRIT DISTRIBUTOR: Give us a lend of your hand there for a second and I'll fix that crinkly old workers hand for you mate. —Kathy McLeish, *ABC TV*, 28th November 2003

length *noun*

the penis, especially when erect *NEW ZEALAND*

- —Sonya Plowman, *Great Kiwi Slang*, p. 113, 2002

▸ **you would not walk the length of yourself**

used of a very lazy person *UK: SCOTLAND*

- He wouldny walk the length of himself since he got that motor an now look at the beef he's carryin. —Michael Munro, *The Patter, Another Blast*, 1988

Len Hutton *noun*

a button *UK*

Rhyming slang, formed from the name of a famous cricketer, 1916–90; probably no longer in use.

- —Ray Puxley, *Cockney Rabbit*, 1992

Len Lott *adjective*

hot *AUSTRALIA*

Rhyming slang alluding to an Australian jockey.

- —Ned Wallish, *The Truth Dictionary of Racing Slang*, p. 46, 1989

Lenny the Lion *noun*

a male homosexual *UK*

Rhyming slang for **IRON** (**IRON HOOF**), which is itself rhyming slang for **POOF** (a male homosexual); formed from the name of a ventriloquist's dummy, a slightly effeminate lion, created by Terry Hall, popular on UK television during the 1950s and 60s.

- —Ray Puxley, *Cockney Rabbit*, 1992

leño *noun*

marijuana; a marijuana cigarette *US, 1955*

Spanish for a **LOG**.

- —Richard A. Spears, *The Slang and Jargon of Drugs and Drink*, p. 312, 1986
- —Mike Haskins, *Drugs*, p. 288, 2003

leños *noun*

phencyclidine, the recreational drug known as PCP or angel dust *US, 1984*

Probably related to **LEÑO** (marijuana).

- —Richard A. Spears, *The Slang and Jargon of Drugs and Drink*, p. 312, 1986

lens *noun*

a dose of LSD; LSD *US*

- —US Department of Justice, *Street Terms*, October 1994

Leo Fender; Leo *adjective*

homosexual *UK*

Rhyming slang for **BENDER** (a homosexual). Leo Fender (1909–91) was an inventer and designer of electric guitars.

- He's a bit Leo. — *Antiquarian Book Review*, p. 18, June 2002
- — Bodmin Dark, *Dirty Cockney Rhyming Slang*, 2003

Leo Sayer *noun*

an event that lasts all day, especially a drinking spree or a rave *UK*

Rhyming slang for 'all-dayer', based on singer/songwriter Leo Sayer (b.1948). Remembered as 'early 90s' by Jonathan Telfer, *Writers News*, 2003.

- — *www.LondonSlang.com*, June 2002

Leo's loot *noun*

the major portion of criminal profits *UK*

A play on 'lion's share'.

- As for the lion's share, Leo's loot, it went phut on dogs and dice. — Charles Raven, *Underworld Nights*, p. 66, 1956

lepping *noun*

in a highly emotional state *IRELAND*

- Mr. Dillon: He did not think he was talking to an omadhaun. Mr. T. Walsh: To whom did he think he was talking, a "lepping" lunatic? — *House of the Oireachtas Parliamentary Debates*, 8th March 1951
- Eddie has bowed out of the managerial scene. "I know there's no-one lepping to get the job, but the players need a change of face, a different voice." — *Carlow Nationalist*, 15th December 2000

lepta *adjective*

eleven *UK*

- — Paul Baker, *Polari*, p. 179, 2002

lergy; lerg *noun*

a completely non-existent disease *US*

- — *American Speech*, p. 304, December 1947

▷ see: DREADED LURGI

Leroy *noun*

used as a term of address by US soldiers for black soldiers from the rural south *US*

- — Linda Reinberg, *In the Field*, p. 127, 1991

les *noun*

a lesbian *UK, 1929*

- The world of the les... the furtive cult of strange loves and fierce passions. — Sloane Britain, *First Person 3rd Sex*, 1959

lesb *adjective*

lesbian *US*

- The leader of the lesb-pack, who has been off trying to capture the third girl, walks into camp just as the two are about to consummate the feelings aroused by the dance. — *Adam Film Quarterly*, p. 9, July 1968

lesbian bed death *noun*

a marked drop in libido experienced in some long-term lesbian relationships *US*

- Obviously, urban folklore tells us, you're suffering from that legendary affliction, Lesbian Bed Death. — *San Francisco Examiner*, p. C1, 20th October 1994
- Some comics call this phenomenon "lesbian bed death." While the phrase is politically incorrect in the extreme, many lesbians report that their experiences bear out the stereotype. — *Los Angeles Times*, p. E2, 31st January 2000

lesbie *noun*

a lesbian *AUSTRALIA*

- — Sidney J. Baker, *The Australian Language*, p. 371, 1966
- [T]hey've only got dogs who do these shows. Lesbies. Look like men. — Charles Whited, *Chiodo*, p. 206, 1973

lesbie friends *noun*

a pair of lesbians *AUSTRALIA*

Punning on **LESBIE** and the phrase 'let's be friends'. Generally used by teenagers as an innuendo.

- She nudged Leith with a 'Lesbie friends', and Leith giggled. — Jenny Pausacker, *What are ya?*, p. 55, 1987

lesbo; lezbo *noun*

lesbian; a lesbian *US, 1927*

Found by Jonathan Lighter in the writings of Ernest 'Papa' Hemingway, 1927.

- This is nothing compared to what Jill Johnston, the country's leading lesbo propagandist dishes out weekly in New York's Village Voice. — *San Francisco Chronicle, Sunday Punch*, p. 4, 6th August 1972
- Ex-whore, ex-addict, ex-con, ex-lesbo. — Robert Deane Pharr, *Giveadamn Brown*, p. 69, 1978
- Halfway through, it threatened to be a lesbo scene[.] — Nicholson Baker, *Vox*, p. 117–118, 1992
- A fat white lezbo songbird would stick out, even in a pus pocket like T.J. — James Ellroy, *Hollywood Nocturnes*, p. 291, 1994
- Or we could turn lesbo. — Anka Radakovich, *The Wild Girls Club*, p. 50, 1994
- Turner had never had acting ambitions but ended up in the lead role as Max, a "carefree single lesbo looking for love." — *Vogue*, p. 91, June 1994
- I'm the lesbo. I used to live here until your daughter threw me out. — *Boys on the Side*, 1995
- Thought so. Lesbos. Must be, knocking us back, all that crap about other guys. — Alan Warner, *Bitter Salvage (Disco Biscuits)*, p. 277, 1996
- ANNETTE: I'd rather concentrate on my studies. SEBASTIAN: You a lesbo? — *Cruel Intentions*, 1999
- Faggy or not, we lesbos always have a cause, and this was a worthwhile one[.] — *The Village Voice*, 7th August 2001
- The show's writers – who are mostly lesbos – seems to be tossing hetero crackers out to entice straight viewers, which is understandable, if really annoying. — *OC (Orange County, California) Weekly*, p. 44, 16th January 2004

les girls *noun*

lesbians *US*

- — *Maledicta*, p. 132, Summer/Winter 1982: 'Dyke diction: the language of lesbians'

lesionaire *noun*

an AIDS patient *US*

Gallows humour to an extreme.

- — *Maledicta*, p. 33, 1988–1989: 'Medical maledicta from San Francisco'

leslie *noun*

a lesbian *US*

- — Dale Gordon, *The Dominion Sex Dictionary*, p. 100, 1967

Leslie Ash *verb*

to urinate *UK*

Rhyming slang for **SLASH**, formed from the name of the British actress (b.1960).

- — Bodmin Dark, *Dirty Cockney Rhyming Slang*, 2003

leso *noun*

a lesbian *AUSTRALIA, 1941*

- While I'm on this unsavoury topic, I'd be a mug if I didn't admit we've got our fair share of lezzos in Australia. — Barry Humphries, *The Traveller's Tool*, p. 20, 1985
- 'Probably think you were lesos,' Claudio warned. — Jenny Pausacker, *What are ya?*, p. 11, 1987
- — Kylie Mole (Maryanne Fahey), *My Diary*, p. 49, 1988
- — Roy Slaven (John Doyle), *Five South Coast Seasons*, p. 75, 1992
- Her skirt was a parachute with women holding the hem, with all these lesoes coming out from underneath the skirt. — *Kink*, p. 51, 1993

leso; lezo; lezzo *adjective*

lesbian *AUSTRALIA*

- Julia is thinking of going lezzo. — Kathy Lette, *Girls' Night Out*, p. 199, 1987
- And those who say otherwise are, in my opinion, dole bludging, stinking, homo, pinko, leso scabs who'd do better to introduce themselves to a bath, have a haircut and get a job. — Roy Slaven (John Doyle), *Five South Coast Seasons*, p. 103, 1992
- Will we ever forget the delirium when we watched in awe as Kimberley stripped and went lezzo – with another chick? — *People*, p. 2, 5th July 1999

lessie *noun*

a lesbian *US, 1938*

- — Dale Gordon, *The Dominion Sex Dictionary*, p. 100, 1967
- I dun' play that there; that's for faggots and sissies, lessies and dykes. — Steve Cannon, *Groove, Bang, and Jive Around*, p. 46, 1969

lessie *adjective*

lesbian *AUSTRALIA*

- Leslie by name, and lessie by nature, hey? — Jenny Pausacker, *What are ya?*, p. 55, 1987

let *verb*

▸ **let down easily; let down gently**

to disappoint someone in as non-hurtful a manner as possible *UK, 1834*

- You're the right person, but it's the wrong time. Are they just trying to let you down gently, or could they really have a point? — *The Guardian*, 10th November 2001

▸ **let fly**
to hit out, to attack physically or verbally *UK, 1859*
- Grumpy investors let fly at directors[.] — *Sydney Morning Herald*, 19th April 2003

▸ **let it all hang out**
to behave in an uninhibited manner; to be free of convention; to hide nothing *US, 1960s*
Originally black musicians' usage; adopted into the counter-culture of the 1960s and 70s, then absorbed into the psycho-babble of 'alternative' and 'new age' therapies, where it remains current.
- [S]uch terms as "sock it to me" and "let it all hang out" portrayed the spontaneous times [late 60s] with precision. — Sean Hutchinson, *Crying Out Loud*, p. 176, 1988

▸ **let off; let one off; let go; let one go**
to fart *UK*
- I'm the kind of sneaky bugger, who lets off and doesn't let on, / I let them go in lifts[.] — Ivor Biggun, *I've Parted (Misprint)*, 1978

▸ **let on**
to reveal a secret *UK, 1725*
- We were told: "The attendance was quite good for mid-week." If they did as well as they were trying to let on, why did they slash the price two days before the concert? — *Irish Examiner*, 6th July 2002
- [N]ever let on how much you have to spend when doing your research. — *The Guardian*, 11th June 2002

▸ **let one go; let one loose**
to fart *US, 1970*
- And then Dino lets one go, and she [the teacher] goes 'Wot's your name?' — Kylie Mole (Maryanne Fahey), *My Diary*, p. 107, 1988
- [He] could be relied upon to 'let one loose' every night just as she was nodding off to sleep. — Gretel Killeen, *Hot Buns and Ophelia get a Bloke*, p. 36, 2000

▸ **let rip**
to let go with considerable, or maximum, force; to shout; to accelerate, *UK, 1843*
- Scowling and barely able to control his rage, Mr Campbell mixed up his syntax as he let rip. — *The Guardian*, 28th June 2003

▸ **let the eel swim upstream**
to have sex *US*
- Another way to say "intercourse" [...] Letting the eel swim upstream[.] — Erica Orloff and JoAnn Baker, *Dirty Little Secrets*, p. 88, 2001

▸ **let you have it**
to attack you, to give you a beating or a severe reprimand *UK, 1848*
The ambiguous nature of the phrase 'Let him have it, Chris' is key to understanding the 1952 murder of a policeman by teenager Chris Craig: did the instruction given by 19-year-old Derek Bentley mean hand over the gun to the police officer, or shoot him? Bentley was executed and posthumously pardoned. The 1991 film of the crime is entitled *Let Him Have It*.

letch; lech *noun*
1 a sudden, powerful sexual urge *UK, 1796*
- In his ten years of marriage he had, like any red-blooded American boy, had an occasional letch for a woman other than his wife. — Max Shulman, *Rally Round the Flag, Boys!*, p. 100, 1957

2 a lecher *US, 1943*
- 'It can't do you any harm to ring this producer.' 'He's a letch,' Janie said. — *Janie Stagestruck (Number 96)*, p. 12, 1972
- 'Jeese, you're a goose.' A goose was better than an lech. — Shane Maloney, *Nice Try*, p. 228, 1998
- [T]he lowest, basest, amoral, dirty wee lech. — Christopher Brookmyre, *Boiling a Frog*, p. 125, 2000
- Not just a lech, yeah, but a beast. — Kevin Sampson, *Clubland*, p. 25, 2002

letch; lech *verb*
to behave lecherously; to ogle *US, 1943*
- I had no idea the Dutchman leched after the kid[.] — Jean Brooks, *The Opal Witch*, p. 124, 1967
- The thing that ate into Arnie worse was that Wendy, a doll he'd been leching after, had rubbished him for Bernie. — Wilda Moxham, *The Apprentice*, p. 55, 1969
- When she walked along Boola Street every man letched and the older women scarified her, as they did a stranger or a new hat, with hard eyes. — Ronald McKie, *The Mango Tree*, p. 97, 1975

letch water *noun*
pre-orgasm penile secretions; semen *UK*
Ultimately comes from 'lechery'.
- — Paul Baker, *Polari*, p. 179, 2002

letchy; lechy *adjective*
lecherous *UK*
- — Jenny Fabian and Johnny Byrne, *Groupie*, 1968
- Don't answer the letchy cunt. — Niall Griffiths, *Kelly + Victor*, p. 296, 2002
- How do you deal with hassle from letchy blokes? — *Mixmag*, p. 73, February 2002

letdown *noun*
a disappointment *UK, 1861*
Originally hyphenated.
- [I]t's the biggest event in the universe ... and then it's all over in five minutes and it's a total letdown. — *The Times Magazine*, p. 7, 2nd March 2002

let George do it!
on the railways, used as a humorous attempt to delegate an unpleasant task *US*
Pullman porters, low men on the food chain of railway workers, were known as George.
- — J. Herbert Lund, *Herb's Hot Box of Railraod Slang*, p. 14, 1975

let in on *verb*
to admit into a secret *UK, 1974*
- In the close-knit world of track and field, only a handful of people would have been let in on the secret that a new 'undetectable' drug was on the market. — *The Observer*, 19th October 2003

let it lay!
forget about it! *US*
- — Marcus Hanna Boulware, *Jive and Slang of Students in Negro Colleges*, 1947

let's be having you!
used as a summons to work *UK, 1984*
This phrase also serves as the foundation for a well-known slang-pun on the location of lesbians: 'Lesbie Avenue'.

let's face it!
used for expressing a requirement for an honest appraisal of the facts when confronting or discussing something; often used as meaningless verbal padding *UK, 1937*
- Let's face it. Punk was rubbish. But perhaps it was always meant to be. — *The Guardian*, 28th May 2002

Let's get ready to rumble!
used for evoking the onset of a competition of some sort *US, early 1990s*
Made famous by Michael Buffer, who introduced boxing, sporting and entertainment events with the signature 'Let's get ready to rumble'. Wildly popular in many contexts.

let's have some!
let's fight!; a call to arms *UK*
- [W]hat you really miss is the Great English Pub Fight... Eleven o'clock? Ding-ding, down yer pint, steam outside, bottle in yer hand – Come on!! Let's 'ave some!! — Bernard Dempsey and Kevin McNally, *Lock, Stock... & Two Sips*, p. 307, 2000

let's squirm, worm
used as an invitation to dance *US*
- — Lou Shelly, *Hepcats Jive Talk Dictionary*, p. 28, 1945

let's talk trash
used as a formulaic greeting *US*
- — *Philadelphia Evening Bulletin*, 11th November 1951

letterbomb *noun*
a piece of e-mail with features that will disrupt the computers of some or all recipients *US*
- — Eric S. Raymond, *The New Hacker's Dictionary*, p. 221, 1991

letter from home *noun*
a black African *US*
- — *American Speech*, p. 154, Spring-Summer 1972: 'An approach to black slang'

letterhack *noun*
a fan who corresponds with many other fans *US*
- — *American Speech*, p. 53, Spring 1978: 'Star trek lives: trekker slang'

letters *noun*
those abbreviations of degree, or degrees, or other educational qualifications, honours or awards for gallantry that are displayed after a person's name *UK, 1961*
- [H]e's got loads of letters after his name. — Beale, 1984

letterzine *noun*

a fan magazine that only publishes letters *US, 1976*

• — *American Speech*, p. 53, Spring 1978: 'Star trek lives: trekker slang'

let the dog see the bone!; let the dog see the rabbit!

a catchphrase used by, or of, someone who wishes to do or see something *UK, 1961*

• "Let the dog see the bone," Fancy said. And running at a rate of knots he crossed the street, and hit the door so hard that he carried away on its hinges[.] — Troy Kennedy Martin, *Z Cars*, p. 149, 1962
• This [room] was locked, and this time Billie had no key. She swore violently. "Just step aside, love," I said. "Let the dog see the rabbit." — Angus Ross, *The London Assignment*, 1972

lettie *noun*

a lesbian *SOUTH AFRICA*

Gay slang, originating among those known in the racial categorisation of South Africa as Cape coloureds.

• A "Priscilla" is a police officer, a "Lettie" a lesbian. — Bart Luirink (translated by Loes Nas), *Moffies*, p. 118, 2000

letties *noun*

lodgings *UK, 1859*

Polari, from parleyaree; the plural of 'letty' (a bed).

• — Paul Baker, *Polari*, p. 179, 2002

lettuce *noun*

money, especially paper money *US, 1903*

• After taxes Jack had just enough lettuce to buy himself an old cow. — Steve Allen, *Bop Fables*, p. 68, 1955
• All I looked at was the lettuce while I sipped a beer. — Red Rudensky, *The Gonif*, p. 96, 1970
• I've got a bundle of lettuce and a clean pair of thunder-bags [underpants] under me daks [trousers]. — Barry Humphries, *Bazza Pulls It Off!*, 1971
• [Y]ou purchased one bottle of sauce up Food Giant. Purchased like gave them lettuce for it. — Jeremy Cameron, *Brown Bread in Wengen*, p. 49, 1999

lettuce leaves *noun*

money, especially one-pound notes *UK*

Used by beatniks of the late 1950s and early 60s; extending the imagery of **LETTUCE** (money). Used in the television soap opera *Coronation Street*, 21st September 1966.

letty *verb*

to sleep *UK*

Polari; from 'letty' (a bed).

• — Paul Baker, *Polari*, p. 179, 2002

leucoddy *noun*

▷ see: **LUCODDY**

level *noun*

▸ **on the level**

honest, truthful, trustworthy *US, 1872*

Also used as an adverb.

• "Are you on the level?" he whispered. "Sorry?" I retorted, a bit indignant. "I mean" – he smiled – "are you on the square?" Then I twigged. This was freemason talk. One of their codes. — Jake Arnott, *He Kills Coppers*, p. 45, 2001

level; level with *verb*

to speak or act honestly, to be frank about something previously concealed, to tell the truth *US, 1921*

• He met her after he left prison and levelled with her about his past. — *The Guardian*, 23rd January 2003

level *adjective*

good, excellent *CANADA*

• "I went to the Bahamas last week." "That's level." — Jack Chambers (Editor), *Slang Bag 93 (University of Toronto)*, p. 4, Winter 1993
• "Never mind me. Things level," he said dismissively[.] — Karline Smith, *Moss Side Massive*, p. 132, 1994

level best *noun*

your absolute best or utmost *US, 1851*

• The twilight of empires can last a long time, but judging from his reckless unilateralism and his economic vandalism, George Bush seems to be determined to do his level best to hasten that decline. — *The Guardian*, 26th March 2003

levels *noun*

legitimate, square, unaltered dice *US*

• — *The Annals of the American Academy of Political and Social Sciences*, p. 127, May 1950

levels on the splonk *noun*

in betting odds, evens *UK*

Used in racing circles, especially amongst bookmakers.

• — *Sunday Telegraph*, 7th May 1967

levels you devils; levels *noun*

in betting odds, evens *UK, 1967*

• Starting favourite at even money ("levels you devils!"), Mustang [...] flopped[.] — John McCririck, *John McCririck's World of Betting*, p. 22, 1991

leviathan *noun*

a heavy backer of horses *AUSTRALIA, 1874*

• — Tom Ellis, *The Science of Turf Investment*, p. 150, 1936
• [H]e was one of the last survivors of the leviathans of the Australian turf whose betting during the last two decades of the 19th century rivalled anything seen on racecourses anywhere in the world. — James Holledge, *The Great Australian Gamble*, p. 81, 1966
• Somewhere in this mess of print you should find a clause saying that the hapless leviathan who was reckless enough to take on myself and Uncle Tom owes us fifty-two dollars. — Gerald Sweeney, *The Plunge*, p. 111, 1981

leviathan *adjective*

(of a bookmaker or gambler) wealthy, heavy betting *AUSTRALIA, 1950*

• Another of the more colourful figures amongst these big starting-price operators was Barney Allen, who rose from small S.P. betting to become the leviathan bookmaker of his day. — Vince Kelly, *The Bogeyman*, p. 127, 1956
• [I]t is reported that leviathan bookmaker, Sol Green, accommodated them to the extent of £100,000 in a single bet for the double. — Maurice Cavanough and Meurig Davies, *Cup Day*, p. 138, 1960
• In the colossal betting era round the turn of the century Barney Allen was probably the foremost leviathan bookmaker in Australia, if not the world, wagering tens of thousands with a careless nod of his head. — James Holledge, *The Great Australian Gamble*, p. 75, 1966

Levy and Frank; levy *noun*

an act of masturbation; also used as a verb *UK*

Rhyming slang for **WANK**, formed, according to Julian Franklyn, *A Dictionary of Rhyming Slang*, 1960, from the name of a well-known firm of public house and restaurant proprietors.

• I'll have a leavy [levy] at the same time and imagine I'm haveing [sic] a bunk up instead of you. — Frank Norman, *Bang To Rights*, p. 153, 1958
• — Ray Puxley, *Cockney Rabbit*, 1992

Lewinsky *noun*

an act of oral sex *US*

Usually in the passive phrase 'get a Lewinsky' but the active 'give good Lewinsky' has been used. In 1995 Monica Lewinsky was a White House intern; she was a central figure in US President Bill Clinton's later attempt to exclude oral sex from a general definition of sexual relations.

• In a recent episode of [...] Law & Order: Special Victims Unit, a detective uses the phrase "getting a Lewinsky" to describe oral sex. — *The Guardian*, 17th October 1999
• — Chris Lewis, *The Dictionary of Playground Slang*, p. 136, 2003

Lex *nickname*

1 the Federal Narcotics Hospital in Lexington, Kentucky *US*

• I'm not a junkie. Lexi is for junkies. I ain't hooked. — Clarence Cooper Jr, *The Scene*, p. 100, 1960
• I think Lex [Lexington – the Federal narcotics hospital/prison] did that for me. — Bruce Jackson, *In the Life*, p. 122, 1972

2 a Lexus car *US*

• — Connie Eble (Editor), *UNC-CH Campus Slang*, p. 5, Fall 1997

lez *noun*

a lesbian *US, 1929*

• — JoAnn Radcliff, *They Call Me Lez*, 1963
• "I wonder if she's a lez," danny is saying. — John Rechy, *Numbers*, p. 63, 1967
• "I want to use Arabell for the lez," said Boris. "Can you get her?" — Terry Southern, *Blue Movie*, p. 73, 1970
• Twosomes, threesomes, lez action. — *Adult Video*, p. 13, August/September 1986
• Every girl I ever gone out wit' has gone lez[.] — Eminem (Marshall Mathers), *Role Model*, 1999
• Greenwood bristles at the insult. Won't be spoken to by a woman like that. "Shut your mouth you fuckin LEZ!" — Jack Allen, *When the Whistle Blows*, p. 140, 2000

lez *verb*

▸ **lez it up**

to behave (sexually) as lesbians *UK*

• Three in a bed! Menage a trois! You two lezzing it up! It'd be great. — Richard Herring, *Talking Cock*, p. 265, 2003

lez *adjective*
lesbian *US*
- I quit working for this outfit when the bad shit that was coming down because too much to take – a friend of the theater-own, whose apartment we were using to film a lez flick – attacked one of the other chicks as she was leaving the pad. — *The Berkeley Tribe*, p. 9, 22th-28th August 1969
- She'll lick Levenson's perineum, but she scruples at lez cunt-sucking. —Josh Alan Friedman, *Tales of Times Square*, p. 121, 1989

lezbo *noun*
▷ see: LESBO

lezo; lezzo *noun*
a lesbian *AUSTRALIA, 1945*
- I never did follow through on beating the hell out of those 'butches' who set me up, but I've never liked out-and-out lezzos ever since. —John O'Day, *Confessions of a Male Prostitute*, p. 91, 1964
- Tough lezzos wi' skin'ead mullets an' tattoos on their knuckles[.] —Ben Elton, *High Society*, p. 217, 2002

lezza *noun*
a lesbian *UK*
- I think she's a lezza, he grins. —Niall Griffiths, *Kelly + Victor*, p. 43, 2002

lezzer *noun*
a lesbian *AUSTRALIA*
- 'Gawd! Look at them two queer!' 'Couple of lezzers if you ask me!' —Barry Humphries, *The Wonderful World of Barry McKenzie*, p. 42, 1968
- This is break-dancing for bears [hairy men] and big truck lezzers who'd need an industrial winch to get them off the floor. —Andrew Fraser, *Attitude*, p. 34, October 2003

lezzie; lezzy *noun*
a lesbian *US, 1938*
Usually offensive.
- —Donald Webster Cory and John P. LeRoy, *The Homosexual and His Society*, p. 265, 1963: 'A lexicon of homosexual slang'
- Lezzy, dike, queer – the pejoratives are heard, but they are out of context, they are simple descriptive words, devoid of contempt and scorn[.] —Donald Webster Cory, *The Lesbian in America*, p. 209, 1964
- Mexican lezzies havin' at each other orally[.] —Lester Bangs, *Psychotic Reactions and Carburetor Dung*, p. 348, 1981
- Butch looks up through bloodshot eyes – was the lezzie scene worth losing five grand for? —Josh Alan Friedman, *Tales of Times Square*, p. 121, 1986
- —Jeff Fessler, *When Drag Is Not a Car Race*, p. 25, 1997
- Non-stop [...] poisonous invective against fucking queers, lezzies – I wouldn't mind fuckin' one of them though[.] —Stuart Browne, *Dangerous Parking*, p. 44, 2000

LF; LF scam *noun*
▷ see: LONG FIRM

LF gear *noun*
the proceeds of a long firm fraud *UK*
- —David Powis, *The Signs of Crime*, 1977
- —Angela Devlin, *Prison Patter*, p. 71, 1996

LG *noun*
▷ see: LIQUID GOLD

liamba; lianda *noun*
cannabis *US, 2001*
Noted as African slang by Simon Worman, *Joint Smoking Rules*, 2001.

liar *verb*
to tell lies *UK*
- The fellas were so convinced I was liaring, they even offered their girfriends as part of the deal. —Wayne Anthony, *Spanish Highs*, p. 23, 1999

liard *noun*
a pathological liar *TRINIDAD AND TOBAGO*
- —Lise Winer, *Dictionary of the English/Creole of Trinidad & Tobago*, 2003

liar's bench *noun*
a settee in front of a country store *US*
- —Charles F. Haywood, *Yankee Dictionary*, p. 99, 1963

lib *noun*
1 *lib*eration *UK, 1970*
Usually allied to a specific political cause, most famously 'women's lib'.
- Was this a victory for women's lib or for Margaret Thatcher? — *The Guardian*, 12th February 1975

2 *lib*erty *UK*
- It's a downright lib! —Angela Devlin, *Prison Patter*, p. 71, 1996

3 Librium™, a branded depressant *UK*
- —Mike Haskins, *Drugs*, p. 283, 2003

lib *verb*
to release from prison *UK*
Abbreviated from 'liberate'.
- Listen, the other bloke just got libbed yesterday, so I haven't had time to clear up. —Christopher Brookmyre, *Boiling a Frog*, p. 52, 2000

libber *noun*
a feminist *US*
From 'Woman's Liberation' as the name for the feminist movement of the late 1960s.
- —Connie Eble (Editor), *UNC-CH Campus Slang*, October 1972
- "Probably a libber," said Rose Rules. —Joseph Wambaugh, *The Choirboys*, p. 319, 1975
- If the men saw her as "The Libber," she adds, she would lose what effectiveness she has. — *The Washington Post*, p. C1, 9th October 1984
- They said these complaints were ridiculous. He was a fine person and we were a bunch of women's libbers. — *Seattle Times*, p. A1, 15th December 2003

libbo *noun*
a liberty *UK*
- He was one of the first to realise that taking libbos [...] was a mug's game[.] —J.J. Connolly, *Layer Cake*, p. 31, 2000

libe; libes *noun*
a library *US, 1915*
- —Collin Baker et al., *College Undergraduate Slang Study Conducted at Brown University*, p. 151, 1968

liberate *verb*
1 to steal *US, 1944*
Coined in irony by US soldiers during World War 2, and then recycled by the political and cultural left of the 1960s.
- [T]he lousy slob ratted on me to the M.P.'s about liberating 10 grand of some kraut's gold hoard back in '45[.] —Mickey Spillane, *Me, Hood!*, p. 15, 1963
- Scavenger Corps and Transport Gang is responsible for garbage collection and the picking up and delivery of items to the various services, as well as liberating anything they think useful for one project or another. — *The Digger Papers*, p. 15, August 1968
- Stew and I liberated their last few copies. —Jerry Rubin, *Do It!*, p. 61, 1970
- In the rear of the Frederick Street Free Frame of Reference was the free store, brimming over with liberated goods to be shared with whoever needed them. —Emmett Grogan, *Ringolevio*, p. 266, 1972
- He had liberated two bennys [overcoats] off hangers and was nonchalantly till tapping (rifling a cash register) men's wear bread. —Iceberg Slim (Robert Beck), *Airtight Willie and Me*, p. 5, 1979

2 to take control of *US*
- The news comes in that Avery Hall, the architecture school, has been liberated. We mark it as such on Grayson's map. —James Simon Kunen, *The Strawberry Statement*, p. 33, 1968

liberated *adjective*
free from narrow, conventional thinking *US*
- It's not very liberated, I know – I want a husband with a decent job, you know. — *Boys on the Side*, 1995

liberati *noun*
a notional grouping of people who promote liberal principles *UK*
Formed with the suffix **-ERATI**. Used, in a derogatory sense, by British Home Secretary David Blunkett, in an interview broadcast on the *Today Show* (BBC Radio 4), 7th July 2004.

liberation *noun*
1 theft in the name of a cause *US*
Said either with irony or a complete lack of humour, depending on the self-righteousness of the speaker.
- Needless to say, we stole where we could, calling it "liberation of urgently-needed materials" and we left many bills unpaid. —Raymond Mungo, *Famous Long Ago*, p. 34, 1970

2 left-wing politics *US*
- We are on strike, of course. There are "liberation classes" but the scene is essentially no more pencils, no more books. —James Simon Kunen, *The Strawberry Statement*, p. 46, 1968

liberty *noun*
a twenty-five-cent piece *US*
From the inscription on the coin.
- —Marcus Hanna Boulware, *Jive and Slang of Students in Negro Colleges*, 1947

liberty act *noun*
in the circus, an act in which horses perform without riders *US*
- —Sherman Louis Sergel, *The Language of Show Biz*, p. 125, 1973

library *noun*
a brakevan (caboose) *US*
• —Norman Carlisle, *The Modern Wonder Book of Trains and Railroading*, p. 265, 1946

lice bin *noun*
a dirty, unsanitary place *US*
• That's why I'm in this lice bin.—Tom Robbins, *Another Roadside Attraction*, p. 15, 1971

license *noun*
freedom to break the law in an area by virtue of having bribed the police *US*
• —Hyman E. Goldin et al., *Dictionary of American Underworld Lingo*, p. 24, 1950
• [W]e pay for them to work, your people give them their license to work.—Richard Condon, *Prizzi's Honor*, p. 217, 1982

-licious *suffix*
used in combination with a general or generic characteristic to describe the object as especially attractive within or with regard to the genre *UK*
• Princess Superstar is the gangsterlicious bad babysitter who's "kinky like pubic hair".—*X-Ray*, p. 84, November 2002

lick *noun*
1 a musical phrase *UK, 1932*
• Many of the younger social and diplomatic sets get a bang out of hot licks.—Jack Lait and Lee Mortimer, *Washington Confidential*, p. 17, 1951
• Some big symphony trumpet player came up and asked me how I done it, said I was doing everything all wrong, but playing licks he couldn't play himself.—Ross Russell, *The Sound*, p. 196, 1961
• '[M]usicians with their "licks" and "chops".—Sean Hutchinson, *Crying Out Loud*, p. 176, 1988
• Excellent melodic ornaments are called 'hot licks'. 'Kinda kung-fu meets dance. That's the lick that, it's got everything'—Diran Abedayo, *My Once Upon A Time*, p. 125, 2000

2 a small amount *US, 1814*
• She can't ride worth a lick anyway.—Terry Southern, *Texas Summer*, p. 136, 1991
• I assume they were resting. I never saw them do a lick of work. —Rhiannon Paine, *Too Late for the Festival*, p. 25, 1999

3 in betting, a huge win *AUSTRALIA*
• In the mid-1960's, punter Peter Huxley, the former secretary of the Rural Bank of NSW, told a court he would need "a big lick" to meet his debts.—Ned Wallish, *The Truth Dictionary of Racing Slang*, p. 6, 1989

4 a robbery *US*
• Smith admitted he heard Stroud and others planning "a lick" (street slang for robbery) at a white house in the country after Payne was at a house in the 1700 block of South Walnut Street.—*South Bend (Indiana) Tribune*, p. D1, 16th July 2002

5 a fast speed *UK, 1847*
• Proceeding at a lick, too, for [...] Wembley took only 300 working days to build.—*The Guardian*, 12th May 2001

6 an intoxicating experience with crack cocaine *UK*
• I remember the first lick I ever had, it was brilliant.—Lanre Fehintola, *Charlie Says...*, p. 112, 2000

7 any mistake, from a slight error to a complete disaster *US*
Vietnam war usage.
• —Linda Reinberg, *In the Field*, p. 127, 1991

8 oral sex *US*
• —Kenn "Naz" Young, *Naz's Underground Dictionary*, p. 43, 1973

9 a serving of ice-cream *NEW ZEALAND*
• —David McGill, *David McGill's Complete Kiwi Slang Dictionary*, p. 79, 1998

▸ **the lick**
anything that is currently considered as stylish, fashionable or best *UK*
• The "new lick" is the Electric Scooter: much quieter than the petrol version[.]—Julian Johnson, *Urban Survival*, p. 222, 2003

lick *verb*
1 to beat, to thrash *UK, 1535*
• Dick Tracy says you're never licked until you quit.—Chester Gould, *Dick Tracy Meets the Night Crawler*, p. 178, 1945
• I want death to know that it ain't shit, I can lick it[.]—Lester Bangs, *Psychotic Reactions and Carburetor Dung*, p. 317, 1980
• You're for a right good licking.—Ian Pattison, *Rab C. Nesbitt*, 1988

2 to shoot and kill *US*
• Two women with Brockington told police he had asked them if they had seen the TV news and told them that he and two other men had "licked" the brother of the girl killed near Tamarind Avenue last year[.]—*Palm Beach (Florida) Post*, p. 1B, 15th September 1994

3 to move or act quickly *BERMUDA*
• —Peter A. Smith and Fred M. Barritt, *Bermewjan Vurds*, 1985

4 to smoke (marijuana) *JAMAICA*
• —Velma Pollard, *Dread Talk*, p. 43, 2000

▸ **lick arse; lick ass**
to behave in a subservient manner *UK, 1959*
A variation of **KISS ARSE**.

▸ **lick butt**
to behave subserviently *US*
A variation of **KISS BUTT**.

▸ **lick down**
1 to physically assault, to force submission *UK*
Elaboration of **LICK** (to beat).
• The paper would look dyam [damn] foolish if we printed a story about some man who claims to be licking down half of the Metropolitan Police Force.—Donald Gorgon, *Cop Killer*, p. 107, 1994

2 to eat quickly *TRINIDAD AND TOBAGO, 1993*
• —Lise Winer, *Dictionary of the English/Creole of Trinidad & Tobago*, 2003

▸ **lick like lizard**
to use a technique of short, quick laps while performing oral sex on a woman *JAMAICA*
Recorded August 2002.

▸ **lick shit**
to lick crack cocaine for a short-lived sensation of intoxication *UK*
• —Angela Devlin, *Prison Patter*, p. 71, 1996

▸ **lick the cat**
to perform oral sex on a woman *US*
• —Erica Orloff and JoAnn Baker, *Dirty Little Secrets*, p. 86, 2001

▸ **lick the dew off her lily**
to engage in oral sex on a woman *US*
• Another way to say "cunnilingus" [...] Licking the dew off her lily[.] —Erica Orloff and JoAnn Baker, *Dirty Little Secrets*, p. 86, 2001

▸ **lick the rock**
to use crack cocaine *UK*
• I know people who lick the rock and, like Es, I've seen what it can do.—Macfarlane, Macfarlane and Robson, *The User*, p. 104, 1996

lick about *verb*
to live a carefree, hedonistic life *BARBADOS*
• —Frank A. Collymore, *Barbadian Dialect*, p. 67, 1965

lick-box *noun*
a person who performs oral sex on women *US*
• —Vincent J. Monteleone, *Criminal Slang*, p. 144, 1949

licked *adjective*
defeated *UK*
• "Knock it off, guys," the prisoner said suddenly, taking the knife and straightening. "We're licked!"—*The Sweeney*, p. 15, 1976

lickety-split *adverb*
speedily, headlong *US, 1831*
In recognisable variations from 1831 and uncertain spelling from 1848.
• They couldn't drive lickety-split all day and see everything they should see.—Jim Thompson, *After Dark, My Sweet*, p. 63, 1955
• Carboot Soul [by Nightmares on Wax] and it's lazy, fumed-up charms will win you over lickety-split.—*Ministry*, May 2002

lickle; likkle *adjective*
little *UK*
Originally childish and twee as 'lickle me' and 'ickle me', and continues to be so. Contemporary use in UK black patois, however, is not cute.
• "Yuh a'right?" "Just a lickle burn," she replied, examining the injury.—Karline Smith, *Moss Side Massive*, p. 45, 1994
• Coupla bods [people] I did some work for. Lickle raasholes [arseholes]!—Diran Abedayo, *My Once Upon A Time*, p. 46, 2000
• [S]moking a lickle draw [marijuana] instead of tooting powders, listening to jungle and chasing young Richards [women]—J.J. Connolly, *Layer Cake*, p. 118, 2000

lick length
used to refuse or reject *UK*
'To lick **LENGTH**' (the penis) is 'to perform oral sex', used here to suggest an extremely unlikely alternative.
- - Worth some dab [amphetamine]? – Lick length. —Mark Powell, *Snap*, p. 17, 2001

lick-mouth *noun*
a gossip *BARBADOS*
- —Frank A. Collymore, *Barbadian Dialect*, p. 67, 1965

lick-mouth *adjective*
salacious, gossip-bearing, inappropriately concerned with the business of others *BARBADOS, 1980*
- —Lise Winer, *Dictionary of the English/Creole of Trinidad & Tobago*, 2003

lick my helmet!
used emphatically to dismiss or reject *UK*
Based on **HELMET** (the head of the penis).
- Fuck them. Yeah, fuck them. They could mind their own business, or lick my helmet. —Frank Skinner, *Frank Skinner*, p. 73, 2001

lick papers *noun*
the thin paper used to roll a marijuana cigarette *US*
A term first applied to paper used to hand-roll tobacco cigarettes, and then later, and briefly, to paper used to roll marijuana cigarettes.

licks *noun*
a beating *UK*
From conventional 'lick' (a blow). Probably since late C18, contemporary usage mainly black.
- Babylon, kiss me raas! You'll never take me alive! Yuh wan' tes' me, well step right in and take some licks! —Donald Gorgon, *Cop Killer*, p. 98, 1994

licorice stick; liquorice stick *noun*
a clarinet *US, 1935*
- She called his clarinet a "licorice stick." Was she corny. —J.D. Salinger, *Catcher in the Rye*, p. 75, 1951
- Well, a-reading, writing, arithmetic / Taught to the tune of a licorice stick / No education is ever complete / Without a boogie-woogie-woogie beat[.] —Bill Haley, *ABC Boogie*, 1954

lid *noun*
1 a hat *US, 1896*
- "My I take your hat?" I snapped out of it long enough to hand over my lid. —Mickey Spillane, *I, The Jury*, p. 63, 1947
- "We don't want to be around when old Mushmouth comes after his lid." —Jim Thompson, *Bad Boy*, p. 363, 1953
- 'Better wear this lid.' He offered me a very battered and shapeless old straw hat. —Nino Culotta (John O'Grady), *They're A Weird Mob*, p. 36, 1957
- The kid with the lid and the proper dark glasses, will soon dig which chick will go for the passes. —Dan Burley, *Diggeth Thou?*, p. 7, 1959
- I picked up my lid and split. —A.S. Jackson, *Gentleman Pimp*, p. 18, 1973
- He was always pressed; nothing but the best / Vines and kicks he had / A thirty-dollar lid and gloves of kid / Man his threads were bad. —Dennis Wepman et al., *The Life*, p. 97, 1976
- The bloke that won it was thrilled pink and I'm down one lid. Cost me $27 for another one. —Sam Weller, *Old Bastards I Have Met*, p. 27, 1979
- My lid was telescoped into a pork-pie, cocked stupidly on the side of my long head. —Iceberg Slim (Robert Beck), *Airtight Willie and Me*, p. 7, 1979
- See, when the Dodgers moved to Los Angeles the general manager donated the old caps to the state. * * * Ever since, when he sees one of those lids he spooks, like he's smelling the flowers on his own grave. —Seth Morgan, *Homeboy*, p. 168, 1990

2 a motorcyle helmet with face protection *US*
- —Connie Eble (Editor), *UNC-CH Campus Slang*, p. 5, Spring 1994

3 a submarine hatch cover *UK*
Reported by John Malin, 1979.

4 in a card game, the top card of the deck *US*
- —George Percy, *The Language of Poker*, p. 52, 1988

5 an approximate measure (variously twenty-two grams, or one to two ounces) of loose, uncleaned marijuana *US, 1966*
Derived from the lid of a tobacco tin, a convenient measure of sufficient marijuana to roll about forty cigarettes.
- The fact that I make more money than the cat who sells one lid of grass a week – now, that's his choice and this is my choice. —Leonard Wolfe (Editor), *Voices from the Love Generation*, p. 187, 1968
- The kidnappings were nothing fancy: a young surfer at the Pompano Pier, lured to a waiting Cadillac with a lid of fresh Colombian red[.] —Carl Hiaasen, *Tourist Season*, p. 178, 1986
- —Angela Devlin, *Prison Patter*, p. 71, 1996
- The $10 lid was fading into the '60s, to be replaced by Bud and Thai stick —Editors of Ben is Dead, *Retrohell*, p. 60, 1997
- He hit you with lids, caps, keys, tabs, nickel bags, blotters, buttons, spoons and everything from milligrams to boatloads. —Robert Sabbag, *A Way with the Spoon [The Howard Marks Book of Dope Stories]*, p. 351, 1998

▷ **see: SAUCEPAN LID**

▸ **on its lid**
(of a vehicle) overturned *US*
Collected by John Thompson of Hendersonville, North Carolina, 2004.

▸ **out of your lid**
drug-intoxicated *UK*
- [T]hey were speeding out of their lids. —Will Birch, *No Sleep Till Canvey Island*, p. 202, 2003

▸ **put the lid on; put the tin lid on**
to conceal something; to bring some activity or enterprise to an (unwelcome) end *UK, 1909*
- [W]hat put the tin lid on it was what she had witnessed over the past half-hour. —Christopher Brookmyre, *The Sacred Art of Stealing*, p. 115, 2002
- [A]ccording to Len, who oversaw such things, Rick's astronomical expenses were threatening to blow us all out of the water. Len said we had to 'put the lid on it' and that he'd 'have a word'. —*The Guardian*, 6th June 2002

lid-poppers *noun*
an amphetamine or other central nervous system stimulant *US*
The 'lid' in question is a head.
- —Eugene Landy, *The Underground Dictionary*, p. 119, 1971
- —Ralph de Sola, *Crime Dictionary*, p. 84, 1982

lid-propper *noun*
an amphetamine or other central nervous system stimulant *US*
- —John B. Williams, *Narcotics and Hallucinogenics*, p. 114, 1967

lids *noun*
units of currency *IRELAND*
- Asked the old man for two hundred lids. —Paul Howard, *Ross O'Carroll-Kelly*, p. 70, 2003

lie *verb*
to talk *US*
- We ain't doing nothin' 'cept sittin around an doin some LYIN'. —Malachi Andrews and Paul T. Owens, *Black Language*, p. 95, 1973

▸ **lie through your teeth**
to lie deliberately *UK*
- Lying through his teeth, he assured her that he had finished with Geraldine, that she had meant nothing to him anyway, he was just using her for sex – the usual old fanny. —Garry Bushell, *The Face*, p. 192, 2001

lie box *noun*
a polygraph *US, 1955*
- Eventually we may end up sitting on the lie box. It's better not to have discussed such things. —Gerald Petievich, *Money Men*, p. 121, 1981

lie-down *noun*
in prison, time spent in the segregation unit *UK*
- —Angela Devlin, *Prison Patter*, p. 71, 1996

lie down *verb*
in pool, to play below your skill level to lure strangers into playing against you for money *US*
- —Mike Shamos, *The Illustrated Encyclopedia of Billiards*, p. 136, 1993

lie low *verb*
to be in hiding; to behave in a manner that ought not to attract attention *UK, 1880*
- I wondered if I should just lie low and not mention this early stumble to anyone. —*The Guardian*, 20th November 2003

lie sheet *noun*
a truck driver's log book *US*
- —Montie Tak, *Truck Talk*, p. 99, 1971

lieut; loot *noun*
a lieutenant *US, 1759*
- "Talk slow, the loot is an edgy type." Lloyd took a deep breath and spoke into the mouthpiece. "Lieutenant, this is Hopkins[.]"—James Ellroy, *Because the Night*, p. 392, 1984
- Telephone for the lieut.—Robert Campbell, *Sweet La-La Land*, p. 237, 1990

lieuty *noun*
a lieutenant *US*
- It was OK that I couldn't tell him much about anything he understood, having been just a "leg," hahaha. That's what his buddy, this second lieuty, calls infantrymen.—Clarence Major, *All-Night Visitors*, p. 175, 1998

life *noun*
life imprisonment *AUSTRALIA, 1833*
- 'It'll be more than slander they charge you with, you mug lair,' snarled the bookie. 'And when they do I hope you get life.'—James Holledge, *The Great Australian Gamble*, p. 142, 1966

▸ **go for your life**
to partake enthusiastically; to go all out *AUSTRALIA, 1920*
- You and your tin-pot court. There's no court in the world big enough to make me give her to you. The Almighty himself couldn't make me do it. Go for your life. See where you get.—D'Arcy Niland, *The Shiralee*, p. 216, 1955

▸ **have a life; get a life**
to enjoy a well-rounded life including work, family, friends and interests *US*
- How come he's not making this trek down memory lane? Or does he have a life?—*Boys on the Side*, 1995

▸ **in the life**
homosexual *US*
- —Donald Webster Cory and John P. LeRoy, *The Homosexual and His Society*, p. 265, 1963: 'A lexicon of homosexual slang'
- —*Male Swinger Number 3*, p. 46, 1981: 'The complete gay dictionary'
- —Paul Baker, *Polari*, p. 178, 2002

▸ **not for the life of you**
expresses the impossibility of your doing, understanding, etc *UK, 1809*
Hyperbole.
- I could not, for the life of me, recall the time of his vanishing.—*The Observer*, 8th October 2000

▸ **the life**
1 the criminal lifestyle; the lifestyle of prostitution *US, 1916*
- If a good gal – a sweethearted dame who had no stomach for the life – had started living with Paul, I'd have objected.—Philip Wylie, *Opus 21*, p. 297, 1949
- I been in the life thirty years and had one pimp or another every single day of it.—John M. Murtagh and Sara Harris, *Cast the First Stone*, p. 112, 1957
- He took me out every night for three weeks after work, and said over and over that he had fallen in love with me at first sight, that he had to marry me and take me out of the life.—Sara Harris, *The Lords of Hell*, p. 32, 1967
- Willie was in the life and he couldn't return to giging (working) everyday, so through friends he began to sell a little pot to make ends meet.—Babs Gonzales, *I Paid My Dues*, p. 96, 1967
- It was an integral part of the Life, and she'd known the Life from childhood.—Nathan Heard, *Howard Street*, p. 166, 1968
- Lots a girls in the life has chillrens.—Robert Gover, *JC Saves*, p. 126, 1968
- I was a con, I loved the life – and to hell with the past and future.—Red Rudensky, *The Gonif*, p. 92, 1970
- I've been outta the life since I left Detroit.—A.S. Jackson, *Gentleman Pimp*, p. 117, 1973
- In the life, a man cannot be involved with words, like who said what about who – for sure you'll be in the middle.—Edwin Torres, *Carlito's Way*, p. 80, 1975
- [S]uch peripheral types as "street cats" and "shadies" are not members, though these groups frequently interact with those who truly belong to the Life.—Dennis Wepman et al., *The Life*, p. 2, 1976
- The hardest thing for me was leaving the life. I still love the life. We were treated like movie stars with muscle.—*Goodfellas*, 1990
- VINCENT: So you're serious, you're really gonna quit? JULES: The life, most definitely.—*Pulp Fiction*, 1994
- The point is: Kip's been living the life.—*Gone in 60 Seconds*, 2000

2 the business and lifestyle of professional wrestling *US*
- It was rough at first, leaving the life, but DiBiase persevered.—*World of Wrestling Magazine*, p. 7, June 1999

▸ **there's life in the old dog yet; there's life in the old girl yet**
he, or she, is still very much alive, and, especially, capable of sexual activity *UK, 1857*
- Oh-ho! Buying gifts for the ladies, eh? There's life in the old dog yet.—Jo Beverley, *Something Wicked*, p. 320, 1997

life and death; life *noun*
breath, especially bad breath *UK*
Rhyming slang.
- —Ray Puxley, *Cockney Rabbit*, 1992

lifeboat *noun*
release from prison as a result of parole board action or a commutation of sentence *US, 1908*
- —Vincent J. Monteleone, *Criminal Slang*, p. 144, 1949
- —Marlene Freedman, *Alcatraz*, 1983
- —Angela Devlin, *Prison Patter*, p. 71, 1996

lifed-up *adjective*
sentenced to life imprisonment *UK*
- I'd fuckin kill him. I'd get lifed up for murder.—Niall Griffiths, *Kelly + Victor*, p. 280, 2002

life in London *noun*
used for describing an easy, carefree lifestyle *TRINIDAD AND TOBAGO, 1991*
- —Lise Winer, *Dictionary of the English/Creole of Trinidad & Tobago*, 2003

life jacket *noun*
a condom *US*
Safe sex saves lives.
- —Pamela Munro, *U.C.L.A. Slang*, p. 55, 1989
- —Kevin Dilallo, *The Unofficial Gay Manual*, p. 242, 1994

life off *verb*
to sentence someone to life imprisonment *UK*
- So he gets lifed off?—J.J. Connolly, *Layer Cake*, p. 168, 2000

life of Riley *noun*
a pleasurable, carefree existence *UK, 1919*
Occasionally spelt 'Reilly'.
- People need to appreciate that you can't work from 25 to 55 and then live the life of Riley to 95[.]—*The Guardian*, 12th July 2002

life on the installment plan *noun*
a series of prison sentences with brief periods of freedom between, which have the cumulative effect of a life sentence *US*
- —Vincent J. Monteleone, *Criminal Slang*, p. 145, 1949
- —John R. Armore and Joseph D. Wolfe, *Dictionary of Desperation*, p. 39, 1976

lifer *noun*
1 a career member of the armed forces *US, 1962*
- There was a lifer in San Diego who was dumped for indebtedness.—Darryl Ponicsan, *The Last Detail*, p. 13, 1970
- And they played songs like "Good Night Irene" and "I Wonder Who's Kissing Her Now" and "I Love You a Bushel and a Peck" – music nobody ever heard of but the gray-headed lifers.—Larry Heinemann, *Paco's Story*, p. 12, 1986
- Oh wowwww – the lifers made a mistake, they cuttin' me some slack.—*Platoon*, 1986
- A collection of "Lifers"; what the hell was I doing there, a reluctant draftee?—Odie Hawkins, *Men Friends*, p. 58, 1989
- Having served in Korea as a dogface grant, he knew a lifer when he saw one.—Joseph Wambaugh, *Finnegan's Week*, p. 27, 1993

2 a prisoner sentenced to penal servitude for life *AUSTRALIA, 1827*
- Among the lifers in Alcatraz, who never again will freely see the light of God's sun or draw a free breath, there are classes.—Jack Lait and Lee Mortimer, *New York Confidential*, p. 16, 1948
- How sweet and truly Christian it would be if every priest, minister and rabbi would be responsible for a lifer and take him out for just one day so he could see his artwork on a sign or perhaps on a license plate[.]—Lenny Bruce, *How to Talk Dirty and Influence People*, p. 71, 1965
- They kept all us lifers in chains.—Patrick White, *A Fringe Of Leaves*, p. 275, 1976
- The North Block cats were more than pets, they were the only living things in a lifer's stone-shrunk world from which he could expect the unconditional reciprocation of his affection.—Seth Morgan, *Homeboy*, p. 44, 1990
- —Angela Devlin, *Prison Patter*, p. 71, 1996

3 a person who has been given a traffic ticket *US*
Ironic usage.
- —Connie Eble (Editor), *UNC-CH Campus Slang*, p. 4, Spring 1984

4 a drug addict *US*
- —Eugene Landy, *The Underground Dictionary*, p. 120, 1971

lifer's dream *noun*
a Soviet-made SKS Type 54 carbine rifle, used by the North Vietnamese and Viet Cong during the Vietnam war *US*
Treasured as the ultimate war trophy by US Marines in Vietnam.

life saver *noun*

heroin *UK*

- —Mike Haskins, *Drugs*, p. 284, 2003

Liffey water *noun*

porter (ale); any dark beer or stout, especially Guinness™ *UK*

Rhyming slang. Later use is heavily influenced by the association of Guinness with water drawn in Dublin from the River Liffey.

- —Julian Franklyn, *A Dictionary of Rhyming Slang*, 1961
- —Ray Puxley, *Cockney Rabbit*, 1992

lift *noun*

1 the act of shoplifting *US, 1791*

- I don't want to go on the lift. Not today, please. —Bernard Wolfe, *The Magic of Their Singing*, p. 25, 1961

2 the early euphoric sensation after using a drug *US*

- —Kenn "Naz" Young, *Naz's Underground Dictionary*, p. 43, 1973

lift *verb*

1 to steal *UK, 1526*

- He could lift a hubcap quicker and more quietly than anyone[.] —S.E. Hinton, *The Outsiders*, p. 11, 1967
- "Well, I don't think she lifted it off him," Raymond said. —Elmore Leonard, *City Primeval*, p. 160, 1980
- I've never lifted anything in my life. Even if I was cold and hungry I'd never steal. —Karline Smith, *Letters to Andy Cole*, p. 141, 1998
- Yeah, so after he threw me out and went to supper, I was just roaming the house looking for liftable objects, if that was gonna be his attitude. —Kenneth Lonergan, *This is Our Youth*, p. 14, 2000

2 to arrest *UK*

- —Christopher Hawke, *For Campaign Service*, 1979
- [A]nother [police car], coming from the other direction, cut in front of us and we were lifted. —Lenny McLean, *The Guv'nor*, p. 22, 1998

3 to work out with weights *US*

- —Connie Eble (Editor), *UNC-CH Campus Slang*, p. 6, November 1990

4 to transfer matter from one periodical to another *UK, 1891*

Used by journalists and printers.

- The script was lifted straight from the book[.] —*The Guardian*, 3rd February 2001

liftbird *noun*

any troop transport plane *US*

Vietnam war usage.

- —Linda Reinberg, *In the Field*, p. 127, 1991

lift doesn't go to the top floor

descriptive of a fool *UK*

- Obviously I start to wonder if his lift goes to the top floor [...] Some nights it feels like every other ride's a frothing loony. —Simon Lewis, *In The Box [britpulp]*, p. 131, 1999

lifted *adjective*

drug-intoxicated *US, 1942*

- Many I got to get high before I can have a haircut. I got to get lifted before I can face it! —John Clellon Holmes, *The Horn*, p. 35, 1958
- —Mike Haskins, *Drugs*, p. 291, 2003

lifter *noun*

an explosive charge *NEW ZEALAND*

Mining slang.

- Seven shots were laid – four lifters and three easers – and 150 lb of gelignite was used. —*Evening Post*, p. 18, 17th February 1965

liftie *noun*

a ski-*lift* operator *CANADA*

- —Mike Fabbro, *Snowboarding*, p. 94, 1996: 'Glossary'

lift-one-drag-one *noun*

a person with a pronounced limp *US*

- The labels were cruel: Gimp, Limpy-go-fetch, Crip, Lift-one-drag one, etc. Pint, Half-a-man, Peewee, Shorty, Lardass, Pork, Blubber, Belly, Blimp. Nuke-knob, Skinhead, Baldy. Four-eyes, Specs, Coke bottles. —*San Francisco Examiner*, p. A15, 28th July 1997

lift-op *noun*

a ski-*lift* operator *US*

- Ninety percent of the time, the lift-op is a snowboarder who might share some local knowledge of the mountain[.] —Jim Humes and Sean Wagstaff, *Boarderlands*, p. 223, 1995

lifts *noun*

hydraulic lifts installed in a car, operated from within the car body to make the car rise or fall suddenly *US*

A key component of a **LOWRIDER**'s car.

- —Edith A. Folb, *runnin' down some lines*, p. 245, 1980

lig *noun*

a music industry social event *UK*

- —Tom Hibbert, *Rockspeak!*, p. 96, 1983

ligger *noun*

a shameless name-dropping hanger-on attached to a rock band *US*

- —Bob Young and Micky Moody, *The Language of Rock 'n' Roll*, p. 88, 1985

light *noun*

a tracer bullet *US*

- "I got light," Coffin Ed said. Grave Digger nodded in the dark and took out his long-barreled, nickelplated .38-caliber revolver and replaced the first three shells with tracer bullets. —Chester Himes, *Cotton Comes to Harlem*, p. 94, 1965

light *verb*

▸ **light a shuck**

to depart suddenly, to move fast *CANADA, 1903*

This phrase is derived from the use of flaming cornhusks for light.

- So I lit a shuck back to my regular old pad and jumped into a different tog. —Bruce Jackson, *Get Your Ass in the Water and Swim Like Me*, p. 86, 1965
- "You lightin' a shuck?" "I have to go," she said. —George Bowering, *Caprice*, p. 196, 1987

▸ **light the rugs**

in drag racing, to accelerate in a fashion that makes the tyres smoke *US*

- —John Lawlor, *How to Talk Car*, p. 69, 1965
- —Lyle K. Engel, *The Complete Book of Fuel and Gas Dragsters*, p. 152, 1968

▸ **light the wienies**

in drag racing, to smoke the tyres when the race begins *US*

- —John Lawlor, *How to Talk Car*, p. 69, 1965

light *adjective*

1 short of funds, especially in the context of a payment owed *US, 1955*

- I had the infantile audacity to cheat. I dealt the Ace of Spades from the bottom of the deck; I stacked the cards, I went "light" in the stud poker pot. —Mario Puzo, *Inside Las Vegas*, p. 146, 1977
- He heard Ricky say, "You're still light," as the old man handed him money. —Elmore Leonard, *Glitz*, p. 172, 1985

2 in poker, owing chips to the collective bet on a hand *US*

- —Albert H. Morehead, *The Complete Guide to Winning Poker*, p. 267, 1967

3 (used of an arrest warrant) susceptible to attack by a skilled defence attorney *US*

- "A light one" meant an arrest affidavit prepared in such a way that a defense lawyer could easily pick holes in it and get the case thrown out. —Peter Maas, *Serpico*, p. 153, 1973

4 unarmed; without a weapon *US*

- He was walking light again. He was stupid, he told himself. Only a stupid cop would let a broad talk him out of his gun. —Joseph Nazel, *Black Cop*, p. 129, 1974

light across the carpet *adjective*

homosexual *UK*

- [H]ere was a boy destined to be "light across the carpet" —Jenny Eclair, *Camberwell Beauty*, p. 193, 2000

light and bitter *noun*

a shitter (in all senses) *UK*

Rhyming slang, formed from a mix of beers.

- —Bodmin Dark, *Dirty Cockney Rhyming Slang*, 2003

light artillery *noun*

1 the equipment needed to inject a drug *US*

- —Hyman E. Goldin et al., *Dictionary of American Underworld Lingo*, p. 125, 1950

2 beans *US*

- —*American Speech*, p. 89, April 1946: 'The language of West Coast culinary workers'

light, bright, damn near white; bright, white and dead white *adjective*

(used of a black person) very light-skinned *US*

Anthony Barthelemy wrote an essay on the politics of genealogy, using this as his title.

- [S]ome stud said, "Light, bright and damn near white; how does that nigger do it?" — Chester Himes, *If He Hollers Let Him Go*, p. 43, 1945
- The light-bright-damn-near-white woman who had been naked in his bed when Iris had called opened the door for him. — Chester Himes, *Cotton Comes to Harlem*, p. 87, 1965
- They'd elect our same old light, bright, damn-near-white Congressman who was always making those pretty promises that never amounted to anything, those bullshit promises. — Claude Brown, *Manchild in the Promised Land*, p. 199, 1965
- Hey, lots a spades runnin with the ofay, making out they's jes bright white an dead right as old El Beejay. — Robert Gover, *JC Saves*, p. 69, 1968
- And always the one in charge was light, bright and almost white. — H. Rap Brown, *Die Nigger Die!*, p. 20, 1969

light colonel *noun*
a lieutenant colonel *US, 1954*
- While the old gent napped away the afternoons upstairs in the White House, a light colonel of Marines had run a secret government in the basement[.] — Richard Condon, *Prizzi's Glory*, p. 139, 1988
- It would mean that they have let poor Ollie, a lowly former light colonel, be a fall guy. — *Chicago Tribune*, p. C3, 26th April 1989
- Don Sheehan of Tewksbury is 71, a retired Air Force light colonel who served from 1956–1979. — *Lowell (Massachusetts) Sun*, 27th September 2003

lightem *noun*
crack cocaine *US*
Evocative of the urging 'light 'em up'.
- — Peter Johnson, *Dictionary of Street Alcohol and Drug Terms*, p. 116, 1993

lighten *verb*
▸ **lighten the tongue**
to avoid Creole and make a point of using conventional English *BELIZE*
- — Richard Allsopp, *Dictionary of Caribbean English Usage*, p. 347, 1996

lighten up *verb*
to become less serious, to calm down; to cease aggravating *US, 1946*
Often an imperative; from the conventional sense 'to relieve (the heart or mind)'.
- [W]hy don't you dweebs go out and get a drink and lighten up. — Howard Stern, *Miss America*, p. 20, 1995
- They hand Shona a spliff, telling her to lighten up and be cool. — Karline Smith, *Letters to Andy Cole*, p. 140, 1998

lighter *noun*
a crewcut haircut *US*
Teen slang.
- — *Newsweek*, p. 28, 8th October 1951

light-fingered *adjective*
inclined to thievery *UK, 1547*
- [T]he old man was notoriously light-fingered. — Richard Russo, *Empire Falls*, p. 185, 2001

lightfoot *noun*
a sneak thief *UK*
- — Angela Devlin, *Prison Patter*, p. 72, 1996

light green *noun*
1 a white person; a Caucasian *US*
Marine usage in Vietnam.
- — Linda Reinberg, *In the Field*, p. 128, 1991

2 marijuana, especially inexpensive, low grade marijuana *US*
- After we checked in, I sent the bellboy out to cop some light green. — A.S. Jackson, *Gentleman Pimp*, p. 33, 1973

lighthouse *noun*
in dominoes, a double played by a player who has no matching pieces *US*
- — Dominic Armanino, *Five-up Domino Games*, p. 3, 1964

light housekeeping *noun*
living together as an unmarried couple *US*
- — Hermese E. Roberts, *The Third Ear*, 1971

lightie *noun*
a child *UK*
- Elaine, the lady of the house and mother to many of Sunday's lighties, had died a month ago. — Diran Adebayo, *My Once Upon A Time*, p. 17, 2000

light infantry *noun*
bedbugs, body lice and/or fleas *US*
- — Vincent J. Monteleone, *Criminal Slang*, p. 145, 1949

light in the loafers *adjective*
homosexual *US, 1967*
A wonderful, old-fashioned, euphemism.
- — Jeff Fessler, *When Drag Is Not a Car Race*, p. 11, 1997

lightning *noun*
any amphetamine, methamphetamine or other central nervous system stimulant *US, 1977*
- — National Institute on Drug Abuse, *What do they call it again?*, 1980
- — Mike Haskins, *Drugs*, p. 279, 2003

lightning and thunder *noun*
whisky and soda *US*
- — Lou Shelly, *Hepcats Jive Talk Dictionary*, p. 28, 1945

lightning bug *noun*
a helicopter equipped with a powerful search light or flares, usually teamed with several gunships *US*
- "Think the flares went up?" Myers asked. A lightning-bug mission involves loading up a Huey with a ridiculous number of aerial flares, whose job it is to be highly flammable. — Dennis Marvicsin and Jerold Greenfield, *Maverick*, p. 252, 1990
- — Linda Reinberg, *In the Field*, p. 81, 1991

lightning flash *noun*
LSD *UK*
A variation on **FLASH**.
- Street names [...] hawk, L, lightning flash, Lucy[.] — James Kay and Julian Cohen, *The Parents' Complete Guide to Young People and Drugs*, p. 141, 1998

lightning hashish *noun*
high quality hashish retained by dealers for their own use *US*
- — Ernest Abel, *A Marijuana Dictionary*, p. 62, 1982

Lightning Joe *nickname*
General Joseph Lawton Collins (1896–1987), who served in the US Army in World War 2, as the Army Chief of Staff during the Korean war, and as an early US presence in Vietnam *US*
Collins earned his nickname when his unit, the 25th Infantry Division, drove the Japanese off Guadalcanal.
- — Gregory Clark, *Words of the Vietnam War*, p. 110, 1990

light off *verb*
to experience an orgasm *US*
- The broad's great in the sack and she lights off real easy. — George V. Higgins, *The Friends of Eddie Doyle*, p. 132, 1971

light of love; love *noun*
a prison *governor* *UK*
Rhyming slang.
- — Angela Devlin, *Prison Patter*, p. 72, 1996

light of my life *noun*
a wife *UK*
Rhyming slang, often with ironic or parodic intent.
- — Ray Puxley, *Fresh Rabbit*, 1998

light on *adjective*
in sparse supply of *AUSTRALIA, 1944*
- — Jim Ramsay, *Cop It Sweet!*, p. 55, 1977
- The thing is, I'm a bit light on for the rent. — James McQueen, *Uphill Runner*, p. 145, 1984

light on her feet *adjective*
(of a man) homosexual *US, 1967*
- It's funny, looking at the bats [boots] on that Brenda [policeman], you wouldn't think she was light on her feet, but she is. — the cast of 'Aspects of Love', Prince of Wales Theatre, *Palare (Boy Dancer Talk) for Beginners*, 1989–92

light out *verb*
to leave, especially in a hurry *US, 1865*
- I stopped for a moment on the highway, put the top down and lit out. — Clancy Sigal, *Going Away*, p. 187–188, 1961

light pipe *noun*
fibre optic cable *US*
- — Eric S. Raymond, *The New Hacker's Dictionary*, p. 222, 1991

light rations *noun*
in horse racing, a drastic diet undertaken by a jockey to lose weight *AUSTRALIA*
- — Ned Wallish, *The Truth Dictionary of Racing Slang*, p. 47, 1989

lights *noun*

1 the eyes *UK, 1820*

- —Malachi Andrews and Paul T. Owens, *Black Language*, p. 106, 1973

2 in poker, the chips owed by a player who bet without sufficient funds to back his bet *US*

- —Peter O. Steiner, *Thursday Night Poker*, p. 413, 1996

lights on but there's nobody home; lights on but nobody home

said of someone who appears to be normal but is empty headed *US*

- I wish I could say the same for you. The lights are on, but nobody's home!—Robert Moore, *King, Warrior, Magician, Lover*, p. 148, 1990

lights out!

used to warn of the presence of police *US*

- Its progress throughout the neighborhood is marked by a steady escort of warning sounds: car alarms set off by drug lookouts, signals from teens on bikes, youthful cries of "Five-oh!" and "Lights out!" – street slang indicating cops are in the neighborhood.—*Chicago Tribune*, p. 1N, 24th May 1997

light stuff *noun*

marijuana or any non-addictive illegal drug *US, 1969*

- —Richard A. Spears, *The Slang and Jargon of Drugs and Drink*, p. 314, 1986
- —Mike Haskins, *Drugs*, p. 288, 2003

light up *verb*

1 to light a cigarette or a pipe, etc *UK, 1861*

- As Private Jamie Ferguson, 20, headed over the border he lit up a huge cigar that he had brought along for the moment.—*The Observer*, 23rd March 2003

2 to share drugs with others *US, 1922*

- I couldn't refuse to light my friends up.—Mezz Mezzrow, *Really the Blues*, p. 215, 1946

3 to shoot someone *US, 1967*

- Whichever way you come into it, they got you; any way you move they can light you up.—Ronald J. Glasser, *365 Days*, p. 41, 1971
- —Ann Lawson, *Kids & Gangs*, p. 56, 1994: 'Common African-American gang slang/phrases'

4 to train a police car's red light on a car *US*

- —*American Speech*, p. 270, December 1962: 'The language of traffic policemen'

lightweight *noun*

1 a person who is not taken as a serious threat *US, 1878*

- A guy's a lightweight, sooner or later it shows. He gets nervous, starts to look around; he thinks, Jesus Christ, maybe I'm over my head. —Elmore Leonard, *Gold Coast*, p. 15, 1981

2 a marijuana smoker who cannot consume as much of the drug as others *US, 2001*

- —Simon Worman, *Joint Smoking Rules*, 2001

light years *noun*

an immeasurably great time, distance or style between one thing and another *UK, 1971*

From the conventional measure of the distance light travels in a year.

- There are some scenes at the beach, but the familiar world of Rio is light years away.—*The Guardian*, 3rd January 2003

like *verb*

▸ like a price

in horse racing, to hold a horse back from winning unless the odds on the horse are high *US*

- Sand Bag won't win in the fifth; his stable likes a price, and he is running at even money.—David W. Maurer, *Argot of the Racetrack*, p. 40, 1951

like *adverb*

1 (preceding an adjective) in the manner described *US, 1959*

- [Teresa] Cornelys's genius was to unite the capital's scattered attractions under one centrally placed roof and to advertise like crazy.—*The Guardian*, 7th December 2003

2 in a manner of speaking; as it were *UK, 1778*

- The long coot was puzzled at first, Nora being so good to him like. —Eric Lambert, *The Veterans*, p. 89, 1954
- Is 'er speakin' voice nice like?—Willie Fennell, *Dexter Gets The Point*, p. 42, 1961
- —Dymphna Cusack, *Picnic Races*, p. 212, 1962
- We thought you might write us a bit of a leaflet, like.—Frank Hardy, *The Outcasts of Foolgarah*, p. 99, 1971
- Even though, like, Tiffany's the spittin' image of him.—Kathy Lette, *Girls' Night Out*, p. 25, 1987
- They, like own this big bridge construction company type of fing[.] —Kathy Lette, *Girls' Night Out*, p. 26, 1987

3 (after an adjective) in the manner described *AUSTRALIA, 1867*

Performing the function of the suffix '- ly'.

- You know, the hokey-pokey has been giving a lot of people pleasure over the last few months, regular like[.]—Roy Slaven (John Doyle), *Five South Coast Seasons*, p. 105, 1992

like

as *UK, 1886*

A conventional C16 usage that is now considered poor or unconventional English.

- [T]he Saudis are not a demonstrating kind of people. They don't go out onto the streets like they do in Egypt and Jordan.—*The Guardian*, 25th March 2003

like

1 used for reducing the specificity, precision or certainty of what is being said *US, 1950*

In the wake of disaster, use of 'like' all but disappears. Linguist Geoffrey Nunberg first observed this after shootings at a San Diego high school in March 2001, and language columnist Jan Freeman of the *Boston Globe* made the same observation after the terrorist attacks in New York and Washington on 11th September 2001. There is no need for distance in certain situations.

- Know what Louie says about Be-bop? Lie-anybody can play mistakes; it's what Louie says, so it must be like-true; right, doll?—George Mandel, *Flee the Angry Strangers*, p. 261, 1952
- "Buster," said Red gratefully, "your timing was like the end, ya know?"—Steve Allen, *Bop Fables*, p. 49, 1955
- The word "like" is a staple of the speech. It is used as a form of punctuation, or it may be used as a compliment, a ploy, and even as a substitution for completing a thought.—Robert George Reisner, *The Jazz Titans*, p. 149, 1957
- For example, the hippies in his circle peppered all their choppy, laconic sentences with the word "like," as though they lived in a world not of events but of similitudes, as though there was no reality for them but reminiscence.—Bernard Wolfe, *The Magic of Their Singing*, p. 125, 1961
- Yeah, man, like I'm the one.—Claude Brown, *Manchild in the Promised Land*, p. 134, 1965
- "Murray the K – well, you know," says Susan, "like, he's what's happening." —Tom Wolfe, *The Kandy-Kolored Tangerine-Flake Streamline Baby*, p. 46, 1965
- [T]he deuces-wild use of the word "like" (as in "like, man, you ain't gonna make it with that chick so like you'd best split") is all ghetto idiom.—Nicholas Von Hoffman, *We Are The People Our Parents Warned Us Against*, p. 111, 1967
- [I]t hit me kind of hard. Like it dispelled my dominant illusion. (We youths say "like" all the time because we mistrust reality. It takes a certain commitment to say something is. Inserting "like" gives you a bit more running room.)—James Simon Kunen, *The Strawberry Statement*, p. 101–102, 1968
- It is all like, like, like ... "like help," as the Californian said when he was drowning. They all use "like" in a way that sets my teeth on edge. —Gore Vidal, *Myra Breckinridge*, p. 54, 1968
- There were a few people like from the Mime Troupe who were living in a communal house.—Leonard Wolfe (Editor), *Voices from the Love Generation*, p. 100, 1968
- As she put it (before I forbade her ever again to say like, and man, and swinger, and crazy, and a groove): "It was, like ethics."—Philip Roth, *Portnoy's Complaint*, p. 175, 1969
- They were also likely to say "like" at odd spaces in conversation.—Odie Hawkins, *Scars and Memories*, p. 61, 1987
- Uttering "like" before any other noun or verb may have sought to give dopers time to think, or express some cosmic simile, but it soon became a tedious habit that stuck to everyone's speech patterns. —Sean Hutchinson, *Cry Out Loud*, p. 177, 1988
- I think you are, like, the funniest person I know.—*Romy and Michele's High School Reunion*, 1997
- Well, me and a buddy go to the video arcade in town and, like, they don't speak English right.—*Austin Powers*, 1997
- You've worn that shirt for, like, three days in a row, man!—*American Pie*, 1999
- She said both of her parents were totally embarrassing, but her dad was like, way beyond?—*American Beauty*, 1999

2 habitually used in informal speech as inconsequential ornamentation *US*

- Uttering "like" before any other noun or verb may have sought to give dopers time to think, or express some cosmic simile, but it soon became a tedious habit that stuck to everyone's speech patterns. —Sean Hutchinson, *Cry Out Loud*, p. 177, 1988
- They, like, go shopping, and sometimes they, like, take things and they, like, think it's cool.—*The Guardian*, p. 23, 10th April 2002

3 used as an introduction to a gesture or expression *US*

- Great movie. Amazing special effects. It was like ... (Strike a taken-aback facial expression) [...] I was so happy, I was like ... (Jump and clap hands.)—Maggie Balistreri, *The Evasion-English Dictionary*, p. 53, 2003

▸ **be like**
used for indicating a quotation, or a paraphrase or what was said, or an interpretation of what was said, or a projection of what was thought but not said *US, 1982*
- I was like, naw man, I got a son on the way. — *Boyz N The Hood*, 1990
- — *American Speech*, p. 215–227, Fall 1990: 'I'm like, "Say what?!": A new quotative in American oral narrative'
- This weekend he called me up and he's all, "Where were you today?" and I'm like, "I'm at my grandmother's house." — *Clueless*, 1995
- — Connie Eble (Editor), *UNC-CH Campus Slang*, p. 6, April 1995
- I got stoned and he comes home and he's like, "This apartment smells like pot all the time." And I'm like, "Yeah, 'cause I always smoking it." So then he's like, "I want that smell out of this house." And then he's like, "No, actually, I want you out of this house." — Kenneth Lonergan, *This is Our Youth*, p. 9, 2000
- And maybe one night me and Lunchbox'll be macking some bitch, and she'll be like, "Oooo! I want to suck youse guys's dicks off. What's your names?" And I'll be like, "Jay and Silent Bob." — Kevin Smith, *Jay and Silent Bob Strike Back*, p. 21, 2001
- This is so not a good thing. I'm like – what? — Kevin Sampson, *Clubland*, p. 107, 2002

like anything *adverb*
with vigour or speed; generally, as an intensifier *UK, 1681*
- The day was hot like anything. — Paroo Nihalini, R.K. Tongue and Priya Hosali, *Indian and British English*, 1979

like a plasterer's radio *adjective*
semen-spattered *UK*
As an example: (after oral sex) 'she had a face like a plasterer's radio'.

like as not; as like as not *adverb*
probably, possibly, likely *UK, 1897*
- [I]f [US presidential advisor, Elliot] Abrams had a hand in drawing up that road map [a peace-plan for the Middle East], as like as not it would show a one-way street ending in a cul-de-sac. — *The Observer*, 30th March 2003

like beef?
do you want to fight? *US*
Hawaiian youth usage.
- — Douglas Simonson, *Pidgin to da Max*, 1981

like butter!
nice, smooth, lovely *US*
A catchphrase from a Mike Meyers *Saturday Night Live* skit.
- — Connie Eble (Editor), *UNC-CH Campus Slang*, p. 5, Spring 1992

like hell!
used as an expression of disbelief or contradiction *UK, 1922*
- For a long time after he'd gone, Fischer sat without moving, staring across the great hall. "Like hell," he muttered then. What in the name of God did Barrett expect him to do? — Richard Matheson, *Hell House*, 1999

like it's my job
used as an intensifier *US*
- I have to pee like it's my job. — Connie Eble (Editor), *UNC-CH Campus Slang*, p. 5, November 2003

likely story
used ironically as an expression of profound disbelief *UK, 1984*
- History is craftily tailored to make us believe that yeoman-farmer Mel [Gibson] could have owned a South Carolina tobacco plantation yet kept no slaves (a likely story), and that slaves were overjoyed at the chance to fight on behalf of their owners. — *The Guardian*, 7th July 2000

like no other *adverb*
extremely *US*
- I'm hungry like no other. — Connie Eble (Editor), *UNC-CH Campus Slang*, p. 7, October 2002

like real
used for expressing doubt *SINGAPORE*
- — Paik Choo, *The Coxford Singlish Dictionary*, p. 66, 2002

like that *adjective*
very close (often described with an accompanying gesture) *UK*
May be figurative, metaphorical or – in print – merely abstract.
- [W]hat's left of the Jenners is like that with what's left of Essex. — John Milne, *Alive and Kicking*, p. 242, 1998
- [F]orever telling the other toe-rags down the boozer about how they and Jimbo were "Like Fuckin That", fingers crossed. — J.J. Connolly, *Layer Cake*, p. 68, 2000

likewise
I agree, especially when reciprocating a compliment *CANADA*
Beale, 1984, notes the (parodic) elaboration 'likewise, I'm sure'.

likkle *adjective*
▷ **see:** LICKLE

l'il *noun*
not much *US*
- "So, what's going on?" "L'il." — Connie Eble (Editor), *UNC-CH Campus Slang*, p. 5, Spring 1987

lil *noun*
the female breast *UK*
Usually in the plural.
- She's got magnificent lils. — Davina McCall, *The Brits*, 20th February 2003

l'il *adjective*
little *UK, 1881*
A colloquial contraction.
- You were just being a pissed, stoned, half-naked little cockteaser, sister! Shaking your lil' ass at those boys[.] — Ben Elton, *High Society*, p. 110, 2002

lilac *adjective*
effeminately homosexual *UK*
- — Clement and La Frenais, *Going Straight*, 1978

lill *noun*
the hand *UK*
- — Paul Baker, *Polari*, p. 179, 2002

Lilley and Skinner *noun*
1 dinner *UK*
Rhyming slang; after the shoe shop, established in 1835.
- Might go on for a bit of Lilley and Skinner after. Fancy coming? — *The Sweeney*, p. 6, 1976

2 a beginner *UK*
- — Julian Franklyn, *A Dictionary of Rhyming Slang*, 1961

Lillian Gish *noun*
1 fish *UK, 1960*
Rhyming slang, based on the name of film actress Lillian Gish (1893–1993).
- I took her for some Lillian Gish / Down at the chippy caff[.] — Ronnie Barker, *Fletcher's Book of Rhyming Slang*, p. 21, 1979

2 an act of urination; urine *UK*
Rhyming slang for **PISH**.
- — Michael Munro, *The Patter, Another Blast*, 1988

Lillian Gished *adjective*
drunk *UK: SCOTLAND*
Glasgow rhyming slang for **PISHED**, formed from the name of film actress Lillian Gish (1893–1993).
- — Michael Munro, *The Patter, Another Blast*, 1988

lillies *noun*
the hands *US, 1973*
- — Joseph E. Ragen and Charles Finston, *Inside the World's Toughest Prison*, p. 807, 1962: 'Penitentiary and underworld glossary'

Lilly; Lily; Lilly F-40 *noun*
a capsule of secobarbital sodium, brand name Seconal™, a barbiturate *US*
From the manufacturer.

lily *noun*
1 the penis *US*
Most commonly heard when describing urination as **KNOCK THE DEW OFF THE LILY**.
- "Raise up, little pud, you're bending my lily," Buck slurred. — Earl Thompson, *Tattoo*, p. 242, 1974

2 an ear-trumpet *UK*
Also used figuratively, as in 'get your lily at the key-hole' (to eavesdrop).
- — Patrick O'Shaughessy, *Market Traders' Slang*, 1979

Lily; Lily Law; Lilly Law; Lillian; Lucy Law *noun*
used as a personification of a police officer, especially a policeman; the police *US, 1949*

An example of **CAMP** trans-gender assignment. Lily Law (and Inspector Beastly) are recorded in the supplement to the 5th edition of *A Dictionary of Slang and Unconventional English*, 1961.

- — *Fact*, p. 26, January-February 1965
- — *American Speech*, p. 57, Spring-Summer 1970: 'Homosexual slang'
- [I]f you see Lilly Law approaching just whistle[.] — Barry Humphries, *Bazza Pulls It Off!*, 1971
- — the cast of 'Aspects of Love', Prince of Wales Theatre, *Palare (Boy Dancer Talk) for Beginners*, 1989–92
- The fairies looked up suddenly and one of them screamed, "There comes Lilly Law!" — Herbert Huncke, *Guilty of Everything*, p. 184, 1990

lily on a dustbin *noun*

something out of place; an incongruous thing *AUSTRALIA, 1943*

- One woman says to look like a lily on a dustbin (or garbage or dirt bin) is to dress inappropriately for an occasion and/or to wear over-fussy, frilly clothes. — Nancy Keesing, *Lily on the Dustbin*, p. 14, 1982

lily pad *noun*

a flat disc of wood *CANADA*

British Columbian logging usage.

- A small cross cut of wood, a "lily pad," from the end of a log was sometimes made to bring the log to proper mill length, or a "log pirate" would do it to remove a company brand. — Tom Parkin, *WetCoast Words*, p. 86, 1989

Lily the Pink; Lilly *noun*

a drink *UK*

Rhyming slang, based on 'Lily the Pink' a popular song which begins: 'We'll drink-a-drink-a-drink'.

- "Oi, Bernie you kant [cunt] where we going for a Lilly?" "A fucking what?" "A facking Lilly the Pink, you slay-agg [slag]! — Kevin Sampson, *Outlaws*, p. 172, 2001

lily-white *noun*

1 the hand *US, 1935*

- It wasn't an Old Master, simply a forgery done by my own lily-whites. — Jonathan Gash, *The Ten Word Game*, p. 46, 2003

2 a unidentified terrorist with no history or past suspicion of criminal activity *UK*

Used during a report on a bomb explosion in Ealing, West London, *BBC Television News*, 3rd March 2001.

lily-white *adjective*

populated entirely by white people; discriminating against black people *US, 1903*

- — Helen Dahlskog (Editor), *A Dictionary of Contemporary and Colloquial Usage*, p. 38, 1972
- The word had its origin with the Lily-white movement in the Republican Party in 1888. — Malachi Andrews and Paul T. Owens, *Black Language*, p. 101, 1973

lily whites *noun*

bed sheets *US*

- I sent a substitute in my place and drove straight for home, to stash my frame beween a deuce of lily-whites. — Mezz Mezzrow, *Really the Blues*, p. 101, 1946

lima *noun*

marijuana *UK, 1998*

Possibly implying Peruvian cultivation.

- — Mike Haskins, *Drugs*, p. 288, 2003

limb *noun*

▸ **on the limb**

in horse racing, said of a horse forced to the outside *US*

- — George Sullivan, *Harness Racing*, p. 104, 1964

▸ **out on a limb**

in a difficult or exposed position *US, 1897*

- Labour MPs who went out on a limb to support the Iraq war are hopping mad that the back-bench rebel Chris Mullin has been rewarded with ministerial office. — *New Statesman*, 30th June 2003

limberneck *noun*

in electric line work, a lineman's helper or groundman *US*

So named because of the need to look upwards all day.

- — A.B. Chance Co., *Lineman's Slang Dictionary*, p. 11, 1980

limbo *noun*

1 a prison *UK, 1590*

- — Hyman E. Goldin et al., *Dictionary of American Underworld Lingo*, p. 126, 1950

2 marijuana cultivated in Columbia *US, 1981*

Possibly derived from the effect of intoxication.

- — Richard A. Spears, *The Slang and Jargon of Drugs and Drink*, p. 315, 1986

limbo log *noun*

in mountain biking, a tree limb overhanging the trail at approximately face height *US*

- — William Nealy, *Mountain Bike!*, p. 161, 1992: 'Bikespeak'

limburger *noun*

a girl who cannot get a date *US*

From the song 'Dance this Mess Around' by the B-52's.

- — Connie Eble (Editor), *UNC-CH Campus Slang*, p. 5, Fall 1984

limby; limbie *noun*

an amputee, especially a member of the armed forces who has lost a limb *NEW ZEALAND*

- There were eight hundred men on the ship including a number of limbies. — William Taylor, *Twilight Hour*, p. 106, 1978

lime *verb*

1 to take part in an informal gathering *TRINIDAD AND TOBAGO, 1941*

- — Lise Winer, *Dictionary of the English/Creole of Trinidad & Tobago*, 2003

2 in the illegal production of alcohol, to whitewash the interior of a fermenter *US*

- We got to lime them boxes. — David W. Maurer, *Kentucky Moonshine*, p. 120, 1974

lime acid *noun*

LSD *US, 1970*

- — Richard A. Spears, *The Slang and Jargon of Drugs and Drink*, p. 315, 1986
- — Mike Haskins, *Drugs*, p. 285, 2003

limer *noun*

an idler *BARBADOS, 1964*

- — Richard Allsopp, *Dictionary of Caribbean English Usage*, p. 349, 1996

limeskin *noun*

a worn-out felt hat *BARBADOS*

- — Frank A. Collymore, *Barbadian Dialect*, p. 67, 1965

limey *noun*

a Briton *US, 1917*

Derives, as an abbreviation of 'lime-juicer', from the compulsory ration of lime juice that was issued in the British Navy; originally used of British immigrants in Australia, New Zealand and South Africa; in this more general sense since 1918.

- [A] new pack of slimy Limeys was coming on over the transistors[.] — Lester Bangs, *Psychotic Reactions and Carburetor Dung*, p. 57, 1970

limey *adjective*

British *AUSTRALIA, 1888*

- My first plunge into foly was getting a limey bike, an insult that i only partially redeemed by destroying it in a high-speed crash and laying me head open. — Hunter S. Thompson, *Hell's Angels*, p. 200, 1966

limit *noun*

the maximum prison sentence for a given offence *US*

- — Vincent J. Monteleone, *Criminal Slang*, p. 146, 1949

▸ **go the limit**

to have sexual intercourse *US, 1922*

- Several times then, she had nearly gone the limit, as they used to call it, but something had always saved her – once a campus policeman but mostly the boy himself, who had scruples. — Mary McCarthy, *The Group*, p. 256, 1960
- — Kenn "Naz" Young, *Naz's Dictionary of Teen Slang*, p. 72, 1993

▸ **the limit**

the degree of anything that is the extreme (or beyond) of what you are prepared to tolerate *US, 1904*

It may be 'the dizzy limit', 'the giddy limit' or 'just about the fucking limit'.

▸ **the sky's the limit**

the possibilities of something are boundless *UK, 1933*

- "The sky's the limit now," said the Swedish goalkeeper Magnus Hedman[.] — *The Guardian*, 13th June 2002

limo *noun*

a *limo*usine *US, 1929*

- The world's comin' to an end, I don't even care / As long as I can have a limo and my orange hair. — Cheech Marin and Tommy Chong, *Earache My Eye!*, 1974
- Had twice seen her come out of the hotel with three guys, one of them a big jig, and another woman and get in the limo he followed to the condo in Ventnor. — Elmore Leonard, *Glitz*, p. 186, 1985

limo *adjective*
luxurious *UK*
From the luxury afforded by a LIMO (a limousine).
- [T]he limo treatment accorded to hot cinema property[.]— *Sunday Express*, p. 7, 30th May 1982

limp *verb*
in poker, to reserve the right to make a bet even though the player has a good hand *US*
- —John Scarne, *Scarne's Guide to Modern Poker*, p. 283, 1979

limp *adjective*
drunk *US*
- —Ralph de Sola, *Crime Dictionary*, p. 84, 1982

limp dick; limp prick *noun*
someone who is weak or cowardly *US, 1970*
The flaccid DICK (penis) as a symbol of impotency.
- Vinnie, you limp dick, I saw you sneak back into your office.—Janet Evanovich, *Seven Up*, p. 37, 2001

limper *noun*
a defective used car *US*
- Then one day I'm sitting there looking at this limper.—Joseph Wambaugh, *The Black Marble*, p. 194, 1978

limp out; limp *verb*
to relax *US*
- —Vann Wesson, *Generation X Field Guide and Lexicon*, p. 106, 1997

limp wrist *noun*
an effeminate man, almost always homosexual; used as a symbol of homosexuality *US*
- Manifestations of this are seen in the number of jokes about the limp wrist set, and the occasional reports of homosexuals.— *Berkshire (Massachusetts) EVening Eagle*, 18th September 1950
- "[A]t the same time depriving him of cunt and subjecting him to homosex stimulation. Then drugs, hypnosis, and -" Benway flipped a limp wrist.—William Burroughs, *Naked Lunch*, p. 27, 1957
- — *Fact*, p. 26, January-February 1965
- Four went to me and a limp-wrist friend / And the fifth went to his main girl.—Dennis Wepman et al., *The Life*, p. 62, 1976
- I reminded her that Boke Kellum was a limp wrist.—Dan Jenkins, *Semi-Tough*, p. 172, 1979
- Comedian Chevy Chase says he was only kidding when he limp wristedly referred to Cary Grant as a "homo" and "what a gal" on a TV talk show[.]— *San Francisco Examiner*, p. 11, 1st September 1982
- He looked like a peroxided limpwrist from Santa Monica Boulevard is what he looked like.—Joseph Wambaugh, *The Delta Star*, p. 130, 1983
- Nervous tittering turned to robust laughter the other night at Nick's as Greg Roman showed his audience that openly gay comics can be funny without campy props, limp wrists and Judy Garland imitations.— *Boston Globe*, p. 51, 22nd june 1993
- Don't you think there are more homos who don't go to bars than those who do? I think that's just a stereotype, like limp wrists or having superb fashion sense.— *Phoenix (Arizona) New Times*, 4th December 2003

limpy-go-fetch *noun*
a disabled person *US*
- The labels were cruel: Gimp, Limpy–go-fetch, Crip, Lift-one-drag one, etc. Pint, Half-a-man, Peewee, Shorty, Lardass, Pork, Blubber, Belly, Blimp. Nuke-knob, Skinhead, Baldy. Four-eyes, Specs, Coke bottles.— *San Francisco Examiner*, p. A15, 28th July 1997

limpy up *adjective*
disabled *BAHAMAS, 1966*
- —John A. Holm, *Dictionary of Bahamian English*, p. 124, 1982

Lincoln *noun*
1 a five-dollar note *US*
- —Lou Shelly, *Hepcats Jive Talk Dictionary*, p. 13, 1945
- Then, when we get out of this cold shack we'll make a pile of Lincolns. —Red Rudensky, *The Gonif*, p. 22, 1970

2 a five-dollar prostitute *US*
- A resident prostitute of any stature won't take his clothes off for less than $10. And frequently they get $15 and $20. Sailors are usually what are called LINCOLNS. They are eager to supplement their income with homosexual acts for as little as five dollars.— *KFRC radio, San Francisco*, 8th November 1965: 'The Market Street proposition'

Lincoln drop *noun*
the small tray near a shop's cash till with pennies which customers may use for making exact payments *US*
- —Anna Scotti and Paul Young, *Buzzwords*, p. 70, 1997

Lincoln Tunnel *noun*
in homosexual usage, a loose anus and rectum *US*
Homage to the tunnel connecting New Jersey and Manhattan.
- — *Male Swinger Number 3*, p. 45, 1981: 'The complete gay dictionary'

line *noun*
1 a dose of powdered cocaine arranged in a line for snorting *US, 1973*
- "Have a line," said the doctor. "Things go better with coke." —Armistead Maupin, *Tales of the City*, p. 300, 1978
- With a razor he cuts the pile into four big lines and then he hands me a rolled up twenty and I lean down and do a line.—Bret Easton Ellis, *Less Than Zero*, p. 32, 1985
- Roy's taken a small sample out of the main stash and he chops two fat lines out on to the mirror.—J.J. Connolly, *Know Your Enemy [britpulp]*, p. 141, 1999
- —Nick Constable, *This is Cocaine*, p. 182, 2002

2 a vein, especially in the context of injecting drugs *US, 1938*
- I bit down on my bottom lip waiting for the stabbing plunge of the needle. He said, "Damn! You got some beautiful lines."—Iceberg Slim (Robert Beck), *Pimp*, p. 131, 1969

3 political philosophy *US*
An important term of the New Left in the US, often modified by 'correct', a precursor of political correctness.
- The Strike Education Committee people were edged out of the Liberation School organization. It became more and more narrow and elitist. A teacher was told he couldn't teach courses because he didn't have the right line.—James Simon Kunen, *The Strawberry Statement*, p. 123–124, 1968

4 an assembly line in a factory *US*
- "De-troit," Buddy said. "I spent three years on the line up there at Chrysler Jefferson till I went crazy and had to quit."—Elmore Leonard, *Out of Sight*, p. 62, 1996

5 collectively, the prostitutes in a brothel who are available for sex at a given moment *US*
- — *Maledicta*, p. 150, Summer/Winter 1986–1987: 'Sexual slang: prostitutes, pedophiles, flagellators, transvestites, and necrophiles'

6 an attractive female *AUSTRALIA, 1941*
- In addition to being 'fabulous drops' these were also 'slashing lines'.—Nino Culotta (John O'Grady), *They're A Weird Mob*, p. 46, 1957

7 a special verbal approach, especially as an introduction to seduction *UK, 1903*
A chat-up line.

8 in the business of dealing with stolen goods, twice the actual price *US*
- Folks, my ticker almost stopped when Buster cracked on you for the line on the stuff. Line means the actual price doubled. It's inside code that jewelers, pawnbrokers and fences use.—Iceberg Slim (Robert Beck), *Trick Baby*, p. 229, 1969

9 the area housing a prison's general population *US*
- —James Harris, *A Convict's Dictionary*, p. 35, 1989
- Why don't they blood test her, yank her off the line?—Seth Morgan, *Homeboy*, p. 256, 1990

10 in sports betting, the points or odds established by a bookmaker that govern the bet *US*
- Even when they're being real generous with the line, I think can beat the spread, I lay off.—John Sayles, *Union Dues*, p. 25, 1977
- —Avery Cardoza, *The Basics of Sports Betting*, p. 44, 1991

11 money *US*
- —David Claerbaut, *Black Jargon in White America*, p. 71, 1972

▸ **do a line**
1 to inhale a measured dose of a powdered drug, especially cocaine *US, 1979*
- —Richard A. Spears, *The Slang and Jargon of Drugs and Drink*, p. 451, 1986
- —Mike Haskins, *Drugs*, p. 291, 2003

2 to make an amorous approach; to date *AUSTRALIA, 1934*
- Now there is a man I could do a line with any time.—Kylie Tennant, *The Honey Flow*, p. 107, 1956
- Pat's with a gross new girl again. Must be doing a line with her.—Noel Hilliard, *The Power of Joy*, p. 266, 1965
- A certain machine-gunner from 'C' company 7RAR was doing a line on a young French/Vietnamese bar girl in the Jade massage parlour in Vung Tau.—Martin Cameron, *A Look at the Bright Side*, 1988

▸ **down the line**
a psychiatric hospital *NEW ZEALAND*
- It was a place nobody mentioned much and was called 'down the line'.—Dell Adsett, *The Magpie Sings*, p. 64, 1963

▸ on the line

1 at risk *US, 1940*

- Our stripes [used symbolically of rank] will be on the line for this. — *Dixon of Dock Green*, 12th March 1968
- Careers on the line as hearings get under way. — *The Guardian*, 11th August 2003

2 at stake, in jeopardy *UK*

- [H]e knows it's his arse on the line — Lanre Fehintola, *Charlie Says...*, p. 99, 2000

3 in combat, especially aerial combat *US*

- When they were done with their first period "on the line" (in combat) and were heading back to the Philippines for a week's break, the deck housing the pilots would be locked off from the rest of the ship[.] — Robert K. Wilcox, *Scream of Eagles*, p. 37, 1990

line crosser *noun*

in the Korean war, a soldier who crossed the main line of resistance to find and retrieve prisoners of war *US*

- By chance someone, perhaps an IBM machine, turned up the fact that earlier in his career, he had been a line crosser in Korea. — David Halberstam, *One Very Hot Day*, p. 91, 1967

line doggy *noun*

an infantry soldier *US, 1967*

- — Linda Reinberg, *In the Field*, p. 128, 1991
- — John Algeo and Adele Algeo, *American Speech*, p. 392, Winter 1991: 'Among the new words'

line duty *noun*

in the language surrounding the Grateful Dead, the hours spent waiting in a queue to buy tickets or to enter a concert venue *US*

- — David Shenk and Steve Silberman, *Skeleton Key*, p. 178, 1994

line forty

used for expressing the price of twenty dollars *US*

- [L]ine forty means the price is twenty dollars[.] — Mezz Mezzrow, *Really the Blues*, p. 220, 1946

line jumper *noun*

an enemy spy who sneaks across allied lines *US*

Korean war usage.

- Roving patrols snoop around anyway, hunting for linejumpers (Korean or Chinese spies that have gotten through out M.I.R. and are trying to cross the river). — Martin Russ, *The Last Parallel*, p. 148, 1957

linemaker *noun*

in a sports betting operation, the oddsmaker *US, 1976*

- — Thomas L. Clark, *The Dictionary of Gambling and Gaming*, p. 119, 1987

linen *noun*

a letter *US*

- For the last six months listeners had "knocked" 2,500 to 3,000 "hunks of linen" a week to the 1290 Club's M.C., young (28), vacant-faced Fred Robbins. — *Time Magazine*, p. 92, 20th January 1947

linen draper; linen *noun*

a newspaper *UK, 1857*

Rhyming slang.

- Obviously what the linens call a national disaster of the first magnitude had occurred[.] — Charles Raven, *Underworld Nights*, p. 74, 1956
- Marchmare's had more publicity in the linens[.] — Derek Raymond (Robin Cook), *The Crust on its Uppers*, p. 23, 1962
- [Y]et another con perpetuated on the Great British Public, just like those geezers in the linens who dole out the 'Spot the Ball' largesse[.] — Andrew Nickolds, *Back to Basics*, p. 55, 1994

liner *noun*

a short promotional statement recorded for a radio station by a famous artist or personality, professing that they listen to that station *US*

Heard on FM radio in San Francisco, California, March 2001.

liners *noun*

cash *US*

- Candy, markers, ammo, liners, stocking stuffer, sweetener, garnish, and pledges are all terms for cash. — Henry Hill and Byron Schreckengost, *A Good Fella's Guide to New York*, p. 123, 2003

lines *noun*

1 cocaine *UK*

A multiple of LINE (a single dose of cocaine); used in contemporary gay society.

- — *Attitude*, p. 60, July 2003: 'New palare lexicon'

2 money *US*

- — Kenn "Naz" Young, *Naz's Underground Dictionary*, p. 44, 1973

▸ do lines

to use cocaine *US*

- — Connie Eble (Editor), *UNC-CH Campus Slang*, p. 3, Fall 2001

▸ get lines

in bodybuilding, to achieve definition, or well-developed and sculpted muscles *US*

- — *American Speech*, p. 199, Fall 1984: 'The language of bodybuilding'

line screw *noun*

a prison guard assigned to a cell block *US*

- — John R. Armore and Joseph D. Wolfe, *Dictionary of Desperation*, p. 39, 1976

line storm *noun*

an equinoctial gale, at the time of the solstice *CANADA*

- A "line storm" is a Nova Scotia name for the "auction gale" or equinoctial storm, especially fierce, at the solstice or "line of crossing" from one season of the year to the next. — Helen Creighton, *Bluenose Magic*, p. 78, 1960

line swine *noun*

a driver who appears oblivious to traffic lanes *US*

- — *American Speech*, p. 270, December 1962: 'The language of traffic policemen'

line-up *noun*

1 serial sex between one person and multiple partners *US, 1913*

- — Dale Kramer and Madeline Karr, *Teen-Age Gangs*, p. 175, 1953
- The "line-up" is a standard part of street life. Boys often "con" a girl into having intercourse, then, regardless of her protests, invite half a dozen other adolescents to share her. — Harrison E. Salisbury, *The Shook-up Generation*, p. 32, 1958
- There is the sexual ambivalence in the gang's exclusion of girls from its activities and then suddenly forcing some luckless girl to submit to the gang "shag," or "lineup," where each member of the gang waits his turn for sexual relations with the female victim. — Herbert Block and Arthur Neiderhoffer, *The Gang*, p. 104, 1958
- So this rape was in fact a line-up? Yes. It was against my will. You have been a party to line-ups on several occasions? I probably have, but if so, I was under the influence of alcohol and I can't remember them. — *Truth*, p. 39, 3rd February 1970
- An old Barnum hand remarked to me that these line-ups remind him very much of Sunday Morning scenes in front of Welsh mining town whore houses[.] — Joe McKennon, *Circus Lingo*, p. 58, 1980
- She turned herself on thinking about having a line-up with them. She fantasised about being gang-banged by the whole tribe[.] — Kevin Sampson, *Powder*, p. 393, 1999

2 the place where waves line up to break *AUSTRALIA*

- — Jack Pollard, *The Australian Surfrider*, p. 18, 1963

3 a display of the prostitutes available for sex in a brothel at a given moment *US*

- As I inspected the lineup, she came in late from doing some shopping in town. — Gerald Paine, *A Bachelor's Guide to the Brothels of Nevada*, p. 106, 1978

line up *verb*

to arrange *US, 1906*

- Now, it seems, they [Everton]'re at it again after lining up a £2.5m approach for West Brom's Jason Koumas. — *The Guardian*, 24th November 2003

line work *noun*

the addition of fine lines or other markings on the design of a card to aid a cheat *US*

- — John Scarne, *Scarne's Guide to Modern Poker*, p. 283, 1979

lingo *noun*

slang or another unconventional English language dialect, jargon or vocabulary *UK, 1859*

Conventional 'lingo' (since 1660) is 'a contemptuous designation for a foreign tongue'.

- It would seem logical to head north, to Manchester, Glasgow, Liverpool [...] Never been there. Don't speak the lingo. Would get lost. — Mark Powell, *Snap*, p. 102, 2001
- [I]t sounds like courtroom lingo. — Kevin Sampson, *Outlaws*, p. 57, 2001

linguist *noun*

a person who enjoys performing oral sex *US*

Leading, inevitably, to cunning puns.

- — Dale Gordon, *The Dominion Sex Dictionary*, p. 101, 1967
- — *Maledicta*, p. 198, Winter 1980: 'A new erotic vocabulary'

linguistic exercise *noun*

oral sex *US*

- — Roger Blake, *The American Dictionary of Sexual Terms*, p. 123, 1964

lingy *noun*
the penis *BAHAMAS*
• —John A. Holm, *Dictionary of Bahamian English*, p. 124, 1982

link *noun*
a police officer, prosecutor or judge who has been bribed *US*
• —R. Frederick West, *God's Gambler*, p. 227, 1964: 'Appendix A'

▸ **the link**
a person who provides what is needed at a particular moment *US*
From the conventional 'missing link'.
• Said to a person walking in with a six-pack. "Man, you are THE LINK." —Connie Eble (Editor), *UNC-CH Campus Slang*, p. 6, Fall 1986

linked *adjective*
1 dating (someone) steadily and exclusively *US*
• —*San Francisco Examiner*, p. 17, 17th June 1966: 'Teen slanguage: real shark'
2 bribed *US*
• —R. Frederick West, *God's Gambler*, p. 227, 1964: 'Appendix A'

Link the Chink *noun*
any Vietnamese person *US*
War usage.
• I had come to view the enemy in Vietnam as a real monster, as a threat to my personal security, something which had to be stopped and squashed. Phrases like "gook" and "link the chink" and "luke the gook," stuff we used in training got solidly into my head. —John Kerry, *The New Soldier*, p. 96, 1971
• —Linda Reinberg, *In the Field*, p. 128, 1991

lion *noun*
1 a greatly respected or revered Rastafarian; a great soul *JAMAICA*
• [T]here were many who shared the views of the old lion dread. —Donald Gorgon, *Cop Killer*, p. 111, 1994
2 in pool, a skilled and competitive player *US*
• —Steve Rushin, *Pool Cool*, p. 20, 1990

Lionel Bart; Lionel *noun*
a fart *UK*
• —Bob Young and Micky Moody, *The Language of Rock 'n' Roll*, p. 90, 1985

Lionel Blair *noun*
a chair *UK*
Rhyming slang, based on the name of UK dancer and entertainer Lionel Blair (b.1931).
• [H]is daughter was sitting by the Jeremiah [fire], on her favourite Lionel Blair. —Ronnie Barker, *Fletcher's Book of Rhyming Slang*, p. 27, 1979

Lionel Blairs; lionels *noun*
flares (trousers with flared legs) *UK*
Rhyming slang, formed from the name of the UK dancer and entertainer (b.1931).
• —Ray Puxley, *Cockney Rabbit*, 1992
• [T]he jolly old sawn-off went out with sideboards and radiograms, three-piece whistles with twenty-four inch lionels[.] —J.J. Connolly, *Layer Cake*, p. 8, 2000

lion food *noun*
mid-management *US*
From a joke, the punch-line of which features a lion boasting of eating one IBM manager a day and nobody noticing.
• —Eric S. Raymond, *The New Hacker's Dictionary*, p. 223, 1991

lion's lair *noun*
a chair *UK*
• —Ray Puxley, *Cockney Rabbit*, 1992

lions roar *noun*
snoring *UK*
Rhyming slang.
• —Ray Puxley, *Cockney Rabbit*, 1992

lions roar *verb*
to snore *UK*
Rhyming slang.
• —Ray Puxley, *Cockney Rabbit*, 1992

lion's share *noun*
a chair *UK*
Rhyming slang.
• —Ray Puxley, *Cockney Rabbit*, 1992

lip *noun*
1 impudence; talking back *UK, 1803*
• Don't you take any lip from him, Governor —Clive Exton, *No Fixed Abode [Six Granada Plays]*, p. 138, 1959
• We took an oath not to hurt anybody on our way up, but we said it was okay to use some lip if you started to slip. —Dan Jenkins, *Life Its Ownself*, p. 53, 1984
• You'll have plenty of lip, arguments, but get 'em outta here. —Josh Alan Friedman, *Tales of Times Square*, p. 52, 1986
• —Connie Eble (Editor), *UNC-CH Campus Slang*, p. 6, March 1986
2 a lawyer, especially a criminal defence lawyer *US, 1929*
From the image of a lawyer as a mouthpiece.
• —Lou Shelly, *Hepcats Jive Talk Dictionary*, p. 13, 1945
• I don't need a bondsman or a lip now. You don't have a 'sheet.' —Iceberg Slim (Robert Beck), *Pimp*, p. 114, 1969
• —Clarence Major, *Dictionary of Afro-American Slang*, p. 77, 1970
3 in the car sales business, a potential buyer *US*
• —Jim Crotty, *How to Talk American*, p. 36, 1997

lip *verb*
1 in horse racing, to win by the slightest of margins *AUSTRALIA*
• —Ned Wallish, *The Truth Dictionary of Racing Slang*, p. 47, 1989
2 to kiss *US*
• —Marcus Hanna Boulware, *Jive and Slang of Students in Negro Colleges*, 1947

lip in *verb*
to interrupt *US, 1899*
• —Hyman E. Goldin et al., *Dictionary of American Underworld Lingo*, p. 127, 1950

lip it *verb*
to stop talking *UK*
• But we lipped it for a bit. They simmered down. —Jeremy Cameron, *Brown Bread in Wengen*, p. 215, 1999

lipkisser *noun*
a regular practitioner of oral sex on women *US*
• —*American Speech*, p. 19, Spring 1985: 'The language of singles bars'

lip-lock *noun*
oral sex performed on a man *US, 1976*
• Why, there's a broad there who'll whip a lip lock on you that'll scorch your shorts and curl the hairs on the back of your neck to look like pig's tails[.] —Larry Heinemann, *Close Quarters*, p. 171, 1977

lip music *noun*
bragging, boasting, teasing *US*
• —William K. Bentley and James M. Corbett, *Prison Slang*, p. 49, 1992

lipo *noun*
liposuction, a surgical procedure for the cosmetic removal of fat *UK*
By elipsis, back to the root of many other biochemical terms.
• PATSY: Surgery. Lipo, on the hips and stomach, bum lift, tit lift, lose a rib. —Jennifer Saunders, *Absolutely Fabulous*, p. 34, 1992

lipper *noun*
a pinch of chewing tobacco *US*
• —Pamela Munro, *U.C.L.A. Slang*, p. 86, 1997

lippie; lippy *noun*
lipstick *AUSTRALIA, 1955*
• —David McGill, *David McGill's Complete Kiwi Slang Dictionary*, p. 80, 1998
• Once a year, usually New Year's Eve, she'd put some lippie on and come down the pub. —Phillip Gwynne, *Deadly Unna?*, p. 157, 1998
• On her lips she wore fuscia lippy[.] —Gretel Killeen, *Hot Buns and Ophelia get shipwrecked*, p. 23, 2001
• [A] woman's right to wear lippy and always be on a diet, yet not be called an airhead. —Alexis Petridis, *The Guardian*, p. 38, 1st June 2002

lippy *adjective*
impudent, impertinent; talkative *US, 1865*
From **LIP** (impudence). With an 1803 UK usage of 'lip' as 'back-chat', the likelihood of an earlier adjective sense is high.
• Listen, you lippy bastard. —George Mandel, *Flee the Angry Strangers*, p. 226, 1952
• [F]acing up to lippy hooligans and getting Kung Fu kicks on the shoulder. —Anthony Masters, *Minder*, p. 8, 1984
• Or it might be a bouncer gives him a clout, says he's too lippy[.] —Nicholas Blincoe, *The Beautiful Beaten-up Irish Boy of the Arndale Centre*, p. 10, 1998
• MACCA: They was gettin' all lippy like... BUNNY: Dey was bad-mouthin' us. —Chris Baker and Andrew Day, *Lock, Stock... & One Big Bullock*, p. 334, 2000
• He told me I was a stupid, lippy 16-year-old. —Jimmy Stockin, *On The Cobbles*, p. 84, 2000

lip read *verb*
to kiss *UK, 1974*
An inspired use of a conventional method of understanding what someone else says and means.

lips *noun*
▸ **your lips are bleeding!**
used sarcastically to someone using big words *AUSTRALIA*
Juvenile.
• —Sidney J. Baker, *Australia Speaks*, 1953

lips!
used as a cry to summon a makeup artist to apply more lipstick to a performer *US*
• —*Adult Video News*, p. 48, August 1995

lip service *noun*
oral sex *US*
• —Xaviera Hollander, *The Best Part of a Man*, 1975

lipsin' *noun*
the act of kissing, snogging *UK*
Collected from teenage boys in August 2002.

lip-sloppy *adjective*
talkative to a fault *US*
• —*Dobie Gillis Teenage Slanguage Dictionary*, 1962

lip spinach *noun*
a moustache *US*
• —Helen Dahlskog (Editor), *A Dictionary of Contemporary and Colloquial Usage*, p. 38, 1972

lipstick *noun*
1 in the new and used car business, purely cosmetic touches *US*
• Some cars just give you a quick lipstick job and try and pass themselves off as new.—Chrysler Corporation, *Of Anchors, Bezels, Pots and Scorchers*, September 1959
• The car was basically lunched, but the service department had added some lipstick.—Stephen Cannell, *King Con*, p. 29, 1997
2 a grease pencil *US*
Used by first aid workers to note tourniquet time on an injured person.
• —*American Speech*, p. 270, December 1962: 'The language of traffic policemen'
▸ **lipstick on your dipstick**
oral sex performed on a man *US*
• —*Current Slang*, p. 20, Spring 1970

lipstick lesbian; lipstick *noun*
a feminine, stylish, upwardly mobile lesbian *US*
• Was it time to relent, to throw in the towel and become a lipstick lesbian?—Armistead Maupin, *Babycakes*, p. 59, 1984
• [A] beautiful Latina lipstick lesbian by the name of Janet Canarias has taken the alderman's seat away from Delvin in the Twenty-seventh[.]—Robert Campbell, *Cat's Meow*, p. 22, 1988
• I even passed up a chance to run for alderman, which maybe was just as well because I had a feeling that Janet Canarias, the Puerto Rican lipstick lesbian who whumped the regular Democratic organization's candidate, would've whumped me too.—Robert Campbell, *In a Pig's Eye*, p. 2, 1991
• —Jeff Fessler, *When Drag Is Not a Car Race*, p. 26, 1997
• People think it's cute, because they've got this fool picture in their heads about lipstick lesbians – like they all resemble Alyssa – while most of them look more like you.—*Chasing Amy*, 1997

Lipton's *noun*
poor quality marijuana *US, 1964*
An allusion to a popular, if weak, tea.
• —Clarence Major, *Dictionary of Afro-American Slang*, p. 77, 1970

lip up!
stop talking!; say nothing! *UK*
A variation of BUTTON YOUR LIP!.
• —Bad Manners, *Lip up Fatty*, 1980

lip work *noun*
oral sex on a woman *US*
• —Dale Gordon, *The Dominion Sex Dictionary*, p. 101, 1967

LIQ *noun*
an off-licence (liquor store) *US*
• —*Current Slang*, p. 9, Fall 1970

liquid *noun*
money, cash *UK*
Abbreviated from 'liquid assets'.
• Kingsley's givin' me a headache. Callin' in my liquid which I ain't got[.]—Nick Barlay, *Curvy Lovebox*, p. 30, 1997

liquid cosh *noun*
any tranquillizer or sedative used by prison authorities to subdue an inmate *UK*
• —Angela Devlin, *Prison Patter*, p. 72, 1996
• [Y]ou're off down to seg [a segregation unit]. Dose of liquid cosh might be in order.—Chris Baker and Andrew Day, *Lock, Stock... & A Good Slopping Out*, p. 426, 2000

liquid courage *noun*
the bravado produced by alcohol *US, 1942*
• —Judi Sanders, *Kickin' like Chicken with the Couch Commander*, p. 15, 1992
• What are you waiting for, run outta liquid courage?—*Kill Bill*, 2003

liquid diet *noun*
used humorously for describing a period when someone is drinking a lot of alcohol *US*
• —Judi Sanders, *Don't Dog by Do, Dude!*, p. 20, 1991

liquid ecstasy; liquid e *noun*
the recreational drug GHB *US*
• People say it's an animo acid, and it's all natural, but it's really a drug, like liquid Ecstasy.—*Los Angeles Times*, p. B1, 3rd November 1993
• —Angela Devlin, *Prison Patter*, p. 72, 1996
• GHB has been marketed as a liquid or powder and has been sold on the street under names such as Grevious Bodily Harm, Georgia Home Boy, Liquid Ecstasy, Liquid X, Liquid E, GHB, GBH, Soap, Scoop, Easy Lay, Salty Water, G-Riffick, [and] Cherry Menth.—*Morbidity and Morality Weekly Report*, p. 281, 4th April 1997
• Backstage, spirits were high and liquid Ecstasy flowed freely. "I got completely and utterly fucked up on the first night."—*Uncut*, p. 54, May 2001

liquid gold; LG *noun*
amyl or butyl nitrate *UK*
From the appearance and brand name.
• —Angela Devlin, *Prison Patter*, p. 71, 1996
• Street names [...] Amyl, liquid gold, locker room[.]—James Kay and Julian Cohen, *The Parents' Complete Guide to Young People and Drugs*, p. 144, 1998

liquid grass *noun*
tetrahydrocannabinol, the purified pyschoactive extract of marijuana *US*
• —*Current Slang*, p. 15, Spring 1971

liquid laugh *noun*
vomiting *AUSTRALIA, 1964*
• Now I've had liquid laughs in bars / And I've hurled from moving cars / And I've chucked where and when it suited me.—Barry Humphries, *The Wonderful World of Barry McKenzie*, p. 15, 1968
• All them liquid laughs I had on the boat have left me feelin' weak as piss!—Barry Humphries, *Bazza Pulls It Off!*, 1971
• Liquid Laughter – Vomit.—Ryan Aven-Bray, *Ridgey Didge Oz Jack Lang*, p. 35, 1983
• —David McGill, *David McGill's Complete Kiwi Slang Dictionary*, p. 80, 1998

liquid lunch *noun*
alcohol but no food for lunch *US, 1963*
• We kicked off with a liquid laugh[.]—Barry Humphries, *A Nice Night's Entertainment*, p. 80, 1964
• Liquid Lunch. Ice with that, sir?—*Code*, p. 103, January 2002

liquid sky *noun*
heroin *US*
• —Carsten Stroud, *Close Pursuit*, p. 269, 1987

liquid sunshine *noun*
rain *UK*
• —Frank McKenna, *A Glossary of Railwaymen's Talk*, 1970

liquid wrench *noun*
alcohol *US*
Like a wrench, alcohol will loosen things.
• —John Vorhaus, *The Big Book of Poker Slang*, p. 25, 1996

liquid X *noun*
the recreational drug GHB *UK*
• Also known as Liquid X, it was manufactured as an anaesthetic for operations, but went out of use because of unpredictable side-effects.—*The Independent*, p. 2, 1st August 1993

- GHB has been marketed as a liquid or powder and has been sold on the street under names such as Grevious Bodily Harm, Georgia Home Boy, Liquid Ecstasy, Liquid X, Liquid E, GHB, GBH, Soap, Scoop, Easy Lay, Salty Water, G-Riffick, [and] Cherry Menth. — *Morbidity and Morality Weekly Report*, p. 281, 4th April 1997

liquored up *adjective*
drunk *US, 1924*
Current use in South Carolina.
- — *e-cyclopaedia*, 20th March 2002

liquorhead *noun*
a drunkard *US, 1923*
- [T]hey shunned guys on the white stuff just like vipers shun liquorheads. — Mezz Mezzrow, *Really the Blues*, p. 248, 1946

liquorice stick *noun*
▷ see: LICORICE STICK

Lisa *noun*
a perfect, idealised girlfriend *US*
- — Judi Sanders, *Faced and Faded, Hanging to Hurl*, p. 25, 1993

listener *noun*
a person whose only role in conversation is to listen and verify what was said *US*
- When Angelo got there, with Charley as his listener, Hanly had brought along a police captain named Kiely from the PC's squad. — Richard Condon, *Prizzi's Honor*, p. 215, 1982

listen up!
used for commanding attention *US*
Almost always heard in the imperative.
- Listen up, don't try to sound pretty. Just belt it out. — *Reno Evening Gazette*, p. 22, 9th November 1962

lister bag *noun*
a water bag *US*
World War 2, Korean and Vietnam war usage.
- Water bags, called "lister bags," were set up on tripods. — Robert Mason, *Chickenhawk*, p. 359, 1983
- Doc, do you have to empty all your iodine bottles into that lister bag? — William B. Hopkins, *One Bugle No Drum*, p. 67, 1986

Listerine *adjective*
anti-American *UK*
The name of a branded antiseptic applied as a punning extension of rhyming slang for SEPTIC TANK (an American).
- — Stephen Fry, *Q.I.*, 13th November 2003

lit *adjective*
drunk *US, 1899*
- Like I said, he was always pretty well lit back in New York. — Raymond Chandler, *The Long Goodbye*, p. 209, 1953
- Nothing is more beautiful than four lit stooges in a graveyard spieling on[.] — John Nichols, *The Sterile Cuckoo*, p. 155, 1965
- — Collin Baker et al., *College Undergraduate Slang Study Conducted at Brown University*, p. 151, 1968

-lit *suffix*
literature, when in combination with a defining style *UK*
- Classified by snooty critics as another one of the trivial "Chick Lit" brigade, she [Jenny Colgan] coined the alternative term Bliggers, meaning Brit Lit It Girls. — *The Guardian*, 28th March 2001

lit crit *noun*
*lit*erary *crit*icism *UK*
- His [Terry Eagleton's] Literary Theory: An Introduction, a punchy synopsis of other writers' ideas first published 20 years ago, must be the best-selling work of lit crit ever. — *The Guardian*, 29th November 2003

lite; -lite *adjective*
denotes a less-substantial version of an original *US, 1962*
In widespread use; a re-spelling of 'light', devised as a commercial strategy to sustain a brand name while advertisng that the product's less-marketable ingredients (sugar, nicotine, etc.) have been reduced.
- That Labour Lite should continue to fortify its centre-right comfort zone [...] was no great surprise. — Christopher Brookmyre, *Boiling a Frog*, p. 18, 2000
- When I saw this episode of The Liver Birds again, it seemed much more shockingly reactionary and joke-lite than memory served. — Stuart Jeffries, *Mrs Slocombe's Pussy*, p. 118, 2000
- The girls are the same. Lowlife lite, they are – no finesse about them. — Kevin Sampson, *Outlaws*, p. 244, 2001
- Radio 1 prides itself of new spelling: def, lite, blak, tekno, dreem and teem. — *The Sunday Times*, p. 13, 23rd June 2002
- Grunge lite [...] A lighter, poppier version of grunge. — *'The Sunday Times Magazine*, p. 50, 1st June 2003: 'The parents' guide to the music maze'

literally *adverb*
used as an intensifier *UK, 1937*
In colloquial use this is generally employed inaccurately or hyperbolically.
- I put everything I owned in the world to fund this legal action – I personally will have literally nothing left. — *The Guardian*, 23rd December 1999

litterbug *noun*
a person who drops litter *US, 1947*
- This city is famous for its gamblers, prostitutes, exhibitionists, Antichrists, alcoholics, sodomites, drug addicts, fetishists, onanists, pornographers, frauds, jades, litterbugs, and lesbians[.] — John Kennedy Toole, *A Confederacy of Dunces*, p. 3, 1980

litter lout *noun*
a person who drops litter *UK, 1927*
- [I]t's comparatively pristine – though litter louts do tend to spoil the place. — Phil Lee, *The Rough Guide to Mallorca*, p. 233, 2001

Little and Large *noun*
margarine *UK*
Rhyming slang for MARGE, formed from the name of a comedy double act.

little bird; little birdie *noun*
an unnamed source *UK*
- Mind you, a little birdie told me he knew one of the reps[.] — Colin Butts, *Is Harry on the Boat?*, p. 44, 1997
- A little bird reckoned you might know something about it. — Diran Adebayo, *My Once Upon A Time*, p. 47, 2000

little bit *noun*
a prostitute *US*
- There's always a little bit at that truck em up stop about this time. — Lanie Dills, *The Official CB Slanguage Language Dictionary*, p. 45, 1976

little black book *noun*
1 an address book containing clients' names and telephone numbers, especially in an illegal enterprise *US*
- Xaviera Hollander admits to paying "$5,000 down" for her little black book when she went out of the business and Hollander went into it. — Leonard Shecter and William Phillips, *On the Pad*, p. 34, 1973
- Police vice squadders who raided Brandy Baldwin's bordello in Forest Hill are chortling over the Little Black Book, which contains some of the more illustrious names in local clubdom. — *San Francisco Chronicle*, p. 21, 8th January 1980

2 a (notional) notebook in which bachelors are reputed to keep girls' telephone numbers *AUSTRALIA, 1984*

little black gun *noun*
the M-16 rifle *US*
Vietnam war usage.
- — Carl Fleischhauer, *A Glossary of Army Slang*, p. 31, 1968

little black worker *noun*
▷ see: BLACK-COATED WORKER

little blister *noun*
a younger sister *AUSTRALIA*
Rhyming slang.
- — James Lambert, *The Macquarie Book of Slang*, 1996

little blues *noun*
capsules of the synthetic opiate oxycodone used recreationally *US*
- Extracts reproduced in the tabloid show Limbaugh referring to "small blue babies" and "the little blues." — *Broward Business Review*, p. 1, 18th November 2003

little bomb *noun*
1 an amphetamine capsule or tablet *UK, 1998*
Possibly a direct translation of Spanish BOMBITA (an amphetamine capsule).
- — Mike Haskins, *Drugs*, p. 279, 2003

2 heroin *UK, 1998*
- — Mike Haskins, *Drugs*, p. 284, 2003

Little Bo Peep *noun*
▷ see: BO PEEP

little boy *noun*
a small, cocktail frankfurter sausage *NEW ZEALAND*
• —Louis S. Leland, *A Personal Kiwi-Yankee Dictionary*, p. 24, 1984
• [T]he kids were wolfing into party pies, sausage rolls and little boys (cheerios in Queensland)[.]—Paul Vautin, *Turn It Up!*, p. 115, 1995

little boy blue *noun*
a prison officer *UK*
Rhyming slang for SCREW.
• —Ray Puxley, *Cockney Rabbit*, 1992

little boys' room *noun*
a toilet, especially one for men *US, 1935*
Juvenile and jocular.
• If I'm at your house, I can never say to you, "Excuse me, where's the toilet?" I have to get hung up with that corrupt facade of "Excuse me, where's the little boys' room?"—Lenny Bruce, *How to Talk Dirty and Influence People*, p. 152, 1965
• FREDDY: So I tell the connection I'll be right back, I'm goin' to the little boys room.—*Reservoir Dogs*, 1992

little brown jug *noun*
a sink or bath *plug*, an electric *plug*; a tampon *UK*
Rhyming slang.
• —Ray Puxley, *Cockney Rabbit*, 1992

little casino *noun*
in a deck of playing cards, the two of spades *US*
• —George Percy, *The Language of Poker*, p. 52, 1988

little cat *noun*
in poker, a hand comprised of five cards between three and eight and no pairs among them *US*
• —Irwin Steig, *Common Sense in Poker*, p. 185, 1963

little D *noun*
a tablet of hydromorphone (trade name Dialudid™), a narcotic analgesic *US*
• —Richard A. Spears, *The Slang and Jargon of Drugs and Drink*, p. 217, 1986

little death *noun*
an orgasm *UK, 1999*
Often in the verb phrase 'have a little death'.
• Five images that will stop the "Little Death". Hold them in your head to mentally prevent nature taking its course.—*Loaded*, p. 9, June 2002

Little Detroit *nickname*
Van Dien, North Vietnam *US*
Like Detroit, Van Dien was highly industrialised.
• —Linda Reinberg, *In the Field*, p. 129, 1991

little Dick; little Dick Fisher *noun*
in craps, a four *US*
• A borrowing from the early C18 language of the game of hazard. A 4 is "Little Dick" or "Little Joe from Kokomo".—Sidney H. Radner, *Radner on Dice*, p. 10, 1957
• —Thomas L. Clark, *The Dictionary of Gambling and Gaming*, p. 119, 1987

little dog *noun*
in poker, a hand comprised of five cards between two and seven and no pairs among them *US*
• —Irwin Steig, *Common Sense in Poker*, p. 185, 1963

little fella *noun*
1 a child (of either gender) *UK*
• They are two boss [wonderful] little fellas, them two.—Kevin Sampson, *Clubland*, p. 113, 2002

2 a tablet of MDMA, the recreational drug best known as ecstasy *UK*
• —Dave Courtney, *Dodgy Dave's Little Black Book*, p. 8, 2001

little friend *noun*
a fighter plane *US, 1944*
• —*American Speech*, p. 310, December 1946: 'More air force slang'

little girls' room *noun*
a toilet, especially one for women *US, 1949*
• She kept saying these very corny, boring things, like calling the can the "little girls' room"...—J.D. Salinger, *Catcher in the Rye*, p. 74, 1951
• —Collin Baker et al., *College Undergraduate Slang Study Conducted at Brown University*, p. 151, 1968
• I gotta go to the little girls' room—Richard Condon, *Prizzi's Money*, p. 112, 1994

little green friends *noun*
marijuana buds *UK*
• —Mike Haskins, *Drugs*, p. 288, 2003

little guy; little man; little people *noun*
a Japanese soldier; a Viet Cong or soldier in the North Vietnamese Army *US, 1950*
• It's kind of dark anyway, but we ain't calling in no medevac bird to tell the little guys and the world where we are, you got it?—Charles Anderson, *The Grunts*, p. 45, 1976
• A little man drags himself away with his rifle under one arm, held level, pushing at the grass with his good leg, pulling with his free arm.—Larry Heinemann, *Close Quarters*, p. 76, 1977
• —Linda Reinberg, *In the Field*, p. 129, 1991

little guy with the helmet *noun*
the penis *US*
• —Erica Orloff and JoAnn Baker, *Dirty Little Secrets*, p. 69, 2001

little Harlem *noun*
a black ghetto *US*
• Baltimore's Little Harlem – Pennsylvania Avenue – is more peaceful than the Negro section of any other large town we ever gandered. —Jack Lait and Lee Mortimer, *Washington Confidential*, p. 272, 1951
• O what times we get when I hit Frisco loaded with loot & maybe Persian hasheesh & we carry wire recorder to little Harlem & also use it to record fucking-sounds in beds, etc.—Jack Kerouac, *Letter to Neal Cassady*, p. 327, 9th October 1951
• "Wheeoo! let's go!" cried Dean, and we jumped in the back seat and clanked to the little Harlem on Folsom Street.—Jack Kerouac, *On the Road*, p. 196, 1957

little help *noun*
a linear amplifier for a citizens' band radio *US*
• —Bill Davis, *Jawjacking*, p. 61, 1977

little Hitler *noun*
a self-important person who wields a small amount of official authority with despotic zeal *UK, 1957*
• That copper. [Re]Member that fat fucker with-a blond hair? Little fuckin Hitler. Squeaky-voiced cunt.—Niall Griffiths, *Sheepshagger*, p. 160, 2001

little house *noun*
an outside toilet *AUSTRALIA, 1886*
• Downstairs, he could smell the black tin in the little house down the yard.—David Ireland, *The Unknown Industrial Prisoner*, p. 80, 1971
• —David McGill, *David McGill's Complete Kiwi Slang Dictionary*, p. 80, 1998
• —Lise Winer, *Dictionary of the English/Creole of Trinidad & Tobago*, 2003

Little Italy *noun*
a neighbourhood populated by a large number of Italian immigrants and Italian-Americans *US*
• A man who had hammered himself off the streets of Little Italy to a position so powerful that for years he dictated to law enforcement agencies[.]—Red Rudensky, *The Gonif*, p. 57, 1970

little Jack Horner *noun*
▷ see: JACK HORNER

little jobs *noun*
urination by a child *AUSTRALIA*
• Oh! You mean when Bazzie did little jobs in the road and the policeman shone his torch at Bazzie's tummy banana...—Barry Humphries, *The Wonderful World of Barry McKenzie*, p. 12, 1968

little Joe *noun*
a roll of four in craps *US, 1890*
Often elaborated with a rhyming place name, in the pattern 'little Joe from Kokomo' (or Chicago, Idaho, Lake Tahoe, Mexico, Ohio, Tokyo).
• "Little Joe from Kokomo," one of the coloured fellows murmured, looking at me.—Chester Himes, *If He Hollers Let Him Go*, p. 32, 1945
• —Frank Garcia, *Marked Cards and Loaded Dice*, p. 262, 1962
• There for a while all I could hear was "snake eyes," "little joes," and "carp out, Lord." It was lovely.—Guy Owen, *The Flim-Flam Man and the Apprentice Grifter*, p. 117, 1972
• —Chris Fagans and David Guzman, *A Guide to Craps Lingo*, p. 15, 1999

little Joe in the snow *noun*
cocaine *US*
• —William K. Bentley and James M. Corbett, *Prison Slang*, p. 49, 1992

little Judas *noun*
the sliding door in a confession box *IRELAND*
• 'Go in peace then, my child,' the priest murmurs. 'Say a prayer for me.' The little Judas slides shut. —Aidan Higgins, *Donkey's Years*, p. 78, 1995

Little Korea *nickname*
Fort Leonard Wood, Missouri *US*
Based on a comparison of the climates.
• —Carl Fleischhauer, *A Glossary of Army Slang*, p. 32, 1968
• Known as a "Little Korea" of climatic extremes, Fort Wood is a place where soldiers swelter in humid summers and freeze in meat-locker winters. —*Newsday (New York)*, p. 4 (Section II), 4th October 1989

little lady *noun*
the wife *AUSTRALIA, 1917*
• [A]nyway, that's the main thing. The little lady had a really good time. —Sandra Jobson, *Blokes*, p. 157, 1984

little lunch *noun*
a mid-morning break at school *AUSTRALIA*
• —Nancy Keesing, *Lily on the Dustbin*, p. 120, 1982

little madam; proper little madam *noun*
a spoilt, conceited or bad-tempered female child *UK, 1787*
• Reese Witherspoon plays Tracy Flick, a smug and prissy little madam, standing unopposed for election as class president[.] —*The Guardian*, 21st August 1999

little man *noun*
1 the penis *UK, 1998*
• —A.D. Peterkin, *The Bald-Headed Hermit & The Artichoke*, 1999

2 a tradesman *UK*
An upper- or middle-class female's patronising term.
• I have a little man deliver from the village twice a week. — Beale, 1984

▷ see: LITTLE GUY

little man in a boat; little man; man in the boat; boy in the boat *noun*
the clitoris *UK, 1896*
The 'little man' or 'boy' represent the clitoris as a small penis, and the vulva is imagined to be boat-shaped.
• —Alan Richter, *Sexual Slang*, p. 28, 1993
• Avoid putting pressure on the little man in the canoe until it seems very aroused. —Anka Radakovich, *The Wild Girls Club*, p. 131, 1994
• It is a small man-in-a-boat – she obviously hasn't masturbated a lot. —Clarence Major, *All-Night Visitors*, p. 8, 1998
• —Erica Orloff and JoAnn Baker, *Dirty Little Secrets*, p. 71, 2001

little Miss Muffet *verb*
used as an emphatic rejection *UK*
Rhyming slang for 'stuff it', formed from the name of a nursery rhyme character.
• You can take your advice and little Miss Muffet up your gonga-pooch. —Ray Puxley, *Cockney Rabbit*, 1992

little muggins *noun*
your child *UK*
From MUGGINS (yourself, as a fool).
• [I]t is you and little muggins will be eating grapes in a noisy hospital ward[.] —James Hawes, *Dead Long Enough*, p. 22, 2000

little Nell *noun*
a door *bell* *UK*
Rhyming slang, formed from the name of a Charles Dickens' heroine.
• —Ray Puxley, *Cockney Rabbit*, 1992

little office *noun*
the toilet *AUSTRALIA*
• I didn't know a man with your commitments had time to visit the 'little office'. —Barry Humphries, *A Nice Night's Entertainment*, p. 185, 1981

little old lady in tennis shoes *noun*
used as a stereotype of an energetic, quirky old woman *US*
In 1972, *Sports Illustrated* titled an article about tennis great Hazel Wightman (1886–1974) 'The Little Old Lady in Tennis Shoes'.
• Which is all well and good, except that the Little Old Lady in Tennis Shoes (a most dreadful symbol for a city) isn't what she used to be[.] —Bill Cardoso, *The Maltese Sangweech*, p. 113, 1984

little people *noun*
▷ see: LITTLE GUY

little peter *noun*
a gas or electric meter *UK*
Rhyming slang.
• —Ray Puxley, *Cockney Rabbit*, 1992

little pigs *noun*
small sausages *US*
• —*American Speech*, p. 88, April 1946: 'The Language of west coast culinary workers'I

little ploughman *noun*
the clitoris *US*
• —*Maledicta*, p. 184, Winter 1980: 'A new erotic vocabulary'

little R *noun*
during the Korean and Vietnam wars, rest and rehabilitation *US*
Distinguished from the BIG R (rotation home).
• Korean Bamboo English —*American Speech*, p. 121, May 1960
• —Linda Reinberg, *In the Field*, p. 129, 1991

littles *noun*
in pool, the solid-coloured balls numbered 1 to 7 *US*
• —Steve Rushin, *Pool Cool*, p. 6, 1990

little Saigon *nickname*
a neigbourhood with a large number of Vietnamese immigrants and businesses *US*
• Do is one of more than a dozen Vietnamese who have set up shop in Clarendon, turning a retailing center once known as "Northern Virginia's downtown" into an area often referred to by Americans as "Little Saigon," the "Mekong Delta" or even the "Ho Chi Min Trail".
— *Washington Post*, p. A1, 23rd September 1979
• The neighborhood is called Little Saigon. In this one-block strip you will find four Vietnamese markets – Pacific Department Store, Mekong Center, Vietnam Market and Saigon Market. —*Washington Post*, p. E1, 17th January 1980
• They say that Vietnamese thugs from Westminster's Little Saigon can strip a radio out of a Mercedes faster than you can tune it to a Dodgers game. —Joseph Wambaugh, *The Golden Orange*, p. 177, 1990

Little Sir Echo *noun*
a person who always agrees with his superiors *AUSTRALIA*
• —Ned Wallish, *The Truth Dictionary of Racing Slang*, p. 47, 1989

little sisters *noun*
a group of US magazines aimed at women *US*
• —Rachel S. Epstein and Nina Liebman, *Biz Speak*, p. 131, 1986

little smoke *noun*
marijuana *UK, 1998*
• —Mike Haskins, *Drugs*, p. 288, 2003

little thing *noun*
a bullet *UK*
• —Dave Courtney, *Dodgy Dave's Little Black Book*, p. 7, 2001

little Tokyo *noun*
an urban neighbourhood with a high concentration of Japanese people *US*
• Only in Little Tokyo the'd have to kill and be killed[.] —Chester Himes, *If He Hollers Let Him Go*, p. 77, 1945
• Filipinois are not concentrated in any section, but many live on N. LaSalle near Little Tokyo. —Jack Lait and Lee Mortimer, *Chicago Confidential*, p. 73, 1950

little white mouse *noun*
a tampon *AUSTRALIA, 1996*
Used euphemistically in mixed company.

little woman *noun*
the wife *UK, 1795*
Intentionally archaic, revoltingly coy, and condescending.
• He still feels free to philander all over the town because he knows his little woman is keeping the home fires burning. —Sue Rhodes, *And when she was bad she was popular*, p. 35, 1968
• Comes home and the little woman sends him to the store. —Elmore Leonard, *Killshot*, p. 106, 1989

little wooden hill *noun*
▷ see: WOODEN HILL

littlie; littley *noun*

a child *AUSTRALIA, 1953*

- Remember when you were a littlie and you used to sneak out in the middle of the night to check the tree and see if Santa had left something? — Paul Vautin, *Turn It Up!*, p. 116, 1995
- 'The "old hands", the "big kids" from Kindergarten 2003 at St Francis Xavier's School in Lurnea, have been playing host to the "littlies", the class of 2004. — *The Catholic Weekly (Australia)*, 23rd November 2003

littl'un *noun*

a child *AUSTRALIA*

- Had the luck to catch a trading schooner making for the Islands, and there was Josh beachcombing away happily on one of them, with a coupla dusky belles dancing attendance on him, and a brood of not so dusky littl'uns rolling around like chocolate balls. — Dymphna Cusack, *Picnic Races*, p. 218, 1962

lit up *adjective*

drunk or drug-intoxicated *US, 1899*

- We were both lit up pretty well when we staggered up from the table that morning. — Donald Goines, *Whoreson*, p. 41, 1972

live *verb*

▸ **live caseo**

to cohabit for sexual purposes *UK*

From 'caseo' (a brothel/overnight hire of a prostitute).

- They picked up a pair of judies who were attracted to their soldierly bearing, and lived caseo with them. — Charles Raven, *Underworld Nights*, p. 45, 1956

▸ **live it up**

to have a good time, to enjoy an extravagent lifestyle *US, 1951*

- [T]ens of thousands of scroungers determined to live it up at the expense of the long-suffering taxpayer[.] — *The Observer*, 3rd August 2003

▸ **live large**

to enjoy a life full of material pleasures *US, 1975*

- He say he gonna be livin' large. — *Stephen Cannell, 'King Con'*, p. 50, 1997
- — Connie Eble (Editor), *UNC-CH Campus Slang*, p. 7, Fall 1999
- The video cemented Jay-Z's reputation as hip-hop's smoothest hustler, and 'big pimpin' became slang for living large. — *New Yorker*, p. 74, 20th August 2001

▸ **live on the smell of an oil rag**

to live on very meagre means *AUSTRALIA, 1903*

- The poor old Poms can live on the smell of an oil rag but we're used to a decent standard of living back home. — Barry Humphries, *The Wonderful World of Barry McKenzie*, p. 38, 1968
- — Barry Humphries, *A Nice Night's Entertainment*, p. 103, 1968

live *adjective*

1 (used of the potential customer of a prostitute) eager to spend money *US*

- Just like to any professional, time is money to the girls and they want to be sure they are latching on to what they call a "live John." — *Screw*, p. 12, 3th November 1969

2 in horse racing, said of a horse that has attracted heavy betting *US*

- It's a way to have some fun – because you've got a "live" horse, one with a lot of money going for it, and you've got an overlay. — Jimmy Snyder, *Jimmy the Greek*, p. 215, 1975

3 extreme, intense, exciting, good *US*

- — *New York Times*, 12th April 1987

4 impressive *US*

- — Trevor Cralle, *The Surfin'ary*, p. 69, 1991

live bait *noun*

one young drug user selling drugs to other young users *US, 1951*

- — *American Speech*, p. 27, February 1952: 'Teen-age hophead jargon'

lived-in look *noun*

a complete mess *US*

- — Collin Baker et al., *College Undergraduate Slang Study Conducted at Brown University*, p. 152, 1968

live gaff *noun*

a premises that is occupied whilst being burgled *UK*

Based on **GAFF** (a place of residence or business).

- He infiltrates – breaks in is much too noisy a word for him – into a live gaff during the small house[.] — Charles Raven, *Underworld Nights*, p. 10, 1956

live gig *verb*

to masturbate; to have sex *UK*

Rhyming slang for **FRIG**.

- — Bodmin Dark, *Dirty Cockney Rhyming Slang*, 2003

live long and prosper

used as a humorous parting *US*

From the original *Star Trek* television series.

- Dinah's pimp Jack was there, and he took the forty and went out saying enjoy yourself my friend and live long and prosper. — William T. Vollman, *Whores for Gloria*, p. 41, 1991

livener *noun*

1 a dose of cocaine *UK*

Abbreviated from conventional 'enlivener', ascribing to cocaine the bracing attributes of a pick-me-up; an earlier (late C19) use was as 'the first drink of the day'.

- There was a decent little stack [of cocaine] there, enough for a bump now and another livener in an hour or so. — Kevin Sampson, *Powder*, p. 128, 1999

2 any alcoholic drink that serves as a pick-me-up *UK, 1887*

live one *noun*

a person worth noticing *US, 1896*

- Tell him you may have a 'live one' out here. — Terry Southern, *Now Dig This*, p. 131, 2001

liverish *adjective*

having symptoms loosely diagnosed as the result of a disordered liver *UK, 1896*

Coined for an advertisment.

- I am, apparently, dehydrated and liverish. And it's my duodenum that has been crying out all this time[.] — *The Observer*, 10th November 2002

Liverpool kiss *noun*

1 a head butt to your opponent's face *UK*

A regional variation of the **GLASGOW KISS**.

- But I can give you the Liverpool Kiss if you like. Or the Geordie Biscuit. [Quoting Keith Richard] — *Courier-Mail*, 8th March 1986
- This was after David Joseph, the Neath player, had head-butted his opponent, or having delivered a 'Liverpool kiss,' as my American pal colourfully described it. — *The Times*, 6th November 1987

2 a blow struck on the mouth *UK*

- — Hy Lit, *Hy Lit's Unbelievable Dictionary of Hip Words for Groovy People*, p. 50, 1968

liver rounds *noun*

used in a hospital as humorous code for a drinking party to be held on hospital grounds *US*

- — *Maledicta*, p. 33, 1988–1989: 'Medical maledicta from San Francisco'

live, spit and die *noun*

LSD *UK*

An elaboration of the initials.

- — Mike Haskins, *Drugs*, p. 285, 2003

liveware *noun*

1 a human being *UK, 1966*

A playful evolution of 'software' and 'hardware'.

- — Karla Jennings, *The Devouring Fungus*, p. 222, 1990

2 a living organism *US*

- Waiter, there's some liveware in my salad. — Eric S. Raymond, *The New Hacker's Dictionary*, p. 226, 1991

live wire *noun*

a male homosexual *UK*

Prison slang, current February 2002.

living daylights; daylights *verb*

life; spirit *UK, 1960*

Ultimately from 'daylights' (the eyes) but here in the consequent sense, 'vitality or vital organs'.

- Enron secured the distinction of being the only corporation to be the subject of an Amnesty International report after it hired goons to beat the living daylights out of villagers protesting against pollution from a power plant in India. — *The Guardian*, 20th January 2002
- 'Al Qaeda [...] was not decimated; it was sufficiently undecimated to murder 34 people, injure 200 and scare the daylights out of Americans everywhere. — Greg Pierce, *The Washington Times*, 29th May 2003

living shit; living crap

used in combination with various transitive verbs to intensify the action to a severe level *US*

- Caldwell on the mound that night for Milwaukie, and i hit the living shit out of his change of speed. — *Playboy*, p. 112, September 1983
- [R]iffs hit like laser bolts as Raymond Herrera ... pounds the living shit out of electronic kit[.] — *Metal Hammer*, p. 4, May 2001

livity *noun*

a vocation or calling in life *JAMAICA, 1992*

A Rastafarian term.

- — Peter Patrick, *Some Recent Jamaican Creole Words*, 2003

livvener *noun*

an alcoholic drink *UK*

Probably from **LIVENER** (a drink that serves as a pick-me-up).

- — Patrick O'Shaughessy, *Market Traders' Slang*, 1979

lizard *noun*

1 an uncooperative, dirty hospital patient with scaly skin *US*

- — *Journal of American Folklore*, p. 568 – 581, January – March 1978: 'The gomer'
- — Sally Williams, *"Strong" Words*, p. 149, 1994

2 the penis *US, 1962*

- — Eugene Landy, *The Underground Dictionary*, p. 121, 1971

3 a mechanical device used by card cheats to hold cards in the player's sleeve *US*

- — George Percy, *The Language of Poker*, p. 53, 1988

▸ **flog the lizard; drain the lizard**

(of a male) to urinate *AUSTRALIA*

- Do you reckon there's time to flog the lizard before me item! — Barry Humphries, *The Wonderful World of Barry McKenzie*, p. 20, 1968
- 7. Drain the lizard – go to the toilet. [in a list of slang] — *Sun-Herald (SundayLife!)*, p. 6, 1998

lizard hit *noun*

the last draw on a water pipe *US*

- It tastes bad and makes you stick your tongue out like a lizard. — Jim Emerson-Cobb, *Scratching the Dragon*, April 1997

lizards *noun*

lizard-skin shoes *US*

- — Edith A. Folb, *runnin' down some lines*, p. 245, 1980

lizard scorcher *noun*

a railway cook *US*

- — Ramon Adams, *The Language of the Railroader*, p. 94, 1977

lizzie *noun*

a lesbian *UK, 1949*

- Another Lesbian moved in with her, and everytime I went to Marian's apartment, there was this huge red-haired Lizzie watching me with her cold fish-eyes full of stupid hate. — William Burroughs, *Junkie*, p. 30 – 31, 1953
- Where the aggressive Lizzie was a guest in the hotel and invited her passive partner up to her room, we would merely notify the desk, so that the next time the woman tried to register in, she would find it difficult. — Dev Collans with Stewart Sterling, *I was a House Detective*, p. 103, 1954
- Those charming young ladies over there are erstwhile lizzies from Cash's old boarding school[.] — Robert Gover, *Poorboy at the Party*, p. 13, 1966

Lizzie *noun*

a car, especially a Ford *US, 1913*

A shortened form of 'Tin Lizzie' (the US stock market nickname for the Ford Motor Company).

- This Lizzie may not look good but she'll run over the top of them mountains like a mountain goat. — Mezz Mezzrow, *Really the Blues*, p. 132, 1946

LK; LK Clark; Elkie Clark *noun*

a mark, a place and time of starting *UK*

Rhyming slang.

- We get off the L.K. at nine. — Julian Franklyn, *A Dictionary of Rhyming Slang*, 1962

LL *noun*

marijuana *UK, 1998*

A play on the name of rap artist and film actor LL Cool J: **COOL** (agreeble) and **J** (a **JOINT**).

- — Mike Haskins, *Drugs*, p. 288, 2003

LLDB *noun*

the special forces of the Army of the Republic of Vietnam *US*

- But in some of the camps, particularly working with the LLDB – Lousy Little Dirty Bastards – the Vietnamese Special Forces, there was a tremendous sense of frustration. — Al Santoli, *To Bear Any Burden*, p. 97, 1985

llesca *noun*

marijuana *US, 1970*

From Portugese *lhesca* (tinder). Similar to **YESCA** which derives in the same way from Spanish.

- — Richard A. Spears, *The Slang and Jargon of Drugs and Drink*, p. 318, 1986
- — Mike Haskins, *Drugs*, p. 288, 2003

Lloyd's List *adjective*

drunk *UK*

Rhyming slang for **PISSED**, formed from the title of the newspaper that reports maritime news.

- — Ray Puxley, *Fresh Rabbit*, 1998

loach *noun*

during the Vietnam war, a light observation helicopter *US*

From the initials LOH.

- — Ronald J. Glasser, *365 Days*, p. 243, 1971
- They flew crews of two men in light observation helicopters, LOH's, except everybody called them loaches. — Dennis Marvicsin and Jerold Greenfield, *Maverick*, p. 179, 1990

load *noun*

1 an ejaculation's-worth of semen *US, 1927*

- I moved my raw and swollen penis, perpetually in dread that my loathsomeness would be discovered by someone stealing up me just as I was in the frenzy of dropping my load. — Philip Roth, *Portnoy's Complaint*, p. 18, 1969
- Carri was really hip to handling a black motherfucker with his over-sized dick and his ability to fuck on after he's dropped his load. — A.S. Jackson, *Gentleman Pimp*, p. 85, 1973
- And when she mounts him, displaying one of the roundest, hottest, most perfect butts in creation (the ancient Greeks would have deified her), it's hard to resist shooting your second load. — *Adult Video*, p. 13, August/September 1986
- She sucked when she was told to suck. To swallow that load you cunt. — Peter Sotos, *Index*, p. 119, 1996
- They'll squirt their load and sit in it just to see how the story ends. — *Boogie Nights*, 1997
- The most honest moment in a man's life is the five minutes after he's blown a load. That's a medical fact. — *Something About Mary*, 1998

2 any sexually transmitted infection *AUSTRALIA, 1936*

- — Thommo, *The Dictionary of Australian Swearing and Sex Sayings*, p. 81, 1985

3 a stock of illegal drugs *UK*

- — Home Office, *Glossary of Terms and Slang Common in Penal Establishments*, July 1978

4 25 bags of heroin *US, 1969*

It is interesting to note that a 'half load' adds up to 15 bags (of heroin).

- — Robert Ashton, *This Is Heroin*, p. 209, 2002

5 a dose of a drug *US*

- [O]n the day of the party he went overboard with a big load and slept through till his mother came home. — Hal Ellson, *The Golden Spike*, p. 67, 1952

6 a codeine pill combined with a Doriden™ sleeping pill, producing an opiate-like effect *US*

- — Geoffrey Froner, *Digging for Diamonds*, p. 41, 1989

7 a state of intoxication *US*

- He seemed like one of those steady, all-day drinkers – always with a load on, but never wobbly. — Marvin Wald and Albert Maltz, *The Naked City*, 1947
- "I saw him in Joe's bar before," Steven said. "He was getting a real load on the way he looked." — Hal Ellson, *Tomboy*, p. 118, 1950
- It's pretty hard to hang around the island without taking on a load. — Jim Thompson, *The Nothing Man*, p. 194, 1954
- A guy gets half a load on. He mouths off. — *Goodfellas*, 1990
- And then he'd go home with his load on, dreaming his dreams, pass out, get up the next day[.] — Richard Price, *Clockers*, p. 379, 1992

8 fabricated evidence *AUSTRALIA*

- — *The (Sydney) Bulletin*, 26th April 1975

9 an inept, ludicrous, stupid or unpleasant person *US, 1950*

- — Collin Baker et al., *College Undergraduate Slang Study Conducted at Brown University*, p. 152, 1968
- Bert Parks was a load! — Howard Stern, *Miss America*, p. ix, 1995

10 a car *US, 1937*

- Boy, with a load like that, would I have me a time. — Irving Shulman, *The Amboy Dukes*, p. 52, 1947
- Cruise around in a load like that with the top down and a pair of shades and some sharp clothes and ya have ta beat the snatch off with a club. — Hubert Selby Jr, *Last Exit to Brooklyn*, p. 28, 1957

11 a car in poor condition *US, 1937*

- — *Cars*, p. 40, December 1953

▸ **get a load of**
to look at; to observe *US, 1922*
• Get a load of the pash-session! Somebody's on a good wicket there. —W.R. Bennett, *Target Turin*, p. 74, 1962
• Gawd, get a load of that mug. —John Wynnum, *Tar Dust*, p. 35, 1962
• —Frank Hardy, *The Yarns of Billy Borker*, p. 147, 1965

▸ **take a load off**
to sit down *US, 1922*
• I gestured to the armchair. 'Take a load off.' —Armistead Maupin, *Maybe the Moon*, p. 155, 1992

load *verb*
1 to fabricate evidence *AUSTRALIA*
• — *The (Sydney) Bulletin*, 26th April 1975
2 to alter (dice); to weight (dice) to score a certain point *US*
• —Frank Garcia, *Marked Cards and Loaded Dice*, p. 262, 1962
• —John S. Salak, *Dictionary of Gambling*, p. 148, 1963

load call *noun*
in a telephone swindle, a repeat call to a recent victim *US*
• —M. Allen Henderson, *How Con Games Work*, p. 221, 1985: 'Glossary'
• —Kathleen Odean, *High Steppers, Fallen Angels, and Lollipops*, p. 133, 1988

loaded *adjective*
1 drunk or drug-intoxicated *US, 1879*
The abbreviated variation of a mainly obsolete range of similes beginning 'loaded to'.
• He's just loaded, honey. — *Rebel Without a Cause*, 1955
• Boy, you are loaded! —Max Shulman, *Rally Round the Flag, Boys!*, p. 143, 1957
• The stumplifter boy, looking like a pellet regurgitated by an owl, woke her up at dawn, so she was again loaded as I shuffled into breakfast. —John Nichols, *The Sterile Cuckoo*, p. 152–153, 1965
• "The coon's loaded," he muttered, craning his neck out the window to look behind us. —Terry Southern, *Now Dig This*, p. 118, November 1968
• Rules of the Black Panther Party No. 7: No party member can have a weapon in his possession while DRUNK or loaded off narcotics or weed. — *The Black Panther*, p. 22, 25th January 1969
• We were riding down market street in the club bus and we were really loaded. —Jamie Mandelkau, *Buttons*, p. 101, 1971
• I'm sorry. Tommy gets loaded. He doesn't mean any disrespect. — *Goodfellas*, 1990
• I wanna get loaded, I wanna get high — *Loaded*, 1990
• He was always getting loaded, beating up my mom, dragging us kids all over creation. — *Slacker*, 1992
• [T]o get as wired and as wasted and as loaded as we can, for as long as we can and whatever transpires. —Darren Francis, *The Sprawl [britpulp]*, p. 307, 1999
• I was getting Nicholson loaded [he laughs] ... really good pot... he was really ripped. —Peter Fonda, *Shaking the Cage*, 1999
2 wealthy *US*
• Jesus, I thought, this dame is loaded, she really is. —Horace McCoy, *Kiss Tomorrow Good-bye*, p. 209, 1948
• With Boo it wouldn't have mattered; she's loaded. —Max Shulman, *Anyone Got a Match?*, p. 264, 1964
• I wish you were going to be loaded. — *Body Heat*, 1980
• Well, a lot of people are jealous because he's loaded. — *Cruel Intentions*, 1999
3 pregnant *US*
• —Malachi Andrews and Paul T. Owens, *Black Language*, p. 50, 1973
4 full of the symptoms of a cold *UK: SCOTLAND*
• Aw ya poor soul, ye're loaded. Away hame tae yer bed wi a hot toddy. —Michael Munro, *The Patter, Another Blast*, p. 42, 1988
5 armed with a gun *US*
• "You loaded?" "The cops lifted my rod and P.I. ticket." —Mickey Spillane, *Kiss Me Deadly*, p. 50, 1952
6 (used of a car) equipped with every possible accessory *US*
• Yah, ya got yer – this loaded here – this has yet independent, uh, yer slipped differential, uh, yer rack and pinion steering, yer alarm and radar. — *Fargo*, 1996

loaded down *adjective*
pregnant *BAHAMAS*
• —John A. Holm, *Dictionary of Bahamian English*, p. 125, 1982

loaded for bear
1 prepared for an emergency, heavily armed *US, 1927*
The term arose in the late C19 as a literal description of a weapon loaded with ammunition suitable for killing a bear, and then in the 1950s came to assume a figurative meaning that dominates today.
• But the O'Sheel woman is coming in loaded for bear this time. —Max Shulman, *Rally Round the Flag, Boys!*, p. 54, 1957
• She looked at the big .45 in Goldy's hand. Her eyes stretched and her lips twitched. But she didn't look surprised. "You-call has sure come loaded for bear." —Chester Himes, *A Rage in Harlem*, p. 140, 1957
• We began the trip into town loaded for bear. —Oscar Zeta Acosta, *The Autobiography of a Brown Buffalo*, p. 173, 1972
• I get out there in Framingham this morning, there's old Tiger Mike Fobarty, got his yellow suit on and he's loaded for bear. —George V. Higgins, *The Rat on Fire*, p. 133, 1981
• Funny how a few hours before we'd been a rifle platoon loaded for bear, and now we were on our ass, hurling firecrackers and not making a dent. —David H. Hackworth, *About Face*, p. 73, 1989
• In one minute there were seventeen blue boys there. all loaded for bear, all knowing exactly what the fuck they were doing, and they were all just there. — *Reservoir Dogs*, 1992
2 in trucking, equipped with a citizens' band radio *US*
With **BEAR** meaning 'police', the trucker with a citizens' band radio is better prepared to evade speeding tickets.
• — *The Official CB Slang Dictionary Handbook*, p. 38, 1976: 'Slingo'

loader *noun*
1 in American casinos, a blackjack dealer who carelessly exposes his down card while dealing *US*
• —Steve Kuriscak, *Casino Talk*, p. 35, 1985
2 an experienced and skilled confidence swindler who makes a second sale to a prior victim *US*
• —Kathleen Odean, *High Steppers, Fallen Angels, and Lollipops*, p. 133, 1988

load exchange *noun*
the passing of semen to its maker, mouth to mouth *US, 1970s*
• —Bruce Rodgers, *The Queens' Vernacular*, p. 76, 1972

loadie *noun*
a drug user *US, 1979*
• The other mechanics were loadies who were always ragging him about his disdain for dope. —James Ellroy, *Suicide Hill*, p. 578, 1986
• —Michael V. Anderson, *The Bad, Rad, Not to Forget Way Cool Beach and Surf Discriptionary*, p. 13, 1988
• Loadies generally hang out on the grassy knoll there. — *Clueless*, 1995

loadies *noun*
dice loaded with weights that affect the roll *US*
• Them metal slugs would take my loadies straight to the bottom of the glass. —Stephen Cannell, *Big Con*, p. 215, 1997

load-in *noun*
the carting in and setting up of equipment before a concert or show *US*
• They were bringing their amps and instrument cases out through the load-in door, a giant illuminated martini glass on the wall above it. —Elmore Leonard, *Be Cool*, p. 62, 1999

load of cock *noun*
nonsense *UK*
• [T]here is no such thing as "time", it's a load of cock, something that man has made to computerize himself[.] —Paul E Willis, *Profane Culture*, p. 141, 1978

load of postholes *noun*
in trucking, an empty trailer *US*
• —Mary Elting, *Trucks at Work*, 1946

load of toffee *noun*
nonsense *UK*
From **TOFFEE** (flattery), but less sweet.
• Just the way he's saying it [...] like a schoolteacher about to give us a load of toffee. —Kevin Sampson, *Outlaws*, p. 223, 2001

load plane *noun*
an aircraft loaded with illegal drugs being smuggled *US*
• There was always a "load plane," carrying pot or Mexican heroin, landing on one of the little desert airstrips, usually at night. —Joseph Wambaugh, *Fugitive Nights*, p. 37, 1992

loads *noun*
dice that have been altered with weights so as to produce a certain score *US*
• —John S. Salak, *Dictionary of Gambling*, p. 148, 1963

loadsa
a large amount of something; a great number of something *UK, 1988*
A slovening of 'loads of'.

- Those previously untouched striped cheeks will bring in loadsa money for you both here and in The States. —Sarah Veitch, *Corrective Measures*, p. 218, 2001
- [H]uge breakfasts (loadsa berries, freshly-squeezed juice, fry-ups). —*The Daily Telegraph*, 27th September 2001

load-up *noun*

a false allegation *AUSTRALIA*

- Grahame Andrew Rogers, 42, of Belmore, claimed he was the victim of a police 'load-up'. —*Illawarra Mercury*, p. 5, 20th June 1996
- Emu said that the prisoner was also sporting a black eye to support his allegation. I knew the allegation was a load-up but the bottom line was that I was going to have to prove it. —William Dodson, *The Sharp End*, p. 81, 2001

load up *verb*

(of the police) to plant incriminating evidence in order to secure a conviction, arrest or the like *AUSTRALIA, 1983*

- Not long after I broke away they tried to stand over a protected sly grog shop, got loaded up by the coppers and did three years. —Clive Galea, *Slipper*, p. 156, 1988

loaf *noun*

1 marijuana *UK*

- —Mike Haskins, *Drugs*, p. 288, 2003

2 a one kilogram unit of hashish *CANADA*

- Once it's collected, the resin is pressed into rectangular, one-kilogram plates (or "loafs") and stamped with a trademark so that buyers will be able to identify it later on. —Suroosh Alvi et al., *The Vice Guide*, p. 113, 2002

loaf *verb*

to strike with the head *IRELAND*

- Jimmy Sr's heart was loafing his breast plate. —Roddy Doyle, *The Van*, p. 261, 1991

loafer *noun*

in horse racing, a horse that does not perform well without constant urging by the jockey *US*

- —Tom Ainslie, *Ainslie's Complete Guide to Thoroughbred Racing*, p. 334, 1976

loaf of bread; loaf *noun*

the head, especially as a source of intelligence *UK, 1925*

Rhyming slang.

- Girls never like separating so we'll have to use our loaves. I've always found the best gambit is to play hide and seek. —Ray Galton and Alan Simpson, *Hancock's Half Hour*, 22nd April 1958
- Look son, why don't you use your loaf and stay away from the mess for a bit. —Graeme Kent, *The Queen's Corporal [Six Granada Plays]*, 1959
- Cor, the currant [sun]'s 'ot today, Oates, me old China [mate]. Don't reckon the loaf of bread can take much more of it. —*The Sweeney*, 1976

loan *noun*

▸ **have a loan of**

to play a joke on someone; to pull someone's leg *AUSTRALIA, 1902*

- Barney wouldn't take a girl to the races with a crowd of fellers. He's havin' a loan of yer. —Ray Lawler, *Summer of the Seventeenth Doll*, p. 70, 1957

loaner *noun*

a piece of equipment that is loaned out while the owner's piece of equipment is being repaired *US, 1926*

- So I dug the loaner out of the motel lot, found a pay phone on P.C.H. and gave old Cal a buzz. —James Ellroy, *Brown's Requiem*, p. 220, 1981
- BB: And I get a loaner if the car's got to stay? SALESMAN: As we discussed, you get a car if the car has to be kept overnight. BB: I get a loaner? —*Tin Men*, 1987

loan shark *noun*

a person who loans money privately with usurious interest rates and criminal collection procedures *UK, 1905*

- And those Monday loan sharks, the six-for-five boys, who make a fine art of collection. —John D. McDonald, *The Neon Jungle*, p. 5, 1953
- I remember once in Chicago when I was working for a loan shark, a very tough outfit, incidentally. —Jim Thompson, *Roughneck*, p. 54, 1954
- Contempt of court, refused to testify before new Jersey State Commission of Investigation on loan-shark activities, sixty days, in and out. —Elmore Leonard, *Glitz*, p. 141, 1985
- You have to understand the loan shark's in business the same as anybody else. —*Get Shorty*, 1995

loan-sharking *noun*

usury with severe repayment terms *US, 1914*

- Yakuza are reputed to traffic in drugs and pornography, manage international prostitution and gambling rings, and engage in loan-sharking and racketeering. —Charles Danziger, *Japan for Starters*, p. 125, 1996

lob *noun*

1 in prison, wages, the weekly pay received by prisoners *UK*

- —Paul Tempest, *Lag's Lexicon*, 1950

2 a prisoner who displays excessive zeal on his job *US*

- —*American Speech*, p. 194, October 1951: 'A Study of Reformatory Argot'

3 a penis *UK, 1890*

Original use as 'a partially erect penis' has been replaced to mean 'an erect penis', as used in the phrase 'to have a lob on'.

4 in a gambling establishment, a hanger-on who runs errands for gamblers *US*

- —John Scarne, *Scarne's Guide to Modern Poker*, p. 283, 1979

5 in horse racing, a horse pulled back by its jockey to prevent it from finishing first, second or third in a race *US, 1935*

- —David W. Maurer, *Argot of the Racetrack*, p. 41, 1951

lob *verb*

1 to throw or chuck; to place roughly; to plonk; to land *AUSTRALIA, 1934*

- Only a villain would lob a rock on the roof when a poor weak woman was alone in a haunted house. —Kylie Tennant, *The Honey Flow*, p. 98, 1956
- —Dymphna Cusack, *Picnic Races*, p. 120, 1962
- 'You black b–' I lobbed him one in the jaw. —Dymphna Cusack, *Black Lightning*, p. 142, 1964
- A week earlier, Thomson had lobbed the mare along well in front as usual. —Gerald Sweeney, *The Plunge*, p. 323, 1981
- An Australian girl with a Greek father who must have once accidentally lobbed it in the right hole[.] —*The Traveller's Tool*, p. 42, 1985

2 (of something airborne) to land *AUSTRALIA, 1943*

- The whole stick lobbed spot-on. —W.R. Bennett, *Target Turin*, p. 69, 1962
- He went sailing over the old wire fence and lobbed on the rockery roughly 40 feet below, in a screaming heap. —Bluey, *Bush Contractors*, p. 271, 1975

3 to arrive at a place; to turn up, especially unexpectedly *AUSTRALIA, 1911*

- In he lobs, bodgied up and smelling like dead horse gully. —Arthur Chipper, *The Aussie Swearer's Guide*, p. 31, 1972
- He would rather pen and ink on his ace until some of his Chinas lobbed. —Ryan Aven-Bray, *Ridgey Didge Oz Jack Lang*, p. 11, 1983
- Okay, lob in half an hour from now in the lounge.' —Kathy Lette, *Girls' Night Out*, p. 95, 1987
- 'The later I lobbed in at The Cardigan and left at about 3.00 with Trace Wickham[.]' —Roy Slaven (John Doyle), *Five South Coast Seasons*, p. 54, 1992

4 (of a racehorse) to win a race *AUSTRALIA*

- The boy hoped like hell that Button Hole would lob for him. —Clive Galea, *Slipper!*, p. 5, 1988

lobby *noun*

a lobster or freshwater crayfish *AUSTRALIA, 1952*

lobby louse *noun*

a non-guest who idles in a hotel lobby *US, 1939*

- It concerned characters inelegantly termed "lobby lice." These were loungers, loafers and larrikins who hung around annoying, and sometimes swindling, desirable patrons. —Dev Collans with Stewart Sterling, *I was a House Detective*, p. 13, 1954

lobe in *verb*

to listen *US*

- —Kenn "Naz" Young, *Naz's Underground Dictionary*, p. 44, 1973

LOBNH

unintelligent *UK*

Doctors' shorthand: an initialism of **LIGHTS ON BUT NOBODY HOME**; recorded in an article about medical slang in British (3 London and 1 Cambridge) hospitals.

- —*Ethics and Behaviour*, August 2003

lobo *noun*

marijuana *US, 1984*

- —Richard A. Spears, *The Slang and Jargon of Drugs and Drink*, p. 319, 1986
- —Mike Haskins, *Drugs*, p. 288, 2003

lob on; lob *noun*

a full or partial erection of the penis *UK, 1896*

- Well, get me dick out and give it a jostle or something, darling, I've had a lob on all the way up here. —Bushell, *The Face*, p. 202, 2001

lob-on *noun*
an erection *UK*
From **LOB** (a penis, especially if erect), hence 'to have a lob on' is 'to have an erection', from which 'lob-on' now stands alone. Acceptable for broadcast in a comedy context by BBC television, *Never Mind The Buzzcocks*, 2000.
- I've got a lob-on like the mole in Thunderbirds, drilling away at my kecks [trousers]. — Kevin Sampson, *Outlaws*, p. 113, 2001

lobster *noun*
1 a twenty-dollar note *AUSTRALIA*
- You finally get to the counter after 15 minutes in the queue, slap your lobster on the laminex and tell the cashier what you want. — *Sydney Morning Herald (Metro)*, p. 5, 26th June 1992

2 in poker, an unskilled and/or inexperienced player *US*
- — George Percy, *The Language of Poker*, p. 53, 1988

3 dried nasal mucus *BAHAMAS*
- — John A. Holm, *Dictionary of Bahamian English*, p. 125, 1982

4 an unexpected and unwelcome erection *UK*
- — Jonathan Blyth, *The Law of the Playground*, p. 115, 2004

lobster claw *noun*
in electric line work, a device formally known as an adjustable insulator fork *US*
- — A.B. Chance Co., *Lineman's Slang Dictionary*, p. 11, 1980

lobster cop *noun*
a fisheries officer *CANADA*
- The mosquitoes also found Allan Robichaud, tall, spare-framed veteran fisheries protection officer – a "lobster cop." — *Star Weekly*, p. 3/1, 22nd August 1959

Lobster Lad *noun*
a young male from Prince Edward Island *CANADA*
- That leaves Nova Scotia and Prince Edward Island presumably in the bag. As long as the opiate of patronage is operated by Handsome Bob Winters for the Bluenoses and Watson Macnaught for the Lobster Lads, no trouble is in sight. — *Pictou Advocate*, p. 4/1, 24th February 1955

lobster shift *noun*
a work shift starting at midnight *US, 1942*
- — Rachel S. Epstein and Nina Liebman, *Biz Speak*, p. 131, 1986
- As punishment, Notch was assigned to work the lobster shift, midnight to eight, along with Mr. Salvo for an unspecified period of time. — Sarah Strohmeyer, *Bubbles Unbound*, p. 329, 2001
- The first was taken up by the Sailfish Diner, a smoky short-order grill favored by cops and cabbies on the lobster shift[.] — Tim Dorsey, *Orange Crush*, p. 217, 2001

lobster skin *noun*
badly sunburnt skin *US*
Hawaiian youth usage.
- — Douglas Simonson, *Pidgin to da Max Hana Hou*, 1982

lob up *verb*
to arrive *AUSTRALIA*
- I've lobbed up with f****** Lizzie in the back seat of the car. — *Sun-Herald*, p. 22, 1990
- [I]t's hard lobbing up for work on Monday when you've been on the wrong end of a flogging. — *Herald Sun*, p. 96, 1st May 1991
- So with great trepidation we lobbed at the theatre and were escorted to our seats[.] — Paul Vautin, *Turn It Up!*, p. 204, 1995

local *noun*
1 a resident of a location, contrasted to the visitor *UK, 1835*
- A woman doesn't count all the miscellaneous dick: the guy she met at the club; that time she fucked Keith Sweat; the local she dubbed in Jamaica. — Chris Rock, *Rock This!*, p. 130, 1997

2 a nearby public house; a public house that has your regular custom *UK*
- Now Danny reasoned that as a result of financial strain Tom might be short on beer, and so he suggested that they, the trio plus Tom, should head for the local[.] — Geoff Wyatt, *Saltwater Saints*, p. 18, 1969
- I went down to the local to watch it on television. — Martin King and Martin Knight, *The Naughty Nineties*, p. 186, 1999

3 a person who surfs in an area and asserts territorial privileges there *US*
- — John M. Kelly, *Surf and Sea*, p. 289, 1965
- Okay, so this is where you tell me all about how locals rule and uppie insects like me shouldn't be surfing your break and all that, right? — *Point Break*, 1991

4 during a massage, hand stimulation of the penis until ejaculation *US*
- — Robert A. Wilson, *Playboy's Book of Forbidden Words*, p. 162, 1972

local *adjective*
pertaining to or representing the essence of Creole culture *TRINIDAD AND TOBAGO, 1983*
- — Lise Winer, *Dictionary of the English/Creole of Trinidad & Tobago*, 2003

localism *noun*
an attitude, defiant if not hostile, of local surfers towards visiting surfers at 'their' beach *US*
- — Trevor Cralle, *The Surfin'ary*, p. 70, 1991

local smokal; local smokel *noun*
local police; a police panda car *US*
Blends **SMOKEY BEAR** (the police) with the model of **LOCAL YOKEL** (a foolish country-dweller).
- — *Complete CB Slang Dictionary*, 1976
- — Peter Chippindale, *The British CB Book*, p. 156, 1981

local talent
a pretty female *US*
- — *American Speech*, p. 304, December 1955: 'Wayne University slang'
- [W]hat local talent there is, ah, to hand, as it were, is spread pretty bloody thin on the ground. — Mike Stott, *Soldiers Talking, Cleanly*, 1978

local white *noun*
a light-skinned person, born in Trinidad *TRINIDAD AND TOBAGO, 1956*
- — Lise Winer, *Dictionary of the English/Creole of Trinidad & Tobago*, 2003

local yokel *noun*
an indigenous inhabitant of a rural area *UK, 1950*
A slightly contemptuous term, originally used by military personnel.
- Organised a darts match against the local yokels. They thrashed us, of course[.] — Beale, 1984
- Stephen O'Mara's Parsifal is best served by the production in the first act, where he plays Parsifal as local yokel who grabs a bunch of communion wafers and munches them through the rest of the scene[.] — *The Guardian*, 29th September 2003

loc'd out *adjective*
psychotic from drug use *US*
- — Kenn "Naz" Young, *Naz's Dictionary of Teen Slang*, p. 73, 1993

loced out; loqued out *adjective*
exciting, crazy *US*
- Did I show you the loqued-out Jeep Daddy got me? — *Clueless*, 1995

locho *adjective*
despicable *TRINIDAD AND TOBAGO, 1989*
From the Hindi *lchcha* (lewd loafer), to the corrupted Anglo-Indian 'loocher'.
- — Lise Winer, *Dictionary of the English/Creole of Trinidad & Tobago*, 2003

loci; lokey *noun*
a small locomotive used for hauling logs or coal *CANADA*
- The trammer now, however – and he has other titles – is the driver of a battery or trolley-powered engine known as an electric mule, a motor or (more frequently) a "loci". — Charles Crate, *The Language of Hardrock Mining*, p. 4, 1964
- Through gaps she could see the railway yards. Locis were hauling rakes of trucks. — Noel Hilliard, *Maori Woman*, p. 25, 1974

lock *noun*
1 control; complete control *US, 1966*
- Slim was a bitch that I really had to put the locks on, or I could blow her to anyone of those rich actors. — A.S. Jackson, *Gentleman Pimp*, p. 163, 1973

2 a sure thing, a certainty *US, 1942*
- BOOGIE: Game's a lock. BAGEL: Nothing's a lock. — *Diner*, 1982
- The Mets are a fucking lock. I wanna make some money. — *The Bad Lieutenant*, 1992

3 in poker, a hand that cannot lose *US*
- — Anthony Holden, *Big Deal*, p. 302, 1990

4 in bar dice games, a perfect hand that at best can be tied *US*
- — Jester Smith, *Games They Play in San Francisco*, p. 104, 1971

lock *verb*
in prison, to reside in a cell *US, 1931*
- —Hyman E. Goldin et al., *Dictionary of American Underworld Lingo*, p. 128, 1950
- You get to know the guy that locks next to you, or you don't get to know him – it depends.—Herbert Huncke, *Guilty of Everything*, p. 116, 1990

▸ **lock neck**
to choke a robbery victim with one arm while rifling through their pockets with the other hand *TRINIDAD AND TOBAGO, 1959*
- —Lise Winer, *Dictionary of the English/Creole of Trinidad & Tobago*, 2003

lock and load *verb*
to prepare for an imminent confrontation *US, 1949*
Originally military, and originally 'load and lock', then reversed for the sound (perhaps to conform with 'rock and roll') and generalised.
- Accustomed to war with show-biz receptionists, and being in character, all locked-and-loaded, so to speak, Fin said, "I don't know what I said."—Joseph Wambaugh, *Finnegan's Week*, p. 113, 1993

lock-down *noun*
1 in prison, a state of security in which all inmates are locked in their cells *UK*
- [W]hat's the betting that there's going to be a lock-down.—*The Guardian*, 6th September 2001: 'A life inside'

2 any situation in which your complete freedom is restricted *US*
Like 'warden' (girlfriend or wife), jail slang brought home.
- Since I got a girlfriend, she has had me on lock down.—Pamela Munro, *U.C.L.A. Slang*, p. 94, 1997

locked *adjective*
1 drunk *IRELAND*
- —*e-cyclopaedia*, 20th March 2002

2 drug-intoxicated *US*
- —Anna Scotti and Paul Young, *Buzzwords*, p. 137, 1997

3 tense, stressed *US*
- I've had it. This is bottoms. I'm really locked.—Max Shulman, *Guided Tour of Campus Humor*, p. 105, 1955

locker *noun*
1 a safe or a locked compartment within a safe *US*
- —Vincent J. Monteleone, *Criminal Slang*, p. 147, 1949

2 a jail *US*
- —Anna Scotti and Paul Young, *Buzzwords*, p. 137, 1997

locker room *noun*
1 amyl or butyl or isobutyl nitrate as a recreational drug *US*
Popular as a sex-aid in the gay community, the name (possibly deriving from a brand name) reflects the locality of use.
- Street names [...] Amyl, liquid gold, locker room, poppers[.]—James Kay and Julian Cohen, *The Parents' Complete Guide to Young People and Drugs*, p. 144, 1998

2 the group of professional wrestlers under contract with a promoter at any given moment *US*
- I'm sure it would be no problem because there are so many talented guys in our locker room right now. [quoting Francine Fournier] —*World of Wrestling Magazine*, p. 143, June 1999
- Vince said he had confidence in his locker room.—*Chatterbox News*, 8th August 2000

lock-in *noun*
an after-hours and behind locked doors drinking session in a public house *UK*
- [W]e had met at a film show in the East End, which blurred into a lock-in at a pub and a walk back to Holloway[.]—Iain Aitch, *A Fete Worse Than Death*, p. 76, 2003

lock-in-a-sock *noun*
an improvised prison weapon – a combination lock inside in a sock *US*
- —Reinhold Aman, *Hillary Clinton's Pen Pal*, p. 48, 1996

lock-mortal cinch *noun*
in betting, the surest possible certainty *US*
- I thought this was a lock-mortal cinch, so I didn't mind taking his offer of five-to-one.—Jimmy Snyder, *Jimmy the Greek*, p. 40, 1975

lockpicker *noun*
an illegal abortionist *US*
- [W]e got this kid that was about sixteen and her boyfriend knocked her up and the lockpicker hurt her so she hadda go in the hospital. —George V. Higgins, *The Judgment of Deke Hunter*, p. 36, 1976

locks *noun*
knotted hair in the Rastafarian fashion *JAMAICA*
- "That's the truth, bra," laughed Col, his hand going instinctively to his greying locks.—John Williams, *Cardiff Dead*, p. 49, 2000

locksmith *noun*
1 in pool, a betting professional who only plays games that he is sure of winning *US*
- —Steve Rushin, *Pool Cool*, p. 20, 1990

2 a poker player who only plays excellent hands *US*
- —John D. Bell et al., *Loosely Speaking*, p. 13, 1966

lockstep *noun*
an undeviating order; absolute conformity *UK, 1955*
A figurative application of a military style of close-marching.
- The whole book falls in lockstep with the rebarbative Gingrich worldview, and no nuance or doubt will interfere[.]—*The Guardian*, 25th July 2003

lockup *noun*
1 a jail or prison *US, 1839*
- The first time I met Ed was in the county lockup in Tempe, Arizona. —*Raising Arizona*, 1987

2 in pool, a shot that cannot be missed or a game that cannot be lost *US*
- —Steve Rushin, *Pool Cool*, p. 20, 1990

lock-up lattie *noun*
a cell; a jail *UK*
Polari, formed on **LATTIE** (a house, a place).

lock-worker *noun*
a thief who steals from hotel rooms *US*
- If a room-rifler or a lock-worker gets away with a good score at some hotel, he'll keep quiet about it.—Dev Collans with Stewart Sterling, *I was a House Detective*, p. 47, 1954

loco *noun*
marijuana *US, 1982*
An abbreviation of **LOCOWEED**.
- You know I'm like a loco man—Busta Rhymes, *Get Out*, 2000
- —Mike Haskins, *Drugs*, p. 288, 2003

loco *adjective*
crazy *US, 1887*
From the Spanish.
- Here you got some loco doings goin' on here.—Chester Gould, *Dick Tracy Meets the Night Crawler*, p. 106, 1945
- The whites didn't like the Blacks, (we were outnumbered on each shift by fifty to one) the Mexicans didn't like the whites and thought the whites were slightly loco.—Odie Hawkins, *Scars and Memories*, p. 122, 1987

▸ **go loco**
to smoke (and experience the effects of) marijuana *US, 1942*
- —Richard A. Spears, *The Slang and Jargon of Drugs and Drink*, p. 225, 1986
- —Mike Haskins, *Drugs*, p. 290, 2003

loco-mote *verb*
to drive fast *US*
- —*The Official CB Slang Dictionary Handbook*, p. 38, 1976: 'Slingo'

locoweed *noun*
marijuana *US, 1930*
Directly from the name given to several species of poisonous parts of the genera *Astragalus* and *Oxytropis* which may cause frenzied behaviour in grazing stock; ultimately from Spanish *loco* (mad).
- Hashish was used among the ancients to stimulate armies for ruthless killing. It has since become known as locoweed[.]—Jack Lait and Lee Mortimer, *New York Confidential*, p. 102, 1948
- They must be mixing it with loco weed or something.—Chester Himes, *The Real Cool Killers*, p. 51, 1959
- If Horatio Alger had been born near a field of locoweed his story might have been a lot different.—Hunter S. Thompson, *Hell's Angels*, p. 215, 1966
- "Well, I ain't never seen no locoweed make a cow act like that," said Harold[.]—Terry Southern, *Texas Summer*, p. 37, 1991
- —Mike Haskins, *Drugs*, p. 288, 2003

locs; lokes *noun*
sunglasses *US*
- —Pamela Munro, *U.C.L.A. Slang*, p. 87, 1997
- —Judi Sanders, *Da Bomb*, p. 19, 1997

log *noun*
1 a turd *US, 1973*
From a similarity in appearance to a log of wood; possibly also from the shared characteristic of an ability to float. Especially in the phrasal verb **LAY A LOG** (to defecate).
2 a marijuana cigarette *US, 1977*
- —Richard A. Spears, *The Slang and Jargon of Drugs and Drink*, p. 320, 1986
- —Mike Haskins, *Drugs*, p. 288, 2003

3 phencyclidine, the recreational drug known as PCP or angel dust *UK*
4 a carton of cigarettes *US*
- —Lee McNelis, *30 + And a Wake-Up*, p. 9, 1991

5 the counter surface in a bar *US, 1967*
- I saw him pound the bottom of his glass against the log. —Iceberg Slim (Robert Beck), *Pimp*, p. 120, 1969

6 a bar or tavern *US*
- —Jack Lait and Lee Mortimer, *Chicago Confidential*, p. 301, 1950: 'Loop lexicon'

7 a heavy, cumbersome surfboard *US*
- —Grant W. Kuhns, *On Surfing*, p. 118, 1963

8 a dullard *US, 1895*
- A well-dressed man, informal or casual, will stir her memories of those days when she was 'heart whole and fancy free', before she got tied up with the 'log' she married[.] —John O'Grady, *Aussie Etiket*, p. 25, 1971
- —Jim Ramsay, *Cop It Sweet!*, p. 55, 1977

▸ **behind the log**
(used of a betting style in poker) conservative, even when winning *US, 1971*
- —Thomas L. Clark, *The Dictionary of Gambling and Gaming*, p. 16, 1987

LOG *adjective*
without money, *l*ow *o*n *g*reen *US*
- —Jim Crotty, *How to Talk American*, p. 51, 1997

log bird *noun*
a logistical supply helicopter, used to bring fresh supplies and provisions to troops in the field *US*
- The first two log birds arrived, one behind the other. The boonierats unloaded seventy cases of C-rations, batteries for the company's fifteen radios and heavy loads of M-60 belts, fragmentation grenades and new M-16 magazines and cartridges. —John M. Del Vecchio, *The 13th Valley*, p. 321, 1982
- —Linda Reinberg, *In the Field*, p. 129, 1991

log-flogger *noun*
a male masturbator *UK*
- That young log-flogger, however, was not the only one who foresaw dire consequences for his masturbatory habits. —Richard Herring, *Talking Cock*, p. 115, 2003

logger *noun*
an old, wooden surfboard *AUSTRALIA*
- —Nat Young, *Surfing Fundamentals*, p. 127, 1985

logger's smallpox *noun*
facial scars caused by spiked boots *US, 1938*
Lumberjacks' and loggers' use.
- His quiet face looked pretty good to here, even with the loggers' smallpox – the scarring from being stomped in the face by caulked boots. —Susan Holtzer, *Black Diamon*, p. 168, 1997

logic bomb *noun*
code secretly included in a program that causes a computer to fail when certain conditions are met *US*
- —Eric S. Raymond, *The New Hacker's Dictionary*, p. 227, 1991

logjam *noun*
constipation *US*
- —Trevor Cralle, *The Surfin'ary*, p. 70, 1991

logor *noun*
LSD *UK*
- —Mike Haskins, *Drugs*, p. 285, 2003

logy *adjective*
lethargic, without energy *US*
- BOCKRIS: I hate Quaaludes. BURROUGHS: You really feel logy in the morning. It's terrible stuff. —Victor Bockris, *With William Burroughs [The Howard Marks Book of Dope Stories]*, p. 35, 1997

loid *noun*
a strip of celluloid, used to force locks *UK, 1958*
- [P]icking a dead gaff [empty house] and persuading the front door to yield to their trust 'loid. —Charles Raven, *Underworld Nights*, p. 53, 1956
- —John R. Armore and Joseph D. Wolfe, *Dictionary of Desperation*, p. 39, 1976

loiner *noun*
an inhabitant of Leeds in West Yorkshire *UK, 1950*
- Tony Harrison (1937 -) [...] has published poems on his Leeds home background (in The Loiners, 1970; and Continuous, 1982) which are as subtle as they are earthy. —Harry Blamires, *A Short History of English History*, p. 381, 1984

loin landlord *noun*
a male homosexual *UK*
- —Tom Hibbert, *Rockspeak!*, p. 98, 1983

Loisaida *nickname*
the Lower East Side of New York *US*
A Spanish adaptation of English, borrowed back into English.
- Loisada, actually, is the area betwen 14th and Houston Streets from Avenue A east. This sunny, flowery, Spanish-flavored name for the Lower East Side was conferred on an unpromising piece of real estate by our Puerto Rican fellow residents to cheer things— *New York Times*, p. C8, 27th May 1981
- The sidewalk bikers of Loisaida dare you to glare at them, and too many of the dogs are pit bulls in training for their pro season. —*New York Times*, p. 4 (Section 14), 7th September 2003

loked out *adjective*
improved, modified, enhanced *US*
- —Anna Scotti and Paul Young, *Buzzwords*, p. 94, 1997

lokey *noun*
▷ **see: LOCI**

LOL *noun*
(in doctors' shorthand) a *l*ittle *o*ld *l*ady *UK*
Medical slang.
- —Adam T. Fox, St Mary's Hospital, London, 10th October 2002

LOL
used as Internet shorthand to mean '*l*aughing *o*ut*l*oud' *US*
- —Eric S. Raymond, *The New Hacker's Dictionary*, p. 342, 1991
- RUBBERBABY: Hold on.. you want me to get the vibrator? CAPTAINJAPAN: Yes [...] RUBBERBABY: Okay... one more sec. CAPTAINJAPAN: What's going on? RUBBERBABY: ... Extension cord ... lol. —Howard Stern, *Miss America*, p. 37, 1995
- And you don't have to use the horrendous acronym "lol" (laughs out loud, for those of you who are blessedly unenlightened) which makes me want to "pmfttm" (put my fist through the monitor). —Jane Doa, *The Guardian*, 21st June 2004

lola *noun*
cocaine *US*
- —Peter Johnson, *Dictionary of Street Alcohol and Drug Terms*, p. 112, 1993

Lolita *noun*
a young teenage girl objectified sexually; a girl of any age up to the legal age of consent who dresses in a manner that is considered sexually provocative or predatory *UK, 1959*
Generic use of a proper name, after the sexually aware 12-year-old girl in Vladimir Nabokov's controversial 1955 novel *Lolita* and subsequent films in 1962 and 1998.
- One thinks of bouncing a "Lolita" on one's lap, but hardly a big-breasted pom-pom girl of one hundred and thirty pounds. —Angelo d'Arcangelo, *The Homosexual Handbook*, p. 215, 1968
- The idea of making it with a young girl – the Lolita plot – has always been a major turn-on to porno audiences. —Stephen Ziplow, *The Film Maker's Guide to Pornography*, p. 18, 1977
- A natural blonde with soft, sensual lips and that virginal fresh look of an innocent child. A regular Lolita. —Lanre Fehintola, *Charlie Says...*, p. 33, 2000
- [H]ave to deal with all them fucking Lolitas. —Kevin Sampson, *Clubland*, p. 114, 2002

lollapalooza *noun*

an outstanding example of its type *US, 1896*

'Lollapalooza' was adopted as the title for an annual series of peripatetic music festivals that commenced in Phoenix, Arizona in July 1991.

- Lollapalooza dockwalloper, good attentive husband, caring step-father, bowler among blowlers. — Sidney Bernard, *This Way to the Apocalypse*, p. 153, 1965
- [S]he grew up to be a wollapalooza of a drugstore fashion model[.] — Lester Bangs, *Psychotic Reactions and Carburetor Dung*, p. 58, 1970

lollapoloosa *noun*

in bar dice games, a roll that produces no points for the player *US*

- — Jester Smith, *Games They Play in San Francisco*, p. 104, 1971

lollipop *noun*

1 a police officer *UK*

Rhyming slang for **COP**. A shorter variant is 'lolly'.

- — Paul Tempest, *Lag's Lexicon*, 1950
- — Julian Franklyn, *A Dictionary of Rhyming Slang*, 1960
- At the Bastille the lollipop said the fare must pay the price on the meter. — Frank Hardy, *The Yarns of Billy Borker*, p. 96, 1965
- — Frank Hardy, *Hardy's People*, p. 111, 1986

2 in cricket, a delivery that is easy to play *AUSTRALIA*

- I was batting when Nikki sent down a lollipop and whoosh, what a shot. — Paul Vautin, *Turn It Up!*, p. 92, 1995

3 in sport, a clever or ostentatious trick *UK*

Rhyming slang on 'lollipop stick'.

- — Susie Dent, *The Language Report*, p. 53, 2003

4 in trucking, a mile marker at the side of the road *US*

- — Wayne Floyd, *Jason's Authentic Dictionary of CB Slang*, p. 21, 1976

5 marijuana *FIJI*

Recorded by Jan Tent.

6 a sugar daddy (an older man who supports or helps support a young woman) *UK, 1961*

Recorded as being used by 'shopgirls and typists'.

lollipop; lollypop; lolly up; lolly *verb*

to betray to the police *UK, 1933*

Rhyming slang for **SHOP** (to inform on).

- He was lollied. — David Powis, *The Signs of Crime*, 1977
- — Angela Devlin, *Prison Patter*, p. 72, 1996
- I even got word from Roy himself, thanking me for not lollying him up and giving him time to vanish. — J.J. Connolly, *Know Your Enemy [britpulp]*, p. 161, 1999
- [T]rot into the witness box, swear the oath and do the business for regin, lolly your buddy Morty, go Queen's evidence, get him lifedoff — J.J Conolly, *Layer Cake*, 2000

lollipop artist *noun*

a male homosexual *US*

- Next to loneliness the biggest problem the trucker encounters on the highway is the "queer," the lollipop artist, the funny boys. They harass a trucker unmercifully. — Gwyneth A. "Dandalion" Seese, *Tijuana Bear in a Smoke 'Um Up Taxi*, p. 75, 1977

lollipop stop *noun*

a rest stop on a motorway known as a place where male homosexuals may be found for sexual encounters *US*

- Lollipop means penis, the principal activity being fellatio. — Wayne Dynes, *Homolexis*, p. 85, 1985

lolly *noun*

1 money *UK, 1943*

From rhyming slang on 'lollipop' for **DROP** (a bribe).

- [A] big take in real lolly, the proper folding crinkle[.] — Charles Raven, *Underworld Nights*, p. 177, 1956
- [H]e said he doesn't agree with people marrying outside their class – that's the okay jargon for people without much lolly. — Peter Nichols, *Promenade [Six Granada Plays]*, p. 63, 1959
- Do I understand you two could do with a bit of lolly? — Barry Humphries, *Bazz Pulls It Off!*, 1971
- — Angela Devlin, *Prison Patter*, p. 72, 1996
- People don't want to just hand you their lolly for fuck all. They want something for their money[.] — Kevin Sampson, *Outlaws*, p. 72, 2001

2 a sweet *AUSTRALIA, 1854*

- Table in the saloon deck [was] decked out with beer, lollies, nuts and a birthday cake[.] — Les Such, *A Yen for Yokohama*, p. 26, 1963

3 the vagina *BAHAMAS*

- — John A. Holm, *Dictionary of Bahamian English*, p. 125, 1982

4 the head *AUSTRALIA*

- Get outa there you useless big bastard an' stop trampin' down my barley, or I'll lop yer lolly off. — John O'Grady, *Aussie Etiket*, p. 2, 1971

▸ **do your lolly**

to lose self-restraint in anger *AUSTRALIA, 1951*

- The Doc did his lolly. He raced out of the shop door, broom in hand, and lashed into the air. — Kerry Cue, *Crooks, Chooks and Bloody Ratbags*, p. 194, 1983

lollybags *noun*

a pair of men's close-fitting and revealing nylon swimming trunks *AUSTRALIA*

From the resemblance to a paper bag full of sweets.

- Put on your lollybags and lets go for a swim. — *Wordmap (www.abc.net.au/wordmap)*, 2003

lollygag; lallygag *verb*

1 to kiss; to have sex *US, 1868*

- — *American Speech*, p. 55, February 1947: 'Pacific war language'

2 to dawdle, to dally *US, 1869*

- For the next few minutes she lollygagged about the room puffing smoke, picking things up and putting them down and adjusting her frizz in a mirror over the sofa. — Gerald Petievich, *To Die in Beverly Hills*, p. 18, 1983
- I was just taking a couple or three courses, lolly gaggin'. — Odie Hawkins, *Black Casanova*, p. 121, 1984
- You guys lollygag the ball around the infield, ya lollgag your way to first, ya lollygag in an' outta the duggout. — *Bull Durham*, 1988
- STEPHANIE: So what are you up to? ULTIMATE LOSER: Same old same old, just lollygagging around. Stil unemployed. — *Slacker*, 1992

lollypop *noun*

1 an attractive young woman seen only in terms of her sexuality *US*

- [T]he next thing Robbie Hurt knew, he was regaling three wide-eyed lollypops with a story as to how he got his "wound." — Joseph Wambaugh, *Lines and Shadows*, p. 218, 1984

2 a shop *UK*

Rhyming slang.

- When there was a football game in town or a full moon Mort stuck a couple of bashers in the lolly pops[.] — J.J. Connolly, *Layer Cake*, p. 25, 2000

lolly scramble *noun*

a distasteful scramble for a portion of something *NEW ZEALAND*

Lollies as 'sweets', and a 'lolly scramble' was originally a children's party activity where guests frantically gathered sweets thrown in the air.

- — Louis S. Leland, *A Personal Kiwi-Yankee Dictionary*, p. 60, 1984

lolly water *noun*

a soft drink *AUSTRALIA, 1905*

- We're buring up a lot more than we should, with those mucking monsters gargling the stuff like it was free lolly-water at a school picnic[.] — W.R. Bennett, *Target Turin*, p. 51, 1962
- — Wilda Moxham, *The Apprentice*, p. 65, 1969

lolo *noun*

the penis *TRINIDAD AND TOBAGO, 1966*

Childrens' vocabulary.

- — Lise Winer, *Dictionary of the English/Creole of Trinidad & Tobago*, 2003

lo-lo; low-low *noun*

a custom-designed low rider car *US*

- — Pamela Munro, *U.C.L.A. Slang*, p. 87, 1997

London taxi *noun*

the buttocks, the anus *UK*

Rhyming slang for **JACKSY**.

- If you don't leave off you'll get my boot six lace-holes up your London taxi. — Ray Puxley, *Cockney Rabbit*, 1992

London to a brick

used of something that is an almost certainty *AUSTRALIA*

Coined by race-caller Ken Howard (1913–76), literally meaning that one can safely make an odds-on bet of the city of London against a **BRICK** (the sum of ten pounds).

- 'Close: but Magger by a head,' the course announcer Ken Howard says, 'London to a brick on Magger.' — Frank Hardy, *The Yarns of Billy Borker*, p. 108, 1965

- Church keeps his raids mum, but I'll lay London to a brick that half the population of the globe knows that Twenty-one are planning a swoop tonight. —Lance Peters, *The Dirty Half-Mile*, p. 169, 1979
- 'If it's on we're in,' Ambrose said, 'and it's on. London to a brick.' —T.A.G. Hungerford, *Stories From Suburban Road*, p. 213, 1983
- [L]isten to the roar as Tamarama Boy bounds away, two, now three lengths clear and I won't have to bet London to a brick on this result[.] —Clive Galea, *Slipper*, p. 218, 1988
- Bet you London to a brick there will be a minority report. — *West Australian*, p. 11, 3rd October 1992

lonely as a bastard on father's day *adjective*

very lonely *AUSTRALIA*

- I sit around on me bum as lonely as a bastard on father's day!!! —Barry Humphries, *Bazza Pulls It Off!*, 1971

Lone Ranger *noun*

danger *UK*

Never in the sense of 'peril' but rather of 'a chance'.

- Any Lone Ranger of you ever paying me back the dough you owe me? —Ray Puxley, *Cockney Rabbit*, 1992

lonesome *noun*

▸ on your lonesome

alone *AUSTRALIA, 1902*

- That left me eating on my lonesome. —Robert S. Close, *Love Me Sailor*, p. 41, 1945

lone wolf *noun*

a criminal who works alone *US, 1909*

- Mostly he was a loner acting the lone-wolf tough guy, but he was still dangerous for all that. —Brian McDonald, *Elephant Boys*, p. 19, 2000

long *noun*

a rifle *UK*

- I could clearly see that one of them was carrying a long. —Andy McNab, *Immediate Action*, p. 30, 1995

long *adjective*

(used of money) a lot of *US*

- A syndicated outfit with lots of the long green. —Mickey Spillane, *I, The Jury*, p. 70, 1947
- I began to realize that to make long bread one needed to be a singer and look pretty for the girls. —Babs Gonzales, *I Paid My Dues*, p. 40, 1967
- He'd read an item about some black female theatrical star getting thousands a week for her act and bemoan the fact that a brilliant and gorgeous dude like himself was pimping his heart out on a gang of stinking street whores instead of taking off long bread from a glamorous black performer. —Iceberg Slim (Robert Beck), *The Naked Soul of Iceberg Slim*, p. 80, 1971
- Where'd I see this blond bitch before, maybe thinking he was a pay lawyer, because he was well groomed and looked like long money. —Robert Price, *Clockers*, p. 93, 1992

▸ as long as your arm

very long *UK, 1846*

- I could cite a list of countries as long as my arm in which economic systems based on that principle have ended in economic disaster. —Quentin Davies, *Hansard (The United Kingdom Parliament)*, 8th June 1990

long acre *noun*

a baker *UK, 1857*

Rhyming slang.

- Got to get some needle and thread from the long acre [baker]. — *The Sweeney*, p. 9, 1976

long and flexy *adjective*

sexy *UK*

Rhyming slang.

- —Tom Nind, *Rude Rhyming Slang*, p. 14, 2003

long and short *noun*

wine *UK*

Rhyming slang.

- —Ray Puxley, *Cockney Rabbit*, 1992

long bread *noun*

a lot of money *US, 1963*

- I had some long bread in my pockets cause I'd just finished selling some fine pot and had bought some more all rolled up. —Piri Thomas, *Down These Mean Streets*, p. 109, 1967
- I began to realize that to make long bread one needed to be a singer and look pretty for the girls. —Babs Gonzales, *I Paid My Dues*, p. 39–40, 1967

long con *noun*

an elaborate confidence swindle in which the victim is initially allowed to profit, and then returns with a large sum of money which he loses *US*

- In long con the sucker is given a powerful play to convince him that whatever scratch he has is only a drop in the bucket compared to what he can take off from the long con proposition. —Iceberg Slim (Robert Beck), *Trick Baby*, p. 112, 1969
- I think I can pull off that particular long-con pretty good. But you'll all have to watch my back. —Kevin Sampson, *Powder*, p. 248, 1999

long cut *noun*

the pervasive desire for sweets experienced by a drug addict withdrawing from drug use *US*

- —Eugene Landy, *The Underground Dictionary*, p. 121, 1971

long-day/short-day *noun*

in lobstering, a schedule in which more traps are hauled every other day than on the intervening days *US*

- —Kendall Merriam, *The Illustrated Dictionary of Lobstering*, p. 57, 1978

long dedger *adjective*

eleven *UK*

From Italian *undici* (eleven).

- —Paul Baker, *Polari*, p. 179, 2002

long-dick *verb*

to win a woman away from another; to cuckold *US*

- Poor ol' Elroy got long-dicked, and now his wife won't even look at him. —Ken Weaver, *Texas Crude*, p. 71, 1984
- Jerry was happy 'til that salesman long-dicked his woman away form him. —Michael Dalton Johnson, *Talking Trash with Redd Foxx*, p. 57, 1994

long drink *noun*

a sustained, lingering, sexually inquisitive look *US*

- — *Maledicta*, p. 149, Summer/Winter 1982: 'Dyke diction: The language of lesbians'

long drink of water *noun*

a very tall thin person *US, 1936*

- Come on you long drink of water, on your feet with you. —Graeme Kent, *The Queen's Corporal [Six Granada Plays]*, p. 88, 1959
- 'He was a tall, lanky man, the kind my grandma called a long drink of water, and the dog was a dachshund[.] —Louise Bernikow, *Bark If You Love Me*, p. 93, 2000

long end *noun*

a confidence game in which the victim is sent for his money, as opposed to a confidence game in which the spoils are limited to the amount on the victim's person *US*

- "You talk the lingo. What's your pitch?" "The long end. The big-con." —Jim Thompson, *The Grifters*, p. 153, 1963

longer and linger; long and linger *noun*

a finger *UK, 1961*

Rhyming slang, in which, unusually, both nouns are affected in the plural form: 'longers and lingers'; 'longs and lingers'.

- —Ray Puxley, *Cockney Rabbit*, 1992

long eye *noun*

the vulva *AUSTRALIA*

- —James McDonald, *A Dictionary of Obscenity, Taboo and Euphemism*, p. 17, 1988

long-eye *adjective*

covetous *TRINIDAD AND TOBAGO, 1956*

- —Lise Winer, *Dictionary of the English/Creole of Trinidad & Tobago*, 2003

long firm; LF; LF scam *noun*

a commercial fraud in which a good credit rating is first established and then abused *UK, 1869*

- "You're at the long firm again," said Terry. "What're you talking about? I paid for all this lot." —Anthony Masters, *Minder*, p. 61, 1984
- —Angela Devlin, *Prison Patter*, p. 71, 1996
- Long firm fraud [...] became big business. It was brilliantly simple. Go to suppliers, order and pay for goods [...] to set up a trading relationship. Then order the big one on credit and disappear[.] —Brian McDonald, *Elephant Boys*, p. 263, 2000

long green *noun*

a large amount of money *US, 1887*

- A syndicated outfit with lots of the long green. —Mickey Spillane, *I, The Jury*, p. 70, 1947
- He didn't neglect his woman because by keeping "long green" (money) in his slide (pocket) daily, he was always copping her furs[.] —Babs Gonzales, *I Paid My Dues*, p. 97, 1967

- For the second time in my pimping career I could see solid success and lots of long green. — Iceberg Slim (Robert Beck), *Pimp*, p. 275, 1969
- These are not the only avenues to long green and white coke, of course. — Lester Bangs, *Psychotic Reactions and Carburetor Dung*, p. 67, 1971
- I told you not to talk to me until you got some long greens. I might even charge you for talkin' to me like this. — Christina and Richard Milner, *Black Players*, p. 87, 1972

long green line *noun*
an infantry unit marching through the jungle in single file *US*
- — Linda Reinberg, *In the Field*, p. 130, 1991

long-guts *noun*
a tendency to eat too much *GUYANA, 1973*
- — Richard Allsopp, *Dictionary of Caribbean English Usage*, p. 353, 1996

longhair *noun*
1 an intellectual *US, 1919*
- "I never read the Post," said Wilma Hepp. "That longhair stuff is too deep for poor little me." — Max Shulman, *The Zebra Derby*, p. 165, 1946

2 a participant in the 1960s counterculture *US, 1969*
- No one ever asks a fellow longhair how old he is. It's a counter-revolutionary question. — Jerry Rubin, *Do It!*, p. 89, 1970
- In Mexico border guards began turning longhairs back with the words: "No hippies, no Jews; on Presidential orders." — Richard Neville, *Play Power*, p. 204, 1970
- Perched on a rock overlooking the entire field was a group of long-hairs playing bongos and guitars. — Ann Fettamen, *Trashing*, p. 22–23, 1970
- The two guys right behind me were longhairs. Acid people. They'd been picked up for vagrancy, too. — Hunter S. Thompson, *Fear and Loathing in Las Vegas*, p. 174, 1971

3 classical music *US, 1951*
- Until the late 1940s, the jazz concerts in symphony halls and other repositories of long-hair music, had been dominated by the Old Guard. — Robert Sylvester, *No Cover Charge*, p. 279, 1956
- Man, just dig all them fine long-hair records, whole albums of operas and symphonies and stuff. — Ross Russell, *The Sound*, p. 190, 1961

long-handled underwear *noun*
warm underwear with long sleeves and legs *US, 1882*
- All around me, in their double-decker bunks, lay sleeping lumberjacks clad in their sweaty long-handled underwear. — *Toronto Globe and Mail*, p. 33/8, 11th October 1966

longies *noun*
long underwear *US, 1941*
- "Where are you going?" "Home," said Guido, "to pack my longies." — Max Shulman, *Rally Round the Flag, Boys!*, p. 237, 1957

long john *noun*
a sleeveless wet suit *US*
- — Frank Fox, *A Beginner's Guide to Zen and the Art of Windsurfing*, p. 152, 1985: 'A short dictionary of wind surfing terms'

Long John *noun*
a 175 mm gun *US*
- — Linda Reinberg, *In the Field*, p. 130, 1991

long johns *noun*
long-legged underpants *US, 1943*
- [T]he final preparations for the Winter Olympics have included everything from fly-pasts by fighter jets to a demonstration of the importance of long johns. — *The Guardian*, 8th February 2002

long john silver *noun*
a car with one headlight burnt out *US*
- — "Slingo", *The Official CB Slang Dictionary Handbook*, p. 39, 1976

long jump *noun*
an act of sexual intercourse *UK*
- Elvis reckoned he never believed his luck, Paulette got to give him the long jump after that. — Jeremy Cameron, *Brown Bread in Wengen*, p. 60, 1999

long-mouth *adjective*
perpetually hungry *GUYANA*
- — Richard Allsopp, *Dictionary of Caribbean English Usage*, p. 353, 1996

longneck *noun*
a bottle of beer with a long neck *US, 1980*
- They sat in the living room of the house in Delray Beach drinking beer out of longnecks, the only way Dale liked to have his. — Elmore Leonard, *Maximum Bob*, p. 107, 1991
- Could I have a carton of heavy long necks, please? — *Wordmap (www.abc.net.au/wordmap)*, 2003

long-nose *noun*
an American or European *US*
From the Vietnamese, adopted by US soldiers.
- Off limits to me. Off limits to you. Off limits to all long noses. Colonel's orders. — David Halberstam, *One Very Hot Day*, p. 15, 1967

long-nosed Henry *noun*
a Ford Capri car *UK*
Citizens' band radio slang, ascribing the length of the bonnet to Henry Ford's physiognomy.
- — Peter Chippindale, *The British CB Book*, p. 161, 1981

long on *adjective*
having a substantial amount of something *US, 1913*
- Long on spectacle but short on heart[.] — *The Daily Telegraph*, 27th October 2003

long one *noun*
one hundred pounds (£100) *UK*
- On top of all the removal expenses, I had to lay out a long one. 100 pound notes, and I didnt begrudge one of them. — Lenny McLean, *The Guv'nor*, p. 78, 1998

long paddock *noun*
grassed areas along the sides of a public road used for grazing *AUSTRALIA, 1929*
- They are sending their sheep down the long paddock now, the travelling stock routes, to try to get them a feed. — *Sydney Morning Herald*, p. 29, 23rd October 1982

long rats *noun*
special pre-cooked rations used by long-range reconnaissance patrols in the field during the Vietnam war *US, 1973*
- — Gregory Clark, *Words of the Vietnam War*, p. 288–289, 1990

longs *noun*
trousers with long legs *TRINIDAD AND TOBAGO, 1967*
- — Lise Winer, *Dictionary of the English/Creole of Trinidad & Tobago*, 2003

long shoe *noun*
a stylish shoe with a tapered toe *US*
- Y'see, long shoes are success. They're the keen-toed design, right for kickin' a whore in the behind with when she comes up with short money or gits outta line. — Nathan Heard, *Howard Street*, p. 159, 1968

long-shoe game *noun*
a swindle *US, 1955*
- He lived off the hicks from out in the sticks / He was a master of the long-shoe game. — Dennis Wepman et al., *The Life*, p. 86, 1976

longshot *noun*
a venture involving great risk; in horse racing, a bet on a horse with very long odds *UK, 1869*
Originally race track slang.
- Only suckers lay it all in on more than one horse race. They finally agreed on a longshot. — Robert Sylvester, *No Cover Charge*, p. 221, 1956
- It was a long shot all the way. We gave 'em a good run at it. — *48 Hours*, 1982
- A runner at "long" odds with little chance. — David Bennet, *Know Your Bets*, p. 58, 2001

▸ **by a long shot**
by a long way, by a great degree *US, 1848*
Generally as an emphatic negative.
- We continue to maintain that the case is nothing like what's been portrayed by the media, not by a long shot. — *The Guardian*, 12th December 2003

long side *noun*
in sports betting, a bet on the underdog *US*
- For some reason, if you really liked an underdog you went to Phillly. You could always get a half point more on the long side. — Jimmy Snyder, *Jimmy the Greek*, p. 36, 1975

long sight *noun*
▸ **by a long sight**
by a long way *US, 1844*
Generally as an emphatic negative.

long skirt *noun*
a Maxi car *UK*
Citizens' band radio slang; punning the length of a maxi-skirt.
- —Peter Chippindale, *The British CB Book*, p. 161, 1981

long sleeve *noun*
the foreskin *FIJI*
Recorded by Jan Tent in 1993: 'Do Europeans get their long sleeves cut?'.

long spit *noun*
▷ see: BIG SPIT

long streak of cocky's shit *noun*
a tall, thin person *AUSTRALIA*
- —Richard Beckett, *The Dinkum Aussie Dictionary*, p. 34, 1986

long streak of misery *noun*
a very tall thin person (who is not necessarily miserable) *UK*

long streak of piss *noun*
a very tall thin person *UK*
- He was a long, lanky streak of piss that geezer, and a proper wanker to boot. —Dave Courtney, *Raving Lunacy*, p. 145, 2000

longtail *noun*
a single female tourist *BERMUDA*
- —Peter A. Smith and Fred M. Barritt, *Bermewjan Vurds*, 1985

long time no see
used as a greeting after an extended separation *US, 1900*
- "Asterix, old friend, long time no see." "It's been five years. We don't get out so much since poor old Goscinny died." —*The Guardian*, 13th April 2001

long time, no smell
used as an affectionate greeting *US*
Hawaiian youth usage.
- —Douglas Simonson, *Pidgin to da Max Hana Hou*, 1982

Long Tom *noun*
a long-range artillery gun *US*
- —Linda Reinberg, *In the Field*, p. 130, 1991
- It was the only U.S. Army World War II towed artillery weapon with a commonly used nickname: "The Long Tom." —Konrad F. Schreier, *Tanks and Artillery*, p. 102, 1994

long 'un *noun*
a hundred pounds, or a thousand pounds sterling *UK*
- It's fifty "lid" for a week – a long 'un for three weeks. —Anthony Masters, *Minder*, p. 106, 1984
- Invites could exchange hands for a long un or more[.] —Wayne Anthony, *Spanish Highs*, p. 183, 1999

long way *noun*
▸ **by a long way; by a long chalk**
by a great degree or measure *UK*
Often in a (implied) negative context.
- French exports of beef to the UK are tiny and only bear worrying about if we are absolutely sure all modes of BSE transmission within the UK have been stopped off. We are not, by a long chalk. —*The Guardian*, 22nd November 2000
- K.J. Choi[...] holed his second for an eagle at the 11th and finished as well as he has ever done in a major by a long way. —*The Sunday Telegraph*, 25th July 2004

long white roll *noun*
a factory-made cigarette *US*
- —Lou Shelly, *Hepcats Jive Talk Dictionary*, p. 28, 1945

long-winded *adjective*
1 slow in doing something *UK, 1961*
In conventional use when applied to talking.
- Of course, driving in northern Majorca is a long-winded affair, given the narrow hairpin bends and colossal charabancs that wallow from one tourist honeypot to the next[.] —*The Guardian*, 19th January 2002

2 in homosexual usage, said of a man who takes a long time to reach orgasm *US*
- —*Male Swinger Number 3*, p. 48, 1981: 'The complete gay dictionary'

loo *noun*
a lavatory *UK, 1940*
Many possible etymologies, mostly from French sources. Contracted from C18 *bordalou* (a portable ladies' privy, shaped like a sauce-boat and carried in a muff); *l'eau* (water) or the C18 warning-cry 'gardy-loo', from pseudo-French *gare de l'eau* (beware of the water), given when emptying the contents of a chamber pot out of a window into the street beneath; an anglicised *lieu* (the place), as in the frequently mispronounced 'time off in *lieu*/loo'. The only entirely English suggestion is a corruption of 'leeward', the sheltered side of a ship over which excretory functions were sensibly performed. The most convincing possibilites are an abbreviated pun on Waterloo, the London railway station named to commemorate the famous battle of Waterloo in Belgium (1815); and the darkly witty reduction of *l'oubliette* (a secret dungeon, often with a pit below).
- Marchmare would hide his bird's knickers in the loo or somewhere[.] —Derek Raymond (Robin Cook), *The Crust on its Uppers*, p. 30, 1962
- In the loo at the Louvre? —Douglas Rutherford, *The Creeping Flesh*, p. 174, 1963
- In the Cat Flap Club ladies' loo lots of girls were standing around gossiping[.] —Stewart Homes, *Sex Kick [britpulp]*, p. 211, 1999
- [S]he relieved herself in a motorway services loo on the way[.] — *ES Magazine*, p. 3, 22nd June 2001

looder *noun*
a blow *IRELAND*
- He got a right looder —Denis O'Shaughnessy, *Stories of Limerick*, p. 68, 2002

loogie *noun*
phlegm that has been expelled from the respiratory passages *US*
- The body snatcher giggled and snuffled and hacked up a loogie, while Fortney fired up the boat and drove away, wanting to be well clear if the floater should explode. —Joseph Wambaugh, *Floaters*, p. 147, 1996

loogin *noun*
an awkward, unaccomplished person *US, 1919*
- That was the kind of man to be associating with, no McGinty and these loogins from the express company. —James T. Farrell, *Willie Collins*, p. 110, 1946

looie; louie; looey *noun*
1 a gob of phlegm or nasal mucus *US, 1970*
- He hocked such a huge looie that I had a spiderweb of saliva running from my dark glasses onto my hair. —Howard Stern, *Miss America*, p. 340, 1995

2 a lieutenant *US, 1916*
- Hey, you see that new second looey? —Charles Anderson, *The Grunts*, p. 113, 1976
- The next morning some young looey stood in the doorway and called everybody's name. —Larry Heinemann, *Close Quarters*, p. 273, 1977
- "We do all the work," said the louies. —Sandee Shaffer Johnson, *Cadences*, p. 52, 1986

look *noun*
1 appearance; style *US*
- — *American Speech*, p. 147–148, May 1959: 'The use of 'lookl' in the 'language of fashion'

2 in the entertainment industry, the right to review and consider a script or project *US*
- "I go to another studio. Tower has first look, that's all. They turn it down I can take it anywhere I want." —Elmore Leonard, *Be Cool*, p. 6, 1999

look *verb*
▸ **look alive**
to be alert, to bestir yourself, to make haste *UK, 1858*
Often as an imperative.
- "Come on, animator!" chuckled the Belgian. "Look alive!" — *The Guardian*, 19th June 2003

▸ **look at the gate**
to near the end of a prison sentence *US*
- —Inez Cardozo-Freeman, *The Joint*, p. 513–514, 1984

▸ **look at the procter and gamble**
to cheat during an examination or test *US*
A pun alluding to the well-known corporation.
- —Collin Baker et al., *College Undergraduate Slang Study Conducted at Brown University*, p. 152, 1968

▸ **look at you**
to judge by your appearance *UK, 1846*
- There is wildness in David Almond's heart. Not that you'd know it to look at him – a middle-aged man with a teacher's beard and a gentle demeanour. —*The Observer*, 23rd November 2003

▸ **look down your nose at**
to regard someone or something with contempt, to despise *UK, 1921*
- It's possible that Nebuchadnezzar looked down his nose at other Babylonians whose gardens didn't hang, and that medieval monks sniggered privately over one another's herbs. — *The Observer*, 29th June 2003

▸ **look for a hole in the fence**
(used of a racehorse) to perform very poorly, as if the horse would rather find a hole in the fence and return to the stable *US*
- — Tom Ainslie, *Ainslie's Complete Guide to Thoroughbred Racing*, p. 334, 1976

▸ **look like nothing on earth**
to have an appearance that is wretched, or indicative of illness, or that is somehow eccentric or ludicrous *UK, 1927*
- [C]lose up it looks like nothing on earth, but, if you stand back, you get the drift. — Sir Bernard Ingham, *UK Hansard (the Public Administration Committee)*, 23rd October 2003

▸ **look out the window**
in horse racing, to fail to bet on a horse in a race it wins after betting on the horse in a number of previous losing efforts *US*
- — David W. Maurer, *Argot of the Racetrack*, p. 41, 1951

▸ **not look back**
to enjoy a continuing success since a defining moment *UK, 1893*
- Rachael Oliveck was a committed vegetarian and animal rights activist for 14 years. But on Christmas Day she finally cracked, and tucked into some turkey – and she hasn't looked back since[.] — *The Guardian*, 29th January 2003

lookalikie; lookylikey *noun*
a lookalike, a person who looks like another (generally the similarity is to a celebrity and often used to professional advantage) *UK*
- C'mon, let's see which lookalikies yewer all hiding from us. — Niall Griffiths, *Sheepshagger*, p. 106, 2001
- A researcher [...] asks me to appear on the following Monday's show as "a Felix Carter lookylikey". — Andrew Holmes, *Sleb*, p. 189, 2002

looker *noun*
an attractive woman *US, 1892*
- That was some looker what just trotted out of here. — Robert Campbell, *Nibbled to Death by Ducks*, p. 260, 1989

look here!
used as a demand for attention to what is being said *UK, 1861*
- Now look here, Elms! — *The Guardian*, 17th February 1973

lookie *verb*
to look *US*
A diminuitive that introduces a folksy tone; almost always used in the imperative.
- Lookie here, cats. Lookie here at the cat who holds the key to the whole jivin' tomorrow. — Dan Jenkins, *Semi-Tough*, p. 135, 1972

lookie-loo *noun*
1 a customer who enjoys looking at merchandise but has no intention of buying *US, 1978*
- Looky-loos, that breed of bird that made it an evening out going around drooling over items they could never afford. — Robert Campbell, *Juice*, p. 228–229, 1988
- Hopefully there'd be a lot more when the finals got under way, but of course most of the tourists were looky-loos. — Joseph Wambaugh, *Floaters*, p. 17, 1996
- Made famous by a series of commercials for Twentieth Century real estate. — Editors of Ben is Dead, *Retrohell*, p. 115, 1997

2 an inquisitive observer *US*
A Los Angeles term, personified in the character Look-Loo Woman in Quentin Tarantino's 1994 film *Pulp Fiction*.
- — Pamela Munro, *U.C.L.A. Slang*, p. 56, 1989

looking glass *noun*
a car's rear view mirror *US*
- — *American Speech*, p. 270, December 1962: 'The language of traffic policemen'

looking good!
used for expressing approval *US*
A signature line of comedian Freddie Prinze on the television comedy *Chico and the Man* (NBC, 1974–78). Repeated with referential humour.

look of eagles *noun*
in horse racing, the proud look perceived in the eyes of a great racehorse *US*
- — Tom Ainslie, *Ainslie's Complete Guide to Thoroughbred Racing*, p. 334, 1976

look-see *noun*
a viewing, an observation *US, 1854*
- Dusted off and gone home with a million dollars wortha gunge on his pecker, all the way ta Michael Reese Hospital, 'cause some fucken lifer wanted to have a 'look-see.' — Larry Heinemann, *Close Quarters*, p. 168, 1977
- Mario Villalobos, while awaiting the arrival of the shoulder holster kids, had given his crime report another perfunctory looksee. — Joseph Wambaugh, *The Delta Star*, p. 39, 1983
- He might come around for a little look-see. — Anthony Masters, *Minder*, p. 165, 1984
- I approached slowly, slowly, and had a look-see. — Richard Marcinko and John Weisman, *Rogue Warrior*, p. 17, 1992

look-see *verb*
to look around *US, 1868*
- Let's go look-see. — Beale, 1984

looks like rain
used by a criminal to indicate an imminent arrest *UK*
The future isn't sunny.
- — Angela Devlin, *Prison Patter*, p. 72, 1996

look that up in your Funk and Wagnalls!
used for a humorous observation about a word or fact *US*
One of the most popular catchphrases from the US television series *Laugh-In* (1967–73) and repeated referentially.

look up *verb*
1 to visit, usually informally *UK, 1788*
- So when Capitol Records looked him [Lee Hazlewood] up and asked him to work with Frank Sinatra's 25-year-old daughter, he took some convincing. Then Frank paid a visit. — *The Guardian*, 9th May 2002

2 to get better *UK, 1806*
- [Y]our economy is growing at 5% a year and things are looking up[— *The Guardian*, 18th February 2004

look who it isn't
used as a facetious greeting on a surprise meeting *UK*
- Milligan, Taylor and Watson crowd round him [...] MILLIGAN: Look who it isn't. — Graeme Kent, *The Queen's Corporal [Six Granada Plays]*, p. 92, 1959

looky here!
used as a demand for attention to what is being said *US, 1876*
A variation of **LOOK HERE!**.

look you!
used as a demand for attention to what is being said; especially (when spoken by a non-Welsh) as catchphrase of stereotypical Welshness *UK: WALES, 1937*

loo la *adjective*
drunk *UK*
- — *e-cyclopaedia*, 20th March 2002

loomer *noun*
a large wave that suddenly appears seaward *US*
- — John Severson, *Modern Surfing Around the World*, p. 172, 1964

loon *noun*
a madman *US, 1823*
An abbreviation of 'lunatic'.
- [W]hat else could I or any other loon from my peer group ever possibly become schizoid over but a lousy rock 'n' roll album? — Lester Bangs, *Psychotic Reactions and Carburetor Dung*, p. 11, 1971
- I'm thinking, Oh, I always get these loons next to me, what is it about me? — Edward Lin, *Big Julie of Vegas*, p. 213, 1974
- To his awestruck fellow loons back on the ward he offered this modest yet manly explanation: "Just to show em I could take it." — Seth Morgan, *Homeboy*, p. 43, 1990
- He's always been a very good money maker but he's a fuckin' loon. — J.J. Connolly, *Know Your Enemy [britpulp]*, p. 152, 1999

loon *verb*
to fool about; to move to music in an uncontrolled manner *UK*
- — Jenny Fabian and Johnny Byrne, *Groupie*, 1968
- The hippy penchant for play survives in the way sisters [in the Women's Lib movement] enjoy "bopping" and "looning" together, that is, dancing and clowning around for fun. — Angela Carter, *The State of the Language*, 1980

loon about; loon *verb*

to play the fool; to enjoy leisure time in a non-conformist manner: dancing, idling, wandering *UK, 1966*

- [T]he little old lady who, upon catching sight of a looning longhair, muttered, "then I'm for the war"[.] — Richard Neville, *Play Power*, p. 55, 1970
- There were about thirty [Hells] Angels looning about in the front room. — Jamie Mandelkau, *Buttons*, p. 64, 1971

looney tune; loony tune *noun*

a crazy person *US, 1967*

From the television cartoons created by Warner Brothers beginning in 1960. The variant 'looney tunes' is also used as a singular.

- Paul [Simonon]'s loony toon playfulness. — Lester Bangs, *Psychotic Reactions and Carburetor Dung*, p. 238, 1977
- He was the local looney tunes. — Edwin Torres, *After Hours*, p. 370, 1979
- — *American Speech*, Winter 1989
- We've got a top-of-the-line loony-tune either way you cut it. — *Basic Instinct*, 1992
- Behind me a coupla loony tune types pro'ly homeless shiteheads from Mersey[.] — Nick Barlay, *Curvy Lovebox*, p. 18, 1997

looney tunes *adjective*

insane *US, 1971*

- I started to realize that they had decided I was loony-tunes. — Cleo Odzer, *Goa Freaks*, p. 258, 1995
- I've always wanted to be in charge, know where I'm going. Not loony tunes stuff, I'm not thingio. — Kevin Sampson, *Clubland*, p. 20, 2002

loon pants; loons *noun*

casual trousers fashioned with a very wide flare below the knee *UK, 1971*

- In this country, Jean-Paul Sartre is as unfashionable as loon pants. — *The Guardian*, 3rd May 2000

loon shit *noun*

boggy land *CANADA*

- "Loon shit" is so wet that it undulates as you walk on it. In many lakes in Manitoba there are floating islands, complete with small trees, that are composed of loon shit. — Chris Thain, *Cold as a Bay Street Banker's Heart*, p. 99, 1987

loony *noun*

1 a madman *US, 1883*

An abbreviation of 'lunatic'. May also be spelt 'looney'.

- Which one of you claims to be the craziest? Which one is the biggest loony? — Ken Kesey, *One Flew Over the Cuckoo's Nest*, p. 17, 1962
- Maybe the owner had fled with his family to Nevada, leaving the village loony to mind the store and deal with the savages in his own way. — Hunter S. Thompson, *Hell's Angels*, p. 149, 1966
- I smiled stupidly at people passing, as if this loony were my bereaved brother-in-law. — Leonard Cohen, *Beautiful Losers*, p. 45, 1966
- Lobotomy – isn't that for loonies? — *Repo Man*, 1984
- [A]n all-American looney like Michael Jackson? — Howard Stern, *Miss America*, p. 71, 1995
- [E]very other ride's a frothing loony. I've had bearded depressives moaning about killing themselves, psychos begging me to jump lights, and bog-eyed schizos asking to be taken to heaven. — Simon Lewis, *In The Box [britpulp]*, p. 131, 1999

2 a one-dollar coin *CANADA*

- We'd each be allowed to spend one loony so that we'd all be done at the same time. — Suroosh Alvi et al., *The Vice Guide*, p. 9, 2002

loony *adjective*

extremely erratic; mildly crazy *US, 1841*

- Pat, our eldest, and seemingly the least loony of the lot, gave us relatively little trouble. — Jim Thompson, *Roughneck*, p. 135, 1954
- "Too bad she's loony," he said to himself, a little later, "because she sure is pretty. — Max Shulman, *Rally Round the Flag, Boys!*, p. 12, 1957
- He was delighted with himself for having had the foresight to be loony and to have the papers to prove it. — Mary McCarthy, *The Group*, p. 278, 1963
- Archibald Cox (crew-cut) told me that he thought anyone who made a big thing about kids' hair was loony as hell (or something to that effect, I don't remember his exact words). — James Simon Kunen, *The Strawberry Statement*, p. 87, 1968
- "Where's that loony fruit Al Ginsbert?!?" I shouted, rushing to overtake him. — Terry Southern, *Now Dig This*, p. 121, November 1968

loony bin *noun*

a hospital (or other institution) for the treatment of psychiatric problems and mental illness *UK, 1919*

- Throwed his ass in a loonybin, called him insane. — Robert Gover, *JC Saves*, p. 172, 1968
- State Law requires the testimony of two shrinks in order to commit one psycho to the loony bin[.] — Oscar Zeta Acosta, *The Autobiography of a Brown Buffalo*, p. 151, 1972
- Got one kid in the loony bin, and my wife's headed there. — George V. Higgins, *Penance for Jerry Kennedy*, p. 141, 1985

loony bird *noun*

a person who is at least eccentric, at most mentally unstable *US*

- Boy, you pay off that hyphenated loon-bird and pack him in. — Max Shulman, *Anyone Got a Match?*, p. 79, 1964

loony left *noun*

used by 'moderate' politicians to demonise committed socialists as fanatical extremists *UK, 1977*

Combines **LOONY** (mad) with 'left' (the sinister positioning of socialist politics).

- If they want to vote – even if it's for some loony lefty – I'll take them down the polling station. — Andrew Nickolds, *Back to Basics*, p. 77, 1994
- [D]ependable moderate Bob Mellish [...] would have nothing to do with the loony left image of the time [early 1980s]. — Mark Steel, *Reasons to be Cheerful*, p. 129, 2001

loony toons *noun*

LSD *UK*

- — Mike Haskins, *Drugs*, p. 285, 2003

loop *noun*

1 a short pornographic video shown on a recurring cycle *US*

- Back in the neolithic days of 1969, most sex theaters were running loops of ten-minute girlie films. — George Paul Csicsery (Editor), *The Sex Industry*, p. 165, 1973
- A hard-core loop from the late '60s is a classic example. — Kenneth Turan and Stephen E. Zito, *Sinema*, p. 91, 1974
- "There was no feature-length porn at that time. It was only loops." (Quoting Harry Reems). — *Adam Film Quarterly*, p. 23, December 1975
- Loops are the short sex scenes usually shown at peep shows – small, individual projection booths located in the rear of many adult bookshops. — Stephen Ziplow, *The Film Maker's Guide to Pornography*, p. 12, 1977
- Truth be told (watch out), all one gets for the give-bill admission is an assortment of the same boring porn loops shown in Times Square for three dollars less. — Jim Carroll, *Forced Entries*, p. 39, 1987
- Why not make loops for the Fat Man?. — Seth Morgan, *Homeboy*, p. 188, 1990

2 in television and film making, voice recordings that are used with previously recorded video *US*

- But they would talk and Julie would run to the studio where she was doing voice loops for an Italian-made film... — Elmore Leonard, *Gold Coast*, p. 151, 1980
- He recorded two versions of the statement, a thirty-second loop for radio and two fifteen-second sound bites for television. — Carl Hiaasen, *Tourist Season*, p. 143, 1986

3 an intrauterine contraceptive device *US*

- — Helen Dahlskog (Editor), *A Dictionary of Contemporary and Colloquial Usage*, p. 33, 1972
- So I'll say sure, Roddy, whatever you want, let's make a baby. I never told him about wearing the loop. — Carl Hiaasen, *Native Tongue*, p. 214, 1991

4 in table tennis, a shot with topspin *US*

- — Dick Squires, *The Other Racquet Sports*, p. 130, 1971: 'Glossary'

5 the people in a business or enterprise who make critical decisions; the process by which those critical decisions are made *US, 1987*

A person is either 'in the loop' or 'out of the loop'.

- — *American Speech*, Fall 1988
- — Connie Eble (Editor), *UNC-CH Campus Slang*, p. 4, Fall 1997

6 a crazy individual *UK: SCOTLAND*

Sometimes expanded to 'loop-de-loop'.

- Ah canny believe you're hingin aboot wi a loop like that. — Michael Munro, *The Complete Patter*, p. 95, 1996

▸ **in the loop**

to be part of an inner-circle that receives restricted information *UK, 1970*

- The nearest woman to power is Kennedy's secretary Evelyn Lincoln, but there isn't a woman 'in the loop' – to employ a phrase they use in the movie though it was not, I think, current back in 1962. — *The Observer Review*, p. 7, 18th March 2001

Loop *noun*

▸ **the Loop**

the core central area of Chicago *US*

From the elevated railway constructed in 1897 that loops around two square miles of central Chicago.

- He had not been in the Loop at lunchtime in several years. —James T. Farrell, *Willie Collins*, p. 101, 1946
- And the Loop is the heart of Chicago's commerical life, the capital of her civic activities, and the headquarters of her underworld. —Jack Lait and Lee Mortimer, *Chicago Confidential*, p. 11, 1950
- But we forgot that and headed straight for North Clark Street, after a spin in the Loop[.] —Jack Kerouac, *On the Road*, p. 238, 1957
- Mr. Cox, Railroad's Papa, dropped dead while shining a customer's shoes in the Loop barber shop where he had worked for twenty years. —Iceberg Slim (Robert Beck), *Mama Black Widow*, p. 193, 1969

loop-de-loop *noun*
simultaneous, reciprocal oral sex between two people *US*
- —Eugene Landy, *The Underground Dictionary*, p. 121, 1971

looped; looping *adjective*
drunk *US, 1934*
Descriptive of the inability when drunk to maintain a straight line.
- [W]e were more than pretty well looped – we were blind. —John Nichols, *The Sterile Cuckoo*, p. 190, 1965
- —Collin Baker et al., *College Undergraduate Slang Study Conducted at Brown University*, p. 152, 1968
- "They're all pretty well looped." —Charles Whited, *Chiodo*, p. 160, 1973
- —Connie Eble (Editor), *UNC-CH Campus Slang*, p. 5, Fall 1981

looper *noun*
1 a person who is capable of crazy actions *IRELAND*
- "Wood [would] ye go 'way oud [out] of dat [that], ye looper!" shouted the bloke who tried to jump the queue. "Fly home on yer broom, bleedin' state o' ye!" —Donal Ruane, *Tales in a rear view mirror*, p. 132, 2003

2 a wave that breaks over itself, creating a hollow through which a surfer can ride *US*
- —John Severson, *Modern Surfing Around the World*, p. 172, 1964

loopie *noun*
a tourist *NEW ZEALAND*
- Aucklander Geoff Chapple wondered why the South Island word for tourists is loopies. —*Listener*, p. 44, 30th June 1984

loop joint *noun*
an arcade showing recurring pornographic videos in private booths *US*
- A woman in San Francisco who has worked as a stripper in most of the live sex shows all over the West, including loop joints and brothels in Nevada, insists that no connection exists betwen sex and violence[.] —Hunter S. Thompson, *Generation of Swine*, p. 130, 16th June 1986

loop-scoop *verb*
to steal something quickly *US*
- —Bruce Jackson, *Outside the Law*, p. 58, 1972: 'Glossary'
- [T]hat's when you come to the penitentiary they'll go loop-scoop your old lady and get her selling cock and they don't send you any of the money. —Bruce Jackson, *Outside the Law*, p. 157, 1972

loop-the-loop; loop-de-loop; loopers; loop *noun*
soup *UK*
- Gimme some more loopers. —Jack Jones, *Rhyming Cockney Slang*, 1971
- —Ray Puxley, *Cockney Rabbit*, 1992

loopy *adjective*
slightly mad; drunk *UK, 1925*
A conventional 'loop' is an obvious aberration from a straight line.
- Sidney Blackpool was looking for Victor Watson in all this loopy art mix[.] —Joseph Wambaugh, *The Secrets of Harry Bright*, p. 15, 1985
- The fact is, on its loopier side, the New Age bolsters American values[.] —*HQ Magazine*, p. 103, 1996: 'Out of my mind '

loopy juice *noun*
1 an alcoholic drink *UK*
A drink with the 'juice' (power) to make you LOOPY (drunk).
- To understand what happens to you as you quaff an evening's worth of loopy juice, you need to understand what is happening to your brain[.] —*Drugs An Adult Guide*, p. 28, December 2001
- After being banned for a century, the 70 per cent proof French loopy juice, aka The Green Fairy, has become a UK staple —*Sky Magazine*, p. 88, May 2001

2 a strong medication *UK*
- —Angela Devlin, *Prison Patter*, p. 72, 1996

loopy looney juice *noun*
alcohol *UK*
Royal Navy slang; LOOPY (eccentric) plus LOONY (crazy) and JUICE.
- —Nigel Foster, *The Making of a Royal Marine Commando*, 1987

loose *noun*
▸ **on the loose**
(used of a wager) made on credit *AUSTRALIA*
- —Ned Wallish, *The Truth Dictionary of Racing Slang*, p. 59, 1989

loose *adjective*
1 (of a slot machine) advantageous to the gambler, both in terms of the frequency of payouts and a small house advantage *US*
- —J. Edward Allen, *The Basics of Winning Slots*, p. 58, 1984

2 romantically unattached *US*
- —Joan Fontaine et al., *Dictionary of Black Slang*, 1968

loose belly *noun*
diarrhoea *TRINIDAD AND TOBAGO, 1991*
- —Lise Winer, *Dictionary of the English/Creole of Trinidad & Tobago*, 2003

loose bump *noun*
in the military, an unsolicited and unwanted promotion *US*
- —*American Speech*, p. 55, February 1947: 'Pacific war language'

loose cannon *noun*
a person whose actions or words cannot be controlled or predicted *US, 1977*
From the image of a cannon rolling loose on the deck of a fighting ship.
- —*American Speech*, Spring 1983

loose goose *adjective*
something or someone that can be described as loose in whatever sense *US, 1958*
- That Foreman camp was totally whacked out, so uptight compared with Ali, who runs a loose-goose operation. —Bill Cardoso, *The Maltese Sangweech*, p. 299, 1984

loose horse *noun*
a tractor truck without a trailer *US*
- —Montie Tak, *Truck Talk*, p. 101, 1971

loose wig *noun*
a wild demeanour *US*
- —*Look*, p. 49, 24th November 1959

loosey-goosey *adjective*
very loose in any sense *US, 1967*
- I'm lookin' like money, but the best kind, casual, loosey-goosey. —Edwin Torres, *After Hours*, p. 177, 1979
- You take it too serious. I wanna see you loosey goosey up there on the eighteenth tee. —Joseph Wambaugh, *The Secrets of Harry Bright*, p. 150, 1985
- "She'd just jump from one man to the next at the senior meeting," Grandma said. "And I heard she was real loosey-goosey." —Janet Evanovich, *Seven Up*, p. 17, 2001

loosie *noun*
1 an individual cigarette sold over the counter *US*
- —Terry Williams, *Crackhouse*, p. 150, 1992
- —John Fahs, *Cigarette Confidential*, p. 302, 1996: 'Glosssary'

2 in rugby, a loose forward *NEW ZEALAND*
- We are strong in our loosies but are still short of locks and props. —*Dominion*, p. 18, 12th September 1977

loosie goosie *noun*
a sexually promiscuous young woman *US*
- I saw Brad weaving off through the bushes with some Loosie Goosie and I remember laughing and thinking that now I could forget about the little padlock I'd planned on getting him for his zipper. —Beatrice Sparks, *Jay's Journal*, p. 115, 1979

loot *noun*
1 money *US, 1929*
- The owner nixed big crowds out; he never allowed more than five or six parties in the place at any one time, and they had to be packed up with loot. —Mezz Mezzrow, *Really the Blues*, p. 84, 1946
- "How much loot you got?" asked the man. "I beg you pardon?" "Money. How much?" —Max Shulman, *The Many Loves of Dobie Gillis*, p. 30, 1951
- He ran out of loot and marble at the same time. —William "Lord" Buckley, *Nero*, 1951
- He don't need the loot, understand. —Bernard Wolfe, *The Late Risers*, p. 193, 1954
- Take this beat-up bovine to market and don't come back without some real loot. —Steve Allen, *Bop Fables*, p. 54, 1955
- I get 75 cents an hour and it's making more loot for me to hit road with. —Jack Kerouac, *Letter to Allen Ginsberg*, p. 494, 14th July 1955
- I have loot – I can afford. —Colin McInnes, *City of Spades*, 1957

- "Now there is one stud that can really go through loot," Zaida said. — Ross Russell, *The Sound*, p. 67, 1961
- [S]ee that blind man, knock him on the head, steal his wallet and lo and behold you have the loot. — Andrew Oldham, *withdrawn sleeve notes for the 2nd Rolling Stones' album*, 1965
- CHARLIE [Michael Caine]: But it's the family. They're after the loot I got off the last job. — Troy Kennedy Martin, *The Italian Job uncut script*, 1969
- I can't make a song and dance about the loot I've got but, to be fair, I have got some fucking potatoes. — Kevin Sampson, *Outlaws*, p. 109, 2001

2 a lieutenant *US*

- Chilly placed the loot's coffee at his elbow. — Malcolm Braly, *On the Yard*, p. 94, 1967

loot-in *noun*

politically motivated group shoplifting *US*

- [A] department store loot-in was being planned. "We'll choose a shop [...] select the stuff we want, hand the cashier a flower and head towards the door." — Richard Neville, *Play Power*,
- He flipped out over Keith's suggestion that "a thousand children will stage Loot-ins at department stores to strike at the property fetish that underlies genocidal war". — Jerry Rubin, *Do It!*, p. 73, 1970

loot money *noun*

after World War 2, Chinese national currency obtained by looting *US*

- — *American Speech*, p. 31, February 1949: 'A.V.G. Lingo'

lope *verb*

to stroke *US*

- Tompkins had such a peeny pecker he'd of had to lope it with forefinger and thumb. — Earl Thompson, *Tattoo*, p. 294, 1974

▸ **lope your donkey**

(of a male) to masturbate *US*

- "Old Chester going 'Ain't it wooooonderful' while he's loping that old rubber donkey!" — Joseph Wambaugh, *The Secrets of Harry Bright*, p. 171, 1985

▸ **lope your mule**

(of a male) to masturbate *US*

- "Pithead's queer for soap," he told his buddies on the yard. "He sleeps with a bar under his pillow and sniffs it while he lopes his mule". — Malcolm Braly, *On the Yard*, p. 8, 1967

lop-ear *noun*

an easily duped person *US*

- — *The Annals of the American Academy of Political and Social Sciences*, p. 127, May 1950
- Figured we'd cull out, from the lopears arriving, a mark to trim on the "smack." — Iceberg Slim (Robert Beck), *Long White Con*, p. 30, 1977

lop-ear; lop-eared *adjective*

naive, gullible *US, 1863*

- It's easy to steer a lop-eared chump, so long as Mordecai Jones has sized up the mark. — Guy Owen, *The Flim-Flam Man and the Apprentice Grifter*, p. 168, 1972

loper *noun*

1 a resident of Michigan's Lower Peninsula *US*

Upper Peninsula usage.

2 in hot rodding, a big and powerful engine that is noisy when it idles *US*

- — John Edwards, *Auto Dictionary*, p. 99, 1993

lopp *noun*

a perpetually naive and ignorant person *US*

- — James Harris, *A Convict's Dictionary*, p. 35, 1989

loqued out *adjective*

▷ see: LOCED OUT

lord and master *noun*

1 the backside, the buttocks *UK*

Rhyming slang, extending the sequence 'plaster' – **PLASTER OF PARIS – ARIS – ARISTOTLE – BOTTLE; BOTTLE AND GLASS – ARSE**. Sometimes seen in the abbreviated form of 'lord'.

- — Ray Puxley, *Fresh Rabbit*, 1998

2 a plaster (a first aid dressing) *UK*

Rhyming slang.

- — Ray Puxley, *Fresh Rabbit*, 1998

lord and mastered *adjective*

drunk *UK*

Rhyming slang.

- — Ray Puxley, *Fresh Rabbit*, 1998
- We went to every pub in town until we were well and truly lord and mastered. — Bodmin Dark, *Dirty Cockney Rhyming Slang*, 2003

lord boards *noun*

sandals *US*

From paintings of Jesus Christ wearing sandals.

- — Judi Sanders, *Mashing and Munching in Ames*, p. 12, 1994

Lord Jesus *noun*

a curly hairstyle popular with black men and women in the mid-1970s *US*

- It's goodby Afro, hello curls for scads of local hip black men who are part of the international, unisex trend to curly hair. They call the style "a Superfly," "a Lord Jesus" or just "a Curly Do" and they're spending lots of time and money to get the look. — *San Francisco Examiner*, p. 34, 13th April 1975

Lord Lovat!

used as an emphatic rejection of something *UK*

Rhyming slang, pronounced 'Lord love it', formed from the name of a long aristocratic line.

- — Ray Puxley, *Cockney Rabbit*, 1992

Lord love-a-duck!

used as a mild expression of shock or surprise *UK, 1917*

Sometimes varied as 'cor love a duck!' or reduced to 'love a duck!'; it is often regarded as a quintessentially Cockney turn of phrase.

Lord Mayor *verb*

to swear *UK*

Rhyming slang.

- A very common reference to bad language that may be extended to "Lord Mayoring". — Ray Puxley, *Cockney Rabbit*, 1992

Lord Muck *noun*

a man who is, in the speaker's opinion, unjustifiably important or esteemed *UK, 1937*

The earlier counterpart to **LADY MUCK**, although they are often seen as a couple.

- There is a Bang & Olufsen television which we swivelled around to watch like Lord and Lady Muck in our fluffy bathrobes on the verandah. — *The Observer*, 17th August 2003

Lord Sutch *noun*

in a car, the clutch *UK*

Rhyming slang, formed from the name of rock musician and politician Screaming Lord Sutch, 3rd Earl of Harrow, 1940–99.

- — Ray Puxley, *Cockney Rabbit*, 1992

Lord tunderin' Jesus

used as one of many elaborate Nova Scotian curses *CANADA*

- Lord tunderin' Jesus, boy, if dose fellows don't know who Hugh MacLennan is, den what are dey doin' at dat meetin? — Harry Bruce, *Movin' East*, p. 7, 1985

Lord Wigg *noun*

a glutton, an ill-mannered person *UK*

Rhyming slang for 'pig', formed from the name of politician George Cecil Wigg, 1900–83.

- Excuse my Lord Wigg, he's a friend. — Ray Puxley, *Cockney Rabbit*, 1992

Lordy!; lawdy!

Lord!, mildly calling upon God *US, 1853*

- 'Oh, Lordy!.. it's the Fat Slags. — *Roger's Profanisaurus*, p. 98, October 1999
- Oh my God! Lordy! Lordy! I'm in deep shit ain't I? — Jack Allen, *When the Whistle Blows*, p. 203, 2000

Loretta Young; loretta *noun*

the tongue *UK*

Rhyming slang, formed from the name of the US television and film actress, 1914–2000.

- "Hold your Loretta." Keep quiet! — Ray Puxley, *Fresh Rabbit*, 1998

Lorna Doone *noun*

a spoon *UK*

Rhyming slang, formed from the eponymous heroine of R.D. Blackmore's romantic novel, 1869, widely known from many film and television versions.

- — Ray Puxley, *Cockney Rabbit*, 1992

lorra *noun*

▷ see: LOTTA

lorry *noun*

▸ **up the lorry**

in a great deal of trouble *SINGAPORE*

- — Paik Choo, *The Coxford Singlish Dictionary*, p. 114, 2002

Los *noun*
Los Angeles, California *US, 1913*
Border Spanish used in English conversation by Mexican-Americans.
- —George Carpenter Baker, *Pachuco*, p. 42, January 1950
- And then they were offered a ride to "Los," as they refer to Los Angeles on the streets. —Joseph Wambaugh, *Lines and Shadows*, p. 78, 1984

lose *verb*
1 to get rid of *US, 1931*
- —Ralph S. Singleton, *Filmmaker's Dictionary*, p. 98, 1990

2 to fail to understand *UK, 1962*
- No, the majority of sound is radiated from the top and back plates of the violin, which are set in motion by the changes of pressure inside the box, which brings us to the crucial role of the bridge. I'm afraid you've lost me. —*The Guardian*, 1st October 2002

3 (used of a computer program) to fail to work as expected *US*
- —Guy L. Steele et al., *The Hacker's Dictionary*, p. 87, 1983

▸ **lose a load**
to ejaculate *US*
- —*American Speech*, p. 117, May 1964: 'Problems in the study of campus slang'

▸ **lose fire**
(used of a car engine) to stop operating *US*
- It is bad news for a drag race team to see its car lose fire right out of the hole. —Ed Radlauer, *Drag Racing Pix Dix*, p. 34, 1970

▸ **lose it**
1 to lose your mental focus to drugs, rhythmic sound and movement, and temporarily lose touch with the reality beyond the rave *UK*
A refined sense of 'lose it' (to temporarily lose control).
- It was neat that I could see the DJ at Drum Club as he was totally losing it back there and getting us all going too. Plenty of smoke – yeah. —Ben Malbon, *Cool Places*, p. 278, 1998

2 to come off your motorcycle accidently *UK*
- —Douglas Dunford, *Motorcycle Department, Beaulieu Motor Museum*, 1979

▸ **lose the plot**
to lose your grasp of a situation *UK*
- I want to reassure the auld cunt that I haven't lost the plot and it's still Thunderbirds Are Go[.] —Kevin Sampson, *Outlaws*, p. 218, 2001
- The UK media has lost the plot. —*The Times*, 8th April 2003

▸ **lose water**
in bodybuilding, to perspire *US*
Done intentionally before competition in bodybuilding in order to improve muscle definition.
- —*American Speech*, p. 200, Fall 1984: 'The language of body building'

▸ **lose your cool**
to become angry, excited, nervous, etc; to lose your self-possession *US, 1984*
- [T]he damage he [boxer Mike Tyson] did himself last January when he repeatedly lost his cool and swore at several reporters live on air. —*The Guardian*, 16th January 2000

▸ **lose your lunch**
to vomit *US, 1918*
- And I think he would have lost his lunch if he knew that his wife was The Plumber's daughter[.] —Richard Condon, *Prizzi's Money*, p. 47, 1994

lose or win *noun*
the foreskin *UK*
Rhyming slang.
- —Bodmin Dark, *Dirty Cockney Rhyming Slang*, 2003

loser *noun*
1 a socially inept person; a person with consistently bad luck; anyone deemed unacceptable or an outcast *US, 1955*
- —*Washington Post*, 23rd April 1961: 'Man, dig this jazz'
- —Collin Baker et al., *College Undergraduate Slang Study Conducted at Brown University*, p. 153, 1968
- —*American Speech*, p. 62, Spring-Summer 1975

2 a convicted felon *US, 1912*
- —Hyman E. Goldin et al., *Dictionary of American Underworld Lingo*, p. 129, 1950
- Richard Douglas Wilson, white male, age thrity-four. Two-time loser with a Quentin jacket. —James Ellroy, *Blood on the Moon*, p. 83, 1984

3 a hospital patient who dies *US*
- This kid looks like a loser. —*M*A*S*H*, 1970

losersville *noun*
a notional place where all socially inept people live *INDIA*
- Are you with it, catchin' up or still in losersville? —*The Times of India*, 30th September 2002

lossage *noun*
the ongoing effect of a computer malfunction *US*
- Thus (for example) a temporary hardware failure is a loss, but bugs in an important tool (like a compiler) are serious lossage. —Eric S. Raymond, *The New Hacker's Dictionary*, p. 228, 1991

loss-leader *noun*
something displayed prominently, and at a cut-price rate, to encourage further buying of other stock *US, 1922*
- How much of it was practically loss-leader stuff, items that we have to sell in order to compete? —Jim Thompson, *The Grifters*, p. 165, 1963

lossy *adjective*
(used of a data-compression computer program) apt to lose some data *US*
- A "lossy" algorithm (such as JPEG) therefore can't possibly be used to compress a piece of software – if even one bit is mislaid, the program just won't run – but it's just fine when it comes to compressing pictures, viedo, or sound. —Andy Ihnatko, *Cyberspeak*, p. 115, 1997

lost *adjective*
murdered, especially as a victim of 'criminal justice' *US*
- —Joseph E. Ragen and Charles Finston, *Inside the World's Toughest Prison*, p. 808, 1962: 'Penitentiary and underworld glossary'

lost-and-found badge *noun*
a US Army name tag *US*
Gulf war usage.
- —*American Speech*, p. 394, Winter 1991: 'Among the new words'

lost fart in a haunted milk bottle *noun*
the epitome of distraction or indecision *UK*
Royal Navy slang.
- —Rick Jolly, *Jackspeak*, p. 104, 1989

lost in the sauce *adjective*
daydreaming, completely inattentive *US*
- —*Washington Post*, p. 7, 3rd January 1988: 'Say wha?'

lost-it *noun*
a person under the sway of drug intoxication *UK*
- She was more or less able to control her buzz and was contemptuous of lost-its – guys walking around with gormless, grinning faces[.] —Colin Butts, *Is Harry on the Boat?*, p. 249, 1997

lost sailor *noun*
in the language surrounding the Grateful Dead, a follower of the band who has lost all touch with reality *US*
From the title of a Grateful Dead song.
- —David Shenk and Steve Silberman, *Skeleton Key*, p. 182, 1994

lost time *noun*
the reduction of time from a prison sentence for good behaviour *US*
- —Hyman E. Goldin et al., *Dictionary of American Underworld Lingo*, p. 129, 1950

Lost Wages *nickname*
Las Vegas, Nevada *US*
- In the last two years I have lost about $40,000 at 'Lost Wages, Nev.' and Del Mar. —*Los Angeles Times*, p. 22, 5th September 1951
- Las Vegas, or "Lost Wages," as it's known in Westside, is off limits to all Negroes – except entertainers and janitors. —Ed Reid and Ovid Demaris, *The Green Felt Jungle*, p. 136, 1963
- —Ralph de Sola, *Crime Dictionary*, p. 199–200, 1982

losum game *noun*
in the language of carnival workers, a game that for whatever reason should be terminated immediately *US*
- —Gene Sorrows, *All About Carnivals*, p. 21–22, 1985: 'Terminology'

lot *noun*
▸ **do the lot**
to lose all your money *UK, 1961*

▸ **the lot**
a life sentence in prison *NEW ZEALAND, 1997*
- —Harry Orsman, *A Dictionary of Modern New Zealand Slang*, p. 82, 1999

lotion *noun*
alcohol *UK, 1876*
- I can tell he's made up for backing down by pouring even more lotion down him[.] — Ted Lewis, *Jack Carter's Law*, p. 56, 1974

lot lady *noun*
in circus and carnival usage, a local woman who is attracted to and makes herself sexually available to circus or carnival employees *US*
In short, a circus or carnival **GROUPIE**.
- — Don Wilmeth, *The Language of American Popular Entertainment*, p. 162, 1981

lot lizard *noun*
1 an aggressive car salesman *US*
- Floor whores, a.k.a. "Lot Lizards" : Just above the baitfish are the "floor whores," salespeople who have survived by learning to pounce on the first person who walks in cold, without making an appointment. — Remar Sutton, *Don't Get Taken Every Time*, p. 46, 2001

2 a prostitute who works at transport cafes *US, 1987*
- Take your hero, a 12-year-old transvestite "lot lizard" – truck-stop whore – out of the safekeeping of his mother, Sarah[.] — *Village Voice*, p. 89, 11th April 2000
- Truckers who don't want solicitations from hookers, he explains, put a decal on their windshield depicting a lizard behind a red circle with a bar through it. (The creature is a reference to the slang term for truck-stop prostitutes: lot lizards.) — *Riverfront Times (St. Louis)*, 6th August 2003

lot loafer *noun*
in circus and carnival usage, a local resident who loiters as a show is assembled or taken down *US*
- — Don Wilmeth, *The Language of American Popular Entertainment*, p. 107, 1981

lot louce *noun*
a patron of a circus or carnival who spends little or no money *US, 1930*
- — Joe McKennon, *Circus Lingo*, p. 59, 1980

lot of it about
a catchphrase applied to the prevalence of anything *UK*
- There's a lot of it about. They promise porn, wealth and a cure for baldness. But unsolicited emails deliver nothing more than a major headache. — *The Guardian*, 7th October 2002

lotsa *noun*
a large amount *US*
A slovenly contraction of 'lots of'.
- Lotsa Doors and Zeppelin, marijuana and 'ludes[.] — Editors of Ben is Dead, *Retrohell*, p. 95, 1997

lotta; lorra
a large amount *UK, 1906*
A slovening of 'lot of'.
- In a publicity drive for the Liverpool clean streets campaign, litter was described as 'norra lorra fun'. — Tom McArthur, *The Oxford Companion to the English Language*, p. 910, 1992
- Lotta people eating a low-fat diet these days. — Jeffrey Eugenides, *Middlesex*, p. 474, 2002

lottery *noun*
in horse racing, a race with no clear favourite *AUSTRALIA*
- — Ned Wallish, *The Truth Dictionary of Racing Slang*, p. 49, 1989

lottery ticket *noun*
a currency note *UK*
In use at least fifteen years before the lottery was introduced to the UK.
- [They buy] each other a drink and pay for it with greenies, crispies, lottery tickets, drinking vouchers. — Ann Barr and Peter York, *The Official Sloane Ranger Handbook*, p. 117, 1982

lotto *noun*
money *SOUTH AFRICA*
Teen slang.
- — *Sunday Times (South Africa)*, 1st June 2003

Lotusland *noun*
the city of Vancouver, British Columbia and sometimes the whole province of BC *CANADA*
- Vancouver and a lot of the province of British Columbia enjoy a laid-back, mild-weather, relaxed culture–Lotusland, they call it. — *peak/sfu.ca*, 9th May 2002

lou *noun*
a lieutenant *US*
- I heard you talking to the lou. — Charles Whited, *Chiodo*, p. 129, 1973

loud *verb*
to arrest; to be arrested *UK*
English gypsy use.
- Let's jell [leave hastily], bruv, before the gavvers [the police] come and we get loud. — Jimmy Stockin, *On The Cobbles*, p. 67, 2000

loud *adjective*
subject to detection by smell *UK, 1641*
- Heroin smoked with tobacco could not be smelled; hence it was not "as loud" – GI lingo – as grass. — Myra MacPherson, *Long Time Passing*, p. 676, 1984

loud and clear *adjective*
expensive, overpriced, *dear* *UK*
Rhyming slang.

loud and proud *adjective*
(used of a citizens' band radio signal) clear *US*
- — Lanie Dills, *The Official CB Slanguage Language Dictionary*, p. 25, 1976

loud pedal *noun*
the accelerator on a drag racing car or hot rod *US*
- Just be gentle with 'er! Take it easy on the loud pedal! — *Hot Rod Comics*, June 1952

louie *noun*
a left turn *US, 1967*
- — *Current Slang*, p. 6, Spring 1968

▷ see: **LOOIE**

Louisiana lottery *noun*
an illegal numbers game *US*
- — *American Speech*, p. 192, October 1949: 'The argot of number gambling'

Louisville Lip *nickname*
the boxer Mohammed Ali, born Cassius Clay in 1942 in Louisville, Kentucky *US*
- Yes, the Louisville Lip is a loudmouthed braggart. — Eldridge Cleaver, *Soul on Ice*, p. 96, 1968

lounder *noun*
a generous portion of anything *CANADA*
- Two fellows were driving in the winter slush, and to clean the windshield, they stopped and put some snow on it. This didn't quite clean it, so the driver yelled to his friend "Throw another lounder on it!" — Lewis Poteet, *The South Shore Phrase Book*, p. 72–73, 1999

loungecore *noun*
a particular style of easy-listening music *UK*
An ironic combination of 'lounge' music (easy-to-listen but hard to define) and **-CORE**, which is usually suffixed to forms of rock music.
- — Susie Dent, *The Language Report*, p. 43, 2003

lounge lizard *noun*
a male sexual predator who seeks prey to seduce in fashionable bars and parties *US, 1918*
- Campbell Scott, playing the fortysomething lounge lizard anti-hero of this thoroughly outrageous and appallingly hilarious comedy of the singles scene, has a well-slapped-looking face. — *The Guardian*, 15th August 2003

Lou Reed *noun*
amphetamine *UK*
Rhyming slang for **SPEED**. Based, perhaps with more than a hint of irony, on rock singer and songwriter Lou Reed (b.1943).
- — Angela Devlin, *Prison Patter*, p. 21, 1996
- These guys are on a bonus, on Lou Reed as well, driven to get the round done and get away. — J.J. Connolly, *Layer Cake*, p. 251, 2000

louse *noun*
a despicable person *US, 1864*
- What was the louse arrested for? — C.D. Payne, *Youth in Revolt*, p. 301, 1993

louse book *noun*
an illegal betting operation that accepts only very small bets *US*
- — David W. Maurer, *Argot of the Racetrack*, p. 41, 1951

louse cage *noun*
a brakevan (caboose) *US, 1960*
- — Ramon Adams, *The Language of the Railroader*, p. 96, 1977

loused up *adjective*
covered with scars and abcesses from repeated drug injections *US*
• —William D. Alsever, *Glossary for the Establishment and Other Uptight People*, p. 18, December 1970

louse house *noun*
a run-down, shoddy boarding house *UK, 1785*

Lousetown *nickname*
▷ see: L-TOWN

louse up *verb*
to ruin, to spoil *US, 1934*
• [I] don't know why I'm telling you this; it's a sure way to louse up a favourite walk. But it would be wrong in a way not to share it.— *The Guardian*, 28th April 2001

lousy *adjective*
contemptible, shoddy, bad *UK, 1386*
Because of the association with body lice, the term was deemed vulgar if not taboo in the US well into the C20.
• "Well. Go to sleep now. How was your dinner?" "Lousy."—J.D. Salinger, *Catcher in the Rye*, p. 177, 1951
• [T]hey sing the praises of the working man's red-state virtues even while they pummel the workingman's economic chances with outsourcing, new overtime rules, lousy health insurance, and coercive new management techniques.—Thomas Frank, *What's the Matter with Kansas?*, p. 151, 2004

lousy with *adjective*
full of something, rich with something *UK, 1594*
From the prevalence of lice in an infestation. Occasionally, especially in relation to money, 'crawling with'.
• Look at me I'm Sandra Dee / Lousy with virginity / Won't go to bed till I'm legally wed / I can't I'm Sandra Dee—Warren Casey and Jim Jacobs, *Look At Me, I'm Sandra Dee*, 1972

lova *noun*
an unemployed person *SOUTH AFRICA*
Scamto youth street slang (South African townships).
• — *The Times*, p. 39, 12th February 2005

love *noun*
1 used as an endearment, or a form of address (generally to the opposite sex, sometimes considered patronising); also for anything that is charming and admired *UK, 1814*
• Bring the teapot, love, and tea caddy.—John O'Toole, *The Bush and the Tree [Six Granada Plays]*, p. 29, 1960
• You don't call me "love" or "darling". You treat me exactly how you'd treat a man.—Kevin Sampson, *Clubland*, p. 37, 2002

2 crack cocaine *UK, 1998*
• —Mike Haskins, *Drugs*, p. 282, 2003

▷ see: LIGHT OF LOVE

love-a-dove *adjective*
extremely affectionate as a result of intoxication with MDMA, the recreational drug best known as ecstasy *UK*
A play on **LOVEY-DOVEY** and **DOVE** (a type of ecstasy).
• Football thugs turned into love-a dove ravers.—Dave Courtney, *Stop the Ride I Want to Get Off*, p. 147, 1999

love a duck!; luvvaduck!
used as a mild expletive *UK, 1934*
Often preceded by 'Cor!', 'Lord!' or 'Gawd!'; probably a gentling of 'fuck a duck!'.
• Where bold is beautiful we don't give a damn / Love a duck we're common as muck[.]—Ian Dury, *Common as Muck*, 1979

love affair *noun*
cocaine; a mixture of heroin and cocaine *UK*
• —Nick Constable, *This is Cocaine*, p. 181, 2002

love and kisses *noun*
a wife *UK*
Rhyming slang for **MISSUS**.
• —Ray Puxley, *Cockney Rabbit*, 1992

love and marriage *noun*
a carriage *UK*
Rhyming slang, possibly acquired from the 1955 song 'Love and Marriage', lyrics by Sammy Cahn: 'Love and marriage, love and marriage / Go together like a horse and carriage'.
• —Ray Puxley, *Cockney Rabbit*, 1992

love an romancin *noun*
dancing *UK: SCOTLAND*
Glasgow rhyming slang.
• Ma folks are away tae the love an romancin at the Plaza.—Michael Munro, *The Patter, Another Blast*, 1988

love bladder *noun*
a condom *US*
• I turned and saw what the wind and the tide had brought in from Brooklyn and from the city's sewers; a sub-aquatic forest of waving white rubber eels, thousands of love-bladders.—Angelo d'Arcangelo, *The Homosexual Handbook*, p. 219, 1968

love blow *noun*
marijuana *US*
• —Richard A. Spears, *The Slang and Jargon of Drugs and Drink*, p. 322, 1986

love boat *noun*
1 phencyclidine, the recreational drug known as PCP or angel dust *US*
• Asked how many knew about the drug "Lovely" or "Loveboat" – street slang for PCP- nearly all raised their hands.—*Washington Post*, p. B3, 20th November 1983
• —US Department of Justice, *Street Terms*, October 1994

2 marijuana dipped in formaldehyde *US, 1998*
• —Mike Haskins, *Drugs*, p. 288, 2003

love child *noun*
a member of the 1960s counterculture *US*
• "They call themselves love children!" It was in the paper, the whole bullshit trip.—Herbert Huncke, *Guilty of Everything*, p. 169, 1990

love conkers *noun*
the testicles *UK*
Drawing an image of the fruit of the horse chestnut tree while playing on the familiar quotation 'love conquers all'.
• —Richard Herring, *Talking Cock*, p. 30, 2003

love cushion *noun*
your boyfriend or girlfriend *US*
• —Connie Eble (Editor), *UNC-CH Campus Slang*, p. 6, Fall 1986

love doctor *noun*
MDMA, the recreational drug best known as ecstasy *UK*
Descriptive of the way that **ECSTASY** treats your emotions.
• —Mike Haskins, *Drugs*, p. 289, 2003

love drug *noun*
1 MDMA, the recreational drug best known as ecstasy *UK, 1998*
Descriptive of the effect that **ECSTASY** has on your emotions; widely used.
• I participated in the popping of the old love drug, as they called it, and got my boy scouts badge in cuddling everyone[.]—Dave Courtney, *Raving Lunacy*, p. 73, 2000
• I was aware of its reputation as the "love drug", had heard it described as a "four-hour, full-body orgasm" and I found this intriguing[.] —Anonymous *Letter to The Guardian [The Howard Marks Book of Dope Stories]*, p. 229, 14th July 2001
• —Mike Haskins, *Drugs*, p. 289, 2003

2 the recreational drug methaqualone, best known as Quaaludes™ *US*
• By 1972 it was one of the most popular drugs of abuse in the United States and was known as love drug, heroin for lovers, Dr. Jekyll and Mr. Hyde, sopors, sopes, ludes, mandrakes and quacks.'—Marilyn Carroll and Gary Gallo, *Methaqualone*, p. 18, 1985

loved up; luvdup; luvved up *adjective*
under the influence of MDMA, the recreational drug best known as ecstasy, and experiencing the emotional need to share the boundless affection that is associated with the drug *UK*
• Steamer isn't the sort of person who allows people to mess with his apparel even when he's well luvved up[.]—Kevin Williamson, *Heart of the Bass (Disco Biscuits)*, p. 111, 1996
• —Alon Shulman, *The Style Bible*, p. 151, 1999
• Johann and Jorgi enter the yard. They are both loved-up and very touchy, touchy.—Guy Ritchie et al, *Lock, Stock... & Four Stolen Hooves*, p. 53, 2000
• [W]e were also bang into the whole loved-up pill thing as well. So you just befriended someone and made them your fucking partner! Dave Courtney.— *Raving Lunacy*, p. 49, 2000
• Ecstasy created a loved-up vibe[.]—Dave Haslam, *Adventures of the Wheels of Steel*, p. xxiii, 2001

love-'em-and-leave-'em; love 'em and leave 'em *adjective*
used as a description of philandering or a philanderer *UK, 1961*
- [In the film *This Earth is Mine*, 1959] Jean Simmons remarks that love-'em-and-leave-'em Hudson is a "bastard in every sense"[.] — *The Guardian*, 1st March 2003

love factory *noun*
a brothel *US*
- I came through the back way Papa Manny always used when the police raided the old love factory he ran. — Mickey Spillane, *Me, Hood!*, p. 25, 1963

lovefest *noun*
a close, happy relationship *US*
Combines 'love' with **-FEST** (a concentration of).
- Until this new thing about the birthday, we had a lovefest going. — Howard Stern, *Miss America*, p. 172, 1995

love glove *noun*
a condom *US*
- [A]lthough their standards and practices permitted the words 'prophylatctic' and 'contraceptive,' and even a student who calls a condom a 'love glove,' the word 'condom' was not allowed. — *PR Newswire*, 2nd November 1987
- However, even a love glove can't always protect you from herpes simplex, genital warts of hepatitis B. — Lisa Sussman, *Sex in the City*, p. 241, 2003

love handles *noun*
a roll of fat on either side of the body, just above the waist *US*
- — *Current Slang*, p. 20, Spring 1970
- HEATHER: He's got those love handles. — *Clerks*, 1994

love heart *noun*
a tablet of MDMA, the recreational drug best known as ecstasy, possibly mixed with the recreational drug methaqualone, best known as Quaaludes™, identified by an embossed heart; a decongestant sold as MDMA *UK*
These variously coloured tablets are named after a sherbety children's sweet.
- — Macfarlane, Macfarlane and Robson, *The User*, p. 74, 1996
- — Gareth Thomas, *This Is Ecstasy*, p. 56, 2002

love-in *noun*
a communal gathering for a hands-on celebration of inter-personal love *US, 1967*
- Sensationalised love-ins erupted from venues as diverse as Alexandra Palace and the Duke of Bedford's Woburn Abbey Estate. — Richard Neville, *Play Power*, p. 32, 1970

love in a punt *noun*
very weak beer *UK, 1973*
A play on 'fucking near water'.

love it!
used for registering definite approval *UK*
- That's what I like, by the way. Heavenly creatures with down-to-earth vices. BO. Bad breath. Brutal sex drives. Love it. — Kevin Sampson, *Outlaws*, p. 37, 2001

love juice *noun*
semen *UK, 1882*
- — Donald Webster Cory and John P. LeRoy, *The Homosexual and His Society*, p. 265, 1963: 'A lexicon of homosexual slang'
- To man, sperm is "nature's love juice." — Anka Radakovich, *The Wild Girls Club*, p. 110, 1994

love lips *noun*
the vaginal labia *UK*
- Unsexy... coarse... clumsy... I mean your use of "love-lips" – oh dear! And as for "came the morning he took me again", words fail me! — *The Guardian*, 5th July 2003

lovely *noun*
1 an attractive woman *US*
- "When I walk down the fairway I want the lovelies to know it's me for sure," Donny once explained. — Dan Jenkins, *Dead Solid Perfect*, p. 91, 1986

2 phencyclidine, the recreational drug known as PCP or angel dust *US, 1978*
A longer variant is 'lovely high'.
- Asked how many knew about the drug "Lovely" or "Loveboat" – street slang for PCP – nearly all raised their hands. — *Washington Post*, p. B3, 20th November 1983
- — US Department of Justice, *Street Terms*, October 1994
- — Mike Haskins, *Drugs*, p. 288, 2003

lovely and
▷ see: BEAUTIFUL AND

lovelyboy *noun*
used as a form of address *UK: WALES*
Sterotypically Welsh, perhaps as a result of actor Windsor Davies in BBC television comedy series *It Ain't Half Hot Mum*, 1974–81.
- I have limitless time to shut up in, lovelyboy, so you better say something worth shutting up for now. — James Hawes, *Dead Long Enough*, p. 292, 2000

lovely jubbly; luvly jubbly *adjective*
wonderful, fantastic *UK*
Coined by John Sullivan (b.1946) as a catchphrase for the popular character Del Boy in the BBC television comedy, *Only Fools and Horses* (1981–96), possibly inspired by a remembered response to a 'Jubbly', a pyramid-shaped frozen ice popular with children during the 1950s and 60s.
- We're going to the football." [...] "Lovely jubbly! — *ID*, 1994
- All deserted an' that. Just silent distant. Weightless. – Luvly jubbly[.] — Nick Barlay, *Curvy Lovebox*, p. 43, 1997

love muffin *noun*
the vagina *UK*
- However, the category edibility glosses over the variablity within it, which, for FGTs [female genital terms] included frequent reference to meat (e.g., bacon rashers, kebab, meat curtains); fish/seafood (e.g., tuna waterfall; fish, clam); and "sweet tidbits" (e.g. love muffin, fudge, cake-hole). — *Journal of Sex Research*, p. 146, 2001

love muscle *noun*
the penis *US, 1958*
- Put a lip lock on my love muscle. — Ken Weaver, *Texas Crude*, p. 81, 1984
- I have a well-developed love muscle. — Anka Radakovich, *The Wild Girls Club*, p. 228, 1994
- He felt his love muscle bathed in her melting shower. — Stewart Home, *Sex Kick [britpulp]*, p. 220, 1999
- I was far too horrified by their sordid tales of throbbing love muscles and red-hot nubs of womanly passion. — Helen Hastings, *Are Friends Electra [Inappropriate Behaviour]*, p. 4, 2002

love mussel *noun*
the vagina *US*
A neat pun on **LOVE MUSCLE** (the penis) and **FISH** (the vagina).
- — Erica Orloff and JoAnn Baker, *Dirty Little Secrets*, p. 91, 2001

love nest *noun*
1 a secluded room, apartment or house where lovers rendezvous *US, 1919*
- She had not left the apartment above the Paradise Room during the entire week, and would have stayed in the love nest for the rest of her life had Duke only asked her. — Donald Goines, *Inner City Hoodlum*, p. 85, 1975

2 the vagina *US*
- In addition to oral moves, some women occasionally like a finger or two inserted into the love nest. — Anka Radakovich, *The Wild Girls Club*, p. 131, 1994
- — Erica Orloff and JoAnn Baker, *Dirty Little Secrets*, p. 71, 2001

love nuggets *noun*
marijuana *UK*
- — Mike Haskins, *Drugs*, p. 288, 2003

love nuts *noun*
testicles that ache because of sexual stimulation that has not led to ejaculation; sexual frustration *US*
- — Eugene Landy, *The Underground Dictionary*, p. 122, 1971
- He then had to walk around for two days with his love-nuts trapped in glassware[.] — *FHM*, p. 250, June 2003

love off *verb*
to love greatly *UK*
- She loves her guy off but she has to stoop to survive. — Diran Abedayo, *My Once Upon A Time*, p. 134, 2000

love pill *noun*
a capsule of MDA, a synthetic amphetamine *US*
- — William D. Alsever, *Glossary for the Establishment and Other Uptight People*, p. 19, December 1970

love plank *noun*
the penis *UK*
Popularised in the film *Kevin & Perry Go Large* (2000).
- KEVIN: Suck my candy! PERRY: Lick my love plank! — Richard Topping, *Havin' It Large*, p. 49, 2000

love pole *noun*
the penis
- His love pole lingered a moment at the embouchement, then gilded past into the clinging folds of her sheath. —Stewart Home, *Sex Kick [britpulp]*, p. 220, 1999

love potion #9 *noun*
MDMA, the recreational drug best known as ecstasy *UK*
Descriptive of the effect that **ECSTASY** has on your emotions, from a 1959 song by Lieber and Stoller.
- —Mike Haskins, *Drugs*, p. 289, 2003

love pump *noun*
the penis *US*
Popularised if not coined for the film *This Is Spinal Tap*.
- Lick My Love Pump! [picture caption]—*Loaded*, June 2003
- This piece is called "Lick My Love Pump". —Christopher Guest, *This Is Spinal Tap*, 1984

lover *noun*
1 used as a form of address to someone who is not the speaker's lover *UK*
Possibly West Country dialect, certainly used as a characteristic of stereotypical West Country **MUMMERSET** speech.
- [The Landlord] grinned and fetched me a drink. "Have that one on me, me lover," he said. —Archie Hill, *A Cage of Shadows*, 1973

2 any sex offender *US*
- —Hyman E. Goldin et al., *Dictionary of American Underworld Lingo*, p. 130, 1950

loverboy; lover boy; lover man *noun*
a sexually promiscuous man, or one who tries hard to be so *US, 1952*
- Shah Rukh Khan smirking for his latest loverboy role[.]—*The Observer*, 7th April 2002
- Harvey Keitel is the sympathetic cop, Brad Pitt a lover-man. —*The Guardian*, 15th September 2003

lover cover *noun*
in drag racing, a protective shield between a driver's legs to prevent injury in the event of an engine explosion *US*
- —John Edwards, *Auto Dictionary*, p. 100, 1993

love rocket *noun*
the penis *UK*
- What do men actually say about their love rockets? —Richard Herring, *Talking Cock*, p. 6, 2003

lover's leap *noun*
in backgammon, the customary play with a first roll of 6–5: moving a back man 11 points *US*
- — Jacoby and John Crawford, *The Backgammon Book*, p. 242, 1970

lovers' nuts *noun*
testicles that ache because of sexual stimulation that has not led to ejaculation; sexual frustration *US, 1961*
- —Helen Dahlskog (Editor), *A Dictionary of Contemporary and Colloquial Usage*, p. 8, 1972

lover's speed; speed for lovers *noun*
MDMA, the recreational drug best known as ecstasy *UK*
MDMA is an amphetamine derivative that encourages empathy that is often confused with feelings of love.
- —Mike Haskins, *Drugs*, p. 289, 2003

lover's tiff; lovers' tiff *noun*
a sexually transmitted infection *UK*
Rhyming slang for 'syph' (syphilis), but applied more widely.
- —Ray Puxley, *Cockney Rabbit*, 1992

love sacks *noun*
the testicles *UK*
- —*A–Z of Rude Health*, 11th January 2002

love sausage *noun*
the penis *US*
- —Erica Orloff and JoAnn Baker, *Dirty Little Secrets*, p. 69, 2001

love, security and devotion *noun*
LSD *US*
A sobriquet formed from the drug's initials.
- —William D. Alsever, *Glossary for the Establishment and Other Uptight People*, p. 18, December 1970

love spuds; spuds *noun*
the testicles *UK, 1998*
- A Scottish farmer faces legal charges after his wife [...] discovered him spuds-deep in her Rhodesian Ridgeback. —*Loaded*, p. 30, June 2003

lovesteak *noun*
the penis *US*
- —Pamela Munro, *U.C.L.A. Slang*, p. 56, 1989

love tap *noun*
in motor racing, minor yet intentional contact between cars *US*
- —John Edwards, *Auto Dictionary*, p. 100, 1993

love trumpet *noun*
the penis *US*
Especially in the phrase 'blowing the love trumpet' (performing oral sex).
- —Erica Orloff and JoAnn Baker, *Dirty Little Secrets*, p. 83, 2001

love truncheon *noun*
the penis *UK*
From the shape and purpose; humorous yet aggressive.
- I batter her twat with my love truncheon. —Stewart Home, *Sex Kick [britpulp]*, p. 202, 1999

love up *verb*
to engage in sexual activity short of intercourse *TRINIDAD AND TOBAGO, 1964*
- Sly Stone covered "Que Sera Sera" because the papers thought he was loving Doris Day up[.]—Paolo Hewitt, *Heaven's Promise*, p. 121, 1999
- —Lise Winer, *Dictionary of the English/Creole of Trinidad & Tobago*, 2003

love weed; loveweed *noun*
marijuana *US, 1938*
- —Richard A. Spears, *The Slang and Jargon of Drugs and Drink*, p. 322, 1986
- —Simon Worman, *Joint Smoking Rules*, 2001
- —Mike Haskins, *Drugs*, 2003

lovey *noun*
used as an endearment, or an over-familiar or patronising form of address *UK, 1731*
In conventional use until late C19, thereafter colloquial.
- You see, lovey, I'm his guvnor and I pay his stamps. —Anthony Masters, *Minder*, p. 10, 1984

lovey-dovey *adjective*
extremely affectionate, sentimental, romantic *US, 1886*
Heard at the turn of the century, then obsolete; heard again in the late 1940s. When not a genuine endearment, it tends to be used contemptuously.
- All this lovey-dovey crap. Wanting everything so perfect. I might've known this was the old brush-off. —Horace McCoy, *Kiss Tomorrow Good-bye*, p. 309, 1948
- The HIP merchants were naturally afraid that Emmett and the Diggers might seize upon the moment to disturb their sweet, lovey dovey courtship of the media[.]—Emmett Grogan, *Ringolevio*, p. 267, 1972
- "My parents have never been so lovey-dovey... They were going at it for hours," he confided. —C.D. Payne, *Youth in Revolt*, p. 456, 1993
- Fine, go round there, give her one [have sex] and be all lovey dovey with her. —Danny King, *The Burglar Diaries*, p. 115, 2001
- Having entranced their public with a lovey-dovey hit entitled 'A Kiss At The End Of The Rainbow', they separated. —*The Guardian*, 30th November 2003

low *noun*
a depression, a state of depression (mental, physical or commercial) *UK, 1961*
The opposite of **HIGH**.

low and slow *adjective*
describing the manner in which lowriders drive their cars, low to the ground and at a crawl *US*
- —Jennifer Blowdryer, *Modern English*, p. 65, 1985

lowball *noun*
in the used car business, a knowingly deflated price *US, 1961*
- If a customer wants too much for his trade-in, a salesman may use the low ball to shock him back to reality. —Peter Mann, *How to Buy a Used Car Without Getting Gypped*, p. 193, 1975

low bandwith *adjective*
lacking useful information *US*
- —Christian Crumlish, *The Internet Dictionary*, p. 114, 1995

lowbrow *noun*
a person who is not, or has no pretentions to be, of above-average intellectual capability or aesthetic refinement *US, 1903*
- —Lawrence W. Levine, *Highbrow/Lowbrow*, 1990

lowbrow *adjective*
of little or no intellectual interest or aesthetic refinement *US, 1903*
- This is all pretty lowbrow stuff, and if you don't enjoy infantile humour then stay away[.]— *The Croydon Guardian*, 12th September 2003

lowbush moose *noun*
in Alaska, a snowshoe rabbit *US*
- —Jim Crotty, *How to Talk American*, p. 8, 1997

low camp *noun*
a coarsely ostentatious style, often unintentional *US*
An elaboration of **CAMP** (flamboyance).
- "Cut the low camp, bitch!" Chi-Chi barked furiously at Echoes and Encores, shoving the queen's hand roughly away from her shoulder. —John Rechy, *City of Night*, p. 355, 1963

lowdown *noun*
detailed information *US, 1907*
- The New York Times [...] just wanted the low-down on Mum, Dad and the whole royal shebang. — *The Guardian*, 20th November 1998

lower 48 *noun*
in Alaska, all states except Alaska *US*
- — *American Speech*, p. 256–258, Fall 1984: 'Terms for 'Not Alaska' in Alaskan English'

lower 49 *noun*
in Alaska, all states except Alaska *US*
- — *American Speech*, p. 256–258, Fall 1984: 'Terms for 'Not Alaska' in Alaskan English'

lower deck *noun*
the genitals, male or female *US*
- —Dale Gordon, *The Dominion Sex Dictionary*, p. 102, 1967

lower states *noun*
in Alaska, all states except Alaska *US*
- — *American Speech*, p. 256–258, Fall 1984: 'Terms for 'Not Alaska' in Alaskan English'

lowest form of life; lowest form of animal life *noun*
used to categorise or insult the despised, the overlooked and the most junior *UK, 1961*
- He [Tony Blair] had not even been a Parliamentary Private Secretary, lowest form of life on the Ministerial food chain. — *The Observer*, 6th May 2001

low-flyer *nickname*
Famous Grouse™ whisky *UK: SCOTLAND*
After the characteristic behaviour of the feathered grouse.
- —Michael Munro, *The Complete Patter*, p. 95, 1996

lowgrade *verb*
to disparage with great effect *US*
- You keep talking that way bout my pardner and I'm gonna LOW GRADE you. —Malachi Andrews and Paul T. Owens, *Black Language*, p. 85, 1973

low-hangers *noun*
testicles that dangle well below the body *US*
Used in *Sex and the City*, a late 1990s television comedy to indicate testicles that may get in the way of sexual penetration.

lowheel *noun*
a street-walking prostitute; any prostitute; a promiscuous woman *AUSTRALIA, 1939*
Inferring that the heels are worn down from persistent street-walking.

low-hung *adjective*
possessing a large penis *US*
- Because you're low-hung and she's high-strung! —Jim Thompson, *Pop. 1280*, p. 191, 1964

lowie *noun*
1 a period of clinical depression *UK*
Liverpool usage. Also spelt 'lowey'.
- I've felt this lowie coming on and now it's pure crashing down on us, a fucking murderous black downer. —Kevin Sampson, *Outlaws*, p. 69, 2001
- I'm not down. Not havin a lowey. —Niall Griffiths, *Kelly + Victor*, p. 143, 2002
- One thing I'd never done though, even in the wake of a mammoth post-binge lowie, was take it out on myself. — *The Guardian*, 12th June 2003

2 a prostitute; a promiscuous woman *AUSTRALIA, 1944*
From **LOWHEEL**.

Lowies *noun*
Lowenbrau™ beer *US*
- —Lillian Glass with Richard Liebmann-Smith, *How to Deprogram Your Valley Girl*, p. 27, 1982

low-low *noun*
▷ see: **LO-LO**

low maintenance *adjective*
(used of a person) not requiring a great deal of attention or emotional support *US*
A term that did not achieve anywhere near the fame of its cousin **HIGH MAINTENANCE**.
- And Ingrid Bergman is low maintenance?— *When Harry Met Sally*, 1989

low-man feed *noun*
in pinball, an understanding among friends playing a game that the person with the lowest score on one game will pay for the next game *US*
- —Bobbye Claire Natkin and Steve Kirk, *All About Pinball*, p. 113, 1977

low man on the totem pole *noun*
in poker, the player with the worst hand *US*
- —George Percy, *The Language of Poker*, p. 54, 1988

low marble count *noun*
low intelligence *US*
- —Sally Williams, *"Strong" Words*, p. 148, 1994

low neck; low neck and short sleeves *noun*
an uncircumcised penis *US, 1941*
- — *Male Swinger Number 3*, p. 48, 1981: 'The complete gay dictionary'

low on the totem pole; low on the totem *adjective*
occupying an unimportant position in a hierarchy *UK, 1974*
- Brinsley Schwarz were pretty low on the totem pole for me at that point. —Will Birch, *No Sleep Till Canvey Island*, p. 68, 2003

low pass *noun*
a preliminary review of a situation *US*
US naval aviator usage.
- — *United States Naval Institute Proceedings*, p. 108, October 1986

low-rate *verb*
to denigrate; to insult *US, 1906*
- Why's he say it like that? Tryin t'lowrate me? —Robert Gover, *JC Saves*, p. 77, 1968
- Now it was their turn to scoff and low-rate me. —Guy Owen, *The Flim-Flam Man and the Apprentice Grifter*, p. 63, 1972

low rent *adjective*
cheap, inferior; despicable *US, 1957*
- Joey low class. Joey low rent. No way Joey could have hold on her[.] —Joel Rose, *Kill Kill Faster Faster*, p. 104, 1997

lowrider *noun*
1 a young person who restores and drives a car with a hydraulic system that lowers the car's chassis to just above the ground *US, 1963*
A lifestyle and art form in the American southwest, especially among Mexican-American youth.
- Low Rider. A Los Angeles nickname for ghetto youth. —Eldridge Cleaver, *Soul on Ice*, p. 4, 1968
- — *Current Slang*, p. 33, Fall 1968
- —Oscar Zeta Acosta, *The Revolt of the Cockroach People*, 1973
- "That lowrider shit is dead." —James Ellroy, *Suicide Hill*, p. 700, 1986

2 a person wearing trousers without a belt and very low on the waist *US*
- —Anna Scotti and Paul Young, *Buzzwords*, p. 105, 1997

low road *noun*
the railway from Glasgow to Dalry *UK*
Surely formed from the famous Scottish song 'Loch Lomond': 'O ye'll tak the high road and I'll tak the low road, / And I'll be in Scotland afore ye'.
- —Harvey Sheppard, *Dictionary of Railway Slang*, 1970

lows *noun*
in pool, the solid-coloured balls numbered 1 to 7 *US*
- — Steve Rushin, *Pool Cool*, p. 15, 1990

low side *noun*
in craps, all the points below seven *US*
- — *The Annals of the American Academy of Political and Social Sciences*, p. 127, May 1950

low-tech *adjective*
using basic technology
Combines 'low' (basic) with an abbreviation.

low wines *noun*
in the illegal production of alcohol, the low-proof distillate produced by the first run of a still *US*
- — David W. Maurer, *Kentucky Moonshine*, p. 120, 1974

lox *verb*
to refill an aircraft's stock of liquid oxygen, used for breathing at high altitudes *CANADA*
- "LOX" is the acronym for liquid oxygen. To "lox" an aircraft is to replenish its supply, a dangerous procedure as it is cold enough to destroy flesh and high flammable. "After the aircraft is refuelled, send the Safety Systems guy to lox it." — Tom Langeste, *Words on the Wing*, p. 177, 1995

loxed; loxed out *adjective*
in a diminished state of consciousness after a heart attack or respiratory arrest *US*
An abbreviation of '*l*ack *o*f o*x*ygen'.
- — *Maledicta*, Summer/Winter 1978: 'Common patient-directed pejoratives used by medical personnel'

loxion *noun*
a neighbourhood *SOUTH AFRICA*
Township slang, from 'location'.
- — Patrick Neate, *Where You're At*, p. 103, 2003

loyal to the dollar *adjective*
bribed and compliant with the intent of the bribe *US*
- Strong competition meant employing more and more backup; the police were no longer "loyal to the dollar" or to the crews they extorted money from. — Terry Williams, *The Cocaine Kids*, p. 123, 1989

L-plate; L-plater *noun*
a prisoner serving a life sentence *UK*
A play on L for 'life' and the L-plates that signify learner-drivers.
- — Angela Devlin, *Prison Patter*, p. 71, 1996

L's *noun*
a driver's licence *US*
- — Rick Ayers (Editor), *Slang Dictionary*, p. 12, 2001

LSD *noun*
▸ **new LSD**
Vicodin™, a prescription painkiller taken recreationally *US, 1990s*
- Courtney Love has also told of getting stuck into the pills, wittily dubbing them "the new LSD – Lead Singer's Drug". — *Drugs An Adult Guide*, p. 25, December 2001

LSD *nickname*
Lake Shore Drive, Chicago *US*
- Today the new in spot is Rush Street, located just west of LSD (Lake Short Drive), north of Chicago Avenue and south of Division Street. — *Graphic Arts Monthly*, p. 57, April 1985
- — Jim Crotty, *How to Talk American*, p. 47, 1997

l-seven *noun*
▹ see: L7

LT; el tee *noun*
a lieutenant *US*
From the common abbreviation.
- "Could you tell me where I can find the platoon leader?" "Say? The El-tee?" — Larry Heinemann, *Close Quarters*, p. 17, 1977
- The L.T. was kind enough to let us use his office. — Elmore Leonard, *Be Cool*, p. 21, 1999

L-town; Lousetown *nickname*
Klondike City, Yukon Territory *CANADA*
- Poking through the ruins of Lousetown, the old red light district across the river from Dawson City, antique collector Gradelle Leigh of Fairbanks came up with a real find — *Alaska Sportsman*, p. 34/3, March 1963

L train *noun*
▸ **take the L train**
to lose, to fail miserably *US*
- — *Merriam-Webster's Hot Words on Campus Marketing Survey '93*, 1993
- — Evening Sun (Baltimore), 1993

L train!
used for a warning that police are nearby *US*
- — *Washington Post*, p. C5, 7th November 1993

lubage *noun*
marijuana *US, 1998*
A variation of LUBANGE (marijuana).
- — Mike Haskins, *Drugs*, p. 288, 2003

lubange *noun*
marijuana *US, 1982*
Originally East African.
- — Richard A. Spears, *The Slang and Jargon of Drugs and Drink*, p. 324, 1986

lube *noun*
a lubricant *US*
- K is for K-Y, miraculous lube! At any good drugstore, a dollar a tube. — *Screw*, p. 15, 22nd March 1970
- "So by the end of the day I totalled nine anals." "Yeeow! That must've hurt. Lotsa lube I imagine?" "Lotsa lube." — Anthony Petkovich, *The X Factory*, p. 55, 1997
- I kept asking for more lube, but finally Red said, "Honey, you have a ton of lub in your ass." — *The Village Voice*, 2nd November 1999
- Christie Lake recommends "lotsa lube" – Astroglide and Wet are popular brands. — Ana Loria, *1 2 3 Be A Porn Star!*, p. 101, 2000

lube *verb*
to lubricate *US, 1956*
- [W]ent out to the De Soto which I had had oiled, gassed up and lubed yesterday afternoon. — Clancy Sigal, *Going Away*, p. 364, 1961
- If she dry, lube up with this and you'll be good to go. — *Kill Bill*, 2003

lubed *adjective*
drunk *US, 1979*
An abbreviated form of LUBRICATED.
- He buys me drinks up the ying yang, gets me righteously lubed, then splits. — James Ellroy, *Because the Night*, p. 485, 1984
- Sounds like his partner's all lubed up. — *Something About Mary*, 1998

lube job *noun*
the process of lubricating a car or other piece of machinery *US, 1950*
- I hung around outside the De Soto, and when he said I had enough gas as it was, I asked him to give it a lube job while I waited. — Clancy Sigal, *Going Away*, p. 164, 1961

lubra *noun*
an Aboriginal woman *AUSTRALIA, 1830*
Probably from an Australian Aboriginal language. Now only used derogatorily.
- Inside that hut, there were seven of them, he thought, and the old man and his lubra in a space not big enough to swing a ruddy cat. — Jean Brooks, *The Opal Witch*, p. 111, 1967

lubra lips *noun*
large lips *AUSTRALIA*
- [O]ne was ginger haired with a face like she was in the toilet when they were given out and these big lubra lips but she had a twinkle in her blue eyes. — Bluey *Bush Contractors*, p. 302, 1975
- The new Prime Minister of Australia had lubra-lips and hair combed back like surf in full moonlight, and called Shadbolt by his first name. — Murray Bail, *Holden's Performance*, p. 344, 1984

lubricated *adjective*
drunk *US, 1911*
- "Breda," he said, "we're both still a little lubricated. We shouldn't try to communicate right now." — Joseph Wambaugh, *Fugitive Nights*, p. 234, 1992

Luby Lou; Luby *nickname*
a Jewish person *UK*
Rhyming slang; probably formed on Looby Loo, a rag doll character in children's television programme *Andy Pandy*, BBC since 1950.
- [A]ll eyes turned accusingly towards Luby (Luby Lou, the Jew), the only Man United fan in the room. — Erwin James, *The Guardian*, 6th July 2000: 'A life inside'

Lucas *noun*
marijuana *US*
• —Peter Johnson, *Dictionary of Street Alcohol and Drug Terms*, p. 113, 1998

lucifee; lucivee *noun*
a Canada lynx *CANADA*
• Simonds, Hazen and White sent a consignment of furs to Halifax to be shipped to England. It consisted of moose skins, carbou, "lucivers," red fox, cross fox, bear skins. —Jesse Lawson, *Our New Brunswick Story*, p. 256, 1949
• "Lucivee" is English corrupted out of the French phrase "loup cervier," or Canada lynx. —*cbc4kids.ca*, 15th June 2002

luck *noun*
▸ **you never know your luck**
something unexpected may well happen *UK, 1961*
Probably an elaboration of **YOU NEVER KNOW**.
• And you never know your luck – he might even allow a spot of light snogging. —*The Observer*, 17th March 2002

luck into *verb*
to be the beneficiary of good fortune *US, 1920*
• Commissioner Cameron seems O.K. is all I'm trying to say, even though he sort of lucked into the job as a compromise candidate of the owners on the forty-eighth ballot. —Dan Jenkins, *Semi-Tough*, p. 15, 1972

luck money *noun*
a tip or gratuity *US*
• If they stay through, they are besieged for "luck money," as gratuities are known among these habitues and sons of habitues. —Jack Lait and Lee Mortimer, *New York Confidential*, p. 70, 1948

luck out *verb*
to experience some good luck *US, 1945*
• Bush's vast legal team had an inkling that Bush had lucked out during the automatic recount. —David Corn, *The Lies of George W. Bush*, p. 54, 2003

lucky 15 *noun*
a multiple bet, based on a yankee, combining 15 separate bets *UK*
• If you add four singles (A,B,C,D) to your Yankee, that is Lucky 15[.] —John McCririck, *John McCririck's World of Betting*, p. 45, 1991

lucky 31 *noun*
a multiple bet covering five selections to '31 win stakes or 62 each-way stakes' *UK*
• —David Bennet, *Know Your Bets*, p. 61, 2001

lucky 63 *noun*
a multiple bet covering six selections to '63 win stakes or 126 each-way stakes' *UK*
• —David Bennet, *Know Your Bets*, p. 61, 2001

lucky boy; luck boy *noun*
a swindler; a pickpocket *US, 1922*
• And the luck boys were there too. It's easy to spot them when you know what to look for. —Robert Edmond Alter, *Carny Kill*, p. 9, 1966
• They are called lucky because they can't lose. —Sherman Louis Sergel, *The Language of Show Biz*, p. 130, 1973
• —Joe McKennon, *Circus Lingo*, p. 59, 1980

lucky buck *noun*
a casino gambling coupon *US, 1974*
• —Thomas L. Clark, *The Dictionary of Gambling and Gaming*, p. 123, 1987
• —Michael Dalton, *Blackjack*, p. 62, 1991

lucky charm *noun*
the arm *UK*
Rhyming slang.
• —Ray Puxley, *Fresh Rabbit*, 1998

Lucky Country; lucky country *noun*
Australia *AUSTRALIA, 1968*
From *The Lucky Country*, 1964, by Donald Horne, Australian author. Often used ironically.
• [They were trying to] gum up the inner workings and end the trot of the Lucky Country's mixed metaphors. —Frank Hardy, *The Outcasts of Foolgarah*, p. 221, 1971
• If they were born poor, they would probably stay poor in this lucky country. —David Ireland, *The Unknown Industrial Prisoner*, p. 335, 1971
• All migrants usually started their life in the 'Lucky Country' working in some large factory[.] —*Joseph's Coat*, p. 143, 1985
• All of them, young and old, were very employable – except that there are no jobs for them in the lucky country because the capitalists won't invest unless they can make super profits. —Frank Hardy, *Hardy's People*, p. 113, 1986

lucky dip *noun*
1 a chip *UK*
Rhyming slang, noted by Ray Puxley, *Cockney Rabbit*, 1992, who suggests a probable derivation in 'eating a bag of chips'.
2 a whip *UK*
Rhyming slang.
• —Ray Puxley, *Fresh Rabbit*, 1998

lucky lady *noun*
a type of bet in an illegal numbers game lottery *US*
• He played the money row, lucky lady, happy days, true love, sun gonna shine, gold, silver, diamonds, dollars and whiskey. —Chester Himes, *A Rage in Harlem*, p. 23, 1957

lucky last *noun*
in horse racing, the final race of the day *AUSTRALIA*
• —Ned Wallish, *The Truth Dictionary of Racing Slang*, p. 49, 1989

lucky Pierre *noun*
the man (or the woman) sandwiched between the outer layers of a sexually active threesome *US, 1942*
Glorified in the following lyric: 'Pierre gave it to Sheila, / Who must have brought it there. / He got it from François and Jacques, / A-ha, Lucky Pierre!' (Tom Lehrer, 'I Got It From Agnes', 1953). Predominately gay male usage.
• —*Maledicta*, p. 232, 1979: 'Kinks and queens: linguistic and cultural aspects of the terminology for gays'
• —Wayne Dynes, *Homolexis: A Historical and Cultural Lexicon of Homosexuality*, p. 105, 1985
• [C]an be substituted with a female name if the dynamics require it. "Lucky Pauline" has a certain ring to it. —*Sky Magazine*, p. 72, July 2001

lucky shop *noun*
in Victoria; an establishment for betting with the TAB (a legal gambling agency) *AUSTRALIA, 1979*
• So one would have thought that punters would waste little time in hot-footing it to the Lucky Shop to collect what they are rightfully owed. —*Herald*, p. 21, 12th March 1990

lucky stiff *noun*
in blackjack, a poor hand that is transformed by a lucky draw into a winning hand *US*
• —Victor H. Royer, *Casino Gamble Talk*, p. 82, 2003

lucoddy; leucoddy; coddy *noun*
the body *UK*
• There look, Mr Horne. Vada that great butch lucoddy. —Barry Took and Marty Feldman, *Round The Horne*, June 1967
• —Paul Baker, *Polari*, p. 179, 2002
• —*Attitude*, p. 60, July 2003: 'Old palare lexicon'

Lucozade *noun*
a black person *UK*
Rhyming slang for **SPADE** (a black person); formed on the name of a branded drink.
• "Listen, any more of that and I'm going to nick you under the Race Relations Act -" "That's for Lucozades – not for Jerries [Germans]." —Anthony Masters, *Minder*, p. 158, 1984

lu-cu-pu
good night *US*
A short-lived, but intensely used, piece of bebop slang.
• "What do 'Mop-shi-lu' and 'Lu-cu-pu' mean?" I asked Dizzy. —*San Francisco Examiner*, p. Pictorial Review, 3 December 1948
• —Arnold Shaw, *Lingo of Tin-Pan Alley*, p. 14, 1950

Lucy *noun*
an individual cigarette sold over the counter *US*
• —John Fahs, *Cigarette Confidential*, p. 302, 1996: 'Glossary'

Lucy in the Sky with Diamonds; Lucy *noun*
LSD *UK, 1975*
One of the Beatles' most psychedelic songs, '*L*ucy in the *S*ky with *D*iamonds', 1967, has always been seen as a (not very discreet) LSD reference.
• —Angela Devlin, *Prison Patter*, p. 72, 1996
• Street names [...] lightning flash, Lucy, micro dot[.] —James Kay and Julian Cohen, *The Parents' Complete Guide to Young People and Drugs*, p. 141, 1998
• —Mike Haskins, *Drugs*, p. 285, 2003

Lucy Locket *noun*
a pocket *UK, 1971*
Rhyming slang, from a nursery rhyme.
• Take your bleeding hands out of your Lucy Lockets and do some work. —Ray Puxley, *Cockney Rabbit*, 1992

Lucy Law *noun*
▷ see: LILLY

lude; lud *noun*
a tablet of the recreational drug methaqualone, best known as Quaaludes™ or, in a manner not inconsistent with the imprecision of the drug culture, any central nervous system depressant *US, 1973*
Quaalude™ was a brand name for methaqualone, a muscle relaxant and barbiturate substitute introduced in 1965 and made illegal in the US in 1984.
- Still, millions choose to ignore the warnings, and relieve their anxieties with minor tranquilizers like Librium and Valium, or sedate their troubles with more powerful sedative phenobarbital or "purple hearts," Quaaludes or "ludes," and a host of other socalled "downers[.]" — *Washington Post*, p. A7, 30th July 1978
- All right. Just relax. Take a lude. Take a lude. — *Manhattan*, 1979
- The carpeted lobby was littered with fallen rainbows, dexis, bennies, ludes, speed, even some dust, though it had a bad rep these days[.] — Joseph Wambaugh, *The Glitter Dome*, p. 122, 1981
- Laugh at the thought of eating ludes / Laugh at the thought of sniffing glue / Always gonna keep in touch / Never want to use a crutch / I've got the straight edge. — Minor Threat, *Straight Edge*, 1983(?)
- Get some up in Boystown, New York AVenue, those cute guys had anything you wanted, knockout drops, percs, street ludes, all kinds of meth. — Elmore Leonard, *Glitz*, p. 131, 1985
- "You wanna lude, is that it?" He pulls out a Pez dispenser and pulls Daffy Ducks' head back. — Bret Easton Ellis, *Less Than Zero*, p. 21, 1985
- He tried to stop using heroin and then got into an even worse state with ludes and other tranquilizers. — Barry Hoskyns, *Waiting For The Sun*, p. 265, 1996

lúdramán; ludramaun *noun*
an idiot, a stupid person *IRELAND*
From the Irish for 'an idle person'.
- I often wonder what sort of ludramaun leaves their cars in one of those backlots late at night anyways. — Eamonn Sweeney, *Waiting for the Healer*, p. 142, 1997
- For example, the PRO of a youth club could have no qualifications; he or she could be the biggest lúdramán since the sliced pan. — Mr. Glynn, *House of the Oireachtas Parliamentary Debates*, 12th November 1998

luego
used as a farewell *US*
Spanish for 'later'.
- — Connie Eble (Editor), *UNC-CH Campus Slang*, p. 5, Fall 1981

luer *noun*
a glass syringe with a slip-on needle and a solid plunger *US*
- — David Maurer and Victor Vogel, *Narcotics and Narcotic Addiction*, p. 424, 1973

lug *noun*
1 a large, clumsy, dim man *US, 1927*
- Then try to get hold of me and maybe we can ambush the lug. — Mickey Spillane, *I, The Jury*, p. 89, 1947
- I need you to run interference with the lug. Make some small talk with him or something. — *Mallrats*, 1995
- Elliot would walk in and Andy would say, "Hi, you big lug," Or he'd say, "Hi stranger. New in town?" — Elmore Leonard, *Be Cool*, p. 305, 1999

2 a woman who takes lesbian lovers in college and then reverts to heterosexuality after graduation from college *US*
An abbreviation of '*l*esbian *u*ntil *g*raduation'.
- There is even a new term – "lugs," lesbians until graduation. — *New York Times*, p. 7, 5th June 1993
- — Steven Daly and Nalthaniel Wice, *alt.culture*, p. 138, 1995
- — Don R. McCreary (Editor), *Dawg Speak*, 2001

3 the ear *UK, 1507*
- — Lou Shelly, *Hepcats Jive Talk Dictionary*, p. 13, 1945
- Gravy [blood] came out his hooter [nose] and his lugs. — Jeremy Cameron, *Brown Bread in Wengen*, p. 5, 1999
- They were trying to cut his lugs off but the scissors kept on folding over. — Lanre Fehintola, *Charlie Says...*, p. 75, 2000

4 an inhalation of marijuana smoke, especially from a water pipe *UK*
- [T]ake a lug, feel the buzz[.] — Macfarlane, Macfarlane and Robson, *The User*, p. 39, 1996
- Contemplation is the musical equivalent of taking a far-larger-than-is-probably-wise lug from a bong[.] — *Ministry*, May 2002

5 a demand *US, 1929*
- I'm hip to the ways you pimps try to play / And the lugs you drop on a frail. — Dennis Wepman et al., *The Life*, p. 86, 1976

6 luggage *US*
- — Ramon Adams, *The Language of the Railroader*, p. 96, 1977

lug *verb*
to bring, to accompany *UK, 1884*
- When I lug that sucker to you, I'm going to wink at the mark and palm a core sample of those phony rocks as you and Pocket show them to us. — Iceberg Slim (Robert Beck), *Trick Baby*, p. 217, 1969

lugan *noun*
a Lithuanian *US, 1947*
Coined in Chicago.
- — Bill Reilly, *Big Al's Official Guide to Chicagoese*, p. 42, 1982

luger lout *noun*
a German *UK*
Rhyming slang for **KRAUT** formed from the well-known brand of German side-arm and a pun on **LAGER LOUT**.
- — Ray Puxley, *Cockney Rabbit*, 1992

lugger *noun*
1 in a big store confidence swindle, somebody who is assigned to provide background ambience, an extra *US, 1931*
- "John, this is Victoria Hart. She's gonna be a lugger on this hustle." — Stephen Cannell, *King Con*, p. 114, 1997

2 a person who physically transports players to an illegal poker game *US*
- — John Scarne, *Scarne's Guide to Modern Poker*, p. 283, 1979

lughole; lug'ole *noun*
the ear *UK, 1895*
A variation of **LUG** (the ear).
- She'd clout you on the lughole. — Derek Bickerton, *Payroll*, p. 45, 1959
- The likelihood of it getting yanked from your lugholes by street toughs is high, given that the thing [a personal stereo] retails at £280. — *The Guardian*, 17th June 2003

lug in *verb*
(used of a racehorse) to tend to run toward the rail *US*
- — Nate Perlmutter, *How to Win Money at the Races*, p. 120, 1964

luke *noun*
pre-coital vaginal secretions *US, 1960s*
- Luke – Female coital fluid. Corruption of "leucorrhea." — *Fact*, p. 26, January–Feburary 1965

luken *noun*
in circus and carnival usage, a naive, gullible person *US*
- — Don Wilmeth, *The Language of American Popular Entertainment*, p. 164, 1981

Luke the Gook *noun*
during the Korean war, a north Korean; during the Vietnam war, any Vietnamese person *US, 1953*
War usage.
- Yet everyone knew he was there – Old Joe Chink, Luke the Gook, the enemy. — T.R. Fehrenbach, *This Kind of War*, p. 432, 1963
- I had come to view the enemy in Vietnam as a real monster, as a threat to my personal security, something which had to be stopped and squashed. Phrases like "gook" and "link the chink" and "luke the gook," stuff we used in training got solidly into my head. — John Kerry, *The New Soldier*, p. 96, 1971
- — Linda Reinberg, *In the Field*, p. 131, 1991

Luke the Gook's castle *noun*
a fortified North Korean position *US*
- In fact they scoffed at one such Red fortress, as "Luke the Gook's Castle." — Don Lawson, *The United States in the Korean War*, p. 109, 1964

lullaby *verb*
to knock unconscious; to kill *US*
- Money, I want you to escort Mr. Rivera out of the court and off the block. If he tries anything, lullaby him. — *New Jack City*, 1990

lulu *noun*
something that is amazing *US, 1886*
- The funny thing was, though, we were the worst skaters on the whole goddamn rink. I mean the worst. And there were some lulus, too. — J.D. Salinger, *Catcher in the Rye*, p. 129, 1951
- James Baldwin has finally written his own "protest novel," Another Country, and it is a lulu. — Terry Southern, *Now Dig This*, p. 202, 1962
- In Parker Tyler's masterpiece Magic and Myth of the Movies, he refers to James Craig's voice as "some kind of Middle Southnwest drawl, a genuine lulu." — Gore Vidal, *Myra Breckinridge*, p. 10, 1968
- He really caught himself a lulu. — Herbert Huncke, *Guilty of Everything*, p. 16, 1990
- Oshun opened up with a LuLu. I can still remember how shook I was as she talked. — Odie Hawkins, *Lost Angeles*, p. 197, 1994

Lulu's parlor *noun*
a brothel *US*
- My ears are bent in half from the tales of woe I've listened to in Lulu's parlors on both sides of the Atlantic. —Mezz Mezzrow, *Really the Blues*, p. 88, 1946

lumber *noun*
1 the stems of a marijuana plant *US*
- —Ernest L. Abel, *A Marijuana Dictionary*, p. 64, 1982

2 stolen goods *UK*
- Andy agreed to place all the lumber I brought him for 15% of the price he got. —Charles Raven, *Underworld Nights*, p. 164, 1956

3 an action or piece of information intended to cause trouble *UK*
- It wasn't long before he was back with a lumber which he'd picked up from Barney Newbiggin[.] —Charles Raven, *Underworld Nights*, p. 155, 1956

4 a member of the opposite sex that you form an initial liaison with, especially with a view to greater intimacy *UK: SCOTLAND*
- I'm looking for a lumber. —Hamish Imlach, *Cod Liver Oil and the Orange Juice*, 1966
- We were at the jiggin [dance] last night; couldny get a lumber, but. —Michael Munro, *The Original Patter*, p. 43, 1985

5 a non-playing, non-betting observer of a game of chance *US, 1961*
- —George Percy, *The Language of Poker*, p. 54, 1988

▸ **in lumber; in dead lumber**
in trouble *UK, 1967*
- I always thought if we ever got in lumber with the Old Bill [police], it would be me who went down. —Danny King, *The Burglar Diaries*, p. 187, 2001

lumber *verb*
1 to steal *UK*
- [J]ust to make sure the right gear was lumbered. —Charles Raven, *Underworld Nights*, p. 21, 1956

2 to fight *US*
- —Connie Eble (Editor), *UNC-CH Campus Slang*, p. 4, Fall 1982

3 to form an initial liaison with someone sexually attractive, especially with a view to greater intimacy *AUSTRALIA, 1933*
- Ma pal got lumbered by your big brother. —Michael Munro, *The Patter*, p. 43, 1985

4 to encumber with problems or trouble *UK*
- The boys were on to him. He had been lumbered in his turn. —Charles Raven, *Underworld Nights*, p. 156, 1956

5 to arrest *UK, 1812*
First recorded in 1812 (Vaux) meaning 'to jail', from 'lumber' (to pawn).
- 'Yeah, they'd lumber him f'sure, if they caught him wandering round like that!' —W.R. Bennett, *Wingman*, p. 66, 1961
- —James Holledge, *The Great Australian Gamble*, p. 106, 1966
- —Lance Peters, *The Dirty Half-Mile*, p. 167, 1979
- MacGillicuddy could have lumbered them for even having the stuff[.] —Bob Staines, *Wot a Whopper*, p. 30, 1982
- —Ryan Aven-Bray, *Ridgey Didge Oz Jack Lang*, p. 35, 1983
- —William Dodson, *The Sharp End*, p. 34, 2001

lumbered *adjective*
1 arrested, in custody *AUSTRALIA, 1812*
Still in current use.
- — *The (Sydney) Bulletin*, 26th April 1975

2 in (any sort of) trouble; having been given unwelcome responsibility *UK, 1984*
- Other people have one common history, we have two. / Other people are lumbered with one leadership, we are lumbered with two. —Abdula Peshew, translated by Muhamad Tawfiq Ali, *Fratricide*, 1st March 2003

lumbering *noun*
sexual intercourse *AUSTRALIA*
- [H]owever, any lumbering or screwing that had to be done all took place at Davo's until until Colin could get a place of his own or one to share with a mate. —Robert G. Barrett, *Davo's Little Something*, p. 14, 1992

lumberjack *noun*
the back *UK*
Rhyming slang, playing on 'lumbar'.
- —Ray Puxley, *Fresh Rabbit*, 1998

lumberman's strawberries *noun*
prunes *CANADA*
- She set prunes on the table. "These here are known as lumberman's strawberries." —B. Freedman, *Mrs. Mike*, p. 79, 1947

lumber wagon *noun*
an old, dilapidated car *US*
- — *American Speech*, p. 270, December 1962: 'The language of traffic policemen'

lumber yard *noun*
1 the trees around and in a golf course *US*
- —Hubert Pedroli and Mary Tiegreen, *Let the Big Dog Eat!*, p. 57, 2000

2 a prison exercise yard *AUSTRALIA, 1956*
- —Maureen Brooks and Joan Ritchie, *Tassie Terms*, p. 86, 1995

lumins *noun*
rays of the sun *US*
Often found as 'soaking up a few lumins'.
- —Collin Baker et al., *College Undergraduate Slang Study Conducted at Brown University*, p. 154, 1968

lummed up *adjective*
drunk *UK: SCOTLAND*
- The pair a them wis lummed up before they even got tae the reception. —Michael Munro, *The Patter, Another Blast*, p. 42, 1988

lump *noun*
1 a stupid, inept person *UK, 1909*
- [O]f the 150, probably 100 were just a bunch of shtarkers who could pull at one end of a rope that was looped around some poor fucker's neck, while some other lump pulled at the other end. —Richard Condon, *Prizzi's Honor*, p. 118, 1982
- You stupid great lump. —Ray Puxley, *Cockney Rabbit*, 1992

2 a tracking device *UK*
- This was a world of bugs, lumps [tracking devices], phone taps, both landline and mobile, both legal and illegal. —Duncan MacLaughlin, *The Filth*, p. 192, 2002

3 in hot rodding and drag racing, an engine *US*
- — Capitol Records, *Hot Rod Jargon*, 1963

4 a small lunch carried in your pocket *US*
- —Joe McKennon, *Circus Lingo*, p. 59, 1980

lump *verb*
1 to dislike something that must be endured *UK, 1833*
- "This is how it is – you can either like it or lump it" is what the under-sourced book is actually saying. — *The Observer*, 17th February 2002

2 to reluctantly accept *UK, 1791*
Usually in the phrase 'lump it'.
- I know he's disappointed that I don't want to go again, but he's just going to have to lump it. —Greg Williams, *Diamond Geezers*, p. 103, 1997

3 to strike; to hit *UK, 1780*
- —Inez *The Joint*, p. 514, 1984
- Fucking hell, Jim, someone's just lumped me. —Jimmy Stockin, *On The Cobbles*, p. 146, 2000
- I did what any man would do. I lumped him one. —Duncan MacLaughlin, *The Filth*, p. 159, 2002

▸ **lump lips**
to talk on the telephone *US*
Teen slang.
- — *Newsweek*, p. 28, 8th October 1951

lumper *noun*
1 any unskilled worker *UK, 1785*
Originally applied to an unskilled worker who helped load and off-load vessels, and then more generally.
- —John Gould, *Maine Lingo*, p. 171, 1975
- —Ramon Adams, *The Language of the Railroader*, p. 96, 1977
- But for most of his life, he registered at the union hall as a lumper. He'd go down to the hall – Local 70 – each morning and sign in, and they'd ship him out, loading and unloading trucks or ships on the docks in Oakland. —Ralph "Sonny" Barger, *Hell's Angel*, p. 12, 2000

2 in carnival usage, a confederate who is hired to play and win a game in order to generate business *US*
- —Don Wilmeth, *The Language of American Popular Entertainment*, p. 30, 1981

lump of coke; lump *noun*
a man *UK, 1859*
Rhyming slang for **BLOKE**.
- Large gentlemen are often spoken of as "big lumps". —Ray Puxley, *Cockney Rabbit*, 1992

lump of ice *noun*
advice *UK, 1909*
Rhyming slang.
- —Ray Puxley, *Cockney Rabbit*, 1992

lump of lead *noun*
the head *UK, 1857*
Rhyming slang, noted in connection with a hangover.
• —Ray Puxley, *Cockney Rabbit*, 1992

lumps *noun*
the consequences of your actions, punishment or other unpleasantness, either physical or by reprimand *US, 1930*
• After three years of getting his lumps in the small towns, he realized that he didn't have it[.]—Babs Gonzales, *I Paid My Dues*, p. 104, 1967
• Larry is getting his lumps in Portsmouth[.]—Darryl Ponicsan, *The Last Detail*, p. 154, 1970
• "I'll talk to you after class," I said. That's when I would have to tell her the truth; that's when I would get my lumps.—Max Shulman, *The Many Loves of Dobie Gillis*, p. 171, 1981

lumpy gravy *noun*
the Royal Navy *UK, 1984*
Rhyming slang.
• —Ray Puxley, *Cockney Rabbit*, 1992

lumpy jumper *noun*
a female member of the Royal Air Force *UK*
A less than flattering allusion to female breasts. In Royal Air Force use, 2002.

lun *noun*
in Newfoundland, a spot in the lee of the wind *CANADA*
• He had no alternative to the slim chance of safety offered by the "lun" of Cat Harbour, Northern Island.—Michael Harrington, *Sea Stories*, p. 93, 1958

Luna Park bookmaker *noun*
a bookmaker who appears to be operating his business just for fun *AUSTRALIA*
Luna Park was an amusement park on Coney Island, New York, and later in Sydney. The Sydney park has long used the sobriquet 'just for fun' in advertisements.
• —Ned Wallish, *The Truth Dictionary of Racing Slang*, p. 49, 1989

lunar *noun*
the bleed period of the menstrual cycle *US*
Emphasises the monthly rhythm of the cycle.
• — *The Museum of Menstruation and Women's Health*, 2000

lunar occurrence *noun*
the bleed period of the menstrual cycle *US*
• —Collin Baker et al., *College Undergraduate Slang Study Conducted at Brown University*, p. 154, 1968

lunatic patrol *noun*
a police operation to bring a mentally ill person to a hospital *CANADA*
• She knew also of their care of the homesteaders, and of the "lunatic patrol" when the police went out to bring to hospital some man or woman whose reason has toppled before the loneliness of the prairies.—Kenneth Haig, *Brave Harvest*, p. 117, 1945

lunatics *noun*
▸ **the lunatics are running the asylum; the lunatics have taken over the asylum**
used of any situation that is managed by those who are incapable *UK*
• —Fun Boy Three *The Lunatics (Have Taken Over the Asylum)*, 1981

lunatic soup *noun*
alcoholic drink *AUSTRALIA, 1933*
• —Jim Ramsay, *Cop It Sweet!*, p. 56, 1977
• The bots ordered up only the best brands of lunatic soup from the top shelf.—Ryan Aven-Bray, *Ridgey Didge Oz Jack Lang*, p. 15, 1983
• —David McGill, *David McGill's Complete Kiwi Slang Dictionary*, p. 81, 1998

lunch *noun*
1 the male genitals, especially as may be hinted at or imagined when dressed *AUSTRALIA, 1944*
• —Paul Baker, *Polari*, p. 185, 2002
2 oral sex performed on a woman *US*
• — *Adult Video News*, p. 48, August 1995

▸ **do lunch**
to have lunch, usually a working lunch *US*
Hollywood lingo, embraced elsewhere with a sense of mocking.
• —Connie Eble (Editor), *UNC-CH Campus Slang*, p. 3, Spring 1987
• I didn't hang out with the movie crowd, didn't "do lunch" at the latest place or swing with the swingers.—Odie Hawkins, *Lost Angeles*, p. 33, 1994

▸ **drop your lunch**
to fart *AUSTRALIA*
• —Lenie Johansen, *The Dinkum Dictionary*, 1988

▸ **out to lunch**
1 distracted, insensible, foolish, stupid, vacant; being there with the mind elsewhere *US, 1955*
A figurative use of a favourite excuse for someone not being there, in this case extended to 'not all there'.
• — *Washington Post*, 23rd April 1961: 'Man, dig this jazz'
• He was a Neurotic Artist, almost a magician when it came to dealing with cards, but "out to lunch" on the people level.—Odie Hawkins, *Men Friends*, p. 113, 1989
2 knocked from your surfboard by a wave *US*
• —Gary Fairmont R. Filosa II, *The Surfer's Almanac*, p. 191, 1977

lunch *verb*
1 to fail, to do poorly *US*
• — *Current Slang*, p. 5, Winter 1966
2 to cause a car engine to explode, scattering parts on the track or road *US*
An especially common event and term in drag racing.
• The car was basically lunched, but the service department had added some lipstick.—Stephen Cannell, *Big Con*, p. 29, 1997
3 to perform oral sex *UK, 1996*
• —A.D Peterkin, *The Bald-Headed Hermit and the Artichoke*, p. 56, 1999

▸ **get lunched**
to be knocked from your surfboard and thrashed by the ocean *US*
• —Michael V. Anderson, *The Bad, Rad, Not to Forget Way Cool Beach and Surf Discriptionary*, p. 13, 1988

lunch *adjective*
without a care, absent-minded *US*
• — *American Speech*, p. 62, Spring-Summer 1975: 'Razorback slang'

lunchbox *noun*
1 the male genitalia, especially when generously presented in tight clothing *UK*
An indiscreet euphemism that makes people smile; perhaps its most famous usage occurred during track athlete Linford Christie's impressive performance at the 1992 Olympic Games, when he took gold in the 100 metres.
• Jacobs, the cream-cracker people, have been advertising [...] a biscuit described as "every man's dream: an extra one-and-a-half inches in the lunchbox department".—David Rowan, *A Glossary for the 90s*, p. 23, 1996
• That, Gentlemen, is a lunch-box to be proud of.— *The Full Monty*, 1997
• [T]he photo finish in the race between black and white lunchboxes is too close to call.—Richard Herring, *Talking Cock*, p. 250, 2003
2 someone who is completely out of touch *US, 1964*
• —Judi Sanders, *Da Bomb!*, p. 18, 1997

lunch bucket *noun*
a socially inept outcast *US, 1956*
• — *Time*, p. 56, 1st January 1965: 'Students: the slang bag'

lunch hooks *noun*
the hands *US, 1896*
• —Ramon Adams, *The Language of the Railroader*, p. 96, 1977

lunchie *noun*
a lunchtime drink consumed in place of a meal *UK*
• East [...] has popped in for a lunchie at the Lord Nelson in Bethnal Green[.]—Mark Powell, *Snap*, p. 15, 2001

lunchin' *adjective*
foolish *US*
A formation based on OUT TO LUNCH.
• — *Washington Post Magazine*, p. 9, 19th April 1987: 'Say wha?'

lunching *noun*
the act of oral sex *UK*
• Most of the time the lunching breaks down before a full hard-on is reached.—Peter Sotos, *Index*, p. 12, 1996

lunching *adjective*
completely out of touch and unaware of what is happening *US*
An evolved OUT TO LUNCH.
• —Connie Eble (Editor), *UNC-CH Campus Slang*, p. 7, Fall 1999

lunchmeat *noun*

1 in the pornography industry, an extremely appealing and sexual woman *US*

- —*Adult Video News*, p. 48, August 1995

2 in poker, bad cards or a player who proceeds with a bad hand *US*

- —John Vorhaus, *The Big Book of Poker Slang*, p. 26, 1996

lunch out *verb*

1 to perform oral sex *US*

- There, finally, Anthony let down the drawbridge whereby men could touch, or in fact lunch out on the particpating strippers[.]—Josh Alan Friedman, *Tales of Times Square*, p. 41, 1986
- After a while you piss. You have your shithole lunched out.—Peter Sotos, *Index*, p. 14, 1996

2 to experience a pyschotic break during drug intoxication *US*

- "Everybody knows somebody who's 'lunched out' at some point," Faggett said, using street slang to refer to the psychotic reactions often produced in PCPC users.—*Washington Post*, p. B4, 22nd October 1988

lunchpail *noun*

an ugly, stupid and/or despised person *US*

- —Collin Baker et al., *College Undergraduate Slang Study Conducted at Brown University*, p. 154, 1968

lunch tray *noun*

a short snowboard *US*

- —Jim Humes and Sean Wagstaff, *Boarderlands*, p. 223, 1995

lund *noun*

a despicable person *TRINIDAD AND TOBAGO, 1980*

- —Lise Winer, *Dictionary of the English/Creole of Trinidad & Tobago*, 2003

Lunenburg champagne *noun*

rum *CANADA*

Lunenburg, on the Nova Scotia South Shore coast, is long known for its fishing and trading, and the nickname comes from the old three-cornered trade with England and the West Indies – salt fish, rum and lumber.

- —Lewis Poteet, *The South Shore Phrase Book*, p. 73, 1999

Lunenburg pudding *noun*

pork sausage *CANADA*

- In Lunenburg pudding, every part of the pig goes in except the squeal.—Bill Casselman, *Canadian Food Words*, p. 86–87, 1998

lung butter *noun*

phlegm *US*

- It's time to get serious, Wayne reasons, before he "ends up at Great America wiping up hurl and lung butter."—*San Francisco Chronicle*, p. C3, 10th December 1993
- —Chris Lewis, *The Dictionary of Playground Slang*, p. 139, 2003

lunger *noun*

1 phlegm expelled from the lungs *US, 1946*

- Every now and then a car splutters, hacks, coughs, hocks a lunga, rumbles out into the track itself for a practice run.—Tom Wolfe, *The Kandy-Kolored Tangerine-Flake Streamline Baby*, p. 139, 1965
- I'll put a fucking lunger right into the bottom of his espresso cup. —Vincent Patrick, *The Pope of Greenwich Village*, p. X, 1979

2 a person suffering from tuberculosis *US, 1893*

- —Hyman E. Goldin et al., *Dictionary of American Underworld Lingo*, p. 130, 1950

lungs *noun*

the female breasts *US, 1951*

- We decided that if she had gone to TCU, she would have come from Floydada with big lungs and skinny calves and a lot of chewing gum.—Dan Jenkins, *Semi-Tough*, p. 32, 1972
- Their secondary sex characteristics are simply too conspicuous to pass without insult, and we were unmerciful towards them: tits, boobs, knockers, jugs, bubbies, bazooms, lungs, flaps and hooters we called them, and there was no way to be polite about it.—*Screw*, p. 6, 3rd January 1972
- The voice-over said, "A nice body, but a little weak in the lungs." —Elmore Leonard, *52 Pick-up*, p. 10, 1974
- —*Maledicta*, p. 255, Summer/Winter 1981: 'Five years and 121 dirty words later'
- It was probably scads of different pictures, lung shots all, the music a lament for a time when love came cheap.—James Ellroy, *Hollywood Nocturnes*, p. 237, 1994

lunk *noun*

a dolt *US, 1867*

- For they are either simpletons with cow-dung on their boots or they are a con-man's dream, the lunk with larceny in his heart.—Jack Lait and Lee Mortimer, *Washington Confidential*, p. 276, 1951
- He was already just a lunk who had gone broke as a cabaret genius. —Robert Sylvester, *No Cover Charge*, p. 219, 1956

lunkhead *noun*

a dolt *US, 1868*

- When a lunkhead and his twist spat in a night club, it's etiquette for him to dash after her and slip her cab fare.—Jack Lait and Lee Mortimer, *New York Confidential*, p. 222, 1948
- An oversize mob of ignorant, lunkheaded jerks who ruled with fear and got away with it because they had money to back themselves up.—Mickey Spillane, *Kiss Me Deadly*, p. 38, 1952
- That moronic culture of macho lunkheads and pap music fem-bots[.] —Jessica Berens and Kerri Sharp, *Prada sucks! [Inappropriate Behaviour]*, p. ix, 2002

lupper *noun*

the finger *UK*

Polari.

- 'Order lau [place] your luppers on the strillers [musical instrument] bona [well].—Barry Took and Marty Feldman, *Round The Horne*, 4th June 1967

lurgi *noun*

▷ **see:** DREADED LURGI

lurk *noun*

a cunning scheme or stratagem *AUSTRALIA, 1891*

A positive term. When referring to a fraudulent or otherwise illegal activity a 'lurk' is only ever a misdemeanor or a bending of the rules. Commonly refers also to a job that is easy yet sounds like hard work, or has some clever trick to being profitable.

- Ask Dennis an' Pat, matey. They know all the lurks.'—Nino Culotta (John O'Grady), *They're A Weird Mob*, p. 159, 1957
- Stone the crows! That's a bonzer lurk so long as the bastards don't catch us in mid stream.—Barry Humphries, *The Wonderful World of Barry McKenzie*, p. 44, 1968
- You fill out a business return for Income Tax? I hear that's the lurk these days isn't it?—Michael Peters, *Pommie Bastard*, p. 49, 1969
- I'm awake up to all the lurks, mate, don't you worry. I've got all the clues.—Alexander Buzo, *Rooted*, p. 96, 1969
- [F]or every honest lurk man like Chilla there has to be a letter of the law regulation enforcer, a lurk detector like Brown Tongue Parker. —Frank Hardy, *The Outcasts of Foolgarah*, p. 4, 1971
- These men know all the lurks. They're fowls, misfits kicked out of other ships.—J.E. MacDonnell, *Big Bill the Bastard*, p. 112, 1976
- But my main beef about the ID card is that it will rob the poor of the few lurks they still have.—Frank Hardy, *Hardy's People*, p. 120, 1986

lurk *verb*

to read postings on an Internet discussion group without posting your own comments *US, 1984*

- A newbie with the nerve to post in alt.sex.bondage, without taking the time to lurk (read, not post) for several weeks, can expect to be flamed to blackened perfection.—Nancy Tamosaitis, *net.sex*, p. 75, 1995

lurker *noun*

1 a person who reads postings on an Internet discussion group without posting their own comments *US*

- —Eric S. Raymond, *The New Hacker's Dictionary*, p. 229, 1991

2 a market-stallholder who is new to the trade, and who operates in non-traditional markets *UK*

Used by veterans who were 'born to the job'.

- A new breed of market stallholders, known to veterans of the trade as "lurkers", has arrived with a new breed of market.—*Radio Times*, p. 11, 30th July 1983

3 a Canadian pilot waiting in Thompson, Manitoba, for a flying job *CANADA*

- They pump gas, work in dollar stores and convenience stores – the lurkers are eager young men who long to fly and have spent thousands of dollars and hundreds of hours getting qualified.—*CBC News*, 28th October 2002

lurk man; lurk-man *noun*

a man who is adept at obtaining lurks *AUSTRALIA, 1945*

- [F]or every honest lurk man like Chilla there has to be a letter of the law regulation enforcer, a lurk detector like Brown Tongue Parker. —Frank Hardy, *The Outcasts of Foolgarah*, p. 4, 1971
- Frank Griffiths was our master spirit. Like Milo he was something of a lurk-man[.]—Clive James, *Unreliable Memoirs*, p. 99, 1980

lurk merchant *noun*

a person adept at obtaining lurks *AUSTRALIA, 1964*

- — Lance Peters, *The Dirty Half-Mile*, p. 90, 1979
- He reckons there's plenty of blokes, even in our squad, who take a bit of graft and give tip-offs to the lurk merchants. — Lance Peters, *The Dirty Half-Mile*, p. 144, 1979

lurp *noun*

1 a misfit *US*

- — *American Weekly*, p. 2, 14th August 1955

2 a long-range reconnaissance patrol; a member of such a patrol *US, 1968*

From the initials LRRP.

- He led Long-Range Reconnaissance patrollers, Lurps, silently harassing enemy camps and columns for weeks and months on end. — James Mills, *The Underground Empire*, p. 241, 1986

lus *noun*

enthusiasm, appetite *SOUTH AFRICA, 1994*

From 'lust' or synonymous Afrikaans *lus*. Noted with reference to a 'lus for politics' by Penny Silva, *A Dictonary of South African English*, 1996.

lus *adjective*

longing for something; lusting after something *SOUTH AFRICA, 1970*

From Afrikaans *lus* (desirous).

- — Penny Silva, *A Dictionary of South African English*, 1996

luser *noun*

a computer neophyte *US*

- — Christian Crumlish, *The Internet Dictionary*, p. 115, 1995

lush *noun*

1 alcohol *UK, 1790*

At one time deemed obsolete slang, but revived.

- Those hunkies were lush crazy and could they drink. — Mezz Mezzrow, *Really the Blues*, p. 71, 1946
- I have seen junkies kick and hit the lush and wind up dead in a few years. — William Burroughs, *Junkie*, p. 125, 1953
- From the way I was holding up you would have sworn I was immune to the lush. — Louis Armstrong, *Satchmo*, p. 202, 1954
- Got a a big bag of whatzit from Long Island, which helps tone-down lush. — Jack Kerouac, *Letter to Allen Ginsberg*, p. 431, 11th August 1954
- With each week of work, bombed and sapped and charged and stoned with lush, with pot, with benny[.] — Norman Mailer, *Advertisements for Myself*, p. 243, 1955
- No, I'm laying off the lush, all that wine you drink is rotgut, it burns your stomach out, it makes your brain dull. — Jack Kerouac, *The Dharma Bums*, p. 89, 1958
- "I can't make lush at all baby," the girl said. — Ross Russell, *The Sound*, p. 11, 1961
- They came into the camp lushed, but nasty lush: ethyl alcohol coming on like the sleeping bags weren't there, you know? — Richard Farina, *Been Down So Long*, p. 63, 1966
- I had been getting high for four or five years and was convinced, with the zeal of a crusader, that marijuana was superior to lush[.] — Eldridge Cleaver, *Soul on Ice*, p. 4, 1968

2 an alcoholic *US, 1851*

- Used to be a lush. Quit. — Philip Wylie, *Opus 21*, p. 249, 1949
- When I got back to Denver and he married Marilyn was when I got to be a real lush. — John Clellon Holmes, *Go*, p. 126, 1952
- You don't want to be a corny lush like these squares, Cart[.] — George Mandel, *Flee the Angry Strangers*, p. 359, 1952
- Pat was a square, a lush. — Alexander Trocchi, *Cain's Book*, p. 150, 1960
- Nobody can make that shot and you know it. Not even a lucky lush. — *The Hustler*, 1961
- There had been a third child and Big Tom was a confirmed lush now from Gina's nagging. — Clancy Sigal, *Going Away*, p. 67, 1961
- Reckon you're as much a lush with cokes, as some blokes is with hard liquor. — Jean Brooks, *The Opal Witch*, p. 123, 1967
- [T]he rulers of the land seemed all to be lushes. — Eldrige Cleaver, *Soul on Ice*, p. 4, 1968
- A couple of times while they poured alcohol into me as though I were a crazed lush I began to rave[.] — Kevin Mackey, *The Cure*, p. 72, 1970
- I got no time for those chumps crying about how they never had no chance 'cause their mammy was a whore or their daddy was a lush – who wants to hear that shit? — Edwin Torres, *Carlito's Way*, p. 42, 1975

lush *verb*

to drink alcohol excessively *UK, 1811*

- It is uncommon for a Chinese woman to drink, but many Japanese girls lush. — Jack Lait and Lee Mortimer, *Chicago Confidential*, p. 88, 1950
- And, if she needed any more evidence, his lushing on the 5:29 was a matter of record. — Max Shulman, *Rally Round the Flag, Boys!*, p. 76, 1957
- The broads stopped talking to watch Humpty lush. — Dan Burley, *Diggeth Thou?*, p. 14, 1959
- You need something for your nerves and that hard lushing you've been doing. — Iceberg Slim (Robert Beck), *Trick Baby*, p. 262, 1969
- He was there, of course, lushing it up. — Terry Southern, *Now Dig This*, p. 155, 2001

lush *adjective*

1 sexually attractive *UK, 1890*

- She was a lush thrush. — J.E. MacDonnell, *Don't Gimme the Ships*, p. 25, 1960
- Stringy had paired off with a lush little physio from Brisbane. — Barry Humphries, *A Nice Night's Entertainment*, p. 41, 1960
- This month we get cosy with some of the lushest babes on the planet! — *Dolly*, p. 6, 1996
- — Susie Dent, *The Language Report*, p. 19, 2003

2 drunk *UK, 1812*

- Two years ago I was real lush and drinking a quart a day. — John Clellon Holmes, *Go*, p. 113, 1952

3 very good, great, especially nice; attractive *UK*

Reported in mid-1970s use in Wigan, south Lancashire. Used, in 2002, by south Wales schoolchildren to describe an impressive room in an historic house.

- Would you like to hear it?" "Oh rather! That would be absolutely lush." — Kenneth Horne and Richard Murdoch, *Much Binding in the Marsh*, 1953
- I love 'im I do, 'e's dead lush. — Ben Elton, *High Society*, p. 29, 2002
- Get listening to Richie Blackmore's "Rainbow", they're fucking lush, pal. — Stuart Maconies, *Cider with Roadies*, p. 100, 2003

lush!

used for expressing approval *UK*

- — Susie Dent, *The Language Report*, p. 75, 2003

lushed *adjective*

drunk *US, 1927*

- Pineapple, a dock worker from Hawaii, was lushed and nursing a beer at a table. — Emmett Grogan, *Ringolevio*, p. 100, 1972
- He could barely walk, so lushed was he. — Bill Cardoso, *The Maltese Sangweech*, p. 173, 1984

lusher *noun*

a drunkard *US, 1848*

- — *American Speech*, p. 87, May 1955: 'Narcotic argot along the mexican border'

lush green *noun*

money *US*

- — David W. Maurer, *Argot of the Racetrack*, p. 42, 1951

lushhead *noun*

a habitual drinker *UK, 1938*

Combines **LUSH** (an alcoholic) with **-HEAD** (a user).

- "He's a lush-head, an acid-head, a pill-head, an H-head", etc. It was almost as if the hippy really was just his head. — Paul E. Willis, *Profance Culture*, p. 109, 1978

lushhound *noun*

a drunkard *US, 1935*

- We liked things to be easy and relaxed, mellow and mild, not loud or loutish, and the scowling chin-out tension of the lushhounds with their false courage didn't appeal to us. — Mezz Mezzrow, *Really the Blues*, p. 94, 1946

lush puppy *noun*

a young person who drinks to excess *UK*

A play on the branded shoes Hush Puppies™.

- — Tom Hibbert, *Rockspeak!*, p. 99, 1983

lush-roll *verb*

to rob drunkards *US*

- "I'm appealing to you as one Razor Back to another," and he pulled out his Razor Back card, a memo of his lush-rolling youth. — William Burroughs, *Naked Lunch*, p. 177, 1957

lushwell *noun*

a drunkard *US, 1960*

- Only thing about him, he's such a lushwell his liver's probably big as his ass. — Joseph Wambaugh, *The Glitter Dome*, p. 6, 1981

lush-worker *noun*

a thief who preys on drunks who have passed out *US, 1908*

- He was a skillful lush worker, but he had no front. — William Burroughs, *Junkie*, p. 26, 1953

lushy *noun*

a drunkard *US, 1944*

- Besides, the lushies didn't even play good music. — Mezz Mezzrow, *Really the Blues*, p. 94, 1946

lust *noun*

▸ **in lust**

sexually attracted to someone *US, 1963*

A play on the conventional 'in love'.

- —Connie Eble (Editor), *UNC-CH Campus Slang*, p. 3, November 1983

lust dog *noun*

a passionate, promiscuous female *US*

- —*American Speech*, p. 62, Spring-Summer 1975: 'Razorback slang'

lusty wench *noun*

an attractive teenage girl *NEW ZEALAND*

The term assumes a degree of respectability in the girl.

- —Louis S. Leland, *A Personal Kiwi-Yankee Dictionary*, p. 61, 1984

luv *noun*

love, especially as a form of address *UK, 1898*

A variant spelling; also used for reasons of alphabetic economy in text messaging.

- It's not like that, luv.—Mike Hodges, *Get Carter*, p. 8, 1971
- [N]o harm meant luv.—James Hawes, *Dead Long Enough*, p. 39, 2000
- Orl right, luv, calm down.—Jenny Eclair, *Camberwell Beauty*, p. 209, 2000

luvdup; luvved up *adjective*

▷ **see:** LOVED UP

luvly jubbly *adjective*

▷ **see:** LOVELY JUBBLY

luvvaduck!

▷ **see:** LOVE A DUCK!

luvvie; luvvy; luvvie-darling *noun*

1 an actor of either sex, especially one given to public extravagance or theatrical gesture; an actor who is considered intensely serious about theatre work *UK, 1990*

Satirical, gently derogatory, often self-descriptive; from the stereotypical thespianic greeting and form of address 'Luvvie, darling'.

- [T]he luvvie is an artist (Mwa, Mwa, Darling). Emma Thompson is the undisputed queen of the luvvies[.]—Alon Shulman, *The Style Bible*, p. 151, 1999
- So, in a fit of luvvie petulance, I turned the telly off[.]—Frank Skinner, *Frank Skinner*, p. 11, 2001

2 used as a form of address, generally affectionate (usually of the opposite sex, sometimes considered patronsing) *UK*

An extension of LOVE.

- I hope you've got one too, have yoo luvvy?—Kevin Sampson, *Clubland*, p. 131, 2002

lux *adjective*

*lux*urious *US*

- [P]etulant uber-bitches dash champagne glasses on the mirror-polished floors of their super-lux apartments[.]—Jessica Berens and Kerri Sharp, *Prada sucks! [Inappropriate Behaviour]*, p. vii, 2002

L'ville *nickname*

Louisville, Kentucky *US*

- —Don Wilmeth, *The Language of American Popular Entertainment*, p. 164, 1981

lye *noun*

marijuana *US, 1990s*

- Buy a nickel bag / Smoke a little lye / Get high tonight—Busta Rhymes, *Get High Tonight*, 1997

lying squad *noun*

the F*lying* Squad of the Metropolitan Police *UK*

- —Angela Devlin, *Prison Patter*, p. 112, 1996

lyle

▷ **see:** LALLY

lyrics *noun*

1 talk, especially when stretching truth or reality *UK*

A play on 'words'.

- I didn't mean anything by that. It's just lyrics that's all.—Karline Smith, *Moss Side Massive*, p. 93, 1994

2 profanity; disparagement *TRINIDAD AND TOBAGO, 1987*

- —Lise Winer, *Dictionary of the English/Creole of Trinidad & Tobago*, 2003

LZ *noun*

a combat aircraft landing zone, especially an improvised one *US*

- It was 100 degrees when they hit the LZ.—Ronald J. Glasser, *365 Days*, p. 30, 1971

Mm

M *noun*

1 **morphine** *US, 1914*

- More specifically, it was classified as M, C, and H – Mary, Charlie, and Harry – which stood for morphine, cocaine, and heroin. — William J. Spillard and Pence James, *Needle in a Haystack*, p. 147–148, 1945
- Heroin got the drive awright – but there's not a tingle to a ton – you got to get M to get that tingle-tingle. — Nelson Algren, *The Man With The Golden Arm [The Howard Marks Book of Dope Stories]*, p. 45, 1949
- Then his money had run out, those few connections who might advance him a little "M" had vanished or been arrested[.] — John Clellon Holmes, *Go*, p. 198, 1952
- I saw him pack in his moldy room where he'd shot M all this time. — Jack Kerouac, *Letter to John Clellon Holmes*, p. 389, 9th December 1952
- During the early part of the war, imports of H were virtually cut off and the only junk available was prescription M. — William Burroughs, *Junkie*, p. 40, 1953
- That night, Marylou took everything in the books; she took tea, goofballs, benny, liquor, and even asked Old Bull for a shot of M[.] — Jack Kerouac, *On the Road*, p. 148, 1957
- It's not like H or M. Nothing like that! — Ross Russell, *The Sound*, p. 22, 1961
- — Angela Devlin, *Prison Patter*, p. 74, 1996

2 **marijuana** *US, 1955*
Extended from the previous sense.

- — Mike Haskins, *Drugs*, p. 288, 2003

3 **an *MBE* (Member of the Order of the British Empire)** *UK, 1961*
Used by civil servants, suggestive of a casual familiarity with the honour.

M20 *noun*

a meeting place *US*
Citizens' band radio jargon, originally US; UK use is interesting as the M20 is a motorway route to Folkstone.

- — Peter Chippindale, *The British CB Book*, p. 157, 1981

M25 *noun*

a tablet of MDMA, the recreational drug best known as ecstasy *UK*
The initial letter of MDMA leads to the designation of the London orbital motorway (M25) thus memorialising the road's pivotal role in reaching the (often) illegal locations of early raves.

- — Macfarlane, Macfarlane and Robson, *The User*, p. 75, 1996
- Street names [...] M and Ms, MDMA, M25s, New Yorkers[.] — James Kay and Julian Cohen, *The Parents' Complete Guide to Young People and Drugs*, p. 136, 1998

M8 *noun*

used in text messaging to mean 'a mate' *UK*
A variant spelling; one of several constructions in which a syllable pronounced 'ate' is replaced by the homophone 'eight'.

- Capital Radio, too, is developing SMS-driven services. It started trials of Capital M8 (pronounced "mate"), an interactive text-driven service in June. — *The Guardian*, 23rd September 2002

ma *noun*

a mother; used for addressing your mother *UK, 1823*
An abbreviation of 'mama'.

- Made it Ma, top o' the world! — James Cagney, *White Heat*, 1949
- "Goodnight, John Boy!" "'night, ma!" "'night, pa!" — Stuart Jeffries, *Mrs Slocombe's Pussy*, p. 216, 2000
- Just bend over and take it like a slut, okay, Ma? / "Oh, now he's raping his own mother[."] — Eminem (Marshall Mathers), *Kill You*, 2000

Ma *nickname*
▷ **see:** MA STATE

ma'a *noun*

crack cocaine *UK*

- — Mike Haskins, *Drugs*, p. 282, 2003

maaga; maga *adjective*

thin *UK*
From West Indian and UK black patois pronunciation of 'meagre'.

- The two dogs looked well maaga, but fortunately they were chained. — Karline Smith, *Moss Side Massive*, p. 40, 1994

ma and pa *adjective*

(used of a business) small-scale, family-owned *US*

- I pull over at a ma and pa liquor store across the street from City Lights Bookstore, a hangout for sniveling intellectuals and runaway teenyboppers out for a score. — Oscar Zeta Acosta, *The Autobiography of a Brown Buffalo*, p. 36, 1972

ma bubby and Choon *noun*

any two things that are very close to each other *TRINIDAD AND TOBAGO, 1990*

- — Lise Winer, *Dictionary of the English/Creole of Trinidad & Tobago*, 2003

mac *noun*

1 **an automated cash machine** *US*
Originally from the trademarked acronym Money Access Center, then applied to any such device.

- — Claudio R. Salvucci, *The Philadelphia Dialect Dictionary*, p. 47, 1996

2 **a mackintosh, hence any waterproof outercoat** *UK, 1901*
Sometimes spelt 'mack'.

Mac; mac; mack *noun*

1 **used as a term of address for a man whose name is not known by the speaker** *US, 1918*

- That's right, Mac. We all been through the mill too. — Max Shulman, *The Zebra Derby*, p. 144, 1946
- "You're right, Mac." I tipped him a quarter. — Philip Wylie, *Opus 21*, p. 8, 1949
- "Have you got a light, mac?" "No, but I've got a dark brown overcoat." — Bonzo Dog Band, *Big Shot*, 1967

2 **a red McIntosh apple, usually from British Columbia** *CANADA*

- Whether you are serving B.C. "Macs" fresh or in your favorite cooked dishes, you can do so with complete confidence. — *Grande Prairie, Alta Herald Tribune*, p. 3–4, 10th January 1958

mac; mack *verb*

to eat voraciously *US*
From the Big Mac, a hamburger speciality from the McDonald's™ hamburger chain.

- — Judi Sanders, *Cal Poly Slang*, p. 6, 1990
- — Trevor Cralle, *The Surfin'ary*, 1991

macaroni *noun*

1 **an Italian-American or Italian** *UK, 1845*
From the pasta product.

- Then the guy who sent the hitter gets hit, the macaronis are shooting each other, and its hard to tell who's on whose side. — Elmore Leonard, *Glitz*, p. 107–108, 1985

2 **excrement** *UK, 1974*
Rhyming slang for 'pony' (the reduced form of **PONY AND TRAP**), **CRAP** (excrement). Sometimes reduced to 'maca'.

3 **a pony; hence £25** *UK, 1857*
Rhyming slang.

4 **in betting, odds of 25–1** *UK*
From rhyming slang for **PONY** (£25).

- — John McCririck, *John McCririck's World of Betting*, p. 61, 1991

5 **in oil drilling, small-diameter pipe** *US*

- — Jerry Robertson, *Oil Slanguage*, p. 81, 1954

macaroni *verb*

to defecate *UK*
Rhyming slang for ***PONY* AND TRAP** (**CRAP**).

- Now it's up to Charlie to back his flush [a poker hand] or macaroni his strides [trousers]. — Ted Lewis, *Jack Carter's Law*, p. 47, 1974

macaroni and cheese *noun*

marijuana worth $5 and cocaine worth $10 *US*

- — *Detroit News*, p. 5D, 20th September 2002

macaroon *noun*
a black person *UK*
Rhyming slang for **COON**.
- —Ray Puxley, *Cockney Rabbit*, 1992

MacArthur sweep *noun*
a combing of the hair from the side of the head over a bald spot on top of the head *US*
- It was brushed sideways across his skull in a MacArthur sweep. I had a hunch there was nothing under it but bare skull.—Raymond Chandler, *The Long Goodbye*, p. 200–201, 1953

macca; macker *noun*
a recruit in the armed forces *AUSTRALIA, 1944*
Origin unknown.
- Only a macca in the outfit, too. Only been here half as long as us. —John Wynnum, *Jiggin' in the Riggin'*, p. 112, 1965

macca *adjective*
enormous *UK: ENGLAND*
School slang.
- —Chris Lewls, *The Dictionary of Playground Slang*, p. 141, 2003

Maccas *noun*
1 food from a McDonald's™ restaurant *AUSTRALIA, 1996*
- 'Richard says no Maccas while I'm in training,' announced Red. —Shane Maloney, *Nice Try*, p. 232, 1998

2 a McDonald's™ restaurant *AUSTRALIA*
- So anyway, I met up with the family at Maccas[.]—Paul Vautin, *Turn It Up!*, p. 122, 1995

macdaddy *noun*
the very best of something *US*
- —Connie Eble (Editor), *UNC-CH Campus Slang*, p. 7, April 1995

mace *verb*
1 to swindle, to defraud *UK, 1790*
- —Patrick O'Shaughnessy, *Market Traders' Slang*, 1979

2 to owe money *UK*
From the previous sense.
- —Patrick O'Shaughnessy, *Market Traders' Slang*, 1979

3 to steal or cheat, especially by means of the three card trick *UK*
A variation of the sense 'to swindle'.
- —David Powis, *The Signs of Crime*, 1977

MacGuffin *noun*
a device or a gimmick within a film that while often peripheral to the storyline is iconic in and of the overall storytelling *US, 1939*
Coined by film director Alfred Hitchcock (1899–1980).
- [T]he brace of antique rifles that serve as Lock, Stock and Two Smoking Barrels' MacGuffin[.]—Graham Hodges, *Brute Force*, p. 83, 2001

macher *noun*
an important and powerful man *US, 1930*
Yiddish.
- So, here he is, the big macher, the committeeman, the next alderman of the Twenty-seventh, the mayor, the governor[.]—Robert Campbell, *In a Pig's Eye*, p. 50, 1991

machine *noun*
1 a fast and attractive car *US, 1908*
Often pronounced 'ma-chine'.
- —Miss Cone, *The Slang Dictionary (Hawthorne High School)*, 1965
- "This your machine?" she asked, smoothing the Buick's leather seat.—Malcolm Braly, *On the Yard*, p. 5, 1967

2 a machine gun *US*
- —Bill Valentine, *Gang Intelligence Manual*, p. 110, 1995: 'Jamaican gang terminology'

3 a trumpet *UK*
- —Tom Hibbert, *Rockspeak!*, p. 99, 1983

4 in horse racing, a pari-mutuel betting machine *US*
- —Tom Ainslie, *Ainslie's Complete Guide to Thoroughbred Racing*, p. 334, 1976

5 in horse racing, a battery-powered device used to impart a shock to a horse during a race *US*
- —Tom Ainslie, *Ainslie's Complete Guide to Thoroughbred Racing*, p. 334, 1976

Machine *noun*
▸ **the Machine**
in big city politics, the over-arching political organisation that runs all facets of life *US*
- Also it wasn't altogether certain that Bilandic, acting mayor or not acting mayor, was going to be the choice of the Democratic Central Committee aka the Regular Organization aka the Machine.—Robert Campbell, *Boneyards*, p. 12, 1992

machine gun; machine *noun*
a syringe used for injecting an illegal drug *UK*
- —Home Office, *Glossary of Terms and Slang Common in Penal Establishments*, July 1978
- —Sean McConville, *The State of the Language*, 1980

Machine Gun Murphy *noun*
a stereotypical fearless soldier *US*
- A mad minute – everybody gets on line, everybody in the company, and you play Machine Gun Murphy. (From the Congressional Record, 7 April 1971).—John Kerry, *The New Soldier*, p. 60, 1971

machinery *noun*
1 the equipment used to prepare and inject narcotics *US*
- —*Congressional Record*, p. E3982, 6th May 1970
- —Eugene Landy, *The Underground Dictionary*, p. 122, 1971

2 marijuana *US, 1977*
Also simply 'mach'.
- —Richard A. Spears, *The Slang and Jargon of Drugs and Drink*, p. 327, 1986
- —Mike Haskins, *Drugs*, p. 288, 2003

macho *noun*
excessively masculine, virile and brave *US, 1959*
A direct loan from Spanish.
- Listen, I did my time in back seats, the Bay Ridge number, getting fucked over by some Saturday night macho moron.—*Saturday Night Fever*, 1977
- Every man wants to be a macho, macho man / To have the kind of body, always in demand.—Victor Willis, *Macho Man*, 1978
- I'm macho and I'm mean / All the tarts think I'm obscene[.]—Albertos y Lost Trios Paranoias, *23*, 1978
- Look, spare me the macho bullshit about your gun.—*48 Hours*, 1982
- Macho man / Can't cook / Macho man / Can't sew / Macho man / Eats plenty Red Meat—Benjamin Zephaniah, *Man to Man*, 1992
- He was a thirty-year-old brain surgeon, a sensitive guy trapped in a macho body, traveling with another doctor and having a terrible singles' cruise.—Anka Radakovich, *The Wild Girls Club*, p. 75, 1994

machona; mach *noun*
▹ **see: MACON**

Macintoy; Macintrash *noun*
an Apple Macintosh™ computer *US*
- —Eric S. Raymond, *The New Hacker's Dictionary*, p. 230, 1991

Macintyre *noun*
fire *UK*
Rhyming slang.
- —Angela Devlin, *Prison Patter*, p. 74, 1996

mack *noun*
1 a pimp *US, 1903*
- The fee went to the pimps, or macs, who kept wandering downstairs. The girls used to fight over their macs.—Mezz Mezzrow, *Really the Blues*, p. 23, 1946
- For some of our boys was drifters and some of our boys was macks. —Bruce Jackson, *Get Your Ass in the Water and Swim Like Me*, p. 133, 1964
- Mack man is short of Mackerel man; the shortened form is in most common use.—Christina and Richard Milner, *Black Players*, p. 35, 1972
- In being a mack, you're supposedly the supreme being of a man. Man rules woman. In being a mack, you acknowledge this fact.—Susan Hall, *Gentleman of Leisure*, p. 39, 1972
- The whole thing happened because we both were consumed by the desire to get a top-notch fron that would cause us to be two of the youngest major-league mack men in the city of Detroit.—A.S. Jackson, *Gentleman Pimp*, p. 59, 1973
- Like every nigger mack fresh outta big foot country [the deep South], he's sizzling for young white 'ho pussy.—Iceberg Slim (Robert Beck), *Airtight Willie and Me*, p. 24, 1979

2 a person who is a facile and convincing talker *US, 1962*
- And I'm gonna need a female mack to steer Tommy.—Stephen Cannell, *King Con*, p. 119, 1997

3 the speech a pimp makes to recruit a woman as a prostitute *US*
- The initial line a pimp uses in recruiting a girl is often referred to as Mack or Mack talk[.]—Christina and Richard Milner, *Black Players*, p. 35, 1972

4 a male who attracts females *US*

- —Judi Sanders, *Da Bomb!*, p. 19, 1997

▷ **see:** MAC

mack *verb*

1 to speak with a stylish flair and flattery *US, 1968*

- He sure can mack 'em down in five minutes.—Christina and Richard Milner, *Black Players*, p. 35, 1972
- And maybe one night me and Lunchbox'll be macking some bitch, and she'll be like, "Oooo! I want to suck youse guys's dicks off. What's your names?" And I'll be like, "Jay and Silent Bob."—Kevin Smith, *Jay and Silent Bob Strike Back*, p. 21, 2001

2 to work as a pimp *UK, 1887*

- Ice! You ain't heard? I cut loose from that gig. I'm macking and that vision is humping for me.—Iceberg Slim (Robert Beck), *The Naked Soul of Iceberg Slim*, p. 54, 1971
- I know you're macking now, and we both know eight bills will buy a lotta cocaine or take care of anything else that's bugging you. —A.S. Jackson, *Gentleman Pimp*, p. 48, 1973
- Your broad becomes lazy, trifling and slack / And starts signifying about your not having a license to mack.—Dennis Wepman et al., *The Life*, p. 165, 1976

3 to behave with ostentatious style and flair *US*

- A fear of muhfucka flossin' (mackin' or showing off) too hard.—*Hip-Hop Connection*, p. 22, July 2002

4 to kiss *US*

- —Judi Sanders, *Faced and Faded, Hanging to Hurl*, p. 26, 1993
- —Connie Eble (Editor), *UNC-CH Campus Slang*, p. 4, Spring 1993

▷ **see:** MAC

Mack Daddy *noun*

a skilled ladies' man; a pimp *US, 1959*

- So I then go into my Mack Daddy mode cause I'm getting a woodie in my cackies y'know.—*Boyz N The Hood*, 1990
- Is that that nigga Caine out there playin' Mack Daddy in the parking lot?—*Menace II Society*, 1993

macker *noun*

a very large wave *US*

- —Nick Carroll, *The Next Wave*, 1991

▷ **see:** MACCA

mackerel and sprat; mackerel *noun*

a fool *UK*

Rhyming slang for **PRAT** (a fool); however, as this generally appears in the shortened form, an alternative rhyming derivation has appeared: mackerel – fish in the pool – fool.

- [A] pranny is a "right mackerel".—Ray Puxley, *Fresh Rabbit*, 1998
- [T]hey have a loada mackerels hanging round to make them feel good about it, to feel a bit superior[.]—J.J. Connolly, *Layer Cake*, p. 14, 2000

mackerel-snapper *noun*

a Roman Catholic *US, 1850s*

From the practice of eating fish on Fridays.

- Me? I was raised a mackerel-snapper.—*M*A*S*H*, 1970

mack man *noun*

a pimp *US*

- Did those oldhead mackmen think they were the only ones who could drive Hogs?—Clarence Cooper Jr, *The Scene*, p. 68, 1960
- Several cons slightly older than I came in on transfer from the big joint. They claimed to be "mack men."—Iceberg Slim (Robert Beck), *Pimp*, p. 56, 1969
- All the big time New York mack men, hustlers, and whores were there.—Babs Gonzales, *Movin' On Down De Line*, p. 45, 1975
- I thought you were a mackman, a master at the Game; But I peeped your hole card, you're a funny-time lame.—Dennis Wepman et al., *The Life*, p. 39, 1976

Mack the Knife *noun*

any surgeon *US*

- —*Maledicta*, Summer 1980: 'Not sticks and stones, but names: more medical pejoratives'
- —Sally Williams, *"Strong" Words*, p. 150, 1994

Macnamara *noun*

a barrow *UK: SCOTLAND*

Glasgow rhyming slang.

- —Michael Munro, *The Patter, Another Blast*, 1988

macocious *adjective*

inclined to gossip *TRINIDAD AND TOBAGO, 1977*

- —Lise Winer, *Dictionary of the English/Creole of Trinidad & Tobago*, 2003

macon; maconha; machona; mach *noun*

marijuana *US, 1938*

From Brazilian *maconha* (marijuana).

- —Richard A. Spears, *The Slang and Jargon of Drugs and Drink*, p. 327, 1986
- —Mike Haskins, *Drugs*, p. 288, 2003

mac out *verb*

to eat ravenously *US*

- —Mimi Pond, *The Valley Girl's Guide to Life*, p. 59, 1982

Mactown *nickname*

McMurdo Station, Antarctica *ANTARCTICA*

- —*Cool Antarctica*, 2003: 'Antarctic slang'

mad *adjective*

1 exciting, good *US, 1941*

- Nero is havin' a ball, he's diggin' this mad game, he's guicin' up a storm.—William "Lord" Buckley, *Nero*, 1951
- —*American Speech*, p. 302, December 1955: 'Wayne University slang'
- You don't know "Jungle Love?" That shit is the mad notes.—Kevin Smith, *Jay and Silent Bob Strike Back*, p. 9, 2001

2 in homosexual usage, unrestrained and ostentatious *US*

- Loosely used with many shades of meaning.—Anon., *The Gay Girl's Guide*, p. 12, 1949
- —Bruce Rodgers, *The Queens' Vernacular*, p. 129, 1972

3 used as an all-purpose, dramatic intensifier *US, 1972*

- I'm gonna get mad diesel.—*Kids*, 1995
- Vince Carter has mad hops.—Connie Eble (Editor), *UNC-CH Campus Slang*, p. 4, Fall 1996
- —*Newsday*, p. B2, 11th October 1997
- Doing this, we make mad bank.—*Gone in 60 Seconds*, 2000

▸ **like mad**

to an extraordinary extent, very much *UK, 1653*

- [W]e, the workers, were "working" like mad[.]—*The Guardian*, 9th April 2004

mad about *adjective*

enthusiastic about, having a strong liking for, sexually infatuated *UK, 1744*

- It was entirely possible that, being obsessed and mad about him, really nuts over him, I unconsciously thought, if I got pregnant he would love me enough to marry me.—Angela Bonavoglia, *The Choices We Made*, p. 45, 2001

madam *noun*

in a deck of playing cards, a queen *US*

- —George Percy, *The Language of Poker*, p. 55, 1988

Madam de Luce; madam *verb*

to deceive *UK, 1938*

Rhyming slang for 'spruce'. Noted also as a noun by Julian Franklyn, *A Dictionary of Rhyming Slang*, 1960.

- —Ray Puxley, *Cockney Rabbit*, 1992

madame *noun*

1 an older homosexual man *US*

- —*Maledicta*, p. 222, 1979: 'Kinks and queens: linguistic and cultural aspects of the terminology for gays'

2 the victim of an extortion scheme *US*

- —Bill Reilly, *Big Al's Official Guide to Chicagoese*, p. 43, 1982

Madame *nickname*

Madame Ngo Dinh Nhu, sister-in-law of South Vietnamese President Diem *US*

- "The Madame" – beautiful, tough demanding – a former president's sister-in-law was the power behind the throne in creating and enforcing the purity laws.—Tony Zidek, *Choi Oi*, p. 24, 1965

Madame Tussaud *noun*

bald *UK*

Rhyming slang, formed on the name of the famous waxworks' founder.

- Worrying about losing your hair will make you go "Madame Tussaud."—Ray Puxley, *Fresh Rabbit*, 1998

mad as a beetle *adjective*

extremely mad; very angry *AUSTRALIA, 1942*

mad as a boiled...
mentally deranged *UK*
A seemingly endless source of nonsense similes; 'mad as a boiled dictionary compiler' makes as much sense, which is probably the point.
- [A] blinding bloke and really, really funny but also as mad as a boiled banana. — Dave Courtney, *Raving Lunacy*, p. 128, 2000
- He was a blinding geezer but as mad as a boiled fish. — Dave Courtney, *Raving Lunacy*, p. 105, 2000

mad as a brush *adjective*
▷ see: DAFT AS A BRUSH

mad as a Chinaman *adjective*
extremely mad; very angry *AUSTRALIA, 1942*

mad as a cut snake *adjective*
extremely mad *AUSTRALIA, 1932*
Either meaning 'out of one's mind with anger' or 'insane'.
- Despite all this I still liked him. Probably because he was mad. Really mad. Madder than a cut snake. — Phillip Gwynne, *Deadly Unna?*, p. 26, 1998
- At this the lawyers were as mad as a cut snake with Jesus, muttering, 'We've got to do something about this bloke.' — Kel Richards, *The Aussie Bible*, p. 31, 2003

mad as a goanna *adjective*
extremely mad; very angry *AUSTRALIA, 1942*
A goanna is a large lizard.

mad as a gum tree full of galahs *adjective*
totally mad; crazy *AUSTRALIA, 1942*
The galah is a striking native bush parrot noted for loud calls and antic behaviour.
- Mad! He's as mad as a gum tree full of galahs. — Bill Wannan, *Bullockies, Beauts and Bandicoots*, p. 107, 1960
- 'Mad as a gum tree full of galahs,' McGarrity stormed. — Dymphna Cusack, *Picnic Races*, p. 81, 1962

mad as a meat-axe *adjective*
extremely mad *AUSTRALIA, 1946*
Generally meaning 'insane' rather than 'out of one's mind with anger'.
- Mad as a meat-axe, crazy as a loon. — Wilda Moxham, *The Apprentice*, p. 34, 1969
- Your Aunty Edna reckons she had to call the local funny farm. Reckon'd the old girl went as mad as a meataxe. — *The Adventures of Barry McKenzie*, 1972
- — Kerry Cue, *Crooks, Chooks and Bloody Ratbags*, p. 171, 1983
- — Dirk Flinthart, *Brotherly Love*, p. 87, 1995

mad as a satchel of knees *adjective*
insane, crazy *UK*
- Mickey [Rourke] can dispatch opponents with a single rev of his engine [...] he's also mad as a satchel of knees. — *Uncut*, p. 17, July 2003

mad as a snake *adjective*
extremely mad *AUSTRALIA, 1917*
Either meaning 'out of one's mind with anger' or 'insane'.
- He's as mad as a snake. Goes round with a gun scaring people off his property. — Kylie Tennant, *The Honey Flow*, p. 57, 1956
- I was beginning to think she was odd before this, but now I thought the poor kid was as mad as a snake. — Les Such, *A Yen for Yokohama*, p. 78, 1963
- Mon dieu! You must be mad as a snake. — Barry Humphries, *Bazza Pulls It Off!*, 1971

mad as sand *adjective*
mentally deranged *UK*
Liverpool usage.
- Purvis was staring fanatically right into James's face, mad as sand. — Kevin Sampson, *Powder*, p. 106, 1999

mad ball *noun*
in circus and carnival usage, a fortune teller's glass globe *US, 1948*
- — Don Wilmeth, *The Language of American Popular Entertainment*, p. 165, 1981

mad bastard *noun*
a variety of MDMA, the recreational drug best known as ecstasy *UK*
- "What did you take?" " Mad Bastard," said Tom."Oh, they're mental[.]" said Maddy smiling. — Colin Butts, *Is Harry on the Boat?*, p. 207, 1997

mad bomber *noun*
a mortar air delivery system *US*
From the initials MADS.
- — Linda Reinberg, *In the Field*, p. 133, 1991

Madchester *nickname*
Manchester, the UK city that was, between 1989 – 92, more in touch with youth, music and drug fashions than any other *UK*
'Mad' puns on craziness and MDMA (ecstasy).
- "Madchester" brought together 1960s Psychedelia, laddish football-terrace nous and elements of Black American music/street culture. — Sarah Callard and Will Hoon, *Surfers Soulies Skinheads & Skaters*, 1996
- [T]he Madchester foursome's funky-as-fuck classic[.] — *Sky Magazine*, p. 7, May 2001

mad dog *noun*
1 a fearless, aggressive, uninhibited criminal *US*
- The thing he soon had was a small following of other "mad dogs" each with a grievance against one mob leader or another, each with nothing to lose but his life. — Robert Sylvester, *No Cover Charge*, p. 62, 1956

2 any cheap red wine *US, 1974*
Originally applied to Mogen-David wine, later to any cheap wine.
- — Connie Eble (Editor), *UNC-CH Campus Slang*, p. 3, April 1978

mad-dog *verb*
1 to behave in an intensely aggressive fashion, giving the appearance of near insanity *US*
- — William K. Bentley and James M. Corbett, *Prison Slang*, 1992
- Or, worse yet, fronting-off the Asian gangbangers who hung out at South Dove, mad-dogging any rival gang that infringed on their turf. — Joseph Wambaugh, *Floaters*, p. 22, 1996

2 to annoy *NEW ZEALAND*
- — David McGill, *David McGill's Complete Kiwi Slang Dictionary*, p. 71, 1998

maddy *noun*
▸ **throw a maddy**
to have a fit of ill-temper *UK: SCOTLAND, 1985*
- The parkie [park-keeper]'ll take a pure maddy if he catches ye pickin the flooers [flowers]. — Michael Munro, *The Complete Patter*, p. 98, 1996

made *adjective*
1 officially admitted into a crime family *US*
- Everyone knew that Hank had once been on the verge of being "made" by the Mafia – taken on by them as a permanent member. — James Mills, *The Panic in Needle Park*, p. 21, 1966
- But his uncle was a made-guy, a lieutenant with the Mulberry Street crew – a heavy hitter[.] — Edwin Torres, *Carlito's Way*, p. 22, 1975
- A fully made Mafioso. Plus, the guy is a total whackadoo. — Vincent Patrick, *The Pope of Greenwich Village*, p. 138, 1979
- He had been a "made man" in the honored society since he was seventeen[.] — Richard Condon, *Prizzi's Honor*, p. 4, 1982
- As far as Jimmy was concerned, with Tommy being made, it was like we were all being made. We would now have one of our own guys as a member. — *Goodfellas*, 1990
- Watching you in the movie, if I didn't know better I'd have to believe you were a made guy and not acting. — *Get Shorty*, 1995

2 (used of a woman) formerly virginal *US*
- — Vincent J. Monteleone, *Criminal Slang*, p. 150, 1949

made in heaven *noun*
in Bingo, the number sixty-seven *UK*
Rhyming slang.
- — *www.expressbingo.co.uk*, 2003

made in the shade *adjective*
successful, accomplished *US*
- — *Newsweek*, 8th October 1951
- He's got it made in the shade with her. — Frederick Kohner, *Gidget*, p. 114, 1957
- Made in the shade? Hell, as long as any man, white or black, isn't getting his rights in America I'm in danger. — Dick Gregory, *Nigger*, p. 159, 1964
- [T]hey would moo over the view, exclaim "Holy shit" or make some comment about how he had it "made in the shade." — Richard Price, *Clockers*, p. 405, 1992
- Most of us mortals would like nothing better than to have it made it the shade, right? So go buy an awning. — *St. Louis Post-Dispatch*, p. 6, 11th April 1998
- I disagree with you about 'made in the shade.' I think the phrase is a fine piece of folk poetry, the kind that gives American English its vitality. To have it made is to be on Easy Street, to be able to sit around and enjoy life without having to work. — *The Patriot Ledger*, p. 37, 28th February 1998

made of money *adjective*
wealthy *UK, 1786*
- "She can't buy a horse," says Nick. "I mean she's not made of money." — *The Guardian*, 6th October 2002

Ma Deuce *noun*
a Browning .50 caliber machine gun *US, 1982*
- Every tank and personnel carrier had one M2 caliber .50 machine gun, called a Ma Duce. — Harold Coyle, *Team Yankee*, p. 104, 1987
- I've seen these things in John Wayne movies, but this is the first time I've seen a Browning .50-caliber machine gun up close. In the GI vernacular, it's called a Ma Deuce. — *The Cincinnatti Post*, 2nd May 2000

made up *adjective*
happy, satisfied, pleased *UK*
- Into town for a long cold drink and a Big Mac and on to some serious shopping. Made up. — Cath Staincliffe, *Trainers*, p. 61, 1999
- If it's got that little red Prada flash [a fashionable logo] he's made up. — Kevin Sampson, *Outlaws*, p. 13, 2001

mad for it *adjective*
very eager *UK*
The phrase, originating in Manchester in the north of England, gained its wider currency as a catchphrase to justify the excesses of Liam and Noel Gallagher and their band Oasis.
- The absurdity of Liam and Noel's "mad for it" 1968 style anything- is-possiblism is transcended by their unquestionable passion and honesty. — *NME*, 1997
- He was like some garish Ebeneezer Goode, in your face the whole time, driving everybody on – on one, up for it, mad for it, top one. — Kevin Sampson, *Powder*, p. 198, 1999
- Manchester? Mad for it! Fookin top one MANCHEST-AH? — Wayne Anthony, *Spanish Highs*, p. 93, 1999

madhead *noun*
a crazy person *UK*
- I don't want my kids to see their pissed up madhead dad down the pub. — *Q*, p. 98, May 2002

madhouse *noun*
a brakevan (caboose) *US*
- — Ramon Adams, *The Language of the Railroader*, p. 97, 1977

Madison Avenue crash helmet *noun*
a kind of businessman's hat *US*
- [I]n walks a young man wearing a crease-top hat, of the genre known as the Madison Avenue crash helmet, and carrying an attache case. — Tom Wolfe, *The Kandy-Kolored Tangerine-Flake Streamline Baby*, p. 49, 1965

mad keen on *adjective*
very enthusiastic about something or someone *UK, 1949*
- Yanks, as far as she could tell, were mad keen on driving around Irish roads, rain or shine, as if they'd never see a field of grass in their lives. — Nora Roberts, *Heart of the Sea*, p. 99, 2000

madly *adverb*
passionately, fervently, extremely *UK, 1756*
- — *Truly, Madly, Deeply*, 1991
- In other words, you don't have to be madly attractive to find a sexual partner, merely be female. — *The Observer*, 16th July 2000

madman *noun*
a pill of pure MDMA, the recreational drug best known as ecstasy; MDMA in powdered form *UK*
A playful disguise of MaDMAn.
- — Gareth Thomas, *This Is Ecstasy*, p. 54, 2002

Mad Max *noun*
tax *UK*
Rhyming slang, formed on the eponymous hero of three films, 1979–85, set in a post-apocalyptic wasteland; suggesting, perhaps, that taxes will both pay for and survive the apocalypse.
- Postman Pat whistling of a morning as he shoved the old Mad Max demands in through the letter-box[.] — Andrew Nickolds, *Back to Basics*, p. 143–144, 1994

mad mick *noun*
a pick (the tool) *AUSTRALIA, 1919*
Rhyming slang.
- — Jim Ramsay, *Cop It Sweet!*, p. 57, 1977

mad mike *noun*
a mad minute *US*
From the military phonetic alphabet in which 'm' is 'mike'.
- — Linda Reinberg, *In the Field*, p. 133, 1991

mad minute *noun*
an intense, short-lived burst of weapon fire *US, 1917*
- And "mad minutes" is when everyboy on perimeter, around the base camp (you have bunkers all the way around it), opens up and fires away with all their fire power for about a minute, two minutes. — John Kerry, *The New Soldier*, p. 62, 1971
- The "mad-minute," ten seconds long for want of ammunition, was over. — Nelson DeMille, *By the Rivers of Babylon*, p. 232, 1978

mad money *noun*
money set aside to use in an emergency or to splurge *US, 1922*
- I embraced her, got me a big fat juicy taste of honey, gave her some mad money and told her if I wasn't there to cab it on in. — A.S. Jackson, *Gentleman Pimp*, p. 110, 1973
- I could rent something nice and still have a little mad money in the bank. — Armistead Maupin, *Maybe the Moon*, p. 31, 1992
- She went to the closet and reached up next to the ski cap, where she kept her mad money, and found the .32-caliber nickel-plated revolver she'd bought from the horney gas station owner who serviced her car. — Joseph Wambaugh, *Floaters*, p. 127, 1996

mad monkey *noun*
a staff worker at the US Military Army Command, Vietnam *US*
Another of many terms expressing the combat soldier's disdain for those who were in the service but did not see combat.
- — Linda Reinberg, *In the Field*, p. 134, 1991

madon!
used as a moderately profane exclamation *US*
Originally Italian-American usage.
- Madon', you guys think you're still in Red Hook. — Edwin Torres, *Q & A*, p. 146, 1977

Madonna *noun*
someone who has died or is unavoidably doomed to die very soon *UK*
Rhyming slang for **GONER**, formed on the popular US singer Madonna Louise Ciccone (b.1958) rather than the religious icon.
- There he is lying bleeding in the Pickettywitch [ditch] thinking he's a Madonna. — Mervyn Stutter, *Getting Nowhere Fast*, 21st May 2004

madonna claws *noun*
an ugly hand *UK*
Contemporary gay use.
- — *Attitude*, p. 60, July 2003: 'New palare lexicon'

mad out of it *adjective*
drunk or drug-intoxicated *IRELAND*
- It gets you mad out of it, have a good time with it. — Ann Hope (et al.), *The Impact of Alcohol Advertising on Teenagers in Ireland*, p. 4, 2001

mad props *noun*
effusive compliments *US*
- — Linda Meyer, *Teenspeak!*, p. 28, 1994

mad railer *noun*
a racing greyhound that will veer towards the inside rail no matter what its starting position *AUSTRALIA*
- — Ned Wallish, *The Truth Dictionary of Racing Slang*, p. 67, 1989

Madras in the evening, mad arse in the morning
given as a proverbial warning against eating a curry that is spicier than your body can comfortably handle *UK: SCOTLAND*
In Glasgow use.
- — Michael Munro, *The Patter, Another Blast*, 1988

mad skull *noun*
a crazy or mentally unstable person *UK: SCOTLAND*
- Here comes that mad skull next door on his motorbike. — Michael Munro, *The Original Patter*, p. 44, 1985

mad spun *adjective*
deeply under the influence of LSD *US*
- — Jim Crotty, *How to Talk American*, p. 89, 1997

madukes *noun*
a mother *US*
- — Connie Eble (Editor), *UNC-CH Campus Slang*, p. 5, November 2002

mad weed *noun*
green, weak marijuana *JAMAICA, 1979*
- — Thomas H. Slone, *Rasta is Cuss*, p. 55, 2003

mad wey it; mad wi' it *adjective*
drunk; mad with drink *UK: SCOTLAND*
• — *e-cyclopaedia*, 20th March 2002

madwoman *noun*
a pill of pure MDEA, an analogue of MDMA, the recreational drug best known as ecstasy *UK*
Probably as a variation of **MADMAN** (MDMA).
• — Gareth Thomas, *This Is Ecstasy*, p. 54, 2002

madza; madzer; medza; medzer; midzer *adjective*
half *UK*
From Italian *mezzo* (a half). Used, for example, in 'madza beagered' (half-drunk) and 'medzer caroon' (a half-crown).
• — Paul Baker, *Polari*, p. 180, 2002

Mae *noun*
among male homosexuals, a term of endearment *UK*
Probably adopted from the name of glamorous film actress Mae West; used in such conversational gambits as: 'Hello, Mae, how are you today?'. Remembered from the 1960s by a Sheffield correspondent.

Mae West *noun*
1 the chest or the breast *UK*
Rhyming slang, formed from the name of buxom US actress and writer, 1892–1980.
• — Ray Puxley, *Cockney Rabbit*, 1992
• — Susie Dent, *The Language Report*, p. 98, 2003
2 a life-jacket worn by aircrews *UK, 1940*
Military. Remains familiar thanks to its popularity with crossword compilers.
3 in the language of parachuting, a partial inversion of the canopy resulting from a deployment malfunction *US, 1958*
• — Dan Poynter, *Parachuting*, p. 169, 1978: 'The language of parachuting'
4 a French-Canadian sugar roll *CANADA*
• — *Maledicta*, p. 183, 1979: 'Canadian slurs, ethnic and other'

mafia *noun*
used as part of a jocular formation referring to a large number or influential group of people *US*
• The "Hawaiian" mafia was a term we had that referred to the large number of Hawaiians among the Wolfhound ranks. — David H. Hackworth, *About Face*, p. 69, 1989

mafioski *noun*
Russian criminals *UK*
Conventional 'mafia' with the suffix '-ski' to indicate a Russian heritage.
• — David Rowan, *Glossary for the 90s*, 1998

mafu *noun*
marijuana *UK*
• — Mike Haskins, *Drugs*, p. 288, 2003

mag *noun*
1 a magazine, in any sense of the term *UK, 1801*
• For the rest of her career in Hollywood, while her gams are still straight and her figure otherwise, she'll pose cheesecake for fang-mags[.] — Jack Lait and Lee Mortimer, *New York Confidential*, p. 145, 1948
• He was going to publish a mag called The Rebel but it had come out only twice. — James Simon Kunen, *The Strawberry Statement*, p. 97, 1968
• Customers who flocked to the stores in 1967 allegedly asked for more explicit mags and loops. — Josh Alan Friedman, *Tales of Times Square*, p. 75, 1986
• MURTAUGH: What's it take? RIGGS: Fifteen in the mag, one up the pipe. — *Lethal Weapon*, 1987
2 a magnesium steel wheel on a race car *US*
• People even put fake mags over regular car wheels to make their cars look fancy. — Ed Radlauer, *Drag Racing Pix Dix*, p. 36, 1970
3 a magneto, used on drag racing engines with no battery or generator *US*
• — Lyle K. Engel, *The Complete Book of Fuel and Gas Dragsters*, p. 153, 1968
4 a brief conversation; a chat; a gossip *AUSTRALIA, 1895*
• Then we'll prop here and have a mag and a few beers. — Robert G. Barrett, *Davo's Little Something*, p. 257, 1992

Mag *noun*
a Magnum™ pistol *US, 1970*
• Thirty-eights, I'll take a three-fifty-seven mag if I have to. — George V. Higgins, *The Friends of Eddie Doyle*, p. 8, 1971
• He's got a range, he's teaching all these housewives come in how to fire three-fifty-sevens, forty-fives. Can you see it? Broad's making cookies, she's got this big fucking Mag stuck in her apron? — Elmore Leonard, *Split Images*, p. 22, 1981

mag *verb*
to chat; to prattle *UK, 1820*
• Plans are made as I mag with dried-out drunks in the eerie quiet of the Exford gardens. — Kevin Mackey, *The Cure*, p. 46, 1970

maga *adjective*
▷ see: **MAAGA**

maga dog *noun*
a mongrel
West Indian and Rastafarian patois.

magazine *noun*
a six-month sentence to jail *US*
• — Vincent J. Monteleone, *Criminal Slang*, p. 150, 1949

maggie *noun*
1 the Australian magpie, *Gymnorhina tibicen* *AUSTRALIA, 1901*
• Yet I loved looking at my maggies' eggs – the pale blue ones or the pale green ones with reddish spots in a ring at the far end[.] — T.A.G. Hungerford, *Stories From Suburban Road*, p. 61, 1983
2 marijuana *US, 1959*
Variants on the name Maggie, all diminutives of Margaret, play very loosely on marijuana: 'Maggie', 'meg', 'megg', 'meggie', 'meggs'.
• — Richard A. Spears, *The Slang and Jargon of Drugs and Drink*, p. 327, 1986
• — Mike Haskins, *Drugs*, p. 288, 2003

Maggie *noun*
any revolver that fires a cartridge that is more powerful than standard ammunition *US*
• — *American Speech*, p. 194, October 1957: 'Some colloquialisms of the handgunner'

Maggie *nickname*
British Prime Minister (1979–90) Margaret Hilda Thatcher (b.1925) *UK*
The UK wasn't really on first name terms with Mrs Thatcher until she became PM; earlier in her political career, however, she was vilified as 'Maggie Thatcher, milk snatcher'. Also known as 'Attila the hen'.
• Britain was a steady ship – Maggie was at the helm and all was right with the world. — Andrew Nickolds, *Back to Basics*, p. 5, 1994
• The miners, the Falklands, Maggie Maggie Maggie Out Out Out, all that stuff. — James Hawes, *Dead Long Enough*, p. 92, 2000
• God bless Maggie and don't fuck with us. — Ken Lukowiak, *Marijuana Time*, p. 20, 2000
• Each one had a message as we [a protest march] passed their house, like "Give it to Maggie when you get there." — Mark Steel, *Reasons to be Cheerful*, p. 90, 2001

Maggie's drawers *noun*
a red flag indicating a 'miss' on a rifle range *US, 1936*
• — Carl Fleischhauer, *A Glossary of Army Slang*, p. 32, 1968
• — Linda Reinberg, *In the Field*, 1991

Maggie's millions *noun*
the unemployed during the premiership of Margaret Thatcher (1979–90) *UK*
• I mean – look at that lot. Maggie's millions. — Anthony Masters, *Minder*, p. 8, 1984

maggot *noun*
1 a loathsome person *AUSTRALIA*
• An' not a flamin' beep outta you, you sterile maggot, or I'll bend this round y'thick skull. — W.R. Bennett, *Wingman*, p. 114, 1961
2 a white person *US, 1985*
Urban black usage.
• — Carsten Stroud, *Close Pursuit*, p. 273, 1987
3 a repulsive female *AUSTRALIA*
• — Kathy Lette, *Girls' Night Out*, p. 187, 1987
4 in the US Air Force, someone who is very dedicated to service *US*
• — *Seattle Times*, p. A9, 12th April 1998: 'Grunts, squids not grunting from the same dictionary'

▸ **act the maggot**
to play the fool *IRELAND, 1937*
• [D]on't be acting the maggot when Sam comes, there's little enough room in there. — Iris Murdoch, *Something Special*, p. 7, 1957

maggot; maggotted *adjective*
drunk *AUSTRALIA*
• 'Oh my god, you are completely maggot!' 'He was absolutely maggotted last night.' — *Wordmap (www.abc.net.au/wordmap)*, 2003

maggot bag *noun*
a meat pie *AUSTRALIA*
• I'm off to the shop to get a maggot bag. — *Wordmap (www.abc.net.au/wordmap)*, 2003

maggotbox *noun*
an Apple Macintosh™ computer *US*
• — Eric S. Raymond, *The New Hacker's Dictionary*, p. 230, 1991

maggot wagon *noun*
a catering truck *US*
• — Lewis Poteet, *Car & Motorcyle Slang*, p. 125, 1992

maggoty; maggotty *noun*
angry; in a bad mood *AUSTRALIA, 1919*
• — Jim Ramsay, *Cop It Sweet!*, p. 57, 1977

maggs-man *noun*
▷ see: MAGSMAN

magic *adjective*
1 excellent, first class; used for showing approval and enthusiasm *UK*
• [T]hat's crankin', man – fuckin' majeek! — Stuart Browne, *Dangerous Parking*, p. 40, 2000

2 in computing, complicated or not yet understood *US*
• — Guy L Steele, *Coevolution Quarterly*, Spring 1981: 'Computer slang'
• — Guy L. Steele et al., *The Hacker's Dictionary*, p. 88, 1983

magic bean *noun*
a tablet of MDMA, the recreational drug best known as ecstasy *UK*
From the fairystory *Jack and the Beanstalk*.
• But what he forgets to do, right, is buy enough magic beans for everyone. — Kevin Williamson, *Heart of the Bass (Disco Biscuits)*, p. 112, 1996

magic flagon *noun*
marijuana *NEW ZEALAND*
• I've smoked the magic flagon with rock stars, actors, doctors, journalists, negros and aboriginals, to name a few[.] — Redmer YSKA, *New Zealand Green*, p. 162, 1990

magic fudge; fudge *noun*
an intoxicating confection that has marijuana as a central ingredient *UK*
• Ice-cold Foster's lager greedily interspersed with chunks of magic fudge [...] I floated into the "performers' bar" on a cloud of fudge. — Richard Neville, *Play Power*, p. 115, 1970

magic hour *noun*
the time between sundown and dark *US*
A filming term; according to Singleton, 'The light is very warm, the sky is a magical deep blue, and shadows are long' (*Filmmaker's Dictionary*, 1990).

magic money machine *noun*
an automated cash machine *NEW ZEALAND*
Used widely in conversation since the 1990s.

magic mushie *noun*
a hallucinogenic mushroom *AUSTRALIA*
• There was marihuana, hash, LSD, and magic mushies. And there was heroin. — *National Times*, p. 3, 5th December 1982

magic mushroom *noun*
any mushroom with an hallucinogenic effect – the most commonly grown and used in the UK is *Psilocybe Semilanceata* or Liberty Cap mushroom *US, 1968*
• — Walter Way, *The Drug Scene*, p. 110, 1977
• — Angela Devlin, *Prison Patter*, p. 74, 1996
• [A] nice cup of liberty-cap tea ... the name summed it up ... magic mushrooms sounded better as liberty caps[.] — John King, *White Trash*, p. 196, 2001

magic numbers
used as a farewell *US*
Referring to 73 and 88, citizens' band radio code for 'good wishes'.
• — Radio Shack, *CBer's Handy Atlas/Dictionary*, p. 32, 1976

magic roundabout *noun*
used as an informal name for the system whereby a difficult prisoner is contantly moved from prison to prison *UK*
Named after *The Magic Roundabout*, a stop-motion animation, children's and cult television programme first broadcast in the UK in 1965.
• — Angela Devlin, *Prison Patter*, p. 74, 1996

magic smoke *noun*
marijuana *UK, 1998*
• — Mike Haskins, *Drugs*, p. 288, 2003

magic sponge *noun*
a towel or sponge applied to injured players during a game who then have a miraculous recovery *AUSTRALIA*
• I grew up in Brisbane, my father coached junior league for as long as I can remember for East Carina, I sat on the lines and took stats, ran on with the "magic sponge" etc. — *www.1staid.com.au/donna.htm*, 2003

magic up *verb*
to improve, to enhance, to encourage *UK*
• [W]hen the band arrived I was usually there with a plate of sandwiches and a beer and made them feel at home. I wanted to magic the band up a bit so they felt good[.] — Will Birch, *No Sleep Till Canvey Island*, p. 155, 2003

magic wand *noun*
the penis *UK*
• — *The Observer*, 29th June 1969

magistrate's court; magistrate's *noun*
a drink of spirits; an alcoholic drink *UK*
Rhyming slang for SHORT.
• — Ray Puxley, *Cockney Rabbit*, 1992

magnacious *adjective*
excellent, great *US*
An elaboration of 'magnificent'.
• I got up, feeling magnacious, and begin to walk away from the poor fuck lying on the floor[.] — Joel Rose, *Kill Kill Faster Faster*, p. 19, 1997

magnet *noun*
a person who attracts the precedent thing or personality type *US*
• With a voice like that, he's got to be a babe magnet. — *Wayne's World 2*, 1993
• Popular babe magnets include a nice car, stylish clothes, attractive looks, and [the old standby] a fistful of cash. — Vann Wesson, *Generation X Field Guide and Lexicon*, p. 10, 1997
• I think I'm just a weirdo magnet. — *Something About Mary*, 1998
• Here's what a guy who goes by the chick-magnet Net handle of "Wampa-One" thinks about Bluntman and Chronic. — Kevin Smith, *Jay and Silent Bob Strike Back*, p. 20, 2001
• Here he is. Netherley's premier fanny magnet. — Niall Griffiths, *Kelly + Victor*, p. 43, 2002

Magnificent Mile *noun*
a stretch of Michigan Avenue running from the river to Oak Street in Chicago, Illinois *US*
A Chamber of Commerce phrase that took root in the vernacular.
• — Bill Reilly, *Big Al's Official Guide to Chicagoese*, p. 43, 1982
• — Laurence Urdang, *Names and Nicknames of Places and Things*, p. 157, 1987

Magnus Pike; magnus *noun*
a lesbian *UK*
Rhyming slang for DYKE, formed from the name of a British scientist and television presenter.
• Any woman who says no to me has got to be a Magnus. — Bodmin Dark, *Dirty Cockney Rhyming Slang*, 2003

magoo *noun*
in circus usage, a cream or custard pie thrown by clowns at each other *US, 1926*
• — Don Wilmeth, *The Language of American Popular Entertainment*, p. 166, 1981

magsman; maggs-man *noun*
1 a confidence trickster whose prime device is conversation *AUSTRALIA, 1877*
• Then I began to suspect I'd seen one of them on the wharf, and I realized they must have robbed me. A magsman and a pickpocket. — Vince Kelly, *The Bogeyman*, p. 29, 1956

2 a talkative person; a raconteur *AUSTRALIA, 1924*
• A couple of guards at Goulburn were the greatest maggs-men I ever met. — Patsy Adam-Smith, *Folklore of the Australian Railwaymen*, 1969

mag wheel *noun*
a racing car wheel made of magnesium alloy *AUSTRALIA, 1981*
- The kids at teachers college called it a 'Marrickville Mercedes' – a red ET Monaro with a sun roof and mag wheels. —Kathy Lette, *Girls' Night Out*, p. 139, 1987

maha *adjective*
very large *INDIA*
From Sanskrit.
- Fool of Fools. Master-Clown of Clowns. Maha-Idiot of idiots. —Vikram Chandra, *Red Earth and Pouring Rain*, 1995

maharishee *noun*
marijuana *US, 1980s*
- —Jay Robert Nash, *Dictionary of Crime*, 1992

Mahatma Gandhi *noun*
a shandy *UK*
Rhyming slang, formed from the name of the Indian leader, 1869–1948.
- —Ray Puxley, *Cockney Rabbit*, 1992

Mahatma Gandhi; mahatma *adjective*
sexually aroused *UK*
Rhyming slang for **RANDY**, formed from the name of the great Indian leader and pacifist, 1889–1948.

mahogany bomber *noun*
the desk which an office-bound pilot 'flies' *UK*
- —Colin Strong Duff Hart-Davis, *Fighter Pilot*, 1981

mahogany gaspipe *noun*
used as a mock representation of intonations of Irish *IRELAND*
- Cuilín amháin le Loch Garman agus tá sé mahogany gaspipe. Tá sé bore a hole in the bucket[.] —Billy Roche, *The Wexford Trilogy (Poor Beast in the Rain)*, p. 73, 1992

mahooha *noun*
ridiculous political manoeuvres and pointless talk *US, 1930*
- Now that I have the vote, all that mahooha going on in Ottawa and Victoria is my fault, too. —*Toronto Globe and Mail*, p. A15, 7th September 2002

mahoot *noun*
in bar dice games, a roll that produces no points for the player *US*
- —Jester Smith, *Games They Play in San Francisco*, p. 104, 1971

mahoska; hoska *noun*
an addictive drug, especially heroin *US, 1949*
- —David Maurer and Victor Vogel, *Narcotics and Narcotic Addiction*, p. 425, 1973

maid *noun*
1 a black woman (regardless of age or occupation) *SOUTH AFRICA, 1961*
Offensive, demeaning.
- —Penny Silva, *A Dictionary of South African English*, 1996

2 female virginity *TRINIDAD AND TOBAGO, 1972*
Also called 'maiden'.
- —Lise Winer, *Dictionary of the English/Creole of Trinidad & Tobago*, 2003

maiden *noun*
1 in horse racing, a horse that has never won a race *US*
- —David W. Maurer, *Argot of the Racetrack*, p. 42, 1951

2 by extension, a jockey who has never won a race *US*
- She was on the bit, but a maiden was up and he came a cropper. —*San Francisco Chronicle*, p. 54, 21st April 1971

maidenhead *noun*
a woman's toilet *US*
Punning on the hymen and **HEAD** as 'a toilet'.
- —Collin Baker et al., *College Undergraduate Slang Study Conducted at Brown University*, p. 154, 1968

maid training *noun*
the process of instructing, and conditioning the behaviour of, a sexual submissive *UK*
The submissive's menial service becomes part of a sexual relationship (in which an element of transvestism is usually implied); used in a dominant prostitute's advertising matter.
- —Caroline Archer, *Tart Cards*, 2003

mail *noun*
1 an overheard conversation on citizens' band radio *US*
- —Wayne Floyd, *Jason's Authentic Dictionary of CB Slang*, p. 21, 1976

2 in horse racing, information about a horse or race useful for wagering *AUSTRALIA*
- —Ned Wallish, *The Truth Dictionary of Racing Slang*, p. 50, 1989

mail-call; mail *noun*
enemy mortar, rockets or artillery being received *US, 1919*
Coined in World War I, still used by World War 2 veterans in Vietnam.
- —Gregory Clark, *Words of the Vietnam War*, p. 244–245, 1990

main *noun*
any large blood vein *US, 1952*
- They knew he was on drugs, a real horsehead who hit the main. —Hal Ellson, *The Golden Spike*, p. 68, 1952

▸ **the main**
to island dwellers off the coast of Maine, the mainland *US*
- —John Gould, *Maine Lingo*, p. 174, 1975

Main *noun*
▸ **the Main**
St Laurent Street in Montreal *CANADA*
Even though St Catherine Street, running east and west through the centre, has become the main street of the city, St Laurent (or St Lawrence) was originally the centre of shopping, immigrant settlement and the garment district, and so it has held the name.

main *verb*
to inject a drug into a main vein *US, 1952*
- Do you know she was the first one to show him how to main? —Hal Ellson, *The Golden Spike*, p. 52, 1952

main line *noun*
1 any large blood vein, especially the median cephalic vein *US, early 1930s*
- After that it was nothing but the main-line, the high of highs. —Hal Ellson, *The Golden Spike*, p. 228, 1952
- I began shooting in the main line to save stuff and because the immediate kick was better. —William Burroughs, *Junkie*, p. 34, 1953

2 a major vein used for the injection of narcotics, usually heroin *US, 1931*
- Ever pop coke in the mainline? It hits you right in the brain, activating connections of pure pleasure. —William Burroughs, *The Naked Lunch*, 1968
- He could absorb a large amount at one time – mainline – and turn on in a flash. —Herbert Huncke, *The Evening Sun Turned Crimson*, p. 189, 1980
- Shoot me up / In the mainline —Alabama 3 *Hypo Full of Love*, 1997

3 at a horse racing track, the area with the greatest concentration of mutuel betting machines *US*
- —David W. Maurer, *Argot of the Racetrack*, p. 42, 1951

4 the general population of a prison *US*
- "They're making fair time," he said. "We'll eat mainline tonight." —Malcolm Braly, *On the Yard*, p. 28, 1967
- Whisper told the police he walked the mainline eighteen years and was never once bumped. —Seth Morgan, *Homeboy*, p. 124, 1990

mainline *verb*
to inject drugs, especially heroin, into a main vein *US, 1938*
- I want it mainline for one blast. —George Mandel, *Flee the Angry Strangers*, p. 378–379, 1952
- Main-lining her. Capping her straight. —John D. McDonald, *The Neon Jungle*, p. 46, 1953
- But when you main-line, you're gone, man, clear out. —Ross Russell, *The Sound*, p. 205, 1961
- Of course all the students smoke pot and experiment with LSD but only a few main-line[.] —Gore Vidal, *Myra Breckinridge*, p. 39, 1968
- "Don't mainline him, for Chrissake," he, too, shouting at the top of his voice, "we'll have a fucking stiff on our hands." —Terry Southern, *Blue Movie*, p. 190, 1970
- Slumberously evil eyes stare into the camera with an odd malevolence, perhaps due to the powerful "speed ball" (heroin and cocaine in combination) I had mainlined a half hour before I sat for the photographer. —Iceberg Slim (Robert Beck), *The Naked Soul of Iceberg Slim*, p. 239, 1971
- It was also believed that dependency [on heroin] could be avoided by careful and occasional "skin popping" rather than mainlining. —Paul E. Wills, *Profane Culture*, p. 151, 1978
- I ain't been mainlining or anything like that, no skin popping, just snorting[.] —Joel Rose, *Kill Kill Faster Faster*, p. 185–186, 1997

Main Line *nickname*

the wealthy suburbs just to the west of Philadelphia, Pennsylvania, extending from Merion to Bryn Mawr to Paoli *US*

From the Paoli Local commuter train that ran out of the main line of the now-defunct Pennsylvania Railroad, carrying businessmen to work and future lexicographers in blue wool jerseys with five white stripes on each arm to school.

- —Laurence Urdang, *Names and Nicknames of Places and Things*, p. 158, 1987

mainliner *noun*

a drug user who injects the drug into a vein *US, 1934*

- U.S. narcotics agents have told us it is not uncommon to find a 12-year-old Negro child deeply habituated to "main-liners," an extreme form of dope addiction, in which the subject gets no kick out of cocaine and heroin unless he inserts a hypodermic needle into a main artery in the arm or leg. —Jack Lait and Lee Mortimer, *Chicago Confidential*, p. 148, 1950
- While Lukey the Swede, with scars under his sleeve and a mainliner standing among junkies, laughed with his old knowledge of Nothing. —George Mandel, *Flee the Angry Strangers*, p. 313, 1952
- They are all mainliners except Nellie and Fran. They go strictly for the veins. —Willard Motley, *Let No Man Write My Epitaph*, p. 158, 1958
- A junkie, a dope addict, a hop-head, a mainliner – a dope fiend! —James Baldwin, *Blues for Mister Charlie*, p. 45, 1964
- I had jumped from being a careful snorter, content to take my kicks of sniffing through my nose, to a not-so-careful skin-popper, and now was full-grown careless mainliner. —Piri Thomas, *Down These Mean Streets*, p. 200, 1967

main man *noun*

1 an important man *US, 1977*

From circus jargon.

- [L]ocated him as the main man, the cock of the walk, the king of this particular little hill[.] —James Hawes, *Dead Long Enough*, p. 105, 2000

2 a pimp, in relation to a prostitute *US*

- The young man was wearing a cardigan, pants with cuffs, and penny loafers, so it never occurred to Wingnut that he could be a hooker's main man. —Joseph Wambaugh, *The Secrets of Harry Bright*, p. 63, 1985

main pin *noun*

a railway official *US, 1930*

- —Norman Carlisle, *The Modern Wonder Book of Trains and Railroading*, p. 265, 1946

main punch *noun*

a man's favoured girlfriend *US*

- Tommy Blue Eyes and his main punch, what's her name, Charlotte, with her ta-tas sticking out of her sundress like a couple of muskmelons[.] [Quoting James Lee Burke] — *USA Today*, p. 8D, 2nd August 1994

main queen *noun*

a man's primary girlfriend *US*

- —Jack Lait and Lee Mortimer, *New York Confidential*, 1948: 'A glossary of Harlemisms'

main squeeze *noun*

a person's primary partner in romance *US, 1926*

- — *Current Slang*, p. 10, Fall 1970
- —Hermese E. Roberts, *The Third Ear*, 1971
- He remembers how each time the lovers' frequent break-ups sent Reba to him for solace, how each time his secret dream, to move from Reba's play big bro to her main squeeze, had to be deferred[.] —Iceberg Slim (Robert Beck), *Doom Fox*, p. 3, 1978
- I happen to think Willie's main squeeze is sexy. —Joseph Wambaugh, *Floaters*, p. 26, 1996

mainstreeting *noun*

the use of the main street of a town, especially by a politician, for campaigning *CANADA*

- There were handshakes all round, a quiet afternoon walk that Dief [Conservative Prime Minister Diefenbaker] loves to call "Main-streeting," then a ball game after dinner. — *Time (Cdn. ed.)*, p. 11/1, 8th March 1959

maintain *verb*

▸ **maintain your low tones**

do not raise your voice at me *US*

A phrase coined by writers of the 'Coneheads' skits on *Saturday Night Live* in the late 1970s, featuring three Remulakian aliens who lived quiet and normal lives in the suburbs of New Jersey. Most of the Remulakian phrases were too forced for everyday slang, such as 'molten lactate extract of hooved animals' for 'melted cheese', but a few such as this were temporarily in vogue.

main vein *noun*

1 the penis *US*

- Another way to say "penis" [...] The main vein[.] —Erica Orloff and JoAnn Baker, *Dirty Little Secrets*, p. 90, 2001

2 the vagina *UK, 1984*

Usage is recorded as 'especially among drug addicts'.

▸ **stab in the main vein**

from a male perspective, to have sex *UK, 1984*

Formed on MAIN VEIN (the vagina).

mainy *adjective*

fearless, crazy *US*

- You mainy, blood, and I don't want to get caught up in that. —Rick Ayers (Editor), *Berkeley High Slang Dictionary*, p. 31, 2004

mais oui *adverb*

of course, certainly *UK*

An affected usage, adopted directly from French *mais oui* (but yes).

- —Paul Baker, *Polari*, p. 180, 2002

Maizie *noun*

used as a term of address among male homosexuals *US*

- — *Fact*, p. 26, January-February 1965

maj *noun*

*maj*esty *UK*

An informal, generally affectionate, reduction.

- "What have you done, Arthur?" "Written to her Maj requesting a Royal Warrant for my new business[.] —Andrew Nickolds, *Back to Basics*, p. 15, 1994

major *noun*

a dependable, reliable person *US*

- — *American Speech*, p. 97, May 1956: 'Smugglers' argot in the Southwest'

major *verb*

▸ **major in plumbing**

in college, to take nothing but easy courses *US*

An allusion to 'pipes' (easy courses).

- — *American Speech*, p. 304, December 1955: 'Wayne University slang'

major *adjective*

1 very good *US*

- —Connie Eble (Editor), *UNC-CH Campus Slang*, p. 5, Fall 1984

2 absolute *AUSTRALIA*

Used as an intensifier.

- We are talking about a major bod here, and I don't care if half of it is plastic. —Paul Vautin, *Turn It Up!*, p. 129, 1995
- You have the major hots for him but he's taken. — *Dolly*, p. 79, 1996

3 handsome, dressed well *TRINIDAD AND TOBAGO, 1967*

- —Lise Winer, *Dictionary of the English/Creole of Trinidad & Tobago*, 2003

Major Dee *noun*

a maître d' *UK*

Possibly influenced by 'major domo'.

- Morty tells the Major Dee that we are with the Price party. —J.J. Connolly, *Layer Cake*, p. 43, 2000

major-league *adjective*

prominent, accomplished, prestigious *US, 1941*

On 4th September 2000, US presidential candidate George Bush leaned to his running mate Dick Cheney at a campaign stop in Naperville, Illinois, and, pointing to a reporter, said 'There's Adam Clymner – major-league asshole from the *New York Times*'. 'Major-league' had major-league arrived.

- The whole thing happened because we both were consumed by the desire to get a top-notch front that would cause us to be two of the youngest major-league mack men in the city of Detroit. —A.S. Jackson, *Gentleman Pimp*, p. 59, 1973
- She's trouble, Ned. The real thing. Big-time, major league trouble. — *Body Heat*, 1980

major leagues *noun*

the highest level of achievement in a field *US*

- Some planned to make the major league when they saved up a roll, but they were the exception. —Jack Lait and Lee Mortimer, *Washington Confidential*, p. 274, 1951

Major Loder *noun*
soda, especially soda water *UK*
Rhyming slang, formed from the name of a famous racehorse owner in the early part of C20.
- —Julian Franklyn, *A Dictionary of Rhyming Slang*, 1961
- —Ray Puxley, *Fresh Rabbit*, 1998

majorly *adverb*
very much *US, 1983*
- I am majorly, totally, butt-crazy in love with Josh.—*Clueless*, 1995
- Ripped off majorly.—Glyn Parry, *Mosh*, p. 48, 1996
- I would have been so majorly stupid of me to turn him down —*American Beauty*, 1999

Major Stevens *noun*
in betting odds, evens *UK, 1961*
Rhyming slang.
- —Ray Puxley, *Cockney Rabbit*, 1992

mak *noun*
a machete *US*
Critically important during the Vietnam war for hacking through jungles.
- —Gregory Clark, *Words of the Vietnam War*, p. 309, 1990

makable *adjective*
(used of a wave) in surfing, possible to catch for a ride *US*
- —William Desmond Nelson, *Surfing*, p. 222, 1973

make *noun*
an identification *US, 1950*
- Things that I'd never thought about before, like why did it take 'em so long to get a make on me?—A.S. Jackson, *Gentleman Pimp*, p. 113, 1973
- I had everything on him. Prints. Positive make. Everything.—George V. Higgins, *The Judgment of Deke Hunter*, p. 38, 1976

▸ **on the make**
1 in search of sexual company *US, 1929*
- But he didn't want Alice fooling around with a kid who was definitely jail bait and on the make.—Irving Shulman, *The Amboy Dukes*, p. 34, 1947
- She's just another of those rich wives on the make.—Philip Wylie, *Opus 21*, p. 273, 1949
- It's a local tradition. Every Wednesday night. And you don't even have to look like you're on the make.—Armistead Maupin, *Tales of the City*, p. 14, 1978
- Since you're on the make again.—*Sleepless in Seattle*, 1993

2 seeking any opportunity or profit *UK*
- [W]e are just a bunch of useless fucking tossers out on the fucking make.—Shaun Ryder, *Shaun Ryder... in His Own Words*, 1992
- Usually I wave away or dead-head [ignore] prozzies on the make, like[.]—Niall Griffiths, *Kelly + Victor*, p. 67, 2002

▸ **put the make on**
to try to seduce *US*
- An this guy gives me a ride – an that was the first guy ever put the make on me.—John Rechy, *City of Night*, p. 152, 1963

make *verb*
1 to identify (a person) *UK, 1906*
- "We still can't make her." "Could it have been a man dressed like a dame?"—Mickey Spillane, *Kiss Me Deadly*, p. 143, 1952
- "They've made us, Pat," I said. "Get going."—William Burroughs, *Junkie*, p. 80, 1953
- He's a nice, clean-cut gun dealer, is what he is, and if he wanted to, he could probably make half the hoods and forty percent of the bikies in this district.—George V. Higgins, *The Friends of Eddie Doyle*, p. 215, 1971
- The detective said, "He say it was going down when he got home? How about, he looked at the guy but couldn't make him? TV – all that kind of shit comes out of TV. They get to be household words." —Elmore Leonard, *Split Images*, p. 17, 1981
- This part of town, they'll make us for heat the second we walk in. —*48 Hours*, 1982
- I'd never make you as a burglar, not in that outfit.—*Get Shorty*, 1995
- I stayed a couple of cars back so she wouldn't make me[.]—Janet Evanovich, *Seven Up*, p. 162, 2001

2 in planespotting, to record ('collect') an aircraft *UK*
- I should, at this juncture, point out that while trainspotters "cop" engine numbers, planespotters "make" aircraft numbers.—Iain Aitch, *A Fête Worse Than Death*, p. 73, 2003

3 to seduce or have sex with someone *US, 1923*
- Al had had the reputation of making every girl he took out.—James T. Farrell, *Saturday Night*, p. 18, 1947
- Later that night I found out why Tino had put me in the hospital so readily. He was trying to make me.—Chester Himes, *Cast the First Stone*, p. 71, 1952
- He had decided at the start that he was going to make one or other of the Graces sooner or later.—Charles Raven, *Underworld Nights*, p. 119, 1956
- We picked up two girls, a pretty young blonde and a fat brunette. They were dumb and sullen, but we wanted to make them.—Jack Kerouac, *On the Road*, p. 34, 1957

4 to admit someone into membership in an organised crime organisation *US*
- Valachi told the subcommittee that the purpose of a particular meeting in upstate New York had been to make us.—*American Speech*, p. 306, December 1964: 'Lingua Cosa Nostra'

5 to manage to catch and travel on a scheduled vehicle *UK, 1955*
- I arrive at Euston at 8.57, heart pounding, trying against the odds to be stoic but run up the escalators to try to make the train with seconds to spare.—*The Observer*, 19th October 2003

6 to fix a price *UK, 1895*
In stock market use.

7 to steal, to appropriate *UK, 1700*

▸ **as pretty/clever/happy as they make them**
used for indicating an extreme *UK, 1896*
Current examples (found in a quick search of the Internet, December 2003): 'as bad as they make them', 'as American as they make them' and 'as happy as they make them'.

▸ **make a break**
to escape or make an attempted escape from prison *US, 1930*
- —Angela Devlin, *Prison Patter*, p. 74, 1996

▸ **make a bubble; make a jail; make jail; make prison; make years**
to be sentenced to or to serve a jail sentence *TRINIDAD AND TOBAGO, 1937*
- —Lise Winer, *Dictionary of the English/Creole of Trinidad & Tobago*, 2003

▸ **make (a period of time)**
to be sentenced to or to serve a jail sentence *TRINIDAD AND TOBAGO, 1904*
- —Lise Winer, *Dictionary of the English/Creole of Trinidad & Tobago*, 2003

▸ **make ass**
to blunder; to make a spectacle of yourself *US*
Hawaiian youth usage.
- —Douglas Simonson, *Pidgin to da Max*, 1981

▸ **make a thing of; make a thing about**
to make a fuss about something *UK, 1934*
- And last night? It was just a glitch. A bit of cold comfort from the cellar dweller. Let's don't make a thing of it.—*Buffy the Vampire Slayer*, 2003
- I'm just saying if it was Clinton, you don't think they would have made a thing about that?—Bill Maher, *Larry King Live*, 28th January 2004

▸ **make a zeef**
to show off *TRINIDAD AND TOBAGO*
- —Lise Winer, *Dictionary of the English/Creole of Trinidad & Tobago*, 2003

▸ **make fares**
to work as a prostitute *TRINIDAD AND TOBAGO, 1987*
- —Lise Winer, *Dictionary of the English/Creole of Trinidad & Tobago*, 2003

▸ **make fart**
to make life difficult for someone *TRINIDAD AND TOBAGO, 1990*
- —Lise Winer, *Dictionary of the English/Creole of Trinidad & Tobago*, 2003

▸ **make friends**
(among women) to take a lesbian lover *TRINIDAD AND TOBAGO, 1960*
- —Lise Winer, *Dictionary of the English/Creole of Trinidad & Tobago*, 2003

▸ **make good**
to succeed; to meet expectations *US, 1901*
- —David Burton Morris (Director), *Hometown Boy Makes Good*, 1993

▸ **make hole**
to drill for oil *US*
- Working on an oil rig, that's what you do: you make hole.—Ken Weaver, *Texas Crude*, p. 92, 1984

▸ **make it**
1 to have sex *US, 1952*
- I took her home and in her kitchen almost made it on the floor, a Marilyn Monroe type with mouth open and round hips and tight skirt[.]—Jack Kerouac, *Letter to Gary Snyder*, p. 582–583, May 1956
- [E]xchanging existential and lover acts for a crack at making it – "making it" the big expression with her, I can see the little out-

pushing teeth through the little redlips seeing "making it." — Jack Kerouac, *The Subterraneans*, p. 6–7, 1958
- Once, because it seemed logical, Jessica and I had tried to make it, but the chemistry just wasn't there. — Clancy Sigal, *Going Away*, p. 407, 1961
- I'm a good woman; that's why he can't make it with me. — Mary McCarthy, *The Group*, p. 130, 1963
- [Y]ou can go inside and score early, and make it with one of the vagrant girls to prove to yourself that youre still All Right. — John Rechy, *City of Night*, p. 109, 1963
- True, he only made it with Millie, but even so – seventy-five years old!! — Max Shulman, *Anyone Got a Match?*, p. 2, 1964
- He "made it" sexually with her, in two days, he moved in. — Babs Gonzales, *I Paid My Dues*, p. 101, 1967
- It's really very groovy to take her to a movie / Where we make it in the balcony. — The Fugs, *Slum Goddess*, 1968
- Then what's his sex life, who was not married? He masturbates? No, probably not. Makes it with men? Who knows. — *The Digger Papers*, p. 4, August 1968
- Are you trying to tell me you wouldn't care if I made it with your old lady? — Oscar Zeta Acosta, *The Autobiography of a Brown Buffalo*, p. 40, 1972
- They loved to make it in Ingwood Park. — Ed Sanders, *Tales of Beatnik Glory*, p. 18, 1975
- Maybe she got bored, want a little something to do. You see Richard making it with her? — Elmore Leonard, *Switch*, p. 85, 1978
- There were several chicks she made it with. — Herbert Huncke, *The Evening Sun Turned Crimson*, p. 52, 1980
- She makes it with him on the same couch that Kris fucked Hershie. — *Adult Video*, p. 13, August/September 1986
- We didn't make it because you were such good friends. — *When Harry Met Sally*, 1989

2 to leave *US, 1913*
- I'd still say now's the time, man – make it back to the Apple. — Ross Russell, *The Sound*, p. 99, 1961
- Buddy jumped quickly. "Sure, I'll do it!" "Beautiful. Let's make it[.]" — Donald Goines, *Inner City Hoodlum*, p. 108, 1975

3 to be accepted by *US, 1955*
- Laura and I marched but her friend went home because she said the whole thing made her sick – all the hatred – which was a very honest thing to say inasmuch as if you want to make it with the activists, hatred is supposed to be all right with you. — James Simon Kunen, *The Strawberry Statement*, p. 118, 1968

4 to be acceptable *US, 1955*
- Brown shoes don't make it. — Frank Zappa, *Borwn Shoes Don't Make It*, 1967

5 to succeed, to become prosperous, to reach an objective *UK, 1885*
- When Mark [Waugh], younger by minutes, was first selected for the limited-overs team, he whoopingly phoned brother Steve: "I've made it!" Said Steve: "Great, bro, wonderful, which poor sap have they dropped?" Answered Mark, simply: "You." — *The Guardian*, 11th March 2002

▸ **make it up to**
to compensate someone for a loss or a wrong that has been suffered *UK, 1860*
- Look, I'll make it up to you. The next time I see you, I'll fire you. I promise. — *The Guardian*, 26th January 2000

▸ **make like**
1 to behave in a suggested manner *US*
Used in conjunction with 'and' to join a noun and a verb in a pun.
- A favorite pun is "make like a tree and leave." — *Gettysburg (Pennsylvania) Times*, 18th March 1954
- Make like an alligator and drag ass. — *American Speech*, p. 100, May 1954
- Today's expressions include "Make like the wind and blow!", "Make like a tree and leave!" — *American Weekly*, p. 2, 14th August 1955
- — *Maledicta*, p. 39–43, Summer 1980: 'Scram! Or, 101 ways to sack your lover'

2 to behave in the manner of something, to act like *US, 1881*
- Do you want to make like a Hollywood superstar interested in the "spiritual" side of life? — *The Guardian*, 15th November 2003

▸ **make like a boid**
to leave *CANADA*
Teen slang, reported by a Toronto newspaper in 1946, and reported as 'obsolescent or obsolete' by Douglas Leechman, 1959.

▸ **make love**
to steal *CANADA, 1988*
- Poteet lists making love to something as a euphemism for stealing it: "Don't leave that battery charger in the bait shed. Someone might come along and make love to it." A woman [from] Pugwash, 300 miles away, says people use making love the same way. — Harry Bruce, *Down Home*, p. 109, 1988

▸ **make love to the lav**
to vomit into a toilet bowl *AUSTRALIA*
- BARRY: You know cry Ruth! Chuck! Make love to the lav!!! LAW: My God man quick the window!! [BARRY:] RUTH RUTH ROOOOOTH!!! — Barry Humphries, *Bazza Pulls It Offl*, 1971

▸ **make nice**
to be act politely *US*
- I'm gonna make nice there! I'm only gonna challenge him. — *West Side Story*, 1957

▸ **make no bones**
without hesitation, to deal with or react to an awkward or unpleasant situation, no matter how difficult *UK*
- I don't make no bones about this, I'm counting on you to help me. — Joel Rose, *Kill Kill Faster Faster*, p. 141, 1997

▸ **make one**
to plan and carry out an escape attempt from prison *UK, 1974*
- — Angela Devlin, *Prison Patter*, p. 74, 1996

▸ **make one out**
to successfully escape from prison *UK*
- — Angela Devlin, *Prison Patter*, p. 74, 1996

▸ **make smiles**
to have sex *UK*
- Making smiles with Gloria had left me famished. — Jonathan Gash, *The Ten Word Game*, p. 23, 2003

▸ **make the hole**
to rob drunks sleeping on underground platforms and in carriages *US*
- They informed me they were making the hole together as partners — Herbert Huncke, *The Evening Sun Turned Crimson*, p. 112, 1980

▸ **make the show**
in motor racing with qualifying heats, to qualify for the race *US*
- — John Edwards, *Auto Dictionary*, p. 103, 1993

▸ **make time**
to flirt, to attempt to seduce *US, 1953*
- Here was me, with no diamond pinkie ring and walkin' around in my drawers and sneakers, making time with this doll. — Edwin Torres, *Carlito's Way*, p. 93, 1975

▸ **make tracks**
to depart hurriedly *US*
- "I know just what you mean," Jackie replied quickly as he tossed his gun on the seat. "Let's make tracks." — Donald Goines, *Crime Partners*, p. 89, 1978

▸ **make with**
to use, to bring into action *US, 1940*
- OK, George [W. Bush], make with the friendly bombs. — *The Observer*, 17th February 2002

▸ **make your day**
to make a highlight or moment of happiness in an ordinary day; to be the highlight *UK, 1907*
- A lovely gesture, in fact – and one that obviously made his day. — *The Guardian*, 30th June 2003

Make and Break engine *noun*
a massive, one-cylinder boat motor with a flywheel *CANADA*
It is also known as a 'one-lunger' in Nova Scotia and Maine.
- In Make and Break Harbour / the boats are so few. — Stan Rogers, *Fogarty's Cove*, 1977

make-believe *noun*
pretence *UK, 1811*
- Because she was always defending an untenable position. Playing make-believe, pretending everything was nice. — Elmore Leonard, *Switch*, p. 25, 1973

make for *verb*
to steal, to obtain *US, 1936*
- Taking junk hidden by another junkie is known as "making him for his stash." — William Burroughs, *Junkie*, p. 35, 1953

make mine; make it *verb*
used for denoting a requirement (a drink, details of an appointment, an amount, a quantity, a price), generally in response to a question or a proposal *US, 1883*
- [A]nd best of all, a special wing for bartenders. Make mine a straight Scotch! — Philip Stephen Schulz, *Cooking with Fire and Smoke*, p. 32, 1991
- Tommy, have whatever you want but don't make it a double, that's taking the piss. — *The Guardian*, 19th August 2003

make my day

used as a jocular challenge *US*

The phrase entered the popular lexicon in 1983 as a line uttered by the Clint Eastwood character 'Dirty Harry' Callahan in the film *Sudden Impact*.

- "I have only one thing to say to the tax increasers," said President Reagan, delighting in a mock-tough line submitted by one of his writers. "Go ahead and make my day." — *New York Times Magazine*, p. 10, 7th April 1985
- William Hague squared up to his pro-European rebels yesterday by inviting them, Dirty Harry-style, to 'make my day.' — *Daily Mail*, p. 8, 18th October 1999

make out *verb*

1 to kiss with passion and in a sustained fashion *US, 1949*

- "Making out" was nothing more than what used to be called necking or petting. This activity, as older readers will recall, covered a good deal of territory, but always stopped short of fulfillment. — Max Shulman, *Rally Round the Flag, Boys!*, p. 171, 1957
- "He has finesse. No sweaty hands, no making out in drive-in movies." "Making out?" "My God, Larry, where've you been living. I guess you still call it necking." — Frederick Kohner, *Gidget*, p. 71, 1957
- Then we broke up, she telling me I didn't know enough about "making out" to keep her from wanting to date other boys[.] — Phyllis and Eberhard Kronhausen, *Sex Histories of American College Men*, p. 116, 1960
- "Make," "Make out," "Make time"[.] — *American Speech*, p. 229–230, October 1961
- [W]hen they used certain phrases like "making out," they were talking about something else. — Robert Gover, *Poorboy at the Party*, p. 5–6, 1966
- [Y]ou didn't act like it was an invitation to make out for the night. — S.E. Hinton, *The Outsiders*, p. 26, 1967
- Who do you make-out to? Sinatra or Mathis? — *Diner*, 1982
- And now he was downstairs making out with one of the prettiest girls Griffin had ever seen. — Francesca Lia Block, *I Was a Teenage Fairy*, p. 97, 1998

2 to pretend *UK, 1659*

- So one day they had a moody ruck and made out that they had a punch up[.] — Frank Norman, *Bang To Rights*, p. 60, 1958
- I can see him laughing and make out I haven't seen him. — Ian Hebditch, *Weekend, The Sharper Word*, p. 134, 1969

makeover *noun*

a complete transformation of fashion and hairstyle *US*

- SCOTT: I can't believe you'd do this on national television! DR. EVIL: They offered me a free makeover. — *Austin Powers*, 1999
- New clothes, some good stuff [drugs] off Becca's brother, have a make-over, hit the clubs. — Cath Staincliffe, *Trainers*, p. 58, 1999

make the scene with 18

used as a jingle to remind US troops in Vietnam to limit their M-16 rifles to 18 rounds because the rifle sometimes jammed when loaded to its 20-round capacity *US*

- — Linda Reinberg, *In the Field*, p. 134, 1991

make-up *noun*

the final result of any event that is the subject of spread-betting *UK*

- Settlement is based on the difference between the "make up" (the number of runs , goals, minutes, votes or points at the conclusion of the event) and the spread when the bet was placed[.] — David Bennet, *Know Your Bets*, p. 107, 2001

makeup!

used as a nonce interjection *US*

Popularised by Milton Berle in the early days of US television; the running gag was that Berle would be knocked off his feet with sacks of flour or a makeup man with an oversized makeup powder puff after mentioning the word 'makeup'. A meaningless catchphrase that swept the nation.

-making *suffix*

used to create a word that describes something as having the ability to cause the condition of a prefixed adjective *UK, 1930*

A linguistic formula credited to the author Evelyn Waugh, 1903–66.

- [Of a speech by Tony Blair] Strutting, ranting, hand-waving, heart-bleeding, soundbiting, sick-making, an unmitigated hour of puffed-up posturing. — *The Guardian*, 6th October 1999
- [F]unny and happy and sad and anguished and angry-making and joyous and delightful and magical and painful. — *The Guardian*, 15th May 2003

makings *noun*

the tobacco and rolling paper needed to make a cigarette *US, 1905*

- — Frank Prewitt and Francis Schaeffer, *Vacaville Vocabulary*, 1961–1962
- [H]e fumbled with Roxy's makings and rolled a cigarette. — Peter Corris, *Pokerface*, p. 41, 1985

mal *noun*

in parachuting, a *mal*function *UK*

- There's a second reserve canopy in a green container around your waist which you're supposed to yank open by hand if the main one has a "mal"[.] — Duncan MacLaughlin, *The Filth*, p. 44–45, 2002

Malabar Hilton *nickname*

the Long Bay Correctional Complex, Sydney *AUSTRALIA*

- If ever two young tearaways were destined for a return visit to the Malabar Hilton it was us. — Clive Galea, *Slipper*, p. 86, 1988

malad *noun*

a *malad*justed child *UK*

Used by social workers.

- — *New Society*, 20th November 1980

malarkey; malarky; mullarkey *noun*

nonsense *US, 1929*

- "I told you earlier I had this date, but to show you much I care for you I ducked him all these hours to spend them with you." The malarkey! — Jack Lait and Lee Mortimer, *New York Confidential*, p. 167, 1948
- That explained the funny business about the statement... the influential friends malarky. — Martin Waddell, *Otley*, p. 106, 1966
- I'm getting too old for all this malarkey... — Ian Pattison, *Rab C. Nesbitt*, 1988
- You're still not on for this Chippendales malarkey, are you? — *The Full Monty*, 1997
- This mullarkey gives me the horn. — Bernard Dempsey and Kevin McNally, *Lock, Stock... & Two Sips*, p. 310, 2000
- The self delusion, the bitter anger, all that malarky. — Ben Elton, *High Society*, p. 99, 2002

Malcolm Scott *adjective*

hot *UK*

Rhyming slang, of theatrical origins, formed from the name of a female impersonator, 1872–1929.

- — Julian Franklyn, *A Dictionary of Rhyming Slang*, 1960
- — Ray Puxley, *Fresh Rabbit*, 1998

Malcolm X *noun*

a tablet of MDMA, the recreational drug best known as ecstasy *UK*

Uses the adopted name of Malcolm Little, 1925–1965, a leading figure in the US black civil rights movement, to disguise **X** (**ECSTASY**).

- Ah they weedjay cunts wir oan Malcolm X's n aw, pure fuckin buzzin[.] — Irvine Welsh, *The State of the Party (Disco Biscuits)*, p. 33, 1995

male beaver *noun*

featuring shots of the naked male genitals *US*

- I was viewing two hours of male beaver films. — *Screw*, p. 7, 31st July 1969

malehouse *noun*

a homosexual brothel *US*

- I figured theres got to be that malehouse somewhere in Hollywood I heard so much about, an someone'll spot me, sign me up for it. — John Rechy, *City of Night*, p. 137, 1963

male twigs *noun*

low quality marijuana *US*

- Also known as doodley-squat, salt and pepper, and "male twigs," this female-impersonator a/k/a Headache Mary is sometimes advertised as "good commercial"[.] — *Hi Life*, p. 15, 1979

malky *noun*

1 a safety razor used as a weapon; hence an improvised weapon (a broken bottle, etc) *UK: SCOTLAND, 1973*

Possibly rhyming slang, based on Malcolm (Malky) Fraser, for 'razor'.

2 a cut given from a razor as an act of violence; a blow; a beating *UK: SCOTLAND, 1973*

From the previous sense.

- I'll just get right down to it. And give you the severe malky. She nuts the woman. — Ian Pattison, *Rab C. Nesbitt*, 1988

malky *verb*

to attack and cut someone with a razor; to stab *UK: SCOTLAND, 1985*

From the noun sense.

- Hey doll! My boy's been malkied. Is that the chib unit? — Ian Pattison, *Rab C. Nesbitt*, 1990

mallard *noun*

a hundred-dollar note *US*

- —Steve Kuriscak, *Casino Talk*, p. 36, 1985

mall crawl *noun*

an outing to a shopping centre, slowly moving from shop to shop *US*

A play on **PUB-CRAWL** or **BAR-HOP**, with a rhyme to boot.

- —*American Demographics*, September 1996: 'Mall crawl palls'
- The Mall Crawl; Many still enjoy shopping the old-fashioned way. —*The Danbury News-Times*, 7th December 2000

mall crawler *noun*

a person who spends their spare time at shopping centres *US*

- —Kenn "Naz" Young, *Naz's Dictionary of Teen Slang*, p. 76, 1993

mallee *adjective*

▸ **fit as a mallee bull**

extremely fit and healthy *AUSTRALIA, 1960*

mallet *verb*

to smash, to defeat *UK*

Used by the SAS in the Falkland Islands, 1982.

- —*The Listener*, 1st July 1982

mallethead *noun*

a fool, a stupid person, a numbskull *US, 1960*

A variation of **MULLETHEAD**.

- Hay mallethead, have you done them pots yet?—Caroline Aherne and Craig Cash, *The Royle Family*, 1999

mallie *noun*

a young person who spends their free time at shopping centres *US, 1985*

- The other day a friend accused me of having become a "mallie." —*Washington Post*, p. D3, 3rd August 1987
- The Time Out, besides being a classroom for sublimating foreign policy, also is headquarters for "mall rats," a subspecies of teen-ager also known as "mallies." You've seen them. Perhaps your son or daughter is one.—*New York Times*, p. B1, 4th September 1987
- —Kenn "Naz" Young, *Naz's Dictionary of Teen Slang*, 1993
- —Vann Wesson, *Generation X Field Guide and Lexicon*, p. 110, 1997

malling *noun*

the practice of spending hours at a shopping centre, socialising with other young people *US, 1989*

- —*American Speech*, Winter 1990

Mall Madonna *noun*

a girl who spends a lot of time in shopping centres *CANADA*

- It is a noble enough endeavour to give voice to the Mall Madonnas, [with their peculiar] fashion sense and bone chilling grammar, who are a cross between a caustic girl Holden Caulfield and a naive, Windsor [ONT] based Pamela des Barres.—*Toronto Globe and Mail*, p. D11, 6th July 2002

mallowpuff Maori *noun*

a Maori student who excels in school *NEW ZEALAND*

From a branded chocolate-covered marshmallow biscuit – brown on the outside, white on the inside.

- —David McGill, *David McGill's Complete Kiwi Slang Dictionary*, p. 83, 1998

mall rat *noun*

a young person who spends a great deal of time at a shopping centre *US, 1982*

- —*American Speech*, Winter 1990
- You're one of those fucking mallrats; you don't come to the mall to shop or work. You hang out and act like you fucking live here. —*Mallrats*, 1995

malpalant *adjective*

inclined to gossip *TRINIDAD AND TOBAGO*

From the French *mal parlant* (speaking poorly).

- —Lise Winer, *Dictionary of the English/Creole of Trinidad & Tobago*, 2003

malt *noun*

a Maltese; Maltese *UK, 1959*

- [B]ig ones, thin ones, malts, spades, bubbles and the queans that beat 'er black an' blue.—Derek Raymond (Robin Cook), *The Crust on its Uppers*, p. 58, 1962
- "Now, gentlemen," said the Malt guy, suddenly all friendly and shit.—Jake Arnott, *He Kills Coppers*, p. 21, 2001

malt sandwich *noun*

a beer *AUSTRALIA, 1968*

- —David McGill, *David McGill's Complete Kiwi Slang Dictionary*, 1998
- —Bernadette Hince, *The Antarctic Dictionary*, p. 222, 2000

mam *noun*

1 a mother, your mother *UK, 1573*

Probably early C16; mainly childish now, but earlier usage was also familiar or vulgar.

- [O]ur mam used to send me and I couldn't have been more than nine or ten[.]—Livi Michael, *Robinson Street*, p. 23, 1999
- [L]ots of money in the bank so Mam never has to go short[.]—Cath Staincliffe, *Trainers*, p. 58, 1999

2 a lesbian *UK*

- You're more than half a Lizzie, aren't you? I've met lady mams before: one of 'em kept a girl I wanted. It was easy for her: she had the lolly.—John Gloag, *Unlawful Justice*, 1962

mama *noun*

1 used as a term of address towards a woman *US*

- Hey mama, don't you treat me wrong / Come and love your daddy all night long.—Ray Charles, *What'd I say*, 1959
- Hey, mama, what it is!—Carolyn Greene, *70 Soul Secrets of Sapphire*, p. 35, 1973

2 a young woman, a woman *US, 1917*

Originally black usage. Also spelt 'mamma'.

3 in motorcyle clubs and gangs, a female who is available to all the gang members and attached to none *US, 1965*

- There are mamas at any Angel gathering, large or small. They travel as part of the troupe, like oxpeckers, fully understanding what's expected: they are available at any time, in any way, to any Angel, friend or favored guest – individually or otherwise.—Hunter S. Thompson, *Hell's Angels*, p. 171, 1966
- He came and so did guys from a dozen other bike clubs, their mamas in their pussy holders[.]—Nicholas Von Hoffman, *We Are The People Our Parents Warned Us Against*, p. 157, 1967
- Everyone watched with rapt anticipation, especially a pair of biker mommas in dirty T-shirts sitting at a corner booth.—Joseph Wambaugh, *Finnegan's Week*, p. 201, 1993

4 a sexually promiscuous female *UK*

- —David Powis, *The Signs of Crime*, 1977

5 in a lesbian couple, the more traditionally feminine partner *US, 1941*

6 used as a disparaging term of address for an Indian female *SINGAPORE*

- —Paik Choo, *The Coxford Singlish Dictionary*, p. 72, 2002

7 in a deck of playing cards, a queen *US*

- —George Percy, *The Language of Poker*, p. 55, 1988

8 the lead aeroplane in a combat flight formation *US*

- —*American Speech*, p. 123, Summer 1986: 'The language of Naval fighter pilots'

mama!

used for expressing surprise, especially by women *TRINIDAD AND TOBAGO*

- —Lise Winer, *Dictionary of the English/Creole of Trinidad & Tobago*, 2003

mama bear *noun*

a policewoman *US*

A feminisation of **BEAR** (the police).

- —*Complete CB Slang Dictionary*, 1976
- —Peter Chippindale, *The British CB Book*, p. 156, 1981

mama coca *noun*

cocaine *US*

- —R.C. Garrett et al, *The Coke Book*, p. 200, 1984
- —Nick Constable, *This is Cocaine*, p. 81, 2002

mama-jammer *noun*

used as a euphemism for 'motherfucker' *US*

- I'd bought a rifle, which was not illegal at that time, and it was a sweet mama-jammer, too.—H. Rap Brown, *Die Nigger Diel*, p. 109, 1969

mamaloos; mamaloosh *adjective*

dead, dying *CANADA*

The word comes from Chinook jargon *memaloost* (dead).

- The Reverend Thomas Pearne, an Indian, said, "Moses, memaloose (dead)." I knew Moses.—Click Relander, *Drummers and Dreamers*, p. 197, 1956

mama man *noun*
an effeminate man, heterosexual or homosexual *TRINIDAD AND TOBAGO, 1973*
- —Lise Winer, *Dictionary of the English/Creole of Trinidad & Tobago*, 2003

mamapoule *noun*
an effeminate, demanding man *TRINIDAD AND TOBAGO, 1928*
From the French for 'mother hen'.
- —Lise Winer, *Dictionary of the English/Creole of Trinidad & Tobago*, 2003

mamary *noun*
a boy who will not leave his mother's protection *TRINIDAD AND TOBAGO, 1978*
- —Lise Winer, *Dictionary of the English/Creole of Trinidad & Tobago*, 2003

mama-san *noun*
in Southeast Asia usage, a woman whose age demands respect, especially a brothel madam *US, 1946*
The Japanese honorific *san* added to English 'mama'.
- In Saigon, once, I lasted for almost two hours with a Mama-San. —Jack Fritscher, *Some Dance to Remember*, p. 266, 1990

mama shop *noun*
a small neighbourhood grocery shop, especially one owned by Indians *SINGAPORE*
- —Paik Choo, *The Coxford Singlish Dictionary*, p. 72, 2002

mama's lane *noun*
the passing lane of a motorway *US*
So named because the trucker, anxious to see his wife, is driving fast and passing cars.
- —Lanie Dills, *The Official CB Slanguage Language Dictionary*, p. 47, 1976

mama's little helper *noun*
in shuffleboard, a score you are accidentally provided by an opponent *US*
- —Omero C. Catan, *Secrets of Shuffleboard Strategy*, p. 69, 1967: 'Glossary of terms'

mama's mellow *noun*
the calming effect of secobarbital (brand name Seconal™), a barbiturate *US*
- —Eugene Landy, *The Underground Dictionary*, p. 127, 1971

mamby pamby *noun*
a stupid man *TRINIDAD AND TOBAGO, 1956*
- —Lise Winer, *Dictionary of the English/Creole of Trinidad & Tobago*, 2003

mammaries *noun*
the female breasts *UK, 1967*
After the conventional sense of 'mammary' (relating to the female breast).
- Although it may not always seem so, Murdoch's morning mammaries are a symbol of a grown-up culture. — *The Guardian*, 18th November 2000

mammoth *adjective*
huge *UK, 1937*
The stuff of advertising: 'MAMMOTH RUG SALE!' (but who'd want a mammoth rug?).

mamms; mams *noun*
the female breasts *UK*
A reduction of **MAMMARIES**.

mammy *noun*
1 a mother *UK, 1523*
- Bereaved, black-weeded, inconsolable, her mammy has taken to bed. — *The Guardian*, 23rd September 2002

2 in a striptease act, a woman, usually older, who waits backstage, catching a stripper's clothing as she flings it offstage *US*
- —Don Wilmeth, *The Language of American Popular Entertainment*, p. 166, 1981

3 the most; the ultimate example *US*
An English language version of the famous Arabic **MOTHER OF ALL**.
- —Hermese E. Roberts, *The Third Ear*, 1971

▸ **the mammy**
my mother *IRELAND*
There is no indefinite article in Irish. The definite article in Hiberno-English, following and sometimes extending the usage of the indefinite article 'an' in Irish, has some distinctive functions which mark it out from standard English, for example, 'Better give her the both o' them' (Doyle, *The Van*, 1991).
- [T]he new wife, when she moved in, made it clear that certain changes would have to be expedited forthwith or she would ship straight back out and home to The Mammy. —Joseph O'Connor, *The Irish Male at Home and Abroad*, p. 46, 1996

mammy *adjective*
a lot of *US*
Placed after the noun.
- A person with four cartons of cigarettes has cigarettes mammy. —William K. Bentley and James M. Corbett, *Prison Slang*, 1992

mammy-fugger *noun*
used as a euphemism for 'motherfucker' *US*
- Leroy is the dumbest, ugliest, biggest, baddest – I mean really malignant! – black mammyfugger on the playground. —Clarence Major, *All-Night Visitors*, p. 27, 1998

mammy-jammer *noun*
used as a euphemism for 'motherfucker' *US*
- —Kenn "Naz" Young, *Naz's Underground Dictionary*, p. 45, 1973
- —*Maledicta*, p. 11, Summer 1977: 'A word for it!'

mammyjamming *adjective*
used as a euphemism for the intensifier 'motherfucking' *US, 1946*
- Then that mammyjamming night manger put the claw on him for 60, so that left 70. —Bernard Wolfe, *The Late Risers*, p. 169, 1954
- —Robert S. Gold, *A Jazz Lexicon*, p. 200, 1964
- —Kenn "Naz" Young, *Naz's Underground Dictionary*, 1973

mammy mine *noun*
wine *UK: SCOTLAND*
Glasgow rhyming slang.
- —Michael Munro, *The Original Patter*, 1985

mammy-screwing *adjective*
used as a euphemism for 'motherfucking' *US*
- Ma fell in a ditch, starts cussin up a mammy-screwin' storm! —John Rechy, *City of Night*, p. 147, 1963

mammy-sucker *noun*
used as a euphemism for 'motherfucker' *US*
- —Robert A. Wilson, *Playboy's Book of Forbidden Words*, p. 165, 1972

mampy *noun*
a buxom, generously voluptuous woman *JAMAICA*
- The endless crowds of ravers, raggas, mampies, yardies, soul heads, bad bwoys, nice gyals, wannabes, and wasters[.] —Donald Gorgon, *Cop Killer*, p. 114, 1994

mampy *adjective*
(of a woman) buxom, generously proportioned, Rubenesque *JAMAICA*
- [A] large-bottomed, mampy-sized girl dressed in a short, tight, white dress and sequinned baseball boots. —Donald Gorgon, *Cop Killer*, p. 87, 1994

man; mandy *noun*
1 me, myself, I *UK*
English gypsy use, from Romany *mandi*.
- —Jimmy Stockin, *On The Cobbles*, 2000

2 a drug dealer *US, 1942*
- You better find somebody else cause I'm not your man no more. I'm not selling you. —Hal Ellson, *The Golden Spike*, p. 30, 1952
- When I first hit New Orleans, the main pusher – or "the Man," as they say there – was a character called Yellow. —William Burroughs, *Junkie*, p. 75, 1953
- I'm waiting for my man / Twenty-six dollars in my hand. —Velvet Underground, *I'm Waiting for the Man*, 1967
- —*Current Slang*, p. 47, Fall 1968
- Well I pawned my Smith and Wesson / And I went to meet my man / He hangs out down on Alvarado Street / By the Pioneer Chicken Stand. —Warren Zevon, *Carmelita*, 1976
- [T]he first thing we would do in the morning of the check delivery was to rush to the check cashing store, get the bread, grab a taxi and head to see our man and get straight. —Herbert Huncke, *The Evening Sun Turned Crimson*, p. 175, 1980

3 in a deck of playing cards, a king *US*
- —George Percy, *The Language of Poker*, p. 55, 1988

▸ **a man's got to do what a man's got to do; a man's gotta do what a man's gotta do**
homespun philosophy in use as a catchphrase *US, 1977*
Jocular.

- Joey, there comes a time when a man's gotta do what a man's gotta do. You go ahead and catch the plane. I'll catch the next one. —Joseph Jaworski, *Synchronicity*, p. 71, 1998
- What's that old bullshit saying-A man's gotta do what a man's gotta do'? Go for it. —Evelyn Coleman, *What's a Woman Gotta Do*, p. 15, 1998

▸ a man's not a camel

I am thirsty and require a drink *AUSTRALIA*

- 'Hey, Mac, man's not a camel.' There was somebody at the window. 'I'll be there directly,' yelled Mac. —Phillip Gwynne, *Deadly Unna?*, p. 161, 1998

▸ the man

a police officer; an authority figure *US, 1928*

- "You're the man, aint' you?" "Yeah, I'm the man." —Chester Himes, *The Real Cool Killers*, p. 78, 1959
- You never know when the man will bust in. —Alexander Trocchi, *Cain's Book*, p. 74, 1960
- My friends were now "downtown," busy, as they put it, "fighting the man." —James Baldwin, *The Fire Next Time*, p. 31, 1963
- I never let them stop laughing, hit them hard and fast with jokes on processed hair and outer space and marijuana and integration and the numbers racket and long white Cadillacs and The Man downtown[.] —Dick Gregory, *Nigger*, p. 101, 1964
- You just had to keep watching for the Man. He was always looking for cats who were down there jostling. —Claude Brown, *Manchild in the Promised Land*, p. 160–161, 1965
- His adversaries in this continual quest are always the police: the "narcos.," "The Man." —James Mills, *The Panic in Needle Park*, p. 15, 1966
- Step out of line / The Man comes and takes you away. — The Buffalo Sprinfield, *For What It's Worth*, 1967
- I thought maybe you was the man. Them cats work on Sundays too. —Piri Thomas, *Down These Mean Streets*, p. 328, 1967
- For the younger kids, the "man" was school, and for the older ones, employers[.] —Nathan Heard, *Howard Street*, p. 110, 1968
- BILLY: The Man – the Man is at the window. The man is at the window. The Man is at the window. GIRLS: Oh, come on. GEORGE: Oh, the Man is at the window. —Peter Fonda, *Easy Rider*, p. 140, 1969
- I got a job with the poverty program as a neighborhood worker and that's really when I began to see where "the man" was at. —H. Rap Brown, *Die Nigger Die!*, p. 75, 1969
- The Man has got himself a "temporary" restraining order against the printer of the Berkeley Tribe (Walter Press) from further printing of the names and addresses of local narcs. — *The Berkeley Tribe*, p. 4, 15th-21th August 1969
- The Man be cooking up conspiracies again, but the sentences are gonna be a motherfucker – I ain't jiving you. —Edwin Torres, *Carlito's Way*, p. 66, 1975
- —Multicultural Management Program Fellows, *Dictionary of Cautionary Words and Phrases*, 1989
- Kathy said, "I walked up to the door – it was open and I heard a voice inside say, 'It's the Man.' I weigh a hundred and five, but that's who I am, the Man." —Elmore Leonard, *Maximum Bob*, p. 165, 1991
- LUCAS: Corey, the Man is everywhere. LUCAS: The interesting thing about you is you've got the Man right inside you. — *Empire Records*, 1995

▸ yer only man

something that possesses a unique quality *IRELAND*

- As if it does you any good to know things. You're better off in the dark...It's yer only man, the oul dark. —Eamonn Sweeney, *Waiting for the Healer*, p. 212, 1997
- A pint of plain is yer only man if you want a healthy heart. Research presented this week in the US suggests that a pint of stout a day could help reduce the risk of heart attack... — *Irish Times*, 13th November 2003

man *verb*

in team sports, to defend an opponent man-to-man *US*

- "They can Man you with Dreamer," Shoat said, looking at Shake Tiller." —Dan Jenkins, *Semi-Tough*, p. 113, 1972

man and man *noun*

people in general *JAMAICA, 1989*

- —Peter Patrick, *Some Recent Jamaican Creole Words*, 2003

man and wife *noun*

a knife *UK, 1925*

Rhyming slang.

- —Ray Puxley, *Cockney Rabbit*, 1992

man boobs *noun*

flabby chest protrusions of an overweight man *AUSTRALIA*

- Nice man boobies Mick— *Inpress Magazine*, p. 4, April 2002

Manc *noun*

1 *Man*chester in northwest England *UK*

- Some late teens in Manc played the Maileresque hipster[.] —Tony Wilson, *24 Hour Party People*, p. 52, 2002

2 a *Man*cunian; a native of Manchester *UK*

- Why do you Mancs always shit out[?] — Martin King and Martin Knight, *The Naughty Nineties*, p. 62, 1999
- Sounds a bit more Manc that way. —Tony Wilson, *24 Hour Party People*, p. 21, 2002

Manc *adjective*

Mancunian, of Manchester *UK*

- Fuck knows why the Manc boys never got on it theirselves and that – fucking easy-peasy, it were. —Kevin Sampson, *Outlaws*, p. p.15, 2001

Manch *noun*

Manchester *UK*

- Another hour, off the motorway, into the outskirts of Manch[.] —J.J. Connolly, *Layer Cake*, p. 119, 2000

Manchester City; manchester *noun*

the female breast *UK*

Rhyming slang for 'titty' (TIT) noted as 'rare'.

- —Julian Franklyn, *A Dictionary of Rhyming Slang*, 1961
- —Ray Puxley, *Cockney Rabbit*, 1992

Manchester United *noun*

a red and black capsule of MDMA, the recreational drug best known as ecstasy *UK*

Designed and branded in tribute to the football team, but someone got the team colours wrong.

- —Gareth Thomas, *This Is Ecstasy*, p. 55, 2002

Mancy *adjective*

Mancunian, of Manchester *UK*

Perhaps, given Manchester's reputation for wet weather, punning deliberately on MANKY (bad).

- They'll get arseholed on my beer an' then shout out rude Mancy witticisms during me ballads. —Ben Elton, *High Society*, p. 160, 2002

man dem *noun*

male friends *UK*

Used by black urban youths.

- Father, may I go to the library with man dem?— *Live*, p. 39, Winter 2004

M and G track *noun*

in a pornographic film, additions to the sound track amplifying moans and groans *US*

- They [later with editing] put in a groan. The M and G track. —Robert Stoller and I.S. Levine, *Coming Attractions*, p. 121, 1991
- — *Adult Video News*, p. 51, October 1995

mandie *noun*

a tablet of the recreational drug methaqualone, best known as Quaaludes™ *US*

From the trade name Mandrax™.

- —Liz Cutland, *Kick Heroin*, p. 107, 1985
- I took a bunch of mandies and Apolon thought I was dying. —Cleo Odzer, *Goa Freaks*, p. 140, 1995

M & M *noun*

a 9 mm pistol *US*

- Calloway asked him if a robbery was involved, if the people were dead and if "an M&M" was used, street slang for a 9mm pistol. — *Times-Picayune (New Orleans)*, p. B1, 10th November 1999

M and M *noun*

any tablet drugs used for recreational purposes: amphetamine, barbiturate, MDMA, the recreational drug best known as ecstasy *US*

Named for M&Ms (branded in the US since 1940s) the candy-coated chocolate sweets which, in appearance, are similar to multi-coloured pills.

- —Donald Wesson and David Smith, *Barbiturates*, p. 121, 1977
- —Angela Devlin, *Prison Patter*, p. 74, 1996
- Street names [...] love doves, M and Ms, MDMA[.] —James Kay and Julian Cohen, *The Parents' Complete Guide to Young People and Drugs*, p. 136, 1998

mandoo-ed *adjective*

drunk *UK*

- — *e-cyclopaedia*, 20th March 2002

man down!

used in prison for alerting the guards that a prisoner has been injured or fallen ill *US*

- His sweatslick buttocks slipped off and he was on the floor, shrieks percussing his skull; and from a great distance heard Smoothbore shouting at the bars: "MAN DOWN!" —Seth Morgan, *Homeboy*, p. 96, 1990

mandrake *noun*

1 a tablet of the recreational drug methaqualone, best known as Quaaludes™ *US*

From Mandrax™, the trade name for a synthetic non-barbiturate sedative consisting of methaqualone and a small amount of the antihistamine diphenhydramine.

- By 1972 it was one of the most popular drugs of abuse in the United States and was known as love drug, heroin for lovers, Dr. Jekyll and Mr. Hyde, sopors, sopes, ludes, mandrakes and quacks. — Marilyn Carroll and Gary Gallo, *Methaqualone*, 1985

2 a sexually aggressive male homosexual *US*

- — Anon., *King Smut's Wet Dreams Interpreted*, 1978

mandy *noun*

a tablet of Mandrax™, a branded tranquillizer *UK, 1970*

- Another thing with Sandy / What often came in handy / was passing her a Mandy / she didn't half go bandy — Ian Dury, *Billericay Dickie*, 1977
- — Angela Devlin, *Prison Patter*, p. 74, 1996
- Onstage, I've been hit by a grapefruit, beer cans, eggs, spit, money, cigarette butts, mandies, Quaaludes, joints, panties and a fist. — *Jabberrock [quoting Iggy Pop]*, p. 194, 1997
- Lemmy [of Motorhead] would be speeding out of his head and he'd think, "Can't take this any more", and the mandies would comeout and they'd get slower and slower. — Simon Napier-Bell, *Black Vinyl White Powder*, p. 117, 2001

▷ **see:** MAN

mane *noun*

a streak of unmown hay left in the field after it has been cut *CANADA*

- A "mane" is caused by a poor cutter bar on the mowing machine, or by not driving properly. "If your guards don't work, you'll leave a mane for sure." — Lewis Poteet, *Talking Country*, p. 53, 1992

man-eater *noun*

1 a woman with a strong sexual appetite *UK, 1906*

A figurative application of the term for dangerous big cats.

- Watch her, guv – she's a man-eater! — *The Sweeney*, p. 17, 1976
- (Oh-oh, here she comes) Watch out boy she'll chew you up / (Oh-oh, here she comes) She's a maneater. — Hall & Oates, *Maneater*, 1982

2 a homosexual man *US*

- — *Maledicta*, p. 217, 1979: 'Kinks and queens: linguistic and cultural aspects of the terminology for gays'

man fat *noun*

semen *UK*

Reported by Laurie Atkinson, 1974.

Manfred Mann *noun*

a tan, a suntan *UK: SCOTLAND*

Glasgow rhyming slang, formed from the successful 1960s pop group and the South African musician who gave his group his name.

- She's away doon tae the sunbed tae top up the Manfred Mann. — Michael Munro, *The Complete Patter*, 1996

man Friday *noun*

a black soldier who curried favour from white superiors and thereby avoided combat *US*

- — Linda Reinberg, *In the Field*, p. 135, 1991

man from Cairo *noun*

a social security/benefits cheque *UK: SCOTLAND*

Glasgow rhyming slang for **GIRO**.

- — Michael Munro, *The Complete Patter*, 1996

man from the Pru *noun*

a cocaine dealer *UK*

A play on the UK investment firm Prudential Building Society's advertising campaign and Peru as a source country for much of the world's cocaine.

- — Tom Hibbert, *Rockspeak!*, p. 100, 1983

manga *noun*

a comic book or graphic novel *JAPAN*

One of the few Japanese words to be transplanted into English-speaking slang, thanks in large part to the proliferation of pornographic websites on the Internet.

- Many members of Animation Society are cartoon artists and avid comic-book fans who read Japanese comic books called Manga. — *St. Louis Post-Dispatch*, p. 2, 15th July 1993
- Lee's visual palette is, however, all her own, with deep blacks and maroons, a mixture of manga imagery and reality[.] — *Variety*, p. 52, 23rd November 1998
- Nearly half the action in the first volume of "Kill Bill" (the second appears next month), with its rapturous, over-the-top homage to yakuza, manga, and other Japanese genre films, takes place in a surreal movie-land Japan[.] — *New York Times*, p. 1 (Section 2), 4th January 2004

manged *adjective*

damaged without hope of repair *US*

- — Eric S. Raymond, *The New Hacker's Dictionary*, p. 231, 1991

mangia-cake *noun*

a white person, especially British, but very North American (said by an Italian) *CANADA*

- "Mangia" is Italian for "eat," so to an [especially] Toronto Italian, a non-Italian is a "mangia-cake." — *Toronto Globe and Mail*, p. C6, 30th May 1998

mangle *noun*

a bicycle *AUSTRALIA, 1941*

- — Jim Ramsay, *Cop It Sweet!*, p. 57, 1977

mangle and wringer *noun*

a (not especially talented) singer *UK*

Rhyming slang.

- — Ray Puxley, *Cockney Rabbit*, 1992

mangled *adjective*

drunk or drug-intoxicated *UK*

- [W]recked spannered mangled caned[.] — Stuart Walton, *Out of It*, cover, 2001
- — Connie Eble (Editor), *UNC-CH Campus Slang*, p. 6, November 2003

mango *noun*

a fifty-dollar note *NEW ZEALAND*

From the orange colour.

- — David McGill, *David McGill's Complete Kiwi Slang Dictionary*, p. 72, 1998

mango head *noun*

an oval-shaped head *TRINIDAD AND TOBAGO, 1994*

- — Lise Winer, *Dictionary of the English/Creole of Trinidad & Tobago*, 2003

mango madness *noun*

in tropical Australia, a feeling of agitation and oppression experienced leading up to the monsoon season *AUSTRALIA, 1984*

- Oh, no! He's got a touch of mango madness AGAIN! — *Wordmap (www.abc.net.au/wordmap)*, 2003

Manhattan silver; Manhattan white; New York City silver; Subway silver *noun*

marijuana *US, 1975*

Originally, 'a flight of fancy', a genetic variation cultivated from seeds which, having been flushed into the New York City sewage system, were white or silver. A highly potent and purely fictional urban myth; now, also, just another synonym for 'marijuana'.

- — *American Speech*, Winter 1982
- — Mike Haskins, *Drugs*, p. 288, 2003

manhaul *noun*

in Antarctica, an overland trip where a sledge is hauled by people, not vehicles *ANTARCTICA, 1986*

- — Bernadette Hince, *The Antarctic Dictionary*, p. 223, 2000
- — *Cool Antarctica*, 2003: 'Antarctic slang'

manhole *noun*

the vagina *US, 1916*

- — *Maledicta*, p. 25, Summer and Winter 1982: 'Canadian sexual terms'

manhole cover; manhole *noun*

a brother *UK*

Rhyming slang for 'bruvver', perhaps also playing on **MANHOLE** (the vagina) hence, a playfully insulting **CUNT**.

- — Ray Puxley, *Cockney Rabbit*, 1992

manhood *noun*

the penis *UK*

Euphemism.

- Veronica squeezed his manhood so hard he almost winced. — Colin Butts, *Is Harry on the Boat?*, p. 137, 1997

man hunt *noun*

a search for a male as a sexual companion *US*

Humorous use of a term originally meaning 'a search for a criminal or escaped convict'.

- Amy's on a man hunt tonight. — Connie Eble (Editor), *UNC-CH Campus Slang*, p. 4, Fall 1996

man-hunter *noun*
a woman, especially a spinster or a widow, particularly one who has, or is reputed to have, a strong sexual appetite *UK, 1961*
- [Kleopatra's] liaison with Julius Caesar is a considered diplomatic move, not the impulsive act of a man-hunter. — *The Observer*, 10th August 2003

maniac *noun*
a railway mechanic *US, 1930*
- — Ramon Adams, *The Language of the Railroader*, p. 98, 1977
- — Peter Chippindale, *The British CB Book*, 1981

Maniblowba *nickname*
the Canadian province of Manitoba *CANADA*
So named because of the cold, windy winters.
- — Bill Casselman, *Canadian Sayings*, p. 24, 2002

manicou-man *noun*
an effeminate man, especially a homosexual *TRINIDAD AND TOBAGO*
- — Richard Allsopp, *Dictionary of Caribbean English Usage*, p. 369, 1996

manicure *verb*
to prepare marijuana for smoking, trimming the leaves and stems and removing foreign objects *US, 1938*
- — Eugene Landy, *The Underground Dictionary*, p. 127, 1971

manifestation *noun*
in Quebec, demonstration *CANADA*
In a province marked by a tradition of public service strikes, this unconventional use of a French word has had much use for a long time.
- — Victor Trahan, *The City of Montreal Style Guide*, p. n.p., 2002

Manila General *noun*
used as a humorous if xenophobic nickname for any hospital with a largely Filipino staff *US*
- — *Maledicta*, p. 33, 1988–1989: 'Medical maledicta from San Francisco'

man in blue *noun*
a police officer *UK*
- — *Complete CB Slang Dictionary*, 1976
- — Peter Chippindale, *The British CB Book*, p. 156, 1981

man in Kokomo *noun*
in horse racing, any mysterious source of inside information on a horse or race *US*
- — David W. Maurer, *Argot of the Racetrack*, p. 42, 1951

man in the boat *noun*
▷ see: LITTLE MAN IN A BOAT

man in the moon *noun*
a madman, a fool *UK*
Rhyming slang for **LOON**.
- — Ray Puxley, *Cockney Rabbit*, 1992

man in the white coat *noun*
a supposed employee of an insane asylum *AUSTRALIA*
Now generally in the plural: 'men in white coats'.
- I think I'd better phone the man in the white coat. — Willie Fennell, *Dexter Gets The Point*, p. 135, 1961

Manisnowba *nickname*
the Canadian province of Manitoba *CANADA*
Home to long, cold winters.
- — Bill Casselman, *Canadian Sayings*, p. 24, 2002

Mank *noun*
a person from Manchester, a *Man*cunian *UK*
- [T]he character of the Manks and the Mickey Mousers [people from Liverpool] is vastly different. — J.J. Connolly, *Layer Cake*, p. 122, 2000

manked in *adjective*
confined indoors by extreme bad weather *ANTARCTICA, 1986*
- — Bernadette Hince, *The Antarctic Dictionary*, p. 224, 2000

manky *adjective*
1 poor quality, inferior; dirty *UK*
Possibly from French *manque* (a deficiency).
- He would have to have all his teeth out as it seems that they were all mankey. — Frank Norman, *Bang to Rights*, 1958
- [W]e're told what to do by some manky old git with a clipboard[.] — John King, *Human Punk*, p. 8, 2000
- The Mersey is in your veins (is right, yeh, all manky, polluted). — Niall Griffiths, *Kelly + Victor*, p. 48, 2002

2 (of weather) bad *ANTARCTICA, 1989*
A narrowing of the general sense.
- — Bernadette Hince, *The Antarctic Dictionary*, p. 224, 2000
- [T]raversin streets through fumes an dirt-drifts an greasy drizzle. All manky. — Niall Griffiths, *Kelly + Victor*, p. 29, 2002

3 drunk *UK*
Possibly deriving from the previous sense, thus 'under the weather' (tipsy).
- — *e-cyclopaedia*, 20th March 2002

man-love *noun*
male homosexuality *UK*
A very arch euphemism.
- Thanks to "The Hanky Code" you could be asking for man-love without even knowing it. — *The FHM Little Book of Bloke*, p. 144, June 2003: 'Gayness Explained'

manly Alice *noun*
a masculine homosexual man *UK*
- — Paul Baker, *Polari*, p. 180, 2002

man-man *noun*
a male who exhibits a high degree of virility *US*
- — Connie Eble (Editor), *UNC-CH Campus Slang*, p. 5, Spring 1999

manna *noun*
easy-pickings; a heaven-sent opportunity *UK*
A biblical allusion.
- Pure fucking manna, it were [...] – the Garden Festival sent these hordes of tourists and trippers right into our backyard, from all over the world, expressly to be had off. — Kevin Sampson, *Outlaws*, p. 7, 2001

manny *noun*
a tablet of Mandrax™, a branded tranquillizer *UK*
A variation of **MANDY** used, and perhaps coined, by Jenny Fabian and Johnny Byrne, *Groupie*, 1968.

mano *noun*
used as an embellished 'man' as a term of address *US*
- [H]e'd try to right the situation something like this: "Oh, gee, mano," using the hip Mexican appellation. — John Rechy, *Numbers*, p. 33, 1967

mano a mano *noun*
a one-on-one confrontation *US, 1968*
Made quite famous in the US by Colonel Oliver North during the moral collapse of the Reagan presidency, the Iran-Contra debacle of 1986–87. Adapted from bull-fighting, where the term refers to a competition between two matadors and two or more bulls each.
- Mano a mano. No – more like High Noon. Gunfight at the O.K. Corral. — Elmore Leonard, *City Primeval*, p. 119, 1980
- North did issue a crowd-pleasing challenge to terrorist Abu Nidal to meet anywhere, anytime and on equal terms – mano a mano. — *Los Angeles Times*, p. 6 (Calendar), 11th July 1987
- In the mano a mano, as you know from reading your books, each matador fights three bulls alternating. — Odie Hawkins, *The Life and Times of Chester Simmons*, p. 23–24, 1991

man of the cloth *noun*
in pool, a skilled player who makes a living betting on his ability *US*
- — Steve Rushin, *Pool Cool*, p. 20, 1990

man oil *noun*
semen *US*
- — Vincent J. Monteleone, *Criminal Slang*, p. 152, 1949

man o Manishewitz!
used as a jocular, mild oath *US*
From a commercial for Manishewitz kosher wine.
- Man-oh-Manischewitz, they say the snatch grows fine up there. — James Ellroy, *White Jazz*, p. 111, 1992

man on the land *noun*
a farmer or other rural worker *AUSTRALIA, 1911*
- It was not till the introduction of cold storage that the thoughts of the man on the land were turned to fruit-growing, dairying, and the breeding of fat lambs for the overseas market. — Vance Palmer, *The Legend of the Nineties*, p. 22, 1954

man on the moon *noun*
a spoon *UK*
Rhyming slang.
- — Ray Puxley, *Fresh Rabbit*, 1998

manor *noun*
1 a district designated to a specified police authority *UK, 1924*
- I've got my sources of information in every manor in the smoke [London]. — Charles Raven, *Underworld Nights*, p. 91, 1956
- [O]n this manor[.] — Frank Norman, *Bang To Rights*, p. 122, 1958
- "Which manor?" "The local nick [police station]." — Derek Raymond (Robin Cook), *The Crust on its Uppers*, p. 47, 1962
- He's Superintendent of this manor[.] — David Powis, *The Signs of Crime*, 1977
- [T]he Sergeant warned him about operating on "my manor without a licence". — Donald Gorgon, *Cop Killer*, p. 3, 1994
- Putney station was my ground – we don't call it "manor" or "patch", as you may have heard thrown about on TV by screenwriters who haven't done their research properly. — Duncan MacLaughlin, *The Filth*, p. 58, 2002

2 the area where you are born, or where you live and/or are well known *UK*
- [W]ith pressure on him from all over the manor – pressure from the law, from the income-tax boys[.] — Derek Raymond (Robin Cook), *The Crust on Its Uppers*, p. 25, 1962
- I was sitting omy jack [alone], in a dusty old saloon bar deep in the backstreets of the old manor[.] — J.J. Connolly, *Layer Cake*, p. 17, 2000

man overboard!
1 in dominoes, used for announcing the fact that a player is forced to draw a piece *US*
- — Dominic Armanino, *Dominoes*, p. 17, 1959

2 in craps in American casinos, used for announcing that the dice or a die are off the table *US*
- — Steve Kuriscak, *Casino Talk*, p. 66, 1985

man o'war *noun*
a bore *UK*
Rhyming slang.
- — Ray Puxley, *Cockney Rabbit*, 1992

manscaping *noun*
the clipping, shaving and shaping of male body hair for aesthetic effect *US*
Popularised in the US, and then the UK, by the varying national productions of television programme *Queer Eye for the Straight Guy*.
- A worse indignity is to follow: the trimming of excess body hair with clippers, henceforth known as manscaping. — *The Guardian*, 16th July 2004

man-size *adjective*
difficult *US*
- — Lou Shelly, *Hepcats Jive Talk Dictionary*, p. 29, 1945

man's man *noun*
a police informer *US*
From **THE MAN** (the police).
- — Bruce Jackson, *Outside the Law*, p. 59, 1972: 'Glossary'

Manson lamps *noun*
a look full of hate, a murderous look *US*
Formed from a reference to US serial killer Charles Manson and **LAMP** (the eye).
- Don't give me your fucking Manson lamps, just fucking stop. — *Sopranos, Episode 24*, 1999
- But it was nonetheless brimming with brilliant moments, funnylines, witty scene dits, and original characterizations, most notably by David Proval, whose Richie Aprile has shut his "Manson lamps" and sported a leisure suit for the last time. — *Boston Globe*, p. D1, 7th April 2000
- Now they were snarling across the table, giving one another "Manson lamps", as Tony Soprano might say. — Andrew Holmes, *Sleb*, p. 251, 2002

manteca *noun*
heroin *UK*
- — Mike Haskins, *Drugs*, p. 284, 2003

man teef *noun*
a woman who 'steals' another's man *UK*
Combines 'man' and **TEEF** (to steal); current in south London according to *Johnny Vaughan Tonight*, 13th February 2002.

manthrax *noun*
unfaithful men *US*
A combination of 'man' and 'anthrax' coined for *Sex and the City*, a late 1990s television comedy.
- — *The Times*, p. 18, 27th July 2002

mantlepiece *noun*
▸ **you don't look at the mantelpiece when you're poking the fire**
the semi-proverbial catchphrase that means a woman's looks are irrelevant during sexual intercourse *UK, 1961*
- Could he ever be as interested in the girl's image as she is? Of course not – you don't look at the mantelpiece while you're poking the fire. — *The Guardian*, 11th January 2001

manto *noun*
a condom *SOUTH AFRICA*
Teen slang, after South African Health Minister Manto Tshabalala-Msimang.
- — *Sunday Times (South Africa)*, 1st June 2003

man-trap *noun*
an attractive, seductive woman *US*
- She would talk to a really beautiful model, a "man-trap" whom she "happened to know." — Michael Leigh, *The Velvet Underground*, p. 45, 1963

manual exercises *noun*
masturbation *US*
- — Roger Blake, *The American Dictionary of Sexual Terms*, p. 128, 1964

manual release *noun*
manual stimulation of a man's genitals *US*
- The rates are $20 for the manual release, $30 for the manual release with top off, $40 for manual release with top and bottom off. — James Ridgeway, *Red Light*, p. 217, 1996

Man United are playing at home
the bleed period of the menstrual cycle *UK*
The Manchester United football team play in a red strip.
- — *The Museum of Menstruation and Women's Health*, October 2000

man upstairs *noun*
God *US*
Always used with 'the'.
- Mr. McDougall says that the only thing that sustained him and kept him going through the hours in the water was the counsel he received from "the man upstairs." — *The New York Times*, p. BR11, 22nd August 1948
- [T]hinking about the Man Upstairs every once in a while. — Lewis John Carlino, *The Great Santini*, 1979
- "I believe the man upstairs will decide who's going to win this tournament," he said to the press[.] — Dan Jenkins, *Dead Solid Perfect*, p. 138, 1986

man with the minties *noun*
in horse racing, a mythical, anonymous person responsible for a series of bad tips about horses and races *AUSTRALIA*
- — Ned Wallish, *The Truth Dictionary of Racing Slang*, p. 51, 1989

Maoriland *nickname*
New Zealand *AUSTRALIA, 1859*
- The next aspirant to the title is endorsed by no less an authority than Arthur Adams, the writer who came to us from Maoriland round about 1898. — Bill Wannan, *Bullockies, Beauts and Bandicoots*, p. 52, 1960
- — Jim Ramsay, *Cop It Sweet!*, p. 57, 1977

Maori overdrive *noun*
coasting downhill in neutral *NEW ZEALAND*
- — David McGill, *David McGill's Complete Kiwi Slang Dictionary*, p. 72, 1998

Maori screwdriver *noun*
a hammer, especially when used on screws *NEW ZEALAND*
- — David McGill, *David McGill's Complete Kiwi Slang Dictionary*, p. 83, 1998

Maori sidestep *noun*
in rugby, a direct confrontation with a potential tackler, relying on brute force rather than guile or finesse *NEW ZEALAND*
- — David McGill, *David McGill's Complete Kiwi Slang Dictionary*, p. 72, 1998

Maori splice *noun*
any time-saving solution to a problem *NEW ZEALAND*
- — David McGill, *David McGill's Complete Kiwi Slang Dictionary*, p. 83, 1998

Maori time *noun*
a sensibility that is not consumed with worry about punctuality *NEW ZEALAND*
- — Sonya Plowman, *Great Kiwi Slang*, p. 120, 2002

map *noun*

1 the face US, 1899
- Brother, you should have seen their maps when they took one peep at those strutting searchlights up above. — Mezz Mezzrow, *Really the Blues*, p. 168, 1946
- You gotta stop that grinning. Freeze your 'map' and keep it that way. — Iceberg Slim (Robert Beck), *Pimp*, p. 162, 1969

2 a musical score; a piece of sheet music US
- — Clarence Major, *Dictionary of Afro-American Slang*, 1970
- — Arnold Shaw, *Dictionary of American Pop/Rock*, p. 223, 1982

3 a cheque US
- Don't take that guy's map. He's a paperhanger. — John Scarne, *Scarne's Guide to Modern Poker*, p. 284, 1979

map *verb*

to hit, to strike US
- — Terry Williams, *The Cocaine Kids*, p. 137, 1989

Mapes *nickname*

the Maples Inn, a popular bar and music venue in Pointe Claire, Quebec CANADA
- The Maples Inn, known affectionately as "The Mapes," was a favorite spot in the 1960s. People would race the stretch between the Mapes and the Edge [the Edgewater, another nearby party bar.] — *Pointe Claire Chronicle*, p. B1 – B3, 17th July 2002

maple key *noun*

the maple tree seed, which has wings so as to make it twirl in the wind CANADA
- The bridge of your nose was the place to stick maple keys in the spring. — Joan Williamson, *The Latest Morningside Papers*, p. 162, 1989
- More than two hundred years ago, in a forest, a little maple key twirls down and lands on a log. The tree's development is beautifully told in words and pictures. — Jan Thornhill, *A Tree in a Forest*, cover, 1991

map of Tasmania *noun*

the female pubic hair or pubic region AUSTRALIA
- Students: note maps of Tasmania. — Barry Humphries, *Les Patterson's Australia*, p. 10, 1978
- — Barry Humphries, *A Nice Night's Entertainment*, p. 182, 1978
- — Barry Humphries, *The Traveller's Tool*, p. 15, 1985
- You sure you can handle a nice map of Tasmania tonight? — Robert G. Barrett, *Davo's Little Something*, p. 263, 1992

map of Tassie *noun*

the female pubic hair or pubic region AUSTRALIA, 1978
- — Barry Humphries, *A Nice Night's Entertainment*, p. 182, 1978
- According to the mag shag survey, all routes lead to the map of Tassie for our blokes! — *Picture*, p. 9, 5th February 1992

maquillage; maquiage *noun*

makeup, cosmetics UK

From French *maquiller* (to make up the face).
- [B]ona maquillage, I must say. — the cast of 'Aspects of Love', Prince of Wales Theatre, *Palare (Boy Dancer Talk) for Beginners*, 1989 – 92
- — Paul Baker, *Polari*, p. 180, 2002

maracas *noun*

the testicles UK

Rhyming slang for **KNACKERS**.
- You'll get a kick up the maracas if you ain't careful. — Ray Puxley, *Fresh Rabbit*, 1998

marathon *noun*

1 in horse racing, any race that is longer than a mile and a quarter US
- — Tom Ainslie, *Ainslie's Complete Guide to Thoroughbred Racing*, p. 334, 1976

2 any amphetamine, methamphetamine or other central nervous system stimulant US
- National Institute on Drug Abuse, — *What do they call it again?*, 1980

marauder *noun*

a surfer who is indifferent to safety, if not reckless US
- — John Blair, *The Illustrated Discography of Surf Music 1961 – 1965*, p. 124, 1985

marble *noun*

1 a slow-witted person US

Teen slang.
- — *San Francisco News*, p. 6, 25th March 1958

2 a tablet of ethchlorvynol (trade name Placidyl^{TM}), a central nervous system depressant US
- — Richard A. Spears, *The Slang and Jargon of Drugs and Drink*, 1986

▸ **make your marble good**

to improve one's prospects AUSTRALIA, 1928
- He'll be staying behind doing the queen rearing, making his marble good, and I'll be somewhere down in the Pilliga with Mongo[.] — Kylie Tennant, *The Honey Flow*, p. 108, 1956

Marble Arch *noun*

starch UK

Rhyming slang, formed from a famous London landmark.
- — Ray Puxley, *Fresh Rabbit*, 1998

marble halls; marbles *noun*

the testicles UK

Rhyming slang for **BALLS**, perhaps formed after an earlier use of 'marbles' in the same sense (but inspired by a similarity of shape and size).
- — Ray Puxley, *Cockney Rabbit*, 1992

Marblehead turkey *noun*

salt cod US
- In the vicinity of Marblehead, Mass., cod fish is such a common food commodity that the inhabitants refer to it as Marblehead Turkey in the same sense that elsewhere cheese is dubbed Welsh rabbit. — George Earlie Shankle, *American Nicknames*, p. 282, 1955

marble orchard *noun*

a graveyard US, 1925
- — William K. Bentley and James M. Corbett, *Prison Slang*, 1992

marbles *noun*

1 the testicles US, 1916
- — James McDonald, *A Dictionary of Obscenity, Taboo and Euphemism*, p. 7, 1988

2 dice US
- — Frank Garcia, *Marked Cards and Loaded Dice*, p. 262, 1962
- — Thomas L. Clark, *The Dictionary of Gambling and Gaming*, p. 126, 1987

3 money, cash, salary UK, 1864

Theatrical.
- The big marbles are not earned at the Festival Theatres or the Old Vic — uncredited example, *A Dictionary of Slang and Unconventional English*, 1984

▸ **all the marbles**

used as a symbol of complete success US, 1924
- — *American Speech*, p. 294, Autumn-Winter 1975: 'The jargon of barbershop'
- This was for all the marbles, the African club championship. — Bill Cardoso, *The Maltese Sangweech*, p. 298, 1984

▸ **hand in your marbles**

to give up; to die AUSTRALIA, 1908

Variant forms are built on the verb: 'toss in your marbles', 'throw in your marbles', etc.
- But there is one thing I wish I had achieved before I handed in my marbles and jumped the twig. — Barry Humphries, *A Nice Night's Entertainment*, p. 166, 1978

▸ **in the marbles**

in motor racing, in the outside portion of a curve where there is less traction US
- — Lewis Poteet, *Car & Motorcyle Slang*, p. 127, 1992

▸ **lose your marbles**

to become insane, to lose your mind US, 1902
- I actually thought I was about to permanently lose my marbles. — Wayne Anthony, *Spanish Highs*, p. 50, 1999

marbles and conkers; marbles *adjective*

mad, crazy UK

Rhyming slang for **BONKERS**, formed from two games played by children, but probably inspired by phrases like 'lose your marbles' (to become mad).
- — Ray Puxley, *Cockney Rabbit*, 1992

marblish *adjective*

displaying a lack of sportsmanship when losing TRINIDAD AND TOBAGO
- — Lise Winer, *Dictionary of the English/Creole of Trinidad & Tobago*, 2003

marcel *noun*

a hairstyle characterised by deep, regular waves made by a heated curling iron US

After Marcel Grateau (1852 – 1936), a French hairdresser.
- Instantly Teese was on his guard, for the young 'ragheads,' as he called them by dint of their habits of tying kerchiefs about their marcels to keep down sweat and protect the sheens[.] — Clarence Cooper Jr, *Black*, p. 190, 1963

• Those two pimps? That style is just called a process, some call it a marcel.—Joseph Wambaugh, *The New Centurions*, p. 66, 1970
• They flashed big smiles signifying their joy at sporting straight hair via konks or marcels.—Piri Thomas, *Stories from El Barrio*, p. 51, 1978

marching dust *noun*
cocaine *UK*
• —Mike Haskins, *Drugs*, p. 280, 2003

marching orders *noun*
a dismissal from employment or romantic involvement *US, 1856*
From the military use.
• FA Premier League linesman Mike Tingey harshly gave him his marching orders.—*Staines Guardian*, 11th September 2003

marching powder *noun*
cocaine *US*
A shortening of **BOLIVIAN** or **PERUVIAN MARCHING POWDER**.
• A boatload of Marching Powder might get you through this ordeal. —Jay McInerney, *Bright Lights, Big City*, p. 25, 1984

Marcia *noun*
in horse racing, odds of 9–1 *AUSTRALIA*
Rhyming slang based on Marcia Hines, an extremeley popular singer in Australia in the mid-1970s.
• —Ned Wallish, *The Truth Dictionary of Racing Slang*, p. 51, 1989

marconi *noun*
an eavesdropper *UK*
• "Vada the homi macaroni," he hissed. [...] Look at the man listening in, he meant. Marconi being used to indicate a gesture of eavesdropping, hands to the ears like radio headphones.—Jake Arnott, *He Kills Coppers*, p. 52, 2001

mardy *adjective*
sulky, moody *UK, 1903*
English dialect creeping into the mainstream via television programmes like *Coronation Street*.
• I never have your chips, you mardy little arse. First time I ask and ya gob on them.—Paul Fraser and Shane Meadows, *TwentyFourSeven*, p. 8, 1997
• There's no point being a mardy cow. I normally put them off by saying I'm a lesbian.—*Mixmag*, p. 73, February 2002

mardy-arse *noun*
a sulker *UK*
From the dialect word **MARDY** (sulky).
• (DAD EXITS). MAM: He's a big mardy-arse.—Caroline Aherne and Craig Cash, *The Royle Family*, 1999

mardy-arsed *adjective*
sulky, whining, 'spoilt' *UK*
A combination of dialect word **MARDY** (sulky) with '-arsed' (having the characteristics of).
• We're delighted the fruit of our labours will soon grow into a mardy-arsed, rebellious, teenage twat[.]—*X-Ray*, p. 7, November 2002

mare *noun*
1 something good that is hard to believe, a dream *UK*
Amends conventional 'nightmare' (a bad dream) and slang 'nightmare' (something bad).
• KNIGHTY: I don't know, you try and go straight and some bloke just gives you a car. I can't believe it. What a mare. DARCY Yer. What a mare.—Paul Fraser and Shane Meadows, *TwentyFourSeven*, p. 58, 1997
2 something undesirable *IRELAND*
• Christmas in my gaff is a complete mare, and we're talking total here.—Paul Howard, *The Teenage Dirtbag Years*, p. 89, 2001
3 an unpleasant, bad-tempered woman, especially as an insulting term of address *UK, 1303*
• —David Powis, *The Signs of Crime*, 1977

mare and foal *noun*
a bankroll *NEW ZEALAND*
Rhyming slang.
• —David McGill, *David McGill's Complete Kiwi Slang Dictionary*, p. 83, 1998

mares' nest *noun*
a bar for women and their escorts *NEW ZEALAND*
• They could not help being brought into close contact with what some of them coarsely termed the 'cats' bar' or the 'mares' nest.'—*New Zealand Observer*, p. 6, 1st July 1953

Margaret Rose; margaret *noun*
the nose *UK*
Rhyming slang.
• —Ray Puxley, *Fresh Rabbit*, 1998

margarine legs *noun*
used as a symbol of a woman's sexual availability *AUSTRALIA*
• —Kathy Lette, *Girls' Night Out*, p. 187, 1987
• It is a patriarchal society where the males hunt in packs for females with 'margarine legs' (easily spread).—*Sydney Morning Herald*, p. 7, 3rd January 1987

Margarita *noun*
marijuana *US, 1970s*
• —Joel Homer, *Jargon*, p. 196, 1979

Margate sand *noun*
the hand *UK*
Rhyming slang, formed from a seaside resort on the East Coast of England.
• —Ray Puxley, *Cockney Rabbit*, 1992

marge *noun*
margarine *UK, 1919*
• [T]hese are the bread and marge issues of floating pollsters.—*The Guardian*, 14th February 2005

Marge *noun*
the passive, 'feminine' partner in a lesbian relationship *US, 1956*
• —Robert A. Wilson, *Playboy's Book of Forbidden Words*, p. 166, 1972

mari *noun*
a marijuana cigarette *US, 1933*
A clipping of 'marijuana'.
• —Richard A. Spears, *The Slang and Jargon of Drugs and Drink*, p. 331, 1986
• —Mike Haskins, *Drugs*, 2003

Maria *noun*
in a deck of playing cards, the queen of spades *US, 1950*
• —Thomas L. Clark, *The Dictionary of Gambling and Gaming*, p. 126, 1987

Mariah Carey *adjective*
scarey *UK*
Rhyming slang, formed on the name of the popular US singer (b.1970).
• —*The Sunday Times*, 9th May 2004

Maria Monk; maria *noun*
semen *UK*
Rhyming slang for **SPUNK**, based on the name of the authoress of *Awful Disclosures*, 1836, a popular erotic book of its time.
• —Paul Baker, *Polari*, p. 180, 2002

maricon *noun*
a homosexual man *TRINIDAD AND TOBAGO, 1950*
Spanish slang on loan to American slang.
• We took turns sounding his mother for giving birth to a maricon like him.—Piri Thomas, *Down These Mean Streets*, p. 52, 1967
• [A]nd you heard a lot of maricons being pitched back and forth. —Clarence Cooper Jr, *The Farm*, p. 117, 1967
• "Maricon!" he spat. "For why you no tella me what you are?"—Nathan Heard, *Howard Street*, p. 56, 1968
• —Dagoberto Fuentes and Jose Lopez, *Barrio Language Dictionary*, p. 96, 1974
• Don't talk this shit on the phone, Roger, maricon.—Edwin Torres, *Q & A*, p. 180, 1977
• —Carsten Stroud, *Close Pursuit*, p. 273, 1987
• —Lise Winer, *Dictionary of the English/Creole of Trinidad & Tobago*, 2003

Marie Corelli; marie *noun*
television; a television *UK*
Rhyming slang for **TELLY**, formed from the pen name of romantic novelist Mary Mackay, 1855–1924.
• —Jack Jones, *Rhyming Cockney Slang*, 1971
• —David Powis, *The Signs of Crime*, 1977
• —Ray Puxley, *Cockney Rabbit*, 1992

marihooch; marihoochie; marihootee; marihootie *noun*
marijuana *US*
• [I]t was an ace bomber of absolutely atomic North African marihooch[.]—Lester Bangs, *Psychotic Reactions and Carburetor Dung*, p. 80, 1971

marijuana martini *noun*
marijuana smoke blown into, and then inhaled from, a chilled glass *US*
- —Simon Worman, *Joint Smoking Rules*, 2001

marimba *noun*
marijuana *UK*
- —Mike Haskins, *Drugs*, p. 288, 2003

marinate *verb*
1 to relax, to idle *US*
- —*Ebony Magazine*, p. 156, August 2000: 'How to talk to the new generation'

2 to ponder, to debate internally *US*
- —Connie Eble (Editor), *UNC-CH Campus Slang*, p. 7, October 2002

Marine Tiger *noun*
a recent arrival in New York City from Puerto Rico *US*
From the name of a converted C4 troopship that brought many early Puerto Rican immigrants to the US.
- They spoke only Spanish, but he would have known anyhow that they were recent arrivals – Marine Tigers – for only newcomers would play ball barefooted in the street.—Hal Ellson, *The Golden Spike*, p. 82, 1952
- —Dale Kramer and Madeline Karr, *Teen-Age Gangs*, p. 175, 1953
- Later I called her my "marine Tiger," after the ship that brought so many Puerto Ricans to New York.—Piri Thomas, *Down These Mean Streets*, p. 109, 1967

marish and parish *noun*
everyone *TRINIDAD AND TOBAGO, 1987*
- —Lise Winer, *Dictionary of the English/Creole of Trinidad & Tobago*, 2003

mariweegee *noun*
marijuana *US*
A jocular mispronunciation.
- —Clarence Major, *Juba to Jive*, p. 276, 1994

marji *noun*
marijuana *AUSTRALIA*
- —Sidney J. Baker, *Australia Speaks*, 1953

marjoon *noun*
a sweet confection with marijuana as a major ingredient *ALGERIA*
- [A] potent range of improvised narcotics, including marjoon (literally jam, but universally understood to be jam containing cannabis)[.] —Richard Neville, *Play Power*, p. 232, 1970
- Special recommendation: Marjoon – a fudge, blended with the leaves – not the buds – of the plant and which sometimes contains opium as an extra taste treat.—Richard Neville, *Play Power*, p. 304–305, 1970

Marjorie *noun*
marijuana *US*
- —Joel Homer, *Jargon*, p. 196, 1979

mark *noun*
1 a victim, a potential victim of a swindle *UK, 1749*
- She had her eye on a mark – a small man in a dark suit and a country haircut, who had stopped to gawk into the lighted window of a photographic-supply shop.—*Rogue for Men*, p. 45, June 1956
- At another time – hustling – Johnny would have probably encouraged the small mousy man – spotting him as an easy mark.—John Rechy, *Numbers*, p. 127, 1967
- The amount of bread it would cost you would stagger the mark that gigs for a living.—A.S. Jackson, *Gentleman Pimp*, p. 123, 1973
- It is alright to burn one's victims as long as they can be referred to as marks, but never – never – burn the guy you work with and who is your partner.—Herbert Huncke, *The Evening Sun Turned Crimson*, p. 138, 1980
- MOE: What's the best way to qualify a mark? STANLEY: What? MOE: How do you know if you can get the upper hand? How do you know if you're dealing with a guy who's in an inferior position to you, or superior position? How do you know?—*Tin Men*, 1987

2 a number bet on in the lottery game whe-whe *TRINIDAD AND TOBAGO, 1909*
- —Lise Winer, *Dictionary of the English/Creole of Trinidad & Tobago*, 2003

mark *verb*
1 in casino gambling, to place in a stack chips equal to the amount of marker (a loan) extended to a gambler *US*
- —Lee Solkey, *Dummy Up and Deal*, p. 116, 1980

2 to realise, to see, to understand *UK*
- —G.F. Newman, *Sir, You Bastard*, 1970

▸ **mark your card**
to inform; to warn *UK*
From the marking of race cards.
- [T]he Superintendent in charge of the Flying Squad had got wise to the fact that one of his mob was marking Charley's card[.]—Charles Raven, *Underworld Nights*, p. 62, 1956
- Always bustling Andy. Always sarky in the bargain, marking my card.—Jeremy Cameron, *Brown Bread in Wengen*, p. 132, 1999
- Purple's just marking their cards for them.—Kevin Sampson, *Outlaws*, p. 113, 2001

marked wheel *noun*
a rigged roulette wheel *US*
- I learned that a "marked wheel" was a roulette table rigged to activate a pin under a heavy number.—Jimmy Snyder, *Jimmy the Greek*, p. 15, 1975

marker *noun*
1 in a casino or gambling enterprise, an advance with an IOU; by extension, any debt or obligation *US, 1887*
- Never sign a marker or IOU.—Mario Puzo, *Inside Las Vegas*, p. 14, 1977
- No, I owe you a favor. You got my marker. That's the way it is.—Robert Campbell, *The Cat's Meow*, p. 179, 1988
- You signed markers for a hundred and a half, you're over sixty days past due and you haven't told anybody what the problem is.—*Get Shorty*, 1995

2 a person who bets on a number in the lottery game whe-whe *TRINIDAD AND TOBAGO, 1930*
- —Lise Winer, *Dictionary of the English/Creole of Trinidad & Tobago*, 2003

3 a vehicle's number plate *CANADA*
- Another place is the average automobile license office a couple of days before the deadline for new markers.—*Toronto Globe and Mail*, 13th April 1949
- —Hyman E. Goldin et al., *Dictionary of American Underworld Lingo*, p. 136, 1950

market price *noun*
the going rate for sex with a prostitute *US*
- —Ralph de Sola, *Crime Dictionary*, p. 89, 1982

Mark Ramprakash *noun*
a urination *UK*
Rhyming slang for **SLASH**, formed from the name of the English cricketer (b.1969).
- —Tom Nind, *Rude Rhyming Slang*, p. 14, 2003

marks *noun*
signs of intravenous drug use, such as scars or abcesses *US*
- Check this out. I ain't got no fucking marks.—Gerald Petievich, *To Live and Die in L.A.*, p. 221, 1983

Marks and Sparks *nickname*
the retailer Marks and Spencer *UK*
- —*Sunday Times*, 5th April 1964
- The accent came out of Brent Cross Shopping Centre via Marks and Sparks lingerie and Safeway's delicatessen counter.—John Milne, *Alive and Kicking*, p. 144, 1998

Marlboro country *noun*
a remote place; the wilderness *US*
- Sure is marlboro country. Ain't a soul in sight. Nothin but sand and water.—Robert Gover, *JC Saves*, p. 66, 1968

Marlboro man *noun*
a rugged, masculine, handsome cowboy type *US*
Derived from the decades-long advertising campaign for Marlboro cigarettes, featuring ultra-masculine cowboys smoking.
- If you are a boy soprano this will underscore your potential as a Marlboro Man.—*Screw*, p. 11, 15th December 1969
- "He walked in, I thought he was a farmer, or maybe a rancher. He looks like a cowboy, that raw-boned, outdoor type. Wears cowboy boots and a hat with a curled brim." "The Marlboro man," Chip said. "Yeah, except he's real."—Elmore Leonard, *Riding the Rap*, p. 102, 1995

Marley *noun*
a marijuana cigarette *US*
From Bob Marley, Rastafarian and marijuana-lover.
- —Jim Emerson-Cobb, *Scratching the Dragon*, April 1997

Marley's collie *noun*
a potent variety of marijuana, a hybrid of Jamaican sensimillia *JAMAICA, late 1990s*
Named in memory of reggae musician Bob Marley (1945–81), a Rastafarian; **COLLIE** (marijuana).

Marlie-Butt *noun*
a cigarette *AUSTRALIA*
- —John Fahs, *Cigarette Confidential*, p. 302, 1996: 'Glossary'

marmalade dropper *noun*
something shocking, surprising or upsetting, especially a newspaper article *UK*
From the idea that someone, especially a newspaper reader, will be so stunned that breakfast may fall from the fingers.
- —Susie Dent, *The Language Report*, p. 13, 2003

Marmite *noun*
excrement; hence, rubbish *UK*
Rhyming slang for **SHITE**, formed on the name of a branded yeast extract – a brown paste which is apparently an acquired taste.
- —Ray Puxley, *Fresh Rabbit*, 1998

Marmite driller; Marmite miner *noun*
a male homosexual *UK*
Pejorative; a reference to anal sex, based on **MARMITE** (excrement).
- —Chris Lewis, *The Dictionary of Playground Slang*, p. 143, 2003

Marmite motorway *noun*
the rectum *UK*
From **MARMITE** (excrement).
- —Chris Lewis, *The Dictionary of Playground Slang*, p. 144, 2003

Marmon *noun*
morphine *US*
- "Are the Marmon and Cadillac working tonight?" "Yeah." "That Marmon's an eight, isn't it? And Cadillac's a twelve?" —William J. Spillard and Pence James, *Needle in a Haystack*, p. 145, 1945

maroc *adjective*
extremely drunk *UK: SCOTLAND, 1985*
A shortening of the Glasow pronunciation of **MIRACULOUS**.
- Did ye see her last night? Maroc or what? —Michael Munro, *The Complete Patter*, p. 102, 1996

maroon *noun*
a moron *US, 1941*
A malapropism that emphasises the point being made.
- —Judi Sanders, *Faced and Faded, Hanging to Hurl*, p. 26, 1993

marquee player *noun*
a leading or pre-eminent professional athlete with the ability to attract a large audience *US*
- Taube said the team will not go after a "marquee" player like a Herschel Walker or Marcus Dupree. —*United Press International*, 14th March 1984
- The old A.F.L. was able to force a merger with the N.F.L. by signing the top box-office marquee players. (Quoting Leigh Steinberg) —*Playboy*, p. 128, November 1984
- Rod, I say this with great respect, but those players you mentioned are marquee players. —*Jerry Maguire*, 1996

Marrakesh 1 *noun*
a variety of Morrocan hashish *UK*
- The quality is by no means top-notch but Marrakesh 1 has a pleasant sandalwood flavour and an exhilarating effect. —Nick Jones, *Spliffs*, p. 86, 2003

marriage *noun*
in car manufacturing, the installation of the powertrain (the engine, transmission, pinion, ring and differential gears) *US*
- —John Edwards, *Auto Dictionary*, p. 104, 1993

Marrickville Mercedes *noun*
in Sydney, any of various cars popular with New Australians *AUSTRALIA*
From Marrickville, a suburb with a high population of New Australians.
- The kids at teachers college called it a 'Marrickville Mercedes' – a red ET Monaro with a sun roof and mag wheels. —Kathy Lette, *Girls' Night Out*, p. 139, 1987

married *adjective*
1 handcuffed together *US*
- —Joseph E. Ragen and Charles Finston, *Inside the World's Toughest Prison*, p. 808, 1962: 'Penitentiary and underworld glossary'

2 in trucking, part of a two-driver team *US*
- —Montie Tak, *Truck Talk*, p. 104, 1971

3 (used of opium) adulterated with foreign substances *US*
- —*American Speech*, p. 101, May 1956: 'Smugglers' argot in the Southwest'

married quarters *noun*
in prison, the section where men who prefer to adopt a gay lifestyle tend to congregate *UK*
- —Erwin James, *The Guardian*, 25th February 2000: 'A life inside'

married to Mary Fist *adjective*
obsessed with masturbating *US*
- —Hyman E. Goldin et al., *Dictionary of American Underworld Lingo*, p. 137, 1950

marry *verb*
in police work, to serve as partners *US*
- Subtracting the five years with Minifee and then averaging it out, he'd been married to a different cop for maybe a year and half at a time, with lots of space between marriages. —Robert Campbell, *Boneyards*, p. 9–19, 1992

▸ **marry under bamboo**
to be married in Hindu rites *GUYANA*
- —Richard Allsopp, *Dictionary of Caribbean English Usage*, p. 372, 1996

marry and bury *verb*
(of a minister of the local church) to carry a parishioner through life's big events *CANADA*
- "Bury and marry" is a proverbial phrasal way to describe, in rhyme, the main ceremonial cultural activity of a minister. "Was he a minister? Well, he used to marry and bury!" —Vollen Hastings, *manuscript oral history, Brome County Historical Society*, p. ?, 1978

marryjuwanna *noun*
marijuana *US*
A less common example of the many personifications of marijuana intended as humorous.
- Nonetheless the pungent odor of marryjuwanna floated out every open window[.[—Raymond Mungo, *Famous Long Ago*, p. 37, 1970

marry money *verb*
to wed a wealthy man or woman *UK, 1858*
- —Susan Wright, *How to Marry Money*, 1995

Mars and Venus; mars *noun*
the penis *UK*
Rhyming slang.
- —Ray Puxley, *Cockney Rabbit*, 1992

Mars Bar; mars *noun*
1 the penis *UK*
Extended from the shortened form of rhyming slang **MARS AND VENUS** (the penis), playing on the name of a famous branded item of confectionary that helps you 'work, rest and play', apparently.
- —Ray Puxley, *Cockney Rabbit*, 1992

2 a scar *UK*
Rhyming slang, after a popular chocolate confection introduced to the UK in 1932.
- —Michael Munro, *The Original Patter*, 1985
- —Ken Smith, *Inside Time*, p. 234, 1989
- —Angela Devlin, *Prison Patter*, p. 74, 1996
- Fighting at football is one thing, but no-one should have to sport a nasty Mars Bar on their face for the rest of their life for their pains. —Martin King and Martin Knight, *The Naughty Nineties*, p. 139, 1999
- The geezer's got a few naughty Mars Bars. —J.J. Connolly, *Layer Cake*, p. 181, 2000
- I'll give you a mars you carry on! —prison inmate, 5th August 2002

marsh *noun*
in soda fountain usage, a marshmallow *US*
- —*American Speech*, p. 88, April 1946: 'The language of West Coast culinary workers'

marshmallow *noun*
a pillow *US*
- —Wayne Floyd, *Jason's Authentic Dictionary of CB Slang*, p. 21, 1976

marshmallow red; marshmallow *noun*
a barbiturate, a central nervous system depressant *US, 1977*
- —Richard A. Spears, *The Slang and Jargon of Drugs and Drink*, p. 332, 1986
- —Mike Haskins, *Drugs*, p. 283, 2003

marshmallows *noun*
1 the female breasts *US*
- —Eugene Landy, *The Underground Dictionary*, p. 129, 1971

2 the testicles *US*
- —Eugene Landy, *The Underground Dictionary*, p. 129, 1971

mart *noun*
the finger *UK, 1984*
All that remains of old rhyming slang 'Martin-Le-Grand; martin' (the hand); recorded as in gay use about 1970.

mart cover *noun*
a glove *UK*
From **MARTINI** (the hand).
• —Paul Baker, *Polari*, p. 180, 2002

Martens *noun*
heavy-duty boots designed for industrial use and subsequently adopted as fashionwear, initially by skinheads and bootboys, then as a general fashion item for either sex *UK*
An abbreviation of the brand name Doctor Martens™.
• I'm showing off a new pair of DMs today [...] Soon as I got these Martens home I went out back and rubbed them up with a brick[.] —John King, *Human Punk*, p. 5–6, 2000

martin *noun*
▷ **see:** ST. MARTINS-LE-GRAND

martin-eye *noun*
a martini *US*
A jocular embellishment.
• "Fresheners," Nancy said. "Tighteners and fresheners. Sometimes drinkees or martin-eyes." —Elmore Leonard, *The Big Bounce*, p. 88, 1969

Martin Harvey *noun*
an act of pretence intended to mislead *UK*
Circus, etymology unknown.
• [A] nightmare summer which came my way later in my circus career proved to me that he had not been "putting on a Martin Harvey"[.] —Butch Reynolds, *Broken Hearted Clown*, p. 31, 1953

martini *noun*
1 a ring *UK*
• —Paul Baker, *Polari*, p. 180, 2002

2 the hand; the arm *UK*
May be abbreviated to 'mart'.
• Your martinis look really nice in that frock, Albert. —the cast of 'Aspects of Love', Prince of Wales Theatre, *Palare (Boy Dancer Talk) for Beginners*, 1989–92
• Doesn't really go with her big tattooed navvy marts which she waves around a lot to show off her groins[.] —James Gardiner, *Who's a Pretty Boy Then?*, p. 123, 1997
• —Paul Baker, *Polari*, p. 180, 2002

▸ **dry martini**
the left hand *UK*
Based on the popular branded drink.
• —Paul Baker, *Polari*, 2002

▸ **sweet martini**
the right hand *UK*
Based on the popular branded drink.
• —Paul Baker, *Polari*, p. 191, 2002

Marty Wilde *noun*
mild ale *UK*
Rhyming slang, from the stage-name of a singer (b.1939) who had a number of hit records in the late 1950s and early 60s, when mild ale was also a popular choice.
• —Ray Puxley, *Cockney Rabbit*, 1992

marvel *noun*
an impressive person *AUSTRALIA*
Also commonly used ironically.
• 'You know your dad's a bloody marvel,' Blaze would say, enviously. —Kylie Tennant, *The Honey Flow*, p. 33, 1956
• 'Doc,' I laughed, 'you're a bloody marvel.' —*Alvin Purple*, p. 79, 1974
• 'Yeah. You're a bloody marvel,' muttered Davo, getting a bit pissed off at Eddie's lairising[.] —Robert G. Barrett, *Davo's Little Something*, p. 55, 1992

marvellous Melbourne *nickname*
the city of Melbourne, Australia's second biggest city *AUSTRALIA, 1885*
• It's not out at woop woop, but right here in marvellous Melbourne. —*Australian Ultimate*, p. 7, 2003

marvy *adjective*
marvellous *US, 1931*
• Then I took her to a movie. "Gee, that was a marvy movie," she said as we left the theater. —Max Shulman, *The Many Loves of Dobie Gillis*, p. 43, 1951
• Tons of marvy makeup, too, and a most effective hairspray. —*Screw*, p. 13, 6th November 1972
• [Nocl] Lowe would declare that everything on that tour was "marvy"[.] —Will Birch, *No Sleep Till Canvey Island*, p. 270, 2003

marvy-groovy *adjective*
bad *US*
A combination of two clichéd adjectives for 'good', meaning 'bad'.
• —*Current Slang*, p. 4, Spring 1967

Mary *noun*
1 an Australian Aboriginal, Papuan or Islander woman *AUSTRALIA, 1830*
• [S]omeone told him there was some Fuzzies along there with the Yanks, and Lucky went to see if he could get a Mary. —Eric Lambert, *The Veterans*, p. 147, 1954
• Have to get a Mary to come too, though. —Wal Watkins, *Race the Lazy River*, p. 126, 1963

2 any woman of Indian descent *SOUTH AFRICA, 1927*
Offensive, though not originally intended to be so.
• —Jean Branford, *A Dictionary of South African English*, 1978

3 any black woman, especially a domestic worker; any non-white woman *SOUTH AFRICA, 1952*
Offensive, demeaning; from the previous sense.
• —Jean Branford, *A Dictionary of South African English*, 1978

4 used as a term of address from one male homosexual to another *US, 1925*
• —Donald Webster Cory and John P. LeRoy, *The Homosexual and His Society*, p. 265, 1963: 'A lexicon of homosexual slang'
• "Oh, Mary, get off it!" the fatman says impatiently with a fatwave of his hand[.] —John Rechy, *City of Night*, p. 166, 1963
• Oh! That whore! Mary, everybody's had him. —Antony James, *America's Homosexual Underground*, p. 34, 1965
• Well get her, Mary! —Kenneth Marlowe, *The Gay World of Kenneth Marlowe*, p. 41, 1966
• Oh, Mary, don't ask. —Mart Crowley, *The Boys in the Band*, p. 42, 1968

5 a homosexual man who is a Catholic *UK*
• —Paul Baker, *Polari*, p. 180, 2002

6 marijuana *US, 1952*
Simply being on first name terms with **MARY JANE**, **MARY WARNER** and many other similar personifications of marijuana. Also written as lower case.
• —Richard A. Spears, *The Slang and Jargon of Drugs and Drink*, p. 332, 1986
• —Mike Haskins, *Drugs*, p. 288, 2003

7 morphine *US*
• More specifically, it was classified as M, C, and H – Mary, Charlie, and Harry – which stood for morphine, cocaine, and heroin. —William J. Spillard and Pence James, *Needle in a Haystack*, p. 147–8, 1945

Mary and Johnny *noun*
marijuana *US, 1935*
A playful personification of marijuana.
• —Richard A. Spears, *The Slang and Jargon of Drugs and Drink*, p. 332, 1986
• —Mike Haskins, *Drugs*, p. 288, 2003

Mary Ann *noun*
1 a fan (for cooling the air) *UK*
Rhyming slang.
• —Ray Puxley, *Cockney Rabbit*, 1992

2 marijuana *US, 1936*
A personification based on varying the vowel-sounds in 'marijuana', so may also appear as 'Maryanne' or 'Mary Anner'.
• —Richard A. Spears, *The Slang and Jargon of Drugs and Drink*, p. 332, 1986
• —Mike Haskins, *Drugs*, p. 288, 2003

Mary Decker *noun*
a fast-moving police vehicle, especially an armoured vehicle; a minibus, especially one made by Mitsubishi *SOUTH AFRICA, 1985*
Township slang; after the US athlete (b.1958) who failed to win a 1984 Olympic medal in the 3,000 metres, as a result of an incident involving South African athlete, Zola Budd (who was actually running for the UK).

Mary-do-you-wanna-dance *noun*
marijuana *UK*
• [A] few dollars' worth of the cheapest but finest Mary-do-you-wanna-dance in the whole wide world[.] —Ken Lukowiak, *Marijuana Time*, p. 90, 2000

Mary Ellen man *noun*
a pickpocket who distracts the victim by telling a sexually charged story *US*
- —John R. Armore and Joseph D. Wolfe, *Dictionary of Desperation*, 1976

Mary Ellens *noun*
large female breasts *UK*
Rhyming slang for **MELONS**; described as 'fairly modern' by Ray Puxley, *Cockney Rabbit*, 1992, but surely an ironic reference to the music hall song of some 80 years earlier: 'I'm Shy, Mary Ellen, I'm Shy'.

Mary Fist *noun*
used as a personification of male masturbation *US*
- Many of them had been abetted by the fold-out pictures in Playboy, the magazine that, indeed, had verbally implanted the original suggestion in his just-turned-twelve mind with an article, "Doing It Without Chicks" – or, rather, doing it with a surrogate cutely identified as "Mary Fist." —Hyman E. Goldin et al., *Dictionary of American Underworld Lingo*, p. 136, 1950
- Jackie the Priest, who's got himself that good ole girlfriend, Mary Fist. —Gilbert Sorrentino, *Steelwork*, p. 39, 1970
- But I can understand some gazoony without a woman, or with the wrong woman, watching crap like this and having it off with Mary Fist. —Robert Campbell, *In La-La Land We Trust*, p. 175, 1986
- —Donald Harington, *Elektrina*, p. 56, 1993

Mary Green; the Mary *noun*
in any suit of cards, the Queen *UK*
Rhyming slang.
- —Ray Puxley, *Cockney Rabbit*, 1992

Mary Jane *noun*
1 marijuana *US, 1928*
From the disputed presumption that marijuana is formed of two Mexican Spanish names: Maria and Juan or Juanita, hence Mary Jane, and many variants, such as Mary J, Mary Jonas, Mary Juana and so on.
- "Is that really mary-juana, Paul?" Christine asked, speaking in a shocked hush. —John Clellon Holmes, *Go*, p. 86, 1952
- —J. Maclaren-Ross, *Bop in Laugh with Me!*, 1954
- I answered (and remember the pills, the liquor, the maryjane)[.] —John Rechy, *City of Night*, p. 124, 1963
- Mr. Mannheim said, "It isn't hep to call it Mary Jane any more," and the woman in the black bikini said, "Hip." —Evan Hunter, *Last Summer*, p. 117, 1968
- Can't get enough of sweet cocaine / Get enough of Mary Jane —John Martyn, *Over the Hill*, 1973
- But everythin' is funny when your smokin' Mary Jane[.] —Tone Loc, *Chheba Cheeba*, 1989
- She toked big H and maryjane[.] —James Ellroy, *Hollywood Nocturnes*, p. 272, 1994
- The LA-based vocal group [The Mary Jane Girls] took their name from a slang term for marijuana[.] —Simon Warner, *Rockspeak!*, 1996
- [T]hey discovered the new Mary Jane, LSD, grew hair and moustaches and started listening to Jimi Hendrix. —Paolo Hewitt, *The Sharper Word*, p. 12, 1998

2 cocaine *UK*
Rhyming slang.
- Is Mary-Jane coming out tonight? —Angela Devlin, *Prison Patter*, p. 74, 1996

Marylou *noun*
glue *UK*
Rhyming slang.
- —Ray Puxley, *Cockney Rabbit*, 1992

Mary Rose *noun*
a nose, especially a notably large specimen *UK*
Rhyming slang, apparently formed from the name of a sunken ship which was raised with much hoop-la in 1982.
- Cop the Mary Rose on ol' Hugh Jooter over there. —Ray Puxley, *Fresh Rabbit*, 1998

Mary unit *noun*
a motorcyle police officer *US*
- There's going to be a parade led by two hundred Mary units (motorcycle cops), followed by a hundred black-and-whites. —Stephen J. Cannell, *The Tin Collectors*, p. 65, 2001

Mary Warner; Mary Warmer; Mary Weaver; Mary Werner; Mary Worner *noun*
marijuana *US, 1933*
Giving a feminine identity by mispronunciation.
- —Vincent J. Monteleone, *Criminal Slang*, p. 153, 1949
- —Paul Tempest, *Lag's Lexicon*, p. 133, 1950
- Here. Try one of these. This is the real Mary Warner. —Douglas Rutherford, *The Creeping Flesh*, p. 49, 1963
- Well, that was my life and I don't feel ashamed at all. Mary Warner, honey, you sure was good —Louis Armstrong, *quoted in Waiting For The Man, Harry Shapiro*, p. 26, 1999

Mary Worthless *noun*
an older homosexual man *US*
- —*Maledicta*, p. 222, 1979: 'Kinks and queens: linguistic and cultural aspects of the terminology for gays'

masacree *noun*
a massacre *UK, 1823*
- —Arlo Guthrie, *Alice's Restaurant Massacree*, 1969

masala relationship *noun*
a romantic relationship between a black man and an Indian woman *TRINIDAD AND TOBAGO, 1994*
From the film *Mississippi Masala*, alluding to the spice mixture used in Indian cooking.
- —Lise Winer, *Dictionary of the English/Creole of Trinidad & Tobago*, 2003

Masarati *noun*
an improvised pipe for smoking crack cocaine, made from a plastic bottle *US*
- —Terry Williams, *Crackhouse*, p. 150, 1992

mash *noun*
1 mashed potato *UK, 1923*
Also variant 'mashed'.
- Already this month I've made a couple of bangers-and-mash suppers[.] —*The Observer*, 16th November 2003

2 a romantic infatuation; a sweetheart *US, 1877*
- And to me it was just another mash – that's what we called flirting in those days. We would use the expression, "The lady as a mash on you[.]" —Louis Armstrong, *Satchmo*, p. 151, 1954
- The dyke was sending Lor a hundred long-stemmed red roses a day, along with mash notes bearing her nom de plume d'amour: "Your tongue of Fire." —James Ellroy, *Hollywood Nocturnes*, p. 270, 1994

3 any homemade liquor *US*
- —Gary K. Farlow, *Prison-ese*, p. 42, 2002

mash *verb*
1 to beat up, to 'beat to a pulp' *US, 1872*
Derives from conventional 'mash' (to crush, smash utterly).
- I mash his fuckin' nose. Fuckin' joker. Mash it good I'm thinkin'. —Nick Barlay, *Curvy Lovebox*, p. 10, 1997
- [Of a combat-based arcade game] I got fucking mashed, man, and now I ain't got no more money. —Melanie McGrath, *Hard, Soft & Wet*, p. 50, 1998
- Some mad fellas came round and mashed us without green-lighting with yourself, Johnny. —Kevin Sampson, *Outlaws*, p. 76, 2001

2 to flirt aggressively *US, 1877*
- We're liable to get pinched for mashing on Sixty-third. I heard the Law is watching that pretty close. —James T. Farrell, *Saturday Night*, p. 38, 1947

3 to go away *TRINIDAD AND TOBAGO, 1956*
Usually used as a command to dogs.
- —Lise Winer, *Dictionary of the English/Creole of Trinidad & Tobago*, 2003

4 to pass, to hand to someone, to give *US, 1944*
- —Jack Lait and Lee Mortimer, *New York Confidential*, p. 235, 1948: 'A glossary of Harlemisms'
- —Joseph E. Ragen and Charles Finston, *Inside the World's Toughest Prison*, p. 808, 1962: 'Penitentiary and underworld glossary'

mash and dash *verb*
to kiss and run *US*
- —*DePauw University Campus Corner*, 29th January 1996: 'Slang terms at DePauw'

mashed *adjective*
1 drunk *US, 1942*
- —*e-cyclopaedia*, 20th March 2002

2 marijuana-intoxicated *UK*
Extending the previous sense.
- Bein' mashed don't help. —Nick Barlay, *Curvy Lovebox*, p. 24, 1997
- [H]e woz mashed, and he did have de munchies[.] —Sacha Baron-Cohen, *Da Gospel According to Ali G*, 2001

3 astonished *US*
- —Collin Baker et al., *College Undergraduate Slang Study Conducted at Brown University*, p. 155, 1968

mashed potato transmission *noun*
in the used car business, a worn, loose, mushy automatic transmission *US*
- They screwed beauty bolts onto the engine block and coaxed the tired, mashed-potato transmission back to life. —Stephen Cannell, *King Con*, p. 29, 1997

mashed up *adjective*
damaged *UK*
- You should never poke fun at them whass mashed up by life. – No of course- God I've got nothing against dwarfs[.] —Nick Barlay, *Curvy Lovebox*, p. 73, 1997

masheer *adjective*
on Prince Edward Island, used for describing a garment *CANADA*
- "She wore a masheer stylish dress." "It's slang for 'for sure'." —T. K. Pratt, *oral citations in Dictionary of Prince Edward Island English*, p. 96, 1988

masher *noun*
1 an attractive man *IRELAND*
- Her new boyfriend is very handsome, a real masher. —Terence Dolan, *A Dictionary of Hiberno-English*, p. 170, 1999

2 an unsophisticated flirt *US*
- —Sherman Louis Sergel, *The Language of Show Biz*, p. 133, 1973

3 a person who takes sexual pleasure from physical contact with strangers in crowded places *US, 1875*
- — Anon., *King Smut's Wet Dreams Interpreted*, 1978

mash list *noun*
a tally of all those with whom you have had sex *US*
- — *DePauw University Campus Corner*, 29th January 1996: 'Slang terms at DePauw'

mash mouth *adjective*
toothless *TRINIDAD AND TOBAGO, 1987*
- —Lise Winer, *Dictionary of the English/Creole of Trinidad & Tobago*, 2003

mash out *verb*
to complete *US*
- I had did my bit, the whole 1–3–2–6 was mashed out and there's one ting about getting outta a New York penitentiary that amazed me. —A.S. Jackson, *Gentleman Pimp*, p. 132, 1973

mashup *noun*
a creative remixing of separate pieces of recorded dance music *UK*
- [Y]ou get space age bachelor pad music ("Lithuania"), breakbeat cheesetronica mashup ("Midget") or queasy abstract ambience ("Cinematic"). —Peter Marsh reviewing 'A Livingroom Hush' by Jaga Jazzist, *BBCi Jazz*, November 2002

mash up *verb*
1 to beat up, to thrash *UK*
- So they get in debt so they get mash[ed] up and you got a gang war[.] —Jeremy Cameron, *Brown Bread in Wengen*, p. 112, 1999
- Mash up the keeners in the Main Block if you have to! —Jack Allen, *When the Whistle Blows*, p. 50, 2000

2 (of a disc jockey) to mix dance records together *UK*
- Kenny Ken took to the decks and started mashing up the beats. —Dean Cavanagh, *Mile High Meltdown (Disco Biscuits)*, p. 210, 1996

mask *noun*
1 a tight, stretched face resulting from extensive cosmetic surgery *US*
- —Anna Scotti and Paul Young, *Buzzwords*, p. 109, 1997

2 oversized sunglasses *US*
- — *American Speech*, p. 270, December 1962: 'The language of traffic policemen'

mason *noun*
1 an extremely frugal person *US*
A reference to stone walls, a metaphor for frugality.
- — *The Annals of the American Academy of Political and Social Sciences*, p. 127, May 1950

2 a male homosexual who takes the active role in sex *US*
- —Vincent J. Monteleone, *Criminal Slang*, p. 153, 1949

mass *noun*
a lot of, a great many *US*
- We have mass knives in our kitchen. —Judi Sanders, *Mashing and Munching in Ames*, p. 13, 1994

mass *adjective*
a lot of *US*
- I've got mass studying to do tonight. —Connie Eble (Editor), *UNC-CH Campus Slang*, p. 4, March 1981

Massa Charlie *noun*
used as a stereotype of the dominant white male in relation to blacks *US*
- They didn't know Goldberg from Massa Charlies; to them, Goldberg was Massa Charlie. —Claude Brown, *Manchild in the Promised Land*, p. 298, 1965

Massachusetts driver *noun*
in the northeastern US, an inconsiderate and dangerous driver *US*
- —John Gould, *Maine Lingo*, p. 177, 1975

massa day done!
used for reminding someone that the colonial era and slavery are a thing of the past *TRINIDAD AND TOBAGO, 1961*
- —Lise Winer, *Dictionary of the English/Creole of Trinidad & Tobago*, 2003

massage *noun*
sexual services *US*
A euphemism so well known that a legitimate masseuse may hesitate to announce his or her profession.
- Melanie specialising in the moodiest massages in town. —John King, *White Trash*, p. 287, 2001

massage *verb*
to kill *US, 1926*
Vietnam war usage.
- —Linda Reinberg, *In the Field*, p. 136, 1991

masses *noun*
a large amount *UK, 1892*
- The architect CFA Voysey, in particular, designed masses of interestingly-dashed homes like this until his death in 1941[.] —*The Daily Telegraph*, 29th May 2004

mass gas *noun*
a group of tanker aircraft refuelling a group of receiver planes *US*
- — *American Speech*, p. 119, May 1963: 'Air refueling words'

massive *noun*
1 a group of friends or peers *JAMAICA, 1989*
- —Peter Patrick, *Some Recent Jamaican Creole Words*, 2003

2 a gang *UK*
Predominantly West Indian and UK black usage.
- Blue started out as a scout for the massive. —Karline Smith, *Moss Side Massive*, p. 8, 1994
- [Y]our Kru, or your Massive, your Thugs, or Bredrins[.] —Julian Johnson, *Urban Survival*, p. 264, 2003

3 a social grouping with a shared leisure interest, often identified by location *JAMAICA, 1995*
West Indian and UK black usage.
- Dis one gan out to da Stepney massive! —Mark Powell, *Snap*, p. 21, 2001

massive *adjective*
excellent *US*
- —Connie Eble (Editor), *UNC-CH Campus Slang*, p. 6, Spring 1982
- He's only massive. —Terence Dolan, *A Dictionary of Hiberno-English*, 1999

▸ **give it massive**
to enjoy in a very enthusiastic or excessive fashion *UK*
Punning on 'give it large'.
- Giving it massive with the missus —Dave Courtney, *Raving Lunacy*, 2000

massive!
used for expressing enthusiastic approval *NEW ZEALAND*
- —David McGill, *David McGill's Complete Kiwi Slang Dictionary*, p. 72, 1998

massive humanity *noun*
a large crowd *US*
- —Connie Eble (Editor), *UNC-CH Campus Slang*, p. 3, November 1983

Ma State; Ma *nickname*
New South Wales, Australia *AUSTRALIA, 1906*
A tribute to NSW's status as Australia's earliest colony, thus the 'mother state'.

master *adjective*
excellent *TRINIDAD AND TOBAGO, 1956*
- —William K. Bentley and James M. Corbett, *Prison Slang*, 1992
- —Lise Winer, *Dictionary of the English/Creole of Trinidad & Tobago*, 2003

master blaster *noun*

a large piece of crack cocaine *US*

• —Terry Williams, *Crackhouse*, p. 150, 1992

master key *noun*

in law enforcement, a sledge hammer *US*

• So when still no one came they used a sledgehammer – what the strike team called their master key – busted in and here was a woman standing in the living room no doubt the whole time, not saying a word. —Elmore Leonard, *Riding the Rap*, p. 37, 1995

master maniac *noun*

on the railways, a master mechanic *US*

• —J. Herbert Lund, *Herb's Hot Box of Railraod Slang*, p. 144, 1975

mastermind *noun*

a railway official *US*

• —Norman Carlisle, *The Modern Wonder Book of Trains and Railroading*, p. 265, 1946

master of your domain *noun*

a person who can refrain from masturbation for a prolonged period *US*

Coined and popularised by Jerry Seinfeld in an episode of his television comedy *The Contest* that first aired on 18th November 1992.

masturbation *noun*

self-indulgent nonsense *UK*

Used in a euphemistic attempt to avoid **WANK**.

• [Of a strategy under discussion] The dreaded "m" word. It's a load of masturbation. —Elis Jones, *Cross Arts Forum, A Kick Up The Arts*, 8th October 2001

masturbation mansion *noun*

a cinema showing pornographic films *US*

• The early skin-flick houses became known humorously among much of the trade as "masturbation mansions." —Roger Blake, *What you always wanted to know about porno-movies*, p. 78, 1972

mat *noun*

▸ **go to the mat**

to engage in a full-scale struggle *US, 1908*

From wrestling.

• Okay. We're going to the mat. —Edwin Torres, *After Hours*, p. 365, 1979

mataby *noun*

marijuana grown in Zaire *ZAIRE*

• —Sean McConville, *The State of the Language*, 1980

matador *adjective*

a stylish, fashionable, independent woman *TRINIDAD AND TOBAGO, 1956*

• —Lise Winer, *Dictionary of the English/Creole of Trinidad & Tobago*, 2003

Matapedia screwdriver *noun*

a hammer *CANADA*

Matapedia is a small town in Quebec, poised on the border with New Brunswick.

• —Bill Casselman, *Canadian Sayings*, p. 134, 2002

match *noun*

approximately half an ounce of marijuana *US*

An abbreviation of 'matchbox', which contains approximately the same amount.

• —Edith A. Folb, *runnin' down some lines*, p. 246, 1980
• —Angela Devlin, *Prison Patter*, p. 74, 1996

match *verb*

▸ **match dials**

on the railways, to synchronise watches *US*

• —Ramon Adams, *The Language of the Railroader*, p. 99, 1977

match bash *noun*

a drag racing event built around a series of races between two types of vehicles *US*

• Match bashes between FoMoCo and MoPar funny cars have proven especially popular. —John Lawlor, *How to Talk Car*, p. 72, 1965

matchbox *noun*

1 an approximate measure, ½ ounce, 5–10 grams, of marijuana *US*

Derives from the capacity of a matchbox, a convenient measure.

• —Angela Devlin, *Prison Patter*, p. 74, 1996

2 a small house *IRELAND, 1920*

• —Penny Silva, *A Dictionary of South African English*, 1996

matchbox Jimmy *noun*

a cabover truck built by General Motors Corporation *US*

• —Montie Tak, *Truck Talk*, p. 105, 1971

match head; match-head *noun*

1 a small single dose of heroin sold individually *US*

• —Kenn "Naz" Young, *Naz's Dictionary of Teen Slang*, p. 76, 1993

2 a football fan, especially one who goes to the game *UK*

Those interested in a specific football fixture refer to 'the match'; this combines with **-HEAD** (an aficionado). A derisory term punning on the small size of a matchhead.

• I know that a lot of the match-heads have got a bit of a take on me. —Kevin Sampson, *Outlaws*, p. 168, 2001

mate *noun*

1 a good friend; a buddy or chum *UK, 1380*

This word is used to the near exclusion of its various synonyms in Australia. Originally used only by men, but since the 1980s increasingly by women.

• He will talk to anybody and everybody, this Australian, and his real mates are few. For them, he will die. Literally. —Nino Culotta (John O'Grady), *They're A Weird Mob*, p. 158, 1957
• And that's how it is. Leave the skirts alone, and they're all good mates. —Arthur Upfield, *Bony and the Mouse*, p. 51, 1959
• And you call yourself my mate! —John Wynnum, *Jiggin' in the Riggin'*, p. 11, 1965
• You're my mate, aren't you? I mean, you and Gary, you're my old mates. —Alexander Buzo, *Rooted*, p. 88, 1969
• We've always been good mates. I'm a bloke who always does the right thing by a bloke. —Alexander Buzo, *Rooted*, p. 98, 1969
• 'Mate!' Chilla corrected like a long-suffering school-teacher. 'How many times have I got to tell you Australians don't have chums, they have mates.' —Frank Hardy, *The Outcasts of Foolgarah*, p. 1, 1971
• 'Yeah...but you shouldn't cheat on me, mate. We're mates, aren't we?' he asked. —Ward McNally, *Supper at Happy Harry's*, p. 9, 1982
• I didn't understand. I'd done a mate a favour and a mate had done me wrong in return. —John Birmingham, *He Died With a Felafel in his Hand*, p. 101, 1994
• [S]he's the bollocks, she's my best mate, and I'm scared of changing that. — *The Guardian*, 16th June 2002

2 used as a form of address to a stranger *UK, 1450*

Generally used in a friendly manner, but also used when being confrontational.

• 'That's all right, mate,' said the look-out man affably. —Vince Kelly, *The Bogeyman*, p. 13, 1956
• The driver started up and went up the street a little way, and then said, 'Where to, mate?' —Nino Culotta (John O'Grady), *They're A Weird Mob*, p. 15, 1957
• Minutes later, the two contestants dragged back into the bar. 'Geez, mate, yer got a terrific right.' —John Wynnum, *Tar Dust*, p. 37, 1962
• 'You're drinks are finished, mate,' said the barman, glaring at the Texan. —Robert English, *Toxic Kisses*, p. 45, 1979
• Well you're bloody mistaken, mate! —Sandra Jobson, *Blokes*, p. 66, 1984
• You fuckin' messed me up with that weed, I'm tellin' ya mate. —Donald Gorgon, *Cop Killer*, p. 67, 1994

3 in poker, a card that forms a pair *US*

• —George Percy, *The Language of Poker*, p. 56, 1988

maternity blouse *noun*

a large, loose shirt worn untucked by a heavy man *US*

• — *Male Swinger Number 3*, p. 48, 1981: 'The complete gay dictionary'

mateship *noun*

masculine friendship *AUSTRALIA, 1864*

In 1999 Prime Minister John Howard tried to introduce this word into a 'preamble' to the Australian Constitution and came under much criticism and ridicule since it was seen to exclude women – the referendum on the matter was not passed.

• The Legend of the Silent Australian had its origin, I believe, in the mateship of men humping bluey in the outback. —Bill Wannan, *Bullockies, Beauts and Bandicoots*, p. 72, 1960
• So I thinks, a poker school. The mateship of the game of cards was just what I needed. —Frank Hardy, *The Yarns of Billy Borker*, p. 139, 1965
• Earlier I said that there was an undertone of homosexuality in the Australian mateship syndrome. —Sue Rhodes, *Now you'll think I'm awful*, p. 58, 1967
• Borky had lived by..the myth of Australian mateship, which he had abandoned because he didn't have a mate left in the world[.] —Frank Hardy, *The Outcasts of Foolgarah*, p. 167, 1971
• There was true mateship in the club in those days. —Sandra Jobson, *Blokes*, p. 63, 1984
• There isn't as much mateship as there was. —Sandra Jobson, *Blokes*, p. 76, 1984

mate's rates; mate rates *noun*
especially cheap prices applied to one's friends *AUSTRALIA*
- R.U. had picked up a crate of cheap sunnies that had 'fallen off the back of a truck' and was proceeding to sell them off for 'Mate Rates'. — *Nine to Five*, p. 17, 4th March 1996

matey *noun*
a man; a companion; a comrade *US, 1841*
Used as an affectionate form of address; in a friendly way for someone whose name is not known; in a pseudo-friendly manner for patronising effect.
- Next station, doors open, and they step backward off the train. But matey on the deck – they drag him off the train by his feet[.] — Martin King and Martin Knight, *The Naughty Nineties*, p. 55, 1999
- But by that time, it was matey who needed the protecting. — Jimmy Stockin, *On The Cobbles*, p. 157, 2000
- Am I ever more glad to see any gaff anywhere, though? Don't think so, matey. — Kevin Sampson, *Outlaws*, p. 6, 2001

matey *adjective*
friendly *UK, 1915*
Whereas 'matey' as a form of address is generally used of a man, this usage ignores gender.
- We assumed encouragement and expressions of matey consolation about knowing how he felt[.] — Robert S. Close, *With Hooves of Brass*, p. 115, 1961
- I've got quite matey with him. It's a pity that's all he is, but it's better than nothing[.] — Mary Hooper, *(megan)2*, p. 177, 1999

matey boy *noun*
used dismissively, a man *UK*
- [A]s matey boy found out. — Danny King, *The Bank Robber Diaries*, p. 155, 2002

math out *verb*
to render a presentation beyond comprehension by virtue of dense mathematical content *US*
- — Eric S. Raymond, *The New Hacker's Dictionary*, p. 237, 1991

'matic *noun*
an automatic pistol *UK*
- With the local yardies' penchant for 9mm 'matics, the police had no intention of making a house call without their own hardware. — Donald Gorgon, *Cop Killer*, p. 4, 1994

matinee *noun*
1 a sexual encounter in the mid-afternoon *US, 1944*
- Some commuting businessmen, called matinees, reject the night hours altogether and come afternoons between two and four-thirty[.] — John M. Murtagh and Sara Harris, *Cast the First Stone*, p. 2, 1957
- A matinee, and so early in the day. — Robert Leslie, *Confessions of a Lesbian Prostitute*, p. 67, 1965
- The second appointment was a "matinee" with a tried-and-true customer, a man I had known for three years[.] — Sara Harris, *The Lords of Hell*, p. 101, 1967
- Picture, if you will, two young men ... old friends, if an unsatisfactory love affair can make for friendship ... in a room, engaged in the preliminaries of a matinee. — Angelo d'Arcangelo, *The Homosexual Handbook*, p. 7, 1968
- [L]ately I'd just as soon have a cold beer and hot hot matinee with the old Florrie while the kids are at Sunday school. — Frank Hardy, *The Outcasts of Foolgarah*, p. 3, 1971
- From theatrical usage and a 1930s recipe for an ideal marriage: "Once a day, plus matinee." — Robert A. Wilson, *Playboy's Book of Forbidden Words*, p. 167, 1972

2 a repeat robbery of a victim *US*
- — Hyman E. Goldin et al., *Dictionary of American Underworld Lingo*, p. 159, 1950

matlock *noun*
a tooth *UK*
Hence 'matlock mender' (a dentist).
- — Paul Baker, *Polari*, p. 180, 2002

matrimonial peacemaker *noun*
the penis *US*
- — Dale Gordon, *The Dominion Sex Dictionary*, p. 105, 1967

matsakaw; matsakow *noun*
heroin *US, 1977*
- — Mike Haskins, *Drugs*, p. 284, 2003

mattie *noun*
a woman's very close female friend *BARBADOS*
- — Frank A. Collymore, *Barbadian Dialect*, p. 71, 1965

mattress *noun*
a sexually active, promiscuous girl from a nearby village *CANADA*
- The Mattress was the nickname of a girl who was sexy, easy, promiscuous in a nearby village in the Eastern Townships of Quebec. — Lewis Poteet, *Talking Country*, p. 54, 1992

mattresses *noun*
▸ **go to the mattresses; hit the mattresses**
during gang warfare, to retreat in an armed group to a fortified room, apartment or house *US*
- Valachi quoted his boss as saying on one occasion: "We have to go to the mattress again," and explained that mattress derived from the practice of warring gangs of moving rapidly from place to place, holing up for temporary stays wherever necessary and sleeping on only a simple mattress. — *American Speech*, p. 306, December 1964: 'Lingua Cosa Nostra'
- Sonny told his *caporegimes* to go to the mattresses. — Mario Puzo, *The Godfather*, p. 253, 1969
- Some of the heavies in the mob have hit the mattress, the big names are surrounding themselves with soldiers and a few have dropped out of sight entirely. — Mickey Spillane, *Last Cop Out*, p. 84, 1972
- And all we're trying to do is stop the button men from hitting the mattresses. — Joseph Wambaugh, *The Glitter Dome*, p. 181, 1981
- Joe Loop said what the guy was doing they used to call "going to the mattress," hiding out, going to a safe house had enough mattresses for the crew to sleep on. — Elmore Leonard, *Be Cool*, p. 125, 1999

mattress fall *noun*
uterine prolapse *TRINIDAD AND TOBAGO*
- — Lise Winer, *Dictionary of the English/Creole of Trinidad & Tobago*, 2003

mattress joint *noun*
a hotel catering to prostitutes *US*
- When the clerk in a mattress joint like the Beloit was reluctant to furnish the police with a guest's room number, the pressure was really on. — *Rogue for Men*, p. 49, June 1956

Mattress Mary *noun*
used as a personification of the stereotypical sexually loose female *US*
- — *American Speech*, p. 302, December 1955: 'Wayne University slang'

Matty Mattel; Matty Mattel mouse gun *noun*
the M-16 rifle *US, 1978*
Named after the toy manufacturer because many soldiers in Vietnam found the M-16 to be a seriously flawed rifle.
- — Linda Reinberg, *In the Field*, p. 136, 1991
- The following story is one that I tell with some trepidation, since my experience(s) with the "Matty Mattel Mouse Guns" were not pleasant ones. — Dick Culver, *The Saga of the M-16 in Vietnam*, 2000

matzoh ball; matzo ball *noun*
a Jewish dance or party held at Christmas *US*
From a pun on a staple of Jewish cuisine, adopted commercially for a series of events, and from there into wider usage.
- "I met my wife at one of our Matzoh Ball events in 1997," said Andy Rudnick, managing director of the SYJP, who founded the event in 1987. — *New York Daily News*, 22nd December 2002

Maud; Maude *noun*
a male prostitute *UK, 1984*
From the female name. Also used amongst male homosexuals as an adopted name. Probably since the 1940s.

Maud and Ruth *noun*
the truth *UK*
Rhyming slang.
- — Clement and La Frenais, *A Further Stir of Porridge*, 1977

Maugerville slippers *noun*
hip waders *CANADA*
Maugerville is a town on the St John River near Fredericton, New Brunswick.
- — Herb Curtis, *Slow Men Working in Trees*, p. 27, 1991

Maui wowie; Maui wauie; Maui wowee; Maui *noun*
a potent marijuana cultivated in Hawaii *US, 1977*
The island of Maui plus **wow** (a thing of wonder).
- When Pattie Mae returned, she put her hand surreptitiously into Philo's coat pocket and said breathlessly: "One's Colombia Gold, the other's Maui wow-ee." — Joseph Wambaugh, *The Black Marble*, p. 145, 1978

- Those familiar with Fat Freddy will know he would be partial to a bit of Hawaiian (Maui Wowie) which is frosty with green, orange and purple flowers. — Mike Rock, *This Book*, 1999
- — Mike Haskins, *Drugs*, p. 288, 2003

Maui-zowie *noun*

a strain of marijuana *UK, 1970s*

A variation of MAUI WOWIE.

- [A] couple of Thinnies of Mauie-zowie sinsemilla dope[.] — Stuart Browne, *Dangerous Parking*, p. 84, 2000

mauler *noun*

a set of brass knuckles *US*

- "Get rid of the knucks," I said, watching his eyes. He looked surprisingly down at his hand. He slipped the mauler off and threw it casually in the corner. — Raymond Chandler, *The Long Goodbye*, p. 126, 1953

maulsprigging *noun*

a beating *BARBADOS*

- — Frank A. Collymore, *Barbadian Dialect*, p. 72, 1965

Mau-Mau *noun*

a black person who uses the fact that he is black to get his way with guilty white people *US*

- "Your life has been too easy for you to be making it as a jazz musician." "And too white," Mary muttered. "Miss Mau Mau." Hitchcock grinned at her. — Nat Hentoff, *Jazz Country*, p. 17, 1965
- The days of the poverty Mau-Mau were finished. No more blacks intimidating the white men with their African garb and Dark Continent souls. — Donald Goines, *Kenyatta's Last Hit*, p. 6–7, 1975

mau-mau *verb*

to bully, especially using confrontational political arguments that play on racial guilt *US*

Coined as a verb by Tom Wolfe based on the name of a secret society organised to expel European settlers from Kenya.

- Going downtown to mau-mau the bureaucrats got to be the routine practice in San Francisco. — Tom Wolfe, *Radical Chic & Mau-Mauing the Flak Catchers*, p. 97, 1970
- Yeah, yeah it could work if Cynthia wrote the kind of proposal they needed, an airtight, fantastic piece of bureaucratic bullshit ... mau-maued into place by the right kind of militant niggerism. — Odie Hawkins, *The Busting Out of an Ordinary Man*, p. 153, 1985

mauve *noun*

a person who appears to be homosexual *UK*

- [S]he's mauve! — Paul Baker, *Polari*, p. 180, 2002

mauzy *adjective*

in Newfoundland, a foggy, misty day with a gentle ocean breeze *CANADA*

- The Caplin Scull is not just a phenomenon of nature, but also a period of the year, and even a period of the year, and even a special kind of weather – "mauzy," with high humidity, frequent fogs and drizzles, easterly winds. — Harold Horwood, *Newfoundland*, p. 166, 1969

maverick *noun*

a stolen or 'reappropriated' military vehicle *US*

From the western US sense of the word as 'stolen cattle'.

- — Gregory Clark, *Words of the Vietnam War*, p. 317, 1990

mavis *noun*

a male homosexual *SOUTH AFRICA*

Gay slang, formed on the name Mavis and originating among Cape coloureds.

- — Bart Luirink (translated by Loes Nas), *Moffies*, p. 118, 2000

Mavis Fritter *noun*

the anus *UK*

Rhyming slang.

- If I ask you nicely will you take it up the Mavis? — Bodmin Dark, *Dirty Cockney Rhyming Slang*, 2003

maw *noun*

a mother *US, 1826*

- That's me away, Maw. — Ian Pattison, *Rab C. Nesbitt*, 1988

MAW *noun*

an attractive woman who is highly visible at fashionable events *UK*

An acronym of '*m*odel, *a*ctress, *w*hatever', approximately how they describe themselves, punning on 'maw' (the vagina) which is an alternative point of view.

- MAWs look good and go to all the right parties, from Clerkenwell to Los Angeles, but tend not to ask themselves too many of the profound questions of life. — David Rowan, *A Glossary for the 90s*, p. 7, 1998

mawkit *adjective*

▷ see: MOCKIT

max *noun*

1 maximum; a maximum *US, 1851*

- I laid up there in the cell, telling myself, even if I can get this cut down to a lesser charge and stand a better chance of getting a lower max, I still end up doing that max[.] — Herbert Huncke, *Guilty of Everything*, p. 115, 1990
- A year – max – that's all I could do. — Danny King, *The Burglar Diaries*, p. 243, 2001

2 a maximum security prison *US, 1961*

- San Quentin, although it was a prison, wasn't a max, though they had other ways of dealing with screw-ups. — Ralph "Sonny" Barger, *Hell's Angel*, p. 193, 2000

▸ **to the max**

as far as possible, to the limit *US, 1971*

- — Bobby Seale, *A Lonely Rage*, 1978
- I left that scene and returned to my room, uptight to the max! — Bobby Seale, *A Lonely Rage*, p. 121, 1978
- — *Maledicta*, p. 268, Summer/Winter 1981: 'By its slang, ye shall know it: the pessimism of prison life'
- — Connie Eble (Editor), *UNC-CH Campus Slang*, p. 4, Spring 1983
- That's what Marshall had, class. He demonstrated it to the max, on at least one romantic occasion. — Odie Hawkins, *Men Friends*, p. 75, 1989
- My imagination's taxed to the max. — Joseph Wambaugh, *Fugitive Nights*, p. 255, 1992
- This guy is like an angel to them and supports me to the max, with money and all that business. — Donald Gorgon, *Cop Killer*, p. 89, 1994
- I've got a connection to the equipment and the mail order distribution, not to mention those kids I got out there who are hot-fuck-action to the max. — *Boogie Nights*, 1997
- Then after years of doing all sorts of art courses, I got into graffiti, which pissed them off to the max. — *X-Ray*, p. 72, May 2003

max *verb*

to wear *UK*

- But check out his footwear and, chances are, he won't be maxing a pair of fly Nike sneaks. — Patrick Neate, *Where You're At*, p. 112, 2003

max *adjective*

maximum security *US, 1976*

- I knew if we didn't make it Snoopy and I'd get sent here or some other max joint. — Elmore Leonard, *Out of Sight*, p. 58, 1996
- During the 1980s, when the authorities went after the Aryan Brotherhood in earnest and slammed validated AB membes in Pelican Bay and other max lock-up prisons, the NLR filled the void[.] — Bill Valentine, *Gangs and Their Tattoos*, p. 9, 2000

max and relax *verb*

to take things easy, to take leisure with pleasure *US*

- Yes, Clifton was feeling on top of the world, just maxin' and relaxin', feeling copasetic. — Karline Smith, *Moss Side Massive*, p. 188, 1994

max BBs *noun*

a tactic in aerial combat of using the highest rate of fire and filling the air with rounds *US*

- The higher rate of fire was for air-to-air fighting where filling a block of sky with "max BBs" was the way to go. — Gerry Carroll, *North S*A*R*, p. 50, 1991

maxed to the onions *adjective*

extremely large *US*

US military usage during the Vietnam war.

- — *Maledicta*, p. 259, Summer/Winter 1982: 'Viet-speak'

Max Factor *noun*

an actor *UK*

Rhyming slang, formed from the name of a cosmetics company.

- — Ray Puxley, *Cockney Rabbit*, 1992

maximum brilliant *adjective*

extremely good *US*

- — Mimi Pond, *The Valley Girl's Guide to Life*, p. 60, 1982

maxi taxi; maxi *noun*

a van used as a taxi *TRINIDAD AND TOBAGO, 1979*

- — Lise Winer, *Dictionary of the English/Creole of Trinidad & Tobago*, 2003

Max Miller *noun*

a pillow *UK*

Rhyming slang, formed from the name of one of the greats of British stand-up comedy, 1895–1963.

- —Ray Puxley, *Cockney Rabbit*, 1992

max out; max *verb*

1 to reach a limit *US, 1977*

- Mommie's Trust Fund was about to max out[.]—Dan Jenkins, *Life Its Ownself*, p. 124, 1984
- "Well max out with the fifty-buck-a-nighters," Lynn suggested. —Joseph Wambaugh, *Fugitive Nights*, p. 128, 1992
- Our credit cards are maxed.—*Traffic*, 2000

2 to complete a maximum prison sentence *US, 1972*

- —John R. Armore and Joseph D. Wolfe, *Dictionary of Desperation*, 1976
- —Ralph de Sola, *Crime Dictionary*, p. 90, 1982

3 to relax *US*

- —Bradley Elfman, *Breakdancing*, p. 41, 1984

Max Walls; maxies *noun*

the testicles *UK*

Rhyming slang, extended from the name of Max Wall (1908–90), a great British comedian.

- —Ray Puxley, *Cockney Rabbit*, 1992

Maxwell House *noun*

a mouse *UK*

Rhyming slang, formed on an instant-coffee brand.

- —Ray Puxley, *Cockney Rabbit*, 1992

may all your consequences by happy ones

used as a humorous farewell *US*

A catchphrase television sign-off on *Truth or Consequences* (1950–1987), a game show. Repeated with referential humour.

Mayflower *noun*

a Plymouth car *US*

- The term derives from the small replica of the Mayflower once used as a trade mark by Plymouth.—John Lawlor, *How to Talk Car*, p. 72, 1965

Mayne Nickless job *noun*

in horse racing, an extremely large bet *AUSTRALIA*

The amount bet is so staggering that it must have been stolen from a payroll van of Mayne Nickless, Australia's largest corporate provider of health care.

- —Ned Wallish, *The Truth Dictionary of Racing Slang*, p. 51, 1989

mayo *noun*

1 cocaine, heroin, morphine *US*

- —Vincent J. Monteleone, *Criminal Slang*, p. 153, 1949
- —Richard A. Spears, *The Slang and Jargon of Drugs and Drink*, p. 333, 1986
- —Mike Haskins, *Drugs*, p. 280, 2003

2 mayonnaise *US, 1960*

- #8 Whopper, Hold the Mayo[.]—Michael Moore, *Dude, Where's My Country?*, p. 76, 2003

Mayor Hunna; Mayor John *noun*

marijuana *US*

- —Collin Baker et al., *College Undergraduate Slang Study Conducted at Brown University*, p. 156, 1968

maypop *noun*

in the used car business, a tyre that is not guaranteed *US*

Because it may pop at any moment.

- —Connie Eble (Editor), *UNC-CH Campus Slang*, p. 4, Spring 1980
- —Lewis Poteet, *Car & Motorcyle Slang*, p. 127, 1992

May snow *noun*

on Prince Edward Island, a late spring snow, supposed to help cure blindness and sore feet *CANADA*

- Water from a snow in May is a good healer. You could soak your feet in it. It's good for sore eyes.—T. K. Pratt, *oral citations in Dictionary of Prince Edward Island English*, p. 96, 1988

maytag *noun*

a weak prisoner, especially one who does laundry for others as a sign of submission *US*

- —Carsten Stroud, *Close Pursuit*, p. 273, 1987
- —Gary K. Farlow, *Prison-ese*, 2002

may you live in interesting times

used as a curse *US*

Generally jocular. In a speech given in South Africa in 1966, US President John F. Kennedy introduced this allegedly ancient Chinese curse to the world.

- Once, an old Buddhist monk had come up to him while his platoon was digging and said to him, "May you live in interesting times." Young Lieutenant Landry had taken it as a blessing of some sort[.] —Nelson Demille, *Spencerville*, p. 100, 1998

Mazatlans *noun*

beach sandals made with tyre treads for soles *US*

- —Duke Kahanamoku with Joe Brennan, *Duke Kahanamoku's World of Surfing*, p. 174, 1965

mazawatee *adjective*

crazy, foolish *UK*

Rhyming slang for **POTTY**, formed from Mazawatee Tea, an old brand name for tea, perhaps also punning on '(tea)pot'.

- —Ray Puxley, *Cockney Rabbit*, 1992

Mazola party *noun*

group sex, enhanced by the application of vegetable oil to the participants' bodies *US, 1968*

An allusion and tribute to Mazola Corn Oil™.

- —Eugene Landy, *The Underground Dictionary*, p. 129, 1971

mazoola *noun*

money *US, 1951*

- All that mazoola, he kin be jes's dum's dum kin be!—Robert Gover, *One Hundred Dollar Misunderstanding*, p. 23, 1961

mazuma *noun*

1 money *US, 1901*

From Hebrew to Yiddish to English.

- You've brought in a lot of mazuma.—Mickey Spillane, *One Lonely Night*, p. 74, 1951
- A tasteful commercial emblazoned across each English breast and thigh would bring much-needed mazuma into the game.—Andrew Nickolds, *Back to Basics*, p. 140, 1994

2 a female professor *US*

- —Marcus Hanna Boulware, *Jive and Slang of Students in Negro Colleges*, 1947

MB *verb*

to return a carnival customer's money *US*

From '*m*oney *b*ack'.

- —Gene Sorrows, *All About Carnivals*, p. 22, 1985: 'Terminology'

MBNWA *noun*

the extensive use of e-mail to keep in touch with subordinates in business *CANADA*

Initialism for '*m*anagement *b*y *n*ot *w*alking *a*round'.

- They questioned the need for the person in the next cubicle or the manager down the hall to communicate by email. "Some respondents called this MBNWA – management by not walking around – or cited a laziness in not wishing to use other ways of [contact]". —*Toronto Globe and Mail*, p. B3, 26th June 2002

MC; emcee *noun*

1 a master of ceremonies *US, 1790*

- An M.C. is trying to warm us up with bad jokes.—Gore Vidal, *Myra Breckinridge*, p. 122, 1968
- The emcee had a voice that could take the paint off your car.—Carl Hiaasen, *Tourist Season*, p. 150, 1986
- SUZY SONG: And then the powow emcee called for a ladies' choice dance.—*Smoke Signals*, 1998

2 a rap artist *US*

Acronym of '*m*icrophone *c*ontroller'.

- [R]appers like MC Hammer and MC Lyte.—Simon Warner, *Rockspeak!*, p. 289, 1996
- My first album is a combination of eveything I went through during my first couple of years as a frustrated emcee.—Eminem (Marshall Mathers), *Angry Blonde*, p. 3, 2000

MC; emcee *verb*

1 to serve as a master of ceremonies *US, 1937*

- The owner asked my mother to m.c. She was petrified.—Lenny Bruce, *How to Talk Dirty and Influence People*, p. 28, 1965
- I'll close the room and serve them booze, and you and I will emcee, encouraging the people to talk.—Mort Sahl, *Heartland*, p. 56–57, 1976

2 the performance of rap *US*

- The only thing that is not a joke is the passion I have for emceeing. —Eminem (Marshall Mathers), *Angry Blond*, p. 3, 2000

Mc- *prefix*

used in combination with the noun that follows for expressing a cheap, mass-produced product *US, 1984*

From the McDonald's™ hamburger chain.

- McPaper – quickly or poorly written paper. —Connie Eble (Editor), *UNC-CH Campus Slang*, p. 6, Spring 1991

McCoy *noun*

▷ **see:** REAL MCCOY

McFired *adjective*

fired from a low-skill, low-wage menial job *US*

- —Connie Eble (Editor), *UNC-CH Campus Slang*, p. 6, November 2003

McFly *noun*

used as a term of address to someone who does not think often or well *US*

From a character in the *Back to the Future* films.

- —Pamela Munro, *U.C.L.A. Slang*, p. 58, 1989

McGimper *noun*

a pimp *US*

- —Vincent J. Monteleone, *Criminal Slang*, p. 161, 1949

McJob *noun*

a temporary job; a job with little or no future prospects *US*

Characterised as the sort of work available at McDonald's™, the multinational fast-food brand. A term coined and trademark-registered by McDonald's itself in 1983 as a positive expression of an affirmative hiring programme aimed at those with disabilities; by the late 1980s a derisive term for the low-skill, low-wage jobs that were proliferating in the US during the presidency of Ronald Reagan.

- Otherwise the week has been normal, with myself and Claire slogging away at our McJobs – me tending bar at Larry's and maintaining the bungalows (I get reduced rent in return for minor caretaking) and Claire peddling five-thousand-dollar purses to old bags. —Douglas Coupland, *Generation X*, p. 67, 1991
- A job at McDonald's would be a McJob. —Jack Chambers (Editor), *Slang Bag 93 (University of Toronto)*, p. 4, Winter 1993
- [T]o capture how the organizational principles of McDonald's chain of fast-food restaurants, with its emphasis on ruthless efficiency, quantification, predictability, control, and deskilled jobs (often described as "McJobs") is providing an icon for organization through our society. —Gareth Morgan, *Images of Organization*, p. 24, 1997
- —Harry Orsman, *A Dictionary of Modern New Zealand Slang*, p. 86, 1999
- Bunch of kids with crap McJobs getting ready for the big night out. —John Williams, *Cardiff Dead*, p. 188, 2000
- Beyond her role as a slayer, she is forced to leave college and to get a horrible "McJob"in order to provide for Dawn after their mother Joyce dies. —James B. South, *Buffy the Vampire Slayer and Philosophy*, p. 152, 2003
- "McJob" has become a common epithet for work without much redeeming value. —Alissa Quart, *Branded*, p. 15, 2003

McJobber *noun*

a person in temporary employment or employment with little or no prospects *UK*

After MCJOB.

- [C]omputer-controlled by a spotty McJobber[.] —Iain Aitch, *A Fête Worse Than Death*, p. 166, 2003

McLean lane *noun*

in trucking, the right hand or slow lane on a motorway *US*

- —"Slingo", *The Official CB Slang Dictionary Handbook*, p. 40, 1976
- McCleans Trucking Company supposedly have a slow fleet of trucks and rarely in the passing lane, therefore, the driving lane became in trucker lingo "The McCleans Lane." —Gwyneth A. "Dandalion" Seese, *Tijuana Bear in a Smoke 'Um Up Taxi*, p. 16, 1977

McMudhole *nickname*

McMurdo Station, Antarctica *ANTARCTICA*

- —*Cool Antarctica*, 2003: 'Antarctic slang'

McNamara Special *noun*

a transport plane specially equipped for flying dignitaries to Vietnam during the war *US*

- It occurred that same October of 1966 aboard a "McNamara Special" bound for Saigon, one of those windowless KC-135 jet tankers that the Air Force had fitted out for long-distance VIP travel and that the secretary used on his frequent shuttles. —Neil Sheehan, *A Bright Shining Lie*, p. 681, 1988

McNamara's War *noun*

the Vietnam war *US*

Robert Strange McNamara was US Secretary of Defense from 1961 until 1967, much of the Vietnam war.

- Pederson came to call it "MacNamara's War." Many of them did. —Robert K. Wilcox, *Scream of Eagles*, p. 93, 1990

MCP *noun*

a *m*ale *c*hauvinist *p*ig *UK, 1971*

In common usage by those involved in the cause of women's liberation.

McPaper *noun*

a poorly researched, poorly thought out, and poorly written term paper or essay *US*

From McDonald's™, the ubiquitous purveyor of fast-food.

- —Connie Eble (Editor), *UNC-CH Campus Slang*, p. 6, Spring 1991

McPhillips Street Station *nickname*

the intersection of McPhillips Street (Winnipeg) and the Canadian Pacific Railway main line *CANADA*

- There never was a McPhillips Street Station, but at the crossing, men riding the freights back home hopped on the trains. If you ever hear anyone speaking of boarding at the Mcphilips Street Station you know that he was "riding the rails." —Chris Thain, *Cold as a Bay Street Banker's Heart*, p. 101, 1987

McShit *noun*

▸ **go for a McShit**

to use a fast-food outlet's toilet facilities without purchasing from the restaurant's menu *NEW ZEALAND*

Based on McDonalds™ but available at Burger King™, etc.

- If challenged by a pimply staff member, your declaration to them that you'll buy their food afterwards is a McShit with Lies. —*unknown source quoted in private correspondence*, 13th March 2002

McTheatre *noun*

a derisory categorisation of heavily marketed, big-budget, low-brow musical theatre *US, 1996*

- [Tom Stoppard] a leading playwright in England, one of the most popular and frequently produced writer there, (perhaps, with the exception of Sir Andrew Lloyd Webber, the high priest of McTheatre, the most popular). —Ian Johnston, *Lecture on Stoppard, Rosencrantz and Guildenstern Are Dead*, 10th April 1997

MD *noun*

1 Dr. Pepper™ soda *US*

- —*American Speech*, p. 63, February 1967: 'Soda-fountain, restaurant and tavern calls'

2 a managing director *UK, 1963*

Only when spoken as 'em dee'.

MDA *noun*

a synthetic hallucinogen (methylenedioxy-amphetamine) that also contains a central nervous system stimulant *US*

Used as a technical term in the late 1950s, in a slang sense later when the drug became popular, largely with gays.

- "Is my MDA still in your stash box?" "Yeah, Christ, you don't need that for a movie!" —Armistead Maupin, *Tales of the City*, p. 110, 1978

MDB *noun*

a hospital patient with an appalling lack of hygiene *US*

A '*m*ega *d*irt*b*all'.

- —*Maledicta*, p. 33, 1988–1989: 'Medical maledicta from San Francisco'

MDO *noun*

a day missed at work due to a feigned illness *NEW ZEALAND*

An abbreviation of '*M*aori *d*ay *o*ff'.

- —David McGill, *David McGill's Complete Kiwi Slang Dictionary*, p. 72, 1998

me *adjective*

my *UK*

- Get out of me kitchin making a mess of me ironing or by the livin' God I'll skin yer. —Norman Lindsay, *Halfway to Anywhere*, p. 64, 1947
- So I'm sitting there with me Campari talking to the morning staff. —Ted Lewis, *Jack Carter's Law*, p. 156, 1974
- Me missus threw me out of the flat. —Robert G. Barrett, *Davo's Little Something*, p. 48, 1992
- She usually blames it on me sister. —Sara McNamee, *Cool Places*, p. 198, 1998
- Me mum told me not to marry him. And me dad as well. —Claire Mansfield and John Mendelssohn, *Dominatrix*, p. 269, 2002

meal *noun*

a socially inept person *US*

Youth usage.

- —*Time*, 3rd October 1949

meal-a-mat *noun*
a vending machine dispensing food *US*
- —Ramon Adams, *The Language of the Railroader*, p. 99, 1977

meals rejected by Ethiopians; meals refused by Ethiopians *noun*
military MREs (meals ready to eat) *US*
- The Army now calls them MRSs: Meals-Ready-to-Eat. The soldiers call them Meals-Rejected-by-Ethiopians. —*Washington Post*, p. A3, 20th December 1988
- Reservist Carolyn Bowman tells me that the miserable packaged chow officially known as MRE (Meals, Ready to Eat) is translated by the troops as "Meals, Refused by Ethiopians." —*San Francisco Chronicle*, p. B1, 21st September 1990
- —Judi Sanders, *Don't Dog by Do, Dude!*, p. 21, 1991
- "Desert cherries" in "Kevlars" fly the "Sand Box Express" to the "beach" and soon are complaining about "Meals Rejected by Ethiopians" if they can't find a "roach coach" run by "Bedouin Bob." —*Houston Chronicle*, p. 15, 24th January 1991
- —Tom Kelly, *The Retired Officer Magazine*, p. 39, January 1993

meal ticket *noun*
a source of support, especially a person *US, 1899*
- Meal ticket – A sponsor, not quite a john or sugar daddy. —*The Guild Dictionary of Homosexual Terms*, p. 30, 1965
- Patricia don't mean nothing to me excepting a meal ticket to help me and her get out of the life. —Sara Harris, *The Lords of Hell*, p. 54, 1967
- Hip was very careful not to punch her in the face. He didn't want his meal ticket threatened. —Nathan Heard, *Howard Street*, p. 145, 1968
- I'm willing to be your wife. You want a meal ticket, get your ass someplace else. —George V. Higgins, *The Judgment of Deke Hunter*, p. 18, 1976
- All they want is a meal ticket. Give me, take me, bring me, and what have you done for me lately. Period. —Edwin Torres, *After Hours*, p. 346, 1979
- What're things coming to when pimps push their meal tickets off roofs? —Joseph Wambaugh, *The Delta Star*, p. 27, 1983
- Got an address on Amanda Hunsecker's meal ticket. —*Lethal Weapon*, 1987
- She could erase Dillinger's record if she tried. I hear she's Keaton's meal ticket. —*The Usual Suspects*, 1995

mealymouth *noun*
a person who speaks insincerely or with a complete lack of conviction *UK, 1600*
- "Oh, get going, mealymouth," she snarled. —Max Shulman, *The Zebra Derby*, p. 108, 1946

mean *adjective*
excellent *US, 1919*
- The message to "Squaresville" (where nobody exact possibly adults live) is that Frankie [Avalon] is "real mean, man" (very good). —*Look*, p. 49, 24th November 1959
- —Robert George Reisner, *The Jazz Titans*, p. 161, 1960
- —*Time*, p. 56, 1st January 1965: 'Students: The slang bag'
- "How do you lack my crib, man?" "It's mean, Bart." —Charles W. Moore, *A Brick for Mister Jones*, p. 112, 1975

▸ **so mean he wouldn't pay a dime to see the Statue of Liberty piss**
very stingy *CANADA, 1988*
- Another was so mean he wouldn't pay a dime to see the Statue of Liberty piss. —Harry Bruce, p. 108, 1988

▸ **so mean he wouldn't shit away from home**
used for expressing a high degree of stinginess and bad temper *CANADA, 1988*
- A third–my nomination as the heavyweight champion of meanness–was so mean he wouldn't shit away from home. —Harry Bruce, *Down Home*, p. 108, 1988

mean *adverb*
very *US*
- —Ethan Hilderbrant, *Prison Slang*, 1998

mean as black cat shit *adjective*
used for expressing a high degree of stinginess *CANADA, 1988*
- As easily as if he were offering another shot of rum, he said one fellow was as mean as black cat shit. —Harry Bruce, *Down Home*, p. 108, 1988

me and the devil, pretty soon just the devil
in poker, said when all players but two have withdrawn from a hand *US*
- —*American Speech*, p. 100, May 1951

me and you *noun*
1 a menu *UK, 1932*
Rhyming slang, or merely a play on words.
- —Ray Puxley, *Fresh Rabbit*, 1998

2 in Bingo, the number two *UK*
Rhyming slang.
- —Ray Puxley, *Fresh Rabbit*, 1998

meanest *adjective*
best, fastest *US*
- —Miss Cone, *The Slang Dictionary (Hawthorne High School)*, 1965

mean green *noun*
phencyclidine, the recreational drug known as PCP or angel dust *US*
The 'green' is from the parsley or mint on which the drug is at times sprinkled; the 'mean' is reduplicative yet accurately describes the behaviour of most users.
- —Ronald Linder, *PCP*, p. 9, 1981

meanie *noun*
copelandia cyancens or *panaeolus cyanescens*: a mushroom with potent psychactive properties *UK*
A shortening of 'blue meanie'.
- Tarzan pulled out a money bag filled with Meanies and poured them into the kettle. —Wayne Anthony, *Spanish Highs*, p. 72, 1999

meanies *noun*
the police or other authorities of enforcement; specifically those opposed to citizens' band radio *US*
Abbreviated from 'blue meanies'.
- —Peter Chippindale, *The British CB Book*, p. 156, 1981

mean mugging *noun*
hateful glances *US*
- Jackson was 17 when he and three friends were shot on March 4 in what police said then was a case of "mean mugging" – a slang term for hard stares. —*Alameda (California) Times-Star*, 1st January 2004

mean out *adjective*
good; bad *US*
Hawaiian youth usage.
- —Douglas Simonson, *Pidgin to da Max Hana Hou*, 1982

mean reds *noun*
the bleed period of the menstrual cycle *US*
- [T]he mean reds. —*Breakfast at Tiffanys*, 1961
- —*The Museum of Menstruation and Women's Health*, March 2001

meanwhile, back at the ranch
used as a humorous indication that a story is about to change to another thread *US, 1956*
From a clichéd device used in cowboy films.
- "Meanwhile, back at the ranch," said Axel. Snickering. Meanwhile, I said, back at the ranch, generally speaking, things were prosperous[.] —Clancy Sigal, *Going Away*, p. 247, 1961

meany *noun*
an exceedingly mean person *UK, 1927*
The Beatles, in the cartoon film *The Yellow Submarine*, 1968, popularised the term 'the blue meanies' as an intensification for those that cast a blight on joyfulness.
- Meany. What do you want to do, fuck? —Elmore Leonard, *Switch*, p. 113, 1978

me an' you *noun*
in Bingo (also House and Tombola), the number two *UK*
- —Peter Wright, *Cockney Dialect & Slang*, p. 109, 1981

measle sheet *noun*
a military map with a large number of small circled numbers indicating checkpoints *US, 1966*
- —Carl Fleischhauer, *A Glossary of Army Slang*, p. 33, 1968

measly *adjective*
contemptible, of little value, petty *UK, 1864*
- This town needs this measly one-horse institution[.] —*It's a Wonderful Life*, 1946
- Public Enemy's Flavor Flav, who was busted with a measly kilo of hash tucked inside his jacket while riding a bicycle. —*Drugs An Adult Guide*, p. 41, December 2001

meat *noun*
1 the penis *UK, 1595*
- —Donald Webster Cory and John P. LeRoy, *The Homosexual and His Society*, p. 265, 1963: 'A lexicon of homosexual slang'
- I think a man has gotta be a bit large in the meat department to get that wash board effect. —A.S. Jackson, *Gentleman Pimp*, p. 109, 1973

- Ron Jeremy is sucked off before ramming his meat into Patti Petite in Blonde on the Run. — *Adult Video*, p. 15, August/September 1986
- Ultimately, though, it's not the meat, but the motion. — Anka Radakovich, *The Wild Girls Club*, p. 12, 1994

2 the vagina *US*

- — Ruth Todasco et al., *The Intelligent Woman's Guide to Dirty Words*, p. 25, 1973

3 the human body *US, 1834*

- You never played the Horseshoe in McKessport, or Christy's Four-a-day in Minneapolis where the ofay strippers threw their meat right over your head[.] — John Clellon Holmes, *The Horn*, p. 28, 1958

4 a corpse *US*

- — Vincent J. Monteleone, *Criminal Slang*, p. 154, 1949

5 in a hospital, tissue taken for a biopsy *US*

- As in the saying "No meat, no treat," meaning, if you don't know the pathology with a biopsy, you won't know what treatment to go ahead with. — Sally Williams, *"Strong" Words*, p. 150, 1994

6 in motor racing, a large racing tyre *US*

- — John Edwards, *Auto Dictionary*, p. 105, 1993

7 in hot rodding, structural metal in the engine block *US*

- When overboring, it's important not to cut too deeply into the meat. — John Lawlor, *How to Talk Car*, p. 72, 1965

8 a musical instrument's sound before any electronic alteration *UK*

- — Tom Hibbert, *Rockspeak!*, p. 101, 1983

▸ be on a meat-free diet
to be a lesbian *UK*
A euphemism formed on **MEAT** (the penis).

- "She's on a meat free diet, that one," she said. I told Gladys I didn't understand why the caretaker's vegetarianism was worthy of a mention. "No, she's a lesbian," said Gladys. — Kitty Churchill, *Thinking of England*, p. 211, 1995

▸ the meat
athletes; in the entertainment industry, the actors, the performers *US, 1967*

- [A]s the TV presenter, Wilson chose to remain the talent, "the meat" as Americans call it. — Tony Wilson, *24 Hour Party People*, p. 212, 2002

meat and two veg; meat *noun*
used for Reg, a diminutive of the name Reginald *UK*
Rhyming slang; an apparently teasing application of the non-rhyming sense as 'the male genitals'.

- — Ray Puxley, *Cockney Rabbit*, 1992

meat ax *noun*
in television and film making, a rod used on scaffolding to hold light screens *US*

- — Ralph S. Singleton, *Filmaker's Dictionary*, p. 103, 1990

▸ as a meat axe
as hell *AUSTRALIA*

- She was dead, deader than a meat-axe, and it looked like a meat-axe had been used to do her in. — Jon Cleary, *The Long Shadow*, p. 51, 1949
- She was, however, brandishing her horsewhip and looking as mean as a meat-axe. — Lance Peters, *The Dirty Half-Mile*, p. 337, 1979

meatball *noun*

1 a dim-witted, gullible person *US, 1939*

- Well, anyhow, Grady Metcalf, who is one of the really big meatballs of our generation and I hate him like poison, he took me out riding on his motorcyle, and you know what? All of a sudden, he didn't seem like such a meatball! — Max Shulman, *Rally Round the Flag, Boys!*, p. 168, 1957
- And Tony Parisi is nothing but a New York tenement house meatball who made good. — Gerald Petievich, *Shakedown*, p. 63, 1988

2 a false or petty criminal charge *US, 1944*

- That's a meatball rap, you'll get out tomorrow. — Hal Ellson, *The Golden Spike*, p. 240, 1952
- [E]ven Jackson Prison was used to lock-up for all the niggers the police were arresting on a lot of bullshit, meatball charges. — A.S. Jackson, *Gentleman Pimp*, p. 9, 1973
- You guys picked me up on a meatball. I ain't robbed nobody, so you ain't got no case on me. — Donald Goines, *Crime Partners*, p. 103, 1978

3 a coloured light that serves as a visual aid in an optical landing system for an aeroplane landing on an aircraft carrier *US, 1957*

- He had to see the meatball, the yellow light between the two green reference, or datum, lights of the optical landing system. — Stephen Coonts, *Final Flight*, p. 99, 1988
- [H]e could start to discern the "meatball" – a mirrored device reflecting a grapefruit-sized orange light, flanked on either side by a line of smaller green lights. — Robert Wilcox, *Scream of Eagles*, p. 35, 1990
- (Royal Canadian Navy, 1950s to 1969). Finally I broke free of the cloud layer; then all I had to do was fly the meatball down onto the deck. — Oral citation from Tom Langeste, *Words on the Wing*, 1995

4 in horse racing, a combination of cathartics administered to a horse *US*

- — David W. Maurer, *Argot of the Racetrack*, p. 12, 1951

meat book *noun*
at a college or university, a book with the names and photographs of all incoming students *US*

- — *DePauw University Campus Corner*, 29th January 1996: 'Slang terms at DePauw'

meat box *noun*
a prison service van for transporting prisoners *UK*

- — Angela Devlin, *Prison Patter*, p. 76, 1996

meat curtains *noun*
the vagina *UK*

- However, the category edibility glosses over the variablity within it, which, for FGTs [female genital terms] included frequent reference to meat (e.g., bacon rashers, kebab, meat curtains); fish/seafood (e.g., tuna waterfall; fish, clam); and "sweet tidbits" (e.g. love muffin, fudge, cake-hole). — *Journal of Sex Research, Vol. 38, Issue 2*, p. 146, 2001

meat cutter *noun*
a surgeon *US*

- — *Maledicta*, p. 57, Summer 1980: 'Not sticks and stones, but names: more medical pejoratives'

meat district *noun*
an area where sex is available *US*

- Down Forty-Second Street, through the meat district. — Jay McInerney, *Bright Lights, Big City*, p. 13, 1984

meat drapes *noun*
the condition that exists when a tight-fitting pair of trousers, shorts, bathing suit or other garment forms a wedge between a woman's labia, accentuating their shape *US*

meat eater *noun*
a corrupt police officer who aggressively seeks out bribes and other personal advantages *US, 1972*

- — Angela Devlin, *Prison Patter*, p. 76, 1996

meat factory *noun*
a college or university that recruits athletes solely for their athletic ability and without any real expectation that they will graduate *US*

- — Bill Shefski, *Running Press Glossary of Football Language*, p. 68, 1978

meat fleet *noun*
a military hospital ship *US*
Gulf war usage.

- — *American Speech*, p. 394, Winter 1991: 'Among the new words'

meat hangers *noun*
a pair of men's close-fitting and revealing nylon swimming trunks *AUSTRALIA*

- Hey look, that dag's wearing meat-hangers! — *Wordmap (www.abc.net.au/wordmap)*, 2003

meathead *noun*
a stupid person; hence a general derogative implying stupidity *US, 1928*
No brains between the ears, just meat.

- Those meatheads? They don't know their rear from third base. — Max Shulman, *Guided Tour of Campus Humor*, p. 141, 1955
- When a woman's glands is actin' up and she can't control certain urges – they say she's got hot pants! Same as the meathead there. Hot trousers, hot pants, same thing! — Eugene Boe (Compiler), *The Wit & Wisdom of Archie Bunker*, p. 153, 1971
- Chiodo, and his meathead partners could be in a real jam over an incident tonight that I won't go into. — Charles Whited, *Chiodo*, p. 277, 1973
- I was a real misfit. The place was full of jocks, meat heads. — John Robb, *The Nineties (quoting Kurt Cobain)*, p. 20, 1999
- Meathead. Fucking bully. — Kevin Sampson, *Outlaws*, p. 251, 2001

meat hook *noun*
in electric line work, a handline hook *US*

- — A.B. Chance Co., *Lineman's Slang Dictionary*, p. 12, 1980

meat injection *noun*

the sexual insertion of the erect penis *AUSTRALIA, 1942*

- Compared to masturbation or a meat injection, even a Pommy bath-dodger can seem pretty exotic. — Kathy Lette, *Girls' Night Out*, p. 199, 1987

meat mag *noun*

a homoerotic, often pornographic, magazine *US*

- — *Maledicta*, p. 250, 1979: 'Kinks and queens: linguistic and cultural aspects of the terminology for gays'

meat market *noun*

1 a bar or other public place where people congregate in search of sexual companionship *UK, 1957*

- There they rent homes, given them "gay names" like Dora's Domicile Campy Corner, loll in the sun, and at night frequent a dark corner of the beach known as "the meat market." — Antony James, *America's Homosexual Underground*, p. 30, 1965
- — Connie Eble (Editor), *UNC-CH Campus Slang*, p. 4, Spring 1983

2 a modelling agency *US*

- — Helen Dahlskog (Editor), *A Dictionary of Contemporary and Colloquial Usage*, p. 40, 1972

meat parlor *noun*

an establishment where sex is the most important commodity *US*

- In one meat parlor, they have two massage rooms. — *Screw*, p. 14, 6th October 1969

meat-pie *adjective*

of average quality *AUSTRALIA*

- Tamarama boy is a meat pie champ. He has beaten nothing in his two runs and I doubt if he can even run a place. — Clive Galea, *Slipper*, p. 211, 1988

meat puppet *noun*

1 the penis *UK*

- I landed on the handle of the cart and hurt my meat puppet. — Richard Herring, *Talking Cock*, p. 206, 2003

2 a prostitute *US*

- — Anna Scotti and Paul Young, *Buzzwords*, p. 7, 1997

meat rack *noun*

1 a restaurant, bar or other public place where people gather in search of sexual partners *US, 1962*

- — Donald Webster Cory and John P. LeRoy, *The Homosexual and His Society*, p. 265, 1963: 'A lexicon of homosexual slang'
- Soon, we got up, walked around the west side – toward the "meat rack" – the gay part of the park. — John Rechy, *City of Night*, p. 53, 1963
- Laguna Beach, you might say, is the meat-rack of the faggot surfing set. — Roger Gordon, *Hollywood's Sexual Underground*, p. 155, 1966
- The kid from nowhere who may be wanted everywhere, who leans against the railing in Los Angeles' Pershing Square and displays his masculinity on the well-known "meat rack." — Johnny Shearer, *The Male Hustler*, p. 9, 1966
- Our landlord had explained that the "meat rack" (an outdoor sex-supermarket) was only a block or so away. — *Screw*, p. 17, 31st July 1969
- Walk along that park wall at night. It's a meat rack. — Edwin Torres, *Q & A*, p. 116, 1977
- "Every time I see her she's staggering around in some meat rack on Division STreet, wearing Kevin Butler's jersey." — Hunter S. Thompson, *Generation of Swine*, p. 73, 27 January 1986
- What if the tabloids – or, worse yet, some activist – had discovered the virile young star of said movie wagging wienie at the local meat rack. — Armistead Maupin, *Maybe the Moon*, p. 274, 1992

2 Piccadilly in London's West End, an area where homosexuals and homosexual prostitutes offer their services *UK, 1972*

Like so much meat displayed in a butchers.

- "Did you know," I say at last, "that this part of London is known as the Meat-Rack?" "Nah," replies Jez. — Melanie McGrath, *Hard, Soft & Wet*, p. 54, 1998
- Piccadilly very quiet, the Meat Rack nearly empty. — Jake Arnott, *He Kills Coppers*, p. 53, 2001

3 a gymnasium *US*

- — Elementary Electronics, *Dictionary of CB Lingo*, p. 86, 1976

meat seat *noun*

the vagina *UK*

- Abjection was invoked in various ways: through reference to dirtiness (e.g., front bum, dirt box), uncooked (bloody?) meat (e.g., meat seat, chopped liver), vaginal secretions of all types (e.g., slushing fuck pit, the snail trail), smell (e.g. smelly hole, stench trench), and wounds (e.g., gash, gaping axe wound). — *Journal of Sex Research*, p. 146, 2001

meat shot *noun*

1 a photograph or scene in a pornographic film focusing on a penis *US*

- Despite the relative absence of hard-core action in it – some oral sex and an occasional discreet meat shot – Little Sisters ran into some legal trouble[.] — Kenneth Turan and Stephen E. Zito, *Sinema*, p. 129, 1974
- Take, for example, the obsessively repeated meat shot as one such moment of solution. — Linda Williams, *Hard Core*, p. 93, 1989

2 a bullet wound in a muscle, not involving a bone or organ damage *US*

- It looked like just a meat shot – it wasn't as if he was dead or anything. — Richard Price, *Clockers*, p. 516, 1992

meat show *noun*

a striptease act or other performance featuring naked or near-naked women *US, 1943*

- — Don Wilmeth, *The Language of American Popular Entertainment*, p. 168, 1981

Meat Street *nickname*

West 14th Street, New York *US*

An allusion both to the meatpacking industry in the area and the transvestite prostitutes who work there at night.

- — Jim Crotty, *How to Talk American*, p. 236, 1997

meat wagon *noun*

1 an ambulance *US, 1925*

- — Lou Shelly, *Hepcats Jive Talk Dictionary*, p. 47, 1945
- — Peter Chippindale, *The British CB Book*, p. 156, 1981
- And a few minutes later, the ambulance, popularly called "the meat wagon." — Odie Hawkins, *Amazing Grace*, p. 22, 1993

2 a coroner's ambulance *US, 1942*

- I saw a cluster of people on the sidewalk at the front door. There was a city meat wagon on the street. — Iceberg Slim (Robert Beck), *Airtight Willie and Me*, p. 60, 1979
- The squad-car guys didn't know for sure he's dead, so they call EMS. EMS comes, they take one look, call the meat wagon. — Elmore Leonard, *City Primeval*, p. 30, 1980
- By the time I gave it to the meat wagon, the ants had bought it. — Joseph Wambaugh, *Finnegan's Week*, p. 133, 1993
- A shitload of Hollywood division black-and-whites showed up, and the meat wagon removed Miller Treadwell and Special Agent Norris Stensland, D.O.A. — James Ellroy, *Hollywood Nocturnes*, p. 191, 1994

3 medical evacuation equipment, especially a helicopter *US*

- — Linda Reinberg, *In the Field*, p. 137, 1991

4 a prison-service or police vehicle used for confining and transporting prisoners *UK, 1954*

- So when we got swaged [swag] into the meatwagon I asked another geezer the strength of him — Frank Norman, *Bang To Rights*, p. 8, 1958
- — Angela Devlin, *Prison Patter*, p. 76, 1996
- [T]he police arrive, driving their meatwagons on to the green in the middle of the fighting. — Martin King and Martin Knight, *The Naughty Nineties*, p. 109, 1999

meat whistle *noun*

the penis *US, 1965*

- "What're you going to do on the variety show," Red wanted to know. "Perform on the meat whistle?" — Malcolm Braly, *On the Yard*, p. 81, 1967
- "It's not a world sensation," insisted the Everton midfielder [Thomas Gravesen] after he was pictured dangling his meat whistle over the head of Denmark team-mate Claus Jensen. — *Loaded*, p. 30, June 2003

meat with two vegetables; meat and two veg *noun*

the penis and testicles *US*

- — Roger Blake, *The American Dictionary of Sexual Terms*, p. 131, 1964
- — Dale Gordon, *The Dominion Sex Dictionary*, p. 106, 1967
- One storey down / Is the maestro James Brown / Displaying his meat and two veg. — *I'm Sorry I Haven't a Clue, the Official Limerick Collection*, 1998
- — Paul Baker, *Polari*, p. 180, 2002

meaty *adjective*

(used of a wave) powerful *US*

- — Trevor Cralle, *The Surfin'ary*, p. 74, 1991

mebbe *adverb*

maybe *UK, 1825*

From North Country dialect.

- Mebbe I am. Depends, dunnit? — Anthony Masters, *Minder*, p. 70, 1984

mech *noun*

a mechanic *UK, 1918*

mechanic *noun*

1 in the underworld, a specialist for hire *US, 1949*
- "What I mean is I was doing him in a very different way than he said Shelley Orchid was asking about doing you." "I understood you the first time. What's this mechanic's name?" — Robert Campbell, *Boneyards*, p. 249, 1992

2 a hired killer *US*
- — James Harris, *A Convict's Dictionary*, p. 38, 1989

3 in gambling, a cheat who manipulates the cards or dice *US, 1909*
- No better card mechanic ever lived. — Mickey Spillane, *Me, Hood!*, p. 29, 1963
- I'm a first-class crap dealer, I'm a pretty good card mechanic, pretty good dice mechanic. — Bruce Jackson, *Outside the Law*, p. 91, 1972
- Folks said, "Precious, you still a star nine ball player and top craps mechanic?" — Iceberg Slim (Robert Beck), *Long White Con*, p. 167, 1977
- He is a dice hustler, a mechanic. — Gerald Petievich, *To Die in Beverly Hills*, p. 113, 1983
- I mean, all of Nicky's half-assed mechanics, they were all real signal happy. — *Casino*, 1995
- He's ... not a dice mechanic, he's a ... a physicist or some kinda physical engineer, an inventor. — Stephen Cannell, *Big Con*, p. 245, 1997

4 any safety device worn by a circus performer *US*
- Most all performers, both aerial and ground, are trained by aid of mechanics. — Joe McKennon, *Circus Lingo*, p. 61, 1980

5 an accomplished, skilled lover *US*
- "Mechanic" – a man who's good with his bird [penis]; a ladies' man. — *Washington Post*, p. B1, 17th January 1985

mechanical digger; mechanical *noun*

a black person *UK*

Rhyming slang for 'nigger'.
- — Ray Puxley, *Cockney Rabbit*, 1992

mechanic's grip *noun*

in card trickery, a method of holding the deck that favours cheating *US*
- The mechanics grip is one of the most often used for false dealing. — *Card Trick Central*, 2003

Med *noun*

▸ **the Med**

the Mediterranean sea; the lands generally known as the Mediterranean *UK, 1943*
- The first three months right after we were married, then nine months he was in the Med. — Darryl Ponicsan, *The Last Detail*, p. 89, 1970
- It was a different kind of heat from the Med, more industrial and dirty. — Colin Butts, *Is Harry on the Boat?*, p. 80, 1997

med *adjective*

medical *US, 1933*
- [A] drunk med student shagging a corpse as a prank is not considered to be "suffering" from necrophilia. — Katheen Kurrick Bryson, *Lap Dogs and Other Perversions [Inappropriate Behaviour]*, p. 48, 2002

med head *noun*

a member of the military police *NEW ZEALAND*
- — David McGill, *David McGill's Complete Kiwi Slang Dictionary*, p. 72, 1998

media flu *noun*

a runny nose and consequent sniffing as symptoms of cocaine use *UK*

Some symptoms of influenza translated to a profession noted for cocaine use, on the model of 'Asian flu', etc.
- Hel-lo (sniff). – Oh I'm so sorry, just a touch of media flu, you know, darling, sounds like you've got it too, eh? — James Hawes, *White Powder, Green Light*, p. 290, 2002

media whore; meeja whore *noun*

someone prepared to do anything for publicity *UK*
- Drugs have every move or change in pop: hippies and acid, punks and speed, house and E, nearly every fake celeb and media whore in the late nineties and cocaine. — John Robb, *The Nineties*, p. 56, 1999
- Regional accents are represented as quirks, media whores dropping their Ts as they play at being cockneys[.] — John King, *Human Punk*, p. 259, 2000
- In the loo talking absolute shit with a couple of media whores you've never met. — *Ministry*, p. 42, January 2002

medic; medico *noun*

a *medic*al doctor, whether physician or surgeon; someone who uses medical skills in a professional capacity *UK, 1659*
- He OD'd four times on barks [barbs, barbiturates] and four times the medics saved him. — Paul E Willis, *Profane Culture*, p. 184, 1978

medical shot *noun*

in a pornographic film, an extreme close-up of genitals *US*
- Use your first camera from a more or less fixed position, and your hand-held camera for the ever-important closeups, or, as some refer to them, the "medical shots." — Stephen Ziplow, *The Film Maker's Guide to Pornography*, p. 78, 1977

medicate *verb*

to use an illegal drug *US*
- — Connie Eble (Editor), *UNC-CH Campus Slang*, p. 6, Spring 2003

medicine *noun*

1 alcohol; liquor *US, 1847*
- "Let's find a place and get a shot," Powers said. "Oh, hell, forget it. that's bad medicine for us now." — James T. Farrell, *The Life Adventure*, p. 186, 1947

2 illegal drugs or narcotics *US*

Noted in the usage of counterculturalists associated with the Rainbow Nation by Jim Crotty, *How to Talk American*, 1997.
- — John R. Armore and Joseph D. Wolfe, *Dictionary of Desperation*, p. 40, 1976

medicine line *noun*

the border between Canada and the US, especially in the west *CANADA*
- Maybe here on this side of the medicine line we can teach them instead of killing them. — George Bowering, *Caprice*, p. 176, 1987

meditation *noun*

solitary confinement in prison *US*
- — Charles Shafer, *Folk Speech in Texas Prisons*, p. 210, 1990

meditation manor *noun*

a prison cell used for solitary confinement *US*
- — Joseph E. Ragen and Charles Finston, *Inside the World's Toughest Prison*, p. 808, 1962: 'Penitentiary and underworld glossary'

Mediterranean back *noun*

a phoney injured back used as an excuse for taking leave from work *AUSTRALIA, 1972*

A racial slur referring to New Australians, many of whom were from a Greek, Italian or Lebanese background.

medza; medzer *adjective*

▷ **see:** MADZA

medzers *noun*

money *UK, 1933*

Parleyaree, theatrical and polari. Variants include 'medzies', 'metzers', 'metzes', 'metties', 'metzies', 'measures' and 'mezsh'.
- — Paul Baker, *Polari*, p. 180, 2002

meeces *noun*

mice *US*

From the *Huckleberry Hound* television cartoon series of the late 1950s, in which Mr Jinx the beatnik cat regularly described his feelings towards Pixie and Dixie, two mice, as 'I hate those meeces to pieces'.
- — Eric S. Raymond, *The New Hacker's Dictionary*, p. 237, 1991

meeja; meejah; meejer *noun*

media *UK, 1983*

A phonetic slurring in fashionable currency; slightly derogatory and generally used with 'the'.
- I read meeja and wimmen pages for half an hour, then the sport[.] — John Milne, *Alive and Kicking*, p. 127, 1998
- [A] sexually voracious old actress [...], a transvestite [...] and sundry meeja piss artists. — *Uncut*, p. 171, July 2001

mee-maws *noun*

the police *UK: SCOTLAND*

Echoic of a two-tone siren.
- Ah got wakened up in the middle a the night wi the mee-maws gaun [going] doon the street. — Michael Munro, *The Patter, Another Blast*, p. 43, 1988

meemies *noun*

a feeling of anxiety and fear *US, 1946*

A shortened form of the **SCREAMING MEEMIES**.
- It was a night to give you the meemies. — Mickey Spillane, *One Lonely Night*, p. 102, 1951

mee-ow!

▷ **see:** MIAOW!

meese *adjective*

plain *UK*

Recorded in contemporary gay use.

- — *Attitude*, p. 60, July 2003: 'New palare lexicon'

meet *noun*

1 a meeting, especially one convened to discuss illegal matters *UK, 1865*

- Pull up, Lottie, you haven't got a meet on, have you? — Norman Lindsay, *Halfway to Anywhere*, p. 83, 1947
- When I arrived at the cafeteria, where we had our meet, there was Bill sitting at a table, his skinny frame huddled in someone else's overcoat. — William Burroughs, *Junkie*, p. 53, 1953
- But Tom had a meet with Ettie. — Alexander Trocchi, *Cain's Book*, p. 243, 1960
- A meeting (a 'meet') was arranged at a bar on 126th Street and Lexington Avenue. — Leonard Shecter and William Phillips, *On the Pad*, p. 178, 1973
- Midway up the fifties, Earl Bassey sent word he wanted meet with me. — Edwin Torres, *Carlito's Way*, p. 26, 1975
- Tell Cous I said for a big one like this, he's gonna have to risk a meet with me soon, so we can polish the plan to take off that bread. — Iceberg Slim (Robert Beck), *Death Wish*, p. 90, 1977
- Pimples had a meet with a fag who – so he said – was good for a double sawbuck[.] — Herbert Huncke, *The Evening Sun Turned Crimson*, p. 50–51, 1980
- Angelo Partanna had a call from Lieutenant Hanly, bagman for the chief inspector's office, who wanted quick meet. — Richard Condon, *Prizzi's Honor*, p. 215, 1982

2 a session in which musicians collectively improvise; a jam session *US, 1957*

- — Robert George Reisner, *The Jazz Titans*, p. 161, 1960

meet *verb*

in poker, to make a bet equal to the previous bet *US*

- — Anthony Holden, *Big Deal*, p. 302, 1990

meeting *noun*

▸ **take a meeting**

to attend a business meeting *US*

Entertainment industry terminology, used outside the industry in a mocking, pretentious tone.

- Well, you take a meeting with him, I'll take a meeting with you if you'll take a meeting with Freedy. — *Annie Hall*, 1977
- "I took three meetings." "Three? That's marvelous. Three! Do ourself any good?" "I took a meeting with Ivan Kipplinger." — Robert Campbell, *Alice in La-La Land*, p. 131, 1987

meff'd *adjective*

drunk *UK*

- — *e-cyclopaedia*, 20th March 2002

mega *adjective*

great, successful, excellent, special *UK, 1969*

A multi-purpose superlative, from Greek prefix *mega-* (great).

- Just one more little step to relieve megaboredom. — Joseph Wambaugh, *The Delta Star*, p. 126, 1983
- Two weeks later I was off for a seven-day cruise of the high seas, on my way to "mega ship luxury" and "the time of my life." — Anka Radakovich, *The Wild Girls Club*, p. 70, 1994
- I was fuckin' mega. And I was still a smackhead [heroin addict] then, of course. — Shaun Ryder, *Shaun Ryder... in His Own Words*, 1994
- I'm not a fucking baby machine, though we're mega at it. — *Q*, p. 100, May 2002

mega- *prefix*

used for intensifying *US, 1966*

- — *Current Slang*, p. 5, Winter 1966
- Just one little step to relieve megaboredom. — Joseph Wambaugh, *The Delta Star*, p. 126, 1983
- Heather, why can't you just be a friend? Why are you such a megabitch? — *Heathers*, 1988
- Sandy, I'm serious. This mega-grimster is totally scorching me. — *Bill and Ted's Excellent Adventure*, 1989
- This band, "Crucial Taunt," had this megabae for a lead singer. — *Wayne's World*, 1992
- Its glistening polish, blood-crimson striping, and mirror-chrome Centerlines told of regular care by a megabuck detailer. — Jess Mowry, *Way Past Cool*, p. 23, 1992
- I am megafuckin stoked! Totally! — Joseph Wambaugh, *Finnegan's Week*, p. 253, 1993
- Instead, he goads bug-fearing farmers into despoiling the earth (and their Mexican farmworkers) with mega-death herbicides. — C.D. Payne, *Youth in Revolt*, p. 6, 1993
- Everything is "gross" to Georgina; I, of course, am mega-gross[.] — Jenny Eclair, *Camberwell Beauty*, p. 153, 2000

megablast *noun*

a dose of crack cocaine *US*

- — Peter Johnson, *Dictionary of Street Alcohol and Drug Terms*, p. 119, 1993

megabuck *adjective*

very expensive *US*

- Its glistening polish, blood-crimson striping, and mirror-chrome Centerlines told of regular care by a megabuck detailer. — Jess Mowry, *Way Past Cool*, p. 23, 1992

mega dirtball *noun*

a hospital patient with an appalling lack of hygiene *US*

- — *Maledicta*, p. 33, 1988–1989: 'Medical maledicta from San Francisco'

megapenny *noun*

ten thousand dollars (one cent times ten to the sixth power) *US*

- — Eric S. Raymond, *The New Hacker's Dictionary*, p. 237, 1991

megg *noun*

a marijuana cigarette *US, 1942*

- — Mike Haskins, *Drugs*, p. 291, 2003

megger *noun*

in the television and film industries, a director *US*

From the long-gone practice of directors' using megaphones.

- — Tony Miller and Patricia George, *Cut! Print!*, p. 103, 1977

megillah *noun*

all of something *US*

For observant Jews on Purim, the reading of the entire Megillas Esther is deemed an obligation.

- Oh, come on, Frana. Not the whole megilleh. — Bernard Wolfe, *The Late Risers*, p. 134, 1954

MEGO

my eyes glaze over *US, 1977*

- — Eric S. Raymond, *The New Hacker's Dictionary*, p. 237, 1991

Meg Ryan *noun*

a homosexual male *UK*

Rhyming slang for 'iron' (**IRON HOOF**), **POOF** formed from the name of the US film actress (b.1961).

- — Ray Puxley, *Fresh Rabbit*, 1998

meig *noun*

a penny; a five-cent piece *US*

- — Joseph E. Ragen and Charles Finston, *Inside the World's Toughest Prison*, p. 808, 1962: 'Penitentiary and underworld glossary'

Mekong Delta *nickname*

a neighbourhood with a large number of Vietnamese immigrants and businesses *US*

- Do is one of more than a dozen Vietnamese who have set up shop in Clarendon, turning a retailing center once known as "Northern Virginia's downtown" into an area often referred to by Americans as "Little Saigon," the "Mekong Delta" or even the "Ho Chi Min Trail." — *Washington Post*, p. A1, 23rd September 1979

mel *noun*

in the language surrounding the Grateful Dead, a conventional, law-abiding citizen *US*

- — David Shenk and Steve Silberman, *Skeleton Key*, p. 190, 1994

melana cream *noun*

a powerful variety of hashish from the Kulu Valley in Himachel Pradesh *UK*

- — Nick Jones, *Spliffs*, p. 82, 2003

Melba *noun*

▸ **do a Melba**

(especially of an entertainer) to retire and then come out of retirement over and over again *AUSTRALIA, 1971*

Referring to Dame Nellie Melba, 1861–1931, Australian opera singer.

Meldrew *noun*

a middle-aged or elderly man who is a complainer or a moaner, or is characteristically intolerant, pessimistic or curmudgeonly *UK*

Named after Victor Meldrew, the central character in BBC situation comedy *One Foot in the Grave* (from 1990), written by David Renwick and played by Scottish character actor Richard Wilson.

mellow *noun*

a good friend *US*

- It came through, fellows; so tell my mellows / I'll spring 'em, 'cause I've got the price. — Dennis Wepman et al., *The Life*, p. 68, 1976

mellow *verb*
to calm *US, 1974*
- Go inside, have a drink and mellow this off, you understand?—*Boogie Nights*, 1997

mellow *adjective*
1 pleasing, relaxed, good *US, 1938*
- [T]he gauge they picked up on was really in there, and it had them treetop tall, mellow as a cello.—Mezz Mezzrow, *Really the Blues*, p. 75, 1946
- Shorty would take me to groovy, frantic scenes in different chicks' and cats' pads, where with the lights and juke down mellow, everybody blew gage and juiced back and jumped.—Malcolm X and Alex Haley, *The Autobiography of Malcolm X*, p. 56, 1964
- "The smoke [marijuana] is mellow, baby," he answered.—Donald Goines, *Whoreson*, p. 131, 1972
- Uh, not a big deal, it's just relax, just be very mellow.—*Annie Hall*, 1977

2 mildly and pleasantly drunk or drug-intoxicated *UK, 1699*
- [T]he gauge they picked up on was really in there, and it had them treetop tall, mellow as a cello.—Mezz Mezzrow, *Really the Blues*, p. 75, 1946

3 (used of a friend) close *US, 1941*
- But like I said, he's a real big man now but he was and still is my righteous mellow fellow.—A.S. Jackson, *Gentleman Pimp*, p. 88, 1973

mellow d *adjective*
relaxed, enjoyable *US*
A glorious pun on 'melody'.
- —Kenn "Naz" Young, *Naz's Underground Dictionary*, p. 46, 1973

mellow man *noun*
an attractive male *US*
- —*Yank*, p. 18, 24th March 1945

mellow yellow *noun*
1 fried banana skin scrapings, sold for their nonexistent psychoactive effect *US, 1966*
- Electrical banana / Is gonna be a sudden craze / Electrical banana / Is bound to be the very next phase / They call it mellow yellow. —Donovan, *Mellow Yellow*, 1967
- At this printing, mellow yellow is legal and United Fruit Company sales are still cllimbing.—Mary Lay and Nancy Orban, *The Hip Glossary of Hippie Language*, June 1967
- —Eugene Landy, *The Underground Dictionary*, p. 130, 1971
- —Ralph de Sola, *Crime Dictionary*, p. 91, 1982

2 LSD *US, 1971*
- —Richard A. Spears, *The Slang and Jargon of Drugs and Drink*, p. 335, 1986
- —Mike Haskins, *Drugs*, p. 285, 2003

melon *noun*
1 the head *AUSTRALIA, 1907*
- The pigs wouldn't care if every biker in the nation split his melon. —Tom Robbins, *Another Roadside Attraction*, p. 34, 1971
- —Inez Cardozo-Freeman, *The Joint*, p. 515, 1984
- My pimple paled into insignificance compared to the 40 or 50 she had on her melon, poor girl.—Paul Vautin, *Turn It Up!*, p. 30, 1995
- He says Sky Channel wanted a 'rough old melon who's been around for a long time' to do the job.—*Aussie Post*, p. 19, 29th August 1998

2 a fool *AUSTRALIA, 1937*
Probably a shortening of 'melonhead'.
- Never wanted to be taken for a melon.—Jeremy Cameron, *Brown Bread in Wengen*, p. 156, 1999

▸ **bust your melon**
to confuse *US*
Combines 'bust' (to break) with **MELON** (the head).
- Further busting our melons are the predominantly white "redeemers" [.]—*The Source*, p. 148, March 2002

▸ **twist your melon**
to confuse, to scramble your thoughts *UK*
Combines 'twist' (to derange) with **MELON** (the head). First heard in 1990 (see citation); survives as a catchphrase with the meaning barely understood.
- You're twisting my melon man, you know you talk so hip man / You're twisting my melon man.—Happy Mondays, *Step On*, 1990

melon gear *noun*
a crash helmet *US*
- Brainbucket, skid lid, melon gear, crash hat. It doesn't matter what you call it, just as long as you have one – a helmet for hitting the slopes, trails, skating rinks and half-pipes.—*Times Union (Albany, New York)*, p. D1, 23rd December 2003

melon hut; melon *noun*
a prefabricated red field hut *ANTARCTICA*
- —Bernadette Hince, *The Antarctic Dictionary*, p. 228, 2000

melons *noun*
large female breasts *US, 1957*
- —Collin Baker et al., *College Undergraduate Slang Study Conducted at Brown University*, p. 156, 1968
- "Big tits?" "Real melons."—James Ellroy, *Brown's Requiem*, p. 106, 1981
- "What the hell you doing, Bouche?" Barcaloo whispered fiercely, "runnin' a goddamn fruit stand, sittin' around with your melons hanging out like that?"—Robert Campbell, *In La-La Land We Trust*, p. 74, 1986
- I remember lying in bed one morning, staring at my new developments and wondering, "Who ordered the melons?"—Anka Radakovich, *The Wild Girls Club*, p. 136, 1994

meltdown *noun*
the complete and total malfunctioning of a casino slot machine *US*
- The second meltdown I ever experienced occurred when I was playing at the Stardust on a Piggy Bankin' machine of the one dollar denomination.—Charles W. Lund, *Robbing the One-Armed Bandits*, p. 115, 1999

melted butter *noun*
semen *US*
- —*Maledicta*, p. 192, Winter 1980: 'A new erotic vocabulary'

melted out *adjective*
broke; without funds *US*
- —Jack Lait and Lee Mortimer, *New York Confidential*, p. 235, 1948: 'A glossary of Harlemisms'

melton *adjective*
hot *UK*
A pun on 'melting' originally recorded in 1885, however current use is probably freshly coined. Recorded in contemporary gay use.
- —*Attitude*, p. 60, July 2003: 'New palare lexicon'

Melvin *noun*
the condition that exists when someone pulls your trousers or underpants forcefully upwards, forming a wedge between buttock cheeks *US*
- And the guys suddenly pull each of the Cowboys' long underwear up, giving them "Melvins."—*Bill and Ted's Excellent Adventure*, p. 42, 1989
- —*American Speech*, Fall 1990
- "Don't that feel uncomfortable?" Leeds asked. "I mean, do you like giving yourself a Melvin all day long?"—Joseph Wambaugh, *Floaters*, p. 81, 1996
- Can be especially painful if the Melvin-receiver is wearing boxer shorts.—Chris Lewis, *The Dictionary of Playground Slang*, p. 146, 2003

Melvin *verb*
1 to seize someone's testicles and twist them, especially as a girl's revenge for sexual harassment *UK*
Obviously extends from the senses that convey a painful and forceful adjustment to someone's underwear.
- Watch out fer that Kim, she'll melvin yer!—Chris Lewis, *The Dictionary of Playground Slang*, p. 147, 2003

2 to dupe *US*
- —*USA Today*, p. 1D, 5th August 1991: 'A sterling lexicon of the lingo'

Melvyn Bragg; melvyn *noun*
1 a cigarette *UK, 1998*
Rhyming slang for **FAG**, based on the name of author and television presenter Lord Bragg of Wigton (b.1939), noted as 'recently rolled' by Ray Puxley, *Fresh Rabbit*, 1998.
- Oi mate, can I scrounge a Melvyn off you?—*www.LondonSlang.com*, June 2002

2 an act of sexual intercourse *UK*
Rhyming slang for **SHAG**, based on the name of author and television presenter Lord Bragg of Wigton (b.1939); this term came into use shortly after the explicity sexual television adaptation of his 1990 novel *A Time to Dance* was first broadcast in 1992.
- —Ray Puxley, *Cockney Rabbit*, 1992

3 a contemptible person *UK, 1998*
Rhyming slang for **SLAG**, based on the name of author and television presenter Lord Bragg of Wigton (b.1939).

4 a sexually promiscuous woman, a slut *UK*
Rhyming slang.
- —Ray Puxley, *Fresh Rabbit*, 1998

member *noun*

a fellow homosexual *US, 1960s*

- There ain't too many members in Alaska. — Bruce Rodgers, *The Queens' Vernacular*, p. 133, 1972

Memphis dominoes *noun*

dice *US, 1942*

- — *The Annals of the American Academy of Political and Social Sciences*, p. 127, May 1950

memsmeric *adjective*

used for expressing approval *UK*

- — Susie Dent, *The Language Report*, p. 75, 2003

menage à moi *noun*

an act of female masturbation *UK*

- — Michelle Baker and Steven Tropiano, *Queer Facts*, p. 46, 2004

menali *noun*

potent hashish originating in the Himalayas

- Menali is reported to have the highest THC content of any hash in the world. — Mike Rock, *This Book*, 1999

mender *noun*

in circus and carnival usage, a claims adjuster *US*

- — Don Wilmeth, *The Language of American Popular Entertainment*, p. 168, 1981

men in white coats *noun*

1 medical or laboratory personnel *UK, 1967*

2 psychiatric staff *UK, 1968*

Usually humorous, and in a context that questions a person's sanity.

- What I actually want, he thought, is to get this bunny-boiler carted off by the men in white coats. She kissed him on the cheek. "See you later." — Colin Butts, *Is Harry Still on the Boat?*, p. 202, 2003

menopause manor *noun*

in the Canadian Forces, the Sergeants and Warrant Officers' Mess *CANADA*

- The slightly disparaging term "menopause manor" arises from the fact that those who use it are generally older than everyone else. "Where's Warrant Officer Griffiths? "I believe you'll find him having a lemonade in Menopause Manor." — Tom Langeste, *Words on the Wing*, p. 184–185, 1995

mensch; mensh; mench *noun*

an honourable person *US, 1953*

German *mensch* (a person) into Yiddish.

- As a child I often heard it said: "The finest thing you can say about a man is that he is a mensch!" — Leo Rosten, *The Joys of Yiddish*, p. 174, 1968
- You're a mensch, guy, you really are. You're my brother. — Joel Rose, *Kill Kill Faster Faster*, p. 172, 1997
- When the hero (Ricardo Darin) is immediately revealed as a bloated, chain-smoking, workaholic deadbeat dad, we know a tragedy and/or cardiac event will transform him into a life-loving mensch. — *The Village Voice*, 26th March 2002

mensh *noun*

a mention; also, as a verb, to mention *UK, 1984*

- To think about packing in the comp when, for the past 12 months, you haven't had a mensh[.] — *New Statesman*, 12th August 2003

mental *noun*

an outburst of anger or madness *AUSTRALIA, 1979*

- Do ya wanna go down to old Doc's and watch him do a mental? — Kerry Cue, *Crooks, Chooks and Bloody Ratbags*, p. 193, 1983
- That's why she hadn't cared about him toughing her. And why the Chihuahua had chucked a mental about being called a poofter. — Kathy Lette, *Girls' Night Out*, p. 84, 1987

mental *adjective*

1 insane, crazy *UK, 1927*

- I lost you two months ago! We broke up. Are you mental? — *Wayne's World*, 1992
- I know it sounds mental, but sometimes I have more fun vegging out than when I go partying. — *Clueless*, 1995
- [T]he sort [of TV commercial] that makes you mental 'cos it's on twice in every break. — Cath Staincliffe, *Trainers*, p. 55, 1999
- — Connie Eble (Editor), *UNC-CH Campus Slang*, p. 7, Fall 1999
- But everything did go a bit mental when I had that acid. — Dave Courtney, *Raving Lunacy*, p. 11, 2000

2 wonderful, amazing, mind-blowing *UK*

- A totally wicked contest man, completely MEN-TAL. — Melanie McGrath, *Hard, Soft & Wet*, p. 53, 1998
- "That's mental!" – that's the best (or the worst). — Paul Baker, *Polari*, p. 180, 2002
- "See you, Tommy, it's been mental." "Yeah right... You've got a bit of star fruit in your hair." — Ben Elton, *High Society*, p. 70, 2002

▸ **go mental**

to become very enraged, to have a fit of ill-temper *UK: SCOTLAND*

- — Michael Munro, *The Original Patter*, p. 45, 1985

mental blooter *noun*

a spree of any kind of excessive behaviour *UK*

- — Michael Munro, *The Patter, Another Blast*, 1988

mentalist *noun*

a crazy person; a lunatic; an eccentric *UK*

- ALAN: No way you big spastic! You're a mentalist! JED: Come back! I'll rip your bloody head off! — *I'm Alan Partridge (Episode 5)*, 1997
- I'm a mentalist, me. — *The Guardian*, 20th October 2003

mentaller *noun*

a mad or crazy person *UK*

- I'm not very bothered if people watched the documentary and thought I was a bit of a mentaller[.] — Frank Skinner, *Frank Skinner*, p. 131, 2001

mentalness *noun*

a state of madness *UK: SCOTLAND*

- What's gaun [going] on in there the day is nothin but pure mentalness. — Michael Munro, *The Complete Patter*, p. 99, 1996

mental pygmy *noun*

a dolt *US*

- — Mary Swift, *Campus Slang (University of Texas)*, 1968

menu *noun*

1 the list of services available in a brothel *US*

- The menu can help "break the ice" for first-timers, and is a conversation piece[.] — J.R. Schwartz, *The Official Guide to the Best Cat Houses in Nevada*, p. 27, 1993

2 grafitti describing sex preferences and telephone numbers *US*

- — Bruce Rodgers, *The Queens' Vernacular*, p. 133, 1972

merc *noun*

a mercenary *ZIMBABWE, 1967*

With the official US use of the term 'private civilian contractor' instead of 'mercenary' in the invasion and occupation of Iraq, use of the term 'merc' in the future is doubtful.

- C.I.A. used to hire mercs who used this same setup. — *Lethal Weapon*, 1987
- One of the South African mercs picked up the rifle of an Australian soldier seated poolside, handled it admiringly, then peered down the laser scope at a table full of journalists. — *The New Republic*, p. 18, 24th May 2004

Merc *noun*

1 a *Mercedes* car *US*

- Boris met her with the big chauffeured Merk, while Lips Malone, driving a Citroen station wagon, took care of the luggage. — Terry Southern, *Blue Movie*, p. 129, 1970
- Mercs with alloys and dark windows. — Dave Courtney, *Raving Lunacy*, p. 99, 2000
- Eli the Mensch had got shot of all fourteen cars – over a million's worth of Mercs – within two hours of the blag. — Kevin Sampson, *Outlaws*, p. 16, 2001

2 a *Mercury* car *US*

- Now I'm the guy who was in that Merc / An' I'm callin' myself all kind of a jerk. — George Wilson (performed by Arkie Shibley), *Hot Rod Race #4*, 1951
- I started around the car when I heard tires turn into the driveway and while I stood there a light-green Merc drove up behind me[.] — Mickey Spillane, *Kiss Me Deadly*, p. 80, 1952
- Get your big dynaflo Buick off the fucking road and let my chopped and channeled '49 Merc fly. — Abbie Hoffman, *Woodstock Nation*, p. 26–27, 1969

Mercedes *noun*

1 in horse racing, odds of 10–1 *AUSTRALIA*

Rhyming slang, formed from Mercedes Benz.

- — Ned Wallish, *The Truth Dictionary of Racing Slang*, p. 52, 1989

2 a variety of MDMA, the recreational drug best known as ecstasy *UK*

After the luxury car; describing the logo stamped on the pill.

- Names such as Doves, Thunderdomes, MacDonalds, TNTs, Mercedes, Apples and Green Goddesses were adopted to describe the logo stamped on a pill. — Ben Osborne, *The A-Z of Club Culture*, p. 81, 1999

merch *noun*
merchandise *US*
• Whenever we got local merch, we'd usually send it to Palm Springs or Arizona. — *Casino*, 1995
• The merch could bring in five grand or more, depending on audience reaction, how much they like the show. — Elmore Leonard, *Be Cool*, p. 251, 1999

merchant *noun*
a prisoner who sells goods to other prisoners *US*
• [I]nmates have drawn a sharp line between selling and giving and the prisoner who sells when he should give is labelled a merchant or pedlar. — Gresham M. Sykes, *The Society of Captives*, p. 93, 1958

merchant banker; merchant; banker *noun*
a contemptible person *UK, 1992*
Rhyming slang for **WANKER** (a contemptible person), coined in response to **YUPPIE** (a young upwardly mobile professional), many of whom were merchant bankers, moving into the East End of London during the 1980s.
• ["]We ain't had a banker like Helmet in years..." "Merchant Banker, yeah!" "I mean it. I don't like the little shyster[.]" — Kevin Sampson, *Powder*, p. 132, 1999

merck; merk *noun*
cocaine *US, 1969*
From the name of a pharmaceutical company.
• — Richard A. Spears, *The Slang and Jargon of Drugs and Drink*, p. 335, 1986
• — Mike Haskins, *Drugs*, p. 280, 2003

mercy!
used for expressing mild surprise *US*
• — William K. Bentley and James M. Corbett, *Prison Slang*, p. 46, 1992

mercy buckets!
thank you *UK, 1960*
An intentional butchering of the French.
• — *New Society*, 10th March 1983
• — Connie Eble (Editor), *UNC-CH Campus Slang*, p. 6, Spring 1990

mercy Mary!
used for expressing surprise in a melodramatic fashion *US*
• — *American Speech*, p. 58, Spring-Summer 1970: 'Homosexual slang'

mercy Miss Percy!
used for embellishing any exclamation *US*
• When I peer into her peeepers, mercy miss percy, I am sent one time. — Lavada Durst, *The Jives of Dr. Hepcat*, p. 9, 1953

mercy sakes!; mercy's sakes alive!
used euphemistically in citizens' band transmissions to register anger, shock, surprise, etc *US*
• Mercy's sakes alive, looks like we got us a convoy. — C.W. McCall, *Convoy*, 1976

mere gook rule *noun*
a belief during the Vietnam war that a crime commited against a Vietnamese person was not a crime *US*
• At that point the grunts allowed the "Mere Gook Rule" to enter their value system: a crime wasn't a crime if it was committed against a Vietnamese, a Mere Gook. — Charles R. Anderson, *The Grunts*, p. 207, 1976
• [A]n endemic, pervasive feeling in the military that wating "mere gooks" was of no great consequence. — Myra MacPherson, *Long Time Passing*, p. 582, 1984

Merlin the magician; merlin *noun*
a pigeon *UK*
Rhyming slang.
• — Ray Puxley, *Cockney Rabbit*, 1992

merry *noun*
marijuana *US, 1938*
A play on the name Mary, featured in many slang terms for 'marijuana'.

merry and bright *noun*
light, a light *UK*
Rhyming slang.
• — Ray Puxley, *Cockney Rabbit*, 1992

merry dancers *noun*
the northern lights *CANADA*
• In some regions the northern lights are called "the merry dancers." — *Beaver*, p. 13/2, September 1946

merry-go-round *noun*
1 the visits to many different prison offices the day before a prisoner is released *US*
• — Reinhold Aman, *Hillary Clinton's Pen Pal: A Guide to Life and Lingo in Federal Prison*, p. 50, 1996

2 a railway turntable *US*
• — Norman Carlisle, *The Modern Wonder Book of Trains and Railroading*, p. 266, 1946

3 a pound (£1) *UK, 1961*
Rhyming slang; often reduced to 'merry'.
• — Ray Puxley, *Cockney Rabbit*, 1992

merry hell *noun*
▸ **play merry hell; raise merry hell**
to make a disturbance, to complain or quarrel noisily and angrily, to make a din *US, 1911*
• [T]here are people who are happy to have something done about it, as long as it doesn't affect them in any way and who will raise merry hell if it does. — *The Observer*, 12th January 2003

merry laird *noun*
a beard *UK: SCOTLAND*
Glasgow rhyming slang (a good rhyme in the local accent).
• Ah see ye've taken aff the merry laird. — Michael Munro, *The Patter, Another Blast*, 1988

merry old soul *noun*
1 a hole *UK*
Rhyming slang.
• — Ray Puxley, *Cockney Rabbit*, 1992

2 the anus *UK*
Rhyming slang for **ARSEHOLE**; a specialism of the previous sense. Logically, this will, if not already (2004), be applied with irony to any **ARSEHOLE** (a contemptible person).
• — Bodmin Dark, *Dirty Cockney Rhyming Slang*, 2003

merry syphilis and a happy gonnerrhoea
used as a humorous replacement for 'Merry Christmas and Happy New Year' *AUSTRALIA*
• — Thommo, *The Dictionary of Australian Swearing and Sex Sayings*, p. 83, 1985

merry widow *noun*
1 a bust-emphasising corset *US*
• Cass emptied the contents of my bag – a spare bathing suit and the Merry Widow that goes with the spare, on account of that lousy bias-cut uplift arrangement. — Frederick Kohner, *Gidget*, p. 111, 1957

2 in pool, a cue stick with a butt made with a single, unspliced piece of wood *US, 1983*
• — Mike Shamos, *The Illustrated Encyclopedia of Billiards*, p. 149, 1993

mersh *noun*
marijuana that is commercially produced for a mass-market *US*
• — Steven Wishnia, *The Cannabis Companion*, p. 152, 2004

Meryl Streep; meryl *noun*
sleep *UK*
Rhyming slang, formed from the name of the US film actress (b.1949).
• The desire to get your bonce down is to need to get some "Meryl". — Ray Puxley, *Fresh Rabbit*, 1998

mesc; mezc *noun*
mescaline *US, 1970*
• "Poor Chessman" – he muttered, still slight zonked from a late night mesc drop[.] — Ed Sanders, *Tales of Beatnik Glory*, p. 41, 1975
• — Angela Devlin, *Prison Patter*, p. 76, 1996

meself *pronoun*
myself *AUSTRALIA, 1898*
Representing a common Australian pronunciation.
• I'd keep it to meself. — Alexander Buzo, *Norm and Ahmed*, p. 8, 1969

meserole *noun*
▷ see: **MEZZROLL**

mesh *noun*
on a computer keyboard, the # character *US*
• — Guy L. Steele et al., *The Hacker's Dictionary*, p. 93, 1983

meshugge; meshuga; meshuggener; meshigener *adjective*
crazy *US, 1888*
Yiddish.
- The woman laughed at him. "Meshugener!" —Irving Shulman, *The Amboy Dukes*, p. 123, 1947
- Mishuga jobs like that don't grow on trees. —Clancy Sigal, *Going Away*, p. 11, 1961
- [A]ll those mesuggeneh rules and regulations on top of their own private craziness! —Philip Roth, *Portnoy's Complaint*, p. 37, 1969
- But the case's not resolved, 'cause your meshuge counsel's trying to make history first time at bat[.] —Emmett Grogan, *Final Score*, p. 164, 1976
- "Meshugana," Zucker muttered. —Edwin Torres, *Q & A*, p. 155, 1977

mess *noun*
1 a person who is dirty or untidy; a person who is disorganised or incapable of being organised *UK, 1891*
- It's a mess! I am a mess! I'm not working like I used to. —*The Guardian*, 14th May 2003

2 excrement *UK, 1903*
- A lump of bird's mess landed on her hat. —Beale, 1984

3 a large amount *US, 1826*
- I've been to a mess of schools like that – ones you won't find on the approved list of any Parent-Teacher Association. —Mezz Mezzrow, *Really the Blues*, p. 3, 1946

4 drugs *US*
- "How do you get your mess from him?" Benson asked sharply. "You got the guy's address?" "Naw man, he comes up on the corner every day at the same time, two o'clock, you dig. If you want to cop, you had better be up there by then." —Donald Goines, *Crime Partners*, p. 9, 1978

5 in poker, a draw of replacement cards that fails to improve the hand *US*
- —John Scarne, *Scarne's Guide to Modern Poker*, p. 284, 1979

mess; mess with *verb*
to confront; to mess with; to interfere; to bother; to fight *US, 1935*
- Daddy, I don't want to mess with 'em. —William "Lord" Buckley, *Nero*, 1951
- [T]he 'don't-mess-with-me' image of the power-packed rottweiler[.] —*The Guardian*, 18th December 2003
- Don't mess with the press. —*The Guardian*, 11th January 2003

messages *noun*
shopping; hence, message bag, shopping bag *UK: SCOTLAND, 1911*
Dialect.
- If I could buy this high at Viccy wines, I'd have a half bottle in my message bag every day! —Ian Pattison, *Rab C. Nesbitt*, 1988

▸ **do the messages**
to go on a small local shopping trip *AUSTRALIA, 1902*
- When she was down the road doing the messages, Mumma often went up and picked up the earphones, holding them at arm's length, and bending her neck towards them like a flamingo[.] —Ruth Park, *Poor Man's Orange*, p. 95, 1949

mess around *verb*
to engage in sexual foreplay; to have sex *UK, 1896*
- There's a lot of girls out there and you mess around with Stacy, —*Fast Times at Ridgemont High*, 1982
- Maybe you just want to mess around or something. —Kenneth Lonergan, *This is Our Youth*, p. 76, 2000

messed up *adjective*
drunk or drug-intoxicated *US, 1963*
- We could buy a cap, and just four of us all could sit down and snort it, and all of us would be messed up. —Henry Williamson, *Hustler!*, p. 74, 1965
- Man, I am so fucking messed up and ripped! I got off on the first hit, man!? —John Rechy, *The Fourth Angel*, p. 32, 1972
- Strike's father had never been a heavy drinker, and whenever he did get a little messed up, he'd never do anything mean or violent. —Richard Price, *Clockers*, p. 65–66, 1992
- [B]attered s**tfaced f**cked messed up[.] —Stuart Walton, *Out of It*, cover, 2001

messenger *noun*
a bullet *US*
- He wouldn't stop, so I sent a couple of little messengers after him. —*American Speech*, p. 270, December 1962: 'The language of traffic policemen'

messer *noun*
a joker *IRELAND*
- Balls would open the back of the superser as if to turn it on and throw a smelly blanket at the visitor. He thought that was hilarious, he was an awful messer. —Ardal O'Hanlon, *The Talk of the Town*, p. 9, 1998

messorole *noun*
▹ see: **MEZZROLL**

mess up *verb*
to beat someone up *US, 1914*
- —Maria Hinojas, *Crews*, p. 167, 1995: 'Glossary'

messy *adjective*
good *UK*
- —The Big Breakfast, 23rd July 2001
- —*Johnny Vaughan Tonight*, 13th February 2002
- —Julian Johnson, *Urban Survival*, p. 258, 2003

met *noun*
methamphetamine *US*
- —Peter Johnson, *Dictionary of Street Alcohol and Drug Terms*, p. 120, 1993

Met *noun*
▸ **the Met**
London's Metropolitan Police, established in 1829 *UK*
- "You're arrest mad, Fancy," John Watt said. "You're like the ruddy Met, arrest mad. —Troy Kennedy Martin, *Z Cars*, p. 157, 1962
- —Peter Laurie, *Scotland Yard*, p. 325, 1970
- —Angela Devlin, *Prison Patter*, p. 76, 1996
- SAVAK – the Met, bulldozed villages – broken placards, a million in Teheran – eight in Gravesend, one world – one struggle. —Mark Steel, *Reasons to be Cheerful*, p. 32, 2001

meta- *prefix*
used for indicating a higher level than super- or hyper- *UK*
- William Goldman cited [Adam] Sandler's metafame as an indicator of our planet's parlous state. —*The Times*, 7th June 2003

metabolic clinic *noun*
a hospital tea-room *UK*
Medical humour.
- —Adam T. Fox, St Mary's Hospital, London, 10th October 2002

metal, metal detectorist *nouns*
▹ see: **HEAVY METAL, DETECTORIST**

metalhead *noun*
a lover of heavy metal music and the attendant lifestyle *US, 1982*
- You know what really bites; when people watch that cafeteria stuff on TV and see all those Geeks and Metalheads jumping around, they're going to think Uncool is the Rule at Westerburg. —*Heathers*, 1988
- Many of them were making a Cross sign with their forefingers, holding their arms in the air. It was like a well-brought cousin of that daft carry-on with the forefinger and the pinkie that metalheads did. —Christopher Brookmyre, *Not the End of the World*, p. 71, 1998

metal jacket *noun*
a condom *US*
- —Judi Sanders, *Faced and Faded, Hanging to Hurl*, p. 27, 1993

metal mouth *noun*
any person with orthodontia *US*
- When Arnold meets Drummond's daughter, a condescending sort who wears braces, he snaps, "Hi, metal mouth." —*Washington Post*, p. B1, 3rd November 1978
- "Fewer people make fun of me; they want to see them," Shawn said. "And they don't call me as many names as they used to, like 'brace face' and 'metal mouth.'" —*St. Petersburg (Florida) Times*, p. 2D, 9th September 1991
- —Chris Lewis, *The Dictionary of Playground Slang*, p. 41, 2003
- For boomers, taunts like "brace-face," tin grin" and "metal mouth" have made way for more sophisticated teasing. —*Washington Post*, p. F1, 13th January 2004

meter *noun*
twenty-five cents *US*
- —Lou Shelly, *Hepcats Jive Talk Dictionary*, p. 15, 1945
- —Jack Lait and Lee Mortimer, *New York Confidential*, p. 235, 1948

-meter; -ometer *suffix*
the conventional suffix that creates a means of measuring, when used to make a flippant or nonce-word, especially as a measurer of sexual arousal *UK, 1837*
In 2003 a brief search of the Internet revealed 'shagometer', from **SHAG** (to have sex), 'hornometer', from **HORN** (an erection) and 'pain-in-the-assometer'.
- What does she read on your clackometer [an imaginary device for measuring the attractiveness of women/clack]? —Beale, 1984

meter maid *noun*
a policewoman who checks cars on city streets for parking infractions *CANADA*
• Advertisements will be placed next week for four meter maids for Kingston. — *Kingston Whig-Standard*, p. 2/6, 26th March 1965

meter reader *noun*
in the US Air Force, a co-pilot *US*
• — *American Speech*, p. 310, December 1946: 'More Air Force slang'

meth *noun*
1 methamphetamine hydrochloride, a powerful central nervous system stimulant, brand name Methedrine™ *US*
• — J. L. Simmons and Barry Winograd, *It's Happening*, p. 172, 1966: 'glossary'
• Take your average Meth freak, once he's started putting the needle in his arm, it's not too hard to say, well, let's shoot a little smack. — Joan Didion, *Slouching Toward Bethlehem*, p. 116, 1967
• Give me Librium or give me Meth. — Mart Crowley, *The Boys in the Band*, p. 160, 1968
• — Donald Louria, *The Drug Scene*, p. 191, 1971
• 'You two 'ho's still pushing your meth?'; she said conversationally. — Robert Deane Pharr, *Giveadamn Brown*, p. 48, 1978
• Half minute or so of bullshit and, "You looking to get high, my man?" Try and sell him some meth. This town was full of meth. — Elmore Leonard, *Glitz*, p. 96, 1985
• The pills are actually nothing but rounded bits of plastic with a yellow dust of pure meth. — Jim Carroll, *Forced Entries*, p. 29, 1987
• Comes out of jail that very fuckin day and to celebrate OD's on meth. Carked it. The prick. — Niall Griffiths, *Sheepshagger*, p. 55, 2001

2 methadone (a drug prescribed as a substitute for heroin) *US, 1980*
• — Angela Devlin, *Prison Patter*, p. 76, 1996
• And some of that time I was using heroin on top of the meth, which was making it double hard. — Shaun Ryder, *Shaun Ryder... in His Own Words*, 1997
• Methadone that was, not diazepam. Bad fuckin stuff that methy. — Niall Griffiths, *Sheepshagger*, p. 108, 2001

3 marijuana *US*
An abbreviation of **METHOD** (marijuana).
• All right, y'all get ya White Owls, get ya meth, get ya skins (cigarette papers) — Method Man (Clifford Smith), *Method Man*, 1994

mether *noun*
a methylated spirits addict *UK*
• [I]t could just be an old mether in there[.] — Andy McNab, *Immediate Action*, p. 38, 1995

meth head *noun*
a habitual user of methamphetamine *US, 1966*
• She's a meth head and an ex-con and stir crazy as hell. — Joseph Wambaugh, *The Blue Knight*, p. 62, 1973
• Hearn's work world is the world of the southwest county meth-heads, where crank is king, and the only rival to getting high is a pocket full of $100 bills. — *Press Enterprise (Riverside, California)*, p. B1, 14th December 1993
• He stumbled onto the answer soon after, when the meth-heads invited him to go "Dumpster diving" for junk. — *New York Times*, p. 42 (Section 6), 21st December 2003

methical *noun*
marijuana *US*
A combination of **METHOD** and **TICAL**, slang terms for 'marijuana' adopted as aliases by rap artist *Methical*/Method Man.

meth monster *noun*
1 an amphetamine addict *US, 1967*
• — Stephen H. Dill (Editor), *Current Slang*, p. 34, Fall 1968
• — William D. Alsever, *Glossary for the Establishment and Other Uptight People*, p. 30, December 1970

2 any paranoid delusion suffered after sustained methamphetamine use *US*
• — Geoffrey Froner, *Digging for Diamonds*, p. 43, 1989

metho *noun*
1 methylated spirits *AUSTRALIA, 1933*
• Went on the metho, slept in the park, fell apart at the seams. — Alexander Buzo, *Rooted*, p. 96, 1969
• [S]he's wrapped in brown paper; her piss tastes like metho. — *Kink*, p. 29, 1993

2 a habitual drinker of methylated spirits *AUSTRALIA, 1933*
• — Jim Ramsay, *Cop It Sweet!*, p. 58, 1977

Metho *noun*
a Methodist *AUSTRALIA, 1940*
• — Arthur Chipper, *The Aussie Swearer's Guide*, p. 61, 1972
• The Methos in Sydney used to invite me to little suburban gatherings to show how broadminded they were with their tame Chinese but then they'd get uncomfortable. — C.J. Koch, *The Year Of Living Dangerously*, p. 96, 1978

method; method murder *noun*
marijuana *US*
• You can smell the method from across the hall. — Lois Stavsky et al., *A2Z*, p. 68, 1995
• But now it's like when you here the word Method, you don't even think of weed anymore. — Method Man, *Methical fan site*, 2001
• — Mike Haskins, *Drugs*, p. 288, 2003

Methodist hell *noun*
the epitome of heat *US*
• Steve Mitchell sold parlor heaters with the absolute guarantee that they would heat any room hotter than a Methodist Hell. — John Gould, *Maine Lingo*, p. 180, 1975

meths *noun*
methylated spirits *AUSTRALIA, 1981*
• There was butter for burns, cloves for toothache, meths for blisters and cold tea for sunburn. — Kerry Cue, *Crooks, Chooks and Bloody Ratbags*, p. 120, 1983

meth speedball *noun*
methamphetamine mixed with heroin
A combination of **METH** (methamphetamine) and **SPEEDBALL** (cocaine and heroin mixed, or an **UPPER** and **DOWNER** mixed).
• — Robert Ashton, *This Is Heroin*, p. 209, 2002

metric miles *noun*
haemorrhoids *UK*
Rhyming slang for 'piles'.
• — Bodmin Dark, *Dirty Cockney Rhyming Slang*, 2003

metrosexual *noun*
an urban, heterosexual male who, in matters of style or recreation, has similar tastes to those stereotypically associated with women or homosexual men *UK*
• "It's been kept underground for too long," observes one sharply dressed "metrosexual" in his early 20s. — *The Independent*, p. 22, 15th November 1994
• As strong as the "pink pound" of high-income gay men, the "metrosexual" pound is burning a hole in the wallets of a new breed of insecure and "neutered" straight men, desperate to reassert themselves. — *The Guardian*, 16th June 2003

Metro Tux *noun*
in Los Angeles, the police officer's uniform except for his shirt, which is replaced by a white t-shirt *US*
With this slight modification, policemen may drink at a bar without violating the department rule against drinking in uniform.
• — *Los Angeles Times*, p. B8, 19th December 1994

Mex *noun*
1 a Mexican or Mexican-American *US, 1847*
Offensive.
• This Mex, now, was about as defenseless as a man could be. — Jim Thompson, *The Killer Inside*, p. 37, 1952
• The Mex had a black and white checked sport shirt, heavily pleated black slacks without a belt, two-tone black and white buckskin shoes, spotlessly clean. — Raymond Chandler, *The Long Goodbye*, p. 169, 1953
• Anyway, we're driving along the interstate, this Mex tells me how he's been picking oranges half the year and how he's going up to Michigan to pick sugarbeets. — Elmore Leonard, *Killshot*, p. 28, 1989

2 the Spanish language *US, 1858*
• Practically everyone in this area talks some Mex, but I do it better than most. — Jim Thompson, *The Killer Inside*, p. 37, 1952

Mex *adjective*
Mexican *US, 1854*
Offensive.
• I have had two women so far, one American with huge tits and a splendid Mex whore in house. — Jack Kerouac, *Letter to Allen Ginsberg*, p. 353, 10th May 1952
• [G]roups of Mex chicks swaggered around in slacks; mambo blasted from jukeboxes[.] — Jack Kerouac, *On the Road*, p. 93, 1957
• The Mex authorities keep an eye on him all the time and let him blow his loot in that little town where he lives[.] — Mickey Spillane, *Last Cop Out*, p. 10, 1972

Mexi *noun*
low quality marijuana, claimed to be from Mexico *US*
• — Pamela Munro, *U.C.L.A. Slang*, p. 93, 2001

Mexican *noun*
in eastern Australia, a person from a state south of one's own *AUSTRALIA, 1991*
In Queensland it refers to either New South Welshmen or Victorians, whereas in New South Wales it refers to Victorians.
- The election, he kept saying during the campaign, was not about southern banks, Keating, Kirner or other Mexicans, as Queenslanders like to refer to people south of the border.— *Sydney Morning Herald*, p. 1, 21st September 1992

Mexican breakfast *noun*
any combination of a glass of water, a cigarette and the chance to urinate *US, 1960*
- — *Maledicta*, p. 165, 1979: 'A glossary of ethnic slurs in American English'
- If I only stopped for a Mexican breakfast. Coffee and piss.— Dan Jenkins, *Dead Solid Perfect*, p. 239, 1986

Mexican brown *noun*
inferior heroin that originates in Mexico *US, 1975*
The adjective 'Mexican' has a negative value.
- [W]here you could get top-grade smack when everybody else was dealing that Mexican brown[.]— Elmore Leonard, *City Primeval*, p. 64, 1980
- [I]t brushes up against the competition, including Mexican-produced Black Tar, known derisively as Mexican Mud because of its poor quality; the more superior Mexican Brown in powder form; and especially high-grade Colombian White, its biggest rival.— *New York Times*, p. SM29, 23rd June 2002

Mexican Buick *noun*
a Chevrolet *US*
- — *Maledicta*, p. 165, 1979: 'A glossary of ethnic slurs in American English'

Mexican Cadillac *noun*
a Chevrolet *US*
- — *American Speech*, p. 270, December 1962: 'The language of traffic policemen'

Mexican carwash *noun*
a rainstorm *US, 1950*
- — *Maledicta*, p. 165, 1979: 'A glossary of ethnic slurs in American English'

Mexican cashmere *noun*
a cotton sweatshirt *US, 1957*
- — *Maledicta*, p. 165, 1979: 'A glossary of ethnic slurs in American English'

Mexican chrome *noun*
aluminium paint *US, 1955*
- — *Maledicta*, p. 165, 1979: 'A glossary of ethnic slurs in American English'

Mexican cigarette *noun*
a poorly made marijuana cigarette *US*
- — *Maledicta*, p. 58, 1986–1987: 'A continuation of a glossary of ethnic slurs in American English'

Mexican compromise *noun*
a decision in which you lose property but save your life *US*
- — Jerry Robertson, *Oil Slanguage*, p. 83, 1954

Mexican credit card; Mexican filling station *noun*
a siphon used for stealing petrol from a parked car *US*
- — *Maledicta*, p. 165, 1979: 'A glossary of ethnic slurs in American English'

Mexican diamond *noun*
a stone cut and polished to look like a diamond *US*
- — Hyman E. Goldin et al., *Dictionary of American Underworld Lingo*, p. 138, 1950

Mexican fox-trot *noun*
diarrhoea *US*
- — *Maledicta*, p. 165, 1979: 'A glossary of ethnic slurs in American English'

Mexican green *noun*
an inferior marijuana cultivated in Mexico *US, 1961*
- Marijuana with less potency and street value than the brown variety— Jay Robert Nash, *Dictionary of Crime*, 1992
- — Mike Haskins, *Drugs*, p. 288, 2003

Mexican hayride *noun*
a car overloaded with passengers *US*
- — *American Speech*, p. 270, December 1962: 'The language of traffic policemen'

Mexican horse *noun*
brown heroin originating in Mexico *US, 1979*
The source plus **HORSE** (heroin).
- — Robert Ashton, *This Is Heroin*, p. 206, 2002
- — Mike Haskins, *Drugs*, p. 284, 2003

Mexican jumping bean; Mexican red *noun*
a capsule of barbiturate, especially Seconal™, manufactured in Mexico *US*
Named for the capsule's appearance, not its effect, which is sedative.
- — Eugene Landy, *The Underground Dictionary*, p. 131–132, 1971
- The only way we made it was with a great big old bag of Mexican reds and two gallons of Robitussin HC [a branded cough medicine]. Five reds and a slug of HC and you can sleep through anything.— Butch Trucks of the Allman Brothers, *Jabberock*, 1997

Mexican locoweed; Mexican tumbleweed *noun*
marijuana *US, 1969*
- — Richard A. Spears, *The Slang and Jargon of Drugs and Drink*, p. 338, 1986
- — Mike Haskins, *Drugs*, p. 288, 2003

Mexican mud *noun*
brown heroin that originates in the Sierra Madre mountains of Mexico; heroin *US, 1977*
- [I]t brushes up against the competition, including Mexican-produced Black Tar, known derisively as Mexican Mud because of its poor quality; the more superior Mexican Brown in powder form; and especially high-grade Colombian White, its biggest rival.— *New York Times*, p. SM29, 23rd June 2002

Mexican muffler *noun*
a tin can stuffed with steel wool functioning as a car silencer *US, 1953*
- — *Maledicta*, p. 166, 1979: 'A glossary of ethnic slurs in American English'

Mexican mushroom *noun*
psylocybin or psylocin, powerful psychedelic drugs extracted from *Psilocybe mexicana* and *Stropharia cubensis* mushrooms which are native to Mexico *US, 1969*
- — Richard A. Spears, *The Slang and Jargon of Drugs and Drink*, p. 338, 1986

Mexican nose guard *noun*
a jock strap (an athletic support) *US*
An unkind linkage of the penis and nose.
- — *Maledicta*, p. 166, 1979: 'A glossary of ethnic slurs in American English'

Mexican overdrive *noun*
while driving, coasting down a hill in neutral gear *US, 1955*
- — *American Speech*, p. 270, December 1962: 'The language of traffic policemen'
- — *Maledicta*, p. 166, 1979: 'A glossary of ethnic slurs in American English'
- — Lewis Poteet, *Car & Motorcyle Slang*, p. 129, 1992

Mexican paint *noun*
silver paint *US*
- — *American Speech*, p. 100, May 1954

Mexican red *noun*
1 a potent variety of marijuana with a red-brown colour cultivated in Mexico *US, 1971*
- — Richard A. Spears, *The Slang and Jargon of Drugs and Drink*, p. 338, 1986
- — Mike Haskins, *Drugs*, p. 288, 2003

2 a capsule of secobarbitral sodium (trade name Seconal™), a central nervous system depressant *US*
- — Donald Wesson and David Smith, *Barbiturates*, p. 122, 1977

Mexican retread *noun*
a tyre that has been hastily and superficially repaired *US*
- — *American Speech*, p. 270, December 1962: 'The language of traffic policemen'

Mexican shower *noun*
a hurried washing of the face and armpits *US*
- — Ben Applebaum and Derrick Pittman, *Turd Ferguson & The Sausage Party*, p. 44, 2004

Mexican sidewalls *noun*
blackwall tyres that have been painted white *US*
- — *Maledicta*, p. 166, 1979: 'A glossary of ethnic slurs in American English'

Mexican standoff *noun*
1 a situation in which nobody clearly has the advantage or emerges a clear winner *US, 1891*
- It is a Mexican standoff. In a Mexican standoff, both parties narrow their eyes and glare but nobody throws a punch.— Tom Wolfe, *The Pump House Gang*, p. 16, 1968
- Our brothers loaded up. Every cop stopped in his tracks and stepped back. It was like the proverbial Mexican standoff.— Bobby Seale, *A Lonely Rage*, p. 213, 1978
- — *Maledicta*, p. 166, 1979: 'A glossary of ethnic slurs in American English'
- Looks like we got a Mexican standoff.— *Natural Born Killers*, 1994

2 the quitting of a poker game when a player is slightly ahead, slightly behind, or even *US, 1958*

- — John Scarne, *Scarne's Guide to Modern Poker*, p. 284, 1979
- — *Maledicta*, p. 166, 1979: 'A glossary of ethnic slurs in American English'

Mexican straight *noun*

in poker, any hand, a knife and a threat to use the knife *US*
Reminiscent of the simple announcement, 'My Smith and Wesson beats your full house'.

- — *Maledicta*, p. 166, 1979: 'A glossary of ethnic slurs in American English'

Mexican strawberries *noun*

dried beans *CANADA*

- — Bill Casselman, *Canadian Sayings*, p. 66, 2002

Mexican time *noun*

used for denoting a lack of punctuality *US*

- Like Mexican Time and the onetime JPT, Jewish People's time, C.P.T. is a phrase that draws the lines of the ghetto. — Paul Jacobs, *Prelude to a Riot*, p. 12, 1967

Mexican toothache *noun*

dysentery *US, 1960*

- — *Maledicta*, p. 166, 1979: 'A glossary of ethnic slurs in American English'

Mexican traffic light *noun*

a speed bump *US*

- — Lewis Poteet, *Car & Motorcyle Slang*, p. 130, 1992

Mexican tumbleweed *noun*

▷ see: **MEXICAN LOCOWEED**

Mexican Valium *noun*

Rohypnol™ (flunitrazepam), popularly known as the 'date-rape drug' *US*

- Mexican Valium. Ruffie. Quaalude of the '90s. Nicknames abound for the illegal drug Rohypnol that's now hitting the Texas teen scene at $1 to $5 a pill. — *Newsweek*, p. 8, 3rd July 1995
- The drug is called rope, rophies, roofies, roche and Mexican Valium on the streets and is marketted as Rohypnol in South America. — *Daily Oklahoman (Oklahoma City)*, p. 1, 5th September 1995

Mextown *noun*

a neighbourhood with a large population of Mexicans and Mexican-Americans *US*

- We bounced over the railroad tracks in Fresno and hit the wild streets of Fresno Mextown. — Jack Kerouac, *On the Road*, p. 93, 1957

mezz *noun*

marijuana, a marijuana cigarette *US, 1937*
An eponym honouring Milton 'Mezz' Mezzrow, a jazz musician who was better known for his missionary work on behalf of marijuana than his jazz, and who is better remembered for his writing than his jazz.

- I had a trey ounce of mezz and that ain't hay. — *War Medicine*, p. 391, 1944
- New words came into being to meet the situation: the mezz and the mighty mezz, referring, I blush to say, to me and to the tea both. — Mezz Mezzrow, *Really the Blues*, p. 215, 1946

mezzony; mizzony *noun*

the money required for a purchase of marijuana *US, 1930s*
A combination of **MEZZ** (marijuana) and 'money'.

mezzroll; mezz roll; Mezz's roll; meserole; messorole; mezzrow *noun*

an extra-large marijuana cigarette *US, 1944*

- [M]ezzroll, to describe the kind of fat, well-packed, and clean cigarettte I used to roll (this word later got corrupted to meserole and it's still used to mean a certain size and shape of reefer, which is different from the so-called panatella). — Mezz Mezzrow, *Really the Blues*, p. 215, 1946
- The cigarettes came in three qualities: sars-fras, the cheapest kind, sold to thousands of school children at about ten cents each; the panatella, or messerole, retailed at twenty-five cents[.] — Jack Lait and Lee Mortimer, *New York Confidential*, p. 102, 1948
- Even then he had wanted to be an important jazz musician and some of the very good ones were reputed to be regular consumers of the reefer and mezziroll. — Ross Russell, *The Sound*, p. 21, 1961
- — Mike Haskins, *Drugs*, p. 274, 2003

MF; em ef *noun*

a motherfucker *US, 1959*

- Oh shit, I thought, you poor m.f. — Piri Thomas, *Down These Mean Streets*, p. 245, 1967
- Of all people, why'd they kill Malcolm? Why'n't they kill some of them Uncle-Tomming m.f.'s? — Eldridge Cleaver, *Soul on Ice*, p. 51, 1968
- Moze, you get that em-ef out here bore I really does try t'kill him. — Robert Gover, *JC Saves*, p. 15, 1968
- Homos read material about their screwballing aloud, screaming, "THAT MF doesn't know what THE HELL he is talking about!" — Peter Tamony, *Cheesecake*, September 1968
- The Rev. (Carl Davis) pulled out his knife and said Babs here's a tom ass m.f. all the way over in Paris tomming. — Babs Gonzales, *Movin' On Down De Line*, p. 18, 1975

MFI *noun*

1 MI5, the UK's security intelligence agency *UK*
From the name of the retail chain that pioneered self-assembly furniture in the UK, and became the butt of many jokes.

- Box Five and Box Six are how the police refer to MI5 and MI6. The derogatory term for MI5, incidentally, is MFI, as I would later learn when I had to work with them. — Duncan MacLaughlin, *The Filth*, p. 137, 2002

2 a very large myocardial infarction; a major heart attack *UK*
Medical slang, elaborating the conventional abbreviation for the condition, MI, with F for, presumably, **-FUCKING-**. MFI is also a well-known flat-pack furniture retailer.

- — Adam T. Fox, St Mary's Hospital, London, 10th October 2002

MFIC *noun*

the *m*other*f*ucker *i*n *c*harge *US*

- — Carl Fleischhauer, *A Glossary of Army Slang*, p. 33, 1968

mfwic *noun*

in the Canadian military, the Commanding Officer *CANADA*
An abbreviation of '*m*other*f*ucker *w*ho's *i*n *c*harge'.

- Who's the MFWIC [pronounced miff-wick] in this Section? — Tom Langeste, *Words on the Wing*, p. 185, 1995

mf-word *noun*

the word motherfuck, motherfucker or motherfucking *US*

- If you had a nickel for every time these rappers used the "F" word, the "MF" word and the like, you might be almost as rich as they are. — *Chicago Tribune*, 26th July 1992
- The F-word and the MF-word. — *The Times Magazine*, p. 43, 16th February 2002

MIA *adjective*

difficult to locate *US*
From the military label for '*m*issing *i*n *a*ction'.

- — Connie Eble (Editor), *UNC-CH Campus Slang*, p. 7, October 2002

miaow!; mee-ow!

used of a malicious gossiper, or as a commentary on the gossip itself *UK, 1984*
Intended as an impression of a cat's mew, from **CATTY** (spiteful).

mic *noun*

a *mic*rophone *US, 1927*
Pronounced 'mike'.

- Don pops the mike back over his throat hole. — Stuart Browne, *Dangerous Parking*, p. 80, 2000
- [S]he could picture the turntables all right, the mixing desk and mic, the speakers, but not the faces involved. — John King, *White Trash*, p. 18, 2001

▷ see: **MICRODOT**

michael *noun*

the vagina *NEW ZEALAND*

- — David McGill, *David McGill's Complete Kiwi Slang Dictionary*, p. 84, 1998

Michael *noun*

an alcoholic beverage that has been adulterated with a strong tranquillser; the narcotic that is so used *US, 1942*
An abbreviation of **MICKEY FINN**.

Michael Caine; michael *noun*

a pain *UK*
Rhyming slang, formed from the name of the London-born film actor (b.1933).

- Whereby a pest may be a "Michael in the Khyber". — Ray Puxley, *Cockney Rabbit*, 1992

Michael Miles; michaels *noun*

haemorrhoids *UK*
Rhyming slang for 'piles', formed from the name of a popular television 'quiz inquisitor', host of *Take Your Pick*, 1955–68; or, less likely, from a US banjo player.

- You can do what you like down ther, just watch out for my Michaels. — Bodmin Dark, *Dirty Cockney Rhyming Slang*, 2003

michael-muncher *noun*
a person who enjoys performing oral sex on a woman *NEW ZEALAND*
• —David McGill, *David McGill's Complete Kiwi Slang Dictionary*, p. 84, 1998

Michael Schumacher *noun*
tobacco *UK*
Rhyming slang, formed from the name of the German-born world champion Formula 1 racing driver (b.1969); the rhyme, while not perfect, is informed with irony – Michael Schumacher 'has long been associated with Marlboro cigarettes', as noted by Ray Puxley, *Fresh Rabbit*, 1998.

Michael Winner *noun*
dinner *UK*
Rhyming slang, formed from the name of the British film director (b.1935) perhaps better known, in this context, as *The Sunday Times* restaurant critic (with his column: 'Winner's Dinners').
• —Ray Puxley, *Fresh Rabbit*, 1998

Michelle *noun*
in cricket, a score of five wickets taken in an innings *UK*
Rhyming slang, formed on the imperfect rhyme of the name of film actress Michelle Pfeiffer (b.1958), with 'five for...'.
• Warney got a Michelle in the first innings at Edgbaston.—Simon Hughes, *Cricket 4*, 2001

Michigan bankroll *noun*
a single large-denomination note wrapped around small-denomination notes, giving the impression of a great deal of money *US, 1914*
• —*The Annals of the American Academy of Political and Social Sciences*, p. 127, May 1950

Michigan handshake *noun*
a firm handshake that imparts a farewell *US*
Newspaper advice columnist Ann Landers used the term in a column on 27th June 1996, in which she urged 'Embarrassed in Pittsburgh' to give her friend Fred 'a Michigan handshake' 'and tell him to hit the bricks' because he had taken a picture of her sleeping in the nude. Landers' use of the term generated a number of inquiries as to its meaning, and placed the term into the public lexicon. Landers herself pointed to Traverse City, Michigan, in the 1960s as the source of the term.

Michoacan; Michoacan green *noun*
a powerful grade of marijuana, claimed to have been grown in the Mexican state of Michoacan *US, 1973*
• —*American Speech*, Winter 1982

mick *noun*
1 an Irish person or Irish-American *US, 1850*
• It's funny, micks like us fighting each other.—James T. Farrell, *Saturday Night*, p. 52, 1947
• Tell me, Dadier, what do you think of kikes and mockies and micks and donkeys and frogs and niggers, Dadier.—Evan Hunter, *The Blackboard Jungle*, p. 209, 1954
• Iris, meanwhile, was going steady with a young mick named Mike Behan[.]—Charles Raven, *Underworld Nights*, p. 24, 1956
• ACTION: Spics! PEPE: Micks!—*West Side Story*, 1957
• You Irish liar, O'Mally, so you was shooting it all the time. You big Mick.—Graeme Kent, *The Queen's Corporal [Six Granada Plays]*, p. 89, 1959
• Agnew has pointed out that it's a land of opportunity for anyone, whether he's a Mick, as Polack or a Jap.—*Playboy*, p. 62, February 1969
• No sooner we was on the bus back, we had to bail out the windows on to Amsterdam Avenue, a mob of micks was comin' through the door after us.—Edwin Torres, *Carlito's Way*, p. 9, 1975
• A bus, you goddamn whiskey Mick cop, you lost a stolen bus.—*48 Hours*, 1982
• Who would've ever throught a Mick from Columbus Avenue would someday own a layout like this?—Elmore Leonard, *Glitz*, p. 52, 1985
• I don't know about some goddamn slum mick from Brooklyn you decided to marry...—Robert Campbell, *Boneyards*, p. 224, 1992

2 a car that is used in Ireland before being imported into, and reregistered in, England – the documentation on such a vehicle gives the impression of a much newer car *UK*
Car dealers' term.
• —*Woman's Own*, 28th February 1968

3 a prisoner *US*
• —Hyman E. Goldin et al., *Dictionary of American Underworld Lingo*, p. 139, 1950

4 the vagina *NEW ZEALAND*
• —David McGill, *David McGill's Complete Kiwi Slang Dictionary*, p. 84, 1998

5 a young bull, especially if unbranded *AUSTRALIA, 1894*
A shortening of **MICKEY**.
• While the fight was at its height, a little mick jumped out of the mob and covered her.—Sam Weller, *Old Bastards I Have Met*, p. 143, 1979

Mick *noun*
a Catholic *AUSTRALIA, 1902*
From Mick, hypocoristic form of Michael, a common name amongst Catholics in Australia.
• As he was a kind of C. of E. and she was brought up a Mick, Chilla settled the argument by calling on a Foolgarah Methodist sky pilot[.]—Frank Hardy, *The Outcasts of Foolgarah*, p. 22, 1971

mick *adjective*
(used of a school or college course) easy *UK*
• —Helen Dahlskog (Editor), *A Dictionary of Contemporary and Colloquial Usage*, p. 40, 1972

Mick *adjective*
1 Irish *US, 1849*
• Liam knows-a score. Even if ee is a fuckin grumpy Mick cunt.—Niall Griffiths, *Grits*, p. 59, 2000

2 Catholic *AUSTRALIA*
• With my strict Mick upbringing I've always drawn the line at bunging a bird on Diner's.—Barry Humphries, *The Traveller's Tool*, p. 8, 1985

mickey *noun*
1 the vagina *AUSTRALIA, 1969*
Earlier also 'michael' (1950) and 'mick' (1930s).
• ANNOUNCER: Here's a human interest story for you. Her name is ... [He thrusts microphone into GIRL's face] GIRL: [sobbing] Mickey Snatchit. ANNOUNCER: Well, Miss...er...Snatchit. [Eyebrows raised to the audience]—Dorothy Hewett, *The Chapel Perilous*, p. 51, 1972
• She's got a mickey like a vacuum cleaner...drags the marrow clear out of your bones!—Stuart Mills, *Wives and Lovers*, p. 110, 1976
• —David McGill, *David McGill's Complete Kiwi Slang Dictionary*, p. 84, 1998

2 the penis *IRELAND, 1909*
• He's got a lump on his mickey,' his mother said, gazing down on her nearest and dearest. 'His penis,' I said with great authority.—John Fleetwood, *In Stitches*, p. 62, 1994
• [D]o you agree that the average Irish man is an indolent shit-bag who never thinks about anything but his gut and his mickey[?]—Joseph O'Connor, *The Irish Make at Home and Abroad*, p. 128, 1996

3 a young bull, especially if unbranded *AUSTRALIA, 1876*
• I remember getting horned by a mickey in the arse.—Herb Wharton, *Cattle Camp*, p. 185, 1994

4 an ordinary fellow *US, 1949*
• You must be new mickies 'cause you don't call a ship a boat.—Piri Thomas, *Down These Mean Streets*, p. 181, 1967

5 a potato *US, 1936*
• After that, the junkies burn it to get at the brass pipes, and the kids do it for whatever reason kids burn things. Roasting mickeys or something.—Vincent Patrick, *The Pope of Greenwich Village*, p. 108, 1979
• "Also in spring firemen get more calls for fires in empty lots. The kids like to roast mickeys-" "Potatoes," Carlucci says. "Talk about dumb. You think an Irish kid like Jimmy here don't know what's a mickey?"—Robert Campbell, *The Cat's Meow*, p. 48, 1988

6 an alcoholic drink adulterated with knock-out drops *US, 1936*
A shortened form of **MICKEY FINN**.
• Theory was to feed them the sweet talk, and in between all the chit and chat slip them these mickeys[.]—Bernard Wolfe, *The Late Risers*, p. 174, 1954
• Thrills would do anything – his favorite gimmick was a peyote-methedrine mickey in the champagne[.]—Ed Sanders, *Tales of Beatnik Glory*, p. 108, 1975
• Somebody slipped the poor old cat an arsenic mickey.—Robert Campbell, *The Cat's Meow*, p. 139, 1988

▸ **throw a mickey**
to throw a tantrum *AUSTRALIA, 1952*
Perhaps related to **MICKEY** (a young bull).

mickey; mickey out *verb*
to drug someone's drink *US, 1946*
• —Robert C. Prus and C.R.D. Sharper, *Road Hustler*, p. 170, 1977: 'Glossary of terms'

Mickey D's *noun*
a McDonald's™ fast-food restaurant *US, 1977*
• —Connie Eble (Editor), *UNC-CH Campus Slang*, p. 6, Fall 1987
• Dennis, my man, run over to Mickey D's and get me a Big Mac and some fries.—*Heathers*, 1988

- At Mickey D's, I earned $200 a week, and the tax man took out fifty. That was like kicking Monday and Friday in the Ass. —Chris Rock, *Rock This!*, p. 96–97, 1997

Mickey Duff *noun*

▷ see: MICKY DUFF

Mickey Finn; Mickey Flynn; Mickey's *noun*

an alcoholic beverage that has been adulterated with a strong tranquillizer; the narcotic that is so used *US, 1928*

- [F]or the first time in my life I had met up with a great old American institution, the Mickey Finn. —Mezz Mezzrow, *Really the Blues*, p. 294, 1946
- We knocked him out with a small and harmless Mickey Finn and we loaded his pockets with corks. —Robert Sylvester, *No Cover Charge*, p. 211, 1956
- I got back to the base a day late and told my C.O. that I'd been given a mickey finn and couldn't wake up until Monday. —Oscar Zeta Acosta, *The Autobiography of a Brown Buffalo*, p. 130, 1972
- I'm positive someone slipped me a Mickey Finn. —Ian Rankin, *The Falls*, p. 110, 2001
- —Mike Haskins, *Drugs*, p. 283, 2003

Mickey-Finn *verb*

to incapacitate someone with a drink that has been adulterated with a tranquillizer *US*

From the noun.

- The sneaky son-of-a-bitch Mickey-Finned the jerkoff on duty one night, slipping something into his beer. —Christopher Brookmyre, *The Sacred Art of Stealing*, p. 386, 2002

Mickey House *noun*

in poker, an unplayable hand *US*

- —George Percy, *The Language of Poker*, p. 56, 1988

mickey juice *noun*

sexual vaginal secretions *AUSTRALIA*

- —James Lambert, *The Macquarie Book of Slang*, 1996

Mickey man *noun*

a radar operator *US*

- —*American Speech*, p. 310, December 1946: 'More Air Force slang'

Mickey Mouse *noun*

1 a house *UK*

Rhyming slang.

- —Julian Franklyn, *A Dictionary of Rhyming Slang*, 1960
- —Ray Puxley, *Cockney Rabbit*, 1992

2 a Liverpudlian *UK*

Rhyming slang for **SCOUSE**, no doubt informed by the use of 'Mickey Mouse' to mean 'inferior'. Noted in mocking use among London football supporters.

- —Ray Puxley, *Cockney Rabbit*, 1992

3 Famous Grouse™ whisky *UK: SCOTLAND*

Glasgow rhyming slang.

- A Mick Jagger [lager] an a Mickey mouse, barman. —Michael Munro, *The Patter, Another Blast*, 1988

4 a wrist watch *US, 1959*

From the watches with the face of Mickey Mouse first popular in the 1930s.

- I peeped into my skull file and saw that "Roost" note. My "Mickey Mouse" read one-thirty A.M. —Iceberg Slim (Robert Beck), *Pimp*, p. 104, 1969

5 a variety of MDMA, the recreational drug best known as ecstasy, identified by the embossed motif *UK*

- —Gareth Thomas, *This Is Ecstasy*, p. 56, 2002

6 in American casinos, a $2.50 chip *US*

- —Steve Kuriscak, *Casino Talk*, p. 11, 1985

7 an ultra-shortwave radar used for aircraft spotting *US*

From a distance, the apparatus may be said to resemble a mouse.

- —*American Speech*, p. 153, April 1947: 'Radar slang terms'

Mickey Mouse *adjective*

1 inferior, trivial, cheap *US, 1947*

Originally coined to describe inferior dance music, then given a broader sense.

- —Arnold Shaw, *Lingo of Tin-Pan Alley*, p. 10, 1950
- After carefully parking a gleaming Selmer tenor on an adjacent chair, he raised to his lips a straight little soprano sax, the once-despised symbol of Mickey Mouse band leaders. —Albert Goldman, *Freak Show*, p. 285, 1963
- All that pedantic Mickey Mouse chitchat. —Richard Farina, *Been Down So Long*, p. 220, 1966
- All they know is that it feels good to swing to way-out body-rhythms instead of dragassing across the dance floor like zombies to the dead beat of mind-smothered Mickey-Mouse music. —Eldridge Cleaver, *Soul on Ice*, p. 81, 1968
- This Mickey Mouse jive with the pussy and the coke and the booze don't mean nothin'. —Edwin Torres, *Carlito's Way*, p. 21, 1975
- [W]e were required to tally up our individual sales and purchases on an ordinary Mickey Mouse adding machine and see if they matched those of the boss computer. —Terry Southern, *Now Dig This*, p. 32, 1975
- What is this Mickey Mouse shit? —*Full Metal Jacket*, 1987
- [N]o fucker ever died from a diazzy overdose mun. Methadone aye, but not diazepam. Mickey Mouse downer, diazepam. —Niall Griffiths, *Sheepshagger*, p. 108, 2001

2 outmoded, old-fashioned or unnecessarily conventional *US*

- I said something about going steady being a Mickey Mouse institution. —Lawrence Block, *Chip Harrison Scores Again*, p. 240, 1971

3 excellent *AUSTRALIA, 1973*

Rhyming slang for **GROUSE**.

- The real mickey mouse direct drives have been costing anything from $500 to $850 in the shops, restricting them to a small section of the market. —*National Times*, p. 48, 16th June 1979
- Despite the television ecstasies of Mr May of the ABC, outsiders have not been slow to point out that Australia is inexorably becoming one of the Mickey Mouse sporting nations of the world. —*Weekend Australian*, p. 14, 16th October 1982

Mickey Mouse around *verb*

to fool around *US*

School usage.

- —*Washington Post*, 23rd April 1961: 'Man, dig this jazz'

Mickey Mouse boots *noun*

heavy rubber boots issued to soldiers during the Korean war *US, 1952*

- But the temperatures were fast approaching zero at night, and the minute the boys got into position, their sweat-filled, heavy rubber "Mickey Mouse" boots (newly issued and so named for the striking resemblance they bore to those worn by Walt Disney's famous rodent) froze from the inside out. —David H. Hackworth, *About Face*, p. 262, 1989

Mickey Mouse mission *noun*

a simple, undemanding, relatively safe military task *US*

- —Gregory Clark, *Words of the Vietnam War*, p. 327, 1990

Mickey Mouse money *noun*

1 any unfamiliar or foreign currency; an unfeasible amount of any money *US, 1945*

Originally used by the US military for Japanese currency; contemporary usage may be applied to, for instance, the Euro or Scottish banknotes.

- "I write free software to make people (not least myself) happy.[...] I sure as hell don't do it for the f***ing silicon value mickey mouse money stock options," wrote one programmer. —*The Guardian*, 18th May 2000

2 military scrip issued to soldiers in the Korean war *US*

- [O]ur US currency has been substituted by a military script referred to as Mickey Mouse money[.] —Martin Russ, *The Last Parallel*, p. 58, 1957

Mickey Mouse movie *noun*

a pornographic film that shows little or no detailed activity *UK*

- —*New Society*, 12th August 1976

Mickey Mouser; mickey *noun*

a person from Liverpool, a Liverpudlian *UK*

Rhyming slang for **SCOUSER**.

- [T]he character of the Manks [from Manchester] and the Mickey Mousers is vastly different. The Manks are droll, dry, think every cunt's soft, whereas the Mickeys are the gobby, have-the-crack-at-all-costs jokers in the pack. —J.J. Connolly, *Layer Cake*, p. 122, 2000

mickey out *verb*

▷ see: MICKEY

Mickey Rooney *noun*

a madman, a crazy person *UK*

Rhyming slang for **LOONY**, formed from the name of US film actor and entertainer (b.1920).

- —Michael Munro, *The Patter, Another Blast*, 1988
- —Ray Puxley, *Cockney Rabbit*, 1992

mickey's *noun*

LSD *UK*

- —Mike Haskins, *Drugs*, p. 285, 2003

mickey-take; micky-take *verb*
to make fun of someone; to pull someone's leg; to jeer at, to deride *UK, 1959*
From **TAKE THE MICKY** (to mock). Also used as a noun.
• —John Ayto, *The Oxford Dictionary of Slang*, p. 331, 1998

mickey-taking; micky-taking *noun*
an act of derisive taunting *UK*
• CLARKE: Bullied. That's an exaggeration. They take the micky a bit. VALE: What about Bell this evening? Would you call that micky-taking? —Graeme Kent, *The Queen's Corporal [Six Granada Plays]*, p. 106, 1959

mickie *noun*
a bottled alcoholic drink *US, 1914*
• We stole our first mickies together from Gordon's fruit stand. —Claude Brown, *Manchild in the Promised Land*, p. 308, 1965
• "Micky," for a small bottle of liquor, is yet another contribution to drinking English created by Canadians from Mickey Finn, slang for both an Irishman and knock-out drops in a drink. —Bill Casselman, *Canadian Words*, p. 14–15, 1995

Mick Jagger *noun*
lager *UK: SCOTLAND*
Glasgow rhyming slang (a good rhyme in the local accent), formed from the singer with The Rolling Stones (b.1943).
• Three heavies [beers] an a Mick Jagger. —Michael Munro, *The Complete Patter*, 1985
• Are ye corned beef[deaf]? I said sit doon on yer chorus [backside] and we'll have a wee Salvador [drink]. Mine's a Mick Jagger by the way. — *The Guardian*, 29th April 2002

micks *noun*
Michelin™ tyres *US*
• —Montie Tak, *Truck Talk*, p. 106, 1971

Mick's blood *noun*
Guinness™ stout *UK: SCOTLAND*
The quintessential Irish beer.
• —Michael Munro, *The Complete Patter*, p. 100, 1996

Mick-takers *nickname*
Scotland Yard's anti-IRA Intelligence Unit *UK*
A play on **MICKEY-TAKE** (to make fun).
• — *Daily Telegraph*, 30th November 1974

Micky Bliss *noun*
▷ **see: MIKE BLISS**

Micky Duff; Mickey Duff *noun*
unwell, rough *UK*
Rhyming slang, formed from the name of a boxing manager and matchmaker (b.1929).
• You alright? You look a bit Micky Duff. —Ray Puxley, *Fresh Rabbit*, 1998

micky muncher *noun*
a cunnilinguist *AUSTRALIA*
• —Lenie Johansen, *The Dinkum Dictionary*, 1988

microbod *noun*
in caving and pot-holing, a small adult or child with the ability to fit into narrow passages and around difficult corners *UK*
• — David Morrison of Wessex Cave Club, 29th February 2004

microchip *noun*
a Japanese person *UK*
Rhyming slang for **NIP**.
• — Ray Puxley, *Cockney Rabbit*, 1992

microdot; mic; micro; mike *noun*
a small tablet of LSD *UK*
• —Angela Devlin, *Prison Patter*, p. 76, 1996
• I had a trip about then too, a black microdot – it was great. —Macfarlane, Macfarlane and Robson, *The User*, p. 88, 1996
• [W]e share a microdot between us. Her face smudged like a Francis Bacon. —Darren Francis, *The Sprawl [britpulp]*, p. 317, 1999
• Very tiny, often brightly-colored pills called "microdots" or "dots" still appear with some regularity in the underground acid market. —Cam Cloud, *The Little Book of Acid*, p. 38, 1999

Microsloth Windows *nickname*
Microsoft Windows™ *US*
• —Eric S. Raymond, *The New Hacker's Dictionary*, p. 242, 1991

mid-air *noun*
in the language of hang gliding, a collision involving two fliers *US*
• —Erik Fair, *California Thrill Sports*, p. 328, 1992

middle *noun*
1 in sports betting, a combination of bets that produce a win no matter what the outcome of the game *US*
• The wider the "middle" the more beautiful is twenty-to-one. —Jimmy Snyder, *Jimmy the Greek*, p. 208, 1975
• I was grabbing everything I could get on the Bears and giving up 10. Here was a chance for a two-point "middle,k" time honored gambler's trick to win coming and going, to collect on both ends. —Hunter S. Thompson, *Generation of Swine*, p. 73, 1986

2 the waist *UK*
From Old English *middel* and *middil*.
• Her knickers are unflattering – so tight they make her middle bulge – and deliberately awry in order to make her look lopsided. — *The Observer*, 25th August 2002

middle comb *noun*
hair parted in the centre *US*
Hawaiian youth usage.
• —Douglas Simonson, *Pidgin to da Max Hana Hou*, 1982

middle leg *noun*
the penis *UK, 1896*
Still in popular use.
• — *Roger's Profanisaurus*, p. 135, 2002

middle name *noun*
anything which is your passion or speciality or outstanding characteristic may be claimed as your middle name *US, 1905*
• Tony – reform is my middle name – Blair isn't obviously the public sector's friend. — *The Guardian*, 21st October 2003

Middlesex *adjective*
homosexual *US*
A pun on the place.
• Between these two levels of honest if Middlesex entertainment are the atmospheric places gotten up to look very Left Bank[.] —Jack Lait and Lee Mortimer, *New York Confidential*, p. 68–69, 1948

middle-sexed *adjective*
homosexual *US*
• Such habituals always draw the distorted and the perverted and that melange of middle-sexed jobs which nature started but never finished. —Jack Lait and Lee Mortimer, *Chicago Confidential*, p. 65, 1950

middle stump *noun*
the penis *UK, 1937*
From cricket.

middlings *noun*
in the illegal production of alcohol, livestock feed used instead of grain *US*
• —David W. Maurer, *Kentucky Moonshine*, p. 121, 1974

middy; middie *noun*
a ten ounce glass of beer; a serving of beer in such a glass *AUSTRALIA, 1945*
• A middy is a ten-oz. glass and 384 middies are equivalent to twenty-four gallons. —Vince Kelly, *The Bogeyman*, p. 186, 1956
• Those big glasses are called schooners and those small ones are called middies. —Nino Culotta (John O'Grady), *They're A Weird Mob*, p. 25, 1957
• How many middies does a jug hold? —Bazza and Curly, *Betcha Wrong!*, p. 83, 1990

midget *noun*
1 a very young member of a youth gang *US*
• All the midgets and tinys in the Black Spiders had been to the Hall. most of the peewees even! —Joseph Wambaugh, *The Glitter Dome*, p. 110, 1981

2 in motor racing, a small, single-seat, open race car *US*
• —Don Alexander, *The Racer's Dictionary*, p. 41, 1980

midgy *adjective*
small *UK*
Probably derived from 'midget'.
• Only thing stopping me shafting her she reckoned was I was too midgy. —Jeremy Cameron, *Brown Bread in Wengen*, p. 33, 1999

Midland Bank *noun*
an act of masturbation *UK*
Rhyming slang for **WANK**, formed from the name of a high street bank.
- —Ray Puxley, *Fresh Rabbit*, 1998

midnight *noun*
in dice games, a roll of 12 *US, 1919*
- —Gil Jacobs, *The World's Best Dice Games*, p. 198, 1976

midnight auto parts; midnight auto service; midnight auto supply *noun*
stolen car parts; their notional source *US*
- Larry organized his "midnight auto supply" with some cunning[.] —E.R. Linton, *America's Newest Sex Cult*, p. 68, 1966
- —Hy Lit, *Hy Lit's Unbelievable Dictionary of Hip Words for Groovy People*, p. 28, 1968
- —Connie Eble (Editor), *UNC-CH Campus Slang*, March 1974
- Its membership, quite loosely knit, supplied the Midnight auto Parts concern so popular with people who dislike paying list price for their automobile repairs. —George V. Higgins, *Penance for Jerry Kennedy*, p. 125, 1985
- [T]hey tend to have interchangeable parts, creating a profitable black market for stolen replacement parts – the so-called Midnight Auto Supply. —*San Antonio (Texas) Express-News*, p. 1J, 15th June 2002

midnight cowboy *noun*
a homosexual prostitute, originally one who wears cowboy clothes; hence a homosexual man *US*
Brought from gay subculture into wider use by the film *Midnight Cowboy*, 1969. The less subtle, general sense resulted from the film's success.
- The clothes chosen by the fetishists epitomize masculinity: cowboys, sailors, etc. The model acting out the cowboy then is a midnight cowboy[.] —Bruce Rodgers, *The Queens' Vernacular*, 1972
- —*Maledicta*, p. 223, 1979: 'Kinks and queens: linguistic and cultural aspects of the terminology for gays'
- —Peter Chippindale, *The British CB Book*, p. 156, 1981

midnight lab *noun*
a laboratory where illegal drugs are manufactured *US*
- —William D. Alsever, *Glossary for the Establishment and Other Uptight People*, p. 21, December 1970

midnight mass *noun*
an informer *UK*
Rhyming slang (probably from the north of England by the accent required for the rhyme) for **GRASS** (an informer).
- —Angela Devlin, *Prison Patter*, p. 76, 1996

midnight oil *noun*
opium *US*
- —Vincent J. Monteleone, *Criminal Slang*, p. 155, 1949

midnight overdrive *noun*
coasting down a hill with the car or truck in neutral gear *US*
- —Montie Tak, *Truck Talk*, p. 106, 1971

midnight revue *noun*
serial consecutive sex between one person and multiuple partners, usually consensual *US*
- It was the Midnight Revue. Everybody plays jam in that park, gets their trim. We got on her. Seven of us. —Hal Ellson, *Duke*, p. 61, 1949

midnights *noun*
the midnight shift, a work schedule beginning at midnight and ending at 8am *US*
- Just when you had adjusted your metabolism to the 8:00 AM to 4:30 PM shift, it was time to get on the swing shift. And finally midnights. —Odie Hawkins, *Lost Angeles*, p. 11, 1994

midnight shopper *noun*
a burglar *US*
- —Wayne Floyd, *Jason's Authentic Dictionary of CB Slang*, p. 21, 1976

midnight supply man *noun*
a person who traffics in stolen equipment *US*
- —Jerry Robertson, *Oil Slanguage*, p. 83, 1954

midnight toker *noun*
a person who smokes marijuana before retiring to bed *US*
- I'm a smoker / I'm a midnight toker —Steve Miller, *The Joker*, 1973

midrats *noun*
a meal served between midnight and 1am *US, 1973*
An abbreviation of 'midnight rations'.
- —Ethan Dicks, *English, as She is Spoke at McMurdo*, 1196
- —Bernadette Hince, *The Antarctic Dictionary*, p. 229, 2000

midway bonus *noun*
in circus and carnival usage, an extravagant, empty promise *US*
- —Don Wilmeth, *The Language of American Popular Entertainment*, p. 172, 1981

midzer *adjective*
▷ see: **MADZA**

MIG alley *noun*
during the Korean war, airspace controlled by North Korea and its allies *US, 1951*
- This he did, while Sabrejets went thundering north to "MIG Alley" to recover air supremacy. —Robert Leckie, *The Wars of America, Volume II*, p. 389, 1968

mighty *adjective*
excellent *NEW ZEALAND*
- —Louis S. Leland, *A Personal Kiwi-Yankee Dictionary*, p. 65, 1984

mighty *adverb*
very, greatly *UK, 1715*
Often ironic.
- I hear music / Mighty fine music —Chaka Khan, *I Hear Music*, 1982

Mighty Joe Young *noun*
a central nervous system depressant *UK, 1998*
- —Mike Haskins, *Drugs*, p. 283, 2003

mighty mezz *noun*
a generous marijuana cigarette, or simply marijuana *US*
- New words came into being to meet the situation: the mezz and the might mezz, referring, I blush to say, to me and to the tea, both[.] —Mezz Mezzrow, *Really the Blues*, p. 215, 1946

mighty mite *noun*
1 a marijuana variety with large buds *CANADA*
- "Heh." "Mighty Mite seeds." "California Girl cross Durban." "Same." —Brian Preston, *Pot Planet*, p. 232, 2002

2 an airblower used by the military in Vietnam to blow smoke or tear gas into enemy tunnels *CANADA*
Also spelt 'mity-mite'.
- Andrews and Hill started the mity-mite. The small gasoline engine sound like a lawnmower. Hill lit the first smudge pot. —John Del Vecchio, *The 13th Valley*, p. 327, 1982

mighty Quinn *noun*
LSD *US, 1975*
- —Richard A. Spears, *The Slang and Jargon of Drugs and Drink*, p. 340, 1986
- —Mike Haskins, *Drugs*, p. 285, 2003

mike *noun*
1 a microgram (1/1,000,000th of a gram) *US*
The unit of measure for LSD doses, even in the non-metric US.
- —Joe David Brown (Editor), *The Hippies*, p. 219, 1967: 'Glossary of hippie terms'
- "How many mikes?" Papa All wanted to know. "Ahh, I dunno. They'll get ya off." —Nicholas Von Hoffman, *We Are The People Our Parents Warned Us Against*, p. 26, 1967
- —Sidney Cohen, *The Drug Dilemma*, p. 130, 1969
- I had one woman that took four hundred mikes of LSD. —*Los Angeles Free Press*, p. 10, 14th-20th August 1970
- She hung out with me while I was coming on when I had been dosed by what I think was something apporaching 3500 mikes[.] —Stephen Gaskin, *Amazing Dope Tales*, p. 115, 1980
- Crisis-level bummers are less likely to happen on low doses of acid – 100 mikes or less – than on high doses of 150 mikes or more. —Cam Cloud, *The Little Book of Acid*, p. 22, 1999

2 a microdot (of LSD)
- Here was some dude, not even a chemistry major, coming on to you with mikes, grams, bricks, kilos and hundredweights[.] —Robert Sabbag, *A Way with the Spoon [The Howard Marks Book of Dope Stories]*, p. 351, 1998

3 a microphone *US, 1927*
- Shortly after noon the two largest national broadcasting systems installed mikes on the main walk down near the front gates. —Chester Himes, *Cast the First Stone*, p. 145, 1952

4 a minute *US*
From the military phonetic alphabet – 'mike' for 'm', and 'm' for 'minute'.
- Three is inbound from the Sierra Whiskey. Should be here in two zero mikes if they don't hit any shit. —*Platoon*, 1986

5 a person who secretly finances a licensed bookmaker *AUSTRALIA*
- —Ned Wallish, *The Truth Dictionary of Racing Slang*, p. 52, 1989

mike; mike up *verb*
to equip with a microphone *UK, 1984*
- Victoria was miked and sat in a straight-back chair opposite Ted. —Stephen Cannell, *King Con*, p. 82, 1992
- Requests to mike up any electronic keyboard should be met with diplomatic tactics. —Ben Duncan, *The Live Sound Manual*, p. 16, 2002

Mike Bliss; Micky Bliss *noun*
the act of urination; urine *UK, 1961*
Rhyming slang for **PISS**, which leads to **TAKE THE MICKY**, **TAKE THE MICHAEL** and variants such as **TAKE THE PISS** (to jeer).
- —Julian Franklyn, *A Dictionary of Rhyming Slang*, 1961

mike boat *noun*
a military landing craft *US*
- Two motor-drive "mike" boat, each with a capacity for 300 passengers, would be waiting to load them on. —Frank Snepp, *A Decent Interval*, p. 505, 1977
- The mike boat came sliding toward the quay, its diesel engine falling silent as it coasted the last few yards to the early float. —Stephen Coonts, *Final Flight*, p. 252, 1988
- One of the SEAL Two lieutenants, Larry Bailey, took command of a Mike boat – an armored Landing Craft, Medium, or LCM – which held an 81-mike-mike (81 mm mortar), plus pairs of M60 and .50-caliber machine guns. —Richard Marcinko and John Weisman, *Rogue Warrior*, p. 83, 1992

mike check *noun*
oral sex on a male *US*
- —Connie Eble (Editor), *UNC-CH Campus Slang*, p. 6, Spring 1992

mike fright *noun*
an overwhelming fear that confronts an actor when facing a microphone *US*
- —Wilfred Granville, *The Theatre Dictionary*, p. 123, 1952

Mike Hunt
a fictitious name, used as a prank for waiting lists *US*
The announcement 'table for Mike Hunt' sounds very much like 'table for my cunt', thus a source of amusement.
- —Michael Dalton Johnson, *Talking Trash with Redd Foxx*, p. 14, 1994

mike juliet *noun*
marijuana *US*
Vietnam war usage. The military phonetic alphabet for **MJ** (marijuana).
- Why, smoke is M.J., Mike Juliet. Ya know – grass. —Larry Heinemann, *Close Quarters*, p. 26, 1977

Mike Malone *noun*
a telephone *UK*
Rhyming slang.
- —Ray Puxley, *Cockney Rabbit*, 1992

mike-mike *noun*
a millimeter, or a weapon with a calibre measured in millimeters *US, 1967*
From the military phonetic alphabet for 'mm'.
- The C-47 was a standard prop flareship, but many of them carried .20- and .762-mm. guns on their doors, Mike-Mikes that could fire out 300 rounds per second[.] —A.D. Horne, *The Wounded Generation*, p. 59, 1981

mik-e-nik *noun*
a car or truck mechanic *US*
- —Porter Bibb, *CB Bible*, p. 99, 1976

mileage *noun*
1 any extra use or advantage that may be derived from a situation *US, 1955*
- Fingersmith and Affinity got a lot of mileage out of people experiencing lesbian desire for the first time[.] —*The Guardian*, 26th September 2002

2 a record of previous convictions *UK*
- —Angela Devlin, *Prison Patter*, p. 77, 1996

Mile End *noun*
a friend *UK*
Rhyming slang, formed from an area of east London.
- I'd like you to meet a Mile End of mine. —Ray Puxley, *Cockney Rabbit*, 1992

Mile High Club *noun*
a collective noun for people who claim to have had sex on an airborne plane *US, 1972*
Interestingly, the equivalent 'club' on a train is not measured in height but distance travelled: 'the nine mile club'.
- I made a few attempts at trying to charm the hostesses into initiating us into their legendary "Mile High Club" but they weren't wearing it. —Dean Cavanagh, *Mile High Meltdown (Disco Biscuits)*, p. 212, 1996

miles *noun*
▸ **make some miles**
to drive (a truck) *US*
- —Montie Tak, *Truck Talk*, p. 104, 1971

miles *adverb*
much *UK, 1885*
- Walking is miles better in D&G shades. —*The Guardian*, 2nd March 2003

milf; MILF *noun*
a sexually appealing mother *US*
- Dude, that chick's a MILF. What the hell is that? Mom I'd like to fuck. —*American Pie*, 1999
- —Connie Eble (Editor), *UNC-CH Campus Slang*, p. 7, Fall 2001

milk *verb*
1 to exploit, to cheat *UK, 1536*
- The boss catered mostly to Indians who struck oil on the reservation, beefy cattlemen who were sure to be milked, sugar-daddies with their sable-sporting chicken dinners, and butter-and-egg men with plenty of bacon. —Mezz Mezzrow, *Really the Blues*, p. 84, 1946
- Too many people wanna milk it for what it's worth. —*The Bad Lieutenant*, 1992
- I could have milked the situation, but the landlord trusted me[.] —John King, *Human Punk*, p. 193, 2000

2 to masturbate *UK, 1616*
- —Helen Dahlskog (Editor), *A Dictionary of Contemporary and Colloquial Usage*, p. 40, 1972

3 in card games, to draw the top and bottom cards (off a new pack) before the first shuffle *US, 1845*
- —Albert H. Morehead, *The Complete Guide to Winning Poker*, p. 268, 1967

▸ **get off and milk it!**
used for heckling a bicyclist *UK, 1975*
Mainly schoolchildren use. In 1982, Beale complained of 12-year-olds taunting him so.

▸ **milk a rush**
while injecting a drug, to draw blood into the syringe and slowly release the drug into the vein, controlling the immediate effect of the drug *US*
- —Richard A. Spears, *The Slang and Jargon of Drugs and Drink*, p. 340, 1986

▸ **milk it**
to squeeze the shaft of the penis towards the head of the penis *US*
- — Anon., *King Smut's Wet Dreams Interpreted*, 1978

▸ **milk the anaconda**
(of a male) to masturbate *US*
- A signal meant they'd caught some guy milking the anaconda. —Joseph Wambaugh, *The Secrets of Harry Bright*, p. 60–61, 1985

▸ **milk the bushes**
to move a boat by pulling on shore bushes *CANADA, 1940*

▸ **milk the lizard**
(of a male) to masturbate; to cause sexual ejaculation *UK*
- [L]ooks at the pictures and milks his lizard. —Tami Hoag, *The Thin Line*, 1997

▸ **milk the one-eyed aphid**
of a male, to masturbate *UK*
- —Richard Herring, *Talking Cock*, p. 113, 2003

milk?
used as a tease of someone whose demeanour is just a bit catty *US*
- —Kevin Dilallo, *The Unofficial Gay Manual*, p. 242, 1994

milk-ball *noun*
any alcoholic beverage served with milk *US*
- "Ulcer?" Mario Villalobos asked. "Iron stomach," she said. "I just like milk-balls." —Joseph Wambaugh, *The Delta Star*, p. 121, 1983

milk bar *noun*
the female breasts *UK, 1984*
Probably dating from the 1950s when conventional milk bars had their peak of popularity.

milkbar cowboy *noun*
a motorcyclist given to frequenting milk bars *NEW ZEALAND*
A term from the 1950s and 60s.
- We usually ending up at the Centreway, ordering sundaes or sodas and watching the milkbar cowboys revving their motorbikes. —Michael Jackson, *Rainshadow*, p. 113, 1988

milk-drop *noun*
an auction fraud, in which the auctioneer inflates the price of an item by accepting non-existent bids before selling the item to the victim of the fraud *UK*
- Nothing spectacular, such as Sotheby's and Christie's might be proud of in their time-honoured way, just the old familiar milk-drop. —Jonathan Gash, *The Ten Word Game*, p. 61, 2003

milker *noun*
in poker, a player who bets only on a very good hand or with very good odds *US*
- —George Percy, *The Language of Poker*, p. 57, 1988

milkie; milky *noun*
a milkman *UK, 1886*

milking stool *noun*
in electric line work, a yoke used for supporting hot line tension tools *US*
- —A.B. Chance Co., *Lineman's Slang Dictionary*, p. 12, 1980

milk jugs *noun*
▷ see: JUGS

milkman's horse *adjective*
cross, angry *UK*
Rhyming slang (the Cockney accent should be obvious).
- —Julian Franklyn, *A Dictionary of Rhyming Slang*, 1961

milko *noun*
a milk vendor *AUSTRALIA, 1907*
- There were twenty runners in the Cup and the milko got enough entries, 500 in fact, to run 25 sweeps. —Roy Higgins and Tom Prior, *The Jockey Who Laughed*, p. 78, 1982
- Stop messin' with the other man's wife, milko. —John Milne, *Alive and Kicking*, 1998

milk rope *noun*
a pearl necklace *US*
- —*American Speech*, p. 98, May 1956: 'Smugglers' argot in the Southwest'

milk route *noun*
an easy, lucrative sales route *US, 1930*
- To use the contemptuous installment house term, I was handed a "milk route." —Jim Thompson, *Roughneck*, p. 59, 1954

▸ **do the milk route**
as a prostitute, to visit late-night venues in search of customers *US*
- —*Maledicta*, p. 150, Summer/Winter 1986–1987: 'Sexual slang: prostitutes, pedophiles, flagellators, transvestites, and necrophiles'

milk run *noun*
1 a routine trip, especially one that calls at several places *UK, 1942*
Originally military. Also called a 'milk round'.
2 a simple, undemanding, undangerous military task *US, 1943*
- —Gregory Clark, *Words of the Vietnam War*, p. 327, 1990

3 the first run of a ski-lift on a given morning, or the first run down the mountain of the day *US*
- Ambitious skiers will get up early to make the milk run. —*American Speech*, p. 206, October 1963: 'The language of skiers'

milkshake *noun*
1 a solution of baking powder administered to a racehorse to improve its performance *NEW ZEALAND*
- The New Zealand Harness racing Conference is only weeks away from introducing new testing, which it hopes will also kill off another wave of rumours about milkshakes and drugs in the game. —*(Aukland) Sunday Star*, p. B6, 23rd December 1990

2 semen that is sucked and swallowed from a rectum *US*
Interview of Jim Holliday, 12th June 1987.
3 oral sex performed on a male *NEW ZEALAND*
- —David McGill, *David McGill's Complete Kiwi Slang Dictionary*, p. 53, 1998

milkshake *verb*
to administer a milkshake to a horse *NEW ZEALAND*
- [An owner] arranged for racecourse inspector Norm Scott to keep the filly under surveillance to prove he was not milkshaking her. —*(Aukland) Sunday Star*, p. 12, 23rd January 1992

milksop *noun*
a cowardly or effeminate man *UK, 1382*
- But Trixie, deferential as she usually was, would have none of this milksop attitude. —Jim Thompson, *Roughneck*, p. 88, 1954

milksucker *noun*
a young child *US*
- Had so fucking many milksuckers running around she forgot the police department summer camp was taking care a the little prick for a week. —Joseph Wambaugh, *The Choirboys*, p. 37, 1975

milk-train *noun*
a train with an early morning schedule *US, 1853*
- She'd gone out to the rear platform for some fresh air – a rarity on the milk train – and taken a tumble. —Jim Thompson, *The Nothing Man*, p. 268–269, 1954

Milky Way *noun*
a homosexual *UK*
Rhyming slang for **GAY**, created from a galaxy far far away, or, more likely, from a popular chocolate confection with the well-remembered slogan: 'the sweet you can eat between meals without spoiling your appetite'.
- —Ray Puxley, *Fresh Rabbit*, 1998

mill *noun*
1 *milli*metre, especially as a measure of a gun's calibre, or a width of still- and cine-camera film *US, 1960*
- Makes a nine mill look like a fuckin peashooter. —Donald Gorgon, *Cop Killer*, p. 60, 1994

2 one thousand dollars *US*
- —Francis J. Rigney and L. Douglas Smith, *The Real Bohemia*, p. xx, 1961

3 a *mill*ion, especially and usually a million dollars or pounds *US, 1942*
Sometimes simply 'mile'.
- They make, what, about a quarter of a mil in a month? —George V. Higgins, *The Friends of Eddie Doyle*, p. 201, 1971
- We walk away with a mill. Does that turn you on? —Gerald Petievich, *One-Shot Deal*, p. 159, 1981
- "Yeah," said Brain, his mouth full of pot roast, "but two mil a movie must soften the blow." —Armistead Maupin, *Further Tales of the City*, p. 46, 1982
- He likes his ladies, his clothes and a quarter mill a year in his kick. —J.J. Connolly, *Layer Cake*, p. 6, 2000
- They won't scoff at the extra half-mill in my back bin [pocket] and all. —Kevin Sampson, *Outlaws*, p. 235, 2001

4 in hot rodding and drag racing, an engine *US, 1918*
- —*Hot Rod Magazine*, p. 13, November 1948: 'Racing jargon'
- Of course you can always swap mills, buif you have a champagne appetite for speed and a beer bankroll, you can go a long way on a little money by overhauling and tuning up[.] —Edd Byrnes, *Way Out with Kookie*, 1959
- — Capitol Records, *Hot Rod Jargon*, 1963
- Just a little deuce coupe with a flat head mill / But she'll walk a Thunderbird like she's standin' still... — Brian Wilson (Performed by The Beach Boys), *Little Deuce Coupe*, 1963

Millennium Dome *noun*
1 a comb *UK*
Rhyming slang, formed from the famous folly while it was no more than a building site.
- —Ray Puxley, *Fresh Rabbit*, 1998

2 a tele*phone* *UK*
Rhyming slang (that barely rhymes).
- Yeah she gave me a tinkle on the Millenium [sic] Dome last night. —*www.LondonSlang.com*, June 2002

millennium domes *noun*
female breasts that are enhanced to misleading dimensions *UK, 2002*
After the UK's much criticised celebration of 2000 years: the Millennium Dome.

- The contents of a Wonderbra, i.e. like the dome, extremely impressive when viewed from the outside, but there's actually fuck-all in there worth seeing. — Chris Lewis, *The Dictionary of Playground Slang*, p. 149, 2003

Miller time *noun*
hours spent drinking beer after work or play *US*
An advertising slogan by the Miller Brewing Company, expanded to non-product-specific ironic usage.
- Every night the sun goes down and the guy that drives the bulldozer around goes back to the shack and gets his jacket on and goes home for Miller Time. — George V. Higgins, *The Rat on Fire*, p. 80–81, 1981

milling *noun*
the action of fighting a companion, no holds barred, as a test of your ability *UK, 1810*
Military.
- As a young soldier, milling was part of any selection or basic training at that time [1976]. — Andy McNab, *Immediate Action*, p. 13, 1995
- It's known in the military as "milling", or "choose a friend and kick the shit out of him"! — Duncan MacLaughlin, *The Filth*, p. 74, 2002

million *noun*
a certainty, a safe bet *UK*
Probably from gambling odds of 1,000,000–1. Examples: (of a plan) 'It's a million'; (for promotion) 'You're a million'.
- — G.F. Newman, *Sir, You Bastard*, 1970

▸ gone a million
utterly undone; defeated; unable to recover *AUSTRALIA, 1913*
- If they drop their bundles they're gone a million. — Gavin Casey, *It's Harder for Girls*, p. 164, 1941
- During the conversation Hawke, in conveying the common belief of the officers that Whitlam would not survive as Leader, remarked, 'Gough's gone a million'. — Blanche d'Alpuget, *Robert J. Hawke*, p. 297, 1982

▸ look a million; look like a million bucks
to look exquisitely stunning *AUSTRALIA*
- She looked a million with her red hair tied back in a long ponytail with a lime green chiffon scarf. — Robert Campbell, *Alice in La-La Land*, p. 59, 1987
- When he went out dancing he reckoned he felt and looked a million, and he really meant business. — Clive Galea, *Slipper*, p. 11, 1988

million dollar wound *noun*
during war, a wound that was serious enough to get a soldier sent home but not so serious as to affect the rest of their life *US, 1947*
- Some examples of "million dollar wounds" were loss of toes, fingers, hearing, and some stomach wounds. Million dollar wounds were an "automatic ticket" back to The World. — Gregory Clark, *Words of the Vietnam War*, p. 327, 1990

millioni *noun*
millions *UK*
An unnecessary elaboration phonetically similar to Italian *milione* (million).
- D'you know how much twenty millioni weighs? — Kevin Sampson, *Outlaws*, p. 268, 2001

Milli Vanilli *noun*
the penis *UK*
Rhyming slang for **WILLY**, formed from a controversial US music duo of the late 1980s and early 90s.
- — Bodmin Dark, *Dirty Cockney Rhyming Slang*, 2003

Millwall brick *noun*
a weapon made from a tightly rolled newspaper *UK*
Named after, or by association with, Millwall Football Club and the awesome reputation of its 'fans'.
- [A] veritable arsenal of weaponry found its way on to the [football] terraces – bottles, blades, darts, razors in oranges, throwing stars, lead piping and even a "Millwall brick"[.] — Martin Roach (writing of football hooliganism in the 1970s), *Dr. Marten's Air Wair*, 1999

Millwall Reserves; millwalls *noun*
nerves *UK*
Rhyming slang, formed from a London football team.
- He gets right on my Millwalls he does. — Ray Puxley, *Fresh Rabbit*, 1998

Milton Keynes; miltons *noun*
1 **beans, especially baked beans when served on toast** *UK*
Rhyming slang, based on the Buckinghamshire town.
- — Ray Puxley, *Fresh Rabbit*, 1998

2 **homosexuals** *UK*
Rhyming slang for **QUEEN(S)**, based on the Buckinghamshire town.
- — Ray Puxley, *Fresh Rabbit*, 1998

3 **jeans, denims** *UK*
Rhyming slang, based on the Buckinghamshire town.
- — *www.LondonSlang.com*, June 2002

mimeo *noun*
a mimeograph machine; a document produced by mimeograph *US*
- He "couldn't take too many meetings" so was running the mimeo instead. — Ann Fettamen, *Trashing*, p. 2, 1970

Mimeo Minnie *noun*
the stereotypical female office worker *US, 1953*
- — *American Speech*, p. 299, December 1955: 'Women office workers in America'
- 'Mimeo Minnie,' 'Sadie, the Office Secretary,' And Other Women Office Workers in America — *American Speech*, p. 299, December 1955

mimi *noun*
an act of urination *NEW ZEALAND*
From the Maori.
- Have a mimi, grab a couple of half g's and walk back. — Keri Hulme, *The Bone People*, p. 260, 1983

Mimi *noun*
the vagina *US*
A given name punning the centrality of the vagina to the user's perception of herself – 'me me'.
- There's [...]"a ghoulie," "possible," "tamale," "tottita," "Connie," a "Mimi" in Miami, "split knish" in Philadelphia[.] — Eve Ensler, *The Vagina Monologues*, p. 6, 1998

mimic-man *noun*
a Trinidadian who has adopted European or American mannerisms and style *TRINIDAD AND TOBAGO, 1971*
- — Lise Winer, *Dictionary of the English/Creole of Trinidad & Tobago*, 2003

mimi hill *noun*
a stop during a road trip to use the toilet *NEW ZEALAND*
From the Maori for 'urinating'.
- — David McGill, *David McGill's Complete Kiwi Slang Dictionary*, p. 73, 1998

mince *noun*
1 **rubbish, nonsense** *UK: SCOTLAND, 1911*
- He talks a lot a mince. — Michael Munro, *The Original Patter*, p. 46, 1985
- Her timing was mince. — Christopher Brookmyre, *Not the End of the World*, p. 153, 1998
- Edinburgh was doing the donkey work while London made the decisions and took the credit. Absolute mince, of course, and both parties knew it[.] — Christopher Brookmyre, *Boiling a Frog*, p. 28, 2000
- IT has been marketed as a noble tradition, but in reality it's just a load of mince. The world of haggis hurling has been rocked to its tartan roots after the "ancient" art was exposed as a hoax, started by an Irishman to gauge the gullibility of the Scots. — *Sunday Herald*, 25th January 2004

2 **anything unpleasant** *UK: SCOTLAND*
- The back a my jeans is aw mince! — Michael Munro, *The Original Patter*, p. 46, 1985

3 **used in similes for listlessness or unintelligence** *UK: SCOTLAND*
- "He's as thick as mince." [...] "What's up wi you? Ye're sittin there like a pun [pound] a mince." — Michael Munro, *The Original Patter*, p. 46, 1985

4 **Guinness™ stout** *UK: SCOTLAND*
- Gie's a pint a mince, dear. — Michael Munro, *The Patter, Another Blast*, p. 44, 1988

mince *adjective*
used of an unpleasant thing, especially when in the wrong place *UK: SCOTLAND*
- — Michael Munro, *The Original Patter*, p. 46, 1985

minced *adjective*
drunk *UK*
- — *e-cyclopaedia*, 20th March 2002

mincemeat *noun*
▸ make mincemeat of
to defeat absolutely *UK, 1876*
- She didn't do swords or martial arts. But [Katherine] Hepburn would have made mincemeat of Lara Croft and Charlie's Angels[.] — *The Guardian*, 15th August 2003

mince pies; minces *noun*

the eyes *UK, 1857*

Rhyming slang.

- [L]ooking Solie straight in the minces[.] —Frank Norman, *Bang To Rights*, p. 122, 1958
- "One pack dealer's choice," he says, minces all gleaming. —Derek Raymond (Robin Cook), *The Crust on its Uppers*, p. 39, 1962
- Ah, do me minces deceive me or is this the swear and cuss [bus]? — *The Sweeney*, p. 6, 1976
- He was a truly ugly man – his north and south drooped, his mince pies were watery, and he had a big red I suppose. —Ronnie Barker, *A Sermon in Slang*, 1979
- [A] big dog, which lay there looking up at me sad and resentful with huge wet minces[.] —Andrew Nickolds, *Back to Basics*, p. 91–92, 1994
- Old Bill [the police] never believed their mince pies now. —Jeremy Cameron, *Brown Bread in Wengen*, p. 7, 1999

minch *noun*

in circus and carnival usage, an unengaged, low-spending customer *US, 1928*

- —Don Wilmeth, *The Language of American Popular Entertainment*, p. 172, 1981

mincy *adjective*

stupid, silly *UK: SCOTLAND*

- All jumping aboot in your mincy wee running sannies[.] —Ian Pattison, *Rab C. Nesbitt*, 1988

mind *noun*

▸ give someone a piece of your mind

to reprimand, to censure *UK, 1861*

- I wish they'd both walk in right now. I'd give them a piece of my mind. —Dawn Powell and Tim Page, *My Home Is Far Away*, p. 120, 1995

▸ the mind boggles!

a catchphrase used as an ironic comment on any marked absurdity *UK, 1984*

Widely popularised in the *Daily Mirror* cartoon strip *The Perishers*, by Maurice Dodd, from the 1950s in print and the late 70s as an animation.

- [T]he mind boggles as to what US Republicans imagine to be a Churchillian response. — *The Guardian*, 13th September 2001

mind *verb*

1 to work as a bodyguard, especially for a criminal; to look after a criminal activity *UK, 1924*

- A psychotic and mostly silent mobster, Han-gi (Jo Je-hyeon), apparently minding a pimping operation for another hard case doing jail time[.] — *The Guardian*, 11th July 2003

2 to bribe regularly *UK*

- —Peter Laurie, *Scotland Yard*, p. 325, 1970

▸ never mind!; never you mind!

mind your own business!, don't let it trouble you! *UK, 1814*

- I was scared too. Still am scared. Why? Oh, never mind, Baz. It doesn't concern you. — *The Guardian*, 13th November 2004

mind!

pay attention!, note what I say!, used to add emphatic force to a statement *UK, 1779*

mindbender *noun*

1 anything that challenges your knowledge or assumptions *UK, 1963*

- —Eugene Landy, *The Underground Dictionary*, p. 132, 1971
- It goes through to where you're going to escape, and they escape and they're getting away, and while they're getting away clean, suddenly, Bang! – they're caught again. It was a real mind-bender. —Stephen Gaskin, *Amazing Dope Tales*, p. 148, 1980
- Walking the yard was a mind bender. —Gerald Petievich, *Money Men*, p. 35, 1981

2 a hallucinogenic drug *US*

- —Eugene Landy, *The Underground Dictionary*, p. 132, 1971

mindblower *noun*

1 an event, experience or situation that completely surprises or shocks *US, 1968*

- —Eugene Landy, *The Underground Dictionary*, p. 133, 1971

2 a hallucinogenic drug *US, 1973*

- I'm talking about drugs and alcohol and their use and and abuse as mind-blowers and leg-openers. —Xaviera Hollander, *The Best Part of a Man*, 1975

mind-blowing *adjective*

1 of drugs, especially hallucinogenic *UK*

- — *The Observer*, 3rd December 1967

2 amazing, almost unbelievable *UK, 1967*

Hyperbole.

- "That is mind-blowing!" the director enthuses, as Kapoor hops off a log. After a few more attempts to make it more mind-blowing, Kapoor complains that she has been wearing the same costume all day and would like to slip into something else. The director assures her that she looks mind-blowing. Besides, there's nowhere to change. — *The Guardian*, 10th May 2002

mind-boggling *adjective*

astounding *UK, 1964*

- Such a demonstrated potential was both mind-boggling and frightening. —Joseph McMoneagle, *The Stargate Chronicles*, p. 79, 2002

mind detergent *noun*

LSD; any psycho-active drug, legal or otherwise *UK*

Coined during the Cold War, this term is suggestive of brainwashing.

- —Mike Haskins, *Drugs*, p. 285, 2003

minder *noun*

a criminal's bodyguard or enforcer *UK, 1924*

Made very familiar to the UK public with the television series *Minder*, 1979–94.

- [T]he penman, who never drops [passed forged cheques] himself, has to send a minder, known as a topper, to keep an eye on the dropper, make sure he doesn't pocket the crinkle [money][.] —Charles Raven, *Underworld Nights*, p. 81, 1956
- —Angela Devlin, *Prison Patter*, p. 77, 1996

mind fart

▷ see: BRAIN FART

mindfuck *noun*

1 anything that causes an internal paradigm shift *US, 1971*

- —Tom Hibbert, *Rockspeak!*, p. 102, 1983

2 the mental aspects of sex *US*

- Mind fuck: A term originated by freaks to describe the experience of orgasm. — *Screw*, p. 7, 12th October 1970

mindfuck *verb*

to baffle; to manipulate psychologically *US, 1967*

- The prosecutor tried for another few minutes, until the judge called both attorneys up to the bench and politely told the prosecutor to please quit mind-fucking the court[.] —Elmore Leonard, *Swag*, p. 7, 1976
- He's really mind-fucked you. —Jack W. Thomas, *Heavy Number*, p. 105, 1976

mind-fucking *adjective*

having the quality to confuse, puzzle or astound *US, 1971*

Conventional use of 'mind' plus FUCK (to confound).

- [T]aking some fucking psychedelic mind-fucking drug[.] —Dave Courtney, *Raving Lunacy*, p. 11, 2000

mindle *noun*

a stupid girl *UK*

Possibly derived as a shortening of 'mindless'. Recorded in contemporary gay use.

- — *Attitude*, p. 60, July 2003: 'New palare lexicon'

mindless *adjective*

(used of waves) immense and powerful *US*

- —Mitch McKissick, *Surf Lingo*, 1987

mind your back!; mind your backs!

get out of the way!; also used to 'warn' of the presence of a male homosexual *UK, 1983*

- [S]houts of 'mind your backs' to unwitting spectators. — *The Tribune (Chandigarh, India)*, 7th March 2004

mine *noun*

your job *US*

- —Jerry Robertson, *Oil Slanguage*, p. 59, 1954

▸ down the mine

lost *AUSTRALIA*

- Picked up a good tip from a local turf identity. Just as well, though, I lost my shirt on the interstate trots the week before. Went down the mine. —Alexander Buzo, *Rooted*, p. 90, 1969
- No kid, marriage down the mine, himself about to be jettisoned. —B. Selkie, *Lime Juice*, p. 60, 1995

mine *adjective*
a 'minus' attached to a grade *US*
- —Collin Baker et al., *College Undergraduate Slang Study Conducted at Brown University*, p. 157, 1968

mine!
used for acknowledging in shorthand form responsibility for a problem *US*
- —Connie Eble (Editor), *UNC-CH Campus Slang*, p. 5, Fall 1989

minehost; mine host; mine-host *noun*
a tavern keeper, a pub landlord *UK, 1904*
Originally recorded as 'mine host' by Farmer and Henley who considered it colloquial; in its continued use hyphenation was used or implied.
- Take Dave, for instance. As minehost he has no equal, the top man.—Andrew Nickolds, *Back to Basics*, p. 3, 1994

miner *noun*
▸ **the miner's**
silicosis *US*
- And a miner with silicosis had rock on the chest, rock on the box, the miner's con, or, succinctly, the miner's.—*It's an Old Wild West Custom*, p. 136, 1951

miner's con *noun*
silicosis *US*
An abbreviation of 'consumption'.
- And a miner with silicosis had rock on the chest, rock on the box, the miner's con, or, succinctly, the miner's.—*It's an Old Wild West Custom*, p. 136, 1951

ming *noun*
an unpleasant smell *UK: SCOTLAND*
- —Michael Munro, *The Original Patter*, p. 46, 1985

ming *verb*
to stink *UK: SCOTLAND*
- The doors open. We're in. And it fucking mings. The stench inside that gaff is knockout[.]—Kevin Samson, *Outlaws*, p. 77, 2001
- You fucking ming, lad.—Niall Griffiths, *Kelly + Victor*, p. 27, 2002

minge *noun*
1 the vagina *UK, 1903*
From the Latin *mingere* (to urinate) and the mistaken belief that urine passes through the vagina.
- —*Journal of Sex Research*, p. 146, 2001
- If nothing else, most women will feel they have cut their losses if you get down there and lick her minge!—Richard Herring, *Talking Cock*, p. 173, 2003

2 the pubic hair *UK, 1903*
Extends from the previous sense to include the general pubic area. A natural redhead is known as a 'ginger minge'.
- —Louis S. Leland, *A Personal Kiwi-Yankee Dictionary*, p. 66, 1984
- [A] little contest to see who can shave their minge in the most eye-catching way.—Kevin Sampson, *Outlaws*, p. 38, 2001

3 a contemptible person *UK*
Extending the sense as 'vagina', synonymous with **CUNT**.
- Harry Tyler would normally have been ranting aloud about town planning "minges" by now, not to mention poxy women drivers[.] —Garry Bushell, *The Face*, p. 3, 2001

minge bag *noun*
a contemptible woman *UK*
Combines **MINGE** with **BAG** (an unattractive woman).
- It's her – the minge bag.—Alan Bleasdale, *Boys From the Blackstuff*, 1982

minge-muncher *noun*
a person who enjoys performing oral sex on women *NEW ZEALAND*
- —David McGill, *David McGill's Complete Kiwi Slang Dictionary*, p. 73, 1998

minger *noun*
a person who smells bad; hence, an unattractive person of either sex *UK*
From Scottish **MING** (to stink). Pronounced with a hard 'g'.
- This dirty minger was giving me a nosh in an alleyway[.]—*Mixmag*, p. 68, April 2003
- Help! I'm a minger—*The Salon*, 5th February 2003

Minge Whinge *nickname*
The Vagina Monologues by Eve Ensler *UK*
Actors' slang for the widely popular theatre piece.
- Although I would never deny that the Minge Whinge was the inspiration for my idea.—Richard Herring, *Talking Cock*, p. 8, 2003
- However, in contrast to the social taboos that "The Minge Whinge" tried to subvert, men have never had any difficulty talking about their cocks/old boys/trouser snakes, etc.—Jeff Hudson, *Bang*, p. 112, November 2003

ming-ho *adjective*
drunk *UK*
Deriving, perhaps, from **MING** (to stink), thus playing on **STINKING** (very drunk).
- —*e-cyclopaedia*, 20th March 2002

minging *adjective*
1 unattractive, unpleasant; descriptive of anything bad *UK: SCOTLAND, 1985*
Also shortened to 'mingin'. From the verb **MING** (to stink), hence to look **STINKING** (disgusting).
- These pieces [sandwiches], Da. They're minging!—Ian Pattison, *Rab C. Nesbitt*, 1988
- Nice to see a West Country babe on the box instead of those mingin' birds with fake knockers.—Chris Baker and Andrew Day, *Lock, Stock... & Spaghetti Sauce*, p. 260, 2000
- [E]verything he touched turned to cack [shit]. – Not only touched, either; all he had to do was fuckin look at something, mum, an that's be it, bing, brown and mingin.—Niall Griffiths, *Sheepshagger*, p. 12–13, 2001
- Faye is incapable of looking minging. During the day, someone refers to her as "a golden goddess", and it's not a bad description.—*Sky Magazine*, p. 17, May 2001

2 drunk *UK*
Royal Navy slang; from **MING** (to stink) hence **STINKING** (drunk).
- —Nigel Foster, *The Making of a Royal Marine Commando*, 1987

minglewood *noun*
a hollowed cigar refilled with hashish and potent marijuana *US*

mingo *noun*
an unpleasant person *UK*
Perhaps a combination of **MING** (to stink) and **MINGE** (the vagina), or perhaps an evolution of the older sense (1775) of the word as a 'chamberpot'.
- He's still a fucking mingo, by the way[.]—Kevin Simpson, *Outlaws*, p. 9, 2001

mingra *noun*
a police officer *UK*
- Nanty! The mingra's screwing you.—Patrick O'Shaughnessy, *Market Traders' Slang*, 1979

ming-ray *noun*
a mischievous 'game' of spreading a school-fellow's possessions over as wide an area as possible without being noticed by the victim *UK*
Commented on by the Plain English Campaign in October 2003.
- When the victim does notice, the word "ming-ray" is shouted by the attackers, with prolonged emphasis on the "ray".—Chris Lewis, *The Dictionary of Playground Slang*, p. 150, 2003

mingy *adjective*
1 mean, miserly *UK, 1911*
Probably a blend of 'mangy' (shabby) or 'mean', and 'stingy' (mean).
- You rotten mingy old cow.—John Peter Jones, *Feather Pluckers*, p. 18, 1964
- The abandonment of gongs [medals] in most countries reveals how mingy the British were.—*The Australian*, 16th March 2000

2 in pool, a shot that cannot be missed or a game that cannot be lost *US*
- —Steve Rushin, *Pool Cool*, p. 21, 1990

mini *noun*
a mini-skirt, a very short skirt *UK, 1966*
- And girls in minis, mini-minis, shifts, or mumus.—Sidney Bernard, *This Way to the Apocalypse*, p. 63, 1967
- In fact, the mini is only the symbol of a far-ranging change in fashion that has toppled the old dictators of style[.]—Joe David Brown, *Sex in the '60s*, p. 78, 1968

mini-bean *noun*
an amphetamine capsule; a tablet of MDMA, the recreational drug best known as ecstasy *UK*
- —Mike Haskins, *Drugs*, p. 279, 2003

mini-bennie *noun*
an amphetamine or Benzedrine™ (amphetamine sulphate, a central nervous system stimulant) tablet or capsule *US, 1977*
- —Richard A. Spears, *The Slang and Jargon of Drugs and Drink*, p. 340, 1986
- —Mike Haskins, *Drugs*, p. 279, 2003

mini L *noun*
a Pontiac Grand Prix car *US*
A car with a strong resemblance to the El Dorado.
- — *Current Slang*, p. 10, Fall 1970

mini-me *noun*
a smaller version of somebody *UK*
From a character introduced in 1997 in the *Austin Powers* films.
- —Susie Dent, *The Language Report*, p. 13, 2003
- [A]n Anglo-German miniature with her mother's big blue eyes, enthusiasm and frightening formidability, and with my ... er ... nails. I have fairly strong nails. But a mini me? A mini me, with the addition of no bowel control?— *The Guardian*, 27th March 2004

Mini Moke *noun*
a cigar, cigarette or pipe *UK*
Rhyming slang for **SMOKE**, formed on a type of small car.
- —Ray Puxley, *Fresh Rabbit*, 1998

mini-moo *noun*
the vagina *UK*
MOO (an unpleasant woman) playing on Mini-Me, the miniature alter-ego of the villainous Dr Evil in the film *Austin Powers, The Spy Who Shagged Me*, 1999.
- — *Sky Magazine*, July 2001

mini skirt *noun*
a woman *US*
- Truckers expanded the existing slang term of "beaver" into their own vocabulary and "sweet thing" and "mini skirt," two previous names used for females were discarded.—Gwyneth A. "Dandalion" Seese, *Tijuana Bear in a Smoke 'Um Up Taxi*, p. 45, 1977

mini-tanker *noun*
a small mobile beer tank hired for social gatherings *NEW ZEALAND*
- JOHN: Must have been some party. JIM: Great, until someone drove off with the mini-tanker.—Rogere Hall, *Glide Time*, p. 14, 1977

MiniWac *nickname*
Bill Bennett, premier of British Columbia from 1975 to 86 *CANADA*
- Bill, nicknamed "MiniWac," son of W. A. C. "Wacky" Bennett, followed his father's doctrine as premier and leader of the Social Credit party.—Tom Parkin, *WetCoast Words*, p. 93, 1989

mink *noun*
1 a female friend or lover *US, 1899*
- —Anthony Romeo, *The Language of Gangs*, p. 20, 4th December 1962
- —Joan Fontaine et al., *Dictionary of Black Slang*, 1968
- —David Claerbaut, *Black Jargon in White America*, p. 72, 1972

2 a female whose romantic interest in a man is overshadowed by her interest in his financial worth *US*
- — *San Francisco Examiner*, p. III-2, 22nd March 1960
- Deek had girls up all the time ... minks that would never have looked twice at Ty in school or on the street.—Jess Mowry, *Way Past Cool*, p. 33, 1992

minky *noun*
the vagina *UK*
- Nonsense slang referred to vague, inoffensive terms that had little or no means in standard English: terms like biff, foo-foo, minky and winkie in FGTs [female genital terms], and chod, dongce, spondoolies, and winks in MGTs [male genital terms].— *Journal of Sex Research*, p. 146, 2001

Min Min light; Min Min; min min *noun*
a will-o'-the-wisp *AUSTRALIA, 1956*
Probably from an Australian Aboriginal language.
- There's the Min Min Light, for instance, that restless will-'o-the-wisp known to every drover on Queensland Western Plains.—Bill Wannan, *Bullockies, Beauts and Bandicoots*, p. 96, 1960

Minnesota mule *noun*
a prostitute recently arrived in New York City from a small town or city *US*
- — *Maledicta*, p. 151, Summer/Winter 1986–1987: 'Sexual slang: prostitutes, pedophiles, flagellators, transvestites, and necrophiles'

Minnesota strip *nickname*
an area in New York City frequented by prostitutes *US*
- The "Minnesota Strip" – Eighth Avenue between 34th and 55th streets – picked up its nickname in 1972. Many hookers gave Minneapolis as their home city whenever asked, to the point of it becoming a cynical retort, though some undoubtedly told the truth.—Josh Alan Friedman, *Tales of Times Square*, p. 143, 1986
- For the past three years, she's been under the watchful eye of "Sweetpea," a very grimy excuse for a human being who plies the sexual trade on the Minnesota Strip.—Mary Rose McGeady, *Are you out there, God?*, p. 38, 1999

minnie *noun*
a homosexual man *UK*
An example of **CAMP** trans-gender identification.
- —Paul Baker, *Polari*, p. 181, 2002

Minnie *noun*
in lowball or low poker, the lowest possible hand *US*
A personification of 'minimum'.
- —Albert H. Morehead, *The Complete Guide to Winning Poker*, p. 268, 1967

minnie *verb*
to mince *UK*
- —Paul Baker, *Polari*, p. 181, 2002

Minnie Mouse *noun*
of a woman, the pubic hair *UK*
Named after a cartoon character.
- Tommy [Ford of Gucci] can persuade model Louise Pedersen to pose with a 'G' shaved in her Minnie Mouse[.]— *The Guardian*, 24th May 2003

minnow *noun*
a poker player who joins a no-stakes game without sufficient funds *US, 1978*
- —Thomas L. Clark, *The Dictionary of Gambling and Gaming*, p. 130, 1987

minny *noun*
a minimum security jail or prison; the minimum security wing of a jail or prison *US*
- —John R. Armore and Joseph D. Wolfe, *Dictionary of Desperation*, p. 40, 1976

minoo *adjective*
a 'minus' attached to a grade *US*
- —Collin Baker et al., *College Undergraduate Slang Study Conducted at Brown University*, p. 157, 1968

minor-league *adjective*
mediocre, less than impressive *US, 1949*
From the minor leagues in US professional baseball.
- I'm in minor-league shock: my eyes are wide, but my gaze is blank. —James Ellroy, *Hollywood Nocturnes*, p. 5, 1994

minors *noun*
▸ **the minors**
in horse racing, the second and third place finishes *AUSTRALIA*
- —Ned Wallish, *The Truth Dictionary of Racing Slang*, p. 52, 1989

minors!
that's not a problem! *US*
Hawaiian youth usage.
- "But I no mo' money fo' da movies!" "Minors, brah. I get."—Douglas Simonson, *Pidgin to da Max*, 1981

mint *noun*
1 a great deal of money *UK, 1655*
From the coinage of coins.
- I could have made a mint, but I never had a very good brain for money[.]—Jane Green, *Mr Maybe*, p. 1, 1999

2 money *US*
- —Vann Wesson, *Generation X Field Guide and Lexicon*, p. 112, 1997

3 a tablet of MDMA, the recreational drug best known as ecstasy *UK*
- —Angela Devlin, *Prison Patter*, p. 77, 1996

mintage *noun*
a mint-flavoured breath freshener or hard sweet *US*
- —Judi Sanders, *Faced and Faded, Hanging to Hurl*, p. 27, 1993

minted *adjective*

1 very rich *UK*
A play on conventional 'mint' (the place where money is made) and being 'made of money'.
- [H]er boyfriend Angelo had to be minted. Money is power[.] — Wayne Anthony, *Spanish Highs*, p. 168, 1999
- [F]lashing his cash now that he's minted. — Christopher Brookmyre, *The Sacred Art of Stealing*, p. 205, 2002

2 excellent *UK: SCOTLAND*
- Ah hear ye passed yer test. That's minted, wee man. — Michael Munro, *The Patter, Another Blast*, p. 44, 1988

mintie *noun*
a lesbian who plays the aggressive or dominant role *US*
- — Helen Dahlskog (Editor), *A Dictionary of Contemporary and Colloquial Usage*, p. 40, 1972

mintox; mont *adjective*
excellent *UK, 2001*
Noted as being in use since the 1970s.
- — Chris Lewis, *The Dictionary of Playground Slang*, 2003

mint rocks; mints; rocks *noun*
socks *UK*
Rhyming slang; a latter day variation of **ALMOND ROCKS** reflecting the predominant flavour of modern seaside rock.
- — Angela Devlin, *Prison Patter*, p. 77, 1996

mintweed; mint *noun*
phencyclidine, the recreational drug known as PCP or angel dust *US*
- — Ronald Linder, *PCP*, p. 9–10, 1981

minty *adjective*

1 less than good, filthy, bad *UK*
- So nice, that, that feeling of hot water on a minty an ravaged body. — Niall Griffiths, *Kelly + Victor*, p. 189, 2002
- I really don't like it at all. It sounds really minty. (X-Ray: Minty?) Yeah... just a bit rubbish. — *X-RAY*, p. 24, November 2002

2 fashionable, stylish *CANADA*
- From Winnipeg: "D'ja see that Farrah Fawcett-Majors poster? Minty, eh?" Later adopted by some Vancouverites, particularly those associated with a small record company, Mint Records, and incorporated into the phrase "Stay minty" for "stay cool." — Emily *An American's Guide to Canada*, p. 6, 10th November 2002

3 homosexual, effeminate *US, 1965*
- — *Maledicta*, p. 238, Winter 1980: '"Lovely, blooming, fresh and gay": the onomastics of camp'
- Freddy was just a minty cunt. — Kevin Sampson, *Outlaws*, p. 9, 2001

4 excellent *US*
- — *Carmel (California) High School Yearbook*, 1987

miracle *noun*
in the language surrounding the Grateful Dead, an extra ticket for that night's show *US*
- The phrase "I need a miracle!" has become the most common plea for a ticket in the parking lot, both spoken (shouted) and written (colorfully) on cardboard placards[.] — David Shenk and Steve Silberman, *Skeleton Key*, p. 194, 1994

miracle meat *noun*
a penis that is almost as large flaccid as erect *US*
- — *American Speech*, p. 58, Spring-Summer 1970: 'Homosexual slang'

Miracle Mile *nickname*
a stretch of Wilshire Boulevard, a main artery in Los Angeles, California *US*
A nickname coined by an estate agent but then accepted in the vernacular.
- — Laurence Urdang, *Names and Nicknames of Places and Things*, p. 169, 1987

Miracle of the Doughnuts *noun*
an apparition of the image of Christ which occurred in September 1998 at a doughnut shop in Cape Breton *CANADA*
- In what became known as the "Miracle of the Doughnuts" an image of Jesus began appearing nightly on the wall outside the Bras D'Or Tim Hortons. — Will Ferguson, *How to be a Canadian*, p. 154, 2001

miracle rice *noun*
IR8, a high-yielding variety of rice introduced in Vietnam in the 1960s, doubling rice production yields *US*
- The GVN became popular in a sense during the 1960s and early 1980s because of agricultural development programs like the introduction of "miracle rice." — Al Santoli, *To Bear Any Burden*, p. 203, 1985

miraculous *adjective*
extremely drunk *UK: SCOTLAND, 1873*
- — Michael Munro, *The Original Patter*, p. 46, 1985

Miranda *noun*
a warning read or recited to criminal suspects before an interrogation, informing them of their constitutional rights in the situation *US, 1966*
From a 1966 decision of the US Supreme Court.
- — *American Speech*, Fall 1981

mirror *noun*
a military sentry's enemy counterpart *US*
- For each Amerian sentry post there's a Cuban counterpart. They're called mirrors. — *A Few Good Men*, 1992

mirror man; mirror *noun*
a person with decision-making authority who avoids making decisions *AUSTRALIA*
From the stock answer of 'I'll look into it'.
- — *Maledicta*, p. 92, 1986–1987: 'Australian maledicta'
- — Ned Wallish, *The Truth Dictionary of Racing Slang*, p. 52, 1989

misbehave *verb*
to shave *UK*
Rhyming slang.
- When a man says that he going to the bathroom to misbehave you now know what he is doing. Or do you? — Ray Puxley, *Cockney Rabbit*, 1992

mischief *noun*

▸ **do you a mischief**
to cause you trouble or harm *UK, 1385*
- [I]f ever he finds it in his power to do you a mischief, he will be sure to do it. — Fitzroy MacLean, *Highlanders*, p. 141, 1995

mischievious *adjective*
mischievous *UK, 1937*
A frequent solecism in both speech and writing.
- Rajiv Gandhi described the allegations as "false, baseless and mischievious." — *The Guardian*, 3rd February 2001

misdee *noun*
a misdemeanour or minor crime *US*
- You don't have anything on me. A misdee auto-theft. — *Gone in 60 Seconds*, 1992

miserable *adjective*
miserly; stingy *AUSTRALIA, 1903*
- Why do you think we've got the most miserable Social Service benefits, the worst schooling, damn near the worst health of any industrial nation? — David Williamson, *Don's Party*, p. 67, 1973

misery *noun*
low quality coffee *US*
- — Vincent J. Monteleone, *Criminal Slang*, p. 155, 1949

▸ **the misery**
the bleed period of the menstrual cycle *US*
Euphemism.
- — Karen Houppert, *The Curse*, 1999

misery fiddle *noun*
(among Canadian loggers) a cross-cut saw *CANADA*
- The use of a "misery fiddle," a man on each end, is hard, sweaty work. — Bill Casselman, *Canadian Words*, p. 193, 1995

misery guts *noun*
a habitually miserable or complaining person *AUSTRALIA, 1981*
- — Lenie Johansen, *The Dinkum Dictionary*, 1988
- Is old misery guts sitting comfortably? — John King, *White Trash*, p. 211, 2001

misery lights *noun*
the coloured lights on the top of a police car *US*
- The cruiser followed suit, hitting its misery lights as soon as both cars were clear of the mainstream traffic. — Richard Price, *Clockers*, p. 395, 1992

misery machine *noun*
a motorcyle *US*
- — *American Speech*, p. 269, December 1962: 'The language of traffic policemen'

misery parade *noun*
alcoholics pacing on the pavement waiting for an off-licence or bar to open in the morning *US*
- —Christopher Cavanaugh, *AA to Z*, p. 127, 1998

misfeature *noun*
in computing, a feature of a program that was carefully planned but that produces undesirable consequences in a given situation *US*
- —Guy L. Steele et al., *The Hacker's Dictionary*, p. 93, 1983

misfire *noun*
an instance of sexual impotence or premature ejaculation *US*
- —Roger Blake, *The American Dictionary of Sexual Terms*, p. 134, 1964
- Perhaps Al Mackey's misfire at the Chinatown motel was inevitable. —Joseph Wambaugh, *The Glitter Dome*, 1981

mish *noun*
the missionary position for sexual intercourse – man on top of prone woman *US*
- After a steamy run munch and a wicked b.j., they engage in some nut-slappin' mish capped off with – you guess it – major anal penetration. —*Adult Video News*, p. 128, August 1995
- —*Adult Video News*, p. 38, September 1995
- A white guy in his early forties wearing a Gang Bang 2 T-shirt is soon fucking Jaz in the mish pazish. —Anthony Petkovich, *The X Factory*, p. 195, 1997

mishegoss *noun*
nonsense; craziness *US*
- Alex, you are never going to hear such a mishegoss of mixed-up crap and disgusting nonsense as the Christian religion in your entire life. —Philip Roth, *Portnoy's Complaint*, p. 44, 1969
- Steve Beauchampof Manhattan, a 27-year-old actor and writer, said he boxed three to five times a week at the West Side Y, mainly as an outlet for bottled up anger, frustration and "all my mishegoss." —*New York Times*, p. 49, 9th January 1983
- —Leo Rosten, *The Joys of Yinglish*, p. 333, 1989
- That's why Beavis and Butt-head are marketed like Barney the Dinosaur; Howard Stern is king of a trash pile bigger than the Twin Towers; Tonya Harding received all that attention for hatching an evil plot; and the three networks shamelessly scrambled to immortalize the Fisher-Buttafucco mishegoss. —*Newsday (New York)*, p. A34, 19th October 1994
- Joel Schumacher's Phone Booth is based on a script by Larry Cohen that, for bold mishegoss, nearly rivals the B-movie meister's Gold Me To. —*Village Voice*, p. 129, 24th September 2002

miss *noun*
▸ **give something a miss; give it a miss**
to avoid doing something *UK, 1919*
- The scheme doesn't distinguish between regular commuters who have no choice but to come to London and leisure visitors who have the choice to give it a miss. —*The Guardian*, 5th September 2003

miss *verb*
to inject a drug intravenously *UK, 1998*
Humorous use of an antonym.
- —Mike Haskins, *Drugs*, p. 290, 2003

▸ **miss a trick**
to fail to take advantage of a situation *UK, 1943*
- [Jon Snow] said he thought Channel 4 News "missed a trick" in not bidding for the Tony Blair interview marking the prime minister's five years in power. —*The Guardian*, 10th June 2002

▸ **miss out on**
to lose an opportunity, to fail to achieve something *US, 1929*
- Britain's Dean Macey missed out on winning a medal in the decathlon in the Olympic Stadium today. —*The Guardian*, 28th September 2000

▸ **miss the boat**
to lose an opportunity, to be late for something *UK, 1929*
Originally nautical.
- But at least the Spanish have got a new currency [the euro] to ignore. Whereas we've missed the boat so badly it feels like we haven't found the ocean. —*The Guardian*, 3rd January 2002

▸ **miss the bus**
to lose an opportunity *UK, 1915*

▸ **miss the pink and pot the brown**
to engage in heterosexual anal intercourse *UK*
A snooker metaphor playing on 'pink' (the open vagina) and 'brown' (the anus).
- Yeah, y'know, threesomes, missing the pink and potting the brown. —Colin Butts, *Is Harry on the Boat?*, p. 21, 1997

Miss Ann; Missy Ann *noun*
the prototype of the white southern woman *US, 1925*
- This, Miss Ann of the Clansman and Rev. Dixon's finest-dream, here in whose name thousands of blackthroats have been stretched and a million blackballs crushed. —Clarence Cooper Jr, *The Farm*, p. 25–26, 1967
- Is he gonna grow up t'be a big bad see-eye-aye man an keep the world safe fo' Missy Ann's fur coat? —Robert Gover, *JC Saves*, p. 70, 1968
- "What about Miss Ann there?" he said. —Vernon E. Smith, *The Jones Men*, p. 14, 1974

Miss Carrie *noun*
a small supply of drugs carried on the person of a drug addict *US*
Carried to get the addict through a short incarceration in the event of an arrest.
- —David Maurer and Victor Vogel, *Narcotics and Narcotic Addiction*, p. 427, 1973

Miss Clean *noun*
▹ **see: MISTER CLEAN**

misses *noun*
dice that have been weighted, either to throw a seven less (for the opening roll in craps) or more (for subsequent rolls) than normal *US*
- —Frank Garcia, *Marked Cards and Loaded Dice*, p. 262, 1962

Miss Green *noun*
marijuana *US*
- By the way, boy, I am of course indulging in a perfect orgy of Miss Green & can hardly see straight right at this minute, whoo! 3 bombs a day. —Jack Kerouac, *Letter to Neal and Carolyn Cassady*, p. 358, 10th May 1952

missing *noun*
a report of a missing person *US*
- She called in a Missing. Morning of the day we found the body. —Elmore Leonard, *Glitz*, p. 89, 1985

missing link *noun*
zinc *UK: SCOTLAND*
Rhyming slang, used by scrap-dealers in Glasgow.
- —Michael Munro, *The Patter, Another Blast*, 1988

missing you already
used as a farewell *UK*
A popular catchphrase; alas the sincerity of the sentiment is often undermined by sarcasm.
- "Any problems ring me on the mobile, okay? Missing you already," I say. —J.J. Connolly, *Layer Cake*, p. 213, 2000

mission *noun*
1 a search to buy crack cocaine *US*
Another *Star Trek* metaphor.
- —Terry Williams, *Crackhouse*, p. 150, 1992

2 an assignment given to a youth gang member *US*
- —Bill Valentine, *Gang Intelligence Manual*, p. 77, 1995: 'Black street gang terminology'

mission bum; mission stiff *noun*
a tramp who frequents the dining rooms and sleeping quarters offered to the desitute by religious missions *US, 1924*
- We call this Mission Row, because it's where the mission stiffs hang out. —Jack Lait and Lee Mortimer, *Washington Confidential*, p. 32, 1951
- The mission bums watched the policemen, two rookies and a more experienced partner, pass them by[.]235 —Clancy Sigal, *Going Away*, p. x, 1961

Mississippi flush *noun*
in poker, any hand and a revolver *US*
- —Jeffrey McQuain, *Never Enough Words*, p. 55, 1999

Mississippi marbles *noun*
dice *US, 1920*
- —Vincent J. Monteleone, *Criminal Slang*, p. 155, 1949
- —Thomas L. Clark, *The Dictionary of Gambling and Gaming*, p. 130, 1987

Mississippi mudflap *noun*
a hairstyle: the hair is worn short at the front and long at the back *US*
Best known as a **MULLET**.
- —Connie Eble (Editor), *UNC-CH Campus Slang*, p. 4, Spring 2001

Mississippi saxophone *noun*

a harmonica, a mouth organ *US*

- Not for nothing has the blues harp long been nicknamed the "Mississippi Saxophone." Masters and definers of harp style dating back to John Lee (Sonny Boy) Williamson and Little Walter[.] —Dick Shurman, *The Hard Way (by William Clarke)*, p. sleeve notes, 1996

Miss It *noun*

used as a term of address to a person with excessive self esteem *US*

- "Oh, Miss It, you're too much." —Nathan Heard, *Howard Street*, p. 119, 1968

Miss Muggins *noun*

a notional seller of out-of-fashion clothing *BARBADOS*

- —Frank A. Collymore, *Barbadian Dialect*, p. 74, 1965

Missouri marbles *noun*

dice *US*

- —Frank Garcia, *Marked Cards and Loaded Dice*, p. 263, 1962

Missouri pass *noun*

in the US, pulling off a road onto the hard shoulder to pass a vehicle on the right *US*

- —Jeffrey McQuain, *Never Enough Words*, p. 54, 1999

Missouri stop *noun*

a rolling stop at a traffic signal or stop sign *US*

- —Jeffrey McQuain, *Never Enough Words*, p. 54, 1999

Miss Palmer and her five daughters *noun*

masturbation *BAHAMAS, 1971*

- —John A. Holm, *Dictionary of Bahamian English*, p. 134–135, 1982

Miss Piggy *noun*

1 a fat, aggressive, loud homosexual man *US*

An allusion to a main character on the *Muppets* children's television programme.

- —*Maledicta*, p. 236, Winter 1980: '"Lovely, blooming, fresh and gay": the onomastics of camp'

2 a cigarette *UK*

Rhyming slang for **CIGGY**.

- —Ray Puxley, *Fresh Rabbit*, 1998

Miss Priss *noun*

used as a friendly female-to-female term of address *US*

- —Connie Eble (Editor), *UNC-CH Campus Slang*, p. 5, March 1996

Miss Thing *noun*

used as a term of address for someone (female or homosexual male) with excessive self-esteem *US*

- You don't have to yell Miss Thing. —Hubert Selby Jr, *Last Exit to Brooklyn*, p. 58, 1957
- Miss Thing had told me, 'why how ridiculous! – that petuh between your legs simpuhlee does not belong, dear.' —John Rechy, *City of Night*, p. 115, 1963
- "Now, Miss Thing," Lillie retorted in mock indignation. —Nathan Heard, *Howard Street*, p. 119, 1968
- No, there she is – WACKING OFF, Jesus, what more does a guy haveta go thru around this camp. —Paul Glover, *Words from the House of the Dead*, 1974
- Every time he hit on me I would just say, "Miss Rubbber I need five for my room rent," and he'd just say, "Go head Miss Thing, I ain't got no money." —Babs Gonzales, *Movin' On Down De Line*, p. 70, 1975
- —Connie Eble (Editor), *UNC-CH Campus Slang*, p. 4, October 1986
- I guess he's just a fag I guess he's just another one of them Miss Things. —William T. Vollman, *Whores for Gloria*, p. 115, 1991
- You watch it, Miss Thing. —Francesca Lia Block, *I Was a Teenage Fairy*, p. 74, 1998

missus *noun*

1 a wife *AUSTRALIA, 1859*

A phonetic rendering of 'Mrs'; ultimately from 'mistress'. Always modified as either 'the missus', or 'my', 'your', 'his missus'.

- Been doin' the housework fer the missus. She's crook again. —Nino Culotta (John O'Grady), *They're A Weird Mob*, p. 90, 1957
- Look, the boss is all right. So's his missus. —Arthur Upfield, *Bony and the Mouse*, p. 50, 1959
- Him and his missus hit town six months ago. Ten minutes after they got in, she slipped her thirteenth. —Walter Gill, *Petermann Journey*, p. 14, 1968
- Therefore we are not permitted to love the missus of the bloke next door. —John O'Grady, *Aussie Etiket*, p. 49, 1971
- [H]e's half thinking about having a bet or a bevvy [drink] or going home to give his missus stick. —Kevin Sampson, *Outlaws*, p. 91, 2001

2 the 'woman of the house' on a country property *AUSTRALIA, 1889*

Counterpart of the masculine **BOSS**.

- I thought there might be trouble with the missus if I engaged a one-time murderer as nursemaid. —Ion L. Idriess, *Over the Range*, p. 208, 1947
- 'What – because of Sid? Don't be silly.' 'No. 'cos of the missus comin' back.' —Jean Brooks, *The Opal Witch*, p. 59, 1967
- The cowboy's boss was usually the missus[.] —Herb Wharton, *Cattle Camp*, p. 76, 1994

3 lady; madam *AUSTRALIA*

Used as a term of address to an unknown woman.

- [A]ll of a sudden Joe stopped and let out a roaring fart and said 'It's all right, missus, it was only wind.' —Sam Weller, *Old Bastards I Have Met*, p. 131, 1979

Missy Ann *noun*

▷ see: **MISS ANN**

mist *noun*

1 phencyclidine, the recreational drug known as PCP or angel dust *US*

Recorded as a 'current PCP alias' by the US Department of Justice, *Street Terms*, October 1994.

- —*Drummer*, p. 77, 1977

2 the smoke produced when crack cocaine is smoked *US*

- —US Department of Justice, *Street Terms*, October 1994

mista *noun*

mister *UK*

A deliberate misspelling.

- They look at the car an' think no way's mista gangstamuthafucka gonna drive it. —Nick Barlay, *Curvy Lovebox*, p. 84, 1997

mister *noun*

1 the male manager of a homosexual brothel *US*

- There are clandestine call boy rings, operated by discreet male madams (often called "misters" in Miami) who supply male prostitutes to guests at beach hotels. —Johnny Shearer, *The Male Hustler*, p. 123–124, 1966

2 a steady boyfriend or common-law husband *TRINIDAD AND TOBAGO, 1945*

- —Lise Winer, *Dictionary of the English/Creole of Trinidad & Tobago*, 2003

Mister; Mr *noun*

a stereotype of the adjective that follows *US, 1940*

- But I know I have to talk to Chichi if I want any kind of emotional angle, a point of view, because Robbie's such a cold fish. He thinks he's Mr. Personality, but he's basically a very dull person. —Elmore Leonard, *Split Images*, p. 213, 1981

Mister B; Mr B *nickname*

Billy Eckstine (1914–93), jazz vocalist *US, 1948*

- —Robert S. Gold, *A Jazz Lexicon*, p. 211, 1964

Mister B-52; Mr B-52 *nickname*

Lt Colonel John Paul Vann (1934–72), killed in a helicopter crash in Vietnam *US*

- Brig. Gen Nguyen Van Toan, whom Cao Van Vien finally recruited to replace Dzu, and the Vietnamese staff at the Pleiku headquarters nicknamed Vann "Mr. B-52." —Neil Sheehan, *A Bright Shining Lie*, p. 782, 1988

Mister Big; Mr Big *noun*

the head of an organisation, especially a criminal enterprise *US, 1940*

- There's a "Mister Big" in the background. —*The Sweeney*, p. 56, 1976
- They've got Roy booked as Mister Big and me and Tony as just simple, dumb runners[.] —J.J. Connolly, *Know Your Enemy [britpulp]*, p. 159, 1999

Mister Bitchy; Mr Bitchy *noun*

a Mitsubishi car *US*

- —Lewis Poteet, *Car & Motorcyle Slang*, p. 112, 1992

Mister Brown; Mr Brown *noun*

the passive male in homosexual anal sex *US*

- —Hyman E. Goldin et al., *Dictionary of American Underworld Lingo*, p. 35, 1950

Mister Busy; Mr Busy *noun*

in prison, any officer with an antagonistic attitude toward the prisoners *UK*

- —Angela Devlin, *Prison Patter*, p. 77, 1996

Mister C; Mr C *nickname*

Perry Como (b.1912), US singer *US*

- —Arnold Shaw, *Dictionary of American Pop/Rock*, p. 235, 1982

Mister Charles; Mr Charles *noun*

a white man *US*

• But black separatists have gone one step further, and would insist that "Mr. Charles" is even more appropriate[.] — Roger Abrahams, *Positively Black*, p. 32, 1970

Mister Charlie; Mr Charlie *noun*

used as a stereotypical representation of white authority over black people *US, 1928*

A piece of slang used as a gesture of resistance by US black people.

• He talks about Mister Charlie, and he says he's with us – us kids – but he ain't going to do nothing to offend him. — James Baldwin, *Blues for Mister Charlie*, p. 40, 1964
• Goldberg's just as bad as Mr. Charlie. — Claude Brown, *Manchild in the Promised Land*, p. 295, 1965
• "Mr. Charlie, Mr. Charlie. Who the fuck is he?" "That's the name Brew calls the paddies." — Piri Thomas, *Down These Mean Streets*, p. 144, 1967
• Whenever some nigga brings in some money from Mister Charlie, all the other niggas want a piece. — Christina and Richard Milner, *Black Players*, p. 129, 1972

Mister Chatsby; Mr Chatsby *noun*

a non-existent member of a circus administration used to fob off unwelcome visitors *UK*

Possibly an elaboration of **CHAT** (a thing).

• And so the bewildered flattie goes round and round, never finding the mysterious Mr Chatsby who gives away free tickets. — Butch Reynolds, *Broken Hearted Clown*, p. 30, 1953

Mister Clean; Mr Clean; Miss Clean *noun*

a person in the public-eye who maintains an image that is beyond reproach *US*

• Egil Krogh was the White Hose Mr. Clean, so straight an arrow that his friends mockingly called him "Evil Krogh." — Carl Bernstein and Bob Woodward, *All the President's Men*, p. 257, 1974
• The C.E.O. of a nonpublic Wall Street competitor sarcastically remarked that Buffet "came in as Mr. Clean, the open-eyed boy from Omaha." — Roger Lowenstein, *Buffet*, p. 403–404, 1995
• [Rugby player, Martin] Johnson gets my vote for his work rate and the reputation he has forged as captain of England, even if sometimes he's not exactly Mr Clean. — *The Guardian*, 30th December 2002

Mister Dictionary has deserted us yet again

used as a humorous comment on profanity *US*

• CARMEN: Oh, piss of you sad twats!' HAMISH: Oh, dear. Mr Dictionary seems to have deserted us again. — Jennifer Saunders, *Absolutely Fabulous*, 1994
• Popularised and varied in the US by ESPN's Keith Olberman. — Keith Olberman and Dan Patrick, *The Big Show*, p. 20–21, 1997

Mister Fixit; Mr Fixit *noun*

used as an informal title for someone who is able to 'fix' things, whether from a technical knowledge or political influence *UK, 1984*

'Mr' may be replaced with another title as appropriate.

• Maybe help is at hand with rugby league's Mr Fixit, Maurice Lindsay, having just revealed his involvement in negotiations. — *The Observer*, 5th October 2003
• 'Lord Fixit' turns attention to BBC — *The Guardian*, 19th September 2003

Mister Floppy; Mr Floppy *noun*

the penis that has become flaccid when an erection is to be preferred *UK*

• [A]nxiety causes us to say hello to Mr Floppy[.] — Richard Herring, *Talking Cock*, p. 172, 2003

Mister Foot; Mr Foot *noun*

the penis *UK*

An imperial measure of bragging.

• — *Sky Magazine*, July 2001

Mister Geezer; Mr Geezer *noun*

the penis *US*

Both parts of this combination indicate 'a man'.

• Sure would make me feel a lot happier if I didn't have to worry about seeing your Mr Geezer hanging out of your boxer shorts. — Janet Evanovich, *Seven Up*, p. 9, 2001

Mister Green; Mr Green *noun*

money *US*

• "Unless you're ready with the only kind of loving the pimp knows." "What's that?" "Mr. Green." — Gail Sheehy, *Hustling*, p. 49, 1973

Mister Happy; Mr Happy *noun*

1 the penis *US, 1984*

Adopted from the character created by UK cartoonist Roger Hargreaves (1935–88) for his *Mr Men* children's books.

• — Connie Eble (Editor), *UNC-CH Campus Slang*, p. 6, Fall 1987
• Another way to say "penis" [...] Mr Happy[.] — Erica Orloff and JoAnn Baker, *Dirty Little Secrets*, p. 90, 2001
• She reached down and grabbed his cock. "How's Mr Happy?" — Garry Bushell, *The Face*, p. 120, 2001
• RAMU: What are you doing? MAKE-UP GIRL: Giving Mr Happy a shine. He gets more screen time than your face does. — *The Guru*, 2002

2 a nappy *UK: SCOTLAND*

Glasgow rhyming slang.

• It's definitely your turn to change the wee guy's Mr Happy. — Michael Munro, *The Patter, Another Blast*, 1988

Mister Hawkins; Mr Hawkins *noun*

a cold winter wind *US*

An embellishment and personification of **HAWK**.

• — Clarence Major, *Dictionary of Afro-American Slang*, p. 83, 1970

Mister Hyde; Mr Hyde *noun*

an untrustworthy person *UK*

Rhyming slang for **SNIDE**, informed by rhyming slang **JEKYLL AND HYDE** (two-faced) and the character of Mr Hyde in Robert Louis Stevenson's *The Strange Case of Dr Jekyll and Mr Hyde*.

• — Ray Puxley, *Cockney Rabbit*, 1992

Mister Jones; Mr Jones *noun*

used as a personification of the dominant white culture *US*

• — Eugene Landy, *The Underground Dictionary*, p. 133, 1971

Mister Lovely; Mr Lovely *noun*

marijuana *UK*

• — Mike Haskins, *Drugs*, p. 288, 2003

Mister Man; Mr Man *noun*

used as a disparaging term of address *TRINIDAD AND TOBAGO, 1904*

• — Lise Winer, *Dictionary of the English/Creole of Trinidad & Tobago*, 2003

Mister Matey; Mr Matey *noun*

the penis *UK, 2001*

A pet name; possibly a reference to Matey™, a brand name bubble bath for children, marketed in a phallic-shaped character-bottle that is suited to playing games in the bath.

Mister Miggles; Mr Miggles *noun*

heroin *NEW ZEALAND, 1997*

• — Harry Orsman, *A Dictionary of Modern New Zealand Slang*, p. 88, 1999

Mister Money; Mr Money *noun*

a Jewish person *US*

• — Edith A. Folb, *runnin' down some lines*, p. 247, 1980

Mister Nasty; Mr Nasty *noun*

the penis *US*

• A while back, after a short consultation with his johnson [penis], Vinnie agreed to hire Joyce [...] Mr. Nasty was still happy with the decision, but the rest of Vinnie didn't know what to do with Joyce. — Janet Evanovich, *Seven Up*, p. 37, 2001

Mister Nice; Mr Nice *noun*

one of the most powerful hybrid strains of marijuana *UK*

Named in honour of Howard Marks, a campaigner for the legalisation of cannabis. 'Mr Nice' was one of forty-three aliases Marks used in his former career as marijuana smuggler and the one by which he is publicly recognised.

• Mr. Nice from Sensi Seeds[.] — Brian Preston, *Pot Planet*, p. 232, 2002

Mister Period; Mr Period *noun*

used of a personification of the fact that a woman has missed her normal menstrual period *US*

• — *Maledicta*, p. 242, Winter 1980: '"Lovely, blooming, fresh and gay": the onomastics of camp'

Mister Sin; Mr Sin *noun*

a police officer assigned to the vice squad *US*

• — Edith A. Folb, *runnin' down some lines*, p. 247, 1980

Mister Softy; Mr Softy *noun*

a flaccid penis *US*

• — *Adult Video News*, p. 38, September 1995

Mister Speaker; Mr Speaker *noun*
a handgun *US*
• —Lou Shelly, *Hepcats Jive Talk Dictionary*, p. 29, 1945

Mister Television; Mr Television *nickname*
Milton Berle, US comedian of vaudeville, radio and television fame (1908–2002) *US*
Berle was the first superstar of US television, hosting the very popular Tuesday night *Texaco Star Theater*. Berle personified the early days of television; when he died in March 2002, newspaper headlines across the US proclaimed that 'Mr Television' had died.

Mister TFX; Mr TFX *nickname*
Albert W. Blackburn, a special assistant to Secretary of the Defense Robert McNamara in the early 1960s and an advocate of the controversial TFX (Tactical Fighter, Experimental) *US*
• To many persons Blackburn was "Mr. TFX." A Naval Academy graduate, he was an aerodynamics engineer and a test pilot.—Clark R. Mollenhoff, *The Pentagon*, p. 309, 1967

Mister Thirty; Mr Thirty *noun*
a tiger *US*
During the Vietnam war, tigers were occasionaly seen near the end of the lunar month when there was less light at night.
• —Linda Reinberg, *In the Field*, p. 145, 1991

Mister Truman's War *noun*
the Korean war *US*
A Republican party coining.
• Many Republicans were openly critical of the conduct of what they called "Mr. Truman's War."—Don Lawson, *The United States in the Korean War*, p. 94, 1964

Mister Twenty-six; Mr Twenty-six *noun*
a hypodermic needle *US*
• —David Maurer and Victor Vogel, *Narcotics and Narcotic Addiction*, p. 427, 1973

Mister Winky; Mr Winky *noun*
the penis *US*
Especially in the phrase 'giving Mr Winky an oral report' (oral sex).
• —Erica Orloff and JoAnn Baker, *Dirty Little Secrets*, p. 83, 2001

Mister Wood; Mr Wood *noun*
a police truncheon *UK*
From the crime-fighting technology employed at the time. Noted in *Free-Lance Writer*, April 1948.
• He pulled out his truncheon. He bent over and prodded at the prone figure beneath him. "Maybe Mr Wood wants a word, eh?" He swung the club[.]—Jake Arnott, *He Kills Coppers*, p. 79, 2001

Mister Wood in the house; Mr Wood in the house
used to describe a poorly attended circus performance *UK*
It is easier to see the wooden benches than the audience that should be sitting on them.
• Some shops he had had were "multi" (poor) or even "multi kativa" (downright bad) with "Mr. Wood in the house" most days.—Butch Reynolds, *Broken Hearted Clown*, p. 30, 1953

Mister Zippo; Mr Zippo *noun*
the operator of a flame thrower *US*
Vietnam war slang based on the Zippo™ manufacturing company's many cigarette lighters.
• —Linda Reinberg, *In the Field*, p. 142, 1991

mistie; misty *noun*
a tablet of morphine sulphate *NEW ZEALAND*
Probably because the sensation described by users is 'misty'.

mistress *noun*
used as a formal title (often seen with an initial capital) for a dominant woman in a fetishistic or sado-masochistic sexual context *UK, 1921*
A specialised consequence of the conventional uses as 'instructress'.
• —Thomas E. Murray and Thomas R. Murrell, *The Language of Sadomasochism*, 1989
• Some Goddesses borrow an idea from the Queen and order their votaries to shave the Mistress's legs, armpits, and even pubic area. —Lorelei, *The Mistress Manual*, 1996

Mitcham Gypsy *noun*
a person who wishes, or pretends, to be a gypsy *UK*
Mitcham in Surrey is a town where a number of travelling families have taken residence in houses.
• —Jimmy Stockin, *On The Cobbles*, p. 108, 2000

mites and lice *noun*
in poker, a hand with a pair of threes and a pair of twos *US*
• —Albert H. Morehead, *The Complete Guide to Winning Poker*, p. 268, 1967

mitsubishi; mitsi *noun*
a variety of MDMA, the recreational drug best known as ecstasy *UK*
From the Mitsubishi car manufacturer's logo embossed on the tablet.
• Says [DJ] Paul [van Dyk], "I wish they maybe would take one less Mitsubishi and try to get really into the music rather than rely on the Mitsubishi[.]"—Dave Haslam, *Adventures of the Wheels of Steel*, p. 26, 2001
• Mitsubishi, containing caffeine only (in other words, glorified Pro-Plus pills).—Gareth Thomas, *This Is Ecstasy*, p. 81, 2002
• Our weapons of mass elation contain warheads made up from bags of late-90s Mitsis.—*Mixmag*, p. 141, June 2003

Mitsubishi Turbo *noun*
a tablet of PMA, a synthetic hallucinogen, etched with the Japanese car manufacturer's logo *UK*
• —*The Guardian*, 14th January 2001

mitt *noun*
1 the hand *US, 1893*
• The Tennessees and Texases wanted to kill every Negro they could lay their mitts on[.]—Mezz Mezzrow, *Really the Blues*, p. 16, 1946
• Some day, before long, I'm going to have my rod in my mitt and the killer in front of me.—Mickey Spillane, *I, The Jury*, p. 7, 1947
• The Pachuco shivs Mace while the big stoop stands there all goofed off with a rod in his mitt.—Thurston Scott, *Cure it with Honey*, p. 160, 1951
• But the meat of his fleshy mitt snapped ringing against her mouth[.]—George Mandel, *Flee the Angry Strangers*, p. 333, 1952
• You're ver fast with your mitts, Collie.—Jim Thompson, *After Dark, My Sweet*, p. 10, 1955
• He said, "All right, Kid, keep that 'sizzle' [drug] in your mitt, so you can down it in a hurry."—Iceberg Slim (Robert Beck), *Pimp*, p. 135, 1969
• He could rip the gates on store fronts when he was a kiddie burglar with his mitts, didn't need no crowbar.—Edwin Torres, *Carlito's Way*, p. 130, 1975
• [S]haking a handful of beans in the royal mitt.—Andrew Nickolds, *Back to Basics*, p. 19, 1994

2 in poker or other card games, a hand of cards *US, 1896*
• —John Scarne, *Scarne's Guide to Modern Poker*, p. 284, 1979

mitt *verb*
to grab, to seize *US, 1915*
• The judge took one look at him that day in police court and decided that no such demure youth could have "mitted" twenty dollars from the grocer's cash drawer, then shortchanged him with his own money.—Jim Thompson, *Bad Boy*, p. 352, 1953

mitt camp *noun*
a fortune-telling booth in a carnival *US*
• —Joe McKennon, *Circus Lingo*, p. 62, 1980
• Although some MITT CAMPS stick to a simple Fortune, others are as deadly as any rigged game.—Gene Sorrows, *All About Carnivals*, p. 22, 1985

mitten money *noun*
extra money, either in the form of a tip or a bribe *US*
From the practice of sea-going pilots charging an extra fee for winter work.
• —John Gould, *Maine Lingo*, p. 182, 1975

mitt man *noun*
in gambling, a cheat who switches cards *US*
• Besides dice tats and 7UPS, there were volumes for nail nickers and crimpers (card markers), hand muckers and mit men (card switchers), as well as card counters and shiner players.—Stephen Cannell, *Big Con*, p. 143, 1997

mitt reader *noun*
in circus and carnival usage, a fortune teller who reads palms *US*
• —Don Wilmeth, *The Language of American Popular Entertainment*, p. 174, 1981

Mitzi *noun*
a Mitsubishi car *UK*
• There's Mercs, Lexus, Beamers, Mitzis, all kinds of fuck-off four wheel drives and that – pure quality, la.—Kevin Sampson, *Clubland*, p. 2, 2002

mix *noun*
kava, a tranquillity-inducing herbal beverage *FIJI*
• Fiji mix is not so strong as Vanuata mix, eh?—Jan Tent, 1995

▸ **in the mix**
involved with youth gang activity *US*
• —Bill Valentine, *Gang Intelligence Manual*, p. 77, 1995: 'Black Street Gang Terminology'
• Casper's in the mix.—*Kids*, 1995

mix *verb*
to fight *US, 1895*
• We're gonna mix with the PRs.—*West Side Story*, 1957

▸ **mix it**
1 to stir up trouble *US, 1899*
• [T]he screw who's giving evidence against you starts telling a load of bleeding lies and mixing it for you, which happens more than enough times, stand on me.—Frank Norman, *Bang To Rights*, p. 23, 1958

2 to fight *UK, 1900*
• —John Ayto, *The Oxford Dictionary of Slang*, p. 259, 1998

▸ **mix your peanut butter**
to play the active role in anal sex *US*
• —Eugene Landy, *The Underground Dictionary*, p. 133, 1971

mix and muddle *noun*
a cuddle *UK*
Rhyming slang.
• One of life's great annoyances is when you're lying in bed on a cold night, having a nice "mix & muddle" and you have to get up to have a cuddle & kiss (an act of urination).—Ray Puxley, *Cockney Rabbit*, 1992

mixed jive *noun*
crack cocaine *UK*
• —Mike Haskins, *Drugs*, p. 282, 2003

mixed up *adjective*
confused *US, 1884*
• [T]he movie ['Spun'] closes with a deeply dishonest attempt to sell Ross to us as a forgivably vulnerable mixed-up dreamer.—*The Guardian*, 28th November 2003

mixer *noun*
1 a troublemaker, a mischief-maker *UK, 1938*

2 a woman who works in a bar, encouraging customers through flirtation to buy drinks, both for themselves and for her *US*
• —Jack Lait and Lee Mortimer, *Chicago Confidential*, p. 302, 1950: 'Loop lexicon'

mix in *verb*
to join a fight *UK, 1912*

mixing stick *noun*
the gear shift of a truck *US*
• —Roberta Hanley, *American Speech*, p. 273, December 1961: 'Northwest truck drivers' language'
• —Montie Tak, *Truck Talk*, p. 107, 1971

mixmaster *noun*
1 a Cessna O-1 Super Skymaster aircraft, used in forward air control missions in Vietnam *US, 1951*
• —Linda Reinberg, *In the Field*, p. 142, 1991

2 a complex motorway interchange *US*
• —Wayne Floyd, *Jason's Authentic Dictionary of CB Slang*, p. 22, 1976

3 a dance music disc jockey *US*
With variant form 'mixmeister'.
• The Mystro, aka Sean Mather, aka a rising young producer with his first gold record on the wall and ambitions for many more, is currently the first-string varsity mixmeister for WPGC.—*Washington Post*, p. R6, 14th September 1995
• If you're gonna be a mixmeister, you need the right kit.—Richard Topping, *Havin' It Large*, p. 79, 2000
• What's a would-be mixmaster DJ virgin to do?—*The Guardian*, 19th April 2000

mixo *noun*
a bartender *US*
• —Jack Lait and Lee Mortimer, *Chicago Confidential*, p. 302, 1950: 'Loop lexicon'

mixologist *noun*
a bartender *US*
• —Jack Lait and Lee Mortimer, *Chicago Confidential*, p. 302, 1950: 'Loop lexicon'

miz!
that's too bad! *US*
An abbreviation of 'miserable'.
• —Pamela Munro, *U.C.L.A. Slang*, p. 90, 1997

mizzi *noun*
a type of MDMA, the recreational drug best known as ecstasy *UK*
• Oh, these Crowns beat Mizzis anytime!—James Hawes, *Dead Long Enough*, p. 154, 2000

mizzle *verb*
to depart hurriedly *UK, 1781*
• MIZZLE – To leave hurriedly.—Gilbert H. Lawson, *A Dictionary of Australian Words and Terms*, 1924
• Mizzle. Get off. Beat it. Get the hell out of here.—Geoff Wyatt, *Saltwater Saints*, p. 27, 1969

mizzony *noun*
▷ see: MEZZONY

MJ; mj *noun*
marijuana *US, 1966*
From **MARY JANE** (marijuana).
• —Richard A. Spears, *The Slang and Jargon of Drugs and Drink*, p. 342, 1986
• —Mike Haskins, *Drugs*, p. 288, 2003

MLR *noun*
in the Korean war, the main line of resistance or the front *US*
• The front, or front lines, are rarely referred to as such. "MLR" is used instead. It stands for "main line of resistance." In our case the MLR is a deep trench from five to seven feet in depth, running along the ridgeline of the hill mass[.]—Martin Russ, *The Last Parallel*, p. 82, 1957

MMM *noun*
an automated cash machine *NEW ZEALAND*
An abbreviation of **MAGIC MONEY MACHINE**; used widely in conversation in the 1990s.

mo *noun*
1 a moment *UK, 1896*
• Norm'll be along in a mo with the tickets.—*A Hard Day's Night*, 1964
• [M]y favourite names at the mo are Luca, Aidan or Zak.—Mary Hooper, *(megan)2*, p. 44, 1999
• [B]ack in a mo[.]—Kevin Sampson, *Outlaws*, p. 187, 2001
• Listen, yewer not a fuckin ex-junkie, mun, yewer a fuckin junkie who's not using at the mo.—Niall Griffiths, *Sheepshagger*, p. 138, 2001

2 in a prison, a prisoner subject to mental observation *US*
• —*Village Voice*, p. 68, 19th December 2000

3 a moustache *AUSTRALIA, 1894*
• MO. – Contraction of moment and moustache.—Gilbert H. Lawson, *A Dictionary of Australian Words and Terms*, 1924
• I was pushed and hit in the back as I got out of the car by a young screw with a blond mo.—Ray Denning, *Prison Diaries*, p. 127, 1979

4 a month *US, 1928*
• "How long a trip?" Carter asked. "Six moes."—George Mandel, *Flee the Angry Strangers*, p. 89, 1952

5 a homosexual *US, 1968*
• —Kevin Dilallo, *The Unofficial Gay Manual*, p. 242, 1994
• You also might want to make it clear that the Federal Wildlife Marshal's Office is also pro-'mo as well.—Kevin Smith, *Jay and Silent Bob Strike Back*, p. 79, 2001
• I had felt, like everyone else I knew, felt that moes, as we called them, were worthy firing-squad material.—Frank Skinner, *Frank Skinner*, p. 218, 2001

'mo *noun*
a homosexual *US, mid-1960s*
• —Kevin Dilallo, *The Unofficial Gay Manual*, p. 242, 1994

MO *noun*
1 a criminal's method of operating *US*
From the Latin *modus operandi*.
• —Evan Hunter, *The Blackboard Jungle*, p. 160, 1954
• I dig your MO, West, and here's what you are, man, here's just what you are.—Evan Hunter, *The Blackboard Jungle*, p. 160, 1954
• The MO was simple. We'd spend the summer on research trips.—Val McDermid, *Keeping on the Right Side of the Law*, p. 180, 1999

2 marijuana *US, 1977*
Also without the capitals.
• —Richard A. Spears, *The Slang and Jargon of Drugs and Drink*, p. 342, 1986
• —Mike Haskins, *Drugs*, p. 288, 2003

mo' *adjective*

more *US*

- [K]ickin' "mo' ass than a donkey." — *The Source*, p. 175, March 2002

moan *noun*

a complaint or grievance, an instance of spoken complaining *UK, 1911*

Originally military, probably from the verb 'moan' (to grumble).

- But typical topics for a moan in my office include: public transport ("Really? You had a bad time on the tube this morning? Gosh, how unexpected!")[.] — *The Guardian*, 17th November 2003

moaning Minnie *noun*

a persistent grumbler *UK, 1962*

Formed on a girl's name but applied to moaners of either gender.

- I want you to be enthusiastic, not a Moaning Minnie. — Maeve Binchy, *Evening Class*, p. 42, 1998

moan-o-drama *noun*

a romance story in a girls' magazine *CANADA*

- What the waitresses are reading is a True Romance magazine. These are not success stories. True Trash, Hilary calls them. Joanne calls them Moan-o-dramas. — Margaret Atwood, *The New Oxford Book of Canadian Short Stories*, p. 248, 1997

mob *noun*

1 a group of friends *US, 1939*

- We were thinking of getting up a mob to go to the Lal Lal races. — Norman Lindsay, *The Cousin from Fiji*, p. 106, 1945
- He introduced me to his mob, lying around of the beach, some of whom were unfriendly[.] — Clancy Sigal, *Going Away*, p. 132, 1961
- But if you belonged to a mob, you were given a certain amount of respect, depending on the strength of the mob you were in. — William Dick, *A Bunch of Ratbags*, p. 86, 1965

2 a group of people sharing some connection *AUSTRALIA, 1848*

- Captured by your mob? Don't gimme the tom tits. You Ities couldn't capture a bloody grasshopper. — Nino Culotta (John O'Grady), *They're A Weird Mob*, p. 24, 1957
- Look at that mob in there. Yer'd be dead unlucky ter be taken by a shark, with that mob. — Nino Culotta (John O'Grady), *They're A Weird Mob*, p. 65, 1957
- I once heard a Sydney Australian describe the citizens of Melbourne as being 'a weird mob'. — Nino Culotta (John O'Grady), *They're A Weird Mob*, p. 200, 1957
- Boy, have we got something to rock the mob with today! — Robert S. Close, *With Hooves of Brass*, p. 81, 1961
- Don't lump me in with the bloody squatter-mob. — Dymphna Cusack, *Picnic Races*, p. 34, 1965
- A mob of us were night breaming on the Yamba Wall a few years ago[.] — Bob Staines, *Wot a Whopper*, p. 9, 1982

3 a gang of criminals *UK, 1791*

4 a military unit *UK, 1894*

5 a group of surfers *AUSTRALIA*

- — John Severson, *Modern Surfing Around the World*, p. 172, 1964

6 a group of Aboriginal Australians; in Aboriginal English, a tribe, language group or Aboriginal community *AUSTRALIA, 1828*

- Mum's always at me about this Noongar mob, though some of them seem to be related to us in a vague way. — Colin Johnson, *Wild Cat Falling*, p. 10, 1965
- "Where's Dumby?' I asked Clemboy. 'Coming with his mob.' — Phillip Gwynne, *Deadly Unna?*, p. 96, 1998

7 in circus and carnival usage, the men employed by the show as a group *US*

- — Don Wilmeth, *The Language of American Popular Entertainment*, p. 175, 1981

8 a group of animals; a flock or herd *AUSTRALIA, 1828*

- Already she had gleaned that he was a squatter, and had come to this little town to truck a mob of sheep for the city markets. — Barbara Baynton, *Her Bush Sweetheart*, p. 106, 1921
- MOB – Group of larrikins; flock of sheep. — Gilbert H. Lawson, *A Dictionary of Australian Words and Terms*, 1924
- — Ion L. Idriess, *Over the Range*, p. 11, 1947
- On the other side of the scrub Grant could see a mob of about twenty kangaroos. — Kenneth Cook, *Wake in Fright*, p. 75, 1961
- [He] took delivery of 1,300 mixed store cattle and headed back to Quilpie again. They were a pretty bad mob, rushing almost every night. — Herb Wharton, *Cattle Camp*, p. 8, 1994

Mob *noun*

▸ **the Mob**

organised crime; the Mafia *US*

- Her father drives a taxi during the day, and a car for The Mob at night. — Philip Roth, *Portnoy's Complaint*, p. 187, 1969
- I hooked up with a fellow named Art who was right with many of the Italian mob. — A.S. Jackson, *Gentleman Pimp*, p. 102, 1973
- The mob made their thrust into Times Square porn shops in 1968. — Josh Alan Friedman, *Tales of Times Square*, p. 75, 1986
- Those fucking mob assholes. — *The Bad Lieutenant*, 1992

mob *verb*

1 to idle, to relax with friends *US*

- — Bill Valentine, *Gang Intelligence Manual*, p. 77, 1995: 'Black street gang terminology'

2 to surround, yell at and assault *US*

- — *Columbia Missourian*, p. 1A, 19th October 1998

MOB

*m*oney *o*ver *b*itches *US*

- — Ethan Hilderbrant, *Prison Slang*, p. 157, 1998

mobbed up *adjective*

associated with organised crime *US, 1973*

- He was mobbed up with the Pleasant Avenue outfit. — Edwin Torres, *Carlito's Way*, p. 21, 1975
- They liked to pretend they were "mobbed up" – associated with big city organized crime. — Kim Rich, *Johnny's Girl*, p. 62, 1993

mobbie *noun*

1 a female willing to take any and all sexual partners *AUSTRALIA*

- — Thommo, *The Dictionary of Australian Swearing and Sex Sayings*, p. 83, 1985

2 a member of an organised crime organisation *US*

- She happened to know after she had done some checking around that The Plumber was a mobbie. — Richard Condon, *Prizzi's Money*, p. 91, 1994

Mobe *noun*

the Student Mobilization Committee Against the War in Vietnam (SMC), the most powerful and visible anti-war group in the US in the late 1960s and early 70s *US*

- At the convention, the "Mobe" people wanted large, disciplined demonstrations focusing on the war and racism. — J. Anthony Lukas, *The Barnyard Epithet and Other Obscenities*, p. 33, 1970

mob-handed *adjective*

used to denote that the person specified is within a group or accompanied by a gang of people *UK, 1934*

- He [Ian Dury] became very hard in some respects, and he liked to be mob-handed. He liked to have a gang around him. — *The Guardian*, p. 12, 12th March 2002

mobie; moby *noun*

a mobile phone *UK, 1998*

- He's going to dish out new mobies, isn't he? Just as you've got used to your last number he's giving you another new one[.] — Kevin Sampson, *Outlaws*, p. 19, 2001
- Craig's left his moby on the dash[.] — Niall Griffiths, *Kelly + Victor*, p. 49, 2002

mobile *adjective*

sexually attractive *US*

- — *People Magazine*, p. 73, 19th July 1993

mobile parking lot *noun*

a car transporter *US*

- — *Complete CB Slang Dictionary*, 1976
- — Peter Chippindale, *The British CB Book*, p. 156, 1981

moblie *noun*

a mobile phone *UK*

- This crew came up to me and started pressing me [...] if they could go dub dub dub [access the Internet] on me moblie. — Craig Charles, *Word for Word (BBC Radio 4)*, 19th January 2005

moblog; moblogging *noun*

a diary or a miscellany of random observations, text-messages and pictures collected on a mobile phone and posted on the Internet; the act of creating, keeping or updating such a record *UK*

From 'mobile weblog' (see **BLOG**).

- It's the latest trend in weblogging: moblogging – or posting thoughts to your weblog from wherever you might be, via mobile phone or handheld device [...] Living in Japan, he has easy access to the gadgets that make moblogs work. — *The Guardian*, 12th December 2002

moboton *noun*

a splendid example of something *BARBADOS*

- She got a moboton of backside. — Frank A. Collymore, *Barbadian Dialect*, p. 74, 1965

mobs *noun*

a great number *AUSTRALIA, 1927*

- So remember, football teams can kick heaps or mobs of goals but only individuals can kick a bag. —Ivor Limb, *Footy's No Joke!*, p. 8, 1986

Moby *noun*

a completely depillated female pubis *US*

Named for the totally bald-headed musician Moby (Richard Melville Hall, b.1965) .

- A smooth and silky Moby. —Mark Lamarr, *Never Mind the Buzzcocks*, 15th September 2003

moby *adjective*

enormous *US, 1965*

A term brought into the world of computer programming from the model railway club at MIT.

- Computer Slang —Guy L. Steele,, *Coevolution Quarterly*, p. 31, Spring 1981
- "Some MIT undergrads pulled off a moby hack at the Harvard-Yale game." —Guy L. Steele et al., *The Hacker's Dictionary*, p. 94, 1983

Moby Dick *noun*

cocaine *UK*

Refers to the **GREAT WHITE WHALE** in *Moby Dick*, the classic novel by Herman Melville (1819–91). Cocaine, thereby, is claimed to be great and white (and you can have 'a whale of a time'?).

▸ **on the Moby Dick; on the moby**

on sick leave *UK*

Rhyming slang.

- Time away from work due to illness is known as being "on the Moby Dick". —Ray Puxley, *Cockney Rabbit*, 1992

Moby Dick; moby *adjective*

sick *UK, 1992*

Rhyming slang.

- —John Ayto, *The Oxford Dictionary of Rhyming Slang*, 2002

moby grape *noun*

an improvised mechanism for injecting drugs, consisting of a syringe with a rubber bulb from a child's dummy attached to the end *US*

The connection between this term and the late 1960s pyschedelic rock band by the same name seems obvious, yet eludes proof or explanation.

- —Eugene Landy, *The Underground Dictionary*, p. 134, 1971

moccasin telegraph *noun*

passing information through rumour, gossip or the Internet *US, 1908*

The original meaning referred to the use of Indian people as runners to carry messages; it has been adapted to the Internet world.

- The Moccasin Telegraph refers to the exchange of information by word of mouth. —*ammsa.com/ams*, 21st July 2002
- For us Native people who are on the Net as well, the moccasin telegraph has never been so strong. —*nation2nation.org/triciawork*, 21st July 2002

mocker *noun*

clothing; attire *AUSTRALIA, 1953*

Origin unknown. 'Thirty-five' (author of a glossary of Australian prison slang) writing in 1950 gave the definition 'a coat'.

- —Jim Ramsay, *Cop It Sweet!*, p. 59, 1977
- —Ryan Aven-Bray, *Ridgey Didge Oz Jack Lang*, p. 36, 1983

mockered up *adjective*

dressed up *AUSTRALIA, 1938*

mockers *noun*

▸ **put the mockers on**

1 to jinx *AUSTRALIA, 1911*

- He had been a good wartime officer; it was peace put the mockers on him. —David Ireland, *The Unknown Industrial Prisoner*, p. 42, 1971
- —Jim Ramsay, *Cop It Sweet!*, p. 59, 1977

2 to thwart, to frustrate someone's plans *AUSTRALIA, 1949*

A variation of earlier 'put the mock(s) on', which had a sense akin to 'put a jinx on someone'.

mock fighting *noun*

simulated fighting *US*

- And we decided to go to Central Park to do all this mock fighting, you know – you hit but you're not really hitting, but you make the sound by smacking the palm of your open hand. —Piri Thomas, *Stories from El Barrio*, p. 105, 1978

mockit; mawkit *adjective*

very dirty *UK: SCOTLAND, 1911*

Originally meant 'maggoty', now applied equally to actual dirt and notional obscenity.

mockitness *noun*

dirtiness *UK: SCOTLAND*

From **MOCKIT** (very dirty).

- There's no room for mockitness in modrin [modern] business, Lorna. —Ian Pattison, *Rab C. Nesbitt*, 1988

mockney *noun*

an ersatz London accent and vocabulary; someone who affects such artificial speech and background in search of cool *UK, 1989*

A compound of 'mock' (false) and 'Cockney' (the accent and identity of anyone born 'within the sound of Bow bells' or, loosely, an East Ender).

- [T]he guy himself was the usual long-haired public schoolboy with a Mick Jagger mockney accent and dodgy bomber jacket[.] —John Williams, *Cardiff Dead*, p. 94, 2000

mock out *verb*

to imitate *US, 1960*

- —Connie Eble (Editor), *UNC-CH Campus Slang*, p. 7, Spring 1991

mockstick *noun*

a person who is the subject of mockery *BARBADOS*

- —Frank A. Collymore, *Barbadian Dialect*, p. 74, 1965

mocky; mockie *noun*

a Jewish person *US, 1893*

- Tell me, Dadier, what do you think of kikes and mockies and micks and donkeys and frogs and niggers, Dadier. —Evan Hunter, *The Blackboard Jungle*, p. 209, 1954
- He can be pretty quick to yell 'guinea,' 'mockie,' and the rest. Maybe he acts like he's kidding, but underneath there's plenty of hostility. —Ross Russell, *The Sound*, p. 174, 1961
- One in a while you hear, "You mockie bastard!" —Lenny Bruce, *The Essential Lenny Bruce*, p. 35, 1967
- You got it all over everything, you mocky son of a bitch! —Philip Roth, *Portnoy's Complaint*, p. 203, 1969
- No one seems to know where mockie comes from. I never heard mockie until I came to New York[.] —Leo Rosten, *The Joys of Yinglish*, p. 344, 1989
- And those given a name were stuck with it forever: Svade, Svenska, Lugan, Schnapps, Moishe, Stosh, Henie, Mockie, Guinea, Canuck, Bohunk, Pork-dodger, Limey, Greaseball, Krauthead, Dutchie, Squarehead, Grick, Mick, Paddy, Goombah, Polski, Dago, Hunkie, Wop— *San Francisco Examiner*, p. A15, 28th July 1997

mocumentary *noun*

a film or television entertainment in the style of a documentary *US*

- Documentary, docucomedy, mocumentary, whatever. —*CBS News*, 18th February 1990
- [A] digital, shoulder-shot, Blair Witch-style, mocumentary, shoot-em-up, yoofsploitation number based on ecowarriors[.] —James Hawes, *White Powder, Green Light*, p. 5, 2002

mod *noun*

1 a member of the 1960s youth cult that is characterised by its detailed dress sense and use of motor-scooters *UK, 1960*

Abbreviated from 'modernist'. Wittily defined in the 6th edition of *The Dictionary of Slang and Unconventional English*, 1967, as 'a teenager unable to afford a motorcycle, and doing his damnedest with a scooter' and pedantically riposted by David Holloway, who writes in his review of the dictionary: '"Mods" ride scooters because the machines protect their clothes[.]' 'Mod' survives in C21 as a convenient music genre, and as small living-history groups who dress up in period costumes, ride scooters and dance to music marketed as 'Mod'.

- Mods smashing Rockers over the heads with deckchairs. — Martin King and Martin Knight, *The Naughty Nineties*, p. 223, 1999
- The Mod goes to tailors, drives them absolutely mad. He makes so many demands[.] —Paolo Hewitt, *The In Crowd*, 2001

2 in computing, a modification *US*
- —Eric S. Raymond, *The New Hacker's Dictionary*, p. 245, 1991

3 a percent sign (%) on a computer keyboard *US*
- —Eric S. Raymond, *The New Hacker's Dictionary*, p. 39, 1991

modams *noun*
marijuana *US, 1977*
- —Richard A. Spears, *The Slang and Jargon of Drugs and Drink*, p. 342, 1986
- —Mike Haskins, *Drugs*, p. 288, 2003

mod con *noun*
a modern convenience *UK, 1934*
From estate agent jargon.
- "Closed circuit television," he said. "All linked to a central control room." [...] "All mod. cons.," I said.—Martin Waddell, *Otley*, p. 77, 1966
- They put us in some brand new barracks all centrally-heated with showers and every mod con.—Johnny Speight, *It Stands to Reason*, p. 65, 1973

modder *noun*
a modifier *UK*
- But computer "modders" are never satisfied by the results of their customisations.—*FHM*, p. 59, June 2003

moddy boy *noun*
a young male who embraces the fashion and style of the mods *UK*
- —Tom Hibbert, *Rockspeak!*, p. 105, 1983
- The same moddy scooter boys who had attempted to cause grief at the 14-Hour Technicolour Dream[.]—Mick Farren, *Give the Anarchist a Cigarette*, p. 125, 2001

mode *verb*
to show disrespect; to exploit *US*
- —Rick Ayers (Editor), *Slang Dictionary*, p. 12, 2001

model *noun*
a prostitute *UK*
- "Why are you here? Are you a model?" "Certainly not." I'd been around this scene long enough to know a euphemism when I heard one.—Kitty Churchill, *Thinking of England*, p. 227, 1995

model C *adjective*
applied to teenagers in South Africa who attend private schools or mixed-race public schools *SOUTH AFRICA*
- There is your underground street language spoken by youth in the townships, and then there are your upwardly mobile Model C youth who speak a different lingo.—*Sunday Times (South Africa)*, 1st June 2003

model D *noun*
a black student who attends, or attended, a government school in a township *SOUTH AFRICA*
Scamto youth street slang (South African townships).
- —*The Times*, 12th February 2005

modified *adjective*
used of a car that has been in an accident *UK*
- —*Sunday Times*, 9th August 1981

modplod *noun*
a member of the military police *UK*
Combines the acronym MOD (the Ministry of Defence) with 'plod' (the police).
- —Nigel Foster, *The Making of a Royal Marine Commando*, 1987
- Military police stood silently on the other side. The "modplods", the peace people called them.—Jake Arnott, *He Kills Coppers*, p. 276, 2001

mods and rockers; mods *noun*
the female breasts *UK*
Rhyming slang for **KNOCKERS**, formed from two youth gangs who battled their way into 1960s folklore.
- Cor, look at the mods on that[.]—Ray Puxley, *Cockney Rabbit*, 1992

mod squad *noun*
any group of black and white people *US*
An allusion to a US television series (1968–73) that featured three hipper-than-hip juvenile delinquents turned police – Julie, Linc and Pete, one black, one white and one blonde.
- —Eugene Landy, *The Underground Dictionary*, p. 134, 1971

modulate; modjitate *verb*
to talk on a citizens' band radio *US, 1975*
Adopted from technical jargon.
- —*Complete CB Slang Dictionary*, 1976
- —Peter Chippindale, *The British CB Book*, p. 156–157, 1981

moer; moera *verb*
to thrash, to beat-up *SOUTH AFRICA*
Not in polite use.
- If you won't take us to the zoo / Then what the heck else can we do / But go on out and moera all the outjies next door.—Jeremy Taylor, *Ag Plees Deddy (The Ballad of the Southern Suburbs)*, 1960
- —Jean Branford, *A Dictionary of South African English*, 1978

moer
as an expletive, used as an expression of rage or disgust; used as an obscene and abusive form of address; in intensifying phrases, 'the moer', 'moer of a', 'moer and gone', etc, a synonym of hell *SOUTH AFRICA, 1946*
From Afrikaans for 'mother' (of animals) or 'womb'.
- — Partridge, *A Dictionary of the Underworld*, 1950
- —Jean Branford, *A Dictionary of South African English*, 1978

moey *noun*
▷ see: **MOOEY**

mofa *noun*
marijuana *US, 2001*
- —Simon Worman, *Joint Smoking Rules*, 2001

moff *noun*
a hermaphroditic animal *AUSTRALIA*
- 'It's a moff' – he gave the name given by bushmen to bi-sexual animals which are hermaphrodites.—H.G. Lamond, *Big Red*, p. 31, 1953

moffie; mophy *noun*
a homosexual male; a male transvestite *SOUTH AFRICA, 1929*
Deriving, probably, from 'hermaphrodite', but other etymological theories are interesting; *mofrodite* (a castrated Italian opera singer); Dutch *mof* (an article of clothing); English 'mauve' (as a variant of lavender, a colour associated with homosexuality). The word 'moffie' or 'mophy' first appears in South African sea slang in 1929 as 'a delicate, well-groomed young man'.
- There are rumours that Theo is a moffie, a queer, but he is not prepared to believe them.—J.M. Coetzee, *Boyhood*, p. 148, 1997
- He worked in the hotel in Vanderbijlpark as a chef. Moffies often stayed there.—Bart Luirink (translated by Loes Nas), *Moffies*, p. 13, 2000

moffiedom *noun*
homosexual society *SOUTH AFRICA, 1977*
From **MOFFIE** (a homosexual).
- —Penny Silva, *A Dictionary of South African English*, 1996

mofo *noun*
motherfucker *US, 1965*
- I tell you this ... and das vedanya, you goon-spy-KGB-mo-fo!—Jim Carroll, *Forced Entries*, p. 70, 1987
- —Lee McNelis, *30 + And a Wake-Up*, p. 2, 1991
- —Connie Eble (Editor), *UNC-CH Campus Slang*, p. 5, Fall 1997
- Move your ass, mo'fo!—Stuart Browne, *Dangerous Parking*, p. 189, 2000
- —Don R. McCreary (Editor), *Dawg Speak*, 2001

mog *noun*
a cat *UK, 1927*
A docking of **MOGGY**.

mo-gas *noun*
gasoline fuel used for ground vehicles *US*
Vietnam war usage.
- Our bellies bloated with water from the mechanics' Lister bag and streaked with grit and sweat, stinking of the road and grease and mo-gas.—Larry Heinemann, *Close Quarters*, p. 101, 1977

moggie *noun*
Mogodon™, a brand name tranquillizer *UK*
- Mogodon are often called "moggies".—James Kay and Julian Cohen, *The Parents' Complete Guide to Young People and Drugs*, p. 150, 1998
- Loves his fuckin downers, Llŷr does. Moggies, temazzies, mathadone.—Niall Griffiths, *Sheepshagger*, p. 119, 2001

moggy; moggie *noun*
a cat *UK, 1911*
- You didn't catch Brady but you did catch this – a maggot-ridden old moggy!—Patrick McCabe, *The Butcher Boy*, p. 206, 1992
- It was fascinating to watch as after a shot of morphine a docile cat turned into a mad moggy – spitting, hissing and charging around the classroom.—John Fleetwood, *In Stitches*, p. 55, 1994
- There were cats on practically every balcony staring at me through the metal railings with an unwinking – and vaguely sinister – expression. It looked like a moggie Alcatraz.—Liz Evans, *Pussy Galore [Tart Noir]*, p. 264, 2002

mogue *verb*
to deceive, to fool *UK, 1854*
• —Paul Baker, *Polari*, p. 181, 2002

▸ and no mogue?
used to imply a slight incredulity, 'That's true?' *UK*
From 'mogue' (to deceive); since late C19 a tailors' catchphrase that slipped into polari.
• —Paul Baker, *Polari*, p. 162, 2002

mohasky *noun*
marijuana *US, 1938*
Variants include 'mohaska', 'moshky', 'mohasty' and 'mohansky'.
• —Kenn "Naz" Young, *Naz's Underground Dictionary*, p. 46, 1973
• —Richard A. Spears, *The Slang and Jargon of Drugs and Drink*, p. 342, 1986
• —Mike Haskins, *Drugs*, p. 288, 2003

moired *adjective*
drunk *UK*
Probably from conventional 'moiréd' (of materials such as silk, 'watered'), thus 'well watered'.
• —*e-cyclopaedia*, 20th March 2002

mojo *noun*
1 a spell, magic *US, 1926*
• "Does this mean that number sixteen, the hole I just bet Lard Ass Louis Huckle five thousand dollars on, has a mojo on it?" "That be the correct terminology, Balls."—Jimmy Buffett, *Tales from Margaritaville*, p. 120, 1989

2 sexuality, libido, sexual attraction *US*
The song 'Got My Mojo Working' was sung on stage by Ann Cole in 1956 – the lyric continues: 'but it just won't work on you'. In 1971, The Doors released a song entitled 'Mr Mojo Risin''; the title serves as an anagram for the singer Jim Morrison and as an advertisement for his dangerous sexuality. This meaning, however, was not widely appreciated before the second *Austin Powers* film opened in 1999, but it caught on quickly thereafter.
• The mojo is the life force, the essence, the libido, the "right stuff." —*Austin Powers*, 1999
• Felix Carter has worked his mojo on a weak-at-the-knees makeup girl and the day is over.—Andrew Holmes, *Sleb*, p. 104, 2002

3 hard drugs, especially powdered drugs: cocaine, heroin, morphine *US, 1935*
From the sense as 'a kind of magic'; first recorded in this sense as 'morphine'.
• —Haldeen Braddy, *American Speech*, p. 87, May 1955: 'Narcotic argot along the Mexican Border'
• —Richard A. Spears, *The Slang and Jargon of Drugs and Drink*, p. 343, 1986
• —Robert Ashton, *This Is Heroin*, p. 206, 2002
• —Mike Haskins, *Drugs*, p. 284, 2003

4 an early version of the fax machine *US*
Very slow, very cumbersome, but for its day a great advance, almost 'magical', hence the term. Popularised by Hunter S. Thompson's writings.
• It'd sent it on the mojo and they didn't know that had mojos in the building.—Hunter S. Thompson, *Songs of the Doomed*, p. 147, 1990

mojo juice *noun*
liquid dolophine, a drug commonly known as methadone, used for the rehabilitation of heroin addicts *US*
• Mrs. Toto at the door gives me a polite shove and tells me I can start tomorrow morning on the mojo juice.—Jim Carroll, *Forced Entries*, p. 116, 1987

moke *noun*
1 a fool *UK, 1855*
From the conventional sense (a donkey).
• Any moke can shoot jack into a woman make a kid.—Joel Rose, *Kill Kill Faster Faster*, p. 47, 1997

2 a horse *AUSTRALIA, 1863*
• 'What?? Not the war horse – oh, no!' he cried, and then moaned like a moke with the mumps.—Willie Fennell, *Dexter Gets The Point*, p. 104, 1961

moko longer than plantain
used for signalling to a woman that her slip is showing *TRINIDAD AND TOBAGO*
• Because a moko fig is usually shorter than a plantain.—Lise Winer, *Dictionary of the English/Creole of Trinidad & Tobago*, 2003

molasses *noun*
used as a euphemism for 'shit' *UK*
• [G]et him out of the molasses he was in.—Andrew Nickolds, *Back to Basics*, p. 130, 1994

mole *noun*
1 a promiscuous woman *AUSTRALIA, 1965*
Commonly used as a term of disparagement implying promiscuity. Merely a respelling of **MOLL** in the same sense, representing the usual Australian pronunciation.
• Kim loves to make a mountain out of a molehill. And in this case there are two moles.—Kylie and Dannii Boulton, *TV Week*, 1st November 2003

2 in electric line work, a lineman or cable-splicer who works underground *US*
• —A.B. Chance Co., *Lineman's Slang Dictionary*, p. 12, 1980

mole hole *noun*
the underground barracks where air attack alert crews live *US*
• —*American Speech*, p. 119, May 1963: 'Air refueling words'

moll *noun*
1 an unmarried female companion of a criminal *UK, 1823*
• Boniface's moll sat in the driver's seat of a red Vauxhall Astra.—Garry Bushell, *The Face*, p. 245, 2001

2 a promiscuous woman *AUSTRALIA*
Commonly used as a term of contempt, especially amongst teenagers, implying promiscuity. Commonly pronounced to rhyme with 'pole'.
• SALLY: She's already a moll. I can't corrupt her.—Dorothy Hewett, *The Chapel Perilous*, p. 50, 1972
• And they are the biggest molls that ever walked the face of the Earth.—Kathy Lette, *Girls' Night Out*, p. 25, 1987
• The boys in my Greehill gang told me I was a scumbag moll and to fuck off out of my territory.—Kathy Lette, *Girls' Night Out*, p. 188, 1987

3 a prostitute *UK, 1604*
Now obsolete in Britain but survives in Australia.
• Marry you, an amateur moll like you? Marry a crow who deserted her husband and kid!—Dorothy Hewett, *The Chapel Perilous*, p. 75, 1972
• Woman of easy virtue and low social status.—Jim McNeil, *'The Chocolate Frog' and 'The Old Familiar Juice'*, 1973

▸ like a moll at a christening
uncomfortably out of place *AUSTRALIA*
• Get out of the rutting way...You're like a moll at a christening!—Robert S. Close, *Love Me Sailor*, p. 125, 1945

moll buzz *noun*
a female pickpocket *US*
• —Vincent J. Monteleone, *Criminal Slang*, p. 156, 1949

moll-buzzer *noun*
a thief who specialises in snatching handbags from women with children in prams or pushchairs *US, 1859*
• —Don Wilmeth, *The Language of American Popular Entertainment*, p. 175, 1981

molly *noun*
1 an effeminate male homosexual *UK, 1709*
• —Dale Gordon, *The Dominion Sex Dictionary*, p. 97, 1967
• —Paul Baker, *Polari*, p. 181, 2002
• Complete with catchy Top Cat style theme tune, the web's molliest mallard is back onscreen, debating with animal chums Openly Gaytor and Bi-Polar Bear whether he should come out to his parents. —*Guardian Unlimited*, March 2002

2 any central nervous system stimulant *US*
• —Elementary Electronics, *Dictionary of CB Lingo*, p. 87, 1976

3 MDMA, the recreational drug best known as ecstasy *UK*
• —Mike Haskins, *Drugs*, p. 290, 2003

molly-booby *noun*
a foolish person *BARBADOS*
• —Frank A. Collymore, *Barbadian Dialect*, p. 74, 1965

mollycoddle *noun*
an effeminate man, especially an effeminate homosexual man *UK, 1833*
• There were no real two-fisted drinkers any more – only molly-coddles who sipped half-heartedly at their drinks and then went on about their business.—Jim Thompson, *Bad Boy*, p. 302, 1953
• You think religion is for suckers and easy marks and mollycoddles, huh?—*Elmer Gantry*, 1960

molly-dooker *noun*
a left-handed person *AUSTRALIA, 1934*
• While a win for left-hander Graham Marchant would be popular with a big section of the club because a "molly-dooker" has not won the event in a long time, most rate the smooth-swinging Shrimpton as the greatest threat to the hig-hitting Wigzell.—*Busselton-Margaret Times*, p. 16, 29th July 1982

Molly Hogan *noun*
in logging, a wire strand, cut from cable, used as a cotter pin *CANADA*
- A "Molly Hogan" is a strand of wire pushed through a hole and twist-tied in place. It is used to replace a cotter pin, which is easily lost in the bush. The word developed from "molle," French for soft. — Tom Parkin, *WetCoast Words*, p. 94, 1989

Molly Hogan deal *noun*
a deal with a catch, something wrong *CANADA*
- Suddenly, logging sports seem to have become the "in" thing, attracting hordes of ardent admirers, most of whom firmly believe Molly Hogan is the young colleen responsible for causing Clancy to get careless with the boom. — *Canadian Forest Industries*, p. 50/2, October 1966

Molly Maguired *adjective*
tired *UK*
Rhyming slang, formed, probably, from the title of the 1970 film *The Molly Maguires* rather than the C19 originals.
- — Ray Puxley, *Fresh Rabbit*, 1998

Molly Malone; molly *noun*
a telephone *UK*
Rhyming slang, formed from the name of the tragic heroine of the traditional ballad, 'Cockles and Mussels'.
- — Jack Jones, *Rhyming Cockney Slang*, 1971
- — David Powis, *The Signs of Crime*, 1977
- — Ray Puxley, *Cockney Rabbit*, 1992

Molly O'Morgan *noun*
an organ (in any sense) *UK, 1961*
Rhyming slang, originally for 'a barrel organ'.
- — Ray Puxley, *Cockney Rabbit*, 1992

molly the monk *adjective*
drunk *AUSTRALIA, 1966*
Rhyming slang.
- — Jim Ramsay, *Cop It Sweet!*, p. 59, 1977

molo *adjective*
drunk *AUSTRALIA, 1906*
Origin unknown.
- There is also a whole boozey flood of alternatives available, among them blithered, full as a goog, half-cut, molo and snockered. — Arthur Chipper, *The Aussie Swearer's Guide*, p. 52, 1972
- — Jim Ramsay, *Cop It Sweet!*, p. 59, 1977
- — Ryan Aven-Bray, *Ridgey Didge Oz Jack Lang*, p. 36, 1983

Molsonland *nickname*
Canada *CANADA*
- They had the Lynx three months before Virge Carter told them it was built in Oakville, Ontario. He should have known from the name, Lynx, must be the national mammal up there in Molsonland. — William Carpenter, *The Wooden Nickel*, p. 11, 2002

Molson muscle *noun*
the rounded belly of the habitual beer drinker *CANADA*
Molson is one of the two largest breweries in Canada.
- Not a drink itself, but the potbelly one gets from drinking too much beer. — Emily *An American's Guide to Canada*, p. 3, 10th November 2001

mom *noun*
the 'feminine' or 'passive' member of a lesbian relationship *US*
- — John M. Murtagh and Sara Harris, *Cast the First Stone*, p. 261, 1957: 'Glossary'
- — Robert George Reisner, *The Jazz Titans*, p. 161, 1960

mom-and-pop *adjective*
small-time, small-scale *US, 1943*
From the image of a small grocery store owned and operated by a husband and wife.
- Evelle and the Cashier, a late-middle-aged man (perhaps the proprietor of this small mom-and-pop store) face each other across the check-out counter. — *Raising Arizona*, 1987
- You run a mom and pop arms smuggling ring. — Mike Judge and Joe Stillman, *Beavis and Butt-Head Do America*, p. 35, 1997

momgram *noun*
the postcard that many US Marine recruits sent home upon arriving at basic training in Parris Island, South Carolina *US*
- — Linda Reinberg, *In the Field*, p. 143, 1991

momma-hopper *noun*
used as a euphemism for 'motherfucker' *US*
- — *Maledicta*, p. 11, Summer 1977: 'A word for it!'

mommy-o *noun*
used as a term of address for a woman *US*
Far rarer than **DADDY-O**.
- "Mommy-o," said Goldie, heading for the yard, "dis is de place!" — Steve Allen, *Bop Fables*, p. 4, 1955

momo *noun*
1 a motor; a car *UK*
Childish, reduplication of first syllable.
- Bad man follows you, sees you meet other girls in mo-mo car – right? — Alan Bleasdale, *Boys From the Blackstuff*, 1982

2 an idiot *US, 1960*
- Frank hit him in the head with a cueball, shrieking, Looka this fuckin momo! — Gilbert Sorrentino, *Steelwork*, p. 63, 1970

momo boy *noun*
a member of the Mongrel Mob gang *NEW ZEALAND, 1977*
- — Harry Orsman, *A Dictionary of Modern New Zealand Slang*, p. 87, 1999

moms *noun*
a mother *US*
- My moms couldn't sleep; there were four of us out there for her to worry about. — Claude Brown, *Manchild in the Promised Land*, p. 258, 1965
- My moms and pops always wanted Hector and me to go to college[.] — Terry Williams, *The Cocaine Kids*, p. 74, 1989
- I'm glad my moms ain't like your moms. My moms lets me do whatever I want, when I want. — *Mo' Better Blues*, 1990
- Yo pale muthfucka, don't play with me, 'cause I ain't your moms. — *New Jack City*, 1990

momzer; momser *noun*
a bastard; a brute; a detestable man *US*
From the Hebrew for 'bastard'.
- "Momser," his mother said bitterly, "you had to be a regular actor, a comedian." — Irving Shulman, *The Amboy Dukes*, p. 90, 1947
- I'll work on the momser. — Clancy Sigal, *Going Away*, p. 17, 1961
- Joe Licamarito, Marxie's boss, was furous that the momser thought he could get away with such a ripoff[.] — Richard Condon, *Prizzi's Honor*, p. 113–114, 1982

Mon *nickname*
the Monongahela River *US*
- — Sam McCool, *Pittsburghese*, p. 25, 1982

Mona Lisa *noun*
1 a pizza *UK*
Rhyming slang, formed from the English name of the famous portrait by Leonardo da Vinci.
- — Ray Puxley, *Fresh Rabbit*, 1998

2 a freezer *UK*
Rhyming slang.
- — Ray Puxley, *Cockney Rabbit*, 1992
- — Ray Puxley, *Fresh Rabbit*, 1998

monarch *noun*
in a deck of playing cards, a king *US*
- — George Percy, *The Language of Poker*, p. 58, 1988

Monday morning quarterback *noun*
1 in American football, a fan who from the distance of the day after a game knows exactly what should have been done *US*
- — Zander Hollander and Paul Zimmerman, *Football Lingo*, p. 5, 1967

2 a self-styled expert who from the safety of distance knows exactly what should have been done in a given situation in which he was not a participant *US, 1950*
- We are a race of grandstand managers, Monday morning quarterbacks and chronic, incurable kibitzers. — Robert Sylvester, *No Cover Charge*, p. 192, 1956

Monday pill *noun*
the large, orange anti-malarial pill (chloroquine-primaquine) taken once a week by US troops in Vietnam *US*
- — Gregory Clark, *Words of the Vietnam War*, p. 100, 1990

mondo *adjective*
large *US, 1982*
- Therein, instead of yelling 'I love mondo hooters,' they can yell 'I love 44 DDs' or 'I want a 34B.' — Nancy Tamosaitis, *net.sex*, p. 85, 1995

mondo *adverb*
very *US, 1968*
- "Mondo gross!" said Ric. — Jess Mowry, *Way Past Cool*, p. 10, 1992
- The boys are back with something quite unnatural / Mondo weird. — Children on Stun, *Mondo Weird*, 1997

money *noun*
1 someone who is attractive, nice and generally a good catch *US*
Popularised as a catchphrase by the film *Swinges*.
- — Connie Eble (Editor), *UNC-CH Campus Slang*, p. 5, Fall 1997

2 a close friend or trusted colleague *US*
- — William K. Bentley and James M. Corbett, *Prison Slang*, p. 50, 1992
- — Rick Ayers (Editor), *Berkeley High Slang Dictionary*, p. 31, 2004

3 in prison, anything of value in trade *US*
- — John R. Armore and Joseph D. Wolfe, *Dictionary of Desperation*, p. 40, 1976

▸ **have money to burn**
to be rich, to have plenty to spend *US, 1896*
- Businesses alerted to huge profits as study shows dope users have money to burn. — *The Observer*, 2nd February 2003

▸ **in the money**
1 wealthy, especially if exceptionally so; comfortably off *UK, 1902*
- Mystic Meg [an astrologer] et al don't need to look up their stars to know if they're going to be in the money or sleeping on the streets come Wednesday. — *The Guardian*, 18th May 2004

2 in horse racing, finishing first, second or third in a race *US*
- — Nate Perlmutter, *How to Win Money at the Races*, p. 120, 1964

▸ **it's only money**
said to yourself or another, as encouragement to spend or consolation, when faced with an unwanted or unexpected expense *UK, 1984*
- "I'll have that, yes I like that, and – wow! – I must have that". Cost is irrelevant. Who cares if you blow $12.87. It's only money. And keep the 13c change. — *The Guardian*, 3rd March 2003

▸ **money talks and bullshit walks**
used as a humorous suggestion that talk is cheap *US*
- Money talks and bullshit walks and if the first album was a hit then we could have pressed on them, then we could have told them yes. — *This is Spinal Tap*, 1984

▸ **money to stone dogs**
a lot of money *JAMAICA*
Pelting anything handy at foraging stray dogs is a common habit among the poor. Collected in 2001.

▸ **put your money where your mouth is**
to back up your words with a wager or a payment *US, 1942*
- [A] carefully designed auction achieves this end by creating a competitive environment in which the bidders are forced to put their money where their mouth is. — *New Statesman*, 25th March 2002

▸ **you pays your money and you takes your choice!; you pays your money!**
only if you contribute to something in some manner are you entitled to hold an opinion or take advantage of that something *UK*
A catchphrase. Originally, and in its literal sense, a stallholder's cry to customers, recorded in *Punch* in 1846. Familiarity has shortened the phrase without amending its sense.
- As they say, "you pays your money". Mine's on Bushill Bandit in the 14.15. — *The Guardian*, 23rd November 2000

moneybags *noun*
a wealthy individual *IRELAND, 1818*
- You've been named as the moneybags of a stolen car ring. — *The Sweeney*, p. 32, 1976

money ball *noun*
in pool, a shot that if made will win a wager *US*
- — Steve Rushin, *Pool Cool*, p. 21, 1990

money box *noun*
1 a Royal Mail train *UK*
- — Harvey Sheppard, *Dictionary of Railway Slang*, 1970

2 any money that remains after the necessities of life are paid for *NEW ZEALAND*
- — Louis S. Leland, *A Personal Kiwi-Yankee Dictionary*, p. 67, 1984

money for jam *noun*
easily obtained or earned money *AUSTRALIA, 1960*
- — J.E. MacDonnell, *Don't Gimme the Ships*, p. 46, 1960
- — Sue Rhodes, *And when she was bad she was popular*, p. 12, 1968
- 'Money for jam, kid,' he snorted. 'Nine-seven on a bog track over two miles at Flemington. I tell ya stick to selling papers, mate. And don't go giving up your day job to be a full-time punter!' — Clive Galea, *Slipper!*, p. 6, 1988
- [C]ry-babies who wanna keep going on about the good old days, how it was money for jam, "Oh what fun we had!!" — J.J. Connolly, *Layer Cake*, p. 94, 2000

money for old rope *noun*
money easily earned, hence anything gained by little or no effort *UK, 1936*
- Many who go to these events – and I'm one of them – suspect that the organisers are often getting money for old rope. — *The Guardian*, 6th May 2003

money from home *noun*
any money won easily, betting *US*
- — David W. Maurer, *Argot of the Racetrack*, p. 42, 1951

money-getter *noun*
the vagina *US*
- But if it was all her thing, she really had a money getter. — A.S. Jackson, *Gentleman Pimp*, p. 15, 1973

money-grabber *noun*
in motor racing, a driver who enters an event and competes only long enough to claim the fee for appearing and then quits the race *US*
- — John Edwards, *Auto Dictionary*, p. 109, 1993

money in the bank and cattle in the hills *noun*
independently wealthy *US*
- — Jerry Robertson, *Oil Slanguage*, p. 60, 1954

money machine *noun*
a generous person *US*
- — Anna Scotti and Paul Young, *Buzzwords*, p. 49, 1997

moneymaker *noun*
1 the genitals; the buttocks *UK, 1896*
- Shuck my clothes an hop in that fabbroom, take a fullout shower, wash the jail off my skin an the funk outa my moneymaker. — Robert Gover, *JC Saves*, p. 78, 1968
- [P]unch him in the cocksucker and land him on his moneymaker. — *Maledicta*, p. 253, 1979
- London's fashionable set now seemed willing, eager even, to acknowledge and yes, in some cases, shake their moneymakers. — Lauren Laverne, *X-RAY*, August 2003

2 a success *US, 1899*
- The play had been a moneymaker for us when I had Puddin Patterson to block for me. — Dan Jenkins, *Life Its Ownself*, p. 33, 1982

3 a low-priced, reliable truck *US*
- — Montie Tak, *Truck Talk*, p. 108, 1971

money player *noun*
an athlete who performs well in critical situations *US, 1922*
- — Parke Cummings, *Dictionary of Baseball*, p. 35, 1950
- The sina qua non is that he is a good "money player," can play his best when heavy action is riding on the game (as many non-hustlers can't). — Ned Polsky, *Hustlers, Beats, and Others*, p. 55, 1967
- — Zander Hollander and Sandy Padwe, *Basketball Lingo*, p. 68, 1971
- While Allen isn't the post guy Seattle needs, he's the money player that any squad covets. — *Bellingham (Washington) Herald*, p. 1B, 7th January 2004

moneypuker *noun*
an automatic cash machine *CANADA*
- Frank went to get some cash from the moneypuker at Becker's. — Jack Chambers (Editor), *Slang Bag 93 (University of Toronto)*, p. 4, Winter 1993

money rider *noun*
in horse racing, a winning jockey *US*
- — David W. Maurer, *Argot of the Racetrack*, p. 43, 1951

money row *noun*
a type of bet in an illegal numbers game lottery *US*
- He played the money row, lucky lady, happy days, true love, sun gonna shsine, gold, silver, diamonds, dollars and whiskey. — Chester Himes, *A Rage in Harlem*, p. 23, 1957

money shot *noun*

a scene in a pornographic film or photograph of a man ejaculating outside his partner *US*

Perhaps because it is the one shot that justifies the cost of the scene.

- This shot is known as the "come shot." On a porno-movie set it is also referred to as the "money shot." — Stephen Ziplow, *The Film Maker's Guide to Pornography*, p. 78, 1977
- Mark examines the flashlight he and Butch will use to distnguish each orgasm in the barely lit room, when Lev does his "money shot." — Josh Alan Friedman, *Tales of Times Square*, p. 105, 1986
- [I]t was not until the early seventies, with the rise of the hard-core features, that the money shot assumed the narrative function of signaling the climax of a genital event. — Linda Williams, *Hard Core*, p. 93, 1989
- You have to stay back so that we can get the money shot here. — Robert Stoller and I.S. Levine, *Coming Attractions*, p. 157, 1991
- For one thing, although male actors must reach a climax, known as the "money shot," women can, and usually do, fake orgasms. — *Los Angeles Times*, p. 8, 17th February 1991
- LEE: We gotta see arses goin' up and down. MOON: Gotta see that mate. JAMIE: Just not my bollocks 'angin' down. MOON: An' push 'er out the way for the money shot. — Chris Baker and Andrew Day, *Lock, Stock... & Spaghetti Sauce*, p. 239, 2000
- Money shot or no, we know that women have a very different relationship to visual pornography than men. — *The Village Voice*, 22nd August 2000
- TMN is showing everything but the money shot. — *Toronto Star*, p. J4, 27th December 2003

money-spinner *noun*

anything that makes easy profits *UK, 1952*

- Tourism is one of the country's main moneyspinners and employs a large percentage of the population. — *Lonely Planet Fiji*, p. 46, 2003

money talks

those who have money have power *US, 1905*

- News makes headlines, but money talks. — *The Observer*, 20th April 2003

Monfort lane *noun*

the passing lane on a motorway *US*

- The Monforts out of Greely, Colorado, probably the most beautiful company truck on the boulevard, Kenworth's with Cat engines and an average speed of 69 m.p.h., established a home in the passing lane and so some serious trailer truckin' and the passing lane became known as the Monfort lane. — Gwyneth A. "Dandalion" Seese, *Tijuana Bear in a Smoke 'Um Up Taxi*, p. 16, 1977

mong *noun*

1 a fool; used as an all-purpose insult *UK*

Abbreviated from the offensive usage of 'mongoloid' (affected with Down's syndrome).

- — Angela Devlin, *Prison Patter*, p. 77, 1996
- [He] is not just "gross" but a "gimp" and a "retard" and a "mong". — Jenny Eclair, *Camberwell Beauty*, p. 153, 2000
- You should've been up there with that mong. — John King, *Human Punk*, p. 60, 2000
- How's me faverit fuckin half-wit then eh? The world's best inbred backwoods feeb psycho mong? — Niall Griffiths, *Sheepshagger*, p. 73, 2001
- That guy set his hair on fire! He's such a mong! — *Wordmap (www.abc.net.au/wordmap)*, 2003

2 a dog of mixed breed *AUSTRALIA, 1903*

Shortening of 'mongrel'.

- [H]e'd have bought a bit of trouble if the mong had been loose. — Jon Cleary, *The Long Shadow*, p. 50, 1949
- — Jim Ramsay, *Cop It Sweet!*, p. 59, 1977

mong; mong out *verb*

(of drugs) to intoxicate; to become intoxicated *UK*

Derives from the conventional sense of 'mongol' (a person affected by Down's syndrome and can mean 'stupid').

- By now everyone is monging out completely. — Gavin Hills, *White Burger Danny (Disco Biscuits)*, p. 71, 1996
- I'd rather have ten quid's worth of hash, it does a better job [than methadone] keeping me away from the smack, and doesn't mong me out as much. — Jason Parkinson, *Skateboards and Methadone [The Howard Marks Book of Dope Stories]*, p. 206, 2001
- I have a one-hour mental-agility workout, then I start monging the herbs [marijuana]. — *Mixmag*, p. 35, December 2001

monged *adjective*

1 drunk *UK*

- [Y]ou're monged on three halves of shandy. — Ben Elton, *High Society*, p. 12, 2002
- — *e-cyclopaedia*, 20th March 2002

2 being fatigued after drug use

- I'm monged. — Nick Brownlee, *This Is Cannabis*, p. 152, 2002

monged-out; monged *adjective*

intoxicated with MDMA, the recreational drug best known as ecstasy, or, occasionally, another drug

Derives from the conventional sense of 'mongol' (a person affected by Down's syndrome and can mean 'stupid').

- [W]ith a girl either side of him – one monged-out, one merry, both in trouble[.] — Dave Courtney, *Raving Lunacy*, p. 107, 2000
- They're just pure monged day and night, on their way up or on their way down. — Kevin Sampson, *Outlaws*, p. 77, 2001

mongee *noun*

a good student who is socially inept *US*

School usage.

- — *Washington Post*, 23rd April 1961: 'Man, dig this jazz'

mongie *noun*

a member of the Mongrel Mob gang *NEW ZEALAND*

- The Black Power gang were sworn enemies of both the Heads and the Mongies. — Greg Newbold, *The Big Huey*, p. 220, 1982
- [W]hat did you hear Tangitutu say? Don't – us mongie around[.] — *Dominion*, p. 3, 16th August 1983

mongie *adjective*

1 dirty, fusty, evil smelling; nasty *UK*

Reported in use amongst Leicestershire children during the 1970s by Beale, 1984. Presumably expanding the insulting use derived from 'mongoloid'.

2 dull, stupid *UK, 1984*

From 'mongoloid'. Teen slang reported by D. and R. McPheely.

mongish *adjective*

dull, stupid *UK*

From 'mongoloid'.

- — *New Society*, 31st January 1980

mongo *noun*

1 an idiot *US, 1975*

Abbreviated from the offensive usage of 'mongoloid' (affected with Down's syndrome); probably used without thinking.

- [T]he mongos blowing the shit out of the Middle East. — Frank Zappa, *The Real Frank Zappa Book*, p. 293, 1989

2 the vagina *US*

- There's [a...] "horsespot," "nappy dugout," mongo," a "pajama," "fannyboo[".] — Eve Ensler, *The Vagina Monologues*, p. 6, 1998

3 a member of the Mongrel Mob gang *NEW ZEALAND, 1977*

- — Harry Orsman, *A Dictionary of Modern New Zealand Slang*, p. 87, 1999

mongo *adjective*

very large *US*

- — Connie Eble (Editor), *UNC-CH Campus Slang*, p. 7, Fall 1985
- — Judi Sanders, *Don't Dog by Do, Dude!*, p. 21, 1991
- I mean, I notice when they're dressed well or when they're fat or ugly or have mongo bazooms- — Rita Ciresi, *Pink Slip*, p. 52, 1999

mongo *adverb*

in foot-propelled scootering, with the wrong foot *UK*

From **MONGO** (an idiot).

- — Ben Sharpe, *Scooter Crazy*, p. 40, 2000

mongo-footed *adjective*

in foot-propelled scootering, used of someone who pushes with the wrong foot *UK*

From **MONGO** (an idiot).

- — Ben Sharpe, *Scooter Crazy*, p. 40, 2000

Mongolian clusterfuck *noun*

an orgy *US*

- I'm startin' to feel like the bottom man in a Mongolian cluster fuck. — James Elroy, *Suicide Hill*, p. 699, 1986
- Fabulous terminology for group sex, though why it should be restricted to Mongolians is anyone's guess. — *Sky Magazine*, p. 73, July 2001

mongrel *noun*

a contemptible person *AUSTRALIA, 1902*

Without any suggestion of mixed breeding.

- There are some mongrels about, aint there? — Jean Brooks, *The Opal Witch*, p. 142, 1967

mongrel *adjective*
displeasurable; unsatisfying; annoying *AUSTRALIA*
Used as a negative intensifier.
- To George everything was "mongrel". He opined that he wanted his mongrel head read for joining this mongrel outfit, while at the same time he was looking forward to his mongrel leave; and (privately) loved his mongrel life aboard this mongrel ship. —J.E. MacDonnell, *Dit Spinner*, p. 53, 1967
- You rotten, bloody, poofter, commo, mongrel bastard. —Bill Hornadge, *The Ugly Australian*, p. 113, 1973

mongy *adjective*
stupid *UK*
From **MONG**, ultimately 'mongoloid'.
- [S]he says she is a "mongy spaz" and "nobody likes her and she smells". —Jenny Eclair, *Camberwell Beauty*, p. 209, 2000

moniker; monicker *noun*
1 a nickname or sobriquet *UK, 1851*
- From this trick he got this moniker. —William Burroughs, *Junkie*, p. 43, 1953
- True monicker was Early Gibson but he was called Early Riser. —Chester Himes, *Cotton Comes to Harlem*, p. 31, 1965
- This is to say that the hustler's nickname is a monicker, not an alias. —Ned Polsky, *Hustlers, Beats, and Others*, p. 115, 1967
- Kid, you've outgrown 'Young Blood' as a monicker. How about 'Iceberg slim?' —Iceberg Slim (Robert Beck), *Pimp*, p. 221, 1969
- JOHNNY: What d'you think, Mon? MONICA: Me moniker's Monica. —Terry Victor, *Family Affair*, 1991
- Bernie the Bolt, who acquired said moniker on account of his prodigious ability to turn Scotch mist (disappear)[.] —Andrew Nickolds, *Back to Basics*, p. 130, 1994
- They called her "Anne of a Thousand Names." That's the moniker her fellow detectives hung on her because during her police-department career she'd been Anne Zorn, Anne Barlett, Anne Sullivan, Anne Minskey, and now Anne Zorn again. —Joseph Wambaugh, *Floaters*, p. 133, 1996
- And now Marco Pierre White has stuck his moniker on the outside. — *The Guardian*, 13th April 2002

2 a signature *UK, 1851*
Extended from the sense as 'a person's name'.

3 the mark that identifies dice as being from a given casino or gambling house *US*
- — *The Annals of the American Academy of Political and Social Sciences*, p. 128, May 1950

moniker file *noun*
a list of street names or aliases maintained by the police *US*
- The field interrogation cards and moniker file had already been checked by Al Mackey and Martin Welborn for the nickname Mr. Wheels. —Joseph Wambaugh, *The Glitter Dome*, p. 123, 1981
- [T]he "monicker" files on "Bird" and "Birdy" had yielded only the names of a dozen ghetto blacks. —James Ellroy, *Blood on the Moon*, p. 192, 1984
- So what do you want to do? Go down, check the moniker file? —Richard Price, *Clockers*, p. 39, 1992

monk *noun*
a monkey *US, 1841*
- Horses are "prads", lions and tigers "cats", monkeys are "monks" and dogs "buffers". —Butch Reynolds, *Broken Hearted Clown*, p. 32, 1953

▸ **have a monk on**
to be angry *UK*
- The ruperts [officers] had an instant monk on because there were these naked squaddies lying on the grass in star shapes[.] —Andy McNab (writing of the late 1970s/early 80s), *Immediate Action*, p. 215, 1995

▸ **out the monk**
completely drunk *NEW ZEALAND*
- He's out the monk. Really out the Joe. He's made a fair dinkum job of himself today. —Ronald Hugh Morrieson, *Come a Hot Friday*, p. 122, 1964

monkey *noun*
1 an addiction, especially to heroin or another drug *US, 1949*
- [I]f one "has a monkey on his back," meaning the urge is desperate and irresistible, he will be soaked from $50 to $100 a week. —Jack Lait and Lee Mortimer, *Washington Confidential*, p. 114, 1951
- "Old monkey climbing up on your back?" asked the man with the pipe, —William Burroughs, *Junkie*, p. 86, 1953
- Aside from the monkey, I got room rent and meals and all that stuff to take care of. —Clarence Cooper Jr, *The Scene*, p. 67, 1960
- A week in this joint, and another in that, until he burns more bridges behind him, until the monkey on his back grows into a full-sized gorilla? —Ross Russell, *The Sound*, p. 214, 1961
- The only way anyone can help me is that they give me some money to get some shit and get that monkey off my back. —Claude Brown, *Manchild in the Promised Land*, p. 195, 1965
- I wish you all the luck in the world, 'cause, mama, that monkey could very well turn out to be an APE! —A.S. Jackson, *Gentleman Pimp*, p. 73, 1973
- I felt my monkey sandpapering my guts as I went to my pad. —Iceberg Slim (Robert Beck), *Airtight Willie and Me*, p. 55, 1979
- Good luck, my brother, the monkey is a monster. — *New Jack City*, 1990
- Hitched a ride on a monkey's back / Headed west into the black. — Dada, *Dizz Knee Land*, 1992

2 five hundred pounds sterling; five hundred US dollars; five hundred Australian dollars *UK, 1832*
- My share was a monkey[.] —Charles Raven, *Underworld Nights*, p. 22, 1956
- In a month or two I done the monkey, in fact I was skint —Frank Norman, *Bang To Rights*, p. 112, 1958
- You're due a monkey on the purse. Why don't you double it? —Anthony Masters, *Minder*, p. 41, 1984
- He still owes us a monkey from the last run. —Chris Baker and Andrew Day, *Lock, Stock... & One Big Bullock*, p. 333, 2000
- [S]igning a century (?100) or even a monkey (?500) away[.] —Duncan MacLaughlin, *The Filth*, p. 117, 2002

3 fifty pounds sterling *UK, 1950*
A prison variation; the reduction in value from the outside world's 500-unit is an economic reality.
- I bet a Monkey you still don't know what I'm talking about, do you? —Ronnie Barker, *Fletcher's Book of Rhyming Slang*, p. 48, 1979

4 500 shares at £100 each, £50,000 (fifty thousand pounds worth of stock) *UK, C20*

5 a naughty rascal; generally said of someone younger *UK, 1604*
- Got to find the monkey first, then he's out on his ear. —Nicholas Blincoe, *The Beautiful Beaten-up Irish Boy of the Arndale Centre*, p. 2, 1998

6 in circus and carnival usage, a gullible customer who has been swindled *US, 1922*
- —Don Wilmeth, *The Language of American Popular Entertainment*, p. 175, 1981

7 a carnival worker who climbs to assemble rides *US*
- — *American Speech*, p. 281, December 1966: 'More carnie talk from the West Coast'

8 a press photographer *UK*
Journalists' slang, allegedly from the ungainly gait a press photographer adopts to manage all his equipment; a less disingenuous possibility derives the term from the organ grinder and his monkey.
- — *Word of Mouth*, 6th August 2004

9 a gambler who complains to the police about an illegal gambling operation after losing *US*
- — *The Annals of the American Academy of Political and Social Sciences*, p. 128, May 1950

10 a band leader *US, 1942*
A reference to the tuxedo, or **MONKEY SUIT**, worn by many band leaders.
- —Robert S. Gold, *A Jazz Lexicon*, p. 207, 1964

11 a poor poker player *US*
- —George Percy, *The Language of Poker*, p. 58, 1988

12 in motorcyle racing, the passenger in a sidecar who works in tandem with the driver *US*
- —Ed Radlauer, *Motorcylopedia*, p. 42, 1973

13 your boyfriend's or girlfriend's 'other' person *US*
- —Pamela Munro, *U.C.L.A. Slang*, p. 59, 1989

14 a white person *US*
- Tie your girl to the back / Of my Jeep butt naked / Slide her monkey ass down the hill[.] —Pete Rock, *For Pete's Sake*, 1992

15 the vagina *US, 1888*
- —Charles Shafer, *Folk Speech in Texas Prisons*, p. 210, 1990
- —Judi Sanders, *Da Bomb*, p. 11, 1997

16 the penis *US, 1989*
As in phrases **SPANK THE MONKEY** (to masturbate) and **MARINATE THE MONKEY** (to perform oral sex).

17 a two-wheeled trailer designed to carry extra long loads *UK*
- — *British Road Services Magazine*, December 1951

18 in horse racing, a $100 bet *US*
- —David W. Maurer, *Argot of the Racetrack*, p. 43, 1951

19 nonsense *US*
- —Jim Crotty, *How to Talk American*, p. 327, 1997

20 in card games, a face card *US*
- —Steve Kuriscak, *Casino Talk*, p. 38, 1985

▷ **see: MONKEY ON YOUR BACK**

▸ **marinate the monkey**
to perform oral sex *US*
• Another way to say "fellatio" [...] Marinating the monkey[.]—Erica Orloff and JoAnn Baker, *Dirty Little Secrets*, p. 83, 2001

▸ **monkey has a nosebleed**
experiencing the bleed period of the menstrual cycle *US*
From **MONKEY** (the vagina).
• When I was young, menstruation was referred to by my male friends as "The monkey has a nose bleed." — a correspondent, *The Museum of Menstruation and Women's Health*, May 2001

▸ **put it where the monkey put the nuts!; shove them where the monkey shoved his nuts!; stick it where the monkey stuck his nuts!**
used as an angry expression of dismissal or refusal *UK, 1879*
Anatomically: 'in the anus'; figuratively: **UP YOUR ASS/ARSE!**.
• [I]n the kind of proud and angry way in which one might say, "Put it where the monkey put the nuts!" Cash was then too important to him.—J R Ackerley, *My Father and Myself*, p. 49, 1968
• You can take Helford Hall and you can take your precious marriage and you can shove them where the monkey shoved his nuts.—Virginia Henley, *The Pirate and the Pagan*, p. 287, 1990
• [T]ell 'em it's "Please Please Me" or else they can stick their deal where the monkey stuck his nuts.—Larry Kirwan, *Liverpool Fantasy*, p. xvii, 2003

monkey *verb*
to fiddle, to tamper, to fool around with *US, 1876*
• You haven't monkeyed with his car there, have ya?—*Fargo*, 1996

monkey around; monkey about *verb*
to behave foolishly, to waste time *US, 1884*
• I'm sure they won't appreciate it if we start monkeying around with the merchandise.—Charles Harrington Elster and Joseph Elliot, *Tooth and Nail*, p. 233, 1994

monkey bath *noun*
a very hot bath *NEW ZEALAND, 2002*
So hot that when lowering yourself into the water an involuntary (monkey-like?) cry of 'Ooh! Ooh! Aah! Aah!' is emitted.

monkey bite *noun*
1 a bruise on the skin produced by extended sucking *US, 1942*
• —Eugene Landy, *The Underground Dictionary*, p. 103, 1971
• Rule number two: no monkey bites, no hickeys – in fact no leavin' no marks of no kind.—*Kill Bill*, 2003

2 a painful pinch *US*
• The monkey bite – the most painful pinch in the history of the time.—Editors of Ben is Dead, *Retrohell*, p. 91, 1997

monkey boots *noun*
a heavy work shoe embraced as a fashion statement by punks and post-punks *US*
• Other acceptable alterna-shoes you could own were: monkey boots[.]—Editors of Ben is Dead, *Retrohell*, p. 60, 1997

monkey box *noun*
the vagina *US*
Either a combination of **MONKEY** (the vagina) and **BOX** (the vagina) or **MONKEY** (the penis) and **BOX** (the vagina).
• There's [a...] "toadie," "dee dee," "nishi," "dignity," "monkey box[".]—Eve Ensler, *The Vagina Monologues*, p. 6, 1998

monkey business *noun*
mischief; foolishness *US, 1883*
The term is powerfully etched in American culture because of revelations in 1987 that Gary Hart, then a married US Senator campaigning for the presidential nomination, had taken an overnight cruise to Bimini with a stunningly attractive woman, Donna Rice, on the aptly named yacht 'Monkey Business'. Hart withdrew from the race under attack as an adulterer.
• And I guarantee I know how to take care of any you guys who feel like a little monkey business[.]—Evan Hunter, *The Blackboard Jungle*, p. 34, 1954
• Any monkey business is ill-advised.—*The Breakfast Club*, 1985

monkey cage; monkey house; monkey hut; monkey wagon *noun*
a brakevan (caboose) *US*
• —Ramon Adams, *The Language of the Railroader*, p. 101, 1977

monkey dick *noun*
a link sausage *US, 1965*
• —*Maledicta*, p. 284, 1984–1985: 'Food names'

monkey drill; monkey pump *noun*
a hypodermic needle and syringe *US*
• —Richard A. Spears, *The Slang and Jargon of Drugs and Drink*, p. 343–344, 1986

monkey dust *noun*
phencyclidine, the recreational drug known as PCP or angel dust *US*
• —Ronald Linder, *PCP*, p. 9, 1981
• —US Department of Justice, *Street Terms*, October 1994

monkey flush *noun*
in poker, three cards of the same suit, unpaired and without value *US*
• —Irwin Steig, *Common Sense in Poker*, p. 185, 1963

monkey-full *adjective*
drunk *UK*
• —*e-cyclopaedia*, 20th March 2002

monkey house *noun*
a brothel *US*
• —Vincent J. Monteleone, *Criminal Slang*, p. 157, 1949

monkey maze *noun*
a confusing, complicated traffic interchange *US*
• —*American Speech*, p. 271, December 1962: 'The language of traffic policemen'

monkey meat *noun*
in Nova Scotia, the small white edible pods or nuts at the base of the fiddlehead fern *CANADA*
• In Upper Port Latour, NS, chiildren dig up and eat the white pods among the roots of the fiddlehead fern and call it "monkey meat." —Lewis Poteet, *The South Shore Phrase Book*, p. 76, 1999

monkey money *noun*
1 an excessive price to pay; silly money *UK*
Acquired an earlier US usage, now obsolete, as 'foreign money'.
• I told him I was not going to pay monkey money for a ticket[.]—Martin King and Martin Knight, *The Naughty Nineties*, p. 159, 1999

2 the salary paid to film extras in US films shot in Canada *CANADA*
• —Martin Stone, 24th June 2002

3 on the railways, a pass to ride for free *US*
• —Ramon Adams, *The Language of the Railroader*, p. 112, 1977

monkey motion *noun*
in hot rodding and drag racing, unwanted movement in any mechanical device *US*
• A carburettor linkage or a gear shift lever are both apt to develop monkey motion.—John Lawlor, *How to Talk Car*, p. 75, 1965

monkey-on-a-stick *adjective*
a style of horse racing using short stirrups *US*
Popularised by jockey Ted Sloan (1874–1933), whose abnormally short legs made the style – widely used today – a necessary innovation. Also applied in the UK to the riding position adopted on early motorcycles.
• It was not all the "monkey-on-a-stick" type of riding that made the American jockey, Ted Sloan, so successful in England.—*San Francisco Examiner*, p. 17, 28th June 1949
• —Tom Ainslie, *Ainslie's Complete Guide to Thoroughbred Racing*, p. 334, 1976

monkey on your back; monkey *noun*
1 an addiction to drugs, especially heroin *US, 1959*
A tenacious monkey is hard to shake off.
• [A] certain down-at-heel vet growing stooped from carrying a thirty-five-pound monkey on his back.—Nelson Algren, *The Man With The Golden Arm [The Howard Marks Book of Dope Stories]*, p. 43, 1949
• And gave him all the confidence he lacked / With a Purple Heart and a monkey on his back[.]—John Prine, *Sam Stone*, 1971
• Sub us a ten-spot then, mun. A know a fuckin monkey oo needs feedin.—Niall Griffiths, *Grits*, p. 30, 2000

2 in sports, the inability to beat a certain opponent *US*
Used in many sports, but probably most commonly in tennis.
• —Peter Schwed, *How to Talk Tennis*, p. 51, 1988

monkey pants *noun*
a difficult situation *TRINIDAD AND TOBAGO, 1950*
• —Lise Winer, *Dictionary of the English/Creole of Trinidad & Tobago*, 2003

monkey-parade *noun*
an informal but regular event, in some public place, in which (generally) young people, intent on meeting and flirting with the opposite sex, stroll in couples and groups of friends to advertise themselves to others similarly engaged *UK, 1914*
Recorded in London around the beginning of C20. Written of soldiers and girls in Salisbury in the mid-1930s by Spike Mays, *No More Soldiering for Me*, 1971. Remembered in 2004, nostalgically and without prompting, by Mrs Elizabeth Gardiner, of the early and mid-1960s industrial south Wales.

monkey pump *noun*
▷ see: MONKEY DRILL

monkey rum *noun*
illegally manufactured alcohol coloured by molasses *US*
- Moonshine with molasses is monkey rum. — *Chicago Tribune*, p. C3, 21st August 1985

monkey's; monkey's fuck *noun*
a notional article of no value *UK, 1960*
Used in the phrase '(not) give a monkey's fuck', an elaboration of (not) **GIVE A FUCK**; generally reduced to '(not) give a monkey's'.
- I don't give a monkey's who he's gone to see. — Clive Exton, *No Fixed Abode [Six Granada Plays]*, p. 136, 1959
- Roy don't give a fuckin' monkey's. — J.J. Connolly, *Know Your Enemy [britpulp]*, p. 139, 1999
- It was as illegal as they got. But we didn't give a fucking monkey's. — Dave Courtney, *Stop the Ride I Want to Get Off*, p. 146, 1999
- I couldn't give a monkey's whether you've got one baby or ten babies. — Mary Hooper, *(megan)2*, p. 162, 1999
- If it was me, and I had been in Melvins shoes, I'd have handed it over and not given a monkey's. — Danny King, *The Bank Robber Diaries*, p. 14, 2002
- Anyway it's irrelevant. I don't give a monkey's what you do[.] — Colin Butts, *Is Harry Still on the Boat?*, p. 40, 2003

monkey see monkey do!
a catchphrase warning against imitating an action, or of doing something that may be imitated; used teasingly of someone who copies an action; applied to an action that is performed by imitation but without understanding *US, 1977*
- [S]o let em' come to you / the rest of us follow suit / monkey see monkey do / tweedle-de-tweedle-dum[.] — Eminem (Marshall Mathers), *Monkey See, Monkey Do*, 2003

monkey's fist *noun*
a knot tied on the end of a heaving line *US*
- The knot gives some heft for tossing, and a good monkey's fist will have a stone or a piece of metal in it. — John Gould, *Maine Lingo*, p. 183, 1975

monkeyshines *noun*
foolish antics, embarrassing behaviour *US, 1828*
- — Hermese E. Roberts, *The Third Ear*, 1971
- [Lou Reed] actually managed to lasso a great rock 'n' roll band to back up his monkeyshines? — Lester Bangs, *Psychotic Reactions and Carburetor Dung*, p. 169, 1975

monkey's nuts *noun*
cigarette butts *UK, 2001*
Rhyming slang in current use by prison inmates; a possible play on **DOG END** (a cigarette butt) via **DOG'S BOLLOCKS** (the best).

monkeyspunk *noun*
nonsense *UK*
- "Complete monkeyspunk." Liam Gallagher shoots down rumour that Oasis are splitting. — *Q*, p. 22, October 2004

monkey's tail *noun*
a nail (for hammering) *UK, 1934*
Rhyming slang.
- — Ray Puxley, *Cockney Rabbit*, 1992

monkey strap *noun*
a lifeline that secures a helicopter gunner to the helicopter *AUSTRALIA, 1945*
- — Linda Reinberg, *In the Field*, p. 143, 1991

monkey suit *noun*
1 a formal evening dress suit; a tuxedo *US, 1895*
- They wore monkey suits and on them the term was absolutely descriptive. — Mickey Spillane, *Kiss Me Deadly*, p. 101, 1952
- He also said I wouldn't have to wear the "monkey" suit, just stay sharp and clean. — Babs Gonzales, *I Paid My Dues*, p. 20, 1967
- Look at you in those candy ass monkey suits. — *The Blues Brothers*, 1980
- Me in a monkey suit? Nothing elegant about that. — *The Archers*, 21st July 2002

2 any uniform worn by a railway employee on a passenger train *US, 1901*
- — J. Herbert Lund, *Herb's Hot Box of Railraod Slang*, p. 164, 1975

monkey's uncle *noun*
used in non-profane oaths to register surprise *US, 1926*
- "Jesus Christ in Marboro Country, but if this here is Cherry then I'm an unkey's moncle." He tried to say it straight, and muffed it again[.] — Lawrence Block, *No Score [The Affairs of Chip Harrison Omnibus]*, p. 113, 1970

monkey wagon *noun*
▷ see: MONKEY CAGE

Monkey Ward *nickname*
Montgomery Ward, a department store chain *US, 1912*
A play on the sound.
- He was an open apple knocker from the West Side wearing plain Monkey Ward jeans rather than Levi's and high-top horsehide shit kickers. — Earl Thompson, *Tattoo*, p. 55, 1974
- — Bill Reilly, *Big Al's Official Guide to Chicagoese*, p. 44, 1982
- Your little tyke can't possibly network with the right people at pre-K if he's wearing a poly-cotton blend from Monkey Ward. — *Washington Post*, p. C1, 4th October 1987
- The guy at the Foot Locker said I might find some at Monkey Ward's. — *Rocky Mountain News (Denver, Colorado)*, p. 5A, 9th January 1996
- The execs at Monkey Ward (as it was fondly known in those days) liked the story and printed 2.4 million copies that year. — *Chattanooga (Tennessee) Times Free Press*, p. E6, 11th December 2003

monkey wrench *verb*
to repair (a car or truck engine) *US*
- — *American Speech*, p. 273, December 1961: 'Northwest truck drivers' language'

monk-on *noun*
a gloomy, introspective mood *ANTARCTICA*
- — *Cool Antarctica*, 2003: 'Antarctic slang'

mono *noun*
1 mononeucleosis glandular fever *US, 1964*
- "Where's Oeuf, anyway?" "Recuperating from mono in the infirm. There was some rumor about the clap, too." — Richard Farina, *Been Down So Long*, p. 22, 1966
- The girls promised to bring me hot soup and other goodies to get over my mono. — Oscar Zeta Acosta, *The Autobiography of a Brown Buffalo*, p. 39, 1972

2 a black and white television set; a monophonic sound reproduction system *UK, 1970*
An abbreviation of 'monochrome', 'monaural' or 'monophonic'; a term only needed, outside of its jargon application, until colour television and stereo sound were widely available.

monobrow *noun*
two eyebrows joined by hair growth above the nose *AUSTRALIA*
- The Mono Brow look was first popularized by a less than natty dresser called Neanderthal Man. — Ignatius Jones, *True Hip*, p. 42, 1990

monolithic *adjective*
extremely drug-intoxicated *US*
- — Eugene Landy, *The Underground Dictionary*, p. 134, 1971

mono-rump *noun*
the buttocks formed into a single mass by a garment *US*
- It was tightly encased in a girdle so it was an unyielding mono-rump, with less fleshy warmth than a medicine ball. — Earl Thompson, *Tattoo*, p. 232, 1974

monsoon bucket *noun*
a helicopter-borne water container used for aerial bombardment of forest fires *CANADA*
- The "monsoon bucket" was an early 1960s device using a 45-gallon drum with a basketball bunging a hole in the bottom. Modern versions are more sophisticated, and are known as "helibuckets." — Lewis Poteet, *Plane Talk*, p. 116, 1997

monsta *adjective*
formidable; excellent *US*
A deliberate misspelling of **MONSTER** (excellent).
- The Beastie Boys first album, a mish mash of AC/DC riffing and monsta hip hop beats that sounded almost like metal drums. — John Robb, *The Nineties*, p. 238, 1999

monster *noun*
1 something that is extremely and unusually large *UK, 1759*
- Like me, you may be astonished at its size – it's a monster almost 46ft long. — *Sutton Guardian*, 27th June 1998

2 a formidable piece of equipment *US, 1955*
- Tim Cahalan carried the Monster, a PRC-77. This radio was similar to the 25 except it was also a kryptographer, automatically scrambling or descrambling voice transmissions. — John Del Vecchio, *The 13th Valley*, p. 193, 1982
- Resembling a prehistoric reptile, its two huge General Electric J79 engines bulging its sides, humpbacking its 58-foot fuselage, the "brute," or "monster," as the Phantom was sometimes called, was already the talk of the Navy. — Robert K. Wilcox, *Scream of Eagles*, p. 13, 1990
- It's got four wheel drive, dual side airbags and monster sound system. — *Clueless*, 1995

3 an immense wave, surfed by a special and small class of surfers *US*
- — Mitch McKissick, *Surf Lingo*, 1987
- You ride the monsters, you gotta know you're ridin' a line between life and death. — *Break Point*, 1991

4 a string of multiple Claymore mines arranged to detonate sequentially *US*
- — Linda Reinberg, *In the Field*, p. 143, 1991

5 in poker, a great hand or large amount of money bet *US*
- — David M. Hayano, *Poker Faces*, p. 186, 1982

6 any powerful drug; cocaine *US, 1975*
- — Richard A. Spears, *The Slang and Jargon of Drugs and Drink*, p. 344, 1986
- — Nick Constable, *This is Cocaine*, p. 181, 2002
- — Mike Haskins, *Drugs*, p. 280, 2003

7 used as a term of endearment *US*
Teen slang.
- — *Look*, p. 88, 10th August 1954

8 an extremely unattractive woman who is seen as a sex object, especially one who is ravaged by age *UK*
- I'll admit it. I like Monsters. I don't mind saying so. You know exactly where the fuck you are with a Monster. — Kevin Sampson, *Clubland*, p. 65, 2002

9 a sex offender, a convicted paedophile *UK*
Prison usage.
- — Angela Devlin, *Prison Patter*, p. 23, 1996

monster *verb*

1 to make a verbal attack on someone or something; to put pressure on *AUSTRALIA, 1967*
- The only way anybody's ever going to give me a job is if I monster them into it[.] — Val McDermid, *Keeping on the Right Side of the Law*, p. 183, 1999

2 to harass, threaten or victimise someone *AUSTRALIA, 1967*
- — Jim Ramsay, *Cop It Sweet!*, p. 59, 1977
- [S]tudious doctors and lawyers become pests, monstering their patients with fishing feats, true and false[.] — Bob Staines, *Wot a Whopper*, p. 7, 1982

monster *adjective*

1 large, formidable, impressive *US, 1975*
- The last car I stole was a Ford Granada, a monster car. — Shaun Ryder, *Shaun Ryder... in His Own Words*, 1988
- And use the monster cable so we don't get any drop-out. — *Airheads*, 1994
- I intended to give that girl the monster fuck of her young life[.] — Lanre Fehintola, *Charlie Says...*, p. 33, 2000

2 excellent *US*
Originally black usage.
- — Lavada Durst, *The Jives of Dr. Hepcat*, p. 13, 1953
- [I]'m say that that was the fuckin' best best beast of a monster party[.] — Mike Benson, *Room full of Angels (Disco Biscuits)*, p. 25, 1996

monstered *adjective*
drunk *UK*
- — Pete Brown, *Man Walks into a Pub*, 2003

monstering *noun*

1 a severe telling-off
From **MONSTER** (to attack verbally).
- David Montgomery of Mirror Group Newspapers, said recently to have given a "Hitlerian monstering" to a quivering employee. — David Rowan, *A Glossary for the 90s*, p. 122, 1998

2 a sudden swoop by paparazzi photographers on their subject *UK*
- — *Word of Mouth*, 6th August 2004

monster lane *noun*
in the US, the lane used for overtaking; in the UK, the slow lane *US*
- — *Complete CB Slang Dictionary*, 1976
- — Peter Chippindale, *The British CB Book*, p. 157, 1981

monster munch *noun*
the vagina *UK*
Derives, probably, from Monster Munch™, a branded savoury snack food.
- — *Sky Magazine*, July 2001

monster net *noun*
during the Vietnam war, the secure radio network connecting radios in the field and headquarters *US*
- — Gregory Clark, *Words of the Vietnam War*, p. 459, 1990

monster shot *noun*
in pornography, a close-up shot of genitals *US*
- Ugly people in harsh, flat lighting, dominated by the same rear master-shot, "or "monster-shot" as Sid kept shouting[.] — Terry Southern, *Blue Movie*, p. 18, 1970
- And he [Randy] is rock hard. So we go monster shots, the graphic close-up. — Robert Stoller and I.S. Levine, *Coming Attractions*, p. 86, 1991
- — *Adult Video News*, p. 38, September 1995

monster truck *noun*
a pickup truck with oversized wheels and tyres (large enough to drive over and crush a standard passenger car) and an enhanced engine and transmission *US*
Only in America.
- Galante warned four-wheelers who are considering building a monster truck to "be advised about your state laws regarding heights before you spend your money." — *United Press International*, 30th April 1984
- — John Edwards, *Auto Dictionary*, p. 109, 1993
- There were two basic schools of monster trucks. — Editors of Ben is Dead, *Retrohell*, p. 132, 1997

mont *adjective*
▷ see: **MINTOX**

Montana maiden *noun*
a ewe *US, 1970s*
Sheep will be sheep and men will be men. Collected from a former resident of Iowa, March 2001.

monte *noun*

1 a potent marijuana from Mexico; marijuana from South America; marijuana *US, 1980*
From the Spanish for 'bush' – **BUSH** (marijuana) – or clipping of **MONTEZUMA GOLD**.
- — Richard A. Spears, *The Slang and Jargon of Drugs and Drink*, p. 344, 1986
- — Mike Haskins, *Drugs*, p. 288, 2003

2 the three card trick, also known as three card monte *UK*
- — David Powis, *The Signs of Crime*, 1977

▷ see: **FULL MONTY**

Monte *nickname*
Monte Carlo *UK*
- TONY: [...] Have you ever been abroad? Rose shakes her head. TONY: Pity. You'd love Monte. ROSE: Monte? TONY: Monte Carlo. — Alexander Baron, *A Bit of Happiness [Six Granada Plays]*, p. 200, 1959

Monte Cairo *noun*
a social security/benefits cheque *UK*
Rhyming slang for **GIRO**.
- [B]ack at the dole shop before closing time to report Monte Cairo missing. — J.J. Connolly, *Layer Cake*, p. 105, 2000

Montezuma gold *noun*
potent marijuana cultivated in Mexico *US, 1978*
From Montezuma II (1466–1520), the ninth Aztec emperor of Mexico.

montezumas *noun*
bloomers (capacious underpants for women) *UK*
Rhyming slang.
- — Ray Puxley, *Cockney Rabbit*, 1992

Montezuma's revenge *noun*
diarrhoea suffered by tourists in Mexico *US*
Montezuma II (1466–1520), the ninth Aztec emperor of Mexico, famously died as a result of his confrontation with Spanish invaders. Former US President Ronald Reagan in 1981 exhibited what commentator David Brinkley referred to as 'excruciatingly bad taste' by telling a joke about Montezuma's revenge at a state dinner in Mexico City.

- The disorder occurs often in Mexico and has been nicknamed Montzuma's revenge, turista, and "the trots." — *Washington Post, Times Herald*, p. L6, 10th April 1960
- [T]hey admit that, like most AMericans, they suffered a three-day gastric upset described by a variety of names like the Gringo Gallop and Montezuma's revenge. — *Washington Post, Times Herald*, p. AW8, 24th January 1960
- And I'm afraid the wife is bringing back Montezuma's revenge. — Gerald Petievich, *The Quality of the Informant*, p. 167, 1985
- Like a thief, traveler's diarrhea has many aliases. It is euphemistically known as "Turista," Montezuma's Revenge," The Aztec Two Step," "Turkey Trots," and scores more. — *The Patriot Ledger (Quincy, Massachusetts)*, p. 16, 3rd June 1997
- Children face bigger threat from Montezuma's revenge [headline] — *San Francisco Chronicle*, p. C8, 18th August 2002

month in Congress *noun*

a period served in solitary confinement *US*

- — Troy Harris, *A Booklet of Criminal Argot, Cant and Jargon*, p. 19, 1976

monthlies *noun*

the bleed period of the menstrual cycle *UK*

- My mother's voice would drop as she whispered, 'She's got her monthlies' (knowing look). In Australia in the 1980s 'Women's Weekly' magazine changed to being published monthly. This caused no end of jokes that the name could hardly be changed to the "Women's Monthly". — a correspondent, *The Museum of Menstruation and Women's Health*, May 2001

monthly bill *noun*

the bleed period of the menstrual cycle *US*

- — Pamela Munro, *U.C.L.A. Slang*, p. 60, 1989

monthly blues *noun*

the bleed period of the menstrual cycle *US*

- — *American Speech*, p. 298, December 1954: 'The vernacular of menstruation'

monthly evacuations *noun*

the bleed period of the menstrual cycle *US*

- — Karen Houppert, *The Curse*, 1999

monthly flowers *noun*

▷ see: FLOWERS

monthly monster *noun*

the bleed period of the menstrual cycle *US*

- — *The Museum of Menstruation and Women's Health*, October 2000

monthly return *noun*

the bleed period of the menstrual cycle *US*

- — Karen Houppert, *The Curse*, 1999

monthly turns *noun*

the bleed period of the menstrual cycle *US*

- — Karen Houppert, *The Curse*, 1999

monthly visitor *noun*

the bleed period of the menstrual cycle *US*

- — Don R. McCreary (Editor), *Dawg Speak*, 2001

month of Sundays *noun*

a long time, with time passing slowly *US*

- It's only just that minute I think maybe that Marry Ellen is more to me in one night than any other woman's ever been to me in a month of Sundays. — Robert Campbell, *Junkyard Dog*, p. 56, 1986

montrel *noun*

a watch *UK*

From obsolete 'montra' (a watch).

- — Paul Baker, *Polari*, p. 181, 2002

monty *noun*

1 everything required within a given context *UK*

An abbreviation of the FULL MONTY.

- His simp [foolish] thinking had left him with two fingers short of the monty, after he'd sold some nastiness [inferior drugs] instead of the Holyfield[.] — Diran Adebayo, *My Once Upon A Time*, p. 20, 2000

2 a certainty *AUSTRALIA, 1894*

- I was given the drum by the chief gunnery instructor that if I put my name to the dotted line, I'd be a monty to get drafted to the U.S. destroyer. — John Wynnum, *Jiggin' in the Riggin'*, p. 128, 1965
- — Jim Ramsay, *Cop It Sweet!*, p. 59, 1977
- — Ivor Limb, *Footy's No Joke!*, p. 10, 1986

moo *noun*

1 an unpleasant or contemptible woman *UK, 1967*

A variation of **cow**. With the descriptor 'silly' the sense is often softened (foolish woman), or even made affectionate. Widely associated with mid-1960s BBC television bigot, the comic creation Alf Garnett, played by Warren Mitchell.

- Shut up Ffion, you silly moo! Yer crime is going up because yer police numbers is falling under Labour. — *The Guardian*, 16th December 2000

2 a silly person *AUSTRALIA*

- 'Silly, old moo,' says Sister George. — Suzy Jarratt, *Permissive Australia*, p. 53, 1970

3 money *US, 1941*

- — Clarence Major, *Dictionary of Afro-American Slang*, p. 82, 1970

mooch *noun*

1 a person who gives his money to swindlers, a dupe *US, 1927*

- If you get the right rhythm you can work it out even if the mooch is awake. — William Burroughs, *Junkie*, p. 45, 1953
- — Frank Garcia, *Marked Cards and Loaded Dice*, p. 263, 1962
- — Gene Sorrows, *All About Carnivals*, p. 23, 1985: 'Terminology'
- Anyone who succumbs to a sales pitch – due to the hot stuff or a phone call – becomes, in the yaks' slang, a mooch. — Kathleen Odean, *High Steppers, Fallen Angels, and Lollipops*, p. 132, 1988
- Hey, sweetheart, let me handle my end of it. How I get this mooch to cooperate is my business. — Stephen Cannell, *King Con*, p. 140, 1997

2 in the car sales business, a customer who thinks that with arithmetic skills, a calculator and his sharp mind he can outsmart the salesman *US*

- — *American Speech*, p. 312, Autumn-Winter 1975: 'The jargon of car salesmen'
- — Kathleen Odean, *High Steppers, Fallen Angels, and Lollipops: Wall Street Slang*, p. 133, 1988

▸ **on the mooch**

alert for any chance to beg or borrow *UK, 1864*

- An exiled South American gigolo living on the mooch from night club to night club was invariably "the Argentinian cattle baron." — Robert Sylvester, *No Cover Charge*, p. 130, 1956

▸ **the mooch**

idling, scrounging, skulking *UK, 1859*

- [Y]ou went on the mooch with Paddy Clohessy. Your mother is going to kill you[.] — Frank McCourt, *Angela's Ashes*, p. 163, 1999

mooch *verb*

1 to wander without purpose; to loiter *UK, 1851*

- Mooching about Brixton began to get horribly tedious[.] — John Peter Jones, *Feather Pluckers*, p. 19, 1964
- I'm going for a mooch about, see if I can find anyone out there. — Lanre Fehintola, *Charlie Says...*, p. 10, 2000
- We parks up by the Red Triangle and mooch up over to the estate[.] — Kevin Sampson, *Outlaws*, p. 76, 2001
- [H]alf a dozen post-teenage boys in woolly balaclavas mooching around in what looked like a crack house. — *The Guardian*, 2nd May 2001

2 to beg from friends, to sponge *UK, 1857*

- "You still mooching around here?" Dopey said sarcastically. — James T. Farrell, *Saturday Night*, p. 27, 1947
- Russell and I had already sold all our albums for cash, and after I ran out of pocket money I went on an orching of mooching. — Jennifer Blowdryer, *White Trash Debutante*, p. 34, 1997

moocher *noun*

a beggar; one who sponges off others, a freeloader *US, 1851*

- They never had any gum money themselves and were both great moochers. — Larry McMurtry, *The Last Picture Show*, p. 18, 1966
- I feel like a moocher. I don't have a dime. — Darryl Ponicsan, *The Last Detail*, p. 104, 1970
- There's more moochers on one corner in downtown San Diego than in this whole town, I bet. — Joseph Wambaugh, *Finnegan's Week*, p. 55, 1993
- He was a moocher, a card cheat, a country-club golf hustler. — *Casino*, 1995
- They are moochers. "Hey, man, got any bread?" — Rhiannon Paine, *Too Late for the Festival*, p. 207, 1999

mooching *noun*

in British Columbia, very simple, inexpensive fishing *CANADA*

- Mooching just consists of dropping a line over the side of a boat with a weight attached to take it to the required depth, and a herring strip attached to a hook for bait. — *Duncan Cowichan Leader*, p. 7/1, 28th April 1960

moo-cow *noun*

a cow *UK, 1812*

Childish.

- Richard Littlejohn [a columnist on The Sun] tells it like it is: "Aaahh, Tonee [Blair]'s saved the ickle moo-cow. Luvlee. Tonee reely cares, he does." — *The Guardian*, 27th April 2001

mood *noun*

▸ **in the mood**

desiring sex *UK, 1984*

A euphemistic colloquialism.

- — Judith Reichman, *I'm Not in the Mood*, 1999

moodies *noun*

faked tablets of MDMA, the recreational drug best known as ecstasy *UK*

By ellipsis from **MOODY** (fake) and **E** (ecstasy tablets).

- —Angela Devlin, *Prison Patter*, p. 77, 1996

moody; old moody *noun*

1 a fit of sulking *UK*

May be preceded by either 'the' or 'a', often in forms such as: 'pull a/the moody' and 'throw a/the moody'.

- CHARLIE [Michael Caine]: Now don't come that old moody. You know how the game is played.— *The Italian Job [uncut script]*, 1969

2 lies, deceit, especially deceit by flattery, a confidence trick (see, especially, the 1977 citation) *UK, 1934*

- [H]is real speciality is the old international moody.—Derek Raymond (Robin Cook), *The Crust on its Uppers*, p. 23, 1962
- Lies, a deceit, and in another sense, something that goes wrong. "What he said was just a load of old moody" means it was deceitful and false, and "It went moody on us" means that the expected successful result did not materialise.—David Powis, *The Signs of Crime*, 1977
- Geezers with ID cards giving you a lot of old moody about being unemployed[.]—Andrew Nickolds, *Back to Basics*, p. 37, 1994

3 a period of (extreme) moodiness *UK*

- —Jenny Fabian and Johnny Byrne, *Groupie*, 1968

4 in prison, a psychiatrist's man-to-man, or even genial, approach to a prisoner *UK, 1945*

Usually with 'the'.

▸ do a moody

to behave suspiciously *UK*

Prison use.

- [D]oing a moody. "Doing something suspicious."—Home Office, *Glossary of Terms and Slang Common in Penal Establishments*, 1978
- —Sean McConville, *The State of the Language*, 1980

moody *verb*

1 to sulk or be bad-tempered *UK*

- I get so effing cross I could go moodying on for hours[.]—Derek Raymond (Robin Cook), *The Crust on its Uppers*, p. 22, 1962

2 to put into good humour by means of ingratiating talk, to wheedle, flatter or humour *UK, 1934*

- —Patrick O'Shaughnessy, *Market Traders' Slang*, 1979

moody *adjective*

simulated, faked *UK, 1958*

- So one day they had a moody ruck and made out that they had a punch up[.]—Frank Norman, *Bang To Rights*, p. 60, 1958
- "I don't have to tell you," Kenyon went on, "how easy it is to plant moody information about a copper"—N.J. Crisp, *The London Deal*, 1978
- What we market-traders call "a moody ruck" ... an argument two stall-holders pretend to start to get attention, to draw a crowd[.]— *New Society*, 23rd April 1981
- It was floor to ceiling with contraband. Boxed of dodgy perfume (Chanel No 4 was one of the clever ones), TVs, videos, bootleg tapes, five thousand pairs of moody Levi's, Barratt house furnishings, stuff like that.—Dave Courtney, *Raving Lunacy*, p. 21, 2000

Moody and Sankey; moody *noun*

deception, trickery *UK*

Rhyming slang for **HANKY PANKY**, formed on US evangelists Dwight Lyman Moody and Ira D. Sankey, jointly known (and vilified) as Moody and Sankey, who brought their message to the UK in the mid-1870s. This term may well have evolved separately or be bound up with **MOODY; OLD MOODY** (lies, deception).

- —Julian Franklyn, *A Dictionary of Rhyming Slang*, 1961

mooey; moey; mooe *noun*

the mouth *UK, 1859*

From Romany *mooi* (mouth, face).

- He looks up at me, Piggy from Lord of the Flies-style, so I volley him clean in the mooey.— Martin King and Martin Knight, *The Naughty Nineties*, p. 133, 1999
- [T]hey'd throw you some digs and sometimes kick you in the mooey when you were down.—Jimmy Stockin, *On The Cobbles*, p. 118, 2000

mooi *adjective*

pretty, pleasant, fine, nice *SOUTH AFRICA, 1850*

From Afrikaans *mooi* (pretty).

- [H]ow charming the mooi meisies [misses] must have looked on Sundays.—Alan Ryan, *The Reader's Companion to South Africa*, 1999

moo juice *noun*

milk *US, 1942*

- They kept saying they were going to leave the milkman a note telling him to nix our the moo-juice, but they never did find a pencil and paper at the same time[.]—Mezz Mezzrow, *Really the Blues*, p. 122, 1946
- It is ridiculous to hear a child referring to milk as 'moo juice'[.]—*New Idea*, p. 87, 7th October 1989

mook *noun*

an incompetent person who is to be more pitied than despised *US, 1930*

- MARY: He's kind of a mook. MAGDEA: What's a mook. MARY: You know, a mookalone, a schlep.—*Something About Mary*, 1998
- "Mook" is a male, "Crude, loud, obnoxious and in-your-face."—*San Francisco Chronicle*, 27th February 2001
- —Lise Winer, *Dictionary of the English/Creole of Trinidad & Tobago*, 2003

mooksey *adjective*

dim-witted, stupid-looking *TRINIDAD AND TOBAGO, 1993*

- —Lise Winer, *Dictionary of the English/Creole of Trinidad & Tobago*, 2003

moola; moolah; mullah *noun*

money *US, 1939*

- But I'm low in the dough. No moolah, and that's bad.—Hal Ellson, *Duke*, p. 3, 1949
- This seemed odd to many who had trouble figuring why a girl with so much moolah couldn't afford rouge, which she never used.—Lee Mortimer, *Women Confidential*, p. 81, 1960
- Barton, of course, was strapped for moolah at the time and could not share the expense.—Ed Sanders, *Tales of Beatnik Glory*, p. 95, 1975
- Mickey Cohen is Skidsville, U.S.A., and he needs moolah, gelt, the old cashola.—James Ellroy, *White Jazz*, p. 7, 1992
- Now you tell us who paid you the mullah[.]—Jeremy Cameron, *Brown Bread in Wengen*, p. 145, 1999

moo-moo maker *noun*

in Nova Scotia, a livestock caller *CANADA*

- And later last night another offer was made–this time for a "moo-moo maker"–official title of a cattle caller.—*Halifax Chronicle-Herald*, p. 1/8, 10th August 1962

moon *noun*

1 used as a quaint, indefinite measure of time *US*

- I've known the sorry-assed shyster for many a moon.—Gerald Petievich, *Shakedown*, p. 77, 1988

2 a month's imprisonment *UK, 1830*

- [T]he Judge, whose breakfast had agreed with him for a change, gave them only eighteen moon apiece.—Charles Raven, *Underworld Nights*, p. 196, 1956
- I've got eighteen moon to do yet[.]—Frank Norman, *Bang To Rights*, p. 58, 1958
- —Angela Devlin, *Prison Patter*, p. 77, 1996

3 a smooth, convex wheel cover *US*

- —Edith A. Folb, *runnin' down some lines*, p. 247, 1980

4 a flat, circular piece of hashish *US*

5 illegally manufactured alcoholic drink *US, 1928*

An abbreviation of **MOONSHINE**.

- Fellow out in the western part of the state was using it to transport moon.—George V. Higgins, *The Friends of Eddie Doyle*, p. 11, 1971
- Of course it wasn't aged much, and when I swallowed the raw moon, it made my eyes blink and reamed my throat out like Red Devil Lye. —Guy Owen, *The Flim-Flam Man and the Apprentice Grifter*, p. 41, 1972

▸ over the moon

extremely pleased, delighted *UK*

- Wally's over the moon about it[.]—Ted Lewis, *Jack Carter's Law [britpulp]*, p. 49, 1974
- Wait till Arthur hears about this – he'll be over the moon.—Anthony Masters, *Minder*, p. 5, 1984
- Greg was always over the moon when he discovered a girl who liked GHB.—Colin Butts, *Is Harry Still on the Boat?*, p. 163, 2003

▸ the moon

the bleed period of the menstrual cycle *US*

Euphemism.

- —Karen Houppert, *The Curse*, 1999

moon *verb*

1 to flash your exposed buttocks at someone *US, 1963*

From the venerable sense as 'the buttocks'.

- —Collin Baker et al., *College Undergraduate Slang Study Conducted at Brown University*, p. 158, 1968
- — *Current Slang*, p. 4, Spring 1968

- Just two weeks ago a whore had dropped her pants and mooned a customer – he wanted to know if she had pimples on her ass – and caused a three-car collision. — Robert Campbell, *Alice in La-La Land*, p. 259, 1987

2 to experience the bleed period of the menstrual cycle *US*
Emphasises the monthly rhythm of the menstrual cycle.
- — *The Museum of Menstruation and Women's Health*, December 2000

3 to idle, especially to move listlessly *UK, 1848*
Generally combined with 'about', 'along', or 'around'.

4 in a split-pot game of poker, to declare or win both high and low *US*
An abbreviation of 'shoot the moon'.
- — George Percy, *The Language of Poker*, p. 58, 1988

moonbeam *noun*
a flashlight *US*
- — Linda Reinberg, *In the Field*, p. 144, 1991

mooneas *noun*
in the Canadian West, a newcomer, a greenhorn *CANADA*
The word comes from Cree, where it originally meant 'a white man'.
- I was the assistant surveyor and the moneas (tenderfoot) of the outfit. — *Royal Military College Review (Yearbook)*, p. 134/2, 1966

moonie *noun*
1 a deliberately provocative display of a person's naked buttocks *UK*
From the verb **MOON**.
- [S]ome irreverents on the Hill made slack-arsed moonies. — Diran Abedayo, *My Once Upon A Time*, p. 222, 2000

2 any blind, unthinking, unquestioning follower of a philosophy or person *US*
An extension of the early 1970s labelling of followers of the Reverend Sun Myung Moon.
- I hope you're not buying into this banza-bullshit like the rest of Bodhi's moonies. — *Point Break*, 1991

▸ **pull a moonie**
to deliberately display naked buttocks *UK*
From **MOONIE** (a provocative display of naked buttocks); logically you would 'make a moonie', however, among older children and young teenagers in South Wales in 2003, 'pull a moonie' appears to be the predominant form.

moonlight *noun*
a discreet and hurried departure to avoid debts, especially of such an absconding made at night *UK, 1958*
A shortening of **MOONLIGHT FLIT**.

moonlight *verb*
to work a second job, especially at night *US, 1957*
- PERSONNEL OFFICER: You moonlightin'? TRAVIS: No, I want long shifts. — *Taxi Driver*, 1976
- She was a cocktail waitress at Spade's Boardwalk, worked days, ten A.M. to six P.M. Which doesn't mean she couldn't have been moonlighting. — Elmore Leonard, *Glitz*, p. 88, 1985

moonlight express *noun*
trucking by an independent, illegal and inexpensive operation *US*
- — Montie Tak, *Truck Talk*, p. 108, 1971

moonlight flit *noun*
a discreet and hurried departure to avoid debts, especially of such an absconding made at night *UK, 1824*
- A German cruise liner has staged a "moonlight flit" from London's port health authority after a routine inspection revealed that its galleys were infested with cockroaches. — *The Guardian*, 17th September 2003

moonlight flits; moonlights *noun*
the female breasts *UK*
Rhyming slang for **TIT(S)**.
- — Ray Puxley, *Fresh Rabbit*, 1998

moonlight freight *noun*
freight hauled illegally *US*
- — *American Speech*, p. 44, February 1963: 'Trucker's language in Rhode Island'

moonlight requisition *noun*
the notional procedure attached to stolen materials *US, 1946*
- — *American Speech*, p. 55, February 1947: 'Pacific War language'

moon rock *noun*
the combination of heroin and crack cocaine *US, 1989*
- — Terry Wiliams, *Crackhouse*, p. 150, 1992
- — Robert Ashton, *This Is Heroin*, p. 209, 2002

moon rocks *noun*
crack cocaine *UK*
An elaboration of **ROCK**.
- — Mike Haskins, *Drugs*, p. 282, 2003

moonshine *noun*
1 privately and illegally distilled alcohol *UK, 1782*
- [T]hey just talked and drank some of the Southern moonshine I left in the compartment. — Jack Kerouac, *On the Road*, p. 125, 1957
- Sister could put away some booze. I remember seeing her drink a half a mason jar of ol' man White's moonshine. — Odie Hawkins, *Amazing Grace*, p. 78, 1993
- — Nick Brownlee, *This Is Alcohol*, p. 164, 2002

2 an aircraft used for dropping magnesium-based flares to illuminate the ground at night *US*
- — Gregory Clark, *Words of the Vietnam War*, p. 180, 1990

moonshine 1; moonshine 2 *noun*
hybrid varieties of hashish produced in Holland *UK*
- — Nick Jones, *Spliffs*, p. 91, 2003

moonshot *noun*
1 anal sex *US*
- — Robert A. Wilson, *Playboy's Book of Forbidden Words*, p. 170, 1972

2 outdoor sex at night *US*
- [A]nd who was to say that they might not be able to go to the powder room simultaneously, and thereby slip off for a ten-minute moon-shot? — Dan Jenkins, *Dead Solid Perfect*, p. 101, 1986

moonstomp *verb*
an ungainly dance associated with the skinhead youth cult *UK*
Popular with authors looking back to the 1960s and 70s.
- "I want all of you skinheads out there to put your braces together," Wood tugged, "and your boots on your feet and give me some of that old moonstomping!" — Stewart Home, *Sex Kick [britpulp]*, p. 221, 1999
- [T]he whole of the Shed [a stand at Chelsea FC's Stamford Bridge ground] is moon-stomping. — Jake Arnott, *He Kills Coppers*, p. 213–214, 2001

moon-time *noun*
the bleed period of the menstrual cycle *US*
Emphasises the monthly rhythm of the cycle.
- — *The Museum of Menstruation and Women's Health*, December 2000

moonwalk *verb*
to perform a dance-step which, when it is done well, gives the impression of walking forward whilst gliding in reverse *US, 1984*
Popularised by pop singer Michael Jackson (b.1958); it derives from a supposed similarity to walking on the moon.
- [H]ere one is, in a club, off his head, and trying to fucking moonwalk! — Dave Courtney, *Raving Lunacy*, p. 73, 2000

moony *noun*
any slow or romantic dance, or the music for it, played at an organised dance or disco, especially at the end of an evening *UK: SCOTLAND*
- Ah'm that shy Ah hide in the lavvy when a moony comes oan. — Michael Munro, *The Patter, Another Blast*, p. 45, 1988

moop *noun*
a person suffering from chronic disorientation in Arctic regions or Antarctica produced by long days and then long nights *ANTARCTICA, 1959*
- — Bernadette Hince, *The Antarctic Dictionary*, p. 232, 2000

moo poo *noun*
cow manure *AUSTRALIA*
- MOO POO! 3 for $12 Offer also includes poultry manure and mushroom compost. — *Wentworth Courier*, p. 25, 30th March 1994

Moor *noun*
▸ **the Moor**
Dart*moor* prison *UK, 1869*
- [T]he judge gave them all a lagging, and Harry got his first taste of the Moor [HM Prison Dartmoor]. — Charles Raven, *Underworld Nights*, p. 48, 1956
- Your [sic] f...ing lucky, I'm doing a neves. I'm going down the Moor soon that will be the third poxy time. — Frank Norman, *Bang To Rights*, p. 17, 1958

- You know where they'd send us? The Moor. That's where they'd send us. — Derek Bickerton, *Payroll*, p. 31, 1959
- — Angela Devlin, *Prison Patter*, p. 77, 1996
- Vinny's been ghosted down to the Moor. — J.J. Connolly, *Layer Cake*, p. 164, 2000

moose *noun*

1 in the Korean war, a girlfriend, mistress or prostitute *US, 1951*
From the Japanese *musume*.
- — *American Speech*, p. 119, May 1960: 'Korean bamboo English'
- I have been shacked up there now for more than two years with the prettiest little moose you ever did see. — Joseph C. Goulden, *Korea*, p. 142, 1982

2 an unattractive female *IRELAND*
- And her friend was an awful-looking moose apparently. — Joseph O'Connor, *Red Roses and Petrol*, p. 73, 1995
- Trouble was she was a bit of a specky [bespectacled] moose. — Dave Courtney, *Dodgy Dave's Little Black Book*, p. 25, 2001

3 in poker, a large pot *US*
- — John Vorhaus, *The Big Book of Poker Slang*, p. 26, 1996

moose call *noun*
a howling sound emitted by the Lockheed Starfighter *CANADA*
- (RCAF, early 1960s to late 1980s) The "moose call" of the Starfighter was an abrupt and sometimes unnerving change of pitch, caused by the variable exhaust nozzle on the engine. "You call always tell the sound of a CF-104, by the moose call." — Tom Langeste, *Words on the Wing*, p. 188, 1995

moose-eyed *adjective*
infatuated; in love *US*
- — Murry A. Taylor, *Jumping Fire*, p. 457, 2000

moose farm *noun*
a college sorority whose members are perceived as not particularly attractive *US*
- — Mary Swift, *Campus Slang (University of Texas)*, 1968

moose-gooser *noun*
an Alaska Railroad train *US, 1948*
- — Russell Tabbert, *Dictionary of Alaskan English*, p. 225, 1991

moose knuckle *noun*
the condition that exists when a tight-fitting pair of trousers, shorts, bathing suit or other garment forms a wedge between a woman's labia, accentuating their shape *US*
- — Surf Punks, *Oh No! Not Them Again! (liner notes)*, 1988

moose milk *noun*
an improvised alcoholic mixed drink, especially a homebrew Yukon cocktail made of milk and rum *US, 1957*
- Nobody makes Moose Milk like Sergeant Tanchuk makes Moose Milk! — Tom Langeste, *oral citation from Words on the Wing*, p. 188, 1995
- Up north, moose milk is homebrew or rum and milk; a more piquant potion is concocted in the Maritimes – sometimes emulsified fiddlehead [ferns], clam juice, and cheap wine. — Bill Casselman, *Canadian Words*, p. 15, 1995

moose pasture *noun*

1 in the Canadian West, worthless or unproven mining claims *CANADA*
- When prospecting lagged and the bottom fell out of the "moose-pasture" market, Ernie took a semi-skilled job with a local mining company. — *Press*, p. 5, January 1962

2 any worthless (or nonexistent) land sold as part of a confidence swindle *US*
- — M. Allen Henderson, *How Con Games Work*, p. 221, 1985: 'Glossary'

moose pasture con *noun*
a big con in which the victim is induced to invest in a company that appears on the verge of a great secret success *US*
- It's gonna be a Big Store. We're gonna set up a trap. I'm gonna run a moose pasture con on Tommy. — Stephen Cannell, *King Con*, p. 110, 1997

moosh *noun*

1 the mouth *AUSTRALIA, 1916*
After **MUSH**.
- His back was turned towards me, part underneath a bush, / Not tunic, boots, or putties, and I couldn't see his "moosh". — Byron Baly, *Patrolling the Desert*, p. 2, 1916
- Come on now, Sloppy, let's start winding this round your moosh. — John Wynnum, *Tar Dust*, p. 116, 1962

2 jail porridge *AUSTRALIA, 1944*

moosh *verb*
to shove in the face *US*
- The alleged perpetrator called him a 'bitch-ass punk' and mooshed him, causing annoyance and alarm. — *The New Yorker*, p. 35, 10th August 1998

moosh; mush; mushie; mooshy *adjective*
fine, excellent, pleasant, nice, super, etc *ZIMBABWE, 1973*
- — Jean Branford, *A Dictionary of South African English*, 1978
- — Penny Silva, *A Dictionary of South African English*, 1996

mooshay *noun*
a light-skinned person; an unlikeable person *SAINT KITTS AND NEVIS*
Collected by Richard Allsopp.

moot *noun*
the vagina *AUSTRALIA*
Origin unknown.
- I'll sell me moot for half a note. — K. Gilbert, *People are Legends*, p. 11, 1978

moota *noun*
marijuana *US, 1926*
The Mexican Spanish slang *mota* (marijuana) was smuggled north with the drug. Variant spellings include 'moocah', 'mootah', 'mooter', 'mootie', 'mooster', 'mootos', 'motta', 'muta' and 'mutah'.
- Rapp smoked his muta while he played the new guitar[.] — Mezz Mezzrow, *Really the Blues*, p. 52, 1946
- — Richard A. Spears, *The Slang and Jargon of Drugs and Drink*, p. 344, 1986
- [W]e took our pleasure gladly – dimly sensing that with the fragrance of mota in the ear, the world would never be quite the same again. — Sean Hutchinson, *Crying Out Loud*, p. 25, 1988
- — Mike Haskins, *Drugs*, p. 288, 2003

mooters *noun*
a marijuana cigarette *UK*
From **MOOTA**.
- — Mike Haskins, *Drugs*, p. 291, 2003

mop *noun*

1 a head of hair *UK, 1821*
- He was a little bit of a guy, no chubbier than a dime and as lean as hard times, with a mop of dark hair[.] — Mezz Mezzrow, *Really the Blues*, p. 109, 1946
- What do they care if their baldheaded and crew-cut elders don't dig their caveman mops? — Eldridge Cleaver, *Soul on Ice*, p. 81, 1968
- Pop was chopping a study's mop and Mom was in her favorite squat behind the stove[.] — A.S. Jackson, *Gentleman Pimp*, p. 11, 1973

2 your date for an evening *US*
Teen slang.
- — *Look*, p. 88, 10th August 1954

MOP *adjective*
in the military, missing on purpose *US*
- DeTonq was MOP – missing on purpose. DeTonq, a Cajun from Louisiana, spoke passable French and had undoubtedly chosen to terminate his short military career before it terminated him. — Nelson DeMille, *Word of Honor*, p. 150, 1985

mop and bucket!
a general declaration of rejection or dimissal; may also imply resignation to, or acceptance of, a situation *UK*
Rhyming slang for **FUCK IT!**.
- — Ray Puxley, *Cockney Rabbit*, 1992

Mop and Pail *nickname*
the *Toronto Globe and Mail* newspaper *CANADA*
This derogatory nickname is surely jocular, as the newspaper is the foremost national newspaper of Canada.

mop booth *noun*
a private booth where pornographic films are shown for a fee *US*
- If public pudpulling is your thing, try a "spooge booth" or "mop booth." — Rob Cohen, *Etiquette for Outlaws*, p. 73, 2001

mope *noun*

1 a person who is not particularly bright *US, 1919*
From C16 to C19 a part of colloquial speech, 'mope' reappeared 200 years later as slang.
- Alma mater for many a mope majorin' in thievery, roguery, lechery, and mopery. — Edwin Torres, *Carlito's Way*, p. 20, 1975

- Just as a couple of mopes who you knew from the Palm Springs crowd. —Gerald Petievich, *To Live and Die in L.A.*, p. 195, 1983
- I don't suppose you could ever accuse these two mopes of being on the take. —Jim Carroll, *Forced Entries*, p. 93, 1987

2 in hospital usage, a nonsurgeon physician *US*
A derogatory evolution of the term '*m*edical *o*ut*p*atient'.
- —Sally Williams, *"Strong" Words*, p. 151, 1994

3 a thug *US*
- Yeah, right, Joey One-Way, you know, that mope wrote White Man Black Hole. —Joel Rose, *Kill Kill Faster Faster*, p. 35, 1997
- On one of these streets, too, a young housing cop was killed when a Dominican mope tossed a bucket of spackling off a rooftop that landed on the poor patrolman's skull, killing the rookie officer. —Samuel M. Katz, *Anytime Anywhere*, p. 63, 1997
- [A] perp can be a "skell" or a "mope," depending on whether he's a bum or a thug. —*The New Yorker*, p. 35, 10th August 1998

mope *verb*
a stealthy escape *US, 1926*
- —Hyman E. Goldin et al., *Dictionary of American Underworld Lingo*, p. 141, 1950

mope away; mope *verb*
to quit your job in the circus *US*
- Many good workers 'moped' away without any valid reason leaving their pay 'in the wagon'. —Joe McKennon, *Circus Lingo*, p. 62, 1980

moped *noun*
a fat female; a promiscuous female *US*
From a joke, because both are fun but you don't want anybody to see you on one.
- —Connie Eble (Editor), *UNC-CH Campus Slang*, p. 4, Spring 2001

mopery *noun*
incompetence, stupidity *US, 1907*
Collected by Richard Allsopp.
- Alma mater for many a mope majorin' in thievery, roguery, lechery, and mopery. —Edwin Torres, *Carlito's Way*, p. 19–20, 1975

mophy *noun*
▷ see: MOFFIE

mop jockey *noun*
a janitor or custodian *US, 1958*
- —*American Speech*, p. 158–159, May 1960: 'The burgeoning of jockey'
- —Hy Lit, *Hy Lit's Unbelievable Dictionary of Hip Words for Groovy People*, p. 48, 1968

mopp *verb*
to don protective clothing and breathing apparatus against chemical warfare *US*
From the official designation '*m*ission *o*riented *p*rotective *p*osture.'
- —*The Retired Officer Magazine*, p. 39, January 1993

mopper *noun*
a person who tends to wheedle drinks from friends *TRINIDAD AND TOBAGO, 1950*
- —Lise Winer, *Dictionary of the English/Creole of Trinidad & Tobago*, 2003

moppet *noun*
a child *UK, 1601*
- And so appalling has moppet misbehavior become that an extra detail of 30 officers has been assigned on duty around the clock[.] —Jack Lait and Lee Mortimer, *Washington Confidential*, p. 120, 1951

mop-squeezer *noun*
in a deck of playing cards, a queen *US, 1949*
- —*American Speech*, p. 100, May 1951

mopsy *noun*
a girlfriend *TRINIDAD AND TOBAGO, 1938*
- —Lise Winer, *Dictionary of the English/Creole of Trinidad & Tobago*, 2003

moptop *noun*
a youth or a young man who wears his hair in a fringed style popularised by the Beatles in the early 1960s *UK, 1964*
- Even the Beatles, no matter how moptop lovable the Daily Mirror might pretend they were[.] —Mick Farren, *Give the Anarchist a Cigarette*, p. 12, 2001

mop-up *noun*
the end-game of a conflict, in which the stragglers of the losing side are rounded up *UK, 1917*
- Many of those arrested in the mop-up didn't own or ride motorcycles[.] —Hunter S. Thompson, *Hell's Angels*, p. 221, 1966

mop up *verb*
1 to win *UK, 1861*
- Support band the Stereo MCs were mopping up every night and they were nicking the [Happy] Mondays' crown from right under their noses. —John Robb, *The Nineties*, p. 66, 1999

2 to consume drinks bought by others *TRINIDAD AND TOBAGO, 1971*
- —Lise Winer, *Dictionary of the English/Creole of Trinidad & Tobago*, 2003

mop-up boy *noun*
a worker performing janitorial work at an arcade where men masturbate while watching videos *US*
- It's not fair. If you're the mop-up boy at a peep show, it's obvious the government is not working for you. —Chris Rock, *Rock This!*, p. 98, 1997

moragrifa *noun*
marijuana *US, 1966*
- —Richard A. Spears, *The Slang and Jargon of Drugs and Drink*, 1986
- —Mike Haskins, *Drugs*, 2003

moral *noun*
a certainty *UK, 1861*
From the phrase 'a moral certainty'.
- —Nino Culotta (John O'Grady), *They're A Weird Mob*, p. 72, 1957
- [I]f any of your female guests are exceptionally attractive it is a moral he will molest them. —Sue Rhodes, *And when she was bad she was popular*, p. 112, 1968
- —Alexander Buzo, *Rooted*, p. 40, 1969
- —Arthur Chipper, *The Aussie Swearer's Guide*, p. 48, 1972
- —Barry Humphries, *A Nice Night's Entertainment*, p. 147, 1974
- —Jim Ramsay, *Cop It Sweet!*, p. 59, 1977

morale-booster *noun*
any stupid act by the authorities that has the immediate effect of lowering morale *US*
- —*Current Slang*, p. 16, Spring 1968

morale-raising flour *noun*
cocaine *UK*
A play on the name and appearance of self-raising flour.
- [P]roviding a gram of ye olde morale-raising flour in Soho House to keep The Gang smiling[.] —James Hawes, *White Powder, Green Light*, p. 8, 2002

more *noun*
phencyclidine, the recreational drug known as PCP or angel dust *US*
- —US Department of Justice, *Street Terms*, October 1994

more fool
used to describe the subject as foolish for acting in a given manner *UK*
Often as an exclamation.
- LOFTY: He got two years. The others got off, and he carried the can back. TICH: More fool him. CORP: That's what his wife said too. —Clive Exton, *No Fixed Abode [Six Granada Plays]*, p. 121, 1959

more hide than Jessie *adjective*
extremely cheeky *AUSTRALIA, 1951*
- You think I'm a liar. I think you're a bigger one. You got more 'ide than Jessie, the elephant. —J. Gaby, *The Restless Waterfront*, p. 144, 1974

more like; more like it *adjective*
would be nearer, better, more acceptable, more accurate *UK, 1888*
- Popstars? Strop stars, more like. —*The Guardian*, 29th January 2002

more or less *noun*
a dress *UK*
Rhyming slang.
- —Ray Puxley, *Cockney Rabbit*, p. 127, 1992

more power to your elbow!
a catchphrase of encouragement or good wishes *UK, 1860*
Used as a headline.
- —*The Guardian*, 29th November 2003

more pricks than a pincushion
an alleged achievement of a promiscuous woman *AUSTRALIA*
- Your little Aussie rosebud has had more pricks than a pincushion. —Barry Humphries, *Bazza Pulls It Off!*, 1971

more tea, vicar(?)
used humorously to acknowledge a fart or a belch *UK*
- Dartford burps. – More tea, vicar, East whispers, testing to see whether Dartford is awake. —Mark Powell, *Snap*, p. 43, 2001

more than somewhat *adverb*
very, extremely, to a great degree, very much *US, 1930*
Coinage credited to US writer Damon Runyan.
- The bookmakers also attracted him more than somewhat.— *The Observer*, 28th July 1968

Moreton Bay fig; Moreton Bay; Moreton *noun*
1 a busybody *AUSTRALIA, 1944*
Rhyming slang for **GIG**. From the name of a type of large native figtree.
- Swim over here a bit, I want to talk to you but I don't want any Moreton Bays listening in.—Clive Galea, *Slipper*, p. 98, 1988

2 a police informer *AUSTRALIA*
Rhyming slang for **GIG**. May be spelt 'Morton'.
- — *The (Sydney) Bulletin*, 26th April 1975

MORF
used as Internet shorthand to mean '*m*ale *or f*emale' *US*
- —Andy Ihnatko, *Cyberspeak*, p. 125, 1997

morgue *noun*
in circus and carnival usage, a performance or series of performances in a town that fail to attract more than a few customers *US, 1904*
- —Don Wilmeth, *The Language of American Popular Entertainment*, p. 176, 1981

Moriarty; mori *noun*
a *party*, a celebration *UK, 1981*
Rhyming slang; informed, if not inspired, by one of two fictional characters: either the arch-enemy of Sherlock Holmes or the comic creation of Spike Milligan in *The Goons*.
- — Ray Puxley, *Cockney Rabbit*, 1992

Mork and Mindy *adjective*
windy *UK*
Rhyming slang, based on cult US television comedy *Mork and Mindy* (first broadcast 1978–82).
- It's a little bit Mork and Mindy today, innit?— *www.LondonSlang.com*, June 2002

Mormons *noun*
in hold 'em poker, a king and two queens *US*
An allusion to the practice of plural marriage.
- —John Vorhaus, *The Big Book of Poker Slang*, p. 26, 1996

morning *noun*
▸ **the top of the morning!; top of the morning to you!**
used as a cheery greeting *IRELAND, 1815*
A stereotypical Irish-ism.
- No corn beef and cabbage cooking where I come from either ... come from an orphanage, goddamn orphanage, no Irish top-of-the-morning mother there either, just a big son-of-a-bitching German[.]—Lyle Kessler, *Orphans*, 1983

morning after the night before *noun*
a morning hangover; applied generally (as a diagnosis) to someone suffering the effects of drinking to excess *UK, 1922*
- If you dread the morning after the night before when it's still only the evening, you need help.— *The Guardian*, 18th October 2003

morning glory *noun*
1 an erection upon waking up in the morning *UK*
Rhyming slang for **COREY** (the penis), formed from the name of a popular garden flower (*Ipomoea violacea*).
- —Ray Puxley, *Cockney Rabbit*, 1992
- So I wrapped a $50 note around my best friend (he means his DICK readers) and fastened it on with a rubber band. I woke up next morning with my Morning Glory being choked.— Picture, p. 45, 5th February 1992
- —David McGill, *David McGill's Complete Kiwi Slang Dictionary*, 1998
- Elaine stubbed her fag out and sunk under the duvet to nosh amicably on his morning glory.—Garry Bushell, *The Face*, p. 105, 2001

2 an act of sexual intercourse in the morning *AUSTRALIA*
- 'Wouldn't mind a mornin' glory meself,' Splinter answered, 'though I'm gettin' a bit old fer it these days.'—J.E. MacDonnell, *Don't Gimme the Ships*, p. 139, 1960
- —Jim Ramsay, *Cop It Sweet!*, p. 60, 1977

3 a drug addict's first injection of the morning *US*
- —J.E. Schmidt, *Narcotics Lingo and Lore*, p. 114, 1959

4 in horse racing, a horse that runs well in early morning workouts but not during races *US, 1904*
- —Robert Saunders Dowst and Jay Craig, *Playing the Races*, p. 165, 1960

morning line *noun*
in horse racing, the odds established by the racetrack handicapper the morning before a race *US*
- —Mel Heimer, *Inside Racing*, p. 212, 1967

morning prayers *noun*
a daily briefing on the work to be done *UK*
First recorded as 'prayers, family prayers and morning prayers' a World War 2 military term for daily staff conference at HQ.
- "Does the Deputy Aircraft Maintenance Officer have to attend morning prayers?" "At this Wing, everyone attends Morning Prayers!"—Tom Langeste, *oral citation from Words on the Wing*, 1995
- —Martin Fido and Keith Skinner, *The Official Encyclopaedia of New Scotland Yard*, 1999

morning shot *noun*
a drug user's first injection that day *US*
- —Richard A. Spears, *The Slang and Jargon of Drugs and Drink*, p. 347, 1986

morning wood *noun*
an erection experienced upon waking *US*
- —Pamela Munro, *U.C.L.A. Slang*, 1997
- —Don R. McCreary (Editor), *Dawg Speak*, 2001

Moroccan black *noun*
a variety of marijuana *UK*
Named for its source and colour.
- —Angela Devlin, *Prison Patter*, p. 77, 1996

moron *noun*
a stupid person, a fool *US, 1921*
Adopted from the Greek in 1910 to classify a person with an IQ of between 50 and 70; this correct technical sense is now largely avoided.
- Which moron mentioned the justice system?— *The Observer*, 19th January 2003

moron corps *noun*
the US Army during the Vietnam war *US*
The US Armed Forces qualification test passing score was lowered substantially in the late 1960s to help swell the ranks of the army with poor urban black men, poor rural white men and Mexican-Americans.
- —Gregory Clark, *Words of the Vietnam War*, p. 333, 1990

morotgara *noun*
heroin *US, 1977*
- —Richard A. Spears, *The Slang and Jargon of Drugs and Drink*, p. 347, 1986
- —Mike Haskins, *Drugs*, p. 284, 2003

morph *verb*
1 to change body shape or image *UK*
From cinematographic jargon for blending one image into another by means of computer manipulation.
- [Kylie Minogue] Has managed to morph from the cute girl next door to sex kitten extraordinaire.— *Loaded*, p. 18, June 2002

2 to create an electronic message in a manner that gives the appearance of having been sent by someone else *US*
- —Andy Ihnatko, *Cyberspeak*, p. 125, 1997

morphing *noun*
the act of taking morphine *UK*
A shape-changing pun.
- —Angela Devlin, *Prison Patter*, p. 77, 1996

morphy *noun*
an hermaphrodite *BARBADOS*
- —Frank A. Collymore, *Barbadian Dialect*, p. 74, 1965

Morris Minor *noun*
a black eye *UK*
Rhyming slang for 'shiner', formed from a type of car manufactured from 1948–71.
- —Ray Puxley, *Cockney Rabbit*, 1992

mort *noun*
a dolt *NEW ZEALAND, 1997*
Prison usage.
- —Harry Orsman, *A Dictionary of Modern New Zealand Slang*, p. 88, 1999

mortal *adjective*
drunk *UK*
• Shall we get mortal? — Ian Rankin, *Mortal Causes*, 1994

mortal combat *noun*
very potent heroin *US*
• — Jim Crotty, *How to Talk American*, p. 89, 1997
• Probably influenced by the computer/arcade game(s) Mortal Kombat, introduced in 1992, and the subsequent cartoon series and movies. — Robert Ashton, *This Is Heroin*, 2002
• — Mike Haskins, *Drugs*, 2003

mortalled *adjective*
drunk *UK: SCOTLAND*
• He tries tae tell us he only hud wan or two. Away, Ah says, mortalled wisny in it! — Michael Munro, *The Complete Patter*, p. 104, 1996
• — Simon Weston, *Moving On*, 2003

mortaller *noun*
literally a mortal sin, figuratively a terrible thing *IRELAND*
• Raising taxes will be seen as the ultimate mortaller, especially if they take the PDs to the Fianna Fáil bosom. — *Irish Examiner*, 28th May 2002

mortal lock *noun*
in horse racing, a bet that is sure to win *US*
• — David W. Maurer, *Argot of the Racetrack*, p. 41, 1951

mortal nuts *noun*
in poker, a hand that is sure to win *US*
• — John Scarne, *Scarne's Guide to Modern Poker*, p. 284, 1979

morto *adjective*
mortified *IRELAND*
• KATHLEEN: Were you "morto"? SIOBHAN: I wasn't "morto" because it was feminist. I was "morto" because it was my mother! — *Irish Times*, 7th March 2001

MOS *noun*
the typical *m*an *o*n the *s*treet *US*
• — Jim Crotty, *How to Talk American*, p. 417, 1997

MOS *adjective*
in television and film making, said of a scene shot without sound *US*
• The first thing to learn about sound is the expression "MOS," which stands for "mit out sound." I was told that it derives from Otto Preminger's heavy accent. — Stephen Ziplow, *The Film Maker's Guide to Pornography*, p. 75, 1977
• Legend has sit that director Lothar Mendes (a German himself) was the person who coined the term when he instructed the crew to do the next shot 'mit out sound.' — Ralph S. Singleton, *Filmaker's Dictionary*, p. 107, 1990

Moscow *noun*
a pawnshop *AUSTRALIA, 1941*
• We find the English cant term moskeneer, to pawn, which survives in Australia today in the phrase gone to Moscow, which has nothing to do with the Soviet capital, but which simply means "pawned". — Sidney J. Baker, *The Australian Language*, p. 26, 1945
• — Jim Ramsay, *Cop It Sweet!*, p. 60, 1977

Moscow mule *noun*
a cocktail of vodka, lager (or ginger ale) and lime *UK*
'Moscow' in honour of the vodka, 'mule' for the kick.
• — Andrew York, *The Co-Ordinator*, 1967

mos' def!
▷ see: MOST DEF!

mosey *verb*
to move slowly and seemingly aimlessly; to amble *US, 1829*
Introduces a folksy tone.
• I sat down in the lobby and planned a large volume to be entitled "Profiles in Snollygostering" and ate a Suchard chocolate bar and then moseyed into the hotel record shop and asked for a Lennie Tristano. — Clancy Sigal, *Going Away*, p. 74, 1961
• Well, I know you're busy, so I'll mosey on. — Max Shulman, *Anyone Got a Match?*, p. 145, 1964
• "Guess I'll mosey along." Kitty stood. — Seth Morgan, *Homeboy*, p. 235, 1990
• Bobbie told Reggie she was going to mosey over to the post office to buy some stamps, but really, she wanted to get some fresh air. — Joseph Wambaugh, *Finnegan's Week*, p. 32, 1993
• And Connie moseyed over, waited for her opportunity, and buzzed Joyce on the ass with the stun gun. — Janet Evanovich, *Seven Up*, p. 37, 2001

mosey at *verb*
to casually investigate or explore *UK*
Possibly from MOSEY (to amble) combined with the sense of 'nosey' (inquisitive).
• There's fucking dolphins in the Mersey now, by the way. Flipper and that coming up to have a mosey at the pondlife[.] — Kevin Sampson, *Outlaws*, p. 6, 2001

mosh; moshing *noun*
(at a rock music concert, especially hardcore, punk or metal) a violent and ungainly bouncing dance that involves deliberately crashing into other moshers *US*
• Benser on moshing: "Normally we have a pit. In the pit, you mosh." — *Washington Post*, p. C1, 4th June 1987

mosh *verb*
(at a rock music concert, especially hardcore, punk or metal) to jump/dance in a violent and ungainly manner, deliberately crashing into other moshers *US, 1983*
• He got her in effortlessly, even though she was too young to drink, and escorted her to a VIP booth by the stage where Wig Starbuck, punk grandpa of the scene, was playing for the moshing youngsters. — Francesca Lia Block, *I Was a Teenage Fairy*, p. 88, 1998
• The city moshes like joyful sardines to the rhythms of this Scouse troupe[.] — *X-Ray*, p. 84, November 2002

mosher *noun*
a dancer at a rock concert (especially hardcore, punk or metal) who responds to the music with violent and ungainly bouncing – mainly off other moshers; by extension a dedicated fan of a rock genre *UK*
• Over a million moshers can't be wrong. — Sky Channel 885 *TOTALROCK*, March 2002

moshie *noun*
a mosher *AUSTRALIA*
• Some moshies join in. They jump onstage and frisbee my CD-ROMs against the back wall. — Glyn Parry, *Mosh*, p. 3, 1996

moshky *noun*
a marijuana user *US*
• — Eugene Landy, *The Underground Dictionary*, p. 135, 1971

mosh pit *noun*
an area in a dance hall where dancers mosh *US, 1992*
• — *American Speech*, p. 417, Winter 1993: 'Among the new words'
• "Are you ready for my darkness?" [...] Words that can and should only be followed by blood and feathers being launched into the moshpit. — *X-Ray*, June 2003

mosquitos; mosquitoes *noun*
cocaine *US*
• — US Department of Justice, *Street Terms*, August 1994
• — Mike Haskins, *Drugs*, p. 280, 2003

moss *noun*
1 hair *US, 1926*
• Later on he would bring the whole Austin High Gang out to Hollywood an set them up, each one with a hand-picked harem of bathing beauties to manicure his toenails and shampoo his moss. — Mezz Mezzrow, *Really the Blues*, p. 131, 1946
• And did you dig that chick with moss that thick? — Dan Burley, *Diggeth Thou?*, p. 19, 1959
• — Jim Bouton, *Ball Four*, p. 252, 1970
• Decatur said, "The black geechie with the wavy moss." — Iceberg Slim (Robert Beck), *Death Wish*, p. 112, 1977

2 seaweed *BARBADOS*
• — Frank A. Collymore, *Barbadian Dialect*, p. 75, 1965

mossback *noun*
1 an old person with outmoded ideas and values *US, 1878*
• — John Ayto, *The Oxford Dictionary of Slang*, p. 370, 1998
• The scruffy portraiture of J. Jordan Bruns and the fluorescent-lit interiors of Matt Klos will gratify only mossbacks who feared the academy had stopped teaching academic painting. — *Washington Post*, p. C5, 19th August 2004

2 a promiscuous girl *US*
• — Connie Eble (Editor), *UNC-CH Campus Slang*, p. 4, Spring 1982

mossie; mozzie; mozzy *noun*
1 a mosquito *AUSTRALIA, 1936*
• The mossies are big in the Territory. — Frank Hardy, *The Yarns of Billy Borker*, p. 28, 1965

• Now you're protected from the rain, and then underneath that you can put your mozzie net.—Andy McNab, *Immediate Action*, p. 92, 1995

2 a sparrow *SOUTH AFRICA, 1884*

• —Jean Branford, *A Dictionary of South African English*, 1978

most *noun*

▸ the most

the best *US, 1953*

• "And, Grandma," said Red, "your ears are the most, to say the least."—Steve Allen, *Bop Fables*, p. 44, 1955
• Have you seen the new featherweight tone-arms they're producing nowadays? Man, they're absolutely the most!—Peter Nichols, *Promenade [Six Granada Plays]*, p. 68, 1959
• It was the mostest the most could be!—Clarence Cooper Jr, *The Scene*, p. 63, 1960
• Gee, this hound's-tooth is really the most.—Ross Russell, *The Sound*, p. 178, 1961

most *adverb*

very *US*

• We will have a most triumphant time.—*Bill and Ted's Excellent Adventure*, 1989

most def!; mos' def!

used for expressing emphatic agreement *US*

• —Ethan Hilderbrant, *Prison Slang*, 1998
• —Connie Eble (Editor), *UNC-CH Campus Slang*, p. 6, Spring 2003

mostie *noun*

a sexually attractive woman *NEW ZEALAND*

• —David McGill, *David McGill's Complete Kiwi Slang Dictionary*, p. 84, 1998

most ricky tick *adverb*

promptly, immediately *US*

Mock pidgin, used by US soldiers during the Vietnam war.

• Vanish, Joker, most ricky-tick, and take Rafterman with you.—*Full Metal Jacket*, 1987
• —Linda Reinberg, *In the Field*, p. 145, 1991

mot; mott *noun*

a woman, a girlfriend, a wife *UK, 1785*

Liverpool Irish usage.

• Yis should se his mot. Darren's mot. -Is she nice? said Bimbo. -Lovely, said Jimmy Sr. -Fuckin' lovely.—Roddy Doyle, *The Van*, p. 79, 1991
• I tell him I don't feel very well and have to nash. Oh good fuck there's Kelly wavin at me.That new mot, is it?—Niall Griffiths, *Kelly + Victor*, p. 109, 2002

MOT *noun*

a Jewish person identified as such by another Jewish person *US*

• Jews may ask, "Is she M.O.T. [member of our tribe]?" instead of "Is she Jewish?"—Leo Rosten, *The Joys of Yinglish*, p. 152, 1989

MOT *verb*

to conduct an MOT test of a vehicle's roadworthiness *UK*

From the official abbreviation of the Ministry of Transport test, introduced in 1960 and grown more stringent since.

• They [London's minicab drivers] will be vetted for criminal records, have to fit their cars with new technology that can track each job and be required to have their cars MOT'd twice a year.—*The Guardian*, 10th November 2002

mota; moto *noun*

marijuana *US, 1933*

The Mexican Spanish slang *mota* (marijuana) was smuggled north with the drug.

• We wandered off campus to get a pint of rum, something to keep our mota strength at a peak 'til 10.—Odie Hawkins, *Men Friends*, p. 55, 1989

motate *verb*

to move *US*

• Man, when he said that, I needed to motate out of there.—Nicholas Von Hoffman, *We Are The People Our Parents Warned Us Against*, p. 61, 1967

MOT'd *adjective*

of a vehicle, having passed the MOT test, having an MOT certificate *UK, 1984*

motel time

used to signal that a bar is closing and that customers must leave *US*

• —*The Guild Dictionary of Homosexual Terms*, p. 30, 1965

moth *noun*

in horse racing, a groom or racehorse attendant who is attracted to the bright lights of nightlife *AUSTRALIA*

• —Ned Wallish, *The Truth Dictionary of Racing Slang*, p. 53, 1989

mothball *noun*

an ether ball used to start a cold diesel truck engine *US*

• —Montie Tak, *Truck Talk*, p. 109, 1971

mothball *verb*

to take out of service; to set against possible future use *US, 1949*

• Last October PowerGen shocked the Government by mothballing nearly a quarter of its generating capacity and declaring the industry 'bust'.—*The Observer*, 31st August 2003

mother *noun*

1 a man; a thing *US*

A slightly euphemistic **MOTHERFUCKER**; sometimes a low form of abuse, sometimes merely jocular.

• Yeah, Nero was an all-high flip-out-in-orbit mother to end all mothers!—William "Lord" Buckley, *Nero*, 1951
• What I mean is I don't care whether you prove I'm an evil mother, you're lying!—Alexander Trocchi, *Cain's Book*, p. 168, 1960
• Drive, you puny mothers, drive!—Ken Kesey, *One Flew Over the Cuckoo's Nest*, p. 194, 1962
• You see that innocent mother with the red hair; you see him waking up in that bed?—Richard Farina, *Been Down So Long*, p. 93, 1966
• So why not put those dirty mothers in prison too?—Eldridge Cleaver, *Soul on Ice*, p. 4, 1968
• Ah, well, you're talking about the Concorde, one of those big mothers[.]—Terry Southern, *Blue Movie*, p. 61, 1970
• Sticky little mothers, aren't they?—*American Graffiti*, 1973
• Frank had a feeling the people watching the guy were probably thinking, Look at that little mother.—Elmore Leonard, *Swag*, p. 4, 1976
• She dragged him out to the stage, took his jacket off, and they did an old style "guagnanco" that was a mother.—Edwin Torres, *After Hours*, p. 325, 1979
• Then I remembered how the words real mother always were used as an insult in junior high.—Rita Ciresi, *Pink Slip*, p. 4, 1999
• [H]er old man's out of the boob now and he's one fuckin' mean mother.—Garry Bushell, *The Face*, p. 15, 2001

2 used of, or to, a wife if she is also a mother *UK, 1961*

3 a male homosexual in relation to a man whom he has introduced to homosexuality *US, 1946*

• —Anon., *The Gay Girl's Guide*, p. 13, 1949

4 a (very) senior secretary *UK*

Civil service use.

• One very senior secretary – in the jargon, these ladies were known as "mothers".—John Le Carre, *The Honourable Schoolboy*, 1977

5 a drug dealer *US*

• —William D. Alsever, *Glossary for the Establishment and Other Uptight People*, p. 26, December 1970

6 marijuana *US*

Probably an anglicised 'mutha'.

7 heroin; a heroin dealer; a homosexual heroin dealer *US*

Perhaps a euphemistic reduction of **MOTHERFUCKER**.

▸ be mother

to assume reponisbility for dispensing hot drinks or refreshments *UK*

Of either sex but reflecting a general perception of a mother's traditional role.

• Good. Coffee, everybody? George, will you be mother?—Chris Ryan, *The Watchman*, p. 106, 2001

▸ you love your mother better than your father; you love your father better than your mother

between schoolgirls, used as a warning that a slip or petticoat can be seen below the hem of a skirt *UK, 1977*

▸ your mother

used as a self-reference by older homosexual men *US, 1974*

• [P]ull up a chair and tell your mother all about it.—Paul Baker, *Polari*, p. 181, 2002

mother and father of all *noun*

an epic, if not the epic, example *UK*

An elaboration of **MOTHER OF ALL**.

• I had the mother and father of all headaches[.]—Duncan MacLaughlin, *The Filth*, p. 49, 2002

- I can assure you that a splash ride with two children is not the way to nurse the mother and father of all hangovers. — *The Guardian*, 11th June 2002

mother-ass; mother-arse; mudder ass *noun*
used as an abusive term of address or term of reference *TRINIDAD AND TOBAGO, 1958*
- — Lise Winer, *Dictionary of the English/Creole of Trinidad & Tobago*, 2003

mother blood!
used for expressing surprise *BAHAMAS*
Almost certainly a euphemism for 'motherfucker!'.
- — John A. Holm, *Dictionary of Bahamian English*, p. 137, 1982

Mother Brown *nickname*
the West End of London *UK*
Rhyming slang for'town'.
- — Ray Puxley, *Cockney Rabbit*, 1992

Mother Bu *nickname*
▷ **see: BU**

Mother Corp *nickname*
the Canadian Broadcasting Corporation *CANADA*
- Cuts continue at Mother Corp – newscast compromise leaves CBC with a $30 million deficit. — 7th August 2000

mother crusher *noun*
used euphemistically for 'motherfucker' *UK*
- Frig you mother crushers[.] — *Varsity*, p. 26, 14th June 2002

mother-cunt *noun*
used as an abusive term of address or term of reference *TRINIDAD AND TOBAGO, 1972*
- — Lise Winer, *Dictionary of the English/Creole of Trinidad & Tobago*, 2003

mother dear *noun*
methedrine, a central nervous system stimulant *US*
A phonic pun.
- — *Current Slang*, p. 9, Fall 1969

motheren; motherin *noun*
used as a euphemism for 'motherfucker' or 'motherfucking' *US*
- I say ... Oh you motheren heart. Then I say. Motheren wolves. Motheren wolves. Come at me you motherens. — Warren Miller, *The Cool World*, p. 31, 1959
- I can remember 'em all, every motherin' one-night stop. — Ross Russell, *The Sound*, p. 61, 1961
- This Penny was a motherin' danger. — Bernard Wolfe, *The Magic of Their Singing*, p. 68, 1961
- Sooner or later, baby, that shakin gonna pay off, fetch me out some big money from that motherin lounge — Robert Gover, *Here Goes Kitten*, p. 44, 1964
- The worst word of all, a word that even sportsmen disguise as "motheren," Mark didn't even attempt to change. "You mother-fucker!" — Sara Harris, *The Lords of Hell*, p. 176, 1967

motherfather *noun*
used as a euphemism for 'motherfucker' *US*
Used by comedian Redd Foxx on *The Royal Family* (CBS, 1991–92).

motherferyer *noun*
used as a euphemism for 'motherfucker' *US, 1946*
- And it was in Pontiac that I dug that Jim Crow man in person, a motherferyer that would cut your throat for looking. — Mezz Mezzrow, *Really the Blues*, p. 4, 1946

motherflipping *adjective*
used as a euphemism for the intensifier 'motherfucking' *US*
- I wanna find out how come nobody kin truss nobody in this mothahflippin muddlefuggin worl', how come everybody gotta ack mean. — Robert Gover, *One Hundred Dollar Misunderstanding*, p. 190, 1961

mother-for-you *noun*
used as a euphemism for 'motherfucker' *US*
- "I'll be a mother-for-you!" he exclaimed, half choking, more repulsed by the sight of the cut throat than shocked. — Chester Himes, *A Rage in Harlem*, p. 182, 1957

motherfouler *noun*
a motherfucker *US*
- Give it to him, Maceo, coolcrack the motherfouler! — Ralph Ellison, *Invisible Man*, p. 488, 1947

motherfuck *verb*
used to damn or curse *US, 1942*
- Motherfuck you, man. — Piri Thomas, *Seven Long Times*, p. 18, 1974
- "Man, look at my door!" "Motherfuck your door," McDaniel said. — Vernon E. Smith, *The Jones Men*, p. 206, 1974
- Motherfuck JLB, they don't support no hip-hop[.] — Eminem (Marshall Mathers), *Low Down Dirty*, 1998

motherfucker *noun*

1 a despised person *US, 1928*
In 1972, the US Supreme Court reversed the conviction of a man who had used the word 'motherfucker' four times during remarks at a school board meeting attended by some 40 children and 25 women, accepting 'motherfucker' as constitutionally protected speech (Rosenfeld v. New Jersey, 1972).
- Probably the most violent curse-word in American slang. Don't call anyone this even in fun. — James Seligmann, *How to be Happy Though Drafted*, p. 32, 1951
- I'll cut your throat you white mother fucker. — William Burroughs, *Naked Lunch*, p. 40, 1957
- Will you tell these motherfuckers to get off my back? — Alexander Trocchi, *Cain's Book*, p. 166, 1960
- "Good, you m——— f———, I'm glad you can't see." — Nat Hentoff, *The Jazz Life*, p. 168, 1961
- It's these respectable motherfuckers been doing all the dirt. They been stealing the colored folks blind, man. — James Baldwin, *Another Country*, p. 16, 1962
- "Motherfuckers," he says, shaking his head, as if he were passing judgment on all the people crammed into his life. — John Rechy, *City of Night*, p. 178, 1963
- Dare any dirty mother-fucker in this place to come and stop me from stomping this bitch. — Dick Gregory, *Nigger*, p. 22, 1964
- The cat in the corner said, "All you mother-fuckers better keep still, because the next cat who moves is dead." — Claude Brown, *Manchild in the Promised Land*, p. 216, 1965
- I told that motherfucker, I'm going to eat and sleep without you and you're not getting a dime of my money. — Babs Gonzales, *Movin' On Down De Line*, p. 10, 1975
- Anybody who said motherfucker in those days, Jesus, get up and fight or else. — Herbert Huncke, *Guilty of Everything*, p. 31, 1990
- They will fuck you. Over and over again. Motherfucker cocksuckers! — Howard Stern, *Miss America*, p. 434, 1995

2 a fellow, a person *US, 1958*
- The ubiquitous term motherfucker, once a serious curse, is now an all-purpose word whose meaning is entirely dependent on tone and context, as in "I love that motherfucker." — Christina and Richard Milner, *Black Players*, p. 46, 1972
- Originally, a derogatory term. Presently used as a term of either admiration or disgust, depending on the moment and the emotional or intellecutal point of view when written or vocalized. — Robert deCoy, *The Nigger Bible*, p. 33, 1967
- Kick out the jams, Motherfuckers — MC5 *Kick Out The Jams*, 1968
- Myra Breckinridge is a dish, and never forget it, you motherfuckers, as the children say nowadays. — Gore Vidal, *Myra Breckenridge*, 1968
- CARRY ON MOTHERFUCKERS — Richard Neville, *Play Power*, p. 13, 1970
- About that time motherfucker came into style – it came down from black Harlem in a game called "the dozens." — Edwin Torres, *Carlito's Way*, p. 10, 1975
- On the other hand, in the Airborne, the term "motherfucker" unless spoken harshly, was among the highest terms of endearment. — David H. Hackworth, *About Face*, p. 510, 1989
- Check out the big brain on Brett. You a smart motherfucker, that's right, the metric system. — *Pulp Fiction*, 1994
- When [the Las Angeles riot] spread to Beverly Hills, the police started beating motherfuckers. — *Jabberrock [quoting Snoop Doggy Dogg, 1995]*, p. 65, 1997

3 a difficult thing or situation *US, 1958*
- Oh shit me! I wish I was back in Memphis now, ooh baby this is gonna be a motherfucker! — *Platoon*, 1986

4 used as a basis for extreme comparisons *US, 1962*
- [I]'m ready to dance like a motherfucker and I see everything nothing at once and I don't hear music[.] — Mike Benson, *Room full of Angels (Disco Biscuits)*, p. 24, 1996
- We can see for a hundred miles, it's hotter than a motherfucker, and there's not a smidgen of sign. — Rad Miller Jr, *Whattaya Mean I Can't Kill 'Em?*, p. 180, 1998
- Yo, your pop grovvier-than-a-motherfucker. — Paul Beatty, *Tuff*, p. 36, 2000
- Damn, girl, it is hotter than a motherfucker up in here. — Dr Dre, *Bar One*, 2001
- Strange was higher than a motherfucker by the time he finished his beer and could muster no bad will toward anyone. — George Pelecanos, *Hard Revolution*, p. 207, 2004

5 methamphetamine hydrochloride, a powerful central nervous system stimulant *US*
- — Peter Johnson, *Dictionary of Street Alcohol and Drug Terms*, 1993

motherfuckers and beans *noun*
canned beans and frankfurters served as field rations by the US Army *US, 1980*
- — *Maledicta*, p. 255, Summer/Winter 1982: 'Viet-speak'

mother-fucking *noun*
sexual intercourse between a son and his mother *UK*
The literal sense which precedes the rest.
- These women are usually fat with grey hair and tightly packed into puce or black stretch-velour dresses. A man would have to be seriously into mother-fucking to want any of them. — Fiona Pitt-Kethley, *Red Light Districts of the World*, p. 73, 2000

motherfucking *adjective*
used as an emphatic intensifier *US, 1897*
In 1972, the US Supreme Court found the statements 'mother fucking facist pig cops' and 'god damned mother fucking police' to be constitionally protected speech.The following year, the California Supreme embraced 'white motherfucking pig' as constitutionally protected.
- I go 3,000 motherfucking miles, sleep on railroad porches, in Slavation flops, eat out of cans – in Hickey, N.C. — Jack Kerouac, *Letter to John Clellon Holmes*, p. 381, 12th October 1952
- I lived with them all, one right after the mother-fucking other. — John Rechy, *City of Night*, p. 177, 1963
- You ain't nothin but an old supid God damn fool, motherfucking asshole! — Bobby Seale, *A Lonely Rage*, p. 24–25, 1978
- [Y]ou think you are gonna be a megastar and you start acting like this motherfucking cunt. — Shaun Ryder, *Shaun Ryder... in His Own Words*, 1997

motherfucking A!
used for expressing dismay, surprise or strong assent *US*
An embellished **FUCKING A!**.
- "Now you a fuckin' de-tective?" Valetin almost shouted back. The two men were leaning forward, their faces almost touching. "Mother-fuckin'-A right." — Edwin Torres, *Q & A*, p. 40, 1977

motherfugger *noun*
used as a euphemism for 'motherfucker' *US*
- — Norman Mailer, *The Naked and the Dead*, 1948

motherfugging *adjective*
used as a euphemism for 'motherfucking' *US*
Found throughout Norman Mailer, *The Naked and the Dead*, 1948.

motherfukka *noun*
a fellow, a person *UK*
A variant spelling of **MOTHERFUCKER**.
- ['E]y, chill, you Jamaican motherfukka! We jus' dancing wiv ve bitch. — Ben Elton, *High Society*, p. 109, 2002

mothergrabbing *adjective*
used as a euphemism for 'motherfucking' *US, 1958*
- [S]erving (i.e. in films and on TV programs) what he describes as "three mother-grabbin' years." — *Time*, p. 48, 28th June 1963

Mother Green *nickname*
the US Marine Corps *US, 1978*
Coined in Vietnam; sometimes embellished to 'Mother Green and her Killing Machine'.
- — Gregory Clark, *Words of the Vietnam War*, p. 129, 1990

motherhopper *noun*
used as a euphemism for 'motherfucker' *US*
- Maybe they're gonna set me up. Mother hopper. — Edwin Torres, *Q & A*, p. 183, 1977

Mother Hubbard *noun*
a cupboard *UK*
Rhyming slang, formed from a nursery rhyme character.
- Cor, look at the mods on that[.] — Ray Puxley, *Cockney Rabbit*, 1992

motherhugger *noun*
used as a euphemism for 'motherfucker' *US*
- Uptown a whore was a whore; a pimp was a pimp; a dike was a dike; a mother-hugger was a mother-hugger. — Billie Holiday, *Lady Sings the Blues*, p. 101, 1956

motherhumper *noun*
used as a clumsy euphemism for 'motherfucker' *US, 1963*
- The motherhumpers who were wrong, stupid, vulgar, shallow, wrong, wrong, wrong, mothersucking bastards always had it. — Cecil Brown, *The Life & Loves of Mr. Jiveass Nigger*, p. 199, 1969

motherin *noun*
▷ see: **MOTHEREN**

mothering *adjective*
used as an intensifier *US, 1951*
From **MOTHERFUCKING**.

mother-in-law *noun*
1 an enemy aeroplane *US*
- "Mother-in-law at sixteen hundred," Charbonnet responded, referring to bogies approaching from the four o'lock position. — Joe Weber, *Defcon One*, p. 268, 1991

2 a carpenter's saw *UK*
Rhyming slang.
- — Ray Puxley, *Cockney Rabbit*, p. 127, 1992

3 a torn cuticle *BARBADOS*
- — Frank A. Collymore, *Barbadian Dialect*, p. 75, 1965

mother-in-law job *noun*
a racehorse that performs well in long-distance races *AUSTRALIA*
The long-distance horse has staying power, and like a mother-in-law seems to stay forever.
- — Ned Wallish, *The Truth Dictionary of Racing Slang*, p. 53, 1989

motherjumper *noun*
used as an affected euphemism for 'motherfucker' *US*
- "So what?" I said to Chink. "That motherjumper ought to get caught." — Hal Ellson, *Duke*, p. 140, 1949
- "David baby," he yelled happily, throwing out his arms, "you old benevolent motherjumper, I love you." — Richard Farina, *Been Down So Long*, p. 107, 1966
- I wanna tell ya I'm here – you bunch of motherjumpers. — Piri Thomas, *Down These Mean Streets*, p. ix, 1967

motherjumping *adjective*
used as a euphemism for 'motherfucking' *US*
- Them mother-jumping Roaches are in the club room busting it up! — Hal Ellson, *Tomboy*, p. 104, 1950
- He said, "The mother-jumping bastards." — Thurston Scott, *Cure it with Honey*, 1951
- I put them packages next to you, you mother-jumping thief! — Hal Ellson, *The Golden Spike*, p. 19, 1952

Mother Kelly *noun*
1 jelly; a jelly *UK*
Rhyming slang, probably formed from the music hall song 'On Mother Kelly's Doorstep'.
- This vicious looking dog came bounding towards me barking its head off. Well, my legs turned to Mother Kelly. — Ray Puxley, *Cockney Rabbit*, 1992

2 television; a television *UK*
Rhyming slang for **TELLY**, noted as 'more recent' than the previous sense.
- — Ray Puxley, *Cockney Rabbit*, 1992

motherless *adverb*
absolutely, completely; especially in the phrase 'motherless broke' (penniless) *AUSTRALIA, 1898*
- Many farmers are rich in assets but are stone motherless broke. — Mr Clough (Bathurst) *New South Wales Legislative Assembly Hansard*, 27th October 1994

motherless broke *adjective*
completely broke; bankrupt; destitute *AUSTRALIA, 1898*
- He came back, anyway, motherless broke, as he said himself. — Olaf Ruhen, *Naked Under Capricorn*, p. 223, 1958

mother lover *noun*
used as a euphemism for 'motherfucker' *US, 1950*
- He raps me across the back. "Stand straight, you little mother-lover," he says. — Rocky Garciano (with Rowland Barber), *Somebody Up There Likes Me*, p. 202, 1955
- Explain this to me, you hairy-backed mother-lover. — *Ministry*, p. 30, May 2002

mother loving *adjective*
used as a euphemism for 'motherfucking' *US, 1951*
Also used as an infix: 'abso-mother-lovin'-lutely!'.
- Hydrogen fuel, it burns so clean, / throbs in the veins; a mother lovin' machine. — Bette Midler, *Oh Industry*, 1988

motherlumping *adjective*
used as a euphemism for the intensifier 'motherfucking' *US*
- I feel like sayin, Baby way you go off, you musta been saving that one for a mothahlumpin lifetime. —Robert Gover, *One Hundred Dollar Misunderstanding*, p. 36, 1961

mother McCree!
used for expressing disapproval *US*
A signature line of Colonel Sherman Potter on *M*A*S*H* (CBS, 1972–83). Repeated with referential humour.

mother nature *noun*
marijuana *US*
- Hey you smoking Mother Nature! / This is a bust— The Who, *We're Not Gonna Take it*, 1969

mother nature's gift *noun*
the bleed period of the menstrual cycle *US*
- —Karen Houppert, *The Curse*, 1999

Mother Nature's maracas *noun*
the testicles *UK*
- —Richard Herring, *Talking Cock*, p. 30, 2003

mother of all *adjective*
an epic, if not the epic, example *US*
From Saddam Hussein's somewhat hyperbolic prediction that the western invasion of the Persian Gulf in 1991 would be the 'mother of all battles'. Hussein's use of a common Arabic vernacular expression immediately appealed to the American and British ear, with hundreds of variations appearing over several years – 'the mother of all retreats', 'the mother of all confirmation hearings', 'the mother of all eclipses', 'the mother of all government mistakes', etc.
- Saddam Hussein said the war would be "the mother of all battles." Reporters hailed Gen. Norman Schwarzkopf's press briefing as "the mother of all briefings." Oh, brother. — *The Detroit News*, 4th March 1991
- A year ago, when Saddam Hussein predicted the Gulf War would be the "mother of all battles," little did he know what was to follow. Everyone, it seems, has jumped on the "mother of all" bandwagon. — *Los Angeles Times*, p. E1, 29th January 1992
- —Connie Eble (Editor), *UNC-CH Campus Slang*, p. 4, Fall 1993
- [Y]ou looking for the mother of all smacks in the 'ead or what. —Mark Steel, *Reasons to be Cheerful*, p. 209, 2001

mother of God *noun*
LSD *UK*
- —Mike Haskins, *Drugs*, p. 285, 2003

mother of pearl *noun*
cocaine *US*
- DEALER: Hey, man. You wanna cop some blow? / JUNKIE: Sure, watcha got? Dust, flakes or rocks? / DEALER: I got China White, Mother of Pearl...I reflect what you need. —Grandmaster Flash & The Furious Five featuring Melle Mel, *White Lines*, 1983
- Then I remembered the two grams of pure crystal cocaine I had stashed somewhere in the lining of my jacket – two grams of mother of pearl! —Lanre Fehintola, *Charlie Says...*, p. 31, 2000

▸ **the old mother of pearl; my old mother of pearl**
a wife; my wife *UK*
Rhyming slang for 'old girl'.
- —Julian Franklyn, *A Dictionary of Rhyming Slang*, 1960
- —Ray Puxley, *Cockney Rabbit*, 1992

mother of shit!
used for registering surprise, rage, etc *US*
Variation on the prayer 'Mother of Christ'.
- [T]he two cops run into the clearing, guns raised. Seeing the Jocks, they stop. MCCORD: Mother of Shit!. MILNER: Call in! —*Heathers*, 1988

mother-raper *noun*
used as a euphemism for 'motherfucker' *US*
Intended as a euphemism, but one which does not leave much room for the affectionate side of **MOTHERFUCKER**.
- Once he said 'the little one' but mostly he used the word mother-raper which Harlemites apply to everybody, enemies, friends and strangers. —Chester Himes, *The Real Cool Killers*, p. 104, 1959
- The Mississippi voice said furiously: "Goddamn stupid mother-raper!" —Chester Himes, *Cotton Comes to Harlem*, p. 9, 1965

mother-raping *adjective*
used as a euphemism for 'motherfucking' *US, 1932*
- [T]hinking of how he could drive that goddam DeSoto taxicab straight off the mother-raping earth. —Chester Himes, *A Rage in Harlem*, p. 17, 1957
- THE NEW WHITE STRIPES ALBUM SUCKS, YOU SHIT LICKING, SCUM FUCKING MOTHER RAPING ASSHOLES — *Dumb Ass and the Fag (On-line Comic)*, 10th April 2003

mother-robbing *adjective*
used as a euphemism for 'motherfucking' *US*
- When we came out I discovered some mother-robbin' bastard had broken into my car window and taken my horn. —Wingy Manone, *Trumpet on the Wing*, p. 237, 1948

mothers and lovers *noun*
a very small crowd at a competition *AUSTRALIA*
- —Ned Wallish, *The Truth Dictionary of Racing Slang*, p. 54, 1989

motherscratcher *noun*
used as a euphemism for 'motherfucker' *US*
- —Don R. McCreary (Editor), *Dawg Speak*, 2001

mother's day *noun*
1 payday *US, 1965*
Because on payday you pay the money you owe to one mother(fucker) after another.
- — *Current Slang*, p. 17, Summer 1970

2 the day when welfare cheques arrive *US*
- —Malachi Andrews and Paul T. Owens, *Black Language*, p. 51, 1973
- —James Harris, *A Convict's Dictionary*, 1989

motherseller *noun*
used as a euphemism for 'motherfucker' *US*
- Cattle Baron, Oil King, and Mother Seller (Headline)— *Esquire*, p. 6, June 1953

mother's little helper *noun*
1 any tranquillzer; meprobamate (trade names Equanjill™, Meprospan™ and Miltown™), a habit-forming antianxiety agent *US*
- Mother needs something today to calm her down / And though she's not really ill / There's a little yellow pill / She goes running for the shelter of a mother's little helper / And it helps her on her way, gets her through her busy day— Jagger/Richards, *Mother's Little Helper*, 1966
- —Donald Wesson and David Smith, *Barbiturates*, p. 122, 1977

2 amphetamines *UK*
- —Mike Haskins, *Drugs*, p. 279, 2003

mother's pride *noun*
a bride *UK*
Rhyming slang, possibly influenced by Mother's Pride™, a popular brand of sliced bread.
- —Ray Puxley, *Cockney Rabbit*, 1992

mother's ruin; mothers *noun*
gin *UK, 1937*
Some claims have been made that this should be noted as a piece of rhyming slang; the rhyme is certainly slurred enough for gin to be an influence.
- [N]ame your poison / pick a flavour / Moonshine, firewater, Captain Morgan, Johnnie Walker, / Southern Comfort, mother's ruin, happy hours of homeless brewing[.] —Carter The Unstoppable Sex Machine *Anytime, Anyplace, Anywhere*, 1992

Mother Superior *noun*
an older, experienced homosexual man *US, 1941*
- —Dale Gordon, *The Dominion Sex Dictionary*, 1967

mother wit *noun*
common sense *US*
- —David Claerbaut, *Black Jargon in White America*, p. 73, 1972

motion lotion *noun*
motor fuel *US*
- — *Complete CB Slang Dictionary*, 1976
- —Peter Chippindale, *The British CB Book*, p. 157, 1981

motions *noun*
▸ **go through the motions**
to give the appearance of doing something, without actually doing it, or without doing it wholeheartedly; to conform to social expectations for the sake of appearances *UK, 1816*

• Solicitors go through the motions of doing an environmental search on your property[.]— *The Guardian*, 24th November 2002

motivate *verb*

to leave *US, 1955*

• — Connie Eble (Editor), *UNC-CH Campus Slang*, p. 6, Fall 1987

moto *noun*

a motivated self-starter *US*

• — *Washington Post*, 14th October 1993

▷ **see: MOTA**

motor *noun*

a *motor* car *UK*

• — Alexei Sayle, *Ullo John, Got a New Motor?*, 1984
• We look so fuckin' suspect, the sounds [music], the motor, the shades. We look like a fuckin' decoy. — J.J. Connolly, *Know Your Enemy [britpulp]*, p. 151, 1999

motor *verb*

1 to perform a task very well *UK*

• "We really are motoring," executives are telling one another. — *The Observer*, 20th March 1989

2 to leave *US, 1980*

• — Connie Eble (Editor), *UNC-CH Campus Slang*, p. 6, Fall 1987
• I'm going to have to motor if I want to be ready for the funeral tomorrow. — Heathers, 1988
• Let's motor. Be cool. — Jess Mowry, *Way Past Cool*, p. 15, 1992

Motor City *nickname*

Detroit, Michigan *US*

Because of the car manufacturing concerns in Detroit.

• Man, I'll lay it back on you as soon as we pay off in Motor City. — Ross Russell, *The Sound*, p. 135, 1961
• At six p.m. we reached the motor city. — A.S. Jackson, *Gentleman Pimp*, p. 55, 1973

motor crap *noun*

car parts made by Motorcraft, a Ford subsidiary *US*

• — Lewis Poteet, *Car & Motorcyle Slang*, p. 133, 1992

motored out *adjective*

said of a scoring device in pinball which fails to register a score because the scoring register is already in use *US*

• — Bobbye Claire Natkin and Steve Kirk, *All About Pinball*, p. 113, 1977

motorhead *noun*

1 a person with more than a passing interest in the internal combustion engine *US, 1974*

• — Marcel Danesi, *Cool*, p. 58, 1994

2 a fool *US, 1973*

• What the hell do you want me to do, motorhead? — *The Blues Brothers*, 1980

motormouth *noun*

someone who talks without end, or when it would be better not to talk *US, 1963*

• That motormouth better put a hat on when he goes outside else he'll get a sunburned tongue. — Ken Weaver, *Texas Crude*, p. 118, 1984
• Courtney [Love] has motormouth trouble. (Juvenile hall social worker's report, 1978) — *Q*, p. 85, December 2001
• At which Motor-Mouth, true to form, completely ignored her husband's mild protest and giggled: "James Bond! I can see it!" — *The Guardian*, p. 3, 12th June 2003

motor mouth *verb*

to talk incessantly *US*

• The drunk also started screaming about suing for false arrest and police brutality until Prankster Frank got a headache from all the motor-mouthing. — Joseph Wambaugh, *The Secrets of Harry Bright*, p. 66, 1985

motor scooter *noun*

used as a euphemism for 'motherfucker' *US*

• He rides through the jungle tearing limbs off of trees / Alley-oop / Knocking great big monsters dead on their knees / Alley-oop / The cats don't bug him coz they know better / Alley-oop / Coz he's a mean motor-scooter and a bad go-getter. — (Dallas Frazier) The Hollywood Argyles, *Alley-Oop*, 1960

motorsickle *noun*

▷ **see: SICKLE**

motorway *noun*

(when skiing) a broad, easy piste *UK*

• — Ann Barr and Peter York, *The Official Sloane Ranger Handbook*, p. 124, 1982

motorway draw *noun*

marijuana *UK*

Extends **DRAW** (marijuana).

• [G]oing over to the pinball machine and rolling a big chunky spliff [joint] on the glass [...] going out front to smoke his motorway draw on one of the benches[.] — John King, *White Trash*, p. 194, 2001

Motown *noun*

Detroit, Michigan *US, 1971*

After **MOTOR CITY**, thus *'motor town'* from Detroit's motor industry.

motser; motzer; motza *noun*

a large sum of money *AUSTRALIA, 1936*

Presumed to be from Yiddish *matse* (bread): **BREAD** (money). Especially used of gambling winnings.

• — Jim Ramsay, *Cop It Sweet!*, p. 60, 1977

mott *noun*

the female genitalia *UK*

From **MOT** (a woman).

• "Her great big, hairy mott", in a mock-Irish accent was a pun on the insect moth. — Beale (remembering his mid-C20 National Service), 1984

mottled *adjective*

drunk *UK*

• — *e-cyclopaedia*, 20th March 2002

Mott the Hoople *noun*

a scruple *UK*

Rhyming slang, formed from the British rock band of the late 1960s and early 70s.

• [H]e starts thinking what I needs a nice little Tina Turner [earner] [...] Now, having no Mott the Hooples [...] he goes out when it's a bit Dave Clark, dark. — *Getting Nowhere Fast*, 21st May 2004

mouldy *adjective*

drunk *IRELAND*

• As darkness falls, they all pour into the pubs and get mouldy drunk — *Irish Times*, 3rd October 1996

mouldy fig *noun*

a very dull person; specifically, used by young supporters of modern jazz of any jazz aficionado who remains loyal to a traditional form *US, 1945*

• — Robert George Reisner, *The Jazz Titans*, p. 161, 1960

Moulin Rouge *noun*

a stooge (a comedian's assistant) *UK*

Theatrical rhyming slang.

• The late Monsewer Eddie Gray, in drag as a gypsy clairvoyant, used to invite questions from the audience... more accurately, planted Moulin Rouges – stooges. — Red Daniells, 1980

moulonjohn *noun*

▷ **see: MULENYAM**

mouly *noun*

a black person *US*

• Us Italian boys got to stick together or the spics 'n' the moulys here will be runnin' everything. — *New Jack City*, 1990

mount *noun*

in hot rodding, a driver's car *US*

A deliberate and jocular borrowing from horse racing.

• — *Hot Rod Magazine*, p. 13, November 1948: 'Racing jargon'

mount *verb*

▸ **mount the red flag**

to have sex with a woman experiencing the bleed period of the menstrual cycle *US*

• — Robert A. Wilson, *Playboy's Book of Forbidden Words*, p. 176, 1972

mountain canary *noun*

a mule *US*

• — Jim Crotty, *How to Talk American*, p. 216, 1997

mountain dew *noun*

1 whisky, distilled illegally *UK, 1816*

• — Ralph de Sola, *Crime Dictionary*, p. 96, 1982
• — Nick Brownlee, *This Is Alcohol*, p. 164, 2002

2 rum, distilled illegally *TRINIDAD AND TOBAGO, 1926*

• — Lise Winer, *Dictionary of the English/Creole of Trinidad & Tobago*, 2003

mountain goat *noun*

1 **a comic who made his name in the Borscht Belt and then came to New York clubs to perform** *US*

• —Sherman Louis Sergel, *The Language of Show Biz*, p. 141, 1973

2 **a coat** *UK*

Glasgow rhyming slang.

• Ah'm pittin oan ma mountain goat, case it gets hillbilly [chilly] later. —Michael Munro, *The Patter, Another Blast*, 1988

mountain oysters *noun*

lamb or calf testicles as food *US, 1857*

• If I was having special company, I might make up a delicacy. You get some money, you can get mountain oysters – that's the male parts of a lamb. —Earl Conrad, *Rock Bottom*, p. 246, 1952

• In the commissariat department are "dope" (butter) and "mountain oysters" (calves fries). —*Alberta Historical Review*, p. 15/2, 1962

• —David McGill, *David McGill's Complete Kiwi Slang Dictionary*, p. 73, 1998

mountain passes *noun*

spectacles, *glasses* *UK*

Rhyming slang.

• —Julian Franklyn, *A Dictionary of Rhyming Slang*, 1960

• —Ray Puxley, *Cockney Rabbit*, 1992

mountain pay *noun*

working on the railways, overtime *US*

• —Ramon Adams, *The Language of the Railroader*, p. 102, 1977

Mountie *nickname*

1 **a member of the Royal Canadian Mounted Police (the Mounties)** *CANADA, 1914*

A colloquial term in such widespread use, especially via films (and the slogan: 'The Mounties always get their man'), that it is often accepted as conventional.

• Nevertheless, publishers have yet to be convinced that an interesting book can be written about the land of moose and Mounties. "You mention Canada, and their faces go ashen," he [Bill Bryson] said. —*The Guardian*, 2nd June 2003

2 **a student of the prestigious all-girl Dublin secondary school, Mount Anville** *IRELAND*

• I spot Fionn chatting up Fiona, this Mountie who all the goys say is SO thick she carries ID around just to, like, remind her of her name. —Paul Howard, *Ross O'Carroll-Kelly*, p. 193, 2003

mouse *noun*

1 **a bruise** *US, 1842*

• My bed was next to the door so the first thing he saw was the mouse on my cheek. —Robert Gover, *Poorboy at the Party*, p. 54, 1966

• He glanced from the wounded man to Phillips, who had a mouse under one eye. —Leonard Shecter and William Phillips, *On the Pad*, p. 93, 1973

• Nelson had a mouse under his eye and his shirt was almost torn from his body. —Joseph Wambaugh, *Fugitive Nights*, p. 305, 1992

2 **in the used car business, a customer or potential customer** *US*

• —*Esquire*, p. 118, March 1968

3 **the soldier on point in the front of a patrol** *US*

• —Linda Reinberg, *In the Field*, p. 145, 1991

mouse *verb*

to blackmail someone *UK*

• —*Maledicta*, p. 144, Summer/Winter 1986–1987: 'Sexual slang: prostitutes, pedophiles, flagellators, transvestites, and necrophiles'

mouse droppings *noun*

in computing, single pixels on a computer screen that do not reappear when the cursor of the mouse is moved away from the spot *US*

• —Eric S. Raymond, *The New Hacker's Dictionary*, p. 247, 1991

mouse house *noun*

1 **a finance company** *US*

• —*American Speech*, p. 312, Autumn-Winter 1975: 'The jargon of car salesmen'

2 **in the used car business, an enterprise that compartmentalises the different functions in the sales process** *US*

• Mouse houses, also called turnover houses or mills, constitute not more than five percent of the 30,000 franchised dealerships[.] —*Esquire*, p. 119, March 1968

mouse motor *noun*

a small-block Chevrolet V-8 engine *US*

Introduced in 1955, it was relatively small for its power.

• —John Edwards, *Auto Dictionary*, p. 110, 1993

mousetrap *noun*

1 **any strong or inferior hard cheese** *UK, 1947*

From the use of such cheeses to bait mousetraps.

• Monkland Cheese Dairy which sells its own and others' cheeses as Mousetrap Cheese[.] —*The Guardian*, 24th May 2003

2 **a series of exit consoles on websites that link back on themselves, creating an infinite loop** *US*

• The latest tactic used by smut peddlers targeting children on the internet is the pop-up mouse trap, said Hansesn. —*Salt Lake Tribune*, p. B1, 2nd November 2003

3 **in oil drilling, a type of tool used to retrieve objects inadvertently dropped down a hole** *US*

• —Jerry Robertson, *Oil Slanguage*, p. 85, 1954

mousetrap *verb*

to ambush an enemy by drawing them into position with some sort of bait *US*

• This was to prevent a patrol from being "mousetrapped," with rescue forces, in turn, becoming entrapped. —Eric Hammel, *Khe Sanh*, p. 154, 1989

mouth *noun*

1 **back-talk, insults** *UK, 1896*

• I used to give Silky mouth. In Ottawa, you could tell pimps shit. I've learned not to talk back to Silky. —Susan Hall, *Gentleman of Leisure*, p. 164, 1972

2 **a dry or furry mouth caused by too much eating or drinking** *UK, 1937*

Often elaborated on the formula a 'mouth like...' – recorded examples vary from 'the bottom of a bird cage' to 'the inside of a Turkish wrestler's jockstrap'.

3 **a play's reputation** *US*

• —Sherman Louis Sergel, *The Language of Show Biz*, p. 141, 1973

▸ **give off a lot of mouth**

to shout abuse *UK*

• A Paki geezer was giving off a lot of mouth[.] — Martin King and Martin Knight, *The Naughty Nineties*, p. 146, 1999

▸ **have a mouth like a cow's cunt**

to be excessively or indiscreetly talkative *UK*

An exaggerated variation of **BIG MOUTH**, reported by Julian Franklyn, 1967.

▸ **in the mouth**

in poker, said of the first player to act in a given situation *US*

• —John Scarne, *Scarne's Guide to Modern Poker*, p. 281, 1979

▸ **with his mouth wide open**

said of a racehorse that easily wins a race *US*

• —David W. Maurer, *Argot of the Racetrack*, p. 69, 1951

mouth *verb*

to inform on someone to the police *US*

• Instead of throwing it away, he tried to sell it, and he got bused – and he mouthed on everybody he knew. —Claude Brown, *Manchild in the Promised Land*, p. 154, 1965

mouth and trousers *noun*

a braggart *UK*

• So old mouth and trousers gets dressed up like a Jamaican pimp and goes floating round Bermondsey like he owned the place. —John Milne, *Alive and Kicking*, 1998

mouth bet *noun*

in poker, a bet made without putting up the funds, binding among friends *US, 1889*

• —Irwin Steig, *Common Sense in Poker*, p. 185, 1963

mouth breather *noun*

a fool *UK, 1986*

• [W]e have a good ol' laugh at some of the idiot mouth-breathers you'll be meeting in Freshers' Week[.] —*Ministry*, p. 7, October 2002

mouthful *noun*

1 **a word or phrase that is difficult to speak (for reasons of complexity or length, not content)** *UK, 1883*

• Then there's Penny Lancaster, who admits to calling Rod Stewart "Daddy." We can only hope that the nickname came about because "Sugar Daddy" is a bit of a mouthful. —*The Guardian*, 30th October 2003

2 something spoken which has importance or other significance *US, 1916*
From earlier use as 'a long word'.
- "She gave you a mouthful there Smokey," the others laughed. — Joe Morgan, *Eastenders Don't Cry*, p. 59, 1994

▸ give a mouthful
to swear or be otherwise verbally abusive to someone *US, 1941*
- Just before the incident that led to his red card, the linesman had missed a couple of offsides and Matt [Bradford] gave him a mouthful which you just can't do. — *Sutton Guardian*, 5th December 2003

mouth music *noun*
oral sex on a woman *UK*
Noted, with distaste, by David Powis, *The Signs of Crime*, 1977.

mouth off *verb*
to brag; to insult *US, 1958*
Derives from the synonymous verb.
- [R]unning with a mob, throwing the odd punch, mouthing off, running from a mob[.] — Irvine Welsh, *The Naughty Nineties*, p. 10, 1999

mouth open, story jump out
used for explaining why something that was perhaps better unsaid was said *TRINIDAD AND TOBAGO, 1988*
- — Lise Winer, *Dictionary of the English/Creole of Trinidad & Tobago*, 2003

mouthpiece *noun*
1 a lawyer *UK, 1857*
- He went up for a hearing and the judge appointed two more attorneys to the case, and these mouthpieces finally made a deal with the D.A. — Mezz Mezzrow, *Really the Blues*, p. 268, 1946
- "The flagrantly provocational role played by Det,-Constable Silver" gave his mouthpiece something to bite on[.] — Charles Raven, *Underworld Nights*, p. 99, 1956
- "He's out of town, but he's the best mouthpiece fixer in Chi." — Iceberg Slim (Robert Beck), *Long White Con*, p. 179, 1977
- TILLEY: You got a high-priced mouthpiece to speak for ya? BB: I don't need one. I don't expect to win. — *Tin Men*, 1987

2 a spokesperson *UK, 1805*
- Clifford C. H. Tavernier, close to Dawson, is the present Bronzeville mouthpiece. — Jack Lait and Lee Mortimer, *Chicago Confidential*, p. 46, 1950

mouth pig *noun*
a male homosexual who offers his mouth anonymously to any penis that is presented through a glory hole *US*
- Mouth pigs are glory hole faggots. Cocksuckers. Made, not born. Male. — Peter Sotos, *Index*, p. 24, 1996

mouthwashing; mouthwash *noun*
a non-conventional method of drinking Cointreau™ (a branded liqueur) *UK*
See citation for detail, also used as a verb.
- People are creating there own mixes and methods (gun-shots, snorting or mouthwashing anyone?)[...] Swill it around the mouth for 10 seconds, swallow and then immediately suck in a huge breath. One to only do sitting down! — *Sky Magazine*, p. 88, May 2001

mouthy *adjective*
loquacious, too talkative *UK, 1589*
- [F]ootball tends to bring out the mouthy git in me. — Frank Skinner, *Frank Skinner*, p. 81, 2001

move *noun*

▸ get a move on
to hurry *US, 1888*
Often as an imperative.
- Where have you been? We've got to get a move on. — *Slacker*, 1992

▸ on the move
about to commit a crime, especially a burglary *UK*
- — Angela Devlin, *Prison Patter*, p. 82, 1996

▸ put the move on
to make sexual advances *US*
- I'm wondering what to do if he does try to put the moves on me. — Jim Carroll, *Forced Entries*, p. 27, 1987

move *verb*
to sell, especially in bulk *US, 1938*
- Ex-pimp. Moved a couple of ounces, supposed to be a big shot. — Edwin Torres, *After Hours*, p. 190, 1979
- Though the 'vette would be easier to move. Get some plates off another car, drive up to Atlanta, and unload it. — Elmore Leonard, *Stick*, p. 67, 1983
- We gotta move these refrigerators / We gotta move these colour TV's. — Dire Straits, *Money for Nothing*, 1985
- All I need is for you to keep bringing the stuff. I've gut a guy in here from Pittsburgh who'll move it for me. — *Goodfellas*, 1990
- Henry Santoro and Frankie Fish are moving weight in Florida. — *Gone in 60 Seconds*, 2000

▸ get moving
to urgently begin to do or go *UK, 1963*
- Once it was confirmed, after all that delay, I really wanted to get moving[.] — *The Observer*, 3rd March 2002

▸ move the line
in sports betting, to change the point spread that is the basis for betting on one team or the other *US*
- When the guys at the Amorita Club noticed how I was winning they paid me the compliment of favoring the side that I liked. That is, they would move the line. — Jimmy Snyder, *Jimmy the Greek*, p. 28, 1975

▸ move under an ashen sail
to row a boat *CANADA, 1975*
As paddles are often made out of ash wood, to say 'he's moving under an ashen sail' is a jocular way of saying that he is not sailing, but rowing.

move in *verb*
in poker, to bet your entire bankroll *US*
- — John Scarne, *Scarne's Guide to Modern Poker*, p. 284, 1979

movement *noun*
collectively the various organisations fighting for social justice and peace in the US in the 1960s *US*
- The Berkeley "Movement" designs, builds, set, and springs a vicious trap on itself. (Letter to the Editor) — *The Berkeley Barb*, p. 10, 6th May 1966
- He says everybody, including movement people, is completely hung up with status. — James Simon Kunen, *The Strawberry Statement*, p. 93, 1968
- [S]o for a nine-month year it ain't been bad, especially since the in-fighting between movement groups and factions had reached grating proportions. — Abbie Hoffman, *Woodstock Nation*, p. 11, 1969
- Ever since Ed and I have been active in the Movement we've always carried our guns. — H. Rap Brown, *Die Nigger Die!*, p. 81, 1969
- [T]here was a businessman from suburban New Jersey who got $10 plus expenses for attending Movement meetings. — J. Anthony Lukas, *The Barnyard Epithet and Other Obscenities*, p. 62, 1970
- Another man gets up, a white named Gerald Lefcourt, who is chief counsel for the Panther 21, a young man with thick black hair and the muttonchops of the Movement and that great motor inside of him that young courtroom lawyers ought to have. — Tom Wolfe, *Radical Chic & Mau-Mauing the Flak Catchers*, p. 25, 1970
- Everything in the movement, in the underground press, in fact in the whole city of Washington, D.C., changed for the better when she came. — Raymond Mungo, *Famous Long Ago*, p. 57, 1970

mover *noun*
1 someone who imports drugs *US*
- — Mark S. Fleisher, *Beggars & Thieves*, p. 290, 1995: 'Glossary'

2 a police ticket for a moving violation *US*
- Wish I could write a ticket. I haven't got a mover yet this month. — Joseph Wambaugh, *The New Centurions*, p. 293, 1970

3 in casino gambling, a dice cheat who places his bet after a roll has started *US*
- — Frank Garcia, *Marked Cards and Loaded Dice*, p. 263, 1962

mover and shaker *noun*
a powerful person with powerful connections *US, 1972*
- We have wax museums for historical people and show business people and sports people, but nary a thing for the movers and shakers of society. — Armistead Maupin, *Further Tales of the City*, p. 35, 1982
- — *American Speech*, Fall 1985
- Mayor Simmons became one of the movers and shakers in the state's political set up. — Odie Hawkins, *The Life and Times of Chester Simmons*, p. 172, 1991

moves *noun*
sexual advances *US, 1968*
Always used with 'the'.
- Nina, seeking "eternal pleasure," makes the moves on Paul thomas as this sex pro gladly teaches her all he knows. — *Adult Video*, p. 18, August/September 1986
- You know sooner or later he's going to make the moves on her, but you don't know what she's going to do. — Elmore Leonard, *Bandits*, p. 84, 1987

movie job *noun*
sex, especially sex for pay, in a cinema *US*
- "Movie jobs go for five dollars and that's too low," he said. — Johnny Shearer, *The Male Hustler*, p. 79, 1966

movies *noun*
police radar recordings of vehicle speed *US*
- —Bill Davis, *Jawjacking*, p. 66, 1977

movie star drug *noun*
cocaine *UK*
A reference to Hollywood's reputation for excess in the 1980s and 90s.
- —Mike Haskins, *Drugs*, p. 280, 2003

movin' *adjective*
good, pleasurable, fashionable, popular *US*
- —Vann Wesson, *Generation X Field Guide and Lexicon*, p. 114, 1997

moving doctor *noun*
a medical doctor *CANADA*
A jocular back-formation from the initials MD.
- Some [Canadian] MDs are Moving Doctors; they leave for the States immediately upon graduation from a Canadian medical school — *Toronto Globe and Mail*, p. D12, 3rd August 2002

mow *verb*
1 to shave *US*
Usually used in describing a woman shaving her legs or her pubic area.
- —Judi Sanders, *Don't Dog by Do, Dude!*, p. 21, 1991

2 to eat with gusto and stamina *US*
- —Trevor Cralle, *The Surfin'ary*, 1991
- —Judi Sanders, *Da Bomb*, p. 10, 1997

▸ **mow the grass; mow the lawn**
to smoke marijuana *UK, 1998*
Punning on **GRASS** (marijuana).
- —Mike Haskins, *Drugs*, p. 290, 2003

mowed lawn *noun*
a shaved vulva *US*
- —Roger Blake, *The American Dictionary of Sexual Terms*, p. 136, 1964
- —Robert A. Wilson, *Playboy's Book of Forbidden Words*, p. 176, 1972
- —*Maledicta*, p. 131, Summer/Winter 1982: 'Dyke diction: the language of lesbians'

mox; moxy *noun*
a homosexual man *UK*
Recorded in contemporary gay use.
- —*Attitude*, p. 60, July 2003: 'New palare lexicon'

moxen *noun*
a group of homosexual men *UK*
The plural of **MOX**, recorded in contemporary gay use.
- —*Attitude*, p. 60, July 2003: 'New palare lexicon'

moxie *noun*
nerve, courage, gall *US, 1930*
Moxie was the first mass marketed soft drink in the US. Founded in Lowell, Massachusetts in 1884 by Dr Augustin Thompson, Moxie was touted as a patent medicine guaranteed to cure almost any ill including loss of manhood, 'paralysis, and softening of the brain'. These claims were revised with the passage of the Pure Food and Drug Act in 1906. It's sphere of influence was largely in New England.
- But you never had the moxie to see what his world was really like. —Ross Russell, *The Sound*, p. 174, 1961
- Poor Williams was left holding the civic bag; he had taken a gutty stand, his image was all moxie[.] —Hunter S. Thompson, *Hell's Angels*, p. 209, 1966

moxy *adjective*
lousy, very bad *IRELAND*
- "Moxy," he says, describing an ancient performance which he rated somewhere between manky and poxy. "Yeah, moxy." —*Irish Times*, 2nd April 1999

Mozart and Liszt; Mozart *adjective*
drunk *UK, 1945*
Rhyming slang for **PISSED** (drunk).
- He became very elephant's trunk and Mozart [drunk][.] —Ronnie Barker, *Fletcher's Book of Rhyming Slang*, p. 26, 1979

mozz *noun*
bad luck; a jinx *AUSTRALIA, 1924*
A shortening of obsolete 'mozzle', from Hebrew *mazzal* (luck). Generally in the phrase 'to put the mozz on'.
- And that might put the mozz on you. —George Johnston, *My Brother Jack*, p. 274, 1964
- —Jim Ramsay, *Cop It Sweet!*, p. 60, 1977

mozz *verb*
to jinx someone; to bring bad luck to someone *AUSTRALIA, 1941*
- 'Don't mozz a man.' —Frank Hardy, *The Yarns of Billy Borker*, p. 107, 1965

mozzie; mozzy *noun*
▷ **see:** **MOSSIE**

mozzle *noun*
▸ **on the mozzle**
cadging, especially when seeking to borrow something small from a friend or neighbour *UK*
This derives from an obsolete piece of rhyming slang, 'mozzle and brocha' for **ON THE KNOCKER** (used of a door-to-door salesman); ultimately from Yiddish *mazel* (good luck) and *brocha* (a blessing).
- —Ray Puxley, *Cockney Rabbit*, 1992

Mr *and variants*
▷ **see:** **MISTER**

Mr Bates, Mr Mason, Mr Plod *nouns*
▷ **see:** **BATES, BENNY MASON, PLOD**

Mrs *noun*
▸ **the Mrs**
the vagina *UK, 2001*
The conventional abbreviation for 'mistress' meaning 'wife'; pronounced 'missis'.

▷ **see:** **MRS MORE**

Mrs Doyle *noun*
a boil *UK*
Rhyming slang, formed from the name of a character in UK Channel 4 television situation comedy *Father Ted*, 1995–98.
- —Ray Puxley, *Fresh Rabbit*, 1998

Mrs Duckett!
used as a general declaration of rejection or dimissal; may also imply resignation to, or acceptance of, a situation *UK*
Rhyming slang for **FUCK IT!**.
- —Julian Franklyn, *A Dictionary of Rhyming Slang*, 1960
- —Ray Puxley, *Cockney Rabbit*, 1992

Mrs Mop; Mrs Mopp *noun*
1 a woman who works as a cleaner, a charwoman *UK, 1948*
After a character introduced in the fourth series of the 1940s BBC radio comedy *ITMA*; Mrs Mopp, with the catchphrase 'Can I do you now, sir?', was played by Dorothy Summers.
- Looking back at Jane Root's dispatch of everything vaguely cultural on BBC2 [...], it's hard to avoid the conclusion that her appointment was always intended to be funereal – the Mrs Mopp of serious programming, paid to sweep the channel clean of whatever wasn't inconsequential — *The Guardian*, 20th November 2001

2 a shop *UK*
Rhyming slang. Also employed as a verb.
- —Ray Puxley, *Cockney Rabbit*, 1992

Mrs Mopping *noun*
shopping *UK*
Rhyming slang, extended from **MRS MOPP** (a shop).
- —Ray Puxley, *Cockney Rabbit*, 1992

Mrs More; the Mrs *noun*
a floor, the floor *UK*
Rhyming slang, from the music hall song 'Don't Have Any More, Mrs More'.
- One can walk on, sit on and, when drunk, fall on "the Mrs". —Ray Puxley, *Cockney Rabbit*, 1992

Mrs Palm and her five lovely daughters; Mrs Palmer and her five daughters *noun*
the hand (seen in the context of male masturbation) *AUSTRALIA, 1955*
- Old Mrs. Palm and her five flamin' daughters have been workin' overtime lately. —Barry Humphries, *Bazza Pulls It Off!*, 1971
- Oh, Mrs Palm and your five lovely daughters / Thank you for having me and being oh, so kind[.] —Ivor Biggun, *The Winker's Song (Misprint)*, 1978
- Bin shakin' hands with Mrs Palmer and her five daughters for fifty-eight months straight. —Kathy Lette, *Girls' Night Out*, p. 181, 1987

- [Y]ou're telling me they see no pussy for months at a time and they're going [to] be satisfied dating Mrs Palmer and her five daughters? —Harrison Biscuit, *The Search for Savage Henry*, p. 55, 1995

Mrs Ples *nickname*
the skull of an Australopithecine man-ape found at Sterkfontein in 1947 *SOUTH AFRICA, 1959*
Indicating the (possibly wrong) gender and his/her generic name *Ples*ianthropus.
- [H]andled, with white gloves, such famous fossils as "Mrs Ples": an almost complete skull of A. africanus[.] —Bruce Chatwin, *The Songlines*, p. 244, 1988
- We are putting these bones together to start seeing what Mrs Ples would have looked like. —*Sunday Times (South Africa)*, 12th August 2001

MSM *noun*
homosexual males *UK*
Initialism formed from '*m*en who have *s*ex with *m*en'.
- —David Rowan, *A Glossary for the 90s*, 1998

MTF *noun*
a very tactile admirer of young ladies *UK*
Initialism, '*m*ust *t*ouch *f*lesh'. Upper-class society usage.
- Female description of an octopus Sloane. —Ann Barr and Peter York, *The Official Sloane Ranger Handbook*, p. 159, 1982

M to F *adverb*
*M*onday *to F*riday *UK*
- —Angela Devlin, *Prison Patter*, p. 77, 1996

mu *noun*
1 marijuana *US, 1936*
- —Richard A. Spears, *The Slang and Jargon of Drugs and Drink*, p. 350, 1986
- —Mike Haskins, *Drugs*, p. 288, 2003

2 used for expressing the sentiment that 'your question cannot be answered because it depends on incorrect assumptions' *US*
A Japanese word borrowed by computer enthusiasts.
- —Eric S. Raymond, *The New Hacker's Dictionary*, p. 248, 1991

much *adverb*
used for ironic emphasis *US*
- God, Veronica, drool much? His name's Jason Dean. —*Heathers*, 1988
- Rude, much? —*Buffy the Vampire Slayer*, 1992

▸ **not much of a**
of limited quality, quantity or degree *UK, 1889*
- I'm not much of a muff diver, but I can strongly recommend that Kentucky cocktail of Sneaky Pete and strawberry juice. —*The Guardian*, 4th December 2003

▸ **not up to much**
inferior *UK, 1864*
- [H]e's simply not up to much as a manager. —*The Guardian*, 22nd April 2002

much more *adjective*
very good *US*
- —Connie Eble (Editor), *UNC-CH Campus Slang*, p. 6, Spring 1994

mucho *adjective*
much, a lot of *US, 1942*
A direct borrowing from Spanish.
- —Collin Baker et al., *College Undergraduate Slang Study Conducted at Brown University*, p. 160, 1968
- To them I say EAT MUCHO FUCK! —*Ask*, p. 46, 5th May 1979
- With what I'd done already – which apparently, although it amounted to no more than threatening violence, was mucho plenty[.] —Ken Lukowiak, *Marijuana Time*, p. 181, 2000

mucho *adverb*
very *US, 1973*
Directly from Spanish.

much of a muchness *noun*
very similar, of much the same degree, size, value, etc *UK, 1728*
- [Geoff] Dyer fumbles around the world in search of exotic experiences that prove to be much of a muchness. —*The Guardian*, 19th April 2003

muck *noun*
1 semen *UK*
- —*Roger's Profanisaurus*, December 1997
- Mario was very much in the dump-me-muck-and-turf-'em-out camp, whereas Arabella belonged to the doey-eyed-let's-have-a-cuddle-and-plan-the-rest-of-the-day-together school of thought. —Colin Butts, *Is Harry Still on the Boat?*, p. 107, 2003

2 any unpleasant, vile or disgusting thing to eat or drink *UK, 1882*
- If Norman thought she was going to eat this overpriced muck with a perfectly good cold supper waiting in the refrigerator at home and a decent programme on the telly, he could forget it. —P.D. James, *Devices & Desires*, p. 78, 1992

3 bad weather *UK, 1855*
- I've always appreciated knowing where I can get out of the muck and into better visibility. —Jerry A Eichenberger, *Cross-Country Flying*, p. 60, 1994

4 stage makeup *US, 1926*
- —Wilfred Granville, *The Theatre Dictionary*, p. 178, 1952
- —Paul Baker, *Polari*, p. 181, 2002

5 in poker, the pile of discarded cards *US*
- —Anthony Holden, *Big Deal*, p. 302, 1990

▸ **as muck**
very, exceedingly *UK, 1782*
Especially used in the phrase 'common as muck'.

▸ **make a muck of**
to ruin *UK, 1906*
- It was the great and the good, in the shape of the BBC governors, who made a muck of the Gilligan business. —*The Guardian*, 16th February 2004

muck *verb*
1 in poker, to fold, to discard your hand *UK*
- If you fold, you "muck", which is to say you put your cards with the discards. —Dave Scharf, *Winning at Poker*, p. 238, 2003

2 in a casino, to spread playing cards on the table and move them randomly as part of the shuffling process *US*
- —Victor H. Royer, *Casino Gamble Talk*, p. 89, 2003

muck about *verb*
1 to fool around; to trifle with *AUSTRALIA, 1946*
- Did you go mucking about with our things? Did you touch anything in them? —Nourma Handford, *Carcoola Holiday*, p. 150, 1953
- —Harvey E. Ward, *Down Under Without Blunder*, p. 42, 1967

2 to mess someone about *AUSTRALIA*
- And you are not going to muck the captain about. Is that clear? —John Wynnum, *Jiggin' in the Riggin'*, p. 114, 1965

3 to behave amorously towards *AUSTRALIA*
- I got no time for that young feller, but he wouldn't be off hunting with the bucks for days on end if he was mucking about with black girls. —Arthur Upfield, *Bony and the Mouse*, p. 58, 1959

muck-a-muck; muckety-muck *noun*
an important and prominent person *US, 1856*
- All the high mucky-mucks cussed and made fun of him for the way he'd cut up in politics. —Jim Thompson, *The Killer Inside*, p. 152, 1952
- Dames in the upper brackets, muck-a-mucks of dames, with upper bracket noses and knockers and legs and bank accounts. —Bernard Wolfe, *The Late Risers*, p. 48, 1954
- A lot of them are clean-cut high 'muckty mucks' in the white world. —Iceberg Slim (Robert Beck), *Pimp*, p. 176, 1969
- You big muckety-muck slab of- —Clarence Major, *All-Night Visitors*, p. 35, 1998

muck around; muck about *verb*
to fool around *UK, 1856*
- You better have the car while you're on leave. Can't be mucking around in trams! —Eric Lambert, *The Veterans*, p. 65, 1954
- It won't give him so much time to muck around with us if we c'n get right on deck. —W.R. Bennett, *Night Intruder*, p. 28, 1962
- I wouldn't muck around with any doubling round the upper deck. —John Wynnum, *Jiggin' in the Riggin'*, p. 11, 1965
- "Inspector Regan," Jack said, playing it by ear. "We're not mucking about, pig [a police officer]," a third spokesman called. —*The Sweeney*, p. 13, 1976
- Rebecca got jealous that I played wif Vanessa, but that's not fair cos I don't mind when she mucks around wif other kids. —Kylie Mole (Maryanne Fahey), *My Diary*, p. 29, 1988
- You certainly don't muck around, do you? —Shane Maloney, *Nice Try*, p. 104, 1998
- Why did you come here? he asks. – It's London, it's where it all happens. – Are you mucking? —Mark Powell, *Snap*, p. 152, 2001
- Truth be known, Dubya mucked around for most of his schooling, but this never worried anyone too much. —*The Big Issue*, p. 10, 2003

mucked up *adjective*
in disarray; confused; spoiled *US*
A euphemism for **FUCKED UP**.
- Sure, and it's a mucked-up civilization to let a guy like that run around loose in the first place. —Thurston Scott, *Cure it with Honey*, p. 197, 1951

mucker *noun*

1 a friend *UK, 1947*

From **MUCK IN** (to share the circumstances of basic living).

- I'll get you old man [...] You and your mucker. —Clive Exton, *No Fixed Abode [Six Granada Plays]*, p. 134, 1959
- This Jill bitch was calling one of these gits Simon and they were real old muckers, so it seemed. —John Peter Jones, *Feather Pluckers*, p. 45, 1964
- So what can I do for you, assuming you're not here to shoot the shit with your old mucker Jason? —John Williams, *Cardiff Dead*, p. 86, 2000

2 a person who uses sleight-of-hand to cheat at cards *US*

- —Frank Scoblete, *Best Blackjack*, p. 266, 1996

mucker-upper *noun*

a bungler *UK, 1942*

- [H]e is the greatest natural mucker-upper in the history of the redistribution industry. —Charles Raven, *Underworld Nights*, p. 188, 1956

muck in *verb*

to share, on an informal basis, food, accommodation and other facilities, or work *UK, 1919*

Of military origin.

- Some of the parents have mucked in to decorate the children's toilet area with bright jungle scenes. —*The Guardian*, 29th October 2002

mucking *noun*

used as a euphemism for 'fucking' *AUSTRALIA*

A literary euphemism from the days when it was not permissable to reproduce the word 'fuck' in print. Not used in real language.

- We're burning up a lot more [fuel] than we should, with those mucking monsters gargling the stuff like it was lolly-water at a school picnic[.] —W.R. Bennett, *Target Turin*, p. 50, 1962

mucking; muckin' *adverb*

used as an intensifier *UK, 1887*

A euphemistic disguise for **FUCKING**.

- It ought to have been a muckin' great rope, you old bastard. —Charles Raven, *Underworld Nights*, p. 113, 1956

muck out *verb*

to kill *US*

- —Inez Cardozo-Freeman, *The Joint*, p. 516, 1984

muck sack *noun*

a lazy person *US*

- —*American Speech*, p. 154, May 1959: 'Gator (University of Florida) slang'

mucksavage *noun*

a country person *IRELAND*

- Nobody mocked you accent in public unless you were some mucksavage from outside the town. —Ardal O'Hanlon, *The Talk of the Town*, p. 21, 1998

muck stick *noun*

a shovel *US, 1908*

- —Vincent J. Monteleone, *Criminal Slang*, p. 158, 1949
- A phrase developed from mining. Muck is broken rubble blasted from the working face of a mine. —Tom Parkin, *WetCoast Words*, p. 95, 1989

muck truck *noun*

in prison, a food trolley *UK*

- —Angela Devlin, *Prison Patter*, p. 77, 1996

muck-up *noun*

a confusion, a muddle, a botch *UK, 1939*

- The government had been deeply incompetent. They have made such a muck-up, you can only gawp in astonishment. —*The Guardian*, 13th July 2001

muck up *verb*

to botch, to ruin, to interfere *UK, 1886*

- BRIDGER [Noel Coward]: If you muck it up, don't ever think of coming back here, except in one of these [he taps the coffin]. —*The Italian Job*, 1969
- Nothing like a little panic to muck up an investigation. —Carl Hiaasen, *Tourist Season*, p. 60, 1986
- I don't want you – with all due respect, Jerry – I don't want you mucking this up. —*Fargo*, 1996

muck-up day *noun*

the last day of high school where leaving students play pranks, etc *AUSTRALIA*

- As a 17-year-old she achieved one of her earliest publicity stunts by putting her Year 12 muck-up day on television news. —*Sunday Telegraph*, p. 31, 8th May 1994

mucky *adjective*

1 contemptible, sordid *UK, 1683*

An old English regional term that survives in the colloquial vocabulary.

- Do you reckon you want to finish up like one of those mucky buggers that change sex? —Geoff Brown, *I Want What I Want*, p. 73, 1966

2 pornographic, especially when mildly so; lewd *UK, 1972*

From the previous sense as 'sordid'.

mucky pup *noun*

a dirty or untidy child *UK, 1984*

A term of disapproval.

mud *noun*

1 excrement *AUSTRALIA*

- There is, in fact, a comprehensive coded system of rubber sex with 25 variations. These include medical scenes, industrial rubber, boots, diver's gear, enema scenes and mud (scat). —*Kink*, p. 47, 1993

2 unprocessed opium; opium; heroin *US, 1915*

- —Angela Devlin, *Prison Patter*, 1996
- —Mike Haskins, *Drugs*, p. 284, 2003

3 coffee *US, 1875*

- Just ground this morning. —James Harris, *A Convict's Dictionary*, 1989

4 chemical fire retardant dropped from the air *US*

- —Murry A. Taylor, *Jumping Fire*, p. 457, 2000

5 in circus and carnival usage, any cheap merchandise used as a prize *US*

- —Don Wilmeth, *The Language of American Popular Entertainment*, p. 177, 1981

6 on the Internet, a multi-user dungeon, a text-based, networked, multiparticipant virtual reality system *US*

- The appeal of MUDs is really quite simple. —Nancy Tamosaitis, *net.sex*, p. 156, 1995

7 a billiard ball *US*

- —Mike Shamos, *The Illustrated Encyclopedia of Billiards*, p. 152, 1993

▸ **up to mud**

no good *AUSTRALIA, 1931*

- You'll be feeling 'up to mud' yourself, if you have a bad hangover[.] —John O'Grady, *Aussie English*, p. 60, 1965
- 'I wish to Heaven the whole thing was over,' he wrote at that time. Then, 'the game's up to mud'. —Patsy Adam-Smith, *The ANZACS*, p. 137, 1978

mud *verb*

(used of a racehorse) to run well on muddy track conditions *US, 1978*

- —Thomas L. Clark, *The Dictionary of Gambling and Gaming*, p. 132, 1987

mud baby *noun*

faeces *US*

- —Chris Lewis, *The Dictionary of Playground Slang*, p. 153, 2003

mud ball *noun*

a doughnut or other pastry eaten with coffee *US*

Harkened to **MUD** (coffee).

- — "Slingo", *The Official CB Slang Dictionary Handbook*, p. 42, 1976

mud butt *noun*

diarrhoea *US*

- —Connie Eble (Editor), *UNC-CH Campus Slang*, p. 4, April 2004

muddafukka *noun*

a motherfucker (in all senses) *US*

- "Don't call me that," Fergus is wounded. "This is America, remember." "OK, muddafukka." "Much better." —Melanie McGrath, *Motel Nirvana*, p. 12, 1995

mudder *noun*

any athlete who performs well in rainy conditions; a racehorse that performs well on wet or muddy track conditions *US, 1942*

- —David W. Maurer, *Argot of the Racetrack*, p. 43, 1951

mudder ass *noun*

▷ **see: MOTHER-ASS**

muddie *noun*

the mud crab *Scylla serrata* *AUSTRALIA, 1953*

- When Jack eventually arrived home, he found the bucket still in the boot but the muddie had gone. —Bob Staines, *Wot a Whopper*, p. 52, 1982
- —Bob Staines, *Wot a Whopper*, p. 34, 1982

muddlefugging *adverb*
used as a euphemism for the intensifier 'motherfucking' *US*
- It was too muddlefuggin way up t'talk bout right now. —Robert Gover, *One Hundred Dollar Misunderstanding,* p. 152, 1961

muddy feet *noun*
said of someone who needs to urinate *US*
- —Carol Ann Preusse, *Jargon Used by University of Texas Co-Eds,* 1963

muddy fuck *noun*
anal sex that brings forth faeces or faecal stains on the penis *US*
- — *Maledicta,* p. 232, 1979: 'Kinks and queens: linguistic and cultural aspects of the terminology for gays'

muddy trench *noun*
the French *UK*
Rhyming slang, possibly based on 'bloody French'.
- —Ray Puxley, *Cockney Rabbit,* 1992

muddy water *noun*
coffee *UK*
Elaboration of **MUD** (coffee) playing on Muddy Waters, the stage-name of bluesman McKinley Morganfield (1915–83).
- —Peter Chippindale, *The British CB Book,* p. 157, 1981

Muddy York *nickname*
York, a suburb of Toronto *CANADA*
- Once the name of Toronto, the Ontario capital's aboriginal name was restored because York could be confused with New York and because Muddy York was a demeaning reference.— *Toronto Globe and Mail,* p. R2, 29th May 2002

mud flaps *noun*
the condition that exists when a tight-fitting pair of trousers, shorts, bathing suit or other garment forms a wedge between a woman's labia, accentuating their shape *US*

mudge *noun*
a hat *UK*
From a particular type of hat worn by C19 women.
- —Paul Baker, *Polari,* p. 181, 2002

mudguard *noun*
a person whose outward geniality masks a vicious nature *AUSTRALIA*
Both are shiny on the outside and filthy underneath.
- —Ned Wallish, *The Truth Dictionary of Racing Slang,* p. 54, 1989

mudhead *noun*
a fanatic enthusiast for multi-user dungeon computer play *US*
- —Eric S. Raymond, *The New Hacker's Dictionary,* p. 250, 1991

mud hog *noun*
football played in rainy, muddy conditions *TRINIDAD AND TOBAGO, 1992*
- —Lise Winer, *Dictionary of the English/Creole of Trinidad & Tobago,* 2003

mud hook *noun*
1 an anchor *US, 1827*
Nautical use.

2 in the dice game crown and anchor, an anchor *UK, 1961*
From the non-symbolic previous sense.

3 a finger *CANADA, 1968*
Usually in the plural.

mud hop *noun*
a clerk in a railway yard *US, 1929*
- —Ramon Adams, *The Language of the Railroader,* p. 102, 1977

mudkicker *noun*
a prostitute, especially of the street-walking variety *US, 1932*
- Mike would say, "Uh, uh, there's one of them mudkickers again[.]" —Mezz Mezzrow, *Really the Blues,* p. 246, 1946
- She knew her husband Howie and his kind, the mudkickers, the stars, the stables and occasional white call-girls – she had been part of these things. —Clarence Cooper Jr, *The Scene,* p. 91–92, 1960
- She was three-quarter Kelsey with mossy glossy hair / she was a stompdown mudkicker and her mug was fair. —Bruce Jackson, *Get Your Ass in the Water and Swim Like Me,* p. 106, 1964
- The only reason Lou's so good, though, is 'cause she don't turn down no money; that bitch is a real mud-kicker. —Nathan Heard, *Howard Street,* p. 40, 1968
- Idella, Sweet Peter Deeder's #2 mudkicker, eases up to confront to love of her life. —Odie Hawkins, *Ghetto Sketches,* p. 17, 1972
- Why couldn't she be a ready-made mud kicker? —A.S. Jackson, *Gentleman Pimp,* p. 35, 1973
- I remember the time we muscled a mud kicker when we was oh ten ... twelve and got our first blowjob together. —Iceberg Slim (Robert Beck), *Death Wish,* p. 174, 1977

mudlark *noun*
a racehorse that performs well on muddy track conditions *US, 1909*
- That horse is a dud on pasteboard, she's strictly a mudlark.— *San Francisco Chronicle,* p. 54, 21st April 1971
- Van Der Hum as a noted mudlark and his price shortened considerably[.] —Joe Brown, *Just for the Record,* p. 140, 1984

mud mark *noun*
in horse racing, an indication in a past performance report that a horse runs well in muddy track conditions *US*
- —George King, *Horse Racing,* p. 59, 1965

mud-moving *noun*
close-in air support for a ground operation in the Canadian Air Force *CANADA*
- "Mud-moving" has the effect of [throwing] large amounts of soil and debris into the air. —Tom Langeste, *Words on the Wing,* p. 190, 1995

mud puppy *noun*
a very ugly girl *US*
- —Connie Eble (Editor), *UNC-CH Campus Slang,* p. 4, Spring 1983

mud-stick artist *noun*
a member of a railway track crew *US*
- —Ramon Adams, *The Language of the Railroader,* p. 102, 1977

mud turtle *noun*
a black prisoner *US*
- —John R. Armore and Joseph D. Wolfe, *Dictionary of Desperation,* 1976

mud wallow *noun*
a coffee house *UK*
Citizens' band slang, elaborating on **MUD** (coffee).
- So follow me, follow / Down to the hollow / And there let us wallow in glorious mud[.] —Flanders & Swann *The Hippopotamus,* 1959
- —Peter Chippindale, *The British CB Book,* p. 157, 1981

muff *noun*
the vulva; a woman as a sex object *UK, 1699*
- For an instant I saw Chenault standing alone; she looked surprised and bewildered, with that little muff of brown hair standing out against the white skin[.] —Hunter S. Thompson, *Songs of the Doomed,* p. 101, 1962
- But in reality, the muff-happy mogul is merely hidden away in an upstairs chamber watching their sexual escapades via a close circuit TV system, while pulling his weenie[.] —*Adult Video,* p. 12, August/September 1986
- "She's maybe got more moves than your or me got." "That's because she's got a pair of tits and a muff." —Robert Campbell, *Juice,* p. 92, 1988
- What's going on here? In some kind of serious conversation that could be about him. Or else the Indian was getting ready to dive into her muff. Either way, Richie didn't like the looks of it. —Elmore Leonard, *Killshot,* p. 278, 1989
- You know, you're sitting around the pool all day, chasing the muff around. — *Dazed and Confused,* 1993
- Robert learned to "slow down" and to develop a taste for Mary's muff. —Anka Radakovich, *The Wild Girls Club,* p. 115, 1994
- To manicure your muff's mane, you can go the way of the Sex and the City chicks and choose hot wax. — *The Village Voice,* 8th-14th November 2000

▸ **buff the muff**
to manually stimulate a woman's genitals *US*
- I even got to the point where I could pop during sex – but only if somebody was buffing the muff while we were going at it. —Amy Sohn, *Run Catch Kiss,* p. 115, 1999

muff *verb*
to bungle *UK, 1827*
- —Randy Voorhees, *The Little Book of Golf Slang,* p. 74, 1997

muff-dive *verb*
to perform oral sex upon a woman *US, 1948*
- Let's get on to "muff-diving," shall we? —Angelo d'Arcangelo, *The Homosexual Handbook,* p. 209, 1968

- You muff-diving, mother-fucking son of a bitch! — Philip Roth, *Portnoy's Complaint*, p. 118, 1969
- Incidentally Jane Fonda is one piece I would be most glad to muff dive. — *Screw*, p. 5, 7th March 1969
- One reason the sport of muff diving is not practiced more often than women would like it to be is that some men don't know how to do it. — Anka Radakovich, *The Wild Girls Club*, p. 131, 1994
- HOLDEN: So if we'd met a long time ago, say in high school... ALYSSA: I'd still be muff-diving, yes. — *Chasing Amy*, 1997
- He was Olympic Muff Diving Champion, our Gaz at Munich[.] — David Peace, *Nineteen Seventy-Four*, p. 102, 1999

muff-diver *noun*

a person who performs oral sex on a woman *US, 1930*

- Only a muffdiver knows for sure (headline). — *Screw*, p. 12, 27th October 1969
- — *Current Slang*, p. 8, Winter 1969
- The rape guy turned out not to be a rape-o, more like a psycho muff diver. — James Ellroy, *Suicide Hill*, p. 702, 1986
- Jack said to Jimmy I could tell just by looking at you you're a muff diver[.] — William T. Vollman, *Whores for Gloria*, p. 42, 1991
- Men with big noses have the potential to be exemplary muffdivers, but most of them are still unaware of how to use their noses as a sex organ[.] — *The Village Voice*, 16th November 1999
- I'm not much of a muff diver, but I can strongly recommend that Kentucky cocktail of Sneaky Pete and strawberry juice. — *The Guardian*, 4th December 2003

muff-diving *noun*

oral sex performed on a woman *US*

- They're all assholes, they got no class and I actually met one guy who thought going down on a girl was something called "muff-diving" and only perverts did it. — Eve Babitz, *Eve's Hollywood*, p. 149, 1974

muffdruff *noun*

▷ **see:** CHUFFDRUFF

muffin *noun*

a woman objectified sexually *US, 1870*

Probably a disguised **MUFF** (the vagina).

- I know your sort you see Nicky. Men you know they do always like a bit of muffin on the side as you say. Always. — Jeremy Cameron, *Brown Bread in Wengen*, p. 45, 1999

Muffin the Mule; muffin *noun*

a fool *UK*

Rhyming slang, formed from the name of a television puppet who was famous in the 1950s.

- Well how important do you think it was important to score the winning goal in the Cup Final, you muffin? — Ray Puxley, *Fresh Rabbit*, 1998

muff job *noun*

oral sex on a woman *US*

- — Charles Shafer, *Folk Speech in Texas Prisons*, p. 210, 1990

muffler burn *noun*

a bruise on the skin caused by sucking *US*

Hawaiian youth usage.

- I got dis muffler burn las' night Diamon' Head! — Douglas Simonson, *Pidgin to da Max Hana Hou*, 1982

muff mag *noun*

a magazine featuring photographs of naked women, focusing on their pubic hair and vulvas *US*

- (Headline) Muff Mags for the Meat and Potatoes Man — *Screw*, p. 5, 3rd July 1972

muff merchant *noun*

a procurer of prostitutes; a man who makes his living off the earnings of prostitutes *US*

- — *Maledicta*, p. 148, Summer/Winter 1986–1987: 'Sexual slang: prostitutes, pedophiles, flagellators, transvestites, and necrophiles'

muff muncher *noun*

a person who performs oral sex on women; a lesbian *AUSTRALIA*

- Willis Is A Secret Muff-Muncher[.] — Wendy Bacon, *Uni Sex*, p. 51, 1972
- — Barry Humphries, *The Traveller's Tool*, p. 139, 1985

muff-noshing *noun*

oral sex on a woman *US*

- — *Maledicta*, p. 198, Winter 1980: 'A new erotic vocabulary'

muffydile; muffydite *noun*

a person or animal with female and male characteristics *TRINIDAD AND TOBAGO, 1986*

A corruption of 'hermaphrodite'.

- — Lise Winer, *Dictionary of the English/Creole of Trinidad & Tobago*, 2003

mufti squad *noun*

individually anonymous, uniformed enforcers for the police or prison authorities *UK*

Prison usage.

- Then the Mufti squad came in [...] they were ruthless bastards, dressed in black boilersuits and crash helmets with visors[.] — Jimmy Stockin, *On The Cobbles*, p. 141, 2000

mu-fucka; muhfucka *noun*

a motherfucker *UK*

Alternative spelling.

- I hear this stupid mu-fucka talking about Snoop being unloyal. — *Hip-Hop Connection*, p. 10, July 2002
- A fear of muhfucka flossin' (mackin' or showing off) too hard. — *Hip-Hop Connection*, p. 22, July 2002

mug *noun*

1 a man, a bloke *US, 1859*

- "There are ten thousand mugs that hat eme and you know it." — Mickey Spillane, *I, The Jury*, p. 7, 1947
- We won't hit anything, and if we do, it'll be the other mug's fault, and some poor bastard's tough titty. — James T. Farrell, *Saturday Night*, p. 25, 1947
- What do these muggs mean to me? I don't worry about them[.] — Horace McCoy, *Kiss Tomorrow Good-bye*, p. 265, 1948
- At the moment he disapproved thoroughly of himself, not for playing a mugg's game with Boo, or with Nineteen Meyers either, but for letting himself wallow so long in the slough of self-pity. — Max Shulman, *Anyone Got a Match?*, p. 14, 1964
- [T]he door is opened by another mug called Tony Crawford[.] — Ted Lewis, *Jack Carter's Law*, p. 14, 1974
- "Who told you that?" he asked. He sounded concerned. "You did, you mug," said Skin firmly[.] — Greg Williams, *Diamond Geezers*, p. 181–182, 1997

2 a gullible fool, an easy dupe *UK, 1857*

A 'mug' is a vessel into which you can pour anything.

- I'm damned if I know which of us is the mug in this business, Ella. — Norman Lindsay, *The Cousin from Fiji*, p. 207, 1945
- Now look, kid, all we want around here is a 60–40 break. Don't say a word if you catch these mugs stealing; so long as we get sixty cents on the dollar we'll call it even. — Mezz Mezzrow, *Really the Blues*, p. 66, 1946
- [N]o mugs to skin. — Charles Raven, *Underworld Nights*, p. 9, 1956
- [H]e told the locals that he was searching for a tiger that had escaped from a circus, and most of the mugs believed him. — Kylie Tennant, *The Honey Flow*, p. 101, 1956
- They would make him the laughing stock of the whole nick and make him look a right mug. — Frank Norman, *Bang To Rights*, p. 60, 1958
- ROSE: I never knew you had the brains. LEONARD: No. I was the mug. — Alexander Baron, *A Bit of Happiness [Six Granada Plays]*, 1959
- Once again, it was like Scooter said: you had to put up a good front, else you'd never get a mug in tow. — Wilda Moxham, *The Apprentice*, p. 9, 1969
- — Louis S. Leland, *A Personal Kiwi-Yankee Dictionary*, 1984
- The tycoon was a skilful player and the leader was, in the quaint language of the day, a mug. — Frank Hardy, *Hardy's People*, p. 84, 1986
- Do they think we're mugs or what? — J.J. Connolly, *Know Your Enemy [britpulp]*, p. 155, 1999

3 the face, especially an ugly one *UK, 1821*

- The last time I saw that kind of a look it was on a district attorney's mug, and it caused me a lot of inconvenience. — Mezz Mezzrow, *Really the Blues*, p. 72, 1946
- [S]he handed me an apron. Very politely, I laid it on the back of a chair. It just wouldn't go well with my mug. — Mickey Spillane, *I, The Jury*, p. 51, 1947
- I looked at his confident mug; he was going to be a farmer. — Ralph Ellison, *Invisible Man*, p. 106, 1947
- But when he was wrestlin' the newspapers printed his mug a few times. — Marvin Wald and Albert Maltz, *The Naked City*, 1947
- I chopped the mops and shaved the mugs and cuffed the boots of about six hicks before the shop closed. — A.S. Jackson, *Gentleman Pimp*, p. 19, 1973

4 the mouth *AUSTRALIA, 1902*

- Bill had had quite enough of it too, and bundled Peter, as its audience, out into the passage, with a ferocious injunction to shut his mug about it, or get a hiding. — Norman Lindsay, *Halfway to Anywhere*, p. 67, 1947

5 a member of a criminal gang by virtue of brawn not brains *US, 1890*

- [T]he door is opened by another mug called Tony Crawford[.] — Ted Lewis, *Jack Carter's Law*, p. 14, 1974

6 a client of a prostitute *AUSTRALIA, c.1906*

- She get's five per cent if she introduces you to a mug. — Kevin Mackey, *The Cure*, p. 88, 1970

mug *verb*

1 to rob with violence or the threat of violence *UK, 1864*
- He told how he and his brother, Calvin, 17, and Vallejo Caldwell, 16, "mugged" Farley and robbed him of twenty dollars. — Louise Meriwether, *Daddy Was a Number Runner*, p. 126, 1970
- You was drinking, you ended up in the Village, you was mugged, had your wallet taken, you put up a fight and got shot, got it? — Edwin Torres, *Carlito's Way*, p. 91, 1975

2 to stare at *US*
- — *Milwaukee Journal-Sentinel*, 5th March 2001

3 to grimace theatrically, especially while posing for a photograph *UK, 1762*
- Bruce, shown here with his attorney, stops and mugs for the cameraman and promises to stire a little commotion at tomorrow's hearing. — Lenny Bruce, *How to Talk Dirty and Influence People*, p. 160, 1965
- Leslie West thumped guitar [...] with broad, joyously agonized mugging, grimacing and grinning and nodding[.] — Lester Bangs, *Psychotic Reactions and Carburetor Dung*, p. 35, 1970

4 to kiss *US*
- — Marcus Hanna Boulware, *Jive and Slang of Students in Negro Colleges*, 1947
- — *American Speech*, p. 62, Spring-Summer 1975: 'Razorback slang'

5 to photograph a prisoner during the after-arrest process *US, 1899*
- We brought him up to the marshsal's office and mugged him and printed him and then we brought him here. — George V. Higgins, *The Friends of Eddie Doyle*, p. 135, 1971

▸ **mug you off**

to show someone as a fool; to play someone for a fool; to consider someone foolish *UK*

From **MUG** (a fool).
- [Y]ou're mugging me off. That's what you're doing. You're vexing me. — Greg Williams, *Diamond Geezers*, p. 9, 1997
- You may laugh, mock or completely mug me off, and deservedly so[.] — Wayne Anthony, *Spanish Highs*, p. xi, 1999
- I really cocked it up and proper mugged myself off. — Dave Courtney, *Raving Lunacy*, p. 102, 2000
- [T]his lot have really tried to mug me off. — Garry Bushell, *The Face*, p. 92, 2001

mug *adjective*

foolish *AUSTRALIA*

Especially in the terms **MUG COPPER** and **MUG PUNTER**.
- I'd have backed Tully and Lasher to put it over any mug provost. — Eric Lambert, *The Veterans*, p. 12, 1954
- Let 'em be in it if they're mug enough! — Eric Lambert, *The Veterans*, p. 49, 1954
- Any mug politician could do as much. — Dymphna Cusack, *Picnic Races*, p. 200, 1962

mug about *verb*

to kiss and fondle someone *AUSTRALIA*
- Hang it, I'll have to stop mugging you about like this, Ella. — Norman Lindsay, *The Cousin from Fiji*, p. 207, 1945
- — Norman Lindsay, *Halfway to Anywhere*, p. 214, 1947

mug book *noun*

a collection of photographs of criminals consulted by the police *US, 1902*

Reported by Albert Petch, 1969.

mug chop *noun*

a sale of a faulty second-hand car made by a dealer posing as a customer *UK*
- — *Woman's Own*, 28th February 1968

mug cop *noun*

a police officer, viewed as inherently stupid *AUSTRALIA*
- The mug cops line might have been valid once but it is not valid any longer. — Bill Hornadge, *The Ugly Australian*, p. 100, 1971

mug copper *noun*

a police officer, viewed as inherently stupid *AUSTRALIA, 1945*
- Go on, Louis! Bite the bloody mug copper! — Vince Kelly, *The Bogeyman*, p. 25, 1956
- My father was already doing some anticipatory laughing, as Roy went on, 'and this mug copper comes up, and starts having a go at him.' — *Sydney City Hub*, p. 5, 4th April 1996

mug down *verb*

to kiss *US*

From **MUG** (the face) on the model of **CHOW DOWN** (to set to eating).
- Mug down. Suck face. — Jim Humes and Sean Wagstaff, *Boarderlands*, p. 223, 1995

mug gallery *noun*

in a carnival, a concession where people pay to have their picture taken *US*
- — *American Speech*, p. 308–309, December 1960: 'Carnival talk'

mugger *noun*

a criminal who commits street robbery with violence (or the threat of violence) *US, 1863*
- Muggers poop scoop haul [...] But she had the last laugh as she imagined the mugger opening the bag and discovering its contents. — *The Guardian*, 8th October 2003

muggie *noun*

marijuana *UK*

A variation of **MUGGLES** (marijuana).
- — Mike Haskins, *Drugs*, p. 288, 2003

mugging *noun*

a street robbery from a person, especially robbery with violence or the threat of violence *US, 1943*
- — Angela Devlin, *Prison Patter*, p. 77, 1996

muggins *noun*

a fool, an idiot, often with an implication that the fool is a victim (and a fool to be so), a gullible fool *US, 1855*
- It's disgusting, you don't have to tell me, it's disgusting... and naturally, we're the ones left to sort out the mess; it's muggins here who has to -— *The Guardian*, 15th September 2000

muggle *noun*

1 a marijuana cigarette *US, 1933*
- "Ever smoke any muggles?" he asked me. "Man, this is some goldenleaf I brought up from New Orleans, it'll make you feel good, take a puff." — Mezz Mezzrow, *Really the Blues*, p. 51, 1946
- [I]t is commonly called "tea" and the cigarettes made therefrom are called "reefers" or "muggles." — Jack Lait and Lee Mortimer, *New York Confidential*, p. 102, 1948
- Me he charged a buck each – maybe these muggles were fatter, or maybe it's just he knows I'm ready and he's taking advantage. — Bernard Wolfe, *The Late Risers*, p. 168, 1954
- The muggles were going around like crazy, loose lip to loose lip. — Willard Motley, *Let No Man Write My Epitaph*, p. 109, 1958

2 a person with little or no understanding of computers *UK*

The opposite of a **WIZARD**; derived from the *Harry Potter* novels of JK Rowling.
- Our new Senior DBA starts on Monday. She's a muggle. No IT background, understanding or aptitude at all. Last job? Social worker in charge of registering child minders. — *Computer Weekly*, p. 22, 2nd September 1999
- — Susie Dent, *Larpers and Shroomers*, p. 57, 2004

mugglehead *noun*

a marijuana user *US, 1926*
- — *American Speech*, p. 28, February 1952: 'Teen-age hophead jargon'

muggles *noun*

marijuana *US, 1928*
- "How in hell do you get away with it? The muggles, I mean." He looked around. "I only smoke when I feel extra special low." — Raymond Chandler, *Playback*, p. 123, 1958

muggy *adjective*

foolish, in the manner of a mug (a fool, a dupe) *UK*
- Look a' them muggy boneheads. — Nick Barlay, *Curvy Lovebox*, p. 51, 1997
- Babe, I've had it with working for muggy straights [non-criminals]. — Lenny McLean, *The Guv'nor*, p. 61, 1998

muggy-cunt *noun*

a fool *UK*
- Jimmy don't sit down to eat with any muggy-cunts, you know. — J.J. Connolly, *Layer Cake*, p. 34, 2000

mug joint *noun*

in circus and carnival usage, a concession where customers are photographed *US, 1931*
- — Joe McKennon, *Circus Lingo*, p. 63, 1980
- — Don Wilmeth, *The Language of American Popular Entertainment*, p. 178, 1981

mug lair *noun*

a showy but foolish person *AUSTRALIA, 1944*
- Five quid to any mug lair who could knock him down. — Shane Maloney, *Nice Try*, p. 93, 1998

mug money *noun*

in horse racing, money bet by uninformed bettors *AUSTRALIA*

- —Ned Wallish, *The Truth Dictionary of Racing Slang*, p. 54, 1989

mug punter *noun*

a punter, viewed as inherently stupid *AUSTRALIA, 1943*

- For all that the hard-headed businessman was in no danger of developing into a mug punter.—James Holledge, *The Great Australian Gamble*, p. 58, 1966
- —David Powis, *The Signs of Crime*, 1977

mug's game *noun*

a thankless activity *UK, 1910*

- [T]his going with girls was a mug's game, which strong, tough blokes like Bill and Waldo couldn't be bothered with.—Norman Lindsay, *Halfway to Anywhere*, p. 37, 1947
- At the moment he disapproved thoroughly of himself, not for playing a mugg's game with Boo, or with Nineteen Meyers either, but for letting himself wallow so long in the slough of self-pity.—Max Shulman, *Anyone Got a Match?*, p. 14, 1964
- [U]nless you're Jack Nicholson don't try climbing through a transom with a hard-on. It's a mug's game.—Barry Humphries, *The Traveller's Tool*, p. 68, 1985

mug shot *noun*

1 a police photograph of a (convicted) criminal *US, 1950*

Combines **MUG** (the face) and 'shot' (a photograph).

- Haskins shoved the mug shots across his desk.—*The Sweeney*, p. 29, 1976

2 a photographic portrait *UK*

- The first time I met him I was up at his gaff in Hampstead to do a mug shot.—*British Journal of Photography*, 17th November 1978

mugsnapper *noun*

in circus and carnival usage, a travelling photographer *US*

- —Don Wilmeth, *The Language of American Popular Entertainment*, p. 178, 1981

mugsnatcher *noun*

a photographer who operates in the street, fairground or at the seaside *UK*

- —Patrick O'Shaughnessy, *Market Traders' Slang*, 1979

mug's ticker *noun*

a counterfeit Swiss watch *UK*

- —David Powis, *The Signs of Crime*, 1977

mug-up *noun*

a coffee break or snack, at work or home *US, 1958*

- —John Gould, *Maine Lingo*, p. 185, 1975
- —Russell Tabbert, *Dictionary of Alaskan English*, 1991

mug up *verb*

1 to flirt, to kiss *US*

- —Marcus Hanna Boulware, *Jive and Slang of Students in Negro Colleges*, 1947

2 to study hard *UK, 1848*

Also 'mug up on'.

- [R]ecording video pieces and mugging up facts and stats.—John McCririck, *John McCririck's World of Betting*, p. 16, 1991

muhfucka *noun*

▷ see: MU-FUCKA

muhfuh; muhfuhkuh *noun*

motherfuck; motherfucker *US, 1969*

- So MEA CULPA MUHFUH, etc.—Lester Bangs, *Psychotic Reactions and Carburetor Dung*, p. 289, 1979

mujer *noun*

cocaine *US*

Spanish for 'woman'.

- —US Department of Justice, *Street Terms*, August 1994

mukluk telegraph *noun*

a radio show that makes announcements delivering messages to people in rural Alaska who have no telephone or mail service *US, 1945*

The 'mukluk' is 'an insulated boot designed for arctic wear'.

- —Mike Doogan, *How to Speak Alaskan*, p. 44, 1993

mukums *noun*

the female pubic mound *TRINIDAD AND TOBAGO*

- She have a mukums like aplumbay, fat and nice—Lise Winer, *Dictionary of the English/Creole of Trinidad & Tobago*, 2003

mula *noun*

marijuana *US*

- Hey Milton did you bring any mula?—Milton Mezzrow, *Really the Blues*, 1946

mulady *noun*

a ghost, a devil *UK*

English gypsy use from Romany *mûlo* (dead, ghost).

- —Jimmy Stockin, *On The Cobbles*, p. 11, 2000

mulberry bush *noun*

▸ **go round the mulberry bush**

to waste time in a misdirected effort *UK*

From a children's singing game – a perfect example of using up energy in pointless activity.

- Are we all chasing out backsides round the mulberry bush, while Kilroy skidaddles to Timbuctoo via the London Underground?—Troy Kennedy Martin, *Z Cars*, p. 149, 1962

mule *noun*

1 a person who physically smuggles drugs or other contraband *US, 1922*

- How? Simple, he thought, with carefully established networks of "mules" to bring it into the States.—Iceberg Slim (Robert Beck), *Death Wish*, p. 32, 1977
- Now you just stand there where I can see you and give your mule the come-ahead.—Gerald Petievich, *Money Men*, p. 87, 1981
- We're just the mules, comprende?—*Repo Man*, 1984
- Bullshit, I ain't handling no dope. He thought about a mule, a buffer between him and the consequences.—Richard Price, *Clockers*, p. 179, 1992
- An attorney of modest talents stood little chance of landing a billionaire narcotrafficker as a client; Mordecai was lucky to get the occasional mule or offloader.—Carl Hiaasen, *Strip Tease*, p. 198, 1993
- I know what the term "mule" means on the street, but I have never met one so young.—Mary Rose McGeady, *Are you out there, God?*, p. 9, 1999
- It's not like you can put it in a condom up some mule's asshole, right?—*Traffic*, 2000
- More than 10% of the women currently in jail are Jamaican drug mules who swallowed rubber wraps of cocaine and boarded flights to this country.—*The Guardian*, 30th September 2003

2 a Vietnamese who carried supplies for the Viet Cong or the North Vietnamese Army *US*

- These mules made their way down the Ho Chi Minh Trail, or along the numerous resupply routes within South Vietnam transporting their goods on thier backs or by bicycle.—Gregory Clark, *Words of the Vietnam War*, p. 357, 1990

3 in motor racing, a car used for tests and practice *US*

- —John Edwards, *Auto Dictionary*, p. 110, 1993

4 a small, motorised platform used for transporting supplies or personnel *US, 1903*

- A mechanical mule – a heavy weapons carrier that looked nothing like a mule but rather resembled an oversized toy wagon – dodged one of the stacks, went over a curb, and roared down a sidewalk, a 106-mm recoilless rifle bouncing in its flatbed.—Philip Caputo, *A Rumor of War*, p. 41, 1977
- They could be rolled along the ground by eight or ten men, or pulled by small wheeled gas-powered tugs called Mules.—Charlie A. Beckwith and Donald Knox, *Delta Force*, p. 212, 1983
- The rest of the squad would then manhandle the bombs onto the pier – large bombs would be rolled down an incline or removed by electric "mules," and small bombs and boxes of ammunition might be passed hand to hand or transported by hand trucks.—Robert L. Allen, *The Port Chicago Mutiny*, p. 47, 1989

5 a railway brakeman *US, 1929*

- —Ramon Adams, *The Language of the Railroader*, p. 103, 1977

6 an infertile woman *TRINIDAD AND TOBAGO, 1986*

- —Lise Winer, *Dictionary of the English/Creole of Trinidad & Tobago*, 2003

7 marijuana that has been soaked in whisky *US*

- —*American Speech*, p. 87, May 1955: 'Narcotic argot along the Mexican border'

mule nose *noun*

the condition that exists when a tight-fitting pair of trousers, shorts, bathing suit or other garment forms a wedge between a woman's labia, accentuating their shape *US*

mulenyam; moulonjohn *noun*

a black person *US*

From the Italian, referring to an eggplant.

- Have I ever talked about the schwarzes when the schwarzes had gone home? Or spoken about the Moulonjohns when they'd left?—Lenny Bruce, *The Essential Lenny Bruce*, p. 11, 1967

mule's ear *noun*
a hidden mechanism used to control the spin of a roulette wheel *US*
- —Ralph de Sola, *Crime Dictionary*, p. 97, 1982

mule teeth *noun*
in craps, a roll of twelve *US*
- —Chris Fagans and David Guzman, *A Guide to Craps Lingo*, p. 38, 1999

mule train *noun*
in humorous smuggler usage, a car *US*
- Smugglers' Argot in the Southwest—*American Speech*, p. 100, May 1956

mulga *noun*
uninhabited or sparsely populated remote regions of Australia *AUSTRALIA, 1898*
From *mulga* (a type of native acacia), from the Australian Aboriginal language Yuwaalaraay.
- Gary's gone away for the weekend, cavorting in the mulga with the Werris Creek Push.—Alexander Buzo, *Rooted*, p. 87, 1969
- —Ignatius Jones, *The 1992 True Hip Manual*, p. 117, 1992

mulga wire *noun*
an information network utilising word of mouth *AUSTRALIA, 1899*
- No good going to Kalgoorlie because Constable Harmon he send mulga wire to police fellers there to arrest him—Arthur Upfield, *Bony and the Mouse*, p. 168, 1959
- —Jim Ramsay, *Cop It Sweet!*, p. 60, 1977

mull *noun*
marijuana prepared for smoking *AUSTRALIA, 1988*
- Tristram pinched some mull between his fingers and examined it closely.—Linda Jaivin, *Rock n Roll Babes from Outer Space*, p. 124, 1996
- He'd swapped a jaffle maker and a curling wand from Jordan's place for a small stick of mull and a bottle of Stone's green ginger wine. —John Birmingham, *The Tasmanian Babes Fiasco*, p. 204, 1997

mull *verb*
to break up marijuana buds in preparation for smoking *AUSTRALIA*
- —Steven Wishnia, *The Cannabis Companion*, p. 152, 2004

mullah *noun*
an Irish person who is not from Dublin *IRELAND*
- When I got back to Dublin after two weeks of hell, I promised to beat the shite out of every mullah bastard that ever darkened the door of The Joy.—Howard Paul, *The Joy*, p. 44, 1996

▷ **see:** MOOLA

mullarkey *noun*
▷ **see:** MALARKEY

mull bowl *noun*
a bowl used to mull marijuana *AUSTRALIA*
- There were a few flecks left in the mull bowl[.]—Harrison Biscuit, *The Search for Savage Henry*, p. 60, 1995

muller *noun*
an ugly or unattractive person *UK*
Teen slang.
- — Susie Dent, *The Language Report*, p. 77, 2003

muller *verb*
to roundly beat the opposition in a physical fight *UK*
German tailor Franz Müller (executed 1864) was the first person to commit a murder on a British train; his name survives here as a synonym for 'murder' but is used only as an exaggeration.
- You fuckin' cunt I'll muller ya.—Nick Barlay, *Curvy Lovebox*, p. 31, 1997
- Chelsea [...] mullered an unsuspecting and enclosed eastbound train full of West Ham's young lot.— Martin King and Martin Knight, *The Naughty Nineties*, p. 102, 1999
- My dad's gonna muller you[.]—Jimmy Stockin, *On The Cobbles*, p. 48, 2000

mullered *adjective*
1 drunk or drug-intoxicated *UK*
- [R]esting his skull in snot, mullered by half-eight[.]—John King, *Human Punk*, p. 237–238, 2000
- [T]rolleyed, mullered, bombed[.]—Stuart Walton, *Out of It*, cover, 2001

2 dead *UK*
- —Jimmy Stockin, *On The Cobbles*, p. 11, 2000

mullering *noun*
a beating *UK*
- [W]e had a scrap. Give him a righ' mullerin' so she's back with me now.—Nick Barlay, *Curvy Lovebox*, p. 119, 1997

mullet *noun*
1 a hairstyle: the hair is worn short at the front and long at the back *US*
Fashionable in the 1980s and much derided by the fashion-conscious generations that followed.
- The Mullet. Hesher/rocker-style 'do. Short (often spikey) on top and at ears, long in back.— Editors of Ben is Dead, *Retrohell*, p. 136, 1997
- One of these Germans 'ave a mullet?—Chris Baker and Andrew Day, *Lock, Stock... & Spaghetti Sauce*, p. 266, 2000
- It is called "the mullet," or "the hockey haircut." It is the National Hairdo of Canada, a blend of long and short, conservative and rebel, silly and stupid.—Will Ferguson, *How to be a Canadian*, p. 28, 2001
- Tough lezzos wi' skin'ead mullets an' tattoos on their knuckles[.] —Ben Elton, *High Society*, p. 217, 2002
- There's nothing quite so bad as a bad haircut. And perhaps the worst of all is the cut we call The Mullet.— *Grand Royal*, MID-90S

2 a gullible person *US, 1955*
- GARY: So you're a big mover with Diane, are you? BENTLEY: Practically home and hosed. GARY: [...] Big mover with Diane! You mullet!—Alexander Buzo, *Rooted*, 1969
- —Connie Eble (Editor), *UNC-CH Campus Slang*, November 1976
- —Kathleen Odean, *High Steppers, Fallen Angels, and Lollipops*, p. 51, 1988

3 a socially inept outcast *US*
- — *Time Magazine*, p. 46, 24th August 1959

mullethead *noun*
a fool, a stupid person *US, 1857*
- Durmot Mulroney is not a mullethead, but he plays one in "About Schmidt."— *Associated Press*, 1st December 2002

mull head *noun*
a habitual smoker of marijuana *AUSTRALIA*
- —James Lambert, *The Macquarie Book of Slang*, 1996

mullier *noun*
a murderer *UK*
- —Patrick O'Shaughnessy, *Market Traders' Slang*, 1979

mulligan *noun*
a prison guard *US, 1939*
Used with derision by prisoners.
- —Charles Shafer, *Folk Speech in Texas Prisons*, p. 210, 1990

mulligan stew; mulligan *noun*
a stew made without a recipe, relying on ingredients that are left over from previous meals *US, 1904*
- The convicts cooked them into mulligan stews. They tasted fine. —Chester Himes, *Cast the First Stone*, p. 207, 1952
- [H]e lived on dehorn alcohol, mulligan, dayolds, misery[.]—John Clellon Holmes, *The Horn*, p. 159, 1958
- Say, "I even built jungle fires beneath the northern stars / and eaten Mulligan with the dirtiest of bums."—Bruce Jackson, *Get Your Ass in the Water and Swim Like Me*, p. 74, 1965

mulligatawny *noun*
desiring sex *UK*
Rhyming slang for **HORNY**.
- —Ray Puxley, *Fresh Rabbit*, 1998

mullion *noun*
an ugly person *US, 1959*
- If an import is a mullion, she may have to pay her own way.—Jim Bouton, *Ball Four*, p. 252, 1970
- —David Claerbaut, *Black Jargon in White America*, p. 73, 1972

mullock *noun*
mining refuse *AUSTRALIA, 1855*
From British dialect.
- —Jean Brooks, *The Opal Witch*, p. 12, 1967
- I worked like a slave today, I worked alongside your father shifting this filthy mullock.—Jean Brooks, *The Opal Witch*, p. 116, 1967
- —Jim Ramsay, *Cop It Sweet!*, p. 61, 1977

mullock heap *noun*
a mound of mullock *AUSTRALIA, 1859*
- —Norman Lindsay, *Halfway to Anywhere*, p. 137, 1947
- We stumbled over fences, over hills, over logs, and down a mullock heap.—Kerry Cue, *Crooks, Chooks and Bloody Ratbags*, p. 153, 1983

mull up *verb*
to prepare marijuana for smoking *AUSTRALIA*
Refers to cutting it up and, usually, mixing it in tobacco.
- He would like his women wild. Mull up. Rub some dirt back onto the toilet tiles. —Kathy Lette, *Girls' Night Out*, p. 15, 1987

mullygrub *verb*
to sulk *US*
A venerable noun (meaning 'depressed spirits'), now surviving in verb form.
- So your sister Darlene runned off with a albino motorcyle gang president. Mullygrubbin' around the house ain't gonna help. Don't you worry, Tyshonda, we'll find you somebody just as good. —Ken Weaver, *Texas Crude*, p. 118, 1984

multi *noun*
a multiple bet covering seven selections to '120 win stakes or 240 each-way stakes' *UK*
Also known as a 'Super Heinz'.
- —David Bennet, *Know Your Bets*, p. 63, 2001

multi; multie; multy; multa *adjective*
poor, bad *UK, 1887*
Polari; a weakening of **MULTI KATIVA** (very bad). Also used as an expletive and intensifying adjective.
- Some shops he had had were "multi" (poor) or even "multi kativa" (very poor)—Butch Reynolds, *Broken Hearted Clown*, p. 30, 1953

multi; multie; multi; multy *adverb*
very *UK, 1887*
Polari.

multi-coloured yawn *noun*
an act of vomiting; vomit *AUSTRALIA, 1977*

multi kativa; multee kertever; multicattivo *adjective*
very bad *UK, 1859*
Polari; from Italian *molto cattivo* (very bad).
- Some shops he had had were "multi" (poor) or even "multi kativa" (downright bad) with "Mr. Wood in the house" most days. —Butch Reynolds, *Broken Hearted Clown*, p. 30, 1953

multiples *noun*
sex involving multiple people; an orgy *US*
- The Orgy, or multiples. (Mulitples has a more discreet sound, don't you think?)—Angelo d'Arcangelo, *The Homosexual Handbook*, p. 112, 1968

multo *adjective*
many *UK*
- Robbery this grand needs multo blokes and training. —Jonathan Gash, *The Ten Word Game*, p. 105, 2003

mum *noun*
1 a wife or a woman in a long-term relationship *UK*
- —David Powis, *The Signs of Crime*, 1977

2 a woman objectified as unattractive *UK*
A logical extension of the belief that you would not fancy your mother. Current in the City of London during the 1990s.
- —David Rowan, *A Glossary for the 90s*, 1998

mum *adjective*
quiet, silent *UK*
- Lepke threatened to the last hour to "blow the roof off," but died mum. —Jack Lait and Lee Mortimer, *Chicago Confidential*, p. 186, 1950

mum and dad *noun*
a cricket pad *UK*
Rhyming slang, usually in the plural, with both elements pluralised.
- Ready with your mums and dads on. —Steve James, *captain of Glamorgan County Cricket Club*, 18th June 2003

mum and dad *adjective*
mad *UK*
Rhyming slang.
- [Y]ou'd feel justified in thinking that those two people were slightly mum and dad[.]— *The Sweeney*, p. 6, 1976
- —David McGill, *David McGill's Complete Kiwi Slang Dictionary*, p. 86, 1998

mumblage *noun*
stuff *US*
- — *Coevolution Quarterly*, p. 31, Spring 1981: 'Computer slang'

mumble
used as a verbal placeholder when an answer is either too difficult or unknown *US*
- Example: "Don't you think that we could improve LISP performance by using a hybrid reference-count transaction garbage collector, if the cache is big enough and there are some extra cache bits for the microcode to use?" "Well, mumble ... I'll have to think about it." —Guy L. Steele et al., *The Hacker's Dictionary*, p. 96, 1983

mumbler *noun*
a woman wearing a tight-fitting pair of trousers, shorts, bathing suit or other garment that forms a wedge between her labia, accentuating their shape; the trousers in question *UK*
- [Y]ou can see the "lips" moving but can't quite make out what they're saying. — *www.LondonSlang.com*, June 2002
- Barbara showed her the very tight pants she wears for cyling: "We call them mumblers. The lips are moving but you can't hear what's being said." — *Messenger - The City (Australia)*, p. 26, 5th February 2003
- Mumblers: Camel toe - the crotch of obscenely tight pants. The lips move but you can't understand a word. — *Playboy*, p. 19, 1st January 2003

mumbo jumbo *noun*
1 meaningless jargon *UK, 1896*
- Joe Bell showed me his picture in the paper. Blackhand. Mafia. All that mumbo jumbo; but they gave him five years. —Truman Capote, *Breakfast at Tiffany's*, p. 25, 1958
- All this synchronization business and mumbo-jumbo. —J.D. Salinger, *Franny and Zooey*, p. 39, 1961
- [T]he lead singer's twerpy attempts at Doctor John-ish mumbo-jumbo [...] were godawful. —Lester Bangs, *Psychotic Reactions and Carburetor Dung*, p. 98, 1972
- All these shrink and psycho mumbo-jumbo artists is maknig good money on these prison staffs and they don't know shit. —Edwin Torres, *Carlito's Way*, p. 42, 1975
- What kind of mumbo-jumbo bullshit was this?—Bobby Seale, *A Lonely Rage*, p. 134, 1978
- Er yeah. Er all that y've just said, y'know, the mumbo jumbo - what it means is er ... what does it mean?—Alan Bleasdale, *Boys From the Blackstuff*, 1982

2 any religion or religious practice, especially one that has or appears to have its roots in Africa *UK*
- I can smell that damned incense. You are trying to drive me round the bend, with your mumbo jumbo. —Charles Raven, *Underworld Nights*, p. 199, 1956
- "Jesus Christ," Princess Grace says, not liking it at all, him being very much into all kinds of Central American mumbo jumbo lately. —Robert Campbell, *In a Pig's Eye*, p. 22, 1991
- Caleb knows that was a load of mumbo jumbo. Ju-ju bollocks from Maria's dad! —Jack Allen, *When the Whistle Blows*, p. 86, 2000

mummerset *noun*
actor's all-purpose West Country dialect accent and speech *UK, 1984*
A punning blend of 'mummer' (an actor) and 'Somerset'.

mummy; mum *noun*
a mother, your mother *UK*
Affectionate diminutives of 'mother'.
- I feel like everyone's getting at me. First the coppers, then the old man then my mum. —John Peter Jones, *Feather Pluckers*, p. 11, 1964
- What does your mum say?—Sara McNamee, *Cool Places*, p. 198, 1998

mummy bag *noun*
a sleeping bag which can enclose the sleeper's head *US*
- Getting into my mummy bag became a problem. Our army sleeping bags were known as Arctic mummy bags, the name stemming from their Egyptian mummy-like shape. —Jennie Darlington and Jane McIlvaine, *My Antarctic Honeymoon*, p. 275, 1956

mummy dust; whiffle dust *noun*
an imaginary magic powder used by conjurors, manufacturers, marketing professionals and others to enhance their product or presentation *AUSTRALIA*
- —Don Bradmore, Faculty of Business and Economics, *www.legamedia.net*, 2000

mump *verb*
1 to obtain cheap or free goods from tradesmen by virtue of being a police officer *UK*
Metropolitan Police slang; a variation in sense of obsolete 'mump' (to get by begging).
- —Peter Laurie, *Scotland Yard*, p. 325, 1970

2 to take a bribe *UK*
A variation of the previous sense.
- —Angela Devlin, *Prison Patter*, p. 78, 1996

mumper *noun*
a tramp, a vagrant; a beggar *UK, 1665*
Current use as 'a beggar or scrounger' by David Powis, *The Signs of Crime*, 1977.
- The world's streets are littered with derelicts and mumpers living rough. —Jonathan Gash, *The Ten Word Game*, p. 138, 2003

mums *noun*
a mother *UK, 1939*

mumsie; mumsy *noun*
a mother *UK, 1876*
- 'Social services – don't shake my tree, Mumsie, don't beat me Daddy-o ten to the bar – ' and Lithy broke off to do a little dance, which was far more in character. —*The Guardian*, 30th June 2000

mum's the word
used as an injunction to keep quiet *UK, 1704*
'Mum' originates in C16, from the onomatapoeic qualities of speech contained by compressed lips.

mumsy *adjective*
motherly *UK*
- —Bill Naughton, *Alfie Darling*, 1970

mun *noun*
used as a general form of individual address to either gender; also used as a means of stressing what has been said *UK: WALES*
Originally used of a man. Later use is less discerning.
- Buck youer ideas up, mun! —John Edwards, *Talk Tidy*, p. 30, 1985
- [O]h come on mun love it's not that bad[.] —Patrick Jones, *Unprotected Sex*, p. 212, 1999
- Yeh, and the fuckin rest, mun, and the fuckin rest. —Niall Griffiths, *Sheepshagger*, p. 1, 2001

munch *noun*
food *US, 1998*
- Whilst knocking back the munch, we noticed two girls[.] —Wayne Anthony, *Spanish Highs*, p. 3, 1999

▸ **put the munch to**
to kiss with passion if not aggression *US*
- —Peter Smith and Fred M. Barritt, *Bermewjan Vurds*, 1985

munch *verb*
1 to eat *UK, 1923*
- —Judi Sanders, *Kickin' like Chicken with the Couch Commander*, p. 16, 1992

2 to kiss *US*
- —Connie Eble (Editor), *UNC-CH Campus Slang*, p. 7, Fall 1985

3 to fall or be knocked from a surfboard *US*
- —Gary Fairmont R. Filosa II, *The Surfer's Almanac*, p. 190, 1977

4 in computing, to explore flaws in a system's security scheme *US*
- —Eric S. Raymond, *The New Hacker's Dictionary*, p. 251, 1991

▸ **munch the trunch**
to perform oral sex on a man *UK*
Formed on an abbreviation of 'truncheon', as in **LOVE TRUNCHEON**.
- —Chris Lewis, *The Dictionary of Playground Slang*, p. 154, 2003

munched *adjective*
angry *US*
- —Kenn "Naz" Young, *Naz's Dictionary of Teen Slang*, p. 78, 1993

munchie *noun*
1 food, especially a snack or light meal *UK, 1959*
Earliest reference is in 1917 as a brand name for a chocolate confection.
- —Helen Dahlskog (Editor), *A Dictionary of Contemporary and Colloquial Usage*, p. 41, 1972
- —*Verbatim*, p. 280, May 1976
- —Peter Chippindale, *The British CB Book*, p. 157, 1981
- They'd been sent out for munchies, maybe.] —Two Fingers, *Puff (Disco Biscuits)*, p. 218, 1996

2 an injury sustained in a fall from a skateboard or bicycle *US*
- —*Washington Post Magazine*, p. 11, 24th May 1987: 'Say wha?'

munchies *noun*
a sensation of hunger experienced when smoking marijuana *US, 1959*
- —*Current Slang*, p. 10, Fall 1970
- We have just smoked three joints of the most extraordinary dope I have ever had, eaten a five pound pot of chili con carner, two pork chops each and a couple other things, buttered bread and cane syrup. Easily a case of the superduper munchies. —Odie Hawkins, *Black Casanova*, p. 15, 1984
- We get serious munchies and decide on Ratner's for soup and blintzes. —Jim Carroll, *Forced Entries*, p. 25, 1987
- An hour went by, He said Loc I'm kinda hungry / I said oh shit! This brothers got tha munchies —Tone Loc, *Cheeba Cheeba*, 1989
- I got the munchies in a big muthafuckin' way! —*Menace II Society*, 1993
- Well-known to anyone who has ever manned the till at a late-night garage are the "munchies", which hit cannabis users after an hour or so. —*Drugs An Adult Guide*, p. 42, December 2001

munchkin *noun*
1 a child *US, 1971*
In general usage. The Munchkins were diminutive characters created by Frank L. Baum for his book *The Wizard of Oz*, 1900. The film of the book, made in 1939, has proved to be an iconographic touchstone for gay culture (**FRIEND OF DOROTHY**, etc.), hence the following citation.
- [T]onight's concert with those camp munchkins [children], all ogles and pots [teeth] and nante voce [voice]. —the cast of 'Aspects of Love', Prince of Wales Theatre, *Palare (Boy Dancer Talk) for Beginners*, 1989–92

2 an acutely short person *US, 1975*
From the race of small people in Frank Baum's *Wizard of Oz*.
- There's gonna be alotta speculation about a middle-aged fat guy and red-headed munchkin in red snakeskin cowboy boots impersonating officers of the law. —Joseph Wambaugh, *Fugitive Nights*, p. 206, 1992

3 a young computer enthusiast *US*
From diminutive characters in the *Wizard of Oz*.
- —Eric S. Raymond, *The New Hacker's Dictionary*, p. 252, 1991

munchy *noun*
a shark *AUSTRALIA*
- —Trevor Cralle, *The Surfin'ary*, p. 78, 1991

munchy *adjective*
excellent, trendy, fashionable *US*
School usage.
- —*Washington Post*, 23rd April 1961: 'Man, dig this jazz'

Muncie *noun*
in hot rodding, a Chevrolet four-speed gearbox *US*
Built at a Chevrolet plant in Muncie, Indiana.
- —John Lawlor, *How to Talk Car*, p. 75, 1965

mundane *adjective*
unrelated to science fiction *US*
- —*American Speech*, p. 28, Spring 1982: 'The langage of science fiction fan magazines'

mundowie; mundowee *noun*
the foot *AUSTRALIA, 1822*
From the extinct Australian Aboriginal language Dharug (Sydney region).
- —Barbara Baynton, *Human Toll*, p. 248, 1907
- We was runnin' too hard from the common enemy to pick up anything but our mundowies. —Xavier Herbert, *Poor Fellow My Country*, p. 1367, 1975
- I've put me mundoee in it now. —*Wordmap (www.abc.net.au/wordmap)*, 2003

mung *noun*
dirt of any kind *US, 1948*
- Even on a tight cardioid pattern [for recording music], we picked up blobs of low-end mung[.] —Frank Zappa, *The Real Frank Zappa Book*, p. 153, 1989

mung *verb*
1 to beg *UK, 1811*
Used by tramps; from Romany *mang* (to beg).

2 to sell lucky heather *UK*
English gypsy use; a variation of the previous sense.
- The girls get ready to go munging in Southend in the 1950s. —Jimmy Stockin, *On The Cobbles*, p. picture caption, 2000

munga *noun*
food *AUSTRALIA, 1918*
A shortening of **MUNGAREE**. Originally in military speech.
- 'They'll probably send Len to some Pacific island,' Alec offered, by way of comfort, 'where he won't have no work but to answer his fan-mail and wonder what sort of munga there is at the cook-house.' —Kylie Tennant, *Lost Haven*, p. 246, 1946

• Do you know..that in certain parts of the world human beings have resorted to cannibalism when the munga supply runs out? — Geoff Wyatt, *Saltwater Saints*, p. 87, 1969
• — Jim Ramsay, *Cop It Sweet!*, p. 61, 1977
• He decided it was bird shit lime to put the nose bag on for some munga. — Ryan Aven-Bray, *Ridgey Didge Oz Jack Lang*, p. 14, 1983

mungaree *noun*
food *UK, 1861*
From Italian *mangiare* (to eat). Variants include 'mungare', 'munjari', 'munjary' and 'menjarie'.
• [H]e invited me to a cup of "char" and asked me to stop for "menjarie", jerking his thumb at the brown sausages sizzling on his coal stove. — Butch Reynolds, *Broken Hearted Clown*, p. 29, 1953

mungaree *verb*
to eat; hence food *UK*
From Italian *mangiare*, via parleyaree and tramps' slang, into polari. Variants include 'mungarly', 'munja', 'munjarry', 'mangiare', 'manjaree', 'monjaree', 'giare' and 'jarry'.
• [A] naff party where there was nante [no] bevvy [drink] and nante giare[.] — the cast of 'Aspects of Love', Prince of Wales Theatre, *Palare (Boy Dancer Talk) for Beginners*, 1989–92
• — Paul Baker, *Polari*, p. 178, 2002

munge *noun*
darkness *UK*
• — Paul Baker, *Polari*, p. 181, 2002

munge; mung *verb*
in computing, to destroy data, accidentally or maliciously *US*
• — Guy L. Steele et al., *The Hacker's Dictionary*, p. 97, 1983

mungers *noun*
the female breasts, especially when of above average dimensions *UK*
Possibly derived from 'humungous'.
• — Chris Lewis, *The Dictionary of Playground Slang*, p. 154, 2003

mung-pusher *noun*
a poker player who habitually plays hands that have no chance of winning *US*
• — John D. Bell et al., *Loosely Speaking*, p. 13, 1966

mung rag *noun*
a cloth used to wipe up spilled alcohol at a bar; a cloth used to wipe off the penis after masturbating *US*
• — Chris Lewis, *The Dictionary of Playground Slang*, p. 154, 2003

mung up; mung *verb*
to botch, to blunder, to ruin *US*
• — *Current Slang*, p. 11, Summer 1969

munjacake *noun*
a bland, uninteresting person *CANADA*
Italian-Canadian coinage and usage.
• — Jack Chambers (Editor), *Slang Bag 93 (University of Toronto)*, p. 4, Winter 1993

munjon *noun*
an Aboriginal who has little or no contact with white people *AUSTRALIA*
From the Western Australian Aboriginal language Yindjibarndi.
• Davey was a smart young aboriginal who, only three years before, had been a munjon (wild bush blackfellow). — Ion L. Idriess, *Over the Range*, p. 6, 1947

munt; muntu *noun*
a black African *SOUTH AFRICA, 1948*
From Bantu *muntu* (a human being), made abusive and offensive during apartheid.
• My Dad has taught me that in England some foolish man may call me sambo, darkie, boot or munt or nigger, even. — Colin McInnes, *City of Spades*, 1957
• He's a good boy, a good munt. A bloody good kaffir[.] — Obioma Nnaemeka, *The Politics of (M)Othering*, p. 37, 1997
• A war instigated by "uppity blacks," "cheeky kaffirs," "bolshy muntus," "restless natives," "the houts." — Alexandra Fuller, *Don't Let's Go to the Dogs Tonight*, p. 26, 2001

munt *verb*
to be ugly *UK*
• Steady, girlfriend! Guy is single and on the hunt, but you sound like you munt. — *X-Ray*, p. 12, December 2003

munted *adjective*
1 drunk or drug-intoxicated *UK*
• [S]aughtered, trashed, twatted, munted[.] — Stuart Walton, *Out of It*, cover, 2001
2 having become sexually intimate with an unattractive, promiscuous drunk *UK*
Student use; explained as 'to have pulled a **MUNTER**'.

munter; munta; munt *noun*
1 an unattractive person who adds to the personal allure with drunkenness and/or promiscuity, especially but not exclusively of young women *UK, 1998*
Student usage.
• A munter is a drunk minger. — Lucy Kenyon Jones, 7th July 2002
• — Susie Dent, *The Language Report*, p. 77, 2003
• — Chris Lewis, *The Dictionary of Playground Slang*, 2003
2 a useless person or object *NEW ZEALAND*
• Why did Atherton ('Atheron's a munter', the youth next to me insisted) set such defensive fields? — *Evening Post*, p. 4, 3rd February 1997

muppet *noun*
1 a person who is mentally or physically incapacitated or disabled, or considered ugly; someone who represents any permutation of such characteristics; hence, any fool *UK*
Created by Jim Henson (b.1936), *The Muppet Show*, a successful television programme of the 1970s and subsequently in films, introduced the gallery of grotesque puppets on which this allusion is founded.
• — Mike Leigh, *Meantime*, 1983
• We know it ain't you Gumbo, you muppet. — *ID*, 1994
• — Angela Devlin, *Prison Patter*, p. 78, 1996
• "You sure you want to do this?" "You fuckin' muppet, you've spent the last 'alf hour talking me into it. — Colin Butts, *Is Harry on the Boat?*, p. 206, 1997
• What are you two muppets doing with all these pills? — Chris Baker and Andrew Day, *Lock, Stock... & a Fist Full of Jack and Jills*, p. 154, 2000
• Baresi's is a fucking muppet. — John King, *Human Punk*, p. 254, 2000
• Steven watched the office muppets steaming over Blackfriar's Bridge like worker ants and shook his head. — Garry Bushell, *The Face*, p. 135, 2001
2 a magistrate *UK*
Police slang.
• You'd think every Muppet would have the Good Book by his bedside. — Duncan MacLaughlin, *The Filth*, p. 108, 2002

muppet house *noun*
a prison psychiatric unit; a mental hospital *UK*
Extended from **MUPPET** (a person who is mentally incapacitated).
• — Angela Devlin, *Prison Patter*, p. 78, 1996

muppetshop *noun*
a prison workshop *UK*
Extended from **MUPPET** (a person who is mentally incapacitated; a fool) for the mindless nature of the work.
• — Angela Devlin, *Prison Patter*, p. 78, 1996

mural *noun*
a person with many tattoos *US*
• — *Los Angeles Times Magazine*, p. 7, 13th July 1997

murder *noun*
1 something that is extremely good *US, 1927*
• Listen – I was a smash in that fight. Oh, Riff, Riff, I was murder! — *West Side Story*, 1957
2 an absolute nuisance; dreadful trouble *UK, 1857*
• We caused murder in Sevvy Park [...] But we was dead young, in fairness. Seven, eight we was. — Kevin Sampson, *Outlaws*, p. 147, 2001
• The rap page biz [publishing] is murder, dog. — *The Source*, p. 36, March 2002

murder *verb*
to consume voraciously *IRELAND*
• He was murdering the Budweiser, guzzling and belching at the same time to get rid of it so they could go. — Roddy Doyle, *The Van*, p. 255, 1991

▸ **could murder**
to want, to be desirous of something *UK, 1935*
• I could murder a cup of tea. — Katie Fforde, *Wild Designs*, p. 129, 1996

murdered *adjective*
very drunk *UK*
• — Tom Hibbert, *Rockspeak!*, p. 106, 1983

murder house *noun*
a school dental clinic *NEW ZEALAND*
• —Louis S. Leland, *A Personal Kiwi-Yankee Dictionary*, p. 68, 1984

murder one *noun*
a mixture of heroin and cocaine *US*
• — US Department of Justice, *Street Terms*, October 1994
• —Robert Ashton, *This Is Heroin*, p. 209, 2002

murder weed; murder *noun*
marijuana *US, 1935*
Anti-marijuana propaganda adopted into regular slang usage.
• —Lois Stavsky et al., *A2Z*, p. 69, 1995

murder-your-wife brick *noun*
in television and film making, an imitation brick *US*
The imitation brick was first used in the 1965 comedy *How to Murder Your Wife*, starring Jack Lemmon and Virna Lisi.
• —Ralph S. Singleton, *Filmaker's Dictionary*, p. 108, 1990

murk *noun*
coffee *US*
• —Vincent J. Monteleone, *Criminal Slang*, p. 160, 1949

murk *verb*
to shoot with a gun *US*
• "The (expletive) made me murk him for $62," Calhoun told one of the accomplices, using street slang for "shoot."—*Milwaukee Journal Sentinel*, p. 1B, 19th November 2003

murky *adjective*
low-spirited, depressed *US*
• —Anna Scotti and Paul Young, *Buzzwords*, p. 71, 1997

murotogura *noun*
heroin *US*
• —Robert Ashton, *This Is Heroin*, p. 206, 2002

murphy *noun*
1 a potato *UK, 1811*
A belief that potatoes formed the basic diet in Ireland is reflected in this adoption of a common Irish surname.
• I got some baked murphies here I want to warm up,—Clive Exton, *No Fixed Abode [Six Granada Plays]*, p. 119, 1959

2 the condition that exists when someone pulls your trousers or underpants forcefully upwards, forming a wedge between the buttock cheeks *US*
Most commonly known as a 'wedgie'.
• —*American Speech*, Fall 1990

Murphy; Murphy game *noun*
a swindle involving a prostitute and her accomplice, usually entailing robbing the prostitute's customer *US*
• I had heard about jostling and the Murphy for a long time, but I didn't really know what it was all about.—Claude Brown, *Manchild in the Promised Land*, p. 160, 1965
• Years later I discovered that the "Murphy" when played by experts was a smooth short con with a slight risk.—Iceberg Slim (Robert Beck), *Pimp*, p. 36, 1969
• The first thing I know, I'd been rooked out of my jade by the some slick-talkin' Armenian cats runnin' the most sophisticated Murphy I'd ever encountered[.]—Odie Hawkins, *Ghetto Sketches*, p. 83, 1972
• Another source of livelihood for me was a first-class Murphy game I used to run up on 111th Street with the tricks looking for hours.—Edwin Torres, *Carlito's Way*, p. 15, 1975
• I'll take numbers, cop stuff, steal booze or anything of value from three-cent stamps to rockets / I'll play the Murphy to the point of death, and I'll even pick pockets.—Dennis Wepman et al., *The Life*, p. 41, 1976
• If we are going to put down murphy for millions, we got to look like millions.—Robert Deane Pharr, *Giveadamn Brown*, p. 156, 1978
• Passing back into the club, she palmed Joe a twenty, his cut of the Murphy, as any bunko prostitution game was called.—Seth Morgan, *Homeboy*, p. 25, 1990

Murphy man *noun*
the prostitute's male accomplice in a Murphy swindle *US*
• He was a Murphy Man, which meant that he supported himself by posing as a pimp.—James Mills, *The Panic in Needle Park*, p. 34, 1966
• Pimps, muggers, Murphy men, narco, vice and regular fuzz haunt the area waiting for victims—*Screw*, p. 6, 19th July 1971
• By the sleight-of-hand of a Murphy man / Or the words that a con man spoke.—Dennis Wepman et al., *The Life*, p. 80, 1976

Murphy's law *noun*
a cynical 'law' of existence that decrees that 'if something can go wrong it will – and even if it can't, it still might' *US, 1955*
Said to derive from a remark (or philosophy) of Captain E. Murphy at Edwards Air Force Base. The underlying maxim or 'law' is found as early as 1941, as 'an old legend' from Peru in 1952, and in 1957 it is offered as 'an old theatrical saying'. At best, it seems to be the attribution of an old saying to a new, glamorous aviation context.
• After breaking his ankle, crashing his car and being robbed in one afternoon, Anthony [Menchetti] investigates Murphy's Law.—*Edinburgh Festivals (on-line listings)*, 19th August 2003

Murray *noun*
in horse racing, to bet on credit *AUSTRALIA*
Rhyming slang from 'Murray Cod' (a delicious inland fish) to **ON THE NOD** (on credit).
• —Ned Wallish, *The Truth Dictionary of Racing Slang*, p. 54, 1989

▸ on the Murray cod
(of a wager) agreed upon without money changing hands *AUSTRALIA, 1967*
Rhyming slang for **ON THE NOD**. Also in the short form 'on the murray'.
• —Jim Ramsay, *Cop It Sweet!*, p. 61, 1977

Murray Walker; murray *noun*
a talker *UK*
Rhyming slang, based on broadcaster (and, therefore, professional talker) Murray Walker (b.1923).
• —*Antiquarian Book Review*, p. 18, June 2002

muscle *noun*
1 a person or persons using violence and intimidation, usually in the service of another *US, 1942*
• The big hotels and casinos pay a lot of muscle to make sure the high rollers don't have even momentary hassles with 'undesirables.'—Hunter S. Thompson, *Fear and Loathing in Las Vegas*, p. 155, 1971
• He ran the troops – period. He was muscle.—Richard Condon, *Prizzi's Honor*, p. 191, 1982
• A family deal, it was best to get outside help, scummers with no personal interest, muscle you hired by the pound.—Elmore Leonard, *Glitz*, p. 238, 1985
• When he lost, he told the bookies to go fuck themselves. What were they gonna do? Muscle Nicky? Nicky was the muscle.—*Casino*, 1995
• The buttons had driven over from Las Vegas where they worked as freelance muscle.—Stephen Cannell, *Big Con*, p. 251, 1997

2 physical violence *US, 1879*
• "Who's behind all the muscle, Mamie?" I was going too fast for her. "Muscle?" she repeated blankly. "Don't go stupid on me. Who's roughing up the street this time?"—*Rogue for Men*, p. 45, June 1956

▸ on the muscle
threatening, coercive *US, 1859*
• You sure get on the muscle easy. I don't care if you're union or not, long as you know melons.—Elmore Leonard, *Mr. Majestyk*, p. 18, 1974

muscle *verb*
to inject a drug intramuscularly, as opposed to intravenously *US*
• —William D. Alsever, *Glossary for the Establishment and Other Uptight People*, p. 22, December 1970

muscle boy *noun*
a hired intimidator *US*
• From Elizabeth, Jersey, y'know? Muscle boys ... docks.—Mickey Spillane, *Me, Hood!*, p. 44, 1963

muscle car *noun*
a passenger car with a powerful engine, a light chassis and two-door body *US, 1969*
• He tossed him the keys to his former clunker and said, "Ride, daddy, ride," then strolled back to his sleek muscle car.—James Ellroy, *Suicide Hill*, p. 649, 1986
• The Pontiac GTO, introduced in 1964, was considered the first muscle car. By the late sixties, all the domestic manufacturers offered at least one muscle car, resulting in a horsepower race[.]—John Edwards, *Auto Dictionary*, p. 111, 1993
• Today, the few middle-aged men who can still afford to maintain these heaps like to speak wistfully of the muscle car era.—Editors of Ben is Dead, *Retrohell*, p. 137, 1997
• The 1970 Plymouth Road Runner. Proof positive of a single all-powerful Deity. The first bargain-priced muscle car ever.—*Gone in 60 Seconds*, 2000
• Fifteen breathless seconds later, Miles urged her muscle car across the finish line first[.]—*Los Angeles Times*, p. A1, 6th June 2003

muscle-dancing *noun*

a sexually suggestive dance *US*

- Muscle-dancing was introduced in the United States in a big way when the late Sol Bloom, as an entrepreneur at the Chicago World's Fair, celebrating the 400th anniversary of the discovery of America, presented "Little Egypt". — Jack Lait and Lee Mortimer, *Chicago Confidential*, p. 157, 1950

muscle-happy *adjective*

said of a prisoner who concentrates on physical fitness in jail *US*

- — Jack Webb, *The Badge*, p. 221, 1958

muscle in *verb*

to intrude, by force or threat of force, on another's activity or business; to intrude, by subterfuge, on another's activity or business *UK, 1929*

- Last weekend I successfully muscled in on the motorcycle industry's ride to work day by travelling from Witney to Oxford on the back of a vintage Enfield 500. — *The Guardian*, 20th June 2002

muscleman *noun*

an enforcer for a criminal enterprise *US, 1929*

- Billy Mist and a heavyset muscleman came off the elevator, opened the apartment door and went in. — Mickey Spillane, *Kiss Me Deadly*, p. 110, 1952
- Bert was known as a muscleman. — William Burroughs, *Junkie*, p. 58, 1953
- They were in a glamorous business which no longer needed peepholes, locked doors, and muscle men standing by for inevitable trouble. — Robert Sylvester, *No Cover Charge*, p. 225, 1956
- He's a muscle man for a Harlem numbers-raquet operator. — Iceberg Slim (Robert Beck), *Trick Baby*, p. 213, 1969

muscle Mary *noun*

a homosexual man who is a bodybuilder *UK*

- — Paul Baker, *Polari*, p. 180, 2002

muscles *nickname*

used as a form of address for a strong or well-muscled man; also used, with heavy irony, of a weakling *UK, 1984*

musgro *noun*

a police officer *UK*

English gypsy use from Romany *mûskro* (a policeman).

- — Jimmy Stockin, *On The Cobbles*, 2000

mush *noun*

1 the mouth or face *US, 1859*

Sometimes seen as 'moosh'.

- "Boy," he went on," would I like to give that bitch a good sock in the mush!" — Jim Thompson, *The Nothing Man*, p. 265, 1954
- I bring up my left hand and give him a looping shot in the mush. — Rocky Garciano (with Rowland Barber), *Somebody Up There Likes Me*, p. 224, 1955
- [A] moosh of no great beauty. — Ray Puxley, *Cockney Rabbit*, p. 109, 1992
- — Angela Devlin, *Prison Patter*, p. 78, 1996
- Who told you to stop filling that bag, fill that fucking bag or you'll get one in the mush too. — Danny King, *The Bank Robber Diaries*, p. 48, 2002

2 a man; used as a greeting or as a dismissive term of address *US, 1906*

- [T]he mush said he would not go[.] — Butch Reynolds, *Broken Hearted Clown*, p. 28, 1953
- — Angela Devlin, *Prison Patter*, p. 78, 1996
- "We'll have a laugh with this mush," smiled Johnny. — Jimmy Stockin, *On The Cobbles*, p. 74, 2000
- Fuck off, mush, he said, leaning forward. — John King, *White Trash*, p. 63, 2001

3 money *UK*

- I carry me mush in me ruddy pockets, not at home. — Troy Kennedy Martin, *Z Cars*, p. 79, 1962

4 in circus and carnival usage, an umbrella *UK, 1821*

- — Don Wilmeth, *The Language of American Popular Entertainment*, p. 179, 1981

5 a weak, slow wave *US*

- — Gary Fairmont R. Filosa II, *The Surfer's Almanac*, p. 190, 1977

6 in the television and film industries, low-level sound used as background *UK*

- — Oswald Skilbeck, *ABC of Film and TV Working Terms*, p. 87, 1960

mush *verb*

1 to kiss *US, 1926*

- Ten minutes after I made home-sweet-home and laid some Chanel Number Five and some find handmade underwear on my old lady, I mushed her and cut out for the Riverside Towers, on the West Side overlooking the Hudson, where the gang dommied. — Mezz Mezzrow, *Really the Blues*, p. 199, 1946

2 (used of an aeroplane) to run out of airspeed *US, 1935*

- She seemed to be mushing, running out of airspeed. — Stephen Coonts, *Flight of the Intruder*, p. 419, 1986
- He drops down, the trees blur by underneath, the overloaded choppers bump and mush through the heavy air. — Dennis Marvicsin and Jerold Greenfield, *Maverick*, p. 102, 1990

mush *adjective*

▷ see: **MOOSH**

mushburger *noun*

in surfing, a weak, poorly formed wave *US*

- — Michael V. Anderson, *The Bad, Rad, Not to Forget Way Cool Beach and Surf Discriptionary*, p. 13, 1988

musher *noun*

1 a man *UK*

An elaborataion of **MUSH**.

- [S]ome sad fuckin musher would pay yis that much to have ther [sic] arse caned? — Niall Griffiths, *Kelly + Victor*, p. 283, 2002

2 a villain; someone who moves in criminal circles *UK*

Liverpool usage; possibly puns **MUSH** (the face) into **FACE** (a known criminal).

- Every musher in town wants to know the Brennan boys. — Kevin Sampson, *Outlaws*, p. 21, 2001

mushfake *noun*

to manufacture in defiance of prison rules and prohibitions *US*

A term originally applied to the makeshift repair of umbrellas.

- Mush-faking was the major industry within the prison. It was the manufacture of gadgets such as cigarette holders and lighters and jewel boxes and rings and pins and similar items from old bones, toothbrush handles, copper coins, and coin crowns. — Chester Himes, *Cast the First Stone*, p. 80, 1952
- — Troy Harris, *A Booklet of Criminal Argot, Cant and Jargon*, 1976

mushie *noun*

1 a mushroom *AUSTRALIA, 1981*

- You needed the consitution of a wash-house boiler to get through a feed of mushies in our house[.] — Kerry Cue, *Crooks, Chooks and Bloody Ratbags*, p. 165, 1983
- Full hit, bacon, sausages, plum tomatoes [...] Black pudding and all, three fried eggs, mushies, loads of toast. — Kevin Sampson, *Outlaws*, p. 227, 2001

2 an hallucinogenic mushroom, a magic mushroom *UK*

- — Angela Devlin, *Prison Patter*, p. 78, 1996
- [S]tuff yewer face full a mushies during-a season like, just trip yewer fuckin life away on a hillside just for something to fuckin do. — Niall Griffiths, *Sheepshagger*, p. 7, 2001

mushie *adjective*

▷ see: **MOOSH**

mushied-up *adjective*

intoxicated by hallucinogenic mushrooms *UK*

From **MUSHIE** (a mushroom).

- [A] bacchanalian freakout usually the preserve of mushied-up drongos invading Stonehenge for the Solstice. — Kevin Sampson, *Powder*, p. 27, 1999

mushmellow *noun*

the vagina *US*

A clever play on 'marshmallow' (a pink flower and a sweet confection), combining 'mush' (anything soft and moist) and 'mellow' (relaxed, comfortable).

- There's [a...] " mongo," a "pajama," "fannyboo," "mushmellow," "a ghoulie[".] — Eve Ensler, *The Vagina Monologues*, p. 6, 1998

mushmouthed *adjective*

unable to speak clearly *US*

- Sometimes he would be mushmouthed on morphine or pain pills[.] — Lester Bangs, *Psychotic Reactions and Carburetor Dung*, p. 219, 1977

mushrat *noun*

a muskrat *CANADA*

- Grant went on to talk a little answering Bill's questions about how it would be later on. November and the mushrat season open. — Charles Bruce, *The Channel Shore*, p. 117, 1954

mushroom *noun*

1 a person who is given no information *UK, 1979*

From the US witticism/poster and T-shirt slogan: 'I feel like a mushroom: everyone keeps me in the dark and is always feeding me bullshit'.

- [During the Falklands war in 1982] The Royal Fleet Auxiliary crew considered themselves "mushrooms" – they were kept in the dark about almost everything. — *The Guardian*, 2nd July 1982

2 in firefighter usage, a fire that spreads out and downward when reaching a ceiling *US*

- — *American Speech*, p. 275, December 1954: 'Fire terms: additional words and definitions'

3 an innocent bystander killed in crossfire *US, 1988*

- In city after city, police report a startling rise in shootings of innocents – "mushrooms" in street slang – struck by stray bullets. — *New York Times*, p. 24 (Section 4), 24th September 1989
- That was a time when crack dealers talked nonchalantly about "mushroom killings," street slang for bystanders slain crossfires. — *Daily News (New York)*, p. 6, 15th December 1997

mushroom *verb*

(of the felt tip on a pool cue stick) to compress and spread outward *US, 1988*

- — Mike Shamos, *The Illustrated Encyclopedia of Billiards*, p. 152, 1993

mushroom pills *noun*

psilocybin or psilocin, in powder or capsule form *UK*

A strong psychedelic drug extracted from *Psilocybe mexicana* and *Stropharia cubensis* mushrooms. One capsule has an equivalent effect to forty or more **MAGIC MUSHROOM(S)**.

mushy *noun*

a weak, slow wave *US*

- — John Severson, *Modern Surfing Around the World*, p. 175, 1964

mushy *adjective*

sentimental, insipidly or gushingly romantic *US, 1848*

A figurative application of the conventional sense.

- SIDNEY: When's the racing come on? TONY: Shuttup. SIDNEY: Well this is mushy. — Ray Galton and Alan Simpson, *Hancock's Half Hour*, 14th June 1955

musical vegetables *noun*

baked beans *UK*

- — Chris Donald, *Roger's Profanisaurus*, 1988

music stand *noun*

in electric line work, a rack for holding insulated line tools *US*

- — A.B. Chance Co., *Lineman's Slang Dictionary*, p. 12, 1980

Muskoka chair *noun*

an outdoor wooden chair with wide flat armrests and a backrest in a fan shape *CANADA*

This is the Canadian name for what is known in the US as the 'Adirondack chair'. The Muskoka Lakes region is north of Toronto.

muskra *noun*

a police officer *UK*

A corruption of Romany *moskero*; *mooshkero* (a constable).

- — Patrick O'Shaughnessy, *Market Traders' Slang*, 1979

muskrat *noun*

a child *US*

- — Porter Bibb, *CB Bible*, p. 100, 1976

muso *noun*

a musician *AUSTRALIA, 1967*

- He's a gas little muso. Could be one of the greats. — Kevin Mackey, *The Cure*, p. 124, 1970
- Martin's muso friends from Canberra. Oh, God! — Bettina Arndt, *The Australian Way of Sex*, p. 93, 1985
- Crosby loved the anti-pop/anti-muso mentality of the San Francisco bands — Barney Hoskyns, *Waiting For The Sun*, 1996
- He hovers near the musos for a while[.] — Pete McCarthy, *McCarthy's Bar*, 2000

mussie *noun*

a tough woman *UK*

- A woman is often called a "mussie" meaning rather a tough kind of "dame". — Butch Reynolds, *Broken Hearted Clown*, p. 30, 1953

mustache *noun*

a Mustache Pete *US, 1973*

- It started out the young guys hitting the old guys, the mustaches, 'cause they wouldn't get off their ass, make a move on the gambling. — Elmore Leonard, *Glitz*, p. 107, 1985

mustache mob *noun*

first generation immigrants from Sicily or southern Italy *US*

- They never saw no fighter who brought out the 'mustache mob' like I done, not even Primo Carnera who was an Italian from Italy. — Rocky Garciano (with Rowland Barber), *Somebody Up There Likes Me*, p. 339, 1955

Mustache Pete *noun*

an older Italian-American criminal, associated with outdated ways of doing things *US, 1938*

- Georgetti was of the old Mafia school, known as the Mustache Petes. — Ed Reid and Ovid Demaris, *The Green Felt Jungle*, p. 181, 1963
- Between the old Moustache Petes and the new breed bucking their way in, there were no exceptions, no excuses, and if you couldn't cut it, they'd cut you. — Mickey Spillane, *Last Cop Out*, p. 104, 1972
- The two old guys flanking Mazzone – Mustache Petes – had the shirt buttoned to the top but no tie. — Edwin Torres, *Carlito's Way*, p. 101, 1975
- Do I look like a penniless 'Mustache Pete' fresh off the boat? — Iceberg Slim (Robert Beck), *Death Wish*, p. 26, 1977

mustache ride *noun*

an act of oral sex *US, 1981*

- Another way to say "cunnilingus" [...] Giving her a moustache ride[.] — Erica Orloff and JoAnn Baker, *Dirty Little Secrets*, p. 86, 2001

mustache rider *noun*

a woman as the object of oral sex with a man *AUSTRALIA*

- — Thommo, *The Dictionary of Australian Swearing and Sex Sayings*, p. 85, 1985

mustang *noun*

an officer appointed from the enlisted ranks *US, 1878*

- It usually takes only thirty months to make the rank of captain, so fifteen years made Sam a "mustang," an enlisted man who was offered a commission because of his demonstrated leadership and military knowledge. — Charles Anderson, *The Grunts*, p. 30, 1976
- — Linda Reinberg, *In the Field*, p. 147, 1991

mustard *noun*

AIDS [Acquired Immune Deficiency Syndrome], a disease that is transmitted by sexual contact *US*

There are very few synonyms for AIDS despite the huge impact of the disease; the etymology here is uncertain.

- The moral to the story is the mustard's all around / ... I ain't really got AIDS, it's just a motherfucking record. — Sadat X, Fat Joe & Diamond D, *Nasty Hoes*, 1996

mustard *adjective*

excellent, best, skilled, keen *UK, 1925*

From the phrases 'keen as mustard' and 'hot as mustard'.

- Norwich is mustard for munching pies. — *The Guardian*, 18th September 2004

mustard and cress; mustard *noun*

a dress *UK*

Rhyming slang.

- — Ray Puxley, *Fresh Rabbit*, 1998

mustard case *noun*

a supreme show-off *US*

The suggestion is of a **HOT DOG**, dosed with mustard.

- He never had many friends in Motors because the officers assigned there were basically "hot pilot" types – attitude junkies known on the job as "mustard cases." — Stephen J. Cannell, *The Tin Collectors*, p. 169, 2001

mustard chucker *noun*

a pickpocket who spills mustard on the victim as a diversion and excuse to approach *US*

- A mustard chucker, for instance, sprays a victim with mustard. He apologizes profusely and helps to remove it while an accomplice steals the victim's wallet. — *The New York Times*, p. B1, 13th July 1989

mustard keen; mustard *adjective*

very keen *UK*

From the proverbial phrase 'keen as mustard'.

- This society is mustard on contamination offences. — *The Guardian*, 26th February 1979
- Michael Owen is mustard-keen to extend his stay[.] — *The Guardian*, 2nd September 2003

mustard pickle; mustard *noun*

a cripple *UK*

Rhyming slang, imperfectly rhymed.

- — Ray Puxley, *Fresh Rabbit*, 1998

mustard pot *noun*
the vagina *UK, 1896*
Rhyming slang for **TWOT** (**TWAT**).
- —Ray Puxley, *Cockney Rabbit*, 1992

mustard pot; mustard *adjective*
hot *UK*
- Ain't it bloody mustard. I could do the ironing with my feet.—Ray Puxley, *Fresh Rabbit*, 1998

mustard shine *noun*
the application of mustard to the shoes in the hope of throwing tracking dogs off the scent *US*
- —Vincent J. Monteleone, *Criminal Slang*, p. 160, 1949

must be nice!
used for expressing envy or congratulations *US*
Collected from a university student, Evanston, Illinois, in September 2002.

mutant *noun*
a social outcast *US, 1984*
- But it's not fair – she's a mutant, Daddy!—*Ten Things I Hate About You*, 1999

mute *noun*
1 the vagina *UK*
Gay slang.
- —Bruce Rodgers, *Queens' Vernacular*, 1972

2 in horse racing, a pari-mutuel betting machine *US, 1942*
- —Dan Parker, *The ABC of Horse Racing*, p. 147, 1947

mutha *noun*
anything or anyone *US*
An abbreviation of **MOTHERFUCKER**.
- All the way across and all the way back. Strip every last mutha down.—Diran Abedayo, *My Once Upon A Time*, p. 261, 2000

muthafucka *noun*
a motherfucker *US*
Alternative spelling.
- MUTHAFUCKA!—Lester Bangs, *Psychotic Reactions and Carburetor Dung*, p. 288, 1979
- I keep hearing about muthafucking Harry Potter. I'm like, Who is this muthafucker I keep hearing about?—*Q*, p. 25, December 2001

muthafucking *adjective*
used as an all-purpose intensifier *US*
Variant spelling of **MOTHERFUCKING**.
- I keep hearing about muthafucking Harry Potter. I'm like, Who is this muthafucker I keep hearing about?—*Q*, p. 25, December 2001

mutt *noun*
1 a dog, especially a mongrel *US, 1900*
Affectionately disparaging.
- Yo soft mutt, Woody.—Paul Fraser and Shane Meadows, *TwentyFourSeven*, p. 5, 1997

2 a despicable low-life *US, 1899*
- [I]nterviewing an anonymous and endless stream of indigent mutts through the grills of the processing pen, haggling over jail time, accepting collect calls from the coinless phones upon the tiers[.] —Richard Price, *Clockers*, p. 445, 1992

3 a thug, a criminal *US*
- Four-six anti-crime was seen trying to leave the premises, a sector car came on the scene, and here we are.—Samuel M. Katz, *Anytime Anywhere*, p. 217, 1997

4 the American shethbill, a small Antarctic bird *ANTARCTICA*
- — *Cool Antarctica*, 2003: 'Antarctic slang'

Mutt and Jeff *noun*
a pair of men who are physically mismatched, especially in height *US, 1914*
From the popular comic strip.
- Baddest of the bad was Big Jeff from the "Mutt and Jeff" detective team from the Twenty-third. One was a little wop, Lil' Jeff, the other a big mick, Big Jeff; you couldn't call either one Mutt or they'd break yo' ass.—Edwin Torres, *Carlito's Way*, p. 16, 1975
- "You had ... experiences together," Sidney Blackpool said, double-teaming him with Mutt and Jeff.—Joseph Wambaugh, *The Secrets of Harry Bright*, p. 240, 1985
- And turned to see Raji first, holding a pistol in his lap, then Elliot, on the love seat. He laid the jacket over a chair, saying, "Mutt and Jeff, what can I do for you?"—Elmore Leonard, *Be Cool*, p. 339, 1999
- Andrew Hallock and Jeffrey Jones Ragona, doubling as Belshazzar's wise men and Dariu's envious counselors, made a kind of Mutt-and-Jeff pair, visually and even vocally.—*Austin (Texas) American-Statesman*, p. 20, 25th December 2003

Mutt and Jeff; mutton *adjective*
deaf *UK, 1960*
Rhyming slang from the US cartoon strip characters created by Bud Fisher (1855–1954). Mutt first appeared in the *San Francisco Chronicle* in 1907, Jeff was drawn in shortly after and by 1915 the pair were a national phenomenon. Adopted into UK theatrical slang and consequently reduced in pronunciation to 'mutton'.
- Terry turned to Arthur. "He's mutton." "That doesn't mean to say he's not a good doctor, Terence."—Anthony Masters, *Minder*, 1984
- Whoever he is, cunt's mutton.—Kevin Sampson, *Outlaws*, p. 62, 2001

mutter and stutter *noun*
butter *UK*
Rhyming slang.
- —Julian Franklyn, *A Dictionary of Rhyming Slang*, 1960

mutton *noun*
the penis *AUSTRALIA*
- —Barry Humphries, *Bazza Pulls It Off!*, 1971
- —David McGill, *David McGill's Complete Kiwi Slang Dictionary*, p. 74, 1998

mutton flaps *noun*
the *labia majora* *NEW ZEALAND*
- —David McGill, *David McGill's Complete Kiwi Slang Dictionary*, p. 74, 1998

muttonhead *noun*
a railway dispatcher *US*
- —Ramon Adams, *The Language of the Railroader*, p. 103, 1977

mutton-headed *adjective*
stupid *UK, 1768*
- Complacent electors of Gubba and fellow-victims of a clique of mutton-headed creeping crawler nincompoop councillors!—Dymphna Cusack, *Picnic Races*, p. 79, 1962
- He said he would have done the same for anybody, even a great useless, clumsy, splay-footed, mutton-headed galah of an Italian. —John O'Grady, *Gone Fishin'*, p. 57, 1962

mutton merchant *noun*
a male sexual exhibitionist *AUSTRALIA*
- I hope he's not a perve or a mutton merchant!—Barry Humphries, *Bazza Pulls It Off!*, 1971

mutton of the sea *noun*
the hawskbill sea turtle *BAHAMAS*
- —John A. Holm, *Dictionary of Bahamian English*, p. 138, 1982

mutt's nuts *noun*
anything considered to be the finest, the most excellent, the best *UK*
Variation of **DOG'S BOLLOCKS**; **MUTT** (a dog) and **NUTS** (the testicles) combine literally and figuratively to mean 'outstanding'.
- "It's the mutt's nuts," declared [Samuel] Jackson at the gala preview[.]—*Play, The Times*, p. 4, 8th December 2001

muvva *noun*
used as an abbreviation of 'motherfucker' *UK*
A slovening of 'mother'.
- There's some mad muvvas out there.—Garry Bushell, *The Face*, p. 16, 2001

muzzie *adjective*
stupid *UK*
Probably from 'muscle-headed'.
- Not good enough for one of the fucking goons, mind you. Nowhere near good enough for Telford muzzie man.—Kevin Sampson, *Outlaws*, p. 50, 2001

muzzle *noun*
heroin *US, 1959*
- —US Department of Justice, *Street Terms*, October 1994
- —Robert Ashton, *This Is Heroin*, p. 206, 2002

muzzle guzzle *noun*
a party organised around alcholic drink *US*
- —Collin Baker et al., *College Undergraduate Slang Study Conducted at Brown University*, p. 160, 1968

muzzler *noun*
in circus and carnival usage, a person lacking morals *US*
- —Don Wilmeth, *The Language of American Popular Entertainment*, p. 180, 1981

muzzy *noun*
a moustache *UK*
- [H]e had a bad muzzy and a sheepie [curled hair].—Kevin Sampson, *Outlaws*, p. 163, 2001
- [A]s wide as she was tall. Yowge [huge]. Pure fuckin Spacehopper. With a muzzy.—Niall Griffiths, *Kelly + Victor*, p. 43, 2002

mwah!
the vocal accompaniment to a kiss, especially an air-kiss *UK, 1994*
- [S]omeone I can rush up to and go mwah mwah and shriek, "We must do lunch!"—Sophie Kinsella, *Confessions of a Shopaholic*, p. 82, 2001

MX *noun*
Mandrax™, a sedative drug *UK, 1960s*
- Did a burglary after eating too many MX.—Paul E Willis, *Profane Culture*, p. 184, 1978

Myakka gold *noun*
marijuana grown in Florida *US, 2001*
- —Simon Worman, *Joint Smoking Rules*, 2001

myall; Myall *noun*
an Aboriginal who has little or no contact with white people *AUSTRALIA*
From the extinct Australian Aboriginal language Dharug, Sydney region, *mayal* (stranger).
- They reckon her grandmother was a regular Myall.—Dymphna Cusack, *Picnic Races*, p. 142, 1962
- [H]e finished up spending the rest of his life as a Myall, keeping right out of touch of civilization.—Wal Watkins, *Race the Lazy River*, p. 89, 1963

myall *adjective*
(of an Australian Aboriginal) traditional; unaffected by white society *AUSTRALIA*
- Sadie comes from myall black fella tribe y'u know.—Wal Watkins, *Andamooka*, p. 56, 1971
- I was still myall when I left.—Herb Wharton, *Cattle Camp*, p. 28, 1994

my arse!; my ass!
used to register disbelief or contempt *UK, 1933*
- —Joseph A. Weingarten, *An American Dictionary of Slang*, p. 11, 1954
- BOB: Easy, Holy. HOLYGHOST: Easy my ass[.]—Howard Stern, *Miss America*, p. 20, 1995
- JIM: There's nowt you can do abroad you can't do here. BARB: What about having a good time? JIM: Good time my arse! They spend half the bloody time on the khazi having the wild shites.—Caroline Aherne and Craig Cash, *The Royle Family*, 1998–99
- When loyalist gangs hurled stones into Catholic areas, they clearly weren't thinking "transubstantiation my arse".—Mark Steel, *Reasons to be Cheerful*, p. 105, 2001

my arsehole!
used for registering disbelief or contempt *UK*
A variation of **MY ARSE!**.
- HEALTH VISITOR: You don't mind if I wash my hands do you, dear? [...] YOSSER: I know what you've come for. Wash your hands, my arsehole.—Alan Bleasdale, *Boys From the Blackstuff*, 1982
- Murder my fuckin arse'ole.—Niall Griffiths, *Sheepshagger*, p. 239, 2001

my Aunt Fanny!
used as a register for disbelief, sometimes exclamatory *UK*
A euphemism for the bolder **MY ASS!**.
- She's got no more idea how to run this house than my Aunt Fanny. —Monica Dickens, *Thursday Afternoons*, p. 69, 1945

my bad!
used for acknowledging responsibility for and apologising for a mistake *US*
- —Connie Eble (Editor), *UNC-CH Campus Slang*, p. 6, Spring 1989
- Yeah, that was my bad, sorry.—*South Park*, 1999
- "I think you have the wrong number." "Oh. Whups, my bad."—Marty Beckerman, *Death to All Cheerleaders*, p. 134, 2000

my bloody oath!
yes indeed! *AUSTRALIA, 1952*
Intesified form of **MY OATH!**.
- I didn't take her – ' 'My bloody oath you took her!—D.E. Charlwood, *All the Green Year*, p. 102, 1965
- I'll give it to yo', yo' come near me, Nugget...my bloody oath I will[.] —Xavier Herbert, *Poor Fellow My Country*, p. 415, 1975
- —Jim Ramsay, *Cop It Sweet!*, p. 13, 1977
- Your freedom is always very precious to you. Les reflected back on getting arrested on Wednesday night. Yeah. My bloody oath it is. —Robert G. Barrett, *The Wind and the Monkey*, p. 193, 1999

my bust!
used for accepting responsibility for a mistake or error *US*
- —Connie Eble (Editor), *UNC-CH Campus Slang*, p. 2, April 1985

my colonial oath *noun*
my word *AUSTRALIA*
Formerly a common exclamation.
- [A]nd you can take my colonial oath on it, there's nothing too ratty fer sheep ter git up ter.—Dymphna Cusack, *Picnic Races*, p. 139, 1962

my dog ate it
used as a humorous explanation of why a person does not have something that they are supposed to have *US*
From the clichéd student excuse for not having a homework assignment.
- It means, "My dog ate it." It's Latin. It's a joke.—*American Pie*, 1999

my face!
used for expressing embarassment *US*
- —Connie Eble (Editor), *UNC-CH Campus Slang*, p. 6, Spring 2003

my foot!
used for registering an emphatic rejection; used as a direct denial of a point just made *UK*
A polite variation of **MY ARSE!**, often used as a suffix to the repeated point of contention.
- I don't believe a damn word. The Tweets outselling Oasis, my foot! —Kevin Sampson, *Powder*, p. 70, 1999

my hen laid a haddock *nickname*
the Welsh national anthem *UK: WALES*
A phonetic transliteration of the title and first-line of *Mae hen Wlad fy Nhadau* (The Land of my Fathers), first published in 1860. There are a number of humorous variations of the continuing lyric but the first line is a constant; dating from the 1990s, it seems to have been inspired by English politicians' inability to learn the Welsh words.

my hole!
used for registering disbelief or contempt *UK*
- Til death us do part is what thee say. My fuckin hole.—Niall Griffiths, *Kelly + Victor*, p. 39, 2002

my oath!
certainly!, yes indeed! *AUSTRALIA, 1869*
- 'Are you still keen to go out?' 'Yeah my oath.'—Robert G. Barrett, *Davo's Little Something*, p. 24, 1992

MYOB
used in colloquial speech as well as shorthand in Internet discussion groups and text message to mean '*m*ind *y*our *o*wn *b*usiness' *US*
- —Gabrielle Mander, *WAN2TLK? ltl bk of txt msgs*, p. 48, 2002

my old fruit *noun*
▷ see: **OLD FRUIT**

Myrna Loy *noun*
a saveloy *UK*
Rhyming slang, formed from the name of the US film actress, 1905–93.
- —Ray Puxley, *Cockney Rabbit*, 1992

my sainted aunt!
used as an exclamation of trivial delight or shock *UK, 1921*
- Take William (please!), Heinrich's great grandson, whose greatest interest over the years was the specialised growing of flowers suitable for show blooms'. Well, my sainted aunt!—*The Guardian*, 4th December 2003

my son *noun*
▷ see: **SON**

mystery *noun*
a young woman, especially when she is a new arrival in a town or city *UK, 1937*
- It seems that Lew had taken up with a mystery, which is the underworld expression for one of those teen-age girls who drift into London from the provinces.—Charles Raven, *Underworld Nights*, p. 107, 1956

- [T]he little mystery's woken up when she wasn't supposed to. —Derek Raymond (Robin Cook), *The Crust on its Uppers*, p. 50, 1962

mystery bag *noun*

1 a sausage *AUSTRALIA*
So called because the contents are unknown.
- She will also economise with food, serving 'mystery bags' (sausages) or some other cheap but substantial fare to her family. —Nancy Keesing, *Lily on the Dustbin*, p. 21, 1982

2 a meat pie *AUSTRALIA*
- — *Wordmap (www.abc.net.au/wordmap)*, 2003

mystery meat *noun*

cold cuts of suspicious heritage *US, 1918*
- —John D. Bell et al., *Loosely Speaking*, p. Addenda, 1969
- — *Verbatim*, p. 280, May 1976

mystery punter *noun*

a man who spends his time obsessively on the lookout for young women who are newly arrived in a town or city with an intention to live with, and take advantage of, them; such a man is said to be 'mystery mad' *UK*
- —David Powis, *The Signs of Crime*, 1977

Mystic Meg *noun*

1 a leg *UK*
Rhyming slang, formed from a television fortune teller who came to fame in the mid-1990s by association with the National Lottery.
- —Ray Puxley, *Fresh Rabbit*, 1998

2 the penis *UK*
Rhyming slang for **THIRD LEG**; a specialisation of the previous sense.
- —Bodmin Dark, *Dirty Cockney Rhyming Slang*, 2003

mysto *adjective*

mystical *US*
- Then I heard he went mysto, and I thought he was sold out. Later on, I went mysto, and looked him up again. —Stephen Gaskin, *Amazing Dope Tales*, p. 2, 1980

my wave!

used by surfers to express 'ownership' of a wave and to warn other surfers to get out and stay out of the way *US*
- —Trevor Cralle, *The Surfin'ary*, p. 78, 1991

my word *noun*

a piece of excrement *UK*
Rhyming slang for **TURD**.
- —Ray Puxley, *Cockney Rabbit*, 1992

my word!

1 used as an expression of surprise or despair *UK, 1841*
- Oh my word, that water tastes funny. — *The Guardian*, 30th April 2004

2 yes indeed! *AUSTRALIA, 1857*
Shortening of 'upon my word!'.
- —Harvey E. Ward, *Down Under Without Blunder*, p. 42, 1967
- 'My word, that's fine!' I said. 'Now you will make a fortune.' —Harold Lewis, *Crow On A Barbed Wire Fence*, p. 119, 1973

myxo *noun*

the viral disease myxomatosis introduced to control feral rabbits *AUSTRALIA, 1953*
- Despite myxo, family complaints, decomposed carcasses, and fossilised skins, Bush Enterprises Inc. apparently made sufficient profit to justify its existence. —Kerry Cue, *Crooks, Chooks and Bloody Ratbags*, p. 165, 1983

Nn

'n' *conjunction*

and *US, 1858*

An abbreviation; notably (since 1955) in **ROCK 'N' ROLL**.

- Rock 'n' roll has been really bringing me down lately—David Bowie, 1976
- [T]he wives went 'n' all[.]—Greg Williams, *Diamond Geezers*, p. 135, 1997
- The salt 'n' lemon shot ritual—*Sky Magazine*, p. 89, May 2001
- [T]he overly dramatised guns 'n' drugs manner[.]—*X-Ray*, p. 119, November 2002

NAAFI; Naafi *noun*

a military organisation that operates shops and canteens for military personnel; any shop or canteen within that organisation *UK, 1921*

Acronym of *N*avy, *A*rmy and *A*ir *F*orce *I*nstitutes.

naavo *noun*

a secret hiding place *IRELAND*

- [T]he sort of place you'd hide your butts from your da[.]—Terence Dolan, *A Dictionary of Hiberno-English*, 1999

nab *noun*

the police; a police officer *UK, 1813*

- —Babs Gonzales, *Be-Bop Dictionary and History of its Famous Stars*, p. 9, 1949
- We'd all gotten in trouble again and the neighborhood was full of nabs, and plainclothes guys were ganging around.—Hal Ellson, *Duke*, p. 1, 1949
- He couldn't afford to have "Nab" (police) catch anything in his short[.]—Babs Gonzales, *I Paid My Dues*, p. 98, 1967

nab *verb*

1 to catch, to arrest *UK, 1686*

- The men stated that when they nabbed Jack Guzik in 1947, Prendergast shook his head and said, "They won't like it."—Jack Lait and Lee Mortimer, *Chicago Confidential*, p. 236, 1950
- Not because they almost nabbed us, but because of me, see?—John Clellon Holmes, *Go*, p. 122, 1952
- After watching a Catholic video mass I caught the end of "Milton the Monster," which dealt with inept motor-cycle cops trying with consistent unsuccess to nab speeders and also violence.—James Simon Kunen, *The Strawberry Statement*, p. 91, 1968
- CAMERON: We're gonna get nabbed, for sure. FERRIS: No way,k Cameron. Only the meek get nabbed.—*Ferris Buehler's Day Off*, 1986
- No one's nabbed DeChooch, and Kruper hasn't floated in with the tide.—Janet Evanovich, *Seven Up*, p. 53, 2001
- Everytime they nabbed him he was let out to try again[.]—Brian Preston, *Pot Planet*, p. 137, 2002

2 to snatch or steal something *UK, 1665*

- I even nabbed a seat for Passport to the Universe at the Rose Center for Earth and Space, which is so far uptown that the atmosphere has no gravity.—*The Village Voice*, 12th December 2000

nabber *noun*

a police officer *US, 1837*

- —Lavada Durst, *The Jives of Dr. Hepcat*, p. 13, 1953
- A California nabber took me, white slavery was my charge / convicted me and in twenty-four hours in the bighouse I did lodge.—Bruce Jackson, *Get Your Ass in the Water and Swim Like Me*, p. 151, 1965

nabe *noun*

1 a neighbourhood cinema *US, 1935*

- It's time to tour the nabes, gang, and what fun that is!—*The Berkeley Barb*, p. 4, 10th June 1966
- —Sherman Louis Sergel, *The Language of Show Biz*, p. 145, 1973
- [O]ur parents, who probably saw the things at the nabes when they first came out[.]—Lester Bangs, *Psychotic Reactions and Carburetor Dung*, p. 121, 1973

2 a tavern *US*

- These work about as the nabe joints do, which will be set forth as fully hereinafter as our stomachs will allow.—Jack Lait and Lee Mortimer, *Chicago Confidential*, p. 12, 1950

nach *adverb*

▷ **see:** NATCH

naches; nakhes *noun*

proud pleasure *US, 1968*

Yiddish from the Hebrew for 'contentment'.

- A boyla, as we would say, who gave nothing but Naches to his parents.—Vincent Patrick, *Family Business*, p. 274, 1985
- I have such naches: My son is chief of his play group.—Leo Rosten, *The Joys of Yinglish*, p. 350, 1989

nack *noun*

▸ **in the nack**

naked *UK*

- I'm walking around that Aldi, dead fucking slow, in the nack.—Kevin Sampson, *Clubland*, p. 32, 2002

nada *noun*

nothing; none *US, 1914*

From the Spanish, used by English speakers who do not understand Spanish, often heard in the 1980s advertising phrase 'Nothing – nada – zilch'. Recorded in UK gay currency.

- GIANT: If your late ass woulda been here you woulda missed nada. —*Mo' Better Blues*, 1990
- "Has anybody got any porn mags?" "Nada," Thurston says.—Darren Francis, *The Sprawl [britpulp]*, p. 296, 1999
- —*Attitude*, p. 60, July 2003: 'Old palare lexicon'

nad alert; gonad alert *noun*

used as a warning in a hospital that an x-ray is about to be taken *US*

- —Sally Williams, *"Strong" Words*, p. 151, 1994

nada to vada in the larder

refering to a man's genitals, less than averagely endowed *UK*

Polari; a clever combination of **NADA** (nothing) and **VADA** (to see) with a conventional location where meat is stored.

- —Paul Baker, *Polari*, p. 181, 2002

nadger *noun*

in horse racing, a horse's nose or head *AUSTRALIA*

- —Ned Wallish, *The Truth Dictionary of Racing Slang*, p. 55, 1989

nadgers *noun*

the testicles *UK, 1998*

Possibly deriving from 'gonads', and with a similarity to **KNACKERS**, 'nadgers' was an all-purpose nonsense word used by the radio comedy series *The Goon Show* during the 1950s.

- The Pole chose to knock Bowe out by hitting him in the nadgers with a punishing three-punch salvo.—*FHM*, p. 149, June 2003

nads *noun*

the testicles *US, 1964*

From 'gonads'.

- It's such run to read, and, Molet really pumps my nads!—*The Breakfast Club*, 1985
- The photos from Stuart's forthcoming health-related adverts exposing the virtues of playing with your 'nads (to check for lumps) arrive.—*Q*, p. 46, May 2002
- [T]o protect the innocent – ie, his newly shackled nads from the wrath of his young bride.—*FHM*, p. 25, June 2003

naff *adjective*

vulgar, bad, unlovely, despicable; generally contemptible; when used in gay society it may mean heterosexual *UK*

Theatrical and **CAMP** origins but the actual derivation is disputed; possibly an acronym for 'not available for fucking', 'not a fuck' or 'normal as fuck'; or a play on the military acronym NAAFI (Navy, Army and Air Force Institutes) as 'no ambition and fuck-all interest'; otherwise it may originate as back slang for **FANNY** (the vagina or the buttocks), a shortening of 'nawfuckingood' or in the French phrase *rien à faire* (nothing to do).

- Oh, those horrible little naff gnomes.—Barry Took and Marty Feldman, *Round The Horne*, May 1965
- They don't know what naff means exactly but they use it of clothes etc that look wrong, unfashionable, drear.—Ann Barr and Peter York, *The Official Sloane Ranger Handbook*, p. 159, 1982

- The eighties in Rock! was pretty naff. —John Robb, *The Nineties*, p. 227, 1999
- [T]hey don't seem to realise that the seventies was utterly naff the first time round[.] —James Hawes, *Dead Long Enough*, p. 159, 2000
- I actually really hate club scenes in films. I think they're really naff. —*X-Ray*, p. 30, November 2002

naff

used as a euphemism for 'fuck' (in all senses except sexual intercourse/to have sex) *UK*

- —Clement and La Frenais, *A Further Stir of Porridge*, 1977

naffette; naffeen *adjective*

vulgar, bad, despicable, unlovely *UK*

Polari; CAMP variations of NAFF.

- —the cast of 'Aspects of Love', Prince of Wales Theatre, *Palare (Boy Dancer Talk) for Beginners*, 1989–92

naffing *adjective*

used as a euphemism for 'fucking' *UK, 1959*

Extended from NAFF.

naff it up *verb*

to spoil something *UK*

- Now some people have naffed it up by putting out too much power [and] the Tunbridge Wells [CB] breakers resent anything that naffs it up for them locally. —*New Society*, 11th June 1981

naff off *verb*

to go away *UK*

From NAFF; made very familiar in the UK during the 1970s by the prison-set television situation comedy, *Porridge*, written by Clement and La Frenais. Perhaps the social highpoint of this word's history was during the 1982 Badminton Horse Trials when Princess Anne (now Princess Royal) asked the press, 'Why don't you just naff off?'.

nagware *noun*

free computer software that frequently asks the user to send a voluntary payment for further use *US*

- —Christian Crumlish, *The Internet Dictionary*, p. 131, 1995

nah

emphatically no *US*

A variation of pronunciation.

- Nah, better to step over the bodies[.] —Lester Bangs, *Psychotic Reactions and Carburetor Dung*, p. 26, 1971
- Nah. Choochy's no murderer. —Janet Evanovich, *Seven Up*, p. 89, 2001
- I was like nah, even though you look grand[.] —Mike Skinner, *Fit But You Know It*, 2004

nail *noun*

1 a hypodermic needle *US, 1936*

- —David Maurer and Victor Vogel, *Narcotics and Narcotic Addiction*, p. 428, 1973

2 a marijuana cigarette *US, 1978*

Possibly another 'nail in your coffin'.

- —Richard A. Spears, *The Slang and Jargon of Drugs and Drink*, p. 354, 1986
- —Mike Haskins, *Drugs*, p. 288, 2003

▸ **on the nail**

(of a payment) promptly *UK, 1600*

- I want it on the nail, mind you! No shilly-shallying. —Anonymous *Streetwalker*, p. 142, 1959
- All kinds of goods would be ordered in bulk from the manufacturers and paid for on the nail. —Lenny McLean, *The Guv'nor*, p. 18, 1998

nail *verb*

1 to apprehend; to arrest *UK, 1732*

- They'd nail him anyhow, so he waited to bluff it out. —Hal Ellson, *The Golden Spike*, p. 5, 1952
- "Remember our story if we get nailed," Roy said. —William Burroughs, *Junkie*, p. 48, 1953
- They nailed him two months later shacked up in Seattle with a red-headed whore. —Darryl Ponicsan, *The Last Detail*, p. 30, 1970
- Nail this guy and make us all look good. —*48 Hours*, 1982
- Jimmy Swaggart, a 52-year-old howler from Baton Rouge known in some quarters as "the Mick Jagger of TV evangelism," got nailed in a nasty little sting operation down in New Orleans[.] —Hunter S. Thompson, *Generation of Swine*, p. 21, 1988
- I forgot for a minute there it was Gibbs convicted Sonny and nailed you on the dope charge. —Elmore Leonard, *Maximum Bob*, p. 116, 1991
- And we nailed over a thousand of them. —*Point Break*, 1991
- And last month Dougie got nailed for fencing stolen goods out of his house. —Janet Evanovich, *Seven Up*, p. 26, 2001

2 to kill *UK, 1824*

- She's a Commie pig. We're going to nail every last one. —*Harold and Maude*, 1971
- If you can think of a better way for nailing this fucker I'm on for it, believe me. —Chris Ryan, *The Watchman*, p. 227, 2001

3 to have sex *US, 1957*

- ALLISON: He nailed me. CLAIRE: Very nice. ALLISON: I don't think that from a legal standpoint what he did can be construed as rape since I paid him. —*The Breakfast Club*, 1985
- Mary and Robert, married for six years, recounted how Robert first nailed Mary in his car, then just rolled off. —Anka Radakovich, *The Wild Girls Club*, p. 115, 1994
- Name me one chick in our senior class that Rick Derris didn't nail, for Christ's sake. —*Chasing Amy*, 1997
- I decided not to nail her when she was too drunk to remember it. —*Ten Things I Have About You*, 1999
- I wonder if I can nail that dumb bitch. —Marty Beckerman, *Death to All Cheerleaders*, 2000

4 to get right, to master *US, 1989*

- We've never really taken to public speaking, though undoubtedly it is one of those things we simply nail with practice. —Kevin Sampson, *Clubland*, p. 51, 2002

5 (of a wave) to knock a surfer from the surfboard *US*

Always in the passive voice.

- —Gary Fairmont R. Filosa II, *The Surfer's Almanac*, p. 190, 1977

▸ **nail someone's bollocks to the door**

to physically beat up, to figuratively neuter and mentally defeat *UK*

- You robbed me of my natural sense of humour / And then you nailed my bollocks to the door —Ian Dury, *Bed O' Roses No 9*, 1998

▸ **nail the core**

in the language of hang gliding, to find the centre of a thermal and ride it up *US*

- —Erik Fair, *California Thrill Sports*, p. 328, 1992

nailed *adjective*

deranged *US, 1836*

- —*American Speech*, p. 304, December 1955: 'Wayne University slang'

nail-em-and-jail-em *noun*

a police officer *US*

- —Edith A. Folb, *runnin' down some lines*, p. 247, 1980

nailer *noun*

a police officer *US*

- —Kenn "Naz" Young, *Naz's Underground Dictionary*, p. 47, 1973

nail nicker *noun*

in gambling, a cheat who marks cards by nicking them with his fingernails *US*

- Besides dice tats and 7UPS, there were volumes for nail nickers and crimpers (card markers), hand muckers and mit men (card switchers), as well as card counters and shiner players. —Stephen Cannell, *Big Con*, p. 143, 1997

nails *noun*

a disappointment; a failure *US*

Hawaiian youth usage.

- Wow, da prom was nails dees year! —Douglas Simonson, *Pidgin to da Max*, 1981

naked *adjective*

(used of a truck) driving without a trailer *US*

- —CB Roadrunner, *CB Lingo Handbook*, p. 17, 1976

Naked Fanny *nickname*

Nakhon Phanon, Thailand *US, 1967*

Vietnam war humour.

- His former classmate was visiting the Shiloh under an unofficial "liaison" program that brought together navy airmen and the air force types stationed at Nakhom Phanom in Thailand, a place referred to by the military as NKP or "naked fanny." —Stephen Coonts, *Flight of the Intruder*, p. 307, 1986

nakhes *noun*

▷ see: NACHES

Nam *nickname*

Vietnam *US, 1962*

Often used with 'the'. Originally military, then widespread, and now slightly arch.

- She's in love with some fool what's in the Nam. —Steve Cannon, *Groove, Bang, and Jive Around*, p. 29, 1969

- In the Nam the same gold ball drives the colonels and generals into their air-conditioned headquarters offices. — Charles Anderson, *The Grunts*, p. 6, 1976
- He likes to hear stories about Nam. — *Apocalypse Now*, 1979
- He wondered if the canyons at night would make him flash to Nam. — Joseph Wambaugh, *Lines and Shadows*, p. 41, 1984
- Sorry bout that boys – 'sin loi' buddy, you gonna love the Nam, man. — *Platoon*, 1986
- They wore bandanas and fatigues clearly influenced by Apocalypse Now [...] Virtual Nam had taken them over. — Michael Moorcock, *The Spencer Inheritance [britpulp]*, p. 20, 1998
- This is not 'Nam. This is bowling. There are rules. — *The Big Lebowski*, 1998

namby-pamby *noun*
an effeminate male *US*
- — Collin Baker et al., *College Undergraduate Slang Study Conducted at Brown University*, p. 161, 1968

name *noun*
1 an important or famous person *US*
- We've got a lot of names coming in. — *Nashville*, 1975

2 a known criminal *UK*
- "He's not a gangster, you know," said Terry, enjoying the nectarine. "He's a name – he's a face." — Anthony Masters, *Minder*, p. 4, 1984

3 a popular, high-profile professional wrestler *US*
- All they had at this stage was a few 8X10's off the names Rougeau presumably plans to build around. — *Herb's Wrestling Tidbits*, 17th August 1995

▸ **have your name on it**
to be meant for you *UK, 1917*
Originally military, applied to a bullet (or similar) that was destined to hit a particular person; later use is far more general, being used, for instance, when a house-hunter finds the perfect property or, more trivially, of a drink.

▸ **no names – no pack drill**
the guilty party (or parties) will not be named and, therefore, cannot be punished *UK, 1923*
Originally used of, or by, army lower-ranks; now general use.
- But it is interesting, is it not, to observe the kind of language being used – no names, no pack drill, but mainly in the Sun – to chronicle the unhappy goings on in the South Atlantic. — *The Guardian*, 27th May 1982
- [T]hey let it go. No names, no pack drill. And good for me. — Ken Lukowiak, *Marijuana Time*, p. 267, 2000

na mean?
▷ see: KNOWMEAN?

nan; nana; nannie; nanny *noun*
a grandmother, especially as a form of address *UK, 1940*
- [S]he might even have the last ever pictures of her late nan on the film[.] — Danny King, *The Burglar Diaries*, p. 91, 2001

nana *noun*
1 a banana *US, 1929*
- [B]randishing a banana which she pulled from her lunchbox. 'I got a nana!' — Peter Wilmoth, *Glad All Over*, p. 199, 1993

2 the head *NEW ZEALAND*
- — David McGill, *David McGill's Complete Kiwi Slang Dictionary*, p. 87, 1998

▸ **do your nana**
to lose control; to get angry *AUSTRALIA, 1968*
- I did my nana and yelled[.] — Sam Weller, *Old Bastards I Have Met*, p. 59, 1979

▸ **off your nana**
crazy, insane *AUSTRALIA, 1966*

nance *noun*
an effeminate male or homosexual *US, 1910*
Disparaging.
- The club-footed nance son-of-a-bitch. — Horace McCoy, *Kiss Tomorrow Goodbye*, p. 70, 1948
- The nance, in drag, had been hoping to get his hands on this inheritance by finding his mother[.] — Bernard Wolfe, *The Late Risers*, p. 211–212, 1954
- Right away I spotted the nances, they were dolled up like Lady Astor's horses. — Dev Collans with Stewart Sterling, *I was a House Detective*, p. 105, 1954
- The unsophisticated who think of queers as prancing nances with rouged lips and bleached hair may not believe that all pansies do not wear skirts over their pants. — Lee Mortimer, *Women Confidential*, p. 63, 1960
- When he told the director, softly, where to get off, the nance gave him notice. — Mary McCarthy, *The Group*, p. 72, 1963
- — *Fact*, p. 27, January-February 1965
- — Robert A. Wilson, *Playboy's Book of Forbidden Words*, p. 177, 1972
- The little nance of a bartender smiled roguishly[.] — Robert Deane Pharr, *Giveadamn Brown*, p. 151, 1978

nance *verb*
to behave in an exaggeratedly feminine fashion *US, 1968*
- "Ok, Buck," he nanced in a high voice. — Earl Thompson, *Tattoo*, p. 243, 1974

nancy *adjective*
effeminate; homosexual *UK, 1937*
- English friends with nancy accents[.] — John Milne, *Alive and Kicking*, p. 197, 1998

nancy boy *noun*
an effeminate or homosexual man; the former may be construed to be the latter *UK, 1904*
- You could've taken him for a nancy boy, from a distance. — John Peter Jones, *Feather Pluckers*, p. 119, 1964
- [T]hey looked like a bunch of nancies. — *Never Mind The Buzzcocks*, 1999
- if you can't fuck or fight you're a nancy boy[.] — Stuart Browne, *Dangerous Parking*, p. 2, 2000
- I mean if your son is a sensitive sort of a soul who isn't exactly built like a brick shithouse and doesn't appear to have much luck with girls, you could be forgiven for thinking he might turn out to be a nancy-boy. — Alan Titchmarsh, *Trowell and Error*, p. 92, 2002

Nancy Lee *noun*
tea *UK*
Rhyming slang.
- — Julian Franklyn, *A Dictionary of Rhyming Slang*, 1960
- — Ray Puxley, *Cockney Rabbit*, 1992

nancy story *noun*
an elaborate fabrication *TRINIDAD AND TOBAGO, 1858*
From a traditional Caribbean folktale about Anancy.
- — Lise Winer, *Dictionary of the English/Creole of Trinidad & Tobago*, 2003

nan flap *noun*
a pendulous spread of flabby upper arm that is characteristic of some older women *UK*
- — Jonathan Blyth, *The Law of the Playground*, p. 129, 2004

nang *adjective*
excellent *UK*
Used by urban black youths.
- My curried goat and rice was so nang. — *Live*, p. 39, Winter 2004

nanna *adjective*
awful *UK*
- — Paul Baker, *Polari*, p. 183, 2002

nannie; nanny *noun*
a black woman, also as a term of address *SOUTH AFRICA, 1956*
Offensive and demeaning.
- — Jean Branford, *A Dictionary of South African English*, 1978

▷ see: NAN

nanny *noun*
a prostitute who will, by arrangement, dress and treat a client as an infant *UK*
- — Caroline Archer, *Tart Cards*, 2003

nanny goat; nanny *noun*
1 the Horserace Totaliser Board *UK, 1960*
Rhyming slang. The Tote was created by Act of Parliament in 1928 as 'an independent body with a monopoly of horse-race pool betting'; the legislation to allow the Tote to operate as an on-course bookmaker was not in force until 1972.
- — John McCririck, *John McCririck's World of Betting*, p. 61, 1991

2 a coat *UK*
Rhyming slang.
- — Jack Jones, *Rhyming Cockney Slang*, 1971
- — David Hillman, 1974
- — Ray Puxley, *Fresh Rabbit*, 1998

3 the throat *UK*
Rhyming slang.
- — Ray Puxley, *Cockney Rabbit*, 1992

4 a boat *UK, 1989*
Rhyming slang.
- — John Ayto, *The Oxford Dictionary of Rhyming Slang*, p. 262, 2002

▸ **get your nanny goat; get your nanny**
to annoy you *US, 1909*
A variation of **GET YOUR GOAT**.

nanny whamming *noun*

in rodeo, the joke event of goat tying *CANADA*

- —Chris Thain, *Cold as a Bay Street Banker's Heart*, p. 106, 1987

nano *noun*

a very short period of time *US*

An abbreviation of 'nanosecond', used figuratively.

- "Be with you in nano" means you really will be free shortly[.]—Eric S. Raymond, *The New Hacker's Dictionary*, p. 254, 1991

nanoo *noun*

heroin *UK, 1998*

- —Robert Ashton, *This Is Heroin*, p. 206, 2002
- —Mike Haskins, *Drugs*, p. 284, 2003

Nanook *noun*

a polar bear *CANADA*

The word comes from Eskimo.

- Eetuk suddenly whirled around and hissed, "Nanook!" He had spotted a polar bear.—*Weekly Magazine*, p. 17/1, 10th August 1963

nante; nantee; nanti; nanty

no; nothing, none; stop, shut up!; not *UK, 1851*

Polari, from Italian *niente* (nothing, anything). Recorded in contemporary gay use.

- Nante on that stuff, cul [man][.]—Butch Reynolds, *Broken Hearted Clown*, p. 30, 1953
- Great close up of his head – nante riah [hair]. That's your cinema verite.—Barry Took and Marty Feldman, *Round The Horne*, 16th April 1967
- —*Attitude*, p. 60, July 2003: 'New palare lexicon'

nante pile on the carpet *adjective*

bald *UK*

- [Y]ou know, Raoul, the ome-pallone [gay man] with the codalina [bad] bins [glasses] and nante pile on the carpet.—the cast of 'Aspects of Love', Prince of Wales Theatre, *Palare (Boy Dancer Talk) for Beginners*, 1989–92

nante pots in the cupboard *adjective*

toothless *UK*

- —the cast of 'Aspects of Love', Prince of Wales Theatre, *Palare (Boy Dancer Talk) for Beginners*, 1989–92
- —Paul Baker, *Polari*, p. 183, 2002

nanti polari!; nanti panarly!; nantee palaver!; nanti parlaree!

be quiet!, don't talk! *UK*

Imperative; literally, 'no talk'.

- —Paul Baker, *Polari*, p. 183, 2002

nanti that!

stop it!, don't do that! *UK*

Imperative.

- —Paul Baker, *Polari*, p. 183, 2002

nantoise; nantois; nantoisale

no; nothing; none *UK*

A variation of **NANTE**.

- "Nantoise," the omi [man] polaried back[.]—James Gardiner, *Who's a Pretty Boy Then?*, p. 123, 1997
- —Paul Baker, *Polari*, p. 183, 2002

nants

no; nothing; none *UK*

A variation of **NANTE**.

- —*Sunday Times*, 28th May 1950

nanty worster *adjective*

being no worse *UK*

- —Paul Baker, *Polari*, p. 183, 2002

nap *noun*

1 the short, curly hair of a black person *US*

- He continued to rub both the broads' heads, pulled Annette's wig off, exposing her naps, and pulling Virginia's stringy hair.—Steve Cannon, *Groove, Bang, and Jive Around*, p. 133, 1969

2 the hair; your hairstyle *US*

- —Connie Eble (Editor), *UNC-CH Campus Slang*, p. 6, March 1996

3 in horse racing, a tipster's best bet *UK*

- [V]ery few [tipsters] consistently return a profit on their naps – their best bets – through the season.—John McCririck, *John McCririck's World of Betting*, p. 29, 1991

4 a good bet, a sure thing *UK*

From the racing use.

- I'm a Scouser [Liverpudlian] and [...] it's a nap that I'm going to get his [police] undivided attention now.—Kevin Sampson, *Outlaws*, p. 50, 2001

nape *noun*

napalm, a mixture of petrol and a thickening agent for use in flame throwers or incendiary bombs, used extensively by the US during World War 2 and later wars *US, 1968*

- They gonna lay snake and nape right on the perimeter so stay tight in your holes and don't leave 'em.—*Platoon*, 1986
- —Linda Reinberg, *In the Field*, p. 148, 1991

napper *noun*

the head *UK, 1724*

- [M]aybe fate's gonny give you a wee dunt [dent] on the napper with the toecap.—Ian Pattison, *Rab C. Nesbitt*, 1988

napper-wrapper *noun*

a turban *UK*

Based on **NAPPER** (the head).

- —Ray Puxley, *Fresh Rabbit*, p. 85, 1998

napps *noun*

morphine sulphate tablets used to treat cancer patients *IRELAND*

- The auld [old] morphine sulphate tablets, or napps as we call them, wouldn't have been me first choice...The napps are used to treat cancer patients and are every bit as strong as smack.—Howard Paul, *The Joy*, p. 78, 1996

nappy *adjective*

of hair, usually of the hair of a black person, naturally tightly curled, frizzy *US, 1885*

Often derogatory.

- He said I had "nappy" hair, because when it grows, it gets all curly. I got really mad at him, so he kept saying it just to piss me off.—*The Observer*, 21st May 2000

nappy dugout *noun*

(of a black woman) the vagina *US*

The imagery of 'dugout' is twofold: literally 'a trench', and, in baseball, the enclosure in which a batsman prepares to play; combined with **NAPPY** which typically describes Black hair.

- There's [a...] "wee wee," "horsespot," "nappy dugout," mongo[".] —Eve Ensler, *The Vagina Monologues*, p. 6, 1998

nap trap *noun*

a roadside rest area *US*

- —Wayne Floyd, *Jason's Authentic Dictionary of CB Slang*, p. 22, 1976

nar *adjective*

treacherous *US*

An abbreviation of **GNARLY**.

- — Surf Punks, *Oh No! Not Them Again! (liner notes)*, 1988

narc; nark *noun*

1 an undercover narcotics officer *US, 1967*

- I read how the narcs came and busted Jerry Rubin, a founder of the Yippies.—James Simon Kunen, *The Strawberry Statement*, p. 94, 1968
- He [President Nixon] announced in his very first speech, his inaugural address if I remember right, that he was adding three hundred new narks to the team.—Abbie Hoffman, *Woodstock Nation*, p. 68, 1969
- The Man has got himself a "temporary" restraining order against the printer of the Berkeley Tribe (Walter Press) from further printing of the names and addresses of local narcs.—*The Berkeley Tribe*, p. 4, 15th-21st August 1969
- Compared with the way everybody was dressed Gary and I must have looked like a couple of narcs.—Jim Bouton, *Ball Four*, p. 135, 1970
- I'll have you know Glenda is seriously involved with a narc from Palm Beach.—*Body Heat*, 1980
- Come to find out the narcs that requested it from me got caught on a dealing rap themselves.—Herbert Huncke, *Guilty of Everything*, p. 190, 1990

2 a social outcast *US*

- —Pamela Munro, *U.C.L.A. Slang*, p. 95, 2001

narc ark; nark ark *noun*

an undercover narcotic officer's car *US*

- I could just picture me and her getting hauled off to jail in a nark ark.—Joseph Wambaugh, *The Blue Knight*, p. 37, 1973
- Halfway down to Sunset with the loot, the car fishtails and sideswipes a sheriff's nark ark.—James Ellroy, *Suicide Hill*, p. 597, 1986

narco *noun*

1 narcotics *US, 1954*

- Where it began, he couldn't say. Maybe on Patterson's first night with the Narco Squad. — Clarence Cooper Jr, *The Scene*, p. 21, 1960
- [T]wo offays stopped them and informed them they were "Narco" (Narcotics) detectives. — Babs Gonzales, *I Paid My Dues*, p. 100, 1967
- Doin 5 years for Sale of Narco. — Clarence Cooper Jr, *The Farm*, p. 9, 1967
- He had plastic surgery done on his face after he beat that narco rap out there and changed his base. — Mickey Spillane, *Last Cop Out*, p. 42, 1972
- Like if there was a shrink who could turn you off narco for the rest of your life, I'd turn all that bread over to him without even bothering to count it. — Robert Deane Pharr, *Giveadamn Brown*, p. 10, 1978

2 a narcotics detective *US, 1955*

- His adversaries in this continual quest are always the police: the "narcos.," "The Man." — James Mills, *The Panic in Needle Park*, p. 15, 1966
- Take hippies and straights, heads and narcos, put them together for 36 hours – under a church roof. — *Berkeley Barb*, p. 3, 25th February 1967

3 any person involved in the manufacture or distribution of drugs *US, 1958*

An abbreviation of 'narcotics'.

- Soon the narcos' plan of action was apparent. — Chris Ryan, *Stand By, Stand By*, p. 215, 1996

4 the Lexington (Kentucky) Federal Narcotics Hospital *US*

- — *American Speech*, p. 87, May 1955: 'Narcotic argot along the Mexican border'

narcotic *adjective*

wild, intense *US*

- — Connie Eble (Editor), *UNC-CH Campus Slang*, p. 5, Fall 1980

nards *noun*

the male genitals *US*

- — *Current Slang*, p. 21, Spring 1970
- [F]reezing my nards off every weekend. — Frank Zappa, *The Real Frank Zappa Book*, p. 35, 1989

narg *noun*

an Indian *NEW ZEALAND*

- — David McGill, *David McGill's Complete Kiwi Slang Dictionary*, p. 75, 1998

narghile *noun*

a water pipe used for smoking marijuana or hashish *US*

- — William D. Alsever, *Glossary for the Establishment and Other Uptight People*, p. 16, December 1970

nark *noun*

1 a police informer *UK, 1839*

Also spelt 'narc'.

- 'Cos we don't have police-pimps about 'ere, that's why. You Stacey, and you're a bloody nark. — Frank Hardy, *Power Without Glory*, p. 99, 1950
- GRANDPA: That young nark – you know [...] I told you. He's gone to see the governor. I told you. — Clive Exton, *No Fixed Abode [Six Granada Plays]*, p. 136, 1959
- — Angela Devlin, *Prison Patter*, p. 78, 1996

2 an aggravating person *AUSTRALIA, 1846*

- She was hard to please, rather a "nark" as he put it, and easily "needled" (annoyed)[.] — Butch Reynolds, *Broken Hearted Clown*, p. 29, 1953
- Only thing coppers'll do for anyone is make it rotten for them. Prize narks. — John Peter Jones, *Feather Pluckers*, p. 17, 1964

3 a spoilsport *AUSTRALIA, 1927*

- — Lance Peters, *The Dirty Half-Mile*, p. 194, 1979
- I don't want to sound like a nark, but mate, do you know what you are all about? — Clive Galea, *Slipper*, p. 119, 1988
- — Clive Galea, *Slipper*, p. 148, 1988
- 'Sounds like she's turning into a nice nark.' 'She is mate. She'd give a bottle of castor oil the shits.' — Robert G. Barrett, *Davo's Little Something*, p. 217, 1992

4 an awkward customer, one with no intention of buying *UK*

- — Patrick O'Shaughnessy, *Market Traders' Slang*, 1979

5 a spiteful argument *UK*

- — Patrick O'Shaughnessy, *Market Traders' Slang*, 1979
- Our Stephen's half having a nark with Shy. — Kevin Sampson, *Clubland*, p. 112, 2002

6 temper; a fit of annoyance *AUSTRALIA*

- And crikey, if it doesn't get people's nark up, I'm a goanna with two tails. — Miles Franklin, *My Career Goes Bung*, p. 56, 1946
- 'I'm not only fed up to the back teeth, the way the old woman goes on,' said Bill, 'I've got the nark properly this time.' — Norman Lindsay, *Halfway to Anywhere*, p. 79, 1947

7 umbrage *UK*

- He took nark. — Patrick O'Shaughnessy, *Market Traders' Slang*, 1979

▸ **put the nark on**

to discourage *UK*

- — Patrick O'Shaughnessy, *Market Traders' Slang*, 1979

nark *verb*

1 to annoy *UK, 1888*

- I'm a dirty dog, Ella – I shouldn't have said a lousy thing like that to you. But it narked me seeing you with that flash cow. — Norman Lindsay, *The Cousin from Fiji*, p. 218, 1945
- This made me a little narked, then I realised that I was only young and he wouldn't have thought that I was applying for the job myself. — A.B. Facey, *A Fortunate Life*, p. 190, 1981
- The stewardess couldn't help glancing at my dishevelled appearance, which narked me because am always clean underneath[.] — Jonathan Gash, *The Ten Word Game*, p. 40, 2003

2 to thwart *AUSTRALIA, 1891*

- [N]ot to mention the fact that Waldo occupied a room with elder brother, Bags, who might nark the whole thing by waking up and putting them away to Pa Peddler. — Norman Lindsay, *Halfway to Anywhere*, p. 120, 1947

3 to complain, to grumble *UK, 1916*

- There is consistent narking and arguing in the outside world about who gets what, where and when. — David Ervine, *Northern Ireland Assembly*, 15th December 1999

4 to nag *NEW ZEALAND*

- — Louis S. Leland, *A Personal Kiwi-Yankee Dictionary*, p. 69, 1984

5 to act as an informer *UK, 1859*

- [S]ome of the less intellectually fortunate of their sex had a nasty habit of getting involved in the whole only god thing to the extent of narking on their sisters. — *www.bbc.co.uk*, 30th March 2002: 'The guide to life, the universe and everything'

nark ark *noun*

▹ see: NARC ARK

nark it!

be quiet!, stop it!, shut up! *UK, 1925*

- "Nark it, Sonny," said Sapphire, "you've got to move with the times , you know." — Charles Raven, *Underworld Nights*, p. 207, 1956
- BELL: [...] Shall I get Milligan to fetch you a glass of milk? MILLIGAN: Nark it – R.S.M. [Regimental Sergeant Major]. — Graeme Kent, *The Queen's Corporal [Six Granada Plays]*, p. 87–88, 1959

narks *noun*

▸ **the narks**

decompression sickness (a medical condition that may be suffered by deep-sea divers) *UK*

From the medical term 'nitrogen narcosis'. Reported by Wilfred Granville, 1964.

narky *adjective*

bad-tempered, aggravated, annoyed; sarcastic *UK, 1895*

- I got narky. "You can piss off!" I said last week. — Sally Cline, *Couples*, p. 110, 1998
- Don't get narky. — Niall Griffiths, *Kelly + Victor*, p. 142, 2002

narrow *adjective*

serious *UK*

Recorded in use in urban black society.

- "You musta been skinnin' teet' when you opened dat bag mate!" "Nah man, I weren't skinnin' no teet', I was narrow. Dem man coulda bin CIDs! — Courttia Newland, *Society Within*, p. 29, 1999

narrowback *noun*

1 an unskilled, unfit labourer *US*

- Because my parents had been born in America, I was considered a 'narrowback' – someone who wasn't really fit for good labor. — Tip O'Neill with William Novak, *Man of the House*, p. 3, 1987

2 a construction electrician *US*

A term used with derision by power linemen to describe their intra-union rivals.

- — A.B. Chance Co., *Lineman's Slang Dictionary*, p. 12, 1980

narrow yellow *noun*

a military form (OCSA Form 159) used to pass routine actions to staff agencies *US*

- — Department of the Army, *Staff Officer's Guidebook*, p. 62, 1986

narsty *adjective*

disgusting *US*

An embellishment of 'nasty'.

- — Connie Eble (Editor), *UNC-CH Campus Slang*, p. 7, October 2002

nary *adverb*

neither; no *US, 1746*

- Groundhogs eat m'beans up an' I never had nary one t'pick. — Elliot Wigginton, *The Foxfire Book*, p. 28, 1972
- "Any long dresses at all?" he asked. "Nary a one," I replied[.] — Dodie Smith, *I Capture the Castle*, p. 42, 1999

nash *verb*

to leave, especially in a hurry *UK, 1819*

From Romany *nash*, *nasher* (to run).

- I tell him I don't feel very well and have to nash. — Niall Griffiths, *Kelly + Victor*, p. 107, 2002

nash *adjective*

weak, sickly, coddled *CAYMAN ISLANDS*

- — Aarona Booker Kohlman, *Wotcha Say*, p. 25, 1985

Nasho; nasho *noun*

1 a person serving in the National Service, a form of compulsory military service 1951–72 *AUSTRALIA, 1962*

- — William Nagel, *The Odd Angry Shot*, p. 13, 1975
- Whilst this was a fairly harmless task Ace saw it as potentially dangerous and was, therefore, quite taken back by the enthusiasm shown by the eager-to-volunteer 'nashos'. — Martin Cameron, *A Look at the Bright Side*, 1988

2 the National Service *AUSTRALIA, 1962*

Often used in the plural Nashos or Nashoes.

- National Service was designed to turn boys into men and make the Yellow Peril think twice about moving south. It was universally known as Nasho – a typically Australian diminutive. — Clive James, *Unreliable Memoirs*, p. 143, 1980
- After all, what could be worse than being stuck at Woodside for the duration of Nashoes. — Martin Cameron, *A Look at the Bright Side*, 1988

nasodrain *noun*

while surfing, the sudden and violent expulsion of sea water through the nose *US*

- — Trevor Cralle, *The Surfin'ary*, p. 79, 1991

nastiness *noun*

poor quality drugs *UK*

- [H]e'd sold some nastiness instead of some Holyfield[.] — Diran Abedayo, *My Once Upon A Time*, p. 20, 2000

nasturtiums *noun*

aspersions *UK, 1984*

A deliberate malapropism, usually as 'cast nasturtiums'.

nasty *noun*

1 the vagina *NEW ZEALAND*

A usage that calls to mind Grose's definition of C**T – 'a nasty name for a nasty thing'.

- — David McGill, *David McGill's Complete Kiwi Slang Dictionary*, p. 85, 1998

2 the penis *AUSTRALIA*

- He's flashin' his flamin' nasty!!! — Barry Humphries, *Bazza Pulls It Off!*, 1971

3 a violently pornographic or horrific film *UK, 1982*

Often combined as **VIDEO-NASTY** but the content appears to be outlasting the technology.

4 an authority or agency that enforces citizens' band radio regulations *UK*

- — Peter Chippindale, *The British CB Book*, p. 157, 1981

▸ **do the nasty**

to have sex *US, 1977*

A squeamish euphemism applied in a jocular manner.

- — Connie Eble (Editor), *UNC-CH Campus Slang*, p. 3, Spring 1990
- "He really dating your grandma? [...] Think they did the nasty?" I almost ran the car up on the sidewalk. "No! Yuck!" — Janet Evanovich, *Seven Up*, p. 7, 2001
- Another way to say "intercourse" [...] Doing the nasty[.] — Erica Orloff and JoAnn Baker, *Dirty Little Secrets*, p. 63, 2001
- If there is one thing that actually is better than getting walloped on brain-rotting chemical stimulants, then it's doing the nasty/getting your stank on* with a lady/man* (*delete as applicable). — *Ministry*, p. 21, October 2002

▸ **the nasty**

heroin *UK*

- — Angela Devlin, *Prison Patter*, p. 78, 1996

nasty *adjective*

1 excellent *US, 1940*

- — Robert S. Gold, *A Jazz Lexicon*, p. 213, 1964

2 sexy, attractive, appealing; sluttish *US*

A reversal of the conventional sense.

- She be wearin' nasty gear and voguin' like Tina Turner. — *A2Z*, p. 70, 1995
- And they're Nasty, the kind of girls who want their tasty butts spanked before they drink cum! — Peter Sotos, *Index*, p. 54, 1996
- We're a party group, we about being nasty and having parties. — Alex Ogg, *The Hip Hop Years [quoting 'Duke Bootee' Ed Fletcher]*, p. 67, 1999

nasty-assed *adjective*

cruel *US*

- I'm being a nasty-assed woman who rejects men and he's falling in love. — Howard Stern, *Miss America*, p. 19, 1995

nasty boat *noun*

a patrol boat developed for the coastal anti-invasion mission of the Royal Norwegian Navy *US*

The 'nasty' is a technical term adopted to the vernacular.

- — Linda Reinberg, *In the Field*, p. 148, 1991

nasty days *noun*

a woman's menstrual period *BAHAMAS*

- — John A. Holm, *Dictionary of Bahamian English*, p. 140, 1982

nastygram *noun*

any unpleasant or unwanted e-mail *US*

- — Eric S. Raymond, *The New Hacker's Dictionary*, p. 255, 1991

nasty-nasty *noun*

sex *US*

- — Judi Sanders, *Faced and Faded, Hanging to Hurl*, p. 28, 1993

nasty neat *adjective*

cleaner than clean *US*

- — John Gould, *Maine Lingo*, p. 187–188, 1975

nasty piece of work *noun*

an objectionable person *UK, 1961*

- [T]he Sun called him [Peter Mandelson] "a lying, manipulative, oily, two-faced nasty piece of work", although some of his colleagues were less complimentary. — *The Guardian*, 21st May 2001

nasty up *verb*

to ruin or spoil *BARBADOS*

- — Frank A. Collymore, *Barbadian Dialect*, p. 76, 1965

Nat; nat *noun*

in politics, a nationalist *SOUTH AFRICA, 1926*

- Welsh Nats Are Sceptical over Devolution Bill. — *The Daily Telegraph*, 28th July 1977

▷ **see: NAT KING COLE**

natalie *noun*

a black homosexual *SOUTH AFRICA*

Gay slang, formed on the name Natalie, possibly as a play on Natal, and originating among Cape coloureds.

- — Bart Luirink (translated by Loes Nas), *Moffies*, p. 150, 2000

natch *noun*

▸ **on the natch**

withdrawing from drug addiction without medication to ease the pain *US, 1969*

- — Eugene Landy, *The Underground Dictionary*, p. 141, 1971

natch; nach *adverb*

naturally *US*

- — Lou Shelly, *Hepcats Jive Talk Dictionary*, p. 15, 1945
- The best I could do was nod. "Natch. What else?" — Mickey Spillane, *I, The Jury*, p. 21, 1947
- But first let us tell you about 9th Street – NW, natch – and specifically where it crosses Pennsylvania Avenue. — Jack Lait and Lee Mortimer, *Washington Confidential*, p. 30, 1951
- Natch I was hip to the lay the moment I dug his joint... — Terry Southern, *Candy*, p. 212, 1958
- "Like to hear it?" "Natch." — Ross Russell, *The Sound*, p. 176, 1961
- "But Mary-Ann told me he behaved abominably at your house." "Natch!! That's what I like." — Gore Vidal, *Myra Breckinridge*, p. 218, 1968
- Followed in 1980 by 'Kill and Kill Again', natch. — *Sick Puppy*, p. 17, 1998
- Natch, Miss Hines didn't just fall into her own venerable shoes. — *Sydney Scope Magazine*, p. 27, 2001
- Like an unholy mix of Gary Glitter (pre paedo charges, natch), 70s horror soundtracks and Hammond organ[.] — *Ministry*, p. 12, October 2002
- [B]uilder, Brian Walker, is to walk from Land's End to John o'Groats carrying a three-stone pine door – for charidee, natch. — *The Guardian*, p. 5, 28th May 2003

nate *noun*

1 nothing *US*

- — *The Bell (Paducah Tilghman High School)*, p. 8–9, 17th December 1993: 'Tilghmanism: the concealed langage of the hallway'

2 an Alaskan native *US, 1983*

- — Russell Tabbert, *Dictionary of Alaskan English*, p. 53, 1991

nates *noun*

the buttocks *US*

- — J.R. Schwartz, *The Official Guide to the Best Cat Houses in Nevada*, p. 165, 1993: 'Sex glossary'

national *noun*

▸ **on tour with the national**

being moved from prison to prison via the national inter-prison transport system *UK*

A pun appreciated by actors of the National Theatre.

- — Angela Devlin, *Prison Patter*, p. 78, 1996

▸ **the national**

the national inter-prison transport system *UK*

- — Angela Devlin, *Prison Patter*, p. 78, 1996

national debt *noun*

a bet *UK*

Rhyming slang.

- — Julian Franklyn, *A Dictionary of Rhyming Slang*, 1960
- — Ray Puxley, *Cockney Rabbit*, 1992

National Front *noun*

an unpleasant or despicable person *UK*

Rhyming slang for **CUNT**, formed on a political organisation of the extreme right; a neat pun.

- — Ray Puxley, *Cockney Rabbit*, 1992

national game *noun*

the gambling game two-up *AUSTRALIA, 1930*

- — James Holledge, *The Great Australian Gamble*, p. 92, 1966
- For the benefit of the uninitiated, here is a brief resume of the procedure and rules of Australia's "national game". — James Holledge, *The Great Australian Gamble*, p. 100, 1966

national handbag *noun*

unemployment benefit; the local offices from which unemployment benefit is managed *UK*

From **handbag** (money). Recorded as a contemporary gay usage.

- — *Attitude*, p. 60, July 2003: 'New palare lexicon'

National Hunt *noun*

audaciousness; impudence *UK*

Rhyming slang for 'front' (see **MORE FRONT THAN SELFRIDGES**), formed from the official name given to horse racing over jumps.

- [M]ore National Hunt than Cheltenham. — Ray Puxley, *Cockney Rabbit*, 1992

native *noun*

1 a native American Indian *US*

- Whites were seen in quiet conversations with Natives. — Bill Valentine, *Gangs and Their Tattoos*, p. 12, 2000

2 to the employee of a circus or carnival, a local patron *US*

- — Joe McKennon, *Circus Lingo*, p. 64, 1980
- — Don Wilmeth, *The Language of American Popular Entertainment*, p. 181, 1981

native sport *noun*

during the Vietnam war, looking for and killing Viet Cong *US*

- — Linda Reinberg, *In the Field*, p. 148, 1991

Nat King Cole; nat *noun*

1 unemployment benefit; a government office from which unemployment benefit is managed *UK*

Rhyming slang for **THE DOLE**; formed on the name of US singer and musician Nat 'King' Cole, 1919–65. Often in the phrase 'on the Nat'.

- — Julian Franklyn, *A Dictionary of Rhyming Slang*, 1961

2 a mole (on the skin) *UK*

Rhyming slang.

- — Ray Puxley, *Cockney Rabbit*, 1992

3 a bread roll *UK*

Rhyming slang.

- — Ray Puxley, *Cockney Rabbit*, 1992

nato *adjective*

used for describing someone who is not sexually aggressive *US*

- When New York girls speak of a date as N.A.T.O., they mean contempuously, "No Action, Talk Only." — Joe David Brown, *Sex in the '60s*, p. 19, 1968
- — Paik Choo, *The Coxford Singlish Dictionary*, p. 76, 2002

natter *noun*

aimless conversation; incessantly complaining talk *UK, 1943*

From northern English dialect *gnatter* (to grumble in conversation).

- [O]ver our menjarie [food] we had a "natter" about the show. — Butch Reynolds, *Broken Hearted Clown*, p. 29, 1953
- Nothing was bloody good enough for the old cow – it was natter, natter, natter all the bloody time. — Anonymous *Streetwalker*, p. 37, 1959
- [W]e was just standing there, having a natter, and this big fat copper shouts, "Git moving you lot." — John Peter Jones, *Feather Pluckers*, p. 7, 1964

natter *verb*

to engage in aimless conversation, to chat *UK, 1943*

- Luckily, it was the ultra-friendly Sara Cox, who nattered happily away. — *The Observer*, 27th January 2002

natty *noun*

1 any natural light beer *US*

- — Connie Eble (Editor), *UNC-CH Campus Slang*, p. 5, November 2002

2 a wearer of dreadlocks, especially a Rastafarian *JAMAICA, 1976*

- — Culture (Joseph Hill), *Natty Never Get Weary*, 1979

natty *adjective*

1 stylish, smartly neat *UK, 1785*

- The little boys in black leather in Hamburg became the natty showbiz mods who became the flower people[.] — *The Guardian*, 15th April 1970

2 of hair, matted, uncombed, in a condition to be formed into dreadlocks *JAMAICA, 1974*

- Natty Dreadlock in a Babylon: Natty Dread — Bob Marley, *Natty Dread*, 1974

Natty Bo *noun*

National Bohemian™ beer *US*

- — Connie Eble (Editor), *UNC-CH Campus Slang*, p. 6, November 1990

natural *noun*

1 a hairstyle embraced largely by black people, featuring longer, unprocessed, unparted hair *US, 1969*

- [S]ome with fluffy naturals like my sister Angie, some with silky naturals like my sister Betty. — George Jackson, *Soledad Brother*, p. 313, June 1970
- Her once scrawny frame was all softness and curves, and she looked like an African princess, with her hair in a then uncommon Natural. — Iceberg Slim (Robert Beck), *The Naked Soul of Iceberg Slim*, p. 83, 1971
- And take those two dudes with the naturals along with you, — Joseph Wambaugh, *The Blue Knight*, p. 67, 1973
- Wilson loopked up at the tall man wearing the large shades that hid his eyes and the wide-brimmed hat that covered his natural. — Joseph Nazel, *Black Cop*, p. 37, 1974

2 in craps, a winning roll of seven on the first toss *US*

- — Frank Garcia, *Marked Cards and Loaded Dice*, p. 263, 1962

3 Seven-Up™ soda *US*

An allusion to the game of craps, where a seven is a 'natural'.

- — *American Speech*, p. 63, February 1967: 'Soda-fountain, restaurant and tavern calls'

4 in pool, a shot that cannot be missed or a game that cannot be lost *US*

- — Steve Rushin, *Pool Cool*, p. 21, 1990

5 a conventional (as opposed to countercultural) person *UK*

Used by beatniks, and then hippies; generally in the plural.

- — *The Observer*, 3rd December 1967

natural punk *noun*

in prison, a man who had been homosexual outside prison *US*

- — Bruce Jackson, *Outside the Law*, p. 59, 1972: 'Glossary'

nature *noun*

the penis; sexual arousal *US*

- Every time I see that bitch, I feel my nature come up on me. — Gary K. Farlow, *Prison-ese*, p. 45, 2002

nature boy *noun*

a boy in need of a haircut *US*

- — *American Weekly*, p. 2, 14th August 1955

nature calls
used for announcing, and for excusing yourself for, a needed visit to the toilet; the condition of needing to relieve yourself *UK, 1984*
- Wheelchair users in search of a swift half will always be welcome at one Cornish pub. "We are fully accessible," says the landlady confidently. If nature calls, "there are always three strong men here to carry you down". — *The Guardian*, 29th October 2003

nature's scythe *noun*
the penis *UK*
- — Richard Herring, *Talking Cock*, p. 30, 2003

Naughton and Gold *noun*
a cold *UK*
Rhyming slang, formed from a comedy double act that was part of the Crazy Gang, Charlie Naughton, 1887 -1976, and Jimmy Gold, 1886–1967.
- — Julian Franklyn, *A Dictionary of Rhyming Slang*, 1961

naughty *noun*
1 an act of sexual intercourse *AUSTRALIA, 1959*
- It is surely no mistake that this, above all civilised nations in the world, is the only one that refers to the simple sexual act – whether in or out of matrimony, as "having a naughty". — Sue Rhodes, *Now you'll think I'm awful*, p. 32, 1967
- Jeez, you look bonzer tonight, I reckon I could go a little celebration naughty before we adjourn inside!! — Barry Humphries, *The Wonderful World of Barry McKenzie*, p. 11, 1968
- What say yous and me nick out the back for a swift naughty! — Barry Humphries, *The Wonderful World of Barry McKenzie*, p. 21, 1968

2 a physical injury; hence, a disservice *UK, 1984*
- Arthur's done a naughty to the South mob. They won't like that. — Anthony Masters, *Minder*, p. 169, 1984

naughty *verb*
to have sex *AUSTRALIA, 1961*
- — Harry Orsman, *A Dictionary of Modern New Zealand Slang*, p. 90, 1999

naughty *adjective*
1 corrupt or violent *UK*
An archaic sense, used by Shakespeare to describe the criminally wicked, re-emerged in the C20.
- Carter Street was notorious for being a hard and very, very naughty nick. — Dave Courtney, *Raving Lunacy*, p. 30, 2000
- the biggest, naughtiest-looking nice guy you've ever seen — Dave Courtney, *Raving Lunacy*, p. 93, 2000

2 of antique furniture, being passed off as something better or other than it is *UK*
- "Naughty" is the term in the trade for [an antique] piece that has been converted [...] or tampered with, without the alterations being declared. — W. Crawley, *Is it Genuine?*, 1971

naughty Nazi salute *noun*
the fully erect penis *UK*
A parallel with the arm raised stiffly from the body at a similar angle.
- For most of us, failure to execute the naughty Nazi salute is an ego-crushing disaster[.] — Richard Herring, *Talking Cock*, p. 155, 2003

nause; nauze *noun*
an inconvenience, a difficulty, an unpleasant person or thing *UK*
'Nausea' abbreviated and adapted.
- He don't do as he's told – that's the fucking nause. — G.G. Newman, *The Guvnor*, 1977
- — Nigel Foster, *The Making of a Royal Marine Commando*, 1987

nause; nause up *verb*
to spoil *UK*
From **NAUSE** (an inconvenience, an unpleasant thing).
- [I]t went against the grain for all of them to "nause" such a bit of [criminal] business. — Piers Paul Read, *The Train Robbers*, 1978
- He's got a hunch about my retirement plans and he could easily nause the whole thing up. — J.J. Connolly, *Layer Cake*, p. 64, 2000

nausea *noun*
trouble, a fuss *UK*
In military use.
- I'd forgetten about the cap. I knew there'd be a nausea about it. — John Winton, *We Joined the Navy*, 1959
- [M]aking it necessary for pilots to check constantly against drifting into Irish air space with the immense subsequent nausea. — Christopher Hawke, *For Campaign Service*, 1979

Naussie *noun*
a New Australian, especially a recent migrant from Europe *AUSTRALIA*
A blend of 'new' and **AUSSIE**.
- — Sidney J. Baker, *The Drum*, 1959

nautch *noun*
a brothel; a striptease; a sex show of any kind *US, 1872*
American Dialect Society member Douglas G. Wilson has suggested that the term is a mildly anglicised version of the Hindi word for 'a dance'.
- I'm one of the nautch girls. I do a specialty dance. — Robert Edmond Alter, *Carny Kill*, p. 5, 1966
- — Joe McKennon, *Circus Lingo*, p. 64, 1980

Nautics *noun*
▸ **the Nautics**
the Royal Navy *UK*
Used, originally, by the Royal Air Force; shortened from 'nautical'.
- — Paul Brickhill, *The Dam Busters*, 1951

nav *noun*
a *navigator* *US, 1956*
In Royal Navy and Royal Air Force use.

Nava-Joe *noun*
a member of the Navajo Indian tribe *US*
- — *American Speech*, p. 271, December 1963: 'American Indian student slang'

naval engagement *noun*
sexual intercourse *CANADA, 1984*
Used, originally, by naval officers; in speech it's a perfect pun.

navy brat *noun*
the child of a career member of the navy *US*
- Renee was a navy brat, born and raised in San Diego. — Armistead Maupin, *Maybe the Moon*, p. 91, 1992

Navy cake *noun*
homosexual anal sex *US*
- — Roger Blake, *The American Dictionary of Sexual Terms*, p. 139, 1964
- — Anon, *King Smut's Wet Dreams Interpreted*, 1978

naw
no *US*
- I was like, naw man, I got a son on the way. — *Boyz N The Hood*, 1990

nay-nays *noun*
a woman's breasts *US*
- You know, in the backs of those "Fun Shops," you'll see guys looking through racks and racks of pictures of ladies' nay-nays wrapped in cellophane. — Lenny Bruce, *The Essential Lenny Bruce*, p. 219, 1967
- Next comes the bato-twirling face of Desiree Cousteau, whose nay-nays are uncle-handed by then-mustachioed Lous at the Melody. — Josh Alan Friedman, *Tales of Times Square*, p. 31, 1986
- She really and truly was until Baby Jewels nuked her naynay. — Seth Morgan, *Homeboy*, p. 274, 1990
- — J.R. Schwartz, *The Official Guide to the Best Cat Houses in Nevada*, p. 165, 1993: 'Sex glossary'

nay-no
no, said with kindness *US*
From the film *Pootie Tang*.
- — Connie Eble (Editor), *UNC-CH Campus Slang*, p. 5, Spring 2003

Nazi *noun*
a fanatic about the preceding noun *US*
Not coined but rendered wildly popular on the 'Soup Nazi' episode of Jerry Seinfeld's television comedy that first aired on 2nd November 1995.
- Barbara Jane shrugged apologetically. "Clothes Nazi." — Dan Jenkins, *Life Its Ownself*, p. 58, 1984
- SURF NAZI: Blond hair, blue eyes and a one track mind. — Michael V. Anderson, *The Bad, Rad, Not to Forget Way Cool Beach and Surf Discriptionary*, p. 20, 1988
- "If you want to be what I call a jazz nazi, it's true we can be criticized. And what is jazz anyway? We wind up with all these hybrid styles of music that may not be jazz per se but are related and yet hold their own." Pure-bred or mongrel? He cares not. — Catherine Solyum, *Montreal Gazette*, p. A4, 5th July 2002

Nazi *adjective*
unreasonably authoritarian *UK*
- Six o'clock he got us up, Crossley. Nazi bastard. — Niall Griffiths, *Sheepshagger*, p. 86, 2001

Nazi crank *noun*
methamphetamine *UK*
- — Harry Shapiro, *Recreational Drugs*, p. 180, 2004

Nazi go-cart; Nazi go-kart *noun*
a Volkswagen car *US*
Citizens' band radio slang remembering that Volkswagen were German manufacturers before and during World War 2.
- — *Complete CB Slang Dictionary*, p. 76, 1976
- — Peter Chippindale, *The British CB Book*, p. 161, 1981

NBG *adjective*
of no use *UK, 1903*
An abbreviation of '*n*o *b*loody *g*ood'.
- [Richard] Curtis has told questioners in Hay-on-Wye and elsewhere that [Emma] Freud uses the codes NBG (No Bloody Good) and CDB (Could Do Better). — *The Guardian*, 13th November 2003

NDG *adjective*
*n*o *d*amned *g*ood *CANADA*
- "NDG" stands for"No Damned Good." — *Canadian Fiction Magazine*, January 1997

near and far *noun*
1 a bar in a public house *UK, 1909*
Dated rhyming slang that remains a familiar term because of its neat reversal with **FAR AND NEAR** (beer).
- — Ray Puxley, *Cockney Rabbit*, 1992

2 a car *UK*
Rhyming slang.
- — Jack Jones (Ed.), *Rhyming Cockney Slang*, 1971

near-beer *noun*
a beer-like product with a very low alcohol content, legal during Prohibition *US, 1909*
There is some dispute about who said the cleverest thing ever said about 'near bear' – 'The guy who called that near beer is a bad judge of distance'. Thomas A. Dorgan, Phlander Johnson and Luke McLuke have all been given credit for the term.
- Ahern said the banning is part of the current drive on "waterholes," those nonalcoholic bars serving near-beer, soft drinks, and sex. — *San Francisco Examiner*, p. 21, 9th March 1976

near the bone *adjective*
barely within contemporary moral standards of taste *UK, 1941*
- [S]he said, "What's the matter, Frank, hasn't he been calling you recently?" This was a bit too near the bone. — Livi Michael, *Frank and the Flames of Truth*, 2004

near the knuckle *adjective*
barely within contemporary standards of decency *UK, 1909*
- Mrs [Anne] Winterton isn't exactly the first person to use near-the-knuckle humour. Similar jokes were being cracked in pubs within days of the Morecambe Bay disaster. — *The Daily Star*, 27th February 2004

neat *adjective*
1 pleasing, very good *US, 1936*
Found as early as 1808, rejected late in the C19, and then returned to favour in the 1930s. Still heard; inescapably **HOKEY**. Considered as an Americanism in the UK but used by teenagers without irony.
- "Hi, I answered. "That's a neat board." — Frederick Kohner, *Gidget*, p. 27, 1957
- I was up there the other day, it's really a neat scene. — Gurney Norman, *Divine Right's Trip (Last Whole Earth Catalog)*, p. 159, 1971
- There's Kip Pullman. He's so neat. — *American Graffiti*, 1973
- I hate to tell yuh, this is nineteen seventy-five, you know that "neat" went out, I would say, at the turn of the century. — *Annie Hall*, 1977
- It's kinda neat to order a cocktail where there's a tablecloth and a flower and a candle on the table, right? — Joseph Wambaugh, *Finnegan's Week*, p. 204, 1993
- We're having like a really neat open house today from like four to whenever if you care to stop by. — *Sleepless in Seattle*, 1993
- It was neat that I could see the DJ[.] — Ben Malbon, *Cool Places*, p. 278, 1998

2 (used of an alcoholic drink) served without ice or water *UK, 1579*
- He sweated in his shirts till the backs were rotted through, and drank his whiskey neat[.] — John Clellon Holmes, *The Horn*, p. 44, 1958
- Buster was trying to look jaunty but his hands were shaking. "Gimme a Johnny Blc," he said. "Neat." — Joseph Wambaugh, *The Golden Orange*, p. 49, 1990
- He felt warm inside, a nice buzz warming his belly, filled with three straight neat gins and an ice-cold Guinness stout. — Odie Hawkins, *Midnight*, p. 84, 1995

neat as a pin *adjective*
very neat *UK, 1787*
- There are people whose homes and offices appear neat as a pin on the surface. Yet, inside their desk drawers and kitchen cabinets, there is no real system. — Julie Morgenstern, *Organising from the Inside Out*, p. 3, 1998

neato *adjective*
good *US, 1901*
- I asked my sisters if they thought they saw a kid burning, melting, on the engine and they said no, did not?, neato. — Bret Easton Ellis, *Less Than Zero*, p. 76, 1985
- — David McGill, *David McGill's Complete Kiwi Slang Dictionary*, p. 75, 1998
- If they do they're probably too scared of seeming critical of those neato Latinos to even try. — Alisa Valdes-Rodriguez, *The Dirty Girls Social Club*, p. 101, 2003

neatojet *adjective*
excellent *US*
- — Helen Dahlskog (Editor), *A Dictionary of Contemporary and Colloquial Usage*, p. 42, 1972

neb *noun*
1 the nose *UK: SCOTLAND*
- — Michael Munro, *The Original Patter*, p. 48, 1985

2 an act of prying *UK: SCOTLAND*
- You just want them to ask us in so's you can have a good neb round the place. — Michael Munro, *The Original Patter*, p. 48, 1985

3 an inquisitive person *UK: SCOTLAND*
- That aul [old] neb wants tae know aw yer business. — Michael Munro, *The Original Patter*, p. 48, 1985

neb *verb*
to pry *UK: SCOTLAND*
From **NEB** (a nosey person or an instance of prying).
- — Michael Munro, *The Original Patter*, p. 48, 1985

nebbie; neb *noun*
Nembutal™, a branded central nervous system depressant *US, 1963*
- Not even a nebbie. He could have given me one at least. — Hubert Selby Jr, *Last Exit to Brooklyn*, p. 55, 1957
- — Richard A. Spears, *The Slang and Jargon of Drugs and Drink*, p. 357, 1986
- — Mike Haskins, *Drugs*, p. 283, 2003

nebbish; nebish; nebbech *noun*
a hapless individual; an insignificant nobody *UK, 1892*
From Yiddish *ne'bech* (too bad!, alas!) thus Yiddish *nebech* (the poor thing); the many variant spellings – not all of which are listed here – result from the difficulty of pronunciation.
- — Collin Baker et al., *College Undergraduate Slang Study Conducted at Brown University*, p. 161, 1968
- The very same fascist nebbishes that keep you from buying juice [alcohol] in highschool[.] — Lester Bangs, *Psychotic Reactions and Carburetor Dung*, p. 116, 1973
- Harry may really be a five-foot two-inch nebbish with glasses and a case of eczema. — Erica Orloff and JoAnn Baker, *Dirty Little Secrets*, p. 132, 2001

nebby *adjective*
inquisitive, prying *US*
- — Sam McCool, *Pittsburghese*, p. 25, 1982

Nebraska sign *noun*
a completely flat reading on an electrocardiogram *US*
An allusion to the endless flat prairies of Nebraska.
- — Sally Williams, *"Strong" Words*, p. 151, 1994

Nebruary morning *adverb*
never *BARBADOS*
- — Frank A. Collymore, *Barbadian Dialect*, p. 76, 1965

nebular *adjective*
excellent *US*
- — Connie Eble (Editor), *UNC-CH Campus Slang*, p. 5, Fall 1995

necessaries *noun*

▸ **the necessaries**

the male genitals *UK*

• —Roderic Jefferies, *Exhibit No. 13*, 1962

necessary *noun*

1 money, funds *UK, 1897*

• —Francis J. Rigney and L. Douglas Smith, *The Real Bohemia*, p. xvi, 1961

2 a latrine *US*

• —Linda Reinberg, *In the Field*, p. 149, 1991

neck *noun*

1 the throat *UK, 1818*

• [T]he government had decided to forge on with reform of the drinking laws to change the "get it down your neck" culture of binge drinking and to boost the tourism industry. — *The Guardian*, 3rd May 2001

2 a drink *UK*

From the verb sense.

• [I]f you want to take a quick neck before I tie you down, you'd better do it now. —Danny King, *The Bank Robber Diaries*, p. 69, 2002

3 a white prisoner *US*

A shortened 'redneck'.

• —John R. Armore and Joseph D. Wolfe, *Dictionary of Desperation*, p. 41, 1976

4 in horse racing, a distance of less than half a horse-length *US*

• —David W. Maurer, *Argot of the Racetrack*, p. 43, 1951

5 impudence, effrontery, self-confidence *UK, 1894*

From Northumberland dialect.

• Reason? Because Sean says the British Empire has a bloody neck. Will that do? —Maeve Binchy, *Light a Penny Candle*, p. 21, 1982

▸ **get it down your neck; get that down your neck**

to swallow it *UK, 1909*

Often, when in reference to an alcoholic drink, a light-hearted imperative.

▸ **get it in the neck; catch it in the neck; take it in the neck**

to be severely punished or reprimanded *US, 1887*

• It's clear the boss told him to keep a low profile or he'd get it in the neck. — *The Guardian*, 1st April 1988

▸ **get under your neck**

to usurp someone else's prerogative *AUSTRALIA*

• —Ned Wallish, *The Truth Dictionary of Racing Slang*, p. 55, 1989

▸ **neck like a jockey's bollocks**

said of someone who is not afraid to take advantage of a situation for their own gain *IRELAND*

• I'm not coddin' yeh Paddy, he has a neck on him now like a jockey's bollocks, the same fella. —Billy Roche, *The Wexford Trilogy (A Handful of Stars)*, p. 11, 1992

▸ **up to the neck; up to your neck**

deeply *US, 1998*

• He's in the shit. Up to his neck and there's no one he can turn to for help and advice. —Jack Allen, *When the Whistle Blows*, p. 138, 2000

neck *verb*

1 to kiss in a lingering fashion *UK, 1825*

• Couples began to neck publicly. —James T. Farrell, *Saturday Night*, p. 50, 1947
• First Frank necked with one of the girls, then he swapped with Benny. —Irving Shulman, *The Amboy Dukes*, p. 29, 1947
• A couple necking on a flat bench beside the Park wall diddled a battery radio and it began to sing through its nose. —Philip Wylie, *Opus 21*, p. 169, 1949
• We parked down by the riverbank and necked for a couple of hours. Then she said, "My name is Pearl McBride." —Max Shulman, *The Many Loves of Dobie Gillis*, p. 124, 1951
• She starts necking some bastard in the kitchen when she gets tanked up. —J.D. Salinger, *Nine Stories*, p. 117, 1953
• The youth cut off the motor and put his arm around the frizzy-haired girl. They started necking. —Willard Motley, *Let No Man Write My Epitaph*, p. 98, 1958
• We were downstairs in the cellar playroom, her parents were asleep, and we decided to turn out the lights and neck a little. —Phyllis and Eberhard Kronhausen, *Sex Histories of American College Men*, p. 74, 1960
• Neck a lot but don't go to bed with him until married: June, 1954, at St. Paul's On-the-Lake. —Elmore Leonard, *Gold Coast*, p. 6, 1980

2 to swallow *UK, 1514*

• Quarter to ten and you've already necked a bottle. —Geoffrey Fletcher, *Down Among the Meths Men*, p. 18, 1966
• [N]ecking a quick cup of rosie before shooting off to Penge[.] —Greg Williams, *Diamond Geezers*, p. 16, 1997
• I've just necked half a thermos of cold coffee and my haemorrhoids are humming. —Simon Lewis, *In The Box [britpulp]*, p. 128, 1999
• They necked a bottle of champagne and started dancing about. —Wayne Anthony, *Spanish Highs*, p. 82, 1999

3 to drink *AUSTRALIA*

• He's half immersed in lukewarm water, necking blue cocktails and beers[.] — *Sun-Herald (Sunday Life)*, p. 6, 17th May 1998
• East is at the foot of the bed, necking a beverage, fag held between two fingers. —Mark Powell, *Snap*, p. 151, 2001

4 in prison, to swallow a package of drugs with the intention of retrieval after excretion *UK*

• —Angela Devlin, *Prison Patter*, p. 79, 1996

5 to commit suicide *AUSTRALIA*

• It went on and on and when I awoke after the two-hour trip he was still going, threatening to neck himself. —Paul Vautin, *Turn It Up!*, p. 42, 1995

necking *noun*

the act of kissing, caressing and cuddling *UK, 1825*

• The slippery slope is pretty much everything: brightly colored linoleum, necking or petting before marriage, public schools, flesh-colored stockings [...] and so on. — *San Francisco Bay Guardian*, 29th January 2003

necklace; necklace of fire *noun*

a tyre doused or filled with petrol, placed around a victim's neck or shoulders, and set alight *SOUTH AFRICA, 1985*

• Queenstown is unique. It is known as the Necklace Capital of the World. —Antjie Krog, *Country of My Skull*, p. 419, 2000
• [In Lagos] the popular mode of execution was the necklace of fire-a tire around the neck doused with petrol and set on fire. —Chris Abani, *Graceland*, p. 30, 2004

necklace *verb*

to set fire to a car tyre that has been doused in petrol and placed around a victim's neck *SOUTH AFRICA, 1986*

An innocent sounding term for a horrid practice, usually practised black-on-black in the waning days of the white supremacist government in South Africa.

• — *Cape Times*, 12th February 1986
• — *American Speech*, Spring 1989
• A woman guerrilla, of my age, told me how when you necklaced a man – poured gas into a tire, slung it around his neck, and set fire to it – the heat was so great the skull popped like an egg in a microwave oven. —Aidan Hartley, *The Zanzibar Chest*, p. 109, 2003

necklacer *noun*

an executioner who, in the name of some informal justice, kills by means of the necklace *SOUTH AFRICA, 1987*

• Here in the mornings, necklacer and victim sit in the sun to-gether. —Antjie Krog, *Country of My Skull*, p. 419, 2000

necklacing *noun*

an act, or the action, of killing by means of the necklace *SOUTH AFRICA, 1986*

• [Y]oung radicals and older moder-ates-were going at it with necklacings and machetes. —P.J. O'Rourke, *Holidays in Hell*, p. 163, 1988
• Ivorian police stood by and watched the "necklacings," too afraid to intercede. —Robert D Kaplan, *The Ends of the Earth*, p. 14, 1996
• "Necklacing" was a form of black-on-black violence that emerged in the mid-1980s. —Antjie Krog, *Country of My Skull*, p. 63, 2000

neck like a jockey's bollocks

used descriptively of a scrawny neck and analogously for personal qualities of toughness and insensitivity *IRELAND*

• You need tough skin in this job [Irish football coach]. I guess you could say I've got a neck like a jockey's bollocks. — *The Guardian*, 27th May 2002

neck oil *noun*

alcohol, especially beer *UK, 1860*

• [A] few chilled tubes of neck oil[.] —Barry Humphries, *Bazza Pulls It Off!*, 1971
• —Barry Humphries, *The Traveller's Tool*, p. 131, 1985
• The people at KZ must have been delighted, and the EON folk, who came fourth, may also have cracked the odd bottle of neck oil. — *The Herald*, p. 4, 4th April 1988
• (RCAF, WWII) "Neck oil lubricates the throat. —Tom Langeste, *Words on the Wing*, p. 193, 1995

necktie party *noun*

a hanging, especially an extra-judicial lynching *US, 1882*

• Howsoever, it sure looked like I was about to be the guest of honor at a necktie party, when Myra decided to speak up. —Jim Thompson, *Pop. 1280*, p. 98, 1964

- While waiting for his special necktie party, President Woodrow Wilson commuted his death sentence[.] —Red Rudensky, *The Gonif*, p. 21, 1970
- All I could visualize was a lunch party waiting under some tree. But no, it is not to a necktie party he's taking me to, it's to Spankie's home in the suburbs. —Odie Hawkins, *Black Casanova*, p. 70, 1984

necro *noun*
a necrophile *US*
- —*Maledicta*, p. 180, Summer/Winter 1986–1987: 'Sexual slang: prostitutes, pedophiles, flagellators, transvestites, and necrophiles'

nectar *noun*
alcohol *US*
Formerly standard English, now slumming in slang with an archaic tone.
- No sign of nectar, though. —Richard Farina, *Been Down So Long*, p. 35, 1966

nectar *adjective*
excellent *US*
- —Pamela Munro, *U.C.L.A. Slang*, p. 61, 1989

ned *noun*
1 a young hooligan; a petty criminal *UK: SCOTLAND*
- —David Powis, *The Signs of Crime*, 1977

2 a member of a Glasgow/Edinburgh subcultural urban adolescent grouping defined by a hip-hop dress and jewellery sense *UK*
- [V]ariations on their type [chav], also known as Neds, Charvers and Townies, can be spotted across the UK. Their icons are Posh and Becks, Daniella Westbrook, singer Charlotte Church's former boyfriend Stephen Johnson and the pop star Brian Harvey. —*The Independent*, 1st February 2004

Ned *noun*
the personification of malnutrition *BARBADOS*
- —Frank A. Collymore, *Barbadian Dialect*, p. 76, 1965

neddy *noun*
a horse *AUSTRALIA, 1887*
- When the horses were coming around the turn, Grafter could see his neddy had no hope. —Frank Hardy and Athol George Mulley, *The Needy and the Greedy*, p. 15, 1975
- The bookies bet some fancy prices in the belief that the neddy would stand little chance with Huck in the saddle. —Frank Hardy and Athol George Mulley, *The Needy and the Greedy*, p. 32, 1975
- —Frank Hardy, *Hardy's People*, p. 189, 1986
- —David McGill, *David McGill's Complete Kiwi Slang Dictionary*, p. 87, 1998

nederhash *noun*
any or all varieties of hashish produced in the Netherlands *NETHERLANDS*
A compound of Dutch *Nederland* (Netherlands) and **HASH**.
- A nederhash confection[.] —Nick Jones, *Spliffs*, p. 91, 2003

Ned Kelly *noun*
1 a television; television *UK*
Rhyming slang for **TELLY**; based on Australian bushranger Ned Kelly (1854–80). Current in UK prisons in 2002.
- [C]lustered round the Ned Kelly, or having a bit of a ding-dong [a song] round the old Joanna [a piano]. —Ronnie Barker, *Fletcher's Book of Rhyming Slang*, p. 39, 1979

2 the belly *AUSTRALIA, 1945*
Rhyming slang.
- I've got a funny feeling deep down in me old Ned Kelly, that's not the last time I'll set me peepers on that pack of ratbags! —Barry Humphries, *The Wonderful World of Barry McKenzie*, p. 13, 1968
- Judging by the size of his Ned Kelly he'd have to be an acrobat to exercise the ferret [have sex]! —Barry Humphries, *Bazza Pulls It Off!*, 1971

3 a thief *AUSTRALIA*
From Edward 'Ned' Kelly, Australian bushranger and folk hero (1855–80), famed for wearing self-made armour during his final showdown with police.
- Real old Ned Kelly, isn't he? —John O'Grady, *Gone Fishin'*, p. 25, 1962
- NED KELLY: A toll attendant, a prime minister, a charity worker, a real estate man, a policeman, a crook: anybody who separates an Aussie from his Oscar is a Ned Kelly. —Arthur Chipper, *The Aussie Swearer's Guide*, p. 67, 1972

▸ **game as Ned Kelly**
extremely game; courageous *AUSTRALIA, 1938*
- Well, I hand it to you, Ern, you're gamer than Australia's patron saint, Ned Kelly. —Robert S. Close, *Love Me Sailor*, p. 68, 1945
- —Maurice Cavanough and Meurig Davies, *Cup Day*, p. 30, 1960

needies *noun*
gypsies *UK*
English gypsy use.
- —Jimmy Stockin, *On The Cobbles*, p. 11, 2000

needle *noun*
1 a feeling of resentment or irritation *UK, 1873*
Originally tailors' slang.
- He had the needle to me after that and used to ring my library books[.] —Charles Raven, *Underworld Nights*, p. 192, 1956
- This twirl had the needle to one geezer in particular —Frank Norman, *Bang To Rights*, p. 75, 1958
- Why all the bloody needle? —Mike Hodges, *Get Carter*, p. 49, 1971

2 a vehicle's speedometer *US*
- —*Complete CB Slang Dictionary*, p. 9, 1976

▸ **do the needle**
to inject drugs, especially heroin *UK*
- "You shoot up?" I ask. "Yeah, but I ain't done the needle in a long time." —Neil S. Skolnik, *On the Ledge*, p. 110, 1996

▸ **get the needle (at, with or to)**
to become angry or ill-tempered (towards a stated someone or something) *UK, 1874*
- [H]e'd get dead [very] pissed – and at about the same time get the needle to poor old Mrs Marengo[.] —Derek Raymond (Robin Cook), *The Crust on its Uppers*, p. 33, 1962

▸ **on the needle**
using or addicted to drugs injected intravenously *US, 1942*
- —Ralph de Sola, *Crime Dictionary*, p. 107, 1982
- —Angela Devlin, *Prison Patter*, p. 82, 1996

needle *verb*
1 to irritate, to annoy, to provoke *UK, 1873*
- [T]he mush said he would not go until he got the denali that was coming to him. That needled the boss. —Butch Reynolds, *Broken Hearted Clown*, p. 28, 1953
- Don't give them any lip if they come by and needle you. —Iceberg Slim (Robert Beck), *Pimp*, p. 300, 1969

2 in the illegal production of alcohol, to simulate aging by inserting an electric needle into the keg *US*
- That ain't aged likker, it's needled. —David W. Maurer, *Kentucky Moonshine*, p. 121, 1974

needle and pin *noun*
a twin *UK*
Rhyming slang. The plural is 'needles and pins'.
- —Ray Puxley, *Fresh Rabbit*, 1998

needle and thread *noun*
bread *UK, 1859*
Rhyming slang.
- Got to get some needle and thread from the long acre [baker]. —*The Sweeney*, p. 9, 1976

needle beer *noun*
beer which has been fortified with another form of alcohol *US*
- —Joseph E. Ragen and Charles Finston, *Inside the World's Toughest Prison*, p. 809, 1962: 'Penitentiary and underworld glossary'

needle candy *noun*
any drug that can be injected *US*
- —Eugene Landy, *The Underground Dictionary*, p. 139, 1971

needledick *noun*
1 a small, thin penis; a man so equipped *US*
- You paddy motherfuckers never make me feel nothin' with yo' needle dicks. —Joseph Wambaugh, *The New Centurions*, p. 81, 1970
- "Hey Needledick, checked anybody's oil lately?" "Needledick the Bug-Fucker!" —John Sayles, *Union Dues*, p. 20, 1977

2 a despicable man *US*
- "The Southland Militia?" Witherson asked Steel. "Those Rambo needle-dicks? You think they did this?" —Christopher Brookmyre, *Not the End of the World*, p. 221, 1998

needle-dicked *adjective*
endowed with a small penis *UK*
- [F]or some reason the idea of circle jerking [participating in group male masturbation] with a needle-dicked lard-arse didn't appeal. —Kitty Churchill, *Thinking of England*, p. 132, 1995

needle freak *noun*
an intravenous drug user *US*
- "Gypsie's a needle freak, too," someone said to him one day, while he was geezing. —Nicholas Von Hoffman, *We are the People Our Parents Warned Us Against*, p. 153, 1967
- —Ralph de Sola, *Crime Dictionary*, p. 101, 1982

needle jockey *noun*
a nurse or doctor who administers shots *US*
- —*American Speech*, p. 158–159, May 1960: 'The burgeoning of 'jockey''

needleman *noun*
in a confidence swindle, an agent who inspires the victim with confidence in the scheme *US*
- —Kathleen Odean, *High Steppers, Fallen Angels, and Lollipops*, p. 133, 1988

needle park *noun*
a public park or public area where drug addicts gather and inject drugs *US, 1966*
Brought into the idiom by the *Panic in Needle Park* (1966), referring to a traffic island at 74th and Broadway on Manhattan's Upper West Side, where heroin addicts congregated.
- Back-pocket bookies get their pockets picked, hookers and Cadillac pimps get herded off the street, the needle parks and shooting galleries get swept. —Robert Campbell, *Juice*, p. 143, 1988

Needle Park *nickname*
Sherman Square (71st Street and Amsterdam Avenue and Broadway), New York *US*
So named because it was a spot favoured by drug users.
- —Ralph de Sola, *Crime Dictionary*, p. 101, 1982

need-one-take-one *noun*
the small tray near a shop's cash till with pennies which customers may use for making exact payments *US*
- —Anna Scotti and Paul Young, *Buzzwords*, p. 70, 1997

neek *noun*
a socially awkward or unfashionable person *UK*
- And what winds them up even more is that, so often, "neeks" trying to sound cool are demonising and taking the piss out of urban youth. —*The Guardian*, 12th January 2005

neff *adjective*
bad, generally contemptible *UK*
A variation of **NAFF**.
- I'd had a score of jobs, all of them neff, all underpaid and some frighteningly risky. —Jonathan Gash, *The Ten Word Game*, 2003

negatory
no *US, 1955*
Coined in the military, popularised in the US by truck drivers in the 1970s.
- —Connie Eble (Editor), *UNC-CH Campus Slang*, p. 7, Spring 1988
- Negatory. Okay! —*Wayne's World 2*, 1993

neg driving *noun*
the crime of negligent driving *AUSTRALIA*
- Remember the time when Hammo had a prang in his B and got dobbed in for neg driving? —Alexander Buzo, *Rooted*, p. 44, 1969

negotiable grass *noun*
money *US*
- —David W. Maurer, *Argot of the Racetrack*, p. 44, 1951

negrogram *noun*
gossip *TRINIDAD AND TOBAGO*
An effort to euphemise the more popular **NIGGERGRAM**.
- —Lise Winer, *Dictionary of the English/Creole of Trinidad & Tobago*, 2003

negs *noun*
in prison, child neglect *UK*
In *Prison Patter*, 1996, Angela Devlin notes this as 'a rather old-fashioned term'.

neighbor *noun*
the number on either side of the winning number on a roulette wheel *US, 1961*
- —Thomas L. Clark, *The Dictionary of Gambling and Gaming*, p. 135, 1987

neil *noun*
an LSD capsule *CANADA*
An allusion to Neil Young, whose music is suitable for enjoyment by young LSD users.
- —Jack Chambers (Editor), *Slang Bag 93 (University of Toronto)*, p. 4, Winter 1993

neither use nor ornament *adjective*
applied to a useless person or thing *UK*
Contemptuous. Not noted until 1978, however '[D]idn't appear to me to be either useful or ornamental[.]', recorded in 1942, implies an earlier use.
- Just baseball boots, and they're neither use nor ornament in weather like this. —Val McDermid, *The Distant Echo*, p. 52, 2003

nekkid *adjective*
naked *US*
Jocular spelling.
- Jerry's gawking at that near-nekkid hoofer lady[.] —Lester Bangs, *Psychotic Reactions and Carburetor Dung*, p. 124, 1973

nellie *noun*
an obviously homosexual man; an effeminate homosexual man *UK, 1916*
Recorded at least as early as 1916, but not fully emerged until the outing of gay culture.
- —Collin Baker et al., *College Undergraduate Slang Study Conducted at Brown University*, p. 161, 1968
- And if a gay cruise up and down the Hudson River does not strike you as the nadir of nellie narcicssism, it was, at all events, enough to set pleated pants back ten years. —*Screw*, p. 10, 20th November 1972
- Today, for the third day in a row, I was besieged by a mob of hostile nellies midway through the feature because no one was making the reel changes up in the projection booth[.] —Jim Carroll, *Forced Entries*, p. 49, 1987
- Nellie, you're a disgrace to depression. —*As Good As It Gets*, 1997
- Get up, yer big fuckin' nelly! —Chris Ryan, *The Watchman*, p. 274, 2001
- —Paul Baker, *Polari*, p. 183, 2002

nelly *noun*
1 cheap wine *AUSTRALIA, 1941*
Shortening of earlier 'Nelly's death' (1935, *Australian National Dictionary*).
- Refer scornfully to their red ned, nelly or fourpenny dark. This implies poor taste and meanness on their part. —Arthur Chipper, *The Aussie Swearer's Guide*, p. 67, 1972

2 the pelvic muscles *TRINIDAD AND TOBAGO*
- —Lise Winer, *Dictionary of the English/Creole of Trinidad & Tobago*, 2003

nelly; nellie *adjective*
extremely, even outrageously, effeminate *US*
- "Shut your nelly mouth, Mary," said the Negro queen – "or I'll have you eight-sixed out of this bar[.]" —John Rechy, *City of Night*, p. 186, 1963
- Horace had chosen show business because it was best for him since he was so obviously nellie... —Lenny Bruce, *How to Talk Dirty and Influence People*, p. 34, 1965
- I had an address book a mile long, packed with tricks from 'drag queens' to rough trade, old aunties, little nellie queens that stayed home with mother. —Antony James, *America's Homosexual Underground*, p. 78, 1965
- I can do without your goddamn spit all over my telephone, you nellie coward. —Mart Crowley, *The Boys in the Band*, p. 148, 1968
- Carey-Lee, secure in his knowledge that he is loved, does not throw a "bitch fit" when his nellie neighbor, Tommy (Edward Dunn) intimates that something more than a simple "visit" may have taken place while he was away. —*Screw*, p. 20, 27 October 1969
- And he wanted to act what we call nelly, you know, act real feminine. —Bruce Jackson, *In the Life*, p. 400, 1972
- He shed his navy-blue cotton parka, submitted to the indignity of women's skates (white, with nelly-looking tassels) and clopped his way awkwardly to the edge of the rink. —Armistead Maupin, *Tales of the City*, p. 124, 1978

nelly!
used, by effeminate homosexual men, as an exclamation of disgust or contempt *UK*
Remembered, or otherwise dated, as 'mid-1950s', by Beale, 1984.

nellyarda *verb*
to listen *UK*
- —Paul Baker, *Polari*, p. 183, 2002

nelly-assed *adjective*
effeminate *US*
- I may not be the Queen of Sheba, exactly, but I am The Queen of This Meat Rack – and I'll prove it to any nellyassed queen that wants to try me. —John Rechy, *City of Night*, p. 53, 1963

Nelly Bligh; Nelly Bly *noun*
1 a meat pie *AUSTRALIA, 1950*
Rhyming slang, formed on the protagonist of a folk song.
2 a fly *AUSTRALIA*
Rhyming slang.
- Thomas, Stan. I never was one for drinking with the Nelly Blys. —Mary Durack, *Keep Him My Country*, p. 235, 1955

Nelly's room *noun*
▸ **up in Nelly's room behind the wallpaper**
the presumed location of something missing *IRELAND*
- There are certain things you know as a child without anybody ever telling you. Certain things and places. Places like "Up in Nelly's room behind the wallpaper". You knew exactly were it was...It was a safe place. —Bernard Share, *Slanguage*, p. 223, 2003

Nelson Eddy; nelson *adjective*
ready *UK*
Rhyming slang, based on US entertainer Nelson Eddy (1901–67).
- Ain't you Nelson Eddy yet? —Ray Puxley, *Cockney Rabbit*, p. 133, 1992

Nelson Mandela; nelson *noun*
lager, especially the Belgian lager Stella Artois™ *UK*
Rhyming slang on 'Mandela' for 'Stella'. Based on African statesman, Nelson Rolihlahla Mandela (b.1918), emphasising lager drinkers' grasp of world affairs.
- — *www.LondonSlang.com*, June 2002
- — *Antiquarian Book Review*, p. 18, June 2002

nelsons *noun*
cash *UK*
Formed from **NELSON EDDY** (ready), thus **READIES** (cash).
- —John McCririck, *John McCririck's World of Betting*, p. 61, 1991

Nelson's blood *noun*
rum *AUSTRALIA, 1924*
- According to an advertisement in the magazine of the Canadian Forestry Association, Nelson's Blood is rum, Black Diamond Demerara Rum. —*Forest and Outdoors*, December 1952
- What about a small keg of Nelson's blood. —John Wynnum, *Tar Dust*, p. 90, 1962
- [T]he fishermen retired up to the bank to have a drop of Nelsons Blood and await a bite. —Bob Staines, *Wot a Whopper*, p. 35, 1982

nembie; nemby *noun*
a barbiturate, especially Nembutal™ *US, 1950*
- This night, Herman was knocked out on "nembies" and his head kept falling down onto the bar. —William Burroughs, *Junkie*, p. 26, 1953
- —Angela Devlin, *Prison Patter*, p. 79, 1996

nemish *noun*
a capsule of pentobarbital sodium (trade name Nembutal™), a central nervous system depressant *US*
- —Richard Lingeman, *Drugs from A to Z*, p. 182, 1969

nemmie *noun*
a capsule of pentobarbital sodium (trade name Nembutal™), a central nervous system depressant *US, 1950*
- Nembutals are the prostitutes' favorite. Among initiates they are known as goof balls, or nemmies. —Jack Lait and Lee Mortimer, *Washington Confidential*, p. 117, 1951
- —Donald Louria, *Nightmare Drugs*, p. 25, 1966

neo-psycher *noun*
▹ **see: PSYCHER**

Nep; Nepalese *noun*
potent hashish from Nepal *UK*
- Nepalese can be found in Buddhist temples being burnt as incense. It is very strong black hash —Mike Rock, *This Book*, 1999
- [I] skinned up in the Gents. The Nepalese hit before take-off[.] —Howard Marks, *The Howard Marks Book of Dope Stories*, p. 300, 2001

Nepalese blue; Nepalese; Royal Nepalese *noun*
marijuana cultivated in Nepal *UK*
- [T]he tobacco giants who are already reliably rumoured to have registered such names as Nepalese Blue, Acapulco Gold and Panama Red ... the kind of joint one smokes will become a status symbol. —Richard Neville, *Play Power*, p. 132, 1970
- —Nick Jones, *Spliffs*, p. 83, 2003

Nepalese temple balls; Nepalese temple hash *noun*
hashish from Nepal, originally prepared for religious use *US*
- Brian has just scored some rather spectacular hash. 'Nepalese Temple Bells,' they're called. —Terry Southern, *Now Dig This*, p. 223, 1989
- On Independence Day, July 4th, 1975, 500 kilos of hand-pressed Nepalese temple balls, some of the best hashish in the world was flown from Kathmandu via Bangkok and Tokyo to New York. —Howard Marks, *Mr Nice*, p. 143, 1997
- To use in the temple, Buddhist Monks roll the hash into balls which are generally about the size of a football look really rough with bits of twigs, seeds etc. within them. This hash can be mildly hallucinogenic —Mike Rock, *This Book*, 1999

nephew *noun*
a young, passive male homosexual in relation to his older lover *US*
- —Hyman E. Goldin et al., *Dictionary of American Underworld Lingo*, p. 144, 1950

neppy *noun*
a person from northeast Philadelphia *US*
A combination of 'North East Philly'.
- —Claudio R. Salvucci, *The Philadelphia Dialect Dictionary*, p. 47, 1996

Nepsha and Kiah *noun*
a random selection of people from the populace *BARBADOS*
- —Frank A. Collymore, *Barbadian Dialect*, p. 76, 1965

'ner *noun*
dinner *US*
- —John D. Bell et al., *Loosely Speaking*, p. Appendix, 1969

nerd; nurd *noun*
a person lacking in social skills, fashion sense or both *US*
- In Detroit, someone who once would be called a drip or a square is now, regrettably, a nerd, or in a less severe case, a scurve. —*Newsweek*, 8th October 1951
- [A]nyone who is not a nerd (drip) knows that the bug is the family car[.] —*Herald Press (St. Jospeh, Missouri)*, p. 14, 23rd June 1952
- Cats who lack grey matter are nerds or oddballs. —*Frederick (Maryland) Post*, p. 9, 8th February 1954
- — *Time*, p. 56, 1st January 1965: 'Students: the slang bag'
- — *Current Slang*, p. 4, Fall 1966
- I almost never call anyone a nerd – I'm partial to the term "wonk". — *Wasington Post (reprinted from The Nation)*, p. C5, 22nd December 1985

nerdbomber *noun*
a pest *US*
A catchy term from the television programme *Full House*.
- —Connie Eble (Editor), *UNC-CH Campus Slang*, p. 6, Spring 1990

nerd box *noun*
a study cubicle *US*
- —Pamela Munro, *U.C.L.A. Slang*, p. 92, 1997

nerdistan *noun*
a dormitory community for information-and-communication-technology workers *US, 1997*
A play on **NERD** (a dull social stereotype).
- "To some extent it's a nerd activity," she [Marian Bell] admitted. "It's very boring." James Plaskitt, the Warwick & Leamington Labour MP, interjected: "They're all citizens of Nerdistan." — *The Times*, 25th June 2004

nerdly *noun*
a socially inept outcast *US*
- — *Time*, p. 56, 1st January 1965: 'Students: the slang bag'

nerdvana *noun*
the world of computer enthusiasts who surf the Internet every night *CANADA*
- Coined by Jack Kapica of the Toronto Globe and Mail, "nerdvana" is the sterile world of computer users who surf the Internet every night. —Bill Casselman, *Canadian Words*, p. 5, 1995

nerf *verb*
in motor racing, to bump a competitor during a race *US, 1952*
- Nerfing is especially common in short track races involving relatively cheap cars. —John Lawlor, *How to Talk Car*, p. 76, 1965
- —Fred Horsley, *The Hot Rod Handbook*, p. 210, 1965: 'Hot talk – a glossary of hot rod terms'

nerf bar *noun*
in hot rodding, a car bumper *US, 1953*
- — *Good Housekeeping*, p. 143, September 1958: 'Hot-rod terms for teen-age girls'

nerk; nurk *noun*

a contemptible person *UK, 1966*
Possibly compounds **NERD** and **JERK** (a fool) or **BERK** (a fool). A floral tribute in the shape of the word 'nurk' featured in the comedy-documentary *Life Beyond The Box*, BBC 2, 3rd May 2004.
- I don't feel the need to go around proving that I'm more macho than the next ... nerk. — Bruce Dickinson, *Ask*, p. 75, 8th May 1981
- [S]ome shoeshop nerk shows me different shoelaces. — Jonathan Gash, *The Ten Word Game*, p. 30, 2003

nerve *noun*

effrontery, audacity *UK, 1893*
- Mark Thomas [...] points out that we sell Saddam arms to kill our compatriots and then have the nerve to call him mad. — *The Guardian*, 27th June 2001
- You've got a nerve to be asking a favour[.] — The Walkmen *The Rat*, 2004

nerves *noun*

▸ **get on your nerves**
to affect morbidly *UK, 1937*
- [M]y dad used to have a motto that really got on my nerves[.] — *The Guardian*, 24th September 2003

Nervo and Knox *noun*

1 television; a television *UK, 1971*
Rhyming slang for **BOX**, formed from the names of a comedy double act, members of the Crazy Gang, Jimmy Nervo, 1890–1975, and Teddy Knox, 1896–1974.
- — Jack Jones, *Rhyming Cockney Slang*, 1971
- — Ray Puxley, *Cockney Rabbit*, 1992

2 syphilis; a sexually transmitted infection *UK*
Rhyming slang for **POX**, sometimes abbreviated to 'nervo'.
- A dose of the old Nervo. — David Powis, *The Signs of Crime*, 1977

3 socks *UK*
Rhyming slang.
- — Julian Franklyn, *A Dictionary of Rhyming Slang*, 1961
- — Ray Puxley, *Fresh Rabbit*, 1998

nervous *adjective*

excellent, well done *US, 1926*
- — *American Speech*, p. 304, December 1955: 'Wayne University slang'
- According to enthusiasts, this "cat" (man) is "real nervous" (great). — *Look*, p. 49, 24th November 1959
- — Robert George Reisner, *The Jazz Titans*, p. 161, 1960

Nervous Air *nickname*

Service Air, the Canadian military administrative term for the rough and ready travel using military transport *CANADA*
- "How will you get from Comox to Halifax?" "I'm taking Nervous Air." — Tom Langeste, *Words on the Wing*, p. 193–194, 1995

nervous Nellie *noun*

an excessively nervous person *US, 1926*
- Nervous breakdowns were for nervous Nellies. — Shane Maloney, *Nice Try*, p. 154, 1998

nervous wreck *noun*

a cheque *UK*
Rhyming slang.
- — Ray Puxley, *Fresh Rabbit*, 1998

nervy *adjective*

nervous *US, 1891*
- I don't know a thing about her, but she seemed like a nervy kid in a jam and I didn't like the snotty way that cop acted when he stopped the car. — Mickey Spillane, *Kiss Me Deadly*, p. 18–19, 1952

Nessie *nickname*

the Loch Ness monster *UK*
This familiar name for a shadow on which part of the Scottish economy exists developed not long after the newspapers announced, on 2nd May 1933, that a giant marine creature had been seen in Loch Ness. It is interesting to note that Nessie reappears in the papers about the same time each year.
- Environmental damage to Loch Ness may have killed off its most famous resident, a scientist has claimed. — *The Guardian (in a column titled: 'The Silly Season')*, 13th August 2001

nest *noun*

1 a bed *US*
- — Judi Sanders, *Cal Poly Slang*, p. 7, 1990

2 a hairdo *US*
High school student usage.
- — *San Francisco Examiner*, p. 21, 12th December 1961: 'Colloquialisms for your murgatroid handcutts'

nest egg *noun*

money saved for the future *UK, 1700*
- It was obvious, they both agreed, that this last, unexpected stake must somehow be built into a nest egg which would reestablish them both on the bigtime where they belonged. — Robert Sylvester, *No Cover Charge*, p. 221, 1956
- Our houses, cars, jewels, paintings, and alleged objets d'art can be sold, which will give us a nice little nest egg to dip into if we should run short in Birmingham. — Max Shulman, *Anyone Got a Match?*, p. 264, 1964

nester *noun*

a member of the Mexican-American prison gang Nuestra Familia *US*
A corrupted pronunciation of 'Nuestra'.
- Sworn blood brothers, allies to the death against La Nuestra Familia, or Nesters, whose membership represented California's rural chilichokers. — Seth Morgan, *Homeboy*, p. 176, 1990
- — Russell Flores, *Gang Slanging*, p. 131, 1998

Nestle's Quick *noun*

a non-commissioned officer recently arrived in Vietnam after graduation from training school *US*
The short time it took to earn their rank bothered enlisted men, who struck back with this allusion to Nestlé Quik™ (later Nesquik™), a powered milk flavouring.
- — Linda Reinberg, *In the Field*, p. 197, 1991

net *noun*

1 ten; in betting, odds of 10–1 *UK, 1851*
Back slang.
- — John McCririck, *John McCririck's World of Betting*, p. 61, 1991

2 the Internet *US*
- — Connie Eble (Editor), *UNC-CH Campus Slang*, p. 5, Fall 1995
- Claims on the net that he'd ODed in his hotel room[.] — John Williams, *Cardiff Dead*, p. 50, 2000

net and bice *noun*

in betting, odds of 12–1 *UK*
A combination of **NET** (ten) and **BICE** (two) adds up to twelve.
- — John McCririck, *John McCririck's World of Betting*, p. 61, 1991

net and ex *noun*

in betting, odds of 16–1 *UK*
A combination of **NET** (ten) and a slurring of 'six', adding up to sixteen.
- — John McCririck, *John McCririck's World of Betting*, p. 61, 1991

net and rouf *noun*

in betting, odds of 14–1 *UK*
A combination of **NET** (ten) and **ROUF** (four), adding up to fourteen.
- — John McCririck, *John McCririck's World of Betting*, p. 61, 1991

nethead *noun*

in the language surrounding the Grateful Dead, a follower of the band who is part of the Grateful Dead cyber community *US*
- — David Shenk and Steve Silberman, *Skeleton Key*, p. 201, 1994

netiquette *noun*

the protocol, implicit or explicit, observed by members of an Internet discussion group *US*
- By taking the time to see if there is a FAQ, you'll be following Usenet "netiquette," the etiquette rules that have developed over the years to let members of the on-line community peacefully interact. — Nancy Tamosaitis, *net.sex*, p. 5, 1995

netlag *noun*

an inordinate delay in an Internet relay chat *US*
A pun on the standard 'jet lag'.
- — Christian Crumlish, *The Internet Dictionary*, p. 134, 1995

net police *noun*

a participant in an Internet discussion group who, on a self-appointed basis, polices the discussion for protocol and etiquette violations *US*
- — Eric S. Raymond, *The New Hacker's Dictionary*, p. 256, 1991

neuron *noun*

a neurologist *US*

• —Sally Williams, *"Strong" Words*, p. 152, 1994

neutral *noun*

▸ **to put into neutral**

to castrate *NEW ZEALAND*

• Dry humour runs thick through this collection; for example commercial traveler – a ram that jumps the fence into a neighbouring paddock; to put into neutral – to castrate male lambs or calves; career girl – a ewe that refuses to mother her lamb; double-yolker – a ewe carrying twins; body-snatcher – a stock buyer. —*Dominion Post*, p. C6, 22nd November 2002

Nevada lettuce *noun*

a one-thousand-dollar note *US*

Nevada, formerly the only state in the US with legal gambling, is still the most popular gambling destination in the US and the only state with legal brothels.

• —Frank Garcia, *Marked Cards and Loaded Dice*, p. 263, 1962

Nevada nickel *noun*

a five-dollar gambling token *US, 1979*

• —Thomas L. Clark, *The Dictionary of Gambling and Gaming*, p. 135, 1987

never *adverb*

not *UK*

• Told her it was never down to me some geezer came round[.]—Jeremy Cameron, *Brown Bread in Wengen*, p. 4, 1999

never again *noun*

Ben Truman™, a branded beer *UK*

Rhyming slang, from the promise made the morning after the night before.

• —Ray Puxley, *Cockney Rabbit*, 1992

neverendum *noun*

either of the two referenda on Quebec sovereignty or independence *CANADA*

The term is a sarcastic allusion to the independentist government's having called two votes on the subject and vowing to keep calling them till it won.

• Every region will have its own phrases, historical references and cultural icons. Some will need no further explanation: ice-storm syndrome, Celine, angryphones, Big O, neverendum. —*Montreal Gazette*, p. A3, 10th March 1999: 'A special way with words'

never fear – NAME is here

a catchphrase announcement – using the speaker's name, of course – of the speaker's reassuring presence; also used, by the speaker, as a general greeting; or, ironically (and, occasionally, disdainfully) of a third party *UK, 1975*

• Never fear, Dee, self-confessed anorak about Upton Park, Pete Tomlin, is here with the answer. —*The Guardian*, 19th September 2002

never happen!

used for expressing supreme doubt *TRINIDAD AND TOBAGO, 1956*

• —Gregory Clark, *Words of the Vietnam War*, p. 344–345, 1990
• —Lise Winer, *Dictionary of the English/Creole of Trinidad & Tobago*, 2003

never in a pig's ear

never *UK*

Rhyming slang for 'never in a year'.

• —David Powis, *The Signs of Crime*, 1977

nevermind *noun*

▸ **makes no nevermind**

makes no difference *US, 1924*

• My own marriage isn't exactly a bed of roses – true – but that makes no nevermind. —Robert Gover, *JC Saves*, p. 63, 1968

never mind!

1 don't worry; mind your own business *UK*

Semi-exclamatory imperative.

• GRANDPA: [...] We was going to do it together. LOFTY: Oh – well – never mind, Granfer. —Clive Exton, *No Fixed Abode [Six Granada Plays]*, p. 140, 1959

2 used as a humorous admission of misunderstanding *US*

A key signature line of the early years of NBC's *Saturday Night Live*, uttered by the Emily Litella character played by Gilda Radner who would end rants about 'Soviet Jewelry' or 'the deaf penalty' with the humble 'never mind'. Repeated with referential humour.

never-never *noun*

1 hire purchase *UK*

A suggestion that you will never, never pay off your debts, with an ironic reference to J.M. Barrie (1860–1937)'s idealised home for Peter Pan, 'Never Never Land', first realised in 1904.

• [Y]our rotten little cars on the never-never. —John Peter Jones, *Feather Pluckers*, p. 156, 1964
• Worried when he didn't have a TV set; then bought one on the never-never and worried about meeting the payments. —Frank Hardy, *The Yarns of Billy Borker*, p. 87, 1965
• —Frank Hardy, *The Outcasts of Foolgarah*, p. 53, 1971

2 the remote regions of interior Australia *AUSTRALIA, 1833*

Origin unknown. Sometimes upper case.

• NEVER-NEVER – The outback. —Gilbert H. Lawson, *A Dictionary of Australian Words and Terms*, 1924
• —Patsy Adam-Smith, *Folklore of the Australian Railwaymen*, p. 90, 1969
• I followed the tracks out into the Never-Never towards Beetaloo. —Herb Wharton, *Cattle Camp*, p. 11, 1994

never-never country *noun*

the remote regions of interior Australia *AUSTRALIA, 1889*

• There was a sort of transit camp of them at Port Augusta, all heading off to the never-never country where they were sure they'd find work. —Patsy Adam-Smith, *Folklore of the Australian Railwaymen*, p. 180, 1969

never-never land *noun*

1 an imaginary, ideal world *UK, 1900*

From J. M. Barrie's *Peter Pan* novels.

• My heart and beliefs is out there in never-never land when it comes to religion, but I don't want to get into that. —Robert Campbell, *Junkyard Dog*, p. 19, 1986

2 the hire purchase method of payment by instalments *UK*

never pitch a bitch

used in confidence swindles as a humorous rule of thumb meaning 'never try to do a sales job on a woman' *US*

• —M. Allen Henderson, *How Con Games Work*, p. 217, 1985: 'Glossary'

never smarten a sucker up

used by gambling cheats and confidence swindlers as a prime rule of the trade *US*

• —*The Annals of the American Academy of Political and Social Sciences*, p. 128, May 1950

never this year

not a chance *UK*

• A client [...] That would be even nice. But never this year. —Diran Abedayo, *My Once Upon A Time*, p. 5, 2000

never-was *noun*

a person to whom actual achievement has eluded *US, 1891*

• Some guy might boast about how he is going to get out next time and stay out, and some will put him down by saying he'll soon be back, playing marbles like a hasbeen, a nerverwas[.] —Eldridge Cleaver, *Soul on Ice*, p. 43, 1968
• The first four were aging has-beens and never-weres. —Robert Campbell, *Alice in La-La Land*, p. 195, 1987

neves; nevis *noun*

1 in betting, odds of 7–1 *UK*

• —John McCririck, *John McCririck's World of Betting*, p. 61, 1991

2 the number seven *UK, 1851*

Back slang.

3 a prison sentence of seven years *UK*

A specific application of the number seven. Sometimes extended to 'nevis stretch'.

• Your [sic] f...ing lucky, I'm doing a bleeding neves. I'll be going down the Moor soon. —Frank Norman, *Bang To Rights*, p. 17, 1958
• —Angela Devlin, *Prison Patter*, p. 79, 1996

neves and a half *noun*

in betting, odds of 15–2 *UK*

In bookmaker slang **NEVES** is 7–1, here the addition of 'a half' increases the odds to 7½–1or 15–2.

• —John McCririck, *John McCririck's World of Betting*, p. 112, 1991

neves to rouf *noun*

in betting, odds of 7–4 *UK*

A combination of **NEVES** (seven) and **ROUF** (four) when, if used alone, each word signifies more than the number itself. Pronounced 'nevis to roaf'.

• —John McCririck, *John McCririck's World of Betting*, p. 112, 1991

Neville *noun*
a stupid or annoying person; a person lacking in social skills, fashion sense or both *AUSTRALIA*
- As he started to write the ticket I said, 'Turn it up Neville, I was only doin' 101.'—Paul Vautin, *Turn It Up!*, p. 109, 1995

new *noun*
a lager-style beer brewed by the bottom-fermentation method *AUSTRALIA, 1935*
As opposed to **OLD**.
- —Dymphna Cusack, *Picnic Races*, p. 198, 1962
- 'Another pint of new...coming up!' cried the barman, sliding the foaming glass pot along the counter.—John Wynnum, *Jiggin' in the Riggin'*, p. 34, 1965

new!
used for commenting humorously on a new purchase *US*
- For example, when a boy gets a haircut, he is greeted by his friends with an emphatic new!—*American Speech*, p. 274, December 1963: 'American Indian student slang'

new addition *noun*
crack cocaine *UK*
- —Mike Haskins, *Drugs*, p. 282, 2003

newb *noun*
a new user of the Internet; a newcomer to an Internet discussion group or multi-player game *UK*
A shortening of 'newbie'.
- Who's that newb?—*You and Yours*, 30th April 2003

newbie *noun*
1 a new user of the Internet; a new arrival to an Internet discussion group *US*
The general sense 'newcomer' used condescendingly.
- If you're a Net neophyte or "newbie," you'll undoubtedly be tempted to ask questions that have been covered thousands of times before.—Nancy Tamosaitis, *net.sex*, p. 5, 1995
- —Christian Crumlish, *The Internet Dictionary*, p. 134, 1995
- Last night I e-mailed Nancy. >I'm very taken with a nut, I said. / And she e-mailed back >It's a newbie phase, sweetie. Bob was just the same.—Melanie McGrath, *Hard, Soft & Wet*, p. 55, 1998

2 a newcomer *US, 1970*
Originally military.
- Andrews had first come to the attention of the grunts because he was the newest arrival – a "newby" – which meant he couldn't really lead or command anyone[.]—Charles Anderson, *The Grunts*, p. 31, 1976
- A Deadhead who just got "on the bus."—David Shenk and Steve Silberman, *Skeleton Key*, p. 203, 1994
- [A] scrubby teenager approaches and asks whether or not I'm a Warhammer "newbie."—Marty Beckerman, *Death to All Cheerleaders*, p. 91, 2000
- Grizzled veterans like Kate and Liberty are expected to be on hand to inspire the newbies, who will no doubt be thrilled[.]—*ES Magazine*, p. 39, 22nd June 2001

new boy *noun*
used of a man or a corporate entity, a new arrival to an existing community *UK, 1948*
From school usage, applied less accurately in military, business and other closed circles.
- New boy Poland flexes its muscles.—*The Guardian*, 10th December 2003

New Brunswick credit card *noun*
a rubber siphoning hose for stealing petrol *CANADA*
An analogous term is the Texas **OKLAHOMA CREDIT CARD**. People from better-off adjacent states or provinces seem convinced that their poorer neighbours are thieves.
- What's a 'New Brunswick credit card'? In Nova Scotia, it's a length of rubber hose for siphoning gasoline.—*Ottawa Citizen*, p. D4, 6th December 1992: 'Words'

newbug *noun*
a new boy or new girl *UK, 1900*
Originally from Marborough School and only of a boy, now widespread.
- British children still do it to "newbugs".—*The Times*, p. 3, 19th October 2002

newby *verb*
to fail to perform at a critical moment *US*
- —Connie Eble (Editor), *UNC-CH Campus Slang*, p. 7, October 2002

Newcastled *adjective*
filled with Newcastle Brown Ale™; drunk (probably as a result of drinking Newcastle Brown Ale) *UK*
Newcastle Brown Ale was first brewed (in Newcastle) in 1927.
- —*e-cyclopaedia*, 20th March 2002
- [T]he recorder gets clicked off, glasses are freshly Newcastled, and the three of us talk about other important matters—*Independent Online*, 14th February 2003

new chum *noun*
1 a newly arrived immigrant from Britain who has little knowledge of local life and customs *AUSTRALIA*
Originally applied to newly incarcerated prisoners (1812 Vaux), it was applied to migrants as early as 1828 (*Australian National Dictionary*); the opposing term was 'old chum' but this did not survive into the C20.
- 'New chum, eh?,' Vic said. 'Won't have much on him if he's a 51 import.'—Michael Peters, *Pommie Bastard*, p. 89, 1969

2 a novice *AUSTRALIA, 1851*
- Some of us here ain't new chums on tracking, Nat, but the bloke got away by hopping over surface rocks[.]—Arthur Upfield, *Bony and the Mouse*, p. 39, 1959
- Pudding is that strange concoction of a bait that is home made from scraps of bread, sausages and cheese mixed together. However, to the new chum, the term can be quite misleading, as the new wife of a Sydney [fishing] club member found out.—Bob Staines, *Wot a Whopper*, p. 13, 1982

New Delhi *noun*
the belly *UK*
Rhyming slang, formed, possibly, on a sly reference to Indian food.
- —Ray Puxley, *Cockney Rabbit*, 1992

Newf *noun*
a Newfoundlander *CANADA*
- Of course he couldn't have passed me, the ill bred Newf that I am.—*St. John's Evening Telegram*, p. 4–5, 8th May 1958

Newfie *noun*
any person from Newfoundland *US, 1942*
- Newfie jokes are in Canada what Polack jokes are in the United States, since Newfoundlanders are considered notoriously stupid and backward due to their isolation from urban centers.—*Maledicta*, p. 163, Summer/Winter 1978: 'How to hate thy neighbor: a guide to racist maledicta'

Newfie banana *noun*
the root of the cinnamon fern *CANADA*
- The "Newfie banana" is crunchy, and children sometimes dug them up and ate them.—Bill Casselman, *Canadian Food Words*, p. 46, 1988

Newfie Bullet *noun*
a train that traversed the interior of Newfoundland *CANADA*
Ironic.
- A couple of weeks back, I described a rail trip (on the famous (Newfie Bullet) through the great dead heart of the island-province.—*Toronto Globe and Mail*, p. 6/4, 7th December 1965

Newfiejohn *noun*
the city of St John's, Newfoundland *CANADA*
- There's something grimly exciting about St. John's, or "Newfiejohn," as the Navy calls it.—William Pugsley, *Saints, Sinners, and Ordinary Seamen*, p. 32, 1945

new girl *noun*
a new arrival to an existing community *UK*
From school use, applied to a female adult joining military, business or other closed group.
- [A]s an impressionable new girl, I was chatting away to a friendly co-worker in a former job.—*The Guardian*, 3rd November 2003

New Guinea crud *noun*
any skin rash suffered in tropical and jungle environments *US*
- "Jungle rot," "New Guinea crud" or "the creeping crud" are U.S. servicemen's names for any & every kind of tropical skin disease.—*Time*, p. 76, 13th August 1946

new guy *noun*
a freshly arrived soldier to combat *US*
Often embellished to **FUCKING NEW GUY**.
- Being a new guy is a very uncomfortable thing; it's probably the most uncomfortable thing I've ever experienced.—Malcolm Boyd, *My Fellow Americans*, p. 212, 1970
- You listen to Joker, new guy.—*Full Metal Jacket*, 1987

New Hampshire screwdriver *noun*
a hammer *US*
Maine usage, looking down on the workmanship of carpenters from the south.
• —John Gould, *Maine Lingo*, p. 189, 1975

newie *noun*
something new *AUSTRALIA, 1924*
• Time to bung in a newie.—John Wynnum, *Tar Dust*, p. 12, 1962
• Finally: Consumer Culture is Also Really Bad. Gosh, that's a newie. —*Sydney Scope Magazine*, p. 35, 2001

Newington Butts; newingtons *noun*
the stomach, abdomen, guts; in a figurative sense the essential qualities of a person *UK, 1960*
Rhyming slang for **GUTS**. Newington Butts is an area of south London.
• I hate your guts, your Newington Butts—Ian Dury, *Blackmail Man*, 1977
• Her hobsons, low and husky / Made my newingtons go numb.—Ronnie Barker, *Fletcher's Book of Rhyming Slang*, p. 21, 1979

new jack *noun*
a newcomer (especially one likely to be a success) *US, 1988*
• Beanie and Xzibit didn't make the new-jack list because they don't qualify. Both already have two or more albums under their belts. —*The Source*, p. 44, March 2002

new jack swing *noun*
heroin and morphine in concert *UK, 1998*
• —Robert Ashton, *This Is Heroin*, p. 209, 2002
• —Mike Haskins, *Drugs*, p. 293, 2003

new kid *noun*
in roller derby, a skater who has not yet been accepted by other skaters *US*
• A rookie may be a new kid for years – until becoming one of the "family."—Keith Coppage, *Roller Derby to Rollerjam*, p. 126, 1999

new kid on the block *adjective*
in bar dice games, a player just joining an ongoing game *US*
• —Jester Smith, *Games They Play in San Francisco*, p. 104, 1971

Newky brown; Newky *noun*
Newcastle Brown Ale™ *UK, 1984*
As widely used as the beer is appreciated.

new-man-rule *noun*
an unwritten rule among some units of the US Army in Vietnam that a newly arrived soldier would be placed at the front of the unit as pointman *US*
• —Gregory Clark, *Words of the Vietnam War*, p. 346, 1990

new meat *noun*
1 a new student at a school *US, 1962*
• —*American Speech*, p. 272, December 1963: 'American Indian student slang'

2 an inexperienced prison inmate *US, 1938*
• I had visions of ending up in Borstal or prison, or being the new young meat in an overcrowded remand wing.—Andy McNab, *Immediate Action*, p. 9, 1995

3 an inexperienced soldier freshly arrived at the front *US, 1971*
• —Linda Reinberg, *In the Field*, p. 150, 1991

new nip *noun*
a small boy, or a new boy at a school *UK*
• —*The Felstedian*, December 1947

new one
applied to a previously unheard joke or anecdote, or to something seen, or heard of, for the first time *US, 1887*
Generally phrased 'that' or 'it's a new one on' followed by a pronoun or person's name.
• Pat had a perfectly pink fillet of lamb[...] in a lavender jus. It was a new one on me, but boy, does it work. It really did taste of lavender[.]—*The Observer*, 19th August 2001

new pussy *noun*
a woman unknown to gang members *US*
• Usually they were mamas, but now and then what the Angels call "a strange broad" or "new pussy" would show up.—Hunter S. Thompson, *Hell's Angels*, p. 193, 1966

news bunny *noun*
a female television reporter or anchor hired for her cute looks *US*
• And for a least two decades now, stations most everywhere have been clipping their call letters to the microphones that their news bunnies thrust at people they want to interview.—*LosAngeles Times*, p. F1, 16th July 1990

new school *adjective*
(used of rap music) current, modern *US*
The functional reciprocal of **OLD SKOOL**.
• —Pamela Munro, *U.C.L.A. Slang*, p. 95, 2001

news hawk *noun*
a newspaper reporter *US, 1931*
• That four-page hot-tamale sheet had scooped the A.P., the U.P., and the I.N.S., along with Reuters and Tass and all the other globe-circling know-it-all newshawks.—Mezz Mezzrow, *Really the Blues*, p. 167, 1946

new-sick *noun*
a new influenza virus *BARBADOS*
• —Frank A. Collymore, *Barbadian Dialect*, p. 76, 1965

newspaper *noun*
a thirty-day jail sentence *US, 1926*
• —Troy Harris, *A Booklet of Criminal Argot, Cant and Jargon*, p. 20, 1976

newspapers *noun*
LSD *UK*
• —Mike Haskins, *Drugs*, p. 285, 2003

newsstand *noun*
a dealer in pornographic literature and magazines *US*
• "Some S and M. Some kiddie porn. Some-" "Zabano was a newsstand?" "Only retail."—Robert Campbell, *In La-La Land We Trust*, p. 97, 1986

newsy *adjective*
1 full of information, especially of trivial or personal matters *UK, 1832*
• It was quite a "newsy" letter telling me of boys and girls who I had known and about life at home.—Fred Digby, *WW2 Peoples War*, 5th July 2003

2 nosy; too interested in gossip *US*
• —Claudio R. Salvucci, *The Philadelphia Dialect Dictionary*, p. 49, 1996

newszine *noun*
a fan magazine that does not contain any fiction, just news *US, 1976*
• —*American Speech*, p. 53, Spring 1978: 'Star Trek lives: Trekker slang'
• —*American Speech*, p. 28, Spring 1982: 'The langage of science fiction fan magazines'

newted *adjective*
drunk *UK, 1984*
From **PISSED AS A NEWT**.

Newton and Ridley *adjective*
mildly drunk *UK*
Rhyming slang for **TIDDLY**, formed from the name of the fictitious brewery that supplies the drinking requirements of the characters in the long running television soap opera *Coronation Street*.
• —Ray Puxley, *Fresh Rabbit*, 1998

Newton Heath *noun*
teeth *UK*
Rhyming slang from Manchester, formed on an industrial suburb of the city. Reported by Jacob Jaffe, 1959.

new toy *noun*
in the Metropolitan Police, a newly introduced piece of equipment; a new recruit *UK*
• —*The Official Encyclopaedia of New Scotland Yard*, 1999

New Year *noun*
▸ **not know if it's New Year or New York**
applied to anyone who is failing to think clearly (for whatever reason) *UK: SCOTLAND*
• They don't know if it's New Year or New York, hauf [half] these kids leaving school the noo.—Michael Munro, *The Patter, Another Blast*, 1988
• They've seen him out dressed in my clothes / Patently unclear / If it's New York or New Year.—Nick Lowe, *The Beast in Me*, 1994

New York City silver *noun*
▷ **see: MANHATTAN SILVER**

New Yorker *noun*

a variety of MDMA, the recreational drug best known as ecstasy *UK*

A play on **APPLE** (a variety of MDMA) and **THE APPLE** (New York).

- —Angela Devlin, *Prison Patter*, p. 79, 1996
- —Macfarlane, Macfarlane and Robson, *The User*, p. 75, 1996
- Street names [...] M25s, New Yorkers, rhubarb and custard[.]—James Kay and Julian Cohen, *The Parents' Complete Guide to Young People and Drugs*, p. 136, 1998
- —Gareth Thomas, *This Is Ecstasy*, p. 55, 2002

New York kiss *noun*

a punch to the face *US*

- —Jeffrey McQuain, *Never Enough Words*, p. 55, 1999

New York minute *noun*

a very short period of time *US, 1948*

A nod to the impatience associated with New Yorkers.

- Equates to a nanosecond, or that infinitesimal blink of time in New York after the traffic light turns green and before the ol' boy behind you honks his horn.—Ken Weaver, *Texas Crude*, p. 116, 1984
- You tell me yes, I'll go call him at his house right now, get you set up in a New York minute.—Richard Price, *Clockers*, p. 524, 1992
- He hesitated for a New York minute, staring at a spot between Leddy's eyes.—Robert Campbell, *Boneyards*, p. 54, 1992

New York reload *noun*

a second (concealed) pistol; an act of drawing a second gun *US*

Derives from a legal loophole: New York police used not to be allowed the use of a speed loader but a second, concealed gun was apparently permissable.

- The fastest revolver reload is a second revolver, a.k.a. "the New York reload[.]"—Ed Lovette, *Snubby Revolver*, p. 51, 2002

New York Slime *nickname*

the *New York Times* newspaper *US*

- —*CoEvolution Quarterly*, p. 27, Spring 1981

newzak *noun*

trivial news, or broadcast news that exists in the background but is ignored *UK*

A play on 'muzak'.

- —Susie Dent, *The Language Report*, p. 14, 2003

New Zealand green *noun*

a strain of marijuana, known elsewhere as Tasmanian tiger, Thai Buddha and Hawaiian head *NEW ZEALAND*

- "What are they?" "Tasmanian Tiger." "What's the genetic heritage of that?" "In Auckland it was called New Zealand Green[.]"—Brian Preston, *Pot Planet*, p. 96–97, 2002

New Zealand mafia *noun*

a notional organisation of New Zealand professionals in London *NEW ZEALAND, 1986*

- —Harry Orsman, *A Dictionary of Modern New Zealand Slang*, p. 83, 1999

next *noun*

during the Vietnam war, a soldier whose rotation home was due in only a few days *US*

- —Linda Reinberg, *In the Field*, p. 150, 1991

next *adjective*

within a few days of returning to the US after a tour of duty in Vietnam *US*

- —Gregory Clark, *Words of the Vietnam War*, p. 465, 1990

nextish *noun*

the next issue of a single-interest fan magazine *US*

- —*American Speech*, p. 28, Spring 1982: 'The langage of science fiction fan magazines'

nexus *noun*

4-bromo-2,5-dimethoxyphenethyliamine, a mild hallucinogen *US*

- —Steven Daly and Nalthaniel Wice, *alt.culture*, p. 256, 1995

NF *verb*

as an act of racial hatred, to set fire to a property that houses members of an ethnic minority *UK*

Derives from the initials of the National Front, a politically right wing organisation founded on muddled philosophies of racial intolerance and violent intervention.

- They had threatened to 'NF' her house. 'It means torch it – as in "National Front,"' she explains.—*The Guardian G2*, p. 9, 7th June 2005

NF *nickname*

the Nuestra Familia prison gang *US*

- NF enforcers then went after the drug dealers and other big-money crooks.—Bill Valentine, *Gangs and Their Tattoos*, p. 34, 2000

NFG *adjective*

used as shorthand to mean '*n*o *f*ucking *g*ood' *US, 1977*

- [T]he Lucas Opus ignition is NFG and tricky besides.—Carroll Smith, *Tune to Win*, p. 5, 1978
- —Andy Ihnatko, *Cyberspeak*, p. 135, 1997

NFN

doctors' shorthand for the facetious diagnosis: *n*ormal *f*or *N*orfolk *UK*

Recorded in an article about medical slang in British (3 London and 1 Cambridge) hospitals.

- —*Ethics and Behaviour*, August 2003

NG *adjective*

no good *US, 1879*

- —Ralph S. Singleton, *Filmaker's Dictionary*, p. 112, 1990

NHI *adjective*

used for describing a crime against a criminal, especially one involving only black people *US*

An abbreviation of '*n*o *h*umans *i*nvolved'.

- And he called the wagon job "the N.H.I. detail." When you asked him what that stood for he'd say "No Humans Involved," and then he let out with that donkey bray of his.—Joseph Wambaugh, *The Blue Knight*, p. 124, 1973
- As incensed as the public gets at appallingly brutal killlings – the ones that blow away innocents – police expend little sympathy on criminal-to-criminal mayhem. An acronym drifts unwritten about the system; those are NHI crimes – No Human Involved.—*Los Angeles Times*, p. 1 (Metro), 14th May 1989
- The file was the end of the line for prostitutes, vagrants, and such. It was marked "NHI" for "no humans involved."—*Houston Chronicle*, p. 3, 25th Aprili 1993
- And they recoiled at a police report documenting a prostitute's death – it was stamped "NHI" – No Human Involved.—*Kansas City Pitch Weekly*, 30th January 2003

Niagara Falls; niagaras *noun*

the testicles *UK, 1943*

Rhyming slang.

- I'd like to believe that coming upon me in the boudoir nakedly inspecting the Niagaras of another man had sent a sudden rush of jealousy coursing through his veins[.]—Kitty Churchill, *Thinking of England*, p. 22, 1995

nibble *noun*

a non-commital expression of interest *UK*

From the image of a fish trying a bait.

- But never any recognition at all, not a nibble.—Ray Galton and Alan Simpson, *Hancock's Half Hour*, 20th March 1959

nibby *noun*

a walking stick, especially one used in mustering *NEW ZEALAND*

- The high-country musterer covers a lot of dangerous country, day after day, and with nothing to aid him but his nibby or walking stick.—Peter Newton, *Straggle Muster*, p. 94, 1964

nibs *noun*

▸ **his nibs; her nibs**

himself; herself; a self-important person *UK, 1821*

Usually styled as a mock-title.

- Look out. There's his nibs. Back to the galley, slaves.—Derek Bickerton, *Payroll*, p. 21, 1959
- His Nibs asked me a stack of intelligent and searching questions which probably speak for a lot of commoners too.—Barry Humphries, *The Traveller's Tool*, p. 30, 1985
- White with two for his nibs.—Shane Maloney, *Nice Try*, p. 36, 1998
- Tell his nibs he can come through now[.]—Ben Elton, *High Society*, p. 310, 2002

nice and easy *noun*

heroin *US*

- —US Department of Justice, *Street Terms*, October 1994
- —Robert Ashton, *This Is Heroin*, p. 206, 2002

nice as pie *adjective*

very polite, very agreeable *US, 1922*

- If I come on nice as pie to her, whatever else I insinuate, she ain't gonna get in a tizzy and have me electrocuted?—Ken Kesey, *One Flew Over the Cuckoo's Nest*, p. 68, 1962

nice bit *noun*

a prison sentence of three years or more *UK*

• —Angela Devlin, *Prison Patter*, p. 79, 1996

nice enough *noun*

a homosexual male *UK*

Rhyming slang for **PUFF**.

• —Ray Puxley, *Cockney Rabbit*, 1992

nice kitty *noun*

a Christmas bonus *US*

• —Jerry Robertson, *Oil Slanguage*, p. 87, 1954

nice little earner *noun*

a well-paid job or profitable scheme, almost always criminal to some degree *UK*

An elaboration of **EARNER**, made popular by actor George Cole as small-time crook and wheeler-dealer Arthur Daley in *Minder*, 1979–94.

• —Angela Devlin, *Prison Patter*, p. 79, 1996

nicely irrigated with horizontal lubricant *adjective*

drunk *UK*

Some people, when drinking, use too many words.

• —*e-cyclopaedia*, 20th March 2002

nice-nice *adjective*

very attractive *UK*

• "If loving you was a crime, / I'd be in prison a long time, I tell you." "Yes, indeed dat's how me feel when me spy dem nice-nice gyal [girls] up Dalston way.["] —Donald Gorgon, *Cop Killer*, p. 112, 1994

nice one

used in a congratulatory sense to express praise for an action *UK*

• There's a ice-cream van parked up outside ready for business. So is Nood. – Nice one, he says takin' out his cigs. —Nick Barlay, *Curvy Lovebox*, p. 43, 1997
• "Do your flies up," I say, nodding at his middle area, and his gloved hand automatically shoots down to his trousers. "Nice one, sir," he smiles. — Martin King and Martin Knight, *The Naughty Nineties*, p. 21, 1999
• All right? 'Ow ya doin'? Nice one. Sound. Yeah. —Ben Elton, *High Society*, p. 155, 2002

nice one Cyril; nice one *noun*

a squirrel *UK*

Rhyming slang.

• —Ray Puxley, *Cockney Rabbit*, 1992

nice one, Cyril

used for expressing praise *UK*

A very popular catchphrase of the mid-1970s. It originated in a television commercial and was taken up in the early 70s as a football chant by Tottenham Hotspur FC's supporters in celebration of Cyril Knowles, one of the club's leading players.

nice talk *noun*

a line of conversation intended to seduce *UK*

Urban black youth usage.

• So if I'm giving you nice talk and I ask you for your number, you're gonna turn me down because I haven't got a phone? — *The Times Magazine*, 21st June 2003

nice up *verb*

to make something more acceptable or presentable, to improve, to refine *UK*

• [Of Margaret Thatcher's speeches sampled for a piece of dance music] We niced it up. —Charles Bailey, *The Today Programme*, 20th February 2004

nice weather for ducks

wet weather *UK, 1973*

Known in variant forms since 1840.

• The bell goes ting-a-ling. Ting-aling! "Nice weather for ducks!"says the girl behind hte counter. —Zadie Smith, *The Autograph Man*, 2002
• Whimiscal weather forecasters smile blandly through this most catastrophic news, as if nice weather for ducks and a good day at Lord's was all that was at stake. — *The Guardian*, 13th August 2004

nicey nice *adjective*

Extremely nice, even excessively nice *UK, 1859*

A diminutive, childish formation usually used with some degree of mocking or irony.

• Why was she so goddamn nice all the time? Nicey-nice. God. —Elmore Leonard, *Switch*, p. 9, 1978

nick *noun*

1 a prison; a police station *UK*

In either case it is where one is taken after getting 'nicked' (arrested); the former dates from 1882, the latter 1957.

• The most commonly used slang word for any prison —Paul Tempest, *Lag's Lexicon*, 1950
• This is the same in the nick as anywhere else. —Frank Norman, *Bang To Rights*, p. 30, 1958
• The boys down at Chelsea nick every time they clock my boat —Derek Raymond Robin Cook, *The Crust on its Uppers*, 1962
• The Office, Barlow called it. Home, John Watt called it. The Stir,Clink, Bog, Nick, depending on what your are, and where you come from. —Troy Kennedy Martin, *Z Cars*, p. 21, 1962
• A police station or, less commonly, prison —David Powis, *The Signs of Crime*, 1977
• [W]hen I was sat in that cell nearly every copper in that nick came down to have another look at me through the little cell door window. —Dave Courtney, *Raving Lunacy*, p. 255, 2000

2 condition or quality, especially in phrases 'in good nick', 'in poor nick', etc *UK, 1905*

Originally dialect.

• It was heart-breaking for them trying to keep their uniforms up to scratch and all that bullshit without the added effort of keeping them in good nick for pleasure as well. —Johnny Speight, *It Stands to Reason*, p. 67, 1973

3 in horse racing, a mating that results in the sought-after qualities *AUSTRALIA*

• —Ned Wallish, *The Truth Dictionary of Racing Slang*, p. 55, 1989

4 five dollars' worth of marijuana *US*

A shortened form of 'nickel' as in **NICKEL BAG**.

• —Gary K. Farlow, *Prison-ese*, p. 45, 2002

5 in craps, a winning roll of seven on the first toss *US*

• —Frank Garcia, *Marked Cards and Loaded Dice*, p. 263, 1962

6 a nickname *US*

• —Christian Crumlish, *The Internet Dictionary*, p. 137, 1995

▸ **in the nick**

naked *NEW ZEALAND*

• —David McGill, *David McGill's Complete Kiwi Slang Dictionary*, p. 88, 1998

▸ **on the nick**

engaged in thieving *UK*

• In my little yellow jersey, I went out on the nick / South Street Romford, shopping arcade —Ian Dury, *Razzle in My Pocket*, 1977
• I wouldn't say I was always on the nick... —Shaun Ryder, *Shaun Ryder... in His Own Words*, 1989

nick *verb*

1 to arrest, to apprehend *UK, 1622*

• But by the time they had started to look around for someone to nick, the tool had been well got rid of. —Frank Norman, *Bang To Rights*, p. 28, 1958
• You're fucking nicked, my old beauty. You've found to your cost that the standards of the British police force are as high as ever. —Joe Orton, *Loot*, 1966
• CENTURION: You're fuckin' nicked, me old beauty. —Monty Python, *Life of Brian*, 1979

2 in prison, to place on report *UK*

• "You've got no previous convictions," I continued, "you've never been nicked (placed on report), you've done the anger management [...] course. — *The Guardian*, 26th April 2001: 'A life inside'

3 to steal *UK, 1869*

• I starts telling him about nicking cars. —John Peter Jones, *Feather Pluckers*, p. 10, 1964
• Oh yeah, I've got one I think, but I nicked it. —Paul E Willis, *Profane Culture*, p. 156, 1978

4 to win a gamble, possibly by taking an unfair advantage or cheating *UK, 1676*

A variation of earlier obsolete senses: 'to cheat at cards', 'to defraud'.

• Give me a chance to nick a few quid on the horses[.] —Jimmy Stockin, *On The Cobbles*, p. 97, 2000

5 (of a person) to move quickly *AUSTRALIA, 1894*

Followed by an adverb. Perhaps a specialised use of the sense 'to cheat'.

• I just nicked in for a draw. —Robert S. Close, *Love Me Sailor*, p. 107, 1945
• I'll nick into the loungeroom and have a listen at the window. —Willie Fennell, *Dexter Gets The Point*, p. 44, 1961

- I just got to nick out to the Gents for a few jiffs to wring the rattlesnake [urinate]!!! —Barry Humphries, *Bazza Pulls It Off!*, 1971

6 to throw dice *BARBADOS*

- —Frank A. Collymore, *Barbadian Dialect*, p. 77, 1965

▸ **get nicked**

get lost *AUSTRALIA, 1968*

Euphemistic for 'get fucked'.

- You can tell the mob you work for to get nicked[.] —Bluey *Bush Contractors*, p. 23, 1975

▸ **nick a living**

to make enough money to survive *UK*

- I've just come out of a nine stretch [in prison]. Well, I want to keep my nut [head] down, nick a living, and keep a low profile. —Lenny McLean, *The Guv'nor*, p. 112, 1998

▸ **nick the title**

to win a sporting contest and thereby to take the title *UK*

- As soon as I had nicked the title from Roy Shaw they started doing business with me[.] —Lenny McLean, *The Guv'nor*, p. 115, 1998

nick about with *verb*

to go around in the company of, or associate with, someone or some group of people *UK: SCOTLAND*

- How long have ye been nickin aboot wi that mob? —Michael Munro, *The Original Patter*, p. 49, 1985

nick away *verb*

to leave, to steal away *NEW ZEALAND*

- —David McGill, *David McGill's Complete Kiwi Slang Dictionary*, p. 76, 1998

nicked *adjective*

stolen *UK*

From the verb **NICK** (to steal).

- Nicking stuff that can't be reported as nicked. In other words, nicking nicked stuff. —Danny King, *The Burglar Diaries*, p. 212, 2001

nickel *noun*

1 a five-year prison sentence *US*

- Fritz was glad to attract so much attention and he talked complacently about his "nickel" in Lexington. —William Burroughs, *Junkie*, p. 42, 1953
- And they probably got nickels and dimes, and you got an 'Under Pressure' 6-month cure. —Clarence Cooper Jr, *The Farm*, p. 80, 1967
- —Malcolm Braly, *On the Yard*, p. c, 1967
- Well, it's only a nickel, even if they stick it all to you, you can still see the end of it. —Malcolm Braly, *On the Yard*, p. 80, 1967
- I could do a nickel in those places and I wouldn't mind. —Joseph Wambaugh, *The Blue Knight*, p. 29, 1973
- I just did a nickel in Terminal Island. —Gerald Petievich, *Money Men*, p. 33, 1981
- She started to scan the charges against him. "This guy did a nickel in Raiford." —Stephen Cannell, *King Con*, p. 79, 1997
- The Dyar Boys are doing a nickel at Chinio. —*Gone in 60 Seconds*, 2000

2 five dollars *US, 1946*

- "Where's that nickel you owe me, Geo?" Lou said from where he stood at the draining board of the sink. —Alexander Trocchi, *Cain's Book*, p. 165, 1960

3 in American casinos, a five-dollar betting chip *US*

- —Lee Solkey, *Dummy Up and Deal*, p. 116, 1980
- —Steve Kuriscak, *Casino Talk*, p. 39, 1985

4 five hundred dollars *US, 1974*

- —*Bay Sports Review*, p. 8, November 1991

5 a mediocre object or situation *US*

- —Gary Fairmont R. Filosa II, *The Surfer's Almanac*, p. 190, 1977

nickel *adjective*

inferior *US, 1932*

- —David W. Maurer, *Argot of the Racetrack*, p. 44, 1951
- How many times am I gon' have to whip your jive, stinkin' ass before you stop tryin' to be nickel slick? —Odie Hawkins, *Ghetto Sketches*, p. 17, 1972
- Bessie working, Fred Lee chili pimpin' and trying to be nickel slick… —Odie Hawkins, *The Busting Out of an Ordinary Man*, p. 137, 1985

nickel and dime; nickel *noun*

1 time *US*

Rhyming slang.

- There's no nickel like the future. —Ray Puxley, *Fresh Rabbit*, 1998

2 in pool, a table that is five feet by ten feet *US*

- —Mike Shamos, *The Illustrated Encyclopedia of Billiards*, p. 154, 1993

nickel and dime *verb*

to wear down in small increments *US, 1961*

nickel-and-dime *adjective*

small-time, operating on a small scale *US, 1941*

- This is the big time, Ira baby, not like those nickel-and-dime epics you made back in the old days. —Max Shulman, *Anyone Got a Match?*, p. 113, 1964
- But the lemonade syndicate, like copping milk bottles, was nickel and dime. —Piri Thomas, *Down These Mean Streets*, p. 75, 1967
- Just the fact that we have over fifteen grand put up shows we wain't some nickel and dime motherfuckers out here trying to get fix money. —Donald Goines, *El Dorado Red*, p. 90, 1974
- That trio and the woman played every nickel-and-dime base camp, every falling-down mess hall and sleazy, scruffy Enlisted Men's Club south of the 17th Parallel[.] —Larry Heinemann, *Paco's Story*, p. 11, 1986
- You know what our big crime is? We're nickel-and-dime guys. We're small-time hustlers. They got us because we're hustling nickels and dimes. —*Tin Men*, 1987
- Rocco saw a hesitant curl coming into his brow and sensed that the guy knew something was up other than the usual nickel-and-dime bullshit. —Richard Price, *Clockers*, p. 513, 1992

nickel-and-dime pimp *noun*

a small-time pimp *US*

- I am a nickel-and-dime pimp who has been built up in the papers to be more than what I was. The only thing I've ever had was an apartment where I had three girls at one time. And that was a very short time. I mostly had one girl and that's it[.] —Bruce Jackson, *In the Life*, p. 185, 1972

nickel bag *noun*

five dollars' worth of a drug *US*

- Often the junkie pusher will deal "nickel bags" at $5 each, as well as $3 "treys." —James Mills, *The Panic in Needle Park*, p. 20, 1966
- He hit you with lids, caps, keys, tabs, nickel bags, blotters, buttons, spoons and everything from milligrams to boatloads. —Robert Sabbag, *A Way with the Spoon [The Howard Marks Book of Dope Stories]*, p. 350, 1998
- Lemme get a nickel bag. —Kevin Smith, *Jay and Silent Bob Strike Back*, p. 9, 2001
- —Robert Ashton, *This Is Heroin*, p. 206, 2002

nickel-dime-quarter *noun*

poker played with very small bets *US, 1968*

- —Thomas L. Clark, *The Dictionary of Gambling and Gaming*, p. 135, 1987

nickel game *noun*

a game of craps in which the true and correct odds are paid *US*

- —*The Annals of the American Academy of Political and Social Sciences*, p. 128, May 1950

nickel gouger *noun*

the operator of a dishonest carnival game *US*

- —*American Speech*, p. 235, October 1950: 'The argot of outdoor boob traps'

nickel note *noun*

a five-dollar note *US, 1926*

- —Ralph de Sola, *Crime Dictionary*, p. 102, 1982

nickelonian *noun*

a crack cocaine addict *US, 1998*

A play on 'nickelodian', after the **NICKEL BAG** that the addict hungers for.

- —Mike Haskins, *Drugs*, p. 292, 2003

nickel-pincher *noun*

a cheapskate *US*

A variation on the much more common 'penny-pincher'.

- I had always tipped too much – knowing that I had never cared because I'd been brought up amidst nickel pinchers and because I like to please the people around me[.] —Philip Wylie, *Opus 21*, p. 66, 1949

nickels *noun*

in craps, a roll of two fives *US, 1983*

- —Thomas L. Clark, *The Dictionary of Gambling and Gaming*, p. 135, 1987

nickels and dimes *noun*

in hold 'em poker, a five and ten as the first two cards dealt to a player *US, 1981*

- —Thomas L. Clark, *The Dictionary of Gambling and Gaming*, p. 135, 1987

nickel seats *noun*

inexpensive seats at an event, usually far from the action *US*

- —Judi Sanders, *Cal Poly Slang*, p. 7, 1990

nickel's worth *noun*
a five-minute conversation on a citizens' band radio *US*
Five minutes was once the longest conversation allowed at one time.
- —Wayne Floyd, *Jason's Authentic Dictionary of CB Slang*, p. 22, 1976

nick 'em and stick 'em
used of the professional approach of a prison officer who is interested only in the discipline and confinement of prisoners *UK*
- He's a real nick 'em and stick 'em type.—Angela Devlin, *Prison Patter*, p. 80, 1996

nicker *noun*
1 one pound sterling (£1); pounds *UK, 1910*
- [A] lovely full-length pen [mink] that must have been worth every nicker of three grand[.]—Charles Raven, *Underworld Nights*, p. 13, 1956
- Cor strike, what am I doing swilling swipes when there's three hundred nicker (£300) in my pouch.—Derek Bickerton, *Payroll*, p. 119, 1959
- Here's a couple of nicker[.]—Barry Humphries, *Bazza Pulls It Off!*, 1971
- —Angela Devlin, *Prison Patter*, p. 80, 1996
- Nicker, note, quid[.]—Brian McDonald, *Elephant Boys*, p. 203, 2000

2 pounds *AUSTRALIA*
- The salesman goes out and tells this bloke the table will cost him a hundred thousand nicker.—Frank Hardy, *The Yarns of Billy Borker*, p. 93, 1965

nicker bit *noun*
a one-pound coin *UK*
From **NICKER** (£1).
- The pound coin was introduced in 1983 and was immediately nick-named a nicker bit.—Ray Puxley, *Cockney Rabbit*, p. 135, 1992

nicker bits *noun*
diarrhoea *UK*
Rhyming slang for **THE SHITS**, formed from **NICKER BIT** (a £1 coin).
- —Ray Puxley, *Cockney Rabbit*, 1992

nick joint *noun*
a dishonest gambling operation *US, 1978*
- —Thomas L. Clark, *The Dictionary of Gambling and Gaming*, p. 135, 1987

nick-nacker *noun*
an infrequent drug user *US*
- —Inez Cardozo-Freeman, *The Joint*, p. 517, 1984

nick nick
used of catching or arresting, or the act of being caught *UK*
Reduplication of **NICK** (to arrest); directly from the catchphrase popularised in the later 1970s by comedian Jim Davidson (b.1953).
- —Peter Chippindale, *The British CB Book*, p. 157, 1981

nick off *verb*
1 to depart, leave *AUSTRALIA, 1901*
- [O]ld Bluey made sure to nick off before we thought of it.—Ray Slattery, *Mobbs' Mob*, p. 15, 1966

2 to play truant *UK*
Teen slang, recorded by Joanna Williamson, 1982.

3 to take or steal something *AUSTRALIA*
- I remember a girl I thought I could trust who nicked off with a man I was about to elevate to number one position in my life.—Sue Rhodes, *And when she was bad she was popular*, p. 15, 1968

nicks *noun*
▷ see: **NIX**

Nicky Butt *noun*
a testicle *UK*
Rhyming slang for **NUT(S)**, formed from a Manchester United footballer (b.1975).
- —Ray Puxley, *Fresh Rabbit*, 1998

nic-nac party *noun*
a party for a bride-to-be *AUSTRALIA, 1988*
At the party, the gifts for the bride focus on her future home.
- —Maureen Brooks and Joan Ritchie, *Tassie Terms*, p. 99, 1995

niddy-noddy *noun*
a stick about a foot long, with end-pieces, used for wrapping yarn *CANADA*
- A niddy-noddy is a long carved object, connected with spinning, to remove the wool from the bobbin. When in use, as the yarn is guided over the ends of the arms, it nods one way, then the other.—*Toronto Globe and Mail*, p. T2, 30th January 1986

niebla *noun*
phencyclidine, the recreational drug known as PCP or angel dust *US*
Spanish for 'cloud'.
- —US Department of Justice, *Street Terms*, October 1994

nieve *noun*
cocaine *US*
Spanish for 'snow'.
- —Peter Johnson, *Dictionary of Street Alcohol and Drug Terms*, p. 132, 1993

niff *noun*
an unpleasant smell *UK, 1903*
Possibly derives from 'sniff'.

niff *verb*
to smell unpleasantly *UK, 1927*
From the noun sense.
- He snored like a bassoon and niffed like a badger.—Charles Raven, *Underworld Nights*, p. 198, 1956

niffy *adjective*
smelly *UK, 1937*
From Sussex dialect.
- He is also a founder-director of Lawson Lucas Mendelsohn (LLM), a political consultancy whose inaugural brochure in 1997 promised to bring an "ethical" fragrance to the niffy business of parliamentary lobbying.—*The Guardian*, 7th February 2001

nifty *noun*
the sum of fifty pounds sterling (£50) *UK*
Not really rhyming slang, merely a convenient rhyme.
- [Y]our average user, who might spend a nifty per day on the stuff [cocaine].—Wayne Anthony, *Spanish Highs*, p. 46, 1999
- [A] pony £25; a nifty £50[.]—*The Guardian*, 30th October 2002

nifty *adjective*
smart, fashionable, fine, splendid *US, 1805*
Old-fashioned and affected; probably a corrupted 'magnificent'.
- I'm free, and I got a date tonight with the niftiest Polack.—James T. Farrell, *Saturday Night*, p. 30–31, 1947
- [S]ome nifty tomfoolery [jewellery].—Charles Raven, *Underworld Nights*, p. 174, 1956
- Strooby here has a couple of the niftiest damn teen-age boys you'll ever meet.—Dan Jenkins, *Semi-Tough*, p. 142, 1972
- Me and Carri got a nifty studio apartment on 85th Street between West End Avenue and Riverside Drive[.]—A.S. Jackson, *Gentleman Pimp*, p. 153, 1973

nifty fifty *noun*
an act of masturbation *UK*
A rhymed approximation of the number of movements required; often in the phrase 'give it the nifty fifty'.

nifty-keen *adjective*
excellent *US*
- —Helen Dahlskog (Editor), *A Dictionary of Contemporary and Colloquial Usage*, p. 42, 1972

nig *noun*
1 a black person *US, 1828*
A shortened form of **NIGGER**, no less offensive.
- All the dirty old nigs and broken down old men.—John Peter Jones, *Feather Pluckers*, p. 60, 1964
- "How you get along with the nigs?" "Fine," I said. "They're good guys."—Dan Jenkins, *Life Its Ownself*, p. 47, 1984
- Nig – black woman's boyfriend: "Let me introduce you to my new nig." Used only by African Americans.—Connie Eble (Editor), *UNC-CH Campus Slang*, p. 6, Spring 1992

2 an Australian Aboriginal *AUSTRALIA, 1880*
Racially offensive; now not very common.
- When a few wild nigs come in he must 'educate' the most intelligent looking[.]—Ion L. Idriess, *Over the Range*, p. 216, 1947
- —Arthur Upfield, *Bony and the Mouse*, p. 68, 1959

3 a new soldier, either a recruit or one just out of recruit training *UK*
- —*Time Out*, 25th July 1980
- Being the nig (new boy), I had to carry the GPMG [General Purpose Machine Gun].—Andy McNab, *Immediate Action*, p. 22, 1995

Nigel Benn *noun*

a pen *UK*

Rhyming slang, formed from the name of a champion boxer (b.1964).

- —Ray Puxley, *Fresh Rabbit*, 1998

Nigerian *noun*

in homosexual usage, any black man *US*

- —*Maledicta*, p. 52, 1986–1987: 'A continuation of a glossary of ethnic slurs in American English'

Nigerian lager *noun*

Guinness™, the branded stout *UK*

From the deep black colour of the beer.

- —David Powis, *The Signs of Crime*, 1977

Nigerian scam spam *noun*

a swindle that uses e-mail to solicit potential victims to help an African correspondent transfer millions of dollars into an American bank account *US*

- "Nigerian scam spam" – junk e-mail promising fabulous wealth to anyone who will help purported African officials or dignitaries handle some banking chores – is one of the Internet's fastest-growing forms of fraud.—*San Francisco Chronicle*, p. A6, 8th September 2002

nigga *noun*

a black person *US, 1980s*

A deliberate misspelling, reinventing **NIGGER** for exclusive black use; widely used in gangsta rap.

- [C]razy muthafucka named Ice Cube / From the gang called Niggaz With Attitudes—NWA, *Straight Outta Compton*, 1989
- There's two niggas inside me. One wants to live in peace, and the other won't die unless he's free.—*Jabberrock [quoting Tupac Shakur]*, p. 64, 1997

nigger *noun*

1 a black person *UK, 1574*

When used by white speakers, highly offensive; used by black speakers, especially the young, with increasing frequency.

- We could call ourselves nigger all we wanted, but when the white folks did it we wanted to fight.—Chester Himes, *If He Hollers Let Him Go*, p. 76, 1945
- "You got a nigger wife?" she shouted. Fine did not answer. "Are you a Jew?" she screamed. "Yes," Fine answered.—*San Francisco Chronicle*, p. 9, 10th September 1957
- Somewhere in the middle of Missouri, for the first time, this sailor, who never called a woman a woman if he could call her a cunt, and a Negro a nigger (I'd advertised for him in the New York Times), finally boiled over.—Clancy Sigal, *Going Away*, p. 175, 1961
- It's simply that you know when whoever's using it uses it, what he really means is Nigger. It's like the subtle double meaning of the word pussy, and it has the same restriction. I'm all for making Nigger an acceptable social word.—Clarence Cooper Jr, *Black*, p. 98, 1963
- It was real wrong to call somebody a nigger in front of a paddy boy. That's the way they felt. It made me feel a little bad myself.—Claude Brown, *Manchild in the Promised Land*, p. 137, 1965
- The nigger is not a human being. He is somewhere between the white man and the ape. We don't believe in tolerance. We don't believe in getting along with our enemy and the nigger is our enemy. (Quoting KKK leader J. B. Stoner of Atlanta, Georgia).—*San Francisco Chronicle, This World*, p. 6, 18th July 1965
- You want to get a glimpse of what it feels like to be a nigger? Let your hair grow long.—Abbie Hoffman, *Revolution for the Hell of It*, p. 71, 1968
- Aunt Sadie, long hair is our black skin. Long hair turns white middle-class youth into niggers.—Jerry Rubin, *Do It!*, p. 94, 1970
- It's just a word, anyway. Nigger, I mean. It's just a word that some dumb-ass plantation owner made up one time by accident when he tried to pronounce nee-grow.—Dan Jenkins, *Semi-Tough*, p. 3, 1972
- It got so that the women's movement called women the "niggers" of our time and confused gender with class.—Mort Sahl, *Heartland*, p. 50, 1976
- "I got nothing against blacks. It's niggers I don't like." "But don't you see, Charlie? Just using that word makes you prejudiced." "Bullshit. The whole business is a lot more complicated than you give it credit for, Diane."—Vincent Patrick, *The Pope of Greenwich Village*, p. 153, 1979
- Forrest doesn't know what a nigger is. Them's niggers. A nigger, Forrest, is somebody you don't want to be.—*Forrest Gump*, 1992
- "Never underestimate these fucking niggers," his [police] superior cautioned.—Donald Gorgon, *Cop Killer*, p. 3, 1994

2 an Australian Aboriginal *AUSTRALIA, 1845*

Racially offensive.

- 'It's nigger's country, ain't it?' 'Wouldn't feed a bloody rabbit,' agreed someone.—Gavin Casey, *It's Harder for Girls*, p. 57, 1941
- Maybe you're right, but they say Abos spoil 'em and a horse never likes anyone who doesn't smell nigger.—Dymphna Cusack, *Picnic Races*, p. 194, 1962

3 a Maori *NEW ZEALAND, 1858*

- —Harry Orsman, *A Dictionary of Modern New Zealand Slang*, p. 91, 1999

4 a friend *UK*

The word having been reclaimed by the black population, usage in the racially mixed community of St Pauls, Bristol, resulted, in 2003, in white youths emulating black peers and calling their friends, of any skin-colour, 'nigger'. Reported by a greatly encouraged youth worker.

5 in the television and film industries, a screen on a stand used to achieve lighting effects *UK*

- —Oswald Skilbeck, *ABC of Film and TV Working Terms*, p. 89, 1960

▸ **another push and you'd have been a nigger**

used insultingly as a slur on the morals of the subject's mother, implying that she would have sex with anyone of any race *UK, 1961*

niggerati *noun*

a high profile grouping of successful members of black society *UK*

A black coinage, combining **NIGGER** (a black person) and **-ERATI** (a suffix which suggests the fashionable).

- The niggerati ain't the only bunch that's saying something[.]—Diran Abedayo, *My Once Upon A Time*, p. 153, 2000

nigger babies *noun*

dirt specks, especially in the creases of the neck *US, 1970*

- —Claudio R. Salvucci, *The Philadelphia Dialect Dictionary*, p. 50, 1996

nigger bait *noun*

a great deal of chrome on a car *US, 1960*

- —*Maledicta*, p. 168, 1979: 'A glossary of ethnic slurs in American English'

nigger bankroll *noun*

a single large-denomination note wrapped around small-denomination notes, giving the impression of a great deal of money *US*

- —Edith A. Folb, *runnin' down some lines*, p. 248, 1980

nigger bet *noun*

an uncommon amount wagered *US, 1968*

- —Thomas L. Clark, *The Dictionary of Gambling and Gaming*, p. 136, 1987

nigger flicker *noun*

a small knife; a razor blade used as a weapon *US*

- —Edith A. Folb, *runnin' down some lines*, p. 248, 1980

niggergram *noun*

gossip *TRINIDAD AND TOBAGO, 1950*

- —Lise Winer, *Dictionary of the English/Creole of Trinidad & Tobago*, 2003

nigger-hater *noun*

an overt racist *US*

- Honest policemen are afraid to make too many pinches in Negro neighborhoods for fear the pinkos will list them as "nigger-haters" and send their names up above – maybe even to the White House.—Jack Lait and Lee Mortimer, *Washington Confidential*, p. 42, 1951

niggerhead *noun*

1 tobacco, twisted into a plug *US, 1843*

- Groceries–particularly tea and "niggerhead" (a trade tobacco for smoking and chewing)–are his more necessary "luxuries."—Charles Crate, *We Speak for the Silent*, p. 3, 1956

2 an eight-gallon milk can *CANADA*

- In Quebec's Eastern Townships, a nigger head was the eight-gallon milk can. In others, it means (as in the US) a head-sized hummock in moist pasture land, a "moss hump."—Lewis Poteet, *Talking Country*, p. 57, 1992

3 a tuft of grass *US, 1859*

- —Robert O. Bowen, *An Alaskan Dictionary*, p. 23, 1965

4 in lobstering, a winch head *US*

- —Kendall Merriam, *The Illustrated Dictionary of Lobstering*, p. 61, 1978

niggerhead keister *noun*

a steel safe shaped like a ball *US*

- Leo took the cold chisel from the satchel and they both began taking turns breaking up the concrete to pound apart the niggerhead keister for what they could now smell it contained.—Emmett Grogan, *Final Score*, p. 86, 1976

nigger heaven *noun*

1 a simple, perfect happiness *US, 1906*

• — *Maledicta*, p. 165, Summer/Winter 1978: 'How to hate thy neighbor: a guide to racist maledicta'

2 the highest, least expensive seats in a theatre *US, 1866*

• — Don Wilmeth, *The Language of American Popular Entertainment*, p. 182, 1981

nigger in the woodpile *noun*

anything that spoils the perfection of a finished article *US, 1852*

Originally used without any sense that offence might be caused; now taboo.

• Do I cop to my "put downs": of light-skinned people of color, bi people as the "niggers in the woodpile" of heterosexuality, black lesbians who "castigate" other black lesbians for sleeping with white lesbians[.]" — Cheryl Clarke, *This Bridge We Call Home*, p. 234, 2002

niggeritis *noun*

laziness; sloth after eating *TRINIDAD AND TOBAGO, 2001*

• — Lise Winer, *Dictionary of the English/Creole of Trinidad & Tobago*, 2003

nigger-knockers *noun*

heavy work boots *US*

Heard used by a young person from Orinda, California, on Jim Dunbar's KGO radio programme by Peter Tamony on 23rd September 1964.

niggerlip *verb*

to moisten the end of a cigarette with saliva *US, 1940*

• "Light me a cigarette, darling," she said, snatching off a bathing cap and shaking her hair. "I don't mean you, O.J. You're such a slob. You always nigger-lip." — Truman Capote, *Breakfast at Tiffany's*, p. 34, 1958

• — *Maledicta*, p. 168, 1979: 'A glossary of ethnic slurs in American English'

• — Connie Eble (Editor), *UNC-CH Campus Slang*, p. 5, Fall 1987

nigger local *noun*

on the railways, a freight train that makes frequent local stops that involve heavy work for the crew *US, 1916*

• — Ramon Adams, *The Language of the Railroader*, p. 105, 1977

nigger-lover *noun*

a white person who mixes with or admires black people; a white person who believes that all men are created equal *US, 1856*

Originally white usage, it was intended to be offensive and disparaging.

• The Southerners had called me a "nigger-lover" there. — Mezz Mezzrow, *Really the Blues*, p. 18, 1946

• [Y]ou're a Nigger-lover and a Jew-lover and a queer, and you can't even talk good English like a real American. — Rocky Garciano (with Rowland Barber), *Somebody Up There Likes Me*, p. 223, 1955

• A crudely painted sign reading "Go Back to Africa Niggers and Nigger Loves" was staked on the front lawn of Balboard High School. — *San Francisco Chronicle*, p. 9, 22nd May 1963

• "Officer, do you know who I am?" "Some nigger-lover who..." — Dick Gregory, *Nigger*, p. 67, 1964

• Here comes the nigger-lover! — James Baldwin, *Blues for Mister Charlie*, p. 143, 1964

• Cried tears in my bedroom when they chased me home from school / Nigger lover this and nigger lover that. — Teena Marie, *Revolution*, 1981

• [H]e's a goddam nigger-lover ... now, jest shut your hole an' git on over yonder an' check them leg-irons. — Terry Southern, *Texas Summer*, p. 75, 1991

• "He just went right off the deep end," says Spencer. "He calls him a Commie nigger lover – my God! This is a guy who was able to get himself elected to the St. Louis school board because he was smooth enough. So he's been careful in the past." — *Riverfront Times (St. Louis)*, 26th November 2003

nigger-loving *adjective*

used for describing a white person who does not share the speaker's pathological hatred of black people *US, 1879*

• We'll cut your niggerlovin heart out. — Hubert Selby Jr, *Last Exit to Brooklyn*, p. 32, 1957

nigger navel *noun*

a type of daisy *US*

• [P]eople could "nigger-rig" a fence (a type of jerry-rigging) or pick "nigger-navel" flowers (a variety of African daisy with a black button center). — Dina Temple-Raston, *A Death in Texas*, p. 38, 2002

nigger pennies *noun*

an illegal lottery game *US*

• There's what's his name, Wee Willie. Hustling them numbers. Nigger pennies. — John Sayles, *Union Dues*, p. 148, 1977

nigger pool *noun*

an illegal numbers gambling lottery *US*

• — *American Speech*, p. 192, October 1949

nigger rich *adjective*

maintaining outward signs of wealth *US, 1930*

• Anyone who wanted to could be nigger-rich, nigger-important, have their Jim Crow religion, and go to nigger heaven. — Chester Himes, *If He Hollers Let Him Go*, p. 153, 1945

• She called everyone shanty Irish or nigger rich. — Gilbert Sorrentino, *Steelwork*, p. 101, 1970

• [I]ts three nigger-rich occupants were his buddies and all worked at Douglas Aircraft during those hours. — Neal Cassady, *The First Third*, p. 166, 1971

• — Christina and Richard Milner, *Black Players*, p. 304, 1972

• He ain't what you'd call nigger rich, but he's got about ten people working for him. — Donald Goines, *El Dorado Red*, p. 171, 1974

• In the bleak shadow of his mother, getting "nigger rich," and buying a restaurant, going into all kinds of shady businesses – a new Cadillac, a hog, every year? — Clarence Major, *All-Night Visitors*, p. 182, 1998

nigger-rig *verb*

to improvise in a shoddy way *US, 1965*

• — *Maledicta*, p. 168, 1979: 'A glossary of ethnic slurs in American English'

• [P]eople could "nigger-rig" a fence (a type of jerry-rigging). — Dina Temple-Raston, *A Death in Texas*, p. 38, 2002

nigger's lip *noun*

a (potato) chip *UK*

Rhyming slang, noted by Red Daniells, 1980.

niggers' man *noun*

a white person who is less prejudiced than most *BAHAMAS, 1905*

• — John A. Holm, *Dictionary of Bahamian English*, p. 143, 1982

Niggerstan *noun*

any country with a black population *UK*

Racist.

• All the shit of the world comes here, from Pakistan, from Niggerstan and from Coon City. — Donald Gorgon, *Cop Killer*, p. 2, 1994

nigger stick *noun*

a reinforced baton used by police on suspected criminals, criminals and prisoners *US, 1971*

• A hack walked over to our table and pointed with a hard-ass reinforced wooden club that I'd learn was called a "nigger stick," supposedly because it could stand against heads that were anything but white. — Piri Thomas, *Seven Long Times*, p. 72, 1974

nigger sticker *noun*

a long, sharp knife *US, 1969*

• — Ralph de Sola, *Crime Dictionary*, p. 102, 1982

nigger ten *noun*

a cross near where a person has died *BARBADOS*

• — Frank A. Collymore, *Barbadian Dialect*, p. 77, 1965

nigger toe *noun*

a Brazil nut *US, 1896*

• For instance, there's this nut I used to eat when I was a kid, we called a niggertoe. It must have some other name, but I don't know what it is. Does that mean that all us kids were prejudiced because we used to eat niggertoes? — Darryl Ponicsan, *The Last Detail*, p. 78, 1970

nigger toes

black olives *US*

• — *Maledicta*, p. 16, 1996: 'Domino's pizza jargon'

niggertown *noun*

a neighbourhood with a large population of black people *US, 1904*

• It's in Niggertown, on the radio alla time. I say, You know where is Niggertown? — Robert Gover, *One Hundred Dollar Misunderstanding*, p. 131, 1961

• A lot of the other kids in school used to drive over to niggertown at night to try and find black women. — James Baldwin, *Blues for Mister Charlie*, p. 87, 1964

• Every Negro that lives in a city has seen the type a thousand times, the Northern cracker who will go to visit "niggertown," to be amused at "the coons." — Malcolm X and Alex Haley, *The Autobiography of Malcolm X*, p. 147, 1964

• Once I went to a Negro party in Niggertown and took on twelve of them in one night. — John Folger, *Black on White*, p. 32, 1967

• Nine out ten is only livin in milkywhite niggertown anyhow[.] — Robert Gover, *JC Saves*, p. 109, 1968

- So the outfit uses Nigger gorillas like Butcher Knife Brown for the petty knockoffs in Niggertown. —Iceberg Slim (Robert Beck), *Trick Baby*, p. 183, 1969
- In Savannah itself, there are two black neighborhoods: one known by everyone as Nigger Town and the other called New Town. —J. Anthony Lukas, *Don't Shoot – We Are Your Children*, p. 129, 1971

nigger up *verb*
to make many purely decorative, inexpensive, flashy modifications to a car *US*
- —Lewis Poteet, *Car & Motorcyle Slang*, p. 139, 1992

niggerville *noun*
a section of a city or town populated by black people *US, 1857*
Offensive.
- That's all Niggerville there now and wasn't much better then. —Elmore Leonard, *Maximum Bob*, p. 122, 1991

niggle *noun*
a complaint *UK, 1886*
- Length aside, John Williams's music is the only real niggle – his flying-car music here is almost identical to ET's flying-bicycle theme— *The Guardian*, 11th April 2003

niggle *verb*
1 to do something in a finicky, fussy or time-wasting manner *UK, 1893*
Originally, certainly from about 1640, in conventional use; now, according to the *Oxford English Dictionary*, chiefly colloquial.
- He would probably have found something to niggle away at[.]— *The Observer*, 9th November 2003

2 to irritate, to cause a slight but persistent annoyance *UK, 1796*
Generally considered to be a conventional use; included here for its derivatives which are certainly in this dictionary's domain.
- [T]he question, "Will I find another job if I leave this one?", is starting to niggle.— *The Guardian*, 27th January 2003

3 to have sex *US*
- —Joseph E. Ragen and Charles Finston, *Inside the World's Toughest Prison*, p. 809, 1962: 'Penitentiary and underworld glossary'

4 in horse racing, to urge a horse with hands and rein *UK*
- —Rita Cannon, *Let's Go Racing*, p. 72, 1948

niggled *adjective*
annoyed, irritated, especially when made so by disappointment or the pettiness of others *UK, 1878*
From Cumberland dialect.
- But it certainly left the prime minister alarmed – niggled, anxious, thrown off balance.— *The Guardian*, 21st November 2002

niggliness *noun*
irritability; a state of being short-tempered *UK, 1982*
- No, it wasn't niggliness, it was out-and-out huge rows all the time or great sulky silences[.]— *Sunday Herald (Scotland)*, 28th December 2003

niggling *adjective*
petty, persistently irritating *UK, 1854*
- The hooker has yet to return to his best after a niggling knee injury[.]— *The Guardian*, 18th February 2002

niggly *adjective*
1 bad-tempered, especially about trifling concerns; irritable *UK, 1840*
- The hecklers can "get a bit niggly sometimes", says [Don] Ward.— *The Observer*, 11th August 2002
- Though a dull first half had been niggly rather than nasty, there was another unsavoury incident[.]— *The Guardian*, 13th November 2002

2 annoying, irritating *UK, 1840*
- I still enjoyed the army but it was all the niggly bits that pissed me off. —Andy McNab, *Immediate Action*, p. 48, 1995

nigh'-nigh'
▷ see: NIGHTY-NIGHT

night *noun*
▸ it'll be all right on the night; it will all come right on the night
used as an optimistic reassurance that everything will be fine *UK, 1899*
Originally theatrical, expressing the belief that all will be well for the first night. *It'll Be Alright on the Night*, a television programme celebrating the things that go wrong (despite its reassuring title) has been broadcast since 1977.

▸ make a night of
to spend the night in pursuit of (dissolute) pleasures *UK, 1693*
- Anyway. Last Saturday we decide to make a night of it, me and the guys[.]— *The Guardian*, 20th May 2003

night; 'night
good night *UK, 1912*
Elliptical reduction of the customary good wishes at parting or sleep.
- TRISTE: bloody soldiers and good luck....night-night – a time to weep and a time to.... GARY: night -—Patrick Jones, *Unprotected Sex*, p. 221, 1999

night and day *noun*
a play *UK*
Rhyming slang.
- —Julian Franklyn, *A Dictionary of Rhyming Slang*, 1960

night and day *adjective*
grey *UK*
Rhyming slang.
- You'll have me night and day before my time. —Ray Puxley, *Cockney Rabbit*, 1992

night bull *noun*
a prison guard assigned to a night shift *US*
- Other night bulls sit out in the towers above the floodlit walls and blocks. —Malcolm Braly, *On the Yard*, p. 53, 1967

nightcap *noun*
1 the final alcoholic drink of the night *UK, 1818*
- On the evening before, I could have accepted Yvonne's invitation for a nightcap, or accepted the later invitation in her note to me. —Philip Wylie, *Opus 21*, p. 192, 1949
- Come on. Let's have a nightcap together.— *The Graduate*, 1967
- Hey, let's go have a nightcap at my place.— *The Deer Hunter*, 1978
- It was broad daylight when we walked over to my apartment on 79th near Riverside Drive, for a nightcap. —Edwin Torres, *After Hours*, p. 245, 1979
- I was wondering if you would care to join us in a nightcap. —Terry Southern, *Now Dig This*, p. 237, 1984

2 a marijuana cigarette, especially the last one of the day *UK*
No doubt for the relaxant properties of the drug.
- —Angela Devlin, *Prison Patter*, p. 80, 1996

3 in horse racing, the last race of the day *US*
- —David W. Maurer, *Argot of the Racetrack*, p. 44, 1951

nightclub tan *noun*
a pale complexion *UK*
- On Moss Side now Peter Green and I were really getting ourselves a night club tan. We were doing about three or four nights a week in the clubs there[.]—Johnny Speight, *It Stands to Reason*, p. 136, 1973

night cocky *noun*
in prison, a night patrolman *UK*
- On entering the spur during his nine o'clock visit, the "night cocky", as he is affectionately known, will notice a newspaper[.]— *The Guardian*, 17th February 2000: 'A life inside'

night compass *noun*
a chamber pot *CAYMAN ISLANDS*
- —Aarona Booker Kohlman, *Wotcha Say*, p. 25, 1985

nightery; niterie *noun*
a nightclub *US, 1934*
- Crothers is grabbing five bills a week as a nitery comic.— *Capitol News*, p. 15, March 1949
- Your style's more some West End nighterie. Know what I mean? —Anthony Masters, *Minder*, p. 65, 1984
- We jumped out of the cab with our luggage outside Bananas, a suitable niterie[.]—Wayne Anthony, *Spanish Highs*, p. 2, 1999

night eye *noun*
an irregular growth on the inside of a horse's legs, useful as a means of identification *US, 1938*
- —Dean Alfange, *The Horse Racing Industry*, p. 215, 1976

night for night *noun*
in television and film making, a scene set at night that is also shot at night *US*
- They're gonna shoot some night for night. —Elmore Leonard, *Freaky Deaky*, p. 20, 1988

nighthawk *noun*

1 a person who is active late at night *UK, 1818*

- In spite of the weather, nighthawks were finally gathering outside Gentry's[.] — Robert Campbell, *In La-La Land We Trust*, p. 32, 1986

2 a taxi driver who works late at night *US, 1868*

- We at least walk you down to the Merchandise Mart. Then we'll see. Maybe we spot a nighthawk cruising. — Robert Campbell, *Boneyards*, p. 188, 1992

night house *noun*

an illegal lottery operating at night *US*

- He put ninety dollars on numbers in the night house, playing five dollars on each. — Chester Himes, *A Rage in Harlem*, p. 23, 1957

nightie; nighty *noun*

a nightgown *UK, 1871*

- It was strange, in that moment he did feel a little sorry for her, standing there in her see-through nighty and her curlers. — Elmore Leonard, *Gold Coast*, p. 70–71, 1980
- I put my hand under my nightie and onto the gauze covering[.] — Mary Hooper, *(megan)2*, p. 9, 1999
- I'm in my nightie, but that's as far as it goes. — Jenny Eclair, *Camberwell Beauty*, p. 217, 2000

nightingale *noun*

a police informer *US*

From the **SING** metaphor.

- — Hy Lit, *Hy Lit's Unbelievable Dictionary of Hip Words for Groovy People*, p. 51, 1968

night maneuvers *noun*

a social date *US*

- — *Dobie Gillis Teenage Slanguage Dictionary*, 1962

nightmare *noun*

an unpleasant experience; an unpleasant person *UK, 1927*

- [I]f she'd stayed in Hollywood, she'd be a nightmare by now. Kids need boundaries. — *The Observer*, 13th June 2004

night nurse *noun*

a cigarette smoked in the middle of the night by an addict whose body is awakend by the craving for nicotine in the night *US*

- — John Fahs, *Cigarette Confidential*, p. 302, 1996: 'Glosssary'

night rider *noun*

1 a person who enjoys the wild side of life at night *US, 1951*

- I was going home now, home to my kind of people – the cons, killers, thieves and night-riders. — Red Rudensky, *The Gonif*, p. 113, 1970

2 in horse racing, someone who takes a horse out for a night workout in the hope of lessening its performance in a race the next day *US*

- — David W. Maurer, *Argot of the Racetrack*, p. 44, 1951

nights belong to Charlie

used as a rule of thumb by US soldiers in Vietnam, acknowledging the ascendancy of the Viet Cong during the dark *US*

- — Gregory Clark, *Words of the Vietnam War*, p. 350, 1990

night train *noun*

suicide *US*

- He used to say if he ever took the Night Train, he'd never do it with his gun. — James Ellroy, *Because the Night*, p. 501, 1984

night work *noun*

at night, urination or defecation other than in a toilet *TRINIDAD AND TOBAGO, 1959*

- — Lise Winer, *Dictionary of the English/Creole of Trinidad & Tobago*, 2003

nighty-night; night-night; nigh'-nigh'

good night *UK, 1896*

Originally children's vocabulary but now widely used and not always ironically.

- But Keyes didn't remember shutting his eyes and going nighty-night on the cool concrete. — Carl Hiaasen, *Tourist Season*, p. 49, 1986
- TRISTE: bloody soldiers and good luck....night-night – a time to weep and a time to.... GARY: night — Patrick Jones, *Unprotected Sex*, p. 221, 1999
- "Night-night!" What is that! Night-night? I don't remember hearing that since I was five years old. And now I'm a 41-year-old geezer with his wife being told "Night night" by a hotel porter! — Dave Courtney, *Dodgy Dave's Little Black Book*, p. 27, 2001

nig in *verb*

to sneak in without paying *UK*

- I had to nig in to see a picture [movie], and libraries were free. — Jonathan Gash, *The Ten Word Game*, p. 112, 2003

nig-nog *noun*

1 any non-white person *UK, 1959*

Rhyming slang, by virtue of the rhyme with **WOG**, this racist and derogatory term is a compound of **NIGGER** (a black person) and **WOG** (any foreigner); it is not always considered abusive by the speaker. In *Love Thy Neighbour*, a UK television comedy which ran to seven series, 1972–76, the white-skinned characters routinely called their black neighbours **SAMBO(S)** and 'nig-nogs'.

- This means all these nig-nogs are getting up to heaven, and perfectly decent blokes like you and me, who have never even committed adultery, we can't get up there – we're be being kept out by these [New] Guineans. — Peter Cook, *Not Only But Also*, 1965
- [He] had referred to coloured people as "them coons" and "nignogs" in the way that say Alf Garnett does[.] — Johnny Speight, *It Stands to Reason*, p. 232, 1973
- You take it from me, nig-nog. You go stealing white man's motor cars you get white man's stick. — *Scum*, 1979
- Oh look another nig nog up to no good. If they weren't all villains, the police wouldn't stop 'em[.] — Donald Gorgon, *Cop Killer*, p. 40, 1994
- Not something the nig-nogs care for, mind[.] — David Peace, *Nineteen Seventy-Four*, p. 102, 1999

2 a fool; a novice *UK*

Military use, possibly from obsolete slang 'nigmenog' (a fool), probably informed by racist sentiments.

- WATSON: [...] How long have you been a sergeant? VALE: Two days. WATSON: Still a nig-nog. — Graeme Kent, *The Queen's Corporal [Six Granada Plays]*, p. 84, 1959

nigra *noun*

marijuana *UK*

- — Mike Haskins, *Drugs*, p. 288, 2003

-nik *suffix*

a supporter or follower of the precedent activity or principle *US*

- I mean, beatniks and slutniks, they're so dull. — Douglas Rutherford, *The Creeping Flesh*, p. 84, 1963
- A few college hawkniks come by. — Elmore Leonard, *Revolution for the Hell of It*, p. 25, 1968
- Beatniks happened elsewhere – even in Australia [...] The Beats showed it was possible, even glamorous, to throw the gauntlet at the lifestyle of IBM. — Richard Neville, *Play Power*, p. 23–24, 1970

Nike air Jerusulam *noun*

Nike Air Jordans™, a branded sport shoe *UK*

A weak pun replacing Jordan with Jerusulam, current in UK prisons August 2002.

Nike down *verb*

to dress in nothing but Nike™ clothing and shoes *US*

- — Ethan Hilderbrant, *Prison Slang*, p. 90, 1998

Niki Lauda; Niki *noun*

cocaine *UK*

Rhyming slang, Lauda (pronounced 'louder'), for 'powder', based on the name of racing driver Nikolaus Andreas Lauder (b.1949).

- — Bob Young and Micky Moody, *The Language of Rock 'n' Roll*, p. 98, 1985
- It's at times like this I could really handle a bit of Niki. — *www.London-Slang.com*, June 2002

niks *noun*

nothing *UK, 1860*

From Afrikaans into South African English.

- — Penny Silva, *A Dictionary of South African English*, 1996

nimby *noun*

1 used as an acronym for '*n*ot *i*n *m*y *b*ack *y*ard', a description of the philosophy of those who support an idea in principle but do not want to be personally inconvenienced by it *US, 1980*

The acronym followed the phrase by only a year.

- The first time we heard of the neat acronym-like word NIMBY, it was voiced by J. Hamilton Lambert, the county executive of Fairfax County[.] — *Washington Post*, p. B2, 13th February 1983
- Not in my Back Yard – NIMBY for short – an acronym that will symbolize the psychographic marketing profile that will dominate the next decade. — *Financial Post (Toronto)*, p. 9, 17th February 1989

• Whereas NIMBIES promise the development will be Not In My Back Yard, the note says Not Over There Either. —David Rowan, *Glossary for th 90s*, p. 9, 1998

2 a capsule of pentobarbital sodium (trade name Nembutal™), a central nervous system depressant *US, 1962*

• —Richard Lingeman, *Drugs from A to Z*, p. 183, 1969

nimrod *noun*

a fool, a stupid person, a bungler *US, 1932*

Jonathan Lighter writes that 'currency of the term owes much to its appearance in a 1940s Warner Bros. cartoon in which Bugs Bunny refers to the hunter Elmer Fudd as "poor little Nimrod"'. It is not clear that watchers of the cartoon understood the C18 sense of the word as 'a great hunter', but the term has stuck.

• — *USA Today*, 29th September 1983
• —Connie Eble (Editor), *UNC-CH Campus Slang*, p. 4, Spring 1993
• VINCENT: Jules, if you give this nimrod fifteen hundred bucks, I'm gonna shoot 'em on general principle. — *Pulp Fiction*, 1994
• EDDIE: Hey, Brent, have a beer. EDDIE: Nimrod. — *Empire Records*, 1995

Nina; Nina from Carolina; Nina from Pasadena *noun*

in craps, a roll of nine or the nine point *US, 1939*

• —Vincent J. Monteleone, *Criminal Slang*, p. 44, 1949
• — *The Annals of the American Academy of Political and Social Sciences*, p. 128, May 1950
• —Steve Kuriscak, *Casino Talk*, p. 68, 1985

NINA

*n*o *I*rish *n*eed *a*pply *US*

• There were businesses in Boston that needed employees but put up signs in the windows saying NINA, which, as we all knew, meant No Irish Need Apply—Tip O'Neill with William Novak, *Man of the House*, p. 4, 1987

nince *noun*

▷ see: NUNCE

nincompoop *noun*

a foolish person, a simpleton *UK, 1673*

In *A Classical Dictionary of the Vulgar Tongue*, 3rd edition, 1796, Francis Grose defines 'nincumpoop' as 'a foolish fellow' and 'one who never saw his wife's ****', which adds a little bite to its use.

• "Many nincompoops are turned out of our great universities annually," Judge Sullivan said. —Willard Motley, *Let No Man Write My Epitaph*, p. 58, 1958
• Goldie has abandoned his perch as the country's biggest drum'n'bass producer and embarked on a mission to become the country's biggest nincompoop. — *The Guardian*, 12th April 2002

nine *noun*

▷ see: 9

nines *noun*

▸ **to the nines**

to an impressive degree *UK, 1793*

• The local girls dolled themselves up to the nines and tried to look their best for the occasion. —Andy McNab (writing of the late 1970s/early 80s), *Immediate Action*, p. 214, 1995
• [A]ll the women were either stewardesses or local birds done up to the nines[.] —Dave Courtney, *Stop the Ride I Want to Get Off*, p. 125, 1999
• [E]ighty or so boys and girls, mostly E'd to the nines[.] —Tony Wilson, *24 Hour Party People*, p. 189, 2002

nineball *noun*

a socially inept person *US*

• —Anna Scotti and Paul Young, *Buzzwords*, p. 95, 1997

ninebar *noun*

nine ounces of cannabis *UK*

• [A] boy who'd been given a nine-bar on tick hadn't paid up in a month. —Macfarlane, Macfarlane and Robson, *The User*, p. 106, 1996

nine-day blues *noun*

the incubation period for gonorrhea *US*

• — *Maledicta*, p. 228, Summer/Winter 1981: 'Sex and the single soldier'

nine-nickel *noun*

ninety-five *US*

• —Ethan Hilderbrant, *Prison Slang*, p. 90, 1998

nine of hearts *noun*

a racehorse that is not likely to win *US*

• —David W. Maurer, *Argot of the Racetrack*, p. 44, 1951
• —Thomas L. Clark, *The Dictionary of Gambling and Gaming*, p. 136, 1987

ninepennyworth *noun*

a prison term of nine months *UK*

• — *Evening News (London)*, 12th November 1957

niner *noun*

1 an erect penis that is nine inches long *UK*

• I reckon it's gorra be 'eading for a niner. maybe a bit more. And 'e's got a massive bell end. —Colin Butts, *Is Harry on the Boat?*, p. 142, 1997

2 a nine gallon keg of beer *AUSTRALIA, 1957*

• —Nino Culotta (John O'Grady), *They're A Weird Mob*, p. 107, 1957
• One night, as we saw a niner arrive and knew it was on again, we got on the telephone and called every good looking girl we knew. —Sue Rhodes, *Now you'll think I'm awful*, p. 152, 1967

nine-strand splicer *noun*

in oil drilling, a big and strong man *US*

• —Jerry Robertson, *Oil Slanguage*, p. 87, 1954

nineteen *noun*

1 amphetamines *UK*

This may well derive from a shortening of the conventional phrase 'nineteen to the dozen' (very fast) as a play on **SPEED** (amphetamine).

• —Mike Haskins, *Drugs*, p. 279, 2003

2 MDMA, the recreational drug best known as ecstasy *UK*

• —Mike Haskins, *Drugs*, p. 290, 2003

3 nothing at all *US*

From the game of cribbage (a hand with no points).

• —John Gould, *Maine Lingo*, p. 190, 1975

nineteen canteen *noun*

a long time ago *SOUTH AFRICA*

• —Angus Hall, *On the Run*, 1974
• She's been here since nineteen-canteen. —Michael Munro, *The Patter*, p. 49, 1985

nineteen-eighty cell *noun*

a secure prison cell used for prisoners at risk to themselves or others *UK*

From the official paperwork, a '1980 form', which must be completed each time before such a cell may be occupied.

• —Angela Devlin, *Prison Patter*, p. 80, 1996

nineteenth hole *noun*

a golf course bar where golfers retire after a round of golf *US, 1901*

• —Randy Voorhees, *The Little Book of Golf Slang*, p. 79, 1997

nine-to-five *noun*

the usual working day; the rut of daily existence *US, 1936*

Based on an average working day, nine in the morning to five in the afternoon, but applied to regular employment whatever the hours worked, and especially to routine drudgery.

• Workin' 9 to 5, what a way to make a livin' / Barely gettin' by, it's all takin' and no givin' —Dolly Parton, *9 to 5*, 1980
• We weren't married to nine-to-five guys, but the first time I realized how different was when Mickey had a hostess party. — *Goodfellas*, 1990
• Hell no, they thinkin' a nine-to-five nigger working at First Jersey or some damn thing. —Richard Price, *Clockers*, p. 321, 1992
• [S]ome glammed-up babe escaping the nine to five[.] —Dave Courtney, *Raving Lunacy*, p. 93, 2000

nine-trey *noun*

ninety-three *US*

• — *The Bell (Paducah Tilghman High School)*, p. 8–9, 17th December 1993: 'Tilghmanism: the concealed langage of the hallway'

ninety *noun*

1 the 90 mm cannon mounted on an M-48 Patton battle tank *US*

• —Linda Reinberg, *In the Field*, p. 152, 1991

2 the M-67 90 mm recoilless rifle *US*

• —Linda Reinberg, *In the Field*, p. 152, 1991

ninety days *noun*

in dice games, a roll of nine *US, 1909*

• —Frank Garcia, *Marked Cards and Loaded Dice*, p. 263, 1962

ninety-day-wonder *noun*

a recent graduate of the US Army's Officer Candidate School *US, 1917*

- The OCS course was 90 days in length, and field troops referred to OCS graduates as "90 day wonders." —Gregory Clark, *Words of the Vietnam War*, p. 359, 1990

ninety-eight *noun*
▷ see: 98

ninety-in-ninety *noun*
in twelve-step recovery programmes such as Alcoholics Anonymous, used as a prescription for starting recovery – ninety meetings in ninety days *US*
- —Christopher Cavanaugh, *AA to Z*, p. 131, 1998

ninety-niner *noun*
a driver from Canada's prairies driving into mountain (Alberta and British Columbia) roads for the first time *CANADA*
- A prairie driver experiencing road curves roads for the first time. Upon reaching BC, they invariably go ninety on the straight-aways, but slow to 9 kph on the bends. —Tom Parkin, *WetCoast Words*, p. 98, 1989

ninety-six *noun*
reciprocal anal sex *US*
- — Anon., *The Gay Girl's Guide*, p. 13, 1949

ninety-weight *noun*
1 any strong alcohol *US*
- —Lanie Dills, *The Official CB Slanguage Language Dictionary*, p. 50, 1976

2 strong, 90-proof whisky *US*
- — Elementary Electronics, *Dictionary of CB Lingo*, p. 89, 1976

ning nong *noun*
a fool, an idiot *AUSTRALIA, 1957*
Probably a variant of British dialect *ning-nang*, recorded since the 1830s (*English Dialect Dictionary*).
- We're sorry for yer, Nino, old boy. Yer've drawn a ning-nong. —Nino Culotta (John O'Grady), *They're A Weird Mob*, p. 190, 1957
- Jeez, I feel a real ning-nong in this sheilah type frock – if they cop me in this rig-out I reckon I'm a gonner! —Barry Humphries, *The Wonderful World of Barry McKenzie*, p. 44, 1968
- —David McGill, *David McGill's Complete Kiwi Slang Dictionary*, p. 76, 1998

ninny *noun*
1 a fool, a dolt *UK, 1593*
- [P]aying the poor ninny six and a half cents a pound for the lot. —Max Shulman, *The Zebra Derby*, p. 84, 1946
- If you "called" a man, the ninny would have you hauled into court instead of making the proper response with fists and feet. —Jim Thompson, *Bad Boy*, p. 302, 1953

2 the vagina or vulva *BAHAMAS*
- —John A. Holm, *Dictionary of Bahamian English*, p. 143, 1982

nip *noun*
1 a nipple, especially a woman's *US*
The nickname given to the character Elaine Benes (played by Julia Louis-Dreyfus) on *Seinfeld* (NBC, 1990–98) after a snapshot that she took for a Christmas card showed a breast nipple.
- Say, Lil had nips on her titties about the size of your thumb. —Bruce Jackson, *Get Your Ass in the Water and Swim Like Me*, p. 150, 1965
- They are certainly very large, but they are also firm and nicely shaped and they have the good nips. —Dan Jenkins, *Semi-Tough*, p. 158, 1972
- She was a healthy-looking bitch, a jogger type with a great rack ... a couple of real pointers. And I'm not talking about a bra with rubber nipples. I'm talking about a pair of honest-to-Christ pointed nips that must have wieghed as much as silver dollars. —Gerald Petievich, *To Die in Beverly Hills*, p. 93, 1983
- There's a certain kind of uniquely American girl who comes from the Midwest to Greenwich Village – cute as a button, pert derriere, full wet lips, nips in eternal distention, etc., etc. —Terry Southern, *Now Dig This*, p. 1, 1986
- I kept looking at you, your little nips showing in that thin material[.] —Elmore Leonard, *Freaky Deaky*, p. 15, 1988
- See, your nip [nipple] is really hard here. —Robert Stoller and I.S. Levine, *Coming Attractions*, p. 155, 1991
- How big and brown are your nips? —Nicholson Baker, *Vox*, p. 10, 1992

2 a small drink *US, 1736*
- You're just in time to join me in a nip. —Chester Himes, *If He Hollers Let Him Go*, p. 80, 1945

3 in Winnipeg, a hamburger *CANADA*
- Winnipeg's 24-hour, 7-days a week hamburger were Salisbury Houses, who has always called its hamburgers "nips." Winnipeggers still refer to nips when speaking of hamburgers. —Chris Thain, *Cold as a Bay Street Banker's Heart*, p. 106–107, 1987

4 a manoeuvre, especially while driving *BERMUDA*
- —Peter A. Smith and Fred M. Barritt, *Bermewjan Vurds*, 1985

Nip *noun*
1 a Japanese or Japanese-American person *US, 1942*
Shortened from 'Niponese'. Deemed offensive by Multicultural Management Program Fellows, *Dictionary of Cautionary Words and Phrases*, 1989.
- If you ever do get a live Nip, keep him away from Daniels. —Eric Lambert, *The Veterans*, p. 143, 1954
- But if the Nips were all there were left, then the Nips it would have to be. —Earl Thompson, *Tattoo*, p. 4, 1974
- —Edith A. Folb, *runnin' down some lines*, p. 248, 1980

2 a Honda car *UK*
Citizens' band radio slang for the product of a Japanese manufacturer; a specific use of a generally racist term.
- —Peter Chippindale, *The British CB Book*, p. 161, 1981

nip *verb*
1 (of a person) to move quickly *UK, 1825*
- —J.E. MacDonnell, *Don't Gimme the Ships*, p. 92, 1960
- Kate nipped into the driving seat and in a bold minute, roared away from the residency down the hill to the wharf. —John Wynnum, *Tar Dust*, p. 57, 1962
- [N]ipped off on the plane with Anzac Jack. —Derek Raymond (Robin Cook), *The Crust on its Uppers*, p. 20, 1962
- —J.E. MacDonnell, *Big Bill the Bastard*, p. 45, 1976

2 to grab *UK, 1566*
- He nipped me by my coatsleeve and lamped me with a wicked eye. —Bruce Jackson, *Get Your Ass in the Water and Swim Like Me*, p. 85, 1965

3 to open a locked door using a special pair of pliers that can grasp the key from the other side of the door *US*
- —Joseph E. Ragen and Charles Finston, *Inside the World's Toughest Prison*, p. 810, 1962: 'Penitentiary and underworld glossary'

▸ **nip it**
to stop doing something *US*
- —Connie Eble (Editor), *UNC-CH Campus Slang*, p. 4, November 1983

Nip *adjective*
Japanese *AUSTRALIA, 1946*
- The Nip convoy got into Bonn last night. —Paul Lesley, *PT Command*, p. 50, 1963
- —Barry Humphries, *The Traveller's Tool*, p. 87, 1985

nip and tuck *noun*
cosmetic surgery *US*
- She wants a little face lift, I bought her a little nip and tuck. —George V. Higgins, *The Rat on Fire*, p. 170, 1981

nip and tuck *adjective*
in a contest, neck and neck, or alternately holding the lead *US, 1845*
- [T]he battle for the green points jersey is hotting up. Last year this was nip and tuck between the Australian Robbie McEwen and the six-times winner Erik Zabel of Germany[.] — *The Guardian*, 16th July 2003

nip factor *noun*
the degree of coldness *US*
- —Vann Wesson, *Generation X Field Guide and Lexicon*, p. 120, 1997

nip it in the bud!
used for humorously suggesting the emerging presence of a problem *US*
A signature line of deputy Barney Fife, played by Don Knotts, on the situation comedy *Andy Griffith Show* (CBS, 1960–68). Repeated with referential humour.

nipper *noun*
1 a baby or young child *UK, 1859*
- I remember my Grandpa. He used to come to the sea-side with us on holiday. When I was a nipper. —Clive Exton, *No Fixed Abode [Six Granada Plays]*, p. 130, 1959
- Fancy a bloke usin' toilet talk in front of his nippers!! —Barry Humphries, *Bazza Pulls It Off!*, 1971
- Honey, could ya slide over a tad and raise the nipper up? — *Raising Arizona*, 1987
- I used to love climbing trees when I was a nipper[.] —Danny King, *The Burglar Diaries*, p. 139, 2001
- The shop windows have not reflected his twenty-one years from toddler to nipper to snapper to bopper to man. —Mark Powell, *Snap*, p. 105, 2001

2 a young lad employed to do menial tasks for a group of labourers *AUSTRALIA, 1915*
- —Gavin Casey, *It's Harder for Girls*, p. 1, 1941

- They were compelled to employ a full-time "nipper" to clean amenities sheds and take and collect lunch orders. — *West Australian*, p. 9, 7th March 1992

3 a sandfly *BAHAMAS*

- — John A. Holm, *Dictionary of Bahamian English*, p. 143, 1982

4 in target shooting, a shot that just nicks a ring, scoring as if it had fallen within the ring *US*

- — *American Speech*, p. 194, October 1957: 'Some colloquialisms of the handgunner'

5 a railway brakeman *US*

- — Ramon Adams, *The Language of the Railroader*, p. 105, 1977

nippers *noun*

1 the female breasts *US*

- — Collin Baker et al., *College Undergraduate Slang Study Conducted at Brown University*, p. 162, 1968

2 the teeth *US*

- The nippers; I lost 'em. — John Nichols, *The Sterile Cuckoo*, p. 219, 1965

3 thickly knit gloves with no fingers *CANADA*

- "Guess we'll haul back," said Jim at last, slipping a pair of woollen "nippers" over his hands and standing up in the bow of the dory. — Frederick Wallace, *Roving Fisherman*, p. 48, 1955
- — Kendall Merriam, *The Illustrated Dictionary of Lobstering*, p. 62, 1978

4 any cutting tool *US*

- — Hyman E. Goldin et al., *Dictionary of American Underworld Lingo*, p. 145, 1950

5 a special pair of pliers that can grasp the key from the other side of the door *US*

- — Joseph E. Ragen and Charles Finston, *Inside the World's Toughest Prison*, p. 810, 1962: 'Penitentiary and underworld glossary'

nippie *noun*

the nipple *UK*

- Because I want to lick your chocolate button nippies. — Bernadine Evaristo, *Lara*, 1997

nipple gripple; nipple cripple *noun*

a violent gripping and twisting assault on someone's (usually a male's) nipples *UK*

- — Chris Lewis, *The Dictionary of Playground Slang*, p. 158, 2003

nipple palm *noun*

a Nipa palm, found in swampy and marshy land in South Vietnam *US*

- He was in a little mound inside this real heavy stuff, nipple [Nipa] palm that grows around the rivers. — Myra MacPherson, *Long Time Passing*, p. 19, 1984

nipplitis *noun*

(used of a woman) erect nipples *US*

- — Pamela Munro, *U.C.L.A. Slang*, p. 93, 1997

Nippon Clipon *noun*

the Auckland Harbor Bridge *NEW ZEALAND, 1976*

Through Japanese technology, the bridge was expanded from two to four lanes.

- — Louis S. Leland, *A Personal Kiwi-Yankee Dictionary*, p. 70, 1984

nippy *adjective*

1 speedy *UK, 1853*

- [T]he best looking, best finished and best presented of the three PCs. It was slightly nippier than the Acer[.] — *The Guardian*, 29th August 2002

2 chilly *US*

Almost always applied to the weather.

- "Kinda nippy out there, ain't it?" Miss Rabbit commented, attempting to cool the tension out. — Odie Hawkins, *The Busting Out of an Ordinary Man*, p. 118, 1985

nips *adjective*

afraid, anxious *SOUTH AFRICA, 1977*

Probably from **NIP STRAWS**.

- — Penny Silva, *A Dictionary of South African English*, 1996

nip slip *noun*

a photograph revealing at least a part of a woman's nipple *US*

The premise is that the reveal is accidental; major usage of the term on Internet photograph sites.

- Now that some of the initial shock of the Jackson nip slip is over, she said: "The audience decided they wanted to see these artists." — *Daily News (New York)*, p. 6, 26th February 2004
- They still haven't got over Janet Jackson's 'nip slip' here and MTV promised to clean up its act. — *Mail on Sunday (London)*, p. 31, 29th February 2004

nip straws *verb*

to be nervous, anxious or afraid *SOUTH AFRICA, 1970*

From the clenching of the jaw; generally as 'nipping straws'.

- — Penny Silva, *A Dictionary of South African English*, 1996

Nirvana Scotia *noun*

Nova Scotia *CANADA*

- Is this Alberta? No, it's Nirvana Scotia, a land where economic dreams just might come true, if there's a big push from development of the offshore energy industry. — *Halifax Chronicle Herald*, p. D1, 6th June 2002

nishi *noun*

the vagina *US*

- There's [a...] "toadie," "dee dee," "nishi," "dignity," "monkey box[".] — Eve Ensler, *The Vagina Monologues*, p. 6, 1998

nishte; nish; nishta *noun*

nothing *UK*

From German *nichts* (nothing), via Yiddish usage. 'Nishta' is recorded as a contemporary gay usage.

- [I]f I had it would have been for nished [nishte] — Frank Norman, *Bang To Rights*, p. 126, 1958
- Odd period in London – but come to a rub: nishte. — Derek Raymond (Robin Cook), *The Crust on its Uppers*, p. 19, 1962
- "I got nish" e.g. no cigarette, drugs or tobacco. — Angela Devlin, *Prison Patter*, p. 80, 1996
- I just been standin' there through the whole thing sayin' an' doin' nish. — Nick Barlay, *Curvy Lovebox*, p. 35, 1997
- — *Attitude*, p. 60, July 2003: 'New palare lexicon'

nishtoise; nishtoisale *noun*

nothing *UK*

A variation of **NISHTE**.

- — Paul Baker, *Polari*, p. 183, 2002

nit *noun*

a simpleton, a moron, a fool *AUSTRALIA, 1941*

Widespread UK term of abuse since about 1950.

- half a nitwit — Sidney J. Baker, *The Drum*, 1959
- He felt a bloody great nit. — Wilda Moxham, *The Apprentice*, p. 40, 1969

▸ **keep nit**

to act as lookout while an illegal activity takes place *AUSTRALIA, 1903*

- — Norman Lindsay, *Halfway to Anywhere*, p. 119, 1947
- Hustle around and keep nit honey While I fan the mug for money. — Sam Weller, *Old Bastards I Have Met*, p. 125, 1979

nit!

run for it! *AUSTRALIA, 1882*

Used to notify wrongdoers of the approach of authority. Probably a variant of **NIX**.

- To cries of 'Nit, blokes, the bell will go in a minute – here's old Cudgi comin',' Bill and Jobags allowed themselves to be separated, breathing slaughter. — Norman Lindsay, *Halfway to Anywhere*, p. 91, 1947

nite *noun*

night *US, 1928*

Generally in a commercial or advertising context.

- The all nite cafes were shut up, too, though the lights were on. — Geoffrey Fletcher, *Down Among the Meths Men*, p. 68, 1966

niterie *noun*

▷ see: **NIGHTERY**

nit-keeper *noun*

a lookout for an illegal activity *AUSTRALIA, 1935*

- But Thommo's became increasingly hard to catch because its proprietor built up what Chuck described as a 'small army of nit-keepers, cockatoos and top-offs'. — Vince Kelly, *The Bogeyman*, p. 165, 1956
- — Frank Hardy, *The Outcasts of Foolgarah*, p. 49, 1971

nit nit!

be quiet!; used as a warning that someone is listening *UK, 1950*

In prison use.

nitro *noun*

a streetlight bulb *US*

- — A.B. Chance Co., *Lineman's Slang Dictionary*, p. 12, 1980

nitro *adjective*
volatile *US*
Derived from the unstable nature of nitroglycerin.
- But with a nitro fluff like that, there's no bedrock stability. Be careful. Don't shake her up! She could blow us into the pen! —Iceberg Slim (Robert Beck), *Long White Con*, p. 90, 1977

nitrous *noun*
the gas nitrous oxide used as a recreational drug *AUSTRALIA*
- The merest flash of nipple would send him off like a retarded child on a nitrous binge. —John Birmingham, *He Died With a Felafel in his Hand*, p. 76, 1994

nits and buggers *noun*
in poker, a hand with a pair of threes and a pair of twos *US*
- —Albert H. Morehead, *The Complete Guide to Winning Poker*, p. 268, 1967

nits and lice *noun*
in poker, a hand with two low-valued pairs *US*
- —Albert H. Morehead, *The Complete Guide to Winning Poker*, p. 268, 1967

nitto!
stop!; be quiet!; used as a general cry of warning *UK, 1959*
A variation of **NIT NIT!**.
- —Angela Devlin, *Prison Patter*, p. 80, 1996

nitty *adjective*
idiotic *UK*
From **NIT** (a fool), possibly influenced by **NUTTY** (crazy).
- If the girl was nitty enough to contemplate marrying him, she was only getting what she deserved. —Patricia Moyes, *Murder Fantastical*, 1967

nitty-clitty *noun*
oral sex on a woman *US*
A play on **CLIT** (the clitoris) and **NITTY-GRITTY** (the essence of the matter).
- [G]et down to the nitty-clitty. —Xaviera Hollander, *The Best Part of a Man*, 1975

nitty-gritty *noun*
the essence of the matter *US, 1956*
Coined by black people, then spread into wide use. In the early 2000s, the belief that the term originally applied to the debris left at the bottom of slave ships when the slaves were removed from the ship circulated with speed, certainty and outrage. Whether the initial report was an intentional hoax or merely basis-free speculation, it is a false etymology. All authorities agree that the etymology is unknown yet some ill-informed politically correct types consider the word to have racist overtones.
- [W]hen it got down to the nitty-gritty, you could always go to Mister Ben. —Dick Gregory, *Nigger*, p. 35, 1964
- —*Current Slang*, p. 2, Spring 1967
- You finished taking our words, too? What do you know know about nitty-gritty? —Nat Hentoff, *I'm really dragged but nothing gets me down*, p. 27, 1968
- —Burton H. Wolfe, *The Hippies*, p. 205, 1968: 'A hip glossary for the uptight people'
- Sapphire believes in gettin' down to the nitty-gritty; beating around the bush just isn't her style. —Carolyn Greene, *70 Soul Secrets of Sapphire*, p. 39, 1973
- The Real Nitty Gritty —*American Speech*, p. 90–101, Spring-Summer 1974
- "If I used nitty gritty I would face a disciplinary charge," said PC Christ Jefford[.] —*The Guardian*, p. 7, 15th May 2002

nitwit *noun*
a simpleton, a moron, a fool *US, 1914*
- But he will vote Democratic because of Bush's vice presidential candidate, Sen. Dan Quayle of Indiana. "That guy is a nitwit," Drews said. —*Newsday (New York)*, p. 7, 12th October 1988
- "Guess who Carlotta slept with last night?" "Who? Bruno Modjaleski?" "No, nitwit. Sheeni Saunders!" —C.D. Payne, *Youth in Revolt*, p. 466, 1993
- These women have talent – more than enough to survive the bashing of right-wing nitwits like Rosen, Rush Limbaugh, Jerry Falwell and hayseed country music radio stations. (Letter to editor). —*Rocky Mountain News (Denver)*, p. 53A, 9th May 2003

nix; nicks *noun*
nothing; no *UK, 1789*
Probably from colloquial German *nichts* via Dutch (colloquial Afrikaans has *niks*).
- "Nix, Alaric," said Nebbice, releasing me. "It's not necessary." —Max Shulman, *The Zebra Derby*, p. 48, 1946
- Nix, nyet, nein and no. —James Ellroy, *White Jazz*, p. 65, 1992

nix *verb*
to reject, to deny *US, 1903*
- He tried to steer me to a hangout around the corner but I nixed the idea[.] —Mickey Spillane, *One Lonely Night*, p. 23, 1951
- But you got the nerve to nix dough and cold shoulder me, Lock Jaw. —Iceberg Slim (Robert Beck), *Mama Black Widow*, p. 164, 1969

nixer *noun*
work undertaken outside normal work, usually without an employer's knowledge *IRELAND*
- The [ambulance] crews were made up of two fireman doing 'nixers' and other guys who drifted in and out. —John Fleetwood, *In Stitches*, p. 11, 1994
- Some so-called "nixers" were acceptable for off-duty gardai but top of the list of those not tolerated was working in the security industry. —*Irish Times*, 5th July 2001

nixie *noun*
an incorrectly addressed letter *US, 1890*
A term used by railway mail clerks.
- —Ramon Adams, *The Language of the Railroader*, p. 105, 1977

nixies *noun*
a female undergarment with a cut-out crotch permitting vaginal sex while otherwise clothed *US*
- —Anon., *King Smut's Wet Dreams Interpreted*, 1978

Nixon's revenge *noun*
an American Ford car *US*
Citizens' band radio slang; a reference to US President Richard Nixon.
- —*Complete CB Slang Dictionary*, p. 76, 1976
- —Peter Chippindale, *The British CB Book*, p. 161, 1981

nizzel; nizzle *noun*
a close friend *US*
A hip-hop, urban black coinage, formed as a rhyming reduplication of **SHIZZLE** (sure, yes).
- Fa shizzle my nizzle used to dribble down in V-A —Jay-Z *Izzo (HOVA)*, 2001
- —Rick Ayers (Editor), *Berkeley High Slang Dictionary*, p. 32, 2004

nkalafaker *noun*
a person who is not so much to be admired as was originally thought; a confidence trickster *SOUTH AFRICA*
Teen slang.
- You are wack to think it is still phat to say cool and certainly a nkalafaker to think kwaito star Mandoza is still a nkalakatha! —*Sunday Times (South Africa)*, 1st June 2003

nkalakatha *noun*
a trustworthy person *SOUTH AFRICA*
Current teen slang.
- —*Sunday Times (South Africa)*, 1st June 2003

N.O.
no *US*
Spelt for emphasis, usually humorous.
- CAROL: Hey, is this what they call copping a feel? JOHN: What? No. Get up. N.O. Jesus! —*American Graffiti*, 1973

no – about it!; there is no – about it!
by enclosing the active verb from a preceding statement, an absolute negation of that verb *UK, 1924*
- However, he also said that "the ultimate location of the privatised company must remain a decision for the management and owners of that company." That is not the case. There is no "must" about it. —Alun Michael (MP for Cardiff South and Penarth), *Hansard*, 15th April 1991

no-access tool *noun*
a light cleaning brush carried by telephone installers and repair technicians *US*
If for any reason the installer or repair technician would rather not make a particular service call, they sneak up to the door and leave a 'sorry-we-missed-you' tag. In jest, a fellow worker might accuse him of using a light cleaning brush to faintly tap on the door. Collected from a former telephone repair technician, September 2003.

noah *noun*
a shark *US*
Rhyming slang from 'Noah's ark'.
- —Grant W. Kuhns, *On Surfing*, p. 119, 1963

• Some whizz kids have even determined that Harold Holt wasn't sucked off a rock by a Noah. — Barry Humphries, *The Traveller's Tool*, p. 13, 1985
• — Trevor Cralle, *The Surfin'ary*, p. 80, 1991
• So if five noahs got trapped in that itsy bitsy net, then how many are there along the other 20 miles of beaches? — Paul Vautin, *Turn It Up!*, p. 108, 1995

Noah's ark *noun*

1 an informer *UK*
Rhyming slang for **NARK** (an informer); recorded in 1960 by Julian Franklyn with the assertion that it 'has been used in England since the first decade of the C20'. 'Noah's ark' is spoonerised into 'oah's nark', which infers the deeply contemptuous 'whore's nark'.
• — Angela Devlin, *Prison Patter*, p. 80, 1996
• — Harry Orsman, *A Dictionary of Modern New Zealand Slang*, p. 92, 1999

2 a person who accompanies a customer but deters him or her from making a purchase *UK*
Rhyming slang for **NARK** (an awkward customer).
• — Patrick O'Shaughnessy, *Market Traders' Slang*, 1979

3 a spoilsport *AUSTRALIA, 1898*
Rhyming slang for **NARK**.

4 a park *UK*
Rhyming slang.
• — Jack Jones, *Rhyming Cockney Slang*, 1971
• — Ray Puxley, *Fresh Rabbit*, 1998

Noah's ark *adjective*
dark *UK, 1934*
Rhyming slang.
• Cricketers have to up-stumps when it gets too "Noah's ark". — Ray Puxley, *Cockney Rabbit*, 1992

Noah's nobles *noun*
female volunteers from the American Red Cross *US*
Korean war usage; Noah is suggested by the Red Cross initials (ARC).
• — Carl Fleischhauer, *A Glossary of Army Slang*, p. 3, 1968

no ass *adverb*
extremely *GUYANA*
Placed after the verb.
• — Richard Allsopp, *Dictionary of Caribbean English Usage*, p. 408, 1996

no ass!
used for expressing the serious nature of what is being said *TRINIDAD AND TOBAGO, 1974*
• — Lise Winer, *Dictionary of the English/Creole of Trinidad & Tobago*, 2003

nob *noun*

1 a person of rank, position or wealth *UK, 1703*
• It's the young nobs I hates the worst of all with their flat-chested bints [girlfriends]. — John Peter Jones, *Feather Pluckers*, p. 29, 1964
• After my theft, three nobs got together. The Marquis of Wells, his pal Lord Featherstonehaugh (pronounce it Fanshaw to be classy) and the Marquis of Gotham[.] — Jonathan Gash, *The Ten Word Game*, p. 51, 2003

2 a completely reliable and dependable person *AUSTRALIA*
• — Ned Wallish, *The Truth Dictionary of Racing Slang*, p. 81, 1989

3 the penis *UK, 1961*
A variation of **KNOB**.
• Cheryl's just been looking at men's nobs. — Caroline Aherne and Craig Cash, *The Royle Family*, 1999
• The smiling child with his hand on his nob[.] — Frank Skinner, *Frank Skinner*, p. 22, 2001

4 the head *UK*
Probably from **KNOB**; since about 1690 but now feels dated and tired.

nob *verb*
to collect money from an audience after a performance or other attraction *UK, 1851*
Possibly from passing the hat round, a **NOB** (a head) more usually being put in a hat.
• We had had a few "burster" houses lately and he thought the "bunce" must be "bona"[good] – no need to do any "nobbing" here. — Butch Reynolds, *Broken Hearted Clown*, p. 29, 1953

nobber *noun*
a person who collects money for a street entertainer *UK, 1890*
• — Paul Baker, *Polari*, p. 184, 2002

nobber; nobba *adjective*
nine *UK*
Polari; from Spanish *nueve* or Italian *nove*, via parleyaree and lingua franca.
• [Y]ou might like to count to ten in Polari: una, duey, trey, quater, chicker, sey, setter, otto, nobber, dacha. — Michael Quinion, *World Wide Words*, 1996
• — Paul Baker, *Polari*, p. 184, 2002

nobbins *noun*
money collected from an audience, especially money thrown into a boxing ring *UK*
From **NOB** (to collect money from an audience).
• [H]is payment was £3 per fight, plus the nobbins tossed into the ring by an appreciative crowd. After a really good fight the nobbins could amount to the same again or more. — Jimmy Stockin, *On The Cobbles*, p. 88, 2000

nobble *verb*

1 to sabotage, especially to hinder or defeat a rival *UK, 1856*
From horse-tampering.
• He's taken care of... I sent Joe and Vic to nobble him! — *The Sweeney*, p. 42, 1976
• DEREK: Dumpton Cross? Us'll find the lorry easy enough... [To LITTLE MICHAEL] You nobblin' their wagon? [LITTLE MICHAEL smiles proudly.] BRIAN: Good lad. — Chris Baker and Andrew Day, *Lock, Stock... & One Big Bullock*, p. 349, 2000

2 to corrupt, or otherwise tamper with, a jury or jury member *UK, 1856*
• Free to tell the truth at last, he would describe how the sting had been set up; how MI5 had arranged for the jury to be nobbled into declaring a pillar of the community a perjurer.] — *The Observer*, 20th July 2003

3 in horse racing, to drug a horse to impair its performance *UK, 1847*
• — Rita Cannon, *Let's Go Racing*, p. 72, 1948

4 to appropriate dishonestly, to steal *UK, 1854*
• They've nobbled the wages! — Derek Bickerton, *Payroll*, p. 65, 1959

nobbler *noun*

1 a person who drugs racehorses or racing dogs to affect their racing performance *US*
• — Ralph de Sola, *Crime Dictionary*, p. 102, 1982

2 a small glass of spirits *AUSTRALIA, 1842*
• Rita administered a stiff nobbler of gin[.] — Norman Lindsay, *Dust or Polish?*, p. 98, 1950
• — Jim Ramsay, *Cop It Sweet!*, p. 63, 1977

Nobby Hall *noun*
a testicle *UK*
Rhyming slang for **BALL(S)**, formed from the name of the eponymous hero of an old and bawdy song: 'They call him Nobby Hall, Nobby Hall / They call him Nobby Hall, 'coz he's only got one....finger / They call him Nobby Hall, Nobby Hall'.
• — Ray Puxley, *Cockney Rabbit*, 1992

Nobby Stiles; nobbys *noun*
haemorrhoids *UK*
Rhyming slang for 'piles', formed from footballer Norbert 'Nobby' Stiles (b.1942) who was a member of the England team that won the World Cup in 1966.
• — Ray Puxley, *Cockney Rabbit*, 1992
• I've been sitting on a rubber ring all week and my Nobbys still hurt. — Bodmin Dark, *Dirty Cockney Rhyming Slang*, 2003

nob end *noun*
the part of town where the money lives *UK*
• I cuts up quite a few old toffee noses on me way down the nob end of town[.] — John Peter Jones, *Feather Pluckers*, p. 38, 1964

nobhead *noun*
▷ see: **KNOBHEAD**

no biggie
don't worry about it *US*
• But NO BIGGIE / It's so AWESOME / It's like TUBULAR, y'know. — Moon Unit and Frank Zappa, *Valley Girl*, 1982
• — Pamela Munro, *U.C.L.A. Slang*, p. 62, 1989

no bitch!
I don't have to sit in the middle of the back seat of the car! *US*
Quickly shouted after someone else reserves the front passenger seat by shouting 'shotgun!'.
• — Pamela Munro, *U.C.L.A. Slang*, p. 62, 1989

noble *noun*
an influential, respected prisoner *US*
- Those real boss meals are eaten by wheels / Nobles and all of that jazz. —Dennis Wepman et al., *The Life*, p. 61, 1976

noble weed *noun*
marijuana *US*
- —*Current Slang*, p. 21, Spring 1970

nobody *noun*
▸ **like nobody's business**
to an extraordinary extent, very much *UK, 1938*
- While they were on the job they'd work like nobody's business. —Patsy Adam-Smith, *Folklore of the Australian Railwaymen*, p. 19, 1969
- And he can dance in those high heels like nobody's business. —Peaches (Merrill Nisker), *The Wire*, p. 24, October 2003
- She's got it all: the talent and the range. She's got comic timing like nobody's business. She's extraordinarily beautiful[.]—*The Guardian*, 22nd February 2004

nobody's home
said of a person who is empty-headed *US*
An abbreviation of **LIGHTS ON BUT THERE'S NOBODY HOME**.
- He looked the same as always. You know, like nobody's home. —Janet Evanovich, *Seven Up*, p. 157, 2001

no brag, just fact
used for humorously calling attention to having bragged *US*
Cavalry scout Will Sonnett, played by Walter Brennan, used this line to instill fear on the television Western *The Guns of Will Sonnett* (ABC, 1967–69). Repeated with referential humour.

no-brainer *noun*
1 an opinion so easily formed or decision so easily made that no thinking is required *US, 1980*
- —*American Speech*, Summer 1989
- His [The Notorious B.I.G.] demo was [...] a no-brainer. Not surprisingly, calls from labels and industry execs came in shortly after[.]—*The Source*, p. 159, March 2002

2 in croquet, a lucky shot *US*
- —James Charlton and William Thompson, *Croquet*, p. 159, 1977: 'Glossary'

nobs *noun*
shoes *US*
- —Joan Fontaine et al., *Dictionary of Black Slang*, 1968
- —Charles Shafer, *Folk Speech in Texas Prisons*, p. 210, 1990

No Cal *noun*
northern California *US*
- "Ill show you where the No-Cal babes hang," Chuck said. —Francesca Lia Block, *Witch Baby*, p. 104, 1991

no can do, Madame Nhu
used as a humorous if emphatic suggestion that something cannot be done *US*
Madame Nhu was the sister-in-law of South Vietnamese President Diem.
- —Linda Reinberg, *In the Field*, p. 152, 1991

no chance!
used as an emphatic negative, often scornful *UK, 1984*
- MONICA: But it's my chance, Johnny. It's my only chance. JOHNNY: No chance. —Terry Victor, *Family Affair*, 1991

no chance outside *noun*
a non-commissioned officer of the US Army *US*
From the initials NCO and a healthy distrust of military authority.
- —Carl Fleischhauer, *A Glossary of Army Slang*, p. 3, 1968
- We're not all NCO's, which short-timers claim stands for 'No Chance Outside' the military. —Jack Hawkins, *Chopper One #2*, p. 250, 1987

no cigar *adverb*
▷ **see:** **CLOSE BUT NO CIGAR**

nochy *noun*
night *UK*
Polari, from Italian *notte* or Spanish *noche*.
- Bona [good] nochy. —Paul Baker, *Polari*, p. 166, 2002

no comment!
used as a jocular catchphrase *UK*
In imitation of politicians everywhere.
- — Partridge, *A Dictionary of Catch Phrases*, 1977

no comprende
I do not understand *US*
Partial Spanish used by English speakers without regard to their fluency in Spanish, and with multiple variations reflecting their lack of fluency.
- What wall were those Tulls coming off anyhoo? No comprende. —Lester Bangs, *Psychotic Reactions and Carburetor Dung*, p. 132, 1971

nod *noun*
1 a drug-induced state of semi- or unconsciousness *US, 1936*
From 'nod' (a sleep).
- Other opiates are on the market in bottles, each on strong enough to get you into a fairly nice nod, or at least make things comfortably blurred around the edges. —Julian Keeling, *Drugstore Cowboy [The Howard Marks Book of Dope Stories]*, p. 115, 1996
- —Robert Ashton, *This Is Heroin*, p. 209, 2002

2 a new recruit to the Royal Marines *UK*
A variant of 'Noddy', which supposedly derives from a standard issue woollen hat that when worn by recruits looks like Noddy (a children's character)'s hat.
- —Nigel Foster, *The Making of a Royal Marine Commando*, 1987

3 the head *UK*
An abbreviation of **NODDLE** (the head).
- Use your flippin' nod. —Diran Abedayo, *My Once Upon A Time*, p. 272, 2000

4 in horse racing, a very small margin of victory or lead *US*
- A little twitch kept her from dwelling, and on a good cushion she took it by a nod. —*San Francisco Chronicle*, p. 54, 21st April 1971

▸ **nod is as good as a wink; nod is as good as a wink to a blind horse; nod's as good as a wink to a blind bat**
applied to a covert yet comprehensible hint *UK, 1802*
The 'blind bat' variation was created in 1969 for the ground-breaking television comedy series *Monty Python's Flying Circus* and, like many of that programme's catchphrases, remains in circulation.
- Follow me! Follow me! I like that. That's good. A nod's as good as a wink to a blind bat, eh? —Graham Chapman, *The Complete Monty Python Flying Circus*, p. 40, 1989
- "Say what you like," said Mr. Parrish. "A nod's as good as a wink." —Phillip Pullman, *The Tiger in the Well*, p. 84, 1992
- A nod's as good as a wink tae a blind horse, man! When ye read between the lines[.]—Virginia Henley, *Tempted*, p. 462, 1993

▸ **on the nod**
1 lost in mental stupefaction brought on by heroin or other narcotics *US, 1951*
- Pat was sitting at the wheel of my car on the nod. We were on the ferry, crossing from Algiers[.]—William Burroughs, *Junkie*, p. 79, 1953
- She'd sit with them, they'd go on the nod, in the dead silence she'd wait[.]—Jack Kerouac, *The Subterraneans*, p. 29, 1958
- When he has finally injected the heroin (he calls it "shooting up," "taking off," "getting off"), he may or may not go on a "nod" – his eyelids heavy, his mind wandering pleasantly[.]—James Mills, *The Panic in Needle Park*, p. 15, 1966
- He trailed off and almost went into a nod. —Nathan Heard, *Howard Street*, p. 174, 1968
- We all three got really stoned and sat talking or simply going on the nod until the early hours of the morning – finally dropping off to sleep – awakening much later in the day. —Herbert Huncke, *The Evening Sun Turned Crimson*, p. 83, 1980
- Skid rows populated by the homeless. Tenderloins strewn with winos sucking on a bottle in a bag and young dopers on the nod. —Robert Campbell, *Alice in La-La Land*, p. 2, 1987

2 within a committee, to be agreed without argument; to be *nodded* through *UK*
Conventionally, a nod is a sign of assent.
- Just work out the budget and then visit me at my office. I'll put it through on the nod. —Stewart Home, *Sex Kick [britpulp]*, p. 236, 1999

3 (of a wager) agreed upon without money changing hands *AUSTRALIA, 1902*
- He holds out the punters who back the last winner and encourages them to bet up on the nod on the strength of that win. —Clive Galea, *Slipper*, p. 182, 1988
- —Ned Wallish, *The Truth Dictionary of Racing Slang*, p. 56, 1989

▸ **the nod**
official approval *UK*
- Now, these lads are fucking tasty, they are. If it weren't for the nod from Bernie I'd half have the horrors having to deal with the cunts. —Kevin Sampson, *Outlaws*, p. 52, 2001

nod *verb*
to enter a near-coma state after drug use *US, 1958*
- There were only moments to cop and moments to use and moments to nod and cop again. —Clarence Cooper Jr, *The Scene*, p. 39, 1960

nod betting *noun*
betting on credit *AUSTRALIA*
- Nod betting often gained Harry a precious few seconds, reflected in a favourable shading of the odds. —Gerald Sweeney, *The Plunge*, p. 28, 1981

nodder *noun*
the head *UK*
- [An onion] rolled away, first bounce off the Governor's nodder, in the direction of the chokey cells [punishment cells]. —Charles Raven, *Underworld Nights*, p. 200, 1956

noddle *noun*
the head *UK, 1509*
- War and bloodshed and heroes with skill in battle and not much else in their thick noddles. — *The Mists of Avalon*, p. 531, 1982

noddle *verb*
to idle, to waste time *UK*
- In the evenings Robert preferred to "noddle around the house" rather than host corporate dinners. — *The Observer*, 13th July 2003

noddy *noun*
1 in a film or television interview, a brief shot of the interviewer listening or nodding *UK, 1982*
In full, a 'noddy-shot'.
- He recalls, for example, filming a British television interview with Mark Lawson, and being introduced for the first time to the concept of the "noddy"- the TV trick in which, after the camera has been filming the interviewee over the interviewer's shoulder, the positions are reversed, so that footage of the interviewer nodding in response can be spliced into the final broadcast. — *The Guardian*, 4th December 2000

2 a police motorcyclist *UK, 1980*
A back-formation from **NODDY-BIKE**.

Noddy *noun*
a tracked snow vehicle manufactured by the Robin Nodwell Manufacturing Company *ANTARCTICA, 1978*
- —Bernadette Hince, *The Antarctic Dictionary*, p. 241, 2000

noddy *adjective*
1 (used of a computer program) trivial, useless but illustrative of a point *US*
- —Eric S. Raymond, *The New Hacker's Dictionary*, p. 261, 1991

2 foolish *UK, 1971*
From Essex dialect.

noddy-bike; noddy *noun*
a police motorcycle *UK, 1964*
Originally of a light motorcycle used by police before the introduction of the **PANDA CAR**. Generally presumed to come from Noddy, the character created by Enid Blyton (1897–1968), in turn named for 'a simpleton', but that would better describe the driver than the vehicle and Noddy drove a car; more likely to be derived from obsolete Irish *noddy* (a one-horse conveyance) with just a hint of Enid Blyton.
- —Angela Devlin, *Prison Patter*, p. 80, 1996

noddy boat *noun*
a canal-using pleasure boat (not a conventional narrow boat) *UK*
Derisory.
- —John Gagg, *The Canaller's Bedside Book*, 1972

noddy shop *noun*
a prison workshop *UK*
From the nature of the work carried on therein: so basic that it can be understood by children so young that they are still reading *Noddy*, the character created by Enid Blyton (1897–1968).
- —Angela Devlin, *Prison Patter*, p. 80, 1996
- He was down the noddy shop learnin' to weave baskets. —Chris Baker and Andrew Day, *Lock, Stock... & A Good Slopping Out*, p. 438, 2000

noddy suit *noun*
a suit of protective clothing worn against nuclear, biological or chemical threat *UK*
- — *British Army Review*, December 1972

no dice!
1 originally and literally, in a dice game a roll of the dice that does not count because of a rule violation *US*
- — *The Annals of the American Academy of Political and Social Sciences*, p. 128, May 1950

2 positively no *US, 1931*
- I packed up with my family and moved out to Jackson Heights, Long Island, to fight it out in the wilderness of the Borough of Queens. No dice. I tried my damnedest, couldn't make it. —Mezz Mezzrow, *Really the Blues*, p. 270, 1946
- Captain Black came in. "No dice." —Philip Wylie, *Opus 21*, p. 342, 1949
- No dice, Mr. Berin. They hurt me but they didn't scare me. —Mickey Spillane, *My Gun is Quick*, p. 74–75, 1950
- I tried to make myself sleep, but it was no dice. —Jim Thompson, *Savage Night*, p. 67, 1953
- No shirts, no shoes, no dice. — *Fast Times at Ridgemont High*, 1982
- "Officer, how about I give you guys some dollars? How much you need?" No dice. —Elmore Leonard, *Glitz*, p. 59, 1985
- Nice try, Gorgeous, but no dice, I'm afraid. — *The Guardian*, 15th March 2002

nod off *verb*
to fall asleep *UK, 1845*
- But Raymond Betson, 41, and William Cockran, 50, were denied leave to appeal, despite Judge Coombe's admission that he nodded off. He has denied snoring. — *The Guardian*, 22nd January 2004

no doubt!
used as a formulaic expression of agreement *US*
- —Connie Eble (Editor), *UNC-CH Campus Slang*, p. 7, Spring 1988
- — *Newsday*, p. B2, 11th October 1997

nod out *verb*
to fall asleep, especially as a result of recreational drug use *US, 1953*
- —Angela Devlin, *Prison Patter*, p. 80, 1996

no duh!
used for expressing sentiment that what was just said is patently obvious to even the casual observer *US*
- —Mimi Pond, *The Valley Girl's Guide to Life*, p. 60, 1982

no end *adverb*
immensely *UK, 1859*
- Well, at least for the last six months I've had the best time possible and enjoyed myself no end. — *The Times*, 2nd March 2001

no end of *adjective*
a great number or quantity of *UK, 1623*
Colloquial.
- There followed no end of encouraging news[.]— *The Guardian*, 5th December 1998

no fear!
used as an expression of refusal *UK, 1887*
- Trust me, I'm a doctor? No fear. — *The Observer*, 25th November 2001

no flies on
nothing at all wrong or amiss with someone *AUSTRALIA, 1845*
- No flies on Gary, mate, you mark my words. —Alexander Buzo, *Norm and Ahmed*, p. 16, 1969

NoFuck, Virginia *nickname*
Norfolk, Virginia *US*
- "NoFuck Virginia." Recruits learn to say "NoFuck" on their first Cinderella liberty when they have to be back on base by midnight without getting "any." —Maria Flook, *My Sister Life*, p. 62, 1998

nog *noun*
1 a Vietnamese or Korean person or soldier; any Southeast Asian person *AUSTRALIA, 1969*
From **NIG-NOG**.
- Shit it feels good, the local nogs are as scared as all Christ of us. —William Nagel, *The Odd Angry Shot*, p. 5, 1975

2 a short piece of wood inserted between wall studs *NEW ZEALAND*
A variant is 'noggings'.
- —Ronald Bacon, *In the Sticks*, p. 181, 1963
- —Jeremy Salmond, *Old New Zealand Houses*, p. 232, 1986

no gain without pain
used to urge sacrifice *US, 1968*
A catchphrase beloved by athletic coaches as inspiration for bulletin board reading.

noggin *noun*
the head *US, 1859*
- "That tap on the noggin ain't bothered your memory any," he said[.] —Chester Himes, *If He Hollers Let Him Go*, p. 185, 1945
- [T]his one here on my noggin is an African hat; but that don't make no difference. —Cecil Brown, *The Life & Loves of Mr. Jiveass Nigger*, p. 53, 1969
- I clapped my noggin: "What the fuck am I thinking of? That's a great song!" —Lester Bangs, *Psychotic Reactions and Carburetor Dung*, p. 9, 1971

noggy *noun*
a Vietnamese or Korean person or soldier; hence, any Southeast Asian person *AUSTRALIA, 1954*
- N is for NOGGIE, the native of the land. / For the good ones that come here we must put out our hand. —Martin Cameron, *A Look at the Bright Side*, 1988

no go; no-go *noun*
a failure, something that is not good; a hopeless attempt *UK, 1824*
Although the term has an undeniable US 1960s space programme ring to it, it was 140 years old and had crossed the Atlantic before we heard it from NASA's lips.
- There were several dark husky men wearing hats who made Lynn's heart pump for a few seconds, but when he'd get close to them it was always a no-go. —Joseph Wambaugh, *Fugitive Nights*, p. 269, 1992
- If their [Dachshunds'] feet aren't crooked, it's no go. I've got one with front feet that are so turned you can't tell which way he's going. —*New York Daily News*, 27th February 2003

no-go-showboat *noun*
a car that has been restored and modified with an emphasis on its appearance, not its speed *US*
- She's just for looks, man, not for drags / 'Cause it's a no-go showboat... — The Beach Boys, *No-Go Showboat*, 1963

no-go zone *noun*
an area to which access is prohibited or ill-advised *US*
The term came to the attention of Americans in 2004 in the context of the US occupation of Iraq.
- Police are planning to cordon off an area between Independence Avenue and Jefferson Drive from Fourth to 14th Street as a secure "no-go" zone. — *Washington Post*, p. C1, 30th September 1979
- There are 'no-go' zones in Iraq today. You can't hold an election in a 'no go' zone. [Quoting John Kerry]. — *New York Times*, p. A1, 24th September 2004

no great shakes *adjective*
nothing remarkable, important or special *UK, 1819*
- I was no great shakes as a teacher. —J.M. Coetzee, *Disgrace*, 2003

no harm in looking!
used as a motto, excuse or philosophy for a husband or boyfriend who finds the sight of the opposite sex irresistible *UK, 1984*
- No harm in looking if you understand. / she's a one man woman / I'm a one woman man. —Hank Williams Jr, *Early in the Morning and Late at Night (Song)*, 1988

NoHo *nickname*
the neighbourhood in New York City just north of Houston Street *US*
- STEPHIE: Where's this party at, anyway. SoHo? VAL: NoHo. — *200 Cigarettes*, 1999

no holds barred *adjective*
without constraint, 'anything goes' *US, 1942*
Taken from the sport of wrestling.
- [A] no-holds-barred 50-minute adult opus called Plug Me In. — *The Guardian*, 27th September 2000

no-hoper *noun*
1 a worthless person; a person with no prospects *AUSTRALIA, 1944*
- 'Aw, give the kid a go,' argued Joyce. 'He might've been a no-hoper, but he ain't done anything bad since he's been here.' —Arthur Upfield, *Bony and the Mouse*, p. 81, 1959
- You flaming no-hopers worry a man so much you'd make him forget what day it is! —Ray Slattery, *Mobbs' Mob*, p. 19, 1966
- —Jean Brooks, *The Opal Witch*, p. 69, 1967
- We didn't create the pedestrian plaza in Martin Place for the hippies, layabouts and no-hopers. —Bill Hornadge, *The Ugly Australian*, p. 233, 1970
- —Frank Hardy, *The Outcasts of Foolgarah*, p. 57, 1971
- [T]he lads from the corridors of learning are a bunch of "no hopers" when it comes to sex. — *Flame*, p. 9, 1972

2 a horse considered unable to win a race; a rank outsider *AUSTRALIA, 1943*
- Then there was the Saturday he put two bob each way on some no-hoper at Rosehill and the no-hoper had come in at fifty to one[.] —Eric Lambert, *The Veterans*, p. 27, 1954
- In a bellow that could be heard all over the ring he would offer to lay fantastic wagers against horses he believed were no-hopers. —Vince Kelly, *The Bogeyman*, p. 126, 1956

nointer *noun*
in Tasmania, a brat or mischievous child *AUSTRALIA*
Survival of a British dialect word, clipping of 'anointer' in the same sense. Formerly (C16, *Oxford English Dictionary*) the word 'anoint' meant 'to beat soundly', thus 'anointer' would mean 'one who requires anointing/beating'.
- [T]hey came in grade ranging from 'a bit of a nointer' to 'a real nointer', but even the latter was not beyond redemption. — *Mercury*, p. 25, 1st August 1994
- —Maureen Brooks and Joan Ritchie, *Tassie Terms*, p. 100, 1995

noise *noun*
1 foolish talk; nonsense *US, 1871*
- He was giving me all kinds of noise about it and I can't take that from him, baby, I can't take it. —James Mills, *The Panic in Needle Park*, p. 140, 1966
- —Hermese E. Roberts, *The Third Ear*, 1971
- You think I need this noise? —George V. Higgins, *Penance for Jerry Kennedy*, p. 120, 1985
- Fuck that redneck noise, dude. All dem chicks be rappin' how dey losin' der ho's and how dey ain't got no bread for beer. — *Platoon*, 1986

2 heroin *US, 1928*
- —Ralph de Sola, *Crime Dictionary*, p. 103, 1982
- —Richard A. Spears, *The Slang and Jargon of Drugs and Drink*, p. 363, 1986
- —Robert Ashton, *This Is Heroin*, p. 206, 2002
- —Mike Haskins, *Drugs*, p. 284, 2003

noisemaker *noun*
in trucking, a radio *US*
- —Montie Tak, *Truck Talk*, p. 110, 1971

noisemaker *adjective*
producing the impression of force through loud sounds *US*
Professional wrestling usage.
- The stomps are quieter since they're putting more weight on the stomping foot and less on the noisemaker foot. —Sharon Mazer, *Professional Wrestling*, p. 165, 1998

noisenik *noun*
a contemporary musician whose compositions appear (to most auditors) to be formless noise *UK*
The suffix '-nik' forms the person out of the noise.
- From a cred history releasing Bikini Kill and Silverfish's noisenik excursions to a post-mid-nineties almost pop Wiiija, it's been a long and strange decade. —John Robb, *The Nineties*, p. 303, 1999
- Les Savy Fav: US art-rock noiseniks return to London in style —*Kerrang!*, p. 41, 3rd November 2001

noise pollution *noun*
in poker, excessive chatter at the table *US*
- —John Vorhaus, *The Big Book of Poker Slang*, p. 27, 1996

noises *noun*
▸ **make the right noises**
to use unexceptionable platitudes, to pay lip-service *UK, 1976*
- And he [Iain Duncan Smith] made the right noises for a leader who has bet his future on rebranding his party as the party of compassion. — *The Guardian*, 10th July 2002

noise up *verb*
to cause trouble *UK*
- "I'm sorry," he said. "You're the last person I should be noising up, under the circumstances." —Christopher Brookmyre, *Boiling a Frog*, p. 84, 2000

noisy *adjective*
of a television programme, talked-about *US*
- —Susie Dent, *The Language Report*, p. 14, 2003

no joke *noun*
a serious matter; hence, a difficulty *UK, 1809*
- It is no joke playing back-to-back Tests with only two days' rest in 40 C. — *The Guardian*, 3rd January 2004

no kid
seriously *AUSTRALIA, 1946*
Shortening of 'no kidding'.

- Look, Polly, I'm going to walk home with you when the show's over. No kid, you've got to let me. — Norman Lindsay, *Halfway to Anywhere*, p. 224, 1947

no kidding!
honestly!, it's the truth! *UK, 1914*
- "This is one of the greatest days of my life." [...] "No kidding. Sit. Sit." He sounded a little as if he was talking to a dog. — Anthony Masters, *Minder*, p. 9, 1984

no lie!
as unbelievable as what I just said may seem, it is true! *US*
- — Judi Sanders, *Kickin' like Chicken with the Couch Commander*, p. 17, 1992

noly *noun*
a simpleton *UK*
Pronounced to rhyme with 'holy'.
- — Patrick O'Shaughnessy, *Market Traders' Slang*, 1979

nomad *noun*
a member of a motorcyle gang who is not a member of any specific chapter of the gang *US*
- — Paladin Press, *Inside Look at Outlaw Motorcyle Gangs*, p. 36, 1992

no make!
stop what you are doing! *US*
Hawaiian youth usage, shortened from 'no make like that'.
- — Douglas Simonson, *Pidgin to da Max Hana Hou*, 1982

no man's Nam *nickname*
Vietnam *US*
A blend of the historic 'no man's land' and 'Vietnam'.
- — Linda Reinberg, *In the Field*, p. 153, 1991

no-mark *noun*
a nobody; someone who has failed to make a mark *UK*
- Sometimes, when I look at the no-marks calling themselves gangsters in this fucking city, I think I should have gone after it[.] — Kevin Sampson, *Outlaws*, p. 66, 2001

no mention
you're welcome *US*
Hawaiian youth usage.
- — Douglas Simonson, *Pidgin to da Max*, 1981

no more forever *adverb*
never again *US*
Echoing the 1877 surrender speech of Chief Joseph of the Nez Perce nation – 'I will fight no more forever'.
- VICTOR: He retired young, man. He will play basketball no more forever. — *Smoke Signals*, 1998

non *noun*
an socially inept person *US*
An abbreviation of the much longer 'non-factor in the game of life'.
- — Connie Eble (Editor), *UNC-CH Campus Slang*, p. 4, Spring 1983

nonce *noun*
1 a sex offender; a child-molester; a pervert *UK, 1975*
The etymology is uncertain: possibly from dialect *nonce* (good for nothing), or with origins in **NANCY BOY** (homosexual, hence pervert); however, given the prison context of the coinage and the violent disdain in which sex-offenders are held by their fellow inmates, the very existence of one may be considered as little more than 'for the nonce', literally 'for the time-being'. It is also worth noting in this context the rhyme on **PONCE** (someone who lives off immoral earnings), another type held in low-esteem in the pecking order of prison life. It is regrettable that modern society feels the need for this term in wider circulation.
- — Angela Devlin, *Prison Patter*, p. 23, 1996
- [O]ne of their top boys is a convicted child molester and rapist. [...] No nonces. — Martin King and Martin Knight, *The Naughty Nineties*, p. 33, 1999
- [H]e made all the young girls give him a kiss before they were allowed in. A nonce case in my book. — Jimmy Stockin, *On The Cobbles*, p. 121, 2000
- You sick fucking nonce. They're only kids and you want to bum them. — John King, *Human Punk*, p. 81, 2000
- When I first saw the men on the rule – or the "nonces", as they were collectively known – the first thing that struck me was that they were a fucking ugly looking bunch. — Ken Lukowiak, *Marijuana Time*, p. 262, 2000
- They always lump the decent honest criminal like me in with the fucking nonces and perverts. — Danny King, *The Burglar Diaries*, p. 170, 2001
- He's been done for raping his mate's sister, it said so in-a paper. Fuckin freak he was, a nonce like. — Niall Griffiths, *Sheepshagger*, p. 55–56, 2001

2 a police informer, someone who betrays a criminal enterprise *UK*
- We wanted to show that nonce where it was really at; that we were one firm not to be fucked with. — Lanre Fehintola, *Charlie Says...*, p. 130, 2000

3 a fool *UK*
- I'm such a nonce. — *Smack the Pony*, 26th December 2002

nonch *adjective*
utterly relaxed, completely at ease *UK*
From 'nonchalant'. A Teddy Boy usage.
- — *News Chronicle*, 23rd May 1958: 'A glossary for our times'

nondy *noun*
a nondescript vehicle used by the police for maintaining a surveillance *UK*
A shortening of 'nondescript'.
- — *The Official Encyclopaedia of New Scotland Yard*, 1999

non-event *noun*
any unexciting or unsatisfactory event, especially one that fails to fulfill expectations *UK, 1962*
- It is hard to be triumphalist about a non-event[.] — *The Guardian*, 5th January 2003

nong *noun*
a fool *AUSTRALIA, 1944*
Shortening of **NING NONG**.
- — Wilda Moxham, *The Apprentice*, p. 77, 1969
- We're not in the bloody bush, you nong. — John O'Grady, *It's Your Shout, Mate!*, p. 15, 1972
- He wandered among the tables, which were all occupied by the usual assortment of tarts, lairs, nongs, louts, touts and crooked coots. — Lance Peters, *The Dirty Half-Mile*, p. 148, 1979
- — David McGill, *David McGill's Complete Kiwi Slang Dictionary*, p. 77, 1998

non-goer *noun*
a racehorse that is not being run to win *AUSTRALIA*
- Knowing that the horse was a non-goer, the bookie was able to offer better odds and so attract a bigger share of the available money from the punters. — Joe Andersen, *Winners Can Laugh*, p. 148, 1982

nonhacker *noun*
a soldier who cannot keep up with his fellow soldiers; an ineffective, incompetent soldier *US*
Coined in Vietnam and used heavily there. Back-formation from **HACK IT** (to cope with).
- I'd like to know where they get some of them non-hacker and then I'd like to know how they ever got through that OCS. — Charles Anderson, *The Grunts*, p. 113, 1976
- And my orders are to weed out all non-hackers who do not pack the gear to serve in my beloved Corps! — *Full Metal Jacket*, 1987

non-heinous *adjective*
good *US*
- — *USA Today*, p. 1D, 5th August 1991: 'A sterling lexicon of the lingo'

no-no *noun*
1 something that ought not be done *US, 1942*
- "Did you do something, Mona?" "I was honest with a client. The Ultimate No-No." — Armistead Maupin, *Tales of the City*, p. 116, 1978
- "That's a no-no, bro." Johnny gave him the boy scout sign with both hands held high. "Profanity is not for us." — Piri Thomas, *Stories from El Barrio*, p. 5, 1978
- It was stifling in there, so we took off our shirts after we'd been boogying for a while. A major no-no. — Armistead Maupin, *Further Tales of the City*, p. 129, 1982
- That's a no-no, Billy Clyde. Can't plug another network. — Dan Jenkins, *Life Its Ownself*, p. 318, 1984
- I've never seen Crash so angry and frankly, Bull fans, he used a certain word that's a "no-no" with umpires. — *Bull Durham*, 1988

2 an impossibility; a failure; any negative outcome *UK*
Reduplication for stress.
- Whole thing will probably be a ghastly no-no, but everyone will be there. — Simon Brett, *Cast, in Order of Disappearance*, 1975
- Got to leave enough time to spring those contingencies if she deals me a no-no. — Diran Abedayo, *My Once Upon A Time*, p. 140, 2000

no nothing *noun*
nothing whatever *UK, 1884*
- [N]o commitment to join the ERM; no intervention; no change in interest-rate policy; no declaration of intent to lower it; no nothing. — *The Observer*, 30th April 2000

no-no war in never-never land *noun*
the US secret war against Pathet Lao communist forces in Laos *US*
- — Gregory Clark, *Words of the Vietnam War*, p. 458, 1990

nonproducer *noun*
a professional gambler who cannot be counted on to lose a great deal of money while gambling in a casino *US*
- During his stay, hieroglyphics are secretly appended to his name on the hotel register, which catalogue him as a "dropper" (businessman and heavy loser), "producer" (businessman), or "nonproducer" (professional gambler). — Ed Reid and Ovid Demaris, *The Green Jungle*, p. 2, 1963

nonseller *noun*
a plan that almost certainly will be rejected *US*
- — Department of the Army, *Staff Officer's Guidebook*, p. 63, 1986

non speaks *noun*
a state of having been excluded from society *UK*
An example of Eton College illiteracy.
- What other people called sending to Coventry, we called non-speaks. — Andrew Sinclair, *The World of the Public School*, 1977

non starter *noun*
something or someone that has no chance of success *UK, 1934*
- Boycotting national primary and secondary school tests was a legal "non-starter", a teaching union leader claimed today. — *The Guardian*, 5th May 2003

non trier *noun*
a racehorse that is not being run to win *AUSTRALIA*
- Those were the notorious days of crooked trotting practices – of ring-ins and nobbling, of non-triers and interference, of doping and bribery[.] — James Holledge, *The Great Australian Gamble*, p. 119, 1966
- He didn't mind being on a non-trier provided that the horse's connections declared it to be one. — Joe Andersen, *Winners Can Laugh*, p. 123, 1982

nontrivial *adjective*
extremely complex *US*
- It's really a nontrivial solution, but it works. — Andy Ihnatko, *Cyberspeak*, p. 138, 1997

no object
no obstacle, or, not an objection *UK, 1984*
In such phrases as 'distance no object' and 'money no object'.

noodenaddy *noun*
a dithering person; someone who is unable to make up their mind *IRELAND*
- My mother always called him a noodenaddy, but he has his own business now, so it proves people can change — Terence Dolan, *A Dictionary of Hiberno-English*, p. 186, 1999

noodle *noun*

1 the head; the brain; intelligence *UK, 1803*
- I mean using diplomacy, the old noodle. — Edwin Torres, *Q & A*, p. 55, 1977
- But I say he's getting ready for a job, thinking, planning, using his noodle. — Gerald Petievich, *Money Men*, p. 140, 1981
- You've got the noodles. You've got the know how. — Kevin Sampson, *Clubland*, p. 222, 2002

2 the penis *US, 1975*
- "You're just not getting enough?" "None! I got a limp noodle," he whispered. — Joseph Wambaugh, *The Glitter Dome*, p. 255, 1981
- I remembered that time she got boiling mad at me when I made a joke about Al Dante's firm noodle[.] — Rita Ciresi, *Pink Slip*, p. 13, 1999

noodle *verb*

1 to think, to ponder *US, 1942*
- How did I discover the VIP food storage lockers? Just noodlin' around with a trash bag over my shoulder, trying to look efficient. — Odie Hawkins, *Lost Angeles*, p. 102, 1994

2 to play music in a tentative, exploratory fashion *US, 1937*
- Next year you'll find me in Hollywood noodling for the sound tracks. — Ross Russell, *The Sound*, p. 207, 1961

noodles *noun*
brains, intelligence *UK*
An extension of **NOODLE**.
- You've got the noodles. You've got the know how. — Kevin Sampson, *Clubland*, p. 222, 2002

noodnik *noun*
▷ **see: NUDNIK**

noogie *noun*
a blow, usually repeated, to the head with a protuberant knuckle *US, 1972*
A hazing of youth. A recurring skit on *Saturday Night Live* in the 1970s vaulted the phrase 'Noogie Patrol' into great popularity, with a nerdish Todd DiLaMuca (played by Bill Murray) grabbing Lisa Lupner (played by Gilda Radner) for a rash of noogies.
- Here's those fall noogies you ordered! Black and blue is going to be a big color this year, my dear! — *Saturday Night Live*, 7th October 1978
- "Noogie time, noogie time," the morons chanted. — Seth Morgan, *Homeboy*, p. 325, 1990

nook *noun*
▷ **see: NUKE**

nook and cranny *noun*
the buttocks, the backside; the vagina *UK*
Rhyming slang for **FANNY**.
- I slipped on a banana skin and fell flat on me nook and cranny. — Ronnie Barker, *Fletcher's Book of Rhyming Slang*, p. 43, 1979
- You can't roll that tobacco, it's as dry as a nun's nook & cranny. — Ray Puxley, *Cockney Rabbit*, 1992

nookie; nooky *noun*
the vagina; hence a woman as a sex object; sexual intercourse *US, 1928*
- He wanted to be an accountant, and it troubled him that there was no accounting for the costs of nooky. — Bernard Wolfe, *The Late Risers*, p. 47, 1954
- "And speaking of that," Jefferson continued, "should you crave a little nookie while you're in town, just let me know." — Max Shulman, *Anyone Got a Match?*, p. 133, 1964
- Oh boy, I wonder who'd gimme some nookie. — Lenny Bruce, *The Essential Lenny Bruce*, p. 145, 1967
- She sure got hot nookie huh, Sy? — Nathan Heard, *Howard Street*, p. 70, 1968
- What's the matter – got some hot nooky lined up for this afternoon? — Terry Southern, *Now Dig This*, p. 33, 1975
- "Well," said Mona, grinning at him, "a little nookie does you a world of good." — Armistead Maupin, *Tales of the City*, p. 199, 1978
- It's a language unto itself, those romantic utterances made by couples sharing intimate moments of nooky bliss[.] — Anka Radakovich, *The Wild Girls Club*, p. 109, 1994
- We had nookie, so later we had no nookie, he's not always so good at nookie, runs out of steam, know what I mean? — Sally Cline, *Couples*, p. 87, 1998
- [H]e thought he'd get him some nookie upon returning[.] — Erica Orloff and JoAnn Baker, *Dirty Little Secrets*, p. 21, 2001

nookie wood *noun*
in logging, a core of wood soaked with sap and emerging from a rotted stump *CANADA*
- "nookie wood," known also as a pitch stick or pitch spike, was taken home by loggers, to start fires easily in the kitchen stove. Also known as skin wood. — Tom Parkin, *WetCoast Words*, p. 107, 1989

nooky-nooky *noun*
sex *US*
- Man, a whole lot of men have pulled time without digging another man's behind and I'd better get my mind on something else beside nooky-nooky. — Piri Thomas, *Seven Long Times*, p. 149, 1974

nooner *noun*
a bout of sex at about noon *US, 1973*
- And you think you can dance me into a porno movie for a nooner? — Joseph Wambaugh, *The Black Marble*, p. 101, 1978
- "Nooners, for Christ sake?" I said. "Coop, I'm middle-aged." — George V. Higgins, *Penance for Jerry Kennedy*, p. 207, 1985
- Keyes hated to admit it, but that's what covered the rent; he'd gotten damn good at staking out nooner motels[.] — Carl Hiaasen, *Tourist Season*, p. 19, 1986

no-pay *noun*
a person who refuses to repay a debt or loan *US*
- The sports book handle was so tremendous, day in day out, that nobody seemed to stop and think about the losses they were taking on, weak collections and no-pays. — Richard Condon, *Prizzi's Honor*, p. 283, 1982

nope

no, emphatically no *US, 1888*

- ELWOOD: Mind if we fill 'er up? Owner: Nope. I said we're outta gas. — *The Blues Brothers*, 1980
- GRAHAM: She didn't tell you why she was upset? CYNTHIA: Nope. — *Sex, Lies and Videotape*, 1989
- MARGE: I know you don't want to be an accessory to something like that. SHEP: Nope. — *Fargo*, 1996
- "I don't suppose he mentioned Loretta Ricci?" "Nope, not a word about Loretta.["] — Janet Evanovich, *Seven Up*, p. 33, 2001

no prob; no probs

no problem; no problems *AUSTRALIA*

- [W]henever I see a decent jam tart with a good set of top bollocks I'm in like Flynn, NO PROBS! — Barry Humphries, *Bazz Pulls It Off!*, 1971
- — Tom Hibbert, *Rockspeak!*, p. 109, 1983
- So when they blew it up, no prob. Evil is punished. — *Clerks*, 1994
- HITCHHIKER: Thanks for picking me up. TED: No prob. — *Something About Mary*, 1998
- LITTLE LEAGUERS: Can I have your autograph? NUKE: No prob, kids. — *Something About Mary*, 1998
- KAT: Look, I'm sorry that I questioned your motives. I was wrong. PATRIC: No prob. — *Ten Things I Hate About You*, 1999
- No probs. I've told her. — Kevin Sampson, *Outlaws*, p. 106, 2001

no problem

1 that is easy; do not worry about that; okay *AUSTRALIA*

A catchphrase of affable non-concern.

- 'I sure hope we can line up some long-haired chums at the *Gladstone*.' 'No problem.' — John Wynnum, *Jiggin' in the Riggin'*, p. 36, 1965
- — Barry Humphries, *A Nice Night's Entertainment*, p. 147, 1974
- 'Could we collect it here?' I said 'No problem, mate.' — Sam Weller, *Old Bastards I Have Met*, p. 43, 1979

2 you're welcome *US*

At some point in the 1980s, the term 'you're welcome' suddenly vanished from the vocabulary of America's young, replaced suddenly and completely with 'no problem'.

- STACY: Thanks for picking me up. RON: No problem. — *Fast Times at Ridgemont High*, 1982
- TEACHER: Thank you, Simone. SIMONE: No problem whatsoever. — *Ferris Buehler's Day Off*, 1986
- Yes, I'll make sure she's all right. Here's Suzanne. Bye now. No problem. — Sandra Bernhard, *Confessions of a Pretty Lady*, p. 100, 1988
- — Connie Eble (Editor), *UNC-CH Campus Slang*, p. 7, Spring 1991
- WEBB: Thank you for your time. ACE: No problem. — *Casino*, 1995
- COLONEL: Thank you, Eddie. DIRK: No problem. — *Boogie Nights*, 1997

no problemo

no problem *US*

A popular elaboration.

- No problemo. — *The Terminator*, 1991
- SKINNER: Er, one question remains: how do I get out of the army? BART: No problemo. Just make a pass at your commanding officer! — *The Simpsons*, 1994
- The loser retires from the field and runs around the house three times with his underpants on his head. No problemo. — John Birmingham, *He Died With a Felafel in his Hand*, p. 46, 1994
- We're going to the concert. No problemo. — Glyn Parry, *Mosh*, p. 63, 1996
- — Connie Eble (Editor), *UNC-CH Campus Slang*, p. 6, April 1997
- "Thanks for the doughnuts." "Hey, no problemo." — Janet Evanovich, *Seven Up*, p. 251, 2001

noras *noun*

breasts *AUSTRALIA*

- Another survey – this time by British bra makers – found that Pommy sheilas' baps are getting bigger and bigger and that soon the average girlie will sport enormous 38D-sized noras. — *Picture*, p. 9, 5th February 1992

nordle *noun*

marijuana *UK*

- The nordle from Thailand, Thai sticks, is some of the best in the world. — Howard Marks, *Mr Nice*, p. 169, 1997

Norfolk 'n' Chance *nickname*

used as a team name in light hearted contests *UK*

A barely euphemistic rendering of 'no fucking chance'; especially popular among quiz teams. Recorded in 1983 as the winners of the University of Essex Rugby 7's Plate.

no risk!

for sure; with certainty *AUSTRALIA*

- The people'd treat you just like one of their own, no risk. — Alexander Buzo, *Norm and Ahmed*, p. 18, 1969
- 'All I ask is bring her back in one piece, to my place before daylight.' 'No risk, Scooter,' Arnie said happily. — Wilda Moxham, *The Apprentice*, p. 87, 1969
- — Tom Hibbert, *Rockspeak!*, p. 109, 1983
- — Roy Slaven (John Doyle), *Five South Coast Seasons*, p. 35, 1992

nork *noun*

the female breast *AUSTRALIA, 1962*

The suggestion (originally in Baker, *The Australian Language*, 1966) that this derives from Norco, a popular brand of butter which at one time had a picture of a cow with an udder on the packaging, is as far fetched as it sounds, and yet it is the standard folk etymology for this term. Baker also records that 'the form *norg* is reported from Melbourne' and this variant is still in occasional use.

- [T]hen I organise a few nice little Antipodean horn-bags who don't mind flashing their norks in public and haven't got too many bruises on their bums, to mingle with the guests in clean G-strings, carrying trays of cholesterol-enriched Oz dairy produce. — Barry Humphries, *The Traveller's Tool*, p. 111, 1985
- Here she was with tits! And a cute little muff! Proudly proclaiming, 'I am woman, see my norks!' — *People*, p. 2, 5th July 1999
- — Paul Baker, *Polari*, p. 183, 2002
- J G, a university colleague, and a strapping popsy of some 5'10" who wore size 42 D, was always described as having magnificent norgs. She wouldn't have had it any other way. In Victoria the preference was for "norgs" rather than "norks". — *home.iprimus.com.au/glsealy/Forum.htm*, 2003
- Too busy gawping at Imogen Bailey's sandy norks last issue. — *FHM*, p. 28, June 2003

norm; normal *noun*

a *norm*al person; a dully conventional person *US, 1983*

- [T]here was some fellow feeling between us, a kind of esprit de corps against normal people. "The norms," Julian would call them dismissively. "Look at them all, norming about." — Jake Arnott, *He Kills Coppers*, p. 61, 2001

norm *verb*

to behave in an unremarkable or conventional manner *UK*

From **NORM** (an ordinary person).

- [T]here was some fellow feeling between us, a kind of esprit de corps against normal people. "The norms," Julian would call them dismissively. "Look at them all, norming about." — Jake Arnott, *He Kills Coppers*, p. 61, 2001

Normandy Beach; normandy *noun*

a speech *UK*

Rhyming slang.

- [T]he best man goes over the top with a "Normandy" designed to embarrass the bridegroom. — Ray Puxley, *Fresh Rabbit*, 1998

Norma Stockers *noun*

large female breasts *AUSTRALIA*

An intentional, humorous corruption of 'enormous **KNOCKERS**'.

- — James McDonald, *A Dictionary of Obscenity, Taboo and Euphemism*, p. 97, 1988

normie *noun*

someone who is not addicted to anything *US*

Used in twelve-step recovery programmes such as Alcoholics Anonymous.

- — Christopher Cavanaugh, *AA to Z*, p. 132, 1998

Norris McWhirter *noun*

diarrhoea *UK*

Rhyming slang for 'squirter', based on author Norris McWhirter (b.1925).

- — *www.LondonSlang.com*, June 2002

north and south *noun*

the mouth *UK, 1857*

Rhyming slang.

- plenty of dust floating about in the air, which gets in your north and south — Frank Norman, *Bang To Rights*, p. 29, 1958
- He was a truly ugly man – his north and south drooped, his mince pies were watery, and he had a big red I suppose. — Ronnie Barker, *A Sermon in Slang*, 1979

North Circ *nickname*

London's North Circular road *UK*

- [P]igs [police] from all over the North Circ. — Nick Barlay, *Curvy Lovebox*, p. 54, 1997

North End Round *noun*

bologna *CANADA*

- Winnipeg's North End is known as the ethnic area, and on the assumption that this area eats more bologna than steak, "North End round" is a name for bologna. Polish round. Ukrainian round. — Chris Thain, *Cold as a Bay Street Banker's Heart*, p. 107, 1987

norther *noun*

a strong, cold wind from the north *US, 1827*

A Texas phrase to describe a Texas winter weather condition.

- I don't know if many people outside of Texas know what a norther is, but a norther is when the sky turns the color of a battleship and you can feel the icicles stabbing you in the chest. — Dan Jenkins, *Semi-Tough*, p. 52, 1972

northern lights *noun*

1 in British Columbia, a local variety of marijuana *CANADA*

- [He] lit up a person favorite, a cross of two varieties, Northern Lights and Blueberry. — Brian Preston, *Pot Planet*, p. 2, 2002

2 a superior variety of hashish produced in Holland from northern lights marijuana pollen *NETHERLANDS*

- Northern lights is one of the legendary sensimillas, so it takes a while to get your head around the idea of a northern lights hash – probably about the time it takes to smoke a joint of the stuff. — Nick Jones, *Spliffs*, p. 92, 2003

Norwegian steam *noun*

brute physical exertion *US, 1944*

- — *Maledicta*, p. 171, 1979: 'A glossary of ethnic slurs in American English'

NORWICH

written on an envelope, or at the foot of a lover's letter as lovers' code for '(k)*n*ickers *o*ff *r*eady *w*hen *I* *c*ome *h*ome' *UK*

Widely known, and well used by servicemen but, apparently, has not transferred to the coded vocabulary of texting. Used by John Winton in *We Saw the Sea*, 1960.

nose *noun*

1 cocaine *US, 1980*

- Nadeau's wife, Helena, beautiful broad, had a disease, too. Cocaine. Two-hundred-dollar-a-day nose. — Robert Campbell, *Juice*, p. 23, 1988
- — Angela Devlin, *Prison Patter*, p. 80, 1996
- Bit of a drug fiend, I hear. Got a nose for nos. — Andrew Holmes, *Sleb*, p. 295, 2002
- Do you wan't this nose then? — Colin Butts, *Is Harry Still on the Boat?*, p. 159, 2003

2 in horse racing, any very short distance that separates winner from loser *US, 1908*

- — David W. Maurer, *Argot of the Racetrack*, p. 44, 1951

3 an informer *UK, 1789*

- — Angela Devlin, *Prison Patter*, p. 80, 1996

4 an innate ability to find things *UK, 1875*

- What they lack is a daring business man with a nose for a good investment[.] — *The Observer*, 1st February 2004

▷ **see: NOSEY**

▸ **get up your nose**

1 to annoy *UK, 1951*

- But what gets up my nose is that MI5, or whoever, is listening to my private conversations. — *The Guardian*, 29th March 2003

2 to irritate, to anger *US, 1968*

- Then some dippy blouse in a Volvo in front gets up my nose cos of the way she hits the brakes whenever a car comes down the opposite lane. — Nick Barlay, *Curvy Lovebox*, p. 53, 1997

▸ **get your nose bent**

to be convicted of a traffic violation *US*

- — *American Speech*, p. 269, December 1962: 'The language of traffic policemen'

▸ **get your nose cold**

to use and become intoxicated on cocaine *US*

- — Edith A. Folb, *runnin' down some lines*, p. 239, 1980

▸ **have a nose for (someone)**

to be sexually attracted to (someone) *US*

- Suppose I fix you up with Baby here. You always had a nose for her. — John Clellon Holmes, *The Horn*, p. 57, 1958

▸ **have your nose open**

to be strongly attracted to *US*

- That's what I intend to do, only trouble is m'nose opens up and I can't tell what I'm doing. — Jack Kerouac, *On the Road*, p. 257, 1957
- She a fox too. I think Jimmy strung out behind her. His nose is wide open. — Nathan Heard, *Howard Street*, p. 63, 1968
- What about that gray girl in San Jose who had your nose wide open? — Eldridge Cleaver, *Soul on Ice*, p. 9, 1968
- I only told him Glveadamn had my nose open and it wasn't a comfortable feeling. — Robert Deane Pharr, *Giveadamn Brown*, p. 13, 1978
- My nose is still open for that yellow, stinking, skunk, lousy, junkie 'ho. — Iceberg Slim (Robert Beck), *Airtight Willie and Me*, p. 104, 1979
- Most working girls were like that, their noses open wider than their cunts. — Seth Morgan, *Homeboy*, p. 7, 1990

▸ **keep your nose to the grindstone; put your nose to the grindstone**

to be (or start) studying hard, working hard *UK, 1828*

From earlier senses denoting harsh treatment.

- The branch manager gave everyone an update on the bank's overall targets, made a little pep talk, and all would be nose to the grindstone for the rest of the day: sell, sell, sell. — *The Guardian*, 22nd March 2003

▸ **on the nose**

1 exactly *US, 1883*

- This poem [by Saul Bellow] called Wonder hits it right on the nose. — *The Guardian*, 10th September 1997

2 in horse racing, a bet on a horse to finish first *US*

- — Robert Saunders Dowst and Jay Craig, *Playing the Races*, p. 166, 1960

3 (used of a person's bet in an illegal numbers gambling lottery) invariably the same *US*

- — *American Speech*, p. 192, October 1949

4 at the start of a song *US*

- — Arnold Shaw, *Dictionary of American Pop/Rock*, p. 267, 1982

5 smelly *AUSTRALIA*

- 'Christ! Alec,' he complained. 'This bait's a bit on the nose, ain't it?' — Kylie Tennant, *Lost Haven*, p. 86, 1946
- The pommie habit of wearing woollen socks with sandals has given a lot of our Brit visitors the reputation of being on the nose[.] — Barry Humphries, *The Traveller's Tool*, p. 32, 1985

6 (used of ocean water) polluted *AUSTRALIA*

- — Trevor Cralle, *The Surfin'ary*, p. 83, 1991

7 recreational time spent under the influence of inhaled drugs *UK*

Compares with **ON THE TILES** (having a good time under the influence of alcohol).

- [Opiates] will also soothe your nerves after an E too many or a night on the nose – at least that's what my friends tell me. — Julian Keeling, *Drugstore Cowboy [The Howard Marks Book of Dope Stories]*, p. 115, 1996

▸ **put your nose out of joint**

to annoy, to upset your plans, to inconvenience, to disconcert *UK, 1576*

- [It] would hardly put Washington's nose out of joint for the leader of the British Lib Dems to criticise President Bush[.] — *The Guardian*, 26th September 2002

▸ **shove your nose in; stick your nose in**

to interfere, to interpose rudely *UK, 1887*

- What on earth do they think they're doing, sticking their nose in our business? — *The Guardian*, 8th November 2000

nose *verb*

to curry favour through obsequious conduct *US*

A shortening of **BROWN-NOSE**.

- — Collin Baker et al., *College Undergraduate Slang Study Conducted at Brown University*, p. 163, 1968

nose and chin *noun*

a win, a winning bet *UK*

- — Julian Franklyn, *A Dictionary of Rhyming Slang*, 1960
- — Ray Puxley, *Cockney Rabbit*, 1992

nose around *noun*

▷ **see: NOSEY**

nosebag *noun*

1 a lunch box or paper bag with lunch inside *UK, 1873*

- — Jerry Robertson, *Oil Slanguage*, p. 87, 1954
- — Ramon Adams, *The Language of the Railroader*, p. 105, 1977

2 a take-away restaurant, a chip shop *UK*

- — Peter Chippindale, *The British CB Book*, p. 157, 1981

3 a plastic bag used for solvent abuse *UK*

- — Angela Devlin, *Prison Patter*, p. 80, 1996

4 cocaine *UK*

- 20-odd bottles of champagne, untold pills and a good ounce or so of nosebag. — Wayne Anthony, *Spanish Highs*, p. 19, 1999
- Call it your commission on the nosebag. — Colin Butts, *Is Harry Still on the Boat?*, p. 160, 2003

5 in electric line work, a canvas tool pouch *US*
- — A.B. Chance Co., *Lineman's Slang Dictionary*, p. 12, 1980

▸ **put on the nosebag**
to have a meal *AUSTRALIA*
- It sure put us off donning the nosebag. — Roy Slaven (John Doyle), *Five South Coast Seasons*, p. 7, 1992

nosebleed *noun*
a stupid, inept person *US*
Teen slang.
- — *Newsweek*, p. 28, 8th October 1951

nosebleeder *noun*
a heavy user of cocaine by nasal inhalation *UK*
From a physical side-effect experienced by users.
- So obviously being a nose-bleeder from way back I was convinced that this was a sting, right? — Ben Elton, *High Society*, p. 73, 2002

nosebleeds *noun*
the highest seats in an auditorium or a stadium *US, 1978*
Because high altitudes can cause nosebleeds.
- — Judi Sanders, *Cal Poly Slang*, p. 7, 1990
- — David Shenk and Steve Silberman, *Skeleton Key*, p. 207, 1994

nose-burner; nose-warmer *noun*
the still-lit butt of a marijuana cigarette *US*
- — Victor H. Vogel and David W. Maurer, *Narcotics and Narcotic Addiction*, p. 429, 1973

nose candy *noun*
cocaine or, rarely, another powdered drug that can be snorted *US, 1925*
- First thing, the nose candy kids'll be tryin' for the tap. — Mickey Spillane, *Me, Hood!*, p. 40, 1963
- 'All you have to do, see about the grass and some candy.' What? I go, Candy? He goes, 'Nose candy, dummy. They like to have a little gig after, you understand?' — Elmore Leonard, *Touch*, p. 29, 1977
- Superman's brother got pinched for possession of nose candy. — Gerald Petievich, *To Die in Beverly Hills*, p. 62, 1983
- We've been doing nose candy all night. — Armistead Maupin, *Babycakes*, p. 279, 1984
- — Nick Constable, *This is Cocaine*, p. 181, 2002

nose drops *noun*
liquefied heroin; liquefied methadone *UK, 1998*
- — Mike Haskins, *Drugs*, p. 284, 2003

no-see-um *noun*
any small, nearly invisible insect that bites *US, 1842*
- — Robert O. Bowen, *An Alaskan Dictionary*, p. 24, 1965
- No-see-ums are called many different things, mostly unprintable. — Mark Wheeler, *Half Baked Alaska*, p. 104, 1972
- Wiley swatted no-see-'ems in the darkness for three hours until he heard the hum of a passing motorboat. — Carl Hiaasen, *Tourist Season*, p. 359, 1986
- The bain of all those who venture into the bush, "noseeums" are also known across much of Canada, but they were named by the Indians and appear to be at their worst in the western bush. — Chris Thain, *Cold as a Bay Street Banker's Heart*, p. 107, 1987
- [A] number of kids had lit strips of newspaper, making a game of swirling them in loops, trying to smoke away the mosquitoes and no-see-ums. — Richard Price, *Clockers*, p. 384, 1992
- — Mike Doogan, *How to Speak Alaskan*, p. 46, 1993

nosefull *noun*
a strong dose of a powdered drug that is snorted *US*
- No, you my man, only man I know can do it cool, without a nosefull. — Elmore Leonard, *Gold Coast*, p. 22, 1980

nose garbage *noun*
poor quality cocaine *US*
- LEE: I have to hand it to you, this is not nose garbage, this is quality. — *True Romance*, 1993

nose hose *noun*
the tubing used for nastrogastic intubation *US*
- — Sally Williams, *"Strong" Words*, p. 152, 1994

nose job *noun*
cosmetic surgery to enhance the nose *US*
Combines a conventional 'nose' with **JOB** (a medical procedure).
- She's admitted that she lived with Rubirosa – and brags about her boyfriends, but any mention of her age or nose job and she gets hysterical. — Lee Mortimer, *Women Confidential*, p. 83, 1960
- "Bullshit, he's too good-lookin' for a Hebe." "Maybe he got a nose job," countered Perry. — Richard Price, *The Wanderers*, p. 27, 1974

nose kiss *noun*
a head butt *UK*
- He got my hair, pulled up my Judge Dread [head] lined for the butt. Aimed. I heard someone got stiffed off a nose kiss one time. — Jeremy Cameron, *Brown Bread in Wengen*, p. 41, 1999

nose out *verb*
to discover by searching *UK, 1630*
- Some slither quite naturally from [political] party to party, nosing out where power is. — *The Guardian*, 8th July 1988

nose packer *noun*
a cocaine user *US*
- Bruce O'Hara is probably a dope addict, like everybody else in Hollywood. A nose-packer. — Gerald Petievich, *Shakedown*, p. 115, 1988

nose paint *noun*
any alcoholic drink *UK, 1880*
From its effect (as mentioned by the Porter in Shakespeare's *Macbeth*) on the colour of a serious drinker's nose.

nose-picking speed *noun*
an extremely slow pace *US*
US naval aviator usage.
- — *United States Naval Institute Proceedings*, p. 108, October 1986

nose powder; nose stuff *noun*
cocaine, or any other drug that has been powdered for inhalation *US, 1936*
- — Richard A. Spears, *The Slang and Jargon of Drugs and Drink*, p. 363, 1986
- — Mike Haskins, *Drugs*, p. 281, 2003

noser *noun*
an informer *US*
- — William K Bentley and James M. Corbett, *Prison Slang*, p. 36, 1992

nose-ride *verb*
in surfing, to ride on the front of the board *US*
- I've admired your nose-riding for years. — *Apocalypse Now*, 1979

nose-up *noun*
cocaine-taking as a cultural activity *UK*
- You ain't out spunkin your dough down the clubs trying to impress some old sploshers, pissed and on the powder, having the big nose-up. — J.J. Connolly, *Layer Cake*, p. 49, 2000

nosey; nose; nose around *noun*
an act of casual surveillance or inquisition *UK, 1984*
- Ooh, I've allus wanted a nosey in men's bogs. — *The Full Monty*, 1997
- Human nature, I guess, like slowing down to have a good nosey when you pass a big car smash. — Dave Courtney, *Stop the Ride I Want to Get Off*, p. 195, 1999

Nosey O'Grady *noun*
an inquisitive person, usually female *CANADA, 1981*

Nosey Parker; Nosy Parker *noun*
a personification of inquisitiveness *UK*
From **NOSEY** (inquisitive), first recorded in a captioned illustration in 1907. Various etymologies suggest links with peeping Toms and eavesdroppers at the Great Exhibition in Hyde *Park*, a link with Archbishop of Canterbury Matthew *Parker* (1504–75) or the characteristics of rabbits in *parks*. Whatever its true origins 'Nosey Parker' is the source of 'nosey-parkering' (being inquisitive); 'nosey-park' (to be inquisitive); 'nosey-parkerdom', 'nosey-parkery', 'Nosey-Parkerism' (the condition of an inquisitive nature or a demonstration of invasive inquisitiveness); 'nosey-parkerishness' (a tendency towards inquisitive behaviour).
- It was too open and there was no telling what Nosy Parker might be watching from behind some curtained window[.] — Chester Himes, *Come Back Charleston Blue*, p. 49, 1966
- A further gaggle of nosey-parkers stood around waiting for something to happen[.] — Greg Williams, *Diamond Geezers*, p. 203, 1997

nosh *noun*
1 food *US, 1951*
From Yiddish, ultimately German *nachen* (to eat slyly), since early 1960s.
- Indian nosh at a little gaff in Earls Court[.] — Derek Raymond (Robin Cook), *The Crust on its Uppers*, p. 55, 1962
- They keep you clean, and give you nosh, and give you clothes[.] — Mike Stott, *Soldiers Talking, Cleanly*, 1978

- [S]ome of the Indian and Pakistani kids spoon their own: nosh that looks strange[.] —Andrea Ashworth, *Moretti's Super-Swirl*, p. 71, 1999

2 an act of oral sex on a man or, perhaps, a woman *UK*
A punning adoption of the previous sense.
- One thing I cannot stand is a girl looking up at us while she's giving us a nosh. —Kevin Sampson, *Outlaws*, p. 136, 2001
- This dirty minger was giving me a nosh in an alleyway[.] —*Mixmag*, p. 68, April 2003

nosh *verb*

1 to eat; to nibble *US, 1947*
From Yiddish.
- —Connie Eble (Editor), *UNC-CH Campus Slang*, p. 5, March 1979
- A picnic and Chick Ottens noshing bar-b-q'd chicken with his snazzy new face. —James Ellroy, *Hollywood Nocturnes*, p. 260, 1994

2 to perform oral sex *UK*
From the more familiar sense 'to eat'.
- Elaine stubbed her fag out and sunk under the duvet to nosh amicably on his morning glory. —Garry Bushell, *The Face*, p. 105, 2001
- —Paul Baker, *Polari*, p. 184, 2002

3 to kiss in a sustained fashioned *US*
- —Linda Meyer, *Teenspeak!*, p. 30, 1994

no shame!
you act as if nothing embarrasses you! *US*
Hawaiian youth usage.
- —Douglas Simonson, *Pidgin to da Max*, 1981

nosher *noun*
an eater *UK, 1957*
From **NOSH** (to eat).
- Now the local bagel shop has a frequent nosher program. —Jack Trout, *Differentiate or Die*, p. 31, 2000

no shit!
used as emphasis that what has just been said is true *US, 1960*
- —John Ayto, *The Oxford Dictionary of Slang*, p. 340, 1998
- Eddie grinned. "No shit." —Janet Evanovich, *Seven Up*, p. 95, 2001
- "This isn't your scene is it, darling? [...] Pity, you'd have made a luscious mid-period Patti Smith." "No shit!" I said, horrified. —Liza Cody, *Queen of Mean [Tart Noir]*, p. 80, 2002

no shit, Dick Tracy!
used for pointing out that another person has just made an obvious statement *US*
A variant of the more common allusion to Sherlock Holmes, this based on the US cartoon detective.
- "Rats run up inside walls," Proctor said. "No shit, Dick Tracy," Fein said. —George V. Higgins, *The Rat on Fire*, p. 60, 1981

no shit, Sherlock!
used for pointing out that another person has just made an obvious statement *US*
Sherlock Holmes extends **NO SHIT!**.
- —Pamela Munro, *U.C.L.A. Slang*, p. 62, 1989
- RIFF-RAFF: You're wet. JANET: Yes, it's raining. *No shit, Sherlock[.]* —Sal Piro and Michael Hess, *The Official 'Rocky Horror Picture Show' Audience Participation Guide*, p. 14, 1991
- [M]y comments didn't fit a family format. No shit, Sherlock. —Howard Stern, *Miss America*, p. 271, 1995
- "I'm never gonna be able to pay you back." "No shit, Sherlock." —Stephen J. Cannell, *The Tin Collectors*, p. 265, 2001

no-show *noun*
a non-appearance at an appointed time or place *US, 1957*
- [F]ind out why he pulled a no-show on his hearing yesterday. —Janet Evanovich, *Seven Up*, p. 4, 2001

nosh up; nosh *noun*
a meal, a period of eating, meal time *UK*
After **NOSH** (to eat).
- So we has a nosh up, of bacon and eggs and some tinned meat we found. —John Peter Jones, *Feather Pluckers*, p. 17, 1964
- —Angela Devlin, *Prison Patter*, p. 80, 1996

no sir; nossir
used for registering a strong refusal or denial *US, 1856*
- They've become alcoholics, you know, and a lot of them have even turned queer. Not me. Nossir. —*News Herald*, 25th October 1998
- "What like to emigrate?" "Huh?" "To go and live there?" "To go and live there, no sir." —*The Guardian*, 22nd May 2004

no siree; no siree, Bob
absolutely no *US, 1848*
- I couldn't do that. No siree, bob, you little nut. —*Lethal Weapon*, 1987
- This ain't gonna happen! You people will not be allowed to put quality radio shows on our air waves, no siree bob! —Odie Hawkins, *Lost Angeles*, p. 141, 1994
- She'd certainly learn her lesson now. No more stepping out of line for that one, no sirree. —Christopher Brookmyre, *Boiling a Frog*, p. 4, 2000
- I don't believe in generating stacks of wealth for others as a result of my own brilliance. No siree. —Kevin Sampson, *Clubland*, p. 36, 2002

no soap
used for signifying that the deal is off, not a hope, you're wasting your time *US, 1926*
- I tried to get transferred to a day job, but it was no soap. —Jim Thompson, *Bad Boy*, p. 405, 1953
- Terry and I tried to find work at the drive-ins. It was no soap anywhere. —Jack Kerouac, *On the Road*, p. 86, 1957
- They all gave me the same answer after they saw the medical report on me. The answer was no soap. —John Knowles, *A Separate Peace*, p. 182, 1959

no sound, no picture *noun*
a person who does not appear for an appointment *SINGAPORE*
- —Paik Choo, *The Coxford Singlish Dictionary*, p. 77, 2002

no squash *noun*
irreparable brain damage *US*
- —*Maledicta*, p. 68, Summer/Winter 1978: 'Common patient-directed pejoratives used by medical personnel'

nostril *noun*
in horse racing, any very short distance between winner and loser that is shorter even than a nose *US*
- —David W. Maurer, *Argot of the Racetrack*, p. 44, 1951

no surrenders *noun*
suspenders *UK*
Rhyming slang.
- —Bodmin Dark, *Dirty Cockney Rhyming Slang*, 2003

no sweat
no problem; no need to worry *US, 1955*
Therefore no sweat will be produced by fear or exertion.
- —*Washington Post*, 23rd April 1961: 'Man, dig this jazz'
- —*American Speech*, p. 119, May 1963: 'Air refueling words'
- JOHN: Don't you have some homework or somethin' to do? CAROL: No sweat. My mother does it. —*American Graffiti*, 1973
- I said to Titch, the driver, "You will bring us in with the door on the kerb-side, won't you?" "No sweat." —Chris Ryan, *Stand By, Stand By*, p. 69, 1996

no-sweat pill *noun*
a potent anti-bacterial pill *US*
- Remorse hit him the next morning; he went to the flight surgeon, asked for and got some "No Sweat" pills guaranteed to be good for what ailed you, no matter what secret Asian problem that was. —Walter J. Boyne and Steven Thompson, *The Wild Blue*, p. 476, 1986

Nosy Parker *noun*
▷ **see:** NOSEY PARKER

not!
used as a humorous cancellation of what has just been said in jest *US, 1893*
Coined a hundred years before it was broadly popularised by Mike Myers in the 'Wayne's World' sketches on *Saturday Night Live*.
- —Connie Eble (Editor), *UNC-CH Campus Slang*, p. 6, November 1990
- I love the suburbs. Not! —*Wayne's World*, 1992
- 'Yeah, but you've got a boyfriend now.' 'Not,' I said, emphatically, appropriating one of her more asinine pop phrases. —Armistead Maupin, *Maybe the Moon*, p. 226, 1992

not a dry seat in the house
used of a theatre audience that is helpless with laughter or a male audience that is sexually aroused *UK, 1974*
A blend of the drama critic's cliché: 'not a dry eye in the house', and **PISS YOURSELF** (to laugh uproariously).
- Tonight! / You're hot, you take all we got, not a dry seat in the house / Next day, we'll be on our way / Tonight I'm gonna rock you / Tonight! —Spinal Tap, *Tonight! I'm Gonna Rock You Tonight*, 1974

not a hundred miles from *adjective*
very close to *UK, 1821*
• My first call, not a hundred miles from Shoreditch Church, was typical of them all. —Charles Raven, *Underworld Nights*, p. 127, 1956

no-talent assclown *noun*
a socially inept person *US*
From the film *Office Space*.
• —Connie Eble (Editor), *UNC-CH Campus Slang*, p. 7, October 2002

not all there *adjective*
slightly mad, mentally or intellectually disadvantaged *UK, 1864*
• The kind of mistake someone might make if they were a bit simple, a bit doo-lally. Not all there. —Andrew Holmes, *Sleb*, p. 142, 2002

not backward in coming forward
not shy *UK, 1830*
• He [Frankie Hejduk]'s not backward in coming forward but didn't show too much and was subbed for Cobi Jones in the second half. — *The Guardian*, 21st June 2002

not bad *adjective*
rather good, or (either patronisingly or with reservations) quite good *UK, 1909*
• Not bad for an "unknown". — *Sunday Herald (Glasgow)*, 30th November 2003

not bloody likely
used as an emphatic negative *UK*
First used in print (and, presumably, polite society) in George Bernard Shaw's play, *Pygmalion*, 1914.
• [A]n unambiguous rejection risks letting the government's line slide from "not yet" to "not bloody likely". — *The New Statesman*, 12th May 2003

notch *verb*
to wound *US*
Vietnam war usage.
• —Linda Reinberg, *In the Field*, p. 153, 1991

notchback *noun*
a car with a dent in its boot *US*
A play on the conventional 'hatchback'.
• —Lewis Poteet, *Car & Motorcyle Slang*, p. 140, 1992

notch up *verb*
to achieve *UK, 1837*
• Has any player during their career played at all 92 league grounds?" asks Mikey Watts. "If not, who's notched up the most?" — *The Guardian*, 26th September 2003

not cricket *adjective*
unfair *UK*
From the rigid rules of the game, but now always in phrases 'it's not cricket', 'that's not ...', etc.
• [Y]our husband's stuck in a barracks in Derry with nothing but a nudie book and his right hand, and possibly even getting shot at, too, well ... it's not bloody cricket, it it? Eh? —Mike Stott, *Soldiers Talking, Cleanly*, 1978

note *noun*
a one-pound note; the sum of £1 *AUSTRALIA, 1863*
Became obsolete in Australia after the introduction of decimal currency in 1966, but is still used in the UK.
• —Barry Humphries, *A Nice Night's Entertainment*, p. 41, 1960
• Stone the crows! That's highway robbery – that's nearly fifty notes where I come from – if I wasn't bustin' to splash the boots I'd do this Pom over – so help me! —Barry Humphries, *The Wonderful World of Barry McKenzie*, p. 3, 1968
• "You got the wonga, san [son]? Five hundred notes [pounds], right?" —Donald Gorgon, *Cop Killer*, p. 59, 1994
• Nicker, note, quid[.] —Brian McDonald, *Elephant Boys*, p. 203, 2000

note from mother *noun*
official permission *US*
US naval aviator usage.
• — *United States Naval Institute Proceedings*, p. 108, October 1986

no-tell motel *noun*
a motel with discreet management favoured by prostitutes and couples seeking privacy *US, 1974*
• [T]rowing hammerhead sharks into hotel swimming pools, blanket-tossing, building 40-foot high pyramids of empty beer cans on the beach and checking in and out of no-tell motels with handsome Ivy Leaguers. — *Washington Post*, p. B1, 20th April 1977
• It was a no-tell motel all right. It offered closed-circuit television with X-rated shows. —Joseph Wambaugh, *The Delta Star*, p. 186, 1983
• [S]he'd been at it ever since, up and down the coast from Tacoma to Tarzana; in massage parlors, for escort services, in no-tell motels, on street corners. —Seth Morgan, *Homeboy*, p. 4, 1990
• They played the one-room beer joints among the no-tell motels, pawnshops and liquor stores that line the city's shadieset thoroughfare. — *Phoenix New Times*, 11th December 2003

notes *noun*
▸ get good notes
in Quebec, to get good marks or grades *CANADA*
• —Victor Trahan, *The City of Montreal Style Guide*, p. n.p., 2002

not even
no, not at all *US*
• —Jonathan Roberts, *How to California*, p. 173, 1984
• —Pamela Munro, *U.C.L.A. Slang*, p. 62, 1989
• MURRAY: He's gay. CHER: Not even. — *Clueless*, 1995
• What? What are you talking about? I'm not even. — *Chasing Amy*, 1997

not fucking likely
used as an emphatic negative *UK, 1937*
• "He had an open chance, I could've got it in from there." "Not fucking likely, your random 'eaders'll go anywhere but in the net." —Jimmy Osborne, *Crossing the Borders*, 7th November 2000

not half *adverb*
used as a very positive intensifier of the verb to which it is attached *UK, 1851*
Usually as 'can't half', 'doesn't half', 'don't half', etc.
• Nana don't half give it some of that. (GESTURING WITH HIS HAND THAT SHE TALKS TOO MUCH) —Caroline Aherne and Craig Cash, *The Royle Family*, 1999

not half!
used for registering assent, approval, agreement, etc *UK, 1920*
• I grinned. "Not half. I mean, yes, sir." —Jake Arnott, *He Kills Coppers*, p. 145, 2001

not half bad *adjective*
quite good *UK, 1867*
• There's a twist, of course, reminiscent of Roald Dahl's Tales of the Totally Anticipated, but it's not half bad. — *The Guardian*, 30th April 2001

not having any; not having any of *adjective*
refusing to agree *UK, 1902*
• I asked him to come incognito, but he wasn't having any of that. — *The Guardian*, 17th June 1999

nothing *noun*
1 something *US*
Also shortened to 'nothin'. A reversal of sense on the model **BAD** (good); used in hip-hop culture.
• N[oreaga] – I'll jump in the crowd and suck a bitches titties and make her suck my dick after. It's nothing. It's nothing. LSD – It's nothing. N- It's nothing. — *Life Sucks Die*, Spring 2000
• What you wanna do, nigga? (Nothin') What you trying to do? (Nothin') —N.O.R.E. *Nothin*, 2002

2 no more than (the height specified) *AUSTRALIA*
Used to emphasise shortness.
• [He was] skinny as a rake with bulbous eyes, five feet nothing but as game as a terrier and cunning as a fox. —Frank Hardy, *The Outcasts of Foolgarah*, p. 162, 1971

▸ have nothing on
to be greatly inferior to something or someone *US, 1906*
• Stan and Ollie have nothing on Weymouth wits. The double act of chairman Ian Ridley and his manager Steve Claridge were the undoubted stars of BBC2's very funny Football Diaries. — *The Guardian*, 10th May 2004

▸ nothing shaking
nothing happening *US*
• [I]f a wop is deported he goes crazy. There's nothin' shakin' outside the U.S.A. —Edwin Torres, *Carlito's Way*, p. 86, 1975

▸ nothing to write home about; nothing worth writing home about
unremarkable *UK, 1914*
Probably military in origin.
• Moby's taste in literature is nothing to write home about, either. — *The Guardian*, 14th February 2003

▸ thank you for nothing!; thanks for nothing!
used in refusal or dismissal of help or advice: I owe you no thanks for that and scorn the offer *UK, 1969*
• "So Ish-Bosheth gave orders and had her taken away from her husband Paltiel son of Laish" 2 Samuel 3:15 [...] We can imagine her snarling, "Pish-posh, Ish-Bosheth! Thanks for nothing, brother of mine." —Liz Curtis Higgs, *Bad Girls of the Bible*, p. 206, 1999

▸ **you aint seen nothing yet!; you ain't heard nothing yet!**
no matter how impressive or extreme something may be there is better or worse yet to come *US, 1919*
A catchphrase made famous by the singer Al Jolson in the first 'talkie' film, *The Jazz Singer*, 1927. Especially popular with advertising copywriters.
- She looked at me with her big brown eyes and said / you ain't seen nothing yet... / .b-b-b-baby you just aint seen n-nothin yet / Here's somethin your just never gonna forget, / b-b-b-b- baby you just aint seen n-n-nothing yet. — Bachman Turner Overdrive, *Aint Seen Nothing Yet*, 1974

nothing *adjective*
inconsequential *US, 1960*
- — Frank A. Collymore, *Barbadian Dialect*, p. 77, 1965

nothing!
when combined with a (partial) repetition of a statement just made, used in denial of that statement *US, 1883*
- Dictionary of slang? Dictionary, nothing! It's just an excuse for a load of academic porn. — Partridge, 1984

nothing-ass bitch *noun*
used as a stern term of contempt for a woman *US*
- As he did, one of them called out after her – "nothin' ass bitch!" – to the laughter of his fellows. — Christina and Richard Milner, *Black Players*, p. 41, 1972

nothing but a thing *noun*
something that is not important *US*
- — Connie Eble (Editor), *UNC-CH Campus Slang*, p. 4, Spring 1993

nothing but the bacon!
used as a stock answer when greeted with 'what's shakin'?' *US*
- — *Philadelphia Evening Bulletin*, 11th November 1951

nothing but the bottom of the cup; nothing but the bottom of the net
used as a humorous comment on a job well done or a remark well made *US*
Coined by ESPN's Dan Patrick to describe a great shot in golf and basketball.
- — Keith Olberman and Dan Patrick, *The Big Show*, p. 22, 1997

nothing doing!
used as an expression of rejection or denial *UK, 1910*
- I asked him to lend me 5 but he said "Nothing doing"[.] — Paroo Nihalini, R.K. Tongue and Priya Hosali, *Indian and British English*, 1979

nothing flat *adverb*
very quickly *US*
- I went through the pile of chicken in nothing flat. — Mickey Spillane, *I, The Jury*, p. 51, 1947
- He got us to Mount Sinai in nothing flat. — Erich Segal, *Love Story*, p. 117, 1970
- I had only one thought – to get the hell out in nothing flat! — Red Rudensky, *The Gonif*, p. 90, 1970

notice *noun*
a contract to do a job, especially an illegal commission *UK*
- — G.F. Newman, *Sir, You Bastard*, 1970

no tilt!
used as a euphemism for 'no shit!' in expressing surprise or affirmation *US*
- — Tom Hibbert, *Rockspeak!*, p. 109, 1983

no time flat *adverb*
very quickly *US*
- We got there in no time flat. — Jack Kerouac, *On the Road*, p. 21, 1957

not in my name; not in our name
used worldwide by various humanitarian and anti-war protesters as a slogan of disavowal of prevailing attitudes *US*
'Not In My Name' (NITM) was adopted, in November 2000, as the name of a Chicago-based Jewish peace group opposed to Israel's occupation of Palestinian Territories.
- VOICE 1: The state says: VOICE 3: An eye for an eye. VOICE 2a: We say: VOICES: 2,4,5: Not in my name. [...] VOICE 1: The Judge says: VOICE 3: Lethal injection. VOICE 2a: We say: VOICES 2,4,5 and SUPPORTERS: Not in my name! — Living Theatre *Not In My Name (a Protest Play Against the Death Penalty)*, 1994
- Jews Gather To Organize Against Israel's Crackdown on Palestinians. "Not in My Name" — *Village Voice*, 16th–22nd May 2001
- When we see this barbarism, this criminality that Israel perpetrates [...] I am forced to say: Not in my name. — Ronnie Kasrils, *(Jewish) Cabinet Minister, South Africa*, 21st April 2002
- New Video Documentary ... "NOT IN MY NAME" A powerful new documentary film has been launched to tell the story of the US attack on Afghanistan.which we DIDN'T see on our television screens. — Norman Thomas, TV Choice, *Press Release*, March 2002
- President Bush has declared: "you're either with us or against us." Here is our answer: We refuse to allow you to speak for all the American people. We will not give up our right to question. We will not hand over our consciences in return for a hollow promise of safety. We say NOT IN OUR NAME. We refuse to be party to these wars and we repudiate any inference that they are being waged in our name or for our welfare. — over 55,000 signatories, *Not In Our Name, a Statement of Conscience*, 21st March 2003
- We believe that as people living / in Australia it is our / responsibility to resist the injustices done by our government, in our names. / Not in our name / will you wage endless war / there can be no more deaths / no more transfusions of blood for oil. — Ron Gray and 4,916 signatories, *Australian Peace Commitee*, 21st March 2003

not likely!
used for registering refusal *UK, 1893*
- — John Ayto, *The Oxford Dictionary of Slang*, p. 333, 1998

not many
yes, a term of emphatic agreement *UK*
- Is boredom a symptom of mental fatigue? / Not many — Ian Dury, *Jack Shit George*, 1998

not many benny
a great deal, a lot; an intensifying agreement *UK*
- "I'm starting to lose fuckin' patience with him," I says. "Lose patience, not many benny. He'll end up going completely fuckin' mad with Roy, seeing fuckin' cozzers [police] every fuckin' where." — J.J. Connolly, *Know Your Enemy [britpulp]*, p. 151, 1999

not much to look at *adjective*
unattractive, ugly *UK, 1861*
- Well, he's not much to look at, but he's got a great personality[.] — Jeramy Clark and Jerusha Clark, *He's Hot, She's Hot*, p. 42, 2001

not off *adjective*
of a horse – or, more precisely, of a jockey – that is considered not to be trying to win a race *UK*
- — John McCririck, *John McCririck's World of Betting*, p. 61, 1991

not on *adjective*
unacceptable; impossible; not permissible *UK*
- You don't abuse your house guests, Phoebe. It's not on. I mean come to grips. — Ian Pattison, *Rab C. Nesbitt*, 1988

not on your life!
used for registering emphatic refusal or denial *US, 1896*
- Can you remember, let alone describe, one outstanding shot from one [snooker] world championship to the next? Not on your life. — *The Guardian*, 4th May 2004

not on your nelly
used as an absolute denial, refusal or rejection *UK, 1941*
Rhyming slang, 'not on your Nellie Duff' for **PUFF** (breath, hence life), thus **NOT ON YOUR LIFE!**.
- "Wish us luck." "Not on your nelly, mate," she intones, "do you mind!" — Derek Raymond (Robin Cook), *The Crust on its Uppers*, p. 61, 1962
- "It's a big wagon is it?" Kilroy said. "Not on your nelly – it's a five-tonner." — Troy Kennedy Martin, *Z Cars*, p. 145, 1962

no-top *noun*
a convertible with its top down *US*
- — "Slingo", *The Official CB Slang Dictionary Handbook*, p. 43, 1976

not Pygmalion likely!
not very likely! *UK, 1948*
Formed on the shocking-in-its-day 'Not bloody likely!' in George Bernard Shaw's play *Pygmalion*, first seen in London in 1914.
- Would they shout for him to stand trial for treason, this Cold War criminal? Not Pygmalion likely. — John E. Gardner, *Day of Absolution*, 2000

no-trump *noun*
a life prison sentence without chance of parole *US*
- — John R. Armore and Joseph D. Wolfe, *Dictionary of Desperation*, p. 41, 1976

not the full quid *adjective*
lacking *NEW ZEALAND*
• —Louis S. Leland, *A Personal Kiwi-Yankee Dictionary*, p. 71, 1984

nottie *noun*
an unattractive person *US*
A back-formation from **HOTTIE** (an attractive person).
• —Connie Eble (Editor), *UNC-CH Campus Slang*, p. 8, October 2002

not tonight, Josephine!
a catchphrase used by a man to defer his sexual duties to a wife or lover; hence, applied to any postponement *UK, 1960*
Originally a quotation, apocryphally attributed to Napoleon dashing his mistress' hopes. In its current sexual context there is obviously a reliance on jocularity of delivery to deflect any serious subtext. Familiar from a music hall poem: 'I'll tell you in a phrase, my sweet, exactly what I mean: / . . . Not tonight, Josephine' (Colin Curzon, 'Not Tonight, Josephine').
• [Gordon] Brown, too, believes that one day we will be in the euro-zone. He is a "not tonight, Josephine" man, a chancellor with a headache, not a "never" man.—*New Statesman*, 12th November 2001

noughties *noun*
the years 2000 through to 2009 *UK*
• The drink [VRB] is to the Noughties what absinthe was to 1890s France—*GQ*, p. 68, July 2001
• [F]rom the early Fifties to the early Noughties[.]—*Uncut*, p. 110, May 2001
• [S]talking – erotomania, delusional behaviour: whatever we're calling it in the name-it noughties[.]—Andrew Holmes, *Sleb*, p. 124, 2002
• A new survey claims many young professional women in 'The Noughties' decade enjoy pornography and are happy visiting lap-dancing clubs.—*MX News*, p. 8, 5th April 2002
• The early Noughties, oddly, mirror the early Nineties' appetitie for American guitar rock.—*Uncut*, p. 88, May 2002
• In the 2000s (or noughties, oughties, or zips)[.]—*The Language Report*, p. 11, 2003
• True to its name, sex in the noughties seems to be a kinky business[.]—*Attitude*, p. 65, October 2003

novhere *adjective*
unattractive; unpleasing *US*
A mock German or Dutch accent.
• —*American Speech*, p. 304, December 1955: 'Wayne University slang'

Novie boat *noun*
a large, low cost lobster boat built in Nova Scotia *US, 1888*
• —Kendall Merriam, *The Illustrated Dictionary of Lobstering*, p. 62, 1978

now *adjective*
fashionable, in style, current *US*
• "Hey, man," said the stranger, "where you goin' with that here now cow?"—Steve Allen, *Bop Fables*, p. 55, 1955
• [L]ooking uncomfortable in an outdated suit, so outdated that it is almost Now again, and a pair of canary yellow pointed toe shoes.—Odie Hawkins, *Ghetto Sketches*, p. 52, 1972

now *adverb*
soon; in time; in a vaguely specified time *UK: WALES*
A stereotypical example of 'Wenglish' (a blending of English and Welsh typical of the valleys of southeast Wales).
• "I'll be going up to Murrayyfield for the match now, next month." or "I'll see to it now, when I get home..."—John Edwards, *Talk Tidy*, 1985

Now American Friends Take All *noun*
the North American Free Trade Agreement *CANADA*
Back-formation from the agreement's initials.
• NAFTA [is set up] so that now American friends take all. I knew there was a catch in that agreement.—*Toronto Globe and Mail*, p. D12, 3rd August 2002

now and thener *noun*
in horse racing, a horse that is an uneven or inconsistent performer *US*
• —David W. Maurer, *Argot of the Racetrack*, p. 44, 1951

no way!
used for expressing disbelief at that which has just been said *US, 1968*
• —*Current Slang*, p. 21, Spring 1970
• She wonderd if it was possible for her to have gotten a habit in such a short amount of time. "No way," she told herself over and over again, but why did she keep thinking about the dope she had in her purse then?—Donald Goines, *Dopefiend*, p. 31–32, 1971
• No day, no way. No can do.—George V. Higgins, *The Friends of Eddie Doyle*, p. 74, 1971
• —Eugene Landy, *The Underground Dictionary*, p. 140, 1971
• I said, "No-o-o way."—Stephen Gaskin, *Amazing Dope Tales*, p. 165, 1980
• "I suppose you have every reason to regard me as a certified nut case." "No way."—Armistead Maupin, *Further Tales of the City*, p. 162, 1982
• LINDA: I hear some surfer pulled a knife on Mr. Hand this morning. STACY: No way! He just called him a dick.—*Fast Times at Ridgemont High*, 1982
• TED: Whoa! Second base! BILL: No way!—*Bill and Ted's Excellent Adventure*, 1989

no way, Jose
used as a humorous, if emphatic, denial *US*
The catchy reduplication makes this a favourite early in a young person's process of slang acquisition.
• —Connie Eble (Editor), *UNC-CH Campus Slang*, p. 5, March 1981
• No way, Jose. First you have to get rid of this bald girl.—Jay McInerney, *Bright Lights, Big City*, p. 5, 1984
• Joe freaks at the badge and cocked magnum in his face and starts blabbing how a hitchhiker left the stuff in the trunk. No way, Jose, the cop said.—James Ellroy, *Suicide Hill*, p. 597, 1986
• No way, Jose, was I going to phone Carol's parents' house and reverse the charges.—Ken Lukowiak, *Marijuana Time*, p. 327, 2000

now cut that out
used as a humorous attempt to end a tease *US*
A signature line of comedian Jack Benny, heard often on *The Jack Benny Show*, 1950–65. Repeated with referential humour.

no what *adverb*
certainly not *SOUTH AFRICA, 1900*
Adapted from Afrikaans *nee wat*.
• —Penny Silva, *A Dictionary of South African English*, 1996

nowhere *adjective*
1 unaware of what is happening, extremely naive, utterly at a loss *US, 1843*
• —Arnold Shaw, *Lingo of Tin-Pan Alley*, p. 15, 1950
• I think trees are nowhere, and grass is about as dull as it can get.—Max Shulman, *I was a Teen-Age Dwarf*, p. 42, 1959
• Man, if you hadn't heard those spools of Royo Dehn's you were not with it at all, were as square as John Home from Rome, really nowhere.—Ross Russell, *The Sound*, p. 165, 1961
• "I'm sorry," I repeated, "but this scene is nowhere."—John Rechy, *City of Night*, p. 234, 1963
• ... he thought to himself, she was nowhere! I mean, she didn't even know what was happenin' to her when it was comin' down.—Donald Goines, *Inner City Hoodlum*, p. 88, 1975

2 badly defeated in a race; utterly unsuccessful, to be out of the running *US, 1853*
• Although he came nowhere in BBC2's Great Britons poll, [Benjamin] Franklin regarded himself as an Englishman until the war of independence began in his 70th year[.]—*The Guardian*, 27th September 2003

3 without money *GUYANA*
Usually in the phrase 'ain't nowhere'. Collected by Richard Allsopp.

▸ **get nowhere fast**
to try hard to do something and yet be frustrated in your endeavour *UK, 1984*
• [H]oards of disgruntled customers who attempt to complain to Europe's largest low-cost airline and get nowhere fast.—*The Guardian*, 7th January 2002

▸ **the middle of nowhere**
any place that is remote, any place that is an inconvenient distance away from urban 'civilisation' or your personal lifestyle requirements *UK, 1960*
• At first glance, the dreary rows of jerry-built sheds in the middle of nowhere look very much like sheds for factory-farmed animals[.]—*The Guardian*, 3rd January 2003

nowhereness *noun*
the state of complete unawareness of current trends or complete lack of grounding in reality *US*
• I had never seen such nowhereness, no s-h-i-t, why don't he just go somewhere and fade, um.—Jack Kerouac, *The Subterraneans*, p. 29, 1958

now it's time to say good-bye
used as a humorous farewell *US*
A catchphrase television sign-off on *The Mickey Mouse Club* (ABC, 1955–59). Repeated with referential and reverential humour.

now-now *adverb*

in the immediate past; immediately; very soon *SOUTH AFRICA, 1948*

Adopted from synonymous Afrikaans *nou-nou*.

- —Jean Branford, *A Dictionary of South African English*, 1978
- —*Lonely Planet Southern Africa*, 2000

now now

used as a gentle admonition to cease *UK*

- NURSE: Ah there you are Mr Hancock..TONY: Where did you expect me to be? NURSE: Now now. Cheeky monkey.—Ray Galton and Alan Simpson, *Hancock's Half Hour*, 28th June 1959

no worries

1 do not worry about that; everything is all right *AUSTRALIA*

- You'd be all right. No worries there. You could make your way in the world out here.—Alexander Buzo, *Norm and Ahmed*, p. 18, 1969
- 'What are we going to do, seriously,' Tramp asked his friends quietly, 'if Evan doesn't crack it for a win?' 'No worries,' said Evan.—Geoff Wyatt, *Saltwater Saints*, p. 82, 1969
- It's God's own country over there, NO WORRIES!—Barry Humphries, *Bazza Pulls It Off!*, 1971
- —Peter Corris, *Pokerface*, p. 100, 1985
- —Barry Humphries, *The Traveller's Tool*, p. 19, 1985
- Collingwood will win, no worries.—Frank Hardy, *Hardy's People*, p. 87, 1986
- No worries, Len me old son. You can rely on your number one man.—Robert G. Barrett, *Davo's Little Something*, p. 50, 1992
- —John Birmingham, *He Died With a Felafel in his Hand*, p. 128, 1994
- The only problem was that I could not work out whether it was beef or pork, so I therefore asked. 'No worries,' I was told. 'You've been eating grilled lizard!'—Rex Hunt, *Tall Tales – and True*, p. 11, 1994
- 'Was there something that you wanted?' 'No worries, Simpson,' I answered.—Dirk Flinthart, *Brotherly Love*, p. 61, 1995
- 'Cut it out, Chook, you'll get us in trouble,' I squirmed to him. 'No worries Bluey, they'll never know who's doin' it.'—Paul Vautin, *Turn It Up!*, p. 22, 1995
- —Paul Vautin, *Turn It Up!*, p. 67, 1995
- [personal ad] Just drop me a line with a photo and number and I'll get back to you. No worries, trust me, I'm good!—*Lesbians on the Loose*, p. 51, 1997
- —Pamela Munro, *U.C.L.A. Slang*, p. 93, 1997
- —David McGill, *David McGill's Complete Kiwi Slang Dictionary*, p. 76, 1998
- I'd like to invite you to the most dinky-di, ridgy didge, fair dinkum, no worries mate tournament that you could imagine.—*Australian Ultimate*, p. 7, 2003

2 you're welcome *US*

- —Connie Eble (Editor), *UNC-CH Campus Slang*, p. 7, Fall 2001

3 yes indeed; certainly *AUSTRALIA*

- I warmed to Truthful's theme. 'What about the Tax Summit. Were *they* behind that?' 'No worries. They and no other.'—Frank Hardy, *Hardy's People*, p. 35, 1986

nowt *noun*

nothing; a worthless person *UK*

Dialect word from northern England for conventional 'naught'; made popular by the televison programme *Coronation Street*, and in clichéd phrases such as 'nowt so queer as folk'.

- The assistant's seen him but done nowt.—Nicholas Blincoe, *The Beautiful Beaten-up Irish Boy of the Arndale Centre*, p. 9, 1998
- [A]ll of a sudden yew've got absolutely fuck all, no family, no home, no money, nowt.—Niall Griffiths, *Sheepshagger*, p. 11, 2001

now then!

used as a mild rebuke, or a call for attention *UK, 1791*

- Now then, now then, boys and bitches.—*The Guardian*, 21st March 2003

nowty *adjective*

moody, grumpy *UK*

Manchester dialect into wider use.

- You can't say anything in this house without having your head bitten off by that nowty sod.—Caroline Aherne and Craig Cash, *The Royle Family*, 1999

no wucking furries

do not worry about that! *AUSTRALIA*

An intentional Spoonerism of 'no fucking worries', both euphemistic and jocular. Also, in the shortened forms 'no wuckers' and 'no wucks'.

- All that was left to do was pot the black. She did this, no wucken furries at all.—Linda Jaivin, *Rock n Roll Babes from Outer Space*, p. 143, 1996
- 'Sorry, mate. Guess I wuz as full as a family poe [sic.].' 'No wucking furries, matey.'—*Sick Puppy Comix*, p. 13, 1997

now what?

can you top what I just said? *US*

- —Jim Goad, *Jim Goad's Glossary of Northwestern Prison Slang*, December 2001

now you're asking!

used in response to a difficult question *UK*

- "What we can't grasp," Susan said, "is why there's been a revolution in the first place. I mean – what brought things to a head so suddenly?" "Ah," Swann sighed. "Now you're asking."—Francis Clifford, *Acts of Mercy*, 1959

now you're railroading!

used on the railways as an all-purpose expression of praise *US*

- —Ramon Adams, *The Language of the Railroader*, p. 106, 1977

now you tell me!; now he tells me!

used when information that has just been supplied is given too late to be of use *US, 1969*

A Hebraism.

- He'd heard that Pat Kavanagh was last heard of working for Dave Danner. "Now he tells me."—Gavin Lyall, *Blame the Dead*, 1972
- "When did it happen?" "Two weeks ago." "Now you tell me?"—Blaine Littell, *The Dolorosa Deal*, 1973

nozzle *noun*

the penis *US, 1994*

- She sandwiches your nozzle between her tits, massaging it with a slow rhythm.—*Bunker 13 (excerpted in 'The Guardian' under the headline 'The Bad Sex award shortlisted passages')*, 4th December 2003

NRC *adjective*

(by police) *n*obody *r*eally *c*ares *US*

- Everybody jist wants to handle NRC calls and go home at shift change.—Joseph Wambaugh, *Fugitive Nights*, p. 95, 1992

'n stuff

used either as a substitute for 'et cetera' or to complete a sentence that has run out of steam *US*

- —Pamela Munro, *U.C.L.A. Slang*, p. 95, 2001

NT *noun*

in pornography, a scene showing nipple teasing (or torture) *US*

- —Ana Loria, *1 2 3 Be A Porn Star!*, p. 166, 2000: 'Glossary of adult sex industry terms'

NTBH *adjective*

unavailable for sexual encounters; ugly *UK*

Gay usage. The definition varies with the point of view; either way it is an acronym of 'not to be had'.

- —Paul Baker, *Polari*, p. 184, 2002

nu *adjective*

in rock music, new *UK*

- [O]ld and nu collide on genre mashing double-header [...] So if Soil represent the old then Adema must be the face of nu-nu-metal.—*Kerrang!*, p. 40, 20th April 2002

nub *noun*

the clitoris *UK*

- I was far too horrified by their sordid tales of throbbing love muscles and red-hot nubs of womanly passion.—Helen Hastings, *Are Friends Electra [Inappropriate Behaviour]*, p. 4, 2002

nubbies *noun*

short, matted hair on its way to growing into dreadlocks *JAMAICA, 1980*

- —Thomas H. Slone, *Rasta is Cuss*, p. 60, 2003

nubbin *noun*

1 the clitoris *UK*

Making 'rubbin' the nubbin' female masturbation.

- —Michelle Baker and Steven Tropiano, *Queer Facts*, p. 46, 2004

2 the penis *US, 1968*

- —Erica Orloff and JoAnn Baker, *Dirty Little Secrets*, p. 67, 2001

nub bush *noun*

a black female *US*

A shortened 'nubian' and a coarse **BUSH**. Vietnam war usage.

- —Linda Reinberg, *In the Field*, p. 153, 1991

nubian *noun*

in homosexual usage, a black man *US*

- — *Maledicta*, p. 53, 1986–1987: 'A continuation of a glossary of ethnic slurs in American English'

nuddy *adjective*

nude, naked *AUSTRALIA, 1953*

- On the way home we had a dip in the nuddy. — *The Adventures of Barry McKenzie*, 1972
- — Thommo, *The Dictionary of Australian Swearing and Sex Sayings*, p. 70, 1985
- — John Birmingham, *He Died With a Felafel in his Hand*, p. 34, 1994
- — David McGill, *David McGill's Complete Kiwi Slang Dictionary*, p. 77, 1998
- [W]hen he's nuddy on his knees scrubbin the bathroom floor[.] — Niall Griffiths, *Kelly + Victor*, p. 132, 2002

nude *adjective*

(used of a car) stripped of chrome *US*

- They are all, as Tom Wolfe has written, "nude and blind," because they've been stripped of chrome and their headlights are gone. — *San Francisco Chronicle (from the New York Times)*, p. 70, 2nd September 1977

nudge *noun*

in pinball, subtle physical force applied to the machine to affect the trajectory of the ball without activating the tilt mechanism *US*

- — Edward Trapunski, *Special When Lit*, p. 154, 1979

nudge *verb*

1 to nag; to annoy *US*

Yiddish. Various transliterations including 'nudzh', 'nudj' and 'noudge'.

- — Collin Baker et al., *College Undergraduate Slang Study Conducted at Brown University*, p. 163, 1968
- Shout he could shout, squabble he could squabble, and oh nudjh,, could he nudjh! — Philip Roth, *Portnoy's Complaint*, p. 44, 1969

2 to drink (alcohol) heavily *AUSTRALIA, 1979*

- Gwen was never much of a drinker, though her Auntie Kath who's a nun, really used to nudge the turps, and she used to regularly piss herself at Confession. — Barry Humphries, *The Traveller's Tool*, p. 26, 1985

3 in pool, to touch the cue ball with the cue stick accidentally while preparing to shoot *US*

- — Mike Shamos, *The Illustrated Encyclopedia of Billiards*, p. 157, 1993

nudge-nudge *adjective*

gossipy, especially of gossip with a sexual inference *UK*

From **NUDGE NUDGE – WINK WINK!**.

- Victims of a nudge-nudge culture. The number of those who are guilty until proven innocent is growing. — *The Guardian*, 18th January 2003

nudge nudge – wink wink!

used as an indicator of lust or an inference of lewd sexual behaviour *UK*

A catchphrase, originally 'nudge nudge – wink wink – say no more!', written by Eric Idle for BBC television comedy *Monty Python's Flying Circus* ('Is your wife a...goer...eh? Know what I mean? Know what I mean? Nudge nudge. Nudge nudge. Know what I mean? Say no more...know what I mean?'), 1969.

- Woman – a sexual object to be lusted after [...] whistled at on the silver screen and nudge nudge wink wink'd at in every comedy series. — *The Guardian*, 24th May 1979
- But even when I was little there was already a flip side to these legends [the 'Mayflower' Pilgrims], a cultural nudge-nudge, wink-wink, from adults and from sitcoms and movies[.] — Beth Harpaz, *Finding Annie Farrell*, p. 144, 2004

nudger *noun*

1 the penis *UK*

Remembered from the late 1960s by Beale, 1984.

- Did anyone ever find out what happened? To his knob, like? Why it was all mangled like that? [...] Some sheep playing hard to get. Snapped out at the end of is nudger. — Niall Griffiths, *Sheepshagger*, p. 99, 2001

2 a pickpocket *UK*

- — Angela Devlin, *Prison Patter*, p. 81, 1996

nudge show *noun*

a safe family comedy *US*

- Nudge shows are always viewed slightly askance by the industry but actors seldom turn down jobs in them and authors and producers wear smug little smiles as they bank their royalites. — Sherman Louis Sergel, *The Language of Show Biz*, p. 147, 1973

nudie *noun*

a performance or film featuring naked women but no sexual activity *US, 1935*

- Usually the "nudies," in contrast to the old-fashioned sun-bathing, nudist colony, sex-exploitation stuff, have a male actor as the central subject or star. — Michael Milner, *Sex on Celluloid*, p. 18, 1964
- Is he making nudies? girlie films? stag films? — *Porno Films and the People who make them*, p. 18, 1973
- Actually, I had done several nudies before doing Strangers, both as a director and working the crew. (Quoting Bob O'Neil). — *Adam Film Quarterly*, p. 48, August 1975

nudie *adjective*

featuring naked or near-naked women *US, 1966*

- To combat a group of religious zealots hounding her nudie magazine, a female publisher calls on several former centerspread models to seduce some of them. — Kent Smith et al., *Adult Movies*, p. 52, 1982
- Only a card-carrying shithead would show his face at a nudie joint in an election year. — Carl Hiaasen, *Strip Tease*, p. 11, 1993
- [H]e [Larry King] acted like she was a whore and he'd never drooled over a nudie mag in his life. — *The Village Voice*, 25th July 2000

nudie book *noun*

a men's magazine featuring pictures of naked women *UK*

- I gave him back his nudie book / I said I was sorry, I slung my hook[.] — Ian Dury, *Razzle in My Pocket*, 1977
- [Y]our husband's stuck in a barracks in Derry with nothing but a nudie book and his right hand[.] — Mike Stott, *Soldiers Talking, Cleanly*, 1978

nudie booth *noun*

a private enclosure affording privacy while a paying customer views a nude woman or nude women, usually through a glass partition *US*

- RANDAL: You've never been in a nudie booth? DANTE: I guess not. RANDAL: Oh, it's great. You step into this little booth and there's this window between you and this naked woman, and she puts on this little show for like ten bucks. — *Clerks*, 1994

nudie-cutie *noun*

a genre of sex film popular in the 1960s, featuring frolicking, cute, nude women *US*

- The sex exploitation film has long since replaced the "nudie-cuties" in the theatres that cater to adults across the nation. — *Adam Film Quarterly*, p. 13, November 1967

nudnik; noodnik *noun*

a pest, a fool *US, 1925*

- — Nathan Ausubel, *A Treasury of Jewish Folklore*, p. 732, 1948
- "I keep talking to myself." "Now, now," the doctor crooned, "that isn't such a bad habit. why, thousands of people do it" "But, doctor," protested Polanski, "you don't know what a nudnik I am!" — Leo Rosten, *The Joys of Yiddish*, p. 274, 1968
- Immediately that noodnick Penny Crone would broadcast my net worth all over Fox TV. — Howard Stern, *Miss America*, p. 354, 1995

nuff *adjective*

enough *US, 1840*

Once abbreviated, 'enough' could not be spelt 'nough' and understood, hence this phonetic variation. UK school dinner ladies in the 1960s accompanied their service with the question, slovened by repetition, 'nuff?'. Since the 1980s it has been widely used in the black community.

- [T]oday I know of one very bad thing the tea can do to you – it can put you in jail. "Nuff said." — Mezz Mezzrow, *Really the Blues*, p. 214, 1946
- Dem bloodclaat babylon lick down nuff yout' a'ready. — Donald Gorgon, *Cop Killer*, p. 111, 1994
- You don't want a girl that can't give you nuff conversation. — Diran Adebayo, *My Once Upon A Time*, p. 22, 2000

nuff respect

used as a greeting and to register admiration, assent or approbation *UK*

Misspelling of 'enough respect'. West Indian and UK black usage.

- It was signed "Nuff Respect, Phillip". — Donald Gorgon, *Cop Killer*, p. 49, 1994
- Shabs how y'doin'? says Nood stickin' his fist out. – Nuff respec', says Shabs bangin' an' slappin' Nood's fist[.] — Nick Barlay, *Curvy Lovebox*, p. 45, 1997

nuff said

used as an assertion that nothing more needs to be said *US, 1840*

- — Nina Simone, *'Nuff Said*, 1968
- I'm leavin lame niggaz brain dead / Aww fuck it, nuff said — Kool G. Rap & DJ Polo, *Nuff Said*, 1992

nug *noun*

1 a female *US*

• —Judi Sanders, *Faced and Faded, Hanging to Hurl*, p. 15, 1993

2 marijuana *US*
Variant 'nugs'.

• —Jim Emerson-Cobb, *Scratching the Dragon*, April 1997

nugget *noun*

1 a fool, an idiot, especially if prone to violent behaviour or mentally handicapped *US, 1990*
Figurative use of 'nugget' (a lump) for 'the head'.

• "Am I binned?" I said pitifully, remembering how I'd cocked up in the jungle with him. "No, you nugget, Get back on the helicopter[.]" —Andy McNab, *Immediate Action*, p. 117, 1995
• —Angela Devlin, *Prison Patter*, p. 81, 1996
• Nuggets are your bog-standard headcase. —Christopher Brookmyre, *Boiling a Frog*, p. 56, 2000

2 a new, inexperienced soldier or pilot *US, 1966*

• "I hope I don't get a nugget." A nugget was a new man on his first tour of duty. —Stephen Coonts, *Flight of the Intruder*, p. 121, 1986
• Thus, "Frogman" became his nickname as a nugget pilot in the fleet. —Joe Weber, *Defcon One*, p. 21, 1989
• As a rookie or "nugget," Ruliffson felt conspicuous and apprehensive. —Robert K. Wilcox, *Scream of Eagles*, p. 29, 1990
• Welch looked at Andrews and, beaming, said, "A couple of nugget jaygees! How about that, Sam?" —Gerry Carroll, *North S*A*R*, p. 58, 1991

3 an attractive girl *US*

• —Connie Eble (Editor), *UNC-CH Campus Slang*, p. 4, Fall 1998

4 a young enthusiast of heavy metal music *US*

• —Tom Hibbert, *Rockspeak!*, p. 110, 1983

5 an amphetamine tablet *US*

• —US Department of Justice, *Street Terms*, August 1994

6 a piece of crack cocaine *US*

• —US Department of Justice, *Street Terms*, October 1994

7 a one-pound coin *UK*
Prison slang, current February 2002.

nuggets *noun*

the testicles *US, 1963*

• Eyes like cold yellow stone at Mark, a regular Sonny Liston prefight hoodoo glare that would sizzle your average bleeding-heart radical's nuggets to a crisp. —John Sayles, *Union Dues*, p. 281, 1977

nuggety; nuggetty *adjective*

1 (of a person) compact, strong and tough; stocky *AUSTRALIA, 1856*

• —Leonard Mann, *Flesh in Armour*, p. 37, 1932
• —Gavin Casey, *It's Harder for Girls*, p. 13, 1941
• A very plucky, nuggety and tough Rugby League halfback. The harder the game got, the more he liked it. —Roy Slaven (John Doyle), *Five South Coast Seasons*, p. 177, 1992

2 (of an animal) small, sturdy and strong *AUSTRALIA, 1893*

• A nuggety fifteen-footer [crocodile] with a tremendous barrel was shot[.] —Ion L. Idriess, *Over the Range*, p. 197, 1947

nugs *noun*

1 female breasts *US*

• —Judi Sanders, *Mashing and Munching in Ames*, p. 14, 1994

2 great waves for surfing *US*

• —Trevor Cralle, *The Surfin'ary*, p. 81, 1991

nuisance *noun*

▸ **the nuisance**

the bleed period of the menstrual cycle *US*
Euphemism.

• —Karen Houppert, *The Curse*, 1999

nuisance grounds *noun*

a rubbish dump *CANADA*

• St. Rose [Manitoba] nuisance grounds Burning and Scavenging not permitted. —*town.sterosedulac.mb.ca*, 22nd July 2002

nuke; nook *noun*

a nuclear weapon *US, 1958*

• [T]here is "reason to believe" that "two Soviet-manufactured suitcase nukes may have fallen into bin Laden's hands." —John W. Dean, *Worse than Watergate*, p. 123, 2004

nuke *verb*

1 to attack with a nuclear bomb *US, 1962*

• The zealous citizens who sported "Nuke Iraq" T-shirts, or who patriotically roughed up people they took to be Arab-Americans. —Kelly Michelle Askew, *The Anthropology of Media*, p. 139, 2002

2 to lay waste, to ravage, to devastate *US, 1969*
A metaphorical, if less dramatic, sense.

• Part of the fun in preparing touring arrangements is nuking those norms. —Frank Zappa, *The Real Frank Zappa Book*, p. 185, 1989
• Something happened. You got nuked in the last quarter. —*Point Break*, 1991

3 to heat in a microwave oven *US, 1984*

• —Connie Eble (Editor), *UNC-CH Campus Slang*, p. 7, Fall 1988

4 in computing, to delete *US*

• —Eric S. Raymond, *The New Hacker's Dictionary*, p. 263, 1991

nuke and pave *verb*

to reformat the hard drive of a computer *US*

• —Don R. McCreary (Editor), *Dawg Speak*, 2001

nuke-and-puke *noun*

a microwave frozen dinner *US*

• —Connie Eble (Editor), *UNC-CH Campus Slang*, p. 6, November 1990

nuke-knob *noun*

a bald or shaved head *US*

• The labels were cruel: Gimp, Limpy–go-fetch, Crip, Lift-one-drag one, etc. Pint, Half-a-man, Peewee, Shorty, Lardass, Pork, Blubber, Belly, Blimp. Nuke-knob, Skinhead, Baldy. Four-eyes, Specs, Coke bottles. —*San Francisco Examiner*, p. A15, 28th July 1997

numba one *adjective*

▹ see: NUMBER ONE

numba ten

▹ see: NUMBER TEN

number *noun*

1 a person, particularly someone attractive, originally of a woman *US, 1896*

• [A] "number" is a potential or actual or merely desired partner in vagrant sex. —John Rechy, *Numbers*, p. 16, 1967
• Darling, there's nothing I love more than knowing that some big bitch number fancies my arse. Except, perhaps, letting him have it. —Simon Napier-Bell, *Black Vinyl White Powder*, p. 302, 2001
• [C]heck out the butch number over there! —Paul Baker, *Polari*, p. 184, 2002

2 a prostitute's client (especially in a male homosexual context) *US, 1967*

• I have three main trips – hustling, "numbers" and mutual contacts with certain people[.] —John Rechy, *The Sexual Outlaw*, p. 69, 1977

3 a casual sex-partner *US*

• —*American Speech*, p. 58, Spring-Summer 1970: 'Homosexual slang'

4 sex involving more than two people *US*

• —Kenn "Naz" Young, *Naz's Underground Dictionary*, p. 25, 1973

5 a situation *US, 1908*

• I'll do my New York number, and you do your Akrons and your Denvers. —Dan Jenkins, *Semi-Tough*, p. 201, 1972
• "Okay," he said, "now here's a funny number a couple of guys I know run from time to time." —Terry Southern, *Now Dig This*, p. 18, 1981
• An interesting number gets played out these days by fifty-year-old brothers who've had white women play prominent roles in their lives; some of them go into a deep denial mode. —Odie Hawkins, *Lost Angeles*, 1994

6 a job, a position *UK, 1948*

• So she got a number up west. Left home 8.20 in the morning[.] —Jeremy Cameron, *Brown Bread in Wengen*, p. 13, 1999
• [George W.] Bush, whose dad helped him book a cushy number in the Air National Guard —*The Guardian*, 8th April 2003

7 used as a vague catch-all susceptible of several meanings, usually related to sex or drugs *US*

• "I recognized him right away, because him and me did a little number last month on his houseboat in Sausalito." "A little number?" "Fucked." —Armistead Maupin, *Tales of the City*, p. 21, 1978

8 in prison, a sex offender; a convicted paedophile *UK*
Such prisoners are kept apart from the main body of the prison on rule *number* 43.

• —Angela Devlin, *Prison Patter*, p. 23, 1996

9 in craps, any roll except the shooter's point or a seven *US*
- He picked up the dice and throwed six numbers. — *The Annals of the American Academy of Political and Social Sciences*, p. 128, May 1950

10 a marijuana cigarette *US, 1963*
- They light another number, passing it around like tribal Indians. — John Rechy, *The Fourth Angel*, p. 22, 1972
- Think I'll roll another number for the road[.] — Neil Young, *Roll Another Number*, 1975
- [W]e both went to the "john" [lavatory] and knocked up a couple of numbers, which we put to good use before we hit the streets. — Ken Lukowiak, *Marijuana Time*, p. 94, 2000
- — Mike Haskins, *Drugs*, p. 288, 2003

11 a song *UK, 1878*
- When you take off on a number, it sounds as though you never know where you're going to come out, you just going flying off into musical space. — Mezz Mezzrow, *Really the Blues*, p. 330, 1946

▸ do a number on

1 to use emotional pressure, to humiliate *US*
- You really fucked me, Kim / You really did a number on me. — Eminem (Marshall Mathers), *Kim*, 2000

2 to kill *US*
- [S]he can pay back the money and a penalty, because she is Charley's wife and we don't do numbers on wives[.] — Richard Condon, *Prizzi's Honor*, p. 270, 1982

▸ have your number; get your number

to understand you, to know your weaknesses, to be in a position to criticise you *UK, 1853*
- Mr Horne: Yes, I was helping her with her career. Sandy: Oooh! Helping her, that's alright ducky, we've all got your number! — Barry Took and Marty Feldman, *Round The Horne*, April 1967

number 3 *noun*

1 cocaine *US, 1953*
c (cocaine) is the third letter of the alphabet.
- — Richard A. Spears, *The Slang and Jargon of Drugs and Drink*, p. 364, 1986
- — Mike Haskins, *Drugs*, p. 281, 2003

2 heroin *UK*
- — Mike Haskins, *Drugs*, p. 284, 2003

number 8; number eight *noun*
▷ see: 8

number 9 *noun*
MDMA, the recreational drug best known as ecstasy *UK*
- — Mike Haskins, *Drugs*, p. 290, 2003

number cruncher *noun*
a computer designed especially for arithmetic operations *UK, 1966*
- — Robert Kirk Mueller, *Buzzwords*, p. 115, 1974

number dummy; number grabber *noun*
a clerk in a railway yard *US*
- — Norman Carlisle, *The Modern Wonder Book of Trains and Railroading*, p. 266, 1946

numbered off; on the numbers *adjective*
in prison, used of sex offenders, convicted paedophiles, etc *UK*
Such prisoners are kept apart from the main body of the prison on rule *number* 43.
- — Angela Devlin, *Prison Patter*, p. 23, 1996

number four; number 4 *noun*
heroin *UK, 1998*
- — Robert Ashton, *This Is Heroin*, p. 206, 2002
- — Mike Haskins, *Drugs*, p. 284, 2003

number one *noun*

1 yourself, your own interests *UK, 1705*
- [H]e started off thinking of number one. — Robert Rossen, *All the King's Men*, 1949
- Take care of business; look out for number one – one way or the other there'll always be hustlers. — Edwin Torres, *Carlito's Way*, p. 81, 1975
- Hard from years of fights and self-defence and looking after number one. — Kevin Sampson, *Outlaws*, p. 163, 2001

2 urination *UK, 1902*
The plural variant 'number ones' is also used.
- On the other hand, some corresponding euphemistic expressions (e.g., dickie, peepee, weewee, number one, number two, to move the bowels, to pass water, to make love, and so on), obviously evasive in their very structure, do have considerable usage. — *Eros*, p. 69, Autum 1962
- — Collin Baker et al., *College Undergraduate Slang Study Conducted at Brown University*, p. 164, 1968
- I feel like I am five years old. Mama, may I go to the potty? Number one? Number two? — Beatrice Sparks (writing as 'Anonymous'), *Jay's Journal*, p. 137, 1979
- Liquid Gold 5 features women doing number one and (ain't that America!) getting paid for it. — *New Times Los Angeles*, 19th July 2001

3 a closely cropped haircut *UK, 1925*
Originally mililtary, from the most extreme setting on the clippers; it is also possible to have a 'number two', etc.
- [A]s uninformed as Samson when he was napping and was given a number one cut by that sly bint[.] — *The Guardian*, 20th December 2001

number one; numba one *adjective*
the very best *US, 1838*
Although coined in the 1830s in a pure English sense, it took on a pidgin or mock pidgin tone in the C20; very popular in the Vietnam war.
- No!! Wear on Tet! T-E-T! Numbah one holiday! — Ted Zidek, *Choi Oi: The Lighter Side of Vietnam*, p. 75, 1965
- Maybe you like see number-one girl? — *The Berkeley Barb*, p. 1, 5th November 1965
- — Carl Fleischhauer, *A Glossary of Army Slang*, p. 4, 1968
- Baby-san give you number one blow job, you like? Come on G.I. Me suck you guts out. Baby'san love to eat G.I. dick. — *Screw*, p. 5, 15th February 1971
- Or, I can show you some number one souvenirs if you want to save yourself the trip. — Earl Thompson, *Tattoo*, p. 294, 1974
- Dosier here is a Chicago boy, boo-coo hardcore and number-one fuck. — Larry Heinemann, *Close Quarters*, p. 42, 1977
- — Linda Reinberg, *In the Field*, p. 154, 1991

numbers *noun*

1 an illegal lottery based on guessing a number determined by chance each day *US, 1897*
- The whole area was overrun with fay gangsters who got fat on the profits they raked in from the big nightclubs and speakeasies and from the numbers racket. — Mezz Mezzrow, *Really the Blues*, p. 182, 1946
- You got the numbers running in here? — Mickey Spillane, *I, The Jury*, p. 43, 1947
- Where'd you get all that much money? You been playing the numbers? — Ralph Ellison, *Invisible Man*, p. 324, 1947
- Numbers and slot machines and the black market paid off. — Irving Shulman, *The Amboy Dukes*, p. 3, 1947
- With such ancestry, it is no wonder today that "numbers" make one of the biggest businesses in Washington. — Jack Lait and Lee Mortimer, *Washington Confidential*, p. 1, 1951
- There is still money in her. The numbers operators will tell you that. — John D. McDonald, *The Neon Jungle*, p. 5, 1953
- That's the way they are. They gamble and play the numbers. — James T. Farrell, *Kilroy was Here*, p. 64, 1954
- God damn it, you mean to tell me you write numbers in this neighbourhood and you don't know anything about the Moslems? — Chester Himes, *The Real Cool Killers*, p. 72, 1959
- All the people who had a little more nerve than average or didn't care would take numbers. Numbers was the thing; it sort of ran the community. — Claude Brown, *Manchild in the Promised Land*, p. 191, 1965
- Some of them old-time numbers men, all they got to show for their years of working is a little, dinky room[.] — Sara Harris, *The Lords of Hell*, p. 117, 1967
- At that time the numbers were controlled by "Jews" in Newark and they used colored men as runners. — Babs Gonzales, *I Paid My Dues*, p. 7, 1967
- It was an even bigger money-maker than numbers, and Jimmy was in charge. — *Goodfellas*, 1990
- Black people don't play the stock market. We play the numbers. But how do we determine what numbers to play? Dreams. — Chris Rock, *Rock This!*, p. 95, 1997

2 a telephone number *US*
- — Connie Eble (Editor), *UNC-CH Campus Slang*, p. 8, October 2002

▸ by the numbers

precisely, correctly *US, 1918*
- Mace, let's make this one smooth and by the numbers. Okay? — *Airheads*, 1994

▸ do numbers

to urinate or defecate *TRINIDAD AND TOBAGO, 1990*
- — Lise Winer, *Dictionary of the English/Creole of Trinidad & Tobago*, 2003

▸ take the numbers down

in horse racing, to disqualify a horse from a race and announce a new winner *US*
- — Walter Steigleman, *Horseracing*, p. 278, 1947

▸ the numbers
in prison, Rule 43, which allows a prisoner to be kept apart from the main prison community for 'safety of self or others' *UK*
Explained by former Cabinet Minister Jonathan Aitken, describing his prison experience 1999–2000, *Have I Got News for You*, 28th November 2003.

numbers banker *noun*
the operator of an illegal numbers racket or lottery *US*
- A numbers banker?—Chester Himes, *The Real Cool Killers*, p. 102, 1959
- [I]t was generally known that the numbers bankers paid off at higher levels of the police department.—Malcolm X and Alex Haley, *The Autobiography of Malcolm X*, p. 85, 1964
- They couldn't be trusted by numbers bankers any more.—Claude Brown, *Manchild in the Promised Land*, p. 191, 1965

numbers drop *noun*
a place where bets on an illegal lottery are turned in or made *US*
- [E]ntered a grimy tobacco-store which fronted for a numbers drop and and reefer shop.—Chester Himes, *A Rage in Harlem*, p. 36, 1957

numbers game *noun*
sex expressed in numeric terms *US*
The most common is, of course, **69**, with other lesser known variants.
- —Roger Blake, *The American Dictionary of Sexual Terms*, p. 141, 1964
- —Anon., *King Smut's Wet Dreams Interpreted*, 1978

number ten; numba ten *adjective*
the very worst *UK, 1953*
Southeast Asian pidgin, commonly used during the Vietnam war.
- You number Ten, you crazy.—*The Berkeley Barb*, p. 3, 3rd December 1965
- —Carl Fleischhauer, *A Glossary of Army Slang*, p. 4, 1968
- —*Maledicta*, p. 256, Summer/Winter 1982: 'Viet-speak'
- —Linda Reinberg, *In the Field*, p. 154, 1991
- [T]he hooch girl, who cleaned up and took care of the laundry, stopped in her work, shook her broom at me, and started yelling, "You go kill VC! Numba fucking ten."—Paul Young, *First Recon – Second to None*, p. 195, 1992

number ten thousand *adjective*
worse than the very worst *US*
Vietnam war usage.
- —Carl Fleischhauer, *A Glossary of Army Slang*, p. 4, 1968
- No, VC. VC numba fucken ten. VC numba ten thou!—Larry Heinemann, *Close Quarters*, p. 107, 1977
- —Gregory Clark, *Words of the Vietnam War*, p. 356, 1990

number thirteen *noun*
▹ see: 13

number three *noun*
sexual relief, by any means (conventional, non-conventional or unaccompanied) *UK, 1984*
The next in a logical sequence: **NUMBER ONE** (urination); **NUMBER TWO** (defecation).

number two; number twos *noun*
defecation *US, 1936*
Adult usage of children's bathroom vocabulary.
- On the other hand, some corresponding euphemistic expressions (e.g., dickie, peepee, weewee, number one, number two, to move the bowels, to pass water, to make love, and so on), obviously evasive in their very structure, do have considerable usage.—*Eros*, p. 69, Autum 1962
- —Collin Baker et al., *College Undergraduate Slang Study Conducted at Brown University*, p. 164, 1968
- I feel like I am five years old. Mama, may I go to the potty? Number one? Number two?—Beatrice Sparks (writing as 'Anonymous'), *Jay's Journal*, p. 137, 1979

number two *adjective*
applied to illegal or irregular activity *INDIA*
'Number one' is all things legal and above-board.
- A contempt for the edicts of bureaucracy rather than physical mayhem is the mark of a Number Two man.—Nigel Hankin, *Hanklyn-Janklyn*, 2003

number two man *noun*
a skilled card cheat adept at dealing the second card instead of the top card in a deck *US*
- —John Scarne, *Scarne's Guide to Modern Poker*, p. 284, 1979

Numbies *noun*
Players' Number 6™ cigarettes *UK: SCOTLAND*
- Is that you back on the Numbies, aye?—Michael Munro, *The Patter, Another Blast*, p. 49, 1988

numbnuts *noun*
an idiot *US, 1960*
- [A]nybody but a born numbnuts could definitely feel it[.]—Lester Bangs, *Psychotic Reactions and Carburetor Dung*, p. 58, 1970
- —*Current Slang*, p. 21, Spring 1970
- I figured even some numbnuts could find this guy easy.—Leonard Shecter and William Phillips, *On the Pad*, p. 143, 1973
- What is your major malfunction, numbnuts?—*Full Metal Jacket*, 1987
- These numbnuts are laughing, thought Jake Harp.—Carl Hiaasen, *Native Tongue*, p. 317, 1991
- A trillion is more than a billion, numb-nuts.—*Austin Powers*, 1999
- But he didn't need this numb-nut fucking telling him—Tony Wilson, *24 Hour Party People*, p. 47, 2002

Numbo *noun*
Number 6™, a branded cigarette *UK*
- He just takes out a Numbo, sparks up and sits on the swing, enjoying the sunshine and smoking his ciggy.—Kevin Sampson, *Outlaws*, p. 246, 2001

numb out *verb*
to feel or show the effects of crack cocaine *UK*
- —Angela Devlin, *Prison Patter*, p. 81, 1996

numbskull; numskull *noun*
a dolt; a fool *UK, 1742*
- Toliver and his boys were louts and numskulls propped up only by the local Communists[.]—Clancy Sigal, *Going Away*, p. 362, 1961

numerologist *noun*
a person who claims to have devised a winning system for an illegal numbers gambling lottery *US*
- —*American Speech*, p. 192, October 1949

numero uno *noun*
1 the very best *US, 1960*
Spanish for 'number one'.
- I am numero uno in the ant racket.—Peter Cook, *Peter Cook & Co*, 1980
- That moves Cush solidly up to numero uno in the draft.—*Jerry Maguire*, 1996
- Later we're in the limo rumbing down to Manhattan's location numero uno, the fashionably drab meat-packing district.—*The Times Magazine*, p. 45, 16th February 2002

2 yourself *US, 1973*
- Being able to take care of yourself. Looking out for numero uno is more important now than ever.—Emmett Grogan, *Final Score*, p. 162, 1976

nummy *noun*
a fool, a dim-witted person *US, 1902*
A shortened 'numbskull'.
- Heh-heh-heh-heh, the nummies picked a Sunday; everybody was scattered all over the island, getting drunk or getting laid.—Philip Caputo, *A Rumor of War*, p. 39, 1977

nummy *adjective*
delicious *US, 1989*
Probably after **YUMMY** (delicious).
- Hi, fellow sports nut. You look yummy and nummy out of your wrinkled, sweaty uniform.—Anonymous *Annie's Baby*, p. 10, 1998

num-nums *noun*
the female breasts *US*
- —J.R. Schwartz, *The Official Guide to the Best Cat Houses in Nevada*, p. 165, 1993: 'Sex glossary'

numpty; numptie *noun*
a fool *UK: SCOTLAND, 1911*
- [A]ll the numpties that urnie [are not] bright enough for the brain drain.—Ian Pattison, *Rab C. Nesbitt*, 1988
- Beadie should sue the numpties who did his last rewire.—Christopher Brookmyre, *Boiling a Frog*, p. 364, 2000

nunce; nince *noun*
a fool *UK*
Student use; derogatory.

nunga *noun*
the penis *AUSTRALIA*
- —Barry Humphries, *Bazza Pulls It Off!*, 1971

nunga-muncher *noun*
a person who performs oral sex on men *AUSTRALIA*
• [P]om [British] sheilahs [women] are generally speaking – real bonzer nunga-munchers. —Barry Humphries, *Bazza Pulls It Off!*, 1971

nun's cunt *noun*
used as a comparison for something that is cold, dry or tight *CANADA*
Reported by Robin Leech, 1981.
• —Thommo, *The Dictionary of Australian Swearing and Sex Sayings*, p. 26, 1985

nun's fart *noun*
a treat made with leftover piecrust dough, cinnamon and sugar *CANADA*
• The [Quebec Eastern Townships] term "nun's fart" is translated from French – "pet de soeur" – and exhibits the sacreligious irreverence of Quebecois popular culture. —Lewis Poteet, *Talking Country*, p. 57, 1992

nunu; nuzni *noun*
the vagina *TRINIDAD AND TOBAGO, 1994*
• —Lise Winer, *Dictionary of the English/Creole of Trinidad & Tobago*, 2003

nunya *noun*
used for conveying that something is 'none of your business' *US*
• —*Ebony Magazine*, p. 156, August 2000: 'How to talk to the new generation'

nurd *noun*
▷ see: NERD

nurds *noun*
the testicles *US*
• —*Maledicta*, p. 255, Summer/Winter 1981: 'Five years and 121 dirty words later'

Nuremburg trials; nuremburgs *noun*
haemorrhoids *UK*
Rhyming slang for 'piles'.
• —Ray Puxley, *Fresh Rabbit*, 1998
• —Bodmin Dark, *Dirty Cockney Rhyming Slang*, 2003

nurk, nurse *nouns*
▷ see: NERK, WHITE NURSE

nurse *verb*
in a card game, to nervously fondle and adjust your cards *US*
• —George Percy, *The Language of Poker*, p. 59, 1988

nursery *noun*
1 a reformatory for juvenile offenders *US*
• —Hyman E. Goldin et al., *Dictionary of American Underworld Lingo*, p. 147, 1950
2 a gentle slope where beginning skiers practice *US*
• —*American Speech*, p. 206, October 1963: 'The language of skiers'

nursery race *noun*
in horse racing, a relatively short distance race for two-year-olds *US*
• —Tom Ainslie, *Ainslie's Complete Guide to Thoroughbred Racing*, p. 335, 1976

nursery rhyme *noun*
time served in prison *UK*
Rhyming slang.
• Basically Morty didn't have to do that Nursery Rhyme but Freddie couldn't be bothered. —J.J. Connolly, *Layer Cake*, p. 193, 2000

nursery rhymes *noun*
the *Times* *UK*
Rhyming slang; ironically, perhaps, suggesting that some content of the esteemed newspaper is of a similar character to the more newsworthy nursery rhymes.
• —Ray Puxley, *Fresh Rabbit*, 1998

nu-skool *adjective*
applied to a new variation on an old theme *UK*
• —*The Sunday Times Magazine*, p. 51, 1st June 2003: 'The parents' guide to the music maze'

nut *noun*
1 a regular and recurring expense *US, 1909*
• The Embers cost about $20,000 to open, a mild nut in these days of expensive construction. —Robert Sylvester, *No Cover Charge*, p. 283, 1956
• Any idea what my nut amounts to on this outfit? —Ross Russell, *The Sound*, p. 91, 1961
• I asked the driver if he'd made his nut for the day and he glared at me as if I were from the vice squad. —Clancy Sigal, *Going Away*, p. 30, 1961
• I'm worried about Milton and me making that rent. It's a big nut. —Edwin Torres, *After Hours*, p. 434, 1979
• She, from the daily bind of trying to crack the weekly nut. —Odie Hawkins, *Black Casanova*, p. 83, 1984
• We'll be rich. No more nut every week. —*Goodfellas*, 1990
2 an act of sexual intercourse; sex as an activity *US*
Extending back from NUT (an orgasm).
• Nut one, nut two, nut four, five, six / I lost the third nut in the mix – fuck it! —NWA *Findum, Fuckum & Flee*, 1991
• Gimme that, gimme that, gimme that nutt —Eazy-E, *Gimme That Nutt*, 1993
3 an orgasm, especially of a male *US, 1968*
• It's not what you think. It won't take but five minutes for the guy to reach a nut. I mean, it's like takin' candy from a baby. —Donald Goines, *Daddy Cool*, p. 106, 1974
• "What exactly is a sweet nut?" I think the woman must have stared at me for five minutes. "Uhh, it'd be pretty hard to explain it to you, if you've never had one, honey." —Odie Hawkins, *The Life and Times of Chester Simmons*, p. 150, 1991
4 semen *US*
• Back up bitch unless you want nut in your eye —NWA *Findum, Fuckum & Flee*, 1991
5 the female breast *UK*
Usually in the plural.
• Her giving it the tart thing, orange hair, big nuts, glasses. —*The Guardian*, p. 13, 10th April 2002
6 the head; hence, brains, intelligence *UK, 1846*
• Angeline waved her plump little dye-stained hands as she pleaded with her husband. "Look use your nut, Herb. If you had seen that woman's arm you wouldn't be so mad at me[.]" —Caroline Blackwood, *Who Needs It*, 1973
7 a crazy person, an eccentric, a crank *US, 1908*
Probably by back-formation from NUTTY (crazy).
8 an enthusiast *US, 1934*
• Health nuts are not necessarily, as the term may imply, fanatics. —Blythe Camenson, *Careers for Health Nuts & Others Who Like to Stay Fit*, p. 1, 2004
9 a person *UK, 1856*
• I had met him before [...] and had always thought him a pretty shrewd nut. —Charles Raven, *Underworld Nights*, p. 111, 1956
10 in horse racing, a horse picked by a racing newspaper to win a race *US*
• —David W. Maurer, *Argot of the Racetrack*, p. 45, 1951
11 in horse racing, the tax levied on bets by the track and the state *US*
• —Robert V. Rowe, *How to Win at Horse-Racing*, 1990
12 a bankroll *US*
• —David W. Maurer, *Argot of the Racetrack*, p. 45, 1951
13 a rugby ball *NEW ZEALAND*
• —David McGill, *David McGill's Complete Kiwi Slang Dictionary*, p. 77, 1998

▸ **crack the nut**
in gambling, to make enough money to meet the day's expenses *US, 1961*
• —Thomas L. Clark, *The Dictionary of Gambling and Gaming*, p. 53, 1987

▸ **do your nut**
1 to explode with anger *UK, 1919*
• [T]he twirl would do his nut[.] —Frank Norman, *Bang To Rights*, p. 75, 1958
• I begin to think that I'd do my nut if I stayed any longer in this place. —John Peter Jones, *Feather Pluckers*, p. 67, 1964
• The reason Jed was doing his nut was because some of the Munchkins [machine-gun platoon] were out of their trenches. —Ken Lukowiak, *A Soldier's Song*, p. 72, 1993
• [H]is granddaughter who's standing there in a white-bra-gone-grey doing her nut[.] —Greg Williams, *Diamond Geezers*, p. 8, 1997
• Mrs Prakash had done her nut with Michael[.] —P-P Hartnett, *Sad Cunt*, p. 97, 1999
2 to go mad, to feign madness *UK*
• "First offenders or not, you do a blag like that one and that [Dartmoor]'s where you'll end up." "I'd do my nut first. Broadmoor for me." "You'd have to do your nut to start knocking flippin' armoured cars around [...]" —Derek Bickerton, *Payroll*, p. 32, 1959

▸ **make the nut**
to suffice *US*
• We were received in camp with cheers and shouting. Our eight cases made the nut. —Hunter S. Thompson, *Hell's Angels*, p. 184, 1966

▸ nod the nut
to plead guilty *AUSTRALIA*
Formed on **NUT** (the head); from bending the head in unspoken affirmative.
- Nodding the Nut for a Swy and One [a sentence of two years that will reduce to one with good behaviour]. — *The (Sydney) Bulletin*, 26th April 1975

▸ off your nut
1 in a state of drunkenness or drug intoxication *UK, 1860*
Parallel to the sense as 'mad'; possibly the original sense, a variation of **OFF YOUR HEAD**.
- Sometimes clubs are bad because you get people off their nut. — Dave Haslam, *Adventures of the Wheels of Steel*, p. 114, 2001

2 in a state of madness *UK, 1873*
A variation of **OFF YOUR HEAD**.
- "Remember the Salisbury nutcase caught at the grave?" "It's your division," Robins said, "but, it's you that's off your nut, Charlie." — Troy Kennedy Martin, *Z Cars*, p. 12, 1962
- You off your fucking nut? — *Scum*, 1979

▸ on the nut
in horse racing, to have lost a large amount of money betting *US*
- — David W. Maurer, *Argot of the Racetrack*, p. 46, 1951
- As facts are mattered, his luck was shattered / For he was what you'd call "on the nut.". — Dennis Wepman et al., *The Life*, p. 103, 1976

▸ out of your nut
drunk or drug-intoxicated *UK*
A variation of **OUT OF YOUR HEAD**.
- [N]o matter how out of their nuts they all get. — Wayne Anthony, *Spanish Highs*, p. 120, 1999

nut *verb*
1 to head-butt an opponent's face *UK, 1937*
Derives from **NUT** (the head).
- She nuts the woman. She falls into the pond. — Ian Pattison, *Rab C. Nesbitt*, 1988
- I nut him. His glasses break and he falls to his knees. — Martin King and Martin Knight, *The Naughty Nineties*, p. 133, 1999
- Alfonso doesn't say a dicky bird [word], just goes over and nuts Wells between the eyes. — John King, *Human Punk*, p. 6, 2000
- [A] whist drive that ended up with the pensioners nutting each other. — Mark Steel, *Reasons to be Cheerful*, p. 231, 2001

2 to execute *IRELAND*
- [O]ne of the PIRA [Provisional Irish Republican Army]'s top nutting boys[.] — Chris Ryan, *The Watchman*, p. 217, 2001

3 to have sex *US*
- — Eugene Landy, *The Underground Dictionary*, p. 140, 1971

4 to orgasm, especially of a male *US*
- get yo' nails out my back / Slut I'm bout to nut — Dr Dre, *Housewife*, 1999

nut and gut *adjective*
mental and physical *UK*
- He was remanded for "nut and gut" reports from the doctor. — Duncan MacLaughlin, *The Filth*, p. 158, 2002

nutbag *noun*
a mesh restraint used by police to restrain violent people *US*
- Known as the "nut bag," the device is meant ot keep the EDP restrained, calm and alive until he or she can be transported[.] — Samuel M. Katz, *Anytime Anywhere*, p. 61, 1997

nutbox *noun*
a mental hospital *US*
- Just because we had fought the day before and I was the only one who saw the accident, I ended up in the nutbox. — Claude Brown, *Manchild in the Promised Land*, p. 23, 1965

nut buster *noun*
▷ **see:** **NUT SPLITTER**

nutcake *noun*
an eccentric or crazy person *US, 1967*
- "How would I know," he said. "We have nutcakes calling here every night of the week." — Tip O'Neill with William Novak, *Man of the House*, p. 128, 1987

nut case *noun*
an eccentric; a madman *AUSTRALIA, 1944*
Combines **NUT** (a lunatic) with conventional medical use of 'case'.
- "Remember the Salisbury nutcase caught at the grave?" "It's your division," Robins said, "but, it's you that's off your nut, Charlie." — Troy Kennedy Martin, *Z Cars*, p. 12, 1962
- This sheila's a flamin' nut case! I haven't even exercised the ferret yet!!! — Barry Humphries, *The Wonderful World of Barry McKenzie*, p. 42, 1968
- Oh well, I'm a nut case, you know, on a motor bike[.] — Paul E Willis, *Profane Culture*, p. 58, 1978
- "Suit yourself. He's a nut case." A nut case who sells newspaper, Mulcahy thought ruefully. — Carl Hiaasen, *Tourist Season*, p. 44, 1986
- That nutcase was right at my door. — *Airheads*, 1994
- You think the chapter title [Ann Coulter: Nutcase] is a little harsh. But, believe me, in Coulter's case, "nutcase" is more than justified. — Al Franken, *Lies*, p. 5, 2003

nut-chokers *noun*
men's underpants *AUSTRALIA*
Formed on **NUTS** (the testicles).
- [O]nly bastards with really twisted minds would want to take a dekko [look] at my nut-chokers!!! — Barry Humphries, *Bazza Pulls It Off!*, 1971

nutcracker *noun*
1 a stern person; a strict disciplinarian, especially a woman who crushes a man's spirit *US*
- Now this Budka is notorious, worst accident record in the mine and pictures himself as a real nutcracker. Always on your back for chickenshit while the important stuff goes right past him. — John Sayles, *Union Dues*, p. 42, 1977
- I never met a broad yet named Tammy wasn't a nut cracker. — Joseph Wambaugh, *The Golden Orange*, p. 11, 1990

2 a railway roundhouse mechanic *US*
- — Ramon Adams, *The Language of the Railroader*, p. 106, 1977

nutcrackers *noun*
the testicles *UK*
Rhyming slang for **KNACKERS**; extending, and, possibly deliberately, disguising, **NUTS** (the testicles).
- — Ray Puxley, *Fresh Rabbit*, 1998

nutcrusher *noun*
a hard man (or woman); a strict disciplinarian *UK*
Crushed nuts are a standard ingredient in many sweet recipes, hence this readymade pun and variation of **BALLBREAKER**.
- Todd, a Londoner, spoke like a Brooklyn nutcrusher. — Kevin Sampson, *Powder*, p. 114, 1999

nutcut *noun*
the critical point in an enterprise or operation *US*
- I take me a pair of dice and beat that shit, or a deck of cards, of it it comes down to the nutcut, I'll sell a sonofabitch the Brooklyn Bridge. — Bruce Jackson, *In the Life*, p. 146, 1972

nut-cutting *noun*
the most critical and distasteful stage in a project or operation *US, 1968*
An image from the West and cattle raising.
- It's getting to be, as the boys say, nut-cutting time. — Jim Bouton, *Ball Four*, p. 89, 1970
- They's one thing you always do when you're down to the nut-cuttin. — Dan Jenkins, *Semi-Tough*, p. 190, 1972

nut farm *noun*
a hospital for the mentally ill *US, 1940*
- You see them around for a few days after the men don't want them, acting crazy before they go off somewheres else – to the House of Detention or the Bellevue nut farm. — Sara Harris, *The Lords of Hell*, p. 55, 1967

nut flush *noun*
in poker, a hand with all cards of the same suit and an ace as the high card *US*
- — John Scarne, *Scarne's Guide to Modern Poker*, p. 295, 1979

nut hatch *noun*
a mental institution *US, 1942*
- I used to know a tall young bum called Big Slim William Holmes Hubbard my buddy of the nuthouse who planned a break with me with bradknives to get to freights that ran behind nuthatch[.] — Jack Kerouac, *Letter to Neal Cassady*, p. 307, 10th January 1951
- The next crisis occurred when they got married, at which time the family considered putting her, or him, or both, into a nuthatch. — Ed Sanders, *Tales of Beatnik Glory*, p. 20, 1975

nuthouse *noun*
a mental hospital *US, 1906*
- This is the man who went to see Ezra Pound at the nuthouse with Robert Lowell. — Jack Kerouac, *Letter to Allen Ginsberg*, p. 208, 16th July 1949
- They'd put you in a nuthouse, Brownie. They wouldn't give you the gas chamber. — Jim Thompson, *The Nothing Man*, p. 283, 1954

- The Vigilante is prosecuted in Federal Court under a lynch bill and winds up in a Federal Nut House[.] —William Burroughs, *Naked Lunch*, p. 8, 1957
- He'd been close to a month in this nuthouse and it might be a lot better than a work farm[.] —Ken Kesey, *One Flew Over the Cuckoo's Nest*, p. 162, 1962
- Old man, they may be about to lock up in a nuthouse. —Robert Gover, *The Maniac Responsible*, p. 219, 1963
- All you lot oughta be in the nut-house, you're bonkers, stone raving bonkers. —John Peter Jones, *Feather Pluckers*, p. 34, 1964
- There is a nut house locally[.] —Jenny Eclair, *Camberwell Beauty*, p. 217, 2000
- They'd sent him to a nut-house on the south coast. —Diran Adebayo, *My Once Upon A Time*, p. 71, 2000

nut hustle *noun*
a swindle involving a prostitute and a confederate *US*
- The Murphy game is also called the nut hustle. —Burgess Laughlin, *Job Opportunities in the Black Market*, p. 16–1, 1978

nut job *noun*
someone who is mentally unstable *US, 1972*
- These charges have attracted a lot of attention and it seems to be bringing all the nut jobs out of the nut jar. —*Traffic*, 2000

nut man *noun*
a male homosexual *AUSTRALIA*
- —Thommo, *The Dictionary of Australian Swearing and Sex Sayings*, p. 88, 1985

nut mob *noun*
a group operating three-shell games in carnivals *US*
- —*American Speech*, p. 235, October 1950: 'The argot of outdoor boob traps'

nut nectar *noun*
semen *US*
- SHE DRINKS THE FRESH NUT NECTAR DOWN HER THROAT. —Peter Sotos, *Index*, p. 37, 1996

nut-nut *noun*
1 a crazy person *UK*
By reduplication of **NUT** (a crazy person).
- I can see why he don't entertain any nut-nuts. —J.J. Connolly, *Layer Cake*, p. 7, 2000
- Vaz shook his head in disbelief. "You really are a nut-nut. I'm going to sleep." —Colin Butts, *Is Harry Still on the Boat?*, p. 41, 2003

2 in high-low poker, a hand that is the best possible hand either high or low *US*
- —Peter O. Steiner, *Thursday Night Poker*, p. 414, 1996

nut off *verb*
to send a prisoner to a secure psychiatric hospital *UK*
From **NUT** (a crazy person).
- [N]utted off. —Angela Devlin, *Prison Patter*, p. 81, 1996

nut out *verb*
1 to think out; to work out *AUSTRALIA, 1919*
- No. Yer wouldn't know how to nut ut out. —Nino Culotta (John O'Grady), *They're A Weird Mob*, p. 30, 1957
- He could lie up at the ceremonial rocks and nut things out. —Arthur Upfield, *Bony and the Mouse*, p. 176, 1959

2 to act mentally ill *US, 1966*
- But I nutted him out and continued my filing and staffingwork. —Clarence Cooper Jr, *The Farm*, p. 233, 1967
- I could nut out and say that I took my frustrations out on her, but that would only be half true. —Odie Hawkins, *Scars and Memories*, p. 86, 1987

nut player *noun*
in poker, a player who only plays a hand that is excellent as dealt *US*
From **NUTS** (the best possible hand in a given situation).
- —John Scarne, *Scarne's Guide to Modern Poker*, p. 295, 1979

nutrients *noun*
food *US*
- —Kenn "Naz" Young, *Naz's Dictionary of Teen Slang*, p. 83, 1993

nut role *noun*
the act of feigning eccentricity or mild insanity *US*
- I'll 'nut roll' on her. I'll stay outta the pimp role until I case her. I'll go 'Sweet William' on her. —Iceberg Slim (Robert Beck), *Pimp*, p. 144, 1969

nut-role; nut-roll *verb*
to feign mental instability *US*
- Buddha deadpans, nutrolls on them, as the Afro-Lords crack up around him. —Odie Hawkins, *Ghetto Sketches*, p. 81, 1972

nut-runner *noun*
in car repair, a pneumatic wrench *US*
- —John Edwards, *Auto Dictionary*, p. 114, 1993

nuts *noun*
1 the testicles; the scrotum *US, 1863*
- You ever been kneed in the nuts in a brawl, buddy? —Ken Kesey, *One Flew Over the Cuckoo's Nest*, p. 58, 1962
- Gut you wit' that razor I used to shave my nuts wit'[.] —Eminem (Marshall Mathers), *Weed Lacer (Freestyle)*, 1999
- Listen you son of a bitch, if you don't let us in to see this movie I'm gonna kick you square in the nuts. —*South Park*, 1999
- If another one of these chairs hits me in the nuts, I'm gonna go postal. —*Austin Powers*, 1999
- [M]y own nuts are sweating. —John King, *Human Punk*, p. 22, 2000
- [Y]ou wouldn't mind if someone came along and yanked off your nuts, just because having them was slightly inconveniencing them now would you? —Danny King, *The Burglar Diaries*, p. 19, 2001

2 in poker, the best possible winning hand at a given moment *US*
- It's tough to beat that character since he won't bet unless he has the nuts. —Robert C. Prus and C.R.D. Sharper, *Road Hustler*, p. 170, 1977: 'Glossary of terms'
- —John Scarne, *Scarne's Guide to Modern Poker*, p. 285, 1979

3 the advantage in a bet *US*
- If two players of equal speed are playing on an overcoat's table, the overcoat has the nuts. —Steve Rushin, *Pool Cool*, p. 21, 1990

▸ **do your nuts over**
to become infatuated with someone *AUSTRALIA*
- 'Ya know he's done's his nuts over ya.' I drew my legs demurely beneath me. —Kathy Lette, *Girls' Night Out*, p. 167, 1987

▸ **get your nuts off**
to ejaculate *US, 1932*
- One of them noticed the hunchback and gave a derisive snort: "Wha'cha doin', Mac – gittin' yer nuts off?" —Terry Southern, *Candy*, 1958
- When I'd gotten my nuts off about six times, we got hungry. —Claude Brown, *Manchild in the Promised Land*, p. 165, 1965

▸ **have your nuts in the wringer**
to be trapped in a very weak position *UK*
- Still, they had my nuts in the wringer, so I had to tell Val that we were moving. —Lenny McLean, *The Guv'nor*, p. 78, 1998

▸ **the nuts**
excellent, outstanding, very impressive *UK*
Possibly, a shortening of **MUTT'S NUTS**.
- So he ended up with this long, James Bond villain scar which made him look the nuts. —Dave Courtney, *Raving Lunacy*, p. 145, 2000

▸ **the nuts are running the fruitcake**
used of any situation that is managed by those who are incapable *UK*
A neat variation, formed on **NUT** (a mad person) and **FRUITCAKE** (a mad person) of **THE LUNATICS ARE RUNNING THE ASYLUM**.
- Drug abuse wasn't considered fun unless it was a dance with death, groupie culture had reached its orgiastic pinnacle and the nuts were running the fruitcake. —Mick Farren, *Give the Anarchist a Cigarette*, p. 338, 2001

nuts *adjective*
enthusiastic about; having a strong liking for; sexually infatuated *UK, 1785*
- It was entirely possible that, being obsessed and mad about him, really nuts over him, I unconsciously thought, if I got pregnant he would love me enough to marry me. —Angela Bonavoglia, *The Choices We Made*, p. 45, 2001

nuts!
used as an expression of defiance *US, 1910*
From the sense as 'testicles', thus **BALLS!**.
- Say nuts to diabetes. —*Mens Fitness*, August 2003

nut sack *noun*
the scrotum *US, 1971*
- —Pamela Munro, *U.C.L.A. Slang*, p. 96, 2001
- You can pull my nutsack up over my dick, so it looks like a bullfrog. —Kevin Smith, *Jay and Silent Bob Strike Back*, p. 90, 2001

nutso *noun*
a crazy person, an eccentric *US, 1975*
From 'nuts' (crazy).

nutso *adjective*
crazy *US, 1979*
- Lady, pardon me for saying, but I think you're goddamn fucking nutso. —Carl Hiaasen, *Native Tongue*, p. 81, 1991

• The idea of women looking down at their own breasts drives me nutso. —Nicholson Baker, *Vox*, p. 56, 1992

nut splitter; nut buster *noun*
a railway machinist *US, 1903*
• —Norman Carlisle, *The Modern Wonder Book of Trains and Railroading*, p. 266, 1946

nuts to...!
when combined with a name, a noun or a pronoun, used for expressing defiance of that person or thing *UK, 1984*
Used as a euphemism for 'balls to...!'.
• He could have added, "So nuts to you." —*The Guardian*, 12th June 2001

nutsy *adjective*
eccentric, odd, crazy *US, 1923*
• You're not going nutsy on me, are you? You're not going to have one of those nervous breakdowns or anything, are you? —*Nashville*, 1975

nutted *adjective*
drug-intoxicated *UK*
• He'd got home from the Arches in Glasgow totally nutted. —Colin Butts, *Is Harry on the Boat?*, p. 272, 1997
• '[R]emembering a time she was dancing, well and truly nutted[.] —John King, *White Trash*, p. 89, 2001
• The Victorians were, in fact, stoners who liked to get nutted, go stumble dancing and have illicit sex with people they barely knew. —*Ministry*, p. 66, January 2002

nutter *noun*
a crazy person; a lunatic; an eccentric *UK, 1958*
Extended from **NUT** (a lunatic).
• I was called up one afternoon to see the psychiotrist [sic], the reason for this is to find out w[h]ether you are a nutter —Frank Norman, *Bang To Rights*, p. 29, 1958
• I'm one to encourage a nutter. In fact, come to think of it, I'm a bit of a fucking nutter magnet I am. —Dave Courtney, *Raving Lunacy*, p. 125, 2000
• [I]f you see someone wearing more than two badges, they're a nutter. —Frank Skinner, *Frank Skinner*, p. 19, 2001

nutters *adjective*
crazy, wildly mad *UK*
• She looked absolutely nutters. —Peter Dickinson, *The Seventh Raven*, p. 91, 1982

nutty *noun*
any confectionary; used generically for all chocolate and sweets *UK*
Royal Navy slang.
• —Nigel Foster, *The Making of a Royal Marine Commando*, 1987

nutty *adjective*
1 crazy, eccentric *US, 1892*
• That nutty sound: Madness at the Hope & Anchor —*Poster*, 3rd May 1983
• Viv's brother Bobby was the sort of nutter who had lots of nutty mates[.] —John King, *White Trash*, p. 55, 2001
2 excellent *US, 1953*
A variation on 'crazy'.
• "Nutty," said the paper bear, "but you better call GAC. They booked you into the wrong room." —Steve Allen, *Bop Fables*, p. 12, 1955
• —*Swinging Syllables*, 1959

nutty as a fruitcake *adjective*
insane, crazy *UK, 1935*
An elaboration of **NUTTY**.
• For, oh, 1,500 or so years now, the conventional wisdom among scholars has been that Caligula, the Roman empire's third ruler, was probably as nutty as a fruitcake. —*The Guardian*, 29th August 2003

nutty putty *noun*
in electric line work, a compound formally known as Seal-A-Conn, used for covering connectors *US*
• —A.B. Chance Co., *Lineman's Slang Dictionary*, p. 12, 1980

nut up *verb*
1 to lose your composure completely *US, 1972*
• —Gary N. Underwood, *American Speech*, p. 63, Spring-Summer 1975: 'Razorback slang'
• But he nutted up. I was tryin to tell him where the necklace was. —Seth Morgan, *Homeboy*, p. 8, 1990
• —William K. Bentley and James M. Corbett, *Prison Slang*, p. 93, 1992
2 in poker, to shift into a more conservative mode of betting *US*
• —David M. Hayano, *Poker Faces*, p. 186, 1982

nut ward *noun*
the pychiatric ward of a prison *US*
• —Inez Cardozo-Freeman, *The Joint*, p. 517, 1984

nuzni *noun*
▷ see: **NUNU**

NWAB *adjective*
(of a girl) promiscuous, because she will *n*eck *w*ith *a*ny *b*oy *US*
Youth usage.
• —*Time*, 3rd October 1949

n-word *noun*
the word 'nigger' *US*
This clumsy euphemism was popularised during the 1995 O.J. Simpson murder trial by F. Lee Baily's cross examination of Mark Fuhrman about a taped interview that Fuhrman had given in 1985.
• But nagging thoughts of ethnic slurs – black resentment over the "n" word, Irish resentment over the "m" word, Jewish resentment over the "k" word, etc. – held me back. —*St. Petersburg (Florida) Times*, p. 5D, 22nd March 1987
• I just said "nigger" a whole lot. You probably think I just use the N-word, but that rule is just for white folks. Any black person can say "nigger" and get away with it. It's true. —Chris Rock, *Rock This!*, p. 22–23, 1997
• "He goes, 'What you bring these niggers for, in my place?' And that was it for conversation." "The N word," Elaine said. —Elmore Leonard, *Be Cool*, p. 240, 1999
• He said you were nothing more than a stupid – the n word – and that you deserved what you got. —*Cruel Intentions*, 1999
• I'm afraid you need to work more on not saying the F word and the N word. —*South Park*, 1999
• Last year, she demanded that a word be removed from the 2000 census for Russian-speaking Sacramentans because it sounded too much like the N-word. —*Sacramento Bee*, 10th November 2001
• Being able to say the N-word is definitely a guilty pleasure. —Suroosh Alvi et al., *The Vice Guide*, p. 18, 2002

nyaff *noun*
an irritating or contemptible person, especially if that person is short *UK: SCOTLAND*
Probably derived from Scots *nyaff* (of a dog, to bark).
• Get aff ya nyaff! —Michael Munro, *The Original Patter*, p. 50, 1985

nyam *noun*
food; something to eat *UK*
From the verb. West Indian, hence UK black.
• C'mon, let's get some nyams. —Diran Abedayo, *My Once Upon A Time*, p. 234, 2000

nyam *verb*
to eat *JAMAICA*
African origins, from 'yam' (a sweet potato).
• It was dog nyam dog. Fluxy frowned. He didn't fancy himself as dog food. —Karline Smith, *Moss Side Massive*, p. 4, 1994
• —Richard Allsopp, *Dictionary of Caribbean English Usage*, p. 410, 1996

nylon disgusters *noun*
a pair of men's close-fitting and revealing nylon swimming trunks *AUSTRALIA*
• Get your nylon disgusters on and we'll go to the pool. —*Wordmap (www.abc.net.au/wordmap)*, 2003

nymph *noun*
a nymphomaniac *US, 1916*
• —W. Haggard, *The Antagonists*, 1964

nymphet *noun*
a sexually attractive, or sexually adventurous, young girl *UK*
First applied to a real, as opposed to mythic, creature by Vladimir Nabokov, *Lolita*, 1955.
• The thrilling Birgit Nilsson, as the titular necrophiliac nymphet [Salome], is a ravening animal. —*The Guardian*, 5th September 1999

nympho *noun*
a nymphomaniac *US, 1910*
A creature of men's dreams; used to disparage a woman whose sexual appetites may threaten to make the dream come true.
• [M]oody old nymphos like Mrs. Marengo[.] —Derek Raymond (Robin Cook), *The Crust on its Uppers*, p. 33, 1962
• The goal of this type of dwelling is to put us in the mood, to get us turned on like crazed nymphos. —Anka Radakovich, *The Wild Girls Club*, p. 15, 1994
• Nympho is more appropriate, quite honestly. —Francesca Lia Block, *I Was a Teenage Fairy*, p. 99, 1998

Oo

O *noun*

1 an *O*BE (Officer of the Order of the British Empire) *UK, 1961*
Used by civil servants; suggestive of a casual familiarity with the honour.

2 opium *US, 1933*
- [O]n the floor a drunken snoring soldier who'd just eaten some O after lush. — Jack Kerouac, *Letter to Allen Ginsberg*, p. 347, 10th May 1952
- He identified the meth by its effect, and the liquid O by its taste and blackness. — Terry Southern, *Blue Movie*, p. 202, 1970

3 an ovation *US*
Most commonly heard in the term 'standing O'.
- Ed Ray received a hero's reception at the state convention of the School Employees Association, and a tumultus standing-O when he was presented its Man-of-the-Year Award. — Bill Cardoso, *The Maltese Sangweech*, p. 62, 1984

O *nickname*
the Nuestra Familia prison gang *US*
- By now the Nortenos, out of necessity, had formed their own prison gang, a paramilitary organization they called Nuestra Familia (Our Family), also known as the "Organization" or, more simply, the "O.' — Bill Valentine, *Gangs and Their Tattoos*, p. 24, 2000

-o *suffix*
used for making colloquial or slang nouns and nicknames *AUSTRALIA, 1865*
In Australia, where there was no influence from Spanish, this suffix originated from early nominal uses of the cries of various street vendors. Thus the milkman used to sing out 'milk-oh!' and so became the **MILKO**, the rabbit seller cried 'rabbit-oh!' and so became the **RABBIT-O**. It is appended to monosyllablic words or to the first syllable of polysyllabic words.
- Here I know Aub and Tony, Bob and Jacko, Addo, Simmo, Peto and Old Vic, and I would not like to be the man who tried to restrict their physical freedom. — Nino Culotta (John O'Grady), *They're A Weird Mob*, p. 196, 1957
- It's like all these Aussie names – Jacko, and Norm and Cec. — Michael Peters, *Pommie Bastard*, p. 133, 1969
- This was your lame-o idea in the first place. — *Point Break*, 1991
- Musso [Mussolini] repaid the favour by invading in 1939 and tossing him out[.] — Ignatius Jones, *The 1992 True Hip Manual*, p. 15, 1992
- VINCENT: I'm on my way somewhere. I got a dinner engagement. Rain check? LANCE: No problemo. — *Pulp Fiction*, 1994
- When women start pissing like us, that's it, we're finished mate. Extincto. — *The Full Monty*, 1997
- There wasn't a barman in the country that made a better Long Island Tea than Roscoe [Ross], and they were essential high-risk fuel. — William Dodson, *The Sharp End*, p. 206, 2001

OAE *noun*
anybody who has spent at least one winter in Antarctica *ANTARCTICA, 1960*
An abbreviation of '*o*ld *A*ntarctic *e*xplorer'.
- — Bernadette Hince, *The Antarctic Dictionary*, p. 244, 2000
- — *Cool Antarctica*, 2003: 'Antarctic slang'

oafo *noun*
an oaf, a socially inferior fool, a lout *UK, 1959*
A conventional 'oaf' embellished.
- [N]ot to mention the oafos, the things who hate us[.] — Derek Raymond (Robin Cook), *The Crust on its Uppers*, p. 25, 1962

Oak; the Austrian Oak *nickname*
Arnold Schwarzenegger (b.1947), the dominant bodybuilder in the steroid-enhanced 1970s *US*
- — *American Speech*, p. 200, Fall 1984: 'The language of bodybuilding'

oak and ash *noun*
cash *UK*
Rhyming slang.
- — Julian Franklyn, *A Dictionary of Rhyming Slang*, 1960

oaktoe *noun*
the numbing of toes by cold water, creating the sensation that your toes are wooden *US*
Surfing usage.
- — *Transworld Surf*, p. 42, April 2004

OAP
an over-anxious patient *UK*
Doctors' shorthand, playing on the conventional abbreviation for 'old age pensioner'.
- — Adam T. Fox, St Mary's Hospital, London, 10th October 2002

oar *noun*
▶ **put your oar in; put in your oar; shove in your oar**
to interfere in someone else's business *UK, 1730*
- So you had to put your oar in. I might have guessed. — Graeme Kent, *The Queen's Corporal [Six Granada Plays]*, p. 94, 1959

oars and rowlocks *noun*
nonsense *UK*
Rhyming slang for **BOLLOCKS**.
- Thats a load of oars & rowlocks and you know it. — Ray Puxley, *Fresh Rabbit*, 1998

oasis *noun*

1 a bar *US*
- A whole series of Barney Gallant oases wrote history in the Village[.] — Robert Sylvester, *No Cover Charge*, p. 247, 1956

2 in motor racing, a refreshment stand *US*
- — John Lawlor, *How to Talk Car*, p. 77, 1965

oatburner; oatmuncher *noun*
in horse racing, a racehorse that does not perform well *US, 1916*
- — David W. Maurer, *Argot of the Racetrack*, p. 45, 1951

oater *noun*
a cowboy film, story or song *US, 1946*
- — Edd Byrnes, *Way Out with Kookie*, 1959
- I mean, yes, I did make eighteen feature-length oaters, that's true[.] — Gore Vidal, *Myra Breckinridge*, p. 51, 1968

oatie *noun*
▶ **go for an oatie**
to go to the toilet *NEW ZEALAND, 1996*
A darkly humorous Antarctic euphemism recalling Captain Oate's heroic lasts words to his tent-mates in 1912: 'I am going outside, and may be some time'.
- — Harry Orsman, *A Dictionary of Modern New Zealand Slang*, 1999

oatmeal *noun*
a small, mushy wave *US*
- — Trevor Cralle, *The Surfin'ary*, p. 82, 1991

oatmeal Chinaman *noun*
in mining in the Cariboo, a Canadian *CANADA*
- As in Red River, the Canadians had made themselves disliked by their drive and pertinacity, and earned the designation of "oatmeal Chinamen" from the easy-going colonists because of their readiness to work hard. — A. S. Morton, *Kingdom of Canada*, p. 336, 1963

oatmeal savage *noun*
a Scotsman *CANADA*
- We wondered had the strange emigrants from Grand Old Scotland come up to expectations. Somewhere beneath the blanket protections was Mabel Young, no doubt wishing that those oatmeal savages would hasten away. — *Ghost Pine*, p. 106, 1954

oats *noun*

1 sexual gratification *UK, 1923*
Usually in phrases such as: 'have your oats', 'get your oats', 'need', 'want', etc. Perhaps from 'sow your wild oats' (to commit youthful indiscretion).
- Chrissie will not get her oats[.] — George Simms, *Sleep No More*, 1967
- [S]logging all the way across the old Channel every weekend, just to get your oats. — Mike Stott, *Soldiers Talking, Cleanly*, 1978

2 money which a carnival worker steals from his boss *US*
- — Gene Sorrows, *All About Carnivals*, p. 23, 1985: 'Terminology'

3 enthusiasm *US, 1831*
- — Lou Shelly, *Hepcats Jive Talk Dictionary*, p. 15, 1945

▸ **off your oats**
off your food *UK, 1890*
- I make an excuse that this is not an unkind piece of culinary criticism, but that I am just not hungry/off my oats/etc. — *The Times*, 27th January 2003

▸ **on his oats**
(used of a racehorse) racing without the benefit of a stimulant *US*
- — Igor Kushyshyn et al., *The Gambling Times Guide to Harness Racing*, p. 120, 1994

oats and barley; Oats *noun*
Charley or Charlie *UK, 1859*
Rhyming slang. Ostensibly and rarely a man's given name but usually in its older slang senses (a nightwatchman; to make a Charlie of; a ponce; etc.).
- Cor, the currant [sun]'s 'ot today, Oates, me old China. — *The Sweeney*, p. 6, 1976

oat soda *noun*
beer *US*
An evolution of **BARLEY POP**.
- — Connie Eble (Editor), *UNC-CH Campus Slang*, p. 6, Spring 1994

obbo; obo; obbs; obs *noun*
surveillance, observation; a lookout *UK, 1933*
Varying abbreviations for 'observation'.
- [K]eep the obbs on us[.] — Derek Raymond (Robin Cook), *The Crust on its Uppers*, p. 97, 1962
- "Obbo vans" Police slang for unmarked vans from which observation and surveillance can be mounted. — *The Official Encyclopaedia of New Scotland Yard*, 1999

OBE *adjective*
overcome by events; overtaken by events *US*
- — Department of the Army *Staff Officer's Guidebook*, p. 63, 1986
- The plans that they had gone into Hong Kong with were now "OBE," or overcome by events, because now, at the beginning of the fall of '72, President Nixon had finally decided that enough was enough. — Gerry Carroll, *North S*A*R*, p. 154, 1991

OBE
(used of a bettor in debt) *o*wes *b*ookies *e*verywhere *AUSTRALIA*
- — Ned Wallish, *The Truth Dictionary of Racing Slang*, p. 56, 1989

OBH *noun*
someone who smokes marijuana constantly *US*
An abbreviation of '*o*riginal *b*uddha *h*ead'.
- — Lois Stavsky et al., *A2Z*, p. 73, 1995

obies; OB's *noun*
old brown sherry, a drink especially popular among students *SOUTH AFRICA, 1979*
Formed on the initials OB.
- — Penny Silva, *A Dictionary of South African English*, 1996

obit *noun*
an obituary *UK, 1874*
- I been reading the obit page for twenty years, and I haven't found one yet. — Max Shulman, *Rally Round the Flag, Boys!*, p. 134, 1957
- So what's a 46-year-old doing writing obits for a two-bit Florida rag? — *The Guardian*, 6th April 2002

obliterated *adjective*
very drunk *US*
- — Connie Eble (Editor), *UNC-CH Campus Slang*, p. 2, Fall 1987

oblivion *noun*
the state of complete intoxication *US*
- — Connie Eble (Editor), *UNC-CH Campus Slang*, p. 5, Spring 1984

oboy *noun*
marijuana *UK*
Presumably this drug is, on occasion, greeted with an exclamation of delight: 'Oh boy!'.
- — Mike Haskins, *Drugs*, p. 288, 2003

obs *noun*

1 *obs*ervation *UK*
Probably military origin.
- How long have they had us under obs? Weeks? Months? Years? — J.J. Connolly, *Know Your Enemy [britpulp]*, p. 160, 1999

2 in a hospital, *obs*tetrics *UK*
- The obs nob said he'd put a couple of extra stitches in after the episiotomy. — Henry Sloane, *Sloane's Inside Guide to Sex & Drugs & Rock 'n' Roll*, p. 93, 1985
- — Adam T. Fox, St Mary's Hospital, London, 10th October 2002

obscure *adjective*
in computing, completely beyond all understanding *US*
- — Eric S. Raymond, *The New Hacker's Dictionary*, p. 267, 1991

obscuro *adjective*
wierd, strange (or simply obscure) *US*
- Lots of people are buying into a revival of the really obscuro foreign stuff from Italy or Germany[.] — Brian Doherty, *Retrohell*, p. 165, 1997

obzocky *adjective*
lacking grace and coordination *TRINIDAD AND TOBAGO, 1956*
- — Lise Winer, *Dictionary of the English/Creole of Trinidad & Tobago*, 2003

OC *noun*

1 organised crime *US*
- Wops don't make parole – right away they stamp us O.C. or mafia. — Edwin Torres, *Carlito's Way*, p. 140, 1975

2 the synthetic opiate oxycodone used recreationally *US*
- "Hey, I was getting OC's prescribed to be in Pennsylvania; I'm going to get them in Las Vegas," he said. — *The New York Times Magazine*, p. 36, 29th July 2001

OC *nickname*
Orange County, California *US*
Immediately south of Los Angeles.

ocal; opal *noun*
the eye *UK*
Punning variations on **OGLE** (the eye).
- — Paul Baker, *Polari*, p. 185, 2002

occifer *noun*
▷ see: **OSSIFER**

occy; occi *noun*
an octopus *AUSTRALIA, 1968*
- And also in the tentacles of the occi was an unopened can of Cold Gold KB beer! — Bob Staines, *Wot a Whopper*, p. 39, 1982

occy strap; ockie strap *noun*
an elastic strap *AUSTRALIA, 1981*
An abbreviation of 'octopus strap'.
- Gravity yanks my occy strap and I'm returned to sender at slingshot speed. — Glyn Parry, *Mosh*, p. 35, 1996

ocean *noun*

1 in pool, the expansive centre of a table *US*
- — Mike Shamos, *The Illustrated Encyclopedia of Billiards*, p. 159, 1993

2 in oil drilling, salt water encountered while drilling *US*
- — Jerry Robertson, *Oil Slanguage*, p. 89, 1954

ocean liner *noun*
a black eye *UK*
Rhyming slang for **SHINER**.
- — Ray Puxley, *Cockney Rabbit*, 1992

ocean rambler *noun*
a herring; a sardine *UK, 1961*

oceans *noun*
a large amount of something *UK, 1840*
- [T]he oceans of drivel pouring out in honour of the dead former president, Ronald Reagan. — *The Guardian*, 9th June 2004

-ocentric *suffix*
used with humour as a suffix attached to a person's name, suggesting that they believe that the world revolves around them *US*
- Mark never thinks of anyone else. He lives in a Markocentric world. — Connie Eble (Editor), *UNC-CH Campus Slang*, p. 5, Fall 1996

ocker; Ocker *noun*

1 an Australian male who is especially boorish and uncouth; the stereotypical Australian male yob *AUSTRALIA, 1971*
Originally a colloquial nickname for someone named Oscar. It became associated with typical male boorishness in the 1970s partly under the influence of a character named Ocker in the television comedy *The Mavis Bramston Show* (1965–68).
- From Hobart to Cairns to Darwin to Perth and back to Melbourne, one finds the same proportion of boozing, gambling, sport-obsessed, sun-worshipping, racist ockers doing their bit to keep alive the honoured image of our great Australian mindlessness. — Bill Hornadge, *The Ugly Australian*, p. 31, 1975
- Like Bjelke, your good Ocker is not merely complacently nationalistic but also devious and fanatic in his provincialism. — Max Harris, *The Ugly Australian*, p. 46, 1975
- [Y]ou're a selfish, in-turned macho ocker. — Peter Corris, *Pokerface*, p. 156, 1985
- As a battler from way back, I am convinced that your typical Australian is in fact the Aussie Battler – not the Ocker! — Frank Hardy, *Hardy's People*, p. 111, 1986

2 Australian English *AUSTRALIA, 1979*
- 'Uurrgh, what'll I do with this?' It had to be thrown away. I reverted to Ocker and screamed: 'Dice it.' — *Sunday Tasmanian*, p. 8, 1st October 1989

ocker; Ocker *adjective*

characteristic of an ocker *AUSTRALIA, 1972*
- I sidled up to a particularly Ocker character on the edge of a group and nervously explained my mission. — Sandra Jobson, *Blokes*, p. 11, 1984
- Ockers stress the loud-mouthed, ugly side of the Australian male character, whereas the bloke possesses a gentleness and innate decency which is definitely not ocker. — Sandra Jobson, *Blokes*, p. 32, 1984

ockerdom *noun*

the state of being an ocker *AUSTRALIA, 1974*
- Ockerdom has spread like the Spanish flu from its infective source in Queensland. — Max Harris, *The Ugly Australian*, p. 30, 1975
- [O]ver the ensuing months I was to find large numbers of blokes who more than lived up to the worst stereotypes of puerile Ockerdom – such as the blue-singleted labourer I came across in a pub in Albury, who, when I asked what type of woman he preferred, muttered grimly: 'One with no mouth.' — Sandra Jobson, *Blokes*, p. 13, 1984

O club *noun*

in the US armed forces, an officer's club *US*
- Most O' clubs around the country were disgraces, vending sub-standard food to captive clients. — Walter J. Boyne and Steven L. Thompson, *The Wild Blue*, p. 261, 1986
- "Are the beers cold in your O club, Lietuenant Ritchie?" Steve asked. — T.E. Cruise, *Wings of Gold III*, p. 226, 1989

-ocracy *suffix*

when linked with a subject, used to designate (and mock) a grouping that may be dominant, or aspiring to dominance, or pretending superiority within that subject-area *UK, 1860*
A sarcastic or humorous application of '-cracy' (power, rule), found in such words as 'democracy', 'plutocracy', etc. The root in all conventional senses ends with an 'o'; in colloquial or journalistic usage the 'o' is incorporated.
- — Alexander Bard and Jan Soderqvist, *Netocracy*, 2002
- They bought expensive cars, country houses, hired chauffeurs (rather sensible, in some cases) and in general carried on like 17th-century rakes, but this is a common reaction to a Niagara of sudden wealth, and at least "the popocracy" invented their own formal ostentation. — *The Guardian*, 7th September 2002
- The rise of webocracy has already made South Korea a place of exhilarating but unpredictable change. — *The Guardian*, 24th February 2003
- Whether it's America's shift to the right or the rise and rise of America's motor-mouth, talk-show culture, or the popular rebellion against establishment media or the emergence of a new Republican babe-ocracy, Ann Coulter represents it all. — *The Guardian*, 17th May 2003

-ocrat *suffix*

▷ see: -CRAT

ocs *noun*

the synthetic opiate oxycodone used recreationally *US*
- Investigators say the drug, an opiate called OxyContin, sold on the street as "Oxys" orl "Ocs," has spawned a crime wave[.] — *Richmond (Virginia) Times Dispatch*, p. B1, 21st October 2000

octopus *noun*

a sexually aggressive boy *US, 1932*
- — San Francisco Examiner p. 2, 22nd March 1960
- — *American Speech*, p. 273, December 1963: 'American Indian student slang'

OD *noun*

a drug overdose *US, 1959*
- Well, he died. The cat took an O.D., an overdose of heroin. — Claude Brown, *Manchild in the Promised Land*, p. 188, 1965
- [O]ne area in which her brilliance was widely recognized was in the treatment of an OD, an overdose – a shot that unexpectedly contains more heroin than the body can survive. — James Mills, *The Panic in Needle Park*, p. 37, 1966
- About this time the OD's started. — Herbert Huncke, *Guilty of Everything*, p. 178, 1990

OD *verb*

to overdose, to take an excessive dose of a drug, usually heroin *US*
- Frankie's OD'ing up in Marcie's room in the Reynolds. He needs help bad, honey. — James Mills, *The Panic in Needle Park*, p. 37, 1966
- When Janis Joplin O.D.'d one Sunday at the Landmark Motel, John Carpenter wrote a piece for the L.A. Free Press which clung pretty much to the theory, "What else is a Janis Joplin going to do on a Sunday afternoon alone in L.A.?" — Eve Babitz, *Eve's Hollywood*, p. 250, 1974
- He OD'd four times on barks (barbs, barbiturates) and four times the medics saved him. — Paul E. Willis, *Profane Culture*, p. 184, 1978
- I couldn't get hung up with her at that point, going over each time she called and shooting her up, having her collapse, with doubt in mind about whether she had O.D.'d or not. — Herbert Huncke, *The Evening Sun Turned Crimson*, p. 176, 1980
- Charlie Bat probably OD'd in the same corner where I slept. — Francesca Lia Block, *Missing Angel Juan*, p. 291, 1993
- LANCE: The day I bring an O.D.ing bitch to your place, then I gotta give her the shot. — *Pulp Fiction*, 1994
- Most of her favorite singers have o.d.'d anyway. — Francesca Lia Block, *I Was a Teenage Fairy*, p. 146, 1998
- Claims on the net that he'd ODed in his hotel room and the record company had hidden his body[.] — John Williams, *Cardiff Dead*, p. 50, 2000
- Elvis had ODed on being Elvis. — Mick Farren, *Give the Anarchist a Cigarette*, p. 393, 2001

o-dark-hundred *noun*

very early in the morning *US, 1982*
Mock military time.
- We got to Chau Doc at oh dark hundred but didn't land until first light. — Richard Marcinko and John Weisman, *Rogue Warrior*, p. 136, 1992

oday *noun*

money *US, 1928*
A pig Latin construction of DOUGH.
- — Don Wilmeth, *The Language of American Popular Entertainment*, p. 185, 1981

odd *noun*

1 a small number over and above a round number *UK, 1845*
- [T]hree hundred and thirty-odd years later[.] — *The Observer*, 1st July 2001

2 the police; a police-officer *UK*
- [O]ne night he was driving along the Old Kent Road when all-of-a-sudden the odd gongs him down. — Frank Norman, *Bang To Rights*, p. 123, 1958

oddball *noun*

an eccentric *US, 1948*
- Tell me what you have in mind, you fucking oddball[.] — Kevin Sampson, *Powder*, p. 15, 1999

oddball *adjective*

eccentric, peculiar *US, 1957*
- This was a challenge given her oddball approach to the English language. — Rhiannon Paice, *Too Late for the Festival*, p. 31, 1999

oddball trick *noun*

a prostitute's customer who pays for fetishistic sex *US*
- "Oddball tricks are where the money is," Sugarman assures her. — Gail Sheehy, *Hustling*, p. 61, 1973

odd bod *noun*

1 an eccentric *UK, 1955*
- [H]e likes teaching because no one really notices what an oddbod he is. — Jim Munroe, *Angry Young Spaceman*, p. 100, 2001

2 an extra person in a given situation *NEW ZEALAND*
- — Louis S. Leland, *A Personal Kiwi-Yankee Dictionary*, p. 72, 1984

odd-lot *noun*

a police car *UK*
- [T]he odd gongs him down and who should get out of the odd-lot but this boggie [bogey] who he had had the bet with. — Frank Norman, *Bang To Rights*, p. 123, 1958

odds *noun*

1 a vague number, as a part of a greater number *UK*
A variation on **ODD**.
- In eighteen hundred and odds they brought a new bill out in Parli[a]ment — Frank Norman, *Bang To Rights*, p. 120, 1958

2 (of money) small change *UK*
A shortening of 'odd coins'.
- Got any odds, lar? she asks in a Dingle accent so it comes out like: Gahrmy oddzzzm lahhhr? — Niall Griffiths, *Kelly + Victor*, p. 66, 2002

▸ make no odds
to make no difference, not better or worse *UK, 1826*
Originally (from 1776) conventional, now colloquial.
- It makes no odds to me whether I'm bowling at Christchurch, Taunton or Lord's. — *The Observer*, 7th April 2002

▸ over the odds
more than is expected; more than is tolerable *UK, 1922*
- [T]hey were on a fantastic bonus and over the odds take-home pay. — *The Sweeney*, p. 48, 1976

▸ what's the odds?
what's the difference? *UK, 1840*
- The whole world's into bondage. Altzheimers or Armani, spermicidal lubricant or Ralph Lauren, everything on the same level. So he goes further. What's the odds? — *The Guardian*, 25th April 1991

odds *verb*
to risk, to chance; to avoid *UK*
Perhaps deriving from 'to bet against the odds'.
- I couldn't odds it, as it is compulsory — Frank Norman, *Bang To Rights*, p. 41, 1958
- I can't odds being mixed up in crime. — G.F. Newman, *Sir, You Bastard*, 1970

odds and sods *noun*
bits and pieces *UK, 1935*
Now used as a variant of conventional 'odds and ends'; originally military slang for 'miscellaneous men or duties'.
- We can occasionally knock out a few odds and sods ourselves[.] — Danny King, *The Burglar Diaries*, p. 59, 2001

odds-on *adjective*

1 very probable, most likely *UK, 1888*
Adopted from gambling use to denote any form of actuarial or notional likelihood.
- It's odds-on I'll be asked to give a paper. — John A. Scott, *Blair*, p. 50, 1988
- Dumby was a sure-fire odds-on cert. He was unbackable. — Phillip Gwynne, *Deadly Unna?*, p. 132, 1998
- I know that I am odds-on to get my pension. — James Hawes, *Dead Long Enough*, p. 94, 2000

2 in horse racing, said of odds that pay less than even money *US*
- — Les Conklin, *Payday at the Races*, p. 207, 1974

o-dom *noun*
an odometer (a milometer) *US*
- She's got 27 miles on her o-dom. — *Gone in 60 Seconds*, 2000

OD's *noun*
a drab olive military uniform *US*
- What he threw in is the set of o.d.s I had on when I was taken from the Fifth Street station house by the MPs. — Rocky Garciano (with Rowland Barber), *Somebody Up There Likes Me*, p. 203, 1955
- "OD and khaki go with everything," said Jaworski, 23, who's majoring in geology. "Also, military clothes are rugged, hold up well and are comfortable to wear, with their drawstrings and tab closures." — *Atlanta Journal-Constitution*, p. 8M, 4th March 2001

OE *noun*
Old English™ malt liquor *US*
- — Judi Sanders, *Da Bomb*, p. 6, 1997

Oedipus Rex; Oedipus *noun*
sex *UK*
Rhyming slang, based on a king of ancient Thebes used by psychiatrists as a model for the sexual relationship between a boy and his mother.
- [S]omething to rabbit [to talk] to the trouble [a wife] about in the skein [a bed], instead of having to fall back on the old Oedipus all the time. — Ronnie Barker, *Fletcher's Book of Rhyming Slang*, p. 5, 1979

ofaginzy *noun*
a white person *US*
- "May, why don't you come clean, don't nobody fault you for makin' out you's ofaginzy," talking as though he was on the girls' side and knew I was really colored. — Mezz Mezzrow, *Really the Blues*, p. 204, 1946

ofay *noun*
a white person *US, 1925*
Origin unknown. Suggestions of a pig Latin etymology (foe) are implausible. More plausible are suggestions of a basis in an African language or the French *au fait* (socially proper).
- Ofay, of course, is pig Latin for foe. — Mezz Mezzrow, *Really the Blues*, p. 221, 1946
- "You mean those ofays?" — Ralph Ellison, *Invisible Man*, p. 282, 1947
- It was in this period that the "ofays," Harlem's word for whites, began mixing openly. — Jack Lait and Lee Mortimer, *New York Confidential*, p. 97, 1948
- It was a pleasure house, where those rich ofay (white) business men and planters would come from all over the South and spend some awful large amounts of loot. — Louis Armstrong, *Satchmo*, p. 147, 1954
- [T]hey will lay their salves and balms on a sufferer even allowing he's ofay. — Bernard Wolfe, *The Late Risers*, p. 150, 1954
- Hincty little ofay is Harlemese for snotty little white girl. — John M. Murtagh and Sara Harris, *Cast the First Stone*, p. 14, 1957
- Not like some of them ofays come here with race girls. — Willard Motely, *Let No Man Write My Epitaph*, p. 337, 1958
- "I don't know the names of all the ofays who come into my place," Bucky said. — Chester Himes, *The Real Cool Killers*, p. 63, 1959
- The old ofay failing! — Ross Russell, *The Sound*, p. 43, 1961
- She a ofay with red hair and all the time before Patricia come, she think she so sly and wise because she my only white chick in my stable[.] — Sara Harris, *The Lords of Hell*, p. 55, 1967
- In six weeks myself and two of the other musicians had scored with "ofay chicks". — Babs Gonzales, *I Paid My Dues*, p. 15, 1967
- You one of those ofay liberals who's got high hopes[.] — Nathan Heard, *Howard Street*, p. 151, 1968
- I am here to tell you that that ofay boy has really got sex appeal in spades! — Gore Vidal, *Myra Breckinridge*, p. 90, 1968
- [T]he nigers think the ofay boys is getting it, but the truth of the matter is, man, that ain't nobody getting it[.] — Cecil Brown, *The Life & Loves of Mr. Jiveass Nigger*, p. 52, 1969
- I turned around – "Ofay trash dee-stroy my nice bed!" — James Ellroy, *White Jazz*, p. 97, 1992

ofer; o-for *adjective*
used to describe a male pornography performer who either cannot achieve an erection or cannot ejaculate when needed *US*
Borrowing from sports lingo, identifying the performer as 'oh' (zero) for however many tries.
- — *Adult Video News*, p. 38, September 1995

off *noun*

1 the start of a race; the beginning of something, the start of a journey *UK, 1959*
From racing.
- We go forward at them and it turns into a serious off. — Martin King and Martin Knight, *The Naughty Nineties*, p. 128, 1999
- We are ready for the off now and I am looking forward to it. — *The Guardian*, 8th May 2001

2 time off, a day off, etc *SOUTH AFRICA, 1966*
By ellipsis.
- — Jean Branford, *A Dictionary of South African English*, 1978

3 a warning given to an illegal betting operation by corrupt police of a pending raid *US*
- — *Life*, p. 39, 19th May 1952

4 in dominoes, a piece that does not contribute to the value of your hand *US*
- — Dominic Armanino, *Dominoes*, p. 17, 1959

off *verb*

1 to kill *US*
- I hoped he wouldn't bring his snitchfriend with him, because that meant I'd have to off both of them. — Clarence Cooper Jr, *The Farm*, p. 236, 1967
- They run around all the time saying: 'Off the pigs.' — George V. Higgins, *The Friends of Eddie Doyle*, p. 66, 1971
- I mean, offin' somebody might be necessary too. — Odie Hawkins, *Ghetto Sketches*, p. 15, 1972
- [A] lot of the fay chicks would go for his revolutionary bullshit, and if that was the program I'd come on with "right on" and "off the pig" good as Reggie. — Edwin Torres, *Carlito's Way*, p. 81, 1975
- Out on the turb folks are wondering who it was got the spic jealous enough to try offing a dude, you know how it is. — Robert Deane Pharr, *Giveadamn Brown*, p. 14, 1978

- Nah, he didn't set it. Somebody offed him. — *Body Heat*, 1980
- There's come all over the sheets – he got off before he got offed. — *Basic Instinct*, 1992
- As soon as his car came to a halt, man, he just put the gun to his head and blammo! Offed himself, man, blew himself away right there. — *Slacker*, 1992
- Considering how low your self-esteem has got to get before you consider offing yourself[.] — Christopher Brookmyre, *Not the End of the World*, p. 257, 1998

2 to sell, especially contraband *US, 1960*

- "You should be able to off the chips at face value, right?" Sands said. — Gerald Petievich, *Shakedown*, p. 148, 1988
- The Indians [Colombians] have so much coke they can't off [sell] it without finding new markets. — Terry Williams, *The Cocaine Kids*, p. 22, 1989

off *adjective*

1 distant, aloof, negative *UK, about 1555*

- I looked over at her to try to judge her mood, and thought she looked a bit off. — Mary Hooper, *(megan)2*, p. 164–165, 1999

2 having lost interest in; averse to *UK, 1908*

- — *The Guardian*, 5th September 2000

3 disgusting, revolting *AUSTRALIA*

- I reckon it's a bit off, kids like us making out we're Toorak types[.] — Jenny Pausacker, *What are ya?*, p. 70, 1987
- They gawped at the derros and prostitutes and drooled, 'Do something *off*. Go on.' — Kathy Lette, *Girls' Night Out*, p. 85, 1987
- You're so off to her Kez. — Kathy Lette, *Girls' Night Out*, p. 126, 1987
- Imagine that, cleaning the house on your own birthday! I reckon that is off. — Kylie Mole (Maryanne Fahey), *My Diary*, p. 3, 1988
- That's fucken *off*. What's so special about Earthlings anyway? — Linda Jaivin, *Rock n Roll Babes from Outer Space*, p. 99, 1996

4 of a street-prostitute, being with a client (and, therefore, *off* the street where the service is offered for sale) *UK*

- "Tuesday night's always a bad night for me." "Been off yet?" He wants to know because it's a point of honour to him to beat the girls at their own game [...] "Yes, I've been off. Four!" It's always satisfactory to start the night with a client for £4. — Anonymous *Streetwalker*, p. 18–19, 1959

5 not using drugs *US*

- "You mean you're off it?" "Yeah, off it. I'm kicking it." — Hal Ellson, *The Golden Spike*, p. 103, 1952
- "Anyway, I didn't want to come around because I knew you was off. You off completely?" — William Burroughs, *Junkie*, p. 118, 1953

▸ **be off!; be off with you!**

go away! *UK, 1842*

Old-fashioned, but still in use.

- "Sorry to trouble you, Mr Jay," said the snivelling wretch, "but there's something here I don't quite understand." "Be off with you," replied the great man, "that piece was written for only three people in Britain and you are not one of them." — *New Statesman*, 13th September 1999

offbeat *adjective*

unconventional, but not unique *US, 1938*

- They Lived And Loved In The Off-Beat World Of Lesbianism. — Miriam Garner (Marion Zimmer Bradley), *Twilight Lovers*, 1964

off-brand cigarette *noun*

a marijuana cigarette *US*

- — Edith A. Folb, *runnin' down some lines*, p. 248, 1980

off-brand stud *noun*

a male homosexual *US*

- — Anthony Romeo, *The Language of Gangs*, p. 20, 4th December 1962

off-by-one error *noun*

in computing, any simple and basic error, such as starting at 1 instead of 0 *US*

- — Eric S. Raymond, *The New Hacker's Dictionary*, p. 267, 1991

off colour *adjective*

1 applied to jokes that may be considered impolite or indecent *UK, 1875*

- Besides, off colour jokes in medicine have an honourable pedigree[.] — *British Medical Journal*, 27th January 2001

2 unwell *UK, 1876*

- Feeling off colour after a day at the pub. — *The Observer*, 23rd November 2003

offensive potatoes *noun*

canned potatoes *ANTARCTICA*

- — *Cool Antarctica*, 2003: 'Antarctic slang'

offer *verb*

▸ **offer you out**

to challenge (you) to a fight *AUSTRALIA, 1943*

- [I]n the clubs or pubs where someone fancied their chances and offered me out. — Lenny McLean, *The Guv'nor*, p. 92, 1998
- Divall – who wasn't known for his sense of humour – offered him out in the street and both removed their jackets for a stand-up fight[.] — Brian McDonald, *Elephant Boys*, p. 61, 2000
- Adam came to my trailer and offered me out. — Jimmy Stockin, *On The Cobbles*, p. 173, 2000

office *noun*

1 a warning; a private signal *UK, 1818*

- [O]ne player gives the other a prearranged signal (gives him "the offic," as the hustler's argot has it). — Ned Polsky, *Hustlers, Beats, and Others*, p. 58, 1967
- "We'll rap tomorrow after breakfast." "Same office?" "Now what do you think?" — Malcolm Braly, *On the Yard*, p. 38, 1967
- Within five minutes he gave me the "office" that some action was coming down the street. — Iceberg Slim (Robert Beck), *Pimp*, p. 37, 1969

2 any secret signal used by gambling cheats to communicate among themselves *US*

- — *The Annals of the American Academy of Political and Social Sciences*, p. 128, May 1950

3 a hint or tip *AUSTRALIA, 1874*

- Cripes, she looked back twice. Practically gives a bloke the office she's on. — Norman Lindsay, *Halfway to Anywhere*, p. 51, 1947

▸ **give the office**

in prison, to explain the way things are, especially to a new inmate *UK*

- — Angela Devlin, *Prison Patter*, p. 57, 1996

office bike *noun*

a woman who readily has sexual intercourse with fellow staff in an office *AUSTRALIA, 1945*

office hours *noun*

1 minor discipline issued by a US Marine Corps company commander *US, 1898*

- You tell them if anybody pulls this shit again I'm gonna rock them in office hours, and they'll never get promoted in this Company. — Charles Andreson, *The Grunts*, p. 94, 1976

2 in poker, pairs of 9s and 5s, or a straight from 9 to 5 *US*

- — Irwin Steig, *Common Sense in Poker*, p. 185, 1963

office piano *noun*

a typewriter *US*

- — Lou Shelly, *Hepcats Jive Talk Dictionary*, p. 29, 1945
- — Clarence Major, *Dictionary of Afro-American Slang*, p. 87, 1970

officer material *noun*

a mentally deficient enlisted soldier *US, 1945*

- — *American Speech*, p. 238, October 1946: 'World War II slang of maladjustment'

office worker *noun*

a shirker *UK*

Rhyming slang, used by manual labourers, with a subtext of bitter irony.

- — Ray Puxley, *Cockney Rabbit*, 1992

offie; offy *noun*

an off-licence (a shop licensed to sell alcoholic drinks for consumption *off* the premises) *UK*

- "Shall we get something to drink? Would you like that?" Oh yes. I am dispatched to the offie with a fifty pound note[.] — Jenny Knight, *Stupid [britpulp]*, p. 266, 1999
- Hey our Antony, nip down to the offie and get us some ciggies. — Caroline Aherne and Craig Cash, *The Royle Family*, 1999
- Right by the offy. Then left. — David Peace, *Nineteen Seventy-Four*, p. 150, 1999

off it *adjective*

drug-intoxicated *UK*

A variation of **OFF YOUR HEAD**.

- Alaskan weed [..] was – and is – the strongest puff I've ever smoked, or am ever likely to. I was off it. — Wayne Anthony, *Spanish Highs*, p. 111, 1999

offshore *adjective*

foreign *US*

- Any offshore stuff. Do the Rinas have any interests in any banks, any savings and loans? — Stephen Cannell, p. 116, 1997

offsider *noun*
an assistant *AUSTRALIA, 1903*
Originally (late C19) an assistant/apprentice to a bullock-driver who worked on the 'off side'.
- I racked my brains. As offsider to a politician, I meet a lot of people. —Shane Maloney, *Nice Try*, p. 8, 1998

offski *verb*
to go away, to leave *UK*
- I understood you was gonna fetch it here in a van, we trade and offski. —Garry Bushell, *The Face*, p. 12, 2001

off the back of a lorry *adjective*
▷ see: FALLEN OFF THE BACK OF A LORRY

off to another NASA convention
used for humour when someone who has been displaying their ignorance leaves a room *US*
- —Connie Eble (Editor), *UNC-CH Campus Slang*, p. 4, Fall 1991

off-trail *adjective*
unconventional, eccentric *US*
- Of all the weird, off-trail characters I have known, he was the weirdest, the most off-trail. —Jim Thompson, *Roughneck*, p. 33, 1954

Offy *noun*
a racing engine or any other piece of equipment manufactured by Meyer-Drake *US*
- —John Edwards, *Auto Dictionary*, p. 116, 1993

o-for *adjective*
▷ see: OFER

OG *noun*
1 your mother *US, 1878*
An abbreviation of OLD GIRL.
- —David Claerbaut, *Black Jargon in White America*, p. 73, 1972

2 a founding member of a youth gang *US*
An abbreviation of ORIGINAL GANGSTER.
- We had to rush the O.G.'s for that. —*Menace II Society*, 1993

oggin *noun*
the ocean *ANTARCTICA*
- — *Cool Antarctica*, 2003: 'Antarctic slang'

ogle *noun*
the eye *UK, 1676*
Survives mainly as a part of the polari vocabulary; usually in the plural.
- [T]onight's concert with those camp munchkins [children], all ogles and pots [teeth] and nante voce [voice]. —the cast of 'Aspects of Love', Prince of Wales Theatre, *Palare (Boy Dancer Talk) for Beginners*, 1989–92
- —Paul Baker, *Polari*, p. 184, 2002

ogle; ogale *verb*
in homosexual use, to look longingly or amorously at a man *UK, 1682*
From the wider conventional sense first recorded in the 1680s.
- —Paul Baker, *Polari*, p. 184, 2002

ogle and leer *noun*
gonorrhoea *UK*
Rhyming slang.
- —Bodmin Dark, *Dirty Cockney Rhyming Slang*, 2003

ogle fake; ogle riah fake; ogle fake riah *noun*
a false eyelash *UK*
Polari; literally 'articles (of hair) made for the eye'.
- —the cast of 'Aspects of Love', Prince of Wales Theatre, *Palare (Boy Dancer Talk) for Beginners*, 1989–92
- [She] straightened up one ogle fake riah that had come adrift[.] —James Gardiner, *Who's a Pretty Boy Then?*, p. 123, 1996
- —Paul Baker, *Polari*, p. 184, 2002

ogle fakes *noun*
spectacles *UK*
Polari; literally 'articles made for the eye'.
- —Paul Baker, *Polari*, p. 184, 2002

ogle filters *noun*
sunglasses *UK*
Polari; based on OGLE (the eye).
- —Paul Baker, *Polari*, p. 184, 2002

ogle riahs *noun*
eyelashes *UK*
Polari; a combination of OGLE (the eye) and RIAH (the hair).
- —Paul Baker, *Polari*, p. 184, 2002

ogle riders *noun*
the eyebrows or eyelashes *UK*
- —Paul Baker, *Polari*, p. 184, 2002

ogle shades *noun*
glasses; sunglasses *UK*
Polari; based on OGLE (the eye).
- —Paul Baker, *Polari*, p. 184, 2002

Ogopogo *noun*
a legendary monster in Okanagan Lake, British Columbia *CANADA*
- Here, according to hundreds of British Columbians who claim they've seen them – [are] a number of friendly sea monsters, including "Ogopogo." — *Canadian Geographical Journal*, p. 91/1, March 1964

ogoy *noun*
heroin *US, 1977*
- —Richard A. Spears, *The Slang and Jargon of Drugs and Drink*, p. 365, 1986
- —Robert Ashton, *This Is Heroin*, p. 206, 2002
- —Mike Haskins, *Drugs*, p. 284, 2003

oh, behave
used as a catch-all catchphrase, usually in the context of a sexual innuendo *US*
Wildly popular for several years after the release of the first *Austin Powers* film in 1997.
- SUPERMODEL 1: We could have another photo session back at my flat. AUSTIN: Oh, behave! — *Austin Powers*, 1997

oh cringe!, oh dear!
▷ see: CRINGE!, DEAR!

oh, fiddle-faddle!
used as a non-profane expression of frustration *US*
Used with regularity by the Aunt Bee character on *The Andy Griffith Show* (CBS, 1960–68). Repeated with referential humour.

Ohio bag *noun*
one hundred grams of marijuana *US*
Under Ohio's decriminalisation laws, this is the maximum amount for a fine for simple possession.
- —Ernest L. Abel, *A Marijuana Dictionary*, p. 75, 1982

ohmigod!; omigod!
used for expressing surprise or horror *US*
- —Mary Corey and Victoria Westermark, *Fer Shurr! How to be a Valley Girl*, 1982
- "Omigod," she said, eyes wide, the shock obvious on her face. —Janet Evanovich, *Seven Up*, p. 239, 2001

oh my Gawd; oh my good Gawd *adjective*
bald *UK*
Rhyming slang; the second variation is reserved for extreme baldness.
- Oh my Gawd he's gone oh my Gawd. —Ray Puxley, *Cockney Rabbit*, 1992

oh my stars!
used for expressing frustration *US*
Popularised by the sexy blonde witch Samantha on *Bewitched* (ABC, 1964–72). Repeated with referential humour.

oh nelly!
used for humorously expressing surprise or upset *US*
- —Connie Eble (Editor), *UNC-CH Campus Slang*, p. 6, Fall 1997

ohnosecond *noun*
an instant of realisation when you have made a mistake, especially in computing *UK*
A punning combination of 'nanosecond' and the exclamation 'oh no!'.
- —Adam T. Fox, St Mary's Hospital, London 10th October 2002
- — Susie Dent, *The Language Report*, p. 30, 2003

-oholic *suffix*
▷ see: -AHOLIC

oh Rinehart!
▷ see: RINEHART!

oh-shit *noun*
a criticism *US*
• You tried to frame your own prosecutor. The list of 'Oh shits' is awesome.—Stephen Cannell, *Big Con*, p. 398, 1997

oh snap!
used as a mild oath *US*
• —Connie Eble (Editor), *UNC-CH Campus Slang*, p. 8, October 2002

oh the pain, the shame!
used as a humorous comment on humiliation *US*
Coined on the television programme *Lost in Space* (1965–68), and then revived and popularised by Keith Olberman on ESPN.
• —Keith Olberman and Dan Patrick, *The Big Show*, p. 22, 1997

oh yeah?
used in questioning veracity or likelihood, or confirming that a person being addressed has understood or is in agreement *US, 1930*
• Oh yeah – you and whose armoury?—*The Observer*, 17th November 2002

oh-zee
▷ see: oz

oi!; oy!
a meaningless noise used to draw attention or cry in protest *UK, 1936*
Derives from the obsolete 'hoy!', which was a combination of 'ho!' and 'hullo!'.
• I shouted out "Oi, oi," but he didn't say nothing[.]—Greg Williams, *Diamond Geezers*, p. 172, 1997
• Oi, watch it mate. You see that? Nearly took the wing mirror off. Idiot.—Simon Lewis, *In The Box [britpulp]*, p. 128, 1999

oicery *noun*
the sleeping quarters of the officer in charge (OIC) *ANTARCTICA, 1959*
• —Bernadette Hince, *The Antarctic Dictionary*, p. 245, 2000

-oid *suffix*
used as a suffix that embellishes without changing the base word's meaning *US, 1978*
• In the middle of the room was a cheesoid Formica replica-pulpit.—Frank Zappa, *The Real Frank Zappa Book*, p. 81, 1989
• Now fearing I would become the brunt of it, I vowed never to introduce another interesting factoid into the rumor mill again.—Rita Ciresi, *Pink Slip*, p. 107, 1999

oik *noun*
someone considered to be a social inferior; a disagreeable youth *UK, 1925*
Originally a public school coinage used to categorise status: 'a townee'; then generalised as 'working-class'; also used within that circle as general abuse for an unpopular fellow pupil or someone from a rival school. Generated from HOICK (to hawk and spit).
• RODDY [an officer]: What do I not like about the Army? Mmmm. Well ... the, ah, oiks ... soldiers, they're a pretty moderate bunch of specimens[.]—Mike Stott, *Soldiers Talking, Cleanly*, 1978
• Having a dozen sentimental oiks pontificatiing on every decision was quite clearly out of the question[.]—John King, *White Trash*, p. 188, 2001

oil *noun*
1 alcohol *US, 1912*
• Janet didn't drink, so I didn't really need any oil but I picked up a pint of gin anyway[.]—Donald Goines, *Never Die Alone*, p. 113, 1974

2 a potent distillate of marijuana or hashish *US*
• We used to bong up on oil after that[.]—Macfarlane, Macfarlane and Robson, *The User*, p. 88, 1996

3 heroin *UK, 1998*
• —Mike Haskins, *Drugs*, p. 284, 2003

4 news; information about something *AUSTRALIA, 1915*
Metaphorically because oil is essential for the smooth running of a machine.
• He spoke to me out of the side of his mouth. I knew this was genuine. This was the oil.—Sutton Woodfield, *A for Artemis*, p. 29, 1960

5 in horse racing, confidential and reliable information about a horse *AUSTRALIA*
• —Ned Wallish, *The Truth Dictionary of Racing Slang*, p. 34, 1989

6 in pool, extreme spin imparted to the cue ball to affect the course of the object ball or the cue ball after striking the object ball *US, 1912*
• —Mike Shamos, *The Illustrated Encyclopedia of Billiards*, p. 160, 1993

▸ **the oil**
the complete truth, the lowdown *NEW ZEALAND*
• —David McGill, *David McGill's Complete Kiwi Slang Dictionary*, p. 78, 1998

oil *verb*
1 to inject yourself with a drug, especially heroin *US, 1981*
• —Richard A. Spears, *The Slang and Jargon of Drugs and Drink*, p. 366, 1986

2 to bribe *US*
• —Ralph de Sola, *Crime Dictionary*, p. 106, 1982

▸ **oil it**
to study late into the night *US*
• —*American Speech*, p. 63, Spring-Summer 1975: 'Razorback slang'

oil and water king *noun*
aboard ship, the engineer controlling fresh water distillation *US*
• —Hans Halberstadt, *USCG*, p. 129, 1986: 'Glossary'

oil burner *noun*
1 a serious drug addiction *US, 1938*
• —*The New American Mercury*, p. 711, 1950
• We both got oil burners, especially Nina.—Clarence Cooper Jr, *The Scene*, p. 43, 1960
• "You look like you kicked an ass wiper." "An oil burner."—Malcolm Braly, *On the Yard*, p. 31, 1967
• You better cut down on your blows, Terry, or you're going to end up with a oil burner.—Donald Goines, *Dopefiend*, p. 118, 1971
• He knew I had an oil burner but he also knew I never once tried to get him to use during all the time we were running buddies.—A.S. Jackson, *Gentleman Pimp*, p. 102, 1973

2 in trucking, a diesel engine *US*
• —Montie Tak, *Truck Talk*, p. 111, 1971

3 in horse racing, a fast horse *US*
• —David W. Maurer, *Argot of the Racetrack*, p. 46, 1951

oil-burning *adjective*
(used of a drug addiction) severe *US*
• I had this habit, a real bad oil-burning habit—Bruce Jackson, *In the Life*, p. 81, 1972
• Things were so smooth that we both got an oil-burning habit (a habit to end all habits) out of the deal.—Herbert Huncke, *Guilty of Everything*, p. 103, 1990

oil can *noun*
a railway tank wagon *US*
• —Norman Carlisle, *The Modern Wonder Book of Trains and Railroading*, p. 266, 1946

oil-can *verb*
(of a boat) to make a hollow booming sound striking the water *US*
• Won't go fast, but very stable. doesn't oil-can when you go to weather.—Joseph Wambaugh, *The Golden Orange*, p. 74, 1990

oiled; oiled up *adjective*
1 drunk *US, 1737*
• —Lou Shelly, *Hepcats Jive Talk Dictionary*, p. 15, 1945
• "Sit down, Holden," Mr. Antolini said. You could tell he was a little oiled up.—J.D. Salinger, *Catcher in the Rye*, p. 182, 1951
• You know. Drunk stewed, clobbered, gone, liquored up, oiled, stoned, in the bag.—Max Shulman, *Guided Tour of Campus Humor*, p. 106, 1955
• I hope the loudness of Audrey's oiled up voice isn't carrying as far as Peter.—Ted Lewis, *Jack Carter's Law*, p. 61, 1974
• Poor old Ian got himself nicely oiled[.]— Barry Humphries, *The Traveller's Tool*, p. 96, 1985
• Frank was not too oiled to miss that.—George V. Higgins, *Penance for Jerry Kennedy*, p. 47, 1985

2 readied; well-prepared *UK*
• I put my jacket on over the tracksuit, hard man. Ray-Bans [of] course [...] Put my gloves on I got from the army surplus. I was oiled.—Jeremy Cameron, *Brown Bread in Wengen*, p. 183, 1999

oilies *noun*
work clothes *US*
• —Jerry Robertson, *Oil Slanguage*, p. 66, 1954

oil in the can *noun*
in horse racing, a horse believed by its backers to be a sure winner *US*
• —David W. Maurer, *Argot of the Racetrack*, p. 46, 1951

oil leak *noun*

a Sikh *UK*

Rhyming slang.

- —Ray Puxley, *Fresh Rabbit*, 1998

oil merchant *noun*

a smooth-talking swindler *US, 1935*

- —Hyman E. Goldin et al., *Dictionary of American Underworld Lingo*, p. 148, 1950

oil patch *noun*

the oil industry *US, 1980*

- —Rachel S. Epstein and Nina Liebman, *Biz Speak*, p. 159, 1986

oil slick *noun*

a Spaniard *UK*

Rhyming slang for **SPIC**.

- —Ray Puxley, *Cockney Rabbit*, 1992

oil tanker *noun*

used as an all-purpose form of abuse *UK*

Rhyming slang for **WANKER**.

- —Ray Puxley, *Cockney Rabbit*, 1992

oil well *noun*

in a deck of playing cards, an ace *US*

From the visual comparison of an 'A' with an oil well.

- —George Percy, *The Language of Poker*, p. 60, 1988

oily *adjective*

mean-spirited, tough *US*

- —*American Speech*, p. 271, December 1958: 'Ranching terms from Eastern Washington'

oily rag *noun*

1 a worker's assistant *UK*

- [H]e'd probably have bagged the pair, one for himself and one for his oily rag.—Andrew Nickolds, *Back to Basics*, p. 154, 1994

2 a cigarette *UK, 1932*

Rhyming slang for **FAG** (a cigarette). Also shortened to 'oil-rag' and 'oily'.

- Rolled an oily rag.—Viv Stanshall, *Ginger Geezer*, 1981
- —Angela Devlin, *Prison Patter*, p. 81, 1996

oink *noun*

a police officer *US*

A far less common usage than the related **PIG** (police).

- —Clarence Major, *Dictionary of Afro-American Slang*, p. 87, 1970

oink *verb*

to lure by greed *US*

- You can't oink Biff into just anything. He don't need the loot, understand.—Bernard Wolfe, *The Late Risers*, p. 193, 1954

oinseach *noun*

a female fool *IRELAND*

- Not long ago I was having a quiet drink in a certain pub in a certain southern county when the gushing alewife shouted over our heads that a Government minister was on his way and that we should all stand up when he came in the door, like, "as a matter of etiquette". I am glad to be able to report that people fell off bar stools laughing at the poor oinseach, and that your man was completely ignored when he did arrive with his retinue.—*Irish Times*, 10th March 2001

Oirish *adjective*

Irish *UK*

From the stereotypically Irish pronunciation of 'Irish'.

- [H]e'd pay up like the Oirish gentleman he was[.]—Derek Raymond (Robin Cook), *The Crust on its Uppers*, p. 33, 1962
- They've already snapped up the rights to her chirpy Oirish [Irish] romance[.]—*The Guardian*, 11th January 2003

OJ *noun*

1 marijuana *US, 1970*

Possibly, an initialism of 'oint-jay' (**JOINT**).

- —Richard A. Spears, *The Slang and Jargon of Drugs and Drink*, p. 366, 1986
- —Mike Haskins, *Drugs*, p. 288, 2003

2 a marijuana cigarette dipped in liquid opium or heroin *US*

In other words, an '*o*pium *j*oint'. Popular with US troops in Vietnam.

- —William D. Alsever, *Glossary for the Establishment and Other Uptight People*, p. 23, December 1970
- The O-Js were thin, perfectly rolled marijuana cigarettes soaked in an opium solution. Fifty O-Js to a deck.—John Del Vecchio, *The 13th Valley*, p. 31, 1982
- The model for usage of the OJ (opium joint – heroin loaded cigarette) was that of the social group use of marijuana at home. [Referring to the war in Vietnam]—David H. Marlowe, *Psychological and Psychosocial Consequences of Combat and Deployment*, p. 93, 2001
- Opium and marijuana rolled into a cigarette is sometimes called an OJ, which is short for "Opium Joint."—Debra Moraes, *The Little Book of Opium*, p. 19, 2003

3 an *o*nline *j*ockey who hosts Internet discussions *UK*

Initialism, on the model of DJ (disc jockey).

- Not a Simpson, not even a soft drink, but the latest in talk show hosts.—David Rowan, *A Glossary for the 90s*, p. 123, 1998

OK; okay *noun*

1 consent, approval *US, 1841*

- The Chancellor gave his okay to the idea[.]—Randy Neil, *The Official Cheerleader's Handbook*, p. 19, 1979
- McFarlane told Congress last week that Reagan gave his okay for the deal to proceed.—*Chicago Tribune*, p. C1, 14th December 1986
- If the rising payroll-tax burden was imposed on young working people, they would eventually revolt and Social Security would self-destruct of its own weight. The Gipper liked that, and gave his OK.—Holly Sklar, *Raise the Floor*, p. 172, 2001

2 a bribe paid by an illegal gambling establishment to the authorities to stay in business *US*

- —John Scarne, *Scarne's Guide to Modern Poker*, p. 285, 1979

OK; okay *verb*

to approve *US, 1988*

- Scotty signed it and the Judge okayed it.—Bernard Malamud, *The Natural*, p. 42, 1952
- Supervising this entire phase of the operation was a medical officer with a flair for accounting who okayed pulses and checked the figures of the tally clerk.—Joseph Heller, *Catch 22*, p. 80–81, 1961
- His Holiness Sheikh Muhammad Harkon himself okayed my visit to Mecca.—Malcolm X and Alex Haley, *The Autobiography of Malcolm X*, 1964
- McFarlane testifies that Reagan okayed first arm shipment.—*ABC World News Tonight*, 5th December 1986
- Even some of the more incurious might wonder if North okayed his wife's Philadelphia rendezvous with a total stranger who wished to offer her $70,000 because he "loved" her husband.—*Washington Post*, p. A2, 7th July 1987

OK; okay *adjective*

1 comfortable, at ease *US*

Especially common as 'OK about' or 'OK with'.

- To be successful in it as a career ... a girl is going to have to know values as well as skills – how to feel OK about herself and what she's doing.—*Washington Post*, p. C3, 2nd April 1978
- Felt OK about it, actually, strangely enough. I don't recall too much guilty.—*The Oprah Winfrey Show*, 27th October 2004

2 safe, unhurt *US, 1839*

- Not a sound came over the intercom until a few long seconds later, and then the skipper asked if we were all OK.—Ron Smith, *Rear Gunner Pathfinders*, p. 23, 1987
- Are you okay? You don't look good.—Aaron McGruder, *Fresh for '01*, p. 96, 2001
- Are you okay Sir? How's the bird Sir? Where'd you get the feckin' bullet holes Sir?—Samuel Brantley, *Zero Dark Thirty*, p. 69, 2002

3 decent, mediocre, satisfactory *US, 1839*

In 1963, the late Allen Walker Read published his extensive and definitive research on the term, tracing its coinage to 1839 as an abbreviation of 'oll korrect', itself a then-popular slang term.

- MOM: How are you? ANDY: Okay. MOM: Just okay? You sound a little down.—Helen E. Johnson, *Don't Tell Me What to Do, Just Send Money*, p. 61, 2000
- The printed looked okay, but just okay.—Bruce Campbell, *If Chins Could Kill*, p. 74, 2002
- "That's okay," I told her. "I'll be fine."—Sue Monk Kidd, *The Secret Life of Bees*, p. 28, 2002
- The upshot: he hopped on the next plane to L.A. to see me and make sure everything was okay.—Janice Dickson, *Everything ABout Me is Fake*, p. 128, 2004

OK

when appended to a slogan, used as a strengthening affirmative, especially when phrased '*X* rule (or rules) OK' *UK*

Nigel Rees, *Graffiti Lives, OK*, 1979, writes: 'The addition of "OK" to slogans first became noticeable in Northern Ireland during the early 1970s, as in "Provos Rule, OK" referring to the Provisional IRA'.

- Inspectors say inspectors rule OK.—*The Guardian*, 22nd March 2002

OK; okay

used for expressing assent, approval, understanding or agreement *US, 1839*

- Okay. That's Washington. But will it happen elsewhere too? — *Forbes*, p. 35, 15th November 1976
- "Forty-five guys won this game. Okay, that's a cliche, right?" — *Washington Post*, p. F1, 20th December 1979
- I love my clients, okay? — Malcolm Gladwell, *The Tipping Point*, p. 71, 2002
- Okay, Sophie, if you must know, P.S. is a code. — Dan Brown, *The Da Vinci Code*, p. 112, 2003
- Okay, some guys might like it, but they're just lazy. — Greg Behrendt, *He's Just Not That Into You*, p. 16, 2004
- One jugee wrote his essay on a tiny piece of paper and gave it to Father Sturm, who promptly handed it back and sad, "Okay, wise guy, read it." — Tim Russert, *Big Russ and Me*, p. 183, 2004

OK Corral *noun*

a group of men masturbating while watching a female *US*

An extrapolation of the **GUN DOWN** image, alluding to the site of a famous American gun battle in 1881.

- — Gary K. Farlow, *Prison-ese*, p. 46, 2002

oke *noun*

used as an affectionate or patronising term of address or reference to a man or boy *SOUTH AFRICA, 1970*

A shortened form of **OKIE**.

- Oke no 2 was a seriously dishy dreadlocked California model called Pope who's got hand-kissing down to a fine art. — *Sunday Times (South Africa)*, 4th April 2000

okey-doke *noun*

1 a swindle or deception *US*

- Ain't no nigger pimp going to put my ass in a sling. I'm too slick for that 'okee doke.' — Iceberg Slim (Robert Beck), *Pimp*, p. 116, 1969
- Forget about that okey-doke shit – gorilla-ing people, robbing pads. — Edwin Torres, *Carlito's Way*, p. 21, 1975
- So its up to all of us down people to see that cats like Brother Martin, Brother Malcolm, Brother Evers, and others did not go for the whitey oke-e-doke in vain. — Babs Gonzales, *Movin' On Down De Line*, p. 98, 1975

2 a wallet, especially its contents *UK*

Rhyming slang for **POKE** used by pickpockets. Sometimes shortened to 'okey'.

- — Julian Franklyn, *A Dictionary of Rhyming Slang*, 1961

okey-doke

used for communicating agreement *US, 1936*

A shortening of **OKEY-DOKEY**.

- "Based on the book!" Okey-doke. — *The Sporting News*, 4th March 2002

okey-dokey *adjective*

acceptable *US, 1942*

- He shrugs, "That's okee dokee with me." — Iceberg Slim (Robert Beck), *Doom Fox*, p. 122, 1978
- Ged Brennan pulls up outside his cousin's gaff. Okey-dokey. Over to you Paulie, lad. — Kevin Sampson, *Clubland*, p. 248, 2002

okey-dokey

used for communicating agreement *US, 1932*

An old-fashioned, affected, still popular perversion of **OK**.

- KRINKILE: Now what's happened, what's going on, and what are you talking about. DIMES: Okee-dokee. It's like this. — *True Romance*, 1993
- Okee dokey. You should come back in seven days and we should have your results. — *Kids*, 1995
- Okey-dokey, thanks a bunch. — *Fargo*, 1996
- Okey-dokey, so tomorrow night? — *Something About Mary*, 1998
- "Okey-dokey?" The nurse smiles as she opens her eyes. "All clear[.]" — Andrea Ashworth, *Moretti's Super-Swirl*, p. 72, 1999

Oki; Okie *noun*

Okinawa *US, 1945*

Coined in World War 2, still used in Vietnam.

- I just think of that first steam bath I'm going to get on Oki. — Charles Anderson, *The Grunts*, p. 11, 1976

okie; oakie *noun*

used as an affectionate or patronising term of address or reference to a man or boy *SOUTH AFRICA, 1943*

Anglicised form of Afrikaans *outjie*.

- With regards to your "okie" talking to other girls: You talk to other guys, don't you? — *Sunday Times (South Africa)*, 1st December 2002

Okie *noun*

a poor, white resident or native of rural Oklahoma; a poor, white resident or native of the south-central US *US, 1938*

Used with derision or pride but not neutrally. 'Derogatory slang for whites' (Multicultural Management Program Fellows, 1989).

- "He done hit me twice," he snarled in an Okie voice. — Chester Himes, *If He Hollers Let Him Go*, p. 31, 1945
- I am quickly annoyed with people who speak disparagingly of "Okies." — Jim Thompson, *Roughneck*, p. 69, 1954
- So after a few beers in the saloon, where sullen Okies reeled to the music of a cowboy band, Terry and I and Johnny went into a motel room and got ready to hit the sack. — Jack Kerouac, *On the Road*, p. 93, 1957
- You don't know whether she's a hillbilly or an Okie or what. — Truman Capote, *Breakfast at Tiffany's*, p. 68, 1958
- The one thing about the Row was that it was filled with okies, weary old Wobblies, drunkies and dopies far gone, whores on their last legs – they never judged you. — Clancy Sigal, *Going Away*, p. 238, 1961
- Riverbank is divided into three parts, and in my corner of the world there were only three kinds of people: Mexicans, Okies and Americans. — Oscar Zeta Acosta, *The Autobiography of a Brown Buffalo*, p. 78, 1972

Okie blower *noun*

in trucking, an air scoop attached to the air-intake system *US*

- — Montie Tak, *Truck Talk*, p. 111, 1971

Okie chrome *noun*

aluminium paint *US*

- — *American Speech*, p. 272, December 1961: 'Northwest truck drivers' language'

Okie trap *noun*

a confusing, complicated traffic interchange *US*

- — *American Speech*, p. 271, December 1962: 'The language of traffic policemen'

Oklahoma credit card *noun*

a hose used to steal petrol by siphoning it from a parked car *US*

Presenting the myth of Oklahoma as a state filled with poor, crafty and dishonest people.

- — *American Speech*, p. 271, December 1962: 'The language of traffic policemen'

Oklahoma toothbrush *noun*

the penis *US*

In Oklahoma, known as a 'Texas toothbrush'.

- — Michael Dalton Johnson, *Talking Trash with Redd Foxx*, p. 93, 1994

OK Yardie *noun*

a stereotypical Briton of the upper- or middle-class who lives in west London's gangland *UK*

A conflation of 'OK, yah' (a catchphrase cliché of the social grouping) and **YARDIE** (a Jamaican gangster).

- — David Rowan, *A Glossary for the 90s*, p. 9, 1998

-ola *suffix*

a meaningless embellishment of a suffix *US, 1919*

- He borrowed thirty-eight bucks from me once, never paid it back. A lousola. — Marvin Wald and Albert Maltz, *The Naked City*, p. 107, 1947
- Payola — *American Speech*, p. 104–116, May 1961
- Mickey Cohen is Skidsville, U.S.A., and he needs moolah, gelt, the old cashola. — James Elroy, *White Jazz*, p. 7, 1992

olalliechuk *noun*

(on the Pacific coast) a homebrew made from berries *CANADA*

The name comes from Chinook jargon.

- The Indian potlatch was only a heathen festival, where people gathered to feast on native food with ollaliechuk. — *Islander*, p. 6/2, 27th February 1966

old *noun*

a dark lager-style beer brewed by the top-fermentation method *AUSTRALIA, 1935*

As opposed to **NEW**.

- — Dymphna Cusack, *Picnic Races*, p. 198, 1962
- I reckon a middy of old would go down well. — Robert G. Barrett, *Davo's Little Something*, p. 179, 1992

old; ol'; ole *adjective*

1 used to intensify some intensifiers *UK, 1844*

A slight narrowing of use since first recorded in the 1440s as 'grand, great, plentiful' now mainly seen in such constructions as: 'high old time' (1858) and 'gay old boys' (1887).

- [S]tate schools, I used to joke, were so called because they were in a "right old state" [a mess]. — Jenny Eclair, *Camberwell Beauty*, p. 60, 2000

2 old *UK, 1844*
- I said "What's so wrong 'bout a good ol' bombing?" — *The Guardian*, 20th February 2003

3 used as a signal of familiarity with the person so described *US*
As spoken in the southern US, not necessarily indicative of affection, cordiality or good humour.
- I talked to ol' Sully the other day. He's sure a good ol' boy, to be as sorry a sonofabitch as he is. — Ken Weaver, *Texas Crude*, p. 119, 1984

4 tiresome *US, 1864*
- I'd dismount with my AK and check them on foot, but that got old awful quick. — Larry Heinemann, *Close Quarters*, p. 248, 1977

old bag *noun*

1 an unattractive or unloveable old woman *UK, 1949*
Disparaging; possibly a variant of **OLD BAT**, cognisant of the following sense as 'an elderly prostitute' which itself may derive from **OLD BAT**. Ray Puxley, writing in 1992, suggests this may be rhyming slang, formed on 'hag'.
- I had to get the old bag on the end of a string, which I found was only too easy in fact it was a doddle. — Frank Norman, *Bang To Rights*, p. 111, 1958
- An old bag, minus a nose, was drinking quietly in a dirty little entry off Hanbury Street. — Geoffrey Fletcher, *Down Among the Meths Men*, p. 54, 1966
- [of Margaret Thatcher] That's really bad luck isn't it? To have two personalities and for both of them to be rancid old bags. — Mark Steel, *Reasons to be Cheerful*, p. 206, 2001

2 an elderly, slatternly prostitute; hence pejorative for a younger prostitute *UK*
- — Julian Franklyn, *A Dictionary of Rhyming Slang*, 1961

old bastard *noun*

a man; fellow *AUSTRALIA, 1944*
Used as an ironic form of friendly personal address, generally amongst males. Such is the love for this expression amongst working-class Australians, a charity organisation was formed in the 1970s under the name the Australasian Order of Old Bastards. Part of the rules of the order is that 'On encountering other O.B.'s in a bar one must administer a hearty slap on the back, accompanied with the cheerful salutation, "Hello you Old Bastard!". Membership card must be carried at all times. Failure to produce same when challenged by fellow O.B. incurs a penalty of one round of drinks'.
- No doubt about the old bastard – the day you put anything over him will be the day! — J.E. MacDonnell, *Don't Gimme the Ships*, p. 19, 1960
- It's good to see you, you old bastard. — Jean Brooks, *The Opal Witch*, p. 175, 1967
- Line us up a row of nice frosty stubbies will you – you miserable old bastard! — Barry Humphries, *The Wonderful World of Barry McKenzie*, p. 42, 1968
- Harry Rowley, a mate o' mine. Auctioneer. Tell him old Rosella friggen sent yer and ter give yer a job or I'll cut his water off, the old bastard. — D'Arcy Niland, *Dead Men Running*, p. 57, 1969
- He used to win and lose twenty grand in a night and he always had a hundred for me at the door. Didn't you, you old bastard. — Robert English, *Toxic Kisses*, p. 40, 1979
- They slap one another on the back saying things like silly old bastard. — Sandra Jobson, *Blokes*, p. 78, 1984
- But Peter and Jerry were likeable and persistent old bastards and for two years I conspired with them to get their monument afloat. — Shane Maloney, *Nice Try*, p. 253, 1998

old bat *noun*

a disagreeable, middle-aged or elderly woman *UK, 1886*
An elaboration of **BAT** (an ugly woman), originally 'a prostitute'.
- [T]here's Erna, a buttoned-up old bat with a soft spot for the local butcher[.] — *The Scotsman*, 22nd November, 2004

old bill *noun*

1 the penis *UK*
- The horse had an old bill about five foot long and it was practically touching the floor. — Lenny McLean, *The Guv'nor*, p. 44, 1998
- My old bill's up and pointing at me again now. — J.J. Connolly, *Layer Cake*, p. 214, 2000

2 a signal, by hand or word, asking 'Are there any other cheaters in this game?' *US*
- — John Scarne, *Scarne's Guide to Modern Poker*, p. 285, 1979

Old Bill *noun*

a police officer; the police *UK, 1958*
Original usage was singular, now mainly collective. Feasible etymologies, in no particular order of likelihood: i) 'Old Bill', a cartoon strip character created by Bruce Bairnsfeather (1888–1959), was a veteran of World War 1 with a distinctive 'authoritarian-looking' moustache – a status and description shared by many pre-World War 2 policemen.This derivation may be reinforced by the 1917 UK government's advertising campaign, featuring Old Bill dressed as a special constable, using the heading 'Old Bill says...' to disseminate important wartime information. ii) Derived from a blend of popular song 'Won't You Come Home, Bill Bailey' punning with 'The Old Bailey' (London's Central Criminal Court). iii) 'Old Bill' was King William IV (1765–1837), during whose reign (1830–37) the police force is wrongly thought to have been established. iv) 'Kaiser Bill', Kaiser Wilhelm I of Prussia (1797–1888), visited England in 1864 when the police uniform changed to helmet and tunic. v) Constables of the watch were nicknamed for the bills or billhooks that they carried as weapons. vi) In Victorian times the 'old bill' was the bill, or account, presented by police accepting bribes, or for services rendered. vii) New laws are introduced as parliamentary *bills*. viii) The London County Council registered all public service vehicles (police, fire and ambulance) with number plates BYL, leading villains to spot unmarked police cars as 'old Bill'. ix) Similarly, Scotland Yard's 'Flying Squad' (established 1921) was reportedly issued with BYL registrations so that the Squad became known as 'old Bill', and hence the police in general. x) In the 1860s, Limehouse police sergeant Bill Smith, of apocryphal memory, was nicknamed 'Old Bill'.
- "No, I won't," says Bri, with a bit of this spirit Old Bill's been on about, "because I haven't done nothink so get well you know what" — Derek Raymond (Robin Cook), *The Crust On Its Uppers*, p. 48, 1962
- It was wall-to-wall Old Bill that night[.] — Val McDermid, *Keeping on the Right Side of the Law*, p. 178, 1999
- If Old Bill hadn't turned up we'd have murdered them. — Martin King and Martin Knight, *The Naughty Nineties*, 1999
- — Martin Roach, *Dr. Marten's Air Wair*, 1999: 'Glossary of travellers' terms'
- The Old Bill there were as thick as pig shit[.] — Dave Courtney, *Raving Lunacy*, p. 12, 2000
- A certain East End copper who liked his beer. His daughter would be sent to fetch him home from one of a number of local pubs, pushing open the door she would cry: "Anyone seen old Bill?" — *The Bill: Official Website for TV Police Drama*, 2001

old bird *noun*

a mature, older or old woman *UK*
- I've never seen an old bird scoff so much, yet she stayed miniature. — Jonathan Gash, *The Ten Word Game*, p. 131, 2003

old bird *adjective*

of a prisoner, having traditonal values *UK*
- Cody, for all his protestations of having been wrongfully convicted, is classic "old bird". No snitching. No siding with the authorities. — *The Guardian*, 26th July 2001

old blind Bob *noun*

the penis *UK, 1974*

old bloke *noun*

the penis *AUSTRALIA*
- [N]ext thing you know, some bloke's straddling the hatch on the squat with a rope around his old bloke. — Roy Slaven (John Doyle), *Five South Coast Seasons*, p. 9, 1992

Old Blue Eyes *nickname*

Frank Sinatra, US singer (1915–98) *US*
- [T]wo together for old blue eyes' umpteenth farewell concert[.] — Anthony Masters, *Minder*, p. 49, 1984
- Has Ol' Blue Eyes ever been up? — Josh Alan Friedman, *Tales of Times Square*, p. 42, 1986
- The guards grinned and waved, and with her earth-brown hair streaming from under the helmet, Breda sprinted past Tamarisk Country Club , the home of Old Blue Eyes himself. — Joseph Wambaugh, *Fugitive Nights*, p. 55, 1992
- Ol' Blue Eyes did it His Way even after the final curtain fell, leaving a fortune to charities supporting abused children. — Aubrey Dillon-Malone, *I Was A Fugitive From A Hollywood Trivia Factory*, p. 135, 1999

old bollocks *noun*

an older man *UK*
- I really do like the old bollocks for all his faults[.] — J.J. Connolly, *Layer Cake*, p. 88, 2000

old boot; boot *noun*

an unattractive woman, a woman with qualities that are considered unattractive *UK, 1958*
- Ere, you dirty old boot, we know who you are and what you're doing. — Joe Morgan, *Eastenders Don't Cry*, p. 31, 1994

old boy *noun*

1 the penis *US, 1943*

- —Jim Ramsay, *Cop It Sweet!*, p. 65, 1977
- Up until I bolted to be with you, the only stimulation the old boy got was the odd dip in crab emulsion. —Kathy Lette, *Girls' Night Out*, p. 181, 1987

2 used as a friendly form of address to another man *UK*

A colloquial vocative since the C17.

- A job, old boy? —*The Observer*, 11th June 2000

3 an old man *UK, 1500*

- There were only two punters, old boys playing crib. —Garry Bushell, *The Face*, p. 6, 2001

4 a father *UK, 1892*

old boy network; Old Boy network *noun*

a social and, especially, business connection between former public school pupils which is presumed, by those without such a connection, to give unfair advantages in matters of employment and social advancement; also applied to connections made at university, and at other institutions which may be considered as for the privileged *UK, 1959*

- One of Scotland's top businessmen has a piece of advice for young people wishing to follow in his footsteps: get out of Scotland. It is parochial, self-centred and riddled with the old-boy network, he claims. —*The Guardian*, 21st September 2002

old breed *noun*

the First Marine Division, US Marine Corps, which saw service in World War 2, North China, Korea and Vietnam *US*

- —Linda Reinberg, *In the Field*, p. 156, 1991

old cat *noun*

A Morris Minor car *UK*

Citizens' band radio slang.

- —Peter Chippindale, *The British CB Book*, p. 161, 1981

old chap *noun*

1 used as a friendly form of address to another man *UK, 1822*

- I say old chap I don't like to trouble you but I wonder if[.] —Frank Norman, *Bang To Rights*, p. 107, 1958
- Sorry, old chap, but you don't have to come to work on Monday. You're fired. —*The Guardian*, 22nd July 2003

2 the penis *UK*

- [T]he need for safe sex is paramount. A "wise monkey" [condom] is therefore essential to deliver the old chap from evil. —Ray Puxley, *Cockney Rabbit*, p. 201, 1992
- I've shagged some fucking mingers in my time, but I'd rather put a cheese-grater over my knees and crawl around in vinegar than put my old chap..." Before Greg could finish, Arabella had run off in tears. —Colin Butts, *Is Harry Still on the Boat?*, p. 228, 2003

old comic *noun*

a Vauxhall Victor car *UK*

Citizens' band radio slang; it sounds like a name a music hall comedian would use.

- —Peter Chippindale, *The British CB Book*, p. 161, 1981

Old Corncob *nickname*

General Douglas MacArthur (1880–1964) of the US Army *US*

From his love for a corncob pipe.

- —Frank Hailey, *Soldier Talk*, p. 46, 1982

old country *noun*

1 to the US armed forces at the end of Word War 2, the United States *US*

- —*American Speech*, p. 30, February 1949: 'A.V.G. lingo'

2 Beverly Hills, California *US*

Used with irony by transplants, especially Jewish transplants, to the San Fernando Valley. Collected in Los Angeles, March 2004.

Old Country *nickname*

England or the United Kingdom *AUSTRALIA, 1834*

- By the time this reaches you you'll be in the Old Country. —Barry Humphries, *A Nice Night's Entertainment*, p. 23, 1959

old cow *noun*

a despicable old woman *AUSTRALIA, 1864*

- All the same, that old cow Martha must have told Ma something[.] —Norman Lindsay, *Halfway to Anywhere*, p. 68, 1947

old D *noun*

a mother *UK*

Initially 'dear' or 'darling'.

- —Angela Devlin, *Prison Patter*, p. 81, 1996

Old Dart *nickname*

England or the United Kingdom; specifically, London *AUSTRALIA, 1892*

First recorded in use in England in 1832 (Wilkes). 'Dart' represents the pronunciation of the word 'dirt' in the Essex dialect, and so 'Old Dart' would correlate with 'old sod' (one's native district or country).

- A good trip back to the Old Dart, via America. —John Wynnum, *Jiggin' in the Riggin'*, p. 109, 1965
- Not only was it the night of a one-day cricket international between England and Australia in the Old Dart, but it was also the coldest night I can remember. —Rex Hunt, *Tall Tales – and True*, p. 18, 1994

old dear *noun*

an old woman *UK*

- He started telling me how he con[n]ed all this gilt of the old dear. —Frank Norman, *Bang To Rights*, p. 108, 1958
- This snotty old dear on the next table[.] —Dave Courtney, *Stop the Ride I Want to Get Off*, p. 344, 1999

▷ **see:** OUL ONE

old dog *noun*

a Rover car *UK*

- —Peter Chippindale, *The British CB Book*, p. 161, 1981

old face *noun*

a chorus dancer whose long tenure makes her unmarketable *US*

- [T]here are thousands of kids who pound out the soles of their aching feet for five or six years, then discover that at 21 or 22 they've been around the Stem so long the managers call them "old faces" and they no longer can get work. —Jack Lait and Lee Mortimer, *New York Confidential*, p. 140, 1948

old faithful *noun*

the bleed period of the menstrual cycle *US*

- —*American Speech*, p. 298, December 1954: 'The vernacular of menstruation'
- —Karen Houppert, *The Curse*, 1999

old fart *noun*

an old or older person, especially one who is unpleasant or disliked *US*

Often elaborated as 'boring old fart'.

- [B]y old farts I mean all the pantheon of geniuses treated with such reverence: Chuck Berry, who might be the greatest songwriter of all time, is an old fart. Little Richard is an old fart[.] —Lester Bangs, *Psychotic Reactions and Carburetor Dung*, p. 72, 1971
- Is he a boring old fart, or is he a boring old fart?. —Robert G. Barrett, *Davo's Little Something*, p. 213, 1992
- —Barry Cryer and Willie Rushton, *Two Old Farts in the Night*, 1994
- My fellow City Club members. Desperate old farts and despicable yuppies. —Shane Maloney, *Nice Try*, p. 6, 1998
- Wake up lads, if anyone sees this old fart pegged out in our yard, we'll disappear for free. —Chris Baker and Andrew Day, *Lock, Stock... & a Fist Full of Jack and Jills*, p. 192–193, 2000

old-fashioned look *noun*

a glance of quizzical disapproval *UK, 1961*

- Despite my protestations that she did not have anything prepared and would find an hour in the presence of Roxanne, one of my more challenging students, just too much of an experience, she gave me an old-fashioned look. —*The Guardian*, 26th March 2002

old fellow *noun*

1 the penis *AUSTRALIA*

- I won't keep you mates, I'll just give the old fella a swift dekko at the scenery! —Barry Humphries, *The Wonderful World of Barry McKenzie*, p. 14, 1968
- Come again? I'd need a stack of greenies before I flashed the old feller on T.V. —Barry Humphries, *The Wonderful World of Barry McKenzie*, p. 46, 1968
- Chilla cursing under his breath, having just sunk the old fella. —Frank Hardy, *The Outcasts of Foolgarah*, p. 114, 1971
- If you reckon I'm goin' to exhibit the old feller, you've another think coming. —Barry Humphries, *Bazza Pulls It Off!*, 1971
- When she takes off her clothes it'll make the ol' feller stand up. —Dorothy Hewett, *The Chapel Perilous*, p. 59, 1972
- —Lance Peters, *The Dirty Half-Mile*, p. 202, 1979
- I consider whipping out the old feller and pissing all over the office. —Dirk Flinthart, *Brotherly Love*, p. 66, 1995
- I finally freed myself up, pulled the old fella clear of my slacks and pointed it out of harm's way. —Danny King, *The Bank Robber Diaries*, p. 4, 2002

2 a father (regardless of age) *AUSTRALIA*
- Go and enjoy yourself while the old feller rakes in a few more shekels. —Eric Lambert, *The Veterans*, p. 66, 1954

3 used as a friendly form of address to another man; a man *UK, 1825*

old fogey *noun*
a small lump of dried nasal mucus *UK*
Rhyming slang for **BOGEY**.
- Lusting after a page three girL, a Sun reader was heard to remark: "I'd eat her old fogeys I would." —Ray Puxley, *Fresh Rabbit*, 1998

old folks *noun*
1 parents (regardless of age) *AUSTRALIA*
- She's takin' yer to meet the old folks? —Nino Culotta (John O'Grady), *They're A Weird Mob*, p. 175, 1957

2 in circus and carnival usage, monkeys *US*
- —Don Wilmeth, *The Language of American Popular Entertainment*, p. 186, 1981

old fruit; my old fruit *noun*
used as a friendly form of address to another man *UK*
- "Look here, old fruit," writes one Josh Lanolin. "I don't mind the odd typo in your pieces, but I do object to your use of crap (ersatz?) American words when there are well-established British ones." —*The Guardian*, 24th September 2003

old gent *noun*
the penis *UK*
- [M]y old gent's getting twitchy at the very thought[.] —J.J. Connolly, *Layer Cake*, p. 107, 2000

old girl *noun*
1 a mother; a wife *UK, 1887*
- She dragged me off to the house of the Rubettes' lead singer to moan at his old girl. The two mums had a big shouting thing on the landing[.] —Andy McNab, *Immediate Action*, p. 4, 1995

2 an old woman *UK, 1791*
- It's as if, having scribbled down the old girl's life story, Ackroyd has now tied up a Hello! -style deal for the picture rights as well. —*The Observer*, 16th November 2003

old git *noun*
any man who is considered past his prime *UK*
- We're Old Gits, I said. – We actually are Old Gits. It's happened. [...] The next ceremony is the Grand Opening of the pension book. —James Hawes, *Dead Long Enough*, p. 92, 2000

old grannie *noun*
▷ **see: GRANNIE GRUNT**

old grinder *noun*
a promiscuous woman *UK*
- Fuck me, what an old grinder. He knobbed it as well. —John King, *Human Punk*, p. 236, 2000

old hand *noun*
an experienced person, an expert *UK, 1785*
- 'How can you live like this?' asks Linda, who is an old hand at dinosaur digs[.] —*The Observer*, 3rd February 2002

old hat *adjective*
old-fashioned, out-of-date *UK, 1911*
- Thirty: new cool or old hat? —*The Observer*, 6th July 2003

old head *noun*
1 an older prisoner *US*
- [S]ome of us junior types had to argue with many an oldhead[.] —*The Source*, p. 36, March 2002

2 a returning student to a school *US*
- —*American Speech*, p. 272, December 1963: 'American Indian student slang'

old horsey *noun*
strong, illegally manufactured whisky *US*
- It is called corn liquor, white lightning, sugar whiskey, skully cracker, popskull, bush whiskey, stump, stumphole, 'splo, ruckus juice, radiator whiskey, rotgut, sugarhead, block and tackle, wildcat, panther's breath, tiger's sweat, Sweet spirits of cats a-fighting, alley bourbon, city gin, cool water, happy Sally, deep shaft, jump steady, old horsey, stingo, blue John, red eye, pine top, buckeye bark whiskey and see seven stars. —*Star Tribune (Minneapolis)*, p. 19F, 31st January 1999

old house *noun*
on the railways, a warehouse of salvaged parts *US*
- —Ramon Adams, *The Language of the Railroader*, p. 107, 1977

oldie *noun*
1 an older or elderly person *UK, 1874*
- But the oldie's an attractive old geezer. —John Wynnum, *Jiggin' in the Riggin*, p. 57, 1965
- Beer and tobacco are 'straight' drugs, used by the Oldies. —Frank Hardy, *Hardy's People*, p. 100, 1986
- In a world obsessed by 'yoof', culture, cellulite and sag, The Oldie stands aloof, proud and tall. It speaks for those on whom the years sit lightly, those who know full well that age only matters if you are a cheese. The Oldie is not the past, it is the future. —Terry Wogan, *quoted on the Cultural Publications website*, August 2003

2 a song from the past that is still popular *US, 1939*
A shortened form of **GOLDEN OLDIE** or 'oldie but goody'.
- We owe our thanks for these to the wonderful services of the U.S.O. Here's another oldie. —*Apocalypse Now*, 1979

oldies *noun*
parents (regardless of age) *AUSTRALIA, 1964*
- I raved on about how hard it must have been growing up with mega rich oldies. —Kathy Lette, *Girls' Night Out*, p. 43, 1987
- —Robert G. Barrett, *Davo's Little Something*, p. 6, 1992

old iron and grass; old iron *noun*
1 grass *UK*
Rhyming slang.
- An order from an over officious parkie is "Keep off the old iron." —Ray Puxley, *Cockney Rabbit*, 1992

2 a pass *UK*
Rhyming slang, in military use.
- —Ray Puxley, *Cockney Rabbit*, 1992

old Joe *noun*
any sexually transmitted infection *US*
- —Dale Gordon, *The Dominion Sex Dictionary*, p. 111, 1967
- —Anon., *King Smut's Wet Dreams Interpreted*, 1978

old King Cole *noun*
unemployment benefit; a government office from which unemployment benefit is managed *UK, 1960*
Rhyming slang for **THE DOLE**; formed on the name of a nursery rhyme character – he was 'a merry old soul' so this rhyme may be intentionally ironic.
- [I]t's either signing up for the Old-King-Cole or off to Hertfordshire to play on a computer[.] —Andrew Nickolds, *Back to Basics*, p. 104, 1994

old kit bag *noun*
a cigarette *UK*
Rhyming slang for **FAG**; possibly from the song by George Asaf and Felix Powell: 'Pack up your troubles in your old kit bag and smile, smile, smile', 1915 – but still familiar.
- —Ray Puxley, *Fresh Rabbit*, 1998

old lad *noun*
used as a friendly form of address to another man *UK, 1588*

old lady *noun*
1 a mother *US, 1877*
- Inspiration's old lady gave birth to a new brainchild one afternoon at a Rhythm Kings rehearsal[.] —Mezz Mezzrow, *Really the Blues*, p. 54, 1946
- About Benny Bliss's old lady having been in Doctros' Hospital for a checkup[.] —Bernard Wolfe, *The Late Risers*, p. 170, 1954
- 'No, no, man,' Manny says with impatience. 'My old lady – my mother…' —John Rechy, *The Fourth Angel*, p. 40, 1972
- Since my old man left,' he said, 'and my old lady tried to make up for it by smothering me with affection, I've always valued my friendships with men more than my relationships with women. —Helen Garner, *Monkey Grip*, p. 138, 1977

2 a wife, common-law or legal; a girlfriend *US, 1836*
- "Hey, look, baby," I said, "I know you're Capone's old lady – uh, uh, I ain't coming on this tab." —Mezz Mezzrow, *Really the Blues*, p. 24, 1946
- At twelve that night my old lady bailed me out and met me at the door with some goof balls. —William Burroughs, *Junkie*, p. 39, 1953
- Many who would ordinarily take their "old ladies" had left the girls behind in case of a serious clash with the law. —Hunter S. Thompson, *Hell's Angels*, p. 119, 1966
- Hang on – youse blokes. The Doc's got to phone his old lady. —Barry Humphries, *The Wonderful World of Barry McKenzie*, p. 30, 1968
- Not to mention Danny's old lady[.] —Ted Lewis, *Jack Carter's Law [britpulp]*, p. 48, 1974
- [H]e began coming around inviting us out or up to his place to pick up on music and maybe smoke a little pot and keep him and his old lady company[.] —Herbert Huncke, *The Evening Sun Turned Crimson*, p. 90, 1980
- That old lady of mine is unbelievable. She'd turn a baked dinner cold. —Robert G. Barrett, *Davo's Little Something*, p. 217, 1992

3 the more passive member of a same-sex couple *US, 1937*
- After that Blocker referred to him as my old lady. —Chester Himes, *Cast the First Stone*, p. 103, 1952
- I promise not to let no one know about you being my old lady[.] —Piri Thomas, *Down These Mean Streets*, p. 266, 1967
- I don't want to be anybody's old lady anymore. I just want to do my time. — *The Advocate*, p. 14, March 31st-April 13th 1971
- He had looked into the eyes of convicts, wondering if they saw something, and had got propositioned, proposed to and finally picked by a big colored buy, Monroe Ritchie, to be his old lady. —Elmore Leonard, *Glitz*, p. 132, 1985

4 any old woman *UK, 1824*
- An obese young woman appears from the left, mopping the floor in a listless, automatic fashion, while an old lady appears in the distance clutching the railing that lines the wall. — *The Observer*, 20th October 2002

Old Lady of Threadneedle Street *nickname*

the Bank of England *UK, 1797*

From a cartoon by James Gillray.
- Someone had to stand up to intimidators and blackmailers. Who better than the old lady of Threadneedle Street? — *The Guardian*, 3rd July 2001

old lady white; old white lady *noun*

a powdered drug: cocaine, heroin or morphine *US, 1942*
- How long have you been on old lady white? —Douglas Rutherford, *The Creeping Flesh*, p. 102, 1963

old lag *noun*

1 a regular prisoner or one who has become institutionalised, a recidivist *UK, 1950*

From LAG (a prisoner).
- —Angela Devlin, *Prison Patter*, p. 69, 1996

2 a prisoner who has been in jail for a long time *AUSTRALIA, 1950*
- Then they jammed his head in a vice, tightened it up and about ten old lags rooted him. —Robert G. Barrett, *Davo's Little Something*, p. 219, 1992
- —Donald Catchlove, *Ray Denning My Life and Time*, p. 13, 1994

3 a former prisoner *AUSTRALIA, 1812*
- In justice to these gentlemen, let it be said that some of the non-professional owners of racehorses are also reputed to be shady, one wealthy man being pointed out ot me as 'an old lag'—whatever that may be. —J.S. James, *The Vagabond Papers*, p. 142, 1877
- Not going to disturb any peace-loving citizen on the say so of any rough old lag. —John Wynnum, *Jiggin' in the Riggin'*, p. 92, 1965

4 a person who has been contracted to a single employer for a very long time, especially of the armed services *UK*

Humorous use of the sense as 'a convict who has been imprisoned for many years'.
- From time to time us old lags get called on to address the Ruperts [officers][.] —Chris Ryan, *The Watchman*, p. 75, 2001

old man *noun*

1 a father *US, 1811*
- "First I want revenge because their fathers sent my old man to die in the pen." The Crawler's eyes were blazing with hate as he spoke. —Chester Gould, *Dick Tracy Meets the Night Crawler*, p. 40, 1945
- My old man came home from work one night when I felt like I was coming on, and I grabbed the horn to show off while he was eating his supper, but he screamed, "Stop blowing so loud – you sound like a fog horn." —Mezz Mezzrow, *Really the Blues*, p. 50, 1946
- Gee, my old man is going to hit the ceiling. —Irving Shulman, *The Amboy Dukes*, p. 77, 1947
- My old man says them Puerto Ricans is ruinin' free ennaprise. — *West Side Story*, 1957
- "Who's Sugartit's father?" "You mean her old man?" "I mean her father." —Chester Himes, *The Real Cool Killers*, p. 101, 1959
- The thing I wanted to avoid was suddenly and without warning meeting my old man on the subway. —Clancy Sigal, *Going Away*, p. 420, 1961
- The Muncys bought me new in Germany when the old man was stationed over there in the army. —Gurney Norman, *Divine Right's Trip (Last Whole Earth Catalog)*, p. 9, 1971
- Let him see what his old man does for a living. —Carl Hiaasen, *Tourist Season*, p. 20, 1986

2 a boyfriend or husband *UK, 1768*
- An old man is another thing. An old man is like a marriage without the legal binding[.] —Leonard Wolfe (Editor), *Voices from the Love Generation*, p. 243, 1968
- "Who's that in back there?" asked the Greek when Estelle got back to the bus. "My old man." —Gurney Norman, *Divine Right's Trip (Last Whole Earth Catalog)*, p. 67, 1971
- We don't need no piece of paper / From the city hall / Keeping us tied and true / My old man / Keeping away my blues. —Joni Mitchell, *My Old Man*, 1971
- The ho is similar in her role to the hippy chick who holds down a straight job and puts on her neat little dress and makeup in the morning to go out and face the working world, so she can bring home money to her long-haired "old man[.]" —Christina and Richard Milner, *Black Players*, p. 212, 1972
- One old sort [wife] even asked me to kill her old man once. —Danny King, *The Burglar Diaries*, p. 90, 2001

3 a commanding officer, military or police *US, 1830*
- There was a lifer in San Diego who was dumped for indebtedness. The old man got sick of the dunning letters so he had the man discharged and thereby made the matter a non-navy problem. —Darryl Ponicsan, *The Last Detail*, p. 13, 1970
- 'Anyway, the captain says no more of it," Bridget continued, "and another thing the old man says is that you guys are not at any time to push cars with your police vehicle." —Joseph Wambaugh, *The New Centurions*, p. 55, 1970
- —Linda Reinberg, *In the Field: The Language of the Vietnam War*, p. 156, 1991

4 a pimp in relation to a prostitute *US, 1891*
- Clippinger added that he knew all the pimps who had "teams" of girls in southern California, but disliked to hire girls who had "old men" for masters. "Old men" was explained to mean pimps with teams of girls. —Ed Reid and Ovid Demaris, *The Green Felt Jungle*, p. 101, 1963
- [E]ventually he became her real old man instead of her play old man and moved in with her and let her support him and go down on lots of fat cats and high rollers for lots of money[.] —Joseph Wambaugh, *The Choirboys*, p. 190, 1975

5 an elder amongst the Australian Aboriginals *AUSTRALIA, 1848*
- Then he urged the Old Men to 'sing out' those responsible for the death of his son. —Ion L. Idriess, *Over the Range*, p. 26, 1947
- —Bob Ellis and Anne Brooksbank, *Mad Dog Morgan*, p. 59, 1976

6 used as a form of address to another man *UK, 1885*
- One was a man he recognized, who said 'Hello, old man' as the other three crowded round him. — *The Daily Telegraph*, 26th June 2000

7 the penis *UK, 1984*
- He'd balance six half crowns along the length of his "old man". —Lenny McLean, *The Guv'nor*, p. 115, 1998

8 a shark *US*
- —John M. Kelly, *Surf and Sea*, p. 289, 1965

old man comforts *noun*

high-top shoes with ankle support and extra laces *US*
- They called them 'old man comforts' and they were soft and comfortable, but ugly as hell, I guess, to most people. —Joseph Wambaugh, *The Blue Knight*, p. 44, 1973

old man kangaroo; old man 'roo *noun*

an adult male kangaroo *AUSTRALIA, 1834*
- She could stay with any flying doe and'd bail up an old man 'roo in a hundred yards. —Alan Marshall, *I Can Jump Puddles*, p. 100, 1955
- There is no mistaking the old man kangaroo. —Patrick White, *Voss*, p. 279, 1957

old man's aid *noun*

in pool, a device used to support the cue stick for a hard-to-reach shot *US, 1977*

As the terminology suggests, the device is scorned by skilled players.
- —Steve Rushin, *Pool Cool*, p. 22, 1990
- —Mike Shamos, *The Illustrated Encyclopedia of Billiards*, p. 160, 1993

old man's milk *noun*

coconut water mixed with gin *TRINIDAD AND TOBAGO*
- —Lise Winer, *Dictionary of the English/Creole of Trinidad & Tobago*, 2003

old Mick *adjective*

nauseated, sick *UK*

Rhyming slang.
- Blimey, after you've got abaht twelve spoonsfuls down yer, on top o' Christmas dinner, yer don't half feel Old Mick. — *Cinema*, December 1967

Old Miss *nickname*

the University of Mississippi *US*
- He had also been such a tenacious tailback he was almost guaranteed a scholarship to Ole Miss[.] —Jimmy Buffett, *Tales from Margaritaville*, p. 131, 1989

old money *noun*

an earlier system of measuring, when applied to anything except money *UK*
- First the good news: it's going to be a baking hot weekend in many parts of Britain, with the Met Office predicting temperatures up to 27 degrees. In old money, that's the high eighties. — *The Guardian*, 16th June 2000

old moody *noun*
▷ see: MOODY

old navy *noun*
heroin *US*
• — *Detroit News*, p. 5D, 20th September 2002

Old Nick *noun*
mischief *US, 1817*
Nearly obsolete.
• Well, when he was young and full of the Old Nick, maybe, hadn't settled down, on the right amount of caps. — Elmore Leonard, *Stick*, p. 134, 1983

old oak *noun*
London *UK*
Probably rhyming slang for THE SMOKE; used by trainspotters; however, Garth Andrews, a retired deputy head of Records and Archives at the British Railways Board, wrote to this dictionary in May 2003, to suggest that 'this has nothing to do with rhyming slang for "smoke". Old Oak Common was the premier engine shed on the Great Western Railway, providing the motive power for crack expresses out of Paddington'. It is, of course, possible that Old Oak Common provided the inspiration for the rhyme – if rhyme it is.
• [S]landerously called a "crate" because, being an "Old Oak" (London) engine it was seen too frequently. — Colin Clifford, *Each a Glimpse*, 1970
• — Ray Puxley, *Cockney Rabbit*, 1992

old pair *noun*
parents *IRELAND*
• When we were kids, roysh [right], Christian's old pair brought the two of us to Lansdowne Road to see Ireland play. — Paul Howard, *The Teenage Dirtbag Years*, p. 83, 2001

old people *noun*
parents (regardless of age) *AUSTRALIA, 1941*
• [T]hey say that when she went up in the world a bit, she treated the old people something frightful (couldn't have found a nicer old couple anywhere, you couldn't). — Dymphna Cusack, *Picnic Races*, p. 213, 1962

old person's friend *noun*
pneumonia *CANADA*
• — Joseph Ross, *History Cape Negro and Blanche*, p. 58, 1987

old pot and pan; old pot *noun*
▷ see: POT AND PAN

old rag *noun*
a flag *UK*
Rhyming slang.
• — Ray Puxley, *Cockney Rabbit*, 1992

old reliable *noun*
the Ninth Infantry Division, US Army *US*
• — Linda Reinberg, *In the Field*, p. 156, 1991

olds *noun*
parents *AUSTRALIA, 1979*
• Don't suppose anything sordid ever happens to your olds. — Jenny Pausacker, *What are ya?*, p. 54, 1987
• — Kathy Lette, *Girls' Night Out*, p. 38, 1987
• What's the big attraction with dope, anyway? Most of the olds smoke it. — David McGill, *David McGill's Complete Kiwi Slang Dictionary*, p. 79, 1998
• — Phillip Gwynne, *Deadly Unna?*, p. 188, 1998

old sailor *noun*
a Morris Marina car *UK*
Citizens' band radio slang; pun on 'mariner'.
• — Peter Chippindale, *The British CB Book*, p. 161, 1981

old school *noun*
a past generation with an old-fashioned but reliable way of doing things *US*
• [H]e's out of the old school, I think, because he looks like he's out of the old school, shorty, portly, baldy, ruddy-faced, twinkly-eyed. — Jim Bouton, *Ball Four*, p. 13, 1970
• — Connie Eble (Editor), *UNC-CH Campus Slang*, p. 6, Fall 1987
• Fuck that, I'm from the old school. — *Menace II Society*, 1993
• He's costing you money, Debra. He's old school. — *Jerry Maguire*, 1996

old shaky *noun*
a C-124 long-range transport aircraft *US*
• He'd spent another profitless year driving C-124s around the globe, an ancient mariner in Old Shaky, as the aging piston-engines planes were called. — Walter J. Boyne and Steven Thompson, *The Wild Blue*, p. 28, 1986

old skool; old school *noun*
the original style of hip-hop music viewed retrospectively; subsequently, any hip-hop music that could not be categorised as house music; finally, any style of music under the hip-hop umbrella that is not absolutely current *US, 1989*
• — Judi Sanders, *Faced and Faded, Hanging to Hurl*, p. 29, 1993
• — Connie Eble (Editor), *UNC-CH Campus Slang*, p. 6, Spring 1994
• "[O]ld skool flavour", allowing the DJ to play recent records that had the old skool vibe. — Ben Osborne, *The A-Z of Club Culture*, p. 212, 1999
• Make the ultimate old skool escape from warring aunties and pissed-up aggro grannies on Boxing Day. — *Mixmag*, p. 128, December 2001

Oldsmobile *noun*
in hold 'em poker, a nine and an eight as the first two cards dealt to a player *US, 1981*
An allusion to the Oldsmobile 98, a popular model.
• — Thomas L. Clark, *The Dictionary of Gambling and Gaming*, p. 139, 1987

Old Smokey *noun*
the electric chair *US, 1929*
• — Lou Shelly, *Hepcats Jive Talk Dictionary*, p. 31, 1945

old soak; soak *noun*
a drunkard *UK, 1820*
From the verb sense (to drink immoderately).
• Jeffrey Bernard, the old soak Soho columnist and writer, gleefully continuing the tradition of drunken scribery[.] — *Drugs An Adult Guide*, p. 31, December 2001

Old Sod *noun*
Ireland *UK, 1891*
• He sounded like the Old Sod. I thought to myself that all I seem to meet are Dagos and Irish[.] — Red Rudensky, *The Gonif*, p. c, 1970

old sort *noun*
a wife, a husband or any partner in a living-together relationship *UK*
• [M]e an' 'im done time together. 'Is old sort used to smuggle in the baccy for us, in her bra. — Bernard Dempsey and Kevin McNally *Lock, Stock... & Two Sips*, p. 304, 2000
• One old sort even asked me to kill her old man once. — Danny King, *The Burglar Diaries*, p. 90, 2001

Old Sparky *noun*
an electric chair, especially Florida's electric chair *US, 1971*
• Union Correctional, or UCI, is what they used to call Raiford, when they had Old Sparky there. See, wherever the 'lectric chair is, that's your state prison. — Elmore Leonard, *Maximum Bob*, p. 107, 1991

old stager *noun*
a person of considerable age or experience *UK, 1570*
• The consensus considers itself to be leftwing in the best sense. The appellation is one that an old-stager like me is reluctant to grant[.] — *The Guardian*, 16th October 2002

oldster *noun*
an older person *UK, 1848*
• A few of the younger members and some of the oldsters leaned forward, having fallen out of pocket for the real reason for their existence in the Club. — Odie Hawkins, *The Busting Out of an Ordinary Man*, p. 123, 1985
• "Not if I'm a cool oldster like him," Barbie said. — Francesca Lia Block, *I Was a Teenage Fairy*, 1998

old Steve *noun*
heroin *US, 1936*
• — US Department of Justice, *Street Terms*, October 1994
• — Robert Ashton, *This Is Heroin*, p. 206, 2002

old style *noun*
fashion sense that is excessive to the point of ridicule *TRINIDAD AND TOBAGO, 1956*
• — Lise Winer, *Dictionary of the English/Creole of Trinidad & Tobago*, 2003

old sweat *noun*
an old soldier; a veteran police officer *UK, 1919*
• [A] grey-haired PC called Reg, an old sweat with a reputation for being a tiger behind the wheel. — Duncan MacLaughlin, *The Filth*, p. 59, 2002

old thing; dear old thing *noun*
used as a term of address, usually as an endearment *UK, 1864*
• Then Blofeld said, "Aggers, my dear old thing, you're looking frightfully smart today." — *The Guardian*, 8th September 2001

oldtimer's disease *noun*
Alzheimer's disease *US*
• A memo from a Mackay airline office to the airline's airport staff said special assistance would have to be offered to one traveller, who was

suffering from 'old timer's disease' and needed help changing planes. — *Courier-Mail*, p. 2, 26th January 1988
- — *Maledicta*, p. 35, 1988–1989: 'More Milawukee medical maledicta'

old Tom *noun*
an aggressive, 'mannish' lesbian *US*
- — Anon., *King Smut's Wet Dreams Interpreted*, 1978

old white lady *noun*
▷ see: OLD LADY WHITE

old woman *noun*
1 a wife; a woman you cohabit with *UK, 1775*
- his old woman who was a brass on the game down the Baze. — Frank Norman, *Bang To Rights*, p. 8, 1958
- THIRD PRISONER: Say hello to the big world, Charlie. SECOND PRISONER: Remember me to the old woman, Charlie. FIRST PRISONER: Ta-ra, Charlie. — Troy Kennedy Martin, *The Italian Job [uncut script]*, 1969

2 a mother *UK, 1829*

3 a male who behaves like an old woman *AUSTRALIA*
- Jeez, you're an old woman, pop. — Wal Watkins, *Race the Lazy River*, p. 82, 1963

ole *adjective*
▷ see: OLD

ole gal *noun*
a male roommate *US*
- — Marcus Hanna Boulware, *Jive and Slang of Students in Negro Colleges*, 1947

Ole Possum *nickname*
▷ see: POSSUM

o-levels *noun*
oral sex, especially when advertised as a service offered by a prostitute *UK*
A play on the name given to 'ordinary-level' examinations in the British education system. Recorded by Jack Slater, 1978. O-level exams were replaced by the GCSE in 1988 but glossed as current by Caroline Archer, *Tart Cards*, 2003.

olive oil; olive *noun*
silver foil (used in the preparation of heroin) *UK*
Rhyming slang.
- — Angela Devlin, *Prison Patter*, p. 81, 1996

Oliver *noun*
in circus and carnival usage, a police officer *US*
- — Don Wilmeth, *The Language of American Popular Entertainment*, p. 186, 1981

Oliver Reed; Ollie; Olly *noun*
1 tobacco; marijuana *UK*
Rhyming slang for **WEED** (tobacco/marijuana), based on the name of actor Oliver Reed, 1938–99.
- Known as the "dread Ollie" this is a reference to tobacco often used by holier than thou non-smokers. — Ray Puxley, *Cockney Rabbit*, p. 139, 1992

2 amphetamine *UK, 1992*
Rhyming slang for **SPEED** (amphetamine), based on the name of actor Oliver Reed, 1938–99.
- — Angela Devlin, *Prison Patter*, p. 21, 1996

Oliver Twist *adjective*
drunk *UK*
Rhyming slang for **PISSED**, formed from Charles Dickens' eponymous hero.
- — Ray Puxley, *Fresh Rabbit*, 1998

Oliver Twist!; oliver!
a derisive suggestion that accompanies the offensive gesture of a raised middle finger *UK*
An elaboration and extension of **TWIST!**, formed from Charles Dickens' famous hero.

Ollie Beak *noun*
a Sikh *UK*
Rhyming slang, formed from a puppet – a Liverpudlian owl – that used to introduce children's television programmes in the 1960s.
- — Ray Puxley, *Fresh Rabbit*, 1998

Ollie, Molly and Dolly *noun*
in poker, three queens *US*
Collected from William E. Rippe by Peter Tamony in March 1948.

olly; ollie *noun*
in skateboarding, a jumping manoeuvre, the basis of most skating tricks *US*
- — Dan Maley, *Macon Telegraph and News*, p. 9A, 18th June 1989
- — Alon Shulman, *The Style Bible*, p. 181, 1999: 'Skatespeak for going airborne.'
- Sorry, got to olly now. — *The Times*, p. 16, 26th April 2003

Oly *nickname*
Olympia, Washington *US*
- — Jim Crotty, *How to Talk American*, p. 314, 1997

'olyfields *noun*
▷ see: HOLYFIELD'S EAR

om *noun*
MDMA, the recreational drug best known as ecstasy *UK*
Possibly from the Buddhist mantra 'Om', playing on the drug's association with 'trance' (a contemporary dance music genre formed on repetitive rhythms), or, perhaps, an abbreviation of **OMEGA**.
- — Angela Devlin, *Prison Patter*, p. 81, 1996

OM *noun*
a male; a partner; a husband *US*
An abbreviation of 'old man'. Frequent usage by shortwave radio operators, carried over into citizens' band radio slang.
- — Radio Shack, *CBer's Handy Atlas/Dictionary*, p. 35, 1976
- — Dan Maley, *Macon Telegraph and News*, p. 9A, 18th June 1989

-omatic *suffix*
used as an embellishment that adds nothing to the meaning of the word embellished *US*
- I'll have to cram-o-matic for that Chemistry test. — Connie Eble (Editor), *UNC-CH Campus Slang*, p. 4, Fall 1982

omee; omey; omer; ome; homee; homi; homie; homey *noun*
a man; a master; a landlord *UK, 1845*
Polari, from Italian *uomo* (a man).
- The boss and that homie have been having a proper barney over the prad [a horse]. — Butch Reynolds, *Broken Hearted Clown*, p. 28, 1953
- Varda [observe] the dolly [good-looking] ome with the tortured riah [hair][.] — the cast of 'Aspects of Love', Prince of Wales Theatre, *Palare (Boy Dancer Talk) for Beginners*, 1989–92
- He noticed a man earwigging our conversation. "Vada the homi macaroni," he hissed. — Jake Arnott, *He Kills Coppers*, p. 52, 2001
- — Paul Baker, *Polari*, p. 184, 2002

omee-palone; omee-paloney; ome-palone; homee-palone; omi-palome; omie-palome *noun*
a homosexual man *UK*
Polari; a combination of **OMEE** (a man) and **POLONE; PALONE** (a woman).
- We can get you the great omee-palone. He's one of ours[.] — Barry Took and Marty Feldman, *Round The Horne*, June 1966
- [Y]ou know, Raoul, the ome-pallone with the codalina [bad] bins [glasses] and nante pile on the carpet [bald]. — the cast of 'Aspects of Love', Prince of Wales Theatre, *Palare (Boy Dancer Talk) for Beginners*, 1989–92
- FRIEND 2: Varda the omie palome! [...] (Cecil rises to talk with the "omi palome"). — Todd Haynes, *Velvet Goldmine*, 1998
- — Paul Baker, *Polari*, p. 184, 2002

omega *noun*
MDMA, the recreational drug best known as ecstasy *UK*
Possibly a play on 'the end' or, perhaps, an elaboration of **OM**.
- — Angela Devlin, *Prison Patter*, p. 82, 1996

omen *noun*
low grade phencyclidine, the recreational drug known as PCP or angel dust *US*
- — Peter Johnson, *Dictionary of Street Alcohol and Drug Terms*, p. 136, 1993

omigod!
▷ see: OHMIGOD!

omo; OMO *adjective*
used for signalling that a woman's husband is not at home: *old man out* *UK*
OMO™ is an established branded soap powder.
- As soon as a battalion was away over the water, all the singlies were straight over to check out the wives. Boxes of OMO appeared in the windows to advertise Old Man Out. I didn't find it funny. None of the married blokes did. — Andy McNab, *Immediate Action*, p. 51, 1995

omygod *noun*

a Plymouth Omega *US*

- Only one in a series of god-awful domestic-built cars that seemed to gush oil from various sources. — Lewis Poteet, *Car & Motorcyle Slang*, p. 142, 1992

on *adjective*

1 in the bleed period of the menstrual cycle *UK*
Euphemistic abbreviation of, or an alternative to, **ON THE RAG** or 'on (your) period'.
- [E]very eye in the place was centred on some sixteen-year-old virging who'd come to the party and was "on". — Jamie Mandelkau, *Buttons*, p. 91, 1971
- [S]ome of the girls would occasionally tease or try to humiliate a boy by stating "Do you know I'm on". — Shane J. Blackman, *Cool Places*, p. 214, 1998

2 ready and willing *UK, 1888*
- Well, here's your chance. I'll get the script and airline tickets in the post. Are you on for it? — *The Guardian*, 20th February 2002

3 willing to take part *AUSTRALIA, 1880*
- You tell young Ponto Griggs I'm on for a deal with me Port Sadies. — Norman Lindsay, *Halfway to Anywhere*, p. 35, 1947

4 willing to take part in an amorous liaison *AUSTRALIA, 1907*
- — Norman Lindsay, *The Cousin from Fiji*, p. 67, 1945
- 'Blowed if I reckon she's on.' 'Cripes, she looked back twice. Practically gives a bloke the office she's on.' — Norman Lindsay, *Halfway to Anywhere*, p. 51, 1947

5 dating *AUSTRALIA*
- Didn't you know your cousin was on with Darky Tyrrell? — Norman Lindsay, *The Cousin from Fiji*, p. 233, 1945
- I know for a fact that he was on with that young niece of Mickey Finn's[.] — Norman Lindsay, *Halfway to Anywhere*, p. 41, 1947
- I'm on with Simmo now. We're going to make it together. — Alexander Buzo, *Rooted*, p. 42, 1969

6 (of a fight or dispute) begun in earnest *AUSTRALIA, 1945*
- 'Hey listen Pancho, take your hands off me or I'll stick your sombrero up your Khyber.' Well then it's on, abuse is flying but I gave in when he was joined by eight of his mates. — Paul Vautin, *Turn It Up!*, p. 42, 1995

7 persistently asking *AUSTRALIA*
- In the early days the Chinese were always on for you to smuggle opium[.] — Patsy Adam-Smith, *Folklore of the Australian Railwaymen*, p. 281, 1969

8 of a criminal enterprise, underway *UK*

9 possible, feasible, worthy of an attempt *UK, 1935*
Originally recorded in use among billiard and snooker players.

10 having secured a bet *AUSTRALIA, 1903*
- What was the stable on? — Nino Culotta (John O'Grady), *They're A Weird Mob*, p. 73, 1957
- When you're on a horse, you've backed him to win. — John O'Grady, *Aussie English*, p. 65, 1965
- Get on. It can't be beaten. — Paul Vautin, *Turn It Up!*, p. 146, 1995

11 protected from policy action by bribes *US*
- "What's going on?" the controller said. "We're on, man." — Peter Maas, *Serpico*, p. 200, 1973

12 of a food dish, on the menu *UK, 1949*

13 drug-intoxicated *US, 1946*
- "I'm on', Diane announced after four gentle hits[.] — George Mandel, *Flee the Angry Strangers*, p. 254, 1952

▸ not on

not going to happen; forbidden *AUSTRALIA, 1972*
- So then I suggested we go to a romantic parking spot like Penny Spence Point and tool about until dawn. She then threatened to call in Kegs Keegan, so I realised it wasn't on. — Roy Slaven (John Doyle), *Five South Coast Seasons*, p. 54, 1992
- What you've done is that wrong. It's not on. — Kel Richards, *The Aussie Bible*, p. 39, 2003

on *preposition*

1 (used of a drug) under the influence of *US, 1925*
- You don't sound too goddamn sane yourself. What are you on, anyway? — Gurney Norman, *Divine Right's Trip (Last Whole Earth Catalog)*, p. 191, 1971

2 so as to affect or disadvantage *IRELAND, 1880*
- And hey, if Her Majesty may be graciously pleased to lay all that empire stuff on me, why can't she write to me herself. — *The Guardian*, 27th November 2003

3 to the detriment of, or the disadvantage of, or the ruin of, etc *UK*
- [S]he had only gone and got married on me. — Diran Adebayo, *My Once Upon A Time*, p. 115, 2000

4 at or in (a place) *AUSTRALIA, 1853*
- Everything related to Gubba was 'on' not 'in'. You were born 'on' Gubba, worked 'on' Gubba, died 'on' Gubba. — Dymphna Cusack, *Picnic Races*, p. 11, 1962
- — Kel Richards, *The Aussie Bible*, p. 39, 2003

5 to be paid for by *US, 1871*
- The tuna melts are on me. — *The Guardian*, 31st May 2003

▸ be on about

to talk in such a manner that the speaker is not entirely understood or listened to by the auditor *UK, 1984*
As in, 'What's he on about now?'.

▸ be on at

to nag, to constantly reprove *UK, 1974*
- I know I should be better organised, my Dad's always on at me. — *The Guardian*, 8th March 2003

▸ go on about; be on about

to grumble; to complain, especially loudly; to talk on a subject for far too long *UK, 1863*
- Stick it, Mr Blair – and Mrs Queen, stop going on about the empire. — *The Guardian*, 27th November 2003

on and off *noun*

a cough *UK*
Rhyming slang.
- — Ray Puxley, *Fresh Rabbit*, 1998

on bob *adjective*

happy *UK*
Variation of **BOB** (pleasant).
- Steady's on bob. He's fine. — Kevin Sampson, *Outlaws*, p. 217, 2001

once a week *noun*

1 a magistrate *UK*
Rhyming slang for **BEAK**.
- — Julian Franklyn, *A Dictionary of Rhyming Slang*, 1960
- — Ray Puxley, *Cockney Rabbit*, 1992

2 impudence *UK, 1925*
Rhyming slang for **CHEEK**.
- — Dick Clement and Ian La Frenais, *A Further Stir of Porridge*, 1977

once in a blue moon

very rarely *UK*
- LOFTY: Got a wife and four kids in Swindon. TICH: When do you see 'em? LOFTY: Once in a blue moon. — Clive Exton, *No Fixed Abode [Six Granada Plays]*, p. 117, 1959

once-over *noun*

a brief look that assesses something or someone *US, 1913*
- Before finalising any deal, get a reputable mechanic to give it a once over for about 50[.] — *The Guardian*, 7th May 2002

oncer *noun*

1 something or someone unique *AUSTRALIA, 1966*
- A great man, a truly great man, a one-off, unique, a oncer. — Roy Slaven (John Doyle), *Five South Coast Seasons*, p. 121, 1992
- — Rex Hunt, *Tall Tales – and True*, p. 94, 1994

2 a person who has sex only once with any given partner *US*
- — J.D. Mercer, *They Walk in Shadow*, p. 565, 1959: 'Slang vocabulary'
- — Guy Strait, *The Lavendar Lexicon*, 1964

3 a one-pound note *UK, 1931*
- [H]e was counting oncers half the night[.] — Derek Bickerton, *Payroll*, p. 48, 1959
- A flash suit, a flash tie, a flash car, a wad of oncers always in your pocket. — Graham Swift, *Last Orders*, p. 44, 1996

4 an impudent person *UK*
Derives from rhyming slang **ONCE A WEEK** for **CHEEK**.
- — Ray Puxley, *Cockney Rabbit*, 1992

one *noun*

1 an eccentric, amusing or outrageous person *UK, 1880*
- [W]hen Diane jokes with her, she tells her, "You are a one. I thought I was a one, but you're a real one." — *The Guardian*, 31st December 1999

2 a devotee, or an adherent, or a champion, of something *UK, 1888*
- I've never been a one for autographs. — *The Observer*, 20th April 2003

3 a grudge; a score; a blow; a kiss; a drink; an act of sexual intercourse; any non-specified noun *UK, 1830*
By ellipsis of the specific noun.
- [T]he striker owed him one after being sent off at the weekend[.] — *The Guardian*, 9th April 2003

4 a lie; a joke or an anecdote *UK, 1813*

- [Y]ou must have that kind of money on you for the taxi fare. Or are you planning to walk home?" Dave just gave a derisory laugh. "Walk home," Dave repeated. "That's a good one. This guy knows how to have a good time all right – go to a club, have a skinful of beer and then walk home." — *New Statesman*, 26th June 2000

5 an act of urination *TRINIDAD AND TOBAGO, 1987*
An abbreviation of **NUMBER ONE**.

- — Lise Winer, *Dictionary of the English/Creole of Trinidad & Tobago*, 2003

▶ **do one for me; have one for me**
a jocular catchphrase addressed to someone on the way to the lavatory *UK, 1984*

▶ **in one**
in bar dice games, to make a hand in one roll of the dice *US*

- — Jester Smith, *Games They Play in San Francisco*, p. 104, 1971

▶ **on one**
in a state of intoxication as a result of use of MDMA, the recreational drug best known as ecstasy *UK*

- He was like some garish Ebeneezer Goode, in your face the whole time, driving everybody on – on one, up for it, mad for it, top one. Heaven knows. He'd be having it large before the night was out. — Kevin Sampson, *Powder*, p. 198, 1999
- — Mike Haskins, *Drugs*, p. 291, 2003

one *adjective*
used as an emphatic indefinite article *UK, 1828*

- I was one serious kid. — Marlene Winell, *Leaving the Fold*, 1993

one
goodbye *US*
An abbreviation of **ONE LOVE**.

- — Connie Eble (Editor), *UNC-CH Campus Slang*, p. 8, October 2002

one and a half *noun*
a prison sentence of eighteen months *UK, 1961*

one and eight *noun*
a plate (in all uses, conventional or slang) *UK*
Rhyming slang.

- — Ray Puxley, *Cockney Rabbit*, 1992

one and half *noun*
a scarf *UK*
Rhyming slang.

- — Ray Puxley, *Cockney Rabbit*, 1992

one and one *noun*

1 an inhalation of cocaine using both nostrils *UK*

- — Mike Haskins, *Drugs*, p. 277, 2003

2 a dose of heroin accompanied by a dose of cocaine *US*

- — Jim Crotty, *How to Talk American*, p. 89, 1997

3 a bag of deep-fried cod and chips *IRELAND, 1963*

- A one an' one there please...Bimbo sank the cod into the fryer. — Roddy Doyle, *The Van*, p. 207, 1991

one and t'other *noun*

1 a brother *UK*
Rhyming slang.

- one and other — Peter Chippindale, *The British CB Book*, p. 157, 1981

2 a mother *UK, 1932*
Rhyming slang.

one-armed bandit *noun*

1 a slot machine gambling device *US, 1938*

- The night we were there, we saw three fancy one-armed bandits whirring and swallowing. — Jack Lait and Lee Mortimer, *Washington Confidential*, p. 65, 1951

2 a petrol pump *UK*
From a vague similarity in appearance to a fruit machine.

- — Peter Chippindale, *The British CB Book*, p. 156, 1981

3 that part of an automatic warning system mounted in a diesel locomotive's cab *UK*

- — Frank McKenna, *A Glossary of Railwaymen's Talk*, 1970

one away!
used by prison officers to raise the alarm when a prisoner escapes *UK, 1950*

- — Angela Devlin, *Prison Patter*, p. 82, 1996

one day for thief, one day for police
used for expressing the conviction that wrongdoers will eventually be caught *TRINIDAD AND TOBAGO, 1990*

- — Lise Winer, *Dictionary of the English/Creole of Trinidad & Tobago*, 2003

one day job *noun*
a car that can be disassembled and sold in one day after being stolen *US*

- — Lewis Poteet, *Car & Motorcyle Slang*, p. 143, 1992

One Day of the Year *noun*
Anzac Day *AUSTRALIA, 1962*

- [He is] a retired officer of high rank (he's wearing civvies) out late celebrating the One Day of the Year[.] — Frank Hardy, *The Outcasts of Foolgarah*, p. 211, 1971

one day, one day, congotay
one day there will be justice *TRINIDAD AND TOBAGO*

- — Lise Winer, *Dictionary of the English/Creole of Trinidad & Tobago*, 2003

one-digit midget *noun*
during the Vietnam war, a soldier with less than 10 days to serve before his date of expected return from oversees *US*

- Something new was tried in Vietnam – fighting the war in one-year hitches, creating "short-timer's mentality." Various phrases were invented for the remaining length of time in the country. A "one-digit midget" was so "short" that he had anything under — Myra MacPherson, *Long Time Passing*, p. 63, 1984

one-eight-seven *noun*
▷ **see: 187**

one 'em *verb*
in the gambling game two-up, to throw a head and a tail *AUSTRALIA*

- If the pennies are different – showing one tail and one head – it is classed as a no throw, and the cry is: 'He's oned 'em.' — James Holledge, *The Great Australian Gamble*, p. 101, 1966

one-eye *noun*

1 the penis *US, 1961*
A variation of the 'one-eyed bestiary'.

- When Pete had uncovered ol' one eye, he rummaged in his boot and bought out a chain. — Kitty Churchill, *Thinking of England*, p. 198, 1995
- I'm afraid he'll pull the stiff one-eye on me. I need you to chaperone. — *As Good As It Gets*, 1997
- When a woman looks you straight in the one-eye and says, "There's no way you're putting that near my tradesman's," she is really saying, "You're huge!" — *GQ*, p. 117, July 2001

2 in a deck of playing cards, a face card drawn in profile, the jack of hearts, the jack of spades or the king of diamonds *US*

- — Albert H. Morehead, *The Complete Guide to Winning Poker*, p. 268–269, 1967

3 a car with only one headlight working *US*

- — Don Dempsey, *American Speech*, p. 271, December 1962: 'The language of traffic policemen'
- — Bill Valentine, *Gang Intelligence Manual*, p. 130, 1995: 'Asian street gang terminology'

one-eyed *adjective*
used in combination with a variety of suitably shaped or characterised nouns to depict the penis *UK, 1775*

one-eyed jack *noun*
a car with only one headlight working *US*
Collected from a Berkeley, California, middle school, 1998.

one-eyed monster *noun*
the penis *US, 1972*
Neither Cyclops nor the character from the film *Monsters Inc*.

- — Erica Orloff and JoAnn Baker, *Dirty Little Secrets*, 2001

one-eyed snake *noun*
the penis *US*
A short 'one-eyed trouser snake'.

- Once he [St Augustine] tucked the old one-eyed snake away for good, he wrote about his experiences[.] — Erica Orloff and JoAnn Baker, *Dirty Little Secrets*, p. 3, 2001

one-eyed trouser snake *noun*
the penis *AUSTRALIA, 1971*

- — Barry Humphries, *The Traveller's Tool*, p. 105, 1985
- Place your throbbing mythically proportioned one eyed trouser snake into my pulsating ever accommodating love mound until you erupt with jugs full of jism, I do say. — *Kink*, p. 39, 1993

one fifty-one *noun*

▷ **see:** 151

one foot in the grave *adjective*

old, perhaps very old *UK, 1632*

Used as the title of a popular BBC situation comedy about an ageing (but not elderly) couple, written by David Renwick and broadcast from 1990–2000.

one for his nob *noun*

a shilling *UK*

Rhyming slang for **BOB** that fell into disuse following decimalisation in 1971.

- —Julian Franklyn, *A Dictionary of Rhyming Slang*, 1961

one for Ron *noun*

an extra cigarette taken when one is offered *AUSTRALIA, 1966*

Typically the person cadging cigarettes says they'll take one 'and one for Ron', when the person giving the cigarettes asks 'Who is Ron?' the answer given is 'one for later on'.

- I am going to save that one for Ron. —*Wordmap (www.abc.net.au/wordmap)*, 2003

one for the boy *noun*

in horse racing, a bet placed on a horse by the owner and given to the jockey before the race *US*

- —David W. Maurer, *Argot of the Racetrack*, p. 46, 1951

one for the road *noun*

a final drink before leaving a bar *US, 1943*

- Collucci stopped to have one for the road and light chitchat with Mack Rivers at the bar. —Iceberg Slim (Robert Beck), *Death Wish*, p. 234, 1977
- Buddy ordered a couple more Jim Beams with a splash, for the road. —Elmore Leonard, *Out of Sight*, p. 186, 1996

one goer *noun*

a race in which only one horse is being run to win *AUSTRALIA, 1966*

- They were badly run and many of the races were obviously 'one goers'. —Joe Andersen, *Winners Can Laugh*, p. 25, 1982
- —Ned Wallish, *The Truth Dictionary of Racing Slang*, p. 59, 1989

one-hand magazine; one-handed magazine; one-handed literature *noun*

a pornographic magazine *UK*

The image of one hand free.

- I sat and took my ease, / With a sausage roll and a one-handed magazine[.] —Ivor Biggun, *The Winker's Paradise*, 1978

one hitter *noun*

a device designed for holding a single inhalation worth of marijuana *US*

- —Connie Eble (Editor), *UNC-CH Campus Slang*, p. 7, Spring 2003

one hitter quitter; one hitta quitta *noun*

a powerful variety of marijuana *UK*

It takes just one **HIT** (an inhalation) to get an intoxicating effect.

- —Mike Haskins, *Drugs*, p. 288, 2003

one-hit wonder *noun*

a recording artist or group with a single hit song *US*

- One-hit wonders have the lucky combination of a good song and the right timing for their moment in the spotlight. —*The Des Moines Register*, p. E8, 15th May 1994
- Fucking one hit wonder, dime-store Frank Miller's. —*Chasing Amy*, 1997
- Some of rock and roll's most notorious one-hit wonders from the '50s and '60s will soon be attempting comebacks via a proposed variety series called "Rock & Roll Legends Live." —*Las Vegas Review-Journal*, p. 1E, 27th July 1999

one-holed flute *noun*

the penis *UK*

Variation of **FLUTE** (the penis).

one-horse *adjective*

of little consequence, unimportant, inferior, small *US, 1853*

- This town needs this mealy one-horse institution[.] —*It's a Wonderful Life*, 1946

one hundred *noun*

a marijuana cigarette dipped in an opium solution *US*

- —Gregory Clark, *Words of the Vietnam War*, p. 361, 1991

One Hung Low *nickname*

used as a name for a Chinaman *UK, 1984*

Intended to be humorous, as in the imagined book title 'The Ruptured Chinaman' by One Hung Low.

one love

used as a farewell *US*

- —Connie Eble (Editor), *UNC-CH Campus Slang*, p. 8, October 2002

one lunger *noun*

a single cylinder motorcycle *US, 1908*

Motorcyclists' slang, noted by Partridge, 1979.

one man *noun*

first degree manslaughter *US*

- —Ralph de Sola, *Crime Dictionary*, p. 88, 1982

one-nighter *noun*

a sexual relationship lasting a single night *US, 1969*

- He left word, no man gets near you in a serious way or as a one nighter just fooling around or anything like it as long as you live. —Elmore Leonard, *Gold Coast*, p. 45, 1980
- Too many one-nighters, too many faces without meaning. —Odie Hawkins, *Black Casanova*, p. 90, 1984

one-night stand *noun*

a sexual relationship lasting a single night *UK, 1937*

- All those guys – out for a one-night stand! —John Rechy, *Numbers*, p. 101, 1967
- I'm through with one-night stands. —*Bull Durham*, 1988

one-off *noun*

a unique person, object or event *UK*

From manufacturing jargon.

- [G]et the Wurriyas back together again, go to the States. Well, wasn't up for that, of course, but a one-off [date] sounded OK. —John Williams, *Cardiff Dead*, p. 172, 2000
- I don't know how our Gerrard can be so disciplined [...] He's a one-off. —Kevin Sampson, *Outlaws*, p. 248, 2001

one off the wrist; quick one off the wrist *noun*

(of a male) an act of masturbation *UK*

The adjective 'quick' (or occasional variations) does not denote an especially speedy endeavour, its purpose is to elaborate the basic term.

- [T]he kilt, a garment designed obviously for a quick one off the wrist. —Johnny Speight, *It Stands to Reason*, p. 139, 1973
- I found I preferred a swift one off the wrist[.] —Ivor Biggun, *The Winker's Song (Misprint)*, 1978
- And he started to shave / And have one off the wrist / And want to see girls / And go out and get pissed[.] —Monty Python, *Brian Song*, 1979
- Why the fook should they care whether or not a bloke gets a quick one off the wrist before he goes home? —Ben Elton, *High Society*, p. 126, 2002
- The Who themselves saw "[Pictures of] Lily" as little more than a euphemistic quick one off the wrist. —*Uncut*, p. 48, January 2003

one of the original twelve *noun*

an extremely high-ranking officer *US*

US naval aviator usage.

- —*United States Naval Institute Proceedings*, p. 108, October 1986

one of these fine days

at a vague point in the future *UK, 1846*

Minor variations abound: 'some fine day', 'one of these fine mornings', etc.

- [C]ould piracy temptingly prove not just pure history one of these fine days? —*Private Banker International*, May 2002

one of those; one of them *noun*

a homosexual *UK, 1933*

- —John Ayto, *Oxford Dictionary of Slang*, p. 81, 1998

one of those days *noun*

a day when everything seems to go wrong, or is more hectic than usual *UK, 1936*

- The bowlers found it tough to put the ball in the right areas. It was just one of those days. —*The Guardian*, 23rd March 2003

one of us *noun*

a male homosexual *UK, 1961*

Especially in the phrase, 'he's one of us'.

one on!

used as a shouted warning that a train is approaching *UK*

- —Harvey Sheppard, *Dictionary of Railway Slang*, 1970

one-one *noun*
in horse racing or harness racing, the position one off the rail and one behind the challenger *US*
A favoured position, close enough to challenge the lead and benefiting from the wind broken by the challenger.

one-on-one house *noun*
a place where cocaine and heroin can be bought *UK, 1998*
- —Robert Ashton, *This Is Heroin*, p. 210, 2002

one-o-one *adjective*
basic *US*
Alluding to basic college courses such as 'English 101'.
- Do de name Gary Hart ring a bell? Fuckups 101 – you need a refresher course?—Carl Hiaasen, *Strip Tease*, p. 11, 1993

one out
by oneself; on one's own; alone *AUSTRALIA, 1950*
- 'Put your gun away,' Chilla said to Scabby Jack, 'and I'll have you one out!'—Frank Hardy, *The Outcasts of Foolgarah*, p. 83, 1971
- The Scunger does not tub too often and consequently does most of his fishing one out.—Bob Staines, *Wot a Whopper*, p. 24, 1982

one over the eight *adjective*
drunk; the final drink that makes you drunk *UK, 1925*
- People who've had "one over the eight," as the bartenders say, often neglect to lock their doors.—Dev Collans with Stewart Sterling, *I was a House Detective*, p. 32, 1954
- I shay, I jusht met the mosht shintillating bunch of artistsh, but I sheem to have had one over the eight.—*The Observer*, 28th October 2001

one over the pocket *noun*
a woman who is easily available for sex *UK*
Adopted from snooker terminology.
- She's definitely one over the pocket this aul' fox.—Kevin Sampson, *Clubland*, p. 145, 2002

one pen
used by small children to ask foreign tourists for money *INDIA*
A request, sometimes a demand. Derives, perhaps, from a 1961 visit to India by US Vice President Lyndon B. Johnson who handed out ballpoint pens marked with his name.
- —Nigel Hankin, *Hanklyn-Janklyn*, 2003

one-percenter; two-percenter *noun*
used as a self-identification by members of outlaw motorcyle clubs *US*
When the president of the American Motorcyle Association proclaimed that 99% (or later 98%) of motorcylists are 'decent, hardworking, law-abiding citizens', outlaw bikers did the maths and proclaimed themselves the remainder.
- This compact description of rancid, criminal sleaziness is substantially correct except for the hocus-pocus about the one percenters. —Hunter S. Thompson, *Hell's Angels*, p. 9, 1966
- Thirty or so hawgs are parked in front, many of their owners (One Percenters, as they're known) pissing into the night highway.—Bill Cardoso, *The Maltese Sangweech*, p. 243, 1984
- —Lewis Poteet, *Car & Motorcyle Slang*, p. 209–210, 1992
- When the Hollister incident cut deep into their cred, they labeled rowdy, outlaw motorcylists the "one-percenters."—Ralph "Sonny" Barger, *Hell's Angel*, p. 41, 2000

one-piece overcoat *noun*
a condom *UK, 1984*

one-pipper; one pip *noun*
a second lieutenant *UK, 1915*
Army, from the sleeve or shoulder insignia.
- [T]hey would have made you a buckshee [rank but no pay] one-pipper and you could have trotted round for two years having the time of your life.—Graeme Kent, *The Queen's Corporal [Six Granada Plays]*, p. 85, 1959

one-plus-one sale *noun*
heroin and cocaine sold together *UK*
- —Robert Ashton, *This Is Heroin*, p. 210, 2002

one-pub *adjective*
(of a town) small enough to have only one public hotel; inconsequential *AUSTRALIA, 1901*
- Daybreak, a one-pub town owned by Melody Sam.—Arthur Upfield, *Bony and the Mouse*, p. 7, 1959

oner *noun*
a one-pound note *UK, 1889*
- —John Ayto, *The Oxford Dictionary of Slang*, p. 184, 1998

ones *noun*
1 the first landing or floor level in a prison *UK*
- —Angela Devlin, *Prison Patter*, p. 53, 1996
- "But you behave yourself, keep that temper under control and I'll put you on the ones." Lovely – I've got a nice easy job.—Lenny McLean, *The Guv'nor*, p. 193, 1998

2 in the gambling game two-up, a throw of a head and a tail *AUSTRALIA, 1911*
- It curled over slowly, and showed its white-crossed tail. 'Ones,' said the keeper.—John O'Grady, *It's Your Shout, Mate!*, p. 26, 1972

▸ **all the ones**
eleven *UK, 1943*
In Bingo, House or Housey-Housey calling, the formula 'all the' announces a double number.

▸ **on the ones and twos**
in prison, used of a sex offender, convicted paedophile, etc *UK*
A variation of **NUMBERED OFF; ON THE NUMBERS**.
- —Angela Devlin, *Prison Patter*, p. 23, 1996

ones and twos *noun*
shoes *US, 1928*
- —Eugene Landy, *The Underground Dictionary*, p. 142, 1971

one-shot wonder *noun*
a man who is unable to achieve a second erection within a short time after orgasm *UK*
- Sorry, darling. I'm a one-shot wonder. You're not going to get any life out of this for a while.—Colin Butts, *Is Harry on the Boat?*, p. 137, 1997

one-side *verb*
to hit without warning *FIJI*
Recorded by Jan Tent in 1995.

one singer, one song; wan singer, wan song
used as a call for order when many people are contributing to a debate at the same time *UK: SCOTLAND*
Originally shouted at people who, uninvited, join in a singer's song, and, inevitably, fail to add a pleasing harmony. Popularised by Glaswegian actor, comedian and folk-singer, Billy Connolly (b.1942).
- Hey yous, wan singer, wan song, eh? Let the boay speak his piece. —Michael Munro, *The Complete Patter*, 1996

one-skin joint *noun*
a marijuana cigarette made with just one cigarette paper *UK*
- [T]he limousine drivers were sitting around a bed rolling one-skin joints for the drive back to the airport.—Will Birch, *No Sleep Till Canvey Island*, p. 90, 2003

one-skinner *noun*
a marijuana cigarette made with just one cigarette paper *UK*
- [He] started to wrap a one-skinner[.]—Kevin Sampson, *Powder*, p. 31, 1999

one-spot *noun*
a prison sentence of one year *US*
- —Vincent J. Monteleone, *Criminal Slang*, p. 168, 1949

one star artist *noun*
a second lieutenant *NEW ZEALAND, 1910s?*
Military, from the sleeve or shoulder insignia. In World War 1 'one star – one stunt' was an army catchphrase that reflected the frequency with which second lieutenants got killed in their first battle.

onesy *noun*
an act of urination *AUSTRALIA*
- Well it got to the stage where nature was calling with everything it had so I drifted off for a onsey and twoseys and rushed back as soon as I could.—Paul Vautin, *Turn It Up!*, p. 87, 1995

one-time *noun*
the police *US*
- The youth's companion also yelled: "Hey, one time's comin', drop the gun."—*Seattle Times*, p. A1, 29th July 1990
- One-time! Break!—*Menace II Society*, 1993
- —Mark S. Fleisher, *Beggars & Thieves*, p. 290, 1995: 'Glossary'
- While kids in Northwest refer to police as "one-time," Northeast teenagers call them "bo-deen" or "hot dog," and in Southeast they're "po-pos" or good old "feds."—*Washington Post*, p. A1, 20th August 2001

one toke no joke
powerful marijuana *UK*
Rhyming elaboration on **TOKE** (to smoke marijuana).
• One toke no joke – all bud and no fucking seeds! Cowboy's honour, man! — Stuart Browne, *Dangerous Parking*, p. 269, 2000

one-toke weed *noun*
marijuana of such potency that only a few inhalations induce intoxication *US*
• — Ernest L. Abel, *A Marijuana Dictionary*, p. 75, 1982

one to one *noun*
in betting odds, evens *UK*
• — John McCririck, *John McCririck's World of Betting*, p. 112, 1991

one-track mind *noun*
an overwhelming interest in a single topic, especially sex *UK, 1984*
Especially familiar, to some, in the catchphrase 'you've got a one-track mind', and various elaborations along the lines of 'and it's a dirt-track'.
• "Whatever happened to the summer of love?" its happy victims sometimes wonder in this town [San Francisco] where everyone has a one-track mind: food. — *The Guardian*, 17th October 2002

one way *noun*
LSD *US, 1970*
Possibly plays on the type of ticket you would purchase for a conventional 'trip'; **TRIP** (a hallucinatory drug experience).
• — Richard A. Spears, *The Slang and Jargon of Drugs and Drink*, p. 369, 1986
• — Mike Haskins, *Drugs*, p. 285, 2003

one-way *adjective*
heterosexual *US*
• — Roger Blake, *The American Dictionary of Sexual Terms*, p. 145, 1964
• — Dale Gordon, *The Dominion Sex Dictionary*, p. 112, 1967

one-way taxi *noun*
a hearse *UK*
• — Peter Chippindale, *The British CB Book*, p. 157, 1981

one-wire *noun*
an electrician *US*
US Navy usage.
• — *Seattle Times*, p. A9, 12th April 1998: 'Grunts, squids not grunting from the same dictionary'

one-woman show *noun*
(of a female) an act of masturbation *US*
Figurative sense of a theatrical presentation that itself is often critically described as 'intellectual masturbation'.
• — Erica Orloff and JoAnn Baker, *Dirty Little Secrets*, p. 67, 2001

one word from you and he does as he likes
he ignores your commands *UK, 1977*
With various pronominal variations. Especially popular amongst parents and pet-owners.

oney *noun*
one *UK*
• — Paul Baker, *Polari*, p. 185, 2002

on for young and old *adjective*
having begun in earnest *AUSTRALIA, 1951*
• Then it was on for young and old. The boys were fighting everywhere, and a square who had his head out of a car window screamed at us. — William Dick, *A Bunch of Ratbags*, p. 251, 1965
• And then it's on for young and old, no holds barred, and I'm pushing her back across the edge of the couch, and we're kissing, and her moans are rising in pitch. — *Alvin Purple*, p. 13, 1974

onion *noun*
1 one hundred dollars *US*
• — Connie Eble (Editor), *UNC-CH Campus Slang*, p. 7, Fall 1988
2 crack cocaine *UK*
• — Mike Haskins, *Drugs*, p. 282, 2003
3 a native Bermudian *BERMUDA*
• — Peter A. Smith and Fred M. Barritt, *Bermewjan Vurds*, 1985
4 a Ford Orion car *UK*
Motor trade slang, reported by a car salesman, 4th August 2004.
5 an absolutely unskilled skateboarder *UK*
Teen slang; because 'it makes you cry to watch'; recorded by Miss Clare Paterson, 1978.

onion ballad *noun*
a painfully sad song *US*
An allusion to the relationship between onions and tears.
• — Don Wilmeth, *The Language of American Popular Entertainment*, p. 188, 1981

onion church *noun*
the Greek Orthodox church *US*
From the dome on many Greek Orthodox churches.
• — Amy and Denise McFadden, *CoalSpeak*, p. 10, 1997

onion hotel *noun*
a boarding house used by oil field workers *US*
• — Jerry Robertson, *Oil Slanguage*, p. 92, 1954

onion peeler *noun*
a switchblade knife *US*
• — Kenn "Naz" Young, *Naz's Underground Dictionary*, p. 48, 1973

onions *noun*
▸ **get up your onions**
to irritate, to anger *UK*
A variation of **GET UP YOUR NOSE**.
• See thae [those] ginks [men], they get right up my onions, so they dae. — Ian Pattison, *Rab C. Nesbitt*, 1988
▸ **pain in the onions**
an irritation; an annoying person *UK*
• And was your grandfather as big a pain in the onions as you are? — Ian Pattison, *Rab C. Nesbitt*, 1988

on it *adjective*
prepared and ready *US*
• I'd had a couple of blues and I was proper on it. I had a hard-on like a baby's frozen arm. — Dave Courtney, *Raving Lunacy*, p. 117, 2000

onk *noun*
the nose *UK*
• — Paul Baker, *Polari*, p. 185, 2002

onkaparinga; onka *noun*
a finger *AUSTRALIA, 1967*
Rhyming slang from Onkaparinga, a steeplechase track in Australia.
• — *The (Sydney) Bulletin*, 26th April 1975
• — Ned Wallish, *The Truth Dictionary of Racing Slang*, p. 59, 1989

onkus *adjective*
no good *AUSTRALIA, 1918*
Origin unknown.
• Cripes, did he? Pretty onkus for him. — Norman Lindsay, *Halfway to Anywhere*, p. 130, 1947

onliest *adjective*
only *US, 1907*
• I found myself running with a literary ex-pug, a pistol-packing rabbi, and a peewee jockey whose onliest riding crop was a stick of marihuana. — Mezz Mezzrow, *Really the Blues*, p. 69, 1946

only *adverb*
very *US*
Hawaiian youth usage.
• Wow, on'y trippy! — Douglas Simonson, *Pidgin to da Max Hana Hou*, 1982

only suckers beef
used as a catchphrase in Chicago to affirm a guiding principle of that city, that losers should not complain *US*
• Only suckers beef – Chicago is a tough town and not interested in losers. Next to "where's mine?" that's the name of the game here. If you lose, take your lumps and don't bitch. — Bill Reilly, *Big Al's Official Guide to Chicagoese*, p. 45, 1982

On my honor as a Rocket Ranger
used as a humorous oath or pledge *US*
On the US children's television programme *Rod Brown of the Rocket Rangers* (CBS, 1953–54), the children in the television audience were asked to pledge on their honour, among other things, 'to chart my course according to the Constitution of the United States of America'. Used in following years with irony by those who had been children during the dark years of the early 1950s.

on my skin
used as a profound oath of honour by white prisoners *US*
• —James Harris, *A Convict's Dictionary*, p. 35, 1989

OnO
used as an Internet shorthand farewell to mean 'over and out' *US*
• —Andy Ihnatko, *Cyberspeak*, p. 140, 1997

on offer *adjective*
available *UK*
• [W]hen the establishment Mafioso realise how much gilt, paper, cashish, wonga, wedge, corn, cutter, loot, spondos, dollar, readies, shillings, folding, dough, money is on offer[.]—J.J. Connolly, *Layer Cake*, p. 94, 2000

on point *adjective*
alert, ready for anything *UK*
Military; the man 'on point' leads a patrol.
• Fuckin' with the best producer in hip-hop music, I had to be more on point.—Eminem (Marshall Mathers), *Angry Blonde*, p. 4, 2001

Ontario dog *noun*
in Cape Breton, a cattle collie purchased from Ontario for work *CANADA*
• We had seen the ads for "cattle collie dogs" in the Family Herald and were in need of a good young working dog. Sceptical neighbours who thought the idea of paying money for a dog was frivolous would ask "Is that your Ontario dog?"—Alistair MacLeod, *Island*, p. 255, 2000

on the floor, hit the door
▷ **see:** DIE ON THE FLOOR, SEVEN AT THE DOOR

on the hob *noun*
the penis *UK*
Rhyming slang for **KNOB**.
• —Bodmin Dark, *Dirty Cockney Rhyming Slang*, 2003

on the in
in prison *UK*
• Dipshit, who had been "on the in" on and off since he was six, had no chance of parole[.]—Ken Lukowiak, *Marijuana Time*, p. 264, 2000

on the numbers *adjective*
▷ **see:** NUMBERED OFF

on the strength!
seriously! *US*
• —Ellen C. Bellone (Editor), *Dictionary of Slang*, p. 17, 1989

on time *adjective*
excellent *US*
• —William K. Bentley and James M. Corbett, *Prison Slang*, p. 46, 1992

on top *adjective*
1 about to happen *UK*
• —Home Office, *Glossary of Terms and Slang Common in Penal Establishments*, 1978
• [W]hoever was involved would have got wind that it was "on top".
— *The Guardian*, 6th September 2001: 'A life inside'

2 wrong; destroyed or defeated *UK*
• [T]hey're the fuckin' old bill [police], we're fuckin' tumbled [detected], it's on fuckin' top me old son.—J.J. Connolly, *Know Your Enemy [britpulp]*, p. 153, 1999

on top!
used as a warning that a prison officer is close *UK*
From the sense 'something is about to happen'.
• —Angela Devlin, *Prison Patter*, p. 83, 1996

onya
used as praise for a job well done *AUSTRALIA, 1948*
• As I made my way back to the table people were slapping me on the back. 'Well done, Blacky.' 'Onya, Blacky.'—Phillip Gwynne, *Deadly Unna?*, p. 131, 1998

on your bike!
go away! *UK, 1967*
• — *The Listener*, 2nd March 1967
• It's T.H.[8–1] over there. Have ?50–6. On your bike!—John McCririck, *John McCririck's World of Betting*, p. 110, 1991
• On your bike, you silly cunt.—Greg Williams, *Diamond Geezers*, p. 17, 1997

o-o *noun*
a quick inspection, a once-over *US, 1913*
• —Wilfred Granville, *The Theatre Dictionary*, p. 134, 1952

oo-ah *verb*
(used of a woman) to sit or lie with legs spread immodestly *NORFOLK ISLAND*
• —Beryl Nobbs Palmer, *A Dictionary of Norfolk Words and Usages*, p. 32, 1992

oodles *noun*
a large number; a large amount *US, 1867*
• Oodles and oodels of love and kisses, Suzie.—Max Shulman, *Guided Tour of Campus Humor*, p. 71, 1955
• They have oodles of photo albums with pictures taken when they were young[.]—Frederick Kohner, *Gidget*, p. 6, 1957
• No groovey clubs, only rock joints and oodles of prejudice.—Babs Gonzales, *Movin' On Down De Line*, p. 115, 1975
• He had oodles of warm, comedic charm.—Iceberg Slim (Robert Beck), *Airtight Willie and Me*, p. 51, 1979

oo-er!; ooo-er!
used for expressing surprise, disgust or embarrassment *UK, 1912*
• "Oo-er!" she exclaimed, as she dropped into the boat.—Kylie Tennant, *Lost Haven*, p. 366, 1946
• This is a "Cor! Get her!" sort of book ['What Falls Away' by Mia Farrow]. An "Oo-er! Fancy that!" account of a life spent in milieux that to most of us are as alien as the vast fields of Mars.—*New Statesman*, 7th March 1977
• Oo-er. What were you up to then, snogging?—*Girlfriend*, p. 78, 1995

oo-er missus!
used for stressing a sexual innuendo, or as a catchphrase-response to such a double-entendre *UK*
A narrowing of the senses used for **OO-ER!**.
• If only Kenneth Williams and Charles Hawtrey were alive, I'd slip them one for their Christmas stockings. Oo-er missus!—*New Statesman*, 3rd December 2001
• Yesterday he [Melvin Burgess] would not be drawn in, other than to say, "Oo-er missus! Yes, I have been warned to open the paper with care over my breakfast eggy."—*The Guardian (under the headline: 'Children's laureate slates teen 'porn' novel')*, 29th March 2003

ooga-booga-land *noun*
a non-specific African location *UK*
A racist notion based on the presumed phonetics of African tribal chants, probably filtered through a Hollywood reality.
• Now, he's not to keen on the idea of all the old savages coming round [...] while he's down in Ooga-Booga-Land[.]—Danny King, *The Burglar Diaries*, p. 54, 2001

oogley *adjective*
good, excellent *US*
Teen slang.
• —*American Weekly*, p. 2, 14th August 1955

ooh and aah *verb*
to express admiration *US, 1957*
• He made his way across the carpeted casino to where a small crowd had gathered to ooh and aah as Duffy threw his money away with stupid bets on table three.—Stephen Cannell, *Big Con*, p. 205, 1997
• People oooh and aaah. More gather to watch.—Mike Judge and Joe Stillman, *Beavis and Butt-Head Do America*, p. 25, 1997
• [T]hey all gathered around the cot, oohing and aahing and giving little screams of surprise and amazement.—Mary Hooper, *(megan)2*, p. 93, 1999

ooh la la *noun*
a brassiere *UK*
Rhyming slang for 'bra'.
• —Ray Puxley, *Fresh Rabbit*, 1998

ooh-la-la
used as an expression of admiration *US*
• What are we going to tell our friends/When they say ooh-la-la?—The Everly Brothers, *Wake Up Little Susie*, 1957
• "Ooh-la-la," Beano said and looked over at Paper Collar John.
—Stephen Cannell, *King Con*, p. 119, 1997

oojah; oojar; oojamaflip; oojah-ma-flip *noun*
a gadget; a non-specific thing *UK, 1917*
Etymology is unknown, however it has been theorised that it may come from Hindustani, or derive as a corruption of the nautical term 'hook-me-dinghy'; earlier variations include 'ooja-ka-piv' and 'ooja-cum-pivvy'.
• Maybe it is in just such a mood of detachment that the sage at the end of his long pilgrimage through life, ascends on a magic oojamaflip to, um, to celestial, you know, thingummy.—Tim Healey, *Home Truths*, 17th January 2004

Ookpik *noun*
a doll that looks like an owl *CANADA*
- Ookpik was originally "invented" by an unnamed Eskimo at Fort Chimo eight months ago, and northern affairs included him in their handicraft catalogue. — *Calgary Herald*, p. 1–2, 17th January 1964

oolies *noun*
marijuana *UK*
- — Mike Haskins, *Drugs*, p. 288, 2003

ooloo *noun*
a knife used by Eskimo women *CANADA*
- A gas lamp hangs from the centre of the tent. Mother sits chewing, her ooloo in her hand. Bannock is slowly cooking in an iron pot hung above an old camp stove. — *North*, p. 45/2, July-August 1966

oomph *noun*
the quality of sexual attraction; hence enthusiasm, vigour, energy *US, 1937*
Echoic, from the mating bellow (perhaps of a bull).
- The zombie put a little too much oomph into the gesture and his tongue fell to the floor with a soft plop. — Stewart Home, *Sex Kick [britpulp]*, p. 221, 1999

ooo-er!
▷ see: OO-ER!

oonock *noun*
an Eskimo implement for harpooning seals *CANADA*
- Oonock – the Company's staff who follow the sport of seal hunting in the spring are all familiar with this spearhead and its shaft. — *Beaver*, p. 38/2, September 1941

oop north *adjective*
in the North of England *UK*
A parodic use of a non-specific northern accent.
- Manchester United have just equalised. It's all happening oop north. — *The Guardian*, 18th September 2002

oop-pa-a-da
used as a greeting by bebop musicians and followers *US*
A highly stylised greeting, widely publicised in the early years of bop jazz, used sparingly.
- — Babs Gonzales, *Be-Bop Dictionary and History of its Famous Stars*, p. 9, 1949
- — Arnold Shaw, *Lingo of Tin-Pan Alley*, p. 15, 1950

oops!
used in response to an accident or mistake, suggesting an acknowledgement of fault *US*
- When we arrived in Monterey (a coastal town in Northern California), it was freezing cold and rained all the time. Oops. — Frank Zappa, *The Real Frank Zappa Book*, p. 23, 1989

oops-a-daisy!
▷ see: UPSIDAISY!

ooroo
goodbye *AUSTRALIA, 1967*
Variant of **HOOROO**.
- I grew up in NW Tasmania and when leaving the house or farewelling via the telephone, we've said "oo-roo" for as long as I can remember. — *Wordmap (www.abc.net.au/wordmap)*, 2003

ooscuse-me *noun*
▷ see: EXCUSE-ME

ooze *verb*
to move, especially slowly, carefully, without enthusiasm *US, 1929*
- Then, having discovered that my funds totaled slightly over six hundred dollars, I oozed to the floor in a moaning mound. — Max Shulman, *The Many Loves of Dobie Gillis*, p. 29, 1951
- Just on the loose – a half hour at Mary's, let's ooze over to Jo's, say Pete's got a fistful of hot new platters, so let's lend an ear. — Dick Clark, *To Goof or Not to Goof*, p. 103, 1963

op *noun*
1 a surgical *op*eration *UK, 1925*
- I've just had a little op. — Barry Humphries, *A Nice Night's Entertainment*, p. 109, 1968
- Vote Tory and you can take 60% of the cost of your operation out of your local hospital's budget, top it up and buy an op in a carpeted private clinic. — *The Guardian*, 8th October 2003

2 an *op*erator *US, 1930*
- The op behind the counter had the kind of mute, predatory face that belonged in a shooting gallery. — Robert Edmond Alter, *Carny Kill*, p. 2, 1966

3 a private detective; a private *op*erator *US*
- Not only that, but she had a private op's ticket and on occasions when she went out with me on a case, packed a flat .32 automatic – and she wasn't afraid to use it. — Mickey Spillane, *I, The Jury*, p. 11, 1947

4 a military *op*eration *UK*
- [T]he bulk items went ahead by road and ferry, leaving us with only our ops kit[.] — Chris Ryan, *Stand By, Stand By*, p. 61, 1996

op *verb*
to operate; to do; to set up *US, 1953*
- We tried to op a pad downtown, like in the Village, but they Jim Crowed us. — Ross Russell, *The Sound*, p. 123, 1961

OP *adjective*
*o*ther *p*eople's *US*
- — Helen Dahlskog (Editor), *A Dictionary of Contemporary and Colloquial Usage*, p. 43, 1972
- "Got a cigarette?" Mannelli asked, reaching across the desk. "I gave them up two years ago. Now I only smoke O.P.'s ... other people's." — William J. Cavnitz, *One Police Plaza*, p. 81, 1984

opal *noun*
▷ see: OCAL

OPB *noun*
used as an initialism for *o*ther *p*eople's *b*rand, a mythical and humorous brand of cigarettes *US*
- — Clarence Major, *Dictionary of Afro-American Slang*, p. 88, 1970

ope *noun*
opium; heroin *UK, 1929*
An abbreviation of 'opium'.
- — Richard A. Spears, *The Slang and Jargon of Drugs and Drink*, p. 369, 1986
- — Mike Haskins, *Drugs*, p. 284, 2003

open *noun*
in computing, a left parenthesis – the (*US*
- — Eric S. Raymond, *The New Hacker's Dictionary*, p. 268, 1991

open *verb*
1 used of a film actor who is a big enough box office attraction that success of a film project is almost guaranteed, to start and carry such a film production *US*
- The massive box-office success confirmed that she could "open" a movie, and made her a bankable star. — *The Times*, 2nd August 2003

2 to turn on *CANADA*
- — Victor Trahan, *The City of Montreal Style Guide*, 2002

▸ **open the kimono**
of a business, to reveal company accounts, to publish business information *UK, 1998*
Business slang.
- That implies a degree of openness and transparency which is new to most commercial organisations. As one technology-company executive puts it: "You have to be ready to open the kimono." — *The Economist*, 24th June 1999
- — Susie Dent, *The Language Report*, p. 83, 2003

▸ **open the lunchbox**
to fart *US*
- — Anna Scotti and Paul Young, *Buzzwords*, p. 73, 1997

open *adjective*
1 excited; drunk or drug-intoxicated; infatuated *US, 1995*
From **HAVE YOUR NOSE OPEN**.
- A woman or a record both "got me open"[.] — Nelson George, *Hip Hop America*, p. 209, 1998

2 in organised crime, safe for anyone without fear of violence *US*
- Las Vegas has been an "open city" (off limits to mob violence and open to mobs with the proper credentials) since the wild days of Bugsy Siegel. — Ed Reid and Ovid Demaris, *The Green Felt Jungle*, p. 179, 1963

open at both ends *adjective*
in poker, four cards in sequence that could form a five-card straight with a draw at either end of the sequence *US*
- — George Percy, *The Language of Poker*, p. 61, 1988

open door *noun*
in surfing, a wave that breaks such that the surfer can ride away from the peak onto the shoulder *US*
- — Grant W. Kuhns, *On Surfing*, p. 119, 1963
- — Rob Burt, *Surf City, Drag City*, 1986

openers *noun*

▸ **for openers**

to begin with; for starters *AUSTRALIA, 1969*

- —Alexander Buzo, *Rooted*, p. 36, 1969
- 'I'll listen, I think.' 'That'd be smart for openers.'—Peter Corris, *Make Me Rich*, p. 141, 1985

open go *noun*

a total lack of restriction *AUSTRALIA, 1940*

- Letters to the newspapers and to Members of Parliament protested that the wealthy betting-shops and posh restaurants were 'getting an open go.'—Vince Kelly, *The Bogeyman*, p. 124, 1956

open heifer *noun*

a woman looking for a mate *CANADA*

- An open heifer is one that is in heat. Just as the term heifer is sometimes applied to young girls, so can "open heifer" be applied, albeit crudely, to girls who are obviously looking for a boyfriend. —Chris Thain, *Cold as a Bay Street Banker's Heart*, p. 110, 1987

open-kimono *adjective*

characterised by complete honesty and full disclosure *US*

Sometimes formulated as 'open the kimono' or a variation thereon. Ronin International, a computer consulting firm, promises 'open-kimono' in its published mission statement, explaining that the term 'stems from feudal Japanese times where the term signified that the party will hide nothing within his clothing (the kimono was the dominant clothing of that era) that could conceivably be used as a weapon'.

- —Robert Kirk Mueller, *Buzzwords*, p. 117, 1974
- The breakup is forcing AT&T not only to get competitive, but to be willing to open its kimono and talk more thoroughly about its plans.—*Computerworld*, p. 55, 4th July 1984
- —*United States Naval Institute Proceedings*, p. 108, October 1986
- "Developers look at us and think 'corporation' and we want them to know that we embrace open source, an open kimono approach so to speak. That was the reason for our keynote," Shapanka said.—*IDG News Service*, 25th October 2000
- Laura Day Del Cotto, attorney for The United Co., Wilkinson's largest creditor, said debtors who receive court protection while reorganizing their finances have to assume an "open kimono" position when asked for financial data by their creditors.—*Lexington Herald-Leader*, 13th April 2001

open-mike *adjective*

said of a club where anybody may perform briefly and without payment *US*

- [H]e saw me at a club, it was open-mike night, and he gave me some shit about this group he's putting together.—Elmore Leonard, *Be Cool*, p. 56, 1999

open room *noun*

an establishment where it is possible to bet on sporting events and listen to or watch the event as it takes place *US*

- An open room is a gambling room where you can make a bet and then listen to the game or race you've bet on.—Burgess Laughlin, *Job Opportunities in the Black Market*, p. 11–4, 1978

open season *noun*

said when there are a lot of police monitoring vehicle speeds on a stretch of road *US*

- —Lanie Dills, *The Official CB Slanguage Language Dictionary*, p. 51, 1976

open shadow *noun*

in a surveillance operation, a follower who lets himself be spotted *US*

- "I guess you know what an open shadow is." "Sure. One that deliberately lets the subject spot him, then shake him, so that another shadow can pick him up when he thinks he is safe." —Raymond Chandler, *Playback*, p. 86, 1958

open slather *noun*

unrestrained freedom *AUSTRALIA, 1919*

From British dialect *slather* (to spill, to squander).

- Apparently, like a lot of country towns, it was open slather.—Robert English, *Toxic Kisses*, p. 157, 1979

open work *noun*

safecracking *US*

- —Vincent J. Monteleone, *Criminal Slang*, p. 169, 1949

opera *noun*

a travelling show *US*

- —Joe McKennon, *Circus Lingo*, p. 67, 1980

Operation Big Switch *noun*

the final exchange of prisoners of war in Korea in 1953 *US*

- Operation "Big Switch" – the final exchange of prisoners – began in August and ended in September.—Don Lawson, *The United States in the Korean War*, p. 128, 1964

Operation Killer *noun*

a main US offensive in the Korean war, 20th February – 6th March 1951 *US*

- Ridgway pursued, authorizing an advance called "Operation Killer."—Robert Leckie, *The Wars of America, Volume II*, p. 381, 1968

Operation Little Switch *noun*

a preliminary exchange of prisoners of war in Korea in 1953 *US*

- In February, General Clark had suggested that both sides exchange their sick and wounded prisoners. This exchange – known as Operation "Little Switch" – began in late April.—Don Lawson, *The United States in the Korean War*, p. 125, 1964

Operation Yo-Yo *noun*

the battle for Wosan, North Korea, in October 1950 *US*

So named by the US Marines who arrived at Wosan too late to take part in the capture because they had sailed back and forth around Wosan as the harbour was cleared of mines.

- The Marines, disgusted because the war seemed to be passing them by, called this futile sailing back and forth, "Operation Yo-Yo."—Don Lawson, *The United States in the Korean War*, p. 69, 1964
- We circled for five days. Our delay was labeled "Operation Yo-Yo" by those aboard.—William B. Hopkins, *Korea*, p. 51, 1986

operator *noun*

1 someone who is popular, crafty and perhaps manipulative *US, 1944*

- —Collin Baker et al., *College Undergraduate Slang Study Conducted at Brown University*, p. 165, 1968

2 a drug dealer *US*

- —*American Speech*, p. 28, February 1952: 'Teen-Age hophead jargon'

opie switch *noun*

in car repair, an oil pressure switch *US*

- The label on the box reads "O/P Switch."—Lewis Poteet, *Car & Motorcyle Slang*, p. 144, 1992

OPM *noun*

*o*ther *p*eople's *m*oney *US, 1901*

- —Robert Kirk Mueller, *Buzzwords*, p. 118, 1974
- When OPM is "backing" a player, he can afford to play for higher stakes.—Steve Rushin, *Pool Cool*, p. 22, 1990

'oppit

▷ see: HOP IT

oppo *noun*

a friend, a pal *UK, 1939*

Short for '*oppo*site number'.

- 'Your friend seems a nice chap,' she smiled, relaxed now. 'One of the best. We been oppos a long time.'—J.E. MacDonnell, *Don't Gimme the Ships*, p. 39, 1960
- Dingo Hancock was focussing with great evidence of concentration on what his oppo, Sloppy Duggan, was saying.—John Wynnum, *Tar Dust*, p. 34, 1962
- [H]aving cannily put a call in to my old Leicester oppo David Gower beforehand[.]—*The Guardian*, 8th March 2003

opposite *adjective*

obscene, especially of language *SOUTH AFRICA*

- —*Cape Times*, 23rd May 1946

op shop *noun*

a charity store *AUSTRALIA, 1976*

From '*op*portunity shop'.

- I had had enough of cubbing and my uniform went straight to the Op Shop.—Rex Hunt, *Tall Tales – and True*, p. 70, 1994
- Stephen is dressed in a dark grey op-shop sixties suit over a white shirt.—Christos Tsiolkas, *Loaded*, p. 60, 1995

optic *noun*

1 an eye *UK, 1600*

- With his black, stubby jowl and the patch over one optic, he looked like a fat pirate[.]—Gavin Casey, *It's Harder for Girls*, p. 27, 1941
- —J.E. MacDonnell, *Don't Gimme the Ships*, p. 32, 1960
- Cast your optics over these and then have the Writer type 'em out for me.—John Wynnum, *Tar Dust*, p. 101, 1962

- Don't waste time wondering, feller, get the optics screwed to that flamin' screen. —W.R. Bennett, *Night Intruder*, p. 114, 1962
- —John Wynnum, *Jiggin' in the Riggin'*, p. 50, 1965

2 a look *AUSTRALIA, 1974*
Short for **OPTIC NERVE**.
- —Jim Ramsay, *Cop It Sweet!*, p. 66, 1977
- She locked the door too and after taking a quick optic at some of the literature on my locker, I realised I'd been doped up and bunged into the Betty Ford Foundation. — Barry Humphries, *The Traveller's Tool*, p. 67, 1985

optical illusions *noun*
LSD *UK, 1998*
From the effect of the drug.
- —Mike Haskins, *Drugs*, p. 285, 2003

optic nerve *noun*
a look *AUSTRALIA, 1977*
Rhyming slang for **PERV**.
- However, we do like to encourage free enterprise and we want you to be able to rent the tape out to your mates so they can have an optic nerve on female lead Lori Petty[.]— *Tracks*, p. 28, October 1992

orace *noun*
an offensive, despicable person; a clumsy person; a socially awkward person *UK*
Recorded in contemporary gay use.
- — *Attitude*, p. 60, July 2003: 'New palare lexicon'

oral *noun*
oral sex *US*
A 2002 Incident Report from the Sausalito (California) Police Department describes the activities at a local massage parlor as follows: 'Only a few girls will do full service (sexual intercourse) and oral (oral copulation) massages'.

orale
hello *US*
Border Spanish used in English conversation by Mexican-Americans.
- —George Carpenter Baker, *Pachuco*, p. 42, 1950

-orama *suffix*
▷ see: **-RAMA**

or am I?
▷ see: **OR IS HE?**

orange *noun*
a tablet of dextroamphetamine sulphate (trade name Dexedrine™), a central nervous system stimulant *US*
- —John B. Williams, *Narcotics and Hallucinogenics*, p. 115, 1967
- —Mike Haskins, *Drugs*, p. 279, 2003

orange barrel *noun*
a type of LSD *UK*
- —Mike Haskins, *Drugs*, p. 285, 2003

orange bud *noun*
marijuana *UK*
From the colour.
- It's this orange bud, man. No wonder they call it goldfish. It knackers your memory. —Ed Allen and Johnny Vaughan, *'Orrible*, 10th September 2001
- —Nick Jones, *Spliffs*, p. 71, 2003

Orange Crush *noun*
in Canadian prisons, a special squad used to restore calm after a disturbance *CANADA*
- Orange is reserved for the Orange Crush (the special task force used to break up riots). —Suroosh Alvi et al., *The Vice Guide*, p. 207, 2002

orange cube *noun*
a dose of LSD given on a sugar cube *US, 1975*
- —Richard A. Spears, *The Slang and Jargon of Drugs and Drink*, p. 371, 1986
- —Mike Haskins, *Drugs*, p. 285, 2003

orange haze *noun*
a type of LSD *UK*
- —Mike Haskins, *Drugs*, p. 286, 2003

orange line *noun*
heroin *UK*
- —Robert Ashton, *This Is Heroin*, p. 206, 2002
- —Mike Haskins, *Drugs*, p. 284, 2003

orange magic *noun*
a type of LSD *UK*
- —Angela Devlin, *Prison Patter*, p. 83, 1996

orange micro *noun*
a type of LSD *UK*
- —Mike Haskins, *Drugs*, p. 286, 2003

orange peel *noun*
a highly visible orange jacket worn by railway workers *UK*
- —Frank McKenna, *A Glossary of Railwaymen's Talk*, 1970

orange-peel *verb*
(used of freshly applied paint) to wrinkle or form small ridges *US*
- Make it shiny and wet, but don't let it orange-peel or run. —Peter Coyote, *Sleeping Where I Fall*, p. 109, 1998

orange pip; orange *noun*
a Japanese person *UK*
Rhyming slang for **NIP**.
- —Ronnie Barker, *Fletcher's Book of Rhyming Slang*, 1979
- —Ray Puxley, *Cockney Rabbit*, 1992

orange squash; orange *noun*
money *UK*
Rhyming slang for **DOSH**.
- Got no orange[.]—Ray Puxley, *Fresh Rabbit*, 1998

orange sunshine *noun*
a type of LSD *US*
- I finally unwrapped the miniscule tablets and looked them over. Mere spots of orange lay on the wrinkled silver paper – "orange sunshine" it was called – labeled by a counterculture that had the Yankee business sense to use a catchy brand name even then. —Sean Hutchinson, *Crying Out Loud*, p. 55, 1988

orange wedge *noun*
a type of LSD *UK*
- —Mike Haskins, *Drugs*, p. 286, 2003

or are you?
▷ see: **OR IS HE?**

orbit *verb*
to engage in oral sex *US*
- — *American Speech*, p. 20, Spring 1985: 'The language of singles bars'

orbital *noun*
1 a person who lives permanently in the vicinity of one travellers' settlement *UK*
Used by late 1980s–early 90s counterculture travellers.
- —Martin Roach, *Dr. Marten's Air Wair*, 1999: 'Glossary of travellers' terms'

2 a breast *UK*
Recorded in contemporary gay usage
- — *Attitude*, p. 60, July 2003: 'New palare lexicon'

orchestra stalls; orchestras; orchestrals; orks *noun*
the testicles *UK*
Rhyming slang for **BALLS**, based on the front seating in a theatre auditorium. Probably late C19 or early C20 but not recorded until 1960.
- I was lucky I didn't damage my orchestra stalls. —Ronnie Barker, *Fletcher's Book of Rhyming Slang*, p. 43, 1979
- [A]ll body-hugging Lycra and a butcher's [look] at the orchestrals for the ladies. —Andrew Nickolds, *Back to Basics*, p. 138, 1994

orchid *noun*
a beautiful woman *US*
- As the poisonous fumes were snuffing out the life of this Broadway orchid – bride of 29 days – the lobby of her apartment building was filling up[.]—Jack Lait and Lee Mortimer, *New York Confidential*, p. 56, 1948
- We would put up a pot of five dollars each day and the one that "copped" the most "orchids" would win. —Babs Gonzales, *I Paid My Dues*, p. 68, 1967

order; orderly *verb*
1 to go, to leave *UK*
- [She] orderlied over as fast as she could manage[.]—James Gardiner, *Who's a Pretty Boy Then?*, p. 123, 1997
- —Paul Baker, *Polari*, p. 184, 2002

2 to orgasm *UK*
From an earlier sense as 'leave', thus 'to come' (to orgasm).
- —Paul Baker, *Polari*, p. 185, 2002

orderly daughters *noun*
the police *UK*
• —Paul Baker, *Polari*, p. 185, 2002

order of the boot *noun*
dismissal from work; the sack *UK, 1917*
• Strips holds the Empire and Olympic record for sackings, miles ahead of his nearest competitor. This in an industry devoted to the order of the boot is no mean feat.—Sutton Woodfield, *A for Artemis*, p. 2, 1960
• How habitual boozers got order of the boot.—*The Guardian*, 3rd January 2004

ordinary *adjective*
1 not very good; below standard *AUSTRALIA*
• Sipping his coffee, he picked up the TV guide to see what movies were on that night – it was a pretty ordinary lot.—Robert G. Barrett, *Davo's Little Something*, p. 200, 1992
• [Sand] gets into your eyes when it's blowy, it gets stuck to the hairs on my back, it gets up your nose, in your ears and of course, worst of all, it gets up your clacker. Ordinary stuff, isnt it?—Paul Vautin, *Turn It Up!*, p. 95, 1995
2 used by bookmakers for describing a losing day *AUSTRALIA*
• —Ned Wallish, *The Truth Dictionary of Racing Slang*, p. 59, 1989

Oregon boots *noun*
leg irons *US*
• —Vincent J. Monteleone, *Criminal Slang*, p. 169, 1949
• —Inez Cardozo-Freeman, *The Joint*, p. 519, 1984

or else
used for indicating consequences that will be unwelcome *UK*
• I'm going to collar the rats who operate this ring or else!—*The Sweeney*, p. 29, 1976

Oreo *noun*
a black person whose values are seen as white values *US, 1968*
Borrowed from a trade name of a chocolate biscuit with a white filling. Never used kindly.
• —*Current Slang*, p. 21, Spring 1970
• She's a pure Oreo. You know, like the cookie, black outside and white inside.—Iceberg Slim (Robert Beck), *The Naked Soul of Iceberg Slim*, p. 89, 1971
• LIONEL: He's what we call an Oreo cookie. ARCHIE: Oreo cookie? LIONEL: That's right. Black on the outside and white on the inside. ARCHIE: I'm glad you liked him, Lionel.—Eugene Boe (Compiler), *The Wit & Wisdom of Archie Bunker*, p. 71, 1971
• —David Claerbaut, *Black Jargon in White America*, p. 74, 1972
• Which explained, among other things, D'orothea's semi-Caucasian features and her fierce reluctance to deal with her African heritage. She was, in short, an Oreo.—Armistead Maupin, *Tales of the City*, p. 335, 1978
• —Edith A. Folb, *runnin' down some lines*, p. 248, 1980
• —Multicultural Management Program Fellows, *Dictionary of Cautionary Words and Phrases*, 1989

orft *adverb*
off *UK*
A deliberately illiterate pronunciation for jocular effect; especially familiar in 'orft we jolly well go', a catchphrase of broadcaster Jimmy Young (b.1923).
• —Nigel Rees, *Very Interesting... But Stupid!*, 1980

organ *noun*
1 a car radio *US*
From the language of used car sales.
• A bum stove and organ. Phony white shoes.—Joseph Wambaugh, *The Black Marble*, p. 194, 1978
2 the penis *UK, 1903*
Euphemistic.
• Through pornography, real women can be avoided, male anxiety soothed and delusions of phallic prowess indulged, by intimations of the rock-hard, larger-than-life male organ.—*The Guardian*, 8th November 2003

organ-arse *noun*
a person who deliberately farts in company *AUSTRALIA*
• —Peter Furze, *Tailwinds*, p. 131, 1998

organ donor *noun*
a motorcyclist who is not wearing a crash helmet *US*
• —Sally Williams, *"Strong" Words*, p. 153, 1994

organ grinder *noun*
a criminal's bodyguard or enforcer *UK*
Rhyming slang for **MINDER**.
• —Ray Puxley, *Cockney Rabbit*, 1992

organized chicken shit *noun*
Officer Candidate School *US*
From the initials.
• He had been accepted to Organized Chicken Shit, which is how OCS is known in the fleet.—Richard Marcinko and John Weisman, *Rogue Warrior*, p. 55–56, 1992

orgasm!
used for registering any transitory pleasure *UK*
• Then you've got those sad cases who close their eyes and say "Oooh. Orgasm!" when they eat something nice[.]—*The Guardian*, 17th February 2001

orgasmic *adjective*
great, excellent *US*
Hyperbole, probably.
• [B]ecause Ranger was paying, and because Rossini's made orgasmic tiramisu.—Janet Evanovitch, *High Five*, p. 244, 1999
• Good movies are now orgasmic but bad ones still just suck.—*The Times of India*, 30th September 2002

orge *verb*
to indulge in an excess of 'sinful' pleasures, especially of food, drugs, shopping or sex *UK*
Based on 'orgy', informed by 'gorge'.
• "Orgers" [...] are always the last to leave a party having consumed more of everything than everyone.—Alon Shulman, *The Style Bible*, p. 182, 1999

orgy room *noun*
a room designated for group sex *US*
• Returning to the "orgy room," I peeked through the curtains.—*The Advocate*, p. 5, March 1969
• These bars generally consist of a large open space containing a bar and dance floor, and a connected "sex room" or "orgy room" where men practice homosexual sexual acts on each other.—*The Knapp Commission Report on Police Corruption*, p. 140, 1972
• I was in the orgy room. Very late. I had smoked a little pipe of sinsemilla, and I was feeling glorious.—Armistead Maupin, *Babycakes*, p. 253, 1984

Oriental dancer *noun*
in circus and carnival usage, a sexually explicit female dancer *US*
• —Don Wilmeth, *The Language of American Popular Entertainment*, p. 190, 1981

Orient Express *noun*
1 any route used to smuggle opiates from Southeast Asia to Europe, especially via Amsterdam *US*
An allusion to the famed Paris-to-Istanbul train.
• —Ralph de Sola, *Crime Dictionary*, p. 108, 1982
2 the #7 subway line to Flushing, Queens, New York *US*
An allusion to the large number of Asian-Americans who commute on this line.
• —Jim Crotty, *How to Talk American*, p. 237, 1997

orifice *noun*
1 an office *UK, 1984*
Jocular.
2 a (police) officer *UK*
Jocular; certainly since the late 1990s.

original *noun*
1 an unconventional or eccentric person *UK, 1824*
• She is something of an original in LA, being both a smoker, a breed that comes second only to al-Qaeda in terms of public disapprobation, and a non-driver[.]—*The Observer*, 16th December 2001
2 a male prisoner who selects and maintains a primary sexual partner in jail *US*
• There are two classes of homos in here. you have what they call the "original" or "square" and you have what they call the "candy-bar punk".—Bruce Jackson, *In the Life*, p. 359, 1972

original gangster *noun*
a member of the founding generation of a youth gang; somebody who is so committed to a gang that he remains a gang member at all costs *US*
• —Mark S. Fleisher, *Beggars & Thieves*, p. 290, 1995: 'Glossary'

originals *noun*
the clothes worn by a member of Hell's Angels when he is initiated into the gang, and worn thereafter in perpetuity *US*
- These are his "originals," to be worn every day until they rot. — Hunter S. Thompson, *Hell's Angels*, p. 47, 1966

or, in English
used as a humorous bridge between a butchered attempt at verbalisation and an attempt to correct *US*
Coined as a self-parody by ESPN's Keith Olberman.
- — Keith Olberman and Dan Patrick, *The Big Show*, p. 23, 1997

O-ring *noun*
a novice surfer; a dolt *US*
- — *Surfer Magazine*, p. 30, February 1992

orinoco; orinoko *noun*
1 cocoa *UK*
Rhyming slang. Also shortened to 'ori'.
- — Ray Puxley, *Cockney Rabbit*, 1992

2 a poker *UK*
Rhyming slang. Also variant 'orinoker'.
- — Ray Puxley, *Cockney Rabbit*, 1992

or is he?; or am I?; or are you?
a catchphrase added to a statement for rhetorical effect *UK, 1984*
- This man is killing jazz. Or is he? — *The Guardian*, 23rd June 1999

o'river
goodbye *US*
An intentional mispronunciation of the French.
- Showing disdain for scholarly display of bilingual accomplishment. — Connie Eble (Editor), *UNC-CH Campus Slang*, p. 7, Spring 1991

orks *noun*
▷ see: ORCHESTRA STALLS

ornament *noun*
on the railways, a stationmaster *US*
- — Ramon Adams, *The Language of the Railroader*, p. 109, 1977

ornery *adjective*
ill-humoured and uncooperative *US, 1816*
- That ornery old man upstairs is very, very hurt right now[.] — Christopher Paul Curtis, *Bud, Not Buddy*, p. 227, 1999
- A computer support technician may exhibit remarkable diagnostic intuition when your PC is acting ornery. — Mel Levine, *A Mind at a Time*, p. 215, 2002

orphan *noun*
1 in craps, a bet on the table that a gambler has forgotten belongs to him *US*
- — N.B. Winkless, *The Gambling Times Guide to Craps*, p. 97, 1981

2 a computer that has been phased out due to technological advances *US*
- — Rachel S. Epstein and Nina Liebman, *Biz Speak*, p. 162, 1986

orphan Annie; orphan *noun*
the vagina *UK*
Rhyming slang for **FANNY**, formed from the character Little Orphan Annie, introduced to the US in comic strip form in 1924, but best known to British audiences from *Annie* the stage-musical, 1977, and film, 1982.
- [A]void it like an infected orphan. — Ray Puxley, *Fresh Rabbit*, 1998

or something
used as a final tag, a vague et cetera *UK, 1961*
- She dresses like some kind of royal person or something, like that American lady who married the king of Jordan. — *The Guardian*, 2nd August 2003

ort *noun*
the anus *AUSTRALIA, 1952*
Origin unknown.
- Take it from me, there's more ways to kill a cat than fillin' its ort with sand. — John Wynnum, *Tar Dust*, p. 116, 1962

orthopod *noun*
an orthopaedist *UK, 1960*
- — Sally Williams, *"Strong" Words*, p. 135, 1994

or what!?
used as an all-purpose, sentence-ending intensifier *TRINIDAD AND TOBAGO, 1983*
- — Lise Winer, *Dictionary of the English/Creole of Trinidad & Tobago*, 2003

or whatever
used as a non-specific alternative to a previously stated noun *UK, 1967*
- I'd walk down the street, go to a restaurant, or what have you, and people were always coming up to me asking for my autograph or whatever. — Jay Saporita, *Pourin' It All Out*, p. 62, 1980

or what-have-you
used as a non-specific continuation of a list or suggestion of further details *UK, 1948*
- I'd walk down the street, go to a restaurant, or what have you, and people were always coming up to me asking for my autograph or whatever. — Jay Saporita, *Pourin' It All Out*, p. 62, 1980

Osama yo mama
used as a general-purpose insult *US*
Teen slang; combines 'yo mama!' (a general-purpose insult) with the name of Osama bin Laden, presumed to be ultimately responsible for the atrocities of 11th September 2001.
- "It's like 'Osama Yo Mama' as an insult," offered Morgan Hubbard, 17, a senior at Quince High School in Gaithersburg, where students have picked up on the phrase from an Internet game. — *The Washington Post*, 19th March 2002

Oscar *noun*
1 a male homosexual *US*
Surely a reference to Oscar Wilde.
- — Dale Gordon, *The Dominion Sex Dictionary*, p. 115, 1967

2 an offensive, unlikeable person *US, 1905*
- She felt a lot better when she left, but this time I didn't get my sentence reduced for being a Boy Scout. There were a hard lot of oscars in the Bridewell. — Mezz Mezzrow, *Really the Blues*, p. 40, 1946

3 a prejudiced, narrow-minded person *US*
- — Kenn "Naz" Young, *Naz's Underground Dictionary*, p. 48, 1973

4 a handgun *US*
- — Vincent J. Monteleone, *Criminal Slang*, p. 169, 1949

Oscar Asche; Oscar Ash; oscar *noun*
cash; money *AUSTRALIA, 1905*
Rhyming slang, formed on the name of Australian actor, producer and director, Oscar Asche (1871 – 1936).
- [W]hat are we going to do for oscar? — Barry Humphries, *Bazz Pulls It Off!*, 1971
- [A]nybody who separates an Aussie from his Oscar (Oscar Ash: cash) is a Ned Kelly. — Arthur Chipper, *The Aussie Swearer's Guide*, p. 67, 1972
- Just before yer get too close, Dimitri, lay yer oscar on the table. — Lance Peters, *The Dirty Half-Mile*, p. 155, 1979
- Oscar (Ashe =cash) is still about[.] — *Antiquarian Book Review*, p. 18, June 2002

Oscar Slater *adverb*
later *UK: SCOTLAND*
Glasgow rhyming slang, formed from a man who, in 1909, was wrongly convicted of murder in a famous and scandalous travesty of justice; Arthur Conan Doyle, author of the *Sherlock Holmes* stories, took an interest and caused uproar by publishing *The Case of Oscar Slater* in defence of the man.
- See you Oscar Slater. — Michael Munro, *The Original Patter*, 1985

O-sign *noun*
the open mouth of a very sick hospital patient *US, 1980*
Medical wit; an especially humorous image when the 'O-sign' becomes the **Q-SIGN** (as above but with the tongue hanging out).
- — Adam T. Fox, St Mary's Hospital, London, 10th October 2002

Ossie Potter *noun*
water *AUSTRALIA*
Rhyming slang, from the name of a prominent Australian racehorse owner of the 1950s.
- — Ned Wallish, *The Truth Dictionary of Racing Slang*, p. 59, 1989

ossifer; occifer *noun*
a police officer *US, 1819*
An intentional metathesis, spoken in imitation of the slurred speech of intoxication.
- — Connie Eble (Editor), *UNC-CH Campus Slang*, p. 7, Spring 1991
- Take me drunk occifer, I'm home. — Geoff Tibballs (Editor), *The Mammoth Book of Humor*, p. 335, 2000

ossified *adjective*
very drunk *US, 1901*
- [O]ne time they got him loaded in the terminal and they got him on the airplane. He was ossified, that's the only way they could get him on. — Edward Lin, *Big Julie of Vegas*, p. 96, 1974

OT and E *adjective*
*o*ver-*t*ired and *e*motional *UK*
Upper-class society usage to describe children who are behaving unsociably. To be **TIRED AND EMOTIONAL** (drunk) is usually a condition for older family members.
- — Ann Barr and Peter York, *The Official Sloane Ranger Handbook*, p. 159, 1982

other *noun*
sexual intercourse, especially heterosexual but also homosexual *UK*
Mainly used as a **BIT OF THE OTHER**. Partridge, in the 1st edition of his *Dictionary of Slang and Unconventional English*, 1937, suggests that the unqualified term indicates 'homosexuality as a criminal offence' and that the other alternative is 'prostitution'.

other half *noun*
a significant other, husband or wife *UK, 1667*
- — *Complete CB Slang Dictionary*, 1976
- — Peter Chippindale, *The British CB Book*, p. 156, 1981

other lot *noun*
the police *UK*
- — Dave Courtney, *Dodgy Dave's Little Black Book*, p. 9, 2001

Other People *noun*
among criminals, the police *UK*
- [M]aking out we were being targeted by the Other People's Criminal Intelligence outfit, SO11, some of the Yard's top boys. — J.J. Connolly, *Layer Cake*, p. 74, 2000

others *noun*
homosexuals *FIJI*
Recorded by Jan Tent in 1996.

other side *noun*
homosexuality *BARBADOS*
Usually in a phrase such as 'gone over to the other side'. Collected in 1960.

other thing *noun*
▸ **the other thing**
1 the penis *UK, 1923*
Euphemistic.
2 sexual intercourse *UK, 1846*
Euphemistic.

▸ **do the other thing!**
used as an expression of contemptuous dismissal: do as you please! *UK, 1848*
- Because if you can't say something worth knowing, you might as well shut your mouth and do the other thing. — *The Guardian*, 15th July 2000

OTL *adjective*
distracted, foolish, stupid *US*
An abbreviation of **OUT TO LUNCH**.
- — Fred Hester, *Slang on the 40 Acres*, p. 12, 1968

OTOH
used as Internet shorthand to mean '*o*n *t*he *o*ther *h*and' *US*
- — Christian Crumlish, *The Internet Dictionary*, p. 145, 1995

OTR *adjective*
literally, experiencing the bleed period of the menstrual cycle; figuratively, complaining *US*
An initialism of **ON THE RAG**.
- — Collin Baker et al., *College Undergraduate Slang Study Conducted at Brown University*, p. 164, 1968
- — Pamela Munro, *U.C.L.A. Slang*, p. 64, 1989

OTT *adjective*
to excess; beyond the boundaries of conventional expectations; exaggerated *UK*
Ultimately from World War 1 troops leaving the trenches to attack the enemy; 'going over the top'.
- I sorted it out well enough without going OTT. I used a little diplomacy rather than just outright force[.] — Dave Courtney, *Stop the Ride I Want to Get Off*, p. 103, 1999

otto; otter; otta *adjective*
eight; eight (pre-decimal) pence *UK, 1893*
Polari, from Italian *octo* via parleyaree.
- [Y]ou might like to count to ten in Polari: una, duey, trey, quater, chicker, sey, setter, otto, nobber, dacha. — Michael Quinion, *World Wide Words*, 1996

ouc-dai-loi *noun*
▷ **see:** **UC DAI LOI**

ouch *noun*
an injury *US*
- — *American Speech*, p. 271, December 1962: 'The language of traffic policemen'

ouch!
how unfortunate! *US*
- — Pamela Munro, *U.C.L.A. Slang*, p. 94, 1997

ouchy *adjective*
(used of a racehorse) sore *US*
- — Tom Ainslie, *Ainslie's Complete Guide to Thoroughbred Racing*, p. 335, 1976

oudish *adjective*
used for expressing approval *UK*
- — Susie Dent, *The Language Report*, p. 75, 2003

ought hole *noun*
in trucking, the shifting position for the lowest gear *US*
- — Montie Tak, *Truck Talk*, p. 113, 1971

oughties *noun*
the first decade of the 21st century *UK*
- In the 2000s (or noughties, oughties, or zips)[.] — Susie Dent, *The Language Report*, p. 11, 2003

ouija board *noun*
in horse racing, the official odds board at the racetrack *US*
- — David W. Maurer, *Argot of the Racetrack*, p. 47, 1951

oul fella *noun*
a father *IRELAND*
- She hurled threats at me all the way to O'Connell Bridge: she would tell her mammy and my oul' one, her daddy and my oul' fella[.] — Hugh Leonard, *Out After Dark*, p. 68, 1989
- She still wore her wedding ring. The oul fella probably melted his down and sold it to Brendan Stokes for scrap before he headed for the hills. — Eamonn Sweeney, *Waiting for the Healer*, p. 51, 1997

oul one; auld wan; old dear *noun*
a mother *IRELAND*
- She hurled threats at me all the way to O'Connell Bridge: she would tell her mammy and my oul' one, her daddy and my oul' fella[.] — Hugh Leonard, *Out After Dark*, p. 68, 1989
- Ah, you're a tight-fisted mowldy auld bollocks. You'd hire your auld wan out be [by] the hour. — Joseph O'Connor, *The Irish Male at Home and Abroad*, p. 57, 1996
- And you can tell it's the last day of term, roysh [right], because all the boggers are walking around with, like, rucksacks full of dirty washing, bringing it home to their old dears to wash over the holidays. — Paul Howard, *The Teenage Dirtbag Years*, p. 86, 2001

ounce man *noun*
a drug dealer at the wholesale level, buying and selling in ounces *US, 1966*
- — Burgess Laughlin, *Job Opportunities in the Black Market*, p. 3, 1978: 'Glossary'
- All the kilo men and ounce men around town talked about real estate, about getting out, but Strike knew they were all full of shift. — Richard Price, *Clockers*, p. 57, 1992

ounce of baccy; ouncer *noun*
a Pakistani *UK*
Rhyming slang for **PAKI**, formed from a measurement of tobacco.
- — Ray Puxley, *Cockney Rabbit*, 1992

our concrete brethren *noun*
members of the US Air Force *US*
US Army usage.
- — *Seattle Times*, p. A9, 12th April 1998: 'Grunts, squids not grunting from the same dictionary'

our friend with the talking brooch *noun*
a uniformed police officer *UK*
A reference to the police radio worn on the uniform's breast.
- I hope our friend with the talking brooch enjoys it. — the cast of 'Aspects of Love', Prince of Wales Theatre, *Palare (Boy Dancer Talk) for Beginners*, 1989–92

out *noun*
an excuse, an alibi, a means of avoiding responsibility or difficulty *US, 1910*

▸ **on the out**
used of a prisoner when not imprisoned *UK, 1984*
- —Angela Devlin, *Prison Patter*, p. 83, 1996
- So when we were "on the out" we'd meet up in London one day[.] —Ken Lukowiak, *Marijuana Time*, p. 283, 2000
- "That's Ricky Vance," he said. "On the out he was a singer with a promising career ahead of him apparently[.]— *The Guardian*, 11th May 2000: 'A life inside'

out *verb*
1 to disclose another person's homosexuality *US, 1990*
Usually done to a public figure, and most commonly to one who is publicly anti-homosexual, such as J. Edgar Hoover or the cadre of gay men who surrounded Lt Col. Oliver North in the Reagan White House.
- He's petrified he'll be outed if this becomes an issue.—Armistead Maupin, *Maybe the Moon*, p. 216, 1992
- Meanwhile, Kia's lover, Evy (Migdalia Melendez), is outed by her ex-husband[.]— *Vogue*, p. 91, June 1994
- The term's coinage was prompted by Michelangelo Signorile's (b. 1960) "The Secret Gay Life of Malcom Forbes," a March 1990 Outweek story which appeared one month after the millionaire's death.—Steven Daly and Nalthaniel Wice, *alt.culture*, p. 175, 1995
- —Jeff Fessler, *When Drag Is Not a Car Race*, p. 39, 1997
- The lavender fascist practice of forcing gay celebrities and public figures out into the open. This "outing" usually takes the form of magazine articles with fly-poster campaigns.—Alon Shulman, *The Style Bible*, p. 182, 1999
- McConnell, I'm gonna out your ass in two seconds if you don't tell me where she is.— *Cruel Intentions*, 1999

2 to suspend or ban a player or competitor *AUSTRALIA, 1962*
- Their verdict was that it had not been allowed to run on its merits, and Corteen was 'outed' for a year.—James Holledge, *The Great Australian Gamble*, p. 18, 1966
- [He] warned him off all courses during the Stewards' pleasure, while Jack, and automatically his horse, were outed for twelve months. —Joe Andersen, *Winners Can Laugh*, p. 108, 1982

▸ **out someone's light**
to kill *TRINIDAD AND TOBAGO, 1987*
- —Lise Winer, *Dictionary of the English/Creole of Trinidad & Tobago*, 2003

out *adjective*
1 publicly and openly homosexual *UK, 1979*
An abbreviation of the full 'out of the CLOSET'.
- — *American Speech*, Winter 1990
- —Jeff Fessler, *When Drag Is Not a Car Race*, p. 39, 1997
- He's so fucking Out his teeth are chattering – he's extremely gay and one of them that wants you to know it, in all fairness.—Kevin Sampson, *Outlaws*, p. 240, 2001

2 unfashionable; no longer fashionable *UK, 1966*
- "Oh no, sir," he said. "Yellow socks are out," and [George] Melly went away blushing.—Nik Cohn, *Yellow Socks Are Out*, p. 21, 1989

3 no longer imprisoned *UK*
- He's only been out a fortnight and the motor's no older than that. —Ted Lewis, *Jack Carter's Law*, p. 151, 1974

4 experiencing the bleed period of the menstrual cycle *US*
- "I'm out" the Hindu American contributor writes, as in "I'm out of the temple." I can't go in because it's against the Hindu rules.— *The Museum of Menstruation and Women's Health*, December 2000

out
used in farewell *US*
- Allright. Out.— *Menace II Society*, 1993

outa here; outta here *adjective*
about to leave *US, 1980*
- "No," Dawn said, "but I wanted you to know I'm outta here."—Joseph Wambaugh, *Floaters*, p. 42, 1996

out-and-out *adjective*
complete, absolute, thorough-going *UK, 1813*
- An out-and-out Mod and Rocker warfare policy then began.—Jamie Mandelkau, *Buttons*, p. 24, 1971

out-and-outer *noun*
a thorough-going person or thing; an absolute lie *UK, 1812*
- Terrorists keep killing innocent Americans because the White House disregards their political claims, exactly the same way Palestinian terrorists behave with the out-and-outer, Zionist regime of Israel. — *The African Independent*, 15th May 2003

outasight *adjective*
▹ see: OUT OF SIGHT

outback *noun*
the remote regions of Australia *AUSTRALIA, 1893*
- So she fled in terror along the dusty track which led north from the Fields into the remote outback, the centre of Australia.—Jean Brooks, *The Opal Witch*, p. 135, 1967
- Is it like this in the outback too?— *Janie Stagestruck*, p. 81, 1972

▸ **go outback**
to go to the toilet for the purpose of defecation *AUSTRALIA*
- You may speak of a 'movement' or 'sit on the seat' Have a passage or stool – or simply excrete Or say to the others 'I'm going outback.' —Sam Weller, *Old Bastards I Have Met*, p. 34, 1979

outback *adjective*
situated in a remote country area *AUSTRALIA, 1893*
- In an outback pub, the drinkers were giving heaps to a fella named Macquarie[.]—Frank Hardy, *Hardy's People*, p. 175, 1986

out-country *noun*
during the Vietnam war, used for reference to any other country in Southeast Asia *US*
- —Linda Reinberg, *In the Field*, p. 159, 1991

outdoors *adverb*
▸ **all outdoors**
a great amount *US, 1830*
- "Goddamned place costs all outdoors," he said.—George V. Higgins, *Penance for Jerry Kennedy*, p. 172, 1985

outer *noun*
▸ **on the outer**
excluded from the mainstream; out of favour; ostracised *AUSTRALIA, 1902*
- I battled away on the outer for years, but where did it get me? —Alexander Buzo, *Rooted*, p. 76, 1969
- When I met him in 1946, Cornelius was on the outer with the machine because he'd worked too hot, even for John Wren, when Mayor of Richmond.—Frank Hardy, *Hardy's People*, p. 94, 1986

outerlimits *noun*
a combination of crack cocaine and LSD *UK, 1998*
- —Mike Haskins, *Drugs*, p. 293, 2003

outers *noun*
an excuse, an alibi; a means of escape, or of avoiding responsibility *UK*
- Give me outers, guv'nor, and I'll tell you where the gear is. —David Powis, *The Signs of Crime*, 1977

outers *adjective*
drug-intoxicated *UK*
From a number of phrases that commence 'out of'.
- [T]hey were so fuckin untogether, outers all the fuckin time. —J.J. Connolly, *Layer Cake*, p. 16, 2000

outfit *noun*
1 a criminal organisation *US, 1933*
- In one season the outfit netted $6,000,000 in Miami gambling houses.—Jack Lait and Lee Mortimer, *New York Confidential*, p. 186, 1948
- Her old man might have "outfit" friends. If he did we'd be found in an alley with our balls rammed down our throats.—Iceberg Slim (Robert Beck), *Pimp*, p. 254, 1969
- It was strictly a penny-ante operation, said Grana, and the Outfit let it exist because it took some heat off of their own dope syndicate. —Emmett Grogan, *Ringolevio*, p. 158, 1972
- He was mobbed up with the Pleasant Avenue outfit.—Edwin Torres, *Carlito's Way*, p. 21, 1975
- There's no doubt there's a Mafia, a Syndicate, a Unione Siciliana, an Outfit. Whatever people want to call it.—Robert Campbell, *Juice*, p. 236, 1988

2 a still used in the illegal production of alcohol *US*
- —David W. Maurer, *Kentucky Moonshine*, p. 121, 1974

3 heroin *UK*
- —Mike Haskins, *Drugs*, p. 284, 2003

4 the needle and syringe used to inject a drug *US, 1951*
- You got an outfit here?—John D. McDonald, *The Neon Jungle*, p. 73, 1953
- I said, "Please, 'Sweet,' cook it for me and load my outfit. It's inside the candy-striped tie in the closet".—Iceberg Slim (Robert Beck), *Pimp*, p. 100, 1969
- I guess they'll try and make it look like an outfit that a junkie would use, but neither me or my wife use, so I don't see how they can make a case out of it.—Donald Goines, *White Man's Justice, Black Man's Grief*, p. 153, 1973
- Anybody got an outfit up there?— *Drugstore Cowboy*, 1988
- —Angela Devlin, *Prison Patter*, p. 84, 1996

5 a vehicle *US*
Idaho usage.
- —Jim Crotty, *How to Talk American*, p. 213, 1997

out for the count *adjective*
fast asleep *UK, 1984*
From boxing.

out front *adjective*
direct, honest *US*
- —Lewis Yablonsky, *The Hippie Trip*, p. 368, 1968: 'Glossary'
- —David Powis, *The Signs of Crime*, 1977

outgribing *noun*
a written contribution to a single-interest fan magazine *US*
- —*American Speech*, p. 28, Spring 1982: 'The langage of science fiction fan magazines'

outhole *noun*
in pinball, the hole beneath the flippers through which a ball leaves play *US*
- —Bobbye Claire Natkin and Steve Kirk, *All About Pinball*, p. 113, 1977

outhouse *noun*
in poker, a full house (three of a kind and a pair) that is inferior to another full house hand *US*
- —John Vorhaus, *The Big Book of Poker Slang*, p. 28, 1996

outie *noun*
an outward-turned navel *US*
- —John D. Bell et al., *Loosely Speaking*, p. 14, 1966
- Erin's mother had paid a plastic surgeon $1,500 to transform her "outie" belly button to an "innie." —Carl Hiaasen, *Strip Tease*, p. 56, 1993

▸ **be outie**
to leave *US*
- Dee, I'm outie. —*Clueless*, 1995

outlaw *noun*
1 a prostitute working without the services of a pimp *US, 1935*
- I don't tell them other bitzes this, but being a lone outlaw in this life, with the johnlaws up one side an the pimps down the other, everybody mouth-waterin for a taste – well you catchin too much mogo at once[.] —Robert Gover, *JC Saves*, p. 55, 1968
- An outlaw is a ho without a proper pimp. —Christina and Richard Milner, *Black Players*, p. 41, 1972
- Walter's girl was the only one that had a pimp for a man. The other two boosters I drove for were outlaws. —A.S. Jackson, *Gentleman Pimp*, p. 32, 1973
- I have also heard that "outlaws," girls without a connection, are thrown out of that hotel bar and all others in Vegas soon as they are spotted. —Gerald Paine, *A Bachelor's Guide to the Brothels of Nevada*, p. 129–130, 1978

2 a worker who has been identified as an activist troublemaker and thus blacklisted *US*
- —Ramon Adams, *The Language of the Railroader*, p. 109, 1977
- Some show owners prefered crews of these 'outlaws' as most of these breed were highly competant (when sober), and they really had no other place to go. —Joe McKennon, *Circus Lingo*, p. 67, 1980

3 a horse that cannot be tamed or is very difficult to handle *AUSTRALIA, 1900*
- Back in town, he suggested that the blacksmith appear in the film shoeing the outlaw, and the farrier was delighted with the idea. —Vince Kelly, *The Bogeyman*, p. 171, 1956

outlaw *verb*
on the railways, to exceed the 16 hour maximum legal work limit *US*
- —*American Speech*, p. 288, December 1968: 'Addenda to the vocabulary of railroading'

outlaw *adjective*
in roller derby, outside the official Roller Derby League *US*
- —Keith Coppage, *Roller Derby to Rollerjam*, 1999

outlet *noun*
a bootlegger's house *CANADA*
- The euphemism "outlet" for bootlegger is due to the restrictive sale of liquor in Nova Scotia. One may get a regular bottle of beer, but pays a higher price than at the Liquor Commission. Off-premises consumption only, too, but it's closer by. —Lewis Poteet, *The South Shore Phrase Book*, p. 84, 1999

out like a light *adjective*
suddenly and deeply unconscious *UK, 1944*
- A coroner ruled yesterday that a widow who "went out like a light" while being treated by the serial murderer Harold Shipman had been unlawfully killed. —*The Guardian*, 17th August 2000

out of here
used as a farewell *US*
- —Lee McNelis, *30 + And a Wake-Up*, p. 10, 1991

out of it *adjective*
1 crazy, mentally ill *US*
- He's out of it, Bailey. I think the defendant should be remanded for a psychiatric examination. —Edwin Torres, *After Hours*, p. 259, 1979
- —Angela Devlin, *Prison Patter*, p. 84, 1996

2 in an advanced a state of drug- or drink-intoxication *US, 1963*
- —Angela Devlin, *Prison Patter*, p. 84, 1996
- [G]uessing what it's like to be out of it. —Kevin Sampson, *Powder*, p. 6, 1999
- [O]ut-of-it ravers going fucking barmy[.] —Dave Courtney, *Raving Lunacy*, p. 99, 2000
- And when he got out-of-it it wasn't falling on the floor out-of-it, it was talking absolute bollocks out-of-it. —Dave Courtney, *Raving Lunacy*, p. 131, 2000
- They are "up the monument" or "half seas over"; they are "on a bender", "out of it" or "off their tits". —Peter Ackroyd, *London The Biography*, p. 359, 2000
- —Stuart Walton, *Out of It – A Cultural History of Intoxication*, 2001

out of order; bang out of order *adjective*
used to describe behaviour that is unacceptable *UK, 1979*
- You smacked him? – Yeah Char yeah he was well out of order. —Nick Barlay, *Curvy Lovebox*, p. 114, 1997
- Bang out of order. The kid was taking a fucking liberty. —Greg Williams, *Diamond Geezers*, p. 8, 1997
- Fuckin' bang out of order. They're like fuckin' leeches all of them. —Lanre Fehintola, *Charlie Says...*, p. 24, 2000
- [H]e's a silly cunt for doing that, bang out of order for what he's done to his family and friends. —John King, *Human Punk*, p. 219–220, 2000

out of sight; outasight *adjective*
excellent, amazing *US, 1876*
Nearly a hundred years old before being swept up as a core adjective of the 1960s hippie lexicon.
- He gave me some LSD that night and it was outasight. —Abbie Hoffman, *Revolution for the Hell of It*, p. 154, 1968
- GEORGE: Now this is supposed to be the finest whorehouse in the South. These ain't no pork chops. These are U.S. Prime. BILLY: out a site, man. —Peter Fonda, *Easy Rider*, p. 117, 1969
- The high point for me, thus far, was an unbelievable performance by The Quarry, an outasite group of very heavy musicians, Saturday night. —*East Village Other*, 20th August 1969
- They say "This is passport control, your passport please?" I says, "Outasight, outasight, outasight," handed my passport over. —Richard Neville, *Play Power*, p. 241, 1970
- We could be a dynamite team, outasight. —*Saturday Night Fever*, 1977
- "Out of sight!" Jerry Rubin said, as the defendants began to talk among themselves. —Bobby Seale, *A Lonely Rage*, p. 237, 1978
- "outta sight" in the words of James Brown. —Dick Hebdige, *Homegrown Cool; The Style of the Mods*, 1979

out of the money *adjective*
in horse and dog racing, finished below third place *US*
- "Out of the money and tiring at the finish," Ciglianni added. —Robert Campbell, *Juice*, p. 2, 1988

out of this world *adjective*
extraordinary *US, 1928*
- Tony could play the blues out of this world. —Mezz Mezzrow, *Really the Blues*, p. 45, 1946

out of town *adjective*
used to describe behaviour that is unacceptable *US, 1942*
- You're well out of order now, this is well out of town. —The Streets (Mike Skinner), *Dry Your Eyes*, 2004

out of whack *adjective*
out of tune, malfunctioning *US, 1885*
- In the winter of 1982–83, all the Pacific weather patterns got out of whack. The result: deadly droughts scorched India, Indonesia, and Australia while North America was battered by violent storms[.] —Roger Von Oech, *A Kick in the Seat of the Pants*, p. 32, 1986

out-out *verb*
to put out *BARBADOS*
- —Frank A. Collymore, *Barbadian Dialect*, p. 80, 1965

outro *noun*
the concluding section, especially of music or broadcast programmes *UK*
The opposite of **INTRO** (introduction).
- —Vivian Stanshall, *The Intro and the Outro*, 1967

outrun *verb*

▸ **outrun the note**

(of a car) to last longer than it takes to pay off the loan incurred to buy it *US*

• — Lewis Poteet, *Car & Motorcyle Slang*, p. 145, 1992

outs *noun*

in poker, the playing of a weak hand in the hope of a drastic improvement in drawing *US*

• — John Scarne, *Scarne's Guide to Modern Poker*, p. 285, 1979

outside *noun*

1 in Alaska, anywhere in the US other than Alaska *US, 1900*

• As a salesman I had an appointment in Anchorage and spent about 10 days and $700 to get there at the appointed time and date, only to be told my customer was "outside," to which I almost replied, "Why don't you go outside and get him." — Mark Wheeler, *Half Baked Alaska*, p. 111, 1972
• — *American Speech*, p. 256–258, Fall 1984: 'Terms for 'not Alaska' in Alaskan English'
• — Mike Doogan, *How to Speak Alaskan*, p. 47, 1993

2 the world outside the armed forces *US, 1898*

• — *American Speech*, p. 288, December 1962: 'Marine Corps slang'

outside *adjective*

1 out of the ordinary *US*

• That shit's really outside. — Steve Cannon, *Groove, Bang, and Jive Around*, p. 21, 1969

2 (of a child) illegitimate *TRINIDAD AND TOBAGO, 1952*

• — Frank A. Collymore, *Barbadian Dialect*, p. 80, 1965
• — Lise Winer, *Dictionary of the English/Creole of Trinidad & Tobago*, 2003

3 (of a lover) adulterous *TRINIDAD AND TOBAGO, 1971*

• — Lise Winer, *Dictionary of the English/Creole of Trinidad & Tobago*, 2003

4 in surfing, seaward of the swell *US*

• — Grant W. Kuhns, *On Surfing*, p. 119, 1963
• They are just "outside," about one fifth of a mile out from the shore, beyond where the waves start breaking. — Tom Wolfe, *The Pump House Gang*, p. 23, 1968

outside *adverb*

not in prison *US, 1871*

• You were outside, I was inside, you were s'posed to keep in touch with the band. — *The Blues Brothers*, 1980
• I hadn't heard from anyone on the outside, and it began to matter less after a while. — Herbert Huncke, *Guilty of Everything*, p. 122, 1990

▸ **get outside of**

to eat *US, 1869*

• Here, you greedy basket of fruit, you're on short rations, get outside of this. — Wilda Moxham, *The Apprentice*, p. 114, 1969

outside!

used for calling to the attention of other surfers the presence of an approaching series of waves seaward *US*

• — John Severson, *Modern Surfing Around the World*, p. 175, 1964

▷ **see:** COME OUTSIDE!

outside child *noun*

an illegitimate child *CAYMAN ISLANDS*

• — Aarona Booker Kohlman, *Wotcha Say*, p. 25, 1985

outside work *noun*

any external alteration of dice for cheating *US*

• — John S. Salak, *Dictionary of Gambling*, p. 174, 1963

outstanding *adjective*

excellent *US, 1964*

Conventional English converted to slang by attitude and a drawn-out pronunciation.

• "Out-standing!" Bobbie said. — Joseph Wambaugh, *Finnegan's Week*, p. 247, 1993
• Hey, Bea Arthur, outstanding! — *Airheads*, 1994

outta here *adjective*

▷ **see:** OUTA HERE

out there *adjective*

1 in a state of extreme marijuana-intoxication *US*

• He smokes a lot, and when he gets really out there on it makes with cartoon non sequiturs that nobody else can fathom[.] — Lester Bangs, *Psychotic Reactions and Carburetor Dung*, p. 234, 1977
• — Angela Devlin, *Prison Patter*, p. 84, 1996

2 in the alternative society; out of the mainstream *US*

• Barton decided that it would be "out there" to leave the apartment just as it was. — Ed Sanders, *Tales of Beatnik Glory*, p. 91, 1975
• — Connie Eble (Editor), *UNC-CH Campus Slang*, p. 7, April 1995
• [L]etting the reader see he's "out there". With them. — Kevin Sampson, *Powder*, p. 5, 1999

3 crazy, mentally ill *UK*

• — Angela Devlin, *Prison Patter*, p. 84, 1996

out ticket *noun*

in horse racing, a winning bet not presented for payment on the day of the race *US*

• — Bob and Barbara Freeman, *Wanta Bet? A Study of the Pari-Mutuels System in the United States*, p. 291, 1982

out to lunch

weird, being in a state that does not conform to peer-group expectations; distracted; crazy *US, 1955*

• Man, that geezer is seriously out to lunch[.] — Donald Gorgon, *Cop Killer*, p. 79, 1994

oven *noun*

▸ **in the oven**

pregnant *UK, 1937*

Especially in the phrase 'bun in the oven'.

• "That's my kid brother, Benny," Abe used to tell the cabbies, "married six weeks and he's already got one in the oven. A quick worker, I'll tell you." — Mordecai Richler, *"Benny," in Canadian Short Stories*, p. 417–418, 1960
• Poor thing has another one in the oven. — Louise Meriwether, *Daddy Was a Number Runner*, p. 51, 1970
• What about this little crumb-crusher you got in the oven here? — Edwin Torres, *After Hours*, p. 378, 1979
• To have a bun in the oven is to be pregnant. [Th]ey will not be so scared bout gettin another bun in da oven and so consequenshaly be less frigid. — Sacha Baron-Cohen, *Da Gospel According to Ali G*, 2001
• [W]hen my sister found she had one in the oven, she became known as the town slag[.] — Danny King, *The Burglar Diaries*, p. 13, 2001

over *adjective*

1 popular with the audience *US*

Professional wrestling usage.

• Myth: Steve Austin is more over than Hulk Hogan was. Fact: It all depends on how you define the term "over." — Luke Johnston, *The Shooters*, p. 10, 2nd December 1999
• Ric Flair was the most over wrestler at this point of the night. — *Herb's Wrestling Tidbits*, 15th May 2000

2 disgusted by; done with *US*

• — Connie Eble (Editor), *UNC-CH Campus Slang*, p. 4, Spring 1983

overamp *verb*

to overdose on narcotics *US, 1967*

• — William D. Alsever, *Glossary for the Establishment and Other Uptight People*, p. 24, December 1970

over-and-under *noun*

1 a capsule containing both a barbiturate and an amphetamine *US*

• — David Maurer and Victor Vogel, *Narcotics and Narcotic Addiction*, p. 431, 1973

2 an M-16 rifle with an M-79 grenade launcher tube under the rifle barrel *US, 1972*

• I continued, "THE PERFORMANCE OF THE OVER AND UNDER," and proceeded to report that this Rube Goldberg wonder weapon (which was an M-16 with an M-79 fixed underneath) was an ineffective, undesirable piece of shit. — David H. Hackworth, *About Face*, p. 479, 1989

overboard *adjective*

drunk *US*

• At about nine o'clock, half overboard, Legs said he was going to the washroom. — Jack Lait and Lee Mortimer, *New York Confidential*, p. 162, 1948

▸ **go overboard**

1 to be over-enthusiastic about something, to exaggerate *US, 1931*

• It's probably going overboard to say that all men fear impotence. — Bob Berkowitz, *What Men Won't Tell You but Women Need to Know*, p. 122, 1990

2 to refuse or fail to pay a gambling debt *US*

• — Dan Parker, *The ABC of Horse Racing*, p. 146, 1947

over-boogie *verb*

to over-indulge in the pleasures of vice *US*

• [M]y ability to consume vast quantities of things that were supposed to poison me from what one rock'n'roll crowd used to call "over boogie" was tested to the hilt and I thought I was invincible. — Eve Babitz, *L.A. Woman*, p. 49, 1982

overbroke *adjective*
used of betting with no profit margin for the bookmaker *UK*
- [O]n the very best prices available it was "overbroke" by 0.6 per cent. —John McCririck, *John McCririck's World of Betting*, p. 43, 1991

overcoat *noun*
1 a coffin *US*
- —Vincent J. Monteleone, *Criminal Slang*, p. 169, 1949

2 in pool, a player who has mastered the foibles of a particular table *US*
- —Steve Rushin, *Pool Cool*, p. 22, 1990

overcoat maker *noun*
an undertaker *UK*
Rhyming slang, with more than a passing reference to (wooden) **OVERCOAT** (a coffin).
- —Ray Puxley, *Cockney Rabbit*, 1992

overdue *adjective*
used of a criminal who, not having been convicted of a crime, is statistically likely to, or should, be found guilty of something (if there is any justice) *UK*
Police use.
- "Not guilty, not guilty, not guilty. What is the expression here? This man is overdue, yes?" "Well overdue, sir." —Anthony Masters, *Minder*, p. 157, 1984

overfix *verb*
to overdose using a drug *US*
- You all won't believe this, but I ain't ever been overfixed. —Bruce Jackson, *In the Life*, p. 223, 1972

overground *noun*
a commercialised milieu for a previously underground culture *UK*
- Once mod had gone overground, the early pioneers were sidelined. —Dave Haslam, *Adventures of the Wheels of Steel*, p. 76, 2001

overjolt *noun*
a drug overdose *US, 1959*
- Finally, the next morning, he said, he drove her to a patch of grass near Mission Emergency Hospital and then tipped police that she'd had "an over-jolt." —*San Francisco Examiner*, p. 12, 9th March 1962
- —Eugene Landy, *The Underground Dictionary*, p. 144, 1971
- —Tom Hibbert, *Rockspeak!*, p. 115, 1983

overjolt *verb*
to suffer a drug overdose *UK*
- —Tom Hibbert, *Rockspeak!*, p. 115, 1983

overland route *noun*
▸ **to take the overland route**
in horse racing, to race on the outside portion of the track because a horse prefers passing around a pack to accelerating through it *US*
- —Walter Steigleman, *Horseracing*, p. 274, 1947

overlay *noun*
in horse racing, a situation where a horse that should win a race is given higher odds than it should *US*
- In order to catch these "overlays," it is necessary to be well-briefed on a race and to know how the more prominent public selectors – especially those with large followings in the vicinity of the track being played – are picking the race. —George King, *Horse Racing*, p. 11, 1965

over-much *adjective*
astonishing, difficult to believe *US*
- —Collin Baker et al., *College Undergraduate Slang Study Conducted at Brown University*, p. 166, 1968

over my dead body
used as an expression of the strongest will to resist *UK, 1936*
Hyperbole.
- They want to control the [Notting Hill] carnival, allowing only the best-behaved Negroes to take part under stringent conditions [...] Over my dead body, I say. —*New Satesman*, 3rd September 2001

overparted *adjective*
having been cast in a *part* that demands more of an actor than he or she is capable of *UK*
- They end up, as we say of actors who have been cast beyond their abilities, overparted. —*The Guardian*, 12th April 2003

overripe fruit *noun*
an older homosexual man *UK*
- —*Maledicta*, p. 222, 1979: 'Kinks and queens: linguistic and cultural aspects of the terminology for gays'

over-round *adjective*
used of betting when the probable or actual profit margin is entirely in a bookmaker's favour *UK*
- [T]he book for the 1991 Seagram Grand National, for instance, was over-round by 29 per cent[.] —John McCririck, *John McCririck's World of Betting*, p. 43, 1991

overs *noun*
1 more money than you need *UK*
- I fell asleep, dreaming of how life might be when I got overs. I had visions of multimillions[.] —Diran Abedayo, *My Once Upon A Time*, p. 89, 2000

2 surplus or undivided profits from a crime *UK*
- —David Powis, *The Signs of Crime*, 1977
- —Angela Devlin, *Prison Patter*, p. 84, 1996

3 money a bookmaker has overpaid *UK*
- —John McCririck, *John McCririck's World of Betting*, p. 61, 1991

4 a wager at odds better than those prevailing elsewhere; any extravagence *AUSTRALIA*
- —Ned Wallish, *The Truth Dictionary of Racing Slang*, p. 59, 1989

5 in a game of poker, the small amount of money left in the centre of the table after a pot is divided among two or more players, held over for the next hand *US*
- —George Percy, *The Language of Poker*, p. 62, 1988

over there *noun*
in Europe *AUSTRALIA*
Originally used of the military during World War 1.
- Somehow, something gets through when he goes Over There. The Australian doesn't necessarily travel well, but he comes back, once travelled, a much better man. —Sue Rhodes, *Now you'll think I'm awful*, p. 156, 1967

over the shoulder boulder holder *noun*
a brassiere *UK, 1998*
- She flashed at me with her over the shoulder boulder holder clearly visible. —*Wordmap (www.abc.net.au/wordmap)*, 2003

ovies *noun*
overtime pay *UK*
- Pay's wank, but yer can make it up in ovies. —Niall Griffiths, *Kelly + Victor*, p. 141, 2002

ow *noun*
▸ **on the ow**
not in prison *UK*
A shortening of 'on the outside'.
- She has been off the heroin for five days, her first detox "on the ow" [...] for ten years. —*The Times Magazine*, p. 51, 24th October 2002

OW *noun*
a wife, a girfiend *UK*
Citizens' band radio slang, abbreviated from **OLD WOMAN**.
- —Peter Chippindale, *The British CB Book*, p. 157, 1981

owf; owff *verb*
to steal *UK*
- The thieves had used a simple ladder, whish they left against the brickwork after owffing Vincent [Van Gogh]'s View of the Sea at Scheveningen[.] —Jonathan Gash, *The Ten Word Game*, p. 79, 2003

owie *noun*
any minor injury *US*
Children's vocabulary.
- Toddler Has 'Owie" After 3-Story Fall [Caption] —*Chicago Tribune*, p. 9C, 20th May 1988
- "Everybody has an owie," Chang siad. "Every has a bruise, a torn something." —*Honolulu Advertiser*, p. 3D, 27th November 2002
- —Chris Lewis, *The Dictionary of Playground Slang*, p. 164, 2003

o-without *noun*
an act of oral sex performed without the protection of a condom, especially when advertised as a service offered by a prostitute *UK*
From **O-LEVELS** (oral sex).
- —Caroline Archer, *Tart Cards*, 2003

owl *noun*

1 on the railways, anything related to the night, such as a late-night train *US*

- —Norman Carlisle, *The Modern Wonder Book of Trains and Railroading*, p. 266, 1946
- —Ramon Adams, *The Language of the Railroader*, p. 110, 1977

2 marijuana *UK*

A possible play on **HOOTER** (a large marijuana cigarette).

- —Mike Haskins, *Drugs*, p. 288, 2003

owlhead *noun*

a revolver *US, 1927*

Originally referred to a revolver manufactured by Iver Johnson Arms, featuring an owlhead logo; later applied to any revolver.

- He pulled out his owl head all packed with lead.—Dan Burley, *Diggeth Thou?*, p. 11, 1959

Owl Shit Junction *noun*

any extremely remote town *US*

- — *Maledicta*, p. 12, Summer 1977: 'A word for it!'

own *verb*

to dominate; to command complete deference *US*

- No, I promise, no a chance. I own this guy.—*As Good As It Gets*, 1997
- —Connie Eble (Editor), *UNC-CH Campus Slang*, p. 6, Fall 2001

ownio *adjective*

▸ **on your ownio**

alone *IRELAND, 1922*

- No, Terry – in a cell. On your ownio.—Anthony Masters, *Minder*, p. 61, 1984
- They may congregate in the Circus or certain pubs but usually work on their ownio (alone), a term none of them could trace back to the Victorian music-hall ditty, "Oh, oh, Antonio, left me on my ownio." — *Maledicta*, p. 144, Summer/Winter 1986–1987

ownsome *adjective*

▸ **on your ownsome**

alone *UK, 1939*

- George Bush seemed ready to go Saddam-hunting all on his ownsome[.]— *The Guardian*, 16th December 2002

own up *verb*

to admit, to confess *US, 1853*

- Only 2% of those from Luxembourg owned up to being totally ignorant of any other foreign language[.]— *The Guardian*, 20th February 2001

own-way *adjective*

obstinate, mulish *BARBADOS*

- —Frank A. Collymore, *Barbadian Dialect*, p. 80, 1965

Owsley; Owsley acid; owsley *noun*

high quality LSD *US*

From the name of legendary LSD manufacturer Augustus Owsley Stanley III. Other variations include: 'Owsley blue dot'; 'Owsley blues'; 'Owsley power'; 'Owsley purple'; **PURPLE OWSLEY**; 'pink Owsley'; 'white Owsley'; 'Owsley's stuff'; 'Owsleys'.

- The Owsleys are also give away as free samples.—Nicholas Von Hoffman, *We Are The People Our Parents Warned Us Against*, p. 35, 1967
- —William D. Alsever, *Glossary for the Establishment and Other Uptight People*, p. 24, December 1970
- —Richard A. Spears, *The Slang and Jargon of Drugs and Drink*, p. 374, 1986
- —Mike Haskins, *Drugs*, p. 286, 2003

owt *noun*

something, anything *UK, 1847*

A dialect word from northern England for conventional 'aught'; made popular by the televison programme *Coronation Street*, and in clichéd phrases such as 'you don't get owt for nowt'.

- You'll not have owt to show for it / if you don't go for it—Ian Dury, *Cacka Boom*, 1998
- [H]im that never did owt[.]—Livi Michael, *Robinson Street*, p. 28, 1999

owzat?; zat?

as an appeal to a cricket umpire, how's that? *UK, 1934*

- Owzat! The presidential election that just isn't cricket.— *The Guardian*, 15th November 2000

Oxford *noun*

a dollar *AUSTRALIA*

- We all love Americans 'cos they spend lots of Oxfords whenever they come here.—John Blackman, *The Aussie Slang Dictionary*, p. 70, 1990

Oxford bag *noun*

a cigarette *UK*

Rhyming slang for **FAG**.

- You're getting old if you can remember when 20 Oxfords cost an Oxford (25p).—Ray Puxley, *Fresh Rabbit*, 1998

Oxford scholar; Oxford; scholar *noun*

1 (of pre-decimalisation currency) five shillings; (post-1971) 25p *UK, 1938*

Rhyming slang for **DOLLAR** (five shillings). The *Oxford English Dictionary* notes reported usage in southwest England in the 1870s.

- —Brian McDonald, *Elephant Boys*, p. 203, 2000

2 a dollar *AUSTRALIA, 1937*

Rhyming slang.

- Cost a million Oxford scholars, they reckon, and it looks like some monument out of a space serial on the TV.—Frank Hardy, *The Outcasts of Foolgarah*, p. 160, 1971

Oxo cube *noun*

the London Underground *UK, 1960*

Rhyming slang for **THE TUBE**, based on the branded beef extract, manufactured in cube form since 1909.

- I usually go by Oxo cube, but thought this would make a change.—*The Sweeney*, p. 6, 1976
- [J]ump on the Oxo cube, come here and spend the afternoon ironing it out[.]—J.J. Connolly, *Layer Cake*, p. 105, 2000

oxy *noun*

the synthetic opiate oxycodone used recreationally; a capsule of OxyContin™ *US*

- On the street, Oxys, as they are commonly called, fetch about $1 per milligram and usually are dosed in 20-, 40-, or 80-milligram tablets. — *Bangor Daily News*, 14th June 2000
- "When you get the oxy buzz," she says, "it's a great feeling. You're happy. Your body don't hurt."—*New York Times Magazine*, p. 34, 29th July 2001
- Hence, Oxy has a time-release coating that gradually releases the drug over time.—Suroosh Alvi et al., *The Vice Guide*, p. 109, 2002
- About the article "Rush back, reborn" (Nov. 18), regarding the return of Rush "Oxy" Limbaugh. (Letter to Editor)—*Palm Beach Post*, p. 19A, 5th December 2003

oxy *adjective*

having a second-hand or dated appearance *UK*

Derives from the appearance of goods sold in the charity shops of Oxfam.

- Sadly another venerable one-volume work, the annual Pears Cyclopaedia [...] is verging on oxy.— *The Times*, 6th December 2003

oxygen section *noun*

seats in a stadium or coliseum that are high up and far from the action *US*

- —Judi Sanders, *Faced and Faded, Hanging to Hurl*, p. 29, 1993

oy!

▷ see: **OI!**

oy gevalt!

used for expressing a lament, protest, dismay or delight *US*

Yiddish from German.

- —Leo Rosten, *The Joys of Yiddish*, p. 134, 1968
- Terrance and Phillip Movie! Oy gevalt! Not again!— *South Park*, 1999

oyster *noun*

1 the vagina *UK, 1707*

From an image of the labia, but note also the following sense as 'the mouth'.

- Flap dancin' I call it [lap dancing] 'cos if you're lucky they give you the full two sets of fanny lips even though they in't s'posed to[...] You can't get no bearded clam with your oysters, no way!—Ben Elton, *High Society*, p. 119, 2002

2 the mouth, especially as an instrument of homosexual oral sex *UK*

Following from the previous sense.

- [T]urn my oyster up (make me smile).—Paul Baker, *Polari*, p. 194, 2002
- — *Attitude*, p. 60, July 2003: 'Old palare lexicon'

3 a gob of thick phlegm *UK, 1785*

From the appearance. First recorded in *A Classical Dictionary of the Vulgar Tongue*, Francis Grose, 1785, with the further observation 'spit by a consumptive man'.

- — *Maledicta*, p. 33, 1988–1989: 'Medical maledicta from San Francisco'

- Everyone was at it: bogies, fag ash, great oysters of phlegm, and this was a posh place too. —Jenny Eclair, *Camberwell Beauty*, p. 97, 2000
- Big oyster on his face, green, slimy. —Niall Griffiths, *Kelly + Victor*, p. 267, 2002

oyster stew *noun*

cocaine *UK*

- —Nick Constable, *This is Cocaine*, p. 181, 2002
- —Mike Haskins, *Drugs*, p. 281, 2003

oy vey!

used for expressing surprise *US*

Yiddish.

- —Judi Sanders, *Kickin' like Chicken with the Couch Commander*, p. 17, 1992

OZ; oh-zee *noun*

an ounce of marijuana or other drugs *US, 1933*

Spelling out the standard abbreviation for 'ounce'.

- And I'll get Verger to bring some weed to your party. He's gotten an o.z. from a passer up on One Hundred and Twenty-fifth Street. —John Clellon Holmes, *Go*, p. 83, 1952
- [A]n American hipster friend from L.A. laid 5 ozees on me free. —Jack Kerouac, *Letter to Neal and Carolyn Cassady*, p. 359, 27th May 1952
- I had managed with financial assistance to breathe a little life into the scene – had an O.Z. of good amphets to use and sell enough of to make up the cost and possibly even realize a little profit. —Herbert Huncke, *The Evening Sun Turned Crimson*, p. 126, 1980
- Unloading a single O.Z. sometimes took up to an hour. —Nathan McCall, *Makes Me Wanna Holler*, p. 124, 1994

Oz *adjective*

Australian *AUSTRALIA*

- It is still indulged in by a small band of smart-aleck but rather retarded pseudo-intellectuals inhabiting those two polluted jungles of Oz culture, Sydney and Melbourne. —Bill Hornadge, *The Ugly Australian*, p. 234, 1974
- But the evening did not belong to the Geezer alone, as we have some seriously shit hot Oz talent. —*3D World*, p. 9, 2003

Oz *nickname*

Australia *AUSTRALIA, 1908*

Although the pronunciation would always have had a final 'z' (the 's' becomes voiced) it was first recorded as 'Oss' in 1908 (*Australian National Dictionary*), and not as 'Oz' until 1944, which spelling is partially influenced by the immensely popular 1939 film *The Wizard of Oz*. Became common in the 1970s.

- I mind the time I was on Day Dream, West Aus., when it was about petering out. —Norman Lindsay, *Halfway to Anywhere*, p. 177, 1947
- The snow scene's fantastic in Oz. —Barry Humphries, *A Nice Night's Entertainment*, p. 78, 1964
- I should have gone back to Oz donkeys years ago, and chucked in the towel. —Sandra Jobson, *Blokes*, p. 33, 1984

ozone *noun*

1 the highest seats in a stadium or auditorium, farthest from the action *US*

- —Connie Eble (Editor), *UNC-CH Campus Slang*, p. 5, Fall 1980

2 a state of drug or alcohol intoxication *US, 1971*

- —Connie Eble (Editor), *UNC-CH Campus Slang*, November 1976

3 phencyclidine, the recreational drug known as PCP or angel dust *US*

- —US Department of Justice, *Street Terms*, October 1994

4 marijuana *UK*

- —Mike Haskins, *Drugs*, p. 288, 2003

ozoner *noun*

an outdoor cinema *US, 1948*

- —*American Speech*, p. 239, October 1957: 'Outdoor movie talk'

ozone ranger *noun*

a person who appears to live in an inner-world, not necessarily as a result of drug or alcohol consumption *US*

- —Connie Eble (Editor), *UNC-CH Campus Slang*, p. 3, April 1978

ozone theater *noun*

an outdoor cinema *US*

- —*American Speech*, p. 239, October 1957: 'Outdoor movie talk'

Ozzie *adjective*

Australian *AUSTRALIA, 1918*

Variant spelling, representing pronunciation of **AUSSIE**.

- His vowels are 'Ozzie' without offence and the overall effect is that of Austral-English as she should be spoke. —Joe Brown, *Just for the Record*, p. 109, 1984
- [E]very case o' ozzie Chardonnay[.] —Ben Elton, *High Society*, p. 217, 2002

ozzy; ozzie *noun*

▷ **see: HOZZY**

Pp

P *noun*

1 pure or nearly pure heroin *US*

- She could hardly keep her eyes open. The strong P., "pure," that Porky had given her was enough to bring the worse dopefiend into a dreamlike state. — Donald Goines, *Dopefiend*, p. 33, 1971
- 'You selling P, if you wanta deal, Bernie Lee.' — Vernon E. Smith, *The Jones Men*, p. 8, 1974
- — Richard A. Spears, *The Slang and Jargon of Drugs and Drink*, p. 381, 1986

2 a Vietnamese piastre *US*

- — *Time*, p. 34, 10th December 1965
- — Carl Fleischhauer, *A Glossary of Army Slang*, p. 5, 1968
- — *Current Slang*, p. 17, Summer 1970

P *adjective*

1 pretty *US*

Hawaiian youth usage.

- 'Oh, she so P, yeah?' — Douglas Simonson, *Pidgin to da Max Hana Hou*, 1982

2 a price *UK*

- Pukka gear [drugs] pukka fuckin' gear. Gi's a P on twenny[.] — Nick Barlay, *Curvy Lovebox*, p. 60, 1997

-p *suffix*

used for turning a word into a question *US*

- From the LISP convention of appending the letter "P" to denote a predicate (A Boolean-values function). The question should expect a yes/no answer, though it needn't. At dinnertime: "Foodp?" "Yeah." — *CoEvolution Quarterly*, p. 27, Spring 1981

P-38 *noun*

1 a police-issue .38 calibre revolver *US*

- I would climb in the ring with nothing but two P-.38's / And send either one that moved through the pearly gates. — Dennis Wepman et al., *The Life*, p. 157, 1976

2 in Vietnam war usage, the small can-opener included with individual field rations *US*

A humorous application of bureaucratic nomenclature.

- — *Army Times*, p. 1, 19th January 1966
- — Carl Fleischhauer, *A Glossary of Army Slang*, p. 8, 1968

P 45 *noun*

▸ give you your P45

to break off a romantic relationship with someone *UK: SCOTLAND*

A P45 is the form given by an employer to a dismissed employee.

- Ach, him? I gied him his P45 last week. — Michael Munro, *The Complete Patter*, p. 104, 1996

pa *noun*

a father; used to address your father *UK, 1811*

An abbreviation of 'papa'.

- "Goodnight, John Boy!" "'night, ma!" "'night, pa!" — Stuart Jeffries, *Mrs Slocombe's Pussy*, p. 216, 2000

PA *noun*

▷ **see:** PRINCE ALBERT

PA

a prosecuting attorney *US*

- I say, "Hey, you say that, we'll have to go to trial, because the PA ain't gonna negotiate that[.]" — Richard Price, *Clockers*, p. 450, 1992

Pablo *noun*

cocaine *UK*

In memory of Colombian Pablo Escobar (1949–93) of the Medellín Cartel.

- There had been some calls for a trip to a restaurant, but Mearns – whose party, after all, it was – had already had dinner with Pablo [...] and couldn't be bothered[.] — Will Self, *The Sweet Smell of Psychosis*, p. 51, 1996

pacey *adjective*

▷ **see:** PACY

Pachuco *noun*

a young Mexican-American, especially a tough or gang member *US, 1943*

A highly stylised fashion sense, a private language and a rage against white oppression of the 1940s.

- [L]ike maybe Gonzalez the Mexican sort of bum or hanger-on sort of faggish who kept coming up to her place on the strength of some old friendship she'd had with some Tracy Pachucos[.] — Jack Kerouac, *The Subterraneans*, p. 43, 1958

Pacific steroid *noun*

the Southeast Asian plant, taro *NEW ZEALAND*

Common in conversation in New Zealand since the 1990s.

pack *noun*

1 a *pack*age of illegal drugs, especially heroin *US, 1952*

Also variant 'packet'.

- — Richard Horman and Allan Fox, *Drug Awarencess*, 1970
- I been feeling boogy ever since this morning. I didn't do but a five-dollar pack when I woke up. — Donald Goines, *Dopefiend*, p. 97, 1971
- — Robert Ashtom, *This is Heroin*, 2002

2 marijuana *UK*

- — Mike Haskins, *Drugs*, p. 288, 2003

3 in the used car business, a fixed amount that is added to the price the dealer has paid for the car *US*

- The pack is used to pay for overheads and other expenses. — Peter Mann, *How to Buy a Used Car Without Getting Gypped*, p. 194, 1975

▸ go to the pack

to deteriorate *AUSTRALIA, 1919*

- pack, to go to the – To fall away; to collapse. — Gilbert H. Lawson, *A Dictionary of Australian Words and Terms*, 1924
- They all wanted exemptions, and one after another comes up and tells the bloke in charge how everything'll go to the pack unless they're let go home again. — Kylie Tennant, *Lost Haven*, p. 248, 1946
- — Arthur Chipper, *The Aussie Swearer's Guide*, p. 78, 1972
- — Jim Ramsay, *Cop It Sweet!*, p. 68, 1977

pack *verb*

1 to carry a weapon, usually a concealed one *US*

- I'm packing no joint. — Hal Ellson, *Duke*, p. 2, 1949
- — Joseph E. Ragen and Charles Finston, *Inside the World's Toughest Prison*, p. 811, 1962: 'Penitentiary and underworld glossary'
- "This cat is packing a Saturday-night special", someone said. — Charles Whited, *Chiodo*, p. 60, 1973
- — H. Craig Collins, *Street Gangs*, p. 223, 1979
- They're going to think you're packing something. — *Repo Man*, 1984
- He wouldn't be packing today, risk doing two years for nothing. — Elmore Leonard, *Glitz*, p. 175, 1985
- BROIS: This guy's packin'. — *True Romance*, 1993
- You pack a gun? — *Get Shorty*, 1995
- — Don R. McCreary (Editor), *Dawg Speak*, 2001

2 to tuck the male genitals into the left or right trouser leg *US*

- "[M]en in the armed forces are taught to pack it to the left, but you show more meat when you pack it to the right." — Bruce Rodgers, *The Queens' Vernacular*, p. 145, 1972

3 to be fearful *AUSTRALIA*

A shortening of **PACK SHIT**.

- And she was packing about telling her mum[.] — Kylie Mole (Maryanne Fahey), *My Diary*, p. 104, 1988

4 while snowboarding, to hit the snow hard *US*

- — Elena Garcia, *A Beginner's Guide to Zen and the Art of Snowboarding*, p. 122, 1990

5 to take someone along on a motorcyle cruise *US*

- On another occasion, Magoo was packing Mama Beverly on a run to Bakersfield when he ran out of gas. — Hunter S. Thompson, *Hell's Angels*, p. 171, 1966

▸ pack a punch

of a thing, to be powerful *US, 1938*

A figurative use of the pugilistic sense.

- Go west, where television packs a punch. — *The Guardian*, 12th March 2002

▸ **pack a rod**
to carry a gun *US, 1940*
In literature by 1940.
• Lend's packin' a rod. Iron. Fill you full of lead. — Nick Barlay, *Curvy Lovebox*, p. 137, 1997

▸ **pack a sad**
to break off a relationship *NEW ZEALAND*
• Mr. Storey told the National Party's Waikato Division last night it was time the New Zealand Government 'packed a sad' with Paul Keating and his Government. — *Evening Post*, p. 3, 3rd December 1994

▸ **pack a shitty**
1 to sulk *AUSTRALIA*
• — Thommo, *The Dictionary of Australian Swearing and Sex Sayings*, p. 92, 1985
2 to become angry *NEW ZEALAND*
• — David McGill, *David McGill's Complete Kiwi Slang Dictionary*, p. 94, 1998

▸ **pack death**
to be fearful *AUSTRALIA*
• Had me here packing death wondering where you'd got to. — Simon French, *Hey Phantom Singlet*, p. 52, 1975
• — Jenny Pausacker, *What are ya?*, p. 55, 1987

▸ **pack double**
to carry a passenger on a motorcyle *US*
• Ernie and I had a couple of girls ("packing double"), and here I was stuck with a dead bike six hundred miles from home. — Ralph "Sonny" Barger, *Hell's Angel*, p. 30, 2000

▸ **pack 'em; pack them**
to be fearful *AUSTRALIA, 1944*
Euphemistic for PACK THE SHITS.
• 'Ah, stop packing 'em,' said Dinger. 'That sort of thing wouldn't work these days.' — John Wynnum, *Jiggin' in the Riggin'*, p. 12, 1965
• — Jim Ramsay, *Cop It Sweet!*, p. 68, 1977

▸ **pack fudge**
to play the active role in anal sex *US*
• He's been making a nice piece of change for himself by taking the wealthy swells of our clientele into a small sofa-filled room aside the projection booth and packing their fudge for prices only the kin of a true superstar can demand. — Jim Carroll, *Forced Entries*, p. 49, 1987

▸ **pack heat**
to carry a gun *US, 1930*
• You packing any heat, mister? — Mickey Spillane, *Last Cop Out*, p. 73, 1972
• Lend's packin' heat. He's packin' a rod. — Nick Barlay, *Curvy Lovebox*, p. 137, 1997

▸ **pack it**
to be fearful *AUSTRALIA, 1945*
Euphemistic for PACK SHIT.

▸ **pack shit; pack the shits**
to be fearful *AUSTRALIA, 1971*
The metaphor is of one so scared that they are straining not to shit themselves.
• — Jim Ramsay, *Cop It Sweet!*, p. 68, 1977
• John spotted that I was packing the shits and said 'He's alright, Sam. Don't worry about him.' — Sam Weller, *Old Bastards I Have Met*, p. 145, 1979
• My friend was packing shit so we borrowed a ute, this at three in the morning, threw everything in the back and fled. — John Birmingham, *He Died With a Felafel in his Hand*, p. 139, 1994

▸ **pack the cracks**
to endure injections of collagen *US*
• — Anna Scotti and Paul Young, *Buzzwords*, p. 109, 1997

▸ **pack the payment**
in new car sales, to make a sale for a price slightly below what the customer has said they are willing to spend *US*
• — *Doctor's Review*, August 1989

package *noun*
1 a man's genitals as seen through trousers *US*
• — Jeff Fessler, *When Drag Is Not a Car Race*, p. 53, 1997
2 a good-looking woman *US*
• — Lou Shelly, *Hepcats Jive Talk Dictionary*, p. 15, 1945
3 the female posterior *US*
• I gotta have a woman with a nice package. A nice ass. — *Sky Magazine*, p. 51, July 2001
4 a sexually transmitted infection, especially gonorrhea *US*
• — Hyman E. Goldin et al., *Dictionary of American Underworld Lingo*, p. 151, 1950
5 AIDS or HIV *US*
• I wouldn't be associating with him if I were you. He's got the package. — Gary K. Farlow, *Prison-ese*, p. 48, 2002

package of trouble *noun*
the bleed period of the menstrual cycle *US*
• — Karen Houppert, *The Curse*, 1999

pack away *verb*
to consume food or drink with gusto *AUSTRALIA*
• You packed away quite a bit last night. — John O'Grady, *It's Your Shout, Mate!*, p. 53, 1972

Packer-backer-maki *noun*
a beer-drinking, snow-suit wearing, Skoal-chewing, snow-mobile-riding fan of the Green Bay Packer professional football team *US*
Michigan Upper Peninsula usage.

packet *noun*
1 the genitals, especially as may be hinted at or imagined when dressed, usually male *UK*
Gay slang.
• — Paul Baker, *Polari*, p. 185, 2002
2 a large sum of money *UK, 1922*
• Hello handsome, I bet that shirt cost a packet[.] — *The Guardian*, 12th July 2003

packet of three; pack of three *noun*
a packet of three condoms *UK*
A dated semi-euphemism that was widespread before the onset of AIDS and the subsequent positive marketing for condoms.
• — Angela Devlin, *Prison Patter*, p. 84, 1996

pack horse *noun*
a person, usually a guard, who brings contraband into prison *US*
• — Inez Cardozo-Freeman, *The Joint*, p. 519, 1984

packie *noun*
an off-licence *US*
From US states where off-licences are known as 'package stores'.
• — Connie Eble (Editor), *UNC-CH Campus Slang*, p. 4, Fall 1991

pack in; pack up *verb*
to stop; to cease an activity; to retire *US, 1942*
• All croakers [doctors] "pack in" sooner or later. — William Burroughs, *Junkie*, p. 36, 1953
• Let's just pack it in an hour early. — *Heathers*, 1988
• SM: What does your mum say? Phil: She tells us both to pack it in. She usually blames it on me sister. — Sara McNamee, *Cool Places*, p. 198, 1998
• But although it's a five-year project, I'm packing it in next month and coming back home — *The Guardian*, 23rd January 1999

pack of rocks *noun*
a packet of ready-to-smoke marijuana fashioned in the manner of cigarettes *UK*
An abbreviation of 'pack of rockets'.
• — Mike Haskins, *Drugs*, p. 288, 2003

pack out *verb*
to unpack *SOUTH AFRICA, 1969*
• — Jean Branford, *A Dictionary of South African English*, 1978

pack-rape *noun*
rape by a gang of men in succession *AUSTRALIA, 1969*
• Rockers' kicks come from pack rape and wanton destruction. — Suzy Jarratt, *Permissive Australia*, p. 28, 1970

pack-rape *verb*
(of a gang of men) to serially rape a woman *AUSTRALIA, 1965*
• Some-one else told me that it was the Engineering students who gave strong vocal support to the police who were pack-raping Arts students at the first Moratorium. — Patsi Dunn, *Uni Sex*, p. 87, 1972

pack-rapist *noun*
a person who commits pack-rape *AUSTRALIA, 1972*
• — *Patsi Dunn, Uni Sex*, p. 87, 1972
• Criminologists Greg Woods and Paul Ward found in their study of pack rapists that few considered that they had committed a crime. — Anne Summers, *Damned Whores and God's Police*, p. 211, 1975

pack-sack citizen *noun*

a short-term resident of any place, living, as it were, out of a packsack (backpack or rucksack) *CANADA*

- [The logger] was a pack-sack citizen and appeared in Skid Row streets complete with dirty Stanfields and caulk boots which would be later hocked for the last bottle. — *Toronto Globe and Mail*, p. B5–B7, 18th January 1966

pack them *noun*

▷ see: PACK 'EM

pack up *verb*

to cease doing something; to retire from work (of a machine, etc) to stop working because of a fault *UK, 1925*

- His mother died last year and he seriously thought of packing up the game. — *The Guardian*, 7th October 2002
- Rhiannon, the new operator of the cafe, is having her own problems: the oven packed up the day she took over. — *The Guardian*, 2nd September 2003

▸ **pack up shop**

to cease trading *UK*

- The legislature [Scottish Assembly] that packed up shop on Thursday is better than almost anybody hoped for – and certainly not the overblown parish council that some thought it might be. — *The Observer*, 30th March 2003

pacotee *noun*

a sexually available woman *TRINIDAD AND TOBAGO, 1950*

From the French and Spanish for 'inferior goods', at times corrupted back into English as 'pack o' tea'.

- — Lise Winer, *Dictionary of the English/Creole of Trinidad & Tobago*, 2003

pacy; pacey *adjective*

fast, speedy *UK, 1906*

- [T]he pacey wide man's talents during his time in Dutch football. — *The Guardian*, 15th June 2004
- [A] young woman speaking pacy, Americanised English. — *Daily Telegraph*, 5th March 2004

pad *noun*

1 an apartment or house; a room, especially a bedroom *US, 1938*

In the C18, 'pad' referred to a bed. By the 1930s, it took on the new meaning and was spread by jazz musicians. Still heard, with a retro feel.

- I told you about her? The big, red-head, six feet tall, who used to come down to Dennison's morphine-pad on Orchard Street in the old days? — John Clellon Holmes, *Go*, p. 7, 1952
- I know this girl. She's got a pad. I ain't been there but I heard it's all right. — Hal Ellson, *The Golden Spike*, p. 31, 1952
- Then we got like-a whole floor, a cool pad for you'n me, doll. — George Mandel, *Flee the Angry Strangers*, p. 167, 1952
- There were bars, honky-tonks and saloons, and lots of women walking the streets for tricks to take to their "pads" as they called their rooms. — Louis Armstrong, *Satchmo: My Life in New Orleans*, p. 8, 1954
- Red Riding Hood opened the door, stepped inside and looked around the room. "Wowie," she said. "What a crazy pad." — Steve Allen, *Steve Allen's, Bop Fables*, p. 42, 1955
- One day I was hanging around the campus and Chad and Tim Gray told me Dean was staying in a cold-water pad in East Harlem, the Spanish Harlem. — Jack Kerouac, *On the Road*, 1957
- Probably we'll check into a Times Square hotel and look for a pad later in the week. — Ross Russell, *The Sound*, p. 95, 1961
- One agent gave a picture to an agent of a typical "smoker" in an apartment or "pad"[.] — Harry J. Anslinger, *The Murderers*, p. 42, 1961
- But he thought a sister who gave me a "pad," not charging me rent, not even running me out to find "some slave," couldn't be all bad. — Malcolm X and Alex Haley, *The Autobiography of Malcolm X*, p. 44, 1964
- Come in my pad, sport, look around. — Richard Farina, *Been Down So Long*, p. 21, 1966
- I moved into a furnished apartment on "Sunset Boulevard," ten minutes away from his pad. — Babs Gonzales, *I Paid My Dues*, p. 20, 1967
- I quit working for this outfit when the bad shit that was coming down because too much to take – a friend of the theater-owner, whose apartment we were using to film a lez flick – attacked one of the other chicks as she was leaving the pad. — *The Berkeley Tribe*, p. 9, 22nd-28th August 1970
- I got to the boss of pimpdom's pad and when I first saw him I really didn't like what I saw. — A.S. Jackson, *Gentleman Pimp*, p. 134, 1973
- Spencer had a pad on 47th Street. It was one of the coziest pads in New York and one which it was an experience to visit for the first time and to always relax in. — Herbert Huncke, *The Evening Sun Turned Crimson*, p. 41, 1980
- C'mon. Show me the rest of your pad. — *Clueless*, 1995
- [W]e liked the Versace room and the pervy Gucci pad best. — *ES Magazine*, p. 3, 22nd June 2001

2 a bed *UK, 1718*

- You gotta have a date with me before you fall in my pad, darling. — Chester Himes, *If He Hollers Let Him Go*, 1945
- One day along about noon Frank Hitchcock yanked us all out of our pads and took us downstairs. — Mezz Mezzrow, *Really the Blues*, 1946
- A bed is now a pad. "I was in the pad when the phone rang." — *Philadelphia Evening Bulletin*, 11th October 1955

3 a prison cell *US, 1943*

- — Inez Cardozo-Freeman, *The Joint*, p. 519, 1984
- — Angela Devlin, *Prison Patter*, p. 84, 1996

4 a padded cell *UK*

- — Angela Devlin, *Prison Patter*, p. 65, 1996
- They dragged him down the stairs and into the pad – the cooling room for bad boys[.] — Howard Paul, *The Joy*, p. 29, 1996

5 the bribery paid by a criminal enterprise to police *US, 1970*

- The "pad" refers to regular weekly, bi-weekly, or monthly payments, usually picked up by a police bagman and divided among fellow officers. — *The Knapp Commission Report on Police Corruption*, p. 66, 1972
- He could hardly believe his ears, that Stanard would be so indiscreet about the existence of a "pad" – as the systematized police payoffs were called – that he could be that stupid. — Peter Maas, *Serpico*, p. 156, 1973
- A pad is what you're on when you're paying police not to do their job. — Leonard Shecter and William Phillips, *On the Pad*, p. 23, 1973
- How long do you think they can stand it without the pad? — Richard Condon, *Prizzi's Honor*, p. 218, 1982

6 an animal track *AUSTRALIA, 1893*

- We led the horses along an animal pad that zigzagged down the one accessible descent. — Ion L. Idriess, *Over the Range*, p. 79, 1947

▸ **on the pad**

bribed *US, 1971*

- Those who make such payments as well as policemen who receive them are referered to as being "on the pad." — *The Knapp Commission Report on Police Corruption*, p. 66, 1972
- And it seemed the lady needed some help. She wanted to go on the pad. — Leonard Shecter and William Phillips, *On the Pad*, p. 23, 1973
- Kept your mouth shut, right. Never made a wave. Kimo sabe, you was on the pad. — Edwin Torres, *Q & A*, p. 165, 1977
- The badge showed that he was on the inspector's pad and the telephone numbers suggested that he had connections. — Burgess Laughlin, *Job Opportunities in the Black Market*, p. 5–5, 1978
- It used to be a captain was on the pad, he let word filter down through the whole precinct that such and such a location was protected. — Vincent Patrick, *The Pope of Greenwich Village*, p. 38, 1979

pad *verb*

1 to reside *US*

- "And if you aint got a pad any time, spote," he said, "you can pad there too." — John Rechy, *City of Night*, p. 43, 1963
- There's a cat in the Chicken Shack that knows where Ace is paddin at. — Charles W. Moore, *A Brick for Mister Jones*, p. 99, 1975
- He pads in the penthouse in my hotel. — Iceberg Slim (Robert Beck), *Airtight Willie and Me*, p. 161, 1979

2 (used of police) to add to the narcotics confiscated from a suspect in order to render the charge against them more serious *US*

- "[P]adding," or adding to the quantity of narcotics found on an arrested person in order to upgrade an arrest — *The Knapp Commission Report on Police Corruption*, p. 91, 1972

▸ **pad the ring**

in horse racing, to place many small bets on several horses in a race while placing a large bet on one horse away from the track, hoping that the small bets on other horses will drive the odds on your horse up *US*

- — David W. Maurer, *Argot of the Racetrack*, p. 49, 1951

paddle *noun*

on the railways, a semaphore signal *US*

- — Ramon Adams, *The Language of the Railroader*, p. 111, 1977

paddle *verb*

in horse racing, to try hard without success *AUSTRALIA*

- — Ned Wallish, *The Truth Dictionary of Racing Slang*, p. 60, 1989

▸ **paddle the pickle**

(of a male) to masturbate *US*

- — Dale Gordon, *The Dominion Sex Dictionary*, p. 117, 1967

▸ **paddle the pink canoe**

(of a female) to masturbate *UK*

- — Michelle Baker and Steven Tropiano, *Queer Facts*, p. 46, 2004

paddle bull *noun*

a young male moose, whose unbranched antlers look like table tennis bats *CANADA*

- — Tom Parkin, *WetCoast Words*, p. 105, 1989

paddle pop *noun*
a block of ice *NEW ZEALAND*
Rhyming slang.
• —David McGill, *David McGill's Complete Kiwi Slang Dictionary*, p. 81, 1998

paddock-basher *noun*
a worn-out old vehicle used to drive around a country property *AUSTRALIA*
• The survey didn't show much difference between the motives of city and country buyers, he said, because it relates to wagon-style (or non-utility light commercial) vehicles only, not to the "paddock-basher" market where once the Holden "ute" held sway. —*Sydney Morning Herald*, p. 36, 19th February 1983

pad down *verb*
to go to sleep *US*
• —Kenn "Naz" Young, *Naz's Dictionary of Teen Slang*, p. 87, 1993

paddy *noun*
1 a white person *US*
• If it had come down to a point where I had to hit a paddy, I'd have hit him without any thought—Chester Himes, *If He Hollers Let Him Go*, p. 3, 1945
• We ought to beat the hell out of those paddies! —Ralph Ellison, *Invisible Man*, p. 268, 1947
• I told his paddy and solemnly did swear / no more farm for me – to damn many ups out there. —Bruce Jackson, *Get Your Ass in the Water and Swim Like Me*, p. 198, 1966
• — *Current Slang*, p. 4, Fall 1966
• My friend Crutch had told me there were a lot of paddies out there, and they didn't dig Negroes or Puerto Ricans. —Piri Thomas, *Down These Mean Streets*, p. 81, 1967
• [S]he was in L.A. and she was tough and she wanted furniture and a paddy husband. Paddy means white in Pachuco. —Eve Babitz, *Eve's Hollywood*, p. 47, 1974

2 a police officer *US*
• I was made the lookout man and told to stick around out front with my eyes peeled for any signs of John Law. When a paddy showed himself I would tap on the window with a key, and in five seconds a billiard tournament was going full blast. —Mezz Mezzrow, *Really the Blues*, p. 20, 1946

3 a temper, a rage *UK, 1894*
• I knew exactly the reason for his little paddy[.]—Danny King, *The Bank Robber Diaries*, p. 63, 2002

Paddy *noun*
an Irish person *UK, 1780*
• Fuck me, if there's one thing we poor bloody Paddies should have learned, it is never to trust a British fucking leftie liberal bastard. —James Hawes, *Dead Long Enough*, p. 253, 2000
• Besides the paddies, Albany was full of high-profile prisoners. —Jimmy Stockin, *On The Cobbles*, p. 141, 2000
• [A] groaner who didn't like the food and didn't like the Paddies and didn't like the Pakis and didn't like the poofs. —John King, *White Trash*, p. 65, 2001

Paddy *nickname*
used as a nickname for any Irishman *UK*
Diminutive of the name Patrick.
• TAYLOR: You're a dirty old man you are, Paddy. O'MALLY: Aw, shut up. —Graeme Kent, *The Queen's Corporal [Six Granada Plays]*, p. 87, 1959

Paddy and Mick *noun*
a *pick*-axe *UK*
Rhyming slang, drawing on the stereotype of Irish labourers.
• —Ray Puxley, *Fresh Rabbit*, 1998

Paddy and Mick *adjective*
stupid *UK*
Rhyming slang for **THICK**, drawing on an Irish stereotype.
• —Ray Puxley, *Cockney Rabbit*, 1992

paddy hustler *noun*
a criminal who targets white people as victims *US*
• There's lesbians, masochists, hypes, whores, flim flammers, paddy hustlers, hugger muggers, ex-cons of all descriptions, and anybody else with a kink of some kind or other. —Joseph Wambaugh, *The New Centurions*, p. 174, 1970

Paddy McGuigan *noun*
dancing, jigging *UK: SCOTLAND*
Glasgow rhyming slang for 'jiggin', formed on no Irishman in particular.
• We're aw [all] gaun [going] tae the Paddy McGuigan the night. —Michael Munro, *The Complete Patter*, 1996

Paddy McGuire *noun*
a fire *UK: SCOTLAND*
Glasgow rhyming slang, formed on no Irishman in particular.
• Sling another shovel on the Paddy McGuire while ye're up. —Michael Munro, *The Patter, Another Blast*, 1988

Paddy O'Rourke *verb*
to talk *UK*
Rhyming slang; derivation unknown.
• —Ray Puxley, *Fresh Rabbit*, 1998

Paddy's Day *nickname*
St Patrick Day *IRELAND*
A national holiday in Ireland to celebrate St Patrick, Ireland's patron saint.
• They want me over in London the day after tomorrow, which is basically Paddy's Day... —Paul Howard, *Ross O'Carroll-Kelly*, p. 44, 2003

Paddy's pig *noun*
the epitome of ignorance *NEW ZEALAND*
• There's one who reminds me of Crawford from the Dunedin gaol – as ignorant as Paddy's pig. —Ivan Agnew, *Loner*, p. 185, 1974

Paddy's taxi *noun*
a police 'Panda' car *UK*
• — *Public Eye, BBC TV*, 13th August 1969

paddy strength *noun*
in the Vietnam war, the combat strength of a unit, measured by the actual number of troops in the field *US*
• —Gregory Clark, *Words of the Vietnam War*, p. 389, 1990

Paddy's Wigwam *nickname*
the Roman Catholic Metropolitan Cathedral in Liverpool *UK*
'Wigwam' is an obvious simile for the shape of the 1960s building, **PADDY** (an Irishman) reflects a cultural perception of Roman Catholics.
• Nor is the solemn, vast Anglican cathedral, nor its Catholic neighbour 'Paddy's Wigwam', at the other end of the street called Hope. —*The Guardian*, 4th June 2003

paddy wagon *noun*
a police transport van *US, 1909*
• The Navy's shore patrol takes over most of the policing. We saw Navy paddy-wagons in front of Guy's, the Ship's Cafe and the Penguin. —Jack Lait and Lee Mortimer, *Washington Confidential*, p. 33, 1951
• I'm thinkin about Neal, red neons, night, and instead, enroute home, get few beers in the wildest bar in America, corner 3rd and Howard, paddy wagon's there every hour[.]—Jack Kerouac, *Letter to John Clellon Holmes*, p. 338, 8th February 1952
• Three squad cars and a paddy wagon stood ready in the icy morning air[.]—Clarence Cooper Jr, *The Scene*, p. 126, 1960
• A Madera County paddy wagon was parked at the other end of the shopping center, with two cops in the front seat. —Hunter S. Thompson, *Hell's Angels*, p. 143, 1966
• [O]nly to find the place surrounded by cops and paddy wagons. —Jamie Mandelkau, *Buttons*, p. 74, 1971
• —Angela Devlin, *Prison Patter*, p. 84, 1996

Paddy water *noun*
Guinness™ Irish stout *UK*
From **PADDY** (an Irish person).
• My mate here, the one drinking the Paddy water[.]—John King, *Human Punk*, p. 231, 2000

paddywood *noun*
a white person *US*
Not used kindly.
• —Edith A. Folb, *runnin' down some lines*, p. 249, 1980

padiddle *noun*
a car with only one headlight functioning *US*
A childish word for the childish activity of spotting cars with one broken headlight.
• — *Elementary Electronics*, *Dictionary of CB Lingo*, p. 91, 1976
• —Connie Eble (Editor), *UNC-CH Campus Slang*, p. 6, April 1997

padlock *noun*
the penis *UK*
Rhyming slang for **COCK**.
• — *Daily Telegraph*, 17th December 1972

pad mate *noun*
in prison, the inmate with whom a cell is shared *UK*
From **PAD** (a cell).
• —Angela Devlin, *Prison Patter*, p. 84, 1996

pad roll *noun*
a controlled roll of the dice by a skilled cheat, best made on a blanket spread on the ground *US*
- — *The Annals of the American Academy of Political and Social Sciences*, p. 128, May 1950

pad-roll *verb*
to roll dice in a controlled fashion *US*
So called because it can best be made on a blanket, rug or other soft pad.
- — *The Annals of the American Academy of Political and Social Sciences*, p. 128, May 1950
- I could knock, shoot the turn down, or pad-roll. — Donald Goines, *Whoreson*, p. 28, 1972
- And by the time I was eleven / I could pad-roll seven. — Lightnin' Rod, *Hustlers Convention*, p. 6, 1973

padrone; padroni *noun*
a boss (especially in a gangster-related context) *ITALY*
From Italian *padrone* (an owner, master), via films about the mafia. The plural is 'padroni'.
- [H]e called his ex-Provo padroni, and Styx drove into town in his Transit to have a hard little word with Ohn. — James Hawes, *Dead Long Enough*, p. 255, 2000

pads *noun*
tyres *US*
Biker (motorcyle) usage.

pad shark *noun*
a prisoner who steals from others' cells *UK*
From **PAD** (a cell).
- — Angela Devlin, *Prison Patter*, p. 84, 1996

paedie-pump *noun*
a prison-issue training shoe worn by sex offenders *UK*
Based on an abbreviation of 'paedophile'. In use August 2002.

paedo *noun*
used as a short form of paedophilia, paedophile and related terms *UK*
The Greek for 'child', used as the root for many conventional terms, has lately been been associated in the public imagination with the worst of its uses.
- Like an unholy mix of Gary Glitter (pre paedo charges, natch), 70s horror soundtracks and Hammond organ[.] — *Ministry*, p. 12, October 2002

Pag *noun*
the short opera *Pagliacci* by Ruggero Leoncavallo *UK*

page *noun*
one thousand doses of LSD soaked into paper *US*
- A larger piece of paper consisting of ten unseparated sheets – a thousand hits, known as a "page" – is a unit commonly sold wholesale. — Cam Cloud, *The Little Book of Acid*, p. 34, 1999

page biz *noun*
the publishing business *US*
Combines **BIZ** (a business) with a small example.
- This rap page biz is murder, dog. — *The Source*, p. 36, March 2002

page oner *noun*
a screenplay in need of a complete rewrite *US*
- — Anna Scotti and Paul Young, *Buzzwords*, p. 8, 1997

page three girl *noun*
a girl whose scantily clad, or nude, picture appears as a newspaper pin-up *UK, 1975*
From a 'Page Three' feature in *The Sun* but applied far more widely.
- New World Chardonnay: strong, creamy, brazen like a page three girl. — *New Statesman*, 30th September 2002

pagger *verb*
to break or smash; to wreck *UK*
Market traders' use; influenced by **BUGGER** (to ruin).
- — Patrick O'Shaughnessy, *Market Traders' Slang*, 1979

paggered *adjective*
drunk *UK*
From **PAGGER**, hence 'smashed' (drunk).
- — *e-cyclopaedia*, 20th March 2002

pagne *noun*
a hangover caused by drinking cham*pagne* *UK*
A pun.
- [T]he season sees every champagne Charlie and bubbly babe getting wasted on the real stuff. Still, no pagne, no gain. — Alon Shulman, *The Style Bible*, p. 184, 1999

pagoda *noun*
in horse racing, the stand where race officials are seated *US*
- — David W. Maurer, *Argot of the Racetrack*, p. 49, 1951

paid *adjective*
financially stable if not wealthy *US*
- — Connie Eble (Editor), *UNC-CH Campus Slang*, p. 5, Fall 1998

pail *noun*
the stomach *US*
An abbreviation of 'lunch pail' (a container).
- — Lou Shelly, *Hepcats Jive Talk Dictionary*, p. 15, 1945

pain *noun*
an irritation; an annoying person *UK, 1933*
- I think there was a gap there that she is relatively OK about but at times is a pain for her. — Sally Cline, *Couples*, p. 69, 1998
- When people ask me for an autograph, they are often apologetic and say stuff like, "I know this must be a pain"[.] — Frank Skinner, *Frank Skinner*, p. 129, 2001

Pain *noun*
Main Street in Winnipeg, which at its crossing of Portage is the exact centre *CANADA*
'Pain' for 'Main' at the intersection of Portage Street is evocative of windy, very cold winter weather.

pain in the ass; pain in the arse; pain in the backside *noun*
a great nuisance *US, 1934*
- "C'mon, let's get out here," I said. "You give me a royal pain in the ass, if you want to know the truth." — J.D. Salinger, *Catcher in the Rye*, p. 133, 1951
- You give me a pain in the backside you lot, you really do. — Graeme Kent, *The Queen's Corporal [Six Granada Plays]*, p. 94, 1959
- My OCD rituals were beginning to become a real pain in the ass. — Howard Stern, *Miss America*, p. 105, 1995
- It was, as the poets say, a bloody big pain in the arse situation. — Tim Etchells, *Taxi Driver [britpulp]*, p. 193, 1999
- [A] friend in need is a right pain in the arse. — Jenny Eclair, *Camberwell Beauty*, p. 14, 2000

pain in the neck *noun*
1 an irritating nuisance *UK, 1941*
- WATSON: [...] And from then on you're a pain in the neck. VALE: I'm sorry you feel like that about it. — Graeme Kent, *The Queen's Corporal [Six Granada Plays]*, p. 85, 1959

2 a cheque *UK*
Rhyming slang.
- — Ray Puxley, *Cockney Rabbit*, 1992

pain in the net *noun*
a person who posts inflammatory attacks on Internet discussion groups *US*
- — Eric S. Raymond, *The New Hacker's Dictionary*, p. 273, 1991

pain slut *noun*
a person who derives sexual satisfaction from physical and verbal abuse *UK*
- — Jay Wiseman, *SM101: A Realistic Introduction*, 1996: 'Glossary'

paint *noun*
1 makeup *UK, 1660*
- [T]he bird from the cabaret passed me on her way to her loo to get the paint off her boat [face]. — Derek Raymond (Robin Cook), *The Crust on its Uppers*, p. 60, 1962
- The school marm came back with a new coat of paint and a bedroom smile. — Iceberg Slim (Robert Beck), *Trick Baby*, p. 195, 1969

2 the inside rails of a horse racing track *AUSTRALIA*
- Just as he spoke, the leaders swung wide and Magger goes through along the paint and dashes three lengths clear. — Frank Hardy, *The Yarns of Billy Borker*, p. 108, 1965
- Rufe had Ming stuck to the paint. He was surrounded by a wall made of horseflesh. — Wilda Moxham, *The Apprentice*, p. 186, 1969
- — Jim Ramsay, *Cop It Sweet!*, p. 68, 1977
- — Joe Andersen, *Winners Can Laugh*, p. 47, 1982
- — Ryan Aven-Bray, *Ridgey Didge Oz Jack Lang*, p. 39, 1983
- — Ned Wallish, *The Truth Dictionary of Racing Slang*, p. 60, 1989

3 in card games, a face card or a ten *US*
- — Steve Kuriscak, *Casino Talk*, p. 41, 1985

▸ come round on the paint
of a racehorse, to take a bend on the inside *AUSTRALIA*
- — Sidney J. Baker, *The Australian Language*, 1953

paint *verb*
1 to apply makeup *UK, 1382*
- [H]er brown hair was as tousled as a lamb's tail, and her unpainted face was drawn with sleep. — Jim Thompson, *The Killer Inside*, p. 8, 1952
- If you are (tell the truth!) the only girl your age within a fifty-mile radius who is not permitted to paint yourself as well as the town red, you have reason to gripe. — Dick Clark, *To Goof or Not to Goof*, p. 97, 1963
- Their women don't paint themselves. — Piri Thomas, *Down These Mean Streets*, p. 293, 1967

2 in lowball poker, to draw a face card to a hand of four low cards *US*
- — Albert H. Morehead, *The Complete Guide to Winning Poker*, p. 269, 1967

3 in hearts, to play a heart on a non-heart trick *US, 1953*
- — Thomas L. Clark, *The Dictionary of Gambling and Gaming*, 1987

4 to mark a target with laser beams *US*
Gulf war usage.
- — *American Speech*, p. 397, Winter 1991: 'Among the new words'

▸ paint the barn
to apply makeup *CANADA*
- — Bill Casselman, *Canadian Sayings*, p. 37, 2002

▸ paint the bus
to change something's appearance without changing its basic foundations *US*
- — Robert Kirk Mueller, *Buzzwords*, p. 122, 1974

▸ paint the town red
to have a raucous time on the town *US, 1884*
- Let's go out and paint old cow town red. — Jim Thompson, *The Killer Inside*, p. 83, 1952
- I drank liquor, smoked marijuana, painted the Big Apple red with increasing numbers of friends[.] — Malcolm X and Alex Haley, *The Autobiography of Malcolm X*, p. 78, 1964
- Yet there were thousands of girls living between Sunset and Santa Monica in between La Brea and La Cienega who painted the town red like me – and who got away with it. — Eve Babitz, *L.A. Woman*, p. 137, 1982
- James Boyer suggests that if I really want to paint the town red, I should try Bracknell. — *The Guardian*, 20th February 2003

painted pony *noun*
in circus and carnival usage, a zebra *US*
- — Don Wilmeth, *The Language of American Popular Entertainment*, p. 193, 1981

painter *noun*
1 a card cheat who marks cards for identification in another player's hand *US*
- — Frank Scoblete, *Guerrilla Gambling*, p. 320, 1993

2 a firefighter assigned to a hook-and-ladder truck *US*
Owing to the ladder.
- — *American Speech*, p. 273, December 1954: 'Fire terms: additional words and definitions'

painters *noun*
▸ have the painters in; painters are in
to be in the bleed period of the menstrual cycle *UK, 1961*
A euphemistic fact of life.
- I rung her one afternoon to ask her if it's all right to pop over. "It's okay but I've got the painters in," she says. "Well, that's okay, they go home at what? Four of five? They got to take their boots off sometime," I say. "No. Arsenal are at home," she says. — J.J. Connolly, *Layer Cake*, p. 291, 2000
- [A]n important diference between men and women iz sumfin called "da mental cycle" or as doctors call it, "havin de painters in". — Sacha Baron-Cohen, *Da Gospel According to Ali G*, 2001
- Not today, H, I can't, the painters are in. I'll be OK tomorrow. — Garry Bushell, *The Face*, p. 202, 2001
- — *The Museum of Menstruation and Women's Health*, April 2001

paint-stripper *noun*
cheap and nasty alcohol *UK*
- I went over the road and bought a cheap six-pack of Skol and some paint-stripper white wine. — Dave Courtney, *Stop the Ride I Want to Get Off*, p. 29, 1999

paipsey *adjective*
ugly *BARBADOS*
- — Frank A. Collymore, *Barbadian Dialect*, p. 81, 1965

pair *noun*
1 a pair of female breasts *US*
- She had a nice pair though. — Hubert Selby Jr, *Last Exit to Brooklyn*, p. 77, 1957
- Also she had the biggest pair at the Villa Monterey, even when they weren't pushed up by her kitty outfit. — Elmore Leonard, *Swag*, p. 44, 1976

2 a pair of testicles, hence manliness or courage *US*
- You like real clangers? I'll show you a pair that gong like Big Ben! — Joseph Wambaugh, *The Secrets of Harry Bright*, p. 47, 1985
- I can't hear you! Sound off like you got a pair. — *Full Metal Jacket*, 1987

pair of ducks; pair *noun*
in cricket, the score of a batsman who is out for no score in each leg of a match *UK*
From DUCK (zero).
- — Steve James, captain of Glamorgan County Cricket Club, 18th June 2003

pair of fives; pair of nickels *noun*
fifty-five miles an hour, the nearly uniform road speed limit in the US in the mid-1970s *US*
- — Lanie Dills, *The Official CB Slanguage Language Dictionary*, p. 52, 1976

pair of nostrils *noun*
a sawn-off shotgun *UK*
From the appearance of the gun.
- "I know where the shooter is hidden." I looked up. "What sort of gun?" "Pair of nostrils." — Duncan MacLaughlin, *The Filth*, p. 113, 2002

pair of panties *noun*
paragliding *US*
From the French term *parapente* (paragliding).
- — Erik Fair, *California Thrill Sports*, p. 335, 1992

paisan; paisano *noun*
an Italian-American; used as a term of address that evokes a common heritage, especially Italian *US, 1947*
- As I hung up, I spotted the two lean, tough-looking paisanos gazing at me cooped up in the booth. — Malcolm X and Alex Haley, *The Autobiography of Malcolm X*, p. 125, 1964
- Why the old lady? Why, paisan, the same reasons we killed the old man, baby, the same reason. — Donald Goines, *Black Gangster*, p. 80, 1977
- The maitre d' didn't shout, "You back again?" nor did the bartender holler, "What's your poison, paesan"? — Rita Ciresi, *Pink Slip*, p. 88–89, 1999

pajama *noun*
the vagina *US*
Something you slip into at bedtime.
- There's [a...] "horsespot," "nappy dugout," mongo," a "pajama," "fannyboo[".] — Eve Ensler, *The Vagina Monologues*, p. 6, 1998

pajama wagon *noun*
in trucking, a truck cab with a factory-manufactured sleeping compartment *US*
- — Montie Tak, *Truck Talk*, p. 115, 1971

Pak *noun*
Pakistan *UK*
- US maps Kashmir line of action for India, Pak. — *The Economic Times*, 27th October 2004

pakalolo *noun*
a variety of marijuana from Hawaii *US, 1981*
- — Richard A. Spears, *The Slang and Jargon of Drugs and Drink*, p. 376, 1986
- — Mike Haskins, *Drugs*, p. 288, 2003

pakapoo ticket *noun*
something indecipherable or overly complicated *AUSTRALIA, 1951*
Pakapoo is a Chinese gambling game that appears to outsiders to be quite complicated.

Paki; paki; pakki; Pak *noun*
a Pakistani; any Asian or Afro-Asian immigrant; loosely, any native of the Indian subcontinent; Pakistan *UK, 1964*
Derogatory or patronising.
- I'm a Paki, Chink, a half-cocked ponce[.] — Ian Dury, *Blackmail Man*, 1977
- So why do all the council homes go to Pakis? — Greg Williams, *Diamond Geezers*, p. 125, 1997
- [F]uckin' queers, lezzies – I wouldn't mind fuckin' one of them though – pakkies, coons and the cuntin' Common market. — Stuart Browne, *Dangerous Parking*, p. 44, 2000
- There's no way a Paki will defend a white man against another Paki. Not in this lifetime anyway. — Lanre Fehintola, *Charlie Says...*, p. 87, 2000
- [A] groaner who didn't like the food and didn't like the Paddies and didn't like the Pakis and didn't like the poofs[.] — John King, *White Trash*, p. 65, 2001
- — Rajeex Sharma, *Pak Proxy War*, 2002

Paki *adjective*
Pakistani *UK*
• Mandy Sucks Paki Cocks[.]—David Peace, *Nineteen Seventy-Four*, p. 61, 1999

Paki-basher; Pakki-basher *noun*
a violent racist who, usually as part of a group, attacks members of the Asian community *UK*
• Pakistanis living in terror of the "paki-basher" mobs of skinheads — *Evening Standard*, 19th April 1970

Paki-bashing; Pakki-bashing *noun*
an organised or opportunistic assaulting of Asian immigrants by gangs of white youths *UK, 1970*
Political and racist agenda are claimed in an attempt to dignify these attacks by thrill-seeking youths; however, it is worth noting that an average **PAKI-BASHER** is unable to draw a distinction between targeted races. This social phenomenon seems to have originated in London and continues, sporadically, nationwide.

Paki pox *noun*
smallpox *UK*
From ill-informed racist opinion.

Pakistaner *noun*
a big-breasted girl *SOUTH AFRICA*
Teen slang.
• — *Sunday Times (South Africa)*, 1st June 2003

Pakistani black; paki black *noun*
a potent, black-brown marijuana cultivated in Pakistan *UK, 1998*
In other contexts the use of 'Paki' may be seen as derogatory, in this case it is attached to a high quality product.
• —Mike Haskins, *Drugs*, p. 288, 2003

Paklish *adjective*
of Anglo-Pakistani birth *AUSTRALIA*
• Under a Tin-Grey Sari [a novel by Wayne Ashton set in 1967] tells the story of Khalid, a young cook in the employ of an "Anglo-Banglo" or "Paklish" household.— *The Post, Perth, Western Australia*, 4th January 2003

pal *noun*
1 a close friend; used as a term of address, usually sarcastically *UK, 1681*
From the English, Turkish and Transylvanian Romany tongues.
• Okay, pal, I accept the compliment.— *As Good As It Gets*, 1997
2 a studio musician *US*
• —Arnold Shaw, *Dictionary of American Pop/Rock*, p. 271, 1982

palace *noun*
a brakevan (caboose) *US*
• —Norman Carlisle, *The Modern Wonder Book of Trains and Railroading*, p. 266, 1946

Palace of Varieties *nickname*
the House of Commons *UK*
A derisory allusion to a place of entertainment.
• [diary entry 14th November 1996] Back at the Palace of Varieties it's all gone wrong again[.]—Gyles Brandreth, *Breaking the Code*, p. 432, 1999

palare *noun*
▷ **see:** **POLARI**

pal around *verb*
to associate with; to socialise with *US, 1879*
• All I know is that when I was a kid palling around with Mike, it never occurred to me that he was insensitive[.]—Jack Kerouac, *Letter to Neal Cassady*, p. 150, 7th May 1948
• After I'd gotten out of reception, Minetti and I started palling around, and we got tight.—Claude Brown, *Manchild in the Promised Land*, p. 142, 1965
• I was pal-ing around with a lot of wops from downtown and the west Bronx, younger guys like me, not the prejudiced old hoods.—Edwin Torres, *Carlito's Way*, p. 30, 1975

palaver *noun*
business; any activity or business that is complicated or annoying, an unnecessary fuss *UK, 1899*
• It doesn't really make any difference to us whether it comes out on Tuesday or Wednesday or whenever. We just think, what a palaver. — *The Guardian*, 22nd February 1999

palaver *verb*
to talk; to chat; to argue *UK, 1733*
• —Paul Baker, *Polari*, p. 185, 2002

paleets *noun*
used as a male-to-male term of address *TRINIDAD AND TOBAGO, 1976*
An embellished 'pal'.
• —Lise Winer, *Dictionary of the English/Creole of Trinidad & Tobago*, 2003

pale-face *noun*
when spoken by a black person, a white person *US, 1945*
From C18 American Indian usage.
• "Yes, I do like you palefaces," he said.—Max Shulman, *Anyone Got a Match?*, p. 60, 1964

palf *noun*
Palfium, a heroin substitute *IRELAND*
• [B]ut if Squirrel had gone to drama classes instead of spending his evenings casing gaffs, perfecting handbrake turns in stolen cars and developing an unhealthy appetite for palf—Howard Paul, *The Joy*, p. 100, 1996

palintoshed *adjective*
drunk *UK*
• — *e-cyclopaedia*, 20th March 2002

pallatic *adjective*
drunk *UK, late C19?*
A drunken slurring of **PARALYTIC** (drunk).
• He'd've just thought I was pallatic blacking out in his cab like that[.] —Kevin Sampson, *Outlaws*, p. 119, 2001

palled-in *adjective*
cohabiting with a woman *UK*
• —R Samuel, *East End Underworld*, 1981

palliness *noun*
comradeship, the condition of being pals *UK, 1937*
• They gave off a strange air of palliness: Charlie [Kennedy] and Tony [Blair] shared a quiet joke and, when Michael Howard leaned over to find out what the funny was, they smilingly passed it on.—*The Guardian*, 26th November 2003

pallish *adjective*
friendly *UK, 1892*
• [Douglas] Coupland's writing diligently embraces gorge-and-puke, trademark, shopping-mall culture, the whole thing in all its pointlessness, with pallish affection[.]— *The Guardian*, 27th October 1999

Pall Mall *noun*
a girl *UK*
Rhyming slang, formed on the London street; recorded as 'now obsolete' by Julian Franklyn, *A Dictionary of Rhyming Slang*, 1960, who explained the rhyme as 'Cockney dialect makes Paow Maow – Gaow'. Despite Franklyn's assertion, it is apparently still in circulation.
• The word in East End dialect becomes "el", likewise this street in the West End has long been "Pell Mell". Said the right way, however, it rhymes with "gal", which is more the show-bizzy version.—Ray Puxley, *Fresh Rabbit*, 1998

pally *noun*
a friend; a comrade *US*
• Pallies, damper the rapping!—Iceberg Slim (Robert Beck), *Airtight Willie and Me*, p. 29, 1979

pally *adjective*
friendly *UK, 1895*
• I think getting pally with him while the trial was going on kept me quiet as well[.]—Lenny McLean, *The Guv'nor*, p. 213, 1998

pally up *verb*
to make friendly overtures; to make friends *UK*
• [T]here's nothing more scally [in the manner of a hooligan youth] than pallying up to a footballer[.]—Niall Griffiths, *Kelly + Victor*, p. 82, 2002

palm *noun*
napalm *US*
Vietnam war usage
• —Linda Reinberg, *In the Field*, p. 161, 1991

palming *noun*
masturbation *BAHAMAS*
• —John A. Holm, *Dictionary of Bahamian English*, p. 151, 1982

palm oil *noun*

1 a bribe *UK, 1627*

- —Joseph E. Ragen and Charles Finston, *Inside the World's Toughest Prison*, p. 811, 1962: 'Penitentiary and underworld glossary'
- —Angela Devlin, *Prison Patter*, p. 84, 1996

2 a gratuity *US*

- —Vincent J. Monteleone, *Criminal Slang*, p. 171, 1949

palm shiner *noun*

in gambling, an object that reflects the image of cards, small enough to be held in the user's hand *US*

- The other was a "palm shiner," which he used when it wasn't his deal. It was a tiny, upside-down periscope. He could palm it, or hold it cupped in his hand on the green felt table, positioned so he could look down through the space between his fingers. —Stephen J. Cannell, *King Con*, p. 2, 1997

palm-walmer *noun*

a person who tips *US*

- The best palm-walmers are South American diplomats, who apparently have no regard for American money. —Jack Lait and Lee Mortimer, *Washington Confidential*, p. 133, 1951

palone-omee *noun*

a lesbian *UK*

Polari; a combination of 'palone' (a woman) and 'omee' (a man); the reverse order 'omee-palone' means a male homosexual.

- —Paul Baker, *Polari*, p. 185, 2002

palonie *noun*

a circus pony used in comedy routines *UK*

- [O]ne of the basic clown acts in any ring is the "joey's palonie"[.] —Butch Reynolds, *Broken Hearted Clown*, p. 29–30, 1953

palooka *noun*

a person who is mediocre at their craft *US, 1925*

Originally a boxing term.

- —Albert H. Morehead, *The Complete Guide to Winning Poker*, p. 269, 1967
- [L]ow man on the totem pole, a mere jog step above the palooka from the Bronx Home News —Bill Cardoso, *The Maltese Sangweech*, p. 281, 1984
- The Doll Theater, at Seventh and 48th, revolves around an emotionless palooka ramming his three-quarters hard-on into some broad's snatch atop a pink-spotlighted mattress tilted toward the audience. —Josh Alan Friedman, *Tales of Times Square*, p. 189, 1986

palsy-walsy *adjective*

friendly, often with an undertone of insincerity *US, 1937*

- Only this afternoon his gin partner and palsy-walsy competitor Big Ernie had been convicted for wholesaling the main line stuff. —Morton Cooper, *High School Confidential*, p. 110, 1958
- They used to treat you palsy-walsy. —Tom Wolfe, *The Pump House Gang*, p. 71, 1968
- getting palsy-walsy with his fellow students to be invited to dinner and parties —Emmett Grogan, *Ringolevio*, p. 81, 1972
- [I]n other words, the world notes that sometimes we are palsy-walsy with the bad guys and sometimes we want to rip their lungs out, depending on which stance serves our perceived interests at the time. —*Milwaukee Journal Sentinel*, p. 4, 29th September 2002

pal up *verb*

to make friends *US*

- [B]ut to take me into his home – pal up with me – when there was any kind of a chance that I might mean trouble —Jim Thompson, *Savage Night*, p. 83, 1953

pamp *verb*

to place or put something somewhere *UK: SCOTLAND*

- [G]et your act cleaned up and some spondulix pamped [placed] in my purse. —Ian Pattison, *Rab C. Nesbitt*, 1990

pamphlet *noun*

one ounce of a drug *US*

- Less than a pound, so smaller than a book. —Robert Sabbag, *Snowblind: A Brief Career in the Cocaine Trade*, p. 271, 1976

pan *noun*

the face *US, 1923*

- One day even Frankie Riccardi's pan jumped out at me. —Mezz Mezzrow, *Really the Blues*, p. 101, 1946

▸ **on the pan**

(used of a truck driver) summoned to appear before a public utility commission for violations of driving laws *US*

- —*American Speech*, p. 273, December 1961: 'Northwest truck drivers' language'

pan *verb*

1 to criticise something as unsuccessful *US, 1911*

- His novel was refused, his movie was panned / And his big Broadway show was a flop. —Loudon Wainwright III, *The Man Who Couldn't Cry*, 1973

2 to utterly defeat someone in a fight; to thrash someone *UK*

- Fucking panned us, they did. —Kevin Sampson, *Clubland*, p. 68, 2002

3 to beg *US*

An abbreviation of 'panhandle'.

- —Jim Crotty, *How to Talk American*, p. 145, 1997

Panama cut *noun*

a variety of marijuana cultivated in Panama *UK, 1998*

- —Mike Haskins, *Drugs*, p. 288, 2003

Panama gold; Panamanian gold *noun*

a potent, gold-leafed marijuana cultivated in Panama *US, 1968*

- —Richard A. Spears, *The Slang and Jargon of Drugs and Drink*, p. 377, 1986
- —Mike Haskins, *Drugs*, p. 288, 2003

Panama red; Panamanian red *noun*

a potent variety of marijuana cultivated in Panama *US*

- "Gold. It's Acapulco Gold," White Rabbit corrected the doctor, who was mixing up the slang names for different kinds of marijuana. "I mean Panama Red," Goddard corrected himself[.] —Nicholas Von Hoffman, *We Are The People Our Parents Warned Us Against*, p. 23, 1967
- [T]he tobacco giants who are already reliably rumoured to have registered such names as Nepalese Blue, Acapulco Gold and Panama Red ... the kind of joint one smokes will become a status symbol. —Richard Neville, *Play Power*, p. 132, 1970
- But when things get too confusing, honey / You're better off in bed / And I'll be searching all the joints in town for / Panama Red. —Peter Rowan (New Riders of the Purple Sage), *Panama Red*, 1971
- This is some of that Panama Red I've been saving for my exit smoke. —Odie Hawkins, *Men Friends*, p. 56, 1989
- Panama Red runs neck and neck with Acapulco gold and it is the flip of a coin which is best loved. Its colour lives up to its name. —Mike Rock, *This Book*, 1999
- —Mike Haskins, *Drugs*, p. 288, 2003

panatella *noun*

1 a marijuana cigarette *US, 1944*

- About half an inch longer than mine and much thinner, and they called their product "panatella" —Milton Mezzrow, *Really the Blues*, 1946
- The cigarettes come in three qualities: saras-fras, the cheapest kind, sold to thousands of school children at about ten cents each; the panatella, or messerole, retailed at twenty-five cents[.] —Jack Lait and Lee Mortimer, *New York Confidential*, p. 102, 1948

2 potent marijuana, especially that originating in South or Central America *US*

- the best panatella you ever smoked —Billie Holiday, *Lady Sings The Blues*, 1956

panatic *noun*

a devoted, die-hard fan of steelband music *TRINIDAD AND TOBAGO, 1988*

- —Lise Winer, *Dictionary of the English/Creole of Trinidad & Tobago*, 2003

pan breid *adjective*

dead *UK: SCOTLAND*

Glasgow rhyming slang for 'pan bread' (a type of crusty loaf).

- Ye never telt us yer dug [dog] wis pan breid. —Michael Munro, *The Patter, Another Blast*, 1988

pancake *verb*

using hydraulic lifts operated from inside the car, to drop suddenly first the back and then the front of a car *US*

- —Edith A. Folb, *runnin' down some lines*, p. 249, 1980

pancake saddle *noun*

in western Canada, an English saddle *CANADA*

- The western rider who uses the heavy working saddle of the range views the light English saddle with derision – hence the nickname "pancake saddle." —Chris Thain, *Cold as a Bay Street Banker's Heart*, p. 114, 1987

panda car; panda *noun*

a black and white police patrol car, hence a police patrol car *UK, 1996*

The logic is black and white: the car was introduced at a time when the pandas at London Zoo were making headlines.

Pandemonium World Scareways *nickname*

US airline company Pan Am *US*

Most airlines attract jocular variations of their names: Pan Am's include: 'Painful, Nauseating and Miserable' and 'Passengers Always Neglected at Mealtimes'.

• Katie Miles filled us in on the nicknames of the airlines [...] Pan Am was "Pandemonium World Scareways"[.] —Mary Higgins Clark, *Kitchen Privileges*, p. 65–66, 2002

P and Q *noun*

solitary confinement in prison *US*

Abbreviated '*p*eace *and* *q*uiet'.

• —Ralph de Sola, *Crime Dictionary*, p. 110, 1982

• —William K. Bentley and James M. Corbett, *Prison Slang*, p. 11, 1992

pane *noun*

a dose of LSD on a tiny, clear gelatin chip *US*

A shortened form of **WINDOWPANE**.

• —US Department of Justice, *Street Terms*, October 1994

panel-beater *noun*

an employee in a car body shop *AUSTRALIA*

Remembered by Beale in 1984 as Australian, 1950s.

• —Louis S. Leland, *A Personal Kiwi-Yankee Dictionary*, p. 74, 1984

panel house *noun*

a brothel with sliding walls through which thieves steal from the clothes of customers *US, 1848*

• There are also "panel" houses. These work by having the woman help the man take his clothing off and place it in a certain position, probably over a convenient chair. While he is concentrating on thoughts other than his watch and money, a panel slides open, a dark hand comes through the opening and takes everything out of the pockets. —Jack Lait and Lee Mortimer, *New York Confidential*, p. 98–99, 1948

panels of fences *noun*

in horse racing, a long lead *AUSTRALIA*

• —Ned Wallish, *The Truth Dictionary of Racing Slang*, p. 60, 1989

pangonadalot *noun*

heroin *US, 1977*

• —Richard A. Spears, *The Slang and Jargon of Drugs and Drink*, p. 377, 1986

• —Mike Haskins, *Drugs*, p. 284, 2003

panhandle *verb*

to beg *US, 1884*

• Diane reminds old New Yorkers of the fabulous Broadway Rose, who used to panhandle in front of Lindy's until she was carted to the bug house. —Jack Lait and Lee Mortimer, *Washington Confidential*, p. 26–27, 1951

• I get high drunk, drop money on floor, am panhandled, play Ruth Brown wildjump records among drunken alky whores. —Jack Kerouac, *Letter to John Clellon Holmes*, p. 338, 8th February 1952

• I didn't know how to panhandle. —Jack Kerouac, *On the Road*, p. 105, 1957

• Shipped back to the United States for treatment, he had walked off the grounds of the Army hospital and panhandled his way south[.] —Clancy Sigal, *Going Away*, p. 233, 1961

• Panhandling really blows the mind when it's carried on by middle class drop-outs. —Abbie Hoffman, *Revolution for the Hell of It*, p. 34, 1968

• To panhandle man-to-man on the street in this country is a noble, liberating act. —Jerry Rubin, *Do It!*, p. 123, 1970

• An hour's panhandling, and Edward could purchase fresh double-A batteries for his discman[.] —Robert Crais, *L.A. Requiem*, p. 58, 1999

panhandler *noun*

1 a beggar *US, 1897*

• Maybe a panhandler will try to mooch a quarter[.] —Jack Lait and Lee Mortimer, *New York Confidential*, p. 14, 1948

• He was a panhandler and a fruit. A disgrace to the Jewish race. —William Burroughs, *Junkie*, p. 68, 1953

• Chicago: invisible hierarchy of decorticated wops, small of atrophied gangsters, earthbound ghost hits you at North and Halstead, Cicero, Lincoln Park, panhandler of dreams[.] —William Burroughs, *Naked Lunch*, p. 11, 1957

• "I been a panhandler for ten years," he said. —Willard Motley, *Let No Man Write My Epitaph*, p. 73, 1958

• [T]he scattered junkies, the smalltime pushers, the teaheads, the sad panhandlers, the occasional lonely exiled nymphos haunting the entrance to the men's head[.] —John Rechy, *City of Night*, p. 100–101, 1963

2 a nurse *US*

Jocular reference to bedpans.

• —*Complete CB Slang Dictionary*, p. 72, 1976

• —Peter Chippindale, *The British CB Book*, p. 157, 1981

panic *noun*

1 a widespread unavailability of an illegal drug *US, 1937*

• Election is over and the panic is off. —George Mandel, *Flee the Angry Strangers*, p. 55, 1952

• This was the Panic: people dying unseen, scraping the sugary bottoms of cookers, licking the bitter taste away with their tongues, frightened and cursing the unknown torment within their intestines. —Clarence Cooper Jr, *The Scene*, p. 30, 1960

• And then if this really does turn out to be a real bad panic, well then too I'll – we'll – always have stuff. —James Mills, *The Panic in Needle Park*, p. 41, 1966

• Everything was going as good as could be expected, till the panic hit. There was a short go of heroin on account of some big wheeler-dealer with millions of dollars' worth of the stuff had gotten himself busted and this caused a bad shortage. —Piri Thomas, *Down These Mean Streets*, p. 202, 1967

• He puttin' out that weak shit like the panic was on or somethin'. —Nathan Heard, *Howard Street*, p. 117, 1968

• There's been a panic. Until this morning I couldn't cop [buy] any stuff [heroin]. —Iceberg Slim (Robert Beck), *Pimp*, p. 99, 1969

• A panic was on among the junkies. There were still a few people able to connect – but on the whole conditions were bad. —Herbert Huncke, *The Evening Sun Turned Crimson*, p. 84, 1980

2 a very good time *US*

• —*San Francisco News*, p. 6, 25th March 1958

• —Judi Sanders, *Faced and Faded, Hanging to Hurl*, p. 30, 1993

panic button *noun*

any switch or button which activates an emergency alarm, or summons urgent assistance, or stops a mechanical operation *UK, 1971*

• —Angela Devlin, *Prison Patter*, p. 84, 1996

panic flip *noun*

in pinball, the premature activation of a flipper *US*

• —Bobbye Claire Natkin and Steve Kirk, *All About Pinball*, p. 113, 1977

panic merchant *noun*

a person who habitually panics *AUSTRALIA*

• 'I reckon he's a real panic merchant,' grunted Storm. 'He's been scared stiff ever since the briefing.' —W.R. Bennett, *Target Turin*, p. 105, 1962

• —Wilda Moxham, *The Apprentice*, p. 4, 1969

• —Arthur Chipper, *The Aussie Swearer's Guide*, p. 86, 1972

panic stations *noun*

a frenzied state of alarmed or confused thinking *UK, 1961*

A jocular adaptation of the military term 'action stations'.

• [T]he result should ring alarm bells, though it was hardly panic stations. —*The Guardian*, 12th June 2002

pan-loaf *adjective*

of a superior social status or well-to-do *UK: SCOTLAND*

Glasgow rhyming slang for **TOFF** – a good rhyme in the local accent – formed from a type of bread with a soft crust.

• A pan-loaf accent is a posh accent. —Michael Munro, *The Original Patter*, 1985

pannikin boss *noun*

a person with a modest amount of authority; a minor boss; a foreman *AUSTRALIA, 1898*

• [The truck was] manned by other coloureds who by their woolly heads were Melanesian and Polynesian, the usual type of pannikin boss connected with missions. —Xavier Herbert, *Poor Fellow My Country*, p. 232, 1975

panno *noun*

1 a panel van *AUSTRALIA*

• I love pannos! If anyone out there has a very good condition panno, please e-mail or contact me. —*www.homepages.picknowl.com.au*, 1998

• Given that I am a mere 19 years of age and still searching for the eternal buzz, it doesn't surprise me that the mighty panno caught my admiration. —*www.holdensandman.com*, 2003

2 a foreman *AUSTRALIA, 1957*

An abbreviation of **PANNIKIN BOSS**.

• Within a week, he jobbed the panno, snatched his time and bought an air ticket to gay Paree. —Frank Hardy, *The Yarns of Billy Borker*, p. 24, 1965

panoramas *noun*

pyjamas *UK*

Rhyming slang.

• —Ray Puxley, *Cockney Rabbit*, 1992

pan out *verb*

(of an event) to turn out; to result *US, 1871*

A figurative application of panning for gold.

• Had [Russell] Crowe been chained up somewhere, the night might have panned out rather differently. —*The Guardian*, 26th March 2001

pansy *noun*

a male homosexual; an effeminate man *UK, 1929*

• [H]e hates the sight of you all and you're a lot of pansies and why don't I get engaged, like my sister? —Peter Nichols, *Promenade [Six Granada Plays]*, p. 54, 1959

- You want to get yourself down to London if you're a bloody pansy. They're all bloody pansies down there. —Geoff Brown, *I Want What I Want*, p. 71, 1966
- —Angela Devlin, *Prison Patter*, p. 84, 1996

pansy-ass *adjective*
effeminate, weak *US*
- Son of a bitch pansy-assed stool-pusher. — *As Good As It Gets*, 1997
- [Andrew WK] loves kittens but hates "pansy-ass" music, cramming up to 90 studio tracks into his piledriver hedonist anthems. — *Uncut*, January 2002

pansy-boy *noun*
an effeminate male homosexual *AUSTRALIA, 1976*
- I also realised I'm pissed off to see him obviously friendly with the pansy-boy. —Christos Tsiolkas, *Loaded*, p. 124, 1995

pansy-man *noun*
a male homosexual *ANTIGUA AND BARBUDA*
Collected by Richard Allsopp.

pansy patch *nickname*
an area in west Hollywood, California, largely populated by homosexual men since the 1960s *US*
- When one thinks of gay ghettos across the country, his mind leaps to the Pansy Patch of West Hollywood[.] —John Francis Hunter, *The Gay Insider*, p. 172, 1971

Pansy Potters *noun*
the documents given to someone who is dismissed from employment *UK: SCOTLAND*
Glasgow rhyming slang for **JOTTERS**, formed on a comic strip character.
- She'd only been there a year when they gave her her Pansy Potters. —Michael Munro, *The Complete Patter*, 1996: 'Lovely blooming fresh and gay'

pansy prattle *noun*
the snide remarks and witty insults characteristic of male homosexual banter *US*
- — *Maledicta*, p. 237, Winter 1980: '"Lovely, blooming, fresh and gay": the onomastics of camp'

pant *noun*
trousers *INDIA*
- I'm going to wear my blue pant today. —Paroo Nihalini, R.K. Tongue and Priya Hosali, *Indian and British English*, 1979

panther *noun*
a condom *JAMAICA*
The image of a large black beast. Collected from UK prisoners in May, 2002.

panther breath *noun*
strong, illegally manufactured whisky *US*
- It is called corn liquor, white lightning, sugar whisky, skully cracker, popskull, bush whiskey, stump, stumphole, 'splo, ruckus juice, radiator whiskey, rotgut, sugarhead, block and tackle, wildcat, panther's breath, tiger's sweat, Sweet spirits of cats a-fighting, alley bourbon, city gin, cool water, happy Sally, deep shaft, jump steady, old horsey, stingo, blue John, red eye, pine top, buckeye bark whiskey and see seven stars. — *Star Tribune (Minneapolis)*, p. 19F, 31st January 1999

panther juice *noun*
strong, homemade alcohol *US, 1960*
- Then I slurped it up like a hound laps pot likker, rolling the panther juice around on my tongue, smacking my lips over it. —Guy Owen, *The Flim-Flam Man and the Apprentice Grifter*, p. 40, 1972

panther piss *noun*
illegally manufactured, low quality alcohol *US*
- Everywhere there were steam baths, massages, girls, Panther Piss, opium dens, souvenirs, clothes from India[.]— *Screw*, p. 5, 15th February 1971
- —Edith A. Folb, *runnin' down some lines*, p. 249, 1980

panther sweat *noun*
1 surgical spirit and Italian vermouth mixed as a potent drink *UK*
After the US slang for inferior whisky. Reported by a correspondent of Partridge as in Beatnik use around 1959, but not recorded until 1984.
2 low quality whisky *US*
- —Ramon Adams, *The Language of the Railroader*, p. 111, 1977

pantload *noun*
a great deal of something *US*
- —Collin Baker et al., *College Undergraduate Slang Study Conducted at Brown University*, p. 168, 1968
- [A] pantload of good it would do us to raid an empty ship. —Christopher Brookmyre, *Not the End of the World*, p. 358, 1998

pant moustache *noun*
a fringe of pubic hair that escapes the confines of a female's underwear or swimwear *UK*
- —Chris Lewis, *The Dictionary of Playground Slang*, p. 166, 2003

pantomime cow *noun*
a row; an argument *UK*
Rhyming slang.
- —Ray Puxley, *Fresh Rabbit*, 1998

pants *noun*
sex *US*
In the spirit of 'cunt', 'ass' or 'leg', but a bit more restrained.
- When one of Johnny's girls messed up on him – tried to hold back some money or gave somebody some pants and didn't get any money – he sure was hard on them. —Claude Brown, *Manchild in the Promised Land*, p. 114, 1965

▸ **frighten the pants off; scare the pants off**
to frighten or scare someone, especially severely or (when horror is presented as entertainment) thrillingly *UK*
- — *Bournemouth Echo*, 25th October 1967
- Do you like to have the pants frightened off of you? —Terry Victor, *Return of the Menu Monster*, 1992

▸ **get into someone's pants**
to seduce someone; to have sex with someone *US*
- I've been in more guys' pants than you could count. —George Mandel, *Flee the Angry Strangers*, p. 220, 1952
- Because as I mentioned, I didn't try and get into her pants last night, or this morning. —Donald Goines, *Never Die Alone*, p. 109, 1974
- He hoped to deflect her thoughts from the possibility of getting into her pants a bit again. —Earl Thompson, *Tattoo*, p. 473, 1974
- Alfred knows that he wants to get into every pair of pants that he sees on a woman. —George V. Higgins, *The Rat on Fire*, p. 89, 1981
- You know all you'd do is hump her leg for an hour and try to get in her pants. — *Mallrats*, 1995
- I threw my costume in his face and said, 'You're always trying to get in my pants. Here's your chance.' —Kathryn Leigh Scott, *The Bunny Years*, p. 81, 1998

pants *verb*
to pull someone's trousers down as part of a prank or practical joke *US*
- They follow this by "pantsing" the Cowboys – pulling their pants down around their knees. — *Bill and Ted's Excellent Adventure*, p. 42, 1989
- Yeah, and who pantsed me at the tenth grade assembly in front of the world? — *Wayne's World 2*, 1992

pants *adjective*
applied to something that is very easily done *UK: SCOTLAND*
- There's nothin tae it ... it's a skoosh [something easily achieved] ... it's pants. —Michael Munro, *The Complete Patter*, p. 116, 1996

pants and vest; pants *noun*
best bitter beer *UK*
Rhyming slang.
- a pint of pants —Ray Puxley, *Cockney Rabbit*, 1992

pantsful *noun*
a great deal, especially of something bad *US*
A suggestion of a lot of excrement.
- All my stuff is gone. My parents think I'm a sicko. And the whole world knows I've got a crooked dick. Thanks a pantsful, Nick. —C.D. Payne, *Youth in Revolt*, p. 91, 1993

pantsman *noun*
a womaniser *AUSTRALIA, 1968*
- Yet for all that he isn't a pants man. —David Ireland, *The Glass Canoe*, p. 3, 1976
- —Jim Ramsay, *Cop It Sweet!*, p. 68, 1977

pants rabbits *noun*
pubic lice; body lice; fleas *US*
- —Vincent J. Monteleone, *Criminal Slang*, p. 171, 1949
- —Helen Dahlskog (Editor), *A Dictionary of Contemporary and Colloquial Usage*, p. 16, 1972

panty hamster *noun*
the vagina *UK*
• — *www.LondonSlang.com*, June 2002

pantyman *noun*
an effeminate heterosexual man; a homosexual man *TRINIDAD AND TOBAGO, 1993*
• — Lise Winer, *Dictionary of the English/Creole of Trinidad & Tobago*, 2003

pantypop *verb*
to fart *US*
• — Chris Lewis, *The Dictionary of Playground Slang*, p. 166, 2003

panty raid *noun*
a college fad in which male students invade the dormitories of female students, seizing underwar as trophies *US, 1952*
The practice and term faded quickly with the onset of 1960s culture.
• I am dubbed a "deranged anarchist" and Mr. Burke concludes the show with the suggestion that I stick to panty raids, which he says are "more constructive." — James Simon Kunen, *The Strawberry Statement*, p. 64–65, 1968

panty-stretcher *noun*
a heavy woman *US*
Also recorded in UK usage.
• — Elementary Electronics, *Dictionary of CB Lingo*, p. 91, 1976
• — Peter Chippindale, *The British CB Book*, p. 157, 1981

pantywaist *noun*
a weakling or coward; a homosexual man *US, 1936*
• And while the hot-shots were tough, the regulars were no pantywaists. — Jim Thompson, *Bad Boy*, p. 366, 1953
• When I first started going with girls, the guys in the gang called me a sissy and a pantywaist and like that[.] — Max Shulman, *I was a Teen-Age Dwarf*, p. 59, 1959
• There's them pantywaiste Owenses with their lifted pinkies. — Max Shulman, *Anyone Got a Match?*, p. 6, 1964
• — Connie Eble (Editor), *UNC-CH Campus Slang*, p. 6, Fall 1986
• You'll go cruising for me? But won't you just bring home a sissy panty-waist like yourself[?] — Terence Sellers, *Dungeon Evidence*, p. 55, 1997

pantzilla *noun*
Sildenafil citrate marketed as Viagra, an anti-impotence drug taken recreationally for performance enhancement, in combination with other chemicals that stimulate the sexual appetites *UK*
A jocular reference to the monster in your underpants. The monster, of course, is Godzilla.
• — *Sky Magazine*, July 2001

pan up *verb*
to prepare a powdered drug for heating prior to injection *US*
• — Eugene Landy, *The Underground Dictionary*, p. 145, 1971

Panzer *noun*
a Mercedes-Benz car *US*
• — Anna Scotti and Paul Young, *Buzzwords*, p. 40, 1997

pap *verb*
to work as a press photographer who specialises in the sensational and the celebrated *UK*
A back-formation from **PAPARAZZI**.
• We've been out papping. — *Word of Mouth*, 6th August 2004

paparazzi *noun*
press photographers who specialise in the sensational and the celebrated, or a single photographer similarly engaged *UK, 1968*
From the Italian *paparazzo* which is the correct, though rarely used, singular form. Named after a character in *La Dolce Vita*, a 1960 film by Frederico Fellini.
• But wouldn't she resent it if the paparazzi started following her? I guess if they're interested it obviously means that... it's just one of the aspects of being well known, isn't it? — *The Guardian*, 24th September 2003

pape *noun*
a Roman Catholic *UK: SCOTLAND*
A shortening of 'papist'.
• — Michael Munro, *The Original Patter*, 1985

paper *noun*
1 money *US*
• The bitch had to make fair paper, no matter how small a part she had on the program. — Donald Goines, *Never Die Alone*, p. 113, 1974
• — John A. Holm, *Dictionary of Bahamian English*, p. 151, 1982
• You know, this 'paper' [money] thing ain't gonna last forever. — Terry Williams, *The Cocaine Kids*, p. 89, 1989
• Always available Nicky you know that. Prefer it we make some paper out of it you understand. — Jeremy Cameron, *Brown Bread in Wengen*, p. 24, 1999
• [W]hen the establishment Mafioso realise how much gilt, paper, cashish, wonga, wedge, corn, cutter, loot, spondos, dollar, readies, shillings, folding, dough, money is on offer[.] — J.J. Connolly, *Layer Cake*, p. 94, 2000
• He had so many petty thieves, crack-heads and scumbags on his books, changing plastic into paper was a doddle for him. — Danny King, *The Bank Robber Diaries*, p. 53, 2002

2 a cigarette paper *UK, 1950*
• Bony stirred uneasily, and, to conceal it, he began with tobacco and papers. — Arthur Upfield, *Bony and the Mouse*, p. 61, 1959
• Realizing he'd left his tobacco and papers under the truck, Hodge went outside. — Wal Watkins, *Race the Lazy River*, p. 28, 1963
• — Mary Lay and Nancy Orban, *The Hip Glossary of Hippie Language*, June 1967
• Canna Pal ana packeta Drum and papers, mate. — Barry Dickins, *What the Dickins*, p. 54, 1985
• — Angela Devlin, *Prison Patter*, p. 85, 1996

3 personal identification papers *US*
• No running. No face jobs or new paper. — Richard Condon, *Prizzi's Honor*, p. 278, 1982

4 promotional literature produced as part of a telephone sales swindle *US*
• — Kathleen Odean, *High Steppers, Fallen Angels, and Lollipops*, p. 132, 1988

5 a free pass to a performance *UK, 1785*
• — Joe McKennon, *Circus Lingo*, p. 68, 1980

6 a cheque *US*
• She is more upgraded, she knows how to pass paper [forged checks, credit cards], she knows the various houses to go to. — Christina and Richard Milner, *Black Players*, p. 95, 1972
• All the joints on 7th and 8th Avenues and up on Sugar Hill, Tad visited and passed out $1,600 worth of bad paper until he got so sick he had to go the hospital. — Babs Gonzales, *Movin' On Down De Line*, p. 50, 1975

7 a speeding ticket *US*
• — Radio Shack, *CBer's Handy Atlas/Dictionary*, p. 36, 1976

8 a deck of cards that have been marked for cheating *US*
• — Robert C. Prus and C.R.D. Sharper, *Road Hustler*, p. 171, 1977: 'Glossary of terms'
• — John Scarne, *Scarne's Guide to Modern Poker*, p. 286, 1979

9 heroin sold in a paper packet; a folded paper containing any powdered drug *US*
• Like where to pick up a strip of benny or a paper of snow, or anything you want from the outside, if the price is right. — Thurston Scott, *Cure it with Honey*, p. 194, 1951
• Whenever a law needs money for a quick beer, he goes over by Lupita and waits for someone to walk out on the chance he may be holding a paper. — William Burroughs, *Junkie*, p. 101, 1953
• [A] little Negro girl roaming the shuffle restless street of winos, hoodlums, sams, cops, paper peddlers[.] — Jack Kerouac, *The Subterraneans*, p. 56, 1958
• — Angela Devlin, *Prison Patter*, p. 84, 1996

10 probation in lieu of a jail sentence; parole from prison *US*
• With his record, Chester didn't believe he'd get out on paper, but he didn't believe he'd get the same time that Willie got[.] — Donald Goines, *White Man's Justice, Black Man's Grief*, p. 127, 1973
• Marie had a habit of fucking with me late at night out in the streets because she knew I was on paper and couldn't stand to be picked up for cracking her head. — A.S. Jackson, *Gentleman Pimp*, p. 83, 1973
• — William K. Bentley and James M. Corbett, *Prison Slang*, p. 101, 1992

11 an underworld contract to have someone killed *US*
• Rick Masters has paper out on me. There's a price on my head so I asked to be put in protective custody. — Gerald Petievich, *To Live and Die in L.A.*, p. 151, 1983
• The point is, Parisi has paper on me and I'm dead, hon. — Gerald Petievich, *Shakedown*, p. 201, 1988

paper *verb*
▸ **paper the house**
to give away free tickets to an event in order to secure a large audience *UK, 1859*
• — Joe McKennon, *Circus Lingo*, p. 68, 1980
• Vince papered the house with the American servicemen, so the reaction is very much American. — *Herb's Wrestling Tidbits*, 21st May 1992
• We paper the house to assure against empty seats. The idea, keep a buzz going. — Elmore Leonard, *Be Cool*, p. 252, 1999

paper acid *noun*
LSD, especially on blotting paper *US, 1977*
- —Richard A. Spears, *The Slang and Jargon of Drugs and Drink*, p. 378, 1986
- —Mike Haskins, *Drugs*, p. 286, 2003

paper and plastic *noun*
in gambling, a combination of cash and betting chips *US*
A play on the grocery clerk's query to a customer – 'Paper or plastic bag?'.
- —John Vorhaus, *The Big Book of Poker Slang*, p. 28, 1996

paper asshole *noun*
an adhesive reinforcement attached to holes punched on a piece of paper to prevent the page from ripping out of a binder *US*
The object is shaped like a small life buoy, visually evocative to some of an anus. Collected from union negotiating committee members in northern California, September 2002.

paper bag *noun*
▸ **go pop like a paper bag**
(of a woman) to copulate vigorously *AUSTRALIA, 1984*

▸ **you couldn't fight your way out of a paper bag; you couldn't punch your way out of a paper bag**
addressed to (or, in the third person, used of) a person boasting of strength or fighting ability *AUSTRALIA, 1961*

paper bag; paper *verb*
to nag someone *UK*
Rhyming slang.
- I couldn't stand her papering me all night.—Ray Puxley, *Cockney Rabbit*, 1992

paperbag case *noun*
an ugly woman *US*
A suggestion that the paper bag be worn over her head.
- —*Complete CB Slang Dictionary*, p. 72, 1976
- —Peter Chippindale, *The British CB Book*, p. 157, 1981

paper blunt *noun*
a marijuana cigarette *UK*
- —Mike Haskins, *Drugs*, p. 288, 2003

paper boy *noun*
a drug dealer, especially a heroin dealer *US, 1970*
Because heroin is often sold in paper envelopes; punning on a newspaper delivery boy.
- —William D. Alsever, *Glossary for the Establishment and Other Uptight People*, p. 26, December 1970
- —US Department of Justice, *Street Terms*, October 1994
- —Robert Ashton, *This Is Heroin*, p. 210, 2002

papered *adjective*
used of a stadium or an auditorium filled by people given free tickets *US*
- —Bill Shefski, *Running Press Glossary of Football Language*, p. 76, 1978

paper grower *noun*
a recycling bin for paper *CANADA, 1980s*
- It was time to figure out how to collect the paper. I called the Ontario Minister of the Environment, to take them up on their offer of free equipment. Their "paper growers" are cardboard tubes the size of a two-litre ice cream tub.—Terry MacLeod, *In The Latest Morningside Papers*, p. 72, 1989

paper-hang *noun*
the passing of counterfeit money or forged securities *US*
- There's the blow-up bang and the paper-hang / Where some poor chump gets beat.—Dennis Wepman et al., *The Life*, p. 161, 1976

paper-hanger *noun*
1 a criminal whose expertise is the use of fraudulent securities *US*
- "You're not a paper hanger, and you're not a small fry pusher, and you're not even a booster."—Evan Hunter, *The Blackboard Jungle*, p. 160, 1954
- The distrust felt toward paperhangers, for instance, is based on the nature of these offenses and on firsthand experience with the men who commit them.—*Saturday Evening Post*, p. 72, 6th October 1962
- They grabbed a paper hanger in a bank. A broad. She's singing for a deal.—Gerald Petievich, *Money Men*, p. 140, 1981
- —Inez Cardozo-Freeman, *The Joint: Language and Culture in a Maximum Security Prison*, p. 519, 1984
- —Angela Devlin, *Prison Patter*, p. 85, 1996

2 in trucking, a police officer writing a ticket *US*
- —Wayne Floyd, *Jason's Authentic Dictionary of CB Slang*, p. 23, 1976

paper hat *noun*
a fool *UK*
Rhyming slang for **TWAT**.
- —Ray Puxley, *Fresh Rabbit*, 1998

paper mushrooms *noun*
LSD *UK*
LSD on blotting paper having the hallucinogenic properties of **MAGIC MUSHROOM(S)**.
- Street names [...] micro dot, paper mushrooms, penguins[.]—James Kay and Julian Cohen, *The Parents' Complete Guide to Young People and Drugs*, p. 141, 1998

paper-puncher *noun*
used as a jocular description of a handgun target shooter *US*
- —*American Speech*, p. 194, October 1957: 'Some colloquialisms of the handgunner'

paper-pusher *noun*
1 a bureaucrat; in the military, anyone with a desk job and not in combat *US*
- —Linda Reinberg, *In the Field*, p. 161, 1991

2 a person who places counterfeit money into circulation *US*
- He had learned to take the edge off the loneliness by working harder, meeting more paper pushers, pressing more strongly for the hundred-grand buys.—Gerald Petievich, *Money Men*, p. 9, 1981
- Hell, he had chased paper pushers and passers around the city for so long that few streets were unfamiliar to him.—Gerald Petievich, *The Quality of the Informant*, p. 16, 1985

papers *noun*
in prison, a person's background *US*
- A prospect's papers [background] had to be checked and approved by the group's leaders.—Bill Valentine, *Gangs and Their Tattoos*, p. 18, 2000

paper soldier *noun*
a rear-area military personnel who supported those in combat *US*
- —Gregory Clark, *Words of the Vietnam War*, p. 426, 1990

paper time *noun*
the additional years added to a prison sentence because of publicity surrounding the crime, criminal and/or trial *US*
- —Joseph E. Ragen and Charles Finston, *Inside the World's Toughest Prison*, p. 811, 1962: 'Penitentiary and underworld glossary'

paper top *noun*
a convertible car top *US*
- I was changing cars twice a year for seven years. A paper top in the summer and a hard top in the winter.—A.S. Jackson, *Gentleman Pimp*, p. 122, 1973

paperweight *noun*
1 in horse racing, a very small weight allowance in a weight-handicapped event *AUSTRALIA*
- —Ned Wallish, *The Truth Dictionary of Racing Slang*, p. 64, 1989

2 a railway office clerk *US*
- —Norman Carlisle, *The Modern Wonder Book of Trains and Railroading*, p. 266, 1946

paperwork *noun*
1 any alteration of playing cards as part of a cheating scheme *US*
- —Frank Garcia, *Marked Cards and Loaded Dice*, p. 263, 1962

2 a speeding ticket *US*
- —Lanie Dills, *The Official CB Slanguage Language Dictionary*, p. 52, 1976

3 money; currency notes *UK*
- WHERE'S MA FUCKIN' PAPERWORK? Koom shouts in my ear.—Nick Barlay, *Curvy Lovebox*, p. 151, 1997

papes *noun*
1 cigarette rolling papers *US*
- —Anna Scotti and Paul Young, *Buzzwords*, p. 139, 1997

2 money *US*
- —*Ebony Magazine*, p. 156, August 2000: 'How to talk to the new generation'

pappy *noun*
a father *UK, 1763*
A childish, rural ring.
- She were that teasing color of them half-chink gals that got white pappies.—Iceberg Slim (Robert Beck), *Trick Baby*, p. 50, 1969

pappy-mammy *noun*
a homosexual man *TRINIDAD AND TOBAGO, 1956*
- —Lise Winer, *Dictionary of the English/Creole of Trinidad & Tobago*, 2003

pappyshow *noun*
a fool, or someone who presents the appearance of a fool *TRINIDAD AND TOBAGO, 1940*
A corruption of 'puppet show'.
- —Lise Winer, *Dictionary of the English/Creole of Trinidad & Tobago*, 2003

paps *noun*
press photographers who specialise in the sensational and the celebrated *UK*
An abbreviation of **PAPARAZZI**.
- [W]hen suddenly the paps are all over me[.]—Ben Elton, *High Society*, p. 52, 2002

par *noun*
▸ **below par; under par**
less than average or less than projected *UK, 1767*
A term that migrated from conventional English into golf and then back into broader slang usage.
- I called him and told him Petey and I were under par.—Iceberg Slim (Robert Beck), *Death Wish*, p. 56, 1977

para *noun*
1 a *para*trooper *US*
- —Gregory Clark, *Words of the Vietnam War*, p. 391, 1990
- Without a doubt, the major at Sutton Coldfield was my very first breathing example of what we paras called a "crap-hat [non-jumper] Rupert [officer] wanker".—Ken Lukowiak, *Marijuana Time*, p. 12–13, 2000

2 paranoia, especially as a result of drug abuse *UK*
- Oh shit! When the para attacks it messes up my head.—Macfarlane, Macfarlane and Robson, *The User*, p. 39, 1996

para; parro *adjective*
1 paranoid *UK*
- I remember seeing a police car and getting para – walking a bit faster and then running.—Macfarlane, Macfarlane and Robson, *The User*, p. 75, 1996
- Roy used to play the music in motor up real loud, like fuckin' deafening, cos he was so fuckin' para about being bugged in the BM.—J.J. Connolly, *Know Your Enemy [britpulp]*, p. 150, 1999
- He'll never tell you nothing over the phone, mind you [...] Para to fuck he is.—Kevin Sampson, *Outlaws*, p. 4, 2001
- See, Jerry got dead para last month, likes, an fitted an infra-red camera up a tree[.]—Niall Griffiths, *Sheepshagger*, p. 167, 2001
- To get away from her an her parro whingin I go to the toilet[.]—Niall Griffiths, *Kelly + Victor*, p. 285, 2002

2 drunk *AUSTRALIA, 1988*
A shortening of **PARALYTIC**.

parachute *noun*
1 a combination of crack cocaine and phencyclidine, the recreational drug known as PCP or angel dust *UK, 1998*
- —Mike Haskins, *Drugs*, p. 293, 2003

2 heroin *UK*
From its effect of slowing down other drug highs.
- —Robert Ashton, *This Is Heroin*, p. 206, 2002
- —Mike Haskins, *Drugs*, p. 284, 2003

parade *noun*
in a striptease show, the dancer's fully clothed walk across the stage before beginning to strip *US*
- In succession as the Flash or entrance; the Parade or march across the stage, in full costume; the Tease or increasing removal of wearing apparel; and the climactic Strip or denuding down to the G-String[.] —*Saturay Review of Literature*, p. 28, 18th August 1945: 'Take 'em off!'

paradise *noun*
the highest gallery in a theatre *UK*
- —Wilfred Granville, *The Theatre Dictionary*, p. 141, 1952
- —Don Wilmeth, *'The Language of American Popular Entertainment'*, p. 195, 1981

paradise stroke *noun*
(generally plural) the final thrust before male orgasm *UK, 1984*
- — Beale, 1984

paradise white; paradise *noun*
cocaine *UK, 1998*
- —Nick Constable, *This is Cocaine*, p. 181, 2002
- —Mike Haskins, *Drugs*, p. 281, 2003

paraffin lamp; paraffin *noun*
a tramp, a homeless person; used as an insult for someone in need of a wash *UK*
Rhyming slang.
- [A] paraffin lamp, an elephant's trunk[.]—Ian Dury, *Blackmail Man*, 1977
- —Angela Devlin, *Prison Patter*, p. 85, 1996
- [F]eeling like a paraffin lamp waking up among the dustbins. —J.J. Connolly, *Layer Cake*, p. 205, 2000

paraffin oil; paraffin *noun*
style *UK: SCOTLAND*
Glasgow rhyming slang (a good rhyme in a local accent).
- Ye never see Wee Jack gaun oot [going out] withoot a bit a paraffin ile aboot him.—Michael Munro, *The Patter, Another Blast*, 1988
- Pit on the paraffin[.]—*The Guardian*, 29th April 2002

parakeet *noun*
a Puerto Rican *US*
- —Anthony Romeo, *The Language of Gangs*, p. 21, 4th December 1962
- —David Claerbaut, *Black Jargon in White America*, p. 74, 1972

parallel *adjective*
lying down *US*
Hawaiian youth usage.
- —Douglas Simonson, *Pidgin to da Max Hana Hou*, 1982

paralysis by analysis *noun*
inaction produced by over-thinking a situation *US*
- —Dick Squires, *The Other Racquet Sports*, p. 221, 1971: 'Glossary'

paralytic; paraletic *adjective*
very drunk; drunk and incapable *AUSTRALIA, 1891*
'Paraletic' is a phonetic misspelling noted by Sonya Plowman, *Great Kiwi Slang*, p.138, 2002.
- If you don't watch it, Monty, he said to himself, you'll be stone blind raving paralytic drunk.—Derek Bickerton, *Payroll*, p. 120, 1959
- —Randolph Stow, *The Merry-Go-Round in the Sea*, p. 245, 1965
- "[P]iss artists" are "boozy", "fluffy", "well-gone", "legless", "crocked", "wrecked", "paralytic", "rat-arsed", "shit-faced" and "arse-holed". —Peter Ackroyd, *London The Biography*, p. 359, 2000
- —*e-cyclopaedia*, 20th March 2002

parboiled *adjective*
drunk *US, 1960*
- —Ralph de Sola, *Crime Dictionary*, p. 111, 1982

parcel *noun*
a quantity of stolen goods being delivered to the receiver *UK*
A specialisation of the conventional sense.
- —*Now!*, 10th April 1981
- They were supposed to be watchng the Bakers round the clock, waiting for them to go "hands on" the pig parcel.—Garry Bushell, *The Face*, p. 75–76, 2001

pard *noun*
partner *US, 1850*
A definite Western flavour; a highly affected shortening of 'partner'.
- What the hell, pard, you finally gone completely crazy or something?—*Drugstore Cowboy*, 1988
- What's happening, pard?—*Airheads*, 1994
- "Well, you just watch your pard operate," Leeds said, signaling the bartender for another round.—Joseph Wambaugh, *Floaters*, p. 113, 1996
- Jerry Cornelius still felt a surge of affection for his little pard.—Michael Moorcock, *The Spender Inheritance*, 1998

pardner *noun*
used as a term of address, male-to-male *US, 1795*
Used with an intentional folksiness that harkens to cowboy films.
- "You're quite a fly fisherman, pardner," he added.—Chester Gould, *Dick Tracy Meets the Night Crawler*, p. 12, 1945

pardon me for living!; pardon me for breathing!
used as an elaborate mock apology offered in answer for a minor error or trivial criticism *UK, 1961*
- Cap leaned forward and sniffed. "You've been drinking," she said. "Well, pardon me for breathing," said Wendy. "Par- don me for eating and drinking and sleeping and waking and pissing and crapping and doing all the other things that real human beings do.—Reginald Hill, *The Wood Beyond*, p. 70,
- He made a fruitcake face at Lily and said, "Pardon me for living," then let the door shut behind him.—Frederick Barthelme, *Natural Selection*, p. 56, 1991

Paree; Gay Paree *noun*
Paris, France *UK, 1848*
From the French pronunciation.
- [Y]ou hear fellars talk about Times Square and Fifth Avenue, and Charing Cross and gay Paree. —Samuel Selvon, *The Lonely Londoners*, p. 104, 1956
- He's just come back from gay Paree. You should hear his continental yarns. —Barry Humphries, *Bazza Pulls It Off!*, 1971
- [T]he train now departing from Gay Paree to London Waterloo[.] —Andrew Nickolds, *Back to Basics*, p. 86, 1994

parental units *noun*
your parents *US*
- —Connie Eble (Editor), *UNC-CH Campus Slang*, p. 6, Spring 1982
- The parental units called while you were out. —*Cruel Intentions*, 1999

parish bull *noun*
a man with illegitimate children *BERMUDA*
- —Peter A. Smith and Fred M. Barritt, *Bermewjan Vurds*, 1985

park *verb*
1 to (temporarily) place something or someone in a position of some safety or convenience *UK, 1908*
Often extended – in worldwide variations – as an invitation or imperative: 'park your arse!'; 'park your carcass!'; 'park your fanny!'; 'park your frame!' and, the nautically inspired, 'park your stern!'.
- A whiff of the salmon from the skid parked on the sideboard beside the chronometer cases put spit in my mouth. —Robert S. Close, *Love Me Sailor*, p. 65, 1945
- If you're hungry, park yourself at one of the restaurants at the port. —*International Travel News*, May 2003

2 to stay at a place for a short time *AUSTRALIA*
- 'Where do we all park?' Jessie considered. 'For a fortnight we can all be one big happy family. Now, let's see Dexter, you can share with Ashleigh, I'll move in with Janie, my mother can have the spare room, and your other can have our bedroom.' —Willie Fennell, *Dexter Gets The Point*, p. 102, 1961

3 to engage in sexual foreplay in a parked car *US*
- —Collin Baker et al., *College Undergraduate Slang Study Conducted at Brown University*, p. 168, 1968
- —Helen Dahlskog (Editor), *A Dictionary of Contemporary and Colloquial Usage*, p. 16, 1972

4 to give *UK*
A shortening of obsolete **PARKER**.
- —Bruce Rodgers, *The Queens' Vernacular*, 1972

▸ **park a custard**
to vomit *UK*
Upper-class society usage.
- —Ann Barr and Peter York, *The Official Sloane Ranger Handbook*, p. 159, 1982

▸ **park a tiger; park the tiger**
to vomit *AUSTRALIA*
- I'd better stick near the rail in case I need to park the tiger. —Barry Humphries, *Bazza Pulls It Off*, 1971
- There is nothing worse or more inconsiderate than a girl who parks a tiger in your car just after you've got her nicely topped up and ready for action. — Barry Humphries, *The Traveller's Tool*, p. 55, 1985

▸ **park it**
(of a person) to sit down *AUSTRALIA*
- He slapped a fat thigh. 'Come on, park it here, honey.' —John Wynnum, *Tar Dust*, p. 31, 1962

▸ **park the ball**
in pool, to leave the cue ball roughly in the centre of the table after an opening break shot *US, 1992*
- —Mike Shamos, *The Illustrated Encyclopedia of Billiards*, p. 167, 1993

▸ **park your carcass**
(of a person) to sit down *AUSTRALIA, 1977*
- —Jim Ramsay, *Cop It Sweet!*, p. 68, 1977
- 'Park your carcass,' he said. 'Take the load.' —Shane Maloney, *Nice Try*, p. 100, 1998

▸ **where I'd like to park my bike**
said by a man of a woman considered as a sexual object *UK, 2003*
The wheel of a bicycle is held in a slot, which puns on vagina.

parked out *adjective*
in horse racing, said of horses forced to the outside on turns *US*
- —Igor Kushyshyn et al., *The Gambling Times Guide to Harness Racing*, p. 120, 1994

Parker *noun*
a chauffeur *UK*
The name of Lady Penelope's chauffeur in *Thunderbirds* (a cult television series of the early 1960s, relaunched in the 90s) adopted as a generic nickname.
- "Help yourself to drinks," says Parker through the intercom[.] — Martin King and Martin Knight, *The Naughty Nineties*, p. 22, 1999

parker *verb*
to pay; to give *UK, 1914*
From 'parleyaree', an early form of **POLARI**.
- [She] asked if she could parker the omi [man] a bevvy [drink]. —James Gardiner, *Who's a Pretty Boy Then?*, p. 123, 1997
- —Paul Baker, *Polari*, p. 185, 2002

Parkheid smiddy *noun*
the female breast *UK: SCOTLAND*
Glasgow rhyming slang for **DIDDY**, from the local pronunciation of Parkhead Smithy, a famous forge in Glasgow's East End.

parkie; parky *noun*
a park keeper *UK*
- We caused murder in Sevvy Park with the Palm House and the parkies and all that [...] And the parkies had uniforms. —Kevin Sampson, *Outlaws*, p. 147–148, 2001

parking lot *noun*
1 a traffic jam *US*
- — *Complete CB Slang Dictionary*, p. 72, 1976
- —Peter Chippindale, *The British CB Book*, p. 157, 1981

2 the vagina *US*
An obvious pun until you start to seek an appropriate vehicle for the penis.
- —Anthony Scaduto, *Mick Jagger*, 1974

▸ **in the parking lot**
in gambling, without further funds *US*
- —John Vorhaus, *The Big Book of Poker Slang*, p. 24, 1996

parking space *noun*
a grave *UK*
- I interred him at Hither Green in a parking space he'd booked seven years before. —John Milne, *Alive and Kicking*, p. 37–38, 1998

Park Lane No. 2's *noun*
marijuana from Cambodia, often pre-rolled into cigarettes *US, 1970*
The term was coined and popularised by US soldiers in Vietnam.
- —Ernest L. Abel, *A Marijuana Dictionary*, p. 78, 1982

parky *adjective*
of the weather, chilly, cold, very cold *UK, 1895*
- Maybe they're just trying to keep themselves warm. It's a bit parky. — *The Guardian*, 1st July 2002

parlare *noun*
▷ see: **POLARI**

parlay *noun*
crack cocaine *US*
- — US Department of Justice, *Street Terms*, October 1994

parlay *verb*
to socialise at clubs, bars or parties *US*
- — *Ebony Magazine*, p. 156, August 2000: 'How to Talk to the New Generation'

parloo *verb*
to masturbate *NORFOLK ISLAND*
- —Beryl Nobbs Palmer, *A Dictionary of Norfolk Words and Usages*, p. 33, 1992

parlor *noun*
a brakevan (caboose) *US*
- —Norman Carlisle, *The Modern Wonder Book of Trains and Railroading*, p. 266, 1946

parlor maid *noun*
a rear railway brakeman *US*
- —Norman Carlisle, *The Modern Wonder Book of Trains and Railroading*, p. 266, 1946

parlour pink *noun*
a wealthy person who espouses socialist views from the safety of luxury *US, 1920*
- Born in Minneapolis in 1888, like many other parlor pinks, fellow-travelers, Communists and convicted perjurers, he attended Harvard Law School. —Jack Lait and Lee Mortimer, *Washington Confidential*, p. 104, 1951

- That showed that dirty parlor pink. — Robert Gover, *One Hundred Dollar Misunderstanding*, p. 99, 1961
- Besides, no man, not even a parlor pink, liked a girl who carried things around in old cream bottles stuffed into paper bags. — Mary McCarthy, *The Group*, p. 215, 1963

parma violet *noun*

a variety of MDMA, the recreational drug best known as ecstasy *UK*

From the purple colour of the tablet and overall similarity to a sweet of the same name.

- — Gareth Thomas, *This Is Ecstasy*, p. 56, 2002

parnee; parnie; parny *noun*

1 rain; tears *UK, 1859*

Polari, originally Anglo-Indian, from 'parnee' (water).

- [T]he was more graft [hard work] than ever on muddy tobers [grounds] with everything heavy and slippery on account of the parnee. — Butch Reynolds, *Broken Hearted Clown*, p. 31, 1953
- — Paul Baker, *Polari*, p. 185, 2002

2 water *UK, 1859*

Current in English gypsy use, from Romany *pâni* (water).

- — Jimmy Stockin, *On The Cobbles*, p. 11, 2000

parnee *verb*

to rain *UK, 1859*

From the noun sense.

- That summer, he said, had been dreadful; it had parneed (rained) for weeks on end. — Butch Reynolds, *Broken Hearted Clown*, p. 30, 1953

parole dust *noun*

fog *US*

A term coined at the San Quentin state penitentiary just north of San Francisco, where fog invites escape attempts.

- — John R. Armore and Joseph D. Wolfe, *Dictionary of Desperation*, p. 43, 1976

Parra *noun*

in the Sydney region, a visting non-resident of a beachside area *AUSTRALIA*

Derogatory. Perhaps from *Parra*matta, a western suburb of Sydney.

- Dickheads are also known as Parras, Westies, nerds, Brizzoes, Reggie Rev-Heads, veggies and egg rolls. — Phil Jarratt, *Surfing Dictionary*, p. 16, 1985
- Every summer this place is swamped with bloody parras! — *www.abc.net.au/wordmap*, 2003

parro *adjective*

▷ see: PARA

Parry *nickname*

the Paremoremo maximum security prison *NEW ZEALAND, 1982*

- — Harry Orsman, *A Dictionary of Modern New Zealand Slang*, p. 97, 1999

parsley *noun*

1 marijuana *UK*

From the similarity of appearance between one **HERB** and another.

- — Angela Devlin, *Prison Patter*, p. 85, 1996
- — Mike Haskins, *Drugs*, p. 288, 2003

2 phencyclidine, the recreational drug known as PCP or angel dust *US*

Because one method of administration of the drug is to sprinkle it on parsley.

- — Ronald Linder, *PCP: The Devil's Dust*, p. 10, 1981

parsley bud *noun*

in British Columbia, a local variety of marijuana *CANADA*

- This one is really interesting, it's called Parsley Bud. It's going through a bit of stress right now, but all the leaves grow that way. — Brian Preston, *Pot Planet*, p. 6, 2002

part *adjective*

of mixed race *FIJI*

Recorded by Jan Tent in 1995.

partial *noun*

a partial fingerprint *US*

- They look around, find ten keys of base in the garage, actually in a Mercedes that happens to have my prints on the steering wheel and partials on the door handle. — Elmore Leonard, *Out of Sight*, p. 63, 1996

▸ **partial to**

having a fondness or liking for something *UK, 1696*

- I have long thought that the whipping boy of British politics could be partial to the odd whipping himself, but who would ever have suspected that he liked to talk dirty in bed? — *New Statesman*, 8th July 2002

Partick Thistle *noun*

1 a whistle *UK*

Rhyming slang, formed on the name of a Scottish football club; also serves as a verb.

- — Ray Puxley, *Cockney Rabbit*, 1992

2 a variety of MDMA, the recreational drug best known as ecstasy, identified by PT embossed on the tablet *UK*

Disguising PT with the name of a Scottish football team.

- — Gareth Thomas, *This Is Ecstasy*, p. 57, 2002

partied out *adjective*

exhausted from excessive party-going *US*

- Phil, you're partied out. — *Wayne's World*, 1992

partner *noun*

1 a very close associate who can be counted on in almost any situation *US*

- JULES: If Jimmie's ass ain't home, I don't know what the fuck we're gonna do. I ain't got any other partners in 818. — *Pulp Fiction*, 1994

2 any Audi car *UK*

Motor trade slang. A pun on 'Howdy, partner', reported by a car salesman, 4th August 2004.

partridge *noun*

a good-looking girl or woman *US*

- He ganders this partridge and goes right on the beam solid. — Haenigsen, *Jive's Like That*, 1947

parts *noun*

▸ **get parts**

to engage in sexual activity short of intercourse *US*

- After the movie, he started getting parts from her. — Connie Eble (Editor), *UNC-CH Campus Slang*, p. 3, March 1979

parts changer *noun*

in car repair, a mechanic who replaces parts until a problem is solved instead of diagnosing the problem at the outset *US*

- — John Edwards, *Auto Dictionary*, p. 122, 1993

part timer *noun*

a variety of MDMA, the recreational drug best known as ecstasy, identified by PT embossed on the tablet *UK*

- — Gareth Thomas, *This Is Ecstasy*, p. 57, 2002

party *noun*

1 a person *UK*

In conventional use from 1650 but considered to be slang since later C19. Not to be confused with a party to a legal action.

- The mouthpiece (a barrister) was a knowing old party who lived buried deep in the north-eastern suburbs[.] — Charles Raven, *Underworld Nights*, p. 133, 1956
- [M]e and Mort are waiting for a party by the name of Jeremy to turn up[.] — J.J. Connolly, *Layer Cake*, p. 2, 2000

2 a woman; a girlfriend *UK*

Royal Navy slang.

- — Nigel Foster, *The Making of a Royal Marine Commando*, 1987

3 sex, especially with a prostitute *US*

A prostitute euphemism.

- I couldn't hear the words, but they would come out to" "How about a little party, honey?" — *Rogue for Men*, p. 45, June 1956
- I'm accustomed to being accosted with "Wanna' have a party, Joe?" — *Screw*, p. 4, 24th November 1969
- She's gonna say French or half and half or party, and all these words been construed by the black robed pussies that sit on the bench to be words with sexual connotations. — Joseph Wambaugh, *The Choirboys*, p. 250, 1975
- She's sitting there very quietly for a couple of minutes, she goes, 'You want to have a party?' I ask her what kind of party. She goes, 'You know' – and looks around to see if anybody's watching – 'do it, man, have a good time. Me and you.' — Elmore Leonard, *Cat Chaser*, p. 139, 1982
- She explained how she'd turned tricks for years, sometimes getting as much as fifty dollars a party. — Kim Rich, *Johnny's Girl*, p. 100, 1993

party *verb*

1 to enjoy a good time *US, 1922*

From the conventional noun sense.

- I hadn't partied this hard since the state of Texas executed that retard guy. — Michael Moore, *Dude, Where's My Country?*, p. 86, 2003

2 to have sex, especially with a prostitute *US*

- Stick around till this mob clears, babe; I'll party you like you never been partied before. —John Rechy, *City of Night*, p. 355, 1963
- I partied with one girl, one and took home a dose. —Elmore Leonard, *Cat Chaser*, p. 25, 1982
- Me love you long time. You party? —*Full Metal Jacket*, 1987
- Several years ago, while I was on holiday with several girlfriends, tucked away at a seaside Florida bar, the hunky bartender poured us all vodka shots "on the house," and asked if we wanted to "party" after closing. "Define 'party,'" was my retort. —Nancy Tamosaitis, *net.sex*, p. 123, 1995

3 to use drugs *US*

- RICKY: Hey, do you party? LESTER: I'm sorry? RICKY: Do you get high. —*American Beauty*, 1999

par-ty!

used as an exhortation to relax and enjoy yourself *US*

The break between syllables is key.

- Hey guys, par-ty! —*Bull Durham*, 1988

party animal *noun*

a person dedicated to making merry and having a good time *US*

A creature born of the 1990s.

- I was more than game, since Bob's parents have a reputation as party animals. —Elissa Stein and Kevin Leslie, *Chunks*, p. 68, 1997
- "I am not a party animal, " I had told her once, defensively. "Nano," she had replied [...] "you're not even a party vegetable." —Rhiannon Paine, *Too Late for the Festival*, p. 32, 1999
- Girl Thing party animal Linzi's always the one to get the party vibe going[.] —*CD:UK*, p. 5, 2000

party central *noun*

an apartment or house where parties are frequently in progress *US*

- As usual, Golk Links was Party Central that day. —Ralph "Sonny" Barger, *Hell's Angel*, p. 107, 2000

party favors *noun*

drugs *US*

- —Pamela Munro, *U.C.L.A. Slang*, p. 64, 1989

party foul *noun*

a faux pas; a substantial breach of etiquette *US*

- —Connie Eble (Editor), *UNC-CH Campus Slang*, p. 4, Spring 1993
- —Ben Applebaum and Derrick Pittman, *Turd Ferguson & The Sausage Party*, p. 51, 2004

party girl *noun*

a prostitute *US*

- Whores are now "call girls," "party girls" or "company girls." Instead of visiting them, they come to see you. —Lee Mortimer, *Women Confidential*, p. 140, 1960
- —*Maledicta*, p. 150, Summer/Winter 1986–1987: 'Sexual Slang: prostitutes, pedophiles, flagellators, transvestites, and necrophiles'

party hat *noun*

1 the signal light(s) on the roof of a police car *US*

When the light is flashing the police are said to have a 'party hat on'.

- —*Complete CB Slang Dictionary*, p. 72, 1976
- —Peter Chippindale, *The British CB Book*, p. 157, 1981

2 a condom *US*

- —Pamela Munro, *U.C.L.A. Slang*, p. 65, 1989
- —David Rowan, *A Glossary for the 90s*, 1998

party hearty *verb*

to party in a diligent fashion *US*

- as everyone "partied hearty" at New York, New York. —*New York Amsterdam News*, p. 28, 28 July 1979
- Celebrity Party, starring Sandra Bernhard, party hearty, be a party animal!" —Sandra Bernhard, *Confessions of a Pretty Lady*, p. 119, 1988
- Alicante wasn't a great party hearty place. —Odie Hawkins, *The Life and Times of Chester Simmons*, p. 18, 1991
- Well, in spite of what you've heard, it is time to party! Party hearty! —*Wayne's World*, 1992

party lights *noun*

the coloured, flashing lights on top of a police car *US*

- When I see those party lights, I know the party's over for me. —*San Francisco Chronicle*, p. C4, 26th December 1992
- —Bill Valentine, *Gang Intelligence Manual*, p. 130, 1995
- Any police car that flips on its party lights and accelerates is leaped upon by these news choppers[.] —*Houston Press*, 13th May 1999

party line *noun*

the 'official version' that must be adhered to whether truthful or not *UK, 1937*

Originally (1834) a political party's policy; thence into much wider usage.

- [Quentin Crisp] was a patriot for himself–for the individual against the party line, for the Self against the wind, on the long and unsafe road. —*New York Observer*, 29th January 2001

party nap *noun*

a nap taken in anticipation of a night of drinking and partying *US*

- —Ben Applebaum and Derrick Pittman, *Turd Ferguson & The Sausage Party*, p. 9, 2004

party on!

used as an encouragement for revelry *US*

- And ... party on, dudes. —*Bill and Ted's Excellent Adventure*, 1989
- Until then, good night and party on. —*Wayne's World*, 1992

party pack *noun*

a packet of ten rolled marijuana cigarettes for sale in Vietnam during the war *US*

- —Gregory Clark, *Words of the Vietnam War*, p. 392, 1991

party piece *noun*

a woman who makes herself sexually available at Hell's Angels gatherings *UK*

A pun formed on **PIECE** (a woman as a sexual object).

- Women play a distinctly secondary role. They are accepted as wives, girlfriends, or "party pieces". —*The Observer*, 12th September 1982

party pooper; party poop *noun*

a killjoy; a spoilsport *US, 1954*

- —*Newsweek*, p. 28, 8 October 1951
- The bastard. Making me look the party-pooper. —Clancy Sigal, *Going Away*, p. 358, 1961
- [A]n aural document of what happened when the greatest party poopers since Charles Manson went into overdrive. —*Pogo A Go Go*, 1993

party powder *noun*

cocaine *UK*

- I've lost my nasal septum through excessive use of party powder. Does this make me trash? —*Trash*, p. 18, July 2003

party reptile *noun*

an enthusiastic party-goer *US*

- — Levi Straus & Company, *Campus Slang – "Hot," "Hip" and "Wicked"*, p. 2, January 1986

pash *noun*

1 a romanticised affection for someone; an infatuation *UK, 1914*

- I thought I was getting a silly schoolgirl hero-pash on him[.] —John Fowles, *The Collector*, p. 151, 1963

2 a fiancée; the woman you enjoy more than a casual relationship with; the primary girlfriend *US, 1960*

Royal Navy slang; an abbreviated form of 'passion'.

- —Nigel Foster, *The Making of a Royal Marine Commando*, 1987

3 a passionate kiss or kissing session, especially French kissing *AUSTRALIA*

- Get a load of that pash-session! Somebody's on a good wicket back there. —W.R. Bennett, *Target Turin*, p. 74, 1962
- Come on, baby, give your blue-eyed blond boy a pash. —Len Riley, *The Kings Cross Racket*, p. 114, 1967
- Got a pash in the bushes. —Phillip Gwynne, *Deadly Unna?*, p. 59, 1998

pash; pash off *verb*

to kiss someone passionately *AUSTRALIA*

- Wayne pashed me off and I got out of the car. —Kathy Lette and Gabrielle Carey, *Puberty Blues*, p. 104, 1979
- Oh don't worry, yer mother and I used to pash when we were kids. —Kylie Mole (Maryanne Fahey), *My Diary*, p. 5, 1988
- They both came as ghosts and ended up pashing off under a tangle of white sheets on the road in front of the house. —John Birmingham, *He Died With a Felafel in his Hand*, p. 198, 1994
- Their way took them past a small park, a large hospital and onto Oxford Street, where Earth boys stood in the doorways of pubs pashing off other Earth boys, and Earth girls knit their fingers together in lust. —Linda Jaivin, *Rock n Roll Babes from Outer Space*, p. 95, 1996

pashing *noun*

kissing and petting *AUSTRALIA*

- A System of Numbers (One to Fourteen) gives you the clew to the amount of pashing a vergin or near vergin permits and expects. —Dymphna Cusack, *Black Lightning*, p. 51, 1964

pash on *verb*

to spend time kissing and petting *AUSTRALIA*

- For entertainment, they packed the back seats of the Shire Hall each Saturday night to watch the flicks and 'pash on' as soon as the lights went out. —Kerry Cue, *Crooks, Chooks and Bloody Ratbags*, p. 71, 1983
- Xenia bounded up to tell them that Leith had pashed on with Mark Douglas for half an hour, then gone off somewhere with him. —Jenny Pausacker, *What are ya?*, p. 61, 1987

pashpie *noun*

an attractive boy or girl *US*

Teen slang.

- — *Newsweek*, p. 28, 8th October 1951

pash rash *noun*

sore lips or irritation of the area surrounding the mouth as a result of kissing *AUSTRALIA*

- Britney is breaking out in pash rash and there are tongues all over the shop. — *Weekend Australian*, p. 20, 9th November 2002
- [I]f you're one of those guys who gets major five-o'clock shadow, shave it off or don't kiss the girl. Nothing hits the spot pain-wise like pash rash does. If you'd like to experience the effect, then try rubbing your face with sandpaper. — *h2g2*, 2003

pashy *noun*

a passionate kiss *UK*

An elaboration of **PASH**.

- [S]he grabbed me and gave me a big pashy on the mouth, tongues and all. —Ken Lukowiak, *Marijuana Time*, p. 138, 2000

pashy *adjective*

passionate *US*

- —Vincent J. Monteleone, *Criminal Slang*, p. 172, 1949

pasray *verb*

(used of a woman) to sit without care to that which may be seen *TRINIDAD AND TOBAGO*

- —Lise Winer, *Dictionary of the English/Creole of Trinidad & Tobago*, 2003

pass *noun*

an amorous approach to someone; an introductory attempt at seduction *UK, 1928*

- Lloyd George made a pass at anything in a skirt while remaining a political giant. — *The Observer*, 30th December 2001

pass *verb*

to seek acceptance as white because of fair skin colouring *US, 1933*

- I heard of many a cat passin' for white, but this is the first time I ever heard of a white man passin' for colored, and in jail too. —Mezz Mezzrow, *Really the Blues*, p. 312, 1946
- There is no way of calculating how many light-skinned citizens can and do "pass." —Jack Lait and Lee Mortimer, *Washington Confidential*, p. 34, 1951
- The boy (she always spoke of him as a boy) would be able to "pass." After perhaps two hundred years of outrace-breeding, after eight generations, there would be a child of her blood who could pass for white. —Jim Thompson, *The Kill-Off*, p. 48, 1957
- "This Loam," he say, "is one nigga ain't passin' nohow let me tell you." —Richard Farina, *Long Time Coming and a Long Time Gone*, p. 3, 1969
- He told him it was a pity that Papa was so near white and yet so far with too much yellow in his complexion to pass. — *Mama Black Widow*, p. 107, 1969

▸ **pass change**

to bribe *TRINIDAD AND TOBAGO, 1989*

- —Lise Winer, *Dictionary of the English/Creole of Trinidad & Tobago*, 2003

▸ **pass the time of day**

to exchange greetings; to chat and gossip *UK, 1851*

- I enjoy living here, and know everyone on my street: we pass the time of day, talk about the weather, parking, local shopping, the small inane topics that bind a community together. — *New Statesman*, 30th July 2001

pass-by *noun*

a stranger *JAMAICA, 1958*

- —Peter Patrick, *Some Recent Jamaican Creole Words*, 2003

passenger *noun*

1 a member of any group who does not fully contribute and is 'carried' by the rest *UK, 1852*

Originally sporting.

- —John Ayto, *The Oxford Dictionary of Slang*, p. 293, 1998

2 a member of a prison clique *US*

Formed from **CAR** (a clique).

- —James Harris, *A Convict's Dictionary*, p. 36, 1989

passenger stiff *noun*

a railway passenger *US*

- —Ramon Adams, *The Language of the Railroader*, p. 113, 1977

passer *noun*

1 a person who places counterfeit money into circulation *US*

- He remembered searching the streets of Los Angeles years ago for a twenties passer with a star tattoo on the back of his right hand. —Gerald Petievich, *One-Shot Deal*, p. 226, 1981

2 a drug dealer *US*

- And I'll get Verger to bring some weed to your party. He's gotten an o.z. from a passer up on One Hundred and Twenty-fifth Street. —John Clellon Holmes, *Go*, p. 83, 1952

passers *noun*

dice that have been altered so as to roll a seven less often than normal *US*

- — *The Annals of the American Academy of Political and Social Sciences*, p. 129, May 1950

passion-killers *noun*

sensible knickers *UK, 1943*

Originally of military-issue knickers.

- Jean ignored the bra. It was functional. Fair enough. But the briefs she held aloft and proclaimed, "Passion killers." "They're tangas," Gillian said, defensively, proud of knowing the modern technical term for the cut-away pant. "They're brief briefs." —Nicola Barker, *G-String*, p. 70, 2000

passion mark *noun*

a bruise caused by extended sucking *US*

- —Andy Anonymous, *A Basic Guide to Campusology*, p. 14, 1966

passion pit *noun*

a drive-in cinema *US*

Teen slang.

- — *Newsweek*, p. 28, 8 October 1951
- The official name of an outdoor movie theater may be Starview, but the patrons will likely refer to it, because of the lovers attending, as the passion pit. — *American Speech*, p. 239, October 1957

passion wagon *noun*

a panel van or the like used for sexual encounters *AUSTRALIA, 1966*

- He had a car or, should I say, he had a passion-wagon. —Rex Hunt, *Tall Tales – and True*, p. 50, 1994

pass out *verb*

to lose consciousness *UK, 1915*

From an earlier sense 'to die'.

- "Will it be a bestseller?" "Not a chance," replied Bluey before passing out. — *The Guardian*, 20th October 2001

passover *noun*

a seizure *BARBADOS*

- —Frank A. Collymore, *Barbadian Dialect*, p. 82, 1965

passover party *noun*

a party where those who have been passed over for promotion drown their sorrows *US*

- — *Seattle Times*, p. A9, 12th April 1998: 'Grunts, squids not grunting from the same dictionary'

passport *noun*

standing permission from a youth gang to enter the territory which they consider their 'turf' *US*

- —David Claerbaut, *Black Jargon in White America*, p. 74, 1972

past *adjective*

▸ **past it**

because of your age or infirmity, to be no longer able to do that which you used to *UK, 1928*

Applied generally or to a specific inability.

- U know ur past it when u don't use U in ur emails. — *The Guardian*, 17th November 2001
- Are IT professionals past it at 40? — *Computer Weekly*, 7th November 2002

▸ past its sell-by date
no longer of interest; out of fashion *UK*
Adopted from product information on packaged goods.
- Now officially past its sell-by date as the preferred epithet — *GQ*, p. 140, July 2001

pasta *noun*
cocaine *US*
From 'paste', a step in the production process.
- — R.C. Garrett et al., *The Coke Book*, p. 200, 1984
- — Nick Constable, *This is Cocaine*, p. 182, 2002

pasta rocket *noun*
any Italian sports car *US*
Collected from a 19-year-old college student in Berkeley, California, July 2004.

paste *noun*
1 finely crafted fake gems *US*
- — Hyman E. Goldin et al., *Dictionary of American Underworld Lingo*, p. 153, 1950

2 the peanut butter in combat rations *US*
- — Linda Reinberg, *In the Field*, p. 162, 1991

3 crack cocaine *US*
From an intermediary step in the production of crack.
- — US Department of Justice, *Street Terms*, October 1994

paste *verb*
to thrash someone *UK, 1846*
- I felt like pasting him. — Mickey Spillane, *I, The Jury*, p. 91, 1947
- Keep your voice down, this lot'll paste you, just for the exercise. — *A Hard Day's Night*, 1964
- He would have liked to paste that rotten scumbag Emilio, yet in a funny way he liked him. — Richard Price, *The Wanderers*, p. 144, 1974
- So I pasted him. — Armistead Maupin, *Babycakes*, p. 27, 1984

pasteboard *noun*
in horse racing, a dry track in good condition *US*
- That horse is a dud on pasteboard, she's strictly a mudlark. — *San Francisco Chronicle*, p. 54, 21st April 1971

pastie *noun*
a fool; used as a friendly term of abuse *UK*
Possibly from the thick crust of a Cornish pastie. Heard in use among a group of male youths from the West Country on the 14th August 2004.

pasties *noun*
decorative coverings for a female dancer's nipples *US, 1961*
- The girls may wear "pasties" on their breasts, small adhesive ornaments covering their nipples shaped like stars, butterflies, snowflakes, and other poetic forms[.] — Michael Milner, *Sex on Celluloid*, p. 14, 1964
- The night before, Marion Conrad, a 25-year-old dancer in the show, got carried away and discarded her pasties. — *San Francisco Chronicle*, p. 1, 11th October 1964
- [B]ush-league sex compared to L.A.; pasties here – total naked public humping in L.A. — Hunter S. Thompson, *Fear and Loathing in Las Vegas*, p. 41, 1971
- What he won was permission for his female dancers to remove the pasties that, until now, they have worn on their breasts. — *San Francisco Examiner*, p. 3, 28th October 1973
- The strippers rippled their bellies and peeled to their pasties and G-strings. — Josh Alan Friedman, *Tales of Times Square*, p. 40, 1986
- In Atlanta, until the late 1970s, performers had to wear G-strings and pasties, coverings over the nipple. — Marilyn Suriani Futterman, *Dancing Naked in the Material World*, p. 125, 1992
- The 6–3 vote allows local or state governments to require that dancers wear at least pasties and a G-string so long as everyone else also is forbidden to appear naked in public. — *Washington Post*, 30th March 2000
- It's hard to believe Jackson's revealing finale was spontaneous, as under her breakaway leather bustier she was wearing what appeared to be a large sunburst pastie. — *Boston Globe*, p. F1, 3rd February 2004

pasting *noun*
a beating *UK, 1851*
Either physical or figurative.
- [A] couple of the Jefferson crew peeling off and giving the boys a pasting — John King, *Human Punk*, p. 106, 2000
- As ever, British share traders are slavishly following the trend on Wall Street, which took a pasting in the wake of the Greenspan announcement. — *The Guardian*, 21st March 2001
- They [London Labour MPs] are terrified of a pasting for the government at the local elections next May. — *New Statesman*, 15th October 2001

pasto *noun*
marijuana *US, 1980*
From Spanish *pasto* (pasture, grass), thus **GRASS** (marijuana).
- — Richard A. Spears, *The Slang and Jargon of Drugs and Drink*, p. 379, 1986
- — Mike Haskins, *Drugs*, p. 288, 2003

pastry cutter *noun*
a person who applies pressure with the teeth while performing oral sex on a man *UK*
- — Paul Baker, *Polari*, p. 185, 2002

pastry wagon *noun*
a truck owned by the Pacific Intermountain Express *US*
Back-formation from PIE, the company's initials.
- — Wayne Floyd, *Jason's Authentic Dictionary of CB Slang*, p. 24, 1976

pasture *noun*
a place where teenagers engage in various levels of sexual activity in parked cars at night *US*
- — *San Francisco Examiner*, p. III-2, 22 March 1960

▸ out to pasture
incarcerated *US*
- — William K. Bentley and James M. Corbett, *Prison Slang*, p. 28, 1992

Pat *noun*
▸ on your Pat
on your own *AUSTRALIA, 1908*
A shortening of **PAT MALONE**.
- 'Come far?' 'Caidmurra.' 'On your pat?' 'I had a mate, but he got himself pinched.' — D'Arcy Niland, *The Shiralee*, p. 122, 1955
- — Jim Ramsay, *Cop It Sweet!*, p. 65, 1977
- — Ned Wallish, *The Truth Dictionary of Racing Slang*, p. 81, 1989

Pat *nickname*
used as a nickname for an Irish man; also used in jokes which need a stereotypical Irishman as the butt *UK, 1806*
Pat, a diminutive of Patrick, is a stereotypically Irish name.

pat *verb*
▸ pat the pad
to go to bed *US*
- Q: What will you do until then? A: I'm gonna flake out. Q: What? A: Pat the pad, sack out, lay in the sun — Max Shulman, *Guided Tour of Campus Humor*, p. 106, 1955

pata *noun*
▷ see: PEATA

patacca *adjective*
used for describing inferior or fake jewellery, especially of a counterfeit Swiss watch *UK*
An Italian slang term, pronounced 'pataka', meaning 'worthless; rubbish'; used at the less-honest end of the jewellery trade, and amongst air stewards.
- — David Powis, *The Signs of Crime*, 1977

Pat and Mick *noun*
the penis *UK, 1961*
Rhyming slang for **PRICK**, formed from two stereotypical Irish names, often featured in jokes. As the butts of these jokes Pat and Mick are inevitably thick, a characteristic which may well pun here as an implied quality of girth.
- — Ray Puxley, *Fresh Rabbit*, 1998

Pat and Mick *adjective*
sick *UK*
Rhyming slang.
- — Bodmin Dark, *Dirty Cockney Rhyming Slang*, 2003

Pat and Mike *noun*
a bicycle *UK, 1931*
Rhyming slang for 'bike'.

Pat Cash *noun*
to urinate *UK, 1998*
Rhyming slang for **SLASH**, based on the name of Australian tennis player Pat Cash (b.1965).
- — *www.LondonSlang.com*, June 2002
- — Bodmin Dark, *Dirty Cockney Rhyming Slang*, 2003

patch *noun*

1 a district which is the responsibility of a specified police authority; a geographical area designated as the responsiblity of public servants, e.g. probation officers, social workers; an area of specialist reponsibility *UK*
Originally northern and midland police, by the mid-1960s it had become common to all public services.
- Look, Ripley, my patch is the city. I'm not like you – a country officer. Your area is wide open. —John Wainwright, *Death in a Sleeping City*, 1965
- — *The Official Encyclopaedia of New Scotland Yard*, 1999
- Putney station was my ground – we don't call it "manor" or "patch", as you may have heard thrown about on TV by screenwriters who haven't done their research properly. —Duncan MacLaughlin, *The Filth*, p. 58, 2002

2 the territory claimed by a prostitute, a drug dealer or a gang *UK*
- —Angela Devlin, *Prison Patter*, p. 86, 1996

3 a small community *US*
- —Amy and Denise McFadden, *CoalSpeak*, p. 10, 1997

4 the zone assigned to a military reconnaissance team *US*
- —Linda Reinberg, *In the Field*, p. 162, 1991

5 a small piece of material covering a striptease dancer's vulva *US*
- —Sherman Louis Sergel, *The Language of Show Biz*, p. 160, 1973
- A small piece is sometimes used underneath a G-string so that when a stripper works strong, she can remove the G-string and then be "in the patch." —Don Wilmeth, *The Language of American Popular Entertainment*, p. 197, 1981

6 a gang emblem sewn to the back of a member's jacket, signifying full membership in the gang *NEW ZEALAND*
- If a member of the gang lost his patch he has to try and get it back himself. — *Dominion*, p. 3, 17th August 1975

7 in computing, a temporary modification of code to repair an immediate problem *US*
- —Eric S. Raymond, *The New Hacker's Dictionary*, p. 275, 1991

8 in the circus or carnival, the person who adjusted legal problems *US*
- — *American Speech*, p. 308–309, December 1960
- —Joe McKennon, *Circus Lingo*, p. 68, 1980

9 an ad hoc payment to a police officer to allow a crime to take place *US*
- I think you're involved with the wrong people, vice or drugs ... some other street action. You were taking a 'patch' and you took too much. —Stephen J. Cannell, *The Tin Collectors*, p. 193, 2001

10 the proceeds of a crime, confiscated and kept by corrupt police in lieu of arrest *US*
- Instead of busting him, they took his supply as a patch or payoff and said good-bye. It was the beginning of a lot of patches for dope dealers after that. —Thomas Renner and Cecil Kirby, *Mafia Enforcer*, p. 75, 1987

▸ **not a patch on**
not in any way to be compared with *UK, 1860*
- Andre Previn's Carmina Burana is not a patch on his earlier EMI version with the LSO[.] — *The Guardian*, 21st February 2003

patched *adjective*
thirsty *US*
- — *Current Slang*, p. 10, Summer 1968

patches *noun*

1 a prison uniform issued to inmates who have been assessed as potential escapees *UK*
- [H]is denials did not stop his immediate ship-out "in patches" (blue-and-yellow escapee garb). — *The Guardian*, 17th August 2000

2 a prisoner considered likely to attempt an escape *UK*
From the yellow patches worn on the prisoner's jacket and trousers.
- —Angela Devlin, *Prison Patter*, p. 86, 1996

patch money *noun*
in a carnival, the money paid by concession operators to the 'patch' or 'fixer' for adjusting legal problems *US*
- —Gene Sorrows, *All About Carnivals*, p. 24, 1985: 'Terminology'

pate *noun*
a father *US*
Abbreviated from Latin *pater*.
- DAD immediately takes another drag with a wide grin. MOM: (SHAKING HER HEAD) You two... VERONICA: Great pate, but I'm going to have to motor if I want to be ready for the funeral tomorrow. — *Heathers*, 1988

patent *noun*
a multiple bet, gambling on three different horses in separate races in a total of seven bets *UK*
- A 1 patent casts 7, with double that each way. —John McCririck, *John McCririck's World of Betting*, p. 45, 1991
- —David Bennet, *Know Your Bets*, p. 78, 2001

pater *noun*
a father *UK, 1728*
A familiar use of Latin *pater* (a father), mainly as schoolboy slang, and often considered pretentious.

path *adjective*
pathology; pathological *UK, 1937*
Originally medical use now widely known, mainly in 'path lab' (a pathology laboratory).
- —Angela Devlin, *Prison Patter*, p. 86, 1996

pat hand *noun*
in blackjack, a hand with points totalling between 17 and 21 *US*
A 'pat hand' is a potentially winning hand.
- —Avery Cardoza, *Winning Casino Blackjack for the Non-Counter*, p. 74, 1991

pathetic *adjective*
ineffectual, contemptible *UK, 1937*
From the conventional sense (worthy of pity).
- It's self-indulgent! It's narcissistic! It's solipsistic! It's pathetic! I'm pathetic and I'm fat and pathetic! — *Adaptation*, 2003

pathy *noun*
a pathologist *UK*
- —Alan Hunter, *Gently by the Shore*, 1956

patico *noun*
crack cocaine *US*
Spanish slang used by English-speakers who would not know what the word means in Spanish.
- —US Department of Justice, *Street Terms*, October 1994

patient zero *noun*
the first person to transmit a disease *US*
Usually used in the context of AIDS.
- Dubbing Dugas "Patient Zero," researchers for the federal Centers for Disease Control retraced his sexual exploits as he traveled throughout North America[.] — *Associated Press*, 6th October 1987
- — *American Speech*, Summer 1989

Pat Malone *noun*
alone *AUSTRALIA, 1908*
Rhyming slang for 'on your own'.
- Personally, I thought he was a bit off his head, wanting to go back along that road on his Pat Malone[.] —Jon Cleary, *The Long Shadow*, p. 207, 1949

patoot *noun*
the vagina *US*
- Anyways, I get this knife an' some bread and I stuck the knife up her ol' patoot, got a nice gob of clam squirt, an' I spread it on the bread. —Richard Price, *The Wanderers*, p. 37, 1974

patootie *noun*
the arse *US*
- Dammit, if you're going to get a wild hair up your Mexican patootie every time I make a comment about something that's going on, I'm not even going to talk to you —Robert Campbell, *Juice*, p. 82, 1988

pat poke *noun*
the hip pocket *US*
Pickpocket usage.
- —Vincent J. Monteleone, *Criminal Slang*, p. 172, 1949

Pats *nickname*
the New England Patriots professional football team *US*
- It was nine points on the card and I took the Pats because I figure they'll at least stay that close —George V. Higgins, *The Friends of Eddie Doyle*, p. 18, 1971

patsy *noun*

1 a dupe; someone blamed for a crime or accident *US, 1903*
Perhaps the most famous maybe-patsy of the C20 was Lee Harvey Oswald, who told reporters shortly before being killed 'They're

taking me in because of the fact that I lived in the Soviet Union. I'm only a patsy'.

- Supposed somebody took you for a patsy. What would you do? —Mickey Spilane, *Kiss Me Deadly*, p. 26, 1952
- And you know who's the biggest patsy of all? Me – for letting myself get into this mess! —Max Shulman, *Rally Round the Flag, Boys!*, p. 142, 1957
- Come up with an answer and they take the credit... mess things up and you're the patsy. —Mickey Spillane, *Last Cop Out*, 1972
- We know they used you as a patsy, a fall guy —Edwin Torres, *Carlito's way*, 1975
- At least I still have my money and a designated patsy to take the rap for grand theft. —C.D. Payne, *Youth in Revolt*, 1993
- We needed Brent, Justice! He was our patsy! —Keslvin Smith, *Joy and Silent Bob Strike Back*, p. 47, 2001

2 in poker, a hand that requires no draw *US*
Conventionally known as a 'pat hand'.

- —George Percy, *The Language of Poker*, p. 65, 1988

3 a half-gallon jar filled with beer *NEW ZEALAND*
A fairly complicated rhyme: Patsy Riggir is a country music singer, and her last name evokes **RIGGER**, which is another term for a half-gallon jar of beer.

- —David McGill, *David McGill's Complete Kiwi Slang Dictionary*, p. 95, 1998

Patsy Cline; Patsy *noun*
a dose of cocaine prepared for inhaling *UK*
Rhyming slang for **LINE**, based on country and western singer Patsy Cline, 1932–63.

- —Angela Devlin, *Prison Patter*, p. 86, 1996

patsy mouth *noun*
a dryness of the mouth as a result of smoking marijuana or hashish *CANADA*

- —Steven Wishnia, *The Cannabis Companion*, p. 152, 2004

Patsy Palmer and her five daughters *noun*
the hand (seen in the context of male masturbation) *UK*
A variation of **MRS PALM AND HER FIVE LOVELY DAUGHTERS**, formed on the name of an actress who came to prominence playing Bianca in the BBC television soap opera *EastEnders* from 1994–99.

- —Chris Lewis, *The Dictionary of Playground Slang*, p. 166, 2003

patter *noun*
talk, speechifying *UK, 1778*

- He spoke casually, without the formulaic patter of the politician, without the bombast of the preacher. —Marcus Buckingham and Donald O. Clifton, *Now, Discover Your Strengths*, p. 35, 2001

Patty Hearst *noun*
a *first* class degree *UK*
Rhyming slang for 'first', formed from the name of the heiress, who was kidnapped by left-wing extremists, and involved in bank-robbery, before becoming a professional actress (b.1954).

- —Ray Puxley, *Fresh Rabbit*, 1998

Paul Anka *noun*
used as an all-purpose form of abuse *UK*
Rhyming slang for **WANKER**; formed from the name of the US singer (b.1941).

- You get some nasty little Paul Anka who's a bit short of the Duane Eddys[.] —Mervyn Stutter, *Getting Nowhere Fast*, 21st May 2004

Paul Weller *noun*
branded Belgian lager Stella Artois™ *UK*
Rhyming slang for 'Stella', based on the name of musician Paul Weller (b.1958).

- — *www.LondonSlang.com*, June 2002
- — *Antiquarian Book Review*, p. 18, June 2002

pause *verb*
▸ **pause for a cause**
to pull off the motorway to use a toilet *US*

- —Bill Davis, *Jawjacking*, p. 73, 1977

pav *noun*
a *pavlova* *AUSTRALIA, 1966*
A type of meringue desert topped with fruit, named after Russian ballerina Anna *Pavlova*.

- —Kathy Lette, *Girls' Night Out*, p. 213, 1987
- In order to stem the intake of kilojoules out go baked cheesecakes, cream cakes, gateaux, tortes, pavs, lamos – even a simple chocolate slice. — *Mercury*, p. 29, 2nd February 1989

Pavarotti *noun*
ten pounds, £10 *UK*
Punning **TENNER** on 'tenor'; formed on the name of great Italian tenor Luciano Pavarotti (b.1935).

- —Ray Puxley, *Fresh Rabbit*, p. 117, 1998

pavement *noun*
▸ **the pavement**
the streets, especially as an area of criminal operation *UK*

- [Y]ou might have to fit things up a bit to take them off the pavement. —Jake Arnott, *He Kills Coppers*, p. 15, 2001

pavement artist *noun*
a criminal specialising in street fraud *UK*

- [A] whole team of pavement artists doing the three-card trick on Tottenham Court Road. —Jake Arnott, *He Kills Coppers*, p. 17, 2001

pavement oyster *noun*
an expectoration of phlegm that has been deposited in the street *UK*

- We say the world's a pavement oyster... / So we're gonna hoist a Union Jack. —Viv Stanshall, *King Kripple*, 1981

pavement pizza *noun*
a splash of vomit *AUSTRALIA*

- A vision of Revor floated up into his consciousness and he felt a sudden urge to dial a pavement pizza. —Linda Jaivin, *Rock n Roll Babes from Outer Space*, p. 53, 1996

pavement-pounder *noun*
a prostitute who solicits customers on the street *US*

- The Mayfair pavement-pounders were the class of the crop. —Lee Mortimer, *Women Confidential*, p. 178, 1960

pavement princess *noun*
a prostitute, especially one who works at truck stops *US*

- The "pavement princess" is out there doing her "thing," also —Gwyneth A. "Dandalion" Seese, *Tijuana Bear in a Smoke 'Um Up Taxi*, p. 75, 1977
- Russell recognised some of the pavement princesses, whose pitch this normally was[.] —Greg Williams, *Diamond Geezers*, p. 203, 1997

pavement surfing *noun*
being thrown from a motorcyle *US*
Biker (motorcyle) usage.

pavilion *noun*
a brakevan (caboose) *US*

- —Ramon Adams, *The Language of the Railroader*, p. 113, 1977

paw *noun*
the hand *UK, 1605*

- He stuck out a skinny paw and me and I took it. —Mickey Spillane, *I, The Jury*, p. 45, 1947
- When nightclubbing, keep your paw off your lady friend's leg. There's a time and place for everything. —Jack Lait and Lee Mortimer, *New York Confidential*, p. 220, 1948
- Dynamite, baby, but get your paws out of my pocket. —Richard Farina, *Been Down So Long*, p. 119, 1966
- Hey, get your paws off the goods, pal. —Ian Pattison, *Rab C. Nesbitt*, 1988

pawn *noun*
▸ **got out of pawn; got out**
born *UK*

- "When was you got out of pawn?" Or an expectant father may be asked if his imminent happy event has been "got out" yet. —Ray Puxley, *Cockney Rabbit*, 1992

paws up *adjective*
dead *US*
New York police slang.

- There is always a lot of second-guessing following a job where the EDP and some of his hostages end up "paws up." —Samuel M. Katz, *Anytime Anywhere*, p. 336, 1997

pay *noun*
a debtor *US*

- He knew how to convince a slow pay to come up with what was owed. This one was different, a one-shot deal, but based on the same idea: scare the guy enough and he'll pay every time. —Elmore Leonard, *Killshot*, p. 50, 1989

pay *verb*
▸ **get paid**
to commit a successful robbery *US*

- —Carsten Stroud, *Close Pursuit*, p. 272, 1987
- — *Philadelphia Inquirer*, p. C3, 12th May 1991

▸ **pay black**
to pay a blackmailer's extortion *UK*
Combines conventional 'pay' with 'black' (blackmail).

▸ **pay crow tax**
to lose a farm animal by accidental death or disease *CANADA*
- [In Quebec's Eastern Townships] to lose your horse or cow by an accident or disease is "to pay crow tax," as years ago, dead animals were left for wild animals and crows to eat. — Lewis Poteet, *Talking Country*, p. 58, 1992

▸ **pay the grandstand**
in horse racing, to place a bet that will generate a huge earning *AUSTRALIA*
- — Ned Wallish, *The Truth Dictionary of Racing Slang*, p. 60, 1989

▸ **pay through the nose**
to pay a high (financial) price for something *UK, 1672*
- British taxpayers are being asked to pay through the nose for the privilege of a hellish ride[.] — *The Guardian*, 8th February 2002

▸ **pay your dues**
to persevere through hardship *US, 1956*
- He'd kicked his habit. He'd paid his dues. — James Baldwin, *Blues for Mister Charlie*, p. 123, 1964
- He [John Tower] spent twenty-eight years in Washington, but he never paid his dues. — Hunter S. Thompson, *Songs of the Doomed*, p. 268, 6th March 1989

pay and lay *noun*
used for describing the exchange of payment and services involved in prostitution *US*
- I heard Bessie running bath water and I couldn't help wondering if Railhead was just another pay and lay customer like the pullman porters. — Iceberg Slim (Robert Beck), *Mama Black Widow*, p. 166, 1969

pay ball *noun*
in pool, a shot that, if made, wins a wager *US*
- — Mike Shamos, *The Illustrated Encyclopedia of Billiards*, p. 168, 1993

pay dirt *noun*
money; success *UK, 1857*
- This, now, could be pay dirt. — Max Shulman, *Rally Round the Flag, Boys!*, p. 76, 1957

pay-for-play *noun*
sex that is paid for *US*
- Outside of the bar scene, most S&M scenes are pay-for-play affairs. — *Screw*, p. 8, 24th November 1969

pay hole *noun*
in trucking, a truck's highest gear *US*
- — Montie Tak, *Truck Talk*, p. 115, 1971

pay lawyer *noun*
a privately retained lawyer, as contrasted with one provided for indigents by the state *US*
- Where'd I see this blond bitch before, maybe thinking he was a pay lawer, because he was well groomed and looked like long money. — Richard Price, *Clockers*, p. 93, 1992

payola *noun*
1 an illegal payment to a radio station or individual to encourage the playing of a particular song *US, 1938*
The word leapt into the American vocabulary in late 1959 as pay-off scandal after pay-off scandal toppled the first generation of rock 'n' roll disc jockeys. Later broadened to include other forms of bribery.
- — Arnold Shaw, *Lingo of Tin-Pan Alley*, p. 16, 1950
- — *American Speech*, p. 104–116, May 1961: 'Payola'
- If she really liked the record she might hustle it with a little extra effort, but without ever getting hyper about it. Any payola arrangements, if they were made, were left to Artie. — Elmore Leonard, *Touch*, p. 22, 1977

2 reward money for anonymous police informants *UK*
- The names only went down on paper when I needed payola for them – a reward for services rendered which had to go through official channels. — Duncan MacLaughlin, *The Filth*, p. 116–117, 2002

3 oil *US*
- — Ken Weaver, *Texas Crude*, 1984

pay out on *verb*
to upbraid someone for a wrongdoing *AUSTRALIA, 1977*
Originally 'to get revenge; to mete out corporal punishment', from British dialect *pay* (to beat/thrash). Now only referring to verbal dressing down.
- — Jim Ramsay, *Cop It Sweet!*, p. 68, 1977
- — Ryan Aven-Bray, *Ridgey Didge Oz Jack Lang*, p. 40, 1983
- Once you get the lingo down, then you're cruising and you can pay out on everybody else. — *Dolly*, p. 70, July 1989

pay school *noun*
a school charging a tuition fee *US*
- Peanut was being cool and funny with Strike sitting there, but Peanut went to Catholic pay school, his mother was a working woman, and he was scared of her. — Richard Price, *Clockers*, p. 11, 1992

payware *noun*
commercially available computer software *US*
- — Eric S. Raymond, *The New Hacker's Dictionary*, p. 276, 1991

PB *nickname*
Pacific Beach, San Diego, California *US*
- The main street of Pacific Beach, or "P.B.," as the locals called it, fed right onto the pier, under a two-story arch that joined two whitewashed, tealshingled buildings belonging to the Crystal Pier Hotel. — Joseph Wambaugh, *Finnegan's Week*, p. 148, 1993

PB and J *noun*
a peanut butter and jelly (jam) sandwich *US*
A culinary staple of American youth for decades.
- — Connie Eble (Editor), *UNC-CH Campus Slang*, p. 5, Fall 1981
- PB & J with the crusts cut off. Well, Brian, this is a very nutritious lunch, all the food groups are represented. — *The Breakfast Club*, 1985

PC *noun*
1 a latex finger glove used during digital examinations *US*
A '*p*inkie *c*heater'.
- "Good Lord!" said Krankeit exasperated. "If you're going to poke your finger into that girl every three minutes you could at least put a p.c. on." — Terry Southern, *Candy*, p. 97, 1958
- The Language of Nursing — *American Speech*, p. 201, Fall-Winter 1973

2 probable cause to arrest someone *US*
- You're a known hijacker. You're sweating like a guilty motherfucker. That's my P.C. — *The Usual Suspects*, 1995

3 a percentage *US, 1956*
Applied to drug sales.
- — Terry Williams, *Crackhouse*, p. 150, 1992

PC *adjective*
*p*olitically *c*orrect *US, 1986*
Originally used of left-on-left criticism, appropriated and exploited by the right to marginalise any and all dissent from the left.
- — Connie Eble (Editor), *UNC-CH Campus Slang*, p. 7, Spring 1991
- I know not to dick with him when it comes to matters PC. — Armistead Maupin, *Maybe the Moon*, p. 163, 1992
- C'mon. Don't get all p.c. on me. — *Chasing Amy*, 1997
- I'm in the garden of our des-res [desirable residence], PC, five-bedroomed, [...] Right-On Crouch End house. — Stuart Browne, *Dangerous Parking*, p. 317–318, 2000
- I'd never have bet on you goin' all PC and self-righteous on us. — Christopher Brookmyre, *Boiling a Frog*, p. 121, 2000

PCH *nickname*
the Pacific Coast Highway, US route 1 in Los Angeles *US*
- So I dug the loaner out of the motel lot, found a pay phone on P.C.H. and gave old Cal a buzz. — James Ellroy, *Brown's Requiem*, p. 220, 1981
- — Trevor Cralle, *The Surfin'ary*, p. 86, 1991

PCOD *noun*
*p*ussy *c*ut-*o*ff *d*ate *US*
When soldiers were returned to the US from the war in Vietnam, they were tested for sexually transmitted diseases. To be sure that any problems were identified and cured before that test, most stopped having sexual relations before the end of their rotation to avoid any delay in returning home.
- — Linda Reinberg, *In the Field*, p. 164, 1991

P'cola *noun*
Pensacola, Florida, home to a naval air station known as the 'cradle of navy aviation' *US*
- He had tried the old "We who are about to ..." line and failed. The blonde had been around P'cola too long and had heard that bullshit too often. — Gerry Carroll, *North S*A*R*, p. 40, 1991

PCP *noun*
phencyclidine, the recreational drug known as PCP or angel dust *US, 1969*
- — Richard A. Spears, *The Slang and Jargon of Drugs and Drink*, p. 380, 1986

- He was often high on PCP, or happy stick, a potent hallucinogen that could cause disorientation[.] — Alex Kotlowitz, *There Are No Children Here*, p. 232, 1991
- She takes PCP and jumps out the school window, falls two stories, gets up, runs around, dies. — Dave Eggers, *A Heartbreaking Work of Staggering Genius*, p. 250, 2001
- [Paul] Greengard's team treated mice with either amphetamine, LSD or PCP – also known as angel dust. — *The Guardian*, 27th November 2003

PC Plod *noun*

▷ see: PLOD

PD *adjective*

pretty *d*isgusting *UK*

- — Angela Devlin, *Prison Patter*, p. 86, 1996

PDA *noun*

a *p*ublic *d*isplay of *a*ffection *US*

- — *Current Slang*, p. 5, Spring 1968
- — Helen Dahlskog (Editor), *A Dictionary of Contemporary and Colloquial Usage*, p. 43, 1972

P-dogs *noun*

cocaine *UK*

- — Mike Haskins, *Drugs*, p. 281, 2003

P-dope *noun*

relatively (20 – 30%) pure heroin *US*

- — Jim Crotty, *How to Talk American*, p. 95, 1997
- — Robert Ashton, *This Is Heroin*, p. 210, 2002
- — Mike Haskins, *Drugs*, p. 284, 2003

PDQ

*p*retty *d*amn *q*uick *UK, 1875*

- — Helen Dahlskog (Editor), *A Dictionary of Contemporary and Colloquial Usage*, p. 43, 1972
- — Lisa Anne Auerbach, *Retrohell*, p. 249, 1997

p'd up *adjective*

paranoid *UK*

- He's keeping this one extra close to his chest, Ged is, to be fair. Even by his own p'd up standards he's telling us fuck all. — Kevin Sampson, *Outlaws*, p. 227, 2001

pea *noun*

1 in Keno, a small ball with a number between one and 80 painted on it, drawn to establish winning numbers *US*

- — Thomas L. Clark, *The Dictionary of Gambling and Gaming*, p. 152, 1987

2 in pool, a small tally ball used as a scoring device *US*

- — Mike Shamos, *The Illustrated Encyclopedia of Billiards*, p. 168, 1993

3 a bullet *US*

- [B]ecause if they dared do anything else they'd been warned they'd get a couple of peas each in their heads[.] — Robert Campbell, *Juice*, p. 287, 1988

4 a person expected to win; in racing, a favourite *AUSTRALIA, 1911*

- The best his 'pea' could do was finish a modest second. — James Holledge, *The Great Australian Gamble*, p. 36, 1966
- He's had his eye on her for some time, you know, but I'm the pea, she said. — Alexander Buzo, *Rooted*, p. 92, 1969
- — Jim Ramsay, *Cop It Sweet!*, p. 68, 1977
- — Ryan Aven-Bray, *Ridgey Didge Oz Jack Lang*, p. 39, 1983

pea-brain *noun*

a person lacking common sense, intelligence or both *US, 1950*

- Their opinion of this character happily coincided with ours – that he was a pea-brain who needed a lesson in manners[.] — Jim Thompson, *Bad Boy*, p. 345, 1953

pea-brained *adjective*

1 very stupid *UK, 1950*

- [I]nspired by the pea-brained rantings of George Bush and his Bible-bashing cronies[.] — *The Guardian*, 25th July 2003

2 under the influence of LSD *US, 1982*

- — Richard A. Spears, *The Slang and Jargon of Drugs and Drink*, p. 381, 1986
- — Mike Haskins, *Drugs*, p. 286, 2003

peace

goodbye *US*

Dave Garroway, host of the morning television news programme *The Today Show* from 1952 to 61, closed each programme raising one hand and saying the single word 'Peace'. In 1988, comedy host Aresenio Hall, whose programme ran until 1993, began to use the same sign-off, at times embellishing it with 'Peace, and think number one'.

- — Connie Eble (Editor), *UNC-CH Campus Slang*, p. 7, Spring 1991

peace and quiet *noun*

1 solitary confinement in prison *US*

- — Ralph de Sola, *Crime Dictionary*, p. 112, 1982

2 a diet *UK*

Rhyming slang.

- — Ray Puxley, *Cockney Rabbit*, 1992

peacemaker *nickname*

the MX missile *US, 1982*

Originally applied to the Colt .45 revolver, which made peace by death. Applied by US President Reagan and his administration in 1982 to the missile that carries thermonuclear warheads, apparently unaware of the irony of the term.

peacenik *noun*

a person who is opposed to war or a war *US*

- I am a peacenik, but the endeavors of the many peacenik organizations with which I am associated look more and more like prayer wheels whirling in front of a bursting dam. — *Bulletin of the Atomic Scientists*, p. 21 – 22, September 1963
- [A]nd toughs out after peaceniks to beat up[.] — Nicholas Von Hoffman, *We Are The People Our Parents Warned Us Against*, p. 53, 1967
- He probably thought I was a peacenik intellectual disloyal commie, but if so I was a peacenik intellectual disloyal commie with two dollars for him, and that's what counts. — James Simon Kunen, *The Strawberry Statement*, p. 92, 1968
- You're an ageing hippie peacenik, scarred by Vietnam, and fuelled by a hatred of America. — Richard Neville writing in 'The Australian', 1990, *Out Of My Mind*, p. 94, 1996
- [T]hese are no ordinary loved-up peaceniks! — James Hawes, *White Powder, Green Light*, p. 13, 2002

peace 'n' love *adjective*

in the style of 1960s counterculture *UK*

The twin aims of the counterculture packaged as a marketing slogan; often derogatory.

- A plethora of hustlers oozed form the woodwork promoting every imaginable fly-by-night scheme involving hippy-trippy, peace 'n' love garbage. — Mick Farren, *Give the Anarchist a Cigarette*, p. 124, 2001

peace out

used as a farewell *US*

- — Connie Eble (Editor), *UNC-CH Campus Slang*, p. 7, Spring 1992
- — Julian Johnson, *Urban Survival*, p. 258, 2003

peace pill *noun*

a combination of the hallucinogen LSD and the stimulant methedrine *US*

- — Eugene Landy, *The Underground Dictionary*, p. 146, 1971

PeaCe Pill; peace *noun*

phencyclidine, the recreational drug known as PCP or angel dust *US*

A rather clumsy back-formation from the initials.

- — *Drummer*, p. 77, 1977
- — Ronald Linder, *PCP*, p. 10, 1981

peace tab *noun*

a tablete of psilocybin, a mushroom-based hallucinogen *US*

- — Eugene Landy, *The Underground Dictionary*, p. 147, 1971

peace tablet *noun*

a tablet (of any description) with a drop of LSD on it *US, 1982*

- — Richard A. Spears, *The Slang and Jargon of Drugs and Drink*, p. 381, 1986
- — Mike Haskins, *Drugs*, p. 286, 2003

peaceweed *noun*

phencyclidine, the recreational drug known as PCP or angel dust *US*

- — Ronald Linder, *PCP: The Devil's Dust*, p. 10, 1981

peach *noun*

1 an excellent person or thing *UK, 1863*

- Look, Charlotte, you've been a peach and I really mean that. — Darryl Ponicsan, *The Last Detail*, p. 106, 1970
- Just like in boxing – the perfectly timed peach is worth any flurry of punches. — Dave Courtney, *Dodgy Dave's Little Black Book*, p. 95, 2001
- Alan stayed with me at the bar, told me what a peach my Debbie was[.] — Danny King, *The Bank Robber Diaries*, p. 29, 2002

2 a sexually attractive person, usually a woman *UK, 1754*

- This is Fleur. You heard me talk about her, right? Ain't she a peach, boyo? — Joel Rose, *Kill Kill Faster Faster*, p. 37, 1997

3 the vagina *US*

- —Pamela Munro, *U.C.L.A. Slang*, p. 95, 1997

4 a tablet of amphetamine sulphate (trade name Benzedrine™), a central nervous system stimulant *US*

- —John B. Williams, *Narcotics and Hallucinogenics*, p. 115, 1967
- —*Current Slang*, p. 37, Fall 1968
- —Mike Haskins, *Drugs*, p. 279, 2003

peach *verb*

to inform against or on someone *UK*

In conventional use from C16 to mid-C19, thereafter considered slang or colloquial.

- [I]t probably would have become clear to the Klan that someone in the Klan was peaching.—Steve Fayer and Henry Hampton, *Voices of Freedom*, p. 80, 1991

peach picker *noun*

a cabover truck that is built high off the ground *US*

- —Montie Tak, *Truck Talk*, p. 116, 1971

peachy *adjective*

good, pleasing, attractive *UK, 1926*

If used at all, used with irony.

- Some people can be content / Playing Bingo and paying rent / That's peachy for some people.—Stephen Sondheim, *Some People*, 1960
- "Just peachy-keen, Harry baby," said Ira. "Just tickety-boo."—Max Shulman, *Anyone Got a Match?*, p. 19, 1964
- Next thing you know he'll find you keen and peachy, you know? —*Annie Hall*, 1977

peachy-keen *adjective*

excellent *US, 1960*

- [E]verything was going to be peachy keen down here in Dixie[.] —Sandra Brown, *Breath of Scandal*, p. 289, 1991

peacocky *adjective*

used of a racehorse, high-headed *US*

- —Tom Ainslie, *Ainslie's Complete Guide to Thoroughbred Racing*, p. 335, 1976

pea-eye *noun*

an English-speaking person from Canada's Maritime Provinces *US*

From, if awkwardly, 'Prince Edward Island'.

- —John Gould, *Maine Lingo*, p. 43, 1975

peak *verb*

1 to become highly excited; to thrill *AUSTRALIA*

- When I got there everyone was peaking[.]—*Tracks*, p. 49, October 1985
- —Kathy Lette, *Girls' Night Out*, p. 99, 1987

2 (of a wave) to reach its highest point before breaking *AUSTRALIA*

- Sitting on the inside, I could see a set peaking.—Kathy Lette, *Girls' Night Out*, p. 190, 1987

peaker plant *noun*

a power-generating facility that is brought online only during periods of peak demand *US, 2000s*

- To calculate avoided costs through 1996, the PSC staff used the "PROMOD III" computer model with an avoided peaker plant costing $1,800/kw[.]—*Electric Utility Week*, p. 11, 27th January 1986

peak freak *noun*

a casino blackjack gambler who consistently tries to see the dealer's down card *US*

- —Ken Uston, *Million Dollar Blackjack*, p. 320, 1981
- —Michael Dalton, *Blackjack*, p. 67, 1991

peaky *adjective*

feeling unwell, or appearing sickly *UK, 1821*

- Have you got the collywobbles or something? You feeling a bit peaky?—Peter Cook, *Not Only But Also*, 1970
- "You're looking a bit peaky," replied Father Collins, trying to get a glimpse of her underwear. "Are you sure you're not on drugs?"—*The Guardian*, 1st December 2003

peanut *noun*

1 the penis *UK, 2001*

An unusually modest pet name; similar to the derogatory joke-description 'hung like a cashew'.

2 a transvestite *UK*

From northern England, likely to derive from the sense as 'a small penis'.

- He had nothing to do with drag. He had nothing to do with peanuts. I was a peanut. Or was a peanut a transvestite who was not a homosexual?—Geoff Brown, *I Want What I Want*, p. 211, 1966

3 a capsule of a barbiturate or other sedative *US*

- —John B. Williams, *Narcotics and Hallucinogenics*, p. 115, 1967

peanut butter *noun*

low quality, impure amphetamine *US*

- —Geoffrey Froner, *Digging for Diamonds*, p. 47, 1989

peanut gallery *noun*

the least expensive seats in a theatre; more abstractly, an audience *US, 1888*

- Again the peanut gallery responded with nods.—Joseph Nazel, *Black Cop*, p. 96, 1974

peanut grifter *noun*

a small-time swindler *US*

- You're a piker, Marlowe. You're a peanut grifter. You're so little it takes a magnifying glass to see you.—Raymond Chandler, *The Long Goodbye*, p. 64, 1953

peanut heaven *noun*

the uppermost gallery in a theatre or arena *US*

- It was fifteen minutes from the time Siki left his roost in Peanut Heaven, where for two hours his noisy Harlem admirers had been calling the crowd's attention to him, before he reached the ring. —James Fair, *Give Him to the Angels*, p. 89, 1946

peanut poker *noun*

poker played for very small stakes *US*

- —George Percy, *The Language of Poker*, p. 65, 1988

peanuts *noun*

a very small sum of money *US, 1934*

- I'd worked for those people for peanuts, and I'd have stolen from myself quicker than I would have from them.—Jim Thompson, *Savage Night*, p. 121, 1953
- Unlike the big-con operator, whose elaborate scene-setting may involve as much as a hundred thousand dollars, the short-con grifter can run on peanuts.—Jim Thompson, *The Grifers*, p. 22, 1963
- Real estate was going for peanuts in those days. That's the only way to describe it. Peanuts.—Edward Lin, *Big Julie of Vegas*, p. 68, 1974
- "Mom says $800 a month. Can you handle that, Nick?" "Peanuts, Frank."—C.D. Payne, *Youth in Revolt*, p. 466, 1993
- [I]t pays relative peanuts.—*Radio Times*, p. 34, 30th March 2002

peanuts and donkey farts *noun*

in poker, three two's *US*

Collected from William E. Rippe by Peter Tamony in March 1948.

peanut smuggler *noun*

a woman whose nipples, especially when erect, are apparent through her clothing *AUSTRALIA*

- —Chris Lewis, *The Dictionary of Playground Slang*, p. 168, 2003

peanut wagon *noun*

in trucking, a small tractor pulling a large trailer *US*

- —Mary Elting, *Trucks at Work*, 1946

pea-picker *noun*

a gambler who only bets very small sums *UK, 1984*

A pun on 'p' (pence).

pea, pie, and pud *noun*

a meal consisting of a meat pie, peas and mashed potatoes *NEW ZEALAND*

- —Louis S. Leland, *A Personal Kiwi-Yankee Dictionary*, p. 75, 1984

pea pod *noun*

▸ **on your pea pod**

alone *UK: SCOTLAND*

Glasgow rhyming slang on Cockney rhyming slang 'on your tod' (**TOD SLOAN**).

- Ah wis on ma pea pod aw night.—Michael Munro, *The Original Patter*, 1985

pearl *noun*

1 an ampoule of amyl nitrite *US*

- —Eugene Landy, *The Underground Dictionary*, p. 147, 1971

2 cocaine *US*

- —R.C. Garrett et al., *The Coke Book*, p. 200, 1984
- —Nick Constable, *This is Cocaine*, p. 181, 2002

pearl *verb*

▹ **see: PURL**

pearl dive *noun*
when surfing, an occasion when you are forced deep under the water by a wave *US*
- [O]n Malibu Mac's how to get out of a "boneyard" when you're caught in the middle of a set of breakers – and on Scooterboy Miller's hot rod I learned how to avoid a pearl dive. — Frederick Kohner, *Gidget*, p. a, 1957

pearl dive *verb*
to perform oral sex on a woman *US*
From the metaphor of the clitoris as a pearl.
- One orally ambidextrous boyfriend specialized in pearl diving. — Anka Radakovich, *The Wild Girls Club*, p. 130, 1994

pearl-diver *noun*
1 a dishwasher in a restaurant *US, 1913*
- Ed Dunkel said he was an old pearldiver from way back and pitched his long arms into the dishes. — Jack Kerouac, *On the Road*, p. 117, 1957
- Blacks were beaten and killed for jobs like porter, bellboy, stoker, pearl diver, and bootblack. — George Jackson, *Soledad Brother*, p. 243, April 1970
- Bobo also took pride in speaking a lil' Spanish (I think he picked it up from a Mexican busboy, during a three day sentence as a pearldiver). — Odie Hawkins, *Men Friends*, p. 12, 1989

2 a five-pound note; the sum of £5 *UK: SCOTLAND, 1985*
- Ah fun [found] a pearl diver down the settee. — Michael Munro, *The Complete Patter*, 1996

peal diving *noun*
oral sex *US*
- — Vincent J. Monteleone, *Criminal Slang*, p. 173, 1949

pearler *noun*
something exceptional *AUSTRALIA, 1941*
Variant of **PURLER**.
- More to the point think of how many pearlers go unridden spinning their empty way toward scattered shores. — *Tracks*, p. 97, October 1992

Pearl Harbour *adjective*
of weather, cold *UK*
From the Japanese air attack on Pearl Harbour, 7th December 1941; punning **NIP** (Japanese) and the conventional phrase 'a nasty nip in the air' (cold weather). This term seems to have emerged following the 2001 release of the film *Pearl Harbor*.
- — *www.LondonSlang.com*, June 2002
- It's a bit Pearl Harbour out here! — unknown source quoted in private correspondence, 13th March 2002

pearlies *noun*
1 the teeth *UK, 1914*
A shortened form of **PEARLY WHITES**. Also variant 'pearls'.
- I see beginnings of bad congestion at the corners of her pearlies which would lead to decay[.] — Jack Kerouac, *The Subterraneans*, p. 69, 1958
- Since the bathroom was down the hall, Taggarty (now clothed provocatively in pale green babydolls) stood guard outside the door as Vijay and I leaned over the grungy sinks and brushed our pearlies. — C.D. Payne, *Youth in Revolt*, p. 193, 1993
- — Paul Baker, *Polari*, p. 186, 2002

2 a chronic shaking of the bowing arm suffered by violinists *UK, 1974*
- — John Ayto, *The Oxford Dictionary of Slang*, p. 266, 1998

pearl necklace *noun*
semen ejaculated on a woman's throat and breasts, especially after penis–breast contact *US*
- — Brigid Mconville and John Shearlaw, *The Slanguage of Sex*, p. 151, 1984
- Sex Glossary — J.R. Schwartz, *The Official Guide to the Best Cat Houses in Nevada*, p. 165, 1993
- In the indoor sex trade, too, such safer sexual activities as massage, hand release, pearl necklace, and fantasy stimulation are common. — Wendy Chapkis, *Live Sex Acts*, p. 170, 1997
- Pearl necklace: stick you penis between her breasts and go to town (use plenty of lube). — Jamie Goddard, *Lesbian Sex Secrets for Men*, p. 46, 2000
- But she said she was familiar with the pearl necklace and agreed that in porn, women seemed to enjoy the facials. — *New York Observer*, p. 2, 26th January 2004

pearl of a great price *noun*
in horse racing, a pure-bred Arabian racehorse *AUSTRALIA*
- — Ned Wallish, *The Truth Dictionary of Racing Slang*, p. 61, 1989

pearly gate *noun*
a plate *UK*
Rhyming slang.
- — Ray Puxley, *Cockney Rabbit*, 1992

pearly gates *noun*
1 LSD *US, 1971*
- — Richard A. Spears, *The Slang and Jargon of Drugs and Drink*, p. 381, 1986
- — Mike Haskins, *Drugs*, p. 286, 2003

2 morning glory seeds, rumoured to have hallucinogenic powers *US*
- — Eugene Landy, *The Underground Dictionary*, p. 147, 1971

Pearly Girl *noun*
in British Columbia, a local variety of marijuana *CANADA*
- [R]ichly resinous strains like B. C. Kush, White Rhino and Pearly Girl[.] — Brian Preston, *Pot Planet*, p. 2, 2002

pearly king; pearly *noun*
the anus *UK*
Rhyming slang for **RING**, formed on a traditional, well-decorated Cockney character.
- Poke it up your pearly! — Ray Puxley, *Cockney Rabbit*, 1992

pearly whites *noun*
the teeth *US, 1935*
- Nothing's sexier than a mouthful of pearly whites. — *Something About Mary*, 1998

pear-shaped *adjective*
no longer perfect; describing anything that is now wrong *UK*
- Pear-shaped. Now officially past its sell-by date as the preferred epithet for that which has gone wrong. Try "Pete Tong". — *GQ*, p. 140, July 2001

peas and rice boonggy *noun*
large buttocks *BAHAMAS*
- — Patricia Clinton-Meicholas, *More Talkin' Bahamian*, p. 22, 1995

peasant *noun*
1 a person below your station *UK, 1943*
Originally British military slang.
- — Anon., *The Gay Girl's Guide*, p. 13, 1949

2 in circus and carnival usage, a customer who does not show proper appreciation for a performance *US*
- — Don Wilmeth, *The Language of American Popular Entertainment*, p. 197, 1981

peasants *noun*
▸ **the peasants are revolting**
a catchphrase that is applied to a general swell of grumbling, used by more senior officers of junior ranks in the military, of a workforce as distinct from management, of students in relation to their educators, etc *UK, 1984*
A tireless pun on 'revolting'.
- "The peasants are revolting: come at once" was the instruction from the National Theatre, where the large cast rehearsing Tom Stoppard's new trilogy about 19th-century Russia had dragooned director Trevor Nunn into giving them an extended lunch break to watch England play Argentina in the World Cup. — *The Guardian*, 22nd June 2002

pease pudding hot; pease pudding *noun*
nasal mucus *UK*
Rhyming slang for **SNOT**, formed on a traditional rhyme: 'Pease pudding hot / Pease pudding cold / Pease pudding in the pot / Nine days old'. This is *not* a pun on the colour of peas – pease pudding is a golden-hued dish, made from yellow split-peas.
- I need a clean hanky, this one's full of pease pudding. — Ray Puxley, *Cockney Rabbit*, 1992

peashooter *noun*
1 a small-calibre handgun *US*
- — Hyman E. Goldin et al., *Dictionary of American Underworld Lingo*, p. 154, 1950
- We were carrying those peashooters like you got. — Joseph Wambaugh, *The Choirboys*, p. 49, 1975

2 the nose *UK*
Rhyming slang for **HOOTER**.
- — Ray Puxley, *Cockney Rabbit*, 1992

peas-in-a-pot; peas in the pot; peas; peasy *adjective*
hot *UK, 1960*
Rhyming slang.
- London was too peas in a pot for hoisting [shop-lifting] — Charles Raven, *Underworld Nights*, p. 117, 1956
- The drum [place to be robbed] was in Cricklewood, which is generally looked upon as a very peasy [...] manor. — Charles Raven, *Underworld Nights*, p. 167, 1956

peas on a drum *noun*
small female breasts *UK*
- My breasts are small / They always have been / Gnat bites / Peas on a drum / 28B / is how they've been described[.] —Mary Longford, *Body Language*, 1980

pea-soup *noun*
a French-Canadian *CANADA*
In the citation, Richler is referring indirectly to the Montreal hockey team, the Canadiens.
- Besides, looked at closely, come playoff time it was always our pea-soups, which is what we used to call French Canadians in those days, against their – that's to say, Toronto's – English-speaking rough-necks. —Mordecai Richler, *Dispatches from the Sporting Life*, p. 250, 2002

pea-souper *noun*
1 a dense yellowish fog *UK, 1890*
From the adjective PEA-SOUPY.
2 a French-Canadian *CANADA*
This term derives from the ubiquitous Quebec pea-soup, made with ham, still a favourite despite the negative connotations.
- —*Maledicta*, p. 167, Summer/Winter 1978: 'How to hate thy neighbor: a guide to racist maledicta'

pea-soupy; soupy *adjective*
descriptive of dense, yellowish fog *UK, 1860*
- James Stewart gets into that plane in The Glenn Miller Story and says, "It's a little soupy, ain't it." —Frank Skinner, *Frank Skinner*, p. 21, 2001

peasy; peasie *adjective*
used of hair, short and curled tightly *BAHAMAS*
- —John A. Holm, *Dictionary of Bahamian English*, p. 153, 1982

peata; pata *noun*
a spoiled child; a favourite child *IRELAND*
- You're mam's peata and don't say you're not. —Terence Dolan, *A Dictionary of Hiberno-English*, p. 195, 1999 (REPT)

pebble *noun*
a piece of crack cocaine *US*
The ROCK metaphor used again; the plural means crack generally.
- —Terry Williams, *The Cocaine Kids*, p. 137, 1989
- —US Department of Justice, *Street Terms*, October 1994
- Crack is also known as PEBBLES, SCUD, WASH, STONE and ROCK[.] —Macfarlane, Macfarlane and Robson, *The User*, p. 112, 1996

pebble-dash *verb*
to splatter a lavatory bowl with faeces as the result of a dramatic expulsion of diarrhoea *UK*
- —Chris Lewis, *The Dictionary of Playground Slang*, p. 168, 2003

Pebble Mill *noun*
1 a pill, especially one that is taken recreationally *UK*
Rhyming slang, formed from an area of Birmingham that is best known as the address of BBC TV studios, and the title of a programme broadcast from there, 1973–86.
- —Ray Puxley, *Fresh Rabbit*, 1998

2 a slight or perfunctory kiss *UK, 1893*
- —Brent Curtis and John Eldredge, *The Sacred Romance*, p. 131, 1997

3 on the railways, the lunch period *US*
- —Ramon Adams, *The Language of the Railroader*, p. 113, 1977

peck *verb*
1 to eat *UK, 1665*
- So I said to Satin, "Say, girl, feel like pecking?" And I said hi to Jim's rib. "Yeah, daddy," she said. "Order me a chicken dinner[.] —A.S. Jackson, *Gentleman Pimp*, p. 100, 1973
- —Charles Shafer, *Folk Speech in Texas Prisons*, p. 211, 1990

2 to kiss someone in a slight or perfunctory manner *UK, 1969*
- At the front door, Christine surprised me again. She pecked me on the cheek. —James Patterson, *Jack and Jill*, p. 248, 1996

pecker *noun*
1 the penis *UK, 1902*
- We had a stand and wait and watch a wild gay whore playing kittenishly with the pecker of the man she just engaged on the street[.] —Jack Kerouac, *Letter to Neal and Carolyn Cassady*, p. 359, 27 May 1952
- Put your pecker in the clothes wringer and call it a party. —Bernard Wolfe, *The Late Risers*, p. 5, 1954
- How long could you live in a world where everyone knew you didn't have a pecker? —Jim Thompson, *The Nothing Man*, p. 167, 1954
- I can't be takin no all night fer one fast fiver, so I start in playin roun wiff his lil ol pecker. —Robert Gover, *One Hundred Dollar Misunderstanding*, p. 21, 1961
- That ought to get his pecker up. —Mary McCarthy, *The Group*, p. 139, 1963
- She'd just come into a room sometimes and my old pecker would stand up at attention. —James Baldwin, *Blues for Mister Charlie*, p. 151, 1964
- Wow! That thing's the fattest, longest, reddest pecker I've ever seen! —James Harper, *Homo Laws in all 50 States*, p. 77, 1968
- He mutilated the Frenchman like he did the others, only worse. Cut his damn pecker right off. —Mickey Spillane, *Last Cop Out*, p. 123, 1972
- What's the bet she goes for my pecker on the first date? —*Diner*, 1982
- Apples sucks pecker as if the appendage were an aqualung and she desperately need oxygen. —Anthony Petkovich, *The X Factory*, p. 192, 1997

2 by extension, a despicable person *US*
- That pecker actually scored something on his own? —*Heathers*, 1988
- We're not signing with this pecker. —*Airheads*, 1994
- [N]ow, I know I put you through hell, and I know I've been one rough pecker, but from here on end you guys are in my cool book. —Quentin Tarantino, *From Dusk Till Dawn*, p. 77, 1995

3 courage, especially in the phrase 'keep your pecker up' *UK, 1853*
- Good luck, soldier. Keep your pecker up and your head down. —Harry Mazer, *The Last Mission*, p. 49, 1979
- Well – keep your pecker up. See ya next week, sweetie. —Sidney Sheldon, *Naked Face*, p. 169, 1985

pecker checker *noun*
1 a military doctor or medic who inspects male recruits for signs of sexually transmitted disease *US*
- —Dale Gordon, *The Dominion Sex Dictionary*, p. 119, 1967

2 a member of a police vice squad targeting homosexual activity *US*
- Pecker checker pine (Headline) —*Screw*, p. 10, 27th April 1970

pecker-foolish *noun*
used of a woman, overly obsessed with men and sex *US*
- —*Maledicta*, p. 16, Summer 1977: 'Award for it'

peckerhead *noun*
a despicable or offensive person *US, 1802*
Formed from PECKER 'penis', not PECKERWOOD 'racist'.
- You were right about my "peckerhead romanticism." —Jack Kerouac, *Letter to Allen Ginsberg*, p. 91, 23th August 1945
- Man, I tell you, I really put them peckerheads on! —Ross Russell, *The Sound*, p. 73, 1961
- "I know there's a war going on, you overweight peckerhead," said Jefferson to the Honorable Mr. Pettigrew. —Max Shulman, *Anyone Got a Match?*, p. 93, 1964
- I don't expect you ever hunted much, except you and that rascal Jones hunting ignorant peckerheads to chisel out of their hard-earned money. —Guy Owen, *The Flim-Flam Man and the Apprentice Grifter*, p. 54, 1972
- And while a government official and the province's TV and newspapers are hopping made about being called "peckerheads" and worse, they're especially upset with Stern for saying that "all people in Montreal should speak English." —*Daily New (New York)*, p. 48, 4th September 1997
- No matter how worthy the cause – and let's face it, some peckerheads don't care much about the city's kids – passing any type of TIF reform isn't easy. —*Riverfront Times (Missouri)*, 20th June 2001

peckerman *noun*
a rapist *US*
- Who the hell cares about a pocketbook booster when a peckerman has gone beserk? —Robert Campbell, *Sweet La-La Land*, p. 215, 1990

peckerneck *noun*
on the railways, a newly hired apprentice *US*
- —J. Herbert Lund, *Herb's Hot Box of Railraod Slang*, p. 64, 1975

pecker pole *noun*
an undersize tree, not worth logging *CANADA*
- —Tom Parkin, *WetCoast Words*, p. 106, 1989

pecker tracks *noun*
stains from seminal fluid *US*
- I know you're not a pansy, not the way you're leaving pecker tracks all over town. —Max Shulman, *Anyone Got a Match?*, p. 8, 1964
- [D]oing it everyway we could think of any-old place we happened to be, in fact, we did it in so many places that Denver was covered with our pecker-tracks. —Neal Cassady, *The First Third*, p. 153, 1971

- The goofy bastard borrowed my car and when I got it back there was a thirteen-inch pecker track on the back seat. —Ken Weaver, *Texas Crude*, p. 76, 1984
- I said you should be picking my brain instead of trying to follow Tommy's pecker tracks. —Elmore Leonard, *Be Cool*, p. 101, 1999

peckerwood *noun*

1 a non-Italian *US*

- Nick also warned against using outside hit men, especially "peckerwoods" – a term used by Kansas City mobsters for non-Italians. —*U.S. News & World Report*, p. 50, 29th September 1980

2 a white rural southerner, especially an uncouth and racist one *US, 1904*

Not praise. Also shortened variants 'peck', 'pecker' and 'wood'.

- A 'buddy' drinks bilge water, eats crap, and runs rabbits. That's what a peckerwood means when he calls you 'buddy.' —Chester Himes, *If He Hollers Let Him Go*, p. 11, 1945
- I kept looking at the blank walls and seeing the mean, murdering faces of those Southern peckerwoods when they went after Big Six and the others with their knives. —Mezz Mezzrow, *Really the Blues*, p. 16, 1946
- [T]he thing I want to know is who's the peckerwood runs the poker game in this establishment. —Ken Kesey, *One Flew Over the Cuckoo's Nest*, p. 264, 1962
- And, man, you ain't seen a peckerwood until you've seen Lyle Britten. —James Baldwin, *Blues for Mister Charlie*, p. 40, 1964
- And Grandma told me what peckerwoods were. —Claude Brown, *Manchild in the Promised Land*, p. 48, 1965
- Did you know that peckerwood of Pepper's is the bankroll behind the biggest policy wheel in town? —Iceberg Slim (Robert Beck), *Pimp*, p. 67, 1969
- You come back here and kill one racist, red-necked, honkey camel-breathed peckerwood who's been misusing you and your people all your life and that's murder. —H. Rap Brown, *Die Nigger Die!*, p. 38, 1969

Peckham Rye; Peckham *noun*

a tie (an article of menswear) *UK, 1925*

Rhyming slang, after an area of south London.

- Can't wear a whistle [suit] like this without the proper shoes, dicky [shirt] or Peckham, can yer now? —*The Sweeney*, p. 6, 1976

pecks *noun*

food *US*

- [F]ood is "pecks"[.] —Harrison E. Salisbury, *The Shook-up Generation*, p. 160, 1958
- —Kenn "Naz" Young, *Naz's Underground Dictionary*, p. 49, 1973

pecky *adjective*

characterised by well developed chest muscles *US*

- —Jeff Fessler, *When Drag Is Not a Car Race*, p. 86, 1997

pecs *noun*

the pectoralis major muscles *US, 1966*

- The Language of Bodybuilding —*American Speech*, p. 200, Fall 1984
- The obvious choice, when you think about it, given the number of Blenheim films in which he's flashed those lovely silicone pecs[.] —Armistead Maupin, *Maybe the Moon*, p. 291, 1992
- "Spread your pecs and save me a place at the bar," Fortney said. —Joseph Wambaugh, *Floaters*, p. 113, 1996

ped *noun*

a *ped*estrian *UK*

- These people should be made to pay road tax. Fucking peds. —Steve Beard, *The Last Good War [britpulp]*, p. 345, 1999

pedaling with both feet; pedaling *verb*

(used of a vehicle, or driver of that vehicle) to achieve top speed *US*

Conjures a misleading image of pedalling a bicycle; the pedal in question is an accelerator.

- —*Complete CB Slang Dictionary*, p. 73, 1976
- —Peter Chippindale, *The British CB Book*, p. 157, 1981

pedal pusher *noun*

a bicyclist *US, 1934*

- —Peter Chippindale, *The British CB Book*, p. 157, 1981

pedal-pushers *noun*

calf-length trousers for women or girls *US, 1944*

Originally designed to be suitable for a **PEDAL PUSHER** (a bicyclist), and variously in and out of fashion since.

- Hannah is 16, all mouth and pink pedal-pushers. —*The Guardian*, 7th August 2001

pedal to the metal *adjective*

used of a motor vehicle, throttled to the maximum *US*

- —John Edwards, *Auto Dictionary*, p. 123, 1993
- Jerry popped a Hank Williams tape into the dash and put the pedal to the metal. —C.D. Payne, *Youth in Revolt*, p. 57, 1993
- Up front the speedo cable's probably glowing red hot. We're pedal to the metal. —Glyn Parry, *Mosh*, p. 114, 1996
- I push the pedal to the metal an' swerve round her. Save her life why not. —Nick Barlay, *Curvy Lovebox*, p. 68, 1997
- [P]lenty of young geezers on the manor desperate to get behind the wheel of a flash motor, put the pedal to the metal given half a chance. —Greg Williams, *Diamond Geezers*, p. 141, 1997

'ped boy *noun*

a young, male, moped rider; a younger, male, BMX cyclist *UK*

- A 'Ped Boy's Worst Fear? "Road Rash"[.] —Julian Johnson, *Urban Survival*, p. 218, 2003

peddle and crank *verb*

to masturbate *UK*

Rhyming slang for **WANK**.

- —Bodmin Dark, *Dirty Cockney Rhyming Slang*, 2003

peddler *noun*

1 a prisoner who sells goods to other prisoners *US*

- Cuba is what is known in present prison jargon as a peddler. He is a real hustler in the sense that if there is anything in the way of contraband to be obtained within the prison, such as eggs, meat, grease, winter overshoes, coats, shirts, tailor made pants, special hair preparations, after-shave lotions, etc., he is the man to see. —Herbert Huncke, *The Evening Sun Turned Crimson*, p. 157, 1980

2 on the railways, a local freight train *US, 1960*

- —Ramon Adams, *The Language of the Railroader*, p. 113, 1977

peddle run *noun*

in trucking, a job with frequent stops for deliveries *US*

- —Montie Tak, *Truck Talk*, p. 116, 1971

pedestrian spear *noun*

a large, sharp car radiator ornament *US*

- —*American Speech*, p. 271, December 1962: 'The language of traffic policemen'

'ped-head *noun*

a motor-scooter enthusiast *UK*

Apparently derived from 'moped' and **-HEAD** (an enthusiast).

- All these 'ped heads carry mobile phones with them[.] —*The Independent Magazine*, p. 19, 28th August 2004

pedigree *noun*

a person's background *US*

- Now sit down, mister, and listen to me / While I run down my pedigree. —Dennis Wepman et al., *The Life*, p. 130, 1976

pedigree chum *noun*

semen; an orgasm *UK*

Rhyming slang for **COME**, formed on branded dog food Pedigree Chum™.

- —Ray Puxley, *Cockney Rabbit*, 1992

pedlar's pack *noun*

dismissal from employment *UK*

Rhyming slang for 'sack'.

- —Ray Puxley, *Cockney Rabbit*, 1992

pedo *noun*

trouble; nonsense *US*

Border Spanish used in English conversation by Mexican-Americans.

- —Dagoberto Fuentes and Jose Lopez, *Barrio Language Dictionary*, p. 112, 1974

Pedro *noun*

1 cocaine *UK*

Given a Spanish name (Peter) to suggest a South American nationality for the supplier.

- "Do you know Pedro?" he twinkled, tiny dimples puckering his cheeks. He was quite a honey. "Alas, I know him well." "And are you a friend of Pedro?" "Not too close, just at the moment. Sorry." —Kevin Sampson, *Powder*, p. 87, 1999

2 a survival winch mounted on a military helicopter *US*

- "Pedro" could be used to extract downed flyers, or a wire-basket stretcher could be attached to remove casualties when the helicopter was unable to land. —Gregory Clark, *Words of the Vietnam War*, p. 395–396, 1991

pee *noun*

an act of urination; urine *UK, 1902*

- She flashed into consciousness, inspected herself – wrinkle-free! – in the mirror, took a pee and headed for the elevator. —Tom Robbins, *Even Cowgirls Get the Blues*, p. 68, 1976
- "I'm going for a pee," Jisel says. "I need to go too," Dennis says. —Darren Francis, *The Sprawl [britpulp]*, p. 291, 1999

pee *verb*

to urinate *UK, 1879*

- May or can. You can, but you may not. We've come a long ways. In the old days if you had to pee, you peed on a tree with no may or can. That's progress for you. — *Avalon*, 1990
- The consensus of opinion was that it was okay to merely hold the gusset to one side whilst peeing, though this made it difficult to pull off a piece of toilet paper with only one hand. — Kitty Churchill, *Thinking of England*, p. 179, 1995

▸ **pee yourself laughing**

to laugh uproariously *UK*

- — Gerald Kersh, *Clean, Bright, and Slightly Oiled*, 1946

pee halt *noun*

a brief stop during a combat patrol so soldiers could urinate *US*

- — Linda Reinberg, *The Grunts*, p. 164, 1991

peek *noun*

▸ **the peek**

in prison, the observation cell *UK*

- — Paul Tempest, *Lag's Lexicon*, 1950

peekaboo *adjective*

1 said of a garment with decorative holes or slashes *US, 1895*

- Harry turned to the problem at hand – namely, what to do when Angela came downstairs in her peek-a-boo negligee. — Max Shulman, *Rally Round the Flag, Boys!*, p. 101, 1957
- The attempt at a Monroe effect, besides the smiles, is present in the tight jeans, spun-candy hairdoes, peekaboo blouses. — Sidney Bernard, *This Way to the Apocalypse*, p. 222, 1965
- I wear peek-a-boo bras, and corsettes that give me the wildest cleavages. — Roger Gordon, *Hollywood's Sexual Underground*, p. 35, 1966
- Finally Letch noticed Rita behind him, all tarted-up for another evening on the john detail: Day-Glo green satin shorts, knee-high green plastic boots with spike heels, a white peekaboo chemise, a sequined jacket on top. — Joseph Wambaugh, *Floaters*, p. 33, 1996

2 used of a mirror, see-through from outside the room *US*

- I strolled, itchy – over to sweat box row. Standard six-by-eights, peekaboo glass. — James Ellroy, *White Jazz*, p. 110, 1992

peeker *noun*

a thief who operates by observing the numbers given at a cloakroom and then using a counterfeit check to retrieve valuable items that have been checked in *US*

- [A] couple of peekers, suitably dressed for admission to one of the zizzier places, waits across the street from the nightclub entrance. — Dev Collans with Stewart Sterling, *I was a House Detective*, p. 16, 1954

peek freak *noun*

a voyeur *US*

- — Dale Gordon, *The Dominion Sex Dictionary*, p. 119, 1967
- — *American Speech*, p. 58, Spring-Summer 1970: 'Homosexual slang'

peek man *noun*

a lookout during an illegal or forbidden activity in prison *US*

- — John R. Armore and Joseph D. Wolfe, *Dictionary of Desperation*, p. 43, 1976

peel *noun*

a caustic chemical treatment of the skin (dermabrasion) *US*

- — Anna Scotti and Paul Young, *Buzzwords*, p. 107, 1997

peel *verb*

1 to undress *UK, 1785*

2 to perform a striptease *US*

Originally a term used by and with athletes, later by and with stripteasers.

- One gal of our acquaintance who had made a respectable and comfortable living on the road (even in Boston) peeling in night clubs and theaters, was booked into one of our larger cafes. — Jack Lait and Lee Mortimer, *New York Confidential*, p. 38, 1948
- They strut their stuff, peeling, slowly, piece by piece, before the music comes to an end and so does their act. — *Adult Video*, p. 15, August/September 1986

3 to pry something open *US*

- [Y]ou know you're home free, or if you're peeling it you see that smoke come out. — *The Digger Papers*, p. 12, August 1968
- You can't peel it, you can't punch it; they've welded deals all around the outside so you can't get a bit on it with your bar. — Bruce Jackson, *Outside the Law*, p. 95, 1972
- In either case, whether it's in a house or an apartment, you never try to pop the door of the safe itself by peeling it or punching it till the pin hits the back of the safe. — Emmett Grogan, *Ringolevio*, p. 91, 1972
- He'd have to peel it open. He took the big cold chisel from his satchel and placed it in one corner of the first layer, in the crack between the safe door and the frame into which it was fitted. — Emmett Grogan, *Final Score*, p. 99, 1976
- While one man is keeping six, two others are either peeling or blowing the safe. — Thomas Renner and Cecil Kirby, *Mafia Enforcer*, p. 38, 1987
- A couple of hard blows and he peels the steering column. — *Menace II Society*, 1993

4 (used of a pimp) to entice a prostitute away from her current pimp *US*

- Sometimes when this happens, the new pimp presents the old pimp with a banana peel wrapped in newspaper and says, "I just peeled your 'ho." — *Washington Post*, p. C5, 7th November 1993

5 to fire a gun *US*

- I've seen fifteen-year-olds roll pipe bombs under taxis and peel a clip-a'-nines at a passing squad car. — Stephen J. Cannell, *The Tin Collectors*, p. 34, 2001

▸ **get peeled**

when filming a film or television programme, to extend the shooting into overtime for the crew *US*

- — Anna Scotti and Paul Young, *Buzzwords*, p. 8, 1997

▸ **peel caps**

to shoot someone *US*

- All I knew was we was gon' find some 'a them niggas, and peel they caps. — *Menace II Society*, 1993

▸ **peel one off**

to fart *UK*

Perhaps this should be 'peal' for the ringing tones.

- I've whistled in my Y-fronts / I've just peeled one off. — Ivor Biggun, *I've Parted (Misprint)*, 1978

▸ **peel wheels**

to accelerate a car quickly, squealing the tyres and leaving rubber marks on the road *US, 1989*

- — Ellen C. Bellone (Editor), *Dictionary of Slang*, p. 18, 1989

▸ **peel your banana**

to pull back the foreskin of your penis for inspection or as part of masturbating *US*

- — Gary K. Farlow, *Prison-ese*, p. 49, 2002

peeled *adjective*

of the eyes, open, thus alert and observant *US, 1853*

'Keep 'em peeled' is a catchphrase associated with Shaw Taylor, presenter of a television police assistance programme *Police 5* since the early 1970s.

- [K]eep your peepers [eyes] peeled for one of them Groinatex posters. — Barry Humphries, *Bazza Pulls It Off!*, 1971

peeler *noun*

1 a police officer *IRELAND, 1817*

After Robert Peel, as founder of the Irish constabulary.

- The peelers wanted him whacked. We whacked him and that's the end of the story as far as I'm concerned. — *The Guardian*, 19th June 2002

2 a striptease dancer *US*

- The flatfeet tore down the billing and wouldn't let her work. They said she was a peeler. — Jack Lait and Lee Mortimer, *New York Confidential*, p. 163, 1948
- They're not all pimping like crazy for a peeler with the roundest heels in the Borough of Manhattan. — Bernard Wolfe, *The Late Risers*, p. 38, 1954

3 a fast, well-developed wave *US*

- — John Severson, *Modern Surfing Around the World*, p. 175, 1964

peel-off *noun*

a theft of part of a common booty *UK*

Criminal and police slang.

- — John Gosling, *The Ghost Squad*, 1959

peel out *verb*

to accelerate a car suddenly from a stopped position, squealing the tyres on the road *US*

- I just love it when guys peel out. — *American Graffiti*, 1973
- As the Furty junkers descended into the crescent, the line of customer cars peeled out[.] — Richard Price, *Clockers*, p. 512, 1992

peelywally *adjective*

drunk *UK: SCOTLAND*

From Scottish *peelie-wallie* (sickly).

- — *e-cyclopaedia*, 20th March 2002

peeny *adjective*
very small *BARBADOS*
- —Frank A. Collymore, *Barbadian Dialect*, p. 82, 1965

peeny-weeny *adjective*
tiny *TRINIDAD AND TOBAGO, 1993*
- —Lise Winer, *Dictionary of the English/Creole of Trinidad & Tobago*, 2003

peep *noun*
1 a quick glance *UK, 1730*
- Brother, you should have seen their maps when they took one peep at those strutting searchlights up above. —Mezz Mezzrow, *Really the Blues*, p. 168, 1946

2 a two-way mirror *US*
- They have what they call the catwalk, and the peep – hidden mirrors – through which someone is looking down at all times at the dealers. —Jimmy Snyder, *Jimmy the Greek*, p. 218, 1975

3 a clandestine photographer *US*
- —Ralph de Sola, *Crime Dictionary*, p. 113, 1982

4 a sexually desirable woman *US*
An abbreviation of the somewhat coarse ‘*p*erfectly *e*legant *e*atin’ *p*ussy’.
- — *Maledicta*, p. 16, Summer 1977: ‘A word for it’

5 something spoken, especially in a negative context *UK, 1903*
- Try it for yourself, or not another peep out of you. — *New York Post*, 12th March 2003

peep *verb*
1 to look at something, to discover something *US, 1992*
Variation of conventional ‘peep’ (to look).
- Just some fools peepin’ out the ride. — *Menace II Society*, 1993
- [P]eep it or weep. — *Hip-Hop Connection*, p. 24, July 2002
- Peep the “Top 10 Albums” and you’ll see ya boys on that list. — *The Source*, p. 44, March 2002

2 to listen to someone or something *US*
- — *Ebony Magazine*, p. 156, August 2000: ‘How to talk to the new generation’

3 to read music *US*
- —Robert S. Gold, *A Jazz Lexicon*, p. 227, 1964

▸ **peep the holecard**
to gain deep insight into someone’s character *US*
- — *Maledicta*, p. 266, Summer/Winter 1981: ‘By its slang, ye shall know it: the pessimism of prison life’

pee pad *noun*
a motorcyle passenger seat *US*
- Biker (motorcyle) usage, alluding to the fact that protracted riding on the back of a motorcyle will at times cause a female passenger to urinate. — *www.mattsphotos.com/bikerslang.*,

peepe *noun*
the vagina *US*
- There’s [...] a “poochi,” a “poopi,” a “peepe,”, a “poopelu,” a “poopelu,” a “poonani,” a “pal” and a “piche[.”] —Eve Ensler, *The Vagina Monologues*, p. 6, 1998

pee-pee *noun*
1 urine; urination *UK, 1923*
Childish.
- On the other hand, some corresponding euphemistic expressions (e.g., dickie, peepee, weewee, number one, number two, to move the bowels, to pass water, to make love, and so on), obviously evasive in their very structure, do have considerable usage. —*Eros*, p. 69, Autum 1962
- [A] few finely crafted doody [excrement] jokes. Then a little pee-pee humor with a few real farts[.] —Howard Stern, *Miss America*, p. 137, 1995
- Daddy, when I make pee-pee my vulva stings. —Joel Rose, *Kill Kill Faster Faster*, p. 4, 1997

2 the penis *US*
Children’s toilet vocabulary. Also variant ‘pi-pi’.
- I felt my pants zipper being pulled open and cold fingers take my pee-pee out and begin to pull it up and down. —Piri Thomas, *Down These Mean Streets*, p. 61, 1967
- Just slip in your pi-pi and fuck away! —Angelo d’Arcangelo, *The Homosexual Handbook*, p. 90, 1968
- They used to be so closety here that they asked you to leave if you shook your pee-pee too many times finishing off at the urinal. —John Francis Hunter, *The Gay Insider*, p. 165, 1971
- Looking down I saw my “peepee” for the first time grow purplish as it filled with blood. — *Screw*, p. 31, 30th October 1972
- [S]he did day work and left me with a teenaged girl who had me climb up on top of her and pushed my lil’ peepee into a huge, hairy, warm Something. —Odie Hawkins, *Scars and Memories*, p. 40, 1987
- I can’t get by / Where’d he put his pee-pee? —Gerard Allessandrini, *Poor Butterfly [Forbidden Broadway Volume 2]*, 1991

peeper *noun*
1 an eye *UK, 1700*
A definite old-fashioned feel to the term. Popularised in 1938 with the film *Going Places* and the song by Harry Warren: ‘Jeepers, creepers / Where’d you get them peepers?’.
- They sure gave me the glad-hand when they laid their peepers on my new car. —Mezz Mezzrow, *Really the Blues*, p. 88, 1946
- Wait till they focused their bright peepers on that biopsy! —Philip Wylie, *Opus 21*, p. 76, 1949
- [K]eep your peepers peeled for one of them Groinatex posters. —Barry Humphries, *Bazza Pulls It Off!*, 1971
- [P]lenty of young and naked birds buzzing around for them to feast their dirty little peepers on. —Petra Christian, *The Sexploiters*, p. 22, 1973
- Time to wake up, kid, I mean, Bobbie. Open up your peepers. —Joseph Wambaugh, *Finnegan’s Week*, p. 231, 1993

2 a voyeur *UK, 1652*
- I looked down at my own pink tipped pretties and decided that maybe the peepers wouldn’t have much time for me after all. —Petra Christian, *The Sexploiters*, p. 70, 1973
- Otherwise, he comes and goes, like some goddamned peeper. —George V. Higgins, *Penance for Jerry Kennedy*, p. 202, 1985
- “Okay, peepers then.” “Say what?” “Peeping Toms. Guys who get their kicks looking in windows.” —James Ellroy, *White Jazz*, p. 51, 1992
- “Alfred Hitchcock did movies about peepers like you,” Fortney informed him. “And they all ended up in trouble.” —Joseph Wambaugh, *Floaters*, p. 158, 1996

3 a private investigator or private detective *US, 1943*
- “Who’s the house peeper here now?” —Raymond Chandler, *The Little Sister*, p. 44, 1949
- All you are is a peeper —Robert Crais, *L.A. Requiem*, p. 100, 1999
- “One thing, Peeper!” he called after me. I stopped and looked round. “This Bronzini kid ... was murder. Serious stuff. No room here for a private operative, you understand?” —Malcolm Pryce, *Aberystwyth Mon Amour*, p. 33 – 34, 2001

4 a police detective *UK*
From an earlier sense as ‘policeman’.
- —Angela Devlin, *Prison Patter*, p. 87, 1996

5 a card player who tries to see another player’s cards *US*
- —George Percy, *The Language of Poker*, p. 65, 1988

6 a one-way eye-hole in a door allowing the person on the inside to see who is outside; a peephole *US*
- She squinted through the peeper in gloomy twilight at a splindly blonde, who knew she was being observed. —Joseph Wambaugh, *Floaters*, p. 6, 1996

peepers *noun*
1 a vehicle’s headlights *US*
- — *Complete CB Slang Dictionary*, p. 10, 1976

2 night-vision enhancing equipment *US*
- —Linda Reinberg, *In the Field*, p. 164, 1991

peep freak *noun*
a voyeur *US*
- —Xaviera Hollander, *The Best Part of a Man*, 1975

peep-hole special *noun*
sex in a public toilet *US*
- The act itself, performed in the toilets, is considered a “peep-hole special” because hustlers and customers know there are special peepholes in many subway toilets for vice squad surveillance. —Johnny Shearer, *The Male Hustler*, p. 18, 1966

pee pill *noun*
a pill containing an agent that increases the excretion of urine *US*
- [S]tart taking pee-pills again to lose weight[.] —Gore Vidal, *Myra Breckinridge*, p. 22, 1968

peeping Tom *noun*
1 a voyeur; a person who spies on others *UK, 1795*
- I’m watchin’ these three people in all their mess and misery. I felt like a burglar, or a peepin’ Tom. —Edwin Torres, *After Hours*, p. 363, 1979
- As I lay there scrunched under the windowsill catching all the juicy action, I thought to myself, “I am a pervert. A techno Peeping Tom. I need professional help.” —Anka Radakovich, *The Wild Girls Club*, p. 95, 1994

2 in poker or other card games, a player or spectator who tries to see a player’s hand *US*
- —John Vorhaus, *The Big Book of Poker Slang*, p. 28, 1996

3 a variety of MDMA, the recreational drug best known as ecstasy, identified by PT embossed on the tablet *UK*
- —Gareth Thomas, *This Is Ecstasy*, p. 57, 2002

pee pipe *noun*
▷ **see: PISS TUBE**

pee-poor *adjective*
very poor *US*
A variation on the much more common **PISS-POOR**.
- Will you settle for pee-poor guardians of the public gut?—Max Shulman, *Anyone Got a Match?*, p. 74, 1964

peep out *verb*
to look at something carefully; to examine something *US*
- "Peep this out." (Gee Money pulls a tiny vial from the jacket of his sweatsuit.)—*New Jack City*, p. 9, 1990

peeps *noun*
people; friends *US*
A probably coincidental usage, based on accidental English, was popularised in the UK by 'Stavros the Greek kebab seller', a character created by comedian Harry Enfield for Channel 4 television's *Friday Night Live* in 1988.
- —Connie Eble (Editor), *UNC-CH Campus Slang*, p. 6, March 1996
- In the rapgame peeps still fumble over what is fact in 2002.—*Hip-Hop Connection*, p. 14, July 2002

peep show *noun*
an arcade where it is possible to view pornographic videos or a nude woman in private booths; formerly an arcade where it was possible to view photographs of scantily clad women *US, 1947*
- This part of 9th Street is packed solid with "play lands," featuring pin-ball machines, peep show movies and souvenir stands[.]—Jack Lait and Lee Mortimer, *Washington Confidential*, p. 30–31, 1951
- It had about six peep show machines.—*Screw*, p. 4, 22nd March 1970
- Loops are the short sex scenes usually shown at peep shows – small, individual projection booths located in the rear of many adult bookshops.—Stephen Ziplow, *The Film Maker's Guide to Pornography*, p. 12, 1977
- But the pang in his gut leads him past all this to an even greater spectacle – the fantastic, featured "Live Nude Girl" peep show.—Josh Alan Friedman, *Tales of Times Square*, p. 63, 1986
- The peep show has lost its popularity. The buddy window, glory hole.—James Ridgeway, *Red Light*, p. 212, 1996
- If you're the mop-up boy at a peep show, it's obvious the government is not working for you.—Chris Rock, *Rock This!*, p. 98, 1997
- Peep shows (porn booths) were the best part of living in Montreal.—Suroosh Alvi et al., *The Vice Guide*, p. 9, 2002

peep this
look at this *US*
- —Vann Wesson, *Generation X Field Guide and Lexicon*, p. 126, 1997

peer queer *noun*
a male homosexual who takes pleasure in watching others have sex *US*
- —*American Speech*, p. 58, Spring-Summer 1970: 'Homosexual slang'

pee-spout *noun*
the penis *UK*
- Suddenly Andy began to grunt, and Bobby looked at him in time to notice white stuff shooting out of his pee-spout.—Christopher Brookmyre, *Not the End of the World*, p. 176, 1998

peeties *noun*
dice that have been altered with small weights to produce a desired number when rolled *US*
- —Frank Garcia, *Marked Cards and Loaded Dice*, p. 263, 1962

peeve *noun*
alcohol; drink *UK, 1979*
Market traders and English gypsy use.
- —Jimmy Stockin, *On The Cobbles*, p. 11, 2000

peevied *adjective*
drunk *UK*
- —*e-cyclopaedia*, 20th March 2002

peewat *noun*
a person of neither importance nor signficance *TRINIDAD AND TOBAGO, 1982*
- —Lise Winer, *Dictionary of the English/Creole of Trinidad & Tobago*, 2003

peewee; pee wee *noun*
1 the penis *US*
- Smith holding back the bushes for him with his peewee hanging hard as a posicle waiting—Clarence Major, *All-Night Visitors*, p. 39, 1998

2 a very young member of a youth gang *US*
- All the midgets and tinys in the Black Spiders had been to the Hall. Most of the peewees even!—Joseph Wambaugh, *The Glitter Dome*, p. 110, 1981

3 a small, tightly rolled marijuana cigarette *US*
- —Clarence Major, *Dictionary of Afro-American Slang*, p. 90, 1970

4 crack cocaine *US*
- —US Department of Justice, *Street Terms*, October 1994

5 in craps, a roll of three *US*
- —Chris Fagans and David Guzman, *A Guide to Craps Lingo*, p. 11, 1999

pee wee *verb*
in dice games with no bank, to roll the dice to see who will play first *US*
- —*The Annals of the American Academy of Political and Social Sciences*, p. 129, May 1950

peewee *adjective*
composed of children *US, 1877*
- He has volunteered to serve as coach in the local peewee football league, thus assuring another generation of gridiron mediocrity in the valley.—C.D. Payne, *Youth in Revolt*, p. 255, 1993

peg *noun*
1 a look *AUSTRALIA*
- Better have a peg at the news, I s'pose.—Jim McNeil, *The Old Familiar Juice*, p. 100, 1973
- So the day of the big date arrives and I wake up in the morning, drift into the bathroom past the mirror, a quick peg at myself on the run and I stopped in horror.—Paul Vautin, *Turn It Up!*, p. 28, 1995

2 a person's leg *UK, 1878*
- I'm gunner cut that geezer's peg off. See what 'appens.—Chris Baker and Andrew Day, *Lock, Stock... & A Good Slopping Out*, p. 457, 2000

3 heroin *US*
- —US Department of Justice, *Street Terms*, October 1994
- —Robert Ashton, *This Is Heroin*, p. 206, 2002

4 a golf tee *US, 1946*
- —Dawson Taylor, *How to Talk Golf*, p. 52, 1985

▸ **give a peg**
to reconnoitre, especially with criminal intent *AUSTRALIA*
- —*The (Sydney) Bulletin*, 26th April 1975

▸ **on the peg**
of driving, at the speed limit *UK*
Citizens' band radio slang.
- —Peter Chippindale, *The British CB Book*, p. 156, 1981

peg *verb*
1 to watch or look at someone *AUSTRALIA*
- Spends half his time in the dressing room pegging off the blokes in the showers.—Suzy Jarratt, *Permissive Australia*, p. 101, 1970
- —Jim Ramsay, *Cop It Sweet!*, p. 69, 1977
- He pegged her up and down[.]—Ryan Aven-Bray, *Ridgey Didge Oz Jack Lang*, p. 7, 1983
- [A] couple were even pegging over in his direction but quickly looked away when he looked like catching their eye.—Robert G. Barrett, *Davo's Little Something*, p. 256, 1992

2 to identify someone or something *US, 1940*
- He went to the window, caught sight of what she pegged, and motioned Leo over.—Emmett Grogan, *Final Score*, p. 65, 1976
- —H. Craig Collins, *Street Gangs*, p. 223, 1979
- His Smash Hits good looks may have matured into the kind of fizzog that has him pegged for film stardom[.]—Andrew Holmes, *Sleb*, p. 103, 2002

3 to push a disabled motorcyle with a second motorcyle by reaching out and putting your leg on the foot-rest (peg) of the disabled motorcyle *US*
- We decided to "peg" Terry home – I stuck my leg out and put my foot on his foot peg, and pushed Terry home while he leaned his bike into mine, so as to keep them next to each other.—Ralph "Sonny" Barger, *Hell's Angel*, p. 167, 2000

4 to throw something *AUSTRALIA, 1941*
- And we got all these rocks and pegged 'em at 'em.—*Tracks*, p. 83, October 1985

5 to put someone on report *UK, 1948*
Originally military, then recorded in use in borstals and detention centres.
- —Home Office, *Glossary of Terms and Slang Common in Penal Establishments*, July 1978

6 in a card cheating scheme, to prepare a deck for a manoeuvre *US*

- — Frank Garcia, *Marked Cards and Loaded Dice*, p. 263, 1962

7 to fix the market price of something *UK, 1882*
Originally Stock Exchange slang, then more general.

▸ **peg it**

1 to walk; to walk fast; to run; to hurry *UK*
A variation of **LEG IT** formed on **PEG** (the leg).

- When you are pegging it from Groove Armada to Franz Ferdinand, you hardly have time to pick a fight[.] — *The Guardian*, p. 7, 28th June 2004

2 to die *UK*
A variation of **PEG OUT**.

- [A] couple of prayers to the gaffer upstairs and then you pegged it. — Andrew Nickolds, *Back to Basics*, p. 113, 1994

peg away *verb*
to labour persistently; to continue to toil *UK, 1818*

- I've been often referred to rather dismissively as writing "traditional novels" but I just pegged away. — *The Observer*, 17th June 2001

peg boy *noun*
in male homosexual intercourse, a passive partner *US, 1960*

- — Bruce Rodgers, *The Queens' Vernacular*, 1972
- — *The FHM Little Book of Bloke*, p. 142, June 2003: 'Gayness explained'

pegged *adjective*
under surveillance *UK*

- — Angela Devlin, *Prison Patter*, p. 87, 1996

pegged out *adjective*
dead *US*
From **PEG OUT** (to die).

- Wake up lads, if anyone sees this old fart pegged out in our yard, we'll disappear for free. — Chris Baker and Andrew Day, *Lock, Stock... & a Fist Full of Jack and Jills*, p. 192–193, 2000

pegger *noun*
a tooth *BARBADOS*

- — Frank A. Collymore, *Barbadian Dialect*, p. 82, 1965
- — Lise Winer, *Dictionary of the English/Creole of Trinidad & Tobago*, 2003

peggy *noun*
a person employed to make tea and lunch for labourers *AUSTRALIA*

- The billy – a battered and blackened old container with a wire handle on it, or on big jobs a four-gallon kero-tin in similar condition – is filled with water and boiled by the Peggy. — John O'Grady, *Aussie Etiket*, p. 5, 1971

Peggy Lee fastball *noun*
in baseball, a fast ball that is not particularly fast *US*
From Peggy Lee's hit recording of 'Is That All There Is?'.

- McGraw uses a collection of pitches that includes his old faithful, the screwball, and another of his own devise, known as the "Peggy Lee" fastball.That is the offspeed pitch where, according to McGraw, the batter sees it and says, "Is that all there is?" — *New York Times*, p. 4 (Section 5), 21st September 1980
- — Mike Whiteford, *How to Talk Baseball*, p. 116, 1987
- He had an innate ability to pump a crowd, loosen up a tight clubhouse and to reach back for whatever was needed on a Peggy Lee fastball[.] — *Philadelphia Daily News*, 6th January 2004

Peggy's Leg *nickname*
a sweet in the form of a longish stalk; a stick of rock *IRELAND*

- It was to be all or nothing and if only one stripped away the ugly surface one would see the sound United Ireland heart beating beneath the uniform of the RUC man playing a tin whistle, people buying Peggy's Leg at the Oul' Lammas Fair at Ballycastle, all the fun of the fair and so on. — *House of the Oireachtas Parliamentary Debates*, 9th February 1983

peg leg *noun*
a wooden or artificial leg *UK, 1833*

- — Multicultural Management Program Fellows, *Dictionary of Cautionary Words and Phrases*, 1989

peg out
to die *UK, 1855*
Possibly from the game of cribbage, less likely from croquet.

- Blokes always peg out first, they can't stand responsibility, can they? — Jenny Eclair, *Camberwell Beauty*, p. 121, 2000

pegs *noun*

1 tapered trousers very fashionable in the US in the late 1950s and 60s *US*

- Get those fuckin tweeds out of Ware Pratt's and let me see those sweet talking pegs. — Abbie Hoffman, *Woodstock Nation*, p. 27, 1969
- She watched Gus dispassionately as he moved assuredly around the table in hand-stitched baby blue pegs that must have cost twenty-five dollars[.] — Earl Thompson, *Tattoo*, p. 47, 1974

2 the external vaginal lips *TRINIDAD AND TOBAGO*

- When she open she leg I like to see the little fat pegs. — Lise Winer, *Dictionary of the English/Creole of Trinidad & Tobago*, 2003

peke-a-poo *noun*
a crossbreed of a pekinese and a poodle *US*

- [C]ockapoos – or terra-poos, peke-a-poos, or labradoodles. Lots of mixes are out there, great pets one and all. But a breed? No. — Gina Spadafori and Marty Becker, *Dogs for Dummies*, p. 28, 2001

Pekinese *adjective*

▸ **do the Pekinese pop-out**
to become wide-eyed with shock or wonder *US*
An allusion to the appearance of a pedigree Pekinese dog.

- One of them was young, and looked like his eyes were about to do the Pekinese pop-out. — Robert Crais, *L.A. Requiem*, p. 30, 1999

pekkie; perkie *noun*
a black person *SOUTH AFRICA, 1963*
Offensive.

- — Penny Silva, *A Dictionary of South African English*, 1996

pelican *noun*
a water bomber, for firefighting *CANADA*

- The "pelican" is named for its ability to skim along the surface of a lake or waterway, scooping up water which it can then drop on a fire. — Lewis Poteet, *Plane Talk*, p. 127, 1997

pellet *noun*
a tablet or capsule of LSD *US*

- — Gilda and Melvin Berger, *Drug Abuse A-Z*, p. 107, 1990

pelt *noun*
a woman's pubic hair; sex; a woman as a sex object *US*
Building on the vulva-as-**BEAVER** image.

- — *Maledicta*, p. 181, Winter 1980: 'A new erotic vocabulary'
- — Michael Dalton Johnson, *Talking Trash with Redd Foxx*, p. 71, 1994

▸ **stroke the pelt**
(of a female) to masturbate *US*

- Another way to say "the girl is masturbating" – Stroking the pelt[.] — Erica Orloff and JoAnn Baker, *Dirty Little Secrets*, p. 67, 2001

pelt *verb*

▸ **pelt wood**
to thrust with vigour during sex *TRINIDAD AND TOBAGO*

- Man, I just begin to pelt wood when de door open and she man come home. — Lise Winer, *Dictionary of the English/Creole of Trinidad & Tobago*, 2003

pelter *noun*
in poker, a non-standard hand consisting of a 9, a 5, a 2, one card between 5 and 9 and one card between 2 and 5 *US*

- — Irwin Steig, *Common Sense in Poker*, p. 186, 1963

pen *noun*

1 a jail or prison *US, 1884*
Shortened from 'penitentiary'.

- If Bob gets called sure 'nough and listens to you and gets sent to the pen, he's a fool. — Chester Himes, *If He Hollers Let Him Go*, p. 121, 1945
- "First I want revenge because their fathers sent my old man to die in the pen." The Crawler's eyes were blazing with hate as he spoke. — Chester Gould, *Dick Tracy Meets the Night Crawler*, p. 40, 1945
- He's on the lam from a pen back east, crashed out with twenty years to serve of a thirty-year bank-robber rap. — Jim Thompson, *A Swell-Looking Babe*, p. 77, 1954
- Gentlemen, I've worked many pens before, and believe me when I tell you I enjoy entertaining you fellows. — Dick Gregory, *Nigger*, p. 153, 1964
- Yeah, they're from Newark and they done time in the state pen. — Piri Thomas, *Down These Mean Streets*, p. 213, 1967
- Ralph is now doing time in a Federal pen[.] — Babs Gonzales, *I Paid My Dues*, p. 109–110, 1967
- I guess you heard I'm outta the pen now. — *Boyz N The Hood*, 1990
- I'm sorry man, I shoulda picked you up personally at the pen. — *Reservoir Dogs*, 1992

2 a detention or holding room at a jail or courthouse *US*

- I was able to communicate with Mr. Mahoney in the pens. — Edwin Torres, *After Hours*, p. 259, 1979

penalty box *noun*
the area behind the back seat of a SUV or station wagon *US*
- —Ben Applebaum and Derrick Pittman, *Turd Ferguson & The Sausage Party*, p. 52, 2004

pen and ink; pen *noun*
1 a noisome smell; a stink *UK, 1859*
Rhyming slang.
- [P]eople passed by on the other side, to avoid the pen and ink. —Ronnie Barker, *Fletcher's Book of Rhyming Slang*, p. 25, 1979

2 a mink as an item of wardrobe *UK*
Rhyming slang.
- [A] lovely full-length pen that must have been worth every nicker of three grand[.]—Charles Raven, *Underworld Nights*, p. 13, 1956

3 a drink *NEW ZEALAND*
Rhyming slang.
- We wander over to the bar for a pen and ink[.]—*Truth*, p. 19, 21st May 1963

pen and ink; pen *verb*
1 to smell rank; to stink *UK*
Rhyming slang.
- I think you stink / You pen and ink—Ian Dury, *Blackmail Man*, 1977

2 to drink *AUSTRALIA*
- He would rather pen and ink on his ace until some of his Chinas lobbed.—Ryan Aven-Bray, *Ridgey Didge Oz Jack Lang*, p. 11, 1983

pen and pencil set *noun*
in electric line work, a digging bar and spoon shovel *US*
- —A.B. Chance Co., *Lineman's Slang Dictionary*, p. 13, 1980

pen bait *noun*
a girl under the age of sexual consent *US*
A variation on the more common **JAILBAIT**.
- —Roger Blake, *The American Dictionary of Sexual Terms*, p. 111, 1964
- —Dale Gordon, *The Dominion Sex Dictionary*, p. 120, 1967

pencil *noun*
1 the penis *UK, 1937*
Perhaps borrowing a Mark Twain pun: 'the penis mightier than the sword'.
- —Barry Humphries, *Bazza Pulls It Off!*, 1971
- —*Maledicta*, p. 188, Winter 1980: 'A new erotic vocabulary'

2 in a casino, the authority to give a gambler complimentary drinks or meals *US*
Often phrased as 'power of the pencil'.
- Only a few Hosts have the awesome authority of "the Pencil" which authorizes a completely free stay in Vegas. The Pencil is strictly controlled.—Mario Puzo, *Inside Las Vegas*, p. 288, 1977
- —John Scarne, *Scarne's Guide to Modern Poker*, p. 286, 1979

pencil *verb*
to work as a penciller *AUSTRALIA, 1919*

pencil dick *noun*
a thin penis; used, generally, to insult a man by attacking a perception of his masculinity *US, 1998*
- I'm more woman than you'll ever have, pencil dick.—*The Guru*, 2002

penciller *noun*
a bookmaker's clerk who writes out betting tickets *AUSTRALIA, 1891*
- —Jim Ramsay, *Cop It Sweet!*, p. 69, 1977
- —Joe Andersen, *Winners Can Laugh*, p. 171, 1982
- His penciller raced across to view the finish while Walter stood nervously by his stand[.]—Joe Andersen, *Winners Can Laugh*, p. 215, 1982
- —Clive Galea, *Slipper*, p. 26, 1988
- —Ned Wallish, *The Truth Dictionary of Racing Slang*, p. 61, 1989

pencil-neck geek *noun*
a bookish, timid, weak man *US*
The term was popularised, if not coined, by US professional wrestler 'Classy' Freddie Blassie to describe his opponents. Blassie recorded a novelty song so titled, written by Johnny Legend and Pete Cicero, in 1979.
- —Connie Eble (Editor), *UNC-CH Campus Slang*, p. 7, Fall 1985
- —Michael Dalton Johnson, *Talking Trash with Redd Foxx*, p. 98, 1994

pencil-pusher *noun*
1 a person who works with words; a clerk or secretary *US, 1881*
Usually derisive.
- —Lou Shelly, *Hepcats Jive Talk Dictionary*, p. 31, 1945
- [F]or a pencil-pusher he sure could flash plenty of Uncle Sam's I.O.U.'s.—Mezz Mezzrow, *Really the Blues*, p. 69, 1946
- —Jerry Robertson, *Oil Slanguage*, p. 95, 1954
- I just love men who work hard, I mean who work with their hands. Yeah, I hate pencil pushers.—Hubert Selby Jr, *Last Exit to Brooklyn*, p. 204, 1957

2 in the US Air Force, the navigator on a bomber aircraft *US*
- —*American Speech*, p. 310, December 1946: 'More air force slang'

pencil-sharpener *noun*
the vagina *UK*
Corresponds, quite logically, with **PENCIL** (the penis).
- —Chris Lewis, *The Dictionary of Playground Slang*, p. 168, 2003

pencil stiff *noun*
a clerical worker *US*
Derisive.
- [Y]ou can bet nobody's gettin in the shop except a few pencil stiffs. —Hubert Selby Jr, *Last Exit to Brooklyn*, p. 139, 1957

pencil talk *noun*
bargaining over a price in a bazaar carried on by writing down the offer *US*
Vietnam war usage.
- —Carl Fleischhauer, *A Glossary of Army Slang*, p. 6, 1968

pencil-whip *verb*
1 to file constant lawsuits and complaints against prison authorities *US*
- —William K. Bentley and James M. Corbett, *Prison Slang*, p. 103, 1992

2 to write someone a traffic ticket or notice of a criminal infraction *US*
- —Don R. McCreary (Editor), *Dawg Speak*, 2001

pend *verb*
to listen; to pay attention *US*
- —Joan Fontaine et al., *Dictionary of Black Slang*, 1968

pendejo *noun*
a fool *US*
From the Spanish of Mexican-Americans, literally translated as 'a pubic hair'.
- —Dagoberto Fuentes, *Barrio Language Dictionary*, p. 113, 1974
- This scrawny pendejo wheeled a mutant '65 GTO which he claimed could outjump Crystal Blue Persuasion, though the Imp and Goat had never showed down.—Seth Morgan, *Homeboy*, p. 176, 1990

Penelope *noun*
a well-built, attractive, somewhat dim woman *UK*
The personification of a **BIMBO**, probably named after an identified celebrity, recorded in contemporary gay usage.
- —*Attitude*, p. 60, July 2003: 'New palare lexicon'

penetrate *verb*
to understand something after analysis *JAMAICA*
- —Peter Patrick, *Some Recent Jamaican Creole Words*, 2003

penguin *noun*
1 LSD *UK*
Presumably from the picture printed on the blotting paper dose.
- Street names [...] paper mushrooms, penguins, rainbows[.]—James Kay and Julian Cohen, *The Parents' Complete Guide to Young People and Drugs*, p. 141, 1998

2 a prison officer *UK*
From the black and white uniform.
- —Angela Devlin, *Prison Patter*, p. 87, 1996

3 a nun *US*
- You can't lie to a nun. We gotta go in and visit the penguin.—*The Blues Brothers*, 1980
- Girls get raped everyday, and now they're gonna pay 50 G just because these chicks wore penguin suits!—*The Bad Lieutenant*, 1992

▸ **go penguin**
in pool, to enter a formal tournament *US*
A reference to the tuxedo that is mandated by the dress code of some tournaments.
- —Steve Rushin, *Pool Cool*, p. 14, 1990

penguin *adjective*
pregnant *AUSTRALIA*
- —Thommo, *The Dictionary of Australian Swearing and Sex Sayings*, p. 93, 1985

penguin food *noun*
anchovies *US*

Limited usage, but clever.

- — *Maledicta*, p. 17, 1996: 'Domino's pizza jargon'

penguin suit; penguin outfit *noun*

a tuxedo or formal evening dress *UK, 1967*

- An effervescent nightmare of familiar faces and bodies turned into rented penguin outfits and slurpy masks. — Odie Hawkins, *Black Casanova*, p. 24, 1984

penis breath *noun*

used as a general-purpose insult *US*

- The movie E.T. has contributed penis breath, an aggressively weird phrase in perfect harmony with the aggressively weird psyche of the eight-year-old. — Gary Goshgarian (Editor), *Exploring Language*, p. 302, 1986

penitentiary pull *noun*

influence within a prison *US*

- — Ronald Davidson, *New York (letter to editor)*, p. 10, 11 February 1985

penitentiary punk *noun*

a male who starts taking part in homosexual sex in prison *US*

- We classify them two ways: penitentiary punk and free-world punk. — Bruce Jackson, *Outside the Law: A Thief's Primer*, p. 176, 1972

penitentiary turn-out *noun*

a man who begins engaging in homosexual sex in prison *US*

- Now there's only a few natural punks in there that are free-world; the rest of them are penitentiary turnouts. — Bruce Jackson, *Outside the Law*, p. 173, 1972

penman *noun*

a forger *UK, 1865*

- — Joseph E. Ragen and Charles Finston, *Inside the World's Toughest Prison*, 1962: 'Penitentiary and underworld glossary'
- — Angela Devlin, *Prison Patter*, p. 87, 1996

pennies *noun*

a substantial amount of money *UK*

- And like as not he was carrying pennies. — Jeremy Cameron, *Brown Bread in Wengen*, p. 5, 1999

penn'orth of chalk; penn'orth *noun*

a walk *UK, 1938*

Rhyming slang.

- Take a penn'orth, I want to talk to your mother, private like. — Ray Puxley, *Cockney Rabbit*, 1992

Pennsy *nickname*

the Pennsylvania Railroad *US, 1953*

- — *American Speech*, p. 288, December 1968: 'Addenda to the vocabulary of railroading'

Pennsylvania caps *noun*

in trucking, tyres that have been recapped with a seamless tread line *US*

- — Montie Tak, *Truck Talk*, p. 116, 1971

penny *noun*

one dollar *US*

- — David Claerbaut, *Black Jargon in White America*, p. 75, 1972

▸ **the penny drops; the penny's dropped; the penny will drop in minute; did I hear a penny drop?**

used in marking the belated understanding of something, often of a delayed appreciation of humour *UK, 1951*

There are more variations on this theme than are shown here.

- Barry is amazed! Has the penny dropped? — Barry Humphries, *Bazza Pulls It Off!*, 1971
- Stein, and the other members, are unaware that they have entered a cult, because it was disguised as a Marxist-Leninist political organisation dedicated to creating cadres ready to fight for the cause. The penny drops only when she tries to leave the organisation — *New Statesman*, 6th January 2003

penny *verb*

to force pennies into the space between a door and the jam near the hinges, making it difficult or, if done correctly, impossible to open the door from the inside *US*

- — Pamela Munro, *U.C.L.A. Slang*, p. 65, 1989

penny a mile *noun*

a smile *UK, 1960*

Rhyming slang.

- Meanwhile take a butcher's at this lot and keep a penny a mile on your boat race! — *The Sweeney*, p. 7, 1976

penny-ante *adjective*

petty, insignificant *US, 1935*

From a poker game with a one-cent 'ante' or buy-in, an insignificant stake.

- Why he ever started this cheap, penny-ante Building and Loan, I'll never know. — *It's a Wonderful Life*, 1946
- Her father was a penny-ante politician on the South Side[.] — Willard Motley, *Let No Man Write My Epitaph*, p. 125, 1958
- Killing machines like Quick Cicero were inexpendable; not so pennyante players like Frank Stutz. — Seth Morgan, *Homeboy*, p. 98, 1990

penny a pound; penny *noun*

the ground *UK, 1932*

Rhyming slang.

- — Ray Puxley, *Cockney Rabbit*, 1992

penny banger *noun*

a mistake *UK*

Rhyming slang for **CLANGER**.

- — Ray Puxley, *Cockney Rabbit*, 1992

penny black; penny *noun*

1 the back *UK, 1992*

Rhyming slang, based on a famously rare stamp.

2 the floor *UK*

By extension from 'penny black' (the back) via the sense to be knocked on your back, thus onto the floor.

- I sparked him. He hit the penny. — prison inmate, 5th August 2002

penny bun *noun*

1 one, especially in connection with racing odds *UK, 1984*

Rhyming slang.

- — Ray Puxley, *Cockney Rabbit*, 1992

2 the sun *UK*

Rhyming slang.

- — Ray Puxley, *Cockney Rabbit*, 1992

penny for the guy *noun*

a pie *UK*

Rhyming slang, formed from the catchphrase of children collecting funds to celebrate Guy Fawkes' night.

- — Ray Puxley, *Fresh Rabbit*, 1998

penny game *noun*

the gambling game two-up *AUSTRALIA*

- Unlike those quoted above he is now cured and has not played the penny game for more than 10 years. — James Holledge, *The Great Australian Gamble*, p. 104, 1966

penny locket *noun*

a pocket *UK*

Rhyming slang.

- [A]s dry as a snooker player's penny locket. — Ray Puxley, *Fresh Rabbit*, 1998

penny-nickle-nickle *noun*

an M-114 155 mm howitzer *US*

The standard infantry heavy artillery weapon during the Vietnam war.

- — Gregory Clark, *Words of the Vietnam War*, p. 304–305, 1990

penny-pinching *adjective*

frugal *US, 1920*

- Because – you ignor-amus – there's a big difference between his father managing big-time jobs like hospitals and airports and him offering penny-pinching housewives like your sister three rooms for the price of two[.] — Rita Ciresi, *Pink Slip*, p. 249–250, 1999

penny stamp *noun*

a tramp *UK*

Rhyming slang.

- There's no trains. Half a dozen penny stamps and two old Bill walking around the place. — Anthony Masters, *Minder*, p. 125, 1984

pension *noun*

▸ **on a pension**

of a policeman, having been bribed *UK*

- — Angela Devlin, *Prison Patter*, p. 82, 1996

pension run *noun*

in trucking, an easy, undemanding, regular route *US*

- — Montie Tak, *Truck Talk*, p. 117, 1971

Pentagon East *noun*

the US military command in Tan Son Nhut air base, South Vietnam *US*

- [A]bout halfway between the South Vietnamese Air Force headquarters and the huge American military complex that used to be called "Pentagon East" or "Mac V." —Hunter S. Thompson, *Songs of the Doomed*, p. 167, May 1975
- There in the bowels of a sprawling bunkerlike complex known as "Pentagon East," the American generals who made up the United States Military Assistance Command for Vietnam (MACV) had plotted the course of the war[.] —Frank Snepp, *Decent Interval*, p. 10, 1977
- These November briefings, the most elaborate of the war, were held at "Pentagon East." —Neil Sheehan, *A Bright Shining Lie*, p. 694, 1988

penthouse *noun*

a brakevan (caboose) cupola *US*

- —Ramon Adams, *The Language of the Railroader*, p. 113, 1977

pen yan *noun*

opium; heroin *US, 1922*

Originally used of opium only and thought to be from a Chinese term for opium. Many variants, including 'pen yang', 'pan yen', 'pen yen', 'pen yuen', 'pin yen', 'pinyon' and 'pin gon'.

- —Richard A. Spears, *The Slang and Jargon of Drugs and Drink*, p. 382, 1986
- —Mike Haskins, *Drugs*, p. 284, 2003

peon *noun*

an ordinary computer user with no special privileges *US*

- —Christian Crumlish, *The Internet Dictionary*, p. 151, 1995

people *noun*

1 narcotics police *US*

- [C]hased up Exchange Place by a baying pack of People. (Note: People is New Orleans slang for narcotics fuzz.) —William Burroughs, *Naked Lunch*, p. 7–8, 1957

2 a prisoner's closest friends and associates *US*

- —William K. Bentley and James M. Corbett, *Prison Slang*, p. 39, 1992

People *noun*

▸ **the People**

the masses, at least to the extent that the masses support the agenda advocated by the speaker *US*

Egalitarian or communist undertones.

- Ostensibly devoted to the cause of speaking to "The People" at their own level and in their own language (the other way had been tried and failed), the League had become fatally implicated in the way to say it rather than the thing that needed saying. —Clancy Sigal, *Going Away*, p. 303, 1961
- We march down Broadway, explaining in unison that "the streets belong to the People." —James Simon Kunen, *The Strawberry Statement*, p. 49, 1968
- We, as the vanguard of the oppressed masses, realize that we must and will serve the People heart and soul. — *The Black Panter*, p. 14, 6th April 1969

people zapper *noun*

a Vehicle Mounted Active Denial System or VMADS, a tank or jeep-mounted crowd control weapon *US*

- The VMADS, or "people zapper", uses a "directed energy beam", according to a Pentagon spokesperson — *The Observer*, p. 13, 18th March 2001

pep *noun*

1 energy *UK, 1912*

- He was full of pep. Must've had his grande-latte enema. —Jim Uhls, *Fight Club*, 1999

2 pepperoni *US*

- — *Maledicta*, p. 17, 1996: 'Domino's pizza jargon'

3 phencyclidine, the recreational drug known as PCP or angel dust *US*

- —Ralph de Sola, *Crime Dictionary*, p. 112, 1982

pep-em-up *noun*

an amphetamine or other central nervous system stimulant *US*

- —Edith A. Folb, *runnin' down some lines*, p. 249, 1980

pepper *noun*

1 an inexperienced, gullible victim of a gambling cheat *US*

Playing on 'green' as a colour and as a slang badge of inexperience.

- —John Scarne, *Scarne on Dice*, p. 475, 1974

2 cinders spread on a snowy road *US*

- — Elementary Electronics, *Dictionary of CB Lingo*, p. 92, 1976

pepper and salt punter *noun*

a bettor who places bets by telephone from home *AUSTRALIA*

- —Ned Wallish, *The Truth Dictionary of Racing Slang*, p. 61, 1989

pepperbelly *noun*

a Mexican or Mexican-American *US*

- — *Current Slang*, p. 22, Spring 1970

pep pill *noun*

a central nervous system stimulant in a tablet form *US, 1937*

A deceptive yet accurate euphemism that persisted for several decades, especially with students.

- The basic drug involved is some for of the amphetamines, or "pep pills," and they are dangerous. — *San Francisco Chronicle*, p. 5, 13th January 1963
- There are those who claim the outlaws don't need food because they get all their energy from pep pills. —Hunter S. Thompson, *Hell's Angels: A Strange and Terrible Saga*, p. 175, 1966
- Amphetamine, that group of drugs which are called pep pills by squares. They are also called psychic energizers. —Ruth Bronsteen, *The Hippy's Handbook*, p. 12, 1967
- "You know where I buy pep peels?" The Mexican laborer says, inquiring of the coffee-sipping dealers in the House of Do-Nuts on Stanyon Street. —Nicholas Von Hoffman, *We Are The People Our Parents Warned Us Against*, p. 31, 1967
- Greenies are pep pills – dextroamphetamine sulphate – and a lot of baseball players couldn't function without them. —Jim Bouton, *Ball Four*, p. 80, 1970
- And heh says, "Yeah, it's just a pep pill." So he gives me the benny [Benzedrine] and he says, "You'll like them.' —Bruce Jackson, *In the Life*, p. 66, 1972
- [S]cores of Negro youth gangs on pep pills were stealing cars[.] —James Ellroy, *Blood on the Moon*, p. 28, 1984

Pepsi; pepper *noun*

a French-Canadian *CANADA*

Originally directed as an insult, because it was said by anglophones that French-Canadians chose Pepsi™ over Coca-Cola™ because they thought the cans were larger, it has been adopted as a badge of pride, especially in the derived form 'pepper'.

- — *Maledicta*, p. 167, Summer/Winter 1978: 'How to hate thy neighbor: a guide to racist maledicta'
- '[W]e call them Frogs, kebs, or peppers.' —Suroosh Alvi et al., *The Vice Guide*, p. 252, 2002

Pepsi *adjective*

sexually frigid *UK*

Presumably because Pepsi™ is 'best served chilled'.

- — *Sky Magazine*, July 2001

Pepsi habit; Pepsi Cola habit *noun*

the occasional use of a drug, short of an all-out addiction *US*

- —William D. Alsever, *Glossary for the Establishment and Other Uptight People*, p. 5, December 1970
- —Jim Crotty, *How to Talk American*, p. 89, 1997

pep talk *noun*

a brief, emotional speech made to encourage or increase morale *US, 1925*

- I'm not paid to give pep talks. —Carl Hiassen, *Tourist Season*, p. 208, 1986
- Just give yourself a little pep talk, "Must try other people's clean silverware as part of the fun of dining out." — *As Good As It Gets*, 1997

pep up *verb*

to invigorate someone; to strengthen or enhance something *UK, 1925*

- After the dog-ass Jets got Dreamer Tatum, they made a stud trade with Dallas and got Jessie Luker and Gruver Allgood to pep up the offense. —Dan Jenkins, *Semi-Tough*, p. 92, 1972

per *noun*

percentage *US*

- In casino gambling, the percentage – always referred to in Las Vegas as the "per" – is everything. —Edward Lin, *Big Julie of Vegas*, p. 74, 1974

perambulator *noun*

a brakevan (caboose) *US*

- —Ramon Adams, *The Language of the Railroader*, p. 113, 1977

Perce *noun*

▹ **see:** PONGO

percentage *noun*

a profit; an advantage *UK, 1948*

Originally military.

- Regardless of the size of the franchisor, training is an important part of the business. There is, literally, no percentage in it for them if a franchisee fails. — *Success*, July 2000

percentage dice *noun*

dice that have been altered to favour a certain roll *US*

- I learned about percentage dice that are shaved to favor an ace-six – and a plenitude of snake eyes and boxcars. — Jimmy Snyder, *Jimmy the Greek*, p. 15, 1975

percentage joint *noun*

a carnival concession that relies on volume for profit *US*

- — Gene Sorrows, *All About Carnivals*, p. 24, 1985: 'Terminology'

percentage player *noun*

a gambler who appreciates odds and percentages, absorbing losses in the belief that the odds will ultimately favour him *US*

- Yeah, percentage players die broke too, don't they, Bert? — *The Hustler*, 1961

percenter *noun*

an ex-girlfriend *BAHAMAS*

- — John A. Holm, *Dictionary of Bahamian English*, p. 153, 1982

perch *noun*

▸ **drop off the perch; fall off the perch**

to die *UK, 1937*

- "We have two children," he said. "They wouldn't want to share the house after we both fall off the perch so it would have to be sold." — *The Observer*, 27th July 2003

percher *noun*

among the police, an easy arrest or an easy victim; in cricket, a very easy catch *UK*

- — David Powis, *The Signs of Crime*, 1977
- — *The Official Encyclopaedia of New Scotland Yard*, 1999

percia *noun*

cocaine *UK*

- — Mike Haskins, *Drugs*, p. 281, 2003

percolate *verb*

to meander; to be doing fine *US*

- — Lou Shelly, *Hepcats Jive Talk Dictionary*, p. 15, 1945

percolator *noun*

a carburettor *US*

- — Montie Tak, *Truck Talk*, p. 117, 1971

percussion adjustment *noun*

a blow to mechanical equipment with a large hammer *UK*

A jocular term for a popular technique, in Royal Air Force use, 2002.

Percy *noun*

1 the penis *UK*

Used as the title of a 1971 British film comedy about a penis-transplant.

- — Jim Ramsay, *Cop It Sweet!*, p. 69, 1977
- — Richard Herring, *Talking Cock*, p. 30, 2003

2 an effeminate male *US*

- — *American Weekly*, p. 2, 14th August 1955

3 a rock band's road manager *UK*

- — Bob Young and Micky Moody, *The Language of Rock 'n' Roll*, p. 106, 1985

4 cocaine *UK*

- — Dominic Anciano and Ray Burdis, *Love, Honour & Obey*, 1999
- CALL IT... Basuco, gianluca, blow, percy, lady, toot, white[.] JUST DON'T CALL IT... Charlie – too Eighties — *Drugs An Adult Guide*, p. 34, December 2001

percy *adverb*

per se (intrinsically) *UK*

- Now I've got nothing percy about Taking Things Back. — Andrew Nickolds, *Back to Basics*, p. 32, 1994

Percy Pongo *noun*

▷ **see: PONGO**

Percy Thrower *noun*

a telephone *UK*

Rhyming slang for **BLOWER**, formed on the name of television's first 'gardening superstar', 1913–88.

- — Ray Puxley, *Cockney Rabbit*, 1992

perdue *noun*

in poker, an unplayable hand abandoned by a player *US*

From the French for 'lost'.

- — George Percy, *The Language of Poker*, p. 66, 1988

perf *noun*

a performance *UK*

- America hated [Entertaining Mister] Sloane. We ran thirteen perfs. Ugh rotten Yanks! — *The Times Magazine*, 4th September 2004

perf *verb*

to retire someone on medical grounds *NEW ZEALAND*

From the acronym of the *P*olice *E*mployment *R*ehabilitation *F*und.

- Police officers who 'perfed out' received what they had paid in superannuation, plus the employers' contribution and some interest. — *Evening Post*, p. 5, 17th January 1991

perf *adjective*

perfect *AUSTRALIA, 1979*

- Oh well, if the food's perf, he won't notice the plonk. — Kathy Lette, *Girls' Night Out*, p. 12, 1987

perfect high *noun*

heroin *UK, 1998*

- — Robert Ashton, *This Is Heroin*, p. 206, 2002
- — Mike Haskins, *Drugs*, p. 284, 2003

perfection *noun*

perfect surfing conditions *AUSTRALIA*

- Nothing like sitting on the beach watching six to eight foot perfection while waiting for someone to show up to go surfing with. — *Tracks*, p. 143, October 1992

perfecto *adjective*

first-class, perfect, wonderful *US*

A simple embellishment in the Spanish style.

- The one perfecto thing I picked up. — *Heathers*, 1988
- WAYNE: How's it working, Scotty? SCOTT: Perfecto! — *Natural Born Killers*, 1994
- Agility. Mobility. Perfecto. — Kevin Sampson, *Outlaws*, p. 18, 2001

perfects *noun*

dice that are true to an extremely minute tolerance, approximately 1/1000th of a inch *US*

- — *The Annals of the American Academy of Political and Social Sciences*, p. 122, May 1950

perform *verb*

to behave histrionically *AUSTRALIA, 1891*

- [Her last fiance] shot through to London, not before leaving a bun in the oven and Chilla performing about paying for an abortion. — Frank Hardy, *The Outcasts of Foolgarah*, p. 13, 1971
- — Jim Ramsay, *Cop It Sweet!*, p. 69, 1977

performer *noun*

a person who behaves histrionically *AUSTRALIA*

- — Barry Humphries, *A Nice Night's Entertainment*, p. 42, 1960
- — Dymphna Cusack, *Picnic Races*, p. 191, 1962
- Up on the Darwin line we had some rare performers. The best was a guard we called the Native Companion because when he got in a rage he danced like a brolga. — Patsy Adam-Smith, *Folklore of the Australian Railwaymen*, p. 253, 1969

perf surf *noun*

excellent surfing conditions *AUSTRALIA*

- — Kathy Lette, *Girls' Night Out*, p. 188, 1987
- Equipped with the correct paraphernalia, they hang beachside talking loudly about 'flicking out' and 'perf surf'. — *Sydney Morning Herald*, p. 7, 3rd January 1987

perico *noun*

cocaine *US*

Spanish slang, adapted by some English speakers.

- — US Department of Justice, *Street Terms*, August 1994

perish *noun*

▸ **do a perish**

to suffer great deprivation, especially of water or sustenance *AUSTRALIA, 1897*

- And I'd like a refill for all the times I done a perish meself...but some'ow I always managed to strike a soak in the nick o' time. —Coralie Rees, *Spinifex Walkabout*, p. 243, 1953
- [T]here was many a time in my young days I did a perish tramping from one shed to another not knowing where the next quart-pot of water was coming from. —Dymphna Cusack, *Picnic Races*, p. 96, 1962

perisher *noun*

a person *UK, 1896*

Usually contemptuous or pitying. *The Perishers* cartoon strip by Maurice Dodd and Dennis Collins/Bill Melvin has appeared in Mirror Group newspapers since 1957.

- He looked a proper perisher. —Charles Raven, *Underworld Nights*, p. 158, 1956

perishing *adjective*

very cold *UK*

Shortened from 'perishing cold'.

- It is perishing, despite the fact that I am wearing a large number of layers, rather like a millefeuille. —*The Guardian*, 21st May 2003

perishing *infix*

used as an intensifier *UK*

- A girl like Tara would talk to you if you were manager of U perishing 2 [U2, a rock group], wouldn't she? —Kevin Sampson, *Powder*, p. 23, 1999

perjohnny *noun*

a poor white person *BARBADOS*

- —Frank A. Collymore, *Barbadian Dialect*, p. 83, 1965

perk *noun*

1 an advantage, in addition to salary, that is offered by a particular employment *UK, 1869*

An abbreviation of 'perquisite'.

- We don't get any perks at all. —John Wynnum, *Tar Dust*, p. 25, 1962
- He pours some of the champagne into a spare glass. "So have a fringe benefit. I know you earn your perks." —Ted Lewis, *Jack Carter's Law*, p. 67, 1974
- Furthermore, where were all the perks he'd heard about? —Lance Peters, *The Dirty Half-Mile*, p. 29, 1979
- No more perks? —Anthony Masters, *Minder*, p. 127, 1984
- They want to be top dog and get all the perks. —Dave Courtney, *Stop the Ride I Want to Get Off*, p. 8, 1999
- You go for whatever you can get away with, threaten a couple of times to walk out and see if they'll throw in some perks. —Elmore Leonard, *Be Cool*, p. 67, 1999

2 a tablet of Percodan™, a painkiller *US, 1971*

Also variant 'perc'.

- Get some up in Boystown, New York Avenue, those cute guys had anything you wanted, knockout drops, percs, street ludes, all kinds of meth. —Elmore Leonard, *Glitz*, p. 131, 1985
- He remembered a thousand Soledad bull sessions about dope and dry-swallowed two perks and three dexies. —James Ellroy, *Suicide Hill*, p. 749, 1986
- Pop a Perc and have a beer and that's it, sweetness all evening. —Suroosh Alvi et al., *The Vice Guide*, p. 109, 2002

perk *verb*

to vomit *AUSTRALIA, 1941*

- [B]oth of the newly-weds were likely to spend more time perking over the rail than reclining between the nuptial sheeting. —George Blaikie, *Remember Smith's Weekly?*, p. 213, 1966
- —Arthur Chipper, *The Aussie Swearer's Guide*, p. 33, 1972
- —Jim Ramsay, *Cop It Sweet!*, p. 69, 1977

perkie *noun*

▷ see: PEKKIE

perk up *verb*

to recover good spirits or vigour *UK, 1656*

- Monthly Viagra ration perks up Eurocrats —*The Guardian*, 9th August 2002

perky *adjective*

said of a woman with large buttocks but otherwise a slender body *US*

- —Rick Ayers (Editor), *Berkeley High Slang Dictionary*, p. 33, 2004

per-lease

▷ see: PLEASE

perlix *verb*

to flaunt your technical skills *BARBADOS*

- —Frank A. Collymore, *Barbadian Dialect*, p. 83, 1965

perm *noun*

in hairdressing, a permanent wave *UK, 1927*

- He [Rev. Al Sharpton] looks like Bookman from "Good Times" with a damn perm. How can you take anyone seriously with that hair? No matter what he says, you can't take your eyes off the hair. —Chris Rock, *Rock This!*, p. 14, 1997
- He got a bad perm and his hair frizzed out from his head like a fright wig[.] —Simon Napier-Bell, *Black Vinyl White Powder*, p. 206, 2001

perm *verb*

to give hair a permanent wave hair treatment *UK, 1928*

- She was wearing a hat and had had her hair permed and looked like someone's maiden aunt[.] —Alexander Trocchi, *Cain's Book*, p. 164, 1960

perma- *prefix*

permanent; permanently *UK*

Acts as adjective or adverb as required.

- Taking Drugs To Make Music To Take Drugs To: the motto of perma-zonked '80s drone rockers Spaceman 3. —*Q*, p. 51, October 2004

permafried *adjective*

drug-intoxicated *UK*

- —Mike Haskins, *Drugs*, p. 291, 2003

perma-tan *noun*

a *perma*nent sun*tan* *UK*

- The government's white paper on energy policy, published yesterday, had a green tinge that even caused the perma-tan of Jack Cunningham to turn pale. —*The Guardian*, 25th February 2003

perp *noun*

1 a criminal suspect *US*

From 'perpetrator'.

- —Carsten Stroud, *Close Pursuit*, p. 274, 1987
- He clobbered a neighbor of his last night and another person who could be one of your perps, and he's at large. —*Fargo*, 1996
- And these men, to make a living, they cross that bridge every day to a place where everything is upside down, where the cop is the perp and the perp is the victim. —*Copland*, 1997
- The perp(s) doused the Oakland Hills house with gasoline and set fire to the kitchen. —Ralph "Sonny" Barger, *Hell's Angel*, p. 180, 2000
- Shane arrested the perp half a block away as he was trying to stuff the murder weapon down into a Dumpster. —Stephen J. Cannell, *The Tin Collection*, 2001

2 wax and baking soda made to look like crack cocaine *US*

- —US Department of Justice, *Street Terms*, October 1994

perpetrate *verb*

to start a fight *US*

- —Don R. McCreary (Editor), *Dawg Speak*, 2001

perp walk *noun*

a purposeful display of a charged criminal, especially when being transported from jail to court *US*

- [W]hat they call a perp walk, they walk the defendant in front of the cameras to assure the public that the perpetrator has been caught. —Terry Moran, *Court TV*, 20th May 1994

Perry *noun*

a member of a 1970s youth movement identified by a uniform of casual wear *UK*

From the branded Fred *Perry* casual shirts they wore.

- Perries saw themselves as rivals to neo-Mods[.] —Sarah Callard and Will Hoon, *Surfers Soulies Skinheads & Skaters*, 1996

Perry Como *noun*

a homosexual *UK*

Rhyming slang for **HOMO** formed, for no apparent reason other than rhyme, on the popular singer, 1912–2001.

- —Ray Puxley, *Cockney Rabbit*, 1992

pers *adjective*

*pers*onal *UK*

- Nood builds a fat blunt with some pers skunk an' we have a smoke[.] —Nick Barlay, *Curvy Lovebox*, p. 53, 1997

Persian *noun*

heroin purportedly grown in or near Iran *US*

- Well, he also uses Mexican brown. And Persian by the bead! He whiffs it. —Joseph Wambaugh, *The Glitter Dome*, p. 248, 1981

Persian brown *noun*

heroin *US*

- —Peter Johnson, *Dictionary of Street Alcohol and Drug Terms*, p. 143, 1993

Persian mafia *noun*

a group of influential Iranians *US*

- —Pamela Munro, *U.C.L.A. Slang*, p. 96, 1997

Persian rugs *noun*
drugs *UK*
Rhyming slang.
• —Bodmin Dark, *Dirty Cockney Rhyming Slang*, 2003

persnickety *adjective*
fussy, snobbish *US, 1905*
An alteration of 'pernickety'.

personality girl *noun*
a popular woman who works in a bar, encouraging customers through flirtation to buy drinks, both for themselves and for her *US*
• —Jack Lait and Lee Mortimer, *Chicago Confidential*, p. 302, 1950: 'Loop lexicon'

persuader *noun*
1 any weapon, the more deadly the more persuasive *UK, 1796*
• —Inez Cardozo-Freeman, *The Joint*, p. 520, 1984

2 a whip, as used by a bullock driver or a jockey *AUSTRALIA, 1890*
• Then, when jockey Jack Thompson figured in a stirring finish and was about to draw the whip, Ken would say 'the Professor has gone for the persuader'. —Joe Brown, *Just for the Record*, p. 141, 1984

3 a linear amplifier for a citizens' band radio *US*
• —Bill Davis, *Jawjacking*, p. 74, 1977

persuasion *noun*
nationality; sex; kind *UK, 1864*
From the conventional sense (religious belief or opinion).
• Kate Hoey, the sport minister, who is of the female persuasion herself, replied that young women needed to be helped and supported in their sporting activities. — *The Guardian*, 1st February 2000

Peruvian *noun*
cocaine, probably from Peru *UK*
• —Mike Haskins, *Drugs*, p. 281, 2003

Peruvian flake *noun*
a powerful type of cocaine *US, 1984*
From its country of origin.
• —Richard A. Spears, *The Slang and Jargon of Drugs and Drink*, p. 383, 1986
• —Mike Haskins, *Drugs*, p. 281, 2003

Peruvian lady *noun*
cocaine *US*
• —US Department of Justice, *Street Terms*, August 1994

Peruvian marching powder *noun*
cocaine *US*
A variation of **BOLIVIAN/COLOMBIAN MARCHING POWDER**.
• "Peruvian Marching Powder is Peruvian coke," Ryan explained. —Stephen J. Cannell, *The Plan*, p. 374, 1995
• Two kilos of Peruvian marching powder. —Wayne Anthony, *Spanish Highs*, p. 183, 1999
• The dressing room after the show was crowded with fans, celebs, shirttail cousins, groupies, and purveyors of Peruvian marching powder. — Kinky Friedman, *Kinky Friedman's Guide to Texas Etiquette*, p. 188, 2001

Peruvian pink *noun*
a type of cocaine originating in Peru *UK*
• Needless to say, it wasn't Paxo inside the hens, it was 10 kilos of finest Peruvian pink. — *Ministry*, May 2002

perv; perve *noun*
1 a sexual pervert *AUSTRALIA, 1942*
Sometimes 'perv' carries the same force as its origin 'pervert', thus 'someone with a kinky sexual bent', 'a person obsessed with sex', 'a lecher' or 'a homosexual' (by those who regard this as unnatural). Can also be used in a weaker sense to refer to anyone whose sexual behaviour is unwanted.
• 'Just look at that ole secko, will you?' he said disgustedly, and scooping up a stone he ran after it, yelling, 'Merv, Merv, the rotten old perv,' throwing stones at its feet until it slipped into invisibility at the alley end. —Ruth Park, *Poor Man's Orange*, p. 38, 1949
• "Time enough for that when we get the next batch of pervs in." "Pervs?" I asked, curious at the Rita's tone and her use of the term. "I thought this place was a pukka naturist resort." —Petra Christian, *The Sexploiters*, p. 21, 1973
• And whit've I told you about dressing in my claes! Ya wee perv! —Ian Pattison, *Rab C. Nesbitt*, 1988
• Heartbroken Alan was branded a perv and a sicko by townsfolk... — *Picture*, p. 21, 5th February 1992
• Nancy played trombone in Spade Cooley's all-woman band and pen-palled with half the pervs in San Quentin. —James Ellroy, *Hollywood Nocturnes*, p. 23, 1994
• Keep your grubby little hands off, you perv. She doesn't want corrupting by you, she's a nice girl. —Colin Butts, *Is Harry on the Boat?*, p. 113–114, 1997
• But I called the phone company and made my number unpublished anyway, hoping to thwart the next perv's wicked plans. —Amy Sohn, *Run Catch Kiss*, p. 84, 1999
• [Y]ou can't be too careful these days with all the psychos and pervs and that running round town. —Kevin Sampson, *Outlaws*, p. 81, 2001

2 in prison, a sex offender; a convicted paedophile *AUSTRALIA, 1949*
An abbreviation of 'pervert'.
• —Angela Devlin, *Prison Patter*, p. 23, 1996

3 a person watching or staring sexually; a voyeur *AUSTRALIA, 1944*
• —Arthur Chipper, *The Aussie Swearer's Guide*, p. 46, 1972
• —Jim Ramsay, *Cop It Sweet!*, p. 69, 1977
• Teachers are so boring. (They must be perves or somethink that they have to know wot we did.) —Kylie Mole (Maryanne Fahey), *My Diary*, p. 97, 1988

4 a voyeuristic look *AUSTRALIA, 1963*
• I don't mind admitting, Geoff, I was having a bit of a perve. Did she know you could see straight through that thing she was wearing? —David Williamson, *The Club*, p. 48, 1978
• Girl surfers were only tolerated because of their perv value[.] —Kathy Lette, *Girls' Night Out*, p. 189, 1987
• Dino and me were just about to kiss each other goodbye after walking home from school together, and guess wot? I catch Adam having a perve. —Kylie Mole (Maryanne Fahey), *My Diary*, p. 69, 1988

5 a look *AUSTRALIA*
• I went into a newsagent's once after a surf. Me nose all plugged up with water, you know. Anyway, I'm leaning over having a perv at a Tracks mag when – whoosh – out comes fifty litres of snot and ocean all over the magazine rack. —Tim Winton, *Lockie Leonard*, p. 79, 1993

perv; perve *verb*
1 to lust after another person; to behave as a voyeur *AUSTRALIA, 1941*
• —Harry Orsman and Des Hurley, *The Beaut Little Book of New Zealand Slang*, 1994
• [He] had pretended he was asleep so that he could perve at her topless form[.] —Colin Butts, *Is Harry on the Boat?*, p. 135, 1997
• [C]os he likes perving over my missus, the dirty cunt[.] —Dave Courtney, *Raving Lunacy*, p. 61, 2000
• — *Ebony Magazine*, p. 156, August 2000: 'How to talk to the new generation'
• I tried not to perv on it, know mean, but fucking hell, man, them two shiny, beautiful you-know-whats pushing out of her blouse. —Kevin Sampson, *Clubland*, p. 82, 2002

2 to look at or watch sexually *AUSTRALIA, 1944*
• This study of the female nude is NOT perving, it is not pornographic – it is Art. — *Flame*, p. 12, 1972
• —John O'Grady, *It's Your Shout, Mate!*, p. 42, 1972
• —Bettina Arndt, *The Australian Way of Sex*, p. 139, 1985
• — *Kink*, p. 98, 1993
• Simone came to the show to perve at the boys. — *Dolly*, p. 37, 1996
• —Phillip Gwynne, *Deadly Unna?*, p. 58, 1998

3 to look at; to observe *AUSTRALIA, 1984*
• Like to perve on the 'in crowd' now and again. —Kathy Lette, *Girls' Night Out*, p. 85, 1987
• People nearly drove off the road perving at them. —Tim Winton, *Lockie Leonard*, p. 27, 1993
• Doncha know it's rude to perve? —Glyn Parry, *Mosh*, p. 33, 1996

pervert squad *noun*
a police sex crime investigative squad *US*
• It is not uncommon to hear officers from other investigative units refer to the sex crime investigative unit as the "pervert squad," or worse, the "pussy posse." —F.D. Jordan, *Sex Crime Investigations*, p. 9, 1996

perving *noun*
sexual ogling; voyeurism *AUSTRALIA*
• Come summer, a new social hobby for men begins. It is called, with frightening Freudian accuracy "perving". —Sue Rhodes, *Now you'll think I'm awful*, p. 58, 1967

pervy *adjective*
sexually perverted; pornographic *UK, 1944*
• And unlike God's Own Country, where every true blue bloke scores heaps of legover, the Poms just don't get enough. They depend on stories about their pervy politicians to get their kicks. — *People*, p. 4, 30th March 1994
• A pervy Pommy postie copped a year in the clink for stealing a whopping eight mailbags full of sex toys! — *People*, 5th July 1999
• [W]e liked the Versace room and the pervy Gucci pad best[.] — *ES Magazine*, p. 3, 22nd June 2001

- She's stuck that pervy poster of pantless Robbie on her bedroom ceiling. — *Skymail, Sky Magazine*, p. 11, May 2001
- I stood up and recited stumbling tracts of pre-rehearsed Kipling to paralytic pervy uncles. — Helen Hastings, *Are Friends Electra [Inappropriate Behaviour]*, 2002

pesky *adjective*
annoying, disagreeable *US, 1775*
- [T]hat pesky old Constitution keeps getting in the way. — Erica Orloff and JoAnn Baker, *Dirty Little Secrets*, p. 34, 2001

pessimal *adjective*
as bad as bad can be *US*
Computer slang.
- — Guy L. Steele et al., *The Hacker's Dictionary*, p. 101, 1983

pest control *noun*
a psychiatrist; psychiatrists *UK*
Medical slang.
- — Adam T. Fox, St Mary's Hospital, London, 10th October 2002

pet *verb*
▸ **pet the cat**
to stroke the air or water while getting through a difficult moment surfing *US*
- — Trevor Cralle, *The Surfin'ary*, p. 87, 1991

petal *noun*
used as an informal or affectionate term of address *UK*
- "Yes, petal – what do you want to know?" the band-leader says with determined cheerfulness. — *New Society*, 18th September 1980

Pete *noun*
1 a truck manufactured by Peterbilt *US*
- — Montie Tak, *Truck Talk*, p. 117, 1971

2 nitroglycerin *US*
- — Vincent J. Monteleone, *Criminal Slang*, p. 174, 1949

▸ **for Pete's sake**
used as a mild, non-profane oath used in times of exasperation or annoyance *US, 1924*
- Oh, for pete's sake, you two are psychological! — John Clellon Holmes, *Go*, p. 141, 1952
- Oh for Pete's sake. For Pete's s- He's fleein' the interview. — *Fargo*, 1996

pete man *noun*
a criminal specialising in breaking into safes *US, 1931*
- Pete Man wasn't anybody's name. It was slang for safecracker. — Emmett Grogan, *Final Score*, p. 18, 1976

Pete Murray *noun*
a curry *UK*
Rhyming slang, formed on the name of a radio DJ (b.1928).
- — Ray Puxley, *Fresh Rabbit*, 1998

peter *noun*
1 the penis *UK, 1902*
- Just a while ago you were as hard as a little boy's peter in a fifty-cent cat house. — Clarence Cooper Jr, *The Scene*, p. 199, 1960
- Screw's invention of the Peter Meter, a graph for the reviewer to record, in inches, the erection potential of pornographic films. — Richard Neville, *Play Power*, p. 77, 1970
- IF YOU DON'T GIVE ME A SEX CHANGE, I'LL CUT OFF YOUR PETER AND SEW IT ON ME MYSELF!!! — John Waters, *Deperate Living*, p. 161, 1988

2 a cell in a prison or a police station *AUSTRALIA, 1890*
The likely derivation is in the the proper name Peter, which comes from Greek *petros* perhaps influenced by *petra* – with the implication 'firm as a rock'.
- Dolly spent the rest of the day, howling for revenge, in the "peter" at the back of the town. — George Farwell, *Land of Mirage*, p. 122, 1950
- [T]hey smack him in a peter on a charge of receiving. — Charles Raven, *Underworld Nights*, p. 22, 1956
- As I came along the passage leading from the court to the peters a twirl shouted. — Frank Norman, *Bang To Rights*, p. 7, 1958
- [Y]ou can get fined twenty dollars or a month in the peter with or without hard labour. — Frank Hardy, *The Outcasts of Foolgarah*, p. 59, 1971
- — Angela Devlin, *Prison Patter*, p. 87, 1996

3 a safe *US, 1859*
- This peter's a motherfucker. — *Casino*, 1995

Peter and his fuzzy pals *noun*
the male genitals *US*
An elaboration of **PETER** (the penis).
- — Erica Orloff and JoAnn Baker, *Dirty Little Secrets*, p. 69, 2001

peter-crazy *adjective*
obsessed with having sex with men *US*
- I mean, she was peter-crazy anyway. — Bruce Jackson, *In the Life*, p. 399, 1972

peter drops; peter; petes *noun*
specifically, knock-out drops; generally, any central nervous system depressant *US, 1933*
- — Eugene Landy, *The Underground Dictionary*, p. 148, 1971
- — Richard A. Spears, *The Slang and Jargon of Drugs and Drink*, p. 383, 1986
- — Mike Haskins, *Drugs*, p. 283, 2003

peter-eater *noun*
a person who enjoys performing oral sex on men *US*
- — Anon., *King Smut's Wet Dreams Interpreted*, 1978

peter-gazer *noun*
a prisoner who cannot hide his interest in other mens' penises while in the showers *US*
- — Jim Goad, *Jim Goad's Glossary of Northwestern Prison Slang*, December 2001

peter heater *noun*
1 an act of urination while wearing a wetsuit *US*
- — Trevor Cralle, *The Surfin'ary*, p. 87, 1991

2 in Canadian military aviation, the pitot heater *CANADA*
The 'pitot tube' is a small tube pointed forward into the airstream, to compare inside and outside pressure and measure airspeed. In cold weather, it can freeze up and must be heated electrically.
- Don't touch the peter heater while I test it! — Tom Langeste, *Words on the Wing*, p. 211, 1995

peterman *noun*
a safe-breaker *UK, 1900*
- I've known several good petermen – safe-breakers – in my time[.] — Charles Raven, *Underworld Nights*, p. 26, 1956
- I was called on to test my ingenuity with every slick move I had learned as a peterman. — Red Rudensky, *The Gonif*, p. 7, 1970
- Not just for obvious villains – tea-leaves [thieves], petermen, etc. — Andrew Nickolds, *Back to Basics*, p. 37, 1994

Peter O'Toole *noun*
a stool, especially a bar stool *UK*
Rhyming slang, formed from the name of the celebrated Irish actor (b.1932).
- — Ray Puxley, *Fresh Rabbit*, 1998

peter out *verb*
to gradually cease; to come to an end *US, 1854*
- The programme is uneven, with sparky ideas petering out inconclusively. — *The Observer*, 18th January 2004

peter pan *noun*
1 a van *UK*
Rhyming slang, formed from J.M. Barrie's immortal hero Peter Pan.
- — Ray Puxley, *Cockney Rabbit*, 1992

2 a pan used by prostitutes while washing a customer's penis *US*
An crude if smart allusion to J.M. Barrie.
- I puked in her peter pan. — Earl Thompson, *Tattoo*, p. 182, 1974

peter parade *noun*
a mass inspection of soldiers for signs of sexually transmitted infections *US*
- — *American Speech*, p. 55, February 1947: 'Pacific war language'

peter pilot *noun*
a co-pilot, especially one in training *US*
- The co-pilot, or peter pilot, was a new man Brody had only seen around the Turkey Farm a couple times, but his jungle boots were scuffed and he needed a haircut, so he must be an OK kinda dude. — Jack Hawkins, *Chopper One #2: Tunnel Warriors*, 1987

peter pocket *noun*
the vagina *US*
Seen as a container for a **PETER** (penis).
- — Erica Orloff and JoAnn Baker *Dirty Little Secrets*, p. 71, 2001

peter-puffer *noun*
a person who performs oral sex on a man *US*
- Are you a peter-puffer? — *Full Metal Jacket*, 1987

Peters and Lee; peters *noun*
an act of urination *UK*
Rhyming slang for **PEE** or **WEE**, formed from a 1970s recording act.
- —Ray Puxley, *Fresh Rabbit*, 1998

peter thief *noun*
a prisoner who steals from others' cells *AUSTRALIA, 1950*
From **PETER** (a cell).
- —Ryan Aven-Bray, *Ridgey Didge Oz Jack Lang*, p. 40, 1983
- —Angela Devlin, *Prison Patter*, p. 87, 1996

peter thin *noun*
a prisoner who steals from others' cells *UK*
From **PETER** (a cell).
- —Angela Devlin, *Prison Patter*, p. 87, 1996

peter tracks *noun*
stains from seminal fluid *US*
- A few days before, Martha had sneaked into his closet and dribbled motor oil on the crotches of his pants. The stains won't wash out and now all his trousers have permanent peter tracks.—C.D. Payne, *Youth in Revolt*, p. 59, 1993

Pete Tong *noun*
a variety of MDMA, the recreational drug best known as ecstasy, identified by PT embossed on the tablet *UK*
Disguising PT with the name of a UK DJ associated with the **RAVE** scene.
- —Gareth Thomas, *This Is Ecstasy*, p. 57, 2002

Pete Tong *adjective*
wrong *UK*
Rhyming slang, based on the name of popular club and BBC Radio 1 DJ, Pete Tong (b.1960).
- This is where it all went a bit Pete Tong.—Gavin Hills, *White Burger Danny (Disco Biscuits)*, p. 76, 1996
- [T]his is where it really does go Pete Tong.—Kevin Sampson, *Outlaws*, p. 302, 2001
- It all went Pete Tong for Nicola.— BBC TV, *Friends Like These*, 9th June 2001

peth *noun*
*Peth*idine™, a branded central nervous system depressant *UK, 1998*
- —Mike Haskins, *Drugs*, p. 283, 2003

petro *adjective*
anxious, nervous, afraid *US*
- —Connie Eble (Editor), *UNC-CH Campus Slang*, p. 7, Spring 2003

petrol bowsers; petrols *noun*
trousers *AUSTRALIA*
Rhyming slang. Petrol bowser is a proprietary name for a pump.
- This randy Australian bastard passed out cold even before I could get him out of his petrols[.]—Barry Humphries, *Bazza Pulls It Off!*, 1971

petrol head *noun*
1 a motor vehicle enthusiast *AUSTRALIA, 1985*
- —Kathy Lette, *Girls' Night Out*, p. 187, 1987
- I watch the fully-worked classic canary yellow Valiant Charger clean up a fire hydrant. The petrol head keeps going.—Glyn Parry, *Mosh*, p. 105, 1996

2 a fast and reckless driver *NEW ZEALAND*
- Mosts of them are what we call petrol heads who drive rust buckets which pose a real threat to law-abiding motorists.— *Sunday Star-Times*, p. A3, 14th June 1998

petrol tank *noun*
an act of masturbation *UK*
Rhyming slang for **WANK**.
- —Ray Puxley, *Fresh Rabbit*, 1998

Petticoat Lane *noun*
a physical pain; a pain (a nuisance) *UK*
Rhyming slang, formed on London's famous Sunday market.
- —Ray Puxley, *Cockney Rabbit*, 1992

Petula *noun*
central London *UK*
Almost certainly a reference to singer Petula Clark (b.1932) who enjoyed lasting success with the songs 'Downtown' and 'Don't Sleep in the Subway'.
- — *Attitude*, p. 60, July 2003: 'New palare lexicon'

Peyton Place *noun*
the face *UK*
Rhyming slang, formed from the title of 1956 novel by Grace Metalious, probably remembered here for the television drama series, 1964–69.
- —Ray Puxley, *Fresh Rabbit*, 1998

pezzy; pez *adjective*
inferior, of poor quality *UK*
Derives from 'peasant'.
- Your BMX is Pezzy.—Chris Lewis, *The Dictionary of Playground Slang*, p. 169, 2003

PFC *noun*
a *p*rivate *f*ucking *c*itizen *US*
What a private first class became upon his discharge from duty in Vietnam.
- Kalane smiled. "They don't let pfc's in here, Lieutenant." Tyson said, "They do if pfc means private fucking civilian."—Nelson DeMille, *Word of Honor*, p. 356, 1985
- —Gregory Clark, *Words of the Vietnam War*, p. 411, 1990

Pfizer riser *noun*
sildenafil citrate marketed as Viagra™, an anti-impotence drug *US*
Viagra™ is manufactured by Pfizer, and 'riser' is a convenient rhyme that suggests the drug's power to stimulate an erection.
- But men of all ages are swamping doctors' offices, claiming flaccidity and begging for that little blue pill dubbed the "Pfizer Riser."— *New York Times*, p. 15 (Section 4), 26th April 1998
- — *Sky Magazine*, July 2001

PFO *adjective*
a hospital patient who was injured while drunk *AUSTRALIA*
From '*p*issed, *f*ell *o*ver'.
- — *Maledicta*, p. 92, 1986–1987: 'Australian maledicta'
- — *Ethics and Behaviour, Volume 13, number 2*, August 2003

PFQ
*p*retty *f*ucking *q*uick *UK*
A variation of **PDQ** (pretty damn quick).
- [O]ur cricketers seem to go to the crease and from it PFQ against Australia these days.—Ray Puxley, *Fresh Rabbit*, 1998

pfund *noun*
▷ see: **FUNT**

p-funk *noun*
1 heroin *UK, 1998*
After the drug-driven music of George Clinton's *P*arliament-*Funk*adelic.
- —Robert Ashton, *This Is Heroin*, p. 206, 2002
- —Mike Haskins, *Drugs*, p. 284, 2003

2 crack cocaine and phencyclidine mixed for smoking *US*
- —US Department of Justice, *Street Terms*, October 1994
- —Mike Haskins, *Drugs*, p. 293, 2003

PG *noun*
1 paregoric elixir, a flavoured tincture of opium designed to assuage pain *US*
- Now he had no money for junk. He couldn't even raise the price of PG and goof balls to taper off.—William Burroughs, *Junkie*, p. 96, 1953

2 a *p*aying *g*uest *UK*
An initialism.
- What on earth had possessed Father to send him as P.G. to these old fogies?—Douglas Rutherford, *The Creeping Flesh*, p. 11, 1963

PG *adjective*
excellent *US*
An abbreviation of '*p*ast *g*one'.

PG&E *noun*
electric shock treatment *US*
From the electric utility *P*acific *G*as and *E*lectric Company.
- —Frank Prewitt and Francis Schaeffer, *Vacaville Vocabulary*, 1961–1962

PG bag *noun*
a small bag for carrying your personal effects, your *p*ersonal *g*ear *US*
- —Murry A. Taylor, *Jumping Fire*, p. 458, 2000

PGT *adjective*
doctors' shorthand for the facetious diagnosis (applied to a casualty patient): *pissed* (drunk), *got thumped* *UK*
Recorded in an article about medical slang in British (3 London and 1 Cambridge) hospitals.
- — *Ethics and Behaviour*, August 2003

PG Tips *noun*
the lips *UK*
Rhyming slang, formed from a well-known brand of tea; a product which is famously, perhaps not coincidentally, advertised by chimpanzees.
- — Ray Puxley, *Cockney Rabbit*, 1992

phantasmagoria *noun*
an astonishing visual display *UK, 1802*
The term was coined for an 1802 exhibition of optical illusions in London. It was used throughout the C19, forgotten, and then briefly revived in the hippie era of the 1960s and 70s.
- The inside of my mitts were flaming from the palms I slapped. It was phantasmorgoria. They wantonly danced to the funky band's erotic pound. — Iceberg Slim (Robert Beck), *Airtight Willie and Me*, p. 26, 1979

phantom gobbler *noun*
an anonymous giver of oral sex *UK*
- A phantom would usually be a closeted gay man in the Merchant Navy who would go round the cabins at night, lifting the sheets of other sailors to administer oral sex while they slept (or pretended to sleep). — Paul Baker, *Polari*, p. 186, 2002

phantom off *verb*
in surfing, to end a ride voluntarily *AUSTRALIA*
- — Gary Fairmont R. Filosa II, *The Surfer's Almanac*, p. 191, 1977

phantom punch *nickname*
the punch thrown by Muhammed Ali (then Cassius Clay) that was not seen but which knocked out his opponent Sonny Liston on 25th May 1965 *US*
- — Louis Phillips and Burnham Holmes, *The Complete Book of Sports Nicknames*, p. 222, 1998

Phar Lap odds *noun*
in horse racing, very high odds *AUSTRALIA*
Phar Lap (1926–32), one of the greatest racehorses of all time, often ran with very high odds.
- — Ned Wallish, *The Truth Dictionary of Racing Slang*, p. 61, 1989

pharmies *noun*
prescription medication *US*
- — Connie Eble (Editor), *UNC-CH Campus Slang*, p. 7, Spring 2003

pharming *noun*
the mixing and then consumption of the mixed prescription drugs *US*
- In ever-increasing numbers, federally sanctioned, totally licit prescription medications, everything from Adderall to Zoloft, are finding their way onto the streets and into the digestive tracts and nasal passages of the unprescribed, as college students locally and nationwide pop prescription pills for practical and recreational purposes. They call it "pharming". — *The Hartford Advocate*, 19 April 2001

phase 4 *noun*
a pill of MDMA, the recreational drug best known as ecstasy, mixed with sufficient amphetamine for a 4 hour effect *UK*
Similarly, a 'phase 8' has an 8 hour effect.
- — Gareth Thomas, *This Is Ecstasy*, p. 54, 2002

phat *adjective*
excellent, admirable *US*
A deliberate misspelling of **FAT** (good); originally black usage, now widespread via hip-hop culture.
- — Connie Eble (Editor), *UNC-CH Campus Slang*, November 1973
- You can feel its big breakbeat power in The Chemical Brothers' huge phat records[.] — John Robb, *The Nineties*, p. 260, 1999

phat 2 death *adjective*
extremely good *US*
- — Connie Eble (Editor), *UNC-CH Campus Slang*, p. 8, Fall 1999

phat-phat; put-put *noun*
a motorcycle; a three-wheeled motor-scooter taxi *INDIA*
Echoic.
- — Nigel Hankin, *Hanklyn-Janklyn*, 2003

phatty!
great! *US*
- — *Maybeck High School Yearbook (Berkeley, California)*, p. 29, 1997

P-head *noun*
a frequent user of phenobarbital, a central nervous system depressant *US*
- — Ralph de Sola, *Crime Dictionary*, p. 114, 1982

pheasant *noun*
in a gambling cheating scheme, a victim *US*
- — John Scarne, *Scarne on Dice*, p. 461, 1974

pheasant plucker *noun*
a 'pleasant fucker' *UK, 1973*
A popular Spoonerism that is also part of the well-known tongue-twisters: 'I'm not a pheasant plucker / I'm a pheasant plucker's son / And I'm only plucking pheasants / 'Til the pheasant plucker comes' and 'I'm not the pheasant plucker / I'm the pheasant plucker's daughter / And I'm not plucking pheasants / When some pheasant plucker oughta'. Often used ironically with the sense 'unpleasant fucker'.
- It was life as normal at the Pheasant Plucker, the Jolly Sailor and the Bridewell, a row of three union flag-bedecked establishments dedicated to keeping Benidorm's legion of beer-drinking British tourists happy last night. — *The Guardian*, 18th May 2002

phenie *noun*
a capsule of phenobarbital, a central nervous system depressant *US*
- — Eugene Landy, *The Underground Dictionary*, p. 148, 1971

phennie *noun*
a capsule of phenobarbital, a central nervous system depressant *US*
- — Stewart L. Tubbs and Sylvia Moss, *Human Communication*, p. 119, 1974
- — Walter L. Way, *The Drug Scene*, p. 112, 1977

pheno *noun*
a capsule of phenobarbital, a central nervous system depressant *UK, 1966*
- We also dealt for red capsules of phenos, two of which, with hot water, produce a forgetting high[.] — Piri Thomas, *Down These Mean Streets*, p. 258, 1967
- — William D. Alsever, *Glossary for the Establishment and Other Uptight People*, p. 2, December 1970

phenomenon *noun*
a prodigy; a remarkable person, animal or thing *UK, 1803*
- That gentleman will never set foot in Perugia again. He was a phenomenon only when he played against Italy. — *The Guardian*, 20th June 2002

phet freak *noun*
an amphetamine addict *US*
- Within fiften minutes, the A-heads began to flock, and the sound of the trilling flute was heart in the hallway of 28 Allen Street, 'phet-freaks banging most urgently on the door. — Ed Sanders, *Tales of Beatnik Glory*, p. 196, 1975

phew!
used for expressing relief or suffering *UK, 1604*
As the legendary, clichéd tabloid weather headline 'Phew! What a scorcher!'.
- The days of rock hysteria have gone. Phew! but not forever. — Richard Neville, *Play Power*, p. 104, 1970
- All that unearned approval! Phew! Makes you think, eh? — Michael Moorcock, *britpulp*, p. 21, 1998
- Phew!!! Who guffed? — *SMTV LIVE it's wicked*, p. 6, 2000

Philadelphia bankroll *noun*
a single large-denomination note wrapped around small-denomination notes, giving the impression of a great deal of money *US*
- — Hy Lit, *Hy Lit's Unbelievable Dictionary of Hip Words for Groovy People*, p. 47, 1968

Philadelphia lawyer *noun*
a shrewd and skilled lawyer who is not guided by scruples or ethics *US, 1788*
One of many unwarranted slurs on a fine city.
- What in hell are you? a Philadelphia lawyer? — Hubert Selby Jr, *Last Exit to Brooklyn*, p. 36, 1957

- Came one response, "You'll need a Philadelphia lawyer for that one." —Sidney Bernard, *This Way to the Apocalypse*, p. 22, 1968
- Ya gotta have a dozen Philadelphia lawyers to figure out them propositions anyway. —Eugene Boe (Compiler), *The Wit & Wisdom of Archie Bunker*, p. 59, 1971
- "Don't pull that Philadelphia lawyer on me," Serpico replied[.] —Peter Maas, *Serpico*, p. 241, 1973

Philadelphia mafia *noun*
recording artists, record producers and radio personalities based in Philadelphia in the late 1950s *US*
- —Arnold Shaw, *Dictionary of American Pop/Rock*, p. 278, 1982

Philadelphia roll *noun*
a Philadelphia bankroll *US*
- Directly, he took out his wallet again and apologized, peeling off two new ten-spots, flashing a few coarse ones, a real Philadelphia roll. —Guy Owen, *The Flim-Flam Man and the Apprentice Grifter*, p. 172, 1972

phile *noun*
a computer file intended to assist computer hacking *US*
- His own Web and ftp sites contain many questionable "philes" and links themselves. —*Electronic Engineering Times*, 8th January 1996
- The spelling of "phile" is important. It's a homage to phone phreaking[.] —Melanie McGrath, *Hard, Soft & Wet*, p. 79, 1998

philharmonic *noun*
tonic water *UK*
Rhyming slang.
- —Ray Puxley, *Cockney Rabbit*, 1992

Philistine *noun*
a usurer *US*
- —John Scarne, *Scarne on Dice*, p. 475, 1974

Phillies Blunt; Phillies; Philly; Phillie *noun*
a cigar re-made to contain marijuana *US*
Generic usage but originally made with a brand name Phillies Blunt™ cigar.
- The saga of the philly blunt continues[.] —Redman, *How To Roll A Blunt*, 1992
- You got a Phillie? —*Kids*, 1995
- I was instrumental in introducing Phillies Blunts to the UK [...] It was LL Cool J who taught me how to roll a Phillies. I can roll Phillies, Dutch Owls and White Owls. —*Mixmag*, p. 75, April 2003

Philly *noun*
Philadelphia, Pennsylvania *US, 1891*
- Look at a few weeks ago when he was off in Philly. —Ralph Ellison, *Invisible Man*, p. 401, 1947
- Washington wolves go to Philly to howl. —Jack Lait and Lee Mortimer, *Washington Confidential*, p. 256, 1951
- In "Philly" I ran into "Archie Moore". —Babs Gonzales, *I Paid My Dues*, p. 63, 1967
- Vickie had met a young cat who lived in Philly and had pleaded with her to make the scene in Philly with him. —Herbert Huncke, *The Evening Sun Turned Crimson*, p. 57, 1980
- As I explained last night, you know, we're not gonna saturate the New York market. Now Philly, now that's a real rock and roll town. —*This is Spinal Tap*, 1984
- Sal Catalina, getting back, is South Philly. —Elmore Leonard, *Glitz*, p. 108, 1985
- I heard one that that a DJ in Philly was playing like crazy[.] —Frank Zappa, *The Real Frank Zappa Book*, p. 88, 1989

philosopher *noun*
a card cheat *US*
- —Albert H. Morehead, *The Complete Guide to Winning Poker*, p. 270, 1967

Phil the fluter; phil *noun*
a gun *UK*
Rhyming slang for **SHOOTER**, from the eponymous hero of an Irish comic ballad, 'Phil the Fluter's Ball', 1915.
- —Ray Puxley, *Cockney Rabbit*, 1992

Phil the Greek *nickname*
His Royal Highness Prince Philip (b.1921), Duke of Edinburgh, Earl of Merioneth and Baron Greenhich, born Prince of Greece and Denmark *UK*
Probably coined by satirical magazine *Private Eye*; it overlooks the fact that Prince Philip is actually Danish.
- Meanwhile we've let William of Orange, Mary Queen of Scots, Phil the Greek and Princess Michael of Kent take up citizenship. —Andrew Nickolds, *Back to Basics*, p. 12, 1994

phish *noun*
an instance of stealing credit card data on the Internet *US*
- [T]he phish made no mention of my name as it appears on a credit card, no other identifying details, and no date of purchase, but did have contact details if this charge was "in error". —*The Guardian*, 5th February 2004

phish *verb*
to steal credit card data on the Internet *US*
- —*San Francisco Chronicle*, p. D2, 27th July 2003

phishing *noun*
the act of stealing credit card data on the Internet *US*
- The scam is called "phishing" – as in fishing for your password, but spelled differently. —*Florida Times-Union*, p. G3, 16th March 1997
- Phishing by playing on fears of being associated with porn purchases is particularly vile. —*The Guardian*, 5th February 2004

phiz *noun*
1 physics, especially as a subject of study *HONG KONG*
- Even pupils in the Anglo-Chinese schools of Hong Kong talk of chem – and math, geog, phiz, etc. —Beale, 1984

2 the face; the expression on the face *UK, 1688*
An abbreviation of 'physiognomy'. Also variants 'phizz' and 'phyz'.

phizgig *noun*
a police informer *AUSTRALIA*
Variant of **FIZGIG**.
- He used pimps and phizgigs as he saw fit[.] —Vince Kelly, *The Bogeyman*, p. 5, 1956
- He was a former phizgig, or police pimp, who had joined Annie's employ[.] —Lance Peters, *The Dirty Half-Mile*, p. 14, 1979

phizog; physog; fizzog *noun*
the face; the expression on the face *UK, 1811*
An abbreviation of 'physiognomy'.
- Simply arrange these fizzogs in order of ugliness[.] —Ian Pattison, *Rab C. Nesbitt*, 1988
- His Smash Hits good looks may have matured into the kind of fizzog that has him pegged for film stardom[.] —Andrew Holmes, *Sleb*, p. 103, 2002

Phoebe *noun*
in dice games, a roll of five *US*
- —Lou Shelly, *Hepcats Jive Talk Dictionary*, p. 15, 1945
- —Frank Garcia, *Marked Cards and Loaded Dice*, p. 263, 1962

phoenix *noun*
LSD *UK*
- —Mike Haskins, *Drugs*, p. 286, 2003

phone *noun*
in prison, the toilet bowl in a cell *AUSTRALIA*
When the bowl empties of water, it is possible to talk to prisoners in other nearby cells using the pipes to carry the soundwaves.
- I had a bit of a talk to Jim Smith on the phone (the shithouse) last night at about 2 am. —Ray Denning, *Prison Diaries*, p. 66, 1978

phone *verb*
▸ **phone it in**
of an entertainer, to go through the motions; to produce a half-hearted performance *UK*
- They're not phoning it in. —Jack White (of the Rolling Stones in rehearsal), *The One and Only Rolling Stones*, 24th August 2003

phone box *noun*
a temporary latrine *US*
- [T]here were also some of the odd US "phone-box" comfort stations, all of which were literally public conveniences, men staring thoughtfully at the horizon while seated. —Kate Adie (writing of the Gulf War), *The Kindness of Strangers*, p. 335, 2002

phone call *noun*
in prison, a remark that someone wants to talk to you *US*
- —Charles Shafer, *Folk Speech in Texas Prisons*, p. 211, 1990

phonecard deal *noun*
in prison, a trade that values a marijuana cigarette at one phonecard *UK*
- —Angela Devlin, *Prison Patter*, p. 87, 1996

phone phreak; phone freak; phreaker *noun*
a person who electronically and fraudulently manipulates international telephone calls *US*
UK use. The original phone phreaks thought of themselves as telecommunications hobbyists (John Markoff, *Wired Style*, 1996).
- A man suspected of being Captain Crunch, bane of telephone companies around the world and hero of "phone phreaks" across the country, was arrested Tuesday in Jamaica, N.Y. — *San Francisco Examiner*, p. 43, 14th July 1972
- — David Powis, *The Signs of Crime*, 1977

phone phreak; phreak *verb*
to hack into a telecommunications system *US*
A play on 'freak'.
- — Eric S. Raymond, *The New Hacker's Dictionary*, p. 281, 1991
- [A] homage to phone phreaking[.] — Melanie McGrath, *Hard, Soft & Wet*, p. 79, 1998

phone spot *noun*
a telephone location used in a bookmaking operation *US*
- Zoot wants to trade a phone spot to us. — Joseph Wambaugh, *The Blue Knight*, p. 56, 1973

phone wench *noun*
a female customer service representative *US*
- — *Maledicta*, p. 10, 1996: 'Domino's pizza jargon'

phoney; phony *noun*
a person who lacks sincerity and substance *US, 1900*
- So I drank up all the money / Yes, I drank up all the money / With these phonies in this Hollywood bar / These friends of mine in this Hollywood bar. — Warren Zevon, *The French Inhaler*, 1973

phoney; phony *adjective*
fraudulent; fake; without substance *US, 1894*
- If an actor acts it out, I hardly listen. I keep worrying about whether he's going to do something phony every minute. — J.D. Salinger, *Catcher in the Rye*, p. 117, 1951

phoney-baloney *adjective*
utterly false *US*
- Being your own boss and having a phony-baloney job like I do affords me the great excuse of saying "I have to be alone and free from distractions in order to create." — Jimmy Buffett, *Tales from Margaritaville*, p. 4, 1989

phonus balonus *noun*
nonsense *US, 1932*
An elaboration of **PHONEY-BALONEY**.
- They all seem so at ease with the phonus balonus. — Kevin Sampson, *Outlaws*, p. 109, 2001

phony *noun*
a deck of playing cards that is either stacked or marked for cheating *US*
- — John Scarne, *Scarne's Guide to Modern Poker*, p. 287, 1979

phooey
used for registering disbelief or disgust *US, 1929*
- "Phooey. You've just been working at it." — Mickey Spillane, *I, The Jury*, p. 91, 1947

photies *noun*
photographs *UK*
- [I]t's not the photies, it ain't the stories, it's the fucking other thing. — Kevin Sampson, *Clubland*, p. 50, 2002

photo finish; photo; photer *noun*
Guinness™, the branded Irish stout *UK*
Rhyming slang.
- — Julian Franklyn, *A Dictionary of Rhyming Slang*, 1960
- — Ray Puxley, *Cockney Rabbit*, 1992

photog; fotog *noun*
a photographer *US, 1913*
- A battery of photogs will greet her at Union Station. — Jack Lait and Lee Mortimer, *New York Confidential*, p. 144, 1948
- This guy knocked off a couple of men giving her a hard time and a photog happened along who grabbed a pic for the front page of his tabloid. — Mickey Spillane, *Kiss Me Deadly*, p. 62, 1952

photogenic *verb*
to remember something or someone in photographic detail *UK*
- I could photogenic the credit cards and keys. — Angela Devlin, *Prison Patter*, p. 87, 1996

phou gas *noun*
▷ see: **FOO GAS**

phucked *adjective*
drug-intoxicated *UK*
Deliberate misspelling of **FUCKED** (intoxicated) inspired by widespread use of **PHAT** (excellent).
- — Ben Osborne, *The A-Z of Club Culture*, p. 223, 1999

phull on *adjective*
enthusiastic *UK*
Deliberate misspelling of **FULL ON** (absolute) probably inspired by the widespread use of **PHAT** (excellent).
- — Ben Osborne, *The A-Z of Club Culture*, p. 223, 1999

phunky; phungky *adjective*
funky in all its senses, but especially fashionable or as a descriptor of music *UK*
Deliberate misspellings inspired by the widespread use of **PHAT** (excellent).
- — Vanilla Ice, *Phunky Rhymes*, 1994
- — Ben Osborne, *The A-Z of Club Culture*, p. 223, 1999

phus-phus *noun*
whispering, murmuring *TRINIDAD AND TOBAGO, 1984*
- — Lise Winer, *Dictionary of the English/Creole of Trinidad & Tobago*, 2003

phwoar *noun*
a sexually attractive person *UK*
From the lecherous exclamation 'phwoar!'.
- HIP HOP'S fruitiest petite phwoar, Princess Superstar[.] — *X-Ray*, p. 84, November 2002

phwoar!; phoor!; fwoarrrgh!
used for registering an enthusiastic, possibly lecherous, reaction to a sexy someone or something *UK, 1980*
- Phoor, those bloody muscles... where'd he get 'em from, though? Tell you, you couldn't buy a bum like that round here. — *The Full Monty*, 1997
- Phwooar! What a fantastic view of her rump! I can't wait for her to start soaping her charlies [breasts]. — *Roger's Profanisaurus*, p. 31, December 1997
- [F]or the most stunning-looking [boys], no superlative expresses their desirability more than the title of Just Seventeen's regular back-page pin-up: Fwoarrrgh! — David Rowan, *A Glossary for the 90s*, p. 196, 1998
- You'd be looking at images of face-painted kids (aah!) or pretty young women (phwoar – sexy football!). — Irvine Welsh, *The Naughty Nineties*, p. 16, 1999
- [G]etting it on with that tidy bit off the telly (and what a dirty little bitch she must be, eh? Phwoaaar). — Christopher Brookmyre, *Boiling a Frog*, p. 105, 2000
- What about the phwoar-factor? You aren't seriously telling me this is the bloke you see in all those warm, fuzzy private fantasies[.] — Liz Evans, *Barking!*, p. 163, 2001

phy *noun*
methadone *UK, 1971*
An shortening of *Phy*septone™, a branded methadone hydrochloride.
- If you're trying to get off heroin and go into a clinic, they'll put you on methadone – phy – as a substitute. — Donal Ruane, *Tales in a rear view mirror*, p. 113, 2003

physical *adjective*
▸ **get physical**
to become violent *US*
- The mob collector would take the customer outside, where the collector would get physical with him[.] — James Ridgeway, *Red Light*, p. 180, 1996

physical jerks *noun*
physical exercises *UK, 1919*
Originally jocular, now commonplace.
- [T]he band [British Sea Power]'s penchant for performing strenuous physical jerks on stage was only curtailed after Yan injured his back demonstrating "a flying leap landing in a press-up". — *The Guardian*, 25th April 2002

physio *noun*
1 a physiotherapist *AUSTRALIA*
- Stringy had paired off with this lush little physio from Brisbane. — Barry Humphries, *A Nice Night's Entertainment*, p. 41, 1960

2 physiotherapy *AUSTRALIA, 1988*
- I'll see the physios and I'll do as much physio as I can and hopefully I'll come good. — *Herald Sun*, p. 70, 9th July 1992

physog *noun*
▷ see: PHIZOG

physsie *noun*
a physical fitness enthusiast *BARBADOS*
• —Frank A. Collymore, *Barbadian Dialect*, p. 83, 1965

PI *noun*
a pimp *US, 1955*
• —Joseph E. Ragen and Charles Finston, *Inside the World's Toughest Prison*, p. 812, 1962: 'Penitentiary and underworld glossary'
• —Robert S. Gold, *A Jazz Lexicon*, p. 238, 1964

pi *adjective*
pious *UK, 1891*

piano *noun*
▸ **on the piano**
lost *US*
• —Lyle K. Engel, *The Complete Book of Fuel and Gas Dragsters*, p. 152, 1968

▸ **play the piano**
to search for particles of crack cocaine with your fingers in an obsessive and compulsive manner *US*
• —Terry Williams, *Crackhouse*, p. 150, 1992

PIB *noun*
someone who dresses completely in black *US*
A '*p*erson *i*n *b*lack'.
• —Connie Eble (Editor), *UNC-CH Campus Slang*, p. 6, Spring 1990

pic *noun*
1 a picture *UK, 1884*
• This guy knocked off a couple of men giving her a hard time and a photog happened along who grabbed a pic for the front page of his tabloid. —Mickey Spillane, *Kiss Me Deadly*, p. 62, 1952
2 a phonograph record *US*
• —Robert George Reisner, *The Jazz Titans*, p. 162, 1960

Picasso *noun*
a card cheat who marks cards for identification in another player's hand *US*
• —Frank Scoblete, *Guerrilla Gambling*, p. 320, 1993

Picasso arse *noun*
a woman whose knickers are too tight *UK*
The works of celebrated artist Pablo Picasso (1881–1973) inspire this abstract image of a multi-buttocked female.
• —*Roger's Profanisaurus*, p. 158, 2002
• —Chris Lewis, *The Dictionary of Playground Slang*, p. 169, 2003

Piccadilly; picca *adjective*
silly *UK, 1992*
Rhyming slang, based on the famous central London location.

Piccadilly Percy *noun*
mercy *UK*
Rhyming slang.
• [L]et us be thankful for small Piccadilly Percys. —Ronnie Barker, *Fletcher's Book of Rhyming Slang*, p. 39, 1979

piccalilli *noun*
the penis *UK*
Rhyming slang for **WILLY**, formed on a popular pickle.
• —Ray Puxley, *Fresh Rabbit*, 1998

piccaninny *noun*
1 an Australian Aboriginal child *AUSTRALIA, 1817*
Considered offensive.
• —Barbara Baynton, *Human Toll*, p. 119, 1907
• PICCANINNY – A baby, or very young Australian aboriginal. —Gilbert H. Lawson, *A Dictionary of Australian Words and Terms*, 1924
• —Ion L. Idriess, *Over the Range*, p. 208, 1947
• —Patsy Adam-Smith, *Folklore of the Australian Railwaymen*, p. 140, 1969
• 'Gee, it's a piccaninny!' It was a live baby girl, about ten months old. —Herb Wharton, *Cattle Camp*, p. 36, 1994
2 a small black child; children; occasionally any black person *UK, 1785*
From Spanish *pequeño* (small) or Portuguese *pequeno* (small). Originally applied in the West Indies and US without being considered racist; now highly offensive and derogatory or, in a black-on- black context, judgemental and negative. Also variants 'piccanin', 'picaninny', 'pickaninny' and 'pickney'.
• You should have seen her – in her feed-sack dress, like scared and roll-eyed, pickaninny mud on her knees, crooning 'Trouble in Mind' all breathy. —John Clellon Holmes, *The Horn*, p. 83, 1958
• I saw that there were some kinds in it with Pookie – a pickanniny who resembled a baby unicorn what with a pink-ribboned pigtail standing straight up on her head[.] —John Nichols, *The Sterile Cuckoo*, p. 188, 1965
• "Just watch my car," he told Blue, "I don't want no pickney distressing it, seen?" —Karline Smith, *Moss Side Massive*, p. 2, 1994
• [S]hould baby fathers take more responsibility for dem pickney? —Donald Gorgon, *Cop Killer*, p. 89, 1994
• —Lise Winer, *Dictionary of the English/Creole of Trinidad & Tobago*, 2003

piccaninny daylight; piccaninny dawn *noun*
the beginning of dawn; first light *AUSTRALIA, 1866*
• They could sleep here, and be in camp at piccaninny daylight, just after dawn. —Ion L. Idriess, *The Red Chief*, p. 201, 1953
• I like to get away at piccaninny dawn. —Alan Marshall, *I Can Jump Puddles*, p. 183, 1955

piccie; piccy *noun*
a picture *AUSTRALIA*
• As usual, the cream of Melbourne's nouveau riche turned out, goose-pimpled and gruesome, to shiver their way through the Melbourne Cup and get their piccies in the paper. —Sue Rhodes, *Now you'll think I'm Awful*, p. 90, 1967
• —Kathy Lette, *Girls' Night Out*, p. 151, 1987
• —Paul Vautin, *Turn It Up!*, p. 172, 1995

piccolo *noun*
1 the penis, especially as the object of oral sex *US*
• —Dale Gordon, *The Dominion Sex Dictionary*, p. 124, 1967
2 a record player *US*
• We made a number of unsuccessful attempts to locate the ideal piccolo-owning host. —William Burroughs, *Junkie*, p. 30, 1953

piccolo and flute; piccolo *noun*
a suit (of clothes) *UK*
Rhyming slang; a variation of **WHISTLE AND FLUTE**.
• —Julian Franklyn, *A Dictionary of Rhyming Slang*, p. 107, 1960
• Spruced up in me piccolo, me titfer [hat] and me daisys [boots]. —Viv Stanshall, *Ginger Geezer*, 1981

Piccy *noun*
Piccadilly, London *UK*
• [S]he gets nicked along Piccy day before[.] —Derek Raymond (Robin Cook), *The Crust on its Uppers*, p. 58, 1962

piche *noun*
the vagina *US*
• There's [...] a "poochi," a "poopi," a "peepe,", a "poopelu," a "poopelu," a "poonani," a "pal" and a "piche[."] —Eve Ensler, *The Vagina Monologues*, p. 6, 1998

pick *noun*
1 a pickpocket *US*
• —Vincent J. Monteleone, *Criminal Slang*, p. 175, 1949
2 an oversized comb, used for bushy hair *US*
• Other indicators of gang affiliation include articles of clothing, hair ties, or a pick (comb) protruding from a pocket[.] —Bill Valentine, *Gangs and Their Tattoos*, p. 77, 2000
3 a needle and syringe *NEW ZEALAND, 1995*
• —Harry Orsman, *A Dictionary of Modern New Zealand Slang*, p. 98, 1999

▸ **on the pick**
drinking (alcohol) *UK*
Based on **PICK AND CHOOSE**, this is the rhyming slang equivalent of **ON THE BOOZE**.
• —Ray Puxley, *Cockney Rabbit*, 1992

pick *verb*
1 to challenge someone to a fight *AUSTRALIA, 1953*
• Are you picking me, sport? —John Wynnum, *Tar Dust*, p. 24, 1962
• I pick you, Noakes. —Wilda Moxham, *The Apprentice*, p. 63, 1969
• —Phillip Gwynne, *Deadly Unna?*, p. 82, 1998
2 to tease or kid someone *US*
• —Connie Eble (Editor), *UNC-CH Campus Slang*, p. 7, Spring 2003

▸ **pick fruit**
to find and select a homosexual partner *US*
• —Hyman E. Goldin et al., *Dictionary of American Underworld Lingo*, p. 156, 1950

▸ **pick lint**
to focus on petty imperfections in a play or performance *US*
• —Sherman Louis Sergel, *The Language of Show Biz*, p. 128, 1973

▸ **pick the cherry**
to drive through a red traffic light *US*
- —Anna Scotti and Paul Young, *Buzzwords*, p. 40, 1997

▸ **pick up your marbles and go home**
to quit an effort, especially to do so with a lack of good sportsmanship *US*
- In politics, you have two choices if your side isn't winning: You can pick up your marbles and go home, abandoning the game to others, or you can stay, fight and try to do better next time.—*Seattle Post-Intelligencer*, p. A12, 27th September 1991
- "As long as we are meeting and talking," Bagley said, "compromise is entirely possible. But to pick up your marbles and go home, as has been suggested by some on the County Commission, makes reaching a resolution extremely difficult."—*The Orlando Sentinel*, p. B1, 21st March 1999

▸ **pick your arse**
to waste your time *UK*
- We just sit here and pick our arses, do we?—Andy McNab, *Immediate Action*, p. 297, 1995

▸ **pick your brains**
to seek and obtain information from someone with specialist knowledge *UK, 1838*
- He has also "picked the brains" of dozens of top entertainment-industry professionals to fill his book[.]—Michael Saint Nicholas, *An Actor's Guide*, p. Back Cover, 2000

pick and choose; pick *noun*
alcohol, drink *UK*
Rhyming slang for **BOOZE**.
- —Julian Franklyn, *A Dictionary of Rhyming Slang*, 1960

pick and pay *noun*
in a casino, a method of paying off bets in blackjack, in which the dealer evaluates each player's hand and pays or collects that player's bet, and then moves to the next player *US*
- The Aladdin is double deck, pick and pay – ugh!—Lee Solkey, *Dummy Up and Deal*, p. 117, 1980

pick-ed wiss *noun*
urination after a period of discomfort *US*
An intentional Spoonerism of 'a wicked piss'.
- —Collin Baker et al., *College Undergraduate Slang Study Conducted at Brown University*, p. 170, 1968

pick 'em *noun*
in sports betting, a game in which neither team is favoured and the bettor must pick the winner *US*
- The odds were 10 to 11 pick-em that the fight wouldn't go ten rounds[.]—Edward Lin, *Big Julie of Vegas*, p. 179, 1974
- —Michael Knapp, *Bay Sports Review*, p. 8, November 1991

pickem up truck *noun*
a pickup truck *US*
Jocular.
- —Wayne Floyd, *Jason's Authentic Dictionary of CB Slang*, p. 23, 1976

picker *noun*
1 a finger *US*
- —Lou Shelly, *Hepcats Jive Talk Dictionary*, p. 15, 1945

2 a pickpocket *US*
- —*The New American Mercury*, p. 707, 1950

Pickettywitch *noun*
a ditch *UK*
Rhyming slang, jocularly contrived from the name of a UK pop group of the late 1960s and early 70s.
- There he is lying bleeding in the Pickettywitch thinking he's a Madonna [goner].—Mervyn Stutter, *Getting Nowhere Fast*, 21st May 2004

pickle *noun*
1 a predicament; a sorry plight; an unpleasant difficulty *UK, 1562*
- What a pickle!—Lester Bangs, *Psychotic Reactions and Carburetor Dung*, p. 77, 1971
- She found herself in the pickle she'd been in a thousand times when she'd been a kid.—Robert Campbell, *Juice*, p. 129, 1988
- She got herself in a right pickle. So what's she going to do?—Caroline Aherne and Craig Cash, *The Royle Family*, 1999

2 a torpedo *US*
- —*American Speech*, p. 38, February 1948: 'Talking underwater: speech in submarines'

3 a handgun *US*
- —Hyman E. Goldin et al., *Dictionary of American Underworld Lingo*, p. 156, 1950

4 in horse racing, a regular but uninformed bettor *AUSTRALIA*
- —Ned Wallish, *The Truth Dictionary of Racing Slang*, p. 62, 1989

5 in lobstering, the brine that accumulates in a bait box produced by decomposing bait fish and the salt used to preserve the bait fish *US*
- —Kendall Merriam, *The Illustrated Dictionary of Lobstering*, p. 8, 1978

▸ **off your pickle**
drunk *UK*
- —*e-cyclopaedia*, 20th March 2002

pickle *verb*
to embalm a corpse *US*
- —Vincent J. Monteleone, *Criminal Slang*, p. 175, 1949

pickled *adjective*
drunk *UK, 1633*
- I figured they were reeling pickled.—S.E. Hinton, *The Outsiders*, p. 50, 1967
- —Connie Eble (Editor), *UNC-CH Campus Slang*, p. 1, Fall 1987

pickled onion *noun*
a bunion *UK*
Rhyming slang.
- —Ray Puxley, *Fresh Rabbit*, 1998

pickled pork *noun*
chalk *UK*
Rhyming slang.
- —Ray Puxley, *Fresh Rabbit*, 1998

pickled punks *noun*
in a carnival, a side show display of jars, each with a foetus preserved in formaldehyde *US*
- —*American Speech*, p. 308–309, December 1960: 'Carnival talk'

pickle fork *noun*
in electric line work, an insulated line tool formally known as a prong tie stick *US*
- —A.B. Chance Co., *Lineman's Slang Dictionary*, p. 13, 1980

pickle me tit!
used for expressing surprise *NEW ZEALAND, 1964*
- —Harry Orsman, *A Dictionary of Modern New Zealand Slang*, p. 99, 1999

pickle party *noun*
male masturbation *US*
- —Erica Orloff and JoAnn Baker, *Dirty Little Secrets*, p. 65, 2001

pickle, pull and climb *verb*
to drop a load of bombs and then climb to evade groundfire *US*
- Four thousand feet was the hard deck, so the procedure was pickle, pull and climb. This meant release your weapons at 5500 feet, then pull as many g's as it took to get climbing without going below four thousand feet.—William H. LaBarge, *Hornet's Next*, p. 243, 1991

picklepuss *noun*
an overtly and infectiously unhappy person *US*
In the same vein as **SOURPUSS**, with 'pickle' conveying the sour quality.
- He was laughing! Old Picklepuss Kaggs laughed out loud!—Jim Thompson, *The Grifters*, p. 167, 1963

pickle-stabbers *noun*
shoes or boots with sharply pointed toes *CANADA*
- —Bill Casselman, *Canadian Sayings*, p. 51, 2002

pickle tickle *noun*
an act of sexual intercourse *US*
- Giving her a little pickle tickle[.]—Erica Orloff and JoAnn Baker, *Dirty Little Secrets*, p. 88, 2001

pick-me-up *noun*
1 an alcoholic drink *US*
- He picked up the drink Moran sest before him. "Thank you, I believe I will. Little pick-me-up."—Elmore Leonard, *Cat Chaser*, p. 278, 1982
- The 44 Regular fit Winnie okay, but he wasn't used to baggy trousers and big shoulders, and when he stopped at Spoon's Landing for a pick-me-up, Spoon looked him over.—Joseph Wambaugh, *The Golden Orange*, p. 61, 1990

2 a dose of a central nervous system stimulant *US*
- She's at the point of bolting when you ask her if she needs a little pick-me-up.—Jay McInerney, *Bright Lights, Big City*, p. 7, 1984

pick mooch *noun*
in sports betting, a bettor who will not pay for handicapping information, but instead bets as those who have paid for the information bet *US*

pick off *verb*
in poker, to catch a player bluffing *US*
• —John Scarne, *Scarne's Guide to Modern Poker*, p. 287, 1979

pick on *verb*
to tease or victimise someone *UK, 1937*
• I used to feel ashamed of being in the Guides because I knew the boys at school would pick on me. — *The Guardian*, 13th November 2002

pick the bones out of that!
1 used as a challenge to unravel, or retort to, or refute, an argument *UK, 1961*
• She describes how she married Sinatra at 19 (he 50) and got on so well with his second wife, Ava Gardner (who had once had an affair with Mia's father, John Farrow), that Ava declared her "the child she and Frank never had". Pick the bones out of that one — *New Statesman*, 7th March 1977

2 a catchphrase that accompanies expectoration *UK, 1984*

pickup *noun*
1 a short-term sexual partner *US, 1871*
• Many Baltimore Street joints are pointedly pick-up bars. —Jack Lait and Lee Mortimer, *Washington Confidential*, p. 267, 1951
• First, there are the pick-up bars for amateurs only. — *Screw*, p. 12, 3 November 1969

2 a police order to detain and bring a person to the station for questioning *US*
• She decided to bluff; she didn't believe there was a pickup out on her. —Donald Goines, *Black Gangster*, p. 279, 1977

3 in the entertainment industry, a commitment to finance production of a set number of episodes of a television programme *US*
• So the job might be good for several episodes if Harbor Nights got a seven-show pickup. —Joseph Wambaugh, *Finnegan's Week*, p. 2, 1993

pick up *verb*
1 to meet someone and form a casual liaison in which at least one of the pair has sexual ambitions involving the other *UK, 1698*
• Does [DT] Birch really think Monica [Lewinsky] would have given Bill Clinton a second glance if he were the average 50-year-old guy trying to pick her up in a bar? — *Psychology Today*, September 1999

2 to pay a bill, especially when the accounting is for more than one person; to meet the expense of financing or sponsoring something *US, 1945*
• This will leave the taxpayer to pick up the bill for dealing with 50 years of accumulated waste[.] — *The Guardian*, 27th June 2002
• You pick the restaurant and I'll pick up the check. —Peter Conti and David Finkel, *Making Big Money Investing in Foreclosures*, p. 125, 2003
• [T]he government needed to stop private companies from walking away from unprofitable contracts and forcing the public to pick up the tab. — *The Guardian*, 3rd June 2003

3 to smoke marijuana *US*
• It was passed around by Pasternak, who gave instructions on how to "pick up" to Kathryn, and all sipped deeply. —John Clellon Holmes, *Go*, p. 86, 1952

▸ **pick up on**
to comprehend something *US*
• —Lawrence Lipton, *The Holy Barbarians*, p. 317, 1959
• —Burton H. Wolfe, *The Hippies*, p. 205, 1968: 'A hip glossary for the uptight people'

pickup girl *noun*
a street prostitute *AUSTRALIA*
• She could pick out unerringly men from the country, and would represent herself to them as a pick-up girl. —Vince Kelly, *The Bogeyman*, p. 144, 1956
• [H]e was able to afford the higher priced call girls and pick-up girls of the King's Cross area. —James Holledge, *The Call-girl in Australia*, p. 79, 1964

pickup man *noun*
in an illegal lottery, a person who takes bets from players to a central location and pays off winning bets *US*
• Teese, the pickup man. —Clarence Cooper Jr, *Black*, p. 183, 1963

picky *adjective*
used of hair, tightly curled and short *BAHAMAS*
• —John A. Holm, *Dictionary of Bahamian English*, p. 155, 1982

picky-head *noun*
a black person with short hair *BARBADOS*
• —Frank A. Collymore, *Barbadian Dialect*, p. 84, 1965

picky-puck *noun*
a one-cylinder, two-stroke engine; a boat powered by such an engine *CANADA*
• We used to go up and down the coast in our picky-puck, looking for moss. —Blaine Bernard, *Dictionary of Irish Moss*, 1986

picnic *noun*
1 oral sex, especially on a man *US*
• —Roger Blake, *The American Dictionary of Sexual Terms*, p. 161, 1964
• —Robert A. Wilson, *Playboy's Book of Forbidden Words*, p. 192, 1972

2 extended foreplay and/or sexual intercourse *US*
• —Kenn "Naz" Young, *Naz's Dictionary of Teen Slang*, p. 89, 1993

3 sex involving many people and many acts; an orgy *US*
• —Roger Blake, *The American Dictionary of Sexual Terms*, p. 161, 1964
• —Anon., *King Smut's Wet Dreams Interpreted*, 1978

4 a difficult situation *NEW ZEALAND*
• —David McGill, *David McGill's Complete Kiwi Slang Dictionary*, p. 83, 1998

5 something difficult, unpleasant, messy, confusing, etc *AUSTRALIA, 1896*
An ironic use.
• I know, Jimmy – but not on such a large scale as this picnic. Every available fighter-bomber and ground-attack aircraft south of the line's going to be laid on[.] —W.R. Bennett, *Wingman*, p. 120, 1961
• —Jim Ramsay, *Cop It Sweet!*, p. 69, 1977

▸ **no picnic**
a difficult situation or circumstance *UK, 1888*
• Ann Bancroft was no picnic. She wouldn't speak [...] Bette Davis was difficult. John Malkovich was no picnic [...] Ah, you've only got to look at him to know he's not going to be a picnic, haven't you? — *The Guardian*, 4th June 2004

picnic *verb*
(used of fishing boats) to congregate in one area where fish are plentiful *BARBADOS*
• —Frank A. Collymore, *Barbadian Dialect*, p. 84, 1965

pic pac *noun*
in the film industry, a contract to make a set number of films *US*
An abbreviation of 'picture package'.
• —Ralph S. Singleton, *Filmaker's Dictionary*, p. 85, 1990

picture *noun*
a beautiful person or thing *UK, 1815*
Often in the phrase 'pretty as a picture'.
• Look at my girls, ain't they pretty as a picture? —Jimmy Stockin, *On The Cobbles*, p. 76, 2000

▸ **get the picture**
to understand a situation *UK, 1938*
• Hardly Swiftian saeva indignatio, but you get the picture almost at once. — *The Guardian*, 11th May 2002

▸ **in the picture**
aware of what is going on *UK, 1900*
• Yes. Right. Well, keep me in the picture so that we can give you the maximum air support [.] —Jon E. Lewis (Editor), *The Mammoth Book of Elite Forces*, p. 194, 2002

picture card; picture *noun*
in a deck of playing cards, any jack, queen or king *US*
• —Irv Roddy, *Friday Night Poker: Penny Poker for Millions*, p. 217, 1961
• [T]hey would answer, after only a little thought, that it would be the ten. A picture. —Edward Lin, *Big Julie of Vegas*, p. 170, 1974

picture gallery *noun*
in circus and carnival usage, a heavily tattooed person *US, 1960*
• —Don Wilmeth, *The Language of American Popular Entertainment*, p. 200, 1981

picture of the queen *noun*
a sterling currency note *UK*

Basically a copy of US 'picture of Abe' (a $5 note), except that the queen's face appears on all denominations issued in England and Wales.
- "How do you want payin'?" "Pictures of the queen, mate!" — *www.LondonSlang.com*, June 2002

pictures *noun*
money *US*
- The usual sentence for that [armed robbery] is ten to a quarter. How come you got only five? Pictures. The secret of getting less time is pictures [money]. — Bruce Jackson, *In the Life*, p. 30–31, 1972

▸ **take pictures**
to use radar to measure a vehicle's speed *US*
- You got a bear in the mediam at Exit 204 and he's taking pictures for sure. — Lanie Dills, *The Official CB Slanguage Language Dictionary*, p. 68, 1976

picture-taker *noun*
a police officer using radar *US*
- — Wayne Floyd, *Jason's Authentic Dictionary of CB Slang*, p. 23, 1976

picturize *verb*
1 to explain something; to put someone in the picture *UK*
Royal Navy slang.
- — Nigel Foster, *The Making of a Royal Marine Commando*, 1987

2 to film something *INDIA*
- The film was entirely picturized in Madras. — Paroo Nihalini, R.K. Tongue and Priya Hosali, *Indian and British English*, 1979

piddle *noun*
urine; an act of urination *UK, 1901*

piddle *verb*
1 to urinate *UK, 1796*
- I widdle when I piddle / Cos my middle is a riddle. — Ian Dury, *Spasticus (Autisticus)*, 1981

2 to rain *UK, 1887*

3 to steal something *US*
- He was supposed to have piddled some funds, that's what they say. — Norman Mailer, *Advertisements for Myself*, p. 178, 1952

4 in bar dice games, to roll the dice to determine who will go first in the game *US*
- — Jester Smith, *Games They Play in San Francisco*, p. 104, 1971

5 in tiddlywinks, to make a minute change in a pile *US*
- — *Verbatim*, p. 526, December 1977

6 to build something with matchsticks *US*
- The inmate, known on death row for his "piddling" ability – a phrase that refers to crafting items out of matchsticks – gave his handicrafts and remaining supplies to fellow inmates. — *Houston Chronicle*, p. 33A, 23rd March 1989

piddle about *verb*
to busy yourself doing nothing *NEW ZEALAND*
- — Louis S. Leland, *A Personal Kiwi-Yankee Dictionary*, p. 76, 1984

piddle around *verb*
to loaf or fool around *UK, 1545*
- Don't be piddling around with me! — Mickey Spillane, *I, The Jury*, p. 74, 1947
- How about some coffee, okay? Sets a bad example; too much piddling around here already. — Jim Thompson, *The Grifters*, p. 120, 1963
- I did piddle around a little bit with barbiturates, but I loathe them. — Herbert Huncke, *Guilty of Everything*, p. 8, 1990

piddler *noun*
in prison, a prisoner assigned to work in a craft shop *US*
- — Charles Shafer, *Folk Speech in Texas Prisons*, p. 211, 1990

piddling *adjective*
small; trivial, insignificant *UK: SCOTLAND, 1559*
- [A] piddling peon's dream! — Lester Bangs, *Psychotic Reactions and Carburetor Dung*, p. 121, 1973
- I'd tried it [crack cocaine] but only piddling experimental stuff to learn what all the fuss was about. — Lanre Fehintola, *Charlie Says...*, p. 54, 2000
- I'm not wasting this team's reputation or time on chasing piddling amounts. — Duncan MacLaughlin, *The Filth*, p. 188, 2002
- Five million may seem a lot of money but it is a piddling amount, given the range and variety of disciplines involved. — *The Guardian*, 21st February 2002

pie *noun*
1 the vulva *US*
- — *Maledicta*, p. 255, Summer/Winter 1981: 'Five Years and 121 Dirty Words Later'

2 a woman as a sexual object *US*
- — *American Speech*, p. 63, Spring-Summer 1975: 'Razorback Slang'

3 a person who is overweight *UK*
Probably from the chant 'who ate all the pies?'.
- — Susie Dent, *The Language Report*, p. 77, 2003

4 a pizza *US*
An abbreviation of the rarely used, full 'pizza pie'.
- — Amy and Denise McFadden, *CoalSpeak*, p. 11, 1997

pie and chips
used by women as a generic instance of the difference between the sexes, especially with an ironic regard to equal opportunities *UK*
- — Angela Devlin, *Prison Patter*, p. 87, 1996

pie and liquor; pie and licker *noun*
a vicar *UK, 1992*
Rhyming slang.

pie and mash *noun*
1 an act of urination *UK*
Rhyming slang for **SLASH**, noted by David Hillman, 1974.

2 radio interference *UK*
Rhyming slang for citizens' band radio jargon 'hash' (channel interference).
- — Peter Chippindale, *The British CB Book*, p. 157, 1981

3 cash *UK*
Rhyming slang.
- In the cab and courier industry a "pie and mash job" is a fare or job that is not accounted for. — Ray Puxley, *Cockney Rabbit*, 1992

pie and mash *adjective*
showy *UK*
Rhyming slang for **FLASH**.
- Don't think me pie and mash (flash) for giving it Jack the biscuit [behaving like a show-off][.] — private correspondence with a prison inmate, *HMP Blundeston, Suffolk*, January 2002

pie and one *noun*
a son; the sun *UK*
Rhyming slang.
- — Julian Franklyn, *A Dictionary of Rhyming Slang*, 1961
- — Ray Puxley, *Cockney Rabbit*, 1992

pie book *noun*
a railwayman's meal ticket *US*
- — Ramon Adams, *The Language of the Railroader*, p. 114, 1977

pie car *noun*
in the circus, a dining car on the circus train *US*
- — Joe McKennon, *Circus Lingo*, p. 68, 1980

pie card *noun*
a meal ticket; a means of surviving; a union card *US, 1909*
- Matt Sylvester and Johnny Savoy, as paid functionaries, pie-cards, monthly earned $28 and $17 respectively. — Clancy Sigal, *Going Away*, p. 279, 1961

pie cart *noun*
a catering truck *NEW ZEALAND*
- Over the road now I see the pie-cart halted by the kerb. — Gordon Slatter, *A Gun in my Hand*, p. 163, 1959

piece *noun*
1 a woman as a sexual object; sex *US, 1942*
- He had planned on a quick piece on a deserted stairwell. — Evan Hunter, *The Blackboard Jungle*, p. 73, 1954
- I said, "Yeah, man. I just had a nice piece last night, a fine bitch, man." — Claude Brown, *Manchild in the Promised Land*, 1965
- [A] beautiful little piece she is[.] — Gore Vidal, *Myra Breckinridge*, p. 24, 1968
- He said he fucked your cousin, your brother, and your niece / And he had the nerve enough to ask your grandmom for a piece. — Anonymous ("Arthur"), *Shine and the Titanic;The Signifying Monkey; Stackolee*, p. 1, 1971
- Whores ought to carry union cards, they were such great actresses, but this piece wasn't putting on any act at all. — Mickey Spillane, *Last Cop Out*, p. 151, 1972
- We commenced to trade drags on the Camel and fondle and neck, and then we tore off another piece[.] — Larry Heinemann, *Close Quarters*, p. 187, 1977
- Likes to have you around for a quick piece now and then when he feels like it, right? — *Saturday Night Fever*, 1977

2 an ounce of drugs *US, 1936*
- "Everyting, she is ready. I have da pieces – pure stuff." Pieces was an underworld term for ounces. — William J. Spillard and Pence James, *Needle in a Haystack*, p. 77, 1945
- I want to pick up a piece of H. — William Burroughs, *Naked Lunch*, p. 213, 1957
- He used to sell half a piece, a whole piece, two-three-four pieces. — Jeremy Larner and Ralph Tefferteller, *The Addict in the Street*, p. 201, 1964
- He bought heroin in "pieces" (ounces), cut it, bagged it, and handed it over on consignment to a handful of pushers. — James Mills, *The Panic in Needle Park*, p. 19, 1966
- Ya mean ya wanna buy a piece and push it for yourself? — Piri Thomas, *Down These Mean Streets*, p. 201, 1967
- A fin for a number-five cap. A sixteenth for a "C." A piece for a grand. — Iceberg Slim (Robert Beck), *Pimp*, p. 128, 1969
- The dealer-in-weight sells by the piece (about an ounce) to street dealers. The street dealer (or dealer) buys the piece and then steps on it. — Burgess Laughlin, *Job Opportunities in the Black Market*, p. 6–5, 1978

3 cocaine *UK*
- — Mike Haskins, *Drugs*, p. 281, 2003

4 crack cocaine *UK*
- — Mike Haskins, *Drugs*, p. 282, 2003

5 a handgun *US, 1930*
Conventional English from C16 until the late C19, then dormant, then slang, chiefly used in the US.
- It was a bad break for Cheyenne that he had happened to be picked up with a "piece" on him. — Harrison E. Salisbury, *The Shook-up Generation*, p. 8, 1958
- I went up to him, and I said, "I got to get me a piece, baby." — Claude Brown, *Manchild in the Promised Land*, p. 176, 1965
- New York is death on a nigger with a gun, so I'm leaving my piece with you. — A.S. Jackson, *Gentleman Pimp*, p. 41, 1973
- Then I started smoking with both pieces. — Edwin Torres, *Carlito's Way*, p. 32, 1975
- You carry a piece? You need one? — *Taxi Driver*, 1976
- Just back me up like you've got a piece. — *48 Hours*, 1982
- And the big kid reaches in his coat, pulls out a little piece, like a twenty-two. — Terry Williams, *The Cocaine Kids*, p. 119, 1989
- I've been in the field 33 years, fired my piece 23 times in the line of duty, and I got no idea what a blind man fetching bricks has gotta do with being a Special Agent. — *Point Break*, 1991

6 a snack *US*
- — Claudio R. Salvucci, *The Philadelphia Dialect Dictionary*, p. 52, 1996

7 a slice of bread, especially bread and spread; a sandwich *UK: SCOTLAND, 1787*
Originally just 'a slice of bread'. Also seen in English dialect use from Northumbria to Cornwall
- These pieces, Da. They're minging! — Ian Pattison, *Rab C. Nesbitt*, 1988

8 (especially with children) a sandwich *AUSTRALIA*
Used in the south and west of mainland Australia.
- We always referred to a sandwich as a piece. e.g. May I have a piece please? I lived in Adelaide & that was always what we asked for on coming home from school. — *www.abc.net.au/wordmap*, 2003

9 a well executed work of graffiti art *US*
An abbreviation of 'masterpiece'.
- Straddling the middle ground are men like Poke, a 27-year-old West Sider who considers himself a skilled artist – able to quickly get his name up, as well as craft more intricate "pieces," graffiti shorthand for masterpieces. — *Plain Dealer (Cleveland, Ohio)*, p. L1, 29th July 2001

10 a domicile, be it a room, apartment or house *US*
- — Don R. McCreary (Editor), *Dawg Speak*, 2001

piece book *noun*
a graffiti artist's notebook containing ideas, outlines, sketches and plans for future graffiti pieces *US*
- — *Los Angeles Times*, p. B10, 5th January 1990
- — Jim Crotty, *How to Talk American*, p. 140, 1997

piece man *noun*
an armed bodyguard; a hired killer *US*
- I ain't sure, but you figure at least two piece men beside the driver. I don't guess he'd move that much shit round with less than two guns guardin' it. — Vernon E. Smith, *The Jones Men*, p. 23, 1974
- So what's the use of being good at it if she's a piece man? — Richard Condon, *Prizzi's Honor*, p. 81, 1982

piece of ass *noun*
a woman as a sexual object; sexual intercourse *US, 1930*
- We'll all go down to Panama Street and get a piece [of] ass for 48c each – beautiful girls with shapely hips leaning in scabrous lovely doorways[.] — Jack Kerouac, *Letter to John Montgomery*, p. 591, 6th November 1956
- Son, here's twenty dollars; I want you to go to a good whore and get a piece of ass off her. — William Burroughs, *Naked Lunch*, p. 119, 1957
- There's nothing like a piece of ass to inspire rock 'n' roll. — *Ask*, p. 47, 5th May 1979
- He went on to say that "she was a foxy little thing" and "better than your average piece of ass." — Elmore Leonard, *City Primeval*, p. 8, 1980
- She's fifteen, this kid – a great piece of ass. — *Raging Bull*, 1980
- You already got a gun and you owe me a piece of ass. — *48 Hours*, 1982
- I'm the best piece of ass in three states. — *American Beauty*, 1999
- Brother D, how you making it? That's a fine piece of ass you got riding with you. — Robert Bingham, *Lightning on the Sun [The Howard Marks Book of Dope Stories]*, p. 334, 2001

piece of brass *noun*
a prostitute *UK*
Elaboration of **BRASS NAIL; BRASS** (a prostitute), playing on 'piece of arse' (an attractive woman).
- Have you ever paid for a piece of brass, Westy? — Mark Powell, *Snap*, p. 126, 2001

piece of cake *noun*
anything that is considered to be easily achieved or acquired *US, 1936*
Originally Royal Air Force usage.
- — C.H. Ward-Jackson, *It's a Piece of Cake or RAF Slang Made Easy*, 1943
- Hey, Steve, what'd 'ya say! Piece o' cake! — *The Deer Hunter*, 1978
- Right. Piece of cake. I'm very happy. Read the man his rights. — *Lethal Weapon*, 1987

piece of change *noun*
a sum of money *US*
- "This place must have cost you a nice piece of change," I said. — Max Shulman, *The Zebra Derby*, p. 98, 1946
- Saved me a piece of change on this job, kid. You know paint. — *Saturday Night Fever*, 1977
- Man, I can't carry it anymore. I've made my piece of change on it. — Herbert Huncke, *Guilty of Everything*, p. 191, 1990

piece of cunt *noun*
sex with a woman; a woman as a sexual object *US*
- A pat on the back and a piece of cunt without no passion? — Ralph Ellison, *Invisible Man*, p. 373, 1947

piece of duff *noun*
a young male homosexual prostitute, a rent boy *UK*
On the model of **PIECE OF ASS** (a woman as a sex object); from **DUFF** (the buttocks), probably informed by **DUFF** (inferior), and possibly by a rhyme of **PUFF** (a homosexual male).
- — Angela Devlin, *Prison Patter*, p. 88, 1996

piece off *verb*
to divide an ounce of drugs *US*
From **PIECE** (an ounce).
- — Inez Cardozo-Freeman, *The Joint*, p. 520, 1984

piece of leg *noun*
sex *US*
- Apeman is more than likely gettin' him a piece of leg somewhere, and it done got too good for him to let go. — Donald Goines, *Black Gangster*, p. 222, 1977

piece of meat *noun*
a woman as a sexual object; sex *US*
- He said to use slang words like "guys" and "a piece-a meat" when talking about girls and to offer them some chewing gum and take out some cigarettes. — Claude Brown, *Manchild in the Promised Land*, p. 161, 1965
- That's some sweet piece of meat, ain't it? — *Natural Born Killers*, 1994

piece of piss *noun*
anything that can be achieved easily *UK, 1949*
This alliterative variation on **PIECE OF CAKE** was originally Royal Air Force slang.
- — Tom Hibbert, *Rockspeak!*, p. 118, 1983
- I'd done many a credit card fraud on shopkeepers in the past. Piece of piss! — Dean Cavanagh, *Mile High Meltdown (Disco Biscuits)*, p. 207, 1996
- This was going to be a piece of piss. — Shane Maloney, *Nice Try*, p. 99, 1998
- [W]ha' – 'aven't you ever seen a pregnant man before – don't know what allah moaning is about – piece of piss!! — Patrick Jones, *Unprotected Sex*, p. 227, 1999
- — Harry Orsman, *A Dictionary of Modern New Zealand Slang*, p. 99, 1999
- I could do that. Piece of piss. — Dave Courtney, *Raving Lunacy*, p. 95, 2000
- Registering for the True Blue Aussie Hat is a piece of piss — *Australian Ultimate*, p. 7, 2003

piece of pistachio *noun*
anything that can be achieved easily *UK*
Euphemistic elaboration of **PIECE OF PISS**.

- "This going to be an easy one then?" "Should be. Should be a piece of pistachio." — BBC Radio 4, *Life of Cranes*, 21st March 2002

piece of shit *noun*
something disgusting or of very poor quality; a person who is greatly disliked *US*
- Rooney'd never believe Mr. Peterson drives that piece of shit. — *Ferris Buehler's Day Off*, 1986
- "Motherfucking piece of SHIT!" raged Gordon. — Jess Mowry, *Way Past Cool*, p. 4, 1992
- Oh man, I'm gonna need a cherry pie to get the taste of ass out of my mouth from that piece of shit movie. — *South Park*, 1999
- I'm glad I'm no longer anything to do with him. He's a piece of shit. — *Sky Magazine*, p. 15, July 2001
- Things they hate include: Graham Norton, the smell of Mike's farts [...] going to work, their "piece-of-shit" TV", not having any money[.] — Lisa Jewell, *Labia Lobelia [Tart Noir]*, p. 242, 2002

piece of skin; piece of flesh *noun*
an attractive woman *UK*
- I meeting that piece of skin tonight, you know. — Samuel Selvon, *The Lonely Londoners*, p. 103, 1956

piece of steel *noun*
in prison, a homemade knife *UK*
- — Angela Devlin, *Prison Patter*, p. 88, 1996

piece of trade *noun*
a male who self-identifies as a heterosexual but will let homosexual men perform oral sex on him *US*
- Making it with a "hustler" or a "piece of trade" fills this need when everything else has failed. — Antony James, *America's Homosexual Underground*, p. 14, 1965
- The humiliating position he would put himself in when some piece of trade spurned him because he was not able to lay on the requisite bread! — Gore Vidal, *Myra Breckinridge*, p. 97, 1968

piece of wet shit *noun*
something disgusting or of very poor quality; a person who is greatly disliked *US*
A slight intensification of PIECE OF SHIT.
- [E]very chick I've ever met from London just is the biggest piece of wet shit I've ever seen. — *Ask*, p. 45, 5th May 1979

piece of work *noun*
1 a contemptible person *UK, 1928*
- Your dad's a real piece of work. — Carl Hiaasen, *Tourist Season*, p. 210, 1986
- Oh, you're good, Ted. You're a real piece of work. — *Something About Mary*, 1998
- Ralph Sr. was a piece of work: a hardworking, hard-drinking functioning alcoholic. — Ralph "Sonny" Barger, *Hell's Angel*, p. 12, 2000

2 a killing *US*
- "He said if I ever needed a 'piece of work' done just call him, Mr. Clean. He would take care of it," said the undercover detective[.] — *Daily News (New York)*, p. 15, 17th May 2001

piece-o-idiot *noun*
a complete fool *BARBADOS*

pieces of eight; pieces *noun*
weight *UK*
Rhyming slang.
- The aim of dieters is to "do some pieces". — Ray Puxley, *Cockney Rabbit*, 1992

piecey *noun*
a slice of bread with a topping *AUSTRALIA*
Used especially in Victoria.
- My Nanna always called a slice of bread with butter and jam or vegemite on it a "piecey". — *www.abc.net.au/wordmap*, 2003

pie-chopper *noun*
the mouth *US*
- — Lavada Durst, *The Jives of Dr. Hepcat*, p. 13, 1953

piecrust *noun*
a thin layer of hard snow over soft snow *ANTARCTICA, 1911*
- — Bernadette Hince, *The Antarctic Dictionary*, p. 262, 2000

piedras *noun*
crack cocaine *UK, 1998*
From the Spanish for 'hailstones', thus the image of small white rocks.
- — Mike Haskins, *Drugs*, p. 282, 2003

pie-eater *noun*
a person of no consequence *AUSTRALIA, 1944*
Calling to mind an image of someone whose principal fare is the meat pie, in other words, a person with a mundane and narrow view of the world judging by their culinary habits. Hartley claims that the word was coined during World War 2, and referred then specifically to conscripted criminals who deserted and thence scrounged free pies from the army buffet in Hyde Park, Sydney. There may be some truth in this, but there is an example of 'pie-biter' dating to 1911, and so perhaps 'pie-eater' may also predate the war.
- It started when Ted Barnes, the eminent sporting writer, called the Australian cricket team a bunch of pie-eaters. — *Woman's Weekly*, p. 56, 5th September 1956
- To a visitor or newcomer to Australia, it may seem strange that pie eater is a term of opprobium in a nation that must be the world's greatest eaters of pastry. — Arthur Chipper, *The Aussie Swearer's Guide*, p. 47, 1972
- — Jim Ramsay, *Cop It Sweet!*, p. 70, 1977

pie-eating *adjective*
inconsequential *AUSTRALIA, 1944*
- — Arthur Chipper, *The Aussie Swearer's Guide*, p. 9, 1972
- Blind Frieda could see you're a pie-eating drongo and a blithering suds artist. — Ignatius Jones, *The 1992 True Hip Manual*, p. 158, 1992

pie-eyed *adjective*
extremely drunk *US, 1904*
- He said that he had been pie-eyed last night and thrown some sugar bowls at people whose faces he didn't like in Sally Carns's restaurant. — James T. Farrell, *Saturday Night and other stories*, p. 27, 1947
- With the later Senator Karl Mundt, he "used to invent drinks and get pie-eyed." — Bill Cardoso, *The Maltese Sangweech and other herbes*, p. 74, 1984
- Sure enough, at table eight a pie-eyed Volvo salesman was trying to suck the toes off a cocktail waitress. — Carl Hiaasen, *Strip Tease*, p. 9, 1993

pie factory *noun*
a mental institution *US*
- The captain's office has him listed for transfer to the pie factory, and that's no rumor. — Malcolm Braly, *On the Yard*, p. 340, 1967

pie hole *noun*
the mouth *US*
- Look, you, shut your pie hole and get moving. — *Airheads*, 1994
- — Pamela Munro, *U.C.L.A. Slang*, p. 106, 1997
- — Connie Eble (Editor), *UNC-CH Campus Slang*, p. 7, Spring 1998

pie horse *noun*
a racehorse that has performed very poorly *AUSTRALIA*
So named because of the horse's figurative future as the makings of a meat pie.
- — Ned Wallish, *The Truth Dictionary of Racing Slang*, p. 62, 1989

pie in the sky *noun*
unattainable dreams *US*
Often, 'there'll be pie in the sky when you die' denoting an illusory happy ever after; taken from a parody of the hymn 'In the Sweet Bye and Bye': 'You will eat, bye and bye, / In that glorious land in the sky; / Work and pray, live on hay, / You'll get pie in the sky when you die' by radical labour activist Joe Hill (aka Joel Haggstrom and Joseph Hillstrom), 'The Preacher and the Slave', ?1911. Joe Hill was executed in Utah in 1915.
- Yeah, a big casino hotel like in Las Vegas. Probably just pie in the sky stuff, but the girls were getting excited by the idea[.] — John Williams, *Cardiff Dead*, p. 147, 2000

pierced up *adjective*
used of someone who that is ornamented with body piercings *UK*
- [S]ome very pierced up characters and their dogs[.] — Mike Benson, *Room full of Angels (Disco Biscuits)*, p. 26, 1996

piercing *noun*
graffiti *US*
- — Jim Crotty, *How to Talk American*, p. 141, 1997

piercing *adjective*
overbearing *US*
- — Robert George Reisner, *The Jazz Titans*, p. 162, 1960

pier rat *noun*
a surfer with no regard for surf etiquette *US*
- — Gary Fairmont R. Filosa II, *The Surfer's Almanac*, p. 191, 1977

pier six brawl *noun*

an all-out brawl *US, 1929*

- Okay. It's turning into a real pier-six brawl[.] — Steve Allen, *Steve Allen's Private Joke File*, p. 361, 2000
- "It's a Pier-6 brawl," he would warn the TV audience. "We'll be back as soon as order is restored." — *Tampa (Florida) Tribune*, p. 1 (Baylife), 10th November 2003

pies *noun*

the eyes *US*

- — Lou Shelly, *Hepcats Jive Talk Dictionary*, p. 16, 1945

pie taster *noun*

a person who enjoys performing oral sex on women *US*

- — *Maledicta*, p. 255, Summer/Winter 1981: 'Five years and 121 dirty words later'

pie wagon *noun*

a police transport truck or van *US, 1904*

- Two by two they were led from bullpen to pie-wagon, thirty in all. — Hal Ellson, *The Golden Spike*, p. 240, 1952

piff *verb*

to throw something *AUSTRALIA, 1999*

Chiefly used in Victoria; onomatopoeic of something whizzing through the air.

- When I was young, I got in trouble for piffing yonnies at the neighbour's kids. — *www.abc.net.au/wordmap*, 2003

piffle *noun*

nonsense *UK, 1890*

From the verb (to talk or act in a feeble manner)

- BARRY: I don't reckon I feel like brekkie. ERICA: Piffle! — Barry Humphries, *Bazza Pulls It Off!*, 1971
- Piffle. Absolute fuckin piffle. Yewer all just making excuses[.] — Niall Griffiths, *Sheepshagger*, p. 31, 2001

pig *noun*

1 a police officer; in the plural it may mean a number of police personnel or the police in general *UK, 1811*

- I don't know Rubin but I do know narcs and I can't stand them, the ugly Facist brute pigs. — James Simon Kunen, *The Strawberry Statement*, p. 94, 1968
- [I]n front of the Hilton, were the police – or "the Pigs" as they were now known by all. — Terry Southern, *Now Dig This*, p. 127–128, November 1968
- LETTVIN: Why do you insist on calling policemen pigs? ABBIE: Cause on TV we can't call them cocksuckers. — Abbie Hoffman, *Woodstock Nation*, p. 12, 1969
- The Pigs, hogs and the boars of the racist power structure – the Pigs of the police department and the hand tool Pork Chop Nationalists are showing the "essence of swine" within their degenerate souls. — *The Black Panter*, p. 1, 25th January 1969
- Inside the police car was Jack Weinberg, a prisoner of the pigs. But we surrounded the pigs, and they were our prisoners. — Jerry Rubin, *Do It!*, p. 21, 1970
- Some were reluctant at first to call cops "pigs." "Pig" was a Berkeley-San Francisco thing, inspired by the Black Panthers... But we took one look at Czechago's big blue-and-white porkers: "Man, those fat fuckers really do look like pigs." — Jerry Rubin, *Do It!*, p. 170, 1970
- Law-abiding citizens deplore the senseless cry of "Pigs." — Richard Allen (James Moffat), *Author's Notes [britpulp]*, p. 57, 1970
- "So the pigs are driven to desperate acts, like the murder of our deputy chairman, Fred Hampton." (Quoting Don Cox). — Tom Wolfe, *Radical Chic & Mau-Mauing the Flak Catchers*, p. 23, 1970
- In 1958 I escaped from Kern County Jail and fought the pigs, all the way back to the midwestern area of my birth[.] — George Jackson, *Soledad Brother*, p. 41, 1970
- I'll even kiss a Sunset pig / California I'm coming home. — Joni Mitchell, *California*, 1971
- A lot of the fay chicks would go for his revolutionary bullshit, and if that was the program, I'd come on with "Right on" and "Off the pig" good as Reggie. — Edwin Torres, *Carlito's Way*, p. 81, 1975
- "Inspector Regan," Jack said, playing it by ear. "We're not mucking about, pig," a third spokesman called. — *The Sweeney*, p. 13, 1976
- They [the police] march, clearing the street. A throng of gays flanks them. "Pigs, pigs! Fucking pigs! Pigs! Shit pigs! Pigs, pigs, pigs, pigs!" — John Rechy, *The Sexual Outlaw*, p. 181, 1977
- Today's pig is tomorrow's bacon! — John Sayles, *Union Dues*, p. 341, 1977
- A pig was downed, another wounded with numerous shots. — Bobby Seale, *A Lonely Rage*, p. 225, 1978
- I know what you're doing, Campbell; bacon; pig; oink oink; police officers. I used to say that to cops when I was your age. — *Wayne's World*, 1992
- Darryl and Lathrop got jailed for hitting a pig. — *Forrest Gump*, 1992

2 a male chauvinist *US*

- Show the world exactly what a pig Clarence Thomas is. — Armistead Maupin, *Maybe the Moon*, p. 264, 1992
- VERONICA: You've slept with twelve different girls? DANTE: Including you, yes. DANTE: What the hell was that for? VERONICA: You're a pig. — *Clerks*, 1994

3 a person who has a large or indiscriminate appetite *UK, 1546*

A shortened form of 'greedy pig'.

- I'm not saying she was a pig but I was talking to her brother Perky and he said she'd bounced more balls off her forehead than Kenny Dalgleish[.] — Dave Courtney, *Stop the Ride I Want to Get Off*, p. 237, 1999

4 a chorus dancer *US*

- And "pigs" is the backstage slang for chorines. — Jack Lait and Lee Mortimer, *New York Confidential*, p. 159, 1948

5 a promiscuous woman *US*

- — *American Speech*, p. 302, December 1955: 'Wayne University slang'
- Let's shoot through [go] and point percy [the penis] at a few Parisian pigs. — Barry Humphries, *Bazza Pulls It Off!*, 1971
- The rest of us are happy enough going down Rocket's to pull a pig, happy to fuck some old boiler in the car park[.] — John King, *Human Punk*, p. 232, 2000

6 an unattractive female *UK: SCOTLAND*

- Hey Sammy, that wis a pur pig ye were winchin the other night. — Michael Munro, *The Patter, Another Blast*, p. 54, 1988

7 a prostitute *CANADA*

- — Brian Moore, *The Luck of Ginger Coffey*, 1960

8 an inferior or bad example of anything *UK, 1925*

From an earlier sense as 'an unpleasant person'.

- – Pig of a fuckin day, Ianto, eh? – Yeh. – Hate this fuckin weather. — Niall Griffiths, *Sheepshagger*, p. 34, 2001

9 a 'Humber' one-ton 4x4 armoured personnel carrier *UK*

Nicknamed by troops serving in Northern Ireland during the 1970s; taken out of service in the early 1990s.

- Leaving the Belfast supermarket, an armored carrier they called "pigs" drove by like a sightless dinosaur[.] — John Brady, *Stone of the Heart*, p. 104, 1990

10 an M-60 machine gun *US*

Each squad in Vietnam was assigned an M-60, the army's general-purpose machine gun which entered the service in the 1950s. It was designed to be lightweight (23 pounds) and easy to carry. It produced a low 'grunting' sound and thus the porcine allusions.

- I sat with my back to the wire, my feet in the ditch, under the tight heaviness of the flak jacket and belted ammo, worn criss-cross fashion, looking down at the M-60 – the "pig," they called it. — Larry Heinemann, *Close Quarters*, p. 47, 1977
- Lighter, at fifteen pounds, than the old M-60 (that weighed twenty-three pounds dry and was sometimes called "The Pig"), which keeps the gunner feeling cheerful and refreshed after a hard day on the assault. — Hans Halberstadt, *Airborne*, p. 104, 1988

11 in circus usage, an elephant, male or female *UK, 1934*

- [E]lephants are called "bulls" or "pigs". — Butch Reynolds, *Broken Hearted Clown*, p. 32, 1953
- — Don Wilmeth, *The Language of American Popular Entertainment*, p. 36, 1981

12 in a split-pot game of poker, a player who declares both high and low *US*

- — George Percy, *The Language of Poker*, p. 67, 1988

▷ **see:** PIG IN THE MIDDLE

▸ **in pig**

pregnant *UK, 1945*

- It's happened at last, I'm in pig. — Henry Sloane, *Sloane's Inside Guide to Sex & Drugs & Rock 'n' Roll*, p. 73, 1985

▸ **kill your pig**

to spoil your chances of doing something *UK: NORTHERN IRELAND*

- — C. I. Macafee, *A Concise Ulster Dictionary*, p. 193, 1996

pig board *noun*

a surfboard with a narrow, tapered point and a broad tail *US*

- — Grant W. Kuhns, *On Surfing*, p. 120, 1963
- Here, you need a rhino chaser like this one to learn on. Good board. I mean for a pig board. — *Point Break*, 1991

pig book *noun*

a student directory with photographs of each student *US, 1969*

- — *Current Slang*, p. 17, Spring 1971

pig-dog *noun*

a bull terrier *AUSTRALIA*

- Pig dog pups for sale. $40 ea. — *Townsville Daily Bulletin*, p. 29, 3rd April 1982

pig down *verb*
to alter a car's body or frame *US*
- He was the one who installed an oversized engine in it and pigged down the frame. —Mickey Spillane, *I, The Jury*, p. 48, 1947

pigeon *noun*
1 a gullible victim of a swindle *UK, 1593*
- Now my old man is a pigeon when it comes to promoting dough for a pair of skis[.] —Frederick Kohner, *Gidget*, p. 23, 1957
- I suppose I shouldn't tell you because it's not my pigeon and he may have changed since then. —Anonymous *Streetwalker*, p. 142, 1959
- Take a seat, Hawk. We can use a fresh pigeon. — *M*A*S*H*, 1970
- I didn't lose no fortune, but I lost all the money I could get my hands on, it began in the Marine Corps, I met a lot of pigeons in Vietnam. —Joan Didion, *The White Album*, p. 105, 1970
- A "steerman" hunts for "pigeons," unsuspecting amateurs who could be steered into fixed games with professional card players. —Kim Rich, *Johnny's Girl*, p. 61, 1993

2 a young woman, especially an attractive one *UK, 1586*
- There was a pin-up pigeon. She was a twenty-twenty quail. —Haenigsen, *Jive's Like That*, 1947
- When you see a friend with a squab in a cabaret, don't suggest that you and your pigeon move to his table. —Jack Lait and Lee Mortimer, *New York Confidential*, p. 223, 1948

3 a new participant in a twelve-step recovery programme such as Alcoholics Anonymous *US*
- —Christopher Cavanaugh, *AA to Z*, p. 142, 1998

4 an informer *US, 1849*
A shortened form of **STOOL PIGEON**.
- A little pigeon I knew shook his head just enough so I knew they weren't there[.] —Mickey Spillane, *Kiss Me Deadly*, p. 96, 1952
- Now they began contacting their pigeons, but only those on the petty-larceny circuit. —Chester Himes, *Cotton Comes to Harlem*, p. 33, 1965
- His terrible eyes accused Eddie. "You are a pigeon," Marco taunted. "You broke the code." —Sidney Bernard, *This Way to the Apocalypse*, p. 164, 1965
- Collucci said, "Is how you planted the pigeon classified?" —Iceberg Slim (Robert Beck), *Death Wish*, p. 67, 1977
- [W]e knew we had our pigeon. —Duncan MacLaughlin, *The Filth*, p. 112, 2002

5 in horse racing, a losing ticket that someone tries to cash in for winnings *US*
- —Dan Parker, *The ABC of Horse Racing*, p. 147, 1947

6 in shuffleboard, a disc straddling the 7/10 off line *US*
- —Omero C. Catan, *Secrets of Shuffleboard Strategy*, p. 69, 1967: 'Glossary of terms'

7 a urinary bottle used in hospital *IRELAND*
- Nurse, a pigeon, please. —Terence Dolan, *A Dictionary of Hiberno-English*, p. 198, 1999

pigeon *verb*
to betray someone; to inform on someone *US*
- If I thought you'd pigeon I'd kill you. —Chester Himes, *The Real Cool Killers*, p. 50, 1959

pigeon drop *noun*
a swindle in which two confederates pretend to find a wallet and convince a third person to share in the proceeds of the find *US, 1940*
- You some kind of confidence man or dope peddler or something? You trying to work one of those pigeon drops on me? —Ralph Ellison, *Invisible Man*, p. 330, 1947
- Artifice became my bible, as I learned how to play stuff, the shell game, pigeon drop and three card molly. —Donald Goines, *Whoreson*, p. 28, 1972
- What we did, ever so often we'd pull off the pigeon drop for maybe twenty-five dollars, with me planting the leather, or work the twenties for a five. —Guy Owen, *The Flim-Flam Man and the Apprentice Grifter*, p. 151, 1972
- The pigeon drop may have begun in China more than 400 years ago. — *San Francisco Examiner*, p. 40, 19th November 1976
- Spring you get your con games. Your pigeon drops, your Murphys[.] —Robert Campbell, *The Cat's Meow*, p. 47, 1988
- He played the pigeon drop and did three Big Store cons. —Stephen J.L. Cannell, *King Con*, p. 35, 1997
- The victim of a "pigeon drop," an old scam that police say has resurfaced, she gave $5,000 to two people with a fake lottery ticket. — *Palm Beach (Florida) Post*, p. 2B, 31st Januay 2004

pigfoot *noun*
marijuana *US*
- —Robert George Reisner, *The Jazz Titans*, p. 162, 1960

pigfucker *noun*
a despicable person *US*
- Throw me in jail? I'm already there, you stupid pigfucker. —*Natural Born Killers*, 1994

piggie bank *noun*
the stockings worn by an overweight woman *US*
- —Don Wilmeth, *The Language of American Popular Entertainment*, p. 200, 1981

piggies *noun*
▸ **make piggies**
to have sex *US*
- — *Kiss*, 1969: 'Groupie glossary'

pigging *adjective*
used as an all-purpose intensifier, generally to negative effect; euphemistic for 'fucking', 'sodding', etc *UK*
- Now take your pigging money and let me out. —Ted Lewis, *Jack Carter's Law*, p. 7, 1974
- And the pigging radios are still sitting there, in their pigging boxes. —Mike Stott, *Soldiers Talking, Cleanly*, 1978

piggle *noun*
the penis *TRINIDAD AND TOBAGO, 1980*
Children's vocabulary.
- —Thurston Scott, *Cure it with Honey*, p. xx, 1951

piggy *noun*
the toe *UK, 1984*
Childish, from the nursery rhyme 'This little piggy went to market, / This little piggy stayed at home'.
- Now let's get these other piggies wiggling. — *Kill Bill*, 2003

piggyback *verb*
1 in casino blackjack, to place a bet in another player's square *US*
- —Frank Scoblete, *Best Blackjack*, p. 252, 1996

2 to transport loaded tractor trailers on railway flat wagons *US*
- —Montie Tak, *Truck Talk*, p. 118, 1971

piggyback *adjective*
used of a vehicle, stacked on top of another vehicle for transport *US, 1936*
- — *American Speech*, May 1957

piggybacking *noun*
the reclamation of an abandoned building, floor by floor *US*
- Landlords have all but left many buildings for dead in these areas, and dealers either rent several apartments on a floor very cheaply, or "squat" illegally wihtout paying any rent, usually working upward, a practice called "piggybacking." —Terry Williams, *The Cocaine Kids*, p. 53, 1989

piggy bank *noun*
1 savings *UK, 1984*
After the traditional money box.
- I will invest more if I know what is in their piggy bank at all times-even though there are still risks. —Thomas L. Friedman, *The Lexus and the Olive Tree*, p. 174, May 2000

2 a toll booth on a turnpike road *US*
- —Porter Bibb, *CB Bible*, p. 101, 1976

3 an act of masturbation *UK*
Rhyming slang for **WANK**. Also shortened form 'piggy'.
- —Ray Puxley, *Cockney Rabbit*, 1992

piggy in the middle; pig in the middle *noun*
a person caught in the middle of a dispute *UK, 1962*
From the traditional children's game.
- — *The Times*, 27th September 1977
- Piggy in the middle is Tony Blair, trying to make his peace with Europe even as he makes war alongside America. — *The Observer*, 30th March 2003

piggy parts *noun*
ham *US*
- — *Maledicta*, p. 17, 1996: 'Domino's pizza jargon'

pig-ignorant *adjective*
very ignorant *UK, 1972*
- supremely confident in their pig-ignorant arrogance —Ben Elton, *High Society*, p. 269, 2002

pig in knickers *noun*
a very unattractive female *UK: SCOTLAND*
An elaboration of **PIG**.
- —Michael Munro, *The Patter, Another Blast*, p. 54, 1988

pig in shit *noun*

▸ **happy as a pig in shit; like a pig in shit**

very happy *UK, 1944*

- Speaking purely as a director, I was happy as a pig in shit[.] — *The Guardian*, 12th January 2002

pig in the middle; pig *noun*

urine; an act of urination *UK*

Rhyming slang for **PIDDLE** or **WIDDLE**.

- — Ray Puxley, *Cockney Rabbit*, 1992

pig in the wall *noun*

an error in bricklaying in which opposite ends of a new wall meet at different heights *UK*

- — Jack Stern, building instructor, 1978

pig iron *noun*

1 in horse racing, any illegal drug given to a racehorse *AUSTRALIA*

- — Ned Wallish, *The Truth Dictionary of Racing Slang*, p. 62, 1989

2 a carnival ride; the metal assembly of a carnival ride *US*

- — *American Speech*, p. 308–309, December 1960: 'Carnival talk'
- — Joe McKennon, *Circus Lingo*, p. 69, 1980

Pig Iron Express *noun*

the steel-hauling division of Pacific Intermountain Express company *US*

- — Montie Tak, *Truck Talk*, p. 118, 1971

pig iron monkey *noun*

in oil drilling, a derrick construction worker *US*

- — Jerry Robertson, *Oil Slanguage*, p. 84, 1954

pig killer *noun*

phencyclidine, the recreational drug known as PCP or angel dust *US*

- — Ronald Linder, *PCP: The Devil's Dust*, p. 10, 1981
- — *Q Magazine*, p. 75, February 2001

pig-out *noun*

a session of gorging on food *US, 1978*

- I haven't had a good TV-and-junk-food pig-out in ages. — Armistead Maupin, *Further Tales of the City*, p. 156, 1982

pig out *verb*

to eat a lot quickly and messily *US, 1978*

- Fix up a nice big plate of sargassum. We'll pig out. — Carl Hiaasen, *Tourist Season*, p. 260, 1987
- Especially memorable was the marijuana one where Scott Baio pigs out on chocolate ice cream before almost murdering his brother with an oar while rowing on a lake. — Editors of Ben is Dead, *Retrohell*, p. 1, 1997

pig party *noun*

serial consensual sex between one person and multiple partners *UK*

- — James McDonald, *A Dictionary of Obscenity, Taboo and Euphemism*, p. 60, 1988

pigpen *noun*

1 a police headquarters *US*

- — Judi Sanders, *Faced and Faded, Hanging to Hurl*, p. 30, 1993
- — Angela Devlin, *Prison Patter*, p. 88, 1996

2 an illegal gambling operation *US, 1982*

- — Thomas L. Clark, *The Dictionary of Gambling and Gaming*, p. 155, 1987

3 in nine wicket croquet, the crossed centre wickets *US*

- — James Charlton and William Thompson, *Croquet*, p. 159, 1977: 'Glossary'

pig pile *noun*

an orgy with homosexual men *US*

- — Bruce Rodgers, *The Queens' Vernacular*, p. 148, 1972

pig-root *verb*

(of a horse) to prop with the front legs and kick up the back legs *AUSTRALIA, 1900*

- — Ion L. Idriess, *Over the Range*, p. 13, 1947
- — Dymphna Cusack, *Picnic Races*, p. 62, 1962
- But a flip on the nose would swerve him off, cavorting and pig-rooting[.] — Norman Lindsay, *Bohemians at the Bulletin*, p. 34, 1965
- — Wilda Moxham, *The Apprentice*, p. 162, 1969
- — Jim Ramsay, *Cop It Sweet!*, p. 70, 1977
- — Herb Wharton, *Cattle Camp*, p. 136, 1994

pigs *noun*

▸ **pigs to**

to hell with *AUSTRALIA, 1906*

- Pigs to your old man. — Norman Lindsay, *Saturdee*, p. 90, 1934
- Pigs to you, so I will go home. — Norman Lindsay, *Halfway to Anywhere*, p. 30, 1947
- All right, pig's tit to you and pigs to playing mines. — Norman Lindsay, *Halfway to Anywhere*, p. 22, 1947

pigs!

used for registering derision or contempt *AUSTRALIA, 1933*

An abbreviation of **PIG'S ARSE!**.

- 'She's worn out.' Pigs she is.' — Nino Culotta (John O'Grady), *They're A Weird Mob*, 1957
- SUKI: I know you've had a few but don't tell me you've copped a brewer's droop. OZZIE: Pigs I haven't!!! — Barry Humphries, *Bazza Pulls It Off!*, 1971
- — Arthur Chipper, *The Aussie Swearer's Guide*, 1972
- — Jim Ramsay, *Cop it Sweet!*, 1977

pig's arse!

nonsense! *AUSTRALIA, 1951*

Although the earliest record of this exclamation is from 1951, the existence of euphemistic forms such as 'pig's ear' (dating to 1919) show that it was clearly in use much earlier.

- 'Those country lads'll dent a few big reputations this afternoon, you mark my words.' 'Pig's ar....pendix!' — Alexander Buzo, *The Roy Murphy Show*, p. 120, 1971
- — Arthur Chipper, *The Aussie Swearer's Guide*, p. 69, 1972
- — Jim Ramsay, *Cop It Sweet!*, p. 70, 1977
- 'I'll drive,' I offered. 'In a pig's arse, you will. I remember your driving.' — Robert English, *Toxic Kisses*, p. 83, 1979
- — Lance Peters, *The Dirty Half-Mile*, p. 64, 1979
- 'He's almost an Aussie, an' we gotta be loyal,' Snowy said. 'Pig's arse.' — Ward McNally, *Supper at Happy Harry's*, p. 35, 1982
- Pig's arse our beaches are dangerous! We've only lost one Prime Minister to sharks in living memory, and *that's debatable*. — Barry Humphries, *The Traveller's Tool*, p. 13, 1985
- 'We've got nothing yet – but something will turn up.' 'Yeah. Pig's arse.' — Robert G. Barrett, *Davo's Little Something*, p. 179, 1992

pigs' ballroom *noun*

a bar or club where unattractive females congregate *UK: SCOTLAND*

- — Michael Munro, *The Patter, Another Blast*, p. 54, 1988

pig's bum

nonsense *AUSTRALIA*

- 'You've got the hots for her, haven't you?' 'Pig's bum I have.' — Phillip Gwynne, *Deadly Unna?*, p. 184, 1998

pig scabs *noun*

pork scratchings, a packaged snack sold in bars *UK*

- — Chris Lewis, *The Dictionary of Playground Slang*, p. 170, 2003

pig's ear *noun*

beer *AUSTRALIA, 1924*

Rhyming slang. Sometimes shortened to 'pigs' in UK usage.

- PIG'S EAR – Beer. — Gilbert H. Lawson, *A Dictionary of Australian Words and Terms*, 1924
- Nah, not a pint of pig's. — Tommy Steele, *Cinema*, December 1967
- Get some glasses, Flo, we don't drink Rosy Lee or pig's ear tonight, we drink champers. — Frank Hardy, *The Outcasts of Foolgarah*, p. 18, 1971
- — Ryan Aven-Bray, *Ridgey Didge Oz Jack Lang*, p. 39, 1983

▸ **make a pig's ear; make a pig's**

to bungle; to blunder; to make a mess of something *UK, 1954*

- Mistakes, mess, hash – to make a pig's. — Colin Strong and Duff Hart-Davis, *Fighter Pilot*, 1981
- UK makes a pig's ear out of farm policy. — *The Guardian*, 1st August 2002

pig shit run *noun*

a supply transport flight in the early years of US involvement in the Vietnam war, including transport of live farm animals that left reminders of their presence in the planes *US*

- — Gregory Clark, *Words of the Vietnam War*, p. 401, 1990

pig-sick *adjective*

irritated; annoyed and disgusted *UK, 1961*

- We are pig-sick of being mucked about. — *The Guardian*, 11th June 2003

pigskin *noun*

a saddle *AUSTRALIA*

- — Ned Wallish, *The Truth Dictionary of Racing Slang*, p. 62, 1989

pig's Latin *noun*

any coded language used by prison guards *US*

- A truly brilliant pun. — Inez Cardozo-Freeman, *The Joint*, p. 521, 1984

pig's lattie *noun*

a sty *UK*

Polari; a play on **LATTIE** (a house) giving 'pig's house'.

- —Paul Baker, *Polari*, p. 186, 2002

pig slices *noun*

ham *US*

- —*Maledicta*, p. 17, 1996: 'Domino's pizza jargon'

pig station *noun*

in prison, a guard control room *US*

- —Inez Cardozo-Freeman, *The Joint*, p. 521, 1984

pig-sticker *noun*

1 a knife, especially a large knife *UK, 1890*

- The pig-sticker, the switchblade, the knife, for Christ's sake.—Jim Thompson, *Savage Night*, p. 69, 1953
- I said back in my own Kentucky Blue Ridge voice, "I reckon you could hurt me real bad with that there pig sticker."—Sandra Bernard, *Confessions of a Pretty Lady*, 1988

2 a stick with a nail or sharp metal point on one end used for picking up paper litter *US*

- —Reinhold Aman, *Hillary Clinton's Pen Pal: A Guide to Life and Lingo in Federal Prison*, p. 55, 1996

pig's trotter *noun*

a squatter (an unauthorised occupant) *UK*

Rhyming slang.

- —Ray Puxley, *Fresh Rabbit*, 1998

pigsty *noun*

1 a untidy or ill-kept place *UK, 1820*

- [W]hy don't you get this place cleared up! It's a pigsty.—Harold Pinter, *The Birthday Party*, 1965

2 a police station *US*

- —*Complete CB Slang Dictionary*, p. 74, 1976
- —Peter Chippindale, *The British CB Book*, p. 157, 1981
- —Angela Devlin, *Prison Patter*, p. 88, 1996

pigtail *noun*

1 in trucking, an electrical cable that connects the electrical systems of the trailer and the tractor cab *US*

- —Montie Tak, *Truck Talk*, p. 118, 1971

2 in electric line work, an insulated line tool formally known as a spiral link stick *US*

- —A.B. Chance Co., *Lineman's Slang Dictionary*, p. 13, 1980

pig water *noun*

weak, low quality alcohol *US*

- [W]hen he said a double bourbon he didn't mean "no one-and-a-half-ounce shot of pig-water bar whiskey either"[.]—John Clellon Holmes, *The Horn*, p. 39, 1958

pike *noun*

1 a toll road, a toll motorway *US*

- —Montie Tak, *Truck Talk*, p. 118, 1971

2 a railway *US*

- —Norman Carlisle, *The Modern Wonder Book of Trains and Railroading*, p. 266, 1946

3 a glance *US*

- —Hyman E. Goldin et al., *Dictionary of American Underworld Lingo*, p. 157, 1950

pike *verb*

1 in a card game, to peek at an opponent's cards *US*

- —Frank Garcia, *Marked Cards and Loaded Dice*, p. 263, 1962

2 (of a man) to tape the penis and testicles to the body as part of an effort to pass as a woman *US*

- "Why do you pike?" Spinnerman asked. "Don't most of your customers just want you to go down on them?"—Robert Campbell, *Alice in La-La Land*, p. 217, 1987
- A man with as many folds and creases as me, who knows how to pike his pecker, he got a dozen ways.—Robert Campbell, *Boneyards*, p. 139, 1992

pike out *verb*

to back out of a commitment *NEW ZEALAND*

- —Louis S. Leland, *A Personal Kiwi-Yankee Dictionary*, p. 77, 1984
- She was clued in enough to realise the pig was a no-show for the date, and tied herself in knots over whether to go or pike out.—John Birmingham, *He Died With a Felafel in his Hand*, p. 148, 1994

piker *noun*

1 a rank amateur or beginner; a gambler who makes small, cautious bets *US, 1872*

- Willie felt impelled to demonstrate that he was something more than a piker like the others here.—James T. Farrell, *Willie Collins*, p. 107, 1946
- A man who has killed three cops looks down upon a piker who only kidnapped a child or robbed a post office.—Jack Lait and Lee Mortimer, *New York Confidential*, p. 16, 1948
- I gave him a quarter so he wouldn't remember me as a piker.—Mickey Spillane, *My Gun is Quick*, p. 65, 1950
- Now, however, "piker bets" were disallowed.—Jim Thompson, *Bad Boy*, p. 368, 1953
- I winked at the mark and said, "What makes you think we're pikers? We're not afraid to bet even as much as ten dollars or more."—Iceberg Slim (Robert Beck), *Trick Baby*, p. 151, 1969
- Mr. Henry Booth, Donovan's owner. A real wealthy gent. And no piker. Lays out money like it grew on trees.—Wilda Moxham, *The Apprentice*, p. 30, 1969
- I can't recall the half of it, but it made the Yellow Kid and Barney the Patch and your average politician look like pikers looting a Sunday school collection.—Guy Owen, *The Flim-Flam Man and the Apprentice Grifter*, p. 95, 1972

2 a person who opts out of an agreement or abandons someone; a weak, cowardly person *AUSTRALIA, 1950*

A term of high contempt in Australia.

- —Nino Culotta (John O'Grady), *They're A Weird Mob*, p. 203, 1957
- None of you pikers'd give breath to a dyin' man.—John Wynnum, *Tar Dust*, p. 102, 1962
- 'You're ill. Let me take you home.' He looked at me in pure disgust. 'Whaddya mean,' he cried. 'I'm no piker.'—Sue Rhodes, *Now You'll Think I'm Awful*, p. 55, 1967

pikey *noun*

a tramp; a gypsy; a traveller *UK, 1847*

Generally used of travellers by non-travellers. Ultimately from early C16 'pike' (to depart). The actor Brad Pitt played a 'pikey' in the film *Snatch*, written and directed by Guy Ritchie, 2000.

- [T]his pikey-looking geezer introduced himself, threw up a couple of names, and offered me a bit of work. These pikeys aren't proper gypsies, though they like to think they are[.]—Lenny McLean, *The Guv'nor*, p. 69, 1998
- I gave him the keys to my garage to stash the stuff I got from the pikeys (as we called the gipsies).—Dave Courtney, *Raving Lunacy*, p. 13, 2000
- Gypsies, pikeys, travellers or didicois, call them what you will[.]—Jimmy Stockin, *On The Cobbles*, p. 13, 2000

pikkie *noun*

1 a photograph or film *NEW ZEALAND*

- —David McGill, *David McGill's Complete Kiwi Slang Dictionary*, p. 84, 1998

2 a small person, a child, a small child; a small thing *SOUTH AFRICA, 1948*

Directly from Afrikaans *pikkie*. Between children, usage may be contemptuous. Also shortened form 'pik'.

- I don't want to play with her; she's only a pik.—Jean Branford, *A Dictionary of South African English*, 1978
- [A]ll the way back to his days as a barefooted pikkie playing rugby.—*Sunday Times (South Africa)*, 20th December 1998

pilchard *noun*

a fool *UK*

- What am I, a pilchard? I had it delivered. It's been pugged up [hidden] in the room and it goes before we check out.—Garry Bushell, *The Face*, p. 209, 2001

pile *noun*

1 a great deal of money *UK, 1741*

- We all wanna make a fuckin' pile.—Shaun Ryder, *Shaun Ryder... in His Own Words*, 1991

2 in poker, the amount of money (cash and/or chips) a player has in front of him available for betting *US*

- —John Scarne, *Scarne's Guide to Modern Poker*, p. 287, 1979

▸on the pile

in prison *US*

- And half of my life would have been spent on the pile.—Red (Morris) Rudensky and Don Riley, *The Gonif*, p. 133, 1970

pile *verb*

(from the male point of view) to have sex *US*

- There is a certain type who will leave you and his wife alone and tell you to pile her real good.—Eldridge Cleaver, *Soul on Ice*, p. 170, 1968

▸pile it on

to exaggerate; to show-off *US, 1876*

A variation of **PILE ON THE AGONY**.

- I am piling it on, deliberately.—*The Observer*, 25th April 1999

pile driver *noun*

1 a sexual position in which the woman stands on her head and the man enters her directly and powerfully from above *US*
A term (and practice) found more commonly in pornography than real life.
- — *Adult Video News*, p. 38, September 1995
- I like pile driver, that's when you lay down and your legs are over your head. — Anthony Petkovich, *The X Factory*, p. 83, 1997
- For most of the girls, the position that makes us shudder is the pile driver. The girl is upside down with only her head and shoulders on the ground and her bits in the air, and the guy is up and over her, pounding away like a jackhammer. — *Playboy*, p. 132, 1st March 2002

2 the active participant in anal sex *US*
- — *Maledicta*, p. 232, 1979: 'Kinks and queens: linguistic and cultural aspects of the terminology for gays'
- — William K. Bentley and James M. Corbett, *Prison Slang*, p. 60, 1992

3 a hole in a road, jarring to the driver when encountered *US*
- — *American Speech*, p. 271, December 1962: 'The language of traffic policemen'

pile in *verb*

to enter en masse, especially a vehicle or a bar *US, 1841*
- Once in a while, when business was slow at the Martinique, I would knock off early and Bix and I would pile into a cab, bound for the South Side in Chicago[.] — Mezz Mezzrow, *Really the Blues*, p. 82, 1946
- And there we'd be pilin' into Effin Nellie's or Peg-leg Pete's, for a couple of pints of good beer, maybe the first in the week[.] — Alan Bleasdale, *Boys From the Blackstuff*, 1982

pile of rocks *noun*

a type of bet in an illegal numbers game lottery *US*
- Then to be on the safe side he also played jail house, death row, lady come back, two-timing woman, pile of rocks, dark days and trouble. — Chester Himes, *A Rage in Harlem*, p. 23, 1957

pile-on *noun*

an offensive, despicable person; a clumsy person; a socially awkward person *INDIA*
An image, perhaps, of this person as victim.
- [Y]our name has now officially been shifted from geek, nerd or spaced out, to duh, mufar or loser, wannabe and a pile-on[.] — *The Times of India*, 30th September 2002

piles *noun*

crack cocaine *UK, 1998*
- — Mike Haskins, *Drugs*, p. 282, 2003

pileup; pile-up *noun*

a crash involving multiple vehicles *UK*
Originally World War 1 Royal Air Force for 'a plane crash', from an earlier verb sense used by the navy. Widely used by mid-C20, this sense was virtually conventional by the mid-1970s.
- Get in your car, start it, and start drivin' / Over the island and cause a forty-two car pileup[.] — Eminem (Marshall Mathers), *Drug Ballad*, 2000

pilgrim *noun*

1 in northwestern Canada, a tourist or newcomer; also, a cow newly imported to the region *CANADA*
- In stockmen's language, newly imported cattle are "pilgrims," also applied to those unable to "rustle" or hunt for food. — *Alberta Historical Review*, p. 16/2, Autumn 1962
- He complains at some length about pilgrims, the local [Yukon and Alaska Highway] name for tourists, and their driving habits. — *Weekend*, p. 26/1, 6th April 1963

2 a newcomer to a game of poker *US*
- — George Percy, *The Language of Poker*, p. 67, 1988

pill *noun*

1 any central nervous system stimulant *US*
- — *American Speech*, p. 281, December 1966: 'More carnie talk from the west coast'

2 a tablet of MDMA, the recreational drug best known as ecstasy *UK*
A generic usage.
- — Angela Devlin, *Prison Patter*, p. 88, 1996
- Es are often referred to simply as "pills". — Macfarlane, Macfarlane and Robson, *The User*, p. 75, 1996

3 a pellet of opium *US*
- Then he held the pipe bowl close to the top of his special lamp and stuck the pill on the edge of the bowl, drawing the yen hok round and round to stretch the opium[.] — Mezz Mezzrow, *Really the Blues*, p. 98, 1946

4 a cigarette *UK, 1914*
- I leaned back again and lit another pill. — Raymond Chandler, *The Long Goodbye*, p. 54, 1953

5 a rugby ball *NEW ZEALAND*
- — Sonya Plowman, *Great Kiwi Slang*, p. 139, 2002

6 in pool, a small tally ball used as a scoring device *US*
- — Mike Shamus, *The Illustrated Encyclopedia of Billiards*, p. 170, 1993

7 an unpleasant person *UK, 1871*
- — John Ayto, *The Oxford Dictionary of Slang*, p. 223, 1998

▸ **the pill**

1 the contraceptive pill *UK, 1957*
Not in practical currency until the early 1960s.
- The pill, of course, is the big new development in the '60s. — Joe David Brown, *Sex in the '60s*, p. 18, 1968
- All I can say is Thank God for the pill! — *Screw*, p. 7, 12th January 1970
- I didn't always use protection and, I sometimes forgot to take the Pill. — *Mixmag*, p. 99, February 2002

2 the weekly anti-malaria pill taken by US troops in Vietnam *US*
Playing on the birth control pill, then very much in vogue back home.
- — Linda Reinberg, *In the Field*, p. 167, 1991

pillar and post *noun*

a ghost *UK, 1960*
Rhyming slang.
- Whereby the holy trinity becomes "the soap, currant and holy pillar and post". — Ray Puxley, *Cockney Rabbit*, 1992

pilled; pilled up *adjective*

under the influence of central nervous system stimulants or depressants *US*
- Most of the meths men are on drugs, many of them pilled up to the eyeballs. — Geoffrey Fletcher, *Down Among the Meths Men*, p. 31, 1966
- — *American Speech*, p. 282, December 1966: 'More carnie talk from the west coast'
- [S]ix or seven blokes in a ring, all pilled out of their tiny minds[.] — Ian Hebditch, *Weekend, The Sharper Word*, p. 134, 1969
- I figured he was pilled up to the eyeballs. — Jamie Mandelkau, *Buttons*, p. 28, 1971
- I was all pilled up – I had a pill habit at that time with the dope habit. — Bruce Jackson, *In the Life*, p. 76, 1972
- Mods; young boys and girls pilled to the eyeballs — Irish Jack, *History, The Sharper Word*, p. 31, 1998
- "Stutter the words – it makes you sound pilled" and I said, "Oh... like I am!" — Roger Daltrey describing the recording of 'My Generation', 1965, *Uncut*, p. 44, January 2003

pillhead *noun*

a habitual user of amphetamines, barbiturates or MDMA, the recreational drug best known as ecstasy *US*
- I'm not a pill head, I really need these things. Here's my prescription. — Roger Gordon, *Hollywood's Sexual Underground*, p. 46, 1966
- [A] wired-up pillhead, he said to himself[.] — Gerald Petievich, *Shakedown*, p. 38, 1988
- The audience responded to the Who on a number of levels. First there was the aggression. "We were all pillheads," said Daltrey. "We were probably the most aggressive group that's ever happened in England." — Harry Shapiro, *Waiting For The Man*, 1999
- Whilst pillheads hold hands and sing happy songs, pissheads are out the back having a punch-up. — Wayne Anthony, *Spanish Highs*, p. 151, 1999

pillion pussy *noun*

a woman attracted to motorcyclists *NEW ZEALAND, 1956*
A 'pillion' (probably from the Scottish Gaelic or Irish Gaelic for 'rug') is a motorcycle saddle.
- These cowboys roared around on bikes attracting girls known as 'pillion pussies'. — Redmer YSKA, *All Shook Up*, p. 144, 1992
- — Harry Orsman, *A Dictionary of Modern New Zealand Slang*, p. 100, 1999
- Mark your diaries, give John a ring and come along with your wife/partner/friend of the opposite gender/pillion pussy or whatever and join in the fun. — *The Motoring Spirit*, p. 9, May 2001

pillock *noun*

a fool *UK, 1967*
From a variation of dialect *pillicock* or *pillcock* (the penis).
- ["I]s it true what they all say about black men?" "What? That we all make great lawyers, accountants, politicians?" "No, yer pillock, that you've all got cowin' big dadgers [penises]. — Colin Butts, *Is Harry on the Boat?*, p. 19, 1997
- People talk about Paul [McCartney] being a pillock, but John [Lennon] did more things that were worthy of being a pillock, saying things like "We're bigger than God"[.] — *Uncut*, p. 51, July 2001

pillow *noun*

1 a weak, effeminate, gutless male *AUSTRALIA*

- And that pillow Keating has refused to meet me in the toilets hundreds of times after arguments. — Roy Slaven (John Doyle), *Five South Coast Seasons*, p. 136, 1992
- Going down Down Under is the perfect holiday package for birds fed up with the freezing Pommy winter and the deadshit pillows they're forced to have as boyfriends. — *Picture*, p. 9, 5th February 1992
- If, as a male stripper, you don't score bigtime on your first engagement, you are a pillow and a hopeless joke and we don't wish to know you. — *People*, p. 13, 5th July 1999

2 a sealed polyethylene bag of drugs *US*

- — William D. Alsever, *Glossary for the Establishment and Other Uptight People*, p. 25, December 1970

▸ an extra pillow

used as a coded reference for a prostitute arranged by a hotel concierge *UK*

- 'In certain places you can order prostitutes through the concierge, who gets kickbacks,' adds Edward-Jones. 'The slang for it is "an extra pillow."' — *The Times*, 16th April 2005

pillow-biter *noun*

a homosexual male; specifically the passive partner in anal intercourse *AUSTRALIA, 1981*

- Visiting pillow-biters have had a few nasty surprises in my homeland[.] — Barry Humphries, *The Traveller's Tool*, p. 20, 1985
- Why don'tcha piss off ya little Pommy pillow biter. — Kathy Lette, *Girls' Night Out*, p. 83, 1987
- — Angela Devlin, *Prison Patter*, p. 88, 1996
- a fully confirmed fudge-packing pillow-biter — Jenny Eclair, *Camberwell Beauty*, p. 193, 2000
- — Connie Eble (Editor), *UNC-CH Campus Slang*, p. 7, Spring 2003

pillow-biting *adjective*

homosexual *AUSTRALIA, 1985*

- — Barry Humphries, *The Traveller's Tool*, p. 117, 1985
- We hate going around saying our marine mates are a bunch of pillow-biting deviates of the deep. — *Picture*, p. 20, 5th February 1992

pillowcase *noun*

an empty-headed fool *US*

- HEATHER CHANDLER: God-damn Heather, you were with me in Study Hall when I thought of it. Such a pillowcase. HEATHER DUKE: (HURT) I forgot. — *Heathers*, 1988

pillow pigeons *noun*

bedbugs *US*

- — Marcus Hanna Boulware, *Jive and Slang of Students in Negro Colleges*, 1947
- — Helen Dahlskog (Editor), *A Dictionary of Contemporary and Colloquial Usage*, p. 45, 1972

pillow talk *noun*

intimate discussions in bed *US*

Suggests secrets shared, not sexually oriented talk.

- "That message gets delivered in pillow talk, I'm sure," Califano said. — *The Washington Post*, p. A3, 30th May 1977

pill party *noun*

execution in the gas chamber *US*

Pills of cyanide dropped into a bucket of water produce the lethal gas, hence the blackly humorous term.

- — Eugene Landy, *The Underground Dictionary*, p. 150, 1971

pill popper *noun*

a habitual user of drugs in pill form *US, 1979*

- — Angela Devlin, *Prison Patter*, p. 88, 1996

pill-pusher *noun*

1 a doctor, especially a specialist in internal medicine *UK, 1909*

- — *American Speech*, p. 145–148, May 1961: 'The spoken language of medicine; argot, slang, cant'
- — Angela Devlin, *Prison Patter*, p. 88, 1996

2 a pharmacist *US*

- — *Maledicta*, p. 57, Summer 1980: 'Not sticks and stones, but names: more medical pejoratives'

pill-roller *noun*

a doctor *US*

- — *American Speech*, p. 194, 'October 1951: 'A study of reformatory argot'

pills *noun*

the testicles *UK, 1937*

- What have we got these great artistic skill for That other lands would gladly give their pills for? — Barry Humphries, *A Nice Night's Entertainment*, p. 183, 1978
- — James McDonald, *A Dictionary of Obscenity, Taboo and Euphemism*, p. 7, 1988
- Bloody hell, lad, what happened to you? Kicked in the pills? — Niall Griffiths, *Kelly + Victor*, p. 98, 2002

▸ on pills

dieting *US*

Teen slang.

- — *San Francisco News*, p. 6, 25th March 1958

pilly *noun*

an abuser of drugs in pill form *US*

- — *Congressional Record*, p. E3981, 6th May 1970

pilot *noun*

1 a person who remains drug-free to guide another through an experience on a hallucinogenic drug *US*

- Psychedelic adventurers in San Francisco who are on a bad trip can call in a friendly pilot to bring them down safely. — *Berkeley Barb*, p. 6, 9th December 1966

2 a driver of any heavy-load vehicle; a bus driver *UK, 1936*

- — *British Road Services Magazine*, December 1951

3 in horse racing, a jockey *US, 1983*

- — Thomas L. Clark, *The Dictionary of Gambling and Gaming*, p. 155, 1987

4 a pimp *BARBADOS*

- — Frank A. Collymore, *Barbadian Dialect*, p. 84, 1965

pilot error *noun*

in computing, a user's misconfiguration that produces errors that at first appear to be the fault of the program *US*

- — Eric S. Raymond, *The New Hacker's Dictionary*, p. 281, 1991

pim *noun*

the clitoris *TRINIDAD AND TOBAGO*

- — Lise Winer, *Dictionary of the English/Creole of Trinidad & Tobago*, 2003

pimp *noun*

1 a charming man who attracts women *US*

- — Judi Sanders, *Da Bomb!*, p. 21, 1997
- — Connie Eble (Editor), *UNC-CH Campus Slang*, p. 6, April 1997

2 in a deck of playing cards, a jack or knave *US*

- — George Percy, *The Language of Poker*, p. 67, 1988

3 an informer to the police or other authorities *AUSTRALIA, 1899*

- They suspected you were either a policeman or a pimp. — Vince Kelly, *The Bogeyman*, p. 13, 1956
- I'll stake my Davey he didn't tell you he was a Customs pimp? — John Wynnum, *Tar Dust*, p. 75, 1962
- — Jim Ramsay, *Cop It Sweet!*, p. 70, 1977
- — Gerald Sweeney, *The Plunge*, p. 311, 1981

4 cocaine *US*

- — US Department of Justice, *Street Terms*, August 1994
- — Nick Constable, *This is Cocaine*, p. 181, 2002

pimp *verb*

1 to work as a pimp; to exert control over a prostitute *US*

- Then I would pimp her – try to get as much out of her as I could. Sandy's not gettin' pimped. She's with a pimp. She doesn't just want to be part of the group that's getting pimped. — Susan Hall, *Gentleman of Leisure*, p. 56, 1972
- The only thing I had going for me was the fact that Ace wasn't a kid but a man who had pimped long enough to know just how the pimp game goes. — A.S. Jackson, *Gentleman Pimp*, p. 143, 1973
- Just because I didn't want to pimp Amelia or anybody else? — Bobby Seale, *A Lonely Rage*, p. 153, 1978
- Sistahs had a lot of heart and you had to be a lotta pimp to pimp'em. — Odie Hawkins, *Black Chicago*, p. 116, 1992

2 to take advantage of *US, 1942*

- You can start pimping hard on a bitch and then sucker out and blow her, but ain't no way you can turn it around and pimp on Pepper after starting with her like a sucker. — Iceberg Slim (Robert Beck), *Pimp*, p. 65, 1969

3 to act in a stylised, fashionable way *US*

- — *Current Slang*, p. 11, Fall 1970

4 to inform; to betray *AUSTRALIA, 1938*

- Now he'll pimp to the second. — Robert S. Close, *Love Me Sailor*, p. 145, 1945
- 'Don't think you can pimp on me and get away with it!' — Frank Hardy, *Power Without Glory*, p. 197, 1950
- — John A. Holm, *Dictionary of Bahamian English*, p. 155, 1982

5 to win away the affection of another person's date *US*

- — John D. Bell et al., *Loosely Speaking*, p. 14, 1966

▸ **pimp your pipe**
to loan or rent a pipe used for smoking crack cocaine *US*
- —US Department of Justice, *Street Terms*, October 1994

pimp *adjective*
excellent, fashionable, stylish *US*
- "Pimp" as an adjective commonly means "sharp" or "beautiful." —Roger Abrahams, *Positively Black*, p. 92, 1970
- Sometime a group of buddies who ran together, who were "stone pimp," as the phrase went, would move straight into the poverty program. —Tom Wolfe, *Radical Chic & Mau-Mauing the Flak Catchers*, p. 132, 1970

pimp-ass *adjective*
in the manner of a pimp *US*
- I blame the star-fucking pimp-ass parents of these kids[.] —Howard Stern, *Miss America*, p. 69, 1995

pimp-crazy *adjective*
psychologically controlled by a pimp *US*
- A woman who has been abused by several pimps in succession is said to be pimp-crazy. —Christina and Richard Milner, *Black Players*, p. 34, 1972

pimp dust *noun*
cocaine *US*
Before the era of crack cocaine, cocaine was an expensive drug enjoyed only by the wealthy, notably by pimps.
- —Edith A. Folb, *runnin' down some lines*, p. 249, 1980

pimped-up *adjective*
flashy; of a car, laden with flashy accessories, usually not related to the car's performance *US*
- [H]e allowed as how thin, pan-sauteed veal with wild mushroom sauce is "a pimped-up version" of that dish —*Newsday*, 18th June 1993
- Cruz says her kids, an 8-year-old son and 11-year-old daughter, loved the pimped up ride. —*Plain Dealer (Cleveland, Ohio)*, p. L1, 23rd May 2004

pimping *adjective*
expensive, fashionable *US*
- "I wish we had a pimping grill like those guys," Kiefer said of one raft. —*Post-Crescent (Appleton, Wisconsin)*, p. 8B, 13th April 2003

pimple *noun*
a steep hill *UK*
Hauliers' slang.
- —*British Road Service Magazine*, December 1951

pimple and blotch; pimple *noun*
Scotch whisky *UK*
Rhyming Slang for 'Scotch'.
- —Julian Franklyn, *A Dictionary of Rhyming Slang*, 1960
- [A] "drop of pimple". —Ray Puxley, *Cockney Rabbit*, 1992

pimple and wart *noun*
port (wine) *UK*
Rhyming slang, always used in full.
- —Julian Franklyn, *A Dictionary of Rhyming Slang*, 1961
- —Ray Puxley, *Cockney Rabbit*, 1992

pimplie; pimply *noun*
a youth, especially a spotty-faced youth *UK*
- So who were the hits? Would you believe the adolescent pimplies, the two-tone punks, the ethnic minorities. —*British Journal of Photography*, 13th June 1980

pimpmobile; pimp-car *noun*
a large, expensive and ostentatious car, whether or not it is actually owned by a pimp *US*
- [C]arting pimp-mobiles off to the pound if they so much as double-parked to buy cigarettes[.] —Gail Sheehy, *Hustling*, p. 95, 1973
- And me with my pimp-car running off with his sister. —Edwin Torres, *Carlito's Way*, p. 70, 1975
- "Driver of the pimpmobile looks hinky," Francis said as they crossed Pico Boulevard on La Brea, slowly passing a red and white Cadillac convertible. —Joseph Wambaugh, *The Choirboys*, p. 107, 1975
- Single mud-kickers [street prostitutes], black players [pimps] and their interracial stables started to park far out pimpmobiles up and down the block. —Iceberg Slim (Robert Beck), *Airtight Willie and Me*, p. 26, 1979
- He reached out the window of his pimpmobile, and with a manicured right index finger – longer than a broomstick and fitted with two diamond rings set in a bed of sapphires – he crossed her heart. —Seth Morgan, *Homeboy*, p. 17, 1992
- "Yeah," said Champ. "I don't go in for no broke-down pimp-mobile." —Richard Price, *Clockers*, p. 254, 1992
- His recent transformation from gangsta to pimp give him the cred to hustle up a modern iteration of a classic '70s pimpmobile. —*Palm Beach Post*, p. 5D, 27th August 2003

pimp post; pimp rest *noun*
an armrest or console between the driver's seat and the passenger seat of a car *US*
Used for the **GANGSTER LEAN**.
- —Edith A. Folb, *runnin' down some lines*, p. 249, 1980

pimp roll *noun*
a highly stylised manner of walking, projecting an image of control and dispassion *US*
- Now he felt good all the way around, so he walked over to the four corners at Hollywood and Vine, practising the pimp roll that made the black hustlers look so cool. —Robert Campbell, *Sweet La-La Land*, p. 66, 1990
- Waylon did the pimp roll past the table out to the kitchen in the back. —Robert Campbell, *Boneyards*, p. 108, 1992

pimp's arrest *noun*
used to describe a pimp causing the arrest of a prostitute who has left his control *US*
- "Pimp's arrest" occurs when a man seizes his former ho and brings her to jail, forcibly if necessary, and then reclaims his bond money. —Christina and Richard Milner, *Black Players*, p. 101, 1972

pimp shoes; pimping shoes *noun*
flashy, expensive shoes *US*
- A few years ago, pimpin' shoes meant expensive alligator shoes with a long and narrow cut. —Christina and Richard Milner, *Black Players*, p. 34, 1972

pimp slap *verb*
to strike someone forcefully, usually with the back of the hand across the face *US*
- —Pamela Munro, *U.C.L.A. Slang*, p. 97, 1997

pimp steak *noun*
a frankfurter *US*
- — Clarence Major, *Dictionary of Afro-American Slang*, p. 91, 1970

pimp stick *noun*
a cigarette holder *US*
- Society Red took the cigarette holder and waved it with his notion of elegance. "Pretty smooth pimp stick for only three packs". —Malcolm Braly, *On the Yard*, p. 155, 1967

pimp sticks *noun*
wire coathangers used by pimps to beat prostitutes *US*
- When my hand came out it was holding my pimp sticks, two coat hangers twisted together. —Donald Goines, *Whoreson*, p. 199, 1972

pimp suit *noun*
a showy, extravagent, tasteless suit *US*
- He knew he should keep still, but he didn't like Roland's bright blue pimp suit or the big Lone Ranger hat touching the roof of the car. —Elmore Leonard, *Gold Coast*, p. 34, 1980

pimpsy; pimps *adjective*
too easy *UK*
Upper-class society use; possibly the result of silly word play (simple, simps, pimps, pimpsy).
- The course was pimpsy. —Ann Barr and Peter York, *The Official Sloane Ranger Handbook*, p. 159, 1982

pimp title *noun*
a pimp's claim on the loyalty, services and earnings of a prostitute *US*
- He had taken off the 'ho's bread and most likely had massaged her tonsils with his swipe to cop legal pimp title. —Iceberg Slim (Robert Beck), *Airtight Willie and Me*, p. 65, 1979

pimp up *verb*
to add flashy touches to something ; to dress something up *US*
- —Sylvia Carter, *Newsday*, p. 91, 18th June 1993
- —Pamela Munro, *U.C.L.A. Slang*, p. 97, 1997
- Hendsbee pimped us his ride some time ago, with a photo of himself, HRM logo and contact information on the side. —*Halifax (Nova Scotia) Daily News*, p. 6, 11th July 2004
- Every Thursday, the VIP room will be pimped up with rock decor and rock music. —*Chicago Tribune*, p. 59, 17th May 2004

pin *noun*
1 the leg or foot *UK, 1530*
Usually in the plural.
- Soon as I was back on my pins, I began running up to Harlem again[.] —Mezz Mezzrow, *Really the Blues*, p. 283, 1946

- Dolls who must cross their pins at ringside tables should be sure they have nice ones. — Jack Lait and Lee Mortimer, *New York Confidential*, p. 222, 1948
- But I did, for some twenty pages of light blast, violate the ironclad altar of femininity and point out mom's big mouth and little brain, her puffed crop and shaky pins. — Philip Wylie, *Opus 21*, p. 20, 1949
- O'MALLY: [...] Did you see those legs she had on her? BELL: I saw them. O'MALLY: Did you ever see such pins, did you, did you honestly now? — Graeme Kent, *The Queen's Corporal [Six Granada Plays]*, p. 87, 1959
- [H]e couldn't see her legs because she was standing behind a sofa, but if anybody asked him to bet, and he never bet on anything, he would bet that she had absolutely gorgeous pins. — Richard Condon, *Prizzi's Glory*, p. 4, 1988
- I can make it on my own two fucking pins thank you. — William T. Vollman, *Whores for Gloria*, p. 103, 1991
- I don't feel too steady on the ol' pins. — Colin Butts, *Is Harry on the Boat?*, p. 210, 1997
- Nifty on her pins is that 'un. — *The Full Monty*, 1997

2 a hypodermic syringe and needle used for the injection of narcotics *US, 1973*

- — Richard A. Spears, *The Slang and Jargon of Drugs and Drink*, p. 388, 1986

3 a very thin marijuana cigarette *US, 1967*

- — Richard A. Spears, *The Slang and Jargon of Drugs and Drink*, p. 389, 1986
- — Pamela Munro, *U.C.L.A. Slang*, p. 97, 1997
- — Simon Worman, *Joint Smoking Rules*, 2001
- — Mike Haskins, *Drugs*, p. 288, 2003

4 a person who serves as a lookout *US*

- — William K. Bentle and James M.Corbett, *Prison Slang*, p. 40, 1992

▷ **see:** PIN POSITION

pin *verb*

1 to scrutinise someone or something, to look at someone or something intently *US*

- The paddy boy'd just pass by you and say, "Watch it, baby, the Man is on the next corner," or "The Man is pinning you from across the street." — Claude Brown, *Manchild in the Promised Land*, p. 161, 1965
- Last night I pinned the heat, I see them. They were sitting there. — Lenny Bruce, *The Essential Lenny Bruce*, p. 202, 1967
- Shit, them whores you 'pinning' ain't but half the stable. — Iceberg Slim (Robert Beck), *Pimp*, p. 119, 1969
- But Spoon and I just grinned / as we continued to pin / to see who else was there. — Lightnin' Rod, *Hustlers Convention*, p. 43, 1973
- When this queen rolled on the scene and began to pin / With one look at her I could tell she was pure sin. — Dennis Wepman et al., *The Life*, p. 52, 1976

2 to inject a drug *UK*

- — Mike Haskins, *Drugs*, p. 290, 2003

3 to tattoo something with improvised equipment *US*

- Kenny also got himself tattooed while there; a sparkling pair of dice, showing up a winning roll of seven, was pinned into his left forearm[.] — Emmett Grogan, *Ringolevio*, p. 65, 1972

4 (from the male perspective) to have sex *UK*

▸ **pin for home**

on the railways, to leave work and go home *US*

- — Ramon Adams, *The Language of the Railroader*, p. 115, 1977

▸ **pin on**

to fix the blame on someone *UK*

- would not make a premature move against [Kim] Philby, until he could indisputably pin the goods on him. — *Times Literary Supplement*, 7th December 1979

▸ **pin one on**

to consume a drink *AUSTRALIA*

- 'Yer gunna pin one on?' 'What is this pin one on, Joe?' 'Knock one back. Gunna 'ave a drink?' — Nino Culotta (John O'Grady), *They're A Weird Mob*, p. 42, 1957

pin and needle *noun*

a beetle *UK*

Rhyming slang. The plural is 'pins and needles'.

- — Ray Puxley, *Cockney Rabbit*, 1992

pin artist *noun*

an illegal abortionist *US*

- — Joseph E. Ragen and Charles Finston, *Inside the World's Toughest Prison*, p. 812, 1962: 'Penitentiary and underworld glossary'

pin-brain *noun*

an idiot *UK*

- [T]he kind of pin-brains who thought Tommy Slaughter was a good egg[.] — John Milne, *Alive and Kicking*, p. 32, 1998

pinch *noun*

1 an arrest *US, 1900*

- I am glad that the newspaper boys, who later liked to refer to me as an ace narcotic inspector, never heard the story of my first big pinch. — William J. Spillard and Pence James, *Needle in a Haystack*, p. 71, 1945
- Cop across the street, instead of making his pinch, holds onto his big fat belly and roars. — Mezz Mezzrow, *Really the Blues*, p. 197, 1946
- You'll be right behind me every inch of the way, but when the pinch comes I'll get shoved aside and you slap the cuffs on. — Mickey Spillane, *I, The Jury*, p. 10, 1947
- The cops carry him from the curb where he has collapsed and lay him tenderly in a dirty hallway; the magistrates are lenient if a pinch is mandatory[.] — Jack Lait and Lee Mortimer, *New York Confidential*, p. 63, 1948
- I thought it was a pinch. I didn't know it was a shakedown till I got here[.] — Horace McCoy, *Kiss Tomorrow Good-bye*, p. 71, 1948
- At the time the pinch was made Freddie, my other sister, had just been born, and we had other things than crime to talk about. — Jim Thompson, *Bad Boy*, p. 296, 1953
- Except some of the wops – there was one boss did a long bit in a dope pinch[.] — Edwin Torres, *Carlito's Way*, p. 52, 1975
- I have at least two dozen gambling and bookmaking pinches on me. — *Casino*, 1995

2 a technique used by a man to maintain an erection, compressing the base of his penis *US*

- — *Adult Video News September*, p. 38, 1995

3 very potent heroin, bought and used in small amounts *US*

- — Peter Johnson, *Dictionary of Street Alcohol and Drug Terms*, p. 145, 1993

4 a small amount of marijuana *UK*

- — Angela Devlin, *Prison Patter*, p. 88, 1996

5 a five-dollar note or betting chip *US*

- — George Percy, *The Language of Poker*, p. 67, 1988

6 a steep incline *AUSTRALIA, 1846*

- Down several steep pinches the lubra went sprawling[.] — Ion L. Idriess, *Over the Range*, p. 283, 1947

pinch *verb*

1 to arrest someone *UK, 1837*

- We're liable to get pinched for mashing on Sixty-third. I heard the Law is watching that pretty close. — James T. Farrell, *Saturday Night*, p. 38, 1947
- The cop shrugged. "Looks like you're pinched, kid," he told me. — Max Shulman, *The Many Loves of Dobie Gillis*, p. 195, 1951
- Which, when you consider that Emmitt Warring also seems to be immune, makes Georgetown seem like a wonderful place to live in – nobody ever gets pinched there. — Jack Lait and Lee Mortimer, *Washington Confidential*, p. 11, 1951
- A few dollars, an inexpensive wristwatch, a car that would get him pinched before he had it a day. — Jim Thompson, *Roughneck*, p. 150, 1954
- POLICE OFFICIAL: I want to tell you that if this man ever uses a four-letter word in this club again, I'm going to pinch you and everyone in here. If he ever speaks against religion, I'm going to pinch you and everyone in here. — Lenny Bruce, *How to Talk Dirty and Influence People*, p. 146, 1965
- My kidneys ain't too good, but I don't wanna get pinched for pissin' in public. — Edwin Torres, *Q & A*, p. 36, 1977
- "Hands against the wall, spread your legs and don't move a fucking inch." He's been pinched. — Greg Williams, *Diamond Geezers*, p. 207, 1997

2 to steal something *UK, 1656*

- He pinches a shoeshine box for me and we start out working the BMT trains. — Rocky Garciano (with Rowland Barber), *Somebody Up There Likes Me*, p. 28, 1955
- "Pinched. Jobbed. Swiped. Stole," he says, happily. "You know, man, like somebody boosted my threads." — Ken Kesey, *One Flew Over the Cuckoo's Nest*, p. 94, 1962
- Anything that could be pinched could be sold. — Brian McDonald, *Elephant Boys*, p. 9, 2000

3 in horse racing, to win *AUSTRALIA*

A jockey may 'pinch' a race. A bookmaker might manage to 'pinch a little.'

- — Ned Wallish, *The Truth Dictionary of Racing Slang*, p. 62, 1989

▸ **pinch a loaf**

to defecate *US*

- — Michael Dalton Johnson, *Talking Trash with Redd Foxx*, p. 44, 1994

pinch *adjective*

substitute *US*

Back-formation from 'pinch-hit' (in baseball, to bat as substitute).

- The Pinch Rapper is good enough to get a verse to fill the song up. — *Hip-Hop Connection July*, p. 16, 2002

pinch and press *verb*
to cheat at gambling, secretly taking back chips from your bet when dealt a bad hand and adding chips when dealt a good hand *US*
• —Steve Kuriscak, *Casino Talk*, p. 43, 1985

pinche *adjective*
used as an intensifier, roughly the same as 'fucking' *US*
Border Spanish used in English conversation by Mexican-Americans.
• —Dagoberto Fuentes and Jose Lopez, *Barrio Language Dictionary*, p. 115, 1974

pinchers *noun*
shoes, especially tight shoes *US*
• —Lou Shelly, *Hepcats Jive Talk Dictionary*, p. 16, 1945

pinch hit *noun*
a single inhalation of marijuana *US*
• —Peter Johnson, *Dictionary of Street Alcohol and Drug Terms*, p. 143, 1993

pinch pipe *noun*
a small pipe designed to hold enough marijuana for a single inhalation *US*
Small, easily hidden from parents and teachers, and economical.
• —Peter Johnson, *Dictionary of Street Alcohol and Drug Terms*, p. 143, 1993

pin dick *noun*
a male with a small penis *US*
• —Chris Lewis, *The Dictionary of Playground Slang*, p. 171, 2003

pin-drop silence *noun*
absolute silence *INDIA*
Indian English, from the familiar phrase 'so quiet you could hear a pin drop'.
• —K.S. Yadurajan, *Current English*, 2001
• In pin-drop silence, perked on lush cushioned sofas, they sipped chilled glasses of diet chrome[.]— *The Times of India*, 4th March 2004

pine *noun*
marijuana *UK*
• —Mike Haskins, *Drugs*, p. 288, 2003

pineapple *noun*
1 a hand grenade, especially a MK-2 hand grenade or Type 59 grenade *US, 1918*
• —Lou Shelly, *Hepcats Jive Talk Dictionary*, p. 47, 1945
• We'd need some arms and stuff, some real factory-made heaters and a couple of machine guns and maybe some pineapples.—Chester Himes, *The Real Cool Killers*, p. 53, 1959
• All Whiskey j. carried was a knapsack and Claymore bag filled with grenades, both the old pineapples and the newer smooth-side sort[.]—Larry Heinemann, *Close Quarters*, p. 46, 1977
• "MK-two," Franklin said, "they call a pineapple." He looked at Jack, offering him the grenade, and grinned.—Elmore Leonard, *Bandits*, p. 359, 1987
• "Fucking hell!!!!!!" I screamed diving head first into the tarmac as far away from the pineapple as I could possibly sling myself.—Danny King, *The Bank Robber Diaries*, p. 217, 2002

2 a combination of cocaine and heroin *US*
• At this time tooting the boy along with the girl was called "PINEAPPLE."—A.S. Jackson, *Gentleman Pimp*, p. 70, 1973

3 a male homosexual *UK*
Perhaps as a specialisation of fruit, possibly punning on anal sex as 'taking the **ROUGH END OF THE PINEAPPLE**'.
• —Leslie Thomas, *Arthur McCann and all his Women*, 1972

4 a fifty-dollar note *AUSTRALIA, 1992*
From its yellowish colour.
• Could you float me a pineapple?— *www.abc.net.au/wordmap*, 2003

5 a chapel *UK: SCOTLAND*
Glasgow rhyming slang, with a stress on the second and third syllables.
• — *New Society*, 15th April 1982
• He's away to the pineapple.—Michael Munro, *The Original Patter*, 1985

6 in electric line work, a spool insulator *US*
• —A.B. Chance Co., *Lineman's Slang Dictionary*, p. 13, 1980

7 unemployment benefit *UK, 1937*
• —John Ayto, *The Oxford Dictionary of Slang*, p. 200, 1998

pineapple chunk; pineapple *noun*
1 a *bunk* bed; a bunk (an act of running away) *UK*
Noted as 'before 1914' by Julian Franklyn, *A Dictionary of Rhyming Slang*, 1961.
• [T]o "do a pineapple" is to abscond.—Ray Puxley, *Cockney Rabbit*, 1992

2 semen *UK*
Rhyming slang for **SPUNK**.
• —Bodmin Dark, *Dirty Cockney Rhyming Slang*, 2003

Pineapple Express *noun*
a wind from the south, onshore in British Columbia, which is said to have the scent of Hawaiian pineapples and is warm, occasionally blowing in the winter *CANADA*
An explanation for the warmer climate on Canada's west coast than inland.

pineapple juice *noun*
a rain storm in Hawaii *US*
• —Trevor Cralle, *The Surfin'ary*, p. 88, 1991

pine box release; pine box parole *noun*
death while in prison *US*
• "Ya done flipped and gotta yen for a pine box parole 'stead of walkin' through the front gate" Percy taunts[.]—Iceberg Slim (Robert Beck), *Doom Fox*, p. 214, 1978
• —William K. Bentley and James M. Corbett, *Prison Slang*, p. 105, 1992

pine top *noun*
strong, illegally manufactured whisky *US*
• It is called corn liquor, white lightning, sugar whiskey, skully cracker, popskull, bush whiskey, stump, stumphole, 'splo, ruckus juice, radiator whiskey, rotgut, sugarhead, block and tackle, wildcat, panther's breath, tiger's sweat, Sweet spsirits of cats a-fighting, alley bourbon, city gin, cool water, happy Sally, deep shaft, jump steady, old horsey, stingo, bluye John, red eye, pine top, buckeye bark whiskey and see seven stars.— *Star Tribune (Minneapolis)*, p. 19F, 31st January 1999

ping *noun*
1 an attempt; an effort; a shot *AUSTRALIA, 1988*
• Twenty yards from the goal-mouth, he steadied and took a ping. —Shane Maloney, *Nice Try*, p. 273, 1998

2 an injection of a drug *NEW ZEALAND*
• —Greg Newbold, *The Big Huey*, p. 252, 1982

3 the sound caused in a car engine by low quality fuel or bad timing *US*
• —Lewis Poteet, *Car & Motorcyle Slang*, p. 149, 1992

ping *verb*
1 to recognise or identify someone or something *UK*
Royal Navy slang; probably echoic of a radar's noise.
• —Nigel Foster, *The Making of a Royal Marine Commando*, 1987

2 to hit something with a projectile *AUSTRALIA, 1934*
• With his blow-pipe he spattered it, and with his shot-ging he pinged it[.]—Norman Lindsay, *Saturdee*, p. 113, 1934
• [B]ut Toze was keen on wearing a dolphin suit as a means of luring the smug bludgers in close enough so we could ping them sweet as a nut.—Roy Slaven (John Doyle), *Five South Coast Seasons*, p. 5, 1992

3 of a racehorse, to jump well *UK*
• — *www.tiptext.com*, 2003

4 to penalise or fine someone for for breaking a rule or law *AUSTRALIA, 1934*
• Moreover, he pinged Bunky Rodgers for harnessing his very own poodle to a go-cart.—Norman Lindsay, *Saturdee*, p. 98, 1934
• —Ivor Limb, *Footy's No Joke!*, p. 57, 1986
• [There] was a brief mention of a Byron Bay law firm, Quayle and Associates, which had been pinged by the Law Society for hawking a prospectus around Tokyo calling for investors in a golf course and resort development they didn't actually own.—Harrison Biscuit, *The Search for Savage Henry*, p. 19, 1995
• —David McGill, *David McGill's Complete Kiwi Slang Dictionary*, p. 97, 1998

▸ **ping the pill**
to remove a small amount of a drug from a capsule or packet for your later use *US*
• —William D. Alsever, *Glossary for the Establishment and Other Uptight People*, p. 25, December 1970

pinger *noun*
a chunk of gold that makes a noise as it hits the pan *CANADA*

- Each pinch of dust was one dollar and it was pure, whereas in other gold everything above a pinger – that is everything above something that pinged in the pan – was coarse gold. — R.E. Watters, *British Columbia Centennial Anthology*, p. 559, 1958

pingers *noun*
money, especially coins *NEW ZEALAND*
Commonly used in New Zealand since the 1950s.

ping-in-wing; ping in the wing; ping-wing; ping shot *verb*
to inject a drug into the arm *US, 1949*
An elaboration of **PIN** (a syringe) combined with **WING** (the arm).
- — Richard A. Spears, *The Slang and Jargon of Drugs and Drink*, p. 388, 1986
- — Mike Haskins, *Drugs*, p. 290, 2003

ping-pong *noun*
a small photographic portrait *BARBADOS*
- — Frank A. Collymore, *Barbadian Dialect*, p. 84, 1965

pingpong *verb*
(used of a doctor engaged in insurance fraud) to needlessly refer a patient to a number of specialists *US*
- — Ralph de Sola, *Crime Dictionary*, p. 114, 1982

pinhead *noun*
1 a fool; an imbecile *US, 1896*
- LISTEN YA LITTLE PINHEADS, IT [spitting]'S NAUSEATING AND MORONIC[.] — Lester Bangs, *Psychotic Reactions and Carburetor Dung*, p. 230, 1977
- — Joe McKennon, *Circus Lingo*, p. 69, 1980

2 a person whose interest in playing pinball approaches the level of obsession *US*
- — Bobbye Claire Natkin and Steve Kirk, *All About Pinball*, p. 113, 1977

3 an amphetamine user *US*
- — Eugene Landy, *The Underground Dictionary*, p. 150, 1971

4 in the language of snowboarding, a skier *US*
- — Elena Garcia, *A Beginner's Guide to Zen and the Art of Snowboarding*, p. 122, 1990: 'Glossary'

5 a railway brakeman *US*
- — Norman Carlisle, *The Modern Wonder Book of Trains and Railroading*, p. 266, 1946

pink *noun*
1 a white person *US*
- "Was she that big Gawga pink work as a tacker?" Pigmeat asked. — Chester Himes, *If He Hollers Let Him Go*, p. 103, 1945
- In no time at all Konky got on the ball / And had ten whorers – nine pinks and a shade. — Dennis Wepman et al., *The Life*, p. 103, 1976

2 a liberal; a socialist; a communist sympathiser *US, 1927*
- The others got good government jobs, became "contact men" or spoke at meetings and wrote for publications sponsored by rich left-wingers to provide automobiles and other luxuries for the needier pinks. — Jack Lait and Lee Mortimer, *Washington Confidential*, p. 9, 1951
- Rumor had it that there were quite a few pinks in the publishing biz. — Mary McCarthy, *The Group*, p. 185, 1963

3 the open vagina *US*
Widely used in pornography, and beyond.
- — Carrie Fisher, *Surrender the Pink*, 1991
- When I see a naked woman spread out in the centerfold of Playboy or a porn queen sitting atop some stud in reverse-cowgirl position or a sassy stripper showing her pink in a gentleman's all-nude club, one burning question always comes to mind: Who does her pubic hair? — *The Village Voice*, 8–14th November 2000

4 proof of car ownership *US*
A shortened form of **PINK SLIP**.
- You know, a guy goes up to another guy's car and looks it up and down like it has gangrene or something, and he says: 'You wanna go?' Or, if it was a real grudge match for some reason, he'd say, 'You wanna for pink slips?' — Tom Wolfe, *The Kandy-Kolored Tangerine-Flake Streamline Baby*, p. 88, 1965
- We already got the pink. Then we maybe drive it around for a week. — Robert Campbell, *In La-La Land We Trust*, p. 85, 1986

5 a capsule of secobarbital sodium (trade name Seconal™), a central nervous system depressant *US*
- — John B. Williams, *Narcotics and Hallucinogenics*, p. 115, 1967

6 a casino gambling token worth $2.50 *US*
- — Michael Dalton, *Blackjack*, p. 68, 1991

7 in poker, a flush consisting of either hearts or diamonds *US*
- — Irwin Steig, *Common Sense in Poker*, p. 186, 1963

8 in horse racing, a track police officer *US*
Derived from the *Pink*erton Agency.
- — Dan Parker, *The ABC of Horse Racing*, p. 147, 1947

Pink *noun*
a 'detective' from the Pinkerton Agency *US, 1904*
Strikebreaking was among the several roles played by the Pinkerton Agency.
- Taussig company police and out-of-town Pinks were lounging around the courthouse spoiling for blood. — Clancy Sigal, *Going Away*, p. 282, 1961

pink *adjective*
1 homosexual *UK*
Traditionally 'pink for a girl, blue for a boy'. As an absolutely negative association the colour pink was used in Nazi Germany to label homosexuals for segregation, internment and extermination; in post-World War 2 Britain, pink had connotations of effeminacy; in the 1970s politically active homosexuals adopted the colour-coded symbolism and pink slowly took on a generally positive tone both in the gay and wider community; especially as a marketing designation.
- It's a bizarre blend of the uber-butch and the ultra-camp, which is why, perhaps, it has been so inevitably embraced by all types of pink persona. — *Attitude*, p. 34, October 2003

2 white; Caucasian *US*
- "Was she that big Gawga pink work as a tacker?" Pigmeat asked. — Chester Himes, *If He Hollers Let Him Go*, p. 103, 1945
- I ain't pink and I got two strikes against me now. — Mezz Mezzrow, *Really the Blues*, p. 267, 1946

▸ **all pink**
in poker, a flush consisting of all hearts or all diamonds *US*
- — Albert H. Morehead, *The Complete Guide to Winning Poker*, p. 255, 1967

pink 125 *noun*
a tablet of MDMA, the recreational drug best known as ecstasy *UK*
From the colour and the 125 mg dosage.
- — Gareth Thomas, *This Is Ecstasy*, p. 54, 2002

pink-assed *adjective*
somewhat angry *US*
- — *American Speech*, p. 271, December 1962: 'The language of traffic policemen'

pink blotters *noun*
a type of LSD *UK, 1998*
- — Mike Haskins, *Drugs*, p. 286, 2003

Pink Cadillac *noun*
a variety of MDMA, the recreational drug best known as ecstasy *UK*
The colour of the tablet inspires the ultimate in rock 'n' roll luxury transport.
- — Angela Devlin, *Prison Patter*, p. 88, 1996

pink champagne *noun*
1 methamphetamine with a pinkish colour produced by the presence of the stimulant pemoline *US*
- — Geoffrey Froner, *Digging for Diamonds*, p. 69, 1989: 'Types of speed'

2 a mix of cocaine and heroin *UK*
- — Angela Devlin, *Prison Patter*, p. 21, 1996

pinker *noun*
in poker, a timid bettor *US*
- — Albert H. Morehead, *The Complete Guide to Winning Poker*, p. 270, 1967

pinkers *noun*
a pink gin *UK, 1961*
Naval in origin.
- — John Ayto, *The Oxford Dictionary of Slang*, p. 145, 1998

pink eye *noun*
1 cheap, low grade whisky *CANADA*
- At Bender's joint, the price of a pint of pink-eye was a day's hard labor in a mine-head. — William Mowery, *Tales of the Mounted Police*, p. 95, 1953

2 special contact lenses worn by card cheats to see luminous markings on the back of cards *US*
- — George Percy, *The Language of Poker*, p. 67, 1988

Pink Floyd *noun*
a potent type of LSD *UK*
Honouring the rock group Pink Floyd, from their early days in the late 1960s when they were considered avant garde and psychedelic.

- [A] secret compartment held some original super-strong Pink Floyd acid tabs[.] — Wayne Anthony, *Spanish Highs*, p. 67, 1999

pink heart *noun*

an amphetamine tablet *US*

- Also black beauties, pink hearts, et cetera, advertised in the back of magazines like Creem, High Times, Hustler. — Laurel Sterns, *Retrohell*, p. 50, 1997

pinkie *noun*

1 the little finger *UK, 1808*

Originally Scottish, mostly among children, but now widespread. Also variant 'pinky'.

- Why, those little twerps at Webster- I can handle 'em with my pinkie! — Max Shulman, *Rally Round the Flag, Boys!*, p. 48, 1957
- Krankeit took hold of the little finger and held it up. "Which is that?" "Pinky!" the patient said delightedly. — Terry Southern, *Candy*, p. 110, 1958
- Vicariousness institutionalized, dipping their pinkies in. — Clancy Sigal, *Going Away*, p. 72, 1961
- This kind of man can kill you with his pinky. — *Apocalypse Now*, 1979

2 a white person, especially a male *UK*

Recorded in use by black teenagers. David Powis, *The Signs of Crime*, 1977, notes: 'Originally an expression for a light-coloured Negro'.

- By the time they leave school whites have become "pinky", "the grey man" or – less common – "Mr Charlie". — *The Observer*, 10th September 1967

3 a pink-eyed albino *UK*

Also variant 'pinky'.

- — John Gloag, *Unlawful Justice*, 1962

4 the vagina *TRINIDAD AND TOBAGO, 1986*

- — Lise Winer, *Dictionary of the English/Creole of Trinidad & Tobago*, 2003

5 a bruised eye *US, 1970*

- — Claudio R. Salvucci, *The Philadelphia Dialect Dictionary*, p. 52, 1996

6 in Vancouver, a warning ticket *CANADA*

- Vancouver police last year started issuing "pinkies," tickets that give motorists a gentle warning of infraction rather than require them to pay a fine. — *Maclean's*, p. 39/1, 30th June 1962

7 a racing greyhound that races best from the outside position *AUSTRALIA*

- — Ned Wallish, *The Truth Dictionary of Racing Slang*, p. 62, 1989

8 in Newfoundland, cheap wine *CANADA*

- Pinkie [in St. John's] is a cheap wine highly regarded by waterfront connoisseurs, a chaser for screech. — *Maclean's*, p. 63/3, 27th September 1958

9 an early model long-wheel base '110' Land Rover *UK*

Used by the British military.

- We started roaring around in the new 110s with 50mm machine-guns dangling off the back that were replacing the old "pinkies". — Andy McNab (writing of the late 1970s/early 80s), *Immediate Action*, p. 192, 1995

▷ see: PINK SPEEDBALL

pinkie cheater *noun*

a latex finger glove used during digital examinations *US*

- — *American Speech*, p. 201, Fall-Winter 1973: 'The language of nursing'

pinkie-load *noun*

in caving and pot-holing, a piece of equipment so light that it can be picked up by a little finger; hence, a person in a group who is not carrying his or her fair share *UK*

From PINKIE (the little finger).

- — David Morrison of Wessex Cave Club, 29th February 2004

pinkie ring; pinky ring *noun*

a ring worn on the little finger, especially an ostentatious ring worn by a criminal *US, 1975*

- Middle-aged guinea with a full head of dyed-black hair, a diamond pink ring. — Elmore Leonard, *Be Cool*, p. 109, 1999

pinkies *noun*

underwear *US*

- If you answered that sometimes it could be scraped off with a knife, in nothing flat she'd be taking her skirt off and parading around in her pinkies. — Dev Collans with Stewart Sterling, *I was a House Detective*, p. 8, 1954

pink lady *noun*

a capsule of secobarbital sodium (trade name Seconal™), a central nervous system depressant *US*

- — *Current Slang*, p. 37, Fall 1968
- — Norman W. Houser, *Drugs*, p. 13, 1969
- — *American Speech*, p. 152–154, Summer 1982: 'More on nursing terms'

pink lemonade *noun*

cleaning fluid injected intravenously *US*

An often lethal substitute for methedrine.

- — Eugene Landy, *The Underground Dictionary*, p. 150, 1971

pink lint *adjective*

having little or no money, penniless *UK*

Rhyming slang for SKINT.

- — Julian Franklyn, *A Dictionary of Rhyming Slang*, 1961
- — Ray Puxley, *Cockney Rabbit*, 1992

pink mafia *noun*

any group of women banded together, especially lesbians *US*

- Isn't that grounds enough for the little pink mafia to throw you out of their club. — *Chasing Amy*, 1997

pinko *noun*

a liberal; a socialist; a communist *US, 1936*

Originally applied to Communist party members, subsequently (in the late 1950s) to anyone who disagreed with the dominant culture and politics. Also used attributively.

- Haunt of homos, pinkos, nature lovers and nuts. Chicago's version of London's Hyde Park with soap boxers and prosties. — Jack Lait and Lee Mortimer, *Chicago Confidential*, p. 289, 1950
- The Old Left says we work for the CIA. Ex-Marines stomp on us as Pinkos. — Abbie Hoffman, *Revolution for the Hell of It*, p. 27, 1968
- Red Mulvaney came into Lento's, looking for ore Reds, or pinkos at least, to beat up. — Gilbert Sorrentino, *Steelwork*, p. 5, 1970
- Well, he's sniffing around and he's got that whole pinko paper behind him. — Mickey Spillane, *Last Cop Out*, p. 53, 1972
- A script was rushed to him – or rather, his agent, who rejected it in summary fashion as being "thoroughly pinko." — Terry Southern, *Now Dig This*, p. 7, 1986
- It's a relief to know there are some decent adults in this world – even if they are left-wing commie pinkos. — C.D. Payne, *Youth in Revolt*, p. 93, 1993
- [C]ontrary to what that wishy-washy pinko Jesus asshole said, their God isn't all that forgiving. — Christopher Brookmyre, *Not the End of the World*, p. 225, 1998

pink oboe *noun*

the penis *UK*

Coined by satirist Peter Cook (1937–95) for a sketch performed in Amnesty International's *The Secret Policeman's Ball*.

- A self-confessed player of the pink oboe. — Peter Cook, *Entirely a Matter For You*, 1979

pink palace *noun*

1 a homosexual venue *UK*

Combines PINK (homosexual) with an alliterative location.

- The Admiral Duncan [...] is now a pink palace, the one that recently suffered a bombing tragedy. — Brian McDonald, *Elephant Boys*, p. 276, 2000

2 the prison at Hobart *AUSTRALIA*

- — Maureen Brooks and Joan Ritchie, *Tassie Terms*, p. 110, 1995

Pink Panther *noun*

a variety of MDMA, the recreational drug best known as ecstasy, identified by the colour and embossed Pink Panther motif *UK*

- — Gareth Thomas, *This Is Ecstasy*, p. 56, 2002

pink pants *noun*

rubbish *UK*

An elaboration of 'pants' (rubbish).

- — Mervyn Stutter, *Getting Nowhere Fast*, 4th June 2004

pink piccolo *noun*

the penis *UK*

- OK, Steve may have been caught playing YMCA on the pink piccolo – the SICK BASTARD! – but he was still FAMILY. — Garry Bushell, *The Face*, p. 187, 2001

pink puffer *noun*

a patient suffering from emphysema *US*

- — *American Speech*, p. 202, Fall-Winter 1973: 'The language of nursing'

pink-ribbon case *noun*
a criminal case that has been thoroughly and professionally investigated by the police *US*
It is said that the police hand the prosecutor a case like this with a pink ribbon tied around it.
- — *American Speech*, p. 271, December 1962: 'The language of traffic policemen'

pink robots *noun*
a type of LSD *US, 1998*
- — The Flaming Lips, *Yoshimi Battles the Pink Robots*, 2002
- — Mike Haskins, *Drugs*, p. 286, 2003

pink slip *noun*
the proof of car ownership *US*
- And if that ain't enough to make you flip your lid / There's one more thing, I got the pink slip, daddy. — The Beach Boys, *Little Deuce Coupe*, 1963
- You know, a guy goes up to another guy's car and looks it up and down like it has gangrene or something, and he says: 'You wanna go?' Or, if it was a real grudge match for some reason, he'd say, 'You wanna for pink slips?' — Tom Wolfe, *The Kandy-Kolored Tangerine-Flake Streamline Baby*, p. 88, 1965
- A new I.D. don't cost no more than a pink slip. — *Repo Man*, 1984

pink snapper *noun*
the vagina *US*
Combines **PINK** (the open vagina) with 'snapper' (various fish are so-called), thus **FISH** (the vagina); 'snapper' also suggests the image of a mouth that closes.
- — Erica Orloff and JoAnn Baker, *Dirty Little Secrets*, p. 91, 2001

pink speedball; pinkie *noun*
a mixture of pharmaceutical cocaine and Dipipanone, an opiate marketed under the brand name Diconal™ *UK*
- [T]he notorious "pink speedball". This is the most dangerous, yet most intensely euphoric hit known to man [...] I never knew pinkies to be anything else. — Peter McDermott, *The Immaculate Injection [The Howard Marks Book of Dope Stories]*, p. 361, 2001

pink tea *noun*
an effeminate male homosexual *US*
- All the fairies in her town were closet queens or pinkteas[.] — Hubert Selby Jr, *Last Exit to Brooklyn*, p. 60, 1957

pink-top *noun*
a small vial of heroin sealed with a pink plastic cap *US*
The pink plastic cap denotes a variation in purity and price.
- The pink-top I have just clumsily purchased has its particular niches, or target market: the "kids from the counties," as middle-class teenagers from the suburbs are known in Maryland. — *New York Times*, p. SM24, 23rd June 2002

pink torpedo *noun*
the penis, especially when erect *US*
Aggressive imagery.
- My baby fits me like a flesh tuxedo / I love to sink her with my pink torpedo. — Spinal Tap, *Big Bottom*, 1984

Pinkville *noun*
an area in the province of Quang Ngai, South Vietnam *US*
Either named because of the area's appearance on maps or because of the strong presence of communist forces in the area.
- One of the Task Force's main objectives would be keeping pressure on an area a few miles northeast of Quang Ngai known as "Pinkville," the name deriving from the fact that its higher population density caused it to appear red on Army maps. — Seymour Hersh, *My Lai 4*, p. 23, 1970
- My Lai 1, 2, 3, and 4 hamlets were part of the village of son My, known as Pinkville – heavily VC in the fiercely contested province of Quang Ngai. — Myra MacPherson, *Long Time Passing*, p. 581, 1984

pink wedge *noun*
a type of LSD *US, 1970*
- — Richard A. Spears, *The Slang and Jargon of Drugs and Drink*, p. 390, 1986
- — Mike Haskins, *Drugs*, p. 286, 2003

pink witch *noun*
a type of LSD *US, 1970*
- — Richard A. Spears, *The Slang and Jargon of Drugs and Drink*, p. 390, 1986
- — Mike Haskins, *Drugs*, p. 286, 2003

pinky *verb*
in dice games with no bank, to roll the dice to see who will play first *US*
- — *The Annals of the American Academy of Political and Social Sciences*, p. 129, May 1950

Pinky and Perky; pinky *noun*
turkey (meat) *UK*
Rhyming slang, formed on the puppets of twin pigs who, from 1957, became children's televison stars and recording artists.
- — Ray Puxley, *Cockney Rabbit*, 1992

pinky ring *noun*
▷ see: **PINKIE RING**

pinky's out of jail!
your slip is showing! *US*
- — *American Weekly*, p. 2, 14th August 1955

pin-money *noun*
spending money *UK, 1697*
Originally a C16 practice of a husband allotting to his wife a certain amount each year for personal expenses.
- For pin money Sammy did an altogether different sort of cooking. — Seth Morgan, *Homeboy*, p. 126, 1990

pinned *adjective*
1 (used of eyes) constricted after opiate use *US*
- When the heroin addict is high, his pupils are "pinned," constricted. — James Mills, *The Panic in Needle Park*, p. 16, 1966
- I looked in the mirror. Oh shit! Look at my eyes! They were so pinned! You could hardly see black in the middle at all. — Cleo Odzer, *Goa Freaks*, p. 65, 1995
- Consequently, on this visit, when I saw that Emmett's eyes were "pinned" and knew that he was using heroin again, I allowed myself to blow up. — Peter Coyote, *Sleeping Where I Fall*, p. 324, 1998

2 addicted to drugs *US*
From **PIN** (a hypodermic syringe).
- I can see you're pinned, man. — Joel Rose, *Kill Kill Faster Faster*, p. 61, 1997
- They collected eighteen hundred pesetas in all denominations of coin, including a five-hundred from James. "They'll go mad on that," he laughed. "They'll be pinned on smack [heroin or cocaine] before we get the engine running." — Kevin Sampson, *Powder*, p. 201, 1999

pinned up *adjective*
drug-intoxicated *UK*
From **PINNED** (the condition of the pupils when intoxicated).
- — Angela Devlin, *Prison Patter*, p. 88, 1996
- It was his mood swings that gave him away [...] and walking around blatantly "pinned up"[.] — *The Guardian*, 27th June 2002

pinny *noun*
a pinafore *US, 1851*
- I don't normally stand around in a pinny, ironing my pants or nothing. — Danny King, *The Burglar Diaries*, p. 88, 2001

pinny *adjective*
very small *BARBADOS*
- — Frank A. Collymore, *Barbadian Dialect*, p. 82, 1965

pin position; pin *noun*
the front position in an authorised taxi rank *UK*
- — David Powis, *The Signs of Crime*, 1977

pin shot *noun*
an improvised injection of a drug, in which the skin is pricked and an injection made directly into the wound *US*
- — Vincent J. Monteleone, *Criminal Slang*, p. 177, 1949
- — *American Speech*, p. 28, February 1952: 'Teen-age hophead jargon'

pinster *noun*
a bowler *US*
- — Lester V. Berrey and Melvin Van den Bark, *The American Thesaurus of Slang*, p. 633, 1953

pint *noun*
a short person *US*
- The labels were cruel: Gimp, Limpy-go-fetch, Crip, Lift-one-drag one, etc. Pint, Half-a-man, Peewee, Shorty, Lardass, Pork, Blubber, Belly, Blimp. Nuke-knob, Skinhead, Baldy. Four-eyes, Specs, Coke bottles. — *San Francisco Examiner*, p. A15, 28th July 1997

pinta *noun*
1 a pint of milk *UK, 1958*
From the advertising slogan, 'Drinka pinta milka day'.

2 a prison *US*
Spanish slang used by English-speaking Mexican-Americans.
- What was of importance now – here in la pinta [Chicano slang for prison] – was the success of the MRU. — Bill Valentine, *Gangs and Their Tattoos*, p. 27, 2000

pint pot *noun*
a pint glass, usually for draught beer *UK*
• They served Tartan and light and bitter in plastic pint pots. — Dave Courtney, *Stop the Ride I Want to Get Off*, p. 34, 1999

pint-size; pint-sized *adjective*
used of a person's stature, small *UK, 1938*
• Each year, the pint-size Latin lothario [Antonio Banderas] and his statuesque wife [Melanie Griffith] join thousands of other extremely wealthy, often famous, ski addicts who fly in on their personal Lear jets[.] — *The Observer*, 8th December 2002

pin-up *noun*
a photograph or printed reproduction of a sexually attractive person; the person who is the subject of, or has the characteristics required for, such a picture *US, 1941*
Originally, from the fact that such images were pinned up on walls.
• Documents which showed that Lord Byron – genius, freedom fighter, and first of the pin-up poets – was a bisexual were kept from his biographers[.] — *The Guardian*, 20th November 2002

PIO's *noun*
in the language of hang gliding, over-control by the flier *US*
An abbreviation of '*p*ilot-*i*nduced *o*scillations'.

pip *noun*
1 the best, the finest *US, 1897*
From 'pippin' (the best).
• "That place's a pip," I said to the driver. — Horace McCoy, *Kiss Tomorrow Good-bye*, p. 198, 1948
• For years, decades probably, I had sung: He's the boss / He's a pip / He's the championship. / He's the most tip-top / Top Cat! — Stuart Jeffries, *Mrs Slocombe's Pussy*, p. 24–25, 2000
• "That's Choochy, he's a pip," Ziggy said. "Did he really shoot Jesus?" — Janet Evanovich, *Seven Up*, p. 97, 2001

2 a star worn by military officers as an indication of rank *UK, 1917*
• Three months later he got his "pip" as a second lieutenant. — Frederick Forsyth, *The Devil's Alternative*, p. 32, 1980

3 an unidentified spot on a radar screen *US*
• — *American Speech*, p. 154, April 1947: 'Radar slang terms'

4 a woman's menstrual period *US*
• — Don R. McCreary (Editor), *Dawg Speak*, 2001

5 in the whe-whe lottery game, a bet that is close to the winning number *TRINIDAD AND TOBAGO*
• — Lise Winer, *Dictionary of the English/Creole of Trinidad & Tobago*, 2003

▸ **give someone the pip**
to annoy someone *UK, 1896*
• I'm teed off. Things like this give me the pip. — Mickey Spillane, *My Gun is Quick*, p. 16, 1950

pip *verb*
to defeat someone by a narrow margin *UK, 1939*
Sometimes elaborated to 'pip at the post'.
• Jonathan Franzen [...] was this week pipped to a Pulitzer by Richard Russo's Empire Falls. — *The Guardian*, 13th April 2002
• It was a case of unlucky again for Australian stand-up Adam Hills; having being nominated in three consecutive years, he was again pipped at the post. — *The Guardian*, 25th August 2003

pipe *noun*
1 the penis *US*
• — Anthony Romeo, *The Language of Gangs*, p. 21, 4th December 1962
• Like a baton twirler with lots of practice, Annette grabbed Willie's pipe[.] — Steve Cannon, *Groove, Bang, and Jive Around*, p. 7, 1969
• When she said that, my pipe jumped to attention, and I had to have her right then. — A.S. Jackson, *Gentleman Pimp*, p. 36, 1973
• Most of them [...] were "gagging for a bit of Regimental pipe". — Chris Ryan, *The Watchman*, p. 95, 2001

2 any large vein, well suited for drug injection *US*
• But keep off, better, because if you like junk you keep shmeckin and shootin, then the skin pop goes to the big pipe[.] — George Mandel, *Flee the Angry Strangers*, p. 56, 1952
• — Walter L. Way, *The Drug Scene*, p. 112, 1977
• — Gilda and Melvin Berger, *Drug Abuse A-Z*, p. 110, 1990
• — Sally Williams, *"Strong" Words*, p. 154, 1994

3 any wind or reed instrument *US*
• — Robert S. Gold, *A Jazz Lexicon*, p. 230, 1964

4 an exhaust pipe *US*
• Some job, Mike. Got twin pipes in back. — Mickey Spillane, *Kiss Me Deadly*, p. 78, 1952

5 a telephone *UK*
• — *British Road Services Magazine*, December 1951

6 the firing chamber of a handgun *US*
• MURTAUGH: What's it take? RIGGS: Fifteen in the mag, one up the pipe. — *Lethal Weapon*, 1987

7 an electric outlet *BARBADOS*
• — Frank A. Collymore, *Barbadian Dialect*, p. 84, 1965

8 a sufficient measure of marijuana for smoking in a pipe *SOUTH AFRICA, 1970*
Recorded as Afrikaans *pyp* in 1967.
• — Penny Silva, *A Dictionary of South African English*, 1996

9 a measurement of time: the distance that could be travelled between rest periods at which a pipe could be smoked *CANADA*
• The distance of a portage was reckoned at so many pipes. — Vardis Fisher, *Pemmican*, p. 251, 1957

10 the vertical bar (|) on a computer keyboard *US*
• — Eric S. Raymond, *The New Hacker's Dictionary*, p. 41, 1991

11 an academically unchallenging course *US*
• — Collin Baker et al., *College Undergraduate Slang Study Conducted at Brown University*, p. 171, 1968

▸ **do the pipe**
to smoke crack cocaine *US*
• Yeah, but I ain't done the needle in a long time. Lately I been doing the pipe. — Neil S. Skolnik, *On the Ledge*, p. 110, 1996

▸ **on the pipe**
1 addicted to crack cocaine *US*
• — Judi Sanders, *Don't Dog by Do, Dude!*, p. ??, 1991
• The kids around the pool table and video game were mostly here by default, half of them living on the street or with mothers on the pipe. — Richard Price, *Clockers*, p. 26, 1992
• It's disgraceful. Uncle Sam is on the pipe. — Chris Rock, *Rock This!*, p. 97, 1997

2 used of a conversation between two jail cells conducted through plumbing emptied of water *US*
• — William K. Bentley and James M. Corbett, *Prison Slang*, p. 56, 1992

▸ **put that in your pipe and smoke it!; stick that in your pipe and smoke it!**
accept the situation, or what you have been told, whether you wish to or not *UK, 1824*
• Put that in your pipe and smoke it, Mr President. — *The Guardian*, 18th December 2003

▸ **take the pipe**
to commit suicide *US*
• — Ralph de Sola, *Crime Dictionary*, p. 148, 1982

▸ **the pipe**
the Greenwich tunnel (under the River Thames) *UK*
• Greenwich is just through the pipe for me. — Garry Bushell, *The Face*, p. 228, 2001

Pipe *noun*
▸ **The Pipe**
General Douglas MacArthur (1880–1964) of the US Army *US*
From his love of a corncob pipe.
• — Frank Hailey, *Soldier Talk*, p. 46, 1982

pipe *verb*
1 to smoke crack cocaine in a pipe *UK*
• We'd been piping and fooling around with each other most of the night. — Lanre Fehintola, *Charlie Says...*, p. 31, 2000

2 to look at someone or something *UK, 1874*
• — Ray Puxley, *Cockney Rabbit*, p. 190, 1992

3 to fabricate a story *US*
• — John R. Armore and Joseph D. Wolfe, *Dictionary of Desperation*, p. 43, 1976

pipe and drum; pipe *noun*
the anus *UK, 1961*
Rhyming slang for **BUM**, especially in the retort 'up your pipe!'.
• "[P]oke it up your pipe" is a common synonym for "stick it where the sun don't shine". — Ray Puxley, *Cockney Rabbit*, 1992

pipe course *noun*
an easy course in college *US, 1927*
From the older, largely forgotten sense of 'pipe' as 'easy to accomplish'.
- "You are all freshmen," continued Mr. Fitzhugh, "and you may not be familiar with the term 'pipe course.' A pipe course is a course where students can get passing grades without doing much work. This is not a pipe course." — Max Shulman, *The Many Loves of Dobie Gillis*, p. 96, 1951

piped *adjective*
drunk or drug-intoxicated *US*
- — Vincent J. Monteleone, *Criminal Slang*, p. 178, 1949

pipe down *verb*
to be quieter; to shut up *UK*
Often exclamatory. From the nautical sense (to dismiss by sounding the pipe).
- — Miss Cone, *The Slang Dictionary (Hawthorne High School)*, 1965
- "All right, pipe down," Maraney bellowed. — Charles Whited, *Chiodo*, p. 71, 1973
- MR. BIG NOSE: Oh. Right. That's your last warning. MRS. GREGORY: Oh, do pipe down. — Monty Python, *Life of Brian*, 1979

pipehead *noun*
a crack cocaine addict *US*
- He looked away, seeing her two months from now, no more baby fat, stinky, just another pipehead. — Richard Price, *Clockers*, p. 3, 1992
- I've got to help an old lady up off the floor after she's been rolled by three fuckin pipeheads [crack cocaine addicts] for her pension. — Niall Griffiths, *Kelly + Victor*, p. 111, 2002

pipe job *noun*
1 oral sex performed on man *US*
- They come around, ask what time's your meal and take you for a ride. Pipe-job specialists. — Charles Whited, *Chiodo*, p. 66, 1973

2 an elaborate, fanciful fabricated story *US*
- — Carl Fleischhauer, *A Glossary of Army Slang*, p. 6, 1968

pipeline *noun*
1 a citizens' band radio channel which is popular *US*
- — Wayne Floyd, *Jason's Authentic Dictionary of CB Slang*, p. 24, 1976

2 in the era of analogue phone exchanges, any number with a recording, where it was possible to communicate with others calling at the same time *US*
Also known as 'pipelines'.
- — Editors of Ben is Dead, *Retrohell*, p. 153, 1997

3 the rapidly spreading curl of a breaking wave *US*
- — D.S. Halacy, *Surfer!*, p. 216, 1965

pipeliner *noun*
in the era of analogue phone exchanges, a person who called a number with a recording, where it was possible to communicate with others calling at the same time *US*
- All the kids at school who were into this called themselves "pipeliners." — Editors of Ben is Dead, *Retrohell*, p. 153, 1997

pipe-opener *noun*
in horse racing, a short, intense workout several days before a race *US*
- — Tom Ainslie, *Ainslie's Complete Guide to Thoroughbred Racing*, p. 336, 1976

piper *noun*
a crack cocaine addict *TRINIDAD AND TOBAGO, 1993*
- — Lise Winer, *Dictionary of the English/Creole of Trinidad & Tobago*, 2003

pipes *noun*
1 the vocal chords *US*
- I had pitched my pipes dry. — Iceberg Slim (Robert Beck), *Pimp*, p. 165, 1969
- She had lost her pipes and all the jive bitches she'd helped on the way was curving as they thought they'd have to lay some loot on her if they went by. — Babs Gonzales, *Movin' On Down De Line*, p. 51, 1975
- Pipes aren't quite as good as old Harry Bright's, but not so bad for a hoofer. — Joseph Wambaugh, *The Secrets of Harry Bright*, p. 291, 1985

2 the upper arm muscles *US*
- — Pamela Munro, *U.C.L.A. Slang*, p. 97, 1997

pipesmoker *noun*
a homosexual male *US*
An allusion to oral sex.
- — Judi Sanders, *Da Bomb*, p. 11, 1997

pipe up *verb*
1 to commence speaking, especially in a situation which may require a degree of boldness on the speaker's part *UK, 1889*
- At one of these meetings, a spirited red-haired woman piped up that she already had a pretty good idea who she was thank you very much. — *The Guardian*, 30th June 2003

2 to smoke crack cocaine *US*
- Girl wants to pipe up, it's a free country. As long as she's got ten dollars. — Richard Price, *Clockers*, p. 7, 1992

pipickhead *noun*
a stupid person *CANADA*
The word is a combination of the Yiddish *pipick* (navel/belly-button) and the English word.
- Hey, Kermit, you pipickhead, you think it's right for you to strike out on Shabbes? — Mordecai Richler, *Dispatches from the Sporting Life*, p. 24, 2002

pip jockey *noun*
a radar operator *US*
- — *American Speech*, p. 154, April 1947: 'Radar slang terms'

pipped *adjective*
drunk *US*
- — Ralph de Sola, *Crime Dictionary*, p. 115, 1982

pipper *noun*
in Canadian military aviation, an aiming device on a fighter's gunsight *CANADA*
- Once I had the pipper lined up on the enemy tanks, I began firing. — Tom Langeste, *Words on the Wing*, p. 214, 1995

pippie *noun*
the penis *BAHAMAS*
- — John A. Holm, *Dictionary of Bahamian English*, p. 156, 1982

pips *noun*
the female breasts *US*
- Her pips were hanging there because she was naked to the waist. — Joseph Wambaugh, *The Glitter Dome*, p. 164, 1981

pipsqueak; pip-squeak *noun*
an insignificant person *UK, 1910*
- There is a scene where a jumped-up pipsqueak officer tells someone who has been through hell: "Your shoelaces are undone. You're a bloody disgrace." — *The Guardian*, 3rd January 2002

piranha *noun*
a poker player who bets aggressively on any hand with any chance of winning *US*
- — George Percy, *The Language of Poker*, p. 68, 1988

pirate *noun*
an unlicensed taxi driver *UK*
- — David Powis, *The Signs of Crime*, 1977

pirate's dream *noun*
a flat-chested woman *US*
From the association of pirates enjoying sex with captive teenage boys, or perhaps from the punning association of a girl with 'a sunken chest and a box full of treasure'.
- — Robert A. Wilson, *Playboy's Book of Forbidden Words*, p. 140, 1972
- — Pamela Munro, *U.C.L.A. Slang*, p. 66, 1989

pish *noun*
rubbish, nonsense *UK*
- Pish...! It's all pish...! Don't talk to me...! — Ian Pattison, *Rab C. Nesbitt*, 1988
- Angel's Claws, the pish-looking "erotic thriller" la Witherspoon was making her feature film debut in. — Christopher Brookmyre, *Not the End of the World*, p. 142, 1998

pish *verb*
used as an alternative spelling for 'piss' (to urinate); hence, to rain heavily *UK, 1997*
- "Joyously English!" he says, as the rain pishes down. — *The Times Magazine*, 31st May 2003

pished *adjective*
drunk *UK: SCOTLAND*
A variation of PISSED (drunk).
- Here, Ah'm pished. Stick ma car keys behind the bar[.] — Michael Munro, *The Patter – Another Blast*, 1988
- — *e-cyclopaedia*, 20th March 2002

pisher *noun*

a person of no consequence *US, 1968*

Yiddish from German, literally 'a bed-wetter'.

- Call me pisher for five hundred miles. —Vincent Patrick, *Family Business*, p. 273, 1985
- A common saying (common in both senses) is "So call me pisher" or "So let him call me a pisher," which means "I don't care." —Leo Rosten, *The Joys of Yinglish*, p. 381, 1989
- Herbert Haft opens negotiations to buy the Toronto Blue Jays, saying, "I'll bury the little pisher." —*Washington Post*, p. B1, 6th July 1993
- Dean, no longer the exciting insurgent riding to glory on the Internet but a pisher with no past and no neck, poised to lead his party to angry defeat. —*Washington Post*, p. C1, 18th December 2003

piso *adjective*

someone who is miserly with money *UK*

Military usage; derives from Indian currency: a pais or pice is one quarter of an anna which, in turn, is one sixteenth of a rupee.

- —Nigel Foster, *The Making of a Royal Marine Commando*, 1987

piss *noun*

1 alcohol, especially beer *AUSTRALIA, 1945*

- Even if it was crook, it'd be better than bloody Pommy piss—John O'Grady, *It's Your Shout, Mate!*, p. 12, 1972
- —Louis S. Leland, *A Personal Kiwi-Yankee Dictionary*, p. 77, 1984
- They poured piss into us until we couldn't stand and sent us home in one of their own choppers. —Martin Cameron, *A Look at the Bright Side*, 1988
- Free piss always made him happy. —Phillip Gwynne, *Deadly Unna*, p. 117, 1998
- Loutish behaviour is found among them [Australians], but mostly among the men who drink "piss" (what they call beer), not those who like pot. —Brian Preston, *Pot Planet*, p. 88, 2002

2 the act of urination; urine *UK*

The verb produced the noun. Late Middle English then standard English, until it was deemed vulgar during C19. The sound of the word echoes the sound of urination.

- [T]he fellow with the weak bladder immediately began to shout about there not being anything in the statutory rules which said he could not have a piss if he wanted one. —Frank Norman, *Bang To Rights*, p. 40, 1958

▸ on the piss

on a drinking binge *AUSTRALIA, 1965*

- Don't you believe a word of it, Phil – he's on the piss with his mates! —Barry Humphries, *The Wonderful World of Barry McKenzie*, p. 30, 1968
- —Lance Peters, *The Dirty Half-Mile*, p. 107, 1979
- —Louis S. Leland, *A Personal Kiwi-Yankee Dictionary*, p. 73, 1984
- —Peter Corris, *Make Me Rich*, p. 36, 1985
- Cheap Indian meals are like rough women. You fancy them for a clearout after a night on the piss[.] —Martin King and Martin Knight, *The Naughty Nineties*, p. 106, 1999

▸ take the piss out of

to satirise someone or something; to make a joke of someone or something; to send up someone or something *AUSTRALIA*

- Country jokers like to take the piss out of Sydney guys. —David Ireland, *The Glass Canoe*, p. 22, 1976
- Here I was, a brand-new screw, having the piss taken out of me by an elder statesman of the criminal fraternity. —William Dodson, *The Sharp End*, p. 13, 2001

▸ the piss

the hell *AUSTRALIA*

- You're scaring the piss out of every rich man in the district. —Bob Ellis and Anne Brooksbank, *Mad Dog Morgan*, p. 95, 1976
- —Herb Wharton, *Cattle Camp*, p. 79, 1994

piss *verb*

1 to urinate *UK, 1290*

Derives from Old French *pisser* and has been perfectly good English since C13, but from mid-C18 it has been considered a vulgarism.

2 to rain heavily *IRELAND*

- On Wednesday – it was pissing all day – Tuesday – Jimmy Sr. brought Bimbo into town. —Roddy Doyle, *The Van*, p. 88, 1991

3 to accomplish a task easily *UK*

- —Tom Hibbert, *Rockspeak!*, p. 118, 1983

4 to whinge *US*

- I force him to take a lung test. He pisses and moans but finally agrees. —Howard Stern, *Miss America*, p. 222, 1995

▸ I wouldn't piss in your ear if your brain was on fire

I could not care less about you *AUSTRALIA*

- [T]here's a type of ex-pat Australian journo who gets off on shafting his old mates back home, and, frankly, I wouldn't piss in his ear if his brain was on fire —Barry Humphries, *The Traveller's Tool*, p. 110, 1985

▸ I wouldn't piss on you if you were on fire

used for expressing the utmost personal contempt *UK*

- You think you're God's gift / You're a liar / I wouldn't piss on you / If you were on fire —Chumbawumba, *Mouthful*, 1994

▸ piss in someone's pocket

to ingratiate yourself with someone; to flatter someone *AUSTRALIA, 1944*

- If we piss in his pocket, he's just as apt to come our way. —Frank Hardy, *The Outcasts of Foolgarah*, p. 77, 1971
- —Barry Humphries, *A Nice Night's Entertainment*, p. 151, 1975
- —Jim Ramsay, *Cop It Sweet!*, p. 70, 1977

▸ piss in the wind

to engage in a hapless, futile activity *US*

- You're all pissin' in the wind / You don't know it but you are —Neil Young, *Ambulance Blues*, 1974
- —Michael Dalton Johnson, *Talking Trash with Redd Foxx*, p. 106, 1994
- He was pissing in the wind with someone like Trevor[.] —Greg Williams, *Diamond Geezers*, 1997

▸ piss into someone's tent

to impinge upon another's interests *UK*

- The fact you even managed to get the issue discussed is bad enough for these people. We're pissing into their tent, Peter. —Ben Elton, *High Society*, p. 55, 2002

▸ piss it in

to win easily *AUSTRALIA*

- —James Lambert, *The Macquarie Book of Slang*, 1996

▸ piss money against the wall; piss it up the wall

to squander or waste money, especially on drinking *UK, 1785*

- We're just to make sure that the players don't piss the money against the wall. —*Sunday Times (South Africa)*, 24th November 2002

▸ piss on

1 to despise or feel contempt for someone or something *UK*

- Did the captain of the Titanic tell the passengers and crew "Icebergs, I piss on 'em"? I think not. —J.J. Connolly, *Layer Cake*, p. 164, 2000

2 to drink heavily; to continue a drinking binge *AUSTRALIA*

- Midweek afternoon, working hours, I was pissing on in a low-life dump with men named Dikko and Toad. —Shane Maloney, *Nice Try*, p. 241, 1998

▸ piss your trousers; piss your pants

to soil your clothing by accidental urination *UK*

- [A] chronically unwashed man, a louse ridden man or one who has pissed his trousers and farted in them until the very cloth is rotten. —Geoffrey Fletcher, *Down Among the Meths Men*, p. 16, 1966

▸ piss yourself

to laugh uproariously *UK, 1951*

Abbreviated from 'piss yourself laughing', from the notion that loss of physical control is a consequence of overwhelming laughter.

- I crease up. Hysterical. Becca's pissing herself. Kelly doesn't get it. Sad. —Cath Staincliffe, *Trainers*, p. 59, 1999

piss- *prefix*

extremely *AUSTRALIA*

- 'Don't worry,' he murmured, 'just let piss-importance here keep talking, and within another five minutes our problems will be over.' —Criena Rohan, *Down by the Dockside*, p. 104, 1963
- If they don't come to study us after the fifty years of library building, let them stay piss-ignorant. —Max Harris, *The Angry Eye*, p. 111, 1973

piss about *verb*

to play the fool, to waste time; to make a mess of something; to inconvenience someone *UK, 1961*

- [H]e wasted all that money pissing about, and he expected us to go out and work to give them more money so they could piss about more. —*The Guardian*, 7th June 2002

piss and moan *verb*

to complain loud and long *US*

- Six months ago you used to piss and moan something awful, I brought you anything but two-inchers. —George V. Higgins, *The Friends of Eddie Coyle*, p. 34, 1971

piss and punk *noun*

bread and water *US*

- "I was on piss 'n punk for three of the eight days." "What's piss 'n punk?" asks the messenger. "Bread 'n water," Billy tells him. "They don't do that much anymore, though." — Darryl Ponicsan, *The Last Detail*, p. 18, 1970

piss and vinegar *noun*
energy, enthusiam, vigour *US, 1942*
- Fulla piss an' vinegar, buddies; they checked my plugs and cleaned my points[.] — Ken Kesey, *One Flew Over the Cuckoo's Nest*, p. 278, 1962
- I'm feeling heady with excitement and I don't know why. Full of some of the old piss and vinegar[.] — Stuart Browne, *Dangerous Parking*, p. 327, 2000

pissant *noun*
a small person *US, 1946*
- Yeah, I know he's a sawed-off little ol' pissant, but you call him 'Shorty' and he'll stop your heart. — Ken Weaver, *Texas Crude*, p. 121, 1984
- We'll trample on the piss ants! — Kathy Lette, *Girls' Night Out*, p. 156, 1987

pissant *adjective*
insignificant, small-time *US*
- I was ensconced in the relatively decidedly pissant environs of Creem[.] — Lester Bangs, *Psychotic Reactions and Carburetor Dung*, p. 377, 1981

pissaphone *noun*
a funnel-shaped urinal used by the military *AUSTRALIA, 1943*
- Targets included latrine blocks and pissaphones and culminated in the attempted obliteration of the C.O.'s personal thunderbox situated perilously close to his sleeping quarters. — Martin Cameron, *A Look at the Bright Side*, 1988

piss around *verb*
to play the fool, to waste time; to make a mess of something; to inconvenience someone *UK, 1998*
- I felt kind of silly pissing around backstage with my surfboard. — *New York Observer*, 19th February 2001

piss-arse about *verb*
to play the fool, to waste time; to make a mess of something; to inconvenience someone *UK, 1948*

piss artist *noun*
a heavy drinker *AUSTRALIA*
- Oh cripes if anything's happened to mum I'll strangle that old piss artist!!! — Barry Humphries, *The Wonderful World of Barry McKenzie*, p. 35, 1968
- — Michael Dalton Johnson, *Talking Trash with Redd Foxx*, p. 112, 1994
- The names for drunkards and drunkenness in London are many and various – "soaks", "whets", "topers", "piss-heads" and "piss artists"[.] — Peter Ackroyd, *London The Biography*, p. 359, 2000

piss-ass *adjective*
despicable, unworthy, inconsequential *US*
- [B]efore he would work at some pissass job all his life and still wind up on welfare, he would take a gun and rob. — Earl Thompson, *Tattoo*, p. 7, 1974
- [T]hat's when I know he's had a piss-ass day and I'm gonna end up driving him home again. — George V. Higgins, *The Rat on Fire*, p. 74, 1981
- Shit, it was only about seven miles long, I don't know what we needed it for, little piss-ass island. — Elmore Leonard, *Bandits*, p. 272, 1987

piss away *verb*
1 to waste or to squander something *US, 1948*
- "The result," Julie says, "is that the bankroll that should have been there to absorb his losing days, he's pissed away." — Edward Lin, *Big Julie of Vegas*, p. 252, 1974
- And they're broke on Monday, boozing, whoring, pissing away the money all weekend. — *Saturday Night Fever*, 1977
- I had a good time with Gail, but I'm not pushing my luck like that, pissing away everything I got. — George V. Higgins, *The Rat on Fire*, p. 70, 1981
- You've got a Hall of Fame arm but you're pissing it away. — *Bull Durham*, 1988
- And if I gave her the money and her jewels now, you know what she's gonna do? She's gonna piss it all away in about a year[.] — *Casino*, 1995
- Make something of your life, knowledge is power! Don't piss it all away. — John Robb, *The Nineties*, p. 96, 1999

2 to move away, especially at speed *UK*
- [Y]ou're fucking pissing away on an export bonnie or sommat [something]. — Paul E. Willis, *Profane Culture*, p. 15, 1978

piss-can *noun*
a local police station or jail *US*
- — Hyman E. Goldin et al., *Dictionary of American Underworld Lingo*, p. 158, 1950

piss-cutter *noun*
1 a clever, resourceful and tough person *US, 1941*
- He was a real piss cutter, Ol' Tonto. Going all that way into Texas alone. — Clancy Sigal, *Going Away*, p. 108, 1961
- — *Maledicta*, p. 13, Summer 1977: 'A word for it'
- Ain't Delbert a piss cutter? I've seen a lot of guys open beer bottles with their teeth, but he's the only guy I know that eats the caps. — Ken Weaver, *Texas Crude*, p. 122, 1984

2 a person who disparages a friend *BAHAMAS*
- — John A. Holm, *Dictionary of Bahamian English*, p. 156, 1982

3 in oil drilling, the third man on a cable tool rig *US*
- — Jerry Robertson, *Oil Slanguage*, p. 97, 1954

piss down *verb*
to rain heavily *UK, 1950*
- It was raining. Pissing down. — Karline Smith, *Moss Side Massive*, p. 204, 1994
- It was pissing down. — David Peace, *Nineteen Seventy-Four*, p. 30, 1999

piss easy *adjective*
very easy *NEW ZEALAND, 1988*
- [G]etting the Pistols on telly; piss easy at this Northern dream factory. — Tony Wilson, *24 Hour Party People*, p. 29, 2002

pissed *adjective*
1 drunk *UK, 1929*
- Thereupon I'd get a bit pissed and let off a lot of stuff by Yeats and Eliot, then he'd get dead [very] pissed[.] — Derek Raymond (Robin Cook), *The Crust on its Uppers*, p. 33, 1962
- I really stuffed myself, boy, and I'm pissed to the ears, too, on top of it. — Lenny Bruce, *The Essential Lenny Bruce*, p. 15, 1967
- [A]nd then you're half pissed again and useless for the rest of the afternoon. — Mart Crowley, *The Boys in the Band*, p. 41, 1968
- "Is she pissed," you ask. "I wouldn't put it that way," Wade says. "I like that word better the British use it – colloquial for intoxicated." — Jay McInerney, *Bright Lights, Big City*, p. 19, 1984
- "That's not Dennis Conner! Blaze, you're getting pissed!" a Kiwi grinder said. — Joseph Wambaugh, *Floaters*, p. 189, 1996

2 angry, annoyed *US, 1971*
An abbreviation of **PISSED OFF**.
- "Is she pissed," you ask. "I wouldn't put it that way," Wade says. "I like that word better the British use it – colloquial for intoxicated." — Jay McInerney, *Bright Lights, Big City*, p. 19, 1984
- The only thing that gave away how pissed she was, was the tone of her voice. — Francesca Lia Block, *I Was a Teenage Fairy*, p. 98, 1998
- You were right. She's still pissed. — *Ten Things I Hate About You*, 1999
- God'll be pissed. You'll rot in hell. — Janet Evanovich, *Seven Up*, p. 86, 2001

pissed as a bastard *adjective*
very drunk *UK*
- — Pete Brown, *Man Walks into a Pub*, 2003

pissed as a cunt *adjective*
extremely drunk *UK, 1961*
- [W]e went in the dressing room and I was pissed as a cunt. — *Uncut*, March 2000

pissed as a fart; pissed as a brewer's fart *adjective*
very drunk *UK, 1998*
- He turned up in court pissed as a fart, declaring his occupation as "sperm donor". — *Uncut*, p. 20, October 2003

pissed as a newt *adjective*
very drunk *AUSTRALIA, 1977*
- — Jim Ramsay, *Cop It Sweet!*, p. 70, 1977
- I was pissed as a newt by the time Bert Newton announced that I had won a Logie for a TV script[.] — Frank Hardy, *Hardy's People*, p. 73, 1986

pissed as an owl *adjective*
very drunk *AUSTRALIA*
- When he arrived at the luncheon, looking distinguished with his white hair and moustache, but to my practised eye, as pissed as an owl, I took him by the arm and sat him down next to me. — Frank Hardy, *Hardy's People*, p. 162, 1986

pissed as a parrot *adjective*
extremely drunk *AUSTRALIA, 1977*
- — Jim Ramsay, *Cop It Sweet!*, p. 70, 1977
- Hyphen-Hyphen let out a shrill whinny of excitement and off his chair – being pissed as a parrot by this stage. — Derek Maitland, *Breaking Out*, p. 58, 1979
- Gabriel Buchanan was as pissed as a parrot. — Lance Peters, *The Dirty Half-Mile*, p. 81, 1979

pissed as a rat *adjective*
very drunk *UK*
- — *British Journal of Photography*, 29th August 1980

pissed as arseholes *adjective*
extremely drunk *UK, 1984*

• We were still up from the night before and we were pissed as arseholes.—*Q Magazine*, January 1998

pissed as a twat *adjective*
very drunk *UK*
• —Pete Brown, *Man Walks into a Pub*, 2003

pissed off *adjective*
fed up; disgruntled; annoyed; angry *US, 1946*
• You're not pissed off with me, are you?—Helen Garner, *Monkey Grip*, p. 60, 1977
• Dad was still pissed off. I talked to Mum mostly.—Andrew McGahan, *Praise*, p. 81, 1992
• I get pissed off at times when my mates are off to play badminton or something and I can't[.]—Ruth Butler, *Cool Places*, p. 92, 1998
• Roseanne Kreiner was standing on her corner, in the rain, looking totally wet and pissed off.—Janet Evanovich, *Seven Up*, p. 93, 2001

pissed out of your mind; pissed out of your skull *adjective*
very drunk *AUSTRALIA*
• —Alexander Buzo, *Rooted*, p. 43, 1969
• —Frank Hardy, *The Outcasts of Foolgarah*, p. 218, 1971
• —Jim Ramsay, *Cop It Sweet!*, p. 70, 1977
• Truthful Jones came, although admittedly he turned up late and pissed out of his mind.—Frank Hardy, *Hardy's People*, p. 159, 1986
• Look, there's Con and Gavin, pissed out of their brains.—Jenny Pausacker, *What are ya?*, p. 10, 1987
• He was pissed out of his skull.—Doug Anthony Allstars, *Book*, p. 95, 1989
• —Christos Tsiolkas, *Loaded*, p. 28, 1995

pissed up *adjective*
in a drunken condition *UK*
A variation of **PISSED**.
• "All those birds come away on holiday to get pissed up..." "... And get a fuckin' good seeing to."—J.J. Connolly, *Know Your Enemy [britpulp]*, p. 152, 1999
• [T]hey got a bit pissed up and started giving it the large [boasting][ ] —Danny King, *The Burglar Diaries*, p. 206, 2001

piss-elegant *adjective*
conceited, haughty *US*
• So this elegant faggot comes to New York from Cunt Lick, Texas, and he is the most piss elegant fag of them all.—William Burroughs, *Naked Lunch*, p. 128, 1957
• — Florida Legislative Investigation Committee (Johns Committee), *Homosexuality and Citizenship in Florida*, 1964: 'Glossary of homosexual terms and deviate acts'
• That piss-elegant kooze hit me!—Mart Crowley, *The Boys in the Band*, p. 94, 1968
• Like Harold Macmillan's biography. Or Churchill's. Or Noel Coward's. Marbled endpapers. Piss elegant.—John Lahr, *Dame Edna Everage and the Rise of Western Civilisation*, p. 200, 1991

pisser *noun*
1 a urinal *UK, 1961*
• Another gang of kids push some melon into the pisser and I take off.—Tim Winton, *That eye, the sky*, p. 121, 1986
• —Pamela Munro, *U.C.L.A. Slang*, p. 97, 1997
• "Where's this little lot come from then Bogey?" Hangs his head shamefaced and embarrassed. Mutters his reply: "From the pisser down the church hall sir."—Jack Allen, *When the Whistle Blows*, p. 108, 2000

2 the penis; the vagina *UK, 1901*

3 a criminal who urinates in their clothing when caught by authorities *AUSTRALIA*
• Something that always intrigued me was the amount of armed robbers that, literally, wet themselves when we confronted them. They were known among the operators as 'pissahs' and were a prized scalp.—William Dodson, *The Sharp End*, p. 156, 2001

4 an extraordinary person or thing *US, 1943*
• Dreamer Tatum is what we call a pisser. I mean that sumbitch will make your helmet ring when he puts it on you.—Dan Jenkins, *Semi-Tough*, p. 17, 1972

5 an annoyance *US, 1943*
Literally something that will **PISS OFF** (annoy).
• That was a pisser. If Eddie didn't hit one of the stripes, Boomer would have an easy run out.—Walter Tevis, *The Color of Money*, p. 7, 1984
• A little pisser I've known all my life.—*Goodfellas*, 1990
• I mean, the matches go off, burn the hell out of my leg, scare the shit out of me...but the real pisser was blowing, a hole in a brand new pair of jeans.—*Hard Eight*, 1996
• "Well, isn't this a pisser," Grandma said.—Janet Evanovich, *Seven Up*, p. 66, 2001

6 during the Vietnam war, an observer of enemy supply trails *US*
• —Linda Reinberg, *In the Field*, p. 168, 1991

7 solitary confinement in prison *US*
• —Charles Shafer, *Folk Speech in Texas Prisons*, p. 211, 1990

8 a pub *NEW ZEALAND*
• —David McGill, *David McGill's Complete Kiwi Slang Dictionary*, p. 84, 1998

9 an electric pylon *UK*
Perhaps from the sense as 'the penis' after its phallic shape.
• —Edmund Crispin, *Glimpses of the Moon*, 1977

10 a type of cicada which releases a liquid when held *AUSTRALIA, 1980*
• When I flooded the cicada hole I got a pisser.—*www.abc.net.au/wordmap*, 2003

▸ **pull your pisser**
to befool, or mislead, or tease someone *UK, 1969*
A variation of **PULL YOUR LEG**.
• HAICH: [...] Take y'shoes off, Dixie – y'could do with a new pair. DIXIE: Are you pulling my pisser? HAICH: Not unless you keep it in your shoe pal.—Alan Bleasdale, *Boys From the Blackstuff*, 1982
• You and Ollie, split up? Nah, I thought someone was pulling my pisser.—Danny King, *The Burglar Diaries*, p. 185, 2001

piss-fart around *verb*
to waste time *AUSTRALIA, 1988*
• JOE: Now, Eddie, would you like to sit down and help us solve it, or do you two wanna piss fart around?—*Reservoir Dogs*, 1992
• "Dad spoke with a lot of passion about football, but his bottom line was when you go don't piss-fart around, just get in and do it properly," he said.—*The Australian*, 15th September 1999
• —Sonya Plowman, *Great Kiwi Slang*, p. 140, 2002

piss fat *noun*
an erection caused by a full bladder *AUSTRALIA*
• Fat is not the same as Piss-fat. A piss-fat is what you wake up with in the morning because you did not do a wee-wee before you went to bed.—Bettina Arndt, *The Australian Way of Sex*, p. 10, 1984

piss flaps *noun*
the vaginal lips *AUSTRALIA*
Roger's Profanisaurus, 1997, also offers its use as an exclamtion of disappointment: 'Oh *piss-flaps!* I never win the Lottery!'.
• She's got piss flaps like John Wayne's saddle bags.—Thommo *The Dictionary of Australian Swearing and Sex Sayings*, p. 95, 1985
• [N]aked, her breasts pendulous and flabby, her legs spread, her piss flaps all red and hairy and wet[.]—Lisa Jewell, *Labia Lobelia [Tart Noir]*, p. 244, 2002

piss-head *noun*
a drunk; a habitual drinker *UK, 1961*
A combination of **PISS** (alcohol) with **-HEAD** (a user).
• Unfortunately, our informants aren't what you might call the world's most reliable witnesses. Piss-heads from the Royal Hotel across the road.—Shane Maloney, *Nice Try*, p. 135, 1998
• You coming or what, you pisshead?—David Peace, *Nineteen Seventy-Four*, p. 60, 1999
• Whilst pillheads hold hands and sing happy songs, pissheads are out the back having a punch-up.—Wayne Anthony, *Spanish Highs*, p. 151, 1999
• [A] mixed group of mainly British, Aussie and Kiwi pissheads.—John King, *Human Punk*, p. 164, 2000
• The names for drunkards and drunkenness in London are many and various – "soaks", "whets", "topers", "piss-heads" and "piss artists"[.]—Peter Ackroyd, *London The Biography*, p. 359, 2000
• [I]t's just pissheads kicking off[.]—Kevin Sampson, *Outlaws*, p. 66, 2001

piss-hole *noun*
1 the entrance to the urethra *US*
• Sperm spills down from my piss-hole.—Peter Sotos, *Index*, p. 149, 1996

2 a urinal *UK*
• —Frank Norman, *Encounter*, 1959

3 an unpleasant location *UK, 1973*
• [T]his filthy piss hole we call Mother Earth[.]—Howard Stern, *Miss America*, p. x, 1995

piss-hole bandit *noun*
a homosexual man who seeks sexual contact in a public urinal *UK*
• —David Powis, *The Signs of Crime*, 1977

piss house *noun*
a public toilet *US*
• Edith (her sister) & Patricia (my love) walked out of the pisshouse hand in hand (I shan't describe my emotions).—Neal Cassady, *The First Third*, p. 190, 7th March 1947

piss in *verb*

to win or achieve something easily *NEW ZEALAND*

- —David McGill, *David McGill's Complete Kiwi Slang Dictionary*, p. 97, 1998

pissing *adjective*

used as an intensifier, generally denoting disapproval *UK, 1984*

pissing contest *noun*

a duel of unpleasantries *US*

- I made it by not getting involved in pissing contests. —Gerald Petievich, *To Live and Die in L.A.*, p. 78, 1983

pissing match *noun*

a dispute based on mutual negative attacks *US*

From the graphic if vulgar image of two men urinating on each other.

- They treated Strike with respect, but the Homicide was a hawk-eyed motherfucker, and anytime they were under the same roof it was a goddamn pissing match. —Richard Price, *Clockers*, p. 207, 1992

pissing rain *noun*

heavy or persistent rainfall *UK*

- [Y]er [here] in the pissing rain jus' waiting just fucking waiting[.] —Patrick Jones, *Everything Must Go*, p. 167–168, 2000

piss in the hand *noun*

something that is very simple *NEW ZEALAND*

- —Louis S. Leland, *A Personal Kiwi-Yankee Dictionary*, p. 77, 1984

piss it *verb*

to succeed or achieve very easily *UK*

- "It pissed it" equals won the horse-race easily. —Ann Barr and Peter York, *The Official Sloane Ranger Handbook*, p. 159, 1982

piss-off *noun*

an annoyance, an irritation *UK*

- The only piss-off now was [...] having to work quite hard to avoid any eye contact[.] —James Hawes, *Dead Long Enough*, p. 19, 2000

piss off *verb*

1 to depart *UK, 1958*

Also used in an exclamatory or imperative sense.

- So what? I wish you'd piss off. —Frank Norman, *Bang to Rights*, 1958
- He's not giving you any money, so piss off! —Monty Python, *Life of Brian*, 1979
- Paul picked me up by my collar. "Now piss off!" —David Peace, *Nineteen Seventy-Four*, p. 213, 1999
- After her return from maternity leave – which she said Mr Boardman referred to as "pissing off" – she was increasingly excluded from meetings[.] — *The Guardian*, 15th November 2002
- [shouted at magician David Blaine] Fuck off home you fucking Yank. No one wants you here. Piss off back to America — Michael Hann, *The Guardian*, 19th September 2003

2 to irritate or annoy someone *US, 1937*

First recorded in the normally slang-free poetry of Ezra Pound.

- Neuza was pissing me off. —B. Selkie, *Lime Juice*, p. 29, 1995
- [A]ll I took was my Technics stereo system, minus the speakers, because I reckoned they'd piss off my neighbours in a close-quarter environment[.] —Chris Ryan, *Stand By, Stand By*, p. 61, 1996
- [P]eople who pissed him off. —Lee Child, *The Visitor*, p. 128, 2000

3 to get rid of someone *AUSTRALIA*

- For Christ's sake, Sally. Piss him off and come to bed. —Dorothy Hewett, *The Chapel Perilous*, p. 65, 1972
- —Barry Humphries, *The Traveller's Tool*, p. 27, 1985
- —Kathy Lette, *Girls' Night Out*, p. 103, 1987

piss play *noun*

sexual behaviour involving urination and urine *US*

- Red is for fisting, black for heavy s/m, light blue for oral sex, dark blue for anal sex, yellow for piss play, orange for anything goes, purple for piercing, and so on. — *The Village Voice*, 24th November 1999

piss-poor *adjective*

extremely poor or feeble *UK, 1946*

Brought into general usage from British service usage during World War 2.

- From the point of view of human interest, it was a piss-poor day, Donald. —Bernard Wolfe, *The Late Risers*, p. 243, 1954
- I have to tell you the time my father and I and a pisspoor bum from Latimer Street took a trip to Nebraska in the middle of the depression to sell flyswatters. —Jack Kerouac, *On the Road*, p. 207, 1957
- How unlike General Eisenhower he is. Make a piss-poor President? —Tom Robbins, *Another Roadside Attraction*, p. 97, 1971
- "You'd make a piss-poor lawyer," he replied. "Relax. I'll handle this." —Hunter S. Thompson, *Fear and Loathing in Las Vegas*, p. 129, 1971
- "I've played this kid before," Bo said. "He's big, he's almost sixteen. But he's got a piss-poor backhand." —Elmore Leonard, *Switch*, p. 28, 1978
- Listen, I've spent over twenty-five hundred of my own money showing Miskito Indians how to fire an M-60 automatic gun, a piss-poor weapon but all we got. —Elmore Leonard, *Bandits*, p. 268, 1987
- [P]aying shit-loads to the taxman until you finally retire (if you don't die first) with a piss-poor pension[.] —Dave Courtney, *Stop the Ride I Want to Get Off*, p. 379, 1999
- Obviously, some of my weekly twenty-five minutes was piss-poor, but it also threw up some good stuff. —Frank Skinner, *Frank Skinner*, p. 45, 2001

pisspot; piss-pot *noun*

1 a vessel for urine *UK, 1440*

Originally conventional; it slipped into vulgar use during the C18 whilst still being very much a household necessity.

- [S]omething my great-aunt Maria might have mixed up in her piss-pot[.] —Derek Raymond (Robin Cook), *The Crust on its Uppers*, p. 55, 1962

2 a terrible thing or place *US*

- Prob'ly ain't every day they get to meet a real man in a pisspot of a town like this. —Jim Thompson, *Pop. 1280*, p. 54, 1964

3 a drunkard; a despicable person *AUSTRALIA*

Figurative use of the sense as 'a chamber pot'.

- You think I'm one of those old piss-pots who go around the place annoying decent people? —Alexander Buzo, *Norm and Ahmed*, p. 4, 1969
- [Y]ou should be wondering what this tranparent pisspot is doing, in any capacity, whatsoever, in Her majesty's Armed Services[.] —Mike Stott, *Soldiers Talking, Cleanly*, 1978
- "Sweeney," Roscommon said, "you remember that little pisspot named Leonard James that they called Jesse[.]" —George V. Higgins, *The Rat on Fire*, p. 33, 1981
- Quick, Mr Meehan, the old piss-pot's at it again. —Kerry Cue, *Crooks Chooks and Bloody Ratbags*, p. 176, 1983
- Bloody old pisspot. Died of fright. —Peter Corris, *Make Me Rich*, p. 147, 1985
- [A] walking pisspot with a penchant for pork scratchings[.] —Ian Pattison, *Rab C. Nesbitt*, 1988

4 a US military M-1 helmet *US*

- —Gregory Clark, *Words of the Vietnam War*, p. 200, 1990

piss-proud *adjective*

having an erect penis as a result of urinal pressure *UK, 1788*

piss-take *noun*

an act of mockery or teasing *UK, 1977*

- "Buildin' a fuckin' motorway through here. It's a fuckin' piss-take," he said in a broad cockney accent. —Donald Gorgon, *Cop Killer*, p. 64, 1994
- [B]ecause of the close proximity of the crowd to the [football] players, those who were on the receiving end of the piss-take really knew it. If a player was bald, ginger, fat, thin, tall, short [...] he'd receive an ear-bashing for ninety non-stop minutes[.] — Martin King and Martin Knight, *The Naughty Nineties*, p. 113, 1999

piss-take *verb*

to mock; to tease; to deride; to ridicule *UK*

- The average turn at Duckie was absurd, confrontational, piss-taking – a mutant hybrid of pub drag and performance art. — *The Guardian*, p. 15, 14th May 2002

piss-taker *noun*

a mocker; a person who ridicules something *UK, 1976*

- And my brother is a piss-taker of the highest degree. — *Daily Telegraph*, 26th September 2002

piss-taking *noun*

mockery *UK*

- —Peter Crookston *Villain*, 1967

piss-to-windward *noun*

an entirely inept person *BARBADOS*

- Good God, George, look what this piss-to-windward done with your new saw! —Frank A. Collymore, *Barbadian Dialect*, p. 85, 1965

piss tube; pee pipe *noun*

a metal tube partially buried in the ground, into which soldiers urinate *US*

Vietnam war usage.

- I put it in my mouth – what the hell – then turned my head and spit it out over the low sandbag wall in the direction of the piss tube. —Larry Heinemann, *Close Quarters*, p. 251, 1977
- [H]e was standing at the piss tube – those were rocket casings that were driven into the ground at an angle and you stuck your dick in them ... when they filled up, you pissed somewhere else. —Dennis Marvicsin and Jerold Greenfield, *Maverick*, p. 42, 1990

piss-up *noun*
a drinking session *UK, 1952*
- [T]hree parties took place in Foolgarah on the same night. Not political parties (though they could be called that) but grog parties, dings, chevoos, happenings, piss-ups. — Frank Hardy, *The Outcasts of Foolgarah*, p. 181, 1971
- [A] big farewell piss-up the day before[.] — Andy McNab, *Immediate Action*, p. 375, 1995
- Noel Gallagher coming round to Tony Blair's for a piss up, the 'Cool Britannia' image. — Dr Cloonan, *BBCi Nottingham*, February 2003

▸ **couldn't organise a piss-up in a brewery**
used of an inefficient person or organisation *UK, 1984*
Formed on **PISS-UP** (a drinking session).
- All those lame jokes about the Welsh [...] not having the wherewithal to organise a piss-up in a brewery, suddenly fell flat. — *The Guardian*, 12th June 2003

piss up; piss up large *verb*
to drink beer or other alcoholic beverages *NEW ZEALAND*
- — David McGill, *David McGill's Complete Kiwi Slang Dictionary*, p. 84, 1998

piss-weak *adjective*
puny and cowardly *AUSTRALIA, 1971*
- I happen to hate piss-weak bastards like you! — Derek Maitland, *Breaking Out*, p. 39, 1979
- Jesus, Riley, can't you see you need more than just a piss weak sit-in? — Bob Jewson, *Stir*, p. 94, 1980
- — Kathy Lette, *Girls' Night Out*, p. 190, 1987

pisswhacker *noun*
a type of cicada which releases a liquid when held *AUSTRALIA, 1981*

piss-willie *noun*
a despicable coward *US*
- — *Maledicta*, p. 13, Summer 1977: 'A word for it'

pissy *noun*
a heavy drinker *AUSTRALIA*
- Sam, I want to play you up as an old pissy from way back, as I reckon it will suit the character of the book. — Sam Weller, *Old Bastards I Have Met*, p. 122, 1979

pissy *adjective*
1 unpleasant, distasteful *UK*
- Past a coupla pissy bars an' then a coupla pissy alleys. Finally park up round the pissy corner from the pissy dole office. — Nick Barlay, *Curvy Lovebox*, p. 82, 1997
- No more hanging around pissy estates, risking our lives. — Lisa Jewell, *Labia Lobelia [Tart Noir]*, p. 244, 2002

2 puny; insignificant; weak *AUSTRALIA*
- Do you think your pissy little poke will satisfy a swinger? — Bettina Arndt, *The Australian Way of Sex*, p. 85, 1985
- — Kathy Lette, *Girls' Night Out*, p. 133, 1987
- — B. Selkie, *Lime Juice*, p. 30, 1995
- Now beam me down to the 100 Club and out of this kid's pissy dream, you tossers! — Glyn Parry, *Mosh*, p. 102, 1996
- — Shane Maloney, *Nice Try*, p. 145, 1998

3 angered, crotchety, fussy *US, 1973*
- He's all pissy these days. Won't give me nothin' hardly. — Joseph Wambaugh, *Floaters*, p. 7, 1996
- Got pissy with me because I wouldn't let her carry the bag. Started running her fuckin' mouth. — *Jackie Brown*, 1997

4 given to drinking *AUSTRALIA*
- Did you hear about the two pissy brickies who were always broke three or four days before pay-day? — Sam Weller, *Old Bastards I Have Met*, p. 10, 1979

5 drunken *AUSTRALIA*
- Tune in to his pissy platitudes and find out. — Frank Hardy, *The Outcasts of Foolgarah*, p. 146, 1971

pissy *adverb*
extremely *BAHAMAS*
- — John A. Holm, *Dictionary of Bahamian English*, p. 156, 1982

pissy-ass *adjective*
dirty, inconsequential *US*
- How many pissy ass winos have more'n a dollar fifty anytime? — Joseph Wambaugh, *The Choirboys*, p. 308, 1975

pissy-eyed *adjective*
drunk *NEW ZEALAND*
- — David McGill, *David McGill's Complete Kiwi Slang Dictionary*, p. 98, 1998

pistol *noun*
1 the penis *US*
- — Gary K. Farlow, *Prison-ese*, p. 51, 2002

2 a hired gunman *US*
- — R. Frederick West, *God's Gambler*, p. 228, 1964: 'Appendix A'

3 a reliable person *US, 1984*
- He was a pistol... and a helluva reporter. — Mark Dawidziak, *The Night Stalker Companion*, p. 6, 1997

4 a lobster that has lost one or both claws *US*
- — John Gould, *Maine Lingo*, p. 210, 1975
- — Kendall Merriam, *The Illustrated Dictionary of Lobstering*, p. 65, 1978

5 in electric line work, an underground cable terminator *US*
- — A.B. Chance Co., *Lineman's Slang Dictionary*, p. 13, 1980

pistola *noun*
a cigarette enhanced with freebase cocaine *US*
- A pistola is a base and tobacco cigarette made by emptying out and repacking a regular cigarette, or by rolling one. — *Hi Life*, p. 78, 1979

Pistol Pete *noun*
a chronic male masturbator *US*
- — Gary K. Farlow, *Prison-ese*, p. 51, 2002

pistorically; pistoratically *adverb*
very (drunk) *BARBADOS*
- — Frank A. Collymore, *Barbadian Dialect*, p. 85, 1965
- — Lise Winer, *Dictionary of the English/Creole of Trinidad & Tobago*, 2003

pit *noun*
1 the armpit *US, 1965*
- Ingrid with long legs and hairy pits; Marie-Helene with huge breasts[.] — Mark Powell, *Snap*, p. 57, 2001

2 the vein at the antecubital site, opposite the elbow, commonly used for drug injections *US*
- He hasn't even used his pit, which is what they call the original mainline to the heart and one of the best veins to hit. — Jeremy Larner and Ralph Tefferteller, *The Addict in the Street*, p. 167, 1964
- — Eugene Landy, *The Underground Dictionary*, p. 151, 1971
- — Geoffrey Froner, *Digging for Diamonds*, p. 48, 1989

3 Pitocin™, a drug used for inducing labour *US*
- — Sally Williams, *"Strong" Words*, p. 154, 1994

4 phencyclidine, the recreational drug known as PCP or angel dust *US*
- US Department of Justice — *Street Tems*, October 1994

5 the area in a club or concert hall where dancers can slam dance *US*
An abbreviation of **MOSH PIT**.
- Got to punk gigs by himself. Slam in the pit with the boys until the pain sweated out of him[.] — Francesca Lia Block, *Baby Be-Bop*, p. 410, 1995

6 a bed *UK, 1948*
- — *Cool Antarctica*, 2003: 'Antarctic slang'

7 an inside jacket pocket *US*
- — *New York Times Magazine*, p. 88, 16th March 1958

▸ **no pit**
no trouble *US*
From 'armpit' to 'pit' to 'sweat' to 'trouble'.
- — Collin Baker et al., *College Undergraduate Slang Study Conducted at Brown University*, p. 172, 1968

pit *verb*
to sweat under the arms *US*
- — John D. Bell et al., *Loosely Speaking*, p. 15, 1966

PITA
used as Internet shorthand to mean '*p*ain *i*n *t*he *a*ss/arse' *US*
- — Christian Crumlish, *The Internet Dictionary*, p. 153, 1995

pit bull *noun*
a variety of MDMA, the recreational drug best known as ecstasy *UK*
- — Angela Devlin, *Prison Patter*, p. 88, 1996

pitch *noun*
a persuasive or exaggerated sales act or talk *UK, 1876*
- But the Guardian has learned that Mr Blair combined this plea for peace with a sales pitch on behalf of Britain's biggest defence manufacturer, BAE Systems. — *The Guardian*, 21st October 2002

pitch *verb*
to play the active sexual role in a homosexual relationship *US, 1966*
- I've been known to pitch, but I'm no catcher. —Malcolm Braly, *On the Yard*, p. 149, 1967
- The young man walked over and leaned in through the window. "It's thirty; head only, pitch or catch," he said. —James Ellroy, *Blood on the Moon*, p. 133, 1984
- Elaine caught his slight grin and was sure Chili did too. He said, "You pitch or catch, Elliot?" "Mostly pitch." —Elmore Leonard, *Be Cool*, p. 269, 1999

▸ **pitch a stink**
to complain loudly *BAHAMAS*
- —John A. Holm, *Dictionary of Bahamian English*, p. 156, 1982

▸ **pitch a tent**
to have an erection *US*
- —Don R. McCreary (Editor), *Dawg Speak*, 2001

▸ **pitch it strong; pitch it high**
to make a forceful case for something *UK, 1837*
- — *The Tribune (India)*, 23rd June 2000: 'States pitch it high'

▸ **pitch woo; pitch the woo**
to commence a courtship *US, 1867*
- I wouldn't like to pitch woo there. I'd never get the girl warmed up. —Jennie Darlington and Jane McIlvaine, *My Antarctic Honeymoon*, p. 125, 1956

pitch and toss *noun*
a boss *AUSTRALIA, 1945*
Rhyming slang.
- —Julian Franklyn, *A Dictionary of Rhyming Slang*, 1960
- —Ray Puxley, *Cockney Rabbit*, 1992

pitcher *noun*
1 the active partner in homosexual sex *US, 1966*
- — *Maledicta*, p. 231, 1979: 'Kinks and queens: linguistic and cultural aspects of the terminology for gays'
- —H. Max, *Gay (S)language*, p. 32, 1988

2 a dealer in a casino card game *US, 1973*
- —Thomas L. Clark, *The Dictionary of Gambling and Gaming*, p. 157, 1987

pitchhole *noun*
a deep pothole in a road *CANADA*
- All must be loaded skillfully so as not to slide or roll off as the cat train rocks and plunges over the hummocks and pitch holes in the ice and snow roads. —Donalda Dickie, *The Great Golden Plain*, p. 288, 1962

pitch in *verb*
1 to commence work in a vigorous manner; to join in with another, or others, doing such work *US, 1847*
- He's going to be remembered as someone who always wanted to help and always pitched in and always struggled to do his best for everyone. — *The Guardian*, 5th June 2003

2 to start eating; to eat heartily *US, 1937*

pitch up; pitch *verb*
to arrive *UK*
- [T]he local hip hop heads are dubious about whether any of the international stars will actually pitch. —Patrick Neate, *Where You're At*, p. 105, 2003
- When we pitched up in Carmel (of interest solely, it seemed to me, for the fact that Clint Eastwood was then its mayor), the cabal of smokers on the bus hurled ourselves off, unlit cigarettes already in hand[.] — *The Guardian*, 16th April 2003

pit cupcake *noun*
in motor racing, a female hanger-on in search of romance with drivers or members of the pit crew *US*
- —Lewis Poteet, *Car & Motorcyle Slang*, p. 151, 1992

pit girl *noun*
a female casino employee whose job is to provide company and encouragement for heavy-betting gamblers *US*
- Known as "pit girls," their job is to entertain high rollers while the house empties their pockets. —Ed Reid and Ovid Demaris, *The Green Felt Jungle*, p. 95, 1963

pit guard *noun*
an underarm deodorant *US*
- — *Current Slang*, p. 10, Summer 1968

pit lamp *verb*
to engage in illegal jacklighting in hunting; also, to dismiss someone from employment *CANADA*
The first meaning of this slang term comes from the use of a lamp like a miner's lamp.
- A pitlamped logger was one who had just been fired. — *Vancouver Sun*, p. 30A/3, 30th May 1966
- Frank Greenfield once jailed a man for pitlamping deer. — *Wildlife Review*, p. 27/2, March 1967

pit room *noun*
a bedroom *ANTARCTICA*
- —Bernadette Hince, *The Antarctic Dictionary*, p. 244, 2000
- — *Cool Antarctica*, 2003: 'Antarctic slang'

pits *noun*
in a hospital, the medical screening area *US*
- — *Maledicta*, p. 68, Summer/Winter 1978: 'Common patient directed pejoratives used by medical personnel'

▸ **the pits**
the very bottom; the depths; the nadir; the worst *US, 1953*
Perhaps from 'arm*pits*'.
- — *American Speech*, p. 194, October 1965: 'Notes on campus Vocabulary, 1964'
- —Collin Baker et al., *College Undergraduate Slang Study Conducted at Brown University*, p. 173, 1968
- Well, the first year it wasn't so bad, but then it went right downhill. The pits. —John Sayles, *Union Dues*, p. 127, 1977
- DeDe smiled bitterly. "I do. Isn't that the pits?" —Armistead Maupin, *Tales of the City*, p. 165, 1978
- I really was in the pits in '78. — *Ask*, p. 47, 5th May 1979
- You guys are the absolute pits of the world, do you know that? —John McEnroe, 1981
- "Things aren't going so well at home, Nickie?" asked Lacey solicitously. "The pits," I replied. —C.D. Payne, *Youth in Revolt*, p. 117, 1993
- B and B is the pits. —Mary Hooper, *(megan)2*, p. 49, 1999
- I am the pits, the fuckin dregs uv humanity, the lowest ov the fuckin low[.] —Niall Griffiths, *Grits*, p. 11, 2000

pit stop *noun*
1 while driving, a stop at a restaurant, petrol station or rest area to use the lavatory and/or buy food and drink; a visit to the toilet *US*
- —Collin Baker et al., *College Undergraduate Slang Study Conducted at Brown University*, p. 173, 1968
- — *Complete CB Slang Dictionary*, p. 74, 1976
- —Peter Chippindale, *The British CB Book*, p. 157, 1981
- I ain't going to piss in my sock, for God's sake. It ain't natural. How come we can't make a pit stop? —Robert Campbell, *Juice*, p. 87, 1988
- Lloyd took a pit stop at the local off-licence for a six-pack of Tennants before heading to his yard. —Donald Gorgon, *Cop Killer*, p. 13, 1994

2 a short stay in prison, especially one occasioned by a parole violation *US*
- —Inez Cardozo-Freeman, *The Joint*, p. 521, 1984

3 an underarm deodorant *US*
- — *Current Slang*, p. 12, Summer 1969

Pitstop *nickname*
used as a humorous nickname for Pittsburgh, Pennsylvania *US*
- — *Maledicta*, p. 319, Summer/Winter 1981: 'Ridiculing place names'

pitter-patter *verb*
1 to walk in small, quiet steps *US*
- So I pitterpatter over an grab my pocketbook[.] —Robert Gover, *Here Goes Kitten*, p. 128, 1964

2 to talk persuasively or glibly *UK*
- You've got to pitter-patter the punters. —Patrick O'Shaughnessy, *Market Traders' Slang*, 1979

Pittsburgh feathers *noun*
coal *US*
- —Vincent J. Monteleone, *Criminal Slang*, p. 175, 1949

Pitt Street farmer *noun*
(especially in New South Wales) a city person with a small country property, often run at a loss for tax purposes *AUSTRALIA, 1945*
From Pitt Street, a principle street in Sydney.
- —Frank Hardy, *The Outcasts of Foolgarah*, p. 143, 1971
- —Arthur Chipper, *The Aussie Swearer's Guide*, p. 65, 1972

pitty *noun*
a pit bull dog *US*

Formerly known as a Staffordshire Terrier or an American Pit Bull Terrier.

• —Judi Sanders, *Cal Poly Slang*, p. 7, 1990

pitty *adjective*

messy, dirty *US*

• —*American Speech*, p. 64, Spring-Summer 1975: 'Razorback slang'

pity pot *noun*

used in twelve-step recovery programmes such as Alcoholics Anonymous as a name for the imaginary place where the addict sits feeling sorry for himself *US*

• —Christopher Cavanaugh, *AA to Z*, p. 143, 1998

pivvy *noun*

a very small amount *BARBADOS*

• —Frank A. Collymore, *Barbadian Dialect*, p. 85, 1965

pix *noun*

photographs or films *US, 1932*

An abbreviation of the pronunciation of 'pictures'.

• Striking pix is enclosed and you must of course send back without fail as I love it.—Jack Kerouac, *Letter to Neal Cassady*, p. 238, 3rd December 1950
• There have been pussy-lathering scenes and bare, fleshy vulva in plenty of pix.—*Adult Video*, p. 48, August/September 1986

pixie *noun*

1 a male homosexual *US, 1941*

The term was enshrined in US popular/political culture during the McCarthy hearings in April 1954. Joseph Welch, the lawyer for the US Army, demanded to know the origins of a doctored photograph, asking if it had come from a 'pixie', alluding to a suspected homosexual relationship involving Roy Cohn, a member of McCarthy's staff. Senator McCarthy asked Mr Welch to define the term, which he happily did: "I should say, Mr Senator, that a pixie is a close relative of a fairy".

• —G. Legman, *The Language of Homsexuality*, p. 1174, 1941

2 a frequent user of marijuana *UK*

• —Tom Hibbert, *Rockspeak!*, p. 119, 1983

3 an amphetamine tablet *US*

• —US Department of Justice, *Street Terms*, August 1994

4 hair that has been chemically straightened *US*

• —David Claerbaut, *Black Jargon in White America*, p. 75, 1972

pixies *noun*

▸ **away with the pixies**

daydreaming *NEW ZEALAND*

• —David McGill, *David McGill's Complete Kiwi Slang Dictionary*, p. 9, 1998

pixilated *adjective*

whimsical, slightly crazy; befuddled; drunk *US, 1848*

• Stiles does a funny little victory dance. A pixilated hornpipe[.]—Jake Arnott, *He Kills Coppers*, p. 98, 2001

pizlum *noun*

a pig's penis *US*

• About the only part of an old pig we don't eat is his pizlum. That's his auger.—Earl Conrad, *Rock Bottom*, p. 246, 1952

pizza *noun*

1 marijuana *US, 1965*

• —Richard A. Spears, *The Slang and Jargon of Drugs and Drink*, p. 393, 1986
• —Mike Haskins, *Drugs*, p. 288, 2003

2 a large area of grazed skin *UK*

Skateboarders' slang; from the appearance of the wound.

• —David Rowan, *A Glossary for the 90s*, 1998

pizza cutter *noun*

in drag racing, an extremely narrow front wheel *US*

• —John Edwards, *Auto Dictionary*, p. 126, 1993
• You see the shoes on that thing? You've got to get some tires for this. It's a pizza cutter, man.—*Dazed and Confused*, 1993

pizza dude *noun*

the pizza delivery person *US*

• —Connie Eble (Editor), *UNC-CH Campus Slang*, p. 8, Spring 1988

pizzaface *noun*

a person with a bad case of acne *US*

• —*Current Slang*, p. 8, Winter 1971

pizza plate *noun*

in electric line work, an insulated tool attachment formally known as a fork suspension attachment *US*

• —A.B. Chance Co., *Lineman's Slang Dictionary*, p. 13, 1980

pizzazz; pizazz; p'zazz *noun*

energy, vim, vigour, excitement *US, 1937*

• I'm not merchandising my product properly. Knuckleball. It's got no pizzaz.—Jim Bouton, *Ball Four*, p. 173, 1970
• [I]f they ever had any pizazz in the first place[!]—Lester Bangs, *Psychotic Reactions and Carburetor Dung*, p. 37, 1970
• The pizzazz had gone out of our lives.—*Raising Arizona*, 1987

PJ *noun*

an unofficial, unlicensed if not illegal, job *TRINIDAD AND TOBAGO, 1990*

An abbreviation of 'private *j*ob'.

• —Lise Winer, *Dictionary of the English/Creole of Trinidad & Tobago*, 2003

PJ's *noun*

pyjamas *US, 1964*

• I'd never get into my brother's Star Trek pjs.—Kitty Churchill, *Thinking of England*, p. 7, 1995
• Next thing I knew I was stuck at the door, sand in my eyes, wearing my pj's with the feet, talking to some Jehovah's Witnesses.—Chris Rock, *Rock This!*, p. 67, 1997
• AUSTIN: I'll get you some PJs. FELICITY: No, I'm ready for bed.—*Austin Powers*, 1999

PK *noun*

*p*reacher's *k*id *US*

Used without regard to denomination or even religion, applied even to children of rabbis; denotating a certain bond among those who have grown up in the shadow of organised religion.

• When one participant revealed the pressures he felt growing up as a "PK – preacher's kid," George W. chuckled. "You think that's tough? Try being a VPK."—Peter Schweizer, *The Bushes*, p. 335, 2004

placa *noun*

a nickname, especially the artistic representation of the nickname on a public wall *US*

Spanish slang used by English-speaking Mexican-Americans.

• —Dagoberto Fuentes and Jose A. Lopez, *Barrio Language Dictionary*, p. 118, 1974
• When off brands venture into the area and flag red, it's the same thing as coming in to cross out [puto mark] the local gang members' placas.—Bill Valentine, *Gangs and Their Tattoos*, p. 113, 2000

placcy; placky; plakky; plaggy; plazzy *adjective*

plastic *UK*

• Back amongst the ponies and the dogs, the rust and plaggy bags.—David Peace, *Nineteen Seventy-Four*, p. 187, 1999
• She hated all them roid-heads [steroid-users] and plazzy gangsters as much as she hated druggies.—Kevin Sampson, *Outlaws*, p. 45, 2001
• I gets my own one out on to the plazzy sheet[.]—Kevin Sampson, *Clubland*, p. 131, 2002
• [T]he crumpled placcy bottle.—Niall Griffiths, *Kelly + Victor*, p. 309, 2002

place *noun*

▸ **you make the place untidy; you are making the place untidy**

used as an ungracious or jocular invitation to be seated *UK*

• Well, sit down then. You make the place untidy.—Clement and La Frenais, *Going Straight*, 1978

placenta poker *noun*

the penis *UK*

Jocular.

• [M]en only discuss their placenta pokers in humorous tones (for example by referring to them as placenta pokers).—Richard Herring, *Talking Cock*, p. 7, 2003

plague *noun*

▸ **the plague**

1 the bleed period of the menstrual cycle *UK, 1961*

2 HIV *US*

• The reason the topmost range of Quarantine is being used, sir, is because it's an opentiered block and it's widely believed you're as scared of heights as you are of the plague.—Seth Morgan, *Homeboy*, p. 351, 1990
• "This immune-deficiency thing." "The plague," Eve said.—Robert Campbell, *Sweet La-La Land*, p. 128, 1990

plague *verb*

to trouble, torment, tease, bother or annoy someone *UK, 1594*

A weakening of the conventional sense.

- [Ian Huntley] had watched each press conference; daily opened and closed the school, the impromptu press centre; plagued us with questions; courted the media. — *The Guardian*, 18th December 2003

plagued *adjective*
infected with HIV *US*

- You don't want not part of Nefertiti. She's plagued, yeah. — Seth Morgan, *Homeboy*, p. 256, 1990

plaguer *noun*
a person infected with HIV *US*

- Every day plaguers are being paroled to spread it in the real world. — Seth Morgan, *Homeboy*, p. 257, 1990

plain Jane *noun*
1 an unremarkably ordinary or unattractive woman *UK, 1912*

- Nancy could go on playing plain-Jane supporting roles in B films for years. — Anne Edwards, *The Reagans*, p. 14, 2003

2 an innocent looking, performance-enhanced unmarked motorway patrol car *US*

- — Lewis Poteet, *Car & Motorcyle Slang*, p. 151, 1992
- But don't take it from me, go ask any uniform sitting in the front seat of a Plain Jane. — Stephen J. Cannell, *The Tin Collectors*, p. 104, 2001

plait your shit!
used for registering dismissal, either of a notion or a person *AUSTRALIA*

- Shut up and go plait your shit! — Barry Humphries, *Bazza Pulls It Off!*, 1971

plamas *noun*
flattery, exaggeration *IRELAND*

- Yes, it will be said that the manager's description of him as the "greatest player on the planet" had an element of plamas to it. — *Irish Examiner*, 19th August 1999

plane *verb*
in the language of wind surfing, to hydroplane *US*

- — Frank Fox, *A Beginner's Guide to Zen and the Art of Windsurfing*, p. 152, 1985: 'A short dictionary of wind surfing terms'

planet *noun*
when combined with a personal characteristic or interest, applied to a person's narrow or exclusive focus on that characteristic or interest *UK*
A remote place that it is hard to contact.

- 'After years of living on Planet Football, spending money they didn't have and expecting tomorrow to take care of tomorrow, clubs now realise they have to change to survive,' says [Jon] Smith. — *The Observer*, 2nd December 2001
- [H]e had definitely emigrated to Planet Paranoid for good. — Ben Elton, *High Society*, p. 116, 2002

▸ **on another planet**
very drug-intoxicated *UK*

- [T]hey were very tight amongst their own, whacked out on another planet but still aware of their like-minded buddies[.] — Wayne Anthony, *Spanish Highs*, p. 11, 1999

Planet Zog *noun*
a supremely unrealistic place; the home of unrealistic ideas; where daydreamers go *UK*
To be said to have arrived from Planet Zog is 'to have no idea what's going on'.

- The new general secretary of the 700,000-member GMB union turned on Mr Johnson after the minister claimed some union leaders took the "occasional day trip" to the "planet Zog" by demanding far-reaching new rights. — *The Guardian*, 17th April 2003

plank *noun*
1 a stupid person *UK*
The phrase **THICK AS TWO SHORT PLANKS** (stupid) gave rise to the adjective **PLANKY** (stupid), hence 'plank'.

- Get real, you plank. — Martin King and Martin Knight, *The Naughty Nineties*, p. 117, 1999
- I don't do things to humiliate you, you plank. I do what I think is right[.] — Kevin Sampson, *Powder*, p. 26, 1999

2 an electric guitar *UK*
From the instrument's original construction in the late 1940s, and an insult hurled at early Fender guitars.

- [A]dd electric guitars, from entry-level planks up to ostensible alternatives to America's best. — Tony Bacon, *Fuzz and Feedback*, p. 12, 2000

3 a heavy surfboard, especially an older wooden one *US*

- "[N]ever seen a girl on those planks!" — Frederick Kohner, *Gidget*, p. 23, 1957
- — John Severson, *Modern Surfing Around the World*, p. 175, 1964

▸ **make the plank**
in homosexual usage, to take the passive position in anal sex *US*

- — *Male Swinger Number 3*, p. 48, 1981: 'The complete gay dictionary'

▸ **put the plank to**
(from a male perspective) to have sex with someone *UK*
A variation of **PLANK** (to have sex) in which 'plank' is understood to be a 'penis'.

- No way is he putting the plank to the lovely Nina. — Kevin Sampson, *Outlaws*, p. 110, 2001

plank *verb*
1 to have sex with *US*
A 'plank' may be a 'floorboard' or, possibly, a 'table'; hence this probably originates from an occurrence on a wooden surface in much the same way as **BED** (to have sex); it may also be a reference to the erect penis which is, no doubt, 'stiff as a board'.

- — Helen Dahlskog (Editor), *A Dictionary of Contemporary and Colloquial Usage*, p. 45, 1972
- They planked on the cinder riding track near 72nd Street on the west side of Central Park and were interrupted by police horses – again at a critical moment. — Ed Sanders, *Tales of Beatnik Glory*, p. 18, 1975

2 to conceal something *UK: SCOTLAND, 1823*

- Where've yi planked the dosh [money]? — Ian Pattison, *Rab C. Nesbitt*, 1988

plank-spanker *noun*
a guitarist *UK*
From **PLANK** (a guitar).

- What they called their Blue Oyster Cult impression, with multiple "plank spankers" — Brian Hinton, *Elvis Costello*, p. 200, 1998

plank-whacker *noun*
a guitarist *UK*
From **PLANK** (a guitar).

- I disliked that plank-whacker from the start. — Mick Farren, *Give the Anarchist a Cigarette*, p. 58, 2001

planky *adjective*
stupid *UK, 1984*
From **THICK AS TWO SHORT PLANKS**.

plant *noun*
1 a person, such as a magician's assistant, who has been secretly placed in an audience, in order to assist whoever is addressing or manipulating that crowd *US, 1926*

2 a police surveillance action *US*

- Sitting on a "plant" – what cops on TV call a stakeout – is like looking at a small section of a street under a microscope. — William J. Cavnitz, *One Police Plaza*, p. 58, 1984

3 a cell used for solitary confinement *US*

- — John R. Armore and Joseph D. Wolfe, *Dictionary of Desperation*, p. 44, 1976

4 an electrical generator *US*

- — Gene Sorrows, *All About Carnivals*, p. 24, 1985: 'Terminology'

5 the equipment and work animals of a drover or other rural worker travelling through the countryside *AUSTRALIA, 1867*

- Nigger smoke-talks had told him of the patrol and of Felix's mustering plant. — Ion L. Idriess, *Over the Range*, p. 44, 1947
- The rest of us went on with the pack-horse plant and I did the cooking. — Herb Wharton, *Cattle Camp*, p. 59, 1994

plant *verb*
1 to bury a body *US, 1855*

- At least she's having him planted decently. — George Mandel, *Flee the Angry Strangers*, p. 372, 1952

2 to deliver a blow; to drive a ball *UK, 1808*

- Geremi moved to take the kick, but another substitute, Maccarone, beat him to it and planted the ball in the corner of the net. — *The Guardian*, 12th January 2003

3 to station a person for use in an underhand manner *UK, 1693*

4 to incriminate someone suspected of a crime by hiding evidence where it is certain to be found by the appropriate authorities *UK, 1865*

- — Angela Devlin, *Prison Patter*, p. 88, 1996

▸ **plant it**
in motor racing, to accelerate to the fullest extent possible *US*

- — John Lawlor, *How to Talk Car*, p. 81, 1965

plantation *noun*

any small garden *CAYMAN ISLANDS*

- A "plantation' is a small piece of tilled ground whhch has been laboriously cleared from the "bush" with a "machete." —Aarona Booker Kohlman, *Wotcha Say*, p. 22, 1985

planting *noun*

a burial *US*

- He said the honors at poor Joe's planting. —John Sayles, *Union Dues*, p. 266, 1977
- GANG BOSS PLANTING THRONGED BY THOUSANDS. —Richard Condon, *Prizzi's Glory*, p. 91, 1988

plant you now, dig you later

used as a farewell *US*

- Well, so long Hank. Plant y'now, dig y'later. — Haenigsen, *Jive's Like That*, 1947
- —Kenn "Naz" Young, *Naz's Underground Dictionary*, p. 50, 1973

plaque whacker *noun*

a dental hygienist *US*

Collected from an orthodontist in Bangor, Maine, April 2001.

plaster-caster *noun*

a groupie who makes plaster casts of celebrities' penises *US, 1968*

- — *Kiss*, 1969: 'Groupie glossary'
- The most famous incident in the Hendrix mythos was his encounter with Cynthia Plaster Caster, a college drop-out whose thing was immortalizing cocks – rock cocks – in plaster. —*Screw*, p. 15, 5th July 1971
- —Robert A. Wilson, *Playboy's Book of Forbidden Words*, p. 197, 1972
- — *Maledicta*, p. 18, Summer 1977: 'A word for it!'
- —Tom Hibbert, *Rockspeak!*, p. 119, 1983

plastered *adjective*

drunk *US, 1912*

- Fell in the river when he was plastered. —Marvin Wald and Albert Maltz, *The Naked City*, 1947
- I took the pieces out of my coat pocket and showed her. "I was plastered," I said. —J.D. Salinger, *Catcher in the Rye*, p. 163, 1951
- Some genius figured you can't get plastered sitting down, forgetting that many who drink and sit can't stand up again. —Jack Lait and Lee Mortimer, *Washington Confidential*, p. 123, 1951
- Now you're plastered, Mother. —Willard Motley, *Let No Man Write My Epitaph*, p. 181, 1958
- He was plastered, I didn't know how. —Clancy Sigal, *Going Away*, p. 25, 1961
- Pane was high but not plastered. —Piri Thomas, *Down These Mean Streets*, p. 96, 1967
- He assumed the risk when he let you drive his bike knowing you were plastered. —Oscar Zeta Acosta, *The Autobiography of a Brown Buffalo*, p. 138, 1972
- In the UK getting plastered in the pub was about as transcendental as it got. —John Robb, *The Nineties*, p. 56, 1999

plaster of Paris; plaster *noun*

the backside, the buttocks *UK*

Rhyming slang, extending the sequence **ARIS – ARISTOTLE – BOTTLE; BOTTLE AND GLASS – ARSE**.

- —Ray Puxley, *Fresh Rabbit*, 1998

plastic *noun*

1 a credit card; consumer credit in general *US*

- These were fifteen-thousand-a-year guys – not paying with plastic, either: hard-earned green. —Vincent Patrick, *The Pope of Greenwich Village*, p. 13, 1979
- Carol was the Queen of Plastic. She could have written books on how to make two grand a day from a hot American Express card. —Gerald Petievich, *Money Men*, p. 35, 1981
- It costs me fifteen bucks for the cab to LAX and a hundred twenty-nine bucks on my plastic to New Orleans. —Robert Campbell, *In La-La Land We Trust*, p. 262, 1986
- What the sponsor will do is give the kid some plastic and about $500 in cash a week[.] —Dan Jenkins, *Dead Solid Perfect*, p. 22, 1986
- —Judi Sanders, *Faced and Faded, Hanging to Hurl*, p. 30, 1993
- He had so many petty thieves, crack-heads and scumbags on his books, changing plastic into paper was a doddle for him. —Danny King, *The Bank Robber Diaries*, p. 53, 2002

2 a person who is liable to act in an unpredictable manner *UK*

- James is evidently an old-code man, with a sharp eye for separating the diamonds (good guys) from the plastics (flaky ones)[.] —*The Guardian*, p. 4, 13th May 2003

3 a condom *US*

- I always pack the plastic. I ain't goin' out like Willy Lump-Lump. —*Menace II Society*, 1993

▸ **on the plastic**

using stolen credit cards, etc *UK*

- —David Powis, *The Signs of Crime*, 1977
- —Angela Devlin, *Prison Patter*, p. 83, 1996

▸ **pull plastic**

(used of a prisoner) to place your belongings in a plastic rubbish bag when you are transferred *US*

- —Jim Crotty, *How to Talk American*, p. 57, 1997

plastic *adjective*

conventional; superficial; shallow *US*

- Plastic people! / Oh, baby, now / You're such a drag. —Frank Zappa, *Plastic People*, 1967
- You talk about a plastic community. Everything you do reflects on your father. —Nicholas Von Hoffman, *We Are The People Our Parents Warned Us Against*, p. 56, 1967
- When you were a child, did you think of your family as up tight and plastic? —Leonard Wolfe (Editor), *Voices from the Love Generation*, p. 216, 1968
- Not like that plastic fashion show. —Fred Baker, *Events*, p. 39, 1970
- Estelle's hips and her thighs were too thick for anyone ever to call her figure "beautiful" in that plastic sense that Miss America is considered "beautiful." —Gurney Norman, *Divine Right's Trip (Last Whole Earth Catalog)*, p. 41, 1971

plastic badge *noun*

a private security guard *US*

- They were stopped by the plastic badge guarding the east gate[.] —Stephen J. Cannell, *The Tin Collectors*, p. 226, 2001

plastic fantastic *noun*

1 a credit card or credit card transation *NEW ZEALAND*

- Swipe 'n' gripe could well be the cry as we pull out the plastic fantastic in the weeks before Christmas to pay for those parties and presents. — *Sunday Star-Times*, p. A17, 3rd Decembere 1995

2 a yacht with a fibreglass hull *NEW ZEALAND*

- The boat is a development of the racer New Zealand trounced in their first venture in their plastic fantastics, the world championships in February. — *Dominion*, p. 24, 9th October 1986

plastic fantastic *adjective*

wonderful *US*

If not coined, widely popularised by Jefferson Airplane's 1967 song, 'Plastic Fantastic Lover'.

- It's a lot of bread. It's like plastic fantastic. —Fred Baker, *Events*, p. 32, 1970

plastic gangster; plastic *noun*

a tough guy who is not anywhere near as tough as he pretends *UK*

- —Angela Devlin, *Prison Patter*, p. 88, 1996
- I don't just mean toe-rags, Jack the Lads or plastic gangsters. I mean men like the Krays who ruled London's underworld. —Lenny McLean, *The Guv'nor*, p. 2, 1998
- Sometimes it was verbal, and sometimes it was physical, particularly from a little crew of "plastics" (wannabe gangsters) led by a man called Moser. — *The Guardian*, 11th May 2000

plastic hippie *noun*

a person who assumes the outer trappings of the counter-culture without fully immersing himself in it *US*

- [Y]ou began to hear stories out of the Haight saying the "real" hippies were taking flight to rural communes and that ersatz plastic hippies and teeni-boppers had taken over. —Nicholas Von Hoffman, *We Are The People Our Parents Warned Us Against*, p. 119, 1967

plastic job *noun*

cosmetic surgery *US*

- The skin had a glossy look along the scars. A plastic job and a pretty drastic one. —Raymond Chandler, *The Long Goodbye*, p. 3, 1953

plastic money *noun*

a credit card or cards; consumer credit in general *US, 1974*

- But plastic money is still under control of the conventional banking system – at the end of the month when the bills arrive, we settle them through a transfer from a bank account. — *The Guardian*, 4th November 1999

plastics *noun*

prison-issue plastic cutlery *UK*

- —Angela Devlin, *Prison Patter*, p. 88, 1996

plate *noun*

1 a plate of food brought by a guest to a party *AUSTRALIA, 1961*

The notion of 'bringing a plate' to supplement the food laid on by the host is an Australian social tradition.

- All players participating in the Inter-town match this Saturday are asked to bring a plate and be at the Town Tennis Club by 8.50 am. — *Herald*, p. 16, 18th July 1984

2 a badge *US*

- — Vincent J. Monteleone, *Criminal Slang*, p. 178, 1949

3 a phonograph record *US, 1935*

- — Frank A. Collymore, *Barbadian Dialect*, p. 85, 1965
- I genuinely like all those same plates of horrid blare and them for pleasure myself[.] — Lester Bangs, *Psychotic Reactions and Carburetor Dung*, p. 376, 1981

▸ on a plate; on a platter
easily acquired; with little or no effort required *UK, 1935*

- [H]is chin was exposed and presented to me on a plate. BOOF! I whacked him smack on the button. — Dave Courtney, *Stop the Ride I Want to Get Off*, p. 246, 1999

plate *verb*

1 to engage in oral sex *UK, 1968*
Rhyming slang for 'plate of ham', **GAM** (to perform oral sex).

- The various chapter prospects were showing everyone how well they could screw and plate her. — Jamie Mandelkau, *Buttons*, p. 99, 1971

2 to engage in oral stimulation of the anus *UK*

- — *Attitude*, July 2003: 'New palare lexicon'

plate and dish *noun*
a wish *UK*
Rhyming slang.

- — Ray Puxley, *Fresh Rabbit*, 1998

plater *noun*

1 in horse racing, a horse that competes in minor, low-paying races *US, 1923*
From the practice of awarding a silver plate instead of a cash prize.

- — Les Conklin, *Payday at the Races*, p. 207, 1974

2 in horse racing, a farrier *US*

- — Tom Ainslie, *Ainslie's Complete Guide to Thoroughbred Racing*, p. 336, 1976

plates and dishes; plates *noun*
a wife *UK*
Rhyming slang for 'missis'.

- — Julian Franklyn, *A Dictionary of Rhyming Slang*, 1960

plates of meat; plates *noun*
the feet *UK*
Rhyming slang since 1857; abbreviated to 'plates' since 1896.

- Now kindly give me my post and remove your great plates off me foot scraper. — Ray Galton and Alan Simpson, *Hancock's Half Hour*, 13th January 1957
- It's me new daisy roots, they're killing me plates. — *The Sweeney*, p. 6, 1976
- [H]e stared at it, lying there at his plates of meat. — Ronnie Barker, *Fletcher's Book of Rhyming Slang*, p. 26, 1979
- A man with a mission: to get the country back on its plates. — Andrew Nickolds, *Back to Basics*, 1994

plats *noun*
platform shoes *US*

- — Vann Wesson, *Generation X Field Guide & Lexicon*, p. 128, 1997

platter *noun*
a phonograph record *US, 1931*

- — Arnold Shaw, *Lingo of Tin-Pan Alley*, p. 17, 1950
- Just on the loose – a half hour at Mary's, let's ooze over to Jo's, say Pete's got a fistful of hot new platters, so let's lend an ear. — Dick Clark, *To Goof or Not to Goof*, p. 103, 1963

platter pusher *noun*
a radio disc jockey *US*

- — Kenn "Naz" Young, *Naz's Underground Dictionary*, p. 50, 1973

platters of meat; platters *noun*
the feet *UK*
Rhyming slang; an elaboration of **PLATES OF MEAT** since 1923; the abbreviation 'platters' since 1945.

play *noun*

1 sexual activity *US*

- — Connie Eble (Editor), *UNC-CH Campus Slang*, p. 3, Fall 1995

2 a manoeuvre; a tactical move *US*

- You got no right for this kind of play. — *48 Hours*, 1982

3 a legitimate scheme or a criminal venture *US*
From the previous sense.

- They weren't always the smoothest plays either, my adventures in self-banking. — Dave Courtney, *Raving Lunacy*, p. 247, 2000

4 the deception surrounding a confidence swindle *US, 1940*

- Now let's join the others at the ghost town for the final tightening up before the play. — *Long White Con*, p. 33, 1977

5 in horse racing, a bet *US*

- — Igor Kushyshyn et al., *The Gambling Times Guide to Harness Racing*, p. 121, 1994

▸ in play
falling into a confidence swindle *US*

- You did great. You got him here. He's in play. — Stephen J. Cannell, *Big Con*, p. 298, 1997

play *verb*
to work as a pimp; to hustle *US*

- I had class, Grief. I never had any filthy low-life junkie bitches when I was playing. — Iceberg Slim (Robert Beck), *Death Wish*, p. 88, 1977

▸ play ball

1 to have sex *US*
Punning on **BALL** (to have sex) and 'play ball' (to cooperate with).

- "You got game?" continued Cochrane. "You can play some ball?" "My game is excellent," replied Jones with evident pride. — *The Observer*, p. 19, 18th March 2001

2 to stop idling and start working *US*

- — Ramon Adams, *The Language of the Railroader*, p. 116, 1977

3 to cooperate with someone else; occasionally applied to inanimate objects such as computers *US*

- His dossier contains three pages of monikers indicating his proclivity for cooperating with the law, "playing ball" the cops call it. — William Burroughs, *Naked Lunch*, p. 157, 1957

▸ play bingo
to try to determine the reason for a cash shortage by comparing orders with receipts *US*

- — *Maledicta*, p. 8, 1996: 'Domino's pizza jargon'

▸ play catch-up
in an athletic contest, to try to catch up and surpass an opponent that at the moment is leading *US, 1971*

- You try not to play catch-up against the Steelers' super defense. — *Washington Post*, p. D4, 20th October 1977

▸ play checkers
to move from empty seat to empty seat in a cinema, looking for a sexual partner *US*
Homosexual usage.

- — Robert A. Wilson, *Playboy's Book of Forbidden Words*, p. 197, 1972

▸ play dead
to act dumb *US*

- — Lavada Durst, *The Jives of Dr. Hepcat*, p. 13, 1953

▸ play for the other team
to be homosexual *US*

- — Jeff Fessler, *When Drag Is Not a Car Race*, p. 39, 1997
- Although I am confident that I can persuade people to play for the other team – I think everyone's sexuality is a lot more fluid than they think it is or would like to be – I was content with our friendship. — *The Village Voice*, 1st July 2002

▸ play handball
to smoke crack cocaine *US*
A highly euphemistic code.

- — Peter Johnson, *Dictionary of Street Alcohol and Drug Terms*, p. 147, 1993

▸ play hard to get
to resist amorous advances (especially while intending to acquiesce); hence, more generally, to be reluctant to comply with what is expected *UK, 1945*

- For months, the Russians have been virtually pleading for the Ljubljana summit, while the Americans have been playing hard to get. — *The Guardian*, 14th June 2001

▸ play hookey; play hooky
to absent yourself from school or work *US, 1848*

- I played hooky more and more often, spending my school hours in burlesque houses. — Jim Thompson, *Bad Boy*, p. 347, 1953
- [W]hen she was 14 or 13 maybe she'd play hookey from school in Oakland and take the ferry to Market Street[.] — Jack Kerouac, *The Subterraneans*, p. 56, 1958
- Some days we played hooky from school, leaving at lunch time with all the other older boys[.] — Bobby Seale, *A Lonely Rage*, p. 29, 1978

▸ **play inside right**
to be mean with money *UK*
Rhyming slang for **TIGHT**, elaborated into football terminology.
- Is he playing inside right again today? — Ray Puxley, *Fresh Rabbit*, 1998

▸ **play it by ear**
to improvise as circumstances dictate *UK, 1984*
As a musician picking up a tune without sheet music to guide.
- "He's fuzz!" a sharper, older voice said from behind the spot. "Inspector Regan," Jack said, playing it by ear. — *The Sweeney*, p. 13, 1976
- Clearly, Yahoo! is playing it by ear. It doesn't want to alienate users or conservative forces, nor does it want to rule out forever a guaranteed moneyspinner. — *The Guardian*, 7th May 2001

▸ **play it cool**
to remain calm and composed *UK, 1942*
- Hart plays it cool as black clouds gather. — *The Guardian*, 3rd November 1999

▸ **play mums and dads; play dads and mums**
to have sex *UK*
An adult version of a children's game. 'Play fathers and mothers' is also recorded but in the strongest current usages it seems that the female comes first.
- — John Gardner, *Madrigal*, 1967
- Let's all play mums and dads, come on / Where do babies come from, mum? / Shut up you naughty boy / And put your clothes back on. — Hazel O'Connor, *We're All Grown-Up*, 1981

▸ **play past something**
to overcome an obstacle or impediment to progress *US*
- Thus, if someone attempts phony excuses one should "play past that shit" and find out the real reasons behind their actions. — Christina and Richard Milner, *Black Players*, p. 39, 1972
- He played it so good 'til he played past the real New York finest a number of times to my knowledge. — A.S. Jackson, *Gentleman Pimp*, p. 130, 1973
- If anybody ask who you are, tell them it's none of their motherfuckin business. Just play past that shit. — Terry Williams, *The Cocaine Kids*, p. 28, 1989

▸ **play silly buggers**
to be a nuisance; to cause trouble or disruption; to 'mess about' *UK*
- But if I played what he called "silly buggers", he could be very, very hard. Sadly my insinct was telling me that on this case I was going to be playing silly buggers. — Malcolm Pryce, *Aberystwyth Mon Amour*, p. 27, 2001

▸ **play someone cheap**
to assume that someone is stupid *US*
- — Marcus Hanna Boulware, *Jive and Slang of Students in Negro Colleges*, 1947

▸ **play the blocks**
to idle on a street corner *BAHAMAS*
- — John A. Holm, *Dictionary of Bahamian English*, p. 157, 1982

▸ **play the chill**
1 to act calm *US, 1920*
- Blue whispered, "Play the chill for him. Remember, son, he's not bunco, he's only robbery detail." — Iceberg Slim (Robert Beck), *Trick Baby*, p. 13, 1969

2 to snub someone *US*
- — M. Allen Henderson, *How Con Games Work*, p. 222, 1985: 'Glossary'

▸ **play the curbs**
to sell drugs on the street *US*
- — Ellen C. Bellone (Editor), *Dictionary of Slang*, p. 18, 1989

▸ **play the queens**
to have sex with a passive, effeminate male prisoner *US*
- — Inez Cardozo-Freeman, *The Joint*, p. 522, 1984

▸ **play the whale**
to vomit *AUSTRALIA*
- Go on lady, play the whale, but I'll bet youse a greenie [$1 note] it won't look nothin' like what youse had for lunch!!! — Barry Humphries, *Bazza Pulls It Off!*, 1971

▸ **play them as they lay**
used as a wisely humorous acceptance of the need to work with what has been given to you *US*
- You gotta play 'em as they lay, Luther. — *A Few Good Men*, 1992

▸ **play too close**
to take advantage of another's good nature by excessive teasing or abuse *US*
- — William K. Bentley and James M. Corbett, *Prison Slang*, p. 93, 1992

▸ **play took and banjo**
to sing or whistle a secular tune on a Sunday or religious holiday *BARBADOS*
- — *Barbadian Dialect*, p. 15, 1965

▸ **play up to someone**
to humour someone; to flatter someone, to take your cue from another; to behave according to expectations *UK, 1809*
Originally in theatrical use.
- The ailing pontiff – dressed in white robes and frail with Parkinson's disease – has played up to his image as a chief dove in the Iraqi crisis[.] — *The Guardian*, 26th March 2003

▸ **play with yourself**
to masturbate *IRELAND, 1922*
The earliest usage recorded of this sweet little euphemism is by James Joyce.
- He kept right on playing with himself, all through high school, in the face of certain insanity. — Larry McMurtry, *The Last Picture Show*, p. 165, 1966
- I was repeatedly warned from the nuns and priests that I hung around with that masturbation was wrong, that playing with myself would lead to cancer and warts. — *Screw*, p. 2, 29 November 1968
- FRANK: This is your bed. And you're alone, right, and you're playing with yourself. KRISTIN: I don't play with myself. — Fred Baker, *Events*, p. 39, 1970

play around *verb*
to have an extra-marital amorous liaison *US, 1943*
- It seems that Mark was playing around and his wife found out. — Jimmy Stockin, *On The Cobbles*, p. 172, 2000

play-away *noun*
a weekend at someone else's place in the country *UK*
Upper-class society usage; predates BBC television childrens' programme *Playaway*, 1984.
- — Ann Barr and Peter York, *The Official Sloane Ranger Handbook*, p. 159, 1982

playback *noun*
a scheme by which the odds on a particular horse race are engineered lower by heavy betting on that horse *US*
- The explanation was reasonable. Playback – knocking the odds down on a horse by heavy pari-mutuel betting – was common in big-time bookmaking. — Jim Thompson, *The Grifters*, p. 41, 1963

Playboy *noun*
a tablet of MDMA, the recreational drug best known as ecstasy *UK*
- I only took half a Playboy and Connor was saying they're not all that strong. — Colin Butts, *A Bus Could Run You Over*, p. 155, 2004

▸ **the Playboy**
a pubic hairstyle *UK*
- The Playboy[:] All hair is removed from the labia and the buttocks, and only a very narrow strip is left. — *Loaded*, p. 5, June 2002

play dough *noun*
bread found in a US Army combat ration *US*
Word play on the inedible mix of flour, water and salt called 'play dough' and played with by children.
- — Linda Reinberg, *In the Field*, p. 168, 1991

played *adjective*
out of money *US*
- — Connie Eble (Editor), *UNC-CH Campus Slang*, p. 6, Fall 1984

player *noun*
1 a person who takes pride in the number of sexual partners they have, not in the depth of any relationship; a selfish pleasure-seeker *US*
- — *Current Slang*, p. 37, Fall 1968
- They were pimps in those days and not players. — Robert Deane Pharr, *Giveadamn Brown*, p. 15, 1978
- — Edith A. Folb, *runnin' down some lines*, p. 250, 1980

2 a pimp *US*
- He is then no longer a pimp but a player, perhaps even a boss (excellent, tops) player. — Christina and Richard Milner, *Black Players*, p. 34, 1972
- It's almost inevitable that a prostitute ends up with a player. It's hand and glove. — Susan Hall, *Gentleman of Leisure*, p. 4, 1972
- After kicking things like that around with the city's biggest pimps and players and smoking a lotta good pot, I went into the hat shop to get my stumps shined. — A.S. Jackson, *Gentleman Pimp*, p. 27, 1973

3 a schemer; an important figure in a field *US*
- Harry Zimm. The man happens to be a major Hollywood player. — *Get Shorty*, 1995

• George chats away harmlessly, telling the brothers about his days as a sinner, about his days as a player in the criminal underworld of East London and Essex. — Mark Powell, *Snap*, p. 54, 2001

4 a drug user or drug seller *US*

• — Eugene Landy, *The Underground Dictionary*, p. 152, 1971

5 an active member of a terrorist organisation *UK*

Used by police, military and other security services.

• This meant the players could prepare in Dundalk on the other side [of the border], then pop over and shoot at us. — Andy McNab, *Immediate Action*, p. 21, 1995

6 in casino gambling, a craps player *US*

• In Las Vegas parlance, a blackjack player is never called anything except "a twenty-one player" and a craps player is never called anything except "a player." — Edward Lin, *Big Julie of Vegas*, p. 182, 1974

7 a hip-hop artist *US*

Also variant 'playa'.

• — *Touch*, January–February 2002: 'Too short – the original Californian playa'

player hater *noun*

someone who is envious or jealous of another's social success *US*

• — Connie Eble (Editor), *UNC-CH Campus Slang*, p. 6, Spring 1999

player of the pink oboe *noun*

a person who performs oral sex on a man *UK*

Coined by satirist Peter Cook (1937–95) for a sketch performed in Amnesty International's *The Secret Policeman's Ball*.

• [A] scrounger, parasite, pervert, a worm, a self-confessed player of the pink oboe, a man or woman who by his own admission chews pillows. — Peter Cook, *Entirely a Matter for You*, 1979

play-for-pay *adjective*

1 available for paid sex *US*

• That title must have rasied plenty of eyebrows among Hollywood's play-for-pay girls [.] — *Confidential*, p. 17, July 1956

2 receiving compensation while competing as an amateur athlete *US*

• But a few days before the SEC tournament opened, Georgia administrators were forced to cancel the rest of the season and fire coach Jim Harrick because of an academic fraud and play-for-pay scandal. — *Pittsburgh Post-Gazette*, p. C1, 30th December 2003

playground's muddy *noun*

experiencing the bleed period of the menstrual cycle *US*

• Sorry, no sex, playground's muddy. — *The Museum of Menstruation and Women's Health*, January 2001

playing *noun*

amongst women prisoners, homosexual flirtation and involvement *UK*

• — Sean McConville, *The State of the Language*, 1980

playing bingo *adjective*

in prison, said of a sex offender *UK*

From the call of the numbers in **RULE FORTY-THREE**.

• — Angela Devlin, *Prison Patter*, p. 23, 1996

playing with confederate money *adjective*

having silicone breast implants *US*

Very impressive to look at but ultimately valueless. Coined for US television comedy *Seinfeld*, 1993–98.

• — Susie Dent, *The Language Report*, p. 146, 2003

play-lunch *noun*

a mid-morning break at primary school; also, the food eaten during this break *AUSTRALIA*

• [S]hrill cries from the playground announced that the children were out for play-lunch. — Dymphna Cusack, *Picnic Races*, p. 82, 1962

playmates *noun*

the testicles *UK*

• — *A–Z of Rude Health*, 11th January 2002

play out *verb*

1 (of a DJ) to perform in public; (of a dance record) to be included in a DJ's repertoire *UK*

• This is one of those records that I picked up purely for pleasure – I don't know if I've ever played it out. — *Muzik*, p. 24, February 2003

• Once I actually "played out" in a local pub. — *Muzik*, p. 21, February 2003

2 to escape from confinement *US*

• So I was there I guess three or four months and I played out [escaped]. — Bruce Jackson, *In the Life*, p. 110, 1972

play-play *adjective*

make-believe *BARBADOS*

• — Frank A. Collymore, *Barbadian Dialect*, p. 85, 1965

playtime *noun*

a time in a prison's schedule when the inmates are out of their cells mixing with each other *UK*

From school usage.

• — Angela Devlin, *Prison Patter*, p. 88, 1996

plazzy *adjective*

▷ see: **PLACCY**

please; per-lease; puh-lease

used for humorously asking please or expressing scepticism *US*

An affectation popularised in any number of television situation comedies in the mid- to late 1980s and thereafter a staple of US popspeak.

• — Connie Eble (Editor), *UNC-CH Campus Slang*, p. 4, Fall 1990

• Puh-leeeze, Nelson! I'm getting seasick. — Joseph Wambaugh, *Fugitive Nights*, p. 134, 1992

• Oh, puh-leez, why don't you take a handful of F-off pills? — *Austin Powers*, 1999

• "With under eighteens?" He raised his eyebrows. "Per-lease!" — Mary Hooper, *(megan)2*, p. 127, 1999

pleasure and pain *noun*

rain *UK*

Rhyming slang.

• — Julian Franklyn, *A Dictionary of Rhyming Slang*, 1960

pleb *noun*

1 an unsophisticated or uneducated person *UK, 1865*

An abbreviation of conventional 'plebeian' (a lower-class person).

• pseudo-clever tapping of popular culture, letting the journo [journalist] know that he's not a pleb — Kevin Sampson, *Powder*, p. 5, 2000

• I had respect alright. And not just from the plebs. — Danny King, *The Bank Robber Diaries*, p. 18, 2002

2 an annoying person; a nuisance *UK*

A generally derogative application of the sense as 'a plebeian'.

• — Peter Chippindale, *The British CB Book*, p. 158, 1981

pleb; plebbie; plebby *adjective*

of a plebeian character; coarse; uneducated *UK, 1962*

• Tony Banks, the plebby Labour MP[.] — *The Guardian*, 22nd May 2002

pleckie *noun*

a *plec*trum *UK: SCOTLAND*

• — Michael Munro, *The Patter, Another Blast*, p. 55, 1988

pledges *noun*

cash *US*

• Candy, markers, ammo, liners, stocking stuffer, sweetener, garnish, and pledges are all terms for cash. — Henry Hill and Byron Schreckengost, *A Good Fella's Guide to New York*, p. 123, 2003

plenty *adverb*

very *UK, 1934*

• Not that there aren't lots of folks who haven't found themselves plenty upset looking back at the theological steamroller of a Christian education[.] — *Orange County Weekly*, 27th June 2003

• [N]o woman I've ever met thinks her breasts are plenty big enough. — Jeremy Clarkson, *The Times*, 25th May 2003

plenty-plenty *adverb*

to a great extent *BAHAMAS*

• — John A. Holm, *Dictionary of Bahamian English*, p. 157, 1982

plier *noun*

in a confidence swindle or sales scheme, an agent who for a commission locates potential victims *US*

• — Kathleen Odean, *High Steppers, Fallen Angels, and Lollipops*, p. 133, 1988

pliers *noun*

a railway ticket inspector's punch *US*

• — Norman Carlisle, *The Modern Wonder Book of Trains and Railroading*, p. 266, 1946

plimmie *noun*

a plimsoll (a rubber-soled canvas shoe) *UK*

• Seb Coe's decided to follow in the plimmies of the great Christopher Chataway and run for Parliament instead[.] — Andrew Nickolds, *Back to Basics*, p. 138, 1994

pling *noun*

an exclamation mark (!) on a computer keyboard *US*

- —Eric S. Raymond, *The New Hacker's Dictionary*, p. 39, 1991

pling *verb*

in circus and carnival usage, to beg *US*

- —Don Wilmeth, *The Language of American Popular Entertainment*, p. 204, 1981

plink *noun*

cheap wine *AUSTRALIA, 1943*

Variant of **PLONK** with a change of vowel influenced by other couplets such as 'ding dong', 'sing song'.

- He was so far gone down the path to physical and mental ruin that no one had the heart to refuse him a drink when he came begging for one; anything came well to the Kidger, plonk, plink, metho, bombo, or just ordinary whisky.—Ruth Park, *Poor Man's Orange*, p. 107, 1949

plinker *noun*

an inexpensive, simply designed gun marketed for casual use *US*

- —Ralph de Sola, *Crime Dictionary*, p. 115, 1982

plod; plodder; PC Plod; Mr Plod; the plod *noun*

a uniformed police officer; the police *UK, 1977*

Derives from Mr Plod the Policeman, a character in the Noddy stories of Enid Blyton (1897–1968), possibly a pun on 'plodding the beat' or, simply, 'to plod' (to proceed tediously).

- "It's the plods, chucking bricks," said a soul-boy, giggling in disbelief—*New Society*, 16th July 1981
- [T]he local plod has been issued with its new night-sticks[.]—Andrew Nickolds, *Back to Basics*, p. 26, 1994
- I'm too old and fat to be running around the streets and swerving Plod.—Martin King and Martin Knight, *The Naughty Nineties*, p. 121, 1999
- A convoy of 150 plod descended on us, believe it or not.—Dave Courtney, *Stop the Ride I Want to Get Off*, p. 148, 1999
- I pleaded with the plodder in charge that I'd just bought the car[.] —Wayne Anthony, *Spanish Highs*, p. 32, 1999
- So this time these two plods came around.—Dave Courtney, *Raving Lunacy*, p. 12, 2000
- Trevor John Atkins to Mister Plod and Kinky to his confederates. —J.J. Connolly, *Layer Cake*, p. 62, 2000
- [T]wo sergeants, a handful of us lads, and a couple of plonks – women police constables to the rest of the world. We're plods, they're plonks.—Duncan MacLaughlin, *The Filth*, p. 93, 2002

ploddite *noun*

a police officer *UK*

- One's a retired ploddite, dunno what rank.—Jonathan Gash, *The Ten Word Game*, p. 71, 2003

plod shop *noun*

a police station *UK*

- —Angela Devlin, *Prison Patter*, p. 88, 1996

plokta *verb*

in computing, to press keys randomly in an effort to obtain a response from the computer *US*

An acronym of '*p*ress *l*ots *o*f *k*eys *t*o *a*bort'.

- —Eric Raymond et al., *The New Hacker's Dictionary*, p. 284, 1991

plonk *noun*

1 cheap wine *AUSTRALIA, 1930*

Alteration of French *blanc*, from *vin blanc* (white wine); occasionally used of other alcoholic drinks. Ray Puxley, in *Cockney Rabbit*, 1992, endorses the case for rhyming slang 'plink plonk'.

- A bottle of cheap plonk.—Eric Lambert, *The Veterans*, p. 70, 1954
- Beer's the only drink fer a workin' man. Whisky makes yer silly. An' plonk'll rot yer boots.—Nino Culotta (John O'Grady), *They're A Weird Mob*, p. 50, 1957
- As it is, there's still plonk and spirits on the shelves.—Arthur Upfield, *Bony and the Mouse*, p. 22, 1959
- I poured some plonk and we got down to it.—Harrison Biscuit, *The Search for Savage Henry*, p. 13, 1995
- [A] three-course meal washed down with five or six bottles of plonk. —Wayne Anthony, *Spanish Highs*, p. 91, 1999
- Home-made plonk! Plus a little extra something.—Duncan MacLaughlin, *The Filth*, p. 104, 2002

2 alcohol, especially beer *NEW ZEALAND*

- —Louis S. Leland, *A Personal Kiwi-Yankee Dictionary*, p. 78, 1984

3 a woman police constable *UK*

- —Angela Devlin, *Prison Patter*, p. 88, 1996
- [T]wo sergeants, a handful of us lads, and a couple of plonks – women police constables to the rest of the world. We're plods, they're plonks.—Duncan MacLaughlin, *The Filth*, p. 93, 2002

4 the surreptitious wagering of a large amount of money *AUSTRALIA*

- 'Must be one big plonk,' he said. 'Can anyone get in on it?'—Gerald Sweeney, *The Plunge*, p. 418, 1981
- 'Bit of a plonk on your horse mate. Did you get the eleven-to-four they bet out the back?—Clive Galea, *Slipper*, p. 64, 1988
- —Ned Wallish, *The Truth Dictionary of Racing Slang*, p. 63, 1989

plonk *verb*

1 to place something, especially with a lack of finesse *AUSTRALIA, 1942*

- [S]he plonked one [a kiss] on me chops[.]—Barry Humphries, *Bazza Pulls It Off!*, 1971

2 (of a male), to have sex *UK, 1984*

In use among National Servicemen in the 1950s.

3 to wager money *AUSTRALIA*

- So he plonked five dollars on Harry White.—Gerald Sweeney, *The Plunge*, p. 174, 1981

plonker; plonk *noun*

1 the penis *UK*

Not recorded in print before 1947.

- Man with the biggest plonker in the world / (Dingle, dangle, strap it to your ankle)[.]—Ivor Biggun, *John Thomas Allcock*, 1981

2 a fool; used (often humorously) as an everyday form of abuse *UK, 1966*

Euphemistic extension of the previous sense for name-calling as **PRICK**. Popularised from the early 1980s by BBC television situation comedy *Only Fools and Horses*.

- [P]lonker (pa-lon-ka.) n. a person of very low intelligence, prone to cocking up and sending the whole deal down the khazi.—John Sullivan, *The Bible of Peckam /Trotter Dictionary*, p. 3, 1999
- I love my sarong and can easily understand why David Beckham was prepared to look a plonker in one of the tabloids.—Wayne Anthony, *Spanish Highs*, p. 14, 1999
- [W]e forgave him for being such a plonker[.]—James Hawes, *Dead Long Enough*, p. 43, 2000
- "I thought you were one of us." Ace laughed. "I still am you plonker."—Colin Butts, *Is Harry Still on the Boat?*, p. 258, 2003

plonkie *adjective*

foolish; displaying the qualities of a plonker *UK*

- Fucking deadbeat [idler] that I am, plonkie half a fucking playboy that I've become.—Kevin Sampson, *Outlaws*, p. 190, 2001

plonko *noun*

an alcoholic *AUSTRALIA, 1963*

- We could go and see if there's any plonkos under Martin's Bridge and chuck rocks at 'em.—William Dick, *A Bunch of Ratbags*, p. 69, 1965
- —Harvey E. Ward, *Down Under Without Blunder*, p. 43, 1967
- —Arthur Chipper, *The Aussie Swearer's Guide*, p. 67, 1972

ploo *adjective*

a 'plus' attached to a grade *US*

- —Collin Baker et al., *College Undergraduate Slang Study Conducted at Brown University*, p. 174, 1968

plook *noun*

▷ **see: PLUKE**

plooky *adjective*

pimply, spotty *UK: SCOTLAND*

Extended from **PLUKE; PLOOK** (a spot).

- Naw, no the wan wi the plooky face.—Michael Munro, *The Patter*, p. 54, 1985

plootered *adjective*

drunk *UK*

Probably from Scottish *plouter* (to splash in water).

plop *noun*

excrement *US*

- In yore, did farmers rush to shovel the plop?—Bill Cardoso, *The Maltese Sangweech*, p. 134, 1984

plop *verb*

to fall or to drop heavily *UK, 1839*

- I couldn't just plop down and sit on the couch.—Howard Stern, *Miss America*, p. 125, 1995

- I simply shoved him on my bed and made him stay there until I had the time to plop down at the end of the party. —Jennifer Blowdryer, *White Trash Debutante*, p. 82, 1997

plop down *verb*
to lay down forcefully; to lie down with abandon *US*
- Grover came in and plopped down on a bench and sighed. —Dan Jenkins, *Dead Solid Perfect*, p. 104, 1986

ploppy *noun*
an unskilled gambler who describes his systems to all around him *UK*
- —Frank Scoblete, *Best Blackjack*, p. 268, 1996

plot up *verb*
1 to establish a singular, group or gang presence in an area and represent it as the territory of that individual, group or gang *UK*
- Someone said West Ham were plotted up outside the Cold Blow Lane. — Martin King and Martin Knight, *The Naughty Nineties*, p. 96, 1999
- I told you we should have plotted up outside Burns's drum [home]. —J.J. Connolly, *Know Your Enemy [britpulp]*, p. 158, 1999

2 to conceal something *UK*
- A mate of mine, Boris, was in prison and when he came out he wanted to get back a gun that he's plotted up in someone's house[.] —Dave Courtney, *Dodgy Dave's Little Black Book*, p. 81, 2001

plotzed *adjective*
drunk *US, 1962*
From German *plotzen* (to burst) via Yiddish *plotz* (to burst).
- [S]he was drunker than she'd been in years, plotzed, zonked, a mess. —Lester Bangs, *Psychotic Reactions and Carburetor Dung*, p. 364, 1981

plow *noun*
marijuana *UK*
The means by which you become **PLOWED** (drug-intoxicated).
- —Mike Haskins, *Drugs*, p. 288, 2003

▶ **get your plow cleaned**
to be killed in combat *US*
- —Carl Fleischhauer, *A Glossary of Army Slang*, p. 6, 1968

plow *verb*
(used of a male) to have sex *US*
- He's so horny he'd plow a dead alligator or even a live one if somebody'd hold the tail. —Joseph Wambaugh, *The New Centurions*, p. 55, 1970
- Dorsey can plow whoever he wants. — *Ten Things I Hate About You*, 1999

▶ **plow the field**
to drive off the road at a high rate of speed into a field *US*
- — *American Speech*, p. 271, December 1962: 'The language of traffic policemen'

plowboy *noun*
a rustic; an unsophisticated person from the far reaches of the countryside *UK, 1569*
Disparaging.
- New York gets its share, but its tourists include many from fairly alive communities; the plowboys hail from New England or other points not very far away. —Jack Lait and Lee Mortimer, *Washington Confidential*, p. 3, 1951

plowed *adjective*
1 drunk *US*
- "It gets better the more you drink," said Joey, on his third. After a while, everyone was plowed. —Richard Price, *The Wanderers*, p. 141, 1974
- "You have one drink a year, and your low tolerance gets you plowed." —James Ellroy, *Because the Night*, p. 431, 1984
- "I did not get drunk," she said absently. "You and Frank did. You got absolutely plowed." —George V. Higgins, *Penance for Jerry Kennedy*, p. 202, 1985

2 drug-intoxicated *US, 1981*
From the previous sense.
- —Richard A. Spears, *The Slang and Jargon of Drugs and Drink*, p. 394, 1986

plow jockey *noun*
1 a farmer *US, 1951*
- — *American Speech*, p. 158–159, May 1960: 'The burgeoning of 'Jockey''

2 a soldier who cannot keep cadence when marching, who appears to be walking as if behind a plough with one foot in the furrow *US*
- — *American Speech*, p. 238, October 1946: 'World War II slang of maladjustment'

plu *noun*
tea *AUSTRALIA*
- 'Plu?' 'Yeah.' Windy poured the strong tea into a thick cup. —J.E. MacDonnell, *Don't Gimme the Ships*, p. 69, 1960

pluck *noun*
1 wine *US, 1964*
- We went and got some "pluck" (wine) and I told him I was in college. — H. Rap Brown, *Die Nigger Die!*, p. 24, 1969
- But the brothers passed the pluck, putting the top back on after each sip, and conjectured anyway. —Steve Cannon, *Groove, Bang, and Jive Around*, p. 154, 1969
- What about China? I missed that runnin' to the git the pluck. —Odie Hawkins, *Ghetto Sketches*, p. 81, 1972
- Sid Strove said, watching a huddle of winos in front of an abandoned store nip at pints of strong port combined with sweet sherry in a mixture known as "pluck" —Emmett Grogan, *Final Score*, p. 157, 1976
- Mr. Chickens, his four super-obedient hens delicately high-stepping around him and his ace, the Spinning Top Dude, stood under the lengthening shadow of a fire escape, just around an alley corner's edge, trying to defeat the autum evening's chill with a pluck. —Donald Goines, *The Busting Out of an Ordinary Man*, p. 47, 1985
- The first time he showed up he was strolling across the grass sipping pluck from a bottle of Thunderbird[.] —Clarence Major, *All-Night Visitors*, p. 145, 1998

2 the recruiting of a prostitute to work for a pimp; a prostitute recruited to work for a pimp *US*
- While I was ripping and running up and down Hastings trying to catch a pluck from all the whore bars, there was a little girl named Ruth who had been watching me[.] —A.S. Jackson, *Gentleman Pimp*, p. 34, 1973

pluck *verb*
1 to recruit a prostitute into the services of a pimp *US*
- A lotta outlaw girls were there and I felt I'd be able to pluck off one of 'em. —A.S. Jackson, *Gentleman Pimp*, p. 91, 1973

2 (used of a male) to have sex with a virgin *BAHAMAS*
- —John A. Holm, *Dictionary of Bahamian English*, p. 157, 1982

▶ **pluck the chicken**
to swindle a victim in a phony investment or sales scheme *US*
- —Kathleen Odean, *High Steppers, Fallen Angels, and Lollipops*, p. 133, 1988

plucky *adjective*
brave, daring *UK, 1842*
- —Ann Barr and Peter York, *The Official Sloane Ranger Handbook*, p. 159, 1982

plug *noun*
1 a piece of publicity, a promotional pitch *US, 1902*
- Getting these songs before the public, or as the trade terms it, the "plug," is perhaps the soul of the industry. —Jack Lait and Lee Mortimer, *New York Confidential*, p. 32, 1948
- When it begins to rain, the dancers begin an anti-rain dance and it stops. The leader concludes with a plug for his studio, which teaches dance, song, drums, and karate. —James Simon Kunen, *The Strawberry Statement*, p. 48, 1969
- [T]hey started reading from Timothy Leary's Psychedelic Prayer Book. He has published two and I want to put in a plug for both of them. —Richard Neville, *Play Power*, p. 237, 1970

2 a tampon *US*
Understood to be a variation on conventional 'plug', possibly from abbreviation of technical jargon 'catamenial plug' (a tampon).
- — *The Museum of Menstruation and Women's Health*, May 2001

3 a bullet hole *UK*
- —Dave Courtney, *Dodgy Dave's Little Black Book*, p. 7, 2001

4 a poker player with a steady, competent and predictable style of play *US*
- —George Percy, *The Language of Poker*, p. 68, 1988

5 a horse that has seen its best days *US, 1860*
- There are five half-mile tracks in Maryland, which run almost all year with unknown plugs and has-beens, raced by "Gypsy" horsemen. —Jack Lait and Lee Mortimer, *Washington Confidential*, p. 273, 1951

6 a temporary worker *US*
- —Vann Wesson, *Generation X Field Guide and Lexicon*, p. 128, 1997

plug *verb*
1 to support, to endorse, to promote *US, 1927*
- —Lou Shelly, *Hepcats Jive Talk Dictionary*, p. 16, 1945
- But a late development in the business, one which suspiciously smacks of a restraint of trade violation, is the practice of some publishers of giving a stock interest in their firms to noted crooners, band leaders, and disc jockeys, who in return "plug" the latest publications of the companies in which they are interested. —Jack Lait and Lee Mortimer, *New York Confidential*, p. 32, 1948
- "I'm still plugging for you," Owens said. —Jim Bouton, *Ball Four*, p. 348, 1970

2 to shoot someone *US, 1870*

- "Listen, rat" – Benny's face paled – "one more word like that and I'll plug you too. They can only burn me once, and I'd just as soon knock you off to stay alive as not." — Irving Shulman, *The Amboy Dukes*, p. 85, 1947
- Heah, go on over and plug that dame in the belly! Get real kicks! — John Clellon Holmes, *Go*, p. 13, 1952
- Fuck The Politics, Plug The Brits, and by Christ you can name your tune[.] — James Hawes, *Dead Long Enough*, p. 105, 2000
- [H]e pointed his gun at the back of the unconscious driver's head and pulled the trigger. Click! "Shit, I'm out, plug him and let's get going," he said. "Plug him?" — Danny King, *The Bank Robber Diaries*, p. 154, 2002

3 (of a male) to have sex with someone *UK*

- You'd be lookin' old as sin too, if you was floppin' up and down bein' plugged by twenty or thirty tricks a night. — Odie Hawkins, *Ghetto Sketches*, p. 20, 1972
- Then old Buck comes around and plugs her dog fashion while she's goin down on me. — Earl Thompson, *Tattoo*, p. 225, 1974
- I spent four fucking hours at Slater Hawkins last night, trying to plug a chick I wouldn't have sneezed at in college. — Armistead Maupin, *Tales of the City*, p. 218, 1978
- — *Maledicta*, p. 250, 1983: 'A Connotative analysis of synonyms for sexual intercourse'

4 to insert contraband items into the anus during a prison visit *UK*

- — Angela Devlin, *Prison Patter*, p. 89, 1996

5 to engage in a fist fight without any weapons *US*

- — William K. Bentley and James M. Corbett, *Prison Slang*, p. 90, 1992

6 on the railways, to use the reverse gear to help stop a train *US*

- — Ramon Adams, *The Language of the Railroader*, p. 116, 1977

7 to tease or taunt someone *US*

- — Gary K. Farlow, *Prison-ese*, p. 52, 2002

▸ plug in

to help *US*

In the usage of counterculturalists associated with the Rainbow Nation gatherings.

- — Jim Crotty, *How to Talk American*, p. 289, 1997

▸ plug in both ways

(of a male), to be bisexual *UK*

A play on **AC/DC**.

- — D. Kavanagh, *Duffy*, 1980

▸ plug your mug

to stop talking *US*

- — Marcus Hanna Boulware, *Jive and Slang of Students in Negro Colleges*, 1947
- — Clarence Major, *Dictionary of Afro-American Slang*, p. 92, 1970

plug away; plug *verb*

to continue doing something or making an effort, to persist doggedly *UK, 1865*

- I have told the players what I think; now we need to keep plugging away and keep believing. — *The Guardian*, 30th December 2002

plugged in *adjective*

connected to something fashionable *US*

- In order to gain status at the university, a professor or composer in residence has to be plugged into something that's really hot – something fundable[.] — Frank Zappa, *The Real Frank Zappa Book*, p. 189, 1989

plugged nickel *noun*

literally, a five-cent piece that has been altered by the insertion of a plug of base metal; figuratively, something of no value *US*

- But your promises aren't worth a plugged nickel, are they? — Robert Campbell, *Juice*, p. 130, 1988

plugger *noun*

a person whose job it is to promote a record or recording artist *US*

- This singer – he was an old-time song plugger! — William J. Spillard and Pence James, *Needle in a Haystack*, p. 77, 1945

plughole *noun*

▸ go down the plughole

to become lost; to go to waste; to fail *UK, 1973*

A variation of **DOWN THE DRAIN**.

- [diary entry 20th January 1997] If we all go anti-European we'll go glug-glug down the plughole. — Gyles Brandreth, *Breaking the Code*, p. 455, 1999
- When Packet of Three was slowly going down the comedy plughole, the Perrier Award turned up and saved my comedy bacon. — Frank Skinner, *Frank Skinner*, p. 340, 2001

plug-ugly *noun*

a violent, rough person *US, 1856*

- Then the plug-ugly moonshiner was leaning over the tombstone and grabbing me around the neck, hard, — Guy Owen, *The Flim-Flam Man and the Apprentice Grifter*, p. 68, 1972

pluke; plook *noun*

a spot, boil or other pus-filled skin blemish *UK*

Directly from Scottish dialect *plook*.

- He's six foot plus with plooks bustin' out his face an' mouth[.] — Nick Barlay, *Curvy Lovebox*, p. 50, 1997

plum *noun*

1 the testicle *UK*

From its shape and fruitfulness. One notable precursor to its unambiguous sense as a testicle is in the innuendo-laden song 'Please Don't Touch My Plums' by Sammy Cahn, 1913–93, written for the film *The Duchess and the Dirtwater Fox*, 1976, in which it was sung in a Golden Globe-winning performance by Goldie Hawn.

- [A] foolhardy procedure that resulted in him smacking one plum square-on and cutting the other with broken glass — *FHM*, p. 250, June 2003

2 a fool; used as a general term of abuse *UK*

From the previous sense.

- Look you, plums – me an' him're in front of the Fraud Section this mornin' because of you[.] — Alan Bleasdale, *Boys From the Blackstuff*, 1982
- Course he's not, you plum, the squat man said, half laughing. — John King, *White Trash*, p. 148, 2001
- Some plum opens the door, looking at you like, "Er – can I help you?" — Julian Johnson, *Urban Survival*, p. 34, 2003

3 an exceptional person or thing *AUSTRALIA*

- 'I hear his wife is a plum,' Blaze said, kissing his fingers. — Kylie Tennant, *The Honey Flow*, p. 101, 1956
- 'Is this good, by the way?' 'An absolute plum, I reckon.' — John Wynnum, *Jiggin' in the Riggin'*, p. 13, 1965
- There you are, gentlemen, here's a real plum. — Sam Weller, *Old Bastards I Have Met*, p. 93, 1979

4 in marketing, a married man with above-average income who is keen to improve his pension *UK*

A specific sense of the general use of 'plum' as 'something desirable'. The opposite is a **LEMON**.

- — David Rowan, *Glossary for the 90s*, p. 106, 1998

5 in pool, the plum-coloured four-ball *US*

- If you're playing Nine-Ball and you've sunk the 1-, 2- and 3-balls, you'd best pick the plum. — Steve Rushin, *Pool Cool*, p. 23, 1990

6 in pool, an easy shot *US*

- [I]t was an unnecessary shot, because Al really had plums all over the table[.] — Gilbert Sorrentino, *Steelwork*, p. 161, 1970

plumb; plum *adverb*

abolutely; completely; utterly *UK, 1587*

From the earlier, conventional sense (exactly).

- I can't seem to understand what is happening to the United States. But what I can gather is it's just plumb crazy. — *The [Acadiana, Louisiana] Times*, 16th January 2002

plumbay *noun*

the vulva; a woman's pubic mound *TRINIDAD AND TOBAGO*

- — Lise Winer, *Dictionary of the English/Creole of Trinidad & Tobago*, 2003

plumber *noun*

1 a urologist *US*

- — *American Speech*, May 1961: 'The spoken language of medicine; argot, slang, cant'

2 a male pornography performer *US*

- — *Adult Video News*, p. 38, September 1995

3 in the Royal Air Force, an armament tradesman *UK, 1942*

Still in Royal Air Force use, 2002.

4 a golfer who is a good putter *US*

Built on 'drain' in the sense of putting into the hole.

- — Hubert Pedroli and Mary Tiegreen, *Let the Big Dog Eat! A Dictionary of the Secret Language of Golf*, p. 67, 2000

plumbing *noun*

1 the reproductive system *US, 1960*

- Helena had known about sex from a very early age, but treated it as a joke, like what she called your plumbing. — Mary McCarthy, *The Group*, p. 102–103, 1963

- In this dive you almost have to check everybody's plumbing to know whether it's interior or exterior. —Joseph Wambaugh, *The Blue Knight*, p. 44, 1973

2 any wind instrument *US, 1935*

- —Robert S. Gold, *A Jazz Lexicon*, p. 232, 1964

plumbing problem *noun*

the inability of a male pornography performer either to maintain an erection or to ejaculate on demand *US*

- —*Adult Video News*, p. 48, September 1995

plum-in-the-mouth *adjective*

upper-class, privileged *UK, 1926*

- [I]t don't matter what family you're born into either, whether it's a poor one or a plum-in-the-mouth one or a plum-in-the-mouth job. —Dave Courtney, *Stop the Ride I Want to Get Off*, p. 15, 1999
- Klosters (pronounced Close-ters even without a plum in your mouth) surprisingly has youth hostel-style rooms[.]— *The Guardian*, 3rd March 2001

plummer *noun*

a pickpocket *UK*

Misspelling of 'plumber' recorded in prison use August 2002.

plummy *adjective*

used for describing an affectedly upper-class manner of speech *UK, 1926*

The original meaning was 'rich, desirable'.

- I mean, a public school rocker with a plummy BBC accent... hardly. — *The Guardian*, 4th July 2003

plum pud; plum pudd *noun*

good *AUSTRALIA, 1927*

Rhyming slang.

plums *noun*

no sexual contact (when the expectation of intimacy is high) *UK*

Royal Navy slang; derives, possibly, from a 'plum' representing the figure 0 (hence 00 = nothing, nowhere). Alternatively **PLUM** (the testicle) hence **BOLLOCKS** (used as a general negative). A 'plums rating' is a sailor who has little luck with the opposite sex.

- "Howja get on with them birds, Taff?" "Plums, mate, nothing but bleeding plums." —Rick Jolly, *Jackspeak*, p. 219, 1989

plunderphonics *noun*

in music, a style of sampling that alters the original, usually without seeking permission from the copyright holder *CANADA, 1985*

A compound of 'plunder' (to rob) and 'phonic' (of sound). Coinage is credited to electronic music artist John Oswald (b.1953).

plunge *noun*

1 a surreptitious wagering of a great amount on a high-odds horse; a large bet *AUSTRALIA, 1895*

If bookmakers become aware that a great deal of money is being bet on a horse, they shorten the odds.

- [W]hen they became aware that their fellows odds-caller, Joe Thompson, was behind the plunge on Don Juan, the bookmakers speedily reduced the horse's price until he touched favouritism at 3/1. —Maurice Cavanough and Meurig Davies, *Cup Day*, p. 33, 1960
- When I put this to him he spent the next thirty minutes telling us of one catastrophe after another – desperate investments, wild plunges – which had dissipated his fortune[.] —Robert English, *Toxic Kisses*, p. 49, 1979
- [H]e was at his best recently, discussing a plunge on a horse which could not lose at Caulfield. —Roy Higgins and Tom Prior, *The Jockey Who Laughed*, p. 40, 1982
- The way I understand it, there's what's called a big betting plunge due on it, and the owners and trainer don't want to lose the big price they expect. —Ward McNally, *Supper at Happy Harry's*, p. 112, 1982
- He could smell trouble before a bet was laid in the shape of a big plunge or a favourite about to blow out the backdoor. —Clive Galea, *Slipper!*, p. 25, 1988
- The leader of the ring Big Bobby Watson bore the brunt of the plunge. —Clive Galea, *Slipper*, p. 42, 1988

2 a large cumulative amount of money wagered on a competitor *AUSTRALIA*

- Pre-race betting saw a sensational plunge on the New Zealand mystery horse, Wairiki. —Maurice Cavanough and Meurig Davies, *Cup Day*, p. 129, 1960
- —Joe Andersen, *Winners Can Laugh*, p. 158, 1982

plunge *verb*

1 to stab someone; to kill someone by stabbing *UK*

- —Angela Devlin, *Prison Patter*, p. 89, 1996
- I had just got to the door in time to see my two blokes get plunged by this pair of drunken slags. —Lenny McLean, *The Guv'nor*, p. 143, 1998
- You reckon I plunge geezers like for practice, keep my fuckin' hand in? —Jeremy Cameron, *Brown Bread in Wengen*, p. 21, 1999

2 to wager a great deal of money *AUSTRALIA, 1877.*

- He knew that the big betting owners knew that he would always do the right thing by them and they plunged accordingly. —Joe Andersen, *Winners Can Laugh*, p. 112, 1982
- That day, however, he plunged and by the last race had built his bank to £3,000. —James Holledge, *The Great Australian Gamble*, p. 26, 1996

plunger *noun*

a heavy bettor *AUSTRALIA, 1895*

- Some experts would class Eric Connolly as Australia's most spectacular professional plunger of all time. —James Holledge, *The Great Australian Gamble*, p. 14, 1966
- —Gerald Sweeney, *The Plunge*, p. 208, 1981

plungeroo *noun*

a pinball enthusiast *US*

- —Lou Shelly, *Hepcats Jive Talk Dictionary*, p. 16, 1945

plunked *adjective*

pregnant *NEW ZEALAND*

- —Sonya Plowman, *Great Kiwi Slang*, p. 81, 2002

plurry *adjective*

bloody *AUSTRALIA*

The Australian Aboriginal English pronunciation of the word **BLOODY**, occasionally used in a jocular or euphemistic way by non-Aboriginals.

- Well, young fella, we got the plurry hiding we deserved. —Frank Hardy, *Power Without Glory*, p. 543, 1950
- The aboriginal station hand was asked how he got on with the colt he'd been breaking in. 'Boss,' he said, 'that colt was so plurry frisky be bucked off his brand!' —Bill Wannan, *Bullockies, Beauts and Bandicoots*, p. 107, 1960
- Me plurry knees is still raw. —J.E. MacDonnell, *Don't Gimme the Ships*, p. 86, 1960
- BLOODY: Sometimes genteelly written. —Arthur Chipper, *The Aussie Swearer's Guide*, p. 26, 1972

plurry *adverb*

bloody *AUSTRALIA*

- 'He's got plurry good eyesight,' Wheelright conceded. —Murray Bail, *Holden's Performance*, p. 106, 1988

PL-US *noun*

like-minded individuals *UK, 1990s*

Initialism contrived from '*p*eople *l*ike *us*'.

- —Alon Shulman, *The Style Bible*, p. 191, 1999

plus-15s *noun*

(pedestrian) overpasses connecting buildings in Calgary, Alberta *CANADA*

- It's a city that is growing rapidly, with new buildings and "plus-15s" springing up all the time. "Plus-l5s" [is a term] referring to their height above the street–though given the weather they should probably be called minus-15s. — *Montreal Gazette*, p. F2, 29th May 2002

plush *noun*

stuffed animals *US*

- —Gene Sorrows, *All About Carnivals*, p. 24, 1985: 'Terminology'

Plush family *noun*

used as a humorous personification of empty seats in a theatre *UK*

- —Wilfred Granville, *The Theater Dictionary*, p. 14, 1952

plush out *verb*

to completely refurbish a car's upholstery and interior *US*

- Sitting on fat wheels and some sparkling Lorenzo's, the car is plushed out. — *Menace II Society*, 1993
- —Anna Scotti and Paul Young, *Buzzwords*, p. 40, 1997

plus-minus *adverb*

approximately, about *SOUTH AFRICA, 1970*

As the mathematical formula represented by the symbol ±.

- "Their left-handers," says Pollock, "scored plus-minus 1850 runs in six Tests against us last summer[."] — *Sunday Times(South Africa)*, 25th August 2002

Pluto pup *noun*
a deep-fried battered saveloy on a stick *AUSTRALIA*
• No you can't have a pluto pup. — *Opus*, p. 16, August 1986

Pluto water *noun*
a natural mineral water that acts as a strong laxative *US*
• He marched over to the dresser and poured himself another snort of painkiller, downing it like it was Pluto water. — Guy Owen, *The Flim-Flam Man and the Apprentice Grifter*, p. 179, 1972
• The name "Pluto water" was coined in the 1890s by two doctors from Louisville, presumably to shift attention from the odor. "It tastes as bad as it smells, too," grins Gail Spencer, spa director[.] — *Chicago Tribune*, p. C9, 13th January 1985
• Visitors still take mineral springs baths at the 471-room French Lick Springs Resort & Spa, where the so called "Pluto" water was once promoted with the slogan: "When nature won't, Pluto will." — *Deseret Morning News (Salt Lake City)*, p. T3, 14th September 2003

pluty *adjective*
wealthy; upscale *NEW ZEALAND*
An abbreviation of 'plutocratic'.
• — Louis S. Leland, *A Personal Kiwi-Yankee Dictionary*, p. 78, 1984

Plymouth Argyll *noun*
a file (a tool) *UK*
Rhyming slang, formed on the name of a football club.
• — Ray Puxley, *Cockney Rabbit*, 1992

PM *noun*
1 a *p*ost *m*ortem examination of a corpse *US*
• They could find out he had a heart attack – a man his age – when they do the P.M — Robert Campbell, *Nibbled to Death by Ducks*, p. 153, 1989
2 in horse racing, the odds listed before a race *US, 1955*
Also known as the 'PM line'.
• — Thomas L. Clark, *The Dictionary of Gambling and Gaming*, p. 160, 1987

PMJI
used as Internet discussion group shorthand to mean '*p*ardon *m*y *j*umping *i*n' *US*
• — Andy Ihnatko, *Cyberspeak*, p. 154, 1997

PMS *noun*
something or someone irritating or unpleasant *US*
Ascribing the stereotypical symptoms of *pre-m*enstrual *s*yndrome.
• I hate him. He's completely PMS. — Janet Evanovich, *Seven Up*, p. 74, 2001

PMS *verb*
(of a woman) to feel the emotions associated with *pre-m*enstrual *s*yndrome; thus to feel angry, irritable, irrational, anxious, etc *US, 1990*
PMS is the recognised abbreviation for 'pre-menstrual syndrome'.
• I wasn't even strung out and now I was PMSing, too. — Janet Evanovich, *Seven Up*, p. 75, 2001

pneumonia hole *noun*
a car window *US*
• — Kenn "Naz" Young, *Naz's Underground Dictionary*, p. 50, 1973
• Throw some glass in that pneumonia hole! — Ken Weaver, *Texas Crude*, p. 9, 1984

pneumonia sedan *noun*
a truck with no window glass or being driven with the windows down in cold weather *US*
• — Montie Tak, *Truck Talk*, p. 119, 1971

po *noun*
1 a chamber pot *UK, 1880*
From the pronunciation of 'pot' in French *pot de chambre*. Survives, mainly, through the efforts of the antique trade.
2 in pool, position *US*
A horrid contraction, but one that is in actual use.
• — Mike Shamos, *The Illustrated Encyclopedia of Billiards*, p. 174, 1993
3 a promiscuous girl, one who will '*p*ut *o*ut' *US*
• — *American Speech*, p. 273, December 1963: 'American Indian student slang'

PO *noun*
a *p*robation officer or *p*arole *o*fficer *US*
• I says, 'If the PO goes over to the house, it's going to be all over' — James Mills, *The Panic in Needle Park*, p. 53, 1966
• The P.O. asked me if I had a job. — Piri Thomas, *Down These Mean Streets*, p. 319, 1967
• Knowing he could outthink, outgame and outmaneuver any cop, judge or P.O. he got hit with and that his destiny was the dead opposite of every man in the bus, he said, "No, Anne Vanderlinden." — James Ellroy, *Suicide Hill*, p. 573, 1986
• I said to my PO, "Look, I've signed all these – sixteen things you're not supposed to do while out on parole." — Herbert Huncke, *Guilty of Everything*, p. 111, 1990

po' boy *noun*
a public assistance cheque *US*
• — Eugene Landy, *The Underground Dictionary*, p. 152, 1971

pocaution *noun*
contraception *BAHAMAS*
• — John A. Holm, *Dictionary of Bahamian English*, p. 158, 1982

poc doc *noun*
a short television documentary *CANADA*
An abbreviation of '*poc*ket *doc*umentary'.
• A "poc-doc" was a short piece with location sound, on-the-spot-interviews, and narration, for CBC in the sixties. — Bill Casselman, *Canadian Words*, p. 190–191, 1995

pocket *noun*
▸ **in pocket**
in possession of drugs to be sold *US*
• — Geoffrey Froner, *Digging for Diamonds*, p. 48, 1989
▸ **in the pocket**
in poker, dealt face-down *US*
• — Anthony Holden, *Big Deal*, p. 303, 1990
▸ **in your pocket**
of someone else, under your control or direction *UK, 1851*
• Rozzers [police] in his pocket? Big deal. — John Milne, *Alive and Kicking*, p. 36, 1998
▸ **out of pocket**
out of line; inappropriate *US*
• If you get caught smoking pot, you're totally out of pocket, you know what I mean? — Christina and Richard Milner, *Black Players*, p. 264, 1972

pocket *verb*
▸ **pocket the red**
to put the penis in the vagina *UK, 1937*
A pun from the game of billiards. Snooker offers a wider choice of puns with **PINK** and **BROWN**.

pocket billiards *noun*
the manipulation of your testicles for masturbation or comfort, performed by your hand hidden in your trouser pocket *UK, 1940*
Often in the phrase 'play pocket billiards'.

pocket change *noun*
a small amount of drugs when that is all that is left *UK, 2001*
From private correspondence with rock musicians.

pocket club *noun*
a police truncheon *US*
• — *American Speech*, p. 271, December 1962: 'The language of traffic policemen'

pocket engine *noun*
a large pocket watch *TRINIDAD AND TOBAGO, 1939*
• — Lise Winer, *Dictionary of the English/Creole of Trinidad & Tobago*, 2003

pocket man *noun*
in a functionally compartmentalised criminal enterprise, the person who holds the cash *US*
• — Carsten Stroud, *Close Pursuit*, p. 274, 1987

pocket pistol *noun*
a roasted cob of corn *BARBADOS*
• — Frank A. Collymore, *Barbadian Dialect*, p. 86, 1965

pocket pole *noun*
the penis *US*
Plays on branded Pocket Pals™, a range of collectible 'whimsies'.
• — Erica Orloff and JoAnn Baker, *Dirty Little Secrets*, 2001

pocket pool *noun*
used of a man, self-stimulation or masturbation while clothed *US, 1960*
Word play based on ball play; the title of a song by Killer Pussy on the 'Valley Girl' soundtrack.

- —Dale Gordon, *The Dominion Sex Dictionary*, p. 127, 1967
- He was playing "pocket pool" with his other hand. —Iceberg Slim (Robert Beck), *Pimp*, p. 105, 1969
- For chrissake, I'm a cop, Phil. What do you think I do all day, hang around eating tacos with Missy and playing pocket pool? —Robert Campbell, *Juice*, p. 230, 1988

pocket rocket *noun*

1 the 1973 – 74 Oldsmobile Cutlass, the first small car from Oldsmobile *US*

- —Lewis Poteet, *Car & Motorcyle Slang*, p. 152, 1992

2 any small, fast, imported car *US*

- —Connie Eble (Editor), *UNC-CH Campus Slang*, p. 6, Spring 1994

3 an improvised syringe filled with a drug and ready for injection *US*

- —James Harris, *A Convict's Dictionary*, p. p.36., 1989

4 marijuana *UK, 1998*

A pocket-sized means to become **SPACED** (drug-intoxicated).

- —Mike Haskins, *Drugs*, p. 288, 2003

poco loco *adjective*

crazy; eccentric *UK*

Directly from Spanish *poco* (little) and *loco* (mad).

- [Ol' Dirty Bastard]'s revered as something of a genius. The second [thing to know] is that he's bananas. Screwy. Poco loco. Bonkers as conkers. — *Uncut*, p. 20, October 2003

pod *noun*

1 marijuana *US*

- Don't say pot, Dinch. It's the intellectuals from college and all who come on that way. They want to get their hip-cards punched. Say pod, Dincher. —George Mandel, *Flee the Angry Strangers*, p. 26, 1952
- — *American Speech*, p. 304, December 1955: 'Wayne University slang'
- So I put in on him for a sawski and make a meet to sell him some "pod" as he calls it[.] —William Burroughs, *Naked Lunch*, p. 4, 1957
- Sometimes he [Jack Kerouac] lapses into pages of terrifying gibberish that sound like a tape recording of a gang bang with everybody full of pod, juice and bennies all at once. — *The Nation*, p. 61, 23rd February 1957
- Neither will he [the beat] tell you that marijuana used to be called "tea," then "tea pot," then simply "pot," and now simply "pod" all to confuse the square. — *San Francisco Chronicle*, p. 4, 15th June 1958
- Oh, you know, man – the score you was with that time – the one that wanted pod so bad. —John Rechy, *City of Night*, p. 140, 1963

2 a marijuana cigarette *CANADA*

- — *Basic Beatnik (in the 'Daily Colonist', Victoria, BC)*, 16th April 1958

3 the head *US*

- I nudged my pod. —William "Lord" Buckley, *The Ballad of Dan McGroo*, 1960

4 an orthopaedist *US*

- —Sally Williams, *"Strong" Words*, p. 135, 1994

5 the tail of a surfboard *CANADA*

- —Gary Fairmont R. Filosa II, *The Surfer's Almanac*, p. 191, 1977

PO'd *adjective*

angry; *pissed off* *US*

- Some of the girls from the luau stood around and they were sort of p.o.'d on account of being stuck there without transportation home. —Frederick Kohner, *Gidget*, p. 136, 1957
- Oh, God ... extremely PO'ed that hubby's not getting off on the decadent ambience. —Armistead Maupin, *Tales of the city*, p. 144, 1978
- Wow. She is really PO'd. — *Romy and Michele's High School Reunion*, 1997

poddle *verb*

in bowling, to roll the ball into the gutter *US*

- —Frank Bryan, *Tackle Tenpin Bowling This Way*, 1962

poddy *noun*

1 a user of an iPod™ branded digital music player; often used as a nickname for an iPod *UK*

- —Susie Dent, *Larpers and Shroomers*, p. 56, 2004
- Poddies will admit it, too: this is a cult that dares to speak its name. — *The Guardian*, p. 2, 2nd January 2004

2 a young, unbranded calf *AUSTRALIA, 1872*

From British dialect *poddy* (obese).

- The skinny little poddies of a couple of years ago were now but a scarcely credible recollection. —Frank Dalby Davison, *The Wells of Beersheba*, p. 130, 1965

poddy *verb*

to handfeed a young calf, lamb or foal *AUSTRALIA*

- On the way to Widden by steamer, Lady Champion died, and her colt had to be poddied. —Maurice Cavanough and Meurig Davies, *Cup Day*, p. 192, 1960

poddy-dodge *verb*

to steal unbranded cattle *AUSTRALIA, 1919*

poddy-dodger *noun*

a person who steals unbranded cattle *AUSTRALIA, 1919*

- [T]hey are prepared not only to swim but to do other things more intimate with sons of black-marketeers and abortionists and poddy-dodgers providing the cash basis is all right. —Dymphna Cusack, *Picnic Races*, p. 240, 1962
- —Jim Ramsay, *Cop It Sweet!*, p. 71, 1977

poddy-dodging *adjective*

the theft of unbranded cattle *AUSTRALIA, 1919*

- At times Bob would pack up his horses, and he and I would go to distant cattle stations and pick up some cattle from their herds and drive them to our station in the wet lands. "Poddy dodging" this was called, for it is against the law. —W.E. Harney, *Brimming Billabongs*, p. 152, 1947
- —Dymphna Cusack, *Picnic Races*, p. 164, 1962

podge *noun*

a short and fat person; fatness *UK, 1876*

From conventional **PODGY**.

- Dieting is the one thing that women put effort into, the one thing we really know about. If our gender went on Mastermind, 'podge' would be our specialist subject. — *The Observer*, 30th March 2003

podger *verb*

to have sex *UK: SCOTLAND*

A possible conflation of **POKE** and **ROGER**.

- Ah'd podger that aw right! —Michael Munro, *The Complete Patter*, p. 121, 1996

podgy *noun*

a girlfriend, mistress or prostitute *US*

Korean war usage; from the Korean word for 'vulva'.

- —Carl Fleischhauer, *A Glossary of Army Slang*, p. 6, 1968

podgy *adjective*

fat *UK, 1846*

- [B]eautiful Elena despises her podgy sister's shroud of flesh[.] — *The Guardian*, 23rd November 2001

podner *noun*

used as a jocular term of address *US*

Approximating a Western drawl of 'partner'.

- "Not me," Wiley said. "You can't make me, podner." —Carl Hiaasen, *Tourist Season*, p. 374, 1986

pods *noun*

the female breasts *US*

- —Fred Hester, *Slang on the 40 Acres*, 1968

Podunk *noun*

any remote, small town *US*

- —Ramon Adams, *The Language of the Railroader*, p. 116, 1977

podunk *adjective*

worthless, remote *US*

- — *Current Slang*, p. 6, Spring 1968

poegaai *adjective*

exhausted; drunk *SOUTH AFRICA, 1942*

- By the end of the evening he looked absolutely poegaai. —Jean Branford, *A Dictionary of South African English*, 1978

poep *noun*

a fart; faeces; hence, contemptuously, of a person *SOUTH AFRICA, 1969*

- —Jean Branford, *A Dictionary of South African English*, 1978

poep *verb*

to fart *SOUTH AFRICA*

From Afrikaans into impolite South African English.

- Bean soup and how it makes him 'poep'. Now takes a glass of Andrews Liver Salts immediately after a plate of bean soup to minimise the effect. —Athol Fugard, *Notebooks*, p. 84, 1983

poep *adjective*

bad, unpleasant *SOUTH AFRICA, 1970*

From the noun sense as 'faeces'.

- —Penny Silva, *A Dictionary of South African English*, 1996

poetical *adjective*

drunk *UK*

- By now the man-sized swigs had topped up the previous day's excesses and I was feeling fairly poetical —Frank Skinner, *Frank Skinner*, p. 122, 2001

poets' day *noun*
Friday, especially when used as an excuse to finish work early on a Friday *UK, 1984*
An acronym for '*p*iss *o*ff *e*arly – *t*omorrow's *S*aturday' or '*p*ush *o*ff *e*arly – *t*omorrow's *S*aturday'.
- In fact Mr Jones calls Friday Poets day, but of course in further education we don't know what that means. — *The Guardian*, 16th April 2002

po-faced *adjective*
having an impassive expression *UK, 1934*
Influenced by **POKER FACE**, but most likely to derive from **PO** (a chamber pot) or 'poh!' (an old exclamation of rejection).
- A po-faced man with a clipboard was ticking names off his list with as much pleasure as the head of a reform school at registration. — *New Statesman*, 3rd May 2003

pogey *noun*
1 a male homosexual who prefers the passive role in anal sex *US*
- — Hyman E. Goldin et al., *Dictionary of American Underworld Lingo*, p. 161, 1950

2 unemployment insurance or welfare *CANADA, 1976*
- Jeez, guys, what can I do. Here I live in this joint on my pogey money; you think this is the Four Seasons Sheraton? — Hugh Garner, *The Intruders*, p. 34, 1976

pogey bait *noun*
any food with high calorific, low nutritional content *US*
In prison, sweets, cigarettes or other inducements given to men willing to play the passive role in anal sex.
- — Hyman E. Goldin et al., *Dictionary of American Underworld Lingo*, p. 161, 1950
- — William H. McMichael, *Seattle Times*, p. A9, 12th April 1998: 'Grunts, squids not grunting from the same dictionary'

poggled *adjective*
of a car, having had crash damage repaired *UK*
A car dealers' term.
- — *Woman's Own*, 28th February 1968

poggler *noun*
1 a purse; a wallet *UK*
- — David Powis, *The Signs of Crime*, 1977

2 a motor vehicle that has had crash-damage repaired *UK*
A car dealers' term.
- — *BBC Radio 4 News*, 3rd January 1977

pogo *noun*
1 a form of dancing (essentially wildly jumping up and down on the spot) associated with punk rock music *UK*
- We also danced the pogo, which was a great dance for people like Wallace who couldn't really dance[.] — David Bowker, *The Joy of Sexism*, p. 43, 1999
- Sid Vicious, a member of the so-called Bromley Contingent, played drums for the hastily formed Siouxsie and the Banshees, and some observers claimed that he also invented "the pogo" that night [20th], violently jumping up and down to the thrashed guitars. — Martin Roach (writing of football hooliganism in the 1970s), *Dr. Marten's Air Wair*, 1999

2 a contemptible person *AUSTRALIA, 1972*
In army use, a member of the administrative personnel, anyone not in the arms corps . From **POGO STICK**, rhyming slang for **PRICK** but influenced by imagery of aimlessly bouncing around as one does on a pogo-stick.
- Jesus, does he think a man's deaf, bloody RAAF pogo. — William Nagel, *The Odd Angry Shot*, p. 1, 1975

pogo-pogo *noun*
cocaine *US*
- — William D. Alsever, *Glossary for the Establishment and Other Uptight People*, p. 6, December 1970

pogo stick *noun*
1 the penis *UK*
Rhyming slang for **DICK** or **PRICK**, influenced by apt imagery.
- — Bodmin Dark, *Dirty Cockney Rhyming Slang*, 2003

2 a Chinese rocket launcher, used in Vietnam by the Viet Cong *US*
- — *Newsweek*, 25th July 1966
- — Carl Fleischhauer, *A Glossary of Army Slang*, 1968

3 in electric line work, any telescoping insulated line tool *US*
- — A.B. Chance Co., *Lineman's Slang Dictionary*, p. 13, 1980

4 in poker, a player with wildly fluctuating play and success *US*
- — John Vorhaus, *The Big Book of Poker Slang*, p. 29, 1996

pogue *noun*
1 a homosexual male who plays the passive role during anal sex, especially if young *US, 1941*
Deriving perhaps from Irish Gaelic *pogue* (to kiss).
- — *Maledicta*, p. 221, 1979: 'Kinks and queens: linguistic and cultural aspects of the terminology for gays'

2 a member of the armed forces assigned to the rear echelon, safely away from combat; a soldier newly arrived in combat *US*
Seemingly unconnected to the C19 sense as 'purse' with 'pogue-hunter' as 'pickpocket'.
- You're an office pogue. You never been anything but an office pogue. You don't have the slightest idea what goes on in a working police division. — Joseph Wambaugh, *The Choirboys*, p. 10, 1975
- It was the ages-old animosity between front-line infantrymen and the staff and support personnel farther back – the "pogues," those "rear-echelon mother-fuckers!" — Charles Anderson, *The Grunts*, p. 28, 1976
- — *Army*, p. 48, November 1991

pogy *noun*
a jail or prison *US*
- Since I had to get to the pogy to consolidate my plans and since my every move was under suspicion because of my break record, I had to have a clear and painful injury. — Red Rudensky, *The Gonif*, p. 13, 1970

poindexter *noun*
a serious student *US*
- — Connie Eble (Editor), *UNC-CH Campus Slang*, p. 5, March 1981
- Ohmigod, like Hillary's brother is like such a total Poindexter he's skipped two grades. — Mary Corey and Victoria Westermark, *Fer Shurr! How to be a Valley Girl*, 1982
- It's facing to ask rents for money, get airmail, or hang around with poindexters. — *United Press International*, 5th January 1984
- The strongest competition to squid and grimbo as successor term to nerd is dexter, a shortening of poindexter, probably based on a cartoon character. — *New York Times Magazine*, 22nd September 1985
- Imagine the surreal social resonance of watching big southern cops harass a bunch of flannel-wearing Poindexters clutching floppy disks if they were beeper-wearing homeboys blasting "Dre Day" too loudly from a jeep. — *Vibe*, June/July 1994
- A good student who has already met his test-score requirement and a classmate who still hasn't qualified take the test on the same Saturday morning. Poindexter puts Sluggo's name on Poindexter's test, and Sluggo puts Poindexter's on Sluggo's. — *Sports Illustrated*, 7th July 1997

point *noun*
1 a hypodermic needle and syringe *US*
- — Francis J. Rigney and L. Douglas Smith, *The Real Bohemia*, p. xx, 1961
- History is a Scabbie Point / For putting Cash to sleep. — Leonard Cohen, *Beautiful Losers*, p. 238, 1966
- Hawaiian Chuck was handing out hepatitis-infected points to friends who'd burned him. — Nicholas Von Hoffman, *We Are The People Our Parents Warned Us Against*, p. 83, 1967
- — Geoffrey Froner, *Digging for Diamonds*, p. 48, 1989

2 a pen; a pencil *UK*
Gay slang.
- Do you happen to have a point on you? — Bruce Rodgers, *The Queens' Vernacular*, 1972

3 a percentage point *US*
- I was peddling them for thirty points on the dollar. — Gerald Petievich, *Money Men*, p. 40, 1981
- He wants three points over the vig. From me? — *Goodfellas*, 1990
- To begin, I put money out on the streets, chargin' three points a week. — *Casino*, 1995

4 a man who ensures that order reigns at a brothel *US*
- — *Maledicta*, p. 150, Summer/Winter 1986–1987: 'Sexual slang: prostitutes, pedophiles, flagellators, transvestites, and necrophiles'

point *verb*
▸ **point Dennis at the Doulton**
(of a male) to urinate *AUSTRALIA*
Doulton is a manufacturer of china.
- — Barry Humphries, *Bazza Pulls It Off!*, 1971

▸ **point Percy**
(of a male) to urinate *AUSTRALIA*
A familiar shortening of **POINT PERCY AT THE PORCELAIN**.
- I've pointed old percy [urinated], down a couple [of beers]... and bunged a few leg openers into that sheilah [woman] out there!!! — Barry Humphries, *Bazza Pulls It Off!*, 1971

▸ **point Percy at the porcelain**
(of a male) to urinate *AUSTRALIA*
Conventionally 'point **PERCY** (the penis) at *porcelain* (the china of a lavatory)'. Popularised in the UK in the late 1960s and early 70s via a *Private Eye* magazine cartoon strip and two films featuring Barry Mackenzie, an **OCKER** (a loutish Australian) created by Barry Humphries (b.1934). Coincidentally, the famously Australian Mr Humphries appeared in a 1974 film called *Percy's Progress*, about a man who had a penis transplant. All of which lends credence to the unproven assertion that this phrase is an Australian coinage.
- No worries – I'll meet you at the customs. I' ve just got to flash off and point Percy at the porcelain! — Barry Humphries, *The Wonderful World of Barry McKenzie*, p. 37, 1968
- England brings out the wrost in you. It makes you want to talk about pillow biters and pointing percy at the porcelain. — Kathy Lette, *Girls' Night Out*, p. 204, 1987
- [L]ift the toilet lid and point Percy at the Porcelain, Shake Hands with My Friend, Exercise The One-Eyed Trouser Snake. — Stuart Browne, *Dangerous Parking*, p. 280, 2000

▸ **point the bone**
to point blame at someone; to accuse someone *AUSTRALIA, 1943*
Figuratively recalling the Australian Aboriginal ritual practice of pointing a bone at a person in order to wish death upon them.
- The greatest sin against the Australian spirit of mateship is to point the bone at a cobber, i.e. sneak on a friend[.] — Arthur Chipper, *The Aussie Swearer's Guide*, p. 33, 1972
- Go along with this and you get a winning fee plus a nice bonus and there'll be no way Watson or Robertson can point the bone at you. — Clive Galea, *Slipper*, p. 199, 1988
- We are not pointing the bone at any particular club in our submission to the AFL, but we believe 11 clubs is too many to play out of Melbourne. — *Advertiser*, p. 54, 1st May 1991

▸ **point the finger**
to testify on behalf of the prosecution *NEW ZEALAND, 1982*
- — Harry Orsman, *A Dictionary of Modern New Zealand Slang*, p. 101, 1999

▸ **point the finger at**
to identify someone or something as having a specific responsibility *UK, 1833*
- "[A]ll those who bear some responsibility for what happened have dashed for cover at the first whiff of cordite," he [Alex Brummer] said, pointing the finger at the government, the Association of British Insurers and the Financial Services Authority. — *The Guardian*, 11th March 2004

pointer *noun*
1 a criminally inclined youth, especially a youth gang member *US*
- What a "Z"! The astonishing private language of Bay Area teenagers — *San Francisco Examiner: People*, p. 8, 27th October 1963

2 a large facial blemish *US*
- — *Verbatim*, p. 280, May 1976

pointers *noun*
female breasts with prominent pointed nipples *US*
- "She was a healthy-looking bitch, a jogger type with a great rack ... a couple of real pointers. And I'm not talking about a bra with rubber nipples. I'm talking about a pair of honest-to-Christ pointed nips that must have weighed as much as silver dollars. — Gerald Petievich, *To Die in Beverly Hills*, p. 93, 1983
- Boobs, zonkers, headlights, watermelons, sweater puppies, pointers, knockers, jugs, tatas – these are some of the words to describe women's breasts. — Howard Stern, *Miss America*, p. 441, 1995

point-five *noun*
a homosexual *FIJI*
- He was a point-five. I didn't know. I was so embarrassed I just had to walk away. — Jan Tent, 1995

point-out *noun*
a member of a confidence swindle who introduces the intended victim to someone whom he identifies as a former acquaintance with good connections, who then lures the victim further into the swindle *US*
- We'll have a separate point-out meeting in a minute, then I want you to run rehearsals. — Stephen J. Cannell, *Big Con*, p. 342, 1997

pointy-head *noun*
an intellectual *US*
Derogatory.
- Lisa Harper against the pointy-heads. — Lee Child, *The Visitor*, p. 328, 2000

pointy-head; pointy-headed *adjective*
intellectual, if at the expense of common sense *US, 1972*
Derogatory.
- — Sam Donaldson, *Hold On, Mr. President*, p. 215, 1987
- That's pointy-head stuff. — Lee Child, *The Visitor*, p. 329, 2000
- They are hostile to the medical profession (pointy-headed experts), the social services (bureaucrats) and to AA (a cult). — *The Guardian*, 1st January 2001

Poirot *noun*
a Belgian police officer *UK*
After Hercule Poirot, Agatha Christie's famous fictional detective.
- At the tiny airport a pair of glum Poirots in plain clothes met me off the plane. — Duncan MacLaughlin, *The Filth*, p. 203, 2002

poison *noun*
1 a narcotic or an alcoholic drink, especially a person's favourite *US, 1805*
Used in a jocular tone.
- He sat beside me and said, "See, Honey, I remembered your poison: gin and soda." — Iceberg Slim (Robert Beck), *Mama Black Widow*, p. 25, 1969
- So what's your poison? What do you drink? — *The Breakfast Club*, 1985
- I didn't think people said ,"What's your poison" anymore, but I don't hang around these joints so I wouldn't really know. — Robert Campbell, *In a Pig's Eye*, p. 116, 1991
- Yeah, well, some people into dope, some into booze. Pick your poison, you know. — Richard Price, *Clockers*, p. 466, 1992
- The maitre d' didn't shout, You back again? nor did the bartender holler, What's your poison, paesan? — Rita Ciresi, *Pink Slip*, p. 88–89, 1999
- "What's your poison?" Alan said, thrusting his hand into his pocket[.] — Danny King, *The Bank Robber Diaries*, p. 29, 2002

2 narcotics, especially heroin *US*
- — Inez Cardozo-Freeman, *The Joint*, p. 522, 1984
- — Robert Ashton, *This Is Heroin*, p. 206, 2002

poisoner *noun*
a cook to a group of rural workers, especially shearers *AUSTRALIA, 1905*
- A station 'poisoner' in his own kitchen is a dictator indeed. — Ion L. Idriess, *Over the Range*, p. 5, 1947
- — Jim Ramsay, *Cop It Sweet!*, p. 71, 1977

poison shop *noun*
a pharmacy *US*
- We gots to find out first just what poison shops in this town are holding. — *Drugstore Cowboy*, 1988

poke *noun*
1 a wallet or purse *US, 1859*
- I was always as ready as they were, although sometimes I never had a blip in my poke. — Mezz Mezzrow, *Really the Blues*, p. 22, 1946
- When the cluck woke up, he frisked his pockets for his poke. — Jack Lait and Lee Mortimer, *Washington Confidential*, p. 268, 1951
- Had it in his pants pocket. I couldn't find a poke. — William Burroughs, *Junkie*, p. 44, 1953
- Purse snatchers grabbed a poke and ran toward the dark beneath the trestle[.] — Chester Himes, *A Rage in Harlem*, p. 164, 1957
- Fat Girl returned to the room and picked up Bernie's wallet. "Your poke, man." — Ross Russell, *The Sound*, p. 158, 1961
- I flushed them down the toilet, frisked Mario and lifted another $400 from his poke and added it to my pile. — Mickey Spillane, *Me, Hood!*, p. 41, 1963
- Where blood was shed for the sake of bread / And drunks rolled for their poke. — Dennis Wepman et al., *The Life*, p. 80, 1976
- Phil reaching behind Bill, fingers feeling the inside breast pockets of the mark's suit jacket or perhaps the overcoat pockets searching for the wallet – or poke, as Phil referred to it. — Herbert Huncke, *The Evening Sun Turned Crimson*, p. 112, 1980

2 money; a roll of money *US, 1926*
- The other boy he had could do the running and make some poke. — Hal Ellson, *Duke*, p. 65, 1949
- — Hy Lit, *Hy Lit's Unbelievable Dictionary of Hip Words for Groovy People*, p. 30, 1968
- — Clarence Major, *Dictionary of Afro-American Slang*, p. 92, 1970
- Then the mark opens the wallet to find out that they switched the poke on him and he has a wallet full of cut paper. — Stephen J. Cannell, *Big Con*, p. 165, 1997

3 the stomach *US*
- — John Gould, *Maine Lingo*, p. 213, 1975

4 power, especially horsepower *UK*
- [W]ith all that poke under the bonnet[.] — R.T Bickers, *The Hellions*, 1965

5 a punch; a hard hitting verbal thrust *UK, 1788*
Both uses derive from the conventional sense (a thrust, a push).
- Retired Gen. Wesley Clark, hoping to overtake the Vermonter, took a poke at [Howard] Dean's temperament and accused Fox News of conspiring against him in Thursday's debate[.] — *Seattle Times*, 24th January 2003

6 an inhalation of marijuana or opium smoke *US, 1955*
- Go ahead. Take a poke. It won't hurt you. — Thurston Scott, *Cure it with Honey*, p. 60, 1951
- Then some lame was puffing on a joint one night, got next to a kitty and said she had to take a poke. — Edwin Torres, *Carlito's Way*, p. 26, 1975

7 marijuana *UK*
From 'pokeweed', *Phytolacca americana*, a strong smelling shrub native to North America.
- — Mike Haskins, *Drugs*, p. 288, 2003

8 a woman sexually objectified *UK, 1937*

9 a poor person who attempts through demeaning behaviour to be accepted by upper-class people *BAHAMAS*
- — John A. Holm, *Dictionary of Bahamian English*, p. 158, 1982

poke *verb*

1 (from a man's point of view) to have sex with a woman *UK, 1868*
- CARTER: How would have liked it if it had been your daughter, eh? (another punch) Being poked in that film, eh? — Mike Hodges, *Get Carter*, p. 65, 1971
- That's pretty much the story, folks, and after everybody gets to poke each other, in the pool, on the couch, in the bathroom and living room, Mosca performs his fabulous erotic dance[.] — *Adult Video*, p. 13, August/September 1986
- BB: Hey, asshole, here's the ultimate fuck-you. I just poked your wife! — *Tin Men*, 1987
- I'd poke her myself, 'cept last time I tried white stuff I got my neck sliced. — James Ellroy, *White Jazz*, p. 52, 1992
- So, we thought we'd get a little bet on, as to whether he'd actually go in and poke one of the brasses [prostitutes][.] — Will Self, *The Sweet Smell of Psychosis*, p. 22, 1996
- Not Man U-fuckin-nited? Aw please God, don't tell me ye poked one of the Scum. — Niall Griffiths, *Kelly + Victor*, p. 110, 2002

2 used as an emphatic rejection *UK*
Synonymous with **STUFF** or **FUCK IT!**.
- I'm going to start working at Labiarinth later in the week, so you can poke your stupid job. — Colin Butts, *Is Harry Still on the Boat?*, p. 139, 2003

3 to smoke marijuana *US, 1982*
- — Mike Haskins, *Drugs*, p. 290, 2003

4 to inject a drug *UK*
- — Mike Haskins, *Drugs*, p. 290, 2003

▸ **poke borak**
to make fun of someone or something; to deride someone or something; to ridicule someone or something *AUSTRALIA, 1873*
Contextually in this phrase 'borak' means 'rubbish; nonsense'. It has its origins in the Australian Aboriginal language Wathawurung where it expressed negation.
- Makes me ropeable that feller does, poking borak every time he gets a chance. — Dymphna Cusack, *Picnic Races*, p. 21, 1962
- — Arthur Chipper, *The Aussie Swearer's Guide*, p. 77, 1972

▸ **poke mullock at**
to deride someone; to make fun of someone *AUSTRALIA, 1916*
- MULLOCK, TO POKE – To deride. — Gilbert H. Lawson, *A Dictionary of Australian Words and Terms*, 1924
- I heard what you said when you grabbed that rope. Poking mullock at us because we won't go out over an empty hatch. — John Morrison, *Stories of the Waterfront*, p. 23, 1962

▸ **poke squid**
(of a male) to have sex *US*
- What, Rory – you wen poke squid las' night? — Douglas Simonson, *Pidgin to da Max Hana Hou*, 1982

poked *adjective*
exhausted *NEW ZEALAND*
- He had told the boys he'd be out at the lake by nine, it was not good getting up on the skis if you felt poked. — Vincent O'Sullivan, *The Boy, the Bridge, the River*, p. 115, 1978
- — Harry Orsman, *A Dictionary of Modern New Zealand Slang*, p. 101, 1999

pokee *noun*
the vagina *TRINIDAD AND TOBAGO, 1974*
Children's vocabulary.
- — Lise Winer, *Dictionary of the English/Creole of Trinidad & Tobago*, 2003

poker *noun*

1 the erect penis *US*
- Gawd, what a poker it was! — *Screw*, p. 19, 17th November 1969

2 in fencing, any weapon with a stiff, heavy blade *UK*
A derisory term, from the similarity to a conventional poker.
- — E.D. Morton, *Martini A-Z of Fencing*, 1988

pokerarse *noun*
someone who is not relaxed or easy going *IRELAND*
- So off went me and Sausage and Fabian of the Yard. I could see Sausage as white as a ghost in the front, in case I'd make a cod of him again but I wouldn't for I knew that was what pokerarse Fabian wanted. — Patrick McCabe, *The Butcher Boy*, p. 211, 1992

poker face *noun*
a blank expression that gives nothing away *US, 1885*
- [H]e used to give us hysterics up on the bandstand, but we had to sit through it poker-faced and act like we weren't hip. — Mezz Mezzrow, *Really the Blues*, p. 85, 1946
- When the case was called, the courtroom filled with poker-faced orientals. — Jack Lait and Lee Mortimer, *Washington Confidential*, p. 56, 1951
- My old lady, nobody can tell what she thinking about nothing or nobody. She the one and original poker face, you know. — Sara Harris, *The Lords of Hell*, p. 114, 1967
- Again, I with my progressive ideas, played poker as well as they did, losing some and winning some as they did, but rapidly reading all stud card-hands and calculating odds and betting properly against the bluffers and the slick pocker faces[.] — Bobby Seale, *A Lonely Rage*, p. 269, 1978
- Dude. You gotta have a poker face, like me. — *Bill and Ted's Excellent Adventure*, 1989

poker voice *noun*
an even speaking tone that does not reveal any underlying emotion *US*
- McManus didn't know if the chief's last remark was a compliment or a jibe; Braverton was a poker voice all the way. — James Ellroy, *Suicide Hill*, p. 633, 1986

pokey *noun*
a jail *US, 1919*
- I'm gonna do everything in my power to fix it up so he'll think heroin's a new dance when he gets out of the pokey. — Clarence Cooper Jr, *The Scene*, p. 122, 1960
- If it weren't for him I probably would have been thrown in a military pokey for three or six months[.] — Clancy Sigal, *Going Away*, p. 214, 1961
- The cop on the bet warns me that some of them are undesirables, that he's noted a few coming in who had been in the pokey on morals charges. — Antony James, *America's Homosexual Underground*, p. 104, 1965
- But she knew she'd wind up in the pokey[.] — Chester Himes, *Come Back Charleston Blue*, p. 109, 1966
- As I stood on the side of the road my thoughts centered around the prospect of "Pokey" – where a state trooper had once threatened to put me when he caught me hitching at 3 a.m. — James Simon Kunen, *The Strawberry Statement*, p. 80, 1968
- They grab some fat cat who identifies himself as a lawyer and go off to the local pokey to bail out fellow Digger Peter Berg. — Abbie Hoffman, *Revolution for the Hell of It*, p. 34, 1968
- Which is not what I would call a lot of fun, standing there and letting the judge chew you out, but easier to bear than a short stretch in the pokey. — George V. Higgins, *Penance for Jerry Kennedy*, p. 189, 1985
- It was nothing to throw a suspect in the pokey and leave him there[.] — Duncan MacLaughlin, *The Filth*, p. 97, 2002

pokey *adjective*

1 of an enclosed space, small and dark; inadequate *UK, 1849*
- The two pokey little rooms that existed before were knocked through[.] — *The Observer*, 25th April 2004

2 dawdling, slow *US*
From **SLOWPOKE**.
- He said it would take about half an hour. Elvin said, "If you're a pokey driver it might." — Elmore Leonard, *Maximum Bob*, p. 126, 1991
- ... Nelson Hareem, who happened to be dawdling down the street at a poky seventy miles per hour, the speed limit he ordinarily reserved for parking lots and residential driveways. — Joseph Wambaugh, *Fugitive Nights*, p. 111, 1992

pokie *noun*
an electronic poker machine *NEW ZEALAND*
- — Sonya Plowman, *Great Kiwi Slang*, p. 142, 2002
- Pokie addiction has led to hundreds of Australians committing crimes[.] — Max Daly, *The Guardian*, 12th February 2003

pol *noun*

a politician *US, 1942*

- I don't tell him that the world of old pols and patronage is probably doomed. — Robert Campbell, *Junkyard Dog*, p. 6, 1986

Polack; Polak *noun*

a Polish immigrant or a Polish-American *US, 1898*

Disparaging.

- Kate hurriedly intervened to remark that she hoped she would be transferred to a school in a better neighborhood, because now she had to teach dirty Polacks who would never be any good for anything[.] — James T. Farrell, *Saturday Night*, p. 8, 1947
- It's just like I'm really only a Polak, just a damn Polak millhand! — John Clellon Holmes, *Go*, p. 151, 1952
- Come on, you yellow-bellied Polack bas- — *West Side Story*, 1957
- Eat your last can of sauerkraut, Polack, because one of us has to die unless Mister Gregory and his people get out of solitary. — Dick Gregory, *Nigger*, p. 195, 1964
- a nice dumb polack who maybe has that extra something that makes for stardom. — Gore Vidal, *Myra Breckinridge*, p. 25, 1968
- A Polack's day, my father has suggested to me, isn't complete until he has dragged his big dumb feet across the bones of a Jew. — Philip Roth, *Portnoy's Complaint*, p. 142, 1969
- Every Polack in the place is drinking Seven Crown and Strohs. — Elmore Leonard, *The Big Bounce*, p. 48, 1969
- Agnew has pointed out that it's a land of opportunity for anyone, whether he's a Mick, a Polack or a Jap. — *Playboy*, p. 62, February 1969
- He finally confessed to himself that he was nothing but a dumb Polack and he might as well lie back and enjoy it. — Darryl Ponicsan, *The Last Detail*, p. 11, 1970
- In the locker rooms of the Eighteenth District Station and around the cop bars, he called Italians guidos or wops, Poles polacks, Bohemians hunkies, Mexicans spicks or greasers, and African-Americans niggers or darkies. — Robert Campbell, *Boneyards*, p. 10, 1992
- a whining old bag with a Boston accent who starts ranting about Niggers, Kikes, Spics, Wops, Dagos, and Polacks. — Howard Stern, *Miss America*, p. 220, 1995

Polack; Polak *adjective*

Polish *US*

- I had a few before I left Lansing – them Polack chicks that used to come over the bridge. — Malcolm X and Alex Haley, *The Autobiography of Malcolm X*, p. 45, 1964

Polack fiddle *noun*

a bucksaw, a one-man tool *US*

Because of the skill attributed to Polish loggers in handling a bucksaw.

- — John Gould, *Maine Lingo*, p. 213, 1975

Poland-and-China *noun*

a black and white police car *US*

- — *American Speech*, p. 269, December 1962: 'The language of traffic policemen'

polari; palare; parlare *noun*

a slang vocabulary used by theatricals and homosexuals *UK*

Variants include: 'polare' and 'parlaree'. Probably from Italian *parlare* (to talk). This 'language' itself derives in great part from Italian and Romany roots, incorporating back slang, Cockney rhyming slang and Yiddish among its influences. The earliest form, known as 'parleyaree', was used by C17 actors who, as a despised section of society, needed a discreet means of communication; as theatricals achieved a degree of respectability so the use of the language changed and polari emerged. By the late 1930s the tolerance of theatre-life had attracted many homosexuals who, as a despised section of society, needed a discreet means of communication.

- SANDY: Oh – he's got all the palare, hasn't he? JULIAN: I wonder where he picks it up. — Barry Took and Marty Feldman, *Round The Horne*, June 1966
- Aunt Nell [listen to] the naff [poor quality] parlare[.] — the cast of 'Aspects of Love', Prince of Wales Theatre, *Palare (Boy Dancer Talk) for Beginners*, 1989–92
- The Piccadilly palare / Was just silly slang / Between me and the boys in my gang. — Morrissey, *Piccadilly Palare*, 1990
- — Paul Baker, *Polari*, p. 186, 2002

polari; palare; parlare *verb*

to talk, especially to talk in polari *UK*

- "So sister," I polaried. "Will you take a varder [look] at the cartz [genitalia] on the feely-omi [young man] in the naf [poor taste] strides [trousers][.] — James Gardiner, *Who's a Pretty Boy Then?*, p. 123, 1997
- — Paul Baker, *Polari*, p. 186, 2002

polari lobe *noun*

the ear *UK*

- — Paul Baker, *Polari*, p. 186, 2002

polari pipe *noun*

a telephone *UK*

- — Paul Baker, *Polari*, p. 186, 2002

Polaroid *noun*

a police radar unit used for measuring vehicles' speed *US*

- — Lanie Dills, *The Official CB Slanguage Language Dictionary*, p. 55, 1976

polboron *noun*

▷ see: PULBORN

pole *noun*

1 the penis *UK*

- "Bitch," I replied coldly, until you grow a pole you leave the pimping to me." — Donald Goines, *Whoreson*, p. 141, 1972

2 an aircraft's control column *UK*

- — Colin Strong and Duff Hart-Davis, *Fighter Pilot*, 1981

3 in planespotting, a telescope *UK*

- [P]lanespotters "make" aircraft numbers. And a pole is a telescope. — Iain Aitch, *A Fete Worse Than Death*, p. 73, 2003

▸ **up the pole**

1 pregnant *IRELAND, 1922*

- He'd have killed him if he'd put her up the pole; she was too nice a young one to have that sort of thing happen to her, far too nice — Roddy Doyle, *The Van*, p. 100, 1991
- Mr Panda can usually only manage about 20 seconds of un torrid, un sweltering love making. Mrs Panda has not at all been pleased with this performance and pandas up the pole are scarce as hen's teeth. — *Irish Examiner*, 14th April 2002

2 in a bad way; at a disadvantage *AUSTRALIA, 1906*

- He generally thought Ronnie was all up the pole when giving advice to someone. — William Dick, *A Bunch of Ratbags*, p. 92, 1965
- — Jim Ramsay, *Cop It Sweet!*, p. 93, 1977

3 insane *UK, 1896*

- It'd drive me up the pole, just sitting there[.] — John Peter Jones, *Feather Pluckers*, p. 71, 1964

pole *verb*

1 from a male perspective, to have sex *UK, 1984*

2 to steal something *NEW ZEALAND*

- Did you ever hear of a man called Arthur Beaumont who poled three hundred thousand pounds. — John A. Lee, *Shiner Slattery*, p. 140, 1964

▸ **pole on**

to impose on someone; to not do one's fair share of work *AUSTRALIA, 1906*

- This room is cheap and I may need to pole on her for my share of the rent if I'm out of a job. — Norman Lindsay, *Dust or Polish?*, p. 12, 1950
- — Jim Ramsay, *Cop It Sweet!*, p. 72, 1977

poleaxe *verb*

to shock someone into helplessness; to stupify someone *UK*

From the antique weapon that combines an axe and a hammer.

- Tipped as the next big destination by the World Tourism Organisation (WTO), China has been poleaxed by the Sars epidemic. — *The Guardian*, 27th April 2003

poleaxed *adjective*

drunk *UK*

From the sense 'to render helpless; to stupify'.

- — *e-cyclopaedia*, 20th March 2002

pole buddy *noun*

in electric line work, a transformer gin *US*

- — A.B. Chance Co., *Lineman's Slang Dictionary*, p. 14, 1980

polecat *noun*

1 a police car *US*

From the animal's black and white fur.

- — Warren Smith, *Warren's Smith's Authentic Dictionary of CB*, p. 56, 1976

2 in the television and film industries, a lamp support *US*

- — Ralph S. Singleton, *Filmaker's Dictionary*, p. 125, 1990

poleclimbers *noun*

heavy work boots with steel-reinforced toes and arches *US*

- Doc Martens may have taken over a decade to go from exotic cipher to mall staple, but poleclimbers – and their lower-cut relative, logger boots – seemed to to do it overnight. — Steven Daly and Nalthaniel Wice, *alt.culture*, p. 184, 1995

poledad *noun*
an annoying, new-to-the-sport skateboarder *US*
- Those hopsotch poledads and pedestrians too, will bug ya / Shout "Cuyabunga!" now and skate right on through. —Jan Berry and Dean Torrance, *Sidewalk Surfin'*, 1964

pole dance *noun*
a sexual dance performed with a vertical pole as a main prop *US*
- Sure, I appreciate a tasteful pose, an artful fuck, and an athletic pole dance as much as the next woman. — *The Village Voice*, 8th–14th November 2000

pole day *noun*
in motor racing, the first day of qualifying heats when the pole position is decided *US*
- —Hal Higdon, *Finding the Groove*, p. 306, 1973

pole hog *noun*
in Canadian military aviation, a pilot who tries to keep his hand on the control column *CANADA*
- "I hate flying with Hughes! He's such a pole-hog." —Tom Langeste, *Words on the Wing*, p. 216, 1995

pole in the hole *nickname*
the Spire monument in O'Connell Street, Dublin *IRELAND*
- Last Post agents have been combing the streets to compile a list of the best monikers for the world's largest monument. Here's some of our favourites. The syringe in the binge; the pin in the bin; the Bertie pole; the spire in the mire; the poker near Croker; the stilt in the filth; the pole in the hole[.] — *Sunday Business Post*, 26th January 2003

pole jockey *noun*
a telephone or power lineman *US*
- — *American Speech*, p. 158–159, May 1960: 'The Burgeoning of 'Jockey''

pole orchard *noun*
the half-acre of utility poles at the Fort Gordon, Georgia Signal Corps School where linemen are given climbing instruction *US*
- —Carl Fleischhauer, *A Glossary of Army Slang*, p. 7, 1968
- "Prepare to ascend the poles," Staff Sgt. Doug Foster tells a group of soldiers, each harnessed to a 30-foot pole at the fort's Pole Orchard. — *Augusta (Georgia) Chronicle*, p. A1, 15th March 1999

poles *noun*
trousers *US*
Vietnam war slang.
- —Linda Reinberg, *In the Field*, p. 169, 1991

pole work *noun*
utilisation of a pole by a dancer in a sex club *US*
- The five-day Pure Talent School allowed Burana to polish her 'floor work' skills on the dance stage – skills that Burana forthrightly acknowledges she lacked in the early years of her career – and refine her 'pole work.' — *Denver Post*, p. E1, 10th October 2001
- There's no pole work in the series, but props include a chair. — *Los Angeles Times*, p. 1 (Part 6), 27th October 2003

poley; poly *noun*
a hornless cow or bull *AUSTRALIA, 1843*
- —Jim Ramsay, *Cop It Sweet!*, p. 72, 1977
- But he never had time to make it before the poly rushed in and butted him fair up the guts[.] —Sam Weller, *Old Bastards I Have Met*, p. 143, 1979

poley *adjective*
1 of a beast, hornless *AUSTRALIA, 1843*
From British dialect *poly*, *polly*, *poll*, variant of *polled* (de-horned).

2 of a container, missing a handle *AUSTRALIA, 1901*
- Sometimes my mother kept a poley jug of cool water in the zinc-lined chamber of the ice-chest, but we were never allowed to get at it. —Gerald Murnane, *Landscape with Landscape*, p. 31, 1987

polgarize *verb*
during the Vietnam war, to give unrealistic and optimistic reports of the US progress in the war *US*
Named after Thomas Polgar, CIA station chief in Saigon in the early 1970s.
- —Gregory Clark, *Words of the Vietnam War*, p. 405, 1990

po-lice *noun*
the police *US*
By stressing the first syllable, the conventional term becomes unconventional.
- I ain't got nothin' to hide, it just that the PO-lice is always fuckin' over me ever' time I goes outside[.] —Joseph Wambaugh, *The New Centurions*, p. 73, 1970
- Still, it took about six months before we had learned to talk enough "game" to earn their respect as non-squares, and for suspicions that we might be "po-lice" to evaporate. —Christina and Richard Milner, *Black Players*, p. 24, 1972

police discount *noun*
a great, if not complete, reduction in the price of goods or services provided to police in their area of duty *US*
- His "police discounts" had furnished his house princely. —Joseph Wambaugh, *The Choirboys*, p. 60, 1975
- Two detectives argue about whether or not to ask for a "police discount" on cookies they're purchasing for Crosetti's funeral reception. — *Star Tribune (Minneapolis)*, p. 1E, 2nd December 1994
- Reference is made to the Ledger's articles on and preceding Nov. 19, regarding police discounts at restaurants[.] (Letter to Editor). — *The Ledger (Lakeland, Florida)*, p. A22, 20th November 2003

policeman *noun*
in horse racing, a horse entered in a claiming race solely for the purpose of permitting the owner to claim another horse in the race *US*
- —David W. Maurer, *Argot of the Racetrack*, p. 52, 1951

policeman lesion *noun*
in an x-ray, a lesion that is unmissable *UK*
Medical wit; the lesion must be so obvious that a policeman would spot it.
- —Adam T. Fox, St Mary's Hospital, London, 10th October 2002

policeman's helmet *noun*
the glans of the erect penis *UK, 1961*
From a similarity in shape to the traditional headwear of the British constable.

police pimp *noun*
an informer to the police *AUSTRALIA*
- Of all the low species of humanity, Ginger Lil told them, it was her opinion that a police pimp was the lowest. —Vince Kelly, *The Bogeyman*, p. 40, 1956
- And here, suddenly, he was presented as a police pimp, an associate of gangsters, a blackmailer, and an underworld 'heeler' who had been put on the spot. —George Blaikie, *Remember Smith's Weekly?*, p. 188, 1966
- You know this Wendlan is a police pimp? —Bob Ellis and Anne Brooksbank, *Mad Dog Morgan*, p. 7, 1976

police psychology *noun*
brute physical force *US*
- At that time they used interrogation by police psychology – a punch in the mouth, a kick in the ass, a rap in the balls. —Leonard Shecter and William Phillips, *On the Pad*, p. 85, 1973

policy *noun*
an illegal lottery *US, 1843*
Better known as the **NUMBERS** racket.
- Once he got the club over Pepper's head, he would force her to sneak in phony "hit" slips against the policy wheel. —Iceberg Slim (Robert Beck), *Pimp*, 1969
- You know when you been round policy long as me it gets in your blood. —Vernon E. Smith, *The Jones Men*, p. 91, 1974

policy banker *noun*
the operator of an illegal numbers racket or lottery *US*
- Around Harlem, he'd feed off the policy bankers. —Edwin Torres, *Carlito's Way*, p. 17, 1975

polio weed *noun*
extremely potent marijuana *US*
Marijuana so strong as to reduce the user to a 'polio-like' condition.
- [W]e were quite often transformed into Fred Astaire and Noel Coward by the same polio weed[.] —Dan Jenkins, *Life Its Ownself*, p. 22, 1982
- A Garcia term from the '70s; marijauana so potent it induces a state of paralysis. —David Shenk and Steve Silberman, *Skeleton Key*, p. 228, 1994

polis *noun*
the police; a police officer *UK, 1878*
Mainly Scottish and Irish use.
- Andy was having fun watching the polis panic. —Christopher Brookmyre, *The Sacred Art of Stealing*, p. 91, 2002

poli sci *noun*
political science *US*
College shorthand.

- CANDY: Poli Sci. With a home ec minor. MRS. CHASEN: Eh, Poli Sci? CANDY: Political Science. It's all about what's going on. — *Harold and Maude*, 1971

polish *noun*

oral sex performed on a man *NEW ZEALAND*

- Whady want, sailor, all the way or just a polish? — David McGill, *David McGill's Complete Kiwi Slang Dictionary*, p. 86, 1998

polish *verb*

▶ **polish the mug**

to wash your face *US*

- — Joseph E. Ragen and Charles Finston, *Inside the World's Toughest Prison*, p. 813, 1962: 'Penitentiary and underworld glossary'

polish and gloss; polish *verb*

(of a male) to masturbate *UK*

Rhyming slang for **TOSS**.

- She wouldn't go all the way but she didn't mind polishing my Grandfather Clock [penis]. — Ray Puxley, *Cockney Rabbit*, 1992

polisher *noun*

an alcoholic who drinks metal polish *UK*

- He sucked at a tin of metal polish. The polishers are an interesting branch of the alcohol seeking fraternity. — Geoffrey Fletcher, *Down Among the Meths Men*, p. 16, 1966

Polish jew *noun*

a firecracker *US*

- This cynical name for a firecracker comes about, I presume, from German days, because when you set fire to one it leaves the world with a harmless bang, scarcely ever injuring its murderers. — William T. Vollman, *Whores for Gloria*, p. 137, 1991

Polish martini *noun*

a shot of whisky and a glass of beer *US*

- — Bill Reilly, *Big Al's Official Guide to Chicagoese*, p. 28, 1982

Polish matched luggage *noun*

two shopping bags from Goldblatt's, a low-end Chicago department store chain *US*

- — Bill Reilly, *Big Al's Official Guide to Chicagoese*, p. 49, 1982

polish off *verb*

to defeat someone; to finish or get rid of something; to eat something without leaving anything (especially with gusto) *UK, 1873*

- Lahouaine shuffles over after you've polished off your meal, plonks down a tray of mint tea and pulls up a plastic chair. — *The Guardian*, 12th November 2002

Polish smoking jacket *noun*

a sleeveless tee-shirt or undershirt vest *US*

Polish victory lap *noun*

circling a track in the opposite direction to which a race has been run in celebration of victory *US*

A calculated creation in 1988 of driver Alan Kulwicki, who died in an aeroplane crash in 1993.

- Kulwicki resisted the urge to take another unique victory lap, similar to his self-described "Polish victory lap" when he ran backward around Phoenix International Raceway after victory No. 1. — *AutoWeek*, p. 51, 29th October 1990
- But at the end of the night, after leading the final six laps, it was Hornaday who was able to turn his Chevrolet around and take a Polish victory lap in celebration and in tribute to the man for whom the race was named. — *Milwaukee (Wisconsin) Journal Sentinel*, p. 1C, 27th June 2004

political holy water *noun*

alcohol *CANADA*

- In Nova Scotia, alcohol is known as the political drug or "political holy water," from the tradition of purchasing votes with bottles. — Lewis Poteet, *The South Shore Phrase Book*, p. 87, 1999

politician *noun*

in prison, a trusted prisoner given responsibilities and liberties exceeding those of normal prisoners *US*

- [I]t didn't take a day before one of the "politicians" (that was what we called the trustees) slipped me a folded piece of toilet paper. — Mezz Mezzrow, *Really the Blues*, p. 10–11, 1946

politico; politicko *noun*

a politican either ambitious or unscrupulous, or both *UK, 1893*

From the Italian or Spanish.

- I mean he's right – you make it with some big politicko an you got a good thing goin. — Robert Gover, *Here Goes Kitten*, p. 41, 1964
- — Joe David Brown (Editor), *The Hippies*, p. 219, 1967: 'Glossary of hippie terms'
- I kept wondering whether the Pigs were concerned about Liberation News Service (politicos) or Tate BLues Band (hippies) and things like that. — Abbie Hoffman, *Woodstock Nation*, p. 56–57, 1969
- O.K., O.K., sorry 'bout that. You politicos are so touchy. — Ann Fettamen, *Trashing*, p. 68, 1970
- I was a very big politico on my campus and even got asked by the president to leave. — Malcolm Boyd, *My Fellow Americans*, p. 160, 1970
- Baby Jewels gladhanding politicos, grabassing showgirls, squeezed into nightclub booths with minor celebrities, lolling in his box at Candlestick Park — Seth Morgan, *Homeboy*, p. 29, 1990
- [S]howbiz schmoozing is a part of the territory with politicos. — John Robb, *The Nineties*, p. 154, 1999

pollakaun *noun*

a hoard of money; savings *IRELAND*

- She has the auld pollkaun. — Irwin Liam, *North Munster Antiquarian Journal*, p. 79, 2000

Pollard's cellar *noun*

a notional representation of homelessness *BARBADOS*

- — Frank A. Collymore, *Barbadian Dialect*, p. 86, 1965

pollatic *adjective*

drunk *UK*

- — *e-cyclopaedia*, 20th March 2002

pollie *noun*

a politician *AUSTRALIA, 1967*

- — Jim Ramsay, *Cop It Sweet!*, p. 72, 1977
- But the founding fathers overlooked the fact that the strong contingent of Victorian pollies and public servants would act as carriers of the disease over the border. — Lawrence Money, *The Footy Fan's Handbook*, p. 65, 1986
- — Harry Orsman and Des Hurley, *The Beaut Little Book of New Zealand Slang*, 1994

pollutant *noun*

amphetamine; MDMA, the recreational drug best known as ecstasy *UK*

It makes you **POLLUTED** (intoxicated).

- — Mike Haskins, *Drugs*, p. 279, 2003

polluted *adjective*

1 drunk *US*

- One night they come home and get polluted on the beer[.] — George V. Higgins, *The Judgment of Deke Hunter*, p. 121, 1976
- Jon was well beyond tipsy. A few minutes later, and with help from his friends, the bottle was empty. Jon was polluted. — Elissa Stein and Kevin Leslie, *Chunks*, p. 2–3, 1997

2 warped, perverse *US*

- You're so polluted. Talking down to people, making fake notes. — *Heathers*, 1988

polly *noun*

a politician *US*

- — John Scarne, *Scarne on Dice*, p. 475, 1974

Polly Flinder *noun*

1 a window *UK, 1961*

Rhyming slang, noted as a 'shiner's (window cleaner's) term'.

- — Ray Puxley, *Cockney Rabbit*, 1992

2 a cinder, especially when used to describe over-cooked food *UK*

Rhyming slang, formed from the nursery rhyme character Polly Flinders.

- This sausage is burnt to a Polly Flinder. — Ray Puxley, *Cockney Rabbit*, 1992

polly parrot *noun*

a carrot *UK*

Rhyming slang.

- — Ray Puxley, *Cockney Rabbit*, 1992

polo *noun*

a mixture of heroin and a motion-sickness drug *UK*

From the middle syllables in 'sco*pola*mine'.

- — Robert Ashton, *This Is Heroin*, p. 210, 2002

polo mint *noun*

1 without money *UK*

Rhyming slang for **SKINT**, based on the famous 'mint with the hole'.

- I'm a bit polo this week. — *www.LondonSlang.com*, June 2002

2 a girlfriend; a young woman *UK*
Rhyming slang for **BINT**. Also based on the branded mint sweet.
- —Bodmin Dark, *Dirty Cockney Rhyming Slang*, 2003

3 a traffic roundabout *UK*
Citizens' band radio slang, from the similarity of shape with Polo™ branded peppermints.
- —Peter Chippindale, *The British CB Book*, p. 158, 1981

polone; pollone; polony; polonee *noun*
a woman; a girl; an effeminate man *UK, 1934*
Polari. Also variants with an 'a' to include 'palone', 'paloney' and 'palogne'.
- [M]y friend began to talk of his "palone". —Butch Reynolds, *Broken Hearted Clown*, p. 29, 1953
- SANDY: You may have vada'd one of our tiny bijou masterpiecettes, heartface. We made Funny Eek, My Fair Palone. And then we done one on Chopin and his love for George Sanders. —Barry Took and Marty Feldman, *Round The Horne*, April 1967
- [A]ll the hideola [hideous] pallones in cod [bad] drag [clothes]. —the cast of 'Aspects of Love', Prince of Wales Theatre, *Palare (Boy Dancer Talk) for Beginners*, 1989–92
- —Paul Baker, *Polari*, p. 185, 2002

Polski *noun*
a Polish immigrant or Polish-American *US*
- And those given a name were stuck with it forever: Svade, Svenska, Lugan, Schnapps, Moishe, Stosh, Henie, Mockie, Guinea, Canuck, Bohunk, Pork-dodger, Limey, Greaseball, Krauthead, Dutchie, Squarehead, Grick, Mick, Paddy, Goombah, Polski, Dago, Hunkie, Wop[.] —*San Francisco Examiner*, p. A15, 28th July 1997

polvo *noun*
1 phencyclidine, the recreational drug known as PCP or angel dust *US*
- —*Q Magazine*, p. 75, February 2001

2 powdered drugs; heroin; cocaine *UK, 1980*
Directly from Spanish *polvo* (powder): **POWDER** (heroin). Also variant 'polvito'.
- —Mike Haskins, *Drugs*, p. 284, 2003

polvo blanco *noun*
cocaine *UK, 1998*
From Spanish for 'white powder'.
- —Mike Haskins, *Drugs*, p. 281, 2003

poly *noun*
1 a person who loves and has sex with multiple partners *US*
An abbreviation of '*poly*amorous'.
- Not all neo-pagans are polys and not all polys are neo-pagans[.] —*Nerve*, p. 78, October-November 2000

2 a *poly*technic *UK*
- University students often indulge in some old-fashioned snobbery by referring to Nottingham Trent University as 'the poly'. —*Nottingham Evening Post*, 8th June 2002

3 marijuana of a supposedly *Poly*nesian origin *UK*
- Look: you was after the boom poly an' I got two kees. —Nick Barlay, *Curvy Lovebox*, p. 33, 1997

4 a surfboard manufactured with *poly*urethane *US*
- —Grant W. Kuhns, *On Surfing*, p. 120, 1963

▷ see: POLEY

polyster queen *noun*
a girl or woman with no fashion sense *US*
- —Connie Eble (Editor), *UNC-CH Campus Slang*, p. 8, Fall 1985

Pom; pom *noun*
an English person, or more loosely, a person from Britain *AUSTRALIA, 1912*
Shortening of **POMMY**.
- —Michael Peters, *Pommie Bastard*, p. 87, 1969
- Can't put one over on the Poms. —John O'Grady, *It's Your Shout, Mate!*, p. 79, 1972
- There's nothing Australians like so much as a really stupid Pom. —Bill Hornadge, *The Ugly Australian*, p. 94, 1975
- Notice at Bacchus Marsh Lion Park: Do not open the windows of your car. Do not alight from you car. Poms welcome on bicycles. —Bill Hornadge, *The Ugly Australian*, p. 96, 1975
- —Barry Humphries, *The Traveller's Tool*, p. 75, 1985
- Where do Poms hide their money? Under the soap. —Kathy Lette, *Girls' Night Out*, p. 205, 1987
- It was the first punk rock single ever, and every Pom from Tony Blackburn to Billy Connolly swears blind it was the beginning of the whole movement. —Suroosh Alvi et al., *The Vice Guide*, p. 130, 2002

Pom; pom *adjective*
English, or more loosely, British *AUSTRALIA*
- The place was stacked with talent and those pom lasses certainly turn it on[.] —Barry Humphries, *A Nice Night's Entertainment*, p. 40, 1960

Pomland *nickname*
England *AUSTRALIA*
- While Bazza was away in Pomland another male Australian character was born from the typewriters of advertising copywriters. —Sandra Jobson, *Blokes*, p. 31, 1984

Pommified *adjective*
having taken on an English character *AUSTRALIA, 1936*
- They try to become Pommified, or Americanised, as fast as possible and go to some lengths to disguise their origins. —Sandra Jobson, *Blokes*, p. 127, 1984

Pommy; Pommie *noun*
an English person, or more loosely, a person from Britain *AUSTRALIA, 1912*
Originally used of English immigrants to Australia, it is a shortening of the now obsolete 'Pomegranate', rhyming slang for 'immigrant'. The rhyming slang term and the shortened variants 'Pom' and 'Pommy' all appear in the lexical record at the same time. The occasional spelling 'pommygrant' shows the rhyming pronunciation. Although this word carries a definite negative connotation, it also can be used as a term of affectionate abuse (see **POMMY BASTARD** and **WHINGEING POM**). The suggestion that Pommy is actually a respelling of P.O.M.E., standing for the reputed term Prisoner Of Mother England, or P.O.H.M.I.E, standing for Prisoner Of Her Majesty In Exile, and other variations on this theme, are implausible on phonetic grounds and are in themselves anachronistic as acronyms were not a common feature of English in the early part of C20.
- POMMY – English immigrant. —Gilbert H. Lawson, *A Dictionary of Australian Words and Terms*, 1924
- All pommies are bastards, bastards or worse. / And England is the arsehole of the universe. —*The Adventures of Barry McKenzie*, 1972

Pommy; Pommie *adjective*
English, or more loosely, British *AUSTRALIA, 1915*
- A lonely, thirsty figure wanders off into the Pommy night[.] —Barry Humphries, *The Wonderful World of Barry McKenzie*, p. 22, 1968
- He'd have been safe in NSW but he made the mistake of doing one of his murders in England and the Pommie cops grabbed him. —Frank Hardy, *Hardy's People*, p. 82, 1986
- Tragically we have to look at his lily-white pommy feet. —*Large*, p. 10, 2002
- Can you believe what's coming out of these pommie pooves' mouths, Stella? —Claire Mansfield and John Mendelssohn, *Dominatrix*, p. 251, 2002

Pommy bastard *noun*
an English person (stereotypically viewed as noisome to the Australian) *AUSTRALIA, 1951*
- —Michael Peters, *Pommie Bastard*, p. 19, 1969
- But what can you do (I tell them) when a New Australian migrant, a Pommy bastard and a Choom to be exact, moves into your house and marries your beautiful sister-in-law. —Frank Hardy, *The Outcasts of Foolgarah*, p. 23, 1971
- —John O'Grady, *It's Your Shout, Mate!*, p. 11, 1972
- —Bill Hornadge, *The Ugly Australian*, p. 80, 1975
- —Bob Staines, *Wot a Whopper*, p. 53, 1982

pommy cock *noun*
an uncircumcised penis *AUSTRALIA*
- —Thommo, *The Dictionary of Australian Swearing and Sex Sayings*, p. 99, 1985

Pommyland *nickname*
England or the British Isles *AUSTRALIA, 1915*
- —Sandra Jobson, *Blokes*, p. 33, 1984
- —Barry Humphries, *The Traveller's Tool*, p. 132, 1985
- Mervyn toils for the council in Nottinghamshire, Pommyland[.] —*Picture*, p. 21, 6th May 1992

po-mo; postie *noun*
a *post*modernist philosopher *UK*
- —Simon Blackburn, *Start The Week*, 26th May 2003

pomosexual *noun*

a person who will not be defined by his or her sexuality *US, 1997*

A contrived play on '*post-mo*dern' and 'homo*sexual*'. 'Pomosexuality' is first recorded in 1995.

- Almost everyone noticed the word 'pomosexual'. Pomosexuals are "people who don't feel that they should be forced to have their identity defined by their sex lives". — *The Observer*, 26th May 2002

pom-pom *noun*

sex *US*

Used by US soldiers in Japan and the Phillipines.

- — *American Speech*, p. 55, February 1947: 'Pacific war language'

ponce *noun*

1 a pimp *UK, 1872*

- Gabriel knew Mavis was a sucker for ponces. She often had several bludging off her at the one time. — Lance Peters, *The Dirty Half-Mile*, p. 92, 1979
- A toothpick traversed his mouth in sync with the restless eye gunning the street, identifying in less time than it took to name the hookers, hustlers, thieves, and thugs; pennyweight ponces and flyweight flimflammers; diddyboppers, deadbeats and dopefiends. — Seth Morgan, *Homeboy*, p. 12–13, 1990
- — Angela Devlin, *Prison Patter*, p. 89, 1996

2 a despised or unpleasant person *UK, 1953*

- "[H]ow could you trust a man who's stupid enough to trust these ponces, you could see it coming." and Gerald says "Too fucking true, he was a berk." — Ted Lewis, *Jack Carter's Law*, p. 10, 1974
- [L]essons in political opportunism and commercial exploitation and they were learned by a nouveau-ponce-class[.] — Irvine Welsh, *The Naughty Nineties*, p. 14, 1999
- the girls upstairs with the ponces who don't mind dancing to shit music and talking bollocks. — John King, *Human Punk*, p. 110, 2000

3 an effeminate male *AUSTRALIA*

- He'd reckon you were a bit of a ponce if you got dressed up for him. — John O'Grady, *Aussie Etiket*, p. 37, 1971
- If any man deserved a medal it was Frank McBee. Why only a corporal? The old story . . . couldn't stand being given orders by ponces. — Murray Bail, *Holden's Performance*, p. 29, 1988

ponce *verb*

1 to obtain something by poncing, usually money *UK, 1938*

2 to live on the earnings of another's prostitution; to act as a pimp (a prostitute's manager) *UK, 1932*

- — Angela Devlin, *Prison Patter*, p. 89, 1996

3 to scrounge; to sponge *UK, 1915*

A general sense of acquiring something for nothing extended from the previous sense.

- [H]e was a right slag, what with never washing and ponsing [sic] dogend from morning to night. — Frank Norman, *Bang To Rights*, p. 95, 1958

▸ **go out poncing**

(of the police) to search for pimps *UK*

- — Angela Devlin, *Prison Patter*, p. 58, 1996

▸ **ponce off; ponce on**

to live on the earnings of another's prostitution, but not taking any active part in the trade *UK, 1936*

- [H]e'd got nicked for ponceing [poncing] off his old woman who was a brass. — Frank Norman, *Bang To Rights*, p. 8, 1958

ponce about; ponce around *verb*

1 to behave in an exaggeratedly camp manner *AUSTRALIA*

- And to rub my nose in it, I gets a squizz through the curtain at first class and there's Rupert Murdoch and Kerry Packer poncing around with glasses of champagne in their hands. — Barry Humphries, *A Nice Night's Entertainment*, p. 174, 1978
- — Robert G. Barrett, *Davo's Little Something*, p. 16, 1992

2 to act the fool; to show off *UK*

- — Angela Devlin, *Prison Patter*, p. 89, 1996

ponce up *verb*

to dress up smartly; to decorate something *UK, 1965*

Originally military.

- All they believed in was getting ponced up and parading their attractions around the local dance halls. — Johnny Speight, *It Stands to Reason*, p. 66, 1973

poncey *adjective*

1 affectedly stylish *UK, 1964*

- "It's poncy." "He's a bit of a ponce." — Ann Barr and Peter York, *The Official Sloane Ranger Handbook*, p. 159, 1982
- I never go overboard and wear kind of poncey stuff – we like to look well-turned out, nice shirts and smart jeans. — Ben Malbon, *Cool Places*, p. 268, 1998

2 blatantly, affectedly homosexual *NEW ZEALAND*

- — Louis S. Leland, *A Personal Kiwi-Yankee Dictionary*, p. 78, 1984

Poncho *nickname*

a Pontiac car *US*

- — John Lawlor, *How to Talk Car*, p. 81, 1965
- — Lyle K. Engel, *The Complete Book of Fuel and Gas Dragsters*, p. 153, 1968

poncified *adjective*

affectedly stylish; effeminate *UK*

From PONCE.

- Perhaps this place wasn't entirely staffed with poncified fairies after all. — Garry Bushell, *The Face*, p. 95, 2001

pond *noun*

▸ **the pond**

a sea, especially the Atlantic Ocean *UK, 1780*

An ironic understatement of the distance between the UK and the US, shortened from earlier 'great pond' which it replaces.

pond life *noun*

an unintelligent person or people *UK, 1998*

- [H]ave a mosey at [look at] the pondlife in the Britannia. — Kevin Sampson, *Outlaws*, p. 6, 2001
- [P]oxy women drivers who were forever SLOWING DOWN for fellow shoppers, parkers, cyclists, pedestrians, pensioners and all the other pondlife who had nothing better to do all day but HOLD HIM UP! TOSSERS! — Garry Bushell, *The Face*, p. 3, 2001
- "The spotters on Queen's Buildings at Heathrow are pond life," said Tony, talking of one of the most popular vantage points for spotters of passenger aircraft. — Iain Aitch, *A Fete Worse Than Death*, p. 75, 2003

pond scum *noun*

a person with no redeeming features *US*

- Because the People of the great Garden State of New Jersey wanted to put a piece of pond scum like Joe "Dancer" Rina in the yellow brick prison at Rahway? — Stephen J. Cannell, *King Con*, p. 11, 1997
- — Vann Wesson, *Generation X Field Guide and Lexicon*, p. 130, 1997
- While other Holmes show panelists described him last Monday as 'pond scum', Marshall seemed more upset that celebrity Charlotte Dawson accused him of being a failed radio and TV journalist. — *Sunday Star-Timers*, p. C3, 17th August 2003

pone *noun*

in a card game, the player immediately to the right of the dealer *UK, 1901*

- — George Percy, *The Language of Poker*, p. 69, 1988

pong *noun*

an unpleasant smell *AUSTRALIA, 1919*

- What's that pong? — Ian Pattison, *Rab C. Nesbitt*, 1988
- [M]y goodness, what a pong. — Mark Steel, *Reasons to be Cheerful*, p. 227, 2001

pong *verb*

1 to stink *UK, 1927*

- — Louis S. Leland, *A Personal Kiwi-Yankee Dictionary*, p. 78, 1984
- I sniffed at it this morning an was surprised at how much it ponged. Stale BO an that. — Niall Griffiths, *Kelly + Victor*, p. 227, 2002

2 in the theatre, to substitute lines when the correct lines are forgotten *UK*

- — Wilfred Granville, *The Theatre Dictionary*, p. 148, 1952

ponga *noun*

the vagina *BAHAMAS*

- — John A. Holm, *Dictionary of Bahamian English*, p. 158, 1982

Pongo; Percy Pongo; Perce *noun*

a member of the British Army *UK*

The Royal Navy perpetuate the wicked myth that this derives from PONG (a smell) suggesting that soldiers smell and sailors don't. 'Percy' appears to be merely alliterative.

- — Nigel Foster, *The Making of a Royal Marine Commando*, 1987

Pongo Pete *nickname*

General Sir Peter de la Billiere (b.1934), commander of British armoured forces during the Gulf war *UK*

- — *American Speech*, p. 398, Winter 1991: 'Among the new words'

pongy *adjective*

smelly *UK, 1936*

- Vince is wearing a white shirt with silver cuff-links, and pongy after-shave. — Graham Swift, *Last Orders*, p. 18, 1996

ponies *noun*

1 horse races held for ponies *AUSTRALIA*

- Syphilitic from birth, he had started as an apprentice in a racing stable, got too heavy, and began touting at the ponies, became a pickpocket, skilful on difficult jobs, but 'rolled the drunks' as well. —Frank Hardy, *Power Without Glory*, p. 259, 1950
- The ARC took advantage of this situation and instituted special races from which horses above the 14.2 limit were excluded. These meetings became known as 'the ponies'. —Joe Andersen, *Winners Can Laugh*, p. 26, 1982

2 horsepower *US*

- —John Edwards, *Auto Dictionary*, p. 127, 1993

▸ **the ponies**

horse racing *UK, 1961*

- I know guys who go to racetracks who say that about the ponies. —George V. Higgins, *Penance for Jerry Kennedy*, p. 75, 1985
- [T]he sentimental image of the old dear [the Queen Mother] who liked a flutter on the ponies, loved her tipple, waved away her overdraft and was good for a laugh[.] —*The Guardian*, 1st April 2002

▸ **push ponies**

to work as a pimp *US*

- —*Maledicta*, p. 150, Summer/Winter 1986–1987: 'Sexual slang: prostitutes, pedophiles, flagellators, transvestites, and necrophiles'

Ponsford odds *noun*

in horse racing, odds of 100–1 or greater *AUSTRALIA*
An allusion to Bill Ponsford, a high scoring cricket legend.

- —Ned Wallish, *The Truth Dictionary of Racing Slang*, p. 64, 1989

pont *verb*

in the harsh climate of Antarctica, to pose for a photograph, especially in an uncomfortable position *ANTARCTICA, 1911*
Eponym from Herbert George *Pont*ing, photographer on Scott's 1910–13 expedition.

- —Bernadette Hince, *The Antarctic Dictionary*, p. 275, 2000

PONTI; ponti *noun*

in military terms, a *p*erson *o*f *n*o *t*actical *i*mportance *UK*
An acronym.

- Early on we heard that we [journalists] were referred to as PONTIs – an official army acronym, no less. This was it, recognition! A long time later we learned that it represented what the army really thought of us: Persons Of No Tactical Importance. —Kate Adie (writing of the Gulf War), *The Kindness of Strangers*, p. 331, 2002

pontoon *noun*

a period of twenty-one months' imprisonment; also twenty-one years in prison or in military service *UK, 1950*
From the card game 'pontoon' in which the winning hand scores twenty-one.

- I was done to rights, through nobody's fault but my own, and got a pontoon. —Charles Raven, *Underworld Nights*, p. 170, 1956
- This geezer was doing a pontoon —Frank Norman, *Bang To Rights*, p. 145, 1958
- —Angela Devlin, *Prison Patter*, p. 89, 1996

Ponty *nickname*

Pontypridd, Pontypool, Pontefract in West Yorkshire, or any town so constructed *UK: WALES, 1937*
From Welsh *ponty* (bridge of).

- [T]he run-in with the two coppers in Ponty. —David Peace, *Nineteen Seventy Four*, p. 95, 1999
- Duw duw, there's a lot of bother. Me, I was born here in Ponty, Janeylove, and I have never moved. —James Hawes, *White Powder, Green Light*, p. 27, 2002

pony *noun*

1 twenty-five pounds *UK, 1797*

- Here is a pony for any inconvenience you may have been caused. —Charles Raven, *Underworld Nights*, p. 39, 1956
- 'Wot d'you 'ave on him?' 'Put a pony on 'im'. —Nino Culotta (John O'Grady), *They're A Weird Mob*, p. 72, 1957
- I'm about to stuff my pony in my kick [trouser pocket][.] —Derek Raymond (Robin Cook), *The Crust on its Uppers*, p. 39, 1962
- —Ned Wallish, *The Truth Dictionary of Racing Slang*, p. 63, 1989

2 in betting, odds of 25–1 *UK*
Adapted from the previous sense.

- —John McCririck, *John McCririck's World of Betting*, p. 61, 1991

3 a racehorse *US, 1907*
Used especially in the phrase 'play the ponies'.

- He played the ponies, got his tail, smoked cigarettes incessantly, despite his bad lungs, drank, sat up at all-night poker games. —James T. Farrell, *Saturday Night*, p. 12, 1947
- He was married to woman by the name of Lisa, who had a pocketful of busted dreams of her own, but he still took what he could get, still played the ponies and still lost the farm nearly each and every time he tried to be a sport. —Robert Campbell, *Juice*, p. 3–4, 1988
- Apparently, way it went, he invited her to come to Santa Anita to play the ponies with him. —*Get Shorty*, 1995

4 a chorus girl or dancer, especially a small one *UK, 1908*

- The whole Ziegfeld chorus, from the ponies to the showgirls, would be hired to fan us with palm leaves as we lounged around in the sun, reading H.L. Mencken and playing Louis Armstrong records[.] —Mezz Mezzrow, *Really the Blues*, p. 131, 1946
- A new crop of lovelies had come up, were displayed and went on to Hollywood. To mention one, Alice Faye – a Hollywood Restaurant pony. —Jack Lait and Lee Mortimer, *New York Confidential*, p. 28, 1948
- But here the feathers hang tired on the rumps of the floor-show ponies, and there is no self-conscious reading of Proust in satined dressing rooms. —John D. McDonald, *The Neon Jungle*, p. 6, 1953
- Rita batted her rhinestoned eyelashes seductively like the Vegas chorus pony she once, recently, was. —Iceberg Slim (Robert Beck), *Long White Con*, p. 20, 1977

5 a female who moves quickly from sexual relationship to sexual relationship, manipulating and using her partners *US*

- —Connie Eble (Editor), *UNC-CH Campus Slang*, p. 8, Fall 1999

6 crack cocaine *US*

- —US Department of Justice, *Street Terms*, October 1994

7 a Pontiac car *US*

- Pony – Pontiac. —Lyle K. Engel, *The Dodge Book of Performance Cars*, p. 321, 1967

8 in Western Australia, a small glass of beer *AUSTRALIA, 1895*
Now generally 5 fluid ounces, though formerly 4 , or even 2 fluid ounces. Obsolescent.

- 'We got ponies, glasses, middies, an' pots, see,' the first man said. 'Now a pony's four ounces –' The second man said, 'Two to four.' 'All right, two to four. But who the bloody hell drinks two's? You keep quiet while I clue him up. A glass is five ounces, a middy is seven ounces, an' a pot's ten.' —John O'Grady, *It's Your Shout, Mate!*, p. 15, 1972
- Others available were ponies, four ounces; schooners, nine ounces; and pints. But a pint, which is by definition twenty ounces, is not so in South Australian pubs. For some strange reason, known only to South Aussies, a pint of beer is fifteen ounces. —John O'Grady, *It's Your Shout, Mate!*, p. 30, 1972

9 dried nose mucus *BAHAMAS*

- —John A. Holm, *Dictionary of Bahamian English*, p. 158, 1982

10 a literal, line-by-line translation of a work in a foreign (usually classical) language *US, 1827*

- Then she would produce a Virgil pony – a Latina text book with English translations set in smaller type beneath each line of Latin. —Max Shulman, *The Many Loves of Dobie Gillis*, p. 2, 1951

pony *verb*

in horse racing, to send a stable pony out with a racehorse to limber up *US*

- —Dan Parker, *The ABC of Horse Racing*, p. 147, 1947

pony and trap; pony *noun*

an act of defecation; hence excreta; rubbish, nonsense *UK, 1960*
Rhyming slang for **CRAP** (excrement); it can substitute for any sense of 'crap'.

- I'm not going to say it's all for the best, because we know that's a lot of pony-and-trap[.] —Charles Raven, *Underworld Nights*, p. 24, 1956
- Fraser and Nash, pony and trap —Ian Dury, *Blackmail Man*, 1977
- Quiet and slippery, no-one ever went in there for a pony. —Jeremy Cameron, *Brown Bread in Wengen*, p. 30, 1999
- The police went through the usual old pony of taking our names and addresses[.] —Martin King and Martin Knight, *The Naughty Nineties*, p. 89, 1999

pony and trap; pony *verb*

to defecate *UK*
Rhyming slang for **CRAP**; usually reduced to 'pony'.

pony and trap; pony *adjective*

rubbishy, trashy, valueless *UK*
Rhyming slang for **CRAP**.

- —Patrick O'Shaughnessy, *Market Traders' Slang*, 1979
- "The Customer Is Always Right" – that pony old chestnut[.] —Andrew Nickolds, *Back to Basics*, p. 33, 1994
- [T]he place [Blackpool] he various refers to as "kickin'" and "pony". —*Hip-Hop Connection*, p. 34, July 2002

pony pecker *noun*

sausage; unidentified pressed meat *US*

- —Carl Fleischhauer, *A Glossary of Army Slang*, p. 26, 1968

ponyplay *noun*
an animal transformation sexual fetish, in which the dominants train, ride and groom people who dress and act like ponies *US*
- The erotic elements of ponyplay depend on the people involved. — *The Village Voice*, 28th November 2000

pony up *verb*
to contribute your share of a bet or collection *US*
- — John Scarne, *Scarne's Guide to Modern Poker*, p. 287, 1979

poo *noun*
1 faeces, excrement; the act of defecation *UK, 1960*
Childish or jocular. Many variant forms, including 'pooh', 'poo poo' and 'pooh pooh'.
- — *Maledicta*, p. 32, 1988–1989: 'Medical Maledicta from San Francisco'
- Who knew that eating cheese makes good pooh-pooh? — Howard Stern, *Miss America*, p. 245, 1995
- This projectile terd shoots right out of his butt and lands SMACK on her neck .... this poo hits her right on the neck. — *Hard Eight*, 1996
- [N]ever once did I wash my hands after I'd been to the toilet, not even after I'd done a poo. — Jenny Eclair, *Camberwell Beauty*, p. 97, 2000
- [H]e loves his walks, the fresh air and chance to have a sniff, a wee and a poo[.] — John King, *White Trash*, p. 1, 2001
- I really don't want her smelling me poo. — Niall Griffiths, *Kelly + Victor*, p. 28, 2002

2 the buttocks; the anus *BAHAMAS*
- — John A. Holm, *Dictionary of Bahamian English*, p. 158, 1982

▸ **in the poo**
in trouble *AUSTRALIA, 1961*
Euphemistic for **IN THE SHIT**.
- Struth, now I'm really in the poo. — *The Adventures of Barry McKenzie*, 1972
- You'd better leave before she gets back or I'll be in the pooh — David Malouf, *Harland's Half Acre*, p. 226, 1984

poo; pooh *verb*
to defecate *UK, 1963*
- It seemed to me that babies only did four things: eat, wee, poo and cry. — Mary Hooper, *(megan)2*, p. 83, 1999

-poo; -poos *suffix*
used for creating an informal elaboration of a person's name *UK*
- Ikey sticks is head in through thuh window an goes: – Yoo hoo, Paulie poos! — Niall Griffiths, *Grits*, p. 20, 2000

poo and spew syndrome *noun*
amoebic dysentery or similar complaint *AUSTRALIA*
- A particular delicacy offered for sale by the culinary street peddler was a meat and salad roll commonly called the 'heppo' roll. An innocent purchaser, would, no doubt, contract hepatitis and/or the 'poo and spew' syndrome amoebic dysentry [sic]. — Martin Cameron, *A Look at the Bright Side*, 1988

poo butt *noun*
a coward *US*
Recorded as 'black street gang terminology' by Bill Valentine, *Gang Intelligence Manual*, p. 77, 1995.

pooch *noun*
1 a dog *US, 1924*
Also used as a term of address for an unknown dog.
- old women with grotesque young get-ups and peroxided hair, parading their pooches — Jack Lait and Lee Mortimer, *New York Confidential*, p. 13, 1948
- Of course the pooch padded down the steps heading straight for the tree to pee over Letch's. — Joseph Wambaugh, *Floaters*, p. 12, 1996

2 the buttocks *BARBADOS*
- — Frank A. Collymore, *Barbadian Dialect*, p. 86, 1965
- — Lise Winer, *Dictionary of the English/Creole of Trinidad & Tobago*, 2003

Pooch *noun*
a Porsche car *US*
- — John Lawlor, *How to Talk Car*, p. 81, 1965

poochi *noun*
the vagina *US*
Sounds more like a dog – (a **POOCH**) – than the traditional **PUSSY** (the vagina); probably a play on Poochi™, an electronic toy dog promoted with such phrases as: 'The more you play with me the happier I will be!' and 'Feed me my special dog bone whenever I get hungry'.
- There's [...] a "poochi," a "poopi," a "peepe,", a "poopelu," a "poopelu," a "poonani," a "pal" and a "piche[."] — Eve Ensler, *The Vagina Monologues*, p. 6, 1998

pooch out *verb*
to purse your lips *US*
- "[M]ake the dancer face" (eyes closed; lips pooched out – you know the one[.)] — Frank Zappa, *The Real Frank Zappa Book*, p. 159, 1989

poodle; pootle *verb*
to travel or move forward without urgency *UK*
- Things were pootling along nicely. — Kevin Sampson, *Powder*, p. 413, 1999
- I start to feel foolish, pootling around in my hire car[.] — Pete McCarthy, *McCarthy's Bar*, p. 68, 2000

poof; pouf; pouff *noun*
a male homosexual *AUSTRALIA, 1833*
In origin probably connected with French slang *poufiasser*, which Barrère (*Argot and Slang*, 1889) defines as a person 'of either sex whose fondness for the opposite sex leads them into a life of questionable description', that is, presumably, a life of prostitution including homosexual prostitution, and *pouffiace* or *pouffiasse* 'a low prostitute'.
- "You're a little pouf," says she, with a manic tiger grin. — Derek Raymond (Robin Cook), *The Crust on its Uppers*, p. 56, 1962
- He pulls in the pouffs for the place. — Petra Christian, *The Sexploiters*, p. 22, 1973
- [T]hey'd had a little poof called Kieron Beck have his way with the soft furnishings. — *Ted Lewis, 'Jack Carter's Law*, p. 14, 1974
- They ran right into his dingy shop and yelled, 'Doc Jenner is an arsehole and a poof,' then scurried off in every direction. — Kerry Cue, *Crooks, Chooks and Bloody Ratbags*, p. 194, 1983
- — Connie Eble (Editor), *UNC-CH Campus Slang*, p. 7, Fall 1988
- From then on its action, action, action for dykes and poofs. — *Lesbians on the Loose*, p. 41, 1997
- Downside: Dressing up like a champion poof and having to do something more physical than walking to the pub. — *People*, p. 13, 5th July 1999
- A groaner who didn't like the food and didn't like the Paddies and didn't like the Pakis and didn't like the poofs[.] — John King, 2001
- Like "POOFS" reminding us what conditions apply for gay sex being permitted P for Private (the location), O, only two persons to be involved, O, both parties must be over 21 fully consenting; S, for Sane. — Duncan Maclaughlin, *The Fifth*, 2002
- As far as he was concerned, umbrellas were for poofs. — Alan Titchmarsh, *Trowell and Error*, p. 92, 2002

poof *adjective*
of a male homosexual *AUSTRALIA*
- So you and your poof mate are going to see Santana eh? — Robert G. Barrett, *Davo's Little Something*, p. 38, 1992

poof-juice *noun*
after-shave lotion, eau-de-cologne for men *UK*
- I should have guessed when you started wearing this poof-juice. — *The Full Monty*, 1997

poofster *noun*
a homosexual man; an effeminate man *US*
Variation of **POOFTER**.
- [H]usbands on Long Island work full-time, then come home and suddenly turn into POOFSTERS like Mrs. Doubtfire, doing all kind of domestic chores. — Howard Stern, *Miss America*, p. 141, 1995

poofteenth *noun*
a very small amount; an umpteenth *AUSTRALIA, 1996*
- You will need to file a poofteenth off to get it to fit. — *www.abc.net.au/wordmap*, 2003

poofter *noun*
1 a homosexual male *AUSTRALIA, 1903*
Variants include 'pooftah' and 'poofdah'.
- What's wrong with you? They're only bloody poufters when all's said and done, and i told you I'm not trade. — Criena Rohan, *Down by the Dockside*, p. 215, 1963
- — Criena Rohan, *Down by the Dockside*, p. 215, 1963
- Bloody poofdah. — Barry Humphries, *A Nice Night's Entertainment*, p. 95, 1965
- Those big, muscle-bound boneheads who romp so beautifully on our beaches are not regarded as poofters simply because they rather shoot a wave than chat to a bird. — Sue Rhodes, *Now you'll think I'm awful*, p. 106, 1967
- You think I'm a poofter, then, don't you? — Alexander Buzo, *Norm and Ahmed*, p. 4, 1969
- I'd say you were a poofdah!! — Barry Humphries, *Bazz Pulls It Off!*, 1971
- [M]incing pansy, head-shaking poofter[.] — *The Times*, 15th March 1973
- Fackin' [fucking] lesbians and pooftahs running the education system. — Donald Gorgon, *Cop Killer*, p. 109, 1994

• [T]he first thing we saw was a man with pink hair. "For fuck's sake!" cried Pat. "What's this? A poofters' convention?"—Chris Ryan, *Stand By, Stand By*, p. 62, 1996

2 an effeminate looking man, not necessarily homosexual *AUSTRALIA, 1903*
Also variant 'poofta'.
• They'd play around like poofters, with the kid gloves and the soft soap.—D'Arcy Niland, *The Shiralee*, p. 207, 1955
• These kids were cissies and a lot of poofters and I disliked most of them.—William Dick, *A Bunch of Ratbags*, p. 132, 1965
• A real man. What a change after all these pallid poufters.—Barry Oakley, *A Salute to the Great McCarthy*, p. 139, 1970
• Fuckin' wowsers and poofters!—Peter Corris, *Make Me Rich*, p. 105, 1985
• Baz said I'd always been a bit of a poofta and gave me a smack on the forehead and a handful of French Blues.—Stuart Browne, *Dangerous Parking*, p. 4, 2000

3 a contemptible person *AUSTRALIA*
Used as a general term of abuse.
• You'll soon learn that most opposition players, coaches, officials and supporters are poofters.—Ivor Limb, *Footy's No Joke!*, p. 58, 1986

4 a braggart *NEW ZEALAND*
• 'I don't like my boss,' he said. 'He's a stuck-up poofter and he makes mistakes.'—Geoffrey Chevasse, *Integrity*, p. 40, 1990

poofter *adjective*

1 (of a male) homosexual *AUSTRALIA*
• First we got to take a dekko at this poofter mate of yours, don't we?—George Johnston, *My Brother Jack*, p. 109, 1964
• —Bill Hornadge, *The Ugly Australian*, p. 113, 1975
• —Lance Peters, *The Dirty Half-Mile*, p. 162, 1979
• —Sandra Jobson, *Blokes*, p. 33, 1984

2 befitting or suitable for an effeminate homosexual man *AUSTRALIA*
• [H]is local's gone poofter with wine bars and fancy beer gardens with foreign tucker to cater for the ladies.—Sandra Jobson, *Blokes*, p. 16, 1984

poofter bash *verb*
to beat up a male homosexual *AUSTRALIA*
• Many of them suffered this cruel fate while being poofter bashed.—*Union Recorder*, p. 13, 4th October 1983

poofter basher *noun*
a man, usually as part of a group, who beats up homosexual men *AUSTRALIA, 1974*
• Even the poofter bashers in the pubs don't go on so much. People are getting a lot more tolerant.—Sandra Jobson, *Blokes*, p. 145, 1984

poofter bashing; poofter-bashing *noun*
the practice of physically assaulting male homosexuals *AUSTRALIA, 1978*
• They interviewed the same number of skinheads who openly admitted they went out 'poofter bashing'.—Robert G. Barrett, *Davo's Little Something*, p. 93, 1992
• The Valley can be a nasty place sometimes. Usually it's just drunken riots, and the occasional vicious poofter-bashing at two in the morning.—Dirk Flinthart, *Brotherly Love*, p. 55, 1995

poofterism *noun*
male homosexuality *AUSTRALIA*
• [H]e had never fallen into the hands of two human monstrosities like Sodomy and Gomorrah, so called by the wags of Tailboard Alley in Penbay Jail because of their propensity to poofterism and leadership of the queer quarter of the prison staff.—Frank Hardy, *The Outcasts of Foolgarah*, p. 170, 1971
• But European style tended to look like poofterism. The swishy manner told you nothing.—B. Selkie, *Lime Juice*, p. 51, 1995

poofter rorter *noun*

1 in a men's prison, a prisoner who induces another inmate into homosexual relations *AUSTRALIA, 1945*
• —Jim Ramsay, *Cop It Sweet!*, p. 72, 1977

2 a person who entices a male homosexual, especially a prostitute, to a secluded place and then robs them *AUSTRALIA, 1938*

poofy *adjective*
overtly homosexual *AUSTRALIA*
Also variant 'poufy'.
• The Petty Officer Cook's complexion was comparatively peaches and cream beside his weatherbeaten compatriots. And it was to this delicate exterior that he owed his dubious nickname. Nothing else. 'Poofy' Allen was one man in the steamer who positively encouraged seduction.—John Wynnum, *Tar Dust*, p. 22, 1962
• [T]heir sissy umbrellas and pouffy little hats.—John Peter Jones, *Feather Pluckers*, p. 29, 1964
• I don't think I'm as poofy as I'm made out to be.—Boy George, *Ask*, p. 22, 1st May 1982
• [Burt Reynolds] has a sexuality which appeals to men, he's not poofy.—Sandra Jobson, *Blokes*, p. 135, 1984
• [A] way of being friendly without acting poofy like a smelly hippy[.]—John King, *Human Punk*, p. 74, 2000

pooh *noun*
an act of defecation *NEW ZEALAND*
Children's vocabulary.
• —Louis S. Leland, *A Personal Kiwi-Yankee Dictionary*, p. 111, 1984

pooh *verb*
▷ see: **POO**

pooh bah *noun*
an important person *UK, 1888*
The name of a character in the Gilbert and Sullivan light opera *The Mikado*.
• [O]n the second night, September 8, we played before an audience of judges, Democratic bigwigs, attorneys, and local pooh-bahs.—Peter Coyote, *Sleeping Where I Fall*, p. 49, 1998

pooh-bum *noun*
a female fan of a rock band who is willing to have sex with band members *UK*
• —Bob Young and Micky Moody, *The Language of Rock 'n' Roll*, p. 106, 1985

pooh-butt *noun*
a despicable person *US*
• LANCE: Don't bring her here! I'm not even fuckin' joking with you, don't you be bringing some fucked up pooh-butt to my house!—*Pulp Fiction*, 1994

pooh-pooh *verb*
to belittle someone or something; to dismiss someone or something as inconsequential *UK, 1827*
• And he pooh-poohed her angry opinion that the stuff was too old for me.—Jim Thompson, *Bad Boy*, p. 294, 1953
• The kids all pooh-poohed her and told her not to worry so much about a fifty-dollar watch[.]—Larry McMurtry, *The Last Picture Show*, p. 79, 1966
• Barry Norman himself pooh-poohed both movies[.]—Danny King, *The Bank Robber Diaries*, p. 188, 2002

poo-jabber *noun*

1 a male homosexual *AUSTRALIA*
• 'Is he really gay?' 'He is a card carrying poo jabber.'—Helen Barnes, *The Crypt Orchid*, p. 38, 1994

2 a contemptible person *AUSTRALIA*
Used as a mild insult, especially amongst children.
• —James Lambert, *The Macquarie Book of Slang*, 1996

pooker *noun*
a signpost *UK*
English gypsy use from Romany *pûkinger* (to tell).
• —Jimmy Stockin, *On The Cobbles*, p. 11, 2000

pookey; pookie *noun*
used as a term of contempt *IRELAND*
• Pookey Flanagan. That's what we used to call him. He used to sweep the roads.—Murphy Tom, *A Whistle in the Dark*, p. 40, 1989

pooki *noun*
the vagina *US*
• In Westchester they called it a pooki, in New Jersey a twat.—Even Ensler, *The Vagina Monologues*, p. 6, 1998

pooky *noun*
marijuana *US*
• —Rick Ayers (Editor), *Slang Dictionary*, p. 13, 2001

pool *noun*
in horse racing, the total amount bet in the win, place and show bets for a race *US*
• —Walter Steigleman, *Horseracing*, p. 274, 1947

Pool *noun*
▸ **the Pool**
Liverpool *UK*
• A barmpot (madman) from the Pool.—Troy Kennedy Martin, *Z Cars*, p. 18, 1962

pooley *noun*

urine *IRELAND*

- 'Can you do pooley?' Nurse O'Reilly asked us. —Aidan Higgins, *Donkey's Years*, p. 5, 1995

poolhall cowboy *noun*

a pool player who has perfected a reckless manner *US*

- I thought he was a jock. He's a poolhall cowboy. —Elmore Leonard, *Swag*, p. 64, 1976

pool harpy *noun*

a pool player who plays for money, relying on a combination of skill and deceptive behaviour *US*

- Pool-Harpies, it should be mentioned, come in all four of the Hollywood sexes; homosexual, heterosexual, lesbian, bisexual. —Roger Gordon, *Hollywood's Sexual Underground*, p. 17, 1966

pool shark *noun*

an expert pool player who makes a living by feigning a lack of expertise and convincing strangers to play against him *US, 1908*

- Back on Chicago's street-corner haunts you tangled with gamblers and racketeers and poolroom sharks[.] —Mezz Mezzrow, *Really the Blues*, p. 206, 1946
- Why, you're a pool shark. A real pool shark. — *The Hustler*, 1961

poom *verb*

to fart *TRINIDAD AND TOBAGO, 1992*

- —Lise Winer, *Dictionary of the English/Creole of Trinidad & Tobago*, 2003

pooma *noun*

a delapidated car *BARBADOS*

- —Frank A. Collymore, *Barbadian Dialect*, p. 86, 1965

poom bag *noun*

large buttocks *TRINIDAD AND TOBAGO, 1987*

- —Lise Winer, *Dictionary of the English/Creole of Trinidad & Tobago*, 2003

poomp *noun*

to fart *BAHAMAS*

- —John A. Holm, *Dictionary of Bahamian English*, p. 159, 1982

poon *noun*

1 the vagina; a woman; a woman as a sex object; sex with a woman *US*

A shortened form of **POONTANG**.

- You'll find more poon per square inch in hick towns than in any big city on God's green earth. —Max Shulman, *Rally Round the Flag, Boys!*, p. 158, 1957
- You don't have to be wild with the notion to want some poon. —Elmore Leonard, *Gold Coast*, p. 19, 1980
- [I]t's hotter than a nun's poon in here! —Terry Southern, *Texas Summer*, p. 119, 1991
- [H]e was given excess gambling skim to invest as he saw best and opened a call house specializing in underaged poon dressed up as movie stars. —James Ellroy, *Hollywood Nocturnes*, p. 210, 1994

2 a fool; a contemptible person *AUSTRALIA, 1940*

Used as a mild insult.

- —Jim Ramsay, *Cop It Sweet!*, p. 72, 1977
- Gentle Jesus meek and mild", the poon in the dress sitting round with kids and sheep in stained glass windows with his typically Jewish golden ringlets and blue eyes and lovely shiny tiara behind his head. — *Review*, p. 9, 15th October 1981

poonce *noun*

an effeminate male *AUSTRALIA, 1941*

- How did a poonce like Bentley ever crack on to a horny bird like Sandy? —Alexander Buzo, *Rooted*, p. 96, 1969
- —Jim Ramsay, *Cop It Sweet!*, p. 72, 1977

pooner

a male with sexual experience and apparent expertise *US*

- —Collin Baker et al., *College Undergraduate Slang Study Conducted at Brown University*, p. 174–175, 1968

poon light *noun*

in the pornography industry, a light used to illuminate the genitals of the performers *US*

- — *Adult Video News*, p. 50, October 1995

poontang *noun*

the vagina; sex; a woman regarded as a sexual object *US, 1929*

Suggestions that the term comes from an American Indian language, Chinese, Bantu, Peruvian or a Filipinio dialect notwithstanding, it almost certainly comes from the French *putain* (prostitute).

- — *American Speech*, p. 234–235, October 1950: 'Poontang'
- I say to you send me over a simple C.O.D. slice of poontang, and what do I get? —Bernard Wolfe, *The Late Risers*, p. 200, 1954
- He's just enervated on too much pooo-oo-nn tang. —Clancy Sigal, *Going Away*, p. 10, 1961
- Two things we always had in common – liquor and poon-tang. —James Baldwin, *Blues for Mister Charlie*, p. 103, 1964
- Say, "You got to get down on that floor on both your knees / Nibble at this pountang like arat nibbling at cheese." —Roger Abrahams, *Positively Black*, p. 95, 1970
- He dug that young poontang – even though at his age I knew he was shooting blanks. —Edwin Torres, *Carlito's Way*, p. 29, 1975
- Talk about poontang / Right down to your yin yang / Down by the banks of the Ohio. —Roogalator, *Cincinnatti Fatback*, 1976
- The poontang was dope and you know that I rocked her. —Kool Moe Dee, *Go See The Doctor*, 1986
- A highly sensitive condition whereby a man temporarily surrenders power to a woman; the consequence of being hypnotized by hot poontang. —Anka Radakovich, *The Wild Girls Club*, p. 18, 1994

poon up *verb*

to dress in a flashy manner in order to impress *AUSTRALIA*

- All pooned up to race her off. He's a moral tonight! —Arthur Chipper, *The Aussie Swearer's Guide*, p. 48, 1972
- —Jim Ramsay, *Cop It Sweet!*, p. 72, 1977

poony *noun*

the vagina; women as sexual objects *UK*

A variation of **PUNANI**.

- Did you check that poony out? —*Airheads*, 1994
- Position her batty (the posterior) over de subwoofers – at moments of extreme bass de vibrations will stimulate her poony. —Sacha Baron-Cohen, *Da Gospel According to Ali G*, p. 101, 2001

poop *noun*

1 information, news *US, 1942*

Probably from the sense as 'nonsense' (**SHIT**).

- The only catch is that the guy who could identify him is dead and they have to go from the poop he gave them. —Mickey Spillane, *My Gun is Quick*, p. 96, 1950
- I gave him the poop on Karen Sinclair's kidnapping from the hospital. —Mickey Spillane, *Return of the Hood*, p. 125, 1964
- What's the old poop, David? You've been hinting. —Richard Farina, *Been Down So Long*, p. 193, 1966
- Surtees walked me down to the seven-three, talking the whole way. "Putting the poop: to me," as he said. —Larry Heinemann, *Close Quarters*, p. 20, 1977
- Musta heard about a big government contract, what it sounds like. That's the way you make it, get the inside poop. —Elmore Leonard, *Stick*, p. 156, 1983
- The Surgeon General, Doctor Koop/Sposed to give you all the poop. But when he's with PMRC [Parents' Music Resource Center]/The poop he's scoopin' amazes me —Frank Zappa, *Promiscuous*, 1988

2 the buttocks *BAHAMAS*

- —John A. Holm, *Dictionary of Bahamian English*, p. 159, 1982

3 faeces; an act of defecation *US, 1948*

Children's toilet vocabulary.

- She'd even say to Buddy, poop all over his stand, "Buddy go potty?" —Elmore Leonard, *Glitz*, p. 341, 1985
- [W]ith half a dozen stubbies [small bottles] of poop under me arm!!! —Tim Winton, *That eye, the sky*, 1986
- There is quite a series of rhymes in which some unfortunate has to lick up piddle or poop. —Wendy Lowenstein, *Improper Play Rhymes*, p. 49, 1988
- One day, taking a poop, I noticed that "it" was not really coming out but felt suspended over the water. —Sandra Bernard, *Confessions of a Pretty Lady*, p. 19, 1988

4 rubbish, nonsense *UK*

- —Susie Dent, *The Language Report*, p. 77, 2003

5 a pledge to a college fraternity *US*

- — *American Speech*, p. 304, December 1955: 'Wayne University slang'

▸ **in the poop**

in trouble *AUSTRALIA*

- 'Mate. Put that away,' Chilla said, 'every time you open it we get in the poop.' —Frank Hardy, *The Outcasts of Foolgarah*, p. 157, 1971

poop *verb*

1 to defecate *UK*

- Don't put him next to my bed, he might poop on me, and if I'm asleep, I won't be able to wipe it off. —Sally Morgan, *My Place*, p. 58, 1987
- I could drive him [a dog] to my archenemy's [...] house to poop. —Janet Evanovich, *Seven Up*, p. 34, 2001

2 in poker, to raise a bet *US*

- — *American Speech*, p. 100, May 1951

poopadoop *noun*
the rectum *US*
- — *Maledicta*, p. 15, Summer 1977: 'A word for it!'

poop-butt *noun*
a lazy person *US*
- A poop-butt is a lazy person, a "drag-ass." — Christina and Richard Milner, *Black Players*, p. 47, 1972

poop chute; poop shute; poop shooter *noun*
the rectum and anus *US*
- She said she gives aroundn the world or straight French 'cause it's too much trouble to screw and she'll go right up the old poop chute if a guy wants it. — Joseph Wambaugh, *The New Centurions*, p. 238, 1970
- And if you inform him that your poop chute is a one-way street, he's gotta respect that, or he won't get a taste of your sweet lovin'! — *Seattle Weekly*, p. 127, 9th August 2001
- — Chris Lewis, *The Dictionary of Playground Slang*, p. 173, 2003

pooped *adjective*
exhausted *US, 1932*
- I'm half dead with looking for a place. A guy told me about a basement apartment on Kings Highway near Ninety-sixth, but it was a bum steer. So I'm pooped. — Irving Shulman, *The Amboy Dukes*, p. 194, 1947
- Another thing ... well, I guess there isn't another thing, I'm all pooped out and I have to get on with other things. — Jack Kerouac, *Letter to Allen Ginsburg*, p. 142, 2 January 1948
- A couple of cars banged bumpers backing up so they could swing around me and I was too damned pooped even to swear back at some of the stuff they called me. — Mickey Spillane, *My Gun is Quick*, p. 6, 1950
- Not tonight, Simon, I'm pooped. — Joseph Wambaugh, *Floaters*, p. 126, 1996
- I'm really pooped so don't attempt to shag me[.] — Jenny Eclair, *Camberwell Beauty*, p. 51, 2000

poopelu *noun*
the vagina *US*
- There's [...] a "poochi," a "poopi," a "peepe,", a "poopelu," a "poopelu," a "poonani," a "pal" and a "piche[."] — Eve Ensler, *The Vagina Monologues*, p. 6, 1998

pooper *noun*
the rectum and anus *US*
From **POOP** (excrement).
- If ya can't fuck a slut-come-lately in the pooper without a rubber, why not watch strangers do it on film? — Anthony Petkovich, *The X Factory*, p. 10, 1997

pooper-scooper *noun*
an implement for gathering canine excrement, designed to meet the social responsibilities or legal requirements placed upon dog owners *US*
Combines **POOP** (faeces) with a conventional tool. Also shortened forms 'pooper-scoop' and 'poop-scoop'.
- — *New York Times*, p. 28, 26th May 1972
- Bring your pooper-scoopers, boys. The dogs are covereing the red carpet in a sea of shit. — Joseph Wambaugh, *The Black Marble*, p. 136, 1978
- To make it easier on them a pooper scooper was invented, which was like a smaller version of the "lobby pans" they clean up with at amusement parks. — Editors of Ben is Dead, *Retrohell*, p. 163, 1997
- I could drive him [a dog] to my archenemy Joyce Barnhardt's house to poop. This way I didn't have to do the pooper-scooper thing, and I felt like I was accomplishing something. — Janet Evanovich, *Seven Up*, p. 34, 2001

poop file *noun*
a collection of (school, college, university) examinations given in the past *US*
- — *Verbatim*, p. 280, May 1976

poophead *noun*
a boring, conventional person *US*
- Couple old poopheads? — *Rebel Without a Cause*, 1955

poopi *noun*
the vagina *US*
- There's [...] a "poochi," a "poopi," a "peepe,", a "poopelu," a "poopelu," a "poonani," a "pal" and a "piche[."] — Eve Ensler, *The Vagina Monologues*, p. 6, 1998

poo-poo head *noun*
an objectionable person *US*
A variation of **SHITHEAD**, perhaps more insulting by the use of childish 'poo-poo' (excrement).
- I was the only person who was trying to shame this poo-poo head of a husband into behaving. — Howard Stern, *Miss America*, p. 302, 1995

poop-poop *noun*
a slow motorboat *BAHAMAS*
- — John A. Holm, *Dictionary of Bahamian English*, p. 159, 1982

poop pusher *noun*
a male homosexual *UK*
- — Tom Hibbert, *Rockspeak!*, p. 121, 1983

poops *verb*
to fart *TRINIDAD AND TOBAGO, 1987*
- — Lise Winer, *Dictionary of the English/Creole of Trinidad & Tobago*, 2003

poop sheet *noun*
a bulletin or other document containing news and information *US*
- — *American Speech*, p. 121, May 1964: 'Problems in the study of campus slang'
- — *Current Slang*, p. 18, Winter 1970

poopy *adjective*

1 filthy with excrement *US*
From **POOP** (faeces).
- [Y]our baby puts its foot in its poopy diaper while you are trying to change it — Alan and Denise Fields, *Baby Bargains*, p. 121, 2003

2 bad, awful; of poor quality *US*
A euphemistic synonym for **SHITTY**.
- Blue birds are poopy. I want to be a black stallion. — Janet Evanovitch, *Hard Eight*, p. 270, 2002

3 in a bad mood *US*
A euphemistic form of **SHITTY**.
- [B]efore you went and started acting all poopy[.] — Jerry Spinelli, *Maniac Magee*, p. 66, 1990

4 afraid *SOUTH AFRICA*
- Come on. Confess. You were scared, hey! A little bit poopy. I've noticed that. — Athol Fugard, *The Blood Knot*, 1963

poopy suit *noun*
in the Canadian military, any bulky official garment *CANADA*
- Immersion suits and Nuclear-Biological-Chemical Warfare Suits are poopy suits. — Tom Langeste, *Words on the Wing*, p. 217–218, 1995

poor *adjective*
cruel, heartless; lacking good taste *US*
- — Connie Eble (Editor), *UNC-CH Campus Slang*, p. 7, Spring 2003

poor-ass *adjective*
wretched, unimportant *US*
- An army of people out there thinking up ways to torture my poor-ass, gentle, loving vagina. — Eve Ensler, *The Vagina Monologues*, p. 69, 1998

poorboy *noun*
a small bottle of alcohol *US*
- I get in my double bed with bop on the radio, a poorboy half-bottle of Tokay wine, the shades drawn[.] — Jack Kerouac, *Letter to John Clellon Holmes*, p. 381, 12 October 1952
- I figured I needed a poorboy of Tokay wine to complete the cold dusk run to Santa Barbara. — Jack Kerouac, *The Dharma Bums*, p. 6, 1958

poor-donkey *noun*
a sandal of plaited rope or one cut from a piece of tyre or wood *BARBADOS*
- — Richard Allsopp, *Dictionary of Caribbean English Usage*, p. 448, 1996

poor-great *adjective*
foolishly pompous *GUYANA*
- — Richard Allsopp, *Dictionary of Caribbean English Usage*, p. 448, 1996

poor-man blanket *noun*
the sun *BAHAMAS*
- — John A. Holm, *Dictionary of Bahamian English*, p. 159, 1982

poor man's *adjective*
describes the lesser status or inferior quality of someone by comparison and reference to the greater name with which it is combined *UK, 1984*
Only colloquial when applied to people.
- [T]he commercial channel would devote a sizeable chunk of their dead airtime to Tarby's Bar, where [Jimmy Tarbuck] the poor man's Bruce Forsyth would trade lame gags with the poor man's Sammy Davis Jr. (aka his good friend Kenny Lynch). — *The Guardian*, 11th May 2001

poor man's roulette *noun*
the game of craps *US, 1953*
• —Thomas L. Clark, *The Dictionary of Gambling and Gaming*, p. 164, 1987

poor man's velvet *noun*
a drink of mixed stout and cider *UK*
An economic variation of **BLACK VELVET** (stout and champagne); remembered from the 1970s, notwithstanding the drink's amnesiac effects.

poor man's weather glass *noun*
seaweed, especially kelp *CANADA*
• This brown algae is known as the "poor man's weather glass" because it may be used to predict weather. At the approach of rain, the dried fronds go rather sticky, but remain dry and brittle in fine weather. *—Prince Edward Island Dept,. of Environment and Tourism*, p. 35, 1974

poor pearl *noun*
an unpopular girl *US*
• —*San Francisco Examiner*, p. III-2, 22nd March 1960

poor-rakey *noun*
thin, gaunt *BARBADOS*
• —Frank A. Collymore, *Barbadian Dialect*, p. 86, 1965

-poos *suffix*
▷ see: -POO

poot *noun*
1 faeces *US*
Children's vocabulary; a variation of **POOP**.
• —*Maledicta*, p. 255, Summer/Winter 1981: 'Five years and 121 dirty words later'

2 anything which is considered to be contemptible *US*
• "WE" manufacture our baffling, insipid packages of inconsequential poot[.]—Frank Zappa, *The Real Frank Zappa Book*, p. 191, 1989

3 a very small thing; anything at all *US*
Usually heard in the negative, as 'that ain't poot'.
• —Terrence M. Steele, *Streettalk Thesaurus*, p. 23,

poot *verb*
1 to defecate *US*
• I'm gonna light in on him and whip 'im till he poot.—Chester Himes, *If He Hollers Let Him Go*, p. 12, 1945
• Now she squirmed, she scooted, she farted, and she pooted.—Bruce Jackson, *Get Your Ass in the Water and Swim Like Me*, p. 159, 1966

2 to fart *US*
• And when I held it up, their eyes stretched and the whole crowd went so still you could've heard a gnat poot across the river.—Guy Owen, *The Flim-Flam Man and the Apprentice Grifter*, p. 12, 1972
• Beans, beans, the musical fruit; the more you eat, the more you poot.—Peter Furze, *Tailwinds*, p. 140, 1998

3 (used of a hospital patient) to become suddenly more ill, especially without hope of reversing the course *US*
• —*Maledicta*, p. 34, 1988–1989: 'Medical maledicta from San Francisco'

poot-butt *noun*
a lazy fool *US, 1972*
• How you gonna convince this pootbutt that havin' a group that would be beneficial to anybody?—Odie Hawkins, *The Busting Out of an Ordinary Man*, p. 152, 1985

pootenanny; pooties *noun*
the female buttocks *US*
Probably derived from Jamaican **PUNANI** (the vagina).
• —Anna Scotti and Paul Young, *Buzzwords*, p. 27, 1997
• [A] tourist from the Home Counties dancing in jiggling her pooties in front of der face.—Ben Elton, *High Society*, p. 111, 2002

pootie *noun*
the vagina *US*
• [Y]oung supple breasts, a tight firm ass and an uncharted pootie[.] *—Cruel Intentions*, 1999

pootle *verb*
▷ see: POODLE

poov; poove *noun*
food, especially grass for grazing *UK, 1933*
Circus and English gypsy use.

poov; poove *verb*
▸ **poov the gry; poov the grey**
to graze a horse, especially without permission from the land's owner *UK*
English gypsy use; a combination of **POOV** (grass) – thus 'pooving' (grazing) – and **GRY** (a horse).
• [T]hey had been up to their usual trick of poovin' the greys.—John Hillaby, *Journey through Britain*, 1968
• One day he was out in the field pooving the grys when three older boys ambled up and started to throw stones at Dad's horses.—Jimmy Stockin, *On The Cobbles*, p. 60, 2000

poove; pouve *noun*
a homosexual *UK*
Variations of **POOF**.
• Oh, bleeding hell [...] manager's a flaming pouve. A fart catcher. —John Gardner, *Madrigal*, 1967
• Can you believe what's coming out of these pommie pooves' mouths, Stella?—Claire Mansfield and John Mendelssohn, *Dominatrix*, p. 251, 2002

pooze *noun*
the vagina *US*
• Listening to Barry [White]'s unctuous, pooze-ooze voice, it is conceivable that this man is dangerous[.]—Lester Bangs, *Psychotic Reactions and Carburetor Dung*, p. 153, 1975

poozle *noun*
a scavenged object *NEW ZEALAND*
• Leo would spend his sober periods worrying about Jill's poozles – a variety of antiques wiht great sentimental and artistic value.—Tim Shadbolt, *Bullshit and Jellybeans*, p. 57, 1971

poozle *verb*
to strip fixtures from buildings scheduled for demolition *NEW ZEALAND*
• —Louis S. Leland, *A Personal Kiwi-Yankee Dictionary*, p. 79, 1984

pop *noun*
1 an instance or occurrence *US, 1868*
• We get anywhere from three hundred to five hundred a pop, depending on how much the Sioux Falls quarterback Club – or some such thing – can afford.—Dan Jenkins, *Semi-Tough*, p. 62, 1972
• By wearing Via Spiga pumps that cost a hundred dollars a pop with fifty-nine-cent grocery-store label panty hose underneath.—Rita Ciresi, *Pink Slip*, p. 80, 1999

2 an attempt, a try *UK, 1929*
• I'll have a pop at it, of course.—J.B. Priestley, *The Good Companions*, 1929
• We hold back in the stands to allow them [a rival gang] to clear so we can have a pop inside the ground.—Martin King and Martin Knight, *The Naughty Nineties*, p. 127, 1999

3 an arrest *US*
• So the minute the pop comes, one of the guys that was out in front during all this, he offered a ten-flat [ten-year sentence].—Bruce Jackson, *In the Life*, p. 170, 1972
• Do whatever the fuck they want – you know, street pops, raids, whatever.—Richard Price, *Clockers*, p. 269, 1992

4 an attack *UK*
Combination and variation of the senses 'attempt' and 'go'.
• [Y]ou're in no position to have a pop at us.—*Kerrang!*, p. 8, 3rd November 2001

5 an ejaculation *US*
• The eighteen-year-old blonde blew Lev to his first pop, reports Mark, and then was replaced by a short-haired brunette, who brought Larry to number two in under thirty minutes.—Josh Alan Friedman, *Tales of Times Square*, p. 105, 1986
• We want the pop. How much time is left on this cassette? Three minutes. Okay, give us the pop in two forty-five.—Robert Stoller and I.S. Levine, *Coming Attractions*, p. 55, 1991

6 one event of sexual intercourse *US*
• There were plenty of girls for that, you know, if a guy wanted a pop. —*Diner*, 1982

7 in prison, an escape attempt *UK*
• —Angela Devlin, *Prison Patter*, p. 89, 1996

8 a father, especially as a term of address *US, 1838*

9 the 'masculine' or 'active' member of a lesbian relationship *US*
• —John M. Murtagh and Sara Harris, *Cast the First Stone*, p. 262, 1957: 'Glossary'
• —Robert George Reisner, *The Jazz Titans*, p. 163, 1960

10 **a musical genre, characterised as trivial and without serious artistic intent** *US, 1935*
Originally widely used to cover the opposite of 'classical music', now denotes just a particular type of popular music: carefully crafted, packaged or manufactured for mass-market appeal.
- [A] perfect piece of pop schlock. — Barney Hoskyns, *Waiting For The Sun*, p. 138, 1996

11 **any non-alcoholic sparkling drink** *UK, 1812*
From the sound of a bottle being opened.
- From the sound of a bottle being opened. 'I'll be there in shorts and a t-shirt, a bag of sausage rolls and wine gums in one hand, and a stone bottle of ginger pop in the other!' — *The Guardian*, 8th December 2000
- A HAPLESS commuter handed over 400 cash to two men in the street for what he thought was a laptop computer – but turned out to be two bottles of pop. — *Wandsworth Guardian*, 3rd June 2003

12 **champagne** *UK*
- This prat owes me money and he's out spunking it on expensive pop. — Dave Courtney, *Raving Lunacy*, p. 171, 2000

13 **a drink, usually at a bar** *US*
- I seen a couple of guys I know, had a couple of pops, got something down on it. — John Sayles, *Union Dues*, p. 24, 1977
- She says she stopped in there for a pop after she was through working and he was in there again. — Elmore Leonard, *Split Images*, p. 265, 1981
- You better learn to have a pop once in a while or you're gonna fall off the wagon. — *Something About Mary*, 1998

14 **cough syrup containing codeine** *US*
- — William D. Alsever, *Glossary for the Establishment and Other Uptight People*, p. 6, December 1970

15 **an injection of a drug** *US*
- You make it wit me, Diane? If I take a pop, you make it? — George Mandel, *Flee the Angry Strangers*, p. 282, 1952

16 **a strong crowd reaction** *US*
Professional wrestling usage.
- It really sounded like the Cat got the biggest pop of the night. — *Chatterbox News*, 23rd August 2000

▷ **see:** POP GOES THE WEASEL

▸ **go off pop**
to lose your temper *NEW ZEALAND*
- Every chance he got he'd pick on men and go off pop. — Frank Sargeson, *That Summer*, p. 33, 1946

▸ **have a pop at**
to attack verbally *UK*
- I've never had a pop at you for taking drugs before, but this is different. — Wayne Anthony, *Spanish Highs*, p. 78, 1999

▸ **on the pop**
drinking alcohol *UK*
- [A]s soon as we'd dropped my bag off at his flat, out on the pop we did go, big time. — Ken Lukowiak, *Marijuana Time*, p. 319, 2000

pop *verb*

1 **to ejaculate; to experience orgasm** *US*
- She likes them jittery tricks cause they pop fast. — Robert Gover, *One Hundred Dollar Misunderstanding*, p. 20, 1961
- But they'll just open up their pants, and in two or three minutes they'll pop. — John Warren Wells, *Tricks of the Trade*, p. 14, 1970
- I remember the time we muscled a mud kicker when we was oh ten ... twelve and got our first blowjob together. He passed out when he popped. — Iceberg Slim (Robert Beck), *Death Wish*, p. 174, 1977
- The cocks pop and the wads fly as wide-open mouths train to catch the steaming jizz. — *Adult Video*, p. 32, August/September 1986
- Then indeed he did pop all over her, and she went raging out of there with semen all over her hair and face[.] — Robert Stoller and I.S. Levine, *Coming Attractions*, p. 56, 1991
- In fact, we've gone through 15 studs and not one has popped yet. — Anthony Petkovich, *The X Factory*, p. 190, 1997
- I even got to the point where I could pop during sex – but only if somebody was buffing the muff while we were going at it. — Amy Sohn, *Run Catch Kiss*, p. 115, 1999

2 **to have sex with someone** *US*
- Well, did you pop her? You must have jugged her by now, haven't you? — Claude Brown, *Manchild in the Promised Land*, p. 363, 1965
- "Oh, man, I popped her a couple, and blam, I was in love," Bill said. — Cecil Brown, *The Life & Loves of Mr. Jiveass Nigger*, p. 113, 1969
- I'd get more thrill out of popping the dead / Than I got out of you in a nice warm bed. — Dennis Wepman et al., *The Life*, p. 143, 1976
- I'll pop a broad in a minute, but nothing to get tied down to, right, Chappie? — Edwin Torres, *Q & A*, p. 117, 1977

3 **(used of a male) to have sex with a virgin** *BAHAMAS*
- — John A. Holm, *Dictionary of Bahamian English*, p. 159, 1982

4 **to give birth** *US*
- What would rapists be doing going after a woman ready to pop? — Robert Campbell, *Sweet La-La Land*, p. 33, 1990

5 **to fart** *UK*
Childish; used in the US, UK and Australia. Also phrased as 'pop off' and 'pop a whiff'.
- [M]y botty popped. — Peter Furze, *Tailwinds*, p. 141, 1998

6 **to administer medication** *UK*
- They'd have to work with us proper... not pop us full of pills and leave us in a fucking wheelchair. — Shaun Ryder, *Shaun Ryder... in His Own Words*, 1991

7 **to inject a drug** *US*
- I never popped in a vein, Carter. — George Mandel, *Flee the Angry Strangers*, p. 290, 1952
- They want to pop. They want company. — John D. McDonald, *The Neon Jungle*, p. 44, 1953

8 **to take a pill** *US, 1968*
- Also has been known to pop a greenie. — Jim Bouton, *Ball Four*, p. 212, 1970
- I participated in the popping of the old love drug[.] — Dave Courtney, *Raving Lunacy*, p. 73, 2000
- Painkillers – particularly Vicodin – have stormed back onto the drug scene in the States in recent months and are apparently being popped like Smarties at showbiz parties. — *Drugs An Adult Guide, FHM Bionic*, p. 25, December 2001

9 **when using amyl nitrate, to break the glass ampoules containing the gas** *US*
- — Steven Daly and Nalthaniel Wice, *alt.culture*, p. 185, 1995

10 **to inhale a powdered drug** *UK, 1998*
- — Mike Haskins, *Drugs*, p. 291, 2003

11 **to steal something** *US, 1994*
Originally in black use.

12 **to obtain confidential or classified information about someone as part of an investigation** *US*
- — Jim Crotty, *How to Talk American*, p. 52, 1997

13 **to arrest someone** *US*
- That fool had driven across the country with a blond without them. Lucky he got popped in the Apple instead of the lowlands. — Babs Gonzales, *Movin' On Down De Line*, p. 80, 1975
- Elijah glared at him. Motherfucker! and threw the empty whiskey bottle out of the open window and held his hands up for the cuffs. Popped again. — Odie Hawkins, *Chicago Hustle*, p. 100, 1977
- Thought they only popped him with two in the apartment. — Edwin Torres, *After Hours*, p. 208, 1979
- There's nothing to worry about. Carmine got popped. — Gerald Petievich, *To Live and Die in L.A.*, p. 31, 1983
- Popped for possession and sale of cocaine, lowered to some kind of misdemeanor. — James Elroy, *Suicide Hill*, p. 575, 1986

14 **to fire a gun** *UK, 1725*
- I go to this little firing range downtown, pop off a few rounds, and it always makes me feel better. — *American Beauty*, 1999
- He gets popped like twenty-thirty times and all hands is getting zapped — Kevin Sampson, *Clubland*, p. 2, 2002

15 **to hit someone** *US*
- And he did his entire stretch in a series of thirty days at a time in solitary, for popping a guard. — Stephen Gaskin, *Amazing Dope Tales*, p. 191, 1980

16 **to kill someone** *US*
- You keep thinking that they wouldn't pop you out in broad daylight[.] — Mickey Spillane, *Kiss Me Deadly*, p. 90, 1952
- Armand tried to think how his brothers used to say it. They would say they were gonig to do a guy. Or they mnight say so-and-so got popped. Maybe because when you used a suppressor it made a popping sound, like an air rifle. — Elmore Leonard, *Killshot*, p. 74, 1989
- I'm not gonna pop her, Harry. — *Get Shorty*, 1995

17 **to pay for something** *US*
- Yeah, but let me pop for it. — Willard Motley, *Let No Man Write My Epitaph*, p. 73, 1958
- The records and phonograph caught his eye, too. "You pop for all this?" — Ross Russell, *The Sound*, p. 188, 1961

18 **to praise or promote someone or something** *US*
- You don't pop the opposition, Teddy. — Dan Jenkins, *Life Its Ownself*, p. 318, 1984

19 **to applaud and cheer enthusiastically** *US*
Professional wrestling usage.
- [T]he audience pops big enough to blow the roof off. — *Rampage Magazine*, p. 35, September 2000

20 to send an e-mail to someone *UK*
- Ewell Court Park has taken a bit of a hammering with grafitti over the past few weeks. [...] If you have any information as to the identity of these budding artists then give me a buzz or pop me an e-mail. — PC Jane Eames, *Surrey Police*, 27th February 2004

21 to go to or from somewhere, especially swiftly or suddenly *UK, 1530*
Usually used with 'up', 'down', 'in', 'out', 'over', 'about', 'off', 'between', etc.
- [H]e left and popped into town to try to score some puff. — Colin Butts, *Is Harry on the Boat?*, p. 38, 1997

22 in pinball, to win a replay or additional ball, activating the sound effect known as a knocker *US*
- — Bobbye Claire Natkin and Steve Kirk, *All About Pinball*, p. 114, 1977

23 (of a car boot or bonnet) to open remotely *US*
- Pop the trunk, I need my tool. — *Gone in 60 Seconds*, 2000

▸ **pop a cap**
to shoot a gun *US*
- MARSELLUS: I'm prepared to scour the earth for this motherfucker. If Butch goes to Indo China, I want a nigger hidin' in a bowl of rice, ready to pop a cap in his ass. — *Pulp Fiction*, 1965
- Outside of the accidental shot fired by Eddie Cervantes when he used his revolver as a club, nobody had popped a single cap in the canyons. — Joseph Wambaugh, *Lines and Shadows*, p. 101, 1984

▸ **pop a top**
to open a can of beer *US*
An inevitable reduplication with the advent of aluminium cans with pull-tabs in the early 1970s.

▸ **pop corn**
to engage in a swindle or dishonest scheme *US*
- — Mark S. Fleisher, *Beggars & Thieves: Lives of Urban Street Criminals*, p. 290, 1995: 'Glossary'

▸ **pop junk**
to gossip *US*
- — *Frederick (Maryland) Post*, p. B2, 24th May 1990: 'For home boys and zimmers; this dictionary is def!'

▸ **pop smoke**
to detonate a smoke grenade *US*
- El Paso signals Doc Johnson to pop smoke and Doc pulls the pin on a smoke grenade. — John M. Del Vecchio, *The 13th Valley*, p. 632, 1982

▸ **pop the chute**
in sailing, to release the spinnaker *US*
- "Okay!" Winnie shouted. "Let's pop the chute!" — Joseph Wambaugh, *The Golden Orange*, p. 286, 1990

▸ **pop ya collar**
to respect yourself *UK*
- — Susie Dent, *The Language Report*, p. 78, 2003

▸ **pop your clogs**
to die *UK*
Literally, 'to put your shoes in the pawnbroker's' (because you have no further use for them).
- Not a bad way to go though, is it? I mean if you did pop your clogs at an outdoor rave. — Dave Courtney, *Raving Lunacy*, p. 190, 2000
- Then she got pneumonia and popped her clogs. — Jenny Eclair, *Camberwell Beauty*, p. 37, 2000
- When it's time for me to go, I wouldn't mind popping my clogs like that. — Jimmy Stockin, *On The Cobbles*, p. 158, 2000

▸ **pop your nuts**
to ejaculate *US*
- They just want to pop their nuts as fast as they can. — John Warren Wells, *Tricks of the Trade*, p. 14, 1970

▸ **pop your pumpkin**
to lose your temper *US*
- The boss man'd just naturally pop his pumpkin if he found out about it. — Jim Thompson, *Roughneck*, p. 16, 1954

▸ **pop your rocks**
to ejaculate *US*
- [H]ere was this guy looking her in the eye like he wanted something more than to pop his rocks. — John Sayles, *Union Dues*, p. 189, 1977

▸ **pop your water**
to ejaculate *BAHAMAS, 1971*
- — John A. Holm, *Dictionary of Bahamian English*, p. 32, 1982

Pop *nickname*
used as a nickname for any male stage door manager *US*
- — Wilfred Granville, *The Theatre Dictionary*, p. 86, 1952

pop bumper *noun*
in pinball, a bumper that scores and kicks the ball on contact *US*
- — Bobbye Claire Natkin and Steve Kirk, *All About Pinball*, p. 111, 1977

popcorn; poppy *noun*
an erect penis *UK, 1992*
Rhyming slang for **HORN**.
- Looking at her legs, too, I started getting the popcorn. — Martin King and Martin Knight, *The Naughty Nineties*, p. 24, 1999

popcorn pimp *noun*
a small-time pimp; a pimp who fails to live up to pimp standards *US*
- Black pimps never solicit for their women if they are "true pimps," and call a man who does a cigarette pimp, popcorn pimp, or chile pimp. — Christina and Richard Milner, *Black Players*, p. 33, 1972
- One of the bouncers pulled his wallet out. Popcorn pimp, he didn't have fifty dollars. — Edwin Torres, *After Hours*, p. 179, 1979
- — Edith A. Folb, *runnin' down some lines*, p. 250, 1980
- Then there are "popcorn pimps," a term of contempt for men who force women into prostitution, unlike true players who claim to operate with personal magnetism alone. — Terry Williams, *The Cocaine Kids*, p. 102, 1989

pope *noun*
▸ **for the pope**
used of work without pay *US*
- — *American Speech*, p. 42, February 1963: 'Trucker's language in Rhode Island'

Pope *noun*
▸ **The Pope**
Frank Sinatra, US singer (1915–98) *US*
- The latest casino owner in Las Vegas to embark on the hearts-and-flowers route is Francis Albert Sinatra, better known as The Leader, The General, The Dago, The Pope, and Frankie Boy. — Ed Reid and Ovid Demaris, *The Green Felt Jungle*, p. 74, 1963

Pope's phone number *noun*
VAT 69™ Scotch whisky *UK, 1961*
Dating from a time when telephone exchanges were given as the first three letters of the area name, thus '69.'

popeye *noun*
a car or truck with only one headlight working *US*
- — Bill Davis, *Jawjacking*, p. 76, 1977

Popeye the sailor *noun*
a tailor *UK*
Rhyming slang, formed on the cartoon character.
- — Ray Puxley, *Cockney Rabbit*, 1992

pop goes the weasel; pop *noun*
diesel *UK*
Rhyming slang, formed, possibly with an ironic regard to the high costs of motoring, on the traditional rhyme: 'That's the way the money goes, / Pop goes the weasel'.
- — Ray Puxley, *Cockney Rabbit*, 1992

popla *noun*
beer *SOUTH AFRICA, 1977*
- [Y]ou pass out. And then we bring you round with popla and we push some meat down your throat[.] — Andre Brink, *A Dry White Season*, p. 218, 1979

po-po *noun*
the police; a police officer *US*
- — Connie Eble (Editor), *UNC-CH Campus Slang*, p. 8, April 1995
- While kids in Northwest refer to police as "one-time," Northeast teenagers call them"bo-deen" or "hot dog," and in Southeast they're "po-pos" or good old "feds." — *Washington Post*, p. A1, 20th August 2001

pop-off *noun*
someone who talks too much *US*
- To shut up the pop-off cut him down by saying he's a 'jack-wise,' or maybe an 'odd job.' — *Philadelphia Evening Bulletin*, 11th November 1951

pop off *verb*
1 to die *UK, 1764*
- Hey pop ups [unasked-for windows that appear on your computer screen], why don't you pop off? — *The Guardian*, 15th December 2003

2 to brag, to boast; to speak out when discretion would suggest silence *US, 1940*
- I sat back a lot, I didn't pop off a lot. — Bruce Jackson, *In the Life*, p. 69, 1972
- I'ma be another rapper dead / for poppin' off at the mouth with shit I shouldn'ta said[.] — Eminem (Marshall Mathers), *Kill You*, 2000

3 to kill someone *UK, 1824*
- The arrest of serial killer David Berkowitz – who claimed he heard the voice of God through his parents' dog, and the God-Dog told him his duty in life was to pop off women – had been all over the papers that year. —Rita Ciresi, *Pink Slip*, p. 10, 1999

4 to ejaculate *BAHAMAS*
- —John A. Holm, *Dictionary of Bahamian English*, p. 159, 1982

pop-out *noun*
a mass-produced surfboard with little or no handwork involved in the making *US*
- —John Severson, *Modern Surfing Around the World*, p. 178, 1964
- PANCHO: Eighty-five dollars would buy me a popout Tiki surfboard. Q: What's a "popout"? PANCHO: A popout, 'cause it was manufactured – it wasn't made custom-made. —Leonard Wolfe (Editor), *Voices from the Love Generation*, p. 170–171, 1968

poppa *noun*
in prison, a lesbian *US*
- When she saw that I really didn't understand, she explained that "Poppa" was the jailhouse term for Lesbian[.] —Polly Adler, *A House is Not a Home*, p. 264, 1953

poppa-lopper *noun*
used as a euphemism for 'motherfucker' *US*
- —*Maledicta*, p. 11, Summer 1977: 'A word for it!'

pop party *noun*
a party where drug users inject drugs *US*
- —Eugene Landy, *The Underground Dictionary*, p. 152, 1971

popped out *adjective*
drug-intoxicated *US*
- "Dinch, you're popped out." It had begun as reproof, but, she tied a smile to it, remembering that she was just as high as the boy. —George Mandel, *Flee the Angry Stranger*, p. 131, 1954

popper *noun*

1 a finger *US*
- —Marcus Hanna Boulware, *Jive and Slang of Students in Negro Colleges*, 1947

2 a pistol *US*
- —Porter Bibb, *CB Bible*, p. 94, 1976

3 a popcorn wagon *US*
- —Gene Sorrows, *All About Carnivals*, p. 24, 1985: 'Terminology'

4 a pneumatic drill *NEW ZEALAND*
Mining slang.
- For the first time in my life I saw and heard pneumatic drills at work. They were referred to as 'poppers'. —Bill Richards, *Off the Sheep's Back*, p. 85, 1986

5 a fart *UK*
Childish, descriptive. Also called 'multipopper'.
- —Peter Furze, *Tailwinds*, p. 140, 1998

6 a capsule containing vapours of amyl nitrate or (iso)butyl nitrate inhaled as a stimulant *US, 1967*
Often used in the plural form.
- When I use a popper, I feel as though I had ten assholes and I wanted them all filled at once. —Angelo d'Arcangelo, *The Homosexual Handbook*, p. 165, 1968
- And if you're sick of people, what about poppers? —Mart Crowley, *The Boys in the Band*, p. 31, 1968
- I had no pot on hand, my popper supply was low, and, most disappointing of all, I couldn't maintain a hard-on. —John Francis Hunter, *The Gay Insider*, p. 36, 1971
- Amyl nitrite, or "poppers" as they are frequenly known, is one of several drugs that have come to be associated with sex. —*Screw*, p. 9, 28th June 1971
- The use of amyl nitrite, or "poppers", has become very popular, especially with they younger guys who play mostly M. —Larry Townsend, *The Leatherman's Handbook*, p. 30, 1972
- The dressing room of the Rolling Stones is always Groove city – the juice flows, smoke rises, crystals crumble, poppers pop, teenies hang in, and Mick knifes through like a ballet-dancing matador. —Terry Southern, *Now Dig This*, p. 153, 1972
- He unscrewed the poppers bottle, took a couple of huge snorts and rescrewed the lid. —Nicholas Blincoe, *Ardwick Green (Disco Biscuits)*, p. 13, 1996

7 any drug addict *UK*
A very loosely defined, or understood, usage.
- —*Bournemouth Echo*, 28th August 1967
- —Linda Reinberg, *In the Field*, p. 170, 1991

poppet *noun*

1 used as an endearment *UK, 1729*
A 'puppet', hence a 'doll'.
- All right, poppet. You can keep it. —John O'Toole, *The Bush and the Tree*, p. 28, 1960
- Magda, get us some more drinks, will you, poppet. —Jake Arnott, *He Kills Coppers*, p. 221, 2001

2 the object of ridicule *BARBADOS*
- —Frank A. Collymore, *Barbadian Dialect*, p. 86, 1965

popplin *noun*
kindling wood, used to start a fire *CANADA*
- An onomatopoeic word (the sound suggests the meaning], "popplin" combines the sounds made by good dry kindling (popping and crackling) with a rhyme-ending with the word "kindling." —*The Coast Guard*, p. 4, 8th February 1984

poppy *noun*

1 opium *UK, 1935*
Earlier pharmaceutical usage into slang.

2 heroin *UK*
- —Robert Ashton, *This Is Heroin*, p. 206, 2002
- —Mike Haskins, *Drugs*, p. 284, 2003

3 money *UK, 1977*
- Ah'm no wastin fuckin poppy oan a jukey [juke box]. —Irvine Welsh, *The State of the Party (Disco Biscuits)*, p. 31, 1995

▷ **see:** POPCORN

poppy *verb*
to pay *UK*
- —Patrick O'Shaughnessy, *Market Traders' Slang*, 1979

poppycock *noun*
nonsense *US, 1857*
- "I'll nuke Britain, says evil Bin Laden". Poppycock – and dangerous poppycock at that. —*New Statesman*, 8th October 2001

poppy love *noun*
an older Jewish man *US*
- —Carsten Stroud, *Close Pursuit*, p. 274, 1987

poppy pad *noun*
a room or apartment where heroin users congregate *US*
- And behind the respectable facades of the apartment buildings were the plush flesh cibs and poppy pads and circus tents of Harlem. —Chester Himes, *The Real Cool Killers*, p. 61, 1959

pops *noun*

1 used as a term of address for a man, especially an older man *US, 1844*
- "Looks like pops couldn't take it," one of them shouted. —Ralph Ellison, *Invisible Man*, p. 87, 1947
- "Pops," said the stranger, "I can see that when it comes to cows you don't know a hill of beans." —Steve Allen, *Bop Fables*, p. 55, 1955
- [W]e ain't got the same hip-hop knowledge as you, pops. —*Hip-Hop Connection*, p. 9, July 2002

2 father *US*
- "My moms and pops always wanted Hector and me to go to college[.]" —Terry Williams, *The Cocaine Kids*, p. 74, 1989
- Yeah, see, you ain't goin' out like ya pops. —*Menace II Society*, 1993

pop shop *noun*
a place where criminals sell stolen goods *US*
- —Vincent J. Monteleone, *Criminal Slang*, p. 180, 1949

pop shot *noun*
a scene in a pornographic film or photograph depicting a man ejaculating *US*
- Pull it out of her. Wait a minute. Got to change batteries! Okay, go into the pop shot now. —Robert Stoller and I.S. Levine, *Coming Attractions*, p. 55, 1991
- —*Adult Video News*, p. 42, August 1995
- Most of the guys get paid anywhere from $75 to $300 per pop shot. —James Ridgeway, *Red Light*, p. 52, 1996
- [T]he whole world can watch movie scenes with strangely abrupt and implausible endings (the infamous and inexplicable "pop shot"). —*Cult Movies No. 17*, p. 46, 1996
- Sean Michaels, the top black male performer in the industry,had a vasectomy before he started his porn career that cuts down on the power of his pop shots[.] —Ana Loria, *1 2 3 Be A Porn Star!*, p. 68, 2000
- Are facials required, or are you just being politce? JULIA ANN: It's not required at all. I usually ask the director where he wants the pop shot. —*Playboy*, p. 132, 1st March 2002

popsicle *noun*
used as a term of abuse *US*
- Come on you fucking popsicles, let's get that car. — *Repo Man*, 1984

popsie *noun*
an ampoule of amyl nitrite *US*
- — Eugene Landy, *The Underground Dictionary*, p. 152, 1971

popskull *noun*
strong, homemade whisky *US*
- It is called corn liquor, white lightning, sugar whiskey, skully cracker, popskull, bush whiskey, stump, stumphole, 'splo, ruckus juice, radiator whiskey, rotgut, sugarhead, block and tackle, wildcat, panther's breath, tiger's sweat, Sweet spirits of cats a-fighting, alley bourbon, city gin, cool water, happy Sally, deep shaft, jump steady, old horsey, stingo, blue John, red eye, pine top, buckeye bark whiskey and see seven stars. — *Star Tribune (Minneapolis)*, p. 19F, 31st January 1999

popsy; popsie *noun*
a young woman who is the object of a romantic or sexual attraction *UK, 1862*
- Bit of high class popsy, I heard you was a hostess. — Jeremy Cameron, *Brown Bread in Wengen*, p. 176, 1999
- Now, if she had had a huge nose and a tiny mouth she would have been a giant anteater [...] but, by a happy throw of the dice, she is the perfect popsy — *The Guardian*, 12th September 2003

poptastic *adjective*
fantastic *UK*
Created for the BBC television programme *Harry Enfield's Television Programme*, 1990, written by Harry Enfield and Paul Whitehouse for the comedy characters Smashie and Nicey.
- — Susie Dent, *The Language Report*, p. 147, 2003
- I don't like that thought because Jay-Z's so ... So what? Slack and simplistic and poptastic and jiggy. — Patrick Neate, *Where You're At*, p. 34, 2003

pop top *noun*
a truck carrying bottled soft drinks *UK*
Citizens' band radio slang, elaborated on **POP** (a carbonated drink).
- — Peter Chippindale, *The British CB Book*, p. 158, 1981

population *noun*
the general population in a prison *US*
- Back in population I stayed clean, worked out every day, did some reading, a lot of rapping. — Edwin Torres, *Carlito's Way*, p. 46, 1975

pop-up *noun*
1 an electronic advertisement delivered to a computer via the Internet that is superimposed over the original browser window *US*
- "I think if they (AOL) are really concerned about junk mail, if they're truly concerned about members wishes, they would stop sending pop-up (advertisement) screens," Wallace said. — *Central Penn Business Journal*, p. 1, 6th December 1996

2 any mushroom with an hallucinogenic effect *UK*
- I'd once before had a third of a microdot of acid, but that had been nothing compared to what thirty of these little pop-ups were now doing to me. — Ken Lukowiak, *Marijuana Time*, p. 329, 2000

pop-up hell *noun*
an unfriendly web-surfing environment characterised by multiple console advertisements in pop-up windows *US*
A term used frequently on the web but not in conventional print sources.
- — *www.adultquarter.com*, January 2004: 'Glossary of adult internet terms'

porcelain god *noun*
a toilet *US*
- — Connie Eble (Editor), *UNC-CH Campus Slang*, p. 4, October 1986

porcelain king; porcelain queen *noun*
someone who habitually drinks alcohol to the point of vomiting *US*
- — Judi Sanders, *Faced and Faded, Hanging to Hurl*, p. 31, 1993

porch climber *noun*
homemade alcohol or cheap British Columbia wines *CANADA*
- "Porch climber" either as homebrew or cheap wines in gallon jugs, caused one to do all kinds of crazy things like shinney up the verandah posts. — Tom Parkin, *WetCoast Words*, p. 109, 1989

porch monkey *noun*
a black person *US*
Offensive, slurring the stereotype of laziness (porch) and the African jungle (monkey).
- — Connie Eble (Editor), *UNC-CH Campus Slang*, p. 5, March 1981

porcupine head *noun*
in hot rodding and motor racing, the cylinder head on the big-block engines manufactured by Chevrolet *US*
John Edwards, *Auto Dictionary*, 1993, gives a neat etymology: 'When the valve covers are removed, the valve stems appear to stick out at odd angles, like the needles on a porcupine'.

Po' Rican *noun*
Puerto Rican *US*
- You had to go with a gang, 'cause if the wops caught you alone on the balcony, you was a flyin' Po' Rican. — Edwin Torres, *Carlito's Way*, p. 12, 1975

pork *noun*
1 flesh, especially in a sexual context *UK*
- [S]he'd asked him to don oven gloves before scratching her pork. — Will Self, *The Sweet Smell of Psychosis*, p. 13, 1996

2 the genitals, male or female *BAHAMAS*
- — John A. Holm, *Dictionary of Bahamian English*, p. 159, 1982

pork *verb*
to have sex with someone *US*
- — Collin Baker et al., *College Undergraduate Slang Study Conducted at Brown University*, p. 175, 1968
- That mean I can go out to where you live and feel up your wife? Maybe pork her, if she's interested? — George V. Higgins, *The Rat on Fire*, p. 127, 1981
- Porked her right there in the backseat of the car in the prison parking lot. — Gerald Petievich, *Shakedown*, p. 65, 1988
- Nice little kids – nice husand, wasn't porkin' around – no financial problems. — *Basic Instinct*, 1992
- And feature – him and that bottle-blond fruitcake are porking in trailers every chance they get[.] — James Ellroy, *White Jazz*, p. 59, 1992
- This may be due to the fact that, for the man, it is like porking a Hefty trash bag. — Anka Radakovich, *The Wild Girls Club*, p. 86, 1994
- Then again, porking never stopped Jeremy from blabbing his blubbery butt off. — Anthony Petkovich, *The X Factory*, p. 191, 1997
- I've got to get on an pork Emma. — Harry Enfield, *Harry Enfield and His Humorous Chums*, p. 53, 1997
- Nine months, and he hasn't porked you? — Marty Beckerman, *Death to All Cheerleaders*, 2000
- King Charles II was porking everyone in sight. — Erica Orloff and JoAnn Baker, *Dirty Little Secrets*, p. 23, 2001
- [I]f she wasn't at this very moment off porkin some scally in St Luke's Gardens. — Niall Griffiths, *Kelly + Victor*, p. 49, 2002
- But I think maybe Newt [Gingrich] was having some trouble at home with his new wife, the former staffer he started porking while he was still married to his second wife. — Al Franken, *Lies*, p. 111, 2003

pork and bean *noun*
a male homosexual *AUSTRALIA, 1944*
Rhyming slang for **QUEAN**.
- — Jim Ramsay, *Cop It Sweet!*, p. 72, 1977
- — Ryan Aven-Bray, *Ridgey Didge Oz Jack Lang*, p. 39, 1983

pork chop *noun*
in electric line work, a wire grip used for holding a conductor under tension *US*
- — A.B. Chance Co., *Lineman's Slang Dictionary*, p. 14, 1980

Pork Chop Hill *noun*
a hill which was the site of extensive fighting in the final months of the Korean war, from 16th April to 18th April and again from 6th July to 10th July, 1953 *US*
- But despite General Clark's determined effort to avoid costly hill fighting, there were savage battles at "Pork Chop" and "T-Bone" Hills. (They were named for their peculiar shapes.) — Don Lawson, *The United States in the Korean War*, p. 116, 1964

pork chop in a synagogue
used as a simile for anything that is badly, especially embarrassingly, out of place or unwelcome *UK, 1984*

pork-dodger *noun*
a Jewish person *US*
From the dietary restrictions of observant Jews.
- And those given a name were stuck with it forever: Svade, Svenska, Lugan, Schnapps, Moishe, Stosh, Henie, Mockie, Guinea, Canuck, Bohunk, Pork-dodger, Limey, Greaseball, Krauthead, Dutchie, Squarehead, Grick, Mick, Paddy, Goombah, Polski, Dago, Hunkie, Wop — *San Francisco Examiner*, p. A15, 28th July 1997

porker *noun*

1 a fat person *US, 1959*

- Which is not to say that everybody's a porker — Robert Campbell, *In a Pig's Eye*, p. 12, 1991
- She was a big, fat, wobbling porker of a bird[.] — Danny King, *The Burglar Diaries*, p. 75, 2001

2 a police officer *US*

An extension of **PIG**.

- I don't hafta point my shotgun / at them pesky porkers no more[.] — Cypress Hill, *Dr. Greenthumb*, 1998

pork-man *noun*

a white man *UK*

- Don't speak to me you fucking white cunt! What business it yours pork-man! — Jack Allen, *When the Whistle Blows*, p. 51, 2000

pork patrol *noun*

a police car *US*

- — Judi Sanders, *Faced and Faded, Hanging to Hurl*, p. 31, 1993

pork pie *noun*

1 a lie *UK*

Rhyming slang. Now stands alone in the reduced form **PORKY**.

- Well, one hardly presumes that he'll be talking a lot of pork pies, is he? — Anthony Masters, *Minder*, p. 145, 1984

2 a serious bruise *NEW ZEALAND*

- — David McGill, *David McGill's Complete Kiwi Slang Dictionary*, p. 99, 1998

pork pies; porkie pies; porkies *noun*

the eyes *UK*

Rhyming slang.

- I never even clapped my little porkies on him before. — Jeremy Cameron, *Brown Bread in Wengen*, p. 15, 1999

pork scratch *noun*

a match *UK*

Rhyming slang, contrived from the savoury snack pork scratchings.

- — Angela Devlin, *Prison Patter*, p. 89, 1996

pork sword *noun*

the penis *US, 1966*

- — Barry Humphries, *Bazza Pulls It Off!*, 1971
- DUANE: How big is your johnson? RAMU: Johnson? DUANE: Your wand, your pork sword, your baloney pony. — *The Guru*, 2002
- Ulrika: Caught in media glare playing hide the pork sword with Sven. — *Rated*, p. 7, June 2002
- Psychologists agree that, just as women secretly covet our pork swords, men need sheds. — *FHM*, p. 44, June 2003

porky *noun*

1 a lie *UK, 1992*

Abbreviated from rhyming slang **PORK PIE**.

- Either he told me a porky or they've changed their operation[.] — Greg Williams, *Diamond Geezers*, p. 61, 1997
- JULIE BRADLEY: Lied to us today? PHILIP OLIVER: Not yet, but give me time and I'll tell you a porky. — *Sky Magazine*, p. 83, July 2001
- [A] case had folded with the hint that one or the other of us had told porkies. — Duncan MacLaughlin, *The Filth*, p. 124, 2002

2 the vagina *BAHAMAS*

- — John A. Holm, *Dictionary of Bahamian English*, p. 159, 1982

3 a police officer *US*

- — Kenn "Naz" Young, *Naz's Underground Dictionary*, p. 50, 1973

porky *adjective*

obese *UK, 1852*

- Less HGH [human growth hormone] means your body makes less muscle and burns less fat – so welcome, Porky. — *Men's Fitness*, September 2003

Porky Pig *adjective*

big; generous *UK*

Rhyming slang, from the name of a Warner Bros' cartoon character. The sense of 'big' is often heavily ironic.

- Oh, so you've put my name down for a fiver's worth of raffle tickets have you? Well that was Porky Pig of you. — Ray Puxley, *Cockney Rabbit*, 1992

porn; porno *noun*

pornography *UK, 1962*

- — *Current Slang*, p. 11, Summer 1968
- Throughout the book are quotes from some of the peole who are very much involved in the world of porno. — Stephen Ziplow, *The Film Maker's Guide to Pornography*, p. 8, 1977
- Some of my best friends are porn stars. — *Cult Movies No. 17*, p. 46, 1996
- I don't mind shooting [filming] more porno[.] — Stewart Home, *Sex Kick [britpulp]*, p. 235, 1999

porn and prawn *adjective*

of a party, arranged for the purpose of showing pornographic films and catered for with epicurean food including prawns *AUSTRALIA*

- Or is there something more? After 30 years in the adult entertainment industry, supplying hundreds of strippers to Australian porn and prawn functions, Barry Goodwill, from Wildcatz Entertainment Design, is not entirely sure. — *Sydney Morning Herald*, p. 8s, 29th June 1996

pornbroke *noun*

a seller of pornographic literature *UK*

A pun on 'pawnbroker'.

- — *The Times Literary Supplement*, 19th January 1967

pornflakes *noun*

crusty, dried semen *AUSTRALIA*

A pun on the branded name of a popular breakfast cereal, Corn Flakes™.

- — Chris Lewis, *The Dictionary of Playground Slang*, p. 174, 2003

porn flick *noun*

a pornographic film *UK*

- — *The Observer*, 15th November 1970

porn mag; porno mag *noun*

a *porno*graphic *mag*azine *UK, 1972*

- "I'm going to the toilet," Wendall says. "Has anybody got any porno mags?" — Darren Francis, *The Sprawl [britpulp]*, p. 297, 1999

porno *noun*

a *porno*graphic film or video *UK*

- In the corner was a TV and video. That was no good – it made him think of pornos. — Colin Butts, *Is Harry on the Boat?*, p. 1, 1997
- Yer look like someone out of a porno. — Niall Griffiths, *Kelly + Victor*, p. 204, 2002

porno *adjective*

*porno*graphic *US, 1952*

- Screw explains its new device to graphically illustrate our evaluation of sexploitation and porno films. — *Screw*, p. 15, 8th December 1969
- Of course the porno movies are hardly limited to showings at public theaters. — Roger Blake, *What you always wanted to know about porno-movies*, p. 89, 1972
- You know how I told you when Nellie came back to L.A. she started going with this darling guy, Stuart, who makes all those porno movies? — Eve Babitz, *Eve's Hollywood*, p. 247, 1974
- Sometimes you'll pick up a black porno flick and with luck get a real actor – some out-of-work brother that you used to see on TV. You'll be watching and you'll say, "Hey wait a minute, isn't that Sticks from 'Happy Days?'" — Chris Rock, *Rock This!*, p. 26, 1997
- Mab, who'd once made Barbie buy her some porno magazines – purely for research purposes – suddenly recognized the ring and realized what Ken wanted to put in it. — Francesca Lia Block, *I Was a Teenage Fairy*, p. 138, 1998

pornographically *adverb*

used in a sexual context for more than averagely *UK*

- If not PORNOGRAPHICALLY endowed there are positions you can try to make your partner feel more "full". — *Loaded*, p. 12, June 2002

pornshop *noun*

a shop where pornography is sold *UK, 1984*

A pun on 'pawnshop'.

porn weed; horny weed *noun*

marijuana with, allegedly, aphrodisiac properties *UK*

Combines **WEED** (marijuana) with sexual possibilities, **HORNY** (sexually stimulating), **PORN** (pornography) and 'love'.

- ["]What're you two smoking?" The boyfriend tittered. "Porn weed, man. Porn weed." [...] "Porn weed, huh? Mmmmm. Sounds just the ticket." [...] "It's like, you know, it's like smoking pure fuckin MDMA, man! Horny grass! Pure fuckin porn!" — Kevin Sampson, *Powder*, p. 314, 1999
- — Mike Haskins, *Drugs*, p. 288, 2003

porny *adjective*

pornographic *US*

- The San Francisco porny movies are being busted, including the audience. — *The Berkeley Tribe*, p. 24, 22nd – 28th August 1969
- Just how porny can you get? — *Sunday Times*, 29th August 1971

porpoise *noun*
a landing by an aeroplane in which the plane bounces from the main gear to the nose gear *US*
• — *American Speech*, p. 119, May 1963: 'Air refueling words'

porpoise *verb*
in mountain biking, to ride responding to, instead of controlling, the bike *US*
• — William Nealy, *Mountain Bike!*, p. 162, 1992: 'Bikespeak'

Porra; porra *noun*
a person of Portuguese descent *SOUTH AFRICA, 1975*
• — Penny Silva, *A Dictionary of South African English*, 1996

porridge *noun*
1 a sentence of imprisonment; the time served in prison *UK, 1955*
Possibly puns on **STIR** (prison) and the staple prison diet of porridge. The term settled in the wider public conciousness during the 1970s with BBC television prison situation comedy *Porridge*.
• Week excuses that's all you get, when you go away to do a bit of porridge. — Frank Norman, *Bang to Rights*, p. 171, 1958
• — Angela Devlin, *Prison Patter*, p. 89, 1996
• Much as I can hack a few nights in the cells, I really don't fancy straight porridge. — Danny King, *The Burglar Diaries*, p. 235, 2001
• [N]ightmares with dodgy builders, wedding plans, imminent births and ex-employees doing porridge are all mentioned. — Kelly Jones, *Q*, p. 44, May 2002
• Her brother's done porridge, just out. — Jonathan Gash, *The Ten Word Game*, p. 34, 2003
2 the brain *UK*
A visual link between varying consistencies of grey matter.
• 'Course I've no idea what it actually means, but it's still lodged up in the porridge. — Greg Williams, *Diamond Geezers*, p. 136, 1997
3 sludge removed from drains *UK*
• — Harvey Sheppard, *Dictionary of Railway Slang*, 1970

porridge gun *noun*
the penis *UK*
• Isn't it time for men to celebrate their porridge guns outside the murky confines of the water closet? — Richard Herring, *Talking Cock*, p. vii, 2003

porridge pot *noun*
in motor racing, a crash helmet that covers only the top of the head *US*
• — John Lawlor, *How to Talk Car*, p. 82, 1965

porridge wog *noun*
a Scot *UK*
Combines **WOG** (a foreigner) with a stereotypical Scottish dish.
• — *www.LondonSlang.com*, June 2002

port *noun*
1 in New South Wales and Queensland, a suitcase or schoolbag *AUSTRALIA, 1898*
From 'portmanteau'.
• — Jim Ramsay, *Cop It Sweet!*, p. 72, 1977
• I grabbed my shorts and put them on, then ports and the remains of my gear and left. — Bettina Arndt, *The Australian Way of Sex*, p. 37, 1985
2 a railway porter *US*
• — Ramon Adams, *The Language of the Railroader*, p. 117, 1977

portable *noun*
a foot-patrol police officer *US*
• — Carsten Stroud, *Close Pursuit*, p. 274, 1987

Portagee *noun*
a person from Portugal, or of Portuguese heritage *US*
• — *Maledicta*, p. 168, Summer/Winter 1978: 'How to hate thy neighbor: a guide to racist maledicta'

▸ **go Portagee on me**
to back out of an agreement *CANADA*
Portuguese immigrants, mostly fishermen, fishbuyers and sailors, settled near where this phrase is current.
• — Lewis Poteet, *The South Shore Phrase Book*, p. 88, 1999

Portagee beer *noun*
any beer in a quart bottle *BERMUDA*
• — Peter A. Smith and Fred M. Barritt, *Bermewjan Vurds*, 1985

Portagee chrome *noun*
aluminium paint *US*
• — *American Speech*, p. 272, December 1961: 'Northwest truck drivers' language'

Portagee lawnmower *noun*
a goat *US*
• — *Maledicta*, p. 234, 1988–1989: 'The portagee in speech and joke'

Portagee lift *noun*
in manual labour, said when one worker does not carry his fair share *US*
• — *Journal of American Folklore*, p. 211, July–September 1960: 'John Newhaus: wobbly folklorist'

Portagee overdrive *noun*
to coast down a hill while driving *US*
• — *American Speech*, p. 273, 1961: 'Truck drivers' language in the northwest'

port and brandy *adjective*
sexually aroused; feeling lecherous *UK*
Rhyming slang for **RANDY**.
• — Ray Puxley, *Cockney Rabbit*, 1992

portapotty *noun*
a portable toilet, transported to construction sites, campgrounds, outdoor concerts, etc *US*
• WAYNE: Do you know anything about portapotties? GARTH: They look like phone booths, they're usually white, they smell funny. — *Wayne's World 2*, 1993
• Check it out Butt-Head, porta-potties. — Mike Judge and Joe Stillman, *Beavis and Butt-Head Do America*, p. 50, 1997

porthole duff *noun*
homosexual anal sex *UK, 1961*
A naval use – another dish on the **NAVY CAKE** menu; the 'porthole' may refer to the anus or, in specialised use, mean that the passive partner has his 'head out of a porthole'.

portion *noun*
an act of sexual intercourse as something given to a woman *UK*
• Thought you'd still be round that sort's place giving her a second portion. — John King, *Human Punk*, p. 250, 2000
• [S]he's getting all worked up cos she probably ain't had a portion in stretches [years]. — J.J. Connolly, *Layer Cake*, p. 284, 2000

portnoy *noun*
a male masturbator *UK*
A reference to *Portnoy's Complaint*, a novel by Philip Roth, 1969.
• [Suzy Creamcheese's] ascents and descents throughout the afternoon providing a pleasant bonus for us uncomplaining Portnoys below[.] — Richard Neville, *Play Power*, p. 109, 1970

Port of Spaniard *noun*
a resident of Port of Spain, Trinidad *TRINIDAD AND TOBAGO, 1990*
• — Lise Winer, *Dictionary of the English/Creole of Trinidad & Tobago*, 2003

portrait painter *noun*
speed radar; a police officer operating a speed camera *US*
• — *Complete CB Slang Dictionary*, p. 76, 1976
• — Peter Chippindale, *The British CB Book*, p. 158, 1981

port-sider *noun*
a left-handed person *US*
• — Dick Squires, *The Other Racquet Sports*, p. 221, 1971: 'Glossary'

Portuguese parliament *noun*
a meeting where everybody talks and nobody listens *US, 1951*
• — *Maledicta*, p. 234, 1988–1989: 'The Portagee in speech and joke'

Portuguese shop *noun*
a small grocery shop attached to a rum shop, whether or not it is owned by Portuguese people *TRINIDAD AND TOBAGO, 1989*
• — Lise Winer, *Dictionary of the English/Creole of Trinidad & Tobago*, 2003

Portuguese straight *noun*
in poker, a straight formed with different suits, thus without value *US*
Hawaiian youth usage.
• — Douglas Simonson, *Pidgin to da Max Hana Hou*, 1982

porty *noun*
a portable telephone *US*
• Is that your porty or mine? — *Jerry Maguire*, 1996

pos *noun*

position *US*

- Check your fire, check your fire, you're short on our pos! —*Platoon*, 1986

▷ **see: POSS**

POS *noun*

a patient regarded by hospital personnel as a *p*iece *o*f *s*hit *US*

- — *Maledicta*, p. 6, Summer/Winter 1978: 'Common patient-directed pejoratives used by medical 'personnel

pose *verb*

to pretend a station in life that has yet to be achieved *US*

- He gave Irving a fit posing all over the place, then cut out for Florida, where he became a bigtime bookmaker. —Mezz Mezzrow, *Really the Blues*, p. 87, 1946

poser *noun*

a person who imitates that which he is not *US*

- Highway surfer: A 'poser' whose surfboard stays on the roofrack. —Rick Abbott and Mike Baker, *Start Surfing*, p. 85, 1980
- —Connie Eble (Editor), *UNC-CH Campus Slang*, p. 7, November 1990

posh *adjective*

1 being stylish, smart; of the best class; elegant and sophisticated *UK, 1918*

In popular folk etymology, reinforced by the song 'Posh' in the 1968 film *Chitty Chitty Bang Bang*, 'posh' is an acronym of '*p*ort *o*ut *s*tarboard *h*ome', supposedly the location of the 'best' cabins on an England to India P&O line cruise; unfortunately P&O has no record of such a phrase ever being used. Other suggested derivations: a contraction of 'polished', an earlier sense as 'money', and a corruption of Scottish *tosh* (smart). However, this is slang and 'port out starboard home' is the more entertaining etymology and therefore likely to continue as the popular favourite.

- He certainly had a posh accent, and his eyes were set rather too close together in his narrow face. —Chris Ryan, *Stand By, Stand By*, p. 145, 1996
- She was my first-ever posh girlfriend[.] —Frank Skinner, *Frank Skinner*, p. 243, 2001
- An environment which is too clean, too ordered – in short, too "posh" – may unwittingly present a threat[.] — *The Guardian*, 18th July 2002

2 being in possession of drugs *UK*

- Oh, and did you say you were posh tonight, darling? No? Oh, that's a bore. —James Hawes, *White Powder, Green Light*, p. 40, 2002

Posh and Becks; Posh 'n' Becks *noun*

sex *UK*

- —Tom Nind, *Rude Rhyming Slang*, p. 16, 2003
- —Bodmin Dark, *Dirty Cockney Rhyming Slang*, 2003

Posh and Becks; Posh 'n' Becks *nickname*

singer Victoria Beckham and her husband, footballer David Beckham, considered as a single celebrity icon *UK*

- Christened David Robert Joseph Beckham. Now, of course, he is simply the latter half of Posh 'n' Becks, a tabloid monster of gargantuan proportions. — *The Observer*, 8th October 2000
- [A] kids' cocktail menu, with the Posh and Becks – a coke float – presumably being the money-maker. —Iain Aitch, *A Fete Worse Than Death*, p. 294, 2003

poshie *noun*

a posh person *IRELAND*

- D'you know what the poshies call this estate, do you? Pill Hill. —Eamonn Sweeney, *Waiting for the Healer*, p. 62, 1997
- I know what it fookin is, ye little poshie bastard. Gimme it. —Paul Howard, *Ross O'Carroll-Kelly*, p. 23, 2003

posho *noun*

a member of the middle- or upper-classes *UK*

- [I]t's some posho fucker's second home now innit[.] —Niall Griffiths, *Sheepshagger*, p. 17, 2001
- [Blur] may have been art school poshoes [...] but at the height of Britpop, it was all Phil Daniels, footie and whippets. — *X-Ray*, p. 56, April 2003

posh totty *noun*

a sexually attractive upper-class woman *UK*

- Diana Rigg [...] was proper posh-totty, mate, and I had to stay on the sofa a good half hour after watching The Avengers. —Dave Courtney, *Dodgy Dave's Little Black Book*, p. 40, 2001

posh wank *noun*

1 an act of male masturbation while the penis is sheathed in a condom *UK*

Combines **POSH** (upper-class) with **WANK** (to masturbate).

- He reached for the condoms. A posh wank would put the world to rights. —Kevin Sampson, *Powder*, p. 317, 1999

2 used as abuse of a contemptible person, especially one you consider to be of a superior status *UK*

A combination of **POSH** (upper-class) with **WANK** (an act of masturbation); informed by contemporaneous 'posh wank' (the act of masturbation in a condom).

- Ah, shut ya face, you, poshwank! —Kevin Sampson, *Powder*, p. 246, 1999

poshy *adjective*

elegant and sophisticated *UK*

Later variation of **POSH**.

- Dramatically half lit in his poshy university office —James Hawes, *Dead Long Enough*, p. 9, 2000

poshy-poshy *adjective*

extremely elegant and stylish *UK*

Reduplication of **POSHY** for emphasis.

- [S]et off to this poshy-poshy hotel. —BBC Radio Wales, *The Jamie Owen Show*, 15th May 2002

pository

yes, affirmative *US*

Citizens' band radio slang.

- — *Complete CB Slang Dictionary*, p. 76, 1976
- —Peter Chippindale, *The British CB Book*, p. 158, 1981

poss; pos *noun*

a possibility *UK*

- Oh yes, a definite poss. He'll look good alongside Susan. — *A Hard Day's Night*, 1964

poss; pos *adjective*

possible *UK, 1886*

- [J]ust wanted to let you know as soon as poss., can't see us getting the morning flight[.] —James Hawes, *Dead Long Enough*, p. 234, 2000

posse *noun*

1 a group of close friends *US*

- —Peter A. Smith and Fred M. Barritt, *Bermewjan Vurds*, 1985
- —Ellen C. Bellone (Editor), *Dictionary of Slang*, p. 18, 1989
- [T]he DJ [...] read out the address of the after-party. Several of our posse went straight there[.] —Wayne Anthony, *Spanish Highs*, p. 85, 1999

2 a gang *US*

- He acted as lookout for the posse, an early warning system to guard against surprise raids. —Karline Smith, *Moss Side Massive*, p. 8, 1994
- I feel so happy. They want me. I'm going to be a part of their posse. —Karline Smith, *Letters to Andy Cole*, p. 139, 1998
- [Y]our Kru, or your Massive, your Thugs, or Bredrins; Dawgs, Homies, your Clique, or your Posse. —Julian Johnson, *Urban Survival*, p. 264, 2003

possible *noun*

1 the vagina *US*

A probably Freudian etymology.

- There's [a...] a "pajama," "fannyboo," "mushmellow," "a ghoulie," "possible," "tamale[".] —Eve Ensler, *The Vagina Monologues*, p. 6, 1998

2 in target shooting, a perfect score *US*

- — *American Speech*, p. 194, October 1957: 'Some colloquialisms of the handgunner'

3 in poker, any hand that can be completed with the draw of one card *US*

Variant 'possibulletee'.

- — *American Speech*, p. 100, May 1951

possie; possy; pozzie; pozzy *noun*

a position *AUSTRALIA, 1915*

Originally in World War 1 a soldier's chosen position from which to snipe, observe, etc.

- Gawd, just when a man's got a decent possy, he has to leave it! —Leonard Mann, *Flesh in Armour*, p. 49, 1932
- [W]e started on a short course of steady drinking, hanging onto our possies at the bar and letting the mob push about and roar for drinks behind us. —Gavin Casey, *It's Harder for Girls*, p. 168, 1941
- Hang on, that looks a likely pozzie in the vicinity of those parked vehicles. —Barry Humphries, *The Wonderful World of Barry McKenzie*, p. 10, 1968
- He was fairly pooped when he got to the possie where half a dozen other regulars were fishing. —Bob Staines, *Wot a Whopper*, p. 19, 1982

possum *noun*

darling *AUSTRALIA, 1894*

A term of affectionate address.

- Mind you, Possums, banana sandwiches do get horribly brown and squashy on a hot day and the very smell of them used to make me violently sick. — Edna Everage (Barry Humphries), *My Gorgeous Life*, p. 33, 1989

Possum; Ole Possum *nickname*

George Jones, a country singer and songwriter (b.1931) *US*

- "Ricky and Randy. I wanted to call them Hank and George, after Hank Williams and Ole Possum, George Jones?" But Winona got her way, as usual. — Elmore Leonard, *Riding the Rap*, p. 93, 1995
- — George Jones, *Live With The Possum*, 1999

possum belly *noun*

the tool box located on the underside of a brakevan (caboose) *US*

- — Norman Carlisle, *The Modern Wonder Book of Trains and Railroading*, p. 266, 1946

post *noun*

an autopsy *US, 1942*

From the more formal 'post mortem'.

- "What's a post? A post mortem?" "Yeah, an autopsy. They have to determine the cause of death. Even when a man's been shot four times." — Elmore Leonard, *Split Images*, p. 104, 1981

▸ **left at the post**

(of a horse in a race) to lose badly *AUSTRALIA, 1895*

- I saw Moore in Sydney before he sailed, and he assured me that he lost his head entirely when Quiver was left at the post, but that he had no intention of doing anything crooked. — Nat Gould, *On and Off the Turf*, p. 29, 1895
- The Old Huck, was given a mount of a 'rogue' at Newcastle. It had been left at the post and had run off at the turn in every race. — Frank Hardy and Athol George Mulley, *The Needy and the Greedy*, p. 23, 1975
- Jim backed his horse well but it got left at the post, so when he came back to the pub after the races the locals chiaked him. — Frank Hardy and Athol George Mulley, *The Needy and the Greedy*, p. 104, 1975
- It was a memorable event as no fewer than five horses were left at the post. — Joe Brown, *Just for the Record*, p. 31, 1984

post *verb*

to leave someone in the lurch, especially during the commission of a crime *AUSTRALIA*

- — *The (Sydney) Bulletin*, 26th April 1975

▸ **post a flyer**

to use coded language in a conversation to advertise your homosexuality and sexual availability *UK*

- — *Maledicta*, p. 144, Summer/Winter 1986–1987: 'Sexual slang: prostitutes, pedophiles, flagellators, transvestites, and necrophiles'

▸ **post a letter**

to go to the toilet *TRINIDAD AND TOBAGO*

- — Lise Winer, *Dictionary of the English/Creole of Trinidad & Tobago*, 2003

postage stamp *noun*

1 a woman *US*

Citizens' band radio slang, etymology unknown, although licking is almost certainly a component.

- — *Complete CB Slang Dictionary*, p. 76, 1976
- — Peter Chippindale, *The British CB Book*, p. 158, 1981

2 a public house bar counter *UK*

Rhyming slang for **RAMP**. Shortened to 'postage'.

- "Come on, get up the postage", means "It's your round". — Ray Puxley, *Cockney Rabbit*, 1992

3 in horse racing, a very small weight allowance in a weight-handicapped event *AUSTRALIA*

- — Ned Wallish, *The Truth Dictionary of Racing Slang*, p. 64, 1989

postal *adjective*

extremely angry; furious to the point of violence *US, 1994*

From a series of highly publicised workplace shootings by frustrated and furious employees of the US Postal Service.

- Like Josh thinking I was mean was making me postal. — *Clueless*, 1995
- — *American Speech*, p. 304, Fall 1996: 'Among the new words'
- — Connie Eble (Editor), *UNC-CH Campus Slang*, p. 4, April 1997
- If another one of these chairs hits me in the nuts, I'm gonna go postal. — *Austin Powers*, 1999
- Listen to ['The Golden Age of the Grotesque' by Marilyn Manson] when: You've gone postal – and you want someone to blame. — *FHM*, p. 223, June 2003

postcode *adjective*

used for describing any matter in which domestic, economic or political status may be defined by geographic location; where your postal address affects the provision of medical care, education and publicly funded services, or insurance, or credit-rating; especially as 'postcode lottery', 'postcode prescribing' and 'postcode discrimination' *UK*

- Postcode lottery in GP services. — *BBC News*, 26th September 1999
- However, it is important that we end postcode prescribing in the NHS. — Prime Minister Tony Blair, *from the parliamentary record*, 21st June 2000
- The report criticises weak leadership from political and community figures [...] and condemns "postcode" discrimination by private employers[.] — *The Guardian*, 12th December 2001

poster boy *noun*

a very good example of an attitude or condition *US*

Used facetiously.

- CLARENCE: Well, I have to admit, walkin' through the door and seein' these Soldier of Fortune poster boys made me a bit nervous. — *True Romance*, 1993

posteriors *noun*

the penis and testicles *BAHAMAS*

- — John A. Holm, *Dictionary of Bahamian English*, p. 160, 1982

postie *noun*

1 a postman or postwoman *UK, 1887*

- Our postie is an exceptionally nice little chappie. — Barry Humphries, *A Nice Night's Entertainment*, p. 140, 1974
- I'd hear my postie pal's voice ringing in my ears. — *The Guardian*, 9th January 2003

2 The Royal Mail, the Post Office *UK*

- [A] lad from the postie that reckoned he knew when a new batch of Visas was coming in. — Kevin Sampson, *Outlaws*, p. 23, 2001

▷ **see: PO-MO**

postman *noun*

in horse racing, someone who can be counted on for inside tips on horses and races *AUSTRALIA*

A term built on **MAIL** as 'inside information'.

- — Ned Wallish, *The Truth Dictionary of Racing Slang*, p. 64, 1989

postman's knock *noun*

1 a lock *UK*

Rhyming slang, ascribed to burglars when used by lockmakers Chubb's in an advertisement.

- — *Daily Telegraph*, 5th March 1962

2 a clock *UK*

Rhyming slang, sometimes seen in an abbreviated form as 'postman's'.

- — Ray Puxley, *Cockney Rabbit*, 1992

3 in pool, a shot in which the cue ball hits the object ball twice in rapid succession, producing a knock-like sound *US*

- — Mike Shamos, *The Illustrated Encyclopedia of Billiards*, p. 180, 1993

post-mortem *noun*

in poker, an analysis of a hand after it has been played *US*

- — George Percy, *The Language of Poker*, p. 70, 1988

postop *noun*

a transexual who has undergone all surgery necessary to complete a sex change *US*

- As a two-year postop MTF, I can attest life as a woman is no bowl of cherries. — Nancy Tamosaitis, *net.sex*, p. 130, 1995

post up *verb*

to idle *US*

- — *Columbia Missourian*, p. 1A, 19th October 1998

pot *noun*

1 marijuana *US, 1938*

The most popular slang term for marijuana in the 1950s. No agreement on the etymology, with competing conjectures and little supporting evidence.

- But I never blew up a joint in the folks' apartment the whole time I was on pot – that's grass, you know, marijuana. I really never did. — David Hulburi, *H is For Heroin*, p. 47, 1952
- "Pot, H., morphine, and that's all," the girl recited in a toneless voice. — Hal Ellson, *The Golden Spike*, p. 31, 1952
- Don't say pot, Dinch. It's the intellectuals from college and all who come on that way. They want to get their hip-cards punched. Say pod, Dinch. — George Mandel, *Flee the Angry Strangers*, p. 26, 1952

- I learned the new hipster vocabulary; "pot" for weed[.] — William Burroughs, *Junkie*, p. 120, 1953
- Benny, the boy who had been collecting admissions, pushed his way through the crowd to us, his eyes wide with excitement. "Hey, Louie!" he said. "The Gremlins are smoking pot in the toilet!" — *The New Yorker*, p. 127, 21 September 1957
- [A] crazy Isadora Duncan girl with long blue hair on his shoulder smoking pot and talking about Pound and peote — Jack Kerouac, *The Subterraneans*, p. 4, 1958
- I just needs some pot to steady my nerves. — Chester Himes, *The Real Cool Killers*, p. 48, 1959
- Marijuana will be legal some day, because the many law students who now smoke pot will some day become Congressmen and legalize it in order to protect themselves. — Lenny Bruce, *How to Talk Dirty and Influence People*, p. 129, 1965
- There were many guys up there I used to bully on the streets and at Wiltwyck, guys I had sold tea leaves to as pot. — Claude Brown, *Manchild in the Promised Land*, p. 16, 1965
- That aint what the Mex'can called it neither – he called it "pot". — Terry Southern, *Red-Dirt Marijuana and Other Tastes*, 1967
- What do you bring to a hippie "tea party"? Your own "pot"! — Paul Laikin, *101 Hippie Jokes*, 1968
- Once or twice a few had fallen in with pot or tea as it was called then and I picked up for the first time one morning and got so stoned I was unable to move. — Herbert Huncke, *The Evening Sun Turned Crimson*, p. 28–29, 1980
- FREDDY: She agreed to that, and said we'd keep the same arrangement as before, the percent and free pot for me, as long as I helped her out that weekend. — *Reservoir Dogs*, 1992
- But although the police found no pot (I bet that's what Spotty calls it), they decided that possession of Rizlas [branded cigarette papers] is sufficient grounds to demand a more intimate search. — Martin King and Martin Knight, *The Naughty Nineties*, p. 121, 1999
- In every practical sense, government has said it's OK to smoke pot for Christ's sake[.] — Kevin Sampson, *Clubland*, p. 17, 2002

2 heroin

- [Charlie Parker] always had a crowd around him and he gave different jobs to each one. "You go and get my horn. You get me some pot. You do this. You do that." And they would jump. — Kenny Dorham, *recalling the late 1940s, quoted in Waiting For The Man, Harry Shapiro*, 1999

3 in Queensland, Victoria and Tasmania, a 10 fluid ounce glass of beer *AUSTRALIA, 1915*

- We walked out of the station and across the road and had a long, cool pot at the nearest pub. — Gavin Casey, *It's Harder for Girls*, p. 117, 1941
- A pair of twelve-ounce pots tasted all right after the hard half-shift, but insufficient. — Gavin Casey, *It's Harder for Girls*, p. 167, 1941
- The sergeant liked a pot himself and swore by Danny's beer. — Bill Wannan, *Folklore of the Australian Pub*, p. 52, 1972
- 'We got ponies, glasses, middies, an' pots, see,' the first man said. 'Now a pony's four ounces –' The second man said, 'Two to four.' 'All right, two to four. But who the bloody hell drinks two's? You keep quiet while I clue him up. A glass is five ounces, a middy is seven ounces, an' a pot's ten.' — John O'Grady, *It's Your Shout, Mate!*, p. 15, 1972
- I had already learnt Melbourne glass sizes and nomenclature, so different from Adelaide. One asks for a four ounce, a small beer, or a pot. A request for a small beer produces seven ounces, and for a pot ten. — John O'Grady, *It's Your Shout, Mate!*, p. 39, 1972
- 'I'm a stranger in Brisbane. What size beers do you serve, and what do you call them?' She said, 'Five ounce, eight ounce, and ten ounce. We call them small beers, beers, and pots.' — John O'Grady, *It's Your Shout, Mate!*, p. 66, 1972
- ...10 ounces in Vic. and 20 ounces in NSW... — Jim Ramsay, *Cop It Sweet!*, p. 73, 1977
- In one hand, the man had a pot of beer, in the other a notebook, a pencil and a thick wad of banknotes. — Roy Higgins and Tom Prior, *The Jockey Who Laughed*, p. 75, 1982
- Crawley winked at him and handed him the pot. — Peter Corris, *Pokerface*, p. 38, 1985

4 a tooth *UK*
Polari; usually in the plural.

- — the cast of 'Aspects of Love', Prince of Wales Theatre, *Palare (Boy Dancer Talk) for Beginners*, 1989–92
- [D]istract attention from the cod [bad] eke [face] and chronic pots. — James Gardiner, *Who's a Pretty Boy Then?*, p. 123, 1997

5 in poker, all of the chips or money bet on a single hand *US*

- — Oswald Jacoby, *Oswald Jacoby on Poker*, p. 138, 1947

6 the jack in a game of bowls *UK*
In Midlands' use. The southern equivalent is 'kitty'.

- — Mr Maurice Butcher, 1979

7 in electric line work, a transformer *US*
An abbreviation of 'potential transformer'.

- — A.B. Chance Co., *Lineman's Slang Dictionary*, p. 14, 1980

8 a carburettor *US, 1941*

- — *Hot Rod Magazine*, p. 13, November 1948: 'Racing jargon'
- He had twin pots and a Columbia clutch / An' speed that no other car could touch / An' to you folks who don't dig the jive / That's two carburetors and an overdrive. — George Wilson (performed by Bob Williams), *Hot Rod Race*, 1960

9 a hospital patient with many trivial complaints *US*

- — *Maledicta*, p. 56, Summer 1980: 'Not sticks and stones, but names: more medical pejoratives'

▸ not have a pot to piss in; not have a pot to pee in
to be extremely poor *CANADA, 1961*

- After all, following two difficult divorces, he [Phil Tufnell] hasn't, as he told me, "got a pot to piss in" – and in these uncertain times, a man has "to nick a few quid" while he can. — *New Statesman*, 30th June 2003

pot *verb*

1 to shoot or kill someone *US, 1860*

- His partner, Fred, smiled. "You goin' pot the bastard?" he asked with unwarranted glee. — Donald Goines, *Black Gangster*, p. 109, 1977

2 to put a baby on a potty (a chamber pot) *UK, 1961*

▸ pot the white
to have sex *UK*
An allusion to billiards.

- — H.E. Bates, *The Darling Buds of May*, 1955

-pot *suffix*
a person of a type defined or suggested by the word to which it is joined *UK, 1880*
The best known current forms are **FUSSPOT** and **SEXPOT**.

pot A *noun*
a prisoner who has received a minimum of ten years is regarded as a *pot*ential Category *A* prisoner *UK*

- — Angela Devlin, *Prison Patter*, p. 89, 1996

potable *noun*
drinking water *US*

- — Carl Fleischhauer, *A Glossary of Army Slang*, p. 7, 1968

pot and pan; old pot and pan; old pot *noun*
a man; a husband; a father *AUSTRALIA, 1905*
Rhyming slang.

- Where's your old pot and pan, not about? — Frank Hardy, *The Outcasts of Foolgarah*, p. 14, 1971
- — Ray Puxley, *Cockney Rabbit*, 1992

potater juice; potato juice; potata juice *noun*
vodka *US*

- — *Complete CB Slang Dictionary*, p. 76, 1976
- — Peter Chippindale, *The British CB Book*, p. 158, 1981
- Well, maybe after this Russian potata juice ferments I'll relax more. — Joseph Wambaugh, *The Golden Orange*, p. 89, 1990

potato *noun*

1 marijuana *UK*
An elaboration of **POT**.

- I warily put my stuff on the bonnet, leaving the lump of Moroccan potato in the pocket of my jeans. — Wayne Anthony, *Spanish Highs*, p. 57, 1999

2 LSD *UK, 1998*

- — Mike Haskins, *Drugs*, p. 286, 2003

3 a woman *AUSTRALIA, 1959*
Short for **POTATO PEELER**.

potato digger *noun*
an amphibious tracked personnel carrier fitted with a dozer blade used for clearing mines during the Vietnam war *US*

- — Gregory Clark, *Words of the Vietnam War*, p. 291, 1991

potatoed *adjective*
sluggish; in a non-responsive state (possibly as a result of drug use) *UK*

- [T]he spirit was willing, but the body was completely potatoed. — Wayne Anthony, *Spanish Highs*, p. 19, 1999

potatoes *noun*
money *US*
One of life's basics.

- I have got some fucking potatoes. I don't really need no more. — Kevin Sampson, *Outlaws*, p. 109, 2001

potato hook *noun*
in electric line work, an insulated line tool formally known as a fixed prong tie stick *US*
- —A.B. Chance Co., *Lineman's Slang Dictionary*, p. 14, 1980

potato-masher *noun*
a German fragmentation hand grenade *US*
Korean war usage.
- —Frank Hailey, *Soldier Talk*, p. 47, 1982
- We policed up a case of Chinese potato-masher grenades. They were probably World War I German Army vintage and about as effective as cherry bombs, but they made a lot of noise and at least they were something.—David H. Hackworth, *About Face*, p. 73, 1989

potato patch *noun*
a group of neurologically depressed patients *US*
- —*Maledicta*, p. 6, Summer/Winter 1978: 'Common patient-directed pejoratives used by medical personnel'

potato peeler *noun*
a woman *AUSTRALIA, 1971*
Rhyming slang for **SHEILA**.
- I'm that full that if a nice little potato peeler walked past flashing a lovely pair of funbags I ascertain there'd be a sad case of brewer's droop.—*The Adventures of Barry McKenzie*, 1972

potatoes in the mould *adjective*
▷ **see: TATERS IN THE MOULD**

potato soup *noun*
vodka *US*
- —*Current Slang*, p. 17, Summer 1970

potato wagon *noun*
a police van *US, 1970*
- —Claudio R. Salvucci, *The Philadelphia Dialect Dictionary*, p. 53, 1996

pot belly *noun*
in trucking, a trailer with a dropped frame middle used for hauling cattle or hogs *US*
- —Montie Tak, *Truck Talk*, p. 121, 1971

potch *verb*
to spank or smack someone *US*
- And why my mother weeps is because my father refuses to potch my behind, which she promised would be potched.—Philip Roth, *Portnoy's Complaint*, p. 95, 1969

potchkeh *verb*
to dawdle; to spend time inefficiently *US*
Yiddish from German. Also variants 'potchee' and 'potchky'.
- Aly Kahn, supposed to be potchkying around in Paris broken-hearted on account of the Princess Margherita walking out on him, was really in this country[.]—Bernard Wolfe, *The Late Risers*, p. 35, 1954
- We got on the first tee and I watched her get over on the ball and potchee around.—Buddy Hackett, *The Truth About Golf and Other Lies*, p. 120, 1968

pot head *noun*
a user of marijuana *US, 1959*
- Impossible, man, they move like potheads.—Richard Farina, *Been Down So Long*, p. 85, 1966
- The months I spent as a depraved pot-head in Tangier were the healthiest in my life.—Richard Neville, *Play Power*, p. 216, 1970
- I leave you for a few years and you turn into a pothead.—Darryl Ponicsan, *The Last Detail*, p. 98, 1970
- Others came also – 42nd Street hustlers – poets – simple dreamers, thieves, prostitutes, (both male and female) and pimps and wise guys and junkies and pot heads, and just people[.]—Herbert Huncke, *The Evening Sun Turned Crimson*, p. 42, 1980
- So I'm blazing with my friends, man. So I'm a fucking pot head man. What's it to you, huh?—*Dazed and Confused*, 1993
- —Angela Devlin, *Prison Patter*, p. 89, 1996
- Prince Harry's a pothead by all accounts.—Ben Elton, *High Society*, p. 75, 2002

pot hook *noun*
in a deck of playing cards, a nine *US*
- —Albert H. Morehead, *The Complete Guide to Winning Poker*, p. 270, 1967

pot hound *noun*
a despised, inferior person *TRINIDAD AND TOBAGO, 1956*
- —Lise Winer, *Dictionary of the English/Creole of Trinidad & Tobago*, 2003

pot house *noun*
a mad or psychotic person *UK*
- I had blokes around me in those days, nice boys, good to their mothers, desperate to please, but total fuckin pothouses. —J.J. Connolly, *Layer Cake*, p. 56, 2000

Pot. Kettle. Black.
used as Internet shorthand to criticise someone for engaging in precisely the same conduct or reasoning that they are attacking in another *US*
- —Christian Crumlish, *The Internet Dictionary*, p. 156, 1995

potless *adjective*
without money *UK*
- And you, my son, are potless.—Anthony Masters, *Minder*, p. 8, 1984
- Uncle Fred [...] slipped a few quid into my hand as he was going. Smashing bloke, he wouldn't see me potless and it kept me going while I was looking round for some way to earn a few shillings.—Lenny McLean, *The Guv'nor*, p. 48, 1998
- Needless to say the duchess and her family are fuckin potless. —J.J. Connolly, *Layer Cake*, p. 54, 2000

pot-licker *noun*
an older dog *NEW ZEALAND*
- A dog of similar years but just a 'bit of an old pooch' would be more likely referred to as a pot-licker.—Robert Loughnan, *Glossary*, p. 2, 1981

pot likker; pot liquor *noun*
1 tea brewed with marijuana leaves *US*
The intentional spelling error gives a rustic, moonshining feel to the term.
- It is ubiquitous and easily grown, can be smoked in "joints" (cigarettes), baked into cookies, or brewed in tea ("pot likker"]. —*Time*, p. 21, 7 July 1967
- —William D. Alsever, *Glossary for the Establishment and Other Uptight People*, p. 20, December 1970
- —Ernest Abel, *A Marijuana Dictionary*, p. 81, 1982
- —Mike Haskins, *Drugs*, p. 288, 2003

2 strong, homemade whisky *US*
- Then I slurped it up like a hound laps pot likker, rolling the panther juice around on my tongue, smacking my lips over it.—Guy Owen, *The Flim-Flam Man and the Apprentice Grifter*, p. 40, 1972

pot lot *noun*
a used car business specialising in old, inexpensive cars *US*
- —*American Speech*, p. 312, Autumn-Winter 1975: 'The jargon of car salesmen'

pot of glue *noun*
1 a Jew *UK*
Rhyming slang. Also shortened form 'potter'.
- —Ray Puxley, *Cockney Rabbit*, 1992

2 a clue *UK: SCOTLAND*
Glasgow rhyming slang. Shortened forms include 'pot' and 'potter'.
- He hasny got a pot, the stumer that he is.—Michael Munro, *The Patter, Another Blast*, 1988

pot of honey; honey *noun*
money *UK*
Rhyming slang.
- —Julian Franklyn, *A Dictionary of Rhyming Slang*, 1961

pot pig *noun*
a marijuana user who takes more than a fair share *UK*
- Didn't leave much on that lanto, aye? Fuckin potpig yew.—Niall Griffiths, *Sheepshagger*, p. 131, 2001

pots *noun*
a large amount of money *UK, 1871*
- [T]hey have inherited pots of money[.]—*The Guardian*, 12th March 2000

POTS *noun*
*p*lain *o*ld *t*elephone *s*ervice *US*
- —Andy Ihnatko, *Cyberspeak*, p. 155, 1997

pots and dishes *noun*
wishes *UK*
Rhyming slang.
- I greet you all, with my warmest pots and dishes.—Ronnie Barker, *Fletcher's Book of Rhyming Slang*, p. 39, 1979

pot shot *noun*
in poker, an early and aggressive bet designed to drive other players from the field of play *US*
Borrowed from hunting and punning on 'pot' as the collective bets.
- —*American Speech*, p. 100, May 1951

potsy *noun*

a firefighter's or police officer's badge *US*

- —*American Speech*, p. 273, December 1954: 'Fire terms: additional words and definition'
- — *New York Times Magazine*, p. 88, 16th March 1958

potted *adjective*

1 tipsy, drunk *US, 1924*

- We had one guest at the hotel where I worked during the early forties, who got well potted every Saturday night he stayed with us[.] —Dev Collans with Stewart Sterling, *I was a House Detective*, p. 67, 1954
- —Collin Baker et al., *College Undergraduate Slang Study Conducted at Brown University*, p. 175, 1968
- He was potted, plastered, stinko —J. Dowell, *Look-Off Bear*, 1974

2 in a state of marijuana intoxication *US, 1955*

- —Ernest L. Abel, *A Marijuana Dictionary*, p. 82, 1982

potten bush *noun*

hashish *US, 1977*

- —Richard A. Spears, *The Slang and Jargon of Drugs and Drink*, p. 403, 1986
- —Mike Haskins, *Drugs*, p. 288, 2003

pottit heid *adjective*

dead *UK: SCOTLAND*

Glasgow rhyming slang, 'deid' in the local accent, formed from local dialect for 'potted meat'.

- Ah think yer goldfish is pottit heid. —Michael Munro, *The Complete Patter*, 1996
- — *The Guardian*, 29th April 2002

pottsville *noun*

a notional location or state of consciousness imagined by marijuana smokers *US, 2001*

Compared to Utopia, Nirvana and Xanadu.

- —Simon Worman, *Joint Smoking Rules*, 2001

potty *noun*

▸ **go potty**

to use a toilet *US, 1942*

Children's toilet vocabulary.

- I feel like I am five years old. Mama, may I go to the potty? Number one? Number two? —Beatrice Sparks (writing as 'Anonymous'), *Jay's Journal*, p. 137, 1979
- Teddy got up during the night to go the bathroom. "Go potty," his mom called it; woman her age. —Elmore Leonard, *Glitz*, p. 341, 1985
- Everyone go potty – we don't want to have to stop! — *Boys on the Side*, 1995

potty *adjective*

crazy; silly; eccentric *UK, 1920*

From 'pot' (a tankard), hence to be inebriated and to have the characteristics of drunken logic.

- It is a strange feeling being locked up on your jack for a few days, some people go potty —Frank Norman, *Bang To Rights*, p. 25, 1958
- Really, boilers [unattractive old women] are simply potty. —Derek Raymond (Robin Cook), *The Crust on its Uppers*, p. 31, 1962
- "You're potty," said Barney furiously. —John Burke and Stuart Douglass, *The Boys*, p. 96, 1962
- NORM: Don't move, any of you. They've gone potty out there. The whole place is surging with girls. JOHN: Please, can I have one to surge with? — *A Hard Day's Night*, 1964
- He was sport-potty. — *The Sweeney*, p. 22, 1976

potty about

in love, infatuated or obsessed (to some degree) with something or someone *UK, 1923*

- He's potty about you my lovely!!! —Barry Humphries, *Bazza Pulls It Off!*, 1971
- He's fucking potty about films, by the way. —Kevin Sampson, *Outlaws*, p. 227, 2001

potty mouth *noun*

a person prone to use profanity; profanity *US, 1968*

- — *Current Slang*, p. 8, Spring 1969
- —Judi Sanders, *Kickin' like Chicken with the Couch Commander*, p. 18, 1992
- It's come to my attention that you boys have a potty-mouth problem. — *South Park*, 1999
- The People v. Potty Mouth — *New York Times*, 7th April 2002
- After sixteen years of uninterrupted potty mouth from you people, I get slammed? — *The Sopranos (Episode 58)*, 2004

potty talk *noun*

speech that is considered obscenely offensive *US*

From childish 'potty' (a chamber pot or toilet); an almost euphemistic variation of **TOILET TALK**.

- [James O'Connor's] book, which offers alternatives to public potty talk, also offers the kind of advice that could have altered the Michigan tale of the tainted tongue[.] — *The New York Times*, 7th April 2002

pot-walloper *noun*

a person employed to wash dishes *US*

- —John Gould, *Maine Lingo*, p. 217, 1975

pot-wrestler *noun*

a restaurant cook or dishwasher *US, 1860*

- He thought he was somebody when he was nothing but a pot wrestler in a downtown restaurant and hardly able to speak English. —Hal Ellson, *The Golden Spike*, p. 83, 1952

pouf; pouff *noun*

▷ see: **POOF**

poultice *noun*

a large sum of money, especially a large wager *AUSTRALIA, 1904*

- It's only two days to pay day and I've got a poultice in that pay-book of mine. —Eric Lambert, *The Twenty Thousand Thieves*, p. 146, 1951
- 'Reckon 'e pulled 'im?' 'That's wot I reckon. But 'ow yer gunna prove ut?' 'Yer can't prove ut.' 'Somebody slung in a poultice, I bet.' —Nino Culotta (John O'Grady), *They're A Weird Mob*, p. 73, 1957
- I want to know if they're going to accept with him, if he's fit, jumping out of his skin, cleaning up his feed, if he's got the heavy irons on and a big boy up when he's trialled, if the owner's going to be on the course on the day, if the connections are putting a poultice on[.] —Wilda Moxham, *The Apprentice*, p. 30, 1969
- —Frank Hardy, *The Outcasts of Foolgarah*, p. 101, 1971
- —Jim Ramsay, *Cop It Sweet!*, p. 73, 1977

pound *noun*

1 a five-dollar note *US, 1935*

- So I got Manny, I gave him a pound, and I said, listen, Manny, you want to get a job? —Jeremy Larner and Ralph Tefferteller, *The Addict in the Street*, p. 240, 1964
- "Man this is my band and I'ma tired of you just allowing me five dollars a night, give me a twenty" I said, "Look man, here's a pound and that's it". —Babs Gonzales, *I Paid My Dues*, p. 78, 1967
- After finding the fat BR, I removed a few pound notes from the center of it and placed it back in the same way it was when I found it. —A.S. Jackson, *Gentleman Pimp*, p. 12, 1973
- My shirts were from Brooks'; my socks cost a pound / I wore solid gold cufflinks – I knew I was down. —Dennis Wepman et al., *The Life*, p. 36, 1976
- Throw Walter a pound for forgetting the dupes. —Vincent Patrick, *The Pope of Greenwich Village*, p. 15, 1979

2 a five-year jail sentence *US*

- But after you do almost a pound here, like me, you get so you can stand it. —Clarence Cooper Jr, *The Farm*, p. 128, 1967
- It's been a good pound since that went down and that's all you do for seven and a half, ain't it? —A.S. Jackson, *Gentleman Pimp*, p. 130, 1973
- Even did time for a homicide. Did a pound. —Edwin Torres, *Q & A*, p. 88, 1977
- I did a pound at Coxsackie. —Vincent Patrick, *The Pope of Greenwich Village*, p. 28, 1979
- —Angela Devlin, *Prison Patter*, p. 89, 1996

3 an 's' unit (five decibels) in measuring the level of a citizens' band radio signal *US*

- —Lanie Dills, *The Official CB Slanguage Language Dictionary*, p. 63, 1976

4 an amount of heroin worth five dollars *US*

- —Ralph de Sola, *Crime Dictionary*, p. 118, 1982

5 a prison cell used for solitary confinement *AUSTRALIA, 1950*

- —Jim Ramsay, *Cop It Sweet!*, p. 73, 1977
- Got three days in the pound. —Kathy Lette, *Girls' Night Out*, p. 167, 1987
- His alleged assailant was put in the 'pound', a jail within the jail. — *Dominion*, p. 3, 30th June 1993
- —Harry Orsman, *A Dictionary of Modern New Zealand Slang*, p. 101, 1999

6 a jail or prison *US*

- Federal pound. Forty-four months. —Edwin Torres, *Q & A*, p. 66, 1977

7 in poker, a heavy bet *US*

- —George Percy, *The Language of Poker*, p. 70, 1988

▸ **have a pound on yourself**

to be conceited; to think very well of yourself *UK*

From betting terminology.

- She's got a pound on herself all right. Obviously thought he, Mellors, wasn't good enough for her. —Derek Bickerton, *Payroll*, p. 25, 1959

pound *verb*

to drink (alcohol) *US*

- We get there, we pound booze till Carlos shows up[.] —Quentin Tarantino, *From Dusk Till Dawn*, p. 79, 1995

- —Connie Eble (Editor), *UNC-CH Campus Slang*, p. 8, April 1995
- One night, while pounding beers and wearing my favorite Tamany Hall sweatshirt, an underclassman we called Grain asked me if he could buy a sweatshirt like the one I had on. —Elissa Stein and Kevin Leslie, *Chunks*, p. 48, 1997

▸ **pound cotton**
to strain the residue of a narcotic from a bit of cotton used to strain the drug for a previous injection *US*
- "I'll do you good if you lemme pound cotton." By which he meant add more water in her cooker and strain the residue from her cotton, something like percolating coffee grounds a second time. —Seth Morgan, *Homeboy*, p. 64, 1990

▸ **pound ground**
to march *US*
- But at least it isn't the straight-leg infantry. At least I won't have to pound ground. —Larry Heinemann, *Close Quarters*, p. 33, 1977

▸ **pound her pee-hole**
from the male perspective, to have energetic sex *US*
- —Michael Dalton Johnson, *Talking Trash with Redd Foxx*, p. 79, 1994

▸ **pound sand**
to engage in futile behaviour *US*
Usually used as a command, where the term takes on a meaning not unlike 'go fuck yourself'.
- And what happens if I, for once, just tell you people to go pound sand? —Gerald Petievich, *One-Shot Deal*, p. 195, 1981

▸ **pound the bishop**
(used of a male) to masturbate *US*
- I stop pounding the bishop now, lest I cross the finish-line right along with him. —*Adam Film World*, p. 60, 1977

▸ **to get pounded**
while surfing, to be knocked from your surfboard and thrashed by the wave *US*
- —Michael V. Anderson, *The Bad, Rad, Not to Forget Way Cool Beach and Surf Discriptionary*, p. 15, 1988

poundage *noun*
weight that should be lost *US*
- You'll need more exercise than sucking dick to work that poundage off. —Bruce Rodgers, *The Queens' Vernacular*, p. 153, 1972

pound and crown *noun*
a lot of money *TRINIDAD AND TOBAGO, 1993*
- —Lise Winer, *Dictionary of the English/Creole of Trinidad & Tobago*, 2003

pounder *noun*
1 a police officer assigned to foot patrol *US*
- —Lou Shelly, *Hepcats Jive Talk Dictionary*, p. 16, 1945
- We just began to eat when in breezed these two pounders on the bloodhound tip, hunting down the owner of the cab parked out front. —Mezz Mezzrow, *Really the Blues*, p. 32, 1946
- —Jack Lait and Lee Mortimer, *New York Confidential*, p. 236, 1948: 'A Glossary of Harlemisms'
- —Kenn "Naz" Young, *Naz's Under-ground Dictionary*, p. 50, 1973

2 a powerful, hard-breaking wave *US*
- —John Severson, *Modern Surfing Around the World*, p. 178, 1964
- —Douglas Simonson, *Pidgin to da Max Hana Hou*, 1982

3 a 16 ounce can of beer *US*
- Any true-blue region transplant should have a few pounders in the fridge at all times. —Amy and Denise McFadden, *CoalSpeak*, p. 11, 1997

pound note *noun*
a coat *UK*
Rhyming slang, now fallen into disuse, a victim of the pound coin introduced in 1983.
- —Ray Puxley, *Cockney Rabbit*, 1992

pound of butter *noun*
a crazy person; a lunatic; an eccentric *UK*
Rhyming slang for **NUTTER**.
- —Ray Puxley, *Fresh Rabbit*, 1998

pound off *verb*
(used of a male) to masturbate *US*
- But I've been pounding off over this for a week! —Philip Roth, *Portnoy's Complaint*, p. 199, 1969

pounds *noun*
money *US*
- —Hermese E. Roberts, *The Third Ear*, 1971

pounds and pence *noun*
sense *UK*
Rhyming slang, an updated form of **SHILLINGS AND PENCE**.
- If he had a bit more pounds and pence he'd just be daft. —Ray Puxley, *Cockney Rabbit*, 1992

pound to a penny
a certainty, a sure thing *UK*
A ludicrously confident wager.
- It's a certain thing. Pound to penny she'll be on her knees sucking Moby's knob. —Kevin Sampson, *Outlaws*, p. 131, 2001

pour *verb*
to move or place a drunk *UK*
- [I]t was a slightly jaded company of artists who were "poured over the side" into launches. —Francis Worsley, *ITMA*, 1948
- We poured old Nobby onto his plane about three in the morning. —Beale, 1984

▸ **pour on the coal**
to throttle up an engine *US*
A borrowing from steam-powered train engines.
- —Levette J. Davidson, *American Speech*, p. 229, October 1956: 'More United States Air Force slang'
- —Monte Tak, *Truck Talk*, p. 122, 1971
- —John Edwards, *Auto Dictionary*, p. 129, 1993

▸ **pour on the coals**
in trucking, to drive fast *US*
- —Montie Tak, *Truck Talk*, p. 122, 1971

▸ **pour the pork**
(from the male point of view) to have sex *US*
- [S]he told him she just laid a guy across the hall and had seen a gun under his pillow while he was pouring her the pork. —Joseph Wambaugh, *The Blue Knight*, p. 167, 1973

poured into *adjective*
said of someone wearing very tight clothing, usually of a woman, and generally complimentary *UK*
- She was poured into a sky-blue uniform. —Patrick Campbell, *Come Here Till I Tell You*, 1960

pour (it) out *verb*
to urinate *US*
- —Charles Shafer, *Folk Speech in Texas Prisons*, p. 211, 1990

pouve *noun*
▷ see: **POOVE**

poverty pimp *noun*
a person who makes their living from the poverty of others, especially by working for government funded programmes for the poor *US*
The Coalition on Homelessness in San Francisco presents a Poverty Pimp Award each year.
- I could see him at the "Board" meeting, Ron Reinaldo, a voice form the community, who will pull no punches. Jive-ass poverty pimp. —Edwin Torres, *After Hours*, p. 177, 1979
- Poverty pimp. It's rough language, but it's also the perfect description of what happens when people stuff their own pockets with money that's supposed to go to the poor. —*Milwaukee Journal Sentinel*, 1st August 2000

poverty poker *noun*
a style of poker in which a player who loses their bankroll may play for free until they win a hand *US*
- —George Percy, *The Language of Poker*, p. 70, 1988

povo *adjective*
cheaply produced for a poor marketplace *UK*
Derives from 'poverty'.
- - Erm, what's that? -Bottle of whiskey, like you said. -Yeh, exactly, whiskey, not povo headfuck cheap piss like that. —Niall Griffiths, *Sheepshagger*, p. 184, 2001

pow!
used as a register of instant excitement *UK, 1881*
- —John Ayto, *The Oxford Dictionary of Slang*, p. 245, 1998

powder *noun*
a powdered narcotic, usually heroin or cocaine *US*
- There's people down here, Blacks pushing the powder and hustling the chicks, and using their own people to pad their damned pockets. —Donald Goines, *Inner City Hoodlum*, p. 23, 1975

- Powder! What do they mean "powder"? Gunpowder, curry powder, cocaine? I mean, what's on their minds? — Ben Elton and Rik Mayall, *The Young Ones*, 8th May 1984
- "Can you get petty cash?" [...] "Some. Why?" "Sort us some powder?" — Kevin Sampson, *Powder*, p. 59, 1999
- It's-a powders yew want, like. Step on em a few times, yewer laughin. — Niall Griffiths, *Sheepshagger*, p. 73, 2001
- "But if it's powder I want every grain of it." Powder, of course, meaning cocaine and heroin; Class A. — Duncan MacLaughlin, *The Filth*, p. 188, 2002
- "He's trying to get 2 ounces of powder," a caller named Truck told Bellamy[.] — *Orlando Sentinel*, p. B2, 17th August 2002

▸ take a powder

1 to leave *US, 1934*

- First Mrs. Hitchcock packed up and took a powder, and there was hell to pay. — Mezz Mezzrow, *Really the Blues*, p. 66, 1946
- Aren't you glad now we didn't take a powder? — Irving Shulman, *The Amboy Dukes*, p. 88, 1947
- Well, when the cuckoo quacks a dozen she takes a fast powder but loses a slipper. — Haenigsen, *Jive's Like That*, 1947
- He had been five minutes away from being killed and he was taking a quick-acting powder. — Mickey Spillane, *Kiss Me Deadly*, p. 168, 1952
- The vine[rumour-mill] said you're Lancaster the guy who took a powder thirteen years ago. — Iceberg Slim (Robert Beck), *Pimp*, p. 299, 1969

2 to inhale or ingest powdered drugs *US*

- — Ralph de Sola, *Crime Dictionary*, p. 148, 1982

powder *verb*

▸ powder your nose

1 to sniff cocaine *US*

- — Tom Hibbert, *Rockspeak!*, p. 122, 1983
- MIA: Well I'll tell you what, I'll go to the bathroom and powder my nose, while you sit here and think of something to say. — *Pulp Fiction*, 1994
- Iyama ready to powder de nose and to boogie. — Nick Barlay, *Curvy Lovebox*, p. 141, 1997

2 to use the lavatory *UK, 1984*

A euphemism.

- [S]he goes to the bathroom to "powder my nose". — *New Statesman*, 4th June 2001

▸ powder your schnoz

to inhale cocaine *UK*

Variation of POWDER YOUR NOSE with SHNOZ; SCHNOZ (the nose).

- [D]rink too much and powder her schnoz too regularly[.] — James Hawes, *Dead Long Enough*, p. 35, 2000

powderbox *noun*

the vagina *US*

- There's "powderbox," "derriere," a "poochi," a "poopi," a "peepe[".] — Eve Ensler, *The Vagina Monologues*, p. 6, 1998

powder diamonds; powdered diamonds *noun*

cocaine *US, 1977*

From the crystalline appearance, and the cost.

- — Richard A. Spears, *The Slang and Jargon of Drugs and Drink*, p. 404, 1986
- — Mike Haskins, *Drugs*, p. 281, 2003

powdered *adjective*

under the influence of cocaine *US*

- — Sacramento Municipal Utility District, *Glossary of Drugs and Drug Language*, 1986

powdered chalk *noun*

a walk *UK*

Rhyming slang.

- — Ray Puxley, *Cockney Rabbit*, 1992

powder monkey *noun*

1 an explosives expert on a work crew *US*

- — Vincent J. Monteleone, *Criminal Slang*, p. 181, 1949
- — Ramon Adams, *The Language of the Railroader*, p. 118, 1977

2 a cocaine user *UK*

Plays on POWDER (cocaine).

- What is it about being on telly that turns seemingly straightforward people [...] into rampaging powder monkeys. — Rob Fitzpatrick, *Ministry*, p. 41, January 2002

powder puff *noun*

1 an effeminate homosexual male *US*

- Now would chime in the litany of abuse: naughty sissy, baby-boy, not-really-a-boy-but-a-pussy, little faggot, secret cocksucking toy, queer-bait, boy-hole, powder-puff. — Terence Sellers, *Dungeon Evidence*, p. 58, 1997

2 in trucking, a small convex mirror mounted on the outside of the cab *US*

- — Montie Tak, *Truck Talk*, p. 122, 1971

powder puff *adjective*

in various sports, describing an event limited to female competitors *US*

- This is a Le Mans start for the powder puff class. — Ed Radlauer, *Motorcylopedia*, p. 39, 1973
- — Phantom Surfers, *The Exciting Sounds of Model Road Racing (Album cover)*, 1997

powder train *noun*

a US Navy SEALS diver with expertise in underwater explosives *US*

- — Linda Reinberg, *In the Field*, p. 170, 1991

power *noun*

a charge of explosives *US*

- — Vincent J. Monteleone, *Criminal Slang*, p. 182, 1949

power *adjective*

in a concentrated, intense manner *US*

Almost always used mockingly.

- powerstudy: to study hard. — Pamela Munro, *U.C.L.A. Slang*, p. 68, 1989
- "I overslept and had to power walk to class." "I need a power nap before I study." — Connie Eble (Editor), *UNC-CH Campus Slang*, p. 5, Fall 1991
- While I was gassing up the mower, Lacey came out on the patio in a weensy bikini for some al fresco power tanning. — C.D. Payne, *Youth in Revolt*, p. 5, 1993
- But you can go out dancing in this too. It's a total power suit. — *Jackie Brown*, 1997

powerdyke *noun*

a militant feminist, whether she is a lesbian or not *US*

- — Connie Eble (Editor), *UNC-CH Campus Slang*, p. 7, Spring 2003

power hit *noun*

the act of inhaling marijuana smoke and then exhaling it into another's mouth as they inhale *US*

- — Ernest L. Abel, *A Marijuana Dictionary*, p. 82, 1982

power lunch *noun*

a lunch meeting where business or deals, not eating, is the central focus *US*

- — Rachel S. Epstein and Nina Liebman, *Biz Speak*, p. 174, 1986

power pill *noun*

a tablet of any variety of MDMA, the recreational drug best known as ecstasy *UK*

- — Angela Devlin, *Prison Patter*, p. 88, 1996

powerplant *noun*

a variety of marijuana *SOUTH AFRICA*

- — Nick Jones, *Spliffs*, p. 72, 2003

power rangers *noun*

a variety of LSD *UK*

Named after the fantasy television programme.

- — Angela Devlin, *Prison Patter*, p. 90, 1996

power table *noun*

a prominent table at a restaurant, seating at which is a recognition of fame or power *US*

Used in the entertainment industry.

- So if you want to become a power luncher, it's imperative you learn which are the prime areas and power tables of the restaurants you frequent – and how to obtain them. — *Nation's Restaurant News*, 13th February 1984

power trip *noun*

any activity that is motivated by a desire for power *US*

- All these people away on power trips and ego trips. I'm almost to the point of being sick of it, sick of being a Digger. — Nicholas Von Hoffman, *We Are The People Our Parents Warned Us Against*, p. 97, 1967

pow-pow *noun*

powder snow *US*

Snowboarders' usage.

- — Jim Humes and Sean Wagstaff, *Boarderlands*, p. 223, 1995

pow-wow *noun*

a meeting *US, 1812*

Originally an Algonquin word for an 'Indian priest' or 'ceremony'.

- This pow-wow right here is news inside already. — Edwin Torres, *Carlito's Way*, p. 122, 1975

- There was a big pow-wow last night to decide what to do. —Jay McInerney, *Bright Lights, Big City*, p. 100, 1984
- A small group of execs with predominantly Irish and Italian surnames had gathered [...] to say a few prayers that everything was going to work out. Observing this Catholic pow-wow, he hit upon an idea that was less than inspired[.] —Christopher Brookmyre, *Not the End of the World*, p. 208, 1998

pox *noun*

1 syphilis; hence any sexually transmitted infection *UK*
Altered spelling of 'pocks', originally applied to the pustules of any eruptive disease.

2 marijuana; hashish *UK*

- —Angela Devlin, *Prison Patter*, p. 90, 1996
- He laid the block on the bed, then sat next to it, looking at it closely. Hashish. Cannabis. Ash. Rocky. Pox. Call it what you like[.] —Courttia Newland, *Society Within*, p. 27, 1999

3 opium; heroin *US, 1942*

- —Richard A. Spears, *The Slang and Jargon of Drugs and Drink*, p. 404, 1986
- —Mike Haskins, *Drugs*, p. 284, 2003

pox *verb*

to spoil something *UK, 1802*
From an earlier sense, 'to infect with syphilis'.

- [O]n an afternoon like this, when the sky had been poxed with intermittent thunderstorms, the view was good enough. —Stephen King, *The Stand*, p. 160, 1990

poxbottle *noun*

a despicable person *IRELAND*

- -I seen [sic] yeh[you], Bimbo insisted. -Yeh poxbottle fuck yeh; yeh did not! —Roddy Doyle, *The Van*, p. 106, 1991

pox docs *noun*

doctors at a clinic for sexually transmitted diseases *UK*
A happy rhyme enjoyed in the medical profession.

- —Adam T. Fox, St Mary's Hospital, London, 10th October 2002

pox doctor's clerk *noun*

used as the epitome of someone dressed in a flashy manner *AUSTRALIA, 1950*

- —Nino Culotta (John O'Grady), *They're A Weird Mob*, p. 106, 1957
- —John O'Grady, *It's Your Shout, Mate!*, p. 15, 1972
- You say you are just an ordinary bloke who buys all his vegies from us at the Victoria Market, and here you are all dressed up like a pox doctor's clerk. —Rex Hunt, *Tall Tales – and True*, p. 94, 1994

poxy *adjective*

loathsome, objectionable, disgusting *UK, 1922*
From **POX** (syphilis), equating the target of the adjective with venereal diseases.

- —Angela Devlin, *Prison Patter*, p. 90, 1996
- [G]oing home to my poxy little cardboard hotel room[.] —James Hawes, *Dead Long Enough*, p. 218, 2000
- Harry Tyler would normally have been ranting aloud about town planning "minges" by now, not to mention poxy women drivers[.] —Garry Bushell, *The Face*, p. 3, 2001

pozzie *noun*

a location *NEW ZEALAND*

- —Louis S. Leland, *A Personal Kiwi-Yankee Dictionary*, p. 80, 1984

pozzle *noun*

the vagina *US*

- I mean, whoever heard of a man gettin' too much pozzle? —*One Flew Over the Cuckoo's Nest*, 1962

pozzy *noun*

▷ **see: POSSIE**

PP *noun*

1 a person whose regular appearance in a hospital casualty department has earned him the label *p*rofessional *p*atient *US*

- —*Maledicta*, p. 6, Summer/Winter 1978: 'Common patient-directed pejoratives used by medical personnel'

2 influence within a prison *US*
A shortened form of '*p*enitentiary *p*ull'.

- —*New York (letter to editor)*, p. 10, 11th February 1985

PP nine *verb*

to attack someone with a weapon improvised with a PP9 battery, often by concealing the battery in a sock *UK*

- —Angela Devlin, *Prison Patter*, p. 90, 1996

PPP *noun*

a severely debilitated hospital patient, with *p*iss-*p*oor *p*rotoplasm *US*

- —*Maledicta*, p. 6, Summer/Winter 1978: 'Common patient-directed pejoratives used by medical personnel'

PQ *noun*

a half-pint of rum *TRINIDAD AND TOBAGO, 1987*
An abbreviation of '*p*etit *q*uart'.

- —Lise Winer, *Dictionary of the English/Creole of Trinidad & Tobago*, 2003

PR *noun*

1 Puerto Rico *US, 1909*

- I got bored of New York and P.R. Figure I'd check the scene over here. —Edwin Torres, *Carlito's Way*, p. 75, 1975

2 a Puerto Rican *US*
Also attributed as an adjective.

- You're gonna make nice with them PR's from now on. —*West Side Story*, 1957
- P.R.'s dig manhood, don't play sissy. —Abbie Hoffman, *Revolution for the Hell of It*, p. 30, 1968
- The tigers would go to the Cabo and the BC, the down P.R.'s would go to the Palladium. —Edwin Torres, *Carlito's Way*, p. 24, 1975
- Gus is in the hospital.. Some P.R.'s got 'em. —*Saturday Night Fever*, 1977

3 *p*anama *r*ed, a variety of marijuana cultivated in Panama *US, 1969*

- —Richard A. Spears, *The Slang and Jargon of Drugs and Drink*, p. 404, 1986
- —Mike Haskins, *Drugs*, p. 288, 2003

practice bleeding *noun*

engaging in night-training flights off an aircraft carrier *US*

- —*United States Naval Institute Proceedings*, p. 108, October 1986

prad *noun*

a horse *UK*
From Dutch *paard* (a horse). Not recorded separately before 1799 but implied in 'prad-lay' (to steal property from horses), now obsolete, noted in Grose's *Dictionary of the Vulgar Tongue*, 2nd edition, 1788.

- The boss and that homie have been having a proper barney over the prad [a horse]. —Butch Reynolds, *Broken Hearted Clown*, p. 28, 1953

prairie chicken *noun*

a grouse, or a newcomer to the prairies *CANADA*

- Clod-hopper, we call him, and stubble-jumper. And when he drives his fat new Buick to the Coast to winter among us we brand him "prairie chicken." —*Vancouver Sun*, p. 1/1, 4th July 1961
- Saskatchewan is the only province to adopt an official emblem in addition to a flower: in 1945 the prairie chicken, or sharp-tailed grouse, by enactment was made an emblem of Saskatchewan. —*Canadian Weekly*, p. 18/4, 30th March 1963

prairie nigger *noun*

a native American Indian *US*

- Among the townspeople, the epithet used to describe an Indian is "prairie nigger"[.] —*New York Times*, p. C7, 29th September 1989
- Mr. Campbell, a Northern Cheyenne Indian, told the Senate that "there are some places in this country yet where American Indians are called 'prairie niggers'." —*New York Times*, p. B6, 23rd July 1993
- As Liphsa turns to leave the store he hears the clerk mutter "prairie nigger" – a phrase so wounding Lipsha can hardly believe he hears it right. —Allan Chavkin (Editor), *The Chippewa Landscape of Louise Erdrich*, p. 165, 1999
- "I've been called 'blanket ass' and 'prairie nigger' more times than I can count," he said. —*Philadelphia Inquirer*, 7th November 1999
- "There are still places in this country," he added, "where American Indians are called prairie niggers, which is about the most vulgar term I can think of for both groups of people". —*Washington Post*, p. A8, 12th December 2003

prairie oyster *noun*

an anti-hangover tonic: an unbroken raw egg in a glass of dry red wine, or an unbroken raw egg in Worcestershire Sauce and sherry *US, 1883*

- —Oscar A Mendelsohn, *The Dictionary of Drinks and Drinking*, 1966

praise *verb*

▸ **praise the porcelain god**

to vomit *US*

- —Connie Eble (Editor), *UNC-CH Campus Slang*, p. 7, Fall 1986

pram *noun*

▸ **get out of your pram**

to become very angry or over-excited *UK*

- —Richard Clapperton, *Victims Unknown*, 1970

▸ **throw your toys out of the pram**
to become angry; to lose your temper; to become over-excited *UK*
- Allesandro didn't want to hear it, however. He threw a few toys out of the pram and started yelling about respect, the usual shit. —Christopher Brookmyre, *The Sacred Art of Stealing*, p. 328, 2002
- It must have been tempting to throw his toys out of the pram when Brown took responsibility for banking supervision from Threadneedle Street and gave it to the new Financial Services Authority. — *New Statesman*, 7th July 2003

prang *noun*
a car accident or collision *US, 1959*
- —John Lawlor, *How to Talk Car*, p. 83, 1965
- Had a bit of a prang when I swerved to avoid a dog. —Dave Courtney, *Stop the Ride I want to Get Off*, p. 112, 1999

prang *verb*
1 in aviation, to crash-land an aircraft *UK, 1941*
- —Woodford Agee Heflin, *United States Air Force Dictionary*, p. 398, 1956
- — *Current Slang*, p. 17, Summer 1970
- I was pranging the Huey again. So was Len. "Pranging" was an unofficial term we learned in flight school. It was descriptive of both the sound of the deflection of a helicopter's skids during a very hard landing. —Robert Mason, *Chickenhawk*, p. 182, 1983

2 to crash a car *UK, 1952*

3 to make a short call to a mobile telephone with the sole purpose of registering yourself on the receiving phone's 'caller ID' (thus delivering a private signal but avoiding the cost of a connection) *UK*
Reported by John Williams, September 2003.

prannet; prannie; pranny *noun*
a fool; a general term of contempt *UK*
After an obsolete sense of 'prannie' (female genitals, hence **CUNT**).
- She wasn't half a prannet[.] —Ian Dury, *Billericay Dickie*, 1977
- Anyways, this prannet goes in, trudges all the way up three flights[.] —Will Self, *The Sweet Smell of Psychosis*, p. 22, 1996

prat *noun*
1 used as a general insult with no particular meaning beyond the derogatory tone; a fool *UK, 1968*
Variant 'pratt'. From the earlier use as 'buttocks'.
- "Are you a prat?" "Course I'm fucking not a prat. Are you questioning me? Do you think I'm a prat? Who the fuck's going to say, oh yeah, I'm a prat[.]" — *Ask*, p. 33, 1st May 1982
- "It's as good as saying, he's a pratt," said my father. "That's your view," said Joe. "Not everyone's as stick-in-the-mud as you." "Pratt," said my father. "As thick as a docker's sandwich." —John Milne, *Alive and Kicking*, p. 33, 1998
- This prat owes me money[.] —Dave Courtney, *Raving Lunacy*, p. 171, 2000
- I tell him, so he doesn't walk around looking like a prat. —John King, *Human Punk*, p. 109, 2000
- Oh my God, she must only watch BBC. Oh, God. What a prat. —Tony Wilson, *24 Hour Party People*, p. 215, 2002
- The prat wore a black string tie and had cheroots sticking from his pocket. —Jonathan Gash, *The Ten Word Game*, p. 55, 2003
- The poker player, the dodgy salesman and the prat. — *The Guardian*, 2nd May 2003

2 the buttocks *UK, 1567*
- [W]e will just fall on our prats[.] —Dennis L McKiernan, *The Silver Call*, p. 259, 1986

3 the vagina *UK, 1937*
From the earlier sense as 'buttocks'.

4 in horse racing, interference during a race *AUSTRALIA*
- —Ned Wallish, *The Truth Dictionary of Racing Slang*, p. 64, 1989

prat *verb*
to engage in coy or fawning behaviour *US*
- The "Murphy" player will "prat" him to enhance his desire. He will say, "Man, don't be offended, but Aunt Kate, that runs the house don't have nothing but high-class white men coming to her place." —Iceberg Slim (Robert Beck), *Pimp*, p. 38, 1969

prat about *verb*
to mess about; to play the fool *UK, 1961*
From **PRAT** (a fool).
- James Beattie was seen pratting about on his £160,000 speedboat. — *The Guardian*, 19th May 2003

pratfall *noun*
in the theatre, a comedy fall, especially one that lands buttocks-first *UK, 1939*
Often applied figuratively:
- Despite his pratfalls in government, [Ken] Clarke will have far more credibility when he mocks new Labour for its performance on the NHS and schools[.] — *New Statesman*, 30th July 2001
- [Jerry] Lewis's staff have replayed all his old films and TV specials [...] and worked out that their employer made 1,795 professional pratfalls. — *New Statesman*, 30th September 2002
- [Sam] Rockwell's performance is all lovable goofy swagger, radiating the pride that cometh before the pratfall. — *The Guardian*, 19th September 2003

prat in *verb*
in pickpocket usage, to back into the potential victim, getting him into position for a confederate *US*
- —Don Wilmeth, *The Language of American Popular Entertainment*, p. 207, 1981

prat powder *noun*
powdered amphetamine *UK*
From the power of the powder to make you behave like a **PRAT** (a fool).
- Speed, see. Prat powder. I'm not always a tosser, honest. —Ben Elton, *High Society*, p. 173, 2002

pratt *noun*
a woman objectified sexually *UK*
Extended from the sense as 'vagina'.
- The pratt's marked us! [...] Get after her! —G,F. Newman, *The Guvnor*, 1977

pratt boy *noun*
a weak or effeminate person; an outcast *US*
- He was becoming a pratt boy for her. —George Mandel, *Flee the Angry Strangers*, p. 372, 1952

pratty *adjective*
stupid, foolish *UK*
From **PRAT** (a fool).
- It's his pratty mate. —John Milne, *Alive and Kicking*, p. 36, 1998

prawn *noun*
1 a fool; a worthless individual *AUSTRALIA, 1893*
- —Nino Culotta (John O'Grady), *They're A Weird Mob*, p. 135, 1957
- It's not their fault they've got a prawn around the house instead of a man. —Willie Fennell, *Dexter Gets The Point*, p. 86, 1961
- —W.R. Bennett, *Wingman*, p. 68, 1961
- —Louis S. Leland, *A Personal Kiwi-Yankee Dictionary*, p. 80, 1984

2 an ugly person with an attractive body *UK*
- Prawn [...] Tasty body, shame about the face. — *Popbitch*, 19th February 2004

prawnhead *noun*
a fool; a worthless individual *AUSTRALIA*
- Answer me, prawnhead. —W.R. Bennett, *Wingman*, p. 19, 1961
- Prawnhead, a dentist-cum-oyster farmer, offered me something from his plate. —Kathy Lette, *Girls' Night Out*, p. 179, 1987

prawn-headed *adjective*
stupid *AUSTRALIA, 1962*
- —John O'Grady, *Aussie Etiket*, p. 56, 1971

pray *verb*
▸ **pray to the porcelain god; pray to the enamel god**
to vomit into a toilet *US*
- —Connie Eble (Editor), *UNC-CH Campus Slang*, p. 5, Fall 1980

prayer bones *noun*
the knees *US*
- My prayerbones played knock-knock. Jack, I was bad off. —Mezz Mezzrow, *Really the Blues*, p. 179, 1946

prayer meeting *noun*
1 a private dice game *US*
- The next night the boys was having a little prayer meeting when I came by. I didn't have no mind for dice so I didn't get in on it. —Hal Ellson, *Duke*, p. 113, 1949

2 a propaganda session conducted by Viet Cong with South Vietnamese villagers *US*
- —Gregory Clark, *Words of the Vietnam War*, p. 408, 1990

praying John *noun*
a gambler who believes that he can influence the fall of the dice by uttering the right, magical words *US*
- — *The Annals of the American Academy of Political and Social Sciences*, p. 129, May 1950

pre; pre-game; pre-party *verb*
to drink before going to an event where there will be drinking *US*
- — Don R. McCreary (Editor), *Dawg Speak*, 2001

preach *verb*
▸ **preach to the choir**
to talk to those who are already convinced *US*
- — Department of the Army, *Staff Officer's Guidebook*, p. 64, 1986
- Instead, the rally organizers decided to preach to the choir. — *The Boston Herald*, p. 10, 1st June 1996

preacher *noun*
1 a traffic police officer who is too kind-hearted to issue citations *US*
- — *American Speech*, p. 271, December 1962: 'The language of traffic policeman'

2 a log that is partially submerged in a river *US, 1974*
- — Russell Tabbert, *Dictionary of Alaskan English*, p. 223, 1991

preacher's car *noun*
in the used car business, a car with no accessories at all *US*
- — *Esquire*, p. 119, March 1968

preacher's pasttime *noun*
the shell game *US*
- Here we are, ladies and gentlemen! Carnival croquet, the preacher's pastime. — Robert Edmond Alter, *Carny Kill*, p. 34, 1966

precious *adjective*
egregious, arrant; very, exceedingly; especially as an intensifier of something bad or worthless *UK, 1430*
- Now who in the precious hell is Harold M-for-Mother Powers? — Lawrence Block, *No Score [The Affairs of Chip Harrison Omnibus]*, p. 125, 1970
- What good would this do? Precious little. — *Los Angeles Business Journal*, 19th July 2000

pre-cum *noun*
penile secretions prior to orgasm *UK*
A refinement of COME (orgasm/semen).
- But even if you swallow cum or pre-cum, there's almost no chance you'll catch HIV. — David Bell and Gill Valentine, *Mapping Desire*, 1995
- I keep my motion steady, working him, drinking in his heady pre-cum. — Marcy Sheiner (Editor), *Herotica 4*, p. 159, 1996
- [A] thick seminal liquid that you would probably know better as pre-cum. — Richard Herring, *Talking Cock*, p. 26, 2003

predator *noun*
heroin *UK, 1998*
- — Robert Ashton, *This Is Heroin*, p. 206, 2002
- — Mike Haskins, *Drugs*, p. 284, 2003

preemie *noun*
a premature baby *US*
- She got a new baby, one of them preemeys, jist a little tiny bug of a chil'. — Joseph Wambaugh, *The New Centurions*, p. 242, 1970

preesh!
I appreciate that! *US*
- — Connie Eble (Editor), *UNC-CH Campus Slang*, p. 6, Fall 1987

prefab *noun*
a prefabricated house, specifically a temporary dwelling (usually a bungalow) that served as a stop-gap measure in the years immediately following World War 2 *UK*
Some are still in use nearly 60 years later.
- Home is where the heart is, even when it's a prefab [...] Across Britain 156,622 prefabs went up between 1945 and 1949, although Churchill wanted to build up to half a million[.] — *The Guardian*, 19th January 2004

prefab *adjective*
prefabricated *US, 1937*
- — *American Speech*, October 1946
- The commerical little pig laid out for a few bars and then moved into a prefab joint somewhere out of the high-rent district[.] — Steve Allen, *Bop Fables*, p. 21, 1955

preggers *adjective*
pregnant *UK, 1942*
- The girl on the grass beside me is white-faced and Mona Lisa like and she's preggers. — Anonymous, *Go Ask Alice*, p. 103, 1971

preggo *adjective*
pregnant *AUSTRALIA, 1951*
- [A]nother younger one that's good for the cot while the wife's preggo, and might bring in a bit of extra kitty as well, if he handles it right? — Neville Jackson, *No end to the way*, p. 67, 1965
- — Jim Ramsay, *Cop It Sweet!*, p. 73, 1977
- Not even preggo, neither. — Mike Stott, *Soldiers Talking, Cleanly*, 1978
- I tried to make my voice sound casual. "Hey, by the way, Carol's preg-o." — Rita Ciresi, *Pink Slip*, p. 52, 1999

preggy; preggie *adjective*
pregnant *UK, 1938*
- All right, girls. Had enough of the preggy lady? And shall we be pushing on? — John Clifford Mortimer, *Summer's Lease*, p. 244, 1991
- I got preggie with you, Sweetie Pie. — Ellen Gilchrist, *I, Rhoda Manning, Go Hunting with My Daddy*, p. 246, 2002

pregnant duck *noun*
the B-24 Liberator bomber *US*
A nod to the plane's clumsy appearance.
- — *American Speech*, p. 310, December 1946: 'More Air Force slang'

pregnant rollerskate; pregnant skateboard *noun*
a Volkswagen 'Beetle' car *US*
Citizens' band radio slang.
- — *Complete CB Slang Dictionary*, p. 76, 1976
- — Peter Chippindale, *The British CB Book*, p. 161, 1981

prelim *noun*
a preliminary sporting match *UK, 1923*
- I saw him in a pre-lim at the stadium. — Iceberg Slim (Robert Beck), *Long White Con*, p. 201, 1977

prellies *noun*
phenmetrazine, a chemical stimulant marketed as Preludin™, used in the US as a diet drug *UK*
- [The Beatles] kept going by using uppers supplied by the clubs – particularly "Prellies". — *Uncut*, p. 41, February 2002

premie *noun*
a premature sexual ejaculation; a man who is subject to such a thing *US*
- — Xaviera Hollander, *The Best Part of a Man*, 1975

premium *noun*
a brand name manufactured cigarette *US*
- — William K. Bentley and James M. Corbett, *Prison Slang*, p. 65, 1992

prenup *noun*
an agreement entered into before marriage concerning the division of property in the event of divorce *US*
Shortened from 'prenupital'.
- Fierman believes clients can sidestep the pre-nup by declaring, with trembling lip, that it would "undermine the trust and love on which our relationship is built." — *Money*, p. 180, June 1983
- O.J. should have had a prenup. Everyone needs a prenup. — Chris Rock, *Rock This!*, p. 199 – 200, 1997

pre-op *noun*
a transexual who has yet to undergo all surgery necessary to complete a sex change *US*
- A Puerto Rican pre-op transsexual stabs a trick in the eye with a sharp fingernail to grab his cabfare before he pays the driver. — Josh Alan Friedman, *Tales of Times Square*, p. 51, 1986
- Inevitably, the pre-op patients are extremely involved in medical concerns and teminology and seek lots of advice. — *Maledicta*, p. 174, Summer/Winter 1986 – 1987: 'Sexual slang: prostitutes, pecophiles, flagellators, transvestites, and necrophiles'
- Pre-ops wanted for erotic encounters. — Anka Radakovich, *The Wild Girls Club*, p. 43, 1994
- A male-to-female preop posts: "On the way home from the doctor, a bunch of men driving past me shouted out of the window 'DYKE' at me, as loud and offensively as they could." — Nancy Tamosaitis, *net.sex*, p. 130, 1995

pre-op *adjective*
in a hospital, pre-operative *US*
- The pictures were more gruesome than he'd imagined: shots of him unconscious in the pre-op theater, his head swollen, his two middle teeth missing. — Stephen Cannell, *King Con*, p. 86, 1997

prep *verb*
to prepare someone or something *US, 1927*
- [H]e moved from chair to chair with incredible speed and finesse, instructing the nurses on what to do to prep each patient. — Jim Carroll, *Forced Entries*, p. 135, 1987

- But I've already been prepped, in fact told what to do. — Elmore Leonard, *Maximum Bob*, p. 242, 1991

pre-papier *noun*
in Quebec, advance publicity about cultural events (production teams, casts and plays) prior to reviews *CANADA*
This word is a French term adapted fully into English.
- Pre-papier helps sell tickets at the beginning of a play's run. (For instance, last weekend millions of trees gave their lives for the overhyped musical Roméo et Juliette, which had already sold 110,000 tickets.) — *Montreal Gazette*, p. F1, 18th June 2002

pre-party *verb*
▷ see: PRE

prepone *verb*
to rearrange something for a future date *INDIA*
A definite variation of 'postpone'.
- — Susie Dent, *The Language Report*, p. 127, 2003

preppy; preppie *noun*
a well-groomed, well-heeled, conventional young person with upper-class, prep school values *US*
- — Collin Baker et al., *College Undergraduate Slang Study Conducted at Brown University*, p. 176, 1968
- Ollie, you're a preppie millionaire, and I'm a social zero. — Erich Segal, *Love Story*, p. 40, 1970
- [H]e was the only person in the whole joint without an alligator on his shirt. Even the bartender had one. Keyes thought he'd died and gone to Preppie Heaven. — Carl Hiaasen, *Tourist Season*, p. 221, 1986

pres *noun*
▷ see: PREZ

Presbo *noun*
a presbyterian *AUSTRALIA, 1965*
- — Arthur Chipper, *The Aussie Swearer's Guide*, p. 61, 1972

Presbyterian poker *noun*
low-key, low-limit, friendly poker *US*
- — John Vorhaus, *The Big Book of Poker Slang*, p. 30, 1996

prescription *noun*
a marijuana cigarette *UK, 1998*
An assertion that marijuana is just what the doctor ordered.
- — Mike Haskins, *Drugs*, p. 288, 2003

prescriptions *noun*
commercially manufactured drugs used for non-medicinal purposes *US*
- — Edith A. Folb, *runnin' down some lines*, p. 250, 1980

presence *noun*
MDMA, the recreational drug best known as ecstasy *US*
- — Bruce Eisner, *Ectasy*, p. 1, 1989

presento *noun*
during the Korean war, a piece of merchandise used by US servicemen to trade with Koreans for services *US*
- — *American Speech*, p. 118, May 1960: 'Korean bamboo English'

presh *adjective*
good, pleasing *US*
An abbreviation of the conventional 'precious'.
- — Connie Eble (Editor), *UNC-CH Campus Slang*, p. 7, Fall 1986

president *noun*
an established, respected graffiti artist, often the leader of a group *US*
- — Jim Crotty, *How to Talk American*, p. 143, 1997

President *nickname*
Lester Young (1909 – 59), jazz saxophonist *US*
- — Babs Gonzales, *Be-Bop Dictionary and History of its Famous Stars*, p. 9, 1949

press *noun*
1 in betting, a doubling of the bet in effect *US, 1962*
- "I'll give you a press," means I will bet you the same amount as the original bet for the remaining holes. — Dawson Taylor, *How to Talk Golf*, p. 55, 1985
- Then he said we'd play Zark and Ruffin a $50 Nassau. Automatic one-down presses. — Dan Jenkins, *Dead Solid Perfect*, p. 16, 1986

2 cocaine; crack cocaine *UK, 1998*
- — Mike Haskins, *Drugs*, p. 281, 2003

press *verb*
1 to pursue criminal charges *US*
- The Korean lady and her kid moved back out of the country so they couldn't press me. — *Menace II Society*, 1993

2 to dress up *US*
- — Stewart L. Tubbs and Sylvia Moss, *Human Communication*, p. 122, 1974

▸ **press the blocks**
to idle on a street corner *BAHAMAS*
- — John A. Holm, *Dictionary of Bahamian English*, p. 161, 1982

▸ **press the bricks**
to walk *US*
- — Vincent J. Monteleone, *Criminal Slang*, p. 182, 1949

▸ **press the flesh**
to shake hands, especially in a political context *US, 1926*
- [Arnold] Schwarzenegger gets out of his limo with practised ease and spends 20 minutes pressing the flesh, doing photographs and signing autographs. — *New Statesman*, 4th August 2003

▸ **press the meat; press the sausage**
while gambling, to continue betting your winnings after several consecutive wins *US*
- — Victor H. Royer, *Casino Gamble Talk*, p. 89, 2003

▸ **press the sheets**
to sleep in a bed *US*
- — *Complete CB Slang Dictionary*, p. 76, 1976
- — Peter Chippindale, *The British CB Book*, p. 158, 1981

pressed *adjective*
1 worried, stressed *US*
- — Connie Eble (Editor), *UNC-CH Campus Slang*, p. 5, Fall 1989

2 dressed stylishly *US*
- — Edith A. Folb, *runnin' down some lines*, p. 250, 1980

pressed duck *noun*
a human corpse that has been flattened by traffic *US*
A truly grim comparison.
- — *American Speech*, p. 271, December 1962: 'The language of traffic policeman'

pressed ham *noun*
the bare buttocks pressed against a car window as a rude prank *US*
- — Andy Anonymous, *A Basic Guide to Campusology*, p. 20, 1966

pressie; prezzie *noun*
a gift, a *present* *UK, 1937*
- Can we look at our prezzies now? — Elizabeth Jolley, *Mr. Scobie's Riddle*, p. 70, 1983
- "Looked after your Mum when you were away?" "Sure." "Dropped round with a few prezzies?" — Anthony Masters, *Minder*, p. 80, 1984
- It was a pressie, don't tell me you didn't enjoy it. — Mark Powell, *Snap*, p. 59, 2001
- Sees the prezzie. Asks what it is, who it's for and that. — Kevin Samson, *Outlaws*, p. 50, 2001
- It's a secret. And a prezzie. — Niall Griffiths, *Kelly + Victor*, p. 316, 2002

pressure cooker *noun*
a sports car *UK*
Citizens' band radio slang.
- — Peter Chippindale, *The British CB Book*, p. 158, 1981

pressure out *verb*
to lose your composure completely under pressure *US*
Hawaiian youth usage.
- Ey, no tell Lance about hees girlfrien', brah – he going pressure out! — Douglas Simonson, *Pidgin to da Max*, 1981

pressurize *verb*
to intimidate; to threaten; to coerce *US*
- — Jim Goad, *Jim Goad's Glossary of Northwestern Prison Slang*, December 2001

pre-stiff *noun*
a patient close to death *US*
- — Sally Williams, *"Strong" Words*, p. 156, 1994

pretender to the throne *noun*
a heterosexual who is attempting to pass as a homosexual *US*
- — *Maledicta*, p. 235, Winter 1980: '"Lovely, blooming, fresh and gay": the onomastics of camp'

pretendica *noun*
poor quality or counterfeit marijuana *UK, 1998*
A play on 'pretend' mixed with *cannabis indica* (a major genus of marijuana).
• —Mike Haskins, *Drugs*, p. 288, 2003

pretendo *noun*
a poor quality or counterfeit marijuana *UK*
An elaboration of 'pretend'.
• —Mike Haskins, *Drugs*, p. 288, 2003

Pretentious? Moi?
used self-satirically as an admission of pretentious qualities *UK*
A somewhat tired catchphrase.
• Mr Johnson's voice... 'Pretentious? Moi?' Basil stops. He hears a female laugh.—John Cleese and Connie Booth, *Fawlty Towers*, 1975
• "I was playing behind a wall of bricks meant to represent the alienation of the rock star." He flashed her a grin. "Pretentious, moi? I'd gone bonkers, basically."—Wendy Holden, *Farm Fatale*, p. 281, 2001
• Pretentious? Moi? I prefer guitars to synthesisers, and The Beatles to Kylie.—*The Guardian*, 23rd August 2003

pretties *noun*
1 the female breasts *UK*
• I looked down at my own pink tipped pretties and decided that maybe the peepers wouldn't have much time for me after all.—Petra Christian, *The Sexploiters*, p. 70, 1973
2 on a film or television crew, the makeup, hair and wardrobe departments *US*
• —*American Speech*, p. 418, Winter 1997: 'Among the new words'
3 in trucking, state permit stickers affixed on a cab window *US*
• —Montie Tak, *Truck Talk*, p. 122, 1971

pretty *noun*
a youthful, sexually inexperienced male who is the object of an older homosexual's desire *US*
• —*Maledicta*, p. 221, 1979: 'Kinks and queens: linguistic and cultural aspects of the terminology for gays'

pretty boy *noun*
1 an effeminate young man *AUSTRALIA, 1942*
• —Gerald Sweeney, *The Plunge*, p. 331, 1981
• Today, Hawthorn head across the Nullarbor to take on the Perth pretty boys on an arid piece of turf known as Subiaco Oval.—*West Australian*, p. 90, 7th September 1991
2 a sexually active young man *US*
• Pretty boy is a sexually active boy, someone who's been fairly promiscuous.—*Oprah Winfrey Show*, 2nd October 2003

pretty face *noun*
▸ **not just a pretty face**
used, often ironically, when claiming to be intelligent *UK, 1968*
• "She's not just a pretty face," Phillpot went on, "she's clever too." —Miles Tripp, *Woman at Risk*, 1974

pretty pictures *noun*
in computing, graphical representations of statistics *US*
• —Eric S. Raymond, *The New Hacker's Dictionary*, p. 287, 1991

pretty please
an emphatic or wheedling intensification of please *UK, 1959*
• Oh please, Mommy, pretty please? We'll be so good.—Adele Faber and Elaine Mazlish, *How To Talk So Kids Will Listen and Listen So Kids Will Talk*, p. 228, 2000

pretty-print *verb*
in computing, to format code so that it looks attractive *US*
• —Guy L. Steele et al., *The Hacker's Dictionary*, p. 74, 1983

pretzels *noun*
a small amount of money *US*
An evolution from the more common **PEANUTS**.
• —George Percy, *The Language of Poker*, p. 71, 1988

previous *noun*
a criminal record *UK*
An abbreviation of 'previous convictions'.
• I'd seen innocent men, especially those with previous, fitted up and jailed.—Dave Courtney, *Stop the Ride I Want to Get Off*, p. 330, 1999

previous *adjective*
premature; early; hasty *US, 1885*
• [A]lerting Michael Owen ahead of a possible semi would a bit previous, wouldn't it?—*The Guardian*, 18th June 2002

prez; pres *noun*
president *IRELAND, 1922*
• Among those who took advantage of the terminal-type cough to steal away to a more active, and less demanding, corner of the party was Les Harrison, handsome, forty-three-year-old vice-prez of Metropolitan pix[.]—Terry Southern, *Blue Movie*, p. 13, 1970
• After they regained their cool he took the Pres's wife's fur stole and put it over his sweaty shoulders and posed with her for a picture. —Babs Gonzales, *Movin' On Down De Line*, p. 32, 1975
• Sugarfoot was prez of the Ventura chapter of the Satan's Slaves and the business end of a dozen felony warrants[.]—Seth Morgan, *Homeboy*, p. 3, 1990
• [N]one was too great for her to get with / Or even mess with, the Prez she says was next on her list[.]—Salt 'N' Pepa, *Let's Talk About Sex*, 1991

Prez *nickname*
Lester Young (1909–59), jazz saxophonist *US*
Singer Billie Holiday nicknamed Young 'Prez' as a shortened form of 'President of the Tenor Saxophone'.
• Then there was Prez, a husky, handsome blond like a freckled boxer, meticulously wrapped inside his sharkskin plaid suit[.]—Jack Kerouac, *On the Road*, p. 238–239, 1957
• Prez had him a sound on the saxophone like he was getting a chick to lay for him.—Ross Russell, *The Sound*, p. 110, 1961
• He switched after one bar of "D.B. Blues" right into "Meadowland," honking it, dropping Prez's phrasing[.]—Gilbert Sorrentino, *Steelwork*, p. 31, 1970
• In that atmosphere, with the spiraled hints of Bird, Prez, Diz, or Miles cuttin' up on somebody's box, we'd have orgies.—Odie Hawkins, *Black Casanova*, p. 163, 1984

prezzie *noun*
▷ **see: PRESSIE**

prezzies *noun*
paper money *US*
An abbreviation of the common **DEAD PRESIDENTS**.
• —Anna Scotti and Paul Young, *Buzzwords*, p. 58, 1997

prezzo *noun*
a gift or present *AUSTRALIA*
• I trust they appreciate the little prezzo I've brought them!—Barry Humphries, *The Wonderful World of Barry McKenzie*, p. 4, 1968
• By the bye, we brought you a little prezzo.—*The Adventures of Barry McKenzie*, 1972
• The buggers are always wanting to visit. Especially around Christmas. In the hope of cracking it for a presso.—Phillip Adams, *The Unspeakable Adams*, p. 181, 1977

price *noun*
1 a chance *UK*
Sporting slang, from bookmakers quoting a 'price' (betting odds).
• Rendall ran and never had a price.—*news commentary on a cricket match*, 27th July 1977
2 in betting on horse racing, the approximate equivalent odds to $1 *US*
• —David W. Maurer, *Argot of the Racetrack*, p. 52, 1951
3 a discount *US*
A euphemism that saves face for both the seller and buyer.
• Also Brennan gives him a price on sandwiches and a free first round of drinks which everybody thinks is very nice of him.—Robert Campbell, *In a Pig's Eye*, p. 2, 1991

pricey *adjective*
expensive *UK, 1932*
• And the cake is kind of pricey, too. For a cake, I mean.—Nicholas Sparks, *The Wedding*, p. 71, 2003

prick *noun*
1 the penis *UK, 1592*
From the basic sense, 'anything that pricks or pierces'; in conventional English until around 1700. William Shakespeare (1564–1616) played word games with it, Robert Burns (1759–96) used it with vulgar good humour and the Victorians finally hid it away.
• She used candles, Roman candles, and door knobs. Not a prick in the land big enough for her, not one. Men went inside her and curled up.—Henry Miller, *Tropic of Cancer*, p. 7, 1961
• In his anxiety the man has even forgotten to pretend he's standing there for any purpose other than to see Johnny's prick[.]—John Rechy, *Numbers*, p. 41, 1967
• [H]is prick is small and rather dismal-looking.—Gore Vidal, *Myra Breckinridge*, p. 109, 1968
• When the prick stands up, the brain gets buried—Philip Roth, *Portnoy's Complaint*, 1969

2 a despicable man; a fool; used as a general term of offence or contempt, often as an abusive form of address, always of a male or an inanimate object *US, 1929*
Since the 1940s, when qualified by the adjective 'silly', the sense need not be derogatory or contemptuous, as 'you silly prick', 'the silly prick' etc.; an unembellished prick, however, is considered very offensive.
- Old men with white hair and black-ribbon glasses "look right" – no cop, no prick dares question their freedom. —Jack Kerouac, *Letter to Allen Ginsberg*, p. 213, 16 July 1949
- You ever stop to figure that, you dumb prick? —Evan Hunter, *The Blackboard Jungle*, p. 295, 1954
- [F]or every sentient being or living creature these actual pricks kill they will be reborn a thousand times to suffer the horrors of samsara and damn good for 'em too. —Jack Kerouac, *The Dharma Bums*, p. 38, 1958
- We can be just three sailors together, or we can be a prisoner and two pricks. —Darryl Ponicsan, *The Last Detail*, p. 67, 1970
- Miles was a soul man, a sound, a black Bogey. He was also an insufferable prick. —Albert Goldman, *Freak Show*, p. 301, 1971
- "What a prick," Bob says. "What a flaming prick." —Ted Lewis, *Jack Carter's Law*, p. 49, 1974
- arseholes, bastards, fucking cunts and pricks —Ian Dury, *Plaistow Patricia*, 1977
- We cut down that prick of a tree, too. —Chris Ryan, *Stand By, Stand By*, p. 224, 1996
- What I wouldn't give to know what heavy feels like, you insensitive prick. —*Something About Mary*, 1998
- You just smile about it cos you'd look like a prick not to. —Dave Courtney, *Raving Lunacy*, p. 19, 2000

3 a marijuana cigarette *UK, 1970s*
Presumably based on phallic imagery.

pricked off *adjective*
annoyed, angry *US*
- —Fred Hester, *Slang on the 40 Acres*, p. 11, 1968

prickface *noun*
a contemptible person *AUSTRALIA*
- Don't you speak ill of the dead prickface, or I'll drop you so help me!!! —Barry Humphries, *Bazza Pulls It Off!*, 1971

pricklick *noun*
a homosexual male *US*
- —Helen Dahlskog (Editor), *A Dictionary of Contemporary and Colloquial Usage*, p. 46, 1972

prick parade *noun*
a group inspection by a military doctor or medic of male recruits for signs of sexually transmitted disease *US*
- —Roger Blake, *The American Dictionary of Sexual Terms*, p. 168, 1964
- —Dale Gordon, *The Dominion Sex Dictionary*, p. 130, 1967

pricksmith *noun*
a military doctor or medic who inspects male recruits for signs of sexually transmitted disease *US*
- —Dale Gordon, *The Dominion Sex Dictionary*, p. 130, 1967
- —Linda Reinberg, *In the Field*, p. 172, 1991

prick-teaser *noun*
a woman who invites sexual advances but does not fulfil that which she seems to promise *US*
- [H]e was beginning to suspect her of being one of the world's great prick-teasers. —Terry Southern, *Blue Movie*, p. 91, 1970
- She was always a prickteaser. Now she stood so closely the pert tips of her tits radiated warm spots on his chest. —Earl Thompson, *Tattoo*, p. 432, 1974

pride and joy *noun*
a boy, especially a new-born son *UK*
Rhyming slang.
- —Ray Puxley, *Cockney Rabbit*, 1992

pride of Deadwood *noun*
in poker, a hand consisting of aces and eights *US*
From the belief, true or legendary, that when Wild Bill Hickock was shot and killed in Deadwood, Dakota Territory, he was holding a hand consisting of aces and eights, all black.
- —George Percy, *The Language of Poker*, p. 71, 1988

pride of the morning *noun*
the erection experienced by a man upon awakening in the morning *US*
- —Robert A. Wilson, *Playboy's Book of Forbidden Words*, p. 204, 1972

priest's dick *noun*
something of little or no worth *UK*
- I don't give a priest's dick about which of you is telling the truth. —James Hawes, *Dead Long Enough*, p. 258, 2000

prim *verb*
(used of a female) to walk in a sexually inviting fashion *BAHAMAS*
- —John A. Holm, *Dictionary of Bahamian English*, p. 161, 1982

prime *verb*
▸ **prime the spunk gun**
(used of a male) to masturbate *UK*
- —Richard Herring, *Talking Cock*, p. 113, 2003

primed *adjective*
drunk or under the influence of drugs *US*
- —Hyman E. Goldin et al., *Dictionary of American Underworld Lingo*, p. 163, 1950
- —Stephen H. Dill (Editor), *Current Slang*, p. 3, Summer 1966

prime time *noun*
1 time spent with a spouse or lover *US*
Trucker slang, punning on television terminology.
- —Wayne Floyd, *Jason's Authentic Dictionary of CB Slang*, p. 25, 1976

2 cocaine; crack cocaine *UK*
- —Mike Haskins, *Drugs*, p. 281, 2003

primo *noun*
1 a very high grade of marijuana, consisting of a high degree of potent flowering tops of the plants *US, 1971*
- —Ernest L. Abel, *A Marijuana Dictionary*, p. 83, 1982

2 marijuana mixed with crack cocaine *US*
- —Mark S. Fleisher, *Beggars & Thieves: Lives of Urban Street Criminals*, p. 290, 1995: 'Glossary'

3 a conventional tobacco cigarette laced with cocaine and heroin *UK, 1998*
- —Robert Ashton, *This Is Heroin*, p. 210, 2002

4 heroin *UK*
- —Robert Ashton, *This Is Heroin*, p. 206, 2002

primo *adjective*
excellent *US*
- —Gary Fairmont R. Filosa II, *The Surfer's Almanac: An International Surfing Guide*, p. 192, 1977
- "I just like the sandwiches." He was damned if he'd let her peg him as an old preppie finding his roots. "Yeah," she said, "they are primo." —Armistead Maupin, *Further Tales of the City*, p. 99, 1982
- Musta got some primo bondsman. —*48 Hours*, 1982
- [H]e was stoked to the gills, having scored some primo Jamaican herb off a busboy at the hotel. —Carl Hiaasen, *Tourist Season*, p. 169, 1986
- But old Owsley's preemo purple or even windowpane, that stuff could get you in touch with your ancestors. —Elmore Leonard, *Freaky Deaky*, p. 19, 1988
- This is primo advertising. Christ, Igor, we're all over the news! —*Airheads*, 1994
- Jimmy held a carved ivory spoon to my nose. "Try some this way. Primo shit, man." —Cleo Odzer, *Goa Freaks*, p. 85, 1995

Prince Albert; PA; Albert *noun*
a piece of jewellery for a penile piercing; also applied to the piercing itself *UK*
This etymology is the stuff of romantic myth: the procedure and bejewelling is named for Queen Victoria's consort who, it is claimed, endured the embellishment of his member to enhance his Queen's pleasure.
- Hi, my name is Michael, and I wear a P.A. (Prince Albert) [...] When a P.A. is done the urethra is pierced between glans and shaft and the other side of the ring leaves the penis through the tip. —*www.fortune-city.com/village*, 24th June 2001
- [P]oor Prince Albert whose only claim to fame is a penile piercing. —*The Observer*, 9th May 2004

Prince Alberts; Alberts *noun*
rags worn by tramps in the place of socks *AUSTRALIA, 1888*
Folk etymolgy suggests the alleged poverty of Prince Albert before marriage to Queen Victoria.

Prince Charming *nickname*
used ironically of someone who is anything but *UK*
- I would have gone to her place only I had Prince Charming with me[.] —John Milne, *Alive and Kicking*, p. 52, 1998

Prince of Darkness *nickname*
Joseph Lucas, British electrical equipment manufacturer of unreliable headlight systems *US*
- —Lewis Poteet, *Car and Motorcyle Slang*, p. 135, 1997

Princess Di *noun*
a pie *UK*
Rhyming slang, formed on a familiar name for Diana, Princess of Wales, 1961–97; recorded in use before and, following a respectful pause, after her death.
- —Ray Puxley, *Fresh Rabbit*, 1998

Princeton rub; Princeton style *noun*
the rubbing of the penis between the thighs of another boy or man until reaching orgasm *US*
Princeton is a prestigious and cultured East Coast university.
- You know, Uncle, the Princeton Rub?—John Francis Hunter, *The Gay Insider*, p. 158, 1971
- Princeton style – Fucking the thighs.—Bruce Rodgers, *The Queens' Vernacular*, p. 154, 1972
- Princeton rub – Ostensibly reflects the gentlemanly restraint of the Ivy League.—Wayne Dynes, *Homolexis*, p. 116, 1985

pringle *noun*
multiple orgasms *UK*
From the advertising slogan for Pringles™, a savoury snack: 'once you pop you can't stop'.
- —*Sky Magazine*, July 2001

print *verb*
to take the fingerprints of a prisoner during the after-arrest process *US, 1939*
- We brought him up to the marshal's office and mugged him and printed him and then we brought him here.—George V. Higgins, *The Friends of Eddie Doyle*, p. 135, 1971

prior *noun*
a prior arrest or prior conviction *US*
- The guy he killed was running on speed and trailing a lifetime of priors, destined – they told Vincent – to crash and burn or die in jail.—Elmore Leonard, *Glitz*, p. 4, 1985
- With their priors, they're looking at a serious bounce.—*Gone in 60 Seconds*, 2000

Priscilla *noun*
a police officer *SOUTH AFRICA*
Gay slang, using a female name, probably elaborating the initial 'p' for 'police'.
- A "Priscilla" is a police officer, a "Lettie" a lesbian.—Bart Luirink (translated by Loes Nas), *Moffies: Gay Life in Southern Africa*, p. 118, 2000

prison air conditioning *noun*
a wet towel *CANADA*
- "Prison air conditioning" is a wet towel with a large hole in it draped over the torso.—Suroosh Alvi et al., *The Vice Guide*, p. 209, 2002

prison bent; prison gay *adjective*
used of a heterosexual prisoner who adopts a homosexual or lesbian lifestyle for the duration of his or her sentence *UK*
- —Angela Devlin, *Prison Patter*, p. 90, 1996

prissy *adjective*
1 prudish
- Jake, who is the most irritating 12 year old in the world, says: "Don't act so prissy, Jane." He shoves The Joy of Sex at me[.]—*The Guardian*, p. 9, 28th November 2001

2 effeminate *US*
Perhaps a blend of 'prim' and **SISSY**.
- —Monica Dickens, *The Happy Prisoner*, 1946
- After seven meetings, David, a prissy, fifty-year-old confirmed bachelor, was on the verge of dropping out.—Irvin D. Yalom, *Theory and Practice of Group Psychotherapy*, p. 409, 1995

prissy lad *noun*
a homosexual man *US*
- He and another prissy lad were in our cocktail lounge one evening, drinking, making catty and audible cracks about other patrons[.] —Dev Collans with Stewart Sterling, *I was a House Detective*, p. 105, 1954

priv *noun*
a *priv*ilege *UK*
- [L]ose privs.—Angela Devlin, *Prison Patter*, p. 73, 1996

private dance *noun*
a one-on-one sexual performance by a woman for a man *US*
- He had gone to the go-go bar to meet a buddy of his, had one beer, that's all, while he was waiting, minding his own business and this go-go whore came up to his table and started giving him a private dance he never asked for.—Elmore Leonard, *Maximum Bob*, p. 1, 1991
- A United States congressman, you're telling me it's just a private dance party?—Carl Hiaasen, *Strip Tease*, p. 280, 1993
- I wanted my girlfriend to have a full strip-club experience, complete with a private dance.—*The Village Voice*, 21st September 1999

private dick *noun*
a private detective *US, 1912*
Conventional use of 'private' combined with **DICK** (detective).
- The police are keeping a blanket on it, but you being a private dick would have your own sources, wouldn't you?—Malcolm Pryce, *Aberystwyth Mon Amour*, p. 37, 2001

private eye *noun*
a private detective *US, 1938*
- M&S calls in private eye to halt top-level leaks.—*The Guardian*, 28th May 2001

privates *noun*
the genitals of either sex *UK, 1602*
- On one of Schiaparelli's evening dresses, a fastener slices diagonally across the wearer's groin, like an arrow pointing to her privates.—*The Observer*, 23rd November 2003

private slick *noun*
a physician in private practice *US*
- —Sally Williams, *"Strong" Words*, p. 154, 1994

private star *noun*
a private detective *US*
- I'm a private star. I followed somebody down here last night. —Raymond Chandler, *Playback*, p. 123, 1958

privy queen *noun*
a homosexual male who searches for sexual partners in public toilets *US, 1941*

prize *adjective*
describes a prime example (of whatever it is appended to); complete, utter *UK, 1976*
- He also hadn't grown up in Kirkby without being able to recognise a prize dickhead when he saw one.—Colin Butts, *Is Harry on the Boat?*, p. 25, 1997

prize jewels carrier *noun*
the scrotum *UK*
- [A] gaping hole in my prize jewels carrier. I have since paid many visits to hospital[.]—*Mixmag*, p. 11, February 2002

pro *noun*
1 a professional, especially in a field of endeavour that is also enjoyed by amateurs (such as sport or theatre); also used as an Internet domain name for a professional practitioner *UK, 1866*
- You'd get blokes from all walks of life wanting to fight [...] ex-pros, current pros out to make a few quid, and applause-junkies like yours truly.—Dave Courtney, *Stop the Ride I Want to Get Off*, p. 195, 1999

2 a professional prostitute *UK, 1937*
- My gal's a pro and them is just chippies.—Chester Himes, *The Real Cool Killers*, p. 100, 1959
- "Jesus, nine years old," he said, reached over and pinched Candy's nose, "and knew a lot more than a good many pros".—Ken Kesey, *One Flew Over the Cuckoo's Nest*, p. 245, 1962
- Hey, don't do that. I said I wasn't a pro, remember?—*48 Hours*, 1982
- God but she was free with her cunt. So she turned pro, huh?—William T. Vollman, *Whores for Gloria*, p. 138, 1991
- CATHERINE: I wasn't dating him. I was fucking him. GUS: What are you – a pro?—*Basic Instinct*, 1992

prob *noun*
a problem *US*
- Gots a prob with that too?—Jess Mowry, *Way Past Cool*, p. 35, 1992
- [N]o fuckin probs dealin with them.—Niall Griffiths, *Sheepshagger*, p. 73, 2001

probate *noun*
in a criminal case, a sentence of probation *US*
A person who is arrested for the illegal production of alcohol and is sentenced to probation is said to 'get probate'.
- —David W. Maurer, *Kentucky Moonshine*, p. 119, 1974

probie *noun*
a probationary employee *US*
- "You're an academy probie, Dan. You've got seven months of probation ahead." — Charles Whited, *Chiodo*, p. 26, 1973
- — *Maledicta*, p. 56, Summer 1980: 'Not sticks and stones, but names: more medical pejoratives'

procesh *noun*
a procession or graduation parade *NEW ZEALAND*
- The first Massey "Procesh' was held in 1935 and was greeted with enthusiasm[.] — Tom Brooking, *Massey – Its Early Years*, p. 118, 1977

process *noun*
a chemical straightening of curly hair *US*
- After observing all the "down" cats who frequent these Barber shops, he decided to get a process (Hair marcelled). — Babs Gonzales, *I Paid My Dues*, p. 94, 1967
- Those two pimps? That style is just called a process, some call it a marcel. — Joseph Wambaugh, *The New Centurions*, p. 66, 1970

procon *noun*
a *pro*fessionally run fan *con*vention *US*
- — *American Speech*, p. 53, Spring 1978: 'Star Trek lives. Trekker slang'

procure *verb*
▸ **procure for a cause**
to steal something *US*
- — *Current Slang*, p. 22, Spring 1970

prod *noun*
1 the penis *US*
- — *American Speech*, p. 64, Spring-Summer 1975: 'Razorback slang'

2 in horse racing, an illegal, battery-powered device used to impart a shock to a horse during a race *US*
- — Tom Ainslie, *Ainslie's Complete Guide to Thoroughbred Racing*, p. 336, 1976

▸ **on the prod**
looking for something; on the offensive; provoked *US, 1904*
- Once a hooligan mob was on the prod and was quick to call my bluff. — Bruce Jackson, *Get Your Ass in the Water and Swim Like Me*, p. 75, 1966
- I never see him when he ain't on the prod. Maybe this is because he's almost always the man sent out to pick up pieces too ugly for other people to pick up. — Robert Campbell, *Junkyard Dog*, p. 21, 1986
- — Lewis Poteet, *The South Shore Phrase Book*, p. 88, 1999

Prod; Prot *noun*
a Protestant *UK, 1942*
Mainly Catholic use across the UK.
- Aah, a Prod. Christianity's second string, God bless them. — James Ellroy, *White Jazz*, p. 160, 1992
- Neither the Rev William McLeod of the Prods nor Fr Francis Shelley of the Tims seemed to know[.] — Christopher Brookmyre, *Boiling a Frog*, p. 108, 2000

Proddie; Proddy *adjective*
Protestant; a Protestant *UK, 1954*
Mainly Catholic use across the UK.
- Notice you were nae breakin' intae any Proddy church heidquarters. — Christopher Brookmyre, *Boiling a Frog*, p. 46, 2000
- [H]ave you ever wondered why we poor Northern Proddie sods keep our kids out of pubs? — James Hawes, *Dead Long Enough*, p. 89, 2000
- [T]he Proddie cathedral[.] — Kevin Sampson, *Outlaws*, p. 102, 2001

Proddy dog *noun*
a Protestant *AUSTRALIA*
- PRODDY DOGS: State school children of both sexes. God did not love them enough to make the Catholics. — Phillip Adams, *More Unspeakable Adams*, p. 189, 1979
- Tyke: A derogatory term for a Catholic; the opposite end of the religious spectrum to the 'Proddy dog'. — Richard Beckett, *The Dinkum Aussie Dictionary*, p. 54, 1984
- Only don't let them know you're a Catholic. If they ask you, say you're a Proddy-dog. — Hugh Leonard, *Out After Dark*, p. 101, Methuen 1989

proddywhack *adjective*
Protestant *UK*
- [J]ust one more ghastly proddywhack epithet flickering among all the others. — John Milne, *Alive and Kicking*, p. 211, 1998

prodigal boy *noun*
a person who excels at the game of footbagging *US*
- — Jim Crotty, *How to Talk American*, p. 123, 1997

produce *noun*
food *US*
- "Got any produce?" "Food," the great Kahoona explained, noticing my puzzled expression. — Frederick Kohner, *Gidget*, p. 31, 1957

producer *noun*
1 an official requirement that you *produce* your driving licence, motor insurance and any other necessary documentation for police scrutiny *UK*
In police use, form HO/RT/1 (Home Office/Road Traffic/1).
- The cop issued him with a producer, clearly angry that they had found nothing to do the black man on. — Donald Gorgon, *Cop Killer*, p. 39, 1994
- Didn't even get a producer gra'ma [grandma]... Wha' d'y'think o' tha? — Nick Barlay, *Curvy Lovebox*, p. 99, 1997
- — *The Official Encyclopaedia of New Scotland Yard*, 1999
- [A] young Asian dude on a producer, all his documents pukka only he got stopped for being Asian. — Jeremy Cameron, *Brown Bread in Wengen*, p. 17, 1999

2 a serious gambler who, like most gamblers, usually loses *US*
- During his stay, heiroglyphics are secretly appended to his name on the hotel register, which catalogue him as a "dropper" (businessman and heavy loser), "producer" (businessman), or "nonproducer" (professional gambler). — Ed Reid and Ovid Demaris, *The Green felt Jungle*, p. 2, 1963

product *noun*
illegal drugs *US*
- Jack a phone in there and make a deal, talk about the product, it's always the product now[.] — Elmore Leonard, *Cat Chaser*, p. 165, 1982
- I'll even tell you how we move the product. — Jay McInerney, *Bright Lights, Big City*, p. 117, 1984
- But girls could steal too, just disappear around a corner with the product. — Richard Price, *Clockers*, p. 5, 1992
- You'll have more product day after tomorrow, right? — *The Bad Lieutenant*, 1992
- No, man, no product. This is a clean run I'm talking about. No contraband, no kind of shit of any kind like that. — Elmore Leonard, *Riding the Rap*, p. 265, 1995
- I hear he's around Palm Springs. Dealing our product. Product we sold to you for five hundred thousand dollars. — *Get Shorty*, 1995
- — Mark S. Fleisher, *Beggars & Thieves*, p. 290, 1995: 'Glossary'
- We hire drivers with nothing to lose. Then we throw a lot of product at the problem. — *Traffic*, 2000

prof *noun*
a *prof*essor; also as a form of address *US, 1838*
- New bunch now – mess of students with arms like twigs, passel of bald-head profs with vests. — Max Shulman, *Anyone Got a Match?*, p. 225, 1964
- [T]here is no such thing as "experiment" in academic psychology, because that would suggest the prof was in some doubt as to what the results would be. — Christopher Brookmyre, *Not the End of the World*, p. 258, 1998

professional scene *noun*
a sado-masochistic encounter for pay *US*
- — *What Color is Your Handkerchief*, p. 6, 1979

professor *noun*
1 a diligent student *US*
- — *American Speech*, p. 304, December 1955: 'Wayne University slang'

2 a piano player in a brothel *US, 1939*
- — Robert S. Gold, *A Jazz Lexicon*, p. 237, 1964

3 a skilled and experienced poker player *US*
- — John Scarne, *Scarne's Guide to Modern Poker*, p. 287, 1979

proffing *noun*
stealing *UK*
- [T]he noble army tradition of "proffing", conducted on the principle that anything not nailed down or attached with a string may well find itself a new owner. — Kate Adie (writing of the Gulf War), *The Kindness of Strangers*, p. 338, 2002

profile *verb*
1 (used of the police) to stop, question and search someone based on their race and age *US*
- It was only natural to look at a cop car; nothing gave a clocker away to a profiling cop like that stony, straight-ahead stare at a red light. — Richard Price, *Clockers*, p. 24, 1992

2 to act in an arrogant and conceited fashion *US*
- — *Newsday*, p. B2, 11th October 1997

profiles *noun*
in a deck of playing cards, the king of diamonds, jack of spades and jack of hearts, all one-eyed and drawn in profile *US*
- —Irwin Steig, *Common Sense in Poker*, p. 186, 1963

pro from Dover *noun*
an expert *US*
- We're the pros from Dover and we figure to crack that kid's chest and get out to the golf course before it's dark.—*M*A*S*H*, 1970

prog *noun*
a radio or television programme *UK, 1975*
Particularly associated with the *JY Prog* presented by Jimmy Young, a BBC radio DJ and presenter from 1959, especially on Radio 2, which he joined in 1973 until his retirement in 2001.
- Thank you Sammy. It's good to be on the prog.—Anthony Masters, *Minder*, p. 178, 1984

prog *adjective*
*prog*ressive, as used of a school or method *UK*
- —R.C. Benge, *Libraries*, 1969

proggy *adjective*
having the characteristics of progressive house music *UK*
- Psychedelic and proggy business from down under. When any of our epic-touting prog gods make the trip down under, they always seem to come back muttering about how "it's a really good scene, man"[.]—*Ministry*, p. 85, January 2002

program *noun*
the twelve-step Alcoholics Anonymous programme for recovery from alcoholism *US*
- Plus everybody there was on the frigging program anyway.—Robert Stoller and I.S. Levine, *Coming Attractions*, p. 192, 1991

program *verb*
in prison, to follow the rules and avoid trouble in hope of an early release *US*
- —*Maledicta*, p. 265, Summer/Winter 1981: 'By its slang, ye shall know it: the pessimism of prison life'

prohi *noun*
a federal law enforcement official *US*
Used by those in the illegal production of alcohol.
- them goddam, low-down, sonuvabitch prohi bastards.—David W. Maurer, *Kentucky Moonshine*, p. 122, 1974

prole *noun*
a member of the proletariat *US*
- "Good morning, fellow proles," you say, slipping into your seat.—Jay McInerney, *Bright Lights, Big City*, p. 16, 1984
- They call it the new liquid acid, and, to proles like me, it's the best drug in the world.—Suroosh Alvi et al., *The Vice Guide*, p. 91, 2002

prole *adjective*
proletariat; of the working-class *US*
- Spector, while still in his teens, seemed to comprehend the prole vitality of rock and roll that has made it the kind of darling holy beast of intellectuals in the United States.—Tom Wolfe, *The Kandy-Kolored Tangerine-Flake Streamline Baby*, p. 66, 1965

prom *noun*
a dance at a school or college *US, 1894*
- Like takin' carrie to the high school prom / Something's always goin' wrong[.]—Ramones *Endless Vacation*, 1985

promise *noun*
▸ on a promise
having been promised sexual intercourse *AUSTRALIA, 1960*
- —Jim Ramsay, *Cop It Sweet!*, p. 73, 1977
- Will it take long, Sarge? I'm on a promise from me sheila tonight! —Lance Peters, *The Dirty Half-Mile*, p. 32, 1979
- Collingwood will win, no worries – and I'm on a promise from Clara!—Frank Hardy, *Hardy's People*, p. 87, 1986

prommer *noun*
a member of the audience, especially a promenader, at a Henry Wood Promenade Concert (now branded the *BBC Proms*) *UK*
So named by James Loughran, in the conductor's traditional last-night-of the-Proms speech, 11th September 1982.

promo *noun*
public relations; promotional item(s); in the music business, an advance copy of an unreleased tune sent to an influential DJ *US, 1966*
- Got a job doin' radio promo[.]—Frank Zappa, *Bobby Brown Goes Down*, 1979
- [B]lagging promos!—J. Hoggarth, *How To Be a DJ*, p. 25, 2002

promo *adjective*
promotional *US, 1963*
- Man has money, he's connected, knows people, like he must know some indie promo guys.—Elmore Leonard, *Be Cool*, p. 176, 1999

promote *verb*
in the circus or carnival, to obtain illegally something that is badly needed *US*
- —Joe McKennon, *Circus Lingo*, p. 72, 1980

prong *noun*
the penis *US*
- I suppose as the biggest stud in England, he felt it his duty to show the biggest prong.—Angelo d'Arcangelo, *The Homosexual Handbook*, p. 67, 1968
- "He's got the biggest prong I ever saw on a white man", Gorilla said in honest admiration.—Earl Thompson, *Tattoo*, p. 327, 1974

pronger *noun*
the penis *US*
- I doubt if there are very many gigs where he doesn't end up pogoing his pronger in some sweet honey's hive.—Lester Bangs, *Psychotic Reactions and Carburetor Dung*, p. 235, 1977

prong me!
used for registering disbelief, despair, surprise or satisfaction *US*
From **PRONG** (the penis), in the manner and sense of **FUCK ME!**, suggesting that 'prong' is also used for **FUCK** (to have sex, etc).
- —Richard McKenna, *The Sand Pebbles*, 1962

pronto *adverb*
immediately *US, 1911*
From the Spanish.
- I told you to get those leaves swept up! Shake a leg, pronto!—Ian Pattison, *Rab C. Nesbitt*, 1988
- Nelson didn't say a word. He ejected that mother, pronto.—Joseph Wambaugh, *Fugitive Nights*, p. 245, 1992
- We did what we were told to do, pronto, or else we got slammed. —Odie Hawkins, *Black Chicago*, p. 117, 1992
- We're in a car we gotta get off the road pronto!—*Pulp Fiction*, 1994
- Mr Hadden wants you back at base, Scoop. Like pronto. Asap. Etc. —Davis Peace, *Nineteen Seventy-Four*, p. 78, 1999

proof *noun*
an identification card establishing you as old enough to buy alcohol *US*
- —*Esquire*, p. 180, June 1983

proof *verb*
to show identification proving that you are old enough to be where you are, buying what you are buying *US*
- I still look young enough to get proofed in bars.—Jim Carroll, *Forced Entries*, p. 7, 1987

proof shot *noun*
a photograph, or a scene in a pornographic film, of a man ejaculating *US*
- Proof Shot stems from old time producers demanding an external ejaculation of sperm so that the customer saw proof that he popped his wad.—*Adult Video News*, p. 42, August 1995

prop *noun*
1 a proposition *UK, 1871*
- But could he suspect it was because of the Rollers, because the Rollers had shot her a prop, one that was impossible for her to resist: her own freedom?—Clarence Cooper Jr, *The Scene*, p. 22, 1960
- —*Current Slang*, p. 38, Fall 1968
- '"Damn," said Rose, "I thought I was a way-out bitch. / And here you shoot me a prop like I was a witch."—Dennis Wepman et al., *The Life*, p. 40, 1976

2 any portable article used in acting *UK, 1864*
An abbreviation of 'property': theatrical, film making, television, etc.; also used by those seeking to create an impression.
- The play is set in 1910, so at the moment we are working on costumes and finding good props.—*Epsom Guardian*, 19th November 2003

3 in casino gambling, a casino employee who poses as a player to draw interest to a game *US*
An abbreviation of 'proposition player'.
- —Frank Scoblete, *Best Blackjack*, p. 269, 1996

4 the leg *US*
- If my 'props' get cut off I'll wheel myself on a wagon looking for a whore.—*Pimp*, p. 103, 1969

5 a prisoners' strike *NEW ZEALAND*
- After Alofoe's suicide, A Block inmates began a 'prop'.—*New Zealand Times*, p. 5, 12th May 1985

prop *verb*

1 to organise a criminal enterprise *UK*
- I got a big 'un on. Only just been propped.—Charles Raven, *Underworld Nights*, p. 123, 1956

2 to take part in a prison strike *NEW ZEALAND*
- Because we were late starting practice we all decided to prop for ten minutes extra.—Greg Newbold, *The Big Huey*, p. 89, 1982

propellerhead *noun*
an expert computer enthusiast *US*
- A geek has more profound understanding of his or her subject, but the propellerhead has a date for Friday night.—Andy Ihnatko, *Cyberspeak*, p. 157, 1997
- So how did an electronic duo from Bath, England, end up with a name that's California slang for computer nerds? Explains Alex Gifford, founding member of Propellerheads [formed 1996]: "A mate of ours, a Canadian, used it in conversation once and it just went clang["]—*Propellerheads website*, 2002

propeller key *noun*
the command key on an Apple Macintosh™ computer keyboard *US*
- —Eric S. Raymond, *The New Hacker's Dictionary*, p. 288, 1991

proper *noun*
proper respect *US*
- These punks just don't want to give us our proper.—Donald Goines, *El Dorado Red*, p. 110, 1974

proper *adjective*

1 excellent, complete, perfect *UK, 1375*
In conventional use until during the C19.
- I thought he was going to fake him a proper one.—Butch Reynolds, *Broken Hearted Clown*, p. 28, 1953

2 of a criminal, respected *UK*
- —Dave Courtney, *Dodgy Dave's Little Black Book*, p. 9, 2001

proper *adverb*
excellently, superbly; without subterfuge; handsomely *UK*
An intensifier.
- I was proper buzzing.—Dave Courtney, *Raving Lunacy*, p. 4, 2000

proper little madam *noun*
▷ see: LITTLE MADAM

proper lush *adjective*
great, excellent, wonderful *UK, 1999*
An intensified variation of **LUSH**.
- I think Newcastle is proper lush – I mean it's so mint it should TOTALLY win city of culture and that. I love it!—*Talk of the Tyne*, May 2003

propper; prop *noun*
in youth-oriented holiday resorts, a person who encourages custom into clubs and bars *UK*
Probably adapted from a reduction of 'proposition'.
- [S]ome of the other lads join in – y'know, DJs, props, guys on the beach party.—Colin Butts, *Is Harry on the Boat?*, p. 21, 1997
- As Ecstasy overload spread from the '86 contingent of workers, DJs and proppers to the general tanked-up community of '87—Tony Wilson, *24 Hour Party People*, p. 209, 2002

props *noun*

1 proper respect; due credit *US*
Variant 'propers'.
- [S]lackness (X-rated lyrics), that gave me the props, that made me stick[.]—*Chicago Tribune*, p. 6C, 3rd January 1993
- Fluxy had to give the boy his props.—Karline Smith, *Moss Side Massive*, p. 1, 1994
- —Connie Eble (Editor), *UNC-CH Campus Slang*, p. 6, Spring 1994
- Nobody's giving me props. Nobody.—*Jerry Maguire*, 1996
- I gotta give y'all props on the whole "Power 30" issue[.]—*The Source*, p. 44, March 2002
- —Susie Dent, *The Language Report*, p. 78, 2003

2 false breasts *US*
- —Dale Gordon, *The Dominion Sex Dictionary*, p. 131, 1967

prop up *verb*
to suggest or arrange a story or an explanation, especially through a third person. *UK*
- [W]e must prop a story over this.—David Powis, *The Signs of Crime*, 1977

pros *noun*
in circus and carnival usage, a prosecutor *US*
- —Don Wilmeth, *The Language of American Popular Entertainment*, p. 210, 1981

Prosecute Coppers Association *noun*
the Police Complaints Authority *UK*
A cynical alternative meaning for the PCA; in police use.
- [B]efore the villain's sorry arse had hit the floor the PCA – Prosecute Coppers Association – would be racing eagerly to the scene to seize the weapon and suspend the officer.—Garry Bushell, *The Face*, p. 243, 2001

prospect *noun*
a prospective member of a club or gang *US*
- To become a Hell's Angel, there never has been any initiation rite outside of serving as a prospect.—Ralph "Sonny" Barger, *Hell's Angel*, p. 42, 2000

prospect *verb*
over a period of time, to prove yourself to be a worthy recruit before initiation as a full member of a motorcycle club *US*
- While I was prospecting for Harley Pete I had on old BSA-M21 with a sidecar[.]—Jamie Mandelkau, *Buttons*, p. 52, 1971

pross; pros *noun*
a prostitute *UK, 1905*
- The hotel guys like us prosses better than legits.—John M. Murtagh and Sara Harris, *Cast the First Stone*, p. 6, 1957
- Several of her stable prosses were chatting over too hot cups of coffee, eager to break luck, anxious for Leila to tell them where to turn the first trick of their workday.—Emmett Grogan, *Final Score*, p. 68, 1976
- Douche-Mouth Eddie with a pros named Betty / Was calmly digging the scene.—Dennis Wepman et al., *The Life*, p. 57, 1976
- The typical pross was required to make a $200 quota every night for her pimp, in $20 throws.—Josh Alan Friedman, *Tales of Times Square*, p. 143, 1986

pross collar *noun*
an arrest of a prostitute for a direct solicitation *US*
- Even girls who are found guilty on the more serious "pross collars," involving a specific proposal for a specific price made to a plainclothesman, are rarely jailed.—Gail Sheehy, *Hustling*, p. 15, 1973

prossie; prossy; prozzy *noun*
a prostitute *AUSTRALIA, 1941*
- The husband was a wrong'un – sly grog, SP, prozzies, you name it.—Peter Corries, *Make me Rich*, p. 137, 1985
- [O]nly use Mint [-flavoured condoms] if you find yourself with a Prossie in a car-park in L.A.—Simon Nye and Paul Dornan, *The A-Z of Behaving Badly*, 1995
- Isn't King's Cross where all the prossies hang out, Malcolm?—John Milne, *Alive and Kicking*, p. 87, 1998
- "It's a fucking stinky shit-hole," the guard replied, "full of fucking dope-smokers, prozzies and lazy bastard jungle bunnies."—Ken Lukowiak, *Marijuana Time*, p. 89, 2000
- I think of her out in Kensington, between prozzies and bagheads.—Niall Griffiths, *Kelly + Victor*, p. 17, 2002
- Aye, well, we're all prozzies, really. Just depends who your pimp is.—Andrew Holmes, *Sleb*, p. 304, 2002

prosso *noun*
a prostitute *AUSTRALIA*
- He knew that the boys knew that his mother was a prosso, but he couldn't have cared less.—William Dick, *A Bunch of Ratbags*, p. 161, 1965

pross van *noun*
a police van used in mass arrests of prostitutes *US*
- The last pross van to Night Court leaves the precinct at seven.—Gail Sheehy, *Hustling*, p. 89, 1973

prosty; prostie *noun*
a prostitute *US, 1930*
- Haunt of homos, pinkos, nature lovers and nuts. Chicago's version of London's Hyde Park with soap boxers and prosties.—Jack Lait and Lee Mortimer, *Chicago Confidential*, p. 289, 1950
- And then she was on top of me, working me up like a Paris prostie[.]—Roger Gordon, *Hollywood's Sexual Underground*, p. 140, 1966
- Check all stationhouse john/prostie lists – try for information on Lucille's tricks.—James Ellroy, *White Jazz*, p. 54, 1992

Prot *noun*
▷ see: **PROD**

protection *noun*
1 contraception, especially a condom *US*
• —Dale Gordon, *The Dominion Sex Dictionary*, p. 133, 1967
• Oh sure, we'll need protection.—Evan Hunter, *Last Summer*, p. 173, 1968
• Padre, fucking that pig without a rubber is like playing the Rams without a helmet. Hope you got protection.—Joseph Wambaugh, *The Choirboys*, p. 325, 1975
2 an extortion scheme in which the victim pays the extorting party to protect him from crime, especially crime committed by the extorting party *US*
• It was his speciality, selling protection.—Elmore Leonard, *Be Cool*, p. 182, 1999

protein shake *noun*
in the pornography industry, semen that is swallowed *US*
• —*Adult Video News*, p. 51, October 1995

proto *noun*
protection from prosecution by law enforcement *US*
• Do you know why? I'll tell you. I'm working under proto.—William J. Spillard and Pence James, *Needle in a Haystack*, p. 127, 1945

proverbial; proverbials *noun*
used as a general-purpose euphemism *UK, 1984*
Always reliant on context for sense.
• [T]he Donnas [in concert] were tighter than a gnat's proverbial.—*X-Ray*, p. 21, May 2003

provo *noun*
1 a 1960s Dutch counterculture revolutionary *NETHERLANDS*
• Amsterdam 1966 Masses of provos and construction workers besiege offices of the ex-facist newspaper De Telegraaf.—Richard Neville, *Play Power*, p. 20, 1970
2 a military police officer *AUSTRALIA, 1943*
From *prov*ost marshall. Can be used with a capital: 'Provo'.
• —Frank Hardy, *The Outcasts of Foolgarah*, p. 32, 1971
• —Frank Hardy, *The Outcasts of Foolgarah*, p. 131, 1971
• People said his wife had run away with a Yankee provo on R&R from Vietnam.'—Frank Hardy, *Hardy's People*, p. 203, 1986

Provo; Provie; Provvie *noun*
a member of the *Prov*isional wing of the IRA, subsequently *Prov*isional IRA *UK: NORTHERN IRELAND, 1971*
More than a simple abbreviation, Provo is probably influenced by 'provo' (a member of a group of 1960s Dutch political activists) derived from French *provocateur* (an aggressor).
• [H]e called his ex-Provo padroni[.]—James Hawes, *Dead Long Enough*, p. 255, 2000
• [H]e was an IRA-supporting, Provo-loving, Proddy-hating, terrorist-sypathising wannabe Irishman[.]—Christopher Brookmyre, *The Sacred Art of Stealing*, p. 52, 2002

provvy *noun*
an approved school (for juvenile offenders) *UK*
• —Angus Hall, *On the Run*, 1974

prozie *noun*
a branded antidepressant Prozac™ tablet *UK*
• CALL IT... Spikers, prozie JUST DON'T CALL IT... The "Happy" Pill—*Drugs An Adult Guide*, p. 35, December 2001

prozine *noun*
a professionally published fan magazine *US*
• —*American Speech*, p. 53, Spring 1978: 'Star Trek lives: trekker slang'

prozzy *noun*
a girl who is (allegedly) sexually available *UK*
Derogatory; shortened from 'prostitute'.
• We didn't use the word "slapper" in our school in the early Sixties. The most derogatory term you could apply to a girl was "prozzy", and that was reserved for an ugly lass from the back end of Burley.—Alan Titchmarsh, *Trowell and Error*, p. 90, 2002

Pru *noun*
▸ **the Pru**
the Prudential Insurance Company *UK, 1927*
• [T]he top-notch safe-breaker who turns over the strong-room at the Pru[.]—Charles Raven, *Underworld Nights*, p. 85, 1956
• No harm done to the peaceable citizenry like me and you, unless you happened to be the Man from the Pru.—Andrew Nickolds, *Back to Basics*, p. 105, 1994

prune *noun*
the anus *US*
An allusion to the wrinkles found on each.
• She kept it on the mantel when she wasn't cramming it in your mammy's prune.—Malcolm Braly, *On the Yard*, p. 32, 1967
• I guess by now you know what MY FANTASY will be about: the old prune, that tight little chocolate path[.]—*Screw*, p. 6, 20th November 1972
• —Paul Glover, *Words from the House of the Dead*, 1974

prune *verb*
to out-race someone in a car race from a stationary position *US*
• —*American Speech*, p. 271, December 1962: 'The language of traffic policemen'

prune and plum; prune *noun*
the buttocks; occasionally and specifically, the anus, the rectum *UK*
Rhyming slang for **BUM**.
• Prod it up your prune.—Ray Puxley, *Fresh Rabbit*, 1998

prune pusher *noun*
the active participant in anal sex *US*
• —*Maledicta*, p. 232, 1979: 'Kinks and queens: linguistic and cultural aspects of the terminology for gays'

prunes *noun*
testicles; courage *US*
• He had prunes, they whispered to one another. Manny's prunes were big as honeydews. Manny Lopez had balls to the walls!—Joseph Wambaugh, *Lines and Shadows*, p. 141, 1984

pruno *noun*
a potent, homemade alcohol, often made with fermented prune juice *US*
• After Lights Joe uncapped a Maxwell House coffee jar of pruno, as prison hootch was called.—Seth Morgan, *Homeboy*, p. 302, 1990
• They had had "pruno" cocktail parties on all three tiers[.]—Odie Hawkins, *Great Lawd Buddha*, p. 57, 1990
• —William Bentley, *Prison Slang*, p. 70, 1992

Prussian *noun*
a male homosexual who prefers the active role in anal sex *US*
• —Hyman E. Goldin et al., *Dictionary of American Underworld Lingo*, p. 164, 1950

P's *noun*
parents *US*
• —Pamela Munro, *U.C.L.A. Slang*, p. 68, 1989

PS *noun*
*p*enal *s*ervitude *UK, 1923*
An abbreviation. This type of prison sentence was ordered from the C19 until 1948.
• [S]entences were comparatively light, an even three years' p.s. all round.—Charles Raven, *Underworld Nights*, p. 99, 1956

p's and q's *noun*
shoes *UK*
Rhyming slang.
• —Ray Puxley, *Cockney Rabbit*, 1992

▸ **mind your p's and q's**
to be careful, exact, prudent *UK, 1779*
Perhaps, as Farmer and Henley suggest, from 'the old custom of alehouse tally, marking "p" for pint and "q" for quart, care being necessary to avoid over- or under-charging'. Whether the source is in printing, or 'pints and quarts', or learning to read, is unknown.
• It paid to be on your ps n' qs at all times, no tellin' when someone was going to pop in the door and throw a knife, a brick, a bottle, or just simply shoot.—Odie Hawkins, *Chicago Hustle*, p. 177, 1977
• What was liberating was not having to mind my p's and q's. I could mouth off.—*The Guardian*, 15th December 1999
• I don't want to mind my Ps & Qs, whatever they are (note to self: find out what Ps & Qs are).—James Hawes, *White Powder, Green Light*, p. 316, 2002

pseud *noun*
a pretentious, image-conscious person *UK, 1954*
Usage popularised by 'Pseud's Corner' in *Private Eye* magazine.
• —Louis S. Leland, *A Personal Kiwi-Yankee Dictionary*, p. 82, 1984
• Depending on your perspective, this smacks of either fearless groundbreaking or fearful Pseud's Corner pretension.—*The Guardian*, 12th September 2002

pseudo *adjective*
pretentious *UK, 1945*
From the conventional prefix.
• —John Ayto, *The Oxford Dictionary of Slang*, p. 281, 1998

pseudy *adjective*

pretentious *UK, 1989*

A variation of **PSEUDO**.

- What is "political theatre"? Usually it means contemporary plays ranging from the journalistic through the "commitment" play (now not so fashionable) to the ultra-pseudy and obscure. — *The Guardian*, 17th May 2003

psst; psst!

used for attracting someone's attention discretely *IRELAND, 1922*

- They're all selling on commission. If they don't sell, they don't make noithing, so-psst, here he comes!" — Jim Thompson, *The Grifters*, p. 119, 1963
- Often it contains posters, games, coloured comic supplements and always - psst - dirty pictures. — Richard Neville, *Play Power*, p. 173, 1970

psych *noun*

1 psychology; psychiatry *US, 1895*

- I would be up against all those emotional forces the psych books describe. — Erich Segal, *Love Story*, p. 58, 1970

2 a psychiatrist or psychologist *US*

- When I got down to the induction center I said I wanted to see the psych — J. Anthony Lukas, *Don't Shoot - We Are Your Children*, p. 436, 1971

psych; psych up *verb*

to use *psych*ological techniques to stimulate, to enthuse, to excite *US, 1957*

- Peter Mandelson [...] would have seen it as part of the programme to psych up the party staff for the election campaign over which he was, until so recently, in almost complete control. — *The Guardian*, 6th February 2001

psych *adjective*

psychedelic, when used in combination with a type of music or musicans, e.g. 'psych rock' or 'psych band' *UK*

- [Hawkwind]'re one of the only psych bands to have made a good record, namely "Silver Machine". — *X-Ray*, p. 71, November 2003

psyche!

I fooled you! *US*

- Pysche! You thought I forgot about your daughter Mary's wedding. — *New Jack City*, 1990

psyched *adjective*

excited, enthusiastic *US, 1970*

- I'm so psyched for this concert. Aerosmith is going to kick ass! — *Wayne's World 2*, 1993
- My colds and sore throats disappeared. I was psyched. — Howard Stern, *Miss America*, p. 109, 1995

psychedelic martini *noun*

DMT, a short-lasting hallucinogen *US*

- — William D. Alsever, *Glossary for the Establishment and Other Uptight People*, p. 9, December 1970

psycher; neo-psycher *noun*

a musician or fan of psychedelic rock or neo-psychodelia *UK*

From **PSYCH**.

- [O]ther neo-psychers include fellow LA residents The Brian Jonestown Massacre, Spiritualized, and even The Flaming Lips. — *X-Ray*, p. 71, November 2003

psychic energizer *noun*

an amphetamine or other central nervous system stimulant *US*

- Amphetamine, that group of drugs which are called pep pills by squares. They are also called psychic energizers. — Ruth Bronsteen, *The Hippy's Handbook*, p. 12, 1967

psycho *noun*

a psychopath, or someone who is otherwise psychologically disturbed *US, 1942*

- I was an escapee from an insane asylum, a pyscho with a gun, an ex-pug who cold do plenty without a gun if he took a notion. — Jim Thompson, *After Dark, My Sweet*, p. 107, 1955
- I hated what the word meant. I hated the sound of it at once. "psycho" had a sudden mental-ward reality about it, a systematic, diagnostic sound. — John Knowles, *A Separate Peace*, p. 135, 1959
- They're a special breed of psycho. — Robert Gover, *The Maniac Responsible*, p. 211, 1963
- He seemed to balloon with rage, transforming himself from an elder-statesmen dope dealer back to the psycho stickup man from the seventies[.] — Richard Price, *Clockers*, p. 181, 1992
- The way I hear it, Soze is some kind of butcher. A pitiless, psycho, fucked-up butcher. — *The Usual Suspects*, 1995
- He stops the van in the middle of the road an' gets out like a fuckin' psycho. — Nick Barlay, *Curvy Lovebox*, p. 87, 1997
- Mary, he sounds like a psycho. — *Something About Mary*, 1998

psycho *adjective*

1 psychiatric or psychological *US, 1927*

- He's in the pscyho ward. He needs some horse. — Clarence Cooper Jr, *The Scene*, p. 66, 1960
- It's one of those things I hid from the psycho team all these years. — Mickey Spillane, *Last Cop Out*, p. 15, 1972
- I think Riggs is pulling for a psycho pension. — *Lethal Weapon*, 1987
- They always got those signs around hospitals that says QUIET, and if I was to go into that shimmy act, they'd probably throw me into the pyscho ward and I'll never get out. — *Drugstore Cowboy*, 1988
- You're on leave, man. You're on pyscho leave. — *Basic Instinct*, 1992

2 crazy *US, 1936*

An abbreviation of 'psychopathic'.

- Besides being psycho, she was unintelligent and illiterate, practically, and probably wouldn't understand it anyhow. — Robert Gover, *One Hundred Dollar Misunderstanding*, p. 148, 1961

psychobabble *noun*

psychological and pseudo-psychological jargon *US, 1976*

Derogatory. Popularised, but not coined, by R.D. Rosen in *Psychobabble*, 1977.

- Yeah, it's all the psychobabble in that blunt summary. — Bill Cardoso, *The Maltese Sangweech*, p. 111, 1984
- — *American Speech*, p. 373–374, Winter 1984: 'Coinage of psychobabble'
- Please, spare me the psycho-babble father bullshit. — *A Few Good Men*, 1992
- Would you cut the psychobabble bullshit, mom. — *Cruel Intentions*, 1999

psycho block *noun*

an area in a prison where the most violent prisoners are held *US*

- The tiers in Quentin or Folsom they call psycho blocks. — Vincent Patrick, *Family Business*, p. 244, 1985

psychopathic *noun*

traffic *UK*

Rhyming slang, inspired, perhaps, by the state of mind that you (or the driver behind you) get into when stuck in traffic.

- — Ray Puxley, *Fresh Rabbit*, 1998

psych out *verb*

1 to intimidate someone completely on a psychological level *US*

- Arnold was able to totally psyche out any confidence Ferigno had. — *Natural Born Killers*, 1994

2 to lose your mental composure or stability *UK*

- I psyched out! I was punching and kicking him, demanding that he should fight back. — Jamie Mandelkau quoting Ken Kesey, *Buttons*, p. 155–156, 1971

3 to figure out or discover something *US*

- You'll learn to psyche out the regulars. — Armistead Maupin, *Tales of the City*, p. 155, 1978

PT *noun*

1 a woman who promises more sex than she delivers *US*

An abbreviation of **PRICK-TEASER**.

- That goddamn P.T. Listen, once I was with her in this guy's car and — Willard Motley, *Let No Man Write My Epitaph*, p. 179, 1958
- — Helen Dahlskog (Editor), *A Dictionary of Contemporary and Colloquial Usage*, p. 46, 1972
- "She's the biggest little PT in town," a tall girl who reminded Jack of one of the Andrew Sisters turned to advise him. — Earl Thompson, *Tattoo*, p. 42, 1974

2 in sports, playing time *US*

- — Don R. McCreary (Editor), *Dawg Speak*, 2001

PTA *noun*

a hasty washing by a female *US*

In the US, the most common association with PTA is the school-support Parent-Teacher Association. The PTA in question here refers to the woman's *p*ussy, *t*its and *a*ss.

- — Eugene Landy, *The Underground Dictionary*, p. 155, 1971

ptomaine palace *noun*

a restaurant serving inexpensive, low quality food *UK*

- For Steering You Away From That Ptomaine Palace [Headline] — *Chronicle Telegram (Elyria, Ohio)*, 2nd February 1952
- He flatly refused to patronize the local ptomaine palaces. — *Ironwood (Michigan) Daily Globe*, 13th February 1965
- — Wayne Floyd, *Jason's Authentic Dictionary of CB Slang*, p. 25, 1976

- This would be Hardin's speed, she decided: a roadside ptomaine palace that looked, to Colleen, like a woodshed out of God's Little Acre. —Dean Ing, *The Nemesis Mission*, p. 175, 1991
- I jogged across Pacific Coast Highway, after eating dinner at a rustic little ptomaine palace called the Pull Pen, and positioned myself as near as I could to the Doc's stage-table. — *Fling*, March 1991
- The place was a ptomaine palace if ever there was one. A gutache waiting to happen. —Peter Straub, *Black House*, p. 224, 2001
- [T]hese godforsaken ptomaine palaces still teased me with their solid visual credentials. —Gerry Wood, *Tales From Country Music*, p. 90, 2003

ptomaine wagon *noun*
a catering truck *US, 1937*
- —Judi Sanders, *Kickin' like Chicken with the Couch Commander*, p. 19, 1992
- It begins with a catering truck, like hundreds that ply San Diego work sites. Yes, but this is no ordinary roach coach, ptomaine wagon or gedunk truck. — *Los Angeles Times*, p. 1, 8th July 1992

P-town *nickname*
Provincetown, Massachusetts *US*
- It's easy to treat P-town as though it were a simple summer spot where you could go and find a place for some quick and good sex. — *Drummer: America's Mag for the Macho Male*, p. 76, 1980
- —Jeff Fessler, *When Drag Is Not a Car Race*, p. 64, 1997

PU!
used for registering disgust of anything that smells *US, 1960*
A jocular spelling (pronounce each letter) of the two syllable stretching of 'phew'.

pub *noun*
a *pub*lic house, an inn, a tavern *UK, 1859*
- It's got a pub, a small one and not many people. —Max Fatchen, *Chase through the Night*, p. 5, 1976
- As in all Australian pubs at the time, the beer came in two kinds, New and Old[.] —Clive James, *Unreliable Memoirs*, p. 131, 1992
- Alcoholics do run the best pubs —Andrew McGahan,, *Prise*, p. 88, 1992
- His evenings would be mapped out by the various intricate routes from pub to pub that characterised the night out in town. —Malcolm Pryce, *Aberystwyth Mon Amour*, p. 11, 2001

pub band *noun*
a band of musicians who play principally in public hotels *AUSTRALIA*
Pub rock, an umbrella genre for such bands and their music, was popular in the UK in the mid-1970s, and is seen as the precursor to **PUNK ROCK**.
- Besides Chasin' the Train, bands such as The Hippos, Mal Eastick, Doc Span Blues Band and others, are doing well on the live circuit as 'pub bands,' with big followings. — *On The Street*, p. 15, 2nd March 1988

pubber *noun*
a publisher, especially of a single-interest fan magazine *US*
- — *American Speech*, p. 28, Spring 1982: 'The language of science fiction fan magazines'

pub-crawl *noun*
a drinking session that moves from one licensed premises to the next, and so on *UK, 1915*
Combines **PUB** (a public house, licensed for the sale of alcohol) with a less-and-less figurative sense of 'crawl'.
- ROSE: Did you go out with the boys last night? TONY: Usual pub-crawl. ROSE: Hangover? —Alexander Baron, *A Bit of Happiness [Six Granada Plays]*, p. 211, 1959

pub-crawl *verb*
to move in a group from one drinking establishment to the next, drinking at each *UK, 1937*
- They pub-crawled through the night and wound up in a twenty four hour restaurant that was Spain's version of Denny's. —Odie Hawkins, *The Life and Times of Chester Simmons*, p. 34, 1991

pub dog sex *noun*
an act of sex performed under a pub table *UK*

pube *noun*
a high school girl *US*
- — *Current Slang*, p. 9, Winter 1969

▸**get pube**
in the categorisation of sexual activity by teenage boys, to touch a girl's vulva *US*
- Next in order of significant intimacy was "getting silk," which meant touching panty-crotch, and then for the more successful, "getting pube." —Terry Southern, *Now Dig This*, p. 3, 1986

pube *adjective*
*pube*scent *US*
- What a pube punk fantasy! —Lester Bangs, *Psychotic Reactions and Carburetor Dung*, p. 58, 1970
- Real pedophiles try and convince everyone it's OK to boink pre-pub kids —Nancy Tamosaitis, *net.sex*, p. 113, 1995

pubes *noun*
pubic hair *US*
- [T]he camera (voyeur's POV) finds occasion to linger, in a desultory, almost caressing fashion, on her pubes. —Terry Southern, *Blue Movie*, p. 24, 1970
- Making a face, she concentrated on fluffing her pubes with a broken-toothed comb. —Seth Morgan, *Homeboy*, p. 22, 1990
- A year has passed. I'm older. I'm wiser. Garth got pubes. —*Wayne's World 2*, 1993
- I'd first puked about six but had felt well enough to go on, staring at the pubes spinning in the broken toilet bowl. —David Peace, *Nineteen Seventy-Four*, p. 102, 1999
- [T]he baby's still got your pubes stuck behind its ears. —Jenny Eclair, *Camberwell Beauty*, p. 56, 2000
- Probably plaits her pubes into a six inch stumb so she can shake it after having a piss. —Jack Allen, *When the Whistle Blows*, p. 106, 2000
- She told me that women who style their pubes often have a better relationship with their pussies as a result of preening them on a regular basis. — *The Village Voice*, 8th–14th November 2000
- Supposedly she flashes some pubes. That's how she got her name in Spin. —Carl Hiaasen, *Basket Case*, p. 18, 2002
- I sucked Miss's tits and I know what colour pubes she has. — *Sunday Times (South Africa)*, 13th April 2003

pubies *noun*
pubic hairs *US*
- —Collin Baker et al., *College Undergraduate Slang Study Conducted at Brown University*, p. 177, 1968
- He sat up and picked a few pubies like flecks of tobacco from the tip of his tongue —Richard Price, *The Wanderers*, p. 99, 1974
- I'm still missing half my pubies from the first day here and the ones I got left aren't but a half-inch long —John Sayles, *Union Dues*, p. 14, 1977

public relations *noun*
a member of a swindling enterprise who promotes the swindle *US*
- —Robert C. Prus and C.R.D. Sharper, *Road Hustler*, p. 171, 1977: 'Glossary of terms'

pub pet *noun*
a two litre plastic container for draught beer *NEW ZEALAND*
- Depending on regional expressions [draught-beer containers] are variously known as a 'jar', 'peter', 'half-gee' (half-gallon) or the more modern 'pub pet' two-litre plastic bottle. — *Pacific Way*, p. 50, July 1988

puck *noun*
1 in a number of casino games, a disc used to mark a point or position *US*
- —Victor H. Royer, *Casino Gamble Talk*, p. 108, 2003

2 a car brake pad *US*
- —John Edwards, *Auto Dictionary*, p. 131, 1993

pucker *noun*
the anus *US*
- You'll pardon me if I ask you to kiss my pucker. — *The Usual Suspects*, 1995

pucker factor *noun*
the degree of fear or anxiety *US*
From the image of the sphincter tightening in a frightening situation.
- — *Maledicta*, p. 255, Summer/Winter 1982: 'Viet-Speak'
- His eyes are glued to the tube in Saudi Arabia, watchful of any sinister dots that tells him a Scud is on its way and it's time to neutralize it by launching a Patriot missile. Anxieties, which he calls "the pucker factor," are high. — *USA Today*, 1st February 1991

puckeroo *adjective*
useless, broken *NEW ZEALAND*
- —Sonya Plowman, *Great Kiwi Slang*, p. 142, 2002

pucker paint *noun*
lipstick *CANADA*
Teen slang, reported by a Toronto newspaper in 1946, and reported as 'obsolescent or obsolete' by Douglas Leechman, 1959.

pucker palace *noun*
a drive-in cinema *US*
High school student usage.
- — *San Francisco Examiner*, p. 21, 12th December 1961

pucker up *verb*

1 to tighten your rectal and anal muscles *US*
- Well, they like you to squeeze yourself up, you know, so it would be tighter. They call it puckering up. And they like to put it in and bring it out and you just all the time squeezing on it. — Bruce Jackson, *In the Life*, p. 399, 1972

2 to behave sycophantically *UK*
- [H]e was about to pucker up to the God squad [church authorities]. It could not possibly get any worse than this. — Christopher Brookmyre, *Boiling a Frog*, p. 327, 2000

pud *noun*

a pudding *UK, 1943*
- Then for pud we have sponge covered with chocolate icing, fresh fruit salad, yoghurts, and cheese and biscuits. — *The Observer*, 7th December 2003

▸ **pound your pud; pull your pud; pull your pudding**

(of a male) to masturbate *UK, 1944*
- Well don't just lay there in your sleeping bag pullin your puddin, get up and fetch some water. — Jack Kerouac, *The Dharma Bums*, p. 164, 1958
- He picked up Rocky's limp cock, nursed it with his tongue back into a hard-on, and gave him the wildest, frenziedest, freakiest blow job his world had ever seen, while he pounded his own pud. — Steve Cannon, *Groove, Bang, and Jive Around*, p. 186, 1969
- The opportunity for more expansive progress came when a guy pulled on my stiff pud and allowed me to pull his at the same time. — *Screw*, p. 14, 9th May 1969
- I'm a wanker, I'm a wanker / And I'm always pulling my pud. — Ivor Biggun, *The Winker's Song (Misprint)*, 1978
- when I used to really dig pulling my pud to pix of 'em in the magazines. — Lester Bangs, *Psychotic Reactions and Carburetor Dung*, p. 334–335, 1980
- I told him about the first time I pounded my pud and which hand I used. — Joseph Wambaugh, *Lines and Shadows*, p. 329, 1984

pudding *noun*

1 money *US*
- — Kenn "Naz" Young, *Naz's Dictionary of Teen Slang*, p. 89, 1993

2 the penis *UK, 1719*

The abbreviation 'pud' does not appear until the 1930s.

pudding and gravy; the pudding *noun*

the Royal Navy *UK*

Rhyming slang.
- — Julian Franklyn, *A Dictionary of Rhyming Slang*, 1961

pudding-basin *noun*

a hairstyle that looks as though a basin has been inverted over the head and the hair cut up to the rim of the basin *UK, 1951*
- Dear Mo [Mowlam] has her problems and her wig is one of them. Is it just me who thinks the pudding-basin style is a wasted opportunity? — *New Statesman*, 18th July 1997

pudding club *noun*

▸ **in the pudding club**

pregnant *UK, 1890*
- In the pudding club first time and cannae even remember who the father was. — M.C. Beaton, *Death of a Poison Pen*, p. 105, 2004

pudding wagon *noun*

in circus and carnival usage, a frozen custard truck *US*
- — Don Wilmeth, *The Language of American Popular Entertainment*, p. 211, 1981

puddle *noun*

a generous dose of liquid LSD *US*
- — David Shenk and Steve Silberman, *Skeleton Key*, p. 239, 1994

puddle about *verb*

to busy yourself doing nothing *NEW ZEALAND*
- — Louis S. Leland, *A Personal Kiwi-Yankee Dictionary*, p. 76, 1984

puddle-jumper *noun*

1 a small plane making a relatively short journey *US, 1961*
- You have sat next to him in a hundred airport bars, waiting for a connection between Atlanta and Memphis, or Atlanta and Little Rock, or Atlanta and hell (a puddle-jumper). — *Washington Post*, p. A25, 21st June 2001

2 in trucking, a lightweight truck *US*
- — Montie Tak, *Truck Talk*, p. 123, 1971

puddy tat *noun*

a cat *US*

From the Looney Tunes cartoons with Sylvester the cat and Tweety Bird, with Tweety Bird's constant mantra of 'I taut I taw a puddy-tat' (I thought I saw a pussy cat).
- Take a look. The puddy tat's out of the bag. — Carl Hiaasen, *Tourist Season*, p. 331, 1986

pudge *noun*

a short squat person; anything short and thick; someone who is overweight *UK*

A probable variant of **PODGE** (a short and fat person).
- You can always spot the one who's meant to be the songwriter in these [boy] bands. It's the uncomfortable looking pudge who can't dance properly[.] — John Robb, *The Nineties*, p. 280, 1999

pudgy *adjective*

short and fat *UK, 1836*
- the image of the Tudor king that fascinates us today: corpulent, piggy-eyed, monarchical to every pudgy finger — *The Guardian*, 27th May 2004

pud puller *noun*

a male masturbator *US*
- A pudpuller at the movies that night said one of them called the other Joe. — Seth Morgan, *Homeboy*, p. 206, 1990

pudwapper *noun*

a male masturbator; hence, a despicable person *US*

Combines 'pud' (the penis) with 'w(h)ap' (to hit).
- KURT: That pudwapper just stepped on my foot. RAK: Let's kick his ass. — *Heathers*, 1988

puff *noun*

1 a homosexual man; a weak, effeminate man *UK, 1902*

Pejorative; probably a variation of **POOF**.
- I was such a puff. — Boy George, *Ask*, p. 24, 1st May 1982
- KNIGHTY: He keeps calling me a puff. DARCY: It's just [boxing] ring banter, tell him you've slept with his mother. — Paul Fraser and Shane Meadows, *TwentyFourSeven*, p. 95, 1997
- [E]ven trying my hardest I'd get a battering from these blokes. [...] You certainly wouldn't call them "puffs", put it that way. — Dave Courtney, *Raving Lunacy*, p. 45, 2000
- Neither of us wore seatbelts – we thought they were for puffs[.] — Frank Skinner, *Frank Skinner*, p. 221, 2001
- Aw get yewer fuckin coat on boy. Shed's only ten fuckin yards away, don't be such a fuckin puff. — Niall Griffiths, *Sheepshagger*, p. 128, 2001

2 marijuana *UK, 1987*

From **PUFF** (to smoke marijuana). Also variant 'puffy'.
- [H]e left and popped into town to try to score some puff. — Colin Butts, *Is Harry on the Boat?*, p. 38, 1997
- Alaskan weed [..] was – and is – the strongest puff I've ever smoked, or am ever likely to. — Wayne Anthony, *Spanish Highs*, p. 111, 1999
- Most gangsters thought drugs was drugs was drugs, meaning that they thought that smoking puff was the same as injecting heroin in your eye. — Dave Courtney, *Raving Lunacy*, p. 6, 2000
- [S]o we headed through Colnbrook to a house where we could normally score a bit of puff. — Jimmy Stockin, *On The Cobbles*, p. 124, 2000
- [T]he officer on call was from the dog section. His hound went mad at all the puff and the pair [of drug smugglers] were busted[.] — *Ministry*, p. 34, January 2002

3 breath *UK*

A puff of wind.
- I'm just dancing, to be fair, just trying to get away from the cunt long enough to get my puff back – then I can come back and finish the job. — Kevin Sampson, *Outlaws*, p. 201–202, 2001

4 existence; life-span *UK, 1921*
- [Rehearsals for "Waiting for Godot" were] the most gruelling that I have ever experienced in all my puff. — Peter Bull, *I Know the Face, but...*, 1959

5 a charge of explosives *US*
- — Vincent J. Monteleone, *Criminal Slang*, p. 184, 1949

▸ **on your puff**

on your own, alone *UK*
- This boy's jist sittin oan ehs puff readin the News ken? — Irvine Welsh, *The State of the Party (Disco Biscuits)*, p. 33, 1995

puff *verb*

to smoke marijuana *UK*
- I puffed before I smoked any fags. — Macfarlane, Macfarlane and Robson, *The User*, p. 1, 1996
- Cos all the people that puffed were sort of like-minded people anyway, even though they might be from different walks of life, puffing was founded in the sort of anti-establishment, don't-give-a-fuck side of society anyway. — Dave Courtney, *Raving Lunacy*, p. 52, 2000
- — Mike Haskins, *Drugs*, p. 290, 2003

▸ **puff the dragon; puff the magic dragon**

1 to smoke marijuana *UK, 1998*
'Puff, The Magic Dragon', 1963, a song by Peter, Paul and Mary, is, according to a popular myth, about smoking marijuana or a weapon of war – nothing in the lyric sustains this but nevertheless the song inspired this term.
- — Mike Haskins, *Drugs*, p. 290, 2003

2 to perform oral sex on a man *US*
Plays on **DRAGON** (the penis) and the song 'Puff, The Magic Dragon'.
- — Erica Orloff and JoAnn Baker, *Dirty Little Secrets*, p. 83, 2001

puffa; puffa jacket *noun*
an extravagantly bulky jacket generally made of lightweight synthetic materials *UK, 1991*
Surely coined by marketing experts to account for the fashion-garment's puffed-up appearance.
- I do the heavy work, all padded up as usual, wearing a puffa jacket so I look about twice my normal size. — Nicholas Blincoe, *The Beautiful Beaten-up Irish Boy of the Arndale Centre*, p. 1, 1998

puff and dart *noun*
in the dice game crown and anchor, a heart *UK*
Rhyming slang, probably dating from about 1860 but first recorded in 1936.

puff and drag *noun*
a cigarette *UK*
Rhyming slang for **FAG**.
- — Ray Puxley, *Cockney Rabbit*, 1992

puffed *adjective*
exhausted *NEW ZEALAND*
- — Louis S. Leland, *A Personal Kiwi-Yankee Dictionary*, p. 83, 1984

puffer *noun*

1 a marijuana smoker *UK*
- Cannabis can be part of the therapy to get people off heroin [...] Puffers need to know about that[.] — Brian Preston, *Pot Planet*, p. 132, 2002

2 a crack cocaine user *US*
- — US Department of Justice, *Street Terms*, October 1994

3 in drag racing and hot rodding, a supercharger *US*
- — Lyle K. Engel, *The Complete Book of Fuel and Gas Dragsters*, p. 153, 1968

puff-juice *noun*
men's toiletries *UK*
Based on **PUFF** (a male homosexual).
- My dad's only concession to men's toiletries, or "puff-juice" as most local males called it, was his use of Old Spice after-shave. — Frank Skinner, *Frank Skinner*, p. 34, 2001

Puff the Magic Dragon; Puff *nickname*
a C-47 aircraft modified as a gunship and redesignated an AC47, heavily used by the US Air Force in Vietnam *US*
From the gentle 1963 folk song recorded by Peter, Paul and Mary.
- 'Puff the Magic Dragon' is among the many kinds of weapons, old and new, serving in the war against the Viet cong. — *The Berkeley Barb*, p. 6, 28 January 1966
- Belmonte recognized its silhouette; it was the type of plane known as "Puff the Magic Dragon." — Neil Sheehan, *The Arnheiter Affair*, p. 191, 1971
- With the spotting plane came the large support plane, Puff the Magic Dragon. — Charles Anderson, *The Grunts*, p. 131, 1976
- Puff, the DC-3 with the Gattlings, blasted unbroken tongues of fire from the black sky. — Robert Mason, *Chickenhawk*, p. 417, 1983

pug *noun*

1 a boxer; a fighter *UK, 1850s?*
A shortened form of the conventional 'pugilist.'
- Feivel was a former pug, a lightweight who had battled it out with Lew Tendler and Abe Attell[.] — Irving Shulman, *The Amboy Dukes*, p. 53, 1947
- On the main floor, facing Broadway, are two cafes – the Turf, hangout for musicians, and Dempsey's, rendezvous of pugs. — Jack Lait and Lee Mortimer, *New York Confidential*, p. 31, 1948
- Scraggs, a thirty-seven-year-old ex-pug who once fought Bobo Olson, was the oldest Angel then riding[.] — Hunter S. Thompson, *Hell's Angels*, p. 7, 1966
- I was thinkin' myself, among other things, half a pug in them days. — Edwin Torres, *Carlito's Way*, p. 11, 1975

2 a male homosexual *US*
- — William K. Bentley and James M. Corbett, *Prison Slang*, p. 50, 1992

3 in trucking, a cabover tractor *US*
- — Montie Tak, *Truck Talk*, p. 123, 1971

pug *verb*
to fight *US*
- — Ellen C. Bellone (Editor), *Dictionary of Slang*, p. 18, 1989
- — Ann Lawson, *Kids & Gangs*, p. 56, 1994: 'Common African-American gang slang/phrases'

puggie *noun*
a hardened criminal *US*
- Teen-age girls, first offenders, some of them merely awating trial, are heaped in with "institutionalized" old puggies who feel like bigger shots inside than out. — Tom Wolfe, *The Kandy-Kolored Tangerine-Flake Streamline Baby*, p. 309, 1965

puggled *adjective*
given to foolish behaviour; tipsy *UK: SCOTLAND*
- You must've been puggled when you put that shelf up. — Michael Munro, *The Patter*, p. 55, 1985

puggy *noun*
a kitty in a card game; a one-armed bandit; an ATM cash dispenser *UK: SCOTLAND*
From a Scots word for 'monkey'.
- — Michael Munro, *The Original Patter*, p. 55, 1985
- Puzzles, from activating lifts to access new areas, to punching a puggy machine to line up health-boosting hamburgers or V-Medals, help keep the action fresh and let you catch your breath. — *Dundee Evening Telegraph*, 5th November 2003

▸ **full as a puggy**
very drunk; having eaten too much *UK: SCOTLAND, 85*
- — Michael Munro, *The Original Patter*, p. 55, 1985
- Burns is stotting out of a gathering of the Crochallan Fencibles, fu' as a puggy, pickin' his way through the vennels to Potter Row to tickle up his Nancy. — W.Gordon Smith, *Mr Jock*, 1987

▸ **take a puggy**
to become very angry *UK: SCOTLAND*
- The boss'll take a puggy if he sees this. — Michael Munro, *The Original Patter*, p. 55, 1985

puggy work *noun*
hard physical labour *UK: SCOTLAND*
From a Scots word for 'monkey'.
- It's awright fur you, sittin on yer arse giein [giving] oot orders, an it's me that's tae dae [to do] the puggy work. — Michael Munro, *The Patter, Another Blast*, p. 56, 1988

pug-ugly *adjective*
very ugly *UK*
Probably a confusion with **PLUG-UGLY** (a thug); based on the appearance of a **PUG** (a boxer) or the broad wrinkled face of a 'pug' (a breed of dog).
- She's highly intelligent, but pug-ugly. — Pete McCarthy, *McCarthy's Bar*, p. 227, 2000

pug up *verb*
to hide something *UK*
- What am I, a pilchard? I had it delivered. It's been pugged up in the room and it goes before we check out. — Garry Bushell, *The Face*, p. 209, 2001

puh-lease
▹ **see: PLEASE**

puke *noun*

1 vomit *US, 1961*
- Kate spews out some puke and I close my eyes and waits. — Ralph Ellison, *Invisible Man*, p. 5, 1952

2 a despised person *US*
In the mid-C19, the term was applied with some degree of scorn to residents of the state of Missouri; it later gained a broader sense. In *Rogue Warrior*, Richard Marcinko gives a virtual litany of pukes – Academy puke, admin puke, fleet puke, jet puke, puke ensign, staff puke and Team-puke.
- — *American Speech*, p. 282, December 1966: 'More carnie talk from the West Coast'
- The roof is is crowded with kids, some with binoculars. One is yelling, "Scorecard! Scorecard! Can't tell the cops from the pukes without a scorecard." — James Simon Kunen, *The Strawberry Statement*, p. 49, 1968
- Anyway, there were five of us in the park that night and for fifteen minutes we all battle that puke. — Joseph Wambaugh, *The New Centurions*, p. 218–219, 1970
- [H]e wasn't able to picture the great Viceroy Wilson – bad hands, bankrupt and all – rubbing elbow with a bunch of pukes at Pauly's. — Carl Hiaasen, *Tourist Season*, p. 48, 1986
- But until that day you are pukes. You're the lowest form of life on Earth. — *Full Metal Jacket*, 1987
- Me? I don't know, I'm only a staff puke. — Gerry Carroll, *North S*A*R*, p. 237, 1991

puke *verb*

1 to vomit *UK, 1600*

- [Eli] Roth has told of how he puked the first time he saw Alien, and puked again thereafter during dozens of blood-drenched Z-grade gore flicks[.] — *The Guardian*, 26th September 2003

2 in the illegal production of alcohol, to allow the still to boil over *US*

- Don't throw no more wood on that fire, you'll puke the still. — David W. Maurer, *Kentucky Moonshine*, p. 122, 1974

3 while on a combat air mission, to separate out from formation while under attack *US*

- — *American Speech*, p. 124, Summer 1986: 'The language of naval fighter pilots'

▸ **puke your ring up**

to vomit violently *UK*

- Can't drink a fuckin sediment, like, yew'd be over in Bronglais puking yewer ring up. — Niall Griffiths, *Sheepshagger*, p. 133, 2001

puke hole *noun*

a shabby, shoddy, dirty place *US*

- I spotted a paddy hustler taking a guy up the back stairs of the Marlowe Hotel, a sleazy Main Street puke hole used by whores and fruits and paddy hustlers. — Joseph Waubaugh, *The Blue Knight*, p. 203, 1973

pukepot *noun*

a despicable person *US*

- I was filled with loathing for a pukepot like Zoot[.] — Joseph Wambaugh, *The Blue Knight*, p. 56, 1973

puker *noun*

a tourist *US*

In Alaska, an allusion to the tendency of tourists on fishing charters to get seasick.

- — Jim Crotty, *How to Talk American*, p. 10, 1997

puking buzzards *nickname*

the 101st Airborne Division, US Army *US*

From the official nickname of 'Screaming Eagles'.

- — Linda Reinberg, *In the Field*, p. 175, 1991

pukka *adjective*

certain; reliable; genuine; hence excellent; fashionable *UK, c.1776*

Derives from Hindu *pakka* which has the meaning of 'substantial'.

- TAYLOR: We weren't expecting anybody. WATSON [LOOKS UP] This is pukka. This bloke's a replacement for Reed. — Graeme Kent, *The Queen's Corporal [Six Granada Plays]*, p. 83, 1959
- I've got a spare magazine and fifty rounds of useable ammo included in the price, which is a fuckin' pukka bargain. — Donald Gorgon, *Cop Killer*, p. 60, 1994
- [W]hy doesn't one of us put on a suit and pose as a potential buyer? Get the keys from the agent and go along all pukka? — Chris Ryan, *Stand By, Stand By*, p. 94, 1996
- [T]hose ads were just saying to people that Apples were pukka. — Dave Courtney, *Raving Lunacy*, p. 72, 2000

pulborn; pulboron; polboron *noun*

heroin *US, 1977*

Possibly from Spanish *polvo grande* (big powder).

- — Richard A. Spears, *The Slang and Jargon of Drugs and Drink*, p. 404, 1986
- — Mike Haskins, *Drugs*, p. 284, 2003

pull *noun*

1 in policing, an act of temporarily detaining a suspicious person or vehicle for investigation *UK*

Derived from PULL (to arrest).

2 a woman as a sex object *UK*

- — Bob Young and Micky Moody, *The Language of Rock 'n' Roll*, p. 113, 1985

▸ **on the pull**

engaged in a casual or recreational quest for a sexual partner *UK*

- The score [of Verdi's 'A Masked Ball'] indicates that the royal Gustavus visits the seer disguised as a fisherman, or pescator, but [director, Calixto] Bieto has teased out the slang meaning of the Italian word, which translates loosely as "someone out on the pull". — *The Guardian*, 21st February 2002

pull *verb*

1 (of police) to stop a vehicle; to stop someone for questioning *UK*

A broader usage of the earlier sense 'to arrest'.

- — Peter Laurie, *Scotland Yard*, p. 326, 1970
- — Angela Devlin, *Prison Patter*, p. 90, 1996

2 to arrest someone *UK, 1811*

- The courtroom was full 'cause Bud had been pulled. — Dennis Wepman et al., *The Life*, p. 57, 1976

3 to engage in a casual or recreational quest for a sexual partner *UK, 1965*

- I'm not trying to pull you / Even though I would like to[.] — Mike Skinner, *Fit But You Know It*, 2004

4 to recruit someone into prostitution *US*

- It was there he pulled his first ofay girl. — Babs Gonzales, *I Paid My Dues*, p. 99, 1967
- I was traveling with my partner, Cocaine Smitty / On our way to pull some whores in Mexico City. — Dennis Wepman et al., *The Life*, p. 36, 1976

5 to serve time in prison or in the armed forces *US*

- The "elder" man had "pulled his combat time," and this was the way many arguments ended, even arguments about religion and politics, and not about the war at all. — Russell Davis, *Marine at War*, p. 57, 1961
- The *haras* wanted to know how things had been in Comstock, how long I had pulled, and how it had been. — Piri Thomas, *Down These Mean Streets*, p. 312, 1967

6 to leave *US*

- Rudy started the car. "I'm pullin." — Clarence Cooper Jr, *The Scene*, p. 35, 1960

7 (of an adult) to buy beer or cigarettes illegally for a minor *CANADA, 2001*

This term is especially, almost exclusively, used in Saskatchewan.

- Pulling describes when an adult buys liquor or cigarettes for minors. — *An American's Guide to Canada*, p. 9, 10th November 2001

8 (of a jockey) to deliberately ride a racehorse to lose *AUSTRALIA, 1895*

- Jockeys are often accused of pulling horses when they are not in fault, but I am sorry to say I have seen horses deliberately 'stopped'. — Nat Gould, *On and Off the Turf*, p. 123, 1895
- PULLING A HORSE – To prevent a horse from winning a race. — Gilbert H. Lawson, *A Dictionary of Australian Words and Terms*, 1924
- Occasionally, when luck's not with him, he excuses his losses by slamming rotten jockeys who pull their mounts, or race three-wide all the way, or else blames their horses for getting blocked for a run. — Clive Galea, *Slipper!*, p. 7, 1988
- Ooh, you pulled that horse, didn't you. — Herb Wharton, *Cattle Camp*, p. 189, 1994

▸ **pull a fast one**

to do something daring (often a criminal act) and hope to get away with it by being smarter, faster and more deceitful than those set to prevent you; to play a dirty trick *UK, 1943*

Originally military.

- [H]aving treated Bush in the midterm elections largely as a bipartisan figure above politics, they found that Bush pulled a fast one on them and went for the Democratic jugular. — *New Statesman*, 3rd February 2003

▸ **pull a stroke**

to do something daring (often a criminal act) and get away with it by being smarter, faster and more deceitful than those set to prevent you; to play a dirty trick *UK*

- — Peter Laurie, *Scotland Yard*, p. 326, 1970

▸ **pull my mouth**

to try to get me to say something in particular *CANADA*

- "Pulling my mouth" may be modelled on, or an original version of, the familiar "pulling my coat" – US young male slang for "pointing out a pretty girl," or "pointing out a girl showing thigh or cleavage." — Lewis Poteet, *The South Shore Phrase Book*, p. 88, 1999

▸ **pull on**

to tackle someone; to contend with someone; to test someone *AUSTRALIA, 1953*

- I'll pull on the Prime Minister himself if I can't get a permit for my business. — Edwin Morrisby, 30th August 1958

▸ **pull on the rope**

to masturbate a man *US*

- And then you start pulling on the rope or to throw the bad-headed champ [perform oral sex], boy you have reached rock bottom in my opinion. — Bruce Jackson, *In the Life*, p. 171, 1972

▸ **pull out (all) the stops**

to apply maximum effort to the task in hand *UK, 1974*

From the stops that limit the full sound of a pipe-organ.

- She unpacks the china on to the table an' moves a plate of biscuits a millimetre to let us know she pulled out all the stops. — Nick Barlay, *Curvy Lovebox*, p. 71, 1997

▸ **pull pud**
(used of a male) to masturbate *UK*
- I'm not pulling pud here. I know we're gonna be big. — *Airheads*, 1994

▸ **pull someone's covers**
to reveal a person's true character *US*
- — William K. Bentley and James M. Corbett, *Prison Slang*, p. 33, 1970

▸ **pull the head off it**
(of a male) to masturbate *UK*
- I cannot wait for her to fuck off out the house so's I can get into some of them little adverts and pull the fucking head off it. — Kevin Sampson, *Clubland*, p. 50, 2002

▸ **pull the monkey**
to pull a rubber disc through a cess drain in order to clean the drain *UK*
- — Harvey Sheppard, *A Dictionary of Railway Slang*, 1970

▸ **pull the pin**
to resign or retire from a job *US, 1927*
Based on the US railroad imagery of uncoupling train wagons by pulling a pin on the couplers.
- — Norman Carlisle, *The Modern Wonder Book of Trains and Railroading*, p. 267, 1946
- "You're not even considering pulling the pin, are you, Bumper?" asked Seymour[.] — Joseph Wambaugh, *The Blue Knight*, p. 15, 1973
- Pulling the pin at twenty? — James Ellroy, *Because the Night*, p. 308, 1984

▸ **pull the plug**
1 to stop; to finish *UK*
An electrical image.
- J.D: Man Veronica, pull the plug on that shit. — *Heathers*, 1988

2 in submarining, to dive *US*
- — *American Speech*, p. 38, February 1948: 'Talking under water: speech in submarines'

▸ **pull the rein**
to advise *AUSTRALIA*
The 'right rein' is good advice, the 'bad rein', bad advice.
- — Ned Wallish, *The Truth Dictionary of Racing Slang*, p. 65, 1989

▸ **pull the rug out**
to disturb the status quo *UK*
- Suppose he decides to pull the rug out – change his Will – set up with a fresh woman. — Alan Hunter, *Gently in Trees*, 1974

▸ **pull the wool over your eyes**
to deceive you, especially as regards the deceiver's intentions *US, 1842*
- [S]he took pride in the fact that it was impossible to pull the wool over her eyes. — Alice Sebold, *Lucky*, p. 21, 1999

▸ **pull time**
to be sentenced to imprisonment *US, 1950*
- "I don't want to pull any more time," Junior tells me, "but I wouldn't take anything in the world for the experience I had in prison." — Tom Wolfe, *The Kandy-Kolored Tangerine-Flake Streamline Baby*, p. 145, 1965
- I've talked to men who have pulled time all over the country and they say it's the same everywhere. — Malcolm Braly, *On the Yard*, p. 42, 1967
- You got to be a boss crook to pull that kind of time. — Joseph Wambaugh, *The Blue Knight*, p. 71, 1973
- I'd be eighty-two years old when I got out if I pulled every day of it. — Piri Thomas, *Seven Long Times*, p. 61, 1974
- — Angela Devlin, *Prison Patter*, p. 90, 1996

▸ **pull up stakes**
to depart; to move house *AUSTRALIA, 1961*

▸ **pull wires**
to use personal influence to achieve a desired outcome *UK, 1984*
A variation of 'pull strings'.

▸ **pull your coat**
to warn someone; to alert someone, *US*
- Last night Lovis had pulled Mort's coat about something. — Bernard Wolfe, *The Late Risers*, p. 35, 1954
- Then get thee in front on a sudden bunt and I'll pull your coat and let you know that's all she wrote. — Dan Burley, *Diggeth Thou?*, p. 25, 1959
- "I been tryin to pull you coat," Ace said. — Clarence Cooper Jr, *The Scene*, p. 77, 1960
- Say, "I shouldn't pull you coat but I guess I might as well / I'm that wicked bitch they call Kansas City Nell." — Bruce Jackson, *Get Your Ass in the Water and Swim Like Me*, p. 111, 1964
- Shit, man, I been in court before, so you better watch me and let me pull your coat about how to act in front of that judge, and those other white people. — Claude Brown, *Manchild in the Promised Land*, p. 95, 1965
- He pulled my coat to all the aspects of royalties I never knew existed. — Babs Gonzales, *I Paid My Dues*, p. 51, 1967
- Look here, baby, pull my coat to what's going down! — Eldridge Cleaver, *Soul on Ice*, p. 198, 1968
- In case you ain't hip to the Moore School, let me pull your coat to the cracks-on-the-ass bit. — A.S. Jackson, *Gentleman Pimp*, p. 17, 1973
- Phil could pull my coat if the gorilla drove up. — Iceberg Slim (Robert Beck), *Airtight Willie and Me*, p. 30, 1979
- She used to get on the corner and rap with the younger ones and pull their coats to what was happening. — Herbert Huncke, *Guilty of Everything*, p. 4, 1990
- [T]here was no way to pull the Homicide's coat about his brother taking the rap for Buddha Hat without implicating himself. — Richard Price, *Clockers*, p. 423, 1992

▸ **pull your head in**
mind your own business *AUSTRALIA, 1942*
- He is told to pull his head in and is thrown out by two footballers. — Cyril Pearl, *So, you want to be an Australian*, p. 59, 1959
- — J.E. MacDonnell, *Don't Gimme the Ships*, p. 27, 1960
- — Sue Rhodes, *Now you'll think I'm awful*, p. 81, 1967
- — Jim Ramsay, *Cop It Sweet!*, p. 74, 1977

▸ **pull your leg**
1 to tease you; to make fun of you *UK, 1888*

2 to good-naturedly hoax or deceive you *UK, 1888*

▸ **pull your pisser**
to good-naturedly hoax or deceive you *UK, 1984*
A variation of **PULL YOUR LEG**.

▸ **pull your plonker**
1 to fool you; to tease you; to take a liberty with you *UK*
Variation of **PULL YOUR LEG**, similar to **PULL YOUR PISSER**, with **PLONKER** (the penis) supplying the image.
- I find myself involved in a game of ping-pong with a shagged out old slapper who's pulling my plonker to the tune of twenty grand a time. — Bernard Demsey and Kevin McNally, *Lock, Stock... & Two Sips*, p. 289, 2000

2 to waste time *UK*
From the sense 'to masturbate'.
- Well, why don't we stop pullin our plonkers an get someat worked out, all right? — Trevor Griffiths, *Oi For England*, p. 12, 1982

▸ **pull your pud; pull your pudden; pull your pudding**
(of a male) to masturbate *UK, 1944*
- I sat there pulling my pud like a total dip and told her to take her whatchamacallit and go home[.] — Lawrence Block, *No Score [The Affairs of Chip Harrison Omnibus]*, p. 150, 1970

▸ **pull your punches**
to exercise moderation, especially in punishment or blame *UK, 1934*
From boxing.
- Yet, given the scale of the scandal and the length of the 16m inquiry, the judge has pulled his punches. — *The Guardian*, 27th October 2000

▸ **pull your tit**
to good-naturedly hoax or deceive you; to make a fool of you *AUSTRALIA*
- — Edward Lindall, *No Place to Hide*, 1959

▸ **pull your wire**
(of a male) to masturbate *UK, 1937*

pull away *verb*
to divert attention from the scene of of a crime *AUSTRALIA*
- The terms "pullaway" – "tugging a head", "pulling away" or "slewing a head" [or "pulling a head"] mean simply diverting someone's attention from the scene of operations[.] — *The (Sydney) Bulletin*, 26th April 1975

pull down *verb*
1 to earn money *US, 1917*
- He's pulling down six bills a week. — *The Blues Brothers*, 1980
- You pull down four bills a week which is damn good. — *48 Hours*, 1982

2 to rob a place *US*
- FREDD: I robbed a few gas and sips, sold some weed, told him recently I held the shotgun while me and another guy pulled down a poker game in Portland. — *Reservoir Dogs*, 1992

pulled up *adjective*
former *US*
- — Bruce Jackson, *Outside the Law*, p. 59, 1972: 'Glossary'
- She must have been a pulled-up whore or something. — Bruce Jackson, *Outside the Law*, p. 151, 1972

puller *noun*
1 a sneak thief *US*
- — Inez Cardozo-Freeman, *The Joint*, p. 523, 1984

2 a dealer in stolen or smuggled goods *US*
- —*American Speech*, p. 98, May 1956: 'Smugglers' argot in the Southwest'

3 a racehorse that strains to run at full speed *US*
- —Igor Kushyshyn et al., *The Gambling Times Guide to Harness Racing*, p. 121, 1994

4 a crack cocaine user who obsessively/compulsively tugs at different body parts *US*
- —Terry Williams, *Crackhouse*, p. 150, 1992

pulleys *noun*
suspenders *US*
- —Lou Shelly, *Hepcats Jive Talk Dictionary*, p. 16, 1945

pullie; pully *noun*
a pullover, a jumper *UK, 1984*

pull in *verb*
to earn (money) *UK, 1529*
- [A] dollar bet can pull in $2,800 to $3,000.—*The Nassau Guardian*, 3rd November 2003

pulling *noun*
1 casual or recreational questing for a sexual partner *UK*
- I'm the king of pulling and you could learn so much.—Susan Nickson, *Two Pints of Lager and a Packet of Crisps*, 12th April 2004

2 a challenge from a gang, or from one of its members *UK*
Teddy Boys' slang.
- —*The Observer*, 1st March 1959

pulling gear *noun*
in trucking, the gear best suited for climbing a hill *US*
- —Montie Tak, *Truck Talk*, p. 124, 1971

pulling time *noun*
in an illegal numbers gambling lottery, the time of day when the winning number is drawn or selected *US*
- —*American Speech*, p. 193, October 1949

pull off *verb*
1 (used of a male) to masturbate *IRELAND, 1922*
- Every night round about eight thirty he goes over into that lot yonder and pulls himself off with steel wool.—William Burroughs, *Naked Lunch*, p. 175, 1957
- [A]s he listened, he tried to conceal the fact that he was pulling off.—John Rechy, *City of Night*, p. 406, 1963
- I can't and won't believe it: four or five guys sit around in a circle on the floor, and at Smolka's signal, each begins to pull off – and the first one to come gets the pot, a buck a head.—Philip Roth, *Portnoy's Complaint*, p. 194, 1969
- More or less every day, more or less same time, young Gavin comes up here to pull himself off.—Kevin Sampson, *Clubland*, p. 160, 2002

2 to succeed in doing, or effecting, something *UK, 1887*
- Persuading them [George Harrison and Ringo Starr] was to achieve 'the impossible – but one way or another we've pulled it off', [Paul] McCartney said in a later interview.—*The Guardian*, 16th March 1995

pull out of *verb*
to be released *US*
- When the day came for you to pull out of Jackson they would fuck around for five or six hours before you'd be on a bus going home.—A.S. Jackson, *Gentleman Pimp*, p. 132, 1973

pull the other one!; pull the other one – it's got bells on!
used as a sarcastic response, from 'leg-pulling' (a humorous act of bluff or deception) *UK*
The invitation is to pull the other leg.
- —Alan Hunter, *Gently Sahib*, 1964

pull through *noun*
a Jew *UK*
Rhyming slang, noted by David Hillman, 1974.

pull up *verb*
1 (of a jockey) to deliberately ride a racehorse to lose *AUSTRALIA*
- A weight-for-age horse was pulled up in an easy third-class rate sprint, and came out to win a classic within a few days.—Tom Ellis, *The Science of Turf Investment*, p. 18, 1936
- He'll pull Magger up.—Frank Hardy, *The Yarns of Billy Borker*, p. 107, 1965
- 'Not as big a thief as you are,' asserted the bushie. 'You pulled up Bernborough.'—Frank Hardy and Athol George Mulley, *The Needy and the Greedy*, p. 7, 1975
- On race day, the battlers decided to pull up the horse anyway. They told the giant jockey to hook it and he seemed to agree. Their horse led into the straight by three lengths and won by ten. 'You stupid mug!' one of the battlers said to the jockey. 'Our horse will have to carry the grandstand next start.'—Frank Hardy and Athol George Mulley, *The Needy and the Greedy*, p. 46, 1975
- 'How many horses have you pulled up?'—Roy Higgins and Tom Prior, *The Jockey Who Laughed*, p. 71, 1982
- 'No, Jack won't be fit, and I could not trust any Melbourne jockey. He could be paid to pull Archer up in the race.'—Anne Brooksbank, *Archer*, p. 115, 1985

2 to stop (doing something) *US*
- —Bruce Jackson, *Outside the Law*, p. 59, 1972: 'Glossary'

pummel *verb*
to skateboard fearlessly, without regard to the effect on the board or body *US*
- —*San Francisco Sunday Examiner & Chronicle*, p. 20, 2nd September 1984: 'Say it right'

pummelled *adjective*
very drunk *US*
- —Connie Eble (Editor), *UNC-CH Campus Slang*, p. 7, November 1990

pump *noun*
1 the heart *US*
- It's funny how the toughest gorilla gets tame and whimpers like a young pup when he begins to hear his own pump riffing.—Mezz Mezzrow, *Really the Blues*, p. 87, 1946
- He's on sick leave, his pump acting up on him, and I doubt will be back.—Elmore Leonard, *Killshot*, p. 182, 1989

2 a fart *UK: SCOTLAND*
- —Michael Munro, *The Original Patter*, p. 55, 1985

3 a fire hydrant *US*
- He came up 111th Street in his jalopy with the windows down and stuck. "Boys" had the pump on.—Edwin Torres, *After Hours*, p. 164, 1979

4 an illegal linear amplifier for a citizens' band radio *US*
- —Elementary Electronics, *Dictionary of CB Lingo*, p. 98, 1976

pump *verb*
1 to have sex, usually from the male perspective *UK, 1730*
- I glanced once out the backwindow as I pumped.—Jack Kerouac, *Letter to Neal Cassady*, p. 299, 10 January 1951
- I bet she's lying up in bed, just a pumping away, ain't she, boy?—James Baldwin, *Blues for Mister Charlie*, p. 13, 1964
- Think I ought to take along some jelly in case she wants to get pumped in the ass?—Terry Southern, *Now Dig This*, p. 38, 1975
- Swingin' and swingin' my ding-a-ling in / Pumpin' that ass until your back starts stinging—Ultramagnetic MCs *Porno Star*, 1992
- I felt like I was being pumped while driving over speed bumps.—Anka Radakovich, *The Wild Girls Club*, p. 85, 1994
- Man, after all that pumping, I'd be surprised if she can sit on a toilet seat without screaming bloody murder.—Anthony Petkovich, *The X Factory*, p. 200, 1997

2 to exert yourself in a labour *US*
- You're fuckin' out here pumping bottles, I mean, what's your problem?—Richard Price, *Clockers*, p. 522, 1992

3 to obtain a free ride *BARBADOS*
- —Frank A. Collymore, *Barbadian Dialect*, p. 69, 1965

4 to interrogate someone *UK, 1656*
- "Trying to be a little detective," he said [...] "You were trying to pump Harte[.]"—Martin Waddell, *Otley*, p. 133, 1966

5 to fart *UK: NORTHERN IRELAND*

6 to sell drugs, especially crack cocaine *US*
- "He's pumping" means he sells drugs.—*USA Today*, p. 1A, 25th April 1989
- You be pumping that rock, Tre?—*Boyz N The Hood*, 1990
- —US Department of Justice, *Street Terms*, October 1994

7 in poker, to increase a bet made by another player *US, 1983*
- —Thomas L. Clark, *The Dictionary of Gambling and Gaming*, p. 168, 1987

▸ **pump the stump**
to shake hands *US*
- —Marcus Hanna Boulware, *Jive and Slang of Students in Negro Colleges*, 1947

pumped *adjective*
pregnant *US*
- —*Current Slang*, p. 9, Winter 1969

pumped up *adjective*
1 with muscles inflated and defined *US*
- [P]umped-up bouncers who teetered only moments from 'roid rage[.]—Greg Williams, *Diamond Geezers*, p. 37, 1997
- He was all pumped up and looking like an even uglier version of Arnold Schwarzenegger with a red-hot poker up his arse.—Dave Courtney, *Stop the Ride I Want to Get Off*, p. 218, 1999

2 excited, energised *UK, 1791*
Current usage is informed by bodybuilding jargon with muscles 'pumped up' for display.
- I'm more pumped-up for this [fight] than I was over Fonzie.—Kevin Sampson, *Outlaws*, p. 243, 2001

pump gas *noun*
petrol as it is available to the general public, which must be used in some drag racing events *US*
- —Ed Radlauer, *Drag Racing Pix Dix*, p. 42, 1970

pumpie *noun*
a pump-action shotgun *AUSTRALIA*
- A Heckler and Koch submachinegun, two pumpies, two Glock nine mils, ammunition, silencers for the handguns and 500g of pick-me-up powder.—Harrison Biscuit, *The Search for Savage Henry*, p. 46, 1995

pumping *adjective*
1 (used of contemporary dance music, and of the atmosphere it generates) exciting, energetic *UK*
- Ibiza's pumping club scene is equally matched by its private party circuit.—Wayne Anthony, *Spanish Highs*, p. 106, 1999

2 (used of surf conditions) powerful, excellent *US*
- —Gary Fairmont R. Filosa II, *The Surfer's Almanac: An International Surfing Guide*, p. 192, 1977
- [I]t's so sick out there [...] it's really sick, it's pumping.—a British surfer interviewed in Newquay, *Word of Mouth*, 6th August 2004

pump iron; pump *verb*
to exercise by lifting weights *US, 1972*
Sports jargon; possibly from **PUMP UP** (to inflate muscles).
- Then I recorded a provocative voice message under my phony name and said I was entertaining, frequently pumped iron, and got my fashion tips from 60s Italian movies and the old "Star Trek" series. —Anka Radakovich, *The Wild Girls Club*, p. 45, 1994

pump jockey *noun*
a petrol station attendant *US*
- Should a pump jockey risk a beating any more than a teller should risk his or her life to save a bank's insured money?—Hunter S. Thompson, *Hell's Angels*, p. 84, 1966
- See her in a year, straddling some pump-jockey in the front seat of a '46 Ford, knocked up.—Richard Farina, *Been Down So Long*, p. 146, 1966
- A pump jockey will answer to a judge tomorrow on charges he raped a 15-year-old girl at the Hamilton gas station that hired him two months ago.—*Boston Herald*, p. 18, 7th July 2004

pumpkin *noun*
1 used as a sentimental term of address *US*
The affectionate tone of the term of address runs counter to the earlier sense of an 'ineffective, incompetent person'.
- I'm guessing that's what the soprano shriek was about, pumpkin. —*Something About Mary*, 1998

2 in car repair, a pumpkin-shaped differential cover *US*
- —Lewis Poteet, *Car & Motorcyle Slang*, p. 157, 1992

3 in trucking, a flat tyre *US*
- —Montie Tak, *Truck Talk*, p. 124, 1971

pumpkin belly *noun*
the abdomen of a pregnant woman *TRINIDAD AND TOBAGO, 1973*
- —Lise Winer, *Dictionary of the English/Creole of Trinidad & Tobago*, 2003

pumpkin positive *adjective*
unintelligent *UK*
A doctors' joke: if you shine a light in the mouth, the head will light up. Recorded in an article about medical slang in British (3 London and 1 Cambridge) hospitals.
- —*Ethics and Behaviour*, August 2003

pumpkin seed *noun*
a yellow, oblong mescaline tablet *US*
- —Eugene Landy, *The Underground Dictionary*, p. 155, 1971

pumpkin time *noun*
a curfew *US*
An allusion to the Cinderella tale.
- —*Current Slang*, p. 22, Spring 1970

pump monkey *noun*
a petrol station attendant *US*
- So this pump-monkey put the car on the rack and started to gun-squirt grease into the joints.—Clancy Sigal, *Going Away*, p. 164, 1961

pump off *verb*
(of a male) to masturbate *UK, 1937*

pumps *noun*
1 the female breasts *US*
- —Vincent J. Monteleone, *Criminal Slang*, p. 184, 1949

2 trainers, sneakers *BARBADOS*
- —Richard Allsopp, *Dictionary of Caribbean English Usage*, p. 455, 1996

pum-pum *noun*
the vagina *JAMAICA*
- —Flowers & Alvin, *In A De Pum Pum*, 1972
- —Max & Niney, *International Pum Pum*, 1972
- Tidy yuh pum-pum!—Lise Winer, *Dictionary of the English/Creole of Trinidad & Tobago*, 2003

pump up *verb*
1 to increase something, to inflate something, to turn something higher *US*
- That was it for Anne and Ted and I, and we left together as we'd arrived, but pumped up from Ochs.—Jim Carroll, *Forced Entries*, p. 74, 1987
- Turn your radios up! Crank it up so's we can hear it! Come on, pump it up, man!—*Airheads*, 1994

2 when lifting weights, to engorge muscles with blood in order to inflate and define them *US*
- —*American Speech*, p. 201, Fall 1984: 'The language of bodybuilding'

3 to conduct an exhaustive and detailed briefing *US*
- —Department of the Army, *Staff Officer's Guidebook*, p. 64, 1986

4 while gambling, to lose at a steady rate *US*
- —Lee Solkey, *Dummy Up and Deal*, p. 118, 1980

punani *noun*
the vagina; hence a woman regarded as a sexual object; hence sex with a woman *UK*
Probably West Indian. The etymology is uncertain, possibly rooted in **POONTANG** (the vagina, hence sex). Variant spellings include 'punany'; 'punyani'; 'punaany'; 'punanny'; 'pudenany'; 'pun-nanny'; 'punaani'; 'poonani'. Black slang, popularised in the wider community by comedian Ali G (Sacha Baron-Cohen, b.1970) and rap music.
- You only love me when you want punanny.—Charlie Ace, *Punanny*, 1972
- She teased him, laying wide her legs so he could get a brief view of her punnany, then closing them[.]—Donald Gorgon, *Cop Killer*, p. 163, 1994
- [M]e luv punaani bad[.]—Chester Francis-Jackson, *The Official Dancehall Dictionary*, p. 41, 1995
- (Punany, punany) / But your name doesn't matter to me / (punany, punany) / as long as you be giving up the punany.—1-800-Disndat *Punany*, 1995
- There's [...] a "poochi," a "poopi," a "peepe,", a "poopelu," a "poopelu," a "poonani," a "pal" and a "piche[."]—Eve Ensler, *The Vagina Monologues*, p. 6, 1998
- Since the lap-dance bars opened up in town, that's all I'm interested in. Poledance punyani. I fucking love them girls.—Kevin Sampson, *Outlaws*, p. 37, 2001
- BEING FIT DONT JUST MEAN HAVIN GREAT BABYLONS (the breasts) AND A NICE PUNANI.—Sacha Baron-Cohen, *Da Gospel According to Ali G*, 2001

▸ **ride the punani**
to have sex *UK*
West Indian slang popularised in the UK in the late 1990s by comedy character Ali G (Sacha Baron-Cohen).
- —Susie Dent, *The Language Report*, p. 144, 2003

punch *noun*
1 an act of sexual intercourse; a person viewed only in terms of sex *US*
- She was just a punch.—Gerald Petievich, *To Die in Beverly Hills*, p. 137, 1983

2 in volleyball, a one-fist overhead pass or volley *US*
- Glossary—Janet Thigpen, *Power Volleyball*, p. 99, 1985

punch *verb*
1 to open something by force *US, 1931*
Most commonly, but not exclusively, applied to breaking into a safe.
- Billy punched a beer can for the girl[.]—Ken Kesey, *One Flew Over the Cuckoo's Nest*, p. 226, 1962
- and there's no charge in the world like when you see that smoke ... and when you're punching it and you hear that pin hit the back of the safe.—*The Digger Papers*, August 1968
- If you're getting ready to punch a safe, you need one man to hold the punch and another to hit the hammer.—Bruce Jackson, *Outside the Law*, p. 81, 1972

- In either case, whether it's in a house or an apartment, you never try to pop the door of the safe itself by peeling it or punching it till the pin hits the back of the safe. —Emmett Grogan, *Ringolevio*, p. 91, 1972
- He knew he couldn't risk punching it. —Emmett Grogan, *Final Score*, p. 99, 1976

2 to have sex *US*

- —Eugene Landy, *The Underground Dictionary*, p. 155, 1971

3 in a card cheating scheme, to prepare a deck for a manoeuvre *US*

- —Frank Garcia, *Marked Cards and Loaded Dice*, p. 263, 1962

▸ punch it

1 to accelerate to high speed *US*

- "Then I'm gonna punch it," Jack said, "get up to about a hundred and twenty miles an hour…" —Elmore Leonard, *Bandits*, p. 273, 1987

2 to escape (from prison) *US*

- —Charles Shafer, *Folk Speech in Texas Prisons*, p. 212, 1990

▸ punch someone's ticket

1 to kill someone *US*

- I've been to too many autopsies of people killed by burglars – old ladies, housewives with kids, people who had never harmed anyone – to worry about how a career burglar got his ticket punched. —Gerald Petievich, *To Die in Beverly Hills*, p. 65, 1983
- Sure punched his ticket. —Edwin Torres, *Carlito's Way*, p. 69, 1985
- —Michael Dalton Johnson, *Talking Trash with Redd Foxx*, p. 102, 1994

2 to have sex with someone *US*

- Callum, to my amazement, was managing a reasonable facsimile of a leer. 'I'd punch her ticket in a minute.' —Armistead Maupin, *Maybe the Moon*, p. 231, 1992

▸ punch the sun

while driving, to accelerate to make it through an intersection on a yellow light *US*

- —Anna Scotti and Paul Young, *Buzzwords*, p. 41, 1997

Punch and Judy *noun*

deception; an unbelievable story *UK*

Formed on traditional puppet characters whose tale of domestic disharmony and dishonesty, perhaps, informs the sense.

- Don't give me all that old Punch and Judy. —Ray Puxley, *Cockney Rabbit*, 1992

punchboard *noun*

a sexually available and promiscuous woman *US*

A 'punchboard' is a game which used to be found in shops, where for a price the customer punched one of many holes on the board in the hope of winning a prize.

- Claymore Face, the platoon punchboard, was there too. —Larry Heinemann, *Close Quarters*, p. 69, 1977
- There's one woman handler, named Wilma. A punchboard. —Joseph Wambaugh, *The Black Marble*, p. 34, 1978

Punch Bowl *noun*

a valley on the east-central coast of Korea formed by the Taebaek-San Maek Mountains, home to some of the bitterest battles of the war *US*

- The 40th Division was deployed on the east coast, near a large valley called the Punch Bowl. The right flank of the division was on the Punch Bowl's northern rim[.] —David H. Hackworth, *About Face*, p. 238, 1989

punch buggie *noun*

a Volkswagen 'Beetle' car *US*

Shouted by the first child in a car to see it, which entitles him or her to slug all other children playing the game.

- —Connie Eble (Editor), *UNC-CH Campus Slang*, p. 1, April 1997

punch-drunk *adjective*

of a boxer, deranged or debilitated to some degree as a result of punches received *US, 1918*

Hence the condition of being punch-drunk: 'punch-drunkenness'.

- He looks like a punch-drunk pug to me. —Irving Shulman, *The Amboy Dukes*, p. 55, 1947
- [H]e happened to read a newspaper article about the awful dangers of punch-drunkenness. He vowed there and then never to box again. —Charles Raven, *Underworld Nights*, p. 42, 1956

puncher *noun*

a safe cracker *US*

- —Vincent J. Monteleone, *Criminal Slang*, p. 184, 1949

punching bag *noun*

a promiscuous woman *US*

From **PUNCH** in its sexual sense.

- "Linda says she's a regular punchin bag." —Earl Thompson, *Tattoo*, p. 237, 1974

punch-in-the-mouth *noun*

oral sex on a woman *US*

- —*American Speech*, p. 229, October 1967: 'Some special terms used in a University of Connecticut men's dormitory'

punch job *noun*

a safe robbery in which the combination lock is punched out to gain access to the safe *US*

- —Jack Webb, *The Badge*, p. 222, 1958
- The punch job is much faster, three minutes maybe. —Leonard Shecter and William Phillips, *On the Pad*, p. 179, 1973

punch-out *noun*

in Keno, a template with 20 holes punched out for the numbers called in a game, used to compare a player's ticket with the winning numbers *US*

- —John Mechigian, *Encyclopedia of Keno*, p. 111, 1972

punch out *verb*

1 to beat someone up *US*

- Some I punched out when they got carried away and forgot to whom they were talking. —Jamie Mandelkau quoting Ken Kesey, *Buttons*, p. 121, 1969

2 to leave *US*

- —*Seattle Times*, p. A9, 12th April 1998: 'Grunts, squids not grunting from the same dictionary'

3 to eject someone from a fighter plane *US*

- —*American Speech*, p. 124, Summer 1986: 'The Language of Naval Fighter Pilots'

punch-up *noun*

a fist fight *UK, 1958*

- They had a punch up —Frank Norman, *Bang To Rights*, p. 60, 1958
- It might end up with a punch-up after they'd got enough drink inside them[.] —Johnny Speight, *It Stands to Reason*, p. 43, 1973
- —Louis S. Leland, *A Personal Kiwi-Yankee Dictionary*, p. 83, 1984
- Whilst pillheads hold hands and sing happy songs, pissheads are out the back having a punch-up. —Wayne Anthony, *Spanish Highs*, p. 151, 1999
- [H]e was more into burn-ups and punch-ups than kids[.] —John King, *White Trash*, p. 160, 2001

punch up *verb*

to enhance something, especially to enhance a script with humour, more lively dialogue, or the like *US*

In the 1950s, the entertainment industry used the term to mean to increase the volume of the sound track or brightness of the picture. Towards the end of the century, the meaning changed to a writing term.

- The eighth team of writers had been brought in to "punch up" the script, and each page that flew out of a typewriter had made the show less humorous and less charming[.] —Dan Jenkins, *Life Its Ownself*, p. 147, 1984
- "I want you to punch up Skip's piece," Mulcahy said. "Really make it sing." —Carl Hiaasen, *Tourist Season*, p. 201, 1986
- Ian, you want to punch it up a little? You're about as spunky as a corpse up there. —*Airheads*, 1994

punchy *adjective*

discomposed, deranged *UK*

Abbreviated from **PUNCH-DRUNK**.

- By this time the president is punchy with boredom[.] —William Burroughs, *Queer*, p. 45, 1985

punga *noun*

the penis *NEW ZEALAND*

- —David McGill, *David McGill's Complete Kiwi Slang Dictionary*, p. 100, 1998

punishing *adjective*

exhausting, gruelling *UK, 1882*

- No performer today would consider such a punishing schedule; [Duke] Ellington kept it up for five decades. —*New Statesman*, 2nd April 1999

punishment *noun*

severe handling; pain, misery *UK, 1811*

- The punishment you take as an everyday catcher. —*Baseball Digest*, December 2000

▸ **put to the punishment**
in horse racing, to use any physicality such as whipping or kicking to an extreme degree *US*
• —David W. Maurer, *Argot of the Racetrack*, p. 53, 1951

punk *noun*
1 a fan of punk rock music and the associated fashions *UK*
• —Television Personalities, *Part Time Punks*, 1976
2 a young and/or weak man used as a passive homosexual partner, especially in prison *US, 1904*
• A punk, if you want it in plain English, is a boy with smooth skin who takes the place of a woman in a jailbird's love life. —Mezz Mezzrow, *Really the Blues*, p. 15, 1946
• Punks and brats are those prisoners who take the passive role in sodomy; there is no chronological age limit. —Arthur V. Huffman, *New York Mattachine Newsletter*, p. 6, June 1961
• The hacks would hear about it and they would put Tico on A-1 tier where all the faggots were, and he'd be a jailhouse punk. —Piri Thomas, *Down These Mean Streets*, p. 266, 1967
• —John A. Holm, *Dictionary of Bahamian English*, p. 162, 1982
• [D]redge out the best-looking punk you got in this moth-eaten bazaar. —William Burroughs, *Queer*, p. 71, 1985
• Four years fuckin' punks in the ass made you appreciate rib when you get it. —*Reservoir Dogs*, 1992
• Awww c'mon, Bop, let's stop calling lesbians bulldaggers and homosexuals fags and punks. —Odie Hawkins, *Midnight*, p. 160, 1995
3 a child *US*
• —Gene Sorrows, *All About Carnivals*, p. 24, 1985: 'Terminology'
4 a lesbian *BAHAMAS*
• —John A. Holm, *Dictionary of Bahamian English*, p. 152, 1982
5 in horse racing, a mildly talented jockey *US*
• —David W. Maurer, *Argot of the Racetrack*, p. 53, 1951
6 marijuana *UK*
• Got the Skunk, got the Punk, we got the Sess, it's Blessed. —Julian Johnson, *Urban Survival*, p. 170, 2003
7 the middle position in the back seat of a car *US*
• —Edith A. Folb, *runnin' down some lines*, p. 251, 1980

punk *verb*
1 to have anal sex with someone *US*
• I had some Vaseline for my chapped lips and the desk copper leered and asked if we punked each other. —Neal Cassady, *The First Third*, p. 193, 3rd July 1949
• That's the only time I've ever been punked. —Bruce Jackson, *In the Life*, p. 372, 1972
• I used to get punked and bullied on my block[.] —Eminem (Marshall Mathers), *I'm Back*, 2000
2 to assault someone *US*
• He said they shouted and joked about "punking on someone" – street slang for jumping and beating a victim. —*Post-Standard*, p. B1, 10th June 1991

punk *adjective*
poor, lousy, inferior *US, 1896*
• "Oh, man, I don't know what's the matter with me. I fell kind of punk." Jack said, "Punk, I never used the word punk in my life." —Elmore Leonard, *Bandits*, p. 1, 1987

punkasals *noun*
trainers, sneakers *GRENADA*
• —Richard Allsopp, *Dictionary of Caribbean English Usage*, p. 456, 1996

punker *noun*
1 a fan of punk music *US*
• [Y]our child is showing signs of becoming a punker[.] —Frank Zappa, *The Real Frank Zappa Book*, p. 290, 1989
2 a punk rock song *UK*
• 14 pitbull punkers to rip the throats out of any doubters —*X-Ray*, p. 21, May 2003

punkette *noun*
a female follower of punk music and fashion *US*
• There was a puffy punkette girl there. —Lester Bangs, *Psychotic Reactions and Carburetor Dung*, p. 309, 1976–82

punkfucker *noun*
a male prisoner who has sex with homosexual prisoners, especially taking the active role *US*
• My fall partner was a notorious punkfucker in the penitentiary and he got out and he just converted right over to girls with no problem whatsoever. —Bruce Jackson, *Outside the Law*, p. 174, 1972

punk-hunt *verb*
to search for homosexuals and assault them for the sole reason of their homosexuality *US*
• The young Negros rejected the homosexual, and this was Wright alluding to a classic, if cruel, example of a ubiquituous phenomenon in the black ghettos of America: the practice by Negro youth of going "punk-hunting." —Eldridge Cleaver, *Soul on Ice*, p. 106, 1968

punki; punkin *noun*
the vagina *TRINIDAD AND TOBAGO, 1973*
Children's vocabulary.
• —Lise Winer, *Dictionary of the English/Creole of Trinidad & Tobago*, 2003

punk in the bunk *noun*
used for expressing the fact that the speaker has an effeminate homosexual prisoner under his control *US*
• —Inez Cardozo-Freeman, *The Joint*, p. 523, 1984

punk out *verb*
1 to withdraw from a task out of fear *US, 1920*
• But if you're a Jap or a turkey or you're going to punk out it's going to be bad stuff for you. —Hal Ellson, *Duke*, p. 31, 1949
• I made sure, but if you want to punk out, say so. —Hal Ellson, *The Golden Spike*, p. 18, 1952
• The opposite of heart is punking out. —Harrison E. Salisbury, *The Shook-up Generation*, p. 25, 1958
• [H]e just wanted to know whether the private standing in front of him was trying to punk out of that war, or was truly bat-shit. —Emmett Grogan, *Ringolevio*, p. 227, 1972
2 to inform on or betray a compatriot *US*
• —John R. Armore and Joseph D. Wolfe, *Dictionary of Desperation*, p. 44, 1976

punk pill *noun*
any central nervous system depressant *US*
• —*Current Slang*, p. 39, Fall 1968

punk ride *noun*
an amusement ride for children *US*
• —Gene Sorrows, *All About Carnivals*, p. 25, 1985: 'Terminology'

punk rock; punk *noun*
a genre of basic, high-energy rock music that came to prominence in the mid-1970s *US*
• A big part of punk rock is the Great American (or English, really) Teen Sublimation Riff. —Lester Bangs, *Psychotic Reactions and Carburetor Dung*, p. 101, 1972

punks *noun*
an unsophisticated, rural audience *US*
• —Wilfred Granville, *The Theatre Dictionary*, p. 155, 1952

punksy *adjective*
spunky *BARBADOS*
• —Frank A. Collymore, *Barbadian Dialect*, p. 69, 1965

punk tank *noun*
a holding cell in a jail or prison reserved for homosexuals *US*
• They take and put him in the punk tank too, and those people are usually the easiest to turn out. —Bruce Jackson, *Outside the Law*, p. 177, 1972

punny eccy; punny *noun*
in school, a piece of written work given as a punishment *UK: SCOTLAND*
From a shortening of '*pun*ishment *ec*ercise'; used by Glasgow teachers and pupils.
• Ah canny come oot til Ah've finished this punny fur Aul Kipper. —Michael Munro, *The Patter, Another Blast*, p. 57, 1988

punt *noun*
1 a gamble; a chance *AUSTRALIA*
• Bentley took what others might again have called a gamble, a punt, a chance. —J.E. Macdonnel, *Alarm-E-boats!*, p. 147, 1958
• Lacking in-depth surveys, we can only guess at the cause. Well, I'll take a punt. —Suzy Jarratt, *Permissive Australia*, p. 142, 1970
• It was a bit of a punt, but we think it paid off. —*Alice Springs Star*, p. 3, 21st August 1984
• I really think it's a better punt than setting Mike onto the abos. —Harrison Biscuit, *The Search for Savage Henry*, p. 69, 1995
2 gambling *AUSTRALIA*
• Sure he'd had a good weekend on the punt, and sure he had almost gone to Mass. —Clive Galea, *Slipper!*, p. 9, 1988
• There was nothing for it but to go back to the punt full time. —Clive Galea, *Slipper!*, p. 10, 1988

- Did I actually back a winner and finish in front on the punt?—Paul Vautin, *Turn It Up!*, p. 123, 1995

punt *verb*

1 to gamble *UK, 1873*

- anyone who wants to punt on the identity of the Conservative leader at the next election.— *The Guardian*, 20th March 2003

2 to do poorly; to give up in some fashion because you are doing poorly *US*

A metaphor from American football, where a team that has not advanced the ball ten yards after three plays will often choose to punt the ball to its opposition rather than risk giving up field position.

- —Collin Baker et al., *College Undergraduate Slang Study Conducted at Brown University*, p. 178, 1968
- —Eric S. Raymond, *The New Hacker's Dictionary*, p. 291, 1991

3 to vomit *IRELAND*

- You don't want Yer Man (q.v.) the tester to punt his lunch all over yeh.—Joseph O'Connor, *The Irish Male at Home and Abroad*, p. 54, 1996

▸ **punt the pail**

to die *UK: SCOTLAND*

A jocular variation of **KICK THE BUCKET**.

- I'm as feart of punting the pail as the next man.—Ian Pattison, *Rab C. Nesbitt*, 1988

punta-rosa *noun*

a hybrid marijuana from Mexico *MEXICO*

- If you've got the space, punta rosa is easy to grow and consistently delivers bumper harvests—Nick Jones, *Spliffs*, p. 72, 2003

punter *noun*

1 a customer, a consumer; in the plural, an audience *UK, 1965*

- —Tom Hibbert, *Rockspeak!*, p. 127, 1983
- —Bob Young and Micky Moody, *The Language of Rock 'n' Roll*, p. 113, 1985
- There were only two punters, old boys playing crib.—Garry Bushell, *The Face*, p. 6, 2001
- [A] populist entertainer such as Adam Sandler or Martin Lawrence will draw in the punters irrespective of season, or, indeed, quality.— *The Guardian*, 29th November 2002

2 a prostitute's customer *UK, 1970*

- — *Maledicta*, p. 147, Summer/Winter 1986–1987: 'Sexual slang: prostitutes, pedophiles, flagellators, transvestites, and necrophiles
- —Angela Devlin, *Prison Patter*, p. 93, 1996
- I never rob my punters; we've got a bad enough name as it is.—Lanre Fehintola, *Charlie Says...*, p. 49, 2000

3 a gambler *UK, 1873*

- But nothing has so infuriated punters as high minimum stakes[.] —John McCririck, *John McCririck's World of Betting*, p. 67, 1991

4 a drug dealer's customer *UK*

- rushing to and from punters, setting up deals.—Lanre Fehintola, *Charlie Says...*, p. 1, 2000

5 a confidence trickster's victim *UK, 1934*

- —Angela Devlin, *Prison Patter*, p. 93, 1996

pup *noun*

1 a young person *US*

- —R. Frederick West, *God's Gambler*, p. 228, 1964: 'Appendix A'
- An impudent pup the like of him.—Hugh Leonard, *Out After Dark*, p. 38, Methuen 1989

2 the early part (of some specified period) *AUSTRALIA, 1915*

Most commonly in the phrase 'the night's a pup' (the night is still young).

- The season's only a pup.—Wilda Moxham, *The Apprentice*, p. 149, 1969

3 in the television and film industries, a 500 watt light source mounted on a stand *UK*

- —Oswald Skilbeck, *ABC of Film and TV Working Terms*, p. 101, 1960

puppies *noun*

the female breasts *US*

- Mae said her puppies are real, unlike all the other women.—Herb Kunze, *Herb's Wrestling Tidbits*, 27th January 2000

▸ **like two puppies under a blanket; like two puppies fighting under a blanket**

used by men as an appreciation or critical commentary of a female posterior, especially one in undulating motion *UK: SCOTLAND*

- [H]arassing her with his sexist jokes: first, his remark about her buttocks resembling "two puppies fighting under a blanket" while she walks from MacArthur Park to East Los Angeles.—Alicia Gaspar de Alba, *Velvet Barrios*, p. 206, 2003

▸ **the puppies**

greyhound racing or coursing *AUSTRALIA*

A play on **THE DOGS**, noted by Barry Prentice, 1984.

puppies in a box *noun*

in the pornography business, a group of bare-breasted women cavorting *US*

- Um-hmmm. Puppies in a box [four young women playing[.]—Robert Stoller and I.S. Levine, *Coming Attractions*, p. 150, 1991

puppy *noun*

1 a person of a specified type *US*

- [W]anting to know the exact moment the assassins were successful. He was one sick puppy.—Kim Harrison, *Dead Witch Walking*, p. 388, 2004

2 a pit bull terrier, especially a fierce one *US*

New York police slang.

- —Samuel M. Katz, *Anytime Anywhere*, p. 389, 1997: 'The extremely unofficial and completely off-the-record NYPD/ESU truck-two glossary'

3 a small penis *US*

- —Edith A. Folb, *runnin' down some lines*, p. 250, 1980

4 in pool, a shot that cannot be missed or a game that cannot be lost *US*

- —Steven Rushin, *Pool Cool*, p. 24, 1990
- —Mike Shamos, *The Illustrated Encyclopedia of Billiards*, p. 183, 1993

5 a small bottle of wine *US*

- —Edith A. Folb, *runnin' down some lines*, p. 250, 1980

6 a gun *US*

Recorded as 'Jamaican gang terminology' by Bill Valentine, *Gang Intelligence Manual*, p.110, 1995.

puppyfoot *noun*

in a deck of playing cards, a club, especially the ace *US*

- —Albert H. Morehead, *The Complete Guide to Winning Poker*, p. 271, 1967

puppy love *noun*

a youthful infatuation *US, 1834*

- Attracted by her extremely mature figure, I found myself in the throes of "puppy love."—Phyllis and Eberhard Kronhausen, *Sex Histories of American College Men*, p. 72, 1960
- I found it difficult to believe that almost fifteen years had passed since our puppy love affair.—Iceberg Slim (Robert Beck), *Airtight Willie and Me*, p. 58, 1979

puppy lover *noun*

a person who is completely infatuated with someone *US*

- Then we sat on a big red sofa, holding hands like puppie lovers[.] —Red Rudensky, *The Gonif*, p. 114, 1970

puppy paws; puppy feet *noun*

in craps, a ten rolled with a pair of fives *US, 1981*

- —Steve Kuriscak, *Casino Talk*, p. 69, 1985

puppy show *noun*

an act that makes you look foolish *BAHAMAS*

- —Patricia Clinton-Meicholas, *More Talkin' Bahamian*, p. 81, 1995

pup tents *noun*

in circus and carnival usage, overshoes *US*

- —Don Wilmeth, *The Language of American Popular Entertainment*, p. 212, 1981

Purdey *noun*

a Hillman Avenger (a popular car manufactured in the UK from 1969–82) *UK*

Citizens' band radio slang; from the tongue-in-cheek spy adventure television series *The New Avengers* (1976–77) which featured actress Joanna Lumley as Purdey, a character named by the actress after a world-renowned shotgun.

- —Peter Chippindale, *The British CB Book*, p. 161, 1981

pure *noun*

pure, unadulterated heroin *US, 1967*

- Musta' shot some 'pure,' cause a lookout on the sidewalk heard him mumble before he croaked, 'Well kiss my dead mammy's ass if this ain't the best smack I ever shot!'—Iceberg Slim (Robert Beck), *Pimp*, p. 79, 1969
- It ain't my fault Crying Junior gave me pure 'stead a mix.—Charles W. Moore, *A Brick for Mister Jones*, p. 28, 1975
- —Robert Ashton, *This Is Heroin*, p. 206, 2002

pure *adverb*
absolutely, entirely, utterly; used as a general intensifier *UK*
- [O]ne thing pure guaranteed to do my head in is selfish driving. —Kevin Sampson, *Outlaws*, p. 2, 2001

pure!
surely! *US*
- —Connie Eble (Editor), *UNC-CH Campus Slang*, p. 4, Spring 1993

pure-food law *noun*
on the railways, a crew sent to relieve a crew that has reached the maximum work hours allowed by law *US*
- —Ramon Adams, *The Language of the Railroader*, p. 119, 1977

pure laine *noun*
in Quebec, a French person who claims direct ancestry among the original French settlers *CANADA*
The phrase means 'pure wool', but even anglophones say 'pure laine'.

pure love *noun*
LSD *US, 1977*
- —Richard A. Spears, *The Slang and Jargon of Drugs and Drink*, p. 409, 1986
- —Mike Haskins, *Drugs*, p. 286, 2003

pure merino *noun*
a person who can trace their ancestry back to free settlers (as opposed to convict transportees) *AUSTRALIA, 1826*
- Some of them coves orter be doing time instead of puttin' on dog, like they was pure merinos. —Dymphna Cusack, *Picnic Races*, p. 155, 1962

purge *noun*
an alcoholic drink *NEW ZEALAND*
- —Harry Orsman and Des Hurley, *The Beaut Little Book of New Zealand Slang*, 1994

purl; pearl *verb*
(used of the nose of a surfboard) to plunge under the surface of the ocean *US*
- —Grant W. Kuhns, *On Surfing*, p. 120, 1963

purler; pearler *noun*
a thing of outstanding excellence or beauty *AUSTRALIA, 1941*
- Suddenly, somebody hit an absolute pearler from about thirty yards. —Frank Skinner, *Frank Skinner*, p. 88, 2001

purple *noun*
the recreational drug ketamine *US*
- — US Department of Justice, *Street Terms*, October 1994

purple *adjective*
sexually suggestive but not explicit *US*
Not quite **BLUE**.
- I saw 'em this morning, Cab, and they're not bad. A little purple, maybe, but interesting. —Carl Hiaasen, *Tourist Season*, p. 43, 1986

purple death *noun*
inexpensive red wine *NEW ZEALAND*
- The Purple Death has scored a few hits over the festive season. It's a wine with a difference, recommended as 'rough-as-guts' drinking. — *Sunday News*, p. 3, 4th January 1987

purple gnome *noun*
a variety of LSD *UK*
- —Angela Devlin, *Prison Patter*, p. 93, 1996

purple haze *noun*
1 LSD *US*
Whether the drug inspired the song – 'Purple Haze all in my brain' (Jimi Hendrix, 'Purple Haze', 1967) – or the song inspired the branding is uncertain.
- Purple Haze all in my brain. —Jimi Hendrix, *Purple Haze*, 1967
- —Richard A. Spears, *The Slang and Jargon of Drugs and Drink*, p. 409, 1986
- They'd arrive in a Purple-Hazish condition and play a song a few times[.] —Frank Zappa, *The Real Frank Zappa Book*, p. 74, 1989
- —Mike Haskins, *Drugs*, p. 286, 2003

2 a potent variety of marijuana *UK*
Named after the 1967 song by Jimi Hendrix.
- —Angela Devlin, *Prison Patter*, p. 93, 1996
- Other types include Purple Haze, Sumatran Red, Durban Poison and skunk. —Macfarlane, Macfarlane and Robson, *The User*, p. 142, 1996

purple-headed love missile *noun*
the erect penis *UK*
Jocular.
- It is through using such uninspiring diagrams and confusing terminology that the scientific community have managed to disarm the purple-headed love missile. —Richard Herring, *Talking Cock*, p. 27, 2003

purple-headed warrior; purple warrior *noun*
the erect penis *US*
This could almost be the superhero identity into which an ordinary comic book penis transforms.
- —Jessica Vitkus, *Smart Sex*, p. 73, 1998
- — *Sky Magazine*, July 2001
- You know, you don't need to put your Purple-Headed Warrior of Love near me, because I don't care. —Laurence Roy Stains, *What Women Want*, p. 335, 2002
- Doesn't the green-eyed monster play havoc with the purple-headed warrior? —Suzi Parker, *Sex in the South*, p. 257, 2003
- Imagine her surprise when you cuddle up next to her and she feels your purple-headed warrior preparing for a third battle. —Karl Mark, *The Complete A**hole's Guide to Handling Chicks*, p. 258, 2003

purple-headed womb ferret *noun*
the penis *UK*
- — *Red Handed (Cardiff)*, p. 10, Autumn 2003

purple heart *noun*
1 a capsule of phenobarbital (trade name Luminal™), a central nervous system depressant *US*
- —Donald Louria, *Nightmare Drugs*, p. 25, 1966
- [F]or five shillings you can buy enough pills – "purple hearts," "depth bombs" and other lovelies of the pharmacalogical arts. —Tom Wolfe, *The Pump House Gang*, p. 81, 1968

2 a tablet of amphetamine Drinamyl™ used as a recreational drug *US*
From the lilac colour of the pill; playing on the US military decoration awarded to any member of the armed forces wounded by the enemy. Also shortened to 'heart' or 'purple'.
- [W]e'd take a taxi back to her gaff and I'd have a heart and pop off to Winston's. —Derek Raymond (Robin Cook), *The Crust on its Uppers*, p. 33, 1962
- [In the 1980s] Mod revivalists, the [Purple Hearts] took their name from a drug much favoured by followers of the in 1960s youth cult. —Simon Warner, *Rockspeak!*, p. 54, 1996
- —Angela Devlin, *Prison Patter*, p. 21, 1996
- I started finding out about Purple Hearts. At sixpence each, some of these kids were taking 80 or 90 a weekend and having amphetamine psychosis. —Simon Napier-Bell, *Black Vinyl White Powder*, p. 43, 2001

purple-helmeted warrior *noun*
▸ **send in the purple-helmeted warrior**
to have sex *US*
- Another way to say "intercourse" [...] Sending in the purple-helmeted warrior[.] —Erica Orloff and JoAnn Baker, *Dirty Little Secrets*, p. 63, 2001

purple hempstar *noun*
in British Columbia, a local variety of marijuana *CANADA*
- Jorege happily snapped pictures of me sniffing bud-Purple Hempstar, Sweet Skunk, a nameless Afghani indica. —Brian Preston, *Pot Planet*, p. 5, 2002

purple Jesus *noun*
an alcoholic drink based on grape juice *CANADA, 1991*
- He introduced her to a few other couples, danced her perfunctorily around the floor, and proceeded to get very drunk on a mixture of grape juice and straight alcohol that the fraternity brothers called Purple Jesus. —Margaret Atwood, *in The New Oxford Book of Canadian Stories*, p. 263, 1997

Purple Nike Swirl E *noun*
a tablet MDMA, the recreational drug best known as ecstasy, with a Nike logo *UK*
- Ecstasy dealers have taken to branding their tablets with famous logos: there is Big Mac E, Purple Nike Swirl E, X-Files E, and a mixture of uppers and downers called a "Happy Meal" —Naomi Klein, *No Logo*, p. 297, 2001

purple nurple; purple herbie *noun*
a violent gripping and twisting assault on someone's (usually a male's) nipples *UK*
- —Chris Lewis, *The Dictionary of Playground Slang*, p. 177, 2003

purple ohm; purple om *noun*
a type of LSD *UK: NORTHERN IRELAND*
- Stex Kelloggs and The Man With No Nickname tripped courtesy of Purple Ohms (aka Mind, Body and Soul), available from all reputable paramilitaries Province-wide. —J. Kelly, *I Talk to Cows, You Know [The Howard Marks Book of Dope Stories]*, p. 253, 2001

purple Owsley *noun*

a powerful type of LSD *US, 1970*

From its colour and the name of legendary LSD manufacturer Augustus Owsley Stanley III. Other variations include 'purple dot'; 'purple dragon'; 'purple microdot'; 'purple owsky'; **PURPLE OZOLIN** and 'purple wedge'.

- —Richard A. Spears, *The Slang and Jargon of Drugs and Drink*, p. 409, 1986

purple ozolin; purple ozoline; purple ozzy *noun*

a powerful variety of LSD *US*

- —Richard A. Spears, *The Slang and Jargon of Drugs and Drink*, p. 409, 1986
- —Mike Haskins, *Drugs*, p. 286, 2003

purple passion *noun*

red wine *US*

- He remembered the previous Christmas with Heff. Mexican grass and birdbath martinis, stealing the D-Phi car at a purple passion party[.] —Richard Farinia, *Been Down So Long*, p. 24, 1966

purple patch *noun*

a string of good luck *AUSTRALIA*

- —Ned Wallish, *The Truth Dictionary of Racing Slang*, p. 65, 1989

purple piccolo *noun*

the erect penis *UK*

- [T]he Romans were certainly not afraid to worship the purple piccolo. —Richard Herring, *Talking Cock*, p. 65, 2003

purple pickle *noun*

the bar awarded to US Air Force flight officers *US*

- —*American Speech*, p. 310, December 1946: 'More Air Force slang'

purple-suiter *noun*

a military officer assigned to the US Department of Defense *US*

- — Department of the Army, *Staff Officer's Guidebook*, p. 64, 1986

purple Thai *noun*

a variety of marijuana *CANADA*

- Purple Thai, which was itself a cross between Chocolate Thai and Highland Oaxaca Gold[.] —Brian Preston, *Pot Planet*, p. 5, 2002

purple warrior *noun*

▷ see: **PURPLE-HEADED WARRIOR**

purr *noun*

the belly *UK*

English gypsy use.

- He couldn't miss the purr as it hangs like a small sack of coal over my track suit bottoms. —Jimmy Stockin, *On The Cobbles*, p. 112, 2000

purse play *noun*

croquet played for money *US*

- —*American Speech*, p. 418, Winter 1997: 'Among the new words'

pus-ball *noun*

▷ see: **PUSS-BALL**

push *noun*

1 a group of friends or associates; a clique *AUSTRALIA, 1884*

Originally 'push' referred to 'an organised gang of street hoodlums'.

- She brought all that stuff home to Sarah and now she's hurrying to tell Lelia Bunthorpe about me. That means the whole push will hear of it. —Norman Lindsay, *The Cousin from Fiji*, p. 240, 1945
- —Norman Lindsay, *Halfway to Anywhere*, p. 104, 1947
- —Alexander Buzo, *Rooted*, p. 87, 1969
- He is a pathetic Polish young man who has loitered about the fringes of the with-it push crowd for years. —Kevin Mackey, *The Cure*, p. 74, 1970
- I might have known I'd land up shit creek friggin' around with a spooky push like youse lot!! —Barry Humphries, *Bazza Pulls It Off!*, 1971
- —Arthur Chipper, *The Aussie Swearer's Guide*, p. 48, 1972
- —Jim Ramsay, *Cop It Sweet!*, p. 74, 1977

2 in betting, a doubling of the bet in effect *US*

- —Sam Snead and Jerry Tarde, *Pigeons, Marks, Hustlers and Other Golf Bettors You Can Beat*, p. 110, 1986

3 in British Columbia logging, the boss, the foreman *CANADA*

- "Well, I'll tell you," says Pete, "I'd a made her I think / But the push, the damn fool, couldn't lay off the drink." —Robert Swanson, *Rhymes of a Haywire Hooker*, p. 21, 1953

4 in blackjack, a tie between the dealer and a player *US*

- —Jerry L. Patterson, *Blackjack*, p. 20, 1978

5 a radio frequency *US*

As in 'the battalion push'. Vietnam war usage.

- —Carl Fleischhauer, *A Glossary of Army Slang*, p. 9, 1968

▸ **the push**

a dismissal from employment or romantic involvement *UK, 1875*

- Blair decides against the push – believing Short will jump. —*The Guardian*, 11th March 2003

push *verb*

1 to sell something, especially drugs *US, 1938*

- There was a government record of those cases but Sid would sooner have his throat cut than push them at legit prices to the drugstore. —Mezz Mezzrow, *Really the Blues*, p. 21, 1946
- Even during the years when I sold the stuff I never "pushed" it like a salesman pushes vacuum cleaners or Fuller brushes. I had it for anybody who came asking, if he was a friend of mine. —Mezz Mezzrow, *Really the Blues*, p. 214, 1946
- You're pushing junk, it's murder, baby. —George Mandel, *Flee the Angry Strangers*, p. 248, 1952
- Pushing weed looks good on paper, like fur farming or raising frogs. —William Burroughs, *Junkie*, p. 30, 1953
- Somebody is pushing horse and tea again. —John D. McDonald, *The Neon Jungle*, p. 32, 1953
- My grandma pushes tea. —*West Side Story*, 1957
- Everyone knows he pushes – and takes the stuff himself. —John Rechy, *City of Night*, p. 210, 1963
- "I wanna push stuff," I whispered. —Piri Thomas, *Down These Mean Streets*, p. 201, 1967
- Frankie has been dealing for six years without a bust. When I first met him he was pushing the stuff out of a hot-dog pushcart on St. Mark's Place. —Abbie Hoffman, *Woodstock Nation*, p. 66, 1969
- I'm no pusher, Betsy. Honest. I never have pushed. —*Taxi Driver*, 1976
- Of making a few stings, getting bread together, of Whitey contacting his man and connecting for weight in heroin and of pushing. —Herbert Huncke, *The Evening Sun Turned Crimson*, p. 209, 1980
- —Angela Devlin, *Prison Patter*, p. 93, 1996

2 to make a special effort to promote a professional wrestler's image and status *US*

- I know Shane McMahon likes him and has told the writing team to push him, but what does he see in him? —*Inside Wrestling*, 25th August 2000

▸ **push poo-poo**

to take the active role in anal sex *FIJI*

Recorded by Jan Tent in 1997.

▸ **push some leg**

to have sex *US*

- —Tom Hibbert, *Rockspeak!*, p. 127, 1983

▸ **push the boat out**

to be more generous or extravagant than usual, to act generously; especially with money *UK, 1937*

Originally naval slang, used of someone buying a round of drinks.

- Thames did a T.V. documentary based on Sloane Rangers and really pushed the boat out. —Peter York, *Style Wars*, p. 16, 1980
- Milan pushed the boat out to extortionate money to get him and they made him an offer he couldn't refuse. —*The Guardian*, 1st August 2002

▸ **push the bush**

(used of a male) to have sex with a woman *US*

- The bartender spoke slowly, as if to an idiot child. "You know, push the bush? Slake the snake? Drain the train? Siphon the python?" —James Ellroy, *Because the Night*, p. 415, 1984

▸ **push the envelope**

to challenge current parameters *US*

From aviation where **ENVELOPE** is the limit of a plane's range and powers, via 1990s marketing speak.

- Greedy trial sharks push envelope of evolution. —*Daily Princetonian*, 16th November 1998
- They were going to push it. Push it further. Much further. What fucking envelope? We can do anything. —Tony Wilson, *24 Hour Party People*, p. 234, 2002

▸ **push up the daisies; pushing up the daisies**

to be dead, especially dead and buried; use is occasionally extended to the dying *UK, 1918*

An image first sketched as the now dated 'turn up your toes to the daisies' in 1842 – from which we derive 'turn up your toes' (to die). Other variations that have slipped from use: 'under the daisies', 'kick up daisies' and, less certainly, 'grin at the daisy-roots', which may also relate to 'roots' (boots).

- And we're pushing up daisies for half a handful of millennia (we're all pushing up daisies, James), until we're powder finer than talc. —Larry Heinemann, *Paco's Story*, p. 17, 1986

- [W]hen we're pushing up daisies / We all look the same — Chumbawumba *Jacob's Ladder (Not In My Name)*, 2002
- The mortality rate is expected to stay constant for another decade: then baby boomers will start pushing up the daisies. — *The Observer*, 29th September 2002

▸ **push your luck**

to take a risk *UK, c.1911*

- I think he [Tony Blair]'d be pushing his luck if he tried to go for another war pretty soon[.] — *The Guardian*, 21st May 2003

push-bike *noun*

a bicycle *UK, 1913*

The 'push' providing a motive distinction from a motorbike.

- [H]e is bicycling around his airy grounds on an old-fashioned push-bike, his knees bobbing up and down as he pedals[.] — *The Guardian*, 30th May 2003

pushed *adjective*

short of something, usually time or money *UK, 1942*

- I'm a bit pushed at the moment. — Ann Barr and Peter York, *The Official Sloane Ranger Handbook*, p. 159, 1982

pusher *noun*

1 a drug dealer *US, 1935*

- Chico slipped the watch on his wrist and they went looking for Domingo, the pusher, to see if he would want it. — Hal Ellson, *The Golden Spike*, p. 15, 1952
- Those nine people are pushers. They handle retail. — John D. McDonald, *The Neon Jungle*, p. 61, 1953
- What frightened the owners most were the "pushers," the traders in narcotics. — Robert Sylvester, *No Cover Charge*, p. 286, 1956
- Many addicts – especially pushers – wear a rubber band on their wrists (a dealer's band, some call it) which, if hooked properly around a deck of heroin, will send it flying if an approaching detective is spotted. — James Mills, *The Panic in Needle Park*, p. 15, 1966
- Everyone down on the pusher, but he don't push nobody, he only push the dope. He provides a service, that's all – somebody got to do it. — Edwin Torres, *Carlito's Way*, p. 41, 1975
- I'm no pusher, Betsy. Honest. — *Taxi Driver*, 1976
- — Angela Devlin, *Prison Patter*, p. 93, 1996

2 in the circus or carnival, a foreman *US*

- — Joe McKennon, *Circus Lingo*, p. 73, 1980

push-in *noun*

a robbery accomplished by knocking on a door and pushing your way into a house or apartment *US*

- "A push-in," said Yo. "You'll have to explain," said Billy. "I don't live up here in this city. "You push 'em in the door," said Yo. — Tom Lewis, *Game of Honor*, p. 276, 1982
- — Angela Devlin, *Prison Patter*, p. 93, 1996

pushing *adverb*

of years of age, approaching, nearly *UK, 1974*

- Go back less than a year and poor Jacques [Chirac] looks out for the count. Pushing 70, a slick but irreparably sleaze-tainted career flesh-presser[.] — *The Guardian*, 6th March 2003

push in the bush *noun*

vaginal sex *US*

- — *Maledicta*, p. 199, Winter 1980: 'A new erotic vocabulary'

push in the truck *noun*

an instance of sexual intercourse *UK*

Rhyming slang for **FUCK** in the transport industry.

- — Ray Puxley, *Cockney Rabbit*, 1992

pushke *noun*

a drive soliciting funds *CANADA*

The term comes from Yiddish, and derives from a charitable collection box in Jewish homes passed around on Sabbath eve to collect for philanthropic purposes.

- Whenever the left-wing pushke was passed around he came through with a nice check. — Mordecai Richler, *Dispatches from the Sporting Life*, p. 286, 2002

push-me-toe *noun*

any thong sandal *TRINIDAD AND TOBAGO*

- — Lise Winer, *Dictionary of the English/Creole of Trinidad & Tobago*, 2003

push-oline *noun*

gasoline, petrol *US*

- — Bill Davis, *Jawjacking*, p. 79, 1977

push out

in the language of hang gliding, used as an all-purpose greeting or farewell *US*

- — Erik Fair, *California Thrill Sports*, p. 328, 1992

pushover *noun*

1 someone who is gullible or easily manipulated; a person who is easily persuaded into sexual activity *US, 1944*

- A curvy push-over called Three-way Rosie lived up at Tenth and Galena. — Iceberg Slim (Robert Beck), *The Naked Soul of Iceberg Slim*, p. 99, 1971
- a romance with a charming little pushover, good for a few drunken parties. — Ayn Rand, *The Fountainhead*, p. 301, 1996
- Jesus was no pushover and displayed firmness and righteous anger toward the religious establishment[.] — Greg Ogden, *Discipleship Essentials*, p. 134, 1998
- It wasn't that she was a pushover either. She had a finely tuned BS detector[.] — Jay McGraw, *Closing the Gap*, p. 42, 2001

2 something that is easy to do *US, 1906*

- As expected, the general election in the fall was a "pushover". — David McCullough, *Truman*, p. 191, 1993

pushunder *noun*

a chamber pot *BARBADOS*

- — Frank A. Collymore, *Barbadian Dialect*, p. 90, 1965

push water *noun*

petrol or diesel fuel *US*

- — Bill Davis, *Jawjacking*, p. 78, 1977

pushy *adjective*

1 self-assertive, especially when unpleasantly so *US, 1936*

- Taking initiative does not mean being pushy, obnoxious, or aggressive. — Stephen R. Covey, *Seven Habits Of Highly Effective People*, p. 75, 1989

2 used of a woman, in the second stage of labour *US*

- — Sally Williams, *"Strong" Words*, p. 156, 1994

pusillanimous polecat *noun*

used as a general term of disapproval *US*

A term used by George 'Gramps' Miller, played by George Cleveland, on the television drama *Lassie* (CBS, 1954–57). Repeated with referential humour.

puss *noun*

1 the vagina; sex *UK*

- Jack Katt and Tom Smart were there, at a front table, lushing it up and keen for puss. — Terry Southern, *Candy*, p. 151, 1958
- That broad can't move, I'm on her. Look at that, scratching her puss[.] — Elmore Leonard, *Split Images*, p. 192, 1981
- After a minute of urgent, unheard deliberation, she's back in business, and finally strips, though she hides her puss with the dress. — Josh Alan Friedman, *Tales of Times Square*, p. 12, 1986
- How did she smell? Did her puss stink? — *Kids*, 1995

2 a girl or woman; an effeminate man *UK*

- I kicked out this puss I had and said that one's mine, the cute blond — Elmore Leonard, *Maximum Bob*, p. 50, 1991
- An you stop actin like a goddamn puss! — Jess Mowry, *Way Past Cool*, p. 9, 1992

3 a 'feminine' lesbian *UK*

- — David Powis, *The Signs of Crime*, 1977

4 the mouth; the face *US, 1891*

A term hatched simultaneously in Ireland and the US.

- I can slap someone in the puss and they can't do a damn thing. — Mickey Spillane, *I, The Jury*, p. 7, 1947
- Do you want me to explain, innocent puss? — Hal Ellson, *Summer Street*, p. 76, 1953
- Did you see the puss on Bobby Tex? — Edwin Torres, *Q & A*, p. 99, 1977
- Why the long puss? I thought that went well. — Cleo Odzer, *Goa Freaks*, p. 102, 1995

5 a disgruntled facial expression *IRELAND*

From Irish *pus*.

- They are also the people who tell me that my extremist political correctness is not only turning me into a sour puss… — *Limerick Leader*, 10th January 2004

puss-ball; pus-ball *noun*

a contemptible person *UK*

- The only thing that's the size of me, you ugly, badly dressed, ignorant, homophobic puss-ball, is your mouth. — Colin Butts, *Is Harry Still on the Boat?*, p. 262, 2003

puss boots *noun*

trainers, sneakers *JAMAICA*

- — Richard Allsopp, *Dictionary of Caribbean English Usage*, p. 457, 1996

pusser; pusser's *adjective*

official *UK*

Royal Navy slang, adapted from the old navy rank of Purser; used in many combinations.

- Anything done unimaginatively or by the book is done in a "Pussers" manner. — Nigel Foster, *The Making of a Royal Marine Commando*, 1987

pusser's *noun*
rum *UK*
Royal Navy slang; derives from 'pusser's' (official issue), not to be confused with branded Pusser's Rum.
- Stocks of Admiralty-issue pusser's are still held, in stone and wickerwork jars, for ceremonial occasions[.] — Rick Jolly, *Jackspeak*, 1989

pusser's brown *noun*
toilet paper *UK*
Royal Navy slang.

pusser's cow *noun*
tinned milk *AUSTRALIA, 1943*
Naval slang.

pusser's dip *noun*
a candle *UK*
Royal Navy slang; originally 'purser's dip'.

pusser's dirk *noun*
a service clasp-knife *UK, 1960*
Royal Navy slang; a variant of 'pusser's dagger'.

pusser's dust *noun*
instant coffee powder *UK*
Royal Navy slang.
- — Rick Jolly, *Jackspeak*, p. 227, 1988

pusser's fix-all *noun*
WD40™, a multi-purpose lubricant *UK*
Royal Navy slang.
- — Rick Jolly, *Jackspeak*, p. 227, 1988

pusser's hard *noun*
navy-issue soap *UK*
Royal Navy slang.
- [Pusser's hard is] now used exclusively in preference to the old term, pusser's yellow or pusser's Vinolia. — Wilfred Granville, *letter to Eric Partidge*, 1962

pusser's leaf *noun*
navy-issue rolling tobacco *UK*
Royal Navy slang.
- — Rick Jolly, *Jackspeak*, p. 227, 1988

pusser's medal *noun*
a food stain on clothing *UK*
Royal Navy slang.
- — Rick Jolly, *Jackspeak*, p. 227, 1988

pussified *adjective*
effeminate *US*
- — Michael Dalton Johnson, *Talking Trash with Redd Foxx*, p. 115, 1994

pussin *noun*
the vagina; a woman as a sexual object *TRINIDAD AND TOBAGO, 1993*
- — Lise Winer, *Dictionary of the English/Creole of Trinidad & Tobago*, 2003

pussy *noun*
1 the vagina; a woman as a sexual object; sex *UK, 1880*
- [T]he cash customers were hotter than a pussy with the pox. — Mezz Mezzrow, *Really the Blues*, p. 85, 1946
- So if you want to get some-a the best pussy in New York, you let me know. — Claude Brown, *Manchild in the Promised Land*, p. 161, 1965
- We're gonna get you the best homemade pussy in America. — Eve Ensler, *The Vagina Monologues*, p. 83, 1998
- "You know what they're saying about us in Wormwood Scrubs, " Mick [Jagger] confided, "they're saying that when the cops arrived they caught me eating a Mars Bar out of your pussy." — *Uncut*, p. 26, January 2002

2 the mouth (as an object of sexual penetration) *US, 1988*
- the rough trade type that insisted on calling my mouth his pussy — Peter Sotos, *Index*, p. 6, 1996

3 a weak or effeminate boy or man; a coward *US, 1942*
- — Collin Baker et al., *College Undergraduate Slang Study Conducted at Brown University*, p. 179, 1968
- If Ossie did not fight, if he turned over all Harry's narco assets and secrets, then Ossie was a pussy. — Robert Deane Pharr, *Giveadamn Brown*, p. 148, 1978
- When I got the nine millimeter, I told everybody I wanted them to know I was no pussy and not to fuck with me. — Terry Williams, *The Cocaine Kids*, p. 60, 1989
- "I'll fuck you up, right fucking now. You pussy," rants Rush. "Who are you calling pussy, you Goodfella's quoting cunt?" — Two Fingers, *Puff (Disco Biscuits)*, p. 220, 1996
- Ah, fuck ya then, you big pussy. — *Something About Mary*, 1998
- Fight back you little pussy. — *American Beauty*, 1999
- A swagger to make John Wayne look a pussy. — Tony Wilson, *24 Hour Party People*, p. 23, 2002

4 a fur skin or fur garment *UK, 1937*
Criminals' slang.
- Everything was where it was supposed to be, some very fair pussies and nice tom [jewellery][.] — Charles Raven, *Underworld Nights*, p. 169, 1956

5 anchovies *US*
Based on the puerile comparison of the smell of fish and the vagina.
- — *Maledicta*, p. 19, 1996: 'Domino's pizza jargon'

6 the middle position in the back seat of a car *US*
- — Edith A. Folb, *runnin' down some lines*, p. 251, 1980

▸ pet the pussy
(of a female) to masturbate *US*
- Another way to say "the girl is masturbating" [...] Petting the pussy[.] — Erica Orloff and JoAnn Baker, *Dirty Little Secrets*, p. 67, 2001

▸ sling pussy
to work as a prostitute *US*
- Now that she was good for nothing else, she figured why not fulfill Sugarfoot's highest ambition for her and sling pussy on Sunset Strip. — Seth Morgan, *Homeboy*, p. 4, 1990

pussy; pussy in *verb*
to move quietly; to enter unobtrusively *AUSTRALIA*
To a degree synonymous with conventional 'pussyfoot'.
- — *The (Sydney) Bulletin*, 26th April 1975

pussy *adjective*
weak; effeminate; not manly *US*
- [S]willing ice-cold raspberry daiquiris and vodka sours by the pitcherful – pussy drinks, bartenders call them. — Larry Heinemann, *Paco's Story*, p. 11, 1986

pussy-ass *noun*
a weak or effeminate man; a coward *US*
- I taught you, you pussy ass! — Howard Stern, *Miss America*, p. 456, 1995

pussy beard *noun*
female pubic hair *US*
- — Dale Gordon, *The Dominion Sex Dictionary*, p. 135, 1967

pussy bumping *noun*
genital-to-genital lesbian sex *US*
- — Vincent J. Monteleone, *Criminal Slang*, p. 185, 1949

pussycat; pussy cat *noun*
1 the vagina *US*
- — Edith A. Folb, *runnin down some lines*, p. 250, 1980
- Don't wear panties underneath your pajamas, dear; you need to air out your pussycat — Eve Ensler, *The Vagina Monologues*, p. 6, 1998

2 a sexually attractive woman *US*
- — Russ Meyer, *Faster, Pussycat! Kill! Kill!*, 1965

3 a pleasant, surprisingly gentle or amenable person *US*
- They were both hulking figures you'd cross the street to avoid if you didn't know them but Garfield did and knew they both were pussy cats. — Larry Kramer, *Faggots*, p. 124, 1978

pussy cat has a nosebleed
a woman who is in the bleed period of the menstrual cycle *US*
A euphemistic elaboration on **PUSSYCAT** (the vagina).
- — *The Museum of Menstruation and Women's Health*, January 2001

pussyclot; pussyclaat *noun*
someone despicable *JAMAICA*
Combines **PUSSY** (vagina) and 'clot' (West Indian pronunciation of 'cloth') to mean 'sanitary towel'; however 'clot' may be understood conventionally as coagulated blood which intensifies the insult.
- I used to know a Jamaican chap and their swearin' is terrible [...] If they call you a pussyclot, you're a blood clot of a tart's doings, you know ... that's fucking filthy, isn't it. — Paul E. Willis, *Profane Culture*, p. 44–45, 1978

- Yuh fucking bawl [bald] head pussyclaat, yuh[.] — Donald Gorgon, *Cop Killer*, p. 144, 1994
- — Bill Valentine, *Gang Intelligence Manual*, p. 111, 1995

pussy cloth *noun*

any improvised sanitary towel *JAMAICA, 1985*

- — Thomas H. Slone, *Rasta is Cuss*, p. 64, 2003

pussy collar *noun*

a desire for sex *US*

- Yes, dopers and drugmen and daper mocking Dans – the fuzz and pussy and pussy-collared[.] — Clarence Cooper Jr, *Black*, p. 289, 1963

pussycratic *adjective*

obsessed with sex *JAMAICA, 1976*

- — Thomas H. Slone, *Rasta is Cuss*, p. 64, 2003

pussy drunk *noun*

a sex offender; a rapist *UK*

- — Angela Devlin, *Prison Patter*, p. 93, 1996

pussy eater *noun*

a practitioner of oral sex on women *US*

- A bit of the old "slow-down-you're-going-too-fast-yeah-there-like-that-oh-that's-perfect" can turn even the John Wayne Bobbitt of pussy eaters into a Doug Hart. — Suroosh Alvi et al., *The Vice Guide*, p. 25, 2002

pussy fart *noun*

an eruption of trapped air from the vagina during sexual intercourse *US*

- Turning pussy farts into mainstream humor requires intense effort. — Howard Stern, *Miss America*, p. 138, 1995

pussyfence *noun*

a receiver of stolen furs *UK*

- Morry Norris, the Pussyfence, going out on a screwing job[.] — Charles Raven, *Underworld Nights*, p. 21, 1956

pussy finger *noun*

the index finger *US*

- You almost wrecked my pussy finger. — *Saturday Night Fever*, 1977

pussyfoot *verb*

to act with such caution that your behaviour appears evasive or cowardly *US, 1903*

From the cautious progress of cats.

- For Christ's sake, Walter, I can't go around pussyfooting on this. — Robert Campbell, *In La-La Land We Trust*, p. 10, 1986
- To reach the restaurant, we had to cross a corner of the paddy field, jump a ravine, and pussyfoot through a ruin. — Cleo Odzer, *Goa Freaks*, p. 28, 1995
- We always pussy-footed around it or tried to find ways of accommodating it. — Sally Cline, *Couples: Scene From the Inside*, p. 298, 1998
- He said it was time for Boorman to stop pussyfooting around and to take an aggressive stance with consumers[.] — Rita Ciresi, *Pink Slip*, p. 297, 1999

pussyfooter *noun*

a railway police officer *US*

- — Ramon Adams, *The Language of the Railroader*, p. 120, 1977

pussy game *noun*

prostitution *US*

- A pimp is an organizer in the pussy game (prostitution). — Burgess Laughlin, *Job Opportunities in the Black Market*, p. 11–4, 1978

pussy hair *noun*

female pubic hair *US*

- Soon the Tenderloin in San Francisco and Forty-second street in New York were audibly rustling with pussyhair. — *Screw*, p. 4, 13th October 1969
- So guys buy these things to look at pussyhair? — *Screw*, p. 4, 3rd July 1972
- One of the hottest times ever was when I told my lover I wanted to go down on her but I wanted to trim her pussy hair first. — Violet Blue, *The Ultimate Guide to Cunnilingus*, p. 63, 2002

pussy holder *noun*

the passenger seat on a motorcyle *US*

- He came and so did guys from a dozen other bike clubs, their mamas in their pussy holders[.] — Nicholas Von Hoffman, *We Are The People Our Parents Warned Us Against*, p. 157, 1967

pussy hole *noun*

a despicable person or object; used abusively *UK*

A synonym for **CUNT**; seemingly euphemistic but possibly more derogatory than the original **PUSSY** (the vagina), with extra detail.

- He called the number [...] "Yaow, Grangebwai ... Pussyhole!" That's all Jigsy managed to say before a stream of profanities greeted him from down the line. — Karlin Smith, *Moss Side Massive*, p. 230, 1994

pussy hook *noun*

a thief who specialises in stealing furs *UK*

A combination of **PUSSY** (a fur) and **HOOK** (a thief).

- Bluey James and Eddy Barnard, two of the greatest pussy-hooks, got themselves locked in[.] — Charles Raven, *Underworld Nights*, p. 203, 1956

pussy hound *noun*

a man obsessed with sex and women *US*

- You're the most notorious pussy hound in Robber-Homicide[.] — James Ellroy, *Blood on the Moon*, p. 144, 1984
- The Stallion was a weight lifter, a party animal – a real pussy hound – and a damn good shooter. — Richard Marcinko, *Rogue Warrior*, p. 285, 1992
- Rumor still had him as a pussyhound, and a bitter one at that. — Faye Kellerman, *Street Dreams*, p. 16, 2003

pussy lips *noun*

the labia *US*

- [W]ord has come down from above that the exposure of pussylips, clitorae, urethrae, etc., is lewd[.] — *Screw*, p. 4, 13th October 1969
- Ugh. All that hair. Then my pussy lips be black. — Alice Walker, *The Color Purple*, p. 78, 1982

pussy man *noun*

a pimp *US*

- "You cheap pimp." She very drunk, you know, and don't know what she saying at all. "Cheap pussy man." — Sara Harris, *The Lords of Hell*, p. 20, 1967

pussy Nellie; pussy Nelly *noun*

a male homosexual *UK*

Mainly naval usage, apparently from early in the C20.

pussy out *verb*

to back out of a task because of fear *US*

- MR. ORANGE: Don't pussy out on me now, Marvin. We're just gonna sit here and bleed until Joe Cabot sticks his fuckin' head through that door. — *Reservoir Dogs*, 1992
- Don't give me that bullshit. Don't pussy out on me. — *The Bad Lieutenant*, 1992
- SANFORD: All I'm saying is if you're going to be insubordinate, you should go the full nine and not pussy out when it comes to free refreshments. — *Clerks*, 1994
- You're just pussyin' out. [...] You're pussy.You'll be lispin' an' reekin' of KY an' shit soon[.] — Nick Barlay, *Curvy Lovebox*, p. 146, 1997

pussy patrol; pussy posse; pussy squad *noun*

a police vice squad focusing on prostitution *US*

- There was, Stanard grandly pointed out, another option that Serpico could elect – the Times Square prostitution detail, the so-called pussy posse[.] — Peter Maas, *Serpico*, p. 156, 1973
- "You ought to transfer to the vice squad. Pussy posse," Chiodo said. — Charles Whited, *Chiodo*, p. 146, 1973
- — Gail Sheehy, *Hustling*, p. 18, 1973: 'Politicians and pussy posses'
- — Ralph de Sola, *Crime Dictionary*, p. 122, 1982

pussy posse *noun*

1 a police vice squad *UK, 1963*

- What is this? You don't belong to the pussy posse? know all them guys. — Jerome Charyn, *Marilyn the Wild [The Isaac Quartet]*, 1976
- It is not uncommon to hear officers from other investigative units refer to the sex crime investigative unit as the "pervert squad," or worse, the "pussy posse." — F.D. Jordan, *Sex Crime Investigations*, p. 9, 1996

2 a group of female friends *US*

- When you get good news, or when you feel so bad even expensive lipstick doesn't help, you will most likely turn to him, not to one of your "pussy posse." — Jill Corral, *Young Wives' Tales*, p. 108, 2001

pussy queer *noun*

a lesbian *US*

- — *Maledicta*, p. 132, Summer/Winter 1982: 'Dyke diction: the language of lesbians'

pussy-seller *noun*

a prostitute *BAHAMAS*

- — John A. Holm, *Dictionary of Bahamian English*, p. 163, 1982

pussysucker; pussysugger *noun*

the mouth *US*

- Settin over there with that grin on his pussysugger an them love-sick eyes jes a-lickin all over my face[.] — Robert Gover, *Here Goes Kitten*, p. 56, 1964

pussywhip *verb*

(used of a woman) to dominate a man *US*

- I ain't gone never let one of them young oversexed broads get ahold of me and pussywhip me and get off into my bankroll. — Joseph Nazel, *Black Cop*, p. 96, 1974

pussy-whipped *adjective*

dominated by a woman *US, 1956*

- — *Current Slang*, p. 4, Summer 1966
- White men (and square Blacks) are thought to be "pussy-whipped" by their wives, after having been brainwashed by their mothers to accept female dominance as the natural order of things. — Christina and Richard Milner, *Black Players*, p. 180, 1972
- Keep seeing a chick who won't fuck you, you get pussy-whipped without even seeing the pussy. — *Saturday Night Fever*, 1977
- Richie liked the idea, the guy thinking he was mean but actually was pussy-whipped. Yes, dear. Whatever you say, dear. — Elmore Leonard, *Killshot*, p. 107, 1989
- He was very much pussy-whipped, OK? His old lady just ran the whole show[.] — William T. Vollman, *Whores for Gloria*, p. 92, 1991
- [H]e croons the wah-wah ballad "Angle Act" achingly, full of baritone tremolos – quintessentially the pussy-whipped loser in lust with the "noir" goddess who's out to trash his life. — James Ellroy, *Hollywood Nocturnes*, p. 8, 1994
- She wants me to work and then come home and be some pussy whipped, Long Island house husband[.] — Howard Stern, *Miss America*, p. 141, 1995
- [David] Beckham has been grotesquely, massively pussy-whipped by his talentless, ambition-hound of a wife. — *The Guardian*, p. 3, 12th June 2003

pussy whisker *noun*

a pubic hair *US*

- You got a wild pussy whisker up your ass? — Robert Campbell, *In La-La Land We Trust*, p. 87, 1986

pussy willow *noun*

a pillow *UK*

Rhyming slang.

- — *This Week*, 10th March 1968

pussy-wood *noun*

stolen firewood *UK, 1984*

Coalminers' use; noted as a 1970s term by W. Forster, editor of *Pit-Talk*.

put *verb*

to dilute a drug *US*

- You put a half on it 'cause it's a little harder for them to get better closer. But, like if somebody's coming up from Virginia? You put a one, one and a half on it. — Richard Price, *Clockers*, p. 180, 1992

▸ put a (number) on

to dilute a drug by the identified numerical factor *US*

- "Give me that stuff, woman!" Sid ordered. "I got ten pieces, Porky, that you can put a six on." — Donald Goines, *Dopefiend*, p. 185, 1971

▸ put it about

to be sexually promiscuous *UK*

- The simplest explanation was that he had just got tired of Jacqui [...] He was a man who had always put it about a bit. — Simon Brett, *Cast in Order of Disappearance*, 1975

▸ put it on

to declare hostilities with another youth gang *US*

- — Dale Kramer and Madeline Karr, *Teen-Age Gangs*, p. 175, 1953

▸ put it to

to have sex with someone *UK*

- You couldn't see a dame like her going without. Someone must be putting it to her. — Kevin Sampson, *Outlaws*, p. 111, 2001

▸ put me in

give me some drugs *UK*

- — Bob Young and Micky Moody, *The Language of Rock 'n' Roll*, p. 113, 1985

▸ put next to

to introduce one person to another or to acquaint one person with another *US, 1906*

- So you're thinking what if I was to put you next to my dry cleaner. — *Get Shorty*, 1995

▸ put on

to fool someone, to tease someone, to deceive someone *US, 1958*

- I assure these people are not putting me on. They are strictly for real. — *The Daily Colonist (Victoria, British Columbia)*, 18th April 1967
- "It sounds like you're putting me on," Dawn said, "except I know you're not." — Elmore Leonard, *Riding the Rap*, p. 230, 1995

▸ put one on

1 to plan a crime *UK*

- — Angela Devlin, *Prison Patter*, p. 93, 1996

2 to hit or punch someone *UK*

- I could put one on him no bother, but it wouldn't be worth the trouble. — Ted Lewis, *Jack Carter's Law*, p. 117, 1974

▸ put paid to

to put a stop to something *UK, 1919*

- Further delay would put paid to the Irish National Hunt season[.] — *The Guardian*, 23rd March 2001

▸ put yourself about

1 to get around and be seen *UK*

Originally police usage, now widespread probably as a result of television and film crime dramas.

- to swagger about, to impress — Peter Laurie, *Scotland Yard*, p. 326, 1970
- to circulate — David Powis, *The Signs of Crime*, 1977

2 to work as a prostitute *UK*

A variation of the previous sense.

- Glad[ys] put herself about around the King's Cross area. — Red Daniells, *British Journal of Photography*, 1st August 1980

puta *noun*

a sexually promiscuous woman; a prostitute *US*

From Spanish *puta* (a whore).

- Liz had been cheating on her. Liz was becoming a tramp. A little chippy. A puta. — Sheldon Lord, *The Third Way*, 1964

put away *verb*

1 to eat or drink something, especially in large quantities *UK, 1878*

- The truly astonishing thing is the huge amounts of food these people put away day by day. — *The Guardian*, 28th May 2003
- It was obvious that the old pair had had a massive row earlier in the day, you could tell from the atmosphere and the way the old dear was putting away the sherry. — Paul Howard, *The Teenage Dirtbag Years*, p. 121, 2001

2 to put someone in jail *UK, 1883*

3 to bribe a jockey to lose a race *UK*

- — *Sporting Chronicle*, 8th September 1978

put-down *noun*

a verbal belittling or criticism *UK, 1984*

- His [Simon Cowell's] abrasive manner and vicious put-downs on Pop Idol and American Idol have kept viewers on both sides of the Atlantic glued to their screens[.] — *The Guardian*, 3rd October 2003

put down *verb*

1 to belittle someone; to treat someone with humiliating contempt *US, 1958*

- rarely consulting him on matters of foreign policy, and putting him down firmly whenever he came up with any ideas of his own — Peter Hopkirk, *Like Hidden Fire*, p. 16, 1994

2 to euthanise an animal *UK, 1899*

- When Mavis found out her dog had been put down in place of Buddy, she called the Belle Glade sheriff's station. — Elmore Leonard, *Maximum Bob*, p. 157, 1991

3 to implicate someone as guilty *US*

- I didn't know if he wanted to put me down or what! I was scared to go down there. — Henry Williamson, *Hustler!*, p. 115, 1965

put it there

used as a greeting, soliciting a handshake *US*

- "Me too." He extended his hand. "Put it there." — Armistead Maupin, *Tales of the City*, p. 129, 1978

puto *noun*

a male homosexual *US*

Border Spanish used by English-speakers in the American southwest.

- [T]he most derogatory are puto (homosexual), culero (coward), and relaje (informer). — George R. Alvarez, *Semiotic Dynamics of an Ethnic-American Sub-Cultural Group*, p. 9, 1965

puto mark *verb*

to cross something out *US*

Puto is Spanish slang for 'a male prostitute'.

- When off brands venture into the area and flag red, it's the same thing as coming in to cross out [puto mark] the local gang members' placas. — Bill Valentine, *Gangs and Their Tattoos*, p. 113, 2000

put-on *adjective*

affected, insincere *UK, 1621*

- He had listened to some of it again to hear her voice, this girl with the easy drawl, nothing put-on about her. —Elmore Leonard, *Be Cool*, p. 15, 1999
- [D]elirious put-on cackling [...] them cackling noises are pure phoney—Kevin Sampson, p. 244, 2001

put out *verb*

1 to consent to sex *US, 1947*

- [I]t was common knowledge that this little tramp put out for every punk on the block. —Bernard Wolfe, *The Late Risers*, p. 46, 1954
- Nobody likes a cockteaser. Either you put out or you don't. —Hubert Selby Jr, *Last Exit to Brooklyn*, p. 107, 1957
- She's been putting out for a long time now. —Willard Motley, *Let No Man Write My Epitaph*, p. 178, 1958
- Sure, I'd make it with the fruits, take whatever I could from them – but I wouldn't put out. —John Rechy, *City of Night*, p. 207, 1963
- None of the girls put out? —Elmore Leonard, *52 Pick-up*, p. 27, 1974
- That went bye-bye down at Harwich, or wherever they were last summer when she made up her mind to put out. —George V. Higgins, *Penance for Jerry Kennedy*, p. 82, 1985
- She only puts out so people will hang out with her. —*Ferris Buehler's Day Off*, 1986
- "So Taggarty put out?" "Most enthusiastically. We were approaching the consummation of the act when the authorities broke in." —C.D. Payne, *Youth in Revolt*, p. 196, 1993
- We're in the big time now. We're freshmen, where all the girls will be putting out. —*Dazed and Confused*, 1993
- Even if it's true she [Britney Spears] doesn't put out (hah!)[.] —*The Guardian*, p. 8, 12th March 2002

2 to be deserving of some punishment *IRELAND*

- In the hall Robbie roared because Jennifer had hit him a clip he'd been putting out for. —Eamonn Sweeney, *Waiting for the Healer*, p. 61, 1997

put-put *noun*

▷ see: PHAT-PHAT

putrid *adjective*

excellent; brilliant *AUSTRALIA*

- I listen to death metal music and lots of the words come from that, like if something was good I would say it was 'rancid', 'putrid' or 'wicked. —*Herald Sun*, p. 11, 22nd June 1993

put some water on it!

used as a demand that a person using a communal toilet flush to rid the room of the smell of faeces *US*

- —Jim Goad, *Jim Goad's Glossary of Northwestern Prison Slang*, December 2001

putt *verb*

to fart *US*

Also used as a noun; a childish variation of **POOT**, probably coined in the mid-1990s by Sylvia Branzei for *Grossology*.

putter *noun*

in hot rodding, a car that has been customised for show rather than performance and is used for 'putting around' *US*

- —John Edwards, *Auto Dictionary*, p. 132, 1993

put the name in the hat *verb*

to inform *UK*

- —Angela Devlin, *Prison Patter*, p. 93, 1996

putting green *noun*

in pool, the largest regulation-size table *US*

- —Steve Rushin, *Pool Cool*, p. 24, 1990

putt-putt *noun*

a boat or vehicle with a puny motor *US*

- We yelled and kissed each other for a considerable time, and then I started the putt-putt and we ran over to the Bass Derby headquarters and entered our baby. —Max Shulman, *I was a Teen-Age Dwarf*, p. 102, 1959
- Presently, we crossed on the little putt-putt ferry and it didn't take five minutes. —Guy Owen, *The Flim-Flam Man and the Apprentice Grifter*, p. 18, 1972
- Run from museum, bump into Bobby Riggs, just arriving from Las Vegas on Harley-Davidson, 175 cc put-put. —Bill Cardoso, *The Maltese Sangweech*, p. 254, 1984

putty *noun*

▸ up to putty

no good *AUSTRALIA, 1916*

- I had a beaut result with a lady who couldn't read her kitchen scales so her cooking was 'up to putty' she brought her scales in and we worked on them. —*www.aris.com.au*, 2003

put up *verb*

to serve time in prison *US*

- I put up eight years at Sing Sing. —Troy Harris, *A Booklet of Criminal Argot, Cant and Jargon*, p. 21, 1976

put-up job *noun*

a pre-arranged deception *UK, 1838*

- [T]he nauseous "Iraqi boy kisses Blair" story, which warmed the flinty cockles of Alastair Campbell's heart. Ross Benson of the Daily Mail told his Arab translator to tell the lad to kiss that nice Mr PM, and he obliged. So the whole thing was a put-up job—*New Statesman*, 30th June 2003

put up or shut up!

used as a challenge to take action to defend what you say, or be quiet *US, 1878*

- IDS [Iain Duncan Smith] was persuaded to emulate John Major's infamous "put up or shut up" challenge in June 1995. —*New Statesman*, 11th November 2002

put you up to *verb*

to incite, induce or persuade you to do something *UK, 1824*

- "He [Leon Rodin] then changed his story and said the GMB had put him up to it," said David [Henke]. —*The Guardian*, 14th September 2000

putz *noun*

1 the penis *US, 1934*

- Smolka, who is always dragging drinks out of everybody else's bottle of cream soda, and grabbing with his hand at your putz! —Philip Roth, *Portnoy's Complaint*, p. 188, 1969
- With regard to the erection per se there is no relationship between the sized of a non-erect putz and its size at erection (so stop comparing schlongs in the locker room)[.] —*Screw*, p. 8, 8th December 1969
- Then he screamed like his putz was in a vise. —Iceberg Slim (Robert Beck), *Long White Con*, p. 55, 1977
- Bet he'd be naked under the coat. Show his stubby putz to every broad he passed on the street—Joseph Wambaugh, *The Glitter Dome*, p. 176, 1981
- Dave's professional putz was just too big. —Josh Alan Friedman, *Tales of Times Square*, p. 117, 1986

2 by extension, an inept, contemptible person *US, 1964*

- The poor putz had nothing to do with Sparky Harper's death[.] —Carl Hiaasen, *Tourist Season*, p. 182, 1986
- Don't be a putz – who's been to Santiago twice in a year? —*Something About Mary*, 1998
- NBC took offence when Walther Matthau called George Burns a "putz", the word to denote "penis" rather than the more common understanding of "jerk". —Aubrey Dillon-Malone, *I Was a Fugitive from a Hollywood Trivia Factory [on "The Sunshine Boys" (1975)]*, p. 44, 1999

putz *verb*

▸ putz around

to idle; to do nothing; to waste time *US*

- The fish was stone-cold-blooded about collecting for damages after a real accident occurred. He didn't putz around—Emmett Grogan, *Ringolevio*, p. 141, 1972
- What the man says she does, she putzes. Putzes around the house trying to think up things to be done—Elmore Leonard, *Stick*, p. 102, 1983
- They putz around, make it as a big case, call Homicide. —James Ellroy, *L.A. Confidential*, p. 228, 1990

PW *adjective*

dominated by a female *US*

An abbreviation of **PUSSY-WHIPPED**.

- —Andy Anonymous, *A Basic Guide to Campusology*, p. 19, 1966

p-whipped *adjective*

dominated by a female *US*

An abbreviated and euphemised **PUSSY-WHIPPED**.

- Oh my God. You're completely p-whipped. —*Cruel Intentions*, 1999

pyjama cricket; pyjama game *noun*

oneday cricket *AUSTRALIA, 1982*

So-called from the colourful uniforms worn by players instead of the usual cricket whites.

- This cleared the way for the pyjama game which saw some strange results, no really good finishes and the World Series Cup back in Australian hands. —*Sun*, p. 67, 12th February 1986

pyjama-python *noun*

the penis *AUSTRALIA*

- I flashed the old pyjama-python[.] —Barry Humphries, *Bazza Pulls It Off!*, 1971

pylons *noun*

the legs *US*

- —*Time Magazine*, p. 92, 20th January 1947: 'Dicty dictionary'

PYO

*p*ick-*y*our-*o*wn, applied to soft fruits and farm vegetables *UK*

Usually seen in roadside advertising.

• — *New Society*, 19th August 1982

pyro *noun*

a pyromaniac; pyrotechnics *UK, 1977*

• —John Ayto, *The Oxford Dictionary of Slang*, p. 303, 1998

python *noun*

the penis *AUSTRALIA*

• Hand down my tweeds...fingers coiled around my python...tug, tug...dragged off by the skewer...behind the dunnies. —Jack Hibberd, *A Stretch of the Imagination*, p. 15, 1971

Pythonesque *adjective*

of an event, or series of events, more than bizarre but less than surreal *UK, 1979*

From the television comedy series *Monty Python's Flying Circus*, BBC, 1969–74.

• The legal department says we can't use the word "activist" in the (Body Shop) Foundation annual report because of its association with TERRORISM! This really is too Pythonesque for me[.] —John Elkington, *The Chrysalis Economy*, p. 105, 2001

p'zazz *noun*

▷ **see: PIZZAZZ**

Qq

Q *noun*

1 a homosexual *US*
An abbreviation of **QUEER**.
- —Collin Baker et al., *College Undergraduate Slang Study Conducted at Brown University*, p. 179, 1968

2 of drugs, generally marijuana, a quarter of an ounce *UK*
- How many [ecstasy tablets] was you wantin'? – Ten... An' a q. —Nick Barlay, *Curvy Lovebox*, p. 45, 1997

3 the recreational drug methaqualone, best known as Quaaludes™ *US, 1977*
- —Richard A. Spears, *The Slang and Jargon of Drugs and Drink*, p. 412, 1986
- —Mike Haskins, *Drugs*, p. 283, 2003

4 in a deck of playing cards, a queen *US*
- —Michael Dalton, *Blackjack*, p. 71, 1991

5 barbecue *US*
- The term barbecue (a.k.a. Bar-B-Q, BBQ, 'cue, or, to the real aficionados, simply Q) is often used synonymously with grilling. —Omaha Steaks, *Omaha Steaks*, 2001

6 in American casinos, a $25 chip *US, 1983*
An abbreviation of **QUARTER**.
- —Steve Kuriscak, *Casino Talk*, p. 45, 1985
- —Thomas L. Clark, *The Dictionary of Gambling and Gaming*, p. 170, 1987

Q *nickname*

the San Quentin state prison in San Rafael, California *US*
- If you was to run into the front end of a Mack truck on one of these corners, the dings might miss you bad over at Q. —Thurston Scott, *Cure it with Honey*, p. 62, 1951
- Went to Q behind armed robbery. —Joseph Wambaugh, *The Blue Knight*, p. 27, 1973
- Frantically the number was correctly ascertained and the call made again but the assistant warden at Q told her that the cyanide pellets had just been dropped. —Ed Sanders, *Tales of Beatnik Glory*, p. 45, 1975
- Half the people you're going to meet at Q are there because someone ratted them out. —Vincent Patrick, *Family Business*, p. 264, 1985
- Her ex – old man's out of Q. —Robert Campbell, *Sweet La-La Land*, p. 234, 1990
- If you were a troublemaker at Q, they'd keep you inside your cell by welding the door shut. —Ralph "Sonny" Barger, *Hell's Angel*, p. 193, 2000

Q and A

a question and answer session *US*
- LASSARO'S AIDE: Where are we going with this? I thought this was a Q and A about the bridge. —*Copland*, 1997
- Anyway, we went through the usual Q and A. When they asked me who had done it, I said I'd been bitten by a dog. —Dave Courtney, *Stop the Ride I Want to Get Off*, p. 223, 1999

qat *noun*

1 methcathinone *US*
- —Office of National Drug Control Policy, *Drug Facts*, February 2003

2 leaves of *catha edulis,* a stimulant also called k, khat or kat, originating in the Horn of Africa and the Arabian peninsula, legally available in the UK and similar to amphetamine in effect when chewed *UK*
Also known as 'qaadka'.
- —Angela Devlin, *Prison Patter*, p. 93, 1996

Q boat *noun*

an unmarked police car with plain clothes officers *UK*
From the name given to disguised naval vessels in World War 1.
- —David Powis, *The Signs of Crime*, 1977

QE *verb*

to turn *Q*ueen's *E*vidence (to give evidence for the prosecution against your alleged accomplices) *UK*
- —Angela Devlin, *Prison Patter*, p. 93, 1996

Q-ship *noun*

among hot rodders, a high-performing car that appears to be a conventional car *US*
Taken from the early C20 meaning of an armed and camouflaged merchant ship used as a decoy.
- —John Lawlor, *How to Talk Car*, p. 85, 1965

Q-sign *noun*

of a very sick hospital patient, the open mouth with the tongue hanging out *UK*
Medical wit; the 'Q' is an image of the mouth and tongue as described. The **O-SIGN** is not quite as serious.
- —Adam T. Fox, St Mary's Hospital, London, 10th October 2002

QT *noun*

▸ on the QT

quietly, in strict confidence *UK, 1884*
- She told me right in front of my boyfriend and kids that she had heard from one of her stool pigeons that I was screwing four or five guys on the Q.T. —Iceberg Slim (Robert Beck), *Mama Black Widow*, p. 103, 1969
- And that's what we did I organized... on the q.t. of course, a tribal festival that involved the Asantehene. —Odie Hawkins, *The Busting Out of an Ordinary Man*, 1985
- Well, this is only my first charitable donation – $400,000 – to the community; between me and you on the "Q.T.," of course. —*New Jack City*, 1990
- So everything is on the Q-T here. —Howard Stern, *Miss America*, p. 453, 1995

Q tip *noun*

in poker, a queen and a ten *US*
- —John Vorhaus, *The Big Book of Poker Slang*, p. 31, 1996

quack *noun*

1 a doctor of medicine *AUSTRALIA, 1919*
Following an earlier (mid-C17) sense as 'a pretended doctor', abbreviated from 'quacksalver' (one who sells his salves by noisy patter or 'quacking'). The current sense, spread through military use, does not imply any lack of qualification or a degree of salesmanship.
- Would you mind telling me why you called that old quack? —Max Shulman, *Rally Round the Flag, Boys!*, p. 142, 1957
- When the last one had been in to see the quack the screw came out and told us to file back into the reception room. —Frank Norman, *Bang To Rights*, p. 13, 1958
- TRAPPER: But weren't you supposed to meet the surgeons who are going to slice up the Congressman's son? GORMAN: You guys are the quacks? —*M*A*S*H*, 1970
- [S]ome pom [British] quack reckons I got you up the spout [pregnant][.] —Barry Humphries, *Bazza Pulls It Off!*, 1971
- On Saturday morning Paul was telling them about what happened at the quack's. —*Bluey 'Bush Contractors'*, p. 144, 1975
- No, no, the doctor says I should walk and I had some shopping. Not that that quack knows what he's talking about. —*Body Heat*, 1980
- You can pop along to the quack and he'll give you a script for Prozac, or whatever. —Kevin Sampson, *Powder*, p. 117, 1999

2 a hospital patient who feigns symptoms in order to receive attention, prescription medication or both *US*
- —*Maledicta*, p. 6, Summer/Winter 1978: 'Common patient-directed pejoratives used by medical personnel'
- —Sally Williams, *"Strong" Words*, p. 157, 1994

3 in poker, a player who complains loudly when losing *US*
- —John Scarne, *Scarne's Guide to Modern Poker*, p. 288, 1979

4 the recreational drug methaqualone, best known as Quaaludes™ *US*
- By 1972 it was one of the most popular drugs of abuse in the United States and was known as 'love drug', 'heroin for lovers', 'Dr. Jekyll and Mr. Hyde', 'sopors', 'sopes', 'ludes', 'mandrakes and quacks'. —Marilyn Carroll and Gary Gallo, *Methaqualone*, p. 18, 1985

5 a firefighter *US*
New York police slang.

• —Samuel M. Katz, *Anytime Anywhere*, p. 389, 1997: 'The extremely unofficial and completely off-the-record NYPD/ESU truck-two glossary'

6 a novice surfer *US*

• —Gary Fairmont R. Filosa II, *The Surfer's Almanac*, p. 192, 1977

quacker *noun*

a Kawasaki motorcycle *UK*

• —Douglas Dunford, *Motorcycle Department, Beaulieu Motor Museum*, 1979

quackery *noun*

forensic scientists; a forensic science department *UK*
Police use; always used with 'the'. Probably a pun on **QUACK** (a doctor).

• —John Wainwright, *Dig His Grave and Let Him Lie*, 1971

quackie *noun*

a white person *TRINIDAD AND TOBAGO, 1971*

• —Lise Winer, *Dictionary of the English/Creole of Trinidad & Tobago*, 2003

quack-quack *noun*

1 a duck *UK, 1865*
An echoic term, used by, or to, infants.

2 a commotion *TRINIDAD AND TOBAGO, 1982*

• —Lise Winer, *Dictionary of the English/Creole of Trinidad & Tobago*, 2003

quad *noun*

1 a *quad*riplegic *US*

• — *Maledicta*, p. 56, Summer 1980: 'Not sticks and stones, but names: more medical pejoratives'

2 in trucking, a *quad*riplex transmission that provides twenty forward gears and four reverse *US*

• —Montie Tak, *Truck Talk*, p. 126, 1971

3 the recreational drug methaqualone, best known as Quaaludes™ *US, 1980*

• —Richard A. Spears, *The Slang and Jargon of Drugs and Drink*, p. 412, 1986
• —Mike Haskins, *Drugs*, p. 283, 2003

4 a carburettor with four barrels *US*

• —John Lawlor, *How to Talk Car*, p. 85, 1965

5 a clumsy, inept fool *CANADA*
An evolved **SQUARE**.

• —Jack Chambers (Editor), *Slang Bag 93 (University of Toronto)*, p. 5, Winter 1993

quad-fifty *noun*

a quadruple mount .50 calibre machine gun, a devastating truck-drawn trailer-mounted weapon *US*
Originated in World War 2.

• Two "quad-fifties" – four .50 caliber machine guns on a single mount: two of these units – are set up on the hill mass behind us. —Martin Russ, *The Last Parallel*, p. 204, 1957
• "What kind of weapons platoon did you command, sir?" "It was a quad-fifties platoon, as I recall." —Lucian K. Truscott, *Army Blue*, p. 335, 1989

quadruplets *noun*

in poker, four cards of the same rank *US*

• —John Scarne, *Scarne's Guide to Modern Poker*, p. 288, 1979

quads *noun*

1 the quadriceps muscles *US*

• — *American Speech*, p. 201, Fall 1984: 'The language of bodybuilding'

2 in poker, a hand with all four cards of the same rank *US*

• —Peter O. Steiner, *Thursday Night Poker*, p. 416, 1996

quaff *verb*

to drink alcohol *UK*

• I stay loose. I hit the flicks, goof off a little, quaff a few brews with the boys. —Max Shulman, *Guided Tour of Campus Humor*, p. 105, 1955
• —Connie Eble (Editor), *UNC-CH Campus Slang*, p. 4, November 1983

quail *noun*

1 a woman *US, 1859*

• He goes to the jukery to watch and wait and cut a rug with a solid gate: he snatches a quail with hep and class and they go to town cooking with gas! — Haenigsen, *Jive's Like That*, 1947
• I fix him up with the fanciest quail in Greater Manhattan. —Bernard Wolfe, *The Late Risers*, p. 248, 1954

2 a girl under the legal age of consent *US*
A shortened form of **SAN QUENTIN QUAIL**.

• — Radio Shack, *CBer's Handy Atlas/Dictionary*, p. 38, 1976

3 a twenty-five cent betting token used in craps *US, 1983*

• —Thomas L. Clark, *The Dictionary of Gambling and Gaming*, p. 170, 1987

Quaker oat *noun*

a coat *UK, 1932*
Rhyming slang, formed from Quaker Oats™, a brand of porridge.

• —Ray Puxley, *Cockney Rabbit*, 1992

quality *noun*

▸ **the quality**

anyone who is not a member of the travelling community *IRELAND*

• Bridgie sniffed. 'Serves you right,' she said. 'You shouldn't tell the quality notten.' —Seamus Dunne, *The Gardner*, p. 11

quango *noun*

a government-financed, notionally independent body with a powerful interest in a given field of interest *UK, 1973*
An acronym for *Qua*si *N*on-*Go*vernment(al) *O*rganisation or *Qua*si-*A*utonomous *N*ational *G*overnment *O*rganisation.

• MPs launch inquiry into housing quango. — *The Guardian*, 16th January 2004

quanker *noun*

in Nova Scotia, a duck-calling device *CANADA*

• This he does by going to the stairdoor and squawking loudly on the small horn-like instrument made to entice ducks, and called a "Quanker." —Evelyn Richardson, *We Keep a Light*, p. 173, 1945

quare *adjective*

mediocre *UK*

• —Tom Hibbert, *Rockspeak!*, p. 129, 1983

quare hawk *noun*

someone who is unconventional in some way *IRELAND*

• "I've seen some quare hawks in my time but that one takes the biscuit."..."They wouldn't go round in England dressed up like that." —Shane Connaughton, *A Border Station*, p. 32, 1989
• As a matter of fact Kilcrea Park, for a small little place, has produced more than its fair share of quare-hawks – weird types I mean, not faggotts like. —Gaye Shortland, *Mind that 'tis my Brother*, p. 26, 1995

quare one *noun*

wife *IRELAND*

• I have a few pounds put away, see. And if we'd gone to Donoghue's the quare one would have known I had it and I'd have to give her some. — Eamonn Sweeney, *Waiting for the Healer*, p. 96, 1997

quar ice *noun*

water that has oozed through the ground through snow and frozen on the surface *CANADA*

• Quar ice is a Labrador term for ice formed in spring from melt water draining on to a beach, ice foot or fast ice where it refreezes. —*Glossary of Arctic and Subarctic Terms*, 1955

quarked out *adjective*

under the influence of drugs *US*

• Three hours later I was in Dodie's apartment quarked out on ludes, my head hanging off the mattress[.] —Rita Ciresi, *Pink Slip*, p. 96, 1999

quarm *verb*

(used of a man) to behave in an exaggerated, effeminate manner *BAHAMAS*

• —John A. Holm, *Dictionary of Bahamian English*, p. 164, 1982

quart *noun*

1 a twenty-five cent piece *BARBADOS*

• —Frank A. Collymore, *Barbadian Dialect*, p. 90, 1965

2 in poker, four cards of the same suit in sequence *US*

• —John Scarne, *Scarne's Guide to Modern Poker*, p. 288, 1979

quarter *noun*

1 a quarter of an ounce of drugs, especially cocaine *US*

• — *Current Slang*, p. 39, Fall 1968
• —Angela Devlin, *Prison Patter*, p. 94, 1996

2 a quarter of a kilo of drugs *UK*

• —Angela Devlin, *Prison Patter*, p. 94, 1996

3 twenty-five dollars' worth of drugs *US*
Also called a 'quarter bag'.

4 a prison sentence of 25 years *US*

• Say, "I'm gonna see if you can't shake this quarter off your goddamn ass." — Bruce Jackson, *Get Your Ass in the Water and Swim Like Me*, p. 87, 1964

- The usual sentence for that [armed robbery] is ten to a quarter. — Bruce Jackson, *In the Life*, p. 30, 1972
- "You can also pull ten to a quarter in Jackson," Stick said. — Elmore Leonard, *Swag*, p. 16, 1976
- — William K. Bentley and James M. Corbett, *Prison Slang*, p. 23, 1992

5 a jail sentence of three months *UK*
Also referred to as 'quarter bit' and 'quarter stretch'.
- — David Powis, *The Signs of Crime*, 1977
- — Ralph de Sola, *Crime Dictionary*, p. 123, 1982

6 in American casinos, a $25 chip *US*
- — Lee Solkey, *Dummy Up and Deal*, p. 118, 1980
- — Steve Kuriscak, *Casino Talk: A Rap Sheet for Dealers and Players*, p. 11, 1985

7 twenty-five pounds of weights used in lifting *US*
- — James Harris, *A Convict's Dictionary*, p. 37, 1989

8 a cigarette *US*
- A square is a cigarette. And also a quarter. — Willard Motley, *Let No Man Write My Epitaph*, p. 148, 1958

quarter bird *noun*
one quarter pound of cocaine *US*
- Erfort then offered Korey "a quarter bird," street slang for a quarter pound of cocaine, to kill Kuhn, Logan testified. — *Pittsburgh Post-Gazette*, p. B7, 10th November 1999

quarter-deck *verb*
during US Marine Corps basic training, to administer physical discipline or Incentive Physical Training *US*

quarter house *noun*
a place where mid-level heroin dealers do business *US*
- — Burgess Laughlin, *Job Opportunities in the Black Market*, p. 6, 1978: 'Glossary'

quarter rock *noun*
crack cocaine *US*
- — Kenn "Naz" Young, *Naz's Dictionary of Teen Slang*, p. 95, 1993

quart store *noun*
a store that sells beer on the retail level *US*
- — Amy and Denise McFadden, *CoalSpeak*, p. 11, 1997

quartz *noun*
methamphetamine that is smoked *UK, 1998*
- — Mike Haskins, *Drugs*, p. 279, 2003

Quasar *noun*
a woman *US*
A strained allusion to a Quasar television advertising slogan – 'works in a drawer', and then punning on 'drawers' as 'trousers'.
- — Lanie Dills, *The Official CB Slanguage Language Dictionary*, p. 57, 1976

quashie *noun*
a country-dweller; an unsophisticated peasant *UK*
Possibly from C18 *Quashee*, an African name, adopted by white people as a general name for any black person.
- [A] promising football career being ended at the age of twenty by some shitkicker (or "quashie" as Steve preferred it) Millwall reserves stopper lumping him in the knee[.] — Greg Williams, *Diamond Geezers*, p. 31, 1997

Quasimodo *noun*
soda water *UK*
Rhyming slang, formed from 'The Hunchback of Notre Dame'. Noted, with a witty reference to Bells™ whisky, by Ray Puxley, *Cockney Rabbit*, 1992.

quat *noun*
in betting, odds of 4–1 *UK*
- — John McCririck, *John McCririck's World of Betting*, p. 112, 1991

quater *noun*
twenty-five cents *US*
A corruption of 'quarter'.
- — Joe McKennon, *Circus Lingo*, p. 74, 1980

quater; quarter; quaterer *adjective*
four *UK*
Polari, from Italian *quattro*.
- [Y]ou might like to count to ten in Polari: una, duey, trey, quater, chicker, sey, setter, otto, nobber, dacha. — Michael Quinion, *World Wide Words*, 1996

quaver *verb*
1 to dither, especially over whether or not to make a purchase *UK*
- The crowie [old woman] was quavering about. — Patrick O'Shaughnessy, *Market Traders' Slang*, 1979

2 to potter about; to tinker *UK*
- The gorger [man]'s quavering about with the screeve [car]. — Patrick O'Shaughnessy, *Market Traders' Slang*, 1979

quaverer *noun*
a vacillating, or uncertain, customer *UK*
From **QUAVER**.
- — Patrick O'Shaughnessy, *Market Traders' Slang*, 1979

quawk *noun*
uncooked frozen meat or fish *CANADA*
- The fish are thus eaten without cooking, and the mess is called quawk. — Charles Gillham, *Raw North*, p. 117, 1947

quay; quas *noun*
the recreational drug methaqualone, best known as Quaaludes™ *US*
- The great Mandrax! Is that the same as quay? BOCKRIS: Stronger than quay. The English equivalent. They use it a lot for seduction. — Victor Bockris, *With William Burroughs [The Howard Marks Book of Dope Stories]*, p. 35, 1997

quean *noun*
1 an effeminate male homosexual; an ageing passive homosexual *UK, 1935*
- [A]ged queans beating each other black and blue[.] — Derek Raymond (Robin Cook), *The Crust on its Uppers*, p. 33, 1962
- — Home Office, *Glossary of Terms and Slang Common in Penal Establishments*, July 1978

2 a lesbian *UK, 1984*
A term used by male homosexuals.

quean up *verb*
in male homosexual society, to adopt girlish mannerisms and affectations; to use cosmetics and to primp *UK*
Defined as British gay slang by Bruce Rodgers, *The Queen's English*, 1972.

queased out *adjective*
nauseated, sick *US*
- I start to feel a little sick to my stomach. Queased out. — Francesca Lia Block, *Missing Angel Juan*, p. 257, 1993

Quebec wrench *noun*
a beer bottle opener *CANADA*
The high consumption rate of beer in Quebec is the source of this oral slang item.

queber *noun*
a social outcast *US*
- — Mitch McKissick, *Surf Lingo*, 1987

queeb *noun*
a bisexual *US*
- — Michael V. Anderson, *The Bad, Rad, Not to Forget Way Cool Beach and Surf Discriptionary*, p. 15, 1988

queef *noun*
the passing of air from the vagina *US*
- [D]efending this limp-wristed yuppie handjob of an album as if it were High Art, and acting as if the blues were a queef emitted from the loins of Camryn Manheim – when she had a yeast infection[.] — *OC Weekly*, p. 25, 25th October 2002
- — Chris Lewis, *The Dictionary of Playground Slang*, p. 179, 2003

queef *verb*
to expel air from the vagina, intentionally or not *US*
- A friend reported the entertainment sticking a banana in her spicebox, asking him to hold his arms aloft like goalposts, then queefing said banana through the uprights. — *Nerve*, p. 17, October-November 2000
- I want a girl who queefs during sex to be able to laugh about it with her partner instead of blushing in embarrassment[.] — *Ohio University Post*, 7th November 2002

queen *noun*
1 a obviously homosexual male *AUSTRALIA, 1924*
- When the cops cracked down, the pouting queens and Lesbians took to Greenwich Village. — Jack Lait and Lee Mortimer, *New York Confidential*, p. 68, 1948

- The ones that bothered the hotel were the aggressive pansies, the ones the staff usually referred to as "queens." The hip-swishing, wrist-flapping type is strictly trouble in trousers. — Dev Collans with Stewart Sterling, *I was a House Detective*, p. 105, 1954
- They would pretend to be "bait" and allow themselves to be taken home by some queen. — Robert Sylvester, *No Cover Charge*, p. 268, 1956
- [E]ven Camille, a frail queen from a small town in Jersey, longed for rough arms. — Hubert Selby Jr, *Last Exit to Brooklyn*, p. 59, 1957
- It was assumed by the Row that because we ganged together so closely the four of us were confirmed, comradely queens. — Clancy Sigal, *Going Away*, 1961
- — Donald Webster Cory and John P. LeRoy, *The Homosexual and His Society: A View from Within*, p. 266, 1963: 'A lexicon of homosexual slang'
- Old Jewish mothers never know when their sons are faggots. They just miss it somehow. Out-and-out screaming queens – mothers are never hip. — Lenny Bruce, *The Essential Lenny Bruce*, p. 162, 1967
- One of them is a Negro queen named Irving Amadeus. — Gore Vidal, *Myra Breckinridge*, p. 87, 1968
- If there's one thing I'm not ready for, it's five screaming queens singing Happy Birthday. — Mart Crowley, *The Boys in the Band*, 1968
- And that's what the old queen heard in the lav at Maurice's. — Ted Lewis, *Jack Carter's Law*, p. 157, 1974
- All the animals come out at night. Whores, skunk pussies, buggers, queens, fairies, dopers, junkies, sick, venal. — *Taxi Driver*, 1976
- As one old queen – who had the apartment next to Spencer's – told me – "My dear – it was really too much. It was a regular black and tan fantasy." — Herbert Huncke, *The Evening Sun Turned Crimson*, p. 43, 1980
- That dapper old queen whose wrist was always limp [...] could have minced for England. — Stuart Jeffries, *Mrs Slocombe's Pussy*, p. 102, 2000

2 a mother *UK*
As the ruler of the house.
- What's such a big fuckin pain about livin with yer ahl (old) queen? Food cooked for yis, clothes washed an ironed[.] — Niall Griffiths, *Kelly + Victor*, p. 285, 2002

3 a popular girl *US*
- — *Time Magazine*, p. 46, 24th August 1959

4 a girlfriend, mistress or prostitute *US*
- — Carl Fleischhauer, *A Glossary of Army Slang*, p. 9, 1968
- — Lise Winer, *Dictionary of the English/Creole of Trinidad & Tobago*, 2003

5 an enthusiast of the preceding thing or activity *US*
- Do I look like some king of gossip queen? — *Cruel Intentions*, 1999

Queen *noun*

▸ **for the Queen**
used to describe extra days added as punishment to a sentence of imprisonment *UK*
- I had to do five days extra for the Queen. — Angela Devlin, *Prison Patter*, p. 94, 1996

▸ **go Queen's; turn Queen's**
to turn Queen's evidence, that is, to give evidence against co-defendants, usually to your own advantage *UK*
- — Angela Devlin, *Prison Patter*, p. 58, 1996
- In fact he felt the full force of the law after repeatedly refusing to turn Queen's and hand up me, Vince and Sid. — Danny King, *The Bank Robber Diaries*, p. 56, 2002

▸ **the Queen**
the National Anthem *UK, 1952*
Before this we stood for 'the King'.

Queen Anne is dead
a catchphrase retort on old news *UK, 1722*
Later variations – 'Queen Elizabeth and my Lord Baldwin' – have not survived.
- "Kilroy from Walton." "What about him?" "He's broken out and Queen Anne's dead," Jock said. "Get away," Grobe said. — Troy Kennedy Martin, *Z Cars*, p. 139, 1962

queen bee *noun*

1 the alpha male in a group of homosexuals *US*
Punning on **QUEAN**. *The Guild Dictionary of Homosexual Terms*, 1965, offers this definition: 'usually, but not always, an auntie with money, an entourage, and numbers (sex-partners). Frequently he is elderly and, most always, an agreeable person.'

2 a heterosexual woman who seeks out the company of homosexual men *US*
- A man with white tie and dress shirt, naked from the waist down except for black garters, talks to the Queen Bee in elegant tones. (Queen Bees are women who surround themselves with fairies)[.] — William Burroughs, *Naked Lunch*, p. 80, 1957

Queen Charlotte tuxedo *noun*
a heavy grey Stanfield's undershirt *CANADA*
- A Queen Charlotte tuxedo was preferably worn for weeks without washing, and stained to suit the inhabitant's habits. — Tom Parkin, *WetCoast Words*, p. 112, 1989

queenie *noun*
a prostitute *US*
- Rest a us queenies from them eight places up and down the street, we was left high and dry, cause they wasn't gonna open them places up no more. — Robert Gover, *Here Goes Kitten*, p. 153, 1964

Queenie *nickname*
Queensland, Australia *AUSTRALIA, 1994*
- — Maureen Brooks and Joan Ritchie, *Tassie Terms*, p. 115, 1995

Queen Mary *noun*

1 a surfboard that is too big for the surfer using it *US*
Named after the ocean liner, not a royal female.
- — John Severson, *Modern Surfing Around the World*, p. 178, 1964

2 a large tank truck *US*
An ocean liner reference.
- — Jerry Robertson, *Oil Slanguage*, p. 102, 1954

Queen of Mean *nickname*
Leona Helmsley (b.1920), American hotelier and prototype of greed during the Reagan era *US*
- — Jim Crotty, *How to Talk American*, p. 235, 1997

Queen of the Jukebox *nickname*
Dinah Washington (1924–1963), a brilliant vocalist in the jazz, pop and R&B genres *US*
- One year at their dance at the Hilton, their star was the Queen (Dinah). — Babs Gonzales, *Movin' On Down De Line*, p. 45, 1975

Queen of the South *noun*
the mouth *UK*
Rhyming slang, formed from the name of a Scottish football club.
- — Ray Puxley, *Cockney Rabbit*, 1992

Queen's Cowboys *nickname*
the Royal Canadian Mounted Police *CANADA*
- — Tom Parkin, *WetCoast Words*, p. 112, 1989

queen's gaff *noun*
the anus *UK*
An allusion to **WINDSOR CASTLE**, a royal **GAFF** (residence) in Berkshire which also serves as rhyming slang for 'arsehole'.
- — Ray Puxley, *Cockney Rabbit*, p. 201, 1992

Queenslander *noun*
a type of weatherboard house raised on stilts *AUSTRALIA*
- Happens all the time in Brisbane. Old Queenslanders get chopped in two, hauled up onto a flatbed and driven off to some yuppie's farm. — John Birmingham, *He Died With a Felafel in his Hand*, p. 82, 1994

Queen's Necklace *nickname*
in Mumbai, the view after dark of the sparkling lights on Marine Drive (now Netaji Subhash Road) *INDIA*
- Raveena Tandon (right) and a friend enjoy watching the Mumbai skyline and the Queen's Necklace at the Raymond Fashion show 2003 in Mumbai[.] — *The Times of India*, 16th November 2002

Queens Park Ranger *noun*
a stranger *UK*
Rhyming slang, formed from the full name of QPR, the London football club, Queens Park Rangers.
- — Julian Franklyn, *A Dictionary of Rhyming Slang*, 1961
- — Ray Puxley, *Cockney Rabbit*, 1992

queen's row *noun*
an area in a prison reserved for blatantly homosexual prisoners *US*
- If you want to stay off queen's row, you better lay low and do exactly what you're told. — Malcolm Braly, *On the Yard*, p. 296, 1967
- Studies of incarcerated persons have shown that such a person is more likely to get hurt on the "inside," since the code of "QUEEN'S ROW" inmates think that such a person is trying to make light of them by being uncooperative. — Richard Frank, *A Study of Sex in Prison*, p. 24, 1973

Queen Street bushie; Queen Street cowboy; Queen Street ringer *noun*
in Queensland, a city person with pretences to country living, such as dressing like a cowboy or driving a 4WD *AUSTRALIA*
- Did you see that lot of hopeless roo-shooters that just came in? Bloody Queen Street cowboys! — *www.abc.net.au/wordmap*, 2003

queen tank *noun*
a jail holding cell reserved for flamboyantly effeminate homosexual men *US*
- I also can throw handcuffs on you and book you into the queen tank at the county jail. — Gerald Petievich, *Shakedown*, p. 191, 1988

queeny *adjective*
1 blatantly homosexual *US*
- — *Maledicta*, p. 234, 1979: 'Kings and queens: linguistic and cultural aspects of the terminology for gays'
- Today at TVam: Brian Sewell (very queeny)[.] — Gyles Brandreth, *Breaking the Code*, p. 6, 1999

2 showy, melodramatic, affected *US*
- — Pamela Munro, *U.C.L.A. Slang*, p. 100, 1997

queer *noun*
1 a homosexual man or a lesbian *US, 1914*
Usually pejorative, but also a male homosexual term of self-reference within the gay underground and subculture.
- I am not a fool! a queer! I am not! — Jack Kerouac, *Letter to Neal Cassady*, p. 167, 3 October 1948
- Is he a queer? Doesn't he act like one though! — John Clellon Holmes, *Go*, p. 25, 1952
- The door was opened by a large, flabby, middle-aged queer with tattooing on his forearms and even on the backs of his hands. — William Burroughs, *Junkie*, p. 21, 1953
- There were plenty of queers. — Jack Kerouac, *On the Road*, p. 73, 1957
- 'And a little hash,' added Jean-baby. 'There was a little hashish in the can, too. Frost shuddered. 'Goddamn queers!' he said. — Terry Southern, *Flash and Filigree*, p. 121, 1958
- There was this queer standing naked in front of him. — Frank Norman, *Bang To Rights*, p. 71, 1958
- The homosexual, who was playing hard to get, came to one masquerade party dressed as Tinkerbelle, the good fairy. He was what the other queers called a screamer. — Phyllis and Eberhard Kronhausen, *Sex Histories of American College Men*, p. 184, 1960
- Then I remembered that was an illiberal thing to say, and argued that even if he was a queer they shouldn't hold it against him. They did. — Clancy Sigal, *Going Away*, p. 150, 1961
- Miss Smith was encompassed by two girl secretaries and a queer. — Mickey Spillane, *Me, Hood!*, p. 28, 1963
- I scarcely heard Lucy as he chattered on and on bringing me up to date on the romances and happenings among the queers I had deserted. — Iceberg Slim (Robert Beck), *Mama Black Widow*, p. 25, 1969
- A cop knelt and kissed the feet of a priest / And a queer threw up at the sight of that[.] — David Bowie, *Five Years*, 1972
- The slogan "Dyke + fag = queer" was common. — William Stewart, *Cassell's Queer Companion*, 1995
- Little did they realise they were dancing [the twist] the way the queers did in Harlem. And black queers at that! — Simon Napier-Bell, *Black Vinyl White Powder*, p. 177, 2001

2 counterfeit money *UK, 1812*
- I was sure that Hertert wanted to use this fellow as a shover of the queer, or the man who was to pass the fake currency. — William J. Spillard and Pence James, *Needle in a Haystack*, p. 54–55, 1945
- The limo back seat is gizmoed, and I copped Jake's hundred and twenty grand in 'queer' and the valises. — Iceberg Slim (Robert Beck), *Long White Con*, p. 212, 1977
- — Joe McKennon, *Circus Lingo*, p. 74, 1980

queer *verb*
to spoil something; to ruin something; to interfere with something *UK, 1812*
- I ain't going to rap and maybe queer things. — Iceberg Slim (Robert Beck), *Pimp*, p. 253, 1969

▸ **queer a pitch**
to spoil a situation or a circumstance; to undermine someone's efforts *UK, 1875*
- But did Mr Prescott improve or queer his pitch by taking issue with the boss over the public sector? — *The Guardian*, 21st June 1999
- There's no binlids [children] to queer the pitch. — Kevin Sampson, *Outlaws*, p. 242, 2001

queer *adjective*
1 homosexual *US, 1914*
Derogatory from the outside, not from within. G. Legman, in his 1941 *The Language of Homosexuality*, notes: 'As an adjective it is the most common in use in America'.
- Not all who call their flats in Greenwich Village "studios" are queer. — Jack Lait and Lee Mortimer, *New York Confidential*, p. 65, 1948
- You mean – if I went and enrolled and asked for a girl teacher – nobody would think I was – queer? — Philip Wylie, *Opus 21*, p. 105, 1949
- You know, he's not queer at all. It was just an imitation. — John Clellon Holmes, *Go*, p. 9, 1952
- In Greenwich Village, Bert had passing relationships with several girls, met a number of queer people, and associated with a group of older and well-known writers. — James T. Farrell, *Ruth and Bertram*, p. 91, 1955
- And Dean told Carlo of unknown people in the West like Tommy Snark, the clubfooted poolhall rotation shark and cardplayer and queer saint. — Jack Kerouac, *On the Road*, p. 8, 1957
- Yeah, let that queer joint over on Division Street operate. — Willard Motely, *Let No Man Write My Epitaph*, p. 247, 1958
- Sometimes I wonder if he's gone queer. — Douglas Rutherford, *The Creeping Flesh*, p. 44, 1963
- Rubber was queer but he weighed 240 and could whip any two cats easily. — Babs Gonzales, *Movin' On Down De Line*, p. 70, 1975
- "Oh, yes. Well, Maurice is as queer as I am." Joe belched. "Excuse me. If not queerer. But he won't acept it.["] — William Burroughs, *Queer*, p. 29–30, 1985
- God, these panites feel great. That don't make me queer, right? — *Bull Durham*, 1988

2 catering to or patronised by homosexuals *US*
- This is a queer bar. You are not a queer. Why do you insist on being in here? — Helen P. Branson, *Gay Bar*, p. 56, 1957

3 driven by deep and perverse sexual desires *US*
- I say, "You not queer, baby. You look around you and you see, you not the only one." — Sara Harris, *The Lords of Hell*, p. 62, 1967

4 not good; out of fashion *US*
Like 'gay', 'queer' has been hijacked from its homosexual context.
- This is so queer! — *Chasing Amy*, 1997

5 counterfeit *US*
- These fast workers make a splendid living peddling queer securities from an office on the sidewalk in front of the Ambassador Hotel, at 14th and K. — Jack Lait and Lee Mortimer, *Washington Confidential*, p. 278, 1951
- I asked for fifties 'cause, you know, they're the hardest to counterfeit and the easiest to spot when they are queer. — Emmett Grogan, *Final Score*, p. 59, 1976
- S'posed to have done time years ago for passing queer twenties and tens. — Gerald Petievich, *Money Men*, p. 12, 1981

▸ **to be queer for**
to be fond of someone or something *US, 1953*
- "I'm queer for Jack," she said. — William Burroughs, *Junkie*, p. 28, 1953
- I'm queer for spades, Bernie, and the sounds, and that one cat. — Ross Russell, *The Sound*, p. 173, 1961

queer and nasty, try another service *nickname*
the Australian airline QANTAS *AUSTRALIA*
Most airlines seem to be the subject of jocular puns. This one is recorded as 'provided by a magazine over fifteen years back' by R.K. Murthi in *The Tribune* (India), 31st August 2002. 'Queers and Nancies Trading as Stewards' had some circulation in the 1980s.

queer as a clockwork orange *adjective*
1 obviously homosexual *UK*
Plays on **QUEER** (unusual/homosexual).
- [The younger brother Damon ... as pretty as a picture and as queer as a clockwork orange. — Petra Christian, *The Sexploiters*, p. 22, 1973
- He's as queer as a clockwork orange. — David Powis, *The Signs of Crime*, 1977
- — Angela Devlin, *Prison Patter*, p. 38, 1996

2 unusual or suspicious *UK*
Predates the novel *Clockwork Orange* (1962) by Anthony Burgess.

queer as a four-speed walking stick *adjective*
unusual; ostentatiously homosexual *UK, 1970s*
Popularised by raconteur 'Blaster' Bates (b.1922).

queer as a left-handed corkscrew *adjective*
unusual; ostentatiously homosexual *UK, 1970s*

queer as a nine-bob note *adjective*
1 ostentatiously homosexual *UK, 1984*
Plays on **QUEER** (unusual/homosexual).

2 unusual or suspicious *UK*
The most 'queer' (unusual) thing about a nine **BOB** (shilling) note is that it has never existed; the phrase survived decimalisation in 1971, which 'bob' failed to do.

queer as a nine-bob watch *adjective*
suspicious *UK*
So cheap it must be suspect.

queer as a three-dollar bill *adjective*
ostentatiously homosexual *US*
- I could tell that feller was queer as a three-dollar bill – been thinking it for years. —Larry McMurtry, *The Last Picture Show*, p. 153, 1966
- Wally's a fag. Queer as a three-dollar bill. —Robert Gover, *JC Saves*, p. 105, 1968
- Big, mean bastards, and every one of them queer as a three-dollar bill. —Vincent Patrick, *The Pope of Greenwich Village*, p. 75, 1979

queer as fuck *adjective*
definitely homosexual; ostentatiously gay *UK*
QUEER (homosexual) plus 'as fuck' (an intensifier); punned in the popular television drama series about gay culture, *Queer As Folk*.

queerbait; queer-bait *noun*
a man who commands the attention of homosexual men, whether he is homosexual or not *US*
- She knew he wouldn't go with her while the others were there, fearing the jeers of queerbait, so was forced to wait and hope the others might leave. —Hubert Selby Jr, *Last Exit to Brooklyn*, p. 45, 1957
- Now would chime in the litany of abuse: naughty sissy, baby-boy, not-really-a-boy-but-a-pussy, little faggot, secret cocksucking toy, queer-bait, boy-hole, powder-puff. —Terence Sellers, *Dungeon Evidence*, p. 58, 1997

queer-bashing *verb*
an attack (usually physical) of a homosexual because of his sexuality *UK, 1970*
- Makin' a big deal aboot him bein' gay just looked like queer-bashin'. —Christopher Brookmyre, *Boiling a Frog*, p. 120, 2000
- Some blokes hang around the Gents and they get bashed in there, Billy continues. That's queer-bashing as well. —John King, *Human Punk*, p. 83, 2000

queer beer *noun*
weak, watery beer *US*
More commonly reduplicated as 'near beer'.
- —Elementary Electronics, *Dictionary of CB Lingo*, p. 99, 1976

queerie *noun*
a homosexual *NEW ZEALAND*
- —David McGill, *David McGill's Complete Kiwi Slang Dictionary*, p. 102, 1998

queer jack *noun*
counterfeit money *US*
- —Vincent J. Monteleone, *Criminal Slang*, p. 187, 1949

queer-rolling *noun*
the practice of attacking and robbing homosexuals *UK, 1977*
- This is called queer-rolling, Billy says, from a bedroom. Turning the dirty bastards over in their own homes. —John King, *Human Punk*, p. 82, 2000

queer's lunch box *noun*
the male crotch *US*
- —Roger Blake, *The American Dictionary of Sexual Terms*, p. 177, 1964

Queer Street *noun*
▸ **in Queer Street; on Queer Street**
experiencing difficulties, especially financial difficulties; in a vulnerable position *UK, 1952*
- LaMotta's on queer street, but he's still standing— *Raging Bull*, 1980
- My body yearned for a couple of Percodans, but I knew that they would put me on Queer Street, and that's not where I wanted to be right now. —Harlan Coben, *Tell No One*, p. 295, 2001

queeve *verb*
to experience a loss of energy *US*
- — *San Francisco Sunday Examiner & Chronicle*, p. 20, 2nd September 1984

quegg *noun*
a homosexual *UK, 2001*
Possibly a compound of QUEER (homosexual or odd) and EGG (a person).
- I know that my helpful, gift-wrapping quegg is watching us every step of the way. —Kevin Sampson, *Outlaws*, p. 241, 2001

Quel Chagrin *noun*
Queen's Counsel *CANADA*
From the initials QC.
- Quel Chagrin ["what a letdown"] is what all QCs say on finding out they will never get to advise the Queen on anything. —*Toronto Globe and Mail*, p. D12, 3rd August 2002

query *noun*
a test or examination *US*
- — *Verbatim*, p. 281, May 1976

ques *noun*
the question mark (?) character on a computer keyboard *US*
- —Eric S. Raymond, *The New Hacker's Dictionary*, p. 294, 1991

queue *noun*
▸ **put on a queue**
(of a woman) to have sex with a line of partners, one after the other *AUSTRALIA*
- [A] generous girl will "put on a queue" behind the sand dunes for a seemingly unlimited line-up of young men. —Richard Neville, *Play Power*, p. 82, 1970

quezzie *noun*
a question *UK*
- She never answers none of the quezzies herself[.] —Kevin Sampson, *Clubland*, p. 112, 2002

quiche-eater *noun*
a sensitive male; an effeminate male *US*
- —Connie Eble (Editor), *UNC-CH Campus Slang*, p. 6, Fall 1984

quick and dirty *adjective*
constructed as quickly as possible *US*
- I can have a quick-and-dirty fix in place tonight, but I'll have to rewrite the whole module to solve the underlying design problem. —Eric S. Raymond, *The New Hacker's Dictionary*, p. 294, 1991

Quickdraw McGraw *noun*
the US Secret Service agent who is closest to the president *US*
Quickdraw McGraw was a Hanna Barbera cartoon that first aired in 1959; ironically, the character Quickdraw McGraw was not a quick draw, but his name has survived, implying that which the character was not.
- That's Quickdraw McGraw, whatever guy has that job, that's what he's called. Keeps within six paces of the president at all times. —Elmore Leonard, *Split Images*, p. 77, 1981

quick-go *noun*
in a sport, a player who does not last very long on a team *US*
- If Unphlet is a no-show or quick-go, then Cal Grote could split playing time with Pearson. — *San Francisco Examiner*, p. 7 (II), 3rd April 1972

quickie *noun*
1 a sexual encounter that is carried out quickly *US*
- We had a quickie; I didn't come & was only telling of the future where there were better bed fucks & us living contentedly as we walked slowly across town again to her home. —Neal Cassady, *The First Third*, p. 201, 5th November 1950
- They range from the lowest, who will come to your room for $5 for a quickie, to the most ultra, who expects $100, plus expenses, as a fee for her company for an evening, and nothing guaranteed. —Jack Lait and Lee Mortimer, *Washington Confidential*, p. 84, 1951
- The rate starts at $100, but many of them can be bargained with, during slow periods of the day, going for a "quickie" for fifty dollars. —Ed Reid and Ovid Demaris, *The Green Felt Jungle*, p. 95, 1963
- We did a stand-up quickie by the refrigerator —Jefferson Poland and Valerie Alison, *The Records of the San Francisco Sexual Freedom League*, p. 60, 1971
- I call this kinda action a quickie. It happens with a guy that's only interested in his kicks and fuck the bitch. —A.S. Jackson, *Gentleman Pimp*, p. 164, 1973
- Sure, Pearl Delight, but it was a quickie, because your old man has a busy day upcoming. —Iceberg Slim (Robert Beck), *Long White Con*, p. 22, 1977
- The rates here start at ten dollars, but once again this is strictly for a quickie. —Gerald Paine, *A Bachelor's Guide to the Brothels of Nevada*, p. 40, 1978
- Inside are six fully pitched camping tents, where quickies are available to the Times Square outdoorsman. —Josh Alan Friedman, *Tales of Times Square*, p. 176, 1986
- EBBY: Got time for another quickie? MILLIE: Jesus,k you got a game to pitch! EBBY: But we got three minutes! — *Bull Durham*, 1988
- He moved his hands over her back, feeling her body beneath the thin T-shirt, Chili thinking, It could be a quickie. —Elmore Leonard, *Be Cool*, p. 321, 1999
- [S]he had come home late and acted very strange. Had never turned down a quickie before. —Jack Allen, *When the Whistle Blows*, p. 38, 2000

2 an alcoholic drink taken hastily *AUSTRALIA*
- I nipped into the pub for a quickie before dinner[.] —Alexander Buzo, *Rooted*, p. 87, 1969

3 something that is accomplished quickly *US, 1940*
- They were riding first-class on a Delta flight from Miami to Dulles; a one-day quickie. —Carl Hiaasen, *Strip Tease*, p. 210, 1993

4 an unexpected, quickly executed manoeuvre or piece of trickery *US*
- —Hyman E. Goldin et al., *Dictionary of American Underworld Lingo*, p. 172, 1950
- —Harry Orsman, *A Dictionary of Modern New Zealand Slang*, p. 105, 1999

quickie *adjective*
carried out quickly *US, 1940*
- It had come to the attention of 60 Minutes that the progressive city of Dallas had spawned a flurry of drive-in divorce centers in which lawyers were handling as many as 175 quickie divorces a day. —Dan Jenkins, *Life Its Ownself*, p. 50, 1984

quick-lunch *noun*
a fast-food small restaurant *CANADA*
- For two years he had done the cooking for the O'Neills, who owned a small quick-lunch. —Morley Callaghan, *Stories*, p. 203, 1959

quickness *noun*
▸ **with a quickness**
as soon as possible *US*
- —Judi Sanders, *Da Bomb!*, p. 31, 1997

quick one *noun*
an unexpected act of betrayal *US*
- —Hyman E. Goldin et al., *Dictionary of American Underworld Lingo*, p. 172, 1950

quick one off the wrist *noun*
▹ see: ONE OFF THE WRIST

quick pussy *noun*
a secure NATO communications system *CANADA*
- "Quick Pussy" (Royal Canadian Air Force, 1960s to early 1980s) was the somewhat lewd nickname for "Fast Cat," a NATO codename for an encrypted system of communications linking headquarters to the air bases armed with nuclear weapons. —Tom Langeste, *Words on the Wing*, p. 227, 1995

quick-smart *adverb*
quickly *AUSTRALIA, 1952*
- You kids get dressed quick-smart and get into the car. —Kerry Cue, *Crooks, Chooks and Bloody Ratbags*, p. 42, 1983

quick-starts *noun*
running shoes *US*
- —Connie Eble (Editor), *UNC-CH Campus Slang*, p. 7, November 1990

quick thinking, Batman!
used for a humorous, if sarcastic, response to another's observation or conclusion *US*
From the *Batman* comic and television series (1966–1968). The television series launched several catchphrases into the vocabulary to a far greater extent than the comic books had.

quick-turn burn *noun*
the refuelling and reloading of an F-18 fighter jet in less than five minutes *US*
- —*Army*, p. 48, November 1991

quid *noun*
1 a pound sterling; pounds sterling *UK, 1688*
Deriving perhaps from Latin *quid* (what?), later suggesting 'the wherewithal'. Note too UK dialect *quid* (a wad of tobacco). The quid has survived decimalisation (1971) and several centuries of inflation; originally coined as 'a guinea' (1 pound, 1 shilling), in C19 it became 'a sovereign'.
- She's got a nice few quid saved up for when I get out [of prison]. —Frank Norman, *Bang To Rights*, p. 58, 1958
- Two fucking quid that toothbrush cost me[.] —Paul Fraser and Shane Meadows, *TwentyFourSeven*, p. 10, 1997

2 some money *AUSTRALIA*
Still in use despite the fact that pounds went out in 1966 when Australia changed over to decimal currency (dollars and cents).
- —Bob Ellis and Anne Brooksbank, *Mad Dog Morgan*, p. 120, 1976
- That visit cost you $120, so when I get a few quid again, I'll be sure to see that you get the $120 back. —Ray Denning, *Prison Diaries*, p. 60, 1978
- —Joe Andersen, *Winners Can Laugh*, p. 43, 1982
- I was desperate for a quid at that time and I didn't care who knew it. —Roy Higgins and Tom Prior, *The Jockey Who Laughed*, p. 65, 1982
- He's pretty genuine, and if he borrows a quid off you he'll pay you back. —Sandra Jobson, *Blokes*, p. 37, 1984

3 five dollars *US*
If a pound is five dollars, so must be a quid.
- —George Percy, *The Language of Poker*, p. 72, 1988

▸ **not the full quid**
without a full complement of intelligence *AUSTRALIA, 1944*
- —Jim Ramsay, *Cop It Sweet!*, p. 75, 1977
- That's Mawbey...he's no good...I mean he's not the full quid. —Angelo Loukakis, *For the Patriarch*, p. 151, 1981
- The interviewer – Ray or maybe Bill – pursued a line of questioning which suggested that anyone who would scream 'I Am A Lonesome Cowboy' couldn't be quite the full quid on the football field. —*Sydney Morning Herald*, p. 16, 21st March 1984

quid deal *noun*
a drug sale involving one pound's worth of drugs, usually marijuana *UK*
- —Tom Hibbert, *Rockspeak!*, p. 129, 1983

quids *noun*
a large amount of money *AUSTRALIA, 1930*
- I got a registered letter here, it might be worth quids. —Lennie Lower, *Here's Luck*, p. 44, 1930
- Had a nice new hat on, Jim. Must have cost her quids! —T.A.G. Hungerford, *Stories from Suburban Road*, p. 166, 1983

▸ **not for quids**
not for anything *AUSTRALIA, 1941*
- —Gavin Casey, *It's Harder for Girls*, p. 95, 1941
- I wouldn't miss this for quids, honest. —W.R. Bennett, *Wingman*, p. 123, 1961
- —Patsy Adam-Smith, *Folklore of the Australian Railwaymen*, p. 119, 1969
- Wouldn't miss it for quids. —*Sun-News Pictorial*, 1986

▸ **wouldn't be dead for quids**
I am generally happy with my life and circumstances *AUSTRALIA, 1986*
- —Robert G. Barrett, *Davo's Little Something*, p. 192, 1992

quids in *adjective*
prospering; at an advantage *UK, 1919*
Figurative use of actual profit measured by the QUID (£1).
- —Ann Barr and Peter York, *The Official Sloane Ranger Handbook*, p. 159, 1982

quietie *noun*
a quiet drink *AUSTRALIA*
- This day many years ago, Gonzo and I were having a couple of quieties, well actually Gonzo was as full as the Warragamba Dam and we got talking to a couple of very attractive young ladies. —Paul Vautin, *Turn It Up!*, p. 136, 1995

quiet-side *adjective*
secret *US*
- —John R. Armore and Joseph D. Wolfe, *Dictionary of Desperation*, p. 45, 1976

quiff *noun*
1 the vagina; a woman as sex object; a prostitute *UK, 1923*
Archaic in the US, but understood in context.
- "Black or blonde," he said. "If it's quiff, it's all the same to Brain-Brain." —Thurston Scott, *Cure it with Honey*, p. 117, 1951
- Gil finds out from Mort Robell that the bum got a date at midnight with some quiff named Becky. —Bernard Wolfe, *The Late Risers*, p. 13, 1954
- Wait a minute – it's some new quiff, isn't it? —*Body Heat*, 1980
- Stroll down the street maybe act like you're drunk or you're a john looking for some quiff. —Elmore Leonard, *Split Images*, p. 23, 1981
- [T]he pilot/mogul had me out bird-dogging quiff: prowling bus depots and train stations for buxom young girls who'd fall prey to RKO contracts in exchange for frequent nighttime visits. —James Ellroy, *Hollywood Nocturnes*, p. 199, 1994

2 by extension, a male homosexual *US*
- We will fuck Reilly in the ass. He's probably a quiff, too. —Edwin Torres, *Q & A*, p. 58, 1977
- Some quiff said Ad Vice was operating the park, which we both know is bullshit. —James Ellroy, *White Jazz*, p. 69, 1992

quill *noun*
1 anything used to snort powdered drugs; the drugs themselves *US, 1935*
- —John B. Williams, *Narcotics and Hallucinogenics*, p. 115, 1967
- But he's got a solid yen for the quill if he can get it. —Iceberg Slim (Robert Beck), *Trick Baby*, p. 213, 1969
- Her fingers trembled slightly as she rolled up a dollar bill, making it into a quill. She stuck one end of the quill in her nose, while she held the other end to the white powder in the package. —Donald Goines, *Dopefiend*, p. 32, 1971

2 cocaine *UK, 1998*
- —Nick Constable, *This is Cocaine*, p. 181, 2002
- —Mike Haskins, *Drugs*, p. 281, 2003

3 heroin *UK*
- —Angela Devlin, *Prison Patter*, p. 94, 1996
- —Robert Ashton, *This Is Heroin*, p. 206, 2002

quill pig *noun*
a porcupine *US*
Michigan Upper Peninsula usage.

quilty *adjective*
luxurious *US*
- Van had a straw, a Corona corona in his jaw / A beige suit looking real quilty. —Dennis Wepman et al., *The Life*, p. 45, 1976

quim *noun*
the vagina; used objectively as a collective noun for women, especially sexually available women *UK, 1735*
- There was a young girl from New York / Who plugged up her quim with a cork. —*Eros*, p. 62, Winter 162
- I'll spring for that if you can guarantee a tight back door and quim. —Iceberg Slim (Robert Beck), *Doom Fox*, p. 6, 1978
- With his pal filling her quim and Butler's dick sliding in and out of her luscious lips, Kari gets a heaping helping of the living needle from both ends at once. —*Adult Video*, p. 65, August/September 1986
- Jokingly, she gave him the finger, then stuck the same digit in her quim. —Anthony Petkovich, *The X Factory*, p. 36, 1997

quimby *noun*
a person completely lacking in social graces *US*
- —Vann Wesson, *Generation X Field Guide and Lexicon*, p. 136, 1997

quimmo *noun*
a fool; an unpleasant individual *UK*
Extending **QUIM** (the vagina) as a synonym for **CUNT**.
- DENVER: pathetic tosser you loser wanker quimmo bender fucker nothing – life fades everything breaks bastard useless dumb cunt —Patrick Jones, *Unprotected Sex*, p. 225, 1999

quince *noun*
an effeminate male; a homosexual *AUSTRALIA, 1941*
- —Jim Ramsay, *Cop It Sweet!*, p. 75, 1977
- —Sonya Plowman, *Great Kiwi Slang*, p. 148, 2002

▸get on your quince
to annoy you *AUSTRALIA, 1941*
- —Jim Ramsay, *Cop It Sweet!*, p. 75, 1977
- For all you know, I may quite like some uncles and aunties of yours that get on your quince. —Phillip Adams, *The Unspeakable Adams*, p. 181, 1977

quinella *noun*
in horse racing, a bet on the first two to finish in either order *US*
- —John McCririck, *John McCririck's World of Betting*, p. 175, 1991

quinine *noun*
in the game of craps, the number nine *US*
- —*The Annals of the American Academy of Political and Social Sciences*, p. 129, May 1950

quint *noun*
in poker, five cards of the same suit in sequence *US*
- —John Scarne, *Scarne's Guide to Modern Poker*, p. 288, 1979

quint major *noun*
in poker, a sequence of five cards, same suit, ending with the face cards *US*
- —George Percy, *The Language of Poker*, p. 72, 1988

quitter *noun*
a suicide *US*
- —Ralph de Sola, *Crime Dictionary*, p. 124, 1982

quiver *noun*
1 a selection of surfboards used for different surf conditions *US*
- —Gary Fairmont R. Filosa II, *The Surfer's Almanac*, p. 192, 1977

2 cocaine *UK*
- [A] limitless supply of alcohol, quiver, pills and trips [LSD][.] —Wayne Anthony, *Spanish Highs*, p. 7, 1999

quivver-giver *noun*
an attractive person *US*
- There's that new pigeon. Boy, she's sure a quivver givver! —Haenigsen, *Jive's Like That*, 1947

quiz *noun*
a roadside sobriety test *US*
- —Wayne Floyd, *Jason's Authentic Dictionary of CB Slang*, p. 25, 1976

quiz room *noun*
a room where the North Vietnamese interrogated US prisoners of war *US*
- —Gregory Clark, *Words of the Vietnam War*, p. 420, 1990

quizzy *adjective*
nosey *NEW ZEALAND*
- —David McGill, *David McGill's Complete Kiwi Slang Dictionary*, p. 90, 1998

quoit *noun*
the anus; the backside *AUSTRALIA, 1919*
- STEWARD'S CHORUS / We expect our Upright Grand Instrument out by this afternoon's delivery. Also, Quoits, Balls, and Games / FUN FOR EVERYONE / that can make fun. —Patsy Adam-Smith, *Folklore of the Australian Railwaymen*, p. 236, 1919
- 'See those blokes sitting on their quoits over there?' he asked Dick. —Eric Lambert, *The Twenty Thousand Thieves*, p. 102, 1951
- An' another thing! If we sit on our quoits for a spell, there'd be a foreman on our hammer geein' us up on wantin' to sack us. —James Gaby, *The Restless Waterfront*, p. 131, 1974
- —Jim Ramsay, *Cop It Sweet!*, p. 75, 1977
- —Sam Weller, *Old Bastards I Have Met*, p. 85, 1979
- [I]f I catch him in Wynyard without a proper exhaust on that motorbike of his I'll kick his quoit for him, right! —Barney Roberts, *Where's Morning Gone?*, p. 84, 1987

quokka soccer *noun*
on Rottnest Island, running around kicking quokkas as a type of entertainment *AUSTRALIA*
The 'quokka' is a small rare native marsupial, *Setonix brachyurus*, of southwestern West Australia.
- Quokka soccer – kicking the delightful quokkas native to Rottnest Island. —Graham Seal, *The Lingo*, p. 27, 1999
- Quokka soccer – to fervently play soccer with one of the many Quokka's on Rottnest Island. Usually followed by a large fine, and being kicked off the island. Most popular during schoolies week. —*www.abc.net.au/wordmap*, 2003
- In 1996, in response to the cruelties of quokka soccer, the Western Australian government imposed a fine of A$10,000 (£4,000) for anyone caught harming the small herbivores. —*www.telegraph.co.uk/news*, 2003

quong *noun*
the testicle *UK*
Usually in the plural.
- —Paul Baker, *Polari*, p. 188, 2002

quorum *noun*
in poker, the agreed-upon minimum number of players to continue a game *US*
- —John Scarne, *Scarne's Guide to Modern Poker*, p. 288, 1979

quote *verb*
in criminal circles, to vouch for someone *UK*
- We can't advertise. I can really only entertain people who are somehow connected, who come to us quoted[.] —J.J. Connolly, *Layer Cake*, p. 10, 2000

quo vadis *noun*
unfashionable or unpopular music *UK*
Probably refers to the 1951 film and the rock group *Status Quo*, formed in 1967 and, in 2003, still working, with the implication that both entertainments are dated. Recorded as a contemporary gay usage in his 'New palare lexicon' by Paul Tierney, *Attitude*, July 2003.

quozzie; quoz *noun*
a disabled or deformed person *UK*
Derived from Quasimodo, 'The Hunchback of Notre Dame'.
- Going swimming, Quozzie? Only swim at night, do yer? —James Herbert, *The Others*, p. 72, 2000

Rr

RA *noun*

▸ **the RA**

the Irish Republican Army *IRELAND*

• [T]hinks he's rock hard. Said he'd get the RA to shoot me[.] — Donal Ruane, *Tales in a rear view mirror*, p. 57, 2003

raas *noun*

1 an arse; hence your being *JAMAICA*

• If there's a God, that cunt's raas will burn in hell. — Donald Gorgon, *Cop Killer*, p. 19, 1994

2 a contemptible person *JAMAICA*

Probable origin in the phrase 'your arse', although some suggest Dutch *raas* (rage). The early, especially West Indian, sense was considered extremely offensive, however modern UK black usage is roughly equivalent to **ARSE** or **ARSEHOLE**. There is a, possibly disingenuous, belief amongst some Jamaicans that Raas was a king of Africa.

• [H]e won't be able to resist thinking about all the sweet-talking raases running after her. — Diran Abedayo, *My Once Upon A Time*, p. 133, 2000

3 nonsense *UK*

From West Indian. Black usage.

• There was also a stout mother who was chiding her son ("Lee, shut your raas before I slap yuh... Lee![")] — Diran Abedayo, *My Once Upon A Time*, p. 174, 2000

▸ **the raas**

used in order to intensify *UK*

Synonymous with 'the hell', 'the fuck', etc.

• Bwoy! Is who the fuck you lookin' at..? Who de raas you fuckin' staring at? — Donald Gorgon, *Cop Killer*, p. 63, 1994

raasclat *noun*

used as an extreme derogative *JAMAICA*

Combines **RAAS** (arse) and 'clat' (West Indian pronunciation of 'cloth') to mean 'a sanitary towel'.

• FRED: What's rassclot mean, then? One called me that. [...] JOE: You know what pussy clot means, you know a tart, if she's, when she's on a period, you know? [...] If they call you a pussyclot, you're a blood clot of a tart's doings, you know. — Paul E Willis, *Profane Culture*, p. 44–45, 1978

• "I know what you am raasclat," said the first youth. "Now hand over your fucking money, guy." — Garry Bushell, *The Face*, p. 257, 2001

raashole *noun*

a contemptible person; used as a general term of abuse *UK*

A cross-cultural variation on **ARSEHOLE**, using West Indian and UK black **RAAS** (an arse).

• At this my friend had finally lost his cool, raging against "Dat lickle raashole!" — Diran Abedayo, *My Once Upon A Time*, p. 17, 2000

raatid *adjective*

▷ see: **RAHTID**

rabbi *noun*

a mentor or protector *US*

• The translation of "I see you got the gold tin, who's your rabbi?" is "I see you have been promoted to detective. Who's your high-ranked sponsor?" — *New York Times*, 15th February 1970

• He did not have, nor did he attempt to develop, any "rabbis" – people in high places in the department – to advance his career[.] — Peter Maas, *Serpico*, p. 110, 1973

• [M]urders were all right as long as you had your rabbi – cops and robbers were all mixed up. — Edwin Torres, *Carlito's Way*, p. 35, 1975

• Now my rabbi, Carmody, comes up with this guy[.] — George V. Higgins, *The Judgment of Deke Hunter*, p. a, 1976

• You mean an Irish guy like you didn't have no rabbi? — Edwin Torres, *Q & A*, p. 17, 1977

• That hasn't changed. Cops still move into slots according to who their rabbis are, and you guys are paying off the rabbis. — Vincent Patrick, *The Pope of Greenwich Village*, p. 39, 1979

• Then comes my Chinaman – who is called a rabbi in New York, a mentor in the colleges and a political sponsor elsewhere – Delvin, who has plenty of jobs to give out since the shit has to be kept moving. — Robert Campbell, *Junkyard Dog*, p. 7–8, 1986

• — William Safire, *Safire's New Political Dictionary*, p. 639, 1993

rabbit *noun*

1 a woman who has a large number of children *JAMAICA*

Collected at a UK prison, August 2002.

2 a man who ejaculates with little stimulation *US*

• — *Maledicta*, p. 150, Summer/Winter 1986–1987: 'Sexual slang: prostitutes, pedophiles, flagellators, transvestites, and necrophiles'

3 a white person *US*

• — Linda Reinberg, *In the Field*, p. 178, 1991

• — Gary K. Farlow, *Prison-ese*, p. 55, 2002

4 a nervous, timid, cautious person *US*

• "Why? Because they all married rabbits." "How very odd!" I exclaimed. "Real rabbits?" "No stupid, they married guys with no drive, no gumption." — Max Shulman, *The Many Loves of Dobie Gillis*, p. 163, 1951

• This rabbit'll do anything not to do time, including wearing a wire. — *True Romance*, 1993

5 a new member of a Rastafarian gang *NEW ZEALAND, 1988*

• — Harry Orsman, *A Dictionary of Modern New Zealand Slang*, p. 106, 1999

6 a prisoner who is known for attempting to escape prison *US*

• He said, "In spite of the rabbit in this man I want him transferred to Ramsey construction immediately." — Bruce Jackson, *In the Life*, p. 322, 1972

7 a person who regularly borrows money from an illegal money lender and pays back promptly *US*

• — Hyman E. Goldin et al., *Dictionary of American Underworld Lingo*, p. 173, 1950

8 on the railways, a side track on a downhill incline used to divert runaway trains and prevent crashes *US*

• — Norman Carlisle, *The Modern Wonder Book of Trains and Railroading*, p. 267, 1946

9 a poor poker player *US*

• — Albert H. Morehead, *The Complete Guide to Winning Poker*, p. 271, 1967

▸ **go like a rabbit**

to demonstrate eagerness during sex *UK*

• I'm gonna do it to you, gonna do it sweet banana, you'll never give up / Yes: Go like a rabbit, gon-na grab it, gon-na do it 'til the night is done — Paul McCartney, *Hi, Hi, Hi*, 1972

▸ **the rabbit died**

used for indicating a state of pregnancy *UK*

From the (former) methodology used to test pregnancy that was introduced in 1949.

▸ **the rabbit's hopping**

experiencing the bleed period of the menstrual cycle *US*

A reversal of the phrase **THE RABBIT DIED** (pregnant).

• A rather promiscuous roommate I once had (a 29-year-old Mid-western Caucasian) always said, "the rabbit's hopping" when she got hers, the period being more reliable than a stick test. — *The Museum of Menstruation and Women's Health*, April 2001

rabbit *verb*

to run away *UK, 1887*

• Frank, why did you rabbit? I can't figure it out. Was someone in camp putting pressure on you? — Malcolm Braly, *On the Yard*, p. 75, 1967

• He was trying to decide whether to rabbit or freeze. — Joseph Wambaugh, *The Blue Knight*, p. 27, 1973

• It was the old man who'd rabbited when he saw me on the ladder. — James Ellroy, *Hollywood Nocturnes*, p. 180, 1994

rabbit and pork; rabbit *noun*

the act of talking; a conversation *UK*

Rhyming slang for 'talk'.

• You won't stop talking, why don't ya give it a rest. / You got more rabbit than Sainsbury's. — Chas 'n' Dave, *Rabbit*, 1980

rabbit and pork; rabbit *verb*

to talk *US, 1941*

Rhyming slang. 'To rabbit on' is 'to talk at length'.

• Bri and he are rabbitin' away about the biz they done[.] — Derek Raymond (Robin Cook), *The Crust on its Uppers*, p. 53, 1962

- She was a peculiar chick. English and well spoken and yet she rabbited on endlessly about pop music and worked as a go-go dancer. — Kevin Mackey, *The Cure*, p. 27, 1970
- [I]t will give something to rabbit to the trouble [wife] about[.] — Ronnie Barker, *Fletcher's Book of Rhyming Slang*, p. 4, 1979
- But how was I to know you'd bend my ear'oles too, with your incessant talking, you're becoming a pest. / Rabbit, Rabbit, Rabbit, Rabbit, etc[.] — Chas 'n' Dave, *Rabbit*, 1980
- He's been rabbiting on lately at the pub about his old Leyland bus having personality and intelligence. — Roy Slaven (John Doyle), *Five South Coast Seasons*, p. 22, 1992

rabbit blood *noun*

a seemingly unstoppable urge to try to escape from prison *US*

- — Hyman E. Goldin et al., *Dictionary of American Underworld Lingo*, p. 173, 1950

rabbit ears *noun*

1 a v-shaped aerial placed on top of a television set *US, 1967*

- Usually she would've gone home by now, but she was wrestling with the rabbit ears on top of the TV, trying to fix the snow on the screen. — Sue Monk Kidd, *The Secret Life of Bees*, p. 19, 2002

2 in a casino Keno game, the two clear plastic tubes through which the number balls are blown *US*

- — Frank Scoblete, *Guerrilla Gambling*, p. 322, 1993

3 an athlete or official who is quick to take offence at teasing *US*

- — Zander Hollander, *Baseball Lingo*, p. 103, 1967
- No rabbit ears, either, though Carroll admits that at least one coach has gotten under her skin. — *Sarasota (Florida) Herald-Tribune*, p. E1, 27th December 2003

rabbiter's breakfast *noun*

a visit to the toilet and a cigarette *NEW ZEALAND, 1975*

- — Harry Orsman, *A Dictionary of Modern New Zealand Slang*, p. 106, 1999

rabbit fever *noun*

the urge to try to escape from prison *US*

- — Joseph E. Ragen and Charles Finston, *Inside the World's Toughest Prison*, p. 814, 1962: 'Penitentiary and underworld glossary'

rabbit food; rabbit's food *noun*

any salad vegetable, especially lettuce *UK, 1936*

A generally dismissive term from the carnivorous lobby.

- The menu is corny – salads are called rabbit food, appetizers "orderves." — Darwin Porter, *Frommer's Portable Charleston*, p. 168, 2003

rabbit hunt *verb*

in poker, to look through undealt cards after a hand is completed to see what might have been *US*

- — Albert H. Morehead, *The Complete Guide to Winning Poker*, p. 271, 1967

rabbit hutch *noun*

the crutch or crotch *UK*

Rhyming slang.

- These bleedin rounders [trousers] is a lot too tight in the rabbit-hutch. — Red Daniells, 1980

rabbit-killer *noun*

a short and vicious punch to the neck, generally with the open hand *AUSTRALIA, 1941*

- I could see him plainly now, and I took a rush and gave him a rabbit-killer that must have nearly broken his neck. — Gavin Casey, *It's Harder for Girls*, p. 19, 1941
- [B]efore they could turn around he was out again, and had accounted for a couple more before he collected the rabbit killer that finally put him out of action. — Criena Rohan, *Down by the Dockside*, p. 255, 1963

rabbit-oh; rabbit-o *noun*

a door-to-door seller of slaughtered rabbits *AUSTRALIA, 1902*

From the cry 'rabbit oh!', used by the vendor to attract attention.

- — Jim Ramsay, *Cop It Sweet!*, p. 76, 1977
- A 'fish-o' was familiar in many areas and, in some, a 'rabbit-o'. — Nancy Keesing, *Lily on the Dustbin*, p. 118, 1984

rabbit season *noun*

spring, when prisoners are inclined to try to escape *US*

- [S]pring was known as rabbit season, and four camp men ran off during the first week of good weather. — Malcolm Braly, *On the Yard*, p. 323, 1967

rabbit's paw; rabbit *verb*

to talk *UK*

Rhyming slang for **JAW**. The shortened form is identical in sense to the shortened form of **RABBIT AND PORK**.

- — Julian Franklyn, *A Dictionary of Rhyming Slang*, 1961

rabbit tracks *noun*

in craps, a six rolled with a pair of threes *US*

- — Steve Kuriscak, *Casino Talk*, p. 68, 1985

rabbit turds *noun*

Italian sausage *US*

Limited usage, but graphic.

- — *Maledicta*, p. 19, 1996: 'Domino's pizza jargon'

race *noun*

1 a single game in an illegal numbers lottery *US*

- You playin' twenty dollars on 526 in the first race? — Clarence Cooper Jr, *Black*, p. 180, 1963

2 a single game of Keno *US, 1973*

- — Thomas L. Clark, *The Dictionary of Gambling and Gaming*, p. 172, 1987

▸ **not in the race**

not having any chance of success *AUSTRALIA, 1904*

- 'So you've never tried to get a job?' 'Sure I did but I wasn't in the race.' — Colin Johnson, *Wild Cat Falling*, p. 43, 1965
- — Arthur Chipper, *The Aussie Swearer's Guide*, p. 78, 1972

▸ **the race**

the game of roller derby *US, 1960s and 70s*

- [S]katers refer to "the race" the way baseball players solemnly refer to their sport as "the game." — Keith Coppage, *Roller Derby to Rollerjam*, p. 127, 1999

race *verb*

▸ **race for pink slips (pinks)**

in drag racing, to compete for the prize of ownership of the opponent's car *US*

▸ **race off**

to conduct a person away to some other place for the purpose of seduction *AUSTRALIA, 1965*

- If I meet a girl who's more interested in girls than boys I'm perfectly ready to be friendly as long as she doesn't try to race me off. — Sue Rhodes, *Now you'll think I'm awful*, p. 106, 1967
- Tom told us you were out somewhere. Said he was going to race us off. — Geoff Wyatt, *Saltwater Saints*, p. 45, 1969
- That's one bird you won't race off. — Wilda Moxham, *The Apprentice*, p. 87, 1969
- — Arthur Chipper, *The Aussie Swearer's Guide*, p. 48, 1972
- — Jim Ramsay, *Cop It Sweet!*, p. 76, 1977
- — Sandra Jobson, *Blokes*, p. 141, 1984
- Cocktail Parties do not start at 9 p.m. and end six hours later in a race to race each other off and/or Park the Tiger. — Ignatius Jones, *The 1992 True Hip Manual*, p. 65, 1992
- An asbestos removalist, Jim 'races the wife off to the bedroom as much as possible'. — *Picture*, p. 58, 5th February 1992

race bird *noun*

an enthusiastic fan of horse racing *US, 1971*

- — Thomas L. Clark, *The Dictionary of Gambling and Gaming*, p. 172, 1987

race face *noun*

in motor racing, the look of total concentration and focus seen on drivers just before a race begins *US*

- — Lewis Poteet, *Car & Motorcyle Slang?*, p. 158,

racehorse *noun*

1 an accomplished, sought-after prostitute *US*

- [A] young what-they-call "racehorse," she'd have run in there, got her $20, and have been back in fifteen minutes. — Bruce Jackson, *Outside the Law*, p. 188, 1972

2 a thinly rolled cigarette *AUSTRALIA, 1944*

- — David McGill, *David McGill's Complete Kiwi Slang Dictionary*, p. 104, 1998
- Mate, that's a bloody racehorse. — *www.abc.net.au/wordmap*, 2003

racehorse Charlie; racehorse Charley *noun*

heroin; cocaine *US, 1936*

Perhaps from the long-ago brand name White Horse.

- I've known many hypes with Racehorse Charlies as a monicker, but never knew why. — David Maurer, *Narcotics and Narcotic Addiction*, p. 436–437, 1973
- — Robert Ashton, *This Is Heroin*, p. 206, 2002
- — Mike Haskins, *Drugs*, p. 281, 2003

race record *noun*

a recording by a black artist; rock 'n' roll before whites discovered rock 'n' roll *US, 1927*

- — Robert S. Gold, *A Jazz Lexicon*, p. 242, 1964

• The music we listened to was called race-records and then rhythm and blues. —Abbie Hoffman, *Woodstock Nation*, p. 24, 1969

racerhead *noun*

in mountain biking, someone who competes in races *US*
A mild put-down to describe riders so into competition that they've lost their perspective on the cosmic absurdity of mountain biking.
• —William Nealy, *Mountain Bike!*, p. 162, 1992

racers *noun*

close-fitting nylon swimwear used for competitive swimming *AUSTRALIA*
So-called because they are used in competitive swimming.
• 'Speedos' and 'racers' were the particular type used in competitive swimming, regardless of brand. — *www.abc.net.au/wordmap*, 2003

races *noun*

▸ **at the races**

unsuccessful, uncompetitive *IRELAND*
• For us lot over here, the old-fashioned Irish-term "at the races", now proves its usefulness, as in "we are not at the races at all." —Bernard Share, *Slanguage*, p. 8, 2003

racetracker *noun*

in horse racing, a person who makes their living in some capacity at racetracks *US*
• —David W. Maurer, *Argot of the Racetrack*, p. 54, 1951

racing stripe *noun*

a faecal stain in the underpants *US*
• —Lee McNelis, *30 + And a Wake-Up*, p. 12, 1991

racing tackle *noun*

amphetamines or other central nervous system stimulants *UK*
• —Tom Hibbert, *Rockspeak!*, p. 129, 1983

rack *noun*

1 a woman's breasts *US*
• Up there near the Section 23 sign. Check the rack on that broad. —Jim Bouton, *Ball Four*, p. 242, 1970
• — *Current Slang*, p. 22, Spring 1970
• — *Verbatim*, p. 281, May 1976
• She was a healthy-looking bitch, a jogger type with a great rack ... a couple of real pointers. And I'm not talking about a bra with rubber nipples. I'm talking about a pair of honest-to-Christ pointed nips that must have wieghed as much as silver dollars. —Gerald Petievich, *To Die in Beverly Hills*, p. 93, 1983
• Two legs, nice rack. — *Ten Things I Hate About You*, 1999

2 a set of antlers *US, 1945*
• Rocky shot a twelve-point buck and laid his deer rifle up in the rack to take a nice picture of it and damned if the buck didn't jump up and run off with the gun and all. —Ken Weaver, *Texas Crude*, p. 123, 1984

3 bed *US, 1955*
• We'll spend twenty-four hours a day in the rack. —John Nichols, *The Sterile Cuckoo*, p. 113, 1965
• I just got in the rack a few hours ago and I'm beat! —Odie Hawkins, *Ghetto Sketches*, p. 177, 1972
• I jumped right out of my fuckin' rack. —Edwin Torres, *Carlito's Way*, p. 121, 1975

4 a room or apartment *US*
• —Kenn "Naz" Young, *Naz's Dictionary of Teen Slang*, p. 97, 1993

5 a maximum security prison cell *US*
• —Ralph de Sola, *Crime Dictionary*, p. 125, 1982

6 a hotel's front desk *US*
• I rang the rack, asked what they had on Mrs. Stehiti. —Dev Collans with Stewart Sterling, *I was a House Detective*, p. 73, 1954

7 a foil-wrapped package of amphetamines *US*
• [Cross Tops] were sold by the $1 unit called a rack in tightly foiled increments of four, five, or ten, depending on the quality of the drugs or the dealer. —Don Bolles, *Retrohell*, p. 50, 1997

8 a packet of five barbiturate capsules or other drugs, give or take several *US*
• —Connie Eble (Editor), *UNC-CH Campus Slang*, October 1972
• —Kenn "Naz" Young, *Naz's Underground Dictionary*, p. 53, 1973
• —Edith A. Folb, *runnin' down some lines*, p. 251, 1980

9 a one-month supply of birth control pills *US*
• —Edith A. Folb, *runnin' down some lines*, p. 251, 1980

10 a six-pack (of beer) *US*
• —Connie Eble (Editor), *UNC-CH Campus Slang*, p. 5, Fall 1991

11 a case (24 cans) of beer *US*
• —Connie Eble (Editor), *UNC-CH Campus Slang*, p. 7, Fall 2000

▸ **hit the rack**

to go to bed; to go to sleep *US*
• The night is young, and I'm not hittin' the rack 'til I get a little action. — *American Graffiti*, 1973
• — *Washington Post*, 14th October 1993

▸ **on the rack**

available for prostitution *US*
• Out on the rack nearly an hour and half and she still hadn't broke luck. —John Sayles, *Union Dues*, p. 182, 1977

rack *verb*

1 to go to sleep *US*
• — *Washington Post*, 14th October 1993

2 to steal *US*
• —Jim Crotty, *How to Talk American*, p. 143, 1997

3 to shoplift *US*
• Real graffiti writers "boost" or "rack" their paint, both slang for stealing. — *Plain Dealer (Cleveland, Ohio)*, p. L1, 29th July 2001

4 to perform well *US*
• I thought I was gonna rack on midterms, but my shovel broke – I forgot I'd even cracked a book. —Max Shulman, *Guided Tour of Campus Humor*, p. 105, 1955

5 to load (a gun) *US*
• —Anna Scotti and Paul Young, *Buzzwords*, p. 140, 1997

6 in the television and film industries, to adjust the camera lens in the middle of a shot to keep the subject in focus *US*
• —Ralph S. Singleton, *Filmaker's Dictionary*, p. 135, 1990

▸ **rack the bars**

to open or close a prison cell door *US*
• —William K. Bentley and James M. Corbett, *Prison Slang*, p. 7, 1992

rack attack *noun*

a nap; sleep *US*
• — *American Speech*, p. 64, Spring-Summer 1975: 'Razorback slang'

racked *adjective*

asleep *US*
• — *American Speech*, p. 64, Spring-Summer 1975: 'Razorback slang'

racked up *adjective*

upset *US*
• —William D. Alsever, *Glossary for the Establishment and Other Uptight People*, p. 26, December 1970

racket *noun*

1 a criminal enterprise; a swindle or a means of deception *UK, 1894*
Any illicit or dubious enterprise may be termed a 'racket' by prefixing the area of criminal operation, hence 'narcotics racket', 'loan-shark racket', etc.
• Now this gal was like me, a racket broad from the word go. —John M. Murtagh and Sara Harris, *Cast the First Stone*, p. 111, 1957
• I wasn't allowed to have a Barbie ("a racket," my parents ruled, "first it's a doll, then a camper van, then the whole mansion") —Naomi Klein, *No Logo*, p. 144, 2001

2 a job, trade or profession *UK, 1891*
A jocular reference: 'What racket are you in?' or 'What's your racket?'.

3 a private, police-only party *US*
• —Carsten Stroud, *Close Pursuit*, p. 275, 1987

4 any rigged carnival game or attraction *US, 1960*
• —Gene Sorrows, *All About Carnivals*, p. 25, 1985: 'Terminology'

racket boy *noun*

a member of an organised criminal enterprise *US*
• He's a walking lesson that it is a mistake to push the racket boys too hard[.] —Raymond Chandler, *The Long Goodbye*, p. 251, 1953

racket jacket *noun*

the jacket of a zoot suit *US*
• —Lou Shelly, *Hepcats Jive Talk Dictionary*, p. 31, 1945

racketty coo *noun*

a Jewish person *AUSTRALIA*
Rhyming slang for 'Jew'.
• I've got a feeling the racketty coo will live[.] —Barry Humphries, *Bazza Pulls It Off!*, 1971

rackety *adjective*
noisy *US*
• —John Gould, *Maine Lingo*, p. 225, 1975

rackey *noun*
a boy who affects a style of dressing reminiscent of a gangster *US*
Teen slang.
• —*American Weekly*, p. 2, 14th August 1955

rack face *noun*
lines on your face left from a blanket, sheet or pillow *US*
• —*DePauw University Campus Corner*, 29th January 1996: 'Slang terms at DePauw'

rack monster *noun*
a person who spends a great deal of time in bed *US*
• —*Verbatim*, p. 281, May 1976

rack off *verb*
to go away *AUSTRALIA, 1975*
Commonly but not exclusively used in the imperative. A euphemistic alternative to **PISS OFF** and **FUCK OFF**. Origin unknown. The *Oxford English Dictionary* (supplement) suggests a connection with 'rack' meaning 'of a horse, to move by alternately raising two legs on one side', but this seems hardly creditable due to the rarity of that term in Australia.
• Rack off y'bastards! —Bob Staines, *Wot a Whopper*, p. 58, 1982
• 'Pickles, rise and shine.' He looked up, his eyes half open. 'Rack off,' he said. —Phillip Gwynne, *Deadly Unna?*, p. 244, 1998

rack off hairy legs!
go away! *AUSTRALIA*
An intensive form of the usual **RACK OFF** with the rather feeble insult 'hairy legs' tacked on.
• —*The Australian Dictionary of Insults and Vulgarities*, 1988

rack out *verb*
to go to sleep *US*
• —Linda Reinberg, *In the Field*, p. 178, 1991

rack up *verb*
1 to accumulate things; to score points *US*
• She could of racked up points on that one. —*Diner*, 1982
2 in a casino or gambling establishment, to have your chips placed in a chip rack to be cashed in *US*
• —David M. Hayano, *Poker Faces*, p. 187, 1982
3 to prepare lines of cocaine *UK*
• He pushes a little bag of kuf over the desk an' Kingsley starts rackin' up lines on his mirror. —Nick Barlay, *Curvy Lovebox*, p. 59, 1997
4 in prison, to return prisoners to their cells *US*
• —Charles Shafer, *Folk Speech in Texas Prisons*, p. 212, 1990

racy bopper *noun*
a female fan of motor racing whose attraction to the sport is a function of her attraction to the race participants *US*
• —John Edwards, *Auto Dictionary*, p. 135, 1993

rad *noun*
1 a political *rad*ical *UK, 1973*
• I know former rads who remain inspiringly committed to eradicating America's inequalities, but even they have nice kitchens and Magellan Fund accounts. —*Newsweek*, p. 47, 2nd September 1996
2 a *rad*iator *UK, 1935*
• [H]e got his rad, he got his cooler, he got the pistons[.] —Jeremy Cameron, *Brown Bread in Wengen*, p. 118, 1999
3 a *rad*io *UK*
• —Angela Devlin, *Prison Patter*, p. 94, 1996

rad *adjective*
extreme; intense; exciting; good *US, 1982*
An abbreviated 'radical'.
• Short for "radical," it is used by Stanford University students with "way" added for emphasis. —Levi Straus & Company, *Campus Slang*, January 1986
• There is a long list of words to say things are going well. On the West Coast, something fantastic is "rad," short for radical. —*New York Times*, 12th April 1987
• —Connie Eble (Editor), *UNC-CH Campus Slang*, p. 7, Fall 1987
• —Michael V. Anderson, *The Bad, Rad, Not to Forget Way Cool Beach and Surf Discriptionary*, p. 15, 1988
• He is the biggest, fastest, raddest wide receiver in the league. —*Jerry Maguire*, 1996

radar *noun*
a petty thief *AUSTRALIA*
Someone who will 'pick up anything'.
• —Ned Wallish, *The Truth Dictionary of Racing Slang*, p. 67, 1989

radar alley *noun*
any stretch of a motorway heavily patrolled by radar; especially, Interstate 90 between Cleveland and the New York state line *US*
• —Montie Tak, *Truck Talk*, p. 127, 1971

radar Charlie *noun*
a poker player with a strong intuitive sense of other players' hands *US*
• —George Percy, *The Language of Poker*, p. 73, 1988

RadCan *noun*
Radio Canada, the francophone side of the Canadian Broadcasting Corporation *CANADA*
The 'Rad' in RadCan suggests 'radical', a view held by Canadian federalists of Radio Canada (pronounced, even by anglophone speakers, in the French way, as 'Raaahdio Canada').
• There is little pressure to settle [the strike and lockout] from Ottawa, where the federal government has always perceived the Rad-Can newsroom as a den of sovereignists. —*Montreal Gazette*, p. A2, 22nd May 2002
• Some people,(not just RadCan employees and union leaders, but also intellectual bien-pensants) are completely bent out of shape. —*Montreal Gazette*, p. B3, 22nd May 2002

raddie *noun*
1 an Italian or Anglo-Italian living in London *UK, 1938*
From the raddled-seeming complexion of some Italians compared to that of a pale Londoner, possibly influenced by **REDDY** (an Italian). Originally used of Italian families in Clerkenwell.
• —David Powis, *The Signs of Crime*, 1977
2 a political *rad*ical *UK*
• He discovered that his acquaintance was a bit of a raddie at heart. —Eric Parr, *Grafters All*, 1964

radge *noun*
a psychotic; a madman *UK*
• [O]ne ay thum's the bratay [betrayed] that radge Keith Allison[.] —Irvine Welsh, *The State of the Party (Disco Biscuits)*, p. 39, 1995

radge *adjective*
1 used in order to express approval *UK*
• — Susie Dent, *The Language Report*, p. 75, 2003
2 mad; psychotic *UK*
• [A] bumfluffed young reporter [...] asks: "It is Glasgow you're from, isnt it?" He [Irvine Welsh] merely smiles. In times past, he would have gone radge at such a slur. Or as radge as a shy, soft-spoken, beamer [blush]-prone guy like him can ever get. —*Scotland on Sunday*, 24th August 2003
3 silly *UK, 1961*
Northen dialect *radgy* (mad).

radgepot *noun*
a fool *UK*
Probably direct from Northern dialect *radge* (mad). Natural derivations are 'radgy' and 'radgified'.
• —Patrick O'Shaughnessy, *Market Traders' Slang*, 1979

radiate *verb*
▸ **radiate a mortgage**
in Quebec, to cancel a mortgage *CANADA*
• —Victor Trahan, *The City of Montreal Style Guide*, p. 120, 2001

radiator whiskey *noun*
strong, homemade whisky *US*
• It is called corn liquor, white lightning, sugar whiskey, skully cracker, popskull, bush whiskey, stump, stumphole, 'splo, ruckus juice, radiator whiskey, rotgut, sugarhead, block and tackle, wildcat, panther's breath, tiger's sweat, Sweet spirits of cats a-fighting, alley bourbon, city gin, cool water, happy Sally, deep shaft, jump steady, old horsey, stingo, blue John, red eye, pine top, buckeye bark whiskey and see seven stars. —*Star Tribune (Minneapolis)*, p. 19F, 31st January 1999

radic *noun*
a police officer, especially armed police *UK*
Shortened from 'eradicator'.
• He had arrived at the same time as the police car that was carrying two radics. —Donald Gorgon, *Cop Killer*, p. 82, 1994

radical *adjective*
extreme; outrageous; good *US*
Originally surfer slang, then migrated into the argot of the San Fernando Valley and then into mainstream US youth slang.
- — Midget Farrelly and Craig McGregor, *The Surfing Life*, p. 191, 1967
- — William Desmond Nelson, *Surfing*, p. 224, 1973
- — Connie Eble (Editor), *UNC-CH Campus Slang*, p. 6, March 1979
- Sometimes he slept on picnic tables at the beach so he could be up at dawn for the most radical waves. — Fracesca Lia Block, *weetzie bat*, p. 32, 1989
- Radical! Head-butt, dude! — *Point Break*, 1991
- Maybe the eighties will be radical, you know? — *Dazed and Confused*, 1993
- — *Sunday Times (South Africa)*, 1st June 2003

'radication squad *noun*
▷ see: ERADICATION SQUAD

radio *noun*
a prisoner who talks loudly and without paying attention to who might be listening *US*
- — Troy Harris, *A Booklet of Criminal Argot, Cant and Jargon*, p. 24, 1976

Radio Ones *noun*
diarrhoea *UK*
Rhyming slang for **THE RUNS**, formed on (the verbal out-pourings of the DJs on) BBC Radio One.
- — Ray Puxley, *Cockney Rabbit*, 1992

radio rental; radio rentals; rentals *adjective*
wonderful, amazing; insane, crazy *UK*
Rhyming slang for **MENTAL**; based on Radio Rentals, a high street shop.
- — *Financial Times*, 7th June 1973
- Ron had totally lost it. Went Radio fucking Rentals. — Greg Williams, *Diamond Geezers*, p. 139, 1997
- Has the guv'nor gone radio rental? Is he feeling Sheridan Morley [poorly]? — Humphrey Lyttleton, *I'm Sorry I Haven't A Clue*, 26th November 2001

radio that!; radio that shit!
used in prison as a demand for quiet *US*
- — *Maledicta*, p. 264, Summer/Winter 1981: 'By its slang, ye shall know it: the pessimism of prison life'

'rado *noun*
a Cadillac El Dorado car *US*
- — Edith A. Folb, *runnin' down some lines*, p. 251, 1980

rad pad *noun*
in skateboarding, a rubber wedge used as a shock pad that changes the angles at which the axle assembly is mounted *US*
- — Laura Torbet, *The Complete Book of Skateboarding*, p. 108, 1976

rads *noun*
the police *UK*
- How it would run, say, rads would come an' take me for a ride[.] — Diran Adebayo, *My Once Upon A Time*, p. 73, 2000

Rafferty's rules; Rafferty rules *noun*
an entire lack of rules altogether *AUSTRALIA, 1918*
From the Irish surname Rafferty, with the implication that the Irish were unruly. Connection with the Northumberland dialect word *raffety* 'irregular; applied by sinkers to stratified deposits', and the Lincolnshire term *raffatory* 'refractory' (see *English Dialect Dictionary*), amount to nothing more than hopeful guesswork.
- I've seen enough of these hole-in-the-wall shivoos where it's Rafferty Rules[.] — Dymphna Cusack, *Picnic Races*, p. 34, 1962
- — Frank Hardy, *The Outcasts of Foolgarah*, p. 21, 1971
- — Jim Ramsay, *Cop It Sweet!*, p. 76, 1977
- But with low mongrels like Watson and Robertson running around it looks like Mr Rafferty might have provided the rules for this game. — Clive Galea, *Slipper*, p. 92, 1988
- 'Rafferty's rules' was the term chief steward John Schreck referred to after censuring jockey James Innes for his ride on Inexplicable in the Tarien Handicap. — *Sun-Herald*, p. 70, 24th September 1989

raffle ticket; raffle *noun*
a mistake *UK*
Rhyming slang for **RICKET**.
- I've made a right raffle. I thought the favourite was in trap 6 and I backed the wrong dog. — Ray Puxley, *Cockney Rabbit*, 1992

raft *noun*
a large amount *US, 1830*
- The state premier, Bob Carr, has also announced that a caution instead of a penalty system would apply for those caught with small amounts of heroin, cocaine, cannabis, amphetamines, and ecstasy in a raft of changes that flowed from a drugs summit held last May. — *British Medical Journal*, 14th August 1999

rag *noun*
1 a sanitary towel *US*
- R is for rag to catch the flow from the womb / it substitutes for Kotex when menstruation is in full bloom. — Bruce Jackson, *Get Your Ass in the Water and Swim Like Me*, p. 213, 1966
- [A] loved one will rebuff you, that's you with the rags on! — Frank Hardy, *The Outcasts of Foolgarah*, p. 17, 1971
- For tomorrow she would have the rags on, and the day off. — Lance Peters, *The Dirty Half-Mile*, p. 3, 1979
- — Edith A. Folb, *runnin' down some lines*, p. 251, 1980

2 the bleed period of the menstrual cycle *US*
- Fellatia passes uptown for a woman and specializes in blowing her johns in the back seat of cabs and if they insist on taking her to their rooms, pleads the rag and blows them there. — John Francis Hunter, *The Gay Insider*, p. 90, 1971
- Many a nut got busted in her butt / For the rag didn't mean a thing. — Dennis Wepman et al., *The Life*, p. 83, 1976

3 a despicable person *US*
- Don't be such a rag. I have to sit here and work up the desire to fuck you later. — *Chasing Amy*, 1997

4 a newspaper, especially a disreputable one *UK, 1889*
- The other rag gave me a good spread and a good going over and they didn't have my picture. — Mickey Spillane, *One Lonely Night*, p. 16, 1951
- I've got a guy coming in – used to work on the labor rag here before it folded[.] — Jim Thompson, *The Nothing Man*, p. 232, 1954

5 a used car that is in very poor condition *US*
- — *American Speech*, p. 309–310, Winter 1980: 'More jargon of car salesmen'

6 a well-worn tyre *US*
- — *American Speech*, p. 273, December 1961: 'Northwest truck drivers' language'
- — Montie Tak, *Truck Talk*, p. 127, 1971

7 a banknote; paper money *UK, 1817*

8 in pool, a cushion *US, 1985*
- — Mike Shamos, *The Illustrated Encyclopedia of Billiards*, p. 186, 1993

9 in horse racing, an outsider (a horse considered unlikely to win a race) *UK*
- [N]ot, as I keep telling owners, that their precious creature is useless: a "rag" in the Derby could be the "jolly" [favourite] next time out in a handicap. — John McCririck, *John McCririck's World of Betting*, p. 61, 1991

10 in poker, a useless card in the dealt hand or a drawn card that does not improve the hand *US, 1978*
- — Edwin Silberstang, *Winning Poker for the Serious Player*, p. 219, 1992

11 in a carnival midway game, a small prize in a plastic bag *US*
- — Gene Sorrows, *All About Carnivals*, p. 25, 1985: 'Terminology'

12 a railway pointsman *US*
- — Norman Carlisle, *The Modern Wonder Book of Trains and Railroading*, p. 267, 1946

▸ **get your rag out**
to lose your temper *UK*
A combination of **LOSE YOUR RAG** and the earlier 'get your shirt out'.
- [H]e had called her a slab-sided cow and that had got her rag out. — Charles Raven, *Underworld Nights*, p. 17, 1956

▸ **lose your rag**
to lose your temper *UK, 1959*
- "Just take your place, Bex," Weasel says, losing his rag a little. — Danny King, *The Burglar Diaries*, p. 100, 2001
- It's just the way it is, son, don't start losing your rag with me! — Mark Powell, *Snap*, p. 28, 2001

▸ **on the rag; have the rag on**
1 experiencing the bleed period of the menstrual cycle *US*
- What's wit' you, you got the rag on or somethin'? — Richard Price, *The Wanderers*, p. 188, 1974
- Is she on the rag or what? — *Airheads*, 1994
- yeah, I'm just waiting because I'm on my rag. — Ana Loria, *1 2 3 Be A Porn Star!*, p. 47, 2000

2 figuratively, to be distracted and irritable *US*
- "You see, zoll- " (That how she said doll.) "-little Flip's got the mean rag on." — John Rechy, *City of Night*, p. 50, 1963
- It's all a matter of which team don't have the rag on. — Dan Jenkins, *Semi-Tough*, p. 48, 1972
- See, he always calls me 'Sergeant' when he's on the rag which is most a the time. — Joseph Wambaugh, *The Choirboys*, p. 259, 1975
- Vinnie was on the rag. He'd pulled a muscle in his leg again and lost a good bust on a chickenshit technicality and then when they reported for work the Captain said they'd have to go an extra four[.] — John Sayles, *Union Dues*, p. 383, 1977

rag *verb*
to mock, bully, tease or ridicule someone *UK, 1808*
- I don't know why they were ragging him – the immediate cause of it. It may have had something to do with who had done most to win the war, or an argument over the relative size of the British and American navies, or British and American cars. — *The Guardian*, 8th March 2003

rag *adjective*
unpleasant, bad *NEW ZEALAND*
- — David McGill, *David McGill's Complete Kiwi Slang Dictionary*, p. 104, 1998

ragamuffin *noun*
the bleed period of the menstrual cycle *AUSTRALIA*
A play on **RAG** (a sanitary towel).
- My boyfriend and I use the phrase, "Are you a ragamuffin yet?" meaning "Have you got your period yet?" or "I've got my ragamuffins" meaning "I've got my period". — a correspondent, *The Museum of Menstruation and Women's Health*, July 2001

rag and bone *noun*
1 a telephone *UK*
Rhyming slang.
- I'm on the rag and bone to San Francisco[.] — Anthony Masters, *Minder*, p. 113, 1984

2 a lavatory pedestal and receptacle, especially the lavatory seat *UK*
Rhyming slang for **THRONE**.
- — Ray Puxley, *Cockney Rabbit*, 1992

rag and boner *noun*
a telephone *UK*
Extended from rhyming slang **RAG AND BONE** (telephone).
- You come here, team-handed, terrorising law-abiding rate-payers who use the facilities of the GPO – to whit a public rag and boner. — Anthony Masters, *Minder*, p. 142, 1984

raga-raga *adjective*
of clothes, worn-out, ragged *JAMAICA*
A variation on conventional 'ragged'.

ragbag *noun*
1 an odd assortment *UK*
- [A] ragbag of protesters – an unlikely alliance reflecting all strata of society[.] — John Robb, *The Nineties*, p. 189, 1999

2 an untidily or shabbily dressed person *UK, 1888*
- The man was all alone in the night – a ragbag with a round, flat face that glowed[.] — Kurt Vonnegut, *Slaughterhouse-Five*, p. 82, 1969

3 in circus and carnival usage, a show that has fallen on hard times or is fundamentally dishonest *US*
- — Don Wilmeth, *The Language of American Popular Entertainment*, p. 215, 1981

rage *noun*
a large wave *US*
- If you want to get aggro, man, this stick can handle your best rage. — *Point Break*, 1991

rage *verb*
1 to enjoy a party with great enthusiasm *US*
- — Connie Eble (Editor), *UNC-CH Campus Slang*, p. 7, Spring 1992
- — Linda Meyer, *Teenspeak!*, p. 30, 1994

2 to dominate someone or something *US*
- — Connie Eble (Editor), *UNC-CH Campus Slang*, p. 5, Spring 1984

-rage *suffix*
when combined with a subject noun, an outburst of enraged hostility within or occasioned by that subject area *UK*
- — Susie Dent, *The Language Report*, p. 17, 2003

rager *noun*
1 a skilled, aggressive surfer or skateboarder *US*
- — Anna Scotti and Paul Young, *Buzzwords*, p. 113, 1997

2 a large party *US*
- — Judi Sanders, *Cal Poly Slang*, p. 8, 1990
- — Vann Wesson, *Generation X Field Guide and Lexicon*, p. 136, 1997

ragga; ragamuffin; raggamuffin *noun*
a ruffian, usually of West Indian racial origin *UK*
Originally a West Indian and UK black term with an approving tone; probably derived from the conventional sense of a 'raggedy' (a disreputable person); ultimately from Ragamoffyn, a demon in the Middle English poem 'Piers Plowman' by William Langland (perhaps 1330–86). The derivation is likely to be influenced by Jamaican 'raga-raga' (ragged) and 'ragamofi' (ragged clothes).
- — Angela Devlin, *Prison Patter*, p. 94, 1996
- [W]e sort of score a pill off these really large raggas there with big Moschino coats on. — Ben Malbon, *Cool Places*, p. 272, 1998

raggagansta; raggagangsta *noun*
a West Indian/UK black gangster *UK*
Compounds **RAGGAMUFFIN** (a ruffian) with **GANGSTA** (a gangster).
- '- Raggaganstamuthafucka. – How y'doing man, says Lendon laughin'. — Nick Barlay, *Curvy Lovebox*, p. 83, 1997

ragged *adjective*
1 without money *US*
- — Charles Shafer, *Folk Speech in Texas Prisons*, p. 212, 1990

2 tired; unwell *AUSTRALIA*
- — D'Arcy Niland, *Call Me...*, 1958

ragged edge *noun*
in hot rodding, drag racing and motor racing, the absolute limit of the car's ability *US*
- A racing vehicle that's running on the ragged edge doesn't have any further margin in performance or handling. — John Lawlor, *How to Talk Car*, p. 86, 1965

raggedy *adjective*
ragged; rough; dishevelled *US, 1890*
- — Malachi Andrews and Paul T. Owens, *Black Language*, p. 52, 1973
- I'll need to use her raggedy ass car the rest of the day. — Donald Goines, *Never Die Alone*, p. 117, 1974
- The basketball courts in Bill Robinson are too raggedy, and the kids need a place to play when it gets cold. — *New Jack City*, 1990

raggedy jack *noun*
in Newfoundland, a homemade pile rug *CANADA*
- The loops were pulled up higher when they hooked [than a regular mat], perhaps to an inch in length. Then the tops of the loops were cut off. This mat was called a 'raggedy jack,' a 'rag-a-jack,' and 'raggedy mat.' — Gerald Pocius, *Textile Traditions of Eastern Newfoundland*, p. 54, 1979

raggedy jacket *noun*
in Newfoundland, a harp seal moulting from the white coat to the bedlamer stage *CANADA*
- Those seals that have some white and some blue-black (known as raggedy jackets) only bring in about $5.00. — *Decks Awash*, p. v.2 p.7, 1976

raggin' *adjective*
dressed in fashionable and expensive clothing *US*
- — *Washington Post Magazine*, p. 13, 26th April 1987: 'Say wha?'

raggy-arse *adjective*
of poor quality *UK*
- [A]ny of your raggy-arse crew lay a finger on Stevie again and it's you that's going to answer[.] — Kevin Sampson, *Clubland*, p. 205, 2002

rag head *noun*
1 an Arab person, or a native of any race that wears a cloth-covering on the head; by extension a native of Muslim countries *US, 1921*
Offensive.
- — Joseph E. Ragen and Charles Finston, *Inside the World's Toughest Prison*, p. 814, 1962: 'Penitentiary and underworld glossary'
- He looked at the rearview mirror thinking, You want to drive, raghead? — Elmore Leonard, *Pronto*, p. 268, 1993
- "You mean this rag-head understands English?" "Most Pakistanis do, Bill." — Howard Marks, *Mr Nice*, p. 262, 1997
- Limbaugh was reacting to a wire story about Sen. Conrad Burns' most recent faux pas, in which the Republican senator described Arabs as "ragheads" during a speech to the Montana Equipment Dealers Association. — *Great Falls (Montana) Tribune*, p. A6, 15th March 1999
- In a series of racist statements that began when the World Trade Center collapsed, Roque announced his murderous plans and told a co-worker that he had been treated rudely at a gasoline station on University Drive by "a towel head or a rag head." — *The Arizona Republic*, p. 1A, 3rd September 2003

2 in circus and carnival usage, a gypsy *US*
- — Don Wilmeth, *The Language of American Popular Entertainment*, p. 215, 1981

raging *adjective*
very good; very exciting *US*
- This is raging! — *Clueless*, 1995

Raging Bull *nickname*
Jake LaMotta (b.1921), a middleweight boxer who fiercely made his presence felt in the ring in the 1940s and 50s *US*

raging queer *noun*
a particularly ostentatious or importunate male homosexual *UK, 1984*
An intensification of **QUEEN** (a male homosexual).

rag joint *noun*
a carnival concession in a canvas booth *US*
- —Gene Sorrows, *All About Carnivals*, p. 25, 1985: 'Terminology'

ragman's coat *noun*
on a woman, an untrimmed and naturally abundant mass of pubic hair *UK*
- [S]he looks quite fit but I bet she's got one like a ragman's coat! —*www.LondonSlang.com*, June 2002

rag order *noun*
chaotic disorder, a mess *UK*
Military.
- The Argentines had left [Port Stanley] in rag order.—*The Observer*, February 1983
- The garden was in rag order, as bad as the van.—Roddy Doyle, *The Van*, p. 113, 1991

rag store *noun*
a big con swindle in which the lure is the promise of wealth from stocks traded based on allegedly inside information *US*
- The same gimmicks are used in the rag store. It's the bogus shares of stock and fake inside market information that trim the sucker in that case.—Iceberg Slim (Robert Beck), *Trick Baby*, p. 119–120, 1969

rag stuffer *noun*
a parachute rigger *US*
- —Linda Reinberg, *In the Field*, p. 178, 1991

ragtime *noun*
the bleed period of a woman's menstrual cycle *US*
A play on **ON THE RAG** (menstruating), after the musical style.
- In the late 1980s [...] an unpleasant middle-aged white guy, would say "It must be ragtime" whenever a female subordinate caused him grief. Thank God I didn't work for him!"—*The Museum of Menstruation and Women's Health*, February 2001

ragtop *noun*
a convertible car *US, 1955*
- —*Good Housekeeping*, p. 143, September 1958: "Hot-rod terms for teen-age girls"
- —Chrysler Corporation, *Of Anchors, Bezels, Pots and Scorchers*, September 1959
- —Tom MacPherson, *Dragging and Driving*, p. 141, 1960
- —*Current Slang*, p. 5, Fall 1966
- Feels like a rag-top day to me.—Jimmy Buffett, *Tales from Margaritaville*, p. 175, 1989
- His head shot up, smashing his mauve fedora flat against the ragtop Cad.—Joseph Wambaugh, *Fugitive Nights*, p. 17, 1990
- Daddy-O meets slinky Jana Ryan, a rich girl with a valid driver's license and a '57 T-Bird ragtop.—James Ellroy, *Hollywood Nocturnes*, p. 6, 1994
- [A] Bentley Azure Mulliner rag-top. The sight of this ghetto-fab machine perked me up considerably[.]—*ES Magazine*, p. 3, 22nd June 2001

rag town *noun*
a town built in prosperous times, bound to fall into poverty with the end of prosperous times *US*
- We had been in many of the same places – the pipeline jobs, the "rag towns" of the south and west.—Jim Thompson, *Roughneck*, p. 65, 1954

ragweed *noun*
1 poor quality marijuana *US, 1969*
After botanical genus *Ambrosia* the which grows wild across North America.

2 poor quality heroin *UK, 1998*
- —Robert Ashton, *This Is Heroin*, p. 210, 2002
- —Mike Haskins, *Drugs*, p. 284, 2003

rag week *noun*
the week of the month when a woman has a menstrual bleed *UK*
Combines **RAG** (a sanitary towel), as in 'on the rag', with conventional 'week' to form a play on university rag week.
- —Sacha Baron-Cohen *Da Gospel According to Ali G*, 2001: 'Rag week'

rah!; rah rah!
used as a cheer, a shouted expression of support or encouragement *US, 1870*
A shortening of 'hurrah!' in college sports use. As 'rah! rah! rah!' it is the climax of a Maori war cry that has been adopted by New Zealand rugby teams.
- Rah! Who'd have freakin' thought it? I was a blackhead with connections.—Diran Abedayo, *My Once Upon A Time*, p. 183, 2000

rah-rah *adjective*
characterised by excessive spirit and enthusiasm, usually associated with college or high school *US, 1914*
- College kids have outgrown all that rah-rah stuff. The war, the A-bomb, the H-bomb – who's thinking about fun and jokes these days?—Max Shulman, *The Many Loves of Dobie Gillis*, p. 24, 1951
- Maybe in some rah-rah campus crowd beer joint I'd just hee-haw and let him slide, but here in the Pink Dragon the beat cops rule by force and fear.—Joseph Wambaugh, *The Blue Knight*, p. 45, 1973
- [S]ome trendy "rah-rah" birds going on about how much they like football[.]—Danny King, *The Burglar Diaries*, p. 122, 2001

rahtid; raatid; rhaatid *adjective*
used as an intensifier that implies anger or strong disapproval *UK*
Urban black usage.
- Here I am trying to sort out family business yet me don't get no rahtid support from you.—Donald Gorgon, *Cop Killer*, p. 18, 1994

rail *noun*
1 a line of cocaine or other powdered drug, laid out for snorting *US*
- You followed the rails of white powder across the mirror in pursuit of a point of convergence[.]—Jay McInerney, *Bright Lights, Big City*, p. 170, 1984
- They have their party, chop some rails, put a movie on.—Elmore Leoanrd, *Maximum Bob*, p. 52, 1991
- —Angela Devlin, *Prison Patter*, p. 94, 1996

2 any railway employee *US*
- —Norman Carlisle, *The Modern Wonder Book of Trains and Railroading*, p. 267, 1946

▸ **on the rail**
in American casinos, observing the gambling but not playing *US*
- —Steve Kuriscak, *Casino Talk*, p. 40, 1985

rail *verb*
to arrest or detain someone *US*
- Okay, so I did a little time, does that mean I get railed every time truck finds its way off the planet?—*The Usual Suspects*, 1995

railbird *noun*
1 in horse racing, an enthusiast who watches morning work-outs, carefully clocking performances *US, 1931*
- —David W. Maurer, *Argot of the Racetrack*, p. 54, 1951

2 in American casinos, a thief who steals chips from inattentive gamblers *US*
- —Steve Kuriscak, *Casino Talk*, p. 46, 1985
- "Guy's acting a little shifty," Roger said. "Could be a railbird, waiting to grab a few chips."—Elmore Leonard, *Glitz*, p. 116, 1985

3 in pool, a spectator *US*
- —Mike Shamos, *The Illustrated Encyclopedia of Billiards*, p. 187, 1993

raildog *noun*
a backstage technician who works with set rigging on a catwalk *US*
- —Connie Eble (Editor), *UNC-CH Campus Slang*, p. 7, Fall 1991

railfield *verb*
a thief who simply grabs shop merchandise and runs from the shop *US*
- Then me and some more guys was railfieldin a radio shop and got caught, and I got sapped up and went to the Hill for eighteen months. I was so scared I never railfielded no more. I kept stealin but I never railfielded.—Clarence Cooper Jr, *The Scene*, p. 135, 1960
- —Clarence Major, *Juba to Jive*, p. 346, 1994

rail job; rail *noun*
a drag racing car with a chassis made of rail-like metal bars; a drag racing car regardless of the chassis construction *US*
- She's hip to everything, man, from customs to rails / And axle grease embedded 'neath her fingernails.—The Beach Boys, *Car Crazy Cutie*, 1963

- Drag City races are the fastest in the nation / Rails are the wildest and the stockers are pretty / I'll get my honey, grab some money / Split to Drag City. — *Drag City*, 1963
- She beats the gassers and the rail jobs and the rail jobs, really drive 'em wild / C'mon and turn it on, wind it up, blow it out, GTO. — John Wilkin, *G.T.O.*, 1964

rail lugger *noun*

in horse racing, a horse that prefers to run near or next to the inside rail *US*

- — Dan Parker, *The ABC of Horse Racing*, p. 148, 1947

rail on; rail *verb*

to criticize or reprimand someone *US*

- — Connie Eble (Editor), *UNC-CH Campus Slang*, p. 7, Fall 1987

railrat *noun*

in the language surrounding the Grateful Dead, a member of the audience who prefers to see the show from as close as possible to the band, right on the rail *US*

- — David Shenk and Steve Silberman, *Skeleton Key*, p. 238, 1994

railroad *verb*

to move your jaw from side to side obsessively and involuntarily after sustained amphetamine use *US*

- — Geoffrey Froner, *Digging for Diamonds*, p. 50, 1989

railroad bible *noun*

a deck of playing cards *US, 1976*

- — Thomas L. Clark, *The Dictionary of Gambling and Gaming*, p. 175, 1987

railroad dick *noun*

a private guard employed by a railway company *US*

- [H]is world became a world of brakies, reefers, redballs, railroad dicks in hard-up midwest towns[.] — John Clellon Holmes, *The Horn*, p. 159, 1958

railroad flat *noun*

an apartment consisting of connected long, narrow rooms *US, 1956*

- Red's apartment was the type known as a "railroad flat." It had no hallway. There was a succession of rooms, one telescoped into the next. — Ross Russell, *The Sound*, p. 105, 1961
- Alan lived in a railroad flat, in one large room of it, with paintings on all the walls. — Clancy Sigal, *Going Away*, p. 417, 1961
- We were freezing our asses off in a fourth-floor railroad flat on Ninety-second Street with a toilet in the hall used to freeze up overnight. — Vincent Patrick, *The Pope of Greenwich Village*, p. 166, 1979

railroad tracks *noun*

the bars on a captain's uniform signifying his office *US*

- — *American Speech*, p. 55, February 1947: 'Pacific War language'
- — Linda Reinberg, *In the Field*, p. 178, 1991

railroad weed *noun*

marijuana, especially of inferior quality *US, 1974*

From the weeds that flourish alongside railway lines, not necessarily **WEED** (marijuana).

- — Richard A. Spears, *The Slang and Jargon of Drugs and Drink*, p. 416, 1986
- — Mike Haskins, *Drugs*, p. 288, 2003

rails *noun*

that part of a racecourse where the rails bookmakers are situated; hence, big-time bookmaking *AUSTRALIA*

- — Gerald Sweeney, *The Plunge*, p. 311, 1981
- — Joe Andersen, *Winners Can Laugh*, p. 148, 1982

rail sandwich *noun*

a surfboard between your legs *US*

- — Dennis Aaberg and John Milius, *Big Wednesday*, p. 211, 1978

rails bookmaker; rails bookie *noun*

one of the more prestigious bookmakers *AUSTRALIA, 1950*

- Among the hard-nosed rails bookmakers, Flint's runners were jokes. — Gerald Sweeney, *The Plunge*, p. 311, 1981
- As soon as Ray left school Joe got him a job with Duvi Goldberg, the rails bookie[.] — Clive Galea, *Slipper*, p. 25, 1988

railway station *noun*

an 'allocation' prison from which prisoners are forwarded *UK*

- They call 'em "railway stations" because you're just parked up waiting to be sent off somewhere. — Dave Courtney, *Stop the Ride I Want to Get Off*, p. 71, 1999

ráiméis *noun*

foolish, nonsensical, ill-founded talk *IRELAND*

- The reply did not address the issues I raised. It was a rambling ráiméis on the series of grant aids available to industry from State agencies — Mr. Creed, *House of the Oireachtas Parliamentary Debates*, 6th February 2001

rain *verb*

▸ **if it was raining ...**

I am extremely unlucky *AUSTRALIA*

- I'm so unlucky that if it was raining mansions I'd get hit on the head with a Mallee lavatory. — Frank Hardy, *The Yarns of Billy Borker*, p. 107, 1965
- Jesus, if it was raining virgins I'd be washed down the gutter with a poofter. — *The Adventures of Barry McKenzie*, 1972
- The difference between a whinger and a genuinely unlucky man is that your whinger would complain in heaven, whereas your unlucky man would, if it were raining mansions, get hit on the head with a Ferntree Gully dunny. — Frank Hardy, *Hardy's People*, p. 33, 1986

▸ **rain pups and pussies**

to rain very hard *US*

- It's fucking raining pups and pussies. — Robert Campbell, *Sweet La-La Land*, p. 279, 1990

rain and pour; rain *verb*

to snore *UK*

Rhyming slang.

- — Ray Puxley, *Cockney Rabbit*, 1992

rainbow *noun*

1 a capsule of amobarbital sodium and secobarbital sodium (trade name Tuinal™), a combination of central nervous system depressants *US*

- — Donald Louria, *Nightmare Drugs*, p. 25, 1966
- The carpeted lobby was littered with fallen rainbows, dexis, bennies, ludes, speed, even some dust, though it had a bad rep these days[.] — Joseph Wambaugh, *The Glitter Dome*, p. 122, 1981

2 in casinos, a bet comprised of different colour and different value betting chips *US*

- — Michael Dalton, *Blackjack*, p. 29, 1991

3 in oil drilling, a very small showing of oil in a hole *US*

- — Jerry Robertson, *Oil Slanguage*, p. 60, 1954

4 a soldier who joins a fighting unit after conflict has ceased *AUSTRALIA, 1919*

Used in both World Wars; a rainbow comes after a storm.

▸ **go up the rainbow**

to experience sexual ecstasy *UK*

- — Richard Allen, *Boot Boys*, 1972

rainbow hand *noun*

a poker hand with cards of all four suits *US, 1950*

- — Thomas L. Clark, *The Dictionary of Gambling and Gaming*, p. 175, 1987

rainbow jumper *noun*

in basketball, a high, arcing jump shot *US*

- He seemingly had the game won when his his 15-foot rainbow jumper over Jabbar sifted through the net with seven seconds to play. — *Washington Post*, p. D1, 12th May 1974

rainbow party *noun*

oral sex on one male by several females, all wearing different colours of lipstick *US*

- A rainbow party is an oral sex party. It's a gathering where oral sex is performed. And a rainbow comes from all – all of the girls put on lipstick and each one puts her mouth around the penis of the gentleman or gentlemen who are there to receive favors and make marks in a different place on the penis, hence the term rainbow. — *Oprah Winfrey Show*, 2nd October 2003

rainbow roll *noun*

a multi-coloured assortment of barbiturate capsules *US*

- — David W. Maurer and Victor Vogel, *Narcotics and Narcotic Addiction*, p. 437, 1973

rainbows *noun*

1 LSD *UK*

Presumably from the pictures printed on the blotting paper dose.

- Street names [...] penguins, rainbows, smilies[.] — James Kay and Julian Cohen, *The Parents' Complete Guide to Young People and Drugs*, p. 141, 1998
- — Mike Haskins, *Drugs*, p. 286, 2003

2 the recreational drug methaqualone, best known as Quaaludes™ *UK*

- — Tom Hibbert, *Rockspeak!*, p. 129, 1983

rain check *noun*

1 a request or promise to take up an invitation at a convenient time; a postponement of any arrangement *US, 1930*
From the ticket given to a spectator at an outdoor event providing for a refund/admission at a later date, should the event be interrupted by rain.
• [L]ast week Andy rang to say that he and Michelle would have to take a rain check because they'd been blackmailed into accepting an invitation from Michelle's parents[.] — *New Statesman*, 9th October 1998

2 the reduction of a criminal penalty; parole, probation *US*
• — Vincent J. Monteleone, *Criminal Slang*, p. 189, 1949

raincoat *noun*
a condom *US*
Figurative use of waterproof wear.
• — *Current Slang*, p. 22, Spring 1970

Raincoat Charlie *noun*
a striptease audience member who masturbates beneath the safety of his raincoat *US*
• — Don Wilmeth, *The Language of American Popular Entertainment*, p. 216, 1981

raincoater *noun*
a stereotypical perverted porngraphy fan *US*
• — Ana Loria, *1 2 3 Be A Porn Star!*, p. 166, 2000: 'Glossary of adult sex industry terms'

raincoat job *noun*
a sexual fetish involving urination on your partner *US*
• — J.R. Schwartz, *The Official Guide to the Best Cat Houses in Nevada*, p. 164, 1993: 'Sex Glossary'

rain dance *noun*
in computing, an action that is expected to be taken but will likely produce no results *US*
• — Robert Kirk Mueller, *Buzzwords*, p. 133, 1974
• I can't boot up the machine. We'll have to wait for Greg to do his rain dance. — Eric S. Raymond, *The New Hacker's Dictionary*, p. 294–295, 1991

rained out *adjective*
postponed *US*
A term from sports, especially baseball, but applied more broadly to refer to, for example, a class on a given day that has been postponed.
• — Connie Eble (Editor), *UNC-CH Campus Slang*, p. 8, April 1995

raining and pouring; raining *noun*
snoring *UK*
Rhyming slang.
• You kept me awake all night with your raining. — Ray Puxley, *Cockney Rabbit*, 1992

rainmaker *noun*
a member of an enterprise whose job includes procuring clients or business by the use of charm *US*
• "Frank is the rainmaker," I Heard Edmund say one night at the annual meeting of the Massachusetts Bar Association[.] — George V. Higgins, *Penance for Jerry Kennedy*, p. 56, 1985
• — Rachel S. Epstein and Nina Liebman, *Biz Speak*, p. 186, 1986
• Beano smiled his boyish rainmaker smile. It brought rain, but only a few drops. — Stephen J. Cannell, *King Con*, p. 73, 1997

rain room *noun*
a shower room *US*
• — Carl Fleischhauer, *A Glossary of Army Slang*, p. 10, 1968
• — Lee McNelis, *30 + And a Wake-Up: A Compendium of Prison Slang Terms and Definitions*, p. 5, 1991
• — Judie Sanders, *Faced and Faded, Hanging at Hurl*, p. 32, 1993

Rainy City *nickname*
Manchester, UK *UK*
• [I]t doesn't take much brain to figure out that Rainy City is Manchester. — Peter Chippindale, *The British CB Book*, p. 169–169, 1981

rainy day woman *noun*
marijuana *US*
This seems to have been inspired by the following lyric: 'Everybody must get stoned' by Bob Dylan, 'Rainy Day Women #12 & 35', 1966.
• — Ralph de Sola, *Crime Dictionary*, p. 125, 1982
• — Mike Haskins, *Drugs*, p. 288, 2003

raise *noun*

1 stake money; a monetary profit *UK*
• Or they'd get up close to someone who'd just made a raise and tax [to rob, to extort] the fuckin' life out of them [...] which is how they came to be up here in Bradford, looking for a raise to open up the way for them. — Lanre Fehintola, *Charlie Says...*, p. 68, 2000

2 parents *US*
• — David Claerbaut, *Black Jargon in White America*, p. 77, 1972

3 the arm *US*
• — Kenn "Naz" Young, *Naz's Underground Dictionary*, p. 53, 1973

raise *verb*

1 (used of a male) to achieve an erection *BAHAMAS, 1971*
• — John A. Holm, *Dictionary of Bahamian English*, p. 165, 1982

2 to identify yourself to a fellow traveller *US*
• Ever notice how many expressions carry over from queers to con men? Like 'raise,' letting someone know you are in the same line? — William Burroughs, *Naked Lunch*, p. 3, 1957

3 to bail someone out of jail *US*
• [S]ince the High One was an undercover bondsman he raised her each time. — A.S. Jackson, *Gentleman Pimp*, p. 121, 1973
• I want to raise. I want out. — Gerald Petievich, *To Live and Die in L.A.*, p. 133, 1983

▸ **raise Cain**
to make a disturbance; to complain or quarrel noisily and angrily *US, 1930*
• Since Democrats can't get the bill they want from the Republican majority, Kennedy favors continuing to raise Cain over the defeat of McCain. — *National Review*, 20th July 1998

▸ **raise hell**
to make a disturbance; to make a din; to cause trouble *US, 1896*
• Raising hell may be good for your health. — *Humanist*, April 2003

▸ **raise sand**
to argue loudly, creating a problem *US*
• There wasn't much raisin' sand at these parties, 'cause the peoples was havin' fun! — Henry Williamson, *Hustler!*, p. 23, 1965

raiser *noun*

1 a lookout who warns confederates of approaching police *US*
• Both of the front doors flew open and two Hawaiian shirts stepped out. The raiser barked "Five-oh" and split. — Richard Price, *Clockers*, p. 441, 1992

2 a criminal who specialises in forging increases in the amount payable to an otherwise legitimate cheque or security *US*
• — Hyman E. Goldin et al., *Dictionary of American Underworld Lingo*, p. 173, 1950

raise up *verb*

1 to make someone angry *US*
• — Don R. McCreary (Editor), *Dawg Speak*, 2001

2 to warn someone *US*
• Strike looked at Peanut now, sulking on the corner, demoted to raising up – looking out for the Fury – a flat twenty-dollar gig, no bottles, no commission. — Richard Price, *Clockers*, p. 4, 1992

3 to be released from prison *US*
• I'll go home to Galvaston n have it n wait on Joe to raise up. — Seth Morgan, *Homeboy*, p. 171, 1990
• — William Bentley, *Prison Slang*, p. 108, 1992

raisinhead *noun*
a black person *US*
Offensive.
• I'm so tired of being called names. I ain't no raisinhead or nothing like that. — Piri Thomas, *Stories from El Barrio*, p. 60, 1978

raisin jack *noun*
a potent and vile alcoholic beverage brewed by letting raisins ferment, usually in prison *US*
• [W]atching mentally impoverished lowlifes get fucked up on raisin-jack[.] — James Ellroy, *Suicide Hill*, p. 574, 1986

raisin picker *noun*
on the railways, a worker from Fresno, California *US*
Fresno is regarded as the raisin capital of the US.
• — J. Herbert Lund, *Herb's Hot Box of Railraod Slang*, p. 70, 1975

raisin snap *noun*
alcohol made from fermented raisins *US*
• Later on she discovered, when a shipmate came to call, that her husband had cooked up some raisin snap in a cookpot stashed behind the boilers. — Robert Campbell, *Juice*, p. 27, 1988

raize *verb*
to annoy or harass someone *US*
• — Trevor Cralle, *The Surfin'ary*, p. 96, 1991

rajah *noun*
an erection *NEW ZEALAND*
• —David McGill, *David McGill's Complete Kiwi Slang Dictionary*, p. 91, 1998

Rajputana *noun*
a banana *UK*
Rhyming slang, formed from a ship that berthed in London's Royal Docks.
• Making love in a French letter [condom] is like eating a Rajputana with the skin on.—Ray Puxley, *Fresh Rabbit*, 1998

rake *noun*
1 an amount of something; a large quantity *IRELAND*
• God, I don't even know where they'd be, love. There's a rake of papers to be gone through—Joseph O'Connor, *Red Roses and Petrol*, p. 26, 1995
• Every place there was a war Ozzie would be. Angola, Mozambique and Biafra and a rake of other spots.—Eamonn Sweeney, *Waiting for the Healer*, p. 113, 1997
2 a comb *US*
• —*San Francisco Examiner*, p. III-2, 22 March 1960
3 in pool, a device used to support the cue stick for a hard-to-reach shot *US*
• —Steve Rushin, *Pool Cool*, p. 24, 1990

rake *verb*
to lower the front end of a car *US*

▸**rake a game**
to charge card players for the privilege of playing *US*
• —Robert C. Prus and C.R.D. Sharper, *Road Hustler*, p. 171, 1977: 'Glossary of terms'

▸**rake the leaves**
to drive at the back of a group of trucks travelling on a motorway together, watching for police from the rear *US*
• —Porter Bibb, *CB Bible*, p. 103, 1976

raked *adjective*
drunk *US*
• —Connie Eble (Editor), *UNC-CH Campus Slang*, p. 6, Spring 1990

rakehell *noun*
an utter scoundrel *UK, 1554*
• Liz is the rakehell from Scarsdale, who bickers her journeyman into defeat.—Sidney Bernard, *This Way to the Apocalypse*, p. 147, 1964

rake-in *noun*
the financial results of an enterprise *US*
• Dopey asked how Phil had gotten the rake-in, and Phil told him. —James T. Farrell, *Saturday Night*, p. 24, 1947

rake in; rake *verb*
to make money, especially in generous quantities or at an enviable speed *UK, 1583*
• It could tour the country, raking it in.—*New Statesman*, 6th June 1997

rake-off *noun*
money obtained from a crime or as a bribe *US, 1899*
• Pa recalled that the old man had made his fortune by rake-offs in the distribution of railway lines during his administration.—Miles Franklin, *My Career Goes Bung*, p. 112, 1946
• Don't be a mug all yer life, Snowy. Back in the States all the sports writers get a rake-off from the promoters. Nothin' crook about it, boy; just good business.—Frank Hardy, *Power Without Glory*, p. 453, 1950
• —Hyman E. Goldin et al., *Dictionary of American Underworld Lingo*, p. 173, 1950
• How much would my rake-off be for getting him a conviction with a fine of a hundred quid. The top-off gets half the fine, doesn't he? —Vince Kelly, *The Bogeyman*, p. 76, 1956
• Indeed, if the Taxation Commissioner declared it a legal profession, just imagine the Treasury rake-off.—*Flame*, p. 12, 1972
• We get to pick up the shares tomorrow and take the rake-off on Friday. Harrison Biscuit,—*The Search for Savage Henry*, p. 30, 1995
• —Angela Devlin, *Prison Patter*, p. 94, 1996

Rakkasans *nickname*
the 3rd Battalion, 187th Infantry Regiment *US*
Distinguished airborne and air assault soldiers in World War 2, Korea, Vietnam and the Persian Gulf. From the Japanese for 'parachute', named during the first four years of occupation duty in Japan.
• We toasted his Rakkasan paratroopers, and then we toasted the Wolfhounds; we even toasted the Chinese, and got so drunk that I slept right through Taijon.—David H. Hackworth, *About Face*, p. 134, 1989

rakli *noun*
a girl; a woman *UK*
Romany in current English gypsy use.
• —Jimmy Stockin, *On The Cobbles*, p. 11, 2000

Raleigh bike *noun*
a lesbian *UK*
Rhyming slang for **DYKE**, formed on a product of a well-known bicycle manufacturer.
• —Ray Puxley, *Cockney Rabbit*, 1992

rally *verb*
to go out drinking *US*
• —Connie Eble (Editor), *UNC-CH Campus Slang*, Fall 1974

ralph *noun*
1 a right turn *US*
• —*Current Slang*, p. 6, Spring 1968
2 vomit *US*
• —*American Speech*, p. 64, Spring-Summer 1975: 'Razorback slang'

ralph *verb*
to vomit *US*
• —*Current Slang*, p. 6, Winter 1966
• —Collin Baker et al., *College Undergraduate Slang Study Conducted at Brown University*, p. 181, 1968
• —Eugene Landy, *The Underground Dictionary*, p. 159, 1971
• Your middle name is Ralph, as in puke.—*The Breakfast Club*, 1985
• I was really bad today. I had two maccacinos. I feel like ralphing. —*Clueless*, 1995

Ralphed up *adjective*
dressed in a smart casual style *UK*
From Ralph Lauren (b.1939), designer of the Polo™ range of casual clothing.
• [S]ome stop-at-nothing Ralphed up hard case comes knocking on the door[.]—Greg Williams, *Diamond Geezers*, p. 8, 1997

ram *noun*
amyl or butyl nitrite *US*
Reflecting popular male gay use, possibly deriving from a brand name.
• Street names [...] poppers, ram, rock hard[.]—James Kay and Julian Cohen, *The Parents' Complete Guide to Young People and Drugs*, p. 144, 1998

ram *verb*
(from a male perspective) to have sex, perhaps violently *UK*
Mainly derived from 'ram' (a male sheep), but the thrusting action echoes 'ram' (to batter with a long pole).
• "I am. I'm going to ram you hard." [...] I pull her towards myself and slams her back to the wall[.]—Kevin Sampson, *Outlaws*, p. 116, 2001

-rama; -erama; -orama *suffix*
used for conveying a superlative quality or quantity *US*
From Greek *orama* (a view).
• —John Lotz, *American Speech*, p. 156–158, May 1954: 'The suffix '-rama''
• —William M. Ryan, *American Speech*, p. 230–233, October 1961: 'A plethorama'
• [G]et him whatever it is they drink, a cokearama?—*A Hard Day's Night*, 1964
• Pyjamarama—*Roxy Music*, 1973
• —Pamela Munro, *U.C.L.A. Slang*, p. 64, 1989
• Upset-O-Rama! (Headline)—*San Francisco Chronicle*, p. 1, 17th March 2001

rama-lama *noun*
rock 'n'roll music *UK*
From the doo-wop song 'Rama Lama Ding Dong' recorded by the Edsels in 1959, and somehow thought to capture the *joie de vivre* of the music.
• It was their turn to incite the riots and play the rama-lama [...] What I didn't have was the knowledge that the rama-lama, like the Corleone family, doesn't let you go that easily.—Mick Farren, *Give the Anarchist a Cigarette*, p. 364, 2001

Rambette *noun*
a female Rambo – reckless, fearless, the warrior woman *US*
• He'd even formed a Pt. Mugu SWAT team – it was unusual in that it contained both men and women – which he lovingly called his Rambo and Rambette SWATs.—Richard Marcinko and John Weisman, *Rogue Warrior*, p. 296, 1992

rambler *noun*
a (portable) radio *UK*
• —Angela Devlin, *Prison Patter*, p. 94, 1996

rambling ROK's *noun*
ground troops of the Army of South Korea (the Republic of Korea) *US*
- When they arrived at their destination, South Korean ground units known as the "Rambling ROK's" were already in possession of the city. —Don Lawson, *The United States in the Korean War*, p. 69, 1964

Rambo *noun*
1 a soldier with too much of a sense of drama and too little intelligence *US*
After the 1982 film starring Sylvester Stallone as an invincible if mentally unstable Vietnam veteran.
- The name "Rambo" (a film version of an invincible Army veteran of Vietnam) is used derisively by soldiers for someone who is braver than he is intelligent. —*Houston Chronicle*, 20th March 1989
- The females often had to become surrogate mothers or big sisters out there in the patrol units at night to all those blue-suited Rambos who temporarily traded testosterone for teddy bears[.] —Joseph Wambaugh, *Fugitive Nights*, p. 49, 1990

2 an intolerant prison officer who would rather punish inmates *UK*
From the 1982 film starring Sylvester Stallone as a military man who uses the most extreme measures to quell his opponents. In use in UK prisons in 2002.

3 heroin *UK, 1998*
- —Robert Ashton, *This Is Heroin*, p. 207, 2002
- —Mike Haskins, *Drugs*, p. 284, 2003

Rambo rag *noun*
a hankerchief worn on the head *US*
Worn by Stallone in the film.
- Other orders prohibit what had threatened to become a desert fashion trend: the wearing of head scarves knotted at the back, prized by soldiers for their anti-dust qualities but disparaged by higher-ups as "Rambo rags." —*Washington Times*, p. 11A, 11th February 1991
- —*Army*, p. 48, November 1991

ramjam *adverb*
absolutely crammed *UK, 1879*
- Meanwhile the room's ramjam packed with gold from the Crimea, Ukraine, and the Caucasus, shimmered and blinded. —Jonathan Gash, *The Ten Word Game*, p. 257, 2003

rammed *adjective*
crammed, stuffed full *UK*
- "Who the chuff's gonna come Sunday afternoons?" "I reckon it'll be rammed." —Nicholas Blincoe, *Ardwick Green (Disco Biscuits)*, p. 3, 1996

rammies *noun*
trousers; pants *AUSTRALIA, 1906*
Rhyming slang. Shortening of 'rammy rousers', rhyming slang for 'trousers'.
- —Jim Ramsay, *Cop It Sweet!*, p. 76, 1977

rammy *noun*
a brawl; a noisy argument, a row; a bustling crowd *UK: SCOTLAND, 1935*
- Hey, gonny youse [will you] keep the rammy doon! —Ian Pattison, *Rab C. Nesbitt*, 1988

rammy *verb*
to take part in crowd violence *UK: SCOTLAND*
- There's too much rammyin at the football these days. —Michael Munro, *The Complete Patter*, p. 128, 1996

ramp *noun*
1 a search of a prisoner or prison cell *AUSTRALIA, 1919*
Conducted to search for contraband, though often carried out with much destruction in order to harass the prisoner.
- The mirror was so small that it was intitially overlooked in several 'ramps' (searches). —William Dodson, *The Sharp End*, p. 37, 2001
- In fact I'd had to up-end him once during a cell ramp in Long Bay's Metropolitan Reception Prison when he refused to comply with a lawful direction. —William Dodson, *The Sharp End*, p. 111, 2001

2 a public house bar counter; hence, a public house *UK, 1935*
From an earlier, more general, sense as a shop counter.
- —John Gosling, *The Ghost Squad*, 1959

ramp *verb*
1 to swindle, to con; to rob, to mug; to make trouble *UK, 1812*
Contemporary use is mainly West Indian and UK black.
- "Listen Jackie," he said in mock patois with a smile, "any fool-fool come trouble you, tell dem they better not ramp wid yuh[."] —Donald Gorgon, *Cop Killer*, p. 79, 1994

2 to pretend *UK*
A variation of the sense 'to swindle, to con'.
- Me from a serious part of town, y'get me? We nah ramp, starr! —Diran Adebayo, *My Once Upon A Time*, p. 39, 2000

3 to search a prisoner or a prison cell *AUSTRALIA, 1919*
- —Jim Ramsay, *Cop It Sweet!*, p. 76, 1977
- Mr Harris, or Harrison, a short screw, has just ramped my cell and started throwing things about on the floor. —Ray Denning, *Prison Diaries*, p. 56, 1978
- —Ryan Aven-Bray, *Ridgey Didge Oz Jack Lang*, p. 41, 1983
- —William Dodson, *The Sharp End*, p. 27, 2001

ramped *adjective*
drunk *US*
- —Connie Eble (Editor), *UNC-CH Campus Slang*, p. 8, Spring 1992

ram-raid; ram-raiding *noun*
a method of robbery that utilises a motor vehicle as a battering ram to gain entry, often using the vehicle to make off with stolen goods *UK*
- Sheep rustling may be a familiar enough crime in rural Wales, but in Northumbria people are currently more concerned with ram raids – that is, raids in which cars are rammed at high speed into a shop which is then fleeced of its goods. —*The Guardian*, 23rd April 1991
- The techniques of ram-raiding are brutal but effective. —Nicholas Jones, *Hackers, Hotting and Hooray Henrys*, p. 52, 1992
- [I]t was mainly ram-raiding or car popping to fund the next buzz. —Macfarlane, Macfarlane and Robson, *The User*, p. 106, 1996

ram-raid *verb*
to rob a premises using a vehicle as a battering ram and driving it through a window or a wall *UK, 1987*
- [A] proper little hooligan nicking cars and joyriding, getting in fights because I was unhappy, ram-raiding shops so she didn't know what to do with me. —John King, *Human Punk*, p. 300–301, 2000
- I couldn't have made more fucking noise if I'd ram-raided the fucking place in an ice-cream van. —Danny King, *The Burglar Diaries*, p. 23, 2001

ramraider *noun*
1 a criminal involved in ram-raiding *UK, 1991*
- Thief! Thief! Burglars! joyriders, ram raiders, walkby shooters; lemme at 'em, I'll rip 'em to shreds! —Diane Duane, *The Wizard's Dilemma*, p. 45, 2001

2 a powerful amphetamine sulphate *UK, 1990s*
- [He] sorts us out some sulph which is this twenny a gee [gram] ramraider guaranteed to bring relatives back from the dead. —Nick Barlay, *Curvy Lovebox*, p. 54, 1997

ramrod *noun*
the penis; the erect penis *UK, 1902*
- My ramrod is me, any man's rod is himself. —Clarence Major, *All-Night Visitors*, p. 4, 1998

Ramsgate Sand; Ramsgate *noun*
the hand *UK*
Rhyming slang, formed on the Kent seaside resort.
- —Ray Puxley, *Cockney Rabbit*, 1992

ram's pasture *noun*
in oil drilling, non-productive land *US*
- —Jerry Robertson, *Oil Slanguage*, p. 59, 1954

ram tube *noun*
in a drag racing car, an injector that forces air into a carburettor *US*
- —Ed Radlouer, *Drag Racing Pix Dix*, p. 29, 1970

ranch *noun*
1 a house *US*
- —Robert George Reisner, *The Jazz Titans*, p. 163, 1960

2 any place where marijuana is sold *US*
- —Lou Shelly, *Hepcats Jive Talk Dictionary*, p. 16, 1945

3 to a trucker, anywhere you spend the night *US*
- —Wayne Floyd, *Jason's Authentic Dictionary of CB Slang*, p. 25, 1976

ranch *verb*
to idle; to spend time doing little *US*
- —Judi Sanders, *Don't Dog by Do, Dude!*, p. 26, 1991

Ranch Hand *noun*

a C-123 aircraft equipped with tanks filled with defoliants used on the Vietnam jungle *US*

- On the other was the motto of the "Ranch Hand" pilots – the men who flew the C-123 defoliation planes: "ONLY YOU CAN PREVENT FORESTS." — Edwin Corley, *Siege*, p. 80, 1969

rancid *adjective*

1 in poor taste *US*

- — Pamela Munro, *U.C.L.A. Slang*, p. 70, 1989

2 excellent; brilliant *AUSTRALIA*

- I listen to death metal music and lots of the words come from that, like if something was good I would say it was 'rancid', 'putrid' or 'wicked'. — *Herald Sun*, p. 11, 22nd June 1993

randan *noun*

a spree of wild, debauched, hedonistic behaviour, especially if heavy drinking is involved *UK: SCOTLAND*

Usually in the phrase 'on the randan'.

- No feelin sae good this mornin? On the randan last night, eh? — Michael Munro, *The Original Patter*, p. 55, 1985

Randolph Scott; Randolph *noun*

a spot *UK, 1992*

Rhyming slang, based on the name of film actor Randolph Scott, 1903–87.

- [P]eople still say they've a Randolph (Scott=spot) on their finger and thumb (buttocks)[.] — *Antiquarian Book Review*, p. 18, June 2002

random *adjective*

ordinary if unexpected *US*

A major word of the 1990s US youth, just a tad to the slang side of conventional English. Noted in the UK by Susie Dent, *The Language Report*, 2003.

- — Collin Baker et al., *College Undergraduate Slang Study Conducted at Brown University*, p. 181, 1968
- — Connie Eble (Editor), *UNC-CH Campus Slang*, p. 4, Fall 1982
- — *Merriam-Webster's Hot Words on Campus Marketing Survey '93*, p. 3, 13th October 1993
- Oh, she met some random guys at the Foot Locker and escorted them right over there. — *Clueless*, 1995

R and R *noun*

1 rest and rehabilitation; rest and recovery; rest and recreation; rest and recuperation; rape and restitution; rape and ruin; rape and run *US, 1953*

Despite disagreement on the 'R's', the meaning is the same – a brief stint away from combat or regular duty.

- Any man who captures a prisoner these days is promised a five-day Rest and Rehabilitation breather in Japan. — Martin Russ, *The Last Parallel*, p. 163, 1957
- He'll be on sick leave for a few weeks. We call it "R & R (Rest and Recuperation)." — Dennis Smith, *Report From Engine Company 82*, p. 46, 1972
- Walker Hill one time belong US Army. that time big R and R place for soldier. R and R mean 'rest and recreation.' — Walter Sheldon, *Gold Bait*, p. 31, 1973
- R&R – rest and recovery leave. — William H. LaBarge and Robert Lawrence Holt, *Sweetwater Gunslinger 201*, p. 281, 1983
- Not a single girl soldier out on manoeuvres looking for a spot of "r and r". — Duncan MacLaughlin, *The Filth*, p. 50, 2002

2 rock 'n' roll *UK, 1977*

- [A] character that had roots back in music hall and '50s R & R[.] — Paul Morley, *Ask*, p. 35, 1986

3 rape and robbery *UK*

A cynical play on the US military 'r and r' (rest and recreation).

- — Angela Devlin, *Prison Patter*, p. 94, 1996

randy *adjective*

1 sexually aroused; feeling lecherous *UK, 1847*

From Scottish dialect *randy*.

- I know what you are thinking dearest!!! You randy so and so. — Barry Humphries, *Bazza Pulls It Off!*, 1971
- [W]ouldn't it be a splendidly compensating irony should randy old Purcell meet his end as the result of a promise made silently to a virgin nun? — Tom Robbins, *Another Roadside Attraction*, p. 168, 1971
- ["]Mel's got another one on the way." "Up the spout [pregnant] again?" said Russell. "You randy old bastard.["] — Greg Williams, *Diamond Geezers*, p. 157, 1997
- [T]here's a big market for videos of rock chicks getting randy in seedy situations. — Stewart Home, *Sex Kick [britpulp]*, p. 206, 1999
- [Mike] Myers, it turns out, is not at all the randy man-about-town he has often played in films [.] — *The Hartford Courant (Connecticut)*, 26th May 1999
- I'm randy as hell. — Kevin Sampson, *Outlaws*, p. 42, 2001

2 homosexual, perhaps seen as a threatening or predatory characteristic *UK*

Public school use, probably deriving from the more general sense as 'lecherous or sexually aroused' when applied in a single-sex environment.

- — *The Sunday Times*, 1st September 1968

randy Andy *nickname*

Prince Andrew; any man named Andrew *UK, 1984*

- They, as well as some of the later lot (Fergie, Randy Andy, Princess Pushy), recall Max Beerbohm's comment on the ill-fated Queen Caroline, 'Fate wrote her a most tremendous tragedy, and she played it in tights'[.] — *The Telegraph (Calcutta)*, 6th December 2003

randy comedown *noun*

a desire for sex as the effects of drug use wear off *UK*

- — Paul Baker, *Polari*, p. 188, 2002

rane *noun*

cocaine; heroin *UK*

- — Mike Haskins, *Drugs*, p. 281, 2003

rang *noun*

a person who is acting very oddly *US*

An abbreviation of 'orangutan'.

- — *American Speech*, p. 282, December 1966: 'More carnie talk from the West Coast'

rangdoodles *noun*

in poker, a temporary increase in the betting limit after a player has won a hand with an agreed-upon, rare and excellent hand *US*

- — Albert H. Morehead, *The Complete Guide to Winning Poker*, p. 271, 1967

Ranger's Bible *noun*

the US Army Ranger handbook, a supplemental training document for long-range reconnaissance patrols *US*

- — Gregory Clark, *Words of the Vietnam War*, p. 424, 1990

rangood *noun*

wild marijuana *UK*

Probably a playful misspelling of **RANGOON**.

- — Mike Haskins, *Drugs*, p. 288, 2003

rangoon *noun*

wild marijuana *US, 1968*

- — Richard A. Spears, *The Slang and Jargon of Drugs and Drink*, p. 416, 1986

Rangoon *noun*

a prune *UK*

Rhyming slang, formed from the Burmese capital.

- — Ray Puxley, *Cockney Rabbit*, 1992

rank *verb*

1 to disparage; to insult, especially in a formulaic or ritual manner *US*

- — Lou Shelly, *Hepcats Jive Talk Dictionary*, p. 16, 1945
- — J. R. Friss, *A Dictionary of Teenage Slang (Mt. Diablo High)*, 1964
- — Collin Baker et al., *College Undergraduate Slang Study Conducted at Brown University*, p. 181, 1968
- Hey, you know; like that's what I come all the fucking way up here for, but if you gon rank me, I'll go somewhere else and spend my money. — Vernon E. Smith, *The Jones Men*, p. 165, 1974
- They knew what 'ranking' and 'snapping' on someone meant. — *New York Amsterdam News*, p. 34, 29 September 1979
- — Inez Cardozo-Freeman, *The Joint*, p. 525, 1984
- There are many different terms for playing the dozens, including "bagging, capping, cracking, dissing, hiking, joning, ranking, ribbing, serving, signifying, slipping, sounding and snapping". — James Haskins, *The Story of Hip-Hop*, p. 54, 2000

2 to bungle or ruin something *US*

- — Hyman E. Goldin et al., *Dictionary of American Underworld Lingo*, p. 174, 1950
- He just hoped Sister Heavenly wouldn't do anything to rank his play. — Chester Himes, *Come Back Charleston Blue*, p. 49, 1966
- But the trouble began when I ranked my hand / And stopped blowing and started to hit. — Dennis Wepman et al., *The Life*, p. 84, 1976

rank *adjective*

unpleasant; stupid; bad-smelling *US*

In the world of bad-is-good alienated youth, 'rank' can be good or bad.

- You always travel in this rank company? — *Rebel Without a Cause*, 1955
- — *Current Slang*, p. 6, Winter 1966
- "Kinds today like things that are rank," he says. — Tom Wolfe, *The Pump House Gang*, p. 99, 1968

- I knew the punk was rank, but Jackson was crazy about him so I stayed on the dummy. — Iceberg Slim (Robert Beck), *The Naked Soul of Iceberg Slim*, p. 122, 1971
- — Pamela Munro, *U.C.L.A. Slang*, p. 70, 1989

ranking *adjective*

1 excellent; admirable *UK*

Also shortened to 'ranks'.

- Dread Broadcast Corp. 93.9FM Tune in if you Rankin'! — John Hind and Stephen Mosco, *(reproduction of a 1982 advertisement) Rebel Radio*, p. vii, 1985

2 average, mediocre *JAMAICA*

- — Velma Pollard, *Dread Talk*, p. 44, 2000

rank out *verb*

to offend or disgust someone by doing something rank *US*

- I've heard the two of you play your little rank out game where one insists the other is gay. — *Chasing Amy*, 1997

ran-tan *noun*

▸ **on the ran-tan**

on a drinking spree *IRELAND*

- And there's Francey's crowd, ten of them on the ran-tan and not a bite of food in the place. — Wesley Burrows, *The Riordans A Personal History*, p. 66, 1977
- Everything was where it was supposed to be except for Johnny. 'He must be on the ran-tan,' Crunch said to himself. — Billy Roche, *Tumbling Down*, p. 7, 1984

rap *noun*

1 a criminal charge *US, 1903*

- This time I'm pinning a murder rap on him, and he won't dodge it. — Chester Gould, *Dick Tracy Meets the Night Crawler*, p. 112, 1945
- He informed me cheerfully that he had strangled one man in Europe for raping his sister, stabbed another to death in a gambling fracas, and was now beating it from the States because of a third murder rap. — Mezz Mezzrow, *Really the Blues*, p. 189, 1946
- For playing at being tough and putting one over on the cops was fun, but now they realized they were facing a real rap[.] — Irving Shulman, *The Amboy Dukes*, p. 159, 1947
- Besides, I was charged in State and State junk raps pile up like any other felony. — William Burroughs, *Junkie*, p. 95, 1953
- I've got a hell of a big income-tax rap hanging over me. — Jim Thompson, *A Swell-Looking Babe*, p. 69, 1954
- I'll go to San Quentin, 'cause, Sal, one more rap of any kind and I go to San Quentin for life – that's the end of me. — Jack Kerouac, *On the Road*, p. 185, 1957
- It'll be hard as hell trying to pin a possession rap on him, and he knows it. — Clarence Coope Jr, *The Scene*, p. 128, 1960
- They were going to bust him and that's a tough rap in California. — Ross Russell, *The Sound*, p. 199, 1961
- Maybe you've taken a couple of raps for hitting the hop over there[.] — Douglas Rutherford, *The Creeping Flesh*, p. 103, 1963
- "How about this chickenshit rap they're holding me on?" she bargained. — Chester Himes, *Cotton Comes to Harlem*, p. 84, 1965
- Just what I needed – get busted for a littering rap on top of six counts of hitchhiking with long hair. — James Simon Kunen, *The Strawberry Statement*, p. 81, 1968
- It was bullshit. The whole rap was a setup. — *The Usual Suspects*, 1995

2 blame or responsibility *US, 1927*

- Y-you m-mean I – I should take the rap for you? — Jim Thompson, *The Killer Inside*, p. 119, 1952

3 a prison sentence *US, 1927*

- He's on the lam from a pen back east, crashed out with twenty years to serve of a thirty-year bank-robber rap. — Jim Thompson, *A Swell-Looking Babe*, p. 77, 1954
- They mentally calculated Murray's age, and they figured this for a prison rap. — Evan Hunter, *The Blackboard Jungle*, p. 79, 1954
- He got sent to Starke on a homicide, shot some dude he was supposed to be bringing in. Doing his rap he was the man up there among the Latinos. — Elmore Leonard, *Riding the Rap*, p. 29, 1995

4 a clever line of improvised chat, speech or conversation *US, 1967*

Black coinage, adopted and popularised by hippies.

- His rap was boss and really got across / When they saw that his eyes were wet. — Dennis Wepman et al., *The Life*, p. 69, 1976
- Our rap was if girls could only look beyond the fact we didn't have good looks [...] they would fall in love with us. — Howard Stern, *Miss America*, p. 4, 1995
- [W]ho else could have come up with the godson's birthday rap, by the way. — Kevin Sampson, *Outlaws*, p. 50, 2001

5 a popular music genre in which a rhythmic lyric is spoken over a musical background *US*

- Hip-hop historians have determined that the first "rap" record (the Fatback Band's "King Tim III [Personality Jock]") preceded the Sugarhill Gang's "Rapper's Delight" by a few months in 1979. — *The Source*, p. 180, March 2002

6 a meandering, unstructured group discussion *US, 1967*

- Please don't dominate the rap, Jack / If you got nothin' to say. — The Grateful Dead, *New Speedway Boogie*, 1970
- The rap was two or three minutes old before D.R. even realized that a strange man and woman had taken over the bus and were driving them away. — Gurney Norman, *Divine Right's Trip (Last Whole Earth Catalog)*, p. 69, 1971

7 the way in which a person expresses himself or herself *US*

- It is true I spend all my time pursuin' good trim and, thank God, have a good rap. — Edwin Torres, *Carlito's Way*, p. 19, 1975

8 a very small amount *US*

- I just didn't give a rap anymore about school. — Leonard Shecter and William Phillips, *On the Pad*, p. 61, 1973

▸ **ride the rap**

to serve a prison sentence without losing control, hope or sanity *US*

- What you have to learn is how to ride the rap, do your own time, but get salty quick as you can. — Elmore Leonard, *Maximum Bob*, p. 108, 1991

rap *verb*

1 to talk without an agenda, aimlessly but honestly *US, 1929*

Found before the 1960s, but truly a word of the 60s.

- Half-breed Joe from Mexico / who was rappin' with Commanche Pete. — Bruce Jackson, *Get Your Ass in the Water and Swim Like Me*, p. 65, 1964
- So I stood there and rapped to them for a little while and then I left. — Henry Williamson, *Hustler!*, p. 49, 1965
- In point of fact he is funny and very glib, and I dig rapping (talking) with him. — Eldridge Cleaver, *Soul on Ice (letter dated 19th September, 1965)*, p. 46, September 1968
- Sarah, I bet you haven't had anybody around like me to rap to, have you? I don't have to tell you how it is, Sarah. You know, I – I love you and I want you to rap[.] — *Easy Rider*, 1969
- I said, "Jack, it's all yours. After I get my ribs I'll duck back into the joint and 'rap' with you." — Iceberg Slim (Robert Beck), *Pimp*, p. 98, 1969
- That's why they call me Rap, 'cause I could rap. (The name stuck beause Ed would always say, "That's my nigger Rap," "Rap my nigger.") — H. Rap Brown, *Die Nigger Die!*, p. 27, 1969
- As Che rapped on for four hours, we fantasized taking up rifles. — Jerry Rubin, *Do It!*, p. 20, 1970
- I confess I enjoyed rapping with them and usually wind up assured that eternal salvation is beyond my reach. — Jim Bouton, *Ball Four*, p. 101, 1970
- Well, as previously reported, old fast-talking Plucky manages to rap his way out of a potentially grim encounter with a pistol-packing padre[.] — Tom Robbins, *Another Roadside Attraction*, p. 86, 1971
- I readily rapped to Zelda, trying to talk cool but nicer than most boastiferous conversations I heard in the Fire Island. — Bobby Seale, *A Lonely Rage*, p. 109, 1978
- He came over to visit and we got to rapping and I told him of our situation. — Herbert Huncke, *Guilty of Everything*, p. 192, 1990

2 to criticise someone *US*

- "They fed me, they clothed me, they sent me to college." "So what are you rapping 'em for?" "Because they filled me full of insecurities." — Max Shulman, *Rally Round the Flag, Boys!*, p. 10, 1957

3 to accuse someone falsely or to seek a more serious sentence for someone than their crime deserves *US*

- I gave the officer that was pressin' charges against me ten dollars, not to turn me loose, but to not rap me. — Henry Williamson, *Hustler!*, p. 68, 1965

4 to perform semi-spoken lyrics over a musical background *US, 1979*

raparazzi *noun*

an elite grouping within hip-hop culture *UK*

Extends **RAP** (the pre-eminent hip-hop music style) on the model of **PAPARAZZI** (photographers who prey on celebrities); the suggestion of preying remains.

- [Princess Superstar's] reach goes beyond the artsy raparazzi to the record-buying masses[.] — *The Times Magazine*, p. 45, 16th February 2002

rape *verb*

in computing, to destroy a program or data without hope of recovering it *US*

- — Eric S. Raymond, *The New Hacker's Dictionary*, p. 297, 1991

rape tools *noun*

the penis and testicles *US*

- — Joseph E. Ragen and Charles Finston, *Inside the World's Toughest Prison*, p. 814, 1962: 'Penitentiary and underworld glossary'

rapid *adjective*

excellent *IRELAND*

- "Wear [sic] ye watchin' de game bud?"..."Any good was it?"... "Bleedin' rapit id [it] was man!" — Donal Ruane, *Tales in a rear view mirror*, p. 229, 2003

rapo; rape-o *noun*

a rapist *US*

- Your rapos, they get ahold of the Bible and they start going to church and they stay there. — Bruce Jackson, *Outside the Law: A Thief's Primer*, p. 143, 1972
- — John R. Armore and Joseph D. Wolfe, *Dictionary of Desperation*, p. 45, 1976
- Joe screamed the words, his voice breaking: "You're a rape-o!" — James Ellroy, *Suicide Hill*, p. 598, 1986

rap parlor *noun*

a brothel in disguise as a massage parlour in disguise as a business where you pay to talk to women *US*

For those entrepreneurs who do not have what it takes to obtain a massage licence.

- — Ralph de Sola, *Crime Dictionary*, p. 126, 1982

rap partner *noun*

in a criminal enterprise, a person who will accept responsibility for a venture gone poorly and serve a jail sentence *US*

- One of the studs was my rap partner in a bit a long time ago. He took the prison sentence, Prince, just so he could cut me loose. — Donald Goines, *Black Gangster*, p. 226, 1977

rapper *noun*

1 a performer of rap lyrics *US, 1979*

- Britain's hidden army of urban teenagers making music in their tower block bedrooms edged closer to the mainstream last night when an 19-year-old rapper [MC Dizzee Rascal from Bow, east London] won the Mercury music prize. — *The Guardian*, 10th September 2003

2 the mouth; the voice *US*

- His voice box screwed up on him a 'dime' ago. He's been the brass nuts here for a double dime, and guess how the bastard lost his 'rapper?' — Iceberg Slim (Robert Beck), *Pimp*, p. 51, 1969

3 the chief witness for the prosecution in a criminal trial *US*

- — Joseph E. Ragen and Charles Finston, *Inside the World's Toughest Prison*, p. 814, 1962: 'Penitentiary and underworld glossary'

rappie *noun*

a partner in crime *US*

- — *Maledicta*, p. 265, Summer/Winter 1981: 'By its slang, ye shall know it: the pessimism of prison life'
- — Lee McNeils, *30 + And a Wake-Up*, p. 3, 1991
- — William K. Bentley and James M. Corbett, *Prison Slang*, p. 41, 1992

rap session *noun*

a group discussion, unstructured and uninhibited *US*

- When the Pigs left we had a heavy rap session about self-defense, land, and whether or not the chickens bar-be-cuing on the open fire were done yet. — Abbie Hoffman, *Woodstock Nation*, p. 57, 1969
- Now dig it, we've all done enough time, or been involved in enough 'git yo' soul!' rap sessions to know how to carry off a group therapy thing, right? — Odie Hawkins, *The Busting Out of an Ordinary Man*, p. 150, 1985

rap sheet *noun*

a record of a person's past arrests and convictions *US, 1960*

- For a long time, my father's FBI rap sheet was all I had by ways of a family history. — Kim Rich, *Johnny's Girl*, p. 27, 1993
- — Angela Devlin, *Prison Patter*, p. 94, 1996

rapt *adjective*

delighted *AUSTRALIA, 1963*

Variant of **WRAPPED**.

- We always had great fishing down in Gippsland and, on this particular occasion, we caught two or three beauties each and were totally rapt in our great day. — Rex Hunt, *Tall Tales – and True*, p. 126, 1994

raptor *noun*

a rap performer who is also an actor *US*

- The biggest raptor ever is, not coincidentally, one of the least street-oriented MCs. — Nelson George, *Hip Hop America*, p. 111, 1998

rapture!

▷ see: **JOY!**

Raquel Welch *noun*

a belch *UK*

Rhyming slang formed from the name of the film actress (b.1940).

- — Ray Puxley, *Cockney Rabbit*, 1992

Raquel Welch *verb*

to belch *UK*

Rhyming slang, formed from the name of the US actress (b.1940); noted by Anthony Haden-Guest, 1971.

rare *adjective*

1 excellent; very enjoyable *UK: SCOTLAND*

- That was a rerr picture [movie]! — Michael Munro, *The Original Patter*, p. 58, 1985
- Ye make a rare cuppa tea, hen. — Michael Munro, *The Complete Patter*, p. 128, 1996

2 of someone, unusual, eccentric *IRELAND*

Sometimes 'wild rare' is also used.

- There's no denying it Francie, you're a rare character! — Patrick McCabe, *The Butcher Boy*, p. 16, 1992

rare as rocking horse shit *adjective*

extremely rare or scarce *AUSTRALIA, 1944*

- Diana had sex before marriage, which was as rare as rocking-horse shit. — Sally Bedell Smith, *Diana in Search of Herself*, p. 72, 1999
- A mate of mine was offered $300 dollars for his XU-1 cap. They're rare as rocking horse shit. — *A Guide to Turbos and Superchargers*, p. 158, 2001

rare groove *noun*

a fashionable style of dance music and its presentation *UK*

Coined by pirate radio presenter Norman Jay.

- The sound of London in the mid-eighties, rare groove essentially described the warehouse party vibe and up-tempo US seventies funk music[.] — Ben Osborne, *The A-Z of Club Culture*, p. 245, 1999
- — *The Sunday Times Magazine*, p. 51, 1st June 2003

raring to go *adjective*

eagerly impatient to get started *US, 1935*

- The Tories were no real threat to Labour – even in West Bromwich, where because of the reintroduction of party politics after the Boothroyd years they should have been raring to go. — *The Guardian*, 24th November 2000

rark-up *noun*

an argument or rebuke *NEW ZEALAND*

- As the talks stretched into weeks, tempers shortened, we weren't having any part of that, so there'd be a bit of a rark up. — *Listener*, p. 23, 14th October 1995

rark up *verb*

to rebuke or annoy someone *NEW ZEALAND*

- One-eyed Canterbury fans will be here in force. We will be rarking it up. — *Evening Post*, p. 1, 13th January 1997

ras!

used for expressing surprise *US*

- — Rick Ayers (Editor), *Berkeley High Slang Dictionary*, p. 35, 2004

rash *noun*

▸ **be all over someone like a rash**

1 to smother someone with affection, kisses, etc *AUSTRALIA*

- He was all over you like a rash, and you were loving every minute of it! — John Wynnum, *Jiggin' in the Riggin'*, p. 69, 1965
- I know how fickle the public are. When you are winning they are all over you like a rash. When you lose they are right up ya. — *Sydney Morning Herald*, p. 26, 22nd April 1996

2 to be easily outdoing an opponent *AUSTRALIA*

- He took him easy, they reckon, all over 'im like a rash. — W.R. Bennett, *Wingman*, p. 98, 1961
- They'll be all over us like a rash. — Phillip Gwynne, *Deadly Unna?*, p. 59, 1998

rashie *noun*

an upper garment worn by surfers *AUSTRALIA, 1996*

Originally worn under a wetsuit in order to prevent **WETTIE RASH**.

raspberry *noun*

1 a disapproving fart-like noise *UK, 1890*

From out-of-date rhyming slang, 'raspberry tart' for **FART**.

- There is no chance of getting into a Friday night performance of Mamma Mia until ooh, March. Saturdays? Late April. Planning that far ahead feels much too provocative, a raspberry to fate. — *The Observer*, 1st February 2004

2 a light grazing of the skin *UK*

Skateboarders' slang; from the appearance.

- — David Rowan, *A Glossary for the 90s*, 1998

3 a sore or abcess on an intravenous drug user from repeated injections in the same spot *US*

- — David Maurer and Victor Vogel, *Narcotics and Narcotic Addiction*, p. 437, 1973

4 a male who trades sex for drugs *US*

- — Mark S. Fleisher, *Beggars & Thieves*, p. 290, 1995: 'Glossary'

raspberryland *nickname*

Tasmania *AUSTRALIA, 1966*

From the crop. Hence, a Tasmanian is called a 'raspberrylander'.

raspberry ripple; raspberry *noun*
a disabled individual *UK*
Rhyming slang for 'cripple'.
- A raspberry ripple, a buckle my shoe. — Ian Dury, *Blackmail Man*, 1977
- Two raspberry ripples in the same band would have been stretching it a bit. — Will Birch, *No Sleep Till Canvey Island*, p. 145, 2003

raspy *adjective*
1 excellent *US*
- — Mimi Pond, *The Valley Girl's Guide to Life*, p. 61, 1982

2 bad, unpleasant *US*
- — Gary Fairmont R. Filosa II, *The Surfer's Almanac*, p. 192, 1977

rass *noun*
the buttocks; hence, used as a term of abuse *JAMAICA, 1790*
From **ARSE**.
- Hey, you rass, not finished yet? — Mark Hemry, *Chasing Danny Boy*, p. 205, 1999

rassle *verb*
▷ see: **WRESTLE**

rasta box *noun*
a large portable stereo system associated, stereotypically, with black youth culture *US*
- Awful tapes were put on a large Rasta box. — P.J. O'Rourke, *Holidays in Hell*, p. 29, 1988

Rastafarian *noun*
MDMA, the recreational drug best known as ecstasy *UK*
Specifically used of any tablet of MDMA stamped with a stylised image of a dreadlocked head.
- — Harry Shapiro, *Recreational Drugs*, p. 211, 2004

rasta weed *noun*
marijuana *US*
Marijuana is famously central to *Rasta*farian ritual.
- I loaned some Rasta weed to somebody. — Stephen J. Cannell, *The Tin Collectors*, p. 58, 2001
- — Mike Haskins, *Drugs*, p. 288, 2003

Rastus *noun*
used as a derogatory personification of a black male *US*
- — Vincent J. Monteleone, *Criminal Slang*, p. 190, 1949

rat *noun*
1 a person who informs on or otherwise betrays compatriots *UK, 1902*
- [H]e stopped me at the beginning of my "pitch" to inform me, boldly and slyly, that he had been a "testifier" and that according to some people he was a rat, traitor and scoundrel. — Clancy Sigal, *Going Away*, p. 271, 1961
- I heard of spitters going down to Honduras and Panama to ice a rat. — Edwin Torres, *Carlito's Way*, p. 44, 1975
- Five narcs ended up in Leavenworth over the incident, including the one who was the rat. — Gerald Petievich, *To Live and Die in L.A.*, p. 164, 1983
- I say the plan became null and void once we found out we got a rat in the house. — *Reservoir Dogs*, 1992
- I'm not a rat. — *The Usual Suspects*, 1995
- At the time we didn't know Tait was a rat working for the federales and just waiting for an excuse to fuck up the club. — Ralph "Sonny" Barger, *Hell's Angel*, p. 233, 2000

2 a despicable person *UK, 1594*
- McCarthy supporters around the country, denouncing him as "a dirty red rat"[.] — Arthur Herman, *Joseph McCarthy*, p. 291, 2000

3 an enthusiast of the preceding activity or thing *US, 1864*
- RINK RAT, Skating rink enthusiast. — Lou Shelly, *Hepcats Jive Talk Dictionary*, p. 31, 1945
- — *Dobie Gillis Teenage Slanguage Dictionary*, 1962
- Up there in Loa Jolla you get a different breed of surf rat. — Joseph Wambaugh, *Finnegan's Week*, p. 205, 1993
- You're one of those fucking mallrats; you don't come to the mall to shop or work. You hang out and act like you fucking live here. — *Mallrats*, 1995
- Couple of young gym rats I know, hang out at the Kronk. — Elmore Leonard, *Out of Sight*, p. 195, 1996
- In a grim twist that could fit into one of his songs, in the past year Zevon has been a gym rat ("I was working out more than Vin Diesel," he says) and assumed that his shortness of breath and the tightness in his chest were side effects of his regimen. — *Los Angeles Times*, 13th September 2002

4 a railway detective *US*
- — Ramon Adams, *The Language of the Railroader*, p. 125, 1977

5 a prostitute *BARBADOS*
- — Frank A. Collymore, *Barbadian Dialect*, p. 91, 1965

▸ **like a rat up a drainpipe; like a rat up a drain**
very swiftly *AUSTRALIA*
Often used with 'up that/her' (see citation) in which case it is usually of a woman objectified in a sexual context.
- [Looking at a poster of a semi-naked female model] Jeez! I could be up that like a rat up a drain! — Barry Humphries, *Bazza Pulls It Off!*, 1971

▸ **like a rat up a rhododendron**
very swiftly *AUSTRALIA*
A jocular variation of **LIKE A RAT UP A DRAIN**.
- Next time I see that sheilah [woman] of yours in Sydney Bazza, I'll be up her like a rat up a rhododendron – no probs!!! — Barry Humphries, *Bazza Pulls It Off!*, 1971

▸ **like a rat up a rope/shoreline**
with great speed *AUSTRALIA*
- [H]e soared up the steps again like a rat up a shoreline. — Robert S. Close, *Love Me Sailor*, p. 209, 1945
- Yer wanner take ut easy. No use goin' like a rat up a rope. — Nino Culotta (John O'Grady), *They're A Weird Mob*, p. 39, 1957

▸ **not give a rat's ass; not give a rat's arse**
to not care at all *US*
- I frankly don't give a rat's ass — George V. Higgins, *The Friends of Eddie Doyle*, p. 115, 1971
- There you go. What am I tellin' you. Who gives a rat's ass about writers? — Robert Campbell, *Alice in La-La Land*, p. 52, 1987
- I mean, so DeBella hated Sweet? Who gives a rat's ass about some fucking group? — Howard Stern, *Miss America*, p. 283, 1995
- I don't give a rat's ass about your or your fuckin' family. — Quentin Tarantino, *From Dusk Till Dawn*, p. 58, 1995
- I don't give a rat's ass if they're working for Jesus Christ! — Robert Crais, *L.A. Requiem*, p. 44, 1999
- 'I think he's on to me too, but I don't give a rat's ass as long as he doesn't try to stop me.' — Vicki Hendricks, *Stormy, Mon Amour [Tart Noir]*, p. 42, 2002

▸ **rat's died up your arse**
used of an especially noxious fart *UK*
- "You dirty bastard, that fucking stinks," complained The Dog. "I think a rat's died up your arse," roared Pyro Joe. — Garry Bushell, *The Face*, p. 238, 2001
- Have you dropped an apple tart [fart] or has a rat died up your Khyber pass? — Bodmin Dark, *Dirty Cockney Rhyming Slang*, p. 17, 2003

rat *verb*
1 to inform *US, 1934*
Perhaps from an earlier political sense of changing political parties.
- And I'm warning you, don't rat to the cops if you want to stay healthy. — Irving Shulman, *The Amboy Dukes*, p. 65, 1947
- I mean, he's got those kids so trained now that they'll rat on their best friend if they hear him curse. — Evan Hunter, *The Blackboard Jungle*, p. 150, 1954
- He had worked for them, had done time in jail because of jobs he did for them, and had never ratted. — James Mills, *The Panic in Needle Park*, p. 21, 1966
- I wasn't blind, and I hadn't ratted on Rocky. — Piri Thomas, *Down These Mean Streets*, p. 39, 1967
- Luce, who had helped organize the Cuba trips and had once gone skinnydipping with Fidel, joined with the FBI and ratted on all of his friends. — Jerry Rubin, *Do It!*, p. 63, 1970
- Unless he's ratting on the Latins or the Blacks – then if he survives the first twenty-four hours, he's all right. — Edwin Torres, *Carlito's Way*, p. 44, 1975
- And I'm not gonna do anything to screw it up, includin' pee in the prison yard, knock up the Warden's daughter or rat on my old partners. — *48 Hours*, 1982
- I've taken four falls and never ratted on anyone in my life. — Gerald Petievich, *To Live and Die in L.A.*, p. 132, 1983
- As long as you done your time nice, you didn't rat anybody out, and you never took it in the ass. — Vincent Patrick, *Family Business*, p. 55, 1985
- PFC William Santiago threatens to rat on Dawson to the Naval Investigative Service. — *A Few Good Men*, 1992
- "See if he'll rat on the guy he works for." "You say 'rat out' now. Yeah, well, he may slip, tell us something." — Elmore Leonard, *Be Cool*, p. 211, 1999
- [W]e wanted to get away before he takes our dabs [fingerprints] and rats to the soshe [Social Security, a UK Government agency]. — Kevin Sampson, *Powder*, p. 28, 1999

2 to rob or loot a person or place *AUSTRALIA, 1898*
- Artie Fethers bent down and souvenired the officer's pistol, and Mick Flyn quickly ratted his pockets. — Leonard Mann, *Flesh in Armour*, p. 56, 1932
- Why none o' yer shipmates would be after rattin' yer ditty bag. — Robert S. Close, *Love Me Sailor*, p. 107, 1945

- 'Do you know,' remarked Ted the stretcher-bearer as he applied the lint, 'some bastard ratted my medical satchel this morning?' — Eric Lambert, *The Veterans*, p. 203, 1954
- — Patsy Adam-Smith, *Folklore of the Australian Railwaymen*, p. 239, 1969

rat *adjective*
disloyal, untrustworthy; *US*
- I was going to get out of this lousy can and catch them rat bastards who shot up Benjy if it was the last thing I did. — Rocky Garciano (with Rowland Barber), *Somebody Up There Likes Me*, p. 160, 1955

rat and mouse *noun*
1 a house *UK*
Rhyming slang; first recorded in *Songs and Slang of the British Soldier: 1914–1918*, John Brophy and Eric Partridge, 3rd edition, 1931. Recorded in the US in 1943.
- [S]itting in your own rat and mouse, clustered around the Ned Kelly[.] — Ronnie Barker, *Fletcher's Book of Rhyming Slang*, p. 39, 1979

2 an informer *UK*
Rhyming slang for **LOUSE** (a despicable person).
- — Julian Franklyn, *A Dictionary of Rhyming Slang*, 1961

rat-arsed; ratarsed *adjective*
drunk *UK, 1982*
- [O]ut witha boys arseholed ratarsed fucked up[.] — Patrick Jones, *Unprotected Sex*, p. 255, 1999
- JAMIE: 'E's rat-arsed. — Chris Baker and Andrew Day, *Lock, Stock... & A Good Slopping Out*, p. 450, 2000
- "[P]iss artists" are "boozy", "fluffy", "well-gone", "legless", "crocked", wrecked", paralytic", "rat-arsed", "shit-faced" and "arse-holed". — Peter Ackroyd, *London The Biography*, p. 359, 2000

ratatouille *noun*
a nightclub that caters to a mix of gay and straight customers *UK*
A culinary allusion.
- — *Attitude*, July 2003: 'New palare lexicon'

ratbag *noun*
a contemptible person *AUSTRALIA, 1890*
A 'ratbag' can be merely a person with odd notions, an eccentric, or someone whose ideas or behaviour verge on the insane.
- BILL: You're just a nobody. The diary of a nobody. TONY: Go on ... up to bed, you ratbag. — *Hancock's Half Hour*, 30th December 1956
- Oh, that's because you bought books written by ratbags. — Willie Fennell, *Dexter Gets The Point*, p. 113, 1961
- Yes, he was a real ratbag, my old man. Mad Dan Gallagher, they used to call him. — Alexander Buzo, *Norm and Ahmed*, p. 19, 1969
- They let any ratbag overtake them at any speed if he wants to. — John O'Grady, *Aussie Etiket*, p. 56, 1971
- RATBAG: An eccentric. — Arthur Chipper, *The Aussie Swearer's Guide*, p. 67, 1972
- [I]t was pretty clear I'd shacked up in the health farm with a Grade A ratbag. — Barry Humphries, *The Traveller's Tool*, p. 44, 1985
- He said the wives of most top executives turned into raving ratbags sooner or later in spite of the fact thay had colour TV, Volvos and a fridge full of Sherry. — Barry Humphries, *The Traveller's Tool*, p. 119, 1985
- Every half-baked ratbag in the district was on the premises[.] — Roy Slaven (John Doyle), *Five South Coast Seasons*, p. 53, 1992

ratbaggery *noun*
behaviour which is eccentric, despicable or otherwise contemptible *AUSTRALIA, 1943*
- Hence ratbaggery, anything un-Aussie or un-normal. — Arthur Chipper, *The Aussie Swearer's Guide*, p. 67, 1972

rat belt *noun*
in computing, a self-locking cable tie *US*
- — Eric S. Raymond, *The New Hacker's Dictionary*, p. 298, 1991

rat bite *noun*
a skin bruise caused by sucking *US*
Hawaiian youth usage.
- — Douglas Simonson, *Pidgin to da Max Hana Hou*, 1982

ratboy *noun*
1 among a group of drug users, a person who will sample any drug before the group uses it *US*
An allusion to the rat as the subject of laboratory experiments.
- — Carsten Stroud, *Close Pursuit: A Week in the Life of an NYPD Homicide Cop*, p. 275, 1987
- — Jim Crotty, *How to Talk American*, p. 96, 1997

2 a member of a subcultural urban adolescent grouping defined by a hip-hop dress and jewellery sense *UK*
- Jack Straw talks tough about juvenile offenders – boasting that ratboys who used to be cautioned and let go are now being seized and dealt with at once. — *The Guardian*, 24th November 2000

rat caper *noun*
a minor crime *CANADA, 1976*
- They ran along the sidewalks, and sometimes to the other side of the cars, bending the chrome steel radio antennas down over the car's hoods. It was a childish, destructive, almost pathological act – the kind of thing Louis Crumlin called a "rat caper." — Hugh Garner, *The Intruders*, p. 44, 1976

ratchet *noun*
any weapon *US*
- In a fourth call, made to friend Larry Morrell, Manor cryptically asked about the "ratchet" – street slang for a weapon – that Morrell was holding for him. — *Rochester (New York) Democrat and Chronicle*, p. 3B, 24th October 2003

ratchet jaw *noun*
a person who talks too much and says too little *US*
- — John Lawlor, *How to Talk Car*, p. 87, 1965

ratchet-mouth *verb*
to talk incessantly *US*
- I never turn the damned CB on anymore. Too many assholes ratchet-mouthin' shit at each other. — George V. Higgins, *The Rat on Fire*, p. 14, 1981

rat-cunning *noun*
craftiness *AUSTRALIA*
- [I] need every last fibre of bloody resistance and rat-cunning[.] — Robert English, *Toxic Kisses*, p. 69, 1979

rat cunning *adjective*
crafty *AUSTRALIA*
- They dispense narcotics with careless disregard for the schemings and plottings of rat cunning junky minds. — Kevin Mackey, *The Cure*, p. 83, 1970

rat-drawn *adjective*
used of shoes, pointed *US*
- Rat-drawn shoes, an old Stetson hat / A '28 Ford and payments on that. — Dennis Wepman et al., *The Life*, p. 135, 1976

rat-eyed *adjective*
drunk *UK*
- I didn't want to say, "oh he had a meet with his ex-wife, got rat-eyed and is sleeping it off on my bathroom floor," did I? — John Milne, *Alive and Kicking*, p. 74, 1998

ratfink; rat fink *noun*
1 a despised person *US, 1964*
Combines **RAT** (someone unpleasant) and **FINK** (someone despised, an informer).
- Boy, will I tell that lying rat fink! — Max Shulman, *Anyone Got a Match?*, p. 28, 1964
- — J. R. Friss, *A Dictionary of Teenage Slang (Mt. Diablo High)*, 1964
- — Hy Lit, *Hy Lit's Unbelievable Dictionary of Hip Words for Groovy People*, p. 33, 1968
- I want you to find that ratfink Eddie DeChooch, and I want you to drag his bony ass back here. — Janet Evanovich, *Seven Up*, p. 3, 2001

2 an informer *US, 1965*
Combines **RAT** (an informer) and **FINK** (an informer).
- "There's a rat fink in this room,"Hugel said, striding around the conference rom and staring at people accusingly. — Bryan Burrough, *Barbarians at the Gate*, p. 366, 1990

rat fuck *noun*
1 a chaotic military disaster *US, 1930*
- Add the excitement of having to shoot rockets and machine guns at the same time and the stiff penalty exacted by your constant rush of adrenaline, never knowing when the routine mission will turn into a legendary Rat Fuck, and you develop a chronic emotional over-draft. — Dennis Marvicsin and Jerold Greenfield, *Maverick*, p. 113, 1990

2 a despicable person *US, 1922*
- [T]hose ratfucks in Chicago can suck my asshole[.] — Lester Bangs, *Psychotic Reactions and Carburetor Dung*, p. 199, 1976

3 a damn *US, 1971*
- — Helen Dahlskog (Editor), *A Dictionary of Contemporary and Colloquial Usage*, p. 48, 1972
- I don't give a rat fuck how much she cries! — Howard Stern, *Miss America*, p. 155, 1995

4 a prank *US*
- — *American Speech*, p. 195, October 1965: 'Notes on campus vocabulary, 1964'

Rat Fuck *noun*
the Reaction Forces of the South Vietnamese Army *US*
- The pilots called the RF's Rat Fucks because they never knew what the hell they'd be flying into. A routine mission could turn into the worst chapter of the book of Revelation in half a second. —Dennis Marvicsin and Jerold Greenfield, *Maverick*, p. 40, 1990

ratfuck *verb*
to pull a prank *US*
- —*American Speech*, p. 195, October 1965: 'Notes on campus vocabulary, 1964'

ratfuck operation *noun*
any operation characterised by poor planning, confusion or chaos *US*
Frequently used in the Vietnam war.
- —Gregory Clark, *Words of the Vietnam War*, p. 107, 1990

rat head *noun*
a person, especially a woman, who conveys a complete lack of taste and finesse *US*
- —Rick Ayers (Editor), *Berkeley High Slang Dictionary*, p. 35, 2004

rat hole *noun*
1 a small, messy, cluttered place *UK, 1812*
- You so hooked up trying to look dirty and live in the nastiest rathole in the ghetto, trying to be a ghetto black[.]—Bobby Seale, *A Lonely Rage*, p. 178, 1978
- You might speak to Mister Fein about this rathole that we live in. —George V. Higgins, *The Rat on Fire*, p. 89, 1981
- Viceroy Wilson didn't belong in a rathole dive on South Beach[.]—Carl Hiaasen, *Tourist Season*, p. 48, 1986
- I go, 'How can you live in a rat hole like this and drive a Cadillac?' and he got pissed. —Elmore Leonard, *Maximum Bob*, p. 235, 1991
- He hoped some junkie would burglarize his goddamn rathole of an apartment so he could make an inflated insurance claim. —Joseph Wambaugh, *Finnegan's Week*, p. 3, 1993
- Do you think I care what rat-hole store in that shit-pit you call the dirt mall has the latest Godzilla bootleg? —*Mallrats*, 1995

2 a railway tunnel *US*
- —J. Herbert Lund, *Herb's Hot Box of Railraod Slang*, p. 92, 1975

rat-hole *verb*
to stash something away, usually secretively *US, 1948*
- But in the process of "rat-holing" – surreptitiously palming an occasional ten or twenty – I often got away with hundreds. —Jim Thompson, *Bad Boy*, p. 368, 1953
- Secretly, in the way of many wives – although she was not legally his wife – she had been rat-holing money for years. —Jim Thompson, *The Grifters*, p. 82, 1963

rat house *noun*
an insane asylum *AUSTRALIA, 1900*
- Ugh! A man would finish up in the rathouse after an evening with her. —John Wynnum, *Jiggin' in the Riggin'*, p. 38, 1965
- —Kevin Mackey, *The Cure*, p. xiv, 1970
- —Frank Hardy, *The Outcasts of Foolgarah*, p. 108, 1971
- —Jim Ramsay, *Cop It Sweet!*, p. 76, 1977
- —Robert G. Barrett, *Davo's Little Something*, p. 161, 1992

rat jacket *noun*
a reputation for being an informer *US*
- You got a rep for protecting your informants. Nobody never got a rat jacket behind your busts. —Joseph Wambaugh, *The Blue Knight*, p. 29, 1973

rat-legged *adjective*
drunk *UK*
A variation of **RAT-ARSED**.
- —*e-cyclopaedia*, 20th March 2002

rat motor *noun*
in hot rodding, a Chevrolet engine, usually 396 cubic inches or larger *US*
- Tires as big as barrels sprout; aluminum rat-motor V-8s of 410 cubes and 750 horses burst through hoods. —Joe Scalzo, *The American Dirt Track Racer*, p. 45, 2001

rat-on *noun*
an erection *NEW ZEALAND, 1995*
- —Harry Orsman, *A Dictionary of Modern New Zealand Slang*, p. 107, 1999

rat out *verb*
to inform on someone *US*
- They're all afraid I'm gonna rat them out. —*Goodfellas*, 1990
- Why would I rat myself out? —*Something About Mary*, 1998
- I rat Cecile out to mommy. —*Cruel Intentions*, 1999

rat pack *noun*
1 in competition surfing, competitors vying for the lead *US*
- —*Competitive Surfing: A Dedicated Approach*, 1988

2 a group of young gang members *US, 1951*
- —Kenn "Naz" Young, *Naz's Dictionary of Teen Slang*, p. 98, 1993

3 a ration of food issued to South African soldiers; a package of food *SOUTH AFRICA, 1984*
- If they took rat packs of mop worms home for their bosses we can expect a rash of severed diplomatic relations in the coming months[.]—*The Sunday Times (South Africa)*, 26th September 1999

rat-pack *verb*
to surround and attack someone *US*
- The batos locos get loaded and start looking for their own kind of action (burning a store, rat-packing a nigger, or stealing some cars for a night of high-speed cruising on the freeways). —Hunter S. Thompson, *Fear and Loathing in Las Vegas*, p. 230, 1971
- Even ten years ago veterans recall "rat packing" each other, kicking and beating en masse, but the guns remained in the background. —*Christian Science Monitor*, p. B2, 16th July 1981
- —Bill Valentine, *Gang Intelligence Manual*, p. 78, 1995
- When we get down and somebody gets rat-packed, people think that's not fair. —Ralph "Sonny" Barger, *Hell's Angel*, p. 40, 2000
- Although such crimes aren't unusual in City Heights, "rat packing," or surrounding and beating a victim, is fairly rare[.]—*San Diego Union-Tribune*, p. B1, 23rd October 2003

rat race *noun*
1 any hectic and non-productive situation, activity or lifestyle *US, 1947*
- —*American Speech*, October 1949
- A going-nowhere ratrace – on a gloriously advanced, technological treadmill. —Robert Gover, *JC Saves*, p. 155, 1968

2 the face *UK*
Rhyming slang.
- —Bodmin Dark, *Dirty Cockney Rhyming Slang*, 2003

rat row *noun*
an area in a jail or prison reserved for police informers who would not be safe in the general population of the facility *US*
- —Ralph de Sola, *Crime Dictionary*, p. 126, 1982

rat run *noun*
a narrow way between buildings; a back alley; a side road, especially if used in a short-cut; a route through back streets that is used by motorists avoiding heavy traffic *UK*
- It is a matter of local pride to know the "back doubles" and "rat runs" well. —David Powis, *The Signs of Crime*, 1977

rats *noun*
combat rations *US*
- Hey Chief, Six says we're getting birds in with mail, rats and water, Man, fucking water! —Charles Anderson, *The Grunts*, p. 84, 1976

rats!
used as an expression of annoyance or dismissal *US, 1886*
- My stars! Thunder and lightning! Rats and blue blazes! Suffering cats! —Audrey Wood, *Elbert's Bad Word*, p. 27, 1988

rats and mice; rats *noun*
1 dice *UK, 1932*
Rhyming slang.
- —*The Annals of the American Academy of Political and Social Sciences*, p. 129, May 1950
- —Ray Puxley, *Cockney Rabbit*, 1992

2 rice *UK*
Rhyming slang.
- Served up in curry houses where chicken and "rats" is much ordered. —Ray Puxley, *Cockney Rabbit*, 1992

rat's coffin *noun*
a meat pie *AUSTRALIA*
- I had a rat's coffin at the footy. —*www.abc.net.au/wordmap*, 2003

ratshit *noun*
a despicable person or thing *US*
- I mean, those two rat shits are a walkin' reminder of just how fucked up our system is. —*Natural Born Killers*, 1994

▶ **go to ratshit**
to go very wrong *UK*
- As the chamber drained of oxygen my ten times table went to ratshit[.]—Andy McNab, *Immediate Action*, p. 148, 1995

ratshit *adjective*

no good; dreadful *AUSTRALIA, 1970*

- —Jim Ramsay, *Cop It Sweet!*, p. 76, 1977
- —Barry Humphries, *A Nice Night's Entertainment*, p. 174, 1978
- —Robert English, *Toxic Kisses*, p. 41, 1979
- But since it's a poison that works by paralysing parts of the nervous system, you don't start to feel ratshit until it starts to wear off. —Ignatius Jones, *The 1992 True Hip Manual*, p. 9, 1992
- Replacing the nicotine patch with a fresh one, I shaved, dressed, ate breakfast and still felt ratshit. —Shane Maloney, *Nice Try*, p. 210, 1998

ratted *adjective*

drunk *UK*

- She committed professional suicide that last time she was on that show, absolutely ratted. —*The Guardian*, 1st October 2002

ratter *noun*

1 a police informer; a traitor to a cause or enterprise *US*

- In other words, you can rat out a ratter but you can't rat out a double-crosser. —Edwin Torres, *Carlito's Way*, p. 80, 1975

2 a thief, especially one who steals opal from another's mine *AUSTRALIA, 1932*

- [heading] End of road for dirty opal ratters. —*The Australian*, p. 3, 2nd January 1997

rattle *noun*

dice *US, 1983*

- —Thomas L. Clark, *The Dictionary of Gambling and Gaming*, p. 176, 1987

▸ **give a rattle**

to have sexual intercourse with a female *IRELAND*

- He's giving her a rattle, no doubt about it. —Paul Howard, *The Teenage Dirtbag Years*, p. 151, 2001

rattle *verb*

to agitate or to unnerve someone *US, 1887*

- Firebug and Happy Jack are playing pool [...] FIREBUG: Eh, Roy? You reckon he's lettin' me win again? [...] ROY: You rattled 'im with yer safety shots —Guy Ritchie et al., *Lock, Stock... & Four Stolen Hooves*, p. 59, 2000

▸ **rattle beads**

to complain *US*

- —*American Speech*, p. 58, Spring-Summer 1970

▸ **rattle your cage**

to annoy or to aggravate you; to arouse your indignation *UK, 1990*

- I know better than to rattle her cage any sooner than I strictly need. —Kevin Sampson, *Clubland*, p. 229, 2002
- What did you do to rattle her cage? —Colin Butts, *Is Harry Still on the Boat?*, p. 273, 2003

▸ **rattle your dags**

to hurry *NEW ZEALAND*

- I'm not overstruck on that new cop – Told me to rattle my dags out of there. —Gordon Slatter, *The Pagan Game*, p. 16, 1968
- —Louis S. Leland, *A Personal Kiwi-Yankee Dictionary*, p. 85, 1984
- "Move along," someone behind them said. "Move! Rattle yer dags! Move, there!" —Elizabeth Jolley, *The Sugar Mother*, p. 161, 1988

rattle and clank; rattle *noun*

a bank *UK*

Rhyming slang.

- —Julian Franklyn, *A Dictionary of Rhyming Slang*, 1962

rattle and hiss; rattle *noun*

an act of urination; urine *UK*

Rhyming slang for **PISS**.

- —Ray Puxley, *Fresh Rabbit*, 1998

rattler *noun*

1 a train *UK, 1871*

- —Norman Carlisle, *The Modern Wonder Book of Trains and Railroading*, p. 267, 1946
- —Don Wilmeth, *The Language of American Popular Entertainment*, p. 217, 1981
- They were foiled by the gates of Glenhuntly, but managed to catch up with the rattler near the Caulfield Racecourse —Kerry Cue, *Crooks, Chooks and Bloody Ratbags*, p. 5, 1983

2 Boston's underground system, the Massachusetts Transit Authority *US*

- —Jim Crotty, *How to Talk American*, p. 29, 1997

rattler-jumping *adjective*

travelling by illegally catching trains *AUSTRALIA*

- I later found out he had seven daughters and wasn't going to trust no rattler-jumping foot-loose school teacher with them. —Patsy Adam-Smith, *Folklore of the Australian Railwaymen*, p. 168, 1969

rattlesnake *noun*

▸ **like a rattlesnake**

of a woman, describes vigorous participation in sexual intercourse *UK*

- The gorgeous contours of her figure stir a hearty lusting in him. Snuggly fitting round her waist. Neat. Trim. Like a rattlesnake, he bets. —Jack Allen, *When the Whistle Blows*, p. 85, 2000

rattlesnakes; rattles *noun*

delirium tremens *UK*

Rhyming slang for **SHAKES**.

- —Ray Puxley, *Cockney Rabbit*, 1992

rattling *adjective*

in an energetic state, possibly as a result of drug abuse *UK*

- I was wondering who might still be switched on. I was rattling. —Lanre Fehintola, *Charlie Says...*, p. 80, 2000

rattling *adverb*

used as an intensifier, especially when describing adventure fiction *UK, 1829*

- Still, the movie is a rattling good yarn and a great adventure[.] —*The Guardian*, 20th July 2000

rattling-cove *noun*

a taxi *UK*

Derived from late C17 – C18 usage (a coachman).

- —Paul Baker, *Polari*, p. 188, 2002

rat trap *noun*

1 a delapidated, shoddy building *UK, 1838*

- "Mister," he said, "there's twelve apartments in this rat-trap and I can't keep track of who comes in and who goes out so long as they're paid up." —Mickey Spillane, *Kiss Me Deadly*, p. 48, 1952

2 a fox hole that accommodated two or three Viet Cong who hid and slept there during the day *US*

- —Gregory Clark, *Words of the Vietnam War*, p. 424, 1990

3 a *Jap*anese person *UK*

Rhyming slang for **JAP**, a pejorative term dating from World War 2 and lingering among veterans of that conflict (especially prisoners of war). Also shortened to 'rat'.

- —Ray Puxley, *Cockney Robbit*, 1992

rat turds *noun*

an Oak Leaf Cluster, a military decoration indicating that the soldier has received another decoration more than once *US*

- —Gregory Clark, *Words of the Vietnam War*, p. 358, 1990

ratty *adjective*

1 wretched, miserable, mean; stained, tattered *US, 1867*

- In the main they was half-witted thugs who hardly had the brains to do up their flies; or ratty little clerks who'd nicked the petty cash[.] —John Peter Jones, *Feather Pluckers*, p. 62, 1964
- Move in with me in a ratty bedsit. —Greg Williams, *Diamond Geezers*, p. 179, 1997
- The blonde guy was getting out, built like a bull in a ratty suit tight on him, too small, and a brightly patterned sportshirt – the kind you saw in stores and wondered who would ever buy a shirt like that —Elmore Leonard, *Be Cool*, p. 222, 1999

2 angry, irritated *UK, 1909*

3 foolish, odd, eccentric *NEW ZEALAND*

- —David McGill, *David McGill's Complete Kiwi Slang Dictionary*, p. 92, 1998

4 crazy *AUSTRALIA, 1895*

- —Gavin Casey, *It's Harder for Girls*, p. 18, 1941
- Macauley recognized him for what he was, and hoped he wasn't too ratty. —D'Arcy Niland, *The Shiralee*, p. 163, 1955
- —Dymphna Cusack, *Picnic Races*, p. 139, 1962
- —Barry Humphries, *A Nice Night's Entertainment*, p. 122, 1968
- —Jim Ramsay, *Cop It Sweet!*, p. 76, 1977

raunch *noun*

in the usage of youthful model road racers (slot car racers), a slow car *US*

- — Phantom Surfers, *The Exciting Sounds of Model Road Racing (Album cover)*, 1997

raunchy *adjective*

1 sexually provocative, risqué; used as a euphemism for pornographic *US, 1967*

- Sexist or raunchy images on television or in advertising could be banned across the European Union under a directive being considered in Brussels. —*The Guardian*, 25th June 2003

2 inept, poorly done; unpleasant, contemptible; dirty *US, 1939*

3 used of music, abrasive, aggressive *US*

- —Arnold Shaw, *Dictionary of American Pop/Rock*, p. 301, 1982

ravaged *adjective*

drunk *UK*

- — *e-cyclopaedia*, 20th March 2002

rave *noun*

1 a party; a bottle party; a party open to the public, often announced and cited clandestinely, featuring drugs, music and sensory overload *UK*

Variant of 'rave up'. First used of wild parties in the late 1950s, then by **MOD(S)** in the 60s; revived in the 80s for parties on such a scale that both UK culture and law were significantly changed.

- —Connie Eble (Editor), *UNC-CH Campus Slang*, p. 8, Spring 1992
- For those of you out there who are over 25, a rave is an illegal party generated by word of mouth. — *Empire Records*, 1995
- Raves have challenged the order of society – enough for them to have been made illegal anyway. —Sarah Champion, *Disco Biscuits*, p. xv, 1997
- This is the birth of Rave culture, of the beatification of the beat, welcome to the Dance Age. —Tony Wilson, *24 Hour Party People*, p. 212, 2002

2 an enthusiastic review *US, 1926*

- Alexis Smith scored a triumph in her first Broadway musical outing, Follies, winning raves even from the critics who disliked the show. —Ken Mandelbaum, *Not Since Carrie*, p. 93, 1991

3 the object of a passionate liking or craze *UK*

- [T]he newest of teenage raves, with beside him his brother[.]—Colin MacInnes, *Absolute Beginners*, 1959

rave *verb*

1 to express an enthusiasm for something *UK, 1704*

- He is an abstract artist in New York city, struggling in the conventional manner, getting roaring drunk and raving about jazz and how much he hates Picasso. — *The Guardian*, 24th May 2004

2 to enjoy the music and other sensations of a rave *US*

- It starts at midnight. Rave on, everybody. — *Empire Records*, 1995
- You can rave on another night. — *Kids*, 1995

3 to persist in discussing something that does not interest anyone else involved in the discussion *US*

- —Guy L Steele, *Coevolution Quartly*, p. 34, spring 1981
- —Karla Jennings, *The Devouring Fungus: Tales of the Computer Age*, p. 223, 1990

rave drug *noun*

any chemical or 'designer' drug associated with dance and club culture *UK*

- I've smoked dope; I've done rave drugs, but I've never tried heroin or cocaine. — *Loaded*, p. 111, June 2003

rave energy *noun*

MDMA, the recreational drug best known as ecstasy *UK*

The rave culture was fuelled by MDMA.

- —Mike Haskins, *Drugs*, p. 290, 2003

raven *adjective*

gluttonous; greedy *GRENADA*

- —Richard Allsopp, *Dictionary of Caribbean English Usage*, p. 468, 1996

raver *noun*

1 a dedicated hedonist, party-goer, sexual-adventurer or drug taker *UK*

Extended from the sense as a 'passionate enthusiast'. Defined as 'a young woman who is enthusiastically promiscuous or merely of a passionate (but not promiscuous) nature' by David Powis, *The Signs of Crime*, 1977.

- They've got no room for ravers / They stop me from groovin', / They bang on me wall. —The Small Faces *Lazy Sunday*, 1968

2 someone who goes to a rave *UK*

- full of other happy, bouncy little ravers—Dave Courtney, *Raving Lunacy*, p. 33, 2000

3 a homosexual male *UK*

- —Angela Devlin, *Prison Patter*, p. 94, 1996

rave-up *noun*

a social gathering *UK*

Used ironically of a mild, as opposed to wild, party, by people old enough to remember the rave-ups of the 1960s.

- Are you going to the rave-up at the vicarage after evensong? — Beale, 1984

ravey *adjective*

characteristic of raving *UK*

- [H]e is cuddling people and asking them to show him their ravey hand movements! — Dave Courtney, *Raving Lunacy*, p. 73, 2000

raving *adjective*

used as an intensifier; complete, excellent, utmost, etc *UK*

- If you don't watch it, Monty, he said to himself, you'll be stone blind raving paralytic drunk. — Derek Bickerton, *Payroll*, p. 120, 1959
- His constant music gives me the raving needle! —Angela Devlin, *Prison Patter*, p. 95, 1996

Ravi Shankar *noun*

a wanker *UK*

Rhyming slang, formed from the name of the celebrated Indian musician (b.1920).

- —Bodmin Dark, *Dirty Cockney Rhyming Slang*, 2003

raw *noun*

crack cocaine *US*

- —US Department of Justice, *Street Terms*, 1994

▸ **in the raw**

naked *US, 1934*

- I got in the sack in the raw. — *Pimp*, p. 110, 1969

raw *adjective*

1 exciting; excellent *US*

- — *Washington Post Magazine*, p. 9, 19th April 1987: 'Say wha?'
- —Trevor Cralle, *The Surfin'ary*, p. 96, 1991
- —Connie Eble (Editor), *UNC-CH Campus Slang*, p. 7, April 1997
- — *San Jose Mercury News*, 11th May 1999

2 naked *US, 1931*

- Though we both wore pajamas, he had insomnia. Now at least I can sleep raw. —Mary McCarthy, *The Group*, p. 130, 1963

3 undiluted *US*

- He says he can cop me some raw stuff. That's what they call pure dope out here. It's supposed to be uncut. —Donald Goines, *Never Die Alone*, p. 116, 1974

4 unembalmed *US*

- — *Maledicta*, p. 180, Summer/Winter 1986–1987: 'Sexual slang: prostitutes, pedophiles, flagellators, tranvestites, and necrophiles'

raw fusion *noun*

heroin *UK*

- —Robert Ashton, *This Is Heroin*, p. 207, 2002
- —Mike Haskins, *Drugs*, p. 284, 2003

rawhide *noun*

heroin *UK*

- —Robert Ashton, *This Is Heroin*, p. 207, 2002
- —Mike Haskins, *Drugs*, p. 284, 2003

rawhide *verb*

to drive those under your supervision to work very hard *US*

- —Joseph E. Ragen and Charles Finston, *Inside the World's Toughest Prison*, p. 814, 1962

raw-jaw *verb*

to ignore someone; to bless someone with silence *US*

- —William K.Bentley and James M.Corbett, *Prison slang*, p. 39, 1992

raw meat *noun*

a new recruit in the US Army *US*

- — *American Speech*, p. 77, February 1948

raw prawn *noun*

a raw deal *AUSTRALIA*

- 'Wheelin' in a few bricks. There's twelve thousand comin' here ter-morrer.' 'Gees,' said Pat. 'Drawn the raw prawn again.' —Nino Culotta (John O'Grady), *They're A Weird Mob*, p. 85, 1957

raymond

yes, affirmative *UK*

Citizens' band radio French *vraiment* (truly, indeed).

- —Peter Chippindale, *The British CB Book*, p. 158, 1981

rays *noun*

radiology *US*

- —Sally Williams, *"Strong" Words*, p. 157, 1994

▸ **bag some rays; catch some rays; cop some rays**

to sunbathe *US*

- And baby go catch some rays in the sunny surf. —Brian Wilson, *Catch a Wave (performed by the Beach Boys)*, 1963

- I learned, with the advent of the "Bennie God" to make an acceptable "bennie machine" out of aluminum foil, and use it on the flat back porch every afternoon during the spring semester to "catch a few rays" while downing some frosties. —John Nichols, *The Sterile Cuckoo*, p. 60, 1965
- —Collin Baker et al., *College Undergraduate Slang Study Conducted at Brown University*, p. 182, 1968

razed *adjective*

drug-intoxicated *UK, 1998*

- —Mike Haskins, *Drugs*, p. 291, 2003

razoo *noun*

1 the smallest amount of money *AUSTRALIA, 1919*

Only ever used in negative contexts, generally 'to not have a razoo,' but also 'not worth a razoo,' 'not get a razoo', etc. Contextually referring to a low value brass coin, the origin of this term remains a mystery despite many guesses over the years. Needless to say no such coin ever existed. Also commonly a 'brass razoo', and formerly spelt 'rahzoo' or 'razzoo' though only rarely.

- —Barry Humphries, *A Nice Night's Entertainment*, p. 24, 1959
- However our mate, the bright barmaid, tells me he hasn't a razzoo and that Edna is keeping him going. —John Wynnum, *Jiggin' in the Riggin'*, p. 43, 1965
- How am I flamin' well going to get back to Earl Court? I haven't got a blessed razoo! —Barry Humphries, *The Wonderful World of Barry McKenzie*, p. 13, 1968
- Jeez Blanchie, I'd give me last razoo to feature with yous right now. —Barry Humphries, *The Wonderful World of Barry McKenzie*, p. 21, 1968
- —Wilda Moxham, *The Apprentice*, p. 10, 1969
- —Jim Ramsay, *Cop It Sweet!*, p. 76, 1977

2 harassment *US*

- The big razoo I can get to home. From my wife —Raymond Chandler, *The Little Sister*, p. 174, 1949

razor *verb*

to slash something with a razor *UK: SCOTLAND*

- I was raised on a diet of violence. Papers screaming about Teddy boys razoring cinema seats[.] —Martin King and Martin Knight, *The Naughty Nineties*, p. 223, 1999

razorback *noun*

a worker on a circus train; any circus worker other than a performer *US, 1904*

Circus historian and linguist Joe McKennon suggested that the term may have derived from the common work command of 'Raise 'er back, let 'er go' when placing circus equipment on train wagons.

- —Joe McKennon, *Circus Lingo*, p. 75, 1980

razor blade; razor *noun*

a black person *UK*

Rhyming slang.

- —G.F. Newman, *Sir, You Bastard*, 1970
- —Ray Puxley, *Cockney Rabbit*, 1992

razored *adjective*

muscular and sculpted *US*

- —*American Speech*, p. 201, Fall 1984: 'The Language of Bodybuilding'

razor edges *noun*

dice that are true to an extremely minute tolerance, approximately 1/1000th of a inch *US*

- —*The Annals of the American Academy of Political and Social Sciences*, p. 129, May 1950

razoring *noun*

an attack on someone with a razor *UK*

From **RAZOR** (to slash with a razor).

- —Angela Devlin, *Prison Patter*, p. 95, 1996

razz *noun*

a telling-off; a harangue *UK*

An Eton school term.

- —J.D.R. McConnell, *Eton: How It Works*, p. 61, 1967

▸ on the razz; on the razzle

a period of drinking, partying and other self-indulgent pleasures *UK, 1915*

Derives from a shortening of 'razzle-dazzle' (excitement). 'Razzle' (a good time) is first recorded in 1908.

- Al Pacino wakes up on a sidewalk in lower Manhattan after a night on the razzle[.] —*The Guardian*, 21st September 2001
- After a night on the razz in Korea with Clare, Cox overslept[.] —*The Times Magazine*, p. 19, 15th June 2002
- I'm not so keen on going out on the razz with a computer nerd. —Colin Butts, *Is Harry Still on the Boat?*, p. 274, 2003

▸ the razz

a beating *IRELAND*

- PAKEY: Padraic O'Dea got the razz. PETEY: He got it allright. Talk about shoein' a wheel...He got at least forty flamin' licks into the kisser an' as many more on top o' the sconce. —John B. Keane, *The Man from Clare*, p. 67, 1962

razz *verb*

to heckle; to show contempt; to jeer *US, 1919*

Short for **RASPBERRY**, a derisive sound.

- That was the way he and Al Herbert always razzed anybody who told them dumb stories. —James T. Farrell, *Saturday Night*, p. 13, 1947
- Then we went back to the house, and after awhile Fay began to razz me a little. —Jim Thompson, *After Dark, My Sweet*, p. 32, 1955
- All amateur try-out turns were razzed regularly even if good. —*The Stage*, 3rd October 1968
- I razzed him about it when we met. —Frank Zappa, *The Real Frank Zappa Book*, p. 195, 1989
- "Take it off, take it off!" the latecoming collegiate mafia began razzing Desdemona. —Seth Morgan, *Homeboy*, p. 136, 1990
- "Did the kids razz you about your suicide attempt?" I asked. —C.D. Payne, *Youth in Revolt*, p. 108, 1993
- Immediately, a half-dozen sailors started razzing Miles, who looked at Anne with approval. —Joseph Wambaugh, *Floaters*, p. 232, 1996

razzberry *noun*

a jeering, derisory, farting noise *US, 1922*

Extends **RAZZ** (to jeer) back to a variation of its source: **RASPBERRY**.

- [D]isappointed at not soliciting more razzberries from the peanut gallery[.] —Lester Bangs, *Psychotic Reactions and Carburetor Dung*, p. 35, 1970
- [H]e now must endure taunts from a jury of unsympathetic razzberry experts[.] —*Saturday Evening Post*, March 2001

razzled *noun*

drunk *UK*

Derives from **ON THE RAZZLE** (having a good time, partying).

- —*e-cyclopaedia*, 20th March 2002

razzle-dazzle *noun*

1 confusion; chaos; bewilderment *US, 1889*

- All this hip shit. You understand what I mean? The casino business, all this razzle-dazzle —Elmore Leonard, *Glitz*, p. 258, 1985

2 sexual intercourse *UK*

- [E]very time we indulged in the full genital razzle-dazzle, we grew closer to each other[.] —Doug Lang, *Freaks*, p. 83, 1973

3 in circus and carnival usage, a prostitute *US*

- —Don Wilmeth, *The Language of American Popular Entertainment*, p. 217, 1981

razzmatazz *noun*

1 old-fashioned, sentimental jazz *US, 1936*

The term was originally used, before use of the word 'jazz', to describe an early jazz-like music.

- [H]e was huddled up more and more at his phonograph at home, listening to all kinds of symphonic razzmatazz like Holst's The Planets and Stravinsky and Ravel. —Mezz Mezzrow, *Really the Blues*, p. 157, 1946

2 a showy outward appearance *UK, 1958*

- [I]n dignity and with style but with no razzamatazz[.] —Maeve Binchy, *Firefly Summer*, p. 552, 1988
- [T]he razzmatazz of contemporary Wall Street[.] —Ron Chernow, *The House of Morgan*, p. front matter, 2001

3 extreme pleasure *US*

- [T]he way they pull their lay hips our ship that they are from the land of razz ma tazz. —Lavada Durst, *The Jives of Dr. Hepcat*, p. 1, 1953

razzy *adjective*

tattered; unkempt *BARBADOS*

- —Frank A. Collymore, *Barbadian Dialect*, p. 92, 1965

RB *noun*

an enthusiastic sportsman whose character is formed by the aggressive pursuit of masculinity and frequently demonstrated by his boorish behaviour and drunken socialising *SOUTH AFRICA, 1991*

An abbreviation of **RUGGER BUGGER**.

- —Penny Silva, *A Dictionary of South African English*, 1996

RC *adjective*

Roman Catholic *UK, 1762*

- For four years, I hitchhiked thirty miles twice a day to attend an R.C. prep school where everybody except me was rich[.] —Raymond Mungo, *Famous Long Ago*, p. 2, 1970

RCH *noun*

a tiny notional unit of measure *US*

An abbreviation of **RED CUNT HAIR**, perceived as a smaller unit even than a simple **CUNT HAIR**.

- —Carl Fleischhauer, *A Glossary of Army Slang*, p. 10, 1968

RCMP *noun*

in Canada, a *R*oman *C*atholic *M*ember of *P*arliament *CANADA*

- —*Maledicta*, p. 264, 1984–1985: 'Miscellaneous nicknames'

RD *noun*

a red-coloured capsule of secobarbital sodium (trade name Seconal™), a central nervous system depressant *US*

An initialised **RED DEVIL**.

- —Donald Wesson and David Smith Barbiturates, *Their Use Misuse and Abuse*, p. 122, 1977

reach *verb*

to be prepared to fight *US*

- —Rick Ayers (Editor), *Berkeley High Slang Dictionary*, p. 35, 2004

▸ **reach out and touch someone**

to telephone *US*

From a 1982 American Telephone and Telegraph advertising slogan.

- Well, then, let's reach out and touch someone, dude! —*Bill and Ted's Excellent Adventure*, 1989

reach-around *noun*

manual stimulation of the passive partner's genitals by the male penetrating from behind *US*

- I'll bet you're the kind of guy that would fuck a person in the ass and not even have the goddamn courtesy to give him a reach around! —*Full Metal Jacket*, 1987
- Replace the "rubbing the clit" part with a reach-around while you're at it. —Suroosh Alvi et al., *The Vice Guide*, p. 42, 2002

read *verb*

1 in poker, to try to discern an opponent's hand *US*

- —John Scarne, *Scarne's Guide to Modern Poker*, p. 288, 1979

2 in sports, to anticipate an opponent's movement *US*

- [A] linebacker has to "read' before he reacts[.] —Dan Jenkins, *Life Its Ownself*, p. 108, 1984

3 in transexual usage, to detect a person's genetic sex *US*

- —*Maledicta*, p. 173, Summer/Winter 1986–1987: 'Sexual slang: prostitutes, pedophiles, flagellators, transvestites, and necrophiles'

▸ **read a shirt**

to look for signs of body lice *US*

- —Don Wilmeth, *The Language of American Popular Entertainment*, 1981

▸ **read between the lines**

said when three fingers are raised in an insolent gesture *UK*

The index finger is the one 'between the lines'; this is, therefore, a catchphrased elaboration of a familiar insulting gesture. Reported by a variety of mothers in Cardiff and Bristol during April 2005 and generally credited to 8-year-old children.

▸ **read (someone) the riot act**

to give someone a very stern lecture or reprimand *UK, 1906*

From a law enacted by George I limiting the activities of groups of 12 or more.

- What I can't understand is why a man with a high temper like yourself wouldn't at least take the opportunity to go over there and tell this goniff what you just told me. Read him the fucking riot act. —Robert Campbell, *Boneyards*, 1992

▸ **read the riot act**

to instruct a prisoner who is about to be released on the legal restrictions concerning firearms *UK*

From the sense 'to give someone a very stern lecture or reprimand'.

- —Angela Devlin, *Prison Patter*, 1996

▸ **you wouldn't read about it**

you wouldn't believe such bad luck! *AUSTRALIA, 1950*

- So they took bloody Tobruk without me, eh? Those Grey Caps and Bludgers! You wouldn't read about it would you? —George Johnston, *My Brother Jack*, 1964
- —Frank Hardy, *The Yarns of Billy Borker*, 1965

readable *adjective*

used of a casino blackjack gambler, sloppy in dealing or generous with body language, in either event revealing to players the strength of his hand *US*

- —Michael Dalton, *Blackjack*, p. 72, 1991

read and write *noun*

a fight *UK, 1857*

Rhyming slang, never used in a shortened form.

- —Ray Puxley, *Cockney Rabbit*, 1992

reader *noun*

1 a book; a magazine; a newspaper *UK*

From the early C18 usage as a 'pocket-book' which moved into the current sense during the mid-C19.

- —Angela Devlin, *Prison Patter*, p. 95, 1996

2 a 'Wanted' poster or handbill *US, 1926*

- We got him on the teletype and they got readers out. —Raymond Cgandler, *Farewell My Lovely*, p. 91, 1940
- I was running snow from the coast to Detroit and there was a reader out on me —Chester Himes, *Cast the First Stone*, p. 14, 1952

3 a counterfeit driving licence *US*

- A popular item on any Midway, a READER usually costs twenty dollars, but it is a cheap investment for someone needing to change identies or unable to obtain his own. —Gene Sorrows, *All About Carnivals*, p. 25, 1985

4 a prescription for a narcotic *US*

- You can't work a cartwheel or a bug to get a reader because the butcher's gumptious to all that —*The New American Mercury*, p. 711, 1950
- —Richard Horman and Allan Fox, *Drug Awareness*, p. 470, 1970

5 a marked card *US, 1894*

- —Albert H. Morehead, *The Complete Guide to Winning Poker*, p. 270, 1967
- He sees through his 'reader' eyeglasses Hicks' hand; space ace in hole with ten showing. —Iceberg Slim (Robert Beck), *Doom Fox*, p. 59, 1978

readers *noun*

1 reading spectacles *UK*

2 special tinted eye glasses used for reading marked cards *US*

- —Steve Kuriscak, *Casino Talk*, p. 46, 1985

readies; reddies *noun*

cash money *UK, 1937*

A variation, not a plural, of **READY**, in turn an abbreviation of 'ready money'.

- We'll need a total shark for a manager and once he's overseen our meteoric rise to the top of the hit parade, we'll have the readies to sue his arse! —Stewart Home, *Sex Kick [britpulp]*, p. 216, 1999
- What's that go for? Sixty grand? Maybe walk away with half that in readies. —Kevin Sampson, *Outlaws*, p. 18, 2001

read my lips

pay attention to what I am saying, for it is the bedrock truth *US*

A pop phrase embraced in a show of bravado by George Bush when he was running for president of the US in 1988: 'Read my lips – no new taxes' and then the gist of endless ridicule when, two years later, he advocated a new tax. Actor Tim Curry named an album that he recorded in 1978 *Read My Lips*, later explaining to William Safire that he took the phrase to mean 'Listen and listen very hard, because I want you to hear what I've got to say'.

- This dramatic use in a formal acceptance speech sealed the phrasal intensifier 'read my lips' into the language. —*New York Times Magazine*, p. 22, 4th September 1988
- Read my lips (as she mouths the word "no"). —*True Romance*, 1993

ready; reddy *noun*

cash money *UK, 1639*

An abbreviation of 'ready money'.

- Not enough reddy in it in my case. —Derek Raymond (Robin Cook), *The Crust on its Uppers*, p. 24, 1962
- Kelly was always short of the ready in Regan's book. —*The Sweeney*, p. 50, 1976
- —Ned Wallish, Geffrey Tolhurist, *The Truth Ddictonary of Racing Slang*, p. 67, 1989
- —Angela Devlin, *Prison Patter*, p. 95, 1996

ready *adjective*
competent *US*
- [H]e's ready, like a boxer poised to take on all comers[.] — Mezz Mezzrow, *Really the Blues*, p. 227, 1946

ready eye *noun*
a police trap *UK*
From **READY-EYED** (well informed or betrayed to the police).
- — Angela Devlin, *Prison Patter*, p. 95, 1996

ready-eye *verb*
(of police) to operate an official surveillance *UK*
- [T]hey can't get out the front door to put a bet on without the Robbery Squad ready-eyeing them there and back. — J.J. Connolly, *Layer Cake*, p. 8, 2000

ready-eyed *adjective*
1 used by criminals of a planned crime that has been betrayed and is therefore a police trap *UK, 1975*
2 in police use, well informed, knowing the detailed truth of a situation *UK, 1977*

ready for Doctor Jesus *adjective*
about to die *US, 1966*
- — Frederic G. Cassidy, *Dictionary of American Regional English, Volume II*, p. 99, 1991

ready, Freddie
used for signalling readiness *US, 1952*
- He would say, "Hey, Bix Six. Everything is A-okay. We are ready, Freddie." You know, he had to add something to whatever you said." — Wallace Terry, *Bloods*, p. 113, 1984

ready-made *noun*
a commercially manufactured cigarette *US*
- Come on down to the bunk and I'll get you a ready-made. — Chester Himes, *Cast the First Stone*, p. 10, 1952

ready rocks; redi rocks *noun*
a form of cocaine prepared for smoking *US*
- — Geoffrey Froner, *Digging for Diamonds*, p. 50, 1989
- They were selling Redi Rocks this evening, precooked nuggets ready to smoke, purer than crack and no mystery ingredients like Raid or formaldehyde. — Richard Price, *Clockers*, p. 72, 1992
- Ready rocks (cocaine) and blows (heroin) can usually be purchased from the same street drug dealers — *The Emergence of Crack Injection Among Injecting Drug Users in Chicago*, June 1995

ready-rolls *noun*
commercially manufactured cigarettes *US*
- — *Newsweek*, p. 98, 8th October 1951
- — Malachi Andrews and Paul T. Owens, *Black Language*, p. 107, 1973

ready-to-run *noun*
in the usage of youthful model road racers (slot car racers), a shop-bought car that has not been modified or enhanced *US*
- — Phantom Surfers, *The Exciting Sounds of Model Road Racing (Album cover)*, 1997

ready whip *noun*
a non-commissioned officer fresh out of training *US*
From the pressurised sweet topping advertised as instant whipped cream.
- — Linda Reinberg, *In the Field*, p. 180, 1991

real *noun*
the truth *US*
- I snarled, "Tell the real, whore." — Donald Goines, *Whoreson*, p. 159, 1972

▸ **on the real**
1 genuine *UK*
Black usage.
- "Well, if you're on the real," I said, "let me warn you I don't do jobs by the hour[.]" — Diran Adebayo, *My Once Upon A Time*, p. 10, 2000

2 seriously *US*
- Now that's some shit on the real! — *Menace II Society*, 1993
- — *Milwaukee Journal-Sentinel*, 5th March 2001

real *adjective*
homosexual *US*
- Don't let Chester's tool belt and boot-cut Wrangler jeans fool you, he's as real as they come. — Jeff Fessler, *When Drag Is Not a Car Race*, p. 13, 1997
- Real girl is used to refer to someone who's not a girl (i.e homosexual man) or a drag queen in the Polari sense. — Paul Baker, *Polari*, p. 188, 2002

real *adverb*
really, truly; hence, used as an intensifier, greatly *UK, 1827*
The *Oxford English Dictionary* offers both Scottish and US origins, but the earliest slang sense is from English writer R.H. Froude.
- Now we all know it's real lonely at the top. — Country Mike (the Beastie Boys), *On Your Way Up Again (the Fowl Song)*, 1999

real bikini *noun*
something that is excellent *US*
Teen slang.
- — *American Weekly*, p. 2, 14th August 1955

real bush *noun*
a white woman *US*
Used by US troops in Vietnam jaded by their experiences with Vietnamese prostitutes.
- — Linda Reinberg, *In the Field*, p. 180, 1991

real case *noun*
a serious medical emergency *US*
- — Sally Williams, *"Strong" Words*, p. 157, 1994

real deal *noun*
1 an authentic item or person; the plain truth *US*
- Always go to where the real people go, that way you'll always know what the real deal is — Odie Hawkins, *The Life and Times of Chester Simmons*, p. 13, 1991
- This baby's the real deal. Daddy's little angel. — *Cruel Intentions*, 1999
- "Ray was the real deal, asswipe," Drucker hissed — Stephen J. Cannell, *The Tin Collectors*, p. 30, 2001
- This album is the real rock deal; the heaviosity of AC/DC spliced with the sassiness of L7[.] — *X-Ray*, p. 21, May 2003

2 a youth gang member who is fully committed to the gang *US*
- — Mark S. Fleisher, *Beggars & Thieves*, p. 291, 1995: 'Glossary'

Real Deal *nickname*
Evander Holyfield (b.1962), three times world heavyweight champion boxer *US*

real estate *noun*
in war, territory to be taken, held, abandoned or lost *US*
- "Real estate" was irrelevant; Ridgway would not advance simply to occupy a few square miles of ground which the Chinese might seize from him a few days later. — Joseph C. Goulden, *Korea*, p. 433, 1982

reality check *noun*
in computing, a simple test of a computer's or program's operating ability *US*
- — Eric S. Raymond, *The New Hacker's Dictionary*, p. 301, 1991

real live *adjective*
genuine, actual *UK, 1887*
Jocular; often used of an inanimate article.
- Seeing the real live tree where the Cheshire cat sat, the real live White Rabbit's hole, the real live croquet lawn... Now, that was – in her own words – "Class, man". — *The Guardian*, 11th May 2002

really!
used for expressing emphatic agreement *US*
- "We got to take care of those people that been takin' care of us!" "REALLY!" — Malachi Andrews and Paul T. Owens, *Black Language*, p. 76, 1973
- — Connie Eble (Editor), *UNC-CH Campus Slang*, April 1977
- "Sorta grabs you, doesn't it?" "Really!" — Odie Hawkins, *The Life and Times of Chester Simmons*, p. 200, 1991

Really Canadian Modest Police *noun*
the Royal Canadian Mounted Police *CANADA*
A back-formation from the initials RCMP.
- George Dew, noting the example given of RCMP as Really Canadian Modest Police, recalled the force's name in French, Gendarmerie Royale du Canada. — *Toronto Globe and Mail*, p. D12, 4th August 2002

real McCoy; McCoy *noun*
the genuine article *US, 1883*
- So he fix up two ropes – one gimmicked to stretch, the other the real McCoy — William Burroughs, *Naked Lunch*, p. 79–80, 1957
- Far as I know it's the McCoy — George V. Higgins, *The Friends of Eddie Doyle*, p. 104, 1971
- "Now," Terry said, "while Czechmate's satisfying himself that stuff is McCoy, I'm inside the South Brooklyn Bank emptying the fifties from our box[.]" — Emmett Grogan, *Final Score*, p. 60, 1976
- "Those are the real McCoys," said Kingsbury. Churrito looked perplexed. "McCoys?" "Her tits, I mean." — Carl Hiaasen, *Native Tongue*, p. 238, 1991

- A friend of mine had himself declared a mininster of hihs own religion. A way to fuck the IRS. Is that what you're doing, or are you the real McCoy? — Quentin Tarantino, *From Dusk Till Dawn*, p. 57, 1995

Real McCoy *noun*
a variety of marijuana *CANADA*
- [T]he Real McCoy, which is a Haze-Skunk cross[.] — Brian Preston, *Pot Planet*, p. 232, 2002

real thing *noun*
▸ **the real thing**
the genuine article *UK, 1939*
Figurative slang from the conventional sense.
- "We say lots of people are funny," said David Letterman. "[But] he [Rich Hall]'s the real thing." — *The Guardian*, 6th March 2003

real world *noun*
the non-pornographic entertainment industry; the world outside the pornography industry *US*
- — *Adult Video News*, p. 38, September 1995

ream *verb*
1 to have anal intercourse *US, 1942*
- Night after night, he rooted, rolled, and reamed. — Tom Robbins, *Jitterbug Perfume*, p. 26, 1984

2 to cheat someone *US, 1933*
Figurative from the more literal sense of poking something up one's rectum. Also variant 'rim'.
- He wouldn't be reamed no sir, not him, because he wasn't the kind of a chump who allowed himself to be chumped by a cheap kike auctioneer. — James T. Farrell, *Willie Collins*, p. 107, 1946

3 to scold or punish someone *US, 1950*
From the sense of 'ream' as widening a hole. 'Ream out' is also used.
- And then Rags reamed her out – real hard. It was pretty rough. — Jim Thompson, *The Kill-Off*, p. 22, 1957
- If they do, they'll get reamed and they know it. — Darryl Ponicsan, *The Last Detail*, p. 22, 1970
- Yeah, Mom already reamed me, alright? — *The Breakfast Club*, 1985

ream *adjective*
excellent *UK*
An intensification of the C19 sense as 'good, genuine, honest'.
- Ream – means the bollocks "Them jeans are buff". — prison inmate, 5th August 2002

ream job *noun*
1 anal sex *US*
- The next time you put an add in your personals section in the back of your magazine about "ream jobs" show a nice brown or black female ass! — David Kerekes, *Critical Vision*, p. 134, 1995

2 a difficult situation *US*
- — Collin Baker et al., *College Undergraduate Slang Study Conducted at Brown University*, p. 183, 1968

rear *noun*
the buttocks *UK, 1796*
Euphemistic.
▸ **get your rear in gear**
to get going *US*
- — Helen Dahlskog (Editor), *A Dictionary of Contemporary and Colloquial Usage*, p. 48, 1972

rear admiral *noun*
a proctologist *US*
- — *American Speech*, p. 201, Fall-Winter 1973: 'The language of nursing'
- — Sally Williams, *"Strong" Words*, p. 157, 1994

rear-area hawk *noun*
an officer stationed away from the field of battle who has strong, bellicose opinions about what should be done in battle *US*
Vietnam war usage.
- He was a rear-area hawk, one of those lily-livered saber-rattling fucks who spouted opinions from the vantage point of his air-conditioned quarters in Saigon about the strategic need for more division-sized month-long sweeps of enemy territory[.] — Lucian K. Truscott, *Army Blue*, p. 89, 1989

rear-area pussy *noun*
a support personnel safely away from combat *US*
Occasionally abbreviated to RAP.
- — Linda Reinberg, *In the Field*, p. 179, 1991

rear-echelon commando *noun*
a soldier assigned to duty safely away from combat *US*
- — *American Speech*, p. 55, February 1947: 'Pacific war language'

rear-echelon motherfucker *noun*
a member of the armed forces serving behind lines well away from combat *US*
Often abbreviated to REMF.
- It was the ages-old animosity between front-line infantrymen and the staff and support personnel farther back – the "pogues," those "rear-echelon mother-fuckers!" — Charles Anderson, *The Grunts*, p. 28, 1976
- The troops developed a series of terms for these officers, the most derisive of which was "rear-echelon motherfucker." — Jay M. Shafritz, *Words on War*, p. 362, 1990

rear-end loader *noun*
a prisoner who hides items in their rectum *AUSTRALIA*
- Some of them – the 'rear-end loaders' – stashed the gear in their anus, the most common items secreted being drugs, money and various types of escape implements. — William Dodson, *The Sharp End*, p. 35, 2001

rear exit *noun*
a retreat or flight from danger *US*
- If the feces really hits the fan, there are three points through which a man can run for the hills – rear exits in the trench called "bug-outs." — Martin Russ, *The Last Parallel*, p. 116, 1957

rear-gunner; rear seat gunner *noun*
a male homosexual *UK*
A masculine image that employs weaponry in a metaphor for anal intercourse.
- NEFARIUS: It's no gay, issi? BACON: Do we look like a pair of rear-gunners? NEFARIUS: Nah, it's jus' I got all this fuckin' gay porn, 'n' I can't sell i' to any o' my contac'. — Guy Ritchie et al, *Lock, Stock... & Four Stolen Hooves*, p. 17, 2000

rearrange *verb*
▸ **rearrange the deck chairs on the Titanic; rearrange the deck chairs**
to focus on petty matters while ignoring major problems *US, 1972*
From the image of the folly of worrying about the arrangement of deck chairs on the Titanic as the ship sank.
- "He's trying to rearrange the deck chairs on the Titanic out of self interest," he told AAP. — *AAP Newsfeed*, 13 February 1998
- Rather than rearrange deck chairs on a sinking ship, the Postal Service should consider more financially sound alternatives — *Business Wire, Inc.*, 26th April 2001
- — *Bremner, Bird and Fortune*, 15th February 2004

reat *adjective*
▷ **see: REET**

reat pleat *noun*
fashionable trousers *US*
Usage by Mexican-American youth (Pachucos) in the south-western US.
- — *Common Ground*, p. 81, Summer 1947

reb *noun*
any poor, rural, white southerner *US*
- — *Maledicta*, p. 168, Summer/Winter 1978: 'How to hate thy neighbor: a guide to racist maledicta'

rebbish *adjective*
poor, white and racist *US*
From the shortened **REB** or **JOHNNY REB**, harkening to Confederate soldiers.
- It was a rebbish neighbourhood, poor white; I'd have felt much better parked in Beverly Hills. — Chester Himes, *If He Hollers Let Him Go*, p. 139, 1945

rebellious henchman *noun*
the penis *UK*
- — Richard Herring, *Talking Cock*, p. 30, 2003

rebel trap *noun*
in pool, the largest regulation-size table *US*
In the US, the large tables were unknown in the south, giving rise to this term in the north.
- — Steve Rushin, *Pool Cool*, p. 24, 1990

rebound *noun*

1 a person with whom you have a romantic relationship in close proximity to the unhappy ending of a prior relationship *US*

- —Pamela Munro, *U.C.L.A. Slang*, p. 102, 1997

2 in trucking, a return trip *US*

- Have a good day today and better day tomorrow and we'll catch you on the rebound[.]—Lanie Dills, *The Official CB Slanguage Language Dictionary*, p. 58, 1976

▸ **on the rebound**

emotionally vulnerable following rejection by a loved-one *UK, 1864*

- Girls sniff out those on the rebound like tracker dogs at customs. —*BBCi*, 25th May 2003

rec *noun*

1 a recreation ground (a municipal park) *UK, 1931*

- [T]hey ran for the safety of the Red Cross "rec", the recreation ground used as their headquarters.—Brian McDonald, *Elephant Boys*, p. 30, 2000

2 in prison, a recommendation given by the judge on sentencing *UK*

- I'd better giv him a rec. of twenty-five years – keep him away from decent people.—Lenny McLean, *The Guv'nor*, p. 187, 1998
- There were others, however, who had been given recommendations (known on prison landings as a "rec") in open court—*The Guardian*, 26th November 2002

recap *noun*

a recapitulation *US, 1926*

- I mean, let's just run it down in a recap—Terry Southern, *Now Dig This*, p. 24, 1981
- REPORTER: I need a recap – Glen Tunney – two years ago – shot a kid holding a water gun.—*Copland*, 1997

recap *verb*

to recapitulate *UK, 1950*

- [Philip K.] Dick recapped years later in his essay How To Build A Universe That Doesn't Fall Apart Two Days Later.—*The Guardian*, 29th June 2002

recce; reccy *noun*

a reconnaissance *UK, 1941*

Originally military; wider usage tends toward vaguer and more figurative shadings of the sense.

- [T]he boss detailed Pat Martin and myself to carry out a preliminary recce of the place.—Chris Ryan, *Stand By, Stand By*, p. 94, 1996
- I didn't find out how to spell "recce" until very recently, and now I find myself on one.—Frank Skinner, *Frank Skinner*, p. 241, 2001

recce *verb*

to go on a reconnaissance; to look around *UK, 1943*

Originally military.

receipt *noun*

in professional wrestling, an arguably unacceptable manoeuvre that is acceptable in the context of justifiable revenge *US*

reck *verb*

to consider; to think *UK*

A shortening of **RECKON**.

- Just your H.T. leads, I reck.—*The Full Monty*, 1997

reckon *verb*

to esteem someone or something as worthwhile *UK*

- JOHN: Gaw, it's depressing in here, isn't it? Funny... (HE PATS THE DOG) 'cos they usually reckon dogs more than people in England, don't they?—*A Hard Day's Night*, 1964

recognize *verb*

to pay attention *US*

- I told him to recognize and stop talking like that to me.—Don R. McCreary (Editor), *Dawg Speak*, 2001

recon *noun*

*recon*naisance *US, 1918*

Often used in an adjectival sense.

- [C]overtly inserting four- to six-man recon teams into enemy territory via a variety of means[.]—Bob Newman, *Marine Special Warfare And Elite Unit Tactics*, p. 11, 1995

recon *verb*

to *recon*noitre *US, 1966*

Shortened for military purposes.

- Scholtes continued to insist on sending his own people in to recon the site[.]—Tom Clancy, *Shadow Warriors*, p. 10, 2002

recon by fire *noun*

in a military situation, random gunfire designed to ascertain the presence of the enemy by return fire *US*

- "Recon by fire" is when you go into an area and you're not exactly sure what is in the area. You want to find out, so you just fire into the jungle or into the surrounding vegetation in the hopes you hit the enemy or something.—John Kerry, *The New Soldier*, p. 62, 1971

record *noun*

▸ **change the record!; put another record on!**

used to demand a change of style, subject or substance in what is being said *UK, 1966*

- Don't hide your face, don't beg and plead / Being sorry for yourself / Put another record on / You're the answer, you're the cause—Julian Lennon, *Get a Life*, 1991

recovery room *noun*

a golf course's bar *US*

- —Hubert Pedroli and Mary Tiegreen, *Let the Big Dog Eat! A Dictionary of the Secret Language of Golf*, p. 71, 2000

rec room *noun*

a recreational room *US, 1962*

A mandatory feature of suburban 1960s life in the US, where the family gathered to watch television, play table tennis, set up model trains, etc.

- It was a snug, knotty-pine bar, more like somebody's rec room than a saloon, and it was cold and rainy outside.—Elmore Leonard, *Glitz*, p. 124, 1985
- We shot pool in the rec room all night the day before our permanent duty stations were posted on the bulletin board.—Odie Hawkins, *Scars and Memories*, p. 78, 1987
- [H]e just suggested that Wilson fuck off to the band rec room across the courtyard[.]—Tony Wilson, *24 Hour Party People*, p. 194, 2002

rectum rocket *noun*

a fast-moving vehicle *UK*

- —Peter Chippindale, *The British CB Book*, p. 158, 1981

recycle *noun*

LSD *UK, 1998*

- —Mike Haskins, *Drugs*, p. 286, 2003

recycle *verb*

▸ **recyle the dice**

in bar dice games, to roll again after a roll that produces no points for the player *US*

- —Jester Smith, *Games They Play in San Francisco*, p. 105, 1971

red *noun*

1 any central nervous system depressant, especially a capsule of Seconal™ or another barbiturate *US*

- I gave her a couple of reds and rocked her into fulfil sleep—Iceberg Slim (Robert Beck), *Airtight Wille and Me*, 1979
- The next step up the scale is Seconal ("reds" or "red devils"), a barbiturate normally used as a sedative.—Hunter S. Thompson, *Hell's Angels*, p. 216, 1966
- "They way they put it is that they drop whites to get out of bed in the morning, or whenever they get up to go to work, and drop reds to go to sleep," Sweeney reported at the conference.—*San Francisco Chronicle*, p. 5, 11th October 1966
- They walking in fours and kicking in doors; dropping Reds and busting heads.—Eldridge Cleaver, *Soul on Ice (letter dated August 15, 1965)*, p. 27, 1968
- What in the world ever became of sweet Jane / She lost her sparkle you know she isn't the same / Living on reds, vitamin C and cocaine—The Grateful Dead, *Trucking*, November 1970
- Someody else do reds, and everyboy share the laughing gas to tie the whole thing together, in honor of Eddie's passing.—Gurney Norman, *Divine Right's Trip (Last Whole Earth Catalog)*, p. 123, 1971
- He has taken reds and now is slumped in a chair, eyes and feet twisted.—Oscar Zeta Acosta, *The Revolt of the Cockroach People*, p. 73, 1973
- [R]eady to go pick him up from the Troubador and lie there next to him all night still in all my clothes, just to make sure nobody took many reds.—Eve Babitz, *L.A. Woman*, p. 142, 1982
- After another day and night of dysoxin-methedrine injections with Gloria, followed in the later hours by palmloads of seconal barbiturate, previously and herewith referred to as "reds," I woke upon the floor[.]—Jim Carroll, *Forced Entries*, p. 35, 1987
- [I]t was enough to gas up the T-bird and score some reds.—Carl Hiaasen, *Strip Tease*, p. 266, 1993
- Barbiturates are also known as BARBS, BLUES, REDS, and SEKKIES. —Macfarlane, Macfarlane and Robson, *The User*, p. 97, 1996

2 marijuana *US*
A generic term for golden-red marijuana, clipping PANAMA RED etc.
• —Ernest L. Abel, *A Marijuana Dictionary*, p. 85, 1982

3 morphine *US*
• They ordered cocaine or morphine by the pieces (ounces) and used the dope peddler's slang or code terms, red or blue identifying morphine or cocaine. —William J. Spillard and Pence James, *Needle in a Haystack*, p. 147, 1945

4 blood *US*
Professional wrestling usage.

5 in a deck of playing cards, any heart or diamond *US*
A flush of hearts or diamonds is referred to as 'all red'.
• —George Percy, *The Language of Poker*, p. 74, 1988

6 in American casinos, a five-dollar betting chip *US*
• —Thomas F. Hughes, *Dealing Casino Blackjack*, p. 74, 1982

7 a penny *US*
• —Hyman E. Goldin et al., *Dictionary of American Underworld Lingo*, p. 176, 1950

8 a liberal; a socialist; a Marxist; a Marxist-Leninist; a Maoist; a Trotskyite; a communist; an anarchist *UK, 1848*

▸ **in the red**
in debt *UK, 1926*
From the use of red ink to show debt in account ledgers.
• [N]ot only as skint as a kipper's backbone, but over £150 in the red[.] —Charles Raven, *Underworld Nights*, p. 66, 1956

red *adjective*

1 made of gold, golden *UK*
In conventional use from C14, slipped into slang during C17. Also in occasional use as a noun.

2 of a mixed (black and white) racial heritage *US*
• In between light negro america and Black negro america (in terms of color), there is a special category of people, who are assigned the name of red niggers. —H. Rap Brown, *Die Nigger Die!*, p. 7, 1969
• Yeah, she was a fine red motherfucker and if you think it was easy for me not to fuck this girl, you're dead wrong. —A.S. Jackson, *Gentleman Pimp*, p. 150, 1973

3 drug-intoxicated *JAMAICA, 1998*
From the *red*dening of the smoker's eyes.
• —Velma Pollard, *Dread Talk: The Language of Rastafari*, p. 44, 2000
• —Mike Haskins, *Drugs*, p. 291, 2003

red and blue *noun*
a capsule of amobarbital sodium and secobarbital sodium (trade name Tuinal™), a combination of central nervous system depressants *US*
• —Norman W. Houser, *Drugs*, p. 13, 1969

red ass *noun*
anger *US*
• —*American Speech*, p. 64, Spring-Summer 1975: 'Razorback slang'

red-ass *verb*
to annoy or tease someone *US*
• —Michael Dalton Johnson, *Talking Trash with Redd Foxx*, p. 123, 1994

red-assed *adjective*
very angry *US*
• —*American Speech*, p. 271, December 1962: 'The language of traffic policemen'
• —Helen Dahlskog (Editor), *A Dictionary of Contemporary and Colloquial Usage*, p. 48, 1972

redback *noun*
in western Canada, a Hereford cow or steer *CANADA*
• I was alone with a stream of red backs moving just a mite too fast for comfort. —Alan Fry, *Ranch on the Cariboo*, p. 25, 1962

red badge of courage *noun*
a notional badge awarded to someone who performs oral sex on a woman who is experiencing the bleed period of the menstrual cycle *US*
• —Michael Dalton Johnson, *Talking Trash with Redd Foxx*, p. 50, 1994

red ball *noun*

1 a fast freight train *US*
• —Norman Carlisle, *The Modern Wonder Book of Trains and Railroading*, p. 267, 1946
• [H]is world became a world of brakies, reefers, redballs, railroad dicks in hard-up midwest towns[.] —John Clellon Holmes, *The Horn*, p. 159, 1958

2 a trail, path or road used by the Viet Cong or North Vietnamese during the Vietnam war *US*
• —Linda Reinberg, *In the Field*, p. 182, 1991

red band; red-band *noun*
a prisoner with privileges; a trusty *UK, 1950*
• I was a Red Band, a trusty, who could move freely about the prison without having to be escorted by a screw. —Charles Raven, *Underworld Nights*, p. 26, 1956
• —Angela Devlin, *Prison Patter*, p. 96, 1996
• Both "red-bands" (trusted prisoners who wear a red armband to indicate their status), they hoped to progress to a less secure prison on the strength of their good conduct[.] —*The Guardian*, 27th April 2000: 'A life inside'

red biddy *noun*
cheap red wine; also a drink of cheap red wine and methylated spirits *UK, 1928*
• With some Red Biddy in a thermos flask, / St Trinian's then were Paradise enow. —James Laver, *The St. Trinian's Story*, p. 59, 1959
• —Ralph de Sola, *Crime Dictionary*, p. 127, 1982

red bike *noun*
the bleed period of the menstrual cycle *AUSTRALIA*
• riding the red bike —a correspondent, *The Museum of Menstruation and Women's Health*, May 2002

red bird *noun*

1 a capsule of secobarbital sodium (trade name Seconal™), a central nervous system depressant *US*
• [W]e have a pretty complete exhibit of the little pills downtown. Bluejays, redbirds, yellow jackets, goofballs, and all the rest of the list. —Raymond Chandler, *The Long Goodbye*, p. 230, 1953
• Well, let's see. I still got some redbirds and yellowjackets. —Emmett Grogan, *Final Score*, p. 81, 1976

2 the AH-1G Cobra helicopter *US*
Used purely as a gunship in the Vietnam war from 1971 until the end of the conflict.
• —Linda Reinberg, *In the Field*, p. 45, 1991

red blanket *noun*
the corpse of a person who has died with massive injuries *US*
• —*Maledicta*, p. 180, Summer/Winter 1986–1987: 'Sexual slang: prostitutes, pedophiles, flagellators, transvestites, and necrophiles'

red board *noun*
in horse racing, the official sign announcing that a race's results stand *US*
• —Walter Steigleman, *Horseracing*, p. 274, 1947

red box *noun*
an ambulance *US*
• —*Complete CB Slang Dictionary*, p. 76, 1976
• —Peter Chippindale, *The British CB Book*, p. 158, 1981

red bread *noun*
payment for donating blood *US*
• —Eugene Landy, *The Underground Dictionary*, p. 35, 1971

red bud *noun*
marijuana *UK*
• —Mike Haskins, *Drugs*, p. 288, 2003

Red Bull *nickname*
Black Label™ beer *SOUTH AFRICA*
Scamto youth street slang (South African townships).
• Black Label beer became tomato and then Red Bull – nothing to do with the energy drink. —Rebecca Harrison, *Reuters*, 8th February 2005

red bullet *nickname*
a capsule of secobarbital sodium (trade name Seconal™), a central nervous system depressant *US*
• —Walter L. Way, *The Drug Scence*, p. 113, 1977

red button *noun*
a foreman *US*
• —*American Speech*, p. 227, October 1955: 'An aircraft production dispatcher's vocabulary'

red can *noun*
a can of Melbourne Bitter™ beer *AUSTRALIA*
• —*www.abc.net.au/wordmap*, 2003

red cap *noun*
a member of the military police *UK, 1931*
From the red-topped cap that forms part of the uniform. Generally familiar from television drama series such as: *Red Cap* (ABC, 1964–66) and *Red Cap* (BBC, 2001–03).

red caps *noun*
crack cocaine *UK, 1998*
- —Mike Haskins, *Drugs*, p. 282, 2003

red cent *noun*
the lowest value denomination, hence the least amount possible *US, c. 1839*
A *copper* cent, thus 'red'.
- I wouldn't give you a red cent for all your rules[.]— *Mr Smith Goes to Washington*, 1939

Red Centre *noun*
the central desert regions of the Australian mainland *AUSTRALIA, 1935*
- Red Centre life, set in mountains, plains, and buoyant winter sunshine, has caught the imagination of the touring public more strikingly than any other Australian environment save the Great Barrier Reef. —Coralie Rees, *Spinifex Walkabout*, p. 240, 1953
- —Jim Ramsay, *Cop It Sweet!*, p. 76, 1977

red chamber club *noun*
the Senate in the Canadian Parliament *CANADA*
The source of the term is that the senate (the 'Red Chamber') has red carpets, leather chairbottoms and desk blotters.
- Diefenbaker picked out an obscure railway conductor from Kenora as the next member of the red chamber club. — *Canada Month*, p. 15/1, January 1963

red chenke *noun*
a light-skinned person; an unlikeable person *ANTIGUA AND BARBUDA*
- —Richard Allsopp, *Dictionary of Caribbean English Usage*, p. 469, 1996

red chicken *noun*
heroin, especially Chinese heroin *US, 1969*
- —Gilda and Melvin Berger, *Drug Abuse A-Z*, p. 114, 1990
- —Robert Ashton, *This Is Heroin*, p. 207, 2002

red cross *noun*
marijuana *UK*
- —Mike Haskins, *Drugs*, p. 288, 2003

red cunt hair *noun*
a very small unit of measure *US*
Sterling Johnson, in *English as a Second F*cking Language*, 1995, notes: 'The term originated with the master carpenters of Cape Cod and is now universally used'.
- —Carl Fleischhauer, *A Glossary of Army Slang*, p. 14, 1968
- It's a thin, red cunt hair away form the "oops" position, so I have a hard time with it. —Marc Animal MacYoung, *Fists, Wits, and a Wicked Right*, p. 25, 1991

redders *noun*
harness racers *AUSTRALIA*
Rhyming slang, from 'red hots' to 'trots'.
- —Ned Wallish, *The Truth Dictionary of Racing Slang*, p. 67, 1989

red devil *noun*
1 a capsule of secobarbital sodium (trade name Seconal™), a central nervous system depressant *US, 1959*
- The next step up the scale is Seconal ("reds" or "red devils"), a barbiturate normally used as a sedative. —Hunter S. Thompson, *Hell's Angels*, p. 216, 1966
- —Donald Louria, *Nightmare Drugs*, p. 25, 1966
- [A] barbiturate, called Red Devils, so called because of the color of the capsule and because they are reputed to possess a vicious kick[.] —Eldridge Cleaver, *Soul on Ice*, p. 27, 1968
- Jack, you're lucky. I just remembered, my sick old man is got some red devils from a script [forged prescription] at his pad. —Iceberg Slim (Robert Beck), *Trick Baby*, p. 268, 1969
- When he got to the car window I bought all the pills he had on him, red devils and secos and a few dexis. —Donald Goines, *Whoreson*, p. 211, 1972

2 a type of amphetamine tablet *UK*
- I've got some powder [cocaine] turning up tomorrow, but all I've got for now are speed pills called Red Devils. —Colin Butts, *Is Harry on the Boat?*, p. 114, 1997

3 heroin *UK*
- —Mike Haskins, *Drugs*, p. 284, 2003

4 a woman's menstrual period *US*
- —*American Speech*, p. 298, December 1954: 'The vernacular of menstruation'

red diaper baby *noun*
a person who was raised by Communist parents who instilled Communist beliefs and values *US*
- They have developed the so-called "red diaper baby" theory to explain it. —Tom Wolfe, *Radical Chic & Mau-Mauing the Flak Catchers*, p. 38, 1970
- Radosh was what radicals call a "red-diaper baby." He grew up in a fellow-traveling household, went to communist-run summer camps, and during college was active with the Labor Youth League[.] —*Washington Post*, p. T8, 22nd July 2001
- I was a red-diaper baby. Born in 1947, the year the House Un-American Activities Committee unleashed its vengeance on the film industry, I learned secrecy at my mother's knee. —*New York Times*, p. 3–8, 8th July 2001

reddies *noun*
▷ see: READIES

red dirt marijuana; red dirt *noun*
uncultivated marijuana *US, 1960*
- "That aint no ordinary loco-weed," said C.K., "...that there is red-dirt marijuana, that's what that is." —Terry Souther, *Red-Dirt Marijuana and Other Tastes*, 1967
- —Mike Haskins, *Drugs*, p. 288, 2003

red doll *noun*
a capsule of secobarbital sodium (trade name Seconal™), a central nervous system depressant *US*
- —Walter L. Way, *The Drug Scene*, p. 113, 1977

red dollars *noun*
US military scrip in Vietnam *US*
- —*Time*, p. 34, 10th December 1965
- —Carl Fleischhauer, *A Glossary of Army Slang*, p. 10, 1968

red dope *noun*
wild cannabis that has been sprayed with a bright red herbicide *US*
The colour plus **DOPE** (marijuana).
- The Oklahoma Bureau of Narcotics And Dangerous Drugs has issued a warning, advising people to stay away from "red dope". — *Mixmag*, p. 32, September 2001

red dot *noun*
▸ **the red dot**
the bleed period of the menstrual cycle *US*
- — *The Museum of Menstruation and Women's Health*, January 2001

red dot special *noun*
the bleed period of the menstrual cycle *US*
- [W]e noticed one day that a product called PMS Tea, an herbal tea for PMS relief, was actually on Red Dot Special at Stop and Shop! We have referred to our periods that way ever since. — *The Museum of Menstruation and Women's Health*, January 2001

red dragon *noun*
a variety of LSD *UK*
- —Angela Devlin, *Prison Patter*, p. 96, 1996

reddy *noun*
an Italian *UK, 1961*
May derive from **RADDIE** (an Italian living in London), or take root in Italian red wine.
▷ see: READY

red-eye *noun*
1 a long, aggressive stare *US*
- —Jennifer Blowdryer, *Modern English*, p. 37, 1985
- —Ann Lawson, *Kids & Gangs*, p. 56, 1994: 'Common African-American gang slang/phrases'

2 an overnight aeroplane flight, arriving at its destination early in the morning *US, 1968*
- Walter, I just put the little guys on the red eye to San Francisco. —Elmore Leonard, *Split Images*, p. 116, 1981
- I'll work in New york for a couple of days then I'll catch like a seven-o'clock plane out then I'll catch the Red-Eye back. —Richard Condon, *Prizzi's Honor*, p. 29, 1982
- I'll take the red-eye tomorrow night after rehearsal. —Dan Jenkins, *Life Its Ownself*, p. 69, 1984
- He had caught the ten p.m. redeye from San Francisco but had not even tried to nap on the plane[.] —Vincent Patrick, *Family Business*, p. 235, 1985
- Tonight. Yeah, the red-eye. I'll be in Arizona on Monday. —*Jerry Maguire*, 1996

3 potent, impure homemade alcohol, especially whisky *US, 1819*
- His animals needs are taken care of by a bowl of soup and as much red-eye as he can drink. —Jack Lait and Lee Mortimer, *Washington Confidential*, p. 33, 1951

4 fermented catsup *US*
A prison concoction.
- —John R. Armore and Joseph D. Wolfe, *Dictionary of Desperation*, p. 45, 1976

5 on the railways, a stop signal *US*
- —Norman Carlisle, *The Modern Wonder Book of Trains and Railroading*, p. 267, 1946

6 in pinball, an activated special scoring device, usually lit in red *US*
- —Bobbye Claire Natkin and Steve Kirk, *All About Pinball*, p. 115, 1977

7 a flashing red light on top of a police car *US*
- — Elementary Electronics, *Dictionary of CB Lingo*, p. 100, 1976

8 the anus *US*
- —Andy Anonymous, *A Basic Guide to Campusology*, p. 20, 1966
- —Collin Baker et al., *College Undergraduate Slang Study Conducted at Brown University*, p. 183, 1968
- Ben over and crack yo daddy some redeye, punk! —Seth Morgan, *Homeboy*, p. 179, 1990

Redfern *noun*
▸ **get off at Redfern**
to practise coitus interruptus *AUSTRALIA, 1956*
Redfern is the railway station immediately prior to Central Station, the principal station in Sydney.

red flag *noun*
1 an obvious indication that all is not well *US, 1968*
- Cap'n, the guard around that boxcar is a red flag. I don't understand why you officers don't recgonize a red flag when you see one. —William B. Hopkins, *One Bugle No Drum*, p. 80, 1986

2 when injecting a drug into a vein, the practice of drawing blood up into the syringe to verify the finding of a vein and to control the pace of the injection *US*
- —Carsten Stroud, *Close Pursuit*, p. 275, 1987

3 a show of menstrual blood on outer clothing; hence, the bleed period of the menstrual cycle *US*
- — *The Museum of Menstruation and Women's Health*, July 2001

▸ **be flying the red flag**
to be in the bleed period of the menstrual cycle *UK*
- You can come over, but I'm flying the red flag. —J.J. Connolly, *Layer Cake*, p. 291, 2000

red flag day *noun*
any day during the bleed period of a woman's menstrual cycle *UK*
- — *The Museum of Menstruation and Women's Health*, November 2000

red flag week *noun*
the bleed period of the menstrual cycle *CANADA*
Also used in Scotland.
- — *The Museum of Menstruation and Women's Health*, September 2000

red goddess *noun*
a firefighting vehicle that is generally used for training but made available (for operation by the military) when regular firefighters and their fire-engines are out of service *UK*
- Red goddesses, fire engines used for training and held in reserve by local authorities, joined the emergency fleet of green goddesses yesterday to cover for the second round of the firefighters' strike. — *The Guardian*, 23rd November 2002

red gunyon *noun*
smashed marijuana seeds or gum hashish smoked in a pipe *US*
- —David W. Maurer and Victor H. Vogel, *Narcotics and Narcotic Addiction*, p. 437, 1973

red head *noun*
a match *US*
- — *Maledicta*, p. 266–267, Summer/Winter 1981: 'By its slang, ye shall know it: the pessimism of prison life'

redheaded aunt from Red Bank *noun*
the bleed period of the menstrual cycle *US*
- —Karen Houppert, *The Curse*, 1999

redheaded friend *noun*
the bleed period of the menstrual cycle *US*
- —Karen Houppert, *The Curse*, 1999

Red Heart *nickname*
the central desert regions of the Australian mainland *AUSTRALIA, 1931*
- He sleeps now in the harsh Red Heart of Australia, so beloved of its people. —Ion L. Idriess, *Flynn of the Inland*, p. 244, 1956

red hot *noun*
1 a variety of MDMA, the recreational drug best known as ecstasy *UK*
- —Angela Devlin, *Prison Patter*, p. 96, 1996

2 a frankfurter *US*
- —Jack Lait and Lee Mortimer, *Chicago Confidential*, p. 302, 1950: 'Loop lexicon'

red hot *adjective*
extremely unfair *AUSTRALIA, 1896*
- RED 'OT – Unfair; extreme. —Gilbert H. Lawson, *A Dictionary of Australian Words and Terms*, 1924
- It's tough, I know. It's bloody red-hot! —Eric Lambert, *The Veterans*, p. 150, 1954

red hots *noun*
1 diarrhoea *UK*
Rhyming slang for **TROTS**.
- —Ray Puxley, *Cockney Rabbit*, 1992

2 trotting races *AUSTRALIA, 1966*
Rhyming slang for **TROTS**.
- —James Holledge, *The Great Australian Gamble*, p. 123, 1966
- —Jim Ramsay, *Cop It Sweet!*, p. 76, 1977
- —Gerald Sweeney, *The Plunge*, p. 46, 1981
- Don't tell me you're hooked on the red-hots again. —Frank Hardy, *Hardy's People*, p. 157, 1986

red Ibo *noun*
a light-skinned person of mixed black and white heritage *JAMAICA*
- —Richard Allsopp, *Dictionary of Caribbean English Usage*, p. 470, 1996

redi rocks *noun*
▹ see: **READY ROCKS**

red Leb *noun*
hashish with a reddish colour produced in the Lebanon *UK*
- It's called Red Leb. From the Lebanon. Red and soft. Feel. —Tony Wilson, *24 Hour Party People*, p. 66, 2002

red-leg *noun*
a poor white person *BARBADOS, 1892*
- —Frank A. Collymore, *Barbadian Dialect*, p. 92, 1965

red-legs *noun*
the artillery *US*
From the red stripes on the trousers of Union artillerymen during the US Civil War.
- —Ronald J. Glasser, *365 Days*, p. 244, 1971

red letter *noun*
a letter that is smuggled out of prison *UK*
- —Angela Devlin, *Prison Patter*, p. 96, 1996

red letter day *noun*
the day each cycle that the menstrual bleed commences *US*
A neat pun on the colour of blood and the date in a calendar.
- — *The Museum of Menstruation and Women's Health*, July 2001

red light *noun*
the bleed period of the menstrual cycle *US*
As in 'red light – stop – there will be no sex'.
- — *American Speech*, p. 298, December 1954: 'The vernacular of menstruation'

red-light *verb*
(used of a police car) to activate flashing lights and pull a vehicle off the road *US*
- — "Slingo", *The Official CB Slang Dictionary Handbook*, p. 49, 1976

red-light *adjective*
pertaining to prostitution *US, 1900*
- The District's "red-light" region may be the largest on earth. —Jack Lait and Lee Mortimer, *Washington Confidential*, p. 21, 1951

red lilly *noun*
a capsule of secobarbital sodium (trade name Seconal™); any central nervous system depressant *US*
From the colour of the capsule and the name of the manufacturer.
- —Donald Wesson and David Smith, *Barbiturates*, p. 121, 1977
- —Stanley M. Aronson, *Providence (Rhode Island) Journal-Bulletin*, p. 6B, 4th August 1997: 'Doctors must know the narcolexicon'

red line *noun*
in the used car business, the minimum which a dealer will accept for a car *US*
- Red line is calculated by adding (1) the amount paid for a car, (2) the pack, (3) any costs incurred in readying the car. Cars are seldom sold as low as red line. —Peter Mann, *How to Buy a Used Car Without Getting Gypped*, p. 194–195, 1975

red lips *noun*
a type of LSD *UK*
Possibly from an image printed on the drug.
- —Mike Haskins, *Drugs*, p. 286, 2003

Red Mary *noun*
the bleed period of the menstrual cycle *US*
- —Edith A. Folb, *runnin' down some lines*, p. 251, 1980

Red Mike *noun*
a woman-hater *CANADA*
Teen slang, reported by a Toronto newspaper in 1946, and reported as 'obsolescent or obsolete' by Douglas Leechman, 1959.

red Mitsubishi *noun*
PMA (*paramethoxyamphetamine*) or PMMA (*paramethoxy-methylamphetamine*) when taken as a recreational drug *UK, 2000*
- They had the Mitsubishi [Japanese car manufacturers] logo, were red, 7mm in diameter and 5mm thick and weighed 230mg. They were sold as "red Mitsubishi" or "killer" (!) —London Toxicology Group February 2002

redneck *noun*
a country-dweller, especially one whose views are considered bigoted by 'sophisticated' citizens *US, 1830*
Generally derogatory.
- I had an entree into the world of redneck small-town Australia[.] —Brian Preston, *Pot Planet*, p. 91, 2002

redneck radio *noun*
citizens' band radio *US*
- —Bill Davis, *Jawjacking*, p. 82, 1977

Red Ned *noun*
cheap red wine *AUSTRALIA, 1941*
- [B]ring half-a-dozen of beer, or a flagon of Red Ned. —John O'Grady, *Aussie Etiket*, p. 11, 1971
- —Arthur Chipper, *The Aussie Swearer's Guide*, p. 67, 1972
- —Jim Ramsay, *Cop It Sweet!*, p. 76, 1977

redner *noun*
▸ **take a redner**
to be embarrassed *IRELAND*
- It didn't take people long to suss out that I was mad into her. The way I'd drop her name, the way I'd take a redner whenever she was around. —Howard Paul, *The Joy*, p. 68, 1996

red nigger *noun*
a native American Indian *US*
- In May 1997, the state says Cilley, 19, and Smith, 20, drove by the home of a Passamaquoddy family in Indian Township in Washington County, yelling "prairie nigger," "red nigger" and "Indian nigger"[.] —*Portland (Maine) Press Herald*, p. 6A, 15th March 1998

red one *noun*
1 in carnival usage, a profitable engagement *US*
- —Sherman Louis Sergel, *The Language of Show Biz*, p. 181, 1973
- —Gene Sorrows, *All About Carnivals*, p. 25, 1985: 'Terminology'

2 a very short distance *US*
A euphemized abbreviation of **RED CUNT HAIR**.
- —A.B. Chance Co., *Lineman's Slang Dictionary*, p. 14, 1980

red onion *noun*
on the railways, an eating establishment *US*
- —Ramon Adams, *The Language of the Railroader*, p. 126, 1977

red-out *noun*
a flood of the colour red in your vision just before you pass out from lack of oxygen *US*
- It causes what is called "red out," a flood of red color in one's eyesight followed by a loss of consciousness. —Robert K. Wilcox, *Scream of Eagles*, p. 147, 1990

red-penny man *noun*
a procurer of prostitutes, a pimp *AUSTRALIA*
- —*The (Sydney) Bulletin*, 26th April 1975

red phosphorus *noun*
smokeable metamphetamine *UK*
From a process in the synthesis of the drug.
- —Mike Haskins, *Drugs*, p. 279, 2003

red pill *noun*
▸ **take the red pill**
to go all-out for the active option *UK*
From a choice between reality and euphoria offered in the film *The Matrix* (1999).
- Are we clubbing? Come on – take the red pill. —*Word*, p. 88, July 2005

red pussy hair *noun*
a very short distance *US*
Slightly less offensive than **RED CUNT HAIR**.
- "That Benzo missed her ass by a red pussy hair." "Why red?" "Don't you know, it's the finest." —Robert Campbell, *Alice in La-La Land*, p. 11, 1987

red-ragger *noun*
a Communist *AUSTRALIA, 1916*
- Old Mother Boag didn't like the idea of her girls going out with a couple of red-raggers. —Shane Maloney, *Nice Try*, p. 108, 1998

red-ragging *adjective*
Communist *AUSTRALIA, 1938*
- Jack McGarity may be a flamin' Bolshevik with red-ragging ideas that are a menace to every honest man[.] —Dymphna Cusack, *Picnic Races*, p. 22, 1962

red rattler *noun*
a type of passenger train with dark red carriages that became noisy when travelling at speed *AUSTRALIA, 1981*
- They always missed the 8.03 a.m. from Ormond, starting their traditional dash from station to station in a race against time and a Victorian Railways red rattler. —Kerry Cue, *Crooks, Chooks and Bloody Ratbags*, p. 5, 1983

red river *noun*
the bleed period of a woman's menstrual cycle *US*
- —*American Speech*, p. 298, December 1954: 'The vernacular of menstruation'

red rock *noun*
granulated heroin originating in China; heroin generally *US, 1969*
- —Gilda and Melvin Berger, *Drug Abuse A-Z*, p. 114, 1990
- —Robert Ashton, *This Is Heroin*, p. 207, 2002

red rock opium *noun*
a mixture of heroin, barbital, strychnine and caffeine *UK*
- —Robert Ashton, *This Is Heroin*, p. 210, 2002

red rum *noun*
1 a variety of heroin *UK*
An allusion to the qualities of the legendary racehorse (steeple-chaser Red Rum won the UK Grand National a record three times). Also rhyming slang for 'dumb' and 'murder' spelt backwards.
- He overdosed on a cocaine and heroin "speedball" made with a particularly lethal strain of heroin nicknamed Red Rum. —*Uncut*, p. 62, May 2001

2 a mixture of heroin, barbital, strychnine and caffeine *UK*
Also known as **RED ROCK OPIUM** from which this may be formed by elision; it is interesting to note with regard to the dangerous nature of this cocktail that 'red rum' is 'murder' backwards.
- —Robert Ashton, *This Is Heroin*, p. 210, 2002

red rush *noun*
amyl nitrite *UK*
- —Angela Devlin, *Prison Patter*, p. 96, 1996

reds *noun*
1 the bleed period of the menstrual cycle *US*
- The reds are in. —Karen Houppert, *The Curse*, 1999

2 a sense of anger *US*

- "It gives me the Reds" means it makes me angry. — *Newsweek*, 8th October 1951

red sails in the sunset

the bleed period of the menstrual cycle *AUSTRALIA*

- What's up, Blanchie, are yous red sails in the sunset or something? — Barry Humphries, *The Wonderful World of Barry McKenzie*, p. 21, 1968
- — Sonya Plowman, *Great Kiwi Slang*, p. 153, 2002

red seal *noun*

a variety of cannabis resin *UK*

Branded with a red seal.

- — Angela Devlin, *Prison Patter*, p. 96, 1996
- — The New Initiatives Project, *The Grass aint always Greena [a report of a Drug Education Programme]*, p. 9, April 1998
- It was red seal and two of us were sick. — *Ministry*, p. 34, October 2002

Red Sea pedestrian *noun*

a Jewish person *UK*

Offensive, intended as jocular; from the crossing of the Red Sea (Exodus 14: 21–22).

- BRIAN: I'm not a Roman, Mum, and I never will be! I'm a Kike! A Yid! A Hebe! A Hook-nose! I'm Kosher, Mum! I'm a Red Sea Pedestrian, and proud of it! — Monty Python, *Life of Brian*, 1979

red shirt *noun*

1 a troublemaker *US*

- "What's a red shirt?" "That's an old expression for troublemaker. If you fell out of line too many times they issued you a red shirt. Then whenever there was trouble on the yard the gun bulls had orders to shoot the cons in the red shirts first." — Malcolm Braly, *On the Yard*, p. 296, 1967

2 a volunteer firefighter *US*

- — *American Speech*, p. 273, December 1954: 'Fire terms: additional words and definitions'

3 a college athlete who, because he did not play in his freshman year, may matriculate and play at the varsity level for a fifth year *US, 1950*

- — Howard B. Bonham, *Football Lingo*, p. 41, 1962
- — *American Speech*, Fall-Winter 1970

4 in roller derby, a skater who engages in rough, 'bad guy' tactics *US*

- If the red-shirt team wins, the skaters on that team must run off the track after the final whistle, partly to make them look cowardly but also for safety reasons, especially if the crowd starts to queue menacingly toward the track. — Keith Coppage, *Roller Derby to Rollerjam*, p. 127, 1999

5 a professional wrestler who is regularly scripted to lose matches to advance the careers of other wrestlers *US*

redskin *noun*

in a deck of playing cards, any face card *US*

- — Albert H. Morehead, *The Complete Guide to Winning Poker*, p. 271, 1967

red snapper *noun*

in blackjack, a dealt hand of two red cards that add up to 21 *US*

- — Frank Scoblete, *Best Blackjack*, p. 272, 1996

Red Sox are in town

experiencing the bleed period of the menstrual cycle *US*

The colour of blood signals this euphemistic adoption of the Boston baseball team.

- — *The Museum of Menstruation and Women's Health*, March 2001

red squad *noun*

a police unit that engages in systematic investigation and record-keeping about leftist political and social action organisations unrelated to criminal conduct *US*

- The antisubversives unit of the Chicago Police Department – known popularly as the Red Squad – has become something of a legend on the shores of Lake Michigan. — J. Anthony Lukas, *The Barnyard Epithet and Other Obscenities*, p. 55, 1970
- In Chicago and Los Angeles and other big cities in the 1960s, police departments had Red Squads that were notorious for spying on leftwing political activists. — *The Progressive*, 14th March 2002

red steer *noun*

a bushfire *AUSTRALIA, 1936*

- [H]adn't he patented the special extinguisher to end the blight of the red steer for all time? — Frank Hardy, *The Outcasts of Foolgarah*, p. 118, 1971

red stuff *noun*

gold *UK*

- Everything was where it was supposed to be, some very fair pussies [furs] and nice tom [jewellery], including quite a bit of "red stuff"[.] — Charles Raven, *Underworld Nights*, p. 169, 1956

reds under the bed *noun*

the communist presence lurking in Western society *UK, 1972*

- Ted Heath had blamed the ruin of the country on "Reds under the bed"[.] — Mark Steel, *Reasons to be Cheerful*, p. 9, 2001

red tape *noun*

excessive formality; bureaucratic obstacles *UK, 1837*

Originally a literal term, referring to the red-coloured tape used in securing legal documents; later used figuratively.

- You know what a stickler she is for procedure – "red-tape" I called it to her – I can tell you she was almost in tears. — Terry Southern, *Flash and Filigree*, p. 55, 1958
- It's a hard life down there so they learn to cut through the U.S. red tape. — Joseph Wambaugh, *Finnegan's Week*, p. 143, 1993

red tide *noun*

1 hordes of communists seen as ready to overwhelm Western civilisation *US*

- From the Korean War, where he got his second Pulitzer, he [Homer Bigart] described a "Red tide" of North Korean soldiers closing in on American troops, "silently and relentlessly, the faces of the Communist infantrymen showing neither fear nor elation." — *The Washington Post*, p. C6, 18th April 1991

2 the bleed period of the menstrual cycle *US*

- — Karen Houppert, *The Curse*, 1999
- — Don R. McCreary (Editor), *Dawg Speak*, 2001

red-top *noun*

a tabloid newspaper at the more populist end of the readership *UK, 1997*

From the red masthead characteristic of such papers.

- Three red-tops (so far) had come up with the "exclusive" ploy[.] — Christopher Brookmyre, *Boiling a Frog*, p. 296, 2000

reducer *noun*

in gin, any card drawn or held for the sole purpose of reducing the number of points in unmatched cards in a hand *US*

- — Irwin Steig, *Play Gin to Win*, p. 141,

red up; rid up *verb*

to clear and clean a table after eating *CANADA*

- In the northern parts of our Maritimes including the Gaspe, to rid up or red up is to clean the table after a meal and make it all tidy for the next meal. — Bill Casselman, *Canadian Food Words*, p. 173, 1998

red wedge *noun*

the bleed period of the menstrual cycle *UK*

Combines 'red', for the colour of blood, with a pun on conventional 'wedge' (something that fills a gap) and 'wedgie' (a trick with underpants) suggesting underwear; the whole being a play on Red Wedge (a 1980s alliance of musicians and actors with the UK Labour party).

- Ladies get da "red wedge" once every three weeks, tho sometimes more often. Mejulie for hexample tells me she has got it at least a couple of times every week. — Sacha Baron-Cohen, *Da Gospel According to Ali G*, 2001

red week *noun*

the bleed period of the menstrual cycle *US*

- — *The Museum of Menstruation and Women's Health*, May 2001

red, white and blue *noun*

a shoe *UK*

Rhyming slang.

- — *Daily Telegraph magazine*, 17th December 1972

red wings *noun*

sexual intercourse or oral sex with a woman who is experiencing the bleed period of the menstrual cycle *US*

From motorcycle gang culture.

- Six or seven of us earned our red wings that evening. — Jamie Mandelkau, *Buttons*, p. 91, 1971
- You got your Red Wings by eating a girl on her period and your Black Wings by eating a black girl. — Ralph "Sonny" Barger, *Hell's Angel*, p. 99, 2000
- "Not today, H, I can't, the painters are in. I'll be OK tomorrow." "I don't mind getting me red wings." "You filthy sod." — Garry Bushell, *The Face*, p. 202, 2001

reeb *noun*

beer *UK, 1859*

Back slang, noted as current in the UK due to its use in the US, possibly reinvigorated by *The Simpsons* television cartoon.

- —David Powis, *The Signs of Crime*, 1977
- —Connie Eble (Editor), *UNC-CH Campus Slang*, p. 7, Fall 1997

reebs *noun*

marijuana *US*

- —Connie Eble (Editor), *UNC-CH Campus Slang*, p. 8, Fall 1988

reeds *noun*

long shorts, favoured by surfers *US*

- —John Blair, *The Illustrated Discography of Surf Music 1961–1965*, p. 124, 1985

reef *noun*

a marijuana cigarette *US*

- I don't touch reefs that come out of the bargain basement. If they're good, then I'm hip—Morton Cooper, *High School Confidential*, p. 69, 1958

reef *verb*

1 to fondle another person's genitals *UK, 1962*

Probably from the earlier sense 'to pick a pocket'.

- The back row of the cinema was occupied with hot bodies reefing each other[.]—Brian McDonald, *Elephant Boys*, p. 224, 2000
- —Paul Baker, *Polari*, p. 188, 2002

2 to remove something from someone's pocket *US*

- —Vincent J. Monteleone, *Criminal Slang*, p. 191, 1949

reefdogger *noun*

a marijuana cigarette *US*

- So like I hide these reefdoggers in a shoebox, like my mom finds them and she's tries to be real cas, right.—Mary Corey and Victoria Westermark, *Fer Shurr! How to be a Valley Girl*, 1982

reefer *noun*

1 a marijuana cigarette *US, 1931*

Almost certainly from the Spanish word meaning 'to twist'. Still used, with a nostalgic air to it.

- Later they smoked the reefers in Panama, and when World War II took them to bases in Ecuador, the hop habit they brought was the answer to a medicine man's prayers.—*Time*, p. 40–41, 14th October 1946
- They're reefers. If you're gonna smoke y'might's well get a kick out it.—Max Shulman, *The Amboy Dukes*, p. 3, 1947
- ... white women learned where they could get a "betl," a "jolt," or a "gow." Reefer-smokers are called "gowsters."—Jack Lait, *New York Confidential*, p. 119, 1948
- I lost ground so fast you'd think I was a juvenile delinquent trying her first reefer.—Philip Wylie, *Opus 21*, p. 287, 1949
- She ran across the rug to the dresser and searched in her purse for the reefers Lukey had given her[.]—George Mandel, *Flee the Angry Strangers*, p. 117, 1952
- Biff took the reefers and held out some bills.—Bernard Wolfe, *The Late Risers*, p. 227, 1954
- Good God! Dirty pictures in the second grade! What's your next project – reefers?—Max Shulman, *Rally Round the Flag, Boys!*, p. 21, 1957
- "He promised to let me have some stuff." "What sort of stuff? Reefers?" "No. A deck of H."—Douglas Rutherford, *The Creeping Flesh*, p. 102, 1963
- Shorty talked to me out of the corner of his mouth: which hustlers – standing around, or playing at this or that table – sold "reefers," or had just come out of prison, or were "second-story men."—Malcolm X and Alex Haley, *The Autobiography of Malcolm X*, p. 45, 1964
- When I came home, Kid and Butch and Danny weren't smoking reefers any more.—Claude Brown, *Manchild in the Promised Land*, p. 102, 1965
- Reefers at that time cost two for fifteen cents, or you could cop a crescent for two bits.—A.S. Jackson, *Gentleman Pimp*, p. 13, 1973
- They all take a drag on their reefers / And say prayers to St. Konky Mohair.—Dennis Wepman et al., *The Life*, p. 107, 1976
- The dried hash crumbled easily onto a Rizla cigarette paper and was mixed with tobacco to be rolled into a joint, which in those days was called a reefer.—Simon Napier-Bell, *Black Vinyl White Powder*, p. 3, 2001

2 marijuana *US, 1931*

- It was like waiting for the accentuated heart beat of your heart when you're on a reefer jag[.[—Mezz Mezzrow, *Really the Blues*, p. 181, 1946
- Two other developments in the street – said to be normal consequences of its jazz madness – are the presence of reefer (marijuana) addicts and homosexuals, of all races.—Jack Lait and Lee Mortimer, *New York Confidential*, p. 45, 1948
- We could sell them for about three or four dollars and buy a bag of reefer. We'd roll up and get high and then go do something crazy... —Claude Brown, *Manchild in the Promised Land*, p. 130, 1965
- I smoked reefer for five years before I even knew what heroin was. —Nathan Heard, *Howard Street*, p. 183, 1968
- We bought three cans of reefer for fifty dollars, and split the rest of the money.—Donald Goines, *Whoreson*, p. 36, 1972
- "I wasn't a college researcher, I was a crazy street whitey," Gravenites said. "Lotta times I carried a pistol. The South Side was my turf. I scored a lot of reefer there..."—*Rolling Stone*, p. 18, 15th March 1973
- It took Bobby Shy the rest of the day to locate a whole lid of Colombian reefer.—Elmore Leonard, *52 Pick-up*, p. 133, 1974
- Man, someone's tokin' some reefer.—*Dazed and Confused*, 1993

3 a refrigerator; a refrigerated railway wagon *US, 1914*

- I'd caught one of these hiball reefer trains and continued the balance of the journey by rail.—Neal Cassady, *The First Third*, p. 203, February 1951
- [W]e didn't know whether they were going east or west or how to find out or what boxcars and flats and de-iced reefers to pick, and so on. —Jack Kerouac, *On the Road*, p. 19, 1957
- One minute you're sleeping it off in the TV room or shootin' craps in the reefer and the next minute you're the sheriff of Cochise.—Darryl Ponicsan, *The Last Detail*, p. 21, 1970
- Cab-over Pete with a reefer on—C.W. McCall, *Convoy*, 1976
- This enabled the refrigerated "reefer" trucks to avoid convoy dust and allowed them more off-loading time at destination.—Shelby L. Stanton, *The Rise and Fall of an American Army*, p. 276, 1985

4 a pickpocket *US*

- —Vincent J. Monteleone, *Criminal Slang*, p. 192, 1949

reefer madness *noun*

a unusually great appetite or determined devotion to the use of marijuana *AUSTRALIA*

An ironic adoption of the title of a 1936 film that famously exposed the immoral excesses of marijuana addicts.

- "I used to smoke ten joints a day, with acid at the weekends..." Soul-searching is a spin-off from reefer madness.—Richard Neville writing in 'Nation Review', 1975, *Out Of My Mind*, p. 33, 1996

reefer room *noun*

in a morgue, a refrigerated room where bodies are stored *US*

- She went past the reefer room where the bodies were frozen after the M.E. had opened them up.—Stephen J. Cannell, *King Con*, p. 62, 1997

reegie *noun*

a police officer in the Regional Crime Squad *UK*

- In desperation, the Reegie place an advertisement in the personal columns of The Sun newspaper[.]—Duncan MacLaughlin, *The Filth*, p. 228–229, 2002

reeker *noun*

a bad-smelling hospital casualty department patient *US*

- —*Journal of American Folklore*, p. 568–581, January–March 1978: 'The gomer'

reek-ho *adjective*

drunk *UK*

- —*e-cyclopaedia*, 20th March 2002

reekstick *noun*

a conventional tobacco cigarette laced with cocaine *UK*

- —Mike Haskins, *Drugs*, p. 293, 2003

reel *verb*

▸ **reel someone in**

to triumph over gullibility, especially regarding a piece of trivial teasing *UK*

Often accompanied by the action of reeling in a fish; sometimes the action may replace the words.

- DENISE: What did you invite him for? He's a right nobhead. Tell you what, if he's going I'm not. DAVE MIMICS REELING IN A FISH. DAVE: Reel her in. One-nil. ALL BUT DENISE LAUGH.—Caroline Aherne and Craig Cash, *The Royle Family*, 1999

reeling and rocking *noun*

a stocking *UK*

Rhyming slang, inspired by the fashions of the rock 'n' roll era; usually seen in pairs.

- —Ray Puxley, *Cockney Rabbit*, 1992

reels *adjective*

without money *AUSTRALIA*

Rhyming slang, from 'reels of cotton' to 'rotten' (without money).

- —Ned Wallish, *The Truth Dictionary of Racing Slang*, p. 67, 1989

reels of cotton *adjective*

rotten *UK*

Rhyming slang.

- —Ronnie Barker, *Fletcher's Book of Rhyming Slang*, 1979
- The job was okay once but since they stopped the overtime it's all gone reels of cotton.—Ray Puxley, *Cockney Rabbit*, 1992

reet; reat *adjective*

good, pleasing *US, 1934*

- "You're really reet," he said as he guided her closer to the curb where they could speak without obstructing the sidewalk. —Irving Shulman, *The Amboy Dukes*, p. 136, 1947
- [O]utdressing everybone on the block in the uniform of the period, pork-pie hat, satin shirt, peg pants, reat jacket. Zoot, man. —Clancy Sigal, *Going Away*, p. 462, 1961

reeve *verb*

to cheat *CANADA*

- As a reeve was a public official in Nova Scotia (some towns even had a hog reeve!), this term as a verb has come to mean "cheat" because of a long-standing tradition of corruption in local politics. —Lewis Poteet, *The South Shore Phrase Book*, p. 91, 1999

ref *noun*

in a sporting contest, a *ref*eree *UK, 1899?*

- He headbutts the Ref, who falls to the floor. —Paul Fraser and Shane Meadows, *TwentyFourSeven*, p. 96, 1997

ref *verb*

in a sporting context, to *ref*eree *UK, 1929?*

- Right, next pair start [boxing]. Tim, you ref[.] —Paul Fraser and Shane Meadows, *TwentyFourSeven*, p. 44, 1997

reffo *noun*

a migrant to Australia who is a refugee from their home country *AUSTRALIA, 1941*

- And since when have you reffos been entitled to teach us Australians about manners. —Barry Humphries, *A Nice Night's Entertainment*, p. 103, 1968
- —Jim Ramsay, *Cop It Sweet!*, p. 77, 1977
- —Barry Humphries, *A Nice Night's Entertainment*, p. 209, 1981
- —Shane Maloney, *Nice Try*, p. 179, 1998

refusenik *noun*

a non-conformist *UK*

Adopted without a full understanding from the name given in 1970s to Jews in the Soviet Union who were refused permission to emigrate to Israel.

- For "homosexual refuseniks", as the Duckie organisers call them[.] — *The Guardian*, p. 15, 14th May 2002

reg *noun*

1 a regular customer or guest *UK*

- And the Billies [customers] are mainly regs and all, too. —Kevin Sampson, *Outlaws*, p. 64, 2001

2 marijuana of average quality *US, 1973*

An abbreviation of 'regular'. The variant 'regs' also exists.

- —Richard A. Spears, *The Slang and Jargon of Drugs and Drink*, p. 421, 1986
- —Mike Haskins, *Drugs*, p. 289, 2003

regale *noun*

a festive occasion *CANADA*

The term is adopted from French, where it has a similar meaning.

- McMillan seized upon the advent of All Saint's Day, November 1, as an excuse for a regale. —B.A. McKelvie, *Fort Langley*, p. 34, 1947

reggaematic *adjective*

in or of a reggae style *UK*

- Now some rant it, some chant it / like me, some do it reggaematic, / Some rap it up and rap it out[.] —Benjamin Zephaniah, *Rappid Rapping*, p. 38, 1992

reggin *noun*

a black person *US*

The offensive **NIGGER** spelt backwards.

- — *Maledicta*, p. 266–267, Summer/Winter 1981: 'By its slang, ye shall know it: the pessimism of prison life'

Reg Grundies; grundies; grunds; reginalds; reggies *noun*

underwear *AUSTRALIA*

Rhyming slang, playing on **UNDIES**, formed from the name Reg Grundy, an Australian televison producer.

- "Just pop all your clothes off and I'll be right back." I should have known she meant everything, even the reginalds. —*Sydney Morning Herald (Good Living)*, p. 1, 7th August 1984
- —David McGill, *David McGill's Complete Kiwi Slang Dictionary*, p. 53, 1998
- You'd have to have a few 'roos loose in the top paddock not to want to come and join us, 'cos it's the most fun you can have with your reg grundies on. — *Australian Ultimate*, p. 7, 2003

Regiment *noun*

▸ **the Regiment**

the SAS (22 Special Air Service regiment) *UK*

- It was only later I found out that to people in it, or who work with it, it's not the "Sass" or even the SAS. It's just called the Regiment. —Andy McNab, *Immediate Action*, p. 32, 1995

regmaker; reggie *noun*

a drink, pick-me-up or medication taken to relieve (or 'cure') a hangover *SOUTH AFRICA, 1954*

A compound of Afrikaans *reg* (right) and English '-maker'.

- And a little "regmaker" for your depressions. —Athol Fugard, *The Road to Mecca*, 1985
- [H]e would drink a bottle of champagne in the mornings as a regmaker for the excesses of the previous night. — *Sunday Times (South Africa)*, 7th November 1999

rego; reggo *noun*

vehicle registration *AUSTRALIA, 1967*

- Hey, don't forget your bloody car reggo Susie. —Kathy Lette, *Girls' Night Out*, p. 144, 1987
- It only passed rego because Deano Davies plays on our side (Deano's old man is the local copper). —Phillip Gwynne, *Deadly Unna?*, p. 15, 1998

regreen *verb*

while working in the office of the US Department of Defense, to receive an update briefing on affairs in the army *US*

- — Department of the Army, *Staff Officer's Guidebook*, p. 64, 1986

regroup *verb*

to recover from a surprise or a setback *US*

- — *Current Slang*, p. 6, Winter 1966

regs *noun*

*reg*ulations *UK*

Military in origin.

- —Angela Devlin, *Prison Patter*, p. 96, 1996
- When prison regs permitted men's families to bring them shoes and clothes from home, I insisted on wearing the sloppy clothes that the system furnished me. —Ralph "Sonny" Barger, *Hell's Angel*, p. 196, 2000

regular *noun*

1 a prisoner who serves his sentence with dignity and strength *US*

- —Paul Glover, *Words from the House of the Dead*, 1974

2 a skateboarder who skates with the left foot to the front *UK*

- —Fabrice le Mao, *Skateboarding*, p. 92, 2004

regular *adjective*

1 complete; absolute; thorough *UK, 1821*

- RAY BONES: (IGNORING HIM) Chili Palmer. (SMILES) Chilly outside. Chili inside. It's a regular fuckin' chili-fest. Hey, waiter – give Mr. Chili Pepper a big fuckin' bowl of chili! —Scott Frank, from the 1991 novel by Elmore Leonard, *Get Shorty*, 1996

2 kind; decent; honest *US*

- What a relief – here was a keeper who talked my language. I was ready to scrub that cell with my tongue for a guy as regular as that. —Mezz Mezzrow, *Really the Blues*, p. 306, 1946

regular P *noun*

crack cocaine *UK, 1998*

- —Mike Haskins, *Drugs*, p. 282, 2003

regulars *noun*

common black ants *BARBADOS*

- —Frank A. Collymore, *Barbadian Dialect*, p. 92, 1965

rehab *noun*

*rehab*ilitation (a medical regime for the cure of alcohol and drug addiction); also, the clinic or hospital environment where *rehab*ilitation takes place *UK, 1961*

Both senses may serve concurrently.

- He's the one who made a small name for himself coming out of rehab a few years back. —John Birmingham, *The Tasmanian Babes Fiasco*, p. 154, 1997
- "May we should book him into rehab." "I heard that, dude. That's a bummer idea. Those people in rehab are weird. They're like real downers. They're all, like, druggies." —Janet Evanovich, *Seven Up*, p. 72, 2001
- Vicodin first hit the news in the US when Friends star Matthew Perry's addiction saw him check in and out of rehab on an almost monthly basis. — *Drugs An Adult Guide*, p. 25, December 2001

rehash *verb*

in the circus or carnival, to resell ticket stubs to patrons and pocket the funds *US*

- —Joe McKennon, *Circus Lingo*, p. 77, 1980

rehitch *verb*
to re-enlist; to re-marry *US*
- Your correspondent is all fluttery at the news that Terry and Sulvia Lennox have rehitched at Las Vegas, the dears. —Raymond Chandler, *The Long Goodbye*, p. 13, 1953

reindeer dust *noun*
any powdered drug; cocaine; heroin *US, 1942*
A play on **SNOW**.
- —Hyman E. Goldin et al., *Dictionary of American Underworld Lingo*, p. 176, 1950
- Do you go for Chinese needlework, reindeer dust [powdered drugs], Texas tea [marijuana] – that kind of stuff? —Douglas Rutherford, *The Creeping Flesh*, p. 49, 1963
- —Robert Ashton, *This Is Heroin*, p. 207, 2002
- —Mike Haskins, *Drugs*, p. 284, 2003

reject *noun*
a socially inept person; a pathetic individual; a person who does not fit in with the fashionable, trendy majority *US*
- —Collin Baker et al., *College Undergraduate Slang Study Conducted at Brown University*, p. 183, 1968
- On their lonesomes they're not total rejects. —Kathy Lette, *Girls' Night Out*, p. 192, 1987

relate *verb*
to understand; to like or appreciate someone or something *US*
A quintessential, over-used vague verb of the 1960s.
- —Lawrence Lipton, *The Holy Barbarians*, p. 317, 1959
- A sister sent in a report that she got kicked out of the party because she refused to relate to a particular brother. —Bobby Seale, *A Lonely Rage*, p. 230, 1978

relay spot *noun*
a room with a telephone used to relay calls placing bets in a bookmaking operation *US*
- "Is it a relay spot? Are you sure?" asked Charlie. —Joseph Wambaugh, *The Blue Knight*, p. 56, 1973

release *noun*
in the coded language of massage parlours, ejaculation *US*
A 2002 Incident Report from the Sausalito (California) Police Department describes the activities at a local massage parlour as follows: 'Every massage ends with some type of "release" (orgasm). The release is accomplished by the employee masturbating the client to an orgasm'.

release *verb*
▸ **release a chocolate hostage**
to defecate *UK*
- I'm just nipping out to release a chocolate hostage. — *www.London-Slang.com*, June 2002

▸ **release the hounds**
to defecate *US*
- —Chris Lewis, *The Dictionary of Playground Slang*, p. 61, 2003

relievers *noun*
shoes *US*
- —Joseph E. Ragen and Charles Finston, *Inside the World's Toughest Prison*, p. 815, 1962: 'Penitentiary and underworld glossary'

re-light *noun*
a cigarette butt retrieved and smoked *US*
- —John Fahs, *Cigarette Confidential*, p. 303, 1996: 'Glossary'

religious issue *noun*
in computing, a topic that is bound to launch an endless debate which cannot be resolved *US*
- —Eric S. Raymond, *The New Hacker's Dictionary*, p. 303, 1991

rellie *noun*
a *rel*ation, a *rel*ative *AUSTRALIA, 1981*
- MAYBE THE RELLIES ARE truly freezing their cojones off back in Tulsa[.] — *Metropolitan [San Francisco]*, 18th January 1999
- my lovely wife [...] and my gorgeous children and all my soft, lairy mates and rellies —Kevin Sampson, *Outlaws*, p. 310, 2001

rello; relo *noun*
a *rel*ative *AUSTRALIA*
- The rellos have departed. —Kathy Lette, *Girls' Night Out*, p. 121, 1987
- Birthdays are spac. All your relos come over (relos are people you hate more than anyone) and you have a rotten day. —Kylie Mole (Maryanne Fahey), *My Diary*, p. 3, 1988

reload *verb*
to give the victim of a confidence trick or fraudulent gambling game a false sense of confidence, then cheat the by-now willing victim of all he or she possesses *UK*
- —David Powis, *The Signs of Crime*, 1977

rels *noun*
*rel*atives *AUSTRALIA, 1991*
- But hang on – you haven't got any rels named 'John'. —Kel Richards, *The Aussie Bible*, p. 12, 2003

Rembrandt *noun*
in poker, a hand of face cards *US*
- —George Percy, *The Language of Poker*, p. 74, 1988

remf *noun*
a soldier assigned to a combat support role *US*
Acronym of a '*r*ear-*e*chelon *m*other*f*ucker'.
- I been humpin ruck in those mountains while you been suckin down whiskey at the NCO club. I know my shit. Man, and I do my job better'n any mother-fucking REMF. —John Del Vecchio, *The 13th Valley*, p. 25, 1982
- Hence those who never went to the front line, but stayed with the echelon were known as "Remfs" or Rear Echelon Mother Fuckers. —Robert McGowan and Jeremy Hands, *Don't Cry For Me Sergeant-Major*, p. 81, 1983
- You're talking like a VC. Jesus, the guy was just some hotdog REMF who wanted a reason to pop some caps somewhere beside the shooting range. —Jack Hawkins, *Chopper One #2*, p. 104, 1987
- He had gone over – become a REMF. As we wandered back toward the platoon tent, Martinez found his voice. "I'd like to have a nice safe job in the rear, but no way could I handle that sucking up business." —Robert Peterson, *Rites of Passage*, p. 473, 1997

Remington warrior *noun*
a rear support troop *US*
Named after the Remington typewriter, the 'warrior's weapon'.
- —Gregory Clark, *Words of the Vietnam War*, p. 426, 1990

remish *noun*
remission (of a prison sentence) *UK*
- —Frank Norman, *Bang to Rights*, 1958

remodel *verb*
in car repair, to damage a vehicle or part severely *US*
- I see you remodeled your front end. —Lewis Poteet, *Car & Motorcycle Slang*, p. 162, 1992

remould *noun*
a sex-change operation *UK*
- —Paul Baker, *Polari*, p. 188, 2002
- —*Attitude*, p. 60, July 2003: 'Old palare lexicon'

Ren and Stimpy *noun*
the female breasts *UK*
Ren and Stimpy are shamelessly gross cartoon characters created by John Kricfalusi, first seen in 1991.
- —*Sky Magazine*, July 2001

Ren Cen *nickname*
the Renaissance Center in Detroit, Michigan *US*
An expensive, bold and risky attempt to revive the dying Detroit central district in the 1970s.

rendered *adjective*
drunk *UK*
- —*e-cyclopaedia*, 20th March 2002

renk *adjective*
impudent; offhand; rude; yobbish *JAMAICA*
Variation of 'rank' (offensive).
- Jigsy listened to Easy-Love, whose attitude had become renk in the last few days. —Karline Smith, *Moss Side Massive*, p. 123, 1994
- [H]e had clearly heard the black driver say "renk" and was familiar enough with Jamaican patois to know what it meant. —Donald Gorgon, *Cop Killer*, p. 39, 1994

Reno *noun*
in bar dice games, two dice that add up to seven *US*
- —Gil Jacobs, *The World's Best Dice Games*, p. 200, 1976

renob *noun*
a person who acts foolishly *US*
- —Don R. McCreary (Editor), *Dawg Speak*, 2001

rent *noun*

1 a youthful, attractive homosexual male prostitute *UK, 1967*

- — Bruce Rodgers, *The Queens' Vernacular*, p. 111, 1972
- — *Maledicta*, p. 220, 1979: 'Kinks and queens: linguistic and cultural aspects of the terminology for gays'

2 road tax *UK*

Motor trade slang, reported by a car salesman, 4th August 2004.

▸ **up me for the rent!**

used to register pleasurable astonishment *AUSTRALIA*

- Up me for the rent sport. If the Mildred Folingsby Marriage Bureau didn't send you. — Barry Humphries, *Bazza Pulls It Off!*, 1971

renta- *prefix*

hired, *rented* *US, 1921*

In commercial usage often used to create a company name, for instance: 'Rentacar' (examples found in Australia, Ireland, Spain, UK, US) and 'Rentavan' (examples found in Australia, Ireland, Mexico, UK). Both 'rentacar' and 'rentavan' are also used informally of a hired vehicle. Other use is often derogatory: 'rentacrowd' (a hired clique), 'rentamob' (a crowd assembled at political demonstration) and 'rentamouth' (a speaker for hire).

- The reply was just another Downing Street rentamissive [an impersonal letter]. — *The Guardian*, 25th June 1982
- The networks and the news agencies already had their seismological rentaquote vacancies filled[.] — Christopher Brookmyre, *Not the End of the World*, p. 58, 1998
- That the revelations of recent weeks might suddenly prove them right is of no consequence to the renta-gobs [hired speakers][.] — *The Guardian*, 25th July 2003

rent-a-cop *noun*

a private security guard *US*

A tad disparaging.

- — Collin Baker et al., *College Undergraduate Slang Study Conducted at Brown University*, p. 183, 1968
- — *Current Slang*, p. 21, Summer 1970
- Shut up, rent-a-cop. — *Repo Man*, 1984
- Rialto started walking through the gate. A uniformed rent-a-cop asked him was he a guest. Rialot put out a folded ten. — Robert Campbell, *Alice in La-La Land*, p. 134–135, 1987
- She had the rentacop half convinced she was looking for a job application in the narcotics box when the real heat arrived. — Seth Morgan, *Homeboy*, p. 181, 1990

rent-a-gob *noun*

a citizens' band radio user who chats on a channel reserved for making contact; a person who talks too much and to little effect *UK*

- — Peter Chippindale, *The British CB Book*, p. 158, 1981

rentals *adjective*

▷ see: RADIO RENTAL

rental units *noun*

parents *US*

PARENTAL UNITS in a neat pun describing parental worth from a youth perspective.

- — Connie C. Eble, *Slang and Sociability*, p. 177, 1996

Rent-a-Svend *nickname*

Canadian politician Svend Robinson, the first openly gay, New Democratic member of Parliament *CANADA*

The controversial Svend Robinson has drawn criticism for his espousal of unpopular causes, such as the Palestinian side in the Arab–Israeli war and gay rights.

- Rent-a-Svend has killed himself as a serious person. — *Toronto Globe and Mail*, p. A2, 4th May 2002

rent-a-tile *noun*

dancing very closely, barely moving your feet *TRINIDAD AND TOBAGO, 1993*

- — Lise Winer, *Dictionary of the English/Creole of Trinidad & Tobago*, 2003

rent boy *noun*

a young male prostitute *UK, 1969*

- — *Maledicta*, p. 223, 1979: 'Kinks and queens: linguistic and cultural aspects of the terminology for gays'
- But people where I come from... rent boy... that's probably the worst thing you could call somebody. — Shaun Ryder, *Shaun Ryder... in His Own Words*, 1991
- [I]f I were a gorgeous rent boy or debonair movie director[.] — James Hawes, *Dead Long Enough*, p. 26, 2000

renter *noun*

a homosexual male prostitute *UK, 1893*

- — *Maledicta*, p. 147, Summer/Winter 1986–1987: 'Sexual slang: prostitutes, pedophiles, flagellators, transvestites, and necrophiles'

rent party *noun*

a party thrown for the purpose of collecting donations from friends to pay your rent *US, 1925*

- They came and went from the apartment houses where the after-hours joints were jumping and the house-rent parties swimming, and the whores plying their trade and the gamblers clipping chumps. — Chester Himes, *A Rage in Harlem*, p. 130, 1957
- — Robert S. Gold, *A Jazz Lexicon*, p. 248, 1964
- I'm gonna play the piano at three rent parties next weekend. — Louise Meriwether, *Daddy Was a Number Runner*, p. 30, 1970
- Every Friday night Bob and Virginia had a rent party. You danced, you drank, and you brought money. — Larry Rivers, *What Did I Do?*, p. 126, 1992

rents *noun*

par*ents* *US*

Teen slang that cuts parents down to size.

- — *Current Slang*, p. 11, Summer 1968
- — Connie Eble (Editor), *UNC-CH Campus Slang*, March 1973
- — *Concord (New Hampshire) Monitor*, p. 17, 23rd August 1983: 'Slang slinging: an intense and awesome guide to prep school slanguage'
- My 'rents drive me nuts, but this year I vow to be their little princess. — *J17*, February 2001

renzos *noun*

Lorenzo™ decorative wheel rims *US*

- Actually all I want is yo 'renzo's and stereo. — *Menace II Society*, 1993

reo *noun*

1 a reinforcement *AUSTRALIA, 1931*

- The reos who had had months of him were choking with resentment and the ex-men obeyed his orders sluggishly, with a weary contempt[.] — Russel Ward, *The Australian Legend*, p. 232, 1966

2 a difficult surfing manoeuvre on the breaking lip of a wave *US*

An abbreviation of 're-entry'.

- — John Conway, *Surfing*, p. 121, 1988
- Barrel after barrel, reo after reo. I don't think I'll ever see another surfer shred that point at Avoca like Sanga did. — *Tracks*, p. 8, October 1992

rep *noun*

1 *rep*utation *US, 1705*

- "Two boys by the name of Charlie Max and Sugar Smallhouse." "They have reps." "So I hear." — Mickey Spillane, *Kiss Me Deadly*, p. 68, 1952
- [B]ut no time for sex, and all the time worrying about his rep. — William Burroughs, *Naked Lunch*, p. 128, 1957
- Shucks, you and me both can put our finger on high society colored ladies here who got their whole rep just by going with some big important white man. — Chester Himes, *The Real Cool Killers*, p. 59, 1959
- A real Cool Cat is hep that he has a rep and has to get going if he plans on showing the chick the jive about loving and the turtle-doving. — Dan Burley, *Diggeth Thou?*, p. 5, 1959
- I'm gonna have to find me some strong cats to get tight with, cats with reps. — Claude Brown, *Manchild in the Promised Land*, p. 136, 1965
- Getting yourself a chick was a rep builder. — Piri Thomas, *Down These Mean Streets*, p. 15, 1967
- I took a few guys out and my rep was made. — Edwin Torres, *Carlito's Way*, p. 21, 1975
- He's got a bad rep, but it's mostly bullshit. — *Cruel Intentions*, 1999
- Tommy had a rep in prison, because of being connected with some of the big criminal families. — Jimmy Stockin, *On The Cobbles*, p. 137, 2000

2 a *rep*etition, or complete cycle of an exercise *US*

- — *American Speech*, p. 201, Fall 1984: 'The language of bodybuilding'
- With me do the exercise for one rep, ant then put the bar down correctly. — Tony Finlay, *Bodybuilding*, p. 42, 1996

3 a *rep*ertory theatre or theatre company; a repertoire *US, 1925*

- After three seasons at Birmingham Rep he [Derek Jacobi] was lured to Stratford upon Avon. — *The Guardian*, 17th October 1991

4 in prison, a written *rep*resentation *UK*

- He could still submit "reps"[.] — *The Guardian*, 13th June 2002

5 a *rep*resentative, often a travelling salesman *UK, 1896*

- He doesn't know that bank has got reps in the Caymans, in the Dutch Antilles, in Hawaii, in Canada, everywhere. — Kevin Sampson, *Outlaws*, p. 250, 2001
- I'd arranged to meet a local train drivers [union] rep. — Mark Steel, *Reasons to be Cheerful*, p. 230, 2001

6 a *rep*ellent *UK*
- I put more cam [camouflage] cream and mozzie [mosquito] rep on my face and hands. — Andy McNab, *Immediate Action*, p. 93, 1995

rep *verb*
1 to *rep*resent someone; to give someone a *rep*utation *UK*
- [U]se your influential status to play good hip-hop and rep the UK properly [...] and stop repping that shit UK garage wannabe bad boy gangsta Junior MAFIA wannabe shit[.] — *Hip-Hop Connection*, p. 9, July 2002

2 to work as a *rep*resentative of a company *UK, 1938*
- You think you know so much about repping, don't you. — Colin Butts, *Is Harry on the Boat?*, p. 179, 1997

Repat *noun*
1 the *Repat*riation Commission which gave assistance to ex-service personnel returning to civilian life *AUSTRALIA, 1920*
- [F]eeling was running pretty high over Effie's case with the Repat and there was talk of us returned men going down to Sydney in a bunch. — Dymphna Cusack, *Picnic Races*, p. 102, 1962

2 a hospital for *repat*riated service personnel *AUSTRALIA*
- The good people here at the Repat have been particularly decent to me for the duration of my stay here[.] — Barry Humphries, *A Nice Night's Entertainment*, p. 109, 1968

repeater *noun*
in horse racing, a horse that won the last race it entered *US*
- — Les Conklin, *Payday at the Races*, p. 207, 1974

repo *noun*
*repo*ssession *US*
- Slim, I been getting a little light weight bad break, so I figured out that angle to keep the repo bastards from copping [taking] my hog [Cadillac] when I ain't in it. — Iceberg Slim (Robert Beck), *The Naked Soul of Iceberg Slim*, p. 126, 1971
- And I profited; my desk was covered with repo orders, ranging in make and model[.] — James Ellroy, *Brown's Requiem*, p. 11, 1981

repo depot *noun*
the Replacement Detachment of any large military force or installation *US*
- — Carl Fleischhauer, *A Glossary of Army Slang*, p. 10, 1968
- — Linda Reinberg, *In the Field*, p. 183, 1991

repo man *noun*
an agent of a finance company who repossesses, by an assortment of techniques, cars which have not been paid for *US*
From '*repo*ssess'.
- BUD: The life of a repo man is always intense. — *Repo Man*, 1984
- That's why they ain't a repo man I know that don't take speed. — *Repo Man*, 1984
- The repo man did not ring the doorbell and say "I've come to take your car." He hooked it up to a wrecker and took it away, as quickly as possible, and in broad daylight, midday. — Lewis Poteet, *Car & Motorcyle Slang*, p. 163, 1992
- I was a repo man also and a bounty hunter. — Elmore Leonard, *Riding the Rap*, p. 23, 1995

repple-depple *noun*
a replacement depot where soldiers arriving in Vietnam were assigned to units and soldiers leaving Vietnam were processed for homecoming *US*
- When a soldier gets out of an army hospital, he will most likely be thrown into a "repple depple." This institution, identified in army regulations as a replacement depot, is a sort of clearing house. — Bill Mauldin, *Up Front*, p. 125, 1945
- — Linda Reinberg, *In the Field*, p. 183, 1991

reppoc; reppock *noun*
a police officer *UK*
Back slang for **COPPER**.
- — Angela Devlin, *Prison Patter*, p. 97, 1996

represent *verb*
1 to serve as a pimp for a prostitute *US*
- I been jumped out here, 'cause like I said my male was in the pen. I didn't have anybody representing me. — William T. Vollman, *Whores for Gloria*, p. 148, 1991

2 to project a positive image and attitude *US*
- — Connie Eble (Editor), *UNC-CH Campus Slang*, p. 7, April 1997

reptile *noun*
a railway pointsman *US*
- — Ramon Adams, *The Language of the Railroader*, p. 126, 1977

Republic of Mali *noun*
cocaine *UK*
Rhyming slang for **CHARLIE** (cocaine).
- — Mike Haskins, *Drugs*, p. 272, 2003

re-rub *noun*
a re-mixed dance music recording *UK*
- Tenaglia's Circuit Boy re-rub sits on the shelf. — *Ministry*, p. 59, January 2002

res *noun*
1 a resident physician in a hospital *US*
- — Sally Williams, *"Strong" Words*, p. 157, 1994

2 a dormitory or residence at a university or college *CANADA*

3 the oily residue in a pipe after crack cocaine has been smoked *US*
- — Terry Williams, *Crackhouse*, p. 151, 1992

resemble *verb*
to resent *UK, 1984*
Usually in the jocular 'I resemble that remark'.
- 'Hello you ugly maggot-ridden bugger,' said one man. The recipient of this jolly welcome looked deeply offended, put his hands on his hips and said 'I resemble remarks like that.' — *The Times*, 24th November 1985
- "Hey, I resemble that remark." Sara Rosen made a pouting face. She was kidding. — James Patterson, *Jack & Jill*, p. 40, 1996

resin *noun*
cannabis resin *UK*
- — Angela Devlin, *Prison Patter*, p. 97, 1996

respec; respect; respeck; rispeck
used for registering approval of someone's action or attitude *UK*
An abbreviation in all variant spellings of 'respect due'; occasionally ironic. Originally West Indian and UK black.
- "My name's Terry." "Respeck Terry, the name's Lloyd." — Donald Gorgon, *Cop Killer*, p. 65, 1994
- They also broke the mics and were presented with the bill at the end of the night – before doing a runner with the suits. Respec. — *Mixmag*, p. 78, December 2001

respect due
used for registering approval of someone's action or attitude *UK, 1998*
Originally West Indian and UK black.

ressie *noun*
a resident DJ *UK*
- [T]his New Year's Eve party [...] will be rocking to house, breakbeat, funk and Latin from the ressies and guests tbc [to be confirmed]. — *Mixmag*, p. 78, December 2001

rest *noun*
▸ **give it a rest**
to stop talking, especially to stop talking about a specific topic *UK, 1984*
Often as an imperative.
- Paul phoned me and said "I hear you're going round saying you're writing a book for me. Give it a rest, would you?" — *The Guardian*, 25th June 2003

rest *verb*
▸ **rest your mouth**
to stop talking *BAHAMAS*
- — John A. Holm, *Dictionary of Bahamian English*, p. 169, 1982

▸ **rest your neck**
to stop talking *US*
- Homeboy, rest your neck; I don't want to hear it! — James Harris, *A Convict's Dictionary*, p. 37, 1989

rest cure *noun*
in the car sales business, sending a car into the shop while the customer waits and then returning it, claiming that work which has not been done has been done *US*
- — *Cars*, p. 41, December 1953

resting *adjective*
of an actor, unemployed *UK*
Originally positive thinking, now arch.

- [A] bloke I recognise from the telly [...] He used to be in the Doctor in the House programmes on TV. Resting, I expect. — Martin King and Martin Knight, *The Naughty Nineties*, p. 104, 1999

rest in peace *noun*
crack cocaine *UK*
Imagery of death.
- — Mike Haskins, *Drugs*, p. 282, 2003

restroom *noun*
a brakevan (caboose) *US*
- — Ramon Adams, *The Language of the Railroader*, p. 126, 1977

result *noun*
1 the winning score in a sporting contest; a victory in any sport *UK, 1981*
Conventionally 'result' means 'outcome', hence a 'good result'; this usage clips and implies the positive adjective, exclusively acquiring the result for victors and so denying losers any achievement.

2 a satisfying or appropriate outcome; an achievement *UK, 1973*
- It's always nice to get a result over those [wheel] clamping cunts, ain't it? — Dave Courtney, *Raving Lunacy*, p. 88, 2000
- And Ian [Dury], he'd be well chuffed. "Result!" he'd go, laughing, the Pearly King chuckling from the Pearly Gates. Yes, Ian. Result. — BP Fallon, *Brand New Boots And Panties*, 2001
- But this is just another case of female stopping play / On otherwise a total result of a holiday[.] — Mike Skinner, *Fit But You Know It*, 2004

3 a successful or profitable robbery *UK*
- I've just had a result. Cop this pony, and buy him some fags. — Lenny McLean, *The Guv'nor*, p. 92, 1998

4 an arrest or a criminal conviction *UK*
- If they [officers] get it right, they get a result, they get a conviction[.] — *The Guardian*, 23rd Septmber 2004

ret *noun*
a cigarette *US*
- — *Current Slang*, p. 9, Winter 1971

retail action *noun*
recreational shopping *US*
- — Anna Scotti and Paul Young, *Buzzwords*, p. 106, 1997

retail therapy *noun*
shopping when considered as an empowering leisure activity *US*
- We've become a nation measuring out our lives in shopping bags and nursing our psychic ills through retail therapy. — *Chicago Tribune*, p. C2, 24th December 1986
- [T]ogether we formulated the Law of Retail Therapy: the larger your size, the further from the city center a woman is forced to forage. — Elizabeth Buchan, *Revenge of the Middle-Aged Woman*, p. 9, 2002

retard *noun*
a slow, dim-witted person *US, 1970*
From 'mentally retarded', but not necessarily indicative of actual mental retardation.
- Like my retard little brother borrows my blow drier to like dry his model airplane, right, and so like I can't find it[.] — Mary Corey and Victoria Westermark, *Fer Shurr! How to be a Valley Girl*, 1982
- What are you thinking? Are you a retard-o, or what? — *Airheads*, 1994
- Everyone thinks I'm a retard. — *Empire Records*, 1995
- [He] is not just "gross" but a "gimp" and a "retard" and a "mong". — Jenny Eclair, *Camberwell Beauty*, p. 153, 2000

retarded *adjective*
1 stupid, foolish *US*
- — Connie Eble (Editor), *UNC-CH Campus Slang*, p. 8, November 2003

2 drunk *US*
- — Connie Eble (Editor), *UNC-CH Campus Slang*, p. 4, Spring 2003

3 in Quebec, delayed, late *CANADA*
- — Victor Trahan, *The City of Montreal Style Guide*, p. 120, 2001

retardo *noun*
a mentally challenged person *US*
- For treating me like a slave! Like a retardo! — James Ellroy, *Brown's Requiem*, p. 190, 1981

retread *noun*
1 in the military: a short-service officer on a second commission; a retired officer recalled to service; a retired officer re-employed as a civilian in an administrative post; an officer who has been promoted from the ranks; an aviator returned to flying duties after a period of ground service *AUSTRALIA, 1943*
The origin is in the new life given to a tyre by the application of a new tread; there is also a pun on 'retired/re-tyred'. The earliest use is for a World War 1 veteran recalled to serve in World War 2.

2 a recently divorced person *US*
- — *American Speech*, p. 20, Spring 1985: 'The language of singles bars'

retread *verb*
in the language surrounding the Grateful Dead, to tape over a tape that has been recorded once *US*
- — David Shenk and Steve Silberman, *Skeleton Key*, p. 246, 1994

retriever *noun*
a prisoner who intimidates other prison inmates for the purpose of 'retrieving' drugs that those inmates are suspected of carrying *UK*
- — Angela Devlin, *Prison Patter*, p. 97, 1996

retro *verb*
to return something or someone from Antarctica to the country of origin *ANTARCTICA*
An abbreviation of 'retrograde'.
- — Ethan Dicks, *English, as She is Spoke at McMurdo*, 2003

retrosexual *noun*
a heterosexual man who enjoys traditional male pastimes and spends as little time and money as possible on his appearance *US*
A play on **METROSEXUAL** (a man with aesthetic tastes), suggesting a throwback to an earlier type.
- [T]he Middle American AWM [angry white man] is an uncomplicated retrosexual, freed from Nineties exhortations to find his feminine side, comfortable with his hairy chest and sagging jeans. — *New Statesman*, 10th May 2004

rette *noun*
a cigarette *US*
- — Anna Scotti and Paul Young, *Buzzwords*, p. 77, 1997

reub *noun*
▷ **see:** RUBE

reunion in my bureau *noun*
in Quebec, a meeting in my office *CANADA*
Both 'reunion' and 'bureau' are used in their French sense in English in Montreal.
- — Victor Trahan, *The City of Montreal Style Guide*, p. 120, 2001

re-up *verb*
to replenish a stack of something; to re-supply something; to re-sign or re-enlist *US, 1906*
Originally a military slang term for re-enlisting.
- — Lou Shelly, *Hepcats Jive Talk Dictionary*, p. 48, 1945
- — *American Speech*, p. 232–234, October 1962: 'Re-Up'
- Harper just got out of the Air Force and they asked him if he wanted to re-up, as they call it. — Jim Bouton, *Ball Four*, p. 20, 1970
- I just might possible re-up and make a twenty-year career of it – but only if I made the rank of staff sergeant before my four-year tour ended. — Bobby Seale, *A Lonely Rage*, p. 107, 1978
- Then I re-upped for another tour. — *Apocalypse Now*, 1979
- He done a year in Japan in the hospital, then when he gets out, the first thing he done is re-up. — *Platoon*, 1986
- "Splib," said Max, "thinks he's gonna re-up on my stuff when he gets the money he says is owed him in the street." — Terry Williams, *The Cocaine Kids*, p. 38, 1989
- "Re-up, re-up," he announced, blaring out the words over the music in his head. — Richard Price, *Clockers*, p. 6, 1992

rev *verb*
to leave, to go *US*
- "Let's rev" means let's go, and the appropriate answer is "reet" (okay). — *Herald Press (St. Jospeh, Missouri)*, p. 14, 23rd June 1952

RevCan *noun*
Revenue Canada, the federal tax collection agency *CANADA*
- Did the boss spring for a hotel room or for your cab fare home? Beware, the kindness of your boss may catch the attention of RevCan (Revenue Canada). — *taxpayer.com.bc*, 22nd July 2002

revenge of the cradle; revenge of the nursery *noun*
Quebec's high birthrate, perceived as being in retaliation for the loss of the province to England by France *CANADA*

- Quebec's answer was a high birthrate, epitomized in an article in a French Canadian nationalist magazine titled "The Revenge of the Cradle." — *Winnipeg Tribune*, p. 6/6, 6th February 1964
- The pro-natality [sic?] suggestions are merely a revival of the traditional "revanche du berceau" (the revenge of the nursery) which led past generations of the nationalists in Quebec to imagine that high birth rates could outstrip hordes of immigrants. — *Toronto Globe and Mail*, p. 8/3, 1st April 1967

revenoo; revenuer; revenooer *noun*

a federal law enforcement official *US*

Used by those in the illegal production of alcohol.

- — David W. Maurer, *Kentucky Moonshine*, p. 123, 1974

Reverend Ronald Knox; the Reverend; the Right Reverend *noun*

syphilis; hence any sexually transmitted infection *UK*

Rhyming slang for **POX**, formed from the Catholic priest and detective storywriter, 1888–1957. Noted by Red Daniells, 1980.

reverse *adjective*

▸ **reverse gears**

to vomit *US*

- — Pamela Munro, *U.C.L.A. Slang*, p. 71, 1989

reverse cowgirl *noun*

a sexual position in which the woman straddles the prone man, facing his feet *US*

- There's a rough scheme before you start: oral, missionary, reverse cowgirl, doggy, then a pop. — Robert Stoller and I.S. Levine, *Coming Attractions*, p. 131, 1991
- Since many men's erections slant upward, doggy style and reverse cowgirl (when you're on top riding him while facing his feet) are ideal. — *Cosmopolitan*, p. 130, 1st January 2001
- When you're working, is there a sexual act or position you won't do. BRITTANY ANDREWS: Reverse cowgirl. I can't stand it. — *Playboy*, p. 132, 1st March 2002
- The Reverse Cowgirl. Best performed wearing your diamante-backed G-string, this back-to-front variation of woman-on-top works wonders for both of you, according to many. — Mandi Norwood, *Sex & the Married Girl*, p. 94, 2003

reverse o *noun*

a position for mutual, simultaneous oral sex between two people, or the act itself, especially when advertised as a service offered by a prostitute *UK*

- — Caroline Archer, *Tart Cards*, 2003

rev-head *noun*

a motor vehicle enthusiast *AUSTRALIA*

- The western suburbs also play host to the 'Rev-heads'. These kids love fast, hot, mag-wheeled cars. Girls who go out with Rev-heads are 'Hubcap biters'. — *Sydney Morning Herald*, p. 7, 3rd January 1987
- We still had our rough edges, our greatcoated winos and barefoot ferals, our ferret-faced teenage mothers and lingerie lunches, our dumb-fuck rev-heads and back-lane chop shops. — Shane Maloney, *Nice Try*, p. 129, 1998
- Two streets away, a rev-head gunned his motor and laid rubber. — Shane Maloney, *Nice Try*, p. 164, 1998

revolt of the admirals *noun*

a highly public clash between the US Navy and the US Air Force in 1949 over basing of the country's strategic airpower *US*

- Republicans were among those who encouraged military dissent in the "revolt of the admirals" against Truman Administration policy in the late 1940s[.] — Clark R. Mollenhoff, *The Pentagon*, p. 411, 1967
- The "Revolt of the Admirals" had broken out; the Navy wanted a much larger share of the Department of Defense's money than it had been appropriated[.] — Stephen E. Ambrose, *Eisenhower*, p. 486, 1983
- Although the so-called "Revolt of the Admirals" in 1949 primarily pitted the US Navy against the fledgling United States Air Force, the roots of this titanic struggle can be traced back to the period between the world wars. — *Air Force Magazine*, May 1990

rev up and fuck off

go away and don't annoy me; don't annoy me *IRELAND*

- 'They're still only young girls,' said Bimbo. -'Kids'. -'Ah, rev up,' said Jimmy Sr. — Roddy Doyle, *The Van*, p. 111, 1991

rewind *noun*

in trucking, a return trip *US*

- — Bill Davis, *Jawjacking*, p. 82, 1977

rex *noun*

a (small) quantity of money *IRELAND*

- Not content with all your loot, you have to milk the last rex from the poor fools, who should on a Sunday be home saying their prayers instead of getting rooked by you. — Shane Connaughton, *A Border Station*, p. 75–76, 1989

Rexall ranger *noun*

someone who wears cowboy clothes but has never worked on a ranch *US*

Rexall is a chain drugstore, giving a touch of specificity to the more common **DRUGSTORE COWBOY**.

- — *Current Slang*, p. 23, Spring 1970

rez *noun*

a Native American Indian reservation *US*

- VELMA: Yeah, you're leaving the rez and going into a whole different country, cousin. — *Smoke Signals*, 1998

RF *verb*

to play a prank *US*

An abbreviation of **RAT-FUCK**.

- — *American Speech*, p. 195, October 1965: 'Notes on campus vocabulary, 1964'
- — *Current Slang*, p. 6, Summer 1967

RFB *noun*

*r*oom, *f*ood and *b*everage – the basic components of a complimentary pass at a casino or hotel *US*

- — Frank Scoblete, *Best Blackjack*, p. 270, 1996

RG *noun*

in homosexual usage, a biological female *US*

A fellow homosexual is a **GIRL**, while a woman is a 'real girl', or RG.

- Eugene Landy, *The Underground Dictionary*, p. 161, 1971

rhaatid *adjective*

▹ **see: RAHTID**

rhine *noun*

heroin *UK, 1998*

Probably by abbrevation of a particular pronunciation.

- — Robert Ashton, *This Is Heroin*, p. 207, 2002
- — Mike Haskins, *Drugs*, p. 284, 2003

rhino *noun*

1 money *UK, 1688*

- — Joseph E. Ragen and Charles Finston, *Inside the World's Toughest Prison*, p. 815, 1962: 'Penitentiary and underworld glossary'
- All HMG has to do to rake in the rhino is [...] bring out every week a new set of stamps[.] — Andrew Nickolds, *Back to Basics*, p. 29, 1994

2 a large and powerful wave *US*

- — Trevor Cralle, *The Surfin'ary*, p. 99, 1991

rhino chaser *noun*

a large surfboard made for big-wave conditions *US*

- — Mitch McKissick, *Surf Lingo*, 1987
- Here, you need a rhino chaser like this one to learn on. — *Point Break*, 1991

RHIP

*r*ank *h*as *i*ts *p*rivileges *US*

- — *Current Slang*, p. 8, Spring 1968

Rhodey *noun*

a white Zimbabwean *SOUTH AFRICA*

Derogatory. A reference to Rhodesia, the country which became Zimbabwe in 1980.

- — *Lonely Planet Southern Africa*, 2000

rhody; rhodie *noun*

a rhododendron *UK, 1851*

- I always clean the car of a Sunday morning and do a bit of pottering around in the garden. Bit worried about those rhodies. — Barry Humphries, *A Nice Night's Entertainment*, p. 18, 1958

rhubarb *noun*

1 nonsense *UK, 1963*

From its use by actors as an 'unintelligible murmur'.

- [T]he acres of rhubarb served up to long-suffering Guardian readers by this reporter[.] — *The Guardian*, 9th September 2002

2 said repeatedly by muttering actors to give the impression of background conversations; hence, spoken nonsense *UK, 1934*
Theatre slang.
• — David Powis, *The Signs of Crime*, 1977

3 a fight; an uproar; a riot *US, 1943*
• — Parke Cummings, *Dictionary of Baseball*, p. 44, 1950
• "It was the only time in my life," remembered an anonymous chap who took part in the rhubarb, "that I was ever kicked in the head by a man spinning in the air above me." — Robert Sylvester, *No Cover Charge*, p. 254, 1956

4 an advance of wages, a loan; as 'rhubarbs': a membership subscription *UK, 1929*
Rhyming slang, pronounced 'roobub', for **SUB** (a subscription).
• — Ray Puxley, *Cockney Rabbit*, 1992

rhubarb and custard *noun*
a variety of MDMA, the recreational drug best known as ecstasy *UK*
From the red and yellow colour of the pill; the syllable 'barb' is possibly an indication that the tablet contains barbiturate.
• — Angela Devlin, *Prison Patter*, p. 97, 1996
• Street names [...] New Yorkers, rhubarb and custard, shamrocks[.] — James Kay and Julian Cohen, *The Parents' Complete Guide to Young People and Drugs*, p. 136, 1998
• — Gareth Thomas, *This Is Ecstasy*, p. 56, 2002

rhubarb pill; rhubarb *noun*
a bill (for payment) *UK*
Rhyming slang, based on a homeopathic remedy for constipation; noted by Julian Franklyn, *A Dictionary of Rhyming Slang*, 1960, who suspected (or perpetrated) the pun 'that both necessitate an outpouring'.
• — Ray Puxley, *Fresh Rabbit*, 1998

rhubarbs *noun*
1 suburbs *UK*
Rhyming slang, pronounced 'roobubs', formed on an elision of 'suburbs'.
• — Julian Franklyn, *A Dictionary of Rhyming Slang*, 1960

2 a variety of LSD *UK*
• — Angela Devlin, *Prison Patter*, p. 97, 1996

rhyme off *verb*
to recite; to talk *UK: SCOTLAND*
From Scottish dialect *rame* (to talk nonsense; to reiterate).
• For one thing, rhyming off the places he'd broken into without getting caught was not the most discreet course of action[.] — Christopher Brookmyre, *Boiling a Frog*, p. 45, 2000

rhythm *noun*
an amphetamine tablet *US*
• — Peter Johnson, *Dictionary of Street Alcohol and Drug Terms*, p. 159, 1993

rhythm and blues; rhythms *noun*
shoes *UK*
Rhyming slang.
• — Ray Puxley, *Fresh Rabbit*, 1998

rhythm method *noun*
a method of cheating while playing a slot machine by controlling the spins of the inner-wheels *US*
Playing on the name of the least successful method of birth control.
• For some time players could beat the machines legitimately with what is called the "rhythm method." — Mario Puzo, *Inside Las Vegas*, p. 220, 1977

riah *noun*
the hair *UK*
Polari back slang.
• Well, I see Samson as huge and all butch, with great bulging thews [muscles] and whopping great lallies [legs], with long blond riah hanging down his Jim and Jack[.] — Barry Took and Marty Feldman, *Round The Horne*, 16th April 1967
• So bona to vada / OH YOU / Your lovely eek [face] and / Your lovely riah. — Morrisey, *Piccadilly Palare*, 1990

riah zhoosher; riah shusher *noun*
a hairdresser *UK*
A combination of **ZHOOSH** (to tidy) with **RIAH** (the hair).
• — Paul Baker, *Polari*, p. 188, 2002

riah-zshumpah *noun*
a hairdresser *UK*
• I went to my riah-zshumpah this morning, you know, Raoul[.] — the cast of 'Aspects of Love', Prince of Wales Theatre, *Palare (Boy Dancer Talk) for Beginners*, 1989–92

rib *noun*
1 a wife or girlfriend *UK, 1589*
From the Biblical creation tale, with Eve springing from Adam's rib.
• — *Current Slang*, p. 40, Fall 1968
• Two of 'em looked like apes, so I picked Walter's rib to sleep with. — A.S. Jackson, *Gentleman Pimp*, p. 32, 1973

2 Rohypnol™ (flunitrazepam), popularly known as the 'date-rape drug' *US*
• On the street the drug has many nicknames; teenagers know it as rope, ribs, or roaches. — *Texas Monthly*, p. 88, September 1995

3 MDMA, the recreational drug best known as ecstasy *UK*
• — Mike Haskins, *Drugs*, p. 290, 2003

rib *verb*
1 to make fun of someone *US, 1930*
• Buck was also a close friend of Louis', and he would rib Zutty now and then about leaving Louis, so that put me on a complex even more. — Mezz Mezzrow, *Really the Blues*, p. 237, 1946
• He started to rib me, called me a square. — Iceberg Slim (Robert Beck), *Pimp*, p. 99, 1969

2 to insult someone in a semi-formal quasi-friendly competition *US*
A variation of 'rib' (to tease).
• There are many different terms for playing the dozens, including "bagging, capping, cracking, dissing, hiking, joning, ranking, ribbing, serving, signifying, slipping, sounding and snapping". — James Haskins, *The Story of Hip-Hop*, p. 54, 2000

ribbon and curl *noun*
a girl *UK*
Rhyming slang.
• — Ray Puxley, *Cockney Rabbit*, 1992

ribbon clerk *noun*
a poker player who withdraws from a hand at any sign of serious betting *US*
• — George Percy, *The Language of Poker*, p. 75, 1988

ribena on toast *adjective*
awful; tasteless; in bad taste *UK*
Possibly a literal translation of a bad taste; coinage is credited to ballet master David Kerr.
• She has a permanent vogue [cigarette] in her screech [mouth] and her droje [clothing] is mega ribena on toast, daughter. — the cast of 'Aspects of Love', Prince of Wales Theatre, *Palare (Boy Dancer Talk) for Beginners*, 1989–92

ribtapper *noun*
a heavy-duty boot *UK: SCOTLAND*
• Spin roon on yir ribtappers[.] — Ian Pattison, *Rab C. Nesbitt*, 1988

ric *verb*
▷ **see: RICK**

Rican *noun*
a Puerto Rican *US*
• Somebody was always jumpin' off the roof too. Usually some Rican who couldn't cut it on the street. — Edwin Torres, *Carlito's Way*, p. 16, 1975

rice *noun*
effort *UK*
Royal Marine slang.
• Give it rice! is like saying: "Let's have more effort!" — Rick Jolly, *Jackspeak*, p. 238, 1989

rice-and-peas boongy *noun*
large buttocks, especially those of a woman *BAHAMAS*

rice-and-ring *verb*
to get married *US*
• He says, "How's about we rice an' ring it?" — Haenigsen, *Jive's Like That*, 1947

rice-a-roni *noun*
in necrophile usage, a badly decomposed corpse *US*
A comparison to the branded soft-boiled rice product.
• — *Maledicta*, p. 180, Summer/Winter 1986–1987: 'Sexual slang: prostitutes, pedophiles, flagellators, transvestites, and necrophiles'

rice bandit *noun*
a Japanese person *AUSTRALIA*
Offensive.
- She found and noted the contacts for Quayle and Associates but there was no trace of the two rice bandits outside the corporate record. —Harrison Biscuit, *The Search for Savage Henry*, p. 70, 1995

rice belly *noun*
the protuding stomach of a child *GUYANA*
- —Richard Allsopp, *Dictionary of Caribbean English Usage*, p. 472, 1996

rice-burner *noun*
a Japanese car or motorcyle *UK*
- —Douglas Dunford, *Motorcycle Department, Beaulieu Motor Museum*, 1979
- —Connie Eble (Editor), *UNC-CH Campus Slang*, p. 6, Fall 1984
- —Lewis Poteet, *Car & Motorcyle Slang*, p. 164, 1992
- Epithets such as "rice burner," and "Jap crap" are frequent. —*Orlando Sentinel Tribune*, p. A1, 28th February 1993

rice eye *noun*
a Japanese person *US*
Hawaiian youth usage, especially in the taunt 'No lie, rice eye'.
- —Douglas Simonson, *Pidgin to da Max Hana Hou*, 1982

rice machine *noun*
a car manufactured in Japan or by a Japanese manufacturer *US*
- —Judi Sanders, *Faced and Faded, Hanging to Hurl*, p. 33, 1993

riceman *noun*
a Chinese person *US*
Offensive.
- —Lou Shelly, *Hepcats Jive Talk Dictionary*, p. 16, 1945

rice paddy Hattie *noun*
any rural Chinese prostitute *US*
- —*American Speech*, p. 31, February 1949: 'A.V.G. Lingo'

rice queen *noun*
a gay man attracted to men of South Asian origin *US*
- —Bruce Rodgers, *The Queens' Vernacular*, p. 171, 1972

ricer *noun*
a person from South Asia *US*
Offensive.
- —Edith A. Folb, *runnin' down some lines*, p. 251, 1980

rice rocket *noun*
a motorcyle made by a Japanese manufacturer *US*
Offensive.
- You could push your rice rocket on Main Street, and it would be left alone. —*Orlando Sentinel Tribune*, p. A1, 28th February 1993
- The newest "rice rockets" can carry 140 horsepower to the rear wheel, and can easily do 180 miles per hour right out of the box. —Ralph "Sonny" Barger, *Hell's Angel*, p. 53, 2000
- —Pamela Munro, *U.C.L.A. Slang*, p. 105, 2001

Richard *noun*
1 any police official, especially a detective *US*
An embellished **DICK**.
- —Hyman E. Goldin et al., *Dictionary of American Underworld Lingo*, p. 177, 1950

2 the penis *UK, 2001*
An extension of **DICK** (the penis), which is the short form of the first name Richard.
- —*Sky Magazine*, July 2001

▸ **had the Richard**
to be ruined or irreparably broken; to be finished *AUSTRALIA, 1967*
In the *Australian National Dictionary* it is claimed that this is from British rhyming slang 'Richard the Third' (the bird), from theatrical slang 'to get the bird' (to get a bad reception on stage), but there is little semantic overlap to warrant this explanation. Rather if something has 'had the dick' then it is 'fucked', and therein lies the metaphor. Richard here is merely euphemistic for **DICK** (the penis). Supporting this explanation are the other variants **HAD THE STICK**, **HAD THE ROD** and of course **HAD THE DICK**.
- —Jim Ramsay, *Cop It Sweet!*, p. 43, 1977
- This pen has just about had the Richard. —Ray Denning, *Prison Diaries*, p. 45, 1978

Richard and Judy *adjective*
moody *UK*
Rhyming slang, formed from husband and wife television presenters Richard Madeley and Judy Finnegan.
- —*The Sunday Times*, 9th May 2004

Richard Burton *noun*
a curtain *UK*
Theatrical rhyming slang, formed from the name of the Welsh actor, 1925–84.
- —Ray Puxley, *Cockney Rabbit*, 1992

Richard the Third; Richard *noun*
1 a young woman; a sweetheart *UK, 1950*
Rhyming slang for **BIRD**.
- —Paul Tempest, *Lag's Lexicon*, 1950
- I walk into a well-known bird-bandit's lair and find a comely Richard flaunting her Arris [buttocks] around the gaff[.] —Anthony Masters, *Minder*, p. 37, 1984
- I'll tell ya where you can collect the Richard, and that'll be my end of the deal. —J.J. Connolly, *Layer Cake*, p. 103, 2000

2 a bird *UK*
Rhyming slang; originally recorded in *Songs and Slang of the British Soldier*, John Brophy and Eric Partridge, 1930. In theatrical use as **THE BIRD** (a farting noise masquerading as criticism).
- And the Richard the Third flew back to its nest. —Ronnie Barker, *Fletcher's Book of Rhyming Slang*, p. 27, 1979

3 a piece of excrement *UK, 1961*
Rhyming slang for **TURD**.
- —Bob Young and Micky Moody, *The Language of Rock 'n' Roll*, p. 119, 1985

Richard Todd *noun*
a portion of fried cod *UK*
Rhyming slang formed on the name of the British actor (b.1919)
- —Ray Puxley, *Cockney Rabbit*, 1992

Richibucto goose *noun*
a fish, salted shad *CANADA, 1939*
Named after a town in Nova Scotia.
- "Richibucto goose" is salt fish as prepared in Richibucto, Kent County, NS. It's a comic reference to common use of this word. —Bill Casselman, *Canadian Food Words*, p. 90, 1998

rich man's drug *noun*
cocaine *US*
Because of its high cost. Although the phrase sounds a bit literary, it was used by those without any particular literary background.
- Cocaine is prestigious to use because it is so expensive; they call it the "rich man's drug." —Christina and Richard Milner, *Black Players*, p. 12, 1972

rick *noun*
1 a mistake *UK*
Probably a shortening of **RICKET** (a mistake).
- —John McCririck, *John McCririck's World of Betting*, p. 61, 1991

2 an accomplice who pretends to be a client in order to encourage trade, originally used of a cheapjack or showman, later of a less than scrupulous bookmaker *UK, 1898*

rick; ric *verb*
to make a mistake *UK*
From **RICK** (a mistake)
- —Angela Devlin, *Prison Patter*, p. 97, 1996

rick *adjective*
fake; spurious *UK*
From the noun.
- It's a rick bet. It don't mean nothing. —*The Sunday Telegraph*, 7th May 1967

ricket *noun*
a mistake *UK*
- It's in the law of averages that if you are chopping all day you must at some time make a ricket and chop your hand or something. —Frank Norman, *Bang To Rights*, p. 29, 1958

▸ **drop a ricket**
to make a mistake *UK*
- I'd dropped a ricket on tape. —Lenny McLean, *The Guv'nor*, p. 188, 1998

rickety-raw *adjective*
attractive, fashionable *US*
- —*Washington Post Magazine*, p. 11, 24th May 1987: 'Say wha?'

Rick Stein *noun*
a fine *UK*
Rhyming slang, formed from the name of the UK television chef (b.1947).
- You could go to prison for that, or incur a very heavy Rick Stein. —Mervyn Stutter, *Getting Nowhere Fast*, 21st May 2004

Rick Witter *noun*
a shitter (in all senses) *UK*
Rhyming slang, formed from the lead singer of Shed Seven.
- —Bodmin Dark, *Dirty Cockney Rhyming Slang*, 2003

Ricky Martin; Ricky *noun*
a side-parting *UK, 2001*
Popney rhyming slang, from popular singer Ricky Martin (b.1971). Popney was contrived for *www.music365.co.uk*, an Internet music site.

Ricky Racer *noun*
a fanatic mountain bike enthusiast who rarely if ever rides *US*
- —Vann Wesson, *Generation X Field Guide and Lexicon*, p. 142, 1997

ricky-ticky; ricky-tick *adjective*
used of a jazz rhythm, old-fashioned, even, boring *US, 1952*
- [H]e had blown complex and minor in the midst of vulgar stomping swing bands, jitterbugs and ricky-ticky-too[.]—John Clellon Holmes, *The Horn*, p. 87, 1958
- [W]hat lifts Tiny Tim miles above the nostalgia, the rickey-tick[.] —Albert Goldman, *Freak Show*, p. 116, 1968
- That ole ricky-tick? That ain't even worth listen to. Ole ricky-tick like that.—Terry Southern, *Texas Summer*, p. 151, 1991

rid *verb*

▸ rid a fit
to get rid of an outfit of clothes *US*
- —Connie Eble (Editor), *UNC-CH Campus Slang*, p. 7, Spring 1994

riddle *verb*
in Newfoundland, to weave up-and-down rods between rails to make a fence *CANADA*
- The fence consisted of three horizontal rails interlaced (riddled) with very slender, peeled rods which alternated in their directions of curvature so that the second opposed the first, the third the second, and so on.—Harold Paddock, *A Dialect Survey of Carbonear, Newfoundland*, p. 195, 1966

riddle-me-ree *noun*
urine; an act of urination *UK*
Rhyming slang for **PEE** or **WEE**; always used in full to avoid confusion with other slang, such as **JIMMY RIDDLE** or **PIDDLE**.
- —Ray Puxley, *Cockney Rabbit*, 1992

riddle me this, Batman
answer this question *US*
From the *Batman* television series (1966–68) and one of its antagonists, The Riddler.
- CLARENCE: Riddle me this, Batman. If you're all so much in love with each other, what the fuck are you doing here?—*True Romance*, 1993
- Well, riddle me this, Batman. How do you feel about the fact that you're never gonna see Mallory again?—*Natural Born Killers*, 1994

riddy *noun*
(as a result of embarrassment) a red face *UK: SCOTLAND*
Glasgow slang.
- —Michael Munro, *The Original Patter*, p. 59, 1985
- They walk away with around eight hundred grand in cash and leave us with bugger all but a communal riddy.—Christopher Brookmyre, *The Sacred Art of Stealing*, p. 202, 2002

ride *noun*
1 a car *US, 1930*
- —Hermese E. Roberts, *The Third Ear*, 1971
- With his unspectacular conservative suits and modest "ride" (a Toyota station wagon) he could easily be your neighbor[.]—Christina and Richard Milner, *Black Players*, p. 151, 1972
- [W]ould you mind parkin' your ride like on the side street from now on?—Vernon E. Smith, *The Jones Men*, p. 73, 1974
- At least until I got the bread to lay down on a far-out ride (maybe a vintage Rolls, fur-trimmed) B.R. (flash cash) and threads to dazzle and lure whores[.]—Iceberg Slim (Robert Beck), *Airtight Willie and Me*, p. 4, 1979
- "Is this your ride?" OI say, "Yeah, you wanna ride wit me?"—*Boyz N The Hood*, 1990
- —John Edwards, *Auto Dictionary*, p. 138, 1993
- Just some fools peepin' out the ride.—*Menace II Society*, 1993
- This is a nice ride, actually.—*Hard Eight*, 1996
- Nice ride. Vintage fenders.—*Ten Things I Hate About You*, 1999

2 a person who you are counting on to drive you somewhere *US*
- —Don R. McCreary (Editor), *Dawg Speak*, 2001

3 a sexually desirable person *UK*
From **RIDE** (to have sex).
- [T]her [sic] all attractive, fuckin rides, like[.]—Niall Griffiths, *Kelly + Victor*, p. 80, 2002

4 an act of sexual intercourse *UK, 1937*

5 a companion, especially a companion who is a fellow gang member *US*
- —*Maledicta*, p. 265, Summer/Winter 1981: 'By its slang, ye shall know it: the pessimism of prison life'

6 a criminal enterprise *US*
- You keep trying to lay this whole ride on Keaton. It wasn't like that. —*The Usual Suspects*, 1995

7 a style of jazz music with an easy-going rhythm *US, 1930*

▸ get a ride
in circus and carnival usage, to receive unfavourable publicity *US*
- —Don Wilmeth, *The Language of American Popular Entertainment*, p. 110, 1981

ride *verb*
1 to have sex *US*
Usually from the female perspective.
- I tied him to the bed, then I rode him. He loved it!—Anka Radakovich, *The Wild Girls Club*, p. 5, 1994
- She probably got the hots so bad for those hunks she rode Al Dante like a horse for days after.—Rita Ciresi, *Pink Slip*, p. 50, 1999

2 (used of a lesbian) to straddle your prone partner, rubbing your genitals together *US*
- Riding is when one girl gets on top of another and their legs are criss-crossed and you just go up and down.—Ruth Allison, *Lesbianism*, p. 39, 1967

3 to engage in sycophantic flattery *US*
- —*Washington Post Magazine*, p. 17, 18th December 1988: 'Say wha?'

4 to irritate or worry someone *US, 1918*
- I'll have that bugger yet – he's been riding me all week.—Beale, 1984

5 to play jazz with a easy-moving rhythm *US, 1929*

▸ let it ride
1 in gambling, to continue a bet from one play to another, increasing the bet with winnings *US*
- —Lee Solkey, *Dummy Up and Deal*, p. 118, 1980
- Let it all ride.—*Diner*, 1982

2 to tolerate something; to take no action about something *UK, 1921*
- [P]eople in high places might make decisions you don't agree with but it's best to let it ride.—*The Guardian*, 13th June 2003

▸ ride a beef
to accept a charge for a crime that you did not commit *US*
- And he let you ride the beef?—Malcolm Braly, *On the Yard*, p. 292, 1967
- 'No sense anybody else riding this beef,' Harold said stubbornly. —Joseph Wambaugh, *The Choirboys*, p. 365, 1975
- Carol would never ride a beef for a man.—Gerald Petievich, *Money Men*, p. 35, 1981

▸ ride a g-string; ride in a g-string
to drive a BMW car *SOUTH AFRICA*
Scamto youth street slang (South African townships).
- Fancy [...] a ride in a g-string?—Rebecca Harrison, *Reuters*, 8th February 2005

▸ ride a pony
to cheat on a test in college or school *US*
- —*Time Magazine*, p. 46, 24th August 1959

▸ ride bitch
to sit in the middle of the front seat in a pickup truck, between the driver and another passenger *US*
- —Lewis Poteet, *Car & Motorcyle Slang*, p. 164–165, 1992

▸ ride dirty
to drive under the influence of alcohol *US*
- —Don R. McCreary (Editor), *Dawg Speak*, 2001

▸ ride ghost
to drive at night without headlights *US*
- —Steven Daly and Nalthaniel Wice, *alt.culture*, p. 120, 1995

▸ ride it
to endure or cope with imprisonment *UK*
• —Angela Devlin, *Prison Patter*, p. 97, 1996

▸ ride it a treat
in horse racing, to ride a skilled and intelligent race *AUSTRALIA*
• —Ned Wallish, *The Truth Dictionary of Racing Slang*, p. 69, 1989

▸ ride old smokey
to be executed by electrocution *US*
• —Hyman E. Goldin et al., *Dictionary of American Underworld Lingo*, p. 177, 1950

▸ ride rubber
to ride in a car *US*
• —Don Wilmeth, *The Language of American Popular Entertainment*, p. 222, 1981

▸ ride Santa's sleigh
to use cocaine *UK*
A phrase that combines **SNOW** as 'cocaine' with 'flying' as 'intoxication'. Private correspondence, 2000.

▸ ride shotgun
1 to act as a security or military escort *UK*
From the time when stage coaches carrying valuables were protected by a man carrying a shotgun who sat on top of the coach alongside the driver.
• [T]he last two Jaguars [aircraft] with Dave riding shotgun between them. —Robert Prest, *F4 Phantom*, 1979

2 to be prepared for any eventuality in business *US*
• —Robert Kirk Mueller, *Buzzwords*, p. 140, 1974

3 to travel in the passenger seat *US, 1921*
• Originally as an armed guard, but later all sense of protection lost. Big Ed and the other doorman riding shotgun hurriedly followed Smokey toward the house. —Donald Goines, *Dopefiend*, p. 168, 1971
• Although you'd probably have to ride in the back seat 'cause his nuts would ride shotgun. — *The Breakfast Club*, 1985
• I could not take off solo in a Jeep while Strauss followed me (Miranda riding shotgun) in his Audi. —Rita Ciresi, *Pink Slip*, p. 331, 1999
• I drove west on Hamilton, toward the river, to Front Street. Lula was in front riding shotgun, and Bob was in back with his head out the window[.] —Janet Evanovich, *Seven Up*, p. 39–40, 2001

4 to oversee and control someone with a firm hand *US*
• 'Cause you did your time there and nobody wasn't constantly riding shotgun on you. —Bruce Jackson, *In the Life*, p. 122, 1972

▸ ride the broom
to threaten someone; to predict harm *US*
• —Charles Shafer, *Folk Speech in Texas Prisons*, p. 212, 1990
• —William K. Bentley and James M. Corbett, *Prison Slang*, p. 36, 1992

▸ ride the bubbles
in hot rodding and drag racing, to rise slightly off the ground as a result of aerodynamics *US*
• —John Lawlor, *How to Talk Car*, p. 88, 1965

▸ ride the bus
to defecate *US*
• —Connie Eble (Editor), *UNC-CH Campus Slang*, p. 7, November 1990

▸ ride the card
to ride a winner on every race at a race meeting *AUSTRALIA*
• George rode the card on New Year's Day, 1923[.] —Joe Brown, *Just for the Record*, p. 200, 1984

▸ ride the circuit
to move someone who has been arrested from stationhouse to stationhouse, making his timely release difficult *US*
• But we dont' have to. We can ride the circuit with you. It might take days. —Raymond Chandler, *The Little Sister*, p. 174, 1949

▸ ride the cotton pony; ride the cotton horse
to experience the bleed period of the menstrual cycle *US*
This 'cotton pony' is a 'sanitary towel'.
• — *American Speech*, p. 298, December 1954: 'The vernacular of menstruation'
• — *Adult Video News*, p. 38, September 1995
• — *The Museum of Menstruation and Women's Health*, April 2002

▸ ride the grub line
to travel and survive by scrounging food wherever it can be found *CANADA*
• But she was not a schoolteacher. Roy Smith was a schoolteacher. She was riding the grub line. —George Bowering, *Caprice*, p. 60, 1987

▸ ride the Hershey Highway
to engage in anal sex *US*
• —Pamela Munro, *U.C.L.A. Slang*, p. 71, 1989

▸ ride the lightning
to be put to death by electrocution *US, 1935*
• ALL RIGHT, RUBY, YOU'RE GONNA RIDE THE LIGHTNING! —Lenny Bruce, *The Essential Lenny Bruce*, p. 206, 1967

▸ ride the pine
to sit on the sidelines of an athletic contest as a substitute player *US, 1938*
• Jake Powell, a part-time outfielder for the New York Yankees, is riding the pine for 10 days for blurting in an impromptu broadcast on the field in Chicago that he spent his winters doing police work and that his speciality was hitting "niggers"[.] — *San Francisco News*, p. 13, 4th August 1938
• —Connie Eble (Editor), *UNC-CH Campus Slang*, p. 8, March 1986
• I'll call the principal for you and tell him his assistant dean of admissions is gonna be at County Jail riding the pine in the detox box. —Stephen J. Cannell, *The Tin Collectors*, p. 98, 2001

▸ ride the pipe
to pilot a jet after engine failure *US*
Korean war usage.

▸ ride the red tide
to experience the bleed period of the menstrual cycle *US*
• —Karen Houppert, *The Curse*, 1999: 'Riding the red tide.'

▸ ride the short bus
to be mentally deficient *US*
From the literally short bus that special education students use in the US.
• Actually, I think our bass player, Frank [Cavanaugh], rode the short bus, but that was 'cause his mom drove it. — *Baltimore Sun*, p. 8, 28th September 1995
• —Chris Lewis, *The Dictionary of Playground Slang*, p. 184, 2003

▸ ride the showing
to tour an area evaluating billboards for potential advertising use *US*
• —Walter Hurst and Donn Delson, *Delson's Dictionary of Radio & Record Industry Terms*, p. 95, 1980

▸ ride the sick book
to feign illness; to malinger *US*
• —Carl Fleischhauer, *A Glossary of Army Slang*, p. 10, 1968

▸ ride the silver steed
to participate in bismuth subcarbonate and neoarsphenamine therapy for syphilis *US*
• — *Maledicta*, p. 227, Summer/Winter 1981: 'Sex and the single soldier'

▸ ride the splinters
to sit on the sidelines of an athletic contest as a substitute player *US*
The 'splinters' are an allusion to the bench which the substitute 'warms' or 'rides'.
• So he just rides the splinters as the Red Sox certainly have no use for him. — *San Francisco Call-Bulletin*, p. 11, 20th June 1949

▸ ride the turtles
to drive on the raised reflective road markers that delineate motorway lanes *US*
• —Jim Crotty, *How to Talk American*, p. 37, 1997

▸ ride the white horse
to experience euphoria after using heroin *US*
• — *American Speech*, p. 88, May 1955: 'Narcotic argot along the mexican border'

▸ ride the wire
to travel by tram *US*
• We didn't trust cabbies, so we got on another trolley, and in one morning I rode the wire more than I had in five years. —Red Rudensky, *The Gonif*, p. 108, 1970

ride along *verb*
in poker, to remain in a game without betting because you have bet your entire bankroll on the hand *US*
• —Albert H. Morehead, *The Complete Guide to Winning Poker*, p. 271, 1967

ride and a rasher *noun*
sexual intercourse followed by breakfast *IRELAND*
• I'd say she'd give you a ride and a rasher if you played your cards right. —Terence Dolan, *A Dictionary of Hiberno-English*, p. 214, 1999

ride man; ride jock; ride monkey *noun*
the operator of a carnival amusement ride *US*
- Most RIDE MEN make below standard wages, sleep in trucks, and seldom have facilities to bathe, but still hold a reputation for being a ladies man. — Gene Sorrows, *All About Carnivals*, p. 25, 1985

ride out *noun*
a group motor-scooter excursion *UK*
- The ride out soon became a wash out as the sunny skies of the last two days were replaced by bursting clouds. — *The New Untouchables*, September 2001

ride out *verb*
to depart *UK*
Used by London teenagers in the late 1950s.
- — *A Glossary for Our Times (New Chronicle)*, 22nd May 1958

rider *noun*
1 a visible, aggressive member of a gang *US*
- I heard legends about one or two female gangbangers who were said to be "riders," an expression of respect used to describe fiercely active gang members. — *Rolling Stone*, p. 80, 12th April 2001

2 a police officer *US*
- Riders was the latest street slang for police, akin to "Po-Po" and "Five-O," according to Vallimont and Miller. — *Alameda (California) Times-Star*, 12th January 2003

3 5 kg of heroin supplied free with a 100 kg shipment of cocaine *UK*
- — Robert Ashton, *This Is Heroin*, p. 210, 2002

4 a cheater *US*
From the phrase **RIDE A PONY** (to cheat on a test).
- — *Time Magazine*, p. 46, 24 August 1959

5 in trucking, a flat tyre on a set of dual tyres *US*
- — Montie Tak, *Truck Talk*, p. 130, 1971

ridge *adjective*
all right; okay *AUSTRALIA, 1938*
Probably a figurative use of now obsolete 'ridge' (gold). Now superseded by **RIDGY DIDGE**.
- I convinced her the whole thing was ridge! — David Ireland, *The Unknown Industrial Prisoner*, p. 130, 1971
- — Jim Ramsay, *Cop It Sweet!*, p. 77, 1977

ridge cottage *noun*
a bunker in the Korean demilitarised zone *US*
Korean war usage.
- — Frank Hailey, *Soldier Talk*, p. 49, 1982

ridge-runner *noun*
any white male from the Appalachian Mountain region in the southern US *US*
- — *Maledicta*, p. 125, Summer 1980: 'Racial and ethnic slurs: regional awareness and variations'

ridgy didge; ridgy-didge *adjective*
all right; okay *AUSTRALIA, 1953*
- — Jim Ramsay, *Cop It Sweet!*, p. 77, 1977
- Once a Kimberley stockman, his Kimberley Moon is as ridgy-didge as they come. — *West Australian*, p. 13, 1991
- I'd like to invite you to the most dinky-di, ridgy didge, fair dinkum, no worries mate tournament that you could imagine. — *Australian Ultimate*, p. 7, 2003
- Lots of other blokes have had a go at telling you what happened – sticking to the ridgy didge, fair dinkum facts, having got the good oil straight from the horse's mouth. — Kel Richards, *The Aussie Bible*, p. 7, 2003

ridiculous *adjective*
excellent *US, 1959*
- — Robert S. Gold, *A Jazz Lexicon*, p. 251, 1964

riding Saint George; the dragon on Saint George *noun*
heterosexual sex with the woman straddling the man, her head upright *US*
- — *Maledicta*, p. 198, Winter 1980: 'A new erotic vocabulary'

riding the waves; riding a wave *adjective*
experiencing drug intoxication *US, 1930*
- — Richard A. Spears, *The Slang and Jargon of Drugs and Drink*, p. 423, 1986
- — Mike Haskins, *Drugs*, p. 291, 2003

rid up *verb*
▷ **see: RED UP**

R-ie *noun*
a Returned Servicemen's League club *AUSTRALIA, 1992*
From the initials *R*SL.

rif *verb*
to separate someone from military service or employment *US*
From the initialism for '*r*eduction *i*n *f*orce'.
- When he didn't make brigadier, he was "rifted" (for "reduction in force": the army's way of controlling its reserve-officer-corps population). — Robert Mason, *Chickenhawk*, p. 195, 1983
- For a while, he had been worried about being Riffed, thrown out before he had his twenty in, not even getting to retire. — Walter Boyne and Steven Thompson, *The Wild Blue*, p. 426, 1986

riff *noun*
1 a rhythmic musical phrase played repeatedly, used in jazz and rock *US, 1935*
Probably an abbreviation of 'refrain'.
- Do you know how he spent years watching the droopy chicks in cathouses, listening to his cellmates moaning low behind the bars, digging the riffs the wheels were knocking out when he rode the rods[.] — Mezz Mezzrow, *Really the Blues*, p. 5, 1946
- The arrangement Ernie Wilkins put behind him for Basie was so great, I used to tell Ernie to copyright his background riffs. — Babs Gonzales, *Movin' On Down De Line*, p. 64, 1975
- A phrase generally repeated ad nauseum by sections of a big band. Deriving from the Riff song, a chorus repeated ad nauseum in The Desert Song. — Peter Clayton and Peter Gammond, *Bluff Your Way In Jazz*, p. 60, 1992
- I know! I'll use the "may I help you" riff. — *Wayne's World*, 1992
- Bo Diddley's Roadrunner was the Smoke On The Water of the mid-60s – the basic riff with which every fifth form guitarist wrestled. — David Hepworth, *Q Rhythm and Blues*, 1993
- future shocked riffs hit like laser bolts — *Metal Hammer*, p. 4, May 2001

2 an oft-repeated argument or point of view *UK*
A figurative usage of the previous sense.
- Another opportunity for the press to go to town on the old "Evil Acid House Music" riff they were so fond of. — Dave Courtney, *Raving Lunacy*, p. 34, 2000

3 the theme or gist of a conversation *UK*
- Harry explained it all on the plane. I say explained, by which I mean a very extended and loud riff. — James Hawes, *Dead Long Enough*, p. 80, 2000
- That's the riff at least, anyway — Kevin Sampson, *Outlaws*, p. 160, 2001

4 a verbal embellishment that adds no meaning to what is being said *US*
- — Ruth Bronsteen, *The Hippy's Handbook*, p. 15, 1967

5 an activity or experience *US*
- [H]e wasn't sure that she and Zack were not going through a sadomasochistic riff for the sake of the camera. — Ed Sanders, *Tales of Beatnik Glory*, p. 208, 1975

6 a refrigerated railway wagon *US*
- — Norman Carlisle, *The Modern Wonder Book of Trains and Railroading*, p. 267, 1946

riff *verb*
1 to repeatedly play a rhythmic musical figure, usually on a piano or guitar *US, 1955*
- [H]e even riffed 'Kashmir' on the Mellotron for a minute. — *NME*, 28th February 2005

2 to brag; to lie *US*
- Some of the same empty yang you riffin' to me? — *New Jack City*, 1990

3 to complain *US*
- — Ellen C. Bellone (Editor), *Dictionary of Slang*, p. 20, 1989

riffage *noun*
rhythmic style(s) of rock music *UK*
- Faith No More riffage with electronic licks[.] — *The Times*, p. 9, 2nd March 2002

riffle *noun*
in a restaurant or soda fountain, to refill (an order) *US*
- — *American Speech*, p. 63, February 1967: 'Soda-fountain, restaurant and tavern calls'

riffology *noun*
in rock music, simple musical learning or skill *UK*
- [S]imple but devastatingly effective three-chord riffology. — John Robb, *The Nineties*, p. 129, 1999

riff on *verb*
to tease someone; to disparage someone or something *US*
- — Maria Hinojas, *Crews*, p. 167, 1995: 'Glossary'

riff-raff *noun*

1 the lowest class *UK, 1470*

- One is for general riffraff; the second is for old-timers; the third is exclusively for sailors. —Jack Lait and Lee Mortimer, *Washington Confidential*, p. 30, 1951
- Mr. Caraballo, the owner, don't cater to no riff-raff. —Edwin Torres, *Carlito's Way*, p. 117, 1975

2 a Welsh person *UK: ENGLAND*
Rhyming slang for **TAFF**.

- —Ray Puxley, *Cockney Rabbit*, 1992

3 a café *UK*
Rhyming slang for **CAFF**.

- —Ray Puxley, *Fresh Rabbit*, 1998

riffs *noun*
music *CANADA*
Teen slang, reported by a Toronto newspaper in 1946, and reported as 'obsolescent or obsolete' by Douglas Leechman, 1959.

rifle range *noun*

1 the ward in a hospital reserved for patients withdrawing from heroin addiction *US*
A pun on **SHOOTING GALLERY**.

- —David Maurer and Victor Vogel, *Narcotics and Narcotic Addiction*, p. 438, 1973

2 change (money) *UK*
Rhyming slang. Shortened form 'rifle'.

- Here's the sausage [and mash, cash]. Look sharp with the rifle. —Red Daniells, 1980
- —Ray Puxley, *Cockney Rabbit*, 1992

rifle spot *noun*
in the television and film industries, a spotlight that produces a long, thin beam of light *US*

- —Ralph S. Singleton, *Filmaker's Dictionary*, p. 141, 1990

rift *noun*
a refrigerated freight railway wagon *US*

- —Ramon Adams, *The Language of the Railroader*, p. 127, 1977

rig *noun*

1 a car, truck or bus *US, 1938*

- And what a driver – a great big tough truckdriver with popping eyes and a hoarse raspy voice who just slammed and kicked at everything and got his rig under way and paid hardly any attention to me. —Jack Kerouac, *On the Road*, p. 16, 1957
- Well, we don't want to take any chances of missing our young friend, or allowing him to see you climb out of this rig. —Donald Goines, *El Dorado Red*, p. 171, 1974

2 the collective equipment used by a musical group in concert *UK*

- —Tom Hibbert, *Rockspeak!*, p. 132, 1983

3 a hypodermic needle and syringe *US, 1969*

- —Richard A. Spears, *The Slang and Jargon of Drugs and Drink*, p. 423, 1986
- "Sweets for my sweet," Rooski softly crooned withdrawing the spent rig. —Seth Morgan, *Homeboy*, p. 64, 1990
- —Peter Johnson, *Dictionary of Street Alcohol and Drug Terms*, p. 160, 1993
- —Mike Haskins, *Drugs*, p. 292, 2003

4 a still used in the illegal production of alcohol *US*

- —David W. Maurer, *Kentucky Moonshine*, p. 123, 1974

5 a holster *US*

- It is a proven LAPD street-cop axiom that any officer in plain clothes who wears a shoulder rig is, by definition, an asshole. —Stephen J. Cannell, *The Tin Collectors*, p. 104, 2001

6 the penis *US*

- "In fact, I believe the reason we couldn't get his rig out [of the plaster cast] was that it wouldn't GET SOFT." —*Screw*, p. 15, 5th July 1971
- —Tom Hibbert, *Rockspeak!*, p. 132, 1983

7 surgically augmented breasts *US*

- —Anna Scotti and Paul Young, *Buzzwords*, p. 110, 1997

8 a bad situation *US*

- —*Maybeck High School Yearbook (Berkeley, California)*, p. 28, 1997

rigger *noun*

1 in the Royal Air Force, an airframe tradesman *UK, 1943*
An official Royal Air Force job title that was dropped as the job description changed in the 1930s yet has continued in colloquial use; still in Royal Air Force use, 2002.

2 a half-gallon jar of beer *NEW ZEALAND*

- —David McGill, *David McGill's Complete Kiwi Slang Dictionary*, p. 92, 1998

rigger mortis *noun*
an ineffectual member of the Royal Canadian Air Force *CANADA*
A 'rigger mortis' is a useless airman, based on **RIGGER** (an airframe tradesman).

- "What's Dennis like?" "He's a real rigger mortis." —Tom Langeste, *Words on the Wing*, p. 232, 1995

rig gig *noun*
a job driving a truck *US*

- —"Slingo", *The Official CB Slang Dictionary Handbook*, p. 50, 1976

right *noun*
in craps, a bet for the shooter *US*

- At the dice table, the professor would bet either on or against the shooter – otherwise known as do or don't, right or wrong – at $1,000 a shot on what may or may not have been a system. —Edward Lin, *Big Julie of Vegas*, p. 47, 1974

right *adjective*

1 intensifies the good or bad character or condition of someone or something; complete, utter *UK*

- I'll give you a right monkey for the good stuff. —Charles Raven, *Underworld Nights*, p. 89, 1956
- I read no matter how bad the book and some are right under the arm, stand on me. —Frank Norman, *Bang To Rights*, p. 25, 1958
- He looks into the camera and goes, "Hi! I'm Glen. As you can see I'm right off my face!" —Dave Courtney, *Raving Lunacy*, p. 139, 2000
- Fuck off. Fuck right off, son. —Niall Griffiths, *Sheepshagger*, p. 104, 2001

2 understanding and accepting the mores of the underworld *US*

- —Hyman E. Goldin et al., *Dictionary of American Underworld Lingo*, p. 177, 1950

▸ **not right in the head**
unsound of mind *UK, 1934*

- I'm not right in the head now. —*The Guardian*, 20th June 1999

right *adverb*
very *CANADA*

- Other intensifiers were "desperate," and "right" as in "right nice". —Harry Bruce, *Down Home*, p. 107, 1988

right

1 used as a greeting or farewell *TRINIDAD AND TOBAGO, 1966*

- —Lise Winer, *Dictionary of the English/Creole of Trinidad & Tobago*, 2003

2 I do not believe you *UK*
Heavily sarcastic, emphasising the negative interpretation. Variants include 'yeah right' and 'aye right'.

- In every language, the lecturer said, you could use two negatives to make a positive – but in English two positives don't make a negative. Cue voice from back of the hall: "Yeah, right." —David Rowan, *A Glossary for the 90s*, p. 196, 1998
- New century. New parliament. New Scotland. Aye, right. —Christopher Brookmyre, *Boiling a Frog*, 2000
- The guy did a palms-up. "No-one knows. Just one of those things." Right. —Janet Evanovich, *Seven Up*, p. 41, 2001

right as rain *adjective*
in good health; satisfactory *UK, 1909*

- Right as rain for two pins, she said. —Richard Francis, *The Rialto*, p. 87, 1999

right enough *adverb*
certainly, indeed *UK, 1885*

- Walk up the hill, past the 'Air Circle' – and right enough, there did seem to be air in it, quite a lot really[.] —*The Observer*, 27th June 1999

righteous *adjective*

1 very good, excellent, fine; honest; satisfactory *US, 1942*
Conventional English with a religious overtone propelled into hip slang by context and emphasis in pronunciation.

- In the late summer of 1924 I got the band together and we headed for the Martinique Inn at Indiana Harbor, righteous and ready. —Mezz Mezzrow, *Really the Blues*, p. 70, 1946
- That from all these ace-stamped studs we double our love kick to that righteous ride for which they cats hard-sounded the last nth bong of the bell of their bell. —William "Lord" Buckley, *The Gettysburg Address*, 1951
- Ah, these righteous dudes, they love to screw it on. —Hunter S. Thompson, *Hell's Angels*, p. 3, 1966
- Owsley makes righteous acid, said the heads. —Tom Wolfe, *The Electric Kool-Aid Acid Test*, p. 188, 1968
- Yes it makes me righteous, yes it makes me feel whole / Yes it makes me mellow down in to my soul. —Van Morrison, *Crazy Love*, 1970

- No offense, but it sounds to me like Cincinnati ain't no healthy place for a righteous dude to be in.—Gurney Norman, *Divine Right's Trip (Last Whole Earth Catalog)*, p. 193, 1971
- 'It'll get you so righteous ripped,' Cob promises Jerry.—John Rechy, *The Fourth Angel*, p. 31, 1972
- Yeahhh, man... George Raft was a sho' 'nuff righteous dude.—Odie Hawkins, *Chicago Hustle*, p. 7, 1977
- C'mon brah, there's a righteous swell.—*Break Point*, 1991

2 used of a drug, relatively pure and undiluted *US*

- I hear it's a very good scene there. Not much heat, beautiful people, no speed freaks, and righteous dope.—Nicholas Von Hoffman, *We Are The People Our Parents Warned Us Against*, p. 47, 1967
- —William D. Alsever, *Glossary for the Establishment and Other Uptight People*, p. 16, December 1970
- So I did these two hits of this acid. It was sa righteous five hundred mikes.—Stephen Gaskin, *Amazing Dope Tales*, p. 133, 1980
- Some, uh, really righteous grass.—George V. Higgins, *Penance for Jerry Kennedy*, p. 228, 1985

righteous bush *noun*

any potent variety of marijuana *US, 1946*

A combination of **RIGHTEOUS** (good) and **BUSH** (marijuana).

- —Richard A. Spears, *The Slang and Jargon of Drugs and Drink*, p. 424, 1986
- —Mike Haskins, *Drugs*, p. 289, 2003

righteous name *noun*

a person's true name *US*

- I never gave a snitch's righteous name since I been on the job.—Joseph Wambaugh, *The Choirboys*, p. 302, 1975

righteous nod *noun*

a refreshing sleep *US*

- —Marcus Hanna Boulware, *Jive and Slang of Students in Negro Colleges*, 1947

right guy *noun*

a dependable, trustworthy and reliable criminal *US*

- —R. Frederick West, *God's Gambler*, p. 228, 1964: 'Appendix A'

right here

used as a set answer to an inquiry as to how you are *BAHAMAS*

- —John A. Holm, *Dictionary of Bahamian English*, p. 169, 1982

rightie *noun*

in craps, a gambler who bets that the shooter will make his point before rolling a seven *US*

- —John Scarne, *Scarne on Dice*, p. 477, 1974

rightio!; righty-o!; righteho!; righty-ho!

all right!; certainly!; gladly! *UK, 1927*

right numbers; right price *noun*

in horse racing, higher than normal odds that merit a wager *US, 1968*

- —Thomas L. Clark, *The Dictionary of Gambling and Gaming*, p. 181, 1987

righto; right-oh

okay!; all right! *AUSTRALIA, 1911*

- RIGHTO – Exclamation of consent.—Gilbert H. Lawson, *A Dictionary of Australian Words and Terms*, 1924
- 'Feel like exploring? It is nearly dinner-time anyway.' 'Right-oh.'—Ion L. Idriess, *Over the Range*, p. 71, 1947
- Oh – righto mate – thanks.—Clive Exton, *No Fixed Abode [Six Granada Plays]*, p. 124, 1959
- 'Righto, Saint Patrick,' Starkey said with a pat on the old man's back. 'We'll see you again.'—D'Arcy Niland, *Dead Men Running*, p. 75, 1969
- He'll be righto again in a minute.—Lance Peters, *The Dirty Half-Mile*, p. 180, 1979
- SHIRLEY: [...] There is a rather fine John Barrymore film on the television tonight that I should hate to miss. JOAN: Righto, Shirl. SHIRLEY: Righto? JOAN: It's my catchphrase. SHIRLEY: Just so long as it's not contagious. WATSON: Righto.—Terry Victor, *The Pedigree Pet*, p. 35, 1981
- Righto, you fellas, one at a time, see if you can belt him.—Herb Wharton, *Cattle Camp*, p. 75, 1994
- Kenny shouted, "Righto, righto, keep it down, we're ready for the off[.]"—Lenny McLean, *The Guv'nor'*, p. 80–81, 1998

right on!

yes; excellent; correct; also used to signal enthusiastic agreement *US*

Originally black usage, perhaps from 'right on the button', 'right on time' or **RIGHTO**. Subsequently adopted by the hippie generation.

- It's good right on, oh it's good right on / Everybody wants it because it's good right on.—Rufus and Ben Quillian, *"Good Right On"*, 1930
- "I have some acid." "Good. Right on."—Doug Lang, *Freaks*, p. 64, 1973
- "Fucking tories," said Mo. "Right on!" Colonel Hira's chubby fist jabbed the air.—Michael Moorcock, *The Spencer Innheritance [britpulp]*, p. 27, 1998

right one *noun*

a person whose behaviour does not conform to expectations *UK, 1981*

- [F]uck me – got a right on yer [here] – look.—Patrick Jones, *Unprotected Sex*, p. 249, 1999

the Right Reverend *noun*

▷ **see: REVEREND RONALD KNOX**

rights *noun*

▸ **do the rights**

to seek or gain revenge *UK*

- —Paul Baker, *Polari*, p. 172, 2002

right-said-Fred *noun*

the head *UK*

Rhyming slang, formed on the name of a pop group who enjoyed success in the early 1990s; the group took its name from the title of a humorous song by Bernard Cribbins which was a top ten hit in 1962.

- If anyone was going to realise that I was out of my right-said-Fred, it would be him.—Ken Lukowiak, *Marijuana Time*, p. 57, 2000

righty *noun*

someone who looks very much like someone else; a double or near double *US*

- —Joseph E. Ragen and Charles Finston, *Inside the World's Toughest Prison*, p. 815, 1962: 'Penitentiary and underworld glossary'

right you are!

certainly!; agreed! *UK, 1864*

- "I'm fine, it's okay. Now are we going to try and leave again? I'll hold on to something this time!" "Right you are, Harry, let's go! Put your foot down Fred!" George grinned.—*The Guardian*, 18th June 2003

rigid *adjective*

drunk *US*

- —Helen Dahlskog (Editor), *A Dictionary of Contemporary and Colloquial Usage*, p. 48, 1972

rigid *adverb*

greatly; used to intensify, especially 'bore', 'scare' and 'shake' *UK, 1943*

Modelled on synonymous **STIFF**, always used after the verb it modifies.

- The Blair Witch Project recaptures the old black magic of the ghost story and scares Peter Bradshaw rigid.—*The Guardian*, 22nd October 1999
- [One guy] bored me rigid then still had the cheek to ask if I wanted to have sex on a nearby building site.—*The Observer*, 30th June 2002
- I've been a fan of Sue Miller's since The Good Mother [...] shook me rigid[.]—*The Guardian Unlimited*, August 2003

rigmarole *noun*

a string of incoherent statements; a disjointed or rambling speech; a trival or almost senseless harangue *UK, 1736*

- In crude code it said, 'Bad Landry rigmarole.'—Iceberg Slim (Robert Beck), *Trick Baby*, p. 56, 1969

rigor mortis *noun*

in croquet, the condition of not being able to hit any opponent's ball on a turn *US*

- —James Charlton and William Thompson, *Croquet*, p. 160, 1977: 'Glossary'

RIH

*r*est *i*n *h*ell *US*

A bitter version of RIP (rest in peace).

- All the photos had R.I.H. scribbled on with a felt-tip pen. Rest in Hell.—Elmore Leonard, *Be Cool*, p. 30, 1999

rile *verb*

to annoy or anger someone *UK, 1836*

- Australia's new 'hairy-chested' attitude riles its east Asian neighbours.—*The Guardian*, 4th December 2002

rim *noun*

▸ **above the rim**

of the highest quality *US*

- —Alonzo Westbrook, *Hip Hoptionary*, p. 1, 2002

rim *verb*

1 to lick, suck and tongue another's anus *US, 1941*

- "Darling, I want to rim you," she whispers.—William Burroughs, *Naked Lunch*, p. 90, 1957
- —Donald Webster Cory and John P. LeRoy, *The Homosexual and His Society*, p. 266, 1963: 'A Lexicon of Homosexual Slang'
- —Dale Gordon, *The Dominion Sex Dictionary*, p. 140, 1967

- Finally, the third man advances to the side of Johnny, licking his chest as the first one did earlier, tongue flitting over his nipples now, then along his back, down, rimming him[.] — John Rechy, *Numbers*, p. 181, 1967
- Rimming is the usual word for it. (Inf.: to rim.) — Angelo d'Arcangelo, *The Homosexual Handbook*, p. 96, 1968
- Your lips are turning blue; you look like you been rimming a snowman. — Mart Crowley, *The Boys in the Band*, p. 94, 1968
- This manipulation of the hungry mouth upon a tender asshole is more commonly known among sexual gourmets as rimming, sometimes pronounced reaming by the lowborn[.] — *Screw*, p. 10, 19th January 1970
- Someone should also caution you that you can get hepatitis from rimming. — John Francis Hunter, *The Gay Insider*, p. 26, 1971
- Or some of them might turn out to scarf and rim [cunnilingus and analingus] to make it. — Bruce Jackson, *In the Life*, p. 120, 1972
- — Terry Southern, *Now Dig This*, p. 52, 25th January 1972
- In the car, Jim raises his body, the other's tongue rims him. — John Rechy, *The Sexual Outlaw*, p. 197, 1977
- — Angela Devlin, *Prison Patter*, p. 97, 1996

2 to swindle someone *US*

- — Vincent J. Monteleone, *Criminal Slang*, p. 194, 1949

rim-jag *verb*

to make an indentation on a playing card with your fingernail or thumbnail to identify the card later in another player's hand *US*

- — George Percy, *The Language of Poker*, p. 75, 1988

rim job *noun*

the licking of a partner's anus for the purposes of sexual pleasure *US*

- Thrills shot from one end of Annette's body to the other, as his tongue ran circles around her behind, giving her a rim job. — Steve Cannon, *Groove, Bang, and Jive Around*, p. 8, 1969
- KYLE'S MOTHER: What was that word, young man? CARTMAN'S MOTHER: Oh, he said rim job. It's when someone licks your ass. — *South Park*, 1999

rimmer *noun*

a person who provides mouth in mouth-to-anus sex *US*

- — *Maledicta*, p. 235, 1979: 'Kinks and queens: linguistic and cultural aspects of the terminology for gays'

rim queen *noun*

a male homosexual who is proficient at mouth-to-anus stimulation *US*

- — *American Speech*, p. 58, Spring-Summer 1970: 'Homosexual slang'

rimrock *verb*

to drive livestock into an enclosure; to entrap someone *CANADA*

- You've got me to thank, boy, for saving you from being rimrocked by a bunch of females in that town. — Richmond Hobson, *Grass Beyond the Mountains*, p. 59, 1951
- With the Vanderhoof stockyards only seven days away, I had a strong feeling that if any outfit could rimrock this drive into the cattle cars, this was the one that would do it. — Richmond Hobson, *Nothing too Good for a Cowboy*, p. 188, 1955

rims *noun*

sunglasses *US*

- — Judi Sanders, *Da Bomb*, p. 13, 1997

rinctum *noun*

an especially violent fit of temper *CANADA*

- She was very angry, a heavenly rinctum! — *Dalhousie Review*, p. 43, Fall 1953

Rinehart!; Oh Rinehart!

used as a shout to announce the onset of a student disturbance, started in fun but not always ending as such *US, 1933*

Specific to Harvard University, honouring John Rinehart, Harvard Law School class of 1903.

- In 1900 a new cry, 'Oh Rinehart!' first sounded through Harvard Yard and in the following years became the high-explosive summons for book-disgruntled students. — *American Speech*, p. 293, December 1958

ring *noun*

1 a telephone call *UK, 1900*

- Give me a ring in a couple of hours. I'll be at the office. — Mickey Spillane, *My Gun is Quick*, p. 100, 1950

2 the anus *UK, 1949*

From the shape.

- I've never liked anyone enough to want to put me entire arm up ther [sic] ring. — Niall Griffiths, *Kelly + Victor*, p. 236, 2002

3 a circular area where the game of two-up takes place *AUSTRALIA, 1896*

- In the lantern light of the two-up ring they pitted skill against skill, luck against luck[.] — Frank Hardy, *Power Without Glory*, p. 334, 1950
- Then he'd make a dinkum spin and if the coins came down heads, the ringie (all ringies worked in with the nob spinners) would immediately turn the pennies over in the ring to show their tails. — Sidney J. Baker, *The Australian Language*, p. 245, 1966
- — Jim Ramsay, *Cop It Sweet!*, p. 77, 1977

4 collectively, the bookmakers at a racecourse *AUSTRALIA, 1877*

- To deceive the ring, all sorts of rumours are circulated. — J.S. James, *The Vagabond Papers*, p. 130, 1877
- — Tom Ellis, *The Science of Turf Investment*, p. 65, 1936
- The ring had overlaid their books to a large amount on the horse. — Maurice Cavanough and Meurig Davies, *Cup Day*, p. 40, 1960
- — Gerald Sweeney, *The Plunge*, p. 3, 1981
- The leader of the ring Big Bobby Watson bore the brunt of the plunge. — Clive Galea, *Slipper*, p. 42, 1988
- The Ring (capital "R") is the main betting ring in the enclosure known as Tattersall's. — David Bennet, *Know Your Bets*, p. 96, 2001

▸ **get a ring in your nose**

in horse racing, to lose all your money betting *US*

- — David W. Maurer, *Argot of the Racetrack*, p. 31, 1951

▸ **put the ring around it**

to confirm something as definite *NEW ZEALAND*

- 'It had better be good weather then,' Latty said. 'You can put the ring around that,' Len said. — Vincent O'SAullivan, *The Boy, the Bridge, the River*, p. 130, 1978

ring *verb*

1 to provide one thing disguised as another *UK, 1812*

- He had the needle to me after that and used to ring my library books, lumbering me with Hegel and Kant when I had applied for Somerset Maugham[.] — Charles Raven, *Underworld Nights*, p. 192, 1956

2 to open and pilfer a cash register *US*

- Butch had warned me many times to never ring a cash register when there was nobody around to keep the person on the counter busy. — Claude Brown, *Manchild in the Promised Land*, p. 31, 1965

3 to shout *BARBADOS*

- — Frank A. Collymore, *Barbadian Dialect*, p. 93, 1965

▸ **ring it on**

to outwit someone *UK*

- They have rung it on us. — David Powis, *The Signs of Crime*, 1977

▸ **ring the bell**

1 to make a successful attempt at something *UK*

Probably from a fairground challenge.

- He had made two or three attempts at suicide, and his last one nearly rang the bell. — Geoffrey Fletcher, *Down Among the Meths Men*, p. 26, 1966

2 to achieve success beyond expectations *US*

- — Hyman E. Goldin et al., *Dictionary of American Underworld Lingo*, p. 179, 1950

▸ **ring the berries**

in ice hockey, to hit the goalie with a hard shot between the legs *CANADA*

- The puck, when you ring the berries, hits a special hard molded plastic protective cup, which gives off a high bong. — George Plimpton, *Open Net*, p. 42, 1985

▸ **ring your chimes**

to strike someone on the head with great force *US*

- If their wives weren't coming down after them it'd be the cops or some sonofabitch wanted to ring their chimes for them. — George V. Higgins, *The Rat on Fire*, p. 102, 1981

ring-a-ding *noun*

an excellent example of something *US*

- In the patois of the Rat Pack, a ring a ding of a scene. — Sidney Bernard, *This Way to the Apocalypse*, p. 153, 1965

ring-a-ling on the ting-a-ling *noun*

a telephone call *US*

- — Hy Lit, *Hy Lit's Unbelievable Dictionary of Hip Words for Groovy People*, p. 33, 1968

ring angel *noun*

a 'blip' on a radar screen, often a flock of birds *US, 1947*

- All unidentified dots [on the radar screen] were originally dubbed "angels" by the radar men [...] Dots in circles that move outward like ripples on a pond are known as "ring-angels". — Jeffrey Boswell (Editor), *Private Lives*, 1970

ringas *noun*
conversation; a conversation *SOUTH AFRICA*
Scamto youth street slang (South African townships).
• — *The Times*, 12th February 2005

ringburner *noun*
an act of defecation that is attended by burning, stinging or other painful sensations in the anus; often applied to the spicy food that causes such effects *UK*
Combines **RING** (the anus) with a conventional sense of 'burn'; upper-class society origins. The following definition is offered by Ann Barr and Peter York in their 1982 *Official Sloane Ranger Handbook*: 'The results of a heavy curry the morning after'.

ringer *noun*
1 a perfect resemblance *US, 1891*
Often intensified with **DEAD**.
• Around 10,000 people – wearing rear-vented Brooks Brothers flannels instead of flashy pinstripes, operating out of the suites in Radio City and the Squibb Building instead of drug-store phone booth, but all of them, in essence, dead ringers for Mort Robel. — Bernard Wolfe, *The Late Risers*, p. 38, 1954
• He was a dead ringer for me. — Angela Devlin, *Prison Patter*, p. 98, 1996
2 an athlete or horse fraudulently entered in a game or race *US, 1890*
• We can balance that by getting ourselves a ringer. — *M*A*S*H*, 1970
• Impressed with Alf's story and his overwhelming confidence, Sam passed the word to Davis that he should pull Three Gulls and back the 'ringer'. — Joe Andersen, *Winners Can Laugh*, p. 173, 1982
• [O]n the day after the race he was put down, but it transpired that this was destroying the evidence in another ringer case. — John McCririck, *John McCririck's World of Betting*, p. 141, 1991
3 a false vehicle registration number plate *US*
• Blackie backed the car deftly into the barn and fixed the "ringers"[.] — Charles Raven, *Underworld Nights*, p. 17, 1956
4 a criminal who builds new cars from the parts of stolen cars *UK*
• — Peter Laurie, *Scotland Yard*, p. 327, 1970
5 a single inhalation of crack cocaine with a strong effect *US*
• — US Department of Justice, *Street Terms*, October 1994
6 a stockman *AUSTRALIA*
• Three of four bookies at the breakfast table were involved and at the next table were a bunch of ringers. — Sam Weller, *Old Bastards I Have Met*, p. 136, 1979
• Every ringer in the place up north, or around 80 percent of them, is shacked up with a gin. — Sandra Jobson, *Blokes*, p. 168, 1984
• — Frank Hardy, *Hardy's People*, p. 132, 1986
• — Herb Wharton, *Cattle Camp*, p. 33, 1994
7 the fastest shearer in a shearing shed *AUSTRALIA, 1871*
• RINGER – The quickest shearer. — Gilbert H. Lawson, *A Dictionary of Australian Words and Terms*, 1924
• They all looked at a white-haired man, their ringer and spokesman, and one nudged him forward. — Bill Wannan, *Folklore of the Australian Pub*, p. 58, 1972
• — Bob Ellis and Anne Brooksbank, *Mad Dog Morgan*, p. 88, 1976
• — Jim Ramsay, *Cop It Sweet!*, p. 77, 1977

ring game *noun*
a game of poker with all seats at the table occupied *US*
• — David M. Hayano, *Poker Faces*, p. 187, 1982

ringie *noun*
the person running a game of two-up *AUSTRALIA, 1941*
• 'Heads,' said George Rand, who acted as ringie. — Frank Hardy, *Power Without Glory*, p. 334, 1950
• — Jim Ramsay, *Cop It Sweet!*, p. 77, 1977

ring-in *noun*
1 an illegal competitor substituted for another in a race *AUSTRALIA, 1918*
• A smartie entered a ring-in for a Maiden Handicap at a bush race meeting. He entered her as an eight-year-old mare unraced. The mare duly bolted in by 10 lengths. — Frank Hardy and Athol George Mulley, *The Needy and the Greedy*, p. 110, 1975
• — Jim Ramsay, *Cop It Sweet!*, p. 77, 1977
• — Roy Higgins and Tom Prior, *The Jockey Who Laughed*, p. 38, 1982
• — Frank Hardy, *Hardy's People*, p. 187, 1986
• '[C]an you dolly up the ring-in so he can pass for Tama?' — Clive Galea, *Slipper*, p. 132, 1988
2 any surreptitious substitute *AUSTRALIA*
• But the pimps had to be trusted to a large extent in police inquiries, and to make sure that they were not ring-ins from the underworld they were screened thoroughly by the police who used them. — Vince Kelly, *The Bogeyman*, p. 71, 1956
3 one who doesn't belong; an outsider *AUSTRALIA*
• She contemplated her description of Buchanan as a feisty fast-talking ring-in from the sticks. — Rodney Hall, *Kisses of the Enemy*, p. 97, 1987

ring in *verb*
1 to illegally substitute a racehorse or greyhound for another in a race; to substitute a phoney in a competition *AUSTRALIA, 1895*
• Some gentlemen who run these picnic race clubs I have found out to be anything but amateurs when it comes to making a book—an amateur book, or course—or ringing in a good one to win a race. — Nat Gould, *On and Off the Turf*, p. 140, 1895
• And I warn you, even if he's losing, I'm not going to ride him with the whip and spur like some of these old pros rung in as honorary amateurs. — Dymphna Cusack, *Picnic Races*, p. 158, 1962
• At Fitzroy a couple of days later it was 'rung-in' as a mediocre galloper named Iron. — James Holledge, *The Great Australian Gamble*, p. 90, 1966
• We had their boats being scrutinised all day and if they was ringing in tethered fish, you tell me how they done it. — Bob Staines, *Wot a Whopper*, p. 28, 1982
• — Ryan Aven-Bray, *Ridgey Didge Oz Jack Lang*, p. 41, 1983
2 to secretly introduce altered dice into a dice game *US*
• — *The Annals of the American Academy of Political and Social Sciences*, p. 130, May 1950

ringing-in *noun*
the illegal substitution of a racehorse or greyhound in a race *AUSTRALIA*
• In the old days, there was a fair bit of ringing-in around the bush racetracks. — Frank Hardy and Athol George Mulley, *The Needy and the Greedy*, p. 21, 1975
• — Joe Andersen, *Winners Can Laugh*, p. 175, 1982

ring-keeper *noun*
the person running a game of two-up *AUSTRALIA, 1896*
• — Vince Kelly, *The Bogeyman*, p. 178, 1956
• The school had a permanent staff of at least 40 – cockatoos, ring-keepers, chuckers-out, doormen, cleaners, clerks and cashiers. — James Holledge, *The Great Australian Gamble*, p. 93, 1966
• — John O'Grady, *It's Your Shout, Mate!*, p. 24, 1972

ring-knocker *noun*
a graduate of one of the US military academies *US*
From the school rings worn by graduates.
• — Linda Reinberg, *In the Field*, p. 184, 1991

ringmaster *noun*
a railway yardmaster *US*
• — Norman Carlisle, *The Modern Wonder Book of Trains and Railroading*, p. 267, 1946

ringpiece *noun*
the anus *UK, 1949*
An **ARSEHOLE** in both the anatomical and figurative senses.
• It was the diminutive Reid herself who had been surgically removed from his ringpiece. — Christopher Brookmyre, *Boiling a Frog*, p. 104, 2000
• He told Mo that he would see him in the recess later and stick his scoop up his foorkin' ringpiece. — *The Guardian*, 9th November 2000
• I'm not kissing his ringpiece, mind you[.] — Kevin Sampson, *Outlaws*, p. 139, 2001
• Your basic dildo is a good way to stretch out a rookie ringpiece, because it has no ridges or things to trigger a cut. — Suroosh Alvi et al., *The Vice Guide*, p. 39, 2002
• [A]bout as stimulating as Thora Hird's ringpiece. — *Ministry*, p. 21, October 2002

ring raider *noun*
a male homosexual *UK*
An allusion to anal intercourse, based on **RING** (the anus).
• — Chris Lewis, *The Dictionary of Playground Slang*, p. 185, 2003

ring-sting *noun*
a burning sensation in and of the anus caused, generally, by spicy food *UK, 1984*
Formed on **RING** (the anus). Occasionally, and originally, known as 'ring-burn'.
• I'm sorry Denise... the last thing I wanted was to be stood at the altar with you with ring-sting. — Caroline Aherne and Craig Cash, *The Royle Family*, 1999
• A Ruby Murray (curry) that induces ring sting and leaves one with an arse like a Jap flag [inflamed]. — *Roger's Profanisaurus*, 2002

ring-stinger *noun*
a curry that produces, as an after-effect, a burning, stinging or other painful sensation in the anus *UK*
- — *Roger's Profanisaurus*, 2002

ringy *adjective*
irritable *US, 1932*
- What do you want that goddamn speed for? You know how ringy it makes you. It turns you into a different person, Bob, and I don't much like that person. — *Drugstore Cowboy*, 1988

rink rat *noun*
a young boy who hangs around ice rinks, totally involved in hockey *US*
- — Lou Shelly, *Hepcats Jive Talk Dictionary*, p. 31, 1945
- — Dobie Gillis, *Teenage Slanguage Dictionary*, 1962
- In Montreal, a rink rat is a kid who spends all his time either playing hockey or watching it being played at the neighbourhood arena. In the Boston Garden, the rink rats were furry rodents, skittering along hallways and under seats. — *Montreal Gazette*, p. A2, 19th April 2002

rinky-dink *noun*
1 something that is second rate, cheap or trivial *US, 1912*
- I had to cook my ass on them stone bleachers, with a Spike Jones band playin' rinky-dink behind me. — Edwin Torres, *After Hours*, p. 197, 1979
- Robbie was smiling sincerely now. It was a con, he was positive. These rinky-dinks were giving him the grim-cop number, Hurd, playing stone-face, and he was supposed to what, break down? — Elmore Leonard, *Split Images*, p. 278, 1981

2 in trucking, the 4000 model White tractor *US*
- — Montie Tak, *Truck Talk*, p. 131, 1971

3 in snooker, the *pink* ball *UK*
- — Ray Puxley, *Cockney Rabbit*, 1992

rinky-dink *adjective*
inexpensive; poorly made; worthless *US, 1912*
- My struggle-buggy was getting to look like a rinky-dinky old tin can on wheels[.] — Mezz Mezzrow, *Really the Blues*, p. 87, 1946
- — Carol Covington, *A Glossary of Teenage Terms*, 1965
- "He was a rinky-dink dope dealer most," Boone continued. — Vernon E. Smith, *The Jones Men*, p. 124, 1974
- Not like those rinkydink toys sold in S&M shops. — Seth Morgan, *Homeboy*, p. 67, 1990

rinse *noun*
a selection of dance tunes mixed into a seamless whole; an event which features such a musical blend *UK*
- Mee' ya down Brickhouse for the rinse na mean [know what I mean], says Deezee[.] — Nick Barlay, *Curvy Lovebox*, p. 101, 1997

rinse *verb*
to mix dance tunes into a seamless whole *UK*
Perhaps because of the wash of sound.
- banging commercial hits that got rinsed around most bars in the immediate vicinity — Wayne Anthony, *Spanish Highs*, p. 162, 1999
- Phoenix were rinsing an easy-listening set of old lovers' and devotional 'revival' tunes. — Diran Abedayo, *My Once Upon A Time*, p. 71, 2000

▸ **rinse arse; rinse skin; rinse tail**
to administer a severe beating *TRINIDAD AND TOBAGO, 1992*
- — Lise Winer, *Dictionary of the English/Creole of Trinidad & Tobago*, 2003

rinsebag *noun*
a plastic bag that once contained amphetamine *US*
- A trace amount of speed remains in the bag; the contents of several of these rinsebags may be combined, in the same manner as cottons, to produce enough drug to achieve a high. — Geoffrey Froner, *Digging for Diamonds*, p. 51, 1989

rinsing!; rinsin'!
excellent; a general-purpose superlative *UK*
The cry of approval offered up to a DJ who is rinsing tunes together (see **RINSE**), adopted by clubbers into wider usage.
- Ibiza! Rinsin'! Large it! Megaaaaaaaaa! — Richard Topping, *Havin' It Large*, p. 93, 2000
- — Susie Dent, *The Language Report*, p. 75, 2003

Rin-Tin-Tin; rinty *noun*
the leg *UK*
Rhyming slang for **PIN**, formed from the name given to several generations of a German Shepherd dog television and film star of the 1930s – 50s and beyond.
- [A] bit lively on his "rintys"[.] — Ray Puxley, *Fresh Rabbit*, 1998

Rio *noun*
Rio de Janeiro *US, 1935*
- It's only a whimsical notion / To fly down to Rio tonight / I probably won't fly down to Rio / But then again I just might — Michael Nesmith, *Rio*, 1977
- Leading soap opera stars joined tens of thousands of Rio residents yesterday to demand more stringent gun controls in Brazil, one of the world's most violent countries. — *The Guardian*, 15th September 2003

riot *noun*
something or someone that is very amusing or greatly funny *UK, 1933*
- — Miss Cone, *The Slang Dictionary (Hawthorne High School)*, 1965
- — Billy Bragg, *Life's a Riot with Spy Vs Spy*, 1983
- In that role, he [Humphrey Lyttleton]'s a riot: the star of the show[.] — *The Guardian*, 23rd May 2001

riot bell *noun*
in prison, any bell *UK*
- — Angela Devlin, *Prison Patter*, p. 98, 1996

riot grrrl; riot girl *noun*
a cultural movement of aggressive young feminists; a member of the riot grrrl movement; the sub-genre of punk rock music associated with the movement *US, 1991*
Lazy journalism seems to be responsible for 'girl/grrl' variations.
- Kathleen Hanna, singer for Bikini Kill, states that the name "riot grrrl" was inspired in 1991 by the Mount Pleasant riots in Washington, D.C.: "During that time, Jean Smith [...] said something like, "We need a girl riot, too." [...] Allison and Molly from Bratmobile [...] heard this and said, "we're going to start a fanzine called Riot Grrrl." — Marion Leonard, *Cool Places*, p. 102 – 103, 1998
- Even The Spice Girls' glib appropriation of the riot grrrl slogan as "Girl Power" was vaguely empowering five year olds in the schoolyard. — John Robb, *The Nineties*, p. 120, 1999

Riot Hyatt; Riot House *nickname*
The Continental Hyatt House, Sunset Boulevard, Los Angeles, famous for its association with rock musicians *US*
- EMI and Book Soup were just down the road with House of Blues and the *Spinal Tap*-legendary Riot Hyatt a walk the other way. — Kevin Sampson, *Powder*, p. 281, 1999
- WILLIAM: You just missed Russell! He says he's at the "Riot House" all week and to call him. — *Almost Famous*, 2000

riot panic *noun*
in circus and carnival usage, enthusiastic applause *US*
- — Don Wilmeth, *The Language of American Popular Entertainment*, p. 224, 1981

rip *noun*
1 a current travelling seawards from shore, usually moving swiftly *US*
An abbreviation of 'rip tide' or 'rip current'.
- He bitched about missing some rad tubes and said that old dorks shouldn't be anywhere near a rip, even a baby rip. — Joseph Wambaugh, *The Golden Orange*, p. 33, 1990

2 a method of breaking into a safe that employs mechanical force and no explosives *US*
- — Hyman E. Goldin et al., *Dictionary of American Underworld Lingo*, p. 179, 1950

3 in a cheating scheme in a dice game, the switching of tampered dice into a game *US*
- — Frank Garcia, *Marked Cards and Loaded Dice*, p. 263, 1962

4 an injustice; an action that is fundamentally unfair *US*
- — Connie Eble (Editor), *UNC-CH Campus Slang*, p. 7, Spring 1982

5 a complaint lodged against a police officer *US*
- — *New York Times*, 15th February 1970

6 a fine or punishment imposed for breaking a police department conduct rule *US*
- I got a five-day rip (fined five days' pay). — *New York Times Magazine*, p. 88, 16th March 1958

7 one pound sterling *UK*
- [A]nything more than a hundred rips'd have to have Keva's counter signature[.] — Kevin Sampson, *Powder*, p. 37, 1999

8 marijuana *UK*
- — Mike Haskins, *Drugs*, p. 289, 2003

9 a coarse, unattractive woman *IRELAND, 1910*
- I'm half in love with aul' rip – I am. — Kevin Sampson, *Clubland*, p. 95, 2002

rip *verb*

1 to cheat or swindle someone *US, 1904*

- "How much did you pay for this man?" I asked her. "Sixty-five." I pressed my lips together. "You got ripped." — Rita Ciresi, *Pink Slip*, p. 18, 1999

2 to steal something *US*

- Most cars you rip are worth two or three hundred dollars. — *Repo Man*, 1984

3 to kill someone *US*

- He probably had him ripped anyway. — Vernon E. Smith, *The Jones Men*, p. 5, 1974

4 to travel quickly *UK*

- [T]he others got drunk and ripped up and down the streets on their bikes. — Jamie Mandelkau, *Buttons*, p. 102, 1971

5 to surf in a bold, skilled manner *US*

- — Brian and Margaret Lowdon, *Competitive Surfing*, 1988

6 to excel *US*

- CHAZZ: You like that Seattle bullshit? CALLER 1: Shroud rips, dude. — *Airheads*, 1994
- "You fully rip," Duck said. — Francesca Lia Block, *Baby Be-Bop*, p. 471, 1995

▸ **rip a new asshole**

to berate someone severely *US*

- She would have some beef with me, real or imagined, and she'd rip me a new asshole or give me the silent treament. — Howard Stern, *Miss America*, p. 168, 1995

▸ **rip into**

to attack someone or something with vigour or gusto *AUSTRALIA, 1970*

Either physically or verbally.

- Ralph Broom ripped into the Graham Kennedy conference in The Sun the next day and tore it to shreds. — Bert Newton, *Bert!*, p. 145, 1977
- The only time we had any chance of getting any affection or attention was at night when it was too dark to check out the tubes. Then he'd rip into you. — Kathy Lette and Gabrielle Carey, *Puberty Blues*, p. 75, 1979

▸ **rip it up**

to enjoy energetically, to dance *US*

- — Little Richard, *Rip It Up*, 1956
- When Bill Haley sung "Let's rip it up, we're gonna rip it up at the joint tonight", it was the best thing kids had ever heard. Whether it meant "let's have some fun", or whether it was really a cry to "rip things up", made little difference, it united the younger generation all over Britain. — Simon Napier-Bell, *Black Vinyl White Powder*, p. 9, 2001

▸ **rip off a piece (of ass)**

to have sex *US*

- "Nice piece of ass," the man said. "You ripping off some of that?" — George V. Higgins, *The Friends of Eddie Coyle*, p. 149, 1971

rip and tear; rip *verb*

to swear *UK, 1937*

Rhyming slang. Possibly an influence on LET RIP (to shout).

- — Ray Puxley, *Cockney Rabbit*, 1992

ripe *adjective*

1 bad-smelling *US*

- Go on in the bathroom and clean yourself up. Man, you smell ripe. — Elmore Leonard, *Riding the Rap*, p. 183, 1995

2 too strong for general acceptability *UK*

- [T]he old lingo's started getting a bit ripe of late[.] — Kevin Sampson, *Powder*, p. 253, 1999

3 used of a girl, over the legal age of consent *US*

- — Michael V. Anderson, *The Bad, Rad, Not to Forget Way Cool Beach and Surf Discriptionary*, p. 16, 1988

4 in the language surrounding the Grateful Dead, poised for enlightenment in the mysteries of the band *US*

- — David Shenk and Steve Silberman, *Skeleton Key*, p. 249, 1994

rip job *noun*

a safe robbery in which the front of the safe is peeled off *US*

- In the rip job you drill a hole in the corner of the safe. Then you peel the front of the door off with a big sectional jimmy or crowbar. — Leonard Shecter and William Phillips, *On the Pad*, p. 179, 1973

rip-off *noun*

1 a copy; an imitation *US, 1970*

- Ignorant people were still writing them [the Count Five] off as nothing more than a Yardbirds rip-off[.] — Lester Bangs, *Psychotic Reactions and Carburetor Dung*, p. 15, 1971

2 a robbery; a theft; a swindle; exploitation *US*

- "It's a rip-off!" Johnny whispered to Buddy. — Donald Goines, *Inner City Hoodlum*, p. 102, 1975

rip off *verb*

1 to steal something *US, 1967*

If the speaker is doing the stealing, the term suggests an act of political heroism; if not, it suggests corporate greed. The subject of this verb can be either the goods stolen, the location or the owner; the subject can split the verb without changing the sense.

- Too bad in a way cause most of us used to rip off the Lion Supermarket when we had to eat and had no dough. — Abbie Hoffman, *Woodstock Nation*, p. 21, 1969
- I was asked, "Are you goood at anything?" I said, "Yeah, ripping off bikes." — Jamie Mandelkau, *Buttons*, p. 77, 1971
- I let her talk me into ripping off a few amphetamines for her. — Beatrice Sparks (writing as 'Anonymous'), *Jay's Journal*, p. 25, 1979
- Many of the catchwords of the day [late 1960s] had a pungent impact. Getting "ripped off," for example, summed up all the indignity of theft. — Sean Hutchinson, *Crying Out Loud*, p. 176, 1988
- The hangers on, the rip-off artists, that is. — *Drugstore Cowboy*, 1988
- I'm just explaining to you what I'm doing here. Case you think I come to rob the place, rip off any of this dusty old shit the man has. — *Get Shorty*, 1995
- He won't give us fuck all. He's a bullshitter. He's just into ripping people off. — Lanre Fehintola, *Charlie Says...*, p. 23, 2000

2 to overcharge someone *UK, 1977*

- [N]umerous companies have ripped their customers off. — *The Guardian*, 22nd February 2003

3 to rape someone *US*

- — Inez Cardozo-Freeman, *The Joint*, p. 526, 1984

rip-off *adjective*

1 in an imitative style, especially with the intention to exploit a commercial advantage *AUSTRALIA, 1973*

- in his big-heeled boots and his Indiana Jones rip-off battered leather coat — James Hawes, *Dead Long Enough*, p. 9, 2000

2 exploitative; cheating *US*

- That 'Dating Game' rip-off thing? Jesus, that guy knows no shame. — *Mallrats*, 1995

rip-off artist *noun*

a swindler; a thief *UK, 1975*

- — R. Carr and T. Tyler, *The Beatles*, 1975
- [E]nterprising rip-off artists have set up shop on street corners and in bazaars selling substandard sunglasses[.] — *The Observer*, 8th August 1999

ripped *adjective*

1 drunk or drug-intoxicated *US*

- She assumed that she must have been stoned. Ripped. Just out of it. — Steve Cannon, *Groove, Bang, and Jive Around*, p. 109, 1969
- [G]o to your concerts just to get ripped and holler[.] — Lester Bangs, *Psychotic Reactions and Carburetor Dung*, p. 67, 1971
- Then I turned around and one of the men passed me a joint and that was it. I wanted to be ripped, smashed, torn up as I had never wanted anything before. — Anonymous, *Go Ask Alice*, p. 71, 1971
- 'It'll get you so righteous ripped,' Cob promises Jerry. — John Rechy, *The Fourth Angel*, p. 31, 1972
- Oh, wow, boy, are you ripped! — Doug Lang, *Freaks*, p. 17, 1973
- Let's get ripped! — John Belushi, *The Blues Brothers*, 1980
- I was shocked. I was also ripped out of my mind. The word on this dope was no exaggeration. — Jim Carroll, *Forced Entries*, p. 48, 1987
- They were both pretty ripped, their eyes shining like glass, and still drinking, a dozen or so longneck beer bottles on a wooden crate they used as a coffee table. — Elmore Leonard, *Maximum Bob*, p. 65, 1991
- JAY: Now I'm gonna head over to Atlantic, drink some beers, get ripped, and – please God – get laid. — *Clerks*, 1994
- I was getting [Jack] Nicholson loaded ... [he laughs]... really good pot ... he was really ripped. — Peter Fonda, *Shaking The Cage*, 1999

2 muscular; lacking body fat; well-sculpted *US*

- — *American Speech*, p. 201, Fall 1984: 'The Language of Bodybuilding'

ripped out of your tits *adjective*

very drunk *UK*

- [G]etting ripped out your tits and having intoxicated sex with highly inappropriate partners[.] — Christopher Brookmyre, *The Sacred Art of Stealing*, p. 63, 2002

ripped to the tits *adjective*

very drunk *US*

- — Connie Eble (Editor), *UNC-CH Campus Slang*, p. 4, November 1983

ripper *noun*

1 a very unattractive (young) woman *UK*
Variant 'old ripper'.
- [They] got horrendously pissed and pulled two old rippers. —Colin Butts, *Is Harry Still on the Boat?*, p. 42, 2003

2 an amphetamine or other central nervous system stimulant *US*
- —Sacramento Muncipal Utility District, *Glossary of Drugs / Drug Language*, 1986
- —Gilda and Melvin Berger, *Drug Abuse A-Z*, p. 115, 1990

3 a skilled skateboarder *US*
- —*San Francisco Sunday Examiner & Chronicle*, p. 20, 2nd September 1984: 'Say It Right'
- —*Macon Telegraph and News*, p. 9A, 18th June 1989

4 a skilled scooter-rider *UK*
- —Ben Sharpe, *Scooter Crazy*, p. 41, 2000

5 in pinball, a ball that is forcefully hit into play *US*
- —Bobbye Claire Natkin and Steve Kirk, *All About Pinball*, p. 115, 1977

ripper *adjective*
intense; extreme; excellent *AUSTRALIA*
- The chances are that you'll cop a dead set ripper masterpiece that'll appreciate at a steady five hundred per cent. —Barry Humphries, *A Nice Night's Entertainment*, p. 147, 1974
- Then he went into this ripper guitar solo. —Jack Chambers (Editor), *Slang Bag 93 (University of Toronto)*, p. 5, Winter 1993

ripper!
used for expressing strong approval *AUSTRALIA*
- [S]he would see if she could get something done my Monday. 'Ripper,' approved Mark. —Jenny Pausacker, *What are ya?*, p. 73, 1987
- —David McGill, *David McGill's Complete Kiwi Slang Dictionary*, p. 93, 1998

ripping *adjective*

1 excellent *UK, 1846*
- —Michael Palin and Terry Jones, *Ripping Yarns*, 1976–79
- —Connie Eble (Editor), *UNC-CH Campus Slang*, p. 8, Spring 1991

2 very angry *US*
- —Collin Baker et al., *College Undergraduate Slang Study Conducted at Brown University*, p. 185, 1968

ripping iron *noun*
a jacket slit up the back *BARBADOS*
- —Frank A. Collymore, *Barbadian Dialect*, p. 93, 1965

rip-rap *noun*
loose, crushed stone used to form embankments *US, 1822*
- They talked about barge lines they'd worked for, about captains and pilots that were pricks, about guys falling overboard, some popping up astern, some not and getting carried downstream to be found on a sandbar or lying cold on the riprap[.] —Elmore Leonard, *Killshot*, p. 260, 1989

riproodling *adjective*
excellent *US*
A rare variant of 'rip-roaring'.
- Frana watched them cross the street and turn the corner, chatting like a couple of riproodling debs. —Bernard Wolfe, *The Late Risers*, p. 132, 1954

rips *noun*
▸ **do rips**
to smoke marijuana *US*
- —Vann Wesson, *Generation X Field Guide and Lexicon*, p. 56, 1997

rip, shit or bust *verb*
to throw yourself wholeheartedly into a task without fear of the consequences *NEW ZEALAND*
- —Harry Orsman, *A Dictionary of Modern New Zealand Slang*, p. 110, 1999

rip-snorter *noun*
a remarkable person; an exceptional thing *US, 1842*
- Bubbles in the bath! / Real rip snorters! —Ivor Biggun, *I've Parted (Misprint)*, 1978

rip track *noun*
on the railways, a hospital *US*
- —Ramon Adams, *The Language of the Railroader*, p. 108, 1977

Rip Van Winkle *verb*
to urinate *UK*
Rhyming slang for **TINKLE** or **SPRINKLE**, formed from the eponymous character in an 1820 story by Washington Irving.
- —Ray Puxley, *Cockney Rabbit*, 1992

rise *noun*
an erection *US*
- —Connie Eble (Editor), *UNC-CH Campus Slang*, p. 8, Spring 1998

rise *verb*
▸ **rise to the occasion**
to achieve an erection when the moment requires it *UK, 1984*
A punning application of a conventional phrase.

rise and shine *noun*
wine *UK*
Rhyming slang.
- —Ray Puxley, *Cockney Rabbit*, 1992

rising damp *noun*
cramp *UK*
Rhyming slang.
- —Ray Puxley, *Cockney Rabbit*, 1992

rispeck
▹ see: **RESPEC**

rissole *noun*

1 the anus *AUSTRALIA, 1971*
Euphemistic for **ARSEHOLE**.

2 a Returned Servicemen's League club *AUSTRALIA*
From a jocular pronunciation of RSL as a vowelless word, punning on 'rissole' (a meat patty).
- 'It's the same guy!' exclaims Sharon. 'He was at the Captain's Flat rissole!' —David Foster, *Plumbum*, p. 106, 1983
- He wished his own trouble and strife would do the same when they went down to the local rissole. —Ryan Aven-Bray, *Ridgey Didge Oz Jack Lang*, p. 14, 1983

▸ **like a rissole**
used as a jocular catchphrase tacked onto the farewell expressions 'catch you round' and 'see you round' *AUSTRALIA*
Punning on 'round' (circular), the shape of a rissole.
- Catch you round like a rissole. —Linda Jaivin, *Rock n Roll Babes from Outer Space*, p. 188, 1996
- 'See ya round,' I said. 'Like a rissole,' said Slogs. —Phillip Gwynne, *Deadly Unna?*, p. 252, 1998

ritual spirit *noun*
MDMA, the recreational drug best known as ecstasy *UK*
- —Mike Haskins, *Drugs*, p. 290, 2003

ritzy *adjective*
classy, stylish, fashionable *US, 1920*
After the Ritz luxury hotels in New York, London and Paris.
- Before long the Goldkette office steered me to a steady job, playing with a small hot band in a ritzy joint called Luigi's Cafe. —Mezz Mezzrow, *Really the Blues*, p. 92, 1946
- I understand she caters to a pretty ritzy clientele. —Mickey Spillane, *I, The Jury*, p. 13, 1947
- Then we gonna buy you a ritzy house ... 'lectric lights! ... a great big slew of snazzy furniture. —Iceberg Slim (Robert Beck), *Airtight Willie and Me*, p. 116, 1979

Riv; Rivie; Rivie hog *noun*
a Buick Riviera car *US*
- —Edith A. Folb, *runnin' down some lines*, p. 252, 1980

river *noun*
in a hand of poker, the final card received by a player *UK*
- —Dave Scharf, *Winning at Poker*, p. 241, 2003
- —*FHM*, p. 147, June 2003

▸ **across the river**
dead *US*
- —Vincent J. Monteleone, *Criminal Slang*, p. 9, 1949

▸ **up the river; upriver**
to a prison *US*
- He had been a pickpocket until a long stretch up the river gave him a turn of mind. —Mickey Spillane, *I, The Jury*, p. 15, 1947
- [T]he poor jerk from Camden you take up the river to the Crossbars Hotel[.] —Darryl Ponicsan, *The Last Detail*, p. 181, 1970
- Or maybe he's storing up memories for his trip upriver, like Butch. —Josh Alan Friedman, *Tales of Times Square*, p. 120, 1986
- Lance would have me sent upriver for a ten-year stretch. —C.D. Payne, *Youth in Revolt*, p. 355, 1993

riverina *noun*
a shilling, hence, 5p *AUSTRALIA, 1943*
Rhyming slang for **DEANER**.
- —Ray Puxley, *Cockney Rabbit*, 1992

river job *noun*
as a result of betting, an enormous loss *AUSTRALIA*
So great is the loss that the bettor thinks of jumping in a river.
• —Ned Wallish, *The Truth Dictionary of Racing Slang*, p. 69, 1989

River Lea *noun*
tea, especially a poor quality cup of tea *UK, 1859*
Rhyming slang, formed on one of London's rivers.
• —Ray Puxley, *Cockney Rabbit*, 1992

River Nile *noun*
a smile *UK*
Rhyming slang.
• Come on, put your boat [face] in the River Nile.—Ray Puxley, *Cockney Rabbit*, 1992

River Ouse; river ooze; the river *noun*
strong drink *UK, 1930*
Rhyming slang for **BOOZE**.
• The sounds were good, the gear was great, the River Ooze was flowing.—Garry Bushell, *The Face*, p. 81, 2001

river rat *noun*
a river-rafting enthusiast *US*
• —Jim Crotty, *How to Talk American*, p. 213, 1997

River Tyne *noun*
wine, especially inferior wine *UK*
Rhyming slang, formed on a major river in the northeast of England.
• —Ray Puxley, *Cockney Rabbit*, 1992

Riviera; Riviera of the south *nickname*
any place in Antarctica perceived to be slightly warmer than the rest of the continent, especially the Antarctic Peninsula or Davis station *ANTARCTICA, 1963*
• —Bernadette Hince, *The Antarctic Dictionary*, p. 288, 2000

rivvel *noun*
among Nova Scotians of German origin, a noodle soup *CANADA*
Like another Lunenburg County word, 'roovled' this word is probably a derivative of the German word *runzeln* (wrinkled).
• —Lewis Poteet, *The South Shore Phrase Book*, p. 92, 1999

Rizla *noun*
a cigarette rolling paper *UK*
A brand name that acquired a generic meaning.
• —Angela Devlin, *Prison Patter*, p. 98, 1996
• [A] packet of ripped cigarette papers! Oh bollocks [...] If they found the Rizlas, our party fund was in danger[.]—Wayne Anthony, *Spanish Highs*, p. 5, 1999
• Dermot puts the magazine to one side an begins to lick an glue Rizlas together.—Niall Griffiths, *Kelly + Victor*, p. 129, 2002

RJR *noun*
inexpensive cigarette tobacco given free to prisoners *US*
An abbreviation of R.J. Reynolds, a major tobacco company.
• —Charles Shafer, *Folk Speech in Texas Prisons*, p. 213, 1990

R 'n' R *noun*
rock 'n' roll *UK*
An initialism.
• [A]s close as you could get to the excitement of the R 'n' R frontline. —John Robb, *The Nineties*, p. 145, 1999

roach *noun*
1 a cockroach *AUSTRALIA*
• The roaches are that big in some parts of Australia they help with the washing up.—Barry Humphries, *The Traveller's Tool*, p. 80, 1985

2 the butt of a marijuana cigarette *US, 1938*
The variant 'roche' also exists.
• —Lou Shelly, *Hepcats Jive Talk Dictionary*, p. 16, 1945
• You don't have to pass a roach to a viper, he'll take it right out of your hand and go to puffin' on it not even thinkin' about who had it in his chops before.—Mezz Mezzrow, *Really the Blues*, p. 214, 1946
• She doubled the empty match cover over backward and put the butt of the cigarette up in the fold to make a crutch, and she brought the cardboard up to her lips and took three deep final drags off the short roach.—Thurston Scott, *Cure it with Honey*, p. 69, 1951
• Everyone who had remained was gathered around the table in a laconic group, rolling new cigarettes out of the collected roaches. —John Clellon Holmes, *Go*, p. 91, 1952
• She finished the marijuana roach and fell to her back on the bed[.] —George Mandel, *Flee the Angry Strangers*, p. 118, 1952
• Save me the roach, man.—Willard Motley, *Let No Man Write My Epitaph*, p. 90, 1958
• Here, you finish the roach. I don't like roaches, they catch me in the throat.—Bernard Wolfe, *The Magic of Their Singing*, p. 77, 1961
• A droopy-eyed Negro hands me a tiny joint, offers what is hardly a roach now: "Turn on?"—John Rechy, *City of Night*, p. 185, 1963
• [A]nd then the stick was gone, burnt to a little bit of a roach.—Piri Thomas, *Down These Mean Streets*, p. 58, 1967
• Don't run, the time approaches / Hotels and midnight coaches / Be sure to hide the roaches.—Graham Nash, *Pre-Road Downs*, 1968
• The bomber in her hand was now a "roach."—Iceberg Slim (Robert Beck), *Pimp*, p. 182, 1969
• Charlotte finishes the roach and puts away her paraphernalia.—Darryl Ponicsan, *The Last Detail*, p. 100, 1970
• Then D.R. took the last drag on the joint, ate the roach as the first hors d'oeuvre of the evening, then set out with his lady to call on the Lone Outdoorsman.—Gurney Norman, *Divine Right's Trip (Last Whole Earth Catalog)*, p. 45, 1971
• Twist up a big bomb of this serious dope / Smoke it down to tha dub or roach tip / So much damn resin it's startin' to drip—Tone Loc, *Cheeba Cheeba*, 1989
• [T]here was still a glimmer of life in the spliff as it made its way down to the cigarette-packet roach.—Donald Gorgon, *Cop Killer*, p. 36, 1994
• Vita snuffed out her jay on white tree bark and stuck the roach in the pocket of her jeans, the jeans cut off at the crotch.—Elmore Leonard, *Be Cool*, p. 51, 1999

3 a still-lit and smokeable cigarette end *UK*
From the previous sense.
• —Angela Devlin, *Prison Patter*, p. 98, 1996

4 Rohypnol™ (flunitrazepam), popularly known as the 'date-rape drug' *US*
From the manufacturer, Hoffman-La Roche. The variant 'roachie' also exists.
• On the street the drug has many nicknames; teenagers know it as rope, ribs, or roaches.—*Texas Monthly*, p. 88, September 1995
• Among the New Words—*American Speech*, p. 193, Summer 1997

5 a police officer *US*
A disliked insect found nearly everywhere.
• —Marlena Kay Nelson, *Rookies to Roaches*, p. 5, 1963

6 an unpopular girl *US*
• —*Time Magazine*, p. 46, 24th August 1959
• —*American Speech*, p. 154, May 1959: 'Gator (University of Florida) Slang'

7 in new car sales, a bad credit risk *US*
• —*Doctor's Review*, August 1989
• —Anna Scotti and Paul Young, *Buzzwords*, p. 41, 1997

roach *verb*
1 to smoke a marijuana cigarette *UK*
• I'll roach a spliff watching the TV throughout[.]—The Streets (Mike Skinner), *Wouldn't Have It Any Other Way*, 2004

2 to have sex with someone's spouse or lover; to cuckold someone *BAHAMAS*
• —John A. Holm, *Dictionary of Bahamian English*, p. 170, 1982

3 in computing, to destroy a program *US*
• Hardware gets toasted or fried, software gets roached.—Eric S. Raymond, *The New Hacker's Dictionary*, p. 305, 1991

roacha *noun*
marijuana *UK*
• —Mike Haskins, *Drugs*, p. 289, 2003

roach and dace *noun*
the face *UK, 1874*
Rhyming slang. A less common variation of **KIPPER AND PLAICE**.
• —Ray Puxley, *Cockney Rabbit*, 1992

roach bender *noun*
someone who smokes marijuana *US, 1942*
An elaboration of the noun and verb senses of **ROACH**.
• —Ernest L. Abel, *A Marijuana Dictionary*, p. 88, 1982

roach clip *noun*
a device, improvised or manufactured, designed to hold the butt of a (marijuana) cigarette and make smoking the final portion possible *US, 1997*
• Roach Clips. Sure, they were mostly decorated alligator clips, but it didn't matter – they were icons, a symbol of an enlightened life. —Bruce Elliot, *Retrohell*, p. 177,
• After several draws, she produces a sequined roach clip for the rest of the joint.—Darryl Ponicsan, *The Last Detail*, p. 99, 1970

- She and Dr. Baker would do it on weekends when he was still in school, using forceps for a roach clip, Keith the only person she knew who could smoke and never crack a smile. — Elmore Leonard, *Maximum Bob*, p. 237, 1991
- Yes I smoke shit, straight off the roach clip. — Cypress Hill, *I Wanna Get High*, 1993
- [Y]ou hear dat? says Shitsky attachin' a roach clip to his spliff. — Nick Barlay, *Curvy Lovebox*, p. 33, 1997

roach coach *noun*

1 a dustcart *UK*

- — Peter Chippindale, *The British CB Book*, p. 158, 1981

2 a catering truck *US*

The reduplicative suggestion is of a lack of hygiene that attracts cockroaches.

- Another depicts workers at the motorized snack bar, which Lai has titled with the workers' slang: "Man Leaning on the Roach Coach at Lunchtime." — *Chicago Tribune*, p. 1C, 6th August 1985
- For the last three years, she has driven the traffic-clogged highways of Tysons corner, dispensing snacks and lunches from my "roach coach." — *Washington Post*, p. D1, 10th October 1985
- — Judi Sanders, *Kickin' like Chicken with the Couch Commander*, p. 19, 1992
- — John Edwards, *Auto Dictionary*, p. 139, 1993
- We need Mexican Popsicle carts downtown, as well as the roach coaches selling tacos. — *Phoenix New Times*, 2nd October 2003

Roachdale College *nickname*

an 'alternative' institution within the University of Toronto, officially named Rochdale College *CANADA, 1969*

Founded in the 1960s, this irreverent nickname captured the flavour of the spirit of the place. Its history is memorialised in an exhibit which includes memoirs of drug use, a Can-Cannabis flag and other 'Counter-Cultural Ephemera'. A **ROACH** is of course in drug slang a 'burnt-down marijuana cigarette butt'.

roached *adjective*

under the influence of Rohypnol™ (flunitrazepam), popularly known as the 'date-rape drug' *US, 1996*

From the name of the manufacturer, Hoffman-La Roche.

- — *American Speech*, p. 193, Summer 1997: 'Among the new words'

roach haven *noun*

a hotel/motel lacking in hygiene *US*

- We got a Winnebago. We don't need those overpriced roach havens. — Quentin Tarantino, *From Dusk Till Dawn*, p. 15, 1995

roach killers *noun*

pointed shoes *US*

- Richie wore roach killers – pointy as a dangerous weapon, curving high over his ankle and low over his heel. — Richard Price, *The Wanderers*, p. 5, 1974

roach motel *noun*

a used car dealership that targets customers with poor credit *US*

- — Jim Crotty, *How to Talk American*, p. 37, 1997

roach wagon *noun*

a catering truck *US*

- Dick Snider watched through binoculars the throngs who played soccer and baseball and bought tamales and soda pop from the Tijuana "roach wagons"[.] — Joseph Wambaugh, *Lines and Shadows*, p. 17, 1984

roachy *noun*

the penis *BAHAMAS*

- — John A. Holm, *Dictionary of Bahamian English*, p. 170, 1982

road *noun*

▸ **the road**

in Roller Derby, anywhere outside the nine San Francisco Bay Area counties, the home of the game *US*

- — Keith Coppage, *Roller Derby to Rollerjam*, 1999

▸ **up the road**

committed for trial before a judge and jury *UK*

- — David Powis, *The Signs of Crime*, 1977

road *verb*

to ride a bicycle on the road in a large Canadian city *CANADA*

- I was roading my bike in Toronto. To road: a verb that describes the gridlocked cars that like to pretend the bicyclists are not there, slaloming around the potholes and sewer grates that make Toronto bicycle lanes so interesting, and avoiding police. — *Toronto Globe and Mail*, p. R1, 17th June 2002

road agent *noun*

a highway patrolman or state police officer *US*

Biker (motorcyle) usage.

road apple *noun*

1 a piece of horse manure *US*

- Road apples are chunks of frozen or dried horse manure, used as pucks in road hockey, also called horse hockey. — Lewis Poteet, *Hockey Talk*, p. 60, 1996

2 a touring performer *US*

- — Don Wilmeth, *The Language of American Popular Entertainment*, p. 224, 1981

roadblock dance *noun*

an unofficial street party *UK*

- Tonight we were going to make some money and have a roadblock dance. — Karline Smith, *Moss Side Massive*, p. 96, 1994

road burn *noun*

in the language surrounding the Grateful Dead, the deteriorated grooming and personal hygiene that serve as physical manifestations of a long tour following the band *US*

- — David Shenk and Steve Silberman, *Skeleton Key*, p. 249, 1994

road dog *noun*

1 an extremely close friend *US*

- — *Houston Chronicle*, 9th April 1989
- Me and my road dog, Tyriqqua, used to steal cars, too, but our main thing was jumpin' people to take what they got. — *Rolling Stone*, p. 86, 12th April 2001

2 in sports betting, a team picked as the underdog playing away from home *US*

- — Wayne Alan Root, *Betting to Win on Sports*, p. 183, 1989

road dope *noun*

amphetamines *UK*

Derives from the drug's use by long-distance drivers.

- — Mike Haskins, *Drugs*, p. 279, 2003

road engineer *noun*

a long-haul truck driver *US*

- — *American Speech*, p. 45, February 1963: 'Trucker's language in Rhode Island'

road face *noun*

a stoic expression giving no sign of emotion *TRINIDAD AND TOBAGO*

- — Lise Winer, *Dictionary of the English/Creole of Trinidad & Tobago*, 2003

road game *noun*

a criminal's field of expertise *US*

- — Inez Cardozo-Freeman, *The Joint*, p. 526, 1984

road head *noun*

oral sex received while driving *US*

- — Don R. McCreary (Editor), *Dawg Speak*, 2001

road helper *noun*

an amphetamine or other central nervous system stimulant *US*

- — *American Speech*, p. 207, Fall 1969: 'Truck driver's jargon'

roadie *noun*

1 a member of a rock band's entourage who is responsible for setting up and dismantling the band's equipment while on tour *UK*

- — Jenny Fabian and Johnny Byrne, *Groupie*, 1968
- — Dr Hook and the Medicine Show, *Roland the Roadie and Gertrude the Groupie*, 1973
- Roadies are usually hired for the duration of a tour and paid a salary. — Jay Saporita, *Pourin' It All Out*, p. 204, 1980
- That's Barry. He used to be a roadie. — *Wayne's World 2*, 1993
- When he came home he was a roadie for different bands, then a roadie for the Boo-Yaa T.R.i.b.e., the famous Samoan rappers, and then hooked up with Raji as a way to get connected in the business end. — Elmore Leonard, *Be Cool*, p. 175, 1999
- VAL: These guys are musicians! STEPHIE: They're roadies, Val! There's a difference! — *200 Cigarettes*, 1999
- While I sit here mired in her bullshit, trying to be a good son, while you're off dropping acid and blowing roadies! — *The Sopranos (Episode 55)*, 2004

2 among mountain-bikers, a derogatory term for a cyclist who only rides on paved surfaces *US*

- A roadie might survive with only a patch kit and a pump, but you will definitely need more[.] — *Mountain Bike Magazine's Complete Guide To Mountain Biking Skills*, p. 96, 1996

3 a final drink before starting a road journey *AUSTRALIA, 1996*
From 'one for the *road*'.

4 a can or bottle of beer drunk while driving *AUSTRALIA, 1996*
Also used as a measure of distance, as in 'It's a three roadie trip'.
- Have a roadie for the trip home. — *www.abc.net.au/wordmap*, 2003

roadie's screwdriver *noun*
a hammer or any blunt instrument used to strike something that is not working *UK*
- — Bob Young and Micky Moody, *The Language of Rock 'n' Roll*, p. 122, 1985

road kill *noun*
literally, an animal or bird carcass on the side of the road; figuratively, an unattractive mess *US, 1979*
- Here, yours is the one that looks like a road kill. Enjoy. — *Break Point*, 1991
- She dropped me like a bad habit and left me for road kill. — *Wayne's World 2*, 1993

road louse *noun*
a chorus dancer who can no longer get work in the major metropolitan dance halls *US*
- [T]hey've got to get jobs in inferior outlying clubs or in out-of-town cafes or road shows, and, typed as a "road louse," there is only one direction for them – down. — Jack Lait and Lee Mortimer, *New York Confidential*, p. 141, 1948

road map *noun*
1 multiple facial lacerations *US*
- — *Maledicta*, p. 34, 1988–1989: 'Medical maledicta from San Francisco'

2 in craps, the dice placed before the shooter with the point needed to win face up *US, 1983*
- — Thomas L. Clark, *The Dictionary of Gambling and Gaming*, p. 182, 1987

3 a peace plan *US, 2002*
Originally, and especially, applied to the Israel–Palestine conflict.
- Bush rips up the road map. — *The Guardian*, 15th April 2004

road pizza *noun*
an animal carcass on the road *CANADA*
- Road pizzas are all those squashed animals you see along the highway. — Chris Thain, *Cold as a Bay Street Banker's Heart*, p. 129, 1987
- — Connie Eble (Editor), *UNC-CH Campus Slang*, p. 9, Spring 1988

road rage *noun*
a driver's violent reaction to the frustrations of traffic hindrances and the discourtesies of other road users *US*
- A fit of "road rage"has landed a man in jail, accused of shooting a woman passenger whose car had "cut him off" on the highway. — *St. Petersburg (Florida) TImes*, p. 1B, 2nd April 1988
- [I]t's all over the front page / You give me road rage[.] — Catatonia *Road Rage*, 1997
- In England, even the janitors suffer Road Rage. — Brian Preston, *Pot Planet*, p. 142, 2002

road rash *noun*
1 scraped, bruised and/or cut skin earned in falls while skateboarding or engaging in activity on the road *US*
- — Albert Cassorla, *The Skateboarder's Bible*, p. 202, 1976
- — Peter Smith and Fred M. Barritt, *Bermewjan Vurds*, 1985

2 scraped, bruised and/or cut skin earned by moped riders in road accidents *UK*
- A 'Ped Boy's Worst Fear? "Road Rash": tarmac and (denim) interfused and woven into skin[.] — Julian Johnson, *Urban Survival*, p. 218, 2003

road rocket; rocket *noun*
an extremely fast motorcycle *UK*
- [W]e used to play a record on the juke box, a fast record, and we used to drive around the block before it finished [...] I used to have a rocket then, a road rocket, and used to get back before it was stopped. — Paul E Willis, *Profane Culture*, p. 37, 1978

road soda *noun*
alcohol drunk in a car on the way to a party or concert *US*
- — Ben Applebaum and Derrick Pittman, *Turd Ferguson & The Sausage Party*, p. 68, 2004

road stake *noun*
enough money to get someone to their next job *US*
- — Robert O. Bowen, *An Alaskan Dictionary*, p. 27, 1965

roadster *noun*
a tramp *US, 1890*
- The other had spike (casual ward) written all over him, a real roadster, and a ruddy hairy one. — Charles Raven, *Underworld Nights*, p. 198, 1956
- [H]e looked more like someone out for a stroll than a "roadster" desperately wanting a ride. — Robin Page, *Down Among the Dossers*, p. 43, 1973

road talk *noun*
gossip; a rumour *BAHAMAS*
- — John A. Holm, *Dictionary of Bahamian English*, p. 170, 1982

road tar *noun*
coffee, especially strong and bitter coffee *US*
- — Wayne Floyd, *Jason's Authentic Dictionary of CB Slang*, p. 26, 1976

road trouble *noun*
problems encountered on the street, usually between a pimp and prostitute *US*
- It was the same nappyheaded bitch that had been giving me the road trouble. — A.S. Jackson, *Gentleman Pimp*, p. 180, 1973

roaf *noun*
▷ see: RUOF

roam *noun*
▸ **on the roam**
away from home *US*
- I went to see your whoring sister, but she was on the roam / I called your dope fiend brother, but the punk had pawned his phone. — Dennis Wepman et al., *The Life*, p. 140, 1976

roarer *noun*
in horse racing, a horse that coughes loudly while galloping *US*
- — Dan Parker, *The ABC of Horse Racing*, p. 148, 1947

roaring forties *nickname*
the latitudes between 40 and 49 degrees south *ANTARCTICA, 1897*
Strong winds from the west produce choppy ocean conditions.
- — Bernadette Hince, *The Antarctic Dictionary*, p. 288, 2000

roaring game *noun*
the sport of curling *CANADA*
- From the sound of the rocks on the ice, curling has been known as "the roaring game." — *www.canadasport.com.ca*, 22nd July 2002

roaring twenty *noun*
a type of amphetamine tablet *UK*
- Drug pushers; sixpence each for French Blues, a shilling for a Roaring Twenty. — Irish Jack (writing of the 1960s), *History, The Sharper Word*, p. 31, 1998

roar up *verb*
(of a male) to have sex *UK*
- Every man and his dog was roaring up this bloke's wife. — Andy McNab, *Immediate Action*, p. 214, 1995

roast *noun*
a person killed by a fire *US*
- His words made the hair prickle on the back of my neck, for I had caught the unmistakable pungent odor of burning human flesh. "Larry," I muttered, "Think we got a roast." — John Barracato with Peter Michelmore, *Arson*, p. 34, 1976

roast *verb*
1 (from an active perspective) to have sex with someone *UK*
- I come straight away, but I think that's a blessing in disguise. If I'd've roasted her for a bit the poor aul' girl'd've had a heart attack. — Kevin Sampson, *Clubland*, p. 90, 2002

2 to criticise someone or something severely; to be mercilessly disparaging of someone or something; to denounce someone *UK, 1782*
- Leonard Bernstein – who had hired white waiters to serve at his fundraising party for the Black Panthers – was famously roasted on the pyre of 'radical chic.' — *The Guardian*, 12th February 1988

3 to earn money after hours, especially when doing so with some degree of dishonesty *JAMAICA, 1990*
- — Peter Patrick, *Some Recent Jamaican Creole Words*, 2003

roast beef *noun*
the teeth *UK*
Rhyming slang.
- I'll knock your roast beef so far down your throat you'll be able to eat your dinner again. — Ray Puxley, *Cockney Rabbit*, 1992

roast beef *verb*
in the used car business, to suggest a higher trade-in value to the dealer management than will be approved, giving the salesman who does so a cushion to fall to the value he expects will be approved *US*
- —Peter Mann, *How to Buy a Used Car Without Getting Gypped*, p. 195, 1975

roasted *adjective*
drunk or drug-intoxicated *US*
- They can pour a whole orchestra's worth of booze in nanoseconds [...] many members were roasted – and so was my music. —Frank Zappa, *The Real Frank Zappa Book*, p. 153, 1989

roastie *noun*
1 a roast potato *UK*
- Potatoes are the obvious choice – roasties in goose fat are about as scrummy an accompaniment as you can get. —*The Observer*, 2nd December 2001

2 a traditional English roast dinner *UK*
- We'll go out for food or something. That new Mexican place. Or make a roastie. —Niall Griffiths, *Kelly + Victor*, p. 39, 2002

roasting *adjective*
1 of an ambient temperature, very hot *UK, 1768*
- The moment you arrive in Phoenix, something seems wrong: the default weather is roasting and the midday air is slothful. —*The Guardian*, 24th October 2003

2 anxious; unhappy *UK*
- —Angela Devlin, *Prison Patter*, p. 98, 1996

roast pork; roast *noun*
a fork *UK*
Rhyming slang.
- —Ray Puxley, *Cockney Rabbit*, 1992

roast pork; roast *verb*
to talk *UK, 1961*
Rhyming slang.
- You don't half roast a load of rubbish. —Ray Puxley, *Cockney Rabbit*, 1992

roast potato; roastie *noun*
a waiter *UK*
Rhyming slang.
- —Ray Puxley, *Cockney Rabbit*, 1992

rob *noun*
▸ **on the rob**
engaged in thievery *UK*
- It was Thatcher's dream of private enterprise gone mad. Europe was awash with Brits on the rob. —John Robb, *The Nineties*, p. 31, 1999
- One night, me, my pal Colin Robinson and by brother Patrick went out on the rob. —Dave Courtney, *Dodgy Dave's Little Black Book*, p. 167, 2001
- A witness told the trial that Barton could get cannabis locally and she would "be on the rob", shoplifting and offering stolen goods in exchange for the drug. —*The Guardian*, 21st January 2004

rob *verb*
to steal *UK*
Unconventional passive usage.
- I remember the European cup final in Paris in 1981, all the stuff that was robbed! [...] By Monday they wouldn't let you into any shops because everything had been robbed! —John Robb, *The Nineties*, p. 30, 1999

▸ **rob the cradle**
to be romantically involved with a young person *US*
- She even gets to robbing the cradle, a little boy or a little girl. —Robert Deane Pharr, *Giveadamn Brown*, p. 120, 1978
- —Connie Eble (Editor), *UNC-CH Campus Slang*, p. 5, Spring 1983

▸ **we wuz robbed; we woz robbed**
used as an excuse for losing *US*
As a jocular exclamation this is a fine example of 'many a true word spoken in jest'; widely used (with serious intent) as an indignant cliché. Apparently coined in 1932 by boxing manager Joe Jacobs when his client, Max Schmeling, lost the world heavyweight title as the result of a controversial split-decision.
- [T]he George Bush "we-was-robbed" Republican wing, which has never been able to forgive Clinton for beating Bush[.] —Andrew Stephen, *New Statesman*, 21st August 1988
- [H]owever much the conservatives might cry "we woz robbed" and complain[.] —David Starkey, *Elizabet*, p. 289, 2000
- Fortunately, we wuz robbed [England lost a football match], and by Friday morning all union flags and Burberry caps are hastily stuffed away. —*The Guardian*, p. 16, 28th June 2004

robber talk *noun*
threatening talk *TRINIDAD AND TOBAGO, 1985*
- —Lise Winer, *Dictionary of the English/Creole of Trinidad & Tobago*, 2003

robe *noun*
in circus and carnival usage, a judge in criminal court *US*
- —Don Wilmeth, *The Language of American Popular Entertainment*, p. 225, 1981

Roberta Flack *noun*
dismissal from employment *UK*
Rhyming slang for **SACK**, formed from the name of the US singer (b.1939).
- —Ray Puxley, *Fresh Rabbit*, 1998

Robert E. Lee *noun*
1 a quay *UK*
Dockers' rhyming slang, formed on the name of the Confederate army general (1807–70).
- —Julian Franklyn, *A Dictionary of Rhyming Slang*, 1961

2 the knee *UK*
Sometimes abbreviated to 'Robert E.' or the simple 'Robert'.
- —Ray Puxley, *Cockney Rabbit*, 1992

3 urine; an act of urination *UK*
Rhyming slang for **PEE** or **WEE**.
- —Ray Puxley, *Fresh Rabbit*, 1998

Robert's your father's brother
everything's all right *UK*
A humorous variation of **BOB'S YOUR UNCLE**.
- [W]ait till the red ones [bills] and/or threats of bumbailiffs arrive – allowing 'em to cop for a chuck of interest – and Robert's your father's brother! —Andrew Nickolds, *Back to Basics*, p. 55, 1994

Robert's your mother's brother
everything's all right *UK*
A humorous variation of **BOB'S YOUR UNCLE**.
- [The insurance company] write his car off, he gets a lump sum from his insurers and Robert's your mother's brother. —Dave Courtney, *Stop the Ride I Want to Get Off*, p. 112, 1999
- Then I come along in the van, back it up, you ride the 'orse in and Robert's yer Mother's brother. —Guy Ritchie et al., *Lock, Stock... & Four Stolen Hooves*, p. 73, 2000

Robin Hood *noun*
wood; a wood; a Woodbine™ cigarette *UK*
Rhyming slang, formed on the name of the legendary hero of Sherwood Forest.
- —Ray Puxley, *Cockney Rabbit*, 1992

Robin Hood *adjective*
good *UK, 1932*
Rhyming slang, formed on the name of the legendary hero of Sherwood Forest.
- Oh that was Robin Hood of you. —Ray Puxley, *Cockney Rabbit*, 1992

Robin Hoods *noun*
merchandise, goods *UK*
Rhyming slang.
- —Ray Puxley, *Cockney Rabbit*, 1992

robin run *noun*
in Canadian maple sugaring, the first flow of the maple tree sap, which is especially sweet *CANADA*
- The robin run in a Canadian sugarbush is the first flowing of maple sap, which is rich in sugar. —Bill Casselman, *Canadian Words*, p. 73, 1995

Robinson Crusoe *verb*
to do so *UK*
Rhyming slang, formed from the eponymous hero of Daniel Defoe's 1719 book.
- —Julian Franklyn, *A Dictionary of Rhyming Slang*, 1960
- "If you don't move your car from the front of my gate I'll call the police." "Well Robinson Crusoe." —Ray Puxley, *Cockney Rabbit*, 1992

rob my pal *noun*
a girl *UK*
Rhyming slang for **GAL**.
- —Julian Franklyn, *A Dictionary of Rhyming Slang*, 1960

robo *noun*

dextromethorphan (DXM), an active ingredient in non-prescription cold and cough medication, often abused for non-medicinal purposes *US*

- Youths' nicknames for DXM: Robo, Skittles, Triple C's, Rojo, Dex, Tussin, Vitamin D. DXM abuse is called "Robotripping" or "Tussing." Users might be called "syrup heads" or "robotards." — *USA Today*, p. 1A, 29th December 2003

robo *verb*

to drink Robitussin™ (a branded cough medicine with codeine) *US, 1993*

- The [Robitussin] trip is more of a buzz to my experience, and to that of my friends. I have been told that high dosages produce hallucinogenic effects similar to 'shrooms and LSD[.] — Nathan Bowen, *alt.drugs*, 13th April 1993
- — *www.addictions.org*, 2004

robodose *verb*

to abuse cough syrups for recreational purposes *US*

From the name of the most popular syrup of abuse, Robitussen™

- — Steven Daly and Nalthaniel Wice, *alt.culture*, p. 207, 1995
- — Vann Wesson, *Generation X Field Guide and Lexicon*, p. 142, 1997

robotard *noun*

a person who abuses for non-medicinal purposes non-prescription medication containing dextromethorphan (DXM) *US*

From the branded cough syrup, Robitussen™.

- Youths' nicknames for DXM: Robo, Skittles, Triple C's, Rojo, Dex, Tussin, Vitamin D. DXM abuse is called "Robotripping" or "Tussing." Users might be called "syrup heads" or "robotards." — *USA Today*, p. 1A, 29th December 2003

robotrip *verb*

to abuse for non-medicinal purposes non-prescription medication containing dextromethorphan (DXM) *US*

From the branded cough syrup, Robitussin™.

- Youths' nicknames for DXM: Robo, Skittles, Triple C's, Rojo, Dex, Tussin, Vitamin D. DXM abuse is called "Robotripping" or "Tussing." Users might be called "syrup heads" or "robotards." — *USA Today*, p. 1A, 29th December 2003

ROC *noun*

the rest of Canada, i.e. all of Canada except Quebec *CANADA, 2002*

- It may not matter to the ROC, but it matters to Quebec. — *Montreal Gazette*, p. A2, 8th April 2002

roca *noun*

1 MDMA, the recreational drug best known as ecstasy *UK*

- — Mike Haskins, *Drugs*, p. 290, 2003

2 crack cocaine *US*

Corrupted Spanish-English for 'rock'.

- — US Department of Justice, *Street Terms*, October 1994

Roche; La Roche; rochie *noun*

Rohypnol™ (flunitrazepam), popularly known as the 'date-rape drug' *US*

Because Roche Pharmaceuticals markets the Rohypnol™ sleeping pill.

- — *American Family Physician*, p. 2619, 1st June 2004

rock *noun*

1 a rhythmic style of (usually) amplified music that provides the umbrella for any number of music genres *US, 1957*

Originally abbreviated from **ROCK 'N' ROLL**; in the US it has continued in use for all forms of driving, rhythmic music. Meanwhile, in the UK early variant forms were called 'beat' or **POP**; not until the mid-1960s was 'rock' used as a title for some contemporary music and then only applied to the more serious music that derived from rock 'n' roll.

- Rock by its very nature defies encapsulation in words, or at least my words [...] "Rock appeals to the intelligence", Chester Anderson once said, "without interference from the intellect." — Richard Neville, *Play Power*, p. 101, 1970

2 a diamond *US, 1908*

- As Duffy served them he noticed that she was ablaze with rocks, and when she reached for money to pay, that she had a roll. — Jack Lait and Lee Mortimer, *Chicago Confidential*, p. 31, 1950
- My wife's got a hundred and fifty grand in rocks and another seventy-five in furs and clothes. — Raymond Chandler, *The Long Goodbye*, p. 65, 1953
- Arvey's engagement present to Lila Leeds was a five-carat rock. — Lee Mortimer, *Women Confidential*, p. 153, 1960
- Profacci bought hot rocks. I knew then it was rocks, phony rocks that he thought were real! — Iceberg Slim (Robert Beck), *Trick Baby*, p. 19, 1969

3 cocaine *US, 1973*

- [I]t's like chopping the rock, laying it out in a big chubby line[.] — Stuart Browne, *Dangerous Parking*, p. 321, 2000
- — Mike Haskins, *Drugs*, p. 281, 2003

4 crack cocaine *US*

Describes the crystalline lumps of purified cocaine.

- — Grandmaster Flash & The Furious Five featuring Melle Mel, *White Lines*, 1983
- I sell the rock with some shake to people who buy quarters [1/4 ounce or seven grams], and pure rock only to my very best customers. — Terry Williams, *The Cocaine Kids*, p. 37, 1989
- You look like you sell rocks. — *Boyz N The Hood*, 1990
- Why go for $3.00 an hour when you can make $500 a day selling rocks for Nino. — *New Jack City*, 1990
- There's a lot of girls out here that do things just for rocks. — William T. Vollman, *Whores for Gloria*, p. 143, 1991
- So what's your gang dealin, fat boy? Rock? — Jess Mowry, *Way Past Cool*, 1992
- Looky here, you want the bitches to really fly high, make your rocks with Cherry Seven-Up. — *True Romance*, 1993
- A $100 bag of coke could pull about $500 in rocks. — *Menace II Society*, 1993
- Don't get me wrong; there is some herb you know, but no rocks, no heroin or ice[.] — Odie Hawkins, *Midnight*, p. 123, 1995
- By the third day he was doing rocks with her, kissing her scabby lips[.] — Kevin Sampson, *Powder*, p. 57, 1999
- Maybe we could show up and smoke a little rock with them to unwind. — *Traffic*, 2000
- You want some crack? Sweet-ass rock. Get you high. — Kevin Smith, *Jay and Slient Bob Strike Back*, p. 90, 2001
- Yeh! Spit-roasted by two crack dealers for a rock! — Niall Griffiths, *Kelly + Victor*, p. 49, 2002
- When crack first began ripping through the 'hood in the mid-80s, word on the street was that the government deliberately pushed rock into the Black community. — *The Source*, p. 74, March 2002
- We got Rocks, we got Bones, we got Brown, we got Stones. — Julian Johnson, *Urban Survival*, p. 170, 2003

5 a pool ball *US*

- — Steve Rushin, *Pool Cool*, p. 24, 1990

6 in the usage of youthful model road racers (slot car racers), a slow car *US*

- — Phantom Surfers, *The Exciting Sounds of Model Road Racing (Album cover)*, 1997

7 a solid, reliable, dependable fellow prisoner *US*

- — John R. Armore and Joseph D. Wolfe, *Dictionary of Desperation*, p. 46, 1976

8 in prison, a predatory homosexual *US*

- I was swinging my feet ever so easy when I dug three rocks watching me, funny like. — Piri Thomas, *Down These Mean Streets*, p. 251, 1967

9 a frugal and stingy person *US*

- — *The Annals of the American Academy of Political and Social Sciences*, p. 130, May 1950

10 a dollar *US, 1950*

- Some old dame stopped me and without me askin' her nothin' she hands me half a rock. — Willard Motley, *Let No Man Write My Epitaph*, p. 73, 1958

11 a packet of brand name manufactured cigarettes, used as a basic medium of exchange in prison *US*

- — William K. Bentley and James M. Corbett, *Prison Slang*, p. 65, 1992

12 a crystal tuning device used in a citizens' band transceiver *US*

- — Porter Bibb, *CB Bible*, p. 103, 1976

Rock *noun*

▸ **the Rock**

1 Gibraltar *UK, 1829*

From Gibraltar's main feature.

- [A] referendum on the Rock showed 99% of voters opposed joint sovereignty with Madrid. — *The Guardian*, 9th November 2002

2 the Alcatraz federal penitentiary, located in San Francisco bay *US*

- You're going to the Rock, Al, a nice long ride to Alcatraz. — Red Rudensky, *The Gonif*, p. 61, 1970
- What was it like to be locked up on The Rock? Well, even if you were a "Machine Gun" Kelly or a "Scarface," at The Rock you were just a number. — Marlene Freedman, *Alcatraz*, 1983

3 Rocky Marciano (1923 – 69), the only undefeated heavyweight champion in boxing history *US*

- Nobody will ever come close to the Rock. I saw him not long before he got killed in the plane crash. —Edwin Torres, *Carlito's Way*, p. 135, 1975

4 Guam *US*
A nickname used by US military pilots during the Vietnamese war.
- —Gregory Clark, *Words of the Vietnam War*, p. 210, 1990

5 Riker's Island jail, New York *US*
- They call them "rocks from The Rock," since they were baked at another jail out on Rikers Island, otherwise known as The Rock. —Ed Sanders, *Tales of Beatnik Glory*, p. 219, 1975
- Rikers prisoners refer to their home as 'the Rock,' but from an archaeological point of view it's more accurate to call this place a dump. — *The Village Voice*, 13th–19th December 2000

6 the island of Newfoundland *CANADA*
This term, almost universal in use in both Newfoundland and the rest of Canada, derives from the stony soil of the island.

rock *verb*

1 to have sex *US, 1922*
- Who did you rock over this week? —George Mandel, *Flee the Angry Strangers*, p. 41, 1952
- you know that I rocked her / But three days later I had to see the doctor —Kool Moe Dee, *Go See The Doctor*, 1986

2 to excel *US*
- The new playhouse rocks, Dotty. —*Jerry Maguire*, 1996
- Cos it's like you're bein' done by a stranger. It rocks. —*Gone in 60 Seconds*, 2000
- "Awesome," I say, adding "you rock." —Marty Beckerman, *Death to All Cheerleaders*, p. 135, 2000

3 to excite someone *US*
- "In other words," I remarked, "whether or not the kid rocks you." —Max Shulman, *Guided Tour of Campus Humor*, p. 161, 1955

4 to work *UK*
- [W]e're rocking again. —Kevin Sampson, *Outlaws*, p. 12, 2001

5 to prepare crack cocaine from powdered cocaine *US*
Recorded as 'Asian street gang terminology' by Bill Valentine, *Gang Intelligence Manual*, 1995.

6 to distress someone; to disturb someone; to startle someone *US, 1940*
- Bush rocked by Senate rebellion on Iraq. —*The Guardian*, 18th October 2003

▸ **rock ass**
to produce rock music that inspires a vigorous audience response *US*
On the model of **KICK ASS** (to behave energetically).
- I was only able to rock ass in '78 because it is inherent to my nature[.] —*Ask*, p. 47, 5th May 1979

▸ **rock the boat**
to upset the status quo; to make difficulties; to cause trouble *UK, 1931*
- Mr Ozawa is known for rocking the boat with his uncompromising statements and political tactics. —*The Guardian*, 8th April 2002

▸ **rock the clock**
in the used car business, to spin the odometer (mileometer) backwards *US*
- In a final act of criminal camouflage, Bob's chief mechanic had rocked the clock back to fifty. —Stephen J. Cannell, *King Con*, p. 29, 1997

▸ **rock the groove**
(of hip-hop music or musicians) to give pleasure *UK*
- Jodeci is rocking the groove, seductively, through Sony speakers. —Karline Smith, *Letters to Andy Cole*, p. 143–144, 1998

rock *adjective*
hard *UK*
- Membership's rock though, Ray says. They're strict as fuck who they'll let in. —Kevin Sampson, *Outlaws*, p. 74, 2001

rockabilly *noun*
a mid-1950s US fashion; a late 1970s British youth fashion and music genre identified as an exaggeration of hillbilly country and western style *US*
An ellision of **ROCK 'N 'ROLL** and 'hillbilly'.
- Rockabilly could be played on cheap instruments by inexperienced musicians[.] —Tony Thorne, *Fads, Fashions & Cults*, p. 226, 1993
- Rockabilly also described a concurrent style epitomized by Elvis in 1956. This look was much smarter[.] —Sarah Callard and Will Hoon, *Surfers Soulies Skinheads & Skaters*, 1996
- [T]he fighting between mods, rockers, skinheads, Pakistanis, suedeheads, Hell's angels, boot boys, greasers, Teds, punks, soulboys, rockabillies, rude boys, casuals and every other shade of herbert going[.] —John King, *Human Punk*, p. 295, 2000

rock and boulder *noun*
the shoulder *UK, 1931*
Rhyming slang.
- —Ray Puxley, *Cockney Rabbit*, 1992

rock and roll *noun*
used of an automatic or semi-automatic weapon, full automatic fire *US*
- Then he stood up, flicked his iron to rock and roll and gave the little zero a long burst through the Playboy mag. —*Apocalypse Now*, 1979
- In other words, you flip the switches on your M-16s from semiautomatic to full automatic – rock and roll, as the men say. —Nelson De Mille, *Cathedral*, p. 382, 1981
- —*Maledicta*, p. 261, Summer/Winter 1982: 'Viet-Speak'
- You peep through that skinny-ass embrasure with your M-16 on full rock and roll[.] —Larry Heinemann, *Paco's Story*, p. 10, 1986
- Sergeant said, "You're on lane four / Set that lever on 'rock and roll.'" —Sandee Shaffer Johnson, *Cadences*, p. 83, 1986

rock and roll; rock 'n' roll *verb*
to begin and perform the task at hand *US*
- —Connie Eble (Editor), *UNC-CH Campus Slang*, p. 7, November 1990
- Little hand says it's time to rock and roll. —*Point Break*, 1991
- Let me make an adjustment here and we'll be ready to rock 'n roll. —*Natural Born Killers*, 1994
- It's God getting ready to rock'n'roll, I'm telling you. —Christopher Brookmyre, *Not the End of the World*, p. 70, 1998

rock ape *noun*

1 a black person *AUSTRALIA, 1972*
Offensive.
- In the small, stifling, white community of Port Moresby, with its neat fibro bungalows and its men servants referred to as Boy to their faces and Rock Ape behind their backs[.] —Blanche d'Alpuget, *Robert J. Hawke*, p. 137, 1982

2 a lout or hooligan *AUSTRALIA*
- —Rex Hunt, *Tall Tales – and True*, p. 64, 1994
- I went across and had the tail between my legs expecting a bit of a barrage from this 'rock ape' who had more tattoos than a wall adorned with graffiti[.] —Rex Hunt, *Tall Tales – and True*, p. 136, 1994

rock attack *noun*
crack cocaine *UK*
An elaboration of **ROCK**.
- —Mike Haskins, *Drugs*, p. 282, 2003

rock bud *noun*
a powerful variety of marijuana *UK*
- —Nick Jones, *Spliffs*, p. 73, 2003

rock cake *noun*
a small bet *UK*
Possibly rhyming slang for 'stake'; or possibly a dismissive comparison to an article of little value.
- —John McCririck, *John McCririck's World of Betting*, p. 60, 1991

rock candy *noun*
diamonds *US*
- —Clarence Major, *Dictionary of Afro-American Slang*, p. 98, 1970

rockchopper *noun*
a Roman Catholic *AUSTRALIA, 1981*
A derogatory term originating amongst Protestants. In earlier use (1908, *Australian National Dictionary*) used of a 'navvy' (i.e. one who breaks up rock), and thus in origin probably a slur labelling all Australian Catholics descendants of Irish Catholic convicts.
- —Ed Campion, *Rockchoppers*, 1982

rock college *noun*
prison *NEW ZEALAND*
- —David McGill, *David McGill's Complete Kiwi Slang Dictionary*, p. 93, 1998

rock crusher *noun*
in poker, a hand that is certain to win *US*
- —George Percy, *The Language of Poker*, p. 76, 1988

rockdance *noun*
walking barefoot over a rocky surface to retrieve a surfboard *US*
- —Grant W. Kuhns, *On Surfing*, p. 120, 1963

rocked out *adjective*
under the influence of crack cocaine *US*
- The guy's sitting there nodding, all rocked out, while I go get a warrant signed. — Elmore Leonard, *Maximum Bob*, p. 164, 1991

rocker *noun*
1 any of the several curved stripes below the three chevrons on the insignia of a sergeant in the US Army or Marine Corps *US, 1944*
- This morning the Duty was a staff sergeant: three stripes and one rocker underneath. — Martin Russ, *The Last Parallel*, p. 19, 1957
- — Carl Fleischhauer, *A Glossary of Army Slang*, p. 11, 1968
- Now they had to call us "sir," although, with the previous summer's experience fresh in our minds, the sight of some old salt with three stripes and a rocker on his sleeves still caused a Pavlovian reaction of terror. — Philip Caputo, *A Rumor of War*, p. 13, 1977

2 a curved patch designating a motorcyle gang or the gang-member's home city or country, worn as part of the colours *US*
A borrowing from the military.
- We'll have everyone running with us wearing the England rocker. — Jamie Mandelkau, *Buttons*, p. 79, 1971
- The patch consisted of the top rocker – three inches wide, red on white – HELL'S ANGELS. The bottom rocker said ENGLAND and between them I carried the small death's head. — Jamie Mandelkau, *Buttons*, p. 81, 1971

3 a member of the 1960s youth cult that is characterised by the use of motorcycles and leathers, and chiefly remembered as the opposite to Mod *UK*
- An out-and-out Mod and Rocker warfare policy then began. — Jamie Mandelkau, *Buttons*, p. 24, 1971
- Mods smashing Rockers over the head with deckchairs — Martin King and Martin Knight, *The Naughty Nineties*, p. 223, 1999

4 a non-surfer who associates with surfers and poses as a surfer *AUSTRALIA*
- — John Severson, *Modern Surfing Around the World*, p. 180, 1964

5 a rock musician/singer *UK*
- The only story competing with Iraq for news space in France involves ageing rocker Johnny Hallyday denying accusations of sexual assault. — *The Guardian*, 17th March 2003

6 a song, or instrumental, exhibiting the rhythmic characteristics of rock 'n' roll *UK*
- — R. Carr and T. Tyler, *The Beatles*, 1975
- [H]is back catalogue of thoughtful country-rockers[.] — *The Guardian*, 5th August 2003

7 the convex curvature of the bottom of a surfboard *US*
- — D.S. Halacy, *Surfer!*, p. 216, 1965

▸ **off your rocker**
crazy *UK, 1897*
- I know it doesn't seem right, but Jake's halfway off his rocker! — Jim Thompson, *Savage Night*, p. 128, 1953
- Are you off your rocker mate? — Barry Humphries, *Bazza Pulls It Off!*, 1971
- "You're nuts, man," Tony stated flatly. "I mean you're really off your goddamn rocker," he said and burst out laughing. — Donald Goines, *Black Gangster*, p. 80, 1977
- The experience was so awful for him that he went completely off his rocker. — Herbert Huncke, *Guilty of Everything*, p. 47, 1990
- [H]e's crazy and off his rocker / Crazier than Slim Shady is off the vodka[.] — Eminem (Marshall Mathers), *The Kids*, 2000

rocker; rokker *verb*
to speak Romany; to talk *UK*
English gypsy use from Romany *roker* (to speak).
- — Jimmy Stockin, *On The Cobbles*, p. 11, 2000

rocket *noun*
1 a marijuana cigarette *US, 1942*
- — Vincent J. Monteleone, *Criminal Slang*, p. 195, 1949
- "Speak to Antonio," Sammy said. "He can always fix you up with a pack of rockets." — Douglas Rutherford, *The Creeping Flesh*, p. 49, 1963
- — Richard A Spears, *The Slang and Jargon of Drugs and Drink*, p. 426, 1986
- — Mike Haskins, *Drugs*, p. 289, 2003

2 a hypodermic needle and syringe *US*
- — Geoffrey Froner, *Digging for Diamonds*, p. 53, 1989

3 a bullet *US*
- 'Bout this time the poor bartender had gone to rest / I pumped six a my rockets in his motherfucken chest. — Bruce Jackson, *Get Your Ass in the Water and Swim Like Me*, p. 47, 1965
- — Roger D. Abrahams, *Deep Down in the Jungle*, p. 262, 1970

4 an Oldsmobile V-8 engine *US*
- — John Lawlor, *How to Talk Car*, p. 88, 1965

5 a tampon *US*
From the shape.
- One word I remember in middle and high school (mid to late 1980s) was the term "rocket" being used for a tampon. — *The Museum of Menstruation and Women's Health*, April 2001

▷ see: ROAD ROCKET

rocket alley *nickname*
Phuoc Binh, South Vietnam *US*
The nickname came from the frequent Viet Cong rocket attacks.
- — Gregory Clark, *Words of the Vietnam War*, p. 400, 1990

rocket burns *noun*
faecal stains in the underwear or on a toilet bowl *CANADA*
- — Bill Casselman, *Canadian Sayings*, p. 44, 2002

rocket cap *noun*
a dome-shaped cap on a vial in which crack cocaine is sold *US*
- — US Department of Justice, *Street Terms*, October 1994

Rocket City *nickname*
Tay Ninh, South Vietnam; Lai Khe, South Vietnam *US*
- Byrom told him that they were under enemy rocket attack and that he had better get used to it, because it happened so often they called Lai Khe "Rocket City." — Peter Goldman and Tony Fuller, *Charlie Company*, p. 35, 1983
- When Donald arrived at Tay Ninh, he discovered the camp was so frequently under attack it had been nicknamed Rocket City. — James Mills, *The Underground Empire*, p. 137, 1986

rocket fuel *noun*
1 phencyclidine, the recreational drug known as PCP or angel dust *US*
- — John R. Armore and Joseph D. Wolfe, *Dictionary of Desperation*, p. 46, 1976
- — *Drummer*, p. 77, 1977

2 a combination of assorted alcoholic beverages *NEW ZEALAND*
- Rocket fuel being a crude concoction of assorted spirits pilfered from their parents' liquor cabinets and mixed together in an innocuous-looking vessel such as a Coke bottle. Rocket fuel is drunk neat and very rapidly induces drunkenness. — *North and South*, p. 53, December 1997

rocket man *noun*
a person who sells syringes to drug addicts *US*
Illegal in the US, but profitable.
- — Geoffrey Froner, *Digging for Diamonds*, p. 53, 1989

rocket ripple *noun*
a barrage of 144 rockets fired from a small cart *US*
Korean war usage.
- It may be ridiculous to call any barrage beautiful, but if one doesn't think about it too hard, a barrage is beautiful – to watch; especially a rocket ripple. — Martin Russ, *The Last Parallel*, p. 280, 1957

rocket science *noun*
any difficult, demanding task *US*
- — Anna Scotti and Paul Young, *Buzzwords*, p. 54, 1997

rocket stains *noun*
faecal stains in the underwear or on a toilet bowl *CANADA*
- — Bill Casselman, *Canadian Sayings*, p. 44, 2002

rock fiend *noun*
a crack cocaine addict *UK*
From **ROCK** (crack cocaine).
- — Mike Haskins, *Drugs*, p. 292, 2003

Rockford Files *noun*
haemorrhoids *UK*
Rhyming slang for 'piles', formed from the title of a US television series, 1975–82.
- — Bodmin Dark, *Dirty Cockney Rhyming Slang*, 2003

rock hard *noun*
amyl or butyl nitrite *UK*
Reflects male use as a sex-aid; possibly derives from a brand name.
- Street names [...] poppers, ram, rock hard, rush[.] — James Kay and Julian Cohen, *The Parents' Complete Guide to Young People and Drugs*, p. 144, 1998

rockhead *noun*

1 a crack cocaine addict *US*

- "I'm Department of Corrections," Kathy said. "What are you?" A rockhead for one thing, no doubt lights popping in this brain. —Elmore Leonard, *Maximum Bob*, p. 65, 1991
- The realization that he hadn't seen a rockhead in three days jolted him. Wowwww! These people ain't into crack. —Odie Hawkins, *Midnight*, p. 62, 1995
- after a heady day's business, dealing with nearly every rock-head in town[.] —Lanre Fehintola, *Charlie Says...*, p. 17, 2000

2 a dim-witted person *US*

- A mule. A rock-head. You know how they get. —Max Shulman, *Rally Round the Flag, Boys!*, p. 3, 1957

rock-hog *noun*

in mining, a tunneller or driller *CANADA*

- They spoke of dynamite and flying rock responsible for the death of many a "rock-hog." —Vera Lysenko, *Yellow Boots*, p. 190, 1954

rockhopper *noun*

an angler who fishes from coastal rocks *AUSTRALIA, 1966*

- —Jim Ramsay, *Cop It Sweet!*, p. 77, 1977
- It was barely first light when they reached the bottom of the cliff but both old 'rockhoppers' still knew their way around. —Robert G. Barrett, *Davo's Little Something*, p. 320, 1992

rock hound *noun*

in oil drilling, a geologist, especially one who focuses on the earth's surface *US*

- —Jerry Robertson, *Oil Slanguage*, p. 105, 1954

rock house *noun*

a premises used for the sale and consumption of crack cocaine *US*

- I said, "Listen homeboy, what you talkin about? / You're mistakin my pad for a rockhouse / Well, I know to you we all look the same / But I'm not the one slingin caine"[.] —Toddy Tee, *Batterram*, 1985
- The rock house nigga. We done served that fool before. —*Menace II Society*, 1993

rocking chair *noun*

1 retirement with a pension *US*

- —Norman Carlisle, *The Modern Wonder Book of Trains and Railroading*, p. 263, 1946

2 in a group of trucks travelling together, the truck in the middle *US*

- —Wayne Floyd, *Jason's Authentic Dictionary of CB Slang*, p. 26, 1976

rocking chair money *noun*

unemployment insurance or Old Age Security *CANADA*

- The somewhat less sophisticated people of the Maritimes have a happier name for Unemployment Insurance: "Rockin' Chair Money." —*Toronto Globe and Mail*, p. 7/1, 22nd April 1959
- Since much labor in Alaska is seasonal, many men draw wages totaling $10,000 to $15,000 a season in construction, and during the long winter months sit back and draw rocking chair money[.] —Robert O. Bowen, *An Alaskan Dictionary*, p. 28, 1965

rocking horse *noun*

sauce, whether the condiment, garnish or impudence *UK*

Rhyming slang.

- —Ronnie Barker, *Fletcher's Book of Rhyming Slang*, 1979
- You've got some bloody rocking horse you have. —Ray Puxley, *Cockney Rabbit*, 1992

Rock Jaw *noun*

Rach Gia, South Vietnam *US*

- —Gregory Clark, *Words of the Vietnam War*, p. 421, 1990

rock jockey *noun*

in the language of paragliding, a hang glider flier *US*

- —Erik Fair, *California Thrill Sports*, p. 336, 1992

rockman *noun*

a dealer in crack cocaine *US, 1989*

- And the Chief of Police says he just might / (Flatten out every house he sees on sight) / Because he say the rockman is takin him for a fool [...] And Mister Rockman, you better stop some day —Toddy Tee, *Batterram*, 1985
- —Ellen C. Bellone (Editor), *Dictionary of Slang*, p. 20, 1989
- —Kenn "Naz" Young, *Naz's Dictionary of Teen Slang*, p. 99, 1993

rock med *noun*

medical treatment targeted for rock 'n' roll concert goers *US*

- —David Shenk and Steve Silberman, *Skeleton Key*, p. 250, 1994

rock 'n' roll *noun*

1 a genre of music with a driving rhythm; an umbrella for most simply rhythmic music produced since the 1950s *US*

The etymology is laden with sexual overtones, thus 'My Man Rocks Me With One Steady Roll', sung by blues singer Trixie Smith in 1924, and a song entitled 'Rock and Roll' is recorded in 1934. It is not until 1954 that the music now recognised as 'rock 'n' roll' is given its identity; coinage is generally credited to US disc jockey Alan Freed.

- —Trixie Smith, *My Man Rocks Me With One Steady Roll*, 1924
- It's right rhythmic rock and roll music that provides plenty of inspiration in Joe Liggins' "Sugar Lump." —*Billboard*, p. 33, 22nd June 1946
- It was Alan Freed, an American DJ in the fifties [...] who started using the phrase to describe "rhythm and blues" played by white musicians rather than black. Then Bill Haley brought rock 'n' roll to the attention of young Britons. —Simon Napier-Bell, *Black Vinyl White Powder*, p. 9, 2001

2 a hole *UK*

Rhyming slang, used practically or figuratively.

- —Ray Puxley, *Cockney Rabbit*, 1992

3 unemployment benefit; any government office from which it is administrated *UK*

Rhyming slang for **THE DOLE**.

- [S]he [Sarah Ferguson]'s given the door. The Royal 'E'. Back on the rock-and-roll. —Andrew Nickolds, *Back to Basics*, p. 13, 1994
- I don't want to wait all my life to get busted like those dickehead cabs parked up right outside the rock an' roll on the high street. —Nick Barlay, *Curvy Lovebox*, p. 85, 1997

rock 'n' roll *verb*

▷ **see: ROCK AND ROLL**

rock 'n' roll!

used as an good-humoured exclamation of dismissal *UK*

- Bob didn't have any cigarette papers and neither did I. [...] But hey, rock 'n' roll! Not to worry, because I might have some in my car[.] —Ken Lukowiak, *Marijuana Time*, p. 316, 2000

rock of ages; rocks *noun*

wages *UK, 1937*

Rhyming slang.

- —Ray Puxley, *Cockney Rabbit*, 1992

rock of Gibraltar *noun*

in shuffleboard, a disc that is well hidden and guarded *US*

- —Omero C. Catan, *Secrets of Shuffleboard Strategy*, p. 71, 1967: 'Glossary of terms'

rock-on *noun*

an erection *UK*

A variation of **HARD-ON** (an erection).

- He made his way over to her as casually as he was able with a semi rock-on in those restrictively snug jeans. —Kevin Sampson, *Powder*, p. 30, 1999

rock on the chest; rock on the box *noun*

silicosis *US*

- And a miner with silicosis had rock on the chest, rock on the box, the miner's con, or, succinctly the miner's. —*It's an Old Wild West Custom*, p. 136, 1951

rockpile *noun*

any prison job *US*

- —Inez Cardozo-Freeman, *The Joint*, p. 527, 1984

rocks *noun*

1 salt *US*

- —Don Wilmeth, *The Language of American Popular Entertainment*, p. 225, 1981

2 money *US*

- —*The Annals of the American Academy of Political and Social Sciences*, p. 130, May 1950

3 dominoes *US*

- —Dominic Armanino, *Dominoes*, p. 16, 1959

4 jewels; pearls *UK, 1937*

From the US sense (diamonds).

5 the testicles *US, 1948*

- Well, he's just a kid, and he always hadda pair of rocks on him, the man. —George V. Higgins, *The Friends of Eddie Coyle*, p. 192, 1971
- "I'm beat to the rocks." "You mean your socks." "I mean my rocks, my nuts, my balls, fachrissakes." —Robert Campbell, *Sweet La-La Land*, p. 24, 1990

6 courage *US*

- Oh yes, planting bombs took a lot of rocks, you had to admire that. —John Sayles, *Union Dues*, p. 176, 1977

▷ **see: ALMOND ROCKS, MINT ROCKS**

▸ **get your rocks off**

1 to ejaculate *US*

- He wiped the blood away and gave her fifty slats [dollars] to get his rocks. — Iceberg Slim (Robert Beck), *Pimp*, p. 293, 1969
- At last he made vulgar use of me to get his rocks off and told me I could leave[.] — Jefferson Poland and Valerie Alison, *The Records of the San Francisco Sexual Freedom League*, p. 153, 1971
- Baths vary in character, from the Wall Street Sauna, where businessmen go to get their rocks off during the lunch hour (it's called "funch"), to the Beacon[.] — *The Village Voice*, 27th September 1976
- The sex scenes cover a wide range of lovin', from the perverse to the passionate, and everybody gets their rocks off. — *Adult Video*, p. 14, August/September 1986

2 to be satisfied with or excited about something *US*

Figurative application of the sense 'to ejaculate'.

- You know, I'm not getting my rocks off. This victory walk SUCKS. — Howard Stern, *Miss America*, p. 291, 1995

▸ **on the rocks**

1 used of a drink, served over ice *US, 1946*

- She gave him a bourbon-on-the-rocks. — Max Shulman, *Anyone Got a Match?*, p. 245, 1964
- Sweetie, will you mix us a nice martini? Beefeater gin, no vermouth, on the rocks, with just the tiniest dash of rock salt. — Gore Vidal, *Myra Breckinridge*, p. 268, 1968

2 in severe trouble *UK, 1889*

- [A]ny scurvy member of the Commons whose reputation is almost on the rocks can run to Sunday service and appear on television pretending to be cleansed, whole and redeemed. — *New Statesman*, 11th April 1997
- A marriage on the rocks[;] Tony Blair left the Labour conference strengthened and Gordon Brown weakened, but their titanic struggle is far from resolved[.] — *The Observer*, 5th October 2003

▸ **shoot your rocks**

to ejaculate *US*

- "There," Gloria said as she closed the door behind her, "don't want those fuckin' honkies to shoot their rocks 'fore they pay!" — Donald Goines, *Inner City Hoodlum*, p. 118, 1975

▸ **the rocks**

a confidence swindle involving fake diamonds *US*

- The Westside mark had een sweet as honeysuckle. He had blown ten grand on our slick version of the rocks. — Iceberg Slim (Robert Beck), *Trick Baby*, p. 11, 1969

rock slinger *noun*

a seller of crack cocaine *US*

- — Kenn "Naz" Young, *Naz's Dictionary of Teen Slang*, p. 99, 1993

rocks of hell *noun*

crack cocaine *UK, 1998*

An elaboration of **ROCK**.

- — Mike Haskins, *Drugs*, p. 282, 2003

rock solvent *noun*

in caving and pot-holing, any explosive *UK*

This is slang with a euphemistic purpose: when communicating by telephone, e-mail, etc., it is thought ill advised to use words like 'explosive'. Noted by David Morrison of Wessex Cave Club, 29th February 2004.

rockspider *noun*

1 an Afrikaner *SOUTH AFRICA, 1970*

Derogatory. Sometimes shortened to 'spider'.

- — Jean Branford, *A Dictionary of South African English*, 1978
- [T]he struggle of the people against the tyranny of the rockspiders, crunchies, hairybacks, ropes, and bloody Dutchmen[.] — Rian Malan, *My Traitor's Heart*, p. 39, 1990

2 a child molester *AUSTRALIA, 1984*

Originally in prison use, but now part of general slang. Baker, 1953, lists as underworld slang: 'a petty thief in a park, who robs the hangbags or other possessions of couples frolicking in parks or other open spaces'.

- Brother Campbell is on the list of the dead, knifed in a public toilet noted for its popularity with arse-bandits and rockspiders. — Dirk Flinthart, *Brotherly Love*, p. 23, 1995
- Rock spiders? They're out from under the pebbles and crawling all over the Net. — *Juice*, p. 94, 1996
- The hatred that general crims have for 'rock spiders' is no secret[.] — William Dodson, *The Sharp End*, p. 19, 2001

rock star *noun*

1 a crack cocaine dealer *US*

- They say 'Beam Me Up, Scotty.' They say, 'I Need a Beam-Me-Up Scotty. You got some? You got some?' And the rock star say, Looky here. Lookyhere. I got a dollar beamer. Dollar Beamer. Three dollar Beamer. — *St. Petersburg (Florida) Times*, p. 1F, 28th February 1988
- "It was mostly old people living there – then the rock stars moved in," Knight said, using street slang to describe the crack dealers. — *Orlando Sentinel Tribune*, p. B3, 22nd May 2001
- — Mike Haskins, *Drugs*, p. 282, 2003

2 a woman who engages in sex for payment in crack cocaine or money to buy crack cocaine; a prostitute addicted to crack cocaine *US*

- — *Washington Post*, p. C5, 7th November 1993
- — Jim Crotty, *How to Talk American*, p. 91, 1997

rock starring *noun*

an act of having sex with a partner in exchange for a payment of crack cocaine *UK*

- — Nick Constable, *This is Cocaine*, p. 182, 2002

rock whore *noun*

a woman who will trade sex for crack cocaine *US*

- This here's a go-go rock whore I'm talking about. Does it to buy crack and get high. — Elmore Leonard, *Maximum Bob*, p. 189, 1991
- DREXEL: You ain't seen nothing like these rock whores. They ass be young man. They got that fine young pussy. Bitches want the rock, they be a freak for you. — *True Romance*, 1993
- You send some hard-headed rock whore and she fucks things up. — *Jackie Brown*, 1997

rock wing *noun*

in the language of paragliding, a hang glider flier *US*

- — Erik Fair, *California Thrill Sports*, p. 335, 1992

rocky *noun*

1 hashish *UK*

Probably from a specific use into generic.

- He laid the block on the bed, then sat next to it, looking at it closely. Hashish. Cannabis. Ash. Rocky. Pox. Call it what you like[.] — Courttia Newland, *Society Within*, p. 27, 1999

2 crack cocaine *UK, 1998*

- An eighth of Charlie [cocaine], five pills [MDMA] and an ounce of rocky. If it's any good we'll be back. — Wayne Anthony, *Spanish Highs*, p. 3, 1999

Rocky *noun*

Coors™ beer *US*

Coors boasts of being brewed with 'pure Rocky Mountain spring water'.

- — *American Speech*, p. 63, February 1967: 'Soda-fountain, restaurant and tavern calls'

rocky black; rocky *noun*

a type of marijuana *UK*

- — Angela Devlin, *Prison Patter*, p. 98, 1996

rocky hash *noun*

a type of marijuana *UK*

- What was you after? – Es an' some rocky hash, says Baggy. — Nick Baclay, *Curvy Lovebox*, p. 45, 1997

Rocky III *noun*

crack cocaine *UK, 1998*

An elaboration of **ROCK**, using the title of a 1982 film.

- — Mike Haskins, *Drugs*, p. 282, 2003

Rocky Mountain deadshot *noun*

pancakes; hotcakes; griddle cakes; flapjacks *CANADA*

- The Rocky Mountain deadshot may be a "full deck," or four pancakes in a stack. — Tom Parkin, *WetCoast Words*, p. 116, 1989

Rocky Mountain Kool Aid *noun*

Coors™ beer *US*

Once available only in Colorado, where it is brewed.

- — Bill Davis, *Jawjacking*, p. 83, 1977

Rocky Mountain oyster *noun*

an animal testicle, usually that of a steer formerly known as a bull, prepared for eating as a regional delicacy *US*

- — John Mariani, *Mariani's Coast-to-Coast Dining Guide*, p. 225, 1986

rocy *noun*

any variety of hashish from Morocco *UK*

- [T]his particular brand of rocy does not live up to its promise. — Nick Jones, *Spliffs*, p. 88, 2003
- Sitting in a deep sweat / thinking / I got to get some rocy for the weekend[.] — Goldie Looking Chain *Soap Bar*, 2004

rod *noun*

1 the penis; the erect penis *UK, 1902*

- It's all right. She's my wife. She needs black rod, is all. — Eldridge Cleaver, *Soul on Ice*, p. 170, 1968
- "The Spirit tells them that they blew the thing, that they should have gotten hold of his Rod – " "His Deick," said Doc. "Yeah." — Cecil Brown, *The Life & Loves of Mr. Jiveass Nigger*, p. 56, 1969
- Jim Tom said, "I'm lucky I inherited the same rod my daddy had. When he died, it took seven days to close the casket." — Dan Jenkins, *Life Its Ownself*, p. 122, 1984
- CHINESE STUDENT: I was distracted by that enormous flying – RACHEL HUNTE: Rod? — *Austin Powers*, 1999

2 a gun, usually a pistol *US, 1903*

A perfect example for those who like to ascribe phallic symbolism to the tools of man's aggression.

- Drop yer rod, Tracy. Yer covered by a machine gun that kin sweep the whole layout. — Chester Gould, *Dick Tracy Meets the Night Crawler*, p. 190, 1945
- In those days guys packed rods like women do lipstick; practically every hip pocket in town was a walking arsenal. — Mezz Mezzrow, *Really the Blues*, p. 32, 1946
- I still have a private cop's license with the privilege to pack a rod, and they're afraid of me. — Mickey Spillane, *I, The Jury*, p. 7, 1947
- I hear they found the rod what knocked off your teacher. — Irving Shulman, *The Amboy Dukes*, p. 262, 1947
- The Pachuco shivs Mace while the big stoop stands there all goofed off with a rod in his mitt. — Thurston Scott, *Cure it with Honey*, p. 160, 1951
- My boys don't carry rods. — Hal Ellson, *The Golden Spike*, p. 70, 1952
- "But what you really need is a rod like this." And he reached into his pocket again and took out a .32 Colt automatic. — Jim Thompson, *Savage Night*, p. 69, 1953
- You couldn't even rob a bank, to rob a bank you needed a rod and to buy a rod you need at least twenty bucks. — Bernard Wolfe, *The Late Risers*, p. 7, 1954
- Lieutenant Anderson asked me last night why we stick to these old-fashioned rods when the new ones are so much better. — Chester Himes, *The Real Cool Killers*, p. 13, 1959
- It worried me to be part of a hustle that required a rod. — Iceberg Slim (Robert Beck), *Pimp*, p. 252, 1969
- — Angela Devlin, *Prison Patter*, p. 98, 1996

3 a hired gunman *US*

- — R. Frederick West, *God's Gambler*, p. 228, 1964: 'Appendix A'

4 a car modified for speed or looks; a hot rod *US, 1945*

- The first was a made one, with a burly blond kind in a souped-up rod. — Jack Kerouac, *On the Road*, p. 79, 1957

5 the draw-rod underneath a railway goods wagon *US, 1904*

- That number is a wonderful example of what happened to the blues when they moved out of the gallion, the work-gang and the levee and rode the rods into big towns like New Orleans, Charleston, Memphis and Chi. — Mezz Mezzrow, *Really the Blues*, p. 45, 1946
- They came riding the rods, in boxcars, or on foot, to the great freight-yard terminals. — Jack Lait and Lee Mortimer, *Chicago Confidential*, p. 53, 1950
- In this jet age, they prefer to transport themselves by motorcyle, the rods, and unrhymed iambics. — Bernard Wolfe, *The Magic of Their Singing*, p. 86, 1961

▸ **had the rod**

wrecked; ruined *AUSTRALIA*

Variant of **HAVE HAD THE DICK**.

- He's had the rod now for sure. — Bluey, *Bush Contractors*, p. 272, 1975

rodadio *noun*

a radio *US*

Trucker embellishment.

- — Wayne Floyd, *Jason's Authentic Dictionary of CB Slang*, p. 26, 1976

rodda *noun*

a Cadillac El Dorado car *US*

- — David Claerbaut, *Black Jargon in White America*, p. 78, 1972

rodded up *adjective*

armed with a handgun or handguns *US*

- — Hyman E. Goldin et al., *Dictionary of American Underworld Lingo*, p. 180, 1950

rodder *noun*

a hot rod enthusiast *US, 1949*

- Many people think that a rodder is a character who spends all his time hotting up his roadster! — *Hod Rod Comics*, June 1952
- Well I guess you might say she's the rodder's dream gal / Always there to help, man, when you need a pal. — The Beach Boys, *Car Crazy Cutie*, 1963

rodeo fuck *noun*

used for describing sex between a man and woman; the man enters the woman from behind, insults her ('you're almost as good as your sister' for example) and then holds on *US*

A term heard mostly in jokes; attributed to Rodney Dangerfield.

- — John-Paul Sousa, *Speaking of Sex*, p. 86, 2002

Rodino *noun*

a Mexican citizen permitted to stay in the US during an immigration amnesty period in the late 1980s *US*

After Congressman Peter Rodino, sponsor of the legislation that made the amnesty possible.

- Abel knew that a real driver would be a gringo, not a former "Rodino" like himself. — Joseph Wambaugh, *Finnegan's Week*, p. 39, 1993

Rodney boater *noun*

a boat-dweller who does not care for the upkeep of the boat-home *UK*

- — D.J. Smith, *Discovering Craft of the Inland Waterways*, p. 81, 1987

rod out *verb*

to install high performance equipment in a car's engine *US*

- — Judi Sanders, *Mashing and Munching in Ames*, p. 16, 1994

Rods; Rod's *nickname*

Harrod's, a department store in Knightsbridge, London *UK*

An abbreviation that seems to be a diminutive. Upper-class society use.

- — Ann Barr and Peter York, *The Official Sloane Ranger Handbook*, p. 159, 1982

Rod the Bod; Rod the Mod *nickname*

rock singer Rod Stewart *US*

- That's when you got my attention, when Rod the Bod takes table five. — Carl Hiaasen, *Strip Tease*, p. 204, 1993

rod walloper *noun*

a male masturbator *AUSTRALIA*

Formed on **ROD** (the penis) with a variation of 'beater'.

- [D]id you hear the one about the poor old rod walloper who overwound his self winding watch. — Barry Humphries, *Bazza Pulls It Off!*, 1971

rod-walloping *noun*

male masturbation *AUSTRALIA*

- Blokes can go blind!!! Rod walloping's got nothin' on what a cove can get from foreign sheilahs. — Barry Humphries, *Bazza Pulls It Off!*, 1971

rofe *noun*

▷ see: **RUOF**

roger *verb*

1 from a male perspective, to have sex *UK, 1711*

From its, now obsolete, use as a slang term for 'the penis'.

- I lay abed till 9 o'clock this morning to bring my wife into temper again and rogered her by way of reconciliation. — David Hackett Fischer, *Albion's Seed*, p. 285, 1991
- Auden fantasised, the wonderfully informative Katherine Bucknell informs us, about being rogered by his father. — *The Observer*, 31st July 1994

2 to acknowledge receipt of a message *US*

- He had "rogered" the transmission but had not shown up for almost forty-five minutes. — Stephen J. Cannell, *The Tin Collectors*, p. 110, 2001

roger!

used for expressing agreement or affirmation *US, 1941*

'R' or 'roger' signified that a message or command had been received.

- That's a roger. — Gerald Petievich, *Money Men*, p. 99, 1981
- "Just watch the show, smartass." "Roger." — Armistead Maupin, *Further Tales of the City*, p. 220, 1982

roger dodger; roger dodge; roger D; roger splodge

yes; affirmative *US*

Variations of **ROGER!** (yes).

- — *Complete CB Slang Dictionary*, p. 80, 1976
- — Peter Chippindale, *The British CB Book*, p. 158, 1981

Roger Hunt *noun*

a cunt in all senses *UK*

Rhyming slang, formed, for no apparent reason other than the rhyme, from the name of a Liverpool and England footballer.

- — Ray Puxley, *Fresh Rabbit*, 1998

rogering *noun*

from a male perspective, sexual intercourse *UK*

From the verb **ROGER** (to have sex).

- Matilda Merriman, notorious for her alleged night of non-stop rogering with a one-time cabinet member — Ian Rankin, *Strip Jack*, p. 86, 1998
- The fifth album from the acceptable face of rampant rogering, Lucky Day [by Shaggy] consists of 14 lovingly crafted dub-pop shagging sonnets[.] — *The Guardian*, 1st November 2002

Roger ramjet *noun*
any speeding and reckless driver *US*
• —Wayne Floyd, *Jason's Authentic Dictionary of CB Slang*, p. 26, 1976

rogue *noun*
1 a horse that is difficult to handle *AUSTRALIA*
• The rogues among the horses and mules sought every chance to break the line and hide under shady trees where sweet grass grew[.] —Ion L. Idriess, *Over the Range*, p. 7, 1947
• —Robert Saunders Dowst and Jay Craig, *Playing the Races*, p. 168, 1960
• —Wilda Moxham, *The Apprentice*, p. 97, 1969
• The Old Huck, was given a mount of a 'rogue' at Newcastle. It had been left at the post and had run off at the turn in every race. —Frank Hardy and Athol George Mulley, *The Needy and the Greedy*, p. 23, 1975
2 in surfing, a wave that appears without warning *US*
• —Gary Fairmont R. Filosa II, *The Surfer's Almanac*, p. 193, 1977

rogue *verb*
to take something without permission *US*
• Who rogued my last beer? —Connie Eble (Editor), *UNC-CH Campus Slang*, p. 5, Spring 1984

rogue *adjective*
strange; threatening *US*
• —Connie Eble (Editor), *UNC-CH Campus Slang*, p. 8, Spring 2003

rogue's badge *noun*
in horse racing, blinkers *US*
Usually worn by horses that do not behave well, hence the label of 'rogue'.
• —Dan Parker, *The ABC of Horse Racing*, p. 148, 1947

rogue's gallery *noun*
a collection of photographs of criminals *US, 1859*
• The butler identified a Rogues Gallery picture of Sam ("Sammy the Hook") Entratta, alias Ippolletti. —Jack Lait and Lee Mortimer, *Chicago Confidential*, p. 18, 1950
• Any day, you can visit the office of Sheriff Ralph Lamb, and you will see on his walls a rogue's gallery of cheaters, identified by their specialties – slots, craps, cards. —Jimmy Snyder, *Jimmy the Greek*, p. 218, 1975

roidhead *noun*
a habitual user of steroids *UK*
An abbreviation of 'ster*oid*' combined with **-HEAD** (a user).
• She hated all them roid-heads[.] —Kevin Sampson, *Outlaws*, p. 45, 2001

roid rage; 'roid rage *noun*
violently ill-tempered behaviour resulting from excessive steroid use *US*
An abbreviation of 'ster*oid*', playing on **ROAD RAGE**.
• But that young athlete should know that there are dozens of other steroid reactions, and that some, such as acne and uncontrollable 'roid rages (aggressive and combative behavior), might cause immediate difficulties. —*FDA Consumer*, p. 16, November 1987
• —*American Speech*, Winter 1989
• [P]umped-up bouncers who teetered only moments from 'roid rage[.] —Greg Williams, *Diamond Geezers*, p. 37, 1997
• "Don't shout at me," she said. "Slow down. Adjust the dose. You're showing all the signs of 'roid rage. —Liza Cody, *Queen of Mean [Tart Noir]*, p. 75, 2002

roids *noun*
anabolic steroids *US*
• Please be advised that no one uses "oids," but rather "roids," instead of steroids. [Letter to the editor] —*New York Times*, p. 78 (Section 6), 21st December 1980
• —Sally Williams, *"Strong" Words*, p. 158, 1994
• I do have that one thing against me, but I'm not on roids, and I don't drink and I've always been able to hold myself in a respectable way wherever I go. [quoting 2 Cold Scorpio] —*Wrestling Flyer*, 1st January 1994
• You probably know of how many guys tested positive on it, it doesn't take a rocket scientist to figure out who was on roids. [quoting Bill Watts] —Herb Kunze, *Herb's Wrestling Tidbits*, 23rd February 1995

rojas *noun*
Malboro™ cigarettes *US*
Spanish for 'red', which is the colour of the packaging.
• —Judi Sanders, *Cal Poly Slang*, p. 8, 1990

rojito *noun*
a red central nervous system depressant, especially Seconal™ *US*
From the Spanish for 'little red one'.
• —Eugene Landy, *The Underground Dictionary*, p. 54, 1971

rojo *noun*
dextromethorphan (DXM), an active ingredient in non-prescription cold and cough medication, often abused for non-medicinal purposes *US*
Spanish for 'red', which is the colour of the cough syrup.
• Youths' nicknames for DXM: Robo, Skittles, Triple C's, Rojo, Dex, Tussin, Vitamin D. DXM abuse is called "Robotripping" or "Tussing." Users might be called "syrup heads" or "robotards." —*USA Today*, p. 1A, 29th December 2003

rojo flow *noun*
the bleed period of the menstrual cycle *US*
A use of the Spanish word *rojo* (red).
• —Don R. McCreary (Editor), *Dawg Speak*, 2001

rokker *verb*
▷ **see: ROCKER**

roko *noun*
a riot, protest or demonstration *INDIA*
• The committee also demanded a judicial inquiry into the attempt on the life of former Finance Minister Kanwaljit Singh during the 'rasta roko' stir at Zirakpur. The peacefully agitating workers at many places in the state were "cane-charged" and humiliated —*The Tribune (India)*, 16th February 2003

rolf *verb*
to vomit *US*
• —Mary Corey and Victoria Westermark, *Fer Shurr! How to be a Valley Girl*, 1982

roll *noun*
1 an act of sexual intercourse *US*
An abbreviation of **ROLL IN THE HAY**.
• Hey, Billy boy, you remember that time in Seattle you and me picked up those two twitches? One of the best rolls I ever had. —Ken Kesey, *One Flew Over the Cuckoo's Nest*, p. 98, 1962
2 a roll of money *US*
• I had just got back with a load of jack / from out where the big shot reside / She lamped my roll, fell heart and soul / and wanted to dance with me. —Bruce Jackson, *Get Your Ass in the Water and Swim Like Me*, p. 101, 1965
• He invested £750 of his 'roll' on a horse he considered a 'good thing' in the opening race. —James Holledge, *The Great Australian Gamble*, p. 36, 1966
3 a single cigarette or marijuana cigarette *FIJI*
• He couldn't leave it and every time he lit another roll he slowly burnt his life away. —*Fiji Times*, 20th March 1993
• In Suva, two Samoan students of the University of the South Pacific were arrested after police found one and a half rolls of marijuana on them aong Carnarvon Street. —*Daily Post*, p. 1, 8th April 1996
4 MDMA, the recreational drug best known as ecstasy *UK*
• —Mike Haskins, *Drugs*, p. 290, 2003
5 ten barbiturate capsules sold as a unit *US*
• —David W. Maurer and Victor Vogel, *Narcotics and Narcotic Addiction*, p. 438, 1973
6 a double-breasted suit *US*
• —Roger D. Abrahams, *Deep Down in the Jungle*, p. 262, 1970

▸ **on a roll**
enjoying continuing success *US, 1976*
• The scent of victory in his nostrils [...] Refreshed in mind and body. On a roll! —Jack Allen, *When the Whistle Blows*, p. 91, 2000

roll *verb*
1 to rob someone, especially with force and especially someone bemused with drink *US, 1873*
• The clip joint would roll a drunk and then toss him, unconscious, out in the parking lot. —Robert Sylvester, *No Cover Charge*, p. 82, 1956
• members of the oldest profession, some of whom are not above rolling a mug for his wallet —Charles Raven, *Underworld Nights*, p. 20, 1956
• She learned how to "roll lushes" and the technique of "boosting" merchandise out of the department stores[.] —John M. Murtagh and Sara Harris, *Cast the First Stone*, p. 27, 1957
• Adolpho had carried away the drunkie's Sterno, replying to my feeble protest, "What in hell, he's lucky, we wain't rolling him." —Clancy Sigal, *Going Away*, p. 237, 1961
• They never worry about a white gal rolling them. —Sara Harris, *The Lords of Hell*, p. 77, 1967
• Joe, you're not very smart, but you can make a living some way besides rolling queers. —Nicholas Von Hoffman, *We Are The People Our Parents Warned Us Against*, p. 25, 1967
• Some black crazy cat threw a cup of coffee at a white drunk and rolled him. —Abbie Hoffman, *Revolution for the Hell of It*, p. 176, 1968
• There were, of course, teen-age gangs who roamed about mugging and rolling drunks[.] —Nathan Heard, *Howard Street*, p. 17, 1968
• Where blood was shed for the sake of bread / And drunks rolled for their poke. —Dennis Wepman et al., *The Life*, p. 80, 1976
• Sometimes I'd roll a stray drunk[.] —Herbert Huncke, *Guilty of Everything*, p. 97, 1990

- I've got to help an old lady up off the floor after she's been rolled by three fuckin pipeheads [crack cocaine addicts] for her pension.—Niall Griffiths, *Kelly + Victor*, p. 111, 2002

2 to avoid paying a bill for services provided by an establishment such as a hotel or restaurant *US*

- —Robert C. Prus and C.R.D. Sharper, *Road Hustler*, p. 171, 1977: 'Glossary of terms'

3 to betray friends by changing sides; to inform on someone *US*
A variation of **ROLL OVER**.

- He knew the big, ugly steroid jockey was just smart enough to figure that Tommy would kill him inch by fucking inch if he ever rolled. —Stephen J. Cannell, *King Con*, p. 20, 1997

4 to leave *US*

- Let's roll, my man.—*Fast Times at Ridgemont High*, 1982
- C'mon, get your gear on, we're rollin'.—*Break Point*, 1991
- Johann looks furtive, eager to get going. JOHANN: Let's roll, Jordi. —Guy Ritchie et al., *Lock, Stock... & Four Stolen Hooves*, p. 54, 2000

5 to arrive on the scene *AUSTRALIA, 1861*

- Seven o'clock: the Fury last rolled on them at four-thirty.—Richard Price, *Clockers*, p. 20, 1992

6 to ride in a car *US*

- Whose Benzo was that I saw you rolling in yesterday?—*Boyz N The Hood*, 1990
- the three of them rolling in the car, still looking for a Maxima—*Menace II Society*, 1993

7 (used of a woman) to walk with a rolling motion of the pelvis *TRINIDAD AND TOBAGO, 1973*

- —Lise Winer, *Dictionary of the English/Creole of Trinidad & Tobago*, 2003

8 in prison, to open a cell *US*

- With grip in hand, Bud called the man / "Roll 'em, Cap, and don't be slow."—Dennis Wepman et al., *The Life*, p. 71, 1976

9 to take MDMA, the recreational drug best known as ecstasy *US*

- Mirranda Fernandes, 22, a waitress who lived alone with her dog, said to a neighbor one day in September 1999 that she wanted "to roll," street slang for taking the drug ecstasy.—*Tampa (Florida) Tribune*, p. 1, 14th February 2001

▸ **roll bones**
to play dice *US*

- —*The Annals of the American Academy of Political and Social Sciences*, p. 130, May 1950

▸ **roll in on**
to attack someone *US*

- AW soldiers would roll in on a white known to have well-off family members.—Bill Valentine, *Gangs and Their Tattoos*, p. 12, 2000

▸ **roll it back**
to decelerate a motorcycle; to close the throttle-twist grip *UK*

- —Douglas Dunford, *Motorcycle Department, Beaulieu Motor Museum*, 1979

▸ **roll on**
let it proceed or happen swiftly *UK, 1901*
Often used in an imperative or exclamatory manner.

▸ **roll the dice**
to take a chance on something *US*

- You want to investigate me, roll the dice, and take your chances. —*A Few Good Men*, 1992

▸ **roll the drums**
in betting, to double the bet in effect *US*

- —Sam Snead and Jerry Tarde, *Pigeons, Marks, Hustlers and Other Golf Bettors You Can Beat*, p. 110, 1986

▸ **roll your own**
to reload your own ammunition *US*

- —*American Speech*, p. 194, October 1957: 'Some colloquialisms of the handgunner'

roll deep *verb*
to go somewhere with a large group of friends; to have a large group of friends *US*

- —Pamela Munro, *U.C.L.A Slang*, p. 107, 2001
- —Connie Eble (Editor), *UNC-CH Campus Slang*, p. 9, October 2002

roller *noun*

1 a police officer *US, 1964*

- Boy, but the next day the roller may run down on ya, take you down to that lonesome old county jail.—Bruce Jackson, *Get Your Ass in the Water and Swim Like Me*, p. 123, 1965
- At noon, two 'rollers' broke the door down.—Iceberg Slim (Robert Beck), *Pimp*, p. 101, 1969
- —Christina and Richard Milner, *Black Players*, p. 10, 1972
- This time, just a few doors from his joint, I dug the rollers round the edge of Winder from Brush Street.—A.S. Jackson, *Gentleman Pimp*, p. 23, 1973
- Now I had a corner just like the rollers got a beat / Right on Eighth Avenue and a Hundred and Fifteenth Street.—Dennis Wepman et al., *The Life*, p. 52, 1976

2 a robber who relies on brute force *US*

- People were waiting to find out who the Greek was betting on, including some people who would make my Ohio River rollers look like choirboys.—Jimmy Snyder, *Jimmy the Greek*, p. 65, 1975

3 a prostitute who takes a client's money without delivering a service *UK*
From **ROLL** (to rob someone).

- —Angela Devlin, *Prison Patter*, p. 98, 1996

4 a Rolls Royce car *UK, 1975*

- Later on he drove a Roller / Chauffering for foreign men[.]—Ian Dury, *My Old Man*, 1977
- —Peter Chippindale, *The British CB Book*, p. 161, 1981
- —Lewis Poteet, *Car & Motorcycle Slang*, p. 167, 1992
- I jumped out the Roller, ran round to his car, jumped in his passenger seat and slammed the door.—Dave Courtney, *Raving Lunacy*, p. 95, 2000
- But we found a bunch of keys on him that could have opened anything from a Roller to a Reliant Robin[.]—Duncan MacLaughlin, *The Filth*, p. 112, 2002

5 in the car sales business, a car that can be driven home the same day it is bought *US*

- I got this floor-pop who's looking for a roller but I can't use the OA for the DP on his old sled – I'd take him to the mouse house but he has no sticks.—*San Francisco Chronicle*, p. 2-1, 31st October 1966

6 a car that is being driven *US*

- "How about rollers?" asked Serge. "How many hot cars do you get rolling?" "Hot rollers? Oh, maybe one a month"—Joseph Wambaugh, *The New Centurions*, p. 42, 1970

7 a machine used to start the engine of a drag racer by spinning the rear wheels while the driver turns on the ignition *US*

- —Ed Radlauer, *Drag Racing Pix Dix*, p. 48, 1970

8 a wave *US*

- —Michael V. Anderson, *The Bad, Rad, Not to Forget Way Cool Beach and Surf Discriptionary*, p. 16, 1988

9 a vein that tends to roll away from a needle *US, 1970*

- —Walter Way, *The Drug Scene*, p. 113, 1977
- He was one of those wiry guys with veins forever; he could even fire at will into the rollers around his wrists and ankles.—Seth Morgan, *Homeboy*, p. 65, 1990

10 a bowler *US*

- —Lester V. Berrey and Melvin Van den Bark, *The American Thesaurus of Slang*, p. 633, 1953

11 a tablet of MDMA, the recreational drug best known as ecstasy *US*

- Tablets of the rave-party drug ecstasy are called "rollers," he added, explaining that ecstasy users often describe their high as "feeling like they're rolling."—*Milwaukee Journal Sentinel*, p. 1B, 9th February 2002

12 a hot dog *US*

- After they had eaten in the formal wardroom (they were fortunate; the meal was real meat in the form of "sliders and rollers," cheeseburgers and hot dogs), they visited Tim's tiny stateroom. —Gerry Carroll, *North S*A*R*, p. 133, 1991

roller-rings *noun*
the police *US*

- —*Washington Post Magazine*, p. 9, 6th September 1987: 'Say Wha?'

rollers *noun*
dice with rounded edges *US*
A roller may be intentionally crafted or not; a naturally occurring roller makes a controlled shot by a cheat difficult.

- —*The Annals of the American Academy of Political and Social Sciences*, p. 130, May 1950

rollerskate; skate *noun*
a small car *UK*

- —*British Road Services Magazine*, December 1951
- —Chrysler Corporation, *Of Anchors, Bezels, Pots and Scorchers*, September 1959
- —*Complete CB Slang Dictionary*, p. 80, 1976
- —Peter Chippindale, *The British CB Book*, p. 158, 1981

roll for the bowl *noun*
toilet paper *US*

- —Lee McNelis, *30 + And a Wake-Up*, p. 11, 1991

rollicks *noun*
▷ **see: TOMMY ROLLOCKS**

rollicking *noun*
a telling-off *UK, 1938*
Probably a euphemistic replacement for synonymous **BOLLOCKING**.

rollie *noun*
1 a hand-rolled cigarette *AUSTRALIA*
- Megaton was smoking a rollie. —Gerard Lee, *True Love and How to Get it*, p. 139, 1981
- —James Harris, *A Convict's Dictionary*, p. 37, 1989
- A joint is simple. Just like the rollies Grandad smoked while seeing off Rommel. —John Birmingham, *He Died With a Felafel in his Hand*, p. 158, 1994
- [T]he monk was one who drank Guinness, smoked rollies and was in the big league of bar-room raconteurs. —John Milne, *Alive and Kicking*, p. 32, 1998
- Once Mick put a rollie in his mouth, it didn't come out, that's where it stayed, stuck to his bottom lip, even when he talked. —Phillip Gwynne, *Deadly Unna?*, p. 95, 1998
- —Phillip Gwynne, *Deadly Unna?*, p. 159, 1998

2 a marijuana cigarette *UK*
A variation of the previous sense.
- [He] felt an incurable urge for a smoke. Nothing too heavy, just a couple of nice pure-grass rollies to set him right. —Kevin Sampson, *Powder*, p. 314, 1999

3 a tablet of Rolypnol™, a brand name for flunitrazepan, a sedative *NEW ZEALAND, 1989*
- —Harry Orsman, *A Dictionary of Modern New Zealand Slang*, p. 111, 1999

rollies *noun*
loose tobacco, used for hand-rolling cigarettes *US*
Prison usage.
- I took out a bag of rollies and rolled one and offered it to him. —Piri Thomas, *Down These Mean Streets*, p. 265, 1967

rolling *adjective*
1 very rich *UK, 1782*
Variants include 'rolling in it' and 'rolling in money'.
- —Ann Barr and Peter York, *The Official Sloane Ranger Handbook*, p. 159, 1982

2 under the influence of MDMA, the recreational drug best known as ecstasy *US, 1996*

rolling bones *noun*
dice *US*
- —*The Annals of the American Academy of Political and Social Sciences*, p. 130, May 1950

rolling hot!
used by helicopter gunship pilots in Vietnam to announce that a strafing attack was about to begin *US*
- —Gregory Clark, *Words of the Vietnam War*, p. 212, 1990

rolling lighthouse *noun*
in trucking, a tractor and trailer embellished with many extra running lights *US*
- —Montie Tak, *Truck Talk*, p. 132, 1971

rollings *noun*
loose cigarette tobacco *US*
- —Lou Shelly, *Hepcats Jive Talk Dictionary*, p. 48, 1945

roll in the hay *noun*
an act of sexual intercourse *US, 1945*
- He uses frig all over the place, and he doesn't even know what he's saying. If a girl uses that word, she knows damn well what she's saying, and you can chalk up another roll in the hay. —Evan Hunter, *The Blackboard Jungle*, p. ,, 146 1954
- We had a few rolls in the hay years ago – nothing much. —Mary McCarthy, *The Group*, p. 349, 1963

roll me in the gutter; roll me *noun*
butter *UK, 1925*
Rhyming slang.
- —Ray Puxley, *Cockney Rabbit*, 1992

rollocks *noun*
the testicles *UK*
Rhyming slang for **BOLLOCKS**. The reduced form of **JIMMY ROLLOCKS**, **JOHNNY ROLLOCKS** and **TOMMY ROLLOCKS**.

roll-on *noun*
a secret lover in addition to your regular partner *SOUTH AFRICA*
Teen slang.
- Roll-on: Replaces umakhwapheni, meaning your bit on the side. —*Sunday Times (South Africa)*, 1st June 2003

roll on *verb*
to travel; to go *US*
Wheeled transport is probably implied.
- "Anyway, where are you off to?" "Me? Oh, not far. I'm just rollin' on home." —Josie Dew, *The Sun In My Eyes*, p. 81, 2001

roll-on, roll-off *noun*
a used, sometimes stolen, car imported for sale *TRINIDAD AND TOBAGO, 2002*
- —Lise Winer, *Dictionary of the English/Creole of Trinidad & Tobago*, 2003

rollout *noun*
in handball, a ball hit off the front wall so low that the ball does not bounce off the floor *US*
- —George J. Zafferano, *Handball Basics*, p. 175, 1977: 'Glossary'

roll out *verb*
to leave *US*
- —Vann Wesson, *Generation X Field Guide and Lexicon*, p. 144, 1997

rollover *noun*
an informant *US*
- Manly began interviewing the rollovers and slowly put together a credible prosecution, thanks to the AW informants. —Bill Valentine, *Gangs and Their Tattoos*, p. 13, 2000

roll over *verb*
to turn against or inform against someone *AUSTRALIA*
- 'ICAC have summonsed Henry and subpoenaed his papers.' 'You think he'll roll over?' —Harrison Biscuit, *The Search for Savage Henry*, p. 15, 1995
- [H]earing that she was now heavy into speedballs, Letch figured she was ripe to roll over on her pimp. —Joseph Wambaugh, *Floaters*, p. 10, 1996
- He rolled over on all the snitches he was doing business with and got 'em brought up. —Elmore Leonard, *Out of Sight*, p. 59, 1996
- He was recovering from these wounds when a fellow Angel, Flash, called to inform him that Moose had rolled over for the police and was testifying against the club. —Peter Coyote, *Sleeping Where I Fall*, p. 126, 1998
- —Bill Valentine, *Gangs and Their Tattoos*, p. a, 2000
- It didn't take long for informants among them to come forward and roll over on the others. —Bill Valentine, *Gangs and Their Tattoos*, p. 13, 2000
- Despite the finding, many people believe that Denning was set up with a 'hot shot' as a payback for rolling over and turning dog. —William Dodson, *The Sharp End*, p. xiv, 2001

Rolls *noun*
a Rolls-Royce car *US, 1928*
- You said the guy had a Rolls. You know how many fucking Rolls are parked out at Seminole? —Elmore Leonard, *Split Images*, p. 172, 1981

Rolls Royce *noun*
the voice, especially a good singing voice *UK*
Rhyming slang.
- —Julian Franklyn, *A Dictionary of Rhyming Slang*, 1960

roll-up *noun*
1 a hand-*roll*ed cigarette *UK, 1950*
A prison coinage.
- —John Fahs, *Cigarette Confidential*, p. 301, 1996: 'Glossary'
- Got there about five minutes before the landlord, little Polish bloke, always had an unlit roll-up nestling in the corner of his mouth. —John Williams, *Cardiff Dead*, p. 131, 2000
- My nephew and me sat on the roof and drew on a roll-up as we watched the goings-on across the street. —Jimmy Stockin, *On The Cobbles*, p. 185, 2000
- —Gary K. Farlow, *Prison-ese*, p. 59, 2002

2 a type of bet where the amount won on one event becomes the stake for the next event *UK*
Better known as an 'accumulator'.
- —David Bennet, *Know Your Bets*, p. 96, 2001

roll up *verb*
1 to arrive *AUSTRALIA, 1920*
- The Augusto Pinochet circus rolled up at a London hospital yesterday[.] — *The Guardian*, 6th January 2000

2 to roll a marijuana cigarette *US*
- —Eugene Landy, *The Underground Dictionary*, p. 162, 1971

rolly *noun*
a match *AUSTRALIA*

Rhyming slang, from Rolly Hatch, a prominent and popular horse racing figure in New Zealand and later Australia.
- —Ned Wallish, *The Truth Dictionary of Racing Slang*, p. 69, 1989

roll-your-own *noun*
a hand-rolled cigarette *NEW ZEALAND*
- —Sonya Plowman, *Great Kiwi Slang*, p. 154, 2002

roly *noun*
a hand-rolled cigarette *UK*
From **ROLL-UP**.
- Skanky had saved the end of his previous roly[.]—James Hawes, *White Powder, Green Light*, p. 282, 2002

roly-poly *adjective*
overweight *UK, 1820*
- Their replacement: a roly-poly high-school teacher. But not just any roly-poly high-school teacher – one I'd met waiting for Duran Duran tickets to go on sale back in the mid-80s[.]—*The Guardian*, 18th May 2002

Roman candle *noun*
1 in homosexual usage, the penis of an Italian or Italian-American *US*
- —*Maledicta*, p. 58, 1986–1987: 'A continuation of a glossary of ethnic slurs in American English'

2 in target shooting, a poorly loaded cartridge that produces a spray of red sparks when detonated *US*
- —*American Speech*, p. 194, October 1957: 'Some colloquialisms of the handgunner'

3 a burst of tracer bullets *US*
- —*American Speech*, p. 272, December 1962: 'The language of traffic policemen'

4 a sandal *UK*
Rhyming slang, formed from a firework.
- —Ray Puxley, *Cockney Rabbit*, 1992

Roman culture *noun*
group sex *US*
- —Dale Gordon, *The Dominion Sex Dictionary*, p. 141, 1967

Roman engagement *noun*
in homosexual usage, anal sex with a woman *US*
- —*Maledicta*, p. 60, 1986–1987: 'A continuation of a glossary of ethnic slurs in American English'

Roman fingers *noun*
the hands of a boy wandering over a girl's body *NEW ZEALAND*
- —Louis S. Leland, *A Personal Kiwi-Yankee Dictionary*, p. 86, 1984

Roman roulette *noun*
birth control by the rhythm method *UK*
A variation of **VATICAN ROULETTE**.
- —Margaret Powell, *Climbing the Stairs*, 1969

romantic ballad *noun*
a salad *UK*
Rhyming slang.
- —Ray Puxley, *Fresh Rabbit*, 1998

rom-com *noun*
*rom*antic *com*edy *UK*
Media jargon that has insinuated itself into mainstream consciousness.
- Rom-com drama owes little to Leone.—*Uncut*, p. 145, October 2002
- Cinema tickets to deplorable, girlie rom-com.—*The FHM Little Book of Bloke*, p. 68, June 2003

romo *noun*
a follower of the New Romantic youth fashion of the early 1980s *UK*
- Then someone – God knows who; romo, goth or casual – dropped in a tape of ... of what?—Patrick Neate, *Where You're At*, p. 2, 2003

romp *noun*
in horse racing, an easy victory *US*
- —Tom Ainslie, *Ainslie's Complete Guide to Thoroughbred Racing*, p. 337, 1976

romp *verb*
1 to excite; to excel; to be lively *US*
- It really romped.—Mezz Mezzrow, *Really the Blues*, p. 236, 1946

2 to win easily *UK, 1881*
Also as 'romp home'.
- Ann Patchett's novel Bel Canto, about a hostage taking which turns into comic opera, romped home despite being rated at only 7–1, lower than any of the other five books shortlisted for the women only awards.—*The Guardian*, 12th June 2002

rompered *noun*
severely beaten *UK: NORTHERN IRELAND, 1974*
Derives from 'romper room'; used by the British military in Northern Ireland to describe a brand of justice dispensed by illegal kangaroo courts.
- —Christopher Hawke, *For Campaign Service*, 1979

rompums *noun*
marijuana *UK*
- —Mike Haskins, *Drugs*, p. 289, 2003

Romulan *noun*
in British Columbia, a local variety of marijuana *CANADA*
A *Star Trek* inspired term.
- Mike had a new strain called Romulan he wanted us to taste. He was planning on entering it in an upcoming Cannabis Cup in Amsterdam.—Brian Preston, *Pot Planet*, p. 7, 2002

ron *noun*
a homosexual Mafia don *US*
- Gay Mafia dons are also called rons and davids.—*New Yorker*, p. 164, 9th September 2002

Ronan Keating *noun*
a beating *UK*
Rhyming slang, formed from the name of the popular Irish singer (b.1977).
- He then gives him a right Ronan Keating and nicks all his Buddy Holly (money).—Mervyn Stutter, *Getting Nowhere Fast*, 21st May 2004

ronies *noun*
pepperoni *US*
- —*Maledicta*, p. 19, 1996: 'Domino's pizza jargon'

Ronnie Biggs *noun*
lodgings *UK*
Rhyming slang for **DIGS**, formed from the name of the 'Great Train Robber' (1929–2005).
- —Ray Puxley, *Cockney Rabbit*, 1992

Ronnie RayGun *nickname*
Ronald Reagan (1911–2004), US President 1981–89 *UK*
A neat pun that refers particularly to Reagan's 'Star Wars' initiative.
- [T]hey grew up with Lech Walesa and Solidarity instead of Ronnie RayGun and the Iron Lady (Margaret Thatcher).—John King, *Human Punk*, p. 137, 2000

ronson *noun*
1 a ponce, a man who lives on the earnings of a prostitute *UK*
Very imperfect rhyming slang, apparently adopted under the influence of high-powered advertising for the branded cigarette lighters.

2 a despised or unpleasant person *UK*
Rhyming slang, formed on a very weak rhyme for **PONCE**.
- —Julian Franklyn, *A Dictionary of Rhyming Slang*, 1960
- —David Powis, *The Signs of Crime*, 1977

roo *noun*
1 a kangaroo *AUSTRALIA, 1898*
By front clipping.
- —Ion L. Idriess, *Over the Range*, p. 80, 1947
- Eh! Dick, John here reckons he wants to have a go at a 'roo with a knife. Will we let him?—Kenneth Cook, *Wake in Fright*, p. 91, 1961
- —Jean Brooks, *The Opal Witch*, p. 136, 1967
- —Jim Ramsay, *Cop It Sweet!*, p. 77, 1977

2 an apprentice station hand working on, and learning how to manage, a cattle or sheep station *AUSTRALIA, 1891*
An abbreviation of 'jackaroo'.
- Every night after Ruby had finished her two-hour watch she would try to waken this roo, but to no avail[.]—Herb Wharton, *Cattle Camp*, p. 53, 1994

-roo *suffix*
used as an meaningless, affected embellishment of a noun *US*
- "Pluto says a buddy-roo of his is making a movie-roo in Venice." —James Ellroy, *Blood on the Moon*, p. 129, 1984

roo bar *noun*
a metal grille attached to the front of a vehicle as protection from kangaroos when driving in the country *AUSTRALIA, 1973*
- Brakes squealed, a landcruise swerved past skidding to the right and its roo bar knocked the girl over into an ungainly tumble across the tarmac like a circus clown.—*OZ-WIDE Tales*, p. 35, 1990

roodle *adjective*
in poker, said of a hand in which the stakes have been temporarily raised *US*
• —Oswald Jacoby, *Oswald Jacoby on Poker*, p. 142, 1947

roody-poo *noun*
someone who is ignorant or unsophisticated *US*
• Cole has played most of this season at No. 3 singles or No. 2 doubles, but he's no tennis roody poo. —*Plain Dealer (Cleveland, Ohio)*, p. 12D, 15th May 1999
• The Rock is a finely tuned machine, and he's more than capable of laying the smack down on every single roody-poo stupid enough to enter the ring against him. — Rock, *The Rock Says*, p. 221, 2000

roody-poo *adjective*
second-rate; shallow *US*
• You mean we're not taking any crap from that roody-poo jabroni Ronald DeChooch. —Janet Evanovich, *Seven Up*, p. 211, 2001

roof *noun*
the flight deck of an aircraft carrier *UK*
• — *Seattle Times*, p. A9, 12th April 1998: 'Grunts, squids not grunting from the same dictionary'

▸ **on the roof**
paid for by the management of the establishment *UK*
A variation of **ON THE HOUSE**.
• – I was just wondering if Uncle Charles was about today? [...] – Uncle C is not only about, but today, for you, he is at home and sitting on the roof [on the house]. —James Hawes, *White Powder, Green Light*, p. 250, 2002

roof *verb*
to break into a building through the roof *US*
• Say it's a two- or three-story building and you've roofed it and you've come in and it's a big old soundproof place[.] —Bruce Jackson, *Outside the Law*, p. 94, 1972

roofer *noun*
Rohypnol™ (flunitrazepam), popularly known as the 'date-rape drug' *US*
• This drug, flunitrazepam, or Rohypnol (known on the street as "roofies" or"roofers") is a powerful sedative[.] — *Teen Magazine*, p. 68, July 1997

roofies; ruffles; roples *noun*
the recreational drug Rohypnol™ (flunitrazepam) *US*
• See if she wasn't stoned-out on roofies. —James Lee Burke, *Cimarron Rose*, p. 277, 1997
• He produces a tobacco tin. Takes out a diamond-shaped purple tablet. Offers it across. "Roofies. One of these and you forget everything man." —Jack Allen, *When the Whistle Blows*, p. 55, 2000
• —Pamela Munro, *U.C.L.A. Slang*, p. 107, 2001

roof-riding *verb*
▷ see: **TRAIN-SURFING**

roof-sniffing *noun*
in caving and pot-holing, the act of moving on your back along a small, water-filled passage with only sufficient air-space for the eyes and nose *UK*
• —David Morrison of Wessex Cave Club, 29th February 2004

rook *noun*
a beginner *US, 1905*
An abbreviation of **ROOKIE**.
• Hey, you're the rook I'm working with tonight. —Charles Whited, *Chiodo*, p. 27, 1973
• Check out the rook! — *Bull Durham*, 1988

rook *verb*
to cheat someone; to swindle someone; to defraud someone *UK, 1590*
• I know exactly what it was worth and that guy just rooked you. —Kenneth Lonergan, *This is Our Youth*, p. 116, 2000

rookety *adjective*
rocky; bumpy *BARBADOS*
• —Frank A. Collymore, *Barbadian Dialect*, p. 93, 1965

rookie *noun*
1 a raw recruit, especially a new recruit in the army or police *UK, 1892*
Probably a perversion of 'recruit'.
• [Jeff Crawford] pioneered the Met's host-family initiative to billet rookie police and prison officers with non-white families. — *The Guardian*, 10th January 2004

2 a novice at a sport; a player in his or her first year with a particular team *US, 1913*
From the wider sense as a 'recruit'.
• [D]efenseman Barret Jackman, our rookie of the year, did a magnificent job of filling some awfully big skates on the Blues' top blue line. — *Hockey Digest*, Summer 2003

3 a college freshman *US*
• —Connie Eble (Editor), *UNC-CH Campus Slang*, p. 6, March 1979

rooly; roolly *adverb*
really *AUSTRALIA*
Representing a pronunciation of young children, though also used to represent supposed uneducated speech.
• Yeah, he treats me roolly good and stuff. —Kathy Lette and Gabriel Carey, *Puberty Blues*, p. 62, 1979
• —Kathy Lette, *Girls' Night Out*, p. 30, 1987
• I rooly think I am adopted[.] —Kylie Mole (Maryanne Fahey), *My Diary*, p. 6, 1988
• I rooly miss you, babe. —Shane Maloney, *Nice Try*, p. 18, 1998

room *noun*
1 in prison, a cell *UK*
• —Angela Devlin, *Prison Patter*, p. 98, 1996

2 a bar or cocktail lounge *US*
• —Clarence Major, *Dictionary of Afro-American Slang*, p. 98, 1970

roomdawg *noun*
a person who shares your room, apartment or house *US*
• —Connie Eble (Editor), *UNC-CH Campus Slang*, p. 9, October 2002

roomdog *noun*
a roommate *US*
• —Connie Eble (Editor), *UNC-CH Campus Slang*, p. 5, Fall 1996

roomie *noun*
1 a roommate *US, 1918*
• "What the hell, roomy," he said. "Let's go to chow." —Ralph Ellison, *Invisible Man*, p. 106, 1947
• Guy's got n'eleven o'clock, roomie won't tell 'im the right Jesuschris' time. —Richard Farina, *Been Down So Long*, p. 94, 1966
• My great roomie, Bob Lasko, has led me down the trail of sin and perdition[.] —Jim Bouton, *Ball Four*, p. 122, 1970
• I called Cruz my old roomie because when we first got out of the police academy twenty years ago, I moved into this big house with him and Socorro. —Joseph Wambaugh, *The Blue Knight*, p. 101, 1973
• "Fuck him," said Mona. "You've got a new roomie now." —Armistead Maupin, *Tales of the City*, p. 72, 1978
• We really became roomies – roommates. —Bobby Seale, *A Lonely Rage*, p. 106, 1978
• She shared an apartment with another schoolteacher, near West End Avenue, the nineties. The roomie was out. —Edwin Torres, *After Hours*, p. 276, 1979

2 a prison cellmate *US*
• —Ralph de Sola, *Crime Dictionary*, p. 130, 1982
• I told two of my old roomies about the coke house, but I didn't say I worked here or nothing. —Terry Williams, *The Cocaine Kids*, p. 40, 1989

room-rifler *noun*
a thief who steals from hotel rooms *US*
• If a room-rifler or a lock-worker gets away with a good score at some hotel, he'll keep quiet about it. —Dev Collans with Stewart Sterling, *I was a House Detective*, p. 47, 1954

'rooms *noun*
mushrooms *US*
• —John D. Bell et al., *Loosely Speaking*, p. Appendix, 1969

rooms *noun*
a roommate *US*
• He'd say things like, "Rooms, tomorrow we go to a bookstore and buy some of those real-estate books." —Jim Bouton, *Ball Four*, p. 227, 1970
• —Connie Eble (Editor), *UNC-CH Campus Slang*, p. 8, Spring 1992

room temperature IQ *noun*
a very low intelligence *US*
• He had a room-temperature I.Q., which made him extremely obliging, hence an excellent artist's model and a pretty fair marine. —Joseph Wambaugh, *The Glitter Dome*, p. 61, 1981
• Even someone with a room temperature IQ would know it was the type of case you could retire on. — *The National Law Journal*, p. 3, 28th November 1983
• — *Maledicta*, p. 118, 1984–1985: 'Milwaukee medical maledicta'
• Either Bush is living up to the rumor of a room temperature IQ or he's getting very bad advice. — *San Diego Union-Tribune*, p. B11, 27th March 2003

room time *noun*
time spent surfing in the breaking hollow of a wave *US*
- —Trevor Cralle, *The Surfin'ary*, p. 102, 1991

'roon *noun*
▷ see: TOSHEROON

rooney *noun*
the penis *US*
- —Collin Baker et al., *College Undergraduate Slang Study Conducted at Brown University*, p. 186, 1968

roost *noun*
1 the highest rows in the highest gallery in a theatre *UK*
- —Wilfred Granville, *The Theatre Dictionary*, p. 166, 1952

2 a residence, be it room, apartment or house *US*
- —Lou Shelly, *Hepcats Jive Talk Dictionary*, p. 16, 1945
- —Clarence Major, *Dictionary of Afro-American Slang*, p. 98, 1970

roost *verb*
to sit *US*
- —Tom Hibbert, *Rockspeak!*, p. 135, 1983

rooster *noun*
1 the buttocks *US*
- "Sorry," the bossman said, not even bothering to get up off his rooster. —Mezz Mezzrow, *Really the Blues*, p. 131, 1946

2 crack cocaine *US*
- —US Department of Justice, *Street Terms*, October 1994

3 a member of the Piru youth gang *US*
- —Ann Lawson, *Kids & Gangs*, p. 56, 1994: 'Common African-American gang slang/phrases'

rooster comb *noun*
a swath of unmown hay left in the field after cutting *CANADA*
- A rooster comb is usually left in the corners of the field, in a sloppy farmer's cutting. —Lewis Poteet, *Talking Country*, p. 61, 1992

rooster tail *noun*
a spray of water directly behind an object or person moving fast through the water *US*
- —John M. Kelly, *Surf and Sea*, p. 292, 1965

root *noun*
1 the penis *US*
- —Collin Baker et al., *College Undergraduate Slang Study Conducted at Brown University*, p. 186, 1968

2 an act of sexual intercourse *AUSTRALIA, 1959*
- [A]rtists in London don't exactly have to chase the odd root. —Barry Humphries, *Bazza Pulls It Off*, 1971
- The old credit card has revolutionised the extramarital root. —Barry Humphries, *The Traveller's Tool*, p. 8, 1985
- I reckon those two sheilas are that hot for a root their arses are nearly on fire. —Robert G. Barrett, *Davo's Little Something*, p. 263, 1992
- You're in man, she'll give you a root. —Christos Tsiolkas, *Loaded*, p. 9, 1995
- Chances of pulling a root: No root for legal reasons, but heaps of blowies. —*People*, p. 13, 5th July 1999
- Love taking it for long periods, sucking, spanking, long roots, etc. —*Sydney Star Observer*, p. 42, 17th June 1999

3 a sexual partner *AUSTRALIA*
Especially used in contexts where a person's sexual abilities are rated; see **DUD ROOT**.
- Find yourself a good woman, something more than just a weekend root[.] —Alexander Buzo, *Norm and Ahmed*, p. 24, 1969
- [Y]ou're not only the best root in Foolgarah but good-natured as well. —Frank Hardy, *The Outcasts of Foolgarah*, p. 196, 1971
- Sally, my dear de facto Sally, always ready, always able. What's known as a good root. —Dorothy Hewett, *The Chapel Perilous*, p. 75, 1972
- She was a moll cause she walked everywhere in her bikini. That meant she was showing off her body and was an easy root. —Kathy Lette and Gabrielle Carey, *Puberty Blues*, p. 5, 1979

4 marijuana; a marijuana cigarette *US, 1959*
- —Richard A. Spears, *The Slang and Jargon of Drugs and Drink*, p. 426, 1986
- —Mike Haskins, *Drugs*, p. 289, 2003

5 an amphetamine or other central nervous system stimulant *US*
- —Eugene Landy, *The Underground Dictionary*, p. 162, 1971

6 a kick *IRELAND*
The variant 'rooter' also exists.
- Well, the sergeant said – 'Which would you prefer, a night in the cells or a few rooters in the behind? —John B. Keane, *The Man from Clare*, p. 45, 1962
- I know the root up the arse his mother would-a gev him, standin' there with a cigar stuck in his fat gob. —Hugh Leonard, *Out After Dark*, p. 38, 1989

root *verb*
1 to copulate with someone *AUSTRALIA, 1958*
- Virgins are very rare, / 'Cos when they get their pubic hair, / They get rooted by the mayor in Mobile. —'S. Hogbotel & S. ffuckes', *Snatches and Lays*, p. 53, 1962
- Such conversations are not about who rooted what sheila after the dinner dance, but are serious discussions about various methods and techniques. —Suzy Jarratt, *Permissive Australia*, p. 57, 1970
- Bump us into Parliament, / Root us anyway, / Shag us into Parliament / On election day. —Dorothy Hewett, *The Chapel Perilous*, p. 62, 1972
- [S]o on me day off I took her down Scarborough an' rooted her up one side of a sandhill an' down the other. —T.A.G. Hungerford, *Stories From Suburban Road*, p. 192, 1983
- I still get that randy sometimes I could root the hair on a barbershop floor. —Barry Humphries, *The Traveller's Tool*, p. 40, 1985
- I told him I didn't root short men and soon after that he moved in. —Kathy Lette, *Girls' Night Out*, p. 61, 1987
- Then they jammed his head in a vice, tightened it up and about ten old lags rooted him. —Robert G. Barrett, *Davo's Little Something*, p. 219, 1992
- Married to a bitch like that. Not a fucking wonder he rooted little boys. —B. Selkie, *Lime Juice*, p. 97, 1995
- From now on, you root 'em, you take their phone calls. —Linda Jaivin, *Rock n Roll Babes from Outer Space*, p. 66, 1996
- You wanna root me or something? —Phillip Gwynne, *Deadly Unna?*, p. 164, 1998

2 to confound someone; to defeat someone *AUSTRALIA, 1944*
- You remember when we were kids those larrikin gangs, the Grey Caps and the Bludgers? You know, and how they always wanted me to join 'em? Well – this'll root you! – I bloody *have*, sport! —George Johnston, *My Brother Jack*, p. 306, 1964

3 to give a hefty blow to someone or something *AUSTRALIA*
- Con rooted him fair up the behind with a boot, and hit him again. —Bluey, *Bush Contractors*, p. 271, 1975

▸ **get rooted**
go away; piss off *AUSTRALIA, 1961*
An analogue to 'get fucked'.
- And as a result of this meaning, the crudest, most direct, most unmistakable brush-off is to tell a man to 'go an' get rooted'. —John O'Grady, *Aussie English*, p. 75, 1965

▸ **root like a rattlesnake**
(usually of a woman) to have sex with vigour and uninhibited enthusiasm *AUSTRALIA, 1969*
- The Pope's a Jew if that Jam Tart [young woman] doesn't root like a rattlesnake. —Barry Humphries, *Bazza Pulls It Off!*, 1971

rootable *adjective*
sexually desirable *AUSTRALIA, 1973*

root around *verb*
to be sexually promiscuous *AUSTRALIA*
- 'I don't want to hear your stupid validation speech for your life of rooting around.' —Gretel Killeen, *Hot Buns and Ophelia get shipwrecked*, p. 47, 2001

rooted *adjective*
wrecked; ruined *AUSTRALIA, 1944*
- Con was lying there saying, 'Jesus, look at it, the friggin boat's rooted.' —Bluey, *Bush Contractors*, p. 299, 1975

rooter *noun*
a person who copulates promiscuously *AUSTRALIA*
- Albie Pewter, nicknamed Pewter the Rooter, denied raping and assaulting the girls and holding them against their will aboard his luxury yacht Quickie III. —*Ribald*, p. 3, 1975
- —David McGill, *David McGill's Complete Kiwi Slang Dictionary*, p. 94, 1998

root for *verb*
to support someone ardently *US*
- I rooted for Olivia Newton-John during the 1974 Eurovision Song Contest[.] —Stuart Jeffries, *Mrs Slocombe's Pussy*, p. 81, 2000

rootin' tootin' oil *noun*
semen *US*
- —Joseph E. Ragen and Charles Finston, *Inside the World's Toughest Prison*, p. 816, 1962: 'Penitentiary and underworld glossary'

root up *verb*
to mess something up *AUSTRALIA*
- Just don't root nothin' up, Davo – that's all. —Robert G. Barrett, *Davo's Little Something*, p. 49, 1992

root ute *noun*
a panel van or the like used for sexual encounters
AUSTRALIA, 2000

rooty-ma-toot *noun*
a suit *UK: SCOTLAND*
Glasgow rhyming slang.
- Should Ah put the rooty-ma-toot for this do? — Michael Munro, *The Patter, Another Blast*, 1988

roovle *noun*
among Nova Scotians of German descent, a wrinkle *CANADA*
In Lunenburg County, the descendants of German soldiers of fortune who were awarded land by King George in the late C18 use unconventional, slightly altered German words in their English conversation. This term is close in sound to 'rivvel' and thus may also come from German *runzeln* (to wrinkle).
- — Lewis Poteet, *The South Shore Phrase Book*, p. 92, 1999

rope *noun*
1 marijuana; hashish; a marijuana cigarette *US, 1944*
Conventional 'rope' is often made from Indian hemp. *Cannabis sativa*, a plant genus that gives us marijuana, is true **HEMP** but sometimes called **INDIAN HEMP** which may well explain the origins of this usage; it is likely that the sense as 'a marijuana cigarette' is influenced by appearance.
- — Richard A. Spears, *The Slang and Jargon of Drugs and Drink*, p. 426, 1986
- — Mike Haskins, *Drugs*, p. 289, 2003

2 Rohypnol™ (flunitrazepam), popularly known as the 'date-rape drug' *US*
- On the street the drug has many nicknames; teenagers know it as rope, ribs, or roaches. — *Texas Monthly*, p. 88, September 1995
- The drug is called rope, rophies, roofies, roche and Mexican Valium on the streets and is marketted as Rohypnol in South America. — *Daily Oklahoman (Oklahoma City)*, p. 1, 5th September 1995

3 a vein used for drug injections *UK*
- — Angela Devlin, *Prison Patter*, p. 98, 1996

4 a thick gold chain necklace *US*
- — Ellen C. Bellone (Editor), *Dictionary of Slang*, p. 20, 1989

5 an Afrikaner *SOUTH AFRICA, 1970*
Contemptuous, insulting; a reference to a rope that is, according to a 1975 informant, 'thick, coarse, twisted, hairy'.
- — Penny Silva, *A Dictionary of South African English*, 1996

6 tough talk *TRINIDAD AND TOBAGO, 1983*
- — Lise Winer, *Dictionary of the English/Creole of Trinidad & Tobago*, 2003

rope *verb*
1 to lure someone into a swindle *US, 1848*
- You've heard me brag that I had once been with the big con. I lied to you, son. I never roped or played the inside. — Iceberg Slim (Robert Beck), *Trick Baby*, p. 39, 1969
- He sends you out to rope suckers in with your ass? — Robert Campbell, *Juice*, p. 233, 1988

2 in a card game, to cheat or mislead someone *US*
- — Steve Kuriscak, *Casino Talk*, p. 48, 1985
- — George Percy, *The Language of Poker*, p. 76, 1988

ropeable *adjective*
livid; splenetic; furious *AUSTRALIA, 1874*
- ROPEABLE – Wild; annoyed. — Gilbert H. Lawson, *A Dictionary of Australian Words and Terms*, 1924
- Makes me ropeable that feller does, poking borak every time he gets a chance. — Dymphna Cusack, *Picnic Races*, p. 21, 1962

rope-a-dope *noun*
1 a defensive tactic employed by Muhammed Ali, resting against the ropes and letting his opponent exhaust himself with punches that Ali evaded or absorbed *US*
- — Louis Phillips and Burnham Holmes, *The Complete Book of Sports Nicknames*, p. 224, 1998

2 a tactic of feigning weakness in order to lure an opponent into an ill-advised offensive *US*
From the boxing sense.
- Carlito, the dude pulled the rope-a-dope on you. — Edwin Torres, *After Hours*, p. 387, 1979

rope dope *noun*
low grade marijuana *US*
- — Nick Brownlee, *This Is Cannabis*, p. 153, 2002

ropehead *noun*
1 a Rastafarian with long matted braids *JAMAICA, 1987*
- — Thomas H. Slone, *Rasta is Cuss*, p. 70, 2003

2 a dark-skinned person *NEW ZEALAND, 1997*
Prison usage.
- — Harry Orsman, *A Dictionary of Modern New Zealand Slang*, p. 111, 1999

roper *noun*
in a confidence swindle, a confederate who identifies and lures the victim into the swindle *US, 1840*
Originally used in the context of gambling houses, and then in confidence swindles.
- You've made it to become a big white con roper. — Iceberg Slim (Robert Beck), *Long White Con*, p. 16, 1977

rophie *noun*
Rohypnol™ (flunitrazepam), popularly known as the 'date-rape drug' *US*
- One rophie salesman says his connection sells them by the thousand, at one dollar per tablet. — *Miami New Times*, 14th July 1993
- The drug is called rope, rophies, roofies, roche and Mexican Valium on the streets and is marketed as Rohypnol in South America. — *Daily Oklahoman (Oklahoma City)*, p. 1, 5th September 1995

roples *noun*
▷ **see: ROOFIES**

ropy; ropey *adjective*
bad; rough; unattractive; unsatisfactory; unwell *UK, 1942*
Originally Royal Air Force use.
- I like ropy bints, they're the ones. — Kevin Sampson, *Clubland*, p. 85, 2002

ro-ro *noun*
1 in prison, a type of educational course that makes it possible for short-term prisoners to complete individual modules *UK*
A figurative application of **RO-RO** (roll on, roll off).
- — Angela Devlin, *Prison Patter*, p. 98, 1996

2 a Rolls Royce car *UK, 1984*

ro-ro *adjective*
roll on, roll off *US*
Said of a containerisation system used to ship military cargo during the Vietnam war.
- Ro-ro container method further increased the Navy's logistical support capabilities. — Gregory Clark, *Words of the Vietnam War*, p. 439, 1990

rort *noun*
1 a confidence trick; an illicit scheme or dodge; a swindle *AUSTRALIA, 1926*
Also used of legitimate practices imputing that they are unfair or a rip-off.
- I was surprised to learn that the first Gallup Polls on the ID Card rort showed about 73 per cent of Australians favoured it. — Frank Hardy, *Hardy's People*, p. 119, 1986
- This explained his muscle bound 'friends' dropping round at midnight to drink Fourex and swap tales of rorts and rampages. — Kathy Lette, *Girls' Night Out*, p. 178, 1987
- Their stoney faces had told the crowd that they had had no part in the rort. — Clive Galea, *Slipper*, p. 190, 1988

2 a wild party; an unrestrained good time; a drunken orgy *AUSTRALIA*
- There'll be plenty to drink, and plenty to eat later. Don't any of youse put on a blue or make a rort out of my house. — Tilly Devine, *Remember Smith's Weekly?*, p. 217, 1950
- 'I hope there's something left over,' Windy said anxiously. 'I feel like a bit of a rort.' — J.E. MacDonnell, *Don't Gimme the Ships*, p. 27, 1960
- Yeah, it sounds like a real rort. — Alexander Buzo, *Norm and Ahmed*, p. 14, 1969
- You belong here as much as anyone else and they've accepted you, invited you into a real rort. — Kevin Mackey, *The Cure*, p. 26, 1970

3 in horse or greyhound racing, a large and unexpected bet *AUSTRALIA*
- — Ned Wallish, *The Truth Dictionary of Racing Slang*, p. 69, 1989

rort *verb*
1 to fraudulently manipulate an organisation, system or the like; to rip someone off; to rig an election *AUSTRALIA, 1919*
- People receiving social welfare benefits under false pretences are 'rorting' the system. — John Blackman, *The Aussie Slang Dictionary*, p. 82, 1990
- Former National Party health and environment minister Leisha Harvey was ordered yesterday to stand trial on 129 charges of rorting State Government funds. — *Advertiser*, p. 1, 1st May 1990

2 to party boisterously *AUSTRALIA*

- Now we don't wanna waste all night rortin' round the pubs like last time. — J.E. MacDonnell, *Don't Gimme the Ships*, p. 136, 1960

3 to engage in petty crime *AUSTRALIA, 1919*

rorter *noun*

a swindler; a cheat *AUSTRALIA, 1926*

rorty *adjective*

wild, boisterous *AUSTRALIA, 1929*

- — J.E. MacDonnell, *Don't Gimme the Ships*, p. 136, 1960
- — Barry Humphries, *A Nice Night's Entertainment*, p. 42, 1960
- One of the hands chipped in, "Pretty rorty parties we've seen, eh Gar.? – Beaut sheilas wandering round – real friendly – we help them in to the carts you know – remember when young Joe got lost in the crinoline!" — *Kings Cross Venus*, p. 13, 1st November 1972
- The buck's night had been a pretty rorty affair[.] — Barry Humphries, *The Traveller's Tool*, p. 26, 1985

Rory O'More; rory *noun*

1 a floor *UK, 1857*

Rhyming slang, on the name of a legendary Irish rebel. The earliest of three uses for the rhyme; however, the second sense, 'a whore' is obsolete.

- Main employment for this is in the sense of being destitute, e.g., "on the Rory". — Ray Puxley, *Cockney Rabbit*, p. 162, 1992

2 a door *UK, 1892*

Rhyming slang, on the name of a legendary Irish rebel. This is the only sense of the word also recorded in the US, where it is sometimes misspelt Rory O'Moore.

- — Angela Devlin, *Prison Patter*, p. 98, 1996

rosa *noun*

an amphetamine tablet *US*

- — US Department of Justice, *Street Terms*, August 1994

Rosa Maria; rosa maria *noun*

marijuana *US, 1938*

- — Ernest L. Abel, *A Marijuana Dictionary*, p. 89, 1982
- In the early twenties, marijuana, muggles, muta, gage, tea, reefer, grifa, Mary Warner, Mary Jane or rosa maria was known almost exclusively to musicians. — Harry Shapiro, *Waiting For The Man*, p. 29, 1999

roscoe *noun*

a handgun *US, 1914*

- Every time I meet a girl I whip out the old roscoe and pretend I'm a New York gangster and scare the hell out of them. — Jack Kerouac, *Letter to Neal Cassady*, p. 127, 13th September 1947
- Then, holding his roscoe or barker on Mr. Mach, the policeman moseyed back to the truck and peered inside. — *San Francisco News*, p. 1, 25th August 1950
- I mean, she stood up, right in the face of my Roscoe! — Robert Gover, *One Hundred Dollar Misunderstanding*, p. 180, 1961
- The dude went mad / an' started to jump bad, pulling his roscoe out his slide. — Lightnin' Rod, *Hustlers Convention*, p. 98, 1973
- You get big respect from the roscoe – it's the only thing people in my business understand. — Vernon E. Smith, *The Jones Men*, p. 70, 1974
- The other man held a cocked Roscoe on us. — James Ellroy, *Hollywood Nocturnes*, p. 109, 1994

roscoe *verb*

to point a handgun at someone and order them not to move *US*

- Why you wants to be roscoeing me, brother? — Vernon E. Smith, *The Jones Men*, p. 115, 1974
- I heard Bailey holler, 'Police,' so I figured he had the suspect roscoed. — Gerald Petievich, *To Die in Beverly Hills*, p. 108, 1983

rose *noun*

1 a tablet of Benzedrine™ (amphetamine sulphate), a central nervous system stimulant *US*

- — John B. Williams, *Narcotics and Hallucinogenics*, p. 114, 1967
- — Mike Haskins, *Drugs*, p. 279, 2003

Roseanne Barr *noun*

a bra *UK*

Rhyming slang, formed from the name of the US actress, comedienne and producer (b.1952).

- — Ray Puxley, *Fresh Rabbit*, 1998

rosebud *noun*

1 the anus *US*

- — *The Guild Dictionary of Homosexual Terms*, p. 39, 1965
- — Bruce Rodgers, *The Queens' Vernacular*, p. 19, 1972

2 a textbook example of a primary lesion *US*

- — *Maledicta*, p. 227, Summer/Winter 1981: 'Sex and the single soldier'

3 following a colostomy, the pink tissue that marks the opening of the intestine on the abdomen *US*

- — *Maledicta*, p. 56, Summer 1980: 'Not Sticks and stones, but names: more medical pejoratives'

4 a potato *UK, 1943*

Rhyming slang for **SPUD**. Sometimes shortened to 'rose'.

- — Ray Puxley, *Cockney Rabbit*, 1992

rosebud *verb*

(of the anus) to become puffy and pronounced *UK*

- Getting slammed on all fours, you asshole rimmed and rosebudded from a plastic fat slimy dildo[.] — Peter Sotos, *Index*, p. 14, 1996

rose garden *noun*

1 in prison, a solitary confinement cell *UK*

- — Home Office, *Glossary of Terms and Slang Common in Penal Establishments*, July 1978
- — Angela Devlin, *Prison Patter*, p. 98, 1996

2 a group of neurologically depressed hospital patients *US*

- — *Maledicta*, p. 69, Summer/Winter 1978: 'Common patient-directed pejoratives used by medical personnel'

Rose Marie *noun*

marijuana *UK*

An anglicisation of **ROSA MARIA**.

- — Mike Haskins, *Drugs*, p. 289, 2003

rose tree trimmer *noun*

a person hired to clean latrines *BARBADOS*

- — Frank A. Collymore, *Barbadian Dialect*, p. 122, 1965

rosewood *noun*

a police nightstick *US*

- — Clarence Major, *Dictionary of Afro-American Slang*, p. 98, 1970

rosey lee; rosie lee; rosie *noun*

tea *UK, 1925*

Rhyming slang; originally military, probably from the 1914–18 war.

- Ever had someone put some snout [cigarette] ash in your rosie? — Derek Raymond (Robin Cook), *The Crust on its Uppers*, p. 21, 1962
- — Angela Devlin, *Prison Patter*, p. 98, 1996
- necking a quick cup of rosie before shooting off to Penge — Greg Williams, *Diamond Geezers*, p. 16, 1997

rosie *noun*

a rubbish bin *UK*

- — Paul Baker, *Polari*, p. 195, 2002

Rosie O'Grady's *noun*

a *ladies'* toilet *UK*

Rhyming slang, originally 'Rosie O'Grady' (a lady) but now used only of a public convenience, formed from the film musical *Sweet Rosie O'Grady*, 1943.

- — Ray Puxley, *Fresh Rabbit*, 1998

Rosie Palm and her five sisters; Rosie Palm; Rosie *noun*

the male hand as the instrument of masturbation *US*

- When you turn out the light – I've got to hand it to me / Looks like it's me and you again tonight Rosie[.] — Jackson Browne and Donald Miller, *Rosie*, 1977
- FRIEND: why don't you be a gentleman and ask Rosey? TED: Who? FRIEND: Rosey Palm, your girlfriend. God knows you spend enough fucking time with her. — *Something About Mary*, 1998

rosiner; roziner; rozener *noun*

a large serving of an alcoholic drink *AUSTRALIA, 1933*

- So you hit yourself with a rozener of rum in a panniken[.] — Sam Weller, *Old Bastards I Have Met*, p. 38, 1979

rosser *noun*

a police officer *AUSTRALIA, 1944*

- 'Yowl!' someone howled. 'The Rossers are on their way up. Blow!' — John Wynnum, *Tar Dust*, p. 36, 1962

Rossy Docks *noun*

socks *UK: SCOTLAND, 1985*

Glasgow rhyming slang, based on local pronunciation of Rothesay.

- Ah'm huntin fur a clean pair a Rossy Docks. — Michael Munro, *The Complete Patter*, 1996

rot *noun*

1 nonsense, rubbish *UK, 1848*

In *Eats, Shoots & Leaves*, 2003, Lynne Truss records the following marginal note, made by a long-ago reader, in the 1st edition of Partridge's *You Have a Point There*: 'Rot! You lazy swine Partridge'.

2 an unidentifed disease or malady *US*

- — *American Speech*, p. 304, December 1947: 'Imaginary diseases in army and navy parlance'

rot *verb*

to be terrible *US*

- That song's awful; it just rots! — Judi Sanders, *Da Bomb*, p. 13, 1997

rotary *adjective*

in circus and carnival usage, emotionally unbalanced *US*

- — Don Wilmeth, *The Language of American Popular Entertainment*, p. 115, 1981

rot corps *noun*

the ROTC, or Reserve Officer Training Corps, found at many colleges *US*

- — Helen Dahlskog (Editor), *A Dictionary of Contemporary and Colloquial Usage*, p. 49, 1972

rote; rout *noun*

in Nova Scotia, the sound of the surf on the shore, a fisherman's locating device *CANADA*

This word, not long in print, descended orally from an Old Norse word *rauta* meaning 'roar'. The different sounds of the surf tell fishermen whose GPS has broken down whether they are near sand, cliff, shingle or gravel beach, and their knowledge of the coastline does the rest.

- The fog was thick, and when Mr. Nickerson stopped the engine and seemed to be listening I asked what he was doing. "I'm listening for the rote," he explained. "The surf breaks with a different sound all along the shore." — Helen Creighton, *A Life in Folklore*, p. 160, 1975

ROTF

used in computer message shorthand to mean '*r*olling *o*n *t*he *f*loor (laughing)' *US*

- — Eric S. Raymond, *The New Hacker's Dictionary*, p. 342, 1991

rotgut *noun*

any unwholesome alcohol *UK, 1633*

- Indiana Harbor was a drinking town, and he must have shoved enough rotgut across the bar to fill Lake Michigan, but he never touched the juice himself. — Mezz Mezzrow, *Really the Blues*, p. 70, 1946
- No Hinky Dink, no Pendergast caters to him, gives him free beer and rot-gut or a kip in the flop on the joint. — Jack Lait and Lee Mortimer, *Washington Confidential*, p. 30, 1951
- They ran up some bottles of rotgut whisky. — Robert Sylvester, *No Cover Charge*, p. 218, 1956
- Somebody passed a bottle of rotgut, the bottom of it. — Jack Kerouac, *On the Road*, p. 24, 1957
- Anything with a buzz in it was in great demand on campus. A pint of "rot gut" whiskey brought from seven and a half to ten dollars, depending on supply. — Iceberg Slim (Robert Beck), *Pimp*, p. 43, 1969
- "Want some wine? I got a jug of rotgut your granny left behind." — C.D. Payne, *Youth in Revolt*, p. 389, 1993
- This ain't Kentucky sipping whiskey. It's Mexican rot gut. — Quentin Tarantino, *From Dusk Till Dawn*, p. 96, 1995

rothe *noun*

two hundred pounds *UK*

Ticket-touting slang, recorded August 2002; possibly an ironic abbreviation of Rothschild (a rich man).

rotheo *noun*

twenty pounds *UK*

Ticket-touting slang, recorded August 2002. From **ROTHE**.

Rothman's-sign *noun*

nicotine-stained fingers as a diagnostic indicator *UK*

An informal medical term, formed on the name of a cigarette manufacturer.

- — Adam T. Fox, St Mary's Hospital, London, 10th October 2002

roti and rum; rum and roti *noun*

a tactic in a political campaign in which voters are given food and drink to encourage their vote *TRINIDAD AND TOBAGO, 1960*

'Roti' is an Indian bread.

- — Lise Winer, *Dictionary of the English/Creole of Trinidad & Tobago*, 2003

rotorhead *noun*

a helicopter pilot or crew member *US*

- With introductions and handshakes all around, the pilots at the table greeted the two rotorheads warmly, as most fixed-wing guys do after one of their own has been pulled out of the water. — Gerry Carroll, *North S*A*R*, p. 36, 1991
- — *The Retired Officer Magazine*, p. 39, January 1993

roto-rooter *noun*

a person who kisses with an active and probing tongue *US*

- — Carol Ann Preusse, *Jargon Used by University of Texas Co-Eds*, 1963

rotted *adjective*

drunk or drug-intoxicated *US*

- — Kenn "Naz" Young, *Naz's Dictionary of Teen Slang*, p. 49, 1993

rotten *adjective*

1 unpleasant *UK*

- Only thing coppers'll do for anyone is make it rotten for them. — John Peter Jones, *Feather Pluckers*, p. 17, 1964

2 ill; depressed; worthless *UK, 1881*

- When you get up and you're feeling rotten and you wonder, 'You know, gee, I feel this badly, do I really want to get on and do the work of the day,' he [Ralph Klein, premier of Alberta, Canada] told reporters. — *The Guardian*, 28th December 2001

3 drunk *AUSTRALIA, 1864*

- — Arthur Chipper, *The Aussie Swearer's Guide*, p. 52, 1972
- — Jim Ramsay, *Cop It Sweet!*, p. 78, 1977
- Well Friday night we go to the Mess and we get rotten. — Sam Weller, *Old Bastards I Have Met*, p. 10, 1979

4 used to intensify a negative quality *UK*

- So my mum turns on me and says I'm trying to turn her Tommy into a rotten little crook like myself. — John Peter Jones, *Feather Pluckers*, p. 11, 1964

rotten row *noun*

a blow *UK*

Rhyming slang, from the name given to the ride in London's Hyde Park.

- [A] Rotten Row to the back of the head[.] — Ray Puxley, *Cockney Rabbit*, 1992

rotten squash *noun*

brain damage *US*

- — *Maledicta*, p. 118, 1984–1985: 'Milwaukee medical maledicta'

rotter *noun*

a despised person *UK, 1894*

- "Shut that panel, you rotter!" he rasped. — Chester Gould, *Dick Tracy Meets the Night Crawler*, p. 216, 1945

rottie *noun*

1 a *Rott*weiler dog *US*

- But you pay $800 for a good rottie, while you can find a Doberman for $30. — *Business Week*, p. 148, 23rd February 1987
- The Rottie is not excitable or quarrelsome; he is faithful, friendly and able. — Andrew De Prisco, *The Mini-Atlas of Dog Breeds*, p. 144, 1990
- Beware of the Rottie — *warning notice on house gate, 2002*

2 a foul mood *NEW ZEALAND*

- — David McGill, *David McGill's Complete Kiwi Slang Dictionary*, p. 61, 1998

rouf *noun*

four; in betting, odds of 4–1 *UK, 1851*

Back slang; pronounced as 'loaf'.

- — John McCririck, *John McCririck's World of Betting*, p. 61, 1991

rouf and a half *noun*

in betting, odds of 9–2 *UK*

In bookmaker slang 'rouf' is 4–1; here the addition of 'a half' increases the odds to $4\frac{1}{2}$–1 or 9–2.

- — John McCririck, *John McCririck's World of Betting*, p. 112, 1991

rough *noun*

turbulent seas following a storm *CANADA*

- The kelp harvesters liked to go out 'after a big rough' because the wash on the ledges, following heavy winds, loosened the clumps of seaweed and allowed them to float. — Hattie Perry, *In and Around Old Barrington*, p. 55, 1979

rough *verb*

1 to rob someone with force or threat of force *US*

- We played this thing for three years and outta all the people we busted, we only had to rough (stick up) three of 'em. — A.S. Jackson, *Gentleman Pimp*, p. 131, 1973

2 to jostle or shove a member of a rival gang *US*

- — *New York Times*, p. 2.15, 1955

▸ **rough it**

to have sex *al fresco* *UK, 2001*

To voluntarily go without such creature comforts as a bed.

▸ **rough it up**

in poker, to bet heavily *US*

- — John Scarne, *Scarne's Guide to Modern Poker*, p. 289, 1979

▸ **rough up the suspect**

(of a male) to masturbate *US*

- "The boy is masturbating" [...] Roughing up the suspect[.] — Erica Orloff and JoAnn Baker, *Dirty Little Secrets*, p. 89, 2001

rough *adjective*

1 unwell *US, 1883*

Dialect.

- He still looks a bit rough these days, despite having sworn off the drink. The problem is that his immune system is gone. — *The Observer*, 25th March 2001

2 good *UK*

On the **BAD** (good) model.

- — Julian Johnson, *Urban Survival*, p. 258, 2003

3 excellent; fashionable, trendy *US*

- — *San Francisco Examiner: People*, p. 8, 27th October 1963: 'What a "Z"! The astonishing private language of Bay Area teenagers'

4 in lowball poker, unfavourable *US*

- — Albert H. Morehead, *The Complete Guide to Winning Poker*, p. 271, 1967

rough as a badger's arse *adjective*

ugly; unsophisticated; unwell, especially as a result of too much drinking *UK*

- Lynn, Liam's first and last girlfriend was a doctor's receptionist and as rough as a badger's arse but such great crack even Winnie's snobbishness dissipated when Lynn told a story. — Denise Mina, *Garnethill*, p. 22, 1998
- [I]t wouldn't translate to this lot. They were rough as badger's arses. — Jenny Colgan, *Talking to Addison*, p. 32, 2003

rough as bags *adjective*

extremely rough; unrefined, uncouth; also, of shabby appearance *AUSTRALIA, 1927*

- [T]he track was laid direct on to the earth. She was as rough as bags. — Patsy Adam-Smith, *Folklore of the Australian Railwaymen*, p. 267, 1969
- — Arthur Chipper, *The Aussie Swearer's Guide*, p. 68, 1972
- — Jim Ramsay, *Cop It Sweet!*, p. 78, 1977

rough as diamonds *adjective*

unsophisticated; unpolished *AUSTRALIA*

A play on **ROUGH DIAMOND**.

- [He] couldn't talk clean in front of sheilahs [women] if he tried. They were rough as diamonds in those days. — Barry Humphries, *Bazza Pulls It Off!*, 1971

rough as guts *adjective*

extremely rough; unrefined; uncouth *AUSTRALIA, 1970*

- And Mac called me 'skipper' – so what the hell's it matter if the landing's as rough as guts? — W.R. Bennett, *Target Turin*, p. 130, 1962
- Her teas are like Bush picnics. Rough as guts. — Arthur Chipper, *The Aussie Swearer's Guide*, p. 48, 1972

rough diamond *noun*

a genuinely good person who is nevertheless unrefined in manners *AUSTRALIA, 1907*

- He was a fine old chap, much appreciated by the rest of us all – a genuine rough diamond. I have met many men who posed in an effort to earn this distinction but they only succeeded in being 'rough' and were minus the attributes of the 'diamond'. — J.P. Osbourne, *Nine Crowded Years*, p. 182, 1921
- — Leonard Mann, *Flesh in Armour*, p. 193, 1932
- I'm afraid you'll have to take my people as you find them, Helen. Jack's a bit of a rough diamond[.] — George Johnston, *My Brother Jack*, p. 224, 1964

rough end of the pineapple *noun*

the raw end of the deal *AUSTRALIA*

- [A]bout the same time as my old drinking mate Sir John Kerr showed Gough what he could do with the rough end of the pineapple (are you with me?) I copped the Cinderella appointment in London as Australian Cultural Attaché[.] — Barry Humphries, *A Nice Night's Entertainment*, p. 180, 1978
- The Queen was shown at the door, anxiously beckoning to an equerry and whispering: 'Psst, what's the rough end of the pineapple mean?' — Bill Hornadge, *The Australian Slanguage*, p. 74, 1980

rough-house *verb*

to brawl in a playful if rowdy and boisterous manner *US, 1900*

- Bill, they won't stop roughhousing. — *Bill and Ted's Excellent Adventure*, 1989

rough hustle *noun*

an amateurish, unpolished swindle *US*

The term does not connote any physical roughness, simply a lack of polish.

- — Robert C. Prus and C.R.D. Sharper, *Road Hustler*, p. 171, 1977: 'Glossary of terms'

roughie *noun*

1 an unrefined person or thing *AUSTRALIA, 1907*

Arthur Chipper notes, in *The Aussie Swearer's Guide*, 1972, that the term is 'Perhaps most commonly assigned to young ladies who aren't good-looking or too well-mannered'.

2 a racehorse or greyhound not expected to win; an outsider *AUSTRALIA, 1922*

- Pat, who was strong on punting but weak on education, collected on a 100–1 winner at Randwick. His mate Mick asked him how he came to pick such a roughie. — Frank Hardy and Athol George Mulley, *The Needy and the Greedy*, p. 45, 1975
- — Jim Ramsay, *Cop It Sweet!*, p. 78, 1977
- — Sam Weller, *Old Bastards I Have Met*, p. 133, 1979
- It was a roughie, a real outsider[.] — Roy Higgins and Tom Prior, *The Jockey Who Laughed*, p. 88, 1982
- — Ned Wallish, *The Truth Dictionary of Racing Slang*, p. 69, 1989

3 a sheep with two seasons of wool growth *FALKLAND ISLANDS (MALVINAS), 1993*

- — Bernadette Hince, *The Antarctic Dictionary*, p. 293, 2000

roughneck *noun*

1 a thug, a lout, a rowdy person *US, 1836*

- I want him to be a gentleman of sorts, not a rough-neck. — Geoff Brown, *I Want What I Want*, p. 164, 1966
- Clubs seem to get a honeymoon period, but then a bunch of roughnecks attach themselves to the night and it goes downhill from there. — Dave Haslam, *Dear Colin*, p. 151, 1999

2 in oil drilling, a skilled oil field worker *US*

- — Jerry Robertson, *Oil Slanguage*, p. 105, 1954

3 on the railways, a brakeman on a goods train *US*

- — Norman Carlisle, *The Modern Wonder Book of Trains and Railroading*, p. 267, 1946

rough off *verb*

to steal something using brute force *US*

- Anyway, a couple of punks tried to rough off the kid's radio and one of them got himself stabbed. — Andrew Vachss, *Flood*, p. 342, 1985

rough rider *noun*

1 a condom of any style or brand thought to bring extra satisfaction to the female partner *JAMAICA*

West Indian and UK black usage, August 2002.

2 an armed guard on a vehicle *US*

- — Linda Reinberg, *In the Field*, p. 187, 1991

rough riding *noun*

sexual intercourse without the protection of a condom *UK, 1961*

rough stuff *noun*

1 violent or sadistic sexual behaviour *US, 1925*

- "No rough stuff or fancy fuckin', boys; Lolita is only sixteen and just startin' out. — Edwin Torres, *Carlito's Way*, p. 15, 1975

2 marijuana that contains unusable detritus *US, 1972*

- — Richard A. Spears, *The Slang and Jargon of Drugs and Drink*, p. 430, 1986
- — Mike Haskins, *Drugs*, p. 289, 2003

rough trade *noun*

a tough, often sadistic male homosexual, especially as a casual sex-partner *US, 1927*

- Basically, a straight one who just likes to be "blown," though a completely homosexual person can assume this role on occasion too. — Anon., *The Gay Girl's Guide*, p. 14, 1949

- So her subjects petitioned the Queen to summon forth her dashing husband and his rough trade friends, for tonight they were daring[.]—Hubert Selby Jr, *Last Exit to Brooklyn*, p. 59, 1957
- "Man, I want to make a score!" a young, rough-trade guy says in loud invitation to any man who wants to go.—Willard Motley, *Let No Man Write My Epitaph*, p. 203, 1958
- "You ever hear of rough trade?" Lewellyn said. "I'm rough trade, very rough."—Bernard Wolfe, *The Magic of Their Singing*, p. 130, 1961
- I had an address book a mile long, packed with tricks from 'drag queens' to rough trade, old aunties, little nellie queens queens that stayed home with mother.—Antony James, *America's Homosexual Underground*, p. 78, 1965
- A street, stud, commonly referred to as "rough trade," will prostitute himself for as little as five dollars.—Johnny Shearer, *The Male Hustler*, p. 17, 1966
- In which case, you will primarily be attracted to the "rough trade" mystique[.]—Angelo d'Arcangelo, *The Homosexual Handbook*, p. 37, 1968
- Almost always rough trade is fellated first after which he turns sour. —Bruce Rodgers, *The Queens' Vernacular*, p. 173, 1972
- How do I know you're not rough trade? Going to beat me up?—Edwin Torres, *Q & A*, p. 169, 1977
- O.K, so the scene gets more rough-trade by the minute.—Armistead Maupin, *Tales of the City*, p. 144, 1978

rough trip *noun*

an unpleasant experience with LSD or another hallucinogen *UK*

- —Tom Hibbert, *Rockspeak!*, p. 135, 1983

rough trot *noun*

a difficult period *AUSTRALIA, 1944*

- Certain local part-time fishing expert had a bit of a rough trot down the Daly last weekend[.]—*News*, p. 7, 2nd April 1982

rough up *verb*

to beat or intimidate someone; to facilitate a street robbery with violence *US*

- —Angela Devlin, *Prison Patter*, p. 99, 1996

roughy *noun*

a manual labourer in a carnival *US*

- —*American Speech*, p. 281, December 1966: 'More carnie talk from the west coast'

round *noun*

an ejaculation *TRINIDAD AND TOBAGO*

- I make three rounds with she.—Lise Winer, *Dictionary of the English/Creole of Trinidad & Tobago*, 2003

round *verb*

to make the rounds *US*

- You can still go rounding. Some stores stay open.—Bernard Wolfe, *The Magic of Their Singing*, p. 25, 1961

roundabout; rounder *noun*

a conditional bet on three selections *UK*

- —David Bennet, *Know Your Bets*, p. 96, 2001

round-brown *noun*

the anus *US*

- We call that a brownie queen. In prison they call it under-yonder and round-brown.—Bruce Jackson, *In the Life*, p. 397, 1972
- "Bend over and show me that round brown," Elwood Banks said. —Joseph Wambaugh, *The Choirboys*, p. 74, 1975

rounder *noun*

1 a migratory, transient worker, especially one living on the edges of legality *US, 1908*

Originally applied to railway workers.

- I'm a piano player and a rounder, a whiskey drinker and a pavement pounder.—Ralph Ellison, *Invisible Man*, p. 176, 1947
- If you've ever been to a carnival, you'll find most people there are "rounders," so to speak. Not that they're all pimps and whores, I'm not saying that, but I am saying that they hustle.—Bruce Jackson, *In the Life*, p. 196, 1972
- Rounders never stay in their pad unless it's for a reason.—Gerald Petievich, *Money Men*, p. 140, 1981

2 a street criminal *CANADA*

- Foote was what they call here in Canada a rounder. It's a term that's been used for more than twenty years to describe street criminals who operate around bars and clubs and hotels[.]—Thomas C. Renner and Cecil Kirby, *Mafia Enforcer*, p. 26, 1987

3 a prisoner associated with traditional Italian-American organised crime *US*

- —William K. Bentley and James M. Corbett, *Prison Slang*, p. 43, 1992

4 a highly skilled professional poker player who travels and plays less skilled players *US*

- —John Scarne, *Scarne's Guide to Modern Poker*, p. 281, 1979
- Rounders, grifters, con artists, and thieves worked the area strip bars and pool halls[.]—Kim Rich, *Johnny's Girl*, p. 48, 1993

rounders *noun*

confusing talk *TRINIDAD AND TOBAGO, 1977*

- —Lise Winer, *Dictionary of the English/Creole of Trinidad & Tobago*, 2003

▷ **see:** ROUND THE HOUSES

round eye *noun*

1 the anus; by extension, a male homosexual who plays the passive role in anal sex *US*

- —Hyman E. Goldin et al., *Dictionary of American Underworld Lingo*, p. 181, 1950
- At thirty-three I was fairly safe from wholesale rape. That is unless I tipped my secret or somebody came in from the street that knew me and told that I was an experienced "round eye."—Iceberg Slim (Robert Beck), *Mama Black Widow*, p. 303, 1969
- —Eugene Landy, *The Underground Dictionary*, p. 25, 1971
- —Bruce Rodgers, *The Queens' Vernacular*, p. 155, 1972
- She had a good round-eye, and that's no lie / How the trickhouse door would swing!—Dennis Wepman et al., *The Life*, p. 83, 1976

2 an American or European *US, 1960*

From the Southeast Asian perspective, adopted by US soldiers in Vietnam to describe themselves.

- The round-eyes are very expensive, they are imported for the politicians and generals[.]—William Wilson, *The LBJ Brigade*, p. 37–38, 1966
- —Carl Fleischhauer, *A Glossary of Army Slang*, p. 11, 1968
- —*Current Slang*, p. 17, Summer 1970
- —Linda Reinberg, *In the Field*, p. 187, 1991

round-eyed *adjective*

American or European, Caucasian *US*

- Now nobody is happy except the command officers; they keep the round-eyed prostitutes[.]—William Wilson, *The LBJ Brigade*, p. 43, 1966
- [A]bout half the round-eyed press corps in Saigon had seriously considered staying on, after South Vietnam finally fell and the PRG took over[.]—Hunter S. Thompson, *Songs of the Doomed*, p. 167, May 1975
- [T]he restaurant proprietor regularly engaged Asian and round-eyed B-girls to solicit drinks from customers.—Joseph Wambaugh, *The Delta Star*, p. 124, 1983

round file *noun*

a wastebasket *US*

- —*American Speech*, p. 65, Spring-Summer 1975: 'Razorback slang'

roundhead *noun*

the circumcised penis *UK*

A visual joke, probably of Royal Navy origin, then polari, or juvenile.

- —Paul Baker, *Polari*, p. 168, 2002

roundheel *noun*

a woman who is easily talked into sexual relations *US, 1943*

Boxing slang from the 1920s for a poor fighter – a 'push-over' – applied later to women of easy virtue.

- —Lou Shelly, *Hepcats Jive Talk Dictionary*, p. 16, 1945
- [N]one of these roundheels that crumb a place up just by walking through the lobby[.]—Jim Thompson, *The Grifters*, p. 18, 1963
- One can dry hump the local roundheels without fear of infection[.] —Seth Morgan, *Homeboy*, p. 44, 1990

round-heeled *adjective*

easily seduced *US, 1957*

- Jefferson Tatum, who never allowed visitors in his house, unless you count Millie and Esther McCabe, the round-heeled twins from packaging[.]—Max Shulman, *Anyone Got a Match?*, p. 95, 1964
- —Jane Juska, *A Round-Heeled Woman*, 2003

round heels *noun*

a promiscuous or sexually compliant woman *US, 1926*

Derogatory; from the anatomical notion that a woman with round heels is more easily put on her back.

- [D]irectly on the round heels of the Food and Drug Administration (FDA) approval of the abortion pill[.]—*Insight on the News*, 23rd October 2000

roundhouse *noun*

a punch that swings round to hit your opponent side-on *US, 1920*

- I'll lift you off your feet so fast with a roundhouse / You'll think I pulled the ground out from underneath you[.]—Eminem (Marshall Mathers), *Fuck the Planet*, 2000

roundie; roundy *noun*
a factory-made cigarette *NEW ZEALAND, 1948*
Prison usage.
- —Harry Orsman, *A Dictionary of Modern New Zealand Slang*, p. 112, 1999

round of drinks *noun*
a small bet relative to the bettor's wealth *AUSTRALIA*
- —Ned Wallish, *The Truth Dictionary of Racing Slang*, p. 69, 1989

round robin *noun*
1 a story begun by one writer and completed by another or multiple writers *US*
- —*American Speech*, p. 29, Spring 1982: 'The langage of science fiction fan magazines'

2 a wager of ten conditional bets on three selections *UK*
- —David Bennet, *Know Your Bets*, p. 96, 2001

round robin shift *noun*
a work schedule in which the worker rotates between several different shifts *US*
- A dude working a round robin shift in a chemical plant has to have someone believe in him most powerfully, that he will escape the situation or else he is doomed.—Odie Hawkins, *Black Casanova*, p. 135, 1984

rounds *noun*
an ejaculation *BAHAMAS*
- —John A. Holm, *Dictionary of Bahamian English*, p. 172, 1982

round sound *noun*
a fashionable, current song *US*
'Round' means nothing, but contrasts with **SQUARE**.
- —*American Speech*, p. 304, December 1955: 'Wayne University slang'

roundtable *noun*
in organised crime, a meeting of leaders convened to discuss and decide with finality pressing business issues *US*
- Tommy, there was a roundtable just before you come out and Mr. A said you done the right thing – so we're gonna move you up[.] —Edwin Torres, *Carlito's Way*, p. 48–49, 1975

round the bend; around the bend *adjective*
mad, crazy; eccentric *UK, 1929*
Probably a naval coinage, widespread by the mid-C20.
- You are trying to drive me round the bend, with your mumbo jumbo.—Charles Raven, *Underworld Nights*, p. 199, 1956
- It's a wonder we haven't all gone round the bend, the way things are in this set up.—Graeme Kent, *The Queen's Corporal [Six Grandada Plays]*, p. 83–84, 1959
- You're round the bloody bend. That's your touble.—Geoff Brown, *I Want What I Want*, p. 71, 1966

round-the-clock *noun*
an elaborate conditional wager on a minimum of three selections *UK*
- —David Bennet, *Know Your Bets*, p. 97, 2001

round the houses; round me's; rounds; rounders *noun*
trousers *UK, 1857*
Rhyming slang on the Cockney pronunciation of 'trousers'. The abbreviation 'round me's' suggests a variation as 'round me houses' – this is not so. In the US the abbreviation 'rounds' was not recorded until 1944.
- And he would put on his almond rocks [socks], and his Dicky Dirt [shirt], and his round the houses, and set off down the frog and toad[.]—Ronnie Barker, *Fletcher's Book of Rhyming Slang*, p. 25, 1979
- These bleedin rounders [trousers] is a lot too tight in the rabbit-hutch.—Red Daniells, 1980

round the twist *adjective*
crazy *UK, 1960*
A variation of **ROUND THE BEND**.
- I reckon I'm goin' round the twist.—Barry Humphries, *Bazza Pulls It Off!*, 1971
- I had guilt that would amaze a Jewish mother and I just about went round the twist.—Kate Pemberton, *The Latest Morningside Papers*, p. 266, 1989

round-up *noun*
in college, a notification of academic deficiency *US*
- —*American Speech*, p. 76–77, February 1968: 'Some notes on flunk notes'

roundy-round *adjective*
used of a motor race track or course oval *US*
- —John Edwards, *Auto Dictionary*, p. 142, 1993

rouse *verb*
▸ **rouse on**
to castigate someone verbally *AUSTRALIA, 1896*
- Old Jack Calahan was rousing on the lubras to hurry with the evening meal.—Ion L. Idriess, *Over the Range*, p. 98, 1947
- —Jim Ramsay, *Cop It Sweet!*, p. 78, 1977
- —Sam Weller, *Old Bastards I Have Met*, p. 49, 1979
- They were always rousing on you for riding the clutch as they took off.—Herb Wharton, *Cattle Camp*, p. 121, 1994

rouseabout
a general assistant on a rural property *AUSTRALIA, 1881*
Hence, also, any general assistant.
- —Lance Corporal Cobber, *The Anzac Pilgrim's Progress*, p. 13, 1914
- ROUSEABOUT – Jack-of-all-trades on a sheep station.—Gilbert H. Lawson, *A Dictionary of Australian Words and Terms*, 1924
- —Leonard Mann, *Flesh in Armour*, p. 37, 1932
- He walked from one end to the other, shouting a word of greeting here and there to shearers and rouseabouts he knew.—Dymphna Cusack, *Picnic Races*, p. 98, 1962
- —Jim Ramsay, *Cop It Sweet!*, p. 78, 1977

roust *verb*
1 to harass someone, especially when done deliberately by the police or other authorities *UK*
- I couldn't remember being rousted recently, and I didn't like it one bit.—James Patterson, *Kiss the Girls*, p. 334, 1995

2 to upbraid someone *AUSTRALIA, 1916*
- The boss was a "birk" (pain in the neck) who kept "rousting" (bawling out) the tentmen[.]—Butch Reynolds, *Broken Hearted Clown*, p. 31, 1953

roustabout *noun*
1 in oil drilling, an unskilled oil field worker *US, 1948*
- —Jerry Robertson, *Oil Slanguage*, p. 105, 1954

2 a general assistant on a rural property *AUSTRALIA, 1940*
Variant of **ROUSEABOUT**.
- It had been Rufe's first job after he left school, roustabout in this pub.—Wilda Moxham, *The Apprentice*, p. 164, 1969
- The roustabout looked at it, woebegone[.]—Bob Ellis and Anne Brooksbank, *Mad Dog Morgan*, p. 88, 1976
- I obtained a job as a roustabout with one of the smaller circuses[.] —Ward McNally, *Supper at Happy Harry's*, p. 90, 1982

rouster *noun*
a rough and ready western Canadian man *CANADA*
This expression is likely derived from **ROUSTABOUT** (an oil field worker), but adapted to describe any rough-hewn male.
- "I will pay for your information, same as I would pay any rouster that came in here with news I can use."—George Bowering, *Caprice*, p. 182, 1987

rousting *noun*
1 a vigorous act of sexual intercourse *UK*
- [T]hey can give a girl a good rousting once in a while[.]—Jeremy Cameron, *Brown Bread in Wengen*, p. 62, 1999

2 an act of deliberate (police) harassment *UK*
- Doing the selfsame job as he does day in, day out, as the rozzers are well aware, and came round to his turn to get a rousting.—*British Journal of Photography*, 28th March 1980

rout *noun*
a wild, rowdy party *US*
- —Collin Baker et al., *College Undergraduate Slang Study Conducted at Brown University*, p. 186, 1968

▹ **see: ROTE**

router *noun*
in horse racing, a horse that performs well in longer races *US*
- —George King, *Horse Racing*, p. 60, 1965

rover *noun*
in a casino, a gambler who moves from game to game, never staying at any one game very long *US, 185*
- —Thomas L. Clark, *The Dictionary of Gambling and Gaming*, p. 185, 1987

row *noun*
▸ **go for a row**
to get into trouble *AUSTRALIA*
- 'You can't have a cigarette, and nor can I,' reprimanded Dinger firmly. 'Otherwise we'll both go for a row, and that would ruin everything.' —John Wynnum, *Jiggin' in the Riggin'*, p. 56, 1965
- Lucky both chicks survived, or he'd really go for a row.—Jenny Pausacker, *What are ya?*, p. 126, 1987

row *verb*
to fight; to battle *UK*
An exaggeration of the sense as 'to argue'.
• [A]ll we spoke of was rowing.— Martin King and Martin Knight, *The Naughty Nineties*, p. 62, 1999

▸ **row down the red river**
to experience the bleed period of the menstrual cycle *US*
• —Don R. McCreary (Editor), *Dawg Speak*, 2001

rowbottom *noun*
a student disturbance, started in fun but not always ending as such *US, 1940*
Specific to the University of Pennsylvania in Philadelphia, claimed to have been named for J.T. Rowbottom, a rowdy member of Penn's Class of 1913.
• Any provocation, particularly that of springtime, is enough to touch off mischief-making riots signaled by the cry "Oh, Rowbottom!" on the Penn campus and the adjacent main streets of Philadelphia. —*American Speech*, p. 293, December 1958
• —Claudio R. Salvucci, *The Philadelphia Dialect Dictionary*, p. 55, 1996

row dog *noun*
in prison, another prisoner whose cell is on the same tier *US*
• —Mark S. Fleisher, *Beggars & Thieves*, p. 291, 1995: 'Glossary'

rowdy *noun*
a person who inhales glue for the psychoactive effect *US*
• —Eugene Landy, *The Underground Dictionary*, p. 162, 1971

rowdy dowdy *noun*
in pickpocketing, the seemingly accidental jostling of victims or potential victims by members of the gang *US*
• —Joseph E. Ragen and Charles Finston, *Inside the World's Toughest Prison*, p. 816, 1962: 'Penitentiary and underworld glossary'

rowed out *adjective*
excluded *UK*
• Occasional cheapskates were simply "rowed out" of the games by not being invited back, a reputation nobody wanted.—Brian McDonald, *Elephant Boys*, p. 18, 2000

rower *noun*
an argument *UK*
• —Angela Devlin, *Prison Patter*, p. 100, 1996

rowers' revenge *noun*
the ritual of throwing the coxswain into the water after a rowing team wins an event *US*
• — Judy's Enterprises, *Coxswain Postcard*, 2001

row in *verb*
to implicate someone in a crime *UK*
• —Peter Laurie, *Scotland Yard*, p. 327, 1970

row out *verb*
1 to contrive the innocence of someone in relation to a particular crime *UK*
• —Peter Laurie, *Scotland Yard*, p. 327, 1970
2 to distance yourself from something or someone *UK*
• But the alternative, rowing out, just wasn't on as far as I was concerned [...] And in any case, trying to row out from a bird like Audrey would be just as dangerous as the present situation.—Ted Lewis, *Jack Carter's Law*, p. 11, 1974

rox *noun*
crack cocaine *US*
A phonetic play on **ROCK(S)**.
• —US Department of Justice, *Street Terms*, October 1994

Roxanne *noun*
cocaine; crack cocaine *US*
A **ROCK** personification.
• —US Department of Justice, *Street Terms*, October 1994
• —Nick Constable, *This is Cocaine*, p. 181, 2002
• —Mike Haskins, *Drugs*, p. 281, 2003

Roy *noun*
a refined and cultured Australian male *AUSTRALIA, 1960*
Counterpart to the **ALF**.
• [T]he young executives, the in-people, call them what you like, the Roys, the jet set, the status symbol seekers from Perisher Valley to Palm Beach, and none of them worth a pinch of shit if it comes to doing an honest day's work[.]—Frank Hardy, *The Outcasts of Foolgarah*, p. 143, 1971

royal *adjective*
effeminately homosexual *UK*
'Queenly'.
• —Paul Baker, *Polari*, 2002

royal blue *noun*
a blue tablet variety of LSD *US, 1971*
• —Richard A. Spears, *The Slang and Jargon of Drugs and Drink*, p. 430, 1986
• —Mike Haskins, *Drugs*, p. 286, 2003

royal crown *noun*
a British Leyland 'Princess' car *UK*
• —Peter Chippindale, *The British CB Book*, p. 161, 1981

Royal Docks *noun*
syphilis; hence any sexually transmitted infection; hence an irritated condition *UK*
Rhyming slang for **POX**.
• Long stationary motorists on the M25 may utter "I've got the Royal Docks of this."—Ray Puxley, *Cockney Rabbit*, 1992

royally *adverb*
greatly, extremely *US*
• —Connie Eble (Editor), *UNC-CH Campus Slang*, p. 9, October 2002

royal mail; royal *noun*
bail *UK, 1961*
Rhyming slang.
• —Angela Devlin, *Prison Patter*, p. 100, 1996

Royal Navy *noun*
gravy *UK*
Rhyming slang. Presumably served in a 'Royal Navy boat'.
• —Ray Puxley, *Cockney Rabbit*, 1992

Royal Navy situation *noun*
a need for money *UK*
A pun on **SUB** (a loan).
• Being in a Royal Navy situation (in need of a sub) I waited till 'er [the speaker's wife] had climbed the wooden hill to Bedfordshire [gone to bed], got on the dog [telephone] and rang the number.—Andrew Nickolds, *Back to Basics*, p. 146–147, 1994

Royal Nepalese *noun*
▷ **see: NEPALESE BLUE**

royal shaft *noun*
monumental mistreatment *US*
• —*Esquire*, p. 180, June 1983

royal temple ball *noun*
hashish and LSD formed into a ball *US, 1978*
• In the center are a dozen hand-pressed balls of Royal temple balls. —Peter Stafford, *Psychedlic Encyclopedia*, p. 216, 1992

royal wedding *noun*
in hold 'em poker, a king and queen, especially of diamonds *US*
• —John Vorhaus, *The Big Book of Poker Slang*, p. 32, 1996

Roy Castle *noun*
the anus *UK*
Rhyming slang for **ARSEHOLE**, used here in its anatomical, non-figurative sense; formed from the name of the multi-talented entertainer, 1932–94.
• [T]he "reeking Roy Castle" of a persistent wind breaker[.]—Ray Puxley, *Fresh Rabbit*, 1998

Roy Rogers *noun*
building tradesmen who are not as skilled as may reasonably be expected *UK*
Rhyming slang on the plural form of **BODGER**. Formed on the name of a famous film cowboy, 1911–98, and thus a play on **COWBOY** (any tradesman who is unreliable, irresponsible and, perhaps, unqualified).
• —Ray Puxley, *Cockney Rabbit*, 1992

roz *noun*
crack cocaine *UK, 1998*
Possibly a misspelling of **ROX**.
• —Mike Haskins, *Drugs*, p. 282, 2003

roziner; rozener *noun*
▷ see: ROSINER

rozzer; roz *noun*
a police officer *UK, 1893*
Possibly from Yiddish *khazer* (a pig). 'Roz' is first recorded in 1971.
- [Y]a sang [informed] to the fuckin' rozzers. Didn't ya? —Nick Barlay, *Curvy Lovebox*, p. 19, 1997
- Rozzers in his pocket? Big deal. —John Milne, *Alive and Kicking*, p. 36, 1998

RPG *noun*
a *r*ole-*p*laying *g*ame *US*
- AppleCat modem information and programming, online role-playing games (RPG) such as Dungeons & Dragons. — *Washington Post*, p. N4, 11th July 1986
- "I'm really into RPGs," he says. "It's a fun thing to collect." —Marty Beckerman, *Death to All Cheerleaders*, p. 92, 2000

RSN
used as Internet shorthand to mean '*r*eal *s*oon *n*ow' *US*
- —Christian Crumlish, *The Internet Dictionary*, p. 172, 1995

RTA *verb*
to return to Australia; to be returned to Australia *AUSTRALIA, 1963*
- —Bernadette Hince, *The Antarctic Dictionary*, p. 294, 2000

RTAer *noun*
a person returning to Australia after expeditioning in Antarctica *AUSTRALIA, 1996*
From RTA.
- —Bernadette Hince, *The Antarctic Dictionary*, p. 295, 2000

RTFM
*r*ead *t*he *f*ucking *m*anual *US*
- —Andy Ihnatko, *Cyberspeak*, p. 166, 1997

ru *noun*
a member of the Piru youth gang *US*
- —Ann Lawson, *Kids & Gangs*, p. 56, 1994: 'Common African-American gang sang/phrases'

rub *verb*

▸ **rub in; rub it in**
to emphasise something annoyingly; to continue to insist, especially in an unkindly or vexing manner *UK, 1870*
- "Everything was just a real bargain," Mario continued, unintentionally rubbing it in. "Every suede jacket." — *New York Observer*, 11th February 2002

▸ **rub off on**
(of abstract qualitities, such as luck or enthusiasm) to transfer from one person to another *US, 1959*
- [T]he textbooks' regimen of good cheer does not seem to have rubbed off on them. Students know when they are being conned. —James W. Loewen, *Lies My Teacher Told Me*, p. 269, 1996
- [H]er enthusiasm clearly rubbed off on Monica[.] — *The Guardian*, 4th July 2003

▸ **rub the magic lamp**
(of a male) to masturbate *US*
- "The boy is masturbating" [...] Rubbing the magic lamp[.] —Erica Orloff and JoAnn Baker, *Dirty Little Secrets*, p. 89, 2001

▸ **rub up the wrong way**
to annoy someone *UK, 1862*
- [Y]ou ought to know by now that you've rubbed so many people up the wrong way that the blame is yours to take. —Desmond Guilfoyle, *The Charisma Effect*, p. 197, 2002

▸ **rub your nose in it**
to humiliate you by reminding you of a mistake *UK, 1963*
- Ender had beaten him, and then rubbed his nose in it by being magnanimous. —Orson Scott Card, *Ender's Game*, p. 88, 1991

rub-a-dub; rub-a-dub-dub; rubberdy; rubbidy; rubba *noun*
a public house *UK, 1932*
Rhyming slang for PUB; from the nursery rhyme 'Rub-a-dub-dub, / Three men in a tub'.
- I'll shoot through [go quickly] for a skinful down the nearest rubbidy! —Barry Humphries, *Bazza Pulls It Off!*, 1971
- Thought I'd take me bird down the rub a dub for a few tiddley winks [drinks]. — *The Sweeney*, p. 6, 1976
- [H]e made his way to the rub-a-dub for a tumble down the sink [drink]. —Ronnie Barker, *Fletcher's Book of Rhyming Slang*, p. 26, 1979
- Bowling down the rubba[.] —Viv Stanshall, *Ginger Geezer*, 1981

rub-a-dub-dubs *nickname*
HMP Wormwood Scrubs (a prison in north London) *UK*
Rhyming slang, in current prison use February 2002.

rubber *noun*

1 a condom *US, 1947*
The most common, and almost only, slang term for a condom in the US.
- Gordon's Novelty Shop, at 428 East Baltimore Street, hands out a business card with a drawing on the reverse side showing a short-skirted cutie standing next to a young soldier in a rainstorm, with the caption: "Don't forget your rubbers." —Jack Lait and Lee Mortimer, *Washington Confidential*, p. 267, 1951
- One of these inexpressible American evenings in a girl's home-parlor, with darkness pressing at the windows, and little lace panties, and little sighs, and noises that make you jump and look over your sweaty shoulder, and the final disposal of the saggy rubber in your handkerchief. —Jack Kerouac, *Letter to Neal Cassady*, p. 287, 10th January 1951
- "Well, later on I went down to Doc Parker's again to get me a rubber." —William Burroughs, *Naked Lunch*, p. 175, 1957
- She went into the bathroom, returned with a rubber. "You never know what the hell you guys have had your pricks in," she said brutally. —John Rechy, *City of Night*, p. 157, 1963
- Well, when some have new chicks going right, they'll come asking you for rubbers. —Malcolm X and Alex Haley, *The Autobiography of Malcolm X*, p. 48, 1964
- She asked me what I meant; rubbers? safes? skins? prophylactics? contraceptives? —John Nichols, *The Sterile Cuckoo*, p. 105, 1965
- There is an awful lot of clap loose in the U.S. – and while rubbers are a drag, the clap is something else again. — *Berkeley Barb*, p. 10, 2nd–8th June 1967
- Since the Pill has come of age, an entire institution which had evolved around the purchasing and using of rubbers has faded into relative obscurity. — *Screw*, p. 21, 22nd March 1970
- I want you to ice the rubber and let him get a shot of pure honey. —A.S. Jackson, *Gentleman Pimp*, p. 47, 1973
- Few men use rubbers in Nevada's clean houses, but you can if you want to. —Gerald Paine, *A Bachelor's Guide to the Brothels of Nevada*, p. 12, 1978
- And the rubbers you hide / In your top left pocket —Gang of Four *At Home He's a Tourist*, 1979
- [S]he still won't learn, what's gonna happen to her if she lets them fuck her without using a rubber. —George V. Higgins, *The Rat on Fire*, p. 26, 1981
- Be a real swell guy and don't be a toad / Wear a rubber before blowing a load. — *Maledicta*, p. 187, 1988–1989
- The only thing I ever touch though is a rubber. I don't give no head without a rubber. I don't fuck without a rubber. —William T. Vollman, *Whores for Gloria*, p. 84, 1991
- What does Magenta do with bloody rubbers? She turns them inside out and uses them again. —Sal Piro and Michael Hess, *The Official 'Rocky Horror Picture Show' Audience Participation Guide*, p. 33, 1991
- Jesus, ain't you learned nuthin yet cept how to slide on a rubber? —Jess Mowry, *Way Past Cool*, p. 33, 1992
- This receptacle is where the studs deposit their used rubbers (perfectly placed, too, as the horrific stench its mouth emits discourages anyone from lingering onstage). —Anthony Petkovich, *The X Factory*, p. 188, 1997

2 balloons *US*
- — *American Speech*, p. 282, December 1966: 'More carnie talk from the west coast'

3 collectively, a car's tyres *US, 1882*
A car might be said to have 'good rubber'.
- Bernie bought new rubber and took the precaution of storing the car in a public garage. —Ross Russell, *The Sound*, p. 122, 1961
- —Lewis Poteet, *Car & Motorcyle Slang*, p. 170, 1992

4 a car *US*
- At sixteen, I didn't have the money to buy a Cadillac, but she had her own fine "rubber," as we called a car in those days. —Malcolm X and Alex Haley, *The Autobiography of Malcolm X*, p. 68, 1964

5 a rubber bullet *US*
- —Ralph de Sola, *Crime Dictionary*, p. 130, 1982

▸ **burn rubber**
to spin a car's wheels in a fast start, leaving rubber tracks on the road *US*
- —Fred Horsley, *The Hot Rod Handbook*, p. 208, 1957
- Dip dropped the gear in gear, burned rubber turning the corner, headed cross town. —Steve Cannon, *Groove, Bang, and Jive Around*, p. 20, 1969
- "Hang on! We're off," and Francine gunned the hot motor and burned rubber as she peeled away from the parking lot. —Vance Donovan, *High Rider*, p. 38, 1969
- "Don't burn rubber. Just go slow," Tommy said from the back seat. —Stephen J. Cannell, *Big Con*, p. 25, 1997

▸ **chirp rubber**
to shift gears in a car in a manner that produces a chirping sound of tyre meeting road *US*
- —John Lawlor, *How to Talk Car*, p. 31, 1965

- Shane tried to make up ground, spinning his wheels, chirping rubber, trying to get around slower traffic. — Stephen J. Cannell, *The Tin Collectors*, p. 222, 2001

▸ **on rubber**

driving a car *US*

- A couple of my boys came up. "You still on rubber, man?" one wanted to know. "That's right," I said. "Say, run me out to Hollywood, man." — Chester Himes, *If He Hollers Let Him Go*, p. 43, 1945

▸ **peel rubber**

to spin a car's wheels in a fast start, leaving rubber tracks on the road *US*

- It left the parking lot swiftly, but without peeling any rubber. — George V. Higgins, *The Friends of Eddie Doyle*, p. 152, 1971
- Can it lay rubber? — *American Graffiti*, 1973
- I didn't know a Plymouth Reliant could peel rubber. — C.D. Payne, *Youth in Revolt*, p. 238, 1993

rubber *adjective*

used of a cheque, unfunded *US*

A back-formation from the metaphor of an unfunded cheque bouncing.

- The guy says, "What can I do? They gave me a rubber check." — Robert Stoller and I.S. Levine, *Coming Attractions*, p. 93, 1991

rubber and rocks *noun*

bacon and eggs *NEW ZEALAND*

Collected during an extensive survey of New Zealand prison slang, 1996–2000.

rubber arms *noun*

the sensation experienced by a surfer paddling into a large wave that might be a little larger than the surfer cares to tackle *US*

- — John Severson, *Modern Surfing Around the World*, p. 180, 1964

rubberband *noun*

a vehicle manufactured by DAF *UK*

Citizens' band radio slang; a slur on DAF technology.

- — Peter Chippindale, *The British CB Book*, p. 161, 1981

rubber bitch *noun*

the inflatable rubber air mattress given to US troops in the field in Vietnam *US*

- — Linda Reinberg, *In the Field*, p. 188, 1991

rubber bum *noun*

a derelict hitchhiker *CANADA*

- Tom Briggs is one of the older hoboes who have switched from the railways to become "rubber bums" – hitch-hikers on long-distance trucks. — *Maclean's*, p. 34/3, 29th July 1961

rubber cheque; rubber check; rubber kite *noun*

a worthless cheque *US, 1931*

An unfunded cheque bounces back from the bank.

- — Angela Devlin, *Prison Patter*, p. 100, 1996

rubber chicken circuit *noun*

the tour made by an after-dinner speaker, with reference to tough chicken as the usual main course *CANADA*

- Next year's rubber-chicken circuit is being sewed up by three Toronto women with a public-speaking agency called Canadian Celebrity Bureau. — *Maclean's*, p. 1/1, 23rd May 1959

rubber cow *noun*

in circus usage, an elephant, male or female *US*

- — Don Wilmeth, *The Language of American Popular Entertainment*, p. 36, 1981

rubber duck *noun*

1 a trifle; something of no value *UK*

Rhyming slang for **FUCK**.

- I couldn't give a rubber duck. — Ray Puxley, *Cockney Rabbit*, 1992

2 an inflatable rubber dinghy *SOUTH AFRICA, 1986*

- I've just got a rubber duck and if I'm not in the boat I am surfing. — *Sunday Times (South Africa)*, 20th July 2003

rubber ducker *noun*

a rubber duck (an inflatable rubber dinghy) enthusiast *SOUTH AFRICA, 1994*

- — Penny Silva, *A Dictionary of South African English*, 1996

rubber duckie *noun*

a short, flexible, rubber-coated vehicle-mounted radio aerial *UK*

A jokey reference to 'Rubber Duck' as referring to the **HANDLE** (a citizens' band radio identity) of the hero of the film *Convoy*, 1975.

- Twig [aerial] city. American truck sports two centre-loaders; British van a rubber duckie and a K40. — Peter Chippindale, *The British CB Book*, p. 117, 1981

rubberdy *noun*

▷ see: **RUB-A-DUB**

rubbered *adjective*

drunk *UK*

- — *e-cyclopaedia*, 20th March 2002

rubber heels; rubber heelers *noun*

the Metropolitan Police internal affairs division at New Scotland Yard *UK*

From the silence and secrecy of its methods.

- Just then a couple more rubber heelers comes stamping up the back stairs. — John Peter Jones, *Feather Pluckers*, p. 111, 1964
- — G.F. Newman, *Sir, You Bastard*, p. 254, 1970
- — Peter Laurie, *Scotland Yard*, p. 327, 1970
- I felt like a fucking rubber-heeler. Checking up on him like that. A fellow officer. — Jake Arnott, *He Kills Coppers*, p. 57, 2001
- It was inevitable that we would come to the attention of CIB, the Met's Internal Affairs Department, known within the force as the "rubber-heelers". — Duncan MacLaughlin, *The Filth*, p. 127, 2002

rubber johnny; rubber johnnie; rubber johney *noun*

a condom *UK*

An elaboration of **JOHNNY**.

- — James McDonald, *A Dictionary of Obscenity, Taboo and Euphemism*, p. 77, 1988
- My mother told me / If I was goody / She would buy me / a rubber johnny[.] — a playground parody of *The Clapping Song*, late 1960s

rubber lip *noun*

a citizens' band radio user who monopolises conversation *US*

- — Wayne Floyd, *Jason's Authentic Dictionary of CB Slang*, p. 26, 1976

rubber man *noun*

in circus and carnival usage, a balloon seller *US*

- — Don Wilmeth, *The Language of American Popular Entertainment*, p. 228, 1981

rubberneck *verb*

to stare with undue interest *US, 1896*

- I rubbernecked around some as we streaked along the avenue[.] — Mezz Mezzrow, *Really the Blues*, p. 174, 1946
- [H]e went on rubber-necking the speed demons. — Bernard Wolfe, *The Late Risers*, p. 183, 1954

rubberneck bus *noun*

a tour bus *US*

- Slowly the rubberneck bus groaned along Maxwell Street, lights out. — Willard Motley, *Let No Man Write My Epitaph*, p. 101, 1958

rubberneck car *noun*

on the railways, an observation carriage *US*

- — Norman Carlisle, *The Modern Wonder Book of Trains and Railroading*, p. 267, 1946

rubbernecker; rubberneck *noun*

a person who stares with curiousity, especially a motorist who slows to view an accident *US, 1934*

- [T]he blues men [meths drinkers] may become exhibitionists. Rubbernecks would attempt to photograph them from the windows of air-conditioned coaches. — Geoffrey Fletcher, *Down Among the Meths Men*, p. 22, 1966
- Back to the street – rubberneckers swarming. — James Ellroy, *White Jazz*, p. 38, 1992
- As soon as you tell people about your separation, they behave like rubberneckers at a car accident — Anka Radakovich, *The Wild Girls Club*, p. 40, 1994
- A few ordinary uniformed officers were standing around trying to disperse the rubberneckers who were disrupting the flow of traffic. — Greg Williams, *Diamond Geezers*, p. 203, 1997

rubber numbers *noun*

very approximate statistics *US*

- These are extremely rubber numbers. It's difficult to verify, especially when you're dropping bombs on people and you don't go back to count bodies. — *The Guardian*, p. 9, 9th April 2003

rubbers *noun*

1 a wet suit; a garment made of rubber or synthetic neoprene worn next to the skin while in cold water *CANADA*

- — Gary Fairmont R. Filosa II, *The Surfer's Almanac*, p. 193, 1977

2 sneakers, trainers *VIRGIN ISLANDS, BRITISH*
- —Richard Allsopp, *Dictionary of Caribbean English Usage*, p. 478, 1996

rubber vag *noun*
in circus and carnival usage, someone who lives in a mobile trailer *US*
- —Don Wilmeth, *The Language of American Popular Entertainment*, p. 228, 1981

rubber walls *adjective*
crazy *US*
In gay use, especially in the phrase 'I'll go rubber walls'.
- —Bruce Rodgers, *The Queens' Vernacular*, 1972

rubbidy *noun*
▷ see: RUB-A-DUB, RUBBITY-DUB

rubbins; rubbings *noun*
rubbing alcohol *US*
A drink of desperation.
- —Joe McKennon, *Circus Lingo*, p. 80, 1980

rubbish *noun*
1 anything of poor quality or little or no worth; nonsense *UK, 1601*
From the sense as 'refuse'.
- I utterly deplore the rubbish you are selling, but I'll defend to the death anyone's right to read it! —John Mortimer, *Rumpole's Return [A First Rumpole Omnibus]*, p. 463, 1980
- rows of bric-brac shops selling rubbish to the tourists —Fiona Duncan, *Insight Guide France*, p. 194, 2002

2 a contemptible person or persons *SOUTH AFRICA, 1941*
- —Penny Silva, *A Dictionary of South African English*, 1996

rubbish *verb*
to criticise someone or something unfavourably; to disparage someone or something; to discard someone or something *AUSTRALIA, 1953*
- The thing that ate into Arnie worse was that Wendy, a doll he'd been leching after, had rubbished him for Bernie. —Wilda Moxham, *The Apprentice*, p. 55, 1969
- [F]or had he not reformed, begun courting a Sunday school teacher, got a job gathering the rubbish of those who had rubbished him? —Frank Hardy, *The Outcasts of Foolgarah*, p. 34, 1971
- —Arthur Chipper, *The Aussie Swearer's Guide*, p. 52, 1972
- —Jim Ramsay, *Cop It Sweet!*, p. 78, 1977

rubbish *adjective*
bad; inferior *UK*
- Frankly, until you come up with a slightly less rubbish band name, you're in no position to have a pop at us. —*Kerrang!*, p. 8, 3rd November 2001

rubbisher *noun*
a person given to detraction *AUSTRALIA*
- Australians are well known as some of the world's most active rubbishers, especially of any talent that happens to be home-grown or dinkum (genuine). —Arthur Chipper, *The Aussie Swearer's Guide*, p. 52, 1972

rubbishing *noun*
an act of denigration *AUSTRALIA*
From RUBBISH (little or no worth).
- I can't ask any of me mates or they'd give me a flamin' rubbishing. —Barry Humphries, *Bazza Pulls It Off!*, 1971

rubbishy *adjective*
of inferior quality *UK, 1824*
- The house is just as he had imagined it would be: rubbishy furniture, a clutter of ornaments (porcelain shepherdesses, cowbells, an ostrich-feather flywhisk)[.] —J. M. Coetzee, *Disgrace*, p. 72–73, 1999

rubbity-dub; rubbity; rubbitty; rubbidy *noun*
a public hotel *AUSTRALIA, 1898*
Rhyming slang for PUB.
- 'Where's Jimmy an' Pat?' 'Down the rubbity.' —Nino Culotta (John O'Grady), *They're A Weird Mob*, p. 104, 1957
- She must have got a draft to another rubbitty. —John Wynnum, *Jiggin' in the Riggin'*, p. 37, 1965
- But like I've just remembered I've got to shoot through to the local rubbidy for a few ice cold beers. —Barry Humphries, *The Wonderful World of Barry McKenzie*, p. 7, 1968

rubby *noun*
a derelict who drinks rubbing alcohol *US*
The word is not to be confused with 'rummy'.
- —Frank Prewitt and Francis Schaeffer, *Vacaville Vocabulary*, 1961–1962
- A "rubby" drinks rubbing alcohol. He can buy it in drugstores on Sunday, when Canadian liquor stores are closed. —Bill Casselman, *Canadian Words*, p. 15, 1995

rubby-dub *noun*
an ignorant soldier from a rural mountain area, a poor candidate to be a good soldier *US*
- —*American Speech*, p. 238, October 1946: 'World War II slang of maladjustment'

rub down *noun*
a cursory search of a prisoner by running hands over clothes and body *UK, 1887*
- —Home Office, *Glossary of Terms and Slang Common in Penal Establishments*, July 1978
- —Angela Devlin, *Prison Patter*, p. 100, 1996

rub down *verb*
to search a prisoner *UK, 1887*

rube; reub *noun*
an unsophisticated, naive, inexperienced person *US, 1896*
From the older, UK 'reuben' (a country bumpkin).
- It sure knocked those rubes out when they heard us play the blues[.] —Mezz Mezzrow, *Really the Blues*, p. 134, 1946
- Baltimore is overrun by rubes. —Jack Lait and Lee Mortimer, *Washington Confidential*, p. 261, 1951
- It used to irritate him, knowing what I had in my head, to hear me talking and acting like any other rube around town. —Jim Thompson, *The Killer Inside*, p. 28, 1952
- A few of the carnys knew who did it but they figured the rube had it coming[.] —Robert Edmond Alter, *Carny Kill*, p. 137, 1966
- I'm not a rube. I know who Tennessee Williams was. —Walter Tevis, *The Color of Money*, p. 52, 1984
- I can't stand this goddamn hotel. Full of American rubes and geeks pissing away Junior's college fund at the blackjack tables. —Carl Hiaasen, *Tourist Season*, p. 164, 1986
- You rubes! You were going for it. —Howard Stern, *Miss America*, p. 280, 1995

rubia de la costa; rubia *noun*
a light-coloured marijuana originating in Columbia *US, 1976*
Directly from Spanish, *rubia* (fair-haired) is used by the Spanish to describe Virginian tobacco, plus *de la costa* (of the coast).
- —Richard A. Spears, *The Slang and Jargon of Drugs and Drink*, p. 431, 1986
- —Mike Haskins, *Drugs*, p. 289, 2003

rubies *noun*
the lips *US*
- —Marcus Hanna Boulware, *Jive and Slang of Students in Negro Colleges*, 1947

Rubik's cubes; rubik's *noun*
pubic hair *UK*
Rhyming slang for PUBES, formed from a puzzling toy.
- You could have knitted a scarf out of her Rubik's. —Bodmin Dark, *Dirty Cockney Rhyming Slang*, 2003

rub joint *noun*
a dance hall where men can, for a small price, dance intimately with women *US*
- —Don Wilmeth, *The Language of American Popular Entertainment*, p. 228, 1981

rub 'n' tug *noun*
a massage that includes masturbation *US*
- If you really got lucky, maybe a wayward stripper took one of your unmarried groomsmen into the coat room of the Armpit Tavern and gave him a rub 'n' tug for an extra twenty-five bucks. —*Nerve*, p. 17, October-November 2000

rub of the brush *noun*
a beverage made from the remnants of drinks in a bar *US*
- Each got a tin-cup of this. It was called "a rub of the brush," because that was how it felt going down. —Jack Lait and Lee Mortimer, *Chicago Confidential*, p. 54, 1950

rub-out *noun*
a killing *US, 1927*
- I paid him back a month later by knocking off a punk that tried to set him for a rub-out when he refused to pay off for protection. —Mickey Spillane, *I, The Jury*, p. 43, 1947
- Had you read about the slaying of a young union leader in New Jersey, a man who was gunned down by a pair of hoods, a rub-out that was clearly tied to the victim's anti-Hoffa activities? —Sidney Bernard, *This Way to the Apocalypse*, p. 127, 1963
- He implied it was a rub-out, an assassination. —Edwin Torres, *Q & A*, p. 73, 1977
- They could always hold gangland rub-outs there. —Dan Jenkins, *Life Its Ownself*, p. 17, 1984

rub out *verb*
1 to kill someone *US, 1848*
- You're scared right now I'm gonna rub you out. —Marvin Wald and Albert Maltz, *The Naked City*, 1947

- The Hook was killed and Tony Indelicato was taken for a ride and rubbed out. —Jack Lait and Lee Mortimer, *Chicago Confidential*, p. 19, 1950
- Ribler had been "quietly rubbed out to prevent his testifying against the Hotsy Totsy Club murderers." —Robert Sylvester, *No Cover Charge*, p. 13, 1956
- Boots thinks you're an all right guy – he don't want you completely rubbed out. —Clarence Cooper Jr, *Black*, p. 279, 1963
- You'd be committing a grave error if you tried to rub us out. —Troy Kennedy Martin, *The Italian Job [uncut script]*, 1969
- Now he had to explain this to a jury of bank tellers and housewives who had sat through four weeks of lurid testimony from the likes of exotic dancer and former Ladd girlfriend "Angel Dust," and ex-cons who talked about rubbing people out by hammering pencils into their ears. —Kim Rich, *Johnny's Girl*, p. 235, 1993

2 to disqualify a competitor *AUSTRALIA, 1902*

- RUB OUT – To disqualify. —Gilbert H. Lawson, *A Dictionary of Australian Words and Terms*, 1924
- [B]oth horse and connections were disqualified. Being 'rubbed out' was not as serious as it appeared. —Joe Andersen, *Winners Can Laugh*, p. 176, 1982

rub up *verb*

to assault someone *US*

- There was a lot of yelling and gesticulating, and a few blows were passed. A couple of the guards got rubbed up a little. —Chester Himes, *Cast the First Stone*, p. 107, 1952

rubyfruit *noun*

the vagina *US*

- — *Maledicta*, p. 147, Summer/Winter 1982: 'Dyke diction: the language of lesbians'

Ruby Murray; ruby *noun*

a curry *UK, 1992*

Rhyming slang, based on popular singer Ruby Murray, 1935–96. In Cardiff, Wales, a local variant is Don Murray, named after the Cardiff City footballer.

- They have morals looser than post-ruby bowels[.] —Andrew Nickolds, *Back to Basics*, p. 83–84, 1994
- If a ruby doesn't take her fancy, try a steak meal. —John Sullivan, *Only Fools and Horses – Bible of Peckham*, p. 133, 1999

ruby rose; ruby *noun*

the nose *UK*

Rhyming slang.

- —Ray Puxley, *Cockney Rabbit*, 1992

ruck *noun*

1 a heated argument; a fight *UK*

Possibly derives from obsolete 'rux' (bad temper, anger, passion, noise) or conventional 'ruckus'.

- So one day they had a moody ruck and made out that they had a punch up. —Frank Norman, *Bang To Rights*, p. 60, 1958
- —Tom Hibbert, *Rockspeak!*, p. 136, 1983
- a smattering of London psychos currently following Chelsea because you get a better class of ruck. — Martin King and Martin Knight, *The Naughty Nineties*, p. 51, 1999

2 a rucksack or backpack *US*

- "You ever been under a ruck? You couldn't even pick my ruck up." —John Del Vecchio, *The 13th Valley*, p. 25, 1982

ruck *verb*

1 to fight, especially as part of a gang *UK*

- No hint whatsoever that this was a top soccer mob who within half an hour would be rucking toe to toe with an equally hard and willing south London firm. — Martin King and Martin Knight, *The Naughty Nineties*, p. 119, 1999

2 to masturbate *UK*

Prison slang.

- —John McVicar, *McVicar by Himself*, 1974

ruck and row; ruck *noun*

a cow, especially in the sense a contemptible woman *UK*

Rhyming slang, formed from a combination of **RUCK** (a fight) and 'row' (a disturbance, a violent quarrel).

- [T]he old ruck next door[.] —Ray Puxley, *Cockney Rabbit*, 1992

rucker *noun*

1 a fighter *UK, 1968*

- They're bigger and older and better fighters, proper ruckers who love a knuckle the same as we love music. —John King, *Human Punk*, p. 95, 2000

2 a customer given to complaining and making a fuss *UK*

A barely euphemistic variation of **FUCKER**, possibly influenced by 'ruckus'. Used by second-hand car dealers.

- — *Woman's Own*, 28th February 1968

rucking *noun*

a severe reprimand *UK*

Mostly in prison use.

- — Frank Norman, *Bang to Rights*, 1958
- I've had him, Jimmy Price, on the phone givin me a ruckin, screamin. —J.J. Connolly, *Layer Cake*, p. 209, 2000

ruck up *verb*

to pick up your rucksack and other combat gear and proceed with a march *US*

Used as a modernised **SADDLE UP**, which has definite overtones of cavalry days.

- —Gregory Clark, *Words of the Vietnam War*, p. 448, 1990

ruckus juice *noun*

strong, homemade whisky *US*

- It is called corn liquor, white lightning, sugar whiskey, skully cracker, popskull, bush whiskey, stump, stumphole, 'splo, ruckus juice, radiator whiskey, rotgut, sugarhead, block and tackle, wildcat, panther's breath, tiger's sweat, Sweet spirits of cats a-fighting, alley bourbon, city gin, cool water, happy Sally, deep shaft, jump steady, old horsey, stingo, blue John, red eye, pine top, buckeye bark whiskey and see seven stars.—
- — *Star Tribune (Minneapolis)*, p. 19F, 31st January 1999

ruco *noun*

a boyfriend or husband *US*

Border Spanish used in English conversation by Mexican-Americans; also used in the feminine 'ruca' (a girlfriend or wife).

- —George Carpenter Baker, *Pachuco*, p. 43, January 1950

ruction *noun*

a disturbance; agitation; disorderly behaviour *UK, 1890*

- Farcical ructions among an astronaut's family as they gather in Florida for a shuttle launch. — *New Statesman*, 3rd December 2001
- A man and a woman, whom I thought at first to be in some state of distress, were shouting and banging on one of the toilet doors which was closed...Oblivious that they were creating a ruction[.] — *Irish Times*, 8th May 2001
- —Lise Winer, *Dictionary of the English/Creole of Trinidad & Tobago*, 2003

ruddy *adjective*

used as an intensifier *UK, 1914*

A rhyming euphemism for **BLOODY** that also puns on the colour red.

- That [pantomime] cow's got a ruddy cheek! — *A London Palladium panto joke from the early 1960s*,
- How was I to know wide girls like them would turn me into a ruddy dreamboat, all three of them? —Charles Raven, *Underworld Nights*, p. 119, 1956
- WATSON: You never know your luck, Milly. MILLIGAN: What, with that ruddy mob? —Graeme Kent, *The Queen's Corporal [Six Granada Plays]*, p. 83, 1959
- A ruddy purse full of sovereigns. —Bill Wannan, *Bullockies, Beauts and Bandicoots*, p. 58, 1960
- Like the sound of a ruddy cannon. —Troy Kennedy Martin, *Z Cars*, p. 6, 1962
- 'Ruddy old bushwhacker, that's what he is, missus!' cried Charlie. —Frank Dalby Davison, *Beersheba*, p. 77, 1965
- This ain't no ruddy secret society were running up here. —Jean Brooks, *The Opal Witch*, p. 40, 1967
- Then they started making the slow ones [records], and that's when I dropped out ... ruddy hell, I could have made that myself. —Paul E Willis, *Profane Culture*, p. 39, 1978

ruddy well *adverb*

certainly, definitely *UK, 1933*

- I never ruddy well laid a finger on her. She's a lying bitch —Johnathan Burke, *Pattern of Shadows*, p. 79, 1965
- PETE SAMPRAS and Andre Agassi ought to feel ashamed of themselves. They won't, of course, but they ruddy well should. — *The Daily Telegraph*, 3rd April 1999

rude *noun*

a youth who steals by mugging *UK*

Adapted from **RUDE BOY** (a Jamaican youth/gangster).

- The kids who jack mobile phones we call "rudes" – rude boys. They're working class, mainly black, though not always [...] it's unusual for rudes to jack [to mug] girls [...] On the whole, rudes don't cross the road to jack you[.] — *The Guardian*, p. 9, 27th February 2002

▸ **in the rude**

naked *UK, 1974*

Light-hearted rhyming euphemism for 'in the nude'.

rude *adjective*

1 sexual; sexy *UK*

Upper-class society use. Not to be confused with **IN THE RUDE** (naked); one condition does not necessarily lead to the next.

- —Ann Barr and Peter York, *The Official Sloane Ranger Handbook*, p. 159, 1982
- Spunked (spent) £600 on a black leather Adidas tracksuit. Very "rude". — *FHM*, p. 16, June 2003

2 attractive *UK*

- — Susie Dent, *The Language Report*, p. 78, 2003

3 intense; superior *US*

Collected from fans of heavy metal music by Seamus O'Reilly, January 1995.

4 used of a computer program, poorly designed *US*

- —Guy L. Steele et al., *The Hacker's Dictionary*, p. 111, 1983

rude!; rudeness!; how rude!; how rudeness!

used for suggesting that the speaker has crossed an etiquette line that is better not breached *US*

- —Pamela Munro, *U.C.L.A. Slang*, p. 51, 1989

rude bits *noun*

genitals *AUSTRALIA*

- [W]e discovered a picture of her in Picture magazine, sitting on a bed next to Ignatius Jones, a couple of lamb chops and T-bones strategically positioned over her rude bits. —John Birmingham, *He Died With a Felafel in his Hand*, p. 191, 1994
- —Gretel Killeen, *Hot Buns and Ophelia get shipwrecked*, p. 27, 2001

rude boy; rude bwoy; rudebwai; rudie *noun*

a Jamaican youth associated with gang activities *JAMAICA*

West Indian and UK black patois.

- Rude bwoy never give up their guns. —Prince Buster (C. Campbell), *Too Hot*, 1967
- Wha'ppen, rudebwai? —Karline Smith, *Moss Side Massive*, p. 119, 1994
- In front of the DJ, malevolence pours off a circle of rude bwoys. —Two Fingers, *Puff (Disco Biscuits)*, p. 224, 1996
- He did the old rude-boy badman routine of kissing his teeth[.] —Dave Courtney, *Raving Lunacy*, p. 80, 2000
- Each time a rudie was busted it triggered a mass stampede, very close to a full-scale wilding. —Mick Farren, *Give the Anarchist a Cigarette*, p. 349, 2001

rudeness *noun*

sex *TRINIDAD AND TOBAGO, 1973*

- —Lise Winer, *Dictionary of the English/Creole of Trinidad & Tobago*, 2003

rude parts *noun*

the most obvious erogenous zones: male and female genitals and posteriors, and female breasts *UK*

Upper-class society use; combines **RUDE** (sexual) with 'private *parts*'.

- —Ann Barr and Peter York, *The Official Sloane Ranger Handbook*, p. 159, 1982

ruderalis skunk *noun*

an extremely potent hydroponic marijuana which is a hybrid of ruderalis (a variety of marijuana from Russia) and skunk *UK*

- —Mick Rock, *This Book*, p. 251, 1999

rudery *noun*

rudeness, impolite or risqué speech or conversation; sexually implicit or explicit gestures or behaviour *UK, 1932*

- Referring to September 11, she says how much she admired all the people involved and that she felt so strongly about it that she gave blow jobs to the rescuers. Now her live audience of young things in San Francisco loved it but is the rest of the country ready for such rudery about a group of people who are normally only referred to in saintly terms? — *The Guardian*, 25th June 2002

Rudolph Hess; rudolph *noun*

a *mess* (a failure) *UK*

Rhyming slang, formed from the name of the high-ranking Nazi officer, 1894–1987.

- He's made a right Rudolph of that! —Ray Puxley, *Fresh Rabbit*, 1998

ruff *noun*

a twenty-five cent piece *US*

- —Lou Shelly, *Hepcats Jive Talk Dictionary*, p. 16, 1945

ruff *adjective*

acceptable, good, cool *US*

- — *National Education Association Today*, April 1985: 'A glossary for rents and other squids'
- Consider that Fatboy Slim's real name is Norman. Which sounds more ruff? Rough? R-u-f-f: it means cool. — *Radio Times*, p. 28, 23rd June 2001

ruffie *noun*

Rohypnol™ (flunitrazepam), popularly known as the 'date-rape drug' *US*

- Mexican Valium. Ruffie. Quaalude of the '90s. Nicknames abound for the illegal drug Rohypnol that's now hitting the Texas teen scene at $1 to $5 a pill. — *Newsweek*, p. 8, 3rd July 1995

ruffle *noun*

the passive participant in lesbian sex or a lesbian relationship *US*

- — *American Speech*, p. 58, Spring-Summer 1970: 'Homosexual slang'

ruffles *noun*

▷ **see: ROOFIES**

ruffneck *noun*

a male or female gangster; a non-conformist or rebellious youth; *UK*

A misspelling of 'roughneck' (a thug). West Indian and UK black use into the US via hip-hop culture.

- This book is dedicated to M and ruffnecks everywhere. —Donald Gorgon, *Cop Killer*, 1994
- Raggamuffins. Ravers. Ruffnecks. HARDCORE GIRLS in black like stormtroopin' death squads. —Nick Barlay, *Curvy Lovebox*, p. 7, 1997

ruff-puff *noun*

a South Vietnamese local defence force *US*

RFs were regional forces, PFs were platoon-size village forces. Quick American minds took RF with PF to form 'ruff-puff'.

- They were PF's, Popular Forces, whom everybody called Ruff Puffs. —Larry Heinemann, *Close Quarters*, p. 83, 1977
- None of the Civil Guards, now called the Regional Forces or RF and referred to derisively by the advisors as "Ruff Puffs," who were supposed to be protecting Cu Chi, stirred. —Neil Sheehan, *A Bright Shining Lie*, p. 511, 1988
- —Gregory Clark, *Words of the Vietnam War*, p. 406, 1990

rug *noun*

1 a hairpiece, especially a poorly executed one *US, 1940*

- At ten p.m. a makeup man from NBC dropped a curly headed rug over my short hair[.] —Mickey Spillane, *Return of the Hood*, p. 100, 1964
- —Ellen C. Bellone (Editor), *Dictionary of Slang*, p. 20, 1989
- And despite the fact that Wilfred wore a black Burt Reynolds toupee, and had do so long before Burt bought his first rug. —Seth Morgan, *Fugitive Nights*, p. 20, 1990
- Hey, Bones, looks like you're gonna have a nice scar up there. Maybe these guys can fit you with a rug, cover it up for ya. — *Get Shorty*, 1995

2 pubic hair, especially on a female *US*

- —Roger Blake, *The American Dictionary of Sexual Terms*, p. 183, 1964
- —Dale Gordon, *The Dominion Sex Dictionary*, p. 141, 1967
- — *Maledicta*, p. 131, Summer/Winter 1982: 'Dyke diction: the language of lesbians'

3 in horse racing, a heavy horse blanket *US*

- —Tom Ainslie, *Ainslie's Complete Guide to Thoroughbred Racing*, p. 337, 1976

rugby ball *noun*

a capsule of Temazepam™, a branded tranquillizer *UK, 1990s*

From the shape.

- Street names [...] "rugby balls" or "temazzies". —James Kay and Julian Cohen, *The Parents' Complete Guide to Young People and Drugs*, p. 150, 1998

rug-cutter *noun*

a great time *US*

- "Hey, Brown," he would shout, "ain't this a rug-cutter?" —Norman Mailer, *Advertisements for Myself*, p. 111, 1951

rug-eater *noun*

a lesbian *US*

- —Jim Crotty, *How to Talk American*, p. 136, 1997

rugger bugger *noun*

an enthusiastic sportsman whose character is formed by the aggressive pursuit of masculinity and frequently demonstrated by his boorish behaviour and drunken socialising *SOUTH AFRICA, 1970*

From 'rugger' (rugby football) but encompassing a wider field of endeavours.

- When the rugger bugger marries he talks to his dog more than his wife. — *The Observer*, 14th December 2003

rug joint *noun*

a well appointed, even luxurious gambling operation *US*

- —John Scarne, *Scarne on Dice*, p. 463, 1974

rug munch *noun*
an instance of oral sex on a woman *US*
- After a steamy rug munch and a wicked b.j., they engage in some nut-slappin' mish capped off with – you guess it – major anal penetration. — *Adult Video News*, p. 128, August 1995

rug-muncher *noun*
a lesbian *US*
From the image of oral sex as 'munching a hairpiece'.
- Maybe that's just what dykes like to do, fuck around with straight guys' heads, just so she can go back to her little rug-muncher club and have a good laugh with all her man-hating cronies about how fucking stupid and easily duped men are! — *Chasing Amy*, 1997

rug out *verb*
to endure a difficult situation *US*
An awkward attempt to render 'rugged' as a verb.
- [E]ven one or two drinks, on top of staying out late... when you get in the gym, you wish you didn't do that. But, you know, you just rugged it out. — *Hip-Hop Connection*, p. 13, July 2002

rug rat *noun*
a young child *US, 1970*
A bit derisive.
- — Kenn "Naz" Young, *Naz's Underground Dictionary*, p. 55, 1973
- Still in Topsiders, mind you, but driving an Audi now and sending a couple of rug rats to the French-American school and swapping notes on their Cuisnarts[.] — Armistead Maupin, *Tales of the City*, p. 245, 1978
- They fuck like minks, raise rugrats, and live happily ever after. — *Basic Instinct*, 1992
- She seems determined to get those rugrats off welfare and with your help I'll bet she does it. — *Something About Mary*, 1998

rug up *verb*
in horse racing, to cover the horse with a blanket after a workout or race *UK*
- — Rita Cannon, *Let's Go Racing*, p. 73, 1948

ruined *adjective*
drunk *UK*
- — *e-cyclopaedia*, 20th March 2002

rule *noun*
▶ **on the rule**
of a prisoner, segregated from the general prison population for that prisoner's protection *UK*
A reference to rule 43 which is, according to HM Prison Service in 2003: 'A now defunct rule that allowed the segregation of prisoners'.
- When I first saw the men on the rule – or the "nonces", as they were collectively known – the first thing that struck me was that they were a fucking ugly looking bunch. — Ken Lukowiak, *Marijuana Time*, p. 262, 2000
- Ricky stood his ground and refused to go "on the rule"[.] — *The Guardian*, 11th May 2000

rule *verb*
used as an expression of supremacy for the preceding collective or plural noun(s) *US*
- You're on top; the greatest, the boss, the leader of the pack; your word is the law because YOU RULE! — Hy Lit, *Hy Lit's Unbelievable Dictionary of Hip Words for Groovy People*, p. 33, 1968
- This guy rules. — *Airheads*, 1994
- — Connie Eble (Editor), *UNC-CH Campus Slang*, p. 7, Spring 1994
- Fuckin' Rod Tidwell – You rule! You rule! — *Jerry Maguire*, 1996
- Cigarettes and beer rule! Huh huh. — Mike Judge and Joe Stillman, *Beavis and Butt-Head Do America*, p. 91, 1997
- — Vann Wesson, *Generation X Field Guide and Lexicon*, p. 168, 1997

rule forty-three; rule 43; the rule *noun*
in prison, a sex offender, or other prisoner, kept apart from the main prison community for 'safety of self or others' *UK*
- — Angela Devlin, *Prison Patter*, p. 23, 1996

rule of five *noun*
a piece of (unofficial) medical lore: if more than five orifices are obscured by plastic tubing then a patient's condition is critical *UK*
- — Adam T. Fox, St Mary's Hospital, London, 10th October 2002

rum *noun*
1 an unsophisticated, unaware person *US*
- They're not a rum, you can't consider them an idiot or a rum, and you can't consider them a character[.] — Bruce Jackson, *Outside the Law*, p. 156, 1972
- — Kenn "Naz" Young, *Naz's Underground Dictionary*, p. 54, 1973

2 a prisoner deemed inferior or too odd by other prisoners *US*
- — Bruce Jackson, *Outside the Law*, p. 59, 1972: 'Glossary'

3 a drunkard *US*
- If that rum is still outside, tell him I said to get the hell away from here. — Clarence Cooper Jr, *The Scene*, p. 93, 1960

rum *adjective*
strange; eccentric; disreputable; questionable *UK, 1774*
- I always knew Hitler was a rum fellow. — *Sunday Times*, 2nd February 2002

rum and roti *noun*
▷ see: **ROTI AND RUM**

rumble *noun*
1 a fight, especially between teenage gangs *US*
- Their activities now range from fighting each other for the pure love of bloodshed (called "rumbles") to highway robbery. — Jack Lait and Lee Mortimer, *New York Confidential*, p. 105, 1948
- — *American Speech*, May 1955
- A rumble! That's the only way. — Max Shulman, *Rally Round the Flag, Boys!*, p. 230, 1957
- And the captain promised me there wouldn't be any rumbles in here. — Chester Himes, *A Rage in Harlem*, p. 207, 1957
- The second test, we had to come off with a rumble – in another town – in other words, a gang war. — Willard Motely, *Let No Man Write My Epitaph*, p. 208, 1958
- Ray was the toast of Paris and although he had a rumble coming up in London in ten weeks with a stud named Turpin, he did his rehearsing in the south of France balling on the beaches and casinos. — Babs Gonzales, *Movin' On Down De Line*, p. 16, 1975

2 a wild party *US*
- — Collin Baker et al., *College Undergraduate Slang Study Conducted at Brown University*, p. 186, 1968

3 a difficult encounter with law enforcement *US*
- — Bruce Jackson, *Outside the Law*, p. 59, 1972: 'Glossary'

4 a concerted police search for narcotics *US*
- — *New York Times Magazine*, p. 88, 16th March 1958

rumble *verb*
1 to fight *US*
- One guy leaning on the bar would make a friendly remark about his neighbor's tie or the style of his haircut, and in nothing flat each one was cussing up a breeze about the other's mother until they began to rumble. — Mezz Mezzrow, *Really the Blues*, p. 70, 1946
- When Ray cut out to London to rumble, he only took his key five cats and left the others at the Claridge Hotel. — Babs Gonzales, *Movin' On Down De Line*, p. 16, 1975
- One time I had to rumble a deaf-mute guy. On me like white-on-rice. — Edwin Torres, *Carlito's Way*, p. 13, 1975

2 in circus and carnival usage, to spoil something *US*
- — Don Wilmeth, *The Language of American Popular Entertainment*, p. 229, 1981

3 to come to an understanding or realisation of something that has been concealed *UK, 1886*
- BBC rumbled as African orphan prank falls flat. — *The Guardian*, 20th November 2000

Rumble in the Jungle *nickname*
the October 1974 heavyweight championship fight between Muhammed Ali and George Foreman in Kinshasa, Zaire, in which Ali knocked Foreman out in the 8th round *US, 1974*
- — Louis Phillips and Burnham Holmes, *The Complete Book of Sports Nicknames*, p. 224, 1998

rumbleseat *noun*
a truck that is not equipped with a citizens' band radio following a truck that is *US*
- — Wayne Floyd, *Jason's Authentic Dictionary of CB Slang*, p. 26, 1976

rumble-tumble *noun*
scrambled eggs *UK*
Originally military.
- — Nigel Hankin, *Hanklyn-Janklyn*, 2003

rum blossom *noun*
a red welt produced from excessive consumption of alcohol *US*
- "[H]e's the kind of guy that doesn't exactly blend into a crowd, with that big nose of his all decorated with rum-blossoms and that scar he got on his cheek[.]" — George V. Higgins, *The Judgment of Deke Hunter*, p. 30, 1976

rum boy *noun*
a drunk *BAHAMAS*
- — John A. Holm, *Dictionary of Bahamian English*, p. 172, 1982

rum, bum and bacca; rum, bum and baccy *noun*
the mythic three graces of a sailor's life *UK*
A (presumed) later variation of 'beer, bum and bacca'. *Rum, Bum and Concertina*, a pun on 'wine, women and song', is the title of the second part of George Melly's autobiography published in 1977. In 1992, the Pogues, reflecting an earlier view of naval life, released an album entitled *Rum, Sodomy and the Lash*.
• — *Sunday Mirror*, 18th March 1973

rumdum; rum-dumb *noun*
a drunk *US, 1891*
• We get up there and sure enough there's the rumdum, some old panhandler who when not mooching used to hang around the lions in front of the Public Library feeding the pigeons. — Bernard Wolfe, *The Late Risers*, p. 266, 1954
• The rum-dumbs would yank themselves together and suddenly remember they'd eaten nothing in ten hours. — Robert Sylvester, *No Cover Charge*, p. 217, 1956

rumdummed *adjective*
extremely drunk *US, 1891*
• Red can't be rumdummed up tonight. This is one night he has to blow. — Ross Russell, *The Sound*, p. 239, 1961

rum goblet; rum goggles *noun*
a large Adam's apple *TRINIDAD AND TOBAGO*
• — Lise Winer, *Dictionary of the English/Creole of Trinidad & Tobago*, 2003

rumin *noun*
▷ see: RUM'UN

rummy *noun*
an alcoholic *US, 1851*
• At this rate, I'll end up being a fuckin' rummy, he warned himself. — Donald Goines, *Never Die Alone*, p. 205, 1974
• He didn't mean to scare the old fart; probably should've just let him go on thinking he was a rummy. — Seth Morgan, *Homeboy*, 1990

rummy *adjective*
1 prone to drink too much, if not alcoholic *US, 1834*
• She and Frannie Halcyon had absolutely nothing to catch up on. Why was this sweet, but rummy, society dowager talking to her like an equal? — Armistead Maupin, *Further Tales of the City*, p. 78, 1982
2 poor; inferior; bad *US*
• Anyway, it was rummy luck for the bastards in this accident. — James T. Farrell, *Saturday Night*, p. 42, 1947

rumored *adjective*
married *UK*
English gypsy use, from Romany *romer* (to marry).
• — Jimmy Stockin, *On The Cobbles*, p. 11, 2000

rump *verb*
to cheat someone *UK*
• The deal was over 2 million worth of bearer bonds for cash and both sides were doing their best to rump the other. — Lenny McLean, *The Guv'nor*, 1998
• "Fuckin' poxy tealeafing [thieving] cows," he goes. "They only fuckin' rumped me on the fuckin' change again them fuckin' cows." — Jeremy Cameron, *Brown Bread in Wengen*, p. 111, 1999

rump bump *noun*
in a sexual dance, a pelvic thrust that emphasises the buttocks moving backwards *US*
• At one point, Mrs. De Carlo turned her back on the enchanted customers to give them some rump bumps that had them shouting for more. — *Confidential*, p. 17, July 1956
• Nor did she give right and left rump bumps that had the men cheering for the overweight Detroit woman who placed fourth. — *Hartford (Connecticut) Courtant*, p. D1, 2nd October 1993

rumper *noun*
in hot rodding, a powerful engine *US*
• — John Lawlor, *How to Talk Car*, p. 89, 1965

rumpo *noun*
sexual intercourse *UK, 1986*
Possibly influenced by (or vice versa) Rambling Syd Rumpo, an innuendo-laden character played by Kenneth Williams in *Round the Horne*, BBC radio, 1965–69.
• Her smell, that wonderful Kara fragrance, played around his nose till it twitched. He had a fleeting image of the cartoon kids in the old Bisto ads. Ah, rumpo, he thought to himself. — Garry Bushell, *The Face*, p. 55, 2001

rump-ordained *adjective*
used for describing a preacher who has no formal theological training or denominational affiliation *US*
• An offshoot of the gambling was a five-dollar-for-ten-dollar loan-sharking business which left a rump-ordained Southern Baptist minister from Oklahoma on his way to being a rich Christian. — Earl Thompson, *Tattoo*, p. 293, 1974

rumpty *adjective*
in poor repair; below standard *NEW ZEALAND*
• It was a pretty rumpty wicket, we didn't take good advantage of it and they did. — *Dominion*, p. 36, 20th September 1995

rumpty pumpty; rumpty *noun*
intimate sexual activity *UK*
A variation of RUMPY-PUMPY with a nursery rhyme feel thanks to Humpty Dumpty.
• [T]he tabloids' latest subtle code word [...] as in "Mike Reid back for rumpty with Babs" – the Sun. — David Rowan, *A Glossary for the 90s*, p. 26, 1998

rumpus *noun*
a brawl; a riot *UK, 1764*
• If the boy got hurt, or if there was any kind of rumpus with the white chick in it, there wouldn't be any way to stop a riot[.] — Chester Himes, *If He Hollers Let Him Go*, p. 77, 1945

rumpy-pumpy *noun*
sexual intercourse *UK*
• — Tom Hibbert, *Rockspeak!*, p. 136, 1983
• I wish I had a horny young man here with me now, who'd really appreciate a nice bitta rumpy-pumpy. — J.J. Connolly, *Layer Cake*, p. 212, 2000

rum-runner *noun*
an importer, transporter and/or purveyor of illegal alcohol, especially rum *US, 1920*
• According to Carroll Mealy, capable and efficient head of the Alcoholic Tax Unit, the rum-runners take this stuff to Washington in 1940 Fords, with Cadillac or racing motors in place of original power. — Jack Lait and Lee Mortimer, *Washington Confidential*, p. 130, 1951

rum-sucker *noun*
a heavy drinker *TRINIDAD AND TOBAGO, 1845*
• — Lise Winer, *Dictionary of the English/Creole of Trinidad & Tobago*, 2003

rumty *noun*
an admirable or excellent person or thing *NEW ZEALAND*
• — David McGill, *David McGill's Complete Kiwi Slang Dictionary*, p. 94, 1998

rum'un; rumun; rumin *noun*
especially in Tasmania, an eccentric person; a character; a scallywag *AUSTRALIA*
• — Harvey E. Ward, *Down Under Without Blunder*, p. 45, 1967

run *noun*
1 a group motorcyle excursion *US*
• A run is a lot of things to the Angels: a party, an exhibition and an exercise in solidarity. — Hunter S. Thompson, *Hell's Angels*, p. 116, 1966
• A motorcyle run is a get-together; a moving power. It's a real show of power and solidarity when you're a Hell's Angel. — Ralph "Sonny" Barger, *Hell's Angel*, p. 1, 2000
2 a period of extended amphetamine use *US*
• — Ruth Bronsteen, *The Hippy's Handbook*, p. 15, 1967
• Speed runs can extend to several months, but usually they are self-limiting and last from 2–3 days. — Geoffrey Froner, *Digging for Diamonds*, p. 53, 1989

▸ **on the run**
escaping from justice; being a fugitive *UK, 1887*
• Fluffies on the run as spikies win battle of the streets. — *The Guardian*, 14th April 2001

run *verb*
1 to associate; to socialise *US*
• I found myself running with a literary ex-pug, a pistol-packing rabbi, and a peewee jockey whose onliest riding crop was a stick of marihuana. — Mezz Mezzrow, *Really the Blues*, p. 69, 1946
• Some big Afro-wearin' gangsters. My dad used to run with 'em. — *Menace II Society*, 1993
2 to smuggle something *UK, 1706*
• — *American Speech*, p. 97, May 1956

▸ **run a pot**
in poker, to make a sustained, pre-planned bluff on a hand *US*
• — Albert H. Morehead, *The Complete Guide to Winning Poker*, p. 272, 1967

▸ **run blues**

to use blue lights in a car's tail lights *US*

- —Jennifer Blowdryer, *Modern English*, 1985

▸ **run hot**

to drive with sirens and flashing lights activated *US*

- There is in fact, no scientific proof that "running hot" – street slang for operating with lights and siren – saves lives.—*USA Today*, p. 1A, 21st March 2002

▸ **run like a hairy goat**

(of a racehorse) to run poorly in a race *AUSTRALIA, 1941*

- When a chosen horse 'runs like a hairy goat' both sexes 'do their dough'[.]—Nancy Keesing, *Lily on the Dustbin*, p. 61, 1982

▸ **run rings round**

to defeat someone with absolute ease *UK, 1891*

- Mr Putin was anything but candid. In fact, he ran rings round the US leader.—*The Guardian*, 5th July 2001

▸ **run speed limit**

to do something with great speed *US*

Hawaiian youth usage.

- —Douglas Simonson, *Pidgin to da Max Hana Hou*, 1982

▸ **run to seed**

with age or lack of care, to become ill-kempt, shabby or undesirable *UK, 1837*

The imagery of the garden.

- Imagination gone mad, fantasy run to seed.—*The Guardian*, 30th November 2002

▸ **run your mouth**

to talk too much *US*

- There was no way to stop the man from running his mouth, from telling one lie after another.—Odie Hawkins, *Chicago Hustle*, p. 7, 1977

▸ **run your neck**

to make threats or boasts which you are not prepared to back up with actions *US*

- —Jim Goad, *Jim Goad's Glossary of Northwestern Prison Slang*, December 2001

runabout *noun*

a small car *UK, 1900*

- [F]rom the front, you could almost mistake the car for a routine runabout[.]—*The Guardian*, 17th December 2002

run along *verb*

to depart; often used as a gentle imperative *UK, 1902*

- You'd better run along now and get to bed! It's way after your bedtime.—Adeline Yen Mah, *Chinese Cinderella*, p. 19, 1999

run-around *noun*

▸ **give the run-around; get the run-around**

to treat someone, or be treated, with contempt, or so as to serve a mere whim; to cause someone trouble, or be caused trouble *US, 1924*

- Scotland Yard detectives [...] consider they have been given the run-around by the royal household in recent weeks.—*The Guardian*, 4th December 2002

run, chicken, run *noun*

the Royal Canadian Regiment *CANADA*

Formed from the initials RCR. Note that 'chicken' does not insinuate cowardice. Rather this insult alludes to a story which alleges that a member of the regiment was found, in flagrante delicto, with a chicken. Members of the RCR counter that he was a cook.

- —Tom Langeste, *Words on the Wing*, p. 238, 1995

rundown *noun*

a complete explanation *US*

- Those pimps back in the joint sure knew basic whorology. I was glad my ears had flapped to all those rundowns.—Iceberg Slim (Robert Beck), *Pimp*, p. 80, 1969

runes *noun*

in computing, any esoteric display character or computer language *US*

- —Eric S. Raymond, *The New Hacker's Dictionary*, p. 307, 1991

run-fast *noun*

on the railways, oil *US*

- —Norman Carlisle, *The Modern Wonder Book of Trains and Railroading*, p. 262, 1946

rung-in *adjective*

substituted; phoney *AUSTRALIA*

- I bet no other eagle ever brought in that much as a rung-in turkey. —Patsy Adam-Smith, *Folklore of the Australian Railwaymen*, p. 152, 1969

run-in *noun*

1 an argumentative or violent encounter *UK*

- the run in with the two coppers in Ponty—David Peace, *Nineteen Seventy-Four*, p. 95, 1999

2 a concealed location used by criminals for the division or transfer of recently stolen goods *UK*

- The normal method was to hire a van from a small lorry-owner, run the van to the warehouse, break in, load the van, take the contents to a "run-in" – usually a shed or a garage in the central London area – and return the van.—John Gosling, *The Ghost Squad*, 1959

run in *verb*

to arrest someone *US*

- —Kenn "Naz" Young, *Naz's Underground Dictionary*, p. 54, 1973

run, Johnny, run *noun*

inexpensive loose cigarette tobacco *US*

Formed from the initials of the R.J. Reynolds tobacco company.

- —Frank Prewitt and Francis Schaeffer, *Vacaville Vocabulary*, 1961–1962
- —Charles Shafer, *Folk Speech in Texas Prisons*, p. 213, 1990

run letter *noun*

a final deportation letter from the US Immigration and Naturalisation Service *US*

- They are noncitizens who either have skipped deportation hearings or disappeared after receiving a final deportation notice – known in street slang as a "run letter," so common is that reaction to its receipt.—*Buffalo (New York) News*, p. B4, 14th January 2002

runner *noun*

1 in an illegal betting operation, a person who physically collects and pays off bets placed with sheet writers *US*

- He don't come around hisself. De runners do all the work.—Mickey Spillane, *I, The Jury*, p. 43, 1947
- I mean today's last number. Ain't you Rine the runner?—Ralph Ellison, *Invisible Man*, p. 491, 1947
- Police-sellers, bookmakers' runners, reefer peddlers and junk salesmen are employed by an organization which protects them also. —Jack Lait and Lee Mortimer, *Washington Confidential*, p. 48–49, 1951
- The daily small army of runners got ten percent of the money they turned in[.]—Malcolm X and Alex Haley, *The Autobiography of Malcolm X*, p. 85, 1964
- If you could be a numbers runner, you'd make about seventy-five dollars a week[.]—Claude Brown, *Manchild in the Promised Land*, p. 191, 1965
- At that time the numbers were controlled by "Jews" in Newark and they used colored men as runners.—Babs Gonzales, *I Paid My Dues*, p. 7, 1967
- I think the flat is a check-in station for so called runners and writers who turn in their bet books and cash, less their earned twenty percent.—Iceberg Slim (Robert Beck), *Mama Black Widow*, p. 97, 1969
- I was glad Daddy was a number runner and not just hanging around the corners like those men.—Louise Meriwether, *Daddy Was a Number Runner*, p. 15, 1970
- Etienne has the best runners in Harlem.—Edwin Torres, *Carlito's Way*, p. 30, 1975
- He was a numbers runner just a few years older than my fourteen. —Piri Thomas, *Stories from El Barrio*, p. 54, 1978
- When his runners and sheet writers called he told them to sit on their totals another day or so and he'd get back to them.—Elmore Leonard, *Pronto*, p. 44, 1993

2 a prison inmate who collects dues for a baron (a powerful criminal whose influence is built on illegal trading) *UK*

- —Home Office, *Glossary of Terms and Slang Common in Penal Establishments*, July 1978

3 someone who carries illegal drugs between dealer and purchaser *US*

- Normally, a runner makes $250 and he's on his own.—Bruce Jackson, *In the Life*, p. 164, 1972
- They've got Roy booked as Mister Big and me and Tony as just simple dumb runners, the Joeys as the top lawman had called us. —J.J. Connolly, *Know Your Enemy [britpulp]*, p. 159, 1999

4 a clerk or collector for a street bookmaker *UK, 1934*

- Watching the increasingly animated signals of Graeme Souness, who might have been auditioning for the job of a bookie's runner, proved a good deal more entertaining[.]—*The Guardian*, 3rd March 2003

5 somebody sent to buy alcohol for others *US*

- —*American Speech*, p. 276, December 1963: 'American Indian student slang'

6 in the television and film industries, an errand-running production assistant *US*

- —Ralph S. Singleton, *Filmaker's Dictionary*, p. 143, 1990

7 a deserter from the armed services; an escapee from prison or borstal *UK, 1959*

- —Angela Devlin, *Prison Patter*, p. 100, 1996

8 in the language surrounding the Grateful Dead, a fan who queues before a show and then quickly claims space for friends who will follow *US*

- —David Shenk and Steve Silberman, *Skeleton Key*, p. 252, 1994

▸ do a runner
to escape by running away; to abscond; to leave hastily *UK, 1981*

- You think I'm going to do a runner?—Anthony Masters, *Minder*, p. 8, 1984
- Steven's does a runner.— *The Guardian*, 7th February 2002

runner and rider *noun*
cider *UK*
Rhyming slang, from the vocabulary of horse racing.

- —Ray Puxley, *Cockney Rabbit*, 1992

runners *noun*
1 sneakers, trainers *AUSTRALIA, 1988*

- —Maureen Brooks and Joan Ritchie, *Tassie Terms*, p. 120, 1995

2 any shoes *US*

- —Connie Eble (Editor), *UNC-CH Campus Slang*, p. 5, Fall 1995

▸ the runners
diarrhoea *US*

- "I got the runners. They came on all of a sudden," I said, going inside, pushing past the men who were coming out.—Horace McCoy, *Kiss Tomorrow Good-bye*, p. 9, 1948

running *noun*
1 diarrhoea *BAHAMAS*

- —John A. Holm, *Dictionary of Bahamian English*, p. 173, 1982

2 MDMA, the recreational drug best known as ecstasy *UK, 1998*

- —Mike Haskins, *Drugs*, p. 290, 2003

running buddy *noun*
a close friend and confederate in crime *US*

- Her running buddy was a burnt-brown color, with red hair, of all things.—Louise Meriwether, *Daddy Was a Number Runner*, p. 26, 1970
- The dope man wants to know why I ain't doing with my running buddy[.]—Vernon E. Smith, *The Jones Men*, p. 150, 1974

running dog *noun*
a servant of the ruling class, subservient to counter-revolutionary powers *US, 1937*
From Chinese communist terminology originally applied to the Kuomintang.

- The People shall smash the glutton roaches running this decadent society and, along with the directing of the Black Panther Party, halt these running dogs and gain true liberation for all.— *The Black Panther*, p. 14, 6th April 1969

running partner *noun*
a close friend joined for criminal and social activities *US*

- For that whole time, I didn't hang out with any of my old running partners.—Claude Brown, *Manchild in the Promised Land*, p. 94, 1965
- Simple pimps have "running partners," and are rarely seen alone, while the boss player almost always arrives and leaves by himself. —Christina and Richard Milner, *Black Players*, p. 104, 1972

runnings *noun*
1 diarrhoea *ANTIGUA AND BARBUDA*

- —Richard Allsopp, *Dictionary of Caribbean English Usage*, p. 482, 1996

2 a sexually transmitted infection with discharge *TRINIDAD AND TOBAGO*

- —Lise Winer, *Dictionary of the English/Creole of Trinidad & Tobago*, 2003

3 whatever is happening or is planned to happen *UK*

- Listen, I've got runnings to sort out so I'd better start making tracks.—Donald Gorgon, *Cop Killer*, p. 22, 1994

run-off *noun*
a prostitute who has attempted to break off from her pimp *US*

- — *Washington Post*, p. C5, 7th November 1993

run of outs *noun*
a succession of losses or failures *AUSTRALIA, 1953*

- After the run of outs I've been having lately, Sheridan's starting to get the crazy notion I'm accident prone.—W.R. Bennett, *Night Intruder*, p. 12, 1962
- —Roy Higgins and Tom Prior, *The Jockey Who Laughed*, p. 13, 1982
- —Roy Slaven (John Doyle), *Five South Coast Seasons*, p. 81, 1992

run-out *noun*
a well-worn tyre *US*

- — *American Speech*, p. 273, December 1961: 'Northwest truck drivers' language'

run out *verb*
▸ run out of road
to fail to keep control of a motor vehicle, especially on a bend, and consequently be involved in an accident *UK*

- —Peter Chippindale, *The British CB Book*, p. 158, 1981

▸ run out of steam
to lose vigour *UK, 1961*

- Britain's long retail boom was indeed running out of steam.— *The Guardian*, 13th August 2002

run-out powder *noun*
the depature of a gambler who has not paid off his gambling debts *US*

- —John Scarne, *Scarne's Guide to Modern Poker*, p. 289, 1979

run-over days *noun*
the first three days of the bleed period of the menstrual cycle *BAHAMAS*

- —John A. Holm, *Dictionary of Bahamian English*, p. 173, 1982

runs *noun*
a sexually transmitted infection with discharge *TRINIDAD AND TOBAGO*

- —Thurston Scott, *Cure it with Honey*, p. xx, 1951

▸ the runs
a case of diarrhoea *US*

- Do you have the runs again?—Rita Ciresi, *Pink Slip*, p. 347, 1999

Runs Empty Only *noun*
a truck manufactured by REO *US*
A back-formation.

- —Montie Tak, *Truck Talk*, p. 135, 1971

runt *noun*
1 in circus and carnival usage, a dwarf or midget *US*

- —Joe McKennon, *Circus Lingo*, p. 80, 1980
- —Don Wilmeth, *The Language of American Popular Entertainment*, p. 230, 1981

2 in poker, a pairless hand *US*

- —Irwin Steig, *Common Sense in Poker*, p. 187, 1963

runts and cunts *noun*
used for expressing disapproval of the composition of the US armed forces in the decades after Vietnam *US*

- Bad Dog, my ass. Five foot three in platforms. It's what the navy's come to: runts 'n cunts.—Joseph Wambaugh, *Finnegan's Week*, p. 31, 1993

runty *adjective*
delicate; sickly *IRELAND*

- [T]he wee runty face on you[.]—Shane Connaughton, *A Border Station*, p. 99, 1989

runway *noun*
a generous dose of powdered cocaine arranged in a line for snorting *UK*
A clever play on a conventional 'runway' (a long straight path used to achieve lift-off).

- The girls sat me down and chopped up two huge runways on a mirror[.]—Wayne Anthony, *Spanish Highs*, p. 27, 1999

run-what-you-brung *noun*
a drag race between amateur drivers driving their own cars *US, 1950s to 70s*

- —Ed Radlauer, *Drag Racing Pix Dix*, p. 48, 1970

ruof; rofe; roaf; rouf *noun*
four *UK, 1863*
Back slang.

rupert *noun*
1 an army officer; any young upper-class type *UK*
A generic based on the perception that Rupert is a popular name in 'quality' families, but note another military use of 'rupert' as 'the penis'. Current usage seems to date from the 1970s.

- [T]here are plenty of first-class Ruperts. Unfortunately, there are also plenty of pricks[.]—Chris Ryan, *Stand By, Stand By*, p. 147, 1996

2 the penis *UK, 1961*
Military; possibly related to the sense as officer.

ruptured duck *noun*
the US armed forces insignia designating honourable discharge *US*
- — *American Speech*, p. 153, April 1946: 'GI words from the separation center and proctology ward'

rush *noun*
1 a sudden and powerful sense of euphoria or energy *US*
Figurative use of the drug term.
- There simply is no rushing thumbing – although I can get a rush off a car stopping for me. — Marge Piaggio, *The Last Supplement to the Whole Earth Catalog*, p. 36, March 1971
- It feels "out there." A major rush. — *Bull Durham*, 1988
- Imagine being one of those guys, legends, and the rush you'd get performing for all those people. — Elmore Leonard, *Be Cool*, p. 265, 1999
- He couldn't remember when he'd last had a rush like that without chemical assistance. — John Williams, *Cardiff Dead*, p. 103, 2000

2 the sudden onset of drug intoxication *US*
- Cocaine and bombitas are both stimulants and combined with heroin, a depressant, they produce an electrifying "rush" or "flash" far more pleasurable to the addict than heroin alone. — James Mills, *The Panic in Needle Park*, p. 36, 1966
- I don't get strung out on any speed; there's no chemical I need. I like the buzz. I like the rush. — Nicholas Von Hoffman, *We are the People Our Parents Warned Us Against*, p. 151, 1967

3 amyl, butyl or isobutyl nitrite *UK*
From the sudden effects of the drug.
- — Angela Devlin, *Prison Patter*, p. 101, 1996
- Street names [...] rock hard, rush, snapper, stag[.] — James Kay and Julian Cohen, *The Parents' Complete Guide to Young People and Drugs*, p. 144, 1998

4 cocaine *UK*
- — Mike Haskins, *Drugs*, p. 281, 2003

5 in poker, an unusual streak of good cards *US*
- — David M. Hayano, *Poker Faces*, p. 187, 1982

rush *verb*
1 to charge an amount of money *UK*

2 to charge for goods or services, especially to overcharge or cheat *UK, 1887*
- What's wrong with rushing the Yanks a pony [£25]? — Andrew Nickolds, *Back to Basics*, p. 16, 1994

3 to be infatuated with someone *BARBADOS*
- Who's the girl your brother's rushing now? — Frank A. Collymore, *Barbadian Dialect*, p. 94, 1965

4 to make sexual advances *TRINIDAD AND TOBAGO, 1934*
- — Lise Winer, *Dictionary of the English/Creole of Trinidad & Tobago*, 2003

▸ **rush the knocks**
in drug sales, to ignore the order of customers and make a sale *US*
- An informal code of conduct mandates dealers at popular drug spots take turns catering to customers, testified Officer Jame "Mike" Gant, a police narcotics expert. Cauley was known to "rush the knocks," street slang for cutting into the rotation and snagging clients out of order. — *Oakland (California) Tribune*, 18th October 2002

rush-and-snatch job *noun*
a search and rescue mission without the complications of enemy fire *US*
- None of the survivors had been down in areas that had been heavily defended. They had been quick rush-and-snatch jobs. — Gerry Carroll, *North S*A*R*, p. 34, 1991

Rushina *noun*
in homosexual usage, a personification of amyl nitrite or butyl nitrite *US*
From **RUSH**, a popular name for amyl nitrite.
- — *Maledicta*, p. 227, Winter 1980: '"Lovely, blooming, fresh and gay": the onomastics of camp'

rushy *adjective*
descriptive of an energetic and euphoric reaction to MDMA, the recreational drug best known as ecstasy *UK*
- "Oh, they're mental," said Maddy smiling. "You get flickery eyes and they're rushy as anything." — Colin Butts, *Is Harry on the Boat?*, p. 207, 1997

Russell Crowe *noun*
an attack *UK*
Rhyming slang for **GO**, formed from the name of the notoriously pugnacious New Zealand-born film actor (b.1964).
- [T]o have a Russell Crowe at someone. — Susie Dent, *The Language Report*, p. 98, 2003

Russell Harty *noun*
a party *UK*
Rhyming slang, formed from the name of the television presenter (1934–88) and noted as not having survived its inspiration by Ray Puxley, *Cockney Rabbit*, 1992.

Russian boots *noun*
leg irons *US*
- — Vincent J. Monteleone, *Criminal Slang*, p. 198, 1949

Russian duck *noun*
an act of sexual intercourse *UK*
Rhyming slang for **FUCK**.
- — Ray Puxley, *Cockney Rabbit*, 1992

Russian jack *noun*
a homemade alcoholic beverage made from sugar, yeast, water and flavouring *FIJI, 1984*
Recorded by Jan Tent.

Russian roast *noun*
a sexual act in which a woman performs oral sex on a man who is, at the same time, being sodomised by another man *UK, 2004*
- — *Popbitch*, 27th May 2004

Russian roulette *noun*
LSD *UK*
- — Angela Devlin, *Prison Patter*, p. 101, 1996

Russki; Russky; Rusky *noun*
a Russian *UK, 1858*
- What's the Russky doing? — Mickey Spillane, *One Lonely Night*, p. 124, 1951
- The only excitement came when Sly beat the huge Russky like a mule. — Hunter S. Thompson, *Generation of Swine*, p. 27, 16 December 1985
- They're not stable, sir. The Russkies. — John Milne, *Alive and Kicking*, p. 97, 1998

Russki *adjective*
Russian *UK, 1859*
- A weasel-faced guy complied; I popped one into the chamber and tucked my Russki roulette piece in my belt. — James Ellroy, *Hollywood Nocturnes*, p. 284, 1994

rust *noun*
faecal stains in the underwear or on a toilet bowl *CANADA*
- — Bill Casselman, *Canadian Sayings*, p. 44, 2002

rust belt *noun*
the northern central US, highly industrialised prior to the economic decline in the US in the 1980s *US*
- Breaking the Rust Belt loose [Headline] — *Milwaukee Journal*, 13th March 1987

rust bucket *noun*
an old, dilapidated vehicle *AUSTRALIA, 1965*
- — Peter Chippindale, *The British CB Book*, p. 161, 1981
- Bit of a rust bucket, but it's good. — Kathy Lette, *Girls' Night Out*, p. 119, 1987
- — Jim Crotty, *How to Talk American*, p. 37, 1997
- — Shane Maloney, *Nice Try*, p. 27, 1998

rustle up *verb*
to obtain something; to organise the supply of something *US, 1891*
- Knowing that every student loves a freebie, Paramount also rustled up a few 'goody bags' that were used to promote the events. — *The Guardian*, 17th January 2004

rusty *adjective*
of a skill, having deteriorated as a result of lack of practice *UK, 1796*
- [I]f, like me, your Chinese is a bit rusty[.] — *The Guardian*, 12th June 2004

rusty bullet wound; rusty bullet hole; rusty sheriff's badge; rusty washer *noun*

the anus *UK*

'Rusty' (brown, the colour associated with the anus) plus a visual metaphor.

- ["]Bradley is referring to the rusty bullet-hole," said Mikey. "The what?" Mario was still struggling. "The chocolate starfish." —Colin Butts, *Is Harry on the Boat?*, p. 21, 1997
- Place two fingers up her rusty bullet hole, then pour baby oil down them. — *GQ*, p. 117, July 2001

rusty dusty *noun*

the buttocks *US, 1942*

- —Robert S. Gold, *A Jazz Lexicon*, p. 259, 1964

rusty fuck *noun*

a notional object of no value whatsoever *US*

- —John D. Bell et al., *Loosely Speaking*, p. 9, 1969

rusty trombone *noun*

a sexual technique in which a man receives oral stimulation of his anus and manual stimulation of his penis at the same time and from the same person *US*

Imagery which becomes apparent if you picture the penis as a trombone's slide and the anus as its mouthpiece.

- WHISKY LIPS: ready to get all wet with your juices. Ever play the rusty trombone? JADEDWOM: what's that? WHISKYLIPS: that's when you blow my a@@ and reach around and stroke. —Cris Burks, *SilkyDreamGirl*, p. 182, 2002

Ruud Gullit *noun*

dismissal from employment *UK*

Rhyming slang for **BULLET**, formed from the name of the Dutch footballer (b.1962) when he was given 'the bullet' as player-manager of Chelsea football club in 1998.

- —Ray Puxley, *Fresh Rabbit*, 1998

RV; r.v. *noun*

a recreational vehicle or large motor home *US, 1967*

- You want to get out of the r.v. business, wasting your talent selling motor homes. —Elmore Leonard, *Touch*, p. 34, 1977

Ryan Giggs *noun*

lodgings *UK*

Rhyming slang for **DIGS**, formed from the name of the Welsh footballer (b.1973).

- —Ray Puxley, *Fresh Rabbit*, 1998

Ss

s- *prefix*

it's, especially preceding a word spelt with an 'n', such as not *snot* and nice *snice* *UK, 1917*

A slovening that allows the childish to say **SNOT**.

• We cannot have that behaviour in this establishment / 'snot worth it Mike, just leave it / Don't touch me, 'snot worth it[.] — Mike Skinner, *Fit But You Know It*, 2004

Sa *noun*

a Samoan *NEW ZEALAND, 1992*

• — Harry Orsman, *A Dictionary of Modern New Zealand Slang*, p. 114, 1999

sa *adjective*

▷ see: **SEY**

sab *verb*

to act as a hunt saboteur *UK*

• — Angela Devlin, *Prison Patter*, p. 101, 1996

• — *Cornwall Hunt Saboteurs*, 2003: 'HOW TO SAB THE HUNT'

saccharine lips *noun*

a glib talker *AUSTRALIA*

Not quite as glib as 'sugar'.

• — Ned Wallish, *The Truth Dictionary of Racing Slang*, p. 71, 1989

sachie *noun*

Versace™ clothing *US*

• — Ethan Hilderbrant, *Prison Slang*, p. 110, 1998

sack *noun*

1 a bed *US, 1942*

Probably related to the C19 sailor's use of 'sack' as a 'hammock'.

• I was pretty well knocked out. I hit the sack early. — Mickey Spillane, *I, The Jury*, p. 9, 1947

• I started to tell her that all during the time she thought I was humped up in the sack with some other dame I was out hustling for her[.] — Horace McCoy, *Kiss Tomorrow Good-bye*, p. 204, 1948

• Got a dread of a cold, lonely sack tonight. — George Mandel, *Flee the Angry Strangers*, p. 65, 1952

• I left the tavern, returned to the dormitory, and put my miserable frame in to the sack. — Max Shulman, *Guided Tour of Campus Humor*, p. 60, 1955

• Terry and I and Johnny went into a motel room and got ready to hit the sack. — Jack Kerouac, *On the Road*, p. 93, 1957

• We'd meet once or twice a week, always on weekends, at the bar, head for the sack and stay there having sex until we were too tired to move. — Antony James, *America's Homosexual Underground*, p. 115, 1965

• She sat on the side of the bed pressing a towel against the wound. I got in the sack in the raw. — Iceberg Slim (Robert Beck), *Pimp*, p. 110, 1969

• I gotta hit the sack. — *The Blues Brothers*, 1980

• One of the things I truly knew was that your father and I were going to have a wonderful time, in the sack I believe you call it. — *Sleepless in Seattle*, 1993

• I think the romance angle in your story is critically important, that it isn't simply a jump in the sack for either of them. — *Get Shorty*, 1995

2 a bag of heroin; hence, heroin *UK, 1998*

• — Angela Devlin, *Prison Patter*, p. 101, 1996

• — Robert Ashton, *This Is Heroin*, p. 207, 2002

3 the scrotum *UK, 1928*

Originally dialect.

• I brought my knee up into his sack and he let go with a surprised look on his bloody face. — Lenny McLean, *The Guv'nor*, p. 83, 1998

• She just hoofed you in the sack and you're going to leave them alone in a jail cell with one inept guard? — *Austin Powers*, 1999

4 courage *US*

A testicular reference.

• — Inez Cardozo-Freeman, *The Joint*, p. 527–528, 1984

5 a coat or jacket *US*

• — David Claerbaut, *Black Jargon in White America*, p. 78, 1972

▸ **in the sack**

used for suggesting sexual activity *US*

Literally 'in bed'.

• That Telly. He sure was good in the sack! — *Kids*, 1995

• Fuckin 'ell, la, you Italians may be gash [useless] in the sack, but yer fucking quick when it comes to catching on. — Colin Butts, *Is Harry on the Boat?*, p. 24, 1997

▸ **the sack**

dismissal from employment *UK, 1841*

• Jack's got the sack after a couple of weeks because he pocketed some of the loot. — John Peter Jones, *Feather Pluckers*, p. 24, 1964

• I got the hoof, man. The sack, the chop, the proverbial bullet. — Doug Lang, *Freaks*, p. 89, 1973

sack *verb*

1 to dismiss someone from employment; to jilt someone *UK, 1841*

• Piers Morgan was tonight sacked as editor of the Daily Mirror[.] — *The Guardian*, 14th May 2004

2 to abruptly stop any activity *UK*

• I'm going to be a better man. I'll sack the caper [lifestyle] – sack snorting the shite, anyway. — Kevin Sampson, *Outlaws*, p. 197, 2001

3 to dispose of something *UK*

• [T]he mobile [phone] would be off for a week or two and then sacked. — Garry Bushell, *The Face*, p. 66, 2001

4 to sleep; to spend the night *US*

• "Got a place to sack?" he asked. — Robert Edmond Alter, *Carny Kill*, p. 8, 1966

▸ **sack it**

to receive an accidental blow to the scrotum *UK*

• If you bail and land with something smashed up between your legs – usually your scoot's steering column – then you've sacked it. — Ben Sharpe, *Scooter Crazy*, p. 42, 2000

sack, back and crack *noun*

a treatment for removing a man's body hair by waxing it and stripping it off *UK*

• Cheeky Victoria Beckham has revealed why husband David is such a smooth operator in the bedroom – it's all down to his intimate waxing sessions. She's joked that David "enjoys" an agonising treatment known as a "sack, back and crack" to remove unwanted body hair. — *Daily Star*, p. 5, 26th December 2003

sack drill *noun*

sleep *US*

• — *American Speech*, p. 76–79, February 1963: 'Marine Corps slang'

sack duty *noun*

sleep *US*

• — *American Speech*, p. 76–79, February 1963: 'Marine Corps slang'

sack hound *noun*

a lazy person, overly fond of sleep *US*

• — *American Speech*, p. 154, May 1959: 'Gator (University of Florida) slang'

sack off *verb*

to reject something *UK*

• People made ther [sic] own entertainment and sacked it all off. — Niall Griffiths, *Kelly + Victor*, p. 14, 2002

sack of garbage *noun*

in bar dice games, a roll that produces no points for the player *US*

• — Jester Smith, *Games They Play in San Francisco*, p. 105, 1971

sack of sauce *noun*

a used condom *US*

• — Pamela Munro, *U.C.L.A. Slang*, p. 104, 1997

sack of shit *noun*

used abusively of an unpleasant person *US*

A conventional 'sack' full of **SHIT** (excrement); probably a revision of **SAD SACK OF SHIT**.

• "Listen, you dickless sack of shit," I said[.] — Janet Evanovich, *Seven Up*, p. 118, 2001

sack out *verb*
to go to bed *US, 1946*
- On his last day in Red Canyon, while Guido was sacked out in his bunk thinking jolly thoughts about all the pleasing prospects ahead, the fly entered the ointment. — Max Shulman, *Rally Round the Flag, Boys!*, p. 18, 1957
- He's in the silk, sacked out with a concrete wig. — William "Lord" Buckley, *The H-Bomb*, 1960
- "If you were a wino," he said, "where would you pick to sack out?" — John Sayles, *Union Dues*, p. 28, 1977

sack rat *noun*
a lazy person, overly fond of sleep *US*
- — *American Speech*, p. 55, February 1947: 'Pacific War language'
- — *American Speech*, p. 154, May 1959: 'Gator (University of Florida) slang'

sack ship *noun*
a big ship used to carry supplies from Europe to the East Coast fisheries *CANADA*
- Its larger vessels, now known as "sack ships," appeared on the scene at St. John's, taking no part in the catching of cod, and serving primarily as freighters and transporters. — W.S. MacNutt, *Atlantic Provinces*, p. 14, 1965

sack weather *noun*
inclement weather during which air missions cannot be flown *US*
- — *American Speech*, p. 30, February 1949: 'A.V.G. lingo'

sacky dacky *noun*
a depressed misfit *US*
- — *American Speech*, p. 238, October 1946: 'World War II slang of maladjustment'

sacrament *noun*
LSD *US*
An arguably pretentious euphemism.
- — Gilda and Melvin Berger, *Drug Abuse A-Z*, p. 116, 1990

sacré bleu!
used for registering shock, frustration, anger, anguish, etc; especially in a context of Frenchness *UK, 1869*
Directly from the French euphemism for *sacré Dieu!* (sacred God!).
- Oh sacré bleu. What is the matter with Jas (besides the obvious)? — Louise Rennison, *Dancing in My Nuddy-Pants*, p. 30, 2002

sacred *adjective*
excellent *US*
- — Trevor Cralle, *The Surfin'ary*, p. 104, 1991

sacred cow; sacred ox *noun*
on the railways, an extra engine used on a mountain *US*
- — Ramon Adams, *The Language of the Railroader*, p. 132, 1977

sacred site *noun*
a place one holds in reverence *AUSTRALIA*
From the meaning as 'a place sacred to Australian Aboriginals'.
- Leith held a map of Central in her head where Xenia's locker and Xenia's form room were her personal sacred sites. — Jenny Pausacker, *What are ya?*, p. 66, 1987

sad *adjective*
terrible *US*
- Anything very bad might also be called "frone" or "sad." — *Women's Digest*, p. 40, September 1945

sad and sorry *noun*
a lorry *UK*
Rhyming slang.
- — Ray Puxley, *Cockney Rabbit*, 1992

sad-ass; sad-assed *adjective*
contemptible *US, 1971*
- Girl, that's a sad-ass state of affairs. — Janet Evanovitch, *High Five*, p. 181, 1999
- [H]e almost looked like just another member of this sad-assed human race. — Thomas Laird, *Black Dog*, p. 155, 2004

sad bastard *noun*
a contemptible person; an ineffectual person *UK*
- Let's face it, you've got to be a bit of an arse to go line dancing. It's a sad bastard occupation, but we don't care. — *Attitude*, p. 35, October 2003

Saddam Hussein *noun*
a pain; an irritation; an annoying person *UK*
Rhyming slang for conventional 'pain', also on a shortened **PAIN IN THE ASS/ARSE**; formed, with all due respect, from the name of the former Iraqi leader.
- — Ray Puxley, *Fresh Rabbit*, 1998

sad day!
used for expressing commiseration with another person's troubles *US*
- — Connie Eble (Editor), *UNC-CH Campus Slang*, p. 7, Spring 1989

saddle *noun*
1 in trucking, the driver's seat *US*
- — Montie Tak, *Truck Talk*, p. 135, 1971

2 in a group of trucks travelling down the motorway together, the truck in the middle *US*
- — Wayne Floyd, *Jason's Authentic Dictionary of CB Slang*, p. 26, 1976

3 a two-part bet in an illegal numbers gambling lottery *US*
- — *American Speech*, p. 193, October 1949

▸ **in the saddle**
1 engaged in sexual intercourse *US*
The term enjoyed widespread popularity in the US during discussions of the 1979 death of former Vice President and New York Governor Nelson Rockefeller.
- The medical literature on sudden, heart-attack death shows that a demise "in the saddle" is very unlikely. — *Maledicta*, p. 59, 1979
- Didn't women have to wait six weeks before you could get back into the saddle? — Odie Hawkins, *Black Casanova*, p. 188, 1984
- He either had a heart attack in the saddle and she had to take him to Charity, or he pulled out. — Elmore Leonard, *Bandits*, p. 338, 1987
- No old guy has looked this sturdy since Nelson Rockefeller. If you recall, Neelson died in the saddle – he didn't need any damn Viagra. — *New York Observer*, 11th January 1999

2 in control *US*
- — Hyman E. Goldin et al., *Dictionary of American Underworld Lingo*, p. 184, 1950

saddle-fuck *verb*
to have sex, the woman astride the prone man *US*
- Again a very pretty chick, this time with beautiful big boobs, is our star, saddle-fucking some weary stud. — *Screw*, p. 23, 6th November 1972

saddler *noun*
a ride on a bicycle's saddle while another person pedals *UK, 1979*

saddles *noun*
the testicles hanging in the scrotum *UK*
Probably from **JOHN WAYNE'S HAIRY SADDLE BAGS**.
- Your mother's got a beard, saddles and a penis too. — Goldie Coloured Chain, *Your Mother's Got a Penis*, 2004

saddle tramp *noun*
1 a person who rides horseback through the countryside *US*
- She was what some people called a saddle tramp, but it was not a good idea to call her that to her face. — George Bowering, *Caprice*, p. 61, 1987

2 a motorcyle gang member *US*
- — James Harris, *A Convict's Dictionary*, p. 37, 1989

saddle up *verb*
1 to pick up your gear and resume a combat patrol *US*
- Pretty soon Sam called again but it was the hated saddle up order. — Charles Anderson, *The Grunts*, p. 75, 1976

2 to engage in mutual oral sex simultaneously *US*
- — *American Speech*, p. 20, Spring 1985: 'The language of singles bars'

saddo *noun*
a pathetic or contemptible individual *UK*
Jocular if not derogatory.
- OK you saddoes it's London, it's Saturday night, we're all wedged up. — Bernard Dempsey and Kevin McNally, *Lock, Stock ... & Two Hundred Smoking Kalashnikovs*, p. 101, 2000
- if you meet one of these laddos or saddos coming round the right-hand side of the bend — James Hawes, *Dead Long Enough*, p. 22, 2000
- desperately trying to engage anyone in conversation so as not to appear a Billy-no-mates saddo — Colin Butts, *Is Harry Still on the Boat?*, p. 5–6, 2003

sadfuck *noun*
a contemptible person *UK*
- [S]ome sadfuck busker who couldn't find a tube station starts in with his sadfuck act. — Nick Barlay, *Curvy Lovebox*, p. 40, 1997

Sadie Masie *noun*
sado-masochism *US*
A jocular personification.
- — *The Guild Dictionary of Homosexual Terms*, p. 40, 1965
- — Roger Gordon, *Hollywood's Sexual Underground*, p. 29, 1966
- A side trip to the "S. & M." (sado-masochistic) or "Sadie-Maisie" homosexual bars — G. Legman, *The Fake Revolt*, p. 30, 1967
- — *Maledicta*, p. 219, 1979: 'Kinks and queens: linguistic and cultural aspects of the terminology for gays'

Sadie the Office Secretary *noun*
used as a personification of the stereotypical female office worker *US, 1953*
- — *American Speech*, p. 299, December 1955: "Mimeo Minnie,' 'Sadie, the Office Secretary,' and other women office workers in America'

Sadie Thompson *verb*
to rape (a man) *US*
- O.A. Jones mumbled, hoping that he would get put in the cops' tank at the county jail because a twenty-four-year-old former surfer, who was also a former cop, would be Sadie Thompson'd in the regular tank within three minutes. — Joseph Wambaugh, *The Secrets of Harry Bright*, p. 33, 1985

sad kecks *noun*
a killjoy *UK*
Pejorative; conventional 'sad' combined with **KECKS** (trousers).
- "Ah, turn it in, sad kecks!" hissed James. — Kevin Sampson, *Powder*, p. 49, 1999

sadlands *noun*
the suburbs of a city *UK*
- [S]at for three hours in a limo crawling through the sadlands of London. — Ben Elton, *High Society*, p. 18, 2002

sad-on *noun*
a bad mood *UK*
Royal Navy slang.
- [T]he Boss got a right sad on that lasted for the rest of the week. — Rick Jolly, *Jackspeak*, p. 245, 1989

sad sack *noun*
a miserable and depressing individual; an inept misfit *US, 1942*
Originally US military.
- — *Newsweek*, p. 28, 8th October 1951
- Jimmy said now listen I used to be a sad sack myself until I met my wife Gloria who made me so happy[.] — William T. Vollman, *Whores for Gloria*, p. 75, 1991
- Scott the Engineer is the Sad Sack of our show. — Howard Stern, *Miss America*, p. 221, 1995
- A well-meaning sad sack who spirals dramatically downward — *The USA Today*, 19th October 2001

sad sack of shit *noun*
a miserable and depressing individual *US*
Abbreviates as **SAD SACK**.
- They've got nothing to do but go fishing, play poker, drink bonded bourbon, and wait for some sad sack of shit like you to show up in the courtroom[.] — Stephen King, *The Stand*, p. 191, 1978
- The cartoon character Sad Sack of course derives his name from the NCO's favorite term for a despised subordinate, a sad sack of shit, a bit of nomenclature reducing the addressee to a bag of noisome matter equipped, as if by some accident, with arms and legs. — Paul Fussell, *Wartime*, p. 91, 1989

safe *noun*

1 the rectum *US*
Referring to the rectum as a depository for drugs to be smuggled into prison.
- — William K. Bentley and James M. Corbett, *Prison Slang*, p. 76, 1992

2 a condom *UK*
- She asked me what I meant; rubbers? safes? skins? prophylactics? contraceptives? — John Nichols, *The Sterile Cuckoo*, p. 105, 1965
- Saul muttered "Have you got a safe? A rubber, a joe, don't be stupid?" — *Islands*, p. 54, 1976
- Meaning she didn't make me wear a safe. — James Ellroy, *White Jazz*, p. 112, 1992
- She'd better have an arsenal of Trojans in her purse just in case he wasn't carrying a safe in his back pocket. — Rita Ciresi, *Pink Slip*, p. 328, 1999

3 in a pickpocketing team, the thief who takes the wallet or object stolen by the wire and leaves the scene with it *US*
- The third partner in the trio might have been either man or woman; his (or her) function was indicated well enough by the name given this important member of the crew; he was called the "safe." — Dev Collans with Stewart Sterling, *I was a House Detective*, p. 48, 1954

▸ **in the safe**
concealed in the anus *UK*
- — Angela Devlin, *Prison Patter*, p. 65, 1996

safe *adjective*

1 worthy of approval *SOUTH AFRICA, 1970*
- — Penny Silva, *A Dictionary of South African English*, 1996

2 hopelessly out of style *US*
Hawaiian youth usage.
- "Oh dat Renton! He so safe! Make be bahf!" — Douglas Simonson, *Pidgin to da Max Hana Hou*, 1982

3 all right; used as an expression of approval or agreement *SOUTH AFRICA, 1981*
- — Penny Silva, *A Dictionary of South African English*, 1996
- Say no to drugs. - Safe. - Wicked. — Nick Barlay, *Curvy Lovebox*, p. 46, 1997
- Safe, man. You're cool. — Diran Abedayo, *My Once Upon A Time*, p. 47, 2000

safe and sound; safe *noun*
the ground *UK*
- [H]appy to get his feet back on the "safe". — Ray Puxley, *Cockney Rabbit*, 1992

safe house *noun*
a room, apartment or house where it is safe to stay, work and hide from the authorities, rival criminals or rival spies *US, 1963*
- Joe Loop said what the guy was doing they used to call "going to the mattress," hiding out, going to a safe house had enough mattresses for the crew to sleep on. — Elmore Leonard, *Be Cool*, p. 125, 1999

safe screw *noun*
a corrupt prison officer *UK*
- — Angela Devlin, *Prison Patter*, p. 101, 1996

safety *noun*

1 a condom *US*
- Can't you recall telling me when I first hit the bricks to always use a safety? — A.S. Jackson, *Gentleman Pimp*, p. 45, 1973

2 a safety pin used for an improvised injection of an illegal drug *US*
- — *American Speech*, p. 29, February 1952: 'Teen-age hophead jargon'

safe word *noun*
a code word, agreed between a sexual dominant and submissive masochistic partner, for use by the masochist as a signal that the current activity should stop *US, 1987*
- "Do you have a safe word with Ben?" she asked. — Kitty Churchill, *Thinking of England*, p. 70, 1995

safey *noun*
in horse racing, a riding assignment for a jockey on a horse that stands little chance of winning *AUSTRALIA*
- — Ned Wallish, *The Truth Dictionary of Racing Slang*, p. 71, 1989

sag *verb*
to wear trousers that are too big and which consequently ride very low on or below the hips *US, 1991*
- "A-WAX", (18), sporting the sagging dickies, with nearly all of his draws showing, looks like a little kid dressed up in his father's clothes. — *Menace II Society*, 1993
- — *The Bell (Paducah Tilghman High School)*, p. 8–9, 17th December 1993: 'Tilghmanism: the concealed language of the hallway'
- — Mark S. Fleisher, *Beggars & Thieves*, p. 291, 1995: 'Glossary'
- — *American Speech*, p. 397, Winter 1995: 'Among the new words'

saga lout *noun*
an elderly person who behaves badly *UK*
Saga is a UK company that supplies a wide range of services to the over-50s; a pun on **LAGER LOUT** (a hooligan fuelled by lager).
- — *The Sunday Times*, 9th May 2004

sage *noun*
a hybrid marijuana *UK*
An initialism of '*S*ativa *A*fghani *g*enetic *e*quilibrium', contrived, perhaps, as a reference to the herb.
- — Nick Jones, *Spliffs*, p. 73, 2003

saggie *noun*
a central nervous system depressant such as Seconal™ *US*
• —Robert George Reisner, *The Jazz Titans*, p. 163, 1960

sag off; sag *verb*
to truant from school or work *UK, 1959*
• I'm saggin skewl. —Frank Shaw, *Lern Yerself Scouse*, p. 45, 1966
• —Angela Devlin, *Prison Patter*, p. 101, 1996

Saigon cowboy *noun*
a rear-echelon troop or civilian who dressed the part of a combat soldier but did not experience combat *US*
• Later that morning, a Chinook came in with a load of newsmen, looking so bad-ass spiffy in their Saigon-cowboy suits – starched tiger fatigues, spit-shined boots, and silly fucking bush hats. —Larry Heinemann, *Close Quarters*, p. 235, 1977
• Saigon cowboys were a breed of rear-echelon soldiers so called for their latest and greatest dressed-to-the-hilt warrior look that they took no closer to the combat zone than absolutely necessary. —David Hackworth and Julie Sherman, *About Face*, p. 579, 1989

Saigon quickstep *noun*
diarrhoea *US*
• —Linda Reinberg, *In the Field*, p. 190, 1991

Saigon Suzie *noun*
used for describing a stereotypical Vietnamese sex worker during the Vietnam war *US*
• Like I believed Saigon Suzie when she swore she loved only me. —Joseph Wambaugh, *Fugitive Nights*, p. 21, 1990

Saigon tea *noun*
a whisky-coloured drink served to bar girls in Vietnam, passing for expensive whisky bought by US servicemen *US*
• —*Life*, p. 33, 25th February 1966
• —Carl Fleischhauer, *A Glossary of Army Slang*, p. 11–12, 1968
• "What? No Saigon tea?" Bung asks in amazement, still trying to climb over my head. —William Nagel, *The Odd Angry Shot*, p. 66, 1975
• She held her glass of Saigon tea with one hand, rubbing the frost with her thumb. —Larry Heinemann, *Close Quarters*, p. 175, 1977
• Always use condoms; obey curfew times; don't hassle the local police (white mice); don't buy the ladies Saigon teas AND never eat the indigenous food. —Martin Cameron, *A Look at the Bright Side*, 1988
• They received a percentage from the drinks of colored water, called "Saigon tea," that the soldiers had to buy them to enjoy their company and dance to the rock 'n' roll music that blared from the bars. —Neil Sheehan, *A Bright Shining Lie*, p. 625, 1988

Saigon Tech *noun*
the war in Vietnam; military service in Vietnam *US*
• —*Current Slang*, p. 13, Summer 1969

sailing *adjective*
1 drunk *US*
• —Collin Baker et al., *College Undergraduate Slang Study Conducted at Brown University*, p. 187, 1968
2 marijuana-intoxicated *US*
• —Peter Johnson, *Dictionary of Street Alcohol and Drug Terms*, p. 163, 1993

sailor's elbow *noun*
an act of ending a relationship with a lover *UK*
An elaboration, perhaps a specialisation, of **ELBOW** (an act of dismissal).
• Well, before long I got the sailor's elbow – nudge, splash – and I was banned from her second floor Camden Town flat[.] —Jonathan Gash, *The Ten Word Game*, p. 61, 2003

sailors on the sea; sailors *noun*
tea *UK, 1961*
• —Julian Franklyn, *A Dictionary of Rhyming Slang*, 1961
• —Ray Puxley, *Fresh Rabbit*, 1998

saint *noun*
an incorruptible prison officer or police officer *UK*
• —Angela Devlin, *Prison Patter*, p. 101, 1996

saint and sinner *noun*
dinner *UK*
Rhyming slang.
• —Ray Puxley, *Cockney Rabbit*, 1992

Saint Loo *nickname*
St Louis, Missouri *US*
• And on into St. Loo, the second or third ugliest city in America, after Indianapolis, Detroit and perhaps El Paso. —Clancy Sigal, *Going Away*, p. 261, 1961

Saint Moritz *noun*
diarrhoea *UK*
Rhyming slang for **THE SHITS**, based on the Swiss resort.
• —Ray Puxley, *Fresh Rabbit*, 1998

Saint Peter *noun*
the penis *UK*
Perhaps because he 'opens the gate to heaven'.
• —Richard Herring, *Talking Cock*, p. 30, 2003

saints preserve us!
used for expressing fear *US*
A signature line of the chief of police on *Batman* (ABC, 1966–68), Chief O'Hara. Repeated with referential humour.

Saint Vitus dance *verb*
to move in a fidgety, jerking manner *UK, 1621*
• He Saint VItus danced to the subway as fast as he could, painfully lugging the load and contemptuously clutching the stupid football close to his side. —Emmett Grogan, *Ringolevio*, p. 93, 1972

sais a ching *noun*
in betting, odds of 6–5 *UK*
A slurring of 'six' combined with **CHING** (five pounds).
• —John McCririck, *John McCririck's World of Betting*, p. 61, 1991

sal *noun*
a friend or pal *BARBADOS*
• —Frank A. Collymore, *Barbadian Dialect*, p. 95, 1965

▷ see: **SAL'TING**

sala *noun*
an idiot *US*
Adopted into hip-hop, urban usage from subtly insulting Hindi *sala* – the literal sense of which is 'a man's wife's brother'; the abusive sense is 'to someone who is not the speaker's wife's brother: the insult lies in the implication that the sister of the person abused is available to the speaker as a wife' (Nigel Hankin, *Hanklyn Janklyn*, 2003). Noted in connection with a legal dispute over rap lyrics by BBC News, 6th June 2003.

salad *noun*
1 marijuana *US*
• —Jim Emerson-Cobb, *Scratching the Dragon*, April 1997
2 a mixture of two or more drugs *US*
• —William D. Alsever, *Glossary for the Establishment and Other Uptight People*, p. 6, December 1970

salad bowl *noun*
a serendipitous mixture of inferior (and, hence, uncommercial) bud and leaf remains of varying marijuana varieties *UK*
Noted as 'cheap and cheerful' by Nick Jones in *Spliffs*, 2003.

salad days *noun*
a period of youthful inexperience and innocence *UK, 1606*
• The Tournament seems forever to remain in its salad days. —Bill Cardoso, *The Maltese Sangweech*, p. 117, 1984
• Big Momma smiled at Robert 30X, formerly called Baby June in his dope fiend salad days, feeling a maternal pride in his superneatness. —Donald Goines, *The Busting Out of an Ordinary Man*, p. 14, 1985

salad dodger *noun*
a person who is overweight *UK*
• [E]ncourage the nation's salad-dodgers to slim. —*Evening Standard*, 13th October 1999

salad parade *noun*
a group of ballet dancers *UK*
• —Wilfred Granville, *The Theatre Dictionary*, p. 170, 1952

salad toss *noun*
any of several sexual practices involving oral–anal stimulation *CANADA*
• If you've got Wet Wipes around, you could even do a little salad tossing but if you're down with that you probably don't need to be reading this. —Suroosh Alvi et al., *The Vice Guide*, p. 41, 2002

salad wagon *noun*
a dustcart *US*
• — *American Speech*, p. 272, December 1962: 'The language of traffic policemen'

salami *noun*
the penis *US*
The image of a large, dark sausage.
• I had been horrified by the drawings in The Joy of Sex, which showed an inexplicably cheerful woman smiling while a giant male salami was stuffed down her throat. — *Nerve*, p. 35, May-June 2000

salaud *noun*
a contemptible person, mainly applied to a French person *UK, 1962*
From French *salaud*, ultimately from French *sale* (dirty).
• "Bah," he said. "The salaud's lucky I didna tear off his head and make him swallow it." — Diana Gabaldon, *Dragonfly in Amber*, p. 172, 1992

saleslady *noun*
a prostitute *US*
• — Joseph E. Ragen and Charles Finston, *Inside the World's Toughest Prison*, p. 816, 1962: 'Penitentiary and underworld glossary'

salesman *noun*
1 a professional wrestler who does a good job of feigning pain, anger or fear *US*
• In the ring, he was a skilled wrestler and a terrific salesman. When he punished an opponent, the crowd never doubted the fury in his face. When he took a beating, his jerk, falls, and cry convinced spectators of his anguish. — Larry Nelson and James Jones, *Stranglehold*, p. 57, 1999
2 in gin, a card discarded to lure a desired card from an opponent *US*
• — Irwin Steig, *Play Gin to Win*, p. 141,

Sally *noun*
a chilled, twelve ounce can of beer *US*
• — Connie Eble (Editor), *UNC-CH Campus Slang*, p. 9, October 2002

Sally Army; Sally Ann; Sally *noun*
the Salvation Army; a Salvation Army hostel *US, 1915*
• [A]fter I had finished my breakfst I left, promising myself never to sleep again in a "sally". — Robin Page, *Down Among the Dossers*, p. 70, 1973
• It's a hotel for the workingman run by the Sallies. — Colleen McCullough, *The Thorn Birds*, p. 65, 1977
• The Sally was Rooski's second home away from the home he never had, the first being jail. — Seth Morgan, *Homeboy*, p. 41, 1990
• I heard the Sally Army's giving tickets to go to Lousy Loughton. — Joe Morgan, *Eastenders Don't Cry*, p. 23, 1994

Sally Gunnell; sally *noun*
a tunnel, especially the Blackwall Tunnel *UK*
Rhyming slang, formed on the name of the British Olympic athlete (b.1966).
• [T]he traffic was backed up from the Sally to the Bow underpass. — Ray Puxley, *Fresh Rabbit*, 1998

salmon *noun*
a twenty-dollar note *AUSTRALIA*
From the orange-red colour.
• — Ryan Aven-Bray, *Ridgey Didge Oz Jack Lang*, p. 43, 1983

salmon and trout; salmon *noun*
1 tobacco; a cigarette *UK, 1974*
Rhyming slang for **SNOUT**.
• — Angela Devlin, *Prison Patter*, p. 101, 1996
• Kids of ten and twelve, smoking salmon and spitting non-stop[.] — J.J. Connolly, *Layer Cake*, p. 119, 2000
2 gout *UK, 1932*
Rhyming slang. Sometimes varied as 'salmon trout'.
• There is even a Salmon Trout club, restricted to gout sufferers. They arrange tours of breweries, distilleries, etc. — Red Daniells, 1980
3 the nose *UK*
Rhyming slang for 'snout'. Noted by David Hillman, 1974.
4 an informer *UK*
Rhyming slang for **SNOUT**.
• — Ray Puxley, *Cockney Rabbit*, 1992
5 a ticket tout *UK, 1932*
Rhyming slang, originally applied to a racecourse tout.
• — Ray Puxley, *Cockney Rabbit*, 1992
6 stout (beer) *UK*
Rhyming slang.
• — Julian Franklyn, *A Dictionary of Rhyming Slang*, 1960

salon *noun*
a semi-private area created by shrubs and trees where homosexual liaisons take place *US*
For example, Coco Chanel's salon was found in a large grove of trees at Land's End in San Francisco.
• — Bruce Rodgers, *The Queens' Vernacular*, p. 176, 1972

saloon *noun*
1 in poker, a hand consisting of three cards of the same rank and a pair *US*
Known conventionally as a 'full house'.
• — George Percy, *The Language of Poker*, p. 78, 1988
2 a brakevan (caboose) *US*
• — Ramon Adams, *The Language of the Railroader*, p. 132, 1977

salt *noun*
1 a sailor, especially an experienced sailor *UK, 1840*
Often in the phrase 'old salt'.
• Up ahead, claims the old salt in the nearby saloon, lies big fish and bigger weather[.] — *The Guardian*, 27th July 2000
2 an experienced veteran in any calling *UK*
• Serge smiled as he remembered how badly the young marines wanted to be salts. — Joseph Wambaugh, *The New Centurions*, p. 36, 1970
3 a woman *UK*
Possibly by extension from obsolete (mid-C17 to mid-C18) 'salt' (the sex act); possibly by abbreviation from obsolete (C19) 'salt-cellar' (the vagina); most likely of unknown etymology.
• ["]Who's that salt over there then?" Harry pipes up. "That's Gammy Gilberts sister." — Ian Hebditch, *Weekend, The Sharper Word*, p. 133, 1969
4 a drunkard *BARBADOS*
• — Frank A. Collymore, *Barbadian Dialect*, p. 95, 1965
5 heroin *US, 1971*
From the appearance of the powdered drug.
• — Peter Johnson, *Dictionary of Street Alcohol and Drug Terms*, p. 163, 1993
• — Robert Ashton, *This Is Heroin*, p. 207, 2002
6 plain tobacco mixed with marijuana *SOUTH AFRICA*
• — C.P. Wittstock, 23rd May 1946

salt *verb*
1 to make something appear to be worth more than it is *US, 1852*
Originally mining slang.
• I salted the graveyard behind St. Pat's over on the Southeast Side with Indian artifacts[.] — Robert Campbell, *Nibbled to Death by Ducks*, p. 65, 1989
2 to swindle someone by baiting them *US*
• — Hyman E. Goldin et al., *Dictionary of American Underworld Lingo*, p. 184, 1950
3 to plant or place something to be found *US*
• — Don Wilmeth, *The Language of American Popular Entertainment*, p. 232, 1981
• "You salted me!" Lopez said with his hand still clutching his shirt pocket. "I'm gonna tell my parole officer you salted me!" — Gerald Petievich, *Shakedown*, p. 92, 1988

salt and pepper *noun*
1 marijuana, especially if of poor quality; marijuana adulterated with oregano *US, 1946*
• Also known as doodley-squat, salt and pepper, and "male twigs," this female-impersonator a/k/a Headache Mary is sometimes advertised as "good commercial"[.] — *Hi Life*, p. 15, 1979
• — Richard A. Spears, *The Slang and Jargon of Drugs and Drink*, p. 431, 1986
• — Mike Haskins, *Drugs*, p. 289, 2003
2 a police car *US*
From the black and white colour scheme of many police cars.
• — Lanie Dills, *The Official CB Slanguage Language Dictionary*, p. 60, 1976
• — Edith A. Folb, *runnin' down some lines*, p. 252, 1980

salt and pepper *adjective*
white and black *US, 1915*
• "Hell, Boston is full of sailors." "Yeah, but how many of them are salt and pepper, toting two .45's in an AWOL bag?" — Darryl Ponicsan, *The Last Detail*, p. 160, 1970
• A salt 'n pepper neighborhood to play in, not too much danger of someone calling the pigs just because a black had been spotted on the block. — Odie Hawkins, *Chicago Hustle*, p. 165, 1977
• Her hair was done in a salt-and-pepper DA. — Armistead Maupin, *Tales of the City*, p. 25, 1978

salt and rob *noun*
assault and robbery *SOUTH AFRICA*
- — *Cape Times*, 23rd May 1946

salt away *verb*
to save money; to hide money and valuables *UK, 1902*
- Money salted away in tax havens runs into hundreds of billions. — *The Observer*, 24th October 1999

salt-banker *noun*
a fishing boat on the Grand Banks carrying enough salt to preserve fish caught, allowing a longer stay on the water *CANADA*
- It was marked by the loss of a Nova Scotia salt-banker which had raced her way into the hearts of the nation. — *Atlantic Advocate*, p. 38, January 1961

salt beef *noun*
an attractive woman married to someone else *BAHAMAS*
- — John A. Holm, *Dictionary of Bahamian English*, p. 174, 1982

saltee; salter; salty; saulty *noun*
a penny *UK, 1859*
From Italian *soldi* (money).
- — Paul Baker, *Polari*, p. 188, 2002

saltie *noun*
a saltwater crocodile *AUSTRALIA, 1951*

sal'ting; saltfish; sal *noun*
the vagina *JAMAICA, 1991*
- Saltfish is renking [offending] me, y'know. — prison inmate, 5th August 2002

salt junk; salted *adjective*
drunk *UK, 1909*
Rhyming slang, from a military and nautical name for 'salted beef'.
- — Ray Puxley, *Cockney Rabbit*, 1992

saltmine *noun*
a workplace *US*
- — Elementary Electronics, *Dictionary of CB Lingo*, p. 103, 1976

salt-rising *adjective*
sourdough retained as leavening for future baking *CANADA*
- Course the cook made salt-risin bread, but he couldn't get nobody to touch it after he got good on pancakes. — John Robins, *A Book of Canadian Humour*, p. 202, 1951

Salt River *noun*
▸ **go up Salt River**
to die *US*
- — Lou Shelly, *Hepcats Jive Talk Dictionary*, p. 25, 1945

salt shaker *noun*
a road-gritting or -salting vehicle *US*
- — *Complete CB Slang Dictionary*, p. 82, 1976
- — Peter Chippindale, *The British CB Book*, p. 158, 1981

salt struck *adjective*
of cod, dressed with enough salt to be pickled *CANADA*
- The fish were left in the stage until they became "salt-struck", then the family removed the fish from salt, washed them, piled them to press out excess water, and finally spread them on the "flakes." — *Canadian Geographic Journal*, p. 129/2, October 1957

salt water *noun*
a US police officer born in Ireland *US*
- — Bill Reilly, *Big Al's Official Guide to Chicagoese*, p. 50, 1982

saltwater taffy *noun*
an attractive woman on the beach *US*
An allusion to a brightly coloured sweet sold at US beaches.
- They were lying in rows, all this Golden Orange saltwater taffy, in taffy-colored French cuts and thong bikinis: lemon, licorice, tangerine, strawberry. They were soft and pliable and tasty[.] — Joseph Wambaugh, *The Golden Orange*, p. 173, 1990

salty *adjective*
1 angry, hostile *US, 1938*
- The soldiers got salty. — Chester Himes, *If He Hollers Let Him Go*, p. 75, 1945
- Ray and Fuzzy were salty with our unhip no-playing piano player, because she broke time on the piano so bad that the strings yelled whoa to the hammers. — Mezz Mezzrow, *Really the Blues*, p. 61, 1946
- And they been sleepin' in crevices and shoe boxes and shelves and holes in the walls ever since and they is very salty with you, Nero. — William "Lord" Buckley, *Nero*, 1951
- But he was in no position to jump salty with Danny[.] — Bernard Wolfe, *The Late Risers*, p. 5, 1954
- All reet, all reet. No call to come on salty. — Ross Russell, *The Sound*, p. 93, 1961
- "Got your ass torn, eh buddy?" "Yeah, the boss man got salty." — Chester Himes, *Cotton Comes to Harlem*, p. 103, 1965
- They were walking by Tiffany's with Mary and me, and some starchy old cat whispered something salty to his wife as they walked by. — Nat Hentoff, *Jazz Country*, p. 122, 1965
- So they salty when you bring a new chick in the stable. — Sara Harris, *The Lords of Hell*, p. 48, 1967
- I get salty standing in a long line for my loving. — Iceberg Slim (Robert Beck), *Pimp*, p. 184, 1969
- Robin, if I had some insurance, I wouldn't be as salty as I am. — A.S. Jackson, *Gentleman Pimp*, p. 111, 1973
- What you have to learn is how to ride the rap, do your own time, but get salty quick as you can. — Elmore Leonard, *Maximum Bob*, p. 108, 1991

2 uncouth; unpleasant *US*
- [He] brought in twenty dry holes before he got cured. That means "get rich", in the salty lingo of the oil fraternity. — William Burroughs, *Queer*, p. 45, 1985

salty dog *noun*
during the Vietnam war, a piece of equipment lost in combat *US*
- — Linda Reinberg, *In the Field*, p. 191, 1991

salty water *noun*
the recreational drug GHB *US*
Caustic soda mixed with industrial cleaner *gamma butyrolactone* produces a *salt* which is dissolved in *water* to produce the clear solution GHB.
- GHB has been marketed as a liquid or powder and has been sold on the street under names such as Grevious Bodily Harm, Georgia Home Boy, Liquid Ecstasy, Liqiud X, Liquid E, GHB, GBH, Soap, Scoop, Easy Lay, Salty Water, G-Riffick, [and] Cherry Menth. — *Morbidity and Morality Weekly Report*, p. 281, 4th April 1997

salute *verb*
▸ **salute the judge**
to win a horse race *AUSTRALIA*
- — Jim Ramsay, *Cop It Sweet!*, p. 79, 1977
- John 'Smokey' McHugh, who nowadays drives pacers, has been another notable rider, who has saluted the judge on four or five occasions in one program. — Joe Brown, *Just for the Record*, p. 200, 1984
- — Clive Galea, *Slipper*, p. 114, 1988
- The John Meagher stable has enjoyed their best season to date with their 100th winner, Dalharaan, saluting the judge at Warwick Farm on Wednesday. — *Sydney Morning Herald*, p. 12, 25th June 1994

Salvador Dali; salvador *noun*
1 cocaine *UK*
Rhyming slang for **CHARLIE** (cocaine).
- We can't bring Salvador Dali through airport security. — James Hawes, *Dead Long Enough*, p. 72, 2000
- — Mike Haskins, *Drugs*, p. 271, 2003

2 a drink *UK: SCOTLAND*
Glasgow rhyming slang for **SWALLY**.
- Are ye corned beef[deaf]? I said sit doon on yer chorus [backside] and we'll have a wee Salvador. Mine's a Mick Jagger [lager] by the way. — *The Guardian*, 29th April 2002

salvation army *adjective*
mad; eccentric *UK*
Rhyming slang for **BARMY**.
- — Ray Puxley, *Cockney Rabbit*, 1992

Salvo *noun*
a Salvation Army officer *AUSTRALIA, 1891*
- — Arthur Chipper, *The Aussie Swearer's Guide*, p. 61, 1972
- — Jim Ramsay, *Cop It Sweet!*, p. 79, 1977
- Everybody respects the Salvos. — Sam Weller, *Old Bastards I Have Met*, p. 137, 1979

Salvosh *noun*
the Salvation Army *UK*
- Now he lives rough in Lincoln's Inn, London, in a cardboard box. The Salvosh feed him most days[.] — Jonathan Gash, *The Ten Word Game*, p. 138, 2003

sam *noun*

1 a federal narcotics agent *US*

An abbreviation of Uncle Sam, the personification of the US federal government.

- —Eugene Landy, *The Underground Dictionary*, p. 164, 1971

2 a *s*outhern *A*ppalachian *m*igrant *US*

- — *Maledicta*, p. 95, Summer/Winter 1981: 'Acrimonious acroynyms for ethnic groups'

Sam and Dave *noun*

a grave *UK*

Rhyming slang, formed from US soul singers Sam Moore and Dave Prater who first came to prominence in the mid-1960s.

- Bound for an early Sam and Dave. —Mervyn Stutter, *Getting Nowhere Fast*, 21st May 2004

Samantha Janus *noun*

the anus *UK*

Rhyming slang based on the name of model and actress Samantha Janus (b.1975).

- — *www.LondonSlang.com*, June 2002

sambie *noun*

a sandwich *AUSTRALIA, 1976*

- Our sambies were packed in greaseproof lunch wrap (where would you buy that today, Possums?) —Edna Everage (Barry Humphries), *My Gorgeous Life*, p. 32, 1989

sambo *noun*

1 a black person *US*

Originally neutral, gradually accepted as taboo and derogatory; popular etymology holds that 'sambo' derives from 'sandboy' as in 'happy as a sandboy'; however Spanish or African origins account for the use from about 1704 as a proper name, slipping into a generic sense later in the C18.

- My Dad has taught me that in England some foolish man may call me sambo, darkie, boot or munt or nigger, even. —Colin McInnes, *City of Spades*, 1957
- Come here, Sambo, and suck this truncheon. —Alan Bleasdale, *Boys From the Blackstuff*, 1982
- Fuck you, Sambo. I'm paying for y'time so shut ya maff [mouth] and do as ya told. —Donald Gorgon, *Cop Killer*, p. 25, 1994
- [W]hite called black "Sambo" and black called white "Honky"[.] —Stuart Jeffries, *Mrs Slocombe's Pussy*, p. 104, 2000
- The bloke and his wife come back [...] to find some scruffy sambo, sleeping off his scotch in the Parker-Knoll[.] —Danny King, *The Burglar Diaries*, p. 41, 2001

2 a sandwich *AUSTRALIA, 1984*

- For a start, he'd never heard of a devon sambo 'til his Aussie fans started writing to him (they don't have devon-the-meat in Canada). — *Dolly*, p. 6s, 1996

Sam Cow and the Duppy *noun*

a random selection of the populace *BARBADOS*

The functional equivalent of 'Tom, Dick and Harry'.

- —Frank A. Collymore, *Barbadian Dialect*, p. 95, 1965

same bat time, same bat channel.

used as a humorous farewell *US*

A catchphrase television sign-off on *Batman* (ABC, 1966–68). Repeated with referential humour.

same-day service *noun*

in computing, a lengthy response time *US*

- —Eric S. Raymond, *The New Hacker's Dictionary*, p. 313, 1991

same difference; same diff *noun*

the same thing, no difference *UK*

- That's not exactly on a par with getting shot, I grant you, but same difference, as they say. —Dave Courtney, *Stop the Ride I Want to Get Off*, p. 120, 1999

same mud, same blood

used for explaining the absence of racism in combat troops *US*

- They shared the same mud. They spilled the same blood. Black and white soldiers soldiering together. —A.D. Horne (Editor), *The Wounded Generation*, p. 167, 1981
- Racism was a minor problem in frontline combat, where the saying went, "Same mud, same blood." In the rear it was a different story. —Myra MacPherson, *Long Time Passing*, p. 663, 1984

same odds *noun*

an equal effect; no difference worth consideration *UK*

From horse racing betting jargon.

- "You mean it's a Federal Reserve sub-branch printing dollars?" "No, it produces notes and coins of the realm." "Same odds. That's real neat." —Howard Marks, *The Howard Marks Book of Dope Stories*, p. 346, 2001

same-old *noun*

an unchanged condition *UK*

An abbreviation of **SAME OLD SAME OLD**.

- [D]espite her same-old, she had that real something – charisma, I guess[.] —Diran Abedayo, *My Once Upon A Time*, p. 195, 2000

same old same old; same-o same-o *noun*

more of the same *US*

- "What's he sayin' now, Thelma?" 'Same-o same-o." —Odie Hawkins, *Ghetto Sketches*, p. 16, 1972
- STEPHANIE: So what are you up to? ULTIMATE LOSER: Same old same old, just lollygagging around. Still unemployed. — *Slacker*, 1992
- "So what's happening, bra?" said Col [...] "Same old, same old," said Mazz. "Still in the music business, yeah?" —John Williams, *Cardiff Dead*, p. 48, 2000
- Same Old, Same Old [Headline] — *Time*, 26th June 2000

same old six and seven

used for expressing a certain lack of progress in life *US*

A borrowing from the game of craps – having established six as the point (the easiest point to make), the shooter rolls a seven, thus losing.

- 'Oh, same old six-and-seven, Ginger,' he said. —Terry Southern, *The Magic Christian*, p. 39, 1959

same shit, different day

used as a stock answer when asked how things are going *US*

- —William K. Bentley and James M. Corbett, *Prison Slang*, p. 47, 1992

samey *adjective*

monotonous; no different *UK, 1929*

- Sales slump at 'safe and samey' M&S. — *The Guardian*, 15th January 2004

samey-same; same same *adjective*

the same *US, 1956*

Korean and Vietnam war usage.

- — *American Speech*, p. 121, May 1960: 'Korean Bamboo English'
- "Why, smoke is M.J., Mike Juliet. Ya know -grass. Same same smoke." —Larry Heinemann, *Close Quarters*, p. 26, 1977
- — *Maledicta*, p. 258, Summer/Winter 1982: 'Viet-Speak'
- Yeah? Well, why go back? Here or there, samey-same. — *Full Metal Jacket*, 1987

Sam Hill *noun*

used as a very quaint euphemism for 'hell' *US, 1839*

- Well, what the Sam Hill, son – it's only money. —Terry Southern, *Blue Movie*, p. 227, 1970
- [W]hat the Sam Hill is this thingumabob supposed to do? —Eric Kraft, *Herb 'n' Lorna*, p. 188, 1989

Sami *noun*

Samoan *NEW ZEALAND*

- —David McGill, *David McGill's Complete Kiwi Slang Dictionary*, p. 96, 1998

sammo *noun*

a sandwich *AUSTRALIA, 1972*

- —Arthur Chipper, *The Aussie Swearer's Guide*, p. 43, 1972
- Lunch was beaut – soup and sammos on the terrace[.] — *Canberra Times*, p. 13, 9th January 1990

sammy *noun*

an Indian man *SOUTH AFRICA, 1906*

An offensive word used as a term of address and reference.

- —Jean Branford, *A Dictionary of South African English*, 1978

Sammy *nickname*

Saddam Hussein *US*

Used by US soldiers during the 1991 war against Iraq.

- — *The Retired Officer Magazine*, p. 39, January 1993

Sammy Hall *noun*

a testicle *UK*

Rhyming slang for **BALL(S)**, apparently formed on a character in a bawdy song.

- —Ray Puxley, *Cockney Rabbit*, 1992

Sammy Lee *noun*
urine; an act of urination *UK*
Rhyming slang for **PEE** or **WEE**, formed on Liverpool and England footballer (b.1959).
- —Ray Puxley, *Fresh Rabbit*, 1998

Samoan family car *noun*
a used police car bought at auction *US*
Hawaiian youth usage.
- —Douglas Simonson, *Pidgin to da Max Hana Hou*, 1982

Sam Sled *noun*
in drag racing, a driver who consistently underperforms *US*
- —John Lawlor, *How to Talk Car*, p. 90, 1965

Samuel Pepys; samuels *noun*
a sensation of dread or unease *UK*
Rhyming slang for **THE CREEPS**, formed from the name of the diarist, 1633–1703.
- A place or a person may give you the "Samuels".—Ray Puxley, *Fresh Rabbit*, 1998

Samurai *noun*
a Japanese man who is abundantly masculine, virile, brave and demeaning towards women *US*
Hawaiian youth usage.
- —Douglas Simonson, *Pidgin to da Max Hana Hou*, 1982

San Antone!
used as a mild oath *US*
- —*American Speech*, p. 100, May 1951: 'The vocabulary of poker'

sana wanga; sana banga *verb*
to have sex *TRINIDAD AND TOBAGO, 1935*
Probably an embellishment of **WANG** (the penis).
- —Lise Winer, *Dictionary of the English/Creole of Trinidad & Tobago*, 2003

San Berdoo; San Berdu *nickname*
▷ see: BERDOO

San Bernaghetto *nickname*
San Bernadino, California *US*
Collected in San Bernadino, August 2004. Numerous Internet usages, but none in print.

sanction *noun*
in organised crime, punishment by death *US*
- He was not a made guy, but an independent contractor that Joe used when he had to do sanctions outside the family.—Stephen J. Cannell, *Big Con*, p. 338, 1997

sand *noun*
1 courage *US*
- —Joseph E. Ragen and Charles Finston, *Inside the World's Toughest Prison*, p. 816, 1962: 'Penitentiary and underworld glossary'

2 cocaine *US*
- The wiretaps recorded a primer of street slang for powder cocaine: white lady, white fingers, soft, fish scales and sand.—*Orlando Sentinel*, p. B2, 17th August 2002

sand *verb*
to mark the edges of playing cards with sandpaper or another abrasive for the purpose of cheating *US*
- —John Scarne, *Scarne's Guide to Modern Poker*, p. 289, 1979

sandbag *noun*
a sanitary towel or tampon *US*
- We always jokingly refer to it as "flooding" and our pads or tampons as "sandbags." The first day, our "floodgates open up".—a contributor, *The Museum of Menstruation and Women's Health*, May 2001

sandbag *verb*
1 to lull someone into a false sense of security, and then suddenly attack them *US, 1940*
Originally a term from poker, used to describe a betting strategy, and then expanded to broader use.
- Now, General, I'm going to sandbag you.—*M*A*S*H*, 1970
- Perfect. Sandbag the father.—*Sleepless in Seattle*, 1993

2 in poker, to decline to raise a bet while holding a good hand in the hope of driving up the bet later in the play *US*
- —Oswald Jacoby, *Oswald Jacoby on Poker*, p. 142, 1947

sandbagger *noun*
1 a person who lulls an opponent into security, and then suddenly attacks *US, 1940*
- Robbie gave him the twelve strokes – the son of a bitch, the sandbagger – and beat him by twenty-six.—Elmore Leonard, *Split Images*, p. 158, 1981

2 in the sport of clayshooting, a competitor 'who by devious methods shoots in a lower class than his true form warrants' *UK*
- —Chris Cradock, *A Manual of Clayshooting*, p. 174, 1983

sandbox *noun*
1 a toilet; a lavatory *US*
A reference to a cat's toilet habits, intended as cute.
- —Collin Baker et al., *College Undergraduate Slang Study Conducted at Brown University*, p. 187, 1968
- —*Complete CB Slang Dictionary*, p. 82, 1976
- —Peter Chippindale, *The British CB Book*, p. 158, 1981

2 in computing, the research and development department *US*
A recognition of the playing nature of research.
- —Eric S. Raymond, *The New Hacker's Dictionary*, p. 313, 1991

Sand Box Express *noun*
military transport to Saudi Arabia or Kuwait during the first Gulf war *US*
- "Desert cherries" in "Kevlars" fly the "Sand Box Express" to the "beach" and soon are complaining about "Meals Rejected by Ethiopians" if they can't find a "roach coach" run by "Bedouin Bob."—*Houston Chronicle*, p. 15, 24th January 1991

sandburner *noun*
a Jeep *UK*
- —Peter Chippindale, *The British CB Book*, p. 161, 1981

sand flea *noun*
someone who associates with surfers at the beach but rarely if ever enters the water *US*
- —John Blair, *The Illustrated Discography of Surf Music 1961–1965*, p. 124, 1985

sandgroper *noun*
a person from the state of Western Australia *AUSTRALIA, 1896*
Western Australia has vast tracts of desert.
- I learnt later – in Sydney – that West Australians are called 'sandgropers', and South Australians are 'crow-eaters'.—John O'Grady, *It's Your Shout, Mate!*, p. 28, 1972
- —Arthur Chipper, *The Aussie Swearer's Guide*, p. 68, 1972

sandhog *noun*
a tunnel construction worker; any underground worker *US, 1903*
- I'm a sand hog. I had a job in the sewers up in Duluth after the war ended[.]—Max Shulman, *The Zebra Derby*, p. 39, 1946
- —Norman Carlisle, *The Modern Wonder Book of Trains and Railroading*, p. 267, 1946
- George "Bama" Lewis, seventy-year-old ex-con man, with his jaws inflated with candied yams, jabbed his fork toward a large painting of slain council member Darrel "The Mole" Miller, in sandhog clothing[.]—Iceberg Slim (Robert Beck), *Death Wish*, p. 82–83, 1977

sandies *noun*
▷ see: SANDY MCNABS

S and J *noun*
a beating by a police officer *US*
An abbreviation of 'sentence and judgment'.
- You wanna go pick up Drucker or Kono or one of Ray's other hamsters ... then go give them some S and J.—Stephen J. Cannell, *The Tin Collectors*, p. 262, 2001

S and M; s-m *noun*
1 sado-masochism *US*
- On another far-out fringe of the "gay" world are the so-called S & M bars.—*Life*, p. 68, 26th June 1964
- S&M is just another equally valid form of love.—Lester Bangs, *Psychotic Reactions and Carburetor Dung*, p. 26, 1971
- The term b & d as an abbreviation for bondage and discipline is gaining currency, certainly in the underground press, for s-m.—Gerald and Caroline Greene, *S-M: The Last Taboo*, p. 205, 1974
- Much of gay S & M is strictly playacting.—John Rechy, *The Sexual Outlaw*, p. 254, 1977
- Eventually me 'n' a friend / Sorta drifted along into S&M[.]—Frank Zappa, *Bobby Brown Goes Down*, 1979
- Melanie's was a decent place, discreet, no drunks allowed, no S&M or kinky stuff[.]—John King, *White Trash*, p. 287, 2001

2 in a sado-masochistic relationship, slave and master (or mistress) *US*
A confusion of meaning with 'sado-masochism' though not of context.
- —John Rechy, *The Sexual Outlaw*, p. 259, 1977

3 sausage and mushrooms *US*
- — *Maledicta*, p. 21, 1996: 'Domino's pizza jargon'

S and M *nickname*
Santa Monica Boulevard in Los Angeles, California *US*
- — *Maledicta*, p. 145, Summer/Winter 1986–1987: 'Sexual slang: prostitutes, pedophiles, flagellators, transvestites, and necrophiles'

sand nigger *noun*
an Arab; an Indian or Pakistani person *US*
Highly offensive.
- "Sand niggers," Big Ed said. "Your A-rabs cause the glut and they cause the gasoline lines." —Dan Jenkins, *Life Its Ownself*, p. 92, 1984
- I know them sand niggers got all kinda sheep and camels runnin loose. —Seth Morgan, *Homeboy*, p. 17, 1990
- I had a couple of sand niggers out there. You know, Arabs. — *Casino*, 1995
- —Connie Eble (Editor), *UNC-CH Campus Slang*, p. 6, Spring 2000

Sandoz; Sandoz's *noun*
LSD *US*
Named after Sandoz Pharmaceuticals, the original Swiss manufacturer of the drug.
- Once, once, I had a white Sandoz. Oh, oh, I can't tell you. Such acid! —Nicholas Von Hoffman, *We Are The People Our Parents Warned Us Against*, p. 34, 1967
- —Richard A. Spears, *The Slang and Jargon of Drugs and Drink*, p. 435, 1986
- —Mike Haskins, *Drugs*, p. 286, 2003

sandpaper *noun*
playing cards that have been altered for cheating by a minute sanding of the edges *US*
- —Frank Garcia, *Marked Cards and Loaded Dice*, p. 263, 1962

sandpaper *verb*
▸ **sandpaper the anchor**
to perform a job that need not and, in fact, cannot be performed *US*
- —John Gould, *Maine Lingo*, p. 241, 1975

sandwich *noun*
1 sex involving more than two people, the specific nature of which varies with use, usually sex between one woman and two men, one penetrating her vagina and one penetrating her anus *US*
A term given a lot of attention in 2000 when actress Cybill Shepherd dedicated a chapter of her autobiography to a description of her having taken the part of the filling in a 'Cybill Sandwich' with two stuntmen.
- I have been invited home to meet one number's lover for a sandwich, have been groped accidentally by platonic acquaintances (I never liked "sister"), and have had many an ego satisfaction. —John Francis Hunter, *The Gay Insider*, p. 102–103, 1971
- — *Maledicta*, p. 232, 1979: 'Kinks and queens: linguistic and cultural aspects of the terminology for gays'
- —Edith A. Folb, *runnin' down some lines*, p. 246, 1980
- It'd be so righteous to be in a Veronica Sawyer-Heather Chandler sandwich. — *Heathers*, 1988
- Pussy/ass penetration has always been known as a SANDWICH. —*Adult Video News*, p. 44, August 1995
- "The Cybill sandwich" turned out to be a positive sexual experience. Having all the pleasure points being attended to simultaneously rather than sequentially made me feel adored, emancipated, and more relaxed about sex. —Cybill Shepherd with Aimee Lee Bail, *Cybill Disobedience*, p. 226, 2000

2 heroin *sandwiched* between layers of cocaine *UK, 1998*
- —Robert Ashton, *This Is Heroin*, p. 210, 2002

▸ **a sandwich short of a picnic (basket)**
not completely sane *UK*
May be 'a sandwich', 'one sandwich', 'two sandwiches' or 'a few sandwiches' *short of a picnic*; all variations of the **NOT ALL THERE** theme. You may also be 'a pork pie' or 'two apples' *short of a picnic*.
- She gave me a sickly little smile that made it clear she thought I was several sandwiches short of a picnic. —Armistead Maupin, *Maybe the Moon*, p. 295, 1992
- Guess I'm just a sick bastard / Who's one sandwich short of a picnic basket[.] —Eminem (Marshall Mathers), *Cum On Everybody*, 1999

sandwich *verb*
1 to rob someone *TRINIDAD AND TOBAGO, 1990*
- —Lise Winer, *Dictionary of the English/Creole of Trinidad & Tobago*, 2003

2 in poker, to surround a player with two confederates whose collusive betting tactics relieve the middle player of his bankroll and drive him from the game *US, 1973*
- —Thomas L. Clark, *The Dictionary of Gambling and Gaming*, p. 188, 1987

sandwich job *noun*
condemnation surrounded on either side by faint praise *US*
- I got my evaluation today. No Waves put it in on my desk so he wouldn't have to face me. It was a 'sandwich job' as usual. —Gerald Petievich, *Money Men*, p. 45, 1981

Sandy *nickname*
a Douglas A-1E Skyraider, especially effective in providing cover for combat rescue missions in Vietnam *US*
- Sandy, the Douglas A-1E was the oldest combat airplane in the Air Force's inventory. —William C. Anderson, *Bat-21*, p. 20, 1980

Sandy McNab; Sandy MacNab *noun*
a taxi *UK*
Rhyming slang for 'cab'.
- —Julian Franklyn, *A Dictionary of Rhyming Slang*, 1960
- He's been driving Sandy McNabs for thirty-five years, so he ought to know. —Frank Hardy, *The Yarns of Billy Borker*, p. 95, 1965
- —Frank Hardy, *The Outcasts of Foolgarah*, p. 81, 1971

Sandy McNabs; sandies *noun*
pubic lice *UK, 1977*
Rhyming slang for **CRABS**.
- A dose of the sandies. Animated dandruff. —Red Daniells, 1980

Sandy Powell *noun*
a towel *UK*
Rhyming slang, formed from the name of the popular northern comedian, 1900–82. Recorded by David Hillman, 1974.

san fairy ann
it doesn't matter, it makes no difference; don't worry *UK, 1927*
From French *ça ne fait rien*.
- Finding God's taboos totalitarian, / Eve adopted a pose of 'San Fairy Ann'[.] — *The Penguin Book of Limericks*, p. 160, 1986

San Fran *nickname*
San Francisco, California *US*
- But this is only after you and I, dear Carlo, go to Texas, dig Old Bull Lee, that gone cat I've never met and both of you've told me so much about, and then I'll go to San Fran. —Jack Kerouac, *On the Road*, p. 48, 1957

San Francisco bomb *noun*
▷ **see: FRISCO SPEEDBALL**

sanga-wanga *noun*
sex *TRINIDAD AND TOBAGO, 1980*
- —Lise Winer, *Dictionary of the English/Creole of Trinidad & Tobago*, 2003

sanger *noun*
a sandwich *AUSTRALIA, 1943*
- The other guy had regained consciousness and discovered his mate had scarfed the whole sanger, hadn't even left him a crust. —John Birmingham, *He Died With a Felafel in his Hand*, p. 165, 1994

sanitary *noun*
a well-built, efficient car *US*
- — *American Speech*, p. 305, December 1956: 'Hot-rodders' jargon again'

sanitary *adjective*
used of a car, built well and without cosmetic frills *US*
A wonderful example of standard English promoted into slang.
- — Fremont Drag Strip, *Guide to Drag Racing*, 1960

sanitary ride *noun*
in a horse race, the tactic of riding away from the rail to avoid the mud flung by the pack of racehorses near the rail *US, 1978*
- —Thomas L. Clark, *The Dictionary of Gambling and Gaming*, p. 189, 1987

sannie *noun*
a shoe or sandal *UK: SCOTLAND, 1985*
From 'sandshoe'.
- All jumping aboot in your mincy wee running sannies[.] —Ian Pattison, *Rab C. Nesbitt*, 1988

▷ **see: SARNIE**

sanny *noun*

a sanitary towel; hence, a tampon *UK*

- —Paul Scott, *The Towers of Silence*, p. 325, 1971

sano; sanno *noun*

a person employed to empty toilet cans from unsewered households *AUSTRALIA*

From '*san*itary'.

- —Frank Hardy, *The Outcasts of Foolgarah*, p. 42, 1971
- 'Look,' Chilla said. 'the Sanos are working overtime.'—Frank Hardy, *The Outcasts of Foolgarah*, p. 91, 1971
- You don't have to be a sanno or garbo (Waste Disposal Men) to rubbish (i.e. belittle or reject or throw away) anything.—Arthur Chipper, *The Aussie Swearer's Guide*, p. 52, 1972

sano *adjective*

used of surf conditions, excellent *US*

- —Michael V. Anderson, *The Bad, Rad, Not to Forget Way Cool Beach and Surf Discriptionary*, p. 18, 1988

San Q *nickname*

the San Quentin state prison, San Rafael, California *US*

- "My man … takes his meals … down at San Q," she replied. "And will be .. for the next … 10 to 20 years."—C.D. Payne, *Youth in Revolt*, p. 182, 1993

San Quentin breakfast *noun*

a male under the age of legal consent as an object of sexual desire *US*

- The man knows he can be sent to San Quentin for having sexual relations with a minor. They are known as "San Quentin breakfast." —*San Francisco Chronicle*, p. 12, 22nd March 1976

San Quentin briefcase *noun*

a large portable stereo system associated, stereotypically, with black youth culture *US*

San Quentin is the most famous of California's state prisons.

- He cranked up his San Quentin briefcase, reawaking its raging rhymes.—Seth Morgan, *Homeboy*, p. 18, 1990

San Quentin quail *noun*

a girl under the age of legal consent *US*

San Quentin is California's largest state prison. In the 1940 film *Go West*, Groucho Marx played a character named S. Quentin Quale, an inside joke.

- —Marcus Hanna Boulware, *Jive and Slang of Students in Negro Colleges*, 1947
- —Jerry Robertson, *Oil Slanguage*, p. 108, 1954
- —Dale Gordon, *The Dominion Sex Dictionary*, p. 137, 1967
- One month to go until I turn 18, free from the stigma of "San Quentin quail."—Jefferson Poland and Valerie Alison, *The Records of the San Francisco Sexual Freedom League*, p. 47, 1971
- Then there was the Flim-Flam Man, a cigar in his mouth, and he hustled me out to face the photographers and a covey of San Quentin quail, all of them pimply-faced and squealing like a stoat being castrated with a rusty knife.—Guy Owen, *The Flim-Flam Man and the Apprentice Grifter*, p. 231, 1972
- "I'm San Quentin Quail, Mr. Winner," Rosalie says.—Oscar Zeta Acosta, *The Revolt of the Cockroach People*, p. 108, 1973
- Sightem spotted by self: middle-aged Volvo with license plates "SQQ," and you'd have to be middle-aged to remember Errol Flynn's painful experience with "San Quentin quail." Just a sec and I'll spin Artie Shaw's Gramercy Seven recording of "When the Quail Come Back to San Quentin".—*San Francisco Chronicle*, p. B1, 19th August 1994
- Hill had a large family in mind when he met Elaine in Linden, N.J., and fell desperately in love when he was 20 and she was "San Quentin Quail" as we used to say. I just assumed she was 17 or 18. My gosh, she was 15.—*Palm Beach (Florida) Post*, p. 1E, 22nd May 2003

Santa Barbara *noun*

in hold 'em poker, an ace and a king as the first two cards dealt to a player *US, 1981*

- An ace and a king are a Santa Barbara. The older term for that is big slick, but a few years ago there was an oil spill off the coast and the California players started called it Santa Barbara.—Thomas L. Clark, *The Dictionary of Gambling and Gaming*, p. 18–19, 1987

Santa Claus rally *noun*

an increase in stock prices between Christmas and the end of the year *US*

- "I think the year-end Santa Claus rally commenced on Tuesday," commented Alfred E. Goldman, vice president of A. G. Edwards & Sons, Inc.—*Wall Street Journal*, p. 19, 23rd December 1976

Santa Marta; Santa Maria *noun*

potent marijuana with a reddish-gold colour, originally cultivated in northern Colombia *US*

- Over the past few years in New York, the magic moniker has been successively, Chiba-Chiba, wacky, red, red wacky, gold and Santa Marta.—*Hi Life*, p. 15, 1979
- —Richard A. Spears, *The Slang and Jargon of Drugs and Drink*, p. 435, 1986
- —Mike Haskins, *Drugs*, p. 289, 2003
- —Nick Jones, *Spliffs*, p. 74, 2003

san toy *noun*

a gang member *UK, 1932*

Rhyming slang for 'boy', as in 'the boys'.

- —Ray Puxley, *Cockney Rabbit*, 1992

sap *noun*

1 a gullible fool *UK, 1815*

- What saps we were!—Max Shulman, *The Zebra Derby*, p. 83, 1946
- "Tomorrow we can go out and get a new radio – if, Wally darling, you'll be a doll and put it in for me?" "You know I will, baby," said Wally. The guy is such a sap.—C.D. Payne, *Youth in Revolt*, p. 121, 1993
- [P]oor saps who are obsessively smitten by clapped-out Jaguars[.] —Jenny Eclair, *Camberwell Beauty*, p. 347, 2000

2 in borstal, a weak trainee who is 'not very bright' *UK*

From the previous sense.

- —Home Office, *Glossary of Terms and Slang Common in Penal Establishments*, July 1978

3 a short club; a police officer's nightstick *US, 1899*

- The Independent has special cops hired by the company, but they don't carry guns. Only saps.—William Burroughs, *Junkie*, p. 45, 1953

sapazzola *noun*

semen *US*

- There's a little jerkoff down there going splooey all over the place! you could hydroplane on all the sapazzola in this freak show!—Joseph Wambaugh, *The Secrets of Harry Bright*, p. 61, 1985

saperoo *noun*

a complete fool *US*

- —Hyman E. Goldin et al., *Dictionary of American Underworld Lingo*, p. 184, 1950

sap gloves *noun*

gloves weighted for maximised damage when used to strike someone *US*

- He wore his old sap gloves with the lead filled palm and padded knuckles (which a sob sister sergeant had caught him beating up a drunk with and which he had been ordered to get rid of).—Joseph Wambaugh, *The Choirboys*, p. 34, 1975

sapper *noun*

1 a Viet Cong or North Vietnamese commando *US*

Members of the North Vietnamese Army's combat engineers, and thus the name, derived from the longstanding UK sense of the word as 'a soldier in the Engineer Corps, the Royal Sappers and Miners'. 'Sappers inside the wire!' was a warning call that US soldiers did not want to hear.

- Now rewrite it and give it a happy ending – say, uh, one kill. Make it a sapper or an officer.—*Full Metal Jacket*, 1987
- The shelling became the worst curse of this DMZ war, worse than the infantry assaults, worse than the ambushes of the convoys, worse than the raids by the sappers (a term Americans applied to NVA and Viet Cong commando-type troops) who stripped to their undershorts and crawled through the barbed wire to toss satchel charges into bunkers and artillery revetments.—Neil Sheehan, *A Bright Shining Lie*, p. 649, 1988

2 during the Vietnam war, an Australian combat engineer, especially one who searched and destroyed enemy tunnels *AUSTRALIA*

- —Gregory Clark, *Words of the Vietnam War*, p. 452, 1990

sap weather *noun*

the period in the spring when maple sap is running *CANADA*

This period is also known as 'sugar weather'.

- Yes, "Sap weather" is really the only sure sign of spring.—*Kingston Whig-Standard*, p. 13/2, 26th March 1963

Saracen Pig, Spartan Dog!

used as a humorous description of an argument *US*

From Woody Allen's 1996 film *What's Up, Tiger Lily?* (followed by *Take this! And this!*), revived and popularised by ESPN's Keith Olberman while broadcasting footage of ice hockey fights.

- —Keith Olberman and Dan Patrick, *The Big Show*, p. 24, 1997

Sarah *noun*

a single, rich and happy woman *UK*

- [W]ith your typical Sarah, there is less waiting in by the phone and more sleeping around[.]—*The Guardian*, p. 38, 1st June 2002

sardine *noun*

1 a shark *US*

Surfer humour.

- —John M. Kelly, *Surf and Sea*, p. 292, 1965

2 a despised person *NEW ZEALAND*

- —Ned Wallish, *The Truth Dictionary of Racing Slang*, p. 71, 1989

sarf London *noun*

south London *UK: WALES*

A jocular attempt to say it correctly.

- [T]ry and recreate a bit of Ibiza in sarf London.—John Robb, *The Nineties*, p. 53, 1999

sarge; sar'nt *noun*

a sergeant, often as a form of addresss *US, 1867*

- "Sar'nt Mellors," says the officer, "we got to get those buggers out of there[.]"—Derek Bickerton, *Payroll*, p. 32, 1959
- OK, Sarge, whatever you want.—Dave Courtney, *Raving Lunacy*, p. 13, 2000
- Uniformed sergeants are "Skip" or "Sarge", or it's first name terms. —Duncan MacLaughlin, *The Filth*, p. 82, 2002

sarky *adjective*

sarcastic *UK, 1912*

- Sarky cow.—Ian Pattison, *Rab C. Nesbitt*, 1988
- He didn't like Dave, said he was too sarky. True enough.—Richard Francis, *The Rialto*, p. 94, 1999
- I wanted to say something sarky[.]—Mary Hooper, *(megan)2*, p. 103, 1999

sarnie; sannie *noun*

a sandwich *UK, 1961*

Reduced from an upper-crust pronunciation of 'sandwich'. In Glasgow a 'sannie' is preferred.

- There's sarnies piled to the ceiling like a big, bread skyscraper.—Dave Courtney, *Raving Lunacy*, p. 139, 2000
- I start chewing the rest of my sarnie[.]—Kevin Sampson, *Outlaws*, p. 122, 2001

sars-fras *noun*

a low grade marijuana cigarette *US*

- The cigarettes come in three qualities: sars-fras, the cheapest kind, sold to thousands of schoool children at about ten cents each[.]—Jack Lait and Lee Mortimer, *New York Confidential*, p. 102, 1948

sarvey; sarvie *noun*

this afternoon *AUSTRALIA*

Only in the phrase 'the sarvey', by metanalysis from 'this arvie'.

- I will go shopping the sarvey.—*www.abc.net.au/wordmap*, 2003

sarvo *noun*

this afternoon *AUSTRALIA, 1942*

Only in the phrase 'the sarvo', by metanalysis of 'this arvo'.

- I've wrapped me Chrissie pressies so the sarvo we can go across to Rotto.—John Blackman, *The Dinkum Dictionary Of Australian English*, p. 7, 1990

sash *noun*

anything used to tie around your arm while injecting a drug *US*

- —Helen Dahlskog (Editor), *A Dictionary of Contemporary and Colloquial Usage*, p. 50, 1972

sashay *verb*

to walk in a casual, often provocative, manner *US, 1928*

A corruption of the French *chasse* (a gliding dance step).

- "Son, I think one of them Arin bastids jus' sashayed by and copped a gander at us" Percy whispers.—Iceberg Slim (Robert Beck), *Doom Fox*, p. 227, 1978

Saskatchewan grunt *noun*

a dessert of berries and dough on top, as in Nova Scotia, but with saskatoon berries *CANADA*

- Somewhere along the way, apparently out in Nova Scotia, the fruit dish with a dough covering, properly called a cobbler, picked up the name grunt. However when made on the prairies with saskatoon berries, the name becomes Saskatchewan grunt.—Chris Thain, *Cold as a Bay Street Banker's Heart*, p. 131, 1987

sass *noun*

disrespectful, flippant back talk *US, 1835*

A corrupted pronunciation of the British **SAUCE**.

- Little Jeff give you sass, Big Jeff look around like he ain't even listening, but if you gave backlip – wap!—Edwin Torres, *Carlito's Way*, p. 17, 1975

sass *verb*

to talk back to someone; to speak to someone with disrespect *US, 1856*

- [F]inally he went to jail for sassing a cop and now he's gone[.]—Jack Kerouac, *Letter to Gary Snyder*, p. 582, May 1956

sassafras *noun*

marijuana *US, 1944*

Adopting the innocent identity and coincidental uses of the sassafras tree (*Sassafras albidum*); a native of North America which is used as a source of natural medicine and tea.

- —Richard A. Spears, *The Slang and Jargon of Drugs and Drink*, p. 436, 1986
- —Mike Haskins, *Drugs*, p. 289, 2003

sassy *noun*

rude speech *BAHAMAS*

Used in the phrase 'give sassies'.

- —John A. Holm, *Dictionary of Bahamian English*, p. 175, 1982

sassy *adjective*

spirited; impudent; used to describe someone who answers back *US, 1833*

- Say now – this one's a real sassy lassie.—William Bast, *The Myth Makers [Six Granada Plays]*, p. 176, 1958
- Which sassy pop diva has an album entitled "Rainbow"? [Mariah Carey]—*CD:UK*, p. 15, 2000

satchel *noun*

▸ **in the satchel**

corrupted; bribed; beholden to someone else *US*

A variation of the more common **IN THE BAG**.

- I got the word to watch out for action on Shank. I think this one is in the satchel.—Rocky Garciano (with Rowland Barber), *Somebody Up There Likes Me*, p. 311, 1955

satchel-swinger *noun*

a bookmaker *AUSTRALIA, 1965*

- —Frank Hardy, *The Yarns of Billy Borker*, p. 103, 1965
- I can assure you that Piping Lane took many thousands of dollars out of the 'satchel swingers' bags.—Joe Brown, *Just for the Record*, p. 128, 1984
- —Ned Wallish, *The Truth Dictionary of Racing Slang*, p. 71, 1989
- —John McCririck, *John McCririck's World of Betting*, p. 61, 1991

sat-com *noun*

*sat*ellite *com*munications *UK*

- Hammond unfurled the aerial of the sat-com radio[.]—Chris Ryan, *The Watchman*, p. 17, 2001

satellite *noun*

1 a prisoner who remains on the fringes of a prison gang without actually joining it *US*

- —William K. Bentley and James M. Corbett, *Prison Slang*, p. 43, 1992

2 a small-stakes poker tournament, the winning of which entitles the player to entry in a higher stakes tournament *US*

- —Anthony Holden, *Big Deal*, p. 304, 1990

satin *noun*

Italian Swiss Colony Silver Satin™ wine *US*

An inexpensive wine.

- —Edith A. Folb, *runnin' down some lines*, p. 253, 1980

satin and lace *noun*

the face *UK*

Rhyming slang.

- —Ray Puxley, *Fresh Rabbit*, 1998

satin and silk *noun*

milk *UK*

Rhyming slang.

- —Michael Munro, *The Original Patter*, 1985
- —Ray Puxley, *Cockney Rabbit*, 1992

Saturday night *noun*

in dominoes, the double blank piece *US*

- —Dominic Armanino, *Dominoes*, p. 17, 1959

Saturday night special *noun*

1 an inexpensive handgun, usually small calibre *US, 1968*

- "This cat is packing a Saturday-night special," someone said.—Charles Whited, *Chiodo*, p. 60, 1973
- Dough-Boy probably told you I don't carry any Saturday Night Specials or crap like that.—*Taxi Driver*, 1976

- It might have been better for him if Pedro's Saturday night special had left him dead. — Piri Thomas, *Stories from El Barrio*, p. 101, 1978
- "What kind of gun is that?" "No kind," Walter said. "Guy shoots the president of the United States with a fucking Saturday-night special." — Elmore Leonard, *Split Images*, p. 77, 1981
- Last year year it was Saturday Night Specials, now it's heavy stuff. — *48 Hours*, 1982

2 in computing, a program designed under intense time restraints *US*

- — Eric S. Raymond, *The New Hacker's Dictionary*, p. 313, 1991

3 a hospital patient who regularly appears in the casualty department at weekends in search of food and a bed *US*

- — *Maledicta*, p. 6, Summer/Winter 1978: 'Common patient-directed pejoratives used by medical 'personnel

Saturday night syndrome *noun*

1 tachycardiac fibrillation *US*

- It used to be called Saturday Night Syndrome, brought on by all-night dancing, carousing, and strenuous sexual activity. — Larry Rivers, *What Did I Do?*, p. 154, 1992

2 prolonged local pressure on a limb with resulting prolonged ischemia (inadequate blood supply) *US*

So named because of the tendency to drink to the point of extreme intoxication and then pass out with a limb dangling across the arm of a chair or the edge of a bed.

3 the stress and fear suffered by preachers who wait until Saturday night to write their Sunday sermon *US*

- In the preaching trade there's that thing called the 'Saturday night syndrome', and what that is, is the anxiety caused by putting off the sermon until Saturday night. Fortunately, I know nothing about that issue! — John M. McCoy, *The Worrying Mind (sermon)*, 7th May 2000

4 the tendency of a restaurant kitchen to fail to live up to its highest potential on the busiest night of the week, Saturday night *US*

- We're not sure whether this was because of the "Saturday night syndrome" or because chicken is something Franco does particularly well. — *Improper Bostonian*, May 2001

sauce *noun*

1 any and all alcohol *US, 1940*

- But the first thing you have to do is cut down on the sauce and build up your health. — William Burroughs, *Junkie*, p. 112, 1953
- Then you make a joy-scene with some fine, hot-ass bitch and a case of sauce to celebrate that you crossed me into the joint. Right? — Iceberg Slim (Robert Beck), *Trick Baby*, p. 268, 1969
- "Oh. You want to sit down and have a drink?" "I'm off the sauce, Connie." — Robert Campbell, *Alice in La-La Land*, p. 265, 1987
- I'm off the sauce. I'm not even smoking anymore. — *Basic Instinct*, 1992

2 in drag racing, a fuel mixed from nitromethane and alcohol *US*

- — Lyle K. Engel, *The Complete Book of Fuel and Gas Dragsters*, p. 153, 1968

3 impudence; impertinence *UK, 1835*

- "Been praying?" she asked eventually. "None of your sauce,"' said Joe. — Angela Huth, *Land Girls*, p. 59, 1998

4 spirit; courage *US*

From the song 'Baby's Got Sauce' by G. Love & Special Sauce.

- — Connie Eble (Editor), *UNC-CH Campus Slang*, p. 7, Fall 1997

▸ **the sauce**

the best *BAHAMAS*

- — John A. Holm, *Dictionary of Bahamian English*, p. 176, 1982

sauce *verb*

to speak impudently or impertinently to someone *UK, 1862*

- Isabella had to slap Francy. She sauced me when I gave an order. — John Jakes, *The Warriors*, p. 132, 1977

saucebox *noun*

an impudent person *UK, 1588*

- Spike's other lovers emerge as similar rentablonde cutouts – adolescent saucebox, cowed student, self-contained artist. — *The Observer*, 23rd March 2003

sauced *adjective*

drunk *US*

- — Connie Eble (Editor), *UNC-CH Campus Slang*, p. 9, Fall 1985

saucepan lid; saucepan; lid *noun*

1 a pound *UK, 1951*

Rhyming slang for **QUID**.

- Here is a saucepan lid – go and buy food. — Ronnie Barker, *Fletcher's Book of Rhyming Slang*, p. 25, 1979
- It's fifty "lid" for a week – a long 'un for three weeks. — Anthony Masters, *Minder*, p. 106, 1984

2 a Jewish person *UK*

Rhyming slang for **YID**.

- — Julian Franklyn, *A Dictionary of Rhyming Slang*, 1960

3 a child *UK, 1960*

Rhyming slang for **KID**.

- "Let go, Ernesto," I said, "You're scaring the saucepan-lids." — John Milne, *Alive and Kicking*, p. 105, 1998

saucepot *noun*

an impudent person *UK*

A variation of **SAUCEBOX**.

- Don't swear at me, you saucepot. — John Milne, *Alive and Kicking*, p. 166, 1998

saucer *noun*

1 a tablet of MDMA, the recreational drug best known as ecstasy *UK*

Perhaps there is an implied pun on flying saucers.

- — Angela Devlin, *Prison Patter*, p. 101, 1996

2 a silver dollar coin *US*

- — Edd Byrnes, *Way Out with Kookie*, 1959

3 in pinball, a scoring hole with a bevelled lip *US*

- — Bobbye Claire Natkin and Steve Kirk, *All About Pinball*, p. 116, 1977

saucer cap *noun*

a US Army wool serge AG-44 service cap *US*

- — Gregory Clark, *Words of the Vietnam War*, p. 453, 1990

saucered and blowed *adjective*

all ready to go; prepared for use in any way *CANADA, 1987*

- The men of the family pour hot tea or coffee into the saucer and blow on it to [cool it]. Once all saucered and blowed it [is] ready to drink, and therefore, anything else that is all ready to go, or prepared, is also all saucered and blowed. — Chris Thain, *Cold as a Bay Street Banker's Heart*, p. 3, 1987

saucy *adjective*

1 attractive; desired *US*

- Those new shoes are hella saucy. — Rick Ayers (Editor), *Berkeley High Slang Dictionary*, p. 36, 2004

2 very drunk *US*

- — Jim Crotty, *How to Talk American*, p. 145, 1997

Saudi cool *adjective*

warm to hot *US*

Gulf war usage.

- — *American Speech*, p. 400, Winter 1991: 'Among the new words'

saulty *noun*

▹ **see: SALTEE**

sausage *noun*

1 the penis *AUSTRALIA, 1944*

- By the time I had left school, I had heard most of the euphemisms. There was dork, eric, muscle, prong, pencil (for having lead in), sausage and tonk. — Bettina Arndt, *The Australian Way of Sex*, p. 10, 1985
- However, if we are sitting on a crowded subway and some creep is standing in front of us shoving his sausage in our face, the penis becomes the ugliest human appendage we have ever seen in our lives. — Anka Radakovich, *The Wild Girls Club*, p. 11, 1994

2 someone foolish or gullible; used as a gently reproving term of address *UK, 1982*

Affectionate, childish and jocular.

- Only joking, you silly sausages! — Dave Courtney, *Stop the Ride I Want to Get Off*, p. 224, 1999
- God, yewer really fuckin scared, aren't yew? Poor sausage. — Niall Griffiths, *Sheepshagger*, p. 254, 2001

3 used, often while reproving or gently chiding a child or lover, as an affectionate form of address, usually qualified with an adjective *UK*

- There he goes, what a character, what a lusty old sausage. — *LAM*, p. 53, 7th September 1982

• "What are you doing here, you silly sausage?" said Mark, and he bent and kissed the tiny bit of Robin that was exposed. —Jacqueline Wilson, *The Lottie Project*, p. 162, 1999

4 marijuana *US, 1968*

• —Ernest L. Abel, *A Marijuana Dictionary*, p. 90, 1982

5 a marijuana cigarette *UK*

• —Home Office, *Glossary of Terms and Slang Common in Penal Establishments*, July 1978

▸ **hide the sausage; sink the sausage**

(of a male) to copulate *AUSTRALIA*

• To engage in congress, or to play cars and garages or hide the sausage. —Barry Humphries, *Bazza pulls it off!*, 1971
• The sinking the sausage rule still applies. (NSW Solicitor quoted by Richard Beckett on divorce law reforms). —Bill Hornadge, *The Ugly Australian*, p. 176, 1973
• —Jim Ramsay, *Cop It Sweet!*, p. 71, 1977
• George would never sink his sausage again. —*Picture*, p. 60, 5th February 1992

▸ **not a sausage**

no money; hence nothing at all *UK, 1938*

From rhyming slang on **SAUSAGE AND MASH** (cash).

• Three hours I waited in that cubicle. Not a dickie bird. Not a sausage. —Richard Herring, *Talking Cock*, p. vi, 2003

sausage and mash *noun*

1 cash; money *UK*

Rhyming slang.

• Hand over your sausage and mash, then you can take the whistle and flute [suit]! —*The Sweeney*, p. 8, 1976

2 a collision *UK*

Rhyming slang for 'crash' or 'smash'.

• —Julian Franklyn, *A Dictionary of Rhyming Slang*, 1961

sausage board *noun*

a surfboard that is rounded at both ends *AUSTRALIA*

• —Jack Pollard, *The Australian Surfrider*, p. 18, 1963

sausage dog *noun*

a dachshund *UK, 1938*

• [A] couple in Somerset had cancelled their holiday in order to pay for a customised wheelchair for their crippled sausage dog, Dotty. We kid you not. —*The Guardian*, 23rd August 2002

sausage fest; sausage party *noun*

a party with far more boys than girls *US*

• —Don R. McCreary (Editor), *Dawg Speak*, 2001
• —Connie Eble (Editor), *UNC-CH Campus Slang*, p. 6, November 2002

sausage grappler *noun*

a male masturbator *AUSTRALIA*

• Yeah, you old sausage grappler!!! —Barry Humphries, *Bazza Pulls It Off!*, 1971

sausage roll *noun*

1 unemployment benefit *UK*

Rhyming slang for **THE DOLE**.

• —*Daily Telegraph*, 17th December 1972

2 a pole *UK*

Rhyming slang.

• To drive someone up the "sausage" is to drive him mad. —Ray Puxley, *Cockney Rabbit*, 1992

3 a Pole *UK*

Rhyming slang.

• —John Gosling, *The Ghost Squad*, 1959

4 the poll (the head), especially in reference to 'Poll Tax' *UK*

Rhyming slang.

• —Ray Puxley, *Cockney Rabbit*, 1992

sausage roll; sausage *verb*

to have sex *UK*

Rhyming slang for **POLE**.

• —Ray Puxley, *Cockney Rabbit*, 1992

sauskee *noun*

in circus and carnival usage, fifteen dollars *US*

• —Don Wilmeth, *The Language of American Popular Entertainment*, p. 232, 1981

savage *adjective*

good; excellent *US*

• —p. 56, 1st January 1965: 'Students: the slang bag' Time
• —Susie Dent, *The Language Report*, p. 75, 2003

Savannah *noun*

in craps, a seven *US, 1983*

• —Thomas L. Clark, *The Dictionary of Gambling and Gaming*, p. 189, 1987

save *verb*

▸ **save me**

please save for me *US*

• Turning to Jimmy, he said, "Save me on that butt, Jim." —Nathan Heard, *Howard Street*, p. 62, 1968

▸ **save right to the blossom**

in British Columbia logging, to fell a tall tree without breaking it *CANADA*

• To be "saved right to the blossom," a tree must be unbroken for its entire length. —Tom Parkin, *WetCoast Words*, p. 120, 1989

saveloy *noun*

a boy, also in the sense 'one of the boys' (a gang member) *UK*

Often heard in the catchphrase greeting, challenge or terrace-chant: 'oi oi saveloy!'.

• —Julian Franklyn, *A Dictionary of Rhyming Slang*, 1961
• —Ray Puxley, *Cockney Rabbit*, 1992

saver *noun*

1 in a pool tournament, an agreement between two or more players to share their winnings *US*

• The effect of a saver is to reduce competitiveness, since a player will still receive money even if he loses. —Mike Shamos, *The Illustrated Encyclopedia of Billiards*, p. 201, 1993

2 a hedging bet *AUSTRALIA, 1891*

• Quite a number of the many followers of the Bradfield stable had a 'saver' on Night Watch mainly on the strength of his good second in the Hotham Handicap[.] —Maurice Cavanough and Meurig Davies, *Cup Day*, p. 165, 1960
• —Wilda Moxham, *The Apprentice*, p. 68, 1969
• —Sam Weller, *Old Bastards I Have Met*, p. 39, 1979
• —Igor Kushyshyn et al., *The Gambling Times Guide to Harness Racing*, p. 211, 1994

savoury rissole *noun*

a lavatory; an unpleasant or dirty place or location *UK*

Rhyming slang for **PISS-HOLE**, formed on an English dish also known as a 'faggot'.

• —Ray Puxley, *Cockney Rabbit*, 1992

savvy *noun*

knowledge; intelligence; experience *US, 1825*

From the Spanish *saber* (to know).

• Common Zen savvy tells us as much. —Terry Southern, *The Magic Christian*, p. 52, 1959
• Them pimps and 'hos offa Rampart Street got their own understanding of one another's crazy shit and savvy of their thing together. —Iceberg Slim (Robert Beck), *Airtight Willie and Me*, p. 24, 1979
• Everybody laughs at that one, because they think it's true, because street savvy says that everybody wears a tag. Everybody can be bought. —Robert Campbell, *Junkyard Dog*, p. 142, 1986

savvy *verb*

to understand *UK, 1785*

Horribly butchered Spanish *saber* (to know), used by a monoglot English speaker trying to make himself understood by a foreigner.

• He moves his leg, look for the bulge. You savvy bulge? —*Get Shorty*, 1995
• But you double-cross me, and I'll come back with dogs – and keep coming back. You savvy? —Duncan MacLaughlin, *The Filth*, p. 198, 2002
• You can go now, Lovejoy. Any more disobedience, you'll have more antics for our amusement. Savvy? —Jonathan Gash, *The Ten Word Game*, p. 153, 2003

-savvy *suffix*

aware, intelligent, informed *UK*

From French *savoir* (to know). Used for forming adjectives, it follows the noun.

• Joe Punter had become a lot more media-savvy recently[.] —Christopher Brookmyre, *Boiling a Frog*, p. 107, 2000

saw *verb*

▸ **saw logs**

to snore *US*

From cartoon illustrations comparing the sounds.

• —Connie Eble (Editor), *UNC-CH Campus Slang*, p. 5, Spring 1980

▸ **saw wood**

in pool, to play with an awkward stroke *US*

• —Steve Rushin, *Pool Cool*, p. 25, 1990

sawbones *noun*
a doctor, especially a surgeon *UK, 1837*
- —Lou Shelly, *Hepcats Jive Talk Dictionary*, p. 48, 1945
- —Ramon Adams, *The Language of the Railroader*, p. 133, 1977
- When that doctor asked me, Son / How'd you get in this condition? I said, "Hey sawbones / I'm just carrying on / An ole family tradition." —Hank Williams Jr, *Family Tradition*, 1979
- Plus we're gonna send for a free specialist so you're not at the mercy of these sorryass state sawbones. —Seth Morgan, *Homeboy*, p. 288, 1990
- HEALY: I got a date tonight with that Mary girl I told you about. SULLY: The sawbones? —*Something About Mary*, 1998

sawbuck *noun*
1 a ten-dollar note *US, 1850*
- Lemme take a sawbuck, man. —Chester Himes, *If He Hollers Let Him Go*, p. 43, 1945
- Through Western Union the Freemans had lucked up on a sawbuck from home, so we were in the chips again. —Mezz Mezzrow, *Really the Blues*, p. 135, 1946
- The two suits I had bought off the rack had had to be altered slightly, but I had given the clerk a sawbuck and he had said they would be delivered this afternoon[.] —Horace McCoy, *Kiss Tomorrow Good-bye*, p. 249, 1948
- He was a kid trying to get a fin or a sawbuck a day to keep his habit up. —Willard Motely, *Let No Man Write My Epitaph*, p. 369, 1958
- "Then Bernie should get 'something extra' every time he solos on Grand Piano Jump." "Say an extra sawbuck," Red went on. —Ross Russell, *The Sound*, p. 91, 1961
- —Joe McKennon, *Circus Lingo*, p. 81, 1980

2 a ten-year prison sentence *US*
- —Hyman E. Goldin et al., *Dictionary of American Underworld Lingo*, p. 185, 1950
- —Joseph E. Ragen and Charles Finston, *Inside the World's Toughest Prison*, p. 816, 1962: 'Penitentiary and underworld glossary'
- —John R. Armore and Joseph D. Wolfe, *Dictionary of Desperation*, p. 47, 1976

sawdust *noun*
1 dynamite *US*
- —Vincent J. Monteleone, *Criminal Slang*, p. 200, 1949

2 dehydrated cabbage *ANTARCTICA*
- —*Cool Antarctica*, 2003: 'Antarctic slang'

sawdust joint *noun*
an unassuming, barebones gambling operation *US*
- Some of the names of the sawdust joints are as direct as their actions. —Ed Reid and Ovid Demaris, *The Green Jungle*, p. 4, 1963
- —John Scarne, *Scarne on Dice*, p. 477, 1974
- —George Percy, *The Language of Poker*, p. 78, 1988

sawdust machine; sawdust pump *noun*
a hand drill *US*
- —A.B. Chance Co., *Lineman's Slang Dictionary*, p. 15, 1980

sawdust nobility *noun*
an owner of a lumber mill or large timber stand *CANADA*
- In each of these ghost towns there must have been a little group of mill and timber owners, a sawdust nobility of the Oak Falls kind. —Thomas Raddall, *Wings*, p. 31, 1956

sawed-off *noun*
a shotgun with a barrel less than 18 inches breech-to-muzzle or 26 inches overall *US*
- —Ralph de Sola, *Crime Dictionary*, p. 134, 1982

sawn-off *noun*
a shotgun with the barrels *sawn-off* to a much shorter length to aid concealment of the weapon and enhance the lethal spread of the shot *UK*
- Parker had a shrewd idea that a sawn-off – a weapon useless except for close quarters work against members of the human race – was illegal anyway. —Derek Bickerton, *Payroll*, p. 48, 1959
- [A] policeman carried no special dispensation from a yard man's 'matic [automatic weapon] or a cockney's sawn-off. —Donald Gorgon, *Cop Killer*, p. 4, 1994
- —Angela Devlin, *Prison Patter*, p. 101, 1996
- [G]o home and get the sawn-off[.] —Dave Courtney, *Raving Lunacy*, p. 224, 2000
- [T]he jolly old sawn-off went out with sideboards and radiograms, three-piece whistles with twenty-four inch lionels[.] —J.J. Connolly, *Layer Cake*, p. 8, 2000

saw-off *noun*
an agreement to compromise with mutual benefits, especially political *CANADA*
- Canada will win saw-off over lumber. —*skchamber.sk.ca/biznews*, 6th June 2002

sawski; sawsky *noun*
a ten-dollar note *US*
From **SAWBUCK**.
- We rigged his room with a one-wayua whorehouse mirror and charged a sawski to watch it. —William Burroughs, *Naked Lunch*, p. 2, 1957
- —Joe McKennon, *Circus Lingo*, p. 81, 1980
- The Manager was right: the Varsity Squad was reaching up, tucking sawskis in her garter belt. —Seth Morgan, *Homeboy*, p. 138, 1990

say *noun*
1 six *UK*
- —Paul Baker, *Polari*, 2002

2 a story *UK*
English gypsy use.
- One say that sticks in my mind concerns my cousin Billy Smith's father, Matty. —Jimmy Stockin, *On The Cobbles*, p. 73, 2000

say *verb*
▸ **say goodbye**
to die *UK*
Apposite imagery for this piece of unusually sentimental rhyming slang.
- —Ray Puxley, *Cockney Rabbit*, 1992

▸ **say Greg**
used for inviting a challenge *TRINIDAD AND TOBAGO*
- If you only say greg I go buss your arse. —Lise Winer, *Dictionary of the English/Creole of Trinidad & Tobago*, 2003

▸ **say your morning prayers**
to vomit in the morning, especially as a result of morning sickness *TRINIDAD AND TOBAGO, 1979*
- —Lise Winer, *Dictionary of the English/Creole of Trinidad & Tobago*, 2003

say *adjective*
▹ see: **SEY**

sayanora
goodbye *US*
- —Collin Baker et al., *College Undergraduate Slang Study Conducted at Brown University*, p. 187, 1968

say dooey *adjective*
eight *UK*
Polari; **SAY** (six) plus **DOOEY** (two).
- —Paul Baker, *Polari*, p. 189, 2002

saying hello to Mr Armitage *adjective*
drunk, perhaps so drunk as to be sick *UK*
Derives either as a tribute to an unknown man or, perhaps, as a reference to lavatory manufacturer Armitage Shanks.
- —*e-cyclopaedia*, 20th March 2002

say kids, what time is it?
used as a humorous call to action *US*
The signature opening of *Howdy Doody Show* (NBC, 1947–60). Repeated often with referential humour.

say now
used as a greeting *US*
- —Malachi Andrews and Paul T. Owens, *Black Language*, p. 86, 1973

say oney *noun*
seven *UK*
Polari; **SAY** (six) plus **ONEY** (one).
- —Paul Baker, *Polari*, p. 189, 2002

say-so *noun*
1 authority *UK, 1637*
- I don't know if he's rippin' us off or not. The thing is, he has too much say-so about the money. —Donald Goines, *Black Gangster*, p. 123, 1977
- We took you to this country. We took you into the paper-hanging business. If I didn't give the say-so, you'd be in the old country. —*Avalon*, 1990

2 a person's word of honour *UK, 1637*
- That's your say-so. I don't take the word of gonnifs, pimps and juicemen. —Robert Campbell, *Juice*, p. 52, 1988

say tray *adjective*
nine *UK*
Polari; **SAY** (six) plus **TRAY** (three).
- —Paul Baker, *Polari*, p. 189, 2002

say what?

1 used as a request to repeat what has just been said *UK*
An Americanism.
- "We're off." The Hispanic detective with Asana looked over. "Say what?" "We're off." — Robert Crais, *L.A. Requiem*, p. 43–44, 1999

2 used for expressing disbelief at what has just been said *US*
- — Connie Eble (Editor), *UNC-CH Campus Slang*, p. 5, Fall 1987

say what and so what?

intended as a clever dismissal of what has just been said *US*
- I say say what and so what. Too bad Wardell's dead, he'd probably want to poke her. — James Ellroy, *White Jazz*, p. 52, 1992

say when!

used to ask *when* enough food has been served or drink been poured *UK, 1889*
By ellipsis.

SBD *adjective*

used of a fart, inaudible but smelly *CANADA*
An abbreviation of '*s*ilent *b*ut *d*eadly'.
- — Bill Casselman, *Canadian Sayings*, p. 62, 2002

sca *noun*

information; news; gossip *IRELAND*
- Come on, Bumper. I want the sca. He's from Abbeytown. Calls himself Snoopy... — Eamonn Sweeney, *Waiting for the Healer*, p. 182, 1997

scab *noun*

1 a strike-breaker *US, 1777*
From earlier usage as 'a generally contemptible person'.
- They're the ones who make scabs out of you. — Ralph Ellison, *Invisible Man*, p. 197, 1947
- It's just the thugs and the scabs fooling you[.] — Woody Guthrie, *Coming into Los Angeles*, 1961
- On the first day of the fifteenth week, skulls were split at the mill gates when truckloads of imported and local scabs staged a lightning assault on depleted picket lines. — Clancy Sigal, *Going Away*, p. 282, 1961
- That wasn't violence, Edith. That was education. It was the only way to teach those fink scabs a lesson! — Eugene Boe (Compiler), *The Wit & Wisdom of Archie Bunker*, p. 29, 1971
- As the baker's strike began, I was allocated a few loaves of (scab) bread, which I kept for the old and the infirm[.] — Mark Steel, *Reasons to be Cheerful*, p. 55, 2001

2 a thief *UK*
Noted as teen slang by Susie Dent, *The Language Report*, 2003.

3 a stingy person; a miser *AUSTRALIA*
- At first I reckoned the lack of food in the fridge was 'cause some cheapskate scabs were not putting into the kitty. — Kathy Lette, *Girls' Night Out*, p. 41, 1987
- [S]he is such a scab, she won't even share the Turkish Delights. — Kylie Mole (Maryanne Fahey), *My Diary*, p. 104, 1988

4 a citizens' band radio operator *US*
A derisive term used by purist shortwave radio operators.
- — Warren Smith, *Warren's Smith's Authentic Dictionary of CB*, p. 61, 1976

5 in western Canada, a saddle *CANADA*
- Throw down that cayuse and cinch my scab down good and hard on him, and I'll be out. — Richmond Hobson, *Grass Beyond the Mountains*, p. 89, 1951

scab *verb*

1 to act as a strike-breaker *US, 1806*
- A mine clerk named Herbert Smith, scabbing in a Colorado Fuel and Iron mine, was brutally beaten near Trinidad. — Russ Kick, *Everything You Know is Wrong*, p. 256, 2002
- Students earned the enmity of the working class by scabbing the jobs of strikers just for fun. — Thomas Frank, *What's the Matter with Kansas?*, p. 204, 2004

2 to search for a possible sex-partner *US*
Hawaiian youth usage.
- — Douglas Simonson, *Pidgin to da Max Hana Hou*, 1982

3 to cadge something *AUSTRALIA*
- In the carry basket was some clothes he said he scabbed from Mrs Musworth at the pub. — Tim Winton, *That eye, the sky*, p. 69, 1986

4 in pinball, to obtain a result through luck, not skill *US*
- — Bobbye Claire Natkin and Steve Kirk, *All About Pinball*, p. 116, 1977

scabby *adjective*

non-union *AUSTRALIA, 1892*
- And what bloody use would it be getting in touch with that scabby turnout? — Frank Hardy, *The Outcasts of Foolgarah*, p. 53, 1971

▸ **I could eat a scabby dog**

used as a declaration of great hunger *UK: SCOTLAND*
In Glasgow use.
- Ah could eat a scabby dug. — Michael Munro, *The Complete Patter*, 1996

scabby eye *noun*

a pie *UK*
Rhyming slang.
- — Ray Puxley, *Cockney Rabbit*, 1992

scabby-headed *adjective*

▸ **I could eat a scabby-headed wean**

used as a declaration of great hunger *UK: SCOTLAND*
In Glasgow use. 'I could eat a scabby-headed cat' is the familiar variant in the English midlands.
- Ah could eat a scabby-heidit wean [a baby; a child]. — Michael Munro, *The Patter, Another Blast*, 1988

scab duty *noun*

especially in Western Australia and New South Wales, the picking up of litter as a school punishment *AUSTRALIA*
- I was regularly sentenced to school detention, time-out and scab duty. — Delphine Jamet, *Streetkid in the City*, p. 108, 2001

scablifter *noun*

a doctor *UK*
- — Angela Devlin, *Prison Patter*, p. 101, 1996

scad!

used in expressing anger *US*
- — Don R. McCreary (Editor), *Dawg Speak*, 2001

scadge *noun*

a tramp *UK: SCOTLAND*
- Don't staun [stand] next yo us, ya scadge. — Michael Munro, *The Complete Patter*, p. 134, 1996

scads *noun*

a large quantity of anything *US*
From an earlier sense specific to money.

scaffle *noun*

phencyclidine, the recreational drug known as PCP or angel dust *US*
- — US Department of Justice, *Street Terms*, October 1994

scag; skag *noun*

1 heroin; cocaine *US, 1967*
- I was snortin' scag / while other kids played tag / and my elders went to church to pray. — Lightnin' Rod, *Hustlers Convention*, p. 8, 1973
- Only a skag high ain't but good the first few times out, then you hooked[.] — Edwin Torres, *Carlito's Way*, p. 10, 1975
- Know where I can cop some skag? — Babs Gonzales, *Movin' On Down De Line*, p. 82, 1975
- When I heard they croaked Charlie I freak out, almost went back to shootin scag. — Charles W. Moore, *A Brick for Mister Jones*, p. 105, 1975
- You copping two bills a week and freebie skag to shoot. — Iceberg Slim (Robert Beck), *Airtight Willie and Me*, p. 173, 1979
- And whether it's brew or skag you do become that sort of bloke. — Shaun Ryder, *Shaun Ryder... in His Own Words*, 1997
- She screeched with pleasure. The skag [cocaine] was kicking in. — Karline Smith, *Promise [britpulp]*, p. 177, 1999
- — Robert Ashton, *This Is Heroin*, p. 207, 2002

2 a cigarette *US*
- — Lou Shelly, *Hepcats Jive Talk Dictionary*, p. 48, 1945

3 inferior alcohol *US*
- — Marcus Hanna Boulware, *Jive and Slang of Students in Negro Colleges*, 1947

4 an unattractive girl or woman *US*
- — *Dobie Gillis Teenage Slanguage Dictionary*, 1962
- — J. R. Friss, *A Dictionary of Teenage Slang (Mt. Diablo High)*, 1964
- — *Current Slang*, p. 5, Spring 1967

scaggy *adjective*

addicted to heroin *UK*
Extended from **SCAG** (heroin).
- Fuck off you scaggy twat. — Tony Wilson, *24 Hour Party People*, p. 176, 2002

scag-hag; skag-hag *noun*

1 a female heroin addict *UK*
Combines **SCAG** (heroin) with conventional 'hag' (a woman), on the model of **FAG-HAG** (a woman smoker).

- These girls were the lost souls, the lowest of the low. Skag-hags and jellyheads[crack addicts], emaciated young girls[.] —Kevin Sampson, *Powder*, p. 55, 1999

2 someone who enjoys the company of heroin users *UK*
A gay coinage; combines **SCAG** (heroin) with conventional 'hag' (a woman), on the model of **FAG-HAG** (someone who enjoys the company of gays).

3 a heterosexual woman who takes pleasure in the company of homosexual men *US*
- —*American Speech*, p. 58, Spring-Summer 1970: 'Homosexual slang'

scag-head; skag-head *noun*
a heroin addict *UK*
A combination of **SCAG** (heroin or cocaine) and **HEAD** (a user).
- He reminded me of a skag-head, face really pale and drawn. —Wayne Anthony, *Spanish Highs*, p. 3, 1999

scag jones; skag jones *noun*
a heroin addiction *US*
- —Ralph de Sola, *Crime Dictionary*, p. 134, 1982

scag nasty; skag nasty *adjective*
repulsive in the extreme *US*
- —Michael Dalton Johnson, *Talking Trash with Redd Foxx*, p. 132, 1994
- —Chris Lewis, *The Dictionary of Playground Slang*, p. 202, 2003

scald *noun*
tea *IRELAND*
- Tea tonight is the usual pot of scald, no fuckin Christmas pudding or Christmas cake. —Paul Howard, *The Joy*, p. 168, 1996

scale *verb*
to ride a bus, train or tram without paying *AUSTRALIA, 1941*
Earlier, since 1904 (*Australian National Dictionary*) used intransitively to mean 'to avoid paying'.
- —Jim Ramsay, *Cop It Sweet!*, p. 79, 1977

scaley *noun*
a signaller in the British military *UK*
- Fraser was going to be running the desk with a couple of scaleys. —Andy McNab (writing of the late 1970s/early 80s), *Immediate Action*, p. 166, 1995

scalie *noun*
a person employed on a vehicle weighbridge *AUSTRALIA, 1976*
- The only thing worse than a queue jumper is a 'scalie', an RTA inspector pursuing trucks hauling more than their legal limit. —*Sydney Morning Herald*, p. 5, 23rd November 1999

Scallicon Valley *nickname*
the Information Technology sector in Liverpool *UK*
A pun on **SCALLY** (a Liverpool rogue, hence a Liverpudlian) and California's mythical Silicon Valley, in the world's eyes the home of computer science.
- YT [yours truly, I] was among the first to get on the Scallicon Valley trail. —Kevin Sampson, *Outlaws*, p. 31, 2001

scally *noun*
a rogue; a hooligan; a rough youth *UK, 1986*
A shortening of **SCALLYWAG** used in Liverpool slang.
- All these little scallies with cricket bats an carving knives wading through the shite. —Niall Griffiths, *Kelly + Victor*, p. 17, 2002

scally *verb*
to behave in a lawless manner *UK*
From the noun sense.
- I can see us, little rats, scallying around that Garden Festival. —Kevin Sampson, *Outlaws*, p. 7, 2001

scallybip *verb*
to burgle a house while the housewife is outside hanging washing on the line to dry *US*
- Around Christmas of that year me and a friend was going to go up through Oklahoma bipping – scallybipping [burglarizing a home when they saw the wife out back hanging clothes], you know. —Bruce Jackson, *In the Life*, p. 82, 1972

scallywag; scallawag; skallywag *noun*
a disreputable fellow *US, 1849*
- You are the father of triplets, sir, you lucky skallywag! —Barry Humphries, *Bazza Pulls It Off!*, 1971
- [H]e's a rascal, no question about it. He's a scallywag – but, I can't buy Arthur, I mean, Daley, as a drug dealer. —Anthony Masters, *Minder*, p. 156, 1984

scalp *noun*
1 the appearance of a pornography performer's photograph on the video box *UK*
From the sense of a 'scalp' as a 'trophy'.
- —*Adult Video News*, p. 51, October 1995

2 a toupee *US*
- —Wilfred Granville, *The Theater Dictionary*, p. 205, 1952

scalp *verb*
1 to buy tickets for an event and resell them, usually outside the event itself *US, 1886*
Originally stock exchange slang, then passed into broader general usage.
- I tell him, picked up once for scalping tickets at the Superdome and fined two hundred books. —Elmore Leonard, *Bandits*, p. 21, 1987

2 to beat up a rival gang member and steal his gang patch *NEW ZEALAND*
- —Harry Orsman, *A Dictionary of Modern New Zealand Slang*, p. 115, 1999

scalper; scalp *noun*
a person who buys tickets for a sporting or entertainment event and resells them at a profit *US, 1869*
- [T]he hawk-eyed scalpers, the hard-boiled New York scouts for Hollywood, the agents of the players or acquisitive agents looking for clients, nervous stockholders in the theater and show and their staffs, comprise the hundreds "out front"[.] —Jack Lait and Lee Mortimer, *New York Confidential*, p. 41, 1948
- —Zander Hollander and Paul Zimmerman, *Football Lingo*, p. 104, 1967
- Scalper? You call me a scalper? I perform a service, my friends. The service costs money. Now do you want the tickets or not. —*Fast Times at Ridgemont High*, 1982
- "You're an expert, Phil. The best scalper in the game," said Arthur with all the respect of one pro for another. Little Phil replied patiently, "I don't like that word scalper, or even tout. I think of myself as a ticket broker." —Anthony Masters, *Minder*, p. 49, 1984
- —Angela Devlin, *Prison Patter*, p. 101, 1996
- As a student in Bronxville I had learned all the tricks – showing up an hour before the performance at Weill to nab five-dollar seats and waiting beneath the overhang at Lincoln Center for the ticket scalpers. —Rita Ciresi, *Pink Slip*, p. 193, 1999

scaly *noun*
an acting detective constable in a Metropolitan Police Crime Squad *UK*
- For some reason we were called "Scalies" – apparently short for "Scaly Aides". It's a word everyone used but no-one seemed to know exactly why. —Duncan MacLaughlin, *The Filth*, p. 106, 2002

scaly leg *noun*
a common prostitute *US*
- See, ordinarily I don't mess with dirty legs, or scaly legs, or whatever you want to call them. Tramps. —Bruce Jackson, *In the Life*, p. 187, 1972

scam *noun*
1 a scheme by which a legitimate business is forced into bankruptcy and taken over by organised crime *US*
- —Bill Reilly, *Big Al's Official Guide to Chicagoese*, p. 50, 1982

2 a scheme to defraud people *US, 1963*
- This kink in the law is rarely prosecuted though, unless it involves a large-scale supply scam. —*Drugs An Adult Guide*, p. 24, December 2001
- The Six Degrees of Separation scam caught up with her at a table that included writers and editors. —Melissa de la Cruz, *How to Become Famous in Two Weeks or Less*, p. 79, 2003

3 a report; the latest information *US*
- —Gary Fairmont R. Filosa II, *The Surfer's Almanac*, p. 193, 1977

scam *verb*
to cheat or defraud someone *US, 1963*
- You're my man. I knew it. I knew soon as you scammed your way in here, got the free ride. —Elmore Leonard, *Glitz*, p. 255, 1985

scammer *noun*
a petty confidence trickster; a fraudster *US, 1972*
- [I]n Utah County it is common for scammers to ensnare their victims by asking them to evaluate the proposed investment[.] —Jon Krakauer, *Under the Banner of Heaven*, p. 272, 2003

scammered *adjective*
drunk *UK*
- —Pete Brown, *Man Walks into a Pub*, 2003

scamp *noun*
a rascal *UK, 1808*
- He put two and two together, remembered that his old running buddy had always been a scamp, and took me in without any questions. —Alice Walker, *The Color Purple*, p. 176, 1982
- MIA: But when you scamps get together, you're worse than a sewing circle. — *Pulp Fiction*, 1994

scampi *noun*
a very attractive man *UK*
Noted in connection with a legal dispute over rap lyrics by *BBC News*, 6th June 2003.
- So let me count the ways in which I love thee / Falling over scampi / A true all fantasy / Telling normal lies / Your love is taking me high —All Saints, *Take the Key*, 1997

scan *verb*
to examine someone or something *US*
- God, scan on Martha Dumptruck. — *Heathers*, 1988

scandal bag *noun*
a plastic shopping bag *JAMAICA*
- —Peter Patrick, *Some Recent Jamaican Creole Words*, 2003

scandalous *adjective*
1 extremely competent *US*
- —William K. Bentley and James M. Corbett, *Prison Slang*, p. 33, 1992

2 mean-spirited *US*
The variant 'scan'lous' also exists.
- —Rick Ayers (Editor), *Slang Dictionary*, p. 14, 2001

scandalous!
used for expressing disbelief or shock *US*
- — *Maybeck High School Yearbook (Berkeley, California)*, p. 29, 1997

Scandi *adjective*
*Scandi*navian *UK*
- The toilet's great – typical Scandi hygiene. —Charlie Hall, *The Box (Disco Biscuits)*, p. 155, 1996

Scandie; Scandy *noun*
a Scandinavian *NEW ZEALAND*
- The place is full of Yanks and Scandies with flags sewn on their back packs. —Maurice Gee, *Prowlers*, p. 41, 1987
- We both like Scandies [...] I've had seven Scandinavian boyfriends. — *The Big Breakfast, Channel 4*, 10th January 2002

Scando-pop *noun*
popular music originating in any Scandinavian country *UK*
- When it comes to Scando-pop, you can't beat the Swedes – or can you? — *Bang*, p. 64, August 2003

scanger; skanger *noun*
a rough, uncouth youth *IRELAND*
- Anyway somewhere along the line my phone must have been robbed...I pick up the phone and dial my number, roysh [right]. This total skanger answers it... —Paul Howard, *Ross O'Carroll-Kelly*, p. 21, 2003

scanties *noun*
skimpy knickers, hence skimpy underwear (usually women's) *UK, 1937*
- I want more photographs of the cast of Hollyoaks in their scanties, shoulders back, tits out, and airbrushed into Mattel-ish perfection. — *The Guardian*, 17th January 2004

scants *noun*
skimpy underpants (usually women's) *UK*
A shortening of SCANTIES.
- —Jenny Fabian and Johnny Byrne, *Groupie*, 1968

Scarborough Fair; scarborough *noun*
hair *UK*
Ephemeral rhyming slang, formed from the title of a 1966 recording by Simon and Garfunkel.
- I like her Scarborough, don't you? —Ray Puxley, *Fresh Rabbit*, 1998

scare *verb*
▸ **scare the shit out of**
to terrify someone *UK, 1961*
- I'd say someone is trying to scare the shit out of more people than just us. —John Hockenberry, *A River Out of Eden*, p. 55, 2001

Scare Air *noun*
any of the many small airlines operating, on land, bush or water, in British Columbia *CANADA*
- Operating on thin profit margins and in notoriously poor weather, the small coastal airlines have been known to press the limits of safety. Survivors of these white-knuckle flights often add "Scare" to the corporate name. —Tom Parkin, *WetCoast Words*, p. 121, 1989

scare cards *noun*
in poker, the strongest cards in a player's hand, exposed to other players accidentally on purpose *US*
- —Peter O. Steiner, *Thursday Night Poker*, p. 417, 1996

scarecrow *noun*
an empty police car parked at the side of a road to deter speeding *US*
- —"Slingo", *The Official CB Slang Dictionary Handbook*, p. 53, 1976

scare-do *noun*
an unflattering or unfashionable hairdo *US*
- —Connie Eble (Editor), *UNC-CH Campus Slang*, p. 7, Spring 1990

scaredy-cat *noun*
a cowardly person *UK, 1933*
Childish.
- "You're just a scaredy-cat." "No I'm not!" —Gary Soto, *Cat's Meow*, p. 52, 1987

Scare Ontario *noun*
Air Ontario *CANADA*
- "Scare Ontario" is an irreverent nickname for this feeder airline. —Lewis Poteet, *Plane Talk*, p. 145, 1997

scarers *noun*
▸ **put the scarers on**
to frighten someone *AUSTRALIA*
- '[Y]ou reckon you can put the scarers on Hardy?' —Peter Corris, *Make Me Rich*, p. 148, 1985

scare up *verb*
to find something by hunting it out; to discover something *US, 1852*
From the hunting of game.
- Both parties have cynically turned the drugs issue into an election beat up, exploiting the victims of drug abuse and addiction to try and scare up a few more votes. — *The Guardian*, 10th March 1999

scarf *noun*
food *US*
- There's plenty on the shelf. Take what you need. If you want coffee or some scarf – help yourself. —Malcolm Braly, *On the Yard*, p. 247, 1967

scarf *verb*
1 to eat, especially to eat greedily and hurriedly *US*
- That, before you know it, it was scarfing time and these port cats is forty-two miles out of town and nobody's got the first biscuit. —William "Lord" Buckley, *The Nazz*, 1951
- In times of crisis, all great mean scarf. —Edwin Torres, *Q & A*, p. 86, 1977
- Tell him not to eat anything. We're gonna scarf when we get there. — *True Romance*, 1993
- scarfing tabs of acid like there was no tomorrow —Barney Hoskyns, *Waiting for the Sun*, p. 155, 1996
- Probably you've been scarfing down doughnuts and all I'm allowed to eat is toast. —Janet Evanovich, *Seven Up*, p. 74, 2001

2 to lick, suck and tongue a woman's vagina *US*
- He said, "All I have to do is scarf her a few times and I get anything I want." Nuttee asked Diehl to explain the word "scarf." "To eat her box, in other words." —Richard Honeycutt, *Candy Mossler*, p. 80, 1966
- Or some of them might turn out to scarf and rim [cunnilingus and analingus] to make it. —Bruce Jackson, *In the Life*, p. 120, 1972

▸ **scarf pussy**
to perform oral sex on a woman *US*
- Scarfing pussy gets great press, but most men know shit about eating out women. — *Screw*, p. 5, 12th June 1972

scarfer *noun*
1 the supporter of a football club *UK*
The supporter's loyalty is advertised by the colours, pattern or insignia of a scarf.
- [T]he '80s casuals might have little knowledge of or contact with the often district-gang-based scarfer mobs of the '70s and late '60s. —Irvine Welsh, *The Naughty Nineties*, p. 13, 1999

2 in the usage of youthful model road racers (slot car racers), a fast car *US*

From **SCARF** (to eat), suggesting that the car 'is eating up' the track.

- — Phantom Surfers, *The Exciting Sounds of Model Road Racing (Album cover)*, 1997

scarfing *noun*

self-asphyxiation as a masturbatory aid *UK, 1994*

- — John Ayto, *Oxford Dictionary of Slang*, p. 78, 1998

scarf up *verb*

to acquire *US*

Extends from **SCARF** (to eat hungrily), possibly playing on **SCARE UP** (to discover).

- If that's your idea of entertainment, scarf up a ticket the next time Jethro Tull hit town. — Lester Bangs, *Psychotic Reactions and Carburetor Dung*, p. 131, 1973

scarlet collar *adjective*

working in the sex industry *US*

Using 'scarlet woman' with the model of 'white collar' and 'blue collar' workers.

- The women and men in the scarlet-collar industries are often exploited by their bosses, abused by patrons, disparaged by the public and harassed by the forces of law and order. — *The Nation*, p. 794, 29th June 1985
- — Susie Dent, *The Language Report*, p. 14, 2003

scarlet sister *noun*

a prostitute *US*

- Many pious people showed up, but so did a swarm of scarlet sisters. — Jack Lait and Lee Mortimer, *Washington Confidential*, p. 88, 1951

scarper *verb*

1 to depart, especially in a hurry *UK, 1844*

Ultimately Italian *scappare* (to run away) or, less likely, rhyming slang for Scapa Flow (to go); via polari into more general usage. Variants include 'scarpa', 'scaper', 'scarpy' and 'scapli'.

- His jills told him to take it out of the horse tent and scarper off their tober [circus ground], John Orderly [quickly]. — Butch Reynolds, *Broken Hearted Clown*, p. 28, 1953
- Then this screw signs the form the copper gives him and the copper scarpers. — John Peter Jones, *Feather Pluckers*, p. 61, 1964
- Scarper, mates – this isn't our fight! — *The Sweeney*, p. 59, 1976
- Has the father of your kid scarpered? — Mary Hooper, *(megan)2*, p. 48, 1999
- [W]e were going to abort the mission and scarpa. — J.J. Connolly, *Layer Cake*, p. 21, 2000
- — Paul Baker, *Polari*, p. 189, 2002

2 to remove something; to dismiss someone *UK*

Circus; a variation of the previous sense

- "I'll scarper him tomorrow", means that I shall get rid of him tomorrow and "scarper that chat" means get rid of that thing. — Butch Reynolds, *Broken Hearted Clown*, p. 31, 1953

scary *adjective*

good *US*

- — *Current Slang*, p. 11, Summer 1969
- — Connie Eble (Editor), *UNC-CH Campus Slang*, p. 5, Spring 1983

scat *noun*

1 excrement, especially as a sexual fetish *US, 1927*

From Greek *skat* (dung).

- — *www.public.diversity.org.uk/deviant*, *Deviants Dictionary*, 1997
- — Paul Baker, *Polari*, p. 189, 2002
- Time he will now spend revisiting the unbelievable Scat pages of that fucking Internet. — Kevin Sampson, *Clubland*, p. 119, 2002

2 sado-masochistic sex play involving defecation *US*

- — *What Color is Your Handkerchief*, p. 7, 1979

3 heroin *US, 1949*

- — John B. Williams, *Narcotics and Hallucinogenics*, p. 116, 1967
- — Eugene Landy, *The Underground Dictionary*, p. 164, 1971
- — Robert Ashton, *This Is Heroin*, p. 207, 2002

4 low quality, low cost whisky *US*

- — Hyman E. Goldin et al., *Dictionary of American Underworld Lingo*, p. 185, 1950

scat *verb*

to travel fast; to leave *US*

Often used as an imperative.

- — *American Speech*, p. 101, May 1954

scattered *adjective*

drunk *UK*

- — *e-cyclopaedia*, 20th March 2002

scatty *adjective*

crazy; slightly mad; feather-brained *UK, 1911*

From '*scat*ter-brained'.

- [Rickie Lee] Jones is as scatty as ever on a reprise of Hicks's I Scare Myself[.] — *The Guardian*, 18th July 2003

scatty-yatty *noun*

an attractive girl *UK*

Noted as teen slang by Susie Dent, *The Language Report*, 2003. Probably acquired from West Indian slang.

scav *verb*

to scavenge; to scrounge *UK*

- Fuckin freeloadin bastard yew are, aye. Scavvin twat. — Niall Griffiths, *Sheepshagger*, p. 132, 2001

scavenger *noun*

in drag racing and hot rodding, a car that wins often, that 'eats up' its competition *US*

- — Lyle K. Engel, *The Complete Book of Fuel and Gas Dragsters*, p. 153, 1968

sceg *noun*

a surfer *AUSTRALIA*

Variant of **SKEG**.

- I don't know if I love Dino or not cos there are these four other guys I like (one is a sceg!). — Kylie Mole (Maryanne Fahey), *My Diary*, p. 99, 1988

scene *noun*

1 a situation *US, 1945*

Robert Gold calls it 'A superfluous word to describe further a person, place, thing, or happening'.

- "Sometimes this whole scene bugs me," Pete said. — John Rechy, *City of Night*, p. 52, 1963
- This scene of going to church on Sunday and playing with the kids, then kissing the wife good-bye Monday morning and heading down to the office to work on maximizing kill-densities or something, is what Hanna Arendt refers to as the banality of evil. — James Simon Kunen, *The Strawberry Statement*, p. 90, 1968
- While there are people camping all over – in the woods and meadows – there are basically two scenes here, the performance area and the Hog Farm/Movement City site. — *East Village Other*, 20th August 1969
- "Two hundred acres," said the Flash. "I was up there the other day, it's really a neat scene." — Gurney Norman, *Divine Right's Trip (Last Whole Earth Catalog)*, p. 159, 1971
- SO, it would be best that the energy that flowed through our scene this summer be work oriented rather than Trip oriented – if you dig what I mean. — *The Last Supplement to the Whole Earth Catalog*, p. 78, March 1971
- The fuckin' scene has ended, and there's no place to go but up. — Donald Goines, *Inner City Hoodlum*, p. 33, 1975
- I have never been able to figure out that whole scene between them. — Herbert Huncke, *Guilty of Everything*, p. 90, 1990
- Milo, boy, you just don't get the scene. — *Airheads*, 1994

2 a personal choice or taste; a favoured setting or milieu *US, 1966*

Originally black usage, then via jazz into hippy circles.

- Hitchcock suddenly scowled and got up. "Teaching life ain't my scene," he said. — Nat Hentoff, *Jazz Country*, p. 17, 1965
- I'm going to make a lot of money / Then I'm going to quit this crazy scene. — Joni Mitchell, *River*, 1971
- Nobody is twisting your arm to buy my book, but nobody should decide for you what is, or is not, your scene… — Richard Allen (James Moffat), *Author's Notes [britpulp]*, p. 62, 1972
- This isn't your kind of scene, Mister Regan. — *The Sweeney*, p. 12, 1976
- Not really his scene. — *Coronation Street*, 18th February 2002

3 a sexual interlude *US*

- I saw her in front of the campfire entertaining a few brothers by having a scene with a dog. — Jamie Mandelkau, *Buttons*, p. 100, 1971

▸ **make the scene**

1 to arrive and participate in a social gathering *US, 1958*

- Carlotta Fugatti made the scene driving a used blue La Salle coupe Bobo had given her. — Iceberg Slim (Robert Beck), *Death Wish*, p. 208, 1977

2 to go where something of interest is happening *US, 1950*

- The Fire Department makes the scene, since smoke seems to be pouring out of one of the classroom buildings, and I sit around and watch them for a while. — James Simon Kunen, *The Strawberry Statement*, p. 52, 1968

3 to have sex *US*

- The folklore of the hustler's world has legendary stories of hustlers who supposedly made the scene with a big-time producer, satisfied the old auntie and ended up as a big star. — Johnny Shearer, *The Male Hustler*, p. 141, 1966

scenester *noun*
a person who is part of contemporary fashionable society *US*
- The scenesters bar to be seen at. — *Bang*, p. 79, November 2003

sceney *adjective*
fashionable; part of the scene *UK*
- — Jenny Fabian and Johnny Byrne, *Groupie*, 1968

scenic route *noun*
in horse racing, running outside the pack on turns *US, 1978*
- — Thomas L. Clark, *The Dictionary of Gambling and Gaming*, p. 189, 1987

sces *noun*
▷ see: SESS

schainer yid; shayner Yid *noun*
an honest and absolutely trustworthy Jewish man *UK*
Yiddish for 'beautiful Jew', especially in the second spelling as noted by Leo Rosten, *The Joys of Yiddish*, 1968 and, among Londoners, in the first spelling, by David Powis, *The Signs of Crime*, 1977.

scheitl; shietel; shyckle; shyker *noun*
a wig *UK*
Polari; from Yiddish *sheytl* (a wig worn by Jewish women who have married in the Orthodox tradition).
- [T]he omi-palone [gay man] with a vogue [cigarette] on and the cod [bad] sheitel. — James Gardiner, *Who's a Pretty Boy Then?*, p. 123,
- I wanted a new scheitl to match the bona bijoux (jewellery) I got off last night's trade[.] — the cast of 'Aspects of Love', Prince of Wales Theatre, *Palare (Boy Dancer Talk) for Beginners*, 1989–92
- — *Attitude*, July 2003: 'New palare lexicon'

scheme *noun*
a housing estate *UK: SCOTLAND, 1985*
- Thur were nae rats in this scheme. Not till youse trendies moved in! — Ian Pattison, *Rab C. Nesbitt*, 1988

scheme-on *noun*
a person's regular opening line in a singles bar *US*
- — *American Speech*, p. 20, Spring 1985: 'The language of singles bars'

sch- *spellings*
▷ see: SH-

schemie *noun*
someone who lives on a council estate *UK: SCOTLAND*
The element of Scotland's social housing system that is popularly known as 'the schemies'.
- [T]here to dwell in perpetual fear of being chibbed [stabbed] and humped by rabid schemies — Christopher Brookmyre, *Boiling a Frog*, p. 3, 2000

schimmel *noun*
among Nova Scotians of German descent, a blond, colourless person *CANADA*
- The Lunenburg County "schimmel," not complimentary, comes from the German "schimmel," "mold, mildew." — Murray Emeneau, *Canadian English*, p. 34–39, 1975

Schindler's List; Schindler's *adjective*
drunk *AUSTRALIA*
Rhyming slang for **PISSED**, formed on the title of a book by Thomas Keneally and a 1993 Oscar-winning film by Steven Spielberg.
- 'Oh, mate,' he replied, 'I was Schindler's.' — *Daily Telegraph*, 24th March 1994
- — Ray Puxley, *Fresh Rabbit*, 1998
- — *www.LondonSlang.com*, June 2002

schinwhars; chinois *noun*
a Chinese person *UK*
- — Paul Baker, *Polari*, p. 189, 2002

schitz; schiz; schizo; skitz; skiz *noun*
anyone who is considered to be mentally ill; generically, a mad person; specifically, a *schizo*phrenic *US, 1945*
- "What do you think is the matter with him?" "I don't know. I expect he's a schitz." "He was talking nonsense after tea." — Geoff Brown, *I Want What I Want*, p. 36, 1966
- bog-eyed schizos asking to be taken to heaven — Simon Lewis, *In The Box [britpulp]*, p. 131, 1999

schitz *verb*
to behave in an abnormal fashion because of sustained methamphetamine use *US*
From 'schiozphrenia'.
- — Peter Johnson, *Dictionary of Street Alcohol and Drug Terms*, p. 165, 1993

schizo; schitzi; schizy; schizzy *adjective*
*schizo*id or *schizo*phrenic; used derogatively of anyone whose behaviour is considered eccentric, illogical or mad *US*
Schizophrenia is a severe mental disorder mistakenly understood by readers of modern thrillers to be little more than a split-personality.
- I was schizy for sure now. — Thurston Scott, *Cure it with Honey*, p. 177, 1951
- The Vigilante copped out as a schizo possession case. — William Burroughs, *Naked Lunch*, p. 8, 1957
- Growing up in Hyde Park, the University of Chicago's stockade on the edge of the Black Belt, Paul led a quietly schizzy life. — Albert Goldman, *Freak Show*, p. 105, 1968
- He went over everything that had been said and came up with ... nothing. She was schizo. — Kevin Sampson, *Powder*, p. 109, 1999

schizz *noun*
a person suffering from *schizo*phrenia *US*
- — *American Speech*, p. 208, Fall-Winter 1973: 'The language of nursing'

schlack *noun*
▷ see: SHLOCK

schlanting *noun*
cheating *AUSTRALIA*
- The win led to allegations of 'schlanting' from Mr Solly, a Victorian MP, as he compared the horse's performance in the previous Herbert Power Handicap. — Joe Andersen, *Winners Can Laugh*, p. 35, 1982

schlemihl *noun*
▷ see: SHLEMIEL

schlump *verb*
to move heavily *US*
- [I]t's just a "hard rock" version of an awful lot of what schlumps around the airwaves these days. — Lester Bangs, *Psychotic Reactions and Carburetor Dung*, p. 271, 1978

schlumph *verb*
to drink alcohol *UK*
- [S]he schlumphed her Vera [gin] down the screech at a rate of knots[.] — James Gardiner, *Who's a Pretty Boy Then?*, p. 123,
- — Paul Baker, *Polari*, p. 189, 2002

schmageggy, schmear *nouns*
▷ see: SHMEGEGGE, SHMEER

schmende *noun*
the vagina *US*
Possibly (a woman's) 'end' elaborated in cod-Yiddish.
- There's [...] a "Mimi" in Miami, "split knish" in Philadelphia, and "schmende" in the Bronx[.] — Eve Ensler, *The Vagina Monologues*, p. 6, 1998

schmick; smick *adjective*
exquisite; immaculate *AUSTRALIA, 1996*
- I have heard "shmick" used by a well travelled local to mean stylish and well done. — *www.abc.net.au/wordmap*, 2003

schmock; shmock *noun*
heroin *UK*
- — Home Office, *Glossary of Terms and Slang Common in Penal Establishments*, July 1978
- — Sean McConville, *The State of the Language*, 1980

schmol *noun*
▷ see: SHMO

schmoogie *noun*
a friend *US*
- — Kenn "Naz" Young, *Naz's Dictionary of Teen Slang*, p. 102, 1993

Schneider *verb*
1 in gin, to win a game leaving an opponent scoreless *US*
Also in the shortened form 'Schnied'.
- — Irwin Steig, *Play Gin to Win*, p. 141,

2 in gambling, to defeat someone completely *US*
- Zigman moved up and whispered to the Floor Manager, "We're gonna Schneider this jerk in less than an hour." — Stephen J. Cannell, *Big Con*, p. 203, 1997

schnockered *adjective*
▷ see: SNOCKERED

schnoink *noun*
a Jewish person *UK*
A deliberately offensive and insulting term used by non-Jews; it appears to be 'oink' (the cry of a pig) dressed up in mock-Yiddish.
- —David Powis, *The Signs of Crime*, 1977

scholar *noun*
▷ see: OXFORD SCHOLAR

schonk *verb*
to hit someone *UK*
- —Paul Baker, *Polari*, p. 189, 2002

school *noun*
1 in poker, a group of players who customarily play together *UK*
- —Albert H. Morehead, *The Complete Guide to Winning Poker*, p. 272, 1967

2 a group of people engaged in a gambling game, especially two-up *AUSTRALIA, 1812*
- On Sundays he controlled a 'school', And played 'two-up' the livelong day[.]—A.B. Paterson, *Rio Grande and Other Verses*, p. 108, 1902
- SCHOOL – Gathering of gamblers.—Gilbert H. Lawson, *A Dictionary of Australian Words and Terms*, 1924
- The games operated every lunch hour, and on paydays as many as 200 players were in the 'school'.—Vince Kelly, *The Bogeyman*, p. 159, 1956

schoolboy *noun*
1 cocaine; codeine; codeine cough syrup *US, 1969*
An inference that these are beginners' drugs.
- —Richard A. Spears, *The Slang and Jargon of Drugs and Drink*, p. 404, 1986
- —Mike Haskins, *Drugs*, p. 281, 2003

2 heroin *UK*
- —Mike Haskins, *Drugs*, p. 284, 2003

schoolboy draw *noun*
in poker, a draw in a highly unlikely attempt to improve a hand *US*
- —George Percy, *The Language of Poker*, p. 79, 1988

schoolcraft *noun*
crack cocaine *UK, 1998*
- —Mike Haskins, *Drugs*, p. 282, 2003

schoolie *noun*
1 a school student *AUSTRALIA, 1994*
- —John Birmingham, *He Died With a Felafel in his Hand*, p. 144, 1994
- 'We always called him 'Swampy' at school. I don't know why.' She looks scornful. 'Yeah, well, that's schoolies for you.'—Dirk Flinthart, *Brotherly Love*, p. 47, 1995
- Everywhere you look there's little posses of hooched-up [drunk] schoolies[.]—Kevin Sampson, *Outlaws*, p. 112, 2001

2 one of a group of a young persons holidaying having just finished high school *AUSTRALIA*
- An original Schoolies T-Shirt that says it all – '12 Years of Hell, One Week of Glory.' A must for all Schoolies. A great souvenir.—*Schoolies Week*, p. 23, 1993

3 a school teacher *AUSTRALIA, 1889*
- It was bloody old Mrs Newby and the girls and that bloody schoolie.—Thomas Keneally, *The Chant of Jimmie Blacksmith*, p. 119, 1972

Schoolies Week *noun*
chiefly in New South Wales and Queensland, a week following final high school exams during which vast numbers of students descend upon certain tourist areas to celebrate *AUSTRALIA, 1984*
- There were plenty of drunken fucked-up kids about – Schoolies Week, according to the Doc[.]—Harrison Biscuit, *The Search for Savage Henry*, p. 50, 1995

schoolmarm tree *noun*
a piece of firewood where two trunks have grown together and crossed; also, the tree itself *CANADA*
- School marm – a forked log or tree.—Robert Swanson, *Rhymes of a Western Logger*, p. 54, 1942
- The "schoolmarm" is a piece of firewood where two trunks have grown together and crossed to form a crotch, so called because "you'll never get them apart." The phrase "schoolmarm tree" occurs in Howard o'Hagan's novel of the Canadian West, Tay John.—Lewis Poteet, *The South Shore Phrase Book*, p. 96, 1999

schoolmate *noun*
a fellow prisoner *US*
- —Vincent J. Monteleone, *Criminal Slang*, p. 201, 1949

school of crime *noun*
a prison *US*
- —Ralph de Sola, *Crime Dictionary*, p. 135, 1982

school of hard knocks
the difficult emotional and physical experiences of growing up, seen as enriching *US, 1912*
The UNIVERSITY OF LIFE for the working-classes.

school solution *noun*
a military tactic as taught in the classroom *US*
- The whole position had been so perfectly chosen and prepared that Scanlon was later to remark that it was the Fort Benning "school solution" of how an outnumbered infantry unit ought to organize a defense.—Neil Sheehan, *A Bright Shining Lie*, p. 274, 1988
- Here lies the bones / Of Ranger Jones / A graduate of this institution / He died last night / In his first fire fight / using the school solution / Therefore, be flexible.—Charlie A. Beckwith and Donald Knox, *Delta Force*, p. 87, 274

schooner *noun*
a 15 fluid ounce glass of beer *AUSTRALIA, 1892*
In South Australia the same name is used for a 10 ounce glass of beer.
- When we get inside order a couple of schooners while I shake hands with the wife's best friend!—Barry Humphries, *The Wonderful World of Barry McKenzie*, p. 28, 1968
- The price of a schooner in those days was eighteen pence.—Bill Wannan, *Folklore of the Australian Pub*, p. 56, 1972
- [W]e are going to take the first copy down to the Steyne at Manly (his current drinking hole) and challenge him to a schooner for every question he can't answer.—Bazza and Curly, *Betcha Wrong!*, p. iii, 1990

schtonker *noun*
anything impressive in its field *UK*
Misspelling of STONKER falsely suggesting a Yiddish etymology.
- An absolute stonker from Ari Linker [Israeli musician].—*Ministry*, p. 97, January 2002

schtook *noun*
▷ see: SHTUCK

schuss *noun*
a dim-witted person *CANADA*
- In Lunenburg County NS, a "schuss" is a halfwit. "Don't listen to her; she's a schuss." From the German "schussel," a careless, slovenly person.—Lewis Poteet, *The South Shore Phrase Book*, p. 96, 1999

schussley; schusslish *adjective*
giddy, silly *CANADA*
- Among Lunenburg County NS German descendants, a person who is "schussley or schusslish" is acting silly, giddy, making a fool of himself. The word is from the German, translated and adapted into English: "schuss" is a fool.—Lewis Poteet, *The South Shore Phrase Book*, p. 96, 1999

schwag; shwag *noun*
marijuana, especially low quality marijuana *US*
- —Connie Eble (Editor), *UNC-CH Campus Slang*, p. 6, Fall 1995
- —Jim Emerson-Cobb, *Scratching the Dragon*, April 1997
- Can you tell the low-thc schwag from the good pot?—Dana Larsen (Editor), *Pot Puzzle Fun Book*, p. 7, 2000
- —Steven Wishnia, *The Cannabis Companion*, p. 153, 2004

schwallied *adjective*
drunk *UK*
- —Pete Brown, *Man Walks into a Pub*, 2003

schwartz *noun*
▷ see: SHVARTZ

schweenie *noun*
the penis *US*
A variation of WEENIE (the penis) using a Yiddish model of reduplication amended with 'sch' or 'schm'.
- I'll slap on some rubber gloves and my schweenie will be hooked right into a rubber tube.—Howard Stern, *Miss America*, p. 49, 1995

schweinhund *noun*
a despicable person *UK, 1941*
From German *schwein* (pig) and *hund* (dog), as used in British propaganda and fiction as one of the few words employed by any Nazi guard to refer to a British prisoner, and hence into the British vocabulary of abuse.

• [S]omebody's jealous of you and hasn't got the nerve to show it out in the open. So the Schweinhund starts a filthy rumor. —Harry Turtledove, *Second Contact*, p. 93, 1999

schwindely *adjective*

among Nova Scotians of German descent, dizzy, unfocused *CANADA*

• In Lunenburg County, someone who is dizzy is called "schwindely." The word is from the German "schwindelig," dizzy. —Lewis Poteet, *The South Shore Phrase Book*, p. 96, 1999

schwing!

used as a vocalisation of the sound a penis makes getting suddenly erect at the passing of a beautiful woman *US*

A gift to teen slang from Mike Myers and his 'Wayne's World' sketches.

• Garth holds up a poster of Claudia Schiffer. WAYNE: Schwing. GARTH: Schwing— *Wayne's World*, 1992

• —Connie Eble (Editor), *UNC-CH Campus Slang*, p. 8, Spring 1992

science fiction *noun*

the US Army Special Forces *US*

From the initials.

• —Linda Reinberg, *In the Field*, p. 192, 1991

scissorbill *noun*

1 in any group setting, an outsider *US*

• —Joseph E. Ragen and Charles Finston, *Inside the World's Toughest Prison*, p. 816, 1962: 'Penitentiary and underworld glossary'

2 a incompetent, stupid or dull logger *CANADA*

• A "scissor-bill," in BC a clumsy logger, is in the US a non-union man. —Tom Parkin, *WetCoast Words*, p. 121, 1989

3 on the railways, a new and incompetent worker *US*

Not praise.

• —Ramon Adams, *The Language of the Railroader*, p. 133, 1977

scissor-fingers *verb*

to shorten a performance *US*

Often accompanied by finger gestures mimicking the use of scissors.

• —Don Wilmeth, *The Language of American Popular Entertainment*, p. 233, 1981

scissors *noun*

marijuana *US, 1977*

• —Richard A. Spears, *The Slang and Jargon of Drugs and Drink*, p. 438, 1986

• —Mike Haskins, *Drugs*, p. 289, 2003

scissor-sister *noun*

a lesbian who engages in vagina-on-vagina sexual contact by spreading her legs as scissor-blades and so conjoining with another woman in a similar position *US*

Adopted as a name by New York band *Scissor Sisters* who found international success in 2004.

scluttery *adjective*

overweight *CANADA*

• In Lunenburg County, the longtime German-descended residents describe a fatty person as "scluttery," and also used to word to describe "shaky, like a bowlful of jello." The word is from the German "schlotterig," "loose, shaky, flabby." —Lewis Poteet, *The South Shore Phrase Book*, p. 96, 1999

scnozz *noun*

▷ **see: SHNOZ**

scobie *noun*

a young uncouth male *IRELAND*

• Who rattled your fucking cage, scobie? —Eamonn Sweeney, *Waiting for the Healer*, p. 224, 1997

scobo *noun*

a black person *US*

• Hell, all scobos is ridiculous. —Ralph Ellison, *Invisible Man*, p. 269, 1947

• — *New York Times Magazine*, p. 62, 23rd August 1964

scody *adjective*

1 excellent *NEW ZEALAND*

• —David McGill, *David McGill's Complete Kiwi Slang Dictionary*, p. 110, 1998

2 disagreeable *US*

• — *San Francisco Examiner*, p. 17, 17 June 1966: 'Teen slanguage: real shark'

scoff *noun*

1 food; a meal *SOUTH AFRICA, 1846*

• [T]hey'll traipse off to make music for Tommy Dorsey or Benny Goodman because the big bands are all the go and can provide them with their scoff. —Mezz Mezzrow, *Really the Blues*, p. 291, 1946

• The newest word for food is "scoff." — *Philadelphia Evening Bulletin*, 11th October 1955

• [T]he blokes tipped in their sachets of beef stew and rice for a communal scoff. —Andy McNab, *Immediate Action*, p. 93, 1995

2 in the Maritime Provinces, a feast *CANADA*

• Went to a scoff on Friday up north–a sort of Newfoundland party/festive occasion/excuse to eat a lot. — *www.electricpenguin.com*, 26th July 2002

scoff *verb*

to eat *US, 1846*

• We sure used to scoff back some during those sessions – my wife Bonnie would come on with a mess of green-apple pies and buttercrust strawberry tarts that were really killers. —Mezz Mezzrow, *Really the Blues*, p. 117, 1946

• "Now, the first thing is scoff, baby, I mean, like eat," Zaida explained and she and the drummer piled into the front seat. —Ross Russell, *The Sound*, p. 15, 1961

• We might could scoff back lightly, in the most minor way, before I uptown. —Bernard Wolfe, *The Magic of Their Singing*, p. 39, 1961

• Scoff is slang for to eat. — *www.probertencyclopedia.com*, 26th July 2002

scoffins *noun*

in circus and carnival usage, food *US*

If **SCOFF** is 'to eat', it is only logical that 'scoffins' are 'that which is eaten'.

• —Don Wilmeth, *The Language of American Popular Entertainment*, p. 233, 1981

scolly *noun*

▷ **see: SKOLLY**

sconce *noun*

the head *UK, 1567*

• I was going to kick him in the belly first, then get one of those quarter beer bottles from the case on the floor and break it over his sconce. —William Burroughs, *Junkie*, p. 27, 1953

scone *noun*

the head *AUSTRALIA, 1945*

• Yer not right in the scone. —Nino Culotta (John O'Grady), *They're A Weird Mob*, p. 19, 1957

• —W.R. Bennett, *Wingman*, p. 115, 1961

▸ duck the scone

to plead guilty *AUSTRALIA, 1984*

Formed on **SCONE** (the head); from bending the head in unspoken affirmative. A variation of **BOW THE CRUMPET** and **NOD THE NUT**.

▸ off your scone

mad *AUSTRALIA, 1958*

A variation of **OFF YOUR HEAD**.

▸ suck your scone in!

mind you own business!; stop talking nonsense! *AUSTRALIA, 1984*

A variation of **PULL YOUR HEAD IN!**.

scone *verb*

to hit someone on the head *AUSTRALIA, 1948*

• Very properly concerned about their children losing an eye, the Goodhew parents would invariably show up just in time to see one of their little darlings sconed by a rock or sliced open by a whizzing piece of fibro. —Clive James, *Unreliable Memoirs*, p. 53, 1980

scone hot *adverb*

vigorously *AUSTRALIA, 1927*

• 'All they do for Tilly is to go her scone-hot.' —George Blaikie, *Remember Smith's Weekly?*, p. 218, 1950

Sconnie *nickname*

a resident of the state of Wisconsin *US*

• —Jim Crotty, *How to Talk American*, p. 208, 1997

scoob *noun*

a beverage *UK*

Gulf war usage.

• — *American Speech*, p. 400, Winter 1991: 'Among the new words'

scoobied *adjective*

drunk *UK*

• —Pete Brown, *Man Walks into a Pub*, 2003

scooby *adjective*

to treat a prisoner unfairly *UK*

From **SCOOBY-DOO** (a prison officer).

• —Angela Devlin, *Prison Patter*, p. 102, 1996

scooby-doo; scooby; scoob *noun*

1 a clue *UK: SCOTLAND*
Rhyming slang, based on a popular animated cartoon character produced by Hannah Barbera since 1969.
- Ah haveny got a scooby. —Michael Munro, *The Original Patter*, 1985
- He didn't have a scoob what the man was talking about. —Christopher Brookmyre, *Not the End of the World*, p. 100, 1998
- I haven't got a fucking Scooby what I'm talking about here. —Kevin Sampson, *Outlaws*, p. 193, 2001
- What the fuck am I doing, standin here? Haven't got a scooby what to say. —Niall Griffiths, *Kelly + Victor*, p. 168, 2002

2 a prison officer *UK*
Rhyming slang for **SCREW** (a prison officer); from the cartoon character.
- —Angela Devlin, *Prison Patter*, p. 102, 1996

3 a look *UK, 2001*
Rhyming slang for 'view'.
- So can I look foward to having a scooby at the script next week? —Charles Robinson, 17th September 2001

4 a marijuana cigarette *US*
Scooby Doo, a popular animated cartoon character produced by Hannah Barbera since 1969, disguises **DOOBY**.
- We [...] went for a stroll along the early evening seafront to smoke some more Scooby-Dooby Doo, where are you. —Ken Lukowiak, *Marijuana Time*, p. 91–92, 2000

scooby snack *noun*

1 marijuana *US*
- —Judi Sanders, *Da Bomb*, p. 13, 1997

2 a drug that acts as a depressant or relaxant, usually Valium™ *US*
- Running around robbing banks / all wacked off of Scooby Snacks! —Fun Loving Criminals, *Scooby Snacks*, 1995

scooby snacks *noun*

1 any food that is hungered for while under the influence of marijuana *US*
From the insatiable appetite of cartoon character Scooby Doo.

2 MDMA, the recreational drug best known as ecstasy *UK*
- —Mike Haskins, *Drugs*, p. 290, 2003

scooch *verb*

while sitting or lying down, to move your body by sliding *US*
- "Awright, honey," Lucille answers, scooching her ample hips around in bed. —Odie Hawkins, *Ghetto Sketches*,
- He nodded yes, yes, I dig coke and scooched himself up in bed, nostrils flared for the cocaine's reception. —Odie Hawkins, *The Busting Out of an Ordinary Man*, p. 154, 1985

scoof *verb*

to steal something *UK: SCOTLAND*
- When Ah came back fae the lavvy some ratbag hud scoofed the Safeways bag Ah left under ma seat. —Michael Munro, *The Complete Patter*, p. 135, 1996

scoop *noun*

1 the latest information or news *US, 1874*
- "What's the scoop for tonight?" said the one called Wally. —Max Shulman, *Rally Round the Flag, Boys!*, p. 171, 1957
- It was Lord Gallo who gave me the scoop on afternoon as I was sitting out in the surf with him waiting for a halfway decent wave to take us in. —Frederick Kohner, *Gidget*, p. 41, 1957
- I'm not even gonna give you a cup of coffee 'till I get the whole scoop and nothing but the scoop. —Darryl Ponicsan, *The Last Detail*, p. 56, 1970
- Sean Hartie's giving everyone the inside scoop. —*Mallrats*, 1995

2 a drink *IRELAND, 1991*
- First alehouse we see, Craig says. – Have a few scoops first[.] —Niall Griffiths, *Kelly + Victor*, p. 53, 2002

3 the convex curvature of the bottom of a surfboard *US*
- —D.S. Halacy, *Surfer!*, p. 216, 1965

4 the recreational drug GHB *US*
- Health officials say mixing the drug, known on the street as "Georgia Home Boy" or "Scoop," with alcohol or other drugs can cause nausea and life-threatening breathing problems. —*Atlanta (Georgia) Journal and Constitution*, p. M1, 15th April 1993
- —Anna Scotti and Paul Young, *Buzzwords*, p. 141, 1997

scoop *verb*

1 to be the first to report a news story *US*
- That four-page hot-tamale sheet had scooped the A.P., the U.P., and the I.N.S., along with Reuters and Tass and all the other globe-circling know-it-all newshawks. —Mezz Mezzrow, *Really the Blues*, p. 167, 1946
- Does the president have a time machine? Have I been scooped on that? —*Austin Powers*, 1999

2 (of a beer enthusiast) to drink any type of beer as a means of collecting and recording that particular brew *UK*
- This practice [a form of trainspotting] is often undertaken by those who also spot beer, or "scoop" on the side. —Iain Aitch, *A Fete Worse Than Death*, p. 55, 2003

3 to kiss someone *US*
- —Vann Wesson, *Generation X Field Guide and Lexicon*, p. 146, 1997

4 to arrest someone *US*
- "We call in his name we got to scoop him." —John Sayles, *Union Dues*, p. 29, 1977

5 in high-low poker, to declare for both high and low *US*
- —John Scarne, *Scarne's Guide to Modern Poker*, p. 289, 1979

scooping *noun*

the practice of collecting and recording different types of beer by the simple expedient of drinking each one *UK*
- Scooping involves "spotting" all the beer you can drink at a real ale festival[.] —Iain Aitch, *A Fete Worse Than Death*, p. 55, 2003

scoot *noun*

1 a foot-propelled scooter *UK*
- If you're a scoot rider who gets his thrills from the trickier stunts, you're definitely a Burly— Ben Sharpe, *Scooter Crazy*, p. 39, 2000

2 a motorcycle *US, 1943*
A shortened 'scooter'.
- Curtis had a big tricked-out scoot, a Harley, he kept in the house. —Elmore Leonard, *Split Images*, p. 48, 1981

3 a dollar *US*
- I found the address of the cab company in the phone book, drove over, and left the dispatcher with an envelope containing fifty scoots. —James Ellroy, *Brown's Requiem*, p. 16, 1981
- That you still owe me ten scoots on last year's World Series pool. —James Ellroy, *Blood on the Moon*, p. 232, 1984

4 an obnoxious drunk *NEW ZEALAND*
- —David McGill, *David McGill's Complete Kiwi Slang Dictionary*, p. 110, 1998

▸ **on the scoot**
on a drinking binge *AUSTRALIA, 1916*
- SCOOT – To clear out; also continued bout of drunkenness. —Gilbert H. Lawson, *A Dictionary of Australian Words and Terms*, 1924
- But when he got on the scoot in town he was a bloody pest. —Sam Weller, *Old Bastards I Have Met*, p. 105, 1979
- —David McGill, *David McGill's Complete Kiwi Slang Dictionary*, p. 79, 1998

scoot *verb*

1 to leave in a hurry *US, 1882*
- You'd better scoot, hadn't you? C'mon, I'll walk you to the door. —Armistead Maupin, *Babycakes*, p. 10, 1984
- [S]he explained she was a lab technician on twenty four hour call and scooted back to the ladies room to phone her escort service and say she couldn't book any tricks that night[.] —Seth Morgan, *Homeboy*, 1990
- We scooted into the dark foyer and I closed and locked the door behind us. —Janet Evanovich, *Seven Up*, p. 44, 2001

2 to slide *UK, 1838*
- Scoot over, goddamnit. —*The Blues Brothers*, 1980

scooter *noun*

marijuana *US*
- —Jim Emerson-Cobb, *Scratching the Dragon*, April 1997

scooter tracks *noun*

faecal stains in underwear *US*
- —Connie Eble (Editor), *UNC-CH Campus Slang*, p. 6, Fall 1989

scooter trash *noun*

a motorcyle gang member *US*
- —James Harris, *A Convict's Dictionary*, p. 37, 1989

scoots *noun*

1 money *US*
- —Judi Sanders, *Da Bomb*, p. 13, 1997

2 diarrhoea *US*
- —*American Speech*, p. 65, Spring-Summer 1975: 'Razorback slang'

scope; scoper; scopey *noun*

an inept, clumsy or stupid individual *UK*

A rebranding of 'spastic' in line with the Spastic Society's 1994 name-change; the change to Scope was intended to avoid the 'most common use of the word "spastic" [which] has insidiously assumed misrepresentation that intends the word as an insult'.

- — *www.LondonSlang.com*, June 2002
- — Chris Lewis, *The Dictionary of Playground Slang*, p. 195, 2003

scope *verb*

to see or to look at someone or something *US, 1974*

- Only a few people had scoped us, but they were cool. — Odie Hawkins, *Lost Angeles*, p. 191, 1994
- Not much. Just, uh, scopin' the babes. — *American Pie*, 1999
- I could stand up there, my back to the wall, and scope the situation below quite comfortably. — Diran Adebayo, *My Once Upon A Time*, p. 72, 2000

▸ **scope on**

to look at or examine someone or something *US*

- Oooh Rene I was scoping on her man. — *Boyz N The Hood*, 1990

scope out *verb*

to investigate something; to examine something; to check something out *US*

- So I hassled and I hustled and I still couldn't scope it out. — Lester Bangs, *Psychotic Reactions and Carburetor Dung*, p. 132, 1973
- You go inside and talk to your dad. I'm gonna scope the place out. — *Bill and Ted's Excellent Adventure*, 1989
- The other guy, Roach, waited in the truck. They were scoping it out, right? — *Break Point*, 1991
- Strike never knew when or where they might be scoping him out. — Richard Price, *Clockers*, p. 4, 1992

scoper; scope jockey *noun*

a pathologist *US*

- — Sally Williams, *"Strong" Words*, p. 159, 1994

scope, scam and scheme

used as a formula for seduction *US*

- — Connie Eble (Editor), *UNC-CH Campus Slang*, p. 4, Fall 1990

scope worker *noun*

in circus and carnival usage, an astrologer *US*

An abbreviation of 'horoscope worker'.

- — Don Wilmeth, *The Language of American Popular Entertainment*, p. 233, 1981

scorch *noun*

a car's performance potential *US*

- Some cars never reach their scorch peak. — Chrysler Corporation, *Of Anchors, Bezels, Pots and Scorchers*, September 1959

scorch *verb*

to stare at someone or something, *US*

- — *USA Today*, p. 1D, 5th August 1991: 'A sterling lexicon of the lingo'

▸ **scorch the iron**

to operate a train at a high rate of speed *US*

- — Ramon Adams, *The Language of the Railroader*, p. 133, 1977

scorcher *noun*

1 a very hot day *UK, 1874*

- Gonna be a scorcher today. — Marvin Wald and Albert Maltz, *The Naked City*, 1947
- A scorcher. It was my father's phrase and came back to me as familiarly, when I opened my eyes, as the heard reveille of my childhood. — Philip Wylie, *Opus 21*, p. 322, 1949
- Ain't this a scorcher, kid? — Jim Thompson, *A Swell-Looking Babe*, p. 67, 1954
- Today was a scorcher. This Chevy doesn't have air conditioning. — *Point Break*, 1991

2 in ball games, an extremely hard shot *UK, 1977*

- [S]ooner or later, out would come another scorcher, which usually also missed the mattress and blasted the bare wall so hard I half expected the ball to stick. — David James Duncan, *The Brothers K*, p. 118, 1992
- [R]ipple the side-netting with a scorcher of a shot from just outside the area. — *The Guardian*, 9th March 2004

scorching *adjective*

extremely hot *UK, 1940*

- Overhead, the sun beats down, one of the few scorching hot days we have had this summer. — *The Guardian*, 17th August 2002

score *noun*

1 a robbery; the proceeds of a robbery *US*

- I was real crazy by then. "Let's pull a score?" I said. — Hal Ellson, *Duke*, p. 68, 1949
- I'd say, "C'mon,man, let's go pull a score." — Claude Brown, *Manchild in the Promised Land*, p. 127, 1965
- Giant scores should be stored in a garage-type warehouse equipped with freezers and its whereabouts known only to the Free Food Gang. — *The Digger Papers*, p. 15, August 1968
- [W]e'd got away with it, hadn't we, we'd got the score, and Tony hadn't grassed and the Securicor man hadn't snuffed it. — Ted Lewis, *Jack Carter's Law*, p. 21, 1974

2 a one-time payment from a criminal to the police to avoid prosecution *US*

- — *The Knapp Commission Report on Police Corruption*, 1972
- A "score" is a one-time payment that an officer might solicit from, for example, a motorist or a narcotics violator. — *The Knapp Commission Report on Police Corruption*, p. 66, 1972

3 a sale, especially of drugs or something else illegal *US, 1914*

- Dincher spoke of the big score he'd make so that he might fill his life with music. — George Mandel, *Flee the Angry Strangers*, p. 170, 1952
- [T]hey go on looking, fabricating preposterous lies about their big scores[.] — William Burroughs, *Junkie*, p. 20, 1953
- Divine Right paid the man with cash he'd got from a big grass score that morning[.] — Gurney Norman, *Divine Right's Trip (Last Whole Earth Catalog)*, p. 9, 1971

4 a prostitute's customer *US*

- And I could spot the scores easily – the men who paid other men sex-money[.] — John Rechy, *City of Night*, p. 35, 1963
- The "scores" frantically wander around the area trying to select the youngest and best-looking hustler. — Johnny Shearer, *The Male Hustler*, p. 44, 1966

5 a sexual conquest *US*

- A score like that, a man could just live on his reputation. — *M*A*S*H*, 1970

6 twenty pounds; twenty dollars *UK, 1929*

- After failing to borrow a 'score' from me he departed, and I was on my own. — James Holledge, *The Great Australian Gamble*, p. 105, 1966
- — Jim Ramsay, *Cop it sweet*, p. 79, 1977
- — Ned Wallish, *The Truth Dictionary of Racing Slang*, p. 72, 1989
- — Brian McDonald (writing of 1960s London underground), *Elephant Boys*, p. 203, 2000

7 in betting, odds of 20–1 *UK*

- — John McCririck, *John McCririck's World of Betting*, p. 112, 1991

▸ **keep score**

to perform the paperwork required of a police team *US*

- "Want to drive or keep score?" asked Light after roll call[.] — Joseph Wambaugh, *The New Centurions*, p. 137, 1970

▸ **the score**

the state of affairs, the current situation *US, 1938*

Often in the verb phrase 'know the score'.

- You know the score, dad. — Alan Bleasdale, *Boys From the Blackstuff*, 1982
- Something passed across Zaffir's face. He knew the score. — Greg Williams, *Diamond Geezers*, p. 9, 1997
- "He knows the score..." he tries to say. — Danny King, *The Burglar Diaries*, p. 117, 2001

score *verb*

1 to obtain something, especially drugs and especially dishonestly *US, 1914*

- We covered Brooklyn, the Bronx, Queens, Jersey City, and Newark. We couldn't even score for pentapon. — William Burroughs, *Junkie*, p. 37, 1953
- He had heard I was in town and wanted to know if I wanted to score. — Alexander Trocchi, *Cain's Book*, p. 19, 1960
- January of 1945 I was out of bread and I hadn't scored musically[.] — Babs Gonzales, *I Paid My Dues*, p. 35, 1967
- I said, "Top, I'm frayed. I sure wish I had a snort of 'gir.' Can you score?" — Iceberg Slim (Robert Beck), *Pimp*, p. 128, 1969
- People too cheap to rent a hotel, people scoring dope, people shooting up, people who want to embarrass you. — *Taxi Driver*, 1976
- Alvy, listen, while you're in California, could you possibly score some coke for me? — *Annie Hall*, 1977
- "I scored a whole pack this time," Pup said[.] — Francesca Lia Block, *Baby Be-Bop*, p. 402, 1995
- Eventually my mate says, "fancy scoring a pill?" and I go "sure, go ahead". So we sort of score a pill off these really large raggas[.] — Ben Malbon, *Cool Places*, p. 272, 1998
- We sometimes went downtown to score. — *Traffic*, 2000

2 to make a sexual conquest *AUSTRALIA, 1907*

- The one time I almost scored was in this hotel. The chick came up to my room after she fell for what I call my innocuous come-on... — Lenny Bruce, *How to Talk Dirty and Influence People*, p. 161, 1965
- On my innumerable business trips I've bumped into plenty of these randy Brit sheilahs and I could have hit the odd one between the legs like a plate of porridge too, but I've never scored with one. — Barry Humphries, *The Traveller's Tool*, p. 99, 1985
- So we could score with the babes. — *Wayne's World 2*, 1993

- Sherman meets a chick for one night and scores. This is just wrong. — *American Pie*, 1999
- She'd better do something about that hair of hers, I thought, if she wanted to score with Strauss tonight. — Rita Ciresi, *Pink Slip*, p. 328, 1999

3 (of a police officer) to extract a one-time bribe from a criminal to avoid prosecution *US*

- The term is also used as a verb, as in "I scored him for $1,500." — *The Knapp Commission Report on Police Corruption*, p. 66, 1972
- It was not his style to score prostitutes. — Leonard Shecter and William Phillips, *On the Pad*, p. 24, 1973

4 (of a horse or rider) to win a race *AUSTRALIA*

- In a bustling finish, Dale got Shiny Star up to score by a nose from the favourite[.] — Wilda Moxham, *The Apprentice*, p. 72, 1969
- He led all the way to score in what I call fine style. — Joe Brown, *Just for the Record*, p. 14, 1984

▸ **score on**
to get the best of someone verbally *US*

- — *American Speech*, p. 275, December 1963: 'American Indian student slang'

score!

1 used as a humorous acknowledgement of a correct answer *US*

- IAN: So Pip's your younger brother? REX: Yup. Score! — *Airheads*, 1994

2 used for expressing joy *US*

- Score! I got an A on my paper. — Connie Eble (Editor), *UNC-CH Campus Slang*, p. 6, November 2002

scorebag *noun*
twenty pounds' worth of a drug *UK*

- — Angela Devlin, *Prison Patter*, p. 102, 1996

scorpion *noun*

1 a variety of MDMA, the recreational drug best known as ecstasy *UK*

- — Angela Devlin, *Prison Patter*, p. 102, 1996

2 cocaine *UK, 1998*

- — Mike Haskins, *Drugs*, p. 281, 2003

3 in dominoes, the 4–4 piece *US*

- — Dominic Armanino, *Dominoes*, p. 17, 1959

scotch *noun*
an improvised place to sleep *BARBADOS*

- — Richard Allsopp, *Dictionary of Caribbean English Usage*, p. 491–92, 1996

Scotch *noun*
in betting odds, even *UK*

- — John McCririck, *John McCririck's World of Betting*, p. 112, 1991

scotch call; scotch ring; scotchie *noun*
a telephone call that is unanswered by pre-arrangement and which acts as a signal or message without entailing the cost of a telephone call *SOUTH AFRICA*

- The little piece here last Tuesday on the Scotch ring, or Scotch call as some readers call it, has prompted three comments and advice[.] — *Dispatch Online*, 31st July 2002

scotch egg; scotch *noun*
the leg *UK*
Rhyming slang; usually plural. John Camden Hotten records 'Scotches, the legs' in 1859 but is probably refering to 'Scotch peg', an obsolete variation.

- [W]earing my head in it's proper place and not between my scotches like a sporran. — Derek Raymond (Robin Cook), *The Crust on its Uppers*, p. 30, 1962
- Her scotches, long and slender / Reached to her kingdom cum [bum][.] — Ronnie Barker, *Fletcher's Book of Rhyming Slang*, p. 21, 1979
- — Ray Puxley, *Cockney Rabbit*, 1992
- — Paul Baker, *Polari*, p. 189, 2002

Scotchman *noun*
a Scotsman *UK*
In conventional use until during C19 and, whilst not strictly incorrect, has been superseded by 'Scotsman' on both sides of the border.

- I was introduced to Ritchie Anderson, the Scotchman who'd helped out when we thought we had aggro at the White Swan. — Lenny McLean, *The Guv'nor*, p. 89, 1998

Scotchman's shout *noun*
a date where each person pays their own way *NEW ZEALAND, 1942*

- — Harry Orsman, *A Dictionary of Modern New Zealand Slang*, p. 115, 1999

scotch mist *noun*
▸ **turn scotch mist**
to vanish; to fade away *UK*

- Berniette Bolt, who acquired said moniker on account of his prodigious ability to turn Scotch mist whenever the long arm in blue [the police] made an appearance. — Andrew Nickolds, *Back to Basics*, 1994

Scotch mist *adjective*
drunk *UK*
Rhyming slang for **PISSED** (drunk), playing on the nebulous sense of Scotch mist and a taste of Scotch (whisky).

Scotch screw *noun*
a nocturnal emission of semen *US*

- — *Maledicta*, p. 60, 1986–1987: 'A continuation of a glossary of ethnic slurs in american english'

Scotch twist *noun*
in handball, a serve that strikes the front wall very near to a corner *US*

- — Peter Tyson and Mort Leve, *Handball*, p. 69, 1972: 'Glossary of handball terms'

Scotland the brave; scotland *noun*
a wave *UK: SCOTLAND*
Glasgow rhyming slang.

- There's wee Mick ower the road giein [giving] us a Scotland. — Michael Munro, *The Patter, Another Blast*, 1988

Scotland the brave; scotland *verb*
to shave *UK*
Rhyming slang.

- [Y]ou should Scotland more often. — Ray Puxley, *Fresh Rabbit*, 1998

Scotsman's grandstand *noun*
a vantage point overlooking a sportsground, permitting viewing with little or no payment. *NEW ZEALAND*

- The Scotsman's grandstand will be there and there will be the ultimate Scotsman's grandstand, a stationary train overlooking the ground. — *Sunday Times*, p. 4, 11th July 1993

scott; scot *noun*
heroin *US, 1971*
Probably a variation of **SCAT** (heroin).

- — Robert Ashton, *This Is Heroin*, p. 207, 2002
- — Mike Haskins, *Drugs*, p. 284, 2003

Scottish *adjective*
sexually uninhibited *CANADA*
The etymology is a mystery.

- [In Canada] "Scottish" is also used liberally as an inducement in the same way we'd use "Swedish". — Fiona Pitt-Kethley, *Red Light Districts of the World*, p. 12, 2000

Scotto- *prefix*
Scottish *UK*

- [T]hat Scotto-Welsh git on the telly[.] — James Hawes, *Dead Long Enough*, p. 10, 2000

Scotty *noun*
crack cocaine; the intoxication produced by crack cocaine *US*
Taken from the catchphrase 'Beam me up, Scotty', first heard in cult science-fiction television series *Star Trek* (1966–69).

- — Terry Williams, *The Cocaine Kids*, p. 137, 1989
- — Terry Williams, *Crackhouse*, p. 151, 1992
- — Mike Haskins, *Drugs*, p. 282, 2003

scouse *noun*
a meat and vegetable stew *UK, 1840*
An abbreviation of 'lobscouse' (a favourite dish of sailors since the C17).

- 'Scouse' is made by frying salt pork, scrap onions, well thickened with flour or add dumplings. — Joseph Ross, *History Cape Negro and Blanche*, p. 55, 1987
- [P]ut a big pan of scouse on[.] — Kevin Sampson, *Clubland*, p. 45, 2002

Scouser; Scouse; scouse *noun*
a person from Liverpool *UK, 1959*

- Wet 'er feet, 'e did. Aw, yus, yus. Aw. Aw. The effin' scouse. — Geoffrey Fletcher, *Down Among the Meths Men*, p. 34, 1966
- I got in a car with a load of Scousers. — Shaun Ryder, *Shaun Ryder... in His Own Words*, 1997
- [I]t's obvious he's twigged I'm a Scouser[.] — Kevin Sampson, *Outlaws*, p. 50, 2001

- Got the time, have you, Scouse? — Kevin Sampson, *Outlaws*, p. 174, 2001
- There are entertainers who are professional scousers. They know who they are, and your readers know too. — *Uncut*, p. 6, February 2002

scout *noun*

a familiar term of address for a male *IRELAND*

- We have the word 'fish' spelt 'gheech'! Gheech and chips, please, my old scout, and a batterburger when you're ready?! — Joseph O'Connor, *The Irish Male at Home and Abroad*, p. 172, 1996

scout around; scout about *verb*

to search and explore a place or area *UK, 1886*

- I was collecting information on the job and often had to search around for it. — *The Guardian*, 20th March 2003

scout's honor *noun*

used as a mocking pledge or oath to tell the truth *US*

A reference to the Boy Scouts of America and their pledge to be truthful.

- Lloyd said "Scout's honor" and started up the car, waggling his eyebrows at Kathleen until she laughed and begged him to stop. — James Ellroy, *Blood on the Moon*, p. 182, 1984

scow *noun*

in trucking, an especially large truck *US*

- — Mary Elting, *Trucks at Work*, 1946

scrabble *noun*

crack cocaine *UK*

Probably derives from scrabbling on the floor for fragments of the drug.

- — Mike Haskins, *Drugs*, p. 282, 2003

scradge *noun*

food *ANTARCTICA*

A British contribution to the slang of the South Pole.

- — *Cool Antarctica*, 2003: 'Antarctic slang'

scrag *verb*

1 to manhandle someone roughly *UK, 1835*

- Maybe I should go and scrag them, too, just like I did Menke. — John Milne, *Alive and Kicking*, p. 112, 1998

2 to murder someone *US, 1930*

- You know, she's hollering Muffo was scragged like Magoo. — George Mandel, *Flee the Angry Strangers*, p. 377, 1952

scraggy *adjective*

shabby *US*

- When we bust in on our pals we found them all kiping in one scraggy room, practically sleeping in layers. — Mezz Mezzrow, *Really the Blues*, p. 177, 1946

scraggy Lou *noun*

influenza *UK*

Rhyming slang for **FLU**.

- I've got the scraggy Lou and I look like her. — Ray Puxley, *Cockney Rabbit*, 1992

scram *noun*

a black person *US, 1940*

scram *verb*

to leave quickly *US, 1928*

Probably a reduction of 'scramble', possibly from German *schrammen* (to run away).

- [A] bookkeeper, no less, who used to beat her up and who scrammed with a lot of her assets. — Jack Lait and Lee Mortimer, *New York Confidential*, p. 187, 1948
- The Inspector wants this fellow to scram. — Horace McCoy, *Kiss Tomorrow Good-bye*, p. 82, 1948
- We have some of the wheels in the Mafia dangling by their you-know-whats and they're scramming for cover. — Mickey Spillane, *Kiss Me Deadly*, p. 140–141, 1952
- Scram, beat it, vamoose, out! Is that plain enough? — *King of Comedy*, 1976
- Atta girl! Let's scram before he regains consciousness! — *The Sweeney*, p. 20, 1976

scram bag *noun*

in circus and carnival usage, a suitcase that is always packed in the event that a hasty departure has become the prudent course of action *US*

- — Don Wilmeth, *The Language of American Popular Entertainment*, p. 233, 1981

scramble *noun*

1 adulterated heroin *US*

- Heroin is called either "bones," referring to a high level of purity, or "scramble," meaning a much less pure version, which is much cheaper. — *Washington Post*, p. B1, 29th July 1984
- — Robert Ashton, *This Is Heroin*, p. 210, 2002

2 crack cocaine *US*

From the effect on the user.

- — US Department of Justice, *Street Terms*, October 1994

3 in motorcyle racing, a race in difficult terrain *US*

- — John Lawlor, *How to Talk Car*, p. 91, 1965

▸ **the scramble**

the chaotic movement of pedestrians as soon as traffic signals permit *AUSTRALIA, 1984*

scramble *verb*

1 to live hand-to-mouth by a variety of hustles *US*

- — Terry Williams, *The Cocaine Kids*, p. 137, 1989

2 to sell drugs *US*

- He beat this kid who was scramblin' for him with a Louisville Slugger, poured gasoline on him and set him on fire after he shorted him $5.00. — *New Jack City*, 1990

scrambled egg; scrambled eggs *noun*

the gold braid insignia on an officer's cap or uniform *UK, 1943*

- They have stripes on the sleeves, scrambled eggs on the peak of the cap and blue socks with yellow stripes. — Jim Bouton, *Ball Four*, p. 98, 1970
- I made him put on his hat. It had a bunch of gold braid, which he called scrambled eggs, on its visor. — Delle Brehan, *Kicks is Kicks*, p. 80, 1970
- the Commandant, with the rank of Commander and a lot of scrambled egg on his shoulders. — Duncan MacLaughlin, *The Filth*, p. 51, 2002

scrambled eggs *noun*

mental confusion or mental illness *US*

- Fred Gil was lying there looking at his littlest daughter, perhaps a bit dazed from the medication, when she said, "Dadd, you don't have scrambled eggs, do you?" — Joseph Wambaugh, *Lines and Shadows*, p. 190, 1984

▸ **have scrambled eggs**

to be drunk *UK*

Rhyming slang for 'scrambled' (out of control) legs.

- — Ray Puxley, *Cockney Rabbit*, 1992

scrambled eggs cap; ham and eggs cap *noun*

a Captain or First Officer's cap, with gold 'scrambled eggs' applique *US*

- The President noted that the general was "with shirt unbuttoned, wearing a greasy ham and eggs cap that evidently had been in use for twenty years." — Joseph C. Goulden, *Korea*, p. 265, 1982
- "That famous scrambled-egg hat didnot look very dashing on that day either. He [General MacArthur] was a beaten man. — Joseph C. Goulden, *Korea*, p. 453, 1982

scrambler *noun*

a street-level drug seller *US*

- Fat Smitty controls the scramblers around the Carter. — *New Jack City*, 1990

scram heat *noun*

the urge to attempt escape from prison *US*

- — Joseph E. Ragen and Charles Finston, *Inside the World's Toughest Prison*, p. 816, 1962: 'Penitentiary and underworld glossary'

scram switch *noun*

in computing, an off switch for use in an emergency *US*

- — Eric S. Raymond, *The New Hacker's Dictionary*, p. 314, 1991

scran *noun*

1 food; a meal *UK, 1916*

Originally naval slang.

- [They] got up for a walk through the town and to find some scran. — Jimmy Stockin, *On The Cobbles*, p. 91, 2000
- I can cook up a scran and all too[.] — Kevin Sampson, *Outlaws*, p. 100, 2001

2 an informer *UK*

Back slang from **NARC** (an undercover narcotic officer).

- — Angela Devlin, *Prison Patter*, p. 102, 1996

scranker *noun*

in the language surrounding the Grateful Dead, a follower of the band who has lost all touch with reality *US*

- — David Shenk and Steve Silberman, *Skeleton Key*, p. 182, 1994

scrap *noun*

1 a fight *UK, 1887*

- MP with the taste for a scrap. — *The Guardian*, 22nd July 1999

2 a problem; a complaint *US*

Hawaiian youth usage.

- — Douglas Simonson, *Pidgin to da Max Hana Hou*, 1982

3 change from a one-pound note or coin *UK*

- — Tom Hibbert, *Rockspeak!*, p. 138, 1983

scrap *verb*

to fight *US*

- — Vann Wesson, *Generation X Field Guide and Lexicon*, p. 148, 1997

scrape *noun*

1 a risky situation *UK, 1709*

- Henry and this girl Beezus got into all kinds of scrapes with their neighbor, who didn't like kids. — Jane Leslie Conly, *Crazy Lady!*, p. 117, 1993

2 a shave *UK, 1859*

Semi-conventional usage.

- It's not that often that you get the time to give your grid [face] a proper fucking scrape. — Kevin Sampson, *Outlaws*, p. 85, 2001

3 a gynaecological dilation and curettage (D&C) of the uterus *UK*

- You would need to have a D and C 'scrape' for the doctor to see the telltale signs. — Suzie Hayman, *Hysterectomy*, p. 25, 1994

4 an abortion *UK, 1968*

- Touch told Mickey she drove to T.J. for a scrape. — James Ellroy, *White Jazz*, p. 295, 1992

scrape *verb*

▸ **scrape the bottom of the barrel; scrape the barrel**

to employ, but not through choice, someone or something of inferior standard *US, 1942*

- "Freeway sniper?" Yawn. "Shark attack?" She must really be scraping the bottom of the barrel. "A broken racehorse leg?" — Chuck Palahniuk, *Survivor*, p. 115, 2000
- I really have scraped the barrel for these two albums. — *The Observer*, 12th October 2003

▸ **scrape the mug**

to shave *US*

- — Joseph E. Ragen and Charles Finston, *Inside the World's Toughest Prison*, p. 816, 1962: 'Penitentiary and underworld glossary'

▸ **scrape the paint**

in horse racing, to race very close to the inside rail *AUSTRALIA*

- — Ned Wallish, *The Truth Dictionary of Racing Slang*, p. 72, 1989

scrape job *noun*

an abortion, especially an illegal one *US*

- — Stephen H. Dill (Editor), *Current Slang*, p. 6, summer 1967
- — Helen Dahlskog (Editor), *A Dictionary of Contemporary and Colloquial Usage*, p. 51, 1972
- A guess: scrape jobs made Lucille sterile. — James Ellroy, *White Jazz*, p. 113, 1992

scrap iron *noun*

1 a potent and dangerous alcoholic concoction made from wood alcohol, mothballs and chlorine *US*

- — William K. Bentley and James M. Corbett, *Prison Slang*, p. 71, 1992

2 in prison, weights for bodybuilding *US*

- — *Maledicta*, p. 266–267, Summer/Winter 1981: 'By its slang, ye shall know it: the pessimism of prison life'

scrap metal; scrap *noun*

a kettle *UK*

Rhyming slang, no longer in use.

- — Ray Puxley, *Cockney Rabbit*, 1992

scrapper *noun*

a fighter *US*

- Alice was pound for pound one of the best scrappers around as well as the President of the Honey Debutantes[.] — Piri Thomas, *Stories from El Barrio*, p. 92–93, 1978

scrap track *noun*

on the railways, a hospital *US*

- — Ramon Adams, *The Language of the Railroader*, p. 133, 1977

scratch *noun*

1 money *US, 1914*

- "How can we make some money?" "I could use some scratch too," he says and throws the dice. — Rocky Garciano (with Rowland Barber), *Somebody Up There Likes Me*, p. 26, 1955
- When he got inside the door, he would shout, "All right you poor ass bastards, it's party time and Joe Evans is in port with enough scratch to burn up a wet elephant." — Iceberg Slim (Robert Beck), *Pimp*, p. 33, 1969
- Say you cop a choice chick and you're really doing great / The scratch is right and the set up looks straight. — Dennis Wepman et al., *The Life*, p. 165, 1976
- — John Scarne, *Scarne's Guide to Modern Poker*, p. 289, 1979
- — Angela Devlin, *Prison Patter*, p. 102, 1996

2 unemployment benefit *IRELAND*

- I was chatting to someone the other day about the dole, otherwise known in more colloquial language as the scratch. — *Kildare Nationalist*, 25th February 2000

3 a masturbatory manipulation of the clitoris *UK*

- Could have been watching Frankie Vaughan [pornography] on the telly and giving herself a scratch. — Ian Dury, *This is What We Find*, 1979

4 a sound or rhythmic effect created by the manipulation of a vinyl recording *US*

- He had a way of rhythmically taking a scratch and making that shit sound musical. — Lois Stavsky et al. (quoting DJ Fuze, July 1994), *A2Z*, p. 89, 1995

5 a drug addict *US*

- — Don R. McCreary (Editor), *Dawg Speak*, 2001

6 rubber marks left on a surface when a car speeds away *US*

- — *Current Slang*, p. 5, Fall 1966

7 an attestation by a superior that a police officer was on his beat at a given time *US*

- waiting at street corners for a sergeant to come by and make the scratch. — Charles Whited, *Chiodo*, p. 291, 1973

scratch *verb*

1 to manipulate a vinyl record to create sounds and rhythms *US*

Scratching, as a technique, was invented in the late 1970s by 13-year-old Theodore Livingstone (later Grand Wizard Theodore) and widely recognised by the mainstream in 1983 with the release of 'Rockit' by Herbie Hancock which featured Grandmixer DST scratching.

- I did the scratching and he was the MC. — Lois Stavsky et al. (quoting DJ Fuze, July 1994), *A2Z*, p. 89, 1995
- [T]echniques like back-spinning, cutting, which was later called scratching[.] — Alex Ogg, *The Hip Hop Years*, p. 27, 1999
- I liked the bit in the middle (of Malcolm McLarens' "Buffalo Girls") that went wucka, wucka, wucka. And he said, "that's scratching, that is". — J. Hoggarth (quoting Prime Cuts), *How To Be a DJ*, p. 81, 2002

2 to sign-on for unemployment benefit *UK*

- informing the dole if guys were scratching and working. — J.J. Connolly, *Layer Cake*, p. 138, 2000

3 to forge *US*

- — Joseph E. Ragen and Charles Finston, *Inside the World's Toughest Prison*, p. 816, 1962: 'Penitentiary and underworld glossary'

4 to erase something; to withdraw a competitor from a competition *UK, 1685*

- No, more like a Formula race car. No, scratch that one, too. — *Natural Born Killers*, 1994

5 to whip someone; to mark someone with a whip *UK*

- [S]ome of the boys, whose backs he had scratched while they were inside, lay in wait for him[.] — Charles Raven, *Underworld Nights*, p. 114, 1956

6 to paddle a surfboard energetically *US*

- — Grant W. Kuhns, *On Surfing*, p. 121, 1963

▸ **scratch gravel**

to leave quickly, especially in a car *US*

- — Hy Lit, *Hy Lit's Unbelievable Dictionary of Hip Words for Groovy People*, p. 51, 1968

▸ **scratch head**

to have sex *TRINIDAD AND TOBAGO*

From the sense of **HEAD** as 'penis'.

- — Lise Winer, *Dictionary of the English/Creole of Trinidad & Tobago*, 2003

▸ **scratch your monkey**

(used of a drug addict) to satisfy your drug habit with an injection or other ingestion of the drug *US*

- — William K. Bentley and James M. Corbett, *Prison Slang*, p. 72, 1992

scratcher *noun*

1 a person who scratches their stylised signature into a window on the underground *US*
- — Jim Crotty, *How to Talk American*, p. 143, 1997

2 a tattoo artist, especially an unlicensed amateur *US*
- — *Los Angeles Times Magazine*, p. 7, 13th July 1997

3 a forger *US*
- — Frank Prewitt and Francis Schaeffer, *Vacaville Vocabulary*, 1961 – 1962

4 a prison warder who is expert in searching a cell *UK*
- — Sean McConville, *The State of the Language*, 1980

5 a rough bed or sleeping bag *NEW ZEALAND*
- after all, getting out of this old scratcher takes a lot of effort. — Ron Helmer, *Stag Party*, p. 56, 1964
- I'll just mosey away up to my scratcher. G'night[.] — Ian Pattison, *Rab C. Nesbitt*, 1988
- Didn't we even have the artist formerly known as Prince (Charles) leppin in and out of the extramarital scratcher with lovely Camilla for years? — Joseph O'Connor, *The Irish Male at Home and Abroad*, p. 125, 1996

scratch house *noun*

an inexpensive boarding house or brothel *US*
- — Joseph E. Ragen and Charles Finston, *Inside the World's Toughest Prison*, p. 817, 1962: 'Penitentiary and underworld glossary'

scratching *noun*

the searching of prison premises *UK*
- — Home Office, *Glossary of Terms and Slang Common in Penal Establishments*, July 1978

scratch man *noun*

a forger *US*
- — Joseph E. Ragen and Charles Finston, *Inside the World's Toughest Prison*, p. 817, 1962: 'Penitentiary and underworld glossary'

scratch off *verb*

to leave, especially in a hurry *US*
- — *American Speech*, p. 229, October 1956: 'More United States Air Force slang'

scratch pad *noun*

very inexpensive lodging *US*
- You'll never toss and turn again in a Bowsery scratchpad, digging the lice and chinches out of your hide. — Mezz Mezzrow, *Really the Blues*, p. 317, 1946

scratch sheet *noun*

a leaflet or pamphlet offering 'inside' tips on horse betting *US*
- — Helen Dahlskog (Editor), *A Dictionary of Contemporary and Colloquial Usage*, p. 19, 1972

scraven *adjective*

gluttonous; greedy *GUYANA*

scrawbee-looby *noun*

a badly scored goal, a fluke or one that barely got past the goalkeeper *IRELAND*
- A scrawbee-looby kind of a goal. — Irwin Liam, *North Munster Antiquarian Journal*, p. 86, 2000

scream *noun*

1 an extremely ridiculous or funny person or thing *US, 1888*
Originally used in theatre slang, now simply melodramatic.
- Oh, Harry, you're a scream. — Max Shulman, *Rally Round the Flag, Boys!*, p. 42, 1957
- It's a scream. You'd love it. — Armistead Maupin, *Tales of the City*, p. 124, 1978
- We made a girl want to consider suicide. What a scream. What a jest. — *Heathers*, 1988

2 an appeal against criminal conviction *UK, 1990s*
Prison slang.
- — David Rowan, *A Glossary for the 90s*, 1998

3 a police search *UK*
- He knew how efficient the Surrey police cordons were once a scream was on. — Charles Raven, *Underworld Nights*, p. 19, 1956

scream *verb*

1 to complain *US*
- — Inez Cardozo-Freeman, *The Joint*, p. 528, 1984

2 to inform the police or prison authorities *UK, 1903*
- — Angela Devlin, *Prison Patter*, p. 102, 1996
- To give him his due, he never screamed, but I think he was well pleased to see me shipped off to Brixton [prison] later on. — Lenny McLean, *The Guv'nor*, p. 211, 1998

▸ **scream like Tarzan; scream like ten Tarzans**

to shout loudly *TRINIDAD AND TOBAGO, 1989*
- — Lise Winer, *Dictionary of the English/Creole of Trinidad & Tobago*, 2003

screamer *noun*

1 a blatant and conspicuous homosexual *US*
- The homosexual, who was playing hard to get, came to one masquerade party dressed as Tinkerbelle, the good fairy. He was what the other queers called a screamer. — Phyllis and Eberhard Kronhausen, *Sex Histories of American College Men*, p. 184, 1960
- In the summer they'd pile into convertibles and head for North Beach, a spot for bawdy screamers and butch hillbilly types. — *Screw*, p. 15, 23th February 1970
- — Jeff Fessler, *When Drag Is Not a Car Race*, p. 14, 1997

2 a hysterical hospital patient *US*
- — *Maledicta*, p. 6, Summer/Winter 1978: 'Common patient-directed pejoratives used by medical personnel'

3 an arrest warrant *US*
- They haven't booked me yet. I'm beginning to think that maybe I can walk out of this when somebody comes up to me and says, "Oh, you're Huncke. We've got a screamer on you." — Herbert Huncke, *Guilty of Everything*, p. 107, 1990

4 a police siren *US*
- Course, if they come it with their screamer full on, just like now. — Jess Mowry, *Way Past Cool*, p. 15, 1992

5 in drag racing and hot rodding, a very fast car *US*
- — *Good Housekeeping*, p. 143, September 1958: 'Hot-rod terms for teen-age girls'

6 a hamburger with hot sauce and onions *US*
- — Amy and Denise McFadden, *CoalSpeak*, p. 12, 1997

7 in typography, an exclamation mark (!) *UK, 1933*
- [K]nown in the newspaper world as a screamer, a gasper, a startler or (sorry) a dog's cock. — Lynne Truss, *Eats, Shoots and Leaves*, p. 136, 2003

screamer and creamer *noun*

a woman who is vocal during sex *US*
- — *Maledicta*, p. 18, Summer 1977: 'A word for it'

screamers *noun*

pieces of metal scrap packed with an artillery shell, which makes a screaming sound as the shell moves through the air *US*
- — Gregory Clark, *Words of the Vietnam War*, p. 454, 1990

screaming *adjective*

1 striking; conspicuous; obvious *US, 1848*
Used as an intensifier since the mid-C19, but in a slangy homosexual sense much more recently.
- I have always made fun of the swishing, screaming, flaunting queens and you have always laughed with me. — *Mattachine Review*, p. 24, March 1960
- — *Fact*, p. 27, January-February 1965
- Old Jewish mothers never know when their sons are faggots. They just miss it somehow. Out-and-out screaming queens – mothers are never hip. — Lenny Bruce, *The Essential Lenny Bruce*, p. 162, 1967
- [S]creaming queen: outrageous homosexual man. — Paul Baker, *Polari*, p. 189, 2002

2 excellent; the best *US*
- That cup of coffee was screamin — James Harris, *A Convict's Dictionary*, p. 37, 1989
- — Jim Goad, *Jim Goad's Glossary of Northwestern Prison Slang*, December 2001

screaming abdabs *noun*

▷ see: ABDABS

screaming area *noun*

in a hospital, the medical screening area *US*
- — *Maledicta*, p. 6, Summer/Winter 1978: 'Common patient-directed pejoratives used by medical personnel'

screaming chickens *noun*

the 101st Airborne Division, US Army *US*
Like the **PUKING BUZZARDS**, a play on the official 'screaming eagles'.
- — Linda Reinberg, *In the Field*, p. 193, 1991

screaming Jimmy *noun*

a large General Motors Corporation diesel truck *US*
A reference to the high-pitched noise of the GMC engine.
- — *American Speech*, p. 272, December 1962: 'The language of traffic policemen'
- — Montie Tak, *Truck Talk*, p. 136, 1971

Screaming Lord Sutch *noun*

the crutch or crotch *UK*

Rhyming slang, formed from the name of rock musician and politician, founder of the Monster Raving Loony Party, David Edward Sutch, 3rd Earl of Harrow, 1940–99. In the 1960s he changed his name by deed poll to Screaming Lord Sutch.

- [I]ll fitting trousers may be said to be a bit tight round the "Screamin' Lord Sutch". — Ray Puxley, *Cockney Rabbit*, 1992

screaming meemies *noun*

hysteria; excessive fear noisily expressed *US, 1927*

- By the time a big company got around to referring one of its employees to a psychiatrist, the screaming meemies had already set in and the patient was often receiving radio beams from Venus. — Carl Hiaasen, *Tourist Season*, p. 40, 1986
- Somebody threw a building block through the plate glass, gave Hetty the screaming meemies. — Robert Campbell, *Alice in La-La Land*, p. 210–211, 1987

screaming shits *noun*

1 a non-existent disease *US*

It is commonly found in expressions such as, 'I'd rather die with the screaming shits'.

- — *American Speech*, p. 305, December 1947: 'Imaginary diseases in army and navy parlance'

2 diarrhoea *US*

Used with 'the'.

- — *Current Slang*, p. 19, Spring 1971

screaming sixties *noun*

the latitudes of 60 to 69 degrees south *ANTARCTICA, 1976*

- — Bernadette Hince, *The Antarctic Dictionary*, p. 299, 2000

screamy *adjective*

melodramatic; exhibitionist; extremely extroverted *US*

Homosexual usage.

- — *Maledicta*, p. 235, 1979: 'Kinks and queens: linguistic and cultural aspects of the terminology for gays'

screech *noun*

1 the mouth, the throat, the face *UK, 1984*

- She has a permanent vogue [cigarette] in her screech and her droje [clothing] is mega ribena on toast [awful], daughter. — the cast of 'Aspects of Love', Prince of Wales Theatre, *Palare (Boy Dancer Talk) for Beginners*, 1989–92
- [S]he schlumphed her Vera [gin] down the screech at a rate of knots[.] — James Gardiner, *Who's a Pretty Boy Then?*, p. 123,
- Oh, shut your screech[.] — Paul Baker, *Polari*, p. 189, 2002

2 dark, strong Jamaican rum imported into Newfoundland *CANADA*

- The Newfoundland-Jamaican relationship goes back a long period of time, i. e. when the Newfs had tons of fish to trade [for screech]. — Emily *An American's Guide to Canada*, p. 3, 10th November 2001

3 powdered lime juice *UK*

Military.

- Each morning we had to drink a mugful of "screech"[.] — Andy McNab, *Immediate Action*, p. 19, 1995

screechie *noun*

in circus and carnival usage, an audio technician *US*

- — Don Wilmeth, *The Language of American Popular Entertainment*, p. 233, 1981

screech-in *noun*

in Newfoundland, an event in which a newcomer is given screech to drink and then asked to sample the ocean temperature with a foot or kiss a cod *CANADA*

- A screech-in is a ceremony we perform at our pub for people who visit our province. — *trapperjohns.com*, 26 July 2002

screel *verb*

to complain loudly *TRINIDAD AND TOBAGO, 1971*

- — Lise Winer, *Dictionary of the English/Creole of Trinidad & Tobago*, 2003
- A blending of 'squeal' and 'scream'. — Lise Winer, *Dictionary of the English/Creole of Trinidad & Tobago*, 2003

screeve *noun*

a car *UK*

- The gorger [man]'s quavering [pottering] about with the screeve. — Patrick O'Shaughnessy, *Market Traders' Slang*, 1979

screw *noun*

1 a prison officer *UK, 1812*

Possibly from an obsolete sense of 'screw' (a skeleton key), hence a 'turnkey' or 'warder', or perhaps from 'thumbscrew' (an instrument of torture used in C17 prisons).

- When the screw came, I'd spit in his face. — William Burroughs, *Junkie*, p. 68, 1953
- They shut me back in my cell and early in the morning the screw whacked my feet with his bat andd woke me up. — Rocky Garciano (with Rowland Barber), *Somebody Up There Likes Me*, p. 112, 1955
- [T]he money which his friends, outside, will bung the screws to pay for his snout [cigarettes] and other little creature comforts. — Charles Raven, *Underworld Nights*, p. 52, 1956
- "What do you mean I'm the prisoner?," said the screw in amazement. — Frank Norman, *Bang To Rights*, p. 103, 1958
- Several prisoners stood in the doorway, watching him. "Somebody call the screw." — Clarence Cooper Jr, *The Scene*, p. 228, 1960
- We clambered out and stood in line to have our handcuffs removed. Two "screws" started at each end of the line unlocking the cuffs. — Iceberg Slim (Robert Beck), *Pimp*, p. 49, 1969
- [E]very screw here is borstal [juvenile offenders' prison]. Every one of us. — *Scum*, 1979
- But one day these screws got to me. — *Raging Bull*, 1980
- — Angela Devlin, *Prison Patter*, p. 102, 1996

2 an act of sexual intercourse *US, 1929*

- If you don't like sleeping, and don't want a screw / Then you should take lots of amphetamine too — The Fugs *New Amphetamine Shreik*, 1965
- After a month of these cheap screws she finally told me she had $25,000 in her personal savings account. — Oscar Zeta Acosta, *The Autobiography of a Brown Buffalo*, p. 155, 1972

3 a sexual partner, potential or actual, of either gender, objectified and gauged *UK, 1937*

- — Alen Richter, *Sexual slang*, p. 193, 1993

4 a wage *UK, 1858*

- — Norman Lindsay, *The Cousin from Fiji*, p. 245, 1945
- I pay his screw. — Arthur Upfield, *Bony and the Mouse*, p. 63, 1959
- The staff drew their screw in golden sovereigns, and the lesser contributors in silver coin. — Norman Lindsay, *Bohemians at the Bulletin*, p. 4, 1965
- Oh the young bloke is getting a good screw, and he likes it. — Harvey E. Ward, *Down Under Without Blunder*, p. 22, 1967

5 a salary *NEW ZEALAND*

- — Louis S. Leland, *A Personal Kiwi-Yankee Dictionary*, p. 89, 1984

6 a mischievous scheme *TRINIDAD AND TOBAGO, 1935*

- — Lise Winer, *Dictionary of the English/Creole of Trinidad & Tobago*, 2003

7 a look *AUSTRALIA, 1907*

- What about nicking in and having a screw through the key hole? — Robert S. Close, *Love Me Sailor*, p. 138, 1945
- So I hid in the shadows and had a screw at the compound. — Alexander Buzo, *Norm and Ahmed*, p. 9, 1969
- — Jim Ramsay, *Cop It Sweet!*, p. 88, 1977

▸ **have a screw loose**

to be or become eccentric, crazy or insane *UK, 1833*

- [A]fter all your mates telling you that you had a screw loose. — Mary Hooper, *(megan)2*, p. 70, 1999
- Everyone seems to have at least one screw loose[.] — *The Guardian*, 3rd April 2003

screw *verb*

1 to have sex *UK, 1725*

- What are you going to screw tonight, eh? Who? Your brother-in-law? — George Mandel, *Flee the Angry Strangers*, p. 50, 1952
- [S]hore, come on with us and we'll all screw ya at ten thousand feet[.] — Jack Kerouac, *The Dharma Bums*, p. 24, 1958
- 'But decent girls don't screw,' Max said. — Willard Motley, *Let No Man Write My Epitaph*, p. 178, 1958
- [H]e wouldn't sure 'nough hurt her like he'd do if he caught her screwing some other nigger. — Chester Himes, *The Real Cool Killers*, p. 59, 1959
- The various chapter prospects were showing everyone how well they could screw and plate her. — Jamie Mandelkau, *Buttons*, p. 99, 1971
- He would've screwed this nanny goat if he couldn't find a nymph. — Tom Robbins, *Another Roadside Attraction*, p. 273, 1971
- I'd bleeding murder anybody you screwed on your own[.] — Ted Lewis, *Jack Carter's Law*, p. 62, 1974
- You see her. You screw her. We go home. — *The Guru*, 2002

2 used dismissively as a synonym for 'fuck' in exclamations and curses *UK, 1949*

- What about the gang? – Screw the gang, go and get those cards. — Mark Powell, *Snap*, p. 81, 2001

3 to burgle *UK, 1812*
A C20 usage from the earlier senses (a skeleton key; and to break into a building using a skeleton key).
- [T]hey had enjoyed a run of luck, screwing country houses in the prosperous Home Counties[.] — Charles Raven, *Underworld Nights*, p. 15, 1956
- lowdown grafting hoods [criminals] who'd set him to work screwing – send him out with a pound of jelly [gelignite]. — Derek Raymond (Robin Cook), *The Crust on its Uppers*, p. 57, 1962
- [T]he coppers sees them going in and thinks they're screwing the place. — John Peter Jones, *Feather Pluckers*, p. 119, 1964
- [W]here are the cunts [the police] when some baghead [junkie]'s trying to screw your house? — Kevin Sampson, *Outlaws*, p. 210, 2001

4 to swindle or cheat someone *UK, 1900*
- — Angela Devlin, *Prison Patter*, p. 102, 1996

5 to ruin something *UK*
Probably a shortening of **SCREW UP**.
- I think they've screwed biology in this country for ever. — *Maclean's*, 17th May 1976

6 to stare at someone; to look at someone accusingly *AUSTRALIA, 1917*
- I saw four Mods come out. They started screwing me. — Jamie Mandelkau, *Buttons*, p. 27, 1971
- Skitzy screwed anyone who dared catch his eye. — Martin King and Martin Knight, *The Naughty Nineties*, p. 145, 1999

7 to leave *US*
- Terminology — Gene Sorrows, *All About Carnivals*, p. 26, 1985

8 in pool, to apply spin to the cue ball to affect the course of the object ball or the cue ball after striking the object ball *US*
- — Steve Rushin, *Pool Cool*, p. 25, 1990

▸ don't screw the crew
a catchphrase injunction: do not have sex with your work-mates *UK*
A corporate updating of **NOT ON YOUR OWN DOORSTEP**.
- But he was almost encouraging you to shag other reps! What about don't screw the crew? — Colin Butts, *Is Harry Still on the Boat?*, p. 28, 2003

▸ screw daft
to have sex to the point of insensibility *UK*
Generally something of a boast.
- [H]e will fuck the arse off her tonight, he thinks, he will shag her senseless, screw her daft[.] — Niall Griffiths, *Grits*, p. 53, 2000

▸ screw the arse off
to have vigorous sex with someone *UK*
- — Peter Crookson, *Villain*, 1967
- "Lucy!" cried The Journalist. "Pipes of Pangalin! I want to screw the arse off you!" "STOP IT!" screamed Dan, and he threw himself at The Journalist — Terry Jones, *Douglas Adam's Starship Titanic*, p. 19, 1998

▸ screw the pooch
to bungle or to ruin something *US*
- [H]is prayer had not been answered, and the Lord let him screw the pooch. — Tom Wolfe, *The Right Stuff*, p. 231, 1979
- You really know how to screw the pooch, Sarge! — John Culbertson, *13 Cent Killers*, p. 62, 2003

▸ screw your brains out
to have sex with great regularity and force *US*
- She didn't talk much but she was quite affectionate. Nearly screwed my brains out is what I'm trying to say. — Tom Robbins, *Another Roadside Attraction*, p. 32, 1971

screwage *noun*
a computer malfunction due to design error *US*
- — Eric S. Raymond, *The New Hacker's Dictionary*, p. 315, 1991

screw around *noun*
to fool around; to waste time *US, 1939*
- Shooting pool and screwing around. — Willard Motley, *Let No Man Write My Epitaph*, p. 85, 1958

screwball *noun*
an odd, eccentric or crazy person *US, 1933*
- You're sure the world's prize screwball. — Irving Shulman, *The Amboy Dukes*, p. 238, 1947
- Kinsey only talked to screwballs and neurotics and people who were inventing stuff to show off. — Philip Wylie, *Opus 21*, p. 113, 1949
- And the only way you'll get me to Scranton is if some screwball hijacks the plane! — Eugene Boe (Compiler), *The Wit & Wisdom of Archie Bunker*, p. 20, 1971

screwball *adjective*
odd, eccentric *US, 1936*
- That screwball pulay of yours with Sugar and Max. — Mickey Spillane, *Kiss Me Deadly*, p. 109, 1952
- "Where'd you get a screwball notion like that?" asks Mule. — Darryl Ponicsan, *The Last Detail*, p. 139, 1970

screwdriver *noun*

1 a principal prison officer *UK, 1950*
An elaboration of **SCREW** (a prison officer).
- — Angela Devlin, *Prison Patter*, p. 102, 1996

2 a person who evades work or duty *UK*
Rhyming slang for **SKIVER**.
- — Ray Puxley, *Cockney Rabbit*, 1992

screwed *adjective*
drunk *UK*
- — *e-cyclopaedia*, 20th March 2002

screwed, blued and tattooed *adjective*
in such misfortune or trouble that there is no likely escape *CANADA, 1969*
- Well, I'll be fucked. Bonnie, knocked up. I'll be screwed, blued and tattooed. I didn't think it could be done. — Edward Abbey, *The Monkey Wrench Gang*, p. 420, 1975
- Looks like we're for it, said Boyd. Screwed, blued and tattooed. This thing's gonna go kablooey any minute now. — Maragaret Atwood, *The Blind Assassin*, p. 352, 2000

screwed up *adjective*

1 troubled, disturbed *UK, 1907*
- The nun goes along on the tour with the boy, this screwed up American kid, holding his rackets, sitting quietly in the grandstands, just watching. — Clancy Sigal, *Going Away*, p. 207, 1961
- "Screwed-up world without laws!" Sylvia muttered disgustedly to herself. — John Rechy, *City of Night*, p. 326, 1963
- Recently, I've gone through a VERY screwed up point in my life[.] — *MUZIK*, p. 9, February 2003

2 spoilt; wrecked; fouled up *US, 1943*
A euphemism for **FUCKED UP**.
- I was next to some really screwed up nutters for a while[.] — Ben Malbon, *Cool Places*, p. 275, 1998

3 being locked in a prison cell *UK*
A pun on **BANGED UP**, via **BANG** (to have sex) and **SCREW** (to have sex).
- — David Powis, *The Signs of Crime*, 1977

screwhead *noun*
a crazy person *UK*
What you are when you **HAVE A SCREW LOOSE**.
- I feel sorry for Stell having to hitch up with the king of the screwheads. — Nick Barlay, *Curvy Lovebox*, p. 80, 1997

screw-hole *noun*
an unpleasant location *UK*
- Nasty – And now look at me, stuck in some screw-hole. — Mark Powell, *Snap*, p. 80, 2001

screwing *adjective*
anxious, unhappy *UK*
Probably from the Jamaican patois verb 'screw' (to frown).
- Leave me alone, I'm screwing! — Angela Devlin, *Prison Patter*, p. 102, 1996
- I had a cris' pair ah Versace jeans dat got bun [burnt] up. I'm screwin' about dat, believe. — Courttia Newland, *Society Within*, p. 11, 1999

screw job *noun*
an exploitation or other maltreatment *US*
- I think this is nothin' but a goddamn screw job. I think it's a shakedown. — *Raising Arizona*, 1987

screw over *verb*
to treat another person with contempt or cruelty in any way; to betray someone; to victimise someone; to cheat someone *UK*
A variation of **SCREW**.
- I'm getting screwed over by some fucker who doesn't care for anything 'cept his own pocket. — John Williams, *Cardiff Dead*, p. 117, 2000

screws *noun*

▸ put the screws on; put the screws to
to put pressure on someone, especially in relation to economic operations or debt recovery *US, 1834*

- The board and venture capitalists start in on the founders and the president, who in turn put the screws to the vice president of sales[.] — Geoffrey A Moore, *Crossing the Chasm*, p. 24, 2002
- Market leader Tesco is putting the screws on suppliers to cut costs so it can keep its own prices down. — *The Scotsman*, 17th January 2004

screwsman *noun*

a housebreaker; a thief *UK, 1812*

Originally 'a thief using a skeleton key'.

- [T]reat this book as a 'Screwsman's Vade Mecum'[.] — Maurice Richardson, *Underworld Nights*, p. 8, 1956

screw-up *noun*

1 an action or circumstance that has been handled badly *US*

- First of all, was a man who had made such a thorough screw-up of his own affairs a suitable mentor for me? — Jim Thompson, *Bad Boy*, p. 335, 1953
- Sorry for the screw-up but since only about ten of us turned up, we decided ... to bugger off to the beach — Reclaim The Streets (RTS), *E-mail report, Darwin, Australia*, 16th May 1998

2 an awkward person; an incompetent, a blunderer; an inadequate person *US*

- It didn't cross his mind that this red-eyed, red-nosed, sweaty, pasty-looking screw-up in the beanie hat was Tommy Hanson. — Ben Elton, *High Society*, p. 130, 2002

screw up *verb*

to bungle; to fail in a task; to perform something poorly *US, 1942*

- You're screwing things up. — Irving Shulman, *The Amboy Dukes*, p. 232, 1947
- Because if I feel down or screwed it up, I'd never live to fumble another one. — Jim Thompson, *Savage Night*, p. 48, 1953
- I'm not going to screw it up just because you people got hot pants. — George V. Higgins, *The Friends of Eddie Doyle*, p. 74, 1971
- I am not flying smoothly, accurately, conservatively. In fact, I am screwing up in a big way — Robert Prest, *F4 Phantom*, 1979
- If you screw up, I can promise you, you're goin' down. *48 Hours*, 1982
- [T]oo busy giving the eye to some little sister hasn't even screwed up her GCSEs [examinations] yet. — John Williams, *Cardiff Dead*, p. 3, 1999

screwy *adjective*

crazy; (very) eccentric *US, 1887*

- [Ol' Dirty Bastard]'s revered as something of a genius. The second [thing to know] is that he's bananas. Screwy. Poco loco. Bonkers as conkers. — *Uncut*, p. 20, October 2003

screw you!

used as contemptuous dismissal *US*

Substituting **SCREW** for **FUCK** in **FUCK YOU!** with the same senses.

- [W]hat her mind was saying was screw you for what you did. But her body was singing a different tune. — John Williams, *Cardiff Dead*, p. 52, 2000

screw your buddy *noun*

in pool, a three-player game in which all players play against all other players *US*

- — Mike Shamos, *The Illustrated Encyclopedia of Billiards*, p. 203, 1993

scribble *verb*

in computing, to inadvertently and detrimentally modify a data structure *US*

- Somebody's disk-compactor program went beserk and scribbled on the i-node table. — Eric S. Raymond, *The New Hacker's Dictionary*, p. 315, 1991

scribe *noun*

a letter *US*

- — Clarence Major, *Dictionary of Afro-American Slang*, p. 101, 1970
- When the door opened and in walked the man / Carrying what looked like a scribe in his hand. — Dennis Wepman et al., *The Life*, p. 139, 1976

scriber *noun*

in the television and film industries, a writer *US*

- — Tony Miller and Patricia George, *Cut! Print!*, p. 134, 1977

scrid *noun*

a very small amount *BARBADOS*

- — Frank A. Collymore, *Barbadian Dialect*, p. 97, 1965

scrilla; skrilla *noun*

money *US*

- — *Columbia Missourian*, p. 1A, 19 October 1998

scrimy *adjective*

despicable; lowdown *US*

- Another kid cut down by a pack of scrimy hoods[.] — Mickey Spillane, *Kiss Me Deadly*, p. 151, 1952

script *noun*

1 a prescription for a narcotic, especially a forged prescription *US, 1936*

- Life telescopes down to junk, one fix and looking forward to the next, "stashes" and "scripts," "spikes" and "droppers." — William Burroughs, *Junkie*, p. 35, 1953
- "From this croaker up on 76th Street. He used to write for me, you know, scripts, prescriptions. I turned a trick with him." — James Mills, *The Panic in Needle Park*, p. 91, 1966
- I just remembered, my sick old man is got some red devils from a script at his pad. — Iceberg Slim (Robert Beck), *Trick Baby*, p. 268, 1969
- [H]e's got a lot of doctors who gamble with him and they write him a scrip once in a while. — Bruce Jackson, *Outside the Law*, p. 107, 1972
- a long list of croakers who wrote scrips for ten, twenty, fifty dollars, depending on what for and how much one wanted. — Emmett Grogan, *Ringolevio*, p. 54, 1972
- We received vials – government sealed with twenty quarter-grain tablets for each script – giving us a total of thirty grains of morphine at the end of our afternoon's work. — Herbert Huncke, *The Evening Sun Turned Crimson*, p. 86, 1980
- Joe told him he only needed to find Rooski this morning, who often cadged [begged] Demerols from Hymie's migraine script. — Seth Morgan, *Homeboy*, p. 59, 1990
- You can pop along to the quack and he'll give you a script for Prozac, or whatever. — Kevin Sampson, *Powder*, p. 117, 1999

2 in prison, a letter *UK*

Possibly from a (medical) prescription seen as a piece of writing with the intention of making you feel better.

- — Angela Devlin, *Prison Patter*, p. 102, 1996

3 a forged cheque *US*

- — Hyman E. Goldin et al., *Dictionary of American Underworld Lingo*, p. 187, 1950

script jockey *noun*

a screenwriter *US*

- The script jockey is one Stanley Shapiro, and he commands $250 Thou per flick. — Sidney Bernard, *This Way to the Apocalypse*, p. 167, 1964

scroat; scrote *noun*

a despicable man *US*

Probably from an abbreviation of 'scrotum'.

- Scrotes! That's what all people are: ignorant filthy disgusting ugly worthless scrotes. — Joseph Wambaugh, *The Choirboys*, p. 33, 1975
- Eventually the officer relented. "Go on then you scrote," he said, by now grinning broadly. — *The Guardian*, 12th July 2001
- Our [the police] job is to get in before the stuff [drugs] can get out. Normally the scroats try to flush it away[.] — Duncan MacLaughlin, *The Filth*, p. 120, 2002

scrod *noun*

1 an ageing motorcyclist who still looks the part but for whom the motorcyle is a stage prop, not a way of life *US*

2 any small fish, usually haddock or cod *CANADA*

This word is part of an old joke: 'Did you get scrod in Boston?' – 'It's the first time I've been asked in the pluperfect subjunctive!'. Boston is a usual destination for Nova Scotia fish.

- Scrod is any undersized fish, too small to sell or fillet. Sometimes it is called "scrod cod or haddock." — Joseph Ross, *History Cape Negro and Blanche*, p. 55, 1987

scrog *verb*

to have sex *US*

- — *Maledicta*, p. 250, 1983: 'A connotative analysis of synonyms for sexual intercourse'

scroggin *noun*

a mixture of dried fruits, chocolate, nuts and grains *NEW ZEALAND*

- Scroggin I can tell you, is the tramper's friend – an energy-sustaining mixture of peanuts, chocolate and raisin. — *Dominion*, p. 10, 9th March 1991

scromp *verb*

to have sex *US*

- — *People Magazine*, p. 72, 19th July 1993

scronies *noun*

pepperoni *US*

- — *Maledicta*, p. 19, 1996: 'Domino's pizza jargon'

scroogie *noun*

a screwdriver *US*

- "Now gimme the scroogie." Danny Pogue checked the street for cards or pedestrians; then he handed Bud Schwartz a nine-inch screwdriver. — Carl Hiaasen, *Native Tongue*, p. 320, 1991

scrot rot *noun*
general discomfort, itchiness or sweatiness of the scrotum and surrounding areas *UK*
• — Chris Lewis, *The Dictionary of Playground Slang*, p. 196, 2003

scrotty *adjective*
dirty; unattractive *UK*
A variation of GROTTY, probably by elision of 'it's grotty'; reported in teenage use by Joanna Williamson, 1982.

scrotum *noun*
▸ **on the scrotum**
alert, prepared *US*
A play on the more common 'on the ball'.
• — *American Speech*, p. 31, February 1949: 'A.V.G. Lingo'

scrounge *noun*
a habitual borrower; a freeloader *UK, 1937*
• If a broad dropped her drawers, right away she lost her rating – even to the scrounge who copped them[.] — Edwin Torres, *Carlito's Way*, p. 11, 1975

scrounge *verb*
to rummage; to search *UK, 1909*
• I scrounged through the mess on his dresser[.] — Janet Evanovich, *Seven Up*, p. 51, 2001

▸ **scrounge off**
to freeload; to sponge off someone *UK*
• I wouldn't spend the rest of me days scrounging off me family. — Clive Exton, *No Fixed Abode [Six Granada Plays]*, p. 122, 1959

scrounger *noun*
a person known for their ability to beg, borrow, buy or steal what is needed *US, 1918*
Respected and valued.
• A "scrounger" in the Marines is a highly experienced artist and not a mere thief. The scrounger's idea is that everything is basically government property, and the government belongs to its citizens. As a citizen in good standing, the scrounger feels entitled to anything he can move. — Russell Davis, *Marine at War*, p. 171, 1961
• He was a decent scrounger; had hustled Haskins for eggs and bacon and No. 10 cans of fruit, and real ground coffee. — Larry Heinemann, *Close Quarters*, p. 228, 1977

scroungy *adjective*
cheap; always in search of help *US*
• — *American Speech*, p. 154, May 1959: 'Gator (University of Florida) slang'

scrub *noun*
1 a contemptible or insignificant person, especially one who does not share your high standards of morality, style or personal hygiene *UK, 1900*
• [A] scrub is checkin' me / But his game is kinda weak / And I know that he cannot approach me / Cuz I'm lookin' like class and he's lookin' like trash[.] — TLC *No Scrubs*, 1999
2 a person attending a dance who is not asked to dance for long periods of time *TRINIDAD AND TOBAGO, 1971*
• — Lise Winer, *Dictionary of the English/Creole of Trinidad & Tobago*, 2003
3 a first year college student *US*
• — Pamela Munro, *U.C.L.A. Slang*, p. 74, 1989
4 a substitute player on a sports team *US, 1892*
• [H]e had benched his regulars and sent in his scrubs, and as a result, the Rockets had been creamed the next three times in a row. — Max Shulman, *Rally Round the Flag, Boys!*, p. 224, 1957
• — Connie Eble (Editor), *UNC-CH Campus Slang*, p. 7, Spring 1990
5 in hip-hop culture, a performer of little or no talent *US*
• I rock ya like Chubb and burn scrubs like a dum-dum[.] — Redman *Headbanger*, 1992

scrub *verb*
to cancel something; to forget something; to reject something *UK, 1943*
A figurative application of the conventional sense 'to erase'; originally recorded in 1828, current use dates from military use in World War 2.
• The team's original objective-the capture of a Covenant ship-had been scrubbed in the face of a new enemy offensive. — Eric Nyland, *First Strike*, p. 2, 2003

▸ **scrub round**
to cancel something; to forget something, especially by agreement *UK, 1943*
• Scrub round it, will you? — Harold Pinter, *The Dumb Waiter*, 1960

scrub-bash *noun*
a journey through thick bushland *AUSTRALIA*
• From the plains the peak is a more formidable proposition, involving a fairly direct scrub-bash and the frontal assault of a few minor cliff faces. — *Tasmanian Tramp*, p. 76, January 1972

scrub bash *verb*
to make a path through thick bushland; to drive a vehicle through bushland *AUSTRALIA, 1964*
• It soon became a mission impossible as Ferrets cannot scrub bash off the roads as fast as vehicles running on the roads. — *Ich Dien*, p. 21, #11 1983

scrub-bashing *noun*
the clearing of bushland *AUSTRALIA*
• 'The old man will get nowhere with his scrub-bashing,' they declared. — Mary Durack, *Kings in Grass Castles*, p. 99, 1959

scrubber *noun*
1 a sexually promiscuous woman *UK, 1959*
• [T]his aged scrubber, Mrs Marengo[.] — Derek Raymond (Robin Cook), *The Crust on its Uppers*, p. 28, 1962
• — Louis S. Leland, *A Personal Kiwi-Yankee Dictionary*, p. 89, 1984
• "Dear oh dear – not the singing scrubber?" "What d'you call her? [...] That is a very special young lady, Terence." — Anthony Masters, *Minder*, p. 67, 1984
• TANYA: Can you believe that guy? He called my mum a scrubber. [SHE PULLS UP HER KNICKERS.] — Bernard Demsey and Kevin McNally, *Lock, Stock... & Two Sips*, p. 289, 2000
2 an unattractive woman *AUSTRALIA, 1977*
• — Jim Ramsay, *Cop It Sweet!*, p. 79, 1977
• I don't like them talking too much, like the last scrubber I had. — Sandra Jobson, *Blokes*, p. 105, 1984
• — Robert G. Barrett, *Davo's Little Something*, p. 45, 1992
3 an inferior horse bred in the country *AUSTRALIA, 1874*
• Mooti was no scrubber either. — Joe Andersen, *Winners Can Laugh*, p. 81, 1982
• This was no scrubber from the bush. — Joe Andersen, *Winners Can Laugh*, p. 176, 1982

scrubout *noun*
a weekly mass cleaning *ANTARCTICA*
• — *Cool Antarctica*, 2003: 'Antarctic slang'

scrubs *noun*
loose-fitting, sterilised clothing worn in hospital operating rooms *US*
• In a holding cell crowded with offenders wearing state-blue uniforms that were like hospital scrubs. — Elmore Leonard, *Maximum Bob*, p. 2, 1991

Scrubs *noun*
▸ **the Scrubs**
Her Majesty's Prison Wormwood Scrubs in west London *UK*
• The Scrubs is what they call an "allocation" prison, one where you go temporarily[.] — Dave Courtney, *Stop the Ride I Want to Get Off*, p. 71, 1999
• This went off in the Scrubs, D-wing[.] — J.J. Connolly, *Layer Cake*, p. 168, 2000

scrub up *verb*
to appear after grooming *AUSTRALIA*
Always followed by a positive adjective or adverb.
• I scrub up good, but basically I look bad. — Barry Dickins, *What the Dickins*, p. 17, 1985

scruffbag *noun*
a scruffy person *UK, 1973*
Originally, 'a down-and-out'.
• [The Beatles] were real scruffbags onstage. — *Uncut*, p. 47, July 2001

scruff puppy *noun*
a girl as the object of social and sexual desire *US*
• — Michael V. Anderson, *The Bad, Rad, Not to Forget Way Cool Beach and Surf Discriptionary*, p. 18, 1988

scruffy and dirty *noun*
in betting, odds of 100–30 *UK*
Rhyming slang.
• — John McCririck, *John McCririck's World of Betting*, p. 59, 1991

scrum *noun*
something of little or no value *AUSTRALIA*
Obsolete rhyming slang for a 'threepenny bit', rhymes on synonymous 'thrums'; back in circulation as the perceived worth of the old coin.
• [N]ow I wouldn't give a scrum, it wouldn't bother me in the slightest[.] — Luke Desforges, *Cool Places*, p. 190, 1998

scrumdiddliumptious *adjective*
extremely delicious or delightful *UK*
An elaboration of **SCRUMPTIOUS**.
- The boy has just got his brand new scrumdiddliumptious candy bar[.] — Craig David, 6th December 2000
- — Chris Lewis, *The Dictionary of Playground Slang*, p. 196, 2003

scrummy; scrummie *adjective*
excellent; delicious *UK, 1915*
An abbreviation of **SCRUMPTIOUS**; often used as an exclamation of delight.
- Well, something smells scrummie. What time were you aiming for eating. — Jennifer Saunders, *Absolutely Fabulous*, p. 120, 1992
- The waiter arrived now with my and Sheba's soup. "How scrummy!" Sheba exclaimed, tasting hers. — Zoe Heller, *What Was She Thinking?*, p. 69, 2003

scrump *verb*
to steal apples from orchards *UK, 1866*
From an old dialect word for a 'withered apple'.
- Maybe it has something to do with those apples we scrumped from the orchard last night[.] — Nick Jones, *The Rough Guide to Travel Health*, p. 244, 2001
- [S]pewing brackish water and half-digested chunks of apple scrumped some hours earlier[.] — Niall Griffiths, *Sheepshagger*, p. 235, 2001

scrumper *noun*
a stealer of apples from orchards *UK, 1946*
- [H]e insisted on wriggling about like a captured scrumper. — Danny King, *The Bank Robber Diaries*, p. 164, 2002

scrumping *noun*
an act of stealing apples from a orchard *UK*
From the verb **SCRUMP**.
- [N]o reason to be helping anyone go scrumping round the Nortrust orchard[.] — Reginald Hill, *Arms and the Women*, p. 298, 1999

scrumptious *adjective*
delicious *UK, 1881*
Often used as an exclamation of delight.
- — *X-Ray*, p. 32, August 2003: 'Truly Scrumptious (headline to an article about singer Holly Golightly)'

scrumpy *noun*
an alcoholic drink of fermented apples; an (often illicitly made or homemade) rough cider *UK, 1904*
West-country dialect, now widely known.
- I learned that most simple of Glastonbury lessons: stay off the scrumpy. — *The Guardian*, 26th May 2003

scruncheons *noun*
in Newfoundland, cut-up pork fat, fried and used to garnish fish and brewis *CANADA*
- "Fish and brewis?" Uncle Jasper's tone was reverent. "And scruncheons?" "And scruncheons. Mary needn't know. And if she does, what odds?" — A. R. Scammell, *My Newfoundland*, p. 23, 1966

scrunch up *verb*
to squeeze in; to huddle *US, 1902*
- You sit scrunched up, bent-backed, and stoop-shouldered on a plain pine plank, staring through a gun slit the size of a mail slot. — Larry Heinemann, *Paco's Story*, p. 10, 1986
- Nadeau was in the corner with Sam's Man, scrunched over into the corner, a Styrofoam cooler full of ice and canned beer on the seat between them... — Robert Campbell, *Juice*, p. 86, 1988

scrungies *noun*
swimming trunks worn for surfing *AUSTRALIA*
- — Trevor Cralle, *The Surfin'ary*, p. 106, 1991

scrunt *verb*
to live at an absolute minimum standard of living *TRINIDAD AND TOBAGO, 1976*
- — Lise Winer, *Dictionary of the English/Creole of Trinidad & Tobago*, 2003

scruples *noun*
crack cocaine *US*
- — US Department of Justice, *Street Terms*, October 1994

scuba diver; scuba *noun*
a five-pound note *UK*
Rhyming slang for **FIVER**.
- — Ray Puxley, *Fresh Rabbit*, 1998

scud *noun*
1 wine *UK: SCOTLAND*
- See's a bottle a Beck's an a glass a red scud. — Michael Munro, *The Complete Patter*, p. 136, 1996

2 crack cocaine *UK*
- Crack is also known as PEBBLES, SCUD, WASH, STONE and ROCK[.] — Macfarlane, Macfarlane and Robson, *The User*, p. 112, 1996

3 a state of nudity *UK: SCOTLAND, 1911*
Variant elaborations include 'scuddy' and 'scuderoony'.
- I've toiled in the scuderoony under my boiler suit at the Parkhead Forge! — Ian Pattison, *Rab C. Nesbitt*, 1988

scud *verb*
to slap someone or deliver someone a glancing blow *UK: SCOTLAND*
- Ah'll scud your lug in a minute. — Michael Munro, *The Original Patter*, p. 61, 1985

scudded *adjective*
drunk *US*
Used by US troops during the 1991 war against Iraq, playing on the missile.
- — *Army*, p. 48, November 1991
- — John Algeo and Adele Algeo, *American Speech*, p. 400, Winter 1991: 'Among the new words'

scudder *noun*
a disagreeable, unlikeable person *US*
- That is, until some feisty scudder comes along begging for trouble and gets my gorge up. — Guy Owen, *The Flim-Flam Man and the Apprentice Grifter*, p. 48, 1972
- A fella did that in a movie where these six scudders wearing black suits go and rob a jewelry store and they all get killed. — Elmore Leonard, *Riding the Rap*, p. 8–9, 1995

scuddy *adjective*
naked *UK: SCOTLAND*
- Went tae this beach an there was aw these scuddy punters[.] — Michael Munro, *The Complete Patter*, p. 136, 1996

scuddy-book *noun*
a pornographic magazine *UK: SCOTLAND*
- Ah was cleanin under his bed an fun [found] a pile a scuddy books, the durty wee devil! — Michael Munro, *The Complete Patter*, p. 136, 1996

scuds *noun*
the female breasts *US*
A comparison with Scud missiles.
- — Don R. McCreary (Editor), *Dawg Speak*, 2001

scuff *noun*
in motor racing, a new racing tyre that has not been broken in *US*
- — John Edwards, *Auto Dictionary*, p. 146, 1993

scuff *verb*
1 in circus and carnival usage, to barely make a living *US*
- — Joe McKennon, *Circus Lingo*, p. 1980, 1981

2 to prepare new racing tyres for a race *US*
- — John Edwards, *Auto Dictionary*, p. 146, 1993

scuffer *noun*
1 a police officer *UK, 1860*
- ten burly scuffers storming into a respectable Bloomsbury bookstore — Mick Farren, *Give the Anarchist a Cigarette*, p. 107, 2001

2 a prostitute *US*
- — Eugene Landy, *The Underground Dictionary*, p. 166, 1971

scuffle *noun*
life, perceived as a struggle *US*
- [N]o matter how tough the scuffle is, it's great to be alive, brother! — Mezz Mezzrow, *Really the Blues*, p. 324, 1946

scuffle *verb*
1 to survive by your ingenuity, not by working *US*
- — Francis J. Rigney and L. Douglas Smith, *The Real Bohemia*, p. xvi, 1961

2 to weed a patch of potatoes without disturbing the plants *CANADA, 1990*
- In a standard dictionary, one definition of that word is "a glancing touch or blow." But when [Prince Edward] Islanders scuffle potatoes, the ground in which they are planted is lightly grazed to remove the weeds without disturbing the seed or plant. — *New Maritimes*, p. 29, March-April 1990

scuffler *noun*

a person who scrounges to earn a living on the fringes of legality *US*

- He said he was a hustler, but he really wasn't nothin' but a goddamn scuffler. —Henry Williamson, *Hustler!*, p. 137, 1965

scuffs *noun*

1 bedroom slippers *US*

So named because of the scuffing sound they make when you walk.

- —Connie Eble (Editor), *UNC-CH Campus Slang*, p. 9, Fall 1985

2 shoes *US*

- —Connie Eble (Editor), *UNC-CH Campus Slang*, p. 7, Fall 1987

scuff up *verb*

to engage in a fist fight *US*

- —William K. Bentley and James M. Corbett, *Prison Slang*, p. 91, 1992

scugly *adjective*

very ugly *US*

- —Carl J. Banks Jr, *Banks Dictionary of the Black Ghetto Language*, 1975

scull *verb*

to quaff or down a drink in one draught *AUSTRALIA, 1984*

Variant spelling of **SKOAL; SKOL**.

- He sculled the rest of the drink and walked out to his ute. —Harrison Biscuit, *The Search for Savage Henry*, p. 64, 1995
- Maybe that time I sculled the two litres of Coke down by the sewage treatment plant something mutated in my brain cells. —Glyn Parry, *Mosh*, p. 53, 1996
- If either of your stubbies is knocked over, you have to scull from your full stubby. —*Australian Ultimate*, p. 8, 2003

scum *noun*

1 a despicable, unlikeable person *US*

- "We'll see about this!" my attorney shouted as we drove away. "You paranoid scum!" —Hunter S. Thompson, *Fear and Loathing in Las Vegas*, p. 45, 1971
- You are scum. I'll be there. —*Sex, Lies and Videotape*, 1989
- Only come lunch some ten ton scum called Blower used to grab the bagels off of him. —Nick Barlay, *Curvy Lovebox*, p. 43, 1997

2 in prison, a sex offender; a convicted paedophile *UK*

- —Angela Devlin, *Prison Patter*, p. 23, 1996

3 semen *US*

- Horse, who was always talking about facts, said, "Man, that can't be scum, 'cause scum is white." Knowing that scum was white, most of the guys said that Horse was right and that it was just dog water." —Claude Brown, *Manchild in the Promised Land*, p. 80–81, 1965
- [A]ll the other girls are having all the fun while she has to scrub the pots, and the floors, and an occasional honied dick, or scum-smeared pussy. —*Adult Video*, p. 73, August/September 1986
- I had to make sure my mother found no stiffened, wrinkled traces of ecstasy's scum. —Larry Rivers, *What Did I Do?*, p. 51, 1992

scumbag *noun*

1 a low, despicable person *US*

The highest profile use of the term in recent years was in late April 1998, when US Congressman Dan Burton publicly called then-President Clinton 'a scumbag'. This was shortly before the revelation that Burton was the father of a child born out of wedlock, a revelation that silenced his public judgments on President Clinton's morality. In May 2004, the word got another 15 minutes of fame when it was used in the family-friendly *Blondie* comic strip, provoking serious outrage among some readers.

- The rotten scumbag. —Hubert Selby Jr, *Last Exit to Brooklyn*, p. 123, 1957
- Ya scum bag, ya didn't have to fight the spic dirty[.] —Piri Thomas, *Down These Mean Streets*, p. 31–32, 1967
- —*Current Slang*, p. 5, Spring 1967
- They call us "scum-bags" and "fairies" and "Jew-bastards" and "commies" and one says, "You pull dese guys' pants off and they ain't got no pecker, just a little piece of flesh." —Abbie Hoffman, *Revolution for the Hell of It*, p. 49, 1968
- Let's get the fuck out of this town. Those scumbags were trying to kill us. —Hunter S. Thompson, *Fear and Loathing in Las Vegas*, p. 34, 1971
- When he flashed on that, on the downright outrageousness of that pack of scumbags paying somebody to snuff him, of even insinuating they'd do such a thing, Emmett began to shake with rage. —Emmett Grogan, *Ringolevio*, p. 349, 1972
- Stick your finger up your ass, you fuckin' scumbag[.] —Edwin Torres, *Q & A*, p. 45, 1977
- Hey! You asswipes, scumbags! —*Saturday Night Fever*, 1977
- And this guy, this scumbag thinks he's Jesus Christ, has got us out in the rain playing nursemaid for the fucking Federals. —John Sayles, *Union Dues*, p. 111, 1977
- They ain't scumbags. They car thieves just like us. —*Repo Man*, 1984
- Hey, don't look at me like I'm some sort of scumbag or something. —Bret Easton Ellis, *Less Than Zero*, p. 189, 1985
- I felt it strange to find a virgin willing to go directly from a public bus to a private scumbag hotel. —Odie Hawkins, *Scars and Memories*, p. 65, 1987
- You don't never learn, do you scumbag? —*Airheads*, 1994
- I'm wearing one of these [a cricket box], you dirty little scumbag. —Paul Fraser and Shane Meadows, *TwentyFourSeven*, p. 45, 1997
- He had so many petty thieves, crack-heads and scumbags on his books, changing plastic into paper was a doddle for him. —Danny King, *The Bank Robber Diaries*, p. 53, 2002

2 a condom *US*

Combines **SCUM** (semen) with a conventional container, however it is not until the 1960s that 'scum' stands apart from this usage.

- According to him and the rest of the boys, the name of the thing was "scum bag." —Phyllis and Eberhard Kronhausen, *Sex Histories of American College Men*, p. 56, 1960
- For men it's the "scum bag" or "rubber" of infamy. —Angelo d'Arcangelo, *The Homosexual Handbook*, p. 219, 1968
- Scumbags Revisited (Headline) —*Screw*, p. 21, 22nd March 1970
- "Do you really use scumbags?" "Yes. I use rubber Trojans every time I fuck." —*Screw*, p. 9, 12th April 1971

3 a prostitute *US*

- —Ruth Todasco et al., *The Intelligent Woman's Guide to Dirty Words*, p. 7, 1973

scumball *noun*

a despicable person *US*

- And I thought we were scumballs. —Carl Hiaasen, *Native Tongue*, p. 353, 1991

scumbucket *noun*

a despised person *US*

- —Connie Eble (Editor), *UNC-CH Campus Slang*, p. 4, November 1983
- The deceased was a well-known scumbucket and they don't usually have the decency to kill themselves. —Carl Hiaasen, *Native Tongue*, p. 222, 1991

scumff *verb*

to massage the genitals through clothing *UK*

Etymology uncertain.

- He's just scumffing her with his four fingers, just fucking rubbing her and grabbing her. —Kevin Sampson, *Outlaws*, p. 134, 2001

scumhead *noun*

a contemptible person *US*

- I know you've been listening to some scumhead[.] —Howard Stern, *Miss America*, p. 276, 1995

scummer *noun*

a despicable lowlife whose services are for hire *US*

Perhaps from the C14 sense of the word as 'a pirate'.

- A family deal, it was best to get outside help, scummers with no personal interest, muscle you hired by the pound. —Elmore Leonard, *Glitz*, p. 238, 1985

scummy *adjective*

unpleasant; despicable *US, 1932*

Figurative use of the conventional sense (polluted).

- The old houses was empty and the outside looked real scummy and unkempt[.] —Bret Easton Ellis, *Less Than Zero*, 1985
- I don't like to have to do this for a living but some cunt's got to do the scummy jobs. —Kevin Sampson, *Outlaws*, p. 57, 2001
- Everyone thought the group was just too scummy or something. —Tony Wilson, *24 Hour Party People*, p. 196, 2002
- YOU FUCKING SCUMMY FUCKED-UP TOERAG BITCH! —Ben Elton, *High Society*, p. 259, 2002

scum of the earth *noun*

an extremely unappealing, unattractive or despicable person *US*

- —Connie Eble (Editor), *UNC-CH Campus Slang*, p. 5, October 1986

scum out *verb*

to live in filth *US*

- —Kenn "Naz" Young, *Naz's Dictionary of Teen Slang*, p. 103, 1993

scumpig *noun*

a low, despicable person *UK*

- La'er scumpig. Don't forget behind your ears. —Nick Barlay, *Curvy Lovebox*, p. 86, 1997

scumpteen *noun*

a vague, large number *US*

- One night Jack "Legs" Diamond fell into the joint with scumpteen of his henchmen and ordered the doors closed, and Jim, it was on. —Mezz Mezzrow, *Really the Blues*, p. 178, 1946

scum-scrubber *noun*
an employee of a pornography arcade whose job is to clean up the semen left by customers *US*
- The adjacent booth is being mopped by professional scum-scrubbers; mop-and-pail Leroys, urban descendants of dung-shoveling stable jockeys. —Josh Alan Friedman, *Tales of Times Square*, p. 64, 1986

scumsucker *noun*
a low, despicable person *US*
- What's going on in this country when a scumsucker like that can get away with sandbagging a doctor of journalism? —Hunter S. Thompson, *Fear and Loathing in Las Vegas*, p. 19, 1971
- Radio talk shows blistered lawmakers for holding secret budget meetings and for the income tax proposal, calling them "scumsuckeers," and other derisive terms. — *The Commercial Appeal (Memphis, Tennessee)*, p. A1, 14th June 2000

scum-sucking *adjective*
despicable *US*
- Dornan vehemently denied his amendment was intended to promote discrimination, characterizing anyone who would attempt to teach racial discrimination to children as a "scum-sucking pig." — *United Press International*, 30th November 1982
- But how many times have you seen an interview of a policeman that tried to save the life of a scum-suckin piece of slime like Earl Rimms? —Joseph Wambaugh, *The Delta Star*, p. 132, 1983
- You put yourself on the line, and you get treated like a scum-sucking pig. — *Pittsburgh Post-Gazette*, p. A8, 17th October 1993
- Conservatives must be willing to accept the fact that the English language does not require the word "liberal" to be preceded by "scum-sucking," "wooly headed" or "pathetic." — *Chattanooga Times Free Press*, p. F2, 16th November 2003

scunds *noun*
a second helping *US*
- —John D. Bell et al., *Loosely Speaking*, p. 16, 1966

scunge *noun*
1 filth *AUSTRALIA, 1966*
- —David McGill, *David McGill's Complete Kiwi Slang Dictionary*, p. 97, 1998

2 a stingy person; a miser *AUSTRALIA*
- They are such scunges, my grandparents. All they give you is flat lemonade and stale biscuits wif worms in them. —Kylie Mole (Maryanne Fahey), *My Diary*, p. 15, 1988

3 a habitual cadger *AUSTRALIA*
- Gloria is a real scunge, she's always borrowing my lipstick. — *www.abc.net.au/wordmap*, 2003

scunge *verb*
to cadge something *NEW ZEALAND*
- To borrow (bot) something with no mention of repaying the favour is to scunge. 'This derro just scunged a fag off me!' —John Blackman, *Best of Aussie Slang*, 1995
- —David McGill, *David McGill's Complete Kiwi Slang Dictionary*, p. 111, 1998

scungeel *noun*
a low-life, a disreputable person *US*
From the Italian *scungili* (squid).
- That's not the only funny fish that comes up in the net. You got two scungeel in there, too. —Edwin Torres, *Q & A*, p. 20, 1977

scungies *noun*
a pair of men's close-fitting and revealing nylon swimming trunks *AUSTRALIA*
- I don't have my togs so I better just wear my scungies. — *www.abc.net.au/wordmap*, 2003

scungy *adjective*
sordid; dirty *AUSTRALIA*
- —Tom Hibbert, *Rockspeak!*, p. 138, 1983
- —David McGill, *David McGill's Complete Kiwi Slang Dictionary*, p. 97, 1998

scunner *noun*
a nuisance *UK: SCOTLAND*
First recorded of persons in 1796, and of things in 1865.
- Look at this. Right scunner in't it, eh? —Ian Pattison, *Rab C. Nesbitt*, 1988

scup *verb*
to swing *US*
Rarely heard.
- No, I don't want no more of them Acme bushings. The shims bust off as soon as you scup 'em… —Max Shulman, *The Many Loves of Dobie Gillis*, p. 183, 1951

scupper *noun*
a promiscuous woman *UK, 1970*
From an earlier sense as 'a prostitute', in turn deriving from 'a hole in a ship's side'.

scupper *verb*
to put an end to something; to thwart someone; to destroy something *UK, 1918*
- Dad lived for our fighting careers and wouldn't want anything to scupper them[.] —Jimmy Stockin, *On The Cobbles*, p. 98, 2000

scurb *noun*
a suburban skateboarder who confines his skateboarding to streets and sidewalks *US*
- — *San Francisco Sunday Examiner & Chronicle*, p. 20, 2nd September 1984: 'Say it right'

scurve *noun*
a graceless person; someone who is disliked *US*
- In Detroit, someone who once would be called a drip or a square is now, regrettably, a nerd, or in a less severe case, a scurve. — *Newsweek*, p. 28, 8th October 1951
- [S]ome jealous scurve (drip, again) is bound to come up with "Well, Jazz-a-boo for you." — *Herald Press (St. Joseph, Missouri)*, p. 14, 23rd June 1952

scurvy *adjective*
1 unkempt; sloppy; ugly *US*
- —Miss Cone, *The Slang Dictionary (Hawthorne High School)*, 1965

2 very thin *US*
- —Don R. McCreary (Editor), *Dawg Speak*, 2001

scuse; 'scuse *verb*
to excuse someone; especially in, or as an abbreviation of, the phrases: excuse me, please excuse me *UK*
In conventional use from C15, and considered a colloquial slovening since the C19.
- Purple Haze was in my brain, / lately things don't seem the same, / actin' funny but I don't know why / 'scuse me while I kiss the sky. —Jimi Hendrix, *Purple Haze*, 1967
- I know just how much I've missed London. "'Scuse." A young woman pushes past me and rushes up to her waiting friends[.] —Jane Green, *Jemima J*, p. 369, 2001

'scuse me *noun*
▷ see: EXCUSE-ME

scut *noun*
1 the end of a cigarette *IRELAND*
- Crunch sucked the last drag from the scut, spat out the loose tobacco that had gathered around his lips and tossed the fag-end away. —Billy Roche, *Tumbling Down*, p. 27, 1984

2 a contemptible person; someone of bad character *IRELAND*
- 'Go lang, ye scut, ye,' said the mother —Patrick Kavanagh, *Tarry Flynn*, p. 34, 1975
- He sorry-for-your-troubled me quickly before dealing with the two scuts who'd blodged the quid. —Eamonn Sweeney, *Waiting for the Healer*, p. 66, 1997

3 any menial medical procedure *US*
- — *Maledicta*, p. 69, Summer/Winter 1978: 'Common patient-directed pejoratives used by medical personnel'

scut *verb*
to ride on the back of a truck or van *IRELAND*
- A couple of kids ran beside him, and one of them kicked the van. They disappeared; Jimmy Sr. knew they were scutting on the back, the fuckers. —Roddy Doyle, *The Van*, p. 150, 1991

scut duty; scut work *noun*
tedious, menial work *US, 1960*
- Scut jobs were the dirty, sometimes degrading, jobs that no one wanted, so they fell to the low men on the "totem pole" or were used as disciplinary assignments. —Gregory Clark, *Words of the Vietnam War*, p. 455, 1990

scuttered *adjective*
drunk *IRELAND*
- — *e-cyclopaedia*, 20th March 2002

scuttlebutt *noun*
gossip, rumours *US, 1901*
From the name of the drinking-water cask found on board a ship, around which sailors gathered to gossip.
- Scuttlebutt down in the catacombs is that a lot of powerful Catholics, including those responsible for the Society of the Felicitator, are unhappy about those reforms. —Tom Robbins, *Another Roadside Attraction*, p. 180, 1971

scutty *adjective*
filthy; decrepit *IRELAND*
- Little scutty houses with whitewashed walls – all flakey...and an outside lav. — Billy Roche, *The Wexford Trilogy (A Handful of Stars)*, p. 11, 1992

scuz *noun*
a dirty, disreputable person *US*
- These guys, at least a few of them, two black guys, and one white, bearded scuz in a dirty buckskin vest and yellow headband, looked radical enough to get violent with an overweight middle-aged copy like myself[.] — Joseph Wambaugh, *The Blue Knight*, p. 64, 1973
- "This state law says to the drug dealers ... the scuz of theh world, the free ride is over," D'Amato said. — *Post Standard (Syracuse, New York)*, p. B3, 9th August 1989
- Indeed, he tries to lean on her as he did on his wife, meanwhile clumsily trying to dissuade her from tying the knot with her scuz of a boyfriend. — *Post and Courier (Charleston, South Carolina)*, p. 9E, 5th January 2003

scuzbag; scuzzbag *noun*
a despicable, undesirable person *US*
A varation of **SCUMBAG**.
- Hit the streets, scuz bag! — John Waters, *Desperate Living*, p. 167, 1099
- — Connie Eble (Editor), *UNC-CH Campus Slang*, p. 6, Fall 1980
- "I'm your partner, scuzzbag!" Dolly yelled at Dilford. — Joseph Wambaugh, *The Delta Star*, p. 169, 1983
- Brad Rowe, playing a conservative scuzzbag in the Nixon White House, gets a phone call. — *Washington Post*, p. C7, 29th April 2000

scuz rag *noun*
during the Vietnam war, a rag used to wipe floors *US*
- — Linda Reinberg, *In the Field*, p. 193, 1991

scuzz *verb*
to be involved in sleazy activities; to keep unpleasant company; to move in low circles *UK*
- Like wha' you been doin' 'part from scuzzin' round town with Nood? – Oh I dunno. Scuzzin' round town with Nood far's I can remember. — Nick Barlay, *Curvy Lovebox*, p. 108, 1997

scuzzball *noun*
a despicable person *US*
- "He wrote about this case," Garcia went on. "About that little scuzzball we arrested." — Carl Hiaasen, *Tourist Season*, p. 19, 1986

scuzzhead *noun*
a despicable person *UK*
- Baba prods me with his foot. -Oi. Scuzzhead. You listenin'? — Nick Barlay, *Curvy Lovebox*, p. 151, 1997

scuzzy *adjective*
disgusting *US, 1968*
- It's a real scuzzy joint. A beer joint that serves food. A real ptomaine tavern. — Joseph Wambaugh, *The New Centurions*, p. 46, 1970
- Anyway, The Toilet is just plain flat-out scuzzy. I totaled a perfectly good pair of Bergdorf Goodman shoes[.] — Armistead Maupin, *Tales of the City*, p. 296, 1978
- — Connie Eble (Editor), *UNC-CH Campus Slang*, p. 7, Spring 1982
- These days Keyes ate alone, or with clients so scuzzy he wanted to gag on the corned beef and rye. — Carl Hiaasen, *Tourist Season*, p. 219, 1986
- [T]here is "nothing worthwhile in St. Louis proper, unless you want to play STD (sexually transmitted disease) roulette with a scuzzy-looking streetwalker[.]" — Nancy Tamosaitis, *net.sex*, p. 81, 1995
- [W]e [black people] clearly all looked the same to his scuzzy ass. — Diran Abedayo, *My Once Upon A Time*, p. 246, 2000
- I've watched nineteen-year-old kids from scuzzy council estates tell pop stars and other household names to fuckin get in line[.] — J.J. Connolly, *Layer Cake*, p. 11, 2000

scwhag *adjective*
inferior; shoddy *US*
- — Connie Eble (Editor), *UNC-CH Campus Slang*, p. 5, Fall 1998

seaboard *adjective*
used of an order for take-away food at a restaurant *US*
- — *American Speech*, p. 232, October 1952: 'The argot of soda jerks'

sea daddy *noun*
in the US Navy, a mentor *US*
- If ever I had a sea daddy, it was Ev Barrett. — Richard Marcinko and John Weisman, *Rogue Warrior*, p. 51, 1992

seafood *noun*
a sailor as an object of homosexual desire *US*
- — Donald Webster Cory and John P. LeRoy, *The Homosexual and His Society*, p. 266, 1963: 'A lexicon of homosexual slang'
- — Florida Legislative Investigation Committee (Johns Committee), *Homosexuality and Citizenship in Florida*, 1964: 'Glossary of homosexual terms and deviate acts'
- You have plenty of clients because of the great number of military men, especially the sailors, which we commonly call "seafood." — *"The Market Street Proposition" (KFRC radio, San Francisco)*, 8th November 1965
- Any kind of seafood will do[.] — Kenneth Marlowe, *The Gay World of Kenneth Marlowe*, p. 31, 1966
- — Robert A. Wilson, *Playboy's Book of Forbidden Words*, p. 219, 1972
- — *Maledicta*, p. 19, 1983: 'Ritual and personal insults in stigmatized subcultures'
- — Paul Baker, *Polari*, p. 189, 2002
- — *Attitude*, p. 60, July 2003: 'Old palare lexicon'

seafood breakfast *noun*
oral sex performed on a woman in the morning *AUSTRALIA*
- — Thommo, *The Dictionary of Australian Swearing and Sex Sayings*, p. 112, 1985

seafood plate
please *US*
An intentionally butchered French *s'il vous plaît*.
- — Connie Eble (Editor), *UNC-CH Campus Slang*, p. 6, Spring 1984

sea-going bellhop *noun*
a member of the US Marine Corps *US, 1960*
Derisive, used by other branches of the armed services to mock the USMC dress uniform.
- I hadn't even finished my second bottle of beer when I began to hear progressively louder comments about 'goddamned dumb jarheads' and 'sea-going bellhops'. — Bruce H. Norton, *Sergeant Major, U.S. Marines*, 1995

seagull *noun*
1 a person who constantly complains *US*
- — Lyle K. Engel, *The Complete Book of Fuel and Gas Dragsters*, p. 153, 1968

2 a casual wharfside worker *AUSTRALIA*
- [H]e was a casual wharfie at the time I'm telling you about, during the Second World War it was, and they call casuals 'seagulls'. — Frank Hardy, *The Yarns of Billy Borker*, p. 115, 1965

3 a person who watches what bets are being made by big spenders and then makes a small bet on the horses favoured by the big spenders *US*
- — *San Francisco Examiner*, p. 52, 13th September 1966

4 a combat pilot who has become reluctant to fly *US*
- The others called them "seagulls" – you have to throw a rock to get them to fly – and "sickbay flight." The Navy let them turn in their wings, or would take them. — Robert K. Wilcox, *Scream of Eagles*, p. 39, 1990

5 a rugby union player who remains outside tight play in the chance that the ball will break loose *NEW ZEALAND, 1975*
- — Harry Orsman, *A Dictionary of Modern New Zealand Slang*, p. 116, 1999

6 chicken *US*
- — Lou Shelly, *Hepcats Jive Talk Dictionary*, p. 48, 1945

seam shooter *noun*
a criminal who specialises in blowing up safes by placing small amounts of explosives in the safe's seams *US*
- — Vincent J. Monteleone, *Criminal Slang*, p. 202, 1949

seam squirrels *noun*
in circus and carnival usage, body lice *US*
- — Don Wilmeth, *The Language of American Popular Entertainment*, p. 217, 1981

Seamus Heaney *noun*
a bikini *UK*
Rhyming slang, formed from the name of the Irish poet (b.1939).
- — Susie Dent, *The Language Report*, p. 98, 2003

Sea of Green *noun*
a marijuana growing technique from British Columbia *CANADA*
- Sea of Green is a growing technique in which a mother plant is selected to supply clones. — Brian Preston, *Pot Planet*, p. 231, 2002

sea pie *noun*
in the Ottawa valley, a Sunday meat dish *CANADA*
- Sea pie is a lumbermen's layered specialty, served with molasses and buns. — Bill Casselman, *Canadian Food Words*, p. 189, 1998

sea pig *noun*
a fat surfer *US*
- — Surf Punks, *Oh No! Not Them Again! (liner notes)*, 1988

sea pussy *noun*
the sea anemone *BAHAMAS*
Based on a visual comparison with the vagina.
- — John A. Holm, *Dictionary of Bahamian English*, p. 178, 1982

sea queen *noun*
a homosexual sailor or ship's steward; a homosexual man with a taste for seamen *UK*
• —Paul Baker, *Polari*, p. 189, 2002

sea rat *noun*
a seagull *US*
• —Trevor Cralle, *The Surfin'ary*, p. 107, 1991

search *verb*
to try to buy illegal drugs *US*
• Spears said he often can't get out of his car without being approached by young men asking "Are you searching?" – street slang for buying drugs. —*Milwaukee Journal Sentinel*, p. 4, 8th January 1997

search and avoid; search and evade *verb*
used by US forces to describe the activities of the South Vietnamese Army *US*
Not praise.
• —Linda Reinberg, *In the Field*, p. 194, 1991

searcher *noun*
a prisoner who intimidates other prison inmates who are suspected of carrying drugs *UK*
• —Angela Devlin, *Prison Patter*, p. 102, 1996

search me
I don't know *US*
• —Marcus Hanna Boulware, *Jive and Slang of Students in Negro Colleges*, 1947

sea stack *noun*
a tall column of granite, created by erosion, just off the shore in the ocean near Newfoundland *CANADA*
• We'd run into Peter the day before, wanting to know the whereabouts of the "sea stack" we'd seen in a photo, a narrow, spectacular column of rock sitting just off the shore. —*Montreal Gazette*, p. H1, 11th May 2002

sea story *noun*
a tale about the teller's exploits, real and imagined *US*
• In the Pacific, telling "sea stories" helped to pass the time and relieve old pressures. I listened to thousands of them. I told them. —Russell Davis, *Marine at War*, p. 165, 1961

seat *noun*
a police officer assigned to ride as a passenger with another officer *US*
• —*New York Times*, 15th February 1970

seat *verb*
to perform anal sex on someone *AUSTRALIA, 1950*
• Hey Horrible Horace have you ever been seated? —Kevin Mackey, *The Cure*, p. 50, 1970

seat back!
used to reserve your seat as you briefly leave the room *US*
• —Connie Eble (Editor), *UNC-CH Campus Slang*, p. 3, Fall 1996

seat cover *noun*
an attractive woman *US*
Citizens' band radio slang.
• —*Official CB Dictionary*, p. 48, 1976
• Check the seat covers[.] —Peter Chippindale, *The British CB Book*, p. 153, 1981

Sea Thing *noun*
the Sea King helicopter, acquired for the Canadian Navy from Sikorsky in 1963 *CANADA*
• The "Sea Thing" or Sea King, is the large antisubmarine helicopter flown from Canadian warships since 1963. The nickname was coined by Tracker pilots of 880 Squadron on carrier HMCS Bonaventure. —Tom Langeste, *Words on the Wing*, p. 243–244, 1995

seatman *noun*
1 in prison, a male homosexual who takes the active role in anal sex *AUSTRALIA*
• —Ryan Aven-Bray, *Ridgey Didge Oz Jack Lang*, p. 45, 1983

2 in circus and carnival usage, a paid customer, employed to show enthusiasm *US*
• —Don Wilmeth, *The Language of American Popular Entertainment*, p. 234, 1981

seat-surf *verb*
to move from empty seat to empty seat in a stadium or auditorium, gradually improving your position *US*
• —David Shenk and Steve Silberman, *Skeleton Key*, p. 255, 1994

Seattle tuxedo *noun*
a clean flannel shirt *US*
• —Jim Crotty, *How to Talk American*, p. 315, 1997

seaweed muncher *noun*
a surfer *AUSTRALIA*
• —Kathy Lette, *Girls' Night Out*, p. 190, 1987
• First off, there are the 'Waxheads'. This is a fierce, amphibious breed – commonly known as 'Seeweed munchers', 'Shark-suckers' or plain old 'Surfies'. —*Sydney Morning Herald*, p. 7, 3rd January 1987

Sebastian Coe; sebastian; seb *noun*
the toe *UK*
Rhyming slang, formed on the name of a celebrated British athlete (b.1956) who went into politics.
• To "have it on your Sebastians (or Sebs)" is to do a runner "a bit lively". —Ray Puxley, *Cockney Rabbit*, 1992

sec *noun*
1 a second *UK, 1909*
• Slipping a hundred G's out of the cash cage takes only a sec- but it's robbery. —Philip Wylie, *Opus 21*, p. 242, 1949
• Wait a sec. —Mickey Spillane, *Kiss Me Deadly*, p. 70, 1952
• Now, shut up a sec, Prudy Sue, and hear me out. —Armistead Maupin, *Further Tales of the City*, p. 35, 1982
• Could you hold this a sec'? —*This is Spinal Tap*, 1984
• "Just a sec," Claire said. —Mary Hooper, *(megan)2*, p. 67, 1999
• Got a sec? We'd like to show you the ropes. —Jonathan Gash, *The Ten Word Game*, p. 150, 2003

2 a capsule of secobarbital sodium (trade name *Seconal*™), a central nervous system depressant *UK*
• —Angela Devlin, *Prison Patter*, p. 102, 1996

seccy *noun*
1 a second *AUSTRALIA*
An elaboration of **SEC** rather than an abbreviation of 'second'.
• Hang on a seccy Silvo! Who's that galah [fool] talking to Erica's nippers [children]? —Barry Humphries, *Bazza Pulls It Off!*, 1971

2 a capsule of secobarbital sodium (trade name Seconal™), a central nervous system depressant *US*
• —Norman W. Houser, *Drugs*, p. 13, 1969
• She turned on once in a while; preferred doriden nembutal, seccies, any of the barbituates and most of all, heroin. —Herbert Huncke, *The Evening Sun Turned Crimson*, p. 189, 1980
• Barbiturates are also known as BARBS, BLUES, REDS, and SEKKIES. —Macfarlane, Macfarlane and Robson, *The User*, p. 97, 1996

secko; secoo; sekko *noun*
a sexual deviant; a sex offender *AUSTRALIA*
• 'Just look at that ole secko, will you?' he said disgustedly, and scooping up a stone he ran after it, yelling, 'Merv, Merv, the rotten old perv,' throwing stones at its feet until it slipped into invisibility at the alley end. —Ruth Park, *Poor Man's Orange*, p. 38, 1949
• 'Gawd,' said Tom, in utter disgust at the display. 'B– seckos,' he muttered. 'B– coppers'll be in here directly and lock the whole b– lot of us up.' —Geoff Wyatt, *Saltwater Saints*, p. 55, 1969

seco *noun*
Seconal™, a barbiturate *US*
• When he got to the car window I bought all the pills he had on him, red devils and secos and a few dexis. —Donadl Goines, *Whoreson*, p. 211, 1972

second *noun*
a close friend *BARBADOS*
• —Frank A. Collymore, *Barbadian Dialect*, p. 98, 1965

second balloon *noun*
a second lieutenant *US*
• —*American Speech*, p. 227, October 1956: 'More United States Air Force slang'

second banana *noun*
a person in a supporting role *US, 1953*
Originally applied to a supporting comedian.
• —*American Speech*, February 1956
• The television experts wonder where Imogene Coca's reconciliation with Sid Caesar will leave Sid's second bananas, Howard Morris and Carl Reiner. —*San Francisco Call-Bulletin*, 31st July 1957
• Not long ago, Art Carney was the most popular second banana on television as the sewer man on the Gleason Show. —*Life*, p. 53, 9th May 1960
• For years one of the most formidable second bananas in the comedy spectrum, Louis Nye comes into his own and attains premium solo status in his current nitery act. —*Variety*, p. 10, 23rd May 1962

- The actor was not the leading-man type, a second banana, maybe. The guy that doesn't get the girl, hard as he tries. —Joseph Wambaugh, *Finnegan's Week*, p. 144, 1993
- Sid [Vicious] could be John's suicidal second banana, eliminating the need for Johnny [Rotten] to carve his own flesh[.] —Mick Farren, *Give the Anarchist a Cigarette*, p. 373, 2001

second base *noun*

1 in a teenage categorisation of sexual activity, a level of foreplay, most usually referring to touching a girl's breasts *US, 1977*
The exact degree varies by region or even school.
- He's too busy going for it with your step-mom! Whoa! Second base! — *Bill and Ted's Excellent Adventure*, 1989

2 in casino games of blackjack, the seat or player in the centre of the table directly across from the dealer *US*
- —Lee Solkey, *Dummy Up and Deal*, p. 119, 1980

3 in a deck of playing cards, the card second from the bottom of the deck *US*
- —George Percy, *The Language of Poker*, p. 79, 1988

Second Chance University *noun*
Sir George Williams University *CANADA*
- Until they were combined to create Concordia in 1974, Loyola was a Jesuit liberal-art college in the west end and Sir George Williams was Second Chance U. It offered a full range of night courses, and enrolment included thousands of working Montrealers. — *Montreal Gazette*, p. A2, 12th September 2002

second-generation joint *noun*
a marijuana cigarette made with the remains of other marijuana cigarettes *US, 1977*

second hat *noun*
an assisant drill instructor, US Marine Corps *US*
Usually the most verbally abusive of the three drill instructors who work together as a team.
- —Linda Reinberg, *In the Field*, p. 194, 1991

second John *noun*
a second lieutenant *US*
- — *American Speech*, p. 227, October 1956: 'More United States Air Force slang'

second nuts *noun*
in poker, a good hand that is beaten by a better hand *US, 1976*
- —Thomas L. Clark, *The Dictionary of Gambling and Gaming*, p. 192, 1987

seconds *noun*

1 sex with someone who has just had sex with someone else *US*
Often preceded by the adjective 'sloppy'.
- That would be kind of you, yes. Unless of course you plan to fall by and watch, take seconds. —Richard Farina, *Been Down So Long*, p. 153, 1966

2 a second helping of food *US*

3 playing cards that have been altered for cheating *US*
- The first offense ever prosecuted in the fledgling community at the junction of the Chicago River and Lake Michicagn was running a swindling cardstore, using "seconds". —Jack Lait and Lee Mortimer, *Chicago Confidential*, p. 124, 1950

▸ **the seconds; touch of the seconds**
second thoughts; a fear of consequences *UK*
Metropolitan Police slang.
- —Nicholas Blake, *The Whisper in the Gloom*, 1954
- —Alan Hunter, *Gently Sahib*, 1964
- —Peter Laurie, *Scotland Yard*, p. 327, 1970
- —David Powis, *The Signs of Crime*, 1977

second second *noun*
in the television and film industries, an additional second assistant director *US*
- —Ralph S. Singleton, *Filmaker's Dictionary*, p. 149, 1990

second-story man *noun*

1 a burglar *US, 1886*
- Viciki living with second-story man in Queens —Jack Kerouac, *Letter to Neal Cassady*, p. 175, 8th December 1948
- He had been released from Riker's Island almost two months before, and had picked up a few dollars steering second-story men to a friend of his from Chicago days. a fence. —John Clellon Holmes, *Go*, p. 198, 1952
- Shorty talked to me out of the corner of his mouth: which hustlers – standing around, or playing at this or that table – sold "reefers," or had just come out of prison, or were "second-story men." —Malcolm X and Alex Haley, *The Autobiography of Malcolm X*, p. 45, 1964
- I had Sal Fusco, a great second-story guy. — *Casino*, 1995

2 a skilled card cheat who deals the second card in a deck *US*
- —George Percy, *The Language of Poker*, p. 79, 1988

second to none *noun*
heroin *UK*
- —Mike Haskins, *Drugs*, p. 284, 2003

secoo *verb*
▷ see: SECKO

secret squirrel *noun*
an intelligence operative *UK*
In military use in Northern Ireland during the 1970s; from the animated cartoon hero created by Hanna Barbera and first seen in his own television show in 1965.
- —Christopher Hawke, *For Campagin Service*, 1979

seditty *adjective*
▷ see: SIDITY

seducing vampires *adjective*
experiencing the bleed period of the menstrual cycle *CANADA*
- — *The Museum of Menstruation and Women's Health*, February 2001

see *noun*
a visual inspection *US*
- Some patrolmen started cooping as soon as the sergeant on patrol made his first "see" – police slang for a visual inspection to make sure all officers in the precinct were properly on duty. —Peter Maas, *Serpico*, p. 63, 1973

see *verb*

1 to understand something; to believe something *US, 1850*
Elaborated in the wordplay: 'I see said the blindman, as he put down his hammer and saw'.

2 to have the ability to read music *UK*
- "He doesn't see too well" refers to a performer who reads music slowly. —Leonard Feather, *Encyclopaedia of Jazz*, 1955

▸ **see a brown friend out to the coast**
to defecate *UK*
- — *www.LondonSlang.com*, June 2002

▸ **see a man about a dog**
to go to the toilet *UK, 1885*
Jocular and euphemistic.
- He leaned closer, winking. "I think I gotta go see a man about a dog. Don't go 'way now.'" —Sue Grafton, *"F" is for Fugitive*, p. 70, 1990
- [Q]uaint traditions, not least closing up for lunch or at some other random time when the owner pops out to see a man about a dog. — *Time Out (Lisbon)*, July 2004

▸ **see it coming a mile off**
to predict an obvious event, often only with the benefit of hindsight *UK, 1966*
An elaboration and intensification of 'see it coming'.
- [T]hey led to the hard news slowly, but I saw it coming from miles off. Any kid can see it coming. —Geoffrey Wolff, *Duke of Deception*, p. 217, 1986
- She must have seen our naive excitement coming a mile off. —Allie Pleiter, *Becoming a Chief Home Officer*, p. 35, 2002

▸ **see red**
to be angry *UK, 1901*
- [H]e saw red and clocked Peggy with a bronze statuette[.] —Charles Raven, *Underworld Nights*, p. 107, 1956

▸ **see Steve**
to use cocaine *US*
- — *American Speech*, p. 29, February 1952: 'Teen-age hophead jargon'

▸ **see the colour of your money**
to see your money; to be paid *UK, 1718*
- Both Abbey National and Barclays like to see the colour of your money before they are prepared to let you borrow more than their respective automatic limits of £250 and £200. — *The Observer*, 29th September 2002

▸ **see you coming**
to take advantage of your gullibility *UK, 1937*
- "That camera; says the Pope,"cost me $100,000!" "Oh," says the Japanese ambassador."They must have seen you coming!" —Jimmy Pritchard, *The New York City Bartender's Joke Book*, p. 60, 2002

seed *noun*

1 a child *US*
- —Ethan Hilderbrant, *Prison Slang*, p. 111, 1998

- [T]he two us in a loft out west or wherever, and our seeds, a-painting and a-scribbling away ... Ha! The mixed-race factor would certainly shake up the gene pool. —Diran Abedayo, *My Once Upn A Time*, p. 205, 2000

2 a person who is hopelessly out of touch with current fashions and trends *US*
A shortened form of **HAYSEED**.
- —Hy Lit, *Hy Lit's Unbelievable Dictionary of Hip Words for Groovy People*, p. 34, 1968

3 in a deck of playing cards, an ace *US*
- —George Percy, *The Language of Poker*, p. 80, 1988

4 in private poker games, a one-dollar betting chip *US, 1971*
- —Thomas L. Clark, *The Dictionary of Gambling and Gaming*, p. 192, 1987

5 a dollar *US*
- It's in hock for fifty seeds. —Ross Russell, *The Sound*, p. 146, 1961

6 the butt of a marijuana cigarette *US*
- —Ernest L. Abel, *A Marijuana Dictionary*, p. 91, 1982

seed money *noun*
money needed to start a business *US, 1943*
- —*American Speech*, Fall-Winter 1974
- That evening, Harold Temple wrote his son a check for $5,000. He called it "seed money." And that was that. —Joseph Wambaugh, *Finnegan's Week*, p. 17, 1993

seeds *noun*
marijuana; a marijuana cigarette *US, 1969*
Usage is generally as a singular noun.
- —Richard A. Spears, *The Slang and Jargon of Drugs and Drink*, p. 442, 1986
- —Mike Haskins, *Drugs*, p. 289, 2003

seeds and stems *noun*
the detritus of marijuana, unsmokeable but a reminder of what was *US*
- —Commander Cody and the Lost Planet Airmen, *Down to Seeds and Stems Again Blues*, 1971
- There wasn't any grass in the apartment anyway. Down to seeds and stems. —Elmore Leonard, *City Primeval*, p. 54, 1980

seed spitter *noun*
the penis *US*
- —Erica Orloff and JoAnn Baker, *Dirty Little Secrets*, p. 69, 2001

seedy *adjective*
1 ill, unwell *UK, 1858*
- "What's the matter? Feeling seedy?" "Don't be ridiculous, Rumpole. We're going to get Erica's cigarettes." —John Mortimer, *Rumpole's Return*, 1980

2 in car repair, rusty *US*
- —Lewis Poteet, *Car & Motorcyle Slang*, p. 175, 1992

seedy rom *noun*
a compact disc (CD-ROM) which is sexually explicit *CANADA*
- "Seedy roms" were first so called by Katherine Kelly and John Karmazyn in the Globe and Mail (4th August 1994), to describe sexually explicit CD-ROMs. —Bill Casselman, *Canadian Words*, p. 5–6, 1995

seeing red *adjective*
experiencing the bleed period of the menstrual cycle *US*
- Are you seeing red? —Karen Houppert, *The Curse*, 1999

seeing-to *noun*
1 the act of sexual intercourse, generally considered as the man *doing it* to the woman *UK*
A sense of aggression is implied; consider the contemporaneous 'seeing-to' (a beating).
- For God's sake take me back to your flat in Knightsbridge and give me the most frightful seeing-to. —Henry Sloane, *Sloane's Inside Guide to Sex & Drugs & Rock 'n' Roll*, p. 41, 1985
- "All those birds come away on holiday to get pissed up [drunk]..." "...And get a fuckin' good seeing to." "A drop of the old debauchery." —J.J. Connolly, *Know Your Enemy [britpulp]*, p. 153, 1999
- Henry was still waiting, though he practised hard enough, giving his pillow a "right seeing to" most nights. —Jenny Eclair, *Camberwell Beauty*, p. 193, 2000

2 a beating *UK*
Often as 'a proper seeing-to'.
- I owe that jumped-up plough-boy a seeing to! —Michael Reeves, *Witchfinder General*, 1968

seek *verb*
▸ **seek the sheets**
to crawl into bed *US*
- —*McCall's*, April 1967

seek and search *noun*
a church *UK*
Rhyming slang.
- —Ray Puxley, *Fresh Rabbit*, 1998

seen!
used for registering agreement or approval *JAMAICA*
Originally West Indian.
- "Rude boy Joshua?" "Seen." —Honeyboy Martin & The Voices, *Dreader than Dread*, 1967
- —Julian Johnson, *Urban Survival*, p. 258, 2003

seen?
understood? *UK*
Originally West Indian.
- "Just watch my car," he told Blue, "I don't want no pickney distressing it, seen?" —Karline Smith, *Moss Side Massive*, p. 2, 1994
- [M]ore time is needed when you don't want the "other" man to understand wha' ah gwan [going on], seen? —Donald Gorgon, *Cop Killer*, p. 99, 1994

see off *verb*
to attend to something; to defeat someone *UK, 1915*
- "Your dinner happened to be getting cold so I saw it off, Bob." "You saw it off! Just like that!" —Troy Kennedy Martin, *Z Cars*, p. 27, 1962
- The BNP literature was overtly racist. But we saw them off in the 1970s and I believe we will see them off again. —*The Guardian*, 23rd November 2002

see seven stars *noun*
strong, illegally manufactured whisky *US*
- It is called corn liquor, white lightning, sugar whisky, skully cracker, popskull, bush whiskey, stump, stumphole, 'splo, ruckus juice, radiator whiskey, rotgut, sugarhead, block and tackle, wildcat, panther's breath, tiger's sweat, Sweet spsirits of cats a-fighting, alley bourbon, city gin, cool water, happy Sally, deep shaft, jump steady, old horsey, stingo, blue John, red eye, pine top, buckeye bark whiskey and see seven stars. —*Star Tribune (Minneapolis)*, p. 19F, 31st January 1999

see the Chaplain!
used for silencing a soldier who complains excessively *US, 1941*
- —Carl Fleischhauer, *A Glossary of Army Slang*, p. 12, 1968

see ya round like a Polo
goodbye *UK*
A variation on **SEE YOU ROUND LIKE A RECORD**, playing on the shape of a Polo™ mint.
- —Angela Devlin, *Prison Patter*, p. 102, 1996

see ya, wouldn't want to be ya
goodbye *US*
- —Connie Eble (Editor), *UNC-CH Campus Slang*, p. 5, Fall 1993

see you around campus
goodbye *US*
Jocular.
- See you around the campus, as they say. Is that what they say? —Dan Jenkins, *Semi-Tough*, p. 127, 1972

see you, Jimmy
used as an aggressive or threatening address to a male stranger *UK*
A cliché in the stereotypical drunken Scotsman's vocabulary. Tartan hats with a wild fringe of ginger hair, intended as a comic representation of the generic Jock, are marketed as 'See You Jimmy hats'.
- The caricature of the Scottish male is in-your-face, "see you Jimmy" aggression. —*The New Statesman*, 15th January 2001

see you later, alligator
goodbye *US*
From the use of **GATOR** as an all-purpose form of male address. A catchphrase to which the automatic response was 'in a while, crocodile'; in vogue around 1956, when Bill Haley and His Comets had great success with the song 'See You Later Alligator' (although the actual call and response in the lyric was a slight variation: 'See you later alligator, after a while crocodile').

see you next Tuesday
used as an insider's code for 'cunt' *UK, 1978*
The 'see you' make the 'cu' and the initials 'nt' follow. *See You Next Tuesday* is the title of Ronald Harwood's 2002 adaptation and translation of Francis Veber's 1993 play *Le Diner De Cons*.

see you round like a record *noun*
goodbye *UK*
- See you 'round like a record, see you round / Check you out, meet ya later[.] — Little Nell *See You Round (Like a Record)*, 1978

seg; seggie *noun*
in prison, segregation; a segregation unit *US*
- If it were up to me, I'd throw him in seg and bury the key. — Malcolm Braly, *On the Yard*, p. 200, 1967
- OLD CON with a white beard looking rather nervous [...] FOLEY: Right Santa, you're off down to seg. — Chris Baker and Andrew Day, *Lock, Stock... & A Good Slopping Out*, p. 426, 2000
- The regular landing cleaner was in the seg unit hiding from drug debts[.] — *The Guardian*, p. 7, 17th October 2002

seggy *noun*
a capsule of secobarbital sodium (trade name Seconal™), a central nervous system depressant *US*
- — John B. Williams, *Narcotics and Hallucinogenics*, p. 116, 1967

sei-cordi box *noun*
a six string guitar *UK*
Polari; a combination of Italian *sei*; **SEY; SEI** (six) and *corda* with **BOX** (a guitar).

seized *verb*
▸ **seized of**
in Quebec, gripped by, seized by (an idea or project, for example) *CANADA*
- Six years ago, Victor Trahan was seized of a dossier to ameliorate the English used by his employer, the city of Montreal. [He] decided to compile helpful rules about English usage. He would produce a style guide for the civil service, he decided. — *Montreal Gazette*, p. A1, 27th July 2002

seizure!
used as a cry of triumph, no matter how petty the success *UK*
Reported as a children's usage, Hay-on-Wye, May 2003.

sekko *noun*
▷ see: **SECKO**

seldom seen *noun*
a queen; the Queen *UK*
Rhyming slang.
- — Ray Puxley, *Cockney Rabbit*, 1992

selecta!
used as an expression of approval or pleasure *UK*
Deriving from a dance music term for a DJ, via **BO SELECTA!** (expressing approval of a DJ's performance). Partly popularised in the UK in the late 1990s by Ali G (comedian Sacha Baron-Cohen).
- — Susie Dent, *The Language Report*, p. 144, 2003

selector; selecta *noun*
a DJ *UK*
A shortening of 'music selector', used in modern dance culture, especially in the term **BO SELECTA!**.

self-love *noun*
masturbation *UK*
- THE SELF-LOVE MIX TAPE – (MUSIC TO LOVE YOURSELF TO) — Paul Sullivan, *Sullivan's Music Trivia*, p. 45, 2003

self-propelled sandbag *noun*
a US Marine *US*
US Army Gulf war usage.
- — *American Speech*, p. 400, Winter 1991: 'Among the new words'

Selina Scott; selina *noun*
a spot (a skin blemish) *UK*
Rhyming slang, formed from the name of a UK television presenter and newspaper columnist.
- [S]proot covered juveniles are actually "Selina" covered juveniles. — Ray Puxley, *Cockney Rabbit*, 1992

sell *verb*
1 to convince someone of something; to trick someone *US*
- [S]he eventually sold them on the idea-and the result was the Easy Spirit Walking Shoe[.] — Kate White, *Why Good Girls Don't Get Ahead But Gutsy Girls Do*, p. 44, 1996

2 to gamble on a result lower than the bookmaker's favoured spread *UK*
- The "spread" in spread-betting is a pair of values, usually a point or two apart, which represent the bookmaker's favoured outcome. The investor has two choices: to bet higher, known as "buying", or bet lower, known as "selling". — David Bennet, *Know Your Bets*, p. 107, 2001

▸ **sell a hog**
to scare someone by bluffing *US*
- — Charles Shafer, *Folk Speech in Texas Prisons*, p. 213, 1990

▸ **sell a pup**
to swindle someone *UK, 1901*

▸ **sell backside**
to prostitute yourself, literally or figuratively *SINGAPORE*
- — Paik Choo, *The Coxford Singlish Dictionary*, p. 94, 2002

▸ **sell Buicks**
to vomit *US*
- — Connie Eble (Editor), *UNC-CH Campus Slang*, p. 4, April 1978
- I charge for the toilet and sell a Buick all over the corner of my cell. — Suroosh Alvi et al., *The Vice Guide*, p. 174, 2002

▸ **sell down the river**
to betray someone *US, 1927*
- Developing countries are about to be sold down the river again and hardly anyone seems to care enough to do anything about it. — *The Guardian*, 18th August 2003

▸ **sell tickets**
to engage in ritualistic, competitive insulting *US*
- — Don R. McCreary (Editor), *Dawg Speak*, 2001

seller *noun*
a gambler who bets on a result lower than the bookmaker's favoured spread *UK*
- Brian is optimistic about Arsenal's chances and decides to be a buyer (bets higher) at £10 per point. Sally, on the other hand, is pessimistic. She is a seller (bets lower), also at £10 per point. — David Bennet, *Know Your Bets*, p. 108, 2001

sell-out *noun*
1 an act of betraying principle or loyalty *US*
- We also got the decade's most spectacular "sellout" – Courtney Love's awe-inspiring sail from junkie punk queen to high-fashion cover girl[.] — Naomi Klein, *No Logo*, p. 82, 2001

2 in pool, a missed shot that leaves your opponent with a good shot *US, 1978*
- — Mike Shamos, *The Illustrated Encyclopedia of Billiards*, p. 204, 1993

sell out *verb*
1 to betray a cause of conviction, especially for financial reward *US, 1888*
Around long before the 1960s, but promoted and glorified in the idealistic haze of the 60s.
- But the gist of it is clear enough. Kesey has sold out to keep from getting a five-year sentence or worse. — Tom Wolfe, *The Electric Kool-Aid Acid Test*, p. 336, 1968
- The gist of the talk from the people was that we had sold them out. — Jamie Mandelkau quoting Ken Kesey, *Buttons*, p. 147, 1969
- It's not selling out. How is it selling out? — Fred Baker, *Events*, p. 19, 1970
- There's two major record companies wants to sign us. Heavy bread. We don't have to sell out, man. Just tone town the sex trip. — Tom Robbins, *Another Roadside Attraction*, p. 98, 1971

2 to vomit after drinking to excess *NEW ZEALAND*
- — Sonya Plowman, *Great Kiwi Slang*, p. 159, 2002

selohssa *noun*
used as a nonce name for a person or company *US*
'Assholes' spelled backwards. Peter Tamony collected examples from the San Francisco telephone directory in 1965, 1966 and 1967. In 1953, Welsh playwright Dylan Thomas introduced the village of 'Llareggub' ('bugger all' backwards) in the play *Under Milkwood*.

semi *noun*
1 a *semi*-detached house *UK, 1912*
- There's lots of semis in Little Smith Street, with their own backyards. — *A Bundle of Yarns*, p. 168, 1986

2 a *semi*-final *US, 1942*
- I am so happy to be here and to play in the semis[.] — *The Guardian*, 28th January 2004

3 a *semi*-trailer *AUSTRALIA, 1956*
- A truckie pulled up at the roadhouse in a big semi and dog with a great load of steel girders on board. — Sam Weller, *Old Bastards I Have Met*, p. 137, 1979

4 the penis in a state between flaccid and erect *US*
- — Judi Sanders, *Mashing and Munching in Ames*, p. 17, 1994
- I'm only getting a semi. — Richard Herring, *Talking Cock*, p. 7, 2003

semi-retired *adjective*
unable to find work *US*
- — *Adult Video News*, p. 51, October 1995

semolina *noun*
a professional cleaner *UK*
Rhyming slang.
- — Ray Puxley, *Cockney Rabbit*, 1992

semolina pilchard *nickname*
Detective Sergeant Norman Pilcher of the Metropolitan Police *UK*
Probably coined by the Beatles. Pilcher secured a small celebrity and lasting notoriety in the late 1960s, by arresting, or attempting to arrest, pop stars such as Brian Jones of the Rolling Stones, and John Lennon and George Harrison of the Beatles, for drug offences, and was himself later imprisoned for corruption.
- That we were never busted at 212 was nothing short of a miracle. We could only suppose that Detective Sergeant Norman Pilcher – the notorious "Semolina Pilchard" from the Beatles' "I Am the Walrus", the scourge of all dopefiend rockers – was too busy chasing luminaries — Mick Farren, *Give the Anarchist a Cigarette*, p. 207, 2001

semper fi
used as a shortened version of the US Marine Corps creed – *semper fidelis* (always faithful) *US*
Used as a greeting, an affirmation, and in practically any situation to mean practically anything.
- Each time one of my men complained, a man from Weapons or a rifle company cried out "Semper Fidelis!" or sometimes the abbreviated version "Semper Fi!" — William B. Hopkins, *One Bugle No Drum*, p. 79, 1986

semper Gumby *adjective*
flexible *US*
- Gulf War usage; a play on the US Marine Corps motto and an allusion to a rubber television character. — *Army*, p. 48, November 1991
- — *American Speech*, p. 400, Winter 1991: 'Among the new words'

sen; sens *noun*
marijuana *UK, 1998*
A clipping of **SENSIMILLIA**.
- — Mike Haskins, *Drugs*, p. 289, 2003

senator *noun*
in a game of poker, a dealer who does not play *US*
- — George Percy, *The Language of Poker*, p. 80, 1988

send *noun*
the phase of a confidence swindle when the victim is sent to retrieve money *US, 1940*

▸ **put on the send**
in a confidence swindle, to send the victim off to retrieve the money that will pass to the swindlers *US*
- Then he put old Hare "on the send" for the cash, as confidence men call it, which doesn't need any lengthy explanation. — Guy Owen, *The Flim-Flam Man and the Apprentice Grifter*, p. 177, 1972

send *verb*
1 to excite someone; to please someone *US, 1935*
- Albert really sent that audience singing Some Sweet Day. — Mezz Mezzrow, *Really the Blues*, p. 26, 1946
- A "solid" driving beat is produced that "sends" the dancers. — William Sansom, *A Public for Jive [The Public's Progress]*, p. 58, 1947
- "Oh, man," she moaned happily, "this beat does it. Man, it sends me." — Robert Gover, *The Maniac Responsible*, p. 84, 1963

2 to produce a drug intoxication *US*
- There are sufficiently strong to "send" the kids. — Jack Lait and Lee Mortimer, *Chicago Confidential*, p. 148, 1950

▸ **send a boy to do a man's work**
in poker, to make a small bet with a good hand in the hope of luring players with inferior hands to continue betting *US*
- — *American Speech*, p. 101, May 1951

▸ **send out a salesman**
in gin, to discard in a manner that is designed to lure a desired card from an opponent *US*
- — Irwin Steig, *Play Gin to Win*, p. 138,

▸ **send packing**
to dismiss someone; to reject someone with immediate effect *UK, 1594*
- [Y]ou will join the ranks of the unemployed and be sent packing back to the ranch. — Michael Moore, *Dude, Where's My Country?*, p. 162, 2003

▸ **send the little sailor to sea**
to have sex *US*
- Another way to say "intercourse" [...] Sending the little sailor into sea[.] — Erica Orloff and JoAnn Baker, *Dirty Little Secrets*, p. 88, 2001

▸ **send to Long Beach**
to flush a toilet *US*
Long Beach is a community to the south of Los Angeles.
- Giving her a proper burial, I flushed the commode. As the saying goes, I sent her to Long Beach. — Eldridge Cleaver, *Soul on Ice*, p. 8, 1968
- — *Current Slang*, p. 41, Fall 1968

send down *verb*
to commit someone to prison *US, 1840*
- He didn't intend to be sent down for this cock up. — Donald Gorgon, *Cop Killer*, p. 9, 1994
- — Angela Devlin, *Prison Patter*, p. 102, 1996

sender *noun*
something or someone that arouses or excites *US, 1935*
Originally (mid-1930s) a jazz term referring to a musician who excites and inspires a jazz band; in the early 1940s extended into general usage. Often emphasised as **SOLID SENDER**.
- [F]inally, he's a solid sender, he can send your spirit soaring and make you real happy[.] — Mezz Mezzrow, *Really the Blues*, p. 227, 1946
- It's a funny thing how life can be such a drag one minute and a solid sender the next. — Louis Armstrong, *Satchmo*, p. 126, 1954

send-off *noun*
1 a funeral *US, 1876*
A specialised use of the sense relating more generally to any journey.
- The funeral was like something out of a film – a proper gangsters send off. — Lenny McLean, *The Guv'nor*, p. 14, 1998
- He gave her a lovely funeral [...] A proper people's send-off. — Michael Moorcock, *The Spencer Inheritance [britpulp]*, p. 32, 1998

2 an occasion at which friendly good wishes are offered to someone leaving a current situation (for a journey or different employment, etc) *US, 1841*
- Despite the early hour, New Yorkers gave Concorde a rousing send off. — *The Guardian*, 24th October 2003

send off *verb*
1 to apprehend or arrest someone *AUSTRALIA*
- The cops are always trying to send him off[.] — Vince Kelly, *The Bogeyman*, p. 110, 1956

2 to steal something *AUSTRALIA*
- Tilly's principle bedroom was transformed into a cloak-room with an ex-boxer as cloak-room attendant to see that 'nothing was sent off.' — George Blaikie, *Remember Smith's Weekly?*, p. 218, 1950

send-up *noun*
a satirical act; a parody *UK, 1958*
From the phrasal verb **SEND UP**.
- [L]ighthearted send-ups of New Age cliches – crystals, guardian angels, regression to past lives, rage cured by hitting pillows, etc. — *Washington Post*, 22nd September 1996

send up *verb*
1 to mock someone or something satirically or parodically *UK, 1931*
- [Ewan] McGregor, who loses neither his charisma nor his personality on stage, makes terrific fun of Malcolm [in the play 'Little Malcolm and His Struggle Against the Eunuchs'] by refusing to send him up. — *Evening Standard (London)*, November 1998

2 to sentence someone to prison *US, 1852*
- This was the master card from the files of the police in the town from which I had been sent up. — Horace McCoy, *Kiss Tomorrow Good-bye*, p. 175, 1948
- He was sent up for his first real bit when he was 16. — Hubert Selby Jr, *Last Exit to Brooklyn*, p. 42, 1957

- You're going to be arrested before you leave this building! I'm going to send you up for this! —Willard Motley, *Let No Man Write My Epitaph*, p. 95, 1958
- I was sent up to Dannemora, a much nicer place than Greenhaven. —Herbert Huncke, *Guilty of Everything*, p. 117, 1990
- I forgot for a minute there it was Gibbs convicted Sonny and nailed you on the dope charge. He's the same one sent me up. —Elmore Leonard, *Maximum Bob*, p. 116, 1991

senile street *noun*
an area in a hospital or nursing home frequented by senile patients *AUSTRALIA*
- —*Maledicta*, p. 92, 1986–1987: 'Australian maledicta'

senior moment *noun*
a short interval in which an older person succumbs to a mental or physical lack of energy or consistency *US*
- When something temporarily goes awry in her recall cells, she waves it away: "Oh, pardon me, I'm having a senior moment." —*Omaha (Nebraska) World Herald*, p. 17, 22nd November 1996
- —Walter A. Atkinson, *Forgive Us Our Senior Moments.*, 2002
- The Queen has predictably been criticised for having a senior moment during a lecture at the end of her state visit to Germany – almost certainly by people who have never fallen asleep themselves in similar circumstances. —*The Guardian*, 6th November 2004

sense; sens *noun*
marijuana *US*
An abbreviation of **SENSIMILLIA**.
- Loose joints. Genuine Hawaiian sens. —Jay McInerney, *Bright Lights, Big City*, p. 108, 1984
- Cause it seems a lot of times, I'm at my best / After some methical or a bowl of sense. —Tone Loc, *Cheeba Cheeba*, 1989

sensi; sensee *noun*
marijuana *JAMAICA*
Clipped from **SENSIMILLIA**.
- —Neville Brown & The Roots Radics, *Babylon Don't Touch My Sensi Dub*, 1983
- "Want a smoke?" she asked, flicking the video off. "Smoke what?" "Anything, coke, black, sensi." —Karline Smith, *Moss Side Massive*, p. 52, 1994
- I held up a pre-rolled big boy, with the minimum tobacco and maximum Jamaican Sensee. —Wayne Anthony, *Spanish Highs*, p. 72, 1999

sensimillia; sinsemilla; sinse *noun*
a very potent marijuana harvested from a hybrid cannabis plant with seedless buds *JAMAICA*
From the Spanish *sin semilla* (seedless). Celebrated in song by 'Cocaine will blow your brain, but sinsemilla is IR-IE!' by Yellowman, quoted in *Waiting For The Man*, Harry Shapiro, 1999.
- As that comforting litany danced in her head, she rolled a joint of her finest sinsemilla and settled back with Boris to enjoy the fire. —Armistead Maupin, *Further Tales of the City*, p. 4, 1982
- —Barrington Levy, *Sensimilea*, 1982
- Mauie-zowie sinsemillia dope and a tab of window pane acid —Stuart Browne, *Dangerous Parking*, p. 84, 2000

seppo *noun*
an American *AUSTRALIA*
From **SEPTIC**.
- [M]aybe some seppos are getting guts and individuality as the last pro contest held in decent surf...showed[.] —*Tracks*, p. 5, October 1985
- Gerlach is a Seppo (Californian) so how he qualifies for an Australian teams event is a matter of some debate. —*Sunday Tasmanian*, p. 49, 1st October 1989
- —Trevor Cralle, *The Surfin'ary*, p. 109, 1991
- —*Sydney Morning Herald*, p. 1, 2002

Sept. 10 *adjective*
petty; inconsequential *US*
Teen slang, post 11th September 2001.
- That's so Sept. 10. —*The Washington Post*, 19th March 2002

September morn
the erect penis *UK*
Rhyming slang for **HORN**.
- —Ray Puxley, *Fresh Rabbit*, 1998

septic *noun*
an American *AUSTRALIA*
Short for **SEPTIC TANK**.
- All of them can understand American accents, but the Septics don't use naughty words on the sacred thanks-for-having-us-in-your-home medium. —Suzy Jarratt, *Permissive Australia*, p. 79, 1970
- —Jim Ramsay, *Cop It Sweet!*, p. 79, 1977

septic tank *noun*
an American *AUSTRALIA, 1967*
Rhyming slang for **YANK**. Certainly derogatory in origin, and demonstrating a general low-level anti-American sentiment prevalent in Australia. In the same way that **POM** demonstrates an anti-English sentiment it is always more joking than serious.
- Septic Tanks don't get VCs. They get purple hearts. —John O'Grady, *Aussie Etiket*, p. 7, 1971
- 'Ed's from Americ.' 'Yeah? What's a bloody Septic Tank doin' out here? Never mind – what're you drinkin', Dusty?' —John O'Grady, *Aussie Etiket*, p. 48, 1971
- —Bob Young and Micky Moody, *The Language of Rock 'n' Roll*, p. 128, 1985
- —John Algeo and Adele Algeo, *American Speech*, p. 400, Winter 1991: 'Among the new words'
- —Ray Puxley, *Fresh Rabbit*, 1998

serenity, tranquility and peace *noun*
STP, a synthetic hallucinogen that appeared on the drug scene in 1967 *US*
Because of its claimed psychedlic powers, the drug was named STP after the engine oil additive (scientifically treated petroleum), with this trinity of virtues produced through back-formation.
- —Carl Chambers and Richard Heckman, *Employee Drug Abuse*, p. 209, 1972

sergeant from K company *noun*
in a deck of playing cards, a king *US*
- —George Percy, *The Language of Poker*, p. 80, 1988

sergeant-major *noun*
in the dice game crown and anchor, a crown *UK, 1925*
From 'crown', an army colloquialism for 'sergeant-major'.

serial speedball *verb*
to use cocaine, cough syrup and heroin in a continual cycle over a 1–2 day period *UK, 1998*
- [S]erial speedballing – doing cocaine, cough syrup and heroin continuously over a couple of days[.] —Robert Ashton, *This Is Heroin*, p. 210, 2002

serio *adverb*
in a serious manner *IRELAND*
This corruption of 'seriously', making use of the familiarising suffix, is especially common in Dublin colloquial speech.
- [R]emembering the joy of going to school in Ireland. Wasn't it fun? Wasn't it grand? I miss it still. Really. Truly. Yes, I do. Serio. And monkeys regularly fly out of my butt. —Joseph O'Connor, *The Irish Male at Home and Abroad*, p. 73, 1996

serious *adjective*

1 used to enhance or intensify *UK*
- "[S]erious eating", "serious drinking". Serious overuse has made it meaningless. —Ann Barr and Peter York, *The Official Sloane Ranger Handbook*, p. 159, 1982
- A client, it seemed. Who knows, maybe one with serious collats [money]. That would be nice. —Diran Adebayo, *My Once Upon A Time*, p. 5, 2000
- The bang-up [a period locked in a prison cell] was costing him serious money. —*The Guardian*, 3rd August 2000
- [They] were forced to resort to "serious ganja [marijuana]" to calm their nerves. —Jim Drury, *Ian Dury and the Blockheads – Song by Song*, p. 88, 2003

2 seriously ill *INDIA*
Indian English.
- Your grandfather is serious, so you had better go to the hospital —Paroo Nihalini, R.K. Tongue and Priya Hosali, *Indian and British English*, 1979

serious chep *noun*
intimate sexual contact; sexual intercourse *IRELAND*
An intensified **CHEP** (a kiss).
- —John Morton, *Skegs and Skangers*, 2001

serious headache *noun*
a gunshot wound to the head *US*
- —Ralph de Sola, *Crime Dictionary*, p. 136, 1982

seriously *adverb*
used to intensify or enhance *US, 1981*
- He's seriously rich. —Ann Barr and Peter York, *The Official Sloane Ranger Handbook*, p. 159, 1982

serpent *noun*
a railway pointsman *US*
From the snake-like 'S' on the pointsman's union pin.
- —Ramon Adams, *The Language of the Railroader*, p. 135, 1977

Serpico; Serpico 21 *noun*

cocaine; crack cocaine *UK, 1998*

From the film *Serpico*, 1973.

- —Mike Haskins, *Drugs*, p. 281, 2003

serve *verb*

1 to insult someone in a semi-formal quasi-friendly competition *AUSTRALIA*

After 'serve' (a criticism).

- There are many different terms for playing the dozens, including "bagging, capping, cracking, dissing, hiking, joning, ranking, ribbing, serving, signifying, slipping, sounding and snapping". —James Haskins, *The Story of Hip-Hop*, p. 54, 2000

2 to humiliate someone; to hit someone *US*

- —Ellen C. Bellone (Editor), *Dictionary of Slang*, p. 21, 1989

3 to sell drugs to someone *US*

- "Yeah, loc, are you serving, cuz?" Glass asked in street slang. —*Los Angeles Times Magazine*, p. 12, 16th September 1990
- I dint serve no one, Big Chief! It's for mah mother's birthday, I swear. —Richard Price, *Clockers*, p. 14, 1992

4 in card games, to deal *US*

- —George Percy, *The Language of Poker*, p. 80, 1988

▸ **serve you right; serves you right**

used as an expression of satisfaction that you have got your just deserts *UK, 1837*

- Then he got in the car, intending to drive away and leave her at the restaurant. "Wouldn't that serve her right?" he thought. —Scott M. Stanley, *A Lasting Promise*, p. 104, 1998

server *noun*

a person who hands crack cocaine to a buyer as part of a multi-layered selling operation *US*

- —US Department of Justice, *Street Terms*, October 1994

service stripes *noun*

bruises, punctures and sores visible on the skin of an intravenous drug user *US*

- —David Maurer and Victor Vogel, *Narcotics and Narcotic Addiction*, p. 440, 1973

serving *noun*

a beating *AUSTRALIA*

- When an Australian says, "I gave him a serving," he doesn't mean cake and ice cream, he means roughly "I beat the crap out of him." —Brian Preston, *Pot Planet*, p. 88, 2002

servo *noun*

a service station *AUSTRALIA*

- We went into a Shell servo to get some change and when we pulled out I couldn't see with the rear vision mirror. —John Birmingham, *He Died With a Felafel in his Hand*, p. 127, 1994
- The only place open was the servo. —Phillip Gwynne, *Deadly Unna?*, p. 25, 1998

sesh *noun*

1 a period of sustained drinking *UK*

A shortening of **SESSION**.

- That was a rare wee sesh last Friday. —Michael Munro, *The Patter*, p. 61, 1985
- Bit too soon to start a sesh innit? —Niall Griffiths, *Sheepshagger*, p. 180, 2001

2 a session *US*

- I mean we like had this way cranking bud sesh and like listened to AC/DC and watched Mommie Dearest with the sound off. —Mary Corey and Victoria Westermark, *Fer Shurr! How to be a Valley Girl*, 1982

sess; sces; sezz *noun*

potent marijuana *US, 1982*

Variations on **SENSIMILLIA**.

- —Richard A. Spears, *The Slang and Jargon of Drugs and Drink*, p. 443, 1986
- Sess. Smoke. Hash, shrooms. —*Kids*, 1995
- Low grade, you're talking bush at one hundred and twenty [...] Indica and sess two hundred plus - —Diran Adebayo, *My Once Upon A Time*, p. 26, 2000
- —Mike Haskins, *Drugs*, p. 289, 2003
- Got the Skunk, got the Punk, we got the Sess, it's Blessed. —Julian Johnson, *Urban Survival*, p. 170, 2003

session *noun*

1 a prolonged period of steady drinking *AUSTRALIA, 1949*

- One winter night, in company with Hookey, they had set out for the mill after a session with Scotty's bombo down at Tenbi. —Robert S. Close, *With Hooves of Brass*, p. 25, 1961
- I took my bottle of Scotch down to the engineers' mess and had a session with the Second, Third and Fourth engineers. —Les Such, *A Yen for Yokohama*, p. 37, 1963
- Max Harris and I have both read this now, and we had a long claret-lubricated session over it on Wednesday[.] —Geoffrey Dutton, *The Outcasts of Foolgarah*, p. 235, 1965
- Back at the pub, in time for the afternoon 'session', my sponsors divided up the loot, and over my protests insisted on splitting it four ways. —John O'Grady, *It's Your Shout, Mate!*, p. 26, 1972
- This time he'd had a real good session and had the tatas bad. —Sam Weller, *Old Bastards I Have Met*, p. 83, 1979
- Clad in Australian flying suits we found a U.S. boozer and settled in for a session. —Martin Cameron, *A Look at the Bright Side*, 1988
- There was this session at the Royal earlier tonight, on account of Darcy. —Shane Maloney, *Nice Try*, p. 190, 1998

2 an instance of sexual intercourse *US*

- —Anna Scotti and Paul Young, *Buzzwords*, p. 29, 1997

3 any period of time spent scooter-riding with friends *UK*

- —Ben Sharpe, *Scooter Crazy*, p. 41, 2000

4 a series of waves *US*

- —Grant W. Kuhns, *On Surfing*, p. 121, 1963

session; sesh *verb*

to concentrate effort on a single objective *US*

- To session a hit means to hit it, unbuckle, hike back up, hit it again, unbuckle, etc. You can session, or sesh, anything from a hit to a particular line down a slope, a bowl, a section of trees, or the local Taco Bell. —Jim Humes and Sean Wagstaff, *Boarderlands*, p. 224, 1995

set *noun*

1 a neighbourhood; a specific place in a neighbourhood where friends congregate *US*

- This was the way people in our set did things. —Claude Brown, *Manchild in the Promised Land*, p. 176, 1965
- Ya baby, I'm going up on the set. —Donald Goines, *Whoreson*, p. 95, 1972
- [T]he player is out "on the set," moving through the "scene" of the city's night life. —Christina and Richard Milner, *Black Players*, p. 12, 1972
- Everybody from Washington Square to Tompkins Square called the streets "the set" - as in "I've been looking for you all over the set, man." —Ed Sanders, *Tales of Beatnik Glory*, p. 192, 1975
- Elijah! heyyyy blood! Wha's happenin'? I heard you was back on the set. Where you been keepin' yourself? —Odie Hawkins, *Chicago Hustle*, p. 122, 1977
- But Slick might be out checking up on her, or one of these chumpas out here on the set might rat on her to him. —John Sayles, *Union Dues*, p. 180–181, 1977
- The group of brothers nodded in return. "You guys know whether or not Kenyatta is on the set?" Billy inquired as he stoped in front of the group. —Donald Goines, *Crime Partners*, p. 48, 1978
- That nigga roll upon the set one more time I swear I'm gonna fuck him up. —*Boyz N The Hood*, 1990

2 a neighbourhood faction of a gang *US*

- Shane knew you didn't usually get a street name unless you'd been "jumped in the set"[.] —Stephen J. Cannell, *The Tin Collectors*, p. 147, 2001
- Claudia had retired from her Crip set after being blinded in a shotgun attack[.] —*Rolling Stone*, p. 77, 12th April 2001

3 a party, especially a party with music *US*

- —*Current Slang*, p. 5, Fall 1966
- The set is on the fifth floor and the floor is creaking an' groaning under the weight of all the coolies that are swinging. —Piri Thomas, *Down These Mean Streets*, p. 59, 1967

4 a group of breaking waves *AUSTRALIA, 1963*

- I stood in the parking lot, watching the sets build. —Kathy Lette, *Girls' Night Out*, p. 188, 1987

5 a woman's breasts *AUSTRALIA*

- 'Hey, Jow, there's a good set,' one will cry. (A 'set', for your information, is a bosom.) —Sue Rhodes, *Now you'll think I'm awful*, p. 58, 1967
- —Collin Baker et al., *College Undergraduate Slang Study Conducted at Brown University*, p. 191, 1968
- Hello, boobs, I'm Alvin Purple, and you're not a bag set either. —*Alvin Purple*, p. 7, 1974

6 in horse or dog racing, a wager or the cumulative amount of wagers taken against a particular contestant *AUSTRALIA*

- Duvi, some of your fellow bagmen have taken a big set against Tamarama Boy, how do you see it? —Clive Galea, *Slipper*, p. 2, 1988

7 a still used in the illegal production of alcohol *US*

- —David W. Maurer, *Kentucky Moonshine*, p. 124, 1974

8 in prison usage, a continuance of a parole hearing *US*

- —*Maledicta*, p. 267, Summer/Winter 1981: 'By its slang, ye shall know It: the pessimism of prison life'

▸ **have a set on**

to be hostile towards someone *AUSTRALIA, 1866*

- It can't be only that they've a set on the Thornes, because they always had it for Old Man Suderman. —Kylie Tennant, *Lost Haven*, p. 133, 1946

set *verb*
to make a bet with someone *AUSTRALIA, 1915*
- [I]f you fancied a bet it was not too hard to find someone to set you. —Clive Galea, *Slipper*, p. 6, 1988

▸ **set (her) down**
in trucking, to make a sudden stop *US*
- —Montie Tak, *Truck Talk*, p. 138, 1971

▸ **set in the woods**
in lobstering, to set traps close to the shore *US*
- —Kendall Merriam, *The Illustrated Dictionary of Lobstering*, p. 76, 1978

▸ **set the centre**
in the gambling game two-up, to ensure that the spinner's wager is covered by the other players *AUSTRALIA, 1930*

▸ **set them up**
to organise a round of drinks *UK*
- BELL: Hey, Milly, set 'em up. MILLIGAN: Cor blimey, where's the fire?—Graeme Kent, *The Queen's Corporal [Six Granada Plays]*, p. 87, 1959

set *adjective*
having a wager settled upon *AUSTRALIA, 1915*
- The keeper said, 'Centre set. All set on the side?'—John O'Grady, *It's Your Shout, Mate!*, p. 25, 1972
- They took some time getting 'set'.—John O'Grady, *It's Your Shout, Mate!*, p. 25, 1972
- McLean said 'I've got fifty to say that's him' and John said 'You're set.'—Sam Weller, *Old Bastards I Have Met*, p. 14, 1979
- Nana Joe's reputation proved to be well founded when he fronted up to the expectant winners and announced that he'd been unable to get set.—Joe Andersen, *Winners Can Laugh*, p. 42, 1982

set about *verb*
to attack or assault someone *UK, 1879*
- Spain's World Cup star couldn't have beaten Depor fullback Romero more comprehensively if he'd set about him with a breeze-block encrusted cricket bat.—*The Guardian*, 2nd September 2002

set back *verb*
to cost, especially to cost a great deal *UK, 1856*
- [An] audacious plan which, if it ever comes to fruition, will set him back a cool £12m.—*The Guardian*, 20th February 2004

set in concrete *adjective*
immutable; unalterable *UK*
A variation of **SET IN STONE**.
- "You have dates," he said, "and so long as you are meeting your targets, those dates are set in concrete.—*The Guardian*, 22nd August 2002

set in stone *adjective*
immutable; unalterable *UK*
A figurative application of the conventional sense.
- Iraq deadline 'not set in stone'.—*Herald Sun (Australia)*, 11th March 2003

set joint *noun*
a carnival game which is rigged to prevent players from winning *US*
- [T]he set joint is peculiar in that it is "set" after all bets are down. —E.E. Steck, *A Brief Examination of an Esoteric Folk*, p. 8, 1968

setter; setta *adjective*
seven; seven (pre-decimal) pence *UK, 1859*
- [Y]ou might like to count to ten in Polari: una, duey, trey, quater, chicker, sey, setter, otto, nobber, dacha.—Michael Quinion, *World Wide Words*, 1996

settle *verb*

▸ **settle your hash**
to subdue you; to silence you; to defeat you; to kill you *UK, 1803*
- A truant officer, he called himself. Some little pansy. I settled his hash for him.—Frank Conroy, *Body and Soul*, 1993

settler *noun*
in an illegal betting operation, the person who determines the final odds on an event after all bets are taken *US, 1964*
- —Thomas L. Clark, *The Dictionary of Gambling and Gaming*, p. 194, 1987

settlers *noun*
dice that have been weighted and which are thrown with an altered cup with great effect by a skilled cheat *US*
- —John S. Salak, *Dictionary of Gambling*, p. 225, 1963

set-up *noun*
1 an organisation or establishment *UK*
- MILLIGAN: Nosey, ain't he? TAYLOR: Wouldn't you be, if you walked into this set up?—Graeme Kent, *The Queen's Corporal [Six Granada Plays]*, p. 85, 1959

2 an arrangement, organisation or situation *US, 1890*
- What sort of set-up have the Yanks got over there, anyway?—Beale, 1984

3 a scheme for the entrapment of a criminal or the incrimination of an innocent *US, 1968*
- [H]e claimed republicans were behind a pipe bomb attack on his car but they denied it, saying it was a set-up.—*The Guardian*, 10th January 2001

4 the equipment used to inject a drug *US*
- The needle had found a vein, and Paddy, with setup firm at his hip, drew his real red blood into the gleaming syringe, where it lost color in boiled heroin.—George Mandel, *Flee the Angry Strangers*, p. 230, 1952

5 a place setting at a dining table *US, 1934*
- How many set-ups for the Smith banquet?—Albert Leechman, 1984

set up *verb*
especially of criminals, to arrange circumstances in such a way that the target of this arrangement is rendered vulnerable; to create a victim; to incriminate someone *US, 1928*
- It was one of their cars and they'd set me up.—Macfarlane, Macfarlane and Robson, *The User*, p. 106, 1996

set-up man *noun*
a criminal who identifies, plans and organises crimes *US*
- They are always looking for a "setup man," someone to plan jobs and tell them exactly what to do.—William Burroughs, *Junkie*, p. 20, 1953
- —Angela Devlin, *Prison Patter*, p. 102, 1996

seven *noun*
1 a telephone number *US*
From the seven digits used in US telephone numbers.
- —Connie Eble (Editor), *UNC-CH Campus Slang*, p. 8, Spring 1998

2 in eastern Australia, a seven fluid ounce glass of beer *AUSTRALIA*
- Mind you, in the bush you'll only get seven ounces. They call it a seven.—John O'Grady, *It's Your Shout, Mate!*, p. 66, 1972

seven and seven *noun*
1 a drink made by mixing equal parts of Seven-Up™ soda and Seagrams Seven Whiskey™ *US*
- Over seven-sevens and whiskey sours they remind each other in silence where they're going[.]—Charles Anderson, *The Grunts*, p. 20, 1976
- BARTENDER: What'll you have, Tony? TONY: Usual – seven and seven.—*Saturday Night Fever*, 1977
- Hey, kid! Get me a seven and seven.—*Goodfellas*, 1990

2 after 1971 in the Vietnam war, seven days of rest and recuperation, followed by seven days of leave *US*
- —Linda Reinberg, *In the Field*, p. 196, 1991

seven and six *noun*
1 a fix (a difficult position) *UK*
Rhyming slang.
- To be in difficulty is to be in a "right old seven and six".—Ray Puxley, *Cockney Rabbit*, 1992

2 a young Mod *UK*
Apparently the **MOD** favoured tee-shirts from Woolworths costing seven shillings and sixpence.
- —Tom Hibbert, *Rockspeak!*, p. 139, 1983

seven and six *verb*
to fix something *UK*
Rhyming slang.
- Leave it to your old man, he'll seven and six it.—Ray Puxley, *Cockney Rabbit*, 1992

seven and sixer *noun*
a married person *UK*
From the cost of a wedding licence, seven shillings and sixpence.
- What they [Mods] hated in others – the tickets [ordinary people], the seven and sixers- is that they settled for so much less.—Paolo Hewitt, *The Sharper Word*, p. 6, 1998

Seven Dials *noun*
haemorrhoids *UK*
Rhyming slang for 'piles', formed on a once notorious area of central London.
- —Ray Puxley, *Fresh Rabbit*, 1998

seven-eleven *noun*
a small amount of money given to a gambler who has lost all their money, either by a casino or his fellow gamblers *US, 1950*
- —Thomas L. Clark, *The Dictionary of Gambling and Gaming*, p. 194, 1987

seven-o *noun*
seventy; 70th Street *US*
- —David Claerbaut, *Black Jargon in White America*, p. 78, 1972

seven out *verb*
in craps, to roll a seven before making your point, thus losing *US*
- When Trish quickly sevens-out, the guy who would have been the next shooter mutters, "Cold as a witch's eyebrows," and turns away. —Edward Lin, *Big Julie of Vegas*, p. 19, 1974
- He sevened out without even throwing a number, much less a pass. —Mario Puzo, *Inside Las Vegas*, p. 261, 1977

seven-ply gasser *noun*
the very best thing *US*
- —Hy Lit, *Hy Lit's Unbelievable Dictionary of Hip Words for Groovy People*, p. 34, 1968

sevens *noun*
▸ **all the sevens**
seventy-seven *UK, 1943*
In Bingo, House or Housey-Housey calling, the formula 'all the' announces a double number.

seventeen-wheeler *noun*
an eighteen-wheel truck with a flat tyre *US*
- —"Slingo", *The Official CB Slang Dictionary Handbook*, p. 54, 1976

seventh cavalry *noun*
any agency that promises or effects an eleventh-hour rescue or last-minute relief from an awkward situation *UK*
- Ah, the boys, the boys, ee sehs. – Seventh bleedin cavalry. Christ a could kiss the both a yer. —Niall Griffiths, *Grits*, p. 21, 2000

seventh wave *noun*
the difficulty that follows many others and proves to be climactic disaster *US*
From the belief that every seventh wave is larger than the six before or after.
- —John Gould, *Maine Lingo*, p. 249, 1975

seven-up *noun*
crack cocaine *US*
A pun on 'coke' as a soft drink and drug.
- —Peter Johnson, *Dictionary of Street Alcohol and Drug Terms*, p. 168, 1993
- —Mike Haskins, *Drugs*, p. 281, 2003

seven-year itch *noun*
a (notional) need to be unfaithful to your spouse after seven years of marriage *UK, 1936*
- [M]arital satisfaction declines, then levels out, and then declines again in the seventh and eighth years as the seven-year itch arises. —Joshua Coleman, *Imperfect Harmony*, p. 19, 2003

severe clear *adjective*
of the weather, perfect for flying *CANADA*
- "Severe clear" is an expression among pilots for "not a cloud in the sky". —Tom Parkin, *WetCoast Words*, p. 122, 1989

severe like *noun*
a strong desire for something *US*
- I have a severe like for this sweater. —Connie Eble (Editor), *UNC-CH Campus Slang*, p. 6, Fall 1984

severely *adverb*
very much *UK, 1854*
- There were people who were severely in to the old jap-slapping [martial arts]. —Andy McNab, *Immediate Action*, p. 380, 1995

sew *verb*
▸ **sew the button on**
in oil drilling, to finish a job *US*
- —Jerry Robertson, *Oil Slanguage*, p. 111, 1954

sewer *noun*
1 a vein, especially a prominent vein suitable for drug injection *US*
- —US Department of Justice, *Street Terms*, October 1994
- Go into a sewer. —Mike Haskins, *Drugs*, p. 290, 2003

2 in pool, a pocket that is receptive to shots dropping *US*
- —Steve Rushin, *Pool Cool*, p. 26, 1990

3 a person who cannot keep a secret *US*
- —*American Weekly*, p. 2, 14th August 1955

sewer hog *noun*
a ditch digger *US*
- —Joseph E. Ragen and Charles Finston, *Inside the World's Toughest Prison*, p. 817, 1962: 'Penitentiary and underworld glossary'

sewer trout *noun*
white fish of unknown origin *US*
- —Lou Shelly, *Hepcats Jive Talk Dictionary*, p. 48, 1945
- Bass there are, and pickerel, and muskenonge, not to mention such sewer trout as catfish, dog fish and pike. —Kenneth Wells, *Cruising the Georgian Bay*, p. 104, 1958
- —*Maledicta*, p. 267, Summer/Winter 1981: 'By its slang, ye shall know it: the pessimism of prison life'
- —Gary K. Farlow, *Prison-ese*, p. 61, 2002

sewing machine *noun*
a small, foreign-made car *US*
Drag racing usage, heard before the great influx of foreign cars into the US.

sewn-up *adjective*
finished *UK*
- Pee, there, is too far gone for you. He's our pal, but he's sewnup. —Geoffrey Fletcher, *Down Among the Meths Men*, p. 38, 1966

sew up *verb*
to organise or achieve a satisfactory conclusion; to ensure a favourable outcome *UK, 1904*
- She's getting paid by the council to make sure that Moby's gaff is sewn up. —Kevin Sampson, *Clubland*, p. 97, 2002

sex *noun*
the genitals *UK, 1938*
A literary nicety as illustrated by Beale in 1984, in the style of 'any piece of classier porn': 'She tried to cover her naked sex with an inadequate hand'.
- His sex was swollen and hot. He was impatient with his clothing. —Sandra Brown, *French Silk*, 1993

sex *verb*
to have sex with someone *US, 1966*
- I gotta girl so there's no need to sex a ho[.] —MC Serch, *Mic Techniques*, 1991
- "You sexing that [woman] then?" I shook my head. —Diran Abedayo, *My Once Upon A Time*, p. 231, 2000

sex appeal *noun*
false breasts *US*
- —Don Wilmeth, *The Language of American Popular Entertainment*, p. 236, 1981

sexational; sexsational *adjective*
very sexy; very sexually attractive *US, 1928*
- [T]he studs headed toward the master bedroom to begin a great gun filled sexy sexsational orgy that none of them would soon forget!!!! —David Sedaris, *Barrel Fever*, p. 23, 1994
- [A]ltogether the outward physicality of the work contributed to the sexational build-up that led to the show's success. —Sally Banes, *Dancing Women*, p. 151, 1998

sex-bomb *noun*
a sexually alluring person, especially a woman, particularly one with exaggerated but stereotypical sexuality *UK, 1963*
- What did James Bond do in the bathroom? When he wasn't sharing the hot tub with sex-bombs whose mascara never dissolved in the steam, that is. —Liz Evans, *Pussy Galore [Tart Noir]*, p. 263, 2002

sexcapade *noun*
a sexual adventure *US*
A combination of 'sex' and 'escapade'.
- I have made private movies out of Justine and other eighteenth-century sexcapades. —Vladimir Nabakov, *Lolita*, p. 292, 1955
- [T]he whole county is privy to the sexcapades of the guy who left the college under the racist cloud[.] —Philip Roth, *The Human Stain*, p. 78, 2000

sex case *noun*
a sex offender *UK*
- — Angela Devlin, *Prison Patter*, p. 23, 1996

sex changer *noun*
a computer cable with either two male or two female connectors *US*
- — Eric S. Raymond, *The New Hacker's Dictionary*, p. 175, 1991

sex down *verb*
to make a thing less appealing *UK*
Derived as an antonym for **SEX UP**.
- Dossier 'sexed down', Campbell tells MPs. — *The Guardian*, 26th June 2003

sexed up *adjective*
sexually aroused *UK, 1942*
- [S]ix men straight from the Raymond Revue bar sexed up to the ears[.] — Nell Dunn, *Up the Junction*, p. 66, 1963

sexile *verb*
to force your roommate from your shared housing while you have sex *US*
- I've been sexiled. — forlorn Tufts student in Tish library, 12.15 am, February 9th (1997), *Nerve*, p. 14, May–June 2000

sex kitten *noun*
an especially attractive young woman who exploits her appeal *UK, 1958*
Coinage apparently inspired by film actress Brigitte Bardot (b.1933).
- — *American Speech*, October 1964
- [T]he sex kitten has turned into a mangy old alley cat, you wouldn't give her a second look. — Jenny Eclair, *Camberwell Beauty*, p. 38, 2000
- Now if you are no sex kitten/stud muffin yourself, just be honest with yourself[.] — Schwartz Pepper, *Everything You Know About Love and Sex is Wrong*, p. 69, 2001

sexo; sex-oh *noun*
1 a sex offender *NEW ZEALAND*
- Maybe he's only laying for me. Maybe he's a sex-oh. — Ronald Hugh Morrieson, *The Scarecrow*, p. 113, 1963

2 a person who is preoccupied with sex *NEW ZEALAND*
- Sefto, you old sexo! How the hell are you? — Gordon Slatter, *A Gun in My Hand*, p. 179, 1959

sexpert *noun*
an expert on sexual behaviour *US, 1924*
Mix 'sex' with an 'expert'.
- These "sexperts" erroneously assume that education will naturally produce sexual happiness. — Tim and Beverly Lahaye, *The Act of Marriage*, p. 73, 1998

sexploitation *noun*
the exploitation of sexual imagery for commercial gain *US*
A combination of 'sex' and 'exploitation'.
- MGM got wind that the sexploitation flick was doing okay on video. — Naomi Klein, *No Logo*, p. 79, 2001

sexpot *noun*
a sexually exciting woman *US, 1957*
- There they were, the sex pots, grown pottier, the once muscular football stars, now into insurance premiums[.] — Odie Hawkins, *Black Casanova*, p. 128, 1984
- [A]fter 1955's The Seven Year Itch she [Marilyn Monroe] wanted serious acting to replace her sexpot image, and went to New York's Actors Studio to work with director Lee Strasberg. — *The Guardian*, 1st June 2001

sexstasy; sextasy *noun*
MDMA, the recreational drug best known as ecstasy, taken with the erection enhancing drug Viagra™ *US*
- The British was 'sexstasy', a pill combining Viagra and Ecstasy, plus a range of super-Ecstasy and powerful Ecstasy-analogue pills[.] — *The Observer*, p. 26, 24th January 1999
- — *Detroit News*, p. 5D, 20th September 2002

sex tank *noun*
a holding cell reserved for homosexual prisoners *US*
- All lonesome tears and Humiliation, Miss Destiny ends up in the sex tank[.] — John Rechy, *City of Night*, p. 104, 1963

Sexton Blake; sexton *noun*
1 a fake; a forgery *UK*
Rhyming slang, formed on the name of a fictional detective who first appeared in 1893 and continued in print well into the 1960s. British artist Tom Keating, 1917–84, famously forged works attributed to Gainsborough, Degas, Boucher, Fragonard, Renoir and Modigliani; in 1976 he confessed to having painted 2000 Sexton Blakes.
- But there's hundreds of Sexton Blakes all over the place. Haven't you read about it in the local rag. — Anthony Masters, *Minder*, p. 126, 1984
- 97% of "genuine antiques" are forgeries, fakes, duff, dud, Sexton Blakes, sham, lookalikes, replicates, all meaning worthless. — Jonathan Gash, *The Ten Word Game*, p. 50, 2003

2 a cake *UK*
Rhyming slang, formed on the fictional detective. Considered obsolete by Julian Franklyn, *A Dictionary of Rhyming Slang*, 1960; however, Ray Puxley, *Cockney Rabbit*, 1992, records it as 'long established'.

3 a 'take' in television and films *UK*
Rhyming slang, formed on the fictional detective.
- — *Daily Telegraph*, 17th December 1972

sex up *verb*
to present a thing in a manner designed to make it more attractive and appealing *UK*
Recorded in 1984 as 'to render a manuscript (more) sexually exciting'.
- What about the allegations first made in this programme that the document in September was "sexed-up" to include that apparent proof of an imminent threat from Iraq that weapons could be used within 45 minutes? — *'Today', BBC Radio 4*, 5th June 2003
- [R]ather than make a simple catch at gully, Murali attempts to sex up the catch for the cameras. — *The Guardian*, 7th March 2003

sex wagon *noun*
a car that appeals to girls *US*
- — *American Speech*, p. 101, May 1954

sexy *adjective*
used to describe anything considered to be desirable, very interesting or influential *UK*
A figurative application of the sense as 'sexually attractive'.
- [T]he only reason for many companies being involved is "sheer fashion", or, in the popular marketing phrase of the moment, sponsorship is "sexy". — *Time Out*, 30th May 1980
- [Journalists] believe McKay [a public relations man] delivers the sexiest stories [about British Leyland] through selected newspapers and carefully-chosen journals. — *Sunday Times*, 18th October 1981
- [I]t shouldn't have been such a surprise that here he was again, encroaching on to managers' turf when it was sexy enough to take his fancy. — Kevin Sampson, *Powder*, p. 37, 1999

sey; sei; sa; say *adjective*
six *UK*
Polari, from Italian *sei*.
- [Y]ou might like to count to ten in Polari: una, duey, trey, quater, chicker, sey, setter, otto, nobber, dacha. — Michael Quinion, *World Wide Words*, 1996
- — Paul Baker, *Polari*, p. 188, 2002

sez *verb*
says *UK, 1844*
- [N]obody gives a shit what anybody sez to A.C. [Alice Cooper] least of all A.C. — Lester Bangs, *Psychotic Reactions and Carburetor Dung*, p. 35, 1970

sezz *noun*
▷ see: **SESS**

shack *noun*
1 a house that exudes wealth and invites burglary *US*
- — Hyman E. Goldin et al., *Dictionary of American Underworld Lingo*, p. 189, 1950

2 especially in Tasmania, and south and west Australia, a holiday house of any size or quality *AUSTRALIA*
- They'd been coming to the Port for ages; their shack was one of the first ones here. We called it a shack but it was bigger and better than our houses. — Phillip Gwynne, *Deadly Unna?*, p. 149, 1998

3 a room, apartment or house *US*
- — *American Speech*, p. 304, December 1955: 'Wayne University slang'

4 any room where a citizens' band radio set is housed *US*
- — Len Buckwalter, *CB Radio*, p. 66, 1976

5 a direct hit on the target by a bomb *US*
- A bulls-eye for an Air Force bomber is a "shack."—*Shreveport Journal*, p. 4B, 1st February 1991

6 a sexual episode *US*
- I heard about your shack with Matt last night.—Connie Eble (Editor), *UNC-CH Campus Slang*, p. 9, April 1995

7 a rear brakeman on a train *US*
- —Ramon Adams, *The Language of the Railroader*, p. 135, 1977

▷ **see:** CHIAC

shack *verb*

1 to live together as an unmarried couple *US, 1935*
Very often used in the variant 'shack up'.
- Who you been shacking with?—George Mandel, *Flee the Angry Strangers*, p. 40, 1952
- Next rite is shacking up with a chick.—Jim Schock, *Life is a Lousy Drag*, 1958
- But the houses had been split up into bed-sized one-room kitchenettes, renting for $25 weekly, at the disposal of frantic couples who wished to shack up for a season.—Chester Himes, *The Real Cool Killers*, p. 61, 1959
- But if I should find out that you and Ira are still shacking up – well, I don't know exactly what I'd do. Nothing out of a Noel Coward comedy, I promise you.—Max Shulman, *Anyone Got a Match?*, p. 179, 1964
- —*The Guild Dictionary of Homosexual Terms*, p. 41, 1965
- She don't go for shackin' up with everybody.—Piri Thomas, *Down These Mean Streets*, p. 164, 1967
- I was 22 years of age and shacking with a chick named Julie, I gave her one "joint" which she stashed and later turned over to the cops – a joint that netted me one of the 5-to-life sentences.—*The Berkeley Tribe*, p. 5, 5th-12th September 1969
- At that time he used stuff for a period of about eighteen months until he ran into some difficulty with a girl he was shacking up with[.] —Herbert Huncke, *The Evening Sun Turned Crimson*, p. 80, 1980
- Yeah, well the only woman of the Indian's we ran into was shacked up with her dyke girlfriend.—*48 Hours*, 1982
- Yeah, Alyssa, who've you been shacking up with?—*Chasing Amy*, 1997
- Now you're shacking up with your therapist!—*200 Cigarettes*, 1999
- His plan was to shack up with some fat girlfriend of his[.]—Lanre Fehintola, *Charlie Says...*, p. 160, 2000

2 to spend the night with someone, sex almost always included *US*
Not the ongoing relationship suggested by the older term SHACK UP.
- —Connie Eble (Editor), *UNC-CH Campus Slang*, p. 5, Fall 1996

shacker *noun*
a sexual partner who spends the night but does not live with you *US*
- —Connie Eble (Editor), *UNC-CH Campus Slang*, p. 9, October 2002

shack house *noun*
a brakevan (caboose) *US*
- —Ramon Adams, *The Language of the Railroader*, p. 136, 1977

shacking *noun*
a party or social gathering *US*
- —*American Speech*, p. 154, Spring-Summer 1972: 'An approach to black slang'

shack job *noun*
a person with whom you are living and enjoying sex without the burdens or blessings of marriage; the arrangement *US*
- —*American Speech*, p. 120, May 1960: 'Korean bamboo English'
- Poor as us, sometimes from mixed marriages and shack jobs.—Joseph Wambaugh, *The New Centurions*, p. 147, 1970

shack rat *noun*
a soldier who has taken up house with a woman *US*
- —*American Speech*, p. 5556, February 1947: 'Pacific War language'
- —John T. Algeo, *American Speech*, p. 120, May 1960: 'Korean bamboo English'

shack-up *noun*
a person with whom you are living and enjoying sex without the burdens or blessings of marriage *US*
- —*American Speech*, p. 120, May 1960: 'Korean bamboo English'

shack up *verb*

1 to take up residence, usually of a temporary nature *US, 1942*
- Besides, Lovis was handy to shack up with on the one night in ten when he felt like shacking up with somebody.—Bernard Wolfe, *The Late Risers*, p. 35, 1954
- I told him he could "shack up" with me for a couple of days so I took him home with me.—Babs Gonzales, *I Paid My Dues*, p. 52, 1967
- I'm better off shacking up at my mum's. She got plenty food, plenty love, plenty money.—Karline Smith, *Moss Side Massive*, p. 21, 1994

2 to provide living quarters for a lover *US*
- However, he might also shack her up or simply shack her.—*American Speech*, p. 120, May 1960: 'Korean bamboo English'

shaddup!
be quiet! *UK, 1959*
A slurring of SHUT UP!.
- Sit your be-hind down, little man, and shaddup!—Zane *Addicted*, 2003

shade *noun*

1 a black person *US, 1865*
Offensive.
- In no time at all Konky got on the ball / And had ten whorers – nine pinks and a shade.—Dennis Wepman et al., *The Life*, p. 103, 1976
- "I reckon this is down to the Brown Brothers, don't you, John." "Who?" "The Shades" I have noticed before that you have to be very current to keep up with young London coppers' slang.—John Milne, *Alive and Kicking*, p. 92, 1998

2 a suntan *US*
- —Anna Scotti and Paul Young, *Buzzwords*, p. 79, 1997

3 a legitimate business that acts as a cover for an illegal enterprise *US*
- Shade is a legal business front that keeps an illegal business out of the bright light of police scrutiny.—Burgess Laughlin, *Job Opportunities in the Black Market*, p. 13–2, 1978

4 detached superiority *US*
- —Kevin Dilallo, *The Unofficial Gay Manual*, p. 245, 1994

shade *verb*

1 to reduce something slightly and gradually *US*
- [H]e would always find a way to shade the odds in his favor.—Stephen J. Cannell, *King Con*, p. 35, 1997

2 to mark the backs of cards with a subtle shading of the existing colour *US*
- —John Scarne, *Scarne's Guide to Modern Poker*, p. 290, 1979

shades *noun*

1 sunglasses *US, 1958*
- —Edd Byrnes, *Way Out with Kookie*, 1959
- —*Swinging Syllables*, 1959
- —Frank A. Collymore, *Barbadian Dialect*, p. 100, 1965
- California, Labor Day weekend ... early, with ocean fog still in the streets, outlaw motorcyclists wearing chains, shades and greasy Levis roll out from damp garages[.]—Hunter S. Thompson, *Hell's Angels*, p. 3, 1966
- I had a minor eye infection and was wearing dark glasses in the bullpen and O'Brien said, "What's with the shades?"—Jim Bouton, *Ball Four*, p. 78, 1970
- He looked at the cap in the mirror, turning his head this way and that to check it out, and pulled the peak down a hair closer to his shades.—Elmore Leonard, *Be Cool*, p. 175, 1999

2 police *IRELAND*
- I reversed slowly and hoped the shades would reckon we had just taken a wrong turn.—Eamonn Sweeney, *Waiting for the Healer*, p. 144, 1997

shade spade *noun*
an Arab *US*
Offensive.
- It didn't matter if they called themselves Arabs, Iranians, Persians, (which was just another name for the goddam Iranians) Iraqis, Saudis, sand niggers, dune coons, shade spades or Kuwaitis. A rag head was a rag head. John hated the goddam camel jockeys.—Robert Crais, *Demolition Angel*, p. 237, 2000

shade-tree mechanic *noun*
an amateur car mechanic of dubious skill, questionable honour and the best of intentions *US*
- —Lewis Poteet, *Car & Motorcycle Slang*, p. 176, 1992
- With that very American combination of style and excess, shade-tree mechanics gave birth to the monster pickup.—Editors of Ben is Dead, *Retrohell*, p. 132, 1997
- Digger, our eccentric and brilliantly inventive shade-tree mechanic, joined the entourage with his step van and tools.—Peter Coyote, *Sleeping Where I Fall*, p. 136, 1998

shadie *noun*
a man, especially a young man, who spends his life on the edges of crime *US*
- [S]uch peripheral types as "street cats" and "shadies" are not members, though these groups frequently interact with those who truly belong to the Life.—Dennis Wepman et al., *The Life*, p. 2, 1976

shadow *noun*

1 a collector for an illegal money lender *US*
- —Hyman E. Goldin et al., *Dictionary of American Underworld Lingo*, p. 189, 1950

2 a truck that is not equipped with a citizens' band radio following one that is *US*
- — Wayne Floyd, *Jason's Authentic Dictionary of CB Slang*, p. 26, 1976

shadows *noun*
dark glasses *US*
- Dark eyeglasses are "shadows." — *Philadelphia Evening Bulletin*, 11th October 1955

shady *adjective*
1 giving an impression of dishonesty; disreputable; not quite honourable *UK, 1862*
- A slavish press connives to hide GW's shady side[.] It's not only his drink-driving arrest Bush has lied about. — *The Guardian*, 6th November 2000

2 detached, aloof *US*
- — Kevin Dilallo, *The Unofficial Gay Manual*, p. 245, 1994
- Look at the cunt now. Half shady with us, can't wait to get away. — Kevin Sampson, *Outlaws*, p. 138, 2001

shady lady *noun*
a prostitute *US*
- — *Complete CB Slang Dictionary*, p. 83, 1976
- — Status Quo, *Shady lady*, 1979
- The shady lady / from shady lane / is lying in my bed again[.] — Deep Purple, *A Touch Away*, 1996

shaft *noun*
1 the penis *UK, 1772*
- With one hand the artist guided his shaft into her welcoming gusset. — Stewart Home, *Sex Kick [britpulp]*, p. 219, 1999

2 an act of sexual intercourse; hence, a woman objectified sexually *UK, 1984*
From the verb.

3 poor treatment *US, 1959*
- Chilly smiled at the shaft. Red was the type of stud that just when you were sure he was a fool and a clown came up with something half sharp. — Malcolm Braly, *On the Yard*, p. 79, 1967
- "Oh ... you got the shaft?" "Well, we parted amiably enough." — Armistead Maupin, *Tales of the City*, p. 70, 1978
- She got the goldmine / I got the shaft — Jerry Reed, *She Got the Goldmine*, 1982

4 a crankshaft *US*
Hot rodder usage.
- — *Hot Rod Magazine*, p. 13, November 1948: 'Racing jargon'

5 the leg *US*
- — Clarence Major, *Dictionary of Afro-American Slang*, p. 102, 1970

shaft *verb*
1 from a male perspective, to have sex *UK*
After **SHAFT** (the penis).
- Cor, shaft me! — Colin Evans, *The Heart of Standing*, 1962
- Only thing stopping me shafting her she reckoned was I was too midgy [small]. — Jeremy Cameron, *Brown Bread in Wengen*, p. 33, 1999

2 to mistreat or abuse *US, 1959*
- Whoever coined the word shafted had me in mind. — Mickey Spillane, *Me, Hood!*, p. 49, 1963
- After all, he intended to shaft Folks for four times the fair market value of his white elephant parcel of land. — *Long White Con*, p. 54, 1977
- I'd rather be upfront about shafting somebody. — *Body Heat*, 1980
- We should try and shaft the Mayor, Lads. Why don't we photograph him in bed in his wildlife snake pants? — Paul Fraser and Shane Meadows, *TwentyFourSeven*, p. 83, 1997
- Know thine enemy, and double know thine employee – for he will shaft you. — Kevin Sampson, *Clubland*, p. 20, 2002

shaft artist *noun*
a person who is prone to cheat or behave unfairly *US*
- — *Maledicta*, p. 14, Summer 1977: 'A word for it!'

shafted *adjective*
in deep trouble; in such deep trouble that your previous position is unrecoverable *UK*
Synonymous with **FUCKED**.
- You would be totally shafted if you shot some old darkie and there was no evidence[.] — Donald Gorgon, *Cop Killer*, p. 8, 1994

shafter *noun*
a single ox in an ox-pull contest or for work *CANADA*
- A "shafter" is a single ox, originally used in Nova Scotia for work but more recently in exhibition ox-pull contests. — *The Ox in Nova Scotia: an exhibition of the desBrisay Museum*, 1985

shafting *noun*
trouble; unfair treatment *UK*
- [W]e owe 'em a shaftin'. After what they done at the races. — Guy Ritchie et al., *Lock, Stock... & Four Stolen Hooves*, p. 61, 2000

shaftsman *noun*
a person who is prone to cheat or behave unfairly *US*
- — *Maledicta*, p. 14, Summer 1977: 'A word for it!'

shafty *adjective*
(used of a thing) fashionable, popular *US*
- A Cadillac convertible is real cool or even shafty, and its driver, particularly if he be cat, or well-dressed, is cool Jonah. — *Newsweek*, p. 28, 8th October 1951

shag *noun*
1 an act of sexual intercourse *UK*
- Take me to a place where the drugs are free, the clubs have no gravity and every shag guarantees an orgasm! — Justin Kerrigan, *Human Traffic*, 1999
- You had a better chance of getting a shag cos the club shut at two[.] — Dave Courtney, *Raving Lunacy*, p. 7, 2000

2 a sexual partner *UK, 1788*
- Yeh yeh, I know how cool I am ... great shag, yeh ... best ever, aye ... I know all that. — Niall Griffiths, *Sheepshagger*, p. 193, 2002

3 a friend *NEW ZEALAND*
- — Louis S. Leland, *A Personal Kiwi-Yankee Dictionary*, p. 90, 1984

4 in trucking, a small trailer used for city driving *US*
- — Montie Tak, *Truck Talk*, p. 139, 1971

▸ **like a shag on a rock**
all alone *AUSTRALIA, 1845*
- They felt I might be lonely, 'perched like a shag on a rock', as they said. — Kylie Tennant, *The Honey Flow*, p. 85, 1956
- 'How did the bike trick work?' 'Great,' said Snow. 'Left him like a shag on a rock.' — Peter Corris, *Pokerface*, p. 115, 1985

shag *verb*
1 to have sex *UK, 1788*
Possibly from obsolete 'shag' (to shake); usage is not gender-specific.
- All you've done is shag your twat, and that ain't nothin'. — *Drugstore Cowboy*, 1988
- [H]e wants to shag you up the arse. — Danny King, *The Burglar Diaries*, p. 166, 2001
- And yet it features three men who, on first impressions, seem more at home browsing around garden centres than snorting, shagging and shooting up. — *Uncut*, p. 44, May 2001

2 to leave *US*
- "Shag, man," she said roughly, "I mean , split – Barbara don't need you guys any more[.]" — John Rechy, *City of Night*, p. 158, 1963
- He was a fag, and so I had to shag. — Dennis Wepman et al., *The Life*, p. 48, 1976
- Same's all them other suckers shaggin off to school ever goddamn mornin. — Jess Mowry, *Way Past Cool*, p. 32, 1992

3 to run someone down; to arrest someone *US*
- I'll bet no other uniformed cop ever takes the trouble to shag him after I'm gone. — Joseph Wambaugh, *The Blue Knight*, p. 48, 1973
- I'm getting the salary of a deputy sheriff to sit here at this computer rather than shagging prisoners[.] — Gerald Petievich, *To Die in Beverly Hills*, p. 111, 1983
- "You gave the kid a five?" Nell asked. "What the hell. I shagged cards more than once. Besides, if I tipped him a buck, I might never see my car again." — Robert Campbell, *Alice in La-La Land*, p. 146, 1987

▸ **shag ass**
to leave *US*
- — *American Speech*, p. 235, October 1964: 'Student slang in Hays, Kansas'
- — Collin Baker et al., *College Undergraduate Slang Study Conducted at Brown University*, p. 192, 1968
- — Helen Dahlskog (Editor), *A Dictionary of Contemporary and Colloquial Usage*, p. 52, 1972

▸ **shag senseless**
to have sex to the point of exhaustion *UK*
Generally used as a boast.
- [H]e will fuck the arse off her tonight, he thinks, he will shag her senseless, screw her daft[.] — Niall Griffiths, *Grits*, p. 53, 2000

shagadelic *adjective*
exciting; great *US*
Combining two clichés of 'swinging sixties London' (from a Hollywood perspective): **SHAG** (to have sex) and 'psychedelic' (of mind-expanding drugs). Usage has added sexual overtones to this

comic coinage which appears just once in the film *Austin Powers, The Spy Who Shagged Me*: 'New case? Very shagadelic, Basil!' (Mike Myers, 1998).

- You've got sexy tits. – Horny, baby, horny. – Shagadelic. Ruby laughed at small boys and words they didn't know the meaning of[.] —John King, *White Trash*, p. 94, 1998

shaganappi *adjective*
worthless *CANADA*

- Thinka anybody having a shaganappi thing like that in their house! —W.O. Mitchell, *Jake and the Kid*, p. 107, 1961

shagbox *noun*
the vagina *UK*

- Women's genitalia were represented as (potential) containers (e.g., bucket, box, hair goblet), places to put things in (e.g., furry letterbox, disk drive, socket, slot), containers for semen (e.g., gism pot, spunk bin, honey pot), and containers for the penis/sex (e.g., willy warmer, wank shaft, shagbox). —*Journal of Sex Research*, p. 146, 2001

shagbucket *noun*
a worthless or despicable person *UK*
Related to obsolete synonym 'shag-bag'.

- DAVE (HEARTFELT): You shag-bucket. —*The Full Monty*, 1997

shagged; shagged out *adjective*
exhausted *UK, 1932*
From **SHAG** (to have sex); compares with **FUCKED** (exhausted).

- Jesus, I'm shagged. —Colin Butts, *Is Harry on the Boat?*, p. 55, 1997
- The horses looked shagged. All of them were drenched with sweat, and steaming. —Dave Courtney, *Stop the Ride I Want to Get Off*, p. 311, 1999

shagger *noun*
a person, especially a male, who has sex *UK*

- [T]elling all hands what you've been up to and what a tidy shagger you are[.] —Kevin Sampson, *Clubland*, p. 81, 2002

shagger's back *noun*
any backache, whether or not produced by over-exertion in sex *AUSTRALIA*

- —James McDonald, *A Dictionary of Obscenity, Taboo and Euphemism*, p. 132, 1988

shagging *adjective*
used as an intensifier *UK*
A direct replacement of **FUCKING**.

- [S]ome horrible old licence-built BAC111 they bought off shagging Ceaucescu[.] —James Hawes, *Dead Long Enough*, p. 72, 2000

-shagging- *infix*
used as an intensifier *UK*

- We might as well be Bela-shaggin'-rus or Iceland or whatever. —Ben Elton, *High Society*, p. 42, 2002
- "Everything alright?" "Tickety-shagging-boo." —*Ultimate Force*, 23rd July 2003

shagging Nora!
used as a register of surprise, anger, amazement, etc *UK*

- Shaggin' nora, listen to that lot. —Trevor Griffiths, *Oi For England*, p. 17, 1982

shagging pad *noun*
a room kept for sexual encounters *AUSTRALIA*

- I even had a Catholic prelate who convinced three generations of choir boys that semen was good for the vocal chords, in between lightning raids on the cathedral poor box to make payments on his Gold Coast shagging pad. —Harrison Biscuit, *The Search for Savage Henry*, p. 6, 1995

shagging room *noun*
in a brothel, a room or cubicle set aside for the business of sex *UK*

- The punter'd take his pick an' up we'd go tae the shaggin' rooms. —Ben Elton, *High Society*, p. 167, 2002

shag-happy *adjective*
obssessed with sex *AUSTRALIA*

- Alongside the Mellor fiasco, Conservative smoothie Cecil Parkinson's own indiscretions seem a bit tame – but they were still enough to see him joining the queue at the dole office with his shag-happy mates. —*People*, p. 7, 30th March 1994

shag me!
used for expressing surprise *NEW ZEALAND*

- —David McGill, *David McGill's Complete Kiwi Slang Dictionary*, p. 98, 1998

shag-merchant *noun*
a man who is only interested in having sex (and not a relationship) *UK*

- Tim Culver was not just a shag-merchant like the rest of them. He might fuck a different girl from one Saturday to the next, but he prided himself on knowing a bit about what he was doing. —Stella Duffy, *Martha Grace [Tart Noir]*, p. 277, 2002

shag-nasty *noun*
an unpopular person *UK, 1961*

shag pad *noun*
a premises used for sexual liaisons *UK*

- They tended to be in mansion blocks that had been divided into self-contained flats, the sort business people used as pieds-a-terre while they were working in London during the week, or as shag pads before going home to their families in the Cotswolds[.] —Andy McNab, *Dark Winter*, p. 103, 2003

shag-rag *noun*
a tabloid newspaper that relies on sexual content for a healthy circulation *UK*
Combines **SHAG** (the sex act) with **RAG** (a newspaper).

- Maybe it was a slow day on the shag-rags. —Christopher Brookmyre, *Boiling a Frog*, p. 198, 2000

shagspot *noun*
a pimple (to which adolescents are prey); hence, also used as a nickname (not necessarily for the afflicted) *UK*

- Excuse me, do you mind not leaving your shag spots in here. —David Sherwin, *If*, 1968
- Feck off ya feckin' owld shagspot, Oy says. —Roger Boylan, *The Great Pint-Pulling Olympiad*, p. 20, 2003

shagtastic *adjective*
wonderful, especially in a sexual context *UK*

- [T]his groovily shagtastic, genuinely groundbreaking show. —*Daily Telegraph*, 26th August 2002

shag wagon; shaggin wagon; shaggin'-wagon *noun*
a panel van, station wagon or the like used for sexual encounters *AUSTRALIA, 1966*

- We went round to pick up his reclaimed Ford, The old shag-wagon[.] —Bruce Dawe, *At Shagger's Funeral*, 1968
- Didja see Hustler posing off in his shag wagon this morning? —Simon French, *Hey Phantom Singlet*, p. 56, 1975
- MICHAEL: 'What other minorities can we discriminate against?' LUKE: 'Let me think! Kooks, doctors..tall people, thieves, esky lids, goat boats, shaggin wagon owners, ex-girl-friends... —*Tracks*, p. 31, 1992
- [It is] the ideal beach-excursion car, if you can handle the 'shaggin'-wagon' jokes. —Dirk Flinthart, *Brotherly Love*, p. 29, 1995
- —David McGill, *David McGill's Complete Kiwi Slang Dictionary*, p. 112, 1998

shag-worthy *adjective*
sexually attractive; sexy *AUSTRALIA*

- But most shag-worthy sheilas kid themselves they need a few romantic preliminaries[.] —Barry Humphries, *The Traveller's Tool*, p. 78, 1985

shaka *adjective*
excellent *US*
Hawaiian youth usage.

- Dat was some shaka weed, brah! —Douglas Simonson, *Pidgin to da Max*, 1981

shaka
used in conjunction with a hand signal emphasising the little finger and thumb, signifying fraternity or a greeting *US*
Hawaiian youth usage.

- —Douglas Simonson, *Pidgin to da Max*, 1981

shake *noun*
1 a moment, an instant of time *UK*
Most often used in all manner of elaborations: 'in a shake' (C19), 'in the shake of a hand' (C19, probably obsolete), 'in a brace of shakes' (mid-C19), 'in a couple of shakes' (mid-C19), 'in two shakes' (late C19); later C20 variations are more whimsical: 'in the shake of a lamb's tail', 'in the shake of a dead lamb's tail', 'in two shakes of a lamb's whiff-whoff' (mid-C20), 'two shakes of a donkey's tail' and 'two shakes of a monkey's tail'.

- Wait just a shake, honey; what are these two little red capsules in here with my vitamin? —Ken Kesey, *One Flew Over the Cuckoo's Nest*, p. 32, 1962
- Give us a couple of shakes to get our breath. —*A Hard Day's Night*, 1964

2 marijuana, especially the resinous matter that is shaken to the bottom during transit or what remains after the buds have been removed *US, 1978*
- A spokesman who identified himself as a "former user," said that "shake," the fine, powdery remants of marijuana processing, costs about $75 per ounce. — *Chicago Tribune*, p. C1, 13th August 1985
- Once stoned on the low-grade green shake, it seemed much safer to stay home. — Sean Hutchinson, *Crying Out Loud*, p. 25, 1988
- — Mike Haskins, *Drugs*, p. 289, 2003
- On a tip, police searched Williamson's Gaston home in August, 2002, and found 13 marijuana plants, 11 gallon-sized bags of marijuana shake and some seeds. — *The Oregonian*, p. C1, 12th September 2003

3 any adulterant added to cocaine powder *US*
- [M]ost suppliers will allow up to 120 grams of shake to a kilo, or 12 percent; kilo-level buyers are usually unhappy if they find more. — Terry Williams, *The Cocaine Kids*, p. 35, 1989

4 a party; a rent party *US, 1946*

5 a blunt demand for money supported by the threat of physical force *US*
A shortened form of **SHAKEDOWN**.
- He was a heavy-set, round-faced, deceptively soft-looking young man who specialized in strong-armn routines and "shakes." — William Burroughs, *Junkie*, p. 58, 1953

▷ **see:** SHAKE AND SHIVER

shake *verb*

1 to search a person's clothing and body *US*
- I told him, "You don't search me. A matron shakes me, but not you." — Bruce Jackson, *In the Life*, p. 84, 1972

2 to get rid of someone or something *US, 1872*
- Nicky couldn't even go for a ride without changing cars at least six times before he could shake all his tails. — *Casino*, 1995

▸ **shake a leg**
to hurry, to get a move on *US, 1904*
Extends from the sense 'to dance'; generally used in the imperative.
- I told you to get those leaves swept up! Shake a leg, pronto! — Ian Pattison, *Rab C. Nesbitt*, 1988

▸ **shake hands**
(of a male) to urinate *AUSTRALIA*
The indirect object has been euphemistically omitted.
- He's not here. Musta gone outside to shake hands. — John Wynnum, *Tar Dust*, p. 37, 1962

▸ **shake hands with an old friend**
1 used by a male as a jocular euphemism when excusing himself to go and urinate *US*
- — Michael Dalton Johnson, *Talking Trash with Redd Foxx*, p. 43, 1994

2 (of a male) to masturbate *UK, 1984*
After the previous sense.

▸ **shake hands with him**
1 (of a male) to urinate *UK, 1984*
An allusion to the penis.

2 (of a male) to masturbate *UK*

▸ **shake hands with Mr Right**
(of a male) to urinate *UK, 1960*
Mr Right is what every woman is searching for, hence this humorous reference to the penis.

▸ **shake hands with my friend**
(of a male) to urinate *UK*
A humorous allusion to the penis; a variation of **SHAKE HANDS WITH AN OLD FRIEND**.
- [P]oint Percy at the Porcelain [to urinate], Shake Hands with My Friend, Exercise The One-Eyed Trouser Snake. Shaking, I hold my terrified dick and try to pass water. — Stuart Browne, *Dangerous Parking*, p. 280, 2000

▸ **shake hands with the Devil**
(of either sex) to masturbate *US*
- — Xaviera Hollander, *The Best Part of a Man*, 1975

▸ **shake hands with the unemployed**
(of a male) to urinate *AUSTRALIA*
The notion behind 'unemployed' is a wry admission that the man in question has not been getting any sex of late.
- [J]ust shooting through [going] to the Gents to shake hands with the unemployed! — Barry Humphries, *Bazza Pulls It Off!*, 1971
- I think I'd better whip out to the utensil and shake hands with the unemployed. — *The Adventures of Barry McKenzie*, 1972
- Billy flung himself up from the table and announced that he was off to shake hands with the unemployed. — Kathy Lette, *Girls' Night Out*, p. 174, 1987

▸ **shake hands with the wife's best friend**
(of a male) to urinate; to masturbate *AUSTRALIA*
- When we get inside order a couple of schooners while I shake hands with the wife's best friend! — Barry Humphries, *The Wonderful World of Barry McKenzie*, p. 28, 1968
- — Barry Humphrie, *The Traveller's Tool*, p. 60, 1985

▸ **shake leg**
to idle *SINGAPORE*
- — Paik Choo, *The Coxford Singlish Dictionary*, p. 95, 2002

▸ **shake the bushes; shake the leaves; shake the trees**
to look for the police, especially so as to warn other drivers *US*
Citizens' band radio slang.
- — *Complete CB Slang Dictionary*, p. 83, 1976
- — Peter Chippindale, *The British CB Book*, p. 159, 1981

▸ **shake the leaves**
in a group of trucks travelling down the motorway together, to drive in the lead position, risking first contact with police watching for speeders *US*
- — Wayne Floyd, *Jason's Authentic Dictionary of CB Slang*, p. 27, 1976

▸ **shake the trees**
to drive in the lead position in a group of trucks travelling on a motorway together in a group effort to avoid speeding tickets while driving fast *US*
- — *Complete CB Slang Dictionary*, p. 11, 1976

▸ **shake them up**
on the railways, to switch wagons or trains *US*
- — Norman Carlisle, *The Modern Wonder Book of Trains and Railroading*, p. 267, 1946

▸ **shake white coconuts from the veiny love tree**
(of a male) to masturbate *UK, 2001*
Coinage credited to surreal BBC comedy *The League of Gentlemen*.

▸ **shake your booty**
to dance in a lively manner *US*
Literally, 'to shake your buttocks'.
- — KC & The Sunshine Band *(Shake, Shake, Shake) Shake Your Booty*, 1978
- Rap, hip-hop... what's the first thing you think of? Great tunes to shake your booty to, but then what? — *The Times Magazine*, p. 43, 16th February 2002

▸ **shake your skirt**
(of a woman) to go dancing *US*
- — Pamela Munro, *U.C.L.A. Slang*, p. 74, 1989

shake and bake *noun*

1 a non-commissioned officer fresh out of training *US*
- The sergeant in charge of rear security was a "shake 'n' bake," like all the squad leaders in the platoon. — Shelby L. Stanton, *The Rise and Fall of an American Army*, p. 314, 1985
- Sergeants who came from the NCO school were also known as "shake-and-bakes," after a television commercial for a product that promised something equally, improbably instantaneous, like fried chicken from the oven. — Lucian K. Truscott, *Army Blue*, p. 22, 1989
- Little did he know there were worse such monikers – within the Army the instant noncoms quickly and forever became known as "shake and bakes." — David H. Hackworth, *About Face*, p. 594, 1989

2 a portable fire shelter used by workers fighting forest fires *US*
- — *American Speech*, p. 205–209, Summer 1991: 'The language of smokejumping – again'

shake and shiver; shake *noun*
a river *UK*
- — Julian Franklyn, *A Dictionary of Rhyming Slang*, 1960
- messing about on the shake — Ray Puxley, *Cockney Rabbit*, 1992

shakedown *noun*

1 a search of a person or place *US, 1914*
- — Paul Glover, *Words from the House of the Dead: Prison Writings from Soledad*, 1974
- That's it? I say, expecting more of a shakedown at this hour. — Ian Caldwell and Dustin Thomason, *The Rule of Four*, p. 167, 2004

2 an act of extortion *US, 1902*
- The "security officer" (refined designation for a house dick) of one of the oldest and most famous hotels in Washington, near the White House, was recently fired because he ran a shakedown racket[.] — Jack Lait and Lee Mortimer, *Washington Confidential*, p. 285–286, 1951

shake down *verb*

1 to search a person or a place *US, 1915*

- People with beards are shaken down thoroughly. —Hunter S Thompson, *Hell's Angels*, p. 210, 1967

2 to extort *US, 1872*

- What's changed? You're still trying to shake me down. —Elmore Leonard, *Glitz*, p. 291, 1985
- He doesn't know if this guy is shaking you down or taking advantage of you. —*Casino*, 1995

shake 'n vac *noun*

an act of male masturbation, especially when performed by one sexual partner upon another *UK*

Shake 'n' Vac™ is a household cleaning product that achieved cult status as the result of a 1970s television commercial. During the all-singing and dancing demonstration, 'Do the Shake 'n' Vac / and put the freshness back' an attractive actress shook the tube-shaped packaging and white powder was scattered – the perfect metaphor.

- Adultery meanz shaggin someone elses bitch. Hobviously it don't refer to receivin a blowie or shake 'n vac. —Sacha Baron-Cohen *Da Gospel According to Ali G*, 2001

shakers *noun*

a bar featuring topless dancers *US*

- —Judi Sanders, *Mashing and Munching in Ames*, p. 17, 1994

shaker wire *noun*

a motion detector system used for perimeter security in prisons *US*

- As soon as they're out you know they're gonna be spotted – the hack in tower seven, or they touch the fence, the shaker wire sets off the alarm[.] —Elmore Leonard, *Out of Sight*, p. 111, 1996

shakes *noun*

any disease or condition characterised by trembling, especially *delirium tremens* *UK, 1782*

- Practically all the men with me were white, either lushheads or junkies, and this morning they all had the shakes and rattles real bad[.] —Mezz Mezzrow, *Really the Blues*, p. 304, 1946
- Most of them were shaving, some had the "shakes" so that it was quite a job, and so as not to cut themselves or face the agony too often, they only shaved when they were on their way uptown to hustle a dime. —Neal Cassady, *The First Third*, p. 54, 1971

shake-up *noun*

a mixture of wine and corn whisky *US*

- —Kenn "Naz" Young, *Naz's Underground Dictionary*, p. 56, 1973

Shakey Isles *nickname*

New Zealand *AUSTRALIA, 1933*

Noted for its earthquakes.

shake your shirt!

hurry up! *NEW ZEALAND*

- —Sonya Plowman, *Great Kiwi Slang*, p. 160, 2002

shakey side *noun*

the west coast of the US, especially California *US*

A term popularised during the citizens' band radio craze of 1976, recognised by many but used by few. A reference to the seismic instability of the west coast.

- —Wayne Floyd, *Jason's Authentic Dictionary of CB Slang*, p. 46, 1976

Shakies *noun*

New Zealand *AUSTRALIA*

From the sobriquet 'the shakey isles'.

- —Ned Wallish, *The Truth Dictionary of Racing Slang*, p. 73, 1989

Shaky *noun*

a Chevrolet car *US*

- —John Lawlor, *How to Talk Car*, p. 92, 1965

shaky jake *nickname*

the Jacobs radial engine, powering Canadian-built variants of the Anson, a training and liaison aircraft *CANADA*

- The Jacobs engine earned a reputation for rough running, therefore the nickname Shaky Jake. —Tom Langeste, *Words on the Wing*, p. 246, 1995

sham *noun*

a streetwise young male; a friend; an untrustworthy individual *IRELAND*

- It's the fly shams I'm talking about. You have to keep watching them all the time. —Murphy Tom, *A Whistle in the Dark*, p. 12, 1989
- The True Tuam Sham talks out of the Left Hand Side of the mouth, with the lower lip rounded in pear-like fashion, with the majority opening to the left. All movements of the lips must be strictly confined to the Left Side. —*Great Tuam Annual "The True Tuam Sham"*, p. 5, 1991
- I'm not killing myself to get you a drink. Don't worry, son, I'm not dying for one. Yet. Drawl. -Pint of Guinness, sham. —Eamonn Sweeney, *Waiting for the Healer*, p. 34, 1997

sham *verb*

during the Vietnam war, to fabricate an injury or aggravate a real injury in the hope of being sent home *US*

- —Linda Reinberg, *In the Field*, p. 197, 1991

sham-battle *verb*

to engage in youth gang warfare *US*

- I ain't club-fighting no more. I ain't sham-battling or nothing else. I'm out. —Hal Ellson, *Duke*, p. 144, 1949

shambolic *adjective*

disordered, chaotic *UK, 1958*

From 'shambles'.

- The testimony of witnesses to an event is notoriously shambolic, especially on its immediate heels. —Lionel Shriver, *We Need to Talk About Kevin*, p. 269, 2003

sham dunk *noun*

in poker, a poor hand that wins a pot as a result of successful bluffing *US*

- —John Vorhaus, *The Big Book of Poker Slang*, p. 32, 1996

shame-face *adjective*

shy *CAYMAN ISLANDS*

- —Aarona Booker Kohlman, *Wotcha Say*, p. 25, 1985

shameful!

used as a humorous admission that you have been cleverly ridiculed *US*

- —*American Speech*, p. 275, December 1963: 'American Indian student slang'

shame out *verb*

to ridicule vociferously *US*

- —*American Speech*, p. 273, December 1963: 'American Indian student slang'

shameration *noun*

the epitome of shame *US*

- —*American Speech*, p. 275, December 1963: 'American Indian student slang'

shammer *noun*

a soldier who prolongs a legitimate absence from the frontline to avoid combat *US*

- The military's own estimate was that, for example, over Christmas in sixty-eight, there were four thousand shammers out of fifteen thousand men in a single division. —Malcolm Boyd, *My Fellow Americans*, p. 210, 1970

shampoo *noun*

1 champagne *UK, 1957*

A soundalike pun.

- [A] glass or two of shampoo before it was off in the chariot up to a grown-ups club in the West End. —Garry Bushell, *The Face*, p. 82, 2001

2 a scene in a pornographic film or photograph depicting a man ejaculating onto a person's hair *US*

- —*Adult Video News*, p. 51, October 1995

shamrock *noun*

MDMA, the recreational drug best known as ecstasy *UK*

- Street names [...] rhubarb and custard, shamrocks, white doves, X[.] —James Kay and Julian Cohen, *The Parents' Complete Guide to Young People and Drugs*, p. 136, 1998
- —Gareth Thomas, *This Is Ecstasy*, p. 57, 2002

shamshes *noun*

good-looking men *UK*

Possibly back slang from 'smashers'.

- Met 2 marines – very charming. Bonar Shamshes. —*Kenneth Williams' Diary*, 24th October 1947

shamus *noun*

a police detective; a private detective *US, 1925*

- What are you afraid of, this dirty two-bit shamus? —Mickey Spillane, *I, The Jury*, p. 20, 1947
- You'll get paid, shamus – if you do a job. —Raymond Chandler, *Playback*, p. 12, 1958

- I want to know so I can call up the shamuses, I want to know so I can blacklist you to the grave. —Clancy Sigal, *Going Away*, p. 265, 1961
- Hey, relax man, I'm a brother shamus. — *The Big Lebowski*, 1998

shanghai *noun*

1 a sudden and unexpected transfer of a prisoner to another facility as a form of punishment *AUSTRALIA, 1977*
- He stood in front of Norton. 'No reprisals, no shanghais, right?' —Bob Jewson, *Stir*, p. 85, 1980

2 a handheld catapult *AUSTRALIA, 1863*
Probably from northern British dialect *shangie*, a variant of *shangan*, from Scottish Gaelic *seangan*: 'a cleft stick for putting on a dog's tail'.
- Man, she's as big as a thundercloud and tossing mountains at us like a nasty little boy with pellets in a finger shanghai. —Dominic Healy, *A Voyage to Venus*, p. 83, 1943
- —Patsy Adam-Smith, *Folklore of the Australian Railwaymen*, p. 225, 1969
- The shanghai was a masterpiece of childhood engineering. The Y-shaped frame was made of clothes-hanger wire reinforced with rubber bands. It had a leather launching-pad and the elasticised armoury was made of bicycle inner tubing linked to form a chain. —Kerry Cue, *Crooks, Chooks and Bloody Ratbags*, p. 114, 1983

shanghai *verb*

1 to abduct someone; to compel someone to do something *US, 1934*
From military usage, 'to transfer forcibly'.
- [T]he shanghai-ing of delegates in cars disguised as cabs[.] —Richard Neville, *Play Power*, p. 54, 1970

2 to transfer a prisoner without warning *AUSTRALIA, 1980*
- —Angela Devlin, *Prison Patter*, p. 102, 1996
- With this in mind I had no doubt that Denning would be expecting to be 'shanghaied' and have his cell sorted out and his gear packed ready to be lifted. —William Dodson, *The Sharp End*, p. xiii, 2001

3 to detail someone to a task; to enlist someone to do something that they are not entirely willing to do *US, 1915*
From US nautical slang describing a method of recruiting sailors consisting of drugs and force.
- Meanwhile, her new boyfriend's out of town, so she's shanghaied yet another guy into her bed – a facistic cop. —C.D. Payne, *Youth in Revolt*, p. 126, 1993

Shania Twain; shania *noun*

a pain *UK*
Rhyming slang, formed from the name of the popular Canadian singer (b.1965).
- — Susie Dent, *The Language Report*, p. 98, 2003
- That could be a right Shania, believe me. —Mervyn Stutter, *Getting Nowhere Fast*, 21st May 2004

shank *noun*

a homemade knife or stabbing and slashing weapon *US*
- Picao, who I dug as no heart, squawked out, "Sticks, shanks, zips – you call it." —Piri Thomas, *Down These Mean Streets*, p. 52, 1967
- I better show you how to make a shank. I could use a spoon. The easiest kind of weapon to make, you how the end of a toothbrush and stick a razor blade in it. —Elmore Leonard, *Maximum Bob*, p. 108, 1991

shank *verb*

to stab someone – especially with a homemade weapon *US, 1955*
- E-magine that cat shanking me like that. —Piri Thomas, *Down These Mean Streets*, p. 114, 1967
- If you send me back there it's the death sentence. I'll get shanked in a week. —Gerald Petievich, *The Quality of the Informant*, p. 35, 1985

shanks's pony *noun*

walking, as a mode of transport *UK, 1898*
Ultimately from 'shank' (the leg).
- Looks like it's shank's pony the rest of the way up the hill, Lois. —Stephen King, *Insomnia*, p. 463, 1994

shant *noun*

a drink; a drinking session *UK*
- "You having a shant later?" We agree to meet at the bar afterwards and get lashed up. — Martin King and Martin Knight, *The Naughty Nineties*, p. 27, 1999

shant *verb*

to drink heavily *UK: SCOTLAND*
- Saturday was the day of rest, especially when you'd been seriously shanting on the Friday night before. —Christopher Brookmyre, *The Sacred Art of Stealing*, p. 69, 2002

shantoozy *noun*

a female singer *UK*
A corruption of *chanteuse*.
- [Britney Spears] the blonde shantoozy from Louisiana— *The Times Magazine*, p. 78, 23rd March 2002

shanty *noun*

1 a brakevan (caboose) *US*
- —Ramon Adams, *The Language of the Railroader*, p. 136, 1977

2 in poker, a hand consisting of three cards of the same rank and a pair *US*
Conventionally known as a 'full house'.
- —George Percy, *The Language of Poker*, p. 80, 1988

shanty Irish *noun*

poor Irish immigrants *US*
- She called everyone shanty Irish or nigger rich. —Gilbert Sorrentino, *Steelwork*, p. 101, 1970
- "Fucking shanty irish sot!" he called toward the bathroom[.] —Vincent Patrick, *The Pope of Greenwich Village*, p. 198, 1979

shantyman's smallpox *noun*

marks from hard physical fighting *CANADA*
- Feet rather than fists were the principal weapons and many a riverman, beaten down in the onset, carried on his face and chest for the rest of his life the scars of "shantyman's smallpox" – the pits and punctures of caulks and cleats. —G. R. Stevens, *The Incompleat Canadian*, p. 38, 1965

shape *noun*

1 a person of unconventional physical appearance *UK: SCOTLAND*
Disparaging.
- Nice lookin, him? He's a wee shape! —Michael Munro, *The Original Patter*, p. 61, 1985

2 a surfboard *AUSTRALIA*
- Pick up your "shape" – that's just another name for a board. —Jack Pollard, *The Australian Surfrider*, p. 19–20, 1963

shape *verb*

1 to improve your behaviour or attitude *UK*
- ALF: I'll have to be shaping. She wouldn't like it if she knew I was here. —John O'Toole, *The Bush and the Tree [Six Granada Plays]*, p. 31, 1960

2 to adopt a fighting stance; to prepare to fight *UK, 1855*
- Me shaping up in 1976. —Jimmy Stockin, *On The Cobbles*, p. picture caption, 2000

shapes *noun*

dice altered by cheats so as to be not true cubes *US*
- —*The Annals of the American Academy of Political and Social Sciences*, p. 130, May 1950
- —Frank Garcia, *Marked Cards and Loaded Dice*, p. 263, 1962
- —Thomas L. Clark, *The Dictionary of Gambling and Gaming*, p. 195, 1987

shape up or ship out!

used as a last warning to someone whose ways need mending *US, 1956*
- You're right, Michael! These folks need to shape up or ship out. —Michael Graham, *Redneck Nation*, p. 95, 2002

shareware *noun*

computer software that is freely available but for which the developer asks a payment *US*
- A $99 CD ROM with more than 3,000 PC-compatible shareware programs has been announced by Alde Publishing. — *InfoWorld*, p. 20, 18th January 1988

shark *noun*

1 an unscrupulous businessman or lawyer given to unethical practice and exploitation *UK, 1713*
Derives from the voracious appetites and predatory behaviour of the fish.
- We need a total shark for a manager[.] —Stewart Home, *Sex Kick [britpulp]*, p. 216, 1999

2 a loan shark *US*
- And then I'd either blow the winnings in a week or go to the sharks to pay back the bookies. — *Goodfellas*, 1990

3 a swindler *UK, 1599*
The variant 'sharkie' also exists.
- One sharkie put up a huge canvas tent and had some little dolly singing inside. —Jamie Mandelkau quoting Ken Kesey, *Buttons*, p. 147, 1971

shark *verb*
in a dice game such as craps, to make a controlled (cheating) throw of the dice *US, 1950*
- —Thomas L. Clark, *The Dictionary of Gambling and Gaming*, p. 195, 1987

shark and tatties *noun*
fish and chips *NEW ZEALAND*
- —Louis S. Leland, *A Personal Kiwi-Yankee Dictionary*, p. 90, 1984

shark bait *noun*
1 a person who swims out past the surf at a beach; a person in shark-infested waters *AUSTRALIA, 1920*
- Windsurfers always sail near surfers because surfers make better shark bait. —*The Dinkum Dictionary Of Australian English*, p. 67, 1990

2 a person with very pale skin *US*
Hawaiian youth usage.
- —Douglas Simonson, *Pidgin to da Max Hana Hou*, 1982

shark city *noun*
Looe, Cornwall *UK*
- Some reflect the main industry or interest of the town – Ellesmere Port has become Motion Lotion [motor fuel] City, Looe in Cornwall is Shark City[.] —Peter Chippindale, *The British CB Book*, p. 169–169, 1981

shark-fucker *noun*
a surfer *AUSTRALIA*
- Surfacing asthmatically, I squirmed back onto my board and paddled out of the impact zone, cursing this shark-fucker. —Kathy Lette, *Girls' Night Out*, p. 190, 1987

sharking *noun*
1 among women, the practice of man-hunting; subsequently also used by men hunting women *UK*
Also used in the verb form 'shark'. In 1999, in answer to the question 'What are you doing tonight?' a professional Soho media-type in her mid-20s offered a non-verbal shorthand: she placed both hands palm to palm above her head in imitation of a shark's fin.
- NO SHARKING —*The legend on a Foster's Lager drinks mat*, 2001
- This is meant to be a comedown trip, not a bleedin sharking one. —Niall Griffiths, *Kelly + Victor*, p. 57, 2002
- His [Augustine's] struggle between promiscuity and monogamy [...] is summed up in the prayer he made, while still in his sharking phase, "God grant me the strength to be chaste... Just not yet." —Richard Herring, *Talking Cock*, p. 67, 2003
- I had to admit / That yeah, yeah you are fit / And yeah I do want it / But I stop sharkin' for a minute to get chips and drinks. —Mike Skinner, *Fit But You Know It*, 2004

2 the illegal loaning of money at extremely high interest rates *US*
- He wore Air corps sunglasses, combed his hair into a gelatinous country pomp and tithed his pay and tithed the vigorish on his sharking. —Earl Thompson, *Tattoo*, p. 293, 1974

shark meat *noun*
an easy victim of a cheat, swindler or hustler *US*
- —Steve Rushin, *Pool Cool*, p. 26, 1990

sharky *adjective*
used of a surfboard nose, pointed *US*
- —Trevor Cralle, *The Surfin'ary*, p. 110, 1991

Sharon; Shaz *noun*
a stereotypical working-class young woman *UK*
Pejorative, in the sense that such a woman is socially unacceptable; from a name widely associated in the 1980s and 90s with that generation and class. Shaz is a diminutive of Sharon.
- [T]hey were charging me £27.50 just for some Sharon to carry the letter down to the post-room once her cuticles had been buffed! —Andrew Nickolds, *Back to Basics*, p. 52, 1994

Sharon Stone; sharon *noun*
a telephone, especially a mobile phone *UK*
Rhyming slang, formed from the name of the US film actress (b.1958).
- Lost your Sharon? Well, leave me the number and if I find it I'll give you a ring. —Ray Puxley, *Fresh Rabbit*, 1998

sharp *noun*
1 in gambling, a cheat *UK, 1797*
A shortened from of **SHARPER**.
- At fifteen, he was an accomplished card sharp, pickpocket and ravishing female impersonator baiting tourist tricks for muggers in the French Quarter. —Iceberg Slim (Robert Beck), *Doom Fox*, p. 46, 1978
- On one wall hung ten or twelve large leather-bound photo albums that had pictures of card sharps. —Stephen Cannell, *King Con*, p. 143, 1997

2 a number sign (#) on a computer keyboard *US*
- —Eric S. Raymond, *The New Hacker's Dictionary*, p. 39, 1991

sharp *adjective*
stylish, fashionable, attractive *US, 1944*
- I wanted to look sharp but I wanted to feel comfortable too. —Chester Himes, *If He Hollers Let Him Go*, p. 136, 1945
- The sidewalks were always jammed, big gamblers and racketeers, dressed sharp as a tack, strutted by with their diamond stickpins[.] —Mezz Mezzrow, *Really the Blues*, p. 5, 1946
- All the hip cats on the corner / They don't look so sharp no mo'. —Jimmy Witherspoon, *Skid Row Blues*, 1947
- He was always sharp then, proud of his clothes, but now they didn't seem to matter too much. —Hal Ellson, *The Golden Spike*, p. 57, 1952
- When it came to personal matters, my mind was strictly on getting "sharp" in my zoot as soon as I left work[.] —Malcolm X and Alex Haley, *The Autobiography of Malcolm X*, p. 65, 1964
- I came back to "New York" so sharp I was bleeding. —Babs Gonzales, *I Paid My Dues*, p. 61, 1967
- He's got three main ambitions – and I happen to think that it's because he's in this country that he only has these main three – one is to drink and look sharp[.] —Nathan Heard, *Howard Street*, p. 160, 1968
- I would dig (deeper than deeply) getting clean once more – not only in the steam-bath sense, but in getting sharp as an Esquire square with a Harlem touch[.] —Eldridge Cleaver, *Soul on Ice*, p. 19, 1968
- It's, like, Santa Claus used ta have this really charp chort, man, y'know? —Cheech Marin and Tommy Chong, *Santa Calus and his Old Lady*, 1971
- We brought in the bread, drank J&B, had the sharp broads. —Edwin Torres, *Carlito's Way*, p. 24, 1975
- Sharp as you can look without turning into a nigger. —*Saturday Night Fever*, 1977
- "I mean, this nigger is sharp!" Elaine said, as I placed the hat on my medium-length, soft natural, then cocked it to the right just a little[.] —Bobby Seale, *A Lonely Rage*, p. 288, 1978

▸ **you are so sharp you'll cut yourself**
used to note someone's (over-)cleverness, also to reprove someone for that over-cleverness; especially implying a sharp-tongued cleverness *UK, 1910*
- Written in Keyes' sparky, so sharp-you'll-cut-yourself style ... with plenty of heart, lots of laughs and a fantastic twist in the tale. —*Cosmopolitan's' review of 'Sushi for Beginners' by Marian Keyes*, 2000

sharp and blunt *noun*
the vagina *UK, 1937*
Rhyming slang for **CUNT**.
- —Ray Puxley, *Cockney Rabbit*, 1992

sharpen *verb*

▸ **sharpen the pencil**
to have sex *US*
Possibly derisory, the use of 'pencil' indicates a small penis.
- Another way to say "intercourse" [...] Sharpening the pencil[.] —Erica Orloff and JoAnn Baker, *Dirty Little Secrets*, p. 88, 2001

▸ **sharpen your pencil**
to reduce the price *UK*
- "Twenty eight grand." Luigi sucked in through his teeth. "Bit steep. Sharpen your pencil a little?" —Colin Butts, *Is Harry on the Boat?*, p. 286, 1997

sharp end *noun*
in any given endeavour, the position which is exposed to the greatest difficuty or criticism; the vanguard *UK, 1976*
From the nautical use as 'the bow of a ship'.
- [New Scotland] Yard unit at sharp end of war against racism —*The Guardian*, 24th February 2000

sharper *noun*
in gambling, a cheater *UK, 1681*
- We got to have sharpers with private licenses hiding information[.] —Raymond Chandler, *The Little Sister*, p. 219, 1949
- The terrier was showing real signs of being a world class sharper, but that was before Beano, using a dead man's I.D., got caught cheating[.] —Stephen J. Cannell, *King Con*, p. 32, 1997

sharpering omee; sharper *noun*
a police officer *UK*
Polari; a variation of **CHARPERER; CHARPERING OMEE**.
- —Paul Baker, *Polari*, p. 190, 2002

sharper's tool *noun*
a fool *UK, 1937*
Rhyming slang.
- —Ray Puxley, *Fresh Rabbit*, 1998

sharpest *adjective*

▸ **not the sharpest tool in the box**

applied to someone of below average intelligence *UK*

- He's not the sharpest tool in the box, but even he's aware that he's in a tight spot here[.] —Andrew Holmes, *Sleb*, p. 17, 2002

sharpie *noun*

1 a gambling cheat *US, 1942*

- The sharpie who got tired of selling the Brooklyn Bridge moved into the District and now sells the Washington Monument. —Jack Lait and Lee Mortimer, *Washington Confidential*, p. 276, 1951
- And do not think that it is the abode, the stomping ground, of only the pimp, sharpie, and floozy set. —John D. McDonald, *The Neon Jungle*, p. 6, 1953
- Just what I said: any of your sharpies here willing to take my five bucks that says that I can get the best of that woman – before the week's up – without her getting the best of me? —Ken Kesey, *One Flew Over the Cuckoo's Nest*, p. 71, 1962
- [H]is latest room had an assortment of bum dice and new-but-marked decks of cards very cleverly packaged and stamped. He was a sharpie. —Mickey Spillane, *Me, Hood!*, p. 23, 1963
- The straight players could never match wits with sharpies and hustlers who loaded dice, marked cards, and used drugs and booze and women to beat the innocent gambler out of his bankroll. —Mario Puzo, *Inside Las Vegas*, p. 42, 1977

2 in pinball, a player who can play for long periods of time without paying because of his ability to win free games *US*

- —Bobbye Claire Natkin and Steve Kirk, *All About Pinball*, p. 116, 1977

3 a stylishly dressed teenage delinquent *AUSTRALIA*

From **SHARP** (stylish). During the 1960s and 70s only, coming after the **BODGIE** and **WIDGIE** and preceding **PUNK ROCK**.

- The sharpies dressed as we did, but did not look for blues, have back-ups or do any of the other real crazy mixed-up things that us cats did for kicks. —William Dick, *A Bunch of Ratbags*, p. 202, 1965

4 an uncircumcised penis *US*

- —Amy Sohn, *Sex and the City*, p. 157, 2002

sharpish *adverb*

quickly *UK, 1984*

- We hit the ground and disappeared sharpish. —Dave Courtney, *Stop the Ride I Want to Get Off*, p. 53, 1999
- [S]o get back up to your room and get some warm clothes on... sharpish! —Colin Butts, *Is Harry Still on the Boat?*, p. 46, 2003

sharps *noun*

a hypodermic needle and syringe *US*

Drug addict usage, borrowed from the medical terminology for any skin-piercing device.

- —US Department of Justice, *Street Terms*, October 1994

sharpshoot *verb*

to question a speaker after a lecture *US*

- —Carl Fleischhauer, *A Glossary of Army Slang*, p. 12–12, 1968

sharpshooter *noun*

1 a man whose wife is always pregnant; a man whose children are of the desired sex *FIJI*

Recorded by Jan Tent in 1994.

2 an intravenous drug user who usually hits a vein on the first attempt to inject a drug *US*

- —Richard A. Spears, *The Slang and Jargon of Drugs and Drink*, p. 445, 1986

3 in electric line work, a narrow blade shovel used in hard dirt *US*

- —A.B. Chance Co., *Lineman's Slang Dictionary*, p. 15, 1980

4 in oil drilling, a long, narrow shovel *US*

- —Jerry Robertson, *Oil Slanguage*, p. 111, 1954

sharp top *noun*

in a deck of playing cards, an ace *US*

- —George Percy, *The Language of Poker*, p. 80, 1988

shasta *noun*

a sexual partner who is not particularly attractive, but who was available at the time *US*

An allusion to Shasta™ soda, not especially liked but available and inexpensive.

- —Don R. McCreary (Editor), *Dawg Speak*, 2001

shat *verb*

▸ **shat along on my uppers**

to have fallen on hard times *CANADA*

- In Nova Scotia, when someone says, in response to "how are you?" "I'm just shatting along on my uppers," he means "hanging, barely, on the edge of the ledge or table, by my upper teeth." —Lewis Poteet, *The South Shore Phrase Book*, p. 99, 1999

▸ **shat it**

to have been frightened into giving up *UK*

A variation in the past tense of **SHIT IT** (to be afraid).

- [Stephen] Hawking, it was rumoured, had considered a book on the subject ["Junkie Logic"], but shat it when he decided he wasn't sure he could pull it off. —Christopher Brookmyre, *Boiling a Frog*, p. 14, 2000

shat on *adjective*

having been insulted and humilated *UK*

The past tense of **SHIT ON**.

- Because people now forget how shat-on and criticised and just generally kicked-about the first ravers were by everyone. —Dave Courtney, *Raving Lunacy*, p. 92, 2000

shattered *adjective*

1 very tired, exhausted *UK, 1930*

- By the third night, I'd be absolutely shattered and have to go to bed at a reasonable time and then get up the following morning and rush like mad to get all the work done. —*The Guardian*, 19th April 2000

2 emotionally battered; depressed *NEW ZEALAND, 1997*

Prison usage.

- —Harry Orsman, *A Dictionary of Modern New Zealand Slang*, p. 118, 1999

3 very drunk *UK*

- [T]hree or four nights on the trot [...] and got absolutely shattered every bastard time. —Colin Evans, *The Heart of Standing*, 1962

shave *noun*

a man with a shaved head; a shaved head *NEW ZEALAND, 1997*

Unlike the **SKINHEAD**, a 'shave' has no racist or Nazi ideology.

- —Harry Orsman, *A Dictionary of Modern New Zealand Slang*, p. 118, 1999

shave *verb*

1 to alter the edges or surfaces of dice for use by a cheat *US*

- —John Savage, *The Winner's Guide to Dice*, p. 91, 1974

2 in hot rodding, to remove body trim from a car prepatory to customising the car *US, 1950s to 70s*

▸ **shave points**

to reduce scoring during a sports contest in furtherance of a gambling conspiracy *US*

- I'm telling you. They're shaving points on the game. This is no bullshit tip. —*Diner*, 1982
- It was like spreading rumors in Boston about Larry Bird shaving points, or priests selling fat young boys out of vans behind Fenway Park. —Hunter S. Thompson, *Generation of Swine*, p. 121, 26th May 1986

shave and a haircut – two bits

describes a particular repeated musical phrase that is characterised by the rhythm of the words in the spoken phrase *US*

This musical **RIFF** is often credited to guitarist Bo Diddley (b.1928) but the rhythm was already familiar as a pattern of raps used for door-knocking.

- Keep on givin' us that shave & a haircut, Bo – we love it! Have a great day!, From all in The Blues Band and The Manfreds, and us here at "Ready", The Blues Band newsletter, and "Groovin'", The Manfreds newsletter. —*on the occasion of Bo Diddley's 70th birthday.*, 1998

shave off *verb*

to deliver a severe reprimand; to rant disapprovingly on any topic *UK*

Royal Navy slang.

- 'ave you ever 'eard 'im shavin' off about them pop singers? —Rick Jolly, *Jackspeak*, 1989

shave off!

used to denote surprise, disgust, frustration or amazement *UK*

The Royal Navy is the only arm of the UK military that may allow a beard to be worn, hence the adoption, as expletive, of the order 'Shave off!'.

- —Nigel Foster, *The Making of a Royal Marine Commando*, 1989

shaver *noun*

1 a discounter of notes, at high interest rates *CANADA*
- The Albertans fought the "St. James Street gang" as dauntlessly as the people of Upper Canada had fought the "Montreal shavers." — A. R. M. Lower, *Colony to Nation*, p. 517, 1946

2 in the Korean war, a booby trap used by South Korean troops to sabotage North Korean transportation carts *US*
- When a group lifted the cart to replace the wheel the booby trap went off. This diabolical device was referred to by the ROKs as 'the shaver' – for the effect it had on one's head. — Joseph C. Goulden, *Korea*, p. 129, 1982

shave-tail *noun*

1 a cigarette stub *US*
- — Vincent J. Monteleone, *Criminal Slang*, p. 205, 1949

2 a newly promoted second lieutenant *US*
- — *Current Slang*, p. 18, Winter 1970

shayner Yid *noun*

▷ see: SCHAINER YID

shaz *noun*

▷ see: SHARON

shazam!; shazzam!

used for registering triumph *US, 1940*

An incantatory ritual from the comic book character created by Bill Parker and C.C. Beck in 1940 – a metaphorically God-like character whose name is called on by the superhero Captain Marvel in moments of crisis; Shazam is an acronym of *S*olomon (wisdom), *H*ercules (strength), *A*tlas (stamina), *Z*eus (power), *A*chilles (courage) and *M*ercury (speed). Further popularised on the *Andy Griffith Show* (CBS, 1960–68) and *Gomer Pyzle, USMC* (CBS, 1964–70) by Jim Nabors.
- Fuck, I'll finish it, send it to Luther Nichols of Doubleday, and, shazam! I'll strike it big. — Oscar Zeta Acosta, *The Autobiography of a Brown Buffalo*, p. 155, 1972
- I suppose the thought that anyone could call "Shazam" and put the world to rights was some solace to boys who could do little to change their surroundings. — Brian McDonald, *Elephant Boys*, p. 23, 2000

she *noun*

1 cocaine *US*
- The She. Yeah, S-h-e. Because if you take cocaine you have no need for a woman. — Willard Motley, *Let No Man Write My Epitaph*, p. 199, 1958
- — R.C. Garrett et al., *The Coke Book*, p. 200, 1984
- — Nick Constable, *This is Cocaine*, p. 181, 2002

2 used of an effeminate homosexual man, he *UK*
- She's an untidy bitch. — Paul Tempest, *Lag's Lexicon*, 1950
- — Donald Webster Cory and John P. LeRoy, *The Homosexual and His Society*, p. 266, 1963: 'A lexicon of homosexual slang'
- The world of queens and malehustlers and what they thrive on, the queens being technically men but no one thinks of them that way – always "she"[.] — John Rechy, *City of Night*, p. 105, 1963
- — Florida Legislative Investigation Committee (Johns Committee), *Homosexuality and Citizenship in Florida*, 1964: 'Glossary of homosexual terms and deviate acts'
- If she [Harold] doesn't like it, she can twirl on it. — Mart Crowley, *The Boys in the Band*, p. 24, 1968
- She's a wicked queen! — Paul Baker, *Polari*, p. 190, 2002

3 the penis *UK, 1922*

An owner's usage, in much the same way a boat or a car is often identified.

shears *noun*

playing cards that have been trimmed for cheating *US, 1961*
- — Thomas L. Clark, *The Dictionary of Gambling and Gaming*, p. 195, 1987

shebang *noun*

any thing, matter or business at issue at the moment *US, 1869*

Usually as 'the whole shebang'. The former senses of 'a hut', 'vehicle' or 'tavern' are all but forgotten.
- Maybe you can get to be boss of the whole shebang! — Jim Thompson, *Roughneck*, p. 114, 1954
- Helen said that after I left Detroit the whole shebang collapsed like a house of cards. — Clancy Sigal, *Going Away*, p. 299, 1961
- If I do, this whole shebang will come apart on me and I won't look too good, will I? — Elmore Leonard, *Killshot*, p. 258, 1989
- A grassy square in the middle of Old Town Plaza was the best part of the whole shebang, as far as Finnegan was concerned. — Joseph Wambaugh, *Finnegan's Week*, p. 141–142, 1993
- Coral is only five and she rides ponies up in Totteridge every Saturday – velvet hat, jods, crop, the whole shebang. — Stuart Browne, *Dangerous Parking*, p. 323, 2000

shebang *verb*

to ingest cocaine by spraying a solution of cocaine and water up the nose *UK*
- — Nick Constable, *This is Cocaine*, p. 182, 2002

shebeen *noun*

an unlicensed drinking place *IRELAND, 1847*

Irish *síbín* (illicit whisky) led to original use in Ireland. Adopted in the C20 for use in South African townships and UK West Indian communities.
- Some of these shebeens would even feature an impromptu live jam session with a local young musician with a hot little band. — Karline Smith, *Moss Side Massive*, p. 109, 1994

she-bill; she-note *noun*

a two-dollar note *US*
- — Claudio R. Salvucci, *The Philadelphia Dialect Dictionary*, p. 57, 1996

shed *noun*

in poker, a hand consisting of three cards of the same rank and a pair *US*

Known conventionally as a 'full house'.
- — George Percy, *The Language of Poker*, p. 80, 1988

▸ off your shed

in a state of mental confusion, insane *UK*

A variation of OFF YOUR HEAD.
- [PCP] sent me a bit off me shed. I was trying to lift up cars[.] — Shaun Ryder, *Shaun Ryder... in His Own Words*, 1991

shed *verb*

in poker, to discard a card or cards *US*
- — Albert H. Morehead, *The Complete Guide to Winning Poker*, p. 272, 1967

shedded *adjective*

drunk *UK*

Recorded by 'e-cyclopaedia', *BBC News*, 20th March 2002, with the somewhat oblique explanation 'as in "My shed has collapsed taking most of the fence with it"'.
- — Susie Dent, *The Language Report*, p. 78, 2003

shedder *noun*

a moulting lobster *US*
- Shedders (or soft-shelled lobsters) bring a lower price than hard-shelled lobsters because their meat is not as firm and is quite watery. — Kendall Merriam, *The Illustrated Dictionary of Lobstering*, p. 77, 1978

shedful *noun*

a great quantity *UK*

A variation of SHED LOAD.
- [We] had croissants and champagne and another shedful of my charlie [cocaine]. — Ben Elton, *High Society*, p. 22, 2002

shed load; shedloads *noun*

a great quantity *UK, 1997*

Probably euphemistic for SHITLOAD rather than a genuinely approximate measure.
- I wasn't to know my dad was going to cark it a couple of years later and leave me a shed load of cash. — Jenny Eclair, *Camberwell Beauty*, p. 30, 2000

shed row *noun*

in horse racing, the row of barns where horses are stabled *US*
- — David W. Maurer, *Argot of the Racetrack*, p. 58, 1951

sheeba *noun*

a sensimilla variety of marijuana; a type of hashish produced from the pollen of the plant *US*

Derived, perhaps, from CHIBA (a marijuana variety).
- Sheeba sensimilla is a beautiful smoke. But the hash produced from it doesn't quite make the grade. — Nick Jones, *Spliffs*, p. 93, 2003

Sheela *noun*

an effeminate man or boy *IRELAND*

Defined by Bernard Share in *Slanguage*, 2003, as a man or boy who takes an interest in 'affairs properly belonging to women'.

sheen *noun*

a car *US*

An abbreviation of 'machine'.
- — *Current Slang*, p. 41, Fall 1968
- — David Claerbaut, *Black Jargon in White America*, p. 79, 1972

Sheena *noun*
a melodramatic black homosexual male *US*
From the comic book, *Sheena, Queen of the Jungle*.
- — *Maledicta*, p. 228, Winter 1980: '"Lovely, blooming, fresh and gay": the onomastics of camp'

sheeny *noun*
a Jewish person *UK, 1816*
- One time in Humboldt Park Leo "Bow" Gistensohn, our leader, didn't like the way a cop down by the lake called him "sheeny." — Mezz Mezzrow, *Really the Blues*, p. 6, 1946
- "Sheeny!" she is screaming. "Hebe!" — Philip Roth, *Portnoy's Complaint*, p. 203, 1969
- — Helen Dahlskog (Editor), *A Dictionary of Contemporary and Colloquial Usage*, p. 53, 1972

sheep *noun*
a woman who volunteers to take part in serial sex with members of a motorcyle club or gang *US*
- — Robert A. Wilson, *Playboy's Book of Forbidden Words*, p. 220, 1972

sheep-dipping *noun*
the use of military equipment or personnel in an intelligence operation under civilian cover *US*
- Those Air Force officers who had "sheep-dipped" – taken a temporary tour of duty with the Agency – had moved quickly up the promotional ladder. — T.E. Cruise, *Wings of Gold III*, p. 64, 1989

sheep-fucker *noun*
a New Zealander *AUSTRALIA*
- Stick to your livestock sheep-fucker. — *Union Recorder*, p. 34, 4th November 1991
- [S]heep fucker – a New Zealander. ...USAGE: 'They're called sheep fuckers because they fuck sheep. Why else would they be called it?'[.] — Bruce Moore, *A Lexicon of Cadet Language*, p. 335, 1993

sheep-herder *noun*
an inferior driver *US*
- — *Complete CB Slang Dictionary*, p. 83, 1976
- — Peter Chippindale, *The British CB Book*, p. 159, 1981

sheepie *noun*
hair permed into a fleece of curls *UK*
- [H]e had a bad muzzy [moustache] and a sheepie. — Kevin Sampson, *Outlaws*, p. 163, 2001

sheep's back *noun*
the wool industry *AUSTRALIA*
- — Dymphna Cusack, *Picnic Races*, p. 150, 1962
- The sheep's back supports Australia, they say; but less and less Australian backs are supporting wool fabrics. — Suzy Jarratt, *Permissive Australia*, p. 112, 1970
- While the nation rode to prosperity on the sheep's back its face was shaded under a mountain of trapped rabbits whose fur was made into felt. — Nancy Keesing, *Lily on the Dustbin*, p. 105, 1984

sheep's eyes *noun*
a look that indicates attraction or sexual interest *UK, 1811*
- [H]e was making sheep's eyes across the room at me from the first. — Barbara Vine, *The Dark-Adapted Eye*, p. 109, 1986

sheepshagger; sheep shagger *noun*
1 a native of Wales *UK*
Literally, 'someone who has sex with sheep'; derogatory.
- KNIGHTY: So where you two from? STUDENT 1: Conway, in Wales. KNIGHTY: Sheep-shagger, ah? STUDENT 1: No, we only moved there a couple of years ago. — Paul Fraser and Shane Meadows, *TwentyFourSeven*, p. 49, 1997
- Fuck off sheep shagger! — Jack Allen, *When the Whistle Blows*, p. 205, 2000
- Any time, sheepshaggers! We'll be waiting! — Niall Griffiths, *Sheepshagger*, p. 19, 2001

2 a New Zealander *UK*
Reflecting the high density of sheep in New Zealand.
- He points his finger straight at Bacon's forehead. ROBBIE: ...him versus the sheepshaggers [...] BACON IS SEATED FACING A LARGE MOUSTACHED NEW ZEALANDER[.] — Bernard Dempsey and Kevin McNally, *Lock, Stock ... & Two Hundred Smoking Kalashnikovs*, p. 102 – 104, 2000

3 an Australian *NEW ZEALAND*
- — Harry Orsman, *A Dictionary of Modern New Zealand Slang*, p. 118, 1999

sheepshagging *adjective*
contemptible *UK*
- [T]hey hated those sheepshagging bastards from Aberdeen. — Christopher Brookmyre, *The Sacred Art of Stealing*, p. 143, 2002

sheepskin *noun*
1 a university diploma *US, 1843*
- Wouldn't have a sheepskin if they paid me. — Robert Gover, *The Maniac Responsible*, p. 25, 1963
- Stevenson said we were discussing the fact that a sheepskin was a handicap in American politics. — Mort Sahl, *Heartland*, p. 51, 1976

2 an executive criminal pardon *US*
- — Joseph E. Ragen and Charles Finston, *Inside the World's Toughest Prison*, p. 817, 1962: 'Penitentiary and underworld glossary'

3 a condom *US*
- — Connie Eble (Editor), *UNC-CH Campus Slang*, p. 5, Fall 1991

sheero *noun*
the head *UK*
English gypsy use.
- Sliding down the wing of my old Corsair. My sheero cracking against the metal rim. — Jimmy Stockin, *On The Cobbles*, p. 30, 2000

sheesh *adjective*
very stylish; unnecessarily ornamented; elaborate; fussy *UK*
Probably from French slang *chichi* (used of affected looks and manners).
- What about this? Very sheesh. — Barry Took and Marty Feldman, *Round The Horne*, June 1967

sheesh!
used as a mild expletive *US*
Euphemistic for, and possibly a slovening of, 'Jesus!'.
- Sheesh, I never thought about it before[.] — Darby Romeo, *Retrohell*, p. 251, 1997

sheet *noun*
1 a police record of arrests and convictions *US, 1958*
Probably a shortened **RAP SHEET**, but earlier sources for 'sheet' than this raise questions.
- Turk had gotten a walk because his sheet wasn't too bad. — Claude Brown, *Manchild in the Promised Land*, p. 17, 1965
- I bet he got a sheet down there damn near long as mine. — Vernon E. Smith, *The Jones Men*, p. 93, 1974
- He'd done read my sheet and put his game down. — Babs Gonzales, *Movin' On Down De Line*, p. 21, 1975
- MR. PINK: One question: Do they have a sheet on you, where you told him you're from. — *Reservoir Dogs*, 1992
- Don't it mean anything I got I got nothing on my sheet the past three years, that I've been clean all that time? — Elmore Leonard, *Riding the Rap*, p. 4, 1995
- — Angela Devlin, *Prison Patter*, p. 102, 1996

2 a one-pound note; £1 in value *UK*
This survived, perhaps surprisingly, the introduction of the coin in 1983.
- — *The Bournemouth Echo*, 20th November 1968
- — Robert Barltrop and Jim Wolveridge, *The Muvver Tongue*, 1980
- And for his last trick he makes five people and the best part of a million sheets disappear. — Christopher Brookmyre, *The Sacred Art of Stealing*, p. 263, 2002

3 a newspaper *US*
- — Don Wilmeth, *The Language of American Popular Entertainment*, p. 237, 1981

4 one hundred doses of LSD soaked into paper *US*
- A "sheet" is one hundred hits on a ten-by-ten-hit piece of paper, a unit often sold on the retail level. — Cam Cloud, *The Little Book of Acid*, p. 34, 1999

sheet *verb*
to charge someone with a criminal offence *UK*
Police use.
- Without doubt the guy can be sheeted[.] — Duncan MacLaughlin, *The Filth*, p. 73, 2002

sheet!
used for registering surprise, rage, etc *US*
May be a euphemism or an emphasised pronunciation of **SHIT!** depending on your needs.
- Christie was just inches away from being the next vice president and Bob Dole is D'Amato's man. Sheeeet! Suck my dick! — Howard Stern, *Miss America*, p. 467, 1995

sheet rocking *noun*
a combination of crack cocaine and LSD *UK*
- — Mike Haskins, *Drugs*, p. 293, 2003

sheets *noun*

a daily report of recent criminal activity, circulated among police going on shift *US*

- I read the sheets this morning ... and they sounded like the same watches. — Donald Goines, *Inner City Hoodlum*, p. 55, 1975

▸ **between the sheets**

in bed, especially in a reference to sex *UK, 1865*

- Tantra between the Sheets illustrates the ultimate techniques to satisfy your partner[.] — Val Sampson, *Tantra Between the Sheets, back cover*, 2003

sheet writer; writer *noun*

in an illegal sports betting operation or lottery; a functionary who takes and records bets *US*

- — *American Speech*, p. 193, October 1949
- Buda was the daughter of a race track sheet-writer, an only child. — Jack Lait and Lee Mortimer, *Chicago Confidential*, p. 15, 1950
- A lot of the junkies started sticking up the numbers writers and sticking up the controllers. — Claude Brown, *Manchild in the Promised Land*, p. 191, 1965
- I think the flat is a check-in station for so called runners or writers who turn in their bet books and cash, less their earned twenty percent. — Iceberg Slim (Robert Beck), *Mama Black Widow*, p. 97, 1969
- You know I'm out of business. So my sheet writers are closing the books, checking the slow pays, I find out this Warren Ganz was using three different names. — Elmore Leonard, *Riding the Rap*, p. 16, 1995

sheezy *noun*

▸ **for sheezy**

a very attractive teenager or young woman *SOUTH AFRICA*

Adopted from **FO' SHEEZY** (certainly).

- — *Sunday Times (South Africa)*, 1st June 2003

she-he *noun*

a transvestite or transgender person *US*

- When she-he finally tired and left the spotlight, a girl got on the bed, undressed, and started to masturbate. — *Screw*, p. 7, 13th April 1970

sheila *noun*

a woman; a girl *AUSTRALIA, 1832*

From the given name Sheila. In the C19 spelt 'shelah' and 'shaler', settling down to its current form in the early part of the C20. Although not highly derogatory it certainly is not complimentary, and many women take exception to it. Women as a rule do not refer to other women as 'sheilas'.

- SHEILA – A young lady. — Gilbert H. Lawson, *A Dictionary of Australian Words and Terms*, 1924
- You *didn't* have a sheila, did you? — Eric Lambert, *The Veterans*, p. 69, 1954
- [W]hen he got back from leave, he told his mates he'd met a 'beaut sheila' and was anxious to get out of the Army to marry her. — Bill Wannan, *Bullockies, Beauts and Bandicoots*, p. 37, 1960
- Oh, Barbara's a bonzer sheila, all right. Trouble is, she's in Bundaberg. — Ray Slattery, *Mobbs' Mob*, p. 76, 1966
- Beaut sheilas wandering round – real friendly – we help them into the carts you know – remember when young Joe got lost in the crinoline! — *Kings Cross Venus*, p. 13, 1st November 1972
- Bloody disgusting, that's what it is, preying on poor screwed-up sheilas. — *Alvin Purple*, p. 102, 1974
- He wipes his mouth with his arm and tells me to have a good time, fuck a few sheilas for him. — Christos Tsiolkas, *Loaded*, p. 116, 1995

sheister *noun*

▷ see: **SHICER**

shekels *noun*

money *US, 1883*

From the ancient Babylonian unit of weight and coin.

- Generally a runner made plenty for himself, taking a chance that the dough he clipped wasn't on the number that pulled in the shekels. — Mickey Spillane, *I, The Jury*, p. 46, 1947
- This is very bad on love-life, and the few still around with loose shekels don't look too longingly at Broadway. — Jack Lait and Lee Mortimer, *New York Confidential*, p. 141, 1948
- And I'd still sacrifice everything. All Freddy's shekels. — Mary McCarthy, *The Group*, p. 352, 1963
- The first step was to place the all-important hat by the fountain to catch the shekels. — Ed Sanders, *Tales of Beatnik Glory*, p. 78, 1975
- One girl was the daughter of a wealthy family from Brooklyn. Lo and behold, the shekels came out. — Herbert Huncke, *Guilty of Everything*, p. 169, 1990

shelf *noun*

1 an informer *AUSTRALIA, 1916*

- These were the stool-pigeons, the shelfs, who were out to make a deal in their own interests with the police whenever it was possible. — Vince Kelly, *The Bogeyman*, p. 70, 1956
- — Ryan Aven-Bray, *Ridgey Didge Oz Jack Lang*, p. 45, 1983

2 solitary confinement *US*

- Stick was confined in the second cell – a holding cell in the isolation unit known as the shelf. — Malcolm Braly, *On the Yard*, p. 61, 1967
- — William K. Bentley and James M. Corbett, *Prison Slang*, p. 11, 1992

3 in circus and carnival usage, an upper sleeping berth *US*

- — Don Wilmeth, *The Language of American Popular Entertainment*, p. 237, 1981

▸ **on the shelf**

unlikely to marry *UK, 1839*

- She didn't seem to go out on many dates, and he couldn't figure out why she was on the shelf. — James T. Farrell, *Saturday Night*, p. 19, 1947

shelf *verb*

to inform on someone *AUSTRALIA, 1936*

- 'You mean you're going to shelf Howie?' 'I'm no stoolie!' — Wilda Moxham, *The Apprentice*, p. 163, 1969
- Nobody here is likely to send you to the nick, they won't shelf you to the police. — Kevin Mackey, *The Cure*, p. 44, 1970

shelf life *noun*

the period of time during which something or someone remains popular or in demand *US*

From the literal sense meaning the period of time during which a product may be stored and remain suitable for use.

- Man, I got a shelf life of ten years, tops! — *Jerry Maguire*, 1996

shelfware *noun*

a computer program bought but not used *US*

- — Eric S. Raymond, *The New Hacker's Dictionary*, p. 318, 1991

shell *noun*

1 a bullet *UK*

From the conventional senses as 'an explosive projectile' or 'cartridge case'.

- — Dave Courtney, *Dodgy Dave's Little Black Book*, p. 7, 2001

2 a person who is somewhat lacking in mental faculties *US*

- — Gary K. Farlow, *Prison-ese*, p. 62, 2002

3 a safe with a thin door and walls *US*

- — Hyman E. Goldin et al., *Dictionary of American Underworld Lingo*, p. 191, 1950

shell *verb*

to move quickly *BARBADOS*

Collymore writes 'Most likely derived from Shell Motor Spirit'.

- — Frank A. Collymore, *Barbadian Dialect*, p. 101, 1965

shellacking *noun*

a beating; a defeat *US, 1931*

- Now Frank 'n' me got our pictures in the paper, and my old man would've given me a shellacking if Sam didn't stop him. — Irving Shulman, *The Amboy Dukes*, p. 101, 1947
- Take a licking, a real shellacking and see how she likes that! — Rocky Garciano (with Rowland Barber), *Somebody Up There Likes Me*, p. 255, 1955

shell back *noun*

a reactionary *UK, 1943*

Originally nautical, meaning 'an experienced sailor'.

- These independent Cornish shell backs need careful wooing[.] — Barry Humphries, *Bazza Pulls It Off!*, 1971

she'll be right

everything will be okay *AUSTRALIA, 1947*

- 'She'll be right,' they would say, summing up their general optimistic attitude to life. — Dymphna Cusack, *Picnic Races*, p. 94, 1962

she'll be sweet

everything will be all right *AUSTRALIA*

- 'Yell if yer want help.' 'She'll be sweet, matey. Nothin' I can't handle.' — Nino Culotta (John O'Grady), *They're A Weird Mob*, p. 155, 1957
- — W.R. Bennett, *Target Turin*, p. 51, 1962

shell-like *noun*

the ear *UK*

Extracted from the phrase **WORD IN YOUR SHELL-LIKE**.

- I go rummaging around in it's shell-like[.] — Andrew Nickolds, *Back to Basics*, p. 94, 1994

Shell Mex *noun*

sex *UK*

Rhyming slang, formed from the oil company.

- [B]lagged a bit of shell mex. — Ray Puxley, *Cockney Rabbit*, 1992

shell out *verb*
to pay *UK, 1801*
• [S]tick a naughty foot on the other side of the rope marked "Strictly Private", then shell out a pony (£25) for a cream tea. —Andrew Nickolds, *Back to Basics*, p. 126, 1994

shells *noun*
money *UK*
Probably adapted from 'clamshell' ($1).
• [W]e have a smoke to celebrate the shells we pulled in. —Nick Barlay, *Curvy Lovebox*, p. 53, 1997

shemale *noun*
a transvestite, transexual or other transgender person; a person with mixed sexual physiology, usually the genitals of a male and surgically augmented breasts *US*
• In hotels these off-beat she-males don't get together in groups, wearing mannish clothes, as they sometimes do in hole-in-the-wall cafes or bohemian eating places. —Dev Collans with Stewart Sterling, *I was a House Detective*, p. 102, 1954
• Like most shemales on the Strip, Olivia's forte was B-drinking. —Seth Morgan, *Homeboy*, p. 14, 1990
• "I'm 47," he says, "and I haven't danced since I was out with a punk rock debutante year ago. She lived on Esplanade Avenue with two shemales." — *Times-Picayune (New Orleans)*, p. 1, 13th November 2003

shemmy *noun*
▷ see: CHEMMY

shemozzle; schemozzle; schlemozzle *noun*
a fuss; an altercation; a difficulty; an unfortunate incident *UK, 1889*
An East End corruption of German *schlimm* (bad) and Hebrew *mazel* (luck), thus Yiddish *schlimazel* (an unlucky person).
• [T]wo write-offs from the latest Hogarth Roundabout schemozzle simply welded together[.] —Andrew Nickolds, *Back to Basics*, p. 65, 1994

shenanigans *noun*
trickery; mischief *US, 1855*
• That's when the shenanigans began. Kefauver had no experience with such shenanigans. —Jack Lait and Lee Mortimer, *Washington Confidential*, p. 197, 1951
• After all my shenanigans, if I'd missed that penalty, the crowd would have crucified me. —Frank Skinner, *Frank Skinner*, p. 27, 2001

she-note *noun*
▷ see: SHE-BILL

shepherd *noun*
a firefighter assigned to a hook-and-ladder truck *US*
Probably named for the hook which he carries, evocative of a shepherd's staff.
• — *American Speech*, p. 273, December 1954: 'Fire terms: additional words and definitions'

shepherd *verb*
in croquet, to guide your ball illegally through the hoop by pushing with your mallet *US*
• —James Charlton and William Thompson, *Croquet*, p. 160, 1977: 'Glossary'

Shepherd's Bush *noun*
1 dismissal from employment *UK*
Rhyming slang for THE PUSH, from an area of west London.
• —Ray Puxley, *Cockney Rabbit*, 1992

2 the face *UK*
Rhyming slang for MUSH (the face), from an area of west London.
• —Ray Puxley, *Fresh Rabbit*, 1998

shepherd's pie; shepherd's *noun*
the sky *UK*
Rhyming slang.
• —Ray Puxley, *Cockney Rabbit*, 1992

shepherd's plaid; shepherds *adjective*
bad *UK, 1932*
Rhyming slang.
• —Ray Puxley, *Fresh Rabbit*, 1998

sherbert; sherbet *noun*
alcoholic drink, especially beer; a drink of beer *AUSTRALIA, 1904*
Originally (late C19) any warm alcoholic drink; ultimately Turkish *sherbet* (a cooling non-alcoholic drink).
• [H]e took to the sherbet, which made him a bigger liability than ever. —Charles Raven, *Underworld Nights*, p. 189, 1956
• Up the bar they got a proper bunch of zombies, sipping their coloured sherberts that had bits of watercress and old lemon peel sticking out of them. —John Peter Jones, *Feather Pluckers*, p. 43, 1964
• 'You've been on the sherbet,' Hugh said, 'haven't you?' —Randolph Stow, *The Merry-Go-Round in the Sea*, p. 258, 1965
• Not to mention calling for more sherbets because the biscuits had given 'em a right Geoff Hurst [thirst]. —Andrew Nickolds, *Back to Basics*, p. 93, 1994
• And he said, "Great," with that same dollop of scorn, before asking me impertinently if I'd been "on the sherbets" last night. —Andrew Holmes, *Sleb*, p. 145, 2002

sherbet dab; sherbet *noun*
a taxi, a *cab* *UK*
Rhyming slang.
• —Ray Puxley, *Fresh Rabbit*, 1998
• "Where do we get the sherbet?" "No, we don't need a cab, mate," said Harry. —Garry Bushell, *The Face*, p. 201, 2001

sherbet dip *noun*
a gratuity, a *tip* *UK*
Rhyming slang.
• —Ray Puxley, *Cockney Rabbit*, 1992

Sheridan Morley *adverb*
unwell *UK*
Rhyming slang for 'poorly'; based on the name of noted author, radio presenter and theatre critic Sheridan Morley (b.1941).
• Has the guv'nor gone radio rental [mental]? Is he feeling Sheridan Morley? —Humphrey Lyttleton, *I'm Sorry I Haven't a Clue*, 26th November 2001

sherm *noun*
1 a marijuana cigarette that has been supplemented with phencyclidine, the recreational drug known as PCP or angel dust *US*
From Shermans™, a cigarette brand.
• —Ralph de Sola, *Crime Dictionary*, p. 137, 1982
• —Richard A. Spears, *The Slang and Jargon of Drugs and Drink*, p. 447, 1986
• This is a Blood hood. Amber live here with her baby and her mother. Her mother be smokin' Sherm all the time. — *Rolling Stone*, p. 80, 12th April 2001

2 crack cocaine *US*
• BIG D: Shit! Nigger, you smoke enough sherm, your dumb ass'll do a lot of crazy ass things. — *True Romance*, 1993

3 a social outcast *US*
• —Connie Eble (Editor), *UNC-CH Campus Slang*, p. 8, Spring 1998

sherman tank; sherman *noun*
1 an American *UK*
Rhyming slang for YANK, based on the main US battle tank of World War 2.
• —Ronnie Barker, *Fletcher's Book of Rhyming Slang*, 1979
• —Bob Young and Micky Moody, *The Language of Rock 'n' Roll*, p. 130, 1985

2 an act of masturbation *UK*
Rhyming slang for WANK.
• Samuel Pepys had, according to his diary, a quick Sherman during the sermon[.] —James Hawes, *Dead Long Enough*, p. 9, 2000

shermed *adjective*
intoxicated with phencyclide, an animal tranquillizer *US*
• For home boys and zimmers; This dictionary is def! —*Frederick (Maryland Post*, p. B2, 24th May 1990
• —Kenn "Naz" Young, *Naz's Dictionary of Teen Slang*, p. 104, 1993

sherms *noun*
1 phencyclidine, the recreational drug known as PCP or angel dust *US*
• —Ronald Linder, *PCP*, p. 10, 1981

2 crack cocaine *US*
• —US Department of Justice, *Street Terms*, October 1994

Sherwin-Williams overhaul *noun*
in the used car business, a paint job and no further effort to repair or restore a car for sale *US*
Sherwin-Williams is a paint manufacturer.
• —Lewis Poteet, *Car & Motorcyle Slang*, p. 177, 1992

she-she *adjective*
effeminate *BARBADOS*
• —Frank A. Collymore, *Barbadian Dialect*, p. 101, 1965

she's right
that's okay; everything is all right *AUSTRALIA, 1938*
- 'You don't mind waiting? We'll only get in the way just now.' 'She's right,' was all I said. — Eric Lambert, *The Veterans*, p. 65, 1954
- 'And thank you very much.' 'She's right, mate.' — Nino Culotta (John O'Grady), *They're A Weird Mob*, p. 105, 1957

sheuch *noun*
the cleft between the buttocks *UK: SCOTLAND*
Glasgow slang from broader Scots *sheuch* (a trench, a ditch).
- He gave um a toe-ender, right in the sheuch! — Michael Munro, *The Complete Patter*, p. 137, 1996

▸ **up the sheuch**
mistaken *UK: SCOTLAND*
- If that's what ye think, ye're up the sheuch, mate. — Michael Munro, *The Complete Patter*, p. 137, 1996

shibby *noun*
a man who does housework *UK: SCOTLAND*
- Mid-Ulster. [Origin unknown] — C. I. Macafee, *A Concise Ulster Dictionary*, p. 299, 1996

shibby *adjective*
positive; pleasing *US*
Probably coined by Phil Ashton for the 2001 film *Dude Where's My Car?* in which it is used as a replacement for nouns, verbs, adjectives, proper names, etc.; the original intention in the film was to use the word to mean 'marijuana'; when all drugs references were removed the word remained. This multi-purpose word is also used as a replacement for any verb, and as a lover's nickname.
- — Susie Dent, *Larpers and Shroomers*, p. 73, 2004

shicer; sheister *noun*
a despicable man; a cheat; a welsher *UK, 1846*
From German *scheisser* (a shitter).
- — David Powis, *The Signs of Crime*, 1977

shick *noun*
a slice, a share, a rake-off *UK*
Perhaps from Schick, a US manufacturer of safety and electric razors since 1926.
- — Jenny Fabian and Johnny Byrne, *Groupie*, 1968

shicker; shickered; schicker *adjective*
drunk *AUSTRALIA, 1898*
From Yiddish *shiker* (drunk); like many words for 'intoxicated' (or the causes thereof), there are a number of understandably inconsistent spellings, including: 'shiker', 'shikker', 'shikkered', 'shikkured' and 'shikkared'.
- [W]e were shickered. — Derek Raymond (Robin Cook), *The Crust on its Uppers*, p. 83, 1962
- Three hours later they are pretty shicker!!! — Barry Humphries, *Bazza Pulls It Off!*, 1971
- I reckon he's too schicker to help out. — Barry Humphries, *Bazza Pulls It Off!*, 1971
- — David McGill, *David McGill's Complete Kiwi Slang Dictionary*, 1998

shield *noun*
a police officer *US*
- He was a true disciple of the field, he never used a hammer / or cracked it by the shield while stickin' in the slammer. — Bruce Jackson, *Get Your Ass in the Water and Swim Like Me*, p. 85, 1965

shietel *noun*
▷ see: **SCHEITL**

shift *verb*
1 to move or be moved from prison to prison *UK*
- I shifted around a lot. — Angela Devlin, *Prison Patter*, p. 104, 1996

2 to engage in sexual activity *IRELAND*
The exact type of sexual activity is not specified, unlike, for example, **RIDE** which implies penetrative sex.
- 'Did you shift?', 'No, you must be joking, only a bunch of oul' tightholes'. — Ardal O'Hanlon, *The Talk of the Town*, p. 69–70, 1998

▸ **shift your arse; shift your ass**
to start moving; to move with speed *UK*
- Christ! We'd better shift our arses. — Chris Ryan, *Stand By, Stand By*, p. 225, 1996

▸ **shift your cock**
(of a man) to start moving; to move with speed *UK*
- FUCKIN' 'ELL. Shift y'cock the Geezer's doin' his nut in there. — Nick Barlay, *Curvy Lovebox*, p. 100, 1997

shiftless *noun*
in the car sales business, equipped with an automatic transmission *US*
- — *Cars*, p. 41, December 1953

shifty *noun*
sex with a prostitute *US*
- — Jerry Robertson, *Oil Slanguage*, p. 112, 1954

shikse; shiksa; shixa *noun*
a Gentile woman *UK, 1892*
- The fault lay with them, because they had never approved Lee-Simon's marryhing a shikseh – and a fair-haired one at that[.] — Clancy Sigal, *Going Away*, p. 375, 1961
- That Alice was so blatantly a shikse caused no end of grief in Heshie's household. — Philip Roth, *Portnoy's Complaint*, p. 60, 1969
- — Ray Puxley, *Cockney Rabbit*, 1992

shikse from Dixie *noun*
the ultimate in Gentile femininity *US*
The reference to Dixie is soley for the rhyme; it does not connote that the woman in question is from the south.
- — Lou Shelly, *Hepcats Jive Talk Dictionary*, p. 37, 1945

shill *noun*
1 in a confidence swindle, a confederate who appears to be prospering as a result of the scheme which is designed to fleece the victim *US, 1940*
- I was never even a shill. I was with it, all right. I was a mere stagehand[.] — Iceberg Slim (Robert Beck), *Trick Baby*, p. 39, 1969

2 a person posing as an enthusiastic and satisfied customer in order to boost sales by a confederate *US, 1916*
- He had the compassion of an icicle, the effrontery of a carnival shill, and the generosity of a pawnbroker. — Mardy Grothe, *Oxymoronica*, p. 152, 2004

shill *verb*
to pose falsely as a satisfied customer or successful gambler in order to encourage genuine customers, gamblers, etc *US, 1914*
- I've shilled for a traveling evangelist. — Max Shulman, *The Zebra Derby*, p. 50, 1946
- You follow a man who shills for Pizza Hut-pizza[.] — Howard Stern, *Miss America*, p. 19, 1995

shillelagh *noun*
1 in hot rodding, a Chevrolet engine, especially a V-8 *US*
Only related to the Irish *blackthorn cudgel* in sound.
- — John Lawlor, *How to Talk Car*, p. 92, 1965

2 in horse racing, a jockey's whip *AUSTRALIA*
- — Ned Wallish, *The Truth Dictionary of Racing Slang*, p. 73, 1989

shillings *noun*
money *UK*
- Now these very same guys do all their shillings on charlie [cocaine], in cold blood, fuck the consequences, grafting all week just to get charged up[.] — J.J. Connolly, *Layer Cake*, p. 10, 2000

shillings and pence; shillings *noun*
sense *UK*
Rhyming slang, updated to **POUNDS AND PENCE** in the wake of 1971's decimalisation.
- He aint got the shillings he was born with. — Ray Puxley, *Cockney Rabbit*, 1992

shilly-shally *verb*
to be undecided; to hesitate *UK, 1782*
Rarely heard in the US, but understood in context.
- We are both young, both well formed, both intelligent. Why shilly-shally? Give me a kiss. — Max Shulman, *The Many Loves of Dobie Gillis*, 1951
- No tan, crisp-ironed shirt, economical manner- no shilly-shallying around, no digressions, no waste, friendly, bright. — Eve Babitz, *Eve's Hollywood*, p. 207, 1974

shilly-shallying *noun*
indecision, hesitation *UK, 1842*
- I like Rocky Graziano's way of belting the bejiminy out of his opponents without any shilly-shallying. — *San Francisco Examiner*, 9th April 1946
- I want it on the nail, mind you! No shilly-shallying. — Anonymous *Streetwalker*, p. 142, 1959
- But after some mental shilly-shallying, he decided against it. — Jim Thompson, *The Grifters*, 1963

shim *noun*

1 a plastic strip used for forcing locks *US, 1968*

- —John Ayto, *Oxford Dictionary of Slang*, p. 91, 1998
- All a thief needs is a shim to open a locking bar, Tobias said.—*Myrtle Beach (Florida) Sun-News*, p. D9, 10th September 2004

2 a person whose sex is not easily guessed on the basis of their hair and clothing *US*

- —William D. Alsever, *Glossary for the Establishment and Other Uptight People*, p. 28, December 1970

shim *verb*

to force a lock with a plastic strip *US, 1972*

- —John Ayto, *Oxford Dictionary of Slang*, p. 94, 1998
- A knife and keys were stolen from a real-estate office entered by shimming a front-door lock.—*Washington Post*, p. T6, 21st August 2001

shimmy *noun*

1 the game chemin de fer *US, 1961*

- —Thomas L. Clark, *The Dictionary of Gambling and Gaming*, p. 196, 1987

2 an undershirt *NORFOLK ISLAND*

Perhaps an abbreviation of 'chemise'.

- —Beryl Nobbs Palmer, *A Dictionary of Norfolk Words and Usages*, p. 39, 1992

shimmy act *noun*

a feigned seizure *US*

- They always got those signs around hospitals that says QUIET, and if I was to go into that shimmy act, they'd probably throw me into the pyscho ward and I'll never get out.—*Drugstore Cowboy*, 1988

shimmy dancer *noun*

a woman who performs sexual dances *US*

- [B]oth those girls are workin' shimmy dancers and hustlers I know from Portland.—Ken Kesey, *One Flew Over the Cuckoo's Nest*, p. 210, 1962

shindig *noun*

a party *US, 1871*

A rural term that moved to the city; it gained wide usage as a result of the musical television programme *Shindig* which aired on ABC from September 1964 until January 1966.

- Man, what a shindig that was. Give me a barrelhouse joint on the South Side any day[.]—Mezz Mezzrow, *Really the Blues*, p. 136, 1946
- At such a rowdy shindig[.]—Charles Raven, *Underworld Nights*, p. 102, 1956
- Well, sir, that was quite a little shindig yesterday, wasn't it?—Max Shulman, *Rally Round the Flag, Boys!*, p. 220, 1957
- As you see, I am off to a shindig. Late already. So if you don't mind, I'll buzz.—John Burke and Stuart Douglass, *The Boys*, p. 58, 1962
- It was an ADMIT TWO in Spanish to some shindig up in the quarter. —Mickey Spillane, *Me, Hood!*, p. 48, 1963
- He preached about how much it meant to him for Carol to be his date at a birthday shindig in his honor at a Southside cabaret.—Iceberg Slim (Robert Beck), *Mama Black Widow*, p. 174, 1969
- I want us both to catch a really big shindig.—Barry Humphries, *Bazza Pulls It Off!*, 1971
- "I don't actually like these shindigs" – his hand casually moving from coat pocket to coat pocket in the pile on the bed.—Ed Sanders, *Tales of Beatnik Glory*, p. 73, 1975
- At least one and perhaps several of the celebrants had made use of Elvira's ladies and the rooms upstairs, the extra service fees being charged to the individual partakers and not to the general cost of the shindig[.]—Robert Campbell, *Boneyards*, p. 181, 1992

shine *noun*

1 a black person *US, 1908*

Abusive in any context.

- Suddenly I heard the school superintendent, who had told me to come, yell, "Bring up the shines, gentlemen! Bring up the little shines!"—Ralph Ellison, *Invisible Man*, p. 18, 1947
- "That's shine music," she said.—Hal Ellson, *Tomboy*, p. 15, 1950
- A Negro sitting opposite us smiled. "The shine is wise," said Roy in my ear.—William Burroughs, *Junkie*, p. 46, 1953
- How did the shine assail him?—Chester Himes, *The Real Cool Killers*, p. 40, 1959
- Get the shine out of here, Carlito.—Edwin Torres, *Carlito's Way*, p. 82, 1975
- Porta whispered, "Jimmy, this shine will be D.O.A. at County[.]" —Iceberg Slim (Robert Beck), *Death Wish*, p. 241, 1977
- Listen, you shine, we 'bout carved up one jungle bunny t'night.—Larry Heinemann, *Close Quarters*, p. 164, 1977
- Let the judge see this poor, rickety old glass of milk jammed in between the shines.—Vincent Patrick, *Family Business*, p. 45, 1985

2 a government bureaucrat *US*

From the shine on the seat of the bureacrat's trousers.

- —Carsten Stroud, *Close Pursuit*, p. 275, 1987

3 alcohol *US, 1933*

- Some of Roland Crowe's buddies were still sloshing around back there in the swamp, driving air boats, guiding hunting and fishing parties, poaching alligators, making shine[.]—Elmore Leonard, *Gold Coast*, p. 33, 1980

4 a still used in the illegal production of alcohol *US*

- —David W. Maurer, *Kentucky Moonshine*, p. 124, 1974

5 an act of oral sex *UK, 2002*

A possible play on spit and polish as a means of getting a shine; it seems only to have been noted in the plural.

▸ **take a shine to**

to take a liking to someone or something *US, 1839*

- Some friends' five year-old daughter took a shine to one of my necklaces. I was fond of it too[.]—*The Guardian*, 17th August 1999

shine *verb*

1 to speak evasively and avoid a subject, often through flattery *US*

- I'm the Finnegan that calls here twice a week hoping to at least hear Orson say there's no work, except that you shine me every time, and I never hear him say anything at all.—Joseph Wambaugh, *Finnegan's Week*, p. 5, 1993

2 to mock someone *US*

- —*Washington Post*, 14th October 1993

3 on the railways, to start a work shift *US*

- —Ramon Adams, *The Language of the Railroader*, p. 136, 1977

▸ **shine for**

to appeal to someone *US*

- He's kind of big and kind of ugly and he's giving the up and down. Right off he don't shine for me.—Hal Ellson, *Duke*, p. 30, 1949

▸ **shine on**

to ignore something completely *US*

- He's in there trying to pick up teenyboppers, but they've all shined him on.—Gerald Petievich, *Money Men*, p. 47, 1981
- No, I shined it on and went to Hawaii.—Sandra Bernard, *Confessions of a Pretty Lady*, p. 80, 1988

shine box *noun*

a nightclub for an exclusively black clientele; a nightclub providing entertainment by black jazz musicians *US*

Combines **SHINE** (a black person) and otherwise obsolete 'box' (a tavern, from French *boîte*).

- "No white folks, brother. Jes' fo' the coloured people. I'se sorry." [...] "Shine box," he said angrily, under his breath.—Raymond Chandler, *Farewell My Lovely*, p. 5, 1940

shine parlor *noun*

an establishment that sells alcohol illegally, by the drink *US*

The 'shine' is an abbreviated **MOONSHINE**.

- Shot-house operators run informal (and illegal) taverns in their own homes (shot-house operators are often women). The houses go by other names too; gold mine, good-time house, blind tiger, shine parlor, or juicejoint.—Burgess Laughlin, *Job Opportunities in the Black Market*, p. 10–9, 1978

shiner *noun*

1 a black eye *US, 1904*

- For a busted smeller, a couple of shiners, and a few creases in the knowledge-box, he made himself ten grand.—Mezz Mezzrow, *Really the Blues*, p. 21, 1946
- He was going to have a couple of very unlovely black eyes. I, who had seen him at a gross disadvantage, was to receive a figurative shiner. —Jim Thompson, *Roughneck*, p. 133, 1954
- But his picture was in the paper. He had quite a 'shiner.'—Mary McCarthy, *The Group*, p. 166, 1963
- I crawled out of it with a sprained thumb and a bloody lip, Pookie picked up a gorgeous shiner.—John Nichols, *The Sterile Cuckoo*, p. 166, 1965
- With your kind of face, the shiner does something, George! Makes it interesting[.]—*The Sweeney*, p. 44, 1976
- "That's a pretty bad shiner," Letch said. "Oliver hit you with his fist or what?"—Joseph Wambaugh, *Floaters*, p. 43, 1996

2 a torch *US*

- —Hyman E. Goldin et al., *Dictionary of American Underworld Lingo*, p. 191, 1950

3 a railway lantern *US*

- —Norman Carlisle, *The Modern Wonder Book of Trains and Railroading*, p. 267, 1946

4 in carnival usage, a diamond *US*

- —Don Wilmeth, *The Language of American Popular Entertainment*, p. 238, 1981

5 in gambling, an object that reflects, enabling the user to cheat by seeing cards as they are dealt *US*

- He had two "shiners" working on the table; one was a money clip that he could lay on the table directly in front of him. It was shiny, but only reflected directly back. — Stephen J.Cannell, *King Con*, p. 2, 1997

shiner player *noun*

in gambling, a cheat who uses a shiny object to reflect the cards as they are dealt *US*

- Besides dice tats and 7UPS, there were volumes for nail nickers and crimpers (card markers), hand muckers and mitt men (card switchers), as well as card counters and shiner players. — Stephen J.Cannell, *Big Con*, p. 143, 1997

shiney *noun*

a clerk *UK*

A reference to the shiny seat of a clerk's trousers – caused by an excess of sitting down. In Royal Air Force use, 2002.

shin fight *noun*

a sham gang fight *US*

- The shin fight simulates gang combat except that knives and guns are now used and blows are not supposed to be struck below the belt or in the face. — Harrison E. Salisbury, *The Shook-up Generation*, p. 25, 1958

shingle *noun*

1 a name plate above a prison cell door *US*

- The name-plate over his cell (a "shingle"), which formerly was white, now becomes blue and, as such, identifies him as someone who has committed a serious infraction of rules. — Arthur V. Huffman, *New York Mattachine Newsletter*, p. 7, August 1961

2 a car number plate *US*

- — John R.Armore and Joseph D. Wolfe, *Dictionary of Desperation*, 1976

3 a lawyer *US*

- I spoke to Iggy Fitelstein. Iggy's the best shingle in New York. — Truman Capote, *Breakfast at Tiffany's*, p. 95, 1958

▸ **a shingle short**

lacking a full complement of intelligence *AUSTRALIA, 1844*

From 'shingle' (a wooden roofing tile), thus 'a shingle short of a roof'.

- Sometimes I think you're a shingle short Bazza. — *The Adventures of Barry McKenzie*, 1972
- — Bob Ellis and Anne Brooksbank, *Mad Dog Morgan*, p. 106, 1976

shining time *noun*

starting time for work *US*

- — Norman Carlisle, *The Modern Wonder Book of Trains and Railroading*, p. 267, 1946

Shinner *noun*

a member of Sinn Fein *IRELAND, 1921*

- As I sat inside the door, the Secretary of State Mo Mowlam suddenly appeared. Not one for protocol, she waved at "the Shinners" and continued down the hall to John Hume's office. — Tom Hayden, *Irish on the Inside*, p. 209, 2003

shinola *noun*

used as a contrast in describing ignorance as not knowing shit from shinola *US, 1940*

Shinola was a patented name (1903) for a boot polish.

- And I don't think the guy knows shit from Shinola about my case[.] — George V. Higgins, *The Judgment of Deke Hunter*, p. 50, 1976
- Paulie, the truth is, this horse don't know shit from Shinola. None of them do. — Vincent Patrick, *The Pope of Greenwich Village*, p. 179, 1979
- His interviewees were hicks who didn't know shit from Shinola. — James Ellroy, *Because the Night*, p. 325, 1984
- Aw, he don't know a cuss word from shinola. — *Raising Arizona*, 1987

shinplaster *noun*

a dollar *CANADA*

- When the Canadian shinplaster plunged to a devaluated discount, the churl's reactionary conservatism crumbled, economically as well as politically. — *Toronto Globe and Mail*, p. 3–4, 29th April 1963

shiny and bright; shiny *adjective*

right *UK*

Rhyming slang.

- A state of satisfaction is quoted as "all shiny". — Ray Puxley, *Cockney Rabbit*, 1992

shiny-arse *noun*

a desk worker *AUSTRALIA, 1945*

Disparaging. During World War 2 used of base personnel who saw no combat.

- I've been signing forms till I got writer's cramp, and the shiny-arses have been round asking a million bloody questions[.] — Eric Lambert, *The Veterans*, p. 16, 1954

shiny buttons *noun*

money *US*

- — Marcus Hanna Boulware, *Jive and Slang of Students in Negro Colleges*, 1947

shiny wing pilot *noun*

a pilot who has just completed his flight instruction training *US*

- — *American Speech*, p. 120, May 1963: 'Air refueling words'

ship *noun*

▸ **on the ship**

in prison, an unofficially worded instruction for immediate transfer to another prison *UK*

- — Angela Devlin, *Prison Patter*, p. 104, 1996

ship; ship out; ship off *verb*

to move or be moved from prison to prison *US, 1950*

- — Angela Devlin, *Prison Patter*, p. 104, 1996

ship driver *noun*

a US Navy officer *US*

Gulf war usage.

- — *American Speech*, p. 88, Spring 1992: 'Gulf War words supplement'

shipfucker *noun*

a rabble rouser; a troublemaker *US*

- Now Dolomite was from San Antone / a rambling shipfucker from the day he was born. — Bruce Jackson, *Get Your Ass in the Water and Swim Like Me*, p. 58, 1970

ship in full sail; ship *noun*

ale *UK, 1857*

Rhyming slang.

- — Ray Puxley, *Cockney Rabbit*, 1992

shipoopi *noun*

a woman *US*

- Remember the halcyon days, when you could get a cheesecake shot of any shipoopi into any paper by announcing she had just been chosen Girl I'd Most Like To Be Snowed In With[?] — Bernard Wolfe, *The Late Risers*, p. 42, 1954
- But a woman who'll wait til the third time around / Head in clouds, feet on the ground / She's the girl he's glad he's found / She's his shipoopi! — Meredith Wilson, *Shipoop i (from the Music Man)*, 1957

shippie *noun*

a prostitute focused on visiting sailors as customers *NEW ZEALAND*

- — Harry Orsman, *A Dictionary of Modern New Zealand Slang*, p. 120, 1999

ship's anchor *noun*

a contemptible person *UK*

Rhyming slang for **WANKER**.

- — Bodmin Dark, *Dirty Cockney Rhyming Slang*, 2003

ship-tick *noun*

in college, a notification of academic deficiency *US*

- — *American Speech*, p. 76–77, February 1968: 'Some notes on flunk notes'

shiralee *noun*

a swag *AUSTRALIA, 1892*

Now only historical.

- And from his shoulder drops the swag, The shiralee, the tether, That through the cruel, stumbling day Drove all his bones together. — Ruth Park, *The Ballad of the Shiralee*, 1955

shirt-lifter *noun*

a male homosexual *AUSTRALIA, 1966*

- Let's face it, for a while Australia's image as a land of culture copped a terrific lot of rubbish and knocking from the expatriate sector, mainly a bunch of know-alls and shirt-lifters, who in my humble viewpoint are lower than the basic wage. — Barry Humphries, *Les Patterson's Australia*, p. [viii], 1978
- Sure, there are any number of frocked-up fruit-baskets, but these kilted Khyber-divers only gown up to look really girly and entertain other shirt-lifters in shady bum bars. — *Picture*, p. 28, 5th February 1992
- I had him down as a shirtlifter, what do you reckon? — Garry Bushell, *The Face*, p. 136, 2001
- [W]e stood out like a pair of shirt-lifters in the sudden silence. — Duncan MacLaughlin, *The Filth*, p. 50, 2002

shirty *adjective*

angry, especially if only temporarily; characteristically ill-tempered *UK, 1897*

From 'shirt' as a symbol of anger in such obsolete phrases as: 'lose your shirt' or 'have your shirt out' (to become angry).

- All right, all right. No need to get shirty. Only having my little joke. — Graeme Kent, *The Queen's Corporal [Six Granada Plays]*, p. 92, 1959

Shishkaberry *noun*

in British Columbia, a local hybrid strain of marijuana *CANADA*

- Shishkaberry is a hybrid developed from a strain called Blueberry. — Brian Preston, *Pot Planet*, p. 5, 2002

shishkebob *noun*

the penis *US*

Rhyming slang for **KNOB** (the penis); based on the appropriately shaped Turkish dish shish kebab (roast meat on a skewer).

- Women all grabbin' at my shishkebob[.] — Eminem (Marshall Mathers), *Cum On Everybody*, 1999

shisty *adjective*

cold-hearted, mean *US*

- — Rick Ayers (Editor), *Berkeley High Slang Dictionary*, p. 38, 2004

shit *noun*

1 heroin *US, 1950*

- It's good shit, not like some of the stuff we've been getting lately. — Alexander Trocchi, *Cain's Book*, p. 9, 1960
- I'm gon beat you wit my gun in your head, nigger, until you go in the hospital. Cause I'd rather see you there than see you on shit. — Claude Brown, *Manchild in the Promised Land*, p. 112, 1965
- "Go easy on it, 'cause it's high-percentage shit"/ Said Bud. "So take it real slow." — Dennis Wepman et al., *The Life*, p. 56, 1976
- Nickie and his friend proceeded to get straight, cooking up their shit. — Herbert Huncke, *The Evening Sun Turned Crimson*, p. 144, 1980
- His father had been unable to figure out any other way to ice Little Phil Terrone, the heaviest shit and boo dealer in the North Bronx. — Richard Condon, *Prizzi's Honor*, p. 4, 1982
- Guess he got hold of some bad shit one night. — Jess Mowry, *Way Past Cool*, p. 35, 1992
- White people who know the difference between good shit and bad shit, this is the house they come to. My shit, I'll take the Pepsi Challenge with Amsterdam shit any ol' day of the fuckin' week. — *Pulp Fiction*, 1994
- YOUNG STUD: This is twice in two days a chick has O.D.'d on me. COLONEL: Well maybe that means you oughta think about getting some new shit, what do you think? — *Boogie Nights*, 1997

2 marijuana *US, 1946*

- Enrique went off and got me about 2 ounces of shit for only $3[.]. — Jack Kerouac, *Letter to Allen Ginsberg*, p. 350, 10th May 1952
- "Man," he breathed, "that was real shit." — Bernard Wolfe, *The Late Risers*, p. 84, 1954
- Well, of course, I been smokin' shit for about seven years now, and my knowledge is pretty fair. — Bruce Jackson, *Get Your Ass in the Water and Swim Like Me*, p. 90, 1964
- Sitting on the couch smoking shit and enjoying yourself? — Lenny Bruce, *The Essential Lenny Bruce*, p. 111–112, 1967
- [He] was doing a year [in prison, in Panama] for selling marijuana. He bought his shit from the guards. — Richard Neville, *Play Power*, p. 224, 1970
- If tha Shit is tha Shit / Cause when it comes to smokin' cheeba / You know my shit is legit — Tone Loc, *Cheeba Cheeba*, 1989
- Yes I smoke shit, straight off the roach clip — Cypress Hill, *I Wanna Get High*, 1993

3 crack cocaine *UK*

- I was licking shit. — Angela Devlin, *Prison Patter*, p. 104, 1996
- He'll do you two for $2,000, and it's good shit too. — Lanre Fehintola, *Charlie Says...*, p. 71, 2000

4 narcotics; drugs in general *US*

- Some kids call all dope "shit" or "junk," terms that were once synonyms for heroin. — Nicholas Von Hoffman, *We Are The People Our Parents Warned Us Against*, p. 65, 1967

5 things; possessions *US*

- They thought it was some strange shit, but glanced at one another, realizing that she liked to fuck. — Steve Cannon, *Groove, Bang, and Jive Around*, 1969
- [P]eople telling you how to do your shit. — Frank Zappa, *The Real Frank Zappa Book*, 1989
- VINCENT: It's the little differences. A lotta the same shit we got here, they got there, but there they're a little different. — *Pulp Fiction*, 1994
- You had to really be into your own shit to own a pair [of trainers], not like now – where they are high street staples. — John Robb, *The Nineties*, p. 28, 1999
- The guitar riff sampled from Guns N' Roses' "Sweet Child O' Mine". Dope shit. — *Muzik*, p. 24, February 2003

6 anything at all *US*

- He didn't recognize shit. — Quentin Tarantino, *From Dusk Till Dawn*, p. 12, 1995

7 nothing; something of no value *IRELAND, 1922*

- Size aint shit, he's from the old school fool. — NWA *Fuck Tha Police*, 1988

8 et cetera *US*

- It's so cool. Like all the cool people live here and shit. — *200 Cigarettes*, 1999

9 used as a basis for extreme comparisons *US*

- Well, sure as shit and taxes, he comes there every night just as regular you can set your watch by him. — William Burroughs, *Naked Lunch*, p. 175, 1957
- Wally did Danny a great big favour once and Danny's a soft as shit and he'd do thirty [years imprisonment] rather than point at me and Wally[.] — Ted Lewis, *Jack Carter's Law [britpulp]*, p. 47–48, 1974
- [T]his is as cool as shit. There can't be anything better than this'. — Ted Nugent, *Ask*, p. 49, 5th May 1979
- As easily as if he were offering another shot of rum, he said one fellow was as mean as black cat shit. — Harry Bruce, *Down Home*, p. 108, 1988
- Brrrr! It's cold as shit lickety-split I think we're here, G[.] — D.A.S-E.F.X. *Hard Like a Criminal*, 1992
- [T]he dumb-as-shit committee[.] — Tony Wilson, *24 Hour Party People*, p. 209, 2002

10 a foul mood *AUSTRALIA*

- You're in a shit because you've been swinging your dick at anything available and missing by yards. — David Williamson, *Don's Party*, p. 63, 1973
- — David McGill, *David McGill's Complete Kiwi Slang Dictionary*, 1998
- 'I was just asking,' said Chris. 'Well dont.' He really was in a shit. — Phillip Gwynne, *Deadly Unna?*, p. 255, 1998

11 trouble *US, 1937*

- We troublemakers would be in deep shit if it weren't for our movement lawyers[.] — Jerry Rubin, *Do It!*, p. 160, 1970
- He's been in and outta shit since he was thirteen, and he's got a couple man-sized charges too. — Vernon E. Smith, *The Jones Men*, p. 123, 1974
- I'm extremely rebellious. I've cut every single day of school so far except one. I'm in deep shit with my mother at all times. — C.D. Payne, *Youth in Revolt*, 1993
- JULES: Listen up man, me an' my homeboy are in some serious shit. We're in a car we gotta get off the road, pronto! — *Pulp Fiction*, 1994

12 a contemptible person *UK, 1508*

Figurative use of excrement, since C16; often in combination as 'regular shit', 'arrogant shit', etc.

- CARTER: You shit. You didn't have the guts to do it yourself, did you? — Mike Hodges, *Get Carter*, p. 65, 1971
- And never believe what the police say because they're shits. — Macfarlane, Macfarlane and Robson, *The User*, p. 50, 1996
- Don't fuck with me, you little shit. — Simon Napier-Bell, *Black Vinyl White Powder*, p. 100, 2001

13 criticism *UK*

- [Mogwai] gave a track ("Summer") to a Levi's advert and got a lot of shit for it. — *X-Ray*, p. 62, June 2003

14 abuse; unfair treatment *UK*

- [The West Indian Youths] think because they've taken so much shit from the police, they're going to dole some back in court. — *New Society*, 24th January 1980

15 nonsense *UK, 1930*

- You can give me a whole ration of shit and this and that, and blah, blah, blah. — George V. Higgins, *The Friends of Eddie Coyle*, p. 75, 1971

16 used as a term of endearment *US*

Especially common in the phrase 'little shit'.

- "Ain't he the cutest little shit?" said Fluffy to Poppy. — Joseph Wambaugh, *The New Centurions*, p. 232, 1970

17 business *US*

- JULES: I apologize for bein' in your shit like I was. — *Pulp Fiction*, 1994

18 in the recording industry, a hit single *US*

- — Arnold Shaw, *Dictionary of American Pop/Rock*, p. 348, 1982

19 excrement; an act of defecation *UK, 1585*

Conventional from the C16, since the C19 has been considered vulgar.

20 used as a meaningless discourse marker *UK*

- [L]oads of blokes wank over her, it don't mean a thing. I mean, shit, even I've wanked over her. — Colin Butts, *Is Harry on the Boat?*, p. 25, 1997

21 a bombardment, especially with shrapnel *UK, 1931*

A military usage recorded in use in the Falkland Islands during 1982 by Robert McGowan and Jeremy Hands, *Don't Cry for Me*, 1983.

▸ **all about like shit in a field**

everywhere *UK*

- Oh hell, it's him again... he's all about like shit in a field. — Caroline Aherne and Craig Cash, *The Royle Family*, 1999

▸ drop in the shit
to get someone blamed and into trouble *UK*
A variation of **LAND IN THE SHIT**; a conventional sense of 'drop' combined with **IN THE SHIT** (in trouble).
- [O]ld big mouth decided to drop us both back into the shit for no good reason. — Danny King, *The Burglar Diaries*, p. 108, 2001

▸ fall in the shit
to get into trouble *UK*
A conventional sense of 'fall' combined with **IN THE SHIT**; leading to the clichéd envy of 'he could fall in the shit and come out smelling of roses'.

▸ get your shit together
to take control of your personal condition; to get your mind and emotions under control; to become organised *US, 1969*
A variation of 'pull yourself together'.
- — Angela Devlin, *Prison Patter*, p. 56, 1996

▸ give a shit
to care, to be concerned – usually in a negative context *UK, 1970s*
- I don't give a shit. Answer it. Get off my back. — *Airheads*, 1994
- "Sorry if you've had to run around a bit," Napoleon didn't give a shit, "but you know how it is.["] — Stewart Home, *Sex Kick [britpulp]*, p. 240, 1999
- "Oh," she said, like she could really, really give a shit. — John Williams, *Cardiff Dead*, p. 85, 2000

▸ have shit for brains
to be stupid; to lack intelligence *AUSTRALIA*
- However the person who supports another team and is described as having 'shit for brains' is a 'proper dick head' and should be ignored. — Ivor Limb, *Footy's No Joke!*, p. 22, 1986

▸ have shit on the liver
to be irritable *AUSTRALIA, 1935*

▸ have your shit together; get your shit together
to be focused, organised, self-confident *US*
- "We've just got to get our shit together," the theme ran, but the issue of "how?" was never resolved and the more important question "why?" was never asked. — Raymond Mungo, *Famous Long Ago*, p. 49, 1970
- Charlie's definitely got his shit together. — *Full Metal Jacket*, 1987

▸ in deep shit
in serious trouble *US*
- Val, listen to me. We are in deep shit, here. — *200 Cigarettes*, 1999

▸ in the shit
1 in considerable trouble *UK, 1937*
You can be **IN DEEP SHIT**, **FALL IN THE SHIT** or **LAND** (someone else) **IN THE SHIT**.
- But if Roy's in the shit he can fuckin' get himself out of it on his fuckin' jack[.] — J.J. Connolly, *Know Your Enemy [britpulp]*, p. 151, 1999
- He's in the shit. Up to his neck and there's no one he can turn to for help and advice. — Jack Allen, *When the Whistle Blows*, p. 138, 2000
- [T]hey usually know they're in the shit and want to do a deal. — Duncan MacLaughlin, *The Filth*, p. 111, 2002

2 in combat *US*
- I am fucking bored to death, man. I gotta get back in the shit. I ain't heard a shot fired in anger in weeks. — *Full Metal Jacket*, 1987

▸ land in the shit
to get someone blamed and into trouble *UK*
A conventional sense of 'land' (to set down) combined with **IN THE SHIT**, generally heard as 'landed (someone) in the shit'.

▸ like shit off a shovel
extremely fast, swift, prompt *UK*
- — Nicholas Blincoe, *The Beautiful Beaten-up Irish Boy of the Arndale Centre*, p. 1, 1998

▸ not for shit
of a person's ability to do something, not at all, by no means, not in any circumstances *UK*
- [S]he can't sing for shit an she looks like my fuckin dad. — Niall Griffiths, *Sheepshagger*, p. 104, 2001

▸ run shit down
to discuss something; to inform someone; to explain something *US*
- This is no "introduction." I'm just glad for the chance to run some shit down, cut up some things, in the context of relating to Jerry. — Eldridge Cleaver, *Do It! (Introduction)*, 1970

▸ talk shit
to say disparaging things *UK*
- CLARENCE: The whole time you were a drunk, did I ever point my finger at you and talk shit? No! — *True Romance*, 1993

▸ the shit
the best *US*
- CHRIS: If I was going to college I'd go to one of them Black colleges they got down south. MONSTER: Yeah, that's the shit. — *Boyz N The Hood*, 1990
- I wish I had a quarterback like you in Arizona. You're the shit. — *Jerry Maguire*, 1996
- You're crispy, you're the shit, you really are, Joey. You're the man. — Joel Rose, *Kill Kill Faster Faster*, p. 141, 1997
- "I love this car," Lula said. "I feel like the shit in this car."' — Janet Evanovitch, *High Five*, 1999
- — Don R. McCreary (Editor), *Dawg Speak*, 2001

▸ the shit will fly
there will be trouble *UK*
- [T]rying to row out from a bird like Audrey would be just as dangerous as the present situation. The shit would fly whatever I did. — Ted Lewis, *Jack Carter's Law*, p. 11, 1974

▸ three kinds of shit
a lot of trouble *AUSTRALIA*
- Man you wouldn't even be asking me along if you didn't think there was going to be three kinds of shit coming down from day one. — Harrison Biscuit, *The Search for Savage Henry*, p. 31, 1995

▸ treat like shit
to treat someone in a disdainful or humiliating manner *UK*
- [S]he was about the only person who didn't treat me like shit, so we formed a friendship[.] — Jane Green, *Mr Maybe*, p. 1, 1999

▸ up to shit
no good; hopeless *AUSTRALIA*
- If a mere mortal like me can see the prison system is up to shit, then why can't the people in power see it? — Ray Denning, *Prison Diaries*, p. 48, 1978
- — Robert G. Barrett, *Davo's Little Something*, p. 216, 1992

▸ when the shit hits the fan; when the shit flies
the moment when a crisis starts, especially if such trouble has been expected *UK, 1966*
- — Todd Rundgren, *When the Shit Hits the Fan/Sunset Blvd*, 1973
- I was proficient. But when the shit hit the fan, all I could think about was that the other character was trying to kill me. — Andy McNab, *Immediate Action*, p. 44, 1995

▸ you're shit and you know you are
used by football fans as a chant to disparage (and enrage) the opposing team and fans *UK*
- [P]roud to be a Londoner and a supporter of West Ham [...] yelling "You're shit and you know you are," at a family of baboons. — Mark Steel, *Reasons to be Cheerful*, p. 2, 2001

shit *verb*
1 to defecate *UK, 1308*
Conventional English for about 400 years from the C14, then, sometime in the C19, slipped into vulgarity.
- The Mafia? I shit 'em. — Barrie Keefe, *The Long Good Friday*, 1979

2 to deceive someone; to lie to someone or stretch the truth *US, 1934*
An abbreviated form of **BULLSHIT**.
- "You're shitting me," says Mule. "I wouldn't shit you. You're my favorite turd," says the chief. — Darryl Ponicsan, *The Last Detail*, p. 17, 1970
- [H]e could picture the guy now: little Jew-boy with a cowboy hat, "Larry, you're shittin' me, aren't you?" — Elmore Leonard, *Mr. Majestyk*, p. 135, 1974
- "You shittin' me?" "Would I shit you? You're my favorite turd." — Richard Price, *The Wanderers*, p. 25, 1974
- Don't shit a shitter. — Elmore Leonard, *Cat Chaser*, 1982
- You're shittin, right? Kip? — *Gone in 60 Seconds*, 2000
- I ain't shittin u. — Sacha Baron-Cohen *Da Gospel According to Ali G*, 2001
- You're shitting me! — *Ministry*, p. 162, May 2002

▸ shit a brick
to have a difficult time accepting something; to react with anger *US*
- All I know is that people were shitting bricks up at his place last Saturday. — Mike Hodges, *Get Carter*, p. 53, 1971
- When I told Woody and the brass about this coup, they practically shit a brick. I'm talkin' an adobe brick. — *Natural Born Killers*, 1994
- Yep, Gil Green shit a brick when he saw the bill. — Stephen J.Cannell, *King Con*, p. 17, 1997
- [H]e nearly shat a brick. Well, not a brick really, more like a lager shandy. — John King, *White Trash*, p. 39, 2001

▸ **shit all over**
to surpass someone or something by a great degree *UK*
- That's what I call a hymn. It shits all over "All Things Bright and Beautiful", doesn't it? — Richard Herring, *Talking Cock*, p. 57, 2003

▸ **shit in**
to win easily or by a large margin *AUSTRALIA*
- The teller picked up a fistful of silver and pushed the lot back and said 'Lady – you SHIT IN.' — Sam Weller, *Old Bastards I Have Met*, p. 66, 1979
- All my men are on and he will shit in. So don't ask me to pull it because I won't. — Clive Galea, *Slipper*, p. 65, 1988

▸ **shit it**
to be very nervous or worried; to be thoroughly frightened *UK*
An allusion to the bowel-loosening effect of terror.
- Whatever he thinks is fine by me. I'm shitting it. — John King, *Human Punk*, p. 114, 2000
- I would've done anything for her. But I was shitting it that she'd tell Ged. — Kevin Sampson, *Outlaws*, p. 104, 2001
- What about me? I'm shitting it, that's what. Just totally and utterly shitting it. — Ben Elton, *High Society*, p. 227, 2002

▸ **shit it in**
to do something with ease *AUSTRALIA*
- Crowds can be heavy, but if you've ever surfed a metropolitan break, you'll shit it in. — *Tracks*, p. 45, October 1992

▸ **shit nickels**
to be very frightened *US*
- — Collin Baker et al., *College Undergraduate Slang Study Conducted at Brown University*, p. 193, 1968

▸ **shit on**
to disparage or abuse someone *UK, 1984*
- Not wanting to shit on the Scousers too much — Tony Wilson, *24 Hour Party People*, p. 164, 2002

▸ **shit or get off the pot**
to get out of the way and let someone else try to do it; make your mind up *CANADA, 1966*
Originally directed at dice players.
- There comes a time in matters like these when you have to shit or get off the pot! The great trouble here is the indecision. — David Gergen, *Eyewitness to Power*, p. 39, 2001

▸ **shit the life out of**
to frighten someone *UK*
Variation of conventional 'scare the life out of' combined with SCARE THE SHIT OUT OF.
- It really shit the life out of us [.] — Dave Courtney, *Stop the Ride I Want to Get Off*, p. 74, 1999

▸ **shit your pants**
1 to soil your underpants by accidental defecation *UK*
- YOU SHIT YOUR PANTS BUT YOU FAIL TO SNIFF ITS SMELL. — *The Guardian*, 23rd March 2001

2 to be terrified *UK*
To lose control over your excretory functions is noted as a symptom of extreme terror; however, this is used figuratively (most of the time), often as an exaggeration.
- He went into this whole story and he sent the letter and he was shitting in his pants, waiting for the FCC to show up. — Howard Stern, *Private Parts*, p. 140, 1994

▸ **shit your shorts**
to behave in a nervous or frightened manner *US*
- That's what people do when they're feelin' scared and insecure. You're shittin' your shorts an' lookin' over your shoulder the whole time[.] — Christopher Brookmyre, *The Sacred Art of Stealing*, p. 7, 2002

▸ **shit yourself**
to be terrified *UK, 1914*
To lose control over your excretory functions is noted as a symptom of extreme terror; it is used here (and most of the time) in a figurative sense, certainly as an exaggeration.
- When I woke up I couldn't see land! I absolutely fucking shat myself. — Dave Courtney, *Raving Lunacy*, p. 238, 2000
- The others shit themselves. — Kevin Sampson, *Outlaws*, p. 1, 2001
- Two blondes grabbed me and tried to take me into the bathroom [...] I bottled it and shat myself. — *The Guardian*, p. 4, 28th June 2004

shit *adjective*
1 inferior; shoddy; valueless; unpleasant; disliked for whatever reason *UK, 1930*
- "I've already told yer I don't give a toss what she's up to." "Even if she's shit at her job?" — Colin Butts, *Is Harry on the Boat?*, p. 127, 1997
- It tasted fucking shit, so fucking shit I found another cup of cold coffee and had another bloody one. — David Peace, *Nineteen Seventy-Four*, p. 100, 1999
- You're fucking Ku-Klux-Klan, you fucking shit cunt. — Wayne Anthony, *Spanish Highs*, p. 69, 1999
- There was a lot of shit pills out there[.] — Dave Courtney, *Raving Lunacy*, p. 72, 2000
- I don't agree with you that New Labour are a disappointment. I knew they'd be shit from the start. — Mark Steel, *Reasons to be Cheerful*, p. 270, 2001
- You're shit and you know you are. — Frank Skinner, *Frank Skinner*, p. 26, 2001

2 unfashionable; in poor taste *UK*
- Wearing glasses is quite trendy now but in those days it was very shit. — Frank Skinner, *Frank Skinner*, p. 32, 2001

3 bad *US*
- I have had the worse shitluck possible with that book and it is the same thing all the time with whatever I do. — Jack Kerouac, *Letter to Neal Cassady*, p. 239, 3rd December 1950
- But that makes me feel shit, too. Shit about the shitty world we live in. — Kevin Sampson, *Outlaws*, 2001
- [T]hings went from bad to really, really shit[.] — Rob Fitzpatrick, *Ministry*, January 2002

4 despicable *US*
- "The fuckers [the police] are just covering the whole park." "Shit bastards!" — John Rechy, *The Sexual Outlaw*, p. 223, 1977

5 good *UK*
- Shit film that... meaning good. Shit means good in Manchester. — Shaun Ryder, *Shaun Ryder... in His Own Words*, 1996

shit!
used for registering annoyance, frustration, despair, etc *UK, 1920*
- David, an editor at [Paul] Gascoigne's publishers, receives a text. He turns ashen. "Oh, no. Shit. Shit. Shit." "Is everything OK?" Georgina the publicist asks him discreetly. "No. No, it's not." He shows her the text. "Shit," she says. " Shit. Shit. Shit." — *The Guardian*, 22nd June 2004

shit a brick!; shit-a-brick!; shit on a brick!
used for expressing annoyance, disgust or shock *AUSTRALIA*
- Shit a brick. There's fifteen and a zac on the clock already. That's nearly a note where I come from. — Barry Humphries, *The Wonderful World of Barry McKenzie*, p. 8, 1968
- The I remembered. Football. Grand final. Wangaroo. The Thumper. Today. Shit-a-brick! — Phillip Gwynne, *Deadly Unna?*, p. 86, 1998

shit-all *noun*
nothing, nothing at all *US*
A variation of FUCK ALL.
- Leo never done much time and certainly didn't do any since he was just a kid that didn't know shit-all from what he was doing so he was always getting caught. — George V. Higgins, *The Rat on Fire*, p. 107, 1981
- Well, nothing recent if it was a conviction for shit-all, because a con for shit-all meant you weren't much of a villain. — Garry Bushell, *The Face*, p. 33, 2001

shit and a shave *noun*
a short sentence of imprisonment *UK*
An inference that the sentence is for no more time than it takes to get ready to go out.
- — Angela Devlin, *Prison Patter*, p. 104, 1996

shit and derision!; shit and corruption!; shit and molasses!
used for registering annoyance and frustration *UK*
Originally air force, describing weather conditions.
- DOCTOR: Oh shit and derision. Sometimes I wish I was a vet. — Alan Bleasedale, *Boys From the Blackstuff*, 1982

shit and git *verb*
to leave quickly *US*
- — Michael Dalton Johnson, *Talking Trash with Redd Foxx*, p. 122, 1994

shit and shinola *noun*
in poker, three two's *US*
- — Peter Tamony, March 1948

shitaree *noun*
a toilet *UK*
- — Kathleen Meyer, *How to Shit in the Woods*, p. 105, 1994

shit-ass; shirt-arse *noun*
a despicable person *US, 1942*
- I had Reggie figured – Earl is a man, a boss, uptown or downtown, where Reggie is a shitass and he knows it. — Edwin Torres, *Carlito's Way*, p. 83, 1975
- — *Maledicta*, p. 13, Summer 1977: 'A word for it!'

shit-ass *adjective*

despicable, of poor quality *US*

- [I]t could've been five, motherfucking shitass car, but it's four, four people in two nights, only one tonight, four. — John Rechy, *Numbers*, p. 107, 1967
- Enough of these shit-ass questions, let's fuck. (Caption) — *Screw*, p. 6, 19th January 1970
- Shit ass punk! — *Airheads*, 1994
- Awww, it's just been a shitass day. Every inch of it hot and miserable. — Quentin Tarantino, *From Dusk Till Dawn*, p. 3, 1995

shitbag *noun*

a despicable person or object *UK*

- I gets to thinking about this manager, and wondering if he really was the sort of shitbag I had him down for. — John Peter Jones, *Feather Pluckers*, p. 84, 1964
- He's a out-and-out shitbag that preys on old ladies and defenceless schoolboys. — Kevin Sampson, *Outlaws*, p. 95, 2001

shitbag *verb*

to denigrate or criticise someone or something *AUSTRALIA*

- As a football supporter there are no restrictions on who you can 'shit bag'. — Ivor Limb, *Footy's No Joke!*, p. 65, 1986

shitball *noun*

a despicable person *US*

- Answer the question, shitball. — *Something About Mary*, 1998

shitbird *noun*

a despicable person *US*

- Sign it shitbird. — Jim Thompson, *The Killer Inside*, p. 167, 1952
- They'd never send a shitbird like you to sea. — Darryl Ponicsan, *The Last Detail*, p. 4, 1970
- "What do you patrol, the fucking barnyard?" said one little shitbird wearing shades[.] — Joseph Wambaugh, *The Blue Knight*, p. 70, 1973
- That could be what happened, a coincidence, and shitbird in the bedroom had nothing to do with it. — Elmore Leonard, *City Primeval*, p. 51, 1980
- I don't want no shitbirds giving me grief at four in the morning. — James Ellroy, *Suicide Hill*, p. 612, 1986
- "I thought you were clean, shitbird." "'Shitbird' went out with vaudeville." — James Ellroy, *White Jazz*, p. 71, 1992
- Last time I saw this shitbird he was flying off in a green and white helicopter. — Stephen J. Cannell, *The Tin Collectors*, p. 288, 2001

shit-blitz *noun*

an intensive media campaign of attack designed to present a negative image of someone or something *UK*

- Matt Drudge [...] is point man in the shit-blitz designed to counter the serious damage [to President George W Bush's credibility] inflicted by Michael Moore. — *The Guardian*, 9th August 2004

shit bowl *noun*

a toilet *US*

- P.S. Tear this up and flush it down the shit bowl. — Piri Thomas, *Down These Mean Streets*, p. 266, 1967
- I was sitting crosslegged and funky on the floor, next to the shitbowl. — Clarence Cooper Jr, *The Farm*, p. 81, 1967

shit box *noun*

1 the anus *UK*

- [S]he won't take it up the shit box. — Colin Butts, *Is Harry on the Boat?*, p. 49, 1997

2 a despicable person *AUSTRALIA*

- Turn back you little shitbox! — Lance Peters, *The Dirty Half-Mile*, p. 16, 1979

3 a small and shoddy dwelling *AUSTRALIA*

- Their mother cleans the toilets at the local primary school and returns home to a small concrete shitbox[.] — Christos Tsiolkas, *Loaded*, p. 43, 1995

4 the Chevrolet Chevette *US*

- — Lewis Poteet, *Car & Motorcycle Slang*, p. 178, 1992

shit-box *adjective*

no good *AUSTRALIA*

- Brian Wilson's voice isn't coming from the taxi's shit-box radio but seems to be emerging from inside my head. — Christos Tsiolkas, *Loaded*, p. 81, 1995

shitbrains; shit-brain *noun*

a stupid person *US*

- I before e except after c, shitbrains. — Darryl Ponicsan, *The Last Detail*, p. 115, 1970

shit-burner *noun*

a person assigned to the task of cleaning out latrines, dousing the spoils with fuel and burning the mixture *US*

Coined during the Vietnam war.

- — Linda Reinberg, *In the Field*, p. 30–31, 1991

shitcan *noun*

1 any rubbish bin *US*

- — *American Speech*, p. 38, February 1948: 'Talking under water: speech in submarines'

2 a cheap car *US*

- [B]lasting down the streets in a souped-up shitcan with some zit-grinnin buddies drinkin the cheapest wine you could find[.] — Lester Bangs, *Psychotic Reactions and Carburetor Dung*, p. 63, 1971

shitcan *verb*

1 to throw something away; to discharge someone from employment *US*

- I was working on my summation – I wrote it all down, then I shitcanned it. — Edwin Torres, *Carlito's Way*, p. 136, 1975
- I would hate to see you get shitcanned and go on welfare. — James Ellroy, *Because the Night*, p. 430, 1984
- "What do you say we shitcan the task force?" the chief said. — Carl Hiaasen, *Tourist Season*, p. 324, 1986
- Shitcan this movie so we don't get called names on the Internet anymore. — Kevin Smith, *Jay and Silent Bob Strike Back*, p. 125, 2001

2 to denigrate or criticise someone *AUSTRALIA, 1950*

- To get canned or 'shit canned' means the footballer is subjected to verbal abuse and denigration from the coach about his poor performance. — Ivor Limb, *Footy's No Joke!*, p. 15, 1986

shitcan *adjective*

rubbishy *UK*

- [T]his is the shitcan end of the movie business. — Christopher Brookmyre, *Not the End of the World*, p. 8, 1998

shit-chute *noun*

the rectum *US*

- — *Maledicta*, p. 15, Summer 1977: 'A word for it!'

shit creek *noun*

▸ **up shit creek; up shit creek without a paddle; up the creek**

stranded, in trouble *US, 1941*

Embellishments abound.

- — Hyman E. Goldin et al., *Dictionary of American Underworld Lingo*, p. 191, 1950
- How about writing a composition for me, for English? I'll be up the creek if I don't got the goddamn thing in by Monday, the reason I ask. — J.D. Salinger, *Catcher in the Rye*, p. 28, 1951
- I'm really up shit creek, there's just no commercial person who can understand what I'm doing. — Jack Kerouac, *Letter to Lucien Carr*, p. 562, 24th February 1956
- If Darden took the money and, by some chance, she didn't trick anymore that night, he'd be up shit's creek without a paddle, in a leaky canoe. — Nathan Heard, *Howard Street*, p. 172, 1968
- — Collin Baker et al., *College Undergraduate Slang Study Conducted at Brown University*, p. 217, 1968
- [T]hose fucking boogs may turn cannibal any minute! Then we'd really be up shit creek. — Terry Southern, *Blue Movie*, p. 182, 1970
- Now listen, sport, my twin brother's up shit creek in a barbed wire canoe without a paddle[.] — Barry Humphries, *Bazza Pulls It Off!*, 1971
- Well, then, I guess you're really up shit creek. — *The Blues Brothers*, 1980
- Then you will be up shit's creek, and you won't have a paddle. — George V. Higgins, *Penance for Jerry Kennedy*, p. 234, 1985
- I'm solo in shit creek innit? — Jeremy Cameron, *Brown Bread in Wengen*, p. 31, 1999

shitcunt *noun*

a contemptible person; used as a harsh term of contempt *UK*

When neither **SHIT** nor **CUNT** is abusive enough this combination may serve.

- [T]hey used to call him Robin Hood / Now he's robbin' fuckin' shit cunt[.] — Ian Dury, *This is What We Find*, 1979
- Half blow up at the snake, go mad, call him all kinds of a shitcunt and tell he's fucking finished and that. — Kevin Sampson, *Outlaws*, p. 292, 2001
- How do I know I ain't gonna drive off the estate with your van and then get a pull from Mr Shitcunt Traffic Cop saying I've got a fucking brake light out? — Garry Bushell, *The Face*, p. 13, 2001

shit disturber *noun*

a troublemaker *US*

- Miller is one of those people who calls himself a "community organizer" and whom other people, both admirers and detractors, call a "s— disturber." — *San Francisco Chronicle*, p. 19, 25th October 1977

- "Hongisto is a great s— disturber," said one Feinstein aide.—*San Francisco Chronicle*, p. 20, 17th August 1979
- —Ralph de Sola, *Crime Dictionary*, p. 134, 1982
- A troublemaker or provocateur. According to Katherine Barber, editor in chief of the Canadian Oxford Dictionary, "shit disturber" is a distinctly Canadian term.—Will Ferguson, *How to be a Canadian*, p. 64, 2001

shite *noun*

excrement; hence rubbish *UK, 1976*

A variation on **SHIT** phonetically similar to German *Scheiße*.

- Your music's shite / It keeps me up all night—Oasis *Married With Children*, 1994
- Anyway, we score these pills, expecting them to be sort of "London-shite" and about an hour later we're staring at each other and coming up SO massively we had to go and sit down[.]—Ben Malbon, *Cool Places*, p. 272, 1998
- More fucking radio shite[.]—Stella Duffy, *Jail Bait [britpulp]*, p. 114, 1999

▸ **give a shite**

to care, to be concerned – usually in a negative context *UK, 1971*

A variation of **GIVE A SHIT**.

- The landlord couldn't give a shite.—Charles de Lint, *Forests of the Heart*, p. 120, 2000

shite *adjective*

1 poor quality, inferior *UK*

- Frankie had annoyed him by making some shite joke about Ron's shoes[.]—Greg Williams, *Diamond Geezers*, p. 139, 1997

2 awful; unhappy; emotionally upset *UK*

- How angry was I? Never in my life have I felt so completely shite. To be tricked like that, abused. I mean honestly, absolutely devastated.—Ben Elton, *High Society*, p. 263, 2002

shite!

used as an expression of frustration, anger, etc *UK, 1937*

shit-eater *noun*

a coprophiliac *US*

- If you're looking for a shit. And shit eaters and shitters and shit fuckers and pissers and piss swallowers, you have very few choices. —Peter Sotos, *Index*, p. 72, 1996

shit-eating *adjective*

sycophantic *UK*

- Most of us had to be sycophants ("shit-eating" we called it).—Steven Piper, *The North Ships*, 1974

shit-eating grin *noun*

a broad smile, ingratiating and unctuous *US, 1957*

- So he kicks it over after 5 minutes and we listen to it cough and miss and Spook went puttin off with a shiteatin grin on his face.—Hubert Selby Jr, *Last Exit to Brooklyn*, p. 101, 1957
- Big Boot, booty-struck, booted it to her from behind, a shit-eating grin on his face.—Steve Cannon, *Groove, Bang, and Jive Around*, p. 193, 1969
- "As opposed to his natural shit-eating grin," Lynn said. "He's a honey."—Elmore Leonard, *Touch*, p. 212, 1977
- I don't know what happened, but she had a big shit-eating grin and kept hugging me.—Larry Heinemann, *Close Quarters*, p. 217, 1977
- What's truly ironic is that he was wearing a shit-eating grin.—*Mallrats*, 1995
- He always have that shit-eating grin?—*Ten Things I Hate About You*, 1999

shite-awful *adjective*

being of very inferior quality *UK: SCOTLAND*

- Efter aw that big build-up it wis a shite-awful gemme.—Michael Munro, *The Complete Patter*, p. 137, 1996

shit eh!

wow! *AUSTRALIA*

- My snow-white knobbly knees and pallid forearms provoked ribald comment from the deeply-tanned citizens in the bar. 'Shit eh? – what is it?'—John O'Grady, *It's Your Shout, Mate!*, p. 78, 1972
- —David McGill, *David McGill's Complete Kiwi Slang Dictionary*, 1998

shitehawk *noun*

a despicable, worthless person *UK*

- [T]he world is full of shite-hawks and envious ne'er-do-wells. —J.J. Connolly, *Layer Cake*, p. 53, 2000
- [T]hey're shitehawks. They'll shoot the car or the house or the back fence instead of shooting the fella.—Kevin Sampson, *Outlaws*, p. 234, 2001

shitehead *noun*

a contemptible person; used as a general term of abuse *UK*

A variation of **SHITHEAD**.

- Behind me a coupla loony tune types pro'ly homeless shiteheads from Mersey start arguin'.—Nick Barlay, *Curvy Lovebox*, p. 18, 1997

shitehole *noun*

▷ **see: SHITHOLE**

shitepoke *noun*

a despicable person *US, 1926*

- Shapian, you shitepoke, when you going to start doing what I'm paying for?—Max Shulman, *Anyone Got a Match?*, p. 227, 1964

shiters *noun*

▸ **put the shiters up**

to frighten someone *UK: SCOTLAND*

- Tell him ye're gauny shop him, just tae put the shitters up the wee nyaff.—Michael Munro, *The Complete Patter*, p. 137–138, 1996

shiters *adjective*

scared *UK*

From **SHIT-SCARED** (terrified) and other variations on the theme.

- Tommy's shiters of Joey.—Niall Griffiths, *Kelly + Victor*, p. 338, 2002

shitey *adjective*

faeces-covered; of poor quality *UK: SCOTLAND*

- holding the warm hand of the boy who always spoke too late, the shitey fatso, the one with the vile lump at the back of his shorts —Andrew O'Hagan, *Glass Cheques*, 1994
- —Michael Munro, *The Complete Patter*, 1996
- Hearing the same shitey remark for the nine hundredth time must be like a ray of sunshine on a cloudy day.—Christopher Brookmyre, *Quite Ugly One Morning*, p. 101, 1996
- Hundreds, no, fuckin millions-a people have a shitey upbringing and they don't turn into killers, do they?—Niall Griffiths, *Sheepshagger*, p. 1, 2001

shit-face *noun*

1 a despised person *UK, 1937*

- Mcginn had said you little shitface to him.—Gilbert Sorrentino, *Steelwork*, p. 17, 1970
- Take your fuckin' hands off me, shit-face, or I'll knock you out, alright?—Paul Fraser and Shane Meadows, *TwentyFourSeven*, p. 98, 1997

2 used as an intensifier of the degree of intoxication *US*

- He went out to the kitchen to rinse the dishcloth and told Elwin why didn't he, instead of standing there getting shit-face drunker than he already was, why didn't he straight up the mess in the kitchen. —Elmore Leonard, *Touch*, p. 6, 1977

shitfaced *adjective*

drunk *US*

- —Collin Baker et al., *College Undergraduate Slang Study Conducted at Brown University*, p. 194, 1968
- One of the guys is asleep. The other is shit-faced.—Leonard Shecter and William Phillips, *On the Pad*, p. 72, 1973
- Jamming the next day we got totally shitfaced[.]—Lester Bangs, *Psychotic Reactions and Carburetor Dung*, p. 219, 1977
- I would've been freezing my balls off except it was summer and anyway I was so shitfaced I was probably good for about twenty below.—George V. Higgins, *The Rat on Fire*, p. 17, 1981
- Tonight, he would find a neighborhood pub that served Scotch eggs and Cornish pasties and get just as shit-faced as the situation required.—Armistead Maupin, *Babycakes*, p. 105, 1984
- [Y]ou go back to your motel with Grover Scomer and pour some Scotch in the trophy and get shit-faced and sing cowboy songs.—Dan Jenkins, *Dead Solid Perfect*, p. 236–237, 1986
- I hope it isn't going to be one of those nights where they get shitfaced and take us to a pasture to tip cows.—*Heathers*, 1988
- "I can only guess," she said, deciding not to accept any more wine. She was getting shit-faced.—Joseph Wambaugh, *Floaters*, p. 44, 1996
- Leave it to you to use big words when you're shitfaced.—*Ten Things I Have About You*, 1999
- I just liked to find an appropriate place for people to get shitfaced. —Dave Courtney, *Raving Lunacy*, p. 39, 2000

shitfire!

used as an oath *US*

- Shitfire! I don't know.—Darryl Ponicsan, *The Last Detail*, p. 78, 1970

shit fit *noun*

1 a bad case of diarrhoea *US*

- No underwear because of shit fit.—Ed Sanders, *Tales of Beatnik Glory*, p. 47, 1975

2 a tantrum *US*

- She has a shit fit and calls him two or three choice names.—Angelo d'Arcangelo, *The Homosexual Handbook*, p. 230, 1968
- Coach has been having shitfits.—John Sayles, *Union Dues*, p. 47, 1977
- I'd always been throwing shitfits over what I saw as concessions to the corporate capitalist music industry[.]—Mick Farren, *Give the Anarchist a Cigarette*, p. 155, 2001

shit-for-brains; shite-for-brains *noun*

an idiot *US*

- Sorry, mate. Shit-for-brains had too much juice [alcohol]. Won't bother you again. — *ID*, 1994
- Hey, shit-for-brains, be careful not to scratch that thing, huh? — *Something About Mary*, 1998
- Foolish fuckin hope tho when a shite-fer-brains like yerself is in on-a conversation, like. — Niall Griffiths, *Sheepshagger*, p. 2, 2001
- He lives in his van with his dog, a Blue Heeler whose name was Shit for Brains, I kid you not. — Brian Preston, *Pot Planet*, p. 90, 2002

shit-for-brains *adjective*

stupid *US*

- And that score was presented in the shit-for-brains 2003 editorial[.] — Al Franken, *Lies*, p. 173, 2003

shit-fuck *noun*

a despicable person *AUSTRALIA*

- Ya sneaky fuckin' trick thief. That's mine, shit-fuck! Mine!! — *Sick Puppy Comix*, p. 13, 1997

shit happens

used for conveying the inevitability of misfortune *US*

A tremendously popular catchphrase in the mid- to late 1980s in the US, spawning dozens of jokes with the predictable punch-line, tee-shirts with lists of various religions' interpretations of the phrase, etc.

- — Connie Eble (Editor), *UNC-CH Campus Slang*, p. 5, Spring 1983
- He might not've hit anybody, but at least they'd know the truth of that old saying, shit happens. When you least expect, too. — Elmore Leonard, *Killshot*, p. 137, 1989

shit-hawk *noun*

a seagull *CANADA*

- — Jack Chambers (Editor), *Slang Bag 93 (University of Toronto)*, p. 6, Winter 1993

shithead *noun*

an objectionable, obnoxious, despised person *UK, 1961*

- And everybody sees him and says, "That shithead, look at him!" — Lenny Bruce, *The Essential Lenny Bruce*, p. 203, 1967
- At the sundial are 500 people ready to follow Mark Rudd (whom they don't particularly like because he always refers to President Kirk as "that shithead") into the Low Library administration building[.] — James Simon Kunen, *The Strawberry Statement*, p. 28, 1968
- The shit-head got a hot-worded letter from me. — *Screw*, p. 13, 27th June 1969
- "'Cause I love you, you shithead," said Fluffy[.] — Joseph Wambaugh, *The New Centurions*, p. 237, 1970
- I had been there with those fuzzy little shitheads – and so, I sensed, had the desk clerk. — Hunter S. Thompson, *Fear and Loathing in Las Vegas*, p. 107, 1971
- Verdun, you dirty bastard, Verdun, you shithead, you're finally gonna get it. — Mickey Spillane, *Last Cop Out*, p. 116, 1972
- Where you gonna go, shithead? — Richard Price, *The Wanderers*, p. 184, 1974
- "Back, Ross!" I said, "Get back, shithead!" — *Scum*, 1979
- I can read a police file, shithead, and quit calling me Jack. — *48 Hours*, 1982
- [T]he sentence could range from fifty push-ups to double-timing around the parade field holding a 9.5-pound M-1 rifle over your head, yelling "I'm a shithead! I'm a shithead!" until you collapsed. — David H. Hackworth, *About Face*, p. 35, 1989
- Oh fuck off, you idiot! Shithead! Tampon dick! — Bernadine Evaristo, *Lara*, 1997
- [T]he girl was a shithead. — Kevin Sampson, *Powder*, p. 98, 1999
- This is insane, Noah. Stop being a total shithead. — Stuart Browne, *Dangerous Parking*, p. 80, 2000
- Word of advice, shithead, don't you ever wake up. — *Kill Bill*, 2003

shitheap *noun*

a motor vehicle that is in poor repair or that lacks power *AUSTRALIA*

- He just thinks he's getting a great deal on his old shitheap. — *Australian Penthouse*, p. 40, July 1984

shitheel *noun*

a despicable person *US, 1935*

- Well, there's going to be a grand jury on these shitheels, and you will appear as a witness against them. — Peter Maas, *Serpico*, p. 217, 1973
- He was a live shitheel and now he's going to be a dead shitheel. — Walter Wagner, *You Must Remember This*, p. 25, 1975
- I've got no respect for a shit-heel like that. — George V. Higgins, *The Rat on Fire*, p. 115, 1981
- I'd like to turn the Corps of Engineers loose on that shitheel place. — Dan Jenkins, *Dead Solid Perfect*, p. 16, 1986
- Keep that in mind – that I loved them – even though they were both world-class shitheels. — James Ellroy, *Hollywood Nocturnes*, p. 199, 1994

shit heroin *noun*

heroin, especially if of poor quality *UK, 1950*

- Shooting up the Peanut Shit. — Leonard Cohen, *Beautiful Losers*, p. 238, 1966
- [I]f we don't take charge of this gizmo for making dynamite out of low-grade shit, you won't be tops no more if somebody else gets hands on it. — Robert Deane Pharr, *Giveadamn Brown*, p. 208, 1978
- — Angela Devlin, *Prison Patter*, p. 104, 1996
- I don't give a fuck what it's called as long as it's good shit. Come to think of it I often call it shit. Y'know. I'm doing some shit. — Robert Ashton, *This Is Heroin*, p. 55, 2002

shithole; shitehole *noun*

1 a bad place; a dirty, run-down or disreputable place *US*

- "Well, we fixed them but good. Opened up with everything we had on the shit-hole," he continued. — *The Berkeley Barb*, p. 2, 3rd December 1965
- "I pity the poor bastards who have to wallow around in this shit hole," she said earnestly. — Jack W. Thomas, *Heavy Number*, p. 67, 1976
- Fucking shithole, that place, it's like, it's like ruined. — *Saturday Night Fever*, 1977
- It was with you and me and we were working in this sleazy shithole motel down in Miami, Florida. — *Repo Man*, 1984
- Or you could get Union Correctional, over west of there not too far. It don't matter which though, they're both shitholes. — Elmore Leonard, *Maximum Bob*, p. 107, 1991
- The insane migrant will pack some bags and leave the shithole they were born in for the promise of better pay and a better life somewhere else. — Christos Tsiolkas, *Loaded*, p. 144, 1995
- We put down to refuel in a shit-hole on the coast[.] — Chris Ryan, *Stand By, Stand By*, p. 61, 1996
- a condemned shithole in the poorest part of Manchester — David Bowker, *The Joy of Sexism*, p. 42, 1999
- VAL: I thought this was the place. STEPHIE: This shit-hole? — *200 Cigarettes*, 1999
- When you come from Workington, a shitehole between the pulp mill and the steel works — Stuart Browne, *Dangerous Parking*, p. 2, 2000
- Amazing how much people love it when you big up their town, no matter what kind o' shitehole it is. — Ben Elton, *High Society*, p. 223–224, 2002
- When he wrote about Afganistan in "The VICE Guide to Evil," it was still an unknown shithole. — Suroosh Alvi et al., *The Vice Guide*, p. 2002, 2002

2 the anus *UK, 1937*

shithook *noun*

1 the hand *US*

- — *Current Slang*, p. 20, Winter 1970

2 a thoroughly unpleasant person *US*

- — Collin Baker et al., *College Undergraduate Slang Study Conducted at Brown University*, p. 193, 1968

3 a CH-47 Chinook helicopter *US*

Vietnam war usage.

- — Linda Reinberg, *In the Field*, p. 197, 1991
- The Chinook was a huge helicopter called the "shit-hook," because it could lift anything. — Mary Reynolds Powell, *A World of Hurt*, p. 55, 2000

shit-hot *noun*

a highly skilled fighter pilot *US, 1983*

- — *American Speech*, p. 124, Summer 1986: 'The language of naval fighter pilots'

shit hot *adjective*

excellent, wonderful *UK, 1961*

A positive sense of **SHIT** intensifies **HOT** (popular, fashionable).

- [T]he Germans were, if nothing else, shit hot when it came to aiming their big guns. — Johnny Speight, *It Stands to Reason*, p. 62, 1973
- He wasn't going to be shit hot. He wasn't going to compete. — Kevin Sampson, *Powder*, p. 17, 1999
- [S]he'd get a band together, with shit-hot PR, someone to push them to number one[.] — Cath Staincliffe, *Trainers*, p. 58, 1999

shithouse *noun*

1 a toilet bowl; a toilet; a lavatory *UK, 1795*

- And I saw the Southern white man who has nothing between him and the lowest Negro except a segregated toilet. No wonder so many of them have shithouse ways. — Dick Gregory, *Nigger*, p. 170, 1964
- I wondered how some guys could take the chance of cooking up and shooting up in any public place like a shithouse[.] — Piri Thomas, *Down These Mean Streets*, p. 117, 1967
- The sound of the Temps still gitting away in the Gumbo House seeped into the shithouse. — Steve Cannon, *Groove, Bang, and Jive Around*, p. 6, 1969
- Well I might not look like much, but no son of a bitch tells me to get my ass out of a public shithouse, you son of a bitch. — Joseph Wambaugh, *The New Centurions*, p. 192, 1970
- So I reached in my slide and came out with two boss threes / And said "Here, girl, go to the shithouse and get the weakness out of your knees." — Dennis Wepman et al., *The Life*, p. 52, 1976

- Stick your head down the shithouse and drink out of that.—Donald Catchlove, *Ray Denning My Life and Time*, 1994

2 a shoddy, dirty, unpleasant place *US*

- At the same time he didn't want to wind up in a "shithouse" precinct like the two-eight (Twenty-eighth) or the two-five (Twenty-fifth). —Leonard Shecter and William Phillips, *On the Pad*, p. 122, 1973
- I'd have had you live like – like somebody. Not in this shithouse. —Edwin Torres, *After Hours*, p. 362, 1979

3 jail or prison *US*

- I thought, "If someone had told me a year ago I'd be back in a shit-house, I'd have thought he was nuts."—Iceberg Slim (Robert Beck), *Pimp*, p. 243, 1969

4 an extremely unpleasant individual *UK*

- Mind you, he was a shithouse with me mother.—Caroline Aherne and Craig Cash, *The Royle Family*, 1999
- Fella's properly a shithouse. He's just a horrible fucking horrible wretch[.]—Kevin Sampson, *Outlaws*, p. 88, 2001

5 a coward *UK*

- To be fair, he's never said he's hard, Paul – but he is a bit of a shithouse.—Kevin Sampson, *Clubland*, p. 66, 2002

▶ **to the shithouse**

to hell *AUSTRALIA*

- Mouche freaked out to the shithouse.—Kathy Lette, *Girls' Night Out*, p. 99, 1987
- One time them Afghans found all this pork and bacon on their camels and chucked the lot to the shithouse.—Herb Wharton, *Cattle Camp*, p. 93, 1994

shithouse *adjective*

1 disgusting, nasty, unpleasant *AUSTRALIA*

- That was a dirty rotten shithouse thing to say.—Barry Humphries, *Bazza Pulls It Off!*, 1971

2 no good; hopeless; abysmal *AUSTRALIA, 1973*

- He's a shithouse bloody driver too.—Sam Weller, *Old Bastards I Have Met*, p. 138, 1979
- If you're really looking forward to seeing someone after a shit-house day, and then she cancels – she don't understand how you feel. —Sandra Jobson, *Blokes*, p. 108, 1984

shithouse rumor *noun*

gossip *US*

A blunt version of the kinder and gentler 'latrine rumor'.

- —Carl Fleischhauer, *A Glossary of Army Slang*, p. 12–12, 1968

shitkicker *noun*

1 a tough, belligerent person *US*

- A shitkicker, you understand, is a gangly male who is all fists in the bunkhouse[.]—Bernard Wolfe, *The Late Risers*, p. 22, 1954
- If somebody played a Lefty Frizell record or some other shitkicker they moaned, made motions with their hands (man! what a fuckin square) and walked out to the street.—Hubert Selby Jr, *Last Exit to Brooklyn*, p. 27, 1957
- But showing his scar is beautiful. That's just where he's at. He's a shitkicker.—Lenny Bruce, *The Essential Lenny Bruce*, p. 60, 1967
- Moke, wearing his new shitkicker image for all to see.—Elmore Leonard, *Stick*, p. 119, 1983
- I met him at a country-western bar. Shit-kicker's paradise, but at least they treat women with respect.—James Ellroy, *Blood on the Moon*, p. 92, 1984
- "Well, he's a shit-kicker," they said, "he's a troublemaker."—Terry Southern, *Now Dig This*, p. 8, 1986
- Couple of shitkickers, but good guys.—Elmore Leonard, *Freaky Deaky*, p. 18, 1988

2 a country-dweller, a peasant *US, 1966*

- a promising football career being ended at the age of twenty by some shitkicker (or "quashie" as Steve preferred it) Millwall reserves stopper lumping him in the knee—Greg Williams, *Diamond Geezers*, p. 31, 1997

3 a person employed to do menial jobs *AUSTRALIA, 1950*

- SH-T-KICKER A short-timer (often employed on sanitary work). — Thirty-five, *The Argot*, 1950
- Suburban shitkicker! Clerk!—Barry Oakley, *A Salute to the Great McCarthy*, p. 168, 1970
- Syd was a mining engineer and Bill and Jack were two experienced miners and I was the shit-kicker.—Sam Weller, *Old Bastards I Have Met*, p. 37, 1979
- —Ryan Aven-Bray, *Ridgey Didge Oz Jack Lang*, p. 45, 1983

4 a prostitute *US*

Far less common than the term **MUDKICKER**.

- Pimps also refer to the women as "cows" and "shitkickers."—Sara Harris, *The Lords of Hell*, p. 47, 1967

5 a fraudster, especially one who adopts a pose of extreme modesty *US*

- —Don Wilmeth, *The Language of American Popular Entertainment*, p. 238, 1981

shitkickers *noun*

heavy work shoes or work boots *US*

- He was an open apple knocker from the West Side wearing plain Monkey Ward jeans rather than Levi's and high-top horsehide shit kickers.—Earl Thompson, *Tattoo*, p. 55, 1974
- "You could bust your ass in those shitkickers you're wearin'," he said.—Jimmy Buffett, *Tales from Margaritaville*, p. 54, 1989
- —Connie Eble (Editor), *UNC-CH Campus Slang*, p. 8, Spring 1989
- Though your shitkickers are big, too, with steel toes.—Elmore Leonard, *Be Cool*, p. 8, 1999

shitless *adverb*

completely, entirely, to a great degree *UK, 1936*

- Thank you [for the applause], we needed that. This is the second time we've ever played in front of people. We're scared shitless.—Stephen Stills of Crosby, Stills and Nash, *Woodstock*, 1969
- The police were scared shitless and the massive crowds of angry protestors chased them for blocks.—*Screw*, p. 16, 25th July 1969
- Look at them now, scared shitless because for a change they're the target and they got nobody to shoot back at.—Mickey Spillane, *Last Cop Out*, p. 43, 1972
- I'm scared shitless, Ferris! What if Rooney guesses my voice?—*Ferris Buehler's Day Off*, 1986
- She's scared shitless, just like I would be after today.—*Boys on the Side*, 1995
- Me, I wasn't scared shitless – quite.—Duncan MacLaughlin, *The Filth*, p. 44, 2002

shitlips *noun*

a person who talks nonsense *US*

Extended from **SHIT** (rubbish, nonsense) with 'lips' representing the mouth that emits it.

- And you can only read about it, shitlips.—Sal Piro and Michael Hess, *The Official 'Rocky Horror Picture Show' Audience Participation Guide*, p. 38, 1991

shit list *noun*

an imagined list of those in disfavour *US, 1942*

- You're on my shit list from now on.—Norman Mailer, *The Naked & Dead*, p. 221, 1948
- If they're playing at Pine Knob usually we get them in the Sheraton, if the group isn't on the hotel's shit list.—Elmore Leonard, *Touch*, p. 28, 1977
- One was on their shit list: an old guy in a nursing home who'd boasted for years to anyone who'd listen that he'd been the Mayor of Munchkinland.—Armistead Maupin, *Maybe the Moon*, p. 56, 1992

shitload *noun*

a great deal of *US*

- I bet you won a shitload on Oakland.—*The Bad Lieutenant*, 1992
- I stared into the brown haze, imaging shitloads of code 2s and 3s thwarted by noxious fumes and bumper-to-bumper revelry.—James Ellroy, *Hollywood Nocturnes*, p. 124, 1994
- I learn he's got money in foreign banks, plus, around five mil in hard cash, plus, loose diamonds and gold coins, a shitload of coins worth around four bills each.—Elmore Leonard, *Out of Sight*, p. 60, 1996
- And since I'm only on the set for a day, I've obviously missed a shitload of good stuff.—Anthony Petkovich, *The X Factory*, p. 14, 1997
- Jesus, you could get in a shitload of trouble for this.—*Cruel Intentions*, 1999
- [T]aking shit from the boss and paying shit-loads to the taxman[.] —Dave Courtney, *Stop the Ride I Want to Get Off*, p. 379, 1999
- [P]aying off a shit load of money you couldn't afford to borrow in the first place[.]—Danny King, *The Burglar Diaries*, p. 18, 2001

shitman

used as an intensifier of what follows *US*

- Shitman, this cat talking make me feel creepy.—Sara Harris, *The Lords of Hell*, p. 15, 1967

shitmobile *noun*

a poor quality motor vehicle *AUSTRALIA*

- The delicate Italian hopped in to our shitmobile and didn't smell a thing.—B. Selkie, *Lime Juice*, p. 91, 1995

shit-nasty *adjective*

very unpleasant *UK*

- There was a shit-nasty DI [Detective Inspector] in charge of us[.]—Jake Arnott, *He Kills Coppers*, p. 15, 2001

shit off!

go away! *UK*

- Oh, shit off, will yer, said Liverpool Jack[.]—Geoffrey Fletcher, *Down Among the Meths Men*, p. 44, 1966

shitogram *noun*

an especially virulent e-mail message *US*

- —Eric S. Raymond, *The New Hacker's Dictionary*, p. 319, 1991

shit on a brick!

▷ see: SHIT A BRICK!

shit on a shingle *noun*

minced or creamed beef on toast *US*

A visual simile in UK military use, possibly of US origin.

• —Kathleen Meyer, *How to Shit in the Woods*, 1994

shit on a string *noun*

an elusive or difficult task *US*

• —*Maledicta*, p. 255, Summer/Winter 1981: 'Five years and 121 dirty words later'

shit order *noun*

a dirty or untidy condition, especially when applied to military accommodation or equipment *UK*

• If we were fighting the desert war [...] they could work in shit order. —D. Hayes, *Tomorrow the Apricots*, 1971

shit-out *noun*

a coward *UK*

• "Shit-outs!" was the last insult I threw over my shoulder[.] —Jimmy Stockin, *On The Cobbles*, p. 121, 2000

shit out *verb*

to run away; to yield *UK*

• "How come United always run from Chelsea?" "Pardon" "You heard. Why do you Mancs always shit out[?]" —Martin King and Martin Knight, *The Naughty Nineties*, p. 62, 1999
• [T]he Victorian bunch weren't shitting out either. —Tony Wilson, *24 Hour Party People*, p. 207, 2002

shit out of luck *adjective*

very unlucky *US*

• —Connie Eble (Editor), *UNC-CH Campus Slang*, p. 5, November 1983

shitpacker *noun*

an anal-sex enthusiast *US*

• Say, there was asshole shellackers and shitpackers / and freaks who drunk blood from a menstruatin' womb. —Bruce Jackson, *Get Your Ass in the Water and Swim Like Me*, p. 146, 1964

shit paper *noun*

toilet paper *US*

• She pulled them halfway up her thighs, twisting her hips, paused, got two small pieces of shit paper and placed one inside her burned out asshole, the other inside the lips of her cunt. —Steve Cannon, *Groove, Bang, and Jive Around*, p. 13, 1969
• —*Maledicta*, p. 195, 1979: 'A taboo-boo word revisited'
• Grunts in the field often carried their "shit paper" under the elastic band that secured the helmet cover or inside the helmet to provide "dry" insurance against sweat and rain. —Gregory Clark, *Words of the Vietnam War*, p. 464, 1990

shitparcel *noun*

a prison officer *UK*

• —Angela Devlin, *Prison Patter*, p. 104, 1996

shitpicker *noun*

a notional menial, demeaning job *US*

• I wouldn't hire a shit-picker on the basis of the I Ching or whatever that book of magic speels is called[.] —Tom Robbins, *Another Roadside Attraction*, p. 129, 1971

shit pie *noun*

a comparative example for anything of no value *UK*

• Your band may well be the hottest thing on eight legs in England, Wheezer, but, boringly, it doesn't mean shit pie here in the States. —Kevin Sampson, *Powder*, p. 292, 1999

shit pit *noun*

a field-latrine *UK*

Military.

• The only place you don't have to go in pairs is to the shit pit, which is just off the side of the patrol area. —Andy McNab (writing of the late 1970s/early 80s), *Immediate Action*, p. 91, 1995

Shitport *nickname*

Norfolk, Virginia *US*

• —Ralph de Sola, *Crime Dictionary*, p. 202, 1982

shitpot *noun*

1 a contemptible, worthless individual *UK, 1937*

• [W]hen someone gets a nice car and some bastard smashed it up because they haven't got one. Shit pots. It's just daft. —Shaun Ryder, *Shaun Ryder... in His Own Words*, 1990

2 a great deal of *US*

• —Collin Baker et al., *College Undergraduate Slang Study Conducted at Brown University*, p. 195, 1968
• Earlier, the LA Free Press let it all hang out and published the whole shitpot full of names. —*The Berkeley Tribe*, p. 4, 15th-21st August 1969
• Yeah, a shitpotful of the crew got deep-sixed. —Darryl Ponicsan, *The Last Detail*, p. 145, 1970

3 marijuana of inferior quality *US, 2001*

A combination of synonyms SHIT and POT.

• —Simon Worman, *Joint Smoking Rules*, 2001

shitpuncher *noun*

a male homosexual *NEW ZEALAND*

• —David McGill, *David McGill's Complete Kiwi Slang Dictionary*, p. 113, 1998

shits *noun*

▸ **for shits and giggles**

for no good reason *US*

Something is done, for example, for shits and giggles.

• —Don R. McCreary (Editor), *Dawg Speak*, 2001

▸ **put the shits up**

to frighten someone *UK*

• [T]hey had been told to scare her, put the shits up her. No more. —Michael Connor, *The Soho Don*, p. 1, 2002

▸ **the shits**

1 diarrhoea *UK, 1947*

• I was excited by the whole thing plus the granola diet didn't do too well, and I had the shits. The first day I was squeezing my legs, I had the shits so bad. —Stephen Ziplow, *The Film Maker's Guide to Pornography*, p. 150, 1977
• Dana Andrews said prunes gave him the runes *Shits.* —Sal Piro and Michael Hess, *The Official 'Rocky Horror Picture Show' Audience Participation Guide*, p. 6, 1991
• If you drink enough, you will cease to be concerned with either your piles or your inevitably on-going case of the shits. —Steven Treanor, *The Guardian*, 18th March 2002

2 the worst *US*

• "Now isn't that the shits," exclaimed Nuclear Phyllis[.] —Tom Robbins, *Another Roadside Attraction*, p. 34, 1971

3 fear *UK, 1967*

Following logically from the earlier sense as 'diarrhoea'.

• —John Ayto, *The Oxford Dictionary of Slang*, p. 267, 1998

shit sandwich *noun*

a troubling, odious situation *US*

• —Stephen H. Dill (Editor), *Current Slang*, Spring 1968
• The review you had on 'Shark Sandwich,' which was merely a two word review – just said "shit sandwich." —*This is Spinal Tap*, 1984
• In other words, it's a huge shit sandwich and we're all gonna have to take a bite. —*Full Metal Jacket*, 1987
• And "shit sandwich" is a good generic negative review for any song, movie, TV show, or music video. —Editors of Ben is Dead, *Retrohell*, p. 141, 1997

shit-scared *adjective*

terrified *UK, 1958*

• I was bigger than a sixpence and worried shit scared. —Johnny Speight, *It Stands to Reason*, p. 62, 1973
• His eyes have a genuine shit-scared look. Practically every juvenile thug known to the police is staring at him in hate. —Jack Allen, *When the Whistle Blows*, p. 150, 2000
• And then you wake up the next morning with the shakes and you're shit-scared for what you got up to. —Andrew Holmes, *Sleb*, p. 107, 2002

shit-shaped *adjective*

used of a prison cell that has been daubed with excrement *UK*

A pun on 'ship-shape'. From private correspondence with a serving prisoner in 2001.

shit, shave, shower, shine

used as a jocular reminder of a man's tasks before going out on the town *US*

Multiple variants, probably coined in the US Marine Corps as a pre-liberty litany.

• Shit, shower 'n shave. —Donald Goines, *The Busting Out of an Ordinary Man*, p. 66, 1985

shitshover *noun*

a male homosexual *UK*

An obvious allusion to anal intercourse.

• —Angela Devlin, *Prison Patter*, p. 104, 1996

shitstabber *noun*
a male homosexual *UK*
- Let's see him talk his way out of that when the words gets round that he's a shit-stabber! — Duncan MacLaughlin, *The Filth*, p. 160, 2002

shit stain *noun*
a stupid, despicable person *US*
- I'm glad it's happened in a place like Montreal, so these bigoted shit stains who call in on sports-talk shows can't blame it all on the blacks. — George Carlin, *Brian Droppings*, p. 48, 1997

shitstain *adjective*
despicable, unpleasant, foolish *US*
- all her shitstain friends that screw with her head all year and tell her I'm a lousy husband — Howard Stern, *Miss America*, p. 155, 1995

shit-stick *noun*
a despised person *US*
- — *American Speech*, p. 298, December 1964
- You're nothing. A fucking shit stick, and if you ever mention my name again, even to a priest, I'll take you out. — Danny King, *The Bank Robber Diaries*, p. 210, 2002

shit sticks!
used as a mildly profane expression of disappointment *US*
- — *American Speech*, p. 298, December 1964

shit-stir *verb*
to tell tales, or spread rumours, with the specific intention of causing trouble *UK*
A limited variation of 'stir the shit'.
- ANTHONY: Hey Dave, Beverly Macca was in the offie [off-licence]. DAVE: What are you telling me for? ANTHONY: Well, you fancy her don't you? DAVE: Stop shit-stirring. — Caroline Aherne and Craig Cash, *The Royle Family*, 1999

shit-stirrer *noun*
a troublemaker; a person who heckles or harasses, especially for the fun of it *AUSTRALIA*
- That'd be him, thought the Dean, a shit-stirrer from way back, trouble is he stirs more shit against us than the class enemy these days. — Frank Hardy, *The Outcasts of Foolgarah*, p. 88, 1971
- But when they get under the control of radical, power-happy, limelighting bloody shit-stirrers, they're dangerous. — Sam Weller, *Old Bastards I Have Met*, p. 56, 1979
- The New Labour politics of stealthily manufactured consensus and straitjacketed news management left slim pickings for the professional shit-stirrer[.] — Christopher Brookmyre, *Boiling a Frog*, p. 197, 2000
- — Gary K. Farlow, *Prison-ese*, p. 63, 2002

shit-stirring *noun*
harassing; heckling; troublemaking *AUSTRALIA*
- Come on, Tich, old mate, we'll go and do a bit of shit-stirring amongst the shitties [sanitary workers]. — Frank Hardy, *The Outcasts of Foolgarah*, p. 91, 1971

shit stompers *noun*
heavy work boots *US*
- — *American Speech*, p. 66, Spring-Summer 1975: 'Razorback slang'

shit stopper *noun*
a prank *US*
- — *Maledicta*, p. 255, Summer/Winter 1981: 'Five years and 121 dirty words later'

shit stoppers *noun*
drain-pipe trousers (a tight-cut, narrow-legged part of a Teddy Boy's 'uniform') *UK*
- "Drainpipes" (or, worse, "shit-stoppers") were what Teddy Boys wore and Teddy Boys were the most laughable [later-1970s] subcult of all, men who would not admit to the passage of time. — Stuart Maconie, *Cider with Roadies*, p. 105, 2003

shitstorm; shit storm *noun*
an extremely serious situation *US*
- They finally got to arguing with each other and created such a shitstorm I lost my quarter-cent-a-pound bonus for not missin' a day[.] — Ken Kesey, *One Flew Over the Cuckoo's Nest*, p. 206, 1962
- Hoss, you ask my wife to dance one more time and you gonna dance yourself into a shit storm. — Ken Weaver, *Texas Crude*, p. 124, 1984
- Everyone looked up – GIs and zips – and knew it was every incoming round left in Creation, a wild and bloody shitstorm, a ball-busting cataclysm. — Larry Heinemann, *Paco's Story*, p. 14, 1986
- Garcia slugged down the coffee; he figured he'd need a gallon of caffeine to brave the waiting shitstorm. — Carl Hiaasen, *Tourist Season*, p. 227, 1986
- [T]he calm before the shit-storm[.] — David Peace, *Nineteen Seventy-Four*, p. 137, 1999
- Look, it's a shit storm here right now. — *Traffic*, 2000
- Dylan brought out the Hawks, and the shitstorm became history. — Mick Farren, *Give the Anarchist a Cigarette*, p. 62, 2001

shit street *noun*
an unpleasant place to be; serious trouble *UK, 1961*
You can be 'in' or 'up' shit street; a similar location to **SHIT CREEK**.
- [I]n shit street. — Angela Devlin, *Prison Patter*, p. 64, 1996
- They were well and truly in shit street[.] — Martin King and Martin Knight, *The Naughty Nineties*, p. 199, 1999
- I'm gonna phone my mum and tell her I'm in shit street: "I can't afford to buy any more drugs mummy." — Lanre Fehintola, *Charlie Says...*, p. 10–11, 2000

shitsure *adverb*
certainly, definitely *US*
- It's one thing to demand technical excellence if you're Duke Ellington or Charles Mingus for that matter for shit fucking sure[.] — Lester Bangs, *Psychotic Reactions and Carburetor Dung*, p. 373, 1981

shittalay *noun*
a Chevrolet car *US*
- — Lewis Poteet, *Car & Motorcyle Slang*, p. 178, 1992

shit-talk *verb*
to engage in bragging, insulting conversation *US*

shitted *adjective*
afraid *UK*
A variation of **SHIT-SCARED**.
- Total silence all round. He's well shitted. — Nick Barlay, *Curvy Lovebox*, p. 20, 1997

shitter *noun*

1 a toilet or bathroom *US, 1969*
- Then one morning I came home and found Slim sitting on the shitter pissy drunk and out cold. — A.S. Jackson, *Gentleman Pimp*, p. 173, 1973
- I sit on the shitter waiting for Miss Thing to do her thing. — Paul Glover, *Words from the House of the Dead*, 1974
- DANTE: My life is in the shitter right about now, so if you don't mind, I'd like to stew a bit. — *Clerks*, 1994

2 the anus *UK*
- How do you take it? says Keef over his shoulder. – In the shitter, I mumble. — Nick Barlay, *Curvy Lovebox*, p. 160, 1997
- Chris gave me a mother-of-pearl trinket box and a pair of ruby studs. Danny gave me one up the shitter. — Jenny Eclair, *Camberwell Beauty*, p. 339, 2000

3 a criminal, usually a burglar, who fetishistically defecates at the scene of the crime *US*
- Anyway, he's a shitter and wouldn't it be nice if somebody would wake up some night and grab a shotgun and catch the bastard squatting on their kitchen table just squeezing out a big one[.] — Joseph Wambaugh, *The New Centurions*, p. 136, 1970
- "In there leaving his calling card," Maurice said, and Kenneth laughed. "White Boy's a shitter." — Elmore Leonard, *Out of Sight*, p. 256, 1996

4 a liar; a braggart; a bluffer *US*
A shortened form of **BULLSHITTER**.
- Don't shit a shitter. — Elmore Leonard, *Cat Chaser*, 1982
- Have you got the bottle [nerve], or are you just another shitter? — Greg Williams, *Diamond Geezers*, p. 144, 1997
- [Y]ou should "never shit a shitter". — Tony Wilson, *24 Hour Party People*, p. 96, 2002

5 a coward *UK*
- You're a shitter, Dave sneers. A fucking shitter. — John King, *Human Punk*, p. 223, 2000
- West Ham mugs. They're all shitters and runners and fucking grasses. — Garry Bushell, *The Face*, p. 155, 2001

6 a horse *US*
- — *American Speech*, p. 270, December 1958: 'Ranching terms from eastern Washington'

7 a prison cell used for solitary confinement *US*
- — Bruce Jackson, *Outside the Law*, p. 60, 1972: 'Glossary'
- They might put us in the shitter [solitary], but I wouldn't get into too much trouble. — Bruce Jackson, *In the Life*, p. 397, 1972
- — Charles Shafer, *Folk Speech in Texas Prisons*, p. 213, 1990

8 the hell *AUSTRALIA*
Used as an intensifier.
- You beat the shitter out of me, Mervyn, fractured my skull. — Jack Hibberd, *A Stretch of the Imagination*, p. 16, 1971

shit the bed!
used for registering wonder or satisfaction *UK*
An elaboration of **SHIT!**.
- Needless to say blood and snot has flown to get this magazine on the shelves, but shit the bed was it worth it. —*X-Ray*, p. 7, November 2002

shit ticket *noun*
a piece of toilet paper *AUSTRALIA*
- He paused and sighed. 'Why're there never any shit tickets when it's *my* turn to have a crap?' —Linda Jaivin, *Rock n Roll Babes from Outer Space*, p. 61, 1996

shitting *adjective*
used as a negative intensifier *UK*
- Aw, yus, shut that shittin' sod hup. —Geoffrey Fletcher, *Down Among the Meths Men*, p. 50, 1966
- [A] calculator, a brass horse and several other shitting little souvenirs[.] —Danny King, *The Burglar Diaries*, p. 120, 2001

shitting in high cotton (and wiping with the leaves)
enjoying prosperous times *US*
- Since ol' Jim Ed's took over his daddy's feed store, he's shittin' in high cotton and wipin' with the leaves. Drivin' a new used car, an' got three-four pairs of shoes. —Ken Weaver, *Texas Crude*, p. 124, 1984

shitting-it *adjective*
scared; very nervous *UK*
- [H]e grabbed hold of the mike off the seriously shitting-it scally MC[.] —Dean Cavanagh, *Mile High Meltdown (Disco Biscuits)*, p. 213, 1996

shittings *noun*
diarrhoea *BAHAMAS*
- —John A. Holm, *Dictionary of Bahamian English*, p. 182, 1982

shitting up *noun*
in prison, a deliberate act of protest by decorating a cell with excrement *UK*
- —Angela Devlin, *Prison Patter*, p. 104, 1996

shit train *noun*
a great number; a lot of *US*
- I refer, of course, to the shit train of eight (8) felony-assault, etc., charges that were brought against me by a maniac neighbor at dawn on Saturday morning[.] —Hunter S. Thompson, *Songs of the Doomed*, p. 283, 1989

shitty *noun*
a bad mood *AUSTRALIA*
- Jesus, he's in a shitty today. —Sam Weller, *Old Bastards I Have Met*, p. 80, 1979

shitty *adjective*
1 awful; of poor quality *US, 1924*
- And then Jenny explained how she had been feeling "absolutely shitty" and gone back to Dr. Sheppard, not for consultation, but confrontation. —Erich Segal, *Love Story*, p. 113, 1970
- If it sounds GOOD to YOU, it's bitchen; and if it sounds BAD to YOU, it's shitty. —Frank Zappa, *The Real Frank Zappa Book*, p. 188, 1989
- Even allowing for the fact that passport photos are always shitty, the eyes in this photo are lifeless. —Stuart Browne, *Dangerous Parking*, p. 13, 2000
- Few ornaments, shitty old gramophone, toaster, not worth the effort. —Danny King, *The Burglar Diaries*, p. 60, 2001
- Well-paid but shitty work[.] —Niall Griffiths, *Kelly + Victor*, p. 46, 2002

2 in a bad mood *AUSTRALIA, 1971*
- Listen, I'm sorry I was a bit shitty when you saw me at St Vincent's. But Christ I was in a lot of pain. —Robert G. Barrett, *Davo's Little Something*, p. 174, 1992
- He'd have a few bites of Milo's Home Brand meat pie and throw the rest away. But if you didn't cook he'd get shitty. —John Birmingham, *He Died With a Felafel in his Hand*, p. 48, 1994
- Chances are it's junk, but if it makes Keating shitty, I'm happy. —Dirk Flinthart, *Brotherly Love*, p. 16, 1995

3 drunk *US*
- —Connie Eble (Editor), *UNC-CH Campus Slang*, p. 4, Spring 2003

shitty end of the stick *noun*
an unfair position to be in; inequitable treatment *UK*
- That bastard's still giving that little girl the shitty end of the stick. —Ted Lewis, *Jack Carter's Law*, p. 53, 1974
- Nigel looked round helplessly. He'd obviously been handed the shitty end of the stick. and was being expected to hand it on to me. —Mick Farren, *Give the Anarchist a Cigarette*, p. 145, 2001

Shitty Mcshit!
used for registering frustration, annoyance, anger, etc *UK*
SHIT! intensified by an elaborated reduplication.
- Anna was so cross, she snapped the stems off two rather smart wineglasses [...] "Shitty Mcshit." Anna was a good swearer. —Jenny Eclair, *Camberwell Beauty*, p. 208, 2000

shit up *verb*
to scare someone *UK*
- A wanter get im out quickly cos churches shit me up a bit now, a always feel like am bein watched, as if am bein judged. —Niall Griffiths, *Grits*, p. 32, 2000
- Fuckin Darren Taylor; shits me up, that bastard does. —Niall Griffiths, *Kelly + Victor*, p. 168, 2002

shitville *noun*
any remote, forsaken town *US*
- —*Maledicta*, p. 12, Summer 1977: 'A word for it!'
- Yes, you found a Johnson, but you waded through Shitville to find him. —William Burroughs, *Queer*, p. 9, 1985

shitwork *noun*
any unglamorous occupation, often dirty work *UK, 1968*
- He complains that everybody wants him to be the one to go to the groceria to buy beer and "do all the shit work because I am the youngest." —Terry Williams, *The Cocaine Kids*, p. 60, 1989
- It is all about loyalty and integrity as well as organization and sheer tough shitwork. —John Robb, *The Nineties*, p. 158, 1999
- Two hours straight shit-work, one-handed typing making it four. —David Peace, *Nineteen Seventy-Four*, p. 169, 1999

shitwrap *noun*
a despicable person *US*
- You're his wife, and you're walking around with the shitwrap who dropped him. —Stephen J. Cannell, *The Tin Collectors*, p. 75, 2001

shiv; chiv; shivvie *noun*
a homemade knife-like weapon, especially one fashioned in prison *US, 1915*
Almost certainly evolved from C17 'chive' (knife).
- "You got a chiv?" he asked. I knew I didn't have one but I fanned myself. "Musta left it in my box," I said. He looked around again, then slipped me his. I didn't look at it, but by its feel it must have been eight inches long. —Chester Himes, *If He Hollers Let Him Go*, p. 34, 1945
- And I don't like you, and if you make a move for your shiv I'm going to beat the piss outa you. —Irving Shulman, *The Amboy Dukes*, p. 209, 1947
- Because they's two of 'em and they got a shiv they're the toughest mugs in the world. —Mickey Spillane, *One Lonely Night*, p. 55, 1951
- "Let's see the shiv," he said. "The what?" "The pig-sticker, the switchblade, the knife." —Jim Thompson, *Savage Night*, p. 69, 1953
- There were wild Negro queers, sullen guys with guns, shiv-packing seamen, thin, non-committal junkies, and an occasional well-dressed middle-aged detective[.] —Jack Kerouac, *On the Road*, p. 131, 1957
- Teddy, I know where you've been, what you learned in there, how to make a shiv, how you settle your differences. —Elmore Leonard, *Glitz*, p. 63, 1985
- [Y]ou would drive a shiv into the zookeeper's heart, so deep. —Howard Stern, *Miss America*, p. 301, 1995
- —Angela Devlin, *Prison Patter*, p. 104, 1996

shiv *verb*
to stab someone *US*
- The Pachuco shivs Mace while the big stoop stands there all goofed off with a rod in his mitt. —Thurston Scott, *Cure it with Honey*, p. 160, 1951
- Do you know who shived him? —Robert Edmond Alter, *Carny Kill*, p. 23, 1966

shivaree *noun*
a group mocking *US, 1805*
- It seemed to Manning that every prisoner in the big yard had joined in the shivaree, just as it seemed to him they were all identical – jeering mouths wrenched open under the round stiff-billed hats. —Malcolm Braly, *On the Yard*, p. 37, 1967

Shiva Skunk *noun*
in British Columbia, a local variety of marijuana *CANADA*
- He toked from a huge fattie consisting of a variety called Shiva Skunk. —Brian Preston, *Pot Planet*, p. 2, 2002

shiver and shake; shiver *noun*
a cake *UK*
Rhyming slang.
- —Ray Puxley, *Fresh Rabbit*, 1998

shivoo *noun*
a party; a celebration *AUSTRALIA, 1844*
From French *chez vous* (at your place).
- He died that night, after the shivoo at Lightfoot's. —D'Arcy Niland, *Dead Men Running*, p. 25, 1969

shivver *noun*

a criminal who attacks victims with a knife *US*

- Then Bull came out with a couple of knives and started showing us how to disarm a would-be shivver in a dark alley. — Jack Kerouac, *On the Road*, p. 154, 1957

shixa *noun*

▷ **see: SHIKSE**

shiznit *noun*

the very best; something of great quality *US*

Used with 'the'. A euphemistic embellishment of **THE SHIT**.

- — Connie Eble (Editor), *UNC-CH Campus Slang*, p. 5, Fall 1996
- Nobody has these babies, no way, not the shiznit. — *Traffic*, 2000
- We sidestep the bling-blingers though to check out some new shiznit. — *X-Ray*, p. 59, April 2003

shizzle; fo' shizzle

certainly; emphatically yes *US*

A hip-hop, urban black coinage; the opening sound of 'sure' elaborated to a pattern; especially in rhyming reduplications, 'fo' shizzle my nizzle' (for sure my nigger), 'fo' shizzle my sizzle' (for sure my sister) and 'fo' shizzle my bizzle' (for sure my brother).

- Mr Justic Lewison ruled that the lyrics in question – "shizzle my nizzle" and "mish mash man" – were not, in fact, intelligible enough to the untrained ear to cause offence. — *Jockey Slut*, August 2003

shizzle my mizzle fizzle dizzle!

used as a contemptuous expression of dismissal *US*

Popular hip-hop cryptography disguising 'suck my mother fucking dick!'.

- "Shizzle my socialist mizzle fizzle dizzle," as [Tony] Benn probably didn't say recently. — *Bang*, November 2003

shizzy *adjective*

great *UK*

- — 7 Seconds *Out the Shizzy*, 1993
- The Thrills [an Irish rock band] are shizzy. — Jo Wiley, *The Glastonbury Festival*, 28th June 2003

shlemiel; schlemiel; schlemihl *noun*

a bungler with chronic bad luck *US*

Yiddish. During the opening montage of the US situation comedy *Laverne and Shirley* (ABC, 1976–83), the lead characters, played by Penny Marshall and Cindy Williams skip down a Milwaukee sidewalk singing '1–2–3–4–5–6–7–8, Shlemiel, shlamazzel, Hassenpepper Incorporated', giving 'shlemiel' its highest profile to date.

- In the Jewish folk-mind, however, the schlemiel is conceived of as an awkward, bungling fellow, plagued not only with "butter-fingers" but with absolutely no skill in coping with any situation in life. — Nathan Ausubel, *A Treasury of Jewish Folklore*, p. 343, 1948
- Despite having done a thousand lunch meetings at Nate 'n Al's, Orson never got the Yiddish right. He said kvel when he meant kvetch, schmutz when he mean schvitz and schlmeil for schlemazel. — Joseph Wambaugh, *Finnegan's Week*, 1993

shlep *noun*

1 stealing from parked cars *US*

- — Hyman E. Goldin et al., *Dictionary of American Underworld Lingo*, p. 192, 1950

2 influence *US*

- He got his kid into the programme because he has shlep with the Board. — *Wordsmith*, 10th May 2002

shlep; schlep *verb*

to move or travel laboriously *IRELAND, 1922*

From Yiddish *schlep* or *schlepen* (to drag).

- Slepp them away from the lunch counters, don't let them use the toilet. — *Esquire*, p. 153, November 1960
- Mazz had schlepped round town, finally finding a place in an arcade with a load of surfing gear[.] — John Williams, *Cardiff Dead*, p. 100, 2000
- [S]he continues to bake chocolate-chip cookies, schlep around with bags from Barnes & Noble and telephone him at the office. — *The Guardian*, 17th June 2000

shlepper; schlepper *noun*

an inconsequential person; a nobody *US, 1934*

- Once I was a schlepper, now I'm Miss Mazeppa. — Stephen Sondheim, *You Gotta Get a Gimmick*, 1960
- My outfit didn't have nothing to do with this Asbury schlepper who is making all this trouble for us. — Richard Condon, *Prizzi's Money*, p. 81, 1994

shlepper bag; schlepper bag *noun*

a tote bag *US*

- Slosberg, a Boca Raton entrepreneur whose interests include the promotional materials business, recently began handing out what he calls the "schlepper bag," a burlap tote bearing his name. — *Palm Beach (Florida) Post*, p. 1B, 17th July 2000

shlimazel; schlimazel *noun*

a person with chronic bad luck *US*

A blend of German and Hebrew, literally translated as 'bad luck'.

- [A] wit has made the follwing neat distinction between these two types: "A schlemihl is a man who spills a bowl of hot soup on a schlimazel." — Nathan Ausubel, *A Treasury of Jewish Folklore*, p. 343, 1948
- Just bring me a cold drink, you old shlimazel. — Joseph Wambaugh, *The Blue Knight*, p. 12, 1973

shlock; schlack; schlock *noun*

shoddy, defective or cheaply made merchandise *US, 1915*

From German to Yiddish to American slang.

- He's been serving time here since 1960, greeting folks with his cane, pointing the way upstairs at the schlock tourist restaurant next to the Winter Garden. — Josh Alan Friedman, *Tales of Times Square*, p. 58, 1986
- Featuring the Standells and the Chocolate Watch band on Mike Curb's soundtrack, it made for a perfect piece of pop schlock. — Barney Hoskyns, *Waiting For The Sun*, p. 138, 1996

shlocker; schlocker *noun*

a cheaply produced horror or thriller film *UK*

A compound of **SHLOCK; SCHLOCK** (something cheap or inferior) and **SHOCKER**.

- Producer of the recent lo-budget/no-budget teenslasher drugs'n'guns cult schlocker, Suzi Got Whacked[.] — James Hawes, *White Powder, Green Light*, p. 3, 2002

shlocky; schlocky *adjective*

shoddy *US*

- A bunch of schlocky broads, the lowest. — Albert Goldman, *Freak Show*, p. 216, 1968
- On the one side – beautiful, witty, perfect – was a Breughel reproduced on fine wool. On the other – campy, tacky, schlocky – were Lurex stripes. — *Harpers & Queen*, October 1976

shlong *noun*

1 the penis *US, 1969*

From the Yiddish. Also spelt 'schlong'.

- His shlong brings to mind the fire hoses coiled along the corridors at school. — Philip Roth, *Portnoy's Complaint*, p. 54, 1969
- With regard to the erection per se there is no relationship between the size of a non-erect putz and its size at erection (so stop comparing schlongs in the locker room)[.] — *Screw*, p. 8, 8th December 1969
- I mean, her old man could've had a shlong that hung down to his knees. — Elmore Leonard, *City Primeval*, p. 191, 1980
- The only hand on your schlong is gonna be yours. — *Diner*, 1982
- Wanting to test the mettle of Dave's 42nd Street schlong, she bit off more than her little box could chew. — Josh Alan Friedman, *Tales of Times Square*, p. 117, 1986
- Because if you didn't, you wouldn't be with me, you'd be with Sheldon the Wonder Schlong. — *When Harry Met Sally*, 1989
- Anyhow, we got forensics to match the punctures in the guy's schlong with the bite pattern of the victim's teeth. — Carl Hiaasen, *Strip Tease*, p. 410, 1993
- There's this talking snake and a naked chick and then this dude puts a leaf on his schlong! Heh heh heh. — Mike Judge and Joe Stillman, *Beavis and Butt-Head Do America*, p. 49, 1997
- The fourteenth-century Queen of Naples, Johanna, particularly liked well-hung men and believed in the size correlation between schnoz and schlong when she chose the big-hootered Prince Andrew of Hungary as her husband. — Richard Herring, *Talking Cock*, p. 224, 2003

2 a hairstyle in which the hair is worn short at the front and long at the back *US*

An ellision of 'short-long'. Better known, perhaps, as a **MULLET**.

shlubby *adjective*

ill-mannered; poorly dressed *US*

Yiddish from the Slavic *zhlob* (a coarse person).

- [A] rather shlubby Steve Lawrence ("sitting in" for Johnny Carson) asked his guest what his friends called him[.] — Albert Goldman, *Freak Show*, p. 67, 1968
- And shlubby guys find a woman and get married every day. — *Paybill*, 8th October 2002

shm-; schm- *prefix*

used for creating a Yiddish-sounding reduplication of an English word, usually with the intention of diminishing the importance of the original word *US, 1929*

- Confusion Schmooshum —*Journal of English and German Philology*, p. 226–227, 1952
- Disguise, schmisguise. So you wear also a gold earring? That's a disguise too? —Bernard Wolfe, *The Late Risers*, p. 218, 1954
- Clues, schmooz. Sure, they're a clue and what the hell you goin' to do with it? —Jim Thompson, *The Nothing Man*, p. 242, 1954
- Ain't we the fancy schmancies? Pink prison bars yet. —John M. Murtagh and Sara Harris, *Cast the First Stone*, p. 241, 1957
- "Fancy-shmancy" was all she said to me on the phone. —Philip Roth, *Goodbye, Columbus*, p. 14, 1959
- —*American Speech*, p. 302–303, December 1961: 'On Yiddish shm-'
- 'Raise, schmaze! Boots beamed at the bearer of good news. —Clarence Cooper Jr, *Black*, p. 249, 1963
- She snarled, "Lonely, schmlonely," folded her arms, slouched deep in her seat, and went to sleep. —John Nichols, *The Sterile Cuckoo*, p. 33, 1965
- Liberal schmiberal. —Lenny Bruce, *The Essential Lenny Bruce*, p. 13, 1967
- He was hanging around a fancy-schmantzy girl named Rebecca Draper[.] — *When Harry Met Sally*, 1989
- Alternate, schmalternate . . . I want you on this appeal, Sidney. —Seth Morgan, *Homeboy*, p. 294, 1990
- Reason, shmeason. You should go give him shit. — *Mallrats*, 1995
- Nowadays, western Europe is overrun by custard tarts that are not frilly at all, fancy-schmantzy Portuguese ones with flakey pastry[.] —Stuart Jeffries, *Mrs Slocombe's Pussy*, p. 4, 2000
- Cover, shmover - you all hated his songs, too. —Kevin Smith, *Jay and Silent Bob Strike Back*, p. 47, 2001

shmagma *noun*

marijuana *UK*

- —Mike Haskins, *Drugs*, p. 289, 2003

shmaltz; schmaltz *noun*

excessive sentimentality, especially in music, writing, etc *US, 1935*

From German *schmaltz* (fat, lard) via Yiddish, with a suggestion of something too greasy to be easily digested.

- Will you be content with that standard box-office schmalz? —J.D. Salinger, *Franny and Zooey*, p. 60, 1961
- [T]he schmaltz side of it which I cringe at[.] — *Ask*, p. 75, 18th December 1982

shmams *noun*

the female breasts *UK*

Derives, apparently, from **MAMMARIES** on the Yiddish model of reduplication ('mams, shmams').

- [T]heir breasts are no longer merely breasts but famous breasts. Celebrity shmams. Hollywood hooters. Tinseltown tumblers. — *The Times*, 2nd August 2003

'shman *noun*

a first year college student, a freshman *US*

- — *New York Times*, 12th April 1987

shmatte; schmatte *noun*

1 the clothing trade *CANADA*

- A few years later my bunch could root for a Jewish player, outfielder Kermit Kitman, who eventually married a Montreal girl and settled here, ending up in the schmata trade. —Mordecai Richler, *Dispatches from the Sporting Life*, p. 97, 2002

2 a less than elegant house dress *US*

Yiddish.

- "A very plain drab person," he said, "who dresses in shmattas". —Philip Roth, *Portnoy's Complaint*, p. 92, 1969

shmear; schmear *noun*

a bribe *US*

- —Hyman E. Goldin et al., *Dictionary of American Underworld Lingo*, p. 185, 1950

shmear; schmear *verb*

to bribe someone *US*

- When the cops were still ticketing you schmeared them fifty a week and had your own private space. —Vincent Patrick, *Family Business*, p. 32, 1985

shmeck; schmeck; shmee *noun*

heroin; cocaine *US, 1932*

From German *schmecken* (to taste), but note an assonant similarity to **SMACK** (heroin).

- 'Let him snort some schmeck!' said Jean-baby, wide-eyed, reaching for her purse. —Terry Southern, *Flash and Filigree*, p. 144, 1958
- Then one night zonked out of my mind on schmeck - pot - benzedrine and seconal - I met a cat I had become friendly with who was a kind of John or mark. —Herbert Huncke, *The Evening Sun Turned Crimson*, p. 46, 1980
- —Mike Haskins, *Drugs*, p. 281, 2003

shmecker; schmecker *noun*

a heroin user *US*

Yiddish, formed from **SHMECK**.

- Like a good shmecker keeps the smell in his own private nose, see? —George Mandel, *Flee the Angry Strangers*, p. 312, 1952
- [W]here the skinpoppers and schmeckers (those who used the needles and those who sniffed the powder), the pushers and the weeheads gathered for sex circuses and to listen to the real cool jive. —Chester Himes, *Come Back Charleston Blue*, p. 150, 1966
- O'Keefe went along, agreeing that the time seemed right for him to become a "schmecker," too. —Emmett Grogan, *Ringolevio*, p. 44, 1972
- Don't have anything to do with Sol. He's a shmecker. —William Burroughs, *Junkie*, p. 67, 1973

shmeckler *noun*

a heroin user or addict *US*

- Dreck written by a shmeckler. —Gerald Petievich, *Shakedown*, p. 133, 1988

shmeer; schmear *noun*

a package or deal *US, 1969*

From the Yiddish.

- You know, big hoop skirt, eight petticoats, high-button shoes, monstro hairpiece, the whole schmear, pretty weird. —Terry Southern, *Blue Movie*, p. 152, 1970
- — *Current Slang*, p. 26, Spring 1970
- The whole team - the busy-bodies. Release, Split, The Samaritans, Mensa, Exist, The London Rape Centre, The Alternative Parents' Group, Gay Rights - the whole shmeer[.] —Anthony Masters, *Minder*, p. 131, 1984

shmegegge; schmageggy *noun*

an incompetent person *US*

An American-born 'Yiddish' word.

- Against a horseplayer, maybe. But against a schmageggy who ain't out of high school, I will do all right. —Jimmy Snyder, *Jimmy the Greek*, p. 16, 1975

shmendrick *noun*

a naive, cowardly person *US*

From the name of a character in an operetta by Abraham Golfaden.

- — *New York Times*, p. B4, 11th August 1980
- "Clyde" - a loser, a shmendrick. — *Washington Post*, p. B1, 17th January 1985
- What a schmendrick he was, sitting around and waiting for us to provide an agenda. — *Atlanta Jounral-Constitution*, p. 12P, 18th December 2003

shmo; schmo; schmol *noun*

a gullible, hapless fool *US, 1948*

An American addition to Yiddish. In August 1948, just as 'shmo' was coming into the American lexicon, US cartoonist Al Capp introduced the 'shmoo' in the *L'il Abner* comic strip. The loveable and selfless 'shmoo' loved to be eaten and tasted like any food desired.

- You copped the 400 because you're an illiterate schmo. —Bernard Wolfe, *The Late Risers*, p. 36, 1954
- Don't be a schmoe. Go along. —Clancy Sigal, *Going Away*, p. 391, 1961
- It just seems that women today are more impressed by the mighty buck than by some schmo who spent the last seventeen years scraping by on Peace Corps wages. — *Something About Mary*, 1998

shmock *noun*

▷ see: SCHMOCK

shmooze; schmooze *noun*

an agreeable conversation; persuasive talk *US, 1939*

- [diary entry 29th June 1993] He sweet-talks them to perfection. Even I fall for his schmooze. —Gyles Brandreth, *Breaking the Code*, 1999

shmooze; schmooze *verb*

to gossip; to chat, to engage in idle talk; to network; to persuade someone indirectly *US, 1897*

Yiddish from the Hebrew.

- We schmoozed around, and then a client burst in from the corridor. —Clancy Sigal, *Going Away*, p. 28, 1961
- [Y]ou automatically think it is something where Jewish widow ladies go and sit out by the swimming pool on nice days like this and schmoos a little. —George V. Higgins, *The Rat on Fire*, p. 148, 1981
- They schmooze the manager, slip him some free goods to make sure he puts the CD on the shelf, try for some in-store airplay and stick this gorgeous shot of Linda Moon in the window. —Elmore Leonard, *Be Cool*, p. 253, 1999
- [S]howbiz schmoozing is a part of the territory with politicos. —John Robb, *The Nineties*, p. 154, 1999

shmoozy *adjective*
chatty; friendly *US*
- Well, Mort's real schmoozy with Biff. — Bernard Book, *The Late Risers*, p. 9, 1954

shmuck; schmuck *noun*
1 a fool; an objectionable person *UK, 1892*
Taken into general usage from Yiddish; the literal meaning is 'penis', hence the original Yiddish usage in this sense had a particularly derogatory tone. The variant 'schmuck' seems to have been adopted in error due to a similarity in sound to Yiddish *schmuck* (jewel).
- Who's afraid of that shmuck? — Irving Shulman, *The Amboy Dukes*, p. 123, 1947
- Which means like be a schmuck. — *West Side Story*, 1957
- I'm no shmuck — Frank Norman, *Bang To Rights*, p. 108, 1958
- You philandering schmuck! — Max Shulman, *Anyone Got a Match?*, p. 254, 1964
- I thought in my arrogance and heartbreak – discarded, unread, considered junk-mail by this schmuck, this moron, this Philistine father of mine! — Philip Roth, *Portnoy's Complaint*, p. 8, 1969
- Better to be king for a night than a schmuck for a lifetime. — *King of Comedy*, 1976
- Asshole! Schmuck! How long does it take you to figure out that nobody knows what they're doing here? — *Apocalypse Now*, 1979
- "Speak English, you shmuck," Wiley snapped. — Carl Hiaasen, *Tourist Season*, p. 105, 1986
- Tell me. Standing on the street, the ultimate schmuck. — *When Harry Met Sally*, 1989
- He even used Yiddishisms like "schmuck." — Kim Rich, *Johnny's Girl*, p. 26, 1993
- Blow the schmuck out of the water! — *Something About Mary*, 1998
- The master rewards the men who made money from the money and punishes the schmuck who didn't. — Al Franken, *Lies*, p. 215, 2003

2 the penis *UK*
- — Richard Herring, *Talking Cock*, p. 30, 2003

shmuck; schmuck *verb*
to make a fool of someone *US*
- He thinks you're being schmucked. — Stephen J. Cannell, *The Tin Collectors*, p. 43, 2001

shmucko; schmucko *noun*
a reprehensible person *AUSTRALIA*
- And reassured each other that your men were either total sleaze schmuckos or hot spunk rats. — Kathy Lette, *Girls' Night Out*, p. 214, 1987

shmutter; schmutter *noun*
clothing, especially a suit *UK*
From Yiddish *shmatte* (a rag), ultimately from Polish *szmatte* (a rag).
- That's a nice schmutter you've got. — David Powis, *The Signs of Crime*, 1977
- Look at his schmutter – not my style, Anthony but he likes it. — Anthony Masters, *Minder*, p. 10, 1984

shmutz; schmutz *noun*
filth; dirt *US*
Yiddish from German.
- "It's clean enough. Look, Aunt Gladys, I'm having a wonderful time." "Schmutz he lives in and I shouldn't worry." — Philip Roth, *Goodbye, Columbus*, p. 54, 1959

shnide *adjective*
▷ **see:** SNIDE

shnitzel; schnitzel *noun*
the penis *US*
- — Dale Gordon, *The Dominion Sex Dictionary*, 1967
- Dick, all I want to do is make serious movies that explore social issues and turn a profit, and slip the schnitzel to Jane DePugh. — James Ellroy, *Hollywood Nocturnes*, p. 80, 1994

shnockered *adjective*
▷ **see:** SNOCKERED

shnook *noun*
an inoffensive, unassertive person; a 'nobody' *US, 1948*
American Yiddish coinage.
- He thinks anything peculiar or unpleasant will just go away if he turns on the radio and some little schnook starts singing. — J.D. Salinger, *Franny and Zooey*, p. 82, 1961
- Jack Benny on radio, 9 October, 1951: "Don't be such an apologetic shnook." — Leo Rosten, *The Joys of Yiddish*, p. 368, 1968
- I'm an average nobody. I get to live the rest of my life like a schnook. — *Goodfellas*, 1990
- Call me crazy, but I like Dougie. He might be a shnook and a schemer, but he was kind of an okay shnook and schemer. — Janet Evanovich, *Seven Up*, p. 50, 2001

shnookered *adjective*
drunk *US*
- — Connie Eble (Editor), *UNC-CH Campus Slang*, p. 9, Fall 1985

shnorrer; schnorrer *noun*
a freeloader *US*
Yiddish from the German for 'begging'.
- What were the characteristics of the schnorrer? He disdained to stretch out his hand for alms like an ordinary beggar. He did not solicit aid – he demanded it. — Nathan Ausubel, *A Treasury of Jewish Folklore*, p. 267, 1948
- I had lunch with him a couple of weeks ago. A real schnorrer, but sort of likeable, and apparently he's hot over there right now. — J.D. Salinger, *Franny and Zooey*, p. 136–137, 1961
- Those schnorer bits: "Oh, you'll do this and this, and here's a bit of schnapps for this and this." — Lenny Bruce, *The Essential Lenny Bruce*, p. 23, 1967

shnoz; schnoz; shnozz; scnozz *noun*
the nose *US, 1942*
A shortening of SHNOZZLE.
- "Go fuck yourself, buster!" Sid roared, gave him a straight shot to the snoz — Terry Southern, *Blue Movie*, p. 250, 1970
- As always, I am in love with the quality of the merchandise. Truly soft on the schnozz. — Gerald Petievich, *To Live and Die in L.A.*, p. 196, 1983
- When do you tape the schnozz? — Howard Stern, *Miss America*, p. 87, 1995
- I guess she's afraid of getting smacked in the shnaz. Can't blame 'er. Quite a hooter on her already. — Anthony Petkovich, *The X Factory*, p. 193, 1997
- It [cocaine] don't do yer schnozz too many favours, either[.] — Garry Bushell, *The Face*, p. 14, 2001
- Gob or shnoz, mun, slong as yew get it down yewer fuckin neck is all that fuckin matters. — Niall Griffiths, *Sheepshagger*, p. 162–163, 2001
- The fourteenth-century Queen of Naples, Johanna, particularly like well-hung men and believed in the size correlation between schnoz and schlong when she chose the big-hootered Prince Andrew of Hungary as her husband. — Richard Herring, *Talking Cock*, p. 224, 2003

shnozzle; shnozzola; schnozzle; schnozzola *noun*
the nose *US, 1930*
- [F]or 3 days my eyes watered with migraine pain from that swollen shnozzola[.] — Jack Kerouac, *Letter to Neal and Gabrielle Kerouac*, p. 399, 25th April 1953
- What a coddy [bad] kaffall [face] dear. Oh vada [observe] the schnozzle on it dear. — David McKenna, *Storm in a Teacup*, 1993

shoat boat *noun*
in trucking, a trailer used for hauling livestock *US*
- — Montie Tak, *Truck Talk*, p. 140, 1971

shock a brew!
have a beer! *US*
An intentional corruption of the Hawaiian SHAKA.
- — Pamela Munro, *U.C.L.A. Slang*, p. 75, 1989

shocked-as *adjective*
very shocked *UK*
- Fonzie looks shocked-as to see my big bald head. — Kevin Sampson, *Outlaws*, p. 113, 2001

shocker *noun*
a person or thing that is shockingly bad *AUSTRALIA*
- Bloody Australians are all shockers – no exceptions! — John Wynnum, *Tar Dust*, p. 50, 1962
- I heard him do "The Girl from Iponema" at the bowling club last time he was in town and it was a shocker. — Roy Slaven (John Doyle), *Five South Coast Seasons*, p. 141, 1992
- I've had plenty of jobs and most of them were shockers. — Paul Vautin, *Turn It Up!*, p. 103, 1995
- Since he left she's dated a steady stream of shockers[.] — *Girlfriend*, p. 100, 1995
- As often as not, when he sank the slipper, the result was an absolute shocker. — Shane Maloney, *Nice Try*, p. 30, 1998

shock jock
a radio personality who tests the limits and tries to win listeners by outrageous language, thoughts or stunts *US*
- There are probably no more than a dozen truly outrageous "shock jocks" at the nation's nearly 10,000 radio stations, yet three of them have worked in Washington. — *Washington Post*, p. F8, 23rd February 1986
- New York's WNEW-FM radio pulled the plug Thursday on shock jocks Opie and Anthony over their sex stunt at St. Patrick's Cathedral. — *New York Daily News*, 23rd August 2003

shock shop *noun*
a room where electric shock therapy is administered *US*
• They didn't take me to the Shock Shop this time. — Ken Kesey, *One Flew Over the Cuckoo's Nest*, p. 8, 1962

shock treatment *noun*
in the used car business, a very low assessment of the value of a customer's trade-in car *US*
• — *American Speech*, p. 309–310, Winter 1980: 'More jargon of car salesmen'

shoddy-doo *noun*
palms slapped in greeting *US*
• "My dear hip friend," the better began / "Here's some splow and a big shoddy-doo." — Dennis Wepman et al., *The Life*, p. 69, 1976

shoddy-dropper *noun*
a vendor of low quality clothing passed off as high quality *AUSTRALIA, 1950*

shoe *noun*
1 a detective *US*
An abbreviation of **GUMSHOE**.
• Told the shoes where to find Robin and her buddy Skip Gibbs. They picked them up in Los Angeles and brought them back for trial. — Elmore Leonard, *Freaky Deaky*, p. 208, 1988

2 a black person *US*
A play on **BOOT**.
• — Robert George Reisner, *The Jazz Titans*, p. 164, 1960

3 in drag and motor racing, a driver *US*
• — Don Alexander, *The Racer's Dictionary*, p. 58, 1980

4 among Quebec anglophones, the Centre Hospitalier Universitaire de Sherbrooke *CANADA*
The word 'shoe' indicates how the acronym CHUS is pronounced, leaving off the last consonant in the French way.

5 a linear amplifier for a citizens' band radio *US*
• — Lanie Dills, *The Official CB Slanguage Language Dictionary*, p. 62, 1976

Shoe *nickname*
Willie Shoemaker (b.1931), the most successful jockey in the history of horse racing in the US *US*

shoebite; shoe-bite *noun*
a blister on the foot caused by a shoe's rubbing *INDIA*
• I've got shoebites from that new pair of shoes. — Paroo Nihalini, R.K. Tongue and Priya Hosali, *Indian and British English*, 1979

shoe boot *noun*
a prostitute *UK*
Rhyming slang.
• — Bodmin Dark, *Dirty Cockney Rhyming Slang*, 2003

shoe clerk *noun*
a poker player who withdraws from a hand at any sign of serious betting *US*
• — John Vorhaus, *The Big Book of Poker Slang*, p. 32, 1996

shoe dog *noun*
a shoe salesman *US*
• — Jim Crotty, *How to Talk American*, p. 263, 1997

shoegazer *noun*
an aficionado of 'serious' introspective rock music; hence the music itself *UK*
• Still, there's Mercury Rev, The Flaming Lips, Sebadoh covering Cold As Ice, and a secret bonus track of some student shoegazer murdering Somewhere Over The Rainbow. — *The Guardian*, 8th December 1999
• Whether you're a fresh-faced student or a long haired ancient there's a scene round town that's perfect for you... SHOEGAZERS. — *Red Handed (Cardiff)*, p. 56, 2003

shoegazing *noun*
'serious', introspective rock music *UK*
• The "sonic cathedral of sound" we know as "shoegazing" is, it seems, ripe for a reappraisal. — *X-Ray*, p. 36, November 2003

shoe laces and collar buttons *noun*
in poker, a hand consisting of a pair of aces and a pair of twos *US*
• — George Percy, *The Language of Poker*, p. 81, 1988

shoe-leather express *noun*
walking *US*
• — Vincent J. Monteleone, *Criminal Slang*, p. 206, 1949
• — Bill Casselman, *Canadian Sayings*, p. 140, 2002

shoemaker *noun*
a boy who is not particularly intelligent *US*
Teen slang.
• — *American Weekly*, p. 2, 14th August 1955

shoes *noun*
1 tyres *US, 1917*
• You see the shoes on that thing? You've got to get some tires for this. — *Dazed and Confused*, 1993

2 car wheel rims *US*
• Dubs, blades, shoes, sneakers, twinkies – street slang for custom wheels – are status symbols, made popular by athletes and rap stars. — *Cincinnati Enquirer*, p. 1B, 29th August 2003

shoes and socks; the shoes *noun*
syphilis; hence any sexually transmitted infection *UK*
Rhyming slang for **POX**.
• — Ray Puxley, *Cockney Rabbit*, 1992

shoestring *noun*
a very small amount of money; a low budget *US, 1904*
• Of these a dozen are highly successful, another half dozen do well, and the rest are mostly shoestring affairs, picking up the ragged edges and discards of the leaders. — Jack Lait and Lee Mortimer, *New York Confidential*, p. 32, 1948

s-h-one-t *noun*
used as a euphemism for 'shit' *UK*
• "S-h-ONE-t!" she'd say, spelling it out[.] — Duncan MacLaughlin, *The Filth*, p. 41, 2002
• You're an s-h-one-t. — *The Alan Clark Diaries*, 19th February 2004

shonk *noun*
a person who engages in dishonest business dealings *AUSTRALIA*
Back-formation from **SHONKY**.
• [W]hat I am saying is stay away from the backyard's and the shonks. — *Truckin' Life*, p. 22, 1982
• Tycho is a shonk, a criminal. — Roy Slaven (John Doyle), *Five South Coast Seasons*, p. 137, 1992

shonker *noun*
the nose *UK*
• [A] super shonker. — Ray Puxley, *Fresh Rabbit*, p. 75, 1998

shonky *noun*
a dishonest person *AUSTRALIA*
• The consular corps wants no shonkies in the business, thank you. — *National Times*, p. 20, 8th December 1979

shonky *adjective*
of an item, phoney; of business dealings, dishonest *AUSTRALIA*
• [T]he Snob's been palmed off shonky notes[.] — B. Breydor, *You Oughta Seen Us!*, p. 186, 1969
• — Barry Humphries, *A Nice Night's Entertainment*, p. 188, 1981
• In London and New York they're a pushover when some crafty dealer wants to flog a bit of shonky slow-moving merchandise. — Barry Humphries, *The Traveller's Tool*, p. 19, 1985
• I need your help, Ross. Nothing shonky you understand, but I'd be grateful if you could call into the surgery. — Clive Galea, *Slipper*, p. 76, 1988

shoo *adjective*
well-dressed *US*
Teen slang.
• — *San Francisco News*, p. 6, 25th March 1958

shoo-fly *noun*
1 a police officer assigned to investigate the integrity of other policemen *US*
• — *New York Times Magazine*, p. 88, 16th March 1958
• [A]lthough Walsh's investigators – or "shoo-flies" – caught countless cops in minor violations of the department's rules and procedures, they somehow turned up very little graft. — Peter Maas, *Serpico*, p. 172, 1973
• The shoofly's looking for you. — Leonard Shecter and William Phillips, *On the Pad*, p. 170, 1973
• I used to do it then figuring the phones in the poolroom or the bar was tapped and Moran's name would get on some shoo-fly tape. — Edwin Torres, *Carlito's Way*, p. 16, 1975
• "But now they flop you for nothing, shoofly all over," Valentin said. — Edwin Torres, *Q & A*, p. 17, 1977

- The key to it would be the Internal Affairs shooflies. —Vincent Patrick, *The Pope of Greenwich Village*, p. 113, 1979

2 on the railways, a temporary track bypassing an unusable section of track *US*

- —Norman Carlisle, *The Modern Wonder Book of Trains and Railroading*, p. 268, 1946

shoofti; shufti *noun*

a look *AUSTRALIA, 1944*

- Take a shoofti at this halo – fulla dents and it would fall around me neck but for me ears. —*Weekend Australian Magazine*, p. 2, 17th March 1984

shoo-in *noun*

a person, idea or thing with no serious competition *US, 1939*

Originally (1935) applied to a fixed horse race and four years later in a more general sense.

- —*American Speech*, October 1950

shook *adjective*

excited; enthusiastic *US*

- —Kenn "Naz" Young, *Naz's Underground Dictionary*, p. 12, 1973

shookon

infatuated with *AUSTRALIA, 1868*

- SHOOK ON – To be friendly. —Gilbert H. Lawson, *A Dictionary of Australian Words and Terms*, 1924
- And if you ask me she's shook on him. —Dymphna Cusack, *Picnic Races*, p. 245, 1962
- —Harry Orsman and Des Hurley, *The Beaut Little Book of New Zealand Slang*, 1994

shook-up *adjective*

alienated; confused; dehumanised *US, 1914*

- Pepito isn't as shook-up as Chocolate. Not yet. But is only fourteen. —Harrison E. Salisbury, *The Shook-up Generation*, p. 53, 1958

shoop *verb*

to have sex *US*

From the song by Salt-N-Pepa.

- —Connie Eble (Editor), *UNC-CH Campus Slang*, p. 7, Spring 1994

shoosh *noun*

silence *AUSTRALIA, 1949*

- But Chilla satisfied that all his fellow outcasts had gathered, had his mind set on something else, 'A bitta shoosh,' he called out then[.] —Frank Hardy, *The Outcasts of Foolgarah*, p. 187, 1971

shoosh *verb*

▸ **shoosh your noise**

to become quiet *UK*

Especially when used as an injunction.

- Look, star. Just take the money and hurry up. They never grief you for ID, so shoosh your noise. —Julian Johnson, *Urban Survival*, p. 268, 2003

shoot *noun*

1 anything legitimate, unscripted or unstaged *US*

- The other key event on the show saw Jim Ross deliver his much awaited hell turn, delivering a "shoot" interview that even put the heroes of that genre, Shane Douglas and Brian Pillman, to shame. —*Herb's Wrestling Tidbits*, 26th September 1996

2 heroin *UK*

- —Robert Ashton, *This Is Heroin*, p. 207, 2002
- —Mike Haskins, *Drugs*, p. 284, 2003

shoot *verb*

1 to ejaculate *IRELAND, 1922*

Most likely a shortened form of the C19 'shooting one's roe'.

- K.B. was always trying to jerk off, and he said he shot one time; but I didn't see it and I didn't believe it. —Claude Brown, *Manchild in the Promised Land*, p. 80, 1965
- The tall, well-dressed man licks Johnny's balls while his hand works Johnny's cock to the point of shooting. —John Rechy, *Numbers*, p. 205, 1967
- I don't care how many broads he uses at once," states Butch to the room at large, "or how he fucks 'em as long as he pulls outta their mouth or cunt before he shoots, so we can see it. —Josh Alan Friedman, *Tales of Times Square*, p. 102, 1986
- The jizz-mopper's job is to clean up the booths afterward, because practically everybody shoots a load against the window, and I don't know if you know this or not, but cum leaves streaks if you don't clean it right away. —*Clerks*, 1994
- 'Cause they fucking shoot you in the eye, the face, the ear. —*Kids*, 1995

2 to inject a drug intravenously *US, 1914*

- I was shooting every day now. —William Burroughs, *Junkie*, p. 33, 1953
- This was earlier, all the junkies in Ross's room tying up and shooting[.] —Jack Kerouac, *The Subterraneans*, p. 27, 1958
- He did suggest maybe the guy would know where to score some H – asking me if I would like to shoot a little stuff. —Herbert Huncke, *The Evening Sun Turned Crimson*, p. 81, 1980
- In the late spring of 1967, she discovered that more kids were shooting crystal methedrine – an extremely potent and dangerous speed – than were tripping the light fantastic on acid. —Barney Hoskyns, *Waiting For The Sun*, p. 150, 1996
- —Mike Haskins, *Drugs*, p. 290, 2003

3 to depart *UK, 1897*

Variants include 'shoot off' and 'shoot out'.

- [N]ecking a quick cup of rosie before shooting off to Penge[.] —Greg Williams, *Diamond Geezers*, p. 16, 1997
- I've got to shoot. Say hello to Ollie for us next time you see him. —Danny King, *The Burglar Diaries*, p. 43, 2001

4 to flirt; to make sexual advances *US*

- All the high powered broads were "shooting" on me. —Babs Gonzales, *I Paid My Dues*, p. 39, 1967

5 to throw or toss something *AUSTRALIA, 1929*

- Then the swing doors of the bar bulged out and someone inside shot a bloke into the gutter. —Gavin Casey, *It's Harder for Girls*, p. 182, 1941
- He glanced at it, expressed no regret in the matter, but shot it into the box where the left-over mail was kept[.] —Frank Dalby Davison, *The Wells of Beersheba*, p. 100, 1965

6 to play *US, 1926*

Usually as 'shoot pool', 'shoot crap', etc.

- Well friday 'bout a week ago / Leroy shootin' dice —Jim Croce, *Bad Bad Leroy Brown*, 1973

7 to drink alcohol in shot glass units *US*

- They go down to bars, shoot tequila and go back up to buy things. —Francesca Lia Block, *Witch Baby*, p. 121, 1991

8 to pick a pocket *US*

- Livin' said, "I wouldn't have shot on you if I had been hip you knew White Folks." —Iceberg Slim (Robert Beck), *Trick Baby*, p. 175, 1969

9 used as an imperative, to start; to continue *US, 1915*

- Mellors leaned over the table and said in a low voice, "Right, kid, shoot." —Derek Bickerton, *Payroll*, p. 25, 1959

10 (used of a plant) to show signs of producing fruit *CAYMAN ISLANDS*

- Or someone will say "That coconut tree starting to shoot." —Aarona Booker Kohlman, *Wotcha Say*, p. 24, 1985

▸ **he shoots, he scores; he shoots, he scores, he wins**

used for registering admiration of a small but telling personal victory *UK*

A cliché of football commentary applied to the ordinary moments of life; always in the third person, even if used of the first person.

- She shoots, she scores, she wins, said Dicky admiringly. —James Hawes, *White Powder, Green Light*, p. 48, 2002

▸ **shoot a beaver**

to look for and see a girl's crotch *US*

- —*Current Slang*, p. 4, Summer 1966

▸ **shoot a blag**

to gossip *TRINIDAD AND TOBAGO*

- —Richard Allsopp, *Dictionary of Caribbean English Usage*, p. 106, 1992

▸ **shoot a good stick**

to play pool well *US*

- You shoot a good stick. —*The Hustler*, 1961

▸ **shoot a jug; shoot a peter**

to break into a safe using explosives *US*

- —Hyman E. Goldin et al., *Dictionary of American Underworld Lingo*, p. 192, 1950

▸ **shoot an air rifle; shoot an air gun**

in pool, to bet without money to back your bet *US*

- When betting an air barrel, or "shooting the air rifle," follow the stewardess's advice and take some time to acquaint yourself with the emergency exits around you. —Steve Rushin, *Pool Cool*, p. 5, 1990
- —Mike Shamos, *The Illustrated Encyclopedia of Billiards*, p. 3, 1993

▸ **shoot an azimuth**

to take a compass bearing *US*

- —Linda Reinberg, *In the Field*, p. 197, 1991

▸ **shoot a wave**

to surf a wave, especially if difficult *US*

- —Grant W. Kuhns, *On Surfing*, p. 121, 1963
- —Frank A. Collymore, *Barbadian Dialect*, p. 101, 1965

▸ **shoot blanks**
(said of a male) to engage in sex with a low or non-existent sperm count *US, 1960*
- He dug that young poontang – even though at his age I knew he was shooting blanks. — Edwin Torres, *Carlito's Way*, p. 29, 1975

▸ **shoot down in flames**
to absolutely defeat in an argument *UK, 1942*

▸ **shoot for two**
to defecate *US*
A combination of basketball terminology and children's bathroom vocabulary.
- — Connie Eble (Editor), *UNC-CH Campus Slang*, p. 9, November 2003

▸ **shoot gravy**
to inject a mixture of blood and drug solution that has been reheated after failing to make a direct hit on the vein *US*
- — David Maurer and Victor Vogel, *Narcotics and Narcotic Addiction*, p. 441, 1973

▸ **shoot it**
to lie *UK*
Euphemistic variation of SHOOT THE SHIT (to tell tall tales).
- You Irish liar, O'Mally, so you was shooting it all the time. You big Mick. — Graeme Kent, *The Queen's Corporal [Six Granada Plays]*, p. 89, 1959

▸ **shoot off your mouth; shoot your mouth off**
to speak with a complete lack of discretion; to speak boastfully *US, 1864*
- You've been shootin' your mouth off all night, and I'm one guy who knows that he can kick the crap outa you. — Irving Shulman, *The Amboy Dukes*, p. 229, 1947
- Winston admits to shooting his mouth off at meetings, going above Sabina to her boss[.] — William Lundin and Kathleen Lundin, *When Smart People Work for Dumb Bosses*, p. 9, 1998

▸ **shoot the breeze**
to chat idly *US, 1919*
- Then the old lady that was around a hundred years and I shot the breeze for a while. — J.D. Salinger, *Catcher in the Rye*, p. 201, 1951
- First, we would sit on a stoop somewhere along the block – shooting the breeze about good marks to rob, about who could beat up who. — Rocky Garciano (with Rowland Barber), *Somebody Up There Likes Me*, p. 54, 1955
- Even if you just want to talk – come in and shoot the breeze. — *Rebel Without a Cause*, 1955
- "Let's get together and shoot the breeze sometime," said Mr. Tupper. — Max Shulman, *Rally Round the Flag, Boys!*, p. 208, 1957

▸ **shoot the bull**
to engage in small talk *US, 1902*
- Well, you could see he really felt pretty lousy about flunking me. So I shot the bull for a while. I told him I was a real moron, and all that stuff. — J.D. Salinger, *Catcher in the Rye*, p. 12, 1951
- Sometimes I visit the shack to shoot the bull and get the latest drawings (news). — Eldridge Cleaver, *Soul on Ice*, p. 44, 1968
- Prince walked beside Red shooting the bull until they reached the mess hall. — Donald Goines, *Black Gangster*, p. 9, 1977

▸ **shoot the con**
to engage in goal-oriented, truth-deficient conversation *US*
- We chewed the rag for quite a while and shot the con for fair / and when it came to spreadin' jive, you could gamble that I was there. — Bruce Jackson, *Get Your Ass in the Water and Swim Like Me*, p. 131, 1965

▸ **shoot the crow; shoot the craw**
to abscond; to depart hurriedly, especially without paying money that is owed *UK, 1887*
- Anyway, here's your gaffer coming. I'd better shoot the craw. — Ian Pattison, *Rab C. Nesbitt*, 1988
- If they hadn't shot the crow like that you could have asked whether it's getting a theatrical release anywhere. — Christopher Brookmyre, *Not the End of the World*, p. 77, 1998

▸ **shoot the curl; shoot the tube**
to surf through the hollow part of a wave *US*
- Shoot it, Gidget. Shoot the curl! — Frederick Kohner, *Gidget*, p. 149, 1957
- — Jack Pollard, *The Australian Surfrider*, p. 20, 1963
- And when I get to Surf City I'll be shootin' the curl / And checkin' out the parties for a surfer girl. — Jan Berry and Dean Torrance, *Surf City*, 1963
- — *Paradise of the Pacific*, p. 27, October 1963

▸ **shoot the doughnut**
to aim artillery strikes at enemy forces encircling a US defensive position *US*
- — Gregory Clark, *Words of the Vietnam War*, p. 465, 1990

▸ **shoot the duck**
to skateboard crouched on one leg with the other leg extended outward *US*
- — Laura Torbet, *The Complete Book of Skateboarding*, p. 105, 1976

▸ **shoot the pier**
to surf, or attempt to surf, through the pilings of a pier *US*
- At Huntington and Malibu / They're shooting the pier / At Rincon they're walking the nose. — Brian Wilson and Mike Love, *Surfin' Safari (performed by the Beach Boys)*, 1962
- — Duke Kahanamoku with Joe Brennan, *Duke Kahanamoku's World of Surfing*, p. 176, 1965

▸ **shoot the scales**
(used of a truck driver) to bypass a weigh station *US*
- — *American Speech*, p. 45, February 1963: 'Trucker's language in Rhode Island'

▸ **shoot the shit; shoot shit**
to engage in idle conversation; to tell lies *UK*
- It sure beats working as an extra, standing out in the sun all day while the director and the star shoot the shit. — Elmore Leonard, *Freaky Deaky*, p. 11, 1988
- She sank down next to Chili on the sofa and put her hand on his knee. "You guys working or just shooting the shit?" — Elmore Leonard, *Be Cool*, p. 256, 1999
- So what can I do for you, assuming you're not here just to shoot the shit with your old mucker Jason? — John Williams, *Cardiff Dead*, p. 86, 2000

▸ **shoot the V**
to make a V-sign (the first and index fingers raised from a clenched fist, knuckles forward) *UK*
'Shoot' as 'to fire a gun' accentuates the aggressive or dismissive nature of this action.
- [T]akes his right hand off the handlebars and shoots the atomic plant the V. — Stuart Browne, *Dangerous Parking*, p. 1, 2000

▸ **shoot the works**
on the railways, to make a sudden, emergency stop *US*
- — Ramon Adams, *The Language of the Railroader*, p. 137, 1977

▸ **shoot your bolt**
to ejaculate *NEW ZEALAND*
- — David McGill, *David McGill's Complete Kiwi Slang Dictionary*, p. 101, 1998
- [F]uckin prove it. Prove yew can shoot yewer bolt an yew never know, Gwenno might even go to bed with you. — Niall Griffiths, *Sheepshagger*, p. 142, 2001

▸ **shoot your cuffs**
(used of a man wearing a suit or sports jacket) to straighten your arms so that the cuffs of the shirt extend beyond the jacket sleeves *UK, 1909*
The modern version of the older (1878) 'shoot your linen'.
- This bald-headed, wrinkle-necked, full bird colonel from the Officer's Candidate Schoool stood at the tend end, shooting his cuffs between handshakes[.] — Larry Heinemann, *Close Quarters*, p. 145, 1977
- "It's a term of art," he replied, shooting his cuffs as he turned to deal with the cash register. — Hunter S. Thompson, *Songs of the Doomed*, p. 203, 1983
- He shot the jacket and shirt cuffs over ihs left wrist, displaying a new Timex watch. — George V. Higgins, *Penance for Jerry Kennedy*, p. 34, 1985
- This is fight night. Shoot cuffs, boy, jack-knife yo' legs. Get down. — *Buzz*, p. 76, May 1994

▸ **shoot your load**
figuratively, to exhaust your resources early in a contest *US*
- The kids were used to hot-shot principals who had shot their loads in the first month and then settled down to letting the school run itself. — Evan Hunter, *The Blackboard Jungle*, p. 78, 1954

▸ **shoot your trap**
to talk too much *US*
- I got sick of hearing him shoot his trap off. — James T. Farrell, *Saturday Night*, p. 34, 1947

▸ **shoot your wad**
to ejaculate *US*
- Did you get any action? Did you slam it to her? Did you stick her? Did you hump her? Did you run it down her throat? Did you jam it up her ass? Did you shoot your wad? — *Screw*, p. 6, 29th May 1972
- Candy makes studs prematurely shoot their wads left and right before they make it to the fuck altar. — Anthony Petkovich, *The X Factory*, p. 192, 1997

shoot!

1 yes! *US*
Hawaiian youth usage.
- "You like manapua, Winton?" "Shoot! I grind 'um!" — Douglas Simonson, *Pidgin to da Max Hana Hou*, 1982

2 used as a euphemism for 'shit' in an exclamation *US, 1934*
- "Shoot," said Danny Pogue. He hadn't said "shoot" since the third grade, but he'd been trying to clean up his language in Molly's presence. —Carl Hiaasen, *Native Tongue*, p. 217, 1991
- Oh shoot, she's tripping [on drugs] —Eminem (Marshall Mathers), *My Fault*, 1999
- "If you are looking for a substitute for every curse word you use ... pick words that sound similar." Shoot!" is a logical substitute because it is a mere vowel away from what really wants to be said." — *The New York Times*, 7th April 2002

shoot and scoot *verb*

to engage in warfare involving brief contact with the enemy and then a quick withdrawal *US*
- It was therefore important for the artillery to keep moving. Shoot 'n scoot was a popular way of putting it. In modern combat you're either quick or you're dead. —Harold Coyle, *Team Yankee*, p. 94, 1987
- The United States, by contrast, practices "hip shooting" or "shoot and scoot," in which guns are moved from position to position, firing at each stop. — *USA Today*, p. 4A, 20 January 1991
- — *American Speech*, p. 400, Winter 1991: 'Among the new words'
- Take potshots and scarper as quickly as possible is what the Iraqis are doing in a tactic known as "shoot and scoot". — *The Guardian*, 4th April 2003

shoot-em-up *noun*

used as a loose category for any film or computer game with violent gunplay as a main element in advancing the story-line *UK*
- [A] digital, shoulder-shot, Blair Witch-style, documentary, shoot-em-up, yoofsploitation number based on ecowarriors[.] —James Hawes, *White Powder, Green Light*, p. 5, 2002

shooter *noun*

1 a gun; a pistol, especially a revolver *UK, 1840*
- [H]olding a shooter in his hand. —Frank Norman, *Bang to Rights*, p. 123, 1958
- When it comes to big-time deviation shooters are a thing you certainly have to consider[.] —Derek Raymond (Robin Cook), *The Crust on its Uppers*, p. 95, 1962
- ERIC: No shooters. Cyril said no shooters, you stupid bastard. PETER: Get stuffed. —Mike Hodges, *Get Carter*, p. 62, 1971
- He's gripping his shooter in his free hand. "Whatever you do, you cunt, don't shoot," I tell him as I follow him through the door. —Ted Lewis, *Jack Carter's Law [britpulp]*, p. 51, 1974
- [T]ime to pull a shooter from his jacket. —Donald Gorgon, *Cop Killer*, p. 74, 1994
- —Angela Devlin, *Prison Patter*, p. 104, 1996

2 a professional killer *US*
- Right now we have word that all the shooters are on the street covering the bosses and just hoping for some action. —Mickey Spillane, *Last Cop Out*, p. 15, 1972

3 a criminal who specialises in breaking into safes *US*
- —Vincent J. Monteleone, *Criminal Slang*, p. 206, 1949

4 an intravenous drug user *US*
- [H]e could tell just by looking at her that she was a shooter, though whether she shot coke or smack he couldn't say[.] —William T. Vollman, *Whores for Gloria*, p. 83, 1991

5 in a functionally compartmentalised illegal drug enterprise, the person who holds and turns over the drugs to buyers *US*
- —Carsten Stroud, *Close Pursuit*, p. 275, 1987

6 a pinball player *US*
- —Bobbye Claire Natkin and Steve Kirk, *All About Pinball*, p. 116, 1977

7 in pinball, the device that propels a ball into the playfield *US*
Known conventionally as a 'plunger'.
- —Roger C. Sharpe, *Pinball!*, p. 159, 1977

8 a television camera operator *US*
- —Rachel S. Epstein and Nina Liebman, *Biz Speak*, p. 205, 1986

shooting gallery *noun*

a place where addicts congregate to buy and inject drugs *US, 1951*
- We have information you're running a regular shooting gallery up here. —William Burroughs, *Junkie*, p. 78, 1953
- We'd drive in with Bull for groceries and Hassel'd disappear. We'd have to go looking for him in every shooting gallery in town. —Jack Kerouac, *On the Road*, p. 158, 1957
- What really tore it was they turned the place into a regular shooting gallery – blowing pot and joy popping all over the place. —Ross Russell, *The Sound*, p. 199, 1961
- A twenty-eight-year-old-man named Teddy operated a Bronx "shooting gallery"[.] —Harry J. Anslinger (US Commissioner of Narcotics), *The Murderers*, p. 180, 1961
- He must be a connection." "Got a shooting gallery's all I knows. —Chester Himes, *Cotton Comes to Harlem*, p. 38, 1965
- When a junkie has a hotel room, the word spreads fast. All his friends and their friends stream in and the place turns into a shooting gallery. —James Mills, *The Panic in Needle Park*, p. 75, 1966
- She was good insurance that he could use the apartment as a shooting gallery while Franchot was at work[.] —Nathan Heard, *Howard Street*, p. 138, 1968
- Old Weeping' fell dead outside a shooting gallery in Saint Paul. —Iceberg Slim (Robert Beck), *Pimp*, p. 79, 1969
- He might rip off one of these little shooting galleries somewhere but he doesn't have the nerve to screw around with McDaniel's stuff. —Vernon E. Smith, *The Jones Men*, p. 58, 1974
- Wow – all these people cutting in and out – this ain't no shooting gallery. —Herbert Huncke, *The Evening Sun Turned Crimson*, p. 144, 1980
- We flew from one gig to the next in this 727 that was outfitted like a kind of low-profile shooting gallery/whorehouse. —Terry Southern, *Now Dig This*, p. 10–11, 1986
- "This picture takes place in back alleys and shooting galleries, Roger," Bama said. —Robert Campbell, *Alice in La-La Land*, p. 200, 1987

shooting match *noun*

all of something; the entire matter *US*
- Meanwhile, if that settlement is not made by April first, I will take over the whole shooting match. —Gore Vidal, *Myra Breckinridge*, p. 107, 1968

shoot it!

in surfing, used to encourage a surfer to catch a wave breaking behind them *US*
- [J]ust then his Lordship has turned his head and saw a bitchen set of waves coming up fast and he yelled, "Shoot it!" which means the wave is breaking behind you[.] —Frederick Kohner, *Gidget*, p. 43, 1957

shoot (someone) out *verb*

to train or prepare someone *US*
- —Bruce Jackson, *Outside the Law*, p. 60, 1972: 'Glossary'

shoot through *noun*

a person who fails to honour an undertaking *UK*
Royal Navy slang, from the verb sense 'to go absent without leave'.
- Shiner didn't turn up – the useless ruddy shoot through. —Rick Jolly, *Jackspeak*, 1989

shoot through *verb*

to depart hastily; to go absent without leave *AUSTRALIA, 1947*
- Anyone'd think you'd shot through with his girl-friend. —W.R. Bennett, *Wingman*, p. 71, 1961
- But like I've just remembered I've got to shoot through to the local rubbidy for a few ice cold beers. —Barry Humphries, *The Wonderful World of Barry McKenzie*, p. 7, 1968
- That's when you discovered us. Stacked on a turn. Went the knuckle. Dorabella shot through, abandoning her white bloomers on a low bough. —Jack Hibberd, *A Stretch of the Imagination*, p. 15, 1971

▸ **shoot through like a Bondi tram**

to depart hastily *AUSTRALIA, 1951*
Referring to trams formerly running from the centre of Sydney to Bondi beach, noted for their speed. Appearing slightly earlier (1945, *Australian National Dictionary*) was the variant 'go through like a Bondi tram'.
- Cripes, old Dominic shot through like a Bondi tram, didn't he? —Barry Humphries, *The Wonderful World of Barry McKenzie*, p. 55, 1968

shoot-up; shoot-up man *noun*

a person who promotes a card game or other activity involved in a swindle *US*
- —Robert C. Prus and C.R.D. Sharper, *Road Hustler*, p. 171, 1977: 'Glossary of terms'

shoot up *verb*

to inject heroin or another drug intravenously *US, 1914*
- Every I time I shoot up, I'm saying to them: 'Fuck you and your system, lames.' —Nathan Heard, *Howard Street*, p. 184, 1968
- I sold my ice at a pawnshop price / And shot up all that dough. —Dennis Wepman et al., *The Life*, p. 84, 1976
- VINCENT: You don't mind if I shoot up here? LANCE: Mi casa, su casa. — *Pulp Fiction*, 1994
- "When was the last time you shot up?" I ask her. —Neil S. Skolnik, *On the Ledge*, p. 111, 1996
- Shoot me up / In the mainline —Alabama 3 *Hypo Full of Love*, 1997
- I slept with this famous female star – once – and before we went to bed, she shot up. — *Radio Times*, p. 33, 30th March 2002

shooty *noun*

a shotgun *US*
Recorded as 'Jamaican gang terminology' by Bill Valentine, *Gang Intelligence Manual*, 1995.

shop *noun*

1 any place of business, where you work *UK*
- This sounded bad. I phoned the shop. It got worse. — Duncan MacLaughlin, *The Filth*, p. 161, 2002

2 any home or apartment where drugs are sold *US*
- "I sold drugs hand-to-hand for him until I could get a higher position," Norton said. "Then I became a lieutenant in my own shop." A shop is street slang for a home where drugs are sold. — *Baltimore Sun*, p. 1B, 31st October 1997

3 a theatrical engagement; a job *UK, 1888*
- From our talk of bona [good] shops and buster [excellent] houses, the little showman got round to making some odious comparisons. — Butch Reynolds, *Broken Hearted Clown*, p. 30, 1953

shop; shop up *verb*

to inform the police authorities against, or reveal the whereabouts of, someone with the expected result of arrest and imprisonment for the subject *UK*
The original (1583) sense 'to imprison' began, during C19, to also mean 'to cause to be imprisoned', which sense survives.
- I pity you if he finds out who shopped him! — *The Sweeney*, p. 17, 1976
- Yeah, love to, shop the both of yer. — Cath Staincliffe, *Trainers*, p. 55, 1999

shop around *verb*

1 to search for and compare different possibilities *UK, 1922*
Extended from the practice of making actual comparisons between shops.
- They're all shopping around for husbands, really. Ones with money. — Christopher Dickey, *Expats*, p. 171, 1991

2 to search for a conversation on a citizens' band radio *US*
- — Wayne Floyd, *Jason's Authentic Dictionary of CB Slang*, p. 27, 1976

shop door *noun*

the fly on a man's trousers *US, 1960s*
- — *The Guild Dictionary of Homosexual Terms*, p. 41, 1965

shopping accident *noun*

an impulse purchase later regretted *CANADA*
- — Jack Chambers (Editor), *Slang Bag 93 (University of Toronto)*, p. 6, Winter 1993

shoppy *noun*

1 a shop assistant; a shop-keeper *UK*
- On the raz tonight then, the shoppy says in a mild Brummy accent. – Party is it? — Niall Griffiths, *Kelly + Victor*, p. 55, 2002

2 a shoplifter *AUSTRALIA*
- — *The (Sydney) Bulletin*, 26th April 1975

shoppying *noun*

shoplifting *AUSTRALIA*
- — *The (Sydney) Bulletin*, 26th April 1975

shoppying job *noun*

an act of shoplifting *AUSTRALIA*
- — *The (Sydney) Bulletin*, 26th April 1975

shore dinner *noun*

a sailor, as seen by a homosexual *US*
- — *Fact*, p. 27, January-February 1965

short *noun*

1 a car, especially a restored older car or hot rod *US, 1914*
- — Babs Gonzales, *Be-Bop Dictionary and History of its Famous Stars*, p. 9, 1949
- "You got your short here?" The Wolf asked. — Willard Motley, *Let No Man Write My Epitaph*, p. 108, 1958
- And I don't think I wanna ride in your short anyway. — Clarence Cooper Jr, *The Scene*, p. 36, 1960
- It happened on the strip where the road is wide / Two cool shorts standin' side by side. — The Beach Boys, *Shutdown*, 1963
- Joe, you have a short, some fronts, and a fine ticker too. — Bruce Jackson, *Get Your Ass in the Water and Swim Like Me*, p. 91, 1964
- [B]ecause three blocks away, a short walk for a sick junkie, are respectable neighborhoods good for burglary and "cracking shorts" (breaking into cars). — James Mills, *The Panic in Needle Park*, p. 19, 1966
- You're hot! You ain't got no business sitting dirty in my 'short.' There's a law, Sucker, that can confiscate a 'short' with stuff in it. — Iceberg Slim (Robert Beck), *Pimp*, p. 64, 1969
- It's, like, Santa Claus used ta have this really sharp short, man, y'know? — Cheech Marin and Tommy Chong, *Santa Calus and his Old Lady*, 1971
- Carlito, they got Mr. Etienne in the back of a short in front of Carl's. — Edwin Torres, *Carlito's Way*, p. 29, 1975
- "This your new short?" Rodney nodded to the Mustang. — Richard Price, *Clockers*, p. 254, 1992

2 a drink of spirits (as opposed to wine, beer, etc), or a spirit and a mixer *UK, 1837*
Used of drinks taken in *short* measures, although the original use is also of undiluted alcohol.
- [T]hey were drinking shorts and, of course, they were surrounded by fawning, gorgeous young women. — *The Guardian*, 16th September 2002

3 the unsmoked butt of a cigarette *UK*
- "Save me shorts, Homes." Joe passed over his Camel stub as they fell in walkin' and talkin'. — Seth Morgan, *Homeboy*, p. 89, 1990
- — Don R. McCreary (Editor), *Dawg Speak*, 2001
- — Gary K. Farlow, *Prison-ese*, p. 63, 2002

4 a brief nap *US*
- — Elementary Electronics, *Dictionary of CB Lingo*, p. 105, 1976

5 in lobstering, a lobster that is not legal size *US*
- — Kendall Merriam, *The Illustrated Dictionary of Lobstering*, p. 79, 1978

6 a railway carriage left between stations *US*
- — Ramon Adams, *The Language of the Railroader*, p. 137, 1977

short *adjective*

1 lacking money; lacking enough money to meet an obligation *US, 1960*
- "Oh, sure, I'm a little short," he drawled on, cruelly unaware of it. — John Clellon Holmes, *The Horn*, p. 120, 1958

2 near the end of a prison sentence or military tour of duty *US*
- I'm so short now I can taste the street, and it's like I can't believe I'm here and the rules and regulations jus aren't meant for me any more. — Piri Thomas, *Down These Mean Streets*, p. 303, 1967
- Sonja is short – I'd be very drugged if she lost goodtime about some dyke production. — Clarence Cooper Jr, *The Farm*, p. 169, 1967
- You're sort of short now, aren't you? — Ronald J. Glasser, *365 Days*, p. 219, 1971
- "Well," I said, "you're a lot shorter now than you were from the jump." — A.S. Jackson, *Gentleman Pimp*, p. 130, 1973
- — *Maledicta*, p. 267, Summer/Winter 1981: 'By its slang, ye shall know it: The pessimism of prison life'
- — *Maledicta*, p. 256, Summer/Winter 1982: 'Viet-speak'
- How many days you short? — *Platoon*, 1986

3 used of an amount of a drug, underweight *US*
- Max knows there is a lot of money out there and you can't have your package short [underweight] like as far off as the last one he gave me. — Terry Williams, *The Cocaine Kids*, p. 37, 1989

▸ **a NOUN (part) short of a NOUN (whole)**

used as the central part of a generally humorous formula – a something short of a greater – that infers a lack of mental capacity, not completely sane, 'not all there' *UK, 1941*
Inspiration for these phrases seems to be universal: 'one planet short of a full galaxy'. Religions account for, among others: 'one candle short of a menorah'; 'two candles short of a mass'; 'a few wafers short of a communion'; 'several fishes short of a miracle'. UK politics and current affairs: 'quite a few red boxes short of a successful Prime Minister'; 'various wheezes short of a Scottish parliament'; 'a few pence short of a euro'; 'a few pence short of a first class stamp'; 'a few digits short of a dialling code'; 'a couple of programmes short of a series'. Sports and games: 'one player short of a cricket team'; 'a couple of cubs short of a full Lion's pack'; 'one helmet short of a huddle'; 'two cards short of a full-house'; 'several pawns short of a full set'; 'several pieces short of a full set'. Animals are also popular: 'two sheep short of a flock'; 'a couple of kangaroos short of a full paddock'. Food and drink: 'several currants short of a bun'; 'one licorice stick short of a Pontefract cake'; 'two bottles short of a crate'; 'a nosebag short of a sack of oats'; 'two luncheon vouchers short of a ploughman's'; 'several prawns short of a cocktail'; 'a few stock-cubes short of a full polar ration'; 'several gondolas short of a Cornetto [a branded ice-cream associated with Venice]'. Fashion: 'three diamond clusters short of a tiara'; 'several gemstones short of a full tiara'; 'more than a Dolce short of a Gabbana [Dolce Gabana is a well-known fashion-house]'. And so on. Two final examples, both with obviously limited circulation but they demonstrate the possibilities: 'a few billion neurons short of a full load'; 'a few shards of pottery short of a full anthropological theory'.
- That whole bunch of weirds are short a few bricks of a full load, a few cards of a full deck, short a few ounces of a full pound, short an inch or two of a full foot, in short – shorted out a little in the brain. Beatrice Sparks (writing as 'Anonymous') — *Jay's Journal*, p. 89, 1979
- My old man thought [...] Joe was a biscuit short of a packet. — John Milne, *Alive and Kicking*, p. 35, 1998

- This geezer Dougie was not exactly what you'd call "together". Several marbles short of a full bag. —Dave Courtney, *Stop the Ride I Want to Get Off*, p. 266, 1999.
- Wu-Tang Clan's Ol' Dirty Bastard [...] he's bananas. Screwy. Poco loco. Bonkers as conkers. Several Wu's short of a Tang Clan in fact. —*Uncut*, p. 20, October 2003
- With his dopey, idiot-savant look he always seems a couple of tunes short of the full iPod. —*The Guardian*, 28th May 2004

▸ a sheep short of a paddock

lacking a full complement of intelligence *AUSTRALIA*

- Being young and willing, I did what I was told, even though I knew that the sergeant-major must have been a sheep short of a paddock. —Rex Hunt, *Tall Tales – and True*, p. 65, 1994

▸ get short

to near the end of a prison sentence or military enlistment *US*

- —*American Speech*, p. 194, October 1951: 'A study of reformatory argot'
- —Inez Cardozo-Freeman, *The Joint*, p. 500, 1984

▸ have short arms and long pockets

to be stingy *AUSTRALIA, 1966*

- They are certainly careful with the moola and they've all got short arms and long pockets, bless their hearts. —Barry Humphries, *The Traveller's Tool*, p. 38, 1985

short-and-curlies *noun*

pubic hair *US*

- —Dale Gordon, *The Dominion Sex Dictionary*, p. 147, 1967
- —Louis S. Leland, *A Personal Kiwi-Yankee Dictionary*, p. 91, 1984

▸ have by the short and curlies

to hold someone at a disadvantage; to exercise complete control over someone *UK, 1948*

Fanciful but convincing imagery in which 'short and curlies' represent pubic hairs; a variation of **HAVE BY THE SHORT HAIRS**.

- They knew they had me by the short and curlies, so they starts to come the old heavy stuff. —John Peter Jones, *Feather Pluckers*, p. 71, 1964
- [N]o coach worth his clipboard would consent to letting a player have him by the short-and-curlies. —Alexander Wolff, *Big Game, Small World*, p. 155, 2003

short-arm *verb*

to perform a rectal examination *US*

- —Sally Williams, *"Strong" Words*, p. 159, 1994

short-arm bandit; short-arm heister *noun*

a rapist *US*

- —Hyman E. Goldin et al., *Dictionary of American Underworld Lingo*, p. 192, 1950

short-arm inspection; small-arm inspection *noun*

an inspection for a sexually transmitted infection *UK, 1919*

Soldiers or prisoners are lined up, each holding his penis. At the command 'Skin it back and milk it down', each man 'milks' down his penis from the base to the tip so that the inspecting doctor can check for pus at the tip of the urethra.

- After the fingerprinting routine and short-arm inspection at Pontiac, we were given numbers and sent to the barber shop[.] —Mezz Mezzrow, *Really the Blues*, p. 10, 1946
- While you were in the Army you must have taken your clothes off thousands of times for small-arm inspection. —Max Shulman, *The Zebra Derby*, p. 132, 1946
- I hear there's a correspondence course in short-arms inspections. —Norman Mailer, *Advertisements for Myself*, p. 110, 1951
- A tall silent screw, dazzling with brass buttons and gold braid on his navy-blue uniform, slashed his lead-loaded cane through the air like a vocal sword directing us to put our bundles on a long bench and to undress for "short arm" inspection[.] —Iceberg Slim (Robert Beck), *Pimp*, p. 50, 1969
- There was a crowd in the kitchen, a mob in the hall / A short-arm inspection by the shithouse wall. —Dennis Wepman et al., *The Life*, p. 110, 1976

short-arm parade *noun*

an inspection of the genitals of a group of men for sexually transmitted infection *AUSTRALIA, 1977*

- [W]e were told to report to hut number so-and-so. "What for?" we enquired naively. "Short arm parade," was the curt reply. Naive was right. I had the idea we were going to get injections of some sort. We didn't. Instead, after entering the hut, we were ordered to strip. Then, a white-coated officer walked down the line, playing cough-and-jiggle while he examined our genitals. —Bettina Arndt, *The Australian Way of Sex*, p. 10, 1984

short-arse; short-ass *noun*

a short person *UK, 1706*

- The performers had a dwarf with them (Michelle didn't know the politically correct term these days, but in her current mood anything above "short-arse" should be considered solicitously polite)[.] —Christopher Brookmyre, *The Sacred Art of Stealing*, p. 77, 2002

short-arsed *adjective*

small, not tall *UK*

Extended from **SHORT-ARSE** (a short person).

- Ah, Greg, you short-arsed little twat. How's the dose? Cleared up yet? —Colin Butts, *Is Harry on the Boat?*, p. 92, 1997

short bus *noun*

used as a reference to the mentally retarded *US*

Referring to the smaller school buses used to transport special education students in the US.

- You know, the guys who ride the short bus. —*Something About Mary*, 1998

short buy *noun*

a purchase of a small amount of drugs *US*

- —*American Speech*, p. 88, May 1955: 'Narcotic argot along the Mexican border'

shortcake *noun*

the act of shortchanging someone deliberately *US*

Used with 'the'.

- —John Scarne, *Scarne on Dice*, p. 478, 1974
- —Joe McKennon, *Circus Lingo*, p. 83, 1980

shortcake *verb*

to shortchange someone *US, 1961*

- "Curly," he says, "that Greek gentleman back there shortcaked me." —Guy Owen, *The Flim-Flam Man and the Apprentice Grifter*, p. 154, 1972
- —Thomas L. Clark, *The Dictionary of Gambling and Gaming*, p. 197, 1987

shortcake artist *noun*

an expert at shortchanging *US*

- —Joe McKennon, *Circus Lingo*, p. 83, 1980

shortchange artist *noun*

a swindler who gives customers too little change *US*

- The shortchange artist works in reverse to the change raise, and simply gives you back less change than you are supposed to get. —W.M. Tucker, *The Change Raisers*, p. 17, 1960

short con *noun*

a confidence game in which the victim is swindled once, without being sent home for a bigger prize *US, 1940*

- Unlike the big con operator, whose elaborate scene-setting may involve as much as a hundred thousand dollars, the short-con grifter can run on peanuts. —Jim Thompson, *The Grifters*, p. 22, 1963
- It's short con because the play for the sucker is short and we can only trim the sucker for the goddamn scratch in his pocket. —Iceberg Slim (Robert Beck), *Trick Baby*, p. 111, 1969
- According to your statement you are a shot-con operator. Run of the mill scams. —*The Usual Suspects*, 1995

short con *verb*

to engage in a short con swindle *US*

- Now all this talk about short-coinin', the Herman was a player too. —Bruce Jackson, *Get Your Ass in the Water and Swim Like Me*, p. 68, 1964

short dog *noun*

a half pint bottle of alcohol; cheap wine *US*

- —*Current Slang*, p. 42, Fall 1968
- Tooner Flats is the area of gangas who spend their last dime on short dogs of T-Bird wine[.] —Oscar Zeta Acosta, *The Revolt of the Cockroach People*, p. 90, 1973
- As I pulled to the curb opposite the Grand Central Market, a wino staggering down Broadway sucking on a short dog saw me, spun around, fell on his ass, dropped his bottle, and got up as though nothing had happened. —Joseph Wambaugh, *The Blue Knight*, p. 123, 1973
- —Edith A. Folb, *runnin' down some lines*, p. 254, 1980
- I stopped at the Mayfair Market to pick up three chilled short dogs. —James Ellroy, *Brown's Requiem*, p. 28, 1981
- —Bill Reilly, *Big Al's Official Guide to Chicagoese*, p. 51, 1982
- The left-hand side of the street featured a grain store, a market, the front window filled with stacks of Tokay and muscatel short dogs, and a clapboard farm-machinery repair shop[.] —James Ellroy, *Hollywood Nocturnes*, p. 177, 1994

short end *noun*

in the television and film industries, unexposed film remaining after cutting off the exposed film *US*

- Many student and experimental films are made from short ends. —Ralph S. Singleton, *Filmaker's Dictionary*, p. 152, 1990

short eyes *noun*
a child molestor *US*
• Punks shooting up a delicatessen on their first heist. Rapists. Short-eyes. —Emmett Grogan, *Final Score*, p. 69, 1976
• —Carsten Stroud, *Close Pursuit*, p. 275, 1987
• Foley turned the lights on and the kid hunched around to look at him, no doubt afraid he was about to get beat up again, the fate of guys with short eyes among a population that felt superior. —Elmore Leonard, *Out of Sight*, p. 14, 1996

short fuse *noun*
an impending deadline *US*
• —Department of the Army, *Staff Officer's Guidebook*, p. 65, 1986

short go; short order *noun*
a drug dose that is smaller than the addict is accustomed to *US*
• —J.E. Schmidt, *Narcotics Lingo and Lore*, p. 166, 1959

short hairs *noun*
▸ **have by the short hairs**
to hold someone at a disadvantage; to exercise complete control over someone *UK, 1888*
A figurative use of the literal meaning 'to hold by the pubic hair'.
• "We had 'im by the short hair," the little one said. —Horace McCoy, *Kiss Tomorrow Good-bye*, p. 60, 1948
• All right, Sheik, you got us by the short hair, but you know you can't get away. —Chester Himes, *The Real Cool Killers*, p. 137, 1959
• I got you by the short hairs now. I'm in and you're out. —Mickey Spillane, *Me, Hood!*, p. 27, 1963
• That Jefferson Tatum – man, has he got the world by the short hairs! —Max Shulman, *Anyone Got a Match?*, p. 6, 1964
• [C]aught by the short hairs by the fickle finger of fate[.] —Gore Vidal, *Myra Breckinridge*, p. 234, 1968
• The government still had me by the short hairs. —Odie Hawkins, *Scars and Memories*, p. 93, 1987

short heist *noun*
an act of masturbation *US*
• There was a prisoner named Tank, a former prize-fighter who was a wealth of terms, like "hack" and "screw" (guards), "undercover faggot," and "short heist" (masturbation). —Piri Thomas, *Seven Long Times*, p. 57, 1974
• Who's that with the funny white collar band? / What's that, a short-heist book in his hand? —Dennis Wepman et al., *The Life*, p. 119, 1976

short house *noun*
a short person *UK*
A euphemistic variation of **SHORT ARSE**.
• RINGO: Hello. GIRL: Get out of it, short house! —*A Hard Day's Night*, 1964

shortie pyjamas *noun*
summer pyjamas with short sleeves and trouser legs *AUSTRALIA, 1987*
• He was wearing shortie pyjamas with aeroplanes all over them. —Phillip Gwynne, *Deadly Unna?*, p. 267, 1998

shortitis *noun*
the mental state of knowing that you have almost finished a prison sentence or military tour of duty *US*
• —Hyman E. Goldin et al., *Dictionary of American Underworld Lingo*, p. 193, 1950
• But I had "shortitis" – the impatience which makes the last few weeks unbearably long[.] —Piri Thomas, *Down These Mean Streets*, p. 301, 1967

short-long *noun*
a hairstyle in which the hair is worn short at the front and long at the back *US*
Most commonly known as a **MULLET**.
• —Don R. McCreary (Editor), *Dawg Speak*, 2001

short of cars *adjective*
on the railways, without a job *US*
• —Ramon Adams, *The Language of the Railroader*, p. 137, 1977

short on *adjective*
less than is adequate, expected or required *UK, 1922*
• [Bill Brown, at the Dun Cow Inn in Sedgefield] preferred former President Bill Clinton and thinks Bush is "a bit short on brains." —*The Scotsman*, 14th November 2003

short ones *noun*
▸ **have by the short ones**
to have absolute control of someone; to force submission *US*
A figurative use of the literal meaning 'to hold by the pubic hair'; a variation on **HAVE BY THE SHORT HAIRS**.
• Now wonder he's got the world by the short ones! —Eugene Boe (Compiler), *The Wit & Wisdom of Archie Bunker*, p. 85, 1971
• [W]e got you by the short ones, and there's nothing you can do about it. —Jack W. Thomas, *Heavy Number*, p. 160, 1976
• Ron [Ronald Reagan] is their Kept Boy. They've got him by the short ones – he must play ball or they'll cut the PR budget[.] —Frank Zappa, *The Real Frank Zappa Book*, p. 293, 1989

short pair *noun*
in poker, a pair of tens or lower *US*
• —Irwin Steig, *Common Sense in Poker*, p. 187, 1963

short round *noun*
gunfire or artillery fired by friendly forces *US*
• We lost our fair share of people from "short rounds" – friendly fire – just plain fuckups. —Al Santoli, *To Bear Any Burden*, p. 134, 1985

shorts *noun*
1 a condition of low or no funds *US, 1932*
• I was still hanging around New York, suffering a bad case of the shorts[.] —Jimmy Snyder, *Jimmy the Greek*, p. 183, 1975
• —Thomas L. Clark, *The Dictionary of Gambling and Gaming*, p. 198, 1987

2 the last portion of a cigarette *US*
• To save someone shorts on a cigarette is to save him a couple of draws at the end. —William K. Bentley and James M. Corbett, *Prison Slang*, p. 65, 1992

3 in poker, a pair that is beaten by a larger pair *US*
• —George Percy, *The Language of Poker*, p. 81, 1988

short short *adverb*
soon *US*
• —*Complete CB Slang Dictionary*, p. 83, 1976
• —Peter Chippindale, *The British CB Book*, p. 159, 1981

short-shorts *noun*
very brief shorts *US*
• Who wears short shorts? She wears short shorts. —The Royal Teens, *Short Shorts*, 1958
• He also didn't need her there dressed in short-shorts and heels, pissing on him in public. —Stephen Cannell, *Big Con*, p. 209, 1997

short skirt *noun*
a Mini car *UK*
Citizens' band radio slang, punning on the length of a mini-skirt.
• —Peter Chippindale, *The British CB Book*, p. 161, 1981

short-sleeves *noun*
in homosexual usage, an uncircumcised penis *US*
• —*Male Swinger Number 3*, p. 48, 1981: 'The complete gay dictionary'

short stick *noun*
a stick notched by a US soldier in Vietnam counting the days until the end of his tour of duty *US*
• A couple of guys were unlimbering their short-sticks, the chunky batons that grunts would carry and notch day by day when their time in-country was running out. —Peter Goldman and Tony Fuller, *Charlie Company*, p. 118, 1983

shortstop *noun*
1 a temporary arrangement or relationship *US*
• Sometimes players deliberately take on a ho they knew will only last a short while. They figure they have nothing to lose, and attempt to get as much "short-stop" money as possible before she leaves. —Christina and Richard Milner, *Black Players*, p. 101, 1972

2 a gambler who makes small and conservative bets *US*
• —*The Annals of the American Academy of Political and Social Sciences*, p. 130, May 1950
• "She was shot in the head by Smitty Cocaine / A notorious shortstop and a practical lame[.] —Dennis Wepman et al., *The Life*, p. 43, 1976

3 in pool, a very skilled player who is just below the highest tier *US*
• Sharks (who use the term pejoratively) beat shortstops, but short-stops beat just about everyone else. —Steve Rushin, *Pool Cool*, p. 26, 1990

4 in a group eating setting, to take a second helping despite an earlier request from another for seconds *US*
• —*American Speech*, p. 56, February 1947: 'Pacific War language'

short time *noun*
a brief session with a prostitute, long enough for sex and nothing more *US*
• Their return English is always questioning, in the few broken phrases they know: "How much you got? "Short time? "All night?" "Costume show?" —Lenny Bruce, *How to Talk Dirty and Influence People*, p. 41, 1965

short-time *verb*

1 to serve the final days of a jail sentence or term of enlistment *US*

- Like when you're short-timin', waitin' on your parole, the cons will provoke you to fight – make you blow your parole. —Edwin Torres, *Carlito's Way*, p. 45, 1975

2 to engage in a quick sexual encounter with a prostitute *US*

- —John T. Algeo, *American Speech*, p. 120, May 1960: 'Korean Bamboo English'
- "To short-time Claymore Face – never mind how God-awful ugly she is, boys, just slip a sandbag over her head – is to guarantee a sovereign cure for everything[.] —Larry Heinemann, *Close Quarters*, p. 245, 1977

short-timer *noun*

1 a soldier near the end of his tour of duty in Vietnam *US*

All but the US Marines served exactly 12 months in Vietnam; the Marines served 13 months.

- — *Harper's*, p. 51, January 1964
- —Carl Fleischhauer, *A Glossary of Army Slang*, p. 14, 1968
- Rodriguez was a genuine "short-timer," with only fourteen days remaining in the Nam. —Charles Anderson, *The Grunts*, p. 84, 1976

2 a prisoner whose release date is approaching *US*

- — *Current Slang*, p. 7, Winter 1966

3 someone whose retirement date is rapidly approaching *US*

- Because Sam had the day off, Fin thought he'd better cover his old pal's ass by making the notifications. Sam had a short-timer's attitude. —Joseph Wambaugh, *Finnegan's Week*, p. 94, 1993

4 a prostitute engaged for a short period of time *US*

- — *American Speech*, p. 120, May 1960: 'Korean bamboo English'

short-timer's calendar *noun*

a calendar showing the days remaining in a soldier's tour of duty in Vietnam *US*

- Most everyone has a short-timers calendar of some sort. —Tony Zidek, *Choi Oi*, p. 124, 1965
- —Carl Fleischhauer, *A Glossary of Army Slang*, p. 14, 1968

shorty *noun*

1 a female, especially an attractive one *US*

- — *Newsday*, p. B2, 11th October 1997
- —Connie Eble (Editor), *UNC-CH Campus Slang*, p. 7, Spring 1999

2 a close friend *US*

- —Anna Scotti and Paul Young, *Buzzwords*, p. 72, 1997

3 in a casino, a shorter-than-expected shift at a table *US*

- I've caught two shorties already tonight. —Lee Solkey, *Dummy Up and Deal*, p. 119, 1980

shot *noun*

1 an opportunity *US*

- I appreciate the shot at the lady, but you didn't introduce me to the shot. —Susan Hall, *Gentleman of Leisure*, p. 53, 1972
- You just don't realize what a shot on the Langford Show can mean. — *King of Comedy*, 1976
- All I want is a shot. Just a fuckin' shot. — *Raging Bull*, 1980
- I've been working my ass off for a shot like this, Bally's Park Place, my charts, and you want me to hide in a hotel room. —Elmore Leonard, *Glitz*, p. 224–225, 1985

2 an attempt *UK, 1756*

- Give it a shot. — *The Blues Brothers*, 1980

3 the right way to do something *AUSTRALIA, 1953*

- The shot's just keep pluggin' along. No sense in bustin' yerself. —Nino Culotta (John O'Grady), *They're A Weird Mob*, p. 39, 1957
- Keep yer 'ands soft, Nino. That's the shot. —Nino Culotta (John O'Grady), *They're A Weird Mob*, p. 83, 1957
- The shot here is to go for one of the bridesmaids and 'line her up' for tomorrow, or the next week. —John O'Grady, *Aussie Etiket*, p. 82, 1971

4 an occurrence or instance; a thing *US*

- About 2 a.m. one morning I met a prostitute downtown who wanted me to pay her fare and 5.00 a "shot." —Phyllis and Eberhard Kronhausen, *Sex Histories of American College Men*, p. 140, 1960
- It seems curious that the first public manifestation of psychedelics was the dances at two and a half a shot. — *Berkeley Barb*, p. 6, 25th November 1966
- I've done too many of these things. Just gimme the whole shot. —Clarence Cooper Jr, *The Farm*, p. 82, 1967
- "Not bad, Molly," Gloria said after examining Leslie up and down. "She's really a fine bitch. We'll pull a hundred a shot!" —Donald Goines, *Inner City Hoodlum*, p. 119, 1975

5 an instance of sexual intercourse *US*

An abbreviation of **SHOT OF COCK**.

- —Carl Fleischhauer, *A Glossary of Army Slang*, p. 14, 1968

6 an ejaculation *US*

- If it'll get me a few hundred miles across country, I'll take a shot in the mouth. —Kevin Smith, *Jay and Silent Bob Strike Back*, p. 27, 2001

7 an injection of drugs *UK, 1929*

- If you really have got a yen I'll give you a shot. —Douglas Rutherford, *The Creeping Flesh*, p. 103, 1963
- Oh can't you see that I'm fading fast? And that this shot will be my last. —The Rolling Stones, *Sister Morphine*, 1971
- —Angela Devlin, *Prison Patter*, p. 105, 1996

8 cocaine *UK*

- —Mike Haskins, *Drugs*, p. 281, 2003

9 Coca-Cola™ *US*

- — *American Speech*, p. 87, April 1946: 'The language of West Coast culinary workers'

10 a single measure of spirits *US*

- Fuck shots! I hope the weed'll outweigh these drinks[.] —Eminem (Marshall Mathers), *Kill You*, 2000

11 a blow, especially a severe one *US*

- Foley said, "I never saw a fighter take as many shots as you did and keep coming back – outside of Rocky Balboa." —Elmore Leonard, *Out of Sight*, p. 6, 1996

12 an illegal move by a gambler *US*

- I had a dozen shots pulled on me today. —Lee Solkey, *Dummy Up and Deal*, p. 119, 1980

13 a competent pickpocket *US*

- —John R. Armore and Joseph D. Wolfe, *Dictionary of Desperation*, p. 49, 1976

14 a person or thing *UK: SCOTLAND*

- [A] homosexual is a "bent shot"[.] —Michael Munro, *The Patter, Another Blast*, p. 64, 1988

15 an incident report describing a prisoner's misconduct *US*

- —John R. Armore and Joseph D. Wolfe, *Dictionary of Desperation*, p. 49, 1976
- —Reinhold Aman, *Hillary Clinton's Pen Pal*, p. 67, 1996

▸ **have a shot at**

to heckle or harass someone *AUSTRALIA, 1947*

- What did you have a shot at her for? —John Wynnum, *Jiggin' in the Riggin'*, p. 38, 1965
- Ah, yes, up to where Danny O'Connell the publican had a shot at Trigger about the raffle. —Frank Hardy, *The Yarns of Billy Borker*, p. 68, 1965
- Aw, take no notice of him. He's only havin' a shot. —John O'Grady, *It's Your Shout, Mate!*, p. 79, 1972

▸ **like a shot**

exceedingly quickly *UK, 1809*

- [T]he Coolboy defence got themselves in a knot and the man with a name better known in show jumping circles – Nick Skelton – was in like a shot to find the net. — *Carlow Nationalist*, 26th November 2003

▸ **make a shot**

to secret something on your body while shoplifting *US*

- They got a blind spot right at the milk and egg department. All you got to do is carry your meat over there and make your shot under the mirror so they can't see you. —Donald Goines, *Dopefiend*, p. 101, 1971

Shot *noun*

▸ **the Shot**

Aldershot (the home of the British Army) *UK, 1925*

- [G]o round to Carol's house, hospitalise the boyfriend and drag her back to "the Shot". —Ken Lukowiak, *Marijuana Time*, p. 179, 2000

shot *adjective*

especially of a mechanical contrivance, broken; wrecked; ruined *AUSTRALIA*

- Finally however, the Plymouth conked out. The carbie was shot. —Kerry Cue, *Crooks, Chooks and Bloody Ratbags*, p. 162, 1983
- It had nothing on the clock but its springs were shot[.] —Peter Corris, *Make Me Rich*, p. 78, 1985

▸ **shot of**

rid of *AUSTRALIA*

- I can't flamin' wait to get shot of these pommy drongos. I've just about had a Ned-Kelly-full of their line of bullsh! —Barry Humphries, *The Wonderful World of Barry McKenzie*, p. 9, 1968
- No, it would be easier to leave, and be shot of the lot of them. —Jessica Anderson, *The Impersonators*, p. 199, 1980

shot!

well done! *BERMUDA*

- —Peter Smith and Fred M. Barritt, *Bermewjan Vurds*, 1985

shotcaller *noun*

the nominal leader of a youth gang *US*

- —Mark S. Fleisher, *Beggars & Thieves*, p. 291, 1995: 'Glossary'

shot down *adjective*

drug-intoxicated *US, 1982*

- —Richard A. Spears, *The Slang and Jargon of Drugs and Drink*, p. 451, 1986
- —Mike Haskins, *Drugs*, p. 291, 2003

shot-for-shot *noun*

an arrangement between two homosexuals in which they switch sex roles to satisfy each other *US*

- —Hyman E. Goldin et al., *Dictionary of American Underworld Lingo*, p. 193, 1950

shotgun *noun*

1 a pipe with air-holes used for smoking marijuana *US, 1977*
The shotgun gives a **BLAST**.

- The shotgun was a tube of seven Coca-Cola cans taped together end-to-end. Grass, bulk marijuana which could be purchased by the sandbag for ten dollars MPC, was burned in the second can.—John Del Vecchio, *The 13th Valley*, p. 132, 1982

2 a ritual of drinking beer, forcing the beer out of the can into the drinker's mouth by opening the down-facing top after puncturing the up-facing bottom *US*

- —Connie Eble (Editor), *UNC-CH Campus Slang*, p. 9, Fall 1988

3 a potent mix of heroin, cocaine, nitroglycerine, phenol and kola nut administered to racehorses as a stimulant *US*

- [T]he trainer gave all his horses a "shotgun" when they went to post.—Harry J. Anslinger, *The Murderers*, p. 227, 1961

4 the front passenger seat in a car *US, 1963*
Also called the 'shotgun seat'. The earliest use of the term, not yet applied to a car, seems to be in the 1939 film *Stagecoach*. To date, the earliest discovered use in the sense of a car is in 1963.

- He got up and staggered to the shotgun seat and tossed me the keys[.]—Robert Gover, *Poorboy at the Party*, p. 180, 1966
- Strike started to walk away, thinking about flex, when the rust-colored Caddy came rolling up again, Rodney at the wheel with his arm flung out along the back of the shotgun seat.—Richard Price, *Clockers*, p. 17, 1992

5 a male passenger in a vehicle equipped with citizens' band radio *UK*

- —Peter Chippindale, *The British CB Book*, p. 159, 1981

6 a police radar unit *US*

- How about it 1–40, we definitely got a bear with a shot gun at Exit 31.—Lanie Dills, *The Official CB Slanguage Language Dictionary*, p. 62, 1976

7 in blackjack, the player to the immediate left of the dealer *US, 1979*

- —Thomas L. Clark, *The Dictionary of Gambling and Gaming*, p. 199, 1987

8 in electric line work, an insulated line tool formally known as a grip-all stick *US*

- —A.B. Chance Co., *Lineman's Slang Dictionary*, p. 15, 1980

9 an unannounced test *US*

- —Collin Baker et al., *College Undergraduate Slang Study Conducted at Brown University*, p. 196, 1968

shotgun *verb*

1 to share marijuana smoke with someone else in the following manner: you blow through a lighted joint or blunt which is held with the burning end in your mouth, while your fellow-smoker inhales the stream of smoke that is produced *US*

- —Connie Eble (Editor), *UNC-CH Campus Slang*, March 1974

2 to smoke an entire marijuana cigarette in one go *AUSTRALIA*

- He lit up, drew the cone and shotgunned it, fighting the burning sensation in his lungs, holding it for as long as he could.—Harrison Biscuit, *The Search for Savage Henry*, p. 60, 1995

3 while treating a hospital patient, to order every possible treatment to avoid being wrong *US*

- —Sally Williams, *"Strong" Words*, p. 159, 1994

shotgun *adjective*

1 used of a house or apartment, having rooms set on both sides of a central hall *US, 1903*

- It was a shotgun flat, one room opening into the other.—Chester Himes, *The Real Cool Killers*, p. 31, 1959
- And you may find yourself / living in a shotgun shack.—Talking Heads, *Once in a Lifetime*, 1980
- It was a warm, lovely, sexy feeling, projected down a long San Francisco shotgun flat, some fifty or sixty feet.—Stephen Gaskin, *Amazing Dope Tales*, p. 2, 1980
- I was living in half a shotgun double on Magazine with hardly any furniture, a job I hated, and I was thinking on and off of getting married.—Elmore Leonard, *Bandits*, p. 20, 1987
- Rodney's apartment looked like every other seventy-five-year-old shotgun flat in Dempsy.—Richard Price, *Clockers*, p. 61, 1992

2 wide-ranging *US*

- You occasionally read about shotgun or scattershot pleadings, but theres's a lot more iffy fishing alleged among litigators than gun-play or even snare-setting.—*The Lawyers Weekly*, 8th July 1994

shotgun!

used as a claim on riding in the front passenger seat of a car *US*

- CARLOS: Shotgun! ANTS: No, I called it. BEAN: When? ANTS: Before we picked you up. BEAN: Man, you can't call it for the whole night. I got it now. Get in the back, punk.—*American Graffiti*, 1973

Shotgun Alley *nickname*

the A Shau Valley, dense jungle terrain near the border of South Vietnam and Laos, southeast of Khe Sanh *US*
A phonetic approximation.

- —Gregory Clark, *Words of the Vietnam War*, p. 1, 1990

shotgun bunk *noun*

a sleeping space into which one must crawl *CANADA*

- Most of the [bunkhouses] had what were called shotgun [or "muzzle-loading"] bunks. Those were on tiers of three high and placed close beside each other. The only way to get in was to crawl in the bottom like going into a tunnel.—*B.C. Digest*, p. 46/3, July-August 1963

shotgun mike *noun*

in the television and film industries, a directional microphone *US*

- —Ralph S. Singleton, *Filmaker's Dictionary*, p. 152, 1990

shotgunner *noun*

a door gunner on an air gunship *US*

- —Gregory Clark, *Words of the Vietnam War*, p. 151, 1990

shot house *noun*

an establishment that sells alcohol illegally, by the drink *US*

- Shot-house operators run informal (and illegal) taverns in their own homes (shot-house operators are often women).—Burgess Laughlin, *Job Opportunities in the Black Market*, p. 10–9, 1978

shot of cock *noun*

sexual intercourse *US*

- —Carl Fleischhauer, *A Glossary of Army Slang*, p. 14, 1968

shot on the swings *noun*

an instance of sexual intercourse *UK: SCOTLAND*

- Good weekend, was it? D'ye get a shot on the swings, aye?—Michael Munro, *The Patter, Another Blast*, p. 70, 1988

shot out *adjective*

in very bad physical shape *US*

- —James Harris, *A Convict's Dictionary*, p. 38, 1989

shot rod *noun*

a fast car *US*
Teen slang.

- —*American Weekly*, p. 2, 14th August 1955

shottie *noun*

a shotgun *US*

- —Anna Scotti and Paul Young, *Buzzwords*, p. 141, 1997

shot to shit *adjective*

ruined, utterly spoiled *UK*

- [H]is former sex life was shot to shit in the face of now and happening fashion.—Mick Farren, *Give the Anarchist a Cigarette*, p. 10, 2001

shotty; shotti *noun*

the front passenger seat in a car *US*
A shortened **SHOTGUN**.

- —Rick Ayers (Editor), *Berkeley High Slang Dictionary*, p. 38, 2004

shotty-gotty!

used as a claim on riding in the front passenger seat of a car *US*
A variation on **SHOTGUN!**.

- —Pamela Munro, *U.C.L.A. Slang*, p. 106, 1997

shoulder *noun*

in betting, odds of 7–4 *UK*
From the **TICK-TACK** signal used by bookmakers.

- —John McCririck, *John McCririck's World of Betting*, p. 61, 1991

shoulder boulder *noun*

an abandoned vehicle on the side of the road *US*

The hard shoulder of the road, rhymed and contrived to make an obstacle.

- — *Complete CB Slang Dictionary*, p. 83, 1976
- — Peter Chippindale, *The British CB Book*, p. 159, 1981

shoulder hopper *noun*

a surfer who surfs in another surfer's right of way *US*

- — Mitch McKissick, *Surf Lingo*, 1987

shoulders *noun*

▸ **on the shoulders**

in betting, odds of 9–2 *UK*

From the **TICK-TACK** signal used by bookmakers.

shouse *noun*

a toilet *AUSTRALIA, 1941*

Euphemistic for **SHITHOUSE**.

- Tell me, what happened after the lightning hit the shouse? — John Wynnum, *Jiggin' in the Riggin'*, p. 53, 1965

shouse *adjective*

no good *AUSTRALIA*

Euphemistic for **SHITHOUSE**.

shout *noun*

1 a drink or round of drinks bought for others; the purchase of a round *AUSTRALIA, 1854*

- When you buy a bloke a beer, it's called a shout, see? — Nino Culotta (John O'Grady), *They're A Weird Mob*, p. 26, 1957

2 your turn to buy drinks for someone else *AUSTRALIA, 1882*

- 'Your shout,' Pincher said amiably, and pushed the empty glasses towards the barmaid's edge of the bar. — J.E. MacDonnell, *Don't Gimme the Ships*, p. 25, 1960
- — Arthur Chipper, *The Aussie Swearer's Guide*, p. 55, 1972

3 your turn to buy anything *AUSTRALIA, 1911*

- Let's buy a Mercedes. But remember, it's *my shout*! You bought the pies[.] — Roy Higgins and Tom Prior, *The Jockey Who Laughed*, p. 94, 1982

4 a call on the police radio *UK*

Derived from conventional 'shout' (used to hail).

- — Peter Laurie, *Scotland Yard*, p. 327, 1970

5 a greeting *US*

- I want to send a shout out to all my friends back home. — Connie Eble (Editor), *UNC-CH Campus Slang*, p. 7, Spring 1999

shout *verb*

1 to buy a round of drink for others *AUSTRALIA, 1854*

- He shouted a round, too, just like any ordinary bloke would. — Alexander Buzo, *Norm and Ahmed*, p. 19, 1969
- However, there was a maximum damage to my bank balanace as I decided to 'shout' drinks. — Rex Hunt, *Tall Tales – and True*, p. 101, 1994

2 to buy something as a present for another *AUSTRALIA, 1949*

- I'm going to call at Kimberley's office and see if he'll shout me a decent lunch. — Willie Fennell, *Dexter Gets The Point*, p. 51, 1961
- We parted after arranging to meet for lunch next day and the Fourth mate shouted a taxi back to Yokohama. — Les Such, *A Yen for Yokohama*, p. 59, 1963
- Reckon I'll shout myself a holiday. — Jean Brooks, *The Opal Witch*, p. 127, 1967

3 to write exclusively in upper case *US*

- — Christian Crumlish, *The Internet Dictionary*, p. 180, 1995

▸ **shout at your shoes**

to vomit *US*

- — *Washington Post*, p. 18, 8th November 1987: 'Say Wha?'

▸ **wouldn't shout if a shark bit you**

to be stingy *AUSTRALIA*

- — Richard Beckett, *The Dinkum Aussie Dictionary*, p. 58, 1986

shout-out *noun*

a greeting; a recognition *US*

- — *San Jose Mercury News*, 11th May 1999

shove *noun*

the member of a pickpocketing team who jostles the victim, diverting his attention so that a confederate can actually pick the victim's pocket *US*

- To do the job well, three persons are necessary: the shove pushed the victim and diverted his attention; the dip goes for the pocket, hip, or otherwise; and the loot is then handed to the wire so that if one of the other two are caught, they would not be caught with the evidence. — Don Wilmeth, *The Language of American Popular Entertainment*, p. 239, 1981

▸ **give the shove**

to dismiss someone from employment or reject the partner in a romantic relationship *UK, 1899*

- When his wife gave him the shove he used the not inconsiderable resources of the Palace to smear her as a mental case and a slut. — *The Guardian*, 25th June 2003

shove *verb*

to have sex *UK*

- So it's dirty, a whitey shoving a dinge? — Alan Hunter, *Gently Coloured*, 1969

▸ **shove it**

used as a harsh rejection of a suggestion *AUSTRALIA, 1941*

A shortened form of 'shove it up your ass'.

- I don't care, if this isnt satisfactory to Grove they can shove it too. — Jack Kerouac, *Letter to Sterling Lord*, p. 588, 7th October 1956
- Look, I'm tired. You take this job; you just take it and shove it. — Claude Brown, *Manchild in the Promised Land*, p. 299, 1965
- Here's one of the few cases where a baseball player has enough courage or money or both to tell baseball to take its one-sided contract and shove it. — Jim Bouton, *Ball Four*, p. 213, 1970

▸ **shove it up the ass**

to reject something completely *US*

- He didn't particularly care about the new guy but he was glad he had shoved it up the boss's ass and broke it off. — Hubert Selby Jr, *Last Exit to Brooklyn*, p. 150, 1957

▸ **shove paper**

to pass counterfeit money or stolen or forged cheques *US*

- "Look," a friend of mine once put it, "shoving paper's too easy. You don't have to know anything but how to write your name, you're risking no danger, you're trading on the trust of gullible people, and you're shooting for nickels." — *Saturday Evening Post*, p. 72, 6th October 1962

▸ **shove shit uphill**

to take the active role in anal intercourse *UK*

- — Angela Devlin, *Prison Patter*, p. 105, 1996

shovel *verb*

▸ **shovel coal**

(of a motor vehicle) to accelerate *US*

An allusion to steam-driven, coal-fired transports.

- — *Complete CB Slang Dictionary*, p. 84, 1976
- — Peter Chippindale, *The British CB Book*, p. 159, 1981

shovel and broom; shovel *noun*

a room *UK*

Rhyming slang.

- — Julian Franklyn, *A Dictionary of Rhyming Slang*, 1960
- — Ray Puxley, *Cockney Rabbit*, 1992

shovel and pick; shovel *noun*

a prison *UK*

Rhyming slang for **NICK**.

- [T]hey've been in and out the shovel since approved school[.] — J.J. Connolly, *Layer Cake*, p. 32, 2000

shovel and tank *noun*

a bank *UK*

Rhyming slang.

- — Julian Franklyn, *A Dictionary of Rhyming Slang*, 1961

shovelhead *noun*

the V-twin Harley Davidson engine, manufactured 1966–83 *US*

Biker (motorcyle) usage.

- What they liked was American shit – softails, shovelheads. Bruce used to say, Harleys are iron horses, man. Fucking iron horses. — Russell Banks, *Rule of the Bone*, p. 46, 1995

shovel pilot *noun*

a manual worker *UK*

- We sub-contract labour. I mean, we're not hiring brain surgeons. They're shovel pilots. Some of them can't even read and write, but by Christ they can shovel ballast. — David Hare, *The Permanent Way*, 2003

shovels and spades *noun*

AIDS *UK*

Rhyming slang.

- — Ray Puxley, *Fresh Rabbit*, 1998

shove off *verb*

to go away *UK, 1909*

Naval coinage, from shoving a boat away; often used as an injunction.

- BELL: [UNDER BREATH] Oh, shove off. — Graeme Kent, *The Queen's Corporal [Six Granada Plays]*, p. 88, 1959

shover *noun*

a person who passes counterfeit money *US*

- I was sure that Hertert wanted to use this fellow as a shover of the queer, or the man who was to pass the fake currency. — William J. Spillard and Pence James, *Needle in a Haystack*, p. 54–55, 1945
- — Frank Garcia, *Marked Cards and Loaded Dice*, p. 264, 1962
- — Joseph E. Ragen and Charles Finston, *Inside the World's Toughest Prison*, p. 817, 1962: 'Penitentiary and underworld glossary'

show *noun*

an opportunity; a chance; an opening *AUSTRALIA, 1876*

- Say I swear off, will you give me a show? I'm dead nuts on you. — Barbara Baynton, *Human Toll*, p. 246, 1907
- Your mate here might have a show though. — John Wynnum, *Jiggin' in the Riggin'*, p. 27, 1965
- — Lance Peters, *The Dirty Half-Mile*, p. 143, 1979
- I've got no show of rememberin' unless you let me have another drink. — Peter Corris, *Make Me Rich*, p. 140, 1985

▷ **see:** SHOW PRICE

show *verb*

to arrive; to make an appearance *US*

- Why do you think I made you wait all this time for before I showed? — Morton Cooper, *High School Confidential*, p. 69, 1958
- "How come her parents didn't show?" the woman continued, lowering her voice, "Show?" repeated Dottie, at a loss – could she mean show dogs or cats? "Turn up for the wedding." — Mary McCarthy, *The Group*, p. 22, 1963

▸ **show hard**

to reveal to other men that you have an erection *US, 1970s*

- For example, a simplified expression of the primary tearoom strategy is frequently inscribed on the walls: "Show hard-get sucked." — Laud Humphreys, *Tearoom Trade*, p. 48, 1975

show and shine *verb*

in car customising, to prepare a car and then exhibit it in a car show *US*

- — John Edwards, *Auto Dictionary*, p. 150, 1993

show-and-tell *noun*

a public display and explanation *US, 1948*

From the name of a school activity for young children.

- I had ventured into a rest room at school, but not wanting to smoke dope, buy drugs, or converse with 20 robust fellows in Raiders jackets hosting a switchblade show-and-tell, I quickly turned around and left. — C.D. Payne, *Youth in Revolt*, p. 107, 1993

showbiz *noun*

the entertainment industry *US, 1945*

A reduction of 'showbusiness'; originally theatrical.

- [W]ho could forget the Tories lining up their showbiz supporters in a sorry role call of personal greed? — John Robb, *The Nineties*, p. 154, 1999

showbizzy *adjective*

used of the stereotypical excesses of showbusiness *UK, 1969*

- [W]e go through a lot of showbizzy things. — Sting (Gordon Sumner), *Ask*, p. 112, 12th April 1980

showboat *verb*

to show off; to pay attention to the performance aspects of a task *US, 1951*

From the C19 river steamers with theatrical performances and melodramatic, showy gamblers.

- The dude was hurt bad in the eleventh [round], but he showboated his way out like 'tweren't nothin'[.] — Edwin Torres, *Carlito's Way*, p. 135, 1975
- It was that showboat lawyer you worked for. — Elmore Leonard, *Bandits*, p. 213, 1987
- Most critics [of Jimi Hendrix] concentrated on the flamboyant showboating, the playing behind his head, the picking with his tongue and teeth[.] — Mick Farren, *Give the Anarchist a Cigarette*, p. 99, 2001

show buddy *noun*

in the language surrounding the Grateful Dead, a friend with whom you team up for Grateful Dead tours *US*

- — David Shenk and Steve Silberman, *Skeleton Key*, p. 224, 1994

showcase *verb*

to show off *US, 1945*

- — Lavada Durst, *The Jives of Dr. Hepcat*, p. 13, 1953
- I liked showcasing with her and I'd take her to all the sets with me[.] — A.S. Jackson, *Gentleman Pimp*, p. 156, 1973

showdown *noun*

1 in prison, private time for sex *US*

- It was pretty hard to get a showdown, any kind of privacy, long enough for intercourse anyway. — Bruce Jackson, *In the Life*, p. 365, 1972

2 in poker, the moment when betting is completed and the players show their hands *US*

- — David M. Hayano, *Poker Faces*, p. 187, 1982

shower *noun*

a worthless collection of people *UK, 1941*

- An absolute shower. — *I'm Alright Jack*, 1959

▸ **not come down in the last shower**

to be aware *AUSTRALIA, 1902*

- 'Ole mother Stein didn't come down in ther last shower.' He shook his head impressively. 'Though 'er's gut a 'ard inside, 'er knows wut side to bite a bun.' — Barbara Baynton, *Human Toll*, p. 217, 1907
- I didn't come down in the last shower. I know who's doing these robberies at the Trades Hall. — Frank Hardy, *Power Without Glory*, p. 273, 1950

shower bath; showers *noun*

ten shillings; hence 50p *UK*

Rhyming slang for '*half* a pound'.

- — Julian Franklyn, *A Dictionary of Rhyming Slang*, 1960
- — Ray Puxley, *Cockney Rabbit*, 1992

shower cap *noun*

a condom *US*

Figurative application of a conventional item.

- — *Current Slang*, p. 13, Summer 1969

shower of shit; shower of shite *noun*

an unpleasant and worthless collection of people *UK*

Derogatory. An elaboration of 'shower'.

- Uh, you shower of shite... it's not funny that. — Caroline Aherne and Craig Cash, *The Royle Family*, 1999
- "One at a time, you shower of shit," I said threateningly. — Jimmy Stockin, *On The Cobbles*, p. 121, 2000

showers *noun*

urination by one person on another, or other acts of urine fetishism, especially when offered or sought in advertisements *UK*

- — Caroline Archer, *Tart Cards*, 2003

shower-spank *verb*

(of a male) to masturbate in the shower *US*

- — Pamela Munro, *U.C.L.A. Slang*, p. 79, 1989

show house *noun*

a homosexual brothel *US*

- — *Male Swinger Number 3*, p. 48, 1981: 'The complete gay dictionary'

showie *noun*

a person who runs or works in a stall or ride at agricultural shows *AUSTRALIA, 1980*

- Some showies pulled him clear and brought him back to the roadhouse where he spent the next couple of hours delirious in front of the fire. — Russell Guy, *What's Rangoon to you is Grafton to me*, p. 62, 1991

show me the money

used as a humorous urging that a statement be backed up *US*

A key catchphrase in the US in the late 1990s.

- TIDWELL: It's a very personal, very important thing. It's a family motto. So I want to share it with you. You ready? JERRY: Yes. TIDWELL: Here it is. "Show me the money." Show. Me. The. Money. — *Jerry Maguire*, 1996

show-off lane *noun*

in trucking, the passing lane of a motorway *US*

- — Porter Bibb, *CB Bible*, p. 104, 1976
- Dandalion, that be you out there in the show off lane? — Gwyneth A. "Dandalion" Seese, *Tijuana Bear in a Smoke 'Um Up Taxi*, p. 27, 1977

show-out *noun*

a discreet signal from an informer to a police officer *UK*

- Another cardinal rule in making contact with a snout was that the detective never made the first move. When you entered the rendezvous and saw your man you waited for the "show-out" – a brief nod – before you joined him. — John Gosling, *The Ghost Squad*, 1959

show out *verb*

to behave ostentatiously *US*

- A cool brother sits inside, both windows rolled down, trying to show out. — *Menace II Society*, 1993
- There's all sorts of Judies in there, mind you, all fucking whacked on cocaine and white wine, all hanging round the lads, showing out for them good style. — Kevin Sampson, *Outlaws*, p. 249, 2001

show pony *noun*
a prissy, prancing fop more concerned with image than performance *AUSTRALIA, 1964*
- However this album is not recommended for show ponies or Nancy boys and will therefore be ignored by a large percentage of readers. — *Opus*, p. 30, August 1989

show price; show *noun*
in gambling racing, the betting odds displayed by a bookmaker at a point in time *UK*
- During the run-up to a race [...] the broadcasting service gives [...] a "show" on that race [...] the prices being offered at that time on the various horses taking part. — *Ladbroke's Pocket Betting Guide*, 1976
- However, investors following the action on a race-by-race basis have the option of betting at the "show price". — David Bennet, *Know Your Bets*, p. 15, 2001

show shop *noun*
a theatre *US*
- — Don Wilmeth, *The Language of American Popular Entertainment*, p. 240, 1981

showstopper *noun*
a proposal that would lead to a breakdown in negotiations; a deal-killer *US*
- "Ouch ... there's a showstopper" – he grinned – "I never thought of that." — Stephen J. Cannell, *King Con*, p. 129, 1997

showtime *noun*
time for something to begin *US*
- NICE GUY EDDIE: It's showtime. Grab your jacket. — *Reservoir Dogs*, 1992
- Showtime! — *Gone in 60 Seconds*, 2000

show-up *noun*
a process used by police to have witnesses to a crime identify the criminals *US*
- I know this black bitch is a cinch ringer for those eight larceny from the person beefs. We oughta take her down and put her on a 'Show Up' or two. — Iceberg Slim (Robert Beck), *Pimp*, p. 177, 1969
- I had him in a regular show-up and I had a few private mug-shot show-ups, and I talked and coaxed and damned near threatened my victims and witnesses. — Joseph Wambaugh, *The Blue Knight*, p. 161, 1973
- Specifically, the defendant aruges that the show up identification must be suppressed on the grounds that the procedure employed by the police was unduly suggestive. — *Daily Record of Rochester (New York)*, 22nd December 2003

show-up box *noun*
a room in a jail where suspects are shown for identification by witnesses *US*
- In the corner of the cell block there may be a second door that leads to the show-up box. One of its walls is wire mesh painted black. On the back wall are ruled lines for height. — Raymond Chandler, *The Long Goodbye*, p. 44, 1953

show us your tits
used as a crass male heckling catchcry *AUSTRALIA*
- [T]he only response Ophelia managed to glean was from a former Prime Minister of Australia who yelled, 'Hey, luv, show us your tits!' — Gretel Killeen, *Hot Buns and Ophelia get a Bloke*, p. 77, 2000

shpilkes *noun*
an inability to sit still *US*
- I should be napping, I guess, but I'm sitting on shpilkes, as Mom used to say about twice a day. — Armistead Maupin, *Maybe the Moon*, p. 289, 1992

SHPOS *noun*
a critically ill hospital patient who fails to follow medical instructions, worsening their own condition; a *s*ub-*h*uman *p*iece *o*f *s*hit *US*
- — *Maledicta*, p. 69, Summer/Winter 1978: 'Common patient-directed pejoratives used by medical personnel'

shpritz; schpritz *verb*
to squirt or spray *US*
Yiddish.
- The Irish got schpritzed and schpritzed and schpritzed. — Lenny Bruce, *The Essential Lenny Bruce*, p. 20, 1967

shrapnel *noun*
the ripple effect in poker of a player completely losing his composure and infecting other players with his poor play *US*
- Brooks went broke, of course, but I caught a little shrapnel. — John Vorhaus, *The Big Book of Poker Slang*, p. 33, 1996

shred *verb*
to perform very well; to excel *US*
- — Gary Fairmont R. Filosa II, *The Surfer's Almanac*, p. 194, 1977
- — *San Francisco Sunday Examiner & Chronicle*, p. 20, 2nd September 1984: 'Say it right'
- — *Carmel (California) High School Yearbook*, 1987
- — Judi Sanders, *Cal Poly Slang*, p. 9, 1990

shredache *noun*
the headache resulting from extreme exertion while surfing *US*
A punned version of the standard 'headache', built on **SHRED** (performing well).
- — *Transworld Surf*, p. 42, April 2004

shredded *adjective*
1 muscular as the result of intense workouts *US*
- — Connie Eble (Editor), *UNC-CH Campus Slang*, p. 5, Spring 2001

2 weary; weak *US*
- FERRIS: How do you feel? CAMERON: Shredded. — *Ferris Buehler's Day Off*, 1986

shredded wheat *adjective*
excellent *UK*
Rhyming slang for **SWEET**, based on the branded breakfast cereal; current in UK prisons February 2002.

shredder *noun*
a snowboarder *US*
- — Jim Humes and Sean Wagstaff, *Boarderlands*, p. 224, 1995

shreddies *noun*
male underpants; army-issue underpants; panties; female underwear *UK*
Originally a reference to the stereotypically disgusting state of bachelor's underwear; Shreddies™, a branded breakfast cereal, are brown and have a woven appearance.
- — *American Speech*, p. 400, Winter 1991: 'Among the new words'
- That didn't stop the guys lying out after lunch and sunbathing in their shreddies. — Chris Ryan, *Stand By, Stand By*, p. 154, 1996
- "All right girls, sorry to burst in on you in your shreddies," and they said, "These ain't our shreddies, Tommy, we're in costume," and it's true, them bras and knickers was their stage costumes. — Ben Elton, *High Society*, p. 82, 2002

shredding *adjective*
extreme; exciting; good *US*
- — *New York Times*, 12th April 1987

shrewd *adjective*
attractive; popular; savvy *US*
- — *Dobie Gillis Teenage Slanguage Dictionary*, 1962

shrewd head *noun*
a cunning or shrewd person *AUSTRALIA, 1915*
- We all began kidding ourselves that we were pretty shrewd heads and pretty smart business men[.] — Gavin Casey, *It's Harder for Girls*, p. 65, 1941
- A shrewd old head was Truthful. — Frank Hardy, *The Yarns of Billy Borker*, p. 32, 1965
- And they tell you in the Bible that Solomon was a shrewd-head. — Frank Hardy, *The Outcasts of Foolgarah*, p. 174, 1971

shrewdie *noun*
1 a cunning or shrewd person *AUSTRALIA, 1904*
- 'Shrewdie Sim' they called him. — Dymphna Cusack, *Picnic Races*, p. 219, 1962
- There was a telephone at the front of the rank and sometimes a shrewdie on the rear of the queue would ring up and send the front cab off on a wild goose chase. — Frank Hardy, *The Yarns of Billy Borker*, p. 97, 1965
- [I]ts ramps and its rackets would make a present-day 'shrewdie' look like a Sunday School teacher. — James Holledge, *The Great Australian Gamble*, p. 28, 1966

2 a clever action *NEW ZEALAND*
- — David McGill, *David McGill's Complete Kiwi Slang Dictionary*, p. 114, 1998

shriek *noun*
1 distilled, concentrated heroin *US*
- — Carsten Stroud, *Close Pursuit*, p. 269, 1987

2 an exclamation mark (!) *US*
- — Guy L. Steele et al., *The Hacker's Dictionary*, p. 115, 1983

shrieking sixties *noun*
the latitudes of 60 to 69 degrees south *ANTARCTICA, 1921*
- — Bernadette Hince, *The Antarctic Dictionary*, p. 313, 2000

shrimp *noun*

1 a short person *UK, 1386*

- A shrimp don't have to be a wimp, but a wimp is always a shrimp, that's what I always say. —Joe Bob Briggs, *Joe Bob Goes to the Drive-In*, p. 21, 1987

2 a small penis *US*

- —Bruce Rodgers, *The Queens' Vernacular*, p. 180, 1972
- —*Sky Magazine*, July 2001

3 marijuana *UK*

- —Mike Haskins, *Drugs*, p. 289, 2003

shrimp job; shrimp *noun*

the act of toe-sucking for sexual pleasure *UK*

A foot-fetishist's view of an appetising similarity between toes and shrimps.

- "How about letting shoot a famous artist giving you a shrimp job?" the Mexican leered [...] Howard got down on his knees and licked the Rock Chick's tootsies. The actress getting the shrimp managed to keep a straight face[.] —Stewart Home, *Sex Kick [britpulp]*, p. 211–212, 1999

shrimp queen; shrimper *noun*

a person with a fetish for the toes *US*

- His favorite territory is your feet. A Shrimp Queen of the first order – and I am not putting him down by using the old-time vernacular, because he's a groovy guy all the way around. I just don't know of another moniker for someone who sucks toes. —John Francis Hunter, *The Gay Insider*, p. 88, 1971

shrink *noun*

a psychiatrist or therapist *US, 1966*

From the longer and older **HEADSHRINKER**.

- And I went up there, I said, "Shrink, I want to kill. I mean, I wanna, I wanna kill." —Arlo Guthrie, *Alice's Restaurant*, 1967
- I'm going to the shrink / So he can help me be a nervous wreck. —Frank Zappa, *Flower Punk*, 1968
- And out of the corner that faint voice of Dr. Serbin, my Jewish shrink butts in. —Oscar Zeta Acosta, *The Autobiography of a Brown Buffalo*, p. 13, 1972
- I think it's because I'm a Leo, but my shrink says I'm pathologically rebellious and self-destructive. —*King of Comedy*, 1976
- And you don't exactly look like a shrink, wearin' that dress. —*48 Hours*, 1982
- You know why you're called a shrink, don't y'? 'Cos y' shrink people[.] —Alan Bleasdale, *Boys From the Blackstuff*, 1982
- You're the shrink. —*Basic Instinct*, 1992
- Get a shrink. Hug a friend. Hug yourself. —*Sleepless in Seattle*, 1993

shrinkage *noun*

the condition of a man's genitals after swimming in cold water *US*

Coined and popularised on an episode of Jerry Seinfeld's television programme (*The Hamptons*) that first aired on 24th May 1994.

shroomer *noun*

a recreational drug user who takes hallucinogenic mushrooms; also, more innocently, a person who gathers wild mushrooms *US*

- High times in magic mushroom business – and it's perfectly legal [...] "The response has been amazing. We're seeing the same groups of shroomers every week." —*The Guardian*, 29th October 2003

shroomers *noun*

mushrooms as a pizza topping *US*

- —*Maledicta*, p. 21, 1996: 'Domino's pizza jargon'

shrooms *noun*

psychoactive mushrooms *US*

- —Connie Eble (Editor), *UNC-CH Campus Slang*, p. 6, Fall 1987
- JAY: I got hits, hash, weed, and later on I'll have 'shrooms. We take cash, or stolen MasterCard and Visa. —*Clerks*, 1994
- One of the grips comes up to me at the premiere and says, "Dude, shrooms." And you know, I didn't know mushrooms, so I took I don't know how many. (Quoting Pauly Shore) —*Spin Magazine*, October 1999

shroud *noun*

from the perspective of a man not accustomed to dressing up, a suit *US*

- —Joseph E. Ragen and Charles Finston, *Inside the World's Toughest Prison*, p. 817, 1962: 'Penitentiary and underworld glossary'

shtarker *noun*

a strong and brave person *US*

Yiddish, from German.

- I don't want no trouble with that starker. —Chester Himes, *The Real Cool Killers*, p. 60, 1959
- With you, I agree. But Detective Canales here's a shtarker. —Emmett Grogan, *Final Score*, p. 165, 1976
- [O]f the 150, probably 100 were justs a bunch of shtarkers who could pull at one end of a rope that was looped around some poor fucker's neck, while some other lump pulled at the other end. —Richard Condon, *Prizzi's Honor*, p. 118, 1982

shtetl *noun*

a predominantly Jewish neighbourhood *UK*

From the German for 'village', originally applied to small Jewish villages in eastern Europe.

- He was also drawn from reality, from Mel's mother and other old-timers who had seen the world change so much it seemed like centuries since they left the shtetl. —Albert Goldman, *Freak Show*, p. 249, 1968

shtick; schtick; shtik; schtik *noun*

1 a theatrical routine, an act; hence a style, routine or behaviour *US, 1961*

From German *stück* (a bit, a piece) into Yiddish, and thence more widespread.

- [W]hy the comic Fyffe Robertson shtick? —*British Journal of Photography*, 1st August 1980
- If leaving them alone is part of the schtick, check in frequently to make sure all is okay. —Rob Cohen, *Etiquette for Outlaws*, 2001
- [T]hey had each settled on their shtik, a signature style they hoped would be as identifying as Zack's drips were. —John Updike, *Seek My Face*, p. 95, 2002
- What was really bothering him was his own response to that fool – his I'm No Pimp schtik. —Charlotte Carter, *Walking Bones*, p. 50, 2002

2 an area of interest *US, 1968*

From the Yiddish for 'piece' or 'play'.

- I can't deal with them digits every day – bad numbers, runners robbing you, all that bookkeeping every day – I'd go crazy. Nah, that ain't my stick. —Edwin Torres, *Carlito's Way*, p. 84, 1975
- No way, man. Konks or marcels ain't my stick. —Piri Thomas, *Stories from El Barrio*, p. 53, 1978

shtuck; schtuck; schtook; stuk *noun*

trouble *UK, 1936*

Not Yiddish despite appearances, although probably formed on the Yiddish model of a reduplicated word commencing with a 'sh' sound, in which case 'shtuck' is a variant of 'stuck' (in a difficult situation).

- —Albertos y Lost Trios Paranoias, *Teenager in Schtuck*, 1977
- Terry put down the phone and turned back to Karen. "We're in stuk. Can't you possibly give me that phone number?" —Anthony Masters, *Minder*, p. 156, 1984
- I would ask for advice if 'm in schtook and he's always done the same[.] —J.J. Connolly, *Layer Cake*, p. 53, 2000
- [I]f God was to burgle my house [...] I'd be all in shtuck because the Old Bill [police] couldn't touch him[.] —Danny King, *The Burglar Diaries*, p. 13, 2001

shtum; shtoom; stumm *adjective*

quiet; saying nothing *UK, 1958*

Anglicised phonetic spelling of synonymous German *stumm* which, it is presumed, reached England through Yiddish.

- Some people in the nick make themselves very bizzie [sic] all the time and think they are very cunning, but I think it's much better to keep shtoom, and to prove my point I came home on the earliest day I possibly could. —Frank Norman, *Bang To Rights*, p. 12, 1958
- [W]e very properly stayed stumm and said nothing. —Derek Raymond (Robin Cook), *The Crust on its Uppers*, p. 105, 1962
- Terry turned to Arthur. "What have you been up to, Arthur?" "Shtum, Terry. Very, very shtum. —Anthony Masters, *Minder*, p. 59, 1984
- Russell kept shtoom. —Greg Williams, *Diamond Geezers*, p. 26, 1997
- Don't try to be clever. Just keep stumm. —Duncan MacLaughlin, *The Filth*, p. 141, 2002

shtunk; shtonk *noun*

a nasty person; a jerk *US*

Yiddish, from German.

- "With all due respects, he's a shtonk," Lubsin said, his puffy eyes expanding into a stare. —Edwin Torres, *Q & A*, p. 131, 1977

shtup *noun*

an act of sexual intercourse *US*

- He gives them all a good shtup. —Josh Alan Friedman, *Tales of Times Square*, p. 42, 1986

shtup; shtoop; schtup *verb*

to have sex *US*

Yiddish from the German for 'to push'.

- It was funny, because when we first got married, I had never slept with a woman before. I had schtupped plenty of women, but I had never slept with one. —Lenny Bruce, *How to Talk Dirty and Influence People*, p. 79, 1965

- With those legs – why of course he was shtupping her ... Wasn't he? —Philip Roth, *Portnoy's Complaint*, p. 92, 1969
- The photography is as honest as a stag film and you see close-ups of the guy shtupping (fucking) the girl's hole. —*Screw*, p. 17, 12th January 1970
- Then when she finds out he [Woody Allen]'s schtupping the girl, he tells Mia [Farrow] he fucked her daughter to instill confidence in her. —Howard Stern, *Miss America*, p. 248, 1995
- I thought he shtupped the one with the black hair[.] —Greg Williams, *Diamond Geezers*, p. 121, 1997

shuck *noun*

1 nonsense; something of little worth *US, 1851*
- [H]ow many times have you heard people say of bands:"Man, what a shuck! I could get up there and cut that shit." —Lester Bangs, *Psychotic Reactions and Carburetor Dung*, p. 38, 1970
- [H]e says it's the same shuck all around[.] —Lawrence Block, *No Score [The Affairs of Chip Harrison Omnibus]*, p. 153, 1970

2 a deception; a tease *US*
- —Lawrence Lipton, *The Holy Barbarians*, p. 317, 1959
- Q: I want to hear about this ethic of the street. The poverty ethic, the Indian ethic. SHIRLY: Somehow I think it's mostly a shuck. —Leonard Wolfe (Editor), *Voices from the Love Generation*, p. 238, 1968

3 in poker, a card that may be discarded and replaced *US*
- —Jim Glenn, *Programmed Poker*, p. 157, 1981

shuck *verb*

to deceive someone in a blustery, teasing manner *US, 1959*
Often used with 'jive'.
- Damn, a rifle in my mouth and him shucking around like that! —A.S. Jackson, *Gentleman Pimp*, p. 94, 1973
- She had paused to shuck and jive on the sidewalk with a grocery clerk. —Iceberg Slim (Robert Beck), *Death Wish*, p. 119, 1977
- Hunter said, "You gonna start shucking me again, Darrold? We're talking about murder, man, not a little half-assed assault." —Elmore Leonard, *City Primeval*, p. 59, 1980

▸ **shuck the ice**

to remove stolen diamonds from their settings *US*
- —Vincent J. Monteleone, *Criminal Slang*, p. 208, 1949

shucker *noun*

a striptease dancer *US*
- —Don Wilmeth, *The Language of American Popular Entertainment*, p. 241, 1981

shuckman *noun*

a swindler *US*
- It was on that Sixth Street to Market, between Central Avenue and Plum / that's the worst old place in ragtown for a shuckman or gun. —Bruce Jackson, *Get Your Ass in the Water and Swim Like Me*, p. 85, 1965

shucks

used as a register of dismay or contempt *US, 1847*
Used where **SHIT!** might do.
- Shucks, even a hard-working nigger wouldn't shoot a white man if he come home and found him in bed with his old lady with his pants down. —Chester Himes, *The Real Cool Killers*, p. 59, 1959
- Shucks. I drove here from Phoenix in a day and a half. —Gurney Norman, *Divine Right's Trip (Last Whole Earth Catalog)*, p. 47, 1971

shucky darn

used as a mock, mild oath *US*
- — "Slingo", *The Official CB Slang Dictionary Handbook*, p. 55, 1976

shuffle *noun*

1 the movement by a surfer forward on the board while surfing, executed without crossing the feet *US*
- —Peter L. Dixon, *The Complete Book of Surfing*, p. 215, 1965

2 counterfeit money *US*
- —Hyman E. Goldin et al., *Dictionary of American Underworld Lingo*, p. 194, 1950

shuffle *verb*

▸ **shuffle off to Buffalo**

to leave *US*
The reference to Buffalo, New York, is for the sake of rhyme and adds nothing to the meaning.
- The dancers high-kick one last time and go shuffling off to Buffalo off the floor. —Robert Campbell, *Junkyard Dog*, p. 132, 1986

▸ **shuffle the deck**

on the railways, to switch wagons onto side tracks at stations along a line *US*
- —Norman Carlisle, *The Modern Wonder Book of Trains and Railroading*, p. 268, 1946

shufti; shuftie; shufty; shoofti *noun*

a quick look *UK, 1943*
Military adoption of Arabic *sufti* (did you see?).
- If we're going to have a shufti at those concert party women we'd better be on our way over. —Graeme Kent, *The Queen's Corporal [Six Granada Plays]*, p. 83, 1959
- "There might be people in there who I don't want to see." "Then have a little shufti[.]" —Anthony Masters, *Minder*, p. 108, 1984
- So she [Queen Elizabeth I] sent off her boys, Walter Raleigh – who invented the bicycle and brought back the first duty-free fags – and Charlie Drake, to have a bit of a shoofti. —Andrew Nickolds, *Back to Basics*, p. 12, 1994
- "I'll nip into town for a shufti," I said as I grabbed my sunglasses[.] —Stuart Browne, *Dangerous Parking*, p. 267, 2000
- Asks if he can have a shuftie in the boot. —Kevin Sampson, *Outlaws*, p. 50, 2001

'shun!

Attention! *UK, 1888*
A military command, abbreviated from the extended delivery 'Atten... shun!'.
- The Sergeants' Mess, roughly prepared for a trial. Drummond, Straw and Vale enter. WATSON: Mess – shun! —Graeme Kent, *The Queen's Corporal [Six Granada Plays]*, p. 101, 1959

shunk; shunkie *noun*

a toilet *UK: SCOTLAND*
- Ma eyebaws are floatin. Gauny [going to] mind ma pint tae Ah nick inty the shunk? —Michael Munro, *The Patter, Another Blast*, p. 64, 1988

shunt *noun*

a car accident *UK, 1959*
- [S]teps have been taken to render the car still safer than it was, with the body now designed to disperse the impact of a shunt by distributing it over a wider area. — *The Guardian*, 18th March 2003

shunt *verb*

in motor racing, to bump a competitor *US*
- —John Lawlor, *How to Talk Car*, p. 94, 1965

shunter *noun*

a drug dealer who becomes addicted and continues to deal in order to fund the habit *UK*
Formed on **PUNTER** (a customer).
- It soon became amateur hour and guys who worked very sensible, very meticulous for the last couple of years started getting outta their heads. They became shunters. —J.J. Connolly, *Layer Cake*, p. 14, 2000

shurrit!

be quiet! *UK*
A phonetic slurring of **SHUT IT!**.
- SWELLS: Are we doing out [anything] or what? NAPPER: Shurrit, will yer! LANDRY: (BIG, RAW, HARD) Never mind "shurrit". What's goin ON? —Trevor Griffiths, *Oi For England*, p. 5, 1982

shurrup!

be quiet! *UK*
A slurring of **SHUT UP!**.
- RINGO Are you as young as that, then? BOYS Shurrup! — *A Hard Day's Night*, 1964

shush *verb*

to steal something *UK*
Polari; a possible variant sense and spelling of **ZHOOSH** (to swallow).
- —Paul Baker, *Polari*, p. 190, 2002

shush bag *noun*

a bag for carrying away stolen property *UK*
Polari; from **SHUSH** (to steal).
- —Paul Baker, *Polari*, p. 190, 2002

shusher *noun*

a person who is employed to keep people quiet on the street outside a nightclub *UK*
From 'shush!' (be quiet!).
- Shusher as in "Shhh"? That's right. Tha's one heck of a funny job you've got – standing outside a nightclub telling people to be quiet. — *The Times Magazine*, p. 12, 4th September 2004

shushing *noun*

the work of keeping people quiet on the street outside a nightclub *UK*
- [Y]ou do a lot of talking? Yeah but shushing's my main job. — *The Times Magazine*, p. 12, 4th September 2004

shush the mush!
be quiet!, shut up! *UK*
A combination of conventional 'shush!' and **MUSH** (the mouth or face).
- — *Pissed on the Job*, 14th January 2004

shush up *verb*
to become quiet *UK*
Often in the imperative. Combines conventional 'shush!' (be quiet!) with **SHUT UP**.
- On holiday. Mrs Morietti is. Now shush up. — Andrea Ashworth, *Moretti's Super-Swirl*, p. 67, 1999

shut *verb*
▸ **shut the gate**
in motor racing, to pass another car and immediately pull in front of the other car, minimising its ability to pass in return *US*
- — John Lawlor, *How to Talk Car*, p. 94, 1965

shut-door *noun*
a rejection; a refusal *UK*
The image of a door being slammed in your face.
- He's had a shut-door about you. — Kevin Sampson, *Outlaws*, p. 223, 2001

shuteye; shut-eye *noun*
sleep *UK, 1896*
- I will say this for my Leonard. He loves his shuteye. Snores the moment his head touches the pillow. — Alexander Baron, *A Bit of Happiness [Six Granada Plays]*, p. 206, 1959
- I think I'll just lie here and have a nice bit of shuteye if it's all the same to you[.] — Derek Bickerton, *Payroll*, p. 125, 1959
- Shuteye on the bus, sneakin' into the woods at the side of the road instead of goin' to a toilet. — Ross Russell, *The Sound*, p. 60, 1961
- Now take your stinking yellow ass upstairs to a bath and some shut-eye. — Iceberg Slim (Robert Beck), *Pimp*, p. 272, 1969
- Lemme get some shut eye cantcha – mon dieu! — Barry Humphries, *Bazza Pulls It Off!*, 1971

shuteyes *noun*
a sex offender *US*
- — Ralph de Sola, *Crime Dictionary*, p. 138, 1982

shut-in *noun*
a person who stays at home and never goes out *US, 1904*
- SHE WAS ALWAYS IN THE FUCKING HOUSE. She'd become a shut-in. — Howard Stern, *Miss America*, p. 6, 1995

shut it!
be quiet! *UK, 1886*
- "Listen, you bitch," he says, still gripping the front of her dress, "you cock-sucking whore. Just fucking shut it or I'll shut it for you." — Ted Lewis, *Jack Carter's Law*, p. 71, 1974
- CARTER: Only because you wouldn't listen, you bastard. REGAN: Now shut it! — *The Sweeney*, 29th November 1976
- Shut it! You don't understand it! / Shut it! That's not the way I planned it. / Shut your mouth till you know the truth. — Dexy's Midnight Runners *Burn It Down*, 1980
- Shuttit you! Where's your mother? — Ian Pattison, *Rab C. Nesbitt*, 1988

shutout *noun*
any situation in which a person fails to score, literally or figuratively *US*
- There was a series of assorted gropes, some moderately successful, some shutouts. — Max Shulman, *Rally Round the Flag, Boys!*, p. 6–7, 1957

shutter *noun*
1 the eyelid *US*
- — Lou Shelly, *Hepcats Jive Talk Dictionary*, p. 17, 1945
- — Clarence Major, *Dictionary of Afro-American Slang*, p. 103, 1970

2 a gunman *UK*
Recorded by a Jamaican inmate in a UK prison, August 2002.

shutterbug *noun*
1 a photography enthusiast; a photographer *US, 1940s*
- The shutterbug's partner could only gape as the 25-ton yacht settled a few more inches, causing the keel to angle up. — Joseph Wambaugh, *Floaters*, p. 2, 1996

2 a photographer who selects subjects for personal sexual gratification, often without the subject's knowledge or consent *US*
- "The guy a weenie wagger?" "Shutterbug." [...] "Another fuckin' perv, be better off with a bullet in his head." — Robert Crais, *L.A. Requiem*, p. 35, 1999

shut the fuck up!
be quiet! *US*
An intensified, very imperative **SHUT UP!** (be quiet!).
- [H]e frantically tore at her dress. "Shut the fuck up!" I guess he interpreted her screaming as insolence[.] — Arthur Nersesian, *The Fuck Up*, p. 76, 1991
- You shut the fuck up, you're getting on my fuckin' nerves. — J.J. Connolly, *Know Your Enemy [britpulp]*, p. 141, 1999
- What's that, I didn't hear you? / Shut the fuck up! / Come on a little louder / Shut the fuck up! — Limp Bizkit *N 2 Gether Now*, 1999
- Shut the fuck up and keep those hands where I can see them. — Robert Crais, *L.A. Requiem*, p. 31, 1999
- [S]hut the fuck up and put up with it. — Mark Steel, *Reasons to be Cheerful*, 2001

shuttup!
be quiet!; stop talking! *UK*
A variation of **SHUT UP!**.
- SIDNEY: When's the racing come on? TONY: Shuttup. SIDNEY: Well this is mushy. — Ray Galton and Alan Simpson, *Hancock's Half Hour*, 14th June 1955

shut up *verb*
to cease talking; to stop making a noise *US, 1840*
Used as a two word exclamation the sense is imperative or (since the 1960s) disbelieving.
- If you two don't shut up we'll all come a tumble. — Frank Norman, *Bang To Rights*, p. 50, 1958

shut up!
used as a humorous, kind, even flirtatious way to change the subject *US*
- — Connie Eble (Editor), *UNC-CH Campus Slang*, p. 4, April 1978

shut UP!
shut up *US*
The difference between the slang 'shut up' and the colloquial is the emphasis on a drawn out 'up' with register rising slightly for the 'up'.
- TED: Remember when she was a senior and we were freshmen? BILL: Shut up, Ted. — *Bill and Ted's Excellent Adventure*, 1989

shut-up sandwich *noun*
a punch in the mouth *CANADA*
- — Bill Casselman, *Canadian Sayings*, p. 130, 2002

shut your crunch!
be quiet! *UK*
- Shut your crunch or I'll shove your choppers down your spudgrinder! — *Undercurrents*, December 1978

shut your face!
be quiet!; shut up! *UK, 1809*
- Verbal Bombs to Avoid [...] you'll do what I tell you to do. Shut your face. This is the only way. It's my way or the highway. — Rod Wallace Kennedy, *The Encouraging Parent*, p. 46, 2001

shut your head!
be quiet!; shut up! *US, 1876*
- "Woman, shut your head," Mrs. Reppler told her. — Stephen King, *Skeleton Crew*, p. 146, 1986

shut your teeth!
be quiet!; stop talking! *UK*
- Shut your teeth, you owd [old] crab. — Jonathan Gash, *The Ten Word Game*, p. 277, 2003

shut your trap!
be quiet! *UK*
From **TRAP** (the mouth).
- TAYLOR: Leave him alone, Paddy. O'MALLY: Shut your trap. — Graeme Kent, *The Queen's Corporal [Six Granada Plays]*, p. 88, 1959

shuzzit *noun*
marijuana *US, 1971*
A discreet variation of **SHIT**.
- — Ernest L. Abel, *A Marijuana Dictionary*, p. 92, 1982

shvartz; schvartz *noun*
a black person; an Indian or Pakistani person *US*
Also seen as 'schwartz', 'schvartze' and ' schvartza'. The Yiddish term *schvartz* (from the German for 'black') is an adjective, with *schvartzer* as the noun for 'a black person'. 'Schvartz' the

adjective became an inside, 'code' word among Jews for 'a black person'.

- As soon as they find out you're Jewish, they wanna have their daughter marry you and not one of the south-of-the-border schwartzas. —Clancy Sigal, *Going Away*, p. 355, 1961
- She irons better even than the schvartze. —Philip Roth, *Portnoy's Complaint*, p. 12, 1969
- [W]henever Ike showed up in the block all the jews would close down yelling to each other, "the swartza is coming," because Ike would steal something off every cart with no sweat. —Babs Gonzales, *Movin' On Down De Line*, p. 1, 1975
- A lot of old ladies in Mattapan worried the shvarzehs are out to rape them. —John Sayles, *Union Dues*, p. 154, 1977
- At first I thought maybe the shvartze sent them to get back the rock. —Seth Morgan, *Homeboy*, p. 99, 1990
- [L]et me now state that those rumors of her leaving me for some shvartze calypso singer are false. —James Ellroy, *White Jazz*, p. 290, 1992
- For the love of Christ, LOSE THAT SCHWARTZE! —Terry Southern, *Now Dig This*, p. 242, 2001
- —Paul Baker, *Polari*, p. 189, 2002

shvartz; schvartz; schwartz; schvartze *adjective*

black, especially as a skin colour *UK*

Derogatory.

- [S]chvartza homie: black man; schvartza palone: black woman. —Paul Baker, *Polari*, p. 189, 2002

shvitz; schvitz *verb*

to perspire *US*

Yiddish, from German.

- Schvitzing like a pig. —Armistead Maupin, *Maybe the Moon*, p. 16, 1992

shvontz; shwantz *noun*

the penis *US*

- — *The Guild Dictionary of Homosexual Terms*, p. 40, 1965
- —Collin Baker et al., *College Undergraduate Slang Study Conducted at Brown University*, p. 189, 1968
- I think this portrays you as a good-looking, hot-headed gavonne who's probably – excuse me, ladies – got a schvanze that's a yard long. —James Ellroy, *Hollywood Nocturnes*, p. 26, 1994

shwag *noun*

▷ see: SCHWAG

shy *verb*

to cook opium pellets for smoking *US*

- "This is what you call shyin', kid," the cook said. This cooks all the poison out of the pill. —Mezz Mezzrow, *Really the Blues*, p. 99, 1946

shy *adjective*

1 having less of something than is desired, required or necessary *US, 1895*

- Chesterton was 137 surplus spaces shy of its stated 390 capacity[.] — *Wandsworth Guardian*, 12th December 2003

2 in debt; owing money *US*

- — *The Annals of the American Academy of Political and Social Sciences*, p. 130, May 1950
- —Irv Roddy, *Friday Night Poker*, p. 220, 1961

shyckle; shyker *noun*

▷ see: SCHEITL

shylock *noun*

1 a person who illegally loans money at very high interest rates and often has violent collection procedures *US, 1930*

The allusion to Shakespeare's usurious money-lender in *Merchant of Venice* cannot be missed.

- Hundreds are in the clutches of the loan-sharks in Maryland and the shylocks, who work their trade right in the government office buildings, exacting 100 percent interest for a one-month loan. —Jack Lait and Lee Mortimer, *Washington Confidential*, p. 72, 1951
- — *American Speech*, p. 306, December 1964: 'Lingua Cosa Nostra'
- Then the Corleone family shylocks were barred from the waterfront piers. —Mario Puzo, *The Godfather*, p. 253, 1969
- We were trying all day to find some shylock so we could get the rest of the money to buy Silky's jewelry. —Susan Hall, *Gentleman of Leisure*, p. 140, 1972
- You think that shylock is going to talk? —Mickey Spillane, *Last Cop Out*, p. 140, 1972
- And now he was in his fifties and the only blind shylock in the world. —Emmett Grogan, *Ringolevio*, p. 100, 1972
- I do collection for Harry once in a while. Harry, or different shylocks call, they want me to lean on some guy. —Elmore Leonard, *Riding the Rap*, p. 23, 1995

2 in circus and carnival usage, the show's office secretary *US*

- —Don Wilmeth, *The Language of American Popular Entertainment*, p. 241, 1981

shylock *verb*

to engage in usurious loan practices *UK, 1930*

- — *American Speech*, p. 306, December 1964: 'Lingua Cosa Nostra'
- Morse had the books and Rose was handling the shylocking. —Mickey Spillane, *Last Cop Out*, p. 10, 1972
- "But," he said, convinced now that he was being shylocked, "how am I going to pay the interest?" —Edward Lin, *Big Julie of Vegas*, p. 85, 1974

shypoo *adjective*

inferior; shoddy *NEW ZEALAND, 1952*

- —Harry Orsman, *A Dictionary of Modern New Zealand Slang*, p. 121, 1999

shyster *noun*

1 a lawyer, especially an unprofessional, dishonest or rapacious lawyer; any dishonest professional *US, 1843*

In his *Origin of the Term Shyster*, slang lexicographer Gerald Cohen demonstrates the craft of slang etymology at its highest: 'coined by New York journalist Mike Walsh'.

- [L]ater on I'll be touchy, you goddamn shyster, you yellow shyster. —Horace McCoy, *Kiss Tomorrow Good-bye*, p. 135, 1948
- If we get a confession, we beat it out of the guy, they say, and some shyster calls us Gestapo in court[.] —Raymond Chandler, *The Little Sister*, p. 218, 1949
- We've already given some shyster defense lawyer enough to go yellin' third-degree. —Jim Thompson, *The Killer Inside*, p. 37, 1952
- Our girl's going to need fancier shysters than I can afford. —Truman Capote, *Breakfast at Tiffany's*, p. 94, 1958
- Two ambulance-chasing shysters were vying with each other for her consent to sue Coffin Ed and the New York police department[.] —Chester Himes, *The Real Cool Killers*, p. 147, 1959
- The next morning I had an appointment with a shyster agent[.] —Babs Gonzales, *I Paid My Dues*, p. 52, 1967
- I mean you're calling this shyster Al, like he's an old friend. —Robert Campbell, *Juice*, p. 155, 1988
- [H]is estranged wife had hired some shyster lawyer[.] —Greg Williams, *Diamond Geezers*, p. 98, 1997

2 a very poorly attended circus performance *UK*

- [B]usiness was so poor that the wooden seating was easier to see than the flatties [audience]. Such a house is called a "shyster". —Butch Reynolds, *Broken Hearted Clown*, p. 30, 1953

siamesed *adjective*

in motor racing and repair, closely connected or joined together *US*

- —John Edwards, *Auto Dictionary*, p. 151, 1993

sib *noun*

a *sib*ling *UK*

- We are just the spoiled kids and younger sibs, born holding our invites to the longest, sexiest party in the history of the world. —James Hawes, *Dead Long Enough*, p. 96, 2000

Siberia *noun*

solitary confinement *US*

- —Inez Cardozo-Freeman, *The Joint*, p. 530, 1984

sice *noun*

in craps, the point and number six *US*

- — *The Annals of the American Academy of Political and Social Sciences*, p. 130, May 1950

Sicilian price *noun*

death, usually slow and painful, as punishment *US*

- [I]f Tommy had been involved in the tat at the Sabre Bay Casino and had stolen money from the dead-drop without an overwhelming pesonal reason, then Tommy would have to pay the Sicilian price. —Stephen J. Cannell, *Big Con*, p. 337, 1997

sick *noun*

withdrawal symptoms suffered by a drug addict *US*

- They were just down junkies and they hit the streets, separately, each one in his own way, trying to scrape together the necessary money to keep the sick off. —Emmett Grogan, *Ringolevio*, p. 51, 1972
- With his own sick coming on Joe was too weak to withhold the junk from another sufferer. —Seth Morgan, *Homeboy*, p. 26, 1990

▸ **on the sick**

in receipt of sickness benefit *UK*

- —Angela Devlin, *Prison Patter*, p. 83, 1996

sick *adjective*

1 suffering the symptoms of withdrawal from a drug addiction *US, 1938*

- But even now the feeling was upon him, not that he was sick, but he would be soon enough if he didn't get it[.] —Hal Ellson, *The Golden Spike*, p. 2, 1952

- When I heard one day that Herman had been arrested I figured I would be next, but I was already sick and did not have the energy to leave town. —William Burroughs, *Junkie*, p. 38, 1953
- He was really sick now, and his stomach was cramping. —Clarence Cooper Jr, *The Scene*, p. 39, 1960
- I remember the times I was sick and you gave me some drugs. —Claude Brown, *Manchild in the Promised Land*, p. 177, 1965
- [B]ecause three blocks away, a short walk for a sick junkie, are respectable neighborhoods good for burglary and "cracking shorts" (breaking into cars). —James Mills, *The Panic in Needle Park*, p. 19, 1966
- Up to Lexington, 125 / Feel sick and dirty, more dead than alive. —Velvet Underground *I'm Waiting for the Man*, 1967
- I didn't know the feeling of being sick 'til I got to the Apple 'cause I had been using cocaine every day and using horse every day, so you can understand how I didn't know I was hooked. —A.S. Jackson, *Gentleman Pimp*, p. 86, 1973
- Say, you like sick, like you need a fix / Perhaps I can do some solids for you. —Dennis Wepman et al., *The Life*, p. 55, 1976
- Everybody soon got wise he wouldn't let you go sick and per result much more was going out than coming in. —Herbert Huncke, *The Evening Sun Turned Crimson*, p. 39, 1980
- "I'm short n sick, Homes," moaned the Whoppa. The old yegg's withdrawal was a palpable effluvium, a contagion bathing Joe with microwaves of misery. —Seth Morgan, *Homeboy*, p. 26, 1990

2 experiencing the bleed period of the menstrual cycle *BAHAMAS*
- —John A. Holm, *Dictionary of Bahamian English*, p. 183, 1982

3 infected with HIV or suffering from AIDS *US*
- Well I ain't sick. I all skinny and shit. —*Boyz N The Hood*, 1990
- "He ain't working now. He's kind of sick." "Oh yeah?" Rocco assumed that sick meant the Virus. —Richard Price, *Clockers*, p. 224, 1992

4 scary *US*
Perhaps from the sensations aroused.
- —Jim Humes and Sean Wagstaff, *Boarderlands*, p. 224, 1995

5 tedious, boring; disaffecting *UK*
- [T]he mood changed to one of indifference and boredom, and typical comments from various individuals [...] were: "What a drag, man, I'm pulling out", or "This sure is a sick scene, man", etc. —Robin Page, *Down Among the Dossers*, p. 12, 1973

6 excellent; wonderful *US*
On the principle that **BAD** means 'good'.
- —Connie Eble (Editor), *UNC-CH Campus Slang*, p. 6, Fall 1987
- —*Macon Telegraph and News*, p. 9A, 18th June 1989
- —Jim Humes and Sean Wagstaff, *Boarderlands*, p. 224, 1995
- —Ben Sharpe, *Scooter Crazy*, p. 41, 2000
- [K]ids say things like "sick" and "dope" when you wear them [fashionable trainers] in the park, then they rob you. —*FHM*, p. 47, June 2003
- At the next set of lights, the daredevil tricks which had horrified the commuters are rewarded with shouts of "Beef!" and "Sick, man!" from his mates. —*The Independent Magazine*, p. 17, 28th August 2004
- [I]t's so sick out there [...] it's really sick, it's pumping. —a British surfer interviewed in Newquay *Word of Mouth*, 6th August 2004

7 in poker, without further funds *US*
- —George Percy, *The Language of Poker*, p. 82, 1988

sick and tired of *adjective*
bored or fed-up with someone or something *UK, 1783*
- We're absolutely sick and tired of putting things out and finding they're not true. —*The Guardian*, 28th March 2003

sick and wrong!
used for conveying a strong disagreement or disapproval *US*
- —Pamela Munro, *U.C.L.A. Slang*, p. 76, 1989

sick as an ANIMAL *adjective*
physically sick, but not necessarily vomiting *UK*
The earliest recorded is 'dog' (1705); followed by 'horse' (1765); 'cat' shows up in 1915, and 'sonofabitch' in 1953. 'Sick as a parrot' is a jocular variation from 1979. On 20th November 2000, Judith Keppel was the first contestant to win a million pounds on the television quiz *Who Wants To Be A Millionaire*; the first question she answered (for £100) was: 'Complete this phrase. As sick as a – Puffin – Penguin – Parrot – Partridge'.
- I am sick as a pig by the time I get a call from Chrissie. —Val McDermid, *Keeping on the Right Side of the Law*, p. 184, 1999

sick-bay commando *noun*
a soldier who feigns illness to avoid combat duty *US*
- —Linda Reinberg, *In the Field*, p. 198, 1991

sickener *noun*
anything that is depressing or disappointing *UK*
- Downer. Fucking sickener. Still now can not get anywhere near comprehending the thing[.] —Kevin Sampson, *Outlaws*, p. 286, 2001

sickest *adjective*
best *TRINIDAD AND TOBAGO, 1987*
- —Lise Winer, *Dictionary of the English/Creole of Trinidad & Tobago*, 2003

sickie; sicky *noun*
a feigned illness cited as grounds for missing work *AUSTRALIA, 1953*
- And then the next day, hungover because of Dave's funeral, everybody 'takes a sickie'. —John O'Grady, *Aussie Etiket*, p. 37, 1971
- On the few occasions he's been too dog-tired to join Mark during the day, he's been known to take a sickie. —*People Magazine*, p. 3, 26th August 1981
- I thought of getting out of it by throwing a 'sickie', but went in the end. —Mike Moore, *Hard Labour*, p. 13, 1987
- I bet she's taken a sickie. —Diran Abedayo, *My Once Upon A Time*, p. 247, 2000
- A Wellington Regional Council worker learned the hard way that not everyone who pulls a sickie can get away with it. —*Listener*, p. 8, 2nd July 2001
- If your conscience won't permit a sickie, then try to get the most out of the leave you do take. —*Sydney Morning Herald*, 12th July 2003

sickle; motorsickle *noun*
a motor*cycle* *US*
Re-pronounced abbreviation punning on **CHOPPER** (a motorcycle).
- And I don't want a tickle / 'Cause I'd rather ride on my motorsickle —Arlo Guthrie, *The Motorcycle Song*, 1967
- Get off my fuckin' sickle, man! —Stuart Browne, *Dangerous Parking*, p. 164, 2000

sickler *noun*
a person suffering from sickle-cell anaemia *US*
- —Sally Williams, *"Strong" Words*, p. 160, 1994

sickness *noun*
the range of symptoms experienced when a drug addict is deprived of the drug *US*
- Warding off the sickness symptoms ... thee sneezing, the flahshees of quick transfer between hot and cold ... the dancing bowels ... I hate the litany. —Jim Carroll, *Forced Entries*, p. 110, 1987

sicko *noun*
an emotionally or psycho-sexually disturbed person; disturbed *US, 1963*
- She's a sicko. Some kinda fruitcake or somethin. She plays with her own clit when I'm lovin her up. —Joseph Wambaugh, *The Black Marble*, p. 290, 1978
- This torrid tribute to the joys of dark meat features a chorus line of ebony beauties bouncing and boffing through a series of raunchy, relentlessly racist, and often unbearably funny skits that mine just about every sick cliche[.] —*Adult Video*, p. 16, August/September 1986
- Heatbroken Alan was branded a perv and a sicko by townsfolk[.] —*Picture*, p. 21, 5th February 1992
- My parents think I'm a sicko. —C.D. Payne, *Youth in Revolt*, p. 91, 1993
- And these assholes are making heroes outta sickos. —*Natural Born Killers*, 1994
- Creator of a gnarly incestual sicko freak scene read by every pretten girl I hung out with[.] —Editors of Ben is Dead, *Retrohell*, p. 5, 1997
- [M]aybe the lady would turn out to be one of those sickos who drifted in off the street to make hoax calls. —Malcolm Pryce, *Aberystwyth Mon Amour*, p. 15, 2001
- I'm blowing the whistle on a sicko bastard who deserves to be strung up and burnt alive[.] —Danny King, *The Burglar Diaries*, p. 169, 2001

sicko *adjective*
depraved *AUSTRALIA, 1993*
- —Glyn Parry, *Mosh*, p. 43, 1996
- If you've been digging David's sicko work in these pages then you're probably gonna want to pick this one up. —*Sick Puppy*, p. 21, 1998

sick pad *noun*
a sanitary towel *US*
- Then the bitch come draggin' it home with her sickpad on / she talkin' shit, "Daddy, you sure is sweet / When you go down to the store bring me back a box a Kotex." —Bruce Jackson, *Get Your Ass in the Water and Swim Like Me*, p. 129, 1966

sick puppy *noun*
a perverted person *US, 1984*
- "This is harmless sport." "You're a sick puppy." —Carl Hiassen, *Strip Tease*, p. 239, 1993

- In your recent letter to the editor of The Anchorage Daily News, you make a strong case that I'm a sick puppy who should probably be put to sleep. — Marty Beckerman, *Death to All Cheerleaders*, p. 36, 2000

sick squid *noun*
six pounds *UK*
A play on on 'six **QUID**'.
- For the price of a poorly octopus (sick squid... geddit?) many an ageing perv (such as myself) can wallow in a joyful amble down memory lane. — David Kerekes, *Headpress 22*, p. 150, 2002

sick to death of *adjective*
bored or fed-up with someone or something *UK, 1890*
- [M]any [trade union] branches are sick to death of government policies[.] — *The Guardian*, 4th February 2004

sid *noun*
▷ see: **'CID**

siddi *noun*
marijuana *UK, 1998*
- — Mike Haskins, *Drugs*, p. 289, 2003

side *noun*
1 a recorded tune or song *US, 1936*
Early gramophone records held one recording on each side.
- We began to record like mad: during the first months of 1945 alone, we made over fifty sides. — Mezz Mezzrow, *Really the Blues*, p. 331, 1946
- Robert threw a Dinah Washington side on real quick. — Hubert Selby Jr, *Last Exit to Brooklyn*, p. 103, 1957
- I have within my comfy shed bottles of rare red wine and lots of sides and tapes of sounds. — Dan Burley, *Diggeth Thou?*, p. 33, 1959
- Then we'll Spin Red's new sides. — Ross Russell, *The Sound*, p. 18, 1961
- Then we went up to my place and started playing some sides and smoking pot. — Claude Brown, *Manchild in the Promised Land*, p. 183, 1965
- "You can't imagine," Jessica said, "how many young editors and labor union people, and even a few cabinet ministers here and there, sat on the floor in our living room asking for another side by Miles or Dizzy or Duke." — Nat Hentoff, *Jazz Country*, p. 29, 1965
- I bought all the latest sides. — Bobby Seale, *A Lonely Rage*, p. 110, 1978
- [Y]ou could buy R&B singles unobtainable elsewhere – all those Lightnin' Slim and Slim Harpo sides on the Excello label. — Frank Zappa, *The Real Frank Zappa Book*, p. 35, 1989

2 a girl *US*
- — *American Speech*, p. 154, Spring-Summer 1972: 'An approach to Black slang'

3 a group of friends *TRINIDAD AND TOBAGO, 1973*
- — Lise Winer, *Dictionary of the English/Creole of Trinidad & Tobago*, 2003

▸ **on the side**
1 describes an extra-marital sexual liaison *US, 1893*
- I can be another woman in your life / I can be the other reason you're out at night / I can be all the things you thought she might / I can be on the side / That would alright, alright, alright[.] — Aaliyah *I Can Be*, 2001

2 of work or commerce, extra to regular or legitimate practice, often discreetly so *UK, 1961*
- A bit on the side? and how to make it[.] Want to earn extra cash? Ignore those get-rich-quick ads[.] — *The Observer*, 2nd May 1999

3 used as an announcement that you are monitoring a citizens' band radio channel; describes someone monitoring a citizens' band radio channel *US, 1976*
- Come back the breaker on the side[.] — Peter Chippindale, *The British CB Book*, p. 18, 1981

▸ **on the ... side**
somewhat; to a noticeable degree *UK, 1713*
- [S]ometimes the cuisine can be a little on the heavy side. — *The Guardian*, 27th April 2002

▸ **over the side**
engaged in private business or sexual liaisons during duty hours *UK*
Originally navy, 'over the side (of a ship)', meaning 'absent without leave'; adopted into police use.
- — Peter Laurie, *Scotland Yard*, p. 325, 1970
- — David Powis, *The Signs of Crime*, 1977

▸ **put on side**
to assume airs and graces *UK, 1878*
Possibly derived from the game of billiards.
- Would you believe that I wore herring tins for shoes once? And my wife Clara – who always liked to put on side – wore condensed milk tins for high heels? — Frank Hardy, *The Yarns of Billy Borker*, p. 49, 1965

side arms *noun*
1 in poker, the lower value pair in a hand consisting of two pairs *US*
- — George Percy, *The Language of Poker*, p. 82, 1988

2 sugar and cream *US*
- — Lou Shelly, *Hepcats Jive Talk Dictionary*, p. 48, 1945

sideboards *noun*
side whiskers *UK, 1857*
- You have described the duke as having small whiskers? – Yes, they were sideboards. Where did you get that name? – I have been in America... You call them sideboards? – Yes, or sideburns. — *The Daily Chronicle*, 7th December 1907
- Everyone always said Joe looked like Elvis. He has his own hair, and the sideboards, and he dyes his hair black, just like Elvis did. — *The Observer*, 11th August 2002

sidebox *verb*
to surround someone in a menacing manner *UK*
- The next day I got sideboxed by three faces [notable criminals] in a club. — *New Statesman*, 20th August 1982

side-buster *noun*
a person whose deeds do not match his description of his deeds *US*
- — James Harris, *A Convict's Dictionary*, p. 38, 1989

side comb *noun*
hair parted on the side *US*
Hawaiian youth usage.
- — Douglas Simonson, *Pidgin to da Max Hana Hou*, 1982

side dish *noun*
a mistress *US*
- — Vincent J. Monteleone, *Criminal Slang*, p. 209, 1949

sidehill winder; sidehill gouger *noun*
a mythical animal whose legs are shorter on one side than the other from years of grazing on a hillside *US*
- — John Gould, *Maine Lingo*, p. 255, 1975
- Ah, you're just bullywhackin' the way you was when you tried to tell me about the side-hill gouger. — George Bowering, *Caprice*, p. 159, 1987

sidekick *noun*
a close friend and accomplice *US, 1906*
- Bull Durham was his sidekick before, but he couldn't see nothing but corona-coronas now. — Mezz Mezzrow, *Really the Blues*, p. 87, 1946
- Here's this honest cop, supposedly, using what he calls leverage, holding my old sidekick, my confidant, the Moose, over my head as a threat. — Elmore Leonard, *Glitz*, p. 330, 1985

sideman *noun*
in a whe-whe lottery game, an assistant to the banker *TRINIDAD AND TOBAGO, 1966*
- — Lise Winer, *Dictionary of the English/Creole of Trinidad & Tobago*, 2003

side-roader *noun*
a rural marijuana thief; a person who grows marijuana in a remote outdoor garden *NEW ZEALAND*
- The drug barons now squared off against the 'side-roaders' in shadowy and ruthless turf wars that fed off regional farm economies and spiralling unemployment. — Redmer Yska, *New Zealand Gree*, p. 158, 1990

'sides *adverb*
in addition; used to introduce a further matter *UK, 1579*
An abbreviation of 'be*sides*'.
- [Y]ou became a pal, like. 'Sides, it would be bad luck to turn you in. — Jake Arnott, *He Kills Coppers*, p. 184, 2001

side squeeze *noun*
a partner in romance other than your primary partner; a romantic affair *US*
- Jagger's spokesman said he hadn't heard anything about Jagger's side squeeze. — *Newsday (New York)*, p. 13, 2nd May 1991

sidewalk pizza *noun*
a puddle of vomit *US*
- I laughed even harder, causing me to toss a sidewalk pizza – much to Bob's delight. — Elissa Stein and Kevin Leslie, *Chunks*, p. 37, 1997

sidewalk Susie *noun*
a prostitute *US*
- — Vincent J. Monteleone, *Criminal Slang*, p. 202, 1949

sideways *adjective*

1 of a sum of money being gambled, split each way (to win or place) *UK*
Racing slang.
- Saucepan [1], sideways, Lanternjaw. —Mark McShane, *The Straight and Crooked*, 1960

2 in motor racing, out of control, whether or not the car is actually sideways to the track traffic *US*
- —Hal Higdon, *Finding the Groove*, p. 308, 1973

sideways trip *noun*
a suicide in prison *US*
- —Inez Cardozo-Freeman, *The Joint*, p. 530, 1984

sidewinder *noun*

1 a South Asian prostitute; a promiscuous South Asian female *US*
The allusion is to a poisonous snake found in North America.
- —Judi Sanders, *Da Bomb*, p. 14, 1997

2 an unknown but very fast horse *CANADA*
- —Fred W. Ludditt, *Campfire Sketches of the Cariboo*, 1974

3 in trucking, a U-model Mack truck with a slightly off-centre driver's compartment *US*
- —Montie Tak, *Truck Talk*, p. 143, 1971

side work *noun*
prostitution *US*
- Despite their assertion that go-go is only a bit of "good clean fun," many strip-club owners tolerate – or even encourage – prostitution (or "side work," as the dancers call it): a blow job or hand job outside in the parking lot[.] —James Ridgeway, *Red Light*, p. 204, 1996

sideys; sidies *noun*
side whiskers *UK, 1967*
An abbreviation of 'sideburns' or 'sideboards'.
- [M]y old mum always told me: Never shag a man with sideys. —James Hawes, *Dead Long Enough*, p. 101, 2000
- [H]e had adopted the aforementioned riotously verdant "sidies" last seen on Jimmy "Wacko" Edwards. —Stuart Maconies, *Cider with Roadie*, p. 33, 2003

sidity; sididy; seditty *adjective*
arrogant, boastful, showing off *US*
- Real siditty affair, you know, all them stuck-up Montclair bitches and everything. —Nathan Heard, *Howard Street*, p. 31, 1968
- You looks some kinda seditty, off by yo'self like this. —Robert Gover, *JC Saves*, p. 17, 1968
- I don't care what your sidity friends think of me. —Christina and Richard Milner, *Black Players*, p. 307, 1972
- —Malachi Andrews and Paul T. Owens, *Black Language*, p. 91, 1973
- You must think you playin me for some kind of fool, think I don't see what'd comin down here, you gettin all sidity on me, think you too good to be out peddlin your butt on the street. —John Sayles, *Union Dues*, p. 184–185, 1977
- It was incredible what was going on, all those sidity people in Boston and Washington of a certain economic class formed these reading groups. —*News and Observer (Raleigh, North Carolina)*, p. 10 (What's Up), 31st January 2003

sieg heils *noun*
haemorrhoids *UK*
Rhyming slang for 'piles'.
- —Bodmin Dark, *Dirty Cockney Rhyming Slang*, 2003

sieve *noun*
a hospital or admitting physician that freely admits patients *US*
- —Sally Williams, *"Strong" Words*, p. 160, 1994

sieve *verb*
to drill holes in a safe for the placement of explosives to be used in opening it *US*
- I decided to use every trick in the drilling business I had ever heard of to sieve it for the soup. —Red Rudensky, *The Gonif*, p. 7, 1970

siff *noun*
syphilis *US*
- There was a young lawyer of note / Who thought he had siff of the throat[.] —Robert A. Wilson, *Playboy's Book of Forbidden Words*, p. 223–224, 1972

sift *verb*
to move swiftly through a crowd *UK*
Adopting conventional 'sift' (to pass through a sieve), perhaps incorporating a gentle pun on 'shift' (to move).
- I sift fast through the crowd takin' in the open bags an' pockets wishin' my fingers were fast too. Siftin's really wha'm good at. Movin'. Skankin'. Disappearin'. —Nick Barlay, *Curvy Lovebox*, p. 21, 1997

SIG
(in doctors' shorthand) a bad-tempered, thoroughly objectionable individual *UK*
An (unofficial) medical initialism: **STROPPY** (bad-tempered) *i*gnorant **GIT** (objectionable individual).
- —Adam T. Fox, St Mary's Hospital, London, 10th October 2002

sight *noun*
a large quantity *UK, 1390*
- They ruined a sight of places. East London, south London, good addresses, wrecked them all so no one else would live there. —Eamonn Sweeney, *Waiting for the Healer*, p. 216, 1997
- Mr McGonigle also said there was "a sight of diesel oil" on the road. —*Irish Examiner*, 12th April 2003

sight *verb*
to understand *BAHAMAS, 1980*
- —John A. Holm, *Dictionary of Bahamian English*, p. 184, 1982

sight *adverb*
very much *UK, 1928*
Often used with 'damn', 'damned' or another intensifier.
- I know what's out there and it's a fuck sight better than this shithole. —Mark Powell, *Snap*, p. 186, 2001

sight-hit *verb*
to stare at someone or something; to ogle someone *INDIA*
- Look at him, sight-hitting the girls again. —Paroo Nihalini, R.K. Tongue and Priya Hosali, *Indian and British English*, 1979

signal-to-noise ratio; s/n ratio *noun*
the amount of useful content found on an Internet site *US*
A figurative use of a technical term.
- A Letterman newsgroup in which most of the postings are pointless discussions of the best Stupid Pet Trick and conjectures about the sexual orientations of the band has a low signal-to-noise ratio. —Andy Ihnatko, *Cyberspeak*, p. 175, 1997

signature *noun*
the backblast of flame or smoke from a weapon *US*
- —Gregory Clark, *Words of the Vietnam War*, p. 468, 1990

signify *verb*
to engage in ritualistic insults, goading and teasing *US, 1932*
Unlike **DOZENS**, signifying does not make a person's mother the subject of the tease.
- "Looks like a flute, don't it? But wait'll you hear the song this little pill sings with it. You play the flute too?" he asked me, signifying to the others, and they all fell out at this funny gag. —Mezz Mezzrow, *Really the Blues*, p. 98, 1946
- Mary Jack commenced signifying with some nasty remarks. —Louis Armstrong, *Satchmo: My Life in New Orleans*, p. 73, 1954
- We take him by the neck and say, 'Don't signify with me!' Bad thing, to signify – y'hear me? —Jack Kerouac, *On the Road*, p. 256, 1957
- He looked like one of the real-gone cats with his signifying walk. —Chester Himes, *Cotton Comes to Harlem*, p. 135, 1965
- Now I ain't signifying, but I never dug you for a punk. —Piri Thomas, *Down These Mean Streets*, p. 110, 1967
- He said sternly, "Grandma, I'm gonna give you a fat mouth if you don't stop signifying and talking shit to me." —Iceberg Slim (Robert Beck), *Mama Black Widow*, p. 298, 1969
- Signifying is more humane. Instead of coming down on somebody's mother, you come down on them. —H. Rap Brown, *Die Nigger Diel*, p. 27, 1969
- He ain't done nuttin' but what you niggers sit around and signify, jive and lie about. —Steve Cannon, *Groove, Bang, and Jive Around*, p. 15, 1969

sign on *verb*
to register unemployed; hence to be unemployed *UK, 1885*
- They will also have to sign on every week for six weeks[.] —*The Guardian*, 10th April 2003

signs *noun*
hand signals showing youth gang affiliation *US*
- —Kenn "Naz" Young, *Naz's Dictionary of Teen Slang*, p. 117, 1993
- —Anna Scotti and Paul Young, *Buzzwords*, p. 143, 1997

Sigourney Weaver *noun*
the vagina *UK*
Rhyming slang for **BEAVER**, formed from the name of the US actress (b.1949).
- —Bodmin Dark, *Dirty Cockney Rhyming Slang*, 2003

sig quote *noun*
in computing, an aphorism automatically included with the user's formatted signature *US*
- —Eric S. Raymond, *The New Hacker's Dictionary*, p. 320, 1991

silencer *noun*
a motorcyle muffler *US*
The UK conventional English 'silencer' is US slang.
- —Ed Radlauer, *Motorcylopedia*, p. 59, 1973

silent *adjective*
of an entry in a criminal's file, unofficial; showing crimes for which the criminal was not charged but probably committed *US*
- Silent beef. When the authorities believe a man guilty of a crime or crimes which they can't prove and must settle for a conviction on a lesser charge, they attach memoranda to the man's record stipulating the uncharged offenses. —Seth Morgan, *Homeboy*, p. 140, 1990

silent but deadly *adjective*
applied to the unpleasant smell that hangs in the air as a result of a silent fart *UK*
Unpleasant but hardly deadly. Anecdotal evidence and experience place this term in the 1970s.
- There's controversy in our office. We all suspect one woman of releasing silent-but-deadly smells. —Teresa Graedon and Joe Graedon, *The People's Pharmacy Guide to Home and Herbal Remedies*, p. 226, 1999
- —Chris Lewis, *The Dictionary of Playground Slang*, p. 202, 2003

silent captain *noun*
in shuffleboard, the scoreboard *US*
- Your SILENT CAPTAIN – the scoreboard – dictates every single shot to be made!!! —Omero C. Catan, *Secrets of Shuffleboard Strategy*, p. 16, 1967

silent death *noun*
an electric train *UK*
By comparison with steam engines, at the date (around 1950) of the introduction of electric trains.
- —Harvey Sheppard, *Dictionary of Railway Slang*, 1970

silent flute *noun*
the penis *UK*
Variation of **FLUTE** (the penis).

silent flute of love *noun*
the erect penis *UK*
- —Richard Herring, *Talking Cock*, p. 30, 2003

silent night *noun*
a *light* ale *UK*
Rhyming slang.
- —Ray Puxley, *Cockney Rabbit*, 1992

silent violent *noun*
an unpleasantly aromatic fart that pollutes without warning, a silent fart *UK*
A variation of **SILENT BUT DEADLY**.
- —Chris Lewis, *The Dictionary of Playground Slang*, p. 202, 2003

silk *noun*
1 a white person *US*
- Every dealer had five or six silks who spent a lot of money. —Clarence Cooper Jr, *The Scene*, p. 70, 1960

2 a homosexual *US*
- —David Claerbaut, *Black Jargon in White America*, p. 77, 1972

3 in the categorisation of sexual activity by teenage boys, a touch of a girl's crotch outside her underwear *US*
- Next in order of significant intimacy was "getting silk," which meant touching panty-crotch, and then for the more successful, "getting pube." —Terry Southern, *Now Dig This*, p. 3, 1986

4 money *US*
- —Hyman E. Goldin et al., *Dictionary of American Underworld Lingo*, p. 195, 1950

5 heroin *UK*
- —Robert Ashton, *This Is Heroin*, p. 207, 2002

▸ **hit the silk; take to silk**
to open a parachute after jumping from a plane *US, 1933*
- —Lou Shelly, *Hepcats Jive Talk Dictionary*, p. 46, 1945
- — *American Speech*, p. 319, October/December 1948: 'Slang of the American paratrooper'

silk *adjective*
1 white-skinned *US*
- I saw the "silk" chicks crane their necks toward the door. —Iceberg Slim (Robert Beck), *Pimp*, p. 127, 1969

2 homosexual *US*
- —Anthony Romeo, *The Language of Gangs*, p. 21, 4th December 1962

silk and satin *noun*
any combination of central nervous system stimulants and central nervous system depressants *US*
- —Edith A. Folb, *runnin' down some lines*, p. 254, 1980

silk department *noun*
the very best *AUSTRALIA*
- —Ned Wallish, *The Truth Dictionary of Racing Slang*, p. 73, 1989

silk glove *noun*
a guard on a passenger train *US*
Not praise.
- —Ramon Adams, *The Language of the Railroader*, p. 138, 1977

silk hat *noun*
in circus and carnival usage, an egocentrist *US*
- —Don Wilmeth, *The Language of American Popular Entertainment*, p. 242, 1981

silkies *noun*
a woman's underpants *US*
- Because she gets candy all the goddamn time from every asshole tryin' to get into her silkies. —Robert Campbell, *In La-La Land We Trust*, p. 180, 1986

silks *noun*
silk or nylon socks *US*
- —David Claerbaut, *Black Jargon in White America*, p. 79, 1972

silk-stocking *adjective*
wealthy *US*
- I worked a silk stocking division out on the west side when I first came out of the academy and I never thought of a Caucasian asshole in terms of race. —Joseph Wambaugh, *The New Centurions*, p. 146, 1970

silky *adjective*
excellent; pleasing; smooth *US*
- Everything was roses. I was contented. And life itself was silky. —A.S. Jackson, *Gentleman Pimp*, p. 43, 1973

silky-straight *noun*
any hairstyle with artificially straightened hair *US*
- The brother was one of those dumb old raghead niggers, probably been in sail the last twenty years and didn't notice nobody wore silky-straights anymore, not even pimps. —Joseph Wambaugh, *The Glitter Dome*, p. 59, 1981

Silky Sullivan *noun*
in horse racing, any horse that comes from far behind to win a race *US*
Ridden by Willie Shoemaker, the original Silky Sullivan came from 30 lengths behind to win the 1958 Santa Anita Derby by three lengths.

silly affairs *noun*
used as a humorous synonym for 'Civil Affairs' *US*
- —Carl Fleischhauer, *A Glossary of Army Slang*, p. 14, 1968

silly as a two-bob watch *adjective*
very silly *NEW ZEALAND*
- —Louis S. Leland, *A Personal Kiwi-Yankee Dictionary*, p. 10, 1984

silly billy *noun*
a fool *UK, 1834*
Formed on Billy, a familiar diminutive of William; originally used as a nickname for William Frederick, Duke of Gloucester (1776–1834) and William IV (1765–1837), then as a popular name for a clown, especially a clown's juvenile stooge.
- Silly billies. A Swindon couple who wanted their wedding day photos to be unusual posed with goofy "hillbilly teeth" in their mouths. — *Western Daily Press*, 26th June 2002

silly bollock; silly bollocks *noun*
a contemptible fool *UK*
- We should start making plans before silly bollocks gets us well and truly fuckin' nicked [arrested]. — J.J. Connolly, *Know Your Enemy [britpulp]*, p. 152, 1999
- Old silly bollock Lucas's outside wiv free uvver geezers. — Colin Butts, *Is Harry Still on the Boat?*, p. 86, 2003

silly cunt *noun*
a fool *UK*
- I felt it was almost my duty, my duty as a silly cunt who likes seeing other people being silly cunts[.] — Dave Courtney, *Raving Lunacy*, p. 12, 2000

silly dust *noun*
a powdered drug *UK*
- You hoovered up some silly dust back in the club, entered a K-hole and don't know what happened. — *Mixmag*, p. 142, June 2003

silly season *noun*
from a police perspective, the summer as a period of counterculture, pop, rock and dance festivals *UK*
From the familiar journalistic sense. Used by late 1980s – early 90s counterculture travellers.
- — Martin Roach, *Dr. Marten's Air Wair*, 1999: 'Glossary of travellers' terms'

silly side bin *noun*
psilocybin or psilocin, in powder or capsule form *UK*
Nonsense pun on the chemical name.

sillyvillian *noun*
a civilian, seen from the cynical eyes of the military *US*
- You know you're needed as much here as among all those sillyvillians. — Herbert Tarr, *The Conversion of Chaplain Cohen*, p. 298, 1963

silly walk *noun*
in computing, an absurd procedure that must be followed *US*
A borrowing from Monthy Python.
- — Eric S. Raymond, *The New Hacker's Dictionary*, p. 321, 1991

sillywatter *noun*
any alcoholic drink, especially in reference to a drinker's foolish behaviour *UK: SCOTLAND*
- Whit? Have you been on the sillywatter? — Michael Munro, *The Complete Patter*, p. 140, 1996

silver *noun*
1 marijuana *UK*
Based on the colour of the leaves.
- [T]hat gummy silver at one hundred and eighty. Indica and sess two hundred plus[.] — Diran Adebayo, *My Once Upon A Time*, p. 26, 2000

2 in American casinos, a silver coin or $1 chip *US*
- — Lee Solkey, *Dummy Up and Deal*, p. 119, 1980
- — Steve Kuriscak, *Casino Talk*, p. 50, 1985

3 money *US*
- — Andy Anonymous, *A Basic Guide to Campusology*, p. 22, 1966

4 a type of bet in an illegal numbers game lottery *US*
- He played the money row, lucky lady, happy days, true love, sun gonna shine, gold, silver, diamonds, dollars and whiskey. — Chester Himes, *A Rage in Harlem*, p. 23, 1957

silver and gold *adjective*
old *UK*
Rhyming slang.
- — Ray Puxley, *Fresh Rabbit*, 1998

silver bike *noun*
a metal syringe *US*
Drug addict usage.
- — William D. Alsever, *Glossary for the Establishment and Other Uptight People*, p. 19, December 1970
- — Walter Way, *The Drug Scene*, p. 114, 1977

silver bullet *noun*
1 an ideal, usually notional, solution to a problem *UK*
From the mythology that a silver bullet is fatal to a werewolf; this symbol was also adopted by the eponymous hero of television Western *The Lone Ranger*, 1956–62.
- [A] biotechnological silver bullet that could solve hunger, malnutrition, and real poverty[.] — *The Guardian*, 25th November 2002

2 a martini *US*
- Five hours, he must've had twenty silver bullets. — Elmore Leonard, *Freaky Deaky*, p. 65, 1988

silver goose *noun*
a proctoscope *US*
- — *Maledicta*, p. 34, 1988–1989: 'Medical maledicta from San Francisco'

silver haze *noun*
a hybrid strain of marijuana *UK*
From the frosty colour of the leaf.
- — Mike Rock, *This Book*, p. 251, 1999
- — Nick Jones, *Spliffs*, p. 75, 2003

silver lady *noun*
a hypodermic needle and syringe *US*
- — Peter Johnson, *Dictionary of Street Alcohol and Drug Terms*, p. 170, 1993

silvermine *verb*
to patrol a casino in search of coins left in the tray of a slot machine or dropped on the floor *US*
- Finally, there's silvermining, which may not be exactly a form of cheating but might qualify as the next thing to it. — Jim Regan, *Winning at Slot Machine*, p. 68, 1985

silver plate
please *US*
Intentionally butchered *s'il vous plaît*.
- — Connie Eble (Editor), *UNC-CH Campus Slang*, p. 8, November 1990

silvers *noun*
any coins *TRINIDAD AND TOBAGO*
- — *Lise Winer, Dictionary of the English/Creole of Trinidad & Tobago*, 2003

silver spoon *noun*
1 used as a metaphor of wealth at birth, especially in the expression 'born with a silver spoon in your mouth' *US*
- My parents were exorbitant. Fllthy rich. And they'd raised me in that silver-spoon tradition. — Oscar Zeta Acosta, *The Autobiography of a Brown Buffalo*, p. 147, 1972

2 the moon *UK*
Rhyming slang.
- — Ray Puxley, *Cockney Rabbit*, 1992

silver surfer *noun*
an elderly or retired person who uses the Internet *UK*
Adopting the identity of cartoon superhero the Silver Surfer, created in 1966 by Stan Lee and Jack Kirby for Marvel Comics; this puns 'silver' (the hair colour) and 'surfer' (someone who browses the Internet).
- I looked at your e-mail. Very impressive [...] You've become a silver surfer. — *The Archers*, 3rd November 2001

silvertail *noun*
1 a member of the privileged class *AUSTRALIA, 1891*
Derogatory.
- We know you want Picnic Races because that'll bring here a lot of fly-by-night, jumped-up, fifth-rate silver-tails from all over the country to fill your new hotel. — Dymphna Cusack, *Picnic Races*, p. 33, 1962
- The silvertails always say the unemployed don't want work[.] — Frank Hardy, *The Yarns of Billy Borker*, p. 13, 1965

2 a prisoner who enjoys privileges *AUSTRALIA, 1950*

silvertail *adjective*
pretentious *AUSTRALIA, 1962*
- The battling punters were closer to the action here and had more in common with these owners and trainers than they had with the silvertail image of the members' enclosure at Randwick. — Joe Andersen, *Winners Can Laugh*, p. 66, 1982

silvery moon *noun*
a black person *UK*
Rhyming slang for **COON**.
- — Ronnie Barker, *Fletcher's Book of Rhyming Slang*, 1979

silvery spoon *noun*
a black person *UK*
Rhyming slang for **COON**.
- A silvery spoon, a bubble and squeak — Ian Dury, *Blackmail Man*, 1977

sim *noun*
a *sim*ulator; a *sim*ulation *UK*
- Each session consists of two sim rides. — Robert Prest, *F4 Phantom: a Pilot's Story*, 1979

simmer down *verb*
to calm down *US, 1871*
- Rebellious spirits may end up manning barricades for real if the present discord between producer Cameron Mackintosh and the Musicians' Union does not simmer down. — *The Guardian*, 22nd January 2004

simoleon *noun*
a dollar *US, 1896*
- If he was to cuss you simoleons out and put you out his car you'd say he was a bad fellow. — Chester Himes, *If He Hollers Let Him Go*, p. 102, 1945
- Not far away, the loft in which I'd earned my eighteen simoleons a week with the other sweated youths. — Philip Wylie, *Opus 21*, p. 289, 1949
- — Frank Garcia, *Marked Cards and Loaded Dice*, p. 264, 1962

simp *noun*
a fool; a *simp*leton *US, 1903*
- Pimps and simps would fall in from here and there and everywhere, grabbing thousand-dollar advances from the madames and leaving their lady friends in pawn. — Mezz Mezzrow, *Really the Blues*, p. 59, 1946
- Gotham gals don't flop for saps, simps, or retail buyers. — Jack Lait and Lee Mortimer, *New York Confidential*, p. 126, 1948
- A rotten ten dollars from a simp like Gregor? — Lawrence Block, *No Score [The Affairs of Chip Harrison Omnibus]*, p. 105, 1970
- [N]oting stuff down was the kind of simp's move that landed a man of my profession in trouble. — Diran Abedayo, *My Once Upon A Time*, p. 6, 2000

simp *adjective*
1 foolish *US*
From **SIMP** (a simpleton).
- His simp thinking had left him with two fingers short of the monty[.] — Diran Abedayo, *My Once Upon A Time*, p. 20, 2000

2 fashionable *US*
- Then I'll put on my simp togs for I will have my gage. — Bruce Jackson, *Get Your Ass in the Water and Swim Like Me*, p. 124, 1965

simple as
very easy *UK*
The familiarity of the phrase 'it is as *simple as* that' has allowed a gradual clipping; first the verb was generally considered unnecessary to express the intention, then 'as' was slurred aside, finally 'that' is understood; it is as simple as that.
- It's easy-peasy to just walk up past the Revolution and get picked up on the corner there. Simple as. — Kevin Sampson, *Outlaws*, p. 249, 2001

simple pimp *noun*
a pimp who fails to live up to the high standards of his fellow pimps *US*
- See, you got so many squares out there trying to pimp, it's pathetic. Would-be pimps. You know what I mean? Simple pimp, that's what we call them. Simple pimp. — Christina and Richard Milner, *Black Players*, p. 61, 1972
- Pimps who do solicit for their women are called popcorn pimps or simple pimps by the boss pimps. — Burgess Laughlin, *Job Opportunities in the Black Market*, p. 11–4, 1978

simple Simon *noun*
1 a diamond (the precious stone; the suit of cards); Double Diamond™ (a branded beer) *UK*
Rhyming slang, formed from a nursery rhyme character.
- — Ray Puxley, *Cockney Rabbit*, 1992

2 psislocybin, a hallucinogenic mushroom *US*
- — William D. Alsever, *Glossary for the Establishment and Other Uptight People*, p. 29, December 1970

simp twister *noun*
in circus and carnival usage, a carousel *US*
- — Don Wilmeth, *The Language of American Popular Entertainment*, p. 243, 1981

sin *noun*
▸ **as sin**
extremely, especially in phrases 'ugly as sin' and 'miserable as sin' *UK, 1821*
- I am angry, I am ill and I am as ugly as sin. — Magazine, *A Song From Under the Floorboards*, 1978
- [A]part from six months in the capital when he was 'miserable as sin', he's remained true to his East Midlands roots. — *The Observer*, 25th August 2002

sin!
used for registering shock or surprise *UK*
Ironic euphemism for **FUCK!**.
- Sin! I can't even think of the last time I saw you two, Dartford says[.] — Mark Powell, *Snap*, p. 37, 2001

sin bin *noun*
1 in team sports, an off-field area a player can be sent to for a period as a punishment for breaking the rules *CANADA*
- High-sticking is a good way to get put in the sin-bin. — Bobby Orr, *Orr on Ice*, p. 165, 1970
- The referee had his work cut out just keeping the game under control without worrying too much about the rules and ended up giving nine players a stint in the sin-bin. — Robert G. Barrett, *Davo's Little Something*, p. 200, 1992

2 in prison, a punishment cell or the punishment block *UK*
- — Angela Devlin, *Prison Patter*, p. 105, 1996

3 a panel van or the like used for sexual encounters *AUSTRALIA*
- They tended not to get on as well with the girlfriend's parents when they turned up in their sinbins. — Sandra Jobson, *Blokes*, p. 75, 1984

▸ **in the sin bin**
ostracised *AUSTRALIA*
- I spent a week in the sin-bin for that one. — Paul Vautin, *Turn It Up!*, p. 116, 1995

sin-bin *verb*
1 to temporarily remove a person from duty or office while they are under investigation for some misdeed *AUSTRALIA, 1983*
- By the time I arrived at Liverpool the balloon had gone up and I'd been sin-binned from taking any further part in the operation, pending the outcome of an inquiry into the photographer's allegation. — William Dodson, *The Sharp End*, p. 191, 2001

2 in team sports, to send a player to the sin bin *AUSTRALIA, 1983*

since Adam was a pup
from time immemorial *AUSTRALIA*
- Hasn't struck a flow since Adam was a pup. — Kylie Tennant, *The Honey Flow*, p. 85, 1956
- — Wilda Moxham, *The Apprentice*, p. 75, 1969
- — Frank Hardy, *Hardy's People*, p. 197, 1986

since Hector was a pup
for a very long time *US, 1904*
- One of the last links with the old days of burlesque in Washington is Abraham Attenson, the portly manager of the Gayety Theater, who has been in burlesque since Hector was a pup. — *Washington Post*, p. 14, 27th March 1977
- We'll go up there and prove it. We haven't lost a case since Hector was a pup. — *Union Leader (Manchester, New Hampshire)*, p. A1, 29th February 2004

since time
from a long time ago *UK*
- [S]ome kind of assumed African identity has been a key signifier of hip hop since time, whether simply an appropriated symbol or a key political or religious agenda. — Patrick Neate, *Where You're At*, p. 88, 2003

sin city *noun*
the neighbourhood in An Khe, Vietnam, housing brothels, bars and other vice dens *US*
- — Carl Fleischhauer, *A Glossary of Army Slang*, p. 15, 1968

Sinead O'Connor; Sinead *noun*
a *doner* kebab *UK, 2001*
Popney rhyming slang, based on the name of Irish singer Sinead O'Connor (b.1966). Popney was contrived for *www.music365.co.uk*, an Internet music site.

sine-died *adjective*
permanently barred (from a bar or sporting endeavour) *UK: SCOTLAND*
From Latin *sine die* (without a day) used in legal language for 'an indefinite adjournment'.
- He's sayin there's nae way you're gettin back in there. Ye're sine-died, he says. — Michael Munro, *The Complete Patter*, p. 140, 1996

sing *verb*
1 to give information or evidence, usually to the police *US, 1929*
- I don't worry about them any more than you do about shaking a guy down and then shooting him in the back to keep him from singing[.] — Horace McCoy, *Kiss Tomorrow Good-bye*, p. 263, 1948
- Note: Dean was "singing" the day she was slain, but clammed up when shown the headlines by his wife. — Jack Lait and Lee Mortimer, *Chicago Confidential*, p. 135, 1950
- Been makin' it all his life singing songs for the cops. — Donald Goines, *Kenyatta's Last Hit*, p. 69, 1975
- They grabbed a paper hanger in a bank. A broad. She's singing for a deal. — Gerald Petievich, *Money Men*, p. 140, 1981

- Yeah they don't know our names, but they can sing about this place. — *Reservoir Dogs*, 1992
- Ya cuntprick, one's saying with harsh breath, ya sang to the fuckin' rozzers. — Nick Barlay, *Curvy Lovebox*, p. 19, 1997

2 in carnival usage, to make a sales pitch *US*
- — Don Wilmeth, *The Language of American Popular Entertainment*, p. 243, 1981

3 in a big store confidence swindle, to provide false information to the intended victim
- How'd you like to take the call and do some singing for us. — Stephen J. Cannell, *Big Con*, p. 195, 1997

▸ **sing in the choir**
to be homosexual *US*
Cute code.
- — Kevin Dilallo, *The Unofficial Gay Manual*, p. 245, 1994

▸ **sing like a canary**
to give information or evidence, usually to the police *US, 1950*
An elaboration of **SING**.
- I heard that the Mafia narcotic syndicate believed this man was "singing like a canary" to us. — Harry J. Anslinger, *The Murderers*, p. 94, 1961

Singapore grey *noun*
hashish purportedly manufactured in Singapore *US*
- My idea was to get into the room, accept the booze and baggage delivery, then smoke my last big chunk of Singapore Grey while watching Walter Cronkite and waiting for my attorney to arrive. — Hunter S. Thompson, *Fear and Loathing in Las Vegas*, p. 109, 1971

singbird *noun*
a police informer *US*
- — Ralph de Sola, *Crime Dictionary*, p. 138, 1982

sing-cerely
used as a humorous closing in letters between singers *US*
- — *American Speech*, p. 301, Autumn-Winter 1975: 'The jargon of barbershop'

singer *noun*
1 in a confidence swindle, a participant who passes information about the false enterprise to the victim *US*
- — M. Allen Henderson, *How Con Games Work*, p. 222, 1985: 'Glossary'
- — Kathleen Odean, *High Steppers, Fallen Angels, and Lollipops*, p. 132, 1988
- There were also "singers" to give background information to Tommy Rina when he was checking Beano out[.] — Stephen J. Cannell, *King Con*, p. 130, 1997

2 in trucking, a recapped tyre *US*
Named after the road noise.
- — Montie Tak, *Truck Talk*, p. 143, 1971

Singin' Johnny *noun*
homebrew *CANADA*
- Singin' Johnny is made by putting ripe black currants and sugar into a liquor bottle in July, filling it with gin, and letting it ferment until Christmas, [to be] served to holiday visitors. — Bill Casselman, *Canadian Food Words*, p. 135, 1998

single eye *noun*
a Japanese person *US*
Hawaiian youth usage.
- — Douglas Simonson, *Pidgin to da Max Hana Hou*, 1982

single-fish *noun*
a urination *UK: SCOTLAND*
Glasgow rhyming slang for **PISH** (a **PISS**).
- Ah'm away fur a single fish. — Michael Munro, *The Patter, Another Blast*, 1988
- Drivers opted to hold it in rather than risk being propositioned, murdered or arrested if they stopped for a quick single-fish. — Christopher Brookmyer, *Boiling a Frog*, p. 297, 2000

single-O *noun*
a criminal, gambling cheat or a prisoner who acts alone *US*
- — Frank Garcia, *Marked Cards and Loaded Dice*, p. 264, 1962
- As he considered it years later he might have done all right if he had stayed on the single-O, but though he had many of the characteristics of a loner he wasn't a true solitary. — Malcolm Braly, *On the Yard*, p. 229, 1967
- — Inez Cardozo-Freeman, *The Joint*, p. 531, 1984
- — Lindsay E. Smith and Bruce A. Walstad, *Sting Shift*, p. 117, 1989: 'Glossary'

single-O *verb*
to operate as a criminal without confederates; to operate selfishly within a criminal enterprise *US*
- — Hyman E. Goldin et al., *Dictionary of American Underworld Lingo*, p. 195, 1950

single-O *adjective*
selfish *US*
- — Hyman E. Goldin et al., *Dictionary of American Underworld Lingo*, p. 195, 1950

singles bar *noun*
a bar that caters to a young, unattached clientele *US, 1969*
- When I used to go to singles bars, I'd wear my San Diego Blood Bank T-shirt just to show all the lonely nurses and schoolteachers that I'm a clean donor. — Joseph Wambaugh, *Finnegan's Week*, p. 154, 1993

single-skinner *noun*
a single fence *UK*
- The fence is high, yet as it's only a single-skinner and there's no razor wire it seems more suited to keeping the curious out than to keeping prisoners in. — *The Guardian*, 27th June 2002

single-stakes-about *noun*
in gambling, a type of conditional bet *UK*
- A bet consiting of two singles, each with an any-to-come [a type of conditional bet] single at the same stake on the other selection. Sometimes denoted by a cross or a series of crosses between the selections (eg £2 A xxx £2 B). — David Bennet, *Know Your Bets*, p. 26, 2001

singlie *noun*
a single man *UK*
- As soon as a battalion was away over the water, all the singlies were straight over to check out the wives. — Andy McNab, *Immediate Action*, p. 51, 1995

Singlish *noun*
a Singaporean adaptation of the English language; a variety of English used in Sri Lanka *SINGAPORE*
- The widespread use of Singlish, a local version of Shakepeare's tongue, is a perpetual worry to the authorities in Singapore[.] — *The Economist*, 20th December 2001

sing on *verb*
in the context of a calypso song, to disparage or tease someone *TRINIDAD AND TOBAGO, 1958*
- — Lise Winer, *Dictionary of the English/Creole of Trinidad & Tobago*, 2003

singular!
great! *US*
- — Connie Eble (Editor), *UNC-CH Campus Slang*, p. 8, Spring 1992

sinistered area *noun*
in Quebec, a disaster area *CANADA*
The French phrase *zone sinestress* is the source of this phrase when used in English in this way.
- — Victor Trahan, *The City of Montreal Style Guide*, p. 120, 2001

sink *noun*
in the language of hang gliding, falling air that increases the speed of descent *US*
- — Dennis Pagen, *Hang Gliding and Flying Skills*, p. 110, 1977: 'Glossary'

▸ **behind the sink**
depleted of funds *US*
- — John Scarne, *Scarne on Dice*, p. 460, 1974

sink *verb*
to down a drink *AUSTRALIA, 1911*
- Lasher's hand grabbed up his beer and he sank it in three gulps. — Eric Lambert, *The Veterans*, p. 15, 1954
- 'Pubs,' he informed them in a voice that brooked no dissent, 'er fer sinkin' piss.' — Linda Jaivin, *Rock n Roll Babes from Outer Space*, p. 245, 1996

▸ **sink the pink**
to have sex *US*
Snooker imagery.
- Another way to say "intercourse" [...] Sinking the pink[.] — Erica Orloff and JoAnn Baker, *Dirty Little Secrets*, p. 88, 2001

sinker *noun*
1 a doughnut *US*
- — Joseph E. Ragen and Charles Finston, *Inside the World's Toughest Prison*, p. 817, 1962: 'Penitentiary and underworld glossary'
- — Don Wilmeth, *The Language of American Popular Entertainment*, p. 243, 1981

2 a dent on a surfboard that requires a resin filler *US*
- — George Colendich, *The Ding Repair Scriptures*, p. 88, 1986

sin loi, motherfucker
sorry about that *US*
Xin loi or *sin loi* is Vietnamese meaning something in the nature of 'sorry about that'. It was widely heard and widely used by US troops in Vietnam.
• —Gregory Clark, *Words of the Vietnam War*, p. 477, 1990

sinner *noun*
a person *IRELAND*
• Dollymount was grand on a good, sunny day but on a rainy day or even just a cloudy one there wasn't a sinner down there to sell a chip to.—Roddy Doyle, *The Van*, p. 223, 1991

sinsemilla; sinse *noun*
▷ see: SENSIMILLIA

sip *verb*
▸ **sip at the fuzzy cup**
to perform oral sex on a woman *US*
• —Edith A. Folb, *runnin' down some lines*, p. 254, 1980

▸ **sip suds; sip on suds**
to drink beer *US*
• —Connie Eble (Editor), *UNC-CH Campus Slang*, p. 5, October 1986

Sip *nickname*
the state of Mississippi *US*
• —*Current Slang*, p. 12, Fall 1970

siphon *verb*
▸ **siphon the python; syphon the python**
1 (of a male) to urinate *AUSTRALIA, 1968*
A jocular construction rhyming a reasonably conventional use of 'syphon' with **PYTHON** (the penis).
• I've just got to nip into the dunnee [a toilet] to syphon the python —Barry Humphries, *Bazza Pulls It Off!*, 1971
• Best go siphon the fackin' python. Big job. Could be a while.—Andrew Holmes, *Sleb*, p. 151, 2002

2 (of a male) to have sex *US*
• The bartender spoke slowly, as if to an idiot child. "You know, push the bush? Slake the snake? Drain the train? Siphon the python?" —James Ellroy, *Because the Night*, p. 415, 1984

Sippie *noun*
a member of the Student Information Processing Board at the Massachusetts Institute of Technology *US, 1990s*
Acronym.
• The Sippies mumble, speculate, cogitate, consider, confer.—Melanie McGrath, *Hard, Soft & Wet*, p. 157, 1998

sipple *adjective*
slippery *TRINIDAD AND TOBAGO, 1973*
• —Lise Winer, *Dictionary of the English/Creole of Trinidad & Tobago*, 2003

sip-sip *verb*
to whisper, especially when gossiping *BAHAMAS*
• —John A. Holm, *Dictionary of Bahamian English*, p. 185, 1982

sir and miss *noun*
syphilis *UK*
Rhyming slang.
• —Bodmin Dark, *Dirty Cockney Rhyming Slang*, 2003

Sir Anthony Blunt; Sir Anthony *noun*
a fool; a despicable fool *UK, 1979*
Rhyming slang for **CUNT**, probably coined by comedian and satirist Peter Cook (1937–95). Sir Anthony Blunt was an art historian and traitor who spied for the Soviet Union ('the fourth man') and, eventually, had his knighthood removed, 1907–83.
• [T]he traitor Sir Anthony Blunt was exposed and within a couple of days a client told me shamefacedly, "I feel a right Sir Anthony". —*Antiquarian Book Review*, p. 18, June 2002

Sir Charles *noun*
the Viet Cong *US*
• —*Maledicta*, p. 254, Summer/Winter 1982: 'Viet-speak'
• We were busting bush in III Corps, looking for "Sir Charles" in an area they called the Hobo Woods.—Lonnie Dotson, *BOOM! Another Landmine*, 2000

Sir Walter Scott *noun*
a pint glass, a pint *pot* *UK*
Rhyming slang, formed from the name of the Scottish novelist and poet, 1777–1832.
• —Ray Puxley, *Cockney Rabbit*, 1992

sis *noun*
1 used as a term of address for a sister *UK, 1656*
• Hey, you're gonna love this place, aren't you sis?—Elmore Leonard, *City Primeval*, p. 145, 1980

2 used as a form of address for a girl or young woman; also (when used by a man of a younger woman) may imply no sexual interest *US, 1859*
• How's little sis? You looked a bit harrassed that day I saw you.—Mary Hooper, *(megan)2*, p. 126, 1999

sissified; sissy; cissy *adjective*
effeminate *US, 1846*
From **SISTER** via **SIS**.
• Jimmy hears this and says in a sissy voice, "Oh really, I hope he doesn't[.]"—John Peter Jones, *Feather Pluckers*, p. 13, 1964
• Unpopular with me were the "cissy" cowboys Roy Rogers and Gene Autry. They also sang. Yuk!—Brian McDonald, *Elephant Boys*, p. 40, 2000

sissy *noun*
an effeminate boy or man, especially a homosexual; a coward *US, 1879*
• Those who come to prison with obvious homosexual tendencies are referred to as "sissies."—*Ebony*, p. 82, July 1951
• You think Jesus was some kind of sissy, eh?—Richard Brooks, *Elmer Gantry*, 1960
• "What?" she yelled. "Get up off me! Give me my drawers! You're nothin' but a goddamn sissy."—Henry Williamson, *Hustler!*, p. 59, 1965
• Why would anybody want to go to bed with a flaming little sissy like you?—Mart Crowley, *The Boys in the Band*, p. 159, 1968
• Nobody was up there except two sissies smoking reefer.—Iceberg Slim (Robert Beck), *Trick Baby*, p. 297, 1969
• Outta the dozen girls that were on the edge only one of 'em looked halfway as good as Satin did and the rest of 'em looked like sissies in drag.—A.S. Jackson, *Gentleman Pimp*, p. 100, 1973
• [M]y father resented the idea – telling her – she was making a god damned sissy out of me – to leave me alone.—Herbert Huncke, *The Evening Sun Turned Crimson*, p. 23, 1980
• He had suspected the guy before, the guy so polite and sounding a little bit like a sissy the way he talked, but looked like a business-man.—Elmore Leonard, *Be Cool*, p. 174, 1999

sissy bar *noun*
1 on a motorcyle or bicycle, a back rest for the passenger seated behind the driver *US*
The suggestion is that a manly man or tough woman has no need for the back rest.
• —*American Speech*, p. 237–238, Fall 1969: 'Sissy bar: the word that made good'
• Tagged for particular critical attention were high handlebars or "ape hangers," the removal of the front wheel brake, the ornamental "sissy bar," a tubular metal backrest rising from the rear of the passenger's section of the seat.—*San Francisco Examiner*, p. 9, 20th February 1970
• —Ed Radlauer, *Motorcylopedia*, p. 59, 1973
• It became a style and look: a bitch bar (sissy bar) so your chick could lay back.—Ralph "Sonny" Barger, *Hell's Angel*, p. 61, 2000

2 a bar patronised by homosexuals *US*
• "They got a few sissy bars not too far from there," the hooker shrugged.—Joseph Wambaugh, *The Delta Star*, p. 154, 1983

sissy stick *noun*
in pool, a mechanical device used to support the cue on hard-to-reach shots *US*
• —Stephen H. Dill (Editor), *Current Slang*, p. 12, Fall 1970
• —Mike Shamos, *The Illustrated Encyclopedia of Billiards*, p. 214, 1993

sissy tank *noun*
a jail holding cell reserved for homosexual prisoners *US*
• Well, they have me in the sissy tank with all the gay people[.]—Joseph Wambaugh, *The Glitter Dome*, p. 156, 1981

sister *noun*
1 used as a form of address for a woman whose name is unknown *US, 1906*
• What's the matter, sister? You ain't saying much.—*It Happened One Night*, 1934

2 a black woman *US*
• But O.J. had the "good-looking-man" factor going for him. Those middle-aged sisters came to court every day and stared at this good-looking man they'd like to fuck.—Chris Rock, *Rock This!*, p. 204,
• Sitting up on the customer's seat was a big fine sister who was popping her fingers and wiggling to the music and smiling at me because our eyes had met.—Eldridge Cleaver, *Soul on Ice*, p. 28, 1968
• And some sister was stepping forward, saying, "Who got guns?!" —Bobby Seale, *A Lonely Rage*, p. 199, 1978
• FLOYD: There used to be a time when sisters didn't know shit about gettin' their pussy licked.—*True Romance*, 1993

3 a form of address between homosexual men *UK*
This **CAMP** adoption of the feminine form is also reflected in the cross-gender assignment of pronouns.
- [T]hey were much too butch pour moi, sister[.] —the cast of 'Aspects of Love', Prince of Wales Theatre, *Palare (Boy Dancer Talk) for Beginners*, 1989–92

4 a fellow homosexual *US*
- Sister – an intimate friend and confidant who is not a lover. —Anon., *The Gay Girl's Guide*, p. 15, 1949
- Right here – behind those trees – my 'sister' will watch out for us. —John Rechy, *City of Night*, p. 194, 1963
- —Florida Legislative Investigation Committee (Johns Committee), *Homosexuality and Citizenship in Florida*, 1964: 'Glossary of homosexual terms and deviate acts'
- When he annexes a new lover he can depend on the fact that his best pal or "sister" as chums are known in the "gay world," is going to do his very best to get the new acquisition into bed. —Antony James, *America's Homosexual Underground*, p. 30, 1965
- I have been invited home to meet one number's lover for a sandwich, have been groped accidentally by platonic acquaintances (I never liked "sister"), and have had many an ego satisfaction. —John Francis Hunter, *The Gay Insider*, p. 102–103, 1971
- Face it, girl, Archie's a sister. —*Chasing Amy*, 1997

5 a female fellow member of a countercultural or underground political movement *US*
- Each service should be performed by a tight gang of brothers and sisters whose commitment should enable them to handle an overload of work with ability and enthusiasm. —*The Digger Papers*, p. 15, August 1968

sister act *noun*
a relationship, usually sexual, between two homosexuals with the same orientation *US*
- —*The Guild Dictionary of Homosexual Terms*, p. 41, 1965

sister girl *noun*
used as a female-to-female term of address, often sternly *US*
- Sister girl, if you don't fix your attitude you're going to fall over it. —Connie Eble (Editor), *UNC-CH Campus Slang*, p. 6, Fall 1989

sister hix *noun*
in craps, a six *US, 1983*
- —Thomas L. Clark, *The Dictionary of Gambling and Gaming*, p. 202, 1987

sisterhood *noun*
the bond that unites male homosexuals *US*
- —*Maledicta*, p. 225, 1979: 'Kinks and queens: linguistic and cultural aspects of the terminology for gays'

sistren *noun*
(of women) friends *UK*
Conventional 'sisters' with religious and political overtones adopted for everyday use by the West Indian and UK black communities.
- [L]ooking out for our bredren, sistren still[.] —Diran Adebayo, *My Once Upon A Time*, p. 21, 2000

sit *noun*
1 in harness racing, the position immediatley behind another horse, thus using the other horse as a wind-break *US*

2 in horse racing, a contract for a jockey to ride a race *AUSTRALIA*
- —Ned Wallish, *The Truth Dictionary of Racing Slang*, p. 74, 1989

sit *verb*
▸ **sit like Miss Queenie**
to sit with your legs crossed as others work *DOMINICA, 1977*

▸ **sit on your hands**
to refrain from applause at a moment when applause would be appropriate *US*
- —Don Wilmeth, *The Language of American Popular Entertainment*, p. 244, 1981

▸ **sit tight**
to stay where you are; especially to remain in place when it would be easier to go *UK*
- [T]he porter buzzed upstairs to see if you were expected. We sat tight while this got done[.] —J.J. Connolly, *Know Your Enemy [britpulp]*, p. 155, 1999

▸ **sit up and beg**
describes elderly cars and old-fashioned bicycles and motorcycles; also the position adopted by drivers of such vehicles *UK, 1979*
- [T]he image of an idealized black sit-up-and-beg bicycle, with a scarf flapping behind you in the wind. —Philippe Delerm, *We Could Almost Eat Outside*, p. 79, 1999

sit-and-grab *noun*
in a carnival, a food concession with seating *US*
- —*American Speech*, p. 308–309, December 1960: 'Carnival talk'

sit-arse *verb*
to wait; to do nothing *UK*
A contraction of 'sit on your arse'.
- They're coming for me, I fucking know it. I'm not gonna sit-arse to find out. —Mark Powell, *Snap*, p. 19, 2001

sit beside her *noun*
a spider *UK*
Rhyming slang that seems to have its origins in the nursery rhyme 'Little Miss Muffet'.
- —Ray Puxley, *Cockney Rabbit*, 1992

sitch *noun*
a situation *US*
- —*Current Slang*, p. 5, Spring 1967
- I'll take full control of the sitch. —Niall Griffiths, *Kelly + Victor*, p. 18, 2002
- I come in and yell, "What's the sitch?" —*Rated*, p. 44, June 2002

sitcom *noun*
a situation comedy *US, 1964*
A protocol for television comedies since the early 1950s in which the humour is drawn from the confluence of characters and situations.
- The fact that he [Colin Powell] was chairman of the Joint Chiefs of Staff makes him the equivalent of a sitcom in a good time slot. Is "Suddenly Susan" any good? We don't know. It's on after "Seinfeld." —Chris Rock, *Rock This!*, p. 16, 1997
- It's a bad week for Davina McCall, who really shouldn't have been persuaded to star in the sub-Friends sitcom Sam's Game (Monday ITV) —*Radio Times*, p. 11, 12th May 2001

sit-down *noun*
1 a meeting or conversation over a meal or while sitting *UK, 1861*
- One only had to see the newspaper photograph of Mr. Shanker as he emerged from a "sit-down" with city officials to know that this "creditor" had been the victim of a very high-class mugging. —Mario Puzo, *Inside Las Vegas*, p. 46, 1977
- At first Strike had enjoyed these sit-downs, but lately this street-corner-prince business had become a little old. —Richard Price, *Clockers*, p. 317, 1992

2 in organised crime, a discussion of a dispute between members of the crime enterprise with a final and binding decision rendered by a leader or group of leaders *US*
- [W]hat are you going to say at the sitdown – that you killed his brother because he refused a drink? —Edwin Torres, *Carlito's Way*, p. 82, 1975
- Spino, his representative, should at the moment be putting it all together for his dream, in a sit-down with the representatives of dissatisfied Mafiosi in families across country. —Iceberg Slim (Robert Beck), *Death Wish*, p. 267, 1977
- —H. Craig Collins, *Street Gangs*, p. 224, 1979
- I got to go into town for a sit-down. —Richard Condon, *Prizzi's Honor*, p. 254, 1982
- Before you could touch a made guy, you had to have a good reason. There had to be a sit-down. —*Goodfellas*, 1990
- So they have the Zip call to suggest a sit-down, like there was a disagreement to discuss. —Elmore Leonard, *Pronto*, p. 345, 1993

3 a base camp or town in the rear, away from combat *US*
Vietnam war use.
- —Gregory Clark, *Words of the Vietnam War*, p. 470, 1990

sit down *verb*
to join a poker game *US*
- —Richard Jessup, *The Cincinnati Kid*, p. 10, 1963

sit-down money *noun*
amongst Australian Aboriginals, government welfare or unemployment benefits *AUSTRALIA, 1978*
- One old man came into town the other day and asked 'Which way my sit-down money?' – that's what they call the unemployment benefit. —Sandra Jobson, *Blokes*, p. 167, 1984

sit hard *verb*
(of ducks) to stay on an egg-nest as long as possible in the approach of danger *CANADA*
- Eider ducks and Old Squaws were "sitting hard" on their eggs and flushed practically in our faces. —*St. Johns Evening Telegram*, p. 21/4, 1st May 1958

sit in *verb*

1 to play by invitation with a band to which the musician does not belong *US, 1936*

- Wednesdays was celebrity night at the Palladium – all the showbiz and Jews doing cha-cha-ca-one-two-three, Marlon Brando sit in on conga (couldn't play to save his ass), out-of-town people – shit like that – all into Latin music.—Edwin Torres, *Carlito's Way*, p. 26, 1975

2 to join a poker game *US*

- —Albert H. Morehead, *The Complete Guide to Winning Poker*, p. 273, 1967

sit on it!

used as an expression of disapproval *US*

Popularised in the 1970s by frequent use on the television series *Happy Days*.

- —Connie Eble (Editor), *UNC-CH Campus Slang*, p. 6, March 1979

sitrep *noun*

a situation report *UK*

Military.

- to get into an area where we could send our sitrep—Andy McNab, *Immediate Action*, p. 102, 1995

sit-still *noun*

in horse racing, a style of riding based on patience *US*

- —Tom Ainslie, *Ainslie's Complete Guide to Thoroughbred Racing*, p. 338, 1976

sitter *noun*

1 a woman who works in a bar, encouraging male customers to drink and to buy them drinks *US*

- —*Maledicta*, p. 150, Summer/Winter 1986–1987: 'Sexual slang: prostitutes, pedophiles, flagellators, transvestites, and necrophiles'

2 a hostess in a brothel, neither prostitute nor madam *AUSTRALIA*

- —Thommo, *The Dictionary of Australian Swearing and Sex Sayings*, p. 119, 1985

3 a person who monitors and comforts an alcohol or drug addict who is going through the initial stages of detoxification *US*

A term used in twelve-step recovery programmes such as Alcoholics Anonymous.

- —Christopher Cavanaugh, *AA to Z*, p. 162, 1998

4 a person who guides another or others through an LSD experience *US, 1966*

An allusion to the practice of babysitting.

- —Richard A. Spears, *The Slang and Jargon of Drugs and Drink*, p. 455, 1986

5 in pool, a ball perched on the lip of a pocket *US, 1924*

- —Mike Shamos, *The Illustrated Encyclopedia of Billiards*, p. 214, 1993

sitting breeches *noun*

the trousers worn (figuratively) by visitors who have overstayed their welcome *BARBADOS*

- —Frank A. Collymore, *Barbadian Dialect*, p. 103, 1965

sitting britches *noun*

the trousers worn (figuratively) by an idler or laggard *US*

- —Charles F. Haywood, *Yankee Dictionary*, p. 153, 1963

sitting down *noun*

in fencing, the 'on-guard/en garde' position *UK*

From the bending of the legs.

- —E.D. Morton, *Martini A-Z of Fencing*, 1988

sitting duck *noun*

1 an easy target *UK, 1944*

Originally military; figurative use of hunting imagery.

- He was a sitting duck for planes[.]—Johnny Speight, *It Stands to Reason*, p. 60, 1973

2 a stolen car discovered by police through serendipitous checking of number plates *US*

- "How often you pick up a sitting duck?" asked Serge, to change the subject, checking a license plate against the numbers on the hot sheet.—Joseph Wambaugh, *The New Centurions*, p. 41, 1970

sitting on a goldmine

used admiringly of a sexually attractive person, especially one who does not take financial advantage of his or her attraction *US*

- —Bruce Rodgers, *The Queens' Vernacular*, 1972
- You'll never win with women because they're sitting on a goldmine. They'll always have the power.—Stephen Ackroyd, *Organizational Misbehaviour*, p. 134, 1999

sit upon *noun*

the posterior *UK, 1961*

Euphemistic.

sitzmark *noun*

among British Columbia skiers, the imprint left in the snow from a skier's fall *CANADA*

- —Tom Parkin, *WetCoast Words*, p. 125, 1989

Siwash *noun*

a stupid person *CANADA*

Originally from Chinook jargon, this term was used by voyageurs for Indians, but over time it has become an insult both to the native peoples and to the person so designated.

- "Anywhere's you goddam stupid Siwash." Chief nodded, staring down at his feet and stifling his anger at being racially insulted.—Hugh Garner, *The Intruders*, p. 108, 1976

Siwash *verb*

to place a non-Indian person on the list of people not allowed to buy alcohol *CANADA*

- As a verb, "siwash" means both to travel light, sleeping in the open, and also in more general use, "being siwashed" means placing a white man on the Interdict (Indian) list.—Tom Parkin, *WetCoast Words*, p. 126, 1989

Siwash blanket *noun*

low cloud cover *CANADA*

- A Siwash blanket portends weather warmer than if the ceiling were higher.—Bill Casselman, *Canadian Food Words*, p. 275, 1998

Siwash logger *noun*

a beachcomber *CANADA*

This term carries on the early derogatory use of siwash for any Indians or their customs.

- "I'm a Siwash logger, am I? Well, I am." At 35, he has worked as a lumberjack, fisherman, and beachcomber, salvaging logs from broken booms.—*Star Weekly*, p. 2, 5th June 1962

Siwash wind *noun*

a storm that comes on quickly *CANADA*

- A Siwash wind is a Pacific Coast localism for any fresh gale that blows up briskly.—Bill Casselman, *Canadian Food Words*, p. 275, 1998

six *noun*

1 a lookout during a crime *US*

- On that job I was "keeping six." That's a safecracker's code for someone who is assigned to watch at a window for cops or to check out and deactivate any alarm system that might screw up the job.—Thomas Renner and Cecil Kirby, *Mafia Enforcer*, p. 38, 1987

2 a six-pack of a beverage *US*

- Gimme a 6 of Diet Cokes and 6 of Budweiser.—*The Bad Lieutenant*, 1992

3 a six fluid ounce glass of beer *AUSTRALIA*

- What do we call them? Fours, sixes and eights.—John O'Grady, *It's Your Shout, Mate!*, p. 56, 1972

4 a unit commander *US*

- Roger that, Six, but the doc says he's in pretty bad shape.—Charles Anderson, *The Grunts*, p. 45, 1976
- Six says torch this place!—*Platoon*, 1986

▸ behind the six

without funds *US*

- —Albert H. Morehead, *The Complete Guide to Winning Poker*, p. 256, 1967

▸ take six

to re-enlist in the military for six years *US*

- —Carl Fleischhauer, *A Glossary of Army Slang*, p. 20, 1968

six-and-eight *noun*

a poor condition *UK*

Rhyming slang for **STATE**.

- Wasn't home till sparrow-fart and my old tiger [wife] was in a right six-and-eight.—Red Daniells, 1980

six-and-eight *adjective*

honest, legitimate *UK, 1959*

Rhyming slang for **STRAIGHT** (honest).

- [H]e's – well, not six-and-eight exactly, but settled down[.]—Derek Raymond (Robin Cook), *The Crust on its Uppers*, p. 41, 1962

six and four *noun*
heroin mixed with other substances *UK*
Probably from the ratio of ingredients.
- —Angela Devlin, *Prison Patter*, p. 105, 1996

sixer *noun*
1 anything that counts or scores as six, especially a six in cricket *UK, 1870*
- "Sometimes four runs, sometimes a sixer," Gibreel told Allie, who was happy to see him laugh. —Salman Rushdie, *The Satanic Verses*, p. 353, 1988

2 a six-pack of beer *US*
- Deek killed his bottle, slipped it back into the sixer, and patted his belly with a satisfied sigh. —Jess Mowry, *Way Past Cool*, p. 40, 1992
- But hey man, know us, we've got a few sixers. You with us? —*Dazed and Confused*, 1993

3 a jail sentence of six months *US*
- —Vincent J. Monteleone, *Criminal Slang*, p. 210, 1949

4 a corporal punishment of six strokes with a cane *UK, 1927*
A variation of SIX OF THE BEST.

sixes *noun*
a small drink of rum *TRINIDAD AND TOBAGO, 1968*
Originally costing six cents.
- —Lise Winer, *Dictionary of the English/Creole of Trinidad & Tobago*, 2003

▸ **all the sixes**
sixty-six *UK, 1943*
In Bingo, House or Tombola the formula 'all the' announces a double number.

six feet under *adjective*
dead and buried *UK, 1942*
- I realized that I was laying the groundwork for playing long after I am six feet under. So, I'll keep acting. —Craig Fass, *Six Degrees of Kevin Bacon*, 1996

six-for-fiver *noun*
a money lender who operates informally to advance workers money on their wages *US*
- At that time, Jake, a former roustabout with the Ringling Brothers Circus, had been a six-for-fiver around the pioneer tent and shack towns. That is, he bought wages from workers in advance of their due date, giving the needy borrower five dollars for each six he had coming. —Jim Thompson, *Bad Boy*, p. 324, 1953

six-four; six-fo' *noun*
▷ see: 64

sixie; sixie from Dixie *noun*
in craps, the number six *US*
- —Steve Kuriscak, *Casino Talk*, p. 68, 1985

six moon *noun*
a six-month prison sentence *UK*
- It was six months, likely to serve three. "Six moon," as they put it in her; or more probably "six moon – canter", in predicting the ease with which they intended to see it out. —Chritopher Brookmyre, *Boiling a Frog*, p. 41, 2000

six o'clock girl *noun*
a thin girl *US*
- —Marcus Hanna Boulware, *Jive and Slang of Students in Negro Colleges*, 1947

six o'clock jump *noun*
an enema given to a patient the night before surgery *US*
- —*American Speech*, p. 154, April 1946: 'GI words from the separation center and proctology ward'

six o'clock swill *noun*
a last minute rush for drinks in a hotel bar prior to six o'clock closing time *AUSTRALIA, 1955*
Now obsolete as opening hours for hotels have been expanded.
- Perhaps it all dates back to the six o'clock swill in those dim dark days of the past when men had to get down as much grog as in the short time available before the pubs shut. —Sue Rhodes, *Now you'll think I'm awful*, p. 55, 1967

six of the best *noun*
a corporal punishment of six strokes with a cane *UK, 1912*
- [I]n one sketch capital punishment is justified as being a mere "six of the best" for a naughty schoolboy[.] —Humphrey Carpenter, *A Great Silly Grin*, 2002
- We give naughty teenagers six of the best and detention, at the same time as we reward ourselves with an A-plus for effort. —*The Big Issue*, p. 10, 2003

six-pack *noun*
1 a well developed and defined abdominal musculature *US*
From the superficial resemblance between the muscles and a six-pack of beer cans.
- —Pamela Munro, *U.C.L.A. Slang*, p. 107, 1997
- I've got six-pack abs. I'm eight inches cut. —Tristan Taorrino, *The Village Voice*, 4th April 2000
- From "Peter Andre's six pack" to "I do knees" – the Body in Young People's Moral Discourse. —Kathryn Backett-Milburn and Linda McKie (editors), *Constructing Gendered Bodies*, p. 141, 2001
- Forget the six-pack. Instead, flaunt your paunch with pride[.] —*The Guardian*, 18th April 2003

2 a car carburettor system with six barrels *US*
- —John Edwards, *Auto Dictionary*, p. 152, 1993

six-packer *noun*
a man with well developed and defined abdominal musculature; a well-built man *SOUTH AFRICA*
Teen slang.
- —*Sunday Times (South Africa)*, 1st June 2003

six-packs *noun*
in craps, a roll of twelve *US*
- —Chris Fagans and David Guzman, *A Guide to Craps Lingo*, p. 38, 1999

sixpennyworth *noun*
a prison term of six months *UK*
- —*Evening News (London)*, 12th November 1957

six, six, and a kick *noun*
military discipline consisting of six months imprisonment, six months forfeiture of pay and a bad-conduct discharge from the service *US*
- —Linda Reinberg, *In the Field*, p. 199, 1991

sixteen *noun*
an M-16 rifle *US*
- They made us switch to the M-16 during our tour. I liked the fourteen much better. The sixteens were unreliable, like a Mattel toy. —Al Santoli, *To Bear Any Burden*, p. 106, 1985

sixteenth *noun*
a sixteenth of an ounce (of drugs) *US*
- How about dilaudid, you got any sixteenths? —*Drugstore Cowboy*, 1988
- There's a sixteenth of personal which is a piece of leb I been savin'[.] —Nick Barlay, *Curvy Lovebox*, p. 89, 1997
- But then a call came over the mobile for a sixteenth, which would mean another $100 in my pocket. —Lanre Fehintola, *Charlie Says...*, p. 1, 2000

six tits *noun*
in poker, three queens *US*
Collected from William E. Rippe by Peter Tamony in March 1948.

six-to-five!; sixty-five!; sixty fifth street!
used as a warning among criminals or swindlers that a police officer is nearby *US*
- —Hyman E. Goldin et al., *Dictionary of American Underworld Lingo*, p. 195, 1950

six to four *noun*
a whore *UK, 1939*
Rhyming slang, from racing odds. Ray Puxley, *Cockney Rabbit*, 1992, wonders if 6–4 is the odds on catching something from one.

six-to-six *noun*
1 a prostitute *FIJI*
From their working hours – evening to dawn. Recorded by Jan Tent in 1996.

2 a conversation between two unit commanders *US*
- —Linda Reinberg, *In the Field*, p. 200, 1991

six-trey *noun*
sixty-three; 63rd Street *US*
- —David Claerbaut, *Black Jargon in White America*, p. 79, 1972

sixty days *noun*
in dice games, a roll of six *US*
- —Frank Garcia, *Marked Cards and Loaded Dice*, p. 264, 1962

sixty-eight *noun*
used as a humorous variation on sixty-nine – you give me oral sex and I'll owe you one *US*
- — *Maledicta*, p. 126, Summer/Winter 1982: 'Dyke diction: the language of lesbians'

sixty-four dollar question; sixty-four thousand dollar question; sixty-four million dollar question *noun*
a question that gets to the heart of the matter *US, 1942*
The US radio quiz show *Take It or Leave It* offered a highest prize of $64, giving rise to the catch-phrase 'sixty-four dollar question'. The phrase gained currency and three decimal places in televised quiz shows on both sides of the Atlantic.
- Now for the sixty-four-dollar question, Mike. — Mickey Spillane, *My Gun is Quick*, p. 58, 1950
- Inevitably, there is one question which every customer puts to a prostitute – what might be called the sixty-four-dollar question. — Polly Adler, *A House is Not a Home*, p. 127, 1953
- Why? Now here we have a $64,000,000 question. — Dick Clark, *To Goof or Not to Goof*, p. 25, 1963
- Because now I'm gonna ask you some sixty-four-thousand-dollar questions and I want the truth[.] — Richard Price, *Clockers*, p. 532, 1992
- But now what? What does Ray do now? That is the sixty-four thousand dollar question. — *Copland*, 1997

sixty-nine; sixty-niner *noun*
▷ see: 69

six-up *noun*
▷ see: 6-UP

six up!
used as a warning in the usage of counterculturalists associated with the Rainbow Nation gatherings and the Grateful Dead that law enforcement officials are approaching *US*
- — David Shenk and Steve Silberman, *Skeleton Key*, p. 262, 1994
- — Jim Crotty, *How to Talk American*, p. 290, 1997

size queen *noun*
a homosexual male or a woman who is attracted to men with large penises *US*
- "I gotta know how big it is before buying," a fairy said to me. Another one with him lisps, "Mary! He'll think we're size queens!" — John Rechy, *City of Night*, p. 365, 1963
- — Guy Strait, *The Lavendar Lexicon*, 1st June 1964
- — *The Guild Dictionary of Homosexual Terms*, p. 42, 1965
- So at the baths the rivalry comes out into the open, and size queens, young or old, have a field day. — John Francis Hunter, *The Gay Insider*, p. 152, 1971
- Two things I detest – size queens and small cocks. — Bruce Rodgers, *The Queens' Vernacular*, p. 182, 1972
- — *Adult Video News*, p. 40, September 1995
- All cocks are the same. Size queens try so hard to put personality where it doesn't belong. — Peter Sotos, *Index*, p. 12, 1996

sizzle *noun*
1 a sister, in the sense as a female companion, especially in the phrase 'fa' shizzle my sizzle' *US*
A hip-hop, urban black coinage, formed as a rhyming reduplication of **SHIZZLE** (sure, yes). After 'fa' shizzle my nizzle' (yes my nigger).

2 an illegal drug *US*
- You don't want to walk through the street with that package of 'sizzle' on you. — Iceberg Slim (Robert Beck), *Pimp*, p. 133, 1969

sizzle *verb*
to be executed by electrocution in the electric chair *US*
- — Ralph de Sola, *Crime Dictionary*, p. 138, 1982

sizzler *noun*
1 in cricket, an exceedingly fast ball; an extremely fast horse, etc *UK, 1961*
- He first dragged down a sizzler at square leg from the bat of the dangerous Lou Vincent to remove him for six. — *New Zealand Herald*, 17th January 2004

2 an unskilled cook *US*
- — John Gould, *Maine Lingo*, p. 256, 1975

sizzle seat *noun*
the electric chair; capital punishment by electrocution *US*
- — Ralph de Sola, *Crime Dictionary*, p. 138, 1982

SK8 *noun*
in text messaging, a skate or to skate *US*
A variant spelling; one of several constructions in which a syllable pronounced 'ate' is replaced by the homophone 'eight'.
- — *SK8 Essentials (Top That Guides)*, 2002
- [Avril] Lavigne hit ["Sk8er Boi"] to sk8 on to silver screen. — *The Guardian*, 28th May 2003

ska *noun*
a rhythmic musical style that evolved into reggae *JAMAICA*
Coinage, in the late 1950s or very early 60s, is generally credited to Jamaican bassist Cluet Johnson when trying to explain the sound and rhythm of ya-ya music; Cluet Johnson is also recorded as using 'skavoovee' and 'love skavoovie' as a nonsensical but American-sounding greeting.
- Ernest Ranglin [...] says the word was coined by musicians "to talk about the skat! skat! skat! scratchin' guitar strum that goes behind." — Timothy White, *Catch a Fire*, 1993
- None of that shite, fucking ska music. — Tony Wilson, *24 Hour Party People*, p. 56, 2002
- [T]he Ninja Tune turntablist balks at nothing in his perusal of vinyl stores in search of a good tune. — *Metro*, p. 23, 17th May 2002

skag *and variants*
▷ see: SCAG

skagged up *adjective*
intoxicated by or addicted to heroin *UK*
- We're meeting half the arseholes in the business and I'm skagged up. — Shaun Ryder, *Shaun Ryder... in His Own Words*, 1993

skallywag *noun*
▷ see: SCALLYWAG

skanger *noun*
a member of a Dublin/Kilkenny subcultural urban adolescent, teenage and young-adult-male grouping that is given to hanging around and causing trouble *IRELAND*
- — John Morton, *Skegs and Skangers*, 2001

skank *noun*
1 a girl whose sole attraction is her immorality and sexual availability *US*
An abusive description possibly derived from 'skunk'.
- If you saw her on the street when she wasn't too sick you probably'd most likely as not wouldn't even know she was a junkie. She's not like these other skanks around here. — James Mills, *The Panic in Needle Park*, p. 25, 1966
- That his sister was a royal skank who fucked for a dime. — Richard Price, *The Wanderers*, p. 33, 1974
- It was a totally kick-ass car. When you had a car like this you didn't mind so much that your boyfriend was boinking a skank. — Janet Evanovitch, *High Five*, 1999

2 a prostitute *US*
- Jeez, what a fuckin' sorry sight. Heroin skank after heroin skank. — Christopher Brookmyre, *The Sacred Art of Stealing*, p. 185, 2002

3 a confidence trick; a fraud *UK*
After **SKANK** (to steal). West Indian, hence UK black.
- [S]he was going to be one of those girls who were always trying to pull a skank. — Donald Gorgon, *Cop Killer*, p. 42, 1994
- — Angela Devlin, *Prison Patter*, p. 105, 1996
- [N]o doubt plotting another quality skank. — Diran Abedayo, *My Once Upon A Time*, p. 20, 2000

4 nastiness, filth *US*
- Virgins, I love 'em. No diseases, no loose as a goose pussy, no skank. — *Kids*, 1995

skank *verb*
1 to work a confidence trick; to operate a fraud; to work behind someone's back *UK*
West Indian and UK black slang which spread into wider criminal circles. An earlier, surviving usage is a dance style, which imagery suggests the possible etymology is of a figurative dance around the victim of the trick.
- Tucker couldn't get his head round it, that this cheeky geezer had tried to so blatantly skank him with a fake fifty. — Dave Courtney, *Raving Lunacy*, p. 101, 2000
- And if I had intended to skank him wouldn't I have been long gone by now[?] — Lanre Fehintola, *Charlie Says...*, p. 108, 2000
- [H]e's been skanking him bad style. — Kevin Sampson, *Clubland*, p. 2, 2002

2 to move to reggae rhythms in a particular loose-limbed style *JAMAICA*
- De tongue plays a beat / De body starts skanking / Dis poetry is quick an childish[.] — Benjamin Zephaniah, *Man to Man*, p. 12, 1992

- [T]he greying rastaman behind the sound decks was happy to skank along with the music as he drew on a pungent stick of sensi. —Karline Smith, *Moss Side Massive*, p. 10, 1994

3 to steal something *UK*

- Backup matches just in case some fucker skanks his three clipper lighters in different colours. —Nick Barlay, *Curvy Lovebox*, p. 34, 1997
- The temptation is there to skank somethin but I don't bother[.] —Niall Griffiths, *Kelly + Victor*, p. 224, 2002
- —Peter Patrick, *Some Recent Jamaican Creole Words*, 2003

skank off *verb*

to play truant *UK, 1990s*

- Skank off school an' go the West End or som'ing. —Nick Barlay, *Curvy Lovebox*, p. 11, 1997

skank-pit *noun*

an unpleasant, distasteful place *US*

- I've got to be crazy letting you drag me back to this skank-pit. —*200 Cigarettes*, 1999

skanky *adjective*

ugly; cheap; nasty *US*

- Watch them on 100th or 117th Street – skanky, dirty, always in pairs like faggots, never no pussy; don't want to know about no pussy, just that spike. —Edwin Torres, *Carlito's Way*, p. 55, 1975
- —Mary Corey and Victoria Westermark, *Fer Shurr! How to be a Valley Girl*, 1982
- —Pamela Munro, *U.C.L.A. Slang*, p. 76, 1989
- Here's another one I had. Real skanky-looking guy, who wants him? —Elmore Leonard, *Maximum Bob*, p. 164, 1991
- This is a room of about 50 skanky groupies and others. —*Wayne's World 2*, 1993

skat; skattie *noun*

used as a term of endearment *SOUTH AFRICA, 1964*

From Afrikaans *schat* (treasure).

- —Jean Branford, *A Dictionary of South African English*, 1978

skate *noun*

1 an easy task *US*

- It wouldn't be a real long hump, but it wouldn't be a real skate either – about six or seven clicks. —Charles Anderson, *The Grunts*, p. 80, 1976
- Normally resupply day was a skate, a day the command cut the boonierats some slack. —John Del Vecchio, *The 13th Valley*, p. 351, 1982

2 an extremely unattractive woman who is seen as a sex object, especially one who is ravaged by age *UK*

Possibly from obsolete 'skate' (an inferior horse) and influenced by the sense 'an unpleasant man'.

- At the end of the day, I like skates. —Kevin Sampson, *Clubland*, p. 65, 2002

3 an unpleasant man *US, 1896*

4 a lazy and/or incompetent worker *US*

US Army usage.

- —*Seattle Times*, p. A9, 12th April 1998: 'Grunts, squids not grunting from the same dictionary'

5 an act of letting someone escape wrongdoing without punishment *US*

- So, feature, Dudley gave Johnny a skate on the fur job and confided some of his own crime gigs to him[.] —James Ellroy, *White Jazz*, p. 302, 1992

6 a tyre *US*

- —"Slingo", *The Official CB Slang Dictionary Handbook*, p. 55, 1976

7 a motorcyle *US*

- —*Current Slang*, p. 12, Winter 1970

▷ **see:** ROLLERSKATE

▸ **do a skate**

to vanish *NEW ZEALAND*

- —David McGill, *David McGill's Complete Kiwi Slang Dictionary*, p. 115, 1998

skate *verb*

1 to get away with something; to escape punishment *US, 1945*

- I'm saying you'll skate – if you curtail your plans with Mickey. —James Ellroy, *White Jazz*, p. 292, 1992
- Leeds sensed that Fortney was as indifferent and lazy as he was. "Wanna let 'em skate?" —Joseph Wambaugh, *Floaters*, p. 81, 1996

2 to win easily *UK: SCOTLAND*

- The Jags'll skate that gemme [game] the morrow [tomorrow]. —Michael Munro, *The Complete Patter*, p. 141, 1996

3 in the used car business, to steal another salesman's sale *US*

- —Peter Mann, *How to Buy a Used Car Without Getting Gypped*, p. 195, 1975

4 to dance *IRELAND*

- —*Great Tuam Annual*, p. 87, 1991

5 to be without money *TRINIDAD AND TOBAGO, 1996*

- —Lise Winer, *Dictionary of the English/Creole of Trinidad & Tobago*, 2003

skate Betty *noun*

a girl who associates with skateboarders, perhaps skateboarding herself *US*

- —*Macon Telegraph and News*, p. 9A, 18th June 1989

skate jockey *noun*

a driver of a small car, especially a sports car *US*

Citizens' band radio slang, combines 'skate' (small car) with another form of 'driver'.

- —*Complete CB Slang Dictionary*, p. 84, 1976
- —Peter Chippindale, *The British CB Book*, p. 159, 1981

skate rat *noun*

a devoted, perhaps skilled skateboarder *US*

- —Pamela Munro, *U.C.L.A. Slang*, p. 76, 1989

skating *adjective*

drunk *UK*

- She had nearly half a bottle – and, boy, was she skating? —Douglas Leechman,

sked *noun*

in remote country regions, a schedule for a radio call *AUSTRALIA, 1946*

- During a 'sked' she could communicate with distant stations as a city child might dangle on the end of a telephone. —Leslie Rees, *Spinifex Walkabout*, p. 226, 1953

sked *verb*

to schedule *US*

A shortening of the US pronunciation.

- Jane Fonda and Marisa Tomei were skedded to appear in "The Vagina Monologues" in Mumbai on Monday[.] —*Variety*, 8th March 2004

skedaddle; skiddadle *verb*

to leave in a hurry *US, 1861*

Originally US Civil War slang, with claims of Swedish and Danish origins probably disproved.

- Are we all chasing our backsides round the mulberry bush, while Kilroy skidaddles to Timbuctoo via the London Underground? —Troy Kennedy Martin, *Z Cars*, p. 149, 1962
- Let's skidaddle down the nearest tube [London underground] and get cracking. —Barry Humphries, *Bazza Pulls It Off!*, 1971
- Our buckboad was skedaddling down a narrow dusty road a short piece from home when a rut in the road flung off a bag of fertilizer. —Iceberg Slim (Robert Beck), *Doom Fox*, p. 117, 1978

Skedaddle Ridge *noun*

a hill in southern New Brunswick *CANADA*

- Skedaddle Ridge reminds us that during the time of the US Civil War, this hill was a favourite spot of American southerners living and working in New England who were in sympathy with the Confederacy, did not wish to fight for the North, and skedaddled. —Bill Casselman, *Canadian Words*, p. 83–84, 1995

skee *noun*

1 whisky, especially low quality, low cost whisky *US*

- —Hyman E. Goldin et al., *Dictionary of American Underworld Lingo*, p. 195, 1950
- —Harry Orsman, *A Dictionary of Modern New Zealand Slang*, p. 122, 1999

2 opium; heroin *US, 1960*

- —Richard A. Spears, *The Slang and Jargon of Drugs and Drink*, p. 456, 1986
- —Mike Haskins, *Drugs*, p. 284, 2003

skeef *noun*

an attractive female *JAMAICA*

- —Velma Pollard, *Dread Talk*, p. 45, 2000

skeef *adverb*

disapprovingly *SOUTH AFRICA, 1969*

From Afrikaans *skeef* (askew).

- What's your response when ordinary girls check you skeef? [...] I don't like women who look skeef. They must understand that I'm still the same person I was before bikes, just maybe having more fun. —*Sunday Times (South Africa)*, 30th March 2002

skeenteen *noun*

used as an imaginary high number *US*

- —Collin Baker et al., *College Undergraduate Slang Study Conducted at Brown University*, p. 197, 1968

skeet *noun*

1 a girl *UK*

- —Julian Johnson, *Urban Survival*, p. 258, 2003

2 in poker, a nonstandard hand consisting of a 9, a 5, a 2, one card between 5 and 9 and one card between 2 and 5 *US*

- —Irwin Steig, *Common Sense in Poker*, p. 187, 1963

skeet *verb*

1 to ejaculate *US*

- —Gary K. Farlow, *Prison-ese*, p. 64, 2002

2 to eject liquid from a syringe *US*

- To emphasize his point, he stuck the works back down in a glass of water sitting next to him and drew up a dropper full of water. He slowly skeeted it out on the floor, making sure the needle wasn't stopped up before loaning it out. —Donald Goines, *Dopefiend*, p. 8, 1971

skeeve *noun*

a disgusting individual *US, 1976*

- You wouldn't believe what this skeeve wrote[.] —Howard Stern, *Miss America*, p. 449, 1995
- —Claudio R. Salvucci, *The Philadelphia Dialect Dictionary*, p. 58, 1996

skeeve; skeeve out *verb*

to disgust *US, 1976*

- —Claudio R. Salvucci, *The Philadelphia Dialect Dictionary*, p. 58, 1996
- And by the way, there is no image – none – that skeevs me out more than that of the hypocritical, hairline-challenged major (Giuliani of New York) having sex with anyone. —*The Village Voice*, 30th May 2000

skeevie *noun*

a disgusting person *US*

Teen slang.

- —*American Weekly*, p. 2, 14th August 1955

skeevie; skeevy *adjective*

disgusting *US*

- —*Philadelphia Magazine*, p. 124, March 1976
- —Claudio R. Salvucci, *The Philadelphia Dialect Dictionary*, p. 58, 1996
- —Connie Eble (Editor), *UNC-CH Campus Slang*, p. 7, March 1996
- Only skeever stoners fart. —Kevin Smith, *Jay and Silent Bob Strike Back*, p. 39, 2001

skeevosa *noun*

a disgusting individual *US*

An extension of SKEEVE (a disgusting individual).

- What a skeevosa! [...] He sounded like the King of Siam, carrying on like a sheik with a concubine. —Howard Stern, *Miss America*, p. 287, 1995

skeeze *verb*

to have sex *US*

- So you skeezin', or what? —*New Jack City*, 1990

skeezer *noun*

a woman who will perform sex for crack cocaine *US*

- Yo, is that the skeezer you met at Frankie's strip joint? —*New Jack City*, 1990
- —Terry Williams, *Crackhouse*, p. 151, 1992
- —Mark S. Fleisher, *Beggars & Thieves: Lives of Urban Street Criminals*, p. 291, 1995: 'Glossary'
- If a girl was labeled a hoe, a skeezer, or a freak by other students, no one seemed willing to defend her. —Nelson George, *Hip Hop America*, p. 177, 1998

skeezix *noun*

a fool *US*

After a character (a foundling, adopted by Walt and Phyllis Rumpus Blossom, who grew up to be the father of Chipper and Clovia) in Frank O. King's newspaper comic strip *Gasoline Alley*.

- Some skeezix from one of the local dailies was up here the other day to do a "human interest" story[.] —Lester Bangs, *Psychotic Reactions and Carburetor Dung*, p. 154, 1975

skeff *noun*

a confidence swindle *TRINIDAD AND TOBAGO, 1975*

- —Lise Winer, *Dictionary of the English/Creole of Trinidad & Tobago*, 2003

skeg *noun*

1 a surfer *AUSTRALIA, 1985*

The variant 'sceg' also exists.

- Surfies – waxheads or skegs to their rival tribes – are Sydney's longest surviving sub-culture. —*Sunday Telegraph*, p. 8, 8th April 1990

2 a member of a subcultural social grouping of pubescent or adolescent girls *IRELAND*

- —John Morton, *Skegs and Skangers*, 2001

3 a fin on a surfboard *US, 1962*

- —Grant W. Kuhns, *On Surfing*, p. 121, 1963
- —*Paradise of the Pacific*, p. 27, October 1963

skeg-first *adverb*

while surfing, said of the beginning of a ride with the tail of the surfboard pointing towards shore *US*

- —Michael V. Anderson, *The Bad, Rad, Not to Forget Way Cool Beach and Surf Discriptionary*, p. 18, 1988

skeg-head *noun*

a surfer *AUSTRALIA, 1988*

- You should go to college. You could go to Kings with the skeg-head here. —Phillip Gwynne, *Deadly Unna?*, p. 187, 1998

skein of thread; skein *noun*

a bed *UK*

Rhyming slang.

- [S]omething to rabbit [to talk] to the trouble about in the skein[.] —Ronnie Barker, *Fletcher's Book of Rhyming Slang*, p. 5, 1979

skeletons fucking on a tin roof

used as a perfect simile for a rattling noise *US, 1961*

- As I moved out the jungle again with my new pack, I sounded like a couple of skeletons fucking on a tin roof and had to stop and repack it. —Thom Jones, *The Pugilist At Rest*, p. 53, 1993

skell; skel *noun*

a vagrant, especially of the thuggish sort *US*

Seemingly related to the C17 'skelder', an honorable cant term for 'a professional beggar' which was long obsolete when 'skell' started to show up in New York in the early 1970s. A favourite word of police television dramas in the 1990s; the screeplay by Gardner Stern for episode 2 of season 2 of *NYPD Blue* that aired in September 1994 was titled *For Whom the Skell Rolls*.

- Of course some a the skells from the bar worked their way up and congratulated and grabbed what they could. —Hubert Selby Jr, *Last Exit to Brooklyn*, p. 102, 1957
- Thus, when one policeman says to another, "Did you collar the skell?", he is asking, "Did you arrest the drunken derelict?" —*New York Times*, 15th February 1970
- I can't tell you damn decoy guys from the rest of the skels. —Charles Whited, *Chiodo*, p. 68, 1973
- See that skell in the dirty sneakers? He can't afford no gun, but he will tire-iron the first john that turns the corner. —Edwin Torres, *Q & A*, p. 19, 1977
- That's what he wanted, to be put out of his misery, like them skells you see in the middle of East Side Highway on a foggy night. —Edwin Torres, *After Hours*, p. 335, 1979
- Three fucking days living in the middle of these skels[.] —Vincent Patrick, *The Pope of Greenwich Village*, p. 121, 1979
- These "skells" are not merely down and out. Many are insane, checked out of New York hospitals in the early 1970's when it was decided that long-term institutionalization was doing them little good. —*New York Times*, p. 6–20, 31st January 1982
- The drug-pitch skells would rather tear off with a wallet than transact an actual exchange, and they make the teenage chicken fags seem like the most discreet commodity on the street. —Josh Alan Friedman, *Tales of Times Square*, p. 51, 1986
- —Carsten Stroud, *Close Pursuit*, p. 276, 1987
- But where was the satisfaction? Even the skells in the cells treated Jimmy like shit, not even regarding him as a real lawyer because he was free. —Richard Price, *Clockers*, p. 445, 1992
- Without me, you, personally, every fuckin' wiseguy skell around'll take a piece of your fuckin' Jew ass. —*Casino*, 1995

skerrick *noun*

a small amount of something *AUSTRALIA, 1854*

From British dialect.

- Although I was very much taken with this idea, all my experience with dentists did not supply one skerrick of fact to support my fiction. —Patsi Dunn, *Uni Sex*, p. 90, 1972

sketch *noun*

1 a situation, an arrangement *UK*

- You know the sketch, ring very early or very late. —J.J. Connolly, *Layer Cake*, p. 92, 2000

2 a term of endearment for someone *IRELAND*

- Noelie always said Johnny was a sound oul sketch. —Eamonn Sweeney, *Waiting for the Healer*, p. 122, 1997

▸ **keep sketch**

to keep watch *IRELAND*

- Back in the supermarket I started robbin' stuff from the other lads' lockers. Jemser, who had started using as well, would keep sketch out the back... —Howard Paul, *The Joy*, p. 50, 1996

sketch *adjective*

suspicious; threatening *US*

- —Connie Eble (Editor), *UNC-CH Campus Slang*, p. 9, Spring 2003

sketchy *noun*
an odd or weird person *UK*
Used amongst foot-powered scooter-riders.
• —Ben Sharpe, *Scooter Crazy*, p. 42, 2000

sketchy *adjective*
dangerous; possibly dangerous *US*
• —Connie Eble (Editor), *UNC-CH Campus Slang*, p. 9, October 2002

skew-whiff; skiwift *adjective*
awry; askew; at the wrong angle *UK, 1754*
• You drop a lobster crate, you know how it'll go skiwift? You see a barn leaning, and you say "the wind blew it skiwift." You got a crate in the water by the wharf, and the boat goes up against it, squash it skiwift! —Dirk van Loon, *Rural Delivery*, 1977
• Now, the trouble with doing your make-up on public transport is that it has a tendency to go a little skew-whiff. — *The Guardian*, 17th May 2003

ski *verb*
in soccer, to kick the ball unnecessarily high in the air *US*
• — Aviation Training Division, U.S. Navy, *The Naval Aviation Physical Training Manual*, p. 136, 1945: 'Glossary'

-ski *suffix*
used in combination to intensify an adjective or adverb *UK: SCOTLAND*
• And there'd maybe be a wee flash of steel, a wee puddle of blood and then offski. —Ian Pattison, *Rab C. Nesbitt*, 1988
• [T]he pizza kid's gone, vanished, goneski, but his moped's still parked at the kerb. —J.J. Connolly, *Know Your Enemy [britpulp]*, p. 145, 1999

ski bum *noun*
a ski enthusiast who spends as much time as possible skiing and as little time as possible working *US*
• — *American Speech*, p. 206, October 1963: 'The language of skiers'

ski bunny *noun*
a female who is learning to ski; a female who visits ski resorts for the company but does not ski *US*
• — *American Speech*, p. 206, October 1963: 'The language of skiers'

skid *noun*
heroin, especially when heavily adulterated *US, 1977*
• —Robert Ashton, *This Is Heroin*, p. 207, 2002
• —Mike Haskins, *Drugs*, p. 284, 2003

skid *verb*
while snowboarding, to slide down a slope sideways *US*
• —Doug Werner, *Snowboarders Start-Up*, p. 114, 1993: 'Glossary'

skid artist *noun*
a getaway driver *UK*
• —Angela Devlin, *Prison Patter*, p. 105, 1996

Skid Blvd. *noun*
a jocular honorific for a living area for poor people *CANADA*
• Their humble hovel on Skid Blvd. has been warmed by a coaliverous furnace. — *Toronto Globe and Mail*, p. 3–4, 29th April 1963

skiddadle *verb*
▷ see: **SKEDADDLE**

skiddies *noun*
1 underpants *UK*
• He was wearing a pair of skiddies, a T-shirt and flip-flops. —Andy McNab, *Immediate Action*, p. 33, 1995

2 faecal marks in underwear *UK*
• CHERYL: What's Dave? Y-fronts or boxers? DENISE: Whatever he wears, they're always full of skiddies. —Caroline Aherne and Craig Cash, *The Royle Family*, 1999

skidge *verb*
attack! *AUSTRALIA*
A command inciting a dog to attack. A variant of **SKITCH!**.
• 'Skidge him, Nip. Kill! Kill!' —Kerry Cue, *Crooks, Chooks and Bloody Ratbags*, p. 67, 1983

skid lid *noun*
1 a safety helmet or crash helmet *US*
• — *Current Slang*, p. 9, Spring 1968
• That's a gorgeous skid lid you got there, boy, but pull it up a little and lemme see those baby blues. —Joseph Wambaugh, *The Blue Knight*, p. 19, 1973
• —Lewis Poteet, *Car & Motorcyle Slang*, p. 180, 1992
• Brainbucket, skid lid, melon gear, crash hat. It doesn't matter what you call it, just as long as you have one – a helmet for hitting the slopes, trails, skating rinks and half-pipes. — *Times Union (Albany, New York)*, p. D1, 23rd December 2003

2 a paratrooper's helmet *US*
• —Linda Reinberg, *In the Field*, p. 200, 1991

skid mark *noun*
a faecal stain on a toilet bowl or underwear *AUSTRALIA*
• Only hope there aren't any skid-marks on me thunder-bags!!! —Barry Humphries, *Bazza Pulls It Off!*, 1971
• —Lee McNelis, *30 + And a Wake-Up*, p. 12, 1991
• Tomorrow, we'll discuss avoiding skid marks in gym class. — *Wayne's World 2*, 1993
• —Pamela Munro, *U.C.L.A. Slang*, p. 113, 2001
• Skid marks are one thing, but worse would have been the embarrassment[.] —Duncan MacLaughlin, *The Filth*, p. 44, 2002
• —Amy Sohn, *Sex and the City*, p. 157, 2002

skidoo *noun*
a snowmobile *CANADA, 1961*
• —Russell Tabbert, *Dictionary of Alaskan English*, p. 230, 1991
• The Skidoo is basically a sled with front skis and a rubber belt on the back with deep treads mounted on a rotor turned by a gasoline engine. Invented by Joseph-Armand Bombardier in 1959, it has been known as snow-bug, Snow Cruiser, and skiscooter —Bill Casselman, *Canadian Words*, p. 21, 1995
• —Bernadette Hince, *The Antarctic Dictionary*, p. 315, 2000

skidoo *verb*
1 to depart hastily *US, 1905*
• [I] turned the lights off, locked the office up, and skidooed down the corridor. —Anthony Frewin, *Sixty-Three Closure*, p. 2, 2000

2 to travel by skidoo (a snowmobile) *CANADA, 1986*
• —Bernadette Hince, *The Antarctic Dictionary*, p. 315, 2000

skid row *noun*
1 in any town, the run-down area where the socially disadvantaged and marginalised tend to congregate *US, 1931*
• Below this intersection, for a third of a mile, is a Skid Row as low and lousy as any in the country, with the usual in the way of flop houses, flea circuses, hoick shops, tattoo parlors[.] —Jack Lait and Lee Mortimer, *Chicago Confidential*, p. 14, 1950
• When on Skid Row, you must do as Skid Row does. You blend in. You take the Row as it leans, and merge into its decaying life[.] —Geoffrey Fletcher, *Down Among the Meths Men*, p. 11, 1966
• And on skid row -if you care to look – you may now and then see among the others a singularly doomed old man. —John Rechy, *The Sexual Outlaw*, p. 162, 1977
• [D]owntown where the food is slop. / Downtown where the hop-heads flop – in the snow / Down on skid row. —Howard Ashman, *Skid Row (Downtown)*, 1982

2 in prison, cells for troublesome prisoners *UK*
• —Angela Devlin, *Prison Patter*, p. 105, 1996

skids *noun*
underpants *UK*
Derives from **SKID MARK(S)** (faecal stains in underwear).
• —Angela Devlin, *Prison Patter*, p. 105, 1996
• Choosing jogging pants, hooded tops, sweatshirts, jeans, boots, clean skids. —Mark Powell, *Snap*, p. 19, 2001

▸ **put the skids under**
(of a person or circumstances) to ensure the imminent dismissal of someone; to dismiss someone from employment *UK, 1948*
• The college president starts at the top, politicians put the skids under him, and he shoots right down to the bottom. —Mary McCarthy, *The Group*, p. 144, 1991

skid shot *noun*
in pool, a shot made with backspin on the cue ball *US*
• —Mike Shamos, *The Illustrated Encyclopedia of Billiards*, p. 215, 1993

skied *adjective*
drug-intoxicated *US*
A play on 'sky' not 'ski', as '**HIGH** in the sky'.
• Most of these sneaker bitches is looking to get skied, not looking for knowledge. —Terry Williams, *The Cocaine Kids*, p. 87, 1989
• —Mike Haskins, *Drugs*, p. 291, 2003

skiff *noun*
an attractive girl *BAHAMAS*
• —John A. Holm, *Dictionary of Bahamian English*, p. 185, 1982

▷ see: **SKIT**

skiffle *noun*

1 a music genre, a sort of poor-man's rock 'n' roll, played on homemade or low budget instruments, popular in the late 1950s *UK, 1957*

Originates in 1930s and 40s US black society; to mean a house-party at which a subscription was charged to cover costs and raise money to meet the rent. Music was played by groups of amateur musicians. From conventional 'scuffle' (an impromptu struggle).

- "[A] shuffle group, or something of that sort." "You mean a skiffle group?" "Something like that." — Douglas Rutherford, *The Creeping Flesh*, p. 27, 1963
- The BBC liked skiffle; it was nicely middle class. There were no electric guitars and it didn't seem dangerous[.] — Simon Napier-Bell, *Black Vinyl White Powder*, p. 11, 2001

2 a very short hairstyle *JAMAICA*

- West Indians sometimes shaved a pencil thin parting in the cut (they called their crop a "skiffle"), and this caught on with UK skins [skinheads]. — Martin Roach, *Dr. Marten's Air Wair*, 1999

skill!

used as a register or exclamation of approval *UK*

- "That new girl at the chippie is skill" or "You've got tickets for the replay? Skill!" — Stuart Maconie, *Cider with Roadies*, p. 100, 2003

skim *noun*

money stolen from a business or enterprise, skimmed from the business funds like cream from milk *US*

- Then there's the secret funds the White House and the CIA control for the Freedom Fighters and their little wars all over the world. At least sixty percent of that is skim. — Richard Condon, *Prizzi's Glory*, p. 263, 1988
- Nobody interfered with the fuckin' skim. — *Casino*, 1995

skim *verb*

to divert a portion of your earnings or winnings to avoid paying taxes or to avoid paying your superiors in the enterprise their share *US, 1966*

- I'm not saying it's skimmed in Washington, but from maker to wearer it's skimmed. — Richard Condon, *Prizzi's Glory*, p. 263, 1988
- He's skimming on them. A sheet writer that used to work for Harry told a friend of mine it's a fact. Twenty years he skimmed like two grand a week over what he made for himself. — Elmore Leonard, *Riding the Rap*, p. 30, 1995

skimaged *adjective*

drunk *UK*

English gypsy use.

- — Jimmy Stockin, *On The Cobbles*, p. 11, 2000

skimmer *noun*

a hat *US*

- — David Claerbaut, *Black Jargon in White America*, p. 79, 1972

skimming *verb*

criminal acquisition of credit or debit card details by use of an electronic reader *UK*

- — Susie Dent, *The Language Report*, p. 19, 2003

skim money *noun*

money taken from an enterprise's net proceeds before any accounting of the proceeds *US*

- "I'm sure you are familiar with the IRS interest in casino ... uh ... funds." "I believe it's called skim money." Glanzmann smiled. — Gerald Petievich, *One-Shot Deal*, p. 258, 1981

skimpy *noun*

in Western Australia and the Northern Territory, a topless barmaid *AUSTRALIA*

- There are skimpies at the Palace Hotel tonight. — *www.abc.net.au/word-map*, 2003

skin *noun*

1 a person *UK*

- He was known far and wide as a decent old skin[.] — Brendan Behan, *Borstal Boy*, 1958

2 an immature or inexperienced young person *UK*

Royal Navy slang.

- [T]he poor kid's just a bit of skin! — Rick Jolly, *Jackspeak*, 1989

3 contact between hands in greeting, acknowledgement or congratulations *US, 1942*

- Open the door and gimme some skin, pig. Or gimme some pigskin, as the case may be. — Steve Allen, *Bop Fables*, p. 25, 1955
- "What it is, my man," he yelled out as he came up and held his hand out for some skin. — Donald Goines, *Cry Revenge*, p. 101, 1974

4 sex *US*

- The numbers were all in, and there wasn't any skin / Crime was on a sudden decrease. — Dennis Wepman et al., *The Life*, p. 57, 1976

5 a woman as a sex object *TRINIDAD AND TOBAGO, 1936*

- — Lise Winer, *Dictionary of the English/Creole of Trinidad & Tobago*, 2003

6 the foreskin *UK, 1961*

7 a condom *US*

Literally, 'an extra layer of (latex) skin'.

- She asked me what I meant; rubbers? safes? skins? prophylactics? contraceptives? — John Nichols, *The Sterile Cuckoo*, p. 105, 1965

8 a thin paper used to roll marijuana or tobacco cigarettes *US*

- — Angela Devlin, *Prison Patter*, p. 105, 1996

9 one dollar *US, 1930*

- Fifty skins was fifty skins. Fifty! For making one lousy phone call! — Bernard Wolfe, *The Late Risers*, p. 159, 1954
- Somebody found a new tailor who could make the greatest pants for 14 skins[.] — Hubert Selby Jr, *Last Exit to Brooklyn*, p. 28, 1957
- I say, Ain you got no skins, no kale? No bread? No bones, no berries, no boys? — Robert Gover, *One Hundred Dollar Misunderstanding*, p. 22, 1961
- He had twelve thousand skins in his pocket when he left here. — Mickey Spillane, *Me, Hood!*, p. 18, 1963
- I've seen him take on a professional twice his size at a carnival and not only stay in for the three minutes to win the twenty-five skins but pin him. — Earl Thompson, *Tattoo*, p. 142, 1974

10 in carnival and amusement park usage, a shirt *US*

- — Don Wilmeth, *The Language of American Popular Entertainment*, p. 244, 1981

11 a wallet *US*

- — Hyman E. Goldin et al., *Dictionary of American Underworld Lingo*, p. 196, 1950

12 a tyre, especially a well-worn one *US, 1954*

- — *Good Housekeeping*, p. 143, September 1958: 'Hot-rod terms for teen-age girls'
- — *American Speech*, p. 273, December 1961: 'Northwest truck drivers' language'

13 fist fighting *US*

- I wanna hold it like we always held it – with skin! — *West Side Story*, 1957

14 an American Indian *US*

An abbreviated form of 'redskin'.

- "Hey, brother, we got a new skin in the yard" means that a new Indian has been assigned to your area of the prison. — James Harris, *A Convict's Dictionary*, p. 38, 1989

▷ **see:** SKINHEAD

▸ **get under your skin**

to irritate; to become constantly irritating *UK, 1896*

- You wonder what's going on, but what really matters is how you feel, whether [Emio] Greco gets under your skin. — *The Guardian*, 21st August 2001

▸ **no skin off your nose**

it makes no difference to you *UK, 1926*

Variations have included: 'no skin off your ear', 'off your ass', 'off your bugle', 'off you' and 'off Jeff' (thus, any person's name).

- It's almost no skin off my nose to do it, so why not do it? — *The Guardian*, 19th January 2001

skin *verb*

1 to inject (a narcotic) into the skin as opposed to a vein *US*

- Even so, he had to shoot in the skin about half the time. But he only gave up and "skinned" a shot after an agonizing half-hour of proving and poking and cleaning out the needle, which would clog up with blood. — Wiliam Burroughs, *Junkie*, p. 51, 1953
- The first time I skinned, like I wouldn't hit the vein, just pick up the spike and shove it in. — Jeremy Larner and Ralph Teffertellerr, *The Addict in the Street*, p. 34, 1964
- I had been skinning morphine and that was the worst habit I ever kicked, believe me. — Bruce Jackson, *In the Life*, p. 72, 1972

2 to swindle someone *US, 1819*

- As this was being written, a gypsy fortune-teller was under indictment charged with using such props as torn diapers, a red candle and a department store ladies' room, to skin three Washington housewives of $450. — Jack Lait and Lee Mortimer, *Washington Confidential*, p. 279, 1951
- To anyone he could buttonhole, he bragged about how he had "stung" this person or "skinned" that one. — Jim Thompson, *Bad Boy*, p. 308, 1953
- [N]o mugs to skin. — Charles Raven, *Underworld Nights*, p. 9, 1956
- [A]fter the patients wouldn't vote he got mad and skinned them so bad at cards that they're all so in debt they're scared to go any deeper[.] — Ken Kesey, *One Flew Over the Cuckoo's Nest*, p. 115–116, 1962

3 to defeat someone *US*
- —Gary K. Farlow, *Prison-ese*, p. 64, 2002

4 in hot rodding, to remove a car's upholstery *US*
- —*Good Housekeeping*, p. 143, September 1958: 'Hot-rod terms for teen-age girls'

5 to surf without a wetsuit *US*
- —Trevor Cralle, *The Surfin'ary*, p. 116, 1991

▸skin a poke
to remove all money and valuables from a stolen wallet *US*
- —Joseph E. Ragen and Charles Finston, *Inside the World's Toughest Prison*, p. 818, 1962: 'Penitentiary and underworld glossary'

▸skin it
to slap hands in greeting *US*
- —*Houston Chronicle*, 9th April 1989

▸skin (it) back
to withdraw the foreskin from your penis, either as part of a medical inspection or masturbation *US*
- —Gary K. Farlow, *Prison-ese*, p. 64, 2002

▸skin teeth
to smile; to grin *JAMAICA*
The image of showing your teeth. West Indian and UK black.
- He had good reason to skin teeth. He was doing exceptionally well[.]—Karline Smith, *Moss Side Massive*, p. 2, 1994
- "You musta been skinnin' teet' when you opened dat bag mate!" "Nah man, I weren't skinnin' no teet', I was narrow. Dem man coulda bin CIDs!—Courttia Newland, *Society Within*, p. 29, 1999

▸skin the cat
to perform oral sex on a woman *US*
- —Connie Eble (Editor), *UNC-CH Campus Slang*, p. 6, Spring 2000

skin *adjective*

1 young, youthful; fresh, new *UK*
Royal Navy slang.
- She's all skin and essence [beauty].—Rick Jolly, *Jackspeak*, 1989

2 used of a film or a publication featuring nudity *UK, 1977*
- The truth is that all but the most prestigious of skin monthlies were produced out of publishing sweatshops, where the only women were serious secretaries, bookkeepers and picture editors.—Mick Farren, *Give the Anarchist a Cigarette*, p. 332, 2001

skin and blister *noun*
a sister *UK, 1925*
Rhyming slang.
- You know she's Superman's big sister / Her X-ray eyes see through my silly ways / Superman's big sister, superior skin and blister / It doesn't seem surprising nowadays... yeah!—Ian Dury, *Superman's Big Sister*, 1981

skin beater *noun*
a drummer *US*
- —Marcus Hanna Boulware, *Jive and Slang of Students in Negro Colleges*, 1947

skin beef *noun*
a prison sentence for an unspecified sexual crime *US*
- —John R. Armore and Joseph D. Wolfe, *Dictionary of Desperation*, p. 49, 1976

skin book *noun*
a sex-themed book *US*
- Where'd you learn that? You really ought be writing skin books. —Darryl Ponicsan, *The Last Detail*, p. 6, 1970

skin boy *noun*
an uncircumcised male *NEW ZEALAND*
- —Harry Orsman, *A Dictionary of Modern New Zealand Slang*, p. 123, 1999

skin chimney *noun*
the vagina *UK*
- —*www.LondonSlang.com*, June 2002

skin complaint *noun*
a bullet wound *US*
- —Ralph de Sola, *Crime Dictionary*, p. 139, 1982

skinder; skinner *noun*
gossip; slanderous rumour *SOUTH AFRICA, 1979*
From the verb.
- Much of the skinder is about families in disarray.—*Sunday Times (South Africa)*, 6th December 1998

skinder; skinner *verb*
to gossip *SOUTH AFRICA, 1942*
From Afrikaans.
- [W]e skindered about a certain leggy socialite[.]—*Sunday Times (South Africa)*, 30th November 2003

skinderer *noun*
a gossip *SOUTH AFRICA, 1993*
From **SKINDER** (to gossip).
- —Penny Silva, *A Dictionary of South African English*, 1996

skindering *noun*
an act of gossiping *SOUTH AFRICA, 1981*
From **SKINDER** (to gossip).
- Meanwhile, in the selfproclaimed lesbian corner, there is plenty of skindering (aided by brandy and Cokes) about the previous week's bar brawl [.]—*Sunday Times (South Africa)*, 18th June 2000

skin diver *noun*

1 a five-pound note; the sum of £5 *UK: SCOTLAND*
Glasgow rhyming slang for **FIVER**.
- Emdy [anybody] got change of a skin diver?—Michael Munro, *The Patter, Another Blast*, 1988

2 a person who performs oral sex on a male *US*
The reverse of a 'muff diver'.
- —*Current Slang*, p. 10, Winter 1969

skin fighting *noun*
a fight between members of rival gangs in which weapons or at least lethal weapons are forbidden *US*
- "A fair fight isn't rough," Two-Bit said. "Blades are rough. So are chains and heaters and pool sticks and rumbles. Skin fighting isn't rough."—S.E. Hinton, *The Outsiders*, p. 28, 1967

skin flick *noun*

1 a pornographic film *US*
- The newest breed in skin flicks is represented by "Babette" which opened in Manhattan recently.—*Screw*, p. 9, 29th November 1968
- —*Current Slang*, p. 12, Summer 1968
- When long-run skin-flicks appealing to heteros (like Censorship in Denmark), the only action is early afternoons.—John Francis Hunter, *The Gay Insider*, p. 148, 1971
- It is typical of the new-new skin flicks in that it goes farther than many in exposing the full nakedness of the female[.]—Roger Blake, *What you always wanted to know about porno-movies*, p. 37, 1972
- I wouldn't even use her [Raquel Welch] in a skin flick I was making. (Quoting Bill Osco).—Kenneth Turan and Stephen E. Zito, *Sinema*, p. 134, 1974
- Every day this cry can be heard echoing down the halls of every distributor of skin flicks.—Stephen Ziplow, *The Film Maker's Guide to Pornography*, p. 45, 1977
- Have you ever thought of starring in skin flicks[?]—Stewart Home, *Sex Kick [britpulp]*, p. 202, 1999

2 a slide used by a dermatologist to illustrate diseases during teaching rounds *US*
- —*Maledicta*, p. 57, Summer 1980: 'Not sticks and stones, but names: more medical pejoratives'

skin-flick house *noun*
a cinema showing pornographic films *US*
- The early skin-flick houses became known humorously among much of the trade as "masturbation mansions."—Roger Blake, *What you always wanted to know about porno-movies*, p. 78, 1972
- Brewer is also a center of racial unrest and urban blight, and it grows more seedy through RA as palatial movie theaters become skin-flick houses.—Jack De Bellis, *The John Updike Encyclopedia*, p. 77, 2000

skinflint *noun*
a mean person *UK, 1700*
- [B]etter to be with a spendthrift than a skinflint.—Marian Keyes, *The Other Side of the Story*, p. 489, 2004

skin flute *noun*
the penis *US*
Often arises in the phrase 'play the skin flute' (to perform oral sex).
- —G. Legman, *The Language of Homsexuality*, p. 1176, 1941
- Oh Christ, could I use her as an accompanist – on the old skin flute!—Gilbert Sorrentino, *Steelwork*, p. 143, 1970
- I reached down and grabbed his "skin flute" and began to blow. —*Screw*, p. 9, 17th May 1971
- I asked her if she'd play 'Flight of the Bumblebee' on my skin flute and she slapped me.—Ken Weaver, *Texas Crude*, p. 73, 1984
- Now she's playin' nighttime skin flute in the Roys R Us parking lot. —Richard Price, *Clockers*, p. 193, 1992
- I heard he plays skin flute with some quiff on the Lawrence Welk program.—James Ellroy, *Hollywood Nocturnes*, p. 34, 1994

skinful *noun*

more than enough alcohol to achieve a drunken state *UK, 1788*

- They [...] don't bother to lock their tomfoolery [jewellery] away, especially if they've had a skinful. —Charles Raven, *Underworld Nights*, p. 11, 1956
- Come on Milly, beddy byes. You've had a skinful tonight. —Graeme Kent, *The Queen's Corporal [Six Granada Plays]*, p. 97, 1959
- I can crack a fat [get an erection] with a flamin' skinful. Let's hit the hay!!! —Barry Humphries, *Bazza Pulls It Off!*, 1971

skin full of *noun*

drunk *US*

- Of course, a forty-nine-year-old cop with a skin full of hooch and only months away from a stroke a heart attack wouldn't be in very good shape to begin with. —Joseph Wambaugh, *The Secrets of Harry Bright*, p. 284, 1985

skin game *noun*

1 in gambling, a rigged game that honest players always lose *US*

- —Frank Garcia, *Marked Cards and Loaded Dice*, p. 264, 1962
- I was head toward a singing career again and could soon kiss the skin game a fond farewell, Lord willing. —Guy Owen, *The Flim-Flam Man and the Apprentice Grifter*, p. 144, 1972
- —George Percy, *The Language of Poker*, p. 83, 1988

2 the science of dermatology *US*

- —*Maledicta*, p. 57, Summer 1980: 'Not sticks and stones, but names: more medical pejoratives'

skingraft *noun*

an intramuscular injection of a drug *US*

- Time was Son only took a skingraft once a week, a little trip t'dreamsville. —Robert Gover, *JC Saves*, p. 16, 1968

skin habit *noun*

a drug addiction based on intramuscular, not intravenous, injections *US*

- It was a skin habit, see, which I got in the last part of of '43. —Bruce Jackson, *In the Life*, p. 72, 1972

skinhead; skin *noun*

1 a member of a youth fashion and gang movement, characterised by close-cropped or shaven scalp and smart utilitarian wear, associated with football hooliganism, racist violence and neo-Nazism *UK, 1969*

Early in the 1970s Richard Allen, a pseudonym of James Moffat (1922–93), published a series of 'youthsploitation' novels under the general title *Skinhead*.

- —William D. Alsever, *Glossary for the Establishment and Other Uptight People*, p. 29, December 1970
- —*Bournemouth Echo*, 2nd January 1971
- How can anyone condemn the skinhead books when, according to the letters received from countless thousand fans, the consensus of opinion is that they – and they alone – present skinheads, suedeheads, boot boys and now smooths as they really are? —Richard Allen, *Author's Notes [britpulp]*, p. 63, November 1972
- No skins will be served —*Time Out*, 13th June 1980
- What is it that provokes skins to punch, kick, nut and razor? —*New Society*, 26th June 1980
- Fuck facist skinhead shit. —Francesca Lia Block, *Baby Be-Bop*, p. 419, 1995
- 4 Skins [...] a band who espoused the street politics of the extreme right. They were made up of skinheads, the close-cropped, heavily booted British youth cult, but their name also framed an anatomical, sexual anti-Semitic pun. —Simon Warner, *Rockspeak!*, p. 33, 1996
- In 1969, Labour Prime Minister Harold Wilson berated some Tory rivals as 'the skinheads of Surbiton'. —Martin Roach, *Dr. Marten's Air Wair*, 1999

2 a British Leyland 'Allegro' car *UK*

Citizens' band radio slang, playing on **AGGRO**.

- —Peter Chippindale, *The British CB Book*, p. 161, 1981

skinhound

a sexually aggressive person *CANADA*

- Huska later told police that the assault was "nothing personal. He's a skinhound – a rapist." —*Montreal Gazette*, p. A7, 6th September 2002

skin house *noun*

a brothel or place where the entertainment is of a sexual nature *US, 1970*

- The various "skin houses" began to flourish as the "adults only" houses of a generation before had never been able to do. —Roger Blake, *What you always wanted to know about porno-movies*, p. 77, 1972
- I'd heard she was hanging out in the skin houses and taxi-dance joints[.] —Joseph Wambaugh, *The Blue Knight*, p. 24, 1973

skin magazine; skin mag *noun*

a magazine featuring photographs of nudes, usually women *US*

- But, mainly, the source of his money has always carried a taint in traditional status terms: Playboy, a "skin magazine," as they say at Yale, and the Playboy Clubs, "those Bunny houses." —Tom Wolfe, *The Pump House Gang*, p. 56, 1968
- I gazed around Roger's room strewn with smudged manuscripts, tattered skin mags, half-empty bottles, and records[.] —Lester Bangs, *Psychotic Reactions and Carburetor Dung*, p. 104, 1972
- Calvin glanced at the rows of skin magazines[.] —Joseph Wambaugh, *The Choirboys*, p. 105, 1975
- It was produced and directed by the managing editor of a bona fide girlie magazine, but the film is more of an adult male fantasy about the skin-magazine business. —Kent Smith et al., *Adult Movies*, p. 51, 1982
- In the coldest weather the boss would leave a pint of cheap whiskey in the drawer along with the stacks of skin magazines (All-Star Tit Queens and Bikes, Black Leather, and Big Broads). —Larry Heinemann, *Paco's Story*, p. 40–41, 1990
- [F]irst came the skin magazines and later, in the dark of night, he found himself climbing a tree in order to peek benenath the shade into a female neighbor's shower room. —*Rocky Mountain News (Denver)*, p. 69A, 5th September 1994
- Chris is inspired by the X-rated skin magazines she finds under her son's bed[.] —*Desert News (Salt Lake City)*, p. C6, 1st January 2004

skin man; skinner *noun*

a sex offender *US*

- —Andreas Schroeder, *Shaking It Rough*, 1976
- —John R. Armore and Joseph D. Wolfe, *Dictionary of Desperation*, p. 49, 1976

skinner *noun*

1 a big win on an unbacked horse or other race competitor; a betting coup *UK, 1874*

- —*Sydney Slang Dictionary*, p. 8, 1882
- —Tom Ellis, *The Science of Turf Investment*, p. 31, 1936
- Grafter had a wonderful book: some backed straw hats, some caps, some hard hitters, some top hats and others panamas. He finished getting a skinner when a big Indian walked out the gate wearing a turban. —Frank Hardy and Athol George Mulley, *The Needy and the Greedy*, p. 37, 1975
- —Jim Ramsay, *Cop It Sweet!*, p. 82, 1977
- 'You must have had a skinner on the Papal election,' I said to The Saint. —Roy Higgins and Tom Prior, *The Jockey Who Laughed*, p. 60, 1982
- —Ryan Aven-Bray, *Ridgey Didge Oz Jack Lang*, p. 43, 1983
- —John McCririck, *John McCririck's World of Betting*, p. 61, 1991
- —David Bennet, *Know Your Bets*, p. 102, 2001

2 a gambling cheat *US*

- —John Scarne, *Scarne on Dice*, p. 479, 1974

3 a police officer *US*

- —Miss Cone, *The Slang Dictionary (Hawthorne High School)*, 1965

skinner *verb*

▷ **see: SKINDER**

skinny *noun*

1 inside information, rumour or fact *US, 1959*

- But I hadn't really, because it turns out the song ["Sky Pilot"] is quite long and the real skinny is at the end – a controversial line: "Thou shalt not kill." —James Simon Kunen, *The Strawberry Statement*, p. 88–89, 1968
- Well, what's the skinny? —Darryl Ponicsan, *The Last Detail*, p. 16, 1970
- [T]he guy was fuckin' obsessed with fuckin' data, you know. obsessed with knowin' the fuckin' skinny on other peoples lives. —James Ellroy, *Because the Night*, p. 486, 1984
- These guys here have got the skinny on the happenin' after hours. —*Clueless*, 1995

2 in circus and carnival usage, a ten-cent piece *US*

- —Don Wilmeth, *The Language of American Popular Entertainment*, p. 244, 1981

skinny *adjective*

1 miserly; niggardly *UK*

- They put me down for a chunk, which I thought was a bit skinny, but I didnt say anything. —Lenny McLean, *The Guv'nor*, p. 117, 1998

2 prepared with low-fat or non-fat milk *US*

- —Connie Eble (Editor), *UNC-CH Campus Slang*, p. 7, April 1997

skinny as a broom; skinny *noun*

a bridegroom *UK*

Rhyming slang.

- [A] "skinny" as he stands at the alter [sic] with his fat and wide [bride]. —Ray Puxley, *Cockney Rabbit*, 1992

skinny-dip *verb*

to swim in the nude *US, 1966*

- Luce, who had helped organize the Cuba trips and had once gone skinnydipping with Fidel, joined with the FBI and ratted on all of his friends. —Jerry Rubin, *Do It!*, p. 63, 1970
- "They going swimming?" "Skinny-dipping," Walter said. —Elmore Leonard, *Split Images*, p. 110, 1981

skinny dipping in the love pond *noun*

from a male perspective, the act of sex without a condom *US*

- —Erica Orloff and JoAnn Baker, *Dirty Little Secrets*, p. 88, 2001

skinny Dugan *noun*

in craps, any combination of seven *US*

- —Steve Kuriscak, *Casino Talk*, p. 51, 1985

skinny end *noun*

in horse racing, a third place finish *AUSTRALIA*

- —Ned Wallish, *The Truth Dictionary of Racing Slang*, p. 74, 1989

skinnymalink *noun*

a thin person *UK: SCOTLAND, 1911*

- —Douglas Kynoch, *Scottish (Doric)-English/English-Scottish (Doric) Concise Dictionary*, p. 82, 1996
- [W]hat the lassie really needed was a big skinnymalink from Lanarkshire. —Christopher Brookmyre, *Not the End of the World*, p. 195, 1998

skinny-minny *adjective*

very thin; small and thin *US*

- [T]his pale white-skinned butt-fucker nancy boy with his cock in his hand, all purple and red and stiff and skinny-minny[.] —Joel Rose, *Kill Kill Faster Faster*, p. 18, 1997

skin one; skin two; skin three *noun*

used as a rating system by US forces in Vietnam for the films shown on base; the system evaluated films on the amount of nudity *US*

Higher ratings reflected higher amounts of nudity.

- —Gregory Clark, *Words of the Vietnam War*, p. 21–22, 1990

skin out *verb*

to clean something out; to finish something *CANADA*

- "It's just about skinned out," she said, of the exhibit of craft in the small building at the Lockeport Dominion Day celebration in 1986. The phrase comes from fish processing, where the last stage in filleting is removing skin and bones. —Lewis Poteet, *The South Shore Phrase Book*, p. 102, 1999

skinpix *noun*

pornographic films *US*

- These "skinpix," as the movie trade paper Variety has dubbed them, have undergone a recent revitalization in terms of production values, level of good taste, and in their profit potential. —Michael Milner, *Sex on Celluloid*, p. 18, 1964

skin pop *noun*

an injection of a drug into the skin or muscle, not into a vein *US*

- Nothing like a skin pop, not scattered like a snort. —George Mandel, *Flee the Angry Strangers*, p. 379, 1952
- That was the first time I ever got high on a skin pop. —James Mills, *The Panic in Needle Park*, p. 44, 1966

skin-pop *verb*

to inject a drug into the skin or muscle, not into a vein *US*

Usually practised in the early stages of drug use.

- But keep off, better, because if you like junk you keep shmeckin and shootin, then the skip pop goes to the big pipe[.] —George Mandel, *Flee the Angry Strangers*, p. 56, 1952
- He said he would stop using drugs altogether rather than start skin-popping. —Claude Brown, *Manchild in the Promised Land*, p. 251, 1965
- I got back to Lino next day and told him what he wanted to hear, that the kid was only sniffin', not skin-poppin', and that he was straightened out. —Edwin Torres, *Carlito's Way*, p. 73–74, 1975
- He skin pops a load of Dilaudid into a forearm, swooms for a moment under the jolt. —Iceberg Slim (Robert Beck), *Doom Fox*, p. 157, 1978
- It was also believed that dependency could be avoided by careful and occasional "skin popping" rather than "mainlining." —Paul E. Willis, *Profane Culture*, p. 171, 1978
- I ain't been mainlining or anything like that, no skin popping, just snorting —Joel Rose, *Kill Kill Faster Faster*, p. 185–186, 1997
- Some young dudes were on my floor skin popping and giggling and listening to Redd Foxx[.] —Clarence Major, *All-Night Visitors*, p. 206, 1998

skin popper *noun*

a drug user who does not inject the drug into a vein *US*

- I had jumped from being a careful snorter, content to take my kicks of sniffing through my nose, to a not-so-careful skin-popper, and now was full-grown mainliner. —Piri Thomas, *Down These Mean Streets*, p. 200, 1967

skin-popping *noun*

an act of injecting a drug subcutaneously, not into a vein *UK*

- —Robin Page, *Down Among the Dossers*, p. 119, 1973

skin-pump *verb*

to inject a drug under the skin, not into a vein *US*

- —*American Speech*, p. 29, February 1952: 'Teen-age hophead jargon'

skins *noun*

drums *UK, 1926*

- Beat the skins and keep 'em thumping! Rock the joint and keep it jumping! —Haenigsen, *Jive's Like That*, 1947
- I was jivin' around with the Latinos, they was bangin' on the skins as usual, timbales, conga and bongos – like a regular fuckin' band. —Edwin Torres, *Carlito's Way*, p. 46, 1975
- —Simon Warner, *Rockspeak!*, p. 297, 1996

skin shake *noun*

a thorough search of a person's body, including orifices *US*

- You take nothing – nothing – inside the walls. Any personal valuables, rings, watches, pens, lighters, will be stored here and returned to you at the time of your release. Throw your smokes away. Now come up here one at a time for a skin shake. —Malcolm Braly, *On the Yard*, p. 33, 1967
- —Paul Glover, *Words from the House of the Dead*, 1974

skin show *noun*

a show featuring women approaching or reaching nudity *US*

- I remember when the slime-balls used to be packed in there solid, asshole to belly button, waiting to look at the skin show in the viewer. —Joseph Wambaugh, *The Blue Knight*, p. 26–27, 1973
- A good SKIN SHOW is a sought after attraction for a Racket Carnival, for the better the FIX, the wilder the show, often including complete nudity and a little body contact as the girls hover at the edge of the stage. —Gene Sorrows, *All About Carnivals*, p. 26, 1985
- The street a midway of skin shows and tacky novelty shops. —Elmore Leonard, *Bandits*, p. 135, 1987
- "Even people who once went to skin shows have classier topless clubs (off the Strip) to visit now," says Sehlinger. —*USA Today*, p. 7D, 25th August 1995
- "This is not a skin show. It's a way of looking at the women and the clothes," said Alison Fenterstock[.] —*Dallas Morning News*, p. 17A, 5th June 2001

skinsman *noun*

1 a drummer *UK*

- —Tom Hibbert, *Rockspeak!*, p. 143, 1983

2 a prolific lover *BARBADOS*

- —Frank A. Collymore, *Barbadian Dialect*, p. 98, 1965

skint *adjective*

having little or no money, penniless *UK, 1925*

Figurative application of conventional 'skinned'.

- Perce was skint when Peter tried to put the touch on him, but he had a nice little job all lined up. —Charles Raven, *Underworld Nights*, p. 44, 1956
- ["]The only civilised thing about it," the Dean continued, "is that they let you sit here, when you're skint". —Colin MacInnes, *Absolute Beginners*, 1959
- My old man don't earn much / In fact he's flippin' skint. —Lonnie Donegan, *My Old Man's a Dustman*, 1960
- I was dead skint and it's bleedin' awful being broke[.] —John Peter Jones, *Feather Pluckers*, p. 85, 1964
- "And you, my son, are potless." "Slightly embarrassed." "Skint." —Anthony Masters, *Minder*, p. 8, 1984
- —Angela Devlin, *Prison Patter*, p. 105, 1996

skint as a kipper's backbone *adjective*

having no money *UK*

An elaboration and intensification of **SKINT** punning on 'skinned', the original derivation.

- [N]ot only as skint as a kipper's backbone, but over £150 in the red[.] —Charles Raven, *Underworld Nights*, p. 66, 1956

skinto *adjective*

having little or no money, penniless *UK: SCOTLAND*

A variation of **SKINT** used in Glasgow.

- OK, wan merr [one more] can a ginger each an that's yer lot. Ye'll have yer aul granda [grandfather] skinto. —Michael Munro, *The Patter, Another Blast*, p. 65, 1988

skin trade *noun*
the sex industry in all its facets *US*
- He didn't get where he was in the skin trade just by scaring pussy to death. —Robert Campbell, *In La-La Land We Trust*, p. 178, 1986
- The skin trade is a universal trade and a lot of people live by it, one way or another. —Robert Campbell, *In a Pig's Eye*, p. 111, 1991

skin two; skin three *noun*
▷ **see:** SKIN ONE

skin up *verb*
1 to roll a marijuana cigarette *UK*
From **SKIN** (cigarette paper).
- [S]kinning up together as I waited for David Holmes[.] —Charlie Hall, *The Box (Disco Biscuits)*, p. 151, 1996
- I'm sat up front with Big John, skinning up —Dave Courtney, *Raving Lunacy*, p. 88, 2000
- The only way we could really find out if it was kosher dope was to skin one up and have a puff or two. —Ken Lukowiak, *Marijuana Time*, p. 65, 2000

2 to expose a woman's genitals and breasts *TRINIDAD AND TOBAGO, 1986*
- —Lise Winer, *Dictionary of the English/Creole of Trinidad & Tobago*, 2003

skinz *noun*
a sexually attractive woman *US*
- — *Washingnton Post*, 14th October 1993

skip *noun*
1 a skipper (a captain, a leader, etc) *UK, 1830*
- Skips toss for jack. —David Bryant, *The Game of Bowls*, p. 71, 1990
- The Canadian film Men With Brooms, about a local curling team, is due to be released in Canada next month. Starring Naked Gun actor Leslie Nielsen as a small-town team skip, it has been described as "Rocky on ice". — *The Guardian*, 22nd February 2002

2 a coach; used as a term of address for a coach *US*
A shortened form of **SKIPPER**.
- Also, instead of calling Joe Schultz Joe I'm calling him Skip, which is what I called Ralph Houk when I first came up. Managers like to be called Skip. —Jim Bouton, *Ball Four*, p. 71, 1970

3 a uniformed police sergeant *UK*
An abbreviation of **SKIPPER** (a US police captain or sergeant).
- Uniformed sergeants are "Skip" or "Sarge", or it's first name terms. —Duncan MacLaughlin, *The Filth*, p. 82, 2002

4 an Anglo-Australian *AUSTRALIA*
From Skip, shortening of Skippy, the name of the kangaroo star of the children's television programme *Skippy, The Bush Kangaroo*.
- The badly-maligned 'Wogs' (Dapto dogs/Chocolate frogs) are finally wreaking revenge on Anglo-Saxon kids. 'Aussies' are 'Skips' or 'Joeys'. — *Sydney Morning Herald*, p. 7, 3rd January 1987

skip *verb*
▸ **skip it**
to forget it; to drop the subject; to dispense with something *US, 1934*
Often used as an imperative.
- The government defended the GCSE today after the head of its exams watchdog said pupils should be able to skip it if schools believed it was a waste of time. — *The Guardian*, 11th August 2003

▸ **skip on**
to leave *US*
- —Pamela Munro, *U.C.L.A. Slang*, p. 77, 1989

▸ **skip the cinders; skip the ties**
to walk along a railway track *US*
- —Ramon Adams, *The Language of the Railroader*, p. 139, 1977

skip *adjective*
Anglo-Australian *AUSTRALIA*
- Some shit skip band is on the radio. —Christos Tsiolkas, *Loaded*, p. 77, 1995

skip and jump *noun*
the heart *UK*
Rhyming slang for **PUMP**.
- —Ray Puxley, *Cockney Rabbit*, 1992

skip-out *noun*
a hotel guest who leavings without paying the bill *US*
- "We have our own organization to take care of skip-outs," he said. —Raymond Chandler, *Playback*, p. 129, 1958

skip out *verb*
to leave in a hurry in order to avoid obligations *UK, 1865*
- They were incandescent when he skipped out of a challenge[.] — *The Guardian*, 21st March 2004

skipper *noun*
1 a police chief, captain or sergeant *US, 1929*
Jocular, from the C14 nautical sense.
- This bust feels like fat city. Any legit L.A.P.D. dick would have taken one of our guys with him on a stakeout. Let's go get the skipper. —James Ellroy, *Because the Night*, p. 375, 1984
- — *The Official Encyclopaedia of New Scotland Yard*, 1999

2 a sport's team captain *UK, 1830*
From the use as 'a ship's captain', originally (in this sense) used of the captain of a curling team.
- Van der Westhuyzen made a clever break and lobbed the ball up for skipper John Smit, who showed great hands and balance to score near the uprights. — *The Observer*, 27th June 2004

3 a mid-level boss in an organised crime enterprise *US*
- The Capos are the middlemen, sometimes called skippers. —Henry Hill and Byron Schreckengost, *A Good Fella's Guide to New York*, p. 8, 2003

4 a prison warden *US*
- —Hyman E. Goldin et al., *Dictionary of American Underworld Lingo*, p. 196, 1950

5 a railway guard *US*
- —Norman Carlisle, *The Modern Wonder Book of Trains and Railroading*, p. 268, 1946

6 a derelict property used as shelter by the homeless *UK*
From the C16 when the original sense was 'a barn' (from Welsh *ysgubor* or Cornish *sciber*), hence 'a bed out of doors' and, finally, the current use.
- [C]ook it over the bums' fire hin the Greatorex Street skipper. —Geoffrey Fletcher, *Down Among the Meths Men*, p. 32, 1966
- —Angela Devlin, *Prison Patter*, p. 105, 1996

7 in poker, a hand with five cards sequenced by twos *US*
- —Irwin Steig, *Common Sense in Poker*, p. 187, 1963

skipper *verb*
1 to live rough *UK, 1845*
From **SKIPPER** (a place of rest for the homeless).
- Where have you been sleeping eh? I've been skippering [sleeping] out for over 20 years, you know what I mean, 20 years. —Robin Page, *Down Among the Dossers*, p. 33, 1973
- —Angela Devlin, *Prison Patter*, p. 105, 1996

2 to move from house to house, staying a few nights at each, with all your worldly possessions in tow *US*
- —Eugene Landy, *The Underground Dictionary*, p. 170, 1971

skippies *noun*
inexpensive shoes *US*
- —Connie Eble (Editor), *UNC-CH Campus Slang*, p. 7, Spring 1990

skippy *noun*
a homosexual male *US*
- —Clarence Major, *Dictionary of Afro-American Slang*, p. 104, 1970

skip rat *noun*
a litter collector *UK*
- —Angela Devlin, *Prison Patter*, p. 105, 1996

skirt *noun*
a woman or women objectified sexually *UK, 1899*
In conventional English usage until the late C19 when Victorians deemed it slang; not necessarily pejorative or contemptuous, however various compounds, some now obsolete, objectify women: 'a light skirt' (a loose woman), a **BIT OF SKIRT** or 'piece of skirt' (a woman as sex object), 'flutter a skirt' (to be a harlot), 'run a skirt' (to keep a mistress) and 'the skirt' (women, collectively).
- It's funny how when you got two skirts going together one of them is always sorta shy and twisted like and the other is always dead brassy. —John Peter Jones, *Feather Pluckers*, p. 40, 1964
- The brother inebriates worried about me for a week or two, undeniably saddened that one of their members should so suddenly go to ruin over a skirt. —John Nichols, *The Sterile Cuckoo*, p. 87, 1965
- Maybe you should have been a lawyer instead of a dumb skirt workin' behind a register. — *48 Hours*, 1982
- Totty. Copping for totty. Skirt. —Henry Sloane, *Sloane's Inside Guide to Sex & Drugs & Rock 'n' Roll*, p. 34, 1985
- Whistler's just got over a skirt that did a number on him. —Robert Campbell, *Alice in La-La Land*, p. 166, 1987
- So what's this skirt's name? — *Chasing Amy*, 1997
- Now I want you to level with me: did you knock this skirt up? — *Something About Mary*, 1998

skit; skiff *noun*

a small amount of snow *CANADA, 1990*

- On PEI, one might hear of a "skit," or "skiff," just a light dusting of snow. — *New Maritimes*, p. 29, March-April 1990

skitch *verb*

in icy winter conditions, to grab the bumper of a passing car and use your feet as skis as you are pulled along *US*

- — Jim Crotty, *How to Talk American*, p. 215, 1997
- I've had some "skitch" on the back of my truck on more than one occasion as I'm driving, which is accompanied by laughter and cheers from their pals. [Letter to the editor] — *Journal and Courier (Lafayette, Indiana)*, p. 10A, 5th September 2004

skitch!

attack! *AUSTRALIA*

A command inciting a dog to attack.

- Joe, running in on an angle, kept yelling, 'Skitch 'im, boy! Skitch 'im!' — Alan Marshall, *I Can Jump Puddles*, p. 130, 1955

skite *noun*

1 a boaster *AUSTRALIA, 1897*

- 'Stinkin' skite,' he muttered at Sam Gudgeon[.] — Norman Lindsay, *Halfway to Anywhere*, p. 29, 1947
- You're a damn' skite. — D.E. Charlwood, *All the Green Year*, p. 30, 1965
- 'Well, I'm Bill Brown, the new Fisheries Inspector.' The skite blinked twice, gulped into his beer and replied, 'Do you know who I am? I'm the biggest bloody liar in Yanco!' — Bob Staines, *Wot a Whopper*, p. 13, 1982
- — Harry Orsman and Des Hurley, *The Beaut Little Book of New Zealand Slang*, 1994

2 boastful talk *AUSTRALIA, 1860*

- Because I slung off at that cow Freddie Parkin putting on skite doing a line with Lottie Treebie. — Norman Lindsay, *Halfway to Anywhere*, p. 97, 1947

3 a glancing blow *UK: SCOTLAND, 1985*

- NESBITT (ANOTHER SKITE): Shuttit you! — Ian Pattison, *Rab C. Nesbitt*, 1988

▸ **on the skite**

engaged in a drinking binge *IRELAND*

- The back door was open and the sink was full of pilchard tins. Da ate pilchards when he was on the skite. — Patrick McCabe, *The Butcher Boy*, p. 43, 1992
- I was on the skite with him on his last night in Boston[.] — Eamonn Sweeney, *Waiting for the Healer*, p. 153, 1997

skite *verb*

1 to boast *AUSTRALIA, 1857*

From British dialect.

- — Gilbert H. Lawson, *A Dictionary of Australian Words and Terms*, 1924
- I said 'Are you going to skite about that?' and he said 'My bloody oath I am.' — Sam Weller, *Old Bastards I Have Met*, p. 51, 1979
- — Louis S. Leland, *A Personal Kiwi-Yankee Dictionary*, p. 93, 1984

2 to hit someone or something with a glancing blow *UK: SCOTLAND, 1911*

- NESBITT (SKITING THEM): No, it bliddy well isnae witty! — Ian Pattison, *Rab C. Nesbitt*, 1988

skitters *noun*

diarrhoea *UK: SCOTLAND*

Recorded as 'skitter' in the *Scots Dialect Dictionary*, 1911.

- Life's not buying off Rab C. Nesbitt with the Birdy song and a dose of the skitters. — Ian Pattison, *Rab C. Nesbitt*, 1988

skittery *adjective*

worthless *IRELAND*

- It was a grand day outside. There were a few skittery bits of cloud lying about the sky, but they didn't care if they ever got anywhere. — Patrick McCabe, *The Butcher Boy*, p. 58, 1992

skittle *verb*

1 to knock someone or something down *AUSTRALIA, 1938*

- As sure as night follows day, people will get skittled and yet we just sit back and accept it. — *Advertiser*, p. 19, 1st May 1991

2 to kill someone *AUSTRALIA*

- If you get skittled, I'll look after the little bugger. — John O'Grady, *Aussie Etiket*, p. 13, 1971

skittle meon *noun*

a sexually available woman *JAMAICA*

Recorded in August 2002.

skittles *noun*

dextromethorphan (DXM), an active ingredient in non-prescription cold and cough medication, often abused for non-medicinal purposes *US*

- Youths' nicknames for DXM: Robo, Skittles, Triple C's, Rojo, Dex, Tussin, Vitamin D. DXM abuse is called "Robotripping" or "Tussing." Users might be called "syrup heads" or "robotards." — *USA Today*, p. 1A, 29th December 2003

skitz; skiz *noun*

▷ see: SCHITZ

skitz *adjective*

used for expressing approval *UK*

- — Susie Dent, *The Language Report*, p. 75, 2003

skive *noun*

an evasion of duty, work or occupation; an instance of such evasion *UK, 1958*

- [W]andering off to the toilet for a skive. Liz went off to the loo with a newspaper[.] — Denise Mina, *Garnethill*, p. 74, 2001

skive *verb*

to evade a duty, work or occupation; to play truant from school *UK, 1919*

Possibly from dialect *skive* (to skim or dart about), more probable is French *esquiver* (to avoid, to slip away). Adopted into military slang during World War 1, and in widespread use by the middle of the century.

- [T]he [school]girls' skiving was not always a happy occasion. Once they were almost caught. — Shane J. Blackman, *Cool Places*, p. 212, 1998

skiver *noun*

a person who evades work or duty, a shirker *UK, 1941*

- Juice, a gobby, penis-ruled skiver so lazy he phones downstairs on his mobile from his bed to tell his ma to bring up more lagers[.] — *The Guardian*, 27th April 2002

skiving *adjective*

work-shy *UK*

From SKIVE (to evade work, to shirk).

- [Y]ou and me and one or two more like that skiving git Jim Taylor[.] — Graeme Kent, *The Queen's Corporal [Six Granada Plays]*, p. 82, 1959

skivvies *noun*

underwear *US, 1918*

Originally applied to an undershirt or vest, now to underwear in general.

- All three, tired at the end of this long day, stand in their skivvies in front of the bed. — Darryl Ponicsan, *The Last Detail*, p. 52, 1970
- So Ordell would have these businessmen stumbling around in their skivvies sneezing, spilling drinks, shit, middle-aged jitterbugs trying to dance sals with the cute ladies who'd be giggling, having some fun with them. — Elmore Leonard, *Switch*, p. 60, 1978
- No, thank you. Nothing. Get your socks and skivvies and let's get out of here before your worst fears come true and we end up at the bottom of the canyon smashed into the roadway by a semi. — Robert Campbell, *Alice in La-La Land*, p. 26, 1987

skivvy *noun*

1 a domestic servant, especially a maid-of-all-work *UK, 1902*

- [T]reatin the mother of yer kids like a fuckin skivvy. — Niall Griffiths, *Kelly + Victor*, p. 40, 2002

2 during the Vietnam war, a prostitute *US*

- — Linda Reinberg, *In the Field*, p. 200, 1991

skivvy *verb*

to perform heavy, boring, menial household chores *UK*

From the noun.

skiwift *adjective*

▷ see: SKEW-WHIFF

skizziest *adjective*

the best *US*

- — *San Francisco Examiner*, p. III-2, 22nd March 1960

skoal; skol *verb*

to drink; to down a drink *US*

- They could skoal two cases of beer in no time flat. — Frederick Kohner, *Gidget*, p. 40, 1957
- [S]he ordered a double alcohol rub and then skolled the lot. — Gretel Killeen, *Hot Buns and Ophelia get a Bloke*, p. 82, 2000

skolly; skollie; scolly *noun*

especially in Cape Town, a non-white street hoodlum or petty criminal *SOUTH AFRICA, 1934*

From Dutch *schullen* (to lie low) via Afrikaans.

- — *Peace Review*, 1st September 2000

skoofer *noun*
a marijuana cigarette *US*
- — Edith A. Folb, *runnin' down some lines*, p. 254, 1980

skookum *adjective*
big; powerful; terrific; smart *CANADA*
- — Robert O. Bowen, *An Alaskan Dictionary*, p. 31, 1965
- From BC Chinook jargon, "skookum" is still in active use among British Columbians to mean "terrific" or "good." — Tom Parkin, *WetCoast Words*, p. 128, 1989
- — Mike Doogan, *How to Speak Alaskan*, p. 52, 1993

skoon *noun*
one dollar *US*
- — George Percy, *The Language of Poker*, p. 83, 1988

skoosh *noun*
1 something that is easily achieved or accomplished *UK: SCOTLAND*
- The drivin test wis a skoosh [...] Four nuthin tae the boys – a pure skoosh-case. — Michael Munro, *The Original Patter*, p. 63, 1985

2 any carbonated soft drink *UK: SCOTLAND, 1985*
- Gie's a slug a yer skoosh. — Michael Munro, *The Original Patter*, p. 63, 1985
- Another sign announced the availability of "Tea, coffee, assorted skoosh." — Val McDermid, *Killing the Shadows*, p. 407, 2000

skooshed *adjective*
drunk *UK: SCOTLAND*
- — Michael Munro, *The Complete Patter*, p. 142, 1996

skop, skiet and donner *noun*
physically violent and threatening behaviour or activity *SOUTH AFRICA, 1970*
From Afrikaans *skop, skiet en donder* (to stop, shoot and beat up). In South African colloquial use: *skop* (to kick, to enjoy yourself); *skiet* (to shoot, to gamble with dice, to lie); **DONDER** (beaten up, also an abusive term of address); *skiet and donder* (used of action entertainment, 'blood and thunder').
- It was heavy, white, bully men who only know how to skop , skiet and donner – and the heavy Venda who knows only how to throw teargas[.] — *Sunday Times (South Africa)*, 8th October 2000

skosh; skoshi *noun*
a small amount *US*
Korean pidgin, used by US soldiers in Korea and brought back to the US as 'skosh'. The word was given a second wind in the 1970s with a radio advertisement for jeans that promised 'just a skosh more room' in the crotch area for men.
- — *Current Slang*, p. 23, Spring 1970
- "Skosh" is an advertising copywriter's way of spelling the Japanese word "sukoshi," meaning "a little." — *Detroit Free Press*, 19th December 1977

SKP *noun*
an escaped prisoner *US*
A play on 'escapee'.
- — *American Speech*, p. 272, December 1962: 'The language of traffic policemen'

skrep *noun*
a worn-out, decrepit prostitute *TRINIDAD AND TOBAGO, 1973*
- — Lise Winer, *Dictionary of the English/Creole of Trinidad & Tobago*, 2003

skrilla *noun*
▷ see: **SCRILLA**

skronk *noun*
in contemporary music, dissonant sounds *UK, 1996*
- — Susie Dent, *The Language Report*, p. 45, 2003

skronky *adjective*
of an electric guitar's sound or style of playing, excitingly raw and basic; hence, applied to fans of such music *US*
- Ferociously lo-fi, they [the Tall Boys] eschew electronics for amphetamine-loaded, skronky guitar riffs, slinky basslines, and relentless, in-your-face drums. — *The Village Voice*, 7th April 2003
- [S]ix months ago, only the skronkiest, most pared-down Detroit-sounding screechrock would have engendered a response[.] — *X-Ray*, p. 35, August 2003

skua *noun*
frozen chicken *ANTARCTICA, 1991*
The 'skua' is a large predatory gull; the comparison with chicken is not in the nature of praise.
- — *Antarctic Vocabulary*, 19th September 1997

skuif; skuifie; skyf; skyfie *noun*
a cigarette, especially a hand-rolled tobacco cigarette, or one containing marijuana *SOUTH AFRICA, 1946*
From Afrikaans *skuif* (a puff of smoke).
- — Partridge, *A Dictionary of the Underworld*, 1950
- He had thought about suicide so often that he had even planned how it would happen: he was going to do a skuif and then gas himself. — Greg Marinovich, *The Bang-Bang Club*, p. 199, 2000

skull *noun*
1 oral sex *US*
- "That's what I need, a little skull," said Fuzzy[.] — Joseph Wambaugh, *The Blue Knight*, p. 139, 1973
- While Willie drove us around, I opted for her far out skull extravaganza. — Iceberg Slim (Robert Beck), *Airtight Willie and Me*, p. 9, 1979
- The Manager gave him all the free bourbon he could guzzle and, if he could still get it up, some Oblivious backbooth skull just to discourage the likes of these two Clevelands from filing complaints. — Seth Morgan, *Homeboy*, p. 25, 1990
- Lizzie's a blast; she's smart, tender, funny and gives great skull. — James Ellroy, *Hollywood Nocturnes*, p. 265, 1994

2 a confidence swindle *TRINIDAD AND TOBAGO, 1979*
- — Lise Winer, *Dictionary of the English/Creole of Trinidad & Tobago*, 2003

3 a passenger in a lorry *UK*
Road hauliers' slang.
- — *British Road Services Magazine*, December 1951

4 in circus and carnival usage, a free ticket *US*
- — Don Wilmeth, *The Language of American Popular Entertainment*, p. 244, 1981

▸ out of your skull
very drunk or drug-intoxicated *UK*
Variation on **OFF YOUR HEAD**.
- [C]oked out of their skulls during the recording of Morrison Hotel[.] — Barney Hoskyns, *Waiting For The Sun*, p. 184, 1996
- — Angela Devlin, *Prison Patter*, p. 84, 1996
- [W]e are stoned out of our skulls[.] — Stuart Browne, *Dangerous Parking*, p. 84, 2000

▸ take a skull
in a dramatic performance, to react slowly to a line *US*
- — Sherman Louis Sergel, *The Language of Show Biz*, p. 97, 1973

skull *verb*
1 to strike someone; to attack someone *IRELAND*
- He's at something I'll skull him. He's a fucking oul man. What could he be at? I'm going to fucking skull him. — Eamonn Sweeney, *Waiting for the Healer*, p. 97, 1997

2 to shun someone *JAMAICA*
- — Peter Patrick, *Some Recent Jamaican Creole Words*, 2003

skull and brains *noun*
oral sex *US*
- — Gary K. Farlow, *Prison-ese*, p. 65, 2002

skull cracker *noun*
strong, homemade whisky *US*
- It is called corn liquor, white lightning, sugar whiskey, skull cracker, popskull, bush whiskey, stump, stumphole, 'splo, ruckus juice, radiator whiskey, rotgut, sugarhead, block and tackle, wildcat, panther's breath, tiger's sweat, Sweet spirits of cats a-fighting, alley bourbon, city gin, cool water, happy Sally, deep shaft, jump steady, old horsey, stingo, blue John, red eye, pine top, buckeye bark whiskey and see seven stars. — *Star Tribune (Minneapolis)*, p. 19F, 31st January 1999

skulldrag *verb*
in prison, to awake a prisoner in the early hours for immediate transfer to another prison *UK*
- — Angela Devlin, *Prison Patter*, p. 105, 1996

skulled *adjective*
drunk *US*
- — *American Speech*, p. 305, December 1955: 'Wayne university slang'
- "He's skulled," McMurphy hissed. "Somebody's gonna have to go out and help him." — Ken Kesey, *One Flew Over the Cuckoo's Nest*, p. 287, 1962

skull-fry *noun*
chemically straightened hair *US*
- — Clarence Major, *Dictionary of Afro-American Slang*, p. 64, 1970

skull fuck *noun*
an intense assault on all the senses *CANADA*
- IT WOULD BE A FUCKING MIND-BENDING, EAR-BLASTING, CUM-DRINKING, STOMACH-CHURNING SKULL FUCK!!! — Suroosh Alvi et al., *The Vice Guide*, p. 113, 2002

skullfuck *verb*
1 to perform oral sex on a man; (from the male perspective) to receive oral sex *CANADA*
- It's important at this point to make sure you avoid getting skull-fucked. Control the tempo yourself. — Suroosh Alvi et al., *The Vice Guide*, p. 30, 2002

2 (notional) to have sex with a head in symbolic victory *US, 2000*
A less realistic variation of the previous sense.
- Corey Taylor [Slipknot] responds: "If he ever f**king says anything to me I will f**king poke his eyes out and skullf**k that little bastard because I don't care anymore, dude." — *Kerrang!*, p. 8, 3rd November 2001

skullie *noun*
a skullcap *US*
- The hats also are sported at underground clubs and at "rave" parties, where, as techno or house music blasts to a peak, the hats are tossed in the air. What are the hats called? Take your pick. Some call them skullies, street slang for skullcap. — *Atlanta Journal and Constitution*, p. L1, 3rd January 1993

skull job *noun*
an act of oral sex *US*
- — Eugene Landy, *The Underground Dictionary*, 1971

skull money *noun*
money earned in illegal ways *UK*
- [O]nce you've got your money in the system, skull money goes to straight money. — J.J. Connolly, *Layer Cake*, p. 21, 2000

skull session *noun*
a group analysis and discussion; a conference *US, 1959*
- I buzzed Dave DePugh's office to pitch a kidnap skull session – the fucker was "out in the field." — James Ellroy, *Hollywood Nocturnes*, p. 77, 1994

skunk *noun*
1 a woman, especially a promiscuous woman with deficiencies in the area of hygiene *US*
- They used to call those kind of girls skunks because they were so dirty. — Claude Brown, *Manchild in the Promised Land*, p. 252, 1965
- "You might as well be a skunk," Chilly said. "What?" "A skunk. A broad." — Malcolm Braly, *On the Yard*, p. 300, 1967

2 an unpleasant man; a contemptible person *UK, 1841*
After the North American animal.
- Leave her 'lone! Come back here, you skunks! You better mind me! — Toni Morrison, *Love*, p. 48, 2003

skunk *verb*
in various games, to defeat an opponent by an overwhelming margin *US, 1843*
- Janie and Speedy, of course, started having fun by skunking them soundly. — Iceberg Slim (Robert Beck), *Long White Con*, p. 62–63, 1977

skunk beer *noun*
inexpensive, bitter, poor quality beer *US*
- We listened to Black Flag, formed bands, tried chewing tobacco, threw up from chewing tobacco, got grounded for swilling skunk beer. — *News and Observer (Raleigh, North Carolina)*, p. E5, 3rd August 1997

skunked *adjective*
drunk *US*
- — Don R. McCreary (Editor), *Dawg Speak*, 2001

skunk juice; skunk juicer; skunk junker *noun*
an illegal linear amplifier for a citizens' band radio *US*
- — Elementary Electronics, *Dictionary of CB Lingo*, p. 108, 1976

skunk oil *noun*
any odorising agent injected into natural gas *US*
- — Jerry Robertson, *Oil Slanguage*, p. 113, 1954

skunk weed; skunk *noun*
an extremely potent variety of marijuana which will produce an hallucinogenic effect; also, good quality marijuana *US, 1982*
- A small dose of the skunk weed, like it's suppose to be[.] — Cypress Hill, *Stoned Raiders*, 1995
- Fucking good skunk. — *Kids*, 1995
- Our favourite drug is weed skunk. Skunk is wicked[.] — Macfarlane, Macfarlane and Robson, *The User*, p. 4, 1996
- [D]at sticky fokkin orange skunk you keep promising and dat most of fokkin town is smokin'[.] — Nick Barlay, *Curvy Lovebox*, p. 33, 1997
- the "paranoia" vibe engendered by the industrial strength cannabis that appeared in the 1990s, so called "skunk" designer dope grown in an artificial environment and genetically engineered to blow your head off — Harry Shapiro, *Waiting For The Man*, p. 199, 1999
- All high-quality fragrant cannabis buds are called Skunk, regardless of whether or not they are related to the Skunk strains developed in Holland[.] — Brian Preston, *Pot Planet*, p. 125, 2002
- — Mike Haskins, *Drugs*, p. 289, 2003
- Got the Skunk, got the Punk, we got the Sess, it's Blessed. — Julian Johnson, *Urban Survival*, p. 170, 2003

sky *noun*
1 in a casino, the ubiquitous overhead surveillance system *US*
An abbreviated form of **EYE IN THE SKY**.
- — Michael Dalton, *Blackjack*, p. 46, 1991

2 a hat *US*
- And his fabulous sky was broke so fly / That the city had it banned. — Dennis Wepman et al., *The Life*, p. 48, 1976

sky *verb*
1 to jump high and with great elan *US*
- — Chuck Wielgus and Alexander Wolff, *The In-Your-Face Basketball Book*, p. 50, 1980
- — Judi Sanders, *Mashing and Munching in Ames*, p. 20, 1994

2 to leave quickly *US*
Vietnam war slang.
- I want to ask you some questions before you sky, Danny. — John Del Vecchio, *The 13th Valley*, p. 534, 1982

sky-blue-pink *noun*
an unknown, indeterminate or fantasy colour *UK, 1942*
Jocular.
- Brrrring! "What colors do you mix to get sky-blue-pink?" Brrrring! "Where can I buy a Danish chair made in Japan?" — Lilian Jackson Braun, *The Cat Who Ate Danish Modern*, p. 167, 1990

sky diver *noun*
a five-pound note; the sum of £5 *UK: SCOTLAND*
Glasgow rhyming slang for **FIVER**.
- — Michael Munro, *The Patter, Another Blast*, 1988

skyf; skyfie *noun*
▷ see: **SKUIF**

sky hook *noun*
1 in oil drilling, a non-existent tool that is often the subject of hazing of new workers *US*
- — Jerry Robertson, *Oil Slanguage*, p. 113, 1954

2 a citizens' band radio antenna *US*
- — Len Buckwalter, *CB Radio*, p. 66, 1976

sky jockey *noun*
a fighter pilot *UK*
Gulf war usage.
- — *American Speech*, p. 401, Winter 1991: 'Among the new words'

sky juice *noun*
a cheap refreshment of flavoured ice *JAMAICA, 1972*
- Big Yout' is saying that is a good thing because it means the sufferer could earn a raise by selling sky juice from his barrow[.] — Donald Gorgon, *Cop Killer*, p. 28, 1994

skylark *verb*
to *park* a vehicle *UK*
Rhyming slang.
- I skylarks along the old West Road there[.] — John Peter Jones, *Feather Pluckers*, p. 39, 1964

sky man *noun*
a preacher *US*
A variant of the more common **SKY PILOT**.
- Let's dig us up a Sky Man who'll tie the knot for us[.] — Dan Burley, *Diggeth Thou?*, p. 35, 1959

sky-nest *noun*
an apartment on an upper floor of an apartment building *US*
- This sky-nest was once occupied by mayors Thompson and Cermak, and was regarded as Chicago's executive mansion. — Jack Lait and Lee Mortimer, *Chicago Confidential*, p. 182, 1950

sky palace *noun*
a church *UK*
The home of a **SKY PILOT** (a preacher).
• —Peter Chippindale, *The British CB Book*, p. 159, 1981

sky-piece *noun*
a hat *US*
• —Jack Lait and Lee Mortimer, *New York Confidential*, p. 236, 1948: 'A glossary of Harlemisms'

sky pilot *noun*
a clergyman, especially in the forces or the prison service *UK, 1887*
Originally nautical slang.
• Jack, I swear I'm no sky-pilot, but a creep pad turns into a confession booth as soon as I squat in it.—Mezz Mezzrow, *Really the Blues*, p. 88, 1946
• This geezer used to have long talks with the sky pilot—Frank Norman, *Bang To Rights*, p. 143, 1958
• A soldier so ill looks at the sky pilot / Remembers the words / Thou shalt not kill / Sky pilot.....sky pilot[.]—Eric Burdon, *Sky Pilot*, 1967
• I gotta twin brother in England called Kevin who's a sky-pilot.—Barry Humphries, *Bazz Pulls It Off!*, 1971
• —Peter Chippindale, *The British CB Book*, p. 159, 1981
• —Angela Devlin, *Prison Patter*, p. 105, 1996

sky rocket; sky *noun*
pocket *UK, 1879*
Rhyming slang.
• [A] rich four-by-twoish [Jewish] merchant [...] put his hand into his sky rocket and took out a Lady Godiva [£5][.]—Ronnie Barker, *Fletcher's Book of Rhyming Slang*, p. 27, 1979

skyrocket *verb*
(of prices or statistics) to increase steeply *US, 1895*
• [A]pplications to join the dark brotherhoods of MI5 and MI6 have skyrocketed since the Beeb started running Spooks. It's been the same at the CIA ever since September 11.—*The Guardian*, 20th July 2002

sky scout *noun*
an air force chaplain *US*
• —Lou Shelly, *Hepcats Jive Talk Dictionary*, p. 48, 1945

skyscraper *noun*
paper; writing paper; toilet paper; a newspaper *UK*
Rhyming slang.
• —Ray Puxley, *Cockney Rabbit*, 1992

sky-shooters *noun*
sunglasses *US*
• He was wearing a bright aloha shirt, khaki shorts, Jesus boots, and mirrored sky-shooters[.]—Kinky Friedman, *Steppin' on a Rainbow*, p. 103, 1997

sky six *noun*
God *US*
From 'sky' (a unit commander).
• That Sky Six ain't cutting no husses this week, Man, not one.—Charles Anderson, *The Grunts*, p. 99, 1976

sky's the limit *noun*
in poker, any game played with no limit on the amount of bets *US*
• —Albert H. Morehead, *The Complete Guide to Winning Poker*, p. 273, 1967

slab *noun*
1 a road; a highway *US*
A specific application of the generally conventional use as 'a broad, solid mass'.
• —*Complete CB Slang Dictionary*, p. 159, 1976
• —Peter Chippindale, *The British CB Book*, p. 159, 1981

2 a thick, dark, cold wave *US*
• —Trevor Cralle, *The Surfin'ary*, p. 116, 1991

3 a sandwich *CANADA*
Teen slang, reported by a Toronto newspaper in 1946, and reported as 'obsolescent or obsolete' by Douglas Leechman, 1959.

4 a cardboard carton of 24 cans or bottles of beer *AUSTRALIA*
• Bodacious tatars a must, slab carrying (silent) mute preferred. Must own VCR. Blank tapes supplied.—*Sydney City Hub*, 1997

5 a phonograph record; any audio recording *US*
• —Robert Kirk Mueller, *Buzzwords*, p. 142, 1974

6 a package of crack cocaine *US*
• Crack isn't usually packaged in vials anymore but in miniature heat-sealed plastic bags, which the dealers call "slabs."—*The New Yorker*, p. 35, 10th August 1998

7 crack cocaine that is heavily adulterated *US*
• —Terry Williams, *Crackhouse*, p. 151, 1992

slab *verb*
in necrophile usage, to engage in sexual activity with a corpse *US*
• —*Maledicta*, p. 180, Summer/Winter 1986–1987: 'Sexual slang: prostitutes, pedophiles, flagellators, transvestites, and necrophiles'

slabbed and slid *adjective*
'dead and gone'; also used in prison of an ex-prisoner who has been forgotten *UK*
• —Paul Tempest, *Lag's Lexicon*, 1950

slab boy *noun*
a necrophile *US*
• —*Maledicta*, p. 178, Summer/Winter 1986–1987: 'Sexual slang: prostitutes, pedophiles, flagellators, transvestites, and necrophiles'

slab house *noun*
a modest restaurant serving barbecued meat *US*
• —Carl J. Banks Jr, *Banks Dictionary of the Black Ghetto Language*, 1975

slabs *noun*
the testicles *UK*
Back slang.
• —Robert Barltrop and Jim Wolveridge, *The Muvver Tongue*, 1980

slack *noun*
1 less than harsh treatment *US*
• —*Current Slang*, p. 43, Fall 1968

2 money *US*
• —David Claerbaut, *Black Jargon in White America*, p. 79, 1972

3 in a military patrol, the soldier immediatley behind the lead soldier in formation *US*
• The slack takes the left overhead and the 90 degrees to his right.—Ronald J. Glasser, *365 Days*, p. 209–210, 1971

slack *verb*
to wear trousers, especially jeans, oversized, baggy and sagging *US*
• —*American Speech*, p. 418, Winter 1993: 'Among the new words'

slack *adjective*
1 of a woman, objectionable; of loose morals *AUSTRALIA, 1977*
• A gutless wonder is about the worst thing you can be in our town. If you're a boy that is. If you're a girl then it's a slack moll.—Phillip Gwynne, *Deadly Unna?*, p. 9, 1998

2 of poor quality, below standard, unacceptable; lewd, vulgar *UK*
• An' you up here blasting out slack music and smoking ganja.—Karline Smith, *Moss Side Massive*, p. 73, 1994
• [T]he usual cross section of late-night London life. Trendy white dance funksters, rude bwoys, soul boys, batty bwoys, ragga gals, slack gals, the drunk and insomniac[.]—Donald Gorgon, *Cop Killer*, p. 88, 1994
• —*Cool Antarctica*, 2003: 'Antarctic slang'

3 unproductive; inefficient; lazy *US*
• I've been so slack for the last month that I've got five hundred pages to read by final exams.—Connie Eble (Editor), *UNC-CH Campus Slang*, p. 4, April 1978
• You've got my new address. I gave it to you the other day. Well write it down this time, you slack bastard[.]—Barry Humphries, *A Nice Night's Entertainment*, p. 185, 1981

4 dreadful; awful; pathetic *NEW ZEALAND, 1981*
• She said it was a pretty slack birthday, and they were only allowed to go on two rides each.—Kylie Mole (Maryanne Fahey), *My Diary*, p. 44, 1988
• —Harry Orsman, *A Dictionary of Modern New Zealand Slang*, p. 124, 1999

5 contemptibly unfair; unkind *AUSTRALIA*
• Don't be slack, he can't help being tall.—June Factor, *Kidspeak*, p. 187, 2000

slack Alice *noun*
a slovenly woman *UK: ENGLAND*
A fictitious friend called Slack Alice featured in the television comedy monologues of Larry Grayson during the early and mid-1970s.
• The cartoon Muse (or Slack Alice as we like to call her) came to my rescue that very same day[.]—*The Guardian*, 26th April 2002

slackarse *noun*

a lazy person *AUSTRALIA, 1971*

- Be a slackarse then. You'll end up with no job and be stuck here forever. —Jenny Pausacker, *What are ya?*, p. 5, 1987

slack-arse *adjective*

tired out, lazy or both *NEW ZEALAND*

- —David McGill, *David McGill's Complete Kiwi Slang Dictionary*, p. 115, 1998

slacker *noun*

a person who avoids work, study and responsibility *US, 1898*
The most recent burst of popularity for the term is not its first.

- [O]ne man returning from R&R and four slackers from the rear. —Charles Anderson, *The Grunts*, p. 140, 1976
- An' you two slackers are in plenty, plenty trouble. —Larry Heinemann, *Close Quarters*, p. 151, 1977
- Sheeni said OK, but she didn't plan to baby "any slackers." —C.D. Payne, *Youth in Revolt*, p. 30, 1993
- —Connie Eble (Editor), *UNC-CH Campus Slang*, p. 7, Spring 1994
- Don't the slackers prefer the grassy knoll over there? —*Clueless*, 1995

Slackers *nickname*

Halifax, Nova Scotia *CANADA*
The following etymology is offered by William Pugsley in his 1945 *Slackers, Sinners, and other Seamen*: so called because of the relatively slack discipline ashore following duty at sea.

slack jaw *noun*

a dolt; a stupid person *US*

- —Michael Dalton Johnson, *Talking Trash with Redd Foxx*, p. 118, 1994

slack man *noun*

in a combat march, the second man in line *US*

- Vega, the second or "slack" man in the line, was the buffer between Chavez's point position and the main body of the unit, fifty meters behind Vega. —Tom Clancy, *Clear and Present Danger*, p. 205, 1989

slackmeister *noun*

someone who has perfected the art of doing nothing *US*

- —Connie Eble (Editor), *UNC-CH Campus Slang*, p. 7, Fall 1987

slackness *noun*

1 lewd and vulgar language *UK*
West Indian and UK black patois.

- "What frigging moment?" she hissed. "Okay, enough of the slackness," Edwards said[.] —Karline Smith, *Moss Side Massive*, p. 171, 1994

2 sexual aggression, promiscuity or perversion *TRINIDAD AND TOBAGO, 1940*

- —Lise Winer, *Dictionary of the English/Creole of Trinidad & Tobago*, 2003

slag *noun*

1 a contemptible person *UK, 1943*

- [H]e was a right slag, what with never washing and ponsing [poncing] [ponce] dogend from morning to night. —Frank Norman, *Bang To Rights*, p. 95, 1958
- The usual slags. The commoners. —Ted Lewis, *Jack Carter's Law*, p. 22, 1974
- Come on you slag! —*The Sweeney*, November 1975
- That's great, guv. That'll keep the slags guessing. —Martin King and Martin Knight, *The Naughty Nineties*, p. 223, 1999
- Pair of lying fucking slags, you ask me. —John Williams, *Cardiff Dead*, p. 83, 2000
- All right then you slag, do you want some [an invitation to fight]? —Mark Steel, *Reasons to be Cheerful*, p. 43, 2001

2 a prostitute; a sexually promiscuous woman *UK, 1958*

- The slag what does she take me for a mug or what? —Frank Norman, *Bang To Rights*, p. 65, 1958
- Slags like your Sandra can get away with it, can't they? —Mike Hodges, *Get Carter*, p. 65, 1971
- The lift smells like the inside of a stripper's G-string which isn't surprising considering the amount of slag traffic it's carried[.] —Ted Lewis, *Jack Carter's Law*, p. 12, 1974
- Oh, Lordy!.. it's the Fat Slags —*Roger's Profanisaurus*, October 1999
- E made me a slag. —*Mixmag*, p. 99, February 2002

3 an unattractive woman *AUSTRALIA, 1988*

- —Clive Galea, *Slipper*, p. 170, 1988
- —Robert G. Barrett, *Davo's Little Something*, p. 275, 1992
- 'Fuck off, ya slags,' snapped the woman, pressing a button labelled 'fit'. —Linda Jaivin, *Rock n Roll Babes from Outer Space*, p. 83, 1996
- You wouldn't kill me ya slag! I'm yer father!! —*Sick Puppy*, p. 16, 1998

4 a petty criminal; petty criminals *UK, 1955*

- —John Ayto, *Oxford Dictionary of Slang*, p. 89, 1998

5 a coward *UK, 1788*
The earliest of many meanings, all of which are pejorative.

- You'v[e] got the guts of a slag[.] —Frank Norman, *Bang To Rights*, p. 50, 1958

6 a negative criticism *AUSTRALIA*

- Yes, it's true you're 'still steadfastly attached to your first wife, but your snipey slag at 'second marriages' is very uncool. —*Sydney Morning Herald*, 12th July 2003

7 an insult *UK: SCOTLAND*

- —Michael Munro, *The Original Patter*, p. 64, 1985

slag *verb*

1 to verbally attack, to slander *UK, 1971*
Variants include 'slag off' and 'slag down'.

- I spent two solid hours slagging down can [armoured car] drivers for burying their vehicles in the mud. —Andy McNab, *Immediate Action*, p. 30, 1995
- —Vann Wesson, *Generation X Field Guide and Lexicon*, p. 152, 1997
- [H]e got jealous and started slagging her off [...] calling her a slag[.] —John King, *White Trash*, p. 55, 2001

2 to spit *AUSTRALIA, 1965*

- I know what it's like to be slagged on. —Kathy Lette, *Girls' Night Out*, p. 163, 1987
- I have gone off Svongo's brother a bit. (I saw him slag on the pavement). —Kylie Mole (Maryanne Fahey), *My Diary*, p. 21, 1988

slag about *verb*

to move around; to come and go *UK*

- Slagging about in all weathers. —*British Journal of Photography*, 1st June 1979

slag-bag *noun*

a contemptible woman *UK*
A rhyming combination of **SLAG** (a contemptible person; a sexually promiscuous woman) and **BAG** (an unattractive woman).

- FUCK! Bitch, whore, slut, slag-bag! —Colin Butts, *Is Harry on the Boat?*, p. 105, 1997

slagging rag *noun*

a parachute that is slow to open or does not open at all *US*

- —Linda Reinberg, *In the Field*, p. 201, 1991

slaggy *noun*

a groupie who is promiscuous and sluttish, even by groupie standards *US*

- —*Kiss*, 1969: 'Groupie glossary'

slaggy *adjective*

sluttish *UK, 1943*

- Bridget Jones, the charmingly slaggy character created by British author Helen Fielding. —Jennifer Baumgardner and Amy Richards, *Manifesta*, p. 36, 2000

slake *verb*

▸ **slake the snake**

(of a male) to have sex *US*

- The bartender spoke slowly, as if to an idiot child. "You know, push the bush? Slake the snake? Drain the train? Siphon the python?" —James Ellroy, *Because the Night*, p. 415, 1984

slam *noun*

1 a jail or prison *US, 1960*
A shortened form of **SLAMMER**; sometimes used as a plural.

- During the Moratorium he was in the slam. —Oscar Zeta Acosta, *The Revolt of the Cockroach People*, p. 204, 1973
- Only plea I ever copped cost me three years in the slams. —Edwin Torres, *Carlito's Way*, p. 10, 1975
- Was it Phyl, my one and only mud-kicker calling from the slams? —Iceberg Slim (Robert Beck), *Airtight Willie and Me*, p. 47, 1979
- One of 'em's in the slam. —*48 Hours*, 1982
- I'm going to find out why they haven't got him in the slam already. —Robert Campbell, *Junkyard Dog*, p. 38, 1986
- He served a year in the slam for income-tax evasion, then returned to the Square, where his stores began to pale next to the newer ones. —Josh Alan Friedman, *Tales of Times Square*, p. 76, 1986
- There're some scary fucking slams you can get sent to, Marion, Lewisburg ... —Elmore Leonard, *Out of Sight*, p. 58, 1996

2 sexual intercourse *US*

- —Connie Eble (Editor), *UNC-CH Campus Slang*, p. 7, Spring 1982

3 in foot-powered scootering, a very hard fall *UK*

- —Ben Sharpe, *Scooter Crazy*, p. 42, 2000

slam *verb*

1 to inject an illegal drug intravenously *US*

- Blaze watched Dawn pulling up the sleeves of the red polyester blouse, examining the tracks where she slammed her speedballs, a mixture of powdered cocaine and Mexican tar heroin. —Joseph Wambaugh, *Floaters*, p. 7, 1996

2 to violently jar a mix of alcoholic spirit (usually a shot of tequila) and carbonated soft drink *UK*
To prepare a **SLAMMER**, from the action of slamming a covered glass containing the mixture down on a hard surface, e.g. a bar counter.
- The Method: Slam it with 7-Up [branded soft drink] or via the salt'n'lemon shot ritual — *Sky Magazine*, p. 89, May 2001

3 to hide prison contraband in your rectum *US*
- Like prisoners everywhere, Rikers inmates use their rectums as a sort of suitcase for weapons, concealing one or two razor blades – or sometimes even 20 or 30 – by "slamming" or "boofing" them. — *Village Voice*, p. 45, 19th December 2000

4 to defecate *US*
- — Don R. McCreary (Editor), *Dawg Speak*, 2001

5 to criticise someone or something harshly *US, 1916*
- Soup kitchens slammed[.] New approach needed to tackle homelessness, says campaigner[.] — *The Guardian*, 7th January 2004

6 to refuse to work *US*
Prison usage.
- — Hyman E. Goldin et al., *Dictionary of American Underworld Lingo*, p. 196, 1950

7 in hot rodding and car customising, to modify a car's suspension so as to lower the body *US*
- — John Edwards, *Auto Dictionary*, p. 154, 1993

8 while riding a surfboard or skateboard, to lose your balance and fall *US*
- — *San Francisco Sunday Examiner & Chronicle*, p. 20, 2nd September 1984: 'Say it right'
- — Nick Carroll, *The Next Wave*, 1991

9 to slam dance *US*
- Go to punk gigs by himself. Slam in the pit with the boys until the pain sweated out of him[.] — Francesca Lia Block, *Baby Be-Bop*, p. 410, 1995

slam bam *noun*

1 homemade whisky *US, 1980s*

2 a hastily prepared sandwich consisting only of bread and bologna *BAHAMAS*
- — Patricia Clinton-Meicholas, *More Talkin' Bahamian*, p. 90, 1995

slambang *verb*
to successfully cheat other gamblers *US*
- — *The Annals of the American Academy of Political and Social Sciences*, p. 130, May 1950

slam-bang *adverb*
with force or noise *UK, 1840*
- I'm only trying to convince you that you can't go slam-bang into this. — Horace McCoy, *Kiss Tomorrow Good-bye*, p. 134, 1948
- I didn't find his conversation very entertaning, he was a pretty dull fellow, until slam bang inthe middle of one of his sentences I said, What did you say your name was again? — Clancy Sigal, *Going Away*, p. 179, 1961

slam book *noun*
a book with a series of questions to which friends write answers *US*
- Slam books were big. You'd pass around a list of questions. "Who's the best looking boy in school." "Who'd you love to date?" "Your favorite song." — *San Francisco Chronicle*, p. 38, 15th December 1969

slam dance *verb*
to dance in a violent manner popular in punk and post-punk settings *US, 1981*
Slam dancing was good fodder for popular television in the US, with the *CHiPs* episode that aired on 31st January 1982 and the *Quincy* episode of 2nd December 1982, both of which centred around the relatively new phenomenon.
- [T]he early Saturday evening mob of U.S. teens and young adults who descend on Tijuana to get drunk, slam-dance in nightclubs, fight, bleed, vomit, and, in general, have a wonderful time. — Joseph Wambaugh, *Finnegan's Week*, p. 266, 1993

slam down *verb*
to confine someone to a jail cell *US*
- — James Harris, *A Convict's Dictionary*, p. 38, 1989

slam dunk *noun*

1 in the language of wind surfing, an unintended, sudden end of a ride when the board steers too hard to windward *US*
- — Frank Fox, *A Beginner's Guide to Zen and the Art of Windsurfing*, p. 154, 1985: 'A short dictionary of wind surfing terms'

2 anything accomplished with ease *US*
- Barbara Molar is my wit. This should be a slam dunk. — Stephen J. Cannell, *The Tin Collectors*, p. 18, 2001

slam-dunk *verb*
to defeat someone convincingly, if not overwhelmingly *US*
From the basketball sense of jamming the ball through the hoop.
- I want to slam-dunk this guy. — *A Few Good Men*, 1992

slam-dunk *adjective*
certain *US*
- [S]he kissed him and told him they were a rockin' slink-chunk, slam-dunk band and that it would be fine. — Francesca Lia Block, *Cherokee Bat*, p. 183, 1992

slam hammer; slam puller *noun*
a tool used by car thieves to pull out the cyclinder of the ignition lock *UK*
- Slide hammer. Sometimes called a "slam hammer" "slam puller" or "Yankee". — David Powis, *The Signs of Crime*, 1977

slammed *adjective*
incarcerated *US*
- — Ralph de Sola, *Crime Dictionary*, p. 139, 1982

slammed back *adjective*
under the influence of heroin *US*
- — Jim Crotty, *How to Talk American*, p. 95, 1997

slammer *noun*

1 a door *US*
- You had to pull up in a diamond-studded limousine, with solid gold fenders and ermine upholstery, before the doorman would even reach for the twister to your slammer. — Mezz Mezzrow, *Really the Blues*, p. 84, 1946
- When he fell back through that tavern slammer / Dad, you shouldda dug the squeals and clamour. — Dan Burley, *Diggeth Thou?*, p. 14, 1959
- I took another sip of coffee and turned around to check her out and saw two of New York's finest coming in the slammer. — A.S. Jackson, *Gentleman Pimp*, p. 151, 1973

2 a jail or prison *US*
Also in UK use.
- My mother had me in the slammer. — George Mandel, *Flee the Angry Strangers*, p. 121, 1952
- He spent twenty-three years in the slammer[.] — William "Lord" Buckley, *The Bad-Rapping of the Marquis de Sade*, 1960
- Some get snuffed, some drop out, some go to the slammer and there's always new guys who've joined. — Hunter S. Thompson, *Hell's Angels*, p. 116, 1966
- "You hang around here you're subject to get put in the slammers," Blue said. — Steve Cannon, *Groove, Bang, and Jive Around*, p. 68, 1969
- After flashing his badge of many numbers, he explained he wouldn't take him to the slammer if his loot was cool enough. — Babs Gonzales, *Movin' On Down De Line*, p. 89, 1975
- I'd hate to throw you in the slammer for conspiracy. — *The Sweeney*, p. 56, 1976
- Or that oatmeal at the Cook County slammer. — *The Blues Brothers*, 1980
- But when Vic asked me how's business, well, you don't lie to man who's just done four years in the slammer for ya. — *Reservoir Dogs*, 1992
- — Angela Devlin, *Prison Patter*, p. 105, 1996
- That meant he was a pusher, and that in turn meant a long spell in the slammer. — Duncan MacLaughlin, *The Filth*, p. 197, 2002

3 solitary confinement *US*
- — Inez Cardozo-Freeman, *The Joint*, p. 531, 1984

4 a mix of alcoholic spirit (usually a shot of tequila) and carbonated soft drink, violently jarred together and gulped down whilst fizzing *UK*
- There are four main ways tequila is served: as a shot, as a slammer, as a cocktail and as a digestif/aperitif[.] — Richard Neill, *Booze*, p. 116, 2001

5 a person who slam dances *US*
- Then he went and stood at the edge of the slammers. — Francesca Lia Block, *Baby Be-Bop*, p. 412, 1995

6 an illegal linear amplifier for a citizens' band radio *US*
- — Elementary Electronics, *Dictionary of CB Lingo*, p. 108, 1976

slammin'; slamming *noun*
MDMA, the recreational drug best known as ecstasy *UK*
- — Mike Haskins, *Drugs*, p. 290, 2003

slamming *adjective*
excellent; beautiful; fabulous *US*
Originally late C19; current usage started in 1980s black society and spread with hip-hop music.

- The Wu[-Tang Clan] is too slammin' for these Cold Killin' labels / Who ain't had hits since I seen Aunt Mable — Genius/GZA *Protect Ya Neck*, 1994
- [A] stable of slammin' hostesses in bunny outfits[.] — Diran Adebayo, *My Once Upon A Time*, p. 34, 2000

slammin', jammin', throw down happy feet!
used for expressing great pleasure *US*
- — Connie Eble (Editor), *UNC-CH Campus Slang*, p. 7, Fall 1986

slam partner *noun*
a partner for sex, pure and simple *US*
- — Judi Sanders, *Faced and Faded, Hanging to Hurl*, p. 36, 1993

slam up *verb*
to imprison someone *US*
- Jist cuz you gonna be slammed up three years dont make her a nun. — Seth Morgan, *Homeboy*, p. 146, 1990

slang *noun*
in carnival and amusement park usage, a watch chain *US*
- — Don Wilmeth, *The Language of American Popular Entertainment*, p. 245, 1981

slang *verb*
1 to sell drugs, especially crack cocaine *US*
- — Judi Sanders, *Don't Dog by Do, Dude!*, p. 29, 1991
- This may happen when the banger is "slangin'" – or selling dope – or when he has been forced to move into enemy territory[.] — Bill Valentine, *Gangs and Their Tattoos*, p. 77, 2000
- His brother is gonna go down, he's steady slangin' outside the apartments. — Rick Ayers (Editor), *Berkeley High Slang Dictionary*, p. 39, 2004

2 to berate someone with abusive language *UK, 1844*
- [T]o go and say sorry to some old girl who'd probably take the chance of slanging him when he got there. — John Burke and Stuart Douglass, *The Boys*, p. 87, 1962
- I got into an argument and slanged them all. — Jamie Mandelkau, *Buttons*, p. 53, 1971

3 to exhibit or perform in a circus, fair or market; to perform on a stage *UK, 1789*
- Lavengro, the Daring, slanged the lion, Ferocious, in "the smallest cage in the world". — Butch Reynolds, *Broken Hearted Clown*, p. 63, 1954
- — Paul Baker, *Polari*, p. 190, 2002

slanged *adjective*
in fetters; in chains *UK, 1812*
- [A] showman in the ring is a "slanger" and animals are always "slanged". — Butch Reynolds, *Broken Hearted Clown*, p. 32, 1953

slanger *noun*
1 a drug dealer *US*
- — Judi Sanders, *Da Bomb*, p. 14, 1997

2 a showman *UK, 1933*
Circus use; from obsolete slang (a travelling show; a single performance of a travelling show).
- A showman who harangues the crowd from outside is a "spieler" or "barker"; a showman in the ring is a "slanger" and animals are always "slanged". — Butch Reynolds, *Broken Hearted Clown*, p. 32, 1953

slanging match *noun*
an exchange of harsh abuse *UK, 1896*
- Eventually John and I had a slanging match with him. — Jamie Mandelkau, *Buttons*, p. 53, 1971
- The situation was aggravated still further by the added fact that men were passing wind with gay abandon and every so often a slanging match would break out. — Robin Page, *Down Among the Dossers*, p. 68, 1973

slangs *noun*
slang words or terms *US*
Hawaiian youth usage.
- — Elizabeth Ball Carr, *Da Kine Talk*, p. 148, 1972

slanguage *noun*
a slang vocabulary *US, 1879*
A jargon-like attempt to dignify slang as a language.
- — Brigid McConville and John Shearlaw, *The Slanguage of Sex*, 1984
- Edgar Wallace, Peter Cheyney and James Hadley Chase followed the American slanguage into the Hard-Boiled school [of fiction.] — Paul Duncan, *Noir Fiction*, p. 25, 2000

slanguist *noun*
a linguist with a special interest in slang; an expert user of a slang vocabulary *US*
An inevitable construction that lends some dignity to a misunderstood academic; it is first recorded in William Safire's *New York Times* column, 26th October 1980, although 'slangist' was recorded in 1885 as 'a user of slang'.
- [N]ot only does the slanguist find ordinary English tame[.] — Gavin Jones, *Strange Talk*, p. 139, 1999
- The inability of slow-witted censors to keep up with the implications of fast talk from "ultra-modern slanguists" made for a fun game of hide-and- seek between the hip and the hapless. — Thomas Doherty, *Pre-Code Hollywood*, p. 181, 1999
- [T]he slanguist John Farmer noted in 1890 that to make the air blue means "to curse; to swear; to use profane language." — William Safire, *No Uncertain Terms*, p. 44, 1999

slant *noun*
a South Asian person *US, 1942*
Offensive.
- ["A]ll these boons just sat there laughing at me." "Boons?" I said. [T]hat's just like a World War II movie where they say "kraut" and "slants" and stuff like that! — Lester Bangs, *Psychotic Reactions and Carburetor Dung*, p. 280, 1978
- Gooks could be both. Slants and slopes were civilians. Dinks could be both. — Nelson DeMille, *Word of Honor*, p. 414, 1985
- By god, when they ain't foolin' around with wars and dope traffic, them slants do pretty good on the cuisine. — Dan Jenkins, *Dead Solid Perfect*, p. 65, 1986
- Oh, there are some soldiers thought Code Six as he watched, soldiers like Jimmy and I were, fighting the fucking GOOKS and SLANTS and SLOPES, soldiers trotting single file across a smoking field. — William T. Vollman, *Whores for Gloria*, p. 36, 1991
- Everybody goes around pretending there's one set of rules. One size fits all. That's not the way. There's one set for crooks and one for coups. Another set for niggers and another for honkies and another for slants. — Robert Campbell, *Boneyards*, p. 268, 1992

slanter *noun*
1 a dishonest trick *AUSTRALIA, 1864*
- He used to delight in telling the story in great detail, claiming it was the greatest 'slanter' in history, and his listener would always say: 'You cleaned up a thousand dollars on a rigged race, eh?' — Frank Hardy and Athol George Mulley, *The Needy and the Greedy*, p. 38, 1975

2 the eye *US*
- — Clarence Major, *Dictionary of Afro-American Slang*, p. 105, 1970

slant-eye *noun*
a person from southern Asia *US*
Offensive.
- — Joseph E. Ragen and Charles Finston, *Inside the World's Toughest Prison*, p. 818, 1962: 'Penitentiary and underworld glossary'

slant six *noun*
a six cylinder engine configured with all six cylinders in line slanted over 30 degrees *US*
Introduced in 1959 for the Plymouth Valiant, it is considered by many to be the most durable engine ever manufactured commercially.
- Its slant-six was a paragon of reliability that could propel it along the road at seventy miles an hour. — Peter Coyote, *Sleeping Where I Fall*, p. 318, 1998

slantville *noun*
a neighbourhood dominated by South Asian people *US*
- Slantville is the N.Y. word for Chinatown. — Richard Farina, *Letter to Peter Tamony*, 24th August 1959

slanty-eyed; slant-eye *noun*
a car of Japanese manufacture *US*
Citizens' band radio slang; a specific application for generally racist terms.
- — *Complete CB Slang Dictionary*, p. 85, 1976
- — Peter Chippindale, *The British CB Book*, p. 161, 1981

slap *noun*
1 a beating *UK*
From the conventional use (to hit with an open hand); as with **SPANK** it is applied with heavy irony.
- That skinny geezer got a proper slap before he legged it out the door. — John King, *White Trash*, p. 149, 2001

2 a prison sentence *UK*
From a conventional 'slap' given as a punishment.
- Wally is off to Albany to serve his sentence, and this time he's copped a six-and-a-half slap. — Jimmy Stockin, *On The Cobbles*, p. 139, 2000

3 theatrical makeup; cosmetics *UK, 1860*
You *slap* it on; theatrical; survives in the face of lighting technology that has made much makeup unnecessary. Also variant 'schlep'.

- [E]ffeminates flaunted their difference and henna and slap went with limp wrists and exaggerated walk and speech. — *Maledicta*, p. 225, Winter 1980
- [She] checked the slap in the mirror behind the bar[.] — James Gardiner, *Who's a Pretty Boy Then?*, p. 123, 1997
- Her face is glowing red so much that you can see it under the white schlep. — J.J. Connolly, *Know Your Enemy [britpulp]*, p. 155, 1999
- Their tawny faces were cosmetic blackface, theatre "slap". — Carol Chillington Rutter, *Enter the Body*, p. 7, 2001
- — Paul Baker, *Polari*, p. 190, 2002

slap *verb*

1 to increase the charge for something; to implement a punitive condition *UK, 1922*

- Slapping capital gains tax on bricks and mortar[.] — *The Guardian*, 23rd October 2003

2 especially in jazz or funk music, to play the double bass or bass guitar by pulling at the strings and letting them 'slap' back *US, 1933*

'Slap-style' is also known as 'thumb-style'.

- Limiting is used only to attenuate a signal's peaks, like those produced when you pop or slap a bass. — Keith Rosier, *Studio Bass Masters*, p. 2, 1999

▸ **slap skins**

1 to have sex *US*

- — Connie Eble (Editor), *UNC-CH Campus Slang*, p. 9, April 1995

2 to slap palms in greeting, farewell or approval *US*

- I slapped skin with them, playing it cool all the way. — Piri Thomas, *Down These Mean Streets*, p. 16, 1967
- We slapped skin all around on the running of our little murder game. — Edwin Torres, *Carlito's Way*, p. 55, 1975
- You'll be slappin' skin with the heavy lifters from south of Hawthorn. — Stephen J. Cannell, *The Tin Collectors*, p. a, 2001

▸ **slap the bacon in the pan**

to have sex *US*

- — Bill Davis, *Jawjacking*, p. 91, 1977

▸ **slap the iron to her**

to put snow chains on a truck's tyres *US*

- — *American Speech*, p. 273, December 1961: 'Northwest truck drivers' language'

▸ **slap the monkey**

(of a male) to masturbate *UK*

A variation of **SPANK THE MONKEY**.

- [E]very lad in the country is slapping his monkey over Emily's knockers [breasts] in GQ magazine[.] — Ben Elton, *High Society*, p. 20, 2002

slap *adverb*

exactly; perfectly *UK, 1829*

- parking this dreadful great orange-and-cream jam-jar [...] slap under a no-parking sign — Derek Raymond (Robin Cook), *The Crust on its Uppers*, p. 23, 1962

slap and tickle *noun*

1 sex *UK*

A little slap and tickle never hurt anyone.

- — Louis S. Leland, *A Personal Kiwi-Yankee Dictionary*, p. 93, 1984

2 a pickle *UK*

Rhyming slang.

- — Ray Puxley, *Cockney Rabbit*, 1992

slap-back *adjective*

self-congratulatory *UK*

- We lacked expertise, a guitar player and any coherent definition beyond that of a ragged, slap-back boho band[.] — Mick Farren, *Give the Anarchist a Cigarette*, p. 48, 2001

slap circuit *noun*

the underworld *US*

- If you're really a hood, then ask around the slap circuit who I am. — Mickey Spillane, *Me, Hood!*, p. 30, 1963

slap-down *noun*

a humiliating situation *US*

- — *55-Plus*, p. 13, 12th February 1986: 'Today's guide to teen slang'

slap down *verb*

to contradict and prevent someone's action, especially when it is done with humiliating effect *UK, 1938*

- Mo Mowlam [...] was slapped down earlier this year when she called for a wider debate on the future of the Royal Family[.] — *The Guardian*, 4th September 2000

slap hammer *noun*

a hammer designed for pulling dents but used to break open the top of a car's steering column to obtain access to the ignition *US*

- He told them he'd spot the car a customer wanted and use a slim jim or lemon pop to get in, a slap hammer to yank the ignition, a side kick to extract steering column locks and usually liquid nitrogen to freeze the alarm system. — Elmore Leonard, *Out of Sight*, p. 56, 1996

slap-happy *adjective*

1 dazed; confused *US, mid-1930s*

- [T]hen for a while I shook Slim, who was wandering a little slap-happy in the street from all the whisky and beer[.] — Jack Kerouac, *On the Road*, p. 34, 1957

2 obsessed with masturbation *US*

- — Joseph E. Ragen and Charles Finston, *Inside the World's Toughest Prison*, p. 818, 1962: 'Penitentiary and underworld glossary'

slaphead *noun*

a bald person, whether naturally so or shaven *UK, 1990*

- Toby, better known as Slaphead, having been bald since he was aged about nine — Andy McNab, *Immediate Action*, p. 222, 1995

slaphead *adjective*

bald-headed *UK, 1990s*

- Some slaphead baby next to me's chokin on a lolly. — Nick Barlay, *Curvy Lovebox*, p. 18, 1997

slap-in-the-chops *noun*

a shot of pure alcohol *BERMUDA*

- — Peter Smith and Fred M. Barritt, *Bermewjan Vurds*, 1985

slap on the wrist *noun*

any minor punishment *UK*

- "Slap on wrist" for scientists who killed mice with loud music — *The Guardian*, 19th August 2002

slapper *noun*

1 a sexually promiscuous woman *UK*

Possibly from **SLAP** (makeup) or, simply, the sound of flesh on flesh.

- It's not got any of the old bitches in it, sad old slags and slappers who've been around forever[.] — Stella Duffy, *Jail Bait [britpulp]*, p. 113, 1999
- [Y]ou couldn't say she's a slapper. She's a sexy girl. — Kevin Sampson, *Outlaws*, p. 236, 2001

2 a small, heavy club *US*

- What caused Typewriter to leave his intentions unfulfilled, flopping straight down in one heap, was an eight-ounce bar of lead tightly bound in burnished leather and cradled in the broad palm of Canale's hand. He returned the slapper to his coat before anyone saw it. — Emmett Grogan, *Final Score*, p. 271, 1976

3 a windscreen wiper *US*

- — *Complete CB Slang Dictionary*, p. 85, 1976
- — Peter Chippindale, *The British CB Book*, p. 159, 1981

slapping *noun*

a beating *UK*

- [J]ust another alleyway slapping[.] — Greg Williams, *Diamond Geezers*, p. 72, 1997

slaps *noun*

plastic flip-flops (sandals) *US*

Skateboarding usage.

- — Albert Cassorla, *The Skateboarder's Bible*, p. 202, 1976

slapsie-maxi *noun*

a taxi *NEW ZEALAND*

Rhyming slang.

- I was caster for Gene Tunney [money] so I took a slapsie maxie to the course. — *Truth*, p. 19, 21st May 1963

slap-slap *noun*

a small police club that fits into a police officer's hand *US*

- — *American Speech*, p. 272, December 1962: 'The language of traffic policemen'

slap-up *adjective*

(of a meal) excellent, generously provisioned, superior *UK, 1889*

Originally (1823) used to describe anything or anyone that was considered excellent.

- [H]e would have been given a pat on the back, maybe even a slap-up dinner. — Frederick Forsyth, *Avenger*, p. 32, 2003
- [T]he local Oxfam group invited the town's bigwigs to a slap-up meal of fairly-traded and local produce. — *The Guardian*, 24th May 2003

slash *noun*

1 a urination *UK, 1950*

- Bloody drongos!! Hope someone catches you bastards having a quiet slash sometime.—Barry Humphries, *The Wonderful World of Barry McKenzie*, p. 11, 1968
- Strewth – why is it whenever a bloke needs a slash some bastard's got there first[?]—Barry Humphries, *Bazza Pulls It Off!*, 1971
- He forced a slash, didn't flush and clumped back downstairs.—Kevin Sampson, *Powder*, p. 224, 1999
- I looked at the gravel and wanted a slash.—David Peace, *Nineteen Seventy-Four*, p. 60, 1999

2 the vagina *US*

- "Snatch," "hole," "kooze, "slash," "pussy" and "crack" were other terms referring variously to women's genitals, to women as individuals, or to women as a species.—*Screw*, p. 5, 3rd January 1972
- She acts like any paid hooker [...] Paid for her slash.—Peter Sotos, *Index*, p. 56, 1996

3 an attractive, white woman *US*

- —Carsten Stroud, *Close Pursuit*, p. 276, 1987

slash *verb*

1 to urinate *UK, 1950*

2 to cut a military-style peaked cap in such a way that the downward angle of the peak is exaggerated *UK*

- The peak of his [a prison officer's] cap has been "slashed" to fit low over the bridge of his nose.—*The Guardian*, 29th January 2001

3 to surf aggressively back and forth across the face of a wave *US*

- —Lee Wardlaw, *Cowabunga!*, p. 156, 1991

slash-and-burn *adjective*

ruthless; unconcerned with the consequences of a tactic *US, 1989*

From a term describing a jungle agricultural practice first recorded in the early 1940s.

- But I do see certain slash-and-burn tactics in the Industry now—Robert Stoller and I.S. Levine, *Coming Attractions*, p. 216, 1991
- —*American Speech*, p. 260, Fall 1993: 'Among the new words'

slasher *noun*

1 a person who takes a perverse pleasure from vandalism by slashing *US*

- A slasher is some warped individual who cuts, rips and mutilates upholstery, leather, curtains, and sometimes employees' uniforms.—Dev Collans with Stewart Sterling, *I was a House Detective*, p. 144, 1954

2 in prison, a self-mutilator *UK*

- —Angela Devlin, *Prison Patter*, p. 105, 1996

3 a surgeon *UK*

Often teamed with anaesthetists as '**GASSERS** and slashers'.

- —Adam T. Fox, St Mary's Hospital, London, 10th October 2002

4 in greyhound racing, a dog that cuts to the inside rail after the first turn *US*

slash-house *noun*

a toilet *AUSTRALIA*

- I was looking for the slash house. Felt like training Thomas at the terracotta[.]—Barry Humphries, *Bazza Pulls It Off!*, 1971

slat *noun*

1 used to denote five shillings, or the post-decimalisation equivalent of 25p *UK*

Originally (1788) 'a half-crown coin'; subsequently, perhaps as a result of inflation, used of a crown (a five-shilling coin) and its value. Thus, pre-1971, 'half-a-slat' was 'a half-crown coin; half-a-crown in value', and so it remained, despite metrication, to represent equivalent values.

- —Patrick O'Shaughnessy, *Market Traders' Slang*, 1979

2 a dollar *US*

- You want the blue too? The bite [cost] is two for fifty slats.—Iceberg Slim (Robert Beck), *Pimp*, p. 92, 1969

3 a jail or prison sentence *US*

- —Kenn "Naz" Young, *Naz's Underground Dictionary*, p. 56, 1973

slate *noun*

marijuana *UK*

- —Angela Devlin, *Prison Patter*, p. 106, 1996

slate *verb*

to criticise someone or something harshly *UK, 1848*

- Did it upset him that, after all that time, so many critics slated it?—*The Guardian*, 19th May 2003

slating *noun*

an instance of harsh criticism *UK, 1870*

- Flintshire social services were lucky to get a metaphorical pat on the back rather than a slating when they took the twins, Belinda and Kimberley, away from the Kilshaws.—*The Guardian*, 9th April 2001

slats *noun*

1 ribs *US, 1898*

- They sometimes wear skirts, but they ask no favors and are likely to kick you in the slats when you ain't looking if you make the mistake of treating them like flowers[.]—Robert Campbell, *Junkyard Dog*, p. 8, 1986

2 prison bars *US*

- —Hyman E. Goldin et al., *Dictionary of American Underworld Lingo*, p. 197, 1950

3 skis *US*

- —*American Speech*, p. 207, October 1963: 'The language of skiers'

slaughter *noun*

a concealed location used by criminals for the division or transfer of recently stolen goods *UK, 1970*

- Superintendent Kneff lost his temper. "If we can't catch 'em, we must find the slaughter," he decreed.—Jeffrey Scott, *Wheelman for the Cleaners in John Creasey's Crime Collection*, 1977
- [We] tucked away the next night's takings in a little lock-up we used as a slaughter[.]—Lenny McLean, *The Guv'nor*, p. 52, 1998
- This breaker's yard was supposed to be their slaughter.—Jake Arnott, *He Kills Coppers*, p. 116, 2001
- Do business this way first, next time you come to my slaughter.—Garry Bushell, *The Face*, p. 12, 2001
- [I]f we lay our hands on a good load being divvied up at a slaughter, it'll be a nice little earner for you.—Duncan MacLaughlin, *The Filth*, p. 116, 2002

slaughter *verb*

1 to utterly defeat someone *UK*

- [C]hoosing a hole and potting the black ... next game up slaughtered by Gal[.]—John King, *White Trash*, p. 194, 2001

2 to severely criticise someone or something *UK*

- It's just in the paper. If I get slaughtered, it doesn't matter. I don't take it seriously.—Shaun Ryder, *Shaun Ryder... in His Own Words*, 1991

3 to use a concealed location for temporary storage, distribution or transfer of recently stolen goods *UK*

- He reckons he knows where it's being slaughtered. I got the address. A scrapyard in Harlesden.—Jake Arnott, *He Kills Coppers*, p. 90, 2001

slaughtered *adjective*

very drunk or drug-intoxicated *US*

- —Pamela Munro, *U.C.L.A. Slang*, p. 77, 1989
- He's not used to getting slaughtered so much these days.—Kevin Sampson, *Outlaws*, p. 172, 2001
- They all rushed out and just started getting slaughtered.—*Varsity*, p. 1, 14th June 2002

slaughterhouse *noun*

1 a premises where a drug dealer stores drugs *UK*

- [He] rents a "slaughterhouse" (place to keep stock); works odd hours; and claims to be a jeweller if stopped and questioned[.]—Julian Johnson, *Urban Survival*, p. 28, 2003

2 a school *US*

Teen slang.

- —*San Francisco News*, p. 6, 25th March 1958

Slaughter on the Water *noun*

the 1995 America's Cup sailing race, a lopsided victory by New Zealand *US*

- They called it "Slaughter on the Water." Dennis Conner had persuaded defeated rival Pact 95 to give him the use of their fast boat, Young America, but nevertheless his team was annihilated in five straight races by Black Magic.—Joseph Wambaughq, *Floaters*, p. 290, 1996

slave *noun*

1 in a sado-masochistic relationship, a person who endures many forms of humiliation, including extreme pain and public displays of submission *US*

- He "loved," he testified, to be his wife's "slave," to be whipped by her and forced to perform cunnilingus for a woman friend or fellatio for a visiting male, while she watched.—Michael Leigh, *The Velvet Underground*, p. 82, 1963

- There is also jealousy among my slaves. In America, I had three slaves, a Wall Street banker, a telephone company executive and a little printer. — *Screw*, p. 5, 8th February 1971
- — Wayne Dynes, *Homolexis*, p. 123, 1985
- — Thomas Murray, *The Language of Sadomasochism*, p. 122–123, 1989

2 a submissive prisoner who performs all types of menial tasks for others *US*
- "In fact, they even assigned him a slave." "A slave?" Novak said. "A gofer. Somebody to carry messages, run errands for him. That kind of shit." — Gerald Petievich, *Shakedown*, p. 85–86, 1988

3 a job *US*
- I didn't mind copping a slave just then because I could use the gold[.] — Mezz Mezzrow, *Really the Blues*, p. 107, 1946
- — Lavada Durst, *The Jives of Dr. Hepcat*, p. 13, 1953
- This slave is a drag, in the bag for some old hag, but strictly nowhere for me, I swear. — Dan Burley, *Diggeth Thou?*, p. 11, 1959
- You mean you just want any slave you can find? — Malcolm X and Alex Haley, *The Autobiography of Malcolm X*, p. 44, 1964
- A guy who worked in the garment center wouldn't say he had a job; he'd say, "Man, like, I got a slave." That's about what it amounted to. — Claude Brown, *Manchild in the Promised Land*, p. 184, 1965
- — Malachi Andrews and Paul T. Owens, *Black Language*, p. 79, 1973
- — Connie Eble (Editor), *UNC-CH Campus Slang*, p. 6, Fall 1980

slave *verb*

to work, especially at a menial job *US*
- "How do you make your bread?" Wilson asked. "Where do you slave? Know what I mean?" — Joseph Nazel, *Black Cop*, p. 178, 1974

slave bracelet *noun*

a bracelet showing romantic devotion to another *US*
- As she approached he took in the slave bracelet she wore around her right ankle[.] — Irving Shulman, *The Amboy Dukes*, p. 136, 1947

slave-driver *noun*

a stern taskmaster *US, 1854*
- Miranda Priestly, the hard-faced, egotistic slave-driver who is narrator Andrea's boss-from-hell[.] — *The Guardian*, 6th December 2003

slave market *noun*

1 any place where day labourers congregate *US*
- Past the slave market where eight wretches sat on a bus bench, not waiting for a bus but talking to motorists who would stop. — Joseph Wambaugh, *The Black Marble*, p. 203, 1978

2 a National Employment Service office *CANADA*
- And the chances are, that he will be a regular customer at the SLAVE MARKET for a few months. — *Voice of the Idle Worker*, p. 2/2, 8th February 1960

slave training *noun*

the process of instructing, and conditioning the behaviour of, a sexual submissive in order that the submissive's menial service and status become part of a sexual relationship, especially when used in a dominant prostitute's advertising matter *UK*
- — Caroline Archer, *Tart Cards*, 2003

slay *verb*

to cause someone to laugh uproariously *UK, 1927*
- [He] proceeded to slay them in the aisles and landed the part[.] — Andy Dougan, *Robin Williams*, p. 51, 1998

slayer *noun*

an assertive young woman *UK*

An allusion to the eponymous lead in the television series *Buffy the Vampire Slayer*. Teen slang.
- — Susie Dent, *The Language Report*, p. 78, 2003

sleaze *noun*

1 sordidness, sleaziness; immorality *UK, 1967*
- [C]ognoscenti of trash, aficionados of sleaze[.] — *Harpers & Queen*, October 1976
- The [play] was dripping showbiz sleaze. — *Sunday Times*, 23rd March 1980
- [T]he Regent Hotel, which is nothing but brown bricks held together with sleaze, where all the mattresses are sealed inside slippery plastic covers[.] — Chuck Palahniuk, *Fight Club*, p. 58, 1999

2 political corruption *US, 1983*
- The Labour party risks an embarrassing fine over "unacceptable" breaches of an anti-sleaze law introduced by Tony Blair to clean up politics. — *The Guardian*, 22nd November 2003

3 a person with low moral standards *US*
- — *Verbatim*, p. 281, May 1976
- Hey you sleaze, my bed! — *The Blues Brothers*, 1980
- "What a sleaze," Alana says, shivering in mock disgust. — Bret Easton Ellis, *Less Than Zero*, p. 29, 1985

sleazebag *noun*

an undesirable, unlikeable person *US*

A useful term when you cannot decide whether to call someone a SCUMBAG or a SLEAZEBALL.
- My guess is that the FDA finally caught up with the sleazebag from Oxnard who was fronting the operation and nailed him with a cease and desist. — Armistead Maupin, *Maybe the Moon*, p. 14, 1992

sleazeball *noun*

an utterly despicable person *US, 1983*
- The sleazeball agent screamed for twenty minutes how Rossi's would be sued. — Seth Morgan, *Homeboy*, p. 292, 1990
- I'm sure you came along here today with the idea that everybody in this business is a sleazeball. Everybody in this business is a sleazeball. But some of them are okay sleazeballs and some of them are asshole sleazeballs. — Christopher Brookmyre, *Not the End of the World*, p. 263, 1998

sleazemeister *noun*

an acknowledged expert on, or practitioner of, sordidness, sleaziness, immorality or political corruption *US*

By a combination of SLEAZE and German *meister* (master).
- "I take it Abernathy tried some cheap sleazemeister tricks at the deposition?" "Like you wouldn't believe." — William Bernhardt, *Deadly Justice*, p. 137, 1993
- [T]ell "sleazemeisters to get lost," as one zealous Seattle Times reporter put it[.] — Paula Gilovich and Traci Vogel, *The Stranger Guide to Seattle*, p. 233, 2001

sleazo *noun*

a despicable, sleazy person *US, 1972*
- He's got this golfcourse job that's really a front, and he's got his hotel and bar that he owns. Really a sleazo racket. — James Ellroy, *Brown's Requiem*, p. 158, 1981
- [T]he outcall office window he'd blown to bits would give him a shot at some kind of file on Vandy – and the rock sleazos she might have run to. — James Ellroy, *Suicide Hill*, p. 807–808, 1986

sleazoid *noun*

a person of low character *US*
- They wondered how the hell he was going to hold together, working for a bunch of sleazoid lawyers and bail bondsmen. — Carl Hiaasen, *Tourist Season*, p. 18, 1986
- Only a queue of sleazoids at the end of the friggin road waiting to have their arses whipped. — Niall Griffiths, *Kelly + Victor*, p. 283, 2002

sleazy *adjective*

1 cheap; inferior; low *US, 1941*
- Your values are pretty sleazy, Phil. — Philip Wylie, *Opus 21*, p. 336, 1949

2 disreputable, especially in a sexually enticing way *UK*
- Half the wardroom were in some sleazy nightclub that was raided. — John Winton, *We Saw the Sea*, 1960
- Nice and sleazy does it every time. — The Stranglers, *Nice and Sleazy*, 1978

sleb *noun*

a celebrity *UK*

A phonetic slurring and reduction.
- Stephen Fry, who has written about his life as a "sleb" in his autobiography (reviewed last week), provides the lengthy forward to Nothing. — *The Independent*, p. 42, 26th October 1997
- — Andrew Holmes, *Sleb*, 2002
- — Susie Dent, *Larpers and Shroomers*, p. 71, 2004

sled *noun*

1 a motorcycle *US*

Biker (motorcycle) usage.

2 a car *US*
- I am not involved with that, those goddamned German sleds. — George V. Higgins, *Penance for Jerry Kennedy*, p. 236, 1985
- "Nice sled, huh?" "Primo." — James Ellroy, *Suicide Hill*, p. 611, 1986

sledge *noun*

a verbal criticism designed to put a player off their game *AUSTRALIA*
- Warne escaped without too many sledges from the crowd when he performed his duties as 12th man on Friday. — *Sun-Herald*, p. 135, 13th August 2000
- And players who wouldn't be intimidated, such as me and Aravinda, would tend to overreact to sledges and end up playing injudicious shots. — Arjuna Ranatunga, *The Observer*, 25th February 2001

sledge *verb*

to needle an opponent in order to put them off their game *AUSTRALIA*

- I've never been one to sledge on the field. — Paul Vautin, *Turn It Up!*, p. 182, 1995
- Dravid pulls Cork's umpteenth bouncer for four, so Cork sledges him. — *The Guardian*, 8th Spetember 2002

sledgehammer *noun*

in pool, a stroke lacking in finesse but full of force *US*

- — Steve Rushin, *Pool Cool*, p. 27, 1990

sledger *noun*

in cricket, a fielder who baits, taunts and abuses an opponent as tactical gamesmanship *UK*

- The finest ever example of giving the sledger a taste of his own medicine doesn't make it here, but I give it to you now: a portly Sri Lankan batsman was asked by a South African why he was "so fucking fat". "Because," replied the batsman calmly, "every time I fuck your wife, she gives me a biscuit. — *The Guardian*, 22nd June 2002

sledgied *adjective*

under the influence of MDMA, the recreational drug best known as ecstasy *UK*

- [S]erious ravers need one or two tablets at an average dose of 100mg to get, in their words, "sledgied" or "monged." — *The Independent*, p. 5, 28th December 1991

sledging *noun*

the practice of needling an opponent in order to put them off their game *AUSTRALIA, 1975*

Originally, and still principally, in cricket, but now also used in reference to other sports.

- The recent tour also saw the term 'sledging' surface in the press. — Frank Hardy, *Hardy's People*, p. 54, 1986
- Mind you, Wally wasn't bad at the sledging caper himself. — Paul Vautin, *Turn It Up!*, p. 181, 1995
- Golf, cricket, football – no sport is safe from the power of sledging. — *The Guardian*, 28th September 2002

sleekit *adjective*

cunning, sly *UK: SCOTLAND, 1911*

Dialect.

- There y'are, sleekit drinker, by the way! — Ian Pattison, *Rab C. Nesbitt*, 1988

sleep *noun*

1 a prison sentence of one year *US*

- — Vincent J. Monteleone, *Criminal Slang*, p. 212, 1949

2 cocaine *US*

Rich irony; if you do, you won't.

- — Carsten Stroud, *Close Pursuit*, p. 277, 1987

sleep *verb*

▸ **sleep with**

to have sex with *UK, 1819*

- A woman is much more comfortable taking her current man around guys she's slept with than a guy is taking his woman around women he's had sex with. ("Slept with"/"sex with." Isn't that it in a nutshell?) — Chris Rock, *Rock This!*, p. 136, 1997

▸ **sleep with the fishes**

to be dead as a result of a murder *US*

- So waking up in the morning is better than sleeping with the fishes. — Gerald Petievich, *Shakedown*, p. 45, 1988

sleep around *verb*

to be sexually promiscuous *US, 1928*

- If a girl sleeps around, she will still get called 'dirty'. But then, who's to know? — *The Observer*, 2nd December 2001

sleeper *noun*

1 a barbiturate capsule; a sleeping tablet *US*

- — Francis J. Rigney and L. Douglas Smith, *The Real Bohemia*, p. xvii, 1961
- — *Current Slang*, p. 43, Fall 1968
- — Carl D. Chambers and Richard D. Heckman, *Employee Drug Abuse*, p. 210, 1972
- — *American Speech*, p. 208, Fall-winter 1973: 'The Language of Nursing'
- Even though the sleeper had only done half its job, Leo was still groggy. — Emmett Grogan, *Final Score*, p. 10, 1976
- — Angela Devlin, *Prison Patter*, p. 106, 1996

2 heroin *UK, 1998*

- — Robert Ashton, *This Is Heroin*, p. 207, 2002
- — Mike Haskins, *Drugs*, p. 284, 2003

3 a book, film, song, etc, that, having failed to sell successfully on its initial release, eventually becomes a 'hit' *UK, 1984*

- Kevin Smith, the brilliant young filmmaker responsible for 1997's underground sleeper hit Chasing Amy, was signed to write a first draft. — Peter Bart, *The Gross*, p. 46, 2000

4 in sports, a player who performs exceptionally well in spite of very low initial expectations *US*

- — Bill Shefski, *Running Press Glossary of Football Language*, p. 99, 1978

5 in betting, uncollected winnings; a stake that is illegally retained by the bookmaker when a bet is won *UK*

- Wally (motto: Wally pays with a smile), had just tried to keep a sleeper for the book, i.e. had omitted to return winning clients their stake-money. — Charles Raven, *Underworld Nights*, p. 70, 1956
- — John McCririck, *John McCririck's World of Betting*, p. 61, 1991

6 in circus and carnival usage, money that a customer overlooks *US*

- — Don Wilmeth, *The Language of American Popular Entertainment*, p. 245, 1981

7 in craps, a bet on the table that a gambler has forgotten is his *US*

- — N.B. Winkless, *The Gambling Times Guide to Craps*, p. 97, 1981

8 in dominoes, an unused piece that rests numbers-down *US*

9 in hot rodding, a conventional-looking, deceptively high-performing car *US*

- — John Lawlor, *How to Talk Car*, p. 94, 1965

10 a train with sleeping carriages *US*

- [H]e would pay off the saxes, slip an extra twenty to the trombone (with a habit and two ulcers to support), pack his elegant suits and gaudy neckwear, and catch a sleeper back to New York[.] — John Clellon Holmes, *The Horn*, p. 131, 1958

11 a rock just below the land surface *CANADA*

- A sleeper is out of sight until struck and turned up by the plough. — Chris Thain, *Cold as a Bay Street Banker's Heart*, p. 140, 1987

sleeper jump *noun*

any long distance move between performances *US*

- — Sherman Louis Sergel, *The Language of Show Biz*, p. 200, 1973

sleeping Bill *noun*

a police truncheon *US*

- — Vincent J. Monteleone, *Criminal Slang*, p. 212, 1949

sleeping policeman *noun*

a speed bump *UK, 1973*

- — Lewis Poteet, *Car & Motorcyle Slang*, p. 181, 1992
- The Briton in his car is just like a Roman in his chariot – apart from the sleeping policemen[.] — Andrew Nickolds, *Back to Basics*, p. 160, 1994

sleeping time *noun*

a very short jail or prison sentence *US*

- — Jay Robert Nash, *Dictionary of Crime*, p. 108, 1992

sleep off *verb*

to serve a short prison sentence without difficulty *US*

- — Hyman E. Goldin et al., *Dictionary of American Underworld Lingo*, p. 197, 1950

sleep on *verb*

to give overnight consideration to something; to put off making a decision until the following day *UK, 1519*

- Go home and sleep on it – Robin Cook's advice to MPs after they threw out all the options for reform. — *The Guardian*, 5th February 2003

sleep-out *noun*

1 an enclosed verandah, or part thereof, fitted with a bed for sleeping *AUSTRALIA, 1927*

- In that case I'll put you in the sleep-out. — Eric Lambert, *The Veterans*, p. 25, 1954
- It was one of those houses where the front door had been boarded up and the verandah converted into a long skinny sleepout. — John Birmingham, *He Died With a Felafel in his Hand*, p. 128, 1994

2 chiefly in Victoria, a separate outbuilding used as sleeping quarters *AUSTRALIA*

- The boys can use the sleep-out if the other rooms are occupied. — *www.abc.net.au/wordmap*, 2003

Sleepy-R *noun*

the Canadian Pacific Railway *CANADA*

- The less than complimentary "Sleepy-R" has the multiple impact of being a takeoff on the sound of the letters CPR, an assessment of the energy of CPR workers, while also sounding like a western cattle brand. — Chris Thain, *Cold as a Bay Street Banker's Heart*, p. 140, 1987

sleepy seeds *noun*
the deposits of mucus formed about the eyes during sleep *US*
- There were still sleepy seeds in his eyes. —Stephen King, *Salem's Lot*, p. 272, 1975

sleet *noun*
crack cocaine *US*
From the drug's resemblance to sleet.
- —US Department of Justice, *Street Terms*, October 1994

sleeve *noun*
a condom *UK*
- —David Rowan, *A Glossary for the 90s*, 1998
- I pulled out of her sopping pussy, and as I lay on my stomach I quickly took off the sleeve and hid it under my pants on the floor. —*Letters to Penthouse XV*, p. 160, 2002

▸ **on the sleeve**
used of someone who injects drugs *UK*
From the need to roll up a sleeve before injecting.
- —Angela Devlin, *Prison Patter*, p. 83, 1996

▸ **put the sleeve on**
to arrest someone *UK*
- —Angela Devlin, *Prison Patter*, p. 93, 1996

sleeve *verb*
to tattoo the lower half of the arm *US*
- —James Harris, *A Convict's Dictionary*, p. 38, 1989

sleeveen *adjective*
sly, devious *IRELAND*
- —Colin Murphy and Donal O'Dea, *The Book of Feckin' Irish Slang*, p. 60, 2004
- The Irish, a sleeveen race if ever there was one, will merely dodge the tollbooths[.] —*Irish Times*, 7th January 2004

sleeves *noun*
a wetsuit of any style *US*
- —Gary Fairmont R. Filosa II, *The Surfer's Almanac*, p. 194, 1977

sleezer *noun*
a person, usually female, who is substandard in some important way *US*
- —Judi Sanders, *Kickin' like Chicken with the Couch Commander*, p. 22, 1992

sleigh ride *noun*
the use of cocaine or heroin; cocaine or heroin *US*
Building on the **SNOW** metaphor.
- —Joseph E. Ragen and Charles Finston, *Inside the World's Toughest Prison*, p. 818, 1962: 'Penitentiary and underworld glossary'
- —David Maurer and Victor Vogel, *Narcotics and Narcotic Addiction*, p. 444, 1973
- —Nick Constable, *This is Cocaine*, p. 181, 2002

sleveen *noun*
in Newfoundland, a person not to be trusted, a rascal *CANADA*
- He's a real sleveen, that fellow. He'd steal the two eyes out o' your head. —Virginia Dillon, *Anglo-Irish Element in the Speech of Southern Newfoundland*, p. 112, 1968

slevered *adjective*
drunk *UK*
Hip-hop, urban slang noted in connection with a legal dispute over rap lyrics by *BBC News*, 6th June 2003.

slew *noun*
a large amount *US, 1839*
- He has toned down all the arch, ironic posturing and compulsive slew of pop-cultural references, allowing a newly meditative, moral tone to emerge. —*The Guardian*, 13th September 2003

slew; slew a head *verb*
to distract someone, especially in the commission of a crime *AUSTRALIA*
- Marg pussies in [enters quietly] to slew the manager. —*The (Sydney) Bulletin*, 26th April 1975

slice *noun*
1 a woman or women, objectified sexually *UK, 1796*
From the phrase 'take a slice' recorded in 1796 as 'to intrigue, particularly with a married woman, because a slice of a cut loaf is not missed'; the etymology is further thought to trace back to the proverbial phrase 'it is safe taking a shive [a slice] of a cut loaf', and 'shive' is easily exchanged with 'swive' (to have sex). Perhaps from an image of the vagina as a slice in the flesh, but also taking a slice of bread as something necessary and in plentiful supply.

2 an act of sexual intercourse (with a woman) *UK*
After the previous sense, possibly influenced by synonymous **PORTION**.
- He'd give his arm to tumble her [and] I wouldn't mind a slice myself, if it comes to that. —Alan Hunter, *Gently Does It*, 1955

▸ **cut off a slice**
to have sex (with a woman) *UK*
A punningly contrived verb form of 'slice' (an act of sexual intercourse).
- There's plenty never gets to see any [girls], you know, let alone cut themselves off a slice. —Red Daniells, 4th January 1980

slice *verb*
▸ **slice bread**
to make a payoff *UK*
- —William D. Alsever, *Glossary for the Establishment and Other Uptight People*, p. 29, December 1970

sliced *adjective*
1 muscular, lacking body fat, well-sculpted *US*
- —*American Speech*, p. 201, Fall 1984: 'The language of bodybuilding'

2 circumcised *US*
- —H. Max, *Gay (S)language*, p. 39, 1988

slice of knuckle pie *noun*
a punch in the mouth *UK*
- —Colin Evans, *The Heart of Standing*, 1962

slice of toast *noun*
a ghost *UK*
Rhyming slang.
- What's the matter? You look like you've seen a slice of toast. —Ray Puxley, *Cockney Rabbit*, 1992

slick *noun*
1 a car tyre without a tread, used in drag racing *US, 1950s?*
Usually heard in the plural.
- Big Cheaters: Stock cars with modifications on the original engine such as multi-carburetion. Racing "slicks" permitted. —Fremont Drag Strip, *Guide to Drag Racing*, 1960
- Chrome reversed rims with whitewall slicks / And it turns a quarter mile in one-o-six. —Brian Wilson and Roger Christian (recorded by the Beach Boys), *Cherry, Cherry Coupe*, 1963
- As the car moves away from the starting line, the slicks begin to bite the road and the dragster accelerates very rapidly. —Ed Radlauer, *Drag Racing Pix Dix*, p. 51, 1970

2 a glossy magazine *US, 1953*
- Sometimes pieces fluttered rejection slips from slick to fanzine[.] —Greil Marcus, *Psychotic Reactions and Carburetor Dung*, 1987

3 in pool, a skilled player who bets on his own ability *US, 1990*
- —Mike Shamos, *The Illustrated Encyclopedia of Billiards*, p. 216, 1993

4 a field of criminal expertise *US*
- —William K. Bentley and James M. Corbett, *Prison Slang*, p. 34, 1992

5 an unarmed aircraft *US*
- They were called "slicks" because, except for an M-60 machine gun in each cargo door, they were unarmed. —Dennis Marvicsin and Jerold Greenfield, *Maverick*, p. 36, 1990

6 a helicopter used for troop transport *US*
- This morning they were inserted by chopper. The slicks moved them inland, keeping about 1500 feet. —Ronald J. Glasser, *365 Days*, p. 30, 1971

slick *adjective*
1 attractive; charming *US*
- —Don R. McCreary (Editor), *Dawg Speak*, 2001

2 in lowball poker, favourable *US*
- —Albert H. Morehead, *The Complete Guide to Winning Poker*, p. 273, 1967

slick chick *noun*
an attractive girl *US*
- —Marcus Hanna Boulware, *Jive and Slang of Students in Negro Colleges*, 1947

slickdick *adjective*
smooth; plausible *UK, 1990s*
Elaboration of conventional 'slick'.
- He pouts his mouth out an' straightens his tie like some slickdick salesman. —Nick Barlay, *Curvy Lovebox*, p. 92, 1997

slicker *noun*

1 a world-wise, sophisticated, urban person *US, 1900*

- He sure wasn't scared at all, and he acted like a slicker. —Chester Gould, *Dick Tracy Meets the Night Crawler*, p. 29, 1945
- "Phil is a real slicker. He's been holding out on us all these years," Beatrice said. —James T. Farrell, *Saturday Night*, p. 23, 1947
- "You know what you are?" she said, huskily. "You're a slicker." —Jim Thompson, *Savage Night*, p. 10, 1953
- His neck was made for a noose, but no noose will replace the gaudy cravate around that slicker's neck. —Willard Motley, *Let No Man Write My Epitaph*, p. 164, 1958
- I tried to tell him a long time ago that these so-called slickers and throughbreds don't mean him no good. —Nathan Heard, *Howard Street*, p. 36, 1968

2 a police officer *US*

- Lookouts shouted warnings, yelling to the dealers inside, using slang terms for police: "Blue and white on State! Slickers on State! I still got slickers on State1[.]" —*Chicago Tribune*, p. C11, 12th April 1998

3 a stolen car with all identification markings erased or removed *US*

- —Hyman E. Goldin et al., *Dictionary of American Underworld Lingo*, p. 197, 1950

4 an oversized, wide, smooth tyre used in racing *US*

- —*Good Housekeeping*, p. 143, September 1958: 'Hot-rod terms for teen-age girls'

slick leggings *noun*

the rubbing of the penis between the thighs of another man until reaching orgasm *US*

- Our prison informants consider this and "slick legging" to be statistically insignificant types of release. —*New York Mattachine Newsletter*, p. 7, June 1961

slicklicker *noun*

an oil spill cleaning machine *CANADA*

- The slicklicker is a machine for cleaning up oil spills, invented and named by Richard Sewell in 1968 at the Canadian Department of National Defence. —Bill Casselman, *Canadian Words*, p. 21, 1995

slick-sleeve *noun*

a US Army private E-1; a US Air Force airman basic; a police recruit *US*

'Slick' because he has no stripes on his sleeve.

- —*Current Slang*, p. 18, Summer 1970
- Goddamn slick-sleeved rookies,' I said, hot as hell[.] —Joseph Wambaugh, *The Blue Knight*, p. 59, 1973
- —Linda Reinberg, *In the Field*, p. 201, 1991

slick superspeed *noun*

methcathinone *US*

From the superior quality of the drug when compared to average SPEED (amphetamine).

- —Office of National Drug Control Policy, *Drug Facts*, February 2003

slick top *noun*

an unmarked police car with no light on its roof *US*

- —Wayne Floyd, *Jason's Authentic Dictionary of CB Slang*, p. 27, 1976

slick-wing *adjective*

used of a pilot in the air force, junior *US*

The wing insignias of the junior pilot do not have a star above them like those of senior and command pilots.

- I didn't drag my ass three thousand miles across the country to have some slick-wing major tell me I'm nuts. —Walter Boyne and Steven Thompson, *The Wild Blue*, p. 235, 1986

slicky; slickey *verb*

to obtain something through ingenious and unorthodox diligence, up to and including theft *US*

An adaptation of pidgin English by United Nations troops in Korea in the early 1950s, from 'slick' (not-quite-honestly smart).

- —Carl Fleischhauer, *A Glossary of Army Slang*, p. 15, 1968

slicky boy *noun*

a thief or swindler *US*

Coined by Koreans, borrowed by US and UN troops in Korea.

- —Frank Hailey, *Soldier Talk*, p. 55, 1982

slide *noun*

a trouser pocket *US, 1932*

- With "six yards" in my slide, I wasn't about to board another bus so I took the "Grand Central" train to New York. —Babs Gonzales, *I Paid My Dues*, p. 29, 1967
- He done had a bath and rubdown, and he got money in his slide. —Nathan Heard, *Howard Street*, p. 67, 1968
- He could have a grand in his slide with most of it being one dollar bills and this egg would break a twenty just for a pack of cigarettes. —A.S. Jackson, *Gentleman Pimp*, p. 98, 1973
- The dude went mad / an' started to jump bad, pulling his roscoe out his slide. —Lightnin' Rod, *Hustlers Convention*, p. 98, 1973
- So I reached in my slide and came out with two boss threes / And said "Here, girl, go to the shithouse and get the weakness out of your knees." —Dennis Wepman et al., *The Life*, p. 52, 1976
- I off the other nineteen, pay Max back his five hundred dollars and take the other fourteen hundnred dollars for my slide[.] —Terry Williams, *The Cocaine Kids*, p. 42, 1989

slide *verb*

1 to depart, to go *US, 1859*

- —John A. Holm, *Dictionary of Bahamian English*, p. 186, 1982
- The train pulled into Kings Cross and Sammy jumped up. "Gotta slide, this is my stop.["] —Paolo Hewitt, *Heaven's Promise*, p. 125, 1999

2 to ride a wave *US*

- —Ross Olney, *The Young Sportsman's Guide to Surfing*, p. 88, 1965

▸ **slide your jive**

to talk freely *CANADA*

Teen slang, reported by a Toronto newspaper in 1946, and reported as 'obsolescent or obsolete' by Douglas Leechman, 1959.

slide *adjective*

used of a college course, easy *US*

- —Connie Eble (Editor), *UNC-CH Campus Slang*, Fall 1974

slide and sluther *noun*

a brother *UK*

Rhyming slang.

- —Ray Puxley, *Fresh Rabbit*, 1998

slider *noun*

1 an electronic device that allows operation between authorised channels on a citizens' band radio *US*

- —"Slingo", *The Official CB Slang Dictionary Handbook*, p. 56, 1976

2 a gambler who slides rather than rolls dice in an effort to control the result *US*

- —Victor H. Royer, *Casino Gamble Talk*, p. 122, 2003

3 a hamburger or cheeseburger *US*

Originally the small hamburgers sold by the White Tower™ chain, later any hamburger.

- —Laurence Urdang, *Names and Nicknames of Places and Things*, p. 232, 1987
- After they had eaten in the formal wardroom (they were fortunate; the meal was real meat in the form of "sliders and rollers," cheeseburgers and hot dogs), they visited Tim's tiny stateroom. —Gerry Carroll, *North S*A*R*, p. 133, 1991

sliders *noun*

men's shorts with an elastic waistband *TRINIDAD AND TOBAGO, 1939*

- —Frank A. Collymore, *Barbadian Dialect*, p. 99, 1965
- —Lise Winer, *Dictionary of the English/Creole of Trinidad & Tobago*, 2003

slide-rule jockey *noun*

a navigator in an aeroplane crew *US, 1959*

- —*American Speech*, p. 158–159, May 1960: 'The burgeoning of 'jockey''

slides *noun*

shoes *US*

- —Joseph E. Ragen and Charles Finston, *Inside the World's Toughest Prison*, p. 818, 1962: 'Penitentiary and underworld glossary'

slim *noun*

a handgun *US*

- —Hyman E. Goldin et al., *Dictionary of American Underworld Lingo*, p. 197, 1950

slime *noun*

1 heroin *US*

- —US Department of Justice, *Street Terms*, October 1994
- —Robert Ashton, *This Is Heroin*, p. 207, 2002

2 British Army Intelligence Corps personnel *UK*

- It seemed the slime had every map, drawing and picture of every ship, aircraft and building in existence. —Andy McNab (writing of the late 1970s/early 80s), *Immediate Action*, p. 244, 1995

slimeball *noun*

a despicable person *US*

- I remember when the slime-balls used to be packed in there solid, asshole to belly button, waiting to look at the skin show in the viewer. — Joseph Wambaugh, *The Blue Knight*, p. 26–27, 1973
- — Mary Corey and Victoria Westermark, *Fer Shurr! How to be a Valley Girl*, 1982
- "My friends tell me Arnold is a rat. I also hear 'slimeball' and 'sleaze' a lot," says [actor Corben] Bernsen[.] — *Chicago Tribune*, p. CN7, 8th April 1987
- Leonard, the little slimeball, had all but promised as much when he'd asked me to perform. — Armistead Maupin, *Maybe the Moon*, p. 33, 1992
- I hate that. Unless it is coming out of the mouths of crocodile pedophile slime balls. — Francesca Lia Block, *I Was a Teenage Fairy*, p. 158, 1998
- An elderly man raised his hand, indicated plaintiff's counsel James Spiering, and said, according to Mall, "I know that slimeball over there from his TV ads." — *National Law Journal*, p. 3, 22nd December 2003

slimedog *noun*

a dirty, offensive person *US*

- — Sally Williams, *"Strong" Words*, p. 139, 1994

slimemouth *noun*

a foul-talking person *US*

- Frank disposed of seven slime-mouths by booking them drunk at the county jail, arrested by U.F. Puck. — Joseph Wambaugh, *The Secrets of Harry Bright*, p. 67, 1985

slim-fast diet *noun*

HIV or AIDS *US*

- — Gary K. Farlow, *Prison-ese*, p. 65, 2002

slim jim *noun*

a device that is slipped into a car door and used to open the door's locking mechanism *US*

- Red Haynes, having used a Slim Jim lock-picking device to gain entry, sat in the front seat of Sands' car. — Gerald Petievich, *Shakedown*, p. 113, 1988
- He told them he'd spot the car a customer wanted and use a slim jim or lemon pop to get in, a slap hammer to yank the ignition, a side kick to extract steering column locks and usually liquid nitrogen to freeze the alarm system. — Elmore Leonard, *Out of Sight*, p. 56, 1996
- And just in case you lose your keys, good sir, I can toss in a complimentary slim-jim, free of charge. — *Gone in 60 Seconds*, 2000

slim off *verb*

to strip to your underwear *US*

- "Make yourself at home." "All right, I'll slim off." — Willard Motely, *Let No Man Write My Epitaph*, p. 210, 1958

slimy *adjective*

having an insincere and ingratiating manner *UK, 1602*

- a newly manufactured legal loophole some slimy RDDB lawyer invented called the "cultural defense" — Michael Savage, *The Enemy Within*, p. 38, 2003

sling *noun*

1 a monetary gift or tip *AUSTRALIA, 1950*

Wilkes records a slightly earlier (1948) variant 'sling back'.

- Gates will get a man-sized sling from the owners. — Wilda Moxham, *The Apprentice*, p. 58, 1969
- The owner of the horse was an undertaker by trade and very light with the sling so the jockey decided to put the horse 'in the bag'. — Frank Hardy and Athol George Mulley, *The Needy and the Greedy*, p. 75, 1975
- A 'sling' from a greatful owner was always appreciated. — Joe Andersen, *Winners Can Laugh*, p. 49, 1982
- The sling was optional and left to the generosity of the owner. — Joe Andersen, *Winners Can Laugh*, p. 113, 1982
- — Clive Galea, *Slipper*, p. 63, 1988
- — Ned Wallish, *The Truth Dictionary of Racing Slang*, p. 75, 1989

2 in horse racing, a gratuity given to the jockey and attendants by the owner after a win *AUSTRALIA*

- — Ned Wallish, *The Truth Dictionary of Racing Slang*, p. 75, 1989

3 a bribe or illegal payment *AUSTRALIA, 1948*

- He's probably bought the pub with all the slings he's taken over the years – the prick. — Robert G. Barrett, *Davo's Little Something*, p. 5, 1992

▸ **beat it for the sling**

to fail to appear in court *AUSTRALIA*

- — *The (Sydney) Bulletin*, 26th April 1975

▸ **in the sling**

said of a woman experiencing her menstrual period *US*

- — *American Speech*, p. 298, December 1954: 'The vernacular of menstruation'

sling *verb*

1 to throw something (or someone) in a specific direction; hence to pass something from one person to another *UK*

Common in the C14 and C15, now dialect or colloquial.

- If shit is flying at you from all directions, [Anthony] Pellicano will catch it and sling it back. — *The Guardian*, 29th November 2002

2 to discard or abandon someone or something; to quit something *UK, 1902*

3 to pay a tip to someone *AUSTRALIA, 1875*

- Though you'd think the Boss had forgotten he'd collect his ten per cent of the purse, plus his cut of Rufe's five, plus any present the owner cared to sling. — Wilda Moxham, *The Apprentice*, p. 72, 1969
- That parrot's got to go. Next thing it will be slinging tips to the newspapers. — Frank Hardy and Athol George Mulley, *The Needy and the Greedy*, p. 30, 1975
- — Joe Andersen, *Winners Can Laugh*, p. 150, 1982
- 'Colletti might sling big Davey,' gloated Watson with a far from pretty laugh, 'but's he's a blow-in, a once-only earner for Billy.' — Clive Galea, *Slipper*, p. 66, 1988

4 to pay a bribe to someone *AUSTRALIA, 1939*

- And some of them have to sling bribes before they can even get a defence contract. — Eric Lambert, *The Veterans*, p. 82, 1954

5 to sell illegal drugs *US*

- When they sling – street slang for selling drugs – they do it alone or maybe with a friend. — *St. Louis Post-Dispatch*, p. F1, 29th March 2001

6 to engage in promiscuous sexual behaviour *BAHAMAS*

- — John A. Holm, *Dictionary of Bahamian English*, p. 187, 1982

▸ **sling hash**

to work as a waitress or short-order cook *US, 1906*

- Maybe some place where she was working, slingin' hash, say, and one of the waitresses passed it around and she got hold of a copy. — Jim Thompson, *The Nothing Man*, p. 176–177, 1954

▸ **sling ink**

to tattoo *US*

- — James Harris, *A Convict's Dictionary*, p. 38, 1989

▸ **sling your hook**

to go, to leave *UK, 1874*

A naval derivation, perhaps inspired by slinging grappling hooks preparatory to swinging across to another ship. Later use seems to be mainly imperative.

- "Go on," said Brewer. "Sling your hooks." — John Burke and Stuart Douglass, *The Boys*, p. 46, 1962
- I gave him back his nudie book / I said I was sorry, I slung my hook[.] — Ian Dury, *Razzle in My Pocket*, 1977
- Go on, sling your fuckin' hook, you're fuckin' wired you cunt. — J.J. Connolly, *Know Your Enemy [britpulp]*, p. 144, 1999

sling-backs *noun*

used generically for high-heeled shoes *UK*

- — Paul Baker, *Polari*, p. 190, 2002

sling-ding *noun*

in fishing, a weight attached to a line of trawl to be set, to moor the end *CANADA*

- These "sling-dings," so-called, were made fast to the first end, and when the whole tub of 2100 feet of line was payed out into the water, an anchor would be used in the last or tub end. — Frederick Wallace, *Roving Fisherman*, p. 68, 1955

slinger *noun*

1 a criminal who passes counterfeit money *UK, 1950*

- — Angela Devlin, *Prison Patter*, p. 106, 1996

2 a striptease artist *US*

- — Don Wilmeth, *The Language of American Popular Entertainment*, p. 246, 1981

sling off *verb*

to speaking disparagingly to someone *AUSTRALIA, 1900*

- You must be mad, thinking I was slinging off at you. — Norman Lindsay, *The Cousin from Fiji*, p. 206, 1945
- — Arthur Chipper, *The Aussie Swearer's Guide*, p. 76, 1972
- They were barely out of court when they started slinging off at one another. — Kerry Cue, *Crooks, Chooks and Bloody Ratbags*, p. 111, 1983

sling out *verb*

to reject something; to eject someone *UK, 1959*

- When she did come home, she slung him out. — *The Observer*, 2nd December 2001

slingshot *noun*

1 a drag racing car design in which the driver is seated behind the rear wheels *US, 1962*

- The slingshot is long and spindly with weak-looking little front wheels and tires... almost as an afterthought the man who guides this projectile is fitted into an iron cage protruding out from the very rear. —Ross Olney, *Kings of the Drag Strip*, p. 77–78, 1968

2 any vehicle that passes others on the motorway at great speed *US*

• —Warren Smith, *Warren's Smith's Authentic Dictionary of CB*, p. 63, 1976

3 in motor racing, a passing method in which the car follows another's draft and then quickly passes *US*

• —Hal Higdon, *Finding the Groove*, p. 309, 1973

4 an extremely skimpy man's bathing suit *US*

• Surrounded by ersatz Indian warriors wearing bright Brazilian slingshots, the princesss proclaimed in song and mime her passionate love. —Carl Hiaasen, *Native Tongue*, p. 229, 1991

slingshotting *noun*

in bungee jumping, a reverse jump, beginning with the cord stretched out, yanking the participant up in the air *US*

• How do I know that this, this, this slingshotting – won't splatter me up against the bottom of the cage like some big hairy bug? —Erik Fair, *California Thrill Sports*, p. 45, 1992

slip *noun*

1 in cricket, a fielder or fielding position close to the wicket keeper *UK, 1816*

• The young fast bowler made 44, and then when he was caught at slip, White took charge and added a further 35 for the last wicket[.] —*The Guardian*, 27th July 2002

2 the price of the fare home given to a punter who has lost all their money *AUSTRALIA, 1977*

• —Ryan Aven-Bray, *Ridgey Didge Oz Jack Lang*, p. 45, 1983

• [O]verseeing the game, watching for any tricks, giving or denying credit and handing out the slips, small handouts which enabled a skint punter to get home. —Clive Galea, *Slipper*, p. 27, 1988

slip *verb*

1 to give birth to a child *AUSTRALIA*

• Him and his missus hit town six months ago. Ten minutes after they got in, she slipped her thirteenth. —Walter Gill, *Petermann Journey*, p. 14, 1968

2 to act inappropriately *US*

• — *The Bell (Paducah Tilghman High School)*, p. 8–9, 17th December 1993: 'Tilghmanism: the concealed langage of the hallway'

3 to insult someone in a semi-formal quasi-friendly competition *US*

• There are many different terms for playing the dozens, including "bagging, capping, cracking, dissing, hiking, joning, ranking, ribbing, serving, signifying, slipping, sounding and snapping". —James Haskins, *The Story of Hip-Hop*, p. 54, 2000

▸ **slip a fatty**

to have sex *UK*

• —Tom Hibbert, *Rockspeak!*, p. 59, 1983

▸ **slip a lock**

to open a locked door by sliding a plastic credit card between the door and jamb and then sliding the lock open *US*

• "Christ, I slipped the lock!" Al Mackey held up his laminated police ID card, the corners chewed by the door latch. —Joseph Wambaugh, *The Glitter Dome*, p. 21, 1981

▸ **slip her a length**

(from the male perspective) to have sex with a woman *UK, 1949*

• What you doing then, slipping her a length? —Greg Williams, *Diamond Geezers*, p. 182, 1997

• She's a fuckin' dyke. But I wouldn't mind slipping her a length of Cockney! —Stuart Browne, *Dangerous Parking*, p. 45, 2000

▸ **slip it to**

(of a male) to have sex with someone *US*

Euphemistic and naughty, both at once.

• I'll bet she won't say no if you try to slip it to her. —Jim Thompson, *The Killer Inside*, p. 51, 1952

• He slips it to the kid good and proper[.] —Angelo d'Arcangelo, *The Homosexual Handbook*, p. 229, 1968

• Could my father have been slipping it to this lady on the side? —Philip Roth, *Portnoy's Complaint*, p. 92, 1969

▸ **slip one to**

(of a male) to have sex with someone *UK*

• [H]e was slipping one to Denise in the travel agent's at the time. —Danny King, *The Burglar Diaries*, p. 79, 2001

slip-and-fall *noun*

a run-of-the-mill, often fraudulent law suit or insurance claim resulting from an injury suffered slipping and falling in a business establishment *US*

• None of his investigators did either, or Karen when she worked surveillance jobs for him: the cute girl following slip-and-fall and whiplash cheaters looking for insurance payoffs. —Elmore Leonard, *Out of Sight*, p. 180, 1996

slip-in *noun*

any lubricant used for facilitating sex, especially anal sex *US*

• —Joseph E. Ragen and Charles Finston, *Inside the World's Toughest Prison*, p. 818, 1962: 'Penitentiary and underworld glossary'

slipper-training *noun*

spanking with an old-fashioned gym shoe, especially when advertised as a service offered by a prostitute *UK*

• —Caroline Archer, *Tart Cards*, 2003

slippery *adjective*

in hot rodding and drag racing, streamlined *US*

• —Lyle K. Engel, *The Complete Book of Fuel and Gas Dragsters*, p. 153, 1968

slippery Anne *noun*

in a deck of playing cards, the queen of spades *US, 1950*

• —Thomas L. Clark, *The Dictionary of Gambling and Gaming*, p. 204, 1987

slippery Sid; slippery *noun*

a Jewish person *UK*

Offensive. Rhyming slang for **YID**.

• You don't have to be a slippery to be a schmuck. —Ray Puxley, *Fresh Rabbit*, 1998

slippings *noun*

any lubricant used in anal sex *US*

• — *Maledicta*, p. 233, 1979: 'Kinks and queens: linguistic and cultural aspects of the terminology for gays'

slipping stick *noun*

a slide rule *US*

• —Jerry Robertson, *Oil Slanguage*, p. 62, 1954

slippy *adjective*

1 quick; spry; nimble *UK, 1885*

From dialect. Perhaps the best known contemporary usage is the song that became the theme of the film *Trainspotting*.

• —Underworld *Born Slippy*, 1993

2 slippery *US*

• —Sam McCool, *Pittsburghese*, p. 32, 1982

slip-slap *noun*

an old shoe, especially a slipper *TRINIDAD AND TOBAGO, 1973*

• —Lise Winer, *Dictionary of the English/Creole of Trinidad & Tobago*, 2003

slip-slop *noun*

a strap sandal with a wooden sole *BARBADOS*

• —Frank A. Collymore, *Barbadian Dialect*, p. 99, 1965

• He is dressed in the usual winemaker's attire, shorts and slip slops, which he has managed to endorse with a slick fashionista message – the slip slops are named; the shorts Armani. —*Sunday Times (South Africa)*, 27th July 2003

slip-sloppy *adjective*

very drunk *CANADA*

• —Connie Eble (Editor), *UNC-CH Campus Slang*, p. 9, Spring 1988

slipstick *noun*

a trombone *US*

• —Clarence Major, *Dictionary of Afro-American Slang*, p. 105, 1970

slip-stick jockey *noun*

a radar technician *US*

• — *American Speech*, p. 154, April 1947: 'Radar slang terms'

slip up *verb*

to make a mistake *US, 1855*

• The cabinet minister appointed to avoid government banana skins was yesterday corrected by the prime minister, chancellor and a foreign office minister after he slipped up over the single currency. — *The Guardian*, 3rd December 2001

S list *noun*

used as a euphemism for 'shit list', a list of enemies *US*

- Watergate prosecutors are on the trial of a roster of people apparently even more in disfavor with the administration known as the "S List." — *San Francisco Chronicle*, p. 6, 18th May 1974

slit *noun*

1 the vagina *UK, 1648*

- Nicole gazed up at him and pulled the lips of her slit taut and up to show him the ragged pear of pinkness inside[.] — William T. Vollman, *Whores for Gloria*, p. 15, 1991
- Shearing our slits is not just for porn stars anymore. — *The Village Voice*, 8th–14th November 2000

2 a person from South Asia *US*

Offensive. From the European perception of South Asian eyes as slanted slits.

- — Edith A. Folb, *runnin' down some lines*, p. 254, 1980

3 a tablet of MDMA, the recreational drug best known as ecstasy *UK*

Possibly from the sense as 'a vagina', punning on **CUNT** (a vein for injecting).

- — Mike Haskins, *Drugs*, p. 290, 2003

slitch *noun*

a despicable and/or promiscuous girl *US*

A blend of **SLUT** and ***BITCH***.

- — Carol Ann Preusse, *Jargon Used by University of Texas Co-Eds*, 1963

slither *noun*

counterfeit coins *US*

- — Ralph de Sola, *Crime Dictionary*, p. 139, 1982

Sloane ranger; Sloane *noun*

a conventional person, part of a fashionable set, born to the privileges of the upper-/middle-class, especially one who dwells in London *UK, 1975*

Coined by Peter York, a playful blend of *Sloane* Square (in Chelsea, London) and The *Lone* Ranger (since the 1930s, a fictional hero of the American West).

- Sloanes are fanatical party givers. — Ann Barr and Peter York, *The Official Sloane Ranger Handbook*, p. 101, 1982

slob *noun*

1 a slovenly person; a fat, lazy person; hence, when the characteristics are applied to the intellect: a simple-minded person, or, when applied to the morals, a delinquent *UK, 1861*

- It didn't matter that she'd been sweating and hadn't brushed her teeth. They were a couple of slobs all right. — John King, *White Trash*, p. 98, 2001

2 anyone of Slavic heritage *US*

Offensive.

- — *Maledicta*, p. 169, Summer/Winter 1978: 'How to hate thy neighbor: a guide to racist maledicta'

3 used as a derogatory nickname for a member of the Bloods youth gang *US*

- — Ann Lawson, *Kids & Gangs*, p. 56, 1994: 'Common African-American gang slang/phrases'

slob; slob out *verb*

to behave in a lazy, slovenly manner *UK*

- If we'd spent the night slobbing on the sofa over a takeaway curry and a bag of Maltesers she'd get the guilts[.] — Andrew Holmes, *Sleb*, p. 189, 2002

slobber *noun*

food; a meal *UK: SCOTLAND*

- Yir getting finest escalope of veal in a bliddy delicate oriental sauce for your slobber, and it's freezing, by the way! — Ian Pattison, *Rab C. Nesbitt*, 1988

slog *noun*

an act or period of hard work *UK, 1888*

- Germans. I mean some of them speak English, but ... it is a slog, really. — Mike Stott, *Soldiers Talking, Cleanly*, 1978

slog *verb*

1 to work hard at something *UK, 1888*

- I mean, it really is a bit of a slog, slogging all the way, across the old Channel every weekend, just to get your oats. — Mike Stott, *Soldiers Talking, Cleanly*, 1978

2 to punch someone *UK, 1824*

- If I'd stood up and slogged him, our steaks would have gone cold. — Dick Francis, *Risk*, p. 130, 1993

3 to walk heavily *UK, 1872*

From obsolete 'foot-slogger' (an infantryman, a pedestrian).

- I parked in my lot and slogged up to my apartment, leaving puddles in my wake. — Janet Evanovich, *Seven Up*, p. 97, 2001

▸ **slog it out**

to work hard at some activity *AUSTRALIA*

An elaboration of **SLOG** (to work hard).

- I came over here after sloggin' it out on the Snowy Mountain Opera Project in Australia. — Barry Humphries, *Bazza Pulls It Off!*, 1971

▸ **slog your guts out**

to work hard at something *UK, 1984*

An intensification of **SLOG**.

- I was slogging my guts out for next to nothing. I began to wonder why. — Peter Woods, *Teacher Skills and Strategies*, 1990

sloo *noun*

a look; a visual examination *AUSTRALIA*

- — Ned Wallish, *The Truth Dictionary of Racing Slang*, p. 75, 1989

sloosh *verb*

to wash in a hurry and in a perfunctory fashion *NORFOLK ISLAND*

- — Beryl Nobbs Palmer, *A Dictionary of Norfolk Words and Usages*, p. 40, 1992

slooze *noun*

a promiscuous female *US*

- — *Verbatim*, p. 281, May 1976

slop *noun*

1 prison food

- — Angela Devlin, *Prison Patter*, p. 106, 1996

2 poorly formed waves for surfing purposes *US*

- — John M. Kelly, *Surf and Sea*, p. 294, 1965
- — Brian and Margaret Lowdon, *Competitive Surfing*, 1988

3 in pool, a shot made unintentionally *US*

- In many games, slop is forbidden. — Steve Rushin, *Pool Cool*, p. 27, 1990

4 in computing, a built-in margin of error in one direction only *US*

- — Guy L. Steele et al., *The Hacker's Dictionary*, p. 115, 1983

5 a second year college student *US*

- — Marcus Hanna Boulware, *Jive and Slang of Students in Negro Colleges*, 1947

slop *verb*

▸ **slop the hogs**

in trucking, to fill a truck radiator with water *US*

- — Montie Tak, *Truck Talk*, p. 147, 1971

slop and flop *noun*

meals and lodging *US*

- The pay was fair – four-fifty a day less a dollar deducted for "slop and flop." — Jim Thompson, *Bad Boy*, p. 390, 1953

slope *noun*

a person from South Asia *US, 1948*

- — *Current Slang*, p. 18, Summer 1970
- One Army intelligence specialist said the pistol slaying of his Chinese interpreter was defended by his superior who said, "She was just a slope, anyway," meaning she was an Asiatic. — Hunter S. Thompson, *Fear and Loathing in Las Vegas*, p. 73, 1971
- 'You want this slope, man?' asks the huge, green-clad black man, walking towards us with the wriggling youth in his vice-like right hand. — William Nagel, *The Odd Angry Shot*, p. 69, 1975
- Yeah – classical stuff – scares the hell out of the slopes – the boys love it. — *Apocalypse Now*, 1979
- — *Maledicta*, p. 125, Summer 1980: 'Racial and ethnic slurs: regional awareness and variations'
- Gooks could be both. Slants and slopes were civilians. Dinks could be both. — Nelson DeMille, *Word of Honor*, p. 414, 1985
- Slopes are resented for their brainpower and mathematical prowess. — *Sydney Morning Herald*, p. 7, 3rd January 1987
- Oh, there are some soldiers thought Code Six as he watched, soldiers like Jimmy and I were, fighting the fucking GOOKS and SLANTS and SLOPES, soldiers trotting single file across a smoking field. — William T. Vollman, *Whores for Gloria*, p. 36, 1991

slopehead *noun*

a Vietnamese; any South Asian *US, 1966*

Derogatory, pejorative, offensive and demeaning.

- And if you don't like it here why don't you go to commie China or North Vietnam with all those slopeheads or Russia??!! — *East Village Other*, p. 2, 15th-21st November 1968

- After all he had been willing to treat them all the same, even niggers and slopeheads. —Joseph Wambaugh, *The Choirboys*, p. 315, 1975
- "Put your money where your mouth is, Slopehead," he said. "Whip it on me!" —Larry Heinemann, *Paco's Story*, p. 6–7, 1986
- Lowest of the hierarchical racist rungs is the 'Slopeheads' (Vietnamese). —*Sydney Morning Herald*, p. 7, 3rd January 1987
- And he'd be damned if any slopeheads were gonna put their greasy yella hands on his boy's birthright. —*Pulp Fiction*, 1994
- I can hear Hugo ranting about giving Hong Kong back to the slopeheads[.] —J.J. Connolly, *Layer Cake*, p. 105, 2000
- But words that came out of the Vietnam War, like 'gook' and 'slopehead,' are only more well-known by Asian Americans. —*San Francisco Examiner*, p. A1, 19th February 2000

slope off *verb*
to depart, especially surreptitiously or in embarrassment *UK, 1861*
- Looks like it's time to slope off while the going is still good. —*The Guardian*, 6th November 2001

slope-out *noun*
an easy task *US*
- If they're parked where that guy says they are it'll be a slopeout. —Hubert Selby Jr, *Last Exit to Brooklyn*, p. 185, 1957

slopey *adjective*
used of a wave, steep *US*
- —Trevor Cralle, *The Surfin'ary*, p. 117, 1991

slopie *noun*
a Chinese person or other South Asian *US*
Offensive.
- —*American Speech*, p. 30, February 1949: 'A.V.G. lingo'

slop out *verb*
1 in prison, to dispose of bodily waste collected in unplumbed toilet facilities *UK*
The first order of the day according to *Lag's Lexicon*, Paul Tempest, 1950; however, according to HM Prison Service in 2003: 'Slopping out was officially ended on 12th April 1996'.
2 to remove and clean plates, bowls, etc, that have been used in a prison cell *UK*
A play on **SLOP** (prison food), and the previous sense.
- —Angela Devlin, *Prison Patter*, p. 106, 1996

slopping out *noun*
in prison, the regular emptying of unplumbed toilet facilities *UK*
- [A] necessary practice known by the revoltingly onomatopoeic term of "slopping out", by which the inmates pissed into any available vessel, then lined up to dispose of it in the morning[.] —Christopher Brookmyre, *Boiling a Frog*, p. 50, 2000

sloppy *adjective*
1 very sentimental *US, 1883*
- "What do you think, Vivian?" Aiden asked. "Killer death robots or sloppy love story?" —Annette Curtis Klause, *Blood and Chocolate*, p. 126, 1999

2 drunk *US*
- —Connie Eble (Editor), *UNC-CH Campus Slang*, p. 7, November 2002

Sloppy Joe *noun*
a multi-layered sandwich from which the fillings ooze *US, 1961*
The name comes from the inevitable mess on fingers and face, the sign of a sloppy eater.
- [S]he discovered the severed penis in her sloppy-joe sandwich[.] —Howard Stern, *Miss America*, p. 239, 1995

sloppy seconds *noun*
sex with someone who has just had sex with someone else *US*
- Hurry up, man. You go first. I'll take sloppy seconds, anytime. —Steve Cannon, *Groove, Bang, and Jive Around*, p. 38, 1969
- Sloppy seconds I think they call it. (Not really sloppy, because she would wash up first, but even so it used to bother me.) —Lawrence Block, *No Score*, p. 82, 1970

slops *noun*
beer *AUSTRALIA, 1944*
- It was a little too sweet for my taste, but the others voted it 'a good drop o' slops'. —John O'Grady, *It's Your Shout, Mate!*, p. 91, 1972

▸ **go slops**
to have sex with a woman who has very recently had sex with another man or other men *AUSTRALIA*
- —Thommo, *The Dictionary of Australian Swearing and Sex Sayings*, p. 60, 1985

slopshoot *noun*
food with little nutritional value but which appeals to popular taste *US*
US Marine Corps slang.
- —Linda Reinberg, *In the Field*, p. 201, 1991

slops merchant *noun*
a habitual drinker of beer *AUSTRALIA*
- He's a real mucking slops merchant, skipper. —W.R. Bennett, *Target Turin*, p. 108, 1962

slopsucker *noun*
a low priority project *US*
- —Eric S. Raymond, *The New Hacker's Dictionary*, p. 322, 1991

slop time *noun*
in prison, meal time *UK*
From **SLOP** (prison food).
- —Angela Devlin, *Prison Patter*, p. 106, 1996

slop up *verb*
to drink to the point of intoxication *US*
- —Joseph E. Ragen and Charles Finston, *Inside the World's Toughest Prison*, p. 818, 1962: 'Penitentiary and underworld glossary'

slosh *noun*
1 a small indeterminate measure of some liquid *UK, 1888*
- Add a small handful of sea salt and a slosh of olive oil. —*The Observer*, 15th July 2001

2 a blow *UK, 1936*
From **SLOSH** (to hit).
3 a drink, especially if watery or weak; tea; coffee; beer; drink in general; hence, sodden or mushy food *UK, 1819*
4 the back-slash (\) on a computer keyboard *US*
- —Eric S. Raymond, *The New Hacker's Dictionary*, p. 40, 1991

slosh *verb*
1 to pour a liquid or a sodden mass carelessly; to swallow a drink, an oyster, etc, carelessly *US, 1875*
Usually combined with an adverb: 'slosh down', 'slosh out', 'slosh over', etc.
- Over the next four days [of Royal Ascot], the better-heeled race goers will put away around 6,000 lobsters and slosh down 120,000 bottles of champagne[.] —*The Guardian*, 17th June 2003

2 to hit someone *UK, 1890*
- The old man gripped the soaking towel as though he was about to slosh Stan with it. —John Burke and Stuart Douglass, *The Boys*, p. 111, 1962

slosh and mud; slosh *noun*
a stud *UK*
Rhyming slang.
- —Ray Puxley, *Fresh Rabbit*, 1998

sloshed *adjective*
drunk *UK, 1946*
- Reed left the mess early, about half past nine, he was pretty well sloshed already. —Graeme Kent, *The Queen's Corporal [Six Granada Plays]*, p. 103, 1959
- —Collin Baker et al., *College Undergraduate Slang Study Conducted at Brown University*, p. 198, 1968
- You could have 143 beers and get sloshed out of your skull, but you were not allowed to enjoy a cocktail before your meal. —Jim Bouton, *Ball Four*, p. 317, 1970
- —Connie Eble (Editor), *UNC-CH Campus Slang*, p. 7, March 1979
- Or Clara might get sloshed tonight, fall off a barstool and crack her head open. —Jay McInerney, *Bright Lights, Big City*, p. 33, 1984
- Frank while semi-sloshed one night in the Last Hurrah, downtown at the Parker House where he was buying drinks, had declared that Maguire was cruel to animals. —George V. Higgins, *Penance for Jerry Kennedy*, p. 56, 1985
- —*Rutgers Alumni Magazine*, p. 21, February 1986
- He kept reaching under the table, where she sat crammed into a booth with seven boozy sailors, so sloshed they'd begun discussing race strategy in the presence of enemy sailors. —Joseph Wambaugh, *Floaters*, p. 187, 1996

sloshing *noun*
a beating; a thrashing *UK, 1931*

sloshy *adjective*
drunk *US*
- —*Washington Post*, 14th October 1993

slot *noun*

1 a prison cell *AUSTRALIA, 1947*
- — *The (Sydney) Bulletin*, 26th April 1975

2 prison *AUSTRALIA, 1976*

3 used as a term of address among jazz lovers of the 1930s and 40s *US*
- Come on slot, get up from there, I got some good gauge you can pick up on. — Mezz Mezzrow, *Really the Blues*, p. 298, 1946

4 the perfect spot to ride a wave *US*
- — John Severson, *Modern Surfing Around the World*, p. 181, 1964

5 a crevasse in the snow *ANTARCTICA*
- — Bernadette Hince, *The Antarctic Dictionary*, p. 319, 2000
- — *Cool Antarctica*, 2003: 'Antarctic slang'

slot *verb*

1 to imprison someone *AUSTRALIA, 1950*
- Oak Task Force detectives had placed the Triads under surveilance over a three-month period and they had finally gathered enough evidence to 'slot' them (lock them up). — William Dodson, *The Sharp End*, p. 146, 2001

2 to shoot someone dead *UK, 1998*
Military.
- [T]he officer slotted Scully from a distance of almost sixty yards. — Michael Dobbs, *Whispers of Betrayal*, 2000

3 to give something *UK*
- James dug out the little wrap [of drugs] Paulie had slotted him last night[.] — Kevin Sampson, *Powder*, p. 128, 1999

slotties *noun*

1 a handbag *UK*
Polari.
- — the cast of 'Aspects of Love', Prince of Wales Theatre, *Palare (Boy Dancer Talk) for Beginners*, 1989–92

2 money *UK*
- Still at least she lent me the slotties to pay for the barouche, bless her. — the cast of 'Aspects of Love', Prince of Wales Theatre, *Palare (Boy Dancer Talk) for Beginners*, 1989–92

slouch *noun*

a lazy non-performer *US, 1796*
- He had hardly been a slouch his junior year, scoring fifteen touchdowns in addition to gaining over a thousand yards rush. — H.G. Bissinger, *Friday Night Lights*, p. 51, 2000

slough *noun*

a jail or prison *US*
- — Hyman E. Goldin et al., *Dictionary of American Underworld Lingo*, p. 198, 1950

slough *verb*

1 to arrest someone *US*
- — Joseph E. Ragen and Charles Finston, *Inside the World's Toughest Prison*, p. 818, 1962: 'Penitentiary and underworld glossary'

2 to close down a poker game *US*
Also used in the variant 'slough up'.
- — John Scarne, *Scarne's Guide to Modern Poker*, p. 290, 1979

slow *verb*

▸ **slow your roll**

to calm down *US*
- Do oor die [we gives a fuck motherfucker]/ So slow your roll, I'm in control. — Snoop Dogg, *For All My Niggaz Bitches*, 1993
- — Bill Valentine, *Gang Intelligence Manual*, p. 78, 1995
- "Slow your roll, now," I told her. "You can't go in there and tell that white man off!" — Yolanda Joe, *Bebe's By Golly Wow*, p. 61, 1998
- But I do care about your health and you've got to slow your roll. — Van Whitfield, *Something's Wrong with Your Scale!*, p. 186, 1999
- i say "do i look like tyra banks? best slow your roll or i'll crop your soht but good!" — Douglas Kearney, *Anansi Meets Peter Park at the Taco Bellon Lexington*, p. 89, 2000

slow boat *noun*

▸ **get someone on a slow boat**

to win all of a person's money by luring them into making ill-advised bets *US*
- — David W. Maurer, *Argot of the Racetrack*, p. 31, 1951

slowcoach *noun*

a slow-moving (or slow-thinking) person *UK, 1837*
- Buck up the treacle-slow batting by recalling middle-order slowcoach Tillekeratne? Brilliant. — *The Guardian*, 3rd February 2003

slow-em-up *noun*

any central nervous system depressant *US*
- — Edith A. Folb, *runnin' down some lines*, p. 254, 1980

slow-me-down *noun*

a sedative tablet *UK*
- The good doctor didn't ask him too many questions. Prescribed more Beta-blockers and Lorazepam. Slow-me-downs and antidepressants. — Jack Allen, *When the Whistle Blows*, p. 45, 2000

slow-mo *adjective*

slow-motion *US*
- But Charlie Bat smiles. It is strange and slow-mo. — Francesca Lia Block, *Missing Angel Juan*, p. 364, 1993

slow-pay *noun*

a person in debt who has been remiss in making repayment *US*
- The reason Ratnoff stalled him on money is that Xaviera was slow pay. — Leonard Shecter and William Phillips, *On the Pad*, p. 32–33, 1973
- I had gotten into a slow-pay situation with two bookmakers in Ohio – they didn't have the money, and yet I had to square other bets I had lost. — Jimmy Snyder, *Jimmy the Greek*, p. 67, 1975
- He had put hundreds of slow-pays in the hospital using a simple trick. — Stephen J. Cannell, *Big Con*, p. 278, 1997

slow pill *noun*

in horse racing, a depressant given to a horse to decrease its performance *US*
- — Dan Parker, *The ABC of Horse Racing*, p. 149, 1947
- The Threat of Two Tests May Eventually Stop the Needling of Winners and the Feeding of "Slow Pills" to Losers [Headline]. — *San Francisco Examiner, American Weekly*, p. 17, 17th July 1949
- Witkin said in a letter to Klein last week he learned of reports that Wallace had been fed a "slow pill" and wanted Palermo's named "cleared." — *San Francisco News*, p. 29, 30th November 1955

slow-play *verb*

1 to stall; to delay *US*
- — William K. Bentley and James M. Corbett, *Prison Slang*, p. 15, 1992

2 in poker, to underbet a hand to lure other players with inferior hands into betting *UK*
- — Anthony Holden, *Big Deal*, p. 305, 1990

slowpoke *noun*

a person who moves slowly or dawdles *US, 1848*
- Ebbie Wexler (who really does look like Nancy's not-too-bright boyfriend, Sluggo) calls back: "Catch us, slowpoke!" — Stephen King, *Black House*, p. 120, 2001

slow set *noun*

in a disco, a set of songs (usually three) played at slow tempo with the purpose of bringing the dancers closer together *IRELAND*
- The lad who boasts of intimately kissing three or four different girls during a slow set at a disco is regarded as a macho male[.] — *Irish Times*, 4th November 1997

slow smolder *noun*

a person whose career is going nowhere fast *US*
US Air Force usage; the opposite of a 'fast burner'.
- — *Seattle Times*, p. A9, 12th April 1998: 'Grunts, squids not grunting from the same dictionary'

slow the row, papa!

take it easy! *US*
- — Marcus Hanna Boulware, *Jive and Slang of Students in Negro Colleges*, 1947

slud *verb*

to fall victim to a chemical warfare attack *US*
From the official military warning that the victim will '*s*alivate, *l*achrymate, *u*rinate and *d*efecate'.
- — *American Speech*, p. 401, Winter 1991: 'Among the new words'
- — *The Retired Officer Magazine*, p. 39, January 1993

sludge *noun*

beer *UK*
- — *A Glossary for Our Times (News Chronicle)*, 22nd May 1958

SLUF *nickname*

an A-7 Corsair attack bomber *US*
An acronym for '*s*hort *l*ittle (or *l*ow) *u*gly *f*ucker (or *f*ellow)'.
- — John Horton, *The Grub Street Dictionary of International Aircraft Nicknames*, p. 119, 1994

sluff *verb*

to play truant *US*

• — *Newsweek*, p. 28, 8th October 1951

slug *noun*

1 a drink *UK, 1756*

• He handed me a man-sized slug of the stuff and set up one for himself. — Mickey Spillane, *I, The Jury*, p. 22, 1947
• This noon, recalling with distaste the nineteen slugs of bourbon he had polished off yesterday, he had promised himself that he would get through one whole day without a snort. — Bernard Wolfe, *The Late Risers*, p. 16, 1954
• Dead Jane was there, had a big bottle of Tokay wine hidden in Mardou's dresser for me and got it out and poured me a big slug[.] — Jack Kerouac, *The Subterraneans*, p. 62, 1958
• [A]fter the fourth pint, and the unease manifests itself as a shudder with each swallow. Every slug brings nearer the end of the day. — Mark Powell, *Snap*, p. 38, 2001

2 a dollar *US*

• — Don Wilmeth, *The Language of American Popular Entertainment*, p. 247, 1981

3 the penis *AUSTRALIA*

Figurative application of the slimy invertebrate found in damp places; the pun on conventional 'slug' (a bullet) into **BULLET** (an ejaculation of semen) is later.

4 an idler *UK, 1425*

Either an abbreviation of 'sluggard' or a comparison to the slow-moving slimy gasteropod or land snail.

• — Connie Eble (Editor), *UNC-CH Campus Slang*, p. 7, Fall 1987

5 a seal *ANTARCTICA, 1940*

A visual similarity.

• — Bernadette Hince, *The Antarctic Dictionary*, p. 319, 2000

6 a group of cards that have been arranged and then inserted into a deck *US*

• — Frank Scoblete, *Best Blackjack*, p. 272, 1996

7 a hospital patient who refuses to participate in therapy or self-help *US*

• — *Maledicta*, p. 34, 1988–1989: 'Medical maledicta from San Francisco'

8 in drag racing and hot rodding, a piston *US*

• — *American Speech*, p. 305, December 1956: 'Hot-Rodders' jargon again'
• — *Good Housekeeping*, p. 143, September 1958: 'Hot-Rod terms for teen-age girls'

9 in the television and film industries, a piece of unusable film that is temporarily used to fill in for footage that will be added *US*

• — Ralph S. Singleton, *Filmaker's Dictionary*, p. 155, 1990

▸ **put the slug on**

to hit someone with your fist *US*

• — Joe McKennon, *Circus Lingo*, p. 73, 1980

slug *verb*

1 to strike someone hard *UK, 1862*

• Stomp King was slugged by his Landlord last Monday because he persisted in playing the piano at 4 a.m. every morning — Frederic Ramsay Junior, *Chicago Documentary*, p. 26, 1944
• MR. BIG NOSE: I'll thump him if he calls me 'Big Nose' again. MR. CHEEKY: Oh, shut up, Big Nose. MR. BIG NOSE: Ah! All right. I warned you. I really will slug you so hard[.] — Monty Python, *Life of Brian*, 1979

2 to drink directly from a bottle *UK: SCOTLAND*

From the noun sense.

• Could you no use a glass instead of sluggin oot the boatle? — Michael Munro, *The Complete Patter*, p. 143, 1996

3 to cheat playing slot machines by inserting something other than the proper coin in the machine *US*

• Next comes the more overt and obvious attempt to play a slot machine for free by inserting foreign coins or slugs, better known as slugging. — Jim Regan, *Winning at Slot Machine*, p. 68, 1985

4 to lie in bed *US*

Verb formation from the more common usage as a noun.

• — Connie Eble (Editor), *UNC-CH Campus Slang*, p. 5, October 1986

slug and snail; slug *noun*

a fingernail, a toenail *UK*

Rhyming slang.

• — Ray Puxley, *Cockney Rabbit*, 1992

slugfest *noun*

a bruising, drawn-out fight; hence, a military engagement at close-quarters *US*

A combination of **SLUG** (to strike) and **-FEST** (a concentration of the preceding noun).

• General Wesley Clark, the former Nato supreme allied commander, warned that US forces will face a "methodical slugfest" in the battle for Baghdad if warplanes have not destroyed the Republican Guard. — *The Guardian*, 5th April 2003
• By moving into Baghdad full force, U.S. hopes to avoid lengthy slugfest. — *USA Today*, p. 2, 8th April 2003

slugger *noun*

1 a brutish fist-fighter *US, 1942*

• [H]e hadn't come up against a slugger. He stuck out a few jabs and I swung some poundhouse punches. — Brian McDonald, *Elephant Boys*, p. 43, 2000

2 a casino cheat who tries to play slot machines with objects other than the proper coin *US*

• The really hard-core "slugger" will counterfeit actual casino dollar tokens, a few of which look almost like the real thing. — Jim Regan, *Winning at Slot Machine*, p. 68, 1985

sluggo *noun*

an extremely skimpy bikini *AUSTRALIA*

• — Trevor Cralle, *The Surfin'ary*, p. 117, 1991

sluggos *noun*

tight-fitting men's nylon swimming briefs *AUSTRALIA*

So called since they display the **SLUG** (the penis).

• By the time the boys surfaced in their sluggoes, I was waxed up and doing warm-up exercises. — Kathy Lette, *Girls' Night Out*, p. 188, 1987
• As I started to walk out of the water I noticed a pair of sluggos getting washed up on the beach some 20 metres away. — Paul Vautin, *Turn It Up!*, p. 96, 1995

slug huggers *noun*

a pair of men's close-fitting and revealing nylon swimming trunks *AUSTRALIA*

• He's wearing slug huggers on the beach. — *www.abc.net.au/wordmap*, 2003

slugout *noun*

a fight, especially between youth gangs *US*

• — *Dobie Gillis Teenage Slanguage Dictionary*, 1962

sluice *noun*

an act of sexual intercourse; sex *UK*

From an earlier sense (the vagina).

• I asked her would she like a sluice. She wasn't quite sure what I meant. — Bill Naughton, *Alfie Darling*, 1970

slum *noun*

1 an apartment or house *US*

The *Oxford English Dictionary* offers several early C19 cites in this sense but deems the term obsolete. Robert Beck (Iceberg Slim) wrote in the language of the streets, not C19 England, suggesting a slang life for the word in the C20 US.

• I forgot, some louse put the heist on your 'slum.' — *Pimp*, p. 116, 1969

2 inexpensive costume jewellery; any low value merchandise *US, 1914*

• The hijacker dumped that slum to the top of the dresser under a bright lamp. It was like the display at Tiffany's. — Iceberg Slim (Robert Beck), *Trick Baby*, p. 24, 1969
• — Clarence Major, *Dictionary of Afro-American Slang*, p. 105, 1970
• — Joe McKennon, *Circus Lingo*, p. 84, 1980
• The price of a Slum can vary from a little over a dollar a gross to almost ten a gross wholesale. — Gene Sorrows, *All About Carnivals*, p. 26, 1985

3 prison food *US*

• — Hyman E. Goldin et al., *Dictionary of American Underworld Lingo*, p. 199, 1950

slum *verb*

1 to visit a poor neighbourhood out of curiousity; to live beneath your station *UK, 1884*

• I want to go slumming down on Central Avenue. — Chester Himes, *If He Hollers Let Him Go*, p. 54, 1945
• On one of my nights off, some of us went slumming. — Helen P. Branson, *Gay Bar*, p. 69, 1957
• "Slumming?" Juan asked in routine. — Willard Motley, *Let No Man Write My Epitaph*, p. 98, 1958
• Why, I said, they must be out slummin', or maybe just pickin' brains. — Ross Russell, *The Sound*, p. 216, 1961

- [E]ven a few well-dressed women, slumming with their well-dressed husbands or escorts – but, usually knowingly slumming. —John Rechy, *City of Night*, p. 247, 1963
- Through "Moms", he got the Negro businessmen and politicans to come when slumming and through his own efforts he got the hustlers and night people. —Babs Gonzales, *I Paid My Dues*, p. 82, 1967
- Eating chitterlings is like going slumming to them. —Eldridge Cleaver, *Soul on Ice*, p. 29, 1968
- A guy and his wife, slumming. Radical chic, vintage 1976. —Armistead Maupin, *Tales of the City*, p. 143, 1978
- You must like slumming, Kareem. What would make a high-class guy like you leave a good computer programming job at Citibank, come uptown and work among a den of thieves? —*New Jack City*, 1990
- These boys do 'Bluntman and Chronic,' which outsells both of our books put together, hence they're never on a panel with the likes of us. They slumming right now. —*Chasing Amy*, 1997

2 to voluntarily mix with social inferiors *UK, 1928*

- I accuse her of slumming with me [...] like she think she better than me. —Joel Rose, *Kill Kill Faster Faster*, p. 11, 1997

slum *adjective*

cheap; shabby; in poor taste *US*

- This fellow was sharp in a black man's kinda fashion and the things he was wearing were far from being slum. —Jackson, *Gentleman Pimp*, p. 158, 1973

slumber slot *noun*

in trucking, a sleeping compartment behind the seat *US*

- —Montie Tak, *Truck Talk*, p. 147, 1971

slumgullion *noun*

a make-shift stew made with whatever ingredients are at hand *US*

- —Charles F. Haywood, *Yankee Dictionary*, p. 154, 1963

slum hustler *noun*

a person who sells fake jewellery *US*

- —Kenn "Naz" Young, *Naz's Underground Dictionary*, p. 56, 1973

slumlord *noun*

a landlord who rents poorly kept-up properties in the ghetto, often with a large profit margin *US, 1953*

- —*American Speech*, December 1961
- We were at the mercy of the rats. The slumlord? Never laid eyes on him. —Odie Hawkins, *Scars and Memories*, p. 17, 1987
- To make matters worse, he never got enough rest because he owned property in Logan Heights and was up half the night doing slumlord collecting. —Joseph Wambaugh, *Floaters*, p. 177, 1996

slummadelic fire *noun*

excellent and exciting rap music *US*

- Every two years the dynamic duo from down South [OutKast] put down the slummadelic fire that makes us bob our head. Ya heard? —*The Source*, p. 42, March 2002

slummy *noun*

small change; coins *UK*

Liverpool use.

- Think you can get me to count out your slummy? —Kevin Sampson, *Outlaws*, p. 86, 2001

slung up *adjective*

relaxed; at ease *US*

- —Connie Eble (Editor), *UNC-CH Campus Slang*, p. 7, Spring 1990

slurp *verb*

▸ slurp at the sideways smile

to perform oral sex on a woman *US*

- Another way to say "cunnilingus" [...] Slurping at the sideways smile[.] —Erica Orloff and JoAnn Baker, *Dirty Little Secrets*, p. 86, 2001

slurpage *noun*

any beverage *US*

- —Vann Wesson, *Generation X Field Guide and Lexicon*, p. 154, 1997

slush *noun*

1 counterfeit paper money *UK, 1924*

- There's hundreds of things you've got to check with slush. Paper, serials, what sort of plates they used[.] —Derek Raymond (Robin Cook), *The Crust on its Uppers*, p. 47, 1962
- —Angela Devlin, *Prison Patter*, p. 106, 1996

2 tea *UK: SCOTLAND*

- We'll have a wee cup a slush if you'll stick the kettle on. —Michael Munro, *The Patter, Another Blast*, p. 66, 1988

▸ in the slush

very drunk *US*

- Instead, the citizen rendered temporarily senseless by booze, or "in the slush" as the street slang goes, is treated more gently here. —*St. Petersburg (Florida) Times*, p. 5D, 26th May 1991

slush box *noun*

an automatic transmission; a car with automatic transmission *AUSTRALIA, 1981*

slush car *noun*

a car with automatic transmission *US*

- —*Good Housekeeping*, p. 143, September 1958: 'Hot-Rod terms for teen-age girls'

slush fund *noun*

1 a discretionary fund, where the source of the money and the exact way in which it is spent is not subject to any accounting or accountability *US, 1874*

- He [George H. Bush] will, of course, need a slush fund – not unlike the one Gordon LIddy and Maurice Stans put together for Nixon in 1972. —Hunter S. Thompson, *Generation of Swine*, p. 188, 8th December 1986

2 money collected by a prisoner's associates for a prisoner's family *UK*

- —Angela Devlin, *Prison Patter*, p. 106, 1996

slushing fuck pit *noun*

the vagina *UK*

- Abjection was invoked in various ways: through reference to dirtiness (e.g., front bum, dirt box), uncooked (bloody?) meat (e.g., meat seat, chopped liver), vaginal secretions of all types (e.g., slushing fuck pit, the snail trail), smell (e.g., smelly hole, stench trench), and wounds (e.g., gash, gaping axe wound). —*Journal of Sex Research*, p. 146, 2001

slush pump *noun*

1 a trombone *US, 1937*

Musicians' slang.

- Slush pump is similarly used in the synthetic style of the 1930s. —Peter Clayton and Peter Gammond, *Jazz A-Z*, p. 220, 1986

2 an automatic transmission; a vehicle with automatic transmission *US, 1960s to 70s*

'Not used so much these days,' noted Clive Graham-Ranger, *Sunday Times*, 9th August 1981.

- —Ross R. Olney, *Kings of the Drag Strip*, p. 188, 1968
- [T]he "slush-pump" automatics compounded the poor performance dramatically. —*How to Build Tri-Five Chevy Trucks*, p. 119, 1999

slush up *verb*

to drink to the point of intoxication *US*

- —Vincent J. Monteleone, *Criminal Slang*, p. 214, 1949

slushy *noun*

a kitchen hand *AUSTRALIA, 1880*

- SLUSHY – A kitchen hand. —Gilbert H. Lawson, *A Dictionary of Australian Words and Terms*, 1924
- I stumbled into the big money when our cook's slushy (officially known as cook's offsider) went crook with a nasty bite[.] —Harold Lewis, *Crow On A Barbed Wire Fence*, p. 176, 1973
- —Ryan Aven-Bray, *Ridgey Didge Oz Jack Lang*, p. 45, 1983
- —Bernadette Hince, *The Antarctic Dictionary*, p. 320, 2000

slushy *adjective*

extremely sentimental *US, 1889*

- I started to wonder how much of a hand the grand master of hotel spin had on the rest of the feature on slushy Valentine's stories. —*The Observer*, 15th February 2004

slut *noun*

1 a promiscuous girl or woman *UK, 1450*

- A girl with few friends who is low in the social hierarchy will get a reputation as a slut for the same behavior that doesn't cost a popular girl anything. —Rosalind Wiseman, *Queen Bees and Wannabes*, p. 39, 2002
- This is when they are most likely to run around with reckless abandon, acting like complete sluts. —Karl Mark, *The Comple A**hole's Guide to Handling Chicks*, p. 48, 2003
- He had ingrained in me the idea that I was just a slut with no self-respect. —Jenna Jameson, *How to Make Love Like a Porn Star*, p. 481, 2004

2 a promiscuous boy or man *US*

- I was a little slut back then, trying to taste all the flavors, so I told her, "Wow, I'd love to fuck in that thing." —Tommy Lee, *The Dirt*, p. 55, 2002

3 a prostitute *US*

- Now that's the kind of girl you ought to be associating with, and not with common sluts like that one. Why, she didn't even look clean. —Joseph Heller, *Catch 22*, p. 297, 1961

- They rarely refer to them other than as whores, sluts, trollops and the like. —Frederick K. Graham, *The Bambo Chest*, p. 71, 2000

4 used as an affectionate female-to-female term of address *US*
Use of the term does not suggest promiscuity.
- —Connie Eble (Editor), *UNC-CH Campus Slang*, p. 4, November 1983

-slut *suffix*
in combination with a sexual fetish or activity, a sexual fetishist or (in pornography) specialist; in such forms as pain-slut, nipple-slut, come-slut, etc *UK*
Intended to, or, at best, tends to, diminish the status of a person so described. Widespread in Internet pornography.

slut-mouth *noun*
a person whose language is often coarse and vulgar *US*
- —Don R. McCreary (Editor), *Dawg Speak*, 2001

slut puppy *noun*
a promiscuous girl *US*
- —Connie Eble (Editor), *UNC-CH Campus Slang*, p. 5, Spring 1990

slutted out *adjective*
broken down; in disrepair *US*
- Son, you want to watch out for those 'mechanic's special' cars in the want ads. Most of 'em are so slutted out it'd take a faith healer to get 'em to start. —Ken Weaver, *Texas Crude*, p. 126, 1984

sluttish *adjective*
sexual in a cheap way *US*
- Sometimes New Yorkers can be a little too direct for a demure girl like me, even one who's realized she's probably more sluttish than demure-ish. —Plum Sykes, *Bergdorf Blondes*, p. 68, 2004

slutty *adjective*
promiscuous; having a sexual appearance *US*
- "A good personality," Reeves begins, "consists of a chick who has a little hard body and who will satisfy all sexual demands without being too slutty about things, and who will essentially keep her dumb fucking mouth shut." —Bret Easton Ellis, *American Psycho*, p. 91, 1991
- "You pig," he said. "You slutty cocktease." —Wally Lamb, *She's Come Undone*, p. 131, 1992

slutwear *noun*
extremely sexually provoking clothing *US*
- —Ana Loria, *1 2 3 Be A Porn Star!*, p. 167, 2000: 'Glossary of adult sex Industry terms'
- America's teen peep show: Has 'slutware' gone too far? [Headline] —*San Francisco Chronicle*, 27th July 2003

sly *adjective*
unfair *UK*
Liverpool usage.
- It's sly on the kids anyway, isn't it? —Kevin Sampson, *Outlaws*, p. 82, 2001
- "Fucking state of that fella's dick, Mam!" "I know, Marie-Rochelle – it's sly, isn't it?" —Kevin Sampson, *Clubland*, p. 32, 2002

sly-boots *noun*
a cunning person *UK, 1700*
Jocular.
- Lew Silver you old sly boots who's your little friend? —Barry Humphries, *Bazza Pulls It Off!*, 1971

sly-grog *noun*
illegally made or supplied alcohol *AUSTRALIA, 1825*
- It was a pity that sailors weren't called as witnesses before the Royal Commission on sly-grog liquor. —J.E. MacDonnell, *Don't Gimme the Ships*, p. 30, 1960
- Most times sly-grog was 15/- a bottle: a mixture of whisky, metho and water. —Patsy Adam-Smith, *Folklore of the Australian Railwaymen*, p. 8, 1969
- George is referring to one of those dreadful sly grog places which are scattered about the city and inner suburbs of Melbourne. —Kevin Mackey, *The Cure*, p. 74, 1970

sly-grogger *noun*
a person selling sly-grog *AUSTRALIA, 1897*
- [T]hey had made a number of attempts to locate the premises and trap the sly-grogger. —Vince Kelly, *The Bogeyman*, p. 8, 1956

sly-groggery *noun*
an establishment selling alcohol without a licence to do so *AUSTRALIA, 1907*
- He was working his way patiently towards the area in which the sly-groggery was somewhere located when he struck trouble. —Vince Kelly, *The Bogeyman*, p. 16, 1956

sly-grogging *noun*
the practice of selling alcohol illicitly *AUSTRALIA, 1952*
- He knew about Fats's sly-grogging. —Wal Watkins, *Andamooka*, p. 41, 1971

sly-grog joint *noun*
an establishment selling alcohol without a licence to do so *AUSTRALIA, 1956*
- There was no doubt Bombo and Hookey had initiated her to Scotty's sly grog joint and she had apparently fallen asleep. —Robert S. Close, *With Hooves of Brass*, p. 50, 1961

sly-grog shop *noun*
an establishment selling alcohol without a licence to do so *AUSTRALIA, 1826*
- Not long after I broke away they tried to stand over a protected sly grog shop, got loaded up by the coppers and did three years. —Clive Galea, *Slipper*, p. 156, 1988

sly mongoose *noun*
an extremely clever and devious person *US*
Hawaiian youth usage.
- —Douglas Simonson, *Pidgin to da Max*, 1981

s-m *noun*
▷ **see:** S AND M

smack *noun*
1 heroin *US, 1942*
Derives, possibly, from Yiddish *shmeker* (a sniffer of drugs).
- Smack, smock, stuff, horse – they're all heroin. —Clarence Cooper Jr, *The Scene*, p. 55, 1960
- I pushed that thought outta my mind, except for the part of the way out feeling when that good-o smack was making it with you[.] —Piri Thomas, *Down These Mean Streets*, p. 206, 1967
- Because when the smack begins to flow / I really don't care anymore. —Velvet Underground *Heroin*, 1967
- [H]e needed it to buy smack. —Nathan Heard, *Howard Street*, p. 171, 1968
- Musta' shot some 'pure,' cause a lookout on the sidewalk heard him mumble before he croaked, "Well kiss my dead mammy's ass if this ain't the best 'smack' I ever shot. —Iceberg Slim (Robert Beck), *Pimp*, p. 79, 1969
- I don't smoke dope no more / I'm through with smack and fucking / Coz Jesus is the lord. —Albertos y Lost Trios Paranoias, *Jesus Wept*, 1976
- They took some smack from a cellophane pack / And they both rolled up their sleeves[.] —Dennis Wepman et al., *The Life*, p. 56, 1976
- Then she did some smack with a Chinese chap. —Ian Dury, *Plaistow Patricia*, 1977
- So you're sickness weighs a ton / And God's name is smack for some[.] —Alice in Chains *God Smack*, 1992
- He's got more money than God and twice as much coke, crank and smack. —*Boogie Nights*, 1997
- I didn't stop taking smack for health reasons. —Shaun Ryder, *Shaun Ryder... in His Own Words*, 1997

2 alcohol *US*
- —Malachi Andrews and Paul T. Owens, *Black Language*, p. 101, 1973

3 disparaging talk *US*
- —*San Jose Mercury News*, 11th May 1999
- —Connie Eble (Editor), *UNC-CH Campus Slang*, p. 7, Spring 2000

4 slang *US*
- —Anna Scotti and Paul Young, *Buzzwords*, p. 79, 1997

5 a swindle based on matching pennies *US*
- It was our interim game between larger scores on the longer rocks, drag and smack con games we played. —Iceberg Slim (Robert Beck), *Trick Baby*, p. 27, 1969

smack *verb*
to murder someone *UK*
- "What you reckon? You reckon they smacked him?" "Nicky let us get one thing straight here. They all the same people. They after the dosh. He dead. Ergo they smacked him innit?" —Jeremy Cameron, *Brown Bread in Wengen*, p. 118, 1999

▸ **smack the pony**
(of a female) to masturbate *UK*
Smack the Pony is an all-women television sketch show, first broadcast on Channel 4 in 1999.
- What would I think if I returned home from work to find her smacking the pony in front of a George Clooney film[?] —Andrew Holmes, *Sleb*, p. 49, 2002

smack *adverb*
precisely *US*
A shortened **SMACK-DAB**.

- Some new guy I'd never seen was on the car, so I figured that if I didn't bump smack into my parents and all I'd be able to say hello to old Phoebe and then beat it and nobody'd even know I'd been around. —J.D. Salinger, *Catcher in the Rye*, p. 157, 1951
- And the assignation hotels are downtown, smack in the middle of everything, very snug.—Jack Lait and Lee Mortimer, *Washington Confidential*, p. 13, 1951
- I want 'em smack in the middle when we got the yucks glued to the chair!—Max Shulman, *Rally Round the Flag, Boys!*, p. 69, 1957
- I'd blow your ass off with a Seminole air boat. Put you smack on the trailer.—Elmore Leonard, *Gold Coast*, p. 77, 1980

smack-bang *adverb*

of a location, exactly, in the middle *UK, 1984*

- [W]hat on earth are they doing putting a map of Great Britain on the fly-leaf that locates Smithfield smack bang on top of Mt Snowdon? — *The Guardian*, 27th November 1987

smack-dab *adverb*

exactly *US, 1892*

At times reversed for comic effect.

- Dab smack on the television where even the idiots who can't read will get the message!—Max Shulman, *Anyone Got a Match?*, p. 48, 1964
- I checked into the James Brown Motor Inn there and ran smack-dab into Ernie Andrews there who had a big hit[.]—Babs Gonzales, *Movin' On Down De Line*, p. 135, 1975
- But close-up pulling the trigger this morning smack-dab up in his face, I know I ain't never gonna forget him and his bloody stump neck.—Iceberg Slim (Robert Beck), *Death Wish*, p. 122, 1977
- They moved to another good groovy lil' house, a place that had a dirty dirveway leading smack dab up to the front porch.—Odie Hawkins, *Black Casanova*, p. 94, 1984

smacked back *adjective*

heroin-intoxicated *US*

- Dilaudid used to be delightful, but now I've got to be smacked-back for all the pain to go.—James Ellroy, *Brown's Requiem*, p. 69, 1981
- —William K. Bentley and James M. Corbett, *Prison Slang*, p. 79, 1992

smacked out *adjective*

in an extreme state of heroin- or cocaine-intoxication *UK*

- —Tom Hibbert, *Rockspeak!*, p. 144, 1983
- —Angela Devlin, *Prison Patter*, p. 106, 1996
- Fucken smacked-out gobshite! Get your head together!—Kevin Sampson, *Powder*, p. 153, 1999

smacker *noun*

1 a loud kiss *UK, 1775*

- When we go into the kitchen she hugs Mary and gives my old man a smacker, which he enjoys even though he's got his doubts about people who love people of the same sex.—Robert Campbell, *Cat's Meow*, p. 36, 1988

2 a one-dollar note *US*

- —Lou Shelly, *Hepcats Jive Talk Dictionary*, p. 17, 1945
- That-sa my horse, boy! I got fifty smackers onna his nose!—Clarence Cooper Jr, *Black*, p. 249, 1963
- We've got 902,000 smackers!—Red Rudensky, *The Gonif*, p. 107, 1970
- —Steve Kuriscak, *Casino Talk*, p. 51, 1985

3 a pound sterling *UK, 1924*

From the previous sense.

smackeroonie *noun*

1 a kiss *UK*

A teenage elaboration of **SMACKER**, noted by Joanna Williamson, 1982.

2 a pound sterling *UK*

An extension of **SMACKER** (a pound), popularised by UK television personality Christ Tarrant (b.1946) on *Who Wants To Be a Millionaire?*, ITV from 1998.

- Or you can quit now and leave with sixty-four thousand crisp smackeroonies. I have the cheque here now[.]—Kevin Sampson, *Clubland*, p. 117, 2002

smackers *noun*

the lips *UK*

- [A] pair of smackers which Mick Jagger would have been proud to own.—Duncan MacLaughlin, *The Filth*, p. 230, 2002

smackhead *noun*

a heroin addict *US, 1972*

A combination of **SMACK** (heroin) and **HEAD** (a user).

- I was fuckin' mega. And I was still a smackhead [heroin addict] then, of course.—Shaun Ryder, *Shaun Ryder... in His Own Words*, 1994
- "Want some saki?" he asked once. "No thanks." "Oh, excuse me, I forgot you were a smack head."—Cleo Odzer, *Goa Freaks*, 1995
- And it isn't as though the smackheads are going to go crying to the UDA [Ulster Defence Association], is it?—Kevin Sampson, *Outlaws*, p. 76, 2001
- Now, it's all smackheads outside the door, saying, "Have you got 20p?"— *The Times Magazine*, p. 49, 24th October 2002

smack in the eye *noun*

a pie *UK*

Rhyming slang.

- —Ray Puxley, *Cockney Rabbit*, 1992

smack up *verb*

1 to attack someone; to beat someone up *AUSTRALIA, 1945*

- Change my pitch up. smack my bitch up.—The Progidy, *Smack My Bitch Up*, 1997
- [T]hose blokes who smacked us up on the bridge.—John King, *Human Punk*, p. 172, 2000

2 to inject oneself with heroin *US*

- Monica and I made daily trips to smack up at Neal's. Heroin cured cocaine frazzle.—Cleo Odzer, *Goa Freaks*, p. 64, 1995

smacky lips *noun*

prolonged kissing *US*

- — *Time*, p. 57, 1st January 1965: 'Students: the slang bag'

smage *verb*

to masturbate *NORFOLK ISLAND*

- —Beryl Nobbs Palmer, *A Dictionary of Norfolk Words and Usages*, p. 40, 1992

small *noun*

one hundred dollars *US*

- Two hundred bucks, two small, two dimes, two C-notes, all blown away.—Robert Campbell, *Juice*, p. 9, 1988

small *adjective*

1 afraid *US*

- "If I was standing there with that guy when I saw him start to get small, I could have done something." Sims meant if he'd been there when the pilot got scared about the DEW Line and the towerless field.—James Mills, *The Underground Empire*, p. 427, 1986

2 drug-intoxicated *US*

Comedian Steve Martin's refrain of 'Let's get small' inspired a wider usage of the term.

- —Connie Eble (Editor), *UNC-CH Campus Slang*, p. 4, April 1978

small-arm inspection *noun*

▷ see: **SHORT-ARM INSPECTION**

small beer *noun*

something or someone of little consequence or importance *UK, 1777*

- But for many surviving on wages of less than £12,000 a year, Tuppen's words are small beer.— *The Guardian*, 4th June 2000

small fortune *noun*

an extravagantly large sum of money *UK, 1874*

- Why giving away a small fortune doesn't make John Paul Getty a saint[.]— *The Guardian*, 22nd April 2003

small fry *noun*

an insignificant thing or things, person or people *UK, 1797*

- American companies are not interested in small fry[.]— *The Guardian*, 20th November 2003

small house *noun*

a latrine *TRINIDAD AND TOBAGO, 1986*

- —Lise Winer, *Dictionary of the English/Creole of Trinidad & Tobago*, 2003

smallie *noun*

1 in Jamaica, a person from any other Caribbean island *JAMAICA*

- Neighbourhood wars heated up between Africans, Jamaicans and "Smallies" from Barbados, Trinidad and St. Kitts. Such was the rivalry between the Jamaicans and their fellow Caribbean islanders, that the "Smallies" often sided with the Africans against the Jamaicans. —Karline Smith, *Moss Side Massive*, p. 213–214, 1994

2 on Trinidad and Tobago, a person from any of the smaller English Caribbean islands northwest of Trinidad and Tobago *TRINIDAD AND TOBAGO, 1945*

- —Lise Winer, *Dictionary of the English/Creole of Trinidad & Tobago*, 2003

small nickel *noun*
fifty dollars or, in a casino, fifty dollars' worth of betting tokens *US, 1961*
- —Thomas L. Clark, *The Dictionary of Gambling and Gaming*, p. 206, 1987

small one *noun*
one hundred dollars *US*
- —George Percy, *The Language of Poker*, p. 83, 1988

small potatoes *adjective*
something of little consequence *US, 1838*
- If I'm small potatoes that's all I want to be. —Mickey Spillane, *Kiss Me Deadly*, p. 65, 1952
- Next to theirs, my sin was pretty small potatoes. —Max Shulman, *I was a Teen-Age Dwarf*, p. 121, 1959

smalls *noun*
1 underwear *UK, 1943*
- watching my smalls churn round [in a washing machine]— *The Guardian*, 3rd July 2001

2 a small amount of money as a bribe *JAMAICA*
- —Peter Patrick, *Some Recent Jamaican Creole Words*, 2003

small suppository in anticipation of the broom handle *noun*
the opening volley in a battle *US*
US naval aviator usage.
- —*United States Naval Institute Proceedings*, p. 108, October 1986

small thing *noun*
▸ **do that small thing**
used in a request for a favour, or to signal compliance with a request *UK, 1984*
- [M]aybe we could ask you, Louis, just to do that small thing for us on health. —Chairperson, *Gauteng Provincial Legislature (South Africa)*, 15th March 2001

small-time *adjective*
insignificant, unimportant; minor *US, 1938*
Of vaudeville origins.
- [H]is small-time narcotics business had elevated him to the position of one of the more affluent rednecks in Ford County. —John Grisham, *Time to Kill*, p. 1, 1989

small-timer *noun*
an insignificant person; someone of trivial importance in any given field *UK, 1935*
- Throughout a multi-faceted directing career, [Michael] Winner has specialised in the genre in which some victimised small-timer picks up a gun and starts offing oppressors. —*The Guardian*, 14th May 1999

smanker *noun*
an unmarried, middle-aged person who has no children objectified as a lifestyle category *UK*
Formed on the acronym of 'single *m*iddle-*a*ged *n*o *k*ids', and probably contrived for marketing purposes.
- —Susie Dent, *The Language Report*, p. 14, 2003

smarm *verb*
to behave in an ingratiating manner; to flatter someone insincerely *UK, 1911*
- Strip away the chat show talk, the gesture politics and the smarming up to every group he meets and you see what Londoners increasingly are seeing – that the emperor has no clothes. —*The Guardian*, 21st April 2000

smarmy *adjective*
smug, self-satisfied; overly sentimental *UK, 1909*
- This guy was built like a brick shithouse, with an elephantine mustache and smoldering brown eyes. What was he doing hooked up to that sort of smarmy Euro-pop? —Armistead Maupin, *Further Tales of the City*, p. 150, 1982
- —Connie Eble (Editor), *UNC-CH Campus Slang*, p. 7, Spring 1987
- "I never wanna see your smarmy face again," Burl Ralston said. "You're never doing business with me after this." —Joseph Wambaugh, *Finnegan's Week*, p. 107, 1993
- [O]dd that someone with a title can be so very smarmy and common[.] —Michael Faber, *The Crimson Petal and the White*, 2003

smart *adjective*
fine; well; alright *UK*
- [J]ust let us know where he's gone and everything will be smart. We'll drop you off home. —Mark Powell, *Snap*, p. 68, 2001

smart alec; smart aleck; smart alick *noun*
an offensively smart person; a know-it-all *US, 1865*
- That was how Winona talked, always a little smart-alecky. —Elmore Leonard, *Pronto*, p. 64, 1993

smart armpit *noun*
a know-all *UK*
Euphemistic for SMART-ARSE.
- Sounds too easy? Okay then, smart armpit, give yourself five seconds to identify each one[.] —*SMTV LIVE it's wicked*, p. 26, 2000

smart-arse; smart-ass *noun*
a person with a conceited view of their own intelligence *AUSTRALIA, 1937*
- No one likes a smartarse[.] —Ignatius Jones, *True Hip*, p. 57, 1990
- 'Why don't you buy your lunch and not be such an old tart?' 'Yeah? And what have you got smart arse?' —Robert G. Barrett, *Davo's Little Something*, p. 8, 1992
- Serves me right for being a smartarse, he thought.. —Chris Ryan, *The Watchman*, p. 66, 2001
- Smartarse is in the genes[.] —Ben Elton, *High Society*, p. 14, 2002

smartarsed; smart-arsed *adjective*
conceited about one's intelligence *US, 1960*
- We don't dig smart-arsed super-studs of either species. —*Searchlight*, p. 16, 1974
- She wanted faith not smartarsed advice. —Frank Moorhouse, *Forty-Seventeen*, p. 161, 1988

smart as a new pin *adjective*
very smartly dressed *UK, 1893*
- Often, as you well know, he was as smart as a new pin. This time, however, he was wearing a baggy suit[.] —Charles Delaunay and Michael James, *Django Reinhardt*, p. 148, 1988

smarter than the average bear
used for a humorous, if at times ironic, observation about another's intelligence *US*
Yogi Bear's boast about himself in the television cartoon series that first aired in 1958.

smart-eye *verb*
to give someone a look that may be aggressive, challenging or disapproving *US*
- Start a fight with the same guy that was smart-eyein' you[.] —Eminem (Marshall Mathers), *Drug Ballad*, 2000

smartie *noun*
1 a shrewd operator; a person who is wise to the various devices used by criminals *AUSTRALIA, 1950*
- So the smarties have got you on a mug's list? —Frank Hardy, *The Yarns of Billy Borker*, p. 59, 1965
- People who had only known him as a 'smartie' and a 'take' were astounded when the racing world turned out in force to give him a slap-up funeral. —James Holledge, *The Great Australian Gamble*, p. 145, 1966
- A smartie entered a ring-in for a Maiden Handicap at a bush race meeting. He entered her as an eight-year-old mare unraced. The mare duly bolted in by 10 lengths. —Frank Hardy and Athol George Mulley, *The Needy and the Greedy*, p. 110, 1975
- Too many smarties think there is a doping ring operating up here. —Clive Galea, *Slipper*, p. 70, 1988

2 an impudent, cheeky person; an offensively smart person *AUSTRALIA*
- We don't like smarties around here, Dale, so just you watch it. —Wilda Moxham, *The Apprentice*, p. 11, 1969
- Told he was speaking to him, the smartie replied, 'That can't be.' —Roy Higgins and Tom Prior, *The Jockey Who Laughed*, p. 92, 1982
- I turned around in horror as I soon realised that some smartie had locked me in the toilet. —Rex Hunt, *Tall Tales – and True*, p. 40, 1994

3 an intelligent person *AUSTRALIA*
- So y' see, sonny, I'm not such a smartie after all. —Ward McNally, *Supper at Happy Harry's*, p. 11, 1982

smarties *noun*
tablets of MDMA, the recreational drug best known as ecstasy *UK*
From a branded multi-coloured confection.
- One of it [MDMA]'s early nicknames, "disco biscuits", was a reflection of how sweet and safe the drug was considered, like "Smarties" (another nickname). —Dave Haslam, *Adventures of the Wheels of Steel*, p. xxv, 2001

smartman *noun*
a man who engages in confidence swindles *TRINIDAD AND TOBAGO*
- —Lise Winer, *Dictionary of the English/Creole of Trinidad & Tobago*, 2003

smart mob *noun*
a group of protesters (or some other demonstration of social unrest) organised and mobilised by text messaging *US*
A play on conventional 'mob' and an abbreviation of 'mobile'; coined by Howard Rheingold for *Smart Mobs*, 2002.
- The people who make up smart mobs co-operate in ways never before possible because they carry devices that possess both communication and (as technology develops) computing capabilities. — *The Times Magazine*, 21st June 2003

smart money *noun*
in horse racing, money bet on the basis of solid, empirical data *US*
- — David W. Maurer, *Argot of the Racetrack*, p. 58, 1951

smart-mouth *verb*
to talk insolently to someone *US, 1968*
- — John Ayto, *The Oxford Dictionary of Slang*, p. 320, 1998

smart pill *noun*
rabbit droppings *AUSTRALIA*
In the US, Michigan Upper Peninsula usage.
- [A] boy and his father were walking through the woods when the son spotted some rabbit droppings. The boy asked his dad: "What are these, Pop?" "They're smart pills, son," said his father. — *Northern Territory (Australia) News*, p. 2, 19th August 2001

smarts *noun*
intelligence *US, 1970*
- If you don't know nothin', the Joint is a great place – me, I had all my smarts long before. — Edwin Torres, *Carlito's Way*, p. 46, 1975
- There's only so many dudes that have enough smarts to pull one off. — Gerald Petievich, *Money Men*, p. 92, 1981
- He's got more learnin than just the paperbooks ridin his hip alla time. That Barker's got street smarts. — Seth Morgan, *Homeboy*, p. 43, 1990
- I guess I had some contacts plus, you know, smarts in certain areas. — Diran Abedayo, *My Once Upon A Time*, p. 72, 2000

smarty *noun*
in horse racing, a person purporting to have inside information but who is not to be trusted *AUSTRALIA*
- — Ned Wallish, *The Truth Dictionary of Racing Slang*, p. 75, 1989

smarty-pants *noun*
a person who is smart, but not quite as smart as they think they are *US, 1941*
- I hope you're proud, Mr. Smartypants Lawyer. — Seth Morgan, *Homeboy*, p. 279, 1990

smash *noun*
1 a great success *UK, 1930*
A shortening of 'smash hit'.
- The single was not a smash but, much to Ian [Parkin]'s delight, outsold Blue and Atomic Kitten in Oxford Street's HMV store. — *Wimbledon Guardian*, 30th April 2004

2 momentum *US*
Air combat slang.
- North Vietnamese ground controllers would lead the MiGs in behind the Phantoms at very low altitude, below radar coverage, building up energy – "smash" was the pilot's term – at supersonic speed[.] — Walter Boyne and Steven Thompson, *The Wild Blue*, p. 523, 1986

3 money; pocket change *US*
- I managed to overcome his original bad impression of me, and soon I was buying his drinks and meals, and he was hitting me for "smash" (change) at regular intervals. — William Burroughs, *Junkie*, p. 26, 1953
- — Allen Geller, *Mr*, p. 9, April 1966: 'The hippie's lexicon'

4 wine *US*
- — Anthony Romeo, *The Language of Gangs*, p. 22, 4th December 1962
- — Hermese E. Roberts, *The Third Ear*, 1971
- — *American Speech*, p. 155, Spring-Summer 1972: 'An approach to Black slang'
- — Edith A. Folb, *runnin' down some lines*, p. 255, 1980

smash *verb*
▸ **smash case**
in computing, to disregard any differentiation between upper and lower case *US*
- — Eric S. Raymond, *The New Hacker's Dictionary*, p. 323, 1991

smash and grab *noun*
1 a black taxi or a minicab *UK*
Rhyming slang.
- — Ray Puxley, *Cockney Rabbit*, 1992

2 a simplistic burglary involving very little planning or thought *US*
- The old man never fenced anything but whiskey from hijackers and clothes from smash-and-grab store burglars. — Iceberg Slim (Robert Beck), *Trick Baby*, p. 17, 1969

smashed *adjective*
1 drunk *US, 1960*
- [H]e would get smashed on two and a half pints of Worthington E from the wood. — Doug Lang, *Freaks*, p. 20, 1973
- She whispers in your ear, 'We go home right now, buddy, or you don't get any.' You have to decide quick. You want to get smashed, have a good time? You do, you're gonna have to wait a month to get laid. — Elmore Leonard, *Killshot*, p. 249, 1989
- — Angela Devlin, *Prison Patter*, p. 106, 1996

2 drug-intoxicated *US, 1967*
- Then I turned around and one of the men passed me a joint and that was it. I wanted to be ripped, smashed, torn up as I had never wanted anything before. — Anonymous, *Go Ask Alice*, p. 71, 1971
- Oh, like the usual. Going to Nautilus, getting smashed, going to this Uva place. — Bret Easton Ellis, *Less Than Zero*, p. 15, 1985
- — Angela Devlin, *Prison Patter*, p. 106, 1996

smash 'em-up *noun*
a vehicle accident *US*
- — "Slingo", *The Official CB Slang Dictionary Handbook*, p. 56, 1976

smasher *noun*
1 a very attractive female *US*
- I knew if I wanted to nail down this little smasher, I would have to move fast. — Max Shulman, *I was a Teen-Age Dwarf*, p. 9, 1959

2 a superlative thing *UK, 1894*
- I turn to the other issue of the day: Europe. Pants, more like. Although The Final Countdown was a smasher. — *The Guardian*, 25th May 2001

3 a baggage handler on a train *US*
- — Ramon Adams, *The Language of the Railroader*, p. 141, 1977

smasheroo *noun*
1 a great success *US, 1948*
An elaboration of **SMASH**.
- In the animated category, there is no smasheroo on the level of Shrek[.] — *The Guardian*, 21st March 2003

2 a good-looking female *US*
- A smasheroo she was – a real zinger. — Max Shulman, *I was a Teen-Age Dwarf*, p. 8, 1959

smash-face *adjective*
physical; aggressive *US, 1990*
- — *American Speech*, p. 88, Spring 1995: 'Among the new words'

smashing *adjective*
fine; excellent; possessed of great charm; large *UK, 1911*
It is often claimed, improbably, that this derives from the Irish phrase *is maith sin* (that's good).
- Young Emma Tierney, a member of the Ennis Lawn Tennis and Badminton Club, was in smashing form at the Junior South of Ireland championships in Limerick during the week. — *Clare Champion*, 2nd July 2002

smash-mouth *noun*
prolonged kissing *US*
- — *Time*, p. 57, 1st January 1965: 'Students: the slang bag'

smash-mouth *verb*
to kiss passionately *US*
- — Collin Baker et al., *College Undergraduate Slang Study Conducted at Brown University*, p. 199, 1968

smash-mouth *adjective*
physical, aggressive *US, 1989*
- — *American Speech*, p. 88, Spring 1995: 'Among the new words'

smazzmo *verb*
to move in an uncoordinated, jerky manner *US*
- [W]e collide and he spazzmos on. — Lester Bangs, *Psychotic Reactions and Carburetor Dung*, p. 257, 1977

smear *noun*
theatrical cosmetics *US*
- — Wilfred Granville, *The Theatre Dictionary*, p. 178, 1952

smear *verb*
to drop napalm on a target *US*
- —Linda Reinberg, *In the Field*, p. 201, 1991

▸ **smear a queer**
to assault a homosexual *US*
- —Kenn "Naz" Young, *Naz's Dictionary of Teen Slang*, p. 108, 1993

smears *noun*
LSD *US*
- —Ralph de Sola, *Crime Dictionary*, p. 139, 1982
- — US Department of Justice, *Street Terms*, October 1994

smeg *noun*
1 used as an all-purpose, non-profane insult *UK*
Used in many different forms – 'smeg!', 'smegging', 'smeghead' – by space castaway Dave Lister on the science fiction comedy television series *Red Dwarf*, BBC since 1988.
2 any viscous matter of unknown origin *US*
The variant 'shmeg' also exists.
- — *Maledicta*, p. 48, 1995: 'Door whore and other New Mexico restaurant slang'

smell *noun*
digital-vaginal contact *US*
- But Buck's havin a little trouble with his. Won't give him smell. —Earl Thompson, *Tattoo*, p. 225, 1974

smell *verb*
▸ **smell Apple pie**
to be near your date of expected return from military service in Vietnam to the US *US*
- —Linda Reinberg, *In the Field*, p. 202, 1991

▸ **smell for water**
to find a spring using a divining rod *CANADA*
- "That's right," said the Gulf Islander. "He witches for wells." In the language of the trade, smelling for water. —*Vancouver Sun*, p. 3/1, 11th April 1960

▸ **smell some gas**
to be transported by motor vehicle *US*
- —Gary K. Farlow, *Prison-ese*, p. 65, 2002

smeller *noun*
the nose *UK, 1700*
- For a busted smeller, a couple of shiners, and a few creases in the knowledge-box he made himself ten grand. —Mezz Mezzrow, *Really the Blues*, p. 21, 1946

smell-fart *noun*
an inquisitive know-it-all *NEW ZEALAND*
- —Harry Orsman and Des Hurley, *The Beaut Little Book of New Zealand Slang*, 1994

smellies *noun*
1 perfume; perfumed deodorants *UK*
- —Paul Baker, *Polari*, p. 190, 2002
- Puttin smellies on; talcum powder, deodorant, white musk body spray. —Niall Griffiths, *Kelly + Victor*, p. 281, 2002

2 anchovies *US*
- — *Maledicta*, p. 21, 1996: 'Domino's pizza jargon'

smell of broken glass *noun*
a strong body odour, especially male *UK*
Probably from the 'sharp' nature of the offending smell.
- —Sean Treacy, *A Smell of Broken Glass*, 1973

smell of clay *noun*
a condition ascribed to a person likely to die soon *UK: SCOTLAND, 1988*
- Wi the smell a clay aff him it's a waste a time him gaun [going] hame. —Michael Munro, *The Complete Patter*, 1996

smellybridge *noun*
the perineum (the area of skin between the anus and the scrotum or vagina) *UK*
- —Adam T. Fox, St Mary's Hospital, London, 10th October 2002

smelly hole *noun*
the vagina *UK*
- Abjection was invoked in various ways: through reference to dirtiness (e.g., front bum, dirt box), uncooked (bloody?) meat (e.g., meat seat, chopped liver), vaginal secretions of all types (e.g., slushing fuck pit, the snail trail), smell (e.g., smelly hole, stench trench), and wounds (e.g., gash, gaping axe wound). —*Journal of Sex Research, Vol. 38, Issue 2.*, p. 146, 2001

smell you!
used for replying to an obvious brag *US*
- —Connie Eble (Editor), *UNC-CH Campus Slang*, p. 9, April 1995

smesh *noun*
in circus and carnival usage, money *US*
- —Don Wilmeth, *The Language of American Popular Entertainment*, p. 248, 1981

smick *adjective*
▹ **see:** SCHMICK

smidge *noun*
the smallest amount *US, 1905*
A shortened SMIDGEN. First recorded in 1905, but popularised by ESPN's Dan Patrick telling viewers that *Sports Center* will resume 'in a smidge'.
- I believe she loved that song, I'd say just a smidge behind Luckenback, Texas. —Elmore Leonard, *City Primeval*, p. 142, 1980

smidgen; smidgin *noun*
a very small amount *US, 1845*
- —Charles F. Haywood, *Yankee Dictionary*, p. 155, 1963
- I guess there would be an excuse for a smidgen of outrage if those nasty agency folk were using clubs to slaughter the unfortunate hogs. — *The Guardian*, 9th April 2003

smile *noun*
something that is amusing *US*
- BOOGIE: What's up, Fen? FENWICK: Just breaking windows, Boog. BOOGIE: What for? FENWICK: It's a smile. —*Diner*, 1982

smile and smirk; smile *noun*
work; also, as a verb: to work *UK*
Rhyming slang.
- [Y]ou may be "smiling" if you are employed or out of "smile" if you're not. —Ray Puxley, *Cockney Rabbit*, 1992

smiley *noun*
1 a simplistic image of a smiling face, used for indicating laughter or happiness *US*
First seen as an icon and later in electronic communications formed with punctuation marks, generally as :) but with multiple variations.
- —Christian Crumlish, *The Internet Dictionary*, p. 2, 1995
- Look back at the two most popular images on T-shirts and caps and bags, and anything else you can stick a patch on to help sell it: the yellow smiley acid face, and the green marijuana leaf. —*Raving Lunacy*, p. 54, 2000

2 a tablet of LSD with the smiley icon printed or etched thereon *UK, 1980s*
- Street names [...] rainbows, smilies, stars[.] —James Kay and Julian Cohen, *The Parents' Complete Guide to Young People and Drugs*, p. 141, 1998

3 a variety of MDMA, the recreational drug best known as ecstasy, identified by the smiley motif embossed on the tablet *UK*
- Smiley – White with acid house face. —Gareth Thomas, *This Is Ecstasy*, p. 57, 2002

4 a large chain with a padlock worn around the arm or neck *US*
- —Jim Crotty, *How to Talk American*, p. 146, 1997

smithereens *noun*
small pieces or fragments; shreds *UK, 1829*
- [I]n one smashing blow, his marriage was blasted to smithereens. —Stephen Arterburn, *Every Man's Battle*, p. 180, 2000
- Everyone assumes we would send up a nuclear warhead and blast it to smithereens. The idea has some problems, however. —Bill Bryson, *A Short History of Nearly Everything*, p. 205, 2003
- I told myself not to get up in the night and walk across the floor unless I wanted to cut my feet to smithereens. —Sue Monk Kidd, *The Secret Life of Bees*, p. 260, 2003

Smitty *noun*
in hot rodding, a silencer packed with fibreglass, increasing the roar of the engine *US*
- —Tom MacPherson, *Dragging and Driving*, p. 141, 1960

smock *noun*
heroin *US*
A corruption of SMACK or the Yiddish SHMECK.
- "What are you in for? Smock?" —Clarence Cooper Jr, *The Scene*, p. 220, 1960

smog *verb*

1 to smoke marijuana *US*

- — Don R. McCreary (Editor), *Dawg Speak*, 2001

2 to execute someone with lethal gas *US*

- — William K. Bentley and James M. Corbett, *Prison Slang*, p. 105, 1992

smoke *noun*

1 a cigarette; a cigar *UK, 1882*

- The white folks sure think they're beautiful, walked up to the drugstore at the corner for a pack of smokes. — Chester Himes, *If He Hollers Let Him Go*, p. 78, 1945
- "I sure need a smoke, boss," he muttered. — Chester Gould, *Dick Tracy Meets the Night Crawler*, p. 57, 1945
- Pat was on the last of his smokes. The dead butts littered the table and his coat was covered with ashes. — Mickey Spillane, *One Lonely Night*, p. 121, 1951
- Getting smokes was the toughest part. — Willard Motley, *Let No Man Write My Epitaph*, p. 20, 1958
- [H]e said in his slowest, deepest drawl how he figured he could use one of the smokes he bought this morning, then ran his hand through the glass. — Ken Kesey, *One Flew Over the Cuckoo's Nest*, p. 190, 1962
- "You got smokes?" he asked impulsively. — Nathan Heard, *Howard Street*, p. 206, 1968
- He pulls a wrinkled pack of smokes from his flannel shirt and lights one. — Larry Heinemann, *Paco's Story*, p. 101, 1986
- MIA: What are you doing? VINCENT: Rollin' a smoke. MIA: Here? VINCENT: It's just tobacco. — *Pulp Fiction*, 1994
- What you have here is pure Havana, a forty-dollar smoke, man. How is it? — Elmore Leonard, *Be Cool*, p. 204, 1999

2 marijuana; heroin; opium; any drug that may be smoked *US, 1946*

- Then you know what smoke is, huh, West? You did a high on smoke, boy? — Evan Hunter, *The Blackboard Jungle*, p. 159, 1954
- They passed it back and forth, getting high. "That's pretty mellow smoke," she announced after a few more hits. — Odie Hawkins, *Chicago Hustle*, p. 161, 1977
- [T]here's definitely a line in the music where they [the Beatles] changed from smoke to acid. — Paul E Willis, *Profane Culture*, p. 146, 1978
- Our smoke was gone and the next day we made plans for replenishing the supply. — Herbert Huncke, *The Evening Sun Turned Crimson*, p. 205, 1980
- G.B. ran back up to his neighborhood (Bed-Sty New Yawk) for a bag of bad smoke over the course of a weekend[.] — Odie Hawkins, *Men Friends*, p. 51, 1989
- Every week they'd be asking me for money to buy coke and smoke. — Terry Williams, *The Cocaine Kids*, p. 79, 1989
- He's really funny, and straight off, he offers me some smoke. — *Clueless*, 1995
- Man, this Likeness Rights shit is more profitable than selling smoke. — *Chasing Amy*, 1997
- [A] narcotic selection box: top quality Peruvian flake [cocaine], California Ecstasy and Caribbean smoke. — Wayne Anthony, *Spanish Highs*, p. 67, 1999
- We fancied some smoke to take the edge of the drink[.] — Jimmy Stockin, *On The Cobbles*, p. 124, 2000

3 a marijuana cigarette *US*

- Our "Sundays" we had off and if we were out of "Smokes" we'd go down to Montreal to "cop"[.] — Babs Gonzales, *I Paid My Dues*, p. 63, 1967
- Buy you a pound of grass and just put it there on the table, roll a smoke any time you want one. — Bruce Jackson, *Outside the Law*, p. 190, 1972
- We got pretty stoned too – it's an excuse to get some in and have a few smokes. — Ben Malbon, *Cool Places*, p. 268, 1998
- To provide the guys in the band with a smoke whenever they needed it, I kept in my my pocket a chunk of hash[.] — Simon Napier-Bell, *Black Vinyl White Powder*, p. 3, 2001

4 crack cocaine when smoked; heroin mixed with crack cocaine when smoked *US*

- — William T. Vollman, *Whores for Gloria*, p. 139, 1991
- — Mike Haskins, *Drugs*, p. 293, 2003

5 denatured alcohol (ethyl alcohol to which a poisonous substance has been added to make it unfit for consumption) mixed with water for drinking *US*

- — Hyman E. Goldin et al., *Dictionary of American Underworld Lingo*, p. 199, 1950

6 toxic, potentially fatal solvents used as substitutes for alcohol for the truly desperate *US*

- If we wanted to make a more legitimate type buck, we could always sell smoke to the bums down on the Bowery. We picked up the pints of smoke – which was alcohol cut with water and some "spirit" pills added – from the neighborhood guy who mixed it in his bathtub. — Rocky Garciano (with Rowland Barber), *Somebody Up There Likes Me*, p. 69, 1955
- The junkman fished a bottle of smoke from his ragged garments. — Chester Himes, *A Rage in Harlem*, p. 123, 1957
- — Ralph de Sola, *Crime Dictionary*, p. 140, 1982

7 a black person *US, 1913*
Offensive.

- And I want the five in my hand, Smoke, before I move. — Elmore Leonard, *Be Cool*, p. 127, 1999

8 a non-commissioned officer commanding an artillery battery *US*

- — Hans Halberstadt, *Airborne*, p. 130, 1988: 'Abridged dictionary of airborne terms'

9 a forest fire *US*

- — *American Speech*, p. 205–209, Summer 1991: 'The language of smokejumping – again'

10 one dollar *US*

- — *American Speech*, p. 66, Spring-Summer 1975: 'Razorback slang'

▸ **bring smoke**
to fire a gun *US*

- If we take them out first, it eliminates any possibility they'll bring smoke during the action. — Stephen J. Cannell, *Big Con*, p. 383, 1997

▸ **in smoke**
in hiding *AUSTRALIA, 1908*

- So there will be big celebrations even though I'm in smoke, even though they are searching for me. — Kevin Mackey, *The Cure*, p. 30, 1970
- King and Matt would go out the back way and go into smoke over at the 'Argent' bar until closing time. — Sam Weller, *Old Bastards I Have Met*, p. 80, 1979

▸ **put smoke**
to fire a single round of artillery to help others mark a target *US*

- — Gregory Clark, *Words of the Vietnam War*, p. 316, 1990

Smoke *noun*

▸ **the Smoke; Big Smoke; Great Smoke; the Smokes**
London; any large city *UK, 1848*
All variations are used with 'the'.

- I've got my sources of information in every manor in the smoke [London]. — Charles Raven, *Underworld Nights*, p. 91, 1956
- [T]hey had to get back to the Smoke Sat. p.m. poor dears. — Henry Sloane, *Sloane's Inside Guide to Sex & Drugs & Rock 'n' Roll*, p. 55, 1985
- So lock, stock and barrel they moved down to the Smoke. — John Robb, *The Nineties*, p. 144, 1999

▸ **up the Smoke**
to London; to central London (from the suburbs) *UK*
Originally tramps' usage; you go '*up* THE SMOKE' (London) even when heading *down* from the north.

smoke *verb*

1 to shoot someone *US, 1926*

- I come in the door smilin' – "Ola, Chucho" – then I started smoking with both pieces. — Edwin Torres, *Carlito's Way*, p. 33, 1975
- Somebody got smoked! Look at the holes in the wall! — *Boyz N The Hood*, 1990
- Bout the Crew gonna smoke us? — Jess Mowry, *Way Past Cool*, p. 21, 1992
- Lloyd pulled the .45 from his waist, pulled the slide back, and clicked off the safety catch. Now he was ready to smoke the motherfucker. — Donald Gorgon, *Cop Killer*, p. 74, 1994
- You shouldn't have smoked the guy. — *Get Shorty*, 1995

2 to drive fast *US*

- — "Slingo", *The Official CB Slang Dictionary Handbook*, p. 57, 1976

3 to defeat someone soundly, especially in a contest of speed *US*

- John Taylor, J.J. Stokes, Andre Rison – I smoke all these fools, and yet they're making the big sweet dollars. — *Jerry Maguire*, 1996

4 to perform oral sex on a man *UK, 1984*
Simple imagery, perhaps influenced by the Freudian notion that smoking is an 'oral' habit.

▸ **smoke a bowl**
to smoke a pipe filled with marijuana *US, 1982*

- — Richard A. Spears, *The Slang and Jargon of Drugs and Drink*, p. 463, 1986
- I've got to *Smoke a bowl.* keep control. — Sal Piro and Michael Hess, *The Official 'Rocky Horror Picture Show' Audience Participation Guide*, p. 15, 1991
- — Mike Haskins, *Drugs*, p. 289, 2003

▸ **smoke a pipe; smoke the pipe**
to surf through the hollow tube of a wave *US*

- — Mitch McKissick, *Surf Lingo*, 1987

▸ **smoke butt**
to curry favour through obsequious behaviour *US*
• Other kids just figured he rode beside Deek all the time and smoked butt. —Jess Mowry, *Way Past Cool*, p. 31, 1992

▸ **smoke it**
to commit suicide by a gunshot wound in the mouth *US*
• I've heard that every sane person contemplates suicide sometime. Well, I made up for all the insane people who never did. I never thought a smoking it – that'd be too dirty, too many reports for other cops. —Joseph Wambaugh, *Lines and Shadows*, p. 329, 1984

▸ **smoke like a chimney**
to smoke cigarettes heavily *UK, 1840*
• There are those who might wonder why a woman with chronic asthma smokes like a chimney, but they will be the people who are not in the terminal stages of motor neurone disease. —*The Observer*, 12th May 2002

▸ **smoke with the devil**
to drive too fast for road conditions *US*
• —"Slingo", *The Official CB Slang Dictionary Handbook*, p. 57, 1976

smokeasy *noun*
a clandestine venue for the illegal sale and consumption of marijuana *UK*
Modelled on SPEAKEASY (a bar that sells alcohol illegally).
• —Steven Wishnia, *The Cannabis Companion*, p. 153, 2004

smoke Canada *noun*
marijuana, presumed to originate in Canada *UK*
• —Mike Haskins, *Drugs*, p. 289, 2003

smoked cheaters *noun*
dark glasses *US*
• Half the cats in Harlem wear their smoke cheaters all night long. —Chester Himes, *The Real Cool Killers*, p. 46, 1959

smoked haddock *noun*
at a racecourse, the paddock *UK*
Rhyming slang.
• —Julian Franklyn, *A Dictionary of Rhyming Slang*, 1961
• —Ray Puxley, *Cockney Rabbit*, 1992

smoked Irishman *noun*
any person with black, brown or coffee-coloured skin *UK*
• —Fritz Spiegl, *Lern Yerself Scouse*, 1966

smoked out *adjective*
1 extremely intoxicated on marijuana or crack cocaine *US*
• The basehead is completely smoked out. —*Menace II Society*, 1993
• —Mike Haskins, *Drugs*, p. 291, 2003
2 without any crack cocaine to smoke *US*
• —*San Diego Union-Tribune*, p. B1, 23rd October 2003

Smoked Scotchman *noun*
a person whose parentage is Scottish and Indian *CANADA*
• They married among the Indians and to this day some of the finest names are perpetuated in Indian tents and their bearers are known locally as Smoked Scotchmen. —George Nelson, *Northern Lights*, p. 516, 1960

smoked Welshman *noun*
any dark-skinned man speaking little English *UK, 1984*
Maybe simple racial stereotyping, but is probably influenced by the fact that an English person attempting a Welsh accent sounds generically Indian.

smoke house *noun*
1 a room where meetings of twelve-step recovery programmes such as Alcoholics Anonymous are held *US*
A term based on the heavy cigarette smoking that is often characteristic of the meetings.
• —Christopher Cavanaugh, *AA to Z*, p. 163, 1998
2 crack cocaine *UK*
• —Mike Haskins, *Drugs*, p. 282, 2003

smoke pole *noun*
a shotgun *CANADA*
• —P. St. Pierre, *Chilicotin Holiday*, 1970

smoker *noun*
1 a social gathering, limited to men, especially one with sexual entertainment; a film shown during such a gathering *UK, 1887*
• If you're real good, we'll let you sing 'Mother Machree' at the police smoker. —Raymond Chandler, *The Long Goodbye*, p. 35, 1953
• [E]ccentric dancer, platinum in the mop and molybdenum in the left ventricle, who gave her all at smokers and stag parties[.] —Bernard Wolfe, *The Late Risers*, p. 37, 1954
• She's given to turning up the speed this way on days like, say, when you got somebody to visit you or when the VFW brings down a smoker show from Portland[.] —Ken Kesey, *One Flew Over the Cuckoo's Nest*, p. 74, 1962
• —Richard Farinia, *Been Down So Long*, 1966: 'Chapter 2: the fraternity smoker type thing'
• "Smokers." "Stag films." "Freak shows." Yes, they're all here, but one cannot expect to find them going on every night, even here. —*Screw*, p. 7, 7th March 1969
• What I got to do is see a man wants to buy some smoker movies. —Elmore Leonard, *52 Pick-up*, p. 146, 1974
• Our elders refer to these movies as "smokers." —Stephen Ziplow, *The Film Maker's Guide to Pornography*, p. 8, 1977
• There were still smokers, stag movies, it wasn't as commonplace, but I guarantee if you wanted to find hard-core in 1930 you could. —Robert Stoller and I.S. Levine, *Coming Attractions*, p. 41, 1991
• How about stags and smokers? You ever been in his company at stags and smokers? —Robert Campbell, *Boneyards*, p. 83, 1992
2 a marijuana smoker *US*
• One agent gave a picture to an agent of a typical "smoker" in an apartment or "pad"[.] —Harry J. Anslinger, *The Murderers*, p. 42, 1961
3 a passenger train carriage in which smoking is permitted *US*
• —Ramon Adams, *The Language of the Railroader*, p. 140, 1977
4 any diesel-powered truck *US*
• —*American Speech*, p. 272, December 1962: 'The language of traffic policemen'
5 a car for sale that a car trader is using for personal transport *UK*
• [D]riving home at night in his "smoker" or just whatever car is left over[.] —*Sunday Times*, 24th October 1965
6 a stolen car *US*
• —Jim Crotty, *How to Talk American*, p. 51, 1997
7 a high mileage car *UK*
A car dealers' term.
• —*Sunday Times*, 9th August 1981

smokestack *noun*
a pile of gambling tokens in the hands of an unskilled gambler *US*
• You know it's only time until that stack turns to smoke. —John Vorhaus, *The Big Book of Poker Slang*, p. 33, 1996

smoke train *noun*
a cigarette *US*
• —Don R. McCreary (Editor), *Dawg Speak*, 2001

smoke-up *noun*
in college, a notification of academic deficiency *US*
• Smoke-Up —W.L. McAtee, *American Speech*, p. 156, May 1961
• —*American Speech*, p. 76–77, February 1968: 'Some notes on flunk notes'

smoke wrench *noun*
in car repair, an oxy-acetylene torch *US*
• —Lewis Poteet, *Car & Motorcyle Slang*, p. 183, 1992

smokey *noun*
1 in prison, a segregation unit *UK*
• —Angela Devlin, *Prison Patter*, p. 106, 1996
2 a Maori *NEW ZEALAND, 1984*
Offensive.
• —Harry Orsman, *A Dictionary of Modern New Zealand Slang*, p. 125, 1999

smokey bear; smokey; bear *noun*
a police officer; the police *US, 1975*
Citizens' band radio slang; from Smokey Bear (aka Smokey the Bear), a caricatured black bear, from Capitan, New Mexico, used since 1950 to promote forest fire prevention. The symbolic bear wears a hat similar to that worn by US highway patrol officers and state troopers. Also used to designate police in various forms: 'smokey beaver' (a policewoman), 'smokey convention' (two or more police cars), 'smokey on four legs' (mounted police), 'smokey with a camera' (police using speed detection equipment), 'smokey with ears' (police with radio), etc.
• Yeah, them smokeys 's thick as bugs on a bumper / They even had a bear in the air[.] —C.W. McCall, *Convoy*, 1976
• —Connie Eble (Editor), *UNC-CH Campus Slang*, April 1977
• —Peter Chippindale, *The British CB Book*, p. 159, 1981
• If there was a Smokey out there tonight, you couldn't prove it by me. —George V. Higgins, *The Rat on Fire*, p. 106, 1981

Smokey the bear *noun*

1 a drill sergeant in the US Army *US*

- — *Time*, p. 31, 10th December 1965
- — Carl Fleischhauer, *A Glossary of Army Slang*, p. 16, 1968

2 a military aircraft used for dropping magnesium-based flares to illuminate the ground at night *US*

- Meanwhile, with a "Smokey the Bear" flareship hovering over the battlefield, dropping flares and lighting the ground like day, Whalen's artillerymen fought like lions for their lives[.] — David Hackworth and Julie Sherman, *About Face*, p. 537, 1989
- — Gregory Clark, *Words of the Vietnam War*, p. 180, 1990

smoking *adjective*

1 excellent; thriving; exciting *US*

- We had the smokinest little seven piece group on the road. — Babs Gonzales, *Movin' On Down De Line*, p. 19, 1975
- — *Washington Post Magazine*, p. 17, 4th October 1987: 'Say Wha?'
- — Ellen C. Bellone (Editor), *Dictionary of Slang*, p. 22, 1989

2 fashionably dressed *US*

- — Terry Williams, *The Cocaine Kids*, p. 138, 1989

smoking gun *noun*

1 unarguable evidence or an unmissable clue *US, 1974*

A term that came into popular use during the President Nixon Watergate scandal in the US in the early 1970s.

- — Angela Devlin, *Prison Patter*, p. 106, 1996

2 a mixture of heroin and cocaine; heroin *UK, 1998*

- — Robert Ashton, *This Is Heroin*, p. 210, 2002
- — Mike Haskins, *Drugs*, p. 284, 2003

smoko *noun*

1 a break from work *AUSTRALIA, 1865*

Originally a break for a cigarette and normally long enough for a hot beverage.

- We had smoko on top of the half deck, in the lee of a lifeboat. — Robert S. Close, *Love Me Sailor*, p. 208, 1945
- Real workers, who use their hard and horny hands, and the muscles of their shoulders, backs and legs, call such pauses for refreshment 'smoko'. — John O'Grady, *Aussie Etiket*, p. 5, 1971
- In the woolstores, smoko was held in the donko, where we'd adjourn after working like billyo. — *Listener*, p. 13, 14th April 1984
- — Bernadette Hince, *The Antarctic Dictionary*, p. 321, 2000

2 marijuana *AUSTRALIA*

- They found a quarter of speed, some fits, some smoko. — Kathy Lette, *Girls' Night Out*, p. 99, 1987

smoky *noun*

an Indian *CANADA*

Offensive.

- Clad in breechclout and moccasins, Itai-Po was no reservation "smoky" but thoroughly an Indian. — William Mowery, *Tales of the Mounted Police*, p. 53, 1953

Smoky Joe *noun*

a military aircraft that marks targets for bomber aircraft with smoke bombs *US*

- — *American Speech*, p. 74, February 1946: 'Some words of war and peace from 1945'

smoo *noun*

the vagina *AUSTRALIA*

- As one nibbled around my choozzies the other worked in my aching smoo. — *Picture*, p. 70, 7th December 1992

smooch *verb*

to kiss in a lingering manner *US, 1932*

- "Nuts," replied Dewey. "College kids are still college kids. They're still smooching and driving convertibles and cutting classes and looking for laughs." — Max Shulman, *The Many Loves of Dobie Gillis*, p. 24, 1951
- You wonder if it's all right for them to do a little smooching? — Elmore Leonard, *The Big Bounce*, p. 33, 1969
- I'm curious to know why a splendid legit gentleman like yourself, with the world smooching your keister, yens to hang it out playing the con and risking the penitentiary? — Iceberg Slim (Robert Beck), *Long White Con*, p. 36–37, 1977

smoochy *adjective*

of music, suitable for slow, romantic dancing *UK, 1966*

- Masters of the three minute pop song whether it be an uptempo number or a smoochy ballad. — *Loughborough Trader*, 15th August 1979

smoochywoochypoochy *noun*

marijuana *UK*

A pet name.

- — Mike Haskins, *Drugs*, p. 289, 2003

smoodge; smooge *verb*

1 to play the sycophant *AUSTRALIA, 1898*

- SMOOGE – To cringe; to fawn. — Gilbert H. Lawson, *A Dictionary of Australian Words and Terms*, 1924
- In groups apart we sat or squatted around our separate trees, little Dick smoodging around Laurie while he was serving out the trackers' tucker. — Ion L. Idriess, *Over the Range*, p. 171, 1947
- That's the sort of stinkin' cow Jobags is, smooging up to big blokes so they can pandy hell out of blokes with tennis balls. — Norman Lindsay, *Halfway to Anywhere*, p. 90, 1947

2 to kiss and cuddle *AUSTRALIA, 1915*

3 to win someone around; to charm someone *AUSTRALIA, 1940*

- I suppose you've already smoodged her into believing that there was nothing in it. — Norman Lindsay, *The Cousin from Fiji*, p. 156, 1945

smoodger; smooger *noun*

a flatterer *AUSTRALIA, 1897*

- SMOOGER – One who fawns. — Gilbert H. Lawson, *A Dictionary of Australian Words and Terms*, 1924
- He was a mean customer, this Grimwade, a petty bureaucrat, and a smooger, to boot. — Frank Dalby Davison, *The Wells of Beersheba*, p. 97, 1965

smoodgingly *adverb*

ingratiatingly *AUSTRALIA*

- 'Nice garden you've got,' McGarrity remarked smoodgingly according to the listeners. — Dymphna Cusack, *Picnic Races*, p. 222, 1962

smooth *noun*

1 a member of the aggressive youth fashion and gang movement that was the final and least notable stage in the evolution of the skinhead *UK*

A **SKINHEAD** with fractionally longer hair became **SUEDEHEAD** which, in turn, grew smooth – and not distinctive enough to survive.

- [S]kinheads, suedeheads, boot boys and now smooths[.] — *Author's Notes [britpulp]*, p. 63, November 1972

2 on the railways, a tip of ten cents *US*

- — Ramon Adams, *The Language of the Railroader*, p. 141, 1977

smooth *verb*

in hot rodding and drag racing, to remove ornaments and hardware from the car body *US*

- — Lyle K. Engel, *The Complete Book of Fuel and Gas Dragsters*, p. 154, 1968

smooth *adjective*

1 used of a man's body, hairless *US*

- — Jeff Fessler, *When Drag Is Not a Car Race*, p. 55, 1997

2 calm *US*

- "What's your name, kid?" "That depends. 'Piri' when I'm smooth and 'Johnny Gringo' when stomping time's around." — Piri Thomas, *Down These Mean Streets*, p. 48, 1967

3 in lowball poker, favourable *US*

- — Albert H. Morehead, *The Complete Guide to Winning Poker*, p. 273, 1967

4 sophisticated, urbane *US*

- — Connie Eble (Editor), *UNC-CH Campus Slang*, p. 9, Spring 1991

smooth

used to intensify a phrasal verb *US*

- That city boy fucked smooth up when he started makin' fun of Shorty. — Ken Weaver, *Texas Crude*, p. 126, 1984

smooth and glassy *adjective*

easy-going *US*

- — Connie Eble (Editor), *UNC-CH Campus Slang*, p. 7, Fall 1984

smoothie *noun*

1 the complete removal of a woman's pubic hair; the result thereof *US*

- Completely bare: sometimes call the Full Monty, the Sphynx, or the Smoothie, this variation on the Brazilian Wax leaves the entire area hair-free. — *Real Simple*, p. 65, May 2001

2 a person who stays calm and avoids trouble *US*

- The decision to cool myself made the next two years the hardest I had done because it meant being a smoothie and staying out of trouble, which in prison is difficult[.] — Piri Thomas, *Down These Mean Streets*, p. 280, 1967

3 a man who is attractive, persuasive, crafty and a bit manipulative *US, 1929*

Often, but not always, pejorative.

- I did try and put a few flaws in but he ended up a bit of a smoothie. Anybody in their right mind would have hated him. — *Metro*, 18th November 2003

4 a skilled gambling cheat *US*
- — R. Frederick West, *God's Gambler*, p. 228, 1964: 'Appendix A'

smooth leg *noun*
a woman *UK*
Citizens' band radio slang.
- — Peter Chippindale, *The British CB Book*, p. 159, 1981

smooth operator *noun*
someone who is attractive, crafty and a bit manipulative *US*
- How'd you come out with that smooth operator? Petey sure picked the right night to run off and join the Navy, eh? — Max Shulman, *The Many Loves of Dobie Gillis*, p. 113, 1951
- No place for beginners or sensitive hearts / When sentiment is left to chance / No place to be ending but somewhere to start / No need to ask. He's a smooth operator. — Sade, *Smooth Operator*, 1985

smooth trade *noun*
an urbane, fashion-conscious homosexual man *US*
- Hustling, or male prostitution, is widespread. Even in the major tourist hotels, where the so-called "smooth trade" operates in the plush bars, for big stakes. — *"The Market Street Proposition" (KFRC radio, San Francisco)*, 8th November 1965
- Smooth trade hustlers are often well-bred, well-dressed and they project an urban air of sophistication and their mannerisms are suave and refined. — Johnny Shearer, *The Male Hustler*, p. 18, 1966

smother *noun*
an overcoat *UK, 1934*
Allied to the practical sense of the coat worn over a pickpocket's arm to mask criminal activity.
- [S]he insisted on our leaving behind three of the finest pen-and-ink [mink] smothers I ever set eyes on. — Charles Raven, *Underworld Nights*, p. 21, 1956
- [He] whips out a pint of scotch where the torch came from in his smother[.] — Derek Raymond (Robin Cook), *The Crust on its Uppers*, p. 53, 1962

smother *verb*
to conceal a person, a thing or a movement *AUSTRALIA, 1932*
- Marg and Ratty Jack was gonna smother with a box. — *The (Sydney) Bulletin*, 26th April 1975

smouch *verb*
to kiss *AUSTRALIA, 1968*
- The Old Digger took no offence, smouching Florrie on the cheek while Moss looked on shyly. — Frank Hardy, *The Outcasts of Foolgarah*, p. 106, 1971

smoush *noun*
a kiss *AUSTRALIA, 1963*
With the long vowel of 'smooch'.
- Reminds me of a widow I knew at Richmond. Whenever I visited her and a plane went over she'd drop whatever she was doing and rush over for a smoush. — David Ireland, *Unknown Industrial Prisoner*, p. 173, 1971

smudge *noun*
1 a photograph *UK, 1931*
Originally photographers' jargon, from blurred pictures.
- There's smudges of us doing really fuckin' everyday sorta shit[.] — J.J. Connolly, *Know Your Enemy [britpulp]*, p. 160, 1999
- "This is fucking great," Sid had said, looking at my piece and the smudge of a semi-clad girl that went with it. — Jake Arnott, *He Kills Coppers*, p. 199, 2001

2 a pornographic magazine or magazines *UK*
Extended from the previous sense.
- — Angela Devlin, *Prison Patter*, p. 106, 1996

3 a photographer, especially a press photographer *UK, 1968*
Shortened from **SMUDGER**.

smudger *noun*
a photographer, especially a press photographer *UK, 1961*
From **SMUDGE** (a photograph).
- [I]t was common malpractice for all smudgers in the 80s to do a spot of moonlighting[.] — Andrew Nickolds, *Back to Basics*, p. 62, 1994

smurf *noun*
1 an ordinary citizen whose personal bank accounts are used to launder drug money *US*
The Smurfs are well known children's cartoon characters, adopted here to suggest the innocent appearance of a money launderer.
- [B]illions of dollars are thought to be passing through the smurf community. — David Rowan, *A Glossary for the 90s*, p. 193, 1998

2 in an Internet discussion group, a frequent poster who adds little in the way of content *US*
- Usually it's something cute and fluffy, posted chiefly to remind everyone that the smurf is part of the gang. — Andy Ihnatko, *Cyberspeak*, p. 177, 1997

Smurf Juice *noun*
the recreational drug GHB *SOUTH AFRICA*
As a marketing strategy the clear liquid is dyed blue, which is the colour of Smurfs™ (internationally known children's characters).

smush *verb*
to crush *US*
A blending of 'crush' and 'smash'.
- "Hey!" the kid cried. "You're smushing me!" — Carl Hiaasen, *Native Tongue*, p. 68, 1991

smut *noun*
pornography *UK, 1698*
- Stagliano sits atop the porn heap like a waggish imp, daring us to step over the line of eroticism and enter the taboo world of no-holes-barred smut. — *The Penthouse Erotic Video Guide*, p. 97, 2003

smut-hound *noun*
a man with a marked predilection for bawdiness or indecent publications; a censor who seeks out such works *US, 1927*
- The Royal Smut-Hound — *Playboy*, January 1966
- You, sir, are nothing but a low-rent smut hound, and you will delete my wife's feet from your Internet before she finds out what you've done with them! — Jonathan Collier, *King of the Hill*, 14th May 2000

smuts *noun*
sexually explicit photographs or postcards *US*
- — Joseph E. Ragen and Charles Finston, *Inside the World's Toughest Prison*, p. 818, 1962: 'Penitentiary and underworld glossary'

snack *noun*
1 a youthful, sexually inexperienced male who is the object of an older homosexual's desire *US*
- — *Maledicta*, p. 156, Summer/Winter 1986–1987: 'Sexual slang: prostitutes, pedophiles, flagellators, transvestites, and necrophiles'

2 something easily accomplished *AUSTRALIA, 1941*

snacker *noun*
aboard a trawler, a deck-boy or odd-job man *UK*
- You'd make a good snacker on a Hull ship. — Steven Piper, *The North Ships*, 1974

snackpack *noun*
the male genitals as seen in a jock strap or tight, skimpy underwear *US*
- — H. Max, *Gay (S)language*, p. 39, 1988

snaffle *verb*
to acquire something for your own *UK, 1902*
- [T]hey had snafled some of his hot jewellery items[.] — Brian McDonald, *Elephant Boys*, p. 66, 2000

snafu *noun*
a chaotic mess *US, 1941*
An initialism of '*s*ituation *n*ormal, *a*ll *f*ucked *u*p' or the more polite '*s*ituation *n*ormal, *a*ll *f*ouled *u*p'.
- "Not only profanity has crept into your speech," she said, "but also the peculiar jargon of the Army." "Snafu," I said, "tarfu, fubar, and weft." — Max Shulman, *The Zebra Derby*, p. 174, 1946
- Now everything was screwed up proper. A real snafu. — Mickey Spillane, *Return of the Hood*, p. 88, 1964
- He yelled at her for a paperwork snafu. — Lee Child, *The Visitor*, p. 201, 2000

snafu *verb*
to bungle something; to reduce something to chaos *US*
From the noun sense.
- He'd ask questions I didn't want to answer. Especially since the pig-heart swap had gotten snafued. — Janet Evanovich, *Seven Up*, p. 201, 2001

snag *noun*
1 a girl, especially an ugly one *US*
- — Anthony Romeo, *The Language of Gangs*, p. 22, 4th December 1962
- — David Claerbaut, *Black Jargon in White America*, p. 80, 1972

2 a tooth *US*
- "Yank the bastards, Doc," he said. "Those snags have whipped me for a lot of action." — Malcolm Braly, *On the Yard*, p. 9, 1967

3 a sausage *AUSTRALIA, 1941*
- What can I do ya for? Coupla snags? Nice juicy chop? — Phillip Gwynne, *Deadly Unna?*, p. 116, 1998

snag *verb*

1 to grab something; to acquire something *US, 1895*
- I can't find my Cranberries CD. I've gotta go to the Quad before somebody snags it. — *Clueless*, 1995

2 to outdo someone *US*
- These cutting contests are just a musical version of the verbal duels. They're staged to see which performer can snag and cap all the others musically. — Mezz Mezzrow, *Really the Blues*, p. 230–231, 1946

snag bag *noun*

a small bag for carrying personal effects *US*
Prison usage.
- I sat down on my snag bag (a cloth bag with whatever junk you carried around) and he squatted next to me. — Piri Thomas, *Down These Mean Streets*, p. 265, 1967

snagged stag *noun*

a boy who is steadily and exclusively dating one girl *US*
- — *San Francisco Examiner*, p. 21, 12th December 1961: 'Colloquialisms for your murgatroid handcuffs'

snaggle tooth *noun*

a young woman or girl with irregular (or missing) teeth *UK, 1909*
Among US boys in 2004 'summer teeths' is a nickname for British girls – some are teeth that point here, some are pointing there.

snail mail *noun*

mail sent by normal postal service *US*
A term that was coined after the advent of electronic mail.
- — Guy L. Steele et al., *The Hacker's Dictionary*, p. 117–118, 1983
- Other terms, like "snail mail," for messages delivered by the United States Postal Service, as opposed to those transported electronically, are more widely comprehensible. — *New York Times*, p. C4, 13th September 1983
- — Connie Eble (Editor), *UNC-CH Campus Slang*, p. 7, April 1997

snail track *noun*

1 a verticle line of hair on the stomach *AUSTRALIA*
- Laser Hair Removals: Under arms $99.95 Bikini lines $99.95 Snail tracks $49.95 — *Beat*, 28th August 2002

2 the residue of vaginal secretions, semen and/or saliva on a woman's thighs after sex *US*
- There was drying snail track on her thigh. — Robert Campbell, *In La-La Land We Trust*, p. 68, 1986
- — *Adult Video News*, p. 51, October 1995

snail trail *noun*

the vagina *UK*
- Abjection was invoked in various ways: through reference to dirtiness (e.g., front bum, dirt box), uncooked (bloody?) meat (e.g., meat seat, chopped liver), vaginal secretions of all types (e.g., slushing fuck pit, the snail trail), smell (e.g., smelly hole, stench trench), and wounds (e.g., gash, gaping axe wound). — *Journal of Sex Research, Vol. 38, Issue 2.*, p. 146, 2001

snake *noun*

1 the penis *US*
- You fucking better get on my team, Gus, or you're gonna have a fucking scar down there where your snake used to play. — Stephen J. Cannell, *King Con*, p. 142, 1997

2 among anglers, a very long rag-worm used as bait *UK*
- — *Bournemouth Echo*, 4th July 1968

3 in electric line work, insulated rubber line hose *US*
- — A.B. Chance Co., *Lineman's Slang Dictionary*, p. 16, 1980

4 a long, serpentine putt *US, 1962*
- — Dawson Taylor, *How to Talk Golf*, p. 61, 1985

5 a subway, an underground system *US*
- — Robert George Reisner, *The Jazz Titans*, p. 165, 1960

6 a surfer who surfs in another surfer's right of way *US*
- — Mitch McKissick, *Surf Lingo*, 1987

7 an informer *US*
- Blood wanted to send two or three snakes (spies or intelligence agents) to check the location and strength of the Rovers. — Harrison E. Salisbury, *The Shook-up Generation*, p. 37, 1958
- — Angela Devlin, *Prison Patter*, p. 106, 1996
- Have you heard about that snake then? — *The Guardian*, 17th February 2000
- "There's an informer on the spur, lads!" he proclaimed, pointing towards the cell where Grady was installing his few intact possessions. "Ssssss," came the reply in chorus. (An informer in prison is known as a grass from the phrase "snake in the grass".) — *The Guardian*, 30th March 2000

8 in foot-powered scootering, another rider who cuts in, especially one who take's another's line into a trick *UK*
- — Ben Sharpe, *Scooter Crazy*, p. 42, 2000

9 an AH-1G Cobra attack helicopter *US*
The US Army's primary gunship in Vietnam.
- They gonna lay snake and nape right on the perimeter so stay tight in your holes and don't leave 'em. — *Platoon*, 1986
- Don't like to me in this kind of mess / Asked the snakes for help and they said yes. — Sandee Shaffer Johnson, *Cadences*, p. 110, 1986
- You're doin' a great job, two six. I have some fast movers and snakes coming your way. — Harold Coyle, *Trial by Fire*, p. 414, 1992

10 a railway pointsman *US*
From the serpentine 'S' on the pointsman's union pin.
- — Norman Carlisle, *The Modern Wonder Book of Trains and Railroading*, p. 268, 1946
- — Ramon Adams, *The Language of the Railroader*, p. 141, 1977

▸ **able to crawl under a snake; lower than a snake's belly**
morally reprehensible; despicable *AUSTRALIA, 1932*
Variations include 'a snake's hips', since World War 2, and 'able to crawl under a snake's belly with a top hat on', 1959.
- To pick on a bloke for a thing like that [a speech defect] well, you could crawl under a snake in a top hat and stilts. — Alex Buzo, *The Roy Murphy Show*, 1971
- You stab me in the back / You're lower than a snake / Your brains are in you're sack / You two-faced fucking fake[.] — *The Kiss of Morning*, 21st October 2002

▸ **the snake**
in firefighting, the hose *UK, 1984*
Used by the London Fire Brigade.

snake *verb*

1 to have sex from the male perspective *US*
- She's been getting snaked by half the fuckin' department. — Stephen J. Cannell, *The Tin Collectors*, p. 9, 2001

2 in snowboarding or skateboarding, to cut in front of someone *US*
- — *San Francisco Sunday Examiner & Chronicle*, p. 20, 2nd September 1984: 'Say it right'
- That Homer snaked the jump and bailed. — Mike Fabbro, *Snowboarding*, p. 95, 1996

3 to go quietly, to move silently *IRELAND*
The variant 'snake off' also exists.
- — Brendan Behan, *Borstal Boy*, 1958

snakebite; snakie *noun*

a mixture of cider and lager *UK*
- If she's been on the snakies aw night it's nae wunner [no wonder] she's honkin her load [vomiting]. — Michael Munro, *The Patter, Another Blast*, p. 66, 1988
- "Yeah. Bit pissed, though," replied Brad. "Fuck me, you're not the only one. I'm caned. Those bloody La Mumbas. What about you?" "Snakebites – cider and lager.["] — Colin Butts, *Is Harry on the Boat?*, p. 113, 1997
- It was more lager now, a lot of pubs refusing to serve snakebite, people going mental on the stuff[.] — John King, *Human Punk*, p. 180, 2000
- Tommy had been in the club for half an hour and had consumed three pints of snakebite in the dark and thunderously noisy anonymity. — Ben Elton, *High Society*, p. 267, 2002

snake-charmer *noun*

in Western Australia, a railway maintenance worker *AUSTRALIA, 1937*
From the prevalence of snakes along railway tracks.
- One snake-charmer on the length at Tuckanarra wrote asking for a transfer to the coast 'to facilitate domestic arragnements.' — Patsy Adam-Smith, *Folklore of the Australian Railwaymen*, p. 90, 1969

snake-eaters *noun*

the US Army Special Forces *US*
From their jungle survival skills.
- — Linda Reinberg, *In the Field*, p. 202, 1991
- Academy grads, he was told, do not become snake-eaters. — Richard Marcinko and John Weisman, *Rogue Warrior*, p. 206, 1992

snake-eye; snake-eye bomb *noun*

during the Vietnam war, one of several aircraft bombs with descent-slowing devices to permit low-level attacks *US*
- The Snakes, or Snake-eyes, were conventional general-purpose bombs fitted with clamshell fins that opened when the weapons were released and acted like parachutes to retard the weapons[.] — Stephen Coonts, *Flight of the Intruder*, p. 279, 1986
- "Snakeye" bombs were fitted with air brakes (drag fins) that deployed when the bomb was released, slowing its descent. — Gregory Clark, *Words of the Vietnam War*, p. 435, 1990

snake eyes *noun*

1 **in dice games, a roll of two one's** *US, 1929*
A visual metaphor.
- —Lou Shelly, *Hepcats Jive Talk Dictionary*, p. 33, 1945
- Abie the Jew bet the dice to win or lose, barring box cars and snake-eyes.—Chester Himes, *A Rage in Harlem*, p. 26, 1957
- —Frank Garcia, *Marked Cards and Loaded Dice*, p. 264, 1962
- Snake eyes! Hoooeee, Cheswicker, where does that put you? That don't put you on my Marvin Gardens by any chance?—Ken Kesey, *One Flew Over the Cuckoo's Nest*, p. 111, 1962
- So I wasn't surprised / when he rolled snake eyes.—Lightnin' Rod, *Hustlers Convention*, p. 61, 1973
- Way it is now C.K.'s natural seven done look like old snake-eyes. —Terry Southern, *Texas Summer*, p. 164, 1991
- The thrower lost immediately if he threw double six, double one (snake eyes) or two and one – these are difficult to repeat and are called craps.—Brian McDonald, *Elephant Boys*, p. 202, 2000

2 **in dominoes, the 1–1 piece** *US*
- —Dominic Armanino, *Dominoes*, p. 17, 1959

3 **in poker, a pair of aces** *US*
- —George Percy, *The Language of Poker*, p. 84, 1988

snake fence *noun*

a rail fence, split cedar, in six or eight interlocking zigzag patterns *US, 1805*
- Even the disappearance of the old wooden "snake fences" on the farms, and their replacement by wire or electric fences, is an example of man's "progress" in the destruction of bird life.—*Kingston Whig-Standard*, p. 4–6, 6th December 1962
- An old standby was known variously as snake, worm, and zigzag. This style of rail fence had no fasteners or posts and was generally fashioned out of rot-resistant cedar. Adaptable to rolling terrain, it required more space, more split rails and repairs.—*Montreal Gazette*, p. B4, 24th August 2002

Snake Gully *noun*

an imaginary remote and backward place *AUSTRALIA, 1945*
- —Arthur Chipper, *The Aussie Swearer's Guide*, p. 66, 1972

snakehead *noun*

a smuggler of Chinese people *US*
Direct translation from a Chinese term.
- [F]amed Manhattan immigration attorney Robert Porges will face a federal trial in March for, among other things, helping snakeheads kidnap and enslave hundreds of asylum-seekers.—*The Source*, p. 144, March 2002

snake juice *noun*

strong liquor, especially of rough quality *AUSTRALIA, 1890*
- SNAKE JUICE – Strong drink.—Gilbert H. Lawson, *A Dictionary of Australian Words and Terms*, 1924
- Some traders charged exorbitant prices for the clothing and gave the 'snake juice' in with the purchases to encourage further spending, —Mary Durack, *Kings in Grass Castles*, p. 183, 1959

Snakenavel, Idaho *noun*

a fictitious rural place *US*
- —Michael Dalton Johnson, *Talking Trash with Redd Foxx*, p. 18, 1994

snake pit *noun*

1 **used in the US military during the conflict in Vietnam for describing any operational headquarters** *US*
- —*Newsweek*, p. 30, 23rd May 1966
- —Carl Fleischhauer, *A Glossary of Army Slang*, p. 16, 1968

2 **a sergeant's mess** *AUSTRALIA, 1941*
- They're sergeants, an' they should have their own blasted snakepit, not clutter our show.—W.R. Bennett, *Wingman*, p. 46, 1961
- Sorrowful and smokeless I sat yearning for the security of the snake-pit I had abandoned.—Martin Cameron, *A Look at the Bright Side*, 1988
- One night I decided to go into Vung Tau to meet an old mate from another unit for a few beers away from the 'snake' pit atmosphere. —Martin Cameron, *A Look at the Bright Side*, 1988

snake ranch *noun*

a bachelor's house *US*
- The Lafayette Escadrille had been actor Victor Mclaglen's summer home – a perfect "snake ranch," as all the Miramar flyers in those days called their bachelor party houses (invite a girl over and show her your "snake").—Robert Wilcox, *Scream of Eagles*, p. 171, 1990

snake room *noun*

a bar *CANADA*
- Snake-room, a side room or a basement where saloon-keepers accommodate doped or drunken people until they recover their senses, presumably a place where they "see snakes."—John Sandilands, *Western Canadian Dictionary*, p. 42/1, 1912
- Drinking and curling are synonymous and many a good rink has lost a crucial Brier game or two in a hotel snake-room.—*Maclean's*, p. 62/1, 7th January 1961

snake's *noun*

an act of urination *AUSTRALIA, 1966*
Shortening of **SNAKE'S HISS**.
- Hey! Are we at Earl Court yet? I could go a snake's!—Barry Humphries, *The Wonderful World of Barry McKenzie*, p. 2, 1968

snake's hiss *noun*

an act of urination *AUSTRALIA, 1966*
Rhyming slang for **PISS**.
- Usually can't negotiate a snakes with another bastard right next door!!!—Barry Humphries, *Bazza Pulls It Off!*, 1971
- The hallway of the timothy where they lobbed smelt of chunder and snakes hiss.—Ryan Aven-Bray, *Ridgey Didge Oz Jack Lang*, p. 9, 1983
- —Ray Puxley, *Cockney Rabbit*, 1992
- —*Sydney Morning Herald*, p. 1, 2002

snakey-snakey *noun*

sexual intercourse *UK*
From **SNAKE** (the penis).
- "So why d'you marry her in the first place?" "Price she put on her virtue. No white dress, no snakey-snakey."—Chris Ryan, *The Watchman*, p. 185, 2001

snaky *adjective*

in a foul mood *AUSTRALIA, 1894*
- She's snaky because I bunged a rock on the roof.—Kylie Tennant, *The Honey Flow*, p. 99, 1956
- —David McGill, *David McGill's Complete Kiwi Slang Dictionary*, p. 117, 1998

snap *noun*

1 **amyl nitrite; an ampoule of amyl nitrite** *UK*
From the sound/action of breaking open the ampoule.
- I feel in my pocket and bring out a darling little snuff box which I keep my snap in. I crack the ampoule and breathe in hard[.]—Derek Raymond (Robin Cook), *The Crust on its Uppers*, p. 74, 1962

2 **an amphetamine tablet** *US*
- —US Department of Justice, *Street Terms*, August 1994

3 **a mouthful of alcohol or a drink taken in one gulp** *CANADA*
- Have a snap, a quick drink: "He had a few snaps before I got home. " Whatever you can get out of the bottle in one try.—T.K. Pratt, *oral citations from the Dictionary of Prince Edward Island English*, p. 140, 1988

4 **a negative statement or taunt, often as part of a rap performance** *US*
- When Dweck walks along 125th Street in Harlem asking people "Got any good snaps?" they all know what he wants.—*The New York Times Magazine*, 15th May 1994
- quick and witty taunts known as "snaps" or "playing the dozens" —James Haskins, *The Story of Hip-Hop*, p. 52–53, 2000

5 **a humorous statement or person** *US*
- —*Current Slang*, p. 13, Fall 1970

6 **something that is simple or easy** *US, 1877*
- It's no snap to explain why I was like that, but let's not try to do it on the run.—*As Good As It Gets*, 1997

7 **in pool, the first shot of the game** *US*
- —Steve Rushin, *Pool Cool*, p. 27, 1990

8 **a photograph** *US, 1894*
- Insetad of Walter having the snaps, we've got them.—Ted Lewis, *Jack Carter's Law*, p. 193, 1974

9 **a snack; a packed meal** *UK*
In dialect from 1642; usage appears to have spread via the railways.

snap *verb*

1 **to insult someone in a semi-formal quasi-friendly competition** *US*
- They knew what 'ranking' and 'snapping' on someone meant.—*New York Amsterdam News*, p. 34, 29th September 1979
- —Ellen C. Bellone (Editor), *Dictionary of Slang*, p. 22, 1989
- It was a summer night and a guy named Al was snapping on Stephan. He was snapping on his whole family – his mother, his father, the car his father was driving, the hat his father was wearing.—*The New York Times Magazine*, 15th May 1994
- There are many different terms for playing the dozens, including "bagging, capping, cracking, dissing, hiking, joning, ranking, ribbing, serving, signifying, slipping, sounding and snapping".—James Haskins, *The Story of Hip-Hop*, p. 54, 2000

2 to realise something suddenly; to experience an epiphany *US*
- He was picked up in drag and they were booking him into the woman's wing of the county jail before they snapped. — Malcolm Braly, *On the Yard*, p. 239, 1967
- — Bruce Jackson, *Outside the Law*, p. 60, 1972: 'Glossary'
- She couldn't have picked up on slang or anything else because I don't use that kind of language. She just snapped after an introduction[.] — Bruce Jackson, *Outside the Law*, p. 150, 1972

3 to flex, and thus contract, the sphincter during anal sex *US*
- — Bruce Rodgers, *The Queens' Vernacular*, p. 32, 1972

▸ **snap in**
to engage in rifle target practice *US*
Korean war usage.
- Following his week of dummy practice, referred to as "snapping-in," we will move to Chappo flats, the huge post rifle range, for qualification[.] — Martin Russ, *The Last Parallel*, p. 10, 1957

▸ **snap out of it**
to stop dreaming; to face reality; to change your mind-set *UK, 1918*
Often used as an imperative.
- When are we going to stop treating people suffering from depression like whiny, red-eyed couch-potato defeatists who could snap out of it if they only turned the temperature up on their stiff upper lip? — *The Guardian*, 27th January 2004

▸ **snap to it**
to urgently begin to do something *UK, 1918*
- [T]he only known way to solve Saturn's tasks: with painstaking exactitude. Snap to it. — *The Observer*, 20th June 2004

▸ **snap your cap**
to lose your sanity *US*
- — Kenn "Naz" Young, *Naz's Underground Dictionary*, p. 57, 1973
- — Charles Shafer, *Folk Speech in Texas Prisons*, p. 215, 1990

snap!
used for registering a (usually minor) concidence *UK*
From the children's card game during which players cry 'snap!' whenever matching cards are exposed.
- NICKY: Where've you been? TRICIA: With Daddy. Where've you? NICKY: With Mother. Talking about marriage. TRICIA: Snap! NICKY: Don't use those dreary schoolgirl expressions the whole time, Trish. You're nineteen now. — Peter Nichols, *Promenade [Six Granada Plays]*, p. 47, 1959

snap cap *noun*
a dummy shotgun cartridge *UK*
- — Chris Cradock, *A Manual of Clayshooting*, p. 175, 1983

snapped up *adjective*
1 under the influence of snap (amyl nitrate) *UK*
- [W]e take snap, and get snapped up, and now snap nearly does knock our blox off [...] we rush about the basement like two toppling lighthouses, snapped to the skies. — Derek Raymond (Robin Cook), *The Crust on its Uppers*, p. 75, 1962

2 very drunk *CANADA*
- In Nova Scotia, someone "all snapped up" is very intoxicated. — Lewis Poteet, *The South Shore Phrase Book*, p. 103, 1999

snapper *noun*
1 the vagina, especially one with exceptional muscular control *US*
- — Xaviera Hollander, *The Best Part of a Man*, 1975

2 a girl or young woman *US*
- Sometimes the Mondos would spend the whole evening in front of Duchesneau's or Sparky's, watching the girls, or "snappers," as they called them. — J. Anthony Lukas, *Don't Shoot – We Are Your Children*, p. 221, 1971

3 an infant *IRELAND*
- Bimbo put his glass down. "Sure, that's wha' we were put down here for. To have snappers." — Bernard Share, *Slanguage*, p. 301, 2003

4 the foreskin *US, 1941*

5 a photographer *UK, 1910*
- Digital snapper[:] Ted Grudowski is a digital/multimedia photographer[.] — *The Guardian*, 19th August 1999

6 in blackjack, an ace and ten-point card dealt as the first two cards to a player *US*
- — Lee Solkey, *Dummy Up and Deal*, p. 120, 1980
- — Steve Kuriscak, *Casino Talk*, p. 51, 1985

7 amyl nitrite; an ampoule of amyl nitrite *US*
- — Joe David Brown (Editor), *The Hippies*, p. 219, 1967: 'Glossary of hippie terms'
- — William D. Alsever, *Glossary for the Establishment and Other Uptight People*, p. 1, December 1970
- "Amy" is a nickname for amyl nitrate (sic). Better known as "poppers." Sometimes called "snappers." — *San Francisco Examiner*, p. 27, 15th December 1976
- Street names [...] rush, snapper, stag[.] — James Kay and Julian Cohen, *The Parents' Complete Guide to Young People and Drugs*, p. 144, 1998

8 a small, fast-breaking wave *AUSTRALIA*
- — Gary Fairmont R. Filosa II, *The Surfer's Almanac*, p. 195, 1977

9 in lobstering, a lobster that is not legal size *US*
- — Kendall Merriam, *The Illustrated Dictionary of Lobstering*, p. 81, 1978

10 a wooden match *US*
- — Clarence Major, *Dictionary of Afro-American Slang*, p. 106, 1970

11 the mythical ingredient in baked beans that can be removed to prevent flatulence *US*
- — John Gould, *Maine Lingo*, p. 263, 1975

▹ see: WHIPPERSNAPPER

snapper-rigged *adjective*
improvised; repaired in a makeshift fashion *CANADA*
Nautical terminology brought ashore in Nova Scotia.
- — Bill Casselman, *Canadian Sayings*, p. 28, 2002

snappers *noun*
the teeth, especially false teeth *UK, 1924*
- Wally, half asleep, from the mug containing the Rabbi's snappers — Charles Raven, *Underworld Nights*, p. 201, 1956

snappy *adjective*
1 fashionably smart *UK, 1881*
Especially as 'snappy dresser'.
- All of the Elephant Gang were snappy dressers. — Brian McDonald, *Elephant Boys*, p. 196, 2000

2 short-tempered; irritable *US, 1834*
- [W]hen your toddler is getting into everything and you find yourself being especially snappy with her[.] — American Academy of Pediatrics, *Caring for Your Baby and Young Child*, p. 284, 1998

▸ **make it snappy; look snappy**
to be quick *UK, 1926*
Often used as an imperative.
- [I]f you'd been on a jaunt in Louisiana, and there'd been alligator on the menu, and you'd ordered it, don't try to tell me you wouldn't have added: 'And make it snappy'? — *The Observer*, 28th December 2003

snaps *noun*
1 praise; recognition *US*
- And I must give her snaps for her courageous fashion efforts. — *Clueless*, 1995
- — Vann Wesson, *Generation X Field Guide and Lexicon*, p. 156, 1997

2 money *US*
- — Judi Sanders, *Da Bomb!*, p. 26, 1997
- — Vann Wesson, *Generation X Field Guide and Lexicon*, p. 156, 1997

3 handcuffs *US*
- — Vincent J. Monteleone, *Criminal Slang*, p. 215, 1949

4 snack food *US*
- — Connie Eble (Editor), *UNC-CH Campus Slang*, p. 5, October 1986

snard lumps *noun*
snow and ice clumps that build up under the fender of the car *CANADA*
In eastern Canada, they have been called 'snowbirds'.
- A snard lump is the collection of ice and snow stuck under the car fender in comparatively warm winter conditions. They keep building up while you are driving, and fall only if you kick them off (in the garage, they form a solid lump behind each wheel). — Chris Thain, *Cold as a Bay Street Banker's Heart*, p. 142, 1987

snarf *verb*
1 to drink or to eat something, especially greedily *UK*
Possibly abbreviated and adapted from an affected UK pronunciation of SNAFFLE (to acquire).
- [E]veryone else snarfed pink champagne[.] — *The Times Magazine*, p. 7, 2nd March 2002

2 to take something; to grab something *US*
- "Snarfing" Tricks — *American Speech*, p. 313–314, December 1968

snark *noun*

a caustic witticism *US*

- [T]hey are also major snark targets, annoying others for seeming to have so much brilliance, youth and charm. — *San Francisco Chronicle*, p. D1, 27th August 2003

snark *verb*

to act grumpily or nastily *US*

- — Connie Eble (Editor), *UNC-CH Campus Slang*, p. 7, April 1997

snarky *adjective*

snide, sarcastic; irritable *UK, 1906*

From the Scottish *snark* (to find fault, to nag).

- She wasn't a cock-teaser, a cold fish, an easy lay or a snarky bitch. — Margaret Atwood, *Dancing Girls*, p. 29, 1977
- Caption on cartoon: The Snarky District — *The New Yorker*, p. 60, 15th January 2001
- We could ask them all kinds of snarky questions in the information session. Like about their interracial dating policy. — Al Franken, *Lies*, p. 261, 2003
- We asked for the more attitude-specific Snarky Pants and the woman helping us said, "Sir, you don't wear snarky. You are snarky." — *San Francisco Chronicle*, p. E1, 27th February 2003

snarler *noun*

a sausage *NEW ZEALAND*

- Are there any more snarlers in the pan? — Ronald Hugh Morrieson, *The Scarecrow*, p. 121, 1963

snarl-up *noun*

a chaotic mess; often applied to a near-gridlock in a traffic system *UK, 1960*

- Egypt's political snarl-up[.] — *The Economist*, 8th February 2001
- My Golf surprised itself by hitting 62mph before creaking to a halt within a minute in a snarl-up near Wolverhampton North services. — *The Guardian*, 9th January 2004

snatch *noun*

1 the vagina; sex; a woman (or women) as a sexual object *UK, 1904*

- Man, he'd be Jack the Ripper with that snatch – they don't call him Don Coyote for nothing. — Bernard Wolfe, *The Late Risers*, p. 30, 1954
- Maybe she got it up her snatch in a finger stall. — William Burroughs, *Naked Lunch*, p. 59, 1957
- The snatch is what got us beat. Each peddler has a woman working with him now and she hides the stuff there. — Willard Motely, *Let No Man Write My Epitaph*, p. 220, 1958
- Maybe Ned would talk about how good her snatch was. — Cecil Brown, *The Life & Loves of Mr. Jiveass Nigger*, p. 50, 1969
- I couldn't figure why Blue would play all that con for young snatch. — Iceberg Slim (Robert Beck), *Trick Baby*, p. 157, 1969
- "A woman's snatch." "A snatch?" "The whole thing, right, all hot and dripping and ready to go." — Philip Roth, *Portnoy's Complaint*, p. 145, 1969
- [N]othing to read but some old Zane Grey paperbacks and not so much as a faint sniff of snatch (pardon me, Amanda, if you are looking on) in the air. — Tom Robbins, *Another Roadside Attraction*, p. 78, 1971
- It was, remember, only '62. Playboy had not yet acknowledged snatch fur, or even snatch. — *Screw*, p. 5, 12th June 1972
- Then we had a boy wanted to see a pussy – he was a boss, had bread, so he put up a hundred dollars for anybody to get his old lady to show her snatch in the visiting room. — Edwin Torres, *Carlito's Way*, p. 123, 1975
- He's spewing his spunk deep inside her seething snatch! — *Adam Film World*, p. 60, 1977
- Clinker did not do anything to me personally, although I got to say a friend of his did, and neither did Clinker's wife, that snatch that'd fuck a flashlight if there was nothing else handy. — George V. Higgins, *The Rat on Fire*, p. 109, 1981
- The Doll Theater, at Seventh and 48th, revolves around an emotionless palooka ramming his three-quarters hard-on into some broad's snatch atop a pink-spotlighted mattress tilted toward the audience. — Josh Alan Friedman, *Tales of Times Square*, p. 189, 1986
- Jesus God in heaven, uh, why did you kill such hot snatch. That's a joke man. — *Heathers*, 1988
- I go for art snatch. I just love the sound of a bird with a posh accent bellowing obscenities[.] — Stewart Home, *Sex Kick [britpulp]*, p. 202, 1999
- For girls in the sex biz, whose pussies are their paychecks, a stylish snatch is just as important as false eyelashes and smudge-proof lipstick. — *The Village Voice*, 8th–14th November 2000

2 a kidnapping *US, 1931*

- He looked at me solemnly. "Is this some kind of a snatch?" — Horace McCoy, *Kiss Tomorrow Good-bye*, p. 282, 1958
- This isn't a ransom snatch. — Mickey Spillane, *Return of the Hood*, p. 117, 1964
- The problem part of any snatch, irregardless, is always the payoff. — Richard Condon, *Prizzi's Honor*, p. 172, 1982
- We do the snatch in broad daylight outside your house. — James Ellroy, *Hollywood Nocturnes*, p. 102, 1994

3 something stolen *UK*

- Watching Blackwell in the hall doing wheelies on his latest snatch gives Caleb a great idea. — Jack Allen, *When the Whistle Blows*, p. 81, 2000

4 an air rescue of ground troops or the crew of a downed aircraft *US*

- Anyway, long short story, we reach the snatch point right near sunset, which is a very nervous-making time to be in the air going anyplace by home, and we spot the smoke coming up. — John Skipp and Craig Spector, *The Scream*, p. 268, 1988

snatch *verb*

to kidnap someone *US, 1932*

- In one of the boldest strokes in gangland annals, he kidnapped Big Frency De Mange, Owney Maddens' top lieutenant, and with him snatched George Immerman, Connie's brother. — Robert Sylvester, *No Cover Charge*, p. 63, 1956
- After them cats from St. Louis snatched me and I had to pay fifty grand to keep them from blowing my head off, I knew I had to have some place to hide. — Charles W. Moore, *A Brick for Mister Jones*, p. 80, 1975
- The woman who was wasted when Finlay got snatched. — Richard Condon, *Prizzi's Honor*, p. 233, 1982

▸ **snatch it**

to quit work taking the wages due *AUSTRALIA, 1911*

- — Jim Ramsay, *Cop It Sweet!*, p. 83, 1977
- — Ryan Aven-Bray, *Ridgey Didge Oz Jack Lang*, p. 45, 1983

▸ **snatch your time**

to quit work taking the wages due *AUSTRALIA, 1916*

- Within a week, he jobbed the panno, snatched his time and bought an air ticket to gay Paree. — Frank Hardy, *The Yarns of Billy Borker*, p. 24, 1965

snatch 22 *noun*

a woman who is considered so sexually unattractive that a man would have to be drunk to attempt sex with her, but too drunk to perform *UK*

A logical knot, formed on **SNATCH** (the vagina); after *Catch 22*, the novel by Joseph Heller, 1961, and the conventional usage it inspired.

- — *Roger's Profanisaurus*, 2002

snatch box *noun*

the vagina *UK, 1961*

An elaboration of **SNATCH**.

snatch box decorated with red roses *noun*

the bleed period of the menstrual cycle *US*

Formed on **SNATCH BOX** (the vagina) with blood imagery.

- — Karen Houppert, *The Curse*, 1999
- — *The Museum of Menstruation and Women's Health*, April 2002

snatcher *noun*

1 a thief *US*

- He's a snatcher but I don't know no sting he's made recently. — Chester Himes, *Cotton Comes to Harlem*, p. 34, 1965

2 a police detective *US*

- — Jack Lait and Lee Mortimer, *New York Confidential*, p. 236, 1948: 'A glossary of Harlemisms'

snatch fur *noun*

female pubic hair *US*

- It was, remember, only '62. Playboy had not yet acknowledged snatch fur, or even snatch. — *Screw*, p. 5, 12th June 1972

snatch hair *noun*

the pubic hair (of either gender) *US*

- My wife would tear out EVERY SNATCH HAIR AND EYEBALL FROM ME, never mind from Sally. — Howard Stern, *Miss America*, p. 234, 1995

snatch hound *noun*

a person who is obsessed with sex and women *US*

- "Is Jonny Duhamel queer?" "Are you nuts? He is the snatch hound to end all snatch hounds." — James Ellroy, *White Jazz*, p. 145, 1992

snatch man *noun*

a press photographer *UK*

- Now Alf's a good snatch man, meaning that his speciality is getting a photo of someone who'd rather not have their face splashed all over the papers. — Jake Arnott, *He Kills Coppers*, p. 118, 2001

snatch patrol *noun*
a combat mission in which the object is to capture enemy troops for interrogation *US*
• A snatch patrol. The squad would capture the two VC and bring them to the outpost. I would interrogate them[.] — Philip Caputo, *A Rumor of War*, p. 299, 1977

snatch-plug *noun*
a tampon *US*
• [M]ost gals use snatch-plugs which have no other utilitarian value that I know of. — *Screw*, p. 6, 4th December 1972

snavel *verb*
to steal something *AUSTRALIA, 1892*
• Peter did it for him, bringing Ponto to Bill's window for Bill to display his goods, and adjudge their value in cigarettes, which Ponto, of course, snavelled from his old man's shop. — Norman Lindsay, *Halfway to Anywhere*, p. 36, 1947
• While I was stuck in Sick Bay, all the good hidin' places got snavelled. — John Wynnum, *Tar Dust*, p. 102, 1962

snazzy *adjective*
stylish; fashionable; smart *US, 1932*
• A gentleman gave us a ride in his snazzy car. — Jack Kerouac, *On the Road*, p. 74, 1957
• Even Sister had to admit he was pretty snazzy, after talking to him for a while. — Mary McCarthy, *The Group*, p. 210, 1963
• "Gee you're the snazziest-looking girl at the party," is a good thing to hear[.] — Dick Clark, *To Goof or Not to Goof*, p. 23, 1963
• Then we gonna buy you a ritzy house ... 'lectric light! ... a great big slew of snazzy furniture. — Iceberg Slim (Robert Beck), *Airtight Willie and Me*, p. 116, 1979
• [U]p and down Collins in snazzy circles and figure eights, honking the horns and flashing the lights[.] — Carl Hiaasen, *Tourist Season*, 1986
• [R]esplendent in off-the-peg snazzy whistle. — Andrew Nickolds, *Back to Basics*, p. 32, 1994

sneak *noun*
1 a schoolchild who tells tales or informs on his or her fellows *UK, 1840*
School slang, from an earlier, more general sense as 'a despicable person, or one who behaves in an underhand manner'.
2 a soft-soled shoe; a running shoe, a trainer *UK, 1862*
• But check out his footwear and, chances are, he won't be maxing a pair of fly Nike sneaks. — Patrick Neate, *Where You're At*, p. 112, 2003

sneak *verb*
1 to tell tales; to inform upon someone *UK, 1897*
School slang.
2 to break into a building *US*
• I figure he was planning the sneak the hotel a little. — Raymond Chandler, *The Little Sister*, p. 58–59, 1949

▸ **sneak a peak**
to take a look at something or someone *US*
• Haven't you ever sneaked a peek at him in his underwear? — *American Beauty*, 1999

sneak *adjective*
▸ **on the sneak tip**
in secret *US*
• — Maria Hinojas, *Crews*, p. 167, 1995: 'Glossary'

sneak-and-peak *adjective*
1 designed to be quiet *US*
• Kind of tough kicking, ain't it, Nick, in those crepe soled, sneak-and-peek shoes you guys wear? — Joseph Wambaugh, *The Blue Knight*, p. 137, 1973
2 undertaken for the purpose of reconnaissance *US*
• But this one was a sneak-and-peak mission and I was the patrol leader. — Elmore Leonard, *The Hunted*, p. 149, 1974

sneaker *noun*
1 a person engaged in an illegal enterprise who does not pay a regular bribe to the police but does when confronted *US*
• He's what you call a sneaker – isn't on the pad, isn't paying anybody. You find him, he pays; you don't, he don't pay. — Leonard Shecter and William Phillips, *On the Pad*, p. 150–151, 1973
2 a smuggler *US*
• — *American Speech*, p. 97, May 1956: 'Smugglers' argot in the Southwest'
3 a linear amplifier for a citizens' band radio *US*
• — Bill Davis, *Jawjacking: The Complete CB Dictionary*, p. 93, 1977
4 in hot rodding or motor racing, an unusually large tyre *US*
• — Lewis Poteet, *Car & Motorcyle Slang*, p. 36, 1992

sneaker bitch *noun*
a person who is too focused on conspicuous consumption, such as high priced trainers *US*
• Most of these sneaker bitches is looking to get skied, not looking for knowledge. — Terry Williams, *The Cocaine Kids*, p. 87, 1989

sneakernet *noun*
in computing, to carry a disk from one computer to another *US*
• — Eric S. Raymond, *The New Hacker's Dictionary*, p. 327, 1991

sneakers *noun*
car wheel rims *US*
• Dubs, blades, shoes, sneakers, twinkies – street slang for custom wheels – are status symbols, made popular by athletes and rap stars. — *Cincinnati Enquirer*, p. 1B, 29th August 2003

sneak go *noun*
any secretive action *AUSTRALIA*
• — Ned Wallish, *The Truth Dictionary of Racing Slang*, p. 33, 1989

sneak-in *noun*
a bar that surreptitiously remains open after the legal closing time *US*
• Washington has hundreds of sneak-ins that remain open all night. — Jack Lait and Lee Mortimer, *Washington Confidential*, p. 13, 1951

sneak job *noun*
housebreaking *UK*
• — Angela Devlin, *Prison Patter*, p. 106, 1996

sneaky *adjective*
used of a recording device, easily hidden *US*
• — Ralph de Sola, *Crime Dictionary*, p. 140, 1982

sneaky beaky *noun*
a spy *UK*
Often used attributively as an adjective.
• How's it going in the Walts, then? You got your sneaky beaky kit yet? — Andy McNab (writing of the late 1970s/early 80s), *Immediate Action*, p. 275, 1995

sneaky man *noun*
a married woman's adulterous sexual partner *BAHAMAS*
• — John A. Holm, *Dictionary of Bahamian English*, p. 188, 1982

sneaky Pete *noun*
1 any potent, potentially fatal, alcoholic concoction, favoured by those whose need outweighs their ability to pay *US*
• Pass me the sneakypete, Muckleroy. — Ralph Ellison, *Invisible Man*, p. 490, 1947
• Down by the river there was some bums that hung around a fire and drank Sneaky Pete all day and sometimes cooked something like stew in a can. — Hal Ellson, *Duke*, p. 151, 1949
• You give off a lungful of Sneaky Pete yaself; I sniffed you out, brother. — George Mandel, *Flee the Angry Strangers*, p. 60, 1952
• They drink wine – sneaky pete, so called because it sneaks up behind and hits you when you don't expect it. — Harrison E. Salisbury, *The Shook-up Generation*, p. 33, 1958
• So drink your Sneaky Pete and then hit the street cause I'm cool like the dawn and really gone! — Dan Burley, *Diggeth Thou?*, p. 45, 1959
• He drank quarts of it a day. Any kind. Gallo, sneaky pete, the distillation of canned heat. — Clancy Sigal, *Going Away*, p. 238, 1961
• Maybe I should make it down to the Bowery, I thought, and lap up some sneaky pete with the rest of the bums. — Piri Thomas, *Down These Mean Streets*, p. 95, 1967
2 marijuana mixed in wine *US*
• — *American Speech*, p. 88, May 1955: 'Narcotic argot along the Mexican border'
3 a member of a US Army long-range reconnaissance patrol unit *US*
• — Gregory Clark, *Words of the Vietnam War*, p. 424, 1990
4 an unannounced in-flight examination by a crew that boards the plane just before take-off *US*
• — *American Speech*, p. 120, May 1963: 'Air refueling words'
5 in pool, an expert player's custom cue, designed to look like an ordinary cue *US*
• — Mike Shamos, *The Illustrated Encyclopedia of Billiards*, p. 217, 1993

sneeze *noun*
pepper *US*
• — *Maledicta*, p. 267, Summer/Winter 1981: 'By its slang, ye shall know it: the pessimism of prison life'

sneeze *verb*
to arrest someone *US*
- —Hyman E. Goldin et al., *Dictionary of American Underworld Lingo*, p. 200, 1950
- —Sherman Louis Sergel, *The Language of Show Biz*, p. 201, 1973

sneeze and squeeze *noun*
cocaine and sex *US*
- A little too early for Odeon, but once we're downtown, it's happy hunting ground for sneeze and squeeze.—Jay McInerney, *Bright Lights, Big City*, p. 44, 1984

sneezed *adjective*
arrested; kidnapped *UK*
- —Angela Devlin, *Prison Patter*, p. 106, 1996

sneeze out *verb*
to confess *UK*
- —Angela Devlin, *Prison Patter*, p. 106, 1996

sneezer *noun*
1 the nose *US*
- —Lou Shelly, *Hepcats Jive Talk Dictionary*, p. 17, 1945

2 in marketing, a person whose opinion the market listens to and trusts *US*
A logical by-product of **VIRAL-MARKETING** (word-of-mouth).
- "Oprah Winfrey is quite probably," says [Seth] Godin, "the most successful sneezer of her generation."—*The Observer*, 26th November 2000

3 a jail or prison *US*
- [A] bit of high class fluff that couldn't stick around long enough to make sure he didn't get tossed in the sneezer by some prowl car boys[.]—Raymond Chandler, *The Long Goodbye*, p. 5, 1953

sneezing powder *noun*
heroin *US*
- "Somebody put some sneezing powder under my nose," the girl told Father Hoodak. Sneezing powder is heroin.—Harrison E. Salisbury, *The Shook-up Generation*, p. 79, 1958

snide *noun*
1 a cunning person; an untrustworthy person; a contemptible person; an informer *UK, 1950*
German *aufschneiden* (to boast, brag), reaching English via Yiddish. Also used in the variant 'shnide'.
- Without being a shnide at that.—Frank Norman, *Bang To Rights*, p. 12, 1958
- —Angela Devlin, *Prison Patter*, p. 106, 1996

2 a stolen pearl *AUSTRALIA, 1933*

snide; shnide; snidey *adjective*
false, counterfeit, sham, bogus; hence mean, contemptible; underhand *UK, 1859*
- [C]ritics ignored or smeared them [the Count Five] with their snidest categorisations[.]—Lester Bangs, *Psychotic Reactions and Carburetor Dung*, p. 15, 1971
- It turns out Clement's American Express Gold Card was a snide.—Dean Cavanagh, *Mile High Meltdown (Disco Biscuits)*, p. 207, 1996
- Snidey E [MDMA]s range from a bit of E mixed with something else to totally snidey Es which can be dog worming tablets[.]—Macfarlane, Macfarlane and Robson, *The User*, p. 74, 1996
- I'd find you [...] new IDs, fresh birth certificates, snide licences, [...] and counterfeit luncheon vouchers.—Dave Courtney, *Stop the Ride I Want to Get Off*, p. 190, 1999

snide *adverb*
secretly; deceitfully *UK*
- Signing on snide like as well.—Niall Griffiths, *Kelly + Victor*, p. 27, 2002

snidey *adjective*
sneering; contemptuous; disdainful *UK*
- Asking me all sorts of questions and making snidey remarks about Henry and Jimmy.—John Peter Jones, *Feather Pluckers*, p. 152, 1964

snidey up *verb*
to adulterate drugs, to prepare fake drugs for sale *UK*
Extended from **SNIDE; SNIDEY** (fake).
- Most worrying of the ingredients that are being used to "snidey up" E [MDMA]s are depressants and anaesthetics.—Macfarlane, Macfarlane and Robson, *The User*, p. 74, 1996

sniff *noun*
1 cocaine *US*
- After some of the fellas would step away from the blackjack table, and the bar, and get ready to buy a fiddy or a hundred dollars' worth of sniff[.]—*New Jack City*, p. 9, 1990
- Fuck Ecstasy, we'll stick with the sniff.—Wayne Anthony, *Spanish Highs*, p. 4, 1999
- Presumably, said promoter then dived right on back into the massive pile of sniff that he had spent the rest of the season ploughing through[.]—*Ministry*, p. 7, October 2002

2 any solvent that can be inhaled for its psychoactive effect *US*
- —Paul Glover, *Words from the House of the Dead*, 1974

3 a sycophant *US*
From an image of the sycophant's brown nose being in the near proximity of an anus.
- —*Current Slang*, p. 10, Spring 1968

4 a girlfriend *UK*
- I'm off for a day out with me new sniff[.]—Niall Griffiths, *Kelly + Victor*, p. 142, 2002

▸ **the sniff**
a recreational hunt for sexually attractive company *UK*
- Maybe he's on the sniff, the girl's boyfriend catches him and leathers him.—Nicholas Blincoe, *The Beautiful Beaten-up Irish Boy of the Arndale Centre*, p. 10, 1998

sniff *verb*
to ingest drugs by nasal inhalation *UK, 1925*
- —Angela Devlin, *Prison Patter*, p. 106, 1996
- —Mike Haskins, *Drugs*, p. 291, 2003

sniffed-up *adjective*
under the influence of cocaine *UK*
- Also, according to sniffed-up logic, the pyramids were built using ancient magic[.]—Wayne Anthony, *Spanish Highs*, p. 106, 1999

sniffer *noun*
1 the nose *UK, 1858*
- Several times the master of ceremonies stuck the pill close to my nose and told me to smell it. Poppa, you never laid your sniffer on anything so fine in all your life.—Mezz Mezzrow, *Really the Blues*, p. 99, 1946
- [T]hey'll go all moody and Beardsley drawing and look down their sniffers at you[.]—Derek Raymond (Robin Cook), *The Crust on its Uppers*, p. 34, 1962

2 an ampoule of amyl nitrite *US*
- —William D. Alsever, *Glossary for the Establishment and Other Uptight People*, p. 1, December 1970

3 a cocaine user *US*
- So while this sniffer's giving you head she just stops in the middle and tells you about a commerical real estate venture?—Robert Campbell, *Juice*, p. 152, 1988

4 a device placed on a vehicle's exhaust pipe to measure the pollutants in the emission *US*
- —John Edwards, *Auto Dictionary*, 1993

5 a claims investigator of unemployment and other benefit fraud *UK*
- We are honoured. Two sniffers from the dole.—Alan Bleasdale, *Boys From the Blackstuff*, 1982

6 a computer program that surreptitiously records user passwords and other log-in data *US, 1994*
- —*American Speech*, p. 192, Summer 1996: 'Among the new words'

7 an outsider who tries to be part of the pornography industry *US*
- —*Adult Video News*, p. 51, October 1995

8 a handkerchief *US*
- —Lou Shelly, *Hepcats Jive Talk Dictionary*, p. 17, 1945

sniffer and snorter *noun*
a reporter *UK*
Rhyming slang.
- —Ray Puxley, *Fresh Rabbit*, 1998

sniffer bag *noun*
a small bag of heroin intended for inhaling *US*
- —*Detroit News*, p. 5D, 20th September 2002

sniffings *noun*
any industrial solvent that is inhaled for its psychoactive effect *US*
- —Inez Cardozo-Freeman, *The Joint*, p. 532, 1984

sniffing snow *noun*
cocaine *UK*
An instructive elaboration of **SNOW** (cocaine).
- This pocket is full of sniffing snow and I'm one generous son of a bitch.—Chris Baker and Andrew Day, *Lock, Stock... & Spaghetti Sauce*, p. 228, 2000

sniff queen *noun*
a homosexual who is a heavy user of amyl nitrite or butyl nitrite during sex *US*

sniffy *adjective*
scornful, disdainful *UK, 1871*
- It is no use, as statisticians, our being sniffy about the slapdash methods of many sociologists[.] — David Salsburg, *The Lady Tasting Tea*, p. 258, 2002

snifter *noun*
1 a small drink of alcoholic liquor; hence, specifically, a brandy glass; more generally, a glass for spirits *US, 1844*
The difference between the senses is not always apparent.
- They understood his predicament, and after calming him with a snifter of Sambuca, gave him advice[.] — Jeffrey Eugenides, *The Virgin Suicides*, p. 80, 1994
- [W]et-headed and fresh from the shower, and she's got a snifter of brandy[.] — Richard Russo, *Straight Man*, p. 53, 1998

2 a single inhaled dose of cocaine *US, 1930*
- Following the snifter, he began preparing a nice skunk spliff[.] — Wayne Anthony, *Spanish Highs*, p. 157, 1999

snig *verb*
to drag something heavy by means of ropes or chains *AUSTRALIA, 1897*
- The machine operators went on strike which left us without means of snigging up the trucks. — Sam Weller, *Old Bastards I Have Met*, p. 57, 1979
- He told her about his fine bullocks, and the huge tree that he intended to fell and snig[.] — Hesba Brinsmead, *Longtime Dreaming*, p. 36, 1982

snip *noun*
1 a bargain *UK, 1926*
- The only part that's no longer a snip is her [Reese Witherspoon's] salary: $15 million for Legally Blonde 2. — *The Times*, 2nd August 2003

2 something that is easily achieved or done; a certainty *UK, 1890*

3 a thing that is more fortunate, excellent or pleasing than might normally be expected *UK, 1952*
In the phrase 'snip of a *thing*'.
- Llaregyb this snip of a morning is wildfruit and warm, the streets, fields, sands and waters springing in the young sun. — Dylan Thomas, *Under Milk Wood*, 1953

4 a ticket collector *UK*
- — Harvey Sheppard, *A Dictionary of Railway Slang*, 1970

▸ **the snip**
any invasive medical procedure that sterilises a patient; a vasectomy, an orchidectomy, etc *UK*
- Bloke goes for the snip, bloke gets wife to take photos of the procedure[.] — *Internet Magazine*, July 2001

snip *verb*
to borrow money on short notice *AUSTRALIA*
- — Ned Wallish, *The Truth Dictionary of Racing Slang*, p. 75, 1989

snipe *noun*
1 the butt of a marijuana cigarette *US, 1969*
In the late C19, a 'snipe' referred to the discarded stub of a cigar or cigarette. It briefly enjoyed standing in the vocabulary of marijuana users before falling victim to **ROACH**.
- — Walter L. Way, *The Drug Scene*, 1977

2 the butt of a cigarette that can still be relit and smoked *US, 1891*
- — Lou Shelly, *Hepcats Jive Talk Dictionary*, p. 17, 1945
- Then the man whose pant-knees and hands were muddy where he had fallen, saw a cigarette snipe on the curb. — Willard Motley, *Let No Man Write My Epitaph*, p. 76, 1958
- — William K. Bentley and James M. Corbett, *Prison Slang*, p. 65, 1992

3 the nose *UK*
From the long straight bill of the bird.
- [R]egal my snipe is, people have said – it's stood up to a lot of punishment without so much as a kink in it, my snipe has. — Kevin Sampson, *Clubland*, p. 227, 2002

4 a sniper's hide *UK: NORTHERN IRELAND*
- A snipe, as the Provos [Provisional IRA] euphemistically called their murderous ambushes[.] — Christopher Hawke, *For Campaign Service*, 1979

5 on board a ship, a crew member, especially an engineering officer *UK, 1918*
- After OCS I was assigned to a small destroyer, the Joseph K. Taussig, as a snipe, or engineering officer, whose domain was the fireroom, where the ship's boilers are located. — Richard Marcinko and John Weisman, *Rogue Warrior*, p. 60, 1992

6 a railway track worker *US*
- — Norman Carlisle, *The Modern Wonder Book of Trains and Railroading*, p. 268, 1946
- — Ramon Adams, *The Language of the Railroader*, p. 142, 1977

snipe *verb*
1 to disparage someone *US*
- — Edith A. Folb, *runnin' down some lines*, p. 255, 1980

2 to snoop; to spy on someone *US*
- — Connie Eble (Editor), *UNC-CH Campus Slang*, p. 10, October 2002

sniper *noun*
1 a person who posts inflammatory attacks on the Internet *US*
- Those Net snipers can be really cruel. — Kevin Smith, *Jay and Silent Bob Strike Back*, p. 124, 2001

2 a sexually promiscuous girl of limited intellect *BAHAMAS*
- — John A. Holm, *Dictionary of Bahamian English*, p. 188, 1982

snippy *adjective*
impatient; argumentative *US, 1848*
Originally used in the UK to mean 'parsimonious' (C18), and then in the US (C19) in the current sense. The term enjoyed a brief moment of fame in the early morning hours of 9th November 2000, when US Vice President Al Gore told future President George Bush, 'You don't have to get snippy with me' as he retracted a concession made several minutes earlier.
- "She was a little snippy snitch," Mickey said. — Elmore Leonard, *Switch*, p. 158, 1978
- Sir, you have no call to get snippy with me. — *Fargo*, 1996
- I sat up and narrowed my eyes at him. "No need to get snippy about it." "Men don't get snippy," Morelli said. "Men get pissed. Women get snippy." — Janet Evanovich, *Seven Up*, p. 105, 2001

snips *noun*
any cutting tool, for example scissors or wire cutters *US*
- — Joseph E. Ragen and Charles Finston, *Inside the World's Toughest Prison*, p. 819, 1962: 'Penitentiary and underworld glossary'

snirt *noun*
a stormy mixture of snow and dirt *CANADA*
- Snirt is descriptive of a unique prairie weather phenomenon–the combination of snow and dirt which can occur during storms at certain times of the year, especially the fall. — Chris Thain, *Cold as a Bay Street Banker's Heart*, p. 142, 1987

snit *noun*
1 a mild temper tantrum *US, 1939*
- "She's going to the same place we are!" said Fortney. "Wanna try again or are you in too much of a snit?" — Joseph Wambaugh, *Floaters*, p. 63, 1996

2 among Nova Scotians of German descent, an apple slice *CANADA*
- In Lunenburg County, "snits" are dried apple slices. The word comes, adapted into English conversation, from the German word "schnitten," "to cut." — Lewis Poteet, *The South Shore Phrase Book*, p. 104, 1999

snitch *noun*
1 an informer, especially a police informer *UK, 1785*
A high profile use of the term was in the motto of the television police drama *Richard Diamond, Private Detective* (1957–60) – 'A detective is only as good as his snitch'.
- You ass-kissing little snitch! — John Waters, *Deperate Living*, p. 166, 1099
- The snitch is comin' out. He trusts you. — Clarence Cooper Jr, *The Scene*, p. 13, 1960
- We're talking to everybody who worked with Iris, might've known her. And we got our snitches to talk to yet. — Elmore Leonard, *Glitz*, p. 89, 1985
- Not the cops. They couldn't smell a dead rat two feet away. But the damn dope fiend snitches could. — *Drugstore Cowboy*, 1988
- You'll be the lowest sort of rat, the prince of snitches, the loudest cooing stool pigeon that ever grabbed his ankles for the man. — *The Usual Suspects*, 1995
- — Angela Devlin, *Prison Patter*, p. 106, 1996

2 a piece of information supplied by a police informer *UK*
- If it was a major snitch, like a significant seizure [of drugs], the reward could go into five figures[.] — Duncan MacLaughlin, *The Filth*, p. 115, 2002

snitch *verb*

1 to inform upon someone *UK, 1801*

- I hope you aren't going to rush over there, break down the door, and tell him I snitched him off. — Gerald Petievich, *Money Men*, p. 143, 1981
- No one knew who'd snitched on her. — William T. Vollman, *Whores for Gloria*, p. 71, 1991

2 to steal something *US, 1904*

- Some mean hack of a keeper nabs a colored boy on the coal gang for snitching a loaf of bread. — Mezz Mezzrow, *Really the Blues*, p. 314, 1946
- My friend on kitchen assignment brought some cookies she snitched. — John M. Murtagh and Sara Harris, *Cast the First Stone*, p. 26, 1957
- It helped to think of old times, carefree days in Hillsborough when she and Binky and Muffy would snitch the keys to Daddy's Mercedes and tool down to the Fillmore to tease the black studs lurking on the street corners. — Armistead Maupin, *Tales of the City*, p. 94, 1978

3 to shoot a marble *NORFOLK ISLAND*

- — Beryl Nobbs Palmer, *A Dictionary of Norfolk Words and Usages*, p. 41, 1992

snitchball *noun*

any game played by prisoners in the protective unit reserved for informers *US*

- — William K. Bentley and James M. Corbett, *Prison Slang*, p. 12, 1992

snitch box *noun*

an in-house prison post box *US*

- — William K. Bentley and James M. Corbett, *Prison Slang*, p. 57, 1992

snitcher *noun*

1 a metal detector *US*

- — Hyman E. Goldin et al., *Dictionary of American Underworld Lingo*, p. 201, 1950

2 a dislike or grudge *NEW ZEALAND, 1953*

- — Harry Orsman, *A Dictionary of Modern New Zealand Slang*, p. 125–126, 1999

snitch jacket *noun*

a reputation for being an informer *US*

- I know you got an army of snitches, but nobody never got a snitch jacket. — Joseph Wambaugh, *The Blue Knight*, p. 29, 1973
- And you'll be in jail wearing a snitch jacket. — Gerald Petievich, *To Die in Beverly Hills*, p. 259, 1983
- On November 5, 1980, while driving (lifting weights) on the lower yard, several of the Aryans spotted a white inmate who was carrying a snitch jacket[.] — Bill Valentine, *Gangs and Their Tattoos*, p. 13, 2000

snitch kite *noun*

a note sent by a prisoner to prison authorities, informing on other prisoners *US*

- Admin was receiving far more snitch kites (notes sent up front to staff when an inmate wants to inform on others). — Bill Valentine, *Gangs and Their Tattoos*, p. 12, 2000

snitty *adjective*

bad-tempered *US, 1978*

- I called Kathleen from the pay phone and rehearsed my snitty but controlled opening line. "Uh, didn't you forget something?" — Anne Lamott, *Hard Laughter*, p. 91, 1979

snob mob *noun*

a group of friends with a very high opinion of themselves *US*

- — *American Speech*, p. 305, December 1955: 'Wayne University slang'

snockered; schnockered; shnockered *adjective*

drunk *US*

- — *American Speech*, p. 304, December 1955: 'Wayne University slang'
- — Collin Baker et al., *College Undergraduate Slang Study Conducted at Brown University*, p. 200, 1968
- Bellamy was so snockered he didn't even blink at the ten-dollar cover. — Carl Hiaasen, *Tourist Season*, p. 2, 1986
- Melvin got properly snockered after two Martinis. — Janet Evanovich, *Seven Up*, p. 143, 2001

snodger *adjective*

great; excellent *AUSTRALIA, 1917*

- And so far as fossickers are concerned, let me tell you those two old coves put a snodger rort over two professional mining crooks who thought they were tricking *them*. — Dymphna Cusack, *Picnic Races*, p. 63, 1962

snog *noun*

a pasionate kiss; a short but intense period of kissing and cuddling *UK, 1959*

- If he defeats George W this week, his victory march can be traced back to the moment when the man – cheerfully considered one of the world's dullest politicians – gathered wife Tipper into a very public snog. — *Sun-Herald (Tempo)*, p. 3, 5th November 2000
- Should they try to get a snog off that woman from an equally rowdy hen party[.] — Iain Aitch, *A Fete Worse Than Death*, p. 159–160, 2003

snog *verb*

to kiss and cuddle *UK, 1945*

- — Tom Hibbert, *Rockspeak!*, p. 145, 1983
- Oo-er. What were you up to then, snogging? — *Girlfriend*, p. 78, 1995
- They can be super cute, fun to hang out with and great to snog, but let's face it, sometimes guys can do and say really stupid things that make us wonder what we ever see in them. — *Dolly*, p. 55, 1996
- [W]henever I snogged Chris, it felt like I was snogging twelve stone of luncheon meat. — Jenny Eclair, *Camberwell Beauty*, p. 31, 2000
- This is actually a very nifty trick she learnt in Botswana while snogging a sheik who was blind[.] — Gretel Killeen, *Hot Buns and Ophelia get shipwrecked*, p. 58, 2001
- So what did you get up to, apart from snogging David Beckham? — *Sky Magazine*, p. 15, July 2001
- He had this engaging way of holding a girl in one arm while he snogged her, so that he could hold his pint and his fag in the other. — Alan Titchmarsh, *Trowell and Error*, p. 127, 2002

snog and fuck *noun*

a public house called the 'Dog and Duck' *UK*

Rhyming slang.

- — Ray Puxley, *Cockney Rabbit*, 1992

snogger *noun*

someone who kisses with passion *UK*

From **SNOG**.

- I've always been a snogger[.] — Jenny Eclair, *Camberwell Beauty*, p. 31, 2000

sno-go *noun*

a snowmobile *US, 1961*

- — Russell Tabbert, *Dictionary of Alaskan English*, p. 230, 1991

snogtastic *adjective*

sexually attractive; kissable *UK*

Elision of **SNOG** (to kiss) and 'fan*tastic*'.

- — David Rowan, *A Glossary for the 90s*, p. 193, 1998

snooge *noun*

in Newfoundland, a way of attaching sled dogs *CANADA*

- [Sled dogs] can also be driven on a "snooge," which is a single long trace with the dogs harnessed to short ones leading off from it at intervals. — *Beaver*, p. 28/1, Autumn 1957

snooker *verb*

1 to trick someone; to place someone in an impossible position *UK, 1915*

From the game played with balls on a billiard table.

- Delvin, knowing he's been snookered, too, gives Cooley half a wink, thanks everybody and turns the chair and the job over to me to another round of spontaneous applause. — Robert Campbell, *In a Pig's Eye*, p. 8, 1991
- "[S]oon as we turn our backs he goes and jumps out a window. I'm telling you, you can't trust nobody anymore." "He snookered us." — Janet Evanovich, *Seven Up*, p. 12, 2001

2 to conceal something or someone *AUSTRALIA, 1950*

- Billy's plan was to 'stay snookered' at my place until we could organise a car and some bugs bunny. — Kathy Lette, *Girls' Night Out*, p. 169, 1987

snookered *adjective*

placed in a deliberately difficult position *UK, 1915*

From the game of snooker.

- But this was a safer way of getting it over with, letting Athena know he was snookered. — Christopher Brookmyre, *The Sacred Art of Stealing*, p. 208, 2002

snookums *noun*

used as an affectionate term of address *US, 1919*

As the *Oxford English Dictionary* so gracefully puts it, 'usually applied to children or lap-dogs'.

- "Just thinking, Nebbice." "About what, snookums? Love?" — Max Shulman, *The Zebra Derby*, p. 91, 1946

snoop *noun*

a detective *US, 1942*

From **SNOOP** (to pry).

- I'm a private snoop! Like you, man! — *The Big Lebowski*, 1998
- The snoop was attempting to shield his face[.] — Stewart Home, *Sex Kick [britpulp]*, p. 215, 1999
- A professional snoop in a world where most people did it as a hobby. — Malcolm Pryce, *Aberystwyth Mon Amour*, p. 11, 2001

snoop *verb*

to pry *US*

- I scrounged through the mess on the dresser and just for the hell of it snooped in his closet. — Janet Evanovich, *Seven Up*, p. 51, 2001

snoop and pry; snoop *verb*

to cry *UK*

Rhyming slang.

- The cause of many a midnight argument is a "snooping" baby. — Ray Puxley, *Cockney Rabbit*, 1992

snooper *noun*

an investigator *US, 1889*

- A private snooper, eh? — Mickey Spillane, *My Gun is Quick*, p. 20, 1950

snoopers *noun*

the flashing lights on top of a police car *US*

- — Lanie Dills, *The Official CB Slanguage Language Dictionary*, p. 65, 1976

snoopy *noun*

the vagina *US*

A pet name; probably from the character Snoopy, a pet beagle, in *Peanuts* cartoon strip by Charles M. Schulz (1922–2000).

- — *Sky Magazine*, p. 57, July 2001

snoose *noun*

damp, grated, chewing snuff *CANADA*

- Just before ya face the old lady ya shove a wad of schnoose in yer mouth. She'll never smell yer breath. — *Vancouver Sun*, p. 7, 22nd April 1951
- Snoose is a Canadian borrowing from Danish where "snustoback" is a moist, chopped snuff, the kind chewed. — Bill Casselman, *Canadian Words*, p. 110, 1995

snoot *noun*

1 the nose *UK, 1861*

- Indeed Dorothy almost poked me in the snoot in Las Vegas recently because I made disparaging remarks about Shattuck and Lewin. — Lee Mortimer, *Women Confidential*, p. 33, 1960

2 cocaine *US*

- — Peter Johnson, *Dictionary of Street Alcohol and Drug Terms*, p. 174, 1993

3 a conceited, snobbish person *AUSTRALIA, 1938*

4 in the television and film industries, a cone attachment that directs light to a specific area *US*

- — Ralph S. Singleton, *Filmaker's Dictionary*, p. 155, 1990

▸ **give you the snoot**

to treat you in a condescending manner *US*

- "I didn't know that," I says, wondering if Betancourt's trying to make chatty conversation or give me the snoot. — Robert Campbell, *Nibbled to Death by Ducks*, p. 179, 1989

snootch *noun*

the vagina *CANADA*

- — Bill Casselman, *Canadian Sayings*, p. 106, 2002
- I wonder what he'd pay for a picture of my snootch. — Queen Latifah, *V Graham Norton*, 28th May 2003

snootchie bootchie nootchies!; snootchie bootchies!

used as an all-purpose, meaning-free catchphrase *US*

The term was apparently coined by actor Jason Mewes in Kevin Smith's films of the 1990s.

- Snootchie bootchie nootchies! — Jason Mewes, *Mallrats*, 1995
- "Snootchie bootchies?" Who the fuck talks like that? That is fucking baby talk! — Jason Mewes, *Chasing Amy*, 1997

snooter *noun*

a habitual drug user who ingests drugs by nasal inhalation *UK*

- — Angela Devlin, *Prison Patter*, p. 106, 1996

snoot full *noun*

enough alcohol to make you drunk *US, 1918*

- Does she light them when she gets a snoot full? — Philip Wylie, *Opus 21*, p. 144, 1949
- Pick up your old man. He's got a snoot full and he's spoiling Tony's wedding. — Iceberg Slim (Robert Beck), *Death Wish*, p. 177, 1977

snooty *adjective*

arrogant, unpleasant, supercilious, snobbish *UK, 1919*

- That Purple Gang was a hard lot of guys, so tough they made Capone's playmates look like a kindergarden class, and Detroit's snooty set used to feel it was really living to talk to them hoodlums without getting their ounce-brains blown out. — Mezz Mezzrow, *Really the Blues*, p. 92, 1946
- The Rediker's social campaign is being managed by Leonard MacBain, elegant publicist and society arbiter of New York's plush El Morocco, where the snootiest people on earth gather. — Jack Lait and Lee Mortimer, *Washington Confidential*, p. 139, 1951
- He was fed up with the snooty ones, the smart ones and the washed-up ones. Like his father. — John Burke and Stuart Douglass, *The Boys*, p. 78–79, 1962
- There ain't nobody snootier than an oilman who's had to sell one of his Cadillacs. — Larry McMurtry, *The Last Picture Show*, p. 53, 1966
- "Your snooty pals are gonna miss you." "Tell them I may come down for the polo matches. I'll see." — Elmore Leonard, *Split Images*, p. 72, 1981
- Well, it's not because of her beauty / and her brand new low cut blouse / It's not because she's so snooty / or a fine famed millionaire — ZZ Top, *If I Could Only Flag Her Down*, 1983
- She's a whimsical, tragical beauty / Uptight and little bit snooty. — Beck, *Nitemare Hippy Girl*, 1994
- I really wanted to walk over there and smack his snooty, wanky, tea-drinking face in and just keep smacking[.] — Danny King, *The Burglar Diaries*, p. 149, 2001

snooze *noun*

1 a short sleep; a doze *UK, 1793*

- [A] one-hour nap in the morning and a one- to two-hour snooze in the afternoon. — William and Martha Sears, *The Baby Book*, p. 355, 2003

2 a bore *US*

- — Anna Scotti and Paul Young, *Buzzwords*, p. 99, 1997

snooze *verb*

to sleep; to doze *UK, 1789*

- Violet snoozed on a mat in the bathroom. — Jan Karon, *A New Song*, p. 321, 2000

▸ **snooze hard**

to sleep deeply *US*

- — Connie Eble (Editor), *UNC-CH Campus Slang*, p. 6, Fall 1995

snoozer *noun*

1 a Pullman sleeping carriage on a passenger train *US*

- — J. Herbert Lund, *Herb's Hot Box of Railraod Slang*, p. 88, 1975

2 in a poker game using the joker, the joker *US, 1950*

Perhaps related to the earlier sense of the word as 'a thief'.

- — Thomas L. Clark, *The Dictionary of Gambling and Gaming*, p. 208, 1987

snoozing and snoring; snooze and snoring *adjective*

boring *UK*

Rhyming slang. Sometimes shortened to 'snoozing'.

- — Ray Puxley, *Cockney Rabbit*, 1992

snop *noun*

marijuana *US, 1969*

- Yeah, they got stoned on giggle-weed, zonked on grifa, zapped on yerba, bombed on boo, they were blitzed with snop, warped on twist, gay on hay, free on V. — *Hi Life*, p. 14, 1979
- — Richard A. Spears, *The Slang and Jargon of Drugs and Drink*, p. 466, 1986
- — Mike Haskins, *Drugs*, p. 289, 2003

snorbs *noun*

the female breasts *US*

- — *Current Slang*, p. 10, Fall 1969

snore-off *noun*

1 a sleep; a nap *AUSTRALIA*

- Hughie was just the same to them as he always was, coming home tired and dirty-faced, ready to snap their heads off till he'd got his boots off and had a snore-off on the couch. — Ruth Park, *Poor Man's Orange*, p. 209, 1949
- — Harry Orsman, *A Dictionary of Modern New Zealand Slang*, p. 126, 1999

2 a place to sleep *AUSTRALIA, 1967*

snore off *verb*

to sleep or fall asleep *AUSTRALIA, 1925*

- 'Where were youse this mornin'?' 'Snorin' orf.' — Nino Culotta (John O'Grady), *They're A Weird Mob*, p. 147, 1957

snore sack *noun*

a sleeping bag *US*

- — Lou Shelly, *Hepcats Jive Talk Dictionary*, p. 48, 1945

snore shelf *noun*

a bed; a sleeping compartment in an over-the-road truck *US*

- If I don't hit the snore shelf pretty soon I'm not going to get up in time to make it to the saltmine. — Radio Shack, *CBer's Handy Atlas/Dictionary*, p. 42, 1976

snorker *noun*

1 a sausage *AUSTRALIA, 1941*

2 the penis *AUSTRALIA*
From the previous sense.
- I don't want to see you exercising the wily old snorker[.] — Barry Humphries, *Bazza Pulls It Off!*, 1971

3 a contemptible fool *US*
From the sense as 'penis', thus synonymous with **PRICK**.
- Okay, Malcolm, Bernie, whoever else manages all those like snorkers and droners all over the place[.] — Lester Bangs, *Psychotic Reactions and Carburetor Dung*, p. 242, 1977

4 in poker, a player who berates the other players when he wins a hand *US*
- — George Percy, *The Language of Poker*, p. 84, 1988

snorrer; snorer *noun*

a difficult customer, a scrounger *UK*
Derived from Yiddish *shnorrer* (a beggar).
- — David Powis, *The Signs of Crime*, 1977
- — Patrick O'Shaughnessy, *Market Traders' Slang*, 1979

snort *noun*

1 a drink of an alcoholic beverage *US, 1889*
- With 3,400 precincts in all, there is as yet no trouble digging up a snort. — Jack Lait and Lee Mortimer, *Chicago Confidential*, p. 141, 1950
- This noon, recalling with distaste the nineteen slugs of bourbon he had polished off yesterday, he had promised himself that he would get through one whole day without a snort. — Bernard Wolfe, *The Late Risers*, p. 16, 1954
- "Howdy, hoss," said Opie genially. "Have a snort." He extended a bottle of whisky to Private Roger Litwhiler. — Max Shulman, *Rally Round the Flag, Boys!*, p. 261, 1957
- There's a pint in the glove compartment. Want a snort? — Raymond Chandler, *Playback*, p. 104, 1958
- Bill reached over toward an almost empty bottle of tequilla and said – "Come on Huncke, have a little snort. It'll make you feel great." — Herbert Huncke, *The Evening Sun Turned Crimson*, p. 119, 1980
- There the barman builds him several drinks – snorts and wets are what the Rangers call them. — Ann Barr and Peter York, *The Official Sloane Ranger Handbook*, p. 117, 1982

2 cocaine *US*
- That's good snort, Vin, you got some more. — Edwin Torres, *Carlito's Way*, p. 108, 1975
- He's got everything aboard, even snort. — Edwin Torres, *Q & A*, p. 150, 1977
- The biggest problem was that there was no snort. Nor any other drugs. — Joseph Wambaugh, *The Secrets of Harry Bright*, p. 44, 1985
- Whistler bumped into Al Lister, an old extra who used to run errands for Suzy, like scoring hash or snort[.] — Robert Campbell, *In La-La Land We Trust*, p. 57, 1986

snort *verb*

1 to ingest drugs by nasal inhalation *US, 1951*
- Then he introduced her to the habit of sniffing heroin – "snorting" is the word used by the addicts. — Harry J. Anslinger (US Commissioner of Narcotics), *The Murderers*, p. 178, 1961
- He's putting a thumb over each nostril and snorting like fuckin' mad to drag up any stray powder that's hangin' around. — J.J. Connolly, *Know Your Enemy [britpulp]*, p. 141, 1999

2 to take a measure of alcohol nasally *UK*
- [A]nyone who came to the villa had to snort alcohol, or they wouldn't be welcome. — Wayne Anthony, *Spanish Highs*, p. 115, 1999
- There is some risk to the nasal septum (à la Daniella Westbrook) as there is with shoving anything up your nose, but I don't know of any cases of such damage from snorting spirits — *Sky Magazine*, p. 89, May 2001

snorter *noun*

a tablespoonful of alcoholic spirit (tequila and vodka are popular) taken nasally *UK*
- — *Sky Magazine*, p. 88, May 2001

snortin' Norton *noun*

a Norton motorcyle *US*
Biker (motorcycle) slang.

snort rag *noun*

a piece of cloth holding a powdered drug *US*
- He felt in his pocket, found a snort rag, stuck it to his nose and got a sniff of some coke. — Steve Cannon, *Groove, Bang, and Jive Around*, p. 138, 1969

snot *noun*

1 nasal mucus *UK, 1425*
Originally conventional English and in common usage; considered to be dialect or vulgar since the C19.
- I can put up with shit and snot and every other gross substance I encounter in this line of work. — Barbara Ehrenreich, *Nickel and Dimed*, p. 112, 2001

2 the residue produced by smoking amphetamine *US*
- — US Department of Justice, *Street Terms*, August 1993

3 an arrogant, conceited and flippant person *US, 1941*
- "Why, you lousy little snot," Hobbs burst out, "how many five-gallon cans of oil have you sold on the black market?" — Norman Mailer, *Advertisements for Myself*, p. 129, 1951
- I still don't want to go and see no play, surrounded by a bunch of pink-faced snots, listening to some berk nattering away for hours[.] — John Peter Jones, *Feather Pluckers*, p. 104, 1964
- Anyway, I was a busy lil' snot in them days. — Edwin Torres, *Carlito's Way*, p. 16, 1975

4 a slut *US*
- "Bitch," Joyce said. "Snot." "Fat ass." "Douche bag." Joyce whirled around and stormed out of the building. — Janet Evanovich, *Seven Up*, p. 144, 2001

▸ **in a snot**

annoyed *IRELAND*
- I don't fuckin' believe dis! Yew [you] are in a snot wit me because of whad I'm wearin'? — Donal Ruane, *Tales in a Rearview Mirror*, p. 172, 2003

snot *verb*

to blow nasal mucus from the nostrils *UK*
- Where was the man [...] when the dog-end who snotted on my coat was about? — Andrew Holmes, *Sleb*, p. 100, 2002

snot and tears *noun*

maudlin misery *SOUTH AFRICA, 1969*
Also in Afrikaans *snot en trane*.
- More than twenty years ago, but I still remember it. Snot and tears. About life in jail. And being scared of dying. — Andre Brink, *A Dry White Season*, p. 54, 1979

snot nose *noun*

1 an arrogant person; a snob *UK*
- [B]eing told what to do and where to go by some half-witted little snot nose like you. — John Peter Jones, *Feather Pluckers*, p. 69, 1964
- I can't believe I acted like such a shitty little snotnose. — Lawrence Block, *Chip Harrison Scores Again*, p. 247, 1971
- So don't come bitchin to me bout some snot-nose seventh grader poppin your ass with a wimpy .22! — Jess Mowry, *Way Past Cool*, p. 42, 1992

2 conceit *US*
- I'll tell you something son. If you don't straight up, the world is gonna have a long party knockin' that snot-nose out of you. — Ken Weaver, *Texas Crude*, p. 127, 1984

snot rag *noun*

1 a handkerchief *UK, 1886*
- Let's give you a bit of a mop down with a clean snot-rag! — Barry Humphries, *Bazza Pulls It Off!*, 1971
- "Say, Pogie, man, let me use your snotrag," I said[.] — Bobby Seale, *A Lonely Rage*, p. 62, 1978
- Careful where you put that snot rag. Why? Thanks to "The Hanky Code" you could be asking for man-love without even knowing it. — *Gayness Explained, The FHM Little Book of Bloke*, p. 144, June 2003

2 an insignificant or contemptible person *UK, 1973*
- [A] gleaming white Fender Telecaster, tantalizingly out of reach in the music shop window. "I was a snot-rag 14-year-old kid, and they wouldn't let me try it until I brought my dad." — Annette Carson, *Jeff Beck*, p. 11, 2001

snotsicle *noun*

frozen mucus hanging from the nose *ANTARCTICA, 1997*
- — Bernadette Hince, *The Antarctic Dictionary*, p. 324, 2000

snotter *noun*

a gob of thick nasal mucus and phlegm *UK: SCOTLAND, 1869*
- — William Graham, *The Scots Word Book*, 1977
- [I]t's just natural, automatic, like, to hawk up a big catarrhal snotter. — Niall Griffiths, *Kelly + Victor*, p. 267, 2002

snotterybeak *noun*

a person with a runny nose *UK*
- Wid sumdy gie Snotterybeak a len [loan] ae a hanky? That sniffin's drivin me up the waw. — Michael Munro, *The Patter, Another Blast*, p. 67, 1988

snottie *noun*

the hagfish *NEW ZEALAND*
From its production of slime.
- — Michael Bradstock, *Fishing – A Guide for Kiwi Kids*, p. 23, 1991

snottily *adverb*

conceitedly, arrogantly, aloofly *UK, 1864*

- [H]e has always been holier-than-thou on this issue and three years ago snottily refused to attend an Olympic champions' dinner because other people there took drugs. — *The Guardian*, 24th April 2003

snotty *adjective*

1 conceited, arrogant, aloof *UK, 1870*

- A jury is cold and impartial like they're supposed to be, while some snotty lawyer makes them pour tears as he tells how his client was insane at the moment or had to shoot in self-defense. — Mickey Spillane, *I, The Jury*, p. 6–7, 1947
- [W]hat hurt most was not that his nose kept dripping and that the back of his head felt as if it had been rammed by a pile driver, but that the kids in the poolroom, those snotty little Tigers, were watching him take a beating from a kid[.] — Irving Shulman, *The Amboy Dukes*, p. 57, 1947
- "None of your business," she said. She can be very snotty sometimes. She can be quite snotty. "I suppose you failed in every single subject again," she said – very snotty. — J.D. Salinger, *Catcher in the Rye*, p. 167, 1951
- — Collin Baker et al., *College Undergraduate Slang Study Conducted at Brown University*, p. 200, 1968
- Snotty bitch. — *Saturday Night Fever*, 1977
- This snotty old dear on the next table[.] — Dave Courtney, *Stop the Ride I Want to Get Off*, p. 344, 1999
- The snotty assistant clearly didn't believe a word[.] — Mary Hooper, *(megan)2*, p. 145, 1999
- Which is a wee bit snotty, like, but so fuckin what. — Niall Griffiths, *Kelly + Victor*, p. 285, 2002

2 dirty with nasal mucus *UK, 1570*

While accepted in conventional usage, the root-word **SNOT** (nasal mucus) is considered vulgar.

- When me nose gets snotty / An me cannot feel me botty / I get de feeling it is time fe go. — Benjamin Zephaniah, *The Cold War*, p. 26, 1992

3 used of a drag racing track surface, slippery *US*

- — John Lawlor, *How to Talk Car*, p. 95, 1965

snotty-nosed *adjective*

contemptible, dirty *UK*

- Dirty little teddy boys. Snotty-nosed layabouts, just you bloody well wait. — John Peter Jones, *Feather Pluckers*, p. 16, 1964

snout *noun*

1 tobacco; a cigarette *UK, 1885*

From 'snout' (the nose), mainly prison use. 'The word originates from the days when smoking was prohibited in prison. When smoking, the lag cupped his hand and pretended to rub his nose[.]' (Paul Tempest, *Lag's Lexicon*, 1950)

- "Have you got any snout on you?" asked the screw with a smile. — Frank Norman, *Bang To Rights*, p. 11, 1958
- — Angela Devlin, *Prison Patter*, p. 106, 1996

2 an informer, especially one who seeks a reward for giving information *UK, 1910*

Derives from a conventional 'snout' (the nose) which is poked into other people's business.

- — Peter Laurie, *Scotland Yard*, p. 328, 1970
- If you can turn a villain into a snout, well, that's the crucial part of being a good thief-taker — Jake Arnott, *He Kills Coppers*, p. 15, 2001

3 a grudge against someone *AUSTRALIA, 1919*

- You got a snout on that kid the first day you saw him working. — Ray Lawler, *Summer of the Seventeenth Doll*, p. 36, 1957

snout-baron *noun*

in prison, a trafficker in tobacco *UK*

SNOUT (tobacco) plus **BARON** (a powerful convict whose influence is built on illegal trading).

- [S]o I'll go into the nick [...] and be a snout-baron. — Derek Raymond (Robin Cook), *The Crust on its Uppers*, p. 188, 1962

snoutery *noun*

a tobacco warehouse *UK*

- This particular night they had screwed [robbed] a big wholesale snoutery at Enfield. — Charles Raven, *Underworld Nights*, p. 185, 1956

snow *noun*

1 a powdered drug, especially cocaine but at times heroin *US, 1914*

- Some of us had taken to sniffing snow not long before; we liked it because it makes your mind very alert, you do so high-jive thinking and talk up a breeze. — Mezz Mezzrow, *Really the Blues*, p. 170, 1946
- Like where to pick up a strip of benny or a paper of snow, or anything you want from the outside, if the price is right. — Thurston Scott, *Cure it with Honey*, p. 194, 1951
- You ever hear of dope? Snow? Junk? Big H? Horse? — John D. McDonald, *The Neon Jungle*, p. 61, 1953
- [T]he hemp makes me limp and I'm ready to go when the cat hollers slow. Like I'm not lame in the brain from a snort of cocaine. — Dan Burley, *Diggeth Thou?*, p. 37, 1959
- [I]t took me only a little while to locate a peddler of "snow" – cocaine. — Malcolm X and Alex Haley, *The Autobiography of Malcolm X*, p. 134, 1964
- He said that they called it "snow" then but that the real name of it was heroin. — Claude Brown, *Manchild in the Promised Land*, p. 104, 1965
- When the wind blows and the rain feels cold / With a head full of snow. — Mick Jagger and K. Richards, *Moonlight Mile*, 1971
- "I need front money for the first load of snow," Mona said. — Gerald Petievich, *The Quality of the Informant*, p. 6, 1985

2 silver; silver money *UK, 1925*

- — Paul Tempest, *Lag's Lexicon*, 1950
- — Frank McKenna, *A Glossary of Railwaymen's Talk*, 1970

3 passes for free admission to a performance; audience members who attend a performance using a free pass *US*

- — Don Wilmeth, *The Language of American Popular Entertainment*, p. 249, 1981

▶ **no snow on your shoes**

in the context of a betting operation, trustworthy *US*

From the belief that someone who has been inside the operation long enough for the snow to have melted off his shoes does not have advance information on a bet.

- — David W. Maurer, *Argot of the Racetrack*, p. 44, 1951

snow *verb*

1 to deceive someone; to flirt insincerely *US, 1943*

- You got it wrong, boy. You mean I'm not snowing you, don't you? — Evan Hunter, *The Blackboard Jungle*, p. 160, 1954
- I walked real close to her and talked to her in this kind of soft, sexy voice that I use when I snow girls. — Max Shulman, *I was a Teen-Age Dwarf*, p. 66, 1959
- I said, 'Why, those slippery bastards have conned me, snowed me into holding their bag.' — Ken Kesey, *One Flew Over the Cuckoo's Nest*, p. 182, 1962
- My lawyer, Jacobs, tries to snow me, but I know it was Kleinfeld broke that wiretape. — Edwin Torres, *After Hours*, p. 163, 1979
- Like somebody gettin snowed? — Robert Campbell, *In La-La Land We Trust*, p. 172, 1986

2 in poker, to bluff or fake *US*

- — Irwin Steig, *Common Sense in Poker*, p. 187, 1963

snow and ice *noun*

a price; in gambling, a starting price *UK*

Rhyming slang.

- Look at the snow and ice of it. — Ray Puxley, *Cockney Rabbit*, 1992

snowball *noun*

1 a variety of MDMA, the recreational drug best known as ecstasy *UK*

- [M]e and Roverto score some Snowball 96s which nearly an hour later are doing fuck all. — Kevin Williamson, *Heart of the Bass (Disco Biscuits)*, p. 114, 1996
- — Angela Devlin, *Prison Patter*, p. 107, 1996
- I do find I can hallucinate a bit on E, especially this one called a "snowball"[.] — Macfarlane, Macfarlane and Robson, *The User*, p. 68, 1996
- Snowballs – Rough-edged, almost spherical pill; don't eat the yellow ones. — Gareth Thomas, *This Is Ecstasy*, p. 55, 2002

2 a mixture of cocaine and heroin *UK*

- I continuously stick my arm out for more, for yet another snowball[.] — Lanre Fehintola, *Charlie Says...*, p. 117, 2000
- Sniffer bag – £3.45 ($5) bag of heroin intended for snorting[.] — Robert Ashton, *This Is Heroin*, p. 210, 2002
- — Mike Haskins, *Drugs*, p. 293, 2003

3 a white person *US*

Offensive.

- — *Maledicta*, p. 125, Summer 1980: 'Racial and ethnic slurs: regional awareness and variations'

4 in hot rodding, a whitewall tyre *US*

- — *Good Housekeeping*, p. 143, September 1958: 'Hot-rod terms for teen-age girls'
- — Tom MacPherson, *Dragging and Driving*, p. 142, 1960

▶ **not a snowball's chance in hell; not a snowball's**

not a chance *UK*

- "Not a chance in hell," Robins said, "not a snowball's chance in hell fire!" — Troy Kennedy Martin, *Z Cars*, p. 11, 1962
- — Clement and La Frenais, *A Further Stir of Porridge*, 1977

snowball *verb*

to pass semen to the donor through a kiss *US*

- —Bruce Rodgers, *The Queens' Vernacular*, p. 76, 1972
- VERONICA: That was Snowball. DANTE: Why do you call him that? VERONICA: Sylvan made it up. It's a blow job thing. DANTE: What do you mean? VERONICA: After he gets a blow job, he likes to have the cum spit back into his mouth while kissing.—*Clerks*, 1994
- Dear Jenna, My girlfried wants to snowball me. I'm a little unwise in such areas.—*FHM*, p. 63, June 2003

snowballing; snowdropping *noun*

after oral sex, passing semen to the donor by kissing *US, 1972*
Originally an exclusively homosexual use.

- Snowballing simply means you unload in your girlfriend's mouth, she swishes it about then spits in yours—*FHM*, p. 63, June 2003

snowballs *noun*

1 crack cocaine *US*

- —Bill Valentine, *Gang Intelligence Manual*, p. 75, 1995

2 dice altered for cheating with only the numbers four, five and six on the faces *US*

- —Frank Scoblete, *Guerrilla Gambling*, p. 327, 1993

snowbanker *noun*

a big American car *CANADA*

- The Canadian tradition of calling big American cars "snowbankers" comes from their being hard to control on icy and snowy roads. —Lewis Poteet, *The South Shore Phrase Book*, p. 104, 1999

snowbird *noun*

1 a person from the northern US or Canada who migrates to Florida or elsewhere in the southern US during winter *US, 1979*
Originally applied to men who enlisted in the army just before winter, and then to workers who flocked south in the winter, and then to tourists.

- He was an innocuous, round little man who was jolliest when Florida was crawling with snowbirds.—Carl Hiaasen, *Tourist Season*, p. 29, 1986
- Not much traffic now, huh? The snowbirds've all gone home. I don't know why anybody wants to live up north.—Elmore Leonard, *Maximum Bob*, p. 48, 1991

2 a cocaine user or addict *US, 1914*
Building on **SNOW** (cocaine) and reaching to pun with the more conventional sense of the term 'snowbird'.

- —Lou Shelly, *Hepcats Jive Talk Dictionary*, p. 17, 1945
- My mother sells hops to the snowbirds.—James T. Farrell, *Saturday Night*, p. 38, 1947
- The little guy's a snowbird and he's hopped.—Mickey Spillane, *Kiss Me Deadly*, p. 96, 1952
- She was one of the few snowbirds who thought she was snowing the snowman and the juiceman. She wasn't snowing anybody.—Robert Campbell, *Juice*, p. 23, 1988
- —Angela Devlin, *Prison Patter*, p. 107, 1996

3 cocaine *UK*

- —Nick Constable, *This is Cocaine*, p. 181, 2002

4 a glob of snow that sticks under a fender *CANADA*

- In the north, a snowbird can be a chunk of ice or frozen snow stuck under the car's fender.—Lewis Poteet, 1978
- We ought only to think of snowbirds as Canadians who head south in the winter.—Bill Casselman, *Canadian Words*, p. 67, 1995

snowblind *adjective*

impaired from excessive cocaine use *UK*

- —Tom Hibbert, *Rockspeak!*, p. 145, 1983

snow-bug *noun*

a motor toboggan, predecessor to the snowmobile *CANADA*

- Snowmobile owners are likely to get their fun going on snow-bug hikes in the bush.—*Star Weekly*, p. 14/1, 19th December 1964
- A Skidoo, a Canadian invention, has been called an 'autoboggan' and a 'motor toboggan', as well as 'snow-bug', 'snowmobile', 'skiscooter' —Bill Casselman, *Canadian Words*, p. 21, 1995

snow bunny *noun*

1 a young woman who hangs around ski resorts in conspicious dress *CANADA*

- December used to be a dull month, but that was before our pretty Canadian snow bunnies gave up hibernation and started brightening up the Canadian snow scene.—*Star Weekly*, p. 39/1, 19th December 1964

2 a Royal Marine trained in arctic warfare *UK*
After the white camouflage suiting. Reported by Marine V. Glynn, 1978.

snowcaine *noun*

cocaine, or a related drug such as benzocaine or lidocaine *US*

- —Peter Johnson, *Dictionary of Street Alcohol and Drug Terms*, p. 175, 1993

snow cap *noun*

cocaine combined and smoked with marijuana *US*

- —Steven Daly and Nalthaniel Wice, *alt.culture*, p. 50, 1995

snow coke *noun*

crack cocaine *UK*
A combination of two terms meaning 'cocaine'.

- —Mike Haskins, *Drugs*, p. 282, 2003

snowcone; snowcones *noun*

cocaine *US*

- —US Department of Justice, *Street Terms*, August 1994
- —Mike Haskins, *Drugs*, p. 281, 2003

snowdrop *noun*

a US military police officer *US*
An allusion to the white helmets, gloves, belts and socks.

- —*American Speech*, p. 75, February 1946: 'Some words of war and peace from 1945'

snow-eater *noun*

in Colorado, warm, dry winds that can quickly melt snow *US*

- —Jim Crotty, *How to Talk American*, p. 211, 1997

snowed *adjective*

cocaine-intoxicated *US*

- —Vincent J. Monteleone, *Criminal Slang*, p. 216, 1949

snowed under *adjective*

over-burdened with work *US, 1984*

- I had three different desks in two different offices and was snowed under by my work.—Dale Carnegie, *How to Stop Worrying and Start Living*, p. 251, 1990

snowflake *noun*

1 a white person *UK*
From racial tension situation comedy *Love Thy Neighbour*, 1972–76.

- [He] would call his racist next door neighbour "snowflake" and "honky" after he had been abused as "nig-nog" and "sambo".—Stuart Jeffries, *Mrs Slocombe's Pussy*, p. 130, 2000

2 cocaine *US*
Also used in the plural.

- —Judi Sanders, *Da Bomb*, p. 14, 1997
- The boys' antidote for feeling rough [...] was to inhale South American snowflakes.—Wayne Anthony, *Spanish Highs*, p. 90, 1999

3 a military mail control record *US*

- —Department of the Army, *Staff Officer's Guidebook*, p. 65, 1986

snowheart *noun*

a variety of MDMA, the recreational drug best known as ecstasy *UK*

- —Angela Devlin, *Prison Patter*, p. 107, 1996

snow hole *noun*

among Nova Scotians living on the coast, the part of the sea from which wind and later snow comes *CANADA*

- The wind is in the snow hole [coming in from the sea and bringing snow], or blowing up for a storm. [Conquerall Banks, German].—Helen Creighton, *Bluenose Magic*, p. 250, 1968

snow job *noun*

deception by flattery *US, 1943*

- Where Affia was holding Velda's hand and Billy mist was giving her a snow job[.]—Mickey Spillane, *Kiss Me Deadly*, p. 102, 1952
- —Evan Hunter, *The Blackboard Jungle*, p. ,, 1954
- "Mr. Dady-yay," Miller said, "s'pose we jus' forget that li'l snowjob, okay?"—Evan Hunter, *The Blackboard Jungle*, p. 92, 1954
- I started in to do a snow job on R.G. – just pour on the old con a mile a minute.—Max Shulman, *I was a Teen-Age Dwarf*, p. 66, 1959
- You better be in touch with one of us by this time next week, or you won't be so lucky next time. We'll let you ass rot in here if you give us a snow job on this shit!—Donald Goines, *Crime Partners*, p. 108, 1978
- I'm thinking you know all there is to know about snow jobs.—Robert Campbell, *In La-La Land We Trust*, p. 172, 1986

snowman *noun*

1 a cocaine dealer *US*

- She was one of the few snowbirds who thought she was snowing the snowman and the juiceman.—Robert Campbell, *Juice*, p. 23, 1988

2 a handsome, popular boy *US*
High school usage.
- — *Washington Post*, 23rd April 1961: 'Man, dig this jazz'

snowmen *noun*
LSD *UK*
- — Mike Haskins, *Drugs*, p. 286, 2003

snow queen *noun*
a black homosexual who is attracted to white men *US*
- — Wayne Dynes, *Homolexis*, p. 119, 1985

snow seal *noun*
a combination of cocaine and amphetamines *UK, 1998*
From **SNOW** (cocaine).
- — Mike Haskins, *Drugs*, p. 293, 2003

snow storm *noun*
▸ **caught in a snow storm**
under the influence of cocaine *US*
- — Vincent J. Monteleone, *Criminal Slang*, p. 46, 1949

snow tank *noun*
an older, large car that is reliable in snow driving *US*
The older and more worn out, the more likely that the car will get you to your destination when road conditions make driving difficult. Michigan Upper Peninsula usage.

snow time *noun*
the infatuation stage of a relationship *US*
- — *Time Magazine*, p. 46, 24th August 1959

snowtubing *noun*
a sporting recreation, racing across snow on an inflated inner-tube *US*
- Day and night ice-skating, ski instruction at all levels of skill, horse-drawn sleigh rides, outdoor barbecues, marshmallow roasts, bonfires, outdoor platform tennis, snowtubing (inner tubes provided by the management) and sports training films are on the agenda. — *New York Times*, p. 20 (Section 11WC), 12th January 1986

Snowturkey *noun*
a member of the Canadian Forces Flying Demonstration Team, the 'Snowbirds' *CANADA*
- The term "Snowturkeys" is not a professional criticism. Rather, it results from envy over the hordes of females who seek the acquaintance of individual Snowbirds. — Tom Langeste, *Words on the Wing*, p. 255, 1995

snow white *noun*
cocaine *US*
- — US Department of Justice, *Street Terms*, August 1993
- — Mike Haskins, *Drugs*, p. 281, 2003

Snow Whites *noun*
tights *UK*
Rhyming slang, formed on the fairytale character Snow White.
- — Ray Puxley, *Cockney Rabbit*, 1992

snozzled *adjective*
drunk *US*
- With a mean boat like the one you got, you'll be a menace to public safety. When you get snozzled, it'll be even worse. — James T. Farrell, *Saturday Night*, p. 23, 1947
- — Ramon Adams, *The Language of the Railroader*, p. 142, 1977

s/n ratio *noun*
▹ **see:** SIGNAL-TO-NOISE RATIO

snubby; snubbie *adjective*
a short-barrelled pistol *UK, 1981*
From 'snub-nosed'.
- — John Ayto, *The Oxford Dictionary of Slang*, p. 177, 1998

snuff *noun*
a murder *US*
- I picked him up and he copped to those Griffith Park snuffs. — James Ellroy, *Hollywood Nocturnes*, p. 67, 1994

▸ **up to snuff**
enough, sufficient, good enough *US*
- I hated the kata, but I knew they had to be up to snuff if I wanted to get my belt. — Odie Hawkins, *Lost Angeles*, p. 63, 1994

snuff; snuff out *verb*
to kill someone *UK, 1932*
In C19 slang, 'to die', and then later the transitive 'to kill'.
- "I'll kill the sonofabitch, Floyd; I'll snuff the bastard," Rudy had said. — Clarence Cooper Jr, *The Scene*, p. 171, 1960
- Kenneth "Country" beamer, vice-president of the San Bernadino chapter, had been snuffed by a truck a few days earlier[.] — Hunter S. Thompson, *Hell's Angels*, p. 13, 1966
- When he flashed on that, on the downright outrageousness of that pack of scumbags paying somebody to snuff him, of even insinuating they'd do such a thing, Emmett began to shake with rage. — Emmett Grogan, *Ringolevio*, p. 349, 1972
- What are you guys gonna do, Buff? Snuff a pig? — Oscar Zeta Acosta, *The Revolt of the Cockroach People*, p. 121, 1973
- That guy I snuffed last night ain't going to take the witness stand too soon. — Gerald Petievich, *Money Men*, p. 91, 1981
- Some of the things these fellas want to do, some of the people they want to snuff! — Carl Hiaasen, *Tourist Season*, p. 171, 1986
- They snuffed my best friend, Peaches Supreme. — Seth Morgan, *Homeboy*, p. 278, 1990
- But maybe they could at least snuff that red-assed dog. — Joseph Wambaugh, *Finnegan's Week*, p. 63, 1993
- Forgive me, Father, because I snuffed Loretta Ricci. — Janet Evanovich, *Seven Up*, p. 85, 2001

snuff-dipper *noun*
a prostitute who works at truckstops *US*
- — Lanie Dills, *The Official CB Slanguage Language Dictionary*, p. 65, 1976

snuffer *noun*
1 a film purporting to depict the actual killing of someone, usually a woman *US*
- They made a snuffer of her. I saw the video. — Seth Morgan, *Homeboy*, p. 278, 1990

2 the nose *US*
- — Lou Shelly, *Hepcats Jive Talk Dictionary*, p. 17, 1945

snuff film; snuff flick; snuff movie *noun*
a film purporting to depict the actual killing of someone, usually a woman *US*
- The film described is what is known in the trades as a "snuff film." This is a film which includes an actual death, murder, or execution scene. — *Adam Film Quarterly*, p. 42, April 1976
- Snuff films are those in which the final sexual act is murder. — Stephen Ziplow, *The Film Maker's Guide to Pornography*, p. 16, 1977
- As far as the Los Angeles Police Department knows, there's never been a snuff film actually verified. — Joseph Wambaugh, *The Glitter Dome*, p. 282, 1981
- In a while, the director and crew of the snuff film ran out of tape, story, patience, and positions. — Robert Campbell, *In La-La Land We Trust*, p. 160, 1986
- So now those nice folks are going to read about her in the paper and maybe even see the snuff flick. — Seth Morgan, *Homeboy*, p. 279, 1990
- Yeah, well, she pretends like she wouldn't care less if I starred in a snuff film or went to Disneyland, but really, she loves me. — Joseph Wambaugh, *Fugitive Nights*, p. 26, 1992
- — Angela Devlin, *Prison Patter*, p. 107, 1996

snuff it *verb*
to die *UK, 1885*
An image of a candle being extinguished.
- There's some poor bugger in your waitin' room who's snuffed it. — Barry Humphries, *Bazza Pulls It Off!*, 1971
- If I do snuff it I can con my way into heaven. — Anthony Masters, *Minder*, p. 137, 1984
- Oh, fuck, no. She's snuffed it, in't she? — Colin Butts, *Is Harry on the Boat?*, p. 152, 1997

snuff muff *noun*
a dead woman used for sex *UK*
From **SNUFF** (to kill), in the adjectival sense found in **SNUFF FILM**, etc., and **MUFF** (the vulva; a woman as a sex object).
- Fact is, Jessie, I've met punters that liked 'em dead, oh yeah, snuff muff. It happens, baby, don't think it don't. Necrohowsyourfather. — Ben Elton, *High Society*, p. 314, 2002

snuff-out *noun*
a fast and violent loss of position on a surfboard, usually followed by a sudden trip below the ocean surface *US*
- — Gary Fairmont R. Filosa II, *The Surfer's Almanac*, p. 195, 1977

snuff powder *noun*
adulterated heroin or a white powdered poison used to injure or kill someone using it in the belief it is heroin *US*
Much better known as a **HOTSHOT**.
- How do you think I know which one slid the snuff powder to Flip? — Clarence Cooper Jr, *The Scene*, p. 183, 1960

snuff stick *noun*
a cigarette *NEW ZEALAND*
• Not with a snuff-stick hanging out of their gates [mouths].—Noel Hilliard, *The Power and the Glory*, p. 76, 1978

snuffy *noun*
any low ranking soldier in the US Army or Marines, performing a servile or degrading task *US*
• —Linda Reinberg, *In the Field*, p. 203, 1991

Snuffy Smith *noun*
in trucking, any driver for the Smith Transfer Company *US*
• —Porter Bibb, *CB Bible*, p. 105, 1976

snug *verb*
in horse racing, to rein the horse in to preserve energy for a sprint later in the race *US*
• —David W. Maurer, *Argot of the Racetrack*, p. 58, 1951
• —Thomas L. Clark, *The Dictionary of Gambling and Gaming*, p. 208, 1987

snuggle-bunny *noun*
a girlfriend *UK*
• The broad – Chris's snuggle-bunny.—Douglas Rutherford, *The Creeping Flesh*, p. 141, 1963

snurgle *verb*
to advance with caution; to crawl forward *UK*
• When the Marines [were] sneaking up on an unsuspecting enemy [it] was called "snurgling".—McGowan and Hands, *Don't Cry For Me*, 1983
• —Nigel Foster, *The Making of a Royal Marine Commando*, 1987

snye *noun*
in the Ottawa valley, a side channel bypassing falls or rapids *CANADA*
• Snye, a side-water channel that [sometimes] rejoins a larger river, creating an island and sometimes helping canoeists get around a rapids, is an Englishing of the Quebecois French "chenail," or channel.—Bill Casselman, *Canadian Words*, p. 105, 1995

SO *noun*
used as Internet discussion group shorthand to mean 'significant other' *US*
• —Andy Ihnatko, *Cyberspeak*, p. 177, 1997

so *adjective*
homosexual *UK*
Dating from the late C19, during the 1930s the pronunciation was affected with a lisp.
• Is he so?—Paul Baker, *Polari*, p. 190, 2002

so *adverb*
very, extremely *US*
Attitude and pronunciation separate the slang sense from the standard sense.
• God, I'm so sure.—*Heathers*, 1988
• We're so ready to leave.—*Clueless*, 1995
• I have been six years without one serious relationship, and I am so not bothered by it.—*New York Observer*, 20th May 2002

▸ **so many women/books/etc, so little time**
used as a humorous expression of regret for lost opportunity *US*
So many variations, so little dictionary space.
• So many things to do and so little to do it with.—Jim Thompson, *Savage Night*, p. 55, 1953
• So many social engagements, so little time.—*Raising Arizona*, 1987
• So many women, so little time.—*Austin Powers*, 1997

so
used within a sentence as introduction to an intensifying repetition *UK, 1935*
Tautological. Originally recorded as a 'proletarian colloquialism', there appears to be a widespread usage in Northern Ireland.
• I have a sower [sore, painful] head, so I have.—John Pepper, *Ulster-English Dictionary*, 1981

soak *noun*
a drunk *UK, 1820*
• The names for drunkards and drunkenness in London are many and various – "soaks", "whets", "topers", "piss-heads" and "piss artists"[.]—Peter Ackroyd, *London The Biography*, p. 359, 2000

soak *verb*
to use something as collateral for a loan *US*
• I had a old raggedy pistol and I was going to soak it to him.—Bruce Jackson, *In the Life*, p. 62, 1972

soaked *adjective*
drunk *US, 1737*
First recorded by Benjamin Franklin in 1737.
• —Collin Baker et al., *College Undergraduate Slang Study Conducted at Brown University*, p. 201, 1968
• —Pamela Munro, *U.C.L.A. Slang*, p. 78, 1989
• Again Rocco thought ahead to the possible trial, the defense bombing out his only witness for being soaked on the night of the murder.—Richard Price, *Clockers*, p. 132, 1992

soaker *noun*
1 a surfer who lingers in the water, rarely catching a wave *US*
• —Trevor Cralle, *The Surfin'ary*, p. 118, 1991
2 a pawnshop *CANADA, 1976*
• "Get out ta one a them little soakers on Queen West, stick a shiv against the kike's throat an get em!" "What's a soaker?" "A pawnshop, you fuckin dummy."—Hugh Garner, *The Intruders*, p. 108, 1976
3 an extremely large halibut *US*
• —Jim Crotty, *How to Talk American*, p. 5, 1997

so-and-so *noun*
1 used as a substitute for a person's name that is either forgotten or that is not important to the point being made *UK, 1596*
• So that's what so-and-so looks like without any clothes on, Jesus.—Elmore Leonard, *Gold Coast*, p. 25, 1980
• They would say they were going to do a guy. Or they might say so-and-so got popped.—Elmore Leonard, *Killshot*, p. 74, 1989
2 used as a euphemism for any derogatory form of address *UK, 1943*
• Cheeky so-and-so.—Caroline Aherne and Craig Cash, *The Royle Family*, 1999
• You cunning old so-and-so—Brian McDonald, *Elephant Boys*, p. 145, 2000

soap *noun*
1 a soap opera, either in the literal sense of a radio or television melodramatic series or in the figurative sense *US, 1943*
• —*American Speech*, December 1961
• The stereo won't work and there's nothing on T.V. except soaps and game shows which I hate.—Beatrice Sparks (writing as 'Anonymous'), *Jay's Journal*, p. 65, 1979
• Senora Sarafina Sanchez Bou-Gomez sat on the worn sofa, watching a Spanish soap, knitting a bit, chewing hard chocolate with the ten teeth she had on the top and the fifteen on the bottom.—Odie Hawkins, *The Life and Times of Chester Simmons*, p. 12, 1991
2 the recreational drug GHB *US*
• The drug's street name is GHB, or "soap," or "liquid ecstasy."—*Dallas Morning News*, p. 27A, 20th December 1995
3 ordinary soap used to fill cracks when using explosives to open a safe *US*
• I never let it impair my business judgment or my work withh the soap and soup.—Red Rudensky, *The Gonif*, p. 93, 1970
4 a bribe *US*
• —Helen Dahlskog (Editor), *A Dictionary of Contemporary and Colloquial Usage*, p. 55, 1972
• —Angela Devlin, *Prison Patter*, p. 107, 1996

soap and flannel *noun*
the National Health Service *UK*
Rhyming slang for 'panel', a term that relates to healthcare under the system that preceded the advent of the NHS in 1946.
• Being out of work through ill health is still known as being on the "soap and flannel".—Ray Puxley, *Cockney Rabbit*, 1992

soap and lather *noun*
a father *UK, 1961*
Rhyming slang. Ray Puxley, *Cockney Rabbit*, 1992, notes that this 'makes the pope the "holy soap"'.

soap and water *noun*
a daughter *UK, 1925*
Rhyming slang.
• —Ray Puxley, *Cockney Rabbit*, 1992

soap bar; soap *noun*
a small block of cannabis resin, often heavily adulterated, especially with animal tranquillizers; thus hashish, especially if adulterated *UK*
From the similarity to a conventional bar of soap.
• —Angela Devlin, *Prison Patter*, p. 107, 1996

- Do you have a soap of puff going spare? —Duncan MacLaughlin, *The Filth*, p. 200, 2002
- Moroccan hashish that, upon arrival in England, is diluted with God knows what – cooking oil, animal tranquillizers, and other extremely unhealthy crap. It's called a soap bar. —Brian Preston, *Pot Planet*, p. 125, 2002
- I'll smoke soap bar till I fucking die. —Goldie Looking Chain *Soap Bar*, 2004

soap box *noun*
a Mini car *UK*
Citizens' band radio slang, from the shape and size.
- —Peter Chippindale, *The British CB Book*, p. 161, 1981

soap-box artist *noun*
a skilled public speaker *NEW ZEALAND, 1938*

soapbox derby syndrome *noun*
any rapidly progressing disease or medical condition *US*
The Soap Box Derby is a downhill coasting race sponsored by the Cub Scouts.
- —*Maledicta*, p. 39, 1983: 'More common patient-directed pejoratives used by medical personnel'

soapdogger *noun*
a person who always seems unwashed *UK: SCOTLAND*
From **DOG** (to dodge, to avoid).
- —Michael Munro, *The Complete Patter*, p. 143, 1996

soaper *noun*
▷ **see: SOPOR**

soap opera *noun*
a never-ending radio or televison drama series, designed to attract long-term audience loyalty and emotional involvement *US, 1939*
The original of the genre, broadcast on US radio from 1932, was *The Puddle Family* sponsored by Procter & Gamble, a soap manufacturer; the product giving the entertainment its identity.
- —*American Speech*, April 1945
- —*American Speech*, April 1947
- A flickering television set that pumped out soap-opera inanities. —John King, *White Trash*, p. 73–74, 2001

soapy *noun*
the balance after a day of betting *AUSTRALIA*
Rhyming slang based on Soapy Vallance, a legendary Australian athlete of the 1930s.
- —Ned Wallish, *The Truth Dictionary of Racing Slang*, p. 75, 1989

soapy *adjective*
dirty; in a mess; in need of a wash *UK*
- —Angela Devlin, *Prison Patter*, p. 107, 1996

soapy bubble; soapy *noun*
trouble *UK*
Rhyming slang, first recorded in Glasgow. Later used as Cockney rhyming slang.
- You're gauna [going to] end up in soapy, pal. —Michael Munro, *The Original Patter*, 1985
- —Ray Puxley, *Fresh Rabbit*, 1998

sob *noun*
one pound sterling *UK, 1970*
Probably a mishearing of **sov** (£1).
- [H]ow much you reckon that suite cost then? Few sobs or what?" —Jeremy Cameron, *Brown Bread in Wengen*, p. 160, 1999

SOB *noun*
1 used as a term of abuse: *s*on *o*f a *b*itch *US, 1918*
- What a bunch of frauds – behind that home-spun exterior there lies the cunning of a real S.O.B. —William Bast, *The Myth Makers [Six Granada Plays]*, p. 179, 1958

2 a *s*ober *o*ld *b*astard *US*
A term used with affection in twelve-step recovery programmes such as Alcoholics Anonymous.
- —Christopher Cavanaugh, *AA to Z*, p. 163, 1998

SOB *adjective*
*s*hort *o*f *b*reath; dyspeptic *US*
- —*Maledicta*, p. 34, 1988–1989: 'Medical maledicta from San Francisco'

sobriety coach *noun*
someone who aids or mentors an alcoholic or a drug addict in the maintenance of a drink- or drug-free life *US*
- Actor Tom Arnold, speaking as Brandon [Davis]'s "sobriety coach," told the Post, "This was a nasty thing for Peter Morton to do to him". —*Las Vegas Review-Journal*, 8th February 2002

sob sister *noun*
a soft-hearted, naive person *US, 1912*
- We'd have caught holy hell from all the sob sisters, male and female, in this town if those punks had turned out to be innocent pranksters. —Chester Himes, *The Real Cool Killers*, p. 150, 1959
- He wore his old sap gloves with the lead filled palm and padded knuckles (which a sob sister sergeant had caught him beating up a drunk with and which he had been ordered to get rid of). —Joseph Wambaugh, *The Choirboys*, p. 34, 1975

sob story *noun*
a sentimental narrative that is told to arouse sympathy *UK, 1913*
- I'm not one for machismo but I'm a sucker for a sob story, so I gave prizes to the girliest looking boy dogs in the ring or the dog with the most tragic tale. —*The Guardian*, 19th June 2004

sob-story artist *noun*
a swindler whose method of operating includes a sentimental narrative of misfortune and an appeal to the emotions of the victim *US*
- The sob-story artists were much more annoying pests. —Dev Collans with Stewart Sterling, *I was a House Detective*, p. 97, 1954

sociable *adverb*
in poolroom betting, for a small wager *US*
- When one player says to another "Let's just play sociable," as often as not he means that they should play for only a dollar or two[.] —Ned Polsky, *Hustlers, Beats, and Others*, p. 47, 1967

social *noun*
a government social worker *US*
- —Maria Hinojas, *Crews*, p. 168, 1995: 'Glossary'

▸ **go social**
to stop fighting *US*
- —Hy Lit, *Hy Lit's Unbelievable Dictionary of Hip Words for Groovy People*, p. 19, 1968

Social *noun*
▸ **on the Social**
receiving Social Security or other state benefits *UK*
- —Angela Devlin, *Prison Patter*, p. 83, 1996

▸ **the Social**
the Department of Health and Social Security (DHSS), reformed as the Department of Social Security (DSS) *UK*
- [T]hey wonder why they get done by the social for fraud. —Nick Barlay, *Curvy Lovebox*, p. 85, 1997

social lubricant *noun*
alcohol *US*
- —Connie Eble (Editor), *UNC-CH Campus Slang*, p. 9, March 1986

socials *noun*
alcoholic beverages *UK*
- —*American Speech*, p. 401, Winter 1991: 'Among the new words'

societ *verb*
to associate with someone *BARBADOS*
- —Frank A. Collymore, *Barbadian Dialect*, p. 99, 1965

society high *noun*
cocaine *UK, 1998*
A neat reversal on 'high society' suggesting the social circles that can afford cocaine.
- —Mike Haskins, *Drugs*, p. 281, 2003

sock *noun*
1 a blow, physical or figurative *UK, 1700*
- [A] riveting finish and a sock in the eye for the self-deluding hosts. —*The Guardian*, 25th March 2003

2 a condom *US*
- —Judi Sanders, *Kickin' like Chicken with the Couch Commander*, p. 22, 1992
- I know of some children who have come to see us for condoms and when I ask them they say they are using it because they go out with men who come to pick them up. They call condoms socks, she said. —*Fiji Times*, p. 1, 29th October 1999

▸ **put a sock in it**
to stop talking *UK, 1919*
Usually as an imperative.

- The gods are like us, only more so [...] their passion is far less bridled than ours. They don't know how to put a sock in it, and they see no logic in reason. — *New Statesman*, 23rd March 1997

sock *verb*

1 to hit or thrash someone *UK, 1700*

- "Why should he sock you?" the lawyer asked. "Why shouldn't he sock me? I was butting in his business, wasn't I?" — John M. Murtagh and Sara Harris, *Cast the First Stone*, p. 116, 1957
- She screams and pops the cross in her mouth and clinches her eyes shut like she's about to get socked[.] — Ken Kesey, *One Flew Over the Cuckoo's Nest*, p. 80, 1962
- "Sock both of the bastards in the Hole!" the warden growled[.] — Odie Hawkins, *The Busting Out of an Ordinary Man*, p. 167, 1985
- How about the other place, where you socked the guy? — Elmore Leonard, *Maximum Bob*, p. 10, 1991

2 to place something somewhere; to hide something *US, 1942*

- I don't know why they sock so much dough in coats when they spend nine-tenths of their time in bed. — Jim Thompson, *Bad Boy*, p. 352, 1953

3 (of a male) to have sex *US*

- Dangerously I was was frantic to sock "it" into every young girl weak enough to go for it. — Iceberg Slim (Robert Beck), *Pimp*, p. 31, 1969

▸ sock it to

1 to attack someone, literally or figuratively *US*

- Flatter 'em first. Now sock it to her. — Max Shulman, *The Zebra Derby*, p. 104, 1946

2 to have sex with a woman *US, 1969*

- Jesus, look at the old bull socking it to her, and she just lies there with a grin on her face. — Lawrence Block, *No Score [The Affairs of Chip Harrison Omnibus]*, p. 115, 1970
- We got in bed and as bad as I wanted to sock it to her, I didn't. — A.S. Jackson, *Gentleman Pimp*, p. 150, 1973

3 used for conveying encouragement and support *US, 1960s*

- Go Fidel! Do your thing! Sock it to 'em! — Abbie Hoffman, *Revolution for the Hell of It*, p. 14, 1968

socket *noun*

the vagina *UK*

- Women's genitalia were represented as (potential) containers (e.g., bucket, box, hair goblet), places to put things in (e.g., furry letterbox, disk drive, socket, slot), containers for semen (e.g., gism pot, spunk bin, honey pot), and containers for the penis/sex (e.g., willy warmer, wank shaft, shagbox). — *Journal of Sex Research*, p. 146, 2001

sock hop *noun*

a dance for teenagers *US*

The term was coined on account of the practice of removing your shoes and dancing in your socks. The practice changed but the term did not.

- Jordan High had thrown a sock hop on a warm Friday night in November. The Stylistics had been hired, and everyone around the school had been looking forward to the dance. — Donald Goines, *Inner City Hoodlum*, p. 80, 1975

socking great *adjective*

very large *UK*

- I really like what you've got – socking great dugongs [breasts]. — Henry Sloane, *Sloane's Inside Guide to Sex & Drugs & Rock 'n' Roll*, p. 48, 1985

sock it to me!

surprise me!; liven things up! *US*

Borrowed from the vocabulary of black jazz musicians. Between 1968 and 70 it was Judy Carne's catchphrase in television variety show *Rown & Martin's Laugh In*.

- Sock it to me, mama. — Otis Redding, *Respect*, July 1967
- Sock it to me one time. — Jimi Hendrix, *Wild Thing*, July 1967

socko *adjective*

excellent; outstanding *US, 1938*

- Now, Sid had spotted Biff right off as a socko shitkicker. — Bernard Wolfe, *The Late Risers*, p. 162, 1954
- Myrtle was a sock attraction, although his performances left much to be desired. — Antony James, *America's Homosexual Underground*, p. 136, 1965
- I didn't mind and the deputy said it was a socko idea, so we counted out the money on the hood of the car. — Hunter S. Thompson, *Hell's Angels*, p. 142, 1966

socko-boffo *adjective*

absolutely excellent; in a showbusiness or film context, in a 'knock-'em-dead' style *US*

A combination of **SOCKO** and **BOFFO**, intensifying either element.

- — *Sunday Telegraph*, 23rd August 1981

socks *noun*

a linear amplifier for a citizens' band radio *US*

From the term **FOOTWARMER** (a linear amplifier in a truck).

- — Porter Bibb, *CB Bible*, p. 105, 1976

▸ give socks

to copulate *IRELAND*

- For three days and nights he gave her socks and a reliable source informed me afterwards that it took three vets and a female member of the Knights of Malta to wipe the smile off her face. — Billy Roche, *Tumbling Down*, p. 40, 1984

▸ your socks off

with great effect; with great commitment *UK*

- Brando acts his socks off (and it looks like he's put them in his mouth) playing the head of a mob family. — Dave Courtney, *Dodgy Dave's Little Black Book*, p. 45, 2001
- From there he [Terry Pratchett] went on to Isaac Asimov and Arthur C Clarke, stuff that would "blow [his] socks off", and feed a child's "delight in the strangeness of the universe". — *The Guardian*, 8th November 2002
- He was very angry. He hated it, it wasn't fair, he worked his socks off for years. — *The Guardian*, 1st September 2003

So Co *noun*

Southern Comfort™ whisky *US*

- — Pamela Munro, *U.C.L.A. Slang*, p. 109, 1997

Socrates' pleasure *noun*

anal sex *US*

- If you want "Socrates' Pleasures" (anal sex), and the lady of your choice declines, complaining about rectal fissures, lesions, poor sphincter control, foreign bodies in the anus, or perforated anal walls, and you're still determiined, ask her to recommend someone else who will oblige you. — J.R. Schwartz, *The Official Guide to the Best Cat Houses in Nevada*, p. 18, 1993

Socred *noun*

a member of the Social Credit party *CANADA*

- And there is the nagging knowledge of the Socred's grand Government House in British Columbia. — *Toronto Globe and Mail*, p. 8–9, 15th January 1966

sod *noun*

1 a sodomite; generally used of a male homosexual *UK, c. 1855*

2 a contemptible man *UK, 1818*

An abbreviation of 'sodomite'.

3 a difficult circumstance; an awkward thing *UK, 1936*

From the previous sense.

- And then there was the bus driver who wouldn't take him on board because he didn't have the exact money. He was a right sod[.] — Mahesh Patel, *Baby Father*, 19th August 2003

4 used as a general form of address *UK, 1942*

- Good on yer, Martha, yer old sod! — Elizabeth O'Connor, *Steak for Breakfast*, 1962

5 a person of the stated characteristic, thus: lucky sod, jammy sod, miserable sod, etc *UK, 1931*

- HARRY: Clever sod, aren't you? CARTER: Only comparatively. — Mike Hodges, *Get Carter*, p. 21, 1971
- Put me down, you big soft sod! — Alan Bleasdale, *Boys From the Blackstuff*, 1982
- Your kids would have an easier life than you, jammy [lucky] sods, with "all the opportunities we never had". — Mark Steel, *Reasons to be Cheerful*, p. 3, 2001

sod!

used for dismissing, or registering exasperation with, whatever or whoever is the subject of this injunction *UK, 1904*

- Sod buying rounds, you're struggling to keep yourself pissed. — *The FHM Little Book of Bloke*, p. 98, June 2003

soda *noun*

1 cocaine *US*

Playing on Coke™ as the most popular soda in the US.

- — Peter Johnson, *Dictionary of Street Alcohol and Drug Terms*, p. 176, 1993

2 something easy to do *AUSTRALIA, 1917*

- [W]e figured if Zelmara had been able to defend herself against a General, a whipper-snapper like Chip Monk would be a soda. — Ray Slattery, *Mobbs' Mob*, p. 122, 1966
- Old Nick had nine peaceful days; but on the tenth there was Jack bashing his ear on what a soda the job had been. — Bill Wannan, *Folklore of the Australian Pub*, p. 34, 1972
- This four-wheel drive was a soda – until I got close to the river, which was almost in flood. — Rex Hunt, *Tall Tales – and True*, p. 127, 1994

sod about *verb*

to play the fool; to potter about; to waste time *UK, 1961*

- We've got to win this. Enough's enough. Stop sodding about, let's get out and get a victory. — *The Guardian*, 7th January 2002

soda jerk *noun*

a person, usually a teenaged boy, who works at a counter at a soda fountain, mixing drinks for customers *US, 1910*

An abbreviation of the earlier (1889) 'soda jerker'.

- "Coke ..." Mandon said to the soda jerk. — Horace McCoy, *Kiss Tomorrow Good-bye*, p. 244, 1948
- [T]hey go on looking, fabricating preposterous lies about their big scores, cooling off as dishwashers, soda jerks, waiters[.] — William Burroughs, *Junkie*, p. 20, 1953
- [M]y wage as a soda-jerk had been five dollars for an approximate thirty-hour week. — Jim Thompson, *Bad Boy*, p. 336, 1953
- It was cool inside, and the soda jerk looked like an angel in his clean, white uniform. — Dick Gregory, *Nigger*, p. 66, 1964

sod-all *noun*

nothing, not a thing *UK, 1958*

- But here they are and there's sod all I can do with them. — Ted Lewis, *Jack Carter's Law*, p. 113, 1974
- Basically she does sod-all, won't lift a finger to help[.] — Jenny Eclair, *Camberwell Beauty*, p. 13, 2000

sod buster *noun*

a business that appears to be legitimate but is in fact a front for criminal activity *US*

- — Bill Reilly, *Big Al's Official Guide to Chicagoese*, p. 52, 1982

sodding *adjective*

used as an all-purpose intensifier, generally to negative effect; interchangeable with bloody, fucking, etc *UK, 1912*

- Now sort me soddin' Giro check out before I knock y' into the disability department. — Alan Bleasdale, *Boys From the Blackstuff*, 1982
- [Y]ou still want me to mention your sodding band? Waddya want – blood. — John Robb, *The Nineties*, p. 2, 1999
- "Absolutely," insists the expert, "it's your sodding water tank!" — *FHM*, p. 31, June 2003

sodding Nora!

used as a register of surprise, anger, amazement, etc *UK*

- Oh, come on, Finn, soddin' nora, what's it matter where where 'e fuckin' met im[.] — Trevor Griffiths, *Oi For England*, p. 8, 1982

sodding well *adverb*

used as an intensifier *UK, 1962*

- What could it be? Just-sodding-well-tell-us. I'm a busy man. — *The Scotsman*, 4th March 2005

sod it!

used for registering resignation, exasperation, aggravation, etc *UK, 1953*

- Sod it, I'm not doing this any more. — Macfarlane, Macfarlane and Robson, *The User*, p. 30, 1996
- [S]he'd almost been feeling like saying sod it and going home[.] — John Williams, *Cardiff Dead*, p. 10, 2000

sod-off *adjective*

very obvious *UK*

- I'm a well-known, well-off film maker living in his big sod-off house. — Stuart Brown, *Dangerous Parking*, p. 323, 2000

sod off!

go away! *UK, 1960*

- Bart's line 'Sod off!' and Willie's rejoinder 'I'll give you something to sod off about!' are not acceptable. This phrase refers to sodomy in spite of your set-up about resodding the lawn. — Matt Groening, *The Guardian*, 1st September 2000

Sodom and Gomorrah; sodom *verb*

to borrow; hence, an act of borrowing *UK*

Cockney rhyming slang, which gives rise to the phrase: 'on the sodom'.

- — Ray Puxley, *Fresh Rabbit*, 1998

sod's law *noun*

a cynical 'law' of existence that decrees that 'if something can go wrong it will' and is therefore named or cited as explanation or justification whenever such circumstances conspire *UK, 1970*

- I suppose it's the parliamentary version of "sod's law". The week you really want a chance to question the prime minister in the House of Commons, parliament is in recess. — *The Guardian*, 28th May 2003

sod this for a game of soldiers!; sod that for a game of soldiers!

used as an emphatic dismissal of any activity or notion that you have no wish to subscribe to *UK, 1979*

- No wonder the Moors never conquered this part of Spain; they probably realised they'd have to abseil down waterfalls and thought: Sod that for a game of soldiers. — *The Guardian*, 18th June 2003

sod this for a lark!; sod that for a lark!

used as an emphatic dismissal of any activity or notion that you have no wish to subscribe to *UK*

- Sod this for a lark. We're tired of going to see band after band at the Pyramid stage[.] — *The Guardian*, p. 2, 28th June 2004

sod you!

used for registering antipathy or hostility towards or dismissal of the person(s) stated *UK, 1904*

- I think they were waiting for a fuller explanation than that, but sod 'em. — Danny King, *The Burglar Diaries*, p. 52, 2001
- For we have caught up with you and your grim cynicism shines through with increasing frequency, so sod you all. — *The Guardian*, 8th December 2002

soft *noun*

1 cocaine *US*

- The wiretaps recorded a primer of street slang for powder cocaine: white lady, white fingers, soft, fish scales and sand. — *Orlando Sentinel*, p. B2, 17th August 2002

2 paper money *US*

- — Hyman E. Goldin et al., *Dictionary of American Underworld Lingo*, p. 201, 1950

3 in the usage of telephone swindlers, a cash sale *US*

- — *American Speech*, p. 150–151, May 1959: 'Notes on the cant of the telephone confidence man'

soft *adjective*

1 denotes all recreational drugs that are loosely categorised as less harmful or addictive *UK*

- Soft drugs were the ones you took to make life more fun, to have a happy moment or boost the party – marijuana, amphetamines and coke. — Simon Napier-Bell, *Black Vinyl White Powder*, p. 124, 2001

2 stupid, dull, half-witted; 'soft in the head' *UK, 1775*

- I don't know what he's good for, the soft cunt. — Kevin Sampson, *Outlaws*, p. 4, 2001

3 in blackjack, said of a hand with an ace where the bettor has the option of treating the ace as 1 point or 11 points *US*

- — Jerry L. Patterson, *Blackjack*, p. 19, 1978

softarse *noun*

a person who is easily imposed upon *UK*

- Last port of call will be a nice cuppa in Co-Zee's with old softarse. — Kevin Sampson, *Clubland*, p. 78, 2002

soft-arsed *adjective*

stupid, dull, half-witted *UK*

- Darren Taylor bottled one of the bouncers for some soft-arsed fuckin reason known only to hisself[.] — Niall Griffiths, *Kelly + Victor*, p. 44, 2002

softball *noun*

any barbiturate or central nervous system depressant *US*

- — Donald Wesson and David Smith, *Barbiturates*, p. 122, 1977

soft cock *noun*

a weak-willed or timid person; a wimp *AUSTRALIA*

- Devised by an ex-Grenadier Guard to sort the men from the soft cocks, the kick-arse event has been running for the past 12 years. — *People*, p. 18, 5th July 1999
- The gaol was home to the Special Care Unit or 'the soft cock unit' as it was aptly known. — William Dodson, *The Sharp End*, p. 40, 2001

soft-cock *adjective*

weak; insipid *AUSTRALIA*

- Limp, soft-cock stuff. What he needed was rock-hard riveting data. — Gerald Sweeney, *The Plunge*, p. 102, 1981

soft-cock rock *noun*

rock music that lacks power and aggression *AUSTRALIA*

Blend of **SOFT COCK** and **COCK ROCK**.

- With immortal classics like *Can I Touch You There* and *Said I Loved You But I Lied* he's bound to have the girlies going wild when he comes to town. Nothing like a bit of soft cock rock, is there? — *Beat*, p. 16, 3rd April 1996

soft con *noun*

a confidence swindle accomplished through charm and warmth *US*

• She flashed her magnificent teeth at him. He smiled in return. "I don't need that soft con, Ruby," he said. —Donald Goines, *Black Gangster*, p. 156, 1977

softcore *noun*

sexual material that does not show insertion, penetration, an erect penis, spread labia or ejaculation *US*

• In soft-core you can show people engaged in sex but not what they're doing it with. —Stephen Ziplow, *The Film Maker's Guide to Pornography*, p. 77, 1977

soft cover *noun*

the official government-issued armed forces baseball cap *US*

Marine usage in the Vietnam war.

• —Gregory Clark, *Words of the Vietnam War*, p. 48, 1990

softly-softly *adjective*

describing a circumspect approach to achieve an objective *UK*

An abbreviation of 'softly softly catchee monkey'. Later use is probably influenced by *Softly Softly*, a BBC television police drama series, 1966–76.

• Shhh, softly, softly boys – remember we don't want to wake him up. — *Evening Standard*, 14th September 1959

• [The police] did try everything, from a good old-fashioned clip round the ear to the softly-softly approach. —Dave Courtney, *Stop the Ride I Want to Get Off*, p. 37, 1999

soft-nose *adjective*

easily learned *US*

A term of derision applied to the 'soft' sciences, for example sociology.

• —Robert Kirk Mueller, *Buzzwords*, p. 144, 1974

soft-on *noun*

a penis flaccid from being sexually turned off *AUSTRALIA*

• You mean with a guy? No way man. Instant soft-on. —Harrison Biscuit, *The Search for Savage Henry*, p. 55, 1995

soft one *noun*

in necrophile usage, a corpse that has yet to stiffen with rigor mortis *US*

• — *Maledicta*, p. 180, Summer/Winter 1986–1987: 'Sexual slang: prostitutes, pedophiles, flagellators, transvestites, and necrophiles'

soft option *noun*

an easier or the easiest choice in any given circumstances *UK, 1923*

Often in a disapproving or derogatory tone.

• Stanley [Falkland Islands' capital] is regarded by the islanders who live outside it as a kind of soft option, a place of bright lights, idleness and decadence. — *Sunday Times*, 13th August 1979

• Education is not a soft option, but a tough option to tackle reoffending rates[.] — *The Guardian*, 15th January 2003

soft parts *noun*

in car repair, parts or equipment that can be expected to wear out and can normally be replaced at a car parts shop *US*

• —Lewis Poteet, *Car & Motorcyle Slang*, p. 185, 1992

soft-pedal *verb*

to proceed in a circumspect, less forceful or subdued manner *UK, 1915*

A figurative application of a piano or organ's volume control.

• The best we can do is soft-pedal it, play it down, stick with the book. —Alan Hunter, *Gently Coloured*, 1969

• an explanation of what had happened, including whether the Government had soft-pedalled on its approach to the Saudis— *The Observer*, 28th April 2002

softplay *verb*

in poker, to play less than ruthlessly against a friend *UK*

• —Anthony Holden, *Big Deal*, p. 305, 1990

soft shoes *noun*

sneakers, trainers *BARBADOS*

soft slugger *noun*

a casino cheat who inserts counterfeit currency into a slot machine *US*

• Soft sluggers use copying machines. In the privacy of their office, they can create choice pieces of imitation currency that will fool many bill acceptors. —Charles W. Lund, *Robbing the One-Armed Bandits*, p. 129, 1999

soft-soap *noun*

flattery, especially as an act of deception or manipulation *US, 1830*

• [Y]our soft soap notwithstanding, what you're really interested in doing is destroying his relationship. —Sanchez Heiman, *New Strategic Selling*, p. 302, 1998

soft-soap *verb*

to flatter or deceive someone *UK, 1840*

• [Boxer, Nigel] Benn was not going to be soft-soaped by the promoter he reckoned had wanted him beaten. — *The Observer*, 4th November 2001

soft time *noun*

a relatively short jail sentence, especially one served in an easy-going prison *US*

• —Marlene Freedman, *Alcatraz*, 1983

soft touch; easy touch *noun*

a person who is easily manipulated or parted from a thing of value; a task that is easily done *US, 1940*

• He didn't mention the rest Rufe had chalked up on his slate. Kev was the softest touch around. —Wilda Moxham, *The Apprentice*, p. 34, 1969

• Maybe I was in a vulnerable or sentimental mood. Maybe I'm a soft touch. —Stephen Fry, *Rescuing the Spectacled Bear*, p. 15, 2002

soft walkers *noun*

sneakers, trainers *ANGUILLA*

• —Richard Allsopp, *Dictionary of Caribbean English Usage*, p. 518, 1992

software rot *noun*

in computing, an imaginary condition in which unused software or software features stop working if not used *US*

• — *Coevolution Quarterly*, p. 34, Spring 1981: 'Computer slang'

• —Guy L. Steele et al., *The Hacker's Dictionary*, p. 118, 1983

softy *noun*

1 a flaccid penis *US*

• — *Adult Video News*, p. 51, October 1995

2 an inexperienced and/or unskilled poker player *US*

• —George Percy, *The Language of Poker*, p. 84, 1988

3 in computing, a programming expert who lacks any substantial understanding of computer hardware *US*

• —Eric S. Raymond, *The New Hacker's Dictionary*, p. 328, 1991

soggy *adjective*

drunk *AUSTRALIA*

• As it is you're half soggy before the day begins. —Norman Lindsay, *The Cousin from Fiji*, p. 114, 1945

soggy Sao *noun*

a game in which a group of men simultaneously masturbate onto a biscuit which is then eaten *AUSTRALIA*

From Sao™, the brand of dry cracker.

• Was I shocked! Not half! Naturally, it was the last time I played a round of soggy Sao with him! — *Sydney Morning Herald*, p. 15, 26th June 1992

• Geoffrey...paraded her through the Halls of St Phineas' College for close on two hours, in and out of the Senior Common Room, several bathrooms and a rather limp game of soggy Sao. — *Union Recorder*, p. 35, 16th March 1992

so help me cripes

good lord! *AUSTRALIA*

• So help me cripes, it takes the cake, a blinkin' lot of old women kicking up a stink about absolutely nothing. —Norman Lindsay, *Halfway to Anywhere*, p. 136, 1947

so help us Fort Knox

used with humour as a pledge or oath *US*

From the US television situation comedy *How to Marry a Millionaire* (1958–60), in which three young women seeking rich husbands pledge to help each other, sealing the pledge with 'So help us Fort Knox', referring to the depository of gold held by the US government. Used with referential humour.

SOHF *noun*

a *s*ense *o*f *h*umour *f*ailure on the part of outsiders who fail to appreciate the graceless antics of the user's social set *UK*

Upper-class society use.

• —Ann Barr and Peter York, *The Official Sloane Ranger Handbook*, p. 159, 1982

so I says
used for effect in introducing a humorous statement *US*
Made famous by Sophie Tucker in her onstage banter about her love life with a fictional Ernie.

soixante-neuf *noun*
mutual and simultaneous oral sex *UK, 1888*
A direct translation into French of synonymous **69**; perhaps with euphemistic intention, or to lend sophistication to the act.
- [B]efore the film came smoking out of the projector we had seen episodes of lesbianism, homosexuality, soixante-neuf, and group sex. — Roger Gordon, *Hollywood's Sexual Underground*, p. 29, 1966
- — *Loaded*, p. 26, June 2002

sol *noun*
solitary confinement *US*
- — William K. Bentley and James M. Corbett, *Prison Slang*, p. 12, 1992

SOL *noun*
ill temper *AUSTRALIA, 1951*
Initialism of '*s*hit *o*n *l*iver'.
- I reckon I've got a reason to have a bit of s.o.l., this is my last trip. — W.R. Bennett, *Night Intruder*, p. 109, 1962

solarist *noun*
a single-minded sunbather *UK*
- [The main aim of] the solarists [...] is not actually see anything [while on package tours overseas], but just go and shove themselves down on a bit of beach, get brick red and come home. — *Radio Times*, 27th October 1979

solar-panel on a sex-machine *noun*
a man's bald-spot *UK*
Jocular.
- An executive in the group pats the shiny saucer of whiteness on top of his skull that has become a standing family joke. "I explain to my son – he's fifteen – that this is really a solar panel for my sex machine." An older, balder man sneers. "There's a whole lot of rationalising going on around this table." — Gail Sheehy, *New Passages*, p. 245, 1995

soldi *noun*
a penny *UK*
From Italian *soldi* (money).
- — Paul Baker, *Polari*, p. 190, 2002

soldier *noun*
1 a regular, low-level member of a criminal organisation who can be counted on to follow orders *US, 1963*
- We got the soldiers out covering everybody and even if we lose a few more, we're going to get somebody sooner or later. — Mickey Spillane, *Last Cop Out*, p. 25, 1972
- The bosses are sitting on millions and they say, you no do-a this, you no do-a that – meanwhile they close the books and the soldiers have to drive trucks on the side to live. — Edwin Torres, *Carlito's Way*, p. 41, 1975
- Every time they broke up a mob score or bounced soldiers and workers around, they planned that the Prizzis had once sold their bank to Robert Finlay. — Richard Condon, *Prizzi's Honor*, p. 234, 1982
- The lookout. Just a guy in the ranks, one of the soldiers. But he wouldn't be there unless someone he worked for was upstairs. — Elmore Leonard, *Glitz*, p. 130, 1985
- He ain't one of Cabot's soldiers either. He's gotta be from outta town. — *Reservoir Dogs*, 1992
- Mazilli played cards with the old-timers and their soldiers almost every day. — Richard Price, *Clockers*, p. 381, 1992

2 a male lookout for a criminal operation *US*
- — *American Speech*, p. 97, May 1956: 'Smugglers' argot in the southwest'

3 a bottle of alcohol; a can of beer *US*
- — Lou Shelly, *Hepcats Jive Talk Dictionary*, p. 17, 1945
- Schoons stood up and chucked his can between two trees into the river. "Look at that old soldier go," he mourned. — John Nichols, *The Sterile Cuckoo*, p. 71, 1965

4 a finger of bread or toast *UK*
- He cut his buttered bread into soldiers to dip into the yolk. — Paul Scott, *Staying On*, 1977

soldier ants; soldiers *noun*
under*pants* *UK*
Rhyming slang.
- — Ray Puxley, *Cockney Rabbit*, 1992

soldier on *verb*
to persevere against peril; to continue doggedly in the face of difficulty or hardship *UK, 1954*
- In Atlantic City, New Jersey, where more high winds were expected, organisers of the Miss America pageant soldiered on, hoping the wooden boardwalk on which it is traditionally held would not be damaged. — *The Guardian*, 20th September 2003

soldier's farewell *noun*
any abusive term of dismissal *UK*
- If they give you a soldier's farewell – well, that's life, isn't it. — Merlin Rees MP (recorded in 1977), *Parliamentary Questions*, 21st July 2004

soldier's wash *noun*
a method or act of washing in which cupped hands are used instead of a flannel *UK*
- — Robert Barltrop and Jim Wolveridge, *The Muvver Tongue*, 1980

sold on *adjective*
convinced by, or enthusiastic about, something *US, 1928*
- East [Germany] not sold on values of the west. — *The Guardian*, 3rd October 2000

soles *noun*
shoes *US*
- — Connie Eble (Editor), *UNC-CH Campus Slang*, p. 6, Fall 1995

solicit *verb*
(of a homosexual man) to walk in public dressed in female clothes – not necessarily for the purposes of prostitution *UK*
An ironic adoption of the stricter legal sense.
- — Paul Baker, *Polari*, p. 190, 2002

solid *noun*
1 a trustworthy, dependable person *US*
- Oh man, the guy a solid. She was a firebrand, that one. Markie a solid. — Joel Rose, *Kill Kill Faster Faster*, p. 36, 1997

2 a favour *US*
- — Connie Eble (Editor), *UNC-CH Campus Slang*, March 1973
- Say, you like sick, like you need a fix / Perhaps I can do some solids for you. — Dennis Wepman et al., *The Life*, p. 55, 1976
- GIANT: "Hey, I'm allergic to smoke. Do me a solid." — *Mo' Better Blues*, 1990
- I know that, but I want to do her a solid. — James Ellroy, *Hollywood Nocturnes*, p. 45, 1994
- Come on Steven, hook me up. Do me this solid. — *Kids*, 1995

solid *adjective*
1 very good *US, 1935*
A jazz term that arrived on the scene with 'swing' in 1935.
- The most action a solid Negro singer will give you is a subdued touch of boogie. — Mezz Mezzrow, *Really the Blues*, p. 27, 1946
- "That Monk is a killer." "Solid." — Irving Shulman, *The Amboy Dukes*, p. 117, 1947
- A "solid" driving beat is produced that "sends" the dancers. — William Sansom, *A Public for Jive [The Public's Progress]*, p. 58, 1947
- Or a hipster: "Everything was solid that year." — Jack Kerouac, *Letter to Neal Cassady*, p. 234, 6 October 1950
- My spunk came running back. "How about tonight?" said I. "Solid," said she. — Max Shulman, *The Many Loves of Dobie Gillis*, p. 211, 1951
- "Solid, man!" Peewee laughed and slammed him across the back with the flat of his hand. — Hal Ellson, *The Golden Spike*, p. 18, 1952
- She said she was cool, just a cold. "I'll be solid in a day or so," she cracked. — A.S. Jackson, *Gentleman Pimp*, p. 183, 1973
- "I don't want to attract no attention." "Solid." — Edwin Torres, *Q & A*, p. 148, 1977
- "That's two dry martinis and two orders of shish kebab. Right, gentlemen?" "Solid, pops[.]" — William Burroughs, *Queer*, p. 49, 1985
- ALYSSA: That was the Buffalo Two-Step. HOLDEN: Very solid. — *Chasing Amy*, 1997

2 especially amongst criminals, loyal; staunch *AUSTRALIA, 1950*
- Duvi's solid dad. — Clive Galea, *Slipper*, p. 3, 1988
- But he also developed concepts of loyalty – of keeping 'solid' – that he only lost track of in the latter years of his life. — Donald Catchlove, *Ray Denning My Life and Time*, p. 6, 1994

3 harsh; severe; unreasonable; unfair *AUSTRALIA, 1915*
- 'I got fined fifty quid, Joe twenty-five.' 'Bit solid, wasn't it?' — Frank Hardy, *Power Without Glory*, p. 60, 1950

4 usually of time, continuously, uninterrupted; complete *UK, 1718*
- For almost four years solid I laid around in The Bunk. — Mezz Mezzrow, *Really the Blues*, p. 245, 1946
- [E]ight hours solid kip [sleep][.] — Derek Raymond (Robin Cook), *The Crust on its Uppers*, p. 39, 1962
- Every fucking fucker in the fucking band [Oasis] and crew had been up for two days straight solid doing coke and crystal meths, right up to showtime. — Simon Napier-Bell, *Black Vinyl White Powder*, p. 318, 2001

solids *noun*
in pool, the solid-coloured balls numbered 1 to 7 *US*
- The other man won it, broke the balls wide and ran half the solids before dogging a thin cut into the corner. — Walter Tevis, *The Color of Money*, p. 114, 1984
- — Steve Rushin, *Pool Cool*, p. 28, 1990

solid sender *noun*
a person, particularly a musician, who is especially inspired or inspiring *US, 1946*
From the jive vocabulary into the rock 'n' roll lexicon.
- Oh my Linda, she's a solid sender / know you better surrender[.] — Buddy Holly, *Slippin' and Slidin'*, 1963

solid six *noun*
in Keno, a bet on a block of three numbers, two rows deep *US, 1973*
- — Thomas L. Clark, *The Dictionary of Gambling and Gaming*, p. 209, 1987

solid sweet!
used as strong approval *US*
- — Connie Eble (Editor), *UNC-CH Campus Slang*, p. 5, Spring 1980

solo box *noun*
a pornographic video cover showing photographs of only one performer *US*
Interview with Jim Holliday, 12th June 1977.

Solomon Gundy *noun*
salt herring in marinade *CANADA*
- Solomon Gundy, a Lunenburg favourite, is chopped fillets of salted herring marinated in vinegar, pickling spices, and onions. The name is a Nova Scotian attempt at the German name, "Salmagundi", influenced by the English nursery rhyme Solomon Grundy. — Bill Casselman, *Canadian Food Words*, p. 92–93, 1998

so long
goodbye *US, 1865*
- Now so long Marianne its time that we began / to laugh and cry and cry and laugh about it all again. — Leonard Cohen, *So Long Marianne*, 1968

so long for now, and spaceman's luck to all of you
used as a humorous farewell *US*
A catchphrase television sign-off on *Tom Corbett, Space Cadet* (1950–55), a children's adventure programme. Repeated with referential humour.

solo sack time *noun*
time spent sleeping alone *US*
- — *American Speech*, p. 310, December 1946: 'More Air Force slang'
- — Albert F. Moe, *American Speech*, p. 76–79, February 1963: 'Marine Corps slang'

solve *noun*
a crime that has been solved *US*
- What the fuck do I care if this goes in as a solve or a beat? — Richard Price, *Clockers*, p. 449, 1992

Somali tea *noun*
1 leaves of *catha edulis*, a stimulant also called qat or qaadka *US*
Originating in the Horn of Africa and the Arabian peninsula, legally available in the UK and similar to amphetamine in effect when chewed.
- — Office of National Drug Control Policy, *Drug Facts*, February 2003

2 methcathinone *US*
- — Office of National Drug Control Policy, *Drug Facts*, February 2003

somatomax *noun*
the recreational drug GHB *US*
In Aldous Huxley's *Brave New World*, 1932, 'soma' is the drug of social conditioning.
- The substance [GHB] is sold in Florida health food stores under such brand names as Gamma Oh, GHM, Gamma Hydrate and Somtomax. — *Orlando (Florida) Sentinel*, p. D1, 9th November 1990

sombitch *noun*
▷ see: SUMBITCH

some *adjective*
exceptional, remarkable *US, 1808*
Used in ironic understatement.
- "They have some hopes if they think the Olympics will transform it now," he said. "There are about six murders a week down here because of all the night-clubs." — *The Guardian*, 15th May 2003

some *adverb*
very *US*
- Some good. — Douglas Simonson, *Pidgin to da Max*, 1981
- We would certainly not conclude an overview of [Prince Edward] Island or Maritime English without some attention to "some" as an intensifier: some good, some hot, some terrible. — T. K. Pratt, *The Garden Transformed*, 1982
- Another word scholar, Lewis J. Poteet, describes a scale of goodness: good, some good, right some good, and right some Jesus good. — Harry Bruce, *Down Home*, p. 107, 1988

somebody up there *noun*
God; a higher power *US*
Used in a jocular and secular vein in expressions such as 'somebody up there likes me'.
- Somebody Up There chuckled. — Max Shulman, *Rally Round the Flag, Boys!*, p. 63, 1957

some cunt from Preston *noun*
country and western music *UK*
Rhyming slang.
- That's what we call country and western. Some cunt from Preston, It's rhyming slang, you dickhead. — Shaun Ryder, *Shaun Ryder... in His Own Words*, 1988

some hope!; some hopes!
used as an expression of hopelessness or extreme scepticism *UK, 1940*
- The anti-angling mob are having things all their own way, and I have been told that as a retired angler I should keep my mouth shut. Some hopes. — Frank James, *www.totalseaangler.com*, 30th November 2001

some mothers do 'ave 'em
used of someone who is clumsy, foolish or laughable *UK, 1960*
A slight variation on a saying from Lancashire: 'don't some mother 'ave 'em?'. Widely popularised as the title of a BBC television comedy series, 1974, and still repeating
- Well the way Guy's mum looked at me, she seemed to think he was as big a prat as I did. Some mothers do 'ave 'em. — Dave Courtney, *Stop the Ride I Want to Get Off*, p. 11, 1999

Somerset Maugham; somerset *adjective*
warm *UK*
Rhyming slang, formed from the name of the British author, 1874–1965.
- — Ray Puxley, *Fresh Rabbit*, 1998

something *noun*
a remarkable thing *UK, 1958*
- "It's quite something to face Mrs Thatcher at your door," he [Ken Clarke] said, "breathing fire under the doorway, coming in to threaten you". — *The Guardian*, 22nd August 2001

▸ **do you want to make something out of it?; do you want to make something of it?**
do you want to fight about it?; do you want to argue about it? *US, 1948*
- "Do you want to make something out of it?" he would say, balling up his fists. — Langston Hughes, *Simple's Uncle Sam*, p. 37, 2000

▸ **have something on**
to have information about someone or something *US, 1919*
- ESSID: "Perhaps I know him. Have they charged them?" KHALED: "They're still in prison." ESSID: "That means they had something on them." — *The Guardian*, 26th October 2001

something *adverb*
used for intensifying *UK*
Amends an adjective into an adverb: 'something cruel', 'something horrible', etc.
- — John Peter Jones, *Feather Pluckers*, p. 18, 1964

something chronic *adverb*
constantly; badly, objectionably, severely, unpleasantly *UK, 1916*
- For the rest of the night, he had the mickey ripped out of him something chronic. — *BBC Sport*, 16th November 2000

something else *adjective*
beyond description; unbelievable *US*
- — Hy Lit, *Hy Lit's Unbelievable Dictionary of Hip Words for Groovy People*, p. 36, 1968

something-something *noun*
sex *US*
- — Connie Eble (Editor), *UNC-CH Campus Slang*, p. 9, November 2003

something strange *noun*
sex with someone other than your regular partner *BERMUDA*
• —Peter Smith and Fred M. Barritt, *Bermewjan Vurds*, 1985

sometime *noun*
a person who cannot be relied upon *US*
• —*Maledicta*, p. 265, Summer/Winter 1981: 'By its slang, ye shall know it: the pessimism of prison life'

sometimesy; sometimey *adjective*
moody; unstable; emotionally inconsistent *US*
• —David Claerbaut, *Black Jargon in White America*, p. 80, 1972
• —Kenn "Naz" Young, *Naz's Underground Dictionary*, p. 57, 1973

sometimish *adjective*
insincere; unreliable *BARBADOS*
• —Frank A. Collymore, *Barbadian Dialect*, p. 100, 1965

sommat *noun*
something *UK*
A phonetic distortion.
• [Y]ou're fucking pissing away on an export bonnie [a motorbike] or sommat.—Paul E Willis, *Profane Culture*, p. 15, 1978

son; my son *noun*
used between contemporary, unrelated males as a familiar form of address *UK, 1914*
Occasionally patronising, used in order to establish social ascendancy.
• Step out of the car, son," said one of them [the police] to me. What is this – fucking role reversal? He's young enough to be my son, the cheeky bastard. What happened to "sir"?—Martin King and Martin Knight, *The Naughty Nineties*, p. 120, 1999
• [I]t's unusual in an office job for the filing clerk to sneak up behind you, boot you in the jaw, shout "Kung Fu, my son", and for everyone to burst out laughing.—Mark Steel, *Reasons to be Cheerful*, p. 7, 2001

son-bitch *noun*
used as a slightly jocular form of son of a bitch *US*
• If he does, he doesn't show it, because the dumb son-bitch keeps doin' it and things like that[.]—George V. Higgins, *The Rat on Fire*, p. 28, 1981

song *noun*
▸ **on song**
in good form, especially in a sporting context *UK*
• Any side on song would have given them the runaround early.—*The Observer*, 1st December 1974
• [Golfer, Phil] Mickelson on song with birdies.—*The Sun-Herald (Sydney)*, 25th January 2004

song *verb*
to advertise a delinquent debtor by putting his name and offence in a song *CANADA*
• Otis Purdy [who ran a store] got his bills paid by "songing" his debtors. If they had heard what he sang about them once, he need only begin with "Come all you jolly jokers, listen to my song.—Helen Creighton, *A Life in Folklore*, p. 161, 1975

song and dance *noun*
1 an elaborate performance or presentation of a story, especially in an effort to persuade *US, 1895*
• The way the john parks his vehicle in front of you, and methodically takes off his gloves, and reaches into his pouch for his notebook and practically stretches and yawns and enjoys the scenery before condescends to come over for the full song and dance.—Clancy Sigal, *Going Away*, p. 402, 1961
• Don't I get a sales talk too, you know, your li'l song 'n dance?—Odie Hawkins, *Chicago Hustle*, p. 132, 1977
• I start giving him a song-and-dance, filling him in on the history of how the Church disposed of the cemetery full of good Catholics[.] —Robert Campbell, *The Cat's Meow*, p. 197, 1988

2 a fuss, an outcry *US, 1895*
Something trivial or of little account is 'nothing to make a song and dance about'.
• I can't make a song and dance about the loot I've got[.]—Kevin Sampson, *Outlaws*, p. 109, 2001

3 a strip search *US*
• —John R. Armore and Joseph D. Wolfe, *Dictionary of Desperation*, p. 50, 1976

4 a chance *UK*
Rhyming slang.
• Any song and dance of a sub till the weekend?—Ray Puxley, *Cockney Rabbit*, 1992

song and dancer *noun*
an opportunist *UK: SCOTLAND*
Glasgow rhyming slang for **CHANCER**.
• Ah hear the new boyfriend's a bit of a song and dancer.—Michael Munro, *The Patter, Another Blast*, 1988

songbird *noun*
1 a female singer *UK, 1886*
• At a time when it was hip to be cool and well-tailored, and female singers were still referred to as "songbirds" and "canaries", the Playboy Club became the most popular nightclub in town.—Kathryn Leigh Scott, *The Bunny Years*, p. 58, 1998

2 a police informer *US*
• It was a cheap revenge since I'd have liked to take care of that filthy songbird myself.—Red Rudensky, *The Gonif*, p. 103, 1970
• —Ralph de Sola, *Crime Dictionary*, p. 141, 1982

songplugger *noun*
a person employed to promote a recorded song by any of a variety of means *US, 1923*
• Even though she was married to a songplugger who was extremely jealous, brooding type, did weightlifting for a hobby.—Bernard Wolfe, *The Late Risers*, p. 35, 1954

sonic *noun*
a type of LSD identified by a picture of computer game hero 'Sonic the Hedgehog' *UK*
• —Angela Devlin, *Prison Patter*, p. 107, 1996

sonk *noun*
a foolish, feeble or otherwise objectionable person *AUSTRALIA, 1922*
Back-formation from **SONKY**.
• 'Been a sonk ever since he was a kid,' Jack said to his glass solemnly.—George Johnston, *My Brother Jack*, p. 115, 1964

sonky *adjective*
foolish, silly; feeble *AUSTRALIA, 1917*
• —Norman Lindsay, *Saturdee*, p. 103, 1934
• "You've got to get rid of those sonky bloody cobbers of yours," he said to me one night.—George Johnston, *My Brother Jack*, p. 65, 1964

sonno *noun*
used generally for addressing a *son*, a boy or a man *AUSTRALIA, 1910s*

sonny *noun*
used for addressing a boy or younger man *UK, 1870*
Often patronising.
• Very important tea is, sonny.—Duncan MacLaughlin, *The Filth*, p. 81, 2002

sonny boy; sonny Jim; sunny Jim *noun*
used to address a boy or younger man *UK*
An elaboration of **SONNY**; often patronising.
• VALE: But you did say it. Mr. Drummond and Sergeant major Straw heard you. MILLIGAN: All right, sonny boy, so I said it.—Graeme Kent, *The Queen's Corporal [Six Granada Plays]*, p. 105, 1959
• GEORGE: I don't care. SIMON: And that pose is out too, Sunny Jim. The new thing is to care passionately, and be right wing.—*A Hard Day's Night*, 1964

son of
a successor of something *UK*
A jocular derivation from the imaginative formula used to title some Hollywood film sequels (a fine example: *Son of Paleface*, 1952, in which Bob Hope played the son of the character he portrayed in *The Paleface*, 1948).
• [T]he camera team dedicated to the production of yet another Son-of-Woodstock[.]—Alex Stuart, *The Bikers*, 1971
• Cheaper seats likely if "Son of Concorde" flies.—*Daily Telegraph*, 29th March 1979
• President Bush's son of star wars has neutralised its first targets in Yorkshire even before the British government has given the formal go-ahead[.]—*The Guardian*, 19th December 2002

sonofabitch; sonuvabitch *noun*
a fellow *US, 1951*
• I'm a handsome sonofabitch / I'm gonna get a good job 'n' be real rich[.]—Frank Zappa, *Bobby Brown Goes Down*, 1979

son of a bitch *noun*

1 a despicable person *UK, 1605*

- Hunt said an obviously drunken George W. approached his family's table in the restaurant and began loudly cursing at him in front of his young child. "You fucking son of a bitch." —J. H. Hatfield, *Fortunate Son*, p. 74, 2001
- "You're trying to ruin me," Rover charged. "My reputation. You son of a bitch." —James Moore, *Bush's Brain*, p. 19, 2003
- Bill O'Reilly, who likes to torment the guests on his top-rated Fox News show, The O'Reilly Factor, rebutting their arguments with sophisticated epithets such as "pinhead" and "vicious son of a bitch." —*Sunday Tribune*, p. 1, 7th September 2003
- [Joseph] Wilson called Cheney a "lying son of a bitch" during a campaign appearance for John Kerry last December. —*National Review*, 9th August 2004

2 used in extreme comparisons *US, 1953*

- We caught a train the next day to Idabelle, Oklahoma. It was hotter than a son of a bitch there. —David Honeyboy Edwards, *The World Don't Owe Me Nothing*, p. 141, 1997

son of a bitch!

used as a mild expletive *US, 1953*

- You like Mickey the Mouse? (little girl kicks her) Ohhh – son-of-a-bitch! —*Paper Moon*, 1973
- Holstein glanced at Pike's shoulder tats, then his face. "Sonofabitch. You're Joe Pike." —Robert Crais, *L.A. Requiem*, p. 38, 1999

son-of-a-bitching *adjective*

used as a somewhat profane intensifier *US, 1930*

- Yeah, perhaps we should get on with the sonofabitchin' meeting at that. —Ken Kesey, *One Flew Over the Cuckoo's Nest*, p. 115, 1962
- It's two-thirty in the son-of-a-bitching morning. —Tom Robbins, *Jitterbug Perfume*, p. 245, 1984
- Best son-of-a-bitching division on God's green earth. —Colin L. Powell, *My American Journey*, p. 204, 1995

son-of-a-bitch with slides *noun*

an expert guest speaker at a medical meeting *US*

- —*Maledicta*, p. 118, 1984–1985: 'Milwaukee medical maledicta'

son of a gun *noun*

a fellow *UK, 1708*

Originally, 'a soldier's bastard', now mildly disparaging or pejorative. Occasionally used as an exclamation of surprise.

- What made you think I wanted to keep you around / While I work my ass off while you just lounge around, huh? / You slump, bum, son of a gun, / And uh, How much you worth? I think negative, done. —Missy Elliott, *Son of a Gun (Remix)*, 2001

sook; sooky; sookie *noun*

a person easily brought to tears; a crybaby *AUSTRALIA, 1941*

- Mummy, don't be a sooky baby, I love you. —Bluey *Bush Contractors*, p. 5, 1975
- Anyway what am I getting all morbid about? I'm being a silly old sookie. —Barry Humphries, *A Nice Night's Entertainment*, p. 143, 1981

sooky *adjective*

apt to burst into tears; weak; timid or cowardly *AUSTRALIA, 1901*

From British dialect (Clydesdale) *sooky* meaning 'effeminate', recorded in the *English Dialect Dictionary* under the word 'soaky'.

sool *verb*

1 to incite someone to attack or go after someone; to spur someone on *AUSTRALIA, 1924*

- Behind the scenes the family, who probably sooled the cops onto me in desperation, have organized things well. —Kevin Mackey, *The Cure*, p. 45, 1970
- And as the leader tired, Button Hole's jockey sooled him to the lead. 'Come on, come on,' the tight-lipped boy urged, 'get moving'. —Clive Galea, *Slipper!*, p. 7, 1988

2 to set a dog onto someone *AUSTRALIA, 1889*

- I sooled the dog on them, but they only climbed trees and laughed from there. —Ion L. Idriess, *Over the Range*, p. 242, 1947

3 (especially of a dog) to attack someone *AUSTRALIA, 1849*

- Midst roars of derisive laughter they jeered at him and shouted to the dog, 'Go on, Louis! Go on, boy! Sool him, Louis! Go on, Louis! Bite the bloody mug copper!' —Vince Kelly, *The Bogeyman*, p. 25, 1956

sooner *noun*

1 a person or thing which fails to perform *AUSTRALIA, 1892*

Because 'they would *sooner* do nothing than something'.

- This was an old sooner of an engine. She'd had it. —Patsy Adam-Smith, *Folklore of the Australian Railwaymen*, p. 117, 1969

2 a mixed-breed dog *BARBADOS*

Because, Collymore writes, 'He'd sooner bark than bite'.

- —Frank A. Collymore, *Barbadian Dialect*, p. 100, 1965

sooty; soot *noun*

a black person *US, 1838*

A derogatory term.

- —Martine Cole, *Maura's Game*, 2002

sooty *noun*

1 a Maori *NEW ZEALAND, 1989*

Offensive.

- —Harry Orsman, *A Dictionary of Modern New Zealand Slang*, p. 127, 1999

2 an engine tradesman in the Royal Air Force *UK*

In Royal Air Force use, 2002.

sooty tunes *noun*

reggae music *UK*

- —Tom Hibbert, *Rockspeak!*, p. 145, 1983

SOP *noun*

in motor racing, *s*eat *o*f the *p*ants *US*

- [A]s in a SOP rally, where instruments can't be used to check time or distance[.] —John Edwards, *Auto Dictionary*, p. 156, 1993

sope *noun*

a tablet of the recreational drug methaqualone, best known as Quaaludes™ *US*

- By 1972 it was one of the most popular drugs of abuse in the United States and was known as love drug, heroin for lovers, Dr. Jekyll and Mr. Hyde, sopors, sopes, ludes, mandrakes and quacks. —Marilyn Carroll and Gary Gallo, *Methaqualone*, p. 18, 1985

soph *noun*

a second year student in high school or college *US, 1778*

An abbreviation of 'sophomore'.

- "He was the only soph on the varsity team, too," Sandy said. —Evan Hunter, *Last Summer*, p. 148, 1968

Sophie *noun*

a girlfriend *US*

Teen slang.

- —*Newsweek*, p. 28, 8th October 1951

sophisticated lady *noun*

cocaine *US*

- —Edith A. Folb, *runnin' down some lines*, p. 255, 1980

sop joint *noun*

a Turkish bath *US*

- He decided to try the sop joint – the bathhouse and masseur's salon on Howard Street[.] —Nathan Heard, *Howard Street*, p. 66, 1968

sopor; soper; soaper *noun*

a tablet of the recreational drug methaqualone, best known as Quaaludes™ *US*

From a brand name, ultimately from 'soporific'.

- —Kenn "Naz" Young, *Naz's Underground Dictionary*, p. 57, 1973
- "Sopors" are both a powerful aphrodisiac and a strong sleep inducer. —Jay Saporita, *Pourin' It All Out*, p. 61, 1980
- By 1972 it was one of the most popular drugs of abuse in the United States and was known as love drug, heroin for lovers, Dr. Jekyll and Mr. Hyde, sopors, sopes, ludes, mandrakes and quacks. —Marilyn Carroll and Gary Gallo, *Methaqualone*, p. 18, 1985
- —Mike Haskins, *Drugs*, p. 283, 2003

soppings *noun*

gravy or sauce *US*

From the act of sopping up with a piece of bread. Southern US.

soppy *adjective*

foolishly sentimental; naive *UK, 1918*

A play on 'sopping wet' (excessively sentimental).

- [W]e meets Henry, who's looking very cheerful, with a soppy smile all over his face. —John Peter Jones, *Feather Pluckers*, p. 27, 1964
- some soppy New-Age hippie type, ten years younger, with a pierced eyebrow —Jenny Eclair, *Camberwell Beauty*, p. 61, 2000
- Ah, it's that new judy. Soppy get's in love. —Niall Griffiths, *Kelly + Victor*, p. 45, 2002

soppy date *noun*

a fool; someone who is foolishly sentimental *UK, 1959*

- I was presented to the Governor, Lord Oxford and Asquith, who looks a soppy date if ever I saw one. —Noel Coward, 24th October 1965

soppy ha'p'orth; soppy 'a'p'orth; soppy apeth *noun*
a fool; someone who is foolishly sentimental *UK, 1984*
An elaboration of **HA'P'ORTH**, and a variation of **SOPPY DATE**; certainly in parental use during the 1950s.

sore *adjective*
angry; bitter; disappointed; disgruntled *UK, 1694*
- You were sore anyway 'cause you didn't want to talk to that grand jury. — Elmore Leonard, *Pronto*, p. 49, 1993

sore as a boil *adjective*
extremely upset *AUSTRALIA, 1955*
- 'She's as sore as a boil,' Joes said, complacently folding his letter away. 'But it'll wear off.' — Kylie Tennant, *The Honey Flow*, p. 45, 1956
- — Ward McNally, *Supper at Happy Harry's*, p. 112, 1982

sore bitch *noun*
a member of a college sorority *US*
- — Mary Swift, *Campus Slang (University of Texas)*, 1968

sore-neck *noun*
the sense of resentment arising from not being invited to a social event *NORFOLK ISLAND*
- — Beryl Nobbs Palmer, *A Dictionary of Norfolk Words and Usages*, p. 41, 1992

sore thumb *verb*
the epitome of something that is patently obvious or conspicuous *US, 1936*
- But people hate strangers on the set, they stand out like a sore thumb don't they? — *The Guardian*, 5th August 1999
- From an appraiser's perspective, the home already sticks out like a financial sore thumb. — Eric Tyson and Ray Brown, *Home Buying for Dummies*, p. 140, 2001
- [Y]ou aint gonna get yourselves far with a boat [face] like that. It's a sore thumb, pal. A sore thumb. — Mark Powell, *Snap*, p. 54, 2001

sorority *noun*
1 male homosexuals collectively as a group *US*
- — *Maledicta*, p. 225, 1979: 'Kinks and queens: Linguistic and cultural aspects of the terminology for gays'

2 a woman's prison *US*
- — Vincent J. Monteleone, *Criminal Slang*, p. 218, 1949

3 a poker game or tournament limited to female players *US*
- — John Vorhaus, *The Big Book of Poker Slang*, p. 34, 1996

Sorority Sal *noun*
a stereotypical sorority member who looks, dresses, talks and lives the part *US*
- — *American Speech*, p. 154, May 1959: 'Gator (University of Florida) slang'

sorority sauce *noun*
ketchup *US*
- — *Maledicta*, p. 284, 1984–1985: 'Food names'

sorostitute *noun*
a member of a college sorority *US*
Derisive, suggesting sexual promiscuity.
- I looked at myself in the mirror once I sobered up and realized that continuing to pledge would end in me becoming a drunken sorostitute. — *Pitt News (University of Pittsburgh)*, 3rd June 1998
- — Connie Eble (Editor), *UNC-CH Campus Slang*, p. 9, Spring 2003

sorrowful tale *noun*
a sentence of three months' imprisonment *UK, 1859*
Rhyming slang for '(three months in) jail'.
- — Angela Devlin, *Prison Patter*, p. 107, 1996

sorry about that
used as a jaded response to something bad that has just happened, especially when caused by the speaker *US*
A keystone of military vernacular during the conflict in Vietnam.
- — *Army Times*, p. 10, 8th December 1965
- — Carl Fleischhauer, *A Glossary of Army Slang*, p. 17, 1968

sorry and sad; sorry *noun*
a father *UK*
Rhyming slang for 'dad'.
- — Ray Puxley, *Fresh Rabbit*, 1998

sorry and sad; sorry *adjective*
bad *UK*
Rhyming slang.
- — Julian Franklyn, *A Dictionary of Rhyming Slang*, 1960
- — Ray Puxley, *Cockney Rabbit*, 1992

- For as many years as anyone can remember, and until finally closed for restoration last June, the Coliseum has been in a sorry state. — *The Guardian*, 2nd February 2004

sorry-ass *adjective*
pathetic; despicable *US*
- She transformed my sorry-ass coochi snorcher and raised it up into a kind of heaven. — Eve Ensler, *The Vagina Monologues*, p. 82, 1998
- If he's alive I get to kick some sorry-ass butt, and if he's dead ... I'm outta there. — Janet Evanovich, *Seven Up*, p. 6, 2001

sort *noun*
1 in combination with an adjective (usually *good* or *bad*), a person of whatever character is indicated *UK, 1869*
- He seemed a good sort: gregarious, stood his round, handsome, no prison record, au fait with the back catalogue of Girls Aloud, but definitely straight[.] — *The Guardian*, 24th January 2004

2 a woman; a companion of the opposite sex *AUSTRALIA, 1933*
- [L]ook at that sort down the front there she aint arf got some top uns[.] — Frank Norman, *Bang To Rights*, p. 144, 1958
- Jimmy Pursey telling some sort he was breaking out of borstal to see her[.] — John King, *Human Punk*, p. 136, 2000
- — Dave Courtney, *Dodgy Dave's Little Black Book*, p. 9, 2001

3 an attractive woman *AUSTRALIA, 1933*
Without a distinguishing epithet this word equates with **GOOD SORT**.
- And if you pick up a sort – don't. If she lets you pick her up it means the Yanks don't want her. — Eric Lambert, *The Veterans*, p. 17, 1954
- What happened to that little sort on the jetty this morning? — John Wynnum, *Jiggin' in the Riggin'*, p. 35, 1965

4 a woman considered in terms of sexual attraction *AUSTRALIA, 1948*
Concentrating on the physical aspect of a person, as opposed to their character. An attractive woman is described as a 'beaut sort', 'great sort', 'grouse sort', 'not a bad sort', 'terrific sort,' etc. An ugly woman can be described as a 'rough sort', 'drack sort', 'awful sort', etc.
- 'It's a wonder she isn't in the movies, a beautiful sort like her.' — Ray Slattery, *Mobb's Mob*, p. 73, 1966
- [P]eople from overseas are devastated, they can't believe that you can see all those superb sorts with nothing on. — Sandra Jobson, *Blokes*, p. 95, 1984

sort *verb*
1 to have sex with someone; to satisfy someone's sexual requirements *UK*
- If Nina Perkins-West is getting sorted then it's not her fella that's doing the honours [...] no way in the world is he sorting Nina. — Kevin Sampson, *Outlaws*, p. 110, 2001

2 to provide someone with drugs *UK*
- And then the guy in the bandanna asked if anyone needed sorting and Harry said yes. — James Hawes, *Dead Long Enough*, p. 150, 2000

3 to beat up a fellow prisoner *UK*
- — Angela Devlin, *Prison Patter*, p. 107, 1996

sorta *adjective*
in a way; to some extent; somehow; one might say *US*
'Sort of' lazily pronounced.
- Well, I was there with my daughter and her husband and I seen you with a laday got sorta red hair. — John Kennedy Tol, *A Confederacy of Dunces*, p. 92, 1980
- [S]orta glam-rock, sorta heavy-metal, sorta post-punk[.] — Barney Hoskyns, *Waiting For The Sun*, p. 328, 1996

sorted *adjective*
provisioned with sufficient drugs *UK*
- — Angela Devlin, *Prison Patter*, p. 107, 1996
- Round at Becca's, well sorted. Her brothers dealing so we can always get hold of something tasty. — Cath Staincliffe, *Trainers*, p. 57, 1999

sort out *verb*
to use violence to resolve a difference with someone *UK, 1937*
- — Ned Wallish, *The Truth Dictionary of Racing Slang*, p. 76, 1989
- So Fletcher says to Christine, "Do you want him sorted out or what?" — Lanre Fehintola, *Charlie Says...*, p. 73, 2000

SOS *noun*
1 the *s*ame *o*ld *s*tuff *US*
- — *American Speech*, p. 272, December 1963: 'American Indian student slang'

2 a *s*omewhat *o*lder *s*tudent *US*
Used by college students to describe, usually unkindly, students in their late twenties or older.

SOS *adjective*

unable to learn; *s*tuck *o*n *s*tupid *US*

- — *Los Angeles Times*, p. B8, 19th December 1994

SOS

between schoolchildren, used as advice that a slip or petticoat can be seen below the hem of a skirt *UK, 1979*

An initialism of 'slip on show', playing on the emergency code 'save our souls'.

sosh *noun*

1 a member of upper-class society *US*

- Like the adults, they developed their own social hierarchy, carving up the town into a variety of cliques: greasers, soshes, basies, and those who feel somewhere in between. — Kim Rich, *Johnny's Girl*, p. 154, 1993

2 a student whose emphasis is on social activities *US*

- — Collin Baker et al., *College Undergraduate Slang Study Conducted at Brown University*, p. 201, 1968
- He wasn't a sosh and he wasn't an athlete and he wasn't a bad ass. — James Ellroy, *Blood on the Moon*, p. 237, 1984

soshe; the soshe *noun*

the Social Security, a UK government agency responsible for welfare payments; the welfare (sickness, old-age, unemployment, etc) payments given by the UK government *UK*

- [W]e know the Minister for Social Security is down there somewhere and we wanted to get away before he takes our dabs [fingerprints] and rats [informs] to the soshe. — Kevin Sampson, *Powder*, p. 28, 1999

soshing *noun*

manipulating someone with criminal intent *US*

Derived from social-engineering.

- Subverting electronic protection was another matter altogether. It required inside help or a skill at soshing – short for social engineering, meaning the con at the front desk or the finesse moves with the housekeeper. — Michael Connelly, *Void Moon*, p. 49, 2000

so-so *adjective*

mediocre *UK, 1570*

- I walked to the car and wondered where in ego hell a skinny black girl who sang funky blues with a so-so voice figured to become a star[.] — Iceberg Slim (Robert Beck), *The Naked Soul of Iceberg Slim*, p. 79, 1971

soss; sossy *noun*

the penis *NEW ZEALAND*

From an abbreviation of 'sausage'.

- — David McGill, *David McGill's Complete Kiwi Slang Dictionary*, p. 117, 1998

sosso *noun*

a sausage *AUSTRALIA*

- Bob made it pretty clear that he was getting what he called "magic sosso's" from Sammy Trimble, and these were apparently sausages that Sam had had about the butchery for weeks and couldn't move. — Roy Slaven (John Doyle), *Five South Coast Seasons*, p. 114, 1992
- — John Blackman, *Best Of Aussie Slang*, p. 180, 1995

sosso roll *noun*

a sausage roll *AUSTRALIA*

- My friend chose a sosso roll which, at sixty cents each, with dead horse [sauce], I thought a bit steep. — Barry Dickins, *What the Dickins*, p. 9, 1985

sot *noun*

an alcoholic dulled by drinking *UK, 1592*

- Ill-matched sots for parents. — Edwin Torres, *Q & A*, p. 194, 1977
- Then Swaggart, crazed by hubris, tried to take out yet another of his rivals – Preacher Gorman from New Orleans, by calling him a sot, a pervert and a dangerous child molester who couldn't help himself. — Hunter S. Thompson, *Generation of Swine*, p. 21, 22nd February 1988

so there!

used at the end of an argumentative or threatening proposition as the final stress *UK*

Abbreviates 'so there you have it', 'so there you are'; often childish.

- HAICH: But you'd be the one who was hurt. SCOTTY: So there. — Alan Bleasdale, *Boys From the Blackstuff*, 1982
- "Yeah," I say, and am tempted to add a "so there", but that would be immature. — Danny King, *The Burglar Diaries*, p. 103, 2001

so? throw party!

used for dismissing the importance of what has just been said *US*

Hawaiian youth usage.

- "Dahlene! I made cheerleadah!" "So? T'row pahty!" — Douglas Simonson, *Pidgin to da Max Hana Hou*, 1982

soul *noun*

the essence of black culture *US*

- "Many, what can anybody see in a gray chick, when colored chicks are so fine; they got so much soul." This was the coming of the "soul" thing too. — Claude Brown, *Manchild in the Promised Land*, p. 172, 1965

soul *adjective*

pertaining to the essence of black culture *US, 1946*

- — *Current Slang*, p. 5, Fall 1966
- Soul. Most times used as an adjective – in conjunction with such activities as eating, politics, music or social exchanges. — Sidney Bernard, *This Way to the Apocalypse*, p. 57, 1968
- The use of "soul" in black parlance drives in this same direction, toward a sense of ethnic unity based on some innate, irrational sense of community, brotherhood. — Roger Abrahams, *Positively Black*, p. 149, 1970
- The AAA gave "Soul Parties." Everyone gretting with the new handshake, doing African dances that looked like overexaggerated gyrations. — Bobby Seale, *A Lonely Rage*, p. 164, 1978

Soul Alley; Soul City; Soulsville *noun*

an area in Saigon with bars and brothels patronised largely by black US soldiers *US*

- — Linda Reinberg, *In the Field*, p. 204, 1991

soulboy *noun*

a member of a mid-1970s youth fashion and music subculture *UK*

- [I]t was soulboys sorting us out that night[.] — John King, *Human Punk*, p. 126, 2000

soul brother *noun*

a black man *US, 1970*

- A certain Soul Brother passing by took out his heat and shot both of them bastards. — Babs Gonzales, *Movin' On Down De Line*, p. 54, 1975

soul-case *noun*

heart and soul *AUSTRALIA, 1901*

- Nice time for *him* to be going gay, I must say, after old man Shadlet keeping him under the thumb for years and that sister Elvira bullying the soul-case out of him ever since. — Norman Lindsay, *The Cousin from Fiji*, p. 216, 1945

soul food *noun*

food associated with southern black culture *US, 1964*

- The emphasis on Soul Food is counter-revolutionary black bourgeois ideology. — Eldridge Cleaver, *Soul on Ice*, p. 29, 1968
- — Clarence Major, *Dictionary of Afro-American Slang*, p. 107, 1970
- Vogue was already preparing a column entitled "Soul Food." — Tom Wolfe, *Radical Chic & Mau-Mauing the Flak Catchers*, p. 31, 1970
- In most European cities there is one swinging pad where there's a piano, records, etc. and good home soul food. — Babs Gonzales, *Movin' On Down De Line*, p. 106, 1975
- We don't even have our own food. Soul food is not black food. It's just some nasty shit they fed to the slaves. You think a ham hock tasted good the first time the white man shoved it in our faces? No. — Chris Rock, *Rock This!*, p. 13, 1997

soulie *noun*

a member of a mid-1970s youth subculture identified by its dedication to soul music; a soulboy or a soulgirl *UK*

- — Sarah Callard and Will Hoon, *Surfers Soulies Skinheads & Skaters*, 1996

soul kiss *noun*

a sustained, open-mouthed kiss *US, 1948*

- Lonely librarians unite in soul kiss of halitosis. — William S. Burroughs, *Naked Lunch*, p. 189, 1959
- They looked at a Roy Lichtenstein blowup of a love-comic panel showing a young blood couple with their lips parted in the moment before a profound, tongue-probing, post-teen, American soul kiss. — Tom Wolfe, *The Painted Word*, p. 72, 1975
- He gave her a long, lingering soul kiss. "Wow!" she said, backing off and gasping for breath. — Jackie Collins, *Dangerous Kiss*, p. 202, 1999

soul kiss *verb*

to give someone a deep and intimate kiss, usually involving tongue or tongues *US*

- — J.D. Salinger, *Catcher in the Rye*, p. 127, 1951

soul sister *noun*

a black woman *US*

- I've also noticed that most of our soul sisters, they marry whitey. — Babs Gonzales, *Movin' On Down De Line*, p. 37, 1975

soulville *noun*

a part of a city inhabited largely by black people *US*

- He hired me to gig for him after I closed in soulville so we just moved downtown to whitey-ville for six more weeks. — Babs Gonzales, *Movin' On Down De Line*, p. 33, 1975

sound *noun*

1 a style of speech, including vocabulary, syntax and attitude *US*

- Naturally, the trigger gang of San Francisco talks the same "sound" as the Rovers of Brooklyn. — Harrison E. Salisbury, *The Shook-up Generation*, p. 158, 1958

2 a taunt or tease; an insult *US*

- "Forget it, Brew. I'm sorry for the sound." — Piri Thomas, *Down These Mean Streets*, p. 122, 1967

sound *verb*

1 to speak or inform; to tease someone; to flirt; to insult someone in a semi-formal quasi-friendly competition *US*

- So, when the Hepcat sounded her, she was bound to beat him down[.] — Dan Burley, *Diggeth Thou?*, p. 34, 1959
- All I want from you is to sound him for me and set up a time and a place to talk[.] — Ross Russell, *The Sound*, p. 58, 1961
- But now I sound her with the truth, just the way it is, the whole truth. — Sara Harris, *The Lords of Hell*, p. 59, 1967
- Alfredo and I had never been too tight and we never seemed to miss a chance to sound each other. — Piri Thomas, *Down These Mean Streets*, p. 109, 1967
- I sound on Joan if she thinks she got time for me to go phone around and see what I can do, get help I guess is what I meant. — *The Digger Papers*, p. 10, August 1968
- I mean, why aren't you sounding on her? It's obvious that you want to. — Cecil Brown, *The Life & Loves of Mr. Jiveass Nigger*, p. 187, 1969
- — Roger D. Abrahams, *Deep Down in the Jungle:*, p. 260, 1970
- She wanted to cop some horse and sounded on Arnie who in turn introduced us. — Herbert Huncke, *The Evening Sun Turned Crimson*, p. 173, 1980
- There are many different terms for playing the dozens, including "bagging, capping, cracking, dissing, hiking, joning, ranking, ribbing, serving, signifying, slipping, sounding and snapping". — Haskins James, *The Story of Hip-Hop*, 2000

2 to glare at or intimidate someone with a look *US*

- — *New York Times*, p. 2, 15th May 1955

sound

that's good; used in a congratulatory sense to express praise for an action *UK*

- All right? 'Ow ya doin'? Nice one. Sound. Yeah. — Ben Elton, *High Society*, p. 155, 2002

sound as a pound *adjective*

reliable; perfectly sound, good or healthy *UK*

- "Don't worry about him, luv. He's sound as a pound." "Yeah?" replied Lesley. "Nice arse, too." — Garry Bushell, *The Face*, p. 113, 2001

sound as a trout *adjective*

perfectly sound, good or healthy *UK, 1635*

- A nice clean statement and no worries: sound as a trout. — James Hawes, *Dead Long Enough*, p. 263, 2000

soundbox *noun*

the throat *US*

- When she wasn't shouting her head off she just moaned way down in her soundbox. — Mezz Mezzrow, *Really the Blues*, p. 74, 1946

sound down *verb*

to speak to someone in a probing or inquiring way *US*

- They wanted to go and get coffee but I had a habit and I knew I was wasting time with them because I'd already been sounded down for money. — Herbert Huncke, *Guilty of Everything*, p. 72, 1990

sound off *verb*

to complain angrily about a particular something; to speak your mind *US, 1918*

- If [Sir David] Frost was sounding off in a promotional video [...] no one could object. — *The Guardian*, 22nd July 2001

sounds *noun*

1 recorded music *US, 1955*

- I have within my comfy shed bottles of rare red wine and lots of sides and tapes of sounds. — Dan Burley, *Diggeth Thou?*, p. 33, 1959
- — Beach Boys *Pet Sounds*, 1966
- I was starved for some sounds that might warp my brain a little. — Lester Bangs, *Psychotic Reactions and Carburetor Dung*, 1971
- I'm more into music, really. Sounds. — Mike Stott, *Soldiers Talking, Cleanly*, 1978
- — Herbert Huncke, *Guilty of Everything*, p. e, 1990
- After the club officially closed up there'd be a small group of us left and we'd sit around smoking pot and listening to sounds – Billie Holiday, Charlie Parker, he had recordings of all the greats. — Herbert Huncke, *Guilty of Everything*, p. 135, 1990
- We look so fuckin' suspect, the sounds, the motor, the shades. We look like a fucking decoy. — J.J. Connolly, *Know Your Enemy [britpulp]*, p. 151, 1999

2 a radio *UK*

From its use as a provider of 'sounds' (music).

- — Angela Devlin, *Prison Patter*, p. 107, 1996

sounds like a personal problem

used for silencing a complaint without sympathy *US*

- — Carl Fleischhauer, *A Glossary of Army Slang*, p. 1, 1968

soundtrack *verb*

to supply the musical accompaniment to an activity *UK*

- [I]n the car going for a night out, or round your mate's house. The album was meant to soundtrack that. — *The Guardian*, p. 12, 26th February 2002

soup *noun*

1 nitroglycerin, or any explosive used for opening a safe *US, 1902*

- What I mean, he doesn't go in for the soup and detonator bit. — Robert Edmond Alter, *Carny Kill*, p. 102, 1966
- I decided to use every trick in the drilling business I had ever heard of to sieve it for the soup. — Red Rudensky, *The Gonif*, p. 7, 1970

2 In the television and film industries, the chemicals used to develop film *US*

- — Ralph S. Singleton, *Filmaker's Dictionary*, p. 157, 1990

3 in hot rodding and drag racing, race fuel *US*

- — *American Speech*, p. 102, May 1954

4 cocaine *US*

- — Mark S. Fleisher, *Beggars & Thieves:*, p. 291, 1995: 'Glossary'

5 foaming water left after a wave breaks *US*

- — Grant W. Kuhns, *On Surfing*, p. 122, 1963
- — *Paradise of the Pacific*, p. 27, October 1963

6 rain *US*

- — Lou Shelly, *Hepcats Jive Talk Dictionary*, p. 17, 1945

7 in shuffleboard, the scoring area of the court *US*

- — Omero C. Catan, *Secrets of Shuffleboard Strategy*, p. 72, 1967: 'Glossary of Terms'

▸ **in the soup**

in grave trouble *US*

- Something's going on, right? You're in the soup, just like me, aren't ya? — Stephen J. Cannell, *The Tin Collectors*, p. 87, 2001

soup and gravy; soup *noun*

a navy *UK, 1960*

- [I]n the Royal soup and gravy, afloat on the high housemaid's knees[.] — Ronnie Barker, *Fletcher's Book of Rhyming Slang*, p. 39, 1979

soup can *noun*

a gas grenade *US*

- Also in the coffin were two SN Speediheat gas grenades for outdoor use, two EN glast dispersion gas grenades, or "soup cans," for indoor work, plus gas masks. — Jon A. Jackson, *The Blind Pig*, p. 7, 1978

souped *adjective*

of a car, power-enhanced *UK*

- The Zephyr was souped; it could beat anything on the highway. — Thurston Scott, *Cure it with Honey*, p. 41, 1951

souped-up *adjective*

usually of a standard model car, supercharged, performance-enhanced *US, 1931*

- Let you be swallowed up by this myth. Let you revel in the souped-up glory. — William Bast, *The Myth Makers [Six Granada Plays]*, p. 174, 1958
- blasting down the streets in a souped-up shitcan with some zit-grinnin buddies drinkin the cheapest wine you could find — Lester Bangs, *Psychotic Reactions and Carburetor Dung*, p. 63, 1971
- little pricks in souped-up E-Reg Polos and that, divvy hatchbacks and that, thinking they're fucking somebodies — Kevin Sampson, *Outlaws*, p. 2, 2001
- I am no great lover of football, but even I can see that to suggest there is little difference between it and the souped-up girly netball ("basketball") [...] is both insane and insulting. — *The Guardian*, p. 3, 12th June 2003

soup job *noun*

a car with many performance-enhancing features *US*

- — Kenn "Naz" Young, *Naz's Dictionary of Teen Slang*, p. 110, 1993

soup jockey *noun*
a cook for a railway work crew *US*
• —J. Herbert Lund, *Herb's Hot Box of Railraod Slang*, p. 82, 1975

soup out *verb*
to ride a wave into the foaming water produced by the breaking wave *US*
• —Grant W. Kuhns, *On Surfing*, p. 122, 1963

soup-plate feet *noun*
large hooves on a horse *UK*
• —Rita Cannon, *Let's Go Racing*, p. 73, 1948

soup-strainer *noun*
a moustache *US*
• With that waxed soup-strainer of his and that slick hair, Johnny took on some grotesque features in my hot mind.—Mezz Mezzrow, *Really the Blues*, p. 181, 1946

soup suit *noun*
a dinner-jacket *US*
• —Jerry Robertson, *Oil Slanguage*, p. 115, 1954

soup up *verb*
to make modifications which increase a car's performance *US, 1933*
• —John Lawlor, *How to Talk Car*, p. 96, 1965
• He had spent a lot of money souping up the Mercury[.]—Larry McMurtry, *The Last Picture Show*, p. 9, 1966

soupy *adjective*
▷ see: **PEA-SOUPY**

sourball *noun*
a person with a sour disposition *US, 1900*
• Well, I just miss being a humorous author – so I just miss being a one hundred per cent sourball.—Philip Wylie, *Opus 21*, p. 32, 1949

sourdough *noun*
1 a person with considerable experience in Alaska *US, 1898*
• —Russell Tabbert, *Dictionary of Alaskan English*, p. 37, 1991
2 in Alaska, homebrew alcohol *US, 1915*
• —Russell Tabbert, *Dictionary of Alaskan English*, p. 89, 1991

sour grape *noun*
rape *NEW ZEALAND*
Prison slang.
• —*NZWords*, p. 2, 2nd October 1999

sourpuss *noun*
a grumbler; a misery; a killjoy *US, 1937*
From the 'sour' look on his or her **PUSS** (face).
• Imagine how an antique must feel, living with a sourpuss like that silly cow.—Jonathan Gash, *The Ten Word Game*, p. 136, 2003

soused *adjective*
drunk *US, 1932*
• "I think I'm a little soused." So he had been drinking.—S.E. Hinton, *The Outsiders*, p. 43, 1967
• I was bombed, man. Three sheets to the wind. Soused.—Gerald Petievich, *To Die in Beverly Hills*, p. 206, 1983
• The reek of liquor spills into the patrol car – the man is soused.—Josh Alan Friedman, *Tales of Times Square*, p. 136, 1986
• —Connie Eble (Editor), *UNC-CH Campus Slang*, p. 9, Fall 1988

south *noun*
▸ **go south**
to palm and hide something, usually dice or cards *US*
• —Frank Garcia, *Marked Cards and Loaded Dice*, p. 262, 1962

South *noun*
▸ **the South**
Antarctica *ANTARCTICA, 1901*
• —Bernadette Hince, *The Antarctic Dictionary*, p. 330, 2000

south 48; south 49 *noun*
in Alaska, all states except Alaska *US*
• —*American Speech*, p. 256–258, Fall 1984: 'Terms for 'Not Alaska' in Alaskan English'

South American snowflakes *noun*
cocaine *UK*
• The boys' antidote for feeling rough [...] was to inhale South American snowflakes.—Wayne Anthony, *Spanish Highs*, p. 90, 1999

South Austin suitcase *noun*
a brown paper bag used to conceal a beer you want to drink on the street *US*
• Another factor these guys consider is the so-called South Austin suitcase, the small brown paper bag the beer should be put in before it leaves the building.—*Austin American-Statesman*, 4th November 2001

South County Indian *noun*
a Portuguese immigrant or Portuguese-American *US*
Rhode Island usage, alluding to the large Portuguese population.
• —*Maledicta*, p. 233, 1988–1989: 'The Portagee in speech and joke'

Southend-on-Sea *noun*
urine; an act of urination *UK*
Rhyming slang for **PEE** or **WEE**, formed from the stereotypical Cockney's traditional seaside resort.
• —Ray Puxley, *Cockney Rabbit*, 1992

Southend Pier *noun*
the ear *UK*
Rhyming slang.
• —Ray Puxley, *Cockney Rabbit*, 1992

southerly buster *noun*
on the east coast, a sudden strong and cooling wind from the south arriving towards evening after a hot day and often bringing rain *AUSTRALIA, 1850*
• —Sam Weller, *Old Bastards I Have Met*, p. 95, 1979
• Now there was a fresh southerly buster blowing up from the harbour.—Lance Peters, *The Dirty Half-Mile*, p. 47, 1979

Southern and Seven *noun*
an alcoholic drink consisting of Southern Comfort™ whisky mixed with Seven-Up™ soda *US*
• Meanwhile he spent his leisure time drinking Southern and Sevens and watching TV with Donna pawing him or listening to her tell him how, after devoting her life to corrections, they had treated her like dirt.—Elmore Leonard, *Killshot*, p. 19, 1989

Southern engineering *noun*
a sloppy job of design or manufacture *US*
• —Ken Weaver, *Texas Crude*, p. 93, 1984

Southern love *noun*
mouth-to-penis contact immediately after the penis is withdrawn from a rectum *US*
• —*Adult Video News*, p. 40, September 1995

Southie *nickname*
an Irish-American enclave in south Boston *US*
An area famous for its support of the Irish Republican Army, its opposition to school busing to achieve racial integration and its anti-homosexual stance.
• A native of Southie, he is no longer popular there.—Bill Cardoso, *The Maltese Sangweech*, p. 147, 1984
• —Laurence Urdang, *Names and Nicknames of Places and Things*, p. 236, 1987

South of France *noun*
a dance *UK*
Rhyming slang.
• —Ray Puxley, *Cockney Rabbit*, 1992

south of the border; south *noun*
order; an orderly condition *UK: SCOTLAND*
Glasgow rhyming slang.
• A wee bit a south fur the singer.—Michael Munro, *The Patter, Another Blast*, 1988

south of the border *adjective*
unacceptable *UK: SCOTLAND*
Glasgow rhyming slang for **OUT OF ORDER**. Michael Munro is also keen to explain that this is not a reference to England but (thanks to Hollywood) Mexico.
• Here, is that no a wee bit south of the border whit he's sayin?—Michael Munro, *The Patter, Another Blast*, 1988

south of the border *adverb*
in or to the area of the genitals, especially a woman's *US*
• On the bottom of the report the doctor noted that "these women were examined from the waist up." The Stars and Stripes headlined the story: DEPENDS ON HOW YOU LOOK AT IT, SAYS JAP DOC WHO DIDN'T GO SOUTH OF BORDER.—*Newsweek*, p. 65, 19th November 1945
• He's not packing very much south of the border.—*America's Sweethearts*, 2001

southpaw *noun*
a left-handed person, especially a left-handed athlete *US, 1891*
• [H]e almost tore my jaw off with a left cross. I hadn't figured him to be a southpaw. — Piri Thomas, *Down These Mean Streets*, p. 260, 1967

South Pole *noun*
the anus *UK*
Rhyming slang for **HOLE**.
• — Ray Puxley, *Cockney Rabbit*, 1992

souvenir *verb*
to take an object as a souvenir *AUSTRALIA, 1918*
Originally World War 1 military slang.
• Neither of us relished going back into the reasonably tough bar to suggest that maybe someone had souvenired Graham Kennedy's cigarette lighter. — Bert Newton, *Bert!*, p. 132, 1977

sov *noun*
one pound sterling (£1) *UK, 1850*
An abbreviation of 'sovereign', which, at one time, was a coin valued at £1; since the departure of the coin as currency it has denoted first a one-pound note, and then a one-pound coin.
• [R]ake in a few sovs by opening up selected corridors of Buck House [Buckingham Palace] to the punters. — Andrew Nickolds, *Back to Basics*, p. 16, 1994

sow belly *noun*
on the railways, a coal tender with a drop bottom *US*
• — Norman Carlisle, *The Modern Wonder Book of Trains and Railroading*, p. 269, 1946

so what?
used for registering dismissal of, or disinterest in, what has gone before *US, 1934*
• I wanted to hear what everyone was getting up to, all the scandal, but when they told me I just thought, so what? — Mary Hooper, *(megan)2*, p. 44, 1999

sox *noun*
socks *UK, 1905*
• [T]rousers with wide stripe, no sox, short boots. — Colin MacInnes, *Absolute Beginners*, 1959

so you feel
that is your opinion, that is what you think *UK*
Recorded in use among young urban blacks.
• "Dat means the money's comin' outta your pocket man, cos' it ain' comin' outta mine." "So you feel," Elisha replied tartly. — Courttia Newland, *Society Within*, p. 3, 1999

sozzled *adjective*
drunk *UK, 1886*
From dialect word *sozzle* (to mix messily).
• They all sat on the grass, some on their sides, others, temporarily less sozzled, sitting with legs crossed like tailors. — Geoffrey Fletcher, *Down Among the Meths Men*, p. 36, 1966
• [H]er sozzled mother drives into a tree and dies[.] — *The Guardian*, 31st May 2003

SP *noun*
1 the latest information *UK, 1974*
Bookmakers abbreviation of jargon 'starting price'.
• "What's the SP on Arthur?" "He's just helping us with our enquiries." — Anthony Masters, *Minder*, p. 155, 1984
• — Angela Devlin, *Prison Patter*, p. 107, 1996
• So what's the SP on the Crab? Can he get us there? — Diran Abedayo, *My Once Upon A Time*, 2000
• [J]ust to see what they've got, what sorta money they're looking for, to get the full SP. — J.J. Connolly, *Layer Cake*, p. 108, 2000
• Cormack's given us a bit of the SP about some of the thinking behind the development and that. — Kevin Sampson, *Clubland*, p. 20, 2002

2 starting price bookmaking *AUSTRALIA, 1941*
• In those days S.P. was illegal but accepted and so long as they did the right thing and kept things in order, the police left them alone. — Sam Weller, *Old Bastards I Have Met*, p. 136, 1979

3 a starting price bookmaker *AUSTRALIA, 1949*
• And the S.P. had paid the full starting price – fifty to one! — Eric Lambert, *The Veterans*, p. 27, 1954
• 'What's the betting on the Cup,' the dark-haired detective asked the SP. — Roy Higgins and Tom Prior, *The Jockey Who Laughed*, p. 75, 1982
• — Joe Andersen, *Winners Can Laugh*, p. 165, 1982

4 an establishment operating starting price bookmaking *AUSTRALIA, 1965*
• This is a restaurant; must be an illegal SP – and it's bloody Sunday! — Frank Hardy, *Hardy's People*, p. 67, 1986

5 the US Navy's Shore Patrol, or internal police *US*
• The Navy's shore patrol takes over most of the policing. We saw Navy paddy-wagons in front of Guy's, the Ship's Cafe and the Penguin. But the SP's seldom make a pinch unless there are fights. — Jack Lait and Lee Mortimer, *Washington Confidential*, p. 33, 1951

SP *adjective*
relating to horse race betting at starting price odds *AUSTRALIA, 1932*
• 'It's an SP job,' I tells him, 'they'll back it off the course.' — Frank Hardy, *The Yarns of Billy Borker*, p. 107, 1965
• Last I heard of him he had sold his violin and was running an SP book in Mildura. — Frank Hardy, *Hardy's People*, p. 89, 1986

SP *adverb*
at starting price odds *AUSTRALIA, 1949*
• Scottish Soldier has been backed SP. It's a certainty. — Frank Hardy and Athol George Mulley, *The Needy and the Greedy*, p. 12, 1975
• There's no point in backing it SP. — Clive Galea, *Slipper*, p. 181, 1988

spa *noun*
a small, privately owned convenience/grocery shop *US*
• — Jim Crotty, *How to Talk American*, p. 29, 1997

Spa *noun*
the Saratoga race track, Saratoga Springs, New York *US*
• — Robert Saunders Dowst and Jay Craig, *Playing the Races:*, p. 169, 1960

spac; spack; spak *noun*
1 a stupid or unfashionable person *AUSTRALIA*
Alteration of **SPASTIC**. Used by schoolchildren.
• I never knew you were such a spak. — *Courier-Mail*, p. 3, 14th May 1988
• But it spins me out to think about how easy it is to be known as a spack. — *Dolly*, p. 70, July 1989

2 a person with spastic paralysis; a person who has any disablement *UK*
• — Barbara Riddick, *Living with Dyslexia*, p. 86, 1996
• — Chris Lewis, *The Dictionary of Playground Slang*, p. 212, 2003

spac *adjective*
stupid; awful *AUSTRALIA*
• Presents are things you are sposed to like, but you never can cos they are usually a book on horses or spac jigsaw puzzles. — Kylie Mole (Maryanne Fahey), *My Diary*, p. 3, 1988
• Just because I didn't do my homework I get yard duty and that's just spack. — June Factor, *Kidspeak*, p. 192, 2000

▸ **go spac**
to lose control in anger *AUSTRALIA*
• Sorry I didn't finish last night, but mum came in and found me writing and went spac cos it was nine-thirty (big deal). — Kylie Mole (Maryanne Fahey), *My Diary*, p. 16, 1988
• According to reports, the model 'went spack', locked herself in her dressing room and refused to come out until the underling had apologised. — *Sydney Morning Herald (Tempo)*, p. 3, February 2000

spac *adverb*
dreadfully *AUSTRALIA*
• He kisses rooly spac. — Kylie Mole (Maryanne Fahey), *My Diary*, p. 51, 1988

spac attack; spack attack *noun*
an instance of idiotic behaviour *UK*
From **SPAC**.
• — Chris Lewis, *The Dictionary of Playground Slang*, p. 212, 2003

spacbrain *noun*
a stupid or unfashionable person *AUSTRALIA*
• And anyway bratface, spacbrain, you won't be able to understand it cos now I am gunna write my dairy [sic] in code. — Kylie Mole (Maryanne Fahey), *My Diary*, p. 11, 1988

spacco *adjective*
▸ **go spacco**
to behave in an idiotic, erratic or hyperactive manner *UK*
From **SPAC**.
• — Chris Lewis, *The Dictionary of Playground Slang*, p. 185, 2003

space *noun*
1 a mental attitude or position *UK*
• [T]he coppers were in the space of picking me out of the mob[.] — Jamie Mandelkau, *Buttons*, p. 56, 1971

2 a year, especially a year in prison *US*
• — Hyman E. Goldin et al., *Dictionary of American Underworld Lingo*, p. 202, 1950

space *verb*

to daydream; to wander off mentally *US*

- Thirty-four, that's freezing, for Christ sake. Yo, Chili, you're spacin'. — *Get Shorty*, 1995

spacebase *noun*

a cigar wrapper filled with phencyclidine and crack cocaine *US*

- — Terry Williams, *Crackhouse:*, p. 151, 1992
- — Mike Haskins, *Drugs*, p. 293, 2003

space cadet *noun*

1 a drug user *UK*

- Not surprised he wants to legalize everything if his own daughter's a bloody space cadet, eh? — Ben Elton, *High Society*, p. 56, 2002

2 a heavily drugged hospital patient *US*

- — *Maledicta*, p. 35, 1988–1989: 'More Milawukee medical maledicta'

space case; space cadet; space head *noun*

a person who is completely out of touch with their surroundings *US*

- — Robert Kirk Mueller, *Buzzwords:*, p. 145, 1974
- He enlisted the assistance of his friend Llazo, a poet and "space cadet." — Ed Sanders, *Tales of Beatnik Glory*, p. 195, 1975
- "Drugs can be fun." He says this matter-of-factly, although he often makes jokes about "space cadets." — *Washington Post*, p. H1, 8th October 1978
- Who would do that? Nobody here would give that space case a drink. — Vincent Patrick, *The Pope of Greenwich Village*, p. 14, 1979
- [T]here's a good proportion of air heads and space cadets in those courses, too. — *Wesleyan Alumnus*, p. 29, Spring 1981
- "Do you see my skirt on your side?" He shook his head slowly. "The other room." "Right. I am such a space case." — Armistead Maupin, *Further Tales of the City*, p. 110, 1982
- Like my mother is like a total space cadet. — Moon Unit and Frank Zappa, *Valley Girl*, 1982
- — *USA Today*, 29th September 1983
- Anna shrugs off Kandi's tantrum with little concern: "She's a space cadet and I'm a space commander." — Josh Alan Friedman, *Tales of Times Square*, p. 11, 1986
- "My family is a bunch o' space cadets, y'know what I mean?" — Odie Hawkins, *The Life and Times of Chester Simmons*, p. 154, 1991
- Oh, and you are such a superficial space cadet. — *Clueless*, 1995

space cookie; space cake *noun*

a sweet confection with marijuana in the recipe *UK, 1998*

- Roger's brought his idea uv a spacecake (uh Spar-bought Swiss roll sliced down thuh middle with resin sprinkled intuh it)[.] — Niall Griffiths, *Grits*, p. 9, 2000
- [P]atrons wander in off the street for a capuccino, a joint, or a space cookie. — Brian Preston, *Pot Planet*, p. 94, 2002

space cowboy *noun*

a disoriented, distracted person *US*

- Comes back such a mindfuck he can't remember. Fuckin space cowboy. — John Sayles, *Union Dues*, p. 313, 1977

spaced *adjective*

1 in a state of drug intoxication, especially as a result of hallucinogen use but loosely of any drug *US*

- — Ruth Bronsteen, *The Hippy's Handbook*, p. 16, 1967
- "You okay?" Ted asks, noticing I'm spaced. "Yeah, i'm finee," I assure him, "I'm just stoned is all." — Jim Carroll, *Forced Entries*, p. 108, 1987
- I was just spaced. I became paranoid at everything. — Bobby Womack, *quoted in Waiting For The Sun*, p. 236, 1996

2 unaware; unfocused; highly distracted *US*

- — Joe David Brown (Editor), *The Hippies*, p. 219, 1967: 'Glossary of hippie terms'
- I was just spaced, my dears, so I stayed only long enough for a sandwich. — *Screw*, p. 15, 22nd December 1969
- — *American Speech*, p. 66, Spring-Summer 1975: 'Razorback slang'
- — *Verbatim*, p. 281, May 1976

spacedancing *noun*

in the language surrounding the Grateful Dead, the freeform dancing practised by band followers *US*

- Freeform gestures involving gentle bending at knees, swaying of the arms, and rocking of the head, combined with expressive movements of the hands. — David Shenk and Steve Silberman, *Skeleton Key:*, p. 267, 1994

spaced out *adjective*

1 drug-intoxicated; disoriented *US, 1970*

Conventionally 'space' is beyond the frontiers of normality.

- Nothing can ever be the same / You're spaced out on sensation / Like you're under sedation — Richard O'Brien, *The Rocky Horror Show*, 1973
- "What did the participants think of the Melchett report on pop festival?" – "Just spaced out" — *The Observer*, 13th June 1976
- [W]e were both sort of really spaced out, the room was swirling and I couldn't tell where I began or anything else[.] — Paul E Willis, *Profane Culture*, p. 142, 1978
- If I didn't know better I'd never come down myself. I was just lying there spaced out in all that beauty of mountain and streams and trees. — Beatrice Sparks (writing as 'Anonymous'), *Jay's Journal*, 1979

2 stupefied from anaesthetic *US*

- — *American Speech*, p. 205, Fall-Winter 1973: 'The language of nursing'

space pill *noun*

MDMA, the recreational drug best known as ecstasy *UK*

- Those space pills, I want to buy them, how much? — J.J. Connolly, *Layer Cake*, p. 256, 2000

spacer *noun*

1 a hallucinogenic recreational drug *UK*

- [H]e's a walking cornucopia of drugs; downers and lifters and speeders and freaked-out spacers. — Alex Stuart, *The Bikers*, 1971

2 a mace cigarette *US*

- and come out in the hallway, lighting cigarets and bullshittin and clinching deals for mae or "spacers" before the hack ran us back to our units — Clarence Cooper Jr, *The Farm*, p. 40, 1967

3 someone who is capable of crazy actions *IRELAND*

- I want to tell him what a focking [fucking] spacer he is, but I don't want to hurt his feelings. — Paul Howard, *Ross O'Carroll-Kelly*, p. 29, 2003

space shake *noun*

a milk-based drink which has marijuana as an important ingredient *UK*

- — Nick Jones, *Spliffs*, p. 252, 2003

space suit *noun*

untearable prison-issue pyjamas *UK*

- — Angela Devlin, *Prison Patter*, p. 107, 1996

spacies *noun*

computerised arcade games *AUSTRALIA*

From *Space Invaders* , one of the earliest popular games of this type. Modelled on **POKIE**.

- Terry Mildner, 14, of Salisbury, often spends time after school and during holidays playing the 'spacies' and watching other people play. — *Courier-Mail*, p. 5, 23th January 1986

spack, spack attack *nouns*

▷ **see:** SPAC, SPAC ATTACK

spacker; spacka; spack *noun*

a stupid person *UK*

A later variation of **SPASTIC** as a general derogative, in juvenile use in the UK.

- Is he king of all the spacks? — Frank Skinner, *Frank Skinner*, p. 163, 2001

spacy; spacey *adjective*

in a state of confusion; denoting an unbalanced normality or a dazed condition; similar to or of a hallucinogenic experience *US, 1970*

Compares a perception of reality to that of being **SPACED** (drug-intoxicated) but does not always describe a drugged state.

- Some spacy kid ... appeared stoned on American TV[.] — *New Scientist*, 7th August 1980
- They gave him a shot at the hospital and he got real spacey. — Carl Hiaasen, *Tourist Season*, p. 127, 1986
- Womack ... remembers the sessions for Riot as "very spacey" — Barney Hoskyns, *Waiting For The Sun*, p. 236, 1996
- We don't talk. Becca is spacey and Kelly is doing something weird[.] — Cath Staincliffe, *Trainers*, p. 63, 1999

spad *nickname*

a Douglas aircraft A-1 Skyraider, used for close air support of ground troops *US*

- "Spad" was the nickname for the prop-driven, A-1 Douglas Skyraider. The A-1 was based on a design so old it reminded the jet jockeys of the famous S.P.A.D. biplane fighter of the First World War. — T.E. Cruise, *Wings of Gold III:*, p. 267, 1989
- The helicopter, a "Big Mother," was joined by two A-1 Skyraiders (also known as "Spads") for protection[.] — Robert K. Wilcox, *Scream of Eagles*, p. 59, 1990

spade *noun*

a black person *US, 1928*

- How in hell did I come to be living with a "spade"? — Mezz Mezzrow, *Really the Blues*, p. 300, 1946

- And down there, with something like that happening and only a few Spades (colored folks) around, it wasn't so good. — Louis Armstrong, *Satchmo*, p. 146, 1954
- We had to look for him in this spade part of town most of the time. — Jack Kerouac, *On the Road*, p. 158, 1957
- The only spades to beat that rap was the fags and junkies. — Ross Russell, *The Sound*, p. 73, 1961
- On the dance floor, spade chicks with classic butts squeezed into gold and orange and red hugging dresses dance with gleaming faced Negro men. — John Rechy, *City of Night*, p. 184, 1963
- We gets down Somerleyton Road, where all the Spades hang out. So Jimmy, whose mum and dad is West Indians, says we might as well go to his house. — John Petter Jones, *Feather Pluckers*, p. 16, 1964
- Why is a white girl like you throwing yourself away with a spade? — Malcolm X and Alex Haley, *The Autobiography of Malcolm X*, p. 94, 1964
- The spade went with a few guys, and then she wanted to quit, but the pregnant one was hot to trot. — Hunter S. Thompson, *Hell's Angels:*, p. 17, 1966
- — J. L. Simmons and Barry Winograd, *It's Happening:*, p. 172, 1966: 'glossary'
- In the Haight the word 'Negro" is almost never used. "Black" is employed by people tinged with New Left polluted understanding, the most common word is "spade." — Nicholas Von Hoffman, *We Are The People Our Parents Warned Us Against*, p. 102, 1967
- Those of us who dropped out before acid have lived/loved with spades & know where it's at, but the new kids don't. — *Berkeley Barb*, p. 7, 3rd March 1967
- Spades, the very soul figures of Hip, of jazz, of the hip vocabulary itself, man and like and dig and baby and scarf and split and later and so fine... — Tom Wolfe, *The Electric Kool-Aid Acid Test*, p. 9, 1968
- The cops put me in the back room. I'm jiving with the spades. — Abbie Hoffman, *Revolution for the Hell of It*, p. 19, 1968
- [S]uddenly I knew – some big spade was going to leap out of the bedroom closet and spring for my heart with his knife. — Philip Roth, *Portnoy's Complaint*, p. 180, 1969
- A spade cat from Port Washington joined the Quarry and tried to tell us what was on his mind. — *East Village Other*, 20th August 1969
- I got to run and find that spade they call Mule. — Darryl Poniscan, *The Last Detail*, p. 12, 1970
- I gave away a copy of my pamphlet and wound up in conversation with the guy who took it, this young spade kid who had the most intense brown eyes I have ever seen. — Gurney Norman, *Divine Right's Trip (Last Whole Earth Catalog)*, p. 121, 1971
- Audrey does her own impression of what the spade chick's doing and wafts across the room towards me. — Ted Lewis, *Jack Carter's Law*, p. 61, 1974
- The black girls are the Mod chicks of today – those little spade chicks you see running around in stacked heels and wedges[.] — Pete Meaden, *The Ace Face's Forgotten Story, The Sharper Word*, p. 165, 1979
- A couple of spade cats cut by[.] — Herbert Huncke, *The Evening Sun Turned Crimson*, p. 132, 1980
- All the way from Swinging London, bringing rather different vibes, came the Who and the wild young "psychedlic Spade" Jimi Hendrix. — Barney Hoskyns, *Waiting for the Sun*, p. 144, 1996

spades *noun*

shoes with pointed toes *US*

Teen slang.

- — *American Weekly*, p. 2, 14th August 1955

▸ **in spades**

to a great degree *US, 1929*

- I'm just talking about that crummy meeting and what that nurse and those other bastards did to you. Did in spades. — Ken Kesey, *One Flew Over the Cuckoo's Nest*, p. 56, 1962
- I am here to tell you that that ofay boy has really got sex appeal in spades! — Gore Vidal, *Myra Breckinridge*, p. 90, 1968
- You'll pay for what you've done! You'll pay in spades! — *Mallrats*, 1995
- These men had that [style] in spades – so crisp and classy. — Dave Courtney, *Stop the Ride I Want to Get Off*, p. 32, 1999
- As it turned out, the house had the space we craved in spades. — Mick Farren, *Give the Anarchist a Cigarette*, p. 54, 2001

spaff *verb*

to ejaculate semen *UK*

- [T]his could indeed be smut even Hitler spaffed over. — *FHM*, p. 47, June 2003

▸ **spaff your load**

to ejaculate semen *UK*

An elaboration of **SPAFF**.

- [Y]our erection lasts longer and it'll feel more explosive when you eventually spaff your load. — *The FHM Little Book of Bloke*, p. 23, June 2003

spag *noun*

spaghetti *UK, 1948*

- Ecker was scared they'd gone too far, but he wasn't going to let this little spag eater know that. — *A Sense of Tradition*, p. 238, 1983

Spag *noun*

an Italian *AUSTRALIA*

From '*spag*hetti'.

- I first met him (we later dubbed him Luigi the Spag, so that's what I'll call him) on a sunny Easter Sunday at Bondi Beach. — Sue Rhodes, *Now you'll think I'm awful*, p. 122, 1967
- The Tennant Creeks and to some extent the Spags cornered the market years ago. — Barry Humphries, *The Traveller's Tool*, p. 80, 1985

spag bol; spag bog *noun*

spaghetti bolognese *UK, 1970*

- Your favourite pasta. — Ann Barr and Peter York, *The Official Sloane Ranger Handbook*, p. 159, 1982
- But Spag Bol doesn't have to be an awful gruel of greyish lumps floating in fluorescent ketchup[.] — Ignatius Jones, *The 1992 True Hip Manual*, p. 121, 1992
- I was doing the Spag Bol when I remembered I'd forgotten a couple of ingredients. — Harry Enfield, *Harry Enfield and His Humorous Chums*, p. 50, 1997

spag fag *noun*

a gay man attracted to Italians *UK*

Combines **SPAG** (an Italian) and **FAG** (a gay man).

spaghetti *noun*

1 in hot rodding, a surfeit of chrome *US*

- — *Good Housekeeping*, p. 143, September 1958: 'Hot-Rod terms for teen-age girls'
- — Tom MacPherson, *Dragging and Driving*, p. 142, 1960

2 in oil drilling, small-diameter piping *US*

- — Jerry Robertson, *Oil Slanguage*, p. 115, 1954

spaghetti *adjective*

Italian *US, 1969*

- The director on this great epic spaghetti picture not only barely speaks English, he hasn't the slighest fucking idea what he's doing. — Elmore Leonard, *Gold Coast*, p. 152, 1980

spaghetti and macaroni *noun*

sado-masochism *US*

Disguising the initialism **S AND M**.

- — Thomas E. Murray and Thomas R. Murrell, *The Language of Sadomasochism*, p. 125, 1989

spaghetti-bender *noun*

an Italian or Italian-American *US*

- There's all kinds of people born there. Colored people, Puerto Ricans like me, an' – even spaghetti-benders like you. — Piri Thomas, *Down These Mean Streets*, p. 25–26, 1967

spaghetti-eater *noun*

an Italian or Italian-American *US*

- — Jack Kerouac, *The Subterraneans*, p. 15, 1958

Spaghetti Junction *nickname*

1 junction 6 of the M6 motorway, the interchange at Gravelly Hill, near Birmingham *UK*

So-called for the complicated pattern of roads; it opened for use in 1972, but was already known by this name in late 1971.

- — *Drive*, New Year 1972
- Perhaps it flirts with the edges of bombast to say so, but I am the MP for Spaghetti Junction. — *The Guardian*, 24th May 2002

2 a motorway overpass 10 kilometres from Durban *SOUTH AFRICA*

- [S]itting on the railing of Spaghetti Junction on the Day of Reconciliation – at the same spot where locals used to hang banners reading "Vaalies go home"[.] — *Sunday Times (South Africa)*, 10th January 1999

spaghetti strap *noun*

very thin shoulder straps on a woman's garment; the garment itself *US, 1972*

- "Sure," Maya said, "and those slippery Republican hatchet men're out there beating the bushes for another smoking bimbo in a spaghetti-strap. Is that any way to win an election?" — Joseph Wambaugh, *Finnegan's Week*, p. 112, 1993

spaghetti western *noun*

a cowboy film about the American 'wild west' produced by the Italian film industry *US, 1973*

- [D]ead, shot full of holes by the new trend of "spaghetti" Westerns. That didn't match the box office figures. — Jane Pattie, *John Wayne ... There Rode a Legend*, p. 193, 2001

spaginzy *noun*

a black person *US*

- — Kenn "Naz" Young, *Naz's Underground Dictionary*, p. 57, 1973

Spahn and Sain and then, dear Lord, two days of rain

used as a humorous entreaty for a bit of luck to accompany a bit of skill or hard work *US, 1948*

Coined by sports writer Gerald Hern in 1948 to describe the strategy of the Boston Braves baseball team – win games pitched by the skilled pitchers Warren Spahn and Johnny Sain and then hope for the best.

- It was Spahn and Sain and then, dear Lord, two days of rain. —Jim Bouton, *Ball Four*, p. 48, 1970

spak *noun*

▷ **see:** SPAC

spam *noun*

unsolicited, unwanted, often fraudulent advertising messages sent by e-mail *US*

- Internet users suffered another "spam attack" last week, this time from a Florida public-access host user who flooded Usenet conferences with ads for a thigh-reducing cream. — *Network World*, p. 2, 30th May 1994

spam *verb*

1 to post e-mail in unwanted quantities, especially advertising matter to people who don't want it *US*

Ultimately from branded tinned meat Spam™ (a compound of spiced ham); popular etymology insists that this usage is inspired by the Monty Python sketch, 1970, set in a café in which nothing but unwanted Spam is served.

- In contrast, the cost to spam an advertisement in thousands of news groups, where it is potentialy read by hundreds of thousands of computer users, is typically less than $50. — *New York Times*, p. 51, 7th May 1994

2 to assign an unpleasant task to someone *UK*

Gulf war usage.

- — *American Speech*, p. 401, Winter 1991: 'Among the new words'

spam can *noun*

1 a Southern Region 4–6–2 passenger locomotive of the 'West Country' class; a class Q freight locomotive also known as a 'biscuit box' *UK*

Railway slang with a derogatory edge; an allusion to the shape. Reported by Clive Hardy, 1979.

2 any metal-skinned light aeroplane *UK*

A derogatory term used by flying club pilots of veteran, fabric-covered aircraft. Reported by Mrs Barbara Huston, 1979, and by John Horton in *The Grub Street Dictionary of International Aircraft Nicknames*, 1994.

spam fritter *noun*

the anus *UK*

Rhyming slang for **SHITTER**.

- I had a vindaloo last night and my spam fritter's been killing me ever since. — Bodmin Dark, *Dirty Cockney Rhyming Slang*, 2003

spam fritters *noun*

the vaginal labia *UK*

A pink highlight of UK cuisine.

- — *Rogers Profanisaurus*, 2002

spam javelin *noun*

the erect penis *UK*

A meat weapon.

- — *Roger's Profanisaurus*, December 1997
- [T]wo anonymous questionnaires all about the spam javelin (one for men, one for women). — Richard Herring, *Talking Cock*, p. 12, 2003
- [Keith Emerson] regales us with lurid tales of "spam javelins" and unorthodox cures for pubic lice. — *Uncut*, p. 15, October 2003

spam lance *noun*

the penis, especially when erect *UK*

- Interfering with himself like. Helping himself along as it were. Giving it six-nil on the old spam lance. — Niall Griffiths, *Sheepshagger*, p. 130, 2001

spam medal *noun*

the Canadian Volunteer Service Medal, given to all Canadian servicemen during World War 2 who volunteered rather than being conscripted *CANADA*

- The term "spam medal" alludes to the fact that most Canadian service members were entitled to this medal, thus making it nearly as common as spam. — Tom Langeste, *Words on the Wing*, p. 257, 1995

spamouflage *noun*

software designed to mask the fact that an e-mail is an unsolicited mass advertisement *US*

- But as spammers adopt increasingly sophisticated "spamouflage" techniques to mask their true nature, these services are struggling to keep up. — *San Francisco Chronicle*, p. A7, 8th September 2002

Spandau Ballet *noun*

an alley *UK*

Rhyming slang, formed from the name of a 1980s UK pop group.

- [H]aving no Mott the Hooples [scruples] he goes out when it's a bit Dave Clark, dark, and mugs some bloke up the Spandau Ballet. — *Getting Nowhere Fast*, 21st May 2004

spang *verb*

to beg on the streets *UK*

Etymology is uncertain, possibly a compound of 'Spare any change?' or, less likely, an abbreviation of 'spangle' (something that glitters, hence a coin).

- — David Rowan, *A Glossary for the 90s*, 1998

spangled *adjective*

drunk *UK*

- — *e-cyclopaedia*, 20th March 2002

Spanic *noun*

in Toronto, a person of South American descent *CANADA*

- Everyone was screaming "spic" and it kind of drew anger towards me. I guess you could say that I am Native Indian but Latins twisted and they say it is a "Spanic" - Spanish People in Control." — Alroy *Cultural Identity and Identity Performance Among Latin American Youths in Toronto*, p. 118, 2001

Spanish archer *noun*

dismissal; a rejection *UK*

An excruciating pun: **ELBOW** (dismissal, a rejection) and 'El Bow'.

- [A]v given Sarah thuh Spanish Archer[.] — Niall Griffiths, *Grits*, p. 45, 2000

Spanish curse *noun*

in dominoes, the 3–3 piece *US*

- — Dominic Armanino, *Dominoes*, p. 17, 1959

Spanish football *noun*

a sexually transmitted infection *UK, 1961*

Navy 'lower decks' usage; possibly a pun on 'dribbling'.

Spanish guitar; spanish *noun*

a cigar *UK*

Rhyming slang.

- — Wilfred Granville, *A Dictionary of Theatrical Terms*, 1952
- — Ray Puxley, *Cockney Rabbit*, 1992

Spanish Main; spanish *noun*

a drain *UK*

Rhyming slang.

- [M]oney down the "Spanish". — Ray Puxley, *Cockney Rabbit*, 1992

Spanish onion *noun*

a bunion *UK*

Rhyming slang

- — Ray Puxley, *Cockney Rabbit*, 1992

Spanish radio station *noun*

used as the epitome of something that is always in the way *TRINIDAD AND TOBAGO, 1984*

- — Lise Winer, *Dictionary of the English/Creole of Trinidad & Tobago*, 2003

Spanish surrealist *noun*

cocaine *UK*

A discreet reference to **SALVADOR DALI** for **CHARLIE** (cocaine).

- [O]ur Spanish surrealist mate is in town + looking very handsome. — James Hawes, *White Powder, Green Light*, p. 42, 2002

Spanish waiter *noun*

a potato *UK*

Rhyming slang.

- — Ray Puxley, *Cockney Rabbit*, 1992

spank *noun*

a beating *UK*

- "And suppose he don''t want to pay?" "Then he gets a spank. And he keeps getting spanked till he does want to pay." — Anthony Masters, *Minder*, p. 80, 1984

spank *verb*

1 to beat someone with violent intent *UK*

Extends from 'spank' (to beat with an open hand).

- [T]he blackest day in Chelsea's terrace history was when they were spanked good and proper inside and outside White Hart Lane[.] — Martin King and Martin Knight, *The Naughty Nineties*, p. 203, 1999

2 to rob someone *US*
- — John R. Armore and Joseph D. Wolfe,, *Dictionary of Desperation*, 1976

3 to fraudulently amend financial accounts *US*
- On the street you call it spanking. In legal business you call it embezzling. In the Chandon family you call it suicide. — Patricia Cornwell, *Black Notice*, 1999

4 (used of a male) to masturbate *US*
- JAY: "Not in me." That's what she says. I gotta pull out and spank it to get it on. — *Clerks*, 1994

5 to slap the inside of the arm to draw out veins for a drug injection *US*
- — Jim Emerson-Cobb, *Scratching the Dragon*, April 1997

▸ **spank the monkey**
(used of a male) to masturbate *US*
- Spanking the monkey. Flogging the bishop. Choking the chicken. Jerking the gherkin. — *American Beauty*, 1999
- Another way to say "the boy is masturbating" [...] Spanking the monkey[.] — Erica Orloff and JoAnn Baker, *Dirty Little Secrets*, 2001

▸ **spank the plank**
1 (of a male) to masturbate *UK*
- — Chris Donald, *Roger's Profanisaurus*, August 1998

2 to play an electric guitar *UK*
- Every self-respecting hard rock fan remembers where they were when they first saw or heard the 'spank-the-plank' pyrotechnics of EVH [Eddie Van Halen]. — *BBC Stoke and Staffordshire*, October 2004

spankadocious *adjective*
▹ see: **SPOKADOCIOUS**

spanked *adjective*
worn out; over-used *US*
- — Connie Eble (Editor), *UNC-CH Campus Slang*, p. 9, Spring 1992

spanking *noun*
a serious beating *UK*
From 'spank' (to hit with the open hand); a blackly humorous understatement of violent intent.
- Most made it back into the relative safety of the station but a few took the sort of spanking that big babies deserve. — Martin King and Martin Knight, *The Naughty Nineties*, p. 182, 1999

spank off *verb*
(of a male) to masturbate *UK*
- Could get that Prince Edward spanking off over the phone, she could. — Kevin Sampson, *Clubland*, p. 132, 2002

spanner *noun*
1 a promiscuous female; a sexually provocative woman *UK*
From the name of the tool used to tighten nuts.
- — Tom Hibbert, *Rockspeak!*, p. 147, 1983
- — *The Sunday Times*, 9th May 2004

2 in prison, a key *UK*
- — Angela Devlin, *Prison Patter*, p. 107, 1996

3 a fool; an idiot *IRELAND*
- You know, the type of spanner who strolls around the office taking imaginary swings – playing 'air-golf' in the same pathetic way he plays sweaty 'air guitar' at the Christmas party — *Irish Business Post*, 21st December 2003

spannered *adjective*
drunk or drug-intoxicated *UK*
- — *The Guardian*, September 2000
- [W]recked spannered mangled caned[.] — Stuart Walton, *Out of It*, cover, 2001

spansula *noun*
a combination of central nervous system depressants and stimulants *US*
- — Eugene Landy, *The Underground Dictionary*, p. 174, 1971

Span-yard *noun*
a Spaniard *UK*
- [H]e never liked the geezer, the Span-yard, always thought he was a slippery, smug cunt, halfa grass. — J.J. Connolly, *Layer Cake*, p. 13, 2000

spar *noun*
1 a friend; a companion *BARBADOS*
Shortening of **SPARRING PARTNER**.
- — Frank A. Collymore, *Barbadian Dialect*, 1965
- Bluebwai, or Blue to his spars, had proved to be a reliable soldier. — Karline Smith, *Moss Side Massive*, p. 1, 1994
- He knew Patrick more on a hail 'n' touch fist basis than as a close spar[.] — Donald Gorgon, *Cop Killer*, p. 53, 1994
- Aright, clart. What're you doing, spar? — Goldie Looking Chain *Soap Bar*, 2004

2 a close male friend *JAMAICA*
- — Peter Patrick, *Some Recent Jamaican Creole Words*, 2003

3 a man *UK*
From the meaning as 'a friend'. Mainly black usage. The variant 'spa' is also used.
- Same motor, dark-haired spa about your age. — John Milne, *Alive and Kicking*, p. 12, 1998

spare *noun*
1 in a social context, any or all unattached members of the opposite sex *UK: SCOTLAND*
- Is there gauny [going to] be any spare at this party? — Michael Munro, *The Patter*, p. 65, 1985

2 a friend *US*
- — Marcus Hanna Boulware, *Jive and Slang of Students in Negro Colleges*, 1947

spare *adjective*
distraught, distracted or distressed; angry; crazy *UK*
- How they nearly drove their old man spare making pets of all the animals. — John Peter Jones, *Feather Pluckers*, p. 49, 1964

▸ **go spare**
to become very angry *UK, 1958*
- I thought she was a sandwich! 'Til she went spare on me hand. — Ringo Starr, *Help!*, 1965

spare me days!
heavens above! *AUSTRALIA, 1915*
With **ME** for 'my'.
- SPARE ME DAYS – Ejaculation of surprise. — Gilbert H. Lawson, *A Dictionary of Australian Words and Terms*, 1924
- Spare me days, what goes on here? — John Wynnum, *Tar Dust*, p. 9, 1962
- Spare me days, how unlucky can a bloke get? — Paul Vautin, *Turn It Up!*, p. 50, 1995

spare prick *noun*
a useless fellow; someone who is surplus to requirements *UK*
A shortening of 'spare prick at a wedding', from the phrase 'standing about like a spare prick at a wedding'.
- Wherever we went I continued to stand out like a spare prick. — *New Society*, p. 205, 4th November 1982

spare rib *noun*
a trivial lie *UK*
Rhyming slang for 'fib'.
- — Ray Puxley, *Fresh Rabbit*, 1998

spare time *noun*
the possession of marijuana *US*
The implication is that you must have spare time if you are to use the marijuana.
- — *www.addictions.org*, 1999

spare tire; spare tyre *noun*
a roll of fat around the waist *US, 1961*
- — *Woman's Realm*, 11th March 1967

spark *verb*
1 to light a cigarette or a marijuana cigarette *US*
Also variant 'spark up'.
- It is one thing to spark up a dubie and get laced at parties, but it is quite another to be fried all day. — *Clueless*, 1995
- Sparked a spliff – I reckoned I'd earned it[.] — Diran Abedayo, *My Once Upon A Time*, p. 270, 2000
- He takes out a Numbo, sparks up and and sits on the swing, enjoying the sunshine and smoking his ciggy. — Kevin Sampson, *Outlaws*, p. 246, 2001
- Order a latte, spark one up and get jazzy. Man. — *Ministry*, p. 10, October 2002
- Decisions, decisions. A line of Charlie [cocaine]? A pill? Or spark up a spliff? — Colin Butts, *Is Harry Still on the Boat?*, 2003

2 to hit someone hard; to knock someone out *UK*
- [A]nother punch connects with my jaw and I'm going down. Don't think I'm sparked because I remember it. — Jimmy Stockin, *On The Cobbles*, p. 29–30, 2000
- I sparked him. He hit the penny. — prison inmate, 5th August 2002

3 to see something or someone *US*
Hawaiian youth usage.
- —Elizabeth Ball Carr, *Da Kine Talk:*, p. 150, 1972

4 in horse racing, to use an electrical device to shock a horse during a race *US*
- —David W. Maurer, *Argot of the Racetrack*, p. 58, 1951

▸ **spark it up**
to smoke marijuana *UK, 1998*
- —Mike Haskins, *Drugs*, p. 290, 2003

sparked *adjective*
knocked out, unconscious *UK*
- —Angela Devlin, *Prison Patter*, p. 107, 1996

sparkers *adjective*
unconscious or deeply asleep *UK*
A variation of **SPARK OUT**.
- She was sparkers.—David Powis, *The Signs of Crime*, 1977

sparkle *noun*
strong and pure methamphetamine with a crystalline appearance *US*
- —Geoffrey Froner, *Digging for Diamonds:*, p. 69, 1989: 'Types of speed'

sparkle plenty *noun*
an amphetamine tablet *US*
Named after a character in the *Dick Tracy* comic strip.
- —Richard Lingeman, *Drugs from A to Z*, 1969

sparkler *noun*
1 a diamond *UK, 1822*
- There were so many buxom madams of both races jammed in there, sporting big sparklers and fancy corsages.—Mezz Mezzrow, *Really the Blues*, p. 91, 1946
- We just sat around feeling the sparklers, counting them, sorting them out according to their size, counting them again until the flashlight went dead.—Rocky Garciano (with Rowland Barber), *Somebody Up There Likes Me*, p. 66, 1955
- When he got into the room where the sparklers were he found a corpse laid out on the bed.—Charles Raven, *Underworld Nights*, p. 191, 1956

2 a tablet of amphetamine *US*
- —US Department of Justice, *Street Terms*, August 1994

sparklers *noun*
clean white socks *US*
Michigan Upper Peninsula usage.

sparkly *adjective*
dishonest; criminal *UK*
An opposite to dull, **STRAIGHT** (honest).
- Because I have an awful lot of sparkly friends it means that you can be guilty by association.—Dave Courtney, *Stop the Ride I Want to Get Off*, p. 385, 1999

sparko *adjective*
1 in a state of unconciousness *UK*
Abbreviated from **SPARK OUT**.
- He was sparko, prostrate on the floor, like the Pope kissing the tarmac.— Martin King and Martin Knight, *The Naught Nineties*, p. 50, 1999
- O'Shea's head became a bloody mess of claret, beer and shards of broken brown glass. "That's it, Doug," said Rhino. "He's sparko." —Garry Bushell, *The Face*, p. 37, 2001

2 psychotic; deranged *UK*
- —Tom Hibbert, *Rockspeak!*, p. 147, 1983

spark out *verb*
to become unconscious; to faint; to die *UK*
The spark of life goes out, to some degree.

spark-out *adjective*
unconscious *UK*
The *spark* of life has (temporarily) gone *out*.
- [S]ome mug laying stark [spark] out on the deck[.]—Frank Norman, *Bang To Rights*, p. 26, 1958

sparkplug *noun*
a tampon *US*
- —Connie Eble (Editor), *UNC-CH Campus Slang*, p. 11, Fall 1999

sparks; sparky; sparkie *noun*
an electrician *UK, 1914*
- Ah'll get that done for ye cheaper than that. Ah know a wee sparkie [electrician] that does homers.—Michael Munro, *The Complete Patter*, p. 77, 1996
- "You working, Russell?" "Yeah, sparky."—Greg Williams, *Diamond Geezers*, p. 35, 1997

spark scene *noun*
a sexual fantasy; the imagined or remembered *scene* that *sparks* or enhances a sexual reaction *UK*
- I still think about it now when I'm wanking or if there's no fireworks with the girl I'm with. It's still my favourite spark scene, me and their Debbi that time.—Kevin Sampson, *Outlaws*, p. 104, 2001

sparky *noun*
a fool; a mentally handicapped person *UK*
Probably derived as a variation of **SPAC; SPACK**.
- —Chris Lewis, *The Dictionary of Playground Slang*, p. 213, 2003

sparky *adjective*
lively *UK*
Electric, giving off sparks.
- This ridiculously hot, dark, noisy little nuthouse full of the sparkiest cunts going[.]—Dave Courtney, *Raving Lunacy*, p. 99, 2000

sparring partner *noun*
a friend; a companion; a husband or wife *UK*
From boxing jargon.

sparrow *noun*
an attractive, single female *BERMUDA*
- —Peter Smith and Fred M. Barritt, *Bermewjan Vurds*, 1985

Sparrow *noun*
in Canada, an Englishman, particularly a Cockney *CANADA*
- Canadians have not been slow to find nicknames for themselves and others. Among them are Spud Islander, peasouper, and for the Englishman, sparrow.—*Vancouver Sun*, p. 12/8, 22nd March 1966

sparrow-fart; sparrow's fart *noun*
dawn *UK, 1886*
- [B]elt round to the agency at sparrow fart!—Barry Humphries, *Bazza Pulls It Off!*, 1971

sparrow grass *noun*
asparagus *CANADA*

sparrow's kneecaps *noun*
undeveloped or non-existent arm muscles *UK*
Parodic, jocular, derisory.
- The muscles of his brawny arms stood out like – sparrow's kneecaps!—Beale, 1984

spastic *noun*
a stupid or uncoordinated person *AUSTRALIA, 1981*
A general term of abuse commonly used by schoolchildren.
- I called him a spastic when he dropped the ball.—June Factor, *Kidspeak*, 2000

spastic *adjective*
incompetent; uncoordinated; unfashionable *US*
A cruel allusion to spastic paralysis.
- You spastic creep!—*American Graffiti*, 1973
- —Ned Wallish, *The Truth Dictionary of Racing Slang*, p. 76, 1989
- I called the boy who smashed the window spastic.—June Factor, *Kidspeak*, p. 193, 2000

spat *noun*
a short, sharp quarrel; a tiff *US, 1804*
- [T]he spat over the pick 'n' mix[.]—Jenny Eclair, *Camberwell Beauty*, p. 43, 2000

spatmobile *noun*
the Toronto airport's Special Assistant Team vehicle *CANADA*
- The "spatmobile" is used to transport passengers with special needs within the airport, usually in the domestic area.—*Horizons*, p. 6, 27th April 1994

spawgee *noun*
a poor white person *BARBADOS*
- —Frank A. Collymore, *Barbadian Dialect*, p. 100, 1965

spaz *noun*

1 a person with spastic paralysis; a person who has any disablement *UK*

• —Chris Lewis, *The Dictionary of Playground Slang*, p. 212, 2003

2 an uncoordinated or incompetent individual; a fool *US*
Contemptuous and derogatory use of '*spas*tic' (a person with spastic paralysis). Also used in the variants 'spazz' and 'spas'.

• —J. R. Friss, *A Dictionary of Teenage Slang (Mt. Diablo High)*, 1964
• —Collin Baker et al., *College Undergraduate Slang Study Conducted at Brown University*, p. 202, 1968
• It's some joke, the old man has been a total spaz since the year one, the coordination of a five-year-old, and here I've got these three – jocks.—John Sayles, *Union Dues*, p. 103, 1977
• He doesn't look like a spaz or anything.—Tim Winton, *That eye, the sky*, p. 80, 1986
• Woody, ya daft spazz. Come on ... off.—Paul Fraser and Shane Meadows, *TwentyFourSeven*, p. 4, 1997
• "Shut up, you spaz," his sister had replied.—Jenny Eclair, *Camberwell Beauty*, p. 223, 2000

spaz; spazzo *adjective*
crazy; foolish *AUSTRALIA, 1966*

• I have got one spazzo brother (spazzo means mentle) and I have two parents, worse luck.—Kylie Mole (Maryanne Fahey), *My Diary*, p. 4, 1988

spaz chariot *noun*
a wheelchair *UK*
From **SPAZ** (a person who has any disablement).

• —Chris Lewis, *The Dictionary of Playground Slang*, p. 213, 2003

spaz cut *noun*
any hairstyle that is alleged to make the wearer look mentally or physically handicapped *UK*
From **SPAZ** (a person with a disablement).

• —Chris Lewis, *The Dictionary of Playground Slang*, p. 213, 2003

spazmo *noun*
an uncoordinated or incompetent individual; a fool *UK*
A variation of **SPASTIC**.

• Just look at you, swotting away for teacher like a total spazmo.—Ben Elton and Rik Mayall, *The Young Ones*, 8th May 1984

spaz out; spazz out *verb*
to act in a very awkward or uncoordinated manner; to lose emotional control *US, 1984*

• They're spazzed out on ganja anyway, they don't give a shit, they're gone.—Elmore Leonard, *Glitz*, p. 113, 1985
• I didn't tell you because I knew you'd spaz out, but the last train left an hour ago.—*200 Cigarettes*, 1999

spazzed *adjective*
drunk *UK*

• [G]etting spazzed off me fucking tits[.]—*Q*, p. 94, May 2002

spazzer *noun*
a spastic (a person with spastic paralysis) *UK*

• What's this fucking spazzer doing squeaking?—Jim Dury [quoting Ian Dury, 1999], *Ian Dury and the Blockheads – Song by Song*, p. 131, 2003

SP betting *noun*
illegal betting at starting price odds *AUSTRALIA, 1936*

• I have had one conviction since 1968: a $500 fine for SP betting. —Murray Farquhar, *Nine Words from the Grave*, p. 86, 1986

SP book *noun*
a starting price bookmaker's ledger *AUSTRALIA, 1948*

• For all I know, he buys drugs wholesale with it, runs massage parlours, operates SP books, imports illegal immigrants, exports protected fauna.—Gerald Sweeney, *The Plunge*, p. 189, 1981

SP bookie; SP bookmaker *noun*
an illegal off-course bookmaker who offers starting price odds *AUSTRALIA, 1938*

• You're right there, of course, sergeant, but an S.P. bookie isn't a criminal, not in the ordinary man's way of thinking, now is he?—Vince Kelly, *The Bogeyman*, p. 99, 1956
• The man in the flat underneath happened to be one of the biggest S.P. bookmakers in Sydney!—George Blaikie, *Remember Smith's Weekly?*, p. 94, 1966
• A husband had just said goodbye to his wife and as he was walking out the front gate, he met the SP bookie.—Frank Hardy and Athol George Mulley, *The Needy and the Greedy*, p. 57, 1975
• Jingling the coins in his pocket the young punter hurries down to the local pub a few minutes before race time to place his bet with the local SP bookie.—Clive Galea, *Slipper!*, p. 6, 1988

SP'd up *adjective*
informed *UK*

• I ain't too fuckin' SP'd up on all that howsyourfather[.]—Jeremy Cameron, *Brown Bread in Wengen*, p. 26, 1999

speak *noun*
a bar where alcohol is served illegally *US, 1930*
A shortened form of **SPEAKEASY**.

• It was during this era that a Yale student, whooping it up in one of the block's posh speaks, wandered from room to room wearing a puzzled frown.—Robert Sylvester, *No Cover Charge*, p. 71, 1956
• [T]he Feds had an uncommonly adept knack of knocking over speaks.—Red Rudensky, *The Gonif*, p. 94, 1970

speak *verb*

▸ **speak the real**
to speak the truth, unpleasant as it might be *US*

• —Ethan Hilderbrant, *Prison Slang*, p. 164, 1998

▸ **speak the same language**
to share a way of thinking about something *UK, 1948*

• The style may be totally different, but [Ian] McCartney and [Peter] Mandelson are speaking the same language about Labour's second term.—*New Statesman*, 14th May 2001

▸ **speak white**
to speak English *US*
Anglophone Canadian usage.

• —*Maledicta*, p. 170, Summer/Winter 1978: 'How to hate thy neighbor: a guide to racist maledicta'

-speak *suffix*
vocabulary or jargon *UK, 1949*
'Newspeak' is the language of Oceania in George Orwell's 1948 novel *1984*. This coinage seeped into the language and, post-1984, provides a neat formula for book titles and media headlines concerned with jargon and slang. 'Jackspeak' 1989, 'Low Speak' 1989, 'Artspeak' 1990, 'Eurospeak' 1992, 'Rockspeak' 1996, 'Freshspeak' 1997, 'Double Speak' 1999, 'Teen Speak' 2001 among others.

• —Connie Eble (Editor), *UNC-CH Campus Slang*, p. 7, Fall 1984
• —*American Speech*, Winter 1984
• —*American Speech*, Summer 1988
• [T]hree AA [Alcoholics Anonymous] meetings kept me on some kind of straight and narrow [...] My head – in Recoveryspeak – was a neighbourhood more dangerous than 135th and Lennox.—Stuart Brown, *Dangerous Parking*, p. 198, 2000
• "Gestapo" is police-speak for the motorbike cops[.]—Duncan MacLaughlin, *The Filth*, p. 87, 2002

speak!
tell me what's on your mind! *US*

• He said, "Speak, speak." So I said, "Well, I want to stay."—Hunter S. Thompson, *Songs of the Doomed*, p. 170, May 1975

speakeasy *noun*
a bar that sells alcohol illegally *US, 1889*

• Bootlegging and speakeasies are out.—Jack Lait and Lee Mortimer, *Chicago Confidential*, p. 145, 1950
• Jesus wouldn't be afraid to walk into this joint or any other speakeasy to preach the gospel.—Richard Brooks, *Elmer Gantry*, 1960

speaker *noun*
a gun *US*

• —Clarence Major, *Dictionary of Afro-American Slang*, p. 107, 1970

speak to the hand
▷ see: **TALK TO THE HAND**

speak up *verb*

▸ **speak up Brown – you're through!; speak up Ginger – you're almost through!**
said, as if on a telephone, as a comment on an audible fart *UK, 1961*
Occasionally heard as 'come on Brown', etc.

spear *noun*

1 a hypodermic needle *US*

• —Francis J. Rigney and L. Douglas Smith, *The Real Bohemia*, p. xx, 1961

2 a firefighter's hook *US*

• —*American Speech*, p. 273, December 1954: 'Fire terms: additional words and definitions'

▸ take the spear
to accept responsibility *US*
Colonel Oliver North popularised the phrase during the moral collapse of the Reagan presidency in 1986 and 87, explaining that while he had said that he would 'take the spear' for the administration's misdeeds in Iran and Nicaragua, he did not mean that he would accept responsibility if criminal prosecution became a possibility.
- Those of us who were won by his performance as an articulate witness may want to rethink our opinions as we watch him perform when it is really time to "take the spear." [Letter to the editor] — *Washington Post*, p. A18, 24th February 1989
- I've taken the spear for a lot of people. — *Gone in 60 Seconds*, 2000

▸ the spear
dismissal from work *AUSTRALIA*

spear *verb*
1 to dismiss someone from employment *AUSTRALIA, 1911*
2 to eject someone from a shop, pub, etc *AUSTRALIA*
- — *The (Sydney) Bulletin*, 26th April 1975

▸ spear the bearded clam
(from a male perspective) to have sex *AUSTRALIA*
Formed on **BEARDED CLAM** (the vagina).
- If youse get jack [bored] of stropping the Mulligan and feel like spearing the bearded clam [...] tell the tart you love her! — Barry Humphries, *Bazza Pulls It Off!*, 1971
- — James McDonald, *A Dictionary of Obscenity, Taboo and Euphemism*, p. 10, 1988

▸ spear the keg
to broach a keg of beer *AUSTRALIA*
- Things went downhill fast after the ceremonial spearing of the keg in the back yard. — John Birmingham, *He Died With a Felafel in his Hand*, p. 53, 1994

spear-carrier *noun*
a non-speaking role in a play; an actor who appears in the background or only plays minor roles *UK, 1984*
- The RSC [Royal Shakespeare Company] was a bit like that. It was fine for lead actors, less good for spear-carriers[.] — *The Guardian*, 4th June 2001

spear-chucker *noun*
1 a black person *US*
Offensive. An allusion to the jungles of Africa.
- — *Current Slang*, p. 10, Winter 1969
- "Spearchukka." "Motherfuckah, ahm gonna chuck a spear at year!" — Richard Price, *The Wanderers*, p. 160, 1974
- — *Maledicta*, p. 125, Summer 1980: 'Racial and ethnic slurs: regional awareness and variations'
- You're not even a name anymore. Just a spear-chucker with a goddamn number stenciled on the back of his prison fatigues. — *48 Hours*, 1982

2 a vocal, aggressive advocate *US*
- When he ran for re-election in 1992, he bragged that "Every lesbian spear chucker in this country is hoping I get defeated." — *NRC Quartler*, Winter 1997

spec *noun*
1 an operational *spec*ification; a detailed description of something *UK, 1956*
- "[G]rade out" – the proportion of a consignment [of fruit] that has to be junked because it doesn't meet the spec[.] — *The Guardian*, 29th May 2004

2 a position, a view-point *UK*
Probably abbreviated from 'spectate'.
- Halfway through the set Wheezer abandoned his usual spec by the mixing desk[.] — Kevin Sampson, *Powder*, p. 351, 1999

3 a pair of eye-glasses *BAHAMAS*
- — John A. Holm, *Dictionary of Bahamian English*, p. 191, 1982

▸ on spec
on the off chance; *spec*ulatively *UK, 1832*
- [S]ometimes they'll go into a likely-looking gaff on spec, so long as they are sure the owners are stinking rich. — Charles Raven, *Underworld Nights*, p. 11, 1956
- [W]e was having to go through a period of going out on spec, which to be honest, I fucking hate. — Danny King, *The Burglar Diaries*, p. 80, 2001

speccy; speckie *noun*
in Australian Rules football, a spectacular catching of the ball *AUSTRALIA, 1989*
- He'd had twice as many kicks as anybody else. Taken heaps of marks, including the speccy of the century. — Phillip Gwynne, *Deadly Unna?*, p. 132, 1998

special *noun*
a potent marijuana cigarette *US, 1938*
- — Ernest L. Abel, *A Marijuana Dictionary*, p. 94, 1982

special *adjective*
applied to a disabled or handicapped person *UK*
More patronising than euphemistic.
- "He's a special person", "He goes to the special school". — Chris Lewis, *The Dictionary of Playground Slang*, p. 213, 2003

special a la coke *noun*
the recreational drug ketamine in powder, capsule or tablet form *US*
- — US Department of Justice, *Street Terms*, October 1994

special friend *noun*
a woman's menstrual period *US*
- — Don R. McCreary (Editor), *Dawg Speak*, 2001

Special K *noun*
ketamine hydrochloride, an anaesthetic used as a recreational drug, in powder, capsule or tablet form *US*
Kellogg's Special K™, a well-known breakfast cereal, is the inspiration for this variation on **K** (ketamine).
- Special K (Ketamine) Cost: $40-$50 per half gram. — *Newsweek*, p. 62, 6th December 1993
- This makes Special K look weak. — *Kids*, 1995
- It reportedly resurfaced as "Special K" last year at Manhattan "rave parties," taking users to mental territory called "K Land" and the "K hole." — *The Record [Bergen County, New Jersey]*, p. A1, 5th December 1995
- — Angela Devlin, *Prison Patter*, p. 107, 1996
- Wha' y'after? Special K. Es... Apples. Got some killer Doves. — Nick Barlay, *Curvy Lovebox*, p. 187, 1997
- Ketamine – a powerful sedative (special K in club parlance), either shoved up your nose on down your gob – is the nastiest of the new breed of drugs. — John Robb, *The Nineties*, p. 59, 1999
- [H]e was totally wired, telling DG it wasn't cocaine but "Special K", or ketamine ... which is more generally used as a horse anaesthetic. — Wayne Anthony, *Spanish Highs*, p. 12, 1999
- Ketamine, Special K. Fucking animal tranquillizer. What you playing at? — Colin Butts, *Is Harry Still on the Boat?*, p. 135, 2003

specimen *noun*
a person of a stated character *UK, 1854*
Generally derogatory.
- I fear that beside the hirsute masculinity of her father I appear a poor specimen. — *The Guardian*, 22nd April 2000

speck *noun*
a black person *US*
Offensive.
- — Edith A. Folb, *runnin' down some lines*, p. 255, 1980

Speck *noun*
▸ the Speck
Tasmania *AUSTRALIA, 1916*
A reference to the shape and size of Tasmania on a map; shortened from obsolete 'Fly-speck Isle'.

speck *verb*
1 to search for gold or opal on the surface of the ground *AUSTRALIA, 1888*
- He had gone specking for gold[.] — Arthur Upfield, *Bony and the Mouse*, p. 46, 1959

2 to place a highly speculative bet on a horse *AUSTRALIA*
- Mr Phillips, however, had no connection with the Bravo stable and merely 'specked' the horse for the sake of the odds. — Maurice Cavanough and Meurig Davies, *Cup Day*, p. 77, 1960
- I specked him at long odds. — Jack Hibberd and Garrie Hutchinson, *The Barracker's Bible*, p. 190, 1984

specker *noun*
1 a speculative bettor *AUSTRALIA*
Agent noun of **SPECK**.
- Some speckers rushed to back the colt for the Melbourne Cup, but the wise ones held off until they knew which horse Mr De Mestre intended to set for the big race. — Maurice Cavanough and Meurig Davies, *Cup Day*, p. 60, 1960

2 one year of a prison sentence *US*
Used in numeric constructions such as 'three-specker' or 'five-specker'.
- — Hyman E. Goldin et al., *Dictionary of American Underworld Lingo*, p. 203, 1950

specking *noun*

an act of randomly searching for houses to burgle *UK*

From **ON SPEC** (speculatively).

- —Angela Devlin, *Prison Patter*, p. 107, 1996

specky *adjective*

bespectacled *UK, 1956*

- Well, the next thing we ken is thit the specky cunt's glassed Tam, cut the side of hes face open. —Irvine Welsh, *The State of the Party (Disco Biscuits)*, p. 33, 1995
- [T]hey were Wristy Specky Swots[.] —James Hawes, *Dead Long Enough*, p. 40, 2000

specs *noun*

1 eye-glasses *UK, 1807*

A shortened form of 'spectacles'.

- "Where your specs, Rooski?" asked Penny, watching him bent two inches over his tray, trolling for vagrant shreds of fowl in the suety paste already setting like concrete. —Seth Morgan, *Homeboy*, p. 45, 1990
- [A] guy in specs with a rash creepin' up his neck[.] —Nick Barlay, *Curvy Lovebox*, p. 103, 1997

2 a person with poor eyesight and thick glasses *US*

- The labels were cruel: Gimp, Limpy-go-fetch, Crip, Lift-one-drag one, etc. Pint, Half-a-man, Peewee, Shorty, Lardass, Pork, Blubber, Belly, Blimp. Nuke-knob, Skinhead, Baldy. Four-eyes, Specs, Coke bottles. — *San Francisco Examiner*, p. A15, 28th July 1997

3 in horse racing, blinkers on a horse *US*

- —David W. Maurer, *Argot of the Racetrack*, p. 59, 1951

spectacles, testicles, wallet and watch

the positions of the hand when making the sign of the cross *UK*

Part Catholic mnemonic, part joke.

- Spectacles, testicles, wallet and watch! —Mike Myers, *Austen Powers: The Spy Who Shagged Me*, 1999
- Spectacles, testicles, wallet, watch. —Stuart Blumberg, *Bad Faith*, 2000

sped *noun*

a social outcast *US*

- — *Newsday*, p. B2, 11th October 1997

speed *noun*

1 an amphetamine, especially Dexedrine™, which is a central nervous system stimulant *US*

- —J. L. Simmons and Barry Winograd, *It's Happening*, p. 173, 1966: 'glossary'
- The profits were might good on the pills and besides with the speed (amphetamine) family the users often got addicted, making more permanent customers. —Abbie Hoffman, *Woodstock Nation*, p. 69, 1969
- When he meets pushers of smack annd speed, as he does not infrequently in his profession, he attempts to convince them that it is a vile and murderous act to peddle chemicals which can ultimately only destroy their imbibers. —Tom Robbins, *Another Roadside Attraction*, p. 58, 1971
- That's why there ain't a repo man I know that don't take speed. —*Repo Man*, 1984
- I tell you I've seen a roomful of cops who had no idea what speed was. "Amphetamine? What the fuck is amphetamine?" —Herbert Huncke, *Guilty of Everything*, 1990
- [As a sop to their pillhead fans [in 1967, the Small Faces] went on Top Of The Pops and sang, "Here comes the nice – he knows what I need – he's always there when I need some speed." The drug squad were too preoccupied to notice. —Simon Napier-Bell, *Black Vinyl White Powder*, p. 93, 2001

2 crack cocaine *UK*

- —Mike Haskins, *Drugs*, p. 282, 2003

3 ability in pool *US*

- The hustler exploits this fact so as to deceive his opponent as to his (the hustler's) true level of skill (true "speed"). —Ned Polsky, *Hustlers, Beats, and Others*, p. 51, 1967
- All hustlers conceal their true speed – or travel below their speed limit – as long as possible, lest they blow their cover or be forced to give weight. —Steve Rushin, *Pool Cool*, p. 27, 1990

speed *verb*

1 to be under the influence of a central nervous system stimulant *US*

- But what usually happened was that I'd be speeding like mad when the downs finally took effect. —Cleo Odzer, *Goa Freaks*, p. 148, 1995

2 in poker, to bet heavily and to bluff often *US, 1983*

- —Thomas L. Clark, *The Dictionary of Gambling and Gaming*, p. 210, 1987

speedball *noun*

1 a mixture of a central nervous system stimulant (especially cocaine) and a narcotic (especially heroin) *US, 1936*

- Goldy shook two small papers of crystal cocaine and morphine into the spoon and cooked a C and M speedball over the flame. —Chester Himes, *A Rage in Harlem*, p. 38, 1957
- One morning you wake up and take a speed ball and feel bugs under your skin. —William Burroughs, *Naked Lunch*, p. 19, 1957
- Leslie thought of copping – four girls and four boys. A speed-ball. —Clarence Cooper Jr, *The Scene*, p. 36, 1960
- Cocaine and bombitas are both stimulants and combined with heroin, a depressant, they produce an electrifying "rush" or "flash" far more pleasurable to the addict than heroin alone. —James Mills, *The Panic in Needle Park*, p. 36, 1966
- And don't take but one, it's all you'll need, it's a speedball. —Chester Himes, *Come Back Charleston Blue*, p. 39, 1966
- He closed his eyes as if he were remembering his last speedball. —Nathan Heard, *Howard Street*, p. 186, 1968
- I started capping "H" with my "C." I'd mix them and shoot speedballs. —Iceberg Slim (Robert Beck), *Pimp*, p. 275, 1969
- Jim was the only guy I knew that had a shooting gallery where you could cop a speedball by buying a half cap of girl and a half cap of boy[.] —A.S. Jackson, *Gentleman Pimp*, p. 98, 1973
- [H]e suggested he try a speedball, which was a "steal" at fifty cents. Barrett wasn't sure exactly what was contained in a speedball and was far too cooled-out to pull a Q & A scene to relieve his ignorance. —Ed Sanders, *Tales of Beatnik Glory*, p. 126, 1975
- —Jim Carroll, *Forced Entries*, 1987
- I have never liked speedballs, the combining of cocaine and heroin in a single shot. —Jim Carroll, *Forced Entries*, p. 1, 1987
- When I was using both stuff and speed, it was something. I've used the expression before – it's the poor man's speedball. —Herbert Huncke, *Guilty of Everything*, p. 190, 1990
- Every morning he woke up to something like morning sickness and had to get his speedball right away, but he wasn't addicted. —William T. Vollman, *Whores for Gloria*, p. 69, 1991
- Then you had John Belushi's speedball death. — Editors of Ben is Dead, *Retrohell*, p. 60, 1997
- He's sitting on his waterbed doing speedballs with some naked Dutch hitchhiker he picked up at the bus stop. —Kenneth Lonergan, *This is Our Youth*, p. 41, 2000
- He overdosed on a cocaine and heroin "speedball" made with a particularly lethal strain of heroin nicknamed Red Rum. — *Uncut*, p. 62, May 2001

2 an alcoholic beverage fortified with a drug *US*

- —Joseph E. Ragen and Charles Finston, *Inside the World's Toughest Prison*, p. 819, 1962: 'Penitentiary and underworld glossary'

3 a rissole *AUSTRALIA, 1965*

- The cook with his speed-balls delightful[.] —Keith Garvey, *Absolutely Australian*, p. 18, 1979

speedball *verb*

to inject or smoke a mixture of cocaine and heroin *UK*

After the noun sense.

- —Robert Ashton, *This Is Heroin*, p. 210, 2002

speedboat *noun*

marijuana *UK, 1998*

- —Mike Haskins, *Drugs*, p. 289, 2003

speedbomb *noun*

amphetamine powder rolled in a cigarette paper (for the purpose of swallowing) *UK*

- Last thing a saw Colm eat apart from speedbombs was a sweaty cheese roll[.] —Niall Griffiths, *Grits*, p. 9, 2000

speed bump *noun*

1 a red bump on the skin sometimes suffered after injecting impure amphetamines *US*

- —Geoffrey Froner, *Digging for Diamonds*, p. 57, 1989
- Signs of long-term use: hair loss, open sores and "speed bumps," or areas on the skin that the user constantly picks. — *The Post-Standard (Syracuse, New York)*, p. B1, 6th February 2004

2 a non-military obstacle that is likely to hinder an army's progress, especially civilians but also used of geographic features *US*

Military jargon.

- Likely human speed bumps are what aid agencies call IDPs, internally displaced persons[.] — *The Guardian*, p. 3, 21st March 2003

speed bumps *noun*

1 small female breasts *US*

- —Chris Lewis, *The Dictionary of Playground Slang*, p. 213, 2003

2 Saudi Arabian troops *US*
Gulf war usage.
- — *American Speech*, p. 401, Winter 1991: 'Among the new words'

speed-dating *noun*
an intensive method of meeting a number of prospective partners, organised so that each meets each for a short period before moving on to 'date' the next *US*
- — Susie Dent, *The Language Report*, p. 9, 2003

speed for lovers *noun*
▷ **see:** LOVER'S SPEED

speedfreak *noun*
a person who is addicted to or compulsively uses amphetamines or methamphetamine *US*
- Sam said he was an ex-speed freak, and that may have been why he gave the impression of spiritual fragility. — Nicholas Von Hoffman, *We Are The People Our Parents Warned Us Against*, p. 15, 1967
- We were turning into a nation of Speed Freaks and Nixon, the used-car dealer from Whittier, California, was becomin the biggest pill pusher of them all!!! — Abbie Hoffman, *Woodstock Nation*, p. 69, 1969
- SUPER JOEL TO DR. SPOCK: "Hey, this march is going too slow for us speed freeks." — Jerry Rubin, *Do It!*, p. 74, 1970
- You had to be to own this joint, which catered to bookmakers, huggermugger whores, paddy hustlers, speed freaks, fruits and fruit hustlers, and ex-cons of both sexes and all ages. — Joseph Wambaugh, *The Blue Knight*, p. 43, 1973
- Did I shoot speed? No, I didn't. Speed kills. I'm not a speedfreak. — Lester Bangs (quoting Lou Reed), *Psychotic Reactions and Carburetor Dung*, p. 177, 1975
- Gloria is a speed freak, in the true sense of the word. She has been on a virtual nonstop run of speed, in one form or another, for the last ten years. — Jim Carroll, *Forced Entries*, p. 29, 1987
- "Speed freaks," said Buell sardonically, and we understood a great deal about the erstwhile tenants. To think that methedrine was a prized and popular drug back then[.] — Sean Hutchinson, *Crying Out Loud*, p. 93, 1988

Speed Gordon *noun*
used as the epitome of trouble or strife *AUSTRALIA*
- As far as I knew that liquor could have been water and we'd have been in more strife than Speed Gordon. — Geoff Mill, *Nobody Dies Biut Me*, p. 98, 1961
- 'Billy M. is hooked,' said one. 'Doing a stack,' enjoined another. 'In more trouble than Speed Gordon,' whispered yet another. — Lew QWright, *Cards, Dice and Pennies*, p. 170, 1967
- All I know is your aunty's in more strife than Speed Gordon. — *Bazza Holds His Own*, 1974

speed hump *noun*
a skindiver *AUSTRALIA*
- The mortal enemy of the tinny driver is the half-submerged skindiver. These are known in the trade as 'speed humps'. — *Sydney Morning Herald*, p. 8s, 29th June 1996

speed jaw *noun*
an aching jaw which is a symptomatic after-effect of amphetamine use *UK*
- If you get speed jaw, use up some of the excess adrenaline by either chewing gun [...] or sucking a lollipop. — *Mixmag*, p. 105, February 2002

speed merchant *noun*
in American football, a fast runner *US*
- — Howard B. Bonham, *Football Lingo*, p. 51, 1962

speed money *noun*
a bribe that purchases official cooperation of bureaucratic machinery *INDIA*
- to root out middlemen and prevent government staff being tempted by speed money — *The Times of India*, 17th July 2002

speedo *noun*
a speedometer *UK, 1934*
- [W]e charge down a country lane and the speedo nips comfortably up to 120 kph. — *Ask*, p. 45, 5th May 1979
- Summers pressed the accelerator hard and the speedo touched 50[.] — Donald Gorgon, *Cop Killer*, p. 4, 1994

speed of heat *noun*
a high speed *US*
US naval aviator usage.
- — *United States Naval Institute Proceedings*, p. 108, October 1986

speedometer *noun*
in computing, a graphic depiction of a computer's current operating speed *US*
- — Eric S. Raymond, *The New Hacker's Dictionary*, p. 332, 1991

speedy *adjective*
of drugs, displaying stimulant qualities; of a person, under the influence of a central nervous system stimulant *UK*
From SPEED (amphetamines).
- "Come on, a nice toot of coke will make you feel better." "I'm too speedy as it is." — Cleo Odzer, *Goa Freaks*, p. 174, 1995
- Now a new drug [amphetamine sulphate] appeared, as speedy as cocaine but much cheaper, and it revitalised the music business. — Simon Napier-Bell, *Black Vinyl White Powder*, p. 158, 2001

speedy dog *nickname*
a Greyhound bus; the Greyhound corporation *US*
- — Kathleen Odean, *High Steppers, Fallen Angels, and Lollipops*, p. 30, 1988

speedy squib *noun*
in horse racing, a horse that runs well for most of the race but does not finish well *AUSTRALIA*
- — Ned Wallish, *The Truth Dictionary of Racing Slang*, p. 76, 1989

Speewah; Speewa *noun*
an imaginary remote country property or locale used as a setting for tall tales *AUSTRALIA, 1890*
Named after an actual place in northwest Victoria.

speiler *noun*
a swindler *AUSTRALIA, 1879*
- It was easy enough to back the winner, but the Gumtreeites find it a much more difficult matter to obtain their money. The 'speilers' cluster together when the favourite wins, and the first backer of the winner, when he asks for his money, is politely told to wait, as an objection is about to be lodged. Of course, no objection is lodged, and the 'speilers' determine to fight their way out of the difficulty. — Nat Gould, *Town and Bush*, p. 222, 1896
- They spoke of 'spielers from the Bland', And 'champions from the Castlereagh', And gave the youth to understand That all these would stop away, And spoil the race, if they should hear That they had got The Trap to fear. — A.B. Paterson, *Rio Grande and Other Verses*, p. 114, 1902
- The spieler likes to put a safe distance between himself and the butt of his jest – and he usually played for big stakes. — Bill Wannan, *Bullockies, Beauts and Bandicoots*, p. 90, 1960
- [C]ampbell Street, Surry Hills, was crowded with its usual clientele of spielers, gamblers, spivs, 'jazz babies' and general crooks. — James Holledge, *The Great Australian Gamble*, p. 151, 1966
- — Sam Weller, *Old Bastards I Have Met*, p. 125, 1979

spell *noun*
a sentence of three months' imprisonment *UK*
- — Angela Devlin, *Prison Patter*, p. 107, 1996

spell *verb*
▸ **spell it out**
to explain something that should be apparent and make it absolutely clear *UK, 1968*
- Now do you understand what was going on last Wednesday – or must I spell it out for you? — *The Guardian*, 18th February 2002

spelling flame *noun*
an inflammatory Internet posting attacking another's spelling *US*
- — Christian Crumlish, *The Internet Dictionary*, p. 184, 1995

spell-o *noun*
a rest period, a break *ANTARCTICA, 1916*
- — Bernadette Hince, *The Antarctic Dictionary*, p. 340, 2000

spelunk *verb*
▸ **spelunk without a partner**
(of a female) to masturbate *US*
Figurative sense of 'spelunking' (caving as a sport), hence this solo exploration of a 'grotto' (the vagina).
- Another way to say "the girl is masturbating" [...] Spelunking without a partner[.] — Erica Orloff and JoAnn Baker, *Dirty Little Secrets*, p. 67, 2001

spelunker *noun*
a caver *US, 1942*
Ultimately from Latin *spelunca* (a cave).
- — John Ayto, *The Oxford Dictionary of Slang*, p. 355, 1998

- In the 1980s, spelunkers entered a deep dive in Romania that had been sealed off from the outside world for a long but unknown period. — Bill Bryson, *A Short History of Nearly Everything*, p. 369, 2003

Spenard divorce *noun*
a shooting of one spouse by the other *US*
- — Robert O. Bowen, *An Alaskan Dictionary*, p. 31, 1965
- The action is named after the Spenard district of Anchorage, where the rite is often conducted in one of the area's many watering holes. — Mike Doogan, *How to Speak Alaskan*, p. 55, 1993

spend *verb*
▸ **spend a penny**
to urinate *UK*
This derives from the charge made for use of a public convenience. The first to charge a penny was opened outside the Royal Exchange, London, in 1855; however, a euphemistic use is not recorded until 1945. Since then prices have risen to beyond a point where the term has any practical meaning.
- [U]nion leaders are seeking a change in the law so that employees can spend a penny whenever they need to, without wages being docked. — *The Guardian*, 21st February 2003

spends *noun*
*spend*ing money *UK*
- Frankie's workin twelve-hour days to get us some spends together. — Niall Griffiths, *Kelly + Victor*, p. 119, 2002

spendy *adjective*
expensive *US*
- — Judi Sanders, *Faced and Faded, Hanging to Hurl*, p. 37, 1993
- Sadly, a twin deck mixing desk can be a bit spendy. Mind you, when you've only got 5.35 in the Post Office account your granny set up for you twelve years ago, anything's a bit spendy. — Richard Topping, *Havin' It Large*, p. 79, 2000

speng *noun*
a fool *UK*
- — Angela Devlin, *Prison Patter*, p. 107, 1996

spent up *adjective*
having no more money *UK*
- I'm spent up and I've got nothing to snort the bastard with. — Nicholas Blincoe, *Ardwick Green (Disco Biscuits)*, p. 13, 1996

sperm wail *noun*
an involuntary cry from a male experiencing an orgasm *UK*
- — *Roger's Profanisaurus*, p. 200, 2002
- — Chris Lewis, *The Dictionary of Playground Slang*, p. 214, 2003

spesh *noun*
Carlsberg Special Brew™ lager *UK*
Phonetic abbreviation of 'special'.
- All I need's a crumpled up can of spesh. — Nick Barlay, *Curvy Lovebox*, p. 155, 1997

spesh *adjective*
special *AUSTRALIA*
- You're probably wondering why, if hemp is so spesh, it hasn't already been used for all these wonderful things! — *Sydney City Hub*, p. 5, 4th July 1996

spew *noun*
1 vomit *US*
- I pulled my shirt over my face, catching about a quart of liquid spew in my T-shirt, which I cradled between my arms. — Elissa Stein and Kevin Leslie, *Chunks*, p. 13, 1997

2 semen *US*
- — Pamela Munro, *U.C.L.A. Slang*, p. 79, 1989

3 a temper tantrum *NEW ZEALAND*
- — David McGill, *David McGill's Complete Kiwi Slang Dictionary*, p. 118, 1998

spew *verb*
1 to vomit *US*
- I told Dennis if he gave me another topic that was political I'd spew burrito chunks. — *Heathers*, 1988
- — Pamela Munro, *U.C.L.A. Slang*, p. 79, 1989
- I'd sing the rest, but I don't want to spew. — *Wayne's World*, 1992

2 to ejaculate *US*
Adopted from the more common sense 'to vomit', suggesting a more than generous ejaculation.
- — Pamela Munro, *U.C.L.A. Slang*, p. 79, 1989

3 to reject an agreement or responsibility *UK*
Possibly a play on synonymous **BLOW OUT**.
- Not workin today? – Nah. Spewed it for today. Called in a sicky. — Niall Griffiths, *Kelly + Victor*, p. 140, 2002

4 to be extremely angry *AUSTRALIA*
- I'd beaten them out the back. They'd be spewing. — Kathy Lette, *Girls' Night Out*, p. 189, 1987
- I am fairdinkum spewing badly. — Kylie Mole (Maryanne Fahey), *My Diary*, p. 3, 1988
- I was talking to Sirro the other day, and he is absolutely spewing about the whole thing[.] — Paul Vautin, *Turn It Up!*, p. 200, 1995
- All the other kids at Little Aths are spewing. — Shane Maloney, *Nice Try*, p. 77, 1998

5 to post an excessive number of messages to an Internet discussion group *US*
- — Christian Crumlish, *The Internet Dictionary*, p. 184, 1995

▸ **spew your guts**
to inform on your friends to the police *UK, 1961*

▸ **spew your guts up**
to vomit violently *UK, 1984*
- He spewed his guts up and passed out. — Kenzaburo Oe, *The Silent Cry*, p. 24, 1994

▸ **spew your ring; spew your ring up**
to vomit violently *UK, 1963*
- An' I thought mibbe it was him that spewed his ring in RE [Religious Education], mind, like the fuckin' Exorcist[.] — Christopher Brookmyre, *One Fine Day in the Middle of the Night*, p. 61, 2003

spewing!
used for expressing anger *AUSTRALIA*
- Went to get the Playboy to bring to school and coodn't find it! I looked everywhere! I bet dad has taken it. Spewin. You just can't trust parents. — Kylie Mole (Maryanne Fahey), *My Diary by Kylie Mole*, p. 31, 1988
- 'Got any dosh?' Tristram shook his head. 'Zilch. I just checked. And my next dole cheque doesn't come in till tomorrow.' 'Spewin'.' Torquil was outraged. — Linda Jaivin, *Rock n Roll Babes from Outer Space*, p. 85, 1996
- — Glyn Parry, *Mosh*, p. 23, 1996

spewsome *adjective*
dreadful; awful *AUSTRALIA*
That is, 'enough to make you vomit'.
- [A] song voicing sympathy for a family of welfare recipients that the government and media picked on for refusing to take mind-deadening jobs requiring ugly haircuts and the wearing of spewsome uniforms. — Linda Jaivin, *Rock n Roll Babes from Outer Space*, p. 198, 1996

sphynx *noun*
the removal by wax of all of a woman's pubic hair; the results thereof *US*
- The Sphynx – it's the name of a hairless cat from Egypt. I must tell you: The Sphynx takes guts and not everyone has a lover who deserves a Sphynx wax. — *Nerve*, p. 20, December 2000–January 2001

spic *noun*
1 a Spanish-speaking person *US, 1913*
Derogatory and offensive.
- What about Puerto Ricans? What about spics, Dadier? — Evan Hunter, *The Blackboard Jungle*, p. 208, 1954
- BERNARDO: With an "American." Who is really a Polack. ANITA: Says the Spic. — *West Side Story*, 1957
- A guy on his way back from an OD, a naked kid in a sink, and some dumb spic broad hustling a guy who's probably too stupid to know she's on junk. Some world. — James Mills, *The Panic in Needle Park*, p. 40, 1966
- Lemme tell you about them rumbles. The wops said no spics could go east of Park Avenue. — Edwin Torres, *Carlito's Way*, p. 8, 1975
- Gus is in the hospital. Some P.R.'s got 'em. Fucking spics! — *Saturday Night Fever*, 1977
- Julio. Great. There are 20,000 spics named "Julio." — *The Bad Lieutenant*, 1992

2 a Spaniard *UK*
This usage reflects the fact that Spain is the closest Spanish-speaking community to the UK.
- The Spanish mobsters led by El Torro are standing listening to Mars Bar [...] HARMLESS: Spics gone? MARS BAR: Yeah... — Chris Baker and Andrew Day, *Lock, Stock... & a Fist Full of Jack and Jills*, p. 189, 2000
- "Can't trust the spicks," he spat with sudden venom. — Jake Arnott, *He Kills Coppers*, p. 44, 2001

3 the Spanish language *US*
- [T]hese guys would crouch around their pile of shredded joy and roll muggles on a twenty-four-hour shift, jabbering away in spic and smoking up all the profits. — Mezz Mezzrow, *Really the Blues*, p. 165, 1946

4 a West Indian *US*
- —Lou Shelly, *Hepcats Jive Talk Dictionary*, p. 17, 1945

5 a railway track worker *US*
Many track workers in the American southwest were Mexican; the racial epithet was applied to Mexican and non-Mexican alike.
- —Ramon Adams, *The Language of the Railroader*, p. 144, 1977

spico *noun*
a Spanish-speaking person *US*
A modestly embellished **SPIC**.
- Rocky and his fellas got to playing a way-out game with me called "One-finger-across-the-neck-inna-slicing-motion," followed by such gentle words as "It won't be long, spico."—Piri Thomas, *Down These Mean Streets*, p. 29, 1967

Spictown *noun*
a Spanish-speaking neighbourhood *US*
- I copped you a sixteenth [of an ounce of heroin] in "Spic" town. You know I gotta love your stinking junkie ass to stick my neck out like that.—Iceberg Slim (Robert Beck), *Pimp*, p. 99, 1969

spide *noun*
a member of a Belfast subcultural urban adolescent grouping that seems to be defined by a hip-hop dress and jewellery sense *UK: NORTHERN IRELAND*
- It's all down to my sartorial transformation. I have morphed into a spide, a boy thug.—*The Observer*, 7th December 2003

spider *noun*
1 in the television and film industries, a device used to support the legs of a tripod on a slippery or uneven surface *UK*
- —Oswald Skilbeck, *ABC of Film and TV Working Terms*, p. 122, 1960

2 in harness racing, a sulky *AUSTRALIA*
- —Ned Wallish, *The Truth Dictionary of Racing Slang*, p. 76, 1989

3 a tall glass of carbonated soft drink with a dollop of ice-cream in the top *AUSTRALIA, 1941*

spider blue *noun*
heroin *US*
Referring probably to the web of blue veins into which heroin users inject the drug.
- —US Department of Justice, *Street Terms*, October 1994
- —Robert Ashton, *This Is Heroin*, p. 207, 2002

spider box *noun*
in the television and film industries, an electrical junction box *US*
- —Ralph S. Singleton, *Filmaker's Dictionary*, p. 158, 1990

spider hole *noun*
a sniper's lair in a cave *US*
Korean war usage.
- Van Horn had asked Louis Bengis to carry a twelve-pound satchel charge, in case we ran across another sniper cave or spider-hole. —Martin Russ, *The Last Parallel*, p. 374, 1957
- This is how we used to booby trap spider holes in the war when we didn't have any demo.—Edward Lee, *Ghouls*, p. 424, 1988

spider's legs *noun*
the pubic hair that can be seen outside the confines of a girl's bikini or underwear *UK*
- —Chris E. Lewis, *The Dictionary of Playground Slang*, 2003

spiel *noun*
1 a long-winded explanation *US, 1896*
- The nurse tried to take my mind off my misery by holding up my appendix and giving me a spiel about it, like a guide taking some sightseers through the Grand Canyon.—Mezz Mezzrow, *Really the Blues*, p. 38–39, 1946
- You give her the main spiel and I'll fill in the details.—Max Shulman, *The Zebra Derby*, p. 103, 1946
- Yeah, I was outside the door while you were going through your spiel.—Mickey Spillane, *I, The Jury*, p. 20, 1947
- He must have hated me behind his spiel, yet he'd ignored me.—Ralph Ellison, *Invisible Man*, p. 445, 1947
- In the morning they'd get the letter at the desk, and he'd give the manager a spiel, and after they got the dough they'd be off.—James T. Farrell, *The Life Adventure*, p. 191, 1947
- In the street, a blend of juke boxes created a weird cacophony, splintered by car horns and the spiel of the hawkers before each club[.]—John Clellon Holmes, *Go*, p. 49, 1952
- The usual routine is to grab someone with junk on him, and let him stew in jail until he is good and sick. Then comes the spiel: "We can get you five years for possession."—William Burroughs, *Junkie*, p. 61, 1953
- He had the whole cookpot spiel worked out; he practiced on Camille and me in the evenings.—Jack Kerouac, *On the Road*, p. 175, 1957
- Old Omar really laid down a righteous spiel!—Ross Russell, *The Sound*, p. 75, 1961
- I was all prepared for a sermon or long spiel about the Muslim thing.—Claude Brown, *Manchild in the Promised Land*, p. 234, 1965
- "We never did try it in the phone booth, did we?" I said, seeking to divert her from the spiel I could feel coming on.—John Nichols, *The Sterile Cuckoo*, p. 174, 1965
- He comes steaming in with his usual spiel about how he's fitted up somebody who wasn't even on the job[.]—Ted Lewis, *Jack Carter's Law [britpulp]*, p. 47, 1974
- I musta been a lawyer in the other life, because I can't resist puttin' down a spiel in the courthouse.—Edwin Torres, *After Hours*, p. 165, 1979
- I don't have to listen to his I-am-a-mad-mobster spiel for much longer—Kelvin Sampson, *Outlaws*, 2001

2 a speech intended to attract customers *US*
- "Carny?" "Yeah." I named a couple of outfits. "Speil?" "Um. And sleight of hand."—Robert Edmond Alter, *Carny Kill*, p. 3, 1966

3 an illegal gambling operation *UK*
- —Angela Devlin, *Prison Patter*, p. 108, 1996

4 a drinking club *UK*
Probably a shortening of **SPIELER**.
- —*Now!*, 10th April 1981

spiel *verb*
to talk, especially at length; to patter *US, 1894*
- One day while he was spieling about his dope, Mike called me over to straighten this gunman out with some golden-leaf and lowrate him once and for all.—Mezz Mezzrow, *Really the Blues*, p. 94, 1946
- [H]e spieled with twinkling eyes, his lips working rapidly.—Ralph Ellison, *Invisible Man*, p. 176, 1947
- I've seen you around and heard you spiel, that's all.—George Mandel, *Flee the Angry Strangers*, p. 5, 1948
- "I'm starving for some carving of beef for a thief," spieled Eddie.—Dan Burley, *Diggeth Thou?*, p. 9, 1959
- John 15X continues spieling ... watching closely as Bam and Baby June lean against each other in pure misery[.]—Odie Hawkins, *Ghetto Sketches*, p. 209, 1972
- Everyone in the room leaned forward a bit as Father Love opened his mouth to spiel.—Donald Goines, *The Busting Out of an Ordinary Man*, p. 76, 1985
- Murikami spieled for a straight hour.—James Ellroy, *Hollywood Nocturnes*, p. 286, 1994

spieler *noun*
1 a facile and smooth speaker *US, 1894*
- If they didn't have a spieler like Kleinfeld around, they would starve to death.—Edwin Torres, *After Hours*, p. 218, 1979
- A man who had a reputation as a spieler (a man who could draw a crowd around him and sell almost anything) welched on a few pounds he owed me over a snooker bet.—Brian McDonald, *Elephant Boys*, p. 206, 2000

2 a person who stands at the door of a business calling out to people passing by, trying to lure them into the business *US, 1894*
- A showman who harangues the crowd from outside is a "spieler" or "barker"[.]—Butch Reynolds, *Broken Hearted Clown*, p. 32, 1953
- "Spielers I don't need," Cochrane told me right off.—Robert Edmond Alter, *Carny Kill*, p. 6, 1966

3 an (illegal) gambling or drinking club *UK, 1931*
- [T]he Berwick Social Club, which is the official name of Dickie Cash's spieler.—Charles Raven, *Underworld Nights*, p. 67, 1956
- He owns a spieler, this character.—Anonymous *Streetwalker*, p. 129, 1959
- flying dodgy kites [passing fraudulent cheques] with each other at bent spielers—Derek Raymond (Robin Cook), *The Crust on its Uppers*, p. 21, 1962
- Spot and Hill ran dozens of spielers in the West End[.]—Brian McDonald, *Elephant Boys*, p. 246, 2000

spiff *noun*
1 a loner *US*
An articulation of the initials SBF (*s*urrounded *by* *f*riends), used with irony.
- —*Carmel (California) High School Yearbook*, 1987

2 a tip, gratuity or commission *US*
- —Anna Scotti and Paul Young, *Buzzwords*, p. 41, 1997

3 a bonus paid by a record company to a promoter who has succeeded in getting a record played *US*
- —Walter Hurst and Donn Delson, *Delson's Dictionary of Radio & Record Industry Terms*, p. 102, 1980

spiff *verb*

to dress up *US, 1979*

Coined in the UK in the 1870s, obsolete by the 1930s, and then resurfaced in the US in the 1970s, used with 'up'.

- Dad just got spiffed up and left the house. He has a date. With a woman! — C.D. Payne, *Youth in Revolt*, p. 299, 1993

spiffed *adjective*

drunk *US*

- "Well, you know," I answered, feigning embarrassment. "I had to get all spiffed. You see, I went to the ballet." — Jim Carroll, *Forced Entries*, p. 20, 1987
- — *e-cyclopaedia*, 20th March 2002

spiffing; spiffin' *adjective*

excellent, first-rate; fashionable or smart *UK, 1872*

Often seen to be dated, redolent of the C19 to mid-C20 upper- and middle-class society, hence current usage tends towards irony. However, it is also current in its original unambiguous sense.

- Hi, Garstang, ready for a spiffin' trip to the seaside[?] — *SM:tv LIVE it's wicked*, p. 27, 2000
- Most agreed that he'd made a spiffing effort to reform. — *The Guardian*, 28th September 2000

spifflicated; spiflicated *adjective*

drunk *US, 1906*

- "Sylvia dead drunk, paralyzed, spifflicated, iced to the eyebrows," I said harshly. — Raymond Chandler, *The Long Goodbye*, p. 25, 1953
- "Damn, Ern," says I, somewhat spiflicated myself, "that's plangent." — Molly Ivins, *Nothin' But Good Times Ahead*, p. 43, 1994

spiffy *adjective*

well-dressed, elegant, sharp *UK, 1853*

- Libby MacAusland had a spiffy apartment in the Village. — Mary McCarthy, *The Group*, p. 181, 1963
- When we got to Japan and climbed down from the plane, everybody was spiffy and scruffy[.] — Larry Heinemann, *Close Quarters*, p. 169, 1977
- Gail was lookin' spiffy. I had her all dolled up in a new wardrobe. — Edwin Torres, *After Hours*, p. 375, 1979
- The Jag got to Fifteenth and turned left, went past that little park there and turned right onto Meridian. When the spiffy dark-green car all of a sudden pulled to a stop across from the Flamingo Terrace apartments, Raylan realized, Jesus, the guy was going to see Joyce Patton. — Elmore Leonard, *Pronto*, p. 84, 1999

spiflicate *verb*

to deal with someone in a way that confounds, silences, dumbfounds or defeats *UK, 1785*

A humorous colloquialism that by mid-C20 survived mainly as a vague threat to children. Recorded as a form of intimidation used among Yorkshire schoolchildren by Iona and Peter Ople, *The Lore and Language of Schoolchildren*, 1959.

- I've seen you somewheres before, though where that somewheres was, spiflicate me if I can call to mind! — Mary Braddon, *The Trail of the Serpent*, p. 343, 2003

spig *noun*

a Spanish-speaking person *US*

A corruption of the prevalent **SPIC**.

- "Sure, I see that spig bfore," Mr. Majestyk said. — Elmore Leonard, *The Big Bounce*, p. 45, 1969

spike *noun*

1 a syringe and needle; a hypodermic needle *US, 1936*

- Life telescopes down to junk, one fix and looking forward to the next, "stashes" and "scripts," "spikes" and "droppers." — William Burroughs, *Junkie*, p. 35, 1953
- "This," he said to Patterson, selecting one of the items, "is what most addicts call a spike. You can see all of it consists of is an everyday eyedropper, a baby's pacifier, tightened at the top with a rubber band, and a size-25 hypodermic needle." — Clarence Cooper Jr, *The Scene*, p. 82, 1960
- They didn't find the heroin but they found two spikes and with his marks and the girl's evidence that was enough. — Alexander Trocchi, *Cain's Book*, p. 106, 1960
- That spike doesn't make you a junkie. — Ross Russell, *The Sound*, p. 230, 1961
- "Willie, my man, I missed my vein," cried Mike with a spike in his arm. — Bruce Jackson, *Get Your Ass in the Water and Swim Like Me*, p. 205, 1962
- "Mainlining" is shooting heroin directly into a vein by means of a hypodermic needle (John S. calls it a "spike"). — Donald Louria, *Nightmare Drugs*, p. 9, 1966
- When he awakes in the morning, he reaches instantly for his "works" – eyedropper, needle ("spike," he calls it), and bottle top ("cooker"). — James Mills, *The Panic in Needle Park*, p. 14, 1966
- Silently they watched him mix a deck of heroin and a deck of cocaine, light the lamp and cook it in a spoon, load the spike. — Chester Himes, *Come Back Charleston Blue*, p. 65, 1966
- Cause it makes me feel like I'm a man / When I put a spike into my vein. — Velvet Underground *Heroin*, 1967
- Hip stayed at a rented room with a junkie girl with whom he'd taken off, after using her spike and giving her a share of his stuff. — Nathan Heard, *Howard Street*, p. 137, 1968
- "Sweet" finally got the "spike" out of the tie lining. I was too weak to shoot the 'H' when he got it cooked. — Iceberg Slim (Robert Beck), *Pimp*, p. 100, 1969
- All the losers went for the spike and the dynamite high behind it. — Edwin Torres, *Carlito's Way*, p. 11, 1975
- We bought two droppers and a couple of spikes – needles – No. 26-half inch and some wires for cleaning them. — Herbert Huncke, *The Evening Sun Turned Crimson*, p. 82, 1980

2 a mixture of heroin and scopolamine or strychnine *UK*

- — Robert Ashton, *This Is Heroin*, p. 210, 2002

3 in a deck of playing cards, an ace *US*

- — George Percy, *The Language of Poker*, p. 84, 1988

4 in volleyball, hitting the ball downward with great force from the top of a jump *US*

- — Bonnie Robison, *Sports Illustrated Volleyball*, p. 95, 1972

5 a casual ward (a temporary accommodation facility for vagrants) *UK, 1866*

- The other had spike (casual ward) written all over him, a real roadster [tramp], and a ruddy hairy one. — Charles Raven, *Underworld Nights*, p. 198, 1956

▸ **the spike**

the hypodermic syringe as a symbol of drug addiction *UK*

- [H]e had tried to get off the "spike" (needle), but had tried most of the other drugs on the black market and now lived by pushing and on Supplementary Benefit. — Robin Page, *Down Among the Dossers*, p. 28, 1973

spike *verb*

1 to adulterate a drink or ply a person with alcohol or drugs *US, 1909*

- So these barrels of near beer were trucked out to the Arrowhead to be spiked. — Mezz Mezzrow, *Really the Blues*, p. 63, 1946
- Almost immediately I was spiked with wine and acid. — Jamie Mandelkau, *Buttons*, p. 68, 1971
- "A little spiked coffee never hurt nobody's incentive," Shoat said. — Dan Jenkins, *Semi-Tough*, p. 136, 1972
- It was me and Wolfie that spiked these local police. — Dave Courtney, *Raving Lunacy*, p. 12, 2000

2 to inject a drug *US, 1935*

- — Robert Ashton, *This Is Heroin*, p. 210, 2002
- [Chet] Baker admits that most of the musicians he played with were on junk [heroin] and that "spiking myself became a gesture as automatic as lighting a cigarette is with you." — Robert Ashton, *This Is Heroin*, p. 28, 2002

3 in American football, to slam the football to the ground in a ritualistic celebration after scoring a touchdown *US*

- — George Sullivan, *Pro Football A to Z*, p. 277, 1975

4 to attach electrical tape on a stage floor to mark positions for props and sets *US*

- — Connie Eble (Editor), *UNC-CH Campus Slang*, p. 7, Fall 1991

spiked *adjective*

in a state of intoxication as the unwitting victim of an adulterated drink or drug *UK*

- I know one bloke who got spiked with seven trips [...] His life went to ruins. I got spiked once too, but I ended up thanking the geezer because I had a wicked time. — Macfarlane, Macfarlane and Robson, *The User*, p. 105, 1996

spiker *noun*

a (branded antidepressant) Prozac™ tablet *UK*

- CALL IT... Spikers, prozie JUST DON'T CALL IT... The "happy" pill — *Drugs An Adult Guide*, p. 35, December 2001

spikes *noun*

1 sports shoes with cleats *US*

- — Judi Sanders, *Da Bomb!*, p. 26, 1997

2 woman's shoes with narrow high heels that taper into a point, formally known as spike-heel shoes *US*

- The kind of jobs I get, I have to wear these killer spikes, they ruin your feet. — Elmore Leonard, *Out of Sight*, p. 142, 1996

spikey; spikie *noun*
an anti-globalisation activist with a philosophy of violent protest *UK*
- Fluffies on the run as spikies win battle of the streets. — *The Guardian*, 14th April 2001

spiky *adjective*
uncompromising in Anglican faith or practice *UK, 1881*
- Noted as theological college slang for 'High church, addicted to ceremonial excess' by — Robert Towler and APB Coxon, *The Fate of the Anglican Clergy*, 1979

spill *verb*
1 to fall off a surfboard *US*
- Do you know he's the only guy besides Duke Kahanamoku who came in on Zero break without spilling? — Frederick Kohner, *Gidget*, p. 41, 1957

2 to talk with energy and no clear agenda *US*
- — Clarence Major, *Dictionary of Afro-American Slang*, p. 107, 1970

▸ **spill the beans**
to tell that which one is not supposed to tell *US*
- Jules knew that he didn't dare have more than one photo session because Cynthia might accidentally spill the beans. — Joseph Wambaugh, *Finnegan's Week*, p. 19, 1993

▸ **spill your guts (out)**
to confess your secrets; to tell all you know *US, 1927*
- [H]e was ready to spill his guts tomorrow[!] — Budd Schulberg, *On the Waterfront*, 1954

spin *noun*
1 a tactical, revisionist interpretation of an event for public consumption *US, 1986*
Although the term came to the forefront during the Reagan presidency, it is an ancient practice that was simply taken to new heights by Reagan's handlers.
- — *American Speech*, Fall 1988

2 an excursion in a car *UK, 1907*
Originally applied to horse training, meaning 'a run of some duration', then to a bicycle ride, and now the present sense.
- I went outside to breathe some cold air and wake up, but figured I'd go for a spin in the auto. — James Simon Kunen, *The Strawberry Statement*, p. 89, 1968
- "You want to take a spin in this little beauty? I'll take you around the block," Doohan said with considerably less enthusiasm. — Robert Campbell, *Juice*, p. 123, 1988
- You guys want to go for a spin? — *Dazed and Confused*, 1993

3 a period of time considered in terms of how you fared during it; an experience; a time of it *AUSTRALIA, 1917*
- Anyway, I'd had a bit of a rough spin over here before, so I reckoned I'd come over again and give it another burl. — Barry Humphries, *The Wonderful World of Barry McKenzie*, p. 38, 1968

4 five years' imprisonment *AUSTRALIA, 1950*

5 a five-pound note; the sum of £5 *AUSTRALIA, 1941*
An abbreviation of **SPINNAKER**. After decimalisation in 1966 also briefly used for $5.
- 'Drive around the block for ten minutes to give me a chance to meet you up at the hospital,' directed Pudden. 'You're on a spin.' — John Wynnum, *Tar Dust*, p. 122, 1962
- — Ned Wallish, *The Truth Dictionary of Racing Slang*, p. 76, 1989

6 a single playing of a song by a radio station *US*
- Yeah, I know we lost the bullet, spins are down slightly, but that record has legs, man. — Elmore Leonards, *Be Cool*, p. 106, 1999

7 a turn at spinning the coins in the gambling game two-up *AUSTRALIA, 1919*
- The division of money was complete now and the School was settling down for the next spin. — Kenneth Cook, *Wake in Fright*, p. 28, 1961

8 a Separation Program Number *US*
The numbers corresponded to several hundred reasons for discharge from the service. Also known as 'spin number'.
- Depending on command whim and caprice, a soldier could also get an even more impairing general discharge with similar "spins" for the same things. — Myra MacPherson, *Long Time Passing*, p. 679, 1984

spin *verb*
1 to manipulate, edit and present information in such a way that it suits political needs or a political agenda *UK*
- The spinners have spun, the plagiarists plagiarised: we are still opposed to Blair's war. — *The Guardian*, 1st March 2003

2 in circus and carnival usage, to speak a language or dialect fluently *US*
- — Don Wilmeth, *The Language of American Popular Entertainment*, p. 251, 1981

3 to search *UK, 1972*
- — Angela Devlin, *Prison Patter*, p. 108, 1996

4 to play a record, especially on the radio *US, 1965*
- Right now you have the unique opportunity of being the very first station on the coast, man, to spin Roadkill, right up to the Top Forty. — Elmore Leonard, *Be Cool*, p. 165, 1999

5 in the language surrounding the Grateful Dead, to tape a concert *US*
- — David Shenk and Steve Silberman, *Skeleton Key*, p. 268, 1994

6 to turn back a car's odometer (mileometer) *US*
- — *American Speech*, p. 309–310, Winter 1980: 'More jargon of car salesmen'

7 to deceive *US*
- Okay, Mike. I'll spin it. Don't bother calling me again, okay? — Mickey Spillane, *Kiss Me Deadly*, p. 120, 1952

8 to leave *US*
- — James Harris, *A Convict's Dictionary*, p. 39, 1989

▸ **spin a dit**
in nautical use, to tell a story, especially a tall story *AUSTRALIA, 1943*
From **DIT** (a tale).
- Kate coughed with self embarrassment, realising that Toggle might spin the odd dit about him. — John Wynnum, *Tar Dust*, p. 22, 1962
- Old Bull Murphy can spin a pretty good dit when it comes to a showdown. — John Wynnum, *Jiggin' in the Riggin'*, p. 21, 1965

▸ **spin a drum; spin**
to search a private premises *UK*
- — David Powis, *The Signs of Crime*, 1977

▸ **spin the shit**
to discuss something *UK*
- I spun the shit with One-of-three-Joses and the others[.] — Andy McNab, *Immediate Action*, p. 374, 1995

spinal *noun*
a paraplegic *US*
- I've seen a lot of spinals, Dude, and this guy is a fake. — *The Big Lebowski*, 1998

spinal tap *noun*
falling over backwards while snowboarding *US*
- Are you perfecting your butt drop of spinal tap? — Elena Garcia, *A Beginner's Guide to Zen and the Art of Snowboarding*, p. 120, 1990

spinbin *noun*
a residential facility for psychiatric treatment *UK: SCOTLAND*
- Her? Oh, she's in the spinbin. I'll never forget the night they took her away. — Michael Munro, *The Patter, Another Blast*, p. 66, 1988

spindle-man *noun*
a game operator in a carnival *US*
- Besides, wouldn't it be at least slightly out of line for a robbery detective and a mere carny spindle-man to exchange gifts? — Iceberg Slim (Robert Beck), *Trick Baby*, p. 14, 1969

spinebash *noun*
a period resting rather than working *AUSTRALIA, 1968*
- He's taken a bit of annual leave and I've been having this spinebash myself. — Murray Bail, *Holden's Performance*, p. 280, 1988

spine-bash *verb*
to loaf *AUSTRALIA, 1958*
- Bloody two weeks I got to spine-bash here. — Jean Brooks, *The Opal Witch*, p. 184, 1967

spinebasher *noun*
a loafer *AUSTRALIA, 1945*
- — Arthur Chipper, *The Aussie Swearer's Guide*, p. 40, 1972
- — Jim Ramsay, *Cop It Sweet!*, p. 84, 1977

spinebashing *noun*
loafing *AUSTRALIA, 1941*
- 'But what do you do?' Alec asked. 'Oh, a bit of drill and a lot of spine-bashing,' Len replied sourly. — Kylie Tennant, *Lost Haven*, p. 343, 1946

spinmeister *noun*
an acknowledged expert in the art of spin *US*
A combination of **SPIN** and German *meister* (master).

- Whenever a U.S. president confronts the Soviets, Americans root for the home team. The spinmeisters can't take all the credit for the burst of patriotic solidarity. — *Newsweek*, p. 23, 27th October 1986
- — Susie Dent, *The Language Report*, p. 41, 2003

spinnable *adjective*

open to persuasion by manipulated information; also, used of information that is suitable for biased interpretation *UK*

- — Susie Dent, *The Language Report*, p. 41, 2003

spinnaker *noun*

a five-pound note; the sum of £5 *AUSTRALIA, 1898*

spinner *noun*

1 in the used car business, a person who is adept at reducing the mileage on a car's odometer (mileometer) *US*

- — Peter Mann, *How to Buy a Used Car Without Getting Gypped*, p. 196, 1975

2 in hot rodding, a showy hubcap *US*

- — *Good Housekeeping*, p. 143, September 1958: "Hot-Rod terms for teen-age girls"
- — Tom MacPherson, *Dragging and Driving*, p. 142, 1960

3 a radio disc jockey *US*

- — Arnold Shaw, *Lingo of Tin-Pan Alley*, p. 20, 1950

4 a person who is mentally unstable after extensive medication *US*

- — James Harris, *A Convict's Dictionary*, p. 39, 1989

5 in the gambling game two-up, the person who tosses the coins *AUSTRALIA, 1911*

- His actions were keenly observed by the 'lucky' spinner[.] — Joe Andersen, *Winners Can Laugh*, p. 51, 1982

6 in air-traffic control, a shift of employment covering absent workers' responsibilities *UK*

- Christ has just finished a rotating shift, "a spinner" they call it, filling for other [air-traffic] controllers when they're having their tea break. — *New Society*, 23rd April 1981

7 in dominoes, a double that may be played on both ends *US*

- — Dominic Armanino, *Dominoes*, p. 20, 1959

8 in poker, a streak of good luck *US*

- — George Percy, *The Language of Poker*, p. 85, 1988

spinny *adjective*

crazy, insane *CANADA, 1992*

- Karen sighed. "Spinny bitches. See you later, A." "Yeah. Later, A," repeated the others[.] — Susan Juby, *Miss Smithers*, p. 176, 2004

spin on it!; spin!

a derisive invitation that accompanies the offensive gesture of a raised middle finger *UK*

- — Chris Lewis, *The Dictionary of Playground Slang*, p. 215, 2003

spin out *verb*

in the gambling game two-up, to throw a pair of tails and hence lose the right to continue spinning *AUSTRALIA, 1951*

- After two more spinners had 'spun out', the keeper announced, 'We've got a guest spinner.' — John O'Grady, *It's Your Shout, Mate!*, p. 25, 1972

spins *noun*

the heightened state of dizziness you feel when you lie down very drunk *US*

- — Judi Sanders, *Faced and Faded, Hanging to Hurl*, p. 37, 1993

spin up *verb*

to roll a cigarette with tobacco or marijuana *UK*

- Spin up a joint, Del. — Jim Drury, *Ian Dury and the Blockheads – Song by Song*, p. 167, 2003

spit *noun*

1 an exact, or near-exact, likeness of someone *UK, 1825*

- Judas the mirror image of Christ and Lazarus the absolute spit of the crucified robber[.] — *The Guardian*, 29th March 2001

2 something of no value *US*

- MOE: I always taught you, BB, never walk out of a place without a signed contract. Somebody's word ain't spit. — *Tin Men*, 1987

3 a small sum of money *US*

- — Steve Kuriscak, *Casino Talk*, p. 52, 1985

4 the payout in coins from a computer poker game *AUSTRALIA*

- — Ned Wallish, *The Truth Dictionary of Racing Slang*, p. 76, 1989

5 in some games of poker, a card turned face-up in the centre of the table which may be used by all players' hands *US*
Also called a 'spit in the ocean'.

- — Irv Roddy, *Friday Night Poker*, p. 221, 1961

spit *verb*

to perform a rap lyric *US*

- I could've spit that line better. — Eminem (Marshall Mathers), *Angry Blonde*, p. 4, 2001
- I got my education on the streets / And I learned how to spit rhymes out with or without beats — Cypress Hill *Memories*, 2001

▸ **spit beef**

to vomit *US*

- — Connie Eble (Editor), *UNC-CH Campus Slang*, p. 4, April 1978

▸ **spit blood**

to be very angry, especially in the phrase 'could spit blood' *UK, 1963*

- — John Ayto, *The Oxford Dictionary of Slang*, p. 255, 1998

▸ **spit bricks**

to be furious *UK*

- Down comes the Scots geezer spitting bricks – and he's got a Samurai sword with him[.] — Duncan MacLaughlin, *The Filth*, p. 147, 2002

▸ **spit chips**

to vent anger verbally *AUSTRALIA, 1947*

- — Arthur Chipper, *The Aussie Swearer's Guide*, p. 48, 1972
- Britons are spitting chips over a new edict by European food watchdogs. — *News*, p. 3, 1st May 1991

▸ **spit cotton**

to salivate while under the influence of heroin *US*

- My mouth was dry, and my spit came out in round white balls – spitting cotton, it's called. — William Burroughs, *Junkie*, p. 29, 1953

▸ **spit lead**

to fire a gun *US*

- — Vincent J. Monteleone, *Criminal Slang*, p. 220, 1949

▸ **spit the dummy; spit the dummy out**

to become furious; to throw a tantrum *AUSTRALIA*
From the image of an upset baby spitting out its dummy and crying.

- Instead Hughes spat his dummy out and refused to have a go and our international sporting image was damaged even further. — *Sunday Mail*, p. 50, 18th March 1984
- I mean, just how much rambling purple prose on the subjects of hashish, heroin and young boys' bottoms can you take before you finally spit the dummy. — Ignatius Jones, *The 1992 True Hip Manual*, p. 31, 1992
- — Kel Richards, *The Aussie Bible*, p. 67, 2003

spit!

be quiet! *US*

- — Hyman E. Goldin et al., *Dictionary of American Underworld Lingo*, p. 203, 1950

spit and drag; spit and a drag *noun*

a cigarette; a cigarette being smoked, especially when the act of smoking is clandestine *UK, 1960*
Rhyming slang for **FAG**.

spit and git *verb*

to accomplish a task quickly *US*

- You talk about spitting and gitting? Those two champeen razor fighters moved like twins. — Guy Owen, *The Flim-Flam Man and the Apprentice Grifter*, p. 120, 1972

spit and image *noun*

an exact likeness of someone or something *UK, 1895*
The surviving form of 'spit and fetch' (image, picture), in which 'spit' is surely the substance of a body, or perhaps its corrupted 'spirit' and the noun with which it is combined represents an outer-appearance ('fetch' is defined by the *Oxford English Dictionary* as 'the apparition, double or wraith of a living person'); 'spit and' has varied in dialect use to *spitten* leading, ultimately, to the conventional synonym: 'spitting image'.

- From the outside, the new [Lincoln] Navigator is the spit and image of the original[.] — *Car and Driver (US)*, June 2002

spit-back *noun*

a technique of spitting a drink back into a glass to give the appearance of consuming more alcohol than you are *US*

- Go back t'my drink, take a sip a whiskey an pssst, spit it back out inta the coke chaser. That's the spit-back. — Robert Gover, *Here Goes Kitten*, p. 19, 1964

spitball *verb*
in the entertainment industry, to offer up a suggestion for discussion; to brainstorm *US, 1955*
- The office believed I had saved her for us by spitballing and I never disenlightened them. —Clancy Sigal, *Going Away*, p. 29, 1961

spit black *noun*
mascara *UK*
Because water is needed to apply.
- —Wilfred Granville, *The Theater Dictionary*, p. 219, 1952

spit box *noun*
in horse racing, the barn where horses are taken after a race to have their saliva tested for the presence of illegal drugs or their metabolites *US*

spit fuck *verb*
to penetrate a rectum or vagina using only saliva as a lubricant *US*
- — *Maledicta*, p. 232, 1979: 'Kinks and queens: linguistic and cultural aspects of the terminology for gays'

spit kit *noun*
in the US submarine corps, an anti-submarine vessel *US*
- — *American Speech*, p. 38, February 1948: 'Talking under water: speech in submarines'

spit out *verb*
to say something that is emotionally difficult to say *UK, 1855*
- Talk to him or her or it / And tell them where they can put it / Spit it out, spit it out[.] —Lou Reed, *Spit It Out*, 1986

spit-roast *noun*
a sexual position in which a woman (or a man) performs oral sex on one man whilst being penetrated by another from behind; the woman (or man) receiving such attention *UK, 1998*
The two erect penises necessary for this activity create the illusory image of a single spit going in one end and out the other. Mainly heterosexual usage.
- That Lucky Pierre had a spit-roast last night. — *Sky Magazine*, p. 73, July 2001

spit-roast *verb*
to have sex as an active participant in the spit-roast position *UK*
- About an hour after she left my room Ace and Hughie ended up spit-roasting her. —Colin Butts, *Is Harry Still on the Boat?*, p. 245, 2003

spit spiders *verb*
to be furious *UK*
- The traffic had ground to a halt at Biggleswade and then crawled all the way up to Normans Cross, by which time Richard was spitting spiders. —Andrew J. Miller, *The Bluebell Girl*, 2001

spits *noun*
sunflower seeds *CANADA*
- You can spit the shells demurely into your hand, you can spit them across the room, or you can spit them anywhere between those two extremes. —Chris Thain, *Cold as a Bay Street Banker's Heart*, p. 146, 1987

spitter *noun*
1 a person who spits out semen after oral sex *AUSTRALIA*
- Chicks are nicknamed bush pigs, swamp hogs, maggots, spitters or swallowers. —Kathy Lette, *Girls' Night Out*, p. 187, 1987

2 a killer *US*
- This little blond guy is raising hell – he's got three or four guys with him, spitters all – the maitre d' is pleading. —Edwin Torres, *Carlito's Way*, p. 27, 1975

3 a wave that sprays from its end as it collapses *US*
- —John Severson, *Modern Surfing Around the World*, p. 182, 1964

spitting feathers *adjective*
1 very thirsty *UK*
- Bring us over a couple of Red Stripes, will you? I'm spitting feathers over here. —Greg Williams, *Diamond Geezers*, p. 39, 1997

2 furiously angry *UK*
- The red-hot passion of the audience had been defused in an instant, leaving [Lou] Reed spitting feathers. —Jim Drury, *Ian Dury and the Blockheads – Song by Song*, p. 66, 2003

spittin' time *noun*
the bleed period of a woman's menstrual cycle *US*
- — *American Speech*, p. 298, December 1954: 'The vernacular of menstruation'

spiv *noun*
a sharply dressed individual who lives by his wits – within the law for preference, and not too far outside the law whenever possible *UK, 1934*
Several possible etymologies vie for credence: an acronym from police records 'Suspected Persons and Itinerant Vagrants'; back slang of the acronym for 'Very Important Persons' (VIPs); dialect *spif* or *spiff* (neat, smart, dandified), which also leads to **SPIFFING** (excellent); *spivic*, an apparently obsolete Romany word for 'sparrow', used to describe those who followed the gypsies and picked up their leavings.
- Mayfair is just top spivs stepping into the slippers of the former gentry[.] —Colin MacInnes, *Absolute Beginners*, 1959
- —Angela Devlin, *Prison Patter*, p. 108, 1996
- [A] self-educated spiv with diamonds in his collar[.] —John King, *White Trash*, p. 88, 2001
- [N]o one who's totally legit. There's kites, dippers, dealers, spivs, all kinds. —Kevin Sampson, *Outlaws*, p. 161, 2001

spivias *noun*
amphetamines; MDMA, the recreational drug best known as ecstasy *UK*
- —Mike Haskins, *Drugs*, p. 279, 2003

spivvery *noun*
petty crime and other behaviour associated with a spiv *UK*
- various forms of casual spivvery on the border-line between work and crime —Charles Raven, *Underworld Nights*, p. 116, 1956

spizz *noun*
a hypodermic needle *US*
- —Francis J. Rigney and L. Douglas Smith, *The Real Bohemia*, p. xx, 1961

SP joint *noun*
an establishment operating starting price bookmaking *AUSTRALIA, 1945*
- He'd been main cockatoo – sentry to the ignorant – at the biggest SP joint in town[.] —Wilda Moxham, *The Apprentice*, p. 24, 1969

splack *noun*
sex *US*
- —Linda Meyer, *Teenspeak!*, p. 29, 1994

splack *verb*
1 to steal a car, especially by shattering the steering column *US*
- They would "splack" cars – breaking into the steering column in seconds – and joy ride all night. — *Orlando (Florida) Sentinel Tribune*, p. A1, 10th October 1993
- There's even street slang for stealing cars such as "new buckets are being splacked." Buckets refer to small cars, such as Dodge neons, and to splack is to steal a car using a screwdriver to break into the steering column and start it. — *Tampa (Florida) Tribune*, p. 1, 6th May 2000

2 to ejaculate in sexual climax *US*
- No, no... I didn't splack. — *Sky Magazine*, p. 51, July 2001

splaff *noun*
a marijuana cigarette laced with LSD *UK*
'A' for **ACID** substitutes the 'i' in **SPLIFF** (a marijuana cigarette).
- Splaff: cannabis joint with a hint of LSD. —Mike Haskins, *Drugs*, p. 289, 2003

splash *noun*
1 an amphetamine or other central nervous system stimulant *US*
- —J. L. Simmons and Barry Winograd, *It's Happening*, p. 173, 1966: 'Glossary'
- —Kenn "Naz" Young, *Naz's Underground Dictionary*, p. 57, 1973

2 a small amount of water added to an alcoholic drink *US*
- Buddy ordered a couple mopre Jim Beams with a splash, for the road. —Elmore Leonard, *Out of Sight*, p. 186, 1996

3 tea (the beverage) *UK, 1960*

4 a bath *US*
- —David Claerbaut, *Black Jargon in White America*, p. 81, 1972

splash *verb*
1 to take a bath *US*
- —David Claerbaut, *Black Jargon in White America*, p. 81, 1972

2 to ejaculate *US*
- The point is that if you usually splash early and you know you're going to get laid, then jerk off. — *Screw*, p. 6, 15th June 1970

▸ **splash the boots**

to urinate *AUSTRALIA*

- Stone the crows! That's highway robbery – that's nearly fifty notes where I come from – if I wasn't bustin' to splash the boots I'd do this Pom over – so help me! —Barry Humphries, *The Wonderful World of Barry McKenzie*, p. 3, 1968

▸ **splash the pot**

in a game of poker, to throw betting tokens directly into the pile of chips in the centre of the table instead of lining them up for other players to see before adding them to the pot *US, 1961*

- —Thomas L. Clark, *The Dictionary of Gambling and Gaming*, p. 210, 1987

splashing *noun*

in a prostitute's advertising, semen, urine and other fluids secreted at orgasm *UK*

- —Caroline Archer, *Tart Cards*, 2003

splash move *noun*

in cheating at dice, a switch of the dice *US*

- The old man nodded. "I'm gonna start with a 'splash move'," indicating he was going to rehearse the switch of the dice first without actually playing them, to see if the Pit Boss would spot it. —Stephen J. Cannell, *Big Con*, p. 196, 1997

splash out *verb*

to spend money extravagantly *UK, 1934*

- [T]hey had splashed out on holidays or luxuries they would not have bought if still married. —*The Guardian*, 18th June 2003

splashover *noun*

a signal leaking from one citizens' band radio channel to another *US*

- — "Slingo", *The Official CB Slang Dictionary Handbook*, p. 58, 1976

splash shot *noun*

a scene in a pornographic film or photograph depicting a man ejaculating *US*

Interview of Jim Holliday, 12th June 1997.

splat *noun*

1 any food not subject to ready identification *US*

From the sound made when it hits the mess kit.

- —Carl Fleischhauer, *A Glossary of Army Slang*, p. 1, 1968

2 the * character on a computer keyboard *US*

- —Guy L. Steele et al., *The Hacker's Dictionary*, p. 119, 1983
- —Eric S. Raymond, *The New Hacker's Dictionary*, p. 332, 1991

splat *verb*

to be killed bungee jumping *US*

- The bungee jumping term for a fatal accident is "zeroing out" or "splatting." Take your pick. —Erik Fair, *California Thrill Sports*, p. 55, 1992

splat hat *noun*

a motorcycle crash helmet *UK*

- —Peter Chippindale, *The British CB Book*, p. 159, 1981

splendiferous; splendacious; splendidious; spledidous *adjective*

excellent; very splendid *US, 1843*

- Libby was not all work and no play; she was managing to have a splendiferous time for herself without overspending her allowance. —Mary McCarthy, *The Group*, p. 189, 1963
- [Y]eah, testify, how many ectoplasmic angels are on your side, give me the splendiferous images of your famous fabulous friggin' self-created self-sustained astral plane! —Anne Rice, *Blood Canticle*, p. 77, 2003
- I didn't need an office. I could afford the most splendiferous office in the city. —Walter Yetnikoff, *Howling at the Moon*, p. 264, 2004

splib *noun*

a black person *US, 1964*

Offensive.

- —Joan Fontaine et al., *Dictionary of Black Slang*, 1968
- —*Current Slang*, p. 45, Fall 1968
- We got some splibs in Central too, but none too many. —Joseph Wambaugh, *The New Centurions*, p. 171, 1970
- All the splibs on the playground knew by Leroy's action that it was Fuck With Junior Time[.] —Clarence Major, *All-Night Visitors*, p. 27, 1998
- —Jim Goad, *Jim Goad's Glossary of Northwestern Prison Slang*, December 2001

splice *verb*

to marry someone *UK, 1710*

- "Now, Mr. Johnson, go ahead and splice them." So the reverend read through his service. —Garald and Lorretta Hausman, *Escape from Botany Bay*, p. 78, 2003

spliced *adjective*

married *US*

- —Anna Scotti and Paul Young, *Buzzwords*, p. 30, 1997

spliff *noun*

1 a marijuana cigarette *JAMAICA, 1936*

- It was slike our friend Slim in British Honduras, who used to buy a fifteen-cent spliff from John Scorn, and turn around and sell it in front of John's house for twenty cents. —Stephen Gaskin, *Amazing Dope Tales*, p. 89, 1980
- I brew a little tea in the mini-kitchen off the living room while the "G" lights a spliff on the big velvet sofa. —Jim Carroll, *Forced Entries*, p. 25, 1987
- Smoking a spliff of high-octaine chronic (street talk for pot) in the back room, he explains his bond to Dre. "He's the bomb," says Snoop. —*People*, p. 77, 23 May 1994
- He takes it [a hat] off to show spliff falls out. —*The Guardian*, p. 2, 28th June 2004

2 marijuana *UK, 1967*

Also used in the variant 'splif'.

- We don't have spliff to do the walk on – so let's not go for the walk. —Macfarlane, Macfarlane and Robson, *The User*, p. 4, 1996
- Blonde birds with their mums' faces toking on dodgy spliff peddled by Trevor's mate Tiny Tony[.] —Greg Williams, *Diamond Geezers*, p. 149, 1997
- —Mike Haskins, *Drugs*, p. 289, 2003

3 a cigarette adulterated with crack cocaine *UK*

- —Nick Constable, *This is Cocaine*, p. 182, 2002

4 a hand-rolled cigarette *UK*

▸ **on the spliff**

a state of marijuana intoxication *UK*

- That ain't on the spliff —BBC TV *Paddington Green*, 13th February 2001

spliff *verb*

to smoke marijuana and be under its influence *UK*

- Paul [Simenon] spliffing in bigeyed space monkey glee playing the new Ramones over and over[.] —Lester Bangs, *Psychotic Reactions and Carburetor Dung*, p. 243, 1977

spliffed; spliffed out; spliffed up *adjective*

in a state of intoxication as a result of smoking marijuana *UK*

- I must be mad, or pissed or spliffed out my fucking brains! —Donald Gorgon, *Cop Killer*, p. 165, 1994
- Oh, some spliffed-up rude boys mounted a GPMG [general-purpose machine gun] on that building across the road[.] —Duncan MacLaughlin, *The Filth*, p. 234, 2002
- [T]his is an essential soundtrack for a spliffed-out nation. Now where did I put that bong... —*Ministry*, May 2002

spliff up *verb*

to prepare a marijuana cigarette; to smoke marijuana in cigarette form *UK*

- Emyr and Col were in the corner spliffing up for a change[.] —John Williams, *Cardiff Dead*, p. 30, 2000

spliff wine *noun*

marijuana wine *UK*

- "No. It's home-grown and home-made!" And that's how I found out about spliff wine. —Duncan MacLaughlin, *The Filth*, p. 104, 2002

spliffy *noun*

a marijuana cigarette *UK*

- Dave lit up a little "spliffy" which he'd knocked together earlier. —Ken Lukowiak, *Marijuana Time*, p. 62, 2000

spliffy *adjective*

in a state of gentle intoxication as a result of smoking marijuana; in a manner that suggests the smoking of marijuana *UK*

Playing on **SQUIFFY** (drunk).

- Fantasy is a set of club tracks simultaneously uptempo and spliffy, indebted to worldbeat, ambient dub, and ragga. —Vladimir Bogdanov, *All Music Guide to Electronica*, p. 568, 2001
- [T]he air grows denser in a spliffy fog. —*Time Out Amsterdam*, p. 39, 2002

splifted *adjective*

marijuana-intoxicated; exhilarated *US*

- —Lois Stavsky et al., *A2Z*, p. 96, 1995

splim *noun*
marijuana *US*
A misreading or simple variation of **SPLIFF**.
- —Ernest Abel, *A Marijuana Dictionary*, p. 94, 1982
- —Richard A. Spears, *The Slang and Jargon of Drugs and Drink*, p. 478, 1986
- —Mike Haskins, *Drugs*, p. 289, 2003

splinky *noun*
the penis *US*
A term apparently coined by the writers of *Mad About You*, a US situation comedy (NBC, 1992–99); repeated with referential humour.

splint *noun*
a marijuana cigarette *US*
- —Jay Robert Nash, *Dictionary of Crime*, p. 360, 1992

splinters *noun*
adversity *US*
- —Jerry Robertson, *Oil Slanguage*, p. 58, 1954

split *noun*
1 the vagina *US*
- —Dale Gordon, *The Dominion Sex Dictionary*, p. 150, 1967

2 a share of mutual property or profits *UK, 1889*
- —John Ayto, *The Oxford Dictionary of Slang*, p. 430, 1998

3 a tranquillizer or other central nervous system depressant *US*
- —Richard Lingeman, *Drugs from A to Z*, p. 226, 1969

4 a decongestant tablet sold as MDMA, the recreational drug best known as ecstasy *UK*
- —Macfarlane, Macfarlane and Robson, *The User*, p. 74, 1996

split *verb*
1 to leave *US, 1956*
Each night, during the 1960s, Philadelphia rock 'n' roll disc jockey Hy Lit ended his broadcast with the mantra, 'Nuff said Ted, solid ahead, time to split the scene and leave it clean'.
- After all, I'm not locked in here. I can split in a year or two if I want to.—Nat Hentoff, *Jazz Country*, p. 139, 1965
- And as I split, I saw her cracking up with kicks.—Eldridge Cleaver, *Soul on Ice*, p. 28, 1968
- —Hy Lit, *Hy Lit's Unbelievable Dictionary of Hip Words for Groovy People*, p. 37, 1968
- WYATT: Let's split. BILLY: Split? WYATT: Yeah.—Peter Fonda, *Easy Rider*, p. 139, 1969
- The police come to break it up. We split into the subway.—Jerry Rubin, *Do It!*, p. 118, 1970
- He told Doyle he had to split in order to make the Ultimate Rendezvous.—Gurney Norman, *Divine Right's Trip (Last Whole Earth Catalog)*, p. 9, 1971
- He saw I was ready to split and asked where I was going.—Jamie Mandelkau, *Buttons*, p. 57, 1971
- I stayed with my oldest sister, 'til her hsuband started to give me those free-loader looks which caused me to split.—A.S. Jackson, *Gentleman Pimp*, p. 21, 1973
- We ate and split, and as we rode, I sat quietly thinking and wondering[.]—Bobby Seale, *A Lonely Rage*, p. 293, 1978
- Joe was now at the door holding it open calling his friends, saying "Come on, Huncke, le's split."—Herbert Huncke, *The Evening Sun Turned Crimson*, p. 135, 1980
- Ferris, let's split, please?—*Ferris Buehler's Day Off*, 1986
- I gotta split. It was really nice meeting you.—*Chasing Amy*, 1997
- Let's just split, Let's just split right now.—*Boogie Nights*, 1997

2 from a male perspective, to have sex *UK, 1937*
Probably more to do with bragging than as a considered threat of violence.
- [W]hen [an army vehicle] passes a girl, aged six years upwards, the usual [soldierly] remark is "Cor, I'd like to split that one".—*New Statesman*, 2nd October 1981

▸ **split a gut**
to exert yourself to the extreme, especially laughing *US*
- "He's split a gut like that every night for years. And it's his only gut."—John Clellon Holmes, *The Horn*, p. 156, 1958

▸ **split on**
to inform on or betray someone *UK, 1795*

▸ **split the breeze**
to drive fast *US*
- —"Slingo", *The Official CB Slang Dictionary Handbook*, p. 58, 1976

▸ **split the difference**
from a male perspective, to have sex *UK*
A punning elaboration of **SPLIT**, reported by Laurie Atkinson, 1974.

▸ **split the scene**
to leave *US*
- [H]e decided the best ting to do for the time being was to split the scene rather than come to the attention of the cops.—Herbert Huncke, *Guilty of Everything*, p. 145, 1990

▸ **split the sheets**
to divorce *US*
- —Wayne Floyd, *Jason's Authentic Dictionary of CB Slang*, p. 28, 1976
- Me and the ol' lady split the sheets a year ago, and now I'm growin' a toenail on my dick from fuckin' my socks.—Ken Weaver, *Texas Crude*, p. 76, 1984

▸ **split the whiskers**
(of a woman) to urinate *AUSTRALIA*
- The blonde's just ducked out to split the whiskers.—Robert G. Barrett, *Davo's Little Something*, p. 258, 1992

▸ **split your sides**
to laugh heartily *UK, 1704*
- [E]verybody was splitting their sides laughing at Professor Trares and his theory of a conspiracy[.]—Michael Kruger (translated by Andrew Shields), *The Cello Player*, p. 83, 2004

split-arse *noun*
a woman *UK, 1998*
Noted as current in the northeast of England by Chris Lewis, *The Dictionary of Playground Slang*, 2003.

split beaver; spread beaver *noun*
the vagina displayed with lips parted *US*
A familiar cliché of pornography.
- Then came the split beaver shot, which is where the girl has lubricated her pussy so that the mons fold apart to reveal the innerlips, clitoris, urethral opening and vagina.—*Screw*, p. 4, 13th October 1969
- —Eugene Landy, *The Underground Dictionary*, p. 31, 1971
- Open-crotch, or "split-beaver" shots of naked young girls abound.—Roger Blake, *What you always wanted to know about porno-movies*, p. 89, 1972
- In the first, which came to be known as the split beaver, the woman spread her legs and exhibited her vagina directly to the cameras, often pulling aside the labia in order to provide a better view of what everyone had come to see.—Kenneth Turan and Stephen E. Zito, *Sinema: American Pornographic Films and the People who Make Them*, p. 77–78, 1974
- —Bill Davis, *Jawjacking*, p. 94, 1977
- Those films were really just "spread beavers."—*Adam Film World*, p. 17, January 1980
- [G]hetto-fabulous rapper Lil' Kim (known for her split beaver shots).—*Village Voice*, p. 33, 21st April 1998
- The Spice Girls, near naked, are singing some dead song in the desert, doing split beaver kicks and throwing metal boomerangs.—Stuart Browne, *Dangerous Parking*, p. 30, 2000

split C-note *noun*
a fifty-dollar note *US*
- As he talked he rubbed Biff's split-C note in his pocket like a rabbit's foot.—Bernard Wolfe, *The Late Risers*, p. 171, 1954

splith *noun*
marijuana prepared and smoked in the fashion of a cigarette *US*
A jocular variation of **SPLIFF**.
- Pass the splith.—Ken Lukowiak, *Marijuana Time*, p. 92, 2000

split knish *noun*
the vagina *US*
A conventional 'knish' is a baked or fried turnover of Russian Jewish origins; 'split' describes the nature of the vagina and exposes the savoury filling.
- There's [...] a "Mimi" in Miami, "split knish" in Philadelphia, and "schmende" in the Bronx[.]—Eve Ensler, *The Vagina Monologues*, p. 6, 1998

split-tail *noun*
a female *US*
- —Hyman E. Goldin et al., *Dictionary of American Underworld Lingo*, p. 203, 1950

split-whisker *noun*
a woman *AUSTRALIA*
- Ah, but he's too good a sailor man to get tangled in split-whisker at sea.—Robert S. Close, *Love Me Sailor*, p. 20, 1945
- —Jim Ramsay, *Cop It Sweet!*, p. 84, 1977

splivins *noun*
amphetamines *US, 1970*
- —Ralph de Sola, *Crime Dictionary*, p. 142, 1982
- —Richard A. Spears, *The Slang and Jargon of Drugs and Drink*, p. 478, 1986
- —Mike Haskins, *Drugs*, p. 279, 2003

splo *noun*
inexpensive, low quality whisky *US*
- —David W. Maurer, *Kentucky Moonshine*, p. 125, 1974
- —Burgess Laughlin, *Job Opportunities in the Black Market*, p. 4, 1978: 'Glossary'

splonk *noun*
in horse race betting, the favourite *UK, 1967*
- [T]he favourite is occasionally known as the "splonk"[.]—John McCririck, *John McCririck's World of Betting*, p. 60, 1991

splooge *noun*
semen *US*
- —Pamela Munro, *U.C.L.A. Slang*, p. 80, 1989
- The slobs could even kiss her (if they so dared, with all that splooge floating about her mug).—Anthony Petkovich, *The X Factory*, p. 183, 1997

splooge *verb*
to ejaculate *US*
- —Pamela Munro, *U.C.L.A. Slang*, p. 80, 1989
- That's right – there is no wacky splooging on her face or in her mouth, which is, of course, considered the Money Shot in almost all straight porn.—*The Village Voice*, 22nd August 2000

splosher *noun*
a drunk *UK*
- You ain't out spunkin your dough down the clubs trying to impress some old sploshers, pissed and on the powder, having the big nose-up.—J.J. Connolly, *Layer Cake*, p. 49, 2000

splow *noun*
palms slapped in greeting *US*
- "My dear hip friend," the letter began / "Here's some splow and a big shoddy-doo."—Dennis Wepman et al., *The Life*, p. 69, 1976

splurge *verb*
to spend money extravagantly; to recklessly use an expensive resource *US, 1934*
- In 1990, the company splurged and built a new three-story high rise.—Peter Lynch and John Rothchild, *Beating the Street*, p. 185, 1994
- That night he splurged and didn't boil meat. Instead he cut a steak off the deer[.]—Gary Paulsen, *Brian's Winter*, p. 117, 1996

SP man *noun*
a starting price bookmaker *AUSTRALIA, 1932*
- —Tom Ellis, *The Science of Turf Investment*, p. 8, 1936
- [T]he S.P. man and the man or woman who sells a few drinks under the lap are fair game for the pimp.—Vince Kelly, *The Bogeyman*, p. 100, 1956

Spock *noun*
used as a term of address for anyone who is coming across as intellectual or superior *US*
From the intellectual and superior character on *Star Trek*.
- —Connie Eble (Editor), *UNC-CH Campus Slang*, p. 4, April 1978

spock *verb*
to examine something or someone *US*
- —Trevor Cralle, *The Surfin'ary*, p. 120, 1991

spod *noun*
a student whose devotion to study excludes all other interests or society, hence an unpopular student; someone who is considered too studious; someone obsessed with computers *UK, 1998*
- [S]he was telling a friend all about him, in not exactly glowing terms. "He's a spod-boy," she said[.]—Andrew Holmes, *Sleb*, p. 169, 2002
- [T]he remixer du jour on apple crumble, Billy Joel and being a spod[.]—*Jockey Slut*, p. 112, August 2003

spoddy *adjective*
obsessively studious and unstylish *UK*
- They're just spoddy planespotter specs.—*Dead Ringers*, December 2001

spodiodi *noun*
1 a mixture of cheap port and whisky *CANADA*
Used (and drunk) by jazz-lovers and musicians.
- —*Basic Beatnik (Daily Colonist)*, 16th April 1959

2 wine *US*
- —Carl J. Banks Jr, *Banks Dictionary of the Black Ghetto Language*, 1975

spoggie; spoggy *noun*
(chiefly in south Australia) the common house sparrow, *passer domesticus* *AUSTRALIA*
- They looked like three spoggies with broken wings.—Max Colwell, *Half Days and Patched Pants*, p. 159, 1975

spoiled water *noun*
any non-alcoholic beverage *US*
- —Joseph E. Ragen and Charles Finston, *Inside the World's Toughest Prison*, p. 819, 1962: 'Penitentiary and underworld glossary'

spoiler *noun*
a team that has no chance of winning a championship but which takes pride if not pleasure in defeating teams that are vying for a championship *US*
- —Howard B. Bonham, *Football Lingo*, p. 52, 1962

spokadocious; spankadocious *adjective*
attractive; fashionable *BAHAMAS*
- —John A. Holm, *Dictionary of Bahamian English*, p. 182, 1982

spoke *adjective*
spoken *UK, 1937*
Especially of language, in the construction 'as she is spoke'.
- Student slang as she is spoke – Your passport to the in-crowd.—*The Guardian*, September 2000

spon *verb*
to tell a lie *UK*
- I was sponning so much I should've been wearing a porkie-pie hat.—Wayne Anthony, *Spanish Highs*, p. 7, 1999

spondonicles; spondonicals; spongs *noun*
a pair of metal tongs for lifting a hot cooking utensil off a fire *AUSTRALIA*
- Lance lost the spondonicles, so we had great difficulty removing the pot from the stove.—*www.abc.net.au/wordmap*, 2003

spondooli *noun*
money *UK*
Variation of **SPONDULICS**.
- Course she grabs the spondooli with both hands.—Nick Barlay, *Curvy Lovebox*, p. 88, 1997

spondulics; spondulix; sponds; spondos *noun*
money *US, 1857*
- Anyway, I wish he'd turn up with the spondulics.—James Joyce, *Dubliners*, p. 94, 1967
- Jack, shekels, mazuma, simoleons, Mr. Green, filthy lucre, even spondulicks – this is the other Why of prostitution.—Gail Sheehy, *Hustling*, p. 11, 1973
- [G]et your act cleaned up and some spondulix pamped [placed] in my purse.—Ian Pattison, *Rab C. Nesbitt*, 1990
- Ask any Dublin taxi driver – assuming every last one of them hasn't fecked off to the Caribbean with the spondulix they made over Christmas!—Joseph O'Connor, *The Irish Male at Home and Abroad*, p. 220, 1996
- [B]ecause he never seemed to flash any of the sponds he claimed to have earned from his various "jobs" and "blags" and because he slept in shop doorways[.]—Howard Paul, *The Joy*, p. 36, 1996
- [W]hen the establishment Mafioso realise how much gilt, paper, cashish, wonga, wedge, corn, cutter, loot, spondos, dollar, readies, shillings, folding, dough, money is on offer[.]—J.J. Connolly, *Layer Cake*, p. 94, 2000

sponge *noun*
1 a group, notional or real, opposed to the gains of the civil rights movement *US, 1965*
The vocalised abbreviation stood for 'Society for the Prevention of Negroes Getting Everything'. The group was more notional than real, but, for example, in 1965 the Student Council of the University of Virginia was petitioned by an organisation calling itself SPONGE for status as an independent organisation eligible to receive Student Council funds.
- A growing Black Nationalist movement often faced off against groups like SPONGE, the acronym for the Society for the Prevention of Negroes Getting Everything.—Gregory S. Bell, *In the Black*, p. 69, 2002

2 a boogie boarder, who rides waves on a small foam board *US*
Used in a disparaging manner by surfers.
- —Trevor Cralle, *The Surfin'ary*, p. 120, 1991

sponge *verb*
1 to obtain something in a parasitic manner *UK, 1673*
- Relatively young and able-bodied, they simply sponged because they preferred not to work.—Jim Thompson, *Roughneck*, p. 144, 1954

- Wadda you think, you can sponge drinks off me all night?—Edwin Torres, *After Hours*, p. 214, 1979

2 in horse racing, to insert a sponge into a horse's nostril just before a race, impeding its breathing during the race *US*

- —David W. Maurer, *Argot of the Racetrack*, p. 59, 1951

spongelled *adjective*

drunk *UK*

- —*e-cyclopaedia*, 20th March 2002

sponger *noun*

a person who obtains things in a parasitic manner *UK, 1677*

- Let's face it, if you were a lazy sponger living in the Czech republic, why would you bother moving your family thousands of miles to claim benefits in an inner-city slum in Britain.—*The Guardian*, 24th February 2004

sponge-worthy *adjective*

used of a man, so sexually desirable as to warrant the use of a contraceptive sponge *US*

Coined and popularised on an episode of Jerry Seinfeld's television comedy show ('The Sponge') that first aired on 7th December 1995.

spongies *noun*

in the usage of youthful model road racers (slot car racers), smooth, soft tyres *US*

- —Phantom Surfers, *The Exciting Sounds of Model Road Racing (Album cover)*, 1997

sponk *noun*

semen *UK*

A variation of **SPUNK**.

- The sponk I rubbed into my belly has gone dry and flaky white, but I'm still half tossing myself off.—Kevin Sampson, *Outlaws*, p. 156, 2001

spoo *noun*

semen *US*

Variant pronunciation of **SPEW** (semen), from **SPEW/SPOO** (to ejaculate).

- Ike had used the word "spoo" – roughly the equivalent of jizz – in a conversation. I don't know where it came from, or if he made it up. In any event "spoo" turned out to be "the mystery word" onstage that night.—Frank Zappa, *The Real Frank Zappa Book*, p. 170, 1989

spoo *verb*

to ejaculate *US*

Variant pronunciation of **SPEW** (to ejaculate), from conventional 'spew' (to vomit), the suggestion therefore is of a copious quantity of semen.

spoof *noun*

1 a hoax, a bluff; an act of hoaxing *UK, 1889*

- Face-to-face confrontations with policemen snarling insults to arrogantly smiling villains enjoying their spoof could be humorous affairs[.]—Brian McDonald, *Elephant Boys*, p. 181, 2000

2 a parody *UK, 1958*

- The Inventor, meanwhile, is a spoof of the kind of movies Georges Melies was making in the early silent era.—*The Guardian*, 6th January 2003

3 semen *AUSTRALIA, 1916*

Rhymes with 'hoof'.

- The amount of spoof is more important to Eternity than the size of your cock.—Paul Radley, *Jack Rivers and Me*, p. 61, 1981

spoof *verb*

1 to hoax; to fool *UK, 1889*

- 'All existing biometrics are capable of being spoofed', Mr Dayman told the Guardian. 'But ours is the hardest to [fool].'—*The Guardian*, 29th July 2003

2 to make a parodic version of something *UK, 1927*

- As the classic mockumentaries Spinal Tap and Bob Roberts proved, it's much easier to spoof something that is already a self-parody.—*The Guardian*, 22nd August 1999

3 to ejaculate *AUSTRALIA, 1992*

spoof *adjective*

parodic; fake; bogus *UK, 1884*

- [Gary] Lineker didn't realise it was actually a spoof commentary[.] —*The Guardian*, 19th June 2002

spoofed *adjective*

used of an electronic message, of a suspect origin *US*

- —Andy Ihnatko, *Cyberspeak*, p. 181, 1997

spoofer *noun*

1 in carnival usage, a large stuffed dog offered as a game prize *US*

- The price of SPOOFERS ranges from ten to fifteen dollars wholesale.—Gene Sorrows, *All About Carnivals*, p. 26, 1985

2 a hoaxer; a bluffer *UK*

- I never slept with her. I never fancied her. She's just a spoofer. —*Q*, p. 86, December 2001

spoofing *noun*

1 the sending of e-mail that claims to come from one organisation but in fact comes from another *US*

Known more fully as 'IP spoofing'.

- Spoofing: Masquerading as another user or program (for example, intruders, worms, and viruses)[.]—*InfoWorld*, p. S6, 11th December 1989

2 the creation of a false website that looks exactly like a real site *US*

More fully known as 'web spoofing'. The attacher can lure an Internet user to the false site, can see everything that the user is doing, and can modify traffic from the user to any web server.

spoof tube *noun*

a cardboard tube filled with scented cloth that masks the smell of exhaled marijuana smoke *US*

- —Chris Lewis, *The Dictionary of Playground Slang*, p. 216, 2003

spoofy *adjective*

spermy *AUSTRALIA*

- IF YOU'RE CUTE, HORNY, ASIAN THIS NICE-LOOKING OZ GUY WOULD LIKE TO TASTE YOUR SPOOFY CUM SOME LUNCHTIME —*toilet graffiti*, 1998

spooge *noun*

1 semen *US*

- —Connie Eble (Editor), *UNC-CH Campus Slang*, p. 8, Fall 1987
- One cock in my face, one inside me, the smell of other men's spooge in my nostrils.—Amy Sohn, *Run Catch Kiss*, p. 116, 1999
- My brain was as soggy as a spooge mop in a porno booth.—Jeffrey McDaniel, *The Splinter Factory*, p. 14, 2002

2 any viscous matter of unknown origin *US*

- —*Maledicta*, p. 48, 1995: 'Door whore and other New Mexico restaurant slang'

3 in computing, code or output which cannot be understood *US*

- —Eric S. Raymond, *The New Hacker's Dictionary*, p. 333, 1991

spooge booth *noun*

a private booth in a pornography arcade *US*

- Sex shops range from smutty bookstores with "spooge booths" to higher-end retailers specializing in erotic tools, toys and garments. —Rob Cohen, *Etiquette for Outlaws*, p. 70, 2001

spook *noun*

1 a black person *US*

Derogatory and offensive.

- Only in Little Tokyo they'd have to kill and be killed, for those spooks down there were some really rugged cats[.]—Chester Himes, *If He Hollers Let Him Go*, p. 77, 1945
- Quite a lot of spooks get done for takeing (sic) charge.—Frank Norman, *Bang to Rights*, p. 143, 1958
- "Listen," she said with no question in her voice, "you on one of them spook kicks?"—Bernard Wolfe, *The Magic of Their Singing*, p. 103, 1961
- You wait until you see a spooks' dance!—Malcolm X and Alex Haley, *The Autobiography of Malcolm X*, p. 47, 1964
- Nevertheless, uneasy white males still continue to tighten their rosy sphincters at the approach of spooks.—Gore Vidal, *Myra Breckinridge*, p. 88, 1968
- I'm what a lot you spooks might think of as a red neck with a terminal case of the dumb-ass.—Dan Jenkins, *Semi-Tough*, p. 7, 1972
- The spooks said no Ricans could go west of Fifth Avenue.—Edwin Torres, *Carlito's Way*, p. 8, 1975
- Some won't take spooks. Hell, don't make no difference to me.—*Taxi Driver*, 1976
- Fucking spook. Clement began thinking of the guy as a Cuban-looking jig.—Elmore Leonard, *City Primeval*, p. 14, 1980
- "A Spook and a Paddy [Irishman] go into a boozer," blah, blah, blah...—J.J. Connolly, *Layer Cake*, p. 151, 2000

2 a ghost *US, 1801*

- The headmasters were Elvis Presley and the spook of Jimmy Dean, and the entrance requirements were completely democratic.—Max Shulman, *Rally Round the Flag, Boys!*, p. 57, 1957

3 a spy *US, 1942*

- The Army was full of spooks.—Earl Thompson, *Tattoo*, p. 633, 1974

- In the spook world they use words like "departure" or "termination" in ways that would not be acceptable in the general business community. —Hunter S. Thompson, *Generation of Swine*, p. 169, 13th October 1986
- [H]e certainly wasn't about to ring Sophie with all these wanky spooks hanging around. —Chris Ryan, *The Watchman*, p. 96, 2001
- Let me tell you, being a spook is the most boring job on the planet. —Duncan MacLaughlin, *The Filth*, p. 137, 2002

4 a drug-addict *UK*
From the addict's ghostly pallor.
- —Frank Norman, *Bang to Rights*, 1958

5 a psychiatrist *US*
- —*American Speech*, p. 145–148, May 1961: 'The spoken language of medicine; argot, slang, cant'

6 in casino blackjack, a player who can spot the dealer's down card *US*
- —Michael Dalton, *Blackjack*, p. 79, 1991

7 in drag racing, a car that crosses the starting line too soon *US, 1960s*
- —Lyle K. Engel, *The Complete Book of Fuel and Gas Dragsters*, p. 154, 1968

spook *verb*

1 to frighten or startle someone *US, 1935*
Also variant 'spook out'.
- "That's why I need you," Raylan said, "help me find a guy I'm looking for without showing myself and spook him." —Elmore Leonard, *Riding the Rap*, p. 286, 1995
- It spooks me out a bit that I can still remember it so clearly. —Frank Skinner, *Frank Skinner*, p. 60, 2001

2 to drive a car without a destination, merely for the pleasure of driving and the social aspects of being seen *US*
- —*Good Housekeeping*, p. 143, September 1958: "Hot-Rod terms for teen-age girls"
- —Tom MacPherson, *Dragging and Driving*, p. 142, 1960

3 in blackjack, to peak and see the dealer's down card *US*
- —Steve Kuriscak, *Casino Talk*, p. 52, 1985

spooked *adjective*

used of playing cards, marked for cheating *US*
- —Richard Jessup, *The Cincinnati Kid*, p. 93, 1963

spooky *adjective*

1 in surfing, difficult or unpredictable *US*
- —Grant W. Kuhns, *On Surfing*, p. 122, 1963

2 fine, good *UK*
West Indian and UK black usage, recorded August 2002.

spool of pipe thread *noun*

used as a mythical task assigned to a newly hired helper *US*
- [H]e was likely to be told next day to go draw a can of striped paint or a left handed monkey wrench or a spool of pipe thread. —Charles F. Haywood, *Yankee Dictionary*, p. 20, 1963

spoon *noun*

1 the amount of a drug needed for a single dose *US*
A measure of heroin, sufficient for a single injection, approximately equal to a standard teaspoon.
- —Kenn "Naz" Young, *Naz's Underground Dictionary*, p. 57, 1973
- —Angela Devlin, *Prison Patter*, p. 108, 1996
- He hit you with lids, caps, keys, tabs, nickel bags, blotters, buttons, spoons and everything from milligrams to boatloads. —Robert Sabbag, *A Way with the Spoon [The Howard Marks Book of Dope Stories]*, p. 351, 1998
- —Robert Ashton, *This Is Heroin*, p. 210, 2002

2 the handle of a hand grenade *US*
From its curved, spoon-like shape.
- He tried to throw a grenade at them, but his hand slipped off the spoon. —Philip Caputo, *A Rumor of War*, p. 204, 1977
- Then he snatched it up again, pinched the halves together, and worked the pink back in, twisting it until the pin just hung there, holding back the spoon just barely. —Larry Heinemann, *Close Quarters*, p. 45, 1977

3 an army cook *US*
- —Linda Reinberg, *In the Field*, p. 207, 1991

4 the dip up at the front nose of a surfboard *US*
- —Grant W. Kuhns, *On Surfing*, p. 122, 1963

5 a dolt *NEW ZEALAND, 1982*
- —Harry Orsman, *A Dictionary of Modern New Zealand Slang*, p. 128, 1999

spoon *verb*

1 to lie behind someone, your face towards their back *US, 1887*
- BRODIE: You know how when someone lays with their back to you and you lay behind them, really close, and you throw one arm over them. T.S.: It's called spooning. —*Mallrats*, 1995

2 to tongue a woman's vagina and clitoris *US*
- —Eugene Landy, *The Underground Dictionary*, p. 175, 1971

spoondoolie *noun*

the penis *UK*
- Nonsense slang referred to vague, inoffensive terms that had little or no means in standard English: terms like biff, foo-foo, minky and winkie in FGTs [female genital terms], and chod, dongce, spondoolies, and winks in MGTs [male genital terms]. —*Journal of Sex Research*, p. 146, 2001

spooney *noun*

an effeminate male who may or may not be homosexual *US*
- —Anon., *King Smut's Wet Dreams Interpreted*, 1978

sport *noun*

used as a term of address, usually male-to-male *AUSTRALIA, 1935*
In Australia an everyday usage. In the US, a self-conscious term that conveys a jocular feeling.
- —Rolf Harris, *Tie Me Kangaroo Down Sport*, 1960
- Come sit in my new pad, sport, look around. —Richard Farina, *Been Down So Long*, p. 21, 1966
- BARRY: See youse later, sport! TORQUIL: Ciaou! And loads of luck! —Barry Humphries, *Bazza Pulls It Off!*, 1971
- "Hey," said the doctor, "you're supposed to be prone, sport." —Armistead Maupin, *Further Tales of the City*, p. 351, 1982
- VERONICA: I was hoping you'd rip my clothes off me, sport. —*Heathers*, 1988
- Your clerk was acting for you, sport. —John Milne, *Alive and Kicking*, p. 103, 1998

sport *verb*

to wear something in order to display it *UK, 1778*
- Before long, he was sporting a pink bandana and making moves on the butch Sylvester. —*The Guardian*, 23rd August 2003

sport fucking *noun*

sex without any pretence of a relationship, although with a competitive edge *US*
- I think what's happened is a recent trend among Fort Worth housewives towards neighborhood sport-fuckin'. —Dan Jenkins, *Dead Solid Perfect*, p. 46, 1986

sporting girl *noun*

a prostitute *US, 1938*
- But have you ever known a pimp to take a barmaid and make a sportin' girl outta her? —A.S. Jackson, *Gentleman Pimp*, p. 156, 1973

sporting house *noun*

a brothel *US, 1894*
- This is a sporting house. If I don't let a white john with money come here, I must have good reasons. —Chester Himes, *The Real Cool Killers*, p. 80, 1959
- "Why hell, woman, time I was his age I'd been to ever cathouse – 'sportin' -house,' we called 'em then – in this county." —Terry Southern, *Texas Summer*, p. 31, 1991

sporting lady *noun*

a prostitute *US*
- Ladies is the polite form, and carries the connotations of "ladies of the evening" and sportin' lady, that is, a kind of gallant euphemism. —Christina and Richard Milner, *Black Players*, p. 37, 1972

sporting life *noun*

1 the business and lifestyle of prostitution and pimping *US*
- His name was famous in sportin' life up 'til the time he died, and then he became a legend. —A.S. Jackson, *Gentleman Pimp*, p. 26, 1973

2 a wife *UK*
Rhyming slang.
- —Ray Puxley, *Cockney Rabbit*, 1992

3 cocaine *US*
From *Porgy and Bess*, in which the character Sportin' Life sells cocaine. Retro and rare. The shortened form is 'sporting'.
- "Sportin' Life," said Mona. "Happy dust. This stuff is an American institution." —Armistead Maupin, *Tales of the City*, p. 46, 1978
- —Mike Haskins, *Drugs*, p. 281, 2003

sportsman *noun*

a pimp *US*

In the mid-C19, the term referred to a gambler. By mid-C20 it was a somewhat grandiose euphemism for 'pimp'.

- She told me one night, just after I got into the life through her, that Bible John was her sportsman. "Sportsman? What's that?" I asked. She shrugged her shoulders. "Fancy word for pimp." —Sara Harris, *The Lords of Hell*, p. 31, 1967
- Tonight we have with us one of the greatest sportsmen of the Middlewest. —Babs Gonzales, *I Paid My Dues*, p. 89, 1967

sportsman's paradise *noun*

a bar favoured by pimps *US*

- —Burgess Laughlin, *Job Opportunities in the Black Market*, p. 6, 1978: 'Glossary'

sporty *adjective*

excellent *BERMUDA*

- —Peter Smith and Fred M. Barritt, *Bermewjan Vurds*, 1985

s'pose; 'spose *verb*

suppose *UK, 1852*

- I mean in the East End it's, like, there is a lot of darkies because it is a working class area I s'pose—*Ask*, p. 74, 8th May 1981
- Huh. S'pose. Well, here you are then. —Will Self, *The Sweet Smell of Psychosis*, p. 4, 1996

spot *noun*

1 a difficult or dangerous position *UK, 1936*

Usually in phrases: 'in a spot' and 'in a bit of a spot'.

- It was Mrs Thatcher being sweetly reasonable with daggered eyes – "but, Mr Day, what you do not appreciate is..." putting poor Sir Robin in a spot: should he start calling her Lady Thatcher? —*The Guardian*, 14th June 1983
- Intel Corp. is in a bit of a spot. The upcoming Itanium processor, the company's successor to its current Pentium 4 flagship product, is a 64-bit processor, yet most applications aren't optimized for a 64-bit processor. —*Electronic News*, 12th March 2001

2 a venue, especially a place of entertainment *UK, 1936*

- Fantastic food and a great location, make this one of the best eating spots around [...] Worth a browse if you want to turn heads when you walk into your favourite night spot. —*The Guardian*, 15th September 2001

3 an apartment or house *US*

- After a while I got tired of creeping downstairs with the around-the-way girls. I had to get my own spot so I could charge it up a bit. —*Style*, p. 96, July 2001

4 a place in a programme of entertainment, or an item of entertainment performed in such a programme *US*

- [Harry Secombe was] a graduate of the famous Windmill Theatre where he worked six comedy spots a day, six days a week, between the nudes. —*The Guardian*, 11th April 2001

5 a large party, a convention or other event that is a promising source for swindle victims *US*

- —Robert C. Prus and C.R.D. Sharper, *Road Hustler*, p. 171, 1977: 'Glossary of terms'

6 of food, a portion or meal that should not be described as extravagant; of abstracts like work, rest and pleasure, a small amount *UK, 1932*

- I told him I was doing a spot of work in the British Library[.] —*New Statesman*, 4th October 1999
- [T]he first thing they do is strip off the pinstripe uniform and dress down to go out for a pint and maybe a spot of dinner at the Bull & Butcher[.] —*The Guardian*, 10th March 2001
- This month W.W. Bellows joins the England Football Manager for a spot of lunch at San Lorenzo's[.] —*The Observer*, 5th May 2002

7 a small measure of drink *UK, 1885*

- Come on in. Spot of whisky before we set out to paint New York? —Anthony Boucher, *The Case of the Baker Street Irregulars*, p. 36, 1995

8 money *US*

- I pulled a five spot from my pocket and slipped it in his shirt pocket. —Mickey Spillane, *I, The Jury*, p. 47, 1947
- Would you have another five-spot to spare? —Bernard Wolfe, *The Late Risers*, p. 31, 1954
- Got to get a three-spot for that mellow chunk of wax, daddy-oh! —Ross Russell, *The Sound*, p. 17, 1961
- Sep,he go an give me a spot, I ain gonna git me no three. —Robert Gover, *One Hundred Dollar Misunderstanding*, p. 25, 1961
- But from the looks of her and the spots I could get for her to work, I felt the fox would be worth the chase[.] —A.S. Jackson, *Gentleman Pimp*, p. 79, 1973

9 a one-hundred-pound note; the sum of £100 *AUSTRALIA, 1945*

After the introduction of decimal currency in 1966, used for $100.

- [T]he police had asked for a two spot ($200) in return[.] —Neil James, *The (Sydney) Bulletin*, 26th April 1975
- —Ryan Aven-Bray, *Ridgey Didge Oz Jack Lang*, p. 45, 1983

10 a prison term, often prefixed with a numeral that denotes the number of years *US, 1901*

11 any of the large suit symbols printed on the face of a playing card *US*

- —Albert H. Morehead, *The Complete Guide to Winning Poker*, p. 274, 1967

12 in a deck of playing cards, an ace *US*

- —George Percy, *The Language of Poker*, p. 85, 1988

13 in poolroom betting, a handicap given in a bet-upon game *US*

- [B]etter players are always willing to give poorer ones a handicap ("spot"). —Ned Polsky, *Hustlers, Beats, and Others*, p. 47, 1967

▸ **put to the spot**

to kill someone who has been lured to a rendezvous *US*

- Dutch Schultz was put on the spot. No sooner had he sat down than the two men who had lured him there dived to the floor, as a man in a green hat stepped out from behind a pillar and gave Schultz all his six bullets in the belly[.] —Jack Lait and Lee Mortimer, *New York Confidential*, p. 18, 1948

spot *verb*

1 to recognise, discover or detect someone or something *US, 1848*

Colloquial.

- [A] local talent scout spotted him [Josh Hartnett] playing Sky Masterson in Guys and Dolls. —*The Guardian*, 21st April 2002

2 to rain in a few scattered drops *UK, 1849*

Originally dialect; 'spotting with rain' is a constant and current feature of UK weather reports.

3 in trucking, to park a truck *US*

- —Mary Elting, *Trucks at Work*, 1946

spot card *noun*

in a deck of playing cards, any card other than an ace or face card *US*

- —Albert H. Morehead, *The Complete Guide to Winning Poker*, p. 274, 1967

spot on *adverb*

absolutely accurate, exact; precisely *UK, 1920*

- Gordon Brown's budget forecast for growth last year of 2–2.5% [...] proved to be spot on[.] —*The Guardian*, 26th February 2004

spot play *noun*

in horse racing, an approach to betting in which the bettor only bets in situations where the odds seem advantageous *US*

- But there are occasions, that are called "spot" plays, where you can have the parimutuel odds working in your favor. —Jimmy Snyder, *Jimmy the Greek*, p. 213, 1975
- —Tom Ainslie, *Ainslie's Complete Guide to Thoroughbred Racing*, p. 338, 1976

spots *noun*

1 dice *UK*

- [T]he groom and his guests crammed into the gents and rolled spots. —Brian McDonald, *Elephant Boys*, p. 201, 2000

2 in circus usage, leopards *US*

- —Don Wilmeth, *The Language of American Popular Entertainment*, p. 253, 1981

spotted dick *adjective*

ill *UK*

Rhyming slang for 'sick', formed on a great British pudding.

- —Ray Puxley, *Cockney Rabbit*, 1992

spotter *noun*

1 a spy hired by an employer to observe and report on employees' activities *US, 1876*

- Not working like hell in school or in a bastard defense plant or shipyard where they had spotters who would turn you in for sleeping on the job or shooting a little crap in one of the storerooms. —Irving Shulman, *The Amboy Dukes*, p. 3, 1947
- By women detectives – spotters, we call 'em. —Jim Thompson, *A Swell-Looking Babe*, p. 2, 1954

2 a criminal who finds or identifies a likely victim for robbery *UK, 1937*

- The information from Leo's spotter was on the money. —Michael Connelly, *Void Moon*, p. 117, 2000

3 a lookout in a drug-selling operation *US*

- And if you do as good a job there as you did as a spotter, well, the sky is the limit. — *New Jack City*, 1990

4 a train*spotter*, a plane*spotter*, a bus-*spotter* or a similar type of hobbyist *US*

Spotter's Guides have been published by Mayflower Books of New York since 1979.

- [F]ar from being a one-dimensional hobby that involves merely underlining the numbers in the National Railway Enthusiasts Association's Spotter's Companion, there are scores of specialists[.] — Iain Aitch, *A Fete Worse Than Death*, p. 55, 2003
- "The spotters on Queen's Buildings at Heathrow are pond life," said Tony, talking of one of the most popular vantage points for spotters of passenger aircraft. "They're real spotter stereotypes with dandruff and -" "Lobotomies," Ray chipped in. — Iain Aitch, *A Fete Worse Than Death*, p. 75, 2003

spotters *noun*

the eyes *US*

- — Lou Shelly, *Hepcats Jive Talk Dictionary*, p. 17, 1945
- — Clarence Major, *Dictionary of Afro-American Slang*, p. 108, 1970

spotters and skinners *noun*

childlike, scratchy handwriting *BARBADOS*

- — Richard Allsopp, *Dictionary of Caribbean English Usage*, p. 525, 1992

spotting it

a method of consuming cannabis resin: pieces of hash, cut to the approximate size of matchheads, are picked up on the end of a lit cigarette; once the drug is burning the smoke given off is inhaled by means of a hollow tube, such as the empty body of a ballpoint pen *UK*

- [T]hree small pieces of hash, which wouldn't have made a quarter of a joint, were pushed in front of me. I was passed the lighted roll-up and empty ball-pen case and off I went. Apparently the name for what I was doing was "spotting it"[.] — Ken Lukowiak, *Marijuana Time*, p. 258, 2000

spotty dog; spotty *noun*

a foreigner *UK*

Rhyming slang for **WOG**.

- [Y]ou can't make up your mind whether you're a spotty [a non-White] or a widow's. — Ronnie Barker, *Fletcher's Book of Rhyming Slang*, p. 24, 1979

spout *noun*

the barrel of a gun *UK, 1943*

Mainly in the phrase 'up the spout'.

- Holds seven cartridges and one up the spout. A real fuckin' John Wayne gun this. — Donald Gorgon, *Cop Killer*, p. 60, 1994

▸ **up the spout**

1 in trouble; close to ruin; bankrupt *UK, 1829*

From the earlier sense (to pawn).

- So there's your infrastructure up the spout and the gang bosses are forced to import cheap foreign labour[.] — Andrew Nickolds, *Back to Basics*, p. 105, 1994

2 of a bullet, in the rifle barrel and ready to fire *UK, 1931*

Often as 'one up the spout'.

- [C]ocked and locked, one up the spout. — Jethro Tull, *Crossfire*, 1980

3 pregnant *UK, 1937*

From the earlier sense (ruined).

- ["]Mel's got another one on the way." "Up the spout again?" said Russell. "You randy old bastard.["] — Greg Williams, *Diamond Geezers*, p. 157, 1997

spout *verb*

to speak *UK*

A broadening of conventional sense (1750s), 'to declaim'.

- [T]he way you were spouting, like. — *A Hard Day's Night*, 1964

spraddle *verb*

to step awkwardly around something or someone *BARBADOS*

A blend of 'sprawl' and 'straddle'.

- Nowadays people in the bus won't move around and you does have to spraddle over them. — Frank A. Collymore, *Barbadian Dialect*, p. 104, 1965

sprag *noun*

1 in school, an informer, a tell-tale *UK*

Commented on by the Plain English Campaign in October 2003.

- — Chris Lewis, *The Dictionary of Playground Slang*, p. 217, 2003

2 chiefly in Queensland, the common house sparrow, *passer domesticus* *AUSTRALIA*

- [T]he sprags gathered in the jacaranda in the close of day. — Gerald Lee, *True Love and How to Get it*, p. 65, 1981

spranksious *adjective*

energetic, playful *BARBADOS*

- — Frank A. Collymore, *Barbadian Dialect*, p. 104, 1965

sprassey; spraser; sprazey; sprowsie; sprouse *noun*

sixpence or 6d; a coin of that value *UK, 1931*

Many variations, ultimately from Shelta *sprazi*. Inflation has rendered the conversion from 6d to 2½p meaningless.

- — Brian McDonald, *Elephant Boys*, p. 202, 2000

spraunce *verb*

to lie; to tell a trivial lie *UK*

- — Lenny McLean, *The Guv'nor*, 1998

sprauncy *adjective*

ostentatious, showy *UK*

- At the darkest end of the wardrobe there was this Flash Suit. A real sprauncy whistle. — *British Journal of Photography*, 13th June 1980

spray *noun*

an aerosol used when inhaling solvents *UK*

- — Angela Devlin, *Prison Patter*, p. 109, 1996

spray *verb*

1 to ejaculate semen onto a sexual partner *UK*

- [I]t comes into my head that I want to spray her. All over her and that, good style. — Kevin Sampson, *Outlaws*, p. 117, 2001

2 to fart *US*

- — Gary K. Farlow, *Prison-ese*, p. 65, 2002

spray and pray *verb*

in a military engagement, to shoot wildly then run *US*

- "They were just spraying and praying," said Warrant Officer Larry Carpenter. — *The Guardian*, 16th April 2003

spread *noun*

1 an assortment of food laid out on a table or served at a social event *UK, 1822*

- Some spread! Grafflings and fortinaxes all over, and pertussmied down the middle. — Bernard Wolfe, *The Late Risers*, p. 257, 1954
- Meanwhile his young wife prepared a magnificent spread in the big ranch kitchen. — Jack Kerouac, *On the Road*, p. 228, 1957
- What kind of spread would they put out over to the Judge's? Some little finger bits and pieces, celery sticks stuffed with cream cheese, potato chips and green dip that worked its way up under the fingernails? — Robert Campbell, *Boneyards*, p. 2, 1992
- [L]adies decked out in their fanciest duds feast on a great spread of food and drink[.] — Rick Steve, *Paris 2004*, p. 128, 2002

2 in sports betting, the margin of victory incorporated into a bet *US, 1973*

- Even when they're being real generous with the line, I think can beat the spread, I lay off. — John Sayles, *Union Dues*, p. 25, 1977
- The spread is nine for game one, but the Celtics will probably win by 14 or 15. — Hunter S. Thompson, *Generation of Swine*, p. 120, 26th May 1986

3 a photograph of a naked woman exposing her genitals *US*

- For those interested in semantics, the pictures with the legs in normal position showing only the pubic bush are called "beaver pictures" but if the legs are spread apart and the camera angle shows the vaginal aperture or clitoris, then it is called "spread. — *Screw*, p. 16, 18th August 1969

4 in pool, the first shot of the game *US*

- — Steve Rushin, *Pool Cool*, p. 27, 1990

spread *verb*

to share information or cards while engaging in a cheating scheme *US, 1968*

- — Thomas L. Clark, *The Dictionary of Gambling and Gaming*, p. 212, 1987

▸ **spread a game**

to start a card game *US*

- — Robert C. Prus and C.R.D. Sharper, *Road Hustler*, p. 171, 1977: 'Glossary of terms'

▸ **spread for**

of a woman, to dispose herself for sex with someone *UK*

Reported by Laurie Atkinson, 1978.

▸ **spread the eagle**

to escape from prison or jail *US*

- — Hyman E. Goldin et al., *Dictionary of American Underworld Lingo*, p. 204, 1950

▸ **spread your shot**
to speak honestly and directly *US*
- —John R. Armore and Joseph D. Wolfe, *Dictionary of Desperation*, p. 51, 1976

spread beaver *noun*
▷ see: SPLIT BEAVER

spread-bet *noun*
a type of gamble against predicted odds *US*

spread-betting *noun*
a form of gambling against a bookmaker's predicted result (see citation) *US*
- The "spread" in spread-betting is a pair of values, usually a point or two apart, which represent the bookmaker's favoured outcome. The investor has two choices: to bet higher, known as "buying", or bet lower, known as "selling".—David Bennet, *Know Your Bets*, p. 107, 2001

spread-eagle *verb*
to spread and stretch out a person's arms and legs *UK, 1826*
- Three squad cars answered the call and within 20 seconds a half dozen cops had Wally out of his car and spread-eagled facedown on the asphalt.—C.D. Payne, *Youth in Revolt*, p. 135, 1993

spreadhead *noun*
a devoted follower of the band Widespread Panic *US*
An evolution of 'deadhead' (a follower of the Grateful Dead).
- —Don R. McCreary (Editor), *Dawg Speak*, 2001

spreading broads *noun*
an act of playing or cheating at cards, especially the manipulating of cards in the three-card trick *UK, 1886*
- —David Powis, *The Signs of Crime*, 1977

spread shot *noun*
a photograph or scene in a pornographic film showing a woman's spread vagina *US*
Recorded in interview with Jim Holliday, 12th June 1997.
- As an example, inspector Guido cited a set of glossy spread shots that sold under the counter for $8.—*Screw*, p. 14, 10th May 1971

spreck up *verb*
(of a male) to orgasm *UK*
A possible pun on 'ejaculate' based on German *sprechen* (to speak).
- I feel like I'm going to spreck up there and then.—Kevin Sampson, *Clubland*, p. 88, 2002

spree boy *noun*
a person who loves fun but not work *BARBADOS*
- —Frank A. Collymore, *Barbadian Dialect*, p. 104, 1965

sprigs *noun*
sparse facial hair *BAHAMAS*
- —John A. Holm, *Dictionary of Bahamian English*, p. 192, 1982

spring *verb*
to escape, or effect someone's escape or release, from prison or detention *US, 1904*
- By this time Bow and Emil Burbacher were sprung from The School and showed up on the Corner again.—Mezz Mezzrow, *Really the Blues*, p. 20, 1946
- Whenever a crowd of fellows were rounded up in a raid on a gambling house or saloon the proprietor knew how to "spring" them, that is, get them out of jail.—Louis Armstrong, *Satchmo*, p. 126, 1954
- As continuity would have it, they are sprung at the same time more or less and take up residence in a flat on the Lower East Side.—William Burroughs, *Naked Lunch*, p. 129, 1957
- So now he's sprung, but he brung his brain with him and he's gonna bring down that whole country.—Edwin Torres, *After Hours*, p. 173, 1979
- —Angela Devlin, *Prison Patter*, p. 108, 1996
- What are you talking about, Rollie? We're springing 'em?—*Gone in 60 Seconds*, 2000

spring buster *noun*
a hole in a road, jarring to the driver when encountered *US*
- —*American Speech*, p. 271, December 1962: 'The language of traffic policemen'

springbutt *noun*
a person who is eager to please *US*
- —*American Speech*, p. 288, December 1962: 'Marine Corps slang'
- We called them "Spring Butts," those eager beavers whose impressive memories had them enthusiastically bouncing out of their chairs and up the road to being first in the class.—David H. Hackworth, *About Face*, p. 214, 1989

spring chicken *noun*
a youthful, attractive boy as the object of sexual desire of an older homosexual man *US*
- —*Maledicta*, p. 220, 1979: 'Kinks and queens: linguistic and cultural aspects of the terminology for gays'

springer *noun*
1 any person in the position to get you out of jail, from a bail bondsman to a lawyer to a judge *US*
- —Hyman E. Goldin et al., *Dictionary of American Underworld Lingo*, p. 204, 1950
- —*Maledicta*, p. 150, Summer/Winter 1986–1987: 'Sexual slang: prostitutes, pedophiles, flagellators, transvestites, and necrophiles'

2 in horse racing, a horse that becomes the betting favourite or nearly the favourite after betting opens on a race *UK*
- —Rita Cannon, *Let's Go Racing*, p. 73, 1948

springy *noun*
a wetsuit covering the body, neck and limbs to the elbows and knees *AUSTRALIA*
- A boy's 'springy' would cost around $80.00.—*Riptide*, p. 86, 1992

springy thingy *noun*
in drag racing, a car with a light structure and thus maximum flexibility *US*
- —John Lawlor, *How to Talk Car*, p. 98, 1965

sprinkle *verb*
to urinate *UK*
- —Ray Puxley, *Cockney Rabbit*, p. 159, 1992

spritz *verb*
to squirt, especially a mist *US, 1917*
- After a vigorous sponge bath, followed by an extra-heavy spritz of deodorant, I dressed quickly and counted out my remaining cash: $43.12.—C.D. Payne, *Youth in Revolt*, p. 55, 1993
- Kay squealed with her mouth full – some club soda spritzed out and hit Leigh.—James Ellroy, *Hollywood Nocturnes*, p. 25, 1994

spritzer *noun*
a fuel injector *US*
- —Lewis Poteet, *Car & Motorcyle Slang*, p. 187, 1992

sprog *noun*
1 a baby; a child *UK, 1706*
From obsolete 'sprag' (a lively young fellow).
- Well, it appears that between us we had a sprog, but she never cracked on about it, and I didn't tumble to it.—John Wynnum, *Jiggin' in the Riggin*, p. 58, 1965
- —Louis S. Leland, *A Personal Kiwi-Yankee Dictionary*, p. 96, 1984
- [T]he monarchy has been a dab hand at the old import/export game, despatching the sprogs round the world to keep associated royal families up to strength.—Andrew Nickolds, *Back to Basics*, p. 12, 1994
- [D]o the lot of them at the earliest possible opportunity, male sprogs especially.—James Hawes, *Dead Long Enough*, p. 81, 2000

2 a recruit *UK, 1941*
Royal Air Force originally, then Royal Navy, now police. Probably derives from obsolete 'sprag' (1706) 'a lively young fellow' but etymological theories abound: a reversal of 'frog spawn' – because it's so very green; a confusion of 'cog and sprocket' – a metaphor with the recruit just a cog (a sprocket) in a wheel; a distortion of 'sprout'; it has also been claimed that a 'sprog' is 'a young gannet'.
- Fifteen years ago I was a fresh-faced sprog straight out of police training college[.]—*FHM*, p. 250, June 2003

3 semen *AUSTRALIA*
- —Gary Simes, *Gay Perspectives*, p. 55, 1992

sprog *verb*
to parent a child *UK*
- You first with the sprogging then, Harry—James Hawes, *Dead Long Enough*, p. 199, 2000

sprogged *adjective*
pregnant *NEW ZEALAND*
- —Louis S. Leland, *A Personal Kiwi-Yankee Dictionary*, p. 96, 1984

sprogie *adjective*
stylish; fashionable *BAHAMAS*
- —John A. Holm, *Dictionary of Bahamian English*, p. 192, 1982

spronce *verb*
to show off, especially by your choice of clothes *UK*
- Spronce was a word much used by girls in London then [the 1960s].—Ben Sonnenberg, *Lost Property*, p. 160, 1991

sproncy; sprauntsy; sprauncy *adjective*
showily dressed; fashionable; showy *UK, 1957*
- It was sproncy to go to South London and sleep with a Jamaican. —Ben Sonnenberg, *Lost Property*, p. 160, 1991
- [T]he main focus for the Lib Dems must be to hold off and challenge the newly sprauncy Tories. — *The Guardian*, 3rd March 2004

sprowsie; sprouse *noun*
▷ see: SPRASSEY

spruik *verb*
to declaim; to hold forth; to make a speech like a showman *AUSTRALIA, 1902*
Exact origin unknown, but no doubt related to some Germanic speech-act verb, such as Dutch *spreken* (to speak) or Yiddish *shpruch* (a saying, a charm).
- Rotten pen pusher Jake is and always will be though he's always spruiking about this university degree he's supposed to have. —Wilda Moxham, *The Apprentice*, p. 31, 1969
- —Jim Ramsay, *Cop It Sweet!*, p. 85, 1977

spruiker *noun*
a speaker employed to attract a crowd to a venue, show or demonstration of a product; a barker *AUSTRALIA, 1902*
- SPRUIKER – A speaker. —Gilbert H. Lawson, *A Dictionary of Australian Words and Terms*, 1924
- A spruiker was up front on a Hollywood tourist bus. —Sam Weller, *Old Bastards I Have Met*, p. 11, 1979
- 'What's the idea of bringing your mate with you? Making sure you win?' the spruiker jeered, and the crowd laughed. —Ward McNally, *Supper at Happy Harry's*, p. 71, 1982

sprung *adjective*
addicted *US*
- —Judi Sanders, *Kickin' like Chicken with the Couch Commander*, p. 23, 1992

sprung on *adjective*
infatuated with *US*
- CHER: Oooh, you knew what? ELTON: That you were totally sprung on me. — *Clueless*, 1995
- —Rick Ayers (Editor), *Berkeley High Slang Dictionary*, p. 39, 2004

SP shop *noun*
an establishment operating starting price bookmaking *AUSTRALIA, 1948*
- The drunk took Bart through a maze of streets and then handed him over to a beautiful young woman, who took him to an S.P. shop, where he was picked up by someone else[.] —George Blaikie, *Remember Smith's Weekly?*, p. 150, 1966

spud *noun*
1 a potato *NEW ZEALAND, 1845*
- I understand why girls won't go / Across a green potato field... / The young fresh spuds have eyes, you know, / And might unto temptation yield. —Norman Lindsay, *Comic Art of Norman Lindsay*, p. 105, 1905
- By the way, the steward tells me it will be the last meal with spuds. —Robert S. Close, *Love Me Sailor*, p. 63, 1945
- CORP: [...] These spuds look like they're about done, Tich. TICH: Oh – righto mate – thanks. —Clive Exton, *No Fixed Abode [Six Granada Plays]*, p. 124, 1959
- I'll flatten him with the spud masher one day. —Les Such, *A Yen for Yokohama*, p. 40, 1963
- —Frank Hardy, *The Yarns of Billy Borker*, p. 14, 1965
- I got some eggs and bread and spuds. —Darryl Ponicsan, *The Last Detail*, p. 59, 1970
- —Bill Wannan, *Folklore of the Australian Pub*, p. 6, 1972
- —Sam Weller, *Old Bastards I Have Met*, p. 21, 1979

2 a trainee *UK*
- We've got a couple of spuds on the shop floor today. —experienced staff member *Starbucks, Bristol*, 25th November 2001

3 a SCUD missile *US*
An obvious rhyme that belittles the enemy's weaponry.
- — *The Retired Officer Magazine*, p. 39, January 1993

spud and onion gang *noun*
a group of wharf workers who load or unload produce *AUSTRALIA*
- —Maureen Brooks and Joan Ritchie, *Tassie Terms*, p. 132, 1995

spud-bashing *noun*
potato peeling; hence, kitchen fatigues *UK*
Military, combining SPUD (a potato) with the suffix -BASHING (vigorous compulsory activity).

spud cocky *noun*
a potato farmer *AUSTRALIA, 1950*

spudge *verb*
to poke a fire's logs, making the fire blaze up *CANADA*
- In Cape Sable Island, to "spudge" the fire is to poke at it, make it burn faster or blaze up. A metaphorical extension means "working hard," especially with an oar. "Like as not the boats is all in; they'd have a hard ol' spudgin' if they was out today." — *The Coast Guard*, p. 4, 22nd February 1984

spud juice *noun*
a potent homemade alcoholic beverage produced by fermenting potatoes *US*
- I got some good spud juice lined up, but it takes five packs to cop. —Donald Goines, *Black Gangster*, p. 12, 1977

spuds *noun*
▷ see: LOVE SPUDS

spun *noun*
in the television and film industries, a light diffuser made with synthetic materials *US*
Originally an abbreviation of 'spun glass', the term was retained when the material changed.
- —Ralph S. Singleton, *Filmaker's Dictionary*, p. 159, 1990

spun *adjective*
1 crazy; disoriented *US*
- —Vann Wesson, *Generation X Field Guide and Lexicon*, p. 158, 1997

2 very drug-intoxicated *US*
- —Jim Crotty, *How to Talk American*, p. 146, 1997

3 excited, enthusiastic *US*
- That was her goal in life, to work "behind the camera." "When it's live, I'm spun," she said. —Dan Jenkins, *Life Its Ownself*, p. 186, 1984

spunk *noun*
1 mettle, courage *UK, 1774*
A word forever associated in the US with actress Mary Tyler Moore; in the initial episode of *The Mary Tyler Moore Show* in 1970, Moore's boss Lou Grant assesses her – 'You've got spunk. I hate spunk!'.
- General Peckem blessed the fates that had sent him a weakling for a subordinate. A man of spunk would have been unthinkable. —Joseph Heller, *Catch 22*, p. 331, 1961
- And it takes a lot of spunk and devotion to be a chaplain. —Darryl Ponicsan, *The Last Detail*, p. 45, 1970
- But then talking to her after changed his mind, seeing this was a good-looking girl up close with a cute figure. She had spunk, too. —Elmore Leonard, *Maximum Bob*, p. 43, 1991
- Imagine gatecrashing that gaff [...] they had more spunk than Monica Lewinsky's dress. —Dave Courtney, *Stop the Ride I Want to Get Off*, p. 396, 1999

2 semen *UK, 1888*
- He's spewing his spunk deep inside her seething snatch! — *Adam Film World*, p. 60, 1977
- The booth smelled of spunk[.] —Richard Price, *Clockers*, p. 393, 1992
- An overweight, faggy-looking Filipino in his early thirties – who was the "floater" at Annabel's gang bang – wipes up any and all spunk sprayed upon Jasmin today. —Anthony Petkovich, *The X Factory*, p. 190, 1997
- [M]e dick spasming like artillery firing shells of what I know must just be spunk but which feels like me innards[.] —Niall Griffiths, *Kelly + Victor*, p. 91, 2002

3 a very attractive person *AUSTRALIA, 1978*
- And Romeo sees Juliet on the balcony, and he goes, 'What a spunk,' and she goes, 'What a spunk[.]' —Kylie Mole (Maryanne Fahey), *My Diary*, p. 72, 1988
- She pursed her lips and blew him a kiss. 'You big spunk.' —Robert G. Barrett, *Davo's Little Something*, p. 47, 1992
- [O]n the first day on the job in the big smoke I had to share a teller's box with a young lady called Kim, a real spunk and my future wife. —Paul Vautin, *Turn It Up!*, p. 82, 1995

spunk *verb*
1 (of a male) to ejaculate *AUSTRALIA*
Also used in the variants 'spunk off' and 'spunk up'.
- I wanted to spunkoff all over her then. — *Searchlight*, p. 8, 1974
- [W]hen the other one turns and smiles at me I almost spunk up in my pants. —John King, *Human Punk*, p. 76, 2000
- What do you want to do now, spunk in his Head and Shoulders? —Danny King, *The Burglar Diaries*, p. 187, 2001

2 to spend or waste money or time *UK*
From 'spunk' (to ejaculate semen), punning on 'spend'.
- I wanted to get it up and running really quickly without spunking any money on it. —Dave Courtney, *Raving Lunacy*, p. 18, 2000

- Spent an afternoon listening to James Beattie debating whether to spunk £3,000 on a Bikkembergs jacket. — *FHM*, p. 16, June 2003
- The putative PM [Tony Blair] spunked away many an hour at university playing guitar[.] — *Bang*, p. 26, November 2003

spunk bin *noun*

the vagina *UK*

- Women's genitalia were represented as (potential) containers (e.g., 'bucket', 'box', 'hair goblet'), places to put things in (e.g., 'furry letterbox', 'disk drive', 'socket', 'slot'), containers for semen (e.g., 'gism pot', 'spunk bin', 'honey pot'), and containers for the penis/sex (e.g., 'willy warmer', 'wank shaft', 'shagbox').' — *Journal of Sex Research*, p. 146, 2001

spunkbubble *noun*

1 used between men as a term of abuse *UK, 1984*

- "Right, spunk bubble," Parlabane said with malicious delight. "Open your mouth." — Christopher Brookmyre, *Quite Ugly One Morning*, p. 208, 2002

2 a sexually attractive person *AUSTRALIA*

- Spunkbubble Sophie Lee has been at a bit of a loose end since Sex came grinding to a halt. The TV program, that is. — *People*, p. 41, 9th December 1992

spunk dust *noun*

used between men as a term of abuse *UK, 1984*

spunker *noun*

used by adolescent girls as a derisory term for any boy of similar maturity *UK*

Demonstrates a very basic grasp of biology: only males produce **SPUNK** (semen).

- Then untold hell breaks out. – You FUCKIN' SPUNKERS. Wan-kaaaahs. — Nick Barlay, *Curvy Lovebox*, p. 45, 1997

spunkette *noun*

a sexually attractive young woman *AUSTRALIA*

- Profumo, a keen pants man, couldn't resist bedding 19-year-old spunkette Christine Keeler after meeting her on a posh country house weekend. — *People*, p. 6, 30th March 1994

spunkiness *noun*

good looks *AUSTRALIA, 1981*

- That kind of spunkiness doesn't come naturally. He must have been taking handsome lessons. — Kathy Lette, *Girls' Night Out*, p. 76, 1987

spunkrat *noun*

a sexually attractive person *AUSTRALIA, 1987*

- — Kathy Lette, *Girls' Night Out*, 1987
- Jason Donovan is a spunkrat. — Kylie Mole (Maryanne Fahey), *My Diary*, p. 12, 1988

spunky *noun*

a sexually attractive person *AUSTRALIA, 1967*

- SYDNEY: Hey Spunkies, earn bread nude modelling. Reply with sample photos. — *Guy*, p. 16, 21st April 1974
- Sydney Guy, own flat, 8" cock, will meet young spunkies for mutual sucks, screws. — *Screw*, p. 12, 4th March 1974
- — Jim Ramsay, *Cop It Sweet!*, p. 85, 1977
- But every Friday night up at the Harbord Diggers disco he'd be holding court, three or four spunkys hanging off each arm[.] — Paul Vautin, *Turn It Up!*, p. 83, 1995

spunky *adjective*

1 brave; spirited; plucky *UK, 1786*

From **SPUNK** (courage).

- "[Y]ou touch my ass again and I'll get someone to shoot you." "Spunky," Ronald said. "I like that." — Janet Evanovich, *Seven Up*, p. 118, 2001

2 sexually attractive *AUSTRALIA, 1973*

- Young spunky guy well hung seeks similar to 40. — *Screw*, p. 12, 4th March 1974
- HI! GREAT WEEK! Mine was really great – back bed-hopping again. Boy, I got some spunky pricks this week – my cunt feels great. — *Screw*, p. 2, 4th March 1974
- [I] used to amuse myself by standing on a chair and looking through the transom above the door at some of the spunky little starlets checking in for a rest. — Barry Humphries, *The Traveller's Tool*, p. 68, 1985
- You can play spin the bottle with spunky rich chicks drunk on $10-a-pop sticky drinks and make suggestive comments about slippery nipples, quick fucks and orgasms. — *People*, p. 14, 5th July 1999

spun out *adjective*

crazy *UK*

- Morty was running around with a team of guys who were seriously spun out. The loonies' loonies. — J.J. Connolly, *Layer Cake*, p. 6–7, 2000

sputnik *noun*

a mixture of marijuana from Pakistan and opium; marijuana *UK*

From 'sputnik' (the Russian satellites, first launched in 1957), hence its use here as something else to take you out of this world.

- Street names [...] shit, skunk, sputnik, wacky backy[.] — James Kay and Julian Cohen, *The Parents' Complete Guide to Young People and Drugs*, p. 133, 1998

squab *noun*

a young girl or woman *US*

From the standard sense (a newly hatched or very young bird).

- The table is so situated that the town's aging and more prosperous squab-hunters who congregate at it nightly can case the door and ogle the bims brought in by younger and more energetic men. — Jack Lait and Lee Mortimer, *New York Confidential*, p. 166, 1948
- The black whore raised her hand above her head. "We got a man wants a squab over here," she singsonged. — Robert Campbell, *Alice in La-La Land*, p. 256, 1987

squab *verb*

to fight *US*

- — *Los Angeles Times*, p. II-6, 11th August 1986

squab job *noun*

a sexually attractive girl below the legal age of consent *US*

- — Roger Blake, *The American Dictionary of Sexual Terms*, p. 111, 1964

squack *noun*

a woman; sex with a woman *US*

- (Caption): WHEN HE GET some fine Ofay squack in the sheets, what he make her do? She suck his joint, man. — *Screw*, p. 15, 30th October 1972

squack *verb*

to ejaculate *US*

- I'm squacking in my pants. — *Airheads*, 1993

squad *noun*

a police car *US*

Known conventionally as a 'squad car'.

- They came and brought the paddy wagon with them, two squads and a paddy wagon. — Henry Williamson, *Hustler!*, p. 104, 1965

Squad *noun*

▸ the Squad

the Flying *Squad* (a unit of the Metropolitan Police, known as the Flying Squad since 1921) *UK*

- — Angela Devlin, *Prison Patter*, p. 109, 1996
- Perhaps the most spectacular, and dangerous, part of the Squad's work is the 'pavement ambush'. — Martin Fido and Keith Skinner, *The Official Encyclopaedia of Scotland Yard*, p. 94, 1999

squaddie; squaddy *noun*

a soldier, usually ranked private *UK, 1933*

From a new recruit's placement in a squad.

- [T]here was a Brit squaddy dead. — Andy McNab, *Immediate Action*, p. 27, 1995
- [K]eeping watch for some ex-squaddie with shards of ice in his heart. — Greg Williams, *Diamond Geezers*, p. 219, 1997
- He's a squaddie serving in Northern Ireland. — John King, *Human Punk*, p. 59, 2000

square *noun*

1 a person with a conventional job and lifestyle; an old-fashioned person *US, 1944*

- A lot of the guys who hung around were squares who worked for their gold, more gamblers than gangsters[.] — Mezz Mezzrow, *Really the Blues*, p. 20, 1946
- 'Coz the good times is over / And the squares don't have no dough — Jimmy Witherspoon, *Skid Row Blues*, 1947
- In Detroit, someone who once would be called a drip or a square is now, regrettably, a nerd, or in a less severe case, a scurve. — *Newsweek*, 8th October 1951
- Let's get out and give the squares a booth. — George Mandel, *Flee the Angry Strangers*, p. 356, 1952
- She's gonna marry this rich jerk from Chicago, a real square. — Jack Kerouac, *The Dharma Bums*, p. 134, 1958
- At each new knock on the door the callers would be screened to keepout such undesirables as square, fuzz, and hip-squares. — Ross Russell, *The Sound*, p. 109, 1961
- I've known squares I was at school with (prefects, monitors, scholarship-winners, all that crap) take jobs in INDUSTRY, as management trainees! — Derek Raymond (Robin Cook), *The Crust on its Uppers*, p. 25, 1962
- Amphetamine, that group of drugs which are called pep pills by squares. They are also called psychic energizers. — Ruth Bronsteen, *The Hippy's Handbook*, p. 12, 1967

- Q: You don't think it's for putting on the squares? RON: I don't think people care that much about the squares. — Leonard Wolfe (Editor), *Voices from the Love Generation*, p. 220, 1968
- We were both popular as squares. — Susan Hall, *Gentleman of Leisure*, p. 44, 1972
- I had out-slicked the law / and taken off a whole lotta squares. — Lightnin' Rod, *Hustlers Convention*, p. 29, 1973

2 a heterosexual *AUSTRALIA, 1960*

- They all want to run around pantsing each other and any one that's normal is a friggin' square. — Robert G. Barrett, *Davo's Little Something*, p. 75, 1992

3 a filling meal *US, 1882*

- He says, "Look, you get three squares a day, don't you?" — Haenigsen, *Jive's Like That*, 1947
- Could he go to Allah for three squares a day? — Clarence Cooper Jr, *Black*, p. 211, 1963
- Have a good dinner, kid. You look as though you haven't had a square in weeks. — Antony James, *America's Homosexual Underground*, p. 46, 1965
- I love the goddam navy. I get three squares a day, a pad to lie down on, roof over my head, tuxedo to wear. We're living high off the hog. — Darryl Ponicsan, *The Last Detail*, p. 33, 1970
- They've been real good to your people – gettin' 'em off the streets, givin' 'em three squares a day, all them fancy uniforms. — Eugene Boe (Compiler), *The Wit & Wisdom of Archie Bunker*, p. 65, 1971
- [W]e can't even afford a fuckin bed and three squares at a state hospital for Clyde. — Joseph Wambaugh, *The Choirboys*, p. 152, 1975
- It was also three squares a day and a clean barracks. — John Sayles, *Union Dues*, p. 70, 1977
- Life in the joint wasn't so bad, he rationalized for a moment, the sun's rays tripping him out, not if you had three squares a day, few hassles, and a chance to write as much as you wanted. — Odie Hawkins, *Great Lawd Buddha*, p. 27, 1990
- All they do is eat three squares a day, they live at home with mommy[.] — *Hip-Hop Connection*, p. 13, July 2002

4 a factory-manufactured cigarette *US*

- A square is a cigarette. And also a quarter. — Willard Motley, *Let No Man Write My Epitaph*, p. 148, 1958
- On the other hand that same San Rafael lass would be just as bewildered as you and I, were she to be strolling across the grounds of Mission High in San Francisco and hear one youth ask another, "Hey man, can you spare a square?" — *San Francisco Examiner*, p. 8, 27th October 1963
- She reached in her purse and pulled out a square / She said "Don't worry, daddy, he's no where." — Bruce Jackson, *Get Your Ass in the Water and Swim Like Me*, p. 50, 1964
- — *Mr.*, p. 8, April 1966: 'The Hippie's lexicon'
- I said, "Hey Jack, how you doing? That sure is a fine 'silk' girl, huh? You got a square to spare?" He flashed a cigarette from his red shirt pocket, handed it to me, and said, "Yeh Kid, she's fine as a Valentine." — Iceberg Slim (Robert Beck), *Pimp*, p. 35, 1969
- — Eugene Landy, *The Underground Dictionary*, p. 67, 1971
- "Got a square, Joe?" Reaching for the Camels on his bedstand, Joe held his breath to wince in pain and was surprised instead to feel only a tightness. — Seth Morgan, *Homeboy*, p. 109, 1990

5 a one-dollar note *US*

- — Kenn "Naz" Young, *Naz's Dictionary of Teen Slang*, p. 110, 1993

▸ on the square

1 honest, truthful, trustworthy *UK, 1872*

Possibly from Masonic symbolism and jargon.

- "Are you on the level?" he whispered. "Sorry?" I retorted, a bit indignant. "I mean" – he smiled – "are you on the square?" Then I twigged. This was freemason talk. One of their codes. — Jake Arnott, *He Kills Coppers*, p. 45, 2001
- The guy was all policeman, 110 per cent on the square. — Garry Bushell, *The Face*, p. 95, 2001

2 in a faithful monogamous relationship with someone *AUSTRALIA, 1944*

- You're not married and you haven't even got sheilas – not ones you're on the square with, anyhow. — Eric Lambert, *The Veterans*, p. 13, 1954

3 being a freemason *UK, 1984*

From symbolism that is employed in freemasonry.

square *verb*

to satisfactorily settle matters or resolve a problem, generally by the use of power and influence, bribery or threat *UK, 1853*

From 'square' (to balance the books).

- They demanded $25,000 to square the rap. — Jack Lait and Lee Mortimer, *Chicago Confidential*, p. 17, 1950
- Opponents were squared and spoils divvied-up. — David Starkey, *Elizabeth*, p. 59, 2000

▸ square it away

to settle matters *AUSTRALIA*

- Diplomatic discretion forbids me to divulge how we squared it away with the police[.] — Barry Humphries, *The Traveller's Tool*, p. 93, 1985

square *adjective*

1 old fashioned; decent and honest; conventional *US, 1946*

- The other patients were a pretty square and sorry lot. Not another junkie in the place. — William Burroughs, *Junkie*, p. 93, 1953
- One of the little pigs was very cool, another was more on the commercial side, and the third was, beyond the shadow of a doubt, square. — Steve Allen, *Bop Fables*, p. 18, 1955
- Dig the square wardrobe! — *Rebel Without a Cause*, 1955
- Their rules were their rules and they disdained square advice. — Robert Sylvester, *No Cover Charge*, p. 285, 1956
- One is Hip or one is Square (the alternative which each new generation coming into American life is beginning to feel), one is a rebel or one conforms[.] — Norman Mailer, *Advertisements for Myself*, p. 339, 1957
- Not only does scuffling often consume more time and brainpower than a square job, but its effect on leisure is more stultifying than any job dissatisfaction would be. — *Dissent*, p. 346, Summer 1961
- Other square situations that you might someday find yourself facing are installation proceedings, when Dad becomes chief of his lodge[.] — Dick Clark, *To Goof or Not to Goof*, p. 167, 1963
- They can tell pimps from square guys. They can tell square girls from prostitutes. — Susan Hall, *Gentleman of Leisure*, p. 4, 1972

2 heterosexual *AUSTRALIA, 1944*

- He looks the square type all right, but not the two-timing type. — Neville Jackson, *No end to the way*, p. 61, 1965

3 in cricket, used to describe fielding positions along an imaginary line extending to the left and right of the batsman's wicket *UK, 1851*

▸ live square

to conduct your life as an honest citizen *AUSTRALIA*

- — *The (Sydney) Bulletin*, 26th April 1975

square as a bear *adjective*

extremely conventional *US*

The bear appears for the rhyming value, nothing else.

- "Daddy-O," she said, "you're square as a bear, but I dig you the most." — Max Shulman, *Rally Round the Flag, Boys!*, p. 48, 1957

square away *verb*

to put in order, to tidy away; hence, to learn *UK, 1909*

- [T]hey'd have had all the cock-ups and found out the little bits and pieces that we needed to know, and squared them all away. — Andy McNab, *Immediate Action*, p. 312, 1995

square-bashing *noun*

military parade-drill *UK, 1943*

From the 'parade-*square*'.

- No more dreams of failure, no more square-bashing with green recruits[.] — Salman Rushdie, *Shame*, p. 210, 1985

square bitch *noun*

any woman who is not a prostitute *US*

- — Christina and Richard Milner, *Black Players*, p. 10, 1972

square box *noun*

in court, a witness box *UK*

- — Angela Devlin, *Prison Patter*, p. 109, 1996

squared *adjective*

craving drugs *US*

- If you're squared, it means you need some stuff. You're not feeling good. — Willard Motley, *Let No Man Write My Epitaph*, p. 148, 1958

square dancing ticket *noun*

a dose of LSD on a square of blotting paper *UK*

- — Mike Haskins, *Drugs*, p. 286, 2003

square-eyed *adjective*

applied contemptuously to someone who watches 'too much' television *UK, 1984*

- — *The Guardian*, 12th January 2004

square from Delaware *noun*

an exceptionally naive, conventional person *US, 1938*

Delaware exists for the rhyme; it is no more or less square than any other state. In the 1930s and 40s, there was a cottage industry in inventing terms along the line of this construction – a 'clown from Allenton', a 'pester from Chester' and so on. The 'square from Delaware' was one of the few that truly worked itself into speech.

- — Lou Shelly, *Hepcats Jive Talk Dictionary*, p. 37, 1945

- Even a square from Delaware should know God ain't going to kiss your ass when you tell him no, you poor boob. —Iceberg Slim (Robert Beck), *Pimp*, p. 134, 1969
- No, man, what we swingers were rebelling against were uptight squares like you, whose bag was money and world domination. — *Austin Powers*, 1997

square grouper *noun*
a brick of compressed marijuana *US*
The name of a notional fish, alluding to the presence of marijuana smugglers in south Florida waters.
- Or I could take the money and invest in a shrimper heading south to do a little "square grouper" fishing and triple my money in a month. —Jimmy Buffett, *Tales from Margaritaville*, p. 172, 1989

squarehead *noun*
1 a German, especially a German soldier in World Wars 1 and 2 *US*
A derogatory term that has lingered, perhaps, through films retelling how we won the war.
- The plucky Allies – Michael Caine, Sylvester Stallone, Ipswich midfielder John Wark – spurn a chance to escape prison-camp just to trounce the squareheads in a rigged soccer joust. Ridiculously moving stuff. —*The Guardian*, 4th November 1999

2 any Scandanavian *US*
Left from the language of the logging camps of the early C20.
- —John Gould, *Maine Lingo*, p. 43, 1975
- —*Maledicta*, p. 171, Summer/Winter 1978: 'How to hate thy neighbor: a guide to racist maledicta'

3 in Quebec, an anglophone *US*
- —*Maledicta*, p. 171, Summer/Winter 1978: 'How to hate thy neighbor: a guide to racist maledicta'

4 a non-criminal *AUSTRALIA, 1890*
- Get this through your squarehead skull. —Kathy Lette, *Girls' Night Out*, p. 163, 1987
- He thinks I'm a squarehead with no idea. —Clive Galea, *Slipper*, p. 155, 1988

square Jane *noun*
an exceptionally conventional woman *US*
- I could read inside the heads of all those square johns. Oh yeah, I could. Square janes, too. —Robert Campbell, *In La-La Land We Trust*, p. 69, 1986

square John *noun*
a decent and law-abiding, if naive, person *US, 1934*
- I clipped a dance moll for a swab, it paid a trey or a fin / but an old squarejohn seen the play come off and he run and told the men. —Bruce Jackson, *Get Your Ass in the Water and Swim Like Me*, p. 85, 1965
- He works longer than "square Johns" who put in their eight hours each day. —Johnny Shearer, *The Male Hustler*, p. 23, 1966
- Still he didn't consider himself a failure, simply because it had never occurred to him he could be confined in any such square john term. —Malcolm Braly, *On the Yard*, p. 4, 1967
- Here this fool had a smart square broad with a progressive square-john husband, infatuated with him. —Iceberg Slim (Robert Beck), *Pimp*, p. 24, 1969
- Of course now, she was no square-john girl. She wasn't a whore, but she had been married to a notoroius pimp and had inherited a bunch of money and they lived real high. —Bruce Jackson, *Outside the Law*, p. 111, 1972
- Vito, you're not a down-the-line square John. —Vincent Patrick, *Family Business*, p. 55, 1985

square joint *noun*
a tobacco cigarette *US*
- —Eugene Landy, *The Underground Dictionary*, p. 67, 1971

square mackerel *noun*
marijuana *US, 1998*
From the shape of packages smuggled by sea.
- —Mike Haskins, *Drugs*, p. 289, 2003

square monicker *noun*
a person's legal, given name *US*
- "What are their family names?" "I don't know none of 'em's square monicker's." —Chester Himes, *The Real Cool Killers*, p. 113, 1959

square name *noun*
a person's legal name, sometimes unknown to his associates who know him only by a nickname *US*
- My first fight was with the Golden Boy of Boxing. His square name was Milo Theodorescu. —Rocky Garciano (with Rowland Barber), *Somebody Up There Likes Me*, p. 271, 1955

square-off *noun*
something that puts matters right; an apology *AUSTRALIA, 1941*
- Well the bloke who has overstayed his leave pass or had a couple too many is going to take the missus a couple of carnations as a square-off[.] —Sam Weller, *Old Bastards I Have Met*, p. 20, 1979

square off *verb*
to settle matters; to make everything right *AUSTRALIA, 1950*
- Probably squaring off to them. —Vince Kelly, *The Bogeyman*, p. 149, 1956
- —Jim Ramsay, *Cop It Sweet!*, p. 85, 1977

square pair *noun*
in craps, an eight rolled with a pair of fours *US*
- —Steve Kuriscak, *Casino Talk*, p. 67, 1985
- —Chris Fagans and David Guzman, *A Guide to Craps Lingo*, p. 28, 1999

squarer *noun*
in circus and carnival usage, a claims adjuster and mender of legal problems *US*
- —Don Wilmeth, *The Language of American Popular Entertainment*, p. 254, 1981

square rigger *noun*
a black person *UK*
Rhyming slang for **NIGGER**. Offensive.
- —Ray Puxley, *Cockney Rabbit*, 1992

square Sam *noun*
an exceedingly honest, upright, conventional person *US*
- A Square Sam myself, I was known to be "strictly okay" and a "right kid." —Jim Thompson, *Bad Boy*, p. 333, 1953

square shooter *noun*
a truthful, direct, honourable person *US, 1914*
- But what with taxes and cost of living, few square shooters can afford such luxury. —Jack Lait and Lee Mortimer, *Washington Confidential*, p. 277, 1951
- I've seen people who were supposed to be square shooters that use signals, they steal money out of the pot. —Kim Rich, *Johnny's Girl*, p. 64, 1993

square time bob *noun*
crack cocaine *UK, 1998*
- —Mike Haskins, *Drugs*, p. 282, 2003

square up *verb*
to return to the path of righteousness after a sojourn in sin *US*
- Soon's I kick this habit I'm gon' square up and git a job. —Nathan Heard, *Howard Street*, p. 78–79, 1968
- Mama, I haven't shot any 'H' in ten years. I haven't had a whore in five years. I squared up. I work every day. —Iceberg Slim (Robert Beck), *Pimp*, p. 29, 1969

square weed *noun*
tobacco *US*
- Choo-Choo fished two Camels from a squashed package in his sweat shirt and lit them, passing one to Sheik. "This square weed on top of gage makes you crazy," he said. —Chester Himes, *The Real Cool Killers*, p. 53, 1959

square-wheeled *adjective*
parked *UK*
Citizens' band radio slang.
- [U]nless you are both square-wheeled [...] you may be moving away from the person you are talking to. —Peter Chippindale, *The British CB Book*, p. 17, 1981

square wife *noun*
in law enforcement, a wife in the literal sense of the word, as opposed to the sense of work partner *US*
- Monk had another wife, a square wife, a wife who'd borne his two children and kept his house and complained every once in a while about the way Wilbur spent more time with Panama than he did with his own wife and kids. —Robert Campbell, *Juice*, p. 4, 1988

square woman *noun*
a woman who is not a prostitute *US*
- But whores ain't like square women. —Sara Harris, *The Lords of Hell*, p. 124, 1967

squarie *noun*
1 especially in nautical parlance, a young woman *AUSTRALIA, 1917*
- You can trap yourself a squarie and we can do the old... —J.E. MacDonnell, *Don't Gimme the Ships*, p. 46, 1960
- Toggle has agreed to lash you up to a couple of little squaries until you find your own feet. —John Wynnum, *Tar Dust*, p. 115, 1962

2 a non-criminal *AUSTRALIA, 1950*

squash *noun*

1 a kiss *US*

Circus and carnival usage.

- — Don Wilmeth, *The Language of American Popular Entertainment*, p. 254, 1981

2 the skull or brain *US*

- — *Maledicta*, p. 118, 1984–1985: 'Milwaukee medical maledicta'

squash it!

forget it! *US*

- — *The Bell (Paducah Tilghman High School)*, p. 8–9, 17th December 1993: 'Tilghmanism: the concealed langage of the hallway'

squash rot *noun*

the medical condition suffered by severe stroke victims *US*

- — *Maledicta*, p. 39, 1983: More common patient-directed pejoratives used by medical personnel

squat *noun*

1 nothing *US, 1967*

A shortened form of **DOODLY-SQUAT**. Often found in double negative constructions.

- Some of them old farts out three, four days a time, you don't say squat to them. — *Saturday Night Fever*, 1977
- She's not hearing squat. — Armistead Maupin, *Babycakes*, p. 36, 1984
- Mark didn't know squat about the management business. — Frank Zappa, *The Real Frank Zappa Book*, p. 79, 1989
- That ain't got squat diddly do, girl. — Seth Morgan, *Homeboy*, p. 21, 1990
- Don't mean squat, dude. She's a bitch, dude, right? — *Airheads*, 1994
- After fucking 251 times on film – and getting her cunt carved and bloodied from unwashed, untrimmed claws – she walked away with squat. Nothing. Niet. Nada penny. — Anthony Petkovich, *The X Factory*, p. 202, 1997

2 an act of defecation *NEW ZEALAND*

- — Sonya Plowman, *Great Kiwi Slang*, p. 88, 2002

3 a seat; a chair *US, 1944*

- Pop was chopping a study's mop and Mom was in her favourite squat behind the store. — A.S. Jackson, *Gentleman Pimp*, 1973
- So we decided we'd liven up the pot / by coppin' a squat. — Lightnin' Rod, *Hustlers Convention*, 1973

squat *verb*

1 to execute someone by electrocution in the electric chair *US*

- — Hyman E. Goldin et al., *Dictionary of American Underworld Lingo*, p. 206, 1950

2 to assemble to discuss and mediate disagreements among prisoners *US*

- — John R. Armore and Joseph D. Wolfe, *Dictionary of Desperation*, p. 51, 1976

squat team *noun*

in prison (especially HMP Holloway), a unit of prison officers trained to discover drugs and other contraband *UK*

- — Angela Devlin, *Prison Patter*, p. 109, 1996

squatter *noun*

a chair *US*

- — Lou Shelly, *Hepcats Jive Talk Dictionary*, p. 17, 1945
- — Clarence Major, *Dictionary of Afro-American Slang*, p. 108, 1970

squat through *verb*

to lower your stance to a squat to maintain control of your surfboard while a wave is cresting over you *US*

- — Duke Kahanamoku with Joe Brennan, *Duke Kahanamoku's World of Surfing*, p. 177, 1965

squatum *noun*

in Newfoundland, homemade berry wine *CANADA*

- "[Christmas] really started the end of August when we picked the whort for squatum," "Squatum," sez I, "what's that?" "Oh shucks" sez the skipper, "whort wine or blueberry wine. The woman had to squat up the berries with a potato masher." — *Evening Telegram*, p. 29, 24th December 1964

squawk *noun*

a complaint, especially a vociferous and indignant one *US, 1909*

- He has therefore developed a trained police corps to protect the Quarter operation from any squawk or complaint, reasonable or otherwise. — Robert Sylvester, *No Cover Charge*, p. 34, 1956
- In other words, I have done all right with the fair sex. I got no squawks in that department. — Edwin Torres, *Carlito's Way*, p. 19, 1975

squawk *verb*

1 to complain *US*

- They don't dare squawk about our location, and the stuff is gone anyhow. — Red Rudensky, *The Gonif*, p. 106, 1970

2 (of an aircraft) to transmit an identification and location signal *US, 1956*

Used among air-traffic controllers.

- — *Listener*, 29th July 1982

squawk book *noun*

a book in which complaints are registered *US*

- — *American Speech*, p. 227, October 1955: 'An aircraft production dispatcher's vocabulary'

squawk box *noun*

1 a low-fidelity public address system *US, 1945*

- The guys went back to talking about the town and the women in the town, and suddenly the LCVP's squawk box burst into static, and a gravelly voice said, "Now hear this. Now hear this." — Evan Hunter, *The Blackboard Jungle*, p. 189, 1954
- The Colonel gave Guido a final scowl and flipped the key on his inter-office squawk box. — Max Shulman, *Rally Round the Flag, Boys!*, p. 120, 1957
- — Carl Fleischhauer, *A Glossary of Army Slang*, p. 1, 1968
- — *Complete CB Slang Dictionary*, p. 88, 1976
- — Peter Chippindale, *The British CB Book*, p. 159, 1981
- Announcements pealing out a squawk box, designed to be heard in every corner of the establishment. — Odie Hawkins, *Black Casanova*, p. 35, 1984
- I was brooding on these things when the pilot came on the squawk-box and said we were turning back to Denver[.] — Hunter S. Thompson, *Generation of Swine*, p. 39, 4th October 1985

2 a citizens' band radio *US*

- — Lawrence Teeman, *Consumer Guide Good Buddy's CB Dictionary*, p. 93, 1976

3 a child hospital patient who persistently cries or complains *US*

- — Sally Williams, *"Strong" Words*, p. 160, 1994

squaw money *noun*

a two-dollar note *CANADA*

- Squaw money – the two-dollar bill – is in disrespect on the prairies, perhaps because it was at one time the standard price of a prostitute — Chris Thain, *Cold as a Bay Street Banker's Heart*, p. 146, 1987

squaw pee *noun*

ginger beer *CANADA*

- Squaw-pee, or ginger beer, is a summer drink, especially during haying. — Lewis Poteet, *Talking Country*, p. 69, 1992

squaw piss *noun*

beer with a low alcohol content *US*

- — *Current Slang*, p. 12, Summer 1968

squaw winter *noun*

the first snowstorm or cold snap, just before Indian summer *CANADA*

squeak *noun*

1 a police informer *US*

- I happen to know you're a goddam squeak. — Hal Ellson, *Tomboy*, p. 136, 1950

2 a cheapskate *US*

- — *San Francisco Examiner*, p. 8, 27th October 1963: 'What a "Z"! The astonishing private language of Bay Area teenagers'

squeak *verb*

to complain *UK*

- "What's this fucking spazzer [spastic] doing squeaking?" Well, I wasn't moaning, I was actually doing the opposite of moaning. I was yelling. — Jim Dury [quoting Ian Dury, 1999], *Ian Dury and the Blockheads – Song by Song*, p. 131, 2003

squeaker *noun*

a very close score in any athletic contest *US*

Often used with irony to describe a large margin of victory.

- — Richard Scholl, *Running Press Glossary of Baseball Language*, p. 73, 1977
- We loved how they won – those late-inning squeakers perfected by the Yankees over the years to break our backs and hearts. — *Boston Globe*, p. A2, 4th January 2004

squeal *noun*

in police work, a person who reports a crime; the call reporting the crime *UK*

- We get a squeal that a nut job has got a knife. — Edwin Torres, *Q & A*, p. 71, 1977

- Fuckin' Elias, man, fuckin' squeal, that's what he is, gonna get everybody in the platoon in shit. — *Platoon*, 1986
- I just spoke to the station commander who caught the squeal. — James Ellroy, *Suicide Hill*, p. 633, 1986
- "Kramer and me caught the squeal." "Why ain't you with the victim?" — Robert Campbell, *Boneyards*, p. 37, 1992

squeal *verb*

1 to inform on someone; to betray someone *US, 1846*

- "I was listenin' to the radio," Crazy hissed, "and you squealed on Benny!" — Irving Shulman, *The Amboy Dukes*, p. 272, 1947
- Charles Becker was executed in Sing Sing for complicity in the murder of Herman Rosenthal, a big-time gambler who squealed to District Attorney Whitman about the tie-up between police and the crime syndicate. — Jack Lait and Lee Mortimer, *New York Confidential*, p. 64, 1948
- James Castle called him a very conceited guy, and one of Stabile's lousy friends went and squealed on him to Stabile. — J.D. Salinger, *Catcher in the Rye*, p. 170, 1951
- Why didn't he tell his jailers about this? He was an ex-con. No con-wise con squeals. — *San Francisco Examiner*, p. 4 (II), 4th August 1957
- That you don't have to suck up to me. I won't squeal. — Leonard Cohen, *Beautiful Losers*, p. 134, 1966
- It's reprehensible to squeal on your own flesh and blood, but it's for his own good. — *Ferris Buehler's Day Off*, 1986

2 from a standstill, to accelerate a car suddenly, squealing the tyres on the road *US*

- — *Newsweek*, p. 28, 8th October 1951

squealer *noun*

1 a police informer *UK, 1865*

- Frank turned to Stan. "You squealer!" he sneered. — Irving Shulman, *The Amboy Dukes*, p. 252, 1947
- A confused old man, he came to Chico's cell twice and asked for the squealer in Number Nineteen, forgetting he'd taken him to deliver his information to those waiting below. — Hal Ellson, *The Golden Spike*, p. 241, 1952
- "Why, you stoolpigeon," I said, hurt-like, "you Puerto Rican squealer." — Piri Thomas, *Down These Mean Streets*, p. 20, 1967

2 in trucking, a device that records time and speed data, used by company officials to assure compliance with laws and regulations *US*

Known conventionally as a 'tachograph'.

- — Montie Tak, *Truck Talk*, p. 153, 1971

3 a baby, especially an illegitimate one *UK, 1865*

- She had left a Montana bordello to run afoul of a spermy gambler who ruined her commercial curves and blew away my heady dreams of mountainous greenbacks by blasting a squealer into her belly. — Iceberg Slim (Robert Beck), *The Naked Soul of Iceberg Slim*, p. 25, 1971

squealers *noun*

bacon *US*

- — *Maledicta*, p. 21, 1996: 'Domino's pizza jargon'

squeegee cop *noun*

in Burnaby, British Columbia, a police undercover officer posing as someone offering to clean windscreens in stopped traffic in order to catch seat-belt violators *CANADA*

- A new undercover threat to look out for: cops posing as squeegee kids. When they find a driver without a seat belt, they signal a spotted hiding nearby. The squeegee cops are careful not to blow their cover. They wash windows and accept donations. — *Toronto Globe and Mail*, p. A1, 19th July 2002

squeegee man *noun*

a street-corner hawker of car windscreen washing services *UK*

- All those years of aggressive beggars and squeegee men in their faces meant upstanding citizens saw nothing[.] — Chris Niles, *Revenge is the Best Revenge [Tart Noir]*, p. 5, 2002

squeegie *noun*

a young person who is hopelessly out of touch with current fashions and trends *US*

Youth usage.

- — *Time*, 3rd October 1949

squeeze *noun*

1 a partner in romance *US, 1980*

A shortening of MAIN SQUEEZE (a man's primary romantic partner).

- — Hermese E. Roberts, *The Third Ear*, 1971
- "She your woman?" "Just a squeeze." — Robert Campbell, *In La-La Land We Trust*, p. 20, 1986
- Renee is in her room now, giggling on the phone with her latest squeeze, a guy named Royal she met at The Sizzler last week. — Armistead Maupin, *Maybe the Moon*, p. 24, 1992
- Maggie as Bad Bob's sister's squeeze – the femme half of a dyke duo. — James Ellroy, *Hollywood Nocturnes*, p. 287, 1994
- I happen to think Willie's main squeeze is sexy. — Joseph Wambaugh, *Floaters*, p. 26, 1996
- Tom Parker-Bowles, son of Prince Charles' squeeze Camilla[.] — *Drugs An Adult Guide*, p. 17, December 2001
- She looked round the room for something to hit Greg and his new squeeze with. — Colin Butts, *Is Harry Still on the Boat?*, p. 266, 2003

2 a benefit; an advantage *UK*

- [S]ome of the muggy-cunt, lowlife, petty criminal, half-a-sex case rubbish play the game cos they wanna earn a little squeeze from the kangas [prison officers]. — J.J. Connolly, *Layer Cake*, p. 39, 2000

3 in prison, a prisoner's application or request which is favourably dealt with *UK*

- — Angela Devlin, *Prison Patter*, p. 109, 1996
- After twenty-three years of mainstream prison life Cody had finally been given a squeeze. — *The Guardian*, 11th January 2001

4 a light sentence of imprisonment *UK*

- — Angela Devlin, *Prison Patter*, p. 109, 1996

5 extortion or graft *US*

- — Vincent J. Monteleone, *Criminal Slang*, p. 222, 1949

▸ **put the squeeze on**

to exert influence on someone *US, 1941*

- Elmer, honey – baby – how could I put the squeeze on you? — Richard Brooks, *Elmer Gantry*, 1960

▸ **the squeeze**

permission to enter *UK*

- Danny knows the bouncers and gets us the squeeze. — Gavin Hills, *White Burger Danny (Disco Biscuits)*, p. 68, 1996

squeeze *verb*

1 to recount or tell something *US*

- — Marcus Hanna Boulware, *Jive and Slang of Students in Negro Colleges*, 1947

2 in poker, to surround a player with two confederates whose collusive betting tactics relieve the middle player of his bankroll and drive him from the game *US, 1949*

- — Thomas L. Clark, *The Dictionary of Gambling and Gaming*, p. 188, 1987

3 while playing cards, to look only at the very edge of a card *US*

- — Albert H. Morehead, *The Complete Guide to Winning Poker*, p. 274, 1967

▸ **squeeze a lemon; squeeze the lemon**

to drive through a traffic light as it changes from yellow to red *US*

- — Connie Eble (Editor), *UNC-CH Campus Slang*, p. 5, Fall 1993
- — Anna Scotti and Paul Young, *Buzzwords*, p. 41, 1997

▸ **squeeze (her) easy**

to slow down a truck *US*

- — Wayne Floyd, *Jason's Authentic Dictionary of CB Slang*, p. 28, 1976

▸ **squeeze one out**

to fart; to defecate; of a male, to masturbate *UK*

▸ **squeeze the breeze**

to close a car window *US*

- — Connie Eble (Editor), *UNC-CH Campus Slang*, p. 6, Fall 1991

▸ **squeeze the cheese**

to fart *US*

- — Judi Sanders, *Faced and Faded, Hanging to Hurl*, p. 38, 1993
- — Peter Furze, *Tailwinds*, p. 54, 1998

▸ **squeeze the lemon**

to urinate *UK, 1984*

▸ **squeeze your head; squeeze**

to defecate *UK, 1984*

squeeze box *noun*

1 an accordion or concertina *UK, 1936*

Musicians' slang.

- Mama's got a squeeze box / She wears on her chest / And when Daddy comes home / He never gets no rest[.] — The Who, *Squeeze Box*, 1975

2 in greyhound racing, the number five starting position (the yellow box) *AUSTRALIA*

- — Ned Wallish, *The Truth Dictionary of Racing Slang*, p. 77, 1989

squeeze cheese *noun*

a pasteurised processed cheese product, semi-solid, sold in a plastic bottle *US*

A clever name for a vile thing.

- They love freeze dried stroganoff, Kraft squeeze cheese, Wyler's fruit mixes, beef jerky, but they only get it when we're backpacking. — *Chicago Tribune*, p. C21, 5th October 1986

squeeze off *verb*

to fire a shot from a gun *US, 1956*

- The guy with the rug was firing at Tommy, suqeezing them off like he was on a target range, the sound of gunfire hitting the air hard... — Elmore Leonard, *Be Cool*, p. 17, 1999

squeezers *noun*

dice that have been squeezed out of shape in a vice for use by cheats *US*

- — *The Annals of the American Academy of Political and Social Sciences*, p. 131, May 1950

squeeze up *verb*

to ejaculate *UK, 1974*

squeezings *noun*

a gel formed with liquid ethanol and saturated calcium acetate solution; when ignited, the alcohol in the gel burns *US*

Used as a source of fuel in portable cooking stoves and as a source of alcohol for truly desperate derelicts who squeeze the gel through sponges and collect the liquid.

- — Joe McKennon, *Circus Lingo*, p. 87, 1980

squib *noun*

1 a coward *AUSTRALIA, 1908*

- SQUIB – A coward. — Gilbert H. Lawson, *A Dictionary of Australian Words and Terms*, 1924
- Biggest squib that ever played. — Frank Hardy, *The Yarns of Billy Borker*, p. 19, 1965

2 in the television and film industries, a small explosive charge that simulates being struck by a bullet *US*

- — John Cann, *The Stunt Guide*, p. 63,: 'Terms and definitions'
- — Ralph S. Singleton, *Filmaker's Dictionary*, p. 160, 1990

3 in target shooting, a hand-loaded cartridge that does not fully detonate *US*

- — *American Speech*, p. 195, October 1957: 'Some colloquialisms of the handgunner'

4 a slow racehorse *AUSTRALIA, 1915*

- — Tom Ellis, *The Science of Turf Investment*, p. 138, 1936
- I'll be offering top odds on Colletti's speedy squib. — Clive Galea, *Slipper*, p. 211, 1988

squib *verb*

1 to act the coward *AUSTRALIA, 1918*

- So the old man had squibbed on it! — Robert S. Close, *Love Me Sailor*, p. 163, 1945
- — Jim Ramsay, *Cop It Sweet!*, p. 85, 1977

2 to fire a gun to frighten rather than to wound *CANADA*

- To "squib the hens out of the porch" is to fire an old muzzle-loader with a small amount of powder to scare off the hens. — Lewis Poteet, *The South Shore Phrase Book*, p. 107, 1999

squid *noun*

1 a serious, dedicated, diligent student *US*

- At San Diego State University, a flattering term for a hard studier is a "study bunny": less so is "squid." — *New York Times*, 12th April 1987

2 a despicable, spineless person *US*

- — Connie Eble (Editor), *UNC-CH Campus Slang*, March 1974
- — *National Education Association Today*, April 1985: 'A glossary for rents and other squids'
- NICHOLSON: Which wasn't too hard, the guy was a real squid. — *True Romance*, 1993

3 an inexperienced, unskilled motorcyclist *US*

Perhaps from the image of flailing arms.

4 a US Navy sailor *US*

From the perspective of the US Marines.

- — Linda Reinberg, *In the Field*, p. 207, 1991

5 a fisherman *US*

- — *Maledicta*, p. 171, Summer/Winter 1978: 'How to hate thy neighbor: a guide to racist maledicta'

6 a Japanese person who is lacking in all social skills *US*

Hawaiian youth usage; highly insulting.

- — Douglas Simonson, *Pidgin to da Max Hana Hou*, 1982

7 one pound sterling (£1) *UK*

A play on **QUID**.

- Oi mate: here's a coupla squids for the box alrigh'. — Nick Barlay, *Curvy Lovebox*, p. 56, 1997
- [A] free record voucher or 15 squid for free. — Sacha Baron-Cohen, *Da Gospel According to Ali G*, 2001

squid *verb*

to study hard *US*

- Studying is squidding or grinding. — Wesleyan Alumnus, p. 29, Spring 1981

squidge *verb*

1 to squeeze; to squelch together so as to make a sucking noise *UK: ENGLAND, 1881*

Originally Isle of Wight dialect.

- They squidge past the giggling women. — *The Full Monty*, 1997

2 in tiddlywinks, to shoot a wink with an oversized wink *US*

- — *Verbatim*, p. 525, December 1977

squidgy black *noun*

a variety of marijuana *UK*

- — Angela Devlin, *Prison Patter*, p. 109, 1996

squidjigger *noun*

in Canada, any resident of the Maritime Provinces *CANADA*

- — *Maledicta*, p. 171, Summer/Winter 1978: 'How to hate thy neighbor: a guide to racist maledicta'

squiffed off *adjective*

annoyed; angry *US*

- Nothing, except a pair of my men are highly squiffed off. — Mickey Spillane, *Kiss Me Deadly*, p. 112, 1952

squiff out *verb*

to lose consciousness as a result of excessive consumption of alcohol *US*

- You squiffed out at The Dancers in a Rolls. Your girl friend ditched you. — Raymond Chandler, *The Long Goodbye*, p. 4, 1953

squiffy *adjective*

drunk *UK, 1855*

Probably from **SKEW-WHIFF** (at the wrong angle).

- I never got squiffy but once ... and it made me horrid sick — Rudyard Kipling, 1900
- She drank wine just like everyone else. We were all slightly squiffy by the end of the afternoon. — *The Guardian*, 17th February 2002

squigg *noun*

a prank *US*

- — Hans Halberstadt, *Airborne*, p. 130, 1988: 'Abridged dictionary of airborne terms'

squiggle *noun*

a tilde (~) on a computer keyboard *US*

- — Eric S. Raymond, *The New Hacker's Dictionary*, p. 41, 1991

squiggles *noun*

during the 1991 US war against Iraq, any writing in the Arabic script *US*

- Only 20 kilometers to "Squiggles." — *Army*, p. 48, November 1991

squiggly *noun*

a sexually attractive woman *BERMUDA*

- — Peter Smith and Fred M. Barritt, *Bermewjan Vurds*, 1985

squillionaire *noun*

a multi-millionaire *UK*

- [T]here is more power for squillionaire sheiks and shahs every time that America's domestic energy production is curbed[.] — *The Economist*, p. 9, 4th March 1978
- [T]he Valley was filled with techno-determinists, swaggering nerd squillionaires who were steadfastly convinced that the money would flow forever. — Cory Doctorow, *A Place So Foreign and Eight More*, p. 222, 2002

squinch-eyed *adjective*

with eyes half closed *US*

- At first he was squinch-eyed but now his eyes blew up like soap-bubbles and panic danced all over his face. — Mezz Mezzrow, *Really the Blues*, p. 96, 1946

squinchy *adjective*

very small *BAHAMAS*

- — John A. Holm, *Dictionary of Bahamian English*, p. 193, 1982

squint *noun*

1 a look; a glance *UK, 1673*
Generally phrased 'have a squint at'.

2 in the car sales business, tinted glass *US*
- — *Cars*, p. 41, December 1953

3 a person lacking in social skills, fashion or both *US*
- "Wouldn't put it past those squints at Internal Affairs," said Montezuma Montez. — Joseph Wambaugh, *The Black Marble*, p. 238, 1978

▶ **on the squint**
on the look-out for something *US*
- Sorry was to move up the platform four or five yards and be on the squint for trouble. — Red Rudensky, *The Gonif*, p. 117, 1970

squire *noun*
used as a familiar form of address to a man *UK, 1961*
- "Are you in the AA [Automobile Association]?" "I told you – I'm trade, squire". — Anthony Masters, *Minder*, p. 41, 1984
- "Are you alright? You'd tell me if you weren't wouldn't you?" "In the pink squire. Never felt better." — Jack Allen, *When the Whistle Blows*, p. 166, 2000

squirm seat *noun*
the chair in which witnesses sit in a courtroom *US*
- — *American Speech*, p. 272, December 1962: 'The language of traffic policemen'

squirrel *noun*

1 a reckless driver who weaves in and out of traffic *US*
- — *American Speech*, p. 272, December 1962: 'The language of traffic policemen'

2 a drug addict who hides drug portions for future use *US*
- Provident junkies, known as squirrels, keep stashes against a bust. — William Burroughs, *Naked Lunch*, p. 9, 1957

squirrel *verb*

1 to smoke cocaine, marijuana and phencyclidine, the recreational drug known as PCP or angel dust *UK*
It makes you nuts; squirrels like nuts.
- — *www.addictions.org*, 1999

2 on the railways, to climb up the side of a coach *US*
- — Ramon Adams, *The Language of the Railroader*, p. 144, 1977

squirrel away *verb*
to hide something; to conceal something for later use; to store something away *UK*
Like the squirrel and his nuts.
- — David Powis, *The Signs of Crime*, 1977
- Nobody will know and then you'll get to squirrel away that half-day for later. — *The Guardian*, 7th July 2003

squirrel cage *noun*
in electric line work, a pole-mounted steel bracket used for supporting a conductor *US*
- — A.B. Chance Co., *Lineman's Slang Dictionary*, p. 16, 1980

squirrel trap *noun*
the vagina *UK*
- The female genitalia were represented as places from which people/things never return (e.g., the Bermuda triangle) or get sucked into (e.g., the black hole, electrolux), hidden dangers (e.g., squirrel trap), and warnings of danger (e.g., hairy growler, bomb doors). — *Journal of Sex Research*, p. 146, 2001

squirrely *adjective*

1 completely obsessed with acquiring and hoarding amphetamine *US*
- A squirrely person may collect and wash rinsebags in order to salvage the residue of speed they had contained. Empty cigarette packs are often mistaken for bags. — Geoffrey Froner, *Digging for Diamonds*, p. 58, 1989

2 in motorcyle racing, difficult to control or out of control *US*
- — Ed Radlauer, *Motorcylopedia*, p. 62, 1973

squirt *noun*

1 a person who is small in stature, character or both *US, 1848*
- Who's the squirt down at the end? — Mickey Spillane, *I, The Jury*, p. 123, 1947
- The pavement heats up now, the Four breaking harder, screaming louder, pushing back the five little squirts, who can't seem to stay out of the way. — Josh Alan Friedman, *Tales of Times Square*, p. 56, 1986
- Little squirt, right? He's a public defender. — Elmore Leonard, *Maximum Bob*, p. 4, 1991

2 twenty-five cents or twenty-five dollars *US*
- — *American Speech*, p. 101, May 1951

3 in the car sales business, windscreen cleaner *US*
- — *Cars*, p. 41, December 1953

squirt *verb*
in pool, to strike the cue ball off centre producing a course in the opposite direction proportional to the degree to which the ball is hit off centre *US, 1978*
- — Mike Shamos, *The Illustrated Encyclopedia of Billiards*, p. 229, 1993

▶ **squirt it into the air**
to test an idea by bringing it up before a group and asking for comments *US*
- — Robert Kirk Mueller, *Buzzwords*, p. 146, 1974

squirt brakes *noun*
hydraulic brakes *US*
- — Fred Horsley, *The Hot Rod Handbook*, p. 211, 1965: 'Hot talk – a glossary of hot rod terms'

squirter *noun*
a scene in a pornographic film or photograph depicting a man ejaculating *US*
- — *Adult Video News*, p. 42, August 1995

squirt racing *noun*
drag racing *US*
- — John Edwards, *Auto Dictionary*, p. 160, 1993

squishy *adjective*
forgetful *US*
Teen slang.
- — *Newsweek*, p. 28, 8th October 1951

squit *noun*
an insignificant person *UK, 1825*
Probably cognate with **SQUIRT**.
- He was an unprepossessing squit and she was a spanking little artifact. — Lindsey Davis, *Ode to a Banker*, p. 74, 2002

squits; the squits *noun*
diarrhoea *UK, 1841*
A shortening of **SQUITTERS**.
- "[O]live oil doesn't agree with me." "Gives you the squits, does it, Grandad?" said Gary. — David Lodge, *Nice Work*, p. 166, 1990

squitters *noun*
diarrhoea *UK, 1664*
From obsolete dialect *squitter* (to squirt).
- He was taken with the squitters after a day of drinking peach-fruit wine and died while on the trots. — Peter Straub and Stephen King, *The Talisman*, p. 509, 2001

squiz; squizz *noun*
a brief look; a peek *AUSTRALIA, 1913*
- SQUIZ – A hurried look — Gilbert H. Lawson, *A Dictionary of Australian Words and Terms*, 1924
- They're not here. I've had a squizz at everyone. — Willie Fennell, *Dexter Gets The Point*, p. 142, 1961
- A quick squiz at an ancient Greek vase leaves no doubt of that! — *Sydney Morning Herald*, 12th July 2003
- Taking a squiz at newborn Kim, he declares her to be 'as plain as an Arrowroot biscuit'! — *TV Week*, p. 28, 1st November 2003

squiz; squizz *verb*
to have a brief look *AUSTRALIA, 1941*
From British dialect (Devon).
- They never squizzed through the fence, or lit fires when the wind was blowing Mumma's way. — Ruth Park, *Poor Man's Orange*, p. 171, 1949

squulch *verb*
to crush *BARBADOS*
- — Frank A. Collymore, *Barbadian Dialect*, p. 104, 1965

Sri Lanka *noun*
a contemptible individual *UK*
Rhyming slang for **WANKER**, apparently inspired by the Sri Lankan cricket team.
- — Ray Puxley, *Fresh Rabbit*, 1998

SRO
standing room only; completely sold-out *US, 1890*
- A month after Zenobia's funeral, the church is again S.R.O. for the wedding of Joe and Reba. — Iceberg Slim (Robert Beck), *Doom Fox*, p. 131, 1978

SS *noun*

1 an injection of drugs into the skin, avoiding a vein *US, 1938*
An initialism of 'skin shot'.
- "What do you usually have?" he inquired over his shoulder. "A V.S. [vein shot] or an S.S." —Douglas Rutherford, *The Creeping Flesh*, p. 104, 1963

2 the Department of Social Security (DSS, previously DHSS) *UK*
An obvious, hard to resist pun on nazi stormtroopers.
- I thought they were snoopers from the SS. —Ian Pattison, *Rab C. Nesbitt*, 1988

ssss... *noun*

an informer *UK*
From the hissing sound of a **SNAKE** (an informer).
- —Angela Devlin, *Prison Patter*, p. 109, 1996
- "There's an informer on the spur, lads!" he proclaimed, pointing towards the cell where Grady was installing his few intact possessions. "Ssssss," came the reply in chorus. — *The Guardian*, 30th March 2000

ssstoned *adjective*

intoxicated with marijuana *UK*
Extends **STONED** to demonstrate the effects of marijuana.
- [Cypress Hill's] music was filled with the ssstoned vibe of draw, the funk beats were slow and heavy like being stoned[.] —John Robb, *The Nineties*, p. 246, 1999

stab *noun*

1 a short and sudden type of scratch (a manipulation of a record to create a musical effect) *UK*
- —J. Hoggarth, *How To Be a DJ*, p. 89, 2002

2 a victim of a knife fight *US*
- — *Maledicta*, p. 15, 1984–1985: 'A medical Christmas song'

▸ **have a stab; make a stab at**

to attempt; to guess *US, 1895*
- [E]verybody be able to make a stab at learning the piano. — *The Guardian*, 26th May 2000
- The Prime Minister knew Mugabe would use the presence of world leaders and the global media to have a stab at him. — *The Observer*, 8th September 2002

stab *verb*

1 to disparage someone with profanity *US*
- —Don R. McCreary (Editor), *Dawg Speak*, 2001

2 in pool, to hit the cue ball with enough backspin so that it stops immediately after striking the object ball *UK, 1873*
- —Mike Shamos, *The Illustrated Encyclopedia of Billiards*, p. 229, 1993

stable *noun*

1 a group of prostitutes working for a single pimp or madam *US, 1937*
- Pell was also responsible for the widespread belief that Hebert maintained a stable of whores in the hotel[.] —Jim Thompson, *Bad Boy*, p. 362, 1953
- Mary thought she might die of jealousy if Bible ever did as Jo-Jo did and got himself a full stable. —John M. Murtagh and Sara Harris, *Cast the First Stone*, p. 17, 1957
- I can rotate my regular stable of boys or, if need be, call on part-time hustlers. —Johnny Shearer, *The Male Hustler*, p. 21, 1966
- I met the broad when I was in San Francisco, I was out on the run / to score me a stable of bitches to work on my pappy's farm. —Bruce Jackson, *Get Your Ass in the Water and Swim Like Me*, p. 112, 1966
- He could watch and keep tabs on his stable of scrawny, junkie whores working the four corners of the intersection. —Iceberg Slim (Robert Beck), *Pimp*, p. 64, 1969
- Rocky has from sixty to seventy-five full and parttime boys in his stable. —John Francis Hunter, *The Gay Insider*, p. 213, 1971
- Many players have several ladies, who constitute their stable. —Christina and Richard Milner, *Black Players: The Secret World of Black Pimps*, p. 40, 1972
- Tony had in his stable of four the best lookin' whore in Harlem, a German war bride. —Edwin Torres, *Carlito's Way*, p. 18, 1975
- City madams are also accustomed to dressing their stable well. —Jan Hutson, *The Chicken Ranch*, p. 84, 1980

2 a group of 'slaves' in the control of, or at the disposal of, a dominatrix; a collection of masochists in the control of a sadist *US*
- —Thomas E. Murray and Thomas R. Murrell, *The Language of Sadomasochism*, 1989

3 by extension, a group of people working for someone *UK, 1942*
- I have a stable of actors and actresses. — *Boogie Nights*, 1997

4 a house or apartment *US*
- — *Ebony Magazine*, p. 156, August 2000: 'How to talk to the new generation'

stable *verb*

(used of a pimp) to induce a prostitute to join other prostitutes working for him *US*
- I never tried to stable her after that. —Iceberg Slim (Robert Beck), *Pimp*, p. 268, 1969

stable boy's favorite *noun*

a controlled throw of dice onto a dirt surface *US, 1974*
- —Thomas L. Clark, *The Dictionary of Gambling and Gaming*, p. 214, 1987

stable of lace *noun*

the prostitutes associated with one pimp *US*
- The women constitute a player's "stable of lace," bound to him by many and varied ties[.] —Dennis Wepman et al., *The Life*, p. 3, 1976

stable sister *noun*

one prostitute in relation to the other prostitutes in a pimp's stable *US*
- Usually the player relies on one to help him recruit new additions, known as stable sisters. —Christina and Richard Milner, *Black Players*, p. 40, 1972

'stache *noun*

a moustache *US*
- Excellent 'stache, Smith. — *Bill and Ted's Excellent Adventure*, 1989

stack *noun*

1 in rock music, an assemblage of loudspeakers *UK*
- —Simon Warner, *Rockspeak!*, p. 297, 1996

2 in pool, the balls assembled inside the rack before a game *US, 1977*
- —Mike Shamos, *The Illustrated Encyclopedia of Billiards*, p. 230, 1993

3 in pool, the clustered pack of balls left at the foot of the table after the first shot of the game *US*
- —Steve Rushin, *Pool Cool*, p. 27, 1990

4 a package of marijuana cigarettes *US*
- — *American Speech*, p. 88, May 1955: 'Narcotic got along the Mexican border'
- —Richard A. Spears, *The Slang and Jargon of Drugs and Drink*, p. 480, 1986
- —Mike Haskins, *Drugs*, p. 289, 2003

5 one thousand dollars *US*
- He claims he could earn a "stack" – street slang for $1000 – for his work. He claims he shot someone in a dispute at a drug house. — *Milwaukee Journal Sentinel*, p. 1A, 17th March 2002

6 money *US*
- —Anna Scotti and Paul Young, *Buzzwords*, p. 80, 1997

7 in trucking, a smokestack from the truck engine *US*
- —Montie Tak, *Truck Talk*, p. 179, 1971

8 a large amount of something *US, 1870*
- There could be a stack of explanations for that initial deployment of the short, sharp blow. — *The Guardian*, 22nd March 2003

stack *verb*

1 to crash a vehicle *AUSTRALIA*
- He had lost his way. Stacked his Harley Davidson. —Jack Hibberd, *A Stretch of the Imagination*, p. 8, 1971

2 to earn a lot of money *US*
- —Vann Wesson, *Generation X Field Guide and Lexicon*, p. 160, 1997

▸ **stack on a blue**

to begin a fight *AUSTRALIA, 1944*
- Now yer might listen t' some sense f' a change 'n stack on a real blue. —Bob Jewson, *Stir*, p. 62, 1980

▸ **stack on an act**

to kick up a fuss *AUSTRALIA*
- But he's stacking on a great act about maintaining the Predictor. —John Wynnum, *Tar Dust*, p. 78, 1962
- —John Wynnum, *Jiggin' in the Riggin'*, p. 54, 1965
- —Jim Ramsay, *Cop It Sweet!*, p. 85, 1977

▸ **stack on a turn**

to kick up a fuss *AUSTRALIA*
- That's when you discovered us. Stacked on a turn. Went the knuckle. Dorabella shot through, abandoning her white bloomers on a low bough. —Jack Hibberd, *A Stretch of the Imagination*, p. 15, 1971
- If God stacks on a turn, what can we do? —Kel Richards, *The Aussie Bible*, p. 20, 2003

stack away *verb*

to eat or drink heartily *AUSTRALIA*

- 'Don't ask me how many [beers] I stacked away that night man, because I just couldn't tell you.'—Barry Humphries, *A Nice Night's Entertainment*, p. 41, 1960

stacked *adjective*

1 possessing large breasts *US, 1942*

Sometimes intensified with phrases such as 'stone to the bone' or rhymed as in 'stacked and packed' (the name of a photographic calendar produced by former Nixon operative G. Gordon Liddy, featuring nearly naked women holding guns).

- Individually they were all interested in dating a girl who was attractive and stacked up like a million[.]—Irving Shulman, *The Amboy Dukes*, p. 207, 1947
- She was stacked. She was pretty.—Jim Thompson, *Savage Night*, p. 74, 1953
- Harry gave the blonde a seven, but you only gave her a six because you didn't think she was stacked enough for a seven.—Max Shulman, *Guided Tour of Campus Humor*, p. 161, 1955
- Well stacked too. Nice behind.—Willard Motely, *Let No Man Write My Epitaph*, p. 297, 1958
- For a non-white, I mean, she was, as they say, ha ha, stacked!—Robert Gover, *One Hundred Dollar Misunderstanding*, p. 29, 1961
- "If you were good-looking or stacked or something, I would," I retaliated.—John Nichols, *The Sterile Cuckoo*, p. 82, 1965
- She was a pretty, well-stacked girl, with black hair and a white softness which set her hair off pretty cool.—Piri Thomas, *Down These Mean Streets*, p. 83, 1967
- Toe's lady, a half something and half something else, with eyes like a cat's and stacked stone to the bone wandered through, fluffing up the pillows on the sofa across from them.—Odie Hawkins, *Chicago Hustle*, p. 152, 1977
- I like women who are aggressive. And stacked.—Anka Radakovich, *The Wild Girls Club*, p. 202, 1994

2 muscular *US*

- —Connie Eble (Editor), *UNC-CH Campus Slang*, p. 10, October 2002

3 used of prison sentences, consecutive, not concurrent *US*

- —Ethan Hilderbrant, *Prison Slang*, p. 121, 1998

4 well-provided; wealthy *UK*

- Everybody was stacked up on pills[.]—Simon Napier-Bell, *Black Vinyl White Powder*, p. 179, 2001

stackhat *noun*

a crash helmet *AUSTRALIA*

- The biggest problem is to get the kids into the stackhats.—*Sunday Mail*, p. 7, 8th August 1985

stack it *verb*

to brag or boast *NEW ZEALAND*

Prison usage.

- —Harry Orsman, *A Dictionary of Modern New Zealand Slang*, p. 129, 1999

stacks *noun*

1 a large amount *US, 1892*

- Yes, he had stacks of money and a girlfriend[.]—*The Guardian*, 26th March 1998

2 a lot of intimate activity with the opposite sex *UK*

- —Nigel Foster, *The Making of a Royal Marine Commando*, 1987

3 in hot rodding, an exhaust system *US*

- —Racing Jargon, p. 13, November 1948: 'Hot Rod Magazine'
- —Tom MacPherson, *Dragging and Driving*, p. 142, 1960

stackup *noun*

a group of waves; a group of surfers on a single wave *US*

- —Gary Fairmont R. Filosa II, *The Surfer's Almanac*, p. 195, 1977

stack up *verb*

on the railways, to have a collision *US*

- —Ramon Adams, *The Language of the Railroader*, p. 145, 1977

staff *noun*

▶ **go to work without a staff**

(of a female) to masturbate *US*

- Another way to say "the girl is masturbating" [...] Going to work without a staff[.]—Erica Orloff and JoAnn Baker, *Dirty Little Secrets*, p. 67, 2001

▶ **meet the staff**

to have sex *US*

Punning on 'staff' (a long stick/weapon/personnel) as 'penis'.

- Another way to say "intercourse" [...] Meeting the staff[.]—Erica Orloff and JoAnn Baker, *Dirty Little Secrets*, p. 63, 2001

stag *noun*

1 at a social function, a man without a date *US, 1905*

- Stags could hang around the kitchen or sit on the bench in front of the basement steps which led to the clubroom until they picked up a date.—Irving Shulman, *The Amboy Dukes*, p. 36, 1947
- We also saw other stags talk to girls with whom they hadn't come in, but with whom they left.—Jack Lait and Lee Mortimer, *Washington Confidential*, p. 14, 1951
- Then you rule out the women. That cuts the total down to sixty or seventy, just the stags.—Jim Thompson, *The Nothing Man*, p. 193, 1954
- Kemp was the only stag.—Hunter S. Thompson, *Songs of the Doomed*, p. 47, 1959
- In back of us, at the door, they were coming in fast, about three stags to every couple.—Mickey Spillane, *Me, Hood!*, p. 62, 1963

2 a male at a stag party *UK*

A back-formation from **STAG PARTY** (a party for men only).

- For most stags and their parties, this part of the night was the do or die moment before the wedding festivities a week or so down the line.—Iain Aitch, *A Fete Worse Than Death*, p. 159, 2003

3 a pornographic film *US*

An elliptical form of **STAG MOVIE**.

- This film was not the scratched, over-printed, sloppy, jerky amateur production typical of most "stags."—Roger Gordon, *Hollywood's Sexual Underground*, p. 43, 1966
- You could see better stuff in any Times Square sex joint than those stags they were turning out.—Mickey Spillane, *Last Cop Out*, p. 21, 1972

4 guard duty *UK, 1943*

Military.

- Surely, he thought, they must have at least some bloke on stag.—Chris Ryan, *The Watchman*, p. 28, 2001

5 amyl or butyl nitrite *UK*

Possibly derived from a brand marketing the drug as a male sex-aid.

- Street names [...] snapper, stag, stud, thrust[.]—James Kay and Julian Cohen, *The Parents' Complete Guide to Young People and Drugs*, p. 144, 1998

6 the butt end of a cigarette *US*

- —Gary K. Farlow, *Prison-ese*, p. 67, 2002

stag dinner *noun*

a males-only dinner featuring sexual entertainment in the form of pornographic films, dancers and/or prostitutes *US*

- Until roughly 1950, the pornographic movie business consisted largely in renting films for showing at stag dinners and the like[.]—Ned Polsky, *Hustlers, Beats, and Others*, p. 201, 1967

stag do; stag night; stag *noun*

a social event for men only *UK*

After **STAG PARTY**.

- One night on the Tattershall Castle all these butcher boys from Smithfield market came on a stag do.—Dave Courtney, *Stop the Ride I Want to Get Off*, p. 114, 1999

stage *verb*

1 to single someone out in front of a crowd *US*

- Yo, teach, stop stagin' me in front of the whole class.—Rick Ayers (Editor), *Berkeley High Slang Dictionary*, p. 39, 2004

2 in drag racing, to bring the front wheels of a car to the starting line preparatory to starting the race *US*

- —Hal Higdon, *Finding the Groove*, p. 309–310, 1973

stage door Johnny *noun*

a man waiting outside the stage door for an actress *US, 1912*

- Some of the regulars send candy backstage, though "Stage Door Johnnies" seem to be an extinct species.—*Screw*, p. 9, 18th April 1969
- You become a stagedoor Johnnie, except that you're not waiting around in the wings, you're waiting in gambling casinos.—Edward Lin, *Big Julie of Vegas*, p. 136, 1974

stage fright *noun*

a *light* ale *UK*

Rhyming slang.

- —David Powis, *The Signs of Crime*, 1977
- —Ray Puxley, *Cockney Rabbit*, 1992

stage mother *noun*

in hospital usage, a mother who coaches their child in answering questions from a doctor and who has a preconceived notion of the diagnosis and appropriate treatment *US*

- —*Maledicta*, p. 69, Summer/Winter 1978: 'Common patient-directed pejoratives used by medical personnel'

stage name *noun*
a criminal's alias *US*
- —Hyman E. Goldin et al., *Dictionary of American Underworld Lingo*, p. 207, 1950

stage stop *noun*
a truck stop *US*
A jocular comparison to the days of stage coaches.
- —Lanie Dills, *The Official CB Slanguage Language Dictionary*, p. 66, 1976

stag fight *noun*
an amateur, extra-legally staged boxing match *US*
- Stag fights were a cash deal. —Rocky Garciano (with Rowland Barber), *Somebody Up There Likes Me*, p. 141, 1955

stag film *noun*
a pornographic film *US*
- As I said, I'd seen stag films before ... but never like these. —Jon Fowler, *Anatomy of Wife-Swapping*, p. 42, 1967
- "Take stag films," he said by way of example, "they're still being made in motels, by guys without any artistic sense." —Malcolm Boyd, *My Fellow Americans*, p. 37, 1970
- The photography is as honest as a stag film and you see close-ups of the guy shtupping (fucking) the girl's hole. —*Screw*, p. 17, 12th January 1970
- If stag films are so depressing, why are they well attended? —Joseph Slade, *The Sexual Scene*, p. 285, December 1971
- Is he making nudies? girlie films? stag films? —*Porno Films and the People who make them*, p. 18, 1973
- After World War II blacks began to perform sexually in stag films[.] —Kenneth Turan and Stephen E. Zito, *Sinema*, p. 91, 1974
- Stallone took it in his stride, readily admitting that he had acted in the stag film when he was broke and desperate. —*Adam Film World*, p. 5, March 1979
- By 1915, the form of the stag film was set. —Kent Smith et al., *Adult Movies*, p. 7, 1982
- Hodas threaded the machines with California stag films of dancing broads flashing tit and cunt, images never exhibited publicly. —Josh Alan Friedman, *Tales of Times Square*, p. 75, 1986

stag flick *noun*
a pornographic film *US*
- [T]hey were going at it in one position, then another, like out of a stag flick. —Robert Gover, *Poorboy at the Party*, p. 156, 1966

stagged-off pants *noun*
among loggers in British Columbia, trousers cut off short *CANADA*
- Loggers cut off their pants at the boot top to rid them of dangerous cuffs which can catch and trip a man. Sometimes trimmed with an axe on a block, the "stagged off pants" symbolize a man's occupation. —Tom Parkin, *WetCoast Words*, p. 135, 1989

stagger soup *noun*
whisky *US*
- —Ramon Adams, *The Language of the Railroader*, p. 145, 1977

stagger-through; stagger *noun*
an early and rough attempt at rehearsing an entire piece of work *UK, 1964*
Theatrical.
- —*Kaleidoscope*, 17th February 1975

stag line *noun*
at a dance, a line of men without dates, waiting to dance *US*
- I met Clothilde at the University of Minnesota's annual Freshman Prom. I was standing in the stag line and I saw her dancing with a fellow halfway across the floor. —Max Shulman, *The Many Loves of Dobie Gillis*, p. 1, 1951

stag movie *noun*
a pornographic film made for and enjoyed by men *US, 1960*
- I mean, our frat has this stag movie (which I, of course, have nothing to do with, no authority over at all). —Robert Gover, *One Hundred Dollar Misunderstanding*, p. 113, 1961
- Now, the stag movie, the dirty movie – the sixteen millimeter reduction print that you drag from lodge hall, the dirty movie that the Kefauver Committee would destroy and then recreate for private parties. —Lenny Bruce, *The Essential Lenny Bruce*, p. 177, 1967
- In general, though, Playboy ads are discreet – no stag movies, no sex manuals. —Joe David Brown, *Sex in the '60*, p. 44, 1968
- One night we were sitting around in Don Mincher's room waiting to look at some stag movies[.] —Jim Bouton, *Ball Four*, p. 241, 1970
- The case against Easy Street was determined by Superior Judge James T. O'Keefe, who enjoined the bar at 2322 El Camino Real from continuing performances of bottomless dancers and waitresses and from showing stag movies. —*San Francisco Examiner*, p. 18, 18th February 1970
- The 8mm porno film is commonly known as the Stag movie. —Stephen Ziplow, *The Film Maker's Guide to Pornography*, p. 8, 1977
- The stag movies go back as far as film itself. —Kent Smith et al., *Adult Movies*, p. 7, 1982
- There were still smokers, stag movies, it wasn't as commonplace, but I guarantee if you wanted to find hard-core in 1930 you could. —Robert Stoller and I.S. Levine, *Coming Attractions*, p. 41, 1991

stag party *noun*
a party for men only, usually organised to view pornography, tell sexual jokes and/or be entertained by strippers or prostitutes *US, 1856*
- [E]ccentric dancer, platinum in the mop and molybdenum in the left ventricle, who gave her all at smokes and stag parties[.] —Bernard Wolfe, *The Late Risers*, p. 37, 1954
- Within the next quarter-hour a stag party had taken over the apartment, several of them in uniform. —Truman Capote, *Breakfast at Tiffany's*, p. 35, 1958
- I mean the whole thing seemed like a wild post-icecream dream, as mentioned above, or (I might as well say it) like a stag party movie. —Robert Gover, *One Hundred Dollar Misunderstanding*, p. 113, 1961
- College fraternities, volunteer fire companies, lodges, businessmen's associations, conventions, bachelor and stag parties comprise the most common customers for this strictly illegal film fare. —Michael Milner, *Sex on Celluloid*, p. 11, 1964
- When sixteen-millimeter film equipment became available, the stag party, or "smoker," was born. —Kent Smith et al., *Adult Movies*, p. 7, 1982
- Whistler had been in Cortez's apartment a few times to little stags that had been lame attempts to make friendships out of poker, beer, and dirty stories. —Robert Campbell, *Alice in La-La Land*, p. 313, 1987

stain *noun*
a contemptible person *UK*
Shortened from WANK-STAIN.
- Mario was a complete and utter stain. —Colin Butts, *Is Harry on the Boat?*, p. 11, 1997
- Fuckin rapist. Fuckin psycho. Fuckin pervert... yew fuckin stain... yew fuckin... mess[.] —Niall Griffiths, *Sheepshagger*, p. 260, 2001

staining *noun*
the bleed period of the menstrual cycle *UK, 1951*
Jilly Cooper, 1980.

stair-dancer *noun*
a thief whose speciality is office buildings with multiple floors *NEW ZEALAND, 1953*
- —Harry Orsman and Des Hurley, *The Beaut Little Book of New Zealand Slang*, 1994

stake *noun*
1. money needed to finance an enterprise or to contribute as a share to finance an enterprise *US, 1738*
   - But I don't have the stake I thought I was gonna. That's why I need you to write me a check. —Elmore Leonard, *City Primeval*, p. 165, 1980
2. in gambling circles, money *US*
   - —Richard Jessup, *The Cincinnati Kid*, p. 34, 1963

stake *verb*
to provide someone with money or other needed resources *US, 1853*
- Okay, and you can stake me to this call, right? —Gurney Norman, *Divine Right's Trip (Last Whole Earth Catalog)*, p. 193, 1971

staked out *adjective*
tired of a necessary but tedious task *BARBADOS*
- —Richard Allsopp, *Dictionary of Caribbean English Usage*, p. 527, 1992

stake driver *noun*
on the railways, an engineer in the engineering department *US*
- —Norman Carlisle, *The Modern Wonder Book of Trains and Railroading*, p. 268, 1946

stakehorse *noun*
in pool, a person who financially backs the wagers of a professional player *US*
- —Steve Rushin, *Pool Cool*, p. 27, 1990

stake-out *noun*
an act of covert surveillance on a stationary target *US, 1942*
- You can imagine you are on a stake-out; you can imagine anything you want, because this is just a Portakabin with tinted windows. —*The Guardian*, 28th May 2002

stake out *verb*
to carry out surveillance of a building or other place *US, 1951*
Extends the imagery of a goat tethered to a stake to bait a trap.

- Seems Henry has been thinking crime for months. He has several places staked out. — John Peter Jones, *Feather Pluckers*, p. 30, 1964
- Haven't done this in a long while, to be fair, staking some cunt out like this. — Kevin Sampson, *Outlaws*, p. 91, 2001

stakey *adjective*

anxious; jumpy; ready to leave *US*

- A term describing a man who has made his stake and doesn't want to stay on the job any longer. — Robert O. Bowen, *An Alaskan Dictionary*, p. 31, 1965

stal; stallie *noun*

a stalactite formation and/or stalagmite formation *UK*

A cavers' and pot-holers' term, noted by George Bliss, 1980.

Stalin Hill *noun*

a hill within the punch bowl basin, occuped by North Korean and Chinese troops during the Korean war *US*

Also refers to hills in North Vietnam and Prague (the site of a statue of Stalin from 1955 to 62).

- We lived right in the shadow of No Name and another high, enemy-held peak the troops called Stalin Hill, both of which looked right down our reverse slope. — David H. Hackworth, *About Face*, p. 272, 1989

stalk *noun*

1 the penis, especially when in a state of erection *UK, 1961*

- Mrs Elizabeth Walk of Lambeth Walk / Had a husband who was jubblified with only half a stalk[.] — Ian Dury, *This is What We Find*, 1979

2 man's obvious sexual appetite; courage; impudence *UK*

Extended from the previous sense.

- He's got plenty of stalk. — David Powis, *The Signs of Crime*, 1977

3 a plastic sheath used for medical examination of the rectum *IRELAND*

- The doctor put on a stalk (a plastic sheath that pulls over the doctor's finger), smeared it with KY jelly and asked the sailor to spread his legs a little so he could examine his bum. — John Fleetwood, *In Stitches*, p. 66, 1994

stalks *noun*

the legs *US*

- — David Claerbaut, *Black Jargon in White America*, p. 81, 1972

stall *noun*

a pickpocket's confederate who distracts the victim *UK, 1591*

- A "cannon" with a tired horse face took the vacant stool in my right. His "stall" took the one on the left. — Iceberg Slim (Robert Beck), *Pimp*, p. 91, 1969
- The stall is the bump man. So he's got to have a newspaper, a magazine. — Leonard Shecter and William Phillips, *On the Pad*, p. 159, 1973

stall *verb*

1 to make excuses; to play for time *UK, 1829*

- Why the Russian president, Vladimir Putin, is stalling is a mystery. — *The Guardian*, 3rd December 2003

2 in pool, to intentionally miss a shot or lose a game *US*

- By "stalling" (deliberately missing some shots, leaving himself out of position, etc.) and by "lemoning" or "lemonading" an occasional game in the session (winning in a deliberately sloppy and seemingly lucky manner, or deliberately losing the game), the hustler keeps his opponent on the hook. — Ned Polsky, *Hustlers, Beats, and Others*, p. 56–57, 1967
- — Steve Rushin, *Pool Cool*, p. 28, 1990

stallion *noun*

an attractive, sensual woman, especially a tall one *US, 1970*

- You got a white woman, a real stallion like Nez here, that's all you need to fight the world. — John Sayles, *Union Dues*, p. 190, 1977
- [T]his Margo stallion has laid some fine trim on this nephew, see? — Robert Deane Pharr, *Giveadamn Brown*, p. 34, 1978
- A real handful of lady if ever there was one, heroic dimensions, but exquisitely put together, about 38–29–42. What used to be called a "stallion" in some circles. — Odie Hawkins, *Scars and Memories*, p. 71, 1987

stall the ball!

stop! *IRELAND*

- How Mother Redcaps stalled the ball — *Irish Times*, 23rd September 1999
- In a nutshell, McCreevy was telling Brennan that the well was beginning to run dry and to stall the ball. — *Carlow Nationalist*, 3rd April 2003

stall the digger!

stop! *IRELAND*

- Stall the digger here for a minute. — Eamonn Sweeney, *Waiting for the Healer*, p. 203, 1997

stall walker *noun*

in horse racing, a nervous jockey who paces before a race *US*

A term originally for a racehorse pacing in the stall.

- — *San Francisco Chronicle*, 19th April 1953

Stamford Hill cowboy *noun*

an orthodox Jewish resident in the Stamford Hill/Stoke Newington area of north London *UK*

From the wide-brimmed black hat that is conventionally worn and the consequent image created by a group with the sun behind them.

- You can feel the constant tension in the streets and bars, where Greeks, Turks, Kurds, West Indians and Africans are all flung together, along with the "Stamford Hill Cowboys"[.] — Duncan MacLaughlin, *The Filth*, p. 146, 2002

stammer and stutter *noun*

butter *UK, 1937*

Rhyming slang.

- — Ray Puxley, *Cockney Rabbit*, 1992

stamper *noun*

a shoe *UK, 1565*

- — Paul Baker, *Polari*, p. 190, 2002

stamping ground *noun*

a territory; an area of responsibility *UK, 1821*

- an area [...] known as a stamping ground for cruising and socializing gays — *The Advocate*, 24th October 1973

stamp on *verb*

to adulterate an illegal drug *UK*

- — Tom Hibbert, *Rockspeak!*, p. 148, 1983

Stan and Ollie *noun*

an umbrella *UK*

Rhyming slang for **BROLLY**, formed on the name of film comedians Stan Laurel and Oliver Hardy.

- — Ray Puxley, *Fresh Rabbit*, 1998

stand *noun*

▷ **see: COCKSTAND**

stand *verb*

in blackjack, to accept your hand without any further cards *US*

- — Lee Solkey, *Dummy Up and Deal*, p. 120, 1980

▸ **stand for**

to endure or tolerate something *US, 1896*

- Mechanical plots and wafer-thin characterisation? Hollywood will never stand for it. — *The Guardian*, 18th February 2000

stand-about *noun*

a idler *INDIA*

A variation of 'layabout', but so literal as to be almost conventional.

- So while 'f beep beep k's' have not quite disappeared from betwixt the lips of the cigarette toting stand-abouts, word has it that Indo-Americanisations has invaded the realm of petty college slang. — *The Times of India*, 30th September 2002

stand-at-ease *noun*

cheese *UK*

Rhyming slang, originally military, current during Word War 1.

- A loaf of Uncle Fred and a pound of stand-at-ease [cheese]. — Ronnie Barker, *Fletcher's Book of Rhyming Slang*, p. 25–26, 1979

stand by for a ramming!

used as a jocular prediction that trouble is impending *US*

- — Michael Dalton Johnson, *Talking Trash with Redd Foxx*, p. 135, 1994

stand from under *noun*

thunder *UK*

Rhyming slang.

- — Julian Franklyn, *A Dictionary of Rhyming Slang*, 1960

stand on it

to accelerate a car to full speed *US, 1960s*

- — Ed Radlauer, *Drag Racing Pix Dix*, p. 52, 1970

stand on me
believe me *UK, 1933*
- [T]he screw who's giving evidence against you starts telling a load of bleeding lies and mixing it for you, which happens more than enough times, stand on me. — Frank Norman, *Bang To Rights*, p. 23, 1958
- — Frank Norman, *Stand on Me*, 1959
- All I have ever sought, stand on me, was to make an iota of profit[.] — Andrew Nickolds, *Back to Basics*, p. 45, 1994

stand-over *noun*
intimidation *AUSTRALIA*
Used attributively.
- Her look-outs were much more scared of her than they were of encounters with hoodlums who tried to get her grog by stand-over methods. — Vince Kelly, *The Bogeyman*, p. 38, 1956
- Using stand-over tactics! — W.R. Bennett, *Wingman*, p. 67, 1961
- She is sixteen and has a seven-month-old baby boy born of her illicit union with a known criminal gunman, hold-up man and stand-over expert. — James Holledge, *The Call-girl in Australia*, p. 50, 1964
- [S]tandover country[.] — D'Arcy Niland, *Dead Men Running*, p. 73, 1969

standover *verb*
to intimidate someone with the threat of violence *AUSTRALIA, 1939*
- You know how Guido and me got busted for trying to stand-over Ma O'Reilly's sly grog joint. — Clive Galea, *Slipper*, p. 85, 1988
- Not long after I broke away they tried to stand over a protected sly grog shop, got loaded up by the coppers and did three years. — Clive Galea, *Slipper*, p. 156, 1988
- It was easy for them to gang up and try to stand over you. — William Dodson, *The Sharp End*, p. 29, 2001

standover man *noun*
a criminal who uses intimidation; a thug *AUSTRALIA, 1939*
- — James Holledge, *The Great Australian Gamble*, p. 147, 1966
- Standover man outside baccarat game watches with amused smile. — Kevin Mackey, *The Cure*, p. 154, 1970
- — Clive Galea, *Slipper*, p. 183, 1988
- — William Dodson, *The Sharp End*, p. 161, 2001

standover merchant *noun*
a criminal who uses intimidation; a thug *AUSTRALIA, 1944*
- — Arthur Chipper, *The Aussie Swearer's Guide*, p. 43, 1972
- The standover merchants were always on the go[.] — William Dodson, *The Sharp End*, p. 31, 2001

stand-read *noun*
an act of *stand*ing and *read*ing magazines, newspapers, etc where they are displayed on a vendor's shelves *UK*
A subtle form of theft.
- He didn't go into Menzies for a stand-read, didn't pick up fries at Burger King. — P-P Hartnett, *Sad Cunt*, p. 102, 1999

stand-to-attention *noun*
a pension *UK*
Rhyming slang, originally military, probably from the early part of C20 and used exclusively of a military pension; now in wider use.
- — Julian Franklyn, *A Dictionary of Rhyming Slang*, 1961
- — Ray Puxley, *Cockney Rabbit*, 1992

stand up *verb*
1 to fail to keep a social appointment or romantic engagement with someone *US, 1902*
- Bob, the rotter who stood her up when she waited for him at a tube station with a pound of sausages. — *The Guardian*, 6th February 2001

2 to refuse to cooperate when questioned by the police; to withstand pressure to confess *US*
- I've done time and I stood up. — George V. Higgins, *The Friends of Eddie Doyle*, p. 75, 1971
- If things went bad, Paulie would stand up. — Vincent Patrick, *The Pope of Greenwich Village*, p. 20, 1979
- — Angela Devlin, *Prison Patter*, p. 109, 1996

stand-up *adjective*
1 loyal to the end, devoted and dependable *US*
Perhaps from boxing, where a stand-up fight was one in which the fighters stood up to each without flinching or evasion. The ultimate praise in the world of organised crime.
- I need some help, I helped you. Are you a standup guy or not. — George V. Higgins, *The Friends of Eddie Doyle*, p. 100, 1971
- They gonna need distributors with brains and with heart – stand-up motherfuckers. — Edwin Torres, *Carlito's Way*, p. 21, 1975
- Tommy always was a stand-up guy. — *Raging Bull*, 1980
- But Tommy's being a real stand-up guy. — Gerald Petievich, *Money Men*, p. 57, 1981
- Placido and Pino Salvaggio. They are stand-up. — Richard Condon, *Prizzi's Glory*, p. 79, 1988
- What happened to you, man? I remember you used to be a stand-up kind of guy. — *Mallrats*, 1995
- He won't talk. Stone is a good kid. Stand-up guy, just like his old man. — *Casino*, 1995

2 solid; pure *US*
- I knew where I could cop a stand up twenty if he wanted it. — A.S. Jackson, *Gentleman Pimp*, p. 123, 1973

stand-up *adverb*
describing someone's play in pool, at your true skill level, not below it *US*
- — Mike Shamos, *The Illustrated Encyclopedia of Billiards*, p. 230, 1993

standy-up *adjective*
used of an on-your-feet position or posture *UK*
- I was bang into it, ramming her doggy-style in that bathtub, but standy-up and that. — Kevin Sampson, *Clubland*, p. 133, 2002

stang *noun*
prospective goods to be stolen *US*
- The law is that who ever finds the stang gets the majority of it. — Henry Williamson, *Hustler!*, p. 130, 1965

'Stang *noun*
a Ford Mustang car *US*
- — Judi Sanders, *Faced and Faded, Hanging to Hurl*, p. 38, 1993

stank *noun*
the vagina; sex *US*
Usually said unkindly.
- — Edith A. Folb, *runnin' down some lines*, p. 255, 1980
- The answer is, it's gonna be interracial, which means it'll offer a few token liberal white broads a chance to give up a lil' stank... — Odie Hawkins, *The Busting Out of an Ordinary Man*, p. 152, 1985

▸ **get your stank on**
(from a female perspective) to have sex *UK*
Reclaiming **STANK** (the vagina) for women.
- If there is one thing that actually is better than getting walloped on brain-rotting chemical stimulants, then it's doing the nasty/getting your stank on* with a lady/man* (*delete as applicable). — *Ministry*, p. 21, October 2002

stanky *adjective*
bad-smelling *US, 1980s*
- stanky – Smelly — Edith A. Folb, *runnin' down some lines*, p. 255, 1980
- As you all remember, in our last meeting we discussed the reasons why the political structure started off stanky and got progressively rotten as time went on. — Donald Goines, *The Busting Out of an Ordinary Man*, p. 26, 1985
- [I]t's like I just been waitin' to fall off my whole stanky life. — Nick Barlay, *Curvy Lovebox*, p. 127, 1997

Stanley *noun*
1 a Pole or Polish-American *US*
Coined in Chicago.
- — Bill Reilly, *Big Al's Official Guide to Chicagoese*, p. 56, 1982

2 an industrial knife with a retractable blade, often used as a discreet weapon *UK*
Although similar tools are manufactured by many other companies, the Stanley brand provides the generic identity.
- Any mug who can pick up a Stanley gets leery, thinks they're a fucking hero. — Greg Williams, *Diamond Geezers*, p. 174, 1997

stanley knife *noun*
a wife *UK*
Rhyming slang, formed from a proprietary cutting tool that is a generic for such tools.
- — Ray Puxley, *Fresh Rabbit*, 1998

stanza *noun*
in horse racing, a single race *US*
- — David W. Maurer, *Argot of the Racetrack*, p. 60, 1951

star *noun*
1 cocaine *US*
Possibly from shortening **STARDUST** (cocaine).
- — Mike Haskins, *Drugs*, p. 281, 2003
- — Office of National Drug Control Policy, *Drug Facts*, February 2003

2 methcathinone *UK*

- —Mike Haskins, *Drugs*, p. 279, 2003

3 a prisoner serving a first custodial sentence *UK*

- —Angela Devlin, *Prison Patter*, p. 109, 1996

4 an asterisk sign (*) on a computer keyboard *US*

- —Eric S. Raymond, *The New Hacker's Dictionary*, p. 39, 1991

5 man; used as a general form of address *JAMAICA*
West Indian, hence UK black. Also spelt 'starr'.

- —Chester Francis-Jackson, *The Official Dancehall Dictionary*, p. 49, 1995
- Yuh lookin' nice y'nuh star! —Courttia Newland, *Society Within*, p. 8, 1999
- Me from serious part of town, y'get me. We nah ramp [pretend], starr. —Diran Adebayo, *My Once Upon A Time*, p. 39, 2000

starch *noun*
semen *US*

- —Dale Gordon, *The Dominion Sex Dictionary*, p. 151, 1967

stardust *noun*

1 cocaine *US*

- —John B. Williams, *Narcotics and Hallucinogenics*, p. 116, 1967

2 phencyclinde *US*
Recorded as a 'current PCP alias'.

- —*Drummer*, p. 77, 1977

starfish *noun*
the anus *UK*
A visual pun.

- [Y]ou'll need to place your fingertips on her perineum (the smooth skin between pussy and starfish) so that you feel her internal contractions. —*Drugs An Adult Guide*, p. 108, December 2001

starfish trooper *noun*
a male homosexual *NEW ZEALAND, 2002*
An allusion to anal sex based on **STARFISH** (the anus), playing on the popular science fiction image of a starship trooper.

starfucker *noun*
anyone who seeks to provide free sexual services to the famous; hence, an ingratiating hanger-on of anyone with celebrity status *UK*

- An English starfucker who is a long-time friend of mine[.] —Richard Neville, *Play Power*, p. 86, 1970
- [as published:] I'm gonna make you scream all night / Yeah starbucker, starbucker star [as recorded:] [...] star fucker star fucker star —Mick Jagger and Keith Richard, *Star Star*, 1972
- —Tom Hibbert, *Rockspeak!*, p. 148, 1983
- He knew it'd work. There isn't a doorman in the world who isn't a starfucker. "Are you guys famous?" —Kevin Sampson, *Powder*, p. 315, 1999
- brokering shag-and-tell memoirs for greedy little starfuckers —Christopher Brookmyre, *Boiling a Frog*, p. 26, 2000

star gazer *noun*

1 on the railways, a brakeman who has misread oncoming signals *US*

- —J. Herbert Lund, *Herb's Hot Box of Railraod Slang*, p. 96, 1975

2 in horse racing, a horse that holds its head too high *UK*

- —Rita Cannon, *Let's Go Racing*, p. 73, 1948

star grade *noun*
in the US military, the rank of general *US*

- Success is measured by promotion. "Star grade" – the rank of general – was the pinnacle. —Joseph C. Goulden, *Korea*, p. 436, 1982

stark bollock naked *adjective*
absolutely naked *UK*
An amended spelling of earlier 'stark ballock naked', 1922.

- [Y]ou with the knife still in you, the woman stark bollock naked holding a plastic bucket under you[.] —Derek Raymond, *He Died With His Eyes Open*, p. 229, 1984
- I'll er... stand in Balham High Road and sing the Moldovan national anthem. Stark bollock naked. —Tony Hawks, p. 3, 2001

stark bollocky; stark bollocky naked; stark ballocky *adjective*
totally naked *AUSTRALIA*

- It's not long before I'm down on the floor, stark ballocky, and they give me this work over. —*Flame Magazine*, p. 6, 1972
- I'll ride stark bollocky naked on a bicycle down Pitt Street in the lunch hour! —Lance Peters, *The Dirty Half-Mile*, p. 151, 1979

starkers *adjective*
totally naked *NEW ZEALAND*

- —Louis S. Leland, *A Personal Kiwi-Yankee Dictionary*, p. 97, 1984
- —Thommo *The Dictionary of Australian Swearing and Sex Sayings*, p. 124, 1985

stark mother naked *adjective*
totally naked *AUSTRALIA*

- When I returned to the lounge he was stark mother naked. —Sue Rhodes, *Now you'll think I'm awful*, p. 123, 1967

stark staring bonkers *adjective*
utterly mad *UK*

- Hogg's remark [in 1964] that anyone voting Labour was 'stark staring bonkers' did the Conservatives no good. —David Childs, *Britain Since 1945*, p. 112, 2001
- I gave her my Mickey Mouse pen. I must be stark staring bonkers. —Jacqueline Wilson, *The Story of Tracy Beaker*, p. 136, 2001

starlight hotel *noun*
sleeping in the open air at night *NEW ZEALAND*

- —David McGill, *David McGill's Complete Kiwi Slang Dictionary*, p. 116, 1998

stars *noun*
LSD *UK*
From the design printed on the dose.

- Street names [...] smilies, stars, strawberries[.] —James Kay and Julian Cohen, *The Parents' Complete Guide to Young People and Drugs*, p. 141, 1998

Starship Enterprise *noun*
a marijuana cigarette *UK*
In the cult televison series *Star Trek* (1966–69) and sequels, the Starship Enterprise is a means 'to boldly go' exploring space – simply a **ROCKET** for the next generation.

- [S]kin up the next Starship Enterprise[.] —*Sky Magazine*, p. 11, May 2001

Starsky and Hutch; starsky *noun*
the crotch *UK*
Rhyming slang, formed from a US television police-action-adventure series, 1976–81.

- —Ray Puxley, *Fresh Rabbit*, 1998
- —Bodmin Dark, *Dirty Cockney Rhyming Slang*, 2003

star's nap *verb*
to borrow something, especially money *UK*
Rhyming slang for **TAP**.

- —Julian Franklyn, *A Dictionary of Rhyming Slang*, 1961

star-spangled powder *noun*
cocaine *UK, 1998*

- —Mike Haskins, *Drugs*, p. 281, 2003

start *verb*

1 to start your menstrual period *US*

- —Don R. McCreary (Editor), *Dawg Speak*, 2001

2 to act as if you want a fight *IRELAND*

- A couple of weeks ago, I was coming out of a chip shop with a bag of chips and this fella comes along and karate kicks the chips out of my hand for absolutely no reason, and then says to me 'Are you startin'?' —Ardal O'Hanlon, *The Talk of the Town*, p. 5, 1998

starter *noun*
a gambler hired by a casino to gamble and thereby create interest in a game *US*

- Today they are used mostly at baccarat tables. They are also called "starters." —Mario Puzo, *Inside Las Vegas*, p. 195, 1977

starter cap *noun*
a condom *US*
To stop anything starting.

- I put the starter cap on the bozack —Kwest Tha Madd Lad, *Lubrication*, 1996

starters *noun*
any lubricant used to facilitate anal sex *UK*

- —Paul Baker, *Polari*, p. 190, 2002

▸ **for starters**
to begin with *UK*

- [L]et's have a baby. Not you having it, for starters. —John Williams, *Cardiff Dead*, p. 94, 2000

starting juice *noun*
pressurised ether in a spray can, used to spray in the carburettor to help start a car that is not inclined to start *US*

- —Lewis Poteet, *Car & Motorcyle Slang*, p. 188, 1992

startler *noun*
in typography, an exclamation mark (!) *UK*
- [K]nown in the newspaper world as a screamer, a gasper, a startler or (sorry) a dog's cock. —Lynne Truss, *Eats, Shoots and Leaves*, p. 136, 2003

star up *verb*
(used of a young prisoner, on turning 21) to be transferred to an adult prison *UK*
- —Angela Devlin, *Prison Patter*, p. 109, 1996
- When he was twenty-one he was "starred up" and transferred from a young offenders' institution to the adult maximum-security dispersal system. —*The Guardian*, 26th October 2000

starver *noun*
a saveloy *AUSTRALIA, 1941*
- Put some tomato sauce on my starvers please. —*www.abc.net.au/wordmap*, 2003

starve the crows!
used for expressing great surprise *AUSTRALIA*
- Starve the crows! Sorry I'm late. She's only ticking over on two cylinders. —Coralie Lees, *Spinifex Walkabout*, p. 175, 1953

starve the lizards!
used for expressing great surprise *AUSTRALIA, 1927*
- Starve the lizards, mates! You fair put the wind up me that time. —Barry Humphries, *The Wonderful World of Barry McKenzie*, p. 17, 1968
- Starve the lizards! No doubt about you sheilas. I mean, one minute you're coming across, now you're not! —*The Adventures of Barry McKenzie*, 1972
- Everyone was staggered and said, 'Well! Starve the lizards! How about that!' —Kel Richards, *The Aussie Bible*, p. 28, 2003

starve the mice!
used for expressing great surprise *AUSTRALIA*
- 'Starve the mice!' Ossie exclaimed. 'What's bitten you, Boss?' —Dymphna Cusack, *Picnic Races*, p. 202, 1962

starving Armenians *noun*
used as an example when parents urge children to finish their dinner *US*
There are endless variations on the theme.
- —*Maledicta*, p. 155, 1979: 'A glossary of ethnic slurs in American English'

starving days *noun*
the first few, unproductive days of a project *US*
A logger term that survived the end of mass logging.
- —John Gould, *Maine Lingo*, p. 274, 1975

stash *noun*
1 a hidden supply of drugs, usually marijuana; the hiding place itself *US, 1942*
- Where is it? Where's your stash, knucklehead? —Alexander Trocchi, *Cain's Book*, p. 106, 1960
- I stopped at the broom-closet stash. I hurled the 'sizzle' [drugs] into the corner on the shelf. —Iceberg Slim (Robert Beck), *Pimp*, p. 155, 1969
- Lady was tipping this broad 20 a day and soon as she found her stash, she ran and told whitey. —Babs Gonzales, *Movin' On Down De Line*, p. 51, 1975
- He didn't shoot me, because I had a stash like you wouldn't believe. —*Apocalypse Now*, 1979
- The stock or "stash" of cocaine is kept in a bag stitched with beads worn by adherents of Santeria[.] —Terry Williams, *The Cocaine Kids*, p. 28, 1989
- SAFFRON[:] I hid your stash. EDINA[:] Where? SAFFRON[:] Down the toilet. —Jennifer Saunders, *Absolutely Fabulous*, p. 58, 1992
- Any other time he would have been riled about losing the stash and the money[.] —Donald Gorgon, *Cop Killer*, p. 3, 1994
- Roy's taken a small sample out of the main stash and he chops two fat lines [of cocaine] out on the mirror. —J.J. Connolly, *Know Your Enemy [britpulp]*, p. 141, 1999

2 in the illegal production of alcohol, a cache of alcohol *US*
- We got ninety gallon left in the stash. —David W. Maurer, *Kentucky Moonshine*, p. 125, 1974

3 ill-gotten or illicit goods kept in a hidden store *UK, 1914*
- —Angela Devlin, *Prison Patter*, p. 109, 1996

4 a person's hiding place *US, 1927*
- If he wasn't home or in his stash, people would say, "Tell that nigger don't come on the street any more until he's got my money." —Claude Brown, *Manchild in the Promised Land*, p. 214, 1965

5 a room, apartment or house *US*
- No Hotel Ritz for us this time; our stash was over some kind of feed store[.] —Mezz Mezzrow, *Really the Blues*, p. 132, 1946

stash *verb*
1 to hide something, especially drugs *US, 1914*
- I got some pod stashed by the subway. —George Mandel, *Flee the Angry Strangers*, p. 26, 1952
- I was learning to hide my stuff carefully – "stash it," as they say in the trade – so Roy and Herman couldn't find it and take some[.] —William Burroughs, *Junkie*, p. 34–35, 1953
- He could have that almost anywhere; there were works stashed at the Garden Bar, the poolroom, near a small bush off the sidewalk on Ninety-second[.] —Clarence Cooper Jr, *The Scene*, p. 12, 1960
- Did anybody see you stash it? —Ross Russell, *The Sound*, p. 239, 1961

2 (used of a prostitute) to retain some of your earnings and not turn them over to your pimp *US*
- "Also during this time, she had a conversation with Daniel Mitchell wherein he told (her) that he would kill her if she ever stashed on him," Corbett said in his report. —*Post-Standard (Syracuse, New York)*, p. B1, 5th January 1989

stash apartment *noun*
an apartment where drugs are hidden *US*
- And it was a lot quicker to serve up bottles out of a bar than to have everybody running in and out of the stash apartment for every ten-dollar sale. —Richard Price, *Clockers*, p. 5, 1992

stash catcher *noun*
an employee of a drug dealer whose job it is to retrieve supplies of drugs that are jetisoned in the event of a police raid *US*
- —Terry Williams, *Crackhouse*, p. 151, 1992

stash pad *noun*
the room, apartment or house where someone hides their drugs *UK*
- —Tom Hibbert, *Rockspeak!*, p. 148, 1983

stat *noun*
1 a statistic *US, 1961*
Usually used in the plural.
- I have the stats on that car, Officer Labeef. —*Repo Man*, 1984
- recording video pieces and mugging up facts and stats —John McCririck, *John McCririck's World of Betting*, p. 16, 1991

2 a *stat*utory tenant *UK*
- —*Sunday Times*, 7th June 1963

3 methcathinone *US*
- —Office of National Drug Control Policy, *Drug Facts*, February 2003

statch *adjective*
statutory *US*
- [H]e had two California convictions for felony statch rape, both complainants thirteen-year-old girls. —James Elroy, *Hollywood Noctunes*, p. 210, 1994

state *noun*
1 a dirty, ill-kempt or poorly preserved condition *UK, 1879*
- [S]tate schools, I used to joke, were so called because they were in a "right old state". —Jenny Eclair, *Camberwell Beauty*, p. 60, 2000

2 a condition of excitement; agitation; anxiety; a state of drunkenness *UK, 1837*
- When I reached the station, my wife was in what is known in domestic circles as "a state". —*The Humorist*, 18th August 1934
- He told the court: I was in a right state. I couldnt think properly. I couldnt stop crying. —*Wanstead and Woodford Guardian*, 22nd December 2000

3 a state prison *US*
- We're talking about McGuire's friendship with Baily, who's doing time in state for second degree murder. —Robert Campbell, *In a Pig's Eye*, p. 58, 1991

State and Perversion *nickname*
in Chicago, the intersection of State and Division Streets *US*
- The corner they call State and Perversion. —Willard Motley, *Let No Man Write My Epitaph*, p. 166, 1958

state college *noun*
a state prison *US*
- —Vincent J. Monteleone, *Criminal Slang*, p. 224, 1949

state electrician *noun*
the executioner in a state using electrocution in the electric chair for capital punishment *US*
- —Ralph de Sola, *Crime Dictionary*, p. 143, 1982

stateful *adjective*
in a nervous or excited condition, 'in a state' *UK*
Teen slang.
- — Susie Dent, *The Language Report*, p. 78, 2003

State of Maine bankroll *noun*
a bankroll made from a real note folded around paper cut to the shape of currency *US*
- — John Gould, *Maine Lingo*, p. 275, 1975

state-of-the-monte *adjective*
state of the art, using up-to-date technology *UK*
Formed with the FULL MONTE (everything).
- Four pot plants and she bought state-of-the-fucking-monte gardening gloves. — Jeremy Cameron, *Brown Bread in Wengen*, p. 5, 1999

state-raised *adjective*
said of a prisoner who has spent most of his life incarcerated *US*
- — William K. Bentley and James M. Corbett, *Prison Slang*, p. 29, 1992

States *noun*
▸ **the States**
in Alaska, all states except Alaska *US*
- — *American Speech*, p. 256–258, Fall 1984: 'Terms for 'Not Alaska' in Alaskan English'

stateside *adjective*
of the US; American *US, 1943*
- Woody Allen [...] is perhaps the only film-maker to unite populist Stateside humour with the European high art of Bergman or Fellini. — *New Statesman*, 17th November 2003

state time *noun*
a prison sentence served in a state prison *US*
More serious than time in COUNTY, and within the state jurisdiction as opposed to federal jurisdiction.
- His sentence wasn't on the sheet – or all the hustles he got away with that Raylan read between the lines – but Louis must have done a few years' state time. — Elmore Leonard, *Riding the Rap*, p. 214, 1995

statey *noun*
a state highway trooper *US*
- Or even one of the Staties, like the one arrested you. — George V. Higgins, *Penance for Jerry Kennedy*, p. 2, 1985
- — Amy and Denise McFadden, *CoalSpeak*, p. 12, 1997

static *noun*
harassment; trouble; complications *US, 1926*
- Hey, look! fool!" she growled into the receiver after having obviously listened to enough bullshit, "don't be givin' me all that static!" — Odie Hawkins, *Chicago Hustle*, p. 29–30,
- That's enough static out of you! — *Rebel Without a Cause*, 1955
- Don't give me any static on that score. — Mart Crowley, *The Boys in the Band*, p. 37, 1968
- — John R. Armore and Joseph D. Wolfe, *Dictionary of Desperation*, p. 51, 1976
- The pair – whose smutty antics have earned them huge ratings – drew heavy static for a contest that rewarded listeners for having sex in public places. — *New York Daily News*, 23rd August 2003

stationery *noun*
free tickets to an athletic or entertainment event *UK*
- — Wilfred Granville, *The Theatre Dictionary*, p. 190, 1952

stations of the cross
a police tactic in which a person who has been arrested is moved from one precinct to another in rapid succession, making it impossible for him to be located and bailed out by his friends and family *US*
- [A]nd the warden wanted to know who was responsible for running a man around the stations of the cross who'd been picked up for nothing more serious than a drunk and disorderly. — Robert Campbell, *Boneyards*, p. 259, 1992

stave *noun*
a drinking session *IRELAND*
- Now as he drew nearer he could hear the faint sound of an accordion and see a band of spruced up wedding guests trooping out of The Small Hotel and into The Rock for a bit of a stave. — Billy Roche, *Tumbling Down*, p. 27, 1984

staving drunk *adjective*
very drunk *CANADA*
This phrase has lasted past the time when alcohol came only in barrels (although swish still does).
- To be "staving drunk" is to be so drunk that you stave in the barrel to get at the grog without pulling the bung. — Lewis Poteet, *The South Shore Phrase Book*, p. 108, 1999

stay *verb*
to reside *US*
- Black People have seldom lived in one area long enough to consider it their own. Black People only STAYED in places. — Malachi Andrews and Paul T. Owens, *Black Language*, p. 101, 1973
- Everybody said we were moving to the 'burbs, and none of my friends wanted us to go where only white people stayed. — Terry Williams, *The Cocaine Kids*, p. 76, 1989

▸ **stay awake**
to use amphetamines or methamphetamine continuously *US*
A vague euphemism.
- — Geoffrey Froner, *Digging for Diamonds*, p. 58, 1989

▸ **stay loose**
to remain calm *US*
- "Well, so long, Jack," she said. "Stay loose." — Max Shulman, *I was a Teen-Age Dwarf*, p. 82, 1959

stay and pray *verb*
in poker, to stay in a hand with a large amount of money bet, hoping for a particular card to be drawn to improve your hand *US*
- — George Percy, *The Language of Poker*, p. 87, 1988

stay-awake *noun*
amphetamine sulphate or any other central nervous system stimulant *US*
- — Peter Johnson, *Dictionary of Street Alcohol and Drug Terms*, p. 180, 1993

stay-behind *adjective*
left to operate in enemy territory *US*
CIA Director Allen Dulles formed 'Operation Stay Behind' shortly after World War 2, building a wide network of anti-communist guerrillas – including many former Nazis – who would fight behind the lines in the event of a Soviet invasion of Europe.
- [A] stay-behind organization of operatives in the event the Communists overran either Japan or Korea[.] — Joseph C. Goulden, *Korea*, p. 456, 1982
- Without "stay-behind assets," intelligence agents, information gathering was slow and tedious. That's where America was in November 1979 – without anyone in Teheran working for it. — Charlie A. Beckwith, *Delta Force*, p. 186, 1983

stayer *noun*
1 in poker, a hand that warrants staying in the game but not raising the bet *US, 1949*
- — Thomas L. Clark, *The Dictionary of Gambling and Gaming*, p. 216, 1987

2 in horse racing, a horse that performs well in longer distance races *US*
- — Tom Ainslie, *Ainslie's Complete Guide to Thoroughbred Racing*, p. 339, 1976

stay-home sauce *noun*
food or drink made with ingredients believed to instil sexual fidelity or attraction *GUYANA*
- — Richard Allsopp, *Dictionary of Caribbean English Usage*, p. 529, 1992

stay-out *noun*
in prison, a confrontational tactic in which prisoners refuse to return to their cells *US*
- — John R. Armore and Joseph D. Wolfe, *Dictionary of Desperation*, p. 52, 1976

stay out of the Koolaid!
mind your own business! *US*
- — Bill Valentine, *Gang Intelligence Manual*, p. 78, 1995

stay put
to remain in place, to stay where you are *US, 1843*
- Pires and Wenger to stay put[.] — *The Guardian*, 31st May 2003

stay up
used as a farewell *US*
- — *Columbia Missourian*, p. 1A, 19th October 1998

stay-wag *noun*
a station wagon *US*
- — Trevor Cralle, *The Surfin'ary*, p. 122, 1991

St Cat's *noun*

in Montreal, Rue St Catherine *CANADA*

- "They know that if they kick us out, we'll just go up to St. Cat's (St. Catherine Street)," said Adam, 20, one of the roughly 30 young squatters in the westernmost part of the park. — *Montreal Gazette*, p. A3, 21st July 2002

STD grab bag *noun*

a person who has had many sexual partners and is likely, therefore, to be a source of sexually transmitted disease *UK*

- —Chris Lewis, *The Dictionary of Playground Slang*, p. 219, 2003

steady *noun*

a steady boyfriend or girlfriend *US, 1897*

- Walter McGrath seemed to be another steady she was heavy on. —Mickey Spillane, *Kiss Me Deadly*, p. 61, 1952
- The Lads and I talked about girls – not their 'steadies' God forbid, but the pert creatures who paraded in pairs and threes along the sea front. —Hugh Leonard, *Out After Dark*, p. 84, 1989
- Apparently you're both on the outs with your steadies. — *Mallrats*, 1995

steady Eddie *noun*

a reliable, dependable, trustworthy person *US*

- The arrest paints a portrait at odds with the middle-aged and balding Dean, a man regarded by his peers as a "very steady Eddie." — *Los Angeles Times*, p. 1 (Part 2), 23rd July 2003

Steak and Kidney *noun*

Sydney *AUSTRALIA, 1905*

Rhyming slang.

- No questions asked about getting that ashore in the old Steak and Kidney! —John Wynnum, *Tar Dust*, p. 27, 1962

steak and kidney pie *noun*

the eye *UK*

Rhyming slang.

- —Julian Franklyn, *A Dictionary of Rhyming Slang*, 1960
- —Ray Puxley, *Cockney Rabbit*, 1992

steak drapes *noun*

the vaginal labia *UK, 1998*

A play on **BEEF CURTAINS**.

- — *www.LondonSlang.com*, June 2002

steal *noun*

something cheap or made available at a cheaper cost *US, 1944*

- Accommodation – usually the biggest single cost for students – is a steal with rooms in halls starting at around £ 28 a week[.] — *The Guardian*, 17th August 2002

steal *verb*

in poker, to win a hand with an inferior hand either through superior bluffing skills or poor estimation by other players *US*

- —John Scarne, *Scarne's Guide to Modern Poker*, p. 291, 1979

▸ **steal the ante**

in poker, to bet aggressively early in a hand, driving out other players and leaving a pot consisting mostly of the buy-in antes *US*

- I decided to slow-play it, figuring that Nick might try to steal the ante. —Jimmy Snyder, *Jimmy the Greek*, p. 198, 1975
- —Edwin Silberstang, *Winning Poker for the Serious Player*, p. 220, 1992

▸ **steal the show**

in a public display, to outshine other performers, to gain most applause *US, 1928*

- With a lingering kiss, and a prime-time declaration of love that brought rousing applause from the audience, a gay couple stole the show at the Tony awards on Sunday night in New York. — *The Guardian*, 10th June 2003

▸ **steal you blind**

to rob you of everything *US, 1976*

An illiterate variation of 'rob you blind'.

- "What if he wakes up before you get home and steals you blind?" "Steals what?" she asked. "My clothes won't fit him[.]" —Sherrilyn Kenyon, *Night Embrace*, p. 23, 2003

stealth bomber *nickname*

Stella Artois™ lager *UK*

Named after the nickname of the US Air Force's B2 Spirit, which is used here to imply invisible strength and a great power to inflict damage.

- Cooking lager? Fackin' poof's drink. Get yourself a Stealth Bomber, mate[.] —Andrew Holmes, *Sleb*, p. 150, 2002

steam *noun*

1 alcohol *AUSTRALIA, 1941*

- Bring us a coupla bottles steam, will yer, Charlie. —John Wynnum, *Tar Dust*, p. 43, 1962

2 hashish *CANADA*

- —Suroosh Alvi et al., *The Vice Guide*, p. 113, 2002

3 in sports betting, a flurry of betting on one side of a bet *US*

- —Michael Knapp, *Bay Sports Review*, p. 11, November 1991

▸ **not give the steam off your turds; not give the steam of your piss**

expresses an absolute refusal to give or be generous *UK*

The predominate style is 'off', rather than 'of'. The term employed for appropriate bodily excretions may be as varied as the user's vocabulary: 'steam off your shit' is a familiar example.

- Dudes who hate them with a vengeance, cos of envy or fear, who wouldn't give 'em the steam of their piss[.] —J.J. Connolly, *Layer Cake*, p. 121, 2000
- Blood form a stone, yew an yewer fuckin gear [drugs] like. Wouldn't give the steam off yewer turds as a Christmas present yew. —Niall Griffiths, *Sheepshagger*, p. 133, 2001

steam *verb*

in gambling, to bet increasingly larger amounts of money in a losing effort to recoup recurring losses *US*

- —Steve Kuriscak, *Casino Talk: A Rap Sheet for Dealers and Players*, p. 53, 1985

steam and cream; steam job *noun*

during the Vietnam war, a bath and sex with a prostitute *US*

- —Linda Reinberg, *In the Field*, p. 209, 1991

steamboat *noun*

a cardboard tube or box with a hole for a marijuana cigarette and a hole for inhaling, used to trap the smoke *US*

- This little contraption is called a steamboat because the roach looks like the smokestack in a steamboat. — *Newsweek*, p. 49, 24th July 1967
- —William D. Alsever, *Glossary for the Establishment and Other Uptight People*, p. 20, December 1970

steamboats *adjective*

1 foolish, silly *UK*

Probably derives as rhyming slang from *Steamboat Willie*, the 1928 animated film that introduced Mickey Mouse.

- Don't be getting seamboats and sloppy. —J.J. Connolly, *Layer Cake*, p. 244, 2000

2 drunk *UK: SCOTLAND*

- Ah've seen the guy totally steamboats in the middle of the day. —Michael Munro, *The Complete Patter*, p. 147, 1996

steame *noun*

a steamed hot dog *CANADA*

- Indeed, steames, as these hot dogs are known, are the National Food of Quebec. —Will Ferguson, *How to be a Canadian*, p. 107, 2001

steamer *noun*

1 a member of a youth gang taking part in a steaming attack *UK*

- In Hackney in east London over a seven-day period, 22 attacks were made by steamers and on another occasion, 30 robberies were carried out in less than half an hour by steamers. — *The Times*, 5th July 1987
- —Nicholas Jones, *Hackers, Hotting and Hooray Henrys*, p. 57, 1992

2 in horse racing, a horse that attracts heavy betting on the morning of a race, at a time before the odds being offered by bookmakers are reduced *UK*

- [T]he trouble with steamers is that for success you need to get on at those fancy morning line prices, and often this is not possible. —John McCririck, *John McCririck's World of Betting*, p. 54, 1991

3 an act of oral sex performed on a man *UK*

- She doesnt go all the way but she'll definitely give you a steamer! —Chris Lewis, *The Dictionary of Playground Slang*, p. 219, 2003

4 a homosexual man, especially one who seeks passive partners *UK, 1958*

Ultimately from **STEAM TUG** (a **MUG**).

- —Paul Baker, *Polari*, p. 190, 2002

5 a prostitute's client *UK*

- —Paul Baker, *Polari*, p. 190, 2002

6 a gambler who increases the size of his bets after losing *US, 1968*

- —Thomas L. Clark, *The Dictionary of Gambling and Gaming*, p. 217, 1987

7 a drinking session *UK: SCOTLAND*

- When wis the last time you wereny on a steamer on a Friday night? —Michael Munro, *The Patter, Another Blast*, p. 68, 1988

8 a full wetsuit covering the torso, legs and arms *AUSTRALIA*

- —Nat Young, *Surfing Fundamentals*, p. 128, 1985

steam in *verb*

to engage in an activity, especially fighting, with absolute commitment *UK, 1961*

- Someone who's going to weigh up all the options rather than just steam in smacking people about.—Greg Williams, *Diamond Geezers*, p. 41, 1997
- [A] tastier West Ham mob appears and steams straight in.—Martin King and Martin Knight, *The Naughty Nineties*, p. 93–94, 1999

steaming *noun*

youth gang activity involving robbing and escaping en masse *UK*

- A new phenomenon that police face is 'steaming'. The American-style crime trend involves gangs of up to 30 people swarming into a shop or bus and stealing en masse.—*The Times*, 5th July 1987
- —Nicholas Jones, *Hackers, Hotting and Hooray Henrys*, p. 57, 1992
- —Angela Devlin, *Prison Patter*, p. 109, 1996

steaming *adjective*

1 used as an intensifier *UK, 1962*

- They got on at Runcorn, bladdered by the way, fucking steaming drunk already[.]—Kevin Sampson, *Clubland*, p. 147, 2002

2 drunk *UK*

- —*e-cyclopaedia*, 20th March 2002

steaming demon *noun*

any large American car *UK*

- —Peter Chippindale, *The British CB Book*, p. 161, 1981

steam packet *noun*

a jacket *UK, 1857*

Rhyming slang.

- —Ray Puxley, *Fresh Rabbit*, 1998

steampigged *adjective*

drunk *UK*

- —*e-cyclopaedia*, 20th March 2002

steam-powered *adjective*

obsolete *US*

- —Eric S. Raymond, *The New Hacker's Dictionary*, p. 334, 1991

steamroller *noun*

1 a thick hand-rolled cigarette *NEW ZEALAND, 1953*

- —Harry Orsman, *A Dictionary of Modern New Zealand Slang*, p. 130, 1999

2 a *bowler* hat *UK*

Rhyming slang. Glossed as: 'A dying piece simply because the headwear of the typical city gent is a thing of the past' by Ray Puxley, *Cockney Rabbit*, 1992.

steam tug; steamer *noun*

a fool; a victim *UK, 1932*

Rhyming slang for **MUG**.

- [I]nside the nick Cecil was a steamer adrift.—Charles Raven, *Underworld Nights*, p. 199, 1956
- There was no more to come from the steam tug.—John McCririck, *John McCririck's World of Betting*, p. 131, 1991
- —Angela Devlin, *Prison Patter*, p. 109, 1996

steeazick *noun*

a marijuana cigarette *US*

- My old friend Henri Cru recently blew into N.Y. with a couple of steeazicks from Panama as big as your thumb.—Jack Kerouac, *Letter to William S. Burroughs*, p. 108, 14th July 1947

steel *noun*

a pistol *US*

A variation of the more common 'iron'.

- —Judi Sanders, *Faced and Faded, Hanging to Hurl*, p. 38, 1993

▸ off the steel

not engaged in railway work *US*

- —Ramon Adams, *The Language of the Railroader*, p. 107, 1977

steel and concrete cure *noun*

the sudden and complete deprivation of drugs to a jailed drug addict, who suffers intensely *US*

- So you might as well get yourself set for the steel-and-concrete and the chuck horrors. I had 'em.—*The New American Mercury*, p. 711, 1950
- The steel and concrete cure is the only cure I recommend for stool pigeons.—David Maurer and Victor Vogel, *Narcotics and Narcotic Addiction*, p. 446, 1973

steel beach

the deck of an aircraft carrier or other warship when used for recreational purposes *US*

- On most cruises, only two days a month are declared holidays when the men can lie around on what some call "the steel beach."—*New York Times*, p. 16, 14th March 1982
- "We work hard, but we play just as hard," said Chief Petty Officer Cole Boarders, of San Francisco, who spends a day off sunning himself at "Steel Beach" on the deck of the Dallas.—*Sun-Sentinel (Fort Lauderdale, Florida)*, p. 1H, 28th March 2004

steel door *noun*

a hospital-admitting physician who admits only the sickest patients *US*

- —Sally Williams, *"Strong" Words*, p. 160, 1994

steelie *noun*

a ball bearing used in a game of marbles *US*

- We had declared that no steelies could be used as toys.—Bobby Seale, *A Lonely Rage*, p. 31, 1978

steelies *noun*

steel-toed boots, especially those made by Doc Marten *US*

- The most sought-after article of clothing, though, was the steelies, 12- to 14-hole, calf-high, steel-toed Doc Marten boots also called DMs or Docs[.]—Bill Valentine, *Gangs and Their Tattoos*, p. 58, 2000

steel pot *noun*

the US military standard-issue M-1 helmet *US*

Vietnam war usage.

- —Carl Fleischhauer, *A Glossary of Army Slang*, p. 19, 1968
- The uniform of the day is shirts, rifles, and steel pots.—Larry Heinemann, *Close Quarters*, p. 62, 1977
- —Gregory Clark, *Words of the Vietnam War*, p. 200, 1990

steely *noun*

1 a steel guitar *UK*

- My mum plays the old steely[.]—Ngaio Marsh, *Death at the Dolphin*, p. 249, 1967

2 in trucking, a brake made with a magnesium-steel brake shoe in a steel drum *US*

- —Montie Tak, *Truck Talk*, p. 154, 1971

steen *noun*

an imaginary large number *US, 1900*

- I ain't seen you in steen million years. How you was?—James T. Farrell, *Saturday Night*, p. 20, 1947

steep *adjective*

1 excessively expensive; over-priced *US*

- "They're going for silly money. Two hundred notes or more." "Bit steep, ain't it?"—Martin King and Martin Knight, *The Naughty Nineties*, p. 159, 1999

2 sought by the police; wanted *US*

- —Bill Valentine, *Gang Intelligence Manual*, p. 111, 1995

steer *noun*

▸ all a steer can do is try

said to justify, humbly, an attempt to do the seemingly impossible *CANADA, 1987*

- As steers are castrated male cattle, when it comes to mating, to try is about all they can accomplish.—Chris Thain, *Cold as a Bay Street Banker's Heart*, p. 2, 1987

steer *verb*

in confidence swindles, to direct the confederate(s) who will swindle the victim *US, 1889*

- The lush was a complete stranger, having been delivered by a cabdriver who steered for various joints, and Tappy had just gotten around to selling him the first bottle of bubbly.—Robert Sylvester, *No Cover Charge*, p. 213, 1956
- What are you steering for this craps joint?—Iceberg Slim (Robert Beck), *Pimp*, p. 94, 1969
- It's easy to steer a lop-eared chump, so long as Mordecai Jones has sized up the mark.—Guy Owen, *The Flim-Flam Man and the Apprentice Grifter*, p. 168, 1972
- He rarely failed to "steer" the mark.—Stephen Cannell, *King Con*, p. 34, 1997

steerage *noun*

economy class on a commercial airliner *US*

- —Rene Foss, *Around the World in a Bad Mood*, p. 34, 2002

steerer *noun*

a person who directs potential customers to an illegal enterprise *US*

- Many are taken on in a variety of tangential roles and work as steerers, touts, guards, runners, and "cop men" – dealers whom suppliers will only sell to on a cash basis. — Terry Williams, *The Cocaine Kids*, p. 33, 1989

steerman *noun*

1 a member of a swindling enterprise who identifies potential victims and directs them into the swindle *US*

- A "steerman" hunts for "pigeons," unsuspecting amateurs who could be steered into fixed games with professional card players. — Kim Rich, *Johnny's Girl*, p. 61, 1993

2 in tandem surfing, the person towards the rear of the surfboard *US*

- The guy behind you is called the "steerman." You're supposed to paddle all the time sort of in the same rhythm as the steerman. — Frederick Kohner, *Gidget*, p. 51, 1957

steeze *noun*

a person's image or style *US*

- — Connie Eble (Editor), *UNC-CH Campus Slang*, p. 9, Spring 2003

Steffi Graf; Steffi *noun*

1 a laugh *UK*

Rhyming slang, formed from the name of the German tennis champion (b.1969).

- You're having a Steffi. — Ray Puxley, *Fresh Rabbit*, 1998
- You're having a Steffi Graf aren't you? — Mervyn Stutter, *Getting Nowhere Fast*, 21st May 2004

2 a bath *UK, 1998*

Rhyming slang, based on the name of the German tennis player Steffi Graf (b.1969).

- I'm off for a Steffi. — *Antiquarian Book Review*, p. 18, June 2002

3 *half* an ounce, especially of drugs *UK*

Rhyming slang.

- — Nick Jones, *Spliffs*, p. 251, 2003

steggies *noun*

steroids *UK*

- [H]alf looks as if he's on the steggies and that, bit of a gymhead. — Kevin Sampson, *Clubland*, p. 101, 2002

Steinie *noun*

a bottle of Steinlager^{TM} beer *NEW ZEALAND*

- — David McGill, *David McGill's Complete Kiwi Slang Dictionary*, p. 119, 1998

stella blue *noun*

a variety of marijuana *UK, 1995*

Possibly named after a 1973 song by the Grateful Dead: 'It seems like all this life / Was just a dream / Stella Blue / Stella Blue'.

- A Cannabis Cup prize winner in 1995, Stella blue has since gone the distance and established itself as a firm favourite in many of Amsterdam's most discerning coffee shops. — Nick Jones, *Spliffs*, p. 75, 2003

stellar *adjective*

very good *US*

A conventional adjective rendered slangy through attitude, pronunciation and application to objects such as hamburgers.

- — Connie Eble (Editor), *UNC-CH Campus Slang*, p. 8, Fall 1986

Stella the Steno *noun*

used as a personification of the stereotypical female office worker *US, 1946*

- — *American Speech*, p. 299, December 1955: 'Mimeo Minnie, Sadie, the office secretary, and other women office workers in America'

stem *noun*

1 a main street or boulevard, especially one frequented by tramps, prostitutes, pimps and their ilk *US, 1914*

- When I hit the main stem, I went down a side street past a little hotel. — Mickey Spillane, *I, The Jury*, p. 25, 1947
- The southeast corner of 50th Street and Seventh Avenue epitomizes the decline of the Stem. — Jack Lait and Lee Mortimer, *New York Confidential*, p. 35, 1948
- You would also be playing your girl against a half-dozen strong, jasper [lesbian] whores on this 'stem. — Iceberg Slim (Robert Beck), *Pimp*, p. 102, 1969
- The stem swirls in a straight line down 47th Street, heading for Buttermilk Bottom, the Fillmore District, Crenshaw, or the dusty, crusty surface of Gwinnett Street in deepest Georgia. — Odie Hawkins, *Ghetto Sketches*, p. 25, 1972
- Yeah, had I been on the stem during the big burn, I'd be one of the many, many niggers that got over the hump. — A.S. Jackson, *Gentleman Pimp*, p. 9, 1973

2 the dominant culture in a society *US*

An abbreviation of 'system'.

- — Bill Valentine, *Gang Intelligence Manual*, p. 111, 1995

3 the penis *US*

- [N]obody to my knowledge spoke of "choad," "rod," stem" or any other more strictly pornographic term. — *Screw*, p. 5, 3rd January 1972

4 a railway track *US*

- — Norman Carlisle, *The Modern Wonder Book of Trains and Railroading*, p. 268, 1946

5 a laboratory pipette used to smoke crack cocaine *US*

- — Terry Williams, *Crackhouse*, p. 152, 1992
- — US Department of Justice, *Street Terms*, October 1994

▸ **on the stem**

performing or inclined to perform oral sex on a man *US*

- — John R. Armore and Joseph D. Wolfe, *Dictionary of Desperation*, p. 42, 1976

▸ **up against the stem**

addicted to smoking marijuana *UK, 1998*

From 'stem' (the non-smokeable part of the marijuana plant).

- — Mike Haskins, *Drugs*, p. 292, 2003

stem *verb*

to beg on the street *US*

- Portland, Oregon's a good town to stem. — Willard Motley, *Let No Man Write My Epitaph*, p. 73, 1958
- Cunningham, who lives in a local homeless shelter, used to spend his days "steming" – street slang for panhandling. — *Christian Science Monitor*, p. 12, 4th June 1992

stemmer *noun*

a beggar *US*

- — Joseph E. Ragen and Charles Finston, *Inside the World's Toughest Prison*, p. 820, 1962: 'Penitentiary and underworld glossary'
- [During the Pope's 2002 visit] "It's not helping very much. I make $10 a day. I'm just not a high-grade stemmer." A stemmer is a panhandler. — *Toronto Globe and Mail*, p. A6, 26th July 2002

stems *noun*

1 the legs *UK, 1860*

- Nor could it have been charming and helpful to her fears and anxieties to have me start out, at the outset of our romance, "kissing her down between the stems[.]" — Jack Kerouac, *The Subterraneans*, p. 75, 1958
- Nice stems! — *Clueless*, 1995

2 marijuana *UK*

An example of **BAD** meaning 'good'; the non-smokeable part of the plant is here adopted as a name for the good.

- — Mike Haskins, *Drugs*, p. 289, 2003

stenchel *noun*

molasses, water and ground ginger, to go on porridge or as a drink in the field *CANADA*

- It was also used as a drink, chiefly in haying time: 1 cup of molasses, 1 cup of vinegar, 2 tbls ginger, 1 gal. water. — T. K Pratt, *oral citation from The Dictionary of Prince Edward Island English*, p. 147, 1988

stench trench *noun*

the vagina *UK*

- — *Roger's Profanisaurus*, December 1997
- Abjection was invoked in various ways: through reference to dirtiness (e.g., front bum, dirt box), uncooked (bloody?) meat (e.g., meat seat, chopped liver), vaginal secretions of all types (e.g., slushing fuck pit, the snail trail), smell (e.g., smelly hole, stench trench), and wounds (e.g., gash, gaping axe wound). — *Journal of Sex Research*, p. 146, 2001

stencil *noun*

a thin and long marijuana cigarette *US*

- — Edith A. Folb, *runnin' down some lines*, p. 255, 1980

stenked *adjective*

drunk *UK: SCOTLAND*

- — Michael Munro, *The Complete Patter*, p. 148, 1996

steno *noun*

a stenographer *US, 1906*

- Under the "El" are sporting goods, music and book stores; shops for the upper crust and cafeterias where lonesome stenos dine. — Jack Lait and Lee Mortimer, *Chicago Confidential*, p. 291, 1950

stenographer *noun*

in a deck of playing cards, a queen *US*

- — George Percy, *The Language of Poker*, p. 87, 1988

step *verb*

▸ **step on**

to dilute a powdered drug *US, 1971*

- I ain't never tried to step on this much heh-rawn in my life. We got a few bags cut but the suitcase is still full. — Vernon E. Smith, *The Jones Men*, p. 48, 1974
- The dealer-in-weight sells by the piece (about an ounce) to street dealers. The street dealer (or dealer) buys the piece and then steps on it. — Burgess Laughlin, *Job Opportunities in the Black Market*, p. 6–5, 1978
- As it is, he's been stepping on it in ever-decreasing moderation[.] — Jim Carroll, *Forced Entries*, p. 11, 1987
- You put a one, one and half on it 'cause stuff is so shitty down there you can step all over the ounce and they still bringing home the best stuff around. — Richard Price, *Clockers*, p. 180, 1992
- [H]is tackle was always of the best – creamy white, rocky, unstepped on[.] — Will Self, *The Sweet Smell of Psychosis*, p. 70, 1996
- A dealer can "step" on his product as much as he wants[.] — Lanre Fehintola, *Charlie Says...*, p. 14, 2000
- It's-a powders yew want, like. Step on em a few times, yewer laughin. — Niall Griffiths, *Sheepshagger*, p. 73, 2001

▸ **step on the gas; step on it**

to hurry; to accelerate; often used as an imperative *US, 1920*

Originally applied just to motor vehicles; the 'it' is the accelerator pedal.

- The defining quality of haste is only now coming into focus in our cultural mirrors, as in the New Yorker cartoons: (1996) man getting into cab – "And step on it. This restaurant may be over any minute"[.] — *The Guardian*, 9th September 2000
- We have been urging the chancellor not to step on the gas as far as the economy is concerned[.] — *The Guardian*, 7th March 2001

▸ **step on your dick**

to commit a self-damaging act *US*

- You just stepped on your dick. — *Maledicta*, p. 171, Winter 1980

▸ **step on your meat**

to engage in self-defeating conduct *US*

- Before you step on your meat, let me draw you a little picture. — Gerald Petievich, *One-Shot Deal*, p. 191, 1981

▸ **step up to the plate**

to rise to a challenge *US*

From the image of a batter in baseball coming up to bat.

- Republican Sen. Fred Thompson of Tennessee, chairman of the committee probing campaign financing, said it was time for Bill Clinton to step up to the plate. — *Gannett News Service*, 10th October 1997

Stephenson's rocket *noun*

a pocket *UK*

Rhyming slang, formed from the early locomotive.

- — Ray Puxley, *Fresh Rabbit*, 1998

Stepin Fetchit *noun*

an black person who curries favour with whites through obsequious behaviour *US*

After the stage name of Lincoln Theodore Monroe Perry (1902–85), a black actor known for his film portrayal of stereotypical black minstrel characters.

- The one thing I knew is that I was not going to write one of those disgraceful high-tech Stepin Fetchit things. — Odie Hawkins, *Lost Angeles*, p. 29, 1994

step off *verb*

to go away *US*

- Bitch, step off! — *Menace II Society*, 1993

stepper *noun*

1 a prostitute; a promiscuous woman *US*

- Mrs. Winroy is quite a stepper – not that I'm saying anything against her, understand? — Jim Thompson, *Savage Night*, p. 4, 1953
- Reba says peevishly, "Trap? Perhaps, Mama, but just briefly for this stepper." — Iceberg Slim (Robert Beck), *Doom Fox*, p. 100, 1978
- — Edith A. Folb, *runnin' down some lines*, p. 256, 1980
- down home gossipers, snuff dippers, exotic religionists, fast steppers, high rollers and just plan ol' folks — Odie Hawkins, *The Busting Out of an Ordinary Man*, p. 141, 1985

2 a gunman *JAMAICA*

- — Velma Pollard, *Dread Talk*, p. 45, 2000

steps *noun*

▸ **up the steps; up the stairs**

on trial *UK, 1931*

The accused goes up the steps/stairs from the cells into the court.

- — Angela Devlin, *Prison Patter*, p. 110, 1996

step to *verb*

to get into a fight *US*

- — *Crews*, p. 168, 1995: 'Glossary'

step up *verb*

to start a fight *US*

- — Don R. McCreary (Editor), *Dawg Speak*, 2001

stern-wheeler *noun*

the passive participant in anal sex *US*

- — *Maledicta*, p. 233, 1979: 'Kinks and queens: linguistic and cultural aspects of the terminology for gays'
- — William K. Bentley and James M. Corbett, *Prison Slang*, p. 58, 1992

Steve Canyon *noun*

any fighter pilot *US*

Vietnam war usage, alluding to the name of a comic strip popular in the US in the 1950s and 60s.

- — Carl Fleischhauer, *A Glossary of Army Slang*, p. 19, 1968

Steve McQueen's *noun*

jeans *UK*

Rhyming slang.

- — *www.LondonSlang.com*, June 2002

Stevie Wonder *noun*

thunder *UK*

Rhyming slang, formed from the name of the US singer and musician (b.1950).

- — Ray Puxley, *Fresh Rabbit*, 1998

stew *noun*

1 an awkward position; an agitated condition *UK, 1806*

- 'The whole country,' he says, 'is in a stew about whether a preferential quota should be admittedly set for blacks and Hispanics over whites with the same scholarly results[.] — Alastair Cooke, *Letter from America*, 23rd March 1999

2 a state of alcohol intoxication *US*

- I was sittin' at the table, gettin' on a might stew / a dead swell dame come sit beside me too. — Bruce Jackson, *Get Your Ass in the Water and Swim Like Me*, p. 131, 1965

3 a drunkard *US*

- Swedes are either teetotalers or wonderful stews. — Jack Lait and Lee Mortimer, *Chicago Confidential*, p. 81, 1950

4 nitroglycerin used to blow open a safe *US*

- — Vincent J. Monteleone, *Criminal Slang*, p. 225, 1949

5 an airline flight attendant *US*

A shortened form of 'stewardess'.

- Terry, a new stewardess who isn't swinging – yet – has a blow up with her mother and leaves home to stay with Gussy, another "stew." — *Adam Film Quarterly*, p. 14, September 1969
- You don't have to go out hunting for a stew. They stay in the same hotels we do. — Jim Bouton, *Ball Four*, p. 204, 1970
- And when I was a stew, 'Oh, she's a stewardess,' and that's that. — John Warren Wells, *Tricks of the Trade*, p. 75, 1970
- I used to sign on with a little blonde stew, Miss Jones. — Edward Lin, *Big Julie of Vegas*, p. 236, 1974
- Here we go to hell, escorted by the tight-hipped, Mabellined, hard-smiling, round-eyed stews from Never-Never Land. — Charles Anderson, *The Grunts*, p. 10, 1976
- Being a stew and all . . . well, you can pick up a lot of art objects in your travels. — Armistead Maupin, *Tales of the City*, p. 5, 1978
- I wake up on a plane and have no idea in the world where we're going. I'm thinking, How do I ask the stew without sounding like an idiot? — Elmore Leonard, *Pronto*, p. 315, 1993

stew *verb*

▸ **stew in your own juice**

to endure the consequences of your actions *UK, 1885*

- [E]veryone else in Washington, the police geniuses especially, stewed in their own juices. — James Patterson, *Jack & Jill*, p. 153, 1996

stewards'; steward's *noun*

an informal investigation of any situation *UK*

Reduced from 'stewards' inquiry' (an authorised investigation by the officials who control horse racing).

- [T]hey held a stewards' there and then. Bags of finger-pointing, blaming and accusing each other of being too old. — Martin King and Martin Knight, *The Naughty Nineties*, p. 110, 1999
- Pre-order you want the works, but then the bill comes and wallop! Everyone has a steward's into it. "Oo ordered the rum baba" and all that caper. — Garry Bushell, *The Face*, p. 43, 2001

Stewart Grainger *noun*
danger *UK*
Rhyming slang, formed from the name of the British film actor.
- Any Stewart Grainger of getting pissed in here today? — Ray Puxley, *Cockney Rabbit*, 1992

stew bum; stewbum *noun*
an alcoholic derelict *US, 1902*
- You ain't nothin' but a skid-row stewbum. — Nathan Heard, *Howard Street*, p. 72, 1968
- He was back in Morning Sections sitting on the bench in the fenced-off section with the stew bums and colored hookers waiting to go before the same judge. — Elmore Leonard, *The Big Bounce*, p. 99, 1969
- You know how these stew bums are. — Mickey Spillane, *Last Cop Out*, p. 56, 1972

stewed *adjective*
drunk *US, 1737*
Another drunk synonym, first recorded by Benjamin Franklin.
- You know. Drunk, stewed, clobbered, gone, liquored up, oiled, stoned, in the bag. — Max Shulman, *Guided Tour of Campus Humor*, p. 106, 1955
- I was suddenly tired. Not stewed or even excited or lonely; just plain tired out. — Clancy Sigal, *Going Away*, p. 182, 1961
- I guess they both reasoned my pardner was still stewed from the Kingfish's gigglesoup. — Guy Owen, *The Flim-Flam Man and the Apprentice Grifter*, p. 116, 1972
- — Ramon Adams, *The Language of the Railroader*, p. 146, 1977

stewed prune *noun*
a tune *UK*
Rhyming slang.
- [D]runkenly humming a stewed prune[.] — Ronnie Barker, *Fletcher's Book of Rhyming Slang*, p. 26, 1979

stewie *noun*
an alcoholic *US*
- — Lou Shelly, *Hepcats Jive Talk Dictionary*, p. 19, 1945

St Gapour *noun*
in Quebec, the alcoholic mixed drink best known as a Singapore Sling *CANADA*
- The use, in English and French in Quebec, of "St. Gapour" for a Singapore Sling is very much in the Quebecois tradition of sacrilegious jokes and nicknames, as well as phony saints. — Lewis Poteet, *Talking Country*, p. 70, 1992

stick *noun*

1 ability in pool *US*
- Hermes Pavolites, one of the three brothers who shot pool in Sal's, fair sticks, hit him a hard uppercut in the Melody Room one night[.] — Gilbert Sorrentino, *Steelwork*, p. 118, 1970
- "Man, you shoot a good stick," Blackjack beamed as he sat back watching Rhodes run the table. — Joseph Nazel, *Black Cop*, p. 149, 1974
- And he would shoot a better stick here tomorrow than he had done in Florida. — Walter Tevis, *The Color of Money*, p. 23, 1984
- — Steve Rushin, *Pool Cool*, p. 28, 1990

2 a cigarette *INDIA*
Indian English.
- "How many cigarettes do you want?" "Oh, just two or three sticks." — Paroo Nihalini, R.K. Tongue and Priya Hosali, *Indian and British English*, 1979
- So why are more women smoking? Ruchira Bose finds reasons to quit the stick[.] — *The Times of India*, 31st May 2002

3 marijuana *UK*
- — Mike Haskins, *Drugs*, p. 289, 2003

4 phencyclidine, the recreational drug known as PCP or angel dust *UK*

5 a truncheon; a riot baton *US, 1929*
In police and prison-service use; narrowing but continuing the sense as 'cudgel', which has been in recorded use since 1377.
- This parade is known as sticks and whistles because the main reason for it is to check up and see that no one comes on duty without his stick and his whistle. — Frank Norman, *Bang To Rights*, p. 158, 1958
- — Angela Devlin, *Prison Patter*, p. 110, 1996
- I managed to draw my stick [truncheon] and lash out at the nearest target[.] — Duncan MacLaughlin, *The Filth*, p. 57, 2002

6 a burglar's pry-bar *UK, 1879*
- — Hyman E. Goldin et al., *Dictionary of American Underworld Lingo*, p. 210, 1950
- To free the safe from its frame with only a "stick", which is not a very delicate tool, without making hell's own row, would take a little time. — Charles Raven, *Underworld Nights*, p. 18, 1956

7 a clarinet *US*
A shortened form of **LICORICE STICK**.
- If I could play that stick like you do I'd be out there runnin' with all them high-powered chicks in all the fines places[.] — Mezz Mezzrow, *Really the Blues*, p. 248, 1946

8 a handgun *UK, 1781*
Recorded in use August 2002.

9 a surfboard *US*
- — John Severson, *Modern Surfing Around the World*, p. 182, 1964
- If you want to get aggro, man, this stick can handle your best rage. — *Point Break*, 1991
- — Pamela Munro, *U.C.L.A. Slang*, p. 111, 1997

10 a skateboard *US*
- — *San Francisco Sunday Examiner & Chronicle*, p. 20, 2nd September 1984: 'Say it right'

11 in horse racing, the whip used by jockeys *US*
- — Tom Ainslie, *Ainslie's Complete Guide to Thoroughbred Racing*, p. 339, 1976

12 a pool player *US*
- — Steve Rushin, *Pool Cool*, p. 28, 1990

13 the game of pool *US*
- Abilene not only had the best car in the country, he also shot the best stick of pool. — Larry McMurtry, *The Last Picture Show*, p. 9, 1966
- — Judi Sanders, *Mashing and Munching in Ames*, p. 19, 1994

14 a set of rules for a game of pool *US*
- — Steve Rushin, *Pool Cool*, p. 28, 1990

15 criticism, especially harsh criticism *UK, 1942*
A softening of the sense 'to beat with a stick'.
- WOMEN drivers are traditional targets for some stick, so why should I be any different? — *Waltham Forest Guardian*, 11th July 2003

16 violent punishment; a severe reprimand *UK, 1856*
Originally 'the stick' (a beating with a stick).
- [T]he worst were the tossers who couldn't take a bit of stick with some honour[.] — Greg Williams, *Diamond Geezers*, p. 7, 1997

17 harsh or extreme demands made of a motor engine *UK*
Usually as 'give it (some) stick'; derives from the sense of the 'cane' as 'punishment'.
- [Y]ou're fucking pissing away on an export bonnie [a motorbike] or sommat, give it almighty stick, you know[.] — Paul E Willis, *Profane Culture*, p. 15, 1978

18 a manually operated car transmission *US, 1960*
A shortened form of 'stick shift'.
- — John Lawlor, *How to Talk Car*, p. 99, 1965

19 in drag and motor racing, tyre traction *US*
- — Don Alexander, *The Racer's Dictionary*, p. 63, 1980

20 a prisoner's personal influence or power *US*
- When a person has a great deal of influence and can get things accomplished, he is said to have a sharp stick. An abundance of stick is referred to as long stick. — William K. Bentley and James M. Corbett, *Prison Slang*, p. 34, 1992

21 a person of a type described *UK, 1784*
- She's a funny old stick but she's been sent from heaven today. — James Herriot, *All Things Bright and Beautiful*, p. 85, 1976

22 a fighter pilot *US*
- — *American Speech*, p. 124, Summer 1986: 'The language of naval fighter pilots'

23 a prostitute *US*
- — Christina and Richard Milner, *Black Players*, p. 308, 1972

24 one thousand dollars *US*
Probably an evolution of **YARD**.
- — Burgess Laughlin, *Job Opportunities in the Black Market*, p. 7, 1978: 'Glossary'

25 in the circus or carnival, a person playing a game or concession with the house's money in an attempt to attract other patrons to play *US*
- — Joe McKennon, *Circus Lingo*, p. 93, 1980
- On the midway, he learned the art of "cake cutting," or shortchanging customers, using "sticks" – carnies posing as customers pretending to win a big prize – and "gaffs" – concealed devices such as magnets used to ensure that the house always won. — Kim Rich, *Johnny's Girl*, p. 37, 1993

▷ see: **BELLY-STICK**

▸ **give it stick; give it some stick**
to enjoy something noisily, and to the utmost *UK, 1984*

▸ **give stick; give some stick**
to energetically criticise someone; to inflict physical damage on something or someone *UK*
- I was giving Dave stick, maybe because I was jealous of him doing so well. —John King, *Human Punk*, p. 194, 2000

▸ **had the stick**
to be ruined or irreparably broken; to be finished *AUSTRALIA, 1953*

▸ **up the stick**
pregnant *AUSTRALIA, 1941*
- She might be up the stick and need a father for her child. —William Dick, *A Bunch of Ratbags*, p. 198, 1965
- I should have known I was up the stick[.] —Jenny Eclair, *Camberwell Beauty*, p. 53, 2000

stick *verb*

1 to stab someone with a knife *US*
- I had been on probation for sticking a guy who'd busted my jaw with brass knuckles made out of ashcan handles. —Edwin Torres, *Carlito's Way*, p. 20, 1975
- Dizzy was always known as a cat that would stick a dude in a minute if they fucked with him. —Babs Gonzales, *Movin' On Down De Line*, p. 52, 1975
- I can't negotiate knives. It takes a lot of anger to stick somebody, you know? That's like real personal. —Richard Price, *Clockers*, p. 390, 1992
- Yeah. And it was in the papers and TV, too. Somebody stuck her. They say it was you. —Joseph Wambaugh, *Floaters*, p. 240, 1996

2 to inject a drug *US*
- Stick your arm for some real fun[.] —Alice in Chains, *God Smack*, 1992

3 to punch or hit someone *US*
- —Connie Eble (Editor), *UNC-CH Campus Slang*, p. 9, Spring 2003

4 (from the male perspective) to have sex *US*
- Did you get any action? Did you slam it to her? Did you stick her? Did you hump her? Did you run it down her throat? Did you jam it up her ass? Did you shoot your wad? —*Screw*, p. 6, 29th May 1972

5 to tolerate or endure someone or something *UK, 1899*
- I'm not making excuses for my dad any more. I can't stick him now. And I especially can't stick her. —Jacqueline Wilson, *The Worry Website*, 2003

6 to burden someone *UK, 1851*
- While music journalists seek the frontman's opinion on burning issues, lead guitarists get stuck with the bloke from International Fretboard and Plectrum Monthly asking about string gauges. —*The Guardian*, 31st January 2003

▸ **stick a hit**
in snowboarding, to achieve impressive height when jumping *US*
- Stick a hit. To land a fat air. —Jim Humes and Sean Wagstaff, *Boarderlands*, p. 224, 1995

▸ **stick beef**
(used of a male) to have sex *BAHAMAS*
- —John A. Holm, *Dictionary of Bahamian English*, p. 194, 1982

▸ **stick fat**
to remain loyal *NEW ZEALAND, 1997*
Prison usage.
- —Harry Orsman, *A Dictionary of Modern New Zealand Slang*, p. 130, 1999

▸ **stick in promise land for**
to threaten someone with a prison sentence *UK*
Prison use.
- —*Encounter*, July 1959

▸ **stick it up**
to treat someone unfairly *AUSTRALIA*
- They'll stitch you up, stick it up you and take you for a dead-set dickhead. —Barry Humphries, *A Nice Night's Entertainment*, p. 147, 1974

▸ **stick like shit to a blanket**
to adhere tenaciously *UK*
- He [a detective following the speaker] sticks as close to me as shit to a blanket. —Gerald Kersh, *Fowler's End*, 1956
- You're stuck with it – stuck, as the saying goes, like shit to the proverbial blanket. —Neville Jackson, *No End to the Way*, p. 65, 1965
- —Frank Hardy, *The Outcasts of Foolgarah*, p. 45, 1971

▸ **stick one on**
to hit someone *UK, 1960*
- I told my players that if I see any sour faces I'm gonna stick one on them[.] —*The Guardian*, 22nd April 2002

▸ **stick to your knitting**
to limit your efforts to doing what you know how to do; in the business world, to avoid the temptation to diversify beyond your company's expertise *US*
- —David Olive, *Business Babble*, p. 141, 1991

▸ **stick with**
to persevere with something; to endure; to remain faithful to someone or something *UK, 1882*
- Weir happy to stick with old routine[.] —*The Guardian*, 16th July 2003

▸ **stick your neck out**
to take a risk *US, 1926*
- I am prepared to really stick my neck out and say: "Arms fair? Booo! People who sell cluster bombs? Bad!" —*The Guardian*, 12th September 2003

▸ **stick your bib in**
to interfere; to meddle *AUSTRALIA, 1952*
- 'Don't stick you bib in,' Father warned[.] —Kerry Cue, *Crooks, Chooks and Bloody Ratbags*, p. 112, 1983

stickability *noun*
perseverance *US, 1888*
- But what I like most is his grit and stickability and stubbornness. That's very Yorkshire. —Tony Horwitz, *Blue Latitudes*, p. 281, 2002

stick and stone; stick *noun*
a bone *UK*
Rhyming slang, generally plural.
- It's my fervent wish that you all make old "sticks". —Ray Puxley, *Cockney Rabbit*, 1992

stick book *noun*
a pornographic book or magazine *AUSTRALIA, 1967*
- —Ryan Aven-Bray, *Ridgey Didge Oz Jack Lang*, p. 45, 1983
- Spilling from beneath the bed was a lurid fan of stick books, DIY gynaecology —Shane Maloney, *Nice Try*, p. 176, 1998

stick bun *noun*
a son *UK*
Rhyming slang.
- —Ray Puxley, *Cockney Rabbit*, 1992

sticker *noun*

1 a knife *UK, 1896*
- One guy tried to hit me with a wooden Keep Off The Grass sign, which he pulled out the ground while he was running from my sticker. —Edwin Torres, *Carlito's Way*, p. 12, 1975
- [He] just stood there for a couple of seconds fingering the handle of the sticker before toppling over[.] —Greg Williams, *Diamond Geezers*, p. 213, 1997

2 a warrant or bill of detainer *US*
- —John R. Armore and Joseph D. Wolfe, *Dictionary of Desperation*, p. 52, 1976

3 a prisoner who is remanded in custody pending a court appearance *UK*
- —David Powis, *The Signs of Crime*, 1977

stick for *verb*
to charge too much for something *UK, 1961*

stick hall *noun*
a pool room *US*
- [A] poolroom is a "stick hall"[.] —Harrison E. Salisbury, *The Shook-up Generation*, p. 160, 1958

stick horse *noun*
in horse racing, a horse that runs best with some encouragement from the jockey and whip *US*
- —Tom Ainslie, *Ainslie's Complete Guide to Thoroughbred Racing*, p. 339, 1976

stickie *nickname*
a member of the 'official' IRA and Sinn Fein *UK: NORTHERN IRELAND, 1972*
- Terrorist organizations Republican: Irish Republican Army. At any given time the Provos (Provisional IRA) and the Stickies (Official IRA) would begin shooting[.] —Laurel Holliday, *Children of the Troubles*, p. 192, 1998
- The republican movement split into 'Officials' (known as stickies) and 'Provisionals'. —*Sunday Business Post*, 18th August 2002

stick Indian *noun*
a backwoods Indian *CANADA*
- To him they were not "characters" or stick Indians, or any of the slighting things that Belile and others of his kind called them. —Hubert Evans, *Mountain Dog*, p. 96, 1956

sticking out *adjective*

good; fashionable *UK*

- — Tom Hibbert, *Rockspeak!*, p. 149, 1983

stick-in-the-mud *noun*

someone who resists change *UK, 1733*

- I've just been painted as some frigid, shrewish stick-in-the-mud, and I've been marked down accordingly. — Christopher Brookmyre, *Boiling a Frog*, p. 37, 2000

stick it up your arse!; stick it in your ear!; stick it up your jumper!

expressions of contemptuous rejection *US, 1960*

- [Describing 'I Am The Walrus', 1967] Choir: six boys singing "Oompah, oompah, stick it up your jumper." — William J Dowdling, *Beatlesongs*, p. 198, 1989
- Fuck you, this is what I'm gonna do, if you don't like it, stick it in your ear. — Peter Biskind, *Easy Riders, Raging Bulls*, p. 195, 1999
- He looked at me with cold hatred and growled, "Ventura, I'm gonna stick this up your ass." — Jesse Ventura, *I Ain't Got Time to Bleed*, p. 128, 2000
- You can take your pieties and your pity and stick them up your scriptural arse. Do you hear me, sir? — Joseph O'Connor, *Star of the Sea*, p. 124, 2003

stick mag *noun*

a pornographic magazine *AUSTRALIA, 1992*

- There are some stick mags under the bed if you wanna look at them. — Phillip Gwynne, *Deadly Unna?*, p. 246, 1998

stickman *noun*

1 a pickpocket, shoplifter or other petty criminal's accomplice who is passed the stolen goods, and also impedes any pursuit *UK, 1861*

West Indian slang.

- — David Powis, *The Signs of Crime*, 1977

2 a marijuana smoker *US*

- — *Mr.*, p. 58, April 1966: 'The hippie's lexicon'

3 a sexually active heterosexual male who prides himself on his skill and prowess *UK*

- — *The Observer*, 5th January 1975
- — David McGill, *David McGill's Complete Kiwi Slang Dictionary*, p. 119, 1998

stick me with a fork – I'm done!

used for expressing submission in the face of a challenge *US*

- "Well, just stick me with a fork, 'cause I'm done," he suddenly burst out with an exaggerated toss of his head. — Donna Hill, *Della's House of Style*, p. 34, 2000

stick of rock *noun*

the penis *UK*

Rhyming slang for **COCK**; a visual pun on a long pink sweet that is made to be sucked.

- — Ray Puxley, *Cockney Rabbit*, 1992

stick of tea *noun*

marijuana prepared and smoked in the fashion of a cigarette *US, 1940*

Combines **STICK** (a cigarette) with **TEA** (marijuana).

- Three highballs [whisky and soda] and three sticks of tea and it took a pipe wrench to get him off the chandelier. — Raymond Chandler, *Farewell My Lovely*, p. 55, 1940
- All you have to do, as every Dirty Old Man knows, is offer them a bar of candy – or a stick of tea. — G. Legman, *The Fake Revolt*, p. 10, 1967

stick out *verb*

to be conspicuous or obvious *UK, 1638*

From 'stick out a mile'. Originally in conventional use, colloquial or slang since mid-C19.

- "There are even rumors about other things as well, if you follow my drift." "Your drift sticks out a mile." — Andre Aciman, *Out of Egypt*, 1996

▸ stick out like dog's balls

to be obvious; to stand out prominently *AUSTRALIA, 1971*

- — Frank Hardy, *The Outcasts of Foolgarah*, p. 228, 1971
- We'll stick out like dogs balls. — Peter Corris, *Pokerface*, p. 129, 1985
- His eyes were sticking out like dog's balls. — Murray Farquhar, *Nine Words from the Grave*, p. 103, 1986

sticks *noun*

1 the countryside *US, 1905*

- He'd gotten so fed up playing corny commercial music in New York that he'd beat it to the sticks with this trio because he could play like he wanted up there. — Mezz Mezzrow, *Really the Blues*, p. 292, 1946
- Ask some young blood from the sticks who goes upstate on some check forgery. — Edwin Torres, *Carlito's Way*, p. 44, 1975
- He lived off the hicks from out in the sticks / He was a master of the long-shoe game. — Dennis Wepman et al., *The Life*, p. 86, 1976
- I mean, we going to set you so far back in the sticks, they going to have to use jackrabbits to bring your mail to you[.] — Bobby Seale, *A Lonely Rage*, p. 267, 1978
- When you were up west with Mods from all over London and the sticks you couldn't help but feel theatrical[.] — Irish Jack, *History*, p. 31, 1979
- You're living out there in the sticks. You don't want to wait for anyone before you cut the turkey! — *Avalon*, 1990
- I mean, it was still way too hot for me to even go near Vegas, so I set up a meeting with the guys way out in the sticks. — *Casino*, 1995

2 goalposts *AUSTRALIA, 1876*

Examples include football (soccer) and Australian Rules football.

- He marked it on his chest, played on and ran for the sticks — Shane Maloney, *Nice Try*, p. 273, 1998
- No matter the placement, power or trajectory of a shot, when [Gordon] Stewart was between the sticks for Tynefield City, he was unbeatable. — *The Observer*, 30th November 2003

3 skis; ski poles *US*

- — *American Speech*, p. 207, October 1963: 'The language of skiers'

4 furniture *US*

- It's a cleaner but he's got no D.P. so I sent him to the happy man and now I find they couldn't get together because he's got no sticks. — *San Francisco Examiner*, p. II-1, 24th February 1956
- I got this floor-pop who's looking for a roller but I can't use the OA for the DP on his old sled – I'd take him to the mouse house but he has no sticks. — *San Francisco Chronicle*, p. 2–1, 31st October 1966
- — *American Speech*, p. 313, Autumn-Winter 1975: 'The jargon of car salesmen'

5 good quality marijuana *UK*

- Low grade, you're talking bush at one hundred and twenty, sticks and that gummy silver at one hundred and eighty. — Diran Adebayo, *My Once Upon A Time*, p. 26, 2000

sticks and stones *noun*

the game of pool *US*

- — Steve Rushin, *Pool Cool*, p. 28, 1990

sticksing *noun*

pickpocketing *UK*

West Indian slang.

- [An 18-year old West Indian girl] talks about the London "sticksing" or "dropstick" scene [...] like a veteran. — *New Society*, 7th July 1977

stick sister *noun*

a woman who shares a sexual partner with another woman *AUSTRALIA*

- But...seein' as we are Stick Sisters, like, right at the moment...What? Ya dunno what I'm on about? — Kathy Lette, *Girls' Night Out*, p. 22, 1987

stickspin *noun*

a scene in a pornographic film in which a woman changes positions without losing her vaginal grip on the man's penis *US*

- — *Adult Video News*, p. 40, September 1995

stickup; stick-up *noun*

1 an armed hold-up *US, 1904*

- A team of tactical operators would also be placed in the hotel that evening and remain there throughout the night to act as an arrest team if and when the stick-up went down. — William Dodson, *The Sharp End*, p. 154, 2001

2 glue used in solvent abuse *UK*

A play on the conventional use of glue.

- — Angela Devlin, *Prison Patter*, p. 110, 1996

stick up *verb*

to rob someone at gunpoint; to hold up a place *AUSTRALIA, 1843*

- One day we got word that the bushranger Morgan was riding along the road, sticking up places. — Eve Langley, *The Pea-Pickers*, p. 257, 1958

stick-up *adjective*

engaged in sex *TRINIDAD AND TOBAGO, 1974*

- — Lise Winer, *Dictionary of the English/Creole of Trinidad & Tobago*, 2003

stick up for *verb*

to champion or defend someone or something *UK, 1837*

- These comics stick up for Rodney King, but they also stick up for Mike Tyson. — *The Guardian*, 31st December 2003

stick-up merchant *noun*
an armed robber *AUSTRALIA*
• Most stick-up merchants are recidivists[.] — William Dodson, *The Sharp End*, p. 18, 2001

sticky *noun*
an inquisitive look *AUSTRALIA, 1974*
Short for **STICKYBEAK**.

sticky *adjective*
1 of a situation, incident, work, etc, unpleasant, very difficult, dangerous *UK, 1915*
• [A] comfort from dawn to midnight, and occasionally at sticky moments in between. — Michel Faber, *The Crimson Petal and the White*, p. 168, 2003
2 in trouble *BARBADOS*
• — Frank A. Collymore, *Barbadian Dialect*, p. 105, 1965
3 of a website, successful at attracting repeated or extended visits from Internet users *UK*
• — Susie Dent, *The Language Report*, p. 19, 2003
4 in volleyball, said of a ball that is briefly, and illegally, held *US*
• — Bonnie Robison, *Sports Illustrated Volleyball*, p. 96, 1972

stickybeak; sticky-beak *noun*
1 an overly inquisitive person *AUSTRALIA, 1920*
• 'Let's peep round the curtain first,' said Allister softly. 'All right, stickybeak.' — Winifred Law, *Through Space to the Planets*, p. 34, 1944
• Mum told us to mind our own business and leave her alone but of course we were sticky-beaks. — Patsy Adam-Smith, *Folklore of the Australian Railwaymen*, p. 148, 1969
• — Arthur Chipper, *The Aussie Swearer's Guide*, p. 54, 1972
• — Sam Weller, *Old Bastards I Have Met*, p. 14, 1979
2 an inquisitive look *AUSTRALIA, 1971*
• By this stage word had spread throughout the hospital so that now hordes of nurses and other doctors were coming to have a sticky-beak. — Doug Anthony Allstars, *Book*, p. 92, 1982

stickybeak; sticky-beak *verb*
to pry *AUSTRALIA, 1933*
• 'I've sticky-beaked enough.' — Jean Brooks, *The Opal Witch*, p. 130, 1967

sticky book *noun*
a pornographic book or magazine *UK*
• Morty's sat in a kinda armchair arrangement that's been made outta boxes of sticky books and sex aids. — J.J. Connolly, *Layer Cake*, p. 25, 2000

sticky buns; the stickys *noun*
diarrhoea *UK*
Rhyming slang for **THE RUNS**.
• I went to India for a month and had the stickys the whole time I was there. — Bodmin Dark, *Dirty Cockney Rhyming Slang*, 2003

sticky dog *noun*
in cricket, a rain-soaked pitch which the sun is drying *UK, 1933*
• — Keith Foley, *A Dictionary of Cricketing Terminology*, p. 360, 1998

sticky end *noun*
▸ **come to a sticky end**
1 (of a person) to end up in prison, or to die an unpleasant (and unnatural) death; (thus, of an abstract or physical thing) to cease to exist, to be destroyed *UK, 1961*
• A profession which depends for its survival on a profession in direct competition is bound to come to a sticky end. — *The Guardian*, 26th October 1999
• [T]he pistol carries an ancient curse that afflicts all those who covet it. Almost everyone who picks up this gun – from the man who made it many years ago to the evil men who seek it now – will come to a sticky end. — *The Guardian*, 5th March 2001
2 to masturbate *AUSTRALIA, 1984*
A pleasing pun.

sticky end of the stick
the least desirable part *TRINIDAD AND TOBAGO, 1987*
• — Lise Winer, *Dictionary of the English/Creole of Trinidad & Tobago*, 2003

sticky finger *verb*
to shoplift *US*
• Jesus, Mary 'n Joseph, you said all you did was sticky finger something from a store! — Darryl Ponicsan, *The Last Detail*, p. 57, 1970

sticky-fingered *adjective*
inclined to thievery *UK, 1890*
• [W]hat if dear old Gramps was a bit of a sticky-fingered felon in his youth? — Bill Bryson, *In a Sunburned Country*, p. 6, 2001

sticky fingers *noun*
1 an inclination to steal *US, 1939*
• There was nobody to run the Inn and keep the books – that is, nobody without sticky fingers. — Mezz Mezzrow, *Really the Blues*, p. 66, 1946
2 a shoplifter *US*
• — Ralph de Sola, *Crime Dictionary*, p. 44, 1982

sticky-icky *noun*
marijuana *US*
• [Amsterdam] a city where you can window shop for sex and sticky-icky. — *The Source*, p. 154, March 2002

sticky toffee *noun*
coffee *UK*
• — Ronnie Barker, *Fletcher's Book of Rhyming Slang*, 1979

sticky wicket *noun*
1 a tricky or uncertain situation *UK*
From the game of cricket; the ball bounces unpredictably on a pitch that is drying out.
• British Prime Minister Tony Blair, maneuvering his way through the sticky wicket of the Middle East, wanted to stress the need to maintain an international coalition. — *The New York Times Magazine*, 18th November 2001
2 in croquet, a difficult shot *US*
• — James Charlton and William Thompson, *Croquet*, p. 161, 1977: 'Glossary'

stiff *noun*
1 a corpse *US, 1859*
• While he's struggling with a big pine box the end falls out and a stiff slides halfway out, conking him on the skull. — Mezz Mezzrow, *Really the Blues*, p. 316, 1946
• Get this stiff outta here. It's a bring down for my live patients. — William Burroughs, *Naked Lunch*, p. 36, 1957
• The homicide lieutenant said, "Well, let's take a look at the stiffs." — Chester Himes, *The Real Cool Killers*, p. 26, 1959
• Looks more like a morgue to me. Those pool tables are the slabs they lay the stiffs on. — *The Hustler*, 1961
• What about the stiffs in your apartment? — Mickey Spillane, *Me, Hood!*, p. 38, 1963
• A funeral detail. Wolfe is gonna escort a stiff home. — Darryl Ponicsan, *The Last Detail*, p. 178, 1970
• It's a flamin' stiff!!! In his birthday suit too, the dirty bastard!!! — Barry Humphries, *Bazza Pulls It Off!*, 1971
• Cart the stiff in and I'll turn over your daughter. — *Ferris Buehler's Day Off*, 1986
• ALYSSA: Two months before she's going to graduate, he's got this job digging graves, and he comes across ... HOLDEN: A stiff. — *Chasing Amy*, 1997
2 an ordinary person; a person who conforms *US*
• He goes, oh it is going round the sixth form that you two are becoming lesbians, and he said, no, really, he goes I don't believe it but you know that the "stiffs" – straight people – do. — Shane J. Blackman, *Cool Places*, p. 214, 1998
3 in any endeavour, a disappointing, poor performer *US*
• — Bill Shefski, *Running Press Glossary of Football Language*, p. 104, 1978
4 a non-player in a gambling establishment *US*
• — John Scarne, *Scarne's Guide to Modern Poker*, p. 291, 1979
5 a poor tipper *US*
• A stiff is a guy who comes down with a hundred or two hundred, whacks you for $1,000 or $1,500 and won't give you a tip. — Edward Lin, *Big Julie of Vegas*, p. 202, 1974
6 a disagreeable person who is likely to try to cheat *US, 1882*
• You can smell them. The big tippers, the stiffs, the trouble makers. — *Taxi Driver*, 1976
7 a tramp; a hobo *UK, 1899*
• The street is a little too fast, flighty and noisy for the old-time bums and stiffs. — Jack Lait and Lee Mortimer, *Washington Confidential*, p. 32, 1951
8 in an illegal betting operation, a person who has agreed to pose as the head of the operation to protect the actual head in the event of a police raid and arrest *US*
• — *Life*, p. 39, 19th May 1952
9 an unskilled pool player *US*
• — Mike Shamos, *The Illustrated Encyclopedia of Billiards*, p. 231, 1993

10 in horse racing, a horse that is favoured to win but is not ridden in an effort to win *US*
- — Dan Parker, *The ABC of Horse Racing*, p. 149, 1947

11 in pool, the cue ball left with no easy shot *US*
- — Mike Shamos, *The Illustrated Encyclopedia of Billiards*, p. 231, 1993

12 a worthless cheque *US*
- — Hyman E. Goldin et al., *Dictionary of American Underworld Lingo*, p. 211, 1950

13 in the usage of telephone swindlers, a payment by cheque *US*
- — *American Speech*, p. 150–151, May 1959: 'Notes on the cant of the telephone confidence man'

14 a clandestine letter; in prison, a letter smuggled into, out of, or between prisons *UK, 1900*
- — Angela Devlin, *Prison Patter*, p. 110, 1996

15 in blackjack, a card with a value of two, three, four, five or six *US*

Combined with a ten-point card, a card that leaves the player in limbo.
- But suppose you have a stiff – a two-card hand that is more than eleven and less than seventeen[.] — Jimmy Snyder, *Jimmy the Greek*, p. 225, 1975
- — Thomas F. Hughes, *Dealing Casino Blackjack*, p. 75, 1982

▸ **the stiff**

money or correspondence to the benefit of a prisoner passed to a prison warder by a prisoner's friend or relative *US, 1875*
- [A]nd for what is known as "the stiff", the money which his friends, outside, will bung the screws to pay for his snout [cigarettes] and other little creature comforts. — Charles Raven, *Underworld Nights*, p. 52, 1956

stiff *verb*

1 to cheat someone; to rob someone; to refuse to pay someone *US, 1950*
- But if she doesn't turn in a tip for every hat, she loses her job on grounds she swiped the money or she is so stupid or icky that she gets stiffed. — Jack Lait and Lee Mortimer, *Washington Confidential*, p. 282, 1951
- She stayed in the cab, what's she gonna do? But she stiffed me. A real skunk. — *Taxi Driver*, 1976
- We're stiffin' people left an' right an' I'm stiffin' him an' out there I just know there's people about to stiff us. — Nick Barlay, *Curvy Lovebox*, p. 87, 1997
- "How about the guy you clocked [hit]?" "He tried to stiff me.["] — Janet Evanovich, *Seven Up*, p. 94, 2001

2 to extort from someone *UK*
- Every time the old man's on the phone, stiff him for all you can get. I'll bet that's what she's telling them. — Roger Busby, *Garvey's Code*, 1978

3 to kill someone *UK*
- — David Powis, *The Signs of Crime*, 1977

4 to fail miserably *US*
- "So you made it and it stiffed," Tommy said. "So? Make another one." — Elmore Leonard, *Be Cool*, p. 4, 1996

5 (of a male) to have sex *UK*

Used in both the passive and active forms.
- — G.F. Newman, *The Guvnor*, 1977

stiff *adjective*

1 of alcoholic liquor, potent or undiluted *UK, 1813*
- After a visit to the purling men's room and a stiff drink at the bar, I started my return march. — Vladimir Nabokov, *Lolita*, p. 235, 1955

2 drunk *US, 1737*
- I'll talk to you when you're not half stiff. — Jim Thompson, *The Nothing Man*, p. 205, 1954

3 excellent *BERMUDA*
- — Peter Smith and Fred M. Barritt, *Bermewjan Vurds*, 1985

4 frustrated; out of luck *AUSTRALIA, 1917*

From earlier sense as 'broke, penniless', 1898 (*Australian National Dictionary*).
- I jolly near forgot their Easter eggs but I shot down the street and caught the little man who told me that if I'd left it another five minutes I would have been stiff. — Barry Humphries, *A Nice Night's Entertainment*, p. 52, 1961
- 'Bad luck,' says Harry, shaking his head at Bung. I screw my nose up and sneer triumphantly at Bung. 'It just goes to show, you don't have to be dead to be stiff, eh?' — William Nagel, *The Odd Angry Shot*, p. 67, 1975

stiff *adverb*

greatly; used to intensify, especially 'bore' and 'scare' *UK, 1905*

After 'stiff' (dead) hence, here, 'to death'; always after the verb it modifies.
- [H]itting little white balls bores him stiff. — *New York Metro*, 14th December 1998
- I appreciate Eamonn paying me the compliment of scaring me stiff. — Michael Palin, *Sahara*, 2002

stiff!

tough luck! *AUSTRALIA*
- 'Hey, I wanted to hear that,' Snow said. 'Stiff,' Crawley snarled. — Peter Corris, *Pokerface*, p. 102, 1985

stiff-assed; stiff-arsed *adjective*

used of a person who behaves in a superior manner and doesn't mix with others *US, 1937*
- But you're one of those stiff-arsed moralists who see a favor as an opportunity to show their piss-green incorruptibility rather than their gratitude. — Peter Barnes, *Laughter*, 1978
- Sure, and would ye rather I was mealy-mouthed like those stiff-assed ponces from London? — Chet Raymo, *Dork of Cork*, p. 343, 1993

stiff bikkies!

used for expressing a lack of sympathy with a bad turn of events *NEW ZEALAND*
- That is stiff bikkies. — *New Zealand Tablet*, p. 22, 1st July 1992

stiff cheddar!

tough luck! *AUSTRALIA*
- 'They don't like it!' 'Stiff cheddar mate!' — Lance Peters, *The Dirty Half-Mile*, p. 286, 1979

stiff cheese!

tough luck! *AUSTRALIA, 1979*
- Senator Harradine said it was just "stiff cheese" that adults would have to go to bed at midnight after watching a movie because he was only interested in protecting children from violence on television. — *West Australian*, p. 26, 7th November 1992

stiffen the crows!

heavens above! *AUSTRALIA, 1932*
- 'Well...! Stiffen the crows!' he cried. 'What do yer know about that?' — Robert S. Close, *With Hooves of Brass*, p. 77, 1961

stiffen the wombats!

heavens above! *AUSTRALIA*
- Stiffen the wombats, Boss! What lardhead's been selling you that tommy-rot? — Dymphna Cusack, *Picnic Races*, p. 97, 1962

stiff-eye *verb*

to look at someone without establishing eye contact *US*
- They walked in stiff-eying the bartenders and waiters who caught their message and acted as though they never had seen them before. — Malcolm X and Alex Haley, *The Autobiography of Malcolm X*, p. 147, 1964

stiffie *noun*

an erection *NEW ZEALAND, 1995*
- — Harry Orsman, *A Dictionary of Modern New Zealand Slang*, p. 130, 1999

stiff luck *noun*

bad luck *AUSTRALIA, 1919*
- 'Stiff luck.' 'Yes. That was a twelve-hundred-and-fifty-mile patrol, and those prisoners had taken some catching.' — Ion L. Idriess, *Over the Range*, p. 74, 1947

stiff one *noun*

any strong alcoholic drink *UK, 1813*
- Helen dropped her compact back in her purse. "C'mon darling. Let's go pour a stiff one at Jean's." — Armistead Maupin, *Tales of the City*, p. 261, 1978

stiff shit!

tough luck! *AUSTRALIA, 1969*
- — Robert English, *Toxic Kisses*, p. 3, 1979
- Fifty dollars, you say? Well, stiff shit! — Robert English, *Toxic Kisses*, p. 60, 1979
- — Peter Corris, *Pokerface*, p. 149, 1985

stiff-toe gang *noun*

the dead *BAHAMAS*
- — Patricia Clinton-Meicholas, *More Talkin' Bahamian*, p. 93, 1995

stiff turps *noun*

bad luck *AUSTRALIA*
- It was just stiff turps that the base admiral had to come aboard and catch him more than half bonkers [drunk] – when he should've been at sea. — J.E. MacDonnell, *Don't Gimme the Ships*, p. 65, 1960

stiff upper lip *noun*

a personal quality characterised as repressed emotion or quiet courage, and regarded as typically British *US, 1815*

In early use you would 'carry' or 'keep' a stiff upper lip; later use is mainly jocular or derisory. Although widely considered a stereotypical British characteristic, actually of US origin.

- TONY: Don't panic man. This is the RAF. Where's that stiff upper lip? KENNETH: Just above this loose flabby chin. —Ray Galton and Alan Simpson, *Hancock's Half Hour*, 30th December 1956
- [P]ass on the example of perennial cheerfulness or a stiff upper lip in the face of disturbing feelings [.] —Daniel Goleman, *Emotional Intelligence*, p. 76, 1997

stiff with *adjective*

closely packed, densely crowded *UK, 1907*

Hyperbole; originally (from C17) a conventional use of 'stiff'.

- Clara has not been without male suitors ("at times the house was stiff with them")[.] — *The Guardian*, 6th January 2004

stiffy *noun*

1 an erection *UK, 1980*

Also variants 'stiffie' and 'stiff'.

- —Connie Eble (Editor), *UNC-CH Campus Slang*, p. 3, Fall 1991
- I got a stiffy for Miss Channel Lock Pliers there. —*Airheads*, 1994
- Holding the moulding pot upright, bend over and plunge your stiffy into the pot... Concentrate on keeping your stiffy. —Kitty Churchill, *Thinking of England*, p. 176, 1995
- —Judi Sanders, *Da Bomb!*, p. 27, 1997
- TRISTE: only had to touch you and you had a stiffy like GARY: the Blackpool tower? —Patrick Jones, *Unprotected Sex*, p. 210, 1999
- Whatever the problem was to start with, it's now the fear that you can't get a stiffy. —*GQ*, p. 119, July 2001
- In the sixteenth century Constanzo Varolio opined that men got stiffies thanks to "erector muscles"[.] —Richard Herring, *Talking Cock*, p. 156, 2003

2 in snowboarding, a stiff-legged jumping manoeuvre *US*

- —Jim Humes and Sean Wagstaff, *Boarderlands*, p. 224, 1995

3 an engraved invitation card *UK*

Upper-class society use; from the unbending quality of the card and the (stiff) formality of the occasion.

- —Ann Barr and Peter York, *The Official Sloane Ranger Handbook*, p. 159, 1982

4 a computer disc *SOUTH AFRICA, 1993*

From the packaging.

- The Boeing 747–400 has 3 NAV systems computers all of which are updated every 28 days by means of a stiffy disk. — *Sunday Times (South Africa)*, 2nd January 2000

stifle *verb*

to silence yourself *US*

A verb popularised by the Archie Bunker character on the television series *All in the Family*.

- Edith, was I talking too fast, or have you got slow ears? Now stifle! —Eugene Boe (Compiler), *The Wit & Wisdom of Archie Bunker*, p. 20, 1971

still *nickname*

a Falkland Islander *UK*

- When the British soldiers arrived to liberate the islands, they nicknamed the islanders 'Bennies' after Benny, the simple soul on Crossroads. But this caused so much upset that the soldiers were banned from using the term, and instead nicknamed them 'Still' – as in 'Still a Benny'. — *The Guardian Weekly*, 17th March 2002

still game *noun*

a card game held on a regular basis with regular players *US*

- —Robert C. Prus and C.R.D. Sharper, *Road Hustler*, p. 171, 1977: 'Glossary of terms'

stilt person; stilt people *noun*

a celebrity *NEW ZEALAND*

- Journalists worthy of the name have a duty to question the behaviour of stilt people, to notice when things look shonky, and to ask embarrassing questions. — *Sunday Star-Times*, p. C8, 17th August 2003

stilts *noun*

the legs *US*

- —Lou Shelly, *Hepcats Jive Talk Dictionary*, p. 19, 1945

stim *noun*

an empty bottle with a refundable deposit *UK*

- [S]alvaging "stims" – empty bottles from gassy drinks like Coca Cola or Cherryade – and taking them down the choggy shop for a refund of two cents a bottle[.] —Andy McNab (writing of the late 1970s/early 80s), *Immediate Action*, p. 216, 1995

stimey *noun*

ten dollars' worth of drugs *US*

From the synonymous **DIME BAG**; a contraction of 'it's a dimey'.

stimp *noun*

the leg *UK*

- —Paul Baker, *Polari*, p. 190, 2002
- —*Attitude*, p. 60, July 2003: 'Old palare lexicon'

stimp cover *noun*

a nylon stocking *UK*

Based on **STIMP** (the leg).

- —Paul Baker, *Polari*, p. 190, 2002

sting *noun*

1 any crime that achieves its purpose by fraud or deception *US, 1930*

- But when I make that big sting, I'll straighten you / If you'll save me a little on the cotton. —Dennis Wepman et al., *The Life*, p. 78, 1976
- He wanted to talk about the sting we're plotting. —*Jackie Brown*, 1997
- I've always told him it's Tom [jewellery] we're bringing in, always blagged it that it's only a little VAT [value added tax] sting and that but he must know in his heart of hearts that that's bullshit. —Kevin Sampson, *Outlaws*, p. 100, 2001

2 a robbery *US, 1940*

- But it wasn't hard at all; it was the sweetest sting in town. —Clarence Cooper Jr, *The Scene*, p. 32, 1960
- You know why I pulled that sting? —Claude Brown, *Manchild in the Promised Land*, p. 410, 1965
- I entered the barbershop and I took a count on the sting: nine bucks and some change. —A.S. Jackson, *Gentleman Pimp*, p. 12–13, 1973
- "I'll cut New York Willie into the action and cop ten percent of the sting." —Iceberg Slim (Robert Beck), *Airtight Willie and Me*, p. 174, 1979
- Of making a few stings, getting bread together, of Whitey contacting his man and connecting for weight in heroin and of pushing. —Herbert Huncke, *The Evening Sun Turned Crimson*, p. 209, 1980

3 a short, sharp chord played to make or disssolve a sense of suspense *US*

- —Sherman Louis Sergel, *The Language of Show Biz*, p. 210, 1973

sting *verb*

1 to swindle someone; to cheat, to rob someone *UK, 1812*

- To anyone he could buttonhole, he bragged about how he had "stung" this person or "skinned" that one. —Jim Thompson, *Bad Boy*, p. 308, 1953
- I saw him the day after Limpy had stung me in the hallway on 149th Street. —Claude Brown, *Manchild in the Promised Land*, p. 176, 1965
- How the hell did you rip it off, Jan? I ain't taught you how to sting. —Donald Goines, *Daddy Cool*, p. 166, 1974

2 in horse racing, to shock a horse with an electrical device during a race *US*

- —David W. Maurer, *Argot of the Racetrack*, p. 60, 1951

▸ sting between the toes

(from a male perspective) to have sex *AUSTRALIA*

- So if youse tell a potato [woman] youse love her she'll let you sting her between the toes with the old pyjama python-shit! —Barry Humphries, *Bazza Pulls It Off!*, 1971

stinger *noun*

1 a pinched nerve *US*

- This would bring about what is commonly known as a singer, a very innocent-sounding word for a sickeningly painful injury. —Mick Foley, *Mankind*, p. 118, 1999
- In the end, the diagnosis was not as frightening as it could have been – the damage was a pinched nerve (called "a stinger"). —Lou Albano and Berg Sugar, *The Complete Idiot's Guide to Professional Wrestling*, p. 56, 1999

2 the penis *US*

- —Dale Gordon, *The Dominion Sex Dictionary*, p. 153, 1967

3 a high velocity, hollow-nose, expanding bullet *US*

- "Stingers and yellowjackets," Parrish said. "Hyper-velocity, hollow-nose expanders. The guy knew what he was doing." —Elmore Leonard, *Split Images*, p. 97, 1981

4 in poker, a sequence of five cards *US*

Known conventionally as a 'straight'.

- —George Percy, *The Language of Poker*, p. 87, 1988

5 a railway brakeman *US*

- Probably derived from the brakeman's custom of applying his brake club to the feet of a sleeping hobo. —Ramon Adams, *The Language of the Railroader*, p. 147, 1977

6 an improvised heating element consisting of exposed wires attached to a small metal plate, used for heating water *US*

- —James Harris, *A Convict's Dictionary*, p. 39, 1989

7 an illegal vote *US*
Chicago Mayor Richard Daley was given credit for delivering Chicago and the state of Illinois to John Kennedy in the 1960 presidential election through extensive use of 'stingers'. Subsequent research dispelled most of these rumours, but Daley enjoyed the power the stories gave him.
- —Bill Reilly, *Big Al's Official Guide to Chicagoese*, p. 56, 1982

8 a radio antenna *US*
- —Wayne Floyd, *Jason's Authentic Dictionary of CB Slang*, p. 29, 1976

stingo *noun*
strong, illegally manufactured whisky *US*
- It is called corn liquor, white lightning, sugar whiskey, skully cracker, popskull, bush whiskey, stump, stumphole, 'splo, ruckus juice, radiator whiskey, rotgut, sugarhead, block and tackle, wildcat, panther's breath, tiger's sweat, Sweet spirits of cats a-fighting, alley bourbon, city gin, cool water, happy Sally, deep shaft, jump steady, old horsey, stingo, blue John, red eye, pine top, buckeye bark whiskey and see seven stars. —*Star Tribune (Minneapolis)*, p. 19F, 31st January 1999

stingy brim *noun*
a hat with a thin brim *US*
- So I slicked up, put on my new stingy brim and went downstairs and breathed deep. —Hal Ellson, *Duke*, p. 1, 1949

stink *noun*
a commotion; a loud complaint *UK, 1812*
- She called up Jane's mother and made a big stink about it. My mother can make a very big stink about that kind of stuff. —J.D. Salinger, *Catcher in the Rye*, p. 76, 1951

▸ **like stink**
desperately hard, extremely fast, very much, etc *UK, 1929*
- This bike goes like stink and handles like a dream. —*The Guardian*, 10th September 2002

stink *verb*
to be aesthetically or morally offensive *US, 1934*
- Hollywood stinks. —Aubrey Dillon-Malone, *I Was A Fugitive From A Hollywood Trivia Factory [quoting Frank Sinatra]*, p. 132, 1999

stink bomb *noun*
in the used car business, a car that won't sell because of a lingering, nauseating smell *US*
- —Lewis Poteet, *Car & Motorcyle Slang*, p. 189, 1992

stinker *noun*
1 an offensive or despicable person or thing *US, 1911*
- This local is a stinker. Christ, don't you know I know it? —Chester Himes, *If He Hollers Let Him Go*, p. 114, 1945
- Now he knew it: he could still battle, still hold his own and beat hell out of the stinkers that came into the poolroom[.] —Irving Shulman, *The Amboy Dukes*, p. 58, 1947
- I think both of them are stinkers. —Philip Wylie, *Opus 21*, p. 273, 1949
- You little stinker. He's given you everything. —*As Good As It Gets*, 1997

2 a corpse that has begun to decompose and, as a result, smell *US*
- Water cops claimed that floaters somehow smelled even worse than stinkers on dry land. —Joseph Wambaugh, *Floaters*, p. 147, 1996

3 an onion *US*
- —Joseph E. Ragen and Charles Finston, *Inside the World's Toughest Prison*, p. 820, 1962: 'Penitentiary and underworld glossary'

4 a cigar *US, 1907*
So known because of the offensive smell the cigar emits.
- "Here, have a guinea stinker. Special tobacco, cured in Torino." —Richard Farina, *Been Down So Long*, p. 237, 1966
- The two old guys flanking Mazzone – Mustache Petes – had the shirt buttoned to the top but no tie – rumped black suits and puffing on guinea stinkers. —Edwin Torres, *Carlito's Way*, p. 101, 1975

5 in dominoes, a player who forces the next player to draw by cutting him off *US*
- —Dominic Armanino, *Dominoes*, p. 20, 1959

6 a strongly worded letter *UK, 1912*
- [A] real stinker can be sent back to the writer. —Margaret Shepherd, *The Art of the Handwritten Note*, p. 1, 2002

stinkeroo *noun*
a complete failure *US, 1934*
Coined by Damon Runyon.
- [T]his year has beena real whizbang stinkeroo[.] —John Nichols, *The Sterile Cuckoo*, p. 174, 1965
- The Grade Z blick is Daddy O – a music/hot rod/romance stinkeroo. —James Ellroy, *Hollywood Nocturnes*, p. 4, 1994

stinker squad *noun*
a police homicide investigative department *US*
- I thought all the guys that worked the Stinker Squads knew each other. —Joseph Wambaugh, *The Glitter Dome*, p. 53, 1981

stink-eye *noun*
a hateful glare *US*
Hawaiian youth usage.
- Wow, you saw da stink-eye she wen geev me? —Douglas Simonson, *Pidgin to da Max*, 1981

stink-finger *noun*
1 the insertion of a finger or fingers into a woman's vagina *UK, 1903*
- I could see a black ugly stud playing "stink finger" with an angel-faced broad in a booth behind me. —Iceberg Slim (Robert Beck), *Pimp*, p. 105, 1969
- A lot of johns don't wna to do much but stinkfinger. They like to hold me tight, cuddle up and talk. —Charles Winick and Paul Kinsie, *The Lively Commerce*, p. 53, 1971
- —Edith A. Folb, *runnin' down some lines*, p. 256, 1980
- —*Maledicta*, p. 127, Summer/Winter 1982: 'Dyke diction: the language of lesbians'

2 the middle finger *UK*
From the vaginal odour occasioned by the finger's predominant use in sexual foreplay.

stink-finger *verb*
to insert a finger or fingers into a woman's vagina *US*
- Papa, unsuccessfuly trying to stink-finger my first girlfriend, Peppy, in the living room, heard my sister and hid behind the piano[.] —Larry Rivers, *What Did I Do?*, p. 51, 1992

stinking *adjective*
1 disgusting, contemptible *UK, 1961*
In conventional use for centuries, but now considered vulgar.
- Fact is, it's a lousy job and the pay's stinking. —John Peter Jones, *Feather Pluckers*, p. 24, 1964
- You swore to me on your life that no matter what, I didn't have to worry. And that was a rotten, stinking, filthy lie, and you deliberately got pregnant. —*CNN*, 27th February 2003

2 drunk, very drunk *US, 1887*
This sense is recorded earlier than **STINKING DRUNK**.
- —D'Arcy Niland, *Call Me When the Cross Turns Over*, 1958

stinking drunk *adjective*
very drunk *UK, 1926*
A combination of two adjectives with the same sense.
- Like fighting, like sex, like taking a bang?? / Think it's time got stinking drunk —Big Black, *Stinking Drunk*, 1987

stinkingly *adverb*
excessively *UK, 1906*
- [P]roduction is contracted out to un-unionised sweatshops in stinkingly corrupt regimes[.] —*The Guardian*, 23rd January 2000

stinking rich; stinking *adjective*
very wealthy *US*
First recorded as 'stinking' in 1940; with 'rich' in 1945.
- Silicon Valley is around the corner. Here, for every stinking rich 65-year-old there is a stinking rich 35-year-old. —*The Guardian*, 13th April 2003

stinking thinking *noun*
the rationalisation of an addiction as 'not that bad' or as something short of an addiction *US*
Used in twelve-step recovery programmes such as Alcoholics Anonymous.
- —Christopher Cavanaugh, *AA to Z*, p. 167, 1998

stinking with money; stinking with it *adjective*
very wealthy *UK, 1961*
A variation of **STINKING RICH**.
- Stinking with money! —*Daily Exelsior (India)*, 12th June 2002

stinko *noun*
alcohol, especially wine *AUSTRALIA*
- This is a little bottle of stinko to go with it. —D'Arcy Niland, *Call Me When the Cross Turns Over*, 1958

stinko *adjective*
exceedingly drunk *US, 1927*
- stinko paralytico —Evelyn Waugh, *Put Out More Flags*, 1942
- stinko profundo —Terence Rattigan, *While The Sun Shines*, 1943
- Can you make it? Are you stinko? —Raymond Chandler, *The Long Goodbye*, p. 6, 1953

- Papa's hair turned almost white and he got stinko more often and he was a little more stooped. —Iceberg Slim (Robert Beck), *Mama Black Widow*, p. 125, 1969
- She wanted to get stinko tonight. —Sandra Brown, *The Witness*, p. 365, 1996

stinkoed *adjective*

drunk *UK*

A variation of **STINKO**.

- CHARLIE[:] Grub's off everyone – let's get stinkoed. —Harry Enfield, *Harry Enfield and His Humorous Chums*, p. 51, 1997

stinkout *noun*

a prank in which bad-smelling material is put in a room, making it uninhabitable *US*

- —*American Speech*, p. 230, October 1967: 'Some special terms used in a University of Connecticut men's dormitory'

stink pot *noun*

the vagina *US*

- —Edith A. Folb, *runnin' down some lines*, p. 256, 1980

stink stiff *noun*

a badly decomposed and smelly corpse *US*

- "Need a couple of uniforms right away on a stink stiff," the sergeant said. —Thomas Larry Adcock, *Precinct 19*, p. 16, 1984

stinkum *noun*

any bad-smelling substance *US*

- "This is one haircut I ain't charging a thin dime for." "If that's the case put some of your stinkum on it. Whatever you figger will fetch the pretty women." —*The Flim-Flam Man and the Apprentice Grifter*, p. 57, 1972
- You can bet he tried everything – smoke, mud, mastodon fat and stinkums too gross to name. —*Arkansas Democrat-Gazette*, p. F1, 2nd September 1999

stinkweed; stink weed *noun*

marijuana *US, 1950*

- —Richard A. Spears, *The Slang and Jargon of Drugs and Drink*, p. 485, 1986
- —Mike Haskins, *Drugs*, p. 289, 2003

stinky *noun*

1 a promiscuous woman *BERMUDA*

- —Peter Smith and Fred M. Barritt, *Bermewjan Vurds*, 1985

2 a female member of the Royal Air Force *UK*

In Royal Air Force use, 2002.

▸ go stinky

to defecate *US*

- He knows I go stinky when I first get up in the mornings[.] —Beatrice Sparks (writing as 'Anonymous'), *Jay's Journal*, p. 72, 1979

stinky pinky *noun*

1 a finger enriched with the aroma of vagina *US*

- My phone rang. "In Framingham, some boys call themselves the Stinky Pinky Pussy Posse," the caller said. Geeze, what happened to the Boy Scouts? As far as the posse goes, suffice it to say that the boys, students at Framingham High School, like to do things with their hands, and we're not talking about building campfires or lean-tos. —*Boston Globe*, p. 25, 7th April 1993
- —Chris Lewis, *The Dictionary of Playground Slang*, p. 221, 2003

2 a party game based on rhymes *US*

An overworked prostitute is a 'sore whore', excretory humour is 'shit wit', etc.

- Stinky-Pinky: There's a new game going the cocktail route. —*San Francisco Examiner*, p. 21, 19th September 1949
- The "currently raging" game ranged here some ten years ago and is properly called "Stinky Pinky." —*Satruday Review of Literature*, p. 25, 4 February 1950
- —*Maledicta*, p. 66–67, Summer 1977: 'A newly printable game of stink-pink (party rhymes)'

stipe *noun*

a stipendiary steward at a racecourse *AUSTRALIA, 1902*

- 'You know very well jockeys are not allowed to bet, Finlay,' one of the stipes said. —Frank Hardy and Athol George Mulley, *The Needy and the Greedy*, p. 97, 1975

stir *noun*

1 a prison or jail *UK, 1851*

Derives from Romany *stariben*, *steripen* thus Welsh *gispy star* (to be imprisoned), *stardo* (imprisoned).

- I've been in the stir and I've had my miseries, but all in all life's been good to me. —Mezz Mezzrow, *Really the Blues*, p. 3, 1946
- When a guy gets out of stir he goes straight sometimes. —Mickey Spillane, *My Gun is Quick*, p. 21, 1950
- Well, Julie wasn't enjoying the can so much. He didn't know nothing about life in stir. —Rocky Garciano (with Rowland Barber), *Somebody Up There Likes Me*, p. 228, 1955
- Few men, once they get outside, keep to the arrangements they make in stir[.] —Charles Raven, *Underworld Nights*, p. 31, 1956
- Long after the turn of the century, a few trickles supplied pig-tailed Chinamen, despondent prostitutes, ex-cons who had picked up the habit in the stir and a few rich fools who would try anything for a bang. —Lee Mortimer, *Women Confidential*, p. 152, 1960
- The Office, Barlow called it. Home, John Watt called it. The Stir,Clink, Bog, Nick, depending on what you are, and where you come from. —Troy Kennedy Martin, *Z Cars*, p. 21, 1962
- You spent thirteen years in stir on a second-degree murder rap. —Chester Himes, *Come Back Charleston Blue*, p. 123, 1966
- Like being in the hole only there's TV and little stuffed animals with you, a half-breed Indian hit man and a female corrections officer, queen of the cons. Shit, I may as well be in stir. —Elmore Leonard, *Killshot*, p. 165, 1989

2 a party *NEW ZEALAND*

- —David McGill, *David McGill's Complete Kiwi Slang Dictionary*, p. 120, 1998

3 teasing *AUSTRALIA*

- [T]he late Bill Bryan (who loved a bit of a "stir") used to fire them up, with great gusto, and then sit back and enjoy the fun. —*Centralian Advocate*, p. 7, 25th January 1985

▸ do stir

to serve time in prison *UK*

- The only felons who did stir were debtors, who were banged up in South London which take my word for it is punishment enough. —Andrew Nickolds, *Back to Basics*, p. 44, 1994

stir *verb*

1 to have sex *US*

- I ain't stirred the old lady for a couple years, but I swear when I'm with Irma I get the urge like a young stallion[.] —Joseph Wambaugh, *The Blue Knight*, p. 96, 1973

2 to tease someone *AUSTRALIA, 1969*

- Stirring the Doc was a ritual. —Kerry Cue, *Crooks, Chooks and Bloody Ratbags*, p. 193, 1983

▸ stir the porridge

(of a man) to have sex with a woman whose vagina is newly awash with the semen of her previous partner(s), especially if the final man in the line; to have sex with a woman who is in a sexual relationship with another man *AUSTRALIA*

The appearance of mixed ejaculate put the coiner in mind of porridge.

- On festive occasions, such as a surf carnival, a generous girl will "put on a queue" behind the sand dunes for a seemingly unlimited line-up of young men. The boy on the end is said to be "stirring the porridge". —Richard Neville, *Play Power*, p. 82, 1970
- I could tell she wasn't interested in a serious relationship. Plus it's not my style to stir a mate's porridge. —Colin Butts, *A Bus Could Run You Over*, p. 306, 2004

▸ stir the shit

to cause trouble, especially by gossiping or telling tales *UK, 1984*

stir bug *noun*

a prisoner crazed by years of incarceration *US*

- —Hyman E. Goldin et al., *Dictionary of American Underworld Lingo*, p. 213, 1950

stir-crazy *adjective*

deranged by incarceration *US, 1908*

- People are talking about you, say you're stir crazy. They're afraid of you. —Edwin Torres, *After Hours*, p. 284, 1979
- Joe only hoped the remitless heat wasn't driving him stir crazy. —Seth Morgan, *Homeboy*, p. 224, 1990

stir-happy *adjective*

adversely affected by imprisonment *UK*

- —John Gosling, *The Ghost Squad*, 1959

Stirling Moss; stirling *noun*

a thing of little or no value *UK*

Rhyming slang for **TOSS**, formed from the champion racing driver, Stirling Moss (b.1929).

- He don't give a Stirling about anyone but himself. —Ray Puxley, *Cockney Rabbit*, 1992

stirrer *noun*
a teaser; a troublemaker *AUSTRALIA, 1966*
- I see here in my notes a quotation attributed to one John Norton, who, I presume, was an Australian of the Victorian era, and something of a 'stirrer'. — John O'Grady, *It's Your Shout, Mate!*, p. 30, 1972
- — Barry Humphries, *The Traveller's Tool*, p. 42, 1985
- — Robert G. Barrett, *Davo's Little Something*, p. 163, 1992
- Needless to say, after this Cyril was marked out as a trouble-maker and a stirrer. — Herb Wharton, *Cattle Camp*, p. 85, 1994
- — B. Selkie, *Lime Juice*, p. 122, 1995

stirrup *noun*
1 in trucking, any device that provides help for climbing up into the cab *US*
- — Montie Tak, *Truck Talk*, p. 157, 1971

2 on the railways, the lowest step on a freight wagon *US*
- — Norman Carlisle, *The Modern Wonder Book of Trains and Railroading*, p. 268, 1946

stir-simple *adjective*
mentally unstable because of incarceration *US*
- "Aw, shut up, you screwball," Glass said. "You're stir-simple." — Chester Himes, *Cast the First Stone*, p. 49, 1952
- — Troy Harris, *A Booklet of Criminal Argot, Cant and Jargon*, p. 29, 1976

stitch *noun*
a confidence trick, often good-natured rather than criminal *UK*
- It would have gone down as one of the great stitches if only he'd remembered that it had poured with rain the whole weekend. — Andy McNab (writing of the late 1970s/early 80s), *Immediate Action*, p. 186, 1995

stitch and bitch *noun*
the (Canadian) Officer's Wives Club at an air base *CANADA*
- "Ian, how come the upper Mess Bar is closed tomorrow?" "The Stitch and Bitch is having a meeting." — Tom Langeste, *oral citation from Words on the Wing*, p. 264, 1995

stitches *noun*
▸ **in stitches**
in the throes of uproarious laughter *UK, 1935*
Deriving from 'stitch' (a sudden pain in the side).
- They were in stitches in Baghdad last night – just as they have been every night for months. While diplomats argue in New York and troops play war games on their border, nearly a thousand Baghdadis gather each evening at the National Theatre on Al Fatah Square[.] — *The Observer*, 23rd February 2003

stitch queen *noun*
a male homosexual wardrobe assistant *US*
- — Sherman Louis Sergel, *The Language of Show Biz*, p. 210, 1973

stitch that!; stitch this!
said at the moment of physical attack with a knife or similar weapon, usually as the climax to a catchphrase threat such as 'Can your wife do first aid? Stitch that!' or 'Are you any good at sewing? Stitch this!' *UK*
- Can your wife/mum do first aid? We'll get her to stitch this up. — Ray Puxley, *Cockney Rabbit*, 1992
- Can your mother sew – Have her stitch' this. — Flotsam & Jetsam *Pick A Window*, 1995
- — Chumbawamba, *Stitch That! [a song about domestic violence]*, 1997

stitch-up *noun*
an act that unjustly places criminal, financial or moral responsibility on someone else *UK, 1984*
- As stitch-ups go, I've got to hand it to them – they've done me good and proper. — Kevin Sampson, *Clubland*, p. 1, 2002

stitch up *verb*
1 (of the police) to incriminate someone, especially by planting false evidence *UK, 1977*
- — Angela Devlin, *Prison Patter*, p. 110, 1996

2 to deliberately take unfair advantage of someone *UK, 1970*
- — Tom Hibbert, *Rockspeak!*, p. 149, 1983
- You see, we didn't give a fuck and, eventually, we got stitched up for it. — Shaun Ryder, *Shaun Ryder... in His Own Words*, 1993
- Nor will they sting me with peak call charges, or stitch me up for line rental every month[.] — Virgin Mobile *advertising leaflet*, June 2001

stitchy *noun*
in circus and carnival usage, a tailor *US*
- — Don Wilmeth, *The Language of American Popular Entertainment*, p. 258, 1981

stivver *verb*
to stagger *CANADA*
- To "stivver" comes from Cape Sable Island, for "to stagger". — *The Dalhousie Review*, p. 46, 1953

STL *adjective*
said of a hospital patient who is in a persistent vegetative state, who is *s*imilar *t*o *l*ettuce *US*
- — Sally Williams, *"Strong" Words*, p. 159, 1994

St Louis *noun*
in circus and carnival usage, second helpings of food *US*
According to Wilmeth, an allusion to the fact that circus engagements in St Louis played in two sections.
- — Don Wilmeth, *The Language of American Popular Entertainment*, p. 255, 1981

St Louis blues; St Louis *noun*
1 shoes *UK*
Rhyming slang, formed from 'St Louis Blues', a song by William Christopher Handy, published in 1914, and now a jazz classic.
- — Red Daniells, 1980
- — Ray Puxley, *Cockney Rabbit*, 1992

2 news; the news *UK: SCOTLAND, 1985*
Glasgow rhyming slang.
- Bung the telly on till we get the St Louis blues. — Michael Munro, *The Complete Patter*, 1996

St Louis stop *noun*
a rolling stop at a traffic signal or stop sign *US*
- — Jeffrey McQuain, *Never Enough Words*, p. 54, 1999

St Martins-le-Grand; St Martin; Martin-le-Grand; martin *noun*
the hand *UK, 1857*
Rhyming slang.
- — Ray Puxley, *Cockney Rabbit*, 1992

stoat *verb*
(of a bet) to win *UK: SCOTLAND*
- If this line stoats Ah'll get ye a doner kebab. — Michael Munro, *The Patter, Another Blast*, p. 69, 1988

stoat down *verb*
to rain very heavily *UK: SCOTLAND*
Formed on Scots *stot* (to bounce).
- It wisnae takin time to rain – it wis stoatin doon. — Michael Munro, *The Complete Patter*, p. 148, 1996

stoated *adjective*
drunk *UK*
- After the show one member of the audience turned to a friend and said enthusiastically: "Let's go get stoated." Proof that student theatre is alive and well in its purest form. — *The Scotsman*, August 1999
- — Pete Brown, *Man Walks into a Pub*, 2003

stoater *noun*
something excellent; a particularly good-looking person, especially a woman *UK: SCOTLAND, 1911*
- — Tom Hibbert, *Rockspeak!*, p. 149, 1983
- A wee stoater! — Michael Munro, *The Original Patter*, p. 66, 1985
- Stella McQueen therefore had a stoater of an alibi for the night Charles McGinty's house had all its windows shot out[.] — Christopher Brookmyre, *One Fine Day in the Middle of the Night*, p. 19, 1999

stoating *adjective*
excellent *UK: SCOTLAND*
From STOATER (a good thing).
- [T]ake a swatch at our stoating discounts[.] — Ian Pattison, *Rab C. Nesbitt*, 1988

stoat-the-baw; stoater *noun*
a paedophile; a child-molester *UK: SCOTLAND*
From Scots for 'bounce-the-ball', possibly an image of a child's head being patted as if bouncing a ball.
- Leave ma wee brither [brother] alane, ya stupit-lookin stoat-the-baw. — Michael Munro, *The Patter, Another Blast*, p. 69, 1988

stocious; stotious *adjective*
drunk *UK, 1937*
Of Anglo-Irish origins.
- In fact, although we were of course only drinking coloured water, I used to feel absolutely stotious afterwards. — John Miller, *Judi Dench with a Crack in her Voice*, p. 265–266, 1998

- Something new had to be coined to cover getting stocious on Bailey's and giving the new Financial Services Advisor a hand-shandy[.] —Christopher Brookmyre, *The Sacred Art of Stealing*, p. 71, 2002

stock *noun*
the prizes in a carnival midway game concession *US*
- —Gene Sorrows, *All About Carnivals*, p. 27, 1985: 'Terminology'

▸ **throw stock**
to distribute prizes in a carnival game *US*
- —*American Speech*, p. 283, December 1966: 'More carnie talk from the West Coast'

-stock *suffix*
used in combination with an entertainer's name (or part thereof) to create a name for a musical festival *UK*
The second syllable of legendary music festival Woodstock, 1969, is taken to lend quality and scale to a current music event. In August 1992, the group Madness reformed after eight years, and hosted and headlined a weekend-long open-air concert called Madstock in London's Finsbury Park. Officially titled 'Big Beach Boutique', Normstock is, or was, a one-day festival of dance music hosted on Brighton beach by DJ Fatboy Slim, real name: *Norm*an Cook. When the crowds in attendance proved to be greater than the authorities expected the parallel to Woodstock was drawn.
- We're gutted. Normstock III is off. What went wrong? —*Mixmag*, p. 16, April 2003

stockbroker's Tudor; stockbroker Tudor *noun*
faux-Tudor architecture *UK, 1938*
- And this house, stockbroker Tudor, if he had not seen it, he knew its kind. —Maureen Howard, *Natural History*, p. 25, 1993

stockholder *noun*
on the railways, any employee who appears to be more concerned about the company than his fellow workers *US*
- Probably derived from the brakeman's custom of applying his brake club to the feet of a sleeping hobo. —Ramon Adams, *The Language of the Railroader*, p. 147, 1977

stockings *noun*
female legs *US*
- —Hermese E. Roberts, *The Third Ear*, 1971

stocking stuffer *noun*
1 in poker, money bet by a player who has withdrawn from the hand *US*
- —John Vorhaus, *The Big Book of Poker Slang*, p. 34, 1996

2 cash *US*
- Candy, markers, ammo, liners, stocking stuffer, sweetener, garnish, and pledges are all terms for cash. —Henry Hill and Byron Schreckengost, *A Good Fella's Guide to New York*, p. 123, 2003

stocks and bonds
a slogan used by prostitutes to advertise bondage services *UK*
A punning euphemism.
- Instead of soliciting passing males, the hookers of London remained out of sight, if not out of mind, advertising their services on discreetly euphemistic postcards in the windows of local newsagents. "French Lessons", "Large Chest for Sale", "Stocks and Bonds". —Mick Farren (recalling London in the late 1960s), *Give the Anarchist a Cigarette*, p. 10, 2001

stocks and shares *noun*
stairs *UK*
Rhyming slang.
- —Ray Puxley, *Cockney Rabbit*, 1992

stocky *noun*
a habitual user of cocaine *UK*
Recorded as 'cokehead' by a Jamaican inmate in a UK prison.

stogie *noun*
1 a cigar *US, 1873*
- Mandon reached in to take out some stogies[.] —Horace McCoy, *Kiss Tomorrow Good-bye*, p. 185, 1948
- "Sue me," he said, taking a good pull on the stogie. —George Mandel, *Flee the Angry Strangers*, p. 96, 1952
- There, after each of us had a mighty sip of toddy and I had been allowed a few puffs from his Pittsburgh stogie, he delivered himself of a lecture. —Jim Thompson, *Bad Boy*, p. 300, 1953
- In his mouth was a twisted stogie; in his hand was the newspaper of the White Citizens Council. —Max Shulman, *Anyone Got a Match?*, p. 208, 1964

2 an extra-large marijuana cigarette *US*
Derives ultimately from Conestoga, a town in Pennsylvania, and the name given to a horse-drawn freight wagon originating in that region in the C18. Conestoga (the town and the wagon) abbreviated to 'Stogy'; 'Stogy drivers', apparently, smoked a coarse cigar which became known as a 'stogie', and by the late C19 a 'stogie' was a generic cheap or roughly made cigar.
- —Edith A. Folb, *runnin' down some lines*, p. 256, 1980
- One matchbox of pot for five bucks, and man, you were really hold; you had a lot of marijuana! We used to roll them in brown paper, three or four of us smoking these stogies as we made our way down the street. —Ralph "Sonny" Barger, *Hell's Angel*, p. 21, 2000

3 a cigarette *US*
- —Lois Stavsky et al., *A2Z*, p. 97, 1995

stokaboka *adjective*
extremely enthusiastic *US*
- —Trevor Cralle et al., *The Surfin'ary*, p. 123, 1991

stoke *verb*
(from a male perspective) to have sex *UK*
Coined for the pun illustrated in the following citation.
- [S]ome old boiler he's been stoking for a couple or three weeks. —Danny King, *The Burglar Diaries*, p. 179, 2001

▸ **stoke the boiler**
in a swindle operated by telephone, to telephone a prospective victim *US*
- —Kathleen Odean, *High Steppers, Fallen Angels, and Lollipops*, p. 132, 1988

stoked *adjective*
1 excited *US*
A major word of the surf lexicon, it was the title and only word in the lyric of a 1963 Beach Boys song written by Brian Wilson.
- —*Paradise of the Pacific*, p. 27, October 1963
- —John Severson, *Modern Surfing Around the World*, p. 182, 1964
- The whole drag racing world was stoked when Don Garlits turned the first officially-timed 200 mph run. —John Lawlor, *How to Talk Car*, p. 101, 1965
- —Miss Cone, *The Slang Dictionary (Hawthorne High School)*, 1965
- —*Time*, p. 57, 1 January 1965
- —Connie Eble (Editor), *UNC-CH Campus Slang*, November 1976
- The band were superb. The Paradise, packed to melting-point with hundreds of stoked Bostonians, took to the Grams from the moment they strolled on stage. —Kevin Sampson, *Powder*, p. 361, 1999
- I'm just fucking stoked I don't have to pay him! —*South Park*, 1999
- [W]e've got a radical future in front of us. I'm so stoked —Me First and the Gimmes Gimmes, *End of the Road*, 2003

2 drug-intoxicated *US*
- As usual Wilson was wrapped safeloy behind his Carrera sunglasses and, as usual, he was stoked to the gills, having scored some prior Jamaican herb off a busboy at the hotel. —Carl Hiaasen, *Tourist Season*, p. 169, 1986

3 drunk *US*
- —J. R. Friss, *A Dictionary of Teenage Slang (Mt. Diablo High)*, 1964

Stoke-on-Trent *adjective*
homosexual *UK*
Rhyming slang for **BENT**, formed from the Staffordshire town.
- —Ray Puxley, *Cockney Rabbit*, 1992
- —Bodmin Dark, *Dirty Cockney Rhyming Slang*, 2003

stoker *noun*
a wave that excites surfers *US*
- —Gary Fairmont R. Filosa II, *The Surfer's Almanac*, p. 182, 1977

Stokey *noun*
Stoke Newington, in north London *UK: ENGLAND*
- The natives have not gone native in Stokey. —John Milne, *Alive and Kicking*, p. 15, 1998

Stolly; Stoli; Stoly *nickname*
*Stoli*chnaya™ vodka *UK, 1998*
- Ab Fab [television comedy Absolutely Fabulous] made the Bolly-Stolly combo famous[.] —*Sky Magazine*, 88 May 2001
- [T]here will be no need to change the labels on bottles of Stolly, a favourite tipple of communist and capitalist leaders alike. —*The Guardian*, 31st July 2003

stomach *noun*
▸ **stomach thinks your throat has been cut**
to be extremely hungry *AUSTRALIA, 1950*

• During that time Jesus didn't have a bite to eat, and by the end his stomach thought his throat had been cut. —Kel Richards, *The Aussie Bible*, p. 22, 2003

stomach Steinway *noun*
the accordion *US*
• A man gyrating with an accordion – pumping his "Stomach Steinway" for all it's worth. —James Ellroy, *Hollywood Nocturnes*, p. 3, 1994
• Some lovers of what Mark Twain dubbed "the stomach Steinway" stubbornly insist it was always stylish so it can't make a comeback. — *The Star-Ledger*, 7th February 1999

stomp *verb*
in computing, to mistakenly overwrite something *US*
• —Eric S. Raymond, *The New Hacker's Dictionary*, p. 335, 1991

stomp-down *adjective*
excellent, admirable *US*
• I'm talking about a stomp-down sophisticated thoroughbred whore like my woman. —Nathan Heard, *Howard Street*, p. 142, 1968
• She was a stomp-down mud-kicker with kelsey hair / A jive-ass bitch but her face was fair. —Dennis Wepman et al., *The Life*, p. 147, 1976

stomper *noun*
1 an aggressive, 'mannish' lesbian *US*
• Known variously as a bull, a stomper, a bad butch, a hard dresser, a truck driver, a diesel dyke, a bull dagger and a half dozen other soubriquets, she is the one who, according to most homosexual girls, gives lesbians a bad name. —Ruth Allison, *Lesbianism*, p. 125, 1967
2 the foot; a shoe, especially a heavy shoe *US*
Also used in the variant 'stomp'.
• I started livin and usin drugs and buyin clothes, strides and stomps that'd set you back a whole month's pay! —Clarence Cooper Jr, *The Scene*, p. 137, 1960
• —Janey Ironside, *A Fashion Alphabet*, p. 134, 1968
• Sucker, first booty 'butt' you don't transport no 'hard' [drugs] in your 'stomp,' keep it in your mitt [hand] so you can down [throw] it fast to the turf. —Iceberg Slim (Robert Beck), *Pimp*, p. 64, 1969
• —David Claerbaut, *Black Jargon in White America*, p. 81, 1972

stompie *noun*
a cigarette butt, especially one saved for smoking later *SOUTH AFRICA, 1947*
• When we heard the news, everybody who had a stompie smoked it, and the warders could not stop the people singing in the night. —Bryce Courtenay, *Power of One*, p. 263, 1989

stomping *noun*
an attack, especially by kicking *UK*
• [He] has a big opinion of himself; he is just about due for a stomping[.] —Alex Stuart, *The Bikers*, 1971

stomp pad *noun*
on a snowboard, the pad between the bindings *US*
• —Doug Werner, *Snowboarders Start-Up*, p. 114, 1993: 'Glossary'

stomps *noun*
shoes *US*
• —Clarence Major, *Dictionary of Afro-American Slang*, p. 109, 1970

stone *noun*
1 a diamond or other precious stone *SOUTH AFRICA, 1884*
• The safe contained a dozen small sacks of stones and maybe a dozen trays. —Red Rudensky, *The Gonif*, p. 82, 1970
• EDDIE: You two take a car each, I'll follow ya. You ditch it, I'll pick you up, then we'll pick up the stones. — *Reservoir Dogs*, 1992
2 an Opel car *UK*
Citizens' band radio slang; pun on 'opal'.
• —Peter Chippindale, *The British CB Book*, p. 161, 1981
3 crack cocaine; a piece of crack cocaine *UK*
A recurring rock metaphor.
• —Angela Devlin, *Prison Patter*, p. 110, 1996
• Crack is also known as PEBBLES, SCUD, WASH, STONE and ROCK[.] —Macfarlane, Macfarlane and Robson, *The User*, p. 112, 1996
• [S]he looked pretty good, turning herself on with that stone. —Lanre Fehintola, *Charlie Says...*, p. 33, 2000
• —Nick Constable, *This is Cocaine*, p. 182, 2002
• —Mike Haskins, *Drugs*, p. 282, 2003
• We got Rocks, we got Bones, we got Brown, we got Stones. —Julian Johnson, *Urban Survival*, p. 170, 2003
4 a state of drug intoxication *US*
• When we got to the concert, I had a strong stone on. —Stephen Gaskin, *Amazing Dope Tales*, p. 155, 1980
5 a billiard ball *US*
• —Steve Rushin, *Pool Cool*, p. 28, 1990
6 in motorcyle racing, a very slow racer *US*
• —John Lawlor, *How to Talk Car*, p. 101, 1965
7 in the usage of youthful model road racers (slot car racers), a slow car *US*
• — Phantom Surfers, *The Exciting Sounds of Model Road Racing (Album cover)*, 1997

stone *verb*
1 to render a drug user intoxicated, especially of marijuana *US, 1952*
2 by extension, to amaze or impress someone *US*
• Allen and I have worked out the pygmy singing & drumbeat that will stone you. —Jack Kerouac, *Letter to Neal Cassady*, p. 238–239, 3rd December 1950

stone *adverb*
completely, utterly *UK, 1928*
• His Lordship and her Ladyship were stone rich and loaded with tomfoolery [jewellery] of all sorts. —Charles Raven, *Underworld Nights*, p. 11, 1956
• If you don't watch it, Monty, he said to himself, you'll be stone blind raving paralytic drunk. —Derek Bickerton, *Payroll*, p. 120, 1959
• Back in New York, stone broke and without any means of support[.] —Malcolm X and Alex Haley, *The Autobiography of Malcolm X*, p. 79–80, 1964
• Stone free to do what I please / Stone free to ride the breeze / Stone free, baby I can't stay. —Jimi Hendrix, *Stone Free*, 1967
• Pathetic ass motherfucker trying to act like he some stone gigolo. —Cecil Brown, *The Life & Loves of Mr. Jiveass Nigger*, p. 148, 1969
• Every black performer will tell you that the Apollo is a stone workhouse. —Albert Goldman, *Freak Show*, p. 60, 1969
• Sometime a group of buddies who ran together, who were "stone pimp," as the phrase went, would move straight into the poverty program. —Tom Wolfe, *Radical Chic & Mau-Mauing the Flak Catchers*, p. 132, 1970
• That de Silva is a stone hood. I ain't taking no chances. —Oscar Zeta Acosta, *The Revolt of the Cockroach People*, p. 115, 1973
• I had me a fabulous Jewish chick name of Honey, a stone freak. —Edwin Torres, *Carlito's Way*, p. 31, 1975
• I'm gonna fix it up and paint it 'til I make it stone cherry wheels. —Iceberg Slim (Robert Beck), *Doom Fox*, p. 97, 1978
• Speaking of other dude's ladyfriends, one of the grooviest and best of the bunch was a stone to the bone sister named Althea. —Odie Hawkins, *Black Casanova*, p. 81, 1984
• Nor do people think that folks want to hear what a stone bore (and we do mean stone, James) sitting bunker guard could be. —Larry Heinemann, *Paco's Story*, p. 9, 1986
• He was a marvelous guy, a stone thief. —Herbert Huncke, *Guilty of Everything*, p. 76, 1990
• It's a stone bloody miracle there's no-one dead. —Ian Drury, *Itinerant Child*, 1998

Stone Age *noun*
in computing, the years from 1943 until the mid-1950s *US*
• —Eric S. Raymond, *The New Hacker's Dictionary*, p. 335, 1991

stonebonker *noun*
in horse racing, a horse sure to win a race *AUSTRALIA*
Popularised by radio race caller Cliff Caller, a fixture in Australia beginning in the mid-1960s.
• —Ned Wallish, *The Truth Dictionary of Racing Slang*, p. 78, 1989

stone-broke *adjective*
▷ **see:** STONY-BROKE

stoned *adjective*
1 intoxicated on a drug, usually marijuana *US*
• To get high again, completely stoned. —Hal Ellson, *The Golden Spike*, p. 60, 1952
• With each week of work, bombed and sapped and charged and stoned with lush, with pot, with benny[.] —Norman Mailer, *Advertisements for Myself*, p. 243, 1955
• "Boy, you're stoned," he said to Bobby. —James Mills, *The Panic in Needle Park*, p. 29, 1966
• Grass is a little less common than cigarettes. When someone says "stoned," he doesn't mean drunk. —James Simon Kunen, *The Strawberry Statement*, p. 171, 1968
• So Laura came to Petrarch's party, to put it stylishly, and got stoned out of her head. —Gore Vidal, *Myra Breckinridge*, p. 59, 1968
• Once or twice a few had fallen in with pot or tea as it was called then and I picked up for the first time one morning and got so stoned I was unable to move. —Herbert Huncke, *The Evening Sun Turned Crimson*, p. 28–29, 1980
2 very drunk *US, 1952*
• I had finished the wine while Terry slept, and I was proper stoned. —Jack Kerouac, *On the Road*, p. 90, 1957

3 exhilarated, unrelated to drugs *US*
- Their ignorance kept me permanently stoned. —Jamie Mandelkau, *Buttons*, p. 82, 1971

stoned out *adjective*
in a state of drug intoxication *US*
An elaboration of **STONED**.
- He must be home, but like stoned out; you know? —George Mandel, *Flee the Angry Strangers*, p. 67, 1952
- You stoned out motherfucking hippie piece of shit! —Stuart Browne, *Dangerous Parking*, p. 85, 2000

stoned out of your playpen *adjective*
highly drug-intoxicated *UK*
- If the army ever found out that I'd been stoned out of my playpen [...] that wasn't likely to go down too well either. —Ken Lukowiak, *Marijuana Time*, p. 177, 2000

stone ginger *adjective*
absolutely certain *NEW ZEALAND, 1936*
From the name of a horse that won virtually every race it ran.
- CARTER: It was all there, I tell you. Stone ginger. REGAN: George, they were scrubbers. Slags. — *The Sweeney*, 29th September 1978

stonehead *noun*
a regular user of marijuana *UK*
A combination of **STONED** (drug-intoxicated) and **HEAD** (a user).
- [W]e're more disorganized than most people because we are all stoneheads[.] —Brian Preston, *Pot Planet*, p. 129, 2002

stone John *noun*
a jail or prison *US*
- —Joseph E. Ragen and Charles Finston, *Inside the World's Toughest Prison*, p. 820, 1962: 'Penitentiary and underworld glossary'

stone jug *noun*
a gullible fool; an easy dupe *UK*
Rhyming slang for 'mug'.
- —Ray Puxley, *Fresh Rabbit*, 1998

stone me!
used for registering surprise or exasperation *UK*
Execution by stoning was current in biblical times, which lends this innocent expletive a mildly blasphemous feel; the inspiration, however, could just as likely be **STONES** (testicles). However obscene the original intention, from the mid-1950s its popularity (and innocence) was spread by comedian Tony Hancock (1924–68) and the BBC.
- Stone me, isn't it marvellous! —Ray Galton and Alan Simpson, *Hancock's Half Hour*, 23rd March 1958
- Gawd [God] stone me! What's the matter now? —Clive Exton, *No Fixed Abode [Six Granada Plays]*, p. 118, 1959
- And stone me, has my Jennifer got a good right hand or what? —Dave Courtney, *Dodgy Dave's Little Black Book*, p. 158, 2001

stone motherless *adjective*
in horse racing, used for describing a horse running a distant last *AUSTRALIA*
- —Ned Wallish, *The Truth Dictionary of Racing Slang*, p. 78, 1989

stoner *noun*
a regular or habitual user of marijuana; a drug user *US*
- Could I get some stoners over here please! — *Heathers*, 1988
- I couldn't tell if he was a drinker, a stoner or a straight. —Howard Marks, *Mr Nice*, p. 1, 1997
- What was that thing the little stoner pulled on the villain in the last issue? — *Chasing Amy*, 1997
- God, what a little stoner. You look so different with long hair. —Kenneth Lonergan, *This is Our Youth*, p. 63, 2000
- "You look like a stoner." "Well, yeah, but that's because you know me." —Janet Evanovich, *Seven Up*, p. 73, 2001
- Hey, can't we do something about those two stoners hanging around outside all the time? —Kevin Smith, *Jay and Silent Bob Strike Back*, p. 10, 2001
- [Y]our average British stoner in the early 90s was a sleepy-eyed student. — *Sky Magazine*, p. 8, July 2001
- I was the West Coast stoner dude. —Brian Preston, *Pot Planet*, p. 1, 2002

stoner moment *noun*
a short interval in which a marijuana user succumbs to a mental or physical lack of energy or consistency *UK*
After **SENIOR MOMENT**.
- —Steven Wishnia, *The Cannabis Companion*, p. 153, 2004

stones *noun*

1 the testicles *UK, 1154*
- They could have heard you squealing over in Cunt Lick County, just a squealing like a stoat with his stones cut off. —William Burroughs, *Naked Lunch*, p. 173, 1957
- Did you see fuckin Monk wade into it? Man has got some hard stones on him! —John Sayles, *Union Dues*, p. 341, 1977
- —Lise Winer, *Dictionary of the English/Creole of Trinidad & Tobago*, 2003

2 courage *US*
From 'stones' as 'testicles' and 'testicles' as 'courage'.
- One caper I've had on the drawing board only I didn't have the stones. —Seth Morgan, *Homeboy*, p. 55, 1990

3 crack cocaine *US*
- —US Department of Justice, *Street Terms*, October 1994
- But the drug of choice now was crack cocaine. Coke. Rock. White. Stones. Charlie. —Lanre Fehintola, *Charlie Says*, p. 129, 2000

4 dominoes *US*
- —Dominic Armanino, *Dominoes*, p. 16, 1959

stone the crows! *verb*
heavens above! *AUSTRALIA, 1927*
- Stone the crows! No wonder he was gettin' fifteen quid a week! —Bill Wannan, *Bullockies, Beauts and Bandicoots*, p. 50, 1960
- 'Stone the crows!' Ossie Gentle reported to Mick, 'you ought ter see him hit the roof!' —Dymphna Cusack, *Picnic Races*, p. 94, 1962
- Stone the crows! That's highway robbery – that's nearly fifty notes where I come from – if I wasn't bustin' to splash the boots I'd do this Pom over – so help me! —Barry Humphries, *The Wonderful World of Barry McKenzie*, p. 3, 1968
- Stone the crows! Look I'm on the verge of doing a little deal with this sheila meself. Couldn't I see you later? — *The Adventures of Barry McKenzie*, 1972
- But, stone the crows, why would the mum of my Big Boss, my Lord, come and see me? —Kel Richards, *The Aussie Bible*, p. 10, 2003

Stonewall Jackson *noun*
used as a soubriquet for an extremely frugal person *US*
Thomas 'Stonewall' Jackson was a general in the Confederate Army, killed by 'friendly fire' in 1863.
- —Frank Garcia, *Marked Cards and Loaded Dice*, p. 264, 1962

stone work *noun*
a jewellery robbery *US*
- —Vincent J. Monteleone, *Criminal Slang*, p. 227, 1949

stoney *adjective*
of drugs, capable of causing intoxication *UK*
From **STONED** (drug-intoxicated). Also known as 'stoney weed'.
- —Mike Haskins, *Drugs*, p. 289, 2003

stoney weed *noun*
marijuana *UK*
A combination of **STONEY** (capable of intoxicating) and conventional 'weed' or 'weed' as marijuana.
- —Mike Haskins, *Drugs*, p. 289, 2003

stonker *noun*

1 anything impressive in its field *UK*
- —Elizabeth Knowles, *Oxford Dictionary of New Words*, 1997
- I've just seen Garcia's goal for Liverpool against Jave – I have to tell you it was an absolute stonker! — *The Guardian*, 5th April 2005

2 the erect penis *UK*
A personal specialisation of something impressive.
- Harry would be on the bed with a stonker, watching Lesley entertain Colin the candle. —Garry Bushell, *The Face*, p. 167, 2001

stonker *verb*

1 to make someone drunk *AUSTRALIA*
- And all that because of stinkin' luck in miscalculating the stonkering effects of beer while being stonkered by it. —Norman Lindsay, *Halfway to Anywhere*, p. 203, 1947

2 to bring a halt to someone or something; to thwart, overcome or stop something *AUSTRALIA*
- He stammered that it wasn't the usual thing and I said it's not the usual thing for a trainee to be bitten by the Kolonel's dog, either, and I want to have a copy in case of any developments. That stonkered them. —Dymphna Cusack, *Black Lightning*, p. 86, 1964

stonkered *adjective*

1 drunk *AUSTRALIA, 1918*

- STONKERED – To be very drunk. —Gilbert H. Lawson, *A Dictionary of Australian Words and Terms*, 1924
- Are you on for getting properly stonkered on beer or are you not? —Norman Lindsay, *Halfway to Anywhere*, p. 180, 1947
- However, everyone was full up to dolly's wax and I was absolutely stonkered[.] —Barry Humphries, *A Nice Night's Entertainment*, p. 85, 1965

2 very tired *NEW ZEALAND*

- —Louis S. Leland, *A Personal Kiwi-Yankee Dictionary*, p. 97, 1984

stonking *adjective*

1 excellent, great; used generally to add positive emphasis to adjectives of size or quality *UK, 1980*

- Ed Wallis, Powergen group chief executive, hailed the transaction, concluded in only seven days, as "a stonking good deal" but rebutted suggestions Powergen had paid a "stonking good" price. —*The Guardian*, 22nd October 2002

2 drunk *UK*

After the previous sense.

- —*e-cyclopaedia*, 20th March 2002

stonk-on *noun*

the erect penis *UK*

- [W]e really have to understand what goes in to making a successful stonk-on. —Richard Herring, *Talking Cock*, p. 156, 2003

stony *adjective*

1 without money *UK, 1886*

A shortened form of **STONY-BROKE**.

- But it was always his lousy luck to be stony when he got a real tip. —James T. Farrell, *Saturday Night*, p. 9, 1947
- —Edd Byrnes, *Way Out with Kookie*, 1959

2 used of a golf ball, extremely close to the hole, such that the making of the putt is a foregone conclusion *US*

From the more conventional but still slangy 'stone dead'.

- —Dawson Taylor, *How to Talk Golf*, p. 63, 1985

stony-broke; stone-broke *adjective*

without money *UK, 1886*

- [T]he BBC Young Playwright of the Year [Pearse Elliott] is on the dole and "stony broke"[.] —*The Guardian*, 4th March 1999

stony lonesome *noun*

prison *US*

- My shit was syrup and I ain't scared to say it. I don't wanna go to stony lonesome, not down in this fuckin country. —Joseph Wambaugh, *Finnegan's Week*, p. 51, 1993

stooge *noun*

1 a performer whose role in an entertainment is as the butt of a leading character's jokes, or straight man or feed *US, 1913*

- [T]he butt of a comic turn is a "stooge"[.] —Butch Reynolds, *Broken Hearted Clown*, p. 32, 1953
- The late Monsewer Eddie Gray, in drag as a gypsy clairvoyant, used to invite questions from the audience... more accurately, planted Moulin Rouges – stooges[.] —Red Daniells, 1980

2 a person in a subservient position *UK, 1937*

- The corporate stooges who nobble serious science[.] —*The Guardian*, 24th February 2004

3 a petty criminal who confesses falsely to a crime committed by a more powerful villain and takes the rap for him *UK*

- —*The Official Encyclopaedia of New Scotland Yard*, 1999

stooge *verb*

to act as someone's lackey *US, 1939*

- You ain't plannin' to stooge, is you? —Nathan Heard, *Howard Street*, p. 139, 1968

stookie *noun*

a stiffly formal person; a fool; a stupid person *UK: SCOTLAND, 1911*

Extends from **STOOKY** (a plastercast).

- Get it yourself ya stookie. —Ian Original Pattison, *Rab C. Nesbitt*, 1988

stooky *noun*

a plastercast on a broken arm or leg *UK: SCOTLAND*

From 'stucco' (a type of plaster).

- —Michael Munro, *The Original Patter*, p. 66, 1985

stool *noun*

a police informer *US, 1906*

A shortened version of **STOOL PIGEON**.

- He protested that he couldn't be a stool. —William J. Spillard and Pence James, *Needle in a Haystack*, p. 39, 1945
- Then we'll cut the word loose on the street Carlito is a stool. —Edwin Torres, *Carlito's Way*, p. 122, 1975

stool *verb*

to inform on *US, 1911*

- If the other rats in this business would let me alone and quit stoolin' to the cops I'd get along. —William J. Spillard and Pence James, *Needle in a Haystack*, p. 192, 1945
- She's that nun who stools for them two darky dicks, ain't she? —Chester Himes, *A Rage in Harlem*, p. 150, 1957
- Here's a rat who stooled on his former policy racketeer bosses. —Chester Himes, *Cotton Comes to Harlem*, p. 15, 1965
- [A]lmost every day in New York City a junkie dies of an overdose, some sold intentionally by pushers who think the addict has been "stooling" to detectives. —James Mills, *The Panic in Needle Park*, p. 39, 1966
- That's the problem. Nobody wants to stool on a brother officer. —Edwin Torres, *Q & A*, p. 138, 1977

stoolie; stooly *noun*

a police informer *US, 1924*

A shortened form of **STOOL PIGEON**.

- Well, it seems that one day some stoolie tipped off the cops that Lil was selling hop in her place[.] —Mezz Mezzrow, *Really the Blues*, p. 249, 1946
- A stoolie got word to me that Mamie Rezik might know something about the missing blonde. —*Rogue for Men*, p. 45, June 1956
- We let you operate because you're a stooly, and that's all. —Chester Himes, *A Rage in Harlem*, p. 74, 1957
- "First guess is that you're figuring a fix for me to turn stoolie," I said. —Mickey Spillane, *Me, Hood!*, p. 12, 1963
- [W]hen Willie finishes his ten year stretch, he'll have to take another city for it, as he is a marked man as a "stoolie" and to come back would mean certain death[.] —Babs Gonzales, *I Paid My Dues*, p. 102, 1967
- With the spics, if a stoolie moves from 111th Street to the Bronx he's out of the jurisdiction[.] —Edwin Torres, *Carlito's Way*, p. 44, 1975
- Collucci said, "Pretend I'm the secret Grand Jury, stoolie cock-sucker!" —Iceberg Slim (Robert Beck), *Death Wish*, p. 213–214, 1977

stool magnet *noun*

a person with bad luck *US*

- —Sally Williams, *"Strong" Words*, p. 161, 1994

stool pigeon *noun*

a police informer *US, 1906*

- Commonly known as stool pigeons in the underworld, these men whom nobody is supposed to like are a narcotic agent's right arm in many instances. —William J. Spillard and Pence James, *Needle in a Haystack*, p. 141, 1945
- I heard that at one time he had been a stool pigeon, but at the time I knew him he was generally considered right. —William Burroughs, *Junkie*, p. 42, 1953
- "I haven't turned stool pigeon." Actually, although I pretended that it was the furthest thing from my thoughts, I was a little worried. There had been rumors of the FBI putting the pressure on him[.] —Clancy Sigal, *Going Away*, p. 265, 1961
- 'Cept that by that time all the heavy people knew it was coming off – yeah, stool pigeons fly in both directions. —Edwin Torres, *Carlito's Way*, p. 26, 1975
- You'll be the lowest sort of rat, the prince of snitches, the loudest cooing stool pigeon that ever grabbed his ankles for the man. —*The Usual Suspects*, 1995
- That is why most editions of Erskine May, the parliamentary rule book, contain a long list of unparliamentary phrases. They include murderer, swine, liar (of course), stool pigeon, guttersnipe, cad, Pecksniffian cant and – you've guessed it – dirty dog. —*The Guardian*, 5th October 2001

stoop *noun*

▷ **see: STUPE**

stoop *adjective*

used of work, usually agricultural, requiring the worker to bend at the waist to work near the ground *US*

- I told him how we'd drifted over into Arkansas, picking cotton, and then down into the Rio Grande Valley for the fruit, and then over into the Imperial for the stoop crops. —Jim Thompson, *Savage Night*, p. 25, 1953
- [W]ho now pay other, less-smart hillbillies to supervise the work of Mexican braceros, whose natural fitness for stoop labor has been explained by the ubiqituous Senator Murphy[.] —Hunter S. Thompson, *Hell's Angels*, p. 14, 1966
- In Georgia, when he got the six-to-eight for intent to rob and kidnap, he did three and a half at Reidsville, most of it stoop labor, all day in the pea fields with them. —Elmore Leonard, *Killshot*, p. 20, 1989

stooper *noun*
in horse racing, a bettor who examines discarded tickets on the ground in the hope of finding a winning bet *US*
- —Dan Parker, *The ABC of Horse Racing*, p. 149, 1947

stoosh *adjective*
pretentious *JAMAICA*
- —Peter Patrick, *Some Recent Jamaican Creole Words*, 2003

stooshie; stushie; stushy *noun*
an uproar *UK: SCOTLAND*
Scottish dialect *stushie*.
- The stooshie was over the fact that the Scottish Secretary had been the one who signed on the dotted line[.] —Christopher Brookmyre, *Boiling a Frog*, p. 28, 2000

stop *noun*
sufficient marijuana for a single joint or pipe; hence, marijuana *SOUTH AFRICA, 1949*
- —Penny Silva, *A Dictionary of South African English*, 1996

stop-and-go *noun*
1 a traffic signal *US*
Michigan Upper Peninsula Usage.
2 the toe *UK*
Rhyming slang. Can be shortened to 'stop'.
- —Ray Puxley, *Cockney Rabbit*, 1992

stop and start *noun*
the heart *UK*
Rhyming slang.
- —Ray Puxley, *Cockney Rabbit*, 1992

stop-at-a-winner *noun*
in gambling, a conditional bet: an instruction to the bookmaker to halt a series of bets when a winning result is recorded *UK*
- Each-way stop-at-a-winner bets continue until one of the selections either occupies or dead-heats for first place. —David Bennet, *Know Your Bets*, p. 26, 2001

stop gun *noun*
on the railways, a torpedo placed on the track to warn a train operator of a problem ahead *US*
- —Ramon Adams, *The Language of the Railroader*, p. 147, 1977

stop it – I like it!
used for registering a guilty pleasure, especially as a pretence that a partner's caresses are unwanted *US*
- Stop stop stop stop stop it I like it (I like it) / stop stop stop stop stop it feels gooood! / You're so wrong I'm getting excited / please don't stop although I know you should. —Rick Derringer, *Rock & Roll Hoochie Koo*, 1970

stop-over *noun*
a short jail sentence, either empirically or in proportion to the crime involved *US*
- —Joseph E. Ragen and Charles Finston, *Inside the World's Toughest Prison*, p. 820, 1962: 'Penitentiary and underworld glossary'

stopper *noun*
1 a central nervous system depressant; a barbiturate *US, 1977*
- —Ralph de Sola, *Crime Dictionary*, p. 144, 1982
- —Richard A. Spears, *The Slang and Jargon of Drugs and Drink*, p. 487, 1986
- —Mike Haskins, *Drugs*, p. 283, 2003

2 air or artillery fire used to prevent enemy ground troops from escaping *US*
- —Gregory Clark, *Words of the Vietnam War*, p. 490, 1990

stoppo driver *noun*
a getaway driver *UK*
- —Angela Devlin, *Prison Patter*, p. 110, 1996

store *noun*
1 a betting operation *US*
- —David W. Maurer, *Argot of the Racetrack*, p. 60, 1951

2 any rigged game or attraction in a carnival *US*
- —Gene Sorrows, *All About Carnivals*, p. 27, 1985: 'Terminology'

3 in a big con swindle, the fake office, poolroom or betting establishment created for the swindle *US, 1940*
- The inside man is the guts of a store. He makes one mistake and he's lost the mark and the score. —Iceberg Slim (Robert Beck), *Trick Baby*, p. 119, 1969

▸ **your store is open**
a catchphrase used to advise that your (trouser) fly is undone *CANADA*
- —D.J. Barr, 1968

store-bought *adjective*
factory-manufactured cigarettes, as opposed to hand-rolled *US*
- George: Oh, no thanks. I got some – uh – store-bought right over here of my own. —Peter Fonda, *Easy Rider*, p. 121, 1969

store choppers *noun*
false teeth *US*
- —John Gould, *Maine Lingo*, p. 279, 1975

store dice *noun*
inexpensive store-bought dice, not milled to casino-level tolerances *US*
- —Frank Garcia, *Marked Cards and Loaded Dice*, p. 264, 1962

store dick *noun*
a department store's private detective *US*
- I got 'em from a lady store-dick in California who used 'em to scratch the ants outta her hot pants. —Clarence Cooper Jr, *The Scene*, p. 196, 1960

stork bite *noun*
a flat pink birthmark or capillary hemangioma *US*
- —Barton D. Schmitt, M.D., *Your Child's Health*, 1991

storked *adjective*
pregnant *US*
- —Lou Shelly, *Hepcats Jive Talk Dictionary*, p. 19, 1945

storm *verb*
1 in hot rodding, to perform very well *US*
- —John Lawlor, *How to Talk Car*, p. 101, 1965

2 to attend a party to which you are not invited *TRINIDAD AND TOBAGO, 1969*
- —Lise Winer, *Dictionary of the English/Creole of Trinidad & Tobago*, 2003

storm carpenter *noun*
an untrained, unskilled, incompetent carpenter *TRINIDAD AND TOBAGO, 1831*
The formation of storm-CRAFT is used with other crafts as well, such as 'storm mason'.
- —Lise Winer, *Dictionary of the English/Creole of Trinidad & Tobago*, 2003

storm damage *noun*
applied to a person of limited intelligence *UK: SCOTLAND*
- Don't pay too much attention to what he says. There's a fair bit a storm damage there. —Michael Munro, *The Patter, Another Blast*, p. 69, 1988

stormer *noun*
1 any excellent thing *UK: SCOTLAND*
- That yer new guitar? It's a stormer. —Michael Munro, *The Original Patter*, p. 66, 1985
- —Michael Munro, *The Complete Patter*, p. 149, 1996

2 an excellent performance in a sports match (hurling, soccer, Gaelic football) *IRELAND*
- Houghton's having a stormer. His cross finds Sheeds, who swings it back across the box. —Howard Paul, *The Joy*, p. 150, 1996

3 a theatrical success *UK*
- It had been a bit of a stormer[.] —Frank Skinner, *Frank Skinner*, p. 3, 2001

4 in hot rodding, a fast car *US*
- —*Good Housekeeping*, p. 143, September 1958: 'Hot-Rod terms for teen-age girls'

storming *adjective*
excellent; exciting *UK*
- Portent is Nic Fanciulli and mate Owen's own Maidstone label, and they've had a string of storming releases. —*Mixmag*, p. 5, April 2003

Stormin' Norman *nickname*
1 US Army General H. Norman Schwarzkopf, commander of the anti-Iraq forces in the Persian Gulf war *US*
- Stormin' Norman In High Command [Headline] —*Washington Post*, p. D1, 28th February 1991

- Every day we were treated to a film demonstartion of such [in]accuracy at work, fronted by Commander-in-Chief Stormin' Norman Schwarzkopf. — Mark Steel, *Reasons to be Cheerful*, p. 211, 2001

2 Norm Van Brocklin (1926–83), quarterback for the Los Angeles Rams during their glory days (1949–57) and then for the Philadelphia Eagles (1958–60) *US*

storm-stayed *adjective*

prevented from reaching home by a storm *CANADA*

- "Storm-stayed" does not mean being closed in (by snow and high winds) here, or not being able to leave your place. Instead [it means] having to be put up for the night at someone else's house, because traveling conditions have deteriorated so much. — Arthur Reddin, *Dln The Latest Morningside Papers*, p. 30, 1989

stotious *adjective*

▷ see: STOCIOUS

stoush *noun*

a fight; a brawl; fighting *AUSTRALIA, 1893*

Possibly a variant of Scottish dialect *stashie* (a commotion, disturbance, quarrel) which was recorded in C19 Aberdeen as 'stash' without the '-ie' suffix. During both World Wars used by servicemen to refer to the war, with a touch of jocular or ironic bravado.

- STOUCH – A fight; to assault. — Gilbert H. Lawson, *A Dictionary of Australian Words and Terms*, 1924
- It was like the old days when I got Ernie into some stoush ashore just for the hell of fighting him out of it. — Robert S. Close, *Love Me Sailor*, p. 149, 1945
- Used to be in the Air Force during the last stouch. — John Wynnum, *Tar Dust*, p. 30, 1962
- 'I joined up a year or so after the stoush finished[.]' — John Wynnum, *Jiggin' in the Riggin'*, p. 57, 1965
- After a most unchildlike stoush, The Wiggles have reclaimed their crown as the most popular children's group from young upstarts Hi-5. — *Sydney Morning Herald*, 4th March 2002

▸ **deal out a stoush**

to assault with violence *AUSTRALIA, 1900*

stoush *verb*

to punch, to hit; to struggle, to battle *AUSTRALIA, 1893*

- Heath Ramsay stoushed with the leaders in last night's 200m butterfly semi-finals[.] — *Sydney Morning Herald*, 18th September 2000

stove *noun*

a truck or car heater *US*

- — Montie Tak, *Truck Talk*, p. 157, 1971
- A bum stove and organ. Phony white shoes. — Joseph Wambaugh, *The Black Marble*, p. 194, 1978

stovebolt *noun*

a Chevrolet or Chevrolet engine *US*

- Originally the term was applied to the old Chevy six, which had connecting rod bolts that looked like ordinary stove bolts. Today, it can mean any Chevrolet or any Chevy engine. — John Lawlor, *How to Talk Car*, p. 101, 1965
- — Lyle K. Engel, *The Complete Book of Fuel and Gas Dragsters*, p. 154, 1968

stovepipe *noun*

1 a distended, gaping anus produced by recent anal intercourse *US*

- — *Adult Video News*, p. 40, September 1995

2 a revolver *US*

- — *American Speech*, p. 195, October 1957: 'Some colloquialisms of the handgunner'

3 a jet aircraft *US*

- — *American Speech*, p. 229, October 1956: 'More United States air force slang'

4 gossip *US*

From the image of railwaymen gathered around a stove gossiping.

- — Ramon Adams, *The Language of the Railroader*, p. 148, 1977

5 a three-part bet in an illegal numbers gambling lottery, in which the bettor must correctly guess two of the three digits in the winning number and have the third digit be one of eight bet on *US*

- — *American Speech*, p. 193, October 1949

stove up *adjective*

injured, ill or exhausted *US, 1901*

- If I weren't so stove up and ailin' critical, I'd bung yo head bigger 'n a Georgia watermelon 'bout you and thet tramp. — Iceberg Slim (Robert Beck), *Doom Fox*, p. 123, 1978
- I been feelin' a little stove up all week, but if I can walk, I can work. — Ken Weaver, *Texas Crude*, p. 129, 1984
- I don't want any parts of surveillance work. Other than following some stove-up cripple walks with a cane. — Elmore Leonard, *Glitz*, p. 320, 1985

stow *verb*

▸ **stow your chant**

to stop talking *US*

- — R. Frederick West, *God's Gambler*, p. 228, 1964: 'Appendix A'

STP *noun*

a type of synthetic hallucinogen *US*

Probably coined as an abbreviation of 'serotonin triphosphate' and as an allusion to the trademark name of a motor oil additive, and later de-abbreviated to '*s*erenity, *t*ranquillity and *p*eace'.

- I could write behind STP, but not behind acid. — Joan Didion, *Slouching Toward Bethlehem*, p. 109, 1967
- STP: free; this is given away, but you have to know somebody. — Ruth Bronsteen, *The Hippy's Handbook*, p. 42, 1967
- Sharon was stoned on STP. — Nicholas Von Hoffman, *We Are The People Our Parents Warned Us Against*, p. 58, 1967
- I swallowed it all, pot, acid, STP, Speed, all in one big, glorious gulp. — Nat Hentoff, *I'm really dragged but nothing gets me down*, p. 22, 1968
- — Burton H. Wolfe, *The Hippies*, p. 206, 1968: 'A hip glossary for the uptight people'
- How does a hippie switch on a radio? He puts STP in the batteries! — Paul Laikin, *101 Hippie Jokes*, 1968
- To a client whom he feels is sound enough to handle it, he also will sell LSD, mescaline, STP, DMT oat pysilocybin. — Tom Robbins, *Another Roadside Attraction*, p. 57–58, 1971
- And I put a definite HOLD on STP; I don't think there's anything wrong with it karmically but it's such a long and juiceless trip that it damages the bearings. — *The Last Supplement to the Whole Earth Catalog*, p. 83, March 1971
- She was tripping on STP one time, and she had a bunch of inner conflicts and ideas that were hanging her up. — Stephen Gaskin, *Amazing Dope Tales*, p. 200, 1980

St Pete *noun*

in shuffleboard, a disc hidden midway on your opponent's side of the court *US*

- — Omero C. Catan, *Secrets of Shuffleboard Strategy*, p. 72, 1967: 'Glossary of terms'

str8 *adjective*

straight, in all its senses *US*

- Str8-G, a rugged L.A. rapper whose lyrics showcase him busting off with his fists and not a gun. — *Billboard*, p. 28, 3rd July 1993
- "It saved my life," the 22-year-old student said of the movement, the fingers of his left hand tattooed with the message STR8. — *Philadelphia Inquirer*, p. A1, 1st October 1995
- — Michelle Baker and Steven Tropiano, *Queer Facts*, p. 13, 2004

str8 draw *noun*

a move in an on-line game of hold 'em poker, when the player gambles on making a straight with the final card *UK*

A variant spelling of a conventional term.

- — *FHM*, p. 147, June 2003

strack; strac *adjective*

professional; neat; clean *US*

Military slang.

- You got zero five to get out of those civvie threads and make a strack troop of yourself. — John Del Vecchio, *The 13th Valley*, p. 46, 1982
- The six bloods from Buffalo graduated basic all spit-shined and strack, the Army honorific for a Class A soldier. — Peter Goldman and Tony Fuller, *Charlie Company*, p. 34, 1983
- I think they take Captain Gardner for a typical HHQ commander, not up to par, not strac enough to command a line company. — Lucian K. Truscott, *Army Blue*, p. 314, 1989

Strad *noun*

a *Strad*ivarius violin *UK, 1884*

- There, to our amazement, he [Gerald Segelman] kept a rare, beautifully decorated Strad. The sagging bedsprings had dented the case and damaged the instrument. — *The Guardian*, 31st August 2002

straddle *noun*

in poker, an increased bet made without looking at your cards *US*

- — George Percy, *The Language of Poker*, p. 87, 1988

straggler *noun*

in horse racing, a winning bet that is not cashed in immediately after a race but, unlike an out ticket, is cashed in before the end of the day *US*

- —Bob and Barbara Freeman, *Wanta Bet?*, p. 295, 1982

straight *noun*

1 a conventional person, blind to the values of a counter-culture *US*

- Most of the hip population slept the mornings out, but the straights in the neighborhood arose to the harmonics of the good morning vibrations and did their straight things. —Nicholas Von Hoffman, *We Are The People Our Parents Warned Us Against*, p. 12, 1967
- There were a few straights but they looked very uptight and out of place. —*Berkeley Barb*, p. 1, 20th January 1967
- Straights shit in their pants when they hear the yippies reveal the most crucial political issue in Amerika today: pay toilets. —Jerry Rubin, *Do It!*, p. 86, 1970
- I saw her in front of the campfire entertaining a few brothers by having a scene [sex] with a dog. Two straights somehow managed to stroll into the scene and froze. —Jamie Mandelkau, *Buttons*, p. 100, 1971
- [R]eaders – people like you, probably – are what we in the criminal world always called "straights". It's not meant as an insult[.] —Dave Courtney, *Stop the Ride I Want to Get Off*, p. 3, 1999

2 a factory-made cigarette *US*

- He took one deep drag and he coughed. "Damned straights make the eyes water." —Thurston Scott, *Cure it with Honey*, p. 35, 1951
- "Naw, just some straights." He walked over to the cigarette machine and got some smokes. —Piri Thomas, *Down These Mean Streets*, p. 211, 1967
- —Eugene Landy, *The Underground Dictionary*, p. 67, 1971
- I walked in the drugstore to cop some straight's and while the girl was getting the smokes, I enjoyed the sound of female voices[.] —A.S. Jackson, *Gentleman Pimp*, p. 68, 1973
- [T]he first time he spoke to me was to ask for a "straight" (an ordinary cigarette, unlike a "joint" which contains "pot") I could not help him[.] —Robin Page, *Down Among the Dossers*, p. 16, 1973
- They give you a bag of sawdust for tobacco, so you learn to scrounge around for cigarettes – to take Joe for a couple of striaghts here, hit Mike for a straight there, so you've got three smokes to knock out the night. —Herbert Huncke, *Guilty of Everything*, p. 122, 1990

3 a house dweller *UK*

Used by late 1980s–early 90s counterculture travellers.

- —Martin Roach, *Dr. Marten's Air Wair*, 1999: 'Glossary of travellers' terms'

4 a heterosexual *US, 1941*

- [T]he pool-playing dykes and femmes sit at tables in one corner away from the juke-box, and the "straights" fill out the rest of the bar. —Roger Gordon, *Hollywood's Sexual Underground*, p. 18, 1966
- And of course a straight arrival like myself causes the heads to flick and the lips to flutter even more. —Ted Lewis, *Jack Carter's Law*, p. 23, 1974
- It was a table in the corner closest to the door, the one where timid straights often perched to watch the freaks at play. —Robert Campbell, *Alice in La-La Land*, p. 270, 1987
- "I don't see why those straights have to stay here tonight," Two complained, his voice muffled because his face was buried in a pillow. —Stewart Home, *Sex Kick [britpulp]*, p. 217, 1999

5 simple vaginal intercourse *US*

- I say, Yoo-hoo, pitty baby, you wanna lil french? Haff an haff? How about jes a straight? I say, Twenty berries an you alla roun the mothahfuggin worl'. —Robert Gover, *One Hundred Dollar Misunderstanding*, p. 21, 1961
- At first she figured she'd play it open-and-shut, bring him off and charge him twenty for a fifteen-dollar straight without dropping anything but her panties. —John Sayles, *Union Dues*, p. 186, 1977
- Half-and-half still costs you more than straight, so if you need the girl's mouth on your dingus to get you up it will set you back a total of thirty dollars[.] —Gerald Paine, *A Bachelor's Guide to the Brothels of Nevada*, p. 26, 1978

6 unadulterated tobacco *UK*

- —Home Office, *Glossary of Terms and Slang Common in Penal Establishments*, July 1978

7 in horse racing, a bet that a horse will win a race *US*

- —Tom Ainslie, *Ainslie's Complete Guide to Thoroughbred Racing*, p. 339, 1976

straight *adjective*

1 heterosexual *US, 1941*

- Back in the days when I was first in the navy, I didn't know a gay guy from a straight guy. —Willard Motely, *Let No Man Write My Epitaph*, p. 210, 1958
- —Donald Webster Cory and John P. LeRoy, *The Homosexual and His Society*, p. 266, 1963: 'A lexicon of homosexual slang'
- Whatever a guy does with other guys, if he does it for money, that don't make him queer. You're still straight. —John Rechy, *City of Night*, p. 45, 1963
- The hostility of the minority "leather" crowd toward the rest of the "gay" world is exceeded by the bitterness of individual homosexuals toward the "straight" world." —*Life*, p. 70, 26th June 1964
- Listen, asshole, what am I going to do? He's straight. —Mart Crowley, *The Boys in the Band*, p. 32, 1968
- The story involves only four characters: two lovers, their "swishy" neighbor, and an old "straight" friend who is a boyhood buddy of one of the lovers. —*Screw*, p. 20, 27th October 1969
- One day he told me that if there was anything that could make him go straight, it was me. —Jefferson Poland and Valerie Alison, *The Records of the San Francisco Sexual Freedom League*, p. 46, 1971
- —*Maledicta*, p. 199, 1983: 'Ritual and personal insults in stigmatized subcultures'
- I like being straight. And I think heterosexuality is making a comeback. —*Boys on the Side*, 1995

2 conventional, not part of the counterculture *US, 1960*

- Of course, they were all straight. They weren't into any crime or stuff like that, as far as I know. —Claude Brown, *Manchild in the Promised Land*, p. 185, 1965
- Another threat is unwanted visitors – the sightseers from "straight" society and the weekend hippies who descend upon them to freeload. —*Life*, p. 16B, 18th July 1969
- Yes, some of us do have straight jobs and others devote more of their time to the movement. —*The Last Supplement to the Whole Earth Catalog*, p. 15, March 1971
- I want to be straight, I want to be straight / I want to create a place of my own in the Welfare State[.] —Ian Dury, *I Want To Be Straight*, 1980
- This is like a real vacation-type vacation that straight people go on. —Cleo Odzer, *Goa Freaks*, p. 74, 1995

3 not currently drug-intoxicated; no longer using drugs *UK, 1967*

- —Angela Devlin, *Prison Patter*, p. 110, 1996
- The terror of facing their daily grind "straight" was unimaginable. —Lanre Fehintola, *Charlie Says...*, p. 170, 2000
- When people are straight they don't come bounding up to you[.] —Dave Haslam, *Adventures of the Wheels of Steel*, p. 114, 2001

4 under the influence of drugs, or at least not suffering from withdrawal symptoms *US, 1946*

- Main-lining her. Capping her straight. —John D. McDonald, *The Neon Jungle*, p. 46, 1953
- I need fifty, Baby, so I can get straight. I been lushed all day. —John Clellon Holmes, *The Horn*, p. 81, 1958
- When they get straight – really feeling good from stuff – they don't want to have nothing to do with no man[.] —Willard Motley, *Let No Man Write My Epitaph*, p. 117, 1958
- You wanna get straight? —Alexander Trocchi, *Cain's Book*, p. 81, 1960
- I don't get high anymore. I just get straight ; I take a cure. I'm just normal, that's all. —Jeremy Larner and Ralph Tefferteller, *The Addict in the Street*, p. 233, 1964
- This is his "wake-up," a morning shot to hold off the anxiety and sickness of withdrawal and get him "straight" enough to start the day. —James Mills, *The Panic in Needle Park*, p. 14, 1966
- But this friend of mine would come over and we'd go to the bathroom and I'd cop a little old fix and be straight for a few days. —Bruce Jackson, *In the Life*, p. 110, 1972
- Enough to keep us straight so we won't have to worry bout coppin' for awhile. —Vernon E. Smith, *The Jones Men*, p. 177, 1974
- Hi, man – my name is Victor – you want to get straight? —Herbert Huncke, *The Evening Sun Turned Crimson*, p. 101, 1980
- I was straight now but still fragile, and just as I settled, the phone rang again. —Peter Coyote, *Sleeping Where I Fall*, p. 62, 1998

5 correct *US*

- —Connie Eble (Editor), *UNC-CH Campus Slang*, p. 6, Fall 1996

6 good, pleasing, acceptable *US*

- A-Wax: Cool, how you feelin' man? Caine: I'm straight. —*Menace II Society*, 1993
- —Don R. McCreary (Editor), *Dawg Speak*, 2001

7 of an utterance, outspoken, straightforward *UK, 1894*

- The need for straight talking[.] —*The Guardian*, 8th July 2002

8 honest, honourable, frank *UK, 1864*

- Foreign Man, a sweet, naive straight man, and an Elvis Presley impression. —Marcus Buckingham and Donald O. Clifton, *Now, Discover Your Strengths*, p. 38, 2001

9 of alcoholic drinks, undiluted *US, 1874*

- He was fueling himself on straight whisky at eleven in the morning. —Andrea Camilleri and Stephen Sartarelli, *The Terra-Cotta Dog*, p. 276, 2003

10 without a 'minus' or 'plus' attached to a grade *US*

- —Collin Baker et al., *College Undergraduate Slang Study Conducted at Brown University*, p. 205, 1968

▸ **go straight**

to abandon a criminal lifestyle in favour of honesty *UK, 1940*

- —Angela Devlin, *Prison Patter*, p. 110, 1996
- [D]oing his usual bit about giving up nicking and going straight[.] —Danny King, *The Burglar Diaries*, p. 73, 2001

straight!
honestly! it's a fact! *UK, 1897*

straight and narrow; straight *noun*
an honest, conventional or virtuous way of life, especially when temptation is resisted *UK, 1930*
Always with 'the'; a shortening of 'the straight and narrow path'.
- Boys and men are kept to the masculine straight and narrow by the threat of being called queer[.] — Diane Richardson, *Theorising Homosexuality*, p. 126, 1996
- Fuckin awful tha would be aye, trine t'stey on-a streyt like an get fuckin gripped with a multi-pack a fuckin Hula Hoops up me fuckin jumper. — Niall Griffiths, *Grits*, p. 60, 2000

straight arrow *noun*
an honest or honourable person *US, 1969*
From the proverbial expression, 'straight as an arrow'.
- Something about his earnestness reassured her. He was such a straight arrow. She thought, He probably will take care of me. — Michael Crichton, *Timeline*, p. 161, 2000

straight as a monk's cock *adjective*
very honest *UK*
- Charge me? TT I'm as straight as a monk's cock you know that. Straighter than bleedin' Snow White. — Jeremy Cameron, *Brown Bread in Wengen*, p. 25, 1999

straight as a stiff *adjective*
very honest or honourable *UK*
An elaboration of STRAIGHT (honest); punning the final posture of a STIFF (a dead body) with the impossibility of the dead being anything other than honest. An interesting comparison with STIFF (to cheat).
- Arthur's straight as a stiff, no problem, no questions. — Kevin Sampson, *Outlaws*, p. 100, 2001

straight as a string *adjective*
used of a racehorse, fully exerting itself *US*
- — Tom Ainslie, *Ainslie's Complete Guide to Thoroughbred Racing*, p. 339, 1976

straight date *noun*
conventional vaginal sex with a prostitute *US*
- At the hotel, if it's a straight date it's usually $10, and a French date, a blow job, is $20. — Bruce Jackson, *Outside the Law*, p. 186, 1972

straight-down-the-line *adjective*
very honest; used to describe someone who sticks to the rules *UK*
An elaboration of STRAIGHT.
- Well known as an absolutely straight-down-the-line copper. — Jake Arnott, *He Kills Coppers*, p. 14, 2001

straight down the line *adverb*
honestly *UK*
- I told them straight down the line. I had nothing to do with it. — Angela Devlin, *Prison Patter*, p. 110, 1996

straight edge *adjective*
reflecting a philosophy that promotes hardcore rock music, abstinence from drugs and abstinence from promiscuous sex *US*
Probably coined by Ian Mackaye in the self-titled song 'Straight Edge' while Mackaye was the singer of the Washington D.C. band Minor Threat.
- I don't think about speed / That's something I just don't need / I've got the straight edge. — Minor Threat, *Stragith Edge*, 1983(?)
- — Connie Eble (Editor), *UNC-CH Campus Slang*, p. 8, March 1996
- It started out hardcore, like Bad Religion, then you got straight-edge, like Minor Threat and surf punk like Agent Orange. — Elmore Leonard, *Be Cool*, p. 197, 1999

straighten *verb*
1 to bribe someone *US, 1923*
- — John Gosling, *The Ghost Squad*, 1959

2 to avenge someone *UK*
A part of TEDDY BOY culture.
- — *The Observer*, 1st March 1959

3 to produce drug intoxication in someone *US*
- Joan told me you could straighten me out. — Morton Cooper, *High School Confidential*, p. 78, 1958
- One bag's not eough to straighten me. — Jeremy Larner and Ralph Tefferteller, *The Addict in the Street*, p. 233, 1964
- Then James Fox came in and said he had his works and that he wanted Johnny to straighten him. — Claude Brown, *Manchild in the Promised Land*, p. 118, 1965
- But when I make that big sting, I'll straighten you / If you'll save me a little on the cotton. — Dennis Wepman et al., *The Life*, p. 78, 1976

▸ **straighten out a curve**
to enter a curve driving too fast and leave the road *US*
- — *American Speech*, p. 272, December 1962: 'The language of traffic policemen'

straightener *noun*
a fist fight to settle an argument, to *straighten* matters out; a fair fight *UK*
A TEDDY BOY term.
- — *The Daily Mail*, 7th February 1959
- — Angela Devlin, *Prison Patter*, p. 110, 1996
- I would've rather had a straightener with him than take any swag back. — Kevin Sampson, *Outlaws*, p. 124, 2001

straighten out *verb*
1 to correct someone; to put someone right *UK, 1956*
- [N]ot only would the snafu have been straightened out more quickly, but the celebrities would have been on the angels. — Bill O'Reilly, *Who's Looking Out for You?*, p. 95, 2003

2 (of a drug addict) to cease drug use *UK*
- Two years ago, the Kirks flew Cameron out to Nairobi [...] to straighten him out. It was a disastrous move – Cameron was soon injecting up to a gramme a day of heroin, purer than he had dreamed possible in England. — *The Guardian*, 19th April 2001

3 to feel the effects of a drug, relieving any pangs of withdrawal *US*
- Like I might find old Joe Schmoe today and buy three bags from him and find that one bag straightens me out. — James Mills, *The Panic in Needle Park*, p. 46, 1966
- How about us getting some speed, see, and then after we're all straightened out, we'll all jump in the car and head down to four-fifty[.] — *Drugstore Cowboy*, 1988

4 to bring someone up to date *US*
- The man at the window there was a fellow countryman of mine downstairs who might straighten me out. — Mezz Mezzrow, *Really the Blues*, p. 191, 1946

straight face *noun*
an facial expression that is hiding amusement or successfully restraining laughter *UK, 1897*
- CEOs would say with straight faces that their companies' revenues and profits would grow[.] — Jack Brennan, *Straght Talk on Investing*, p. 180, 2002
- [A] risible multi-million-dollar lawsuit by a Tennessee woman citing – with a straight face – "outrage, anger, embarrassment and serious injury" on behalf of all 100m viewers. — *The Guardian*, 14th February 2004

straight-faced *adjective*
displaying a facial expression devoid of humour *UK, 1975*
- "Well, I like the other too," he said, deliberately straight-faced, "but yes, I meant that." — Diana Gabaldon, *Outlander*, p. 312, 1992

straight flush wannabe *noun*
in poker, a sequenced hand comprised of all red or all black suits, but not a flush *US*
Impressive looking, but worth no more than any non-flush straight.
- — John Vorhaus, *The Big Book of Poker Slang*, p. 8, 1996

straight-goer *noun*
a dependable, honest person *AUSTRALIA, 1899*
- — Angela Devlin, *Prison Patter*, p. 110, 1996
- Always the straight goer George, never liked a curved copper. — Jeremy Cameron, *Brown Bread in Wengen*, p. 149, 1999
- He was a straight goer when he got out of the army in the 60s[.] — *The Guardian*, p. 7, 17th October 2002

straight-leg *noun*
an infantry soldier, unattached to a mechanised or airborne unit *US, 1951*
- — Carl Fleischhauer, *A Glossary of Army Slang*, p. 19, 1968
- — *Current Slang*, p. 11, Spring 1968
- The artillery dudes and straight-leg grunts and the gooks was doin' it hand to hand. — Larry Heinemann, *Close Quarters*, p. 29, 1977
- "He said he was going up to the wardroom to talk to the straight-legs, Lieutenant," Hardin said. Troops who were not jump-qualified and therefore wore their trousers unbloused at the ankles were called a number of things by the Rangers; "straight-legs" was the least insulting. — Alfred Coppel, *The Burning Mountain*, p. 37, 1983

• Airborne, "straight leg," which is best? / AIRBORNE! AIRBORNE! YES! YES! YES! —Sandee Shaffer Johnson, *Cadences*, p. 91, 1986
• Without preamble, he said, "We have twelve ex-Rangers and a couple of straight legs so far." —Alfred Coppel, *Show Me A Hero*, p. 78, 1987

straight moniker *noun*
a person's legal name *US*
• No one but Pinky and Sister Heavenly knew his straight monicker[.] —Chester Himes, *Come Back Charleston Blue*, p. 51, 1966

straight puda *noun*
the complete, whole truth *US*
• —Fred Hester, *Slang on the 40 Acres*, p. 9, 1968

straights *noun*
straight pool or continuous pocket billiards *US*
• In straights, if you were hot you kept right on going[.] —Walter Tevis, *The Color of Money*, p. 146, 1984
• —Mike Shamos, *The Illustrated Encyclopedia of Billiards*, p. 234, 1993

straight shooter *noun*
a glass or metal device used to smoke crack cocaine *US*
• —Mark S. Fleisher, *Beggars & Thieves*, p. 291, 1995: 'Glossary'

straight trade *noun*
homosexual sex with a man who considers himself heterosexual *US*
• One of the principal arguments that will be made, according to Martin, is that "homosexual behavior, by homosexuals, but especially also by sailors who consider themselves and are generally considered to be heterosexual – 'straight trade' – is widespread. —*The Advocate*, p. 9, 19th January 1972

straight trick *noun*
vaginal sex between a prostitute and customer *US*
• In a joint most of them are straight tricks, but on call about half of them are straight and the other half a little other than straight. Bruce Jackson, *In the Life*, p. 195, 1972

straight up *adjective*
1 used of an alcoholic drink or a drug, undiluted *US, 1973*
• Scotch straight up and a rum and Coke for me. —*Tin Men*, 1987
• If somebody coming in from Jersey City, you give 'em a straight-up ounce 'cause they can get pretty good stuff right in town. —Richard Price, *Clockers*, p. 180, 1992

2 a prison sentence, without reduction for good behaviour or other factors *US*
• He was an orphan and he had just done a two-year "bit" "straight up," his fourth, two months before. —Iceberg Slim (Robert Beck), *Pimp*, p. 36, 1969
• I get busted again, I do five years straight up and not at one of those country-club joints either. —Elmore Leonard, *Riding the Rap*, p. 78, 1995

3 pure, unadulterated *US*
• We're gonna play straight-up rock and roll. —*Empire Records*, 1995

4 used of a person, especially a girl, thin *US*
• —Marcus Hanna Boulware, *Jive and Slang of Students in Negro Colleges*, 1947

straight up!
honestly; used for emphasis *UK*
• We're just going to rot here, straight up for the rest of our born days. —Graeme Kent, *The Queen's Corporal [Six Granada Plays]*, p. 82, 1959
• —*Maledicta*, p. 268, Summer/Winter 1981: 'By its slang, ye shall know it: the pessimism of prison life'
• "Straight up!" added Rac. —Jess Mowry, *Way Past Cool*, p. 13, 1992
• [T]here used to be this girl Laetitia that had hers [pubic bush] done in a Nike swoosh. Straight up. —Kevin Sampson, *Outlaws*, p. 38, 2001

straight up and down *adverb*
entirely *US*
• [T]hey fucked us off, straight up and down. They were just crooks. —Alex Ogg, *The Hip Hop Years [quoting Rodney C of the Funky Four]*, p. 64, 1999

straight up the platform *adverb*
absolutely, completely, entirely *UK*
• Fucking understand you mate, fucking understand you straight up the fucking platform. —Jeremy Cameron, *Brown Bread in Wengen*, p. 19, 1999

straight wire *noun*
the whole truth *NEW ZEALAND*
• —David McGill, *David McGill's Complete Kiwi Slang Dictionary*, p. 120, 1998

strain *verb*
▸ **strain at the leash**
to demonstrate a great eagerness *UK, 1910*
From the characteristic behaviour of a dog.
• Only twelve soldiers were still able to fight, but they weren't exactly straining at the leash. —Joe Haldeman, *The Forever War*, p. 175, 1974

▸ **strain the potatoes; strain the spuds; strain your taters**
to urinate *AUSTRALIA, 1965*
• I gotta get up top and strain the potatoes! —Barry Humphries, *Bazza Pulls It Off!*, 1971
• [T]here is another Army gentleman there, also carrying a bayonetted rifle and wearing a few medals – and straining his spuds in the self-same letter box. —Frank Hardy, *The Outcasts of Foolgarah*, p. 211, 1971

strange *noun*
a new and unknown sexual partner *US*
• Any man figures to get something strange ever' once in a while. —Malcolm Braly, *On the Yard*, p. 110, 1967
• —Connie Eble (Editor), *UNC-CH Campus Slang*, p. 5, November 1983
• Except on days when he yearned for some strange. —Seth Morgan, *Homeboy*, p. 276, 1990
• Once qualifies as strange. More than once you might as well pop your old lady for all the surprises you get with whoo-ers. —James Ellroy, *White Jazz*, p. 111, 1992

strange *adjective*
new, fresh, unknown, especially sexually *US*
• That was what he needed. A strange piece. Been a long time since he fucked anybody but Irene. —Hubert Selby Jr, *Last Exit to Brooklyn*, p. 268, 1957
• Usually they were mamas, but now and then what the Angels call a "strange broad" or "new pussy" would show up. —Hunter S. Thompson, *Hell's Angels*, p. 193, 1966
• He decided to run by the Roost and see if there was some strange cunt hanging around. —Donald Goines, *Black Gangster*, p. 108, 1977

▸ **don't be strange**
don't resist; don't hesitate *UK*
A polari catchphrase, always in the imperative.
• Well, don't be strange, Mr Horne. Sit yourself down. Now what do you fancy? —Barry Took and Marty Feldman, *Round The Horne*, 21st May 1967

strangely weird; strangely *noun*
a beard *UK*
Rhyming slang.
• —Ray Puxley, *Cockney Rabbit*, 1992

stranger *noun*
1 used as a form of address emphasising the fact that the two people have not seen each other for a while *US*
• "Hell, Stranger," Helen said to him. "Hello, Helen," he said, thinking, Why do people call other people stranger when they haven't seen them for a while? Is it to instill guilt that you haven't been attentive enough? —Joseph Wambaugh, *Floaters*, p. 224, 1996

2 in poker, any card added to a hand by draw *US*
• —George Percy, *The Language of Poker*, p. 88, 1988

strangers *noun*
in gin, cards in a hand that do not and cannot form a sequence *US*
• —Irwin Steig, *Play Gin to Win*, p. 142

strange stuff *noun*
a new and different sex-partner *US*
• "Do you want to bust in on the church dance?" Steven said. "It's Friday night. There ought to be some strange stuff there?" —Hal Ellson, *Tomboy*, p. 128, 1950

strangle *verb*
1 to turn something off; to deactivate something *US*
• —*American Speech*, p. 120, May 1963: 'Air refueling words'

2 to prevent a horse from winning a race *AUSTRALIA*
Strictly, and originally, by pulling back on the reins so strongly that the horse is almost strangled.
• —Lawson Glassop, *Lucky Palmer*, 1949
• The general opinion among the jockeys was that Sandy had "strangled" a couple at one stage, but not during the past few months. —Dick Francis, *Dead Cert*, 1962

▸ **strangle a darkie**
to defecate *UK*
• —Bob Young and Micky Moody, *The Language of Rock 'n' Roll*, p. 135, 1985

strap *noun*
1 a naughty or lascivious girl *IRELAND*
• She's a bold strap, that one. —Irwin Liam, *North Munster Antiquarian Journal*, p. 86, 2000

2 a handgun *US*
Recorded in UK prison use, August 2002.
• [P]anic ensued when someone on the steps yelled, "Get the straps" – street slang for guns – and a bottle shattered in the street, frightening Bynoe and causing him to fire wildly, without aim. — *Boston Globe Magazine*, p. 14, 14th November 1991
• — Ethan Hilderbrant, *Prison Slang*, p. 122, 1998

strap *verb*
1 to interrogate someone in a severe manner *UK*
• — Angela Devlin, *Prison Patter*, p. 110, 1996
2 to have sex *US*
Also used in the variant 'strap on'.
• — Eugene Landy, *The Underground Dictionary*, p. 178, 1971

strap-hanger *noun*
1 a passenger on public transport who stands supported by an overhead strap (or other type of grip) *UK, 1905*
• [D]ormitory towns inhabited by commuting "strap-hangers". — Stephen Inwood and Roy Porter, *A History of London*, p. 818, 2000
2 a member of the armed forces, stationed well away from combat, accompanying troops into the field without having a specific role to play *US*
• — Department of the Army, *Staff Officer's Guidebook*, p. 66, 1986
• — Linda Reinberg, *In the Field*, p. 210, 1991

strap-on *noun*
a dildo that is harnessed to a person's body *UK*
• Eve was sitting on the edge of one of the twin beds, stark naked and with a strap-on sticking up from her cunt. — Stewart Home, *Sex Kick [britpulp]*, p. 242, 1999
• When will I have another prime-time opportunity to educate the masses about a particularly crucial but mostly misunderstood aspect of lesbian sexuality like strap-ons? — *The Village Voice*, 27th June 2000

strapped *adjective*
1 armed, especially with a gun *US*
From **STRAP** (a handgun).
• Dog, you strapped? — *Menace II Society*, 1993
• — Vann Wesson, *Generation X Field Guide and Lexicon*, p. 160, 1997
• Members who weren't felons were heavily strapped. — Ralph "Sonny" Barger, *Hell's Angel*, p. 7, 2000
• Yet many of the shocked blacks, few of them strapped (armed), now cowered under tables hoping to save their lives. — Bill Valentine, *Gangs and Their Tattoos*, p. 12, 2000
2 short of money *US, 1857*
Also appears as 'cash-strapped'.
• — Angela Devlin, *Prison Patter*, p. 110, 1996
• How did cash-strapped Yana [Booth] get the wherewithal to train with the Bolshoi? — *The Guardian*, 26th February 2002

straps *noun*
suspenders *US*
• — Lou Shelly, *Hepcats Jive Talk Dictionary*, p. 19, 1945
• — Clarence Major, *Dictionary of Afro-American Slang*, p. 110, 1970

strap up *verb*
to carry a pistol *US*
• — Ethan Hilderbrant, *Prison Slang*, p. 123, 1998

strat *noun*
a cigarette *UK*
• — Angela Devlin, *Prison Patter*, p. 110, 1996

Strat *noun*
a Fender '*Strat*ocaster' guitar, first manufactured in 1954 *US*
• He [Jimi Hendrix] was a gentle, shy guy, basically, who donned his character when he slipped his Strat on. — *Uncut*, p. 53, March 2004

strat *verb*
to deceive someone *BARBADOS*
• — Frank A. Collymore, *Barbadian Dialect*, p. 106, 1965

straw *noun*
1 marijuana; a marijuana cigarette *US, 1971*
Playing on **GRASS** or **HAY**.
• — Richard A. Spears, *The Slang and Jargon of Drugs and Drink*, p. 488, 1986
• — Mike Haskins, *Drugs*, p. 289, 2003
2 a hat *US*
• I'll beat you for your bankroll and your wardrobe too / And I'd beat you for your straw, but all suckers don't chew. — Dennis Wepman et al., *The Life*, p. 148, 1976

strawb *noun*
a strawberry *AUSTRALIA, 1985*

strawberries *noun*
LSD bearing a strawberry design *UK*
• Street names [...] stars, strawberries, sugar[.] — James Kay and Julian Cohen, *The Parents' Complete Guide to Young People and Drugs*, p. 141, 1998

strawberries and cream *noun*
a variety of MDMA, the recreational drug best known as ecstasy, identified by the pink and white colours of a pill *UK*
• — Gareth Thomas, *This Is Ecstasy*, p. 56, 2002

strawberry *noun*
1 a woman who trades sex for crack cocaine *US*
• — Geoffrey Froner, *Digging for Diamonds*, p. 59, 1989
• They would only say that they were investigating a series of crimes that involved women who traded sex for drugs. Since August, 1985, at least nine such women, known in street slang as "strawberries," have been found shot to death. — *Los Angeles Times*, p. 3, 24th February 1989
• The woman that answers is thin and emaciated, a crack addict, pipe in hand an all. This is SHERYL, a strawberry. — *Boyz N The Hood*, p. 48, 1990
• — Judi Sanders, *Kickin' like Chicken with the Couch Commander*, p. 23, 1992
• — Mark S. Fleisher, *Beggars & Thieves*, p. 291, 1995: 'Glossary'
• The "strawberries" or rock whores, who worked farther east on the boulevard, would blow a guy in a doorway just for a taste of rock cocaine. — Joseph Wambaugh, *Floaters*, p. 39, 1996
• [In downtown Los Angeles] Some of the local beer bars have prostitutes known as strawberries. Strawberries are anybody's for a helping of rock cocaine which (in 1994) is worth 4 or 5 dollars. — Fiona Pitt-Kethley, *Red Light Districts of the World*, p. 85, 2000
2 the female nipple *US*
Usually in the plural.
• — *Maledicta*, p. 132, Summer/Winter 1982: 'Dyke diction': the language of lesbians
3 a tablet of mescaline *US, 1971*
From the colour of the tablet.
• — Richard A. Spears, *The Slang and Jargon of Drugs and Drink*, p. 488, 1986
• — Mike Haskins, *Drugs*, p. 283, 2003
4 a bruise or scrape *CANADA, 1921*
• — *American Speech*, p. 158–160, May 1959: 'Smokejumping words'
• Tommy Harper has a pulled thigh muscle and a bad sliding strawberry. — Jim Bouton, *Ball Four*, p. 244, 1970
• — Judi Sanders, *Mashing and Munching in Ames*, p. 19, 1994

strawberry fields; fields; strawberries *noun*
LSD *US*
Named for the drug-inspired imagery that is the Beatles song 'Strawberry Fields Forever', 1966. Strawberry Fields is an area of Liverpool.
• — Richard A. Spears, *The Slang and Jargon of Drugs and Drink*, p. 488, 1986
• — Mike Haskins, *Drugs*, p. 285, 2003

strawberry jam *noun*
1 the corpse of a person who has died with massive injuries *US*
• — *Maledicta*, p. 180, Summer/Winter 1986–1987: 'Sexual slang: prostitutes, pedophiles, flagellators, transvestites, and necrophiles'
2 an unspecified flammable substance *US*
• He'd recognized the slang term 'strawberry jam.' It was GI jargon for gasoline, or napalm, or whatever the flame-throwing tanks were carrying this week. — Jack Hawkins, *Chopper One #2*, p. 57, 1987

strawberry patch *noun*
a brakevan (caboose) seen from the rear at night *US*
From the red lights.
• — Norman Carlisle, *The Modern Wonder Book of Trains and Railroading*, p. 268, 1946

strawberry ripple *noun*
a cripple *UK*
Rhyming slang, from an ice-cream variety.
• He spent months in a wheelchair [...] living in a "strawberry ripple" residential school. — *New Society*, p. 210, 5th August 1982

strawberry shortcake *noun*
amphetamine; MDMA, the recreational drug best known as ecstasy *US*
• — William D. Alsever, *Glossary for the Establishment and Other Uptight People*, p. 1, December 1970
• — Mike Haskins, *Drugs*, p. 279, 2003

strawberry tablet; strawberry *noun*
a variety of MDMA, the recreational drug best known as ecstasy *UK*

From the pink colour of the tablet.
- —Angela Devlin, *Prison Patter*, p. 110, 1996
- —Gareth Thomas, *This Is Ecstasy*, p. 56, 2002

strawberry tart; strawberry *noun*
the heart *UK, 1984*
Rhyming slang.
- —Ray Puxley, *Cockney Rabbit*, 1992

straw boss *noun*
an assistant foreman *US, 1894*
- "Break up that prayer meeting!" the white straw boss yelled. —Richard A. Wright, *Black Boy*, p. 163, 1945
- The shabby Dutchman, the straw boss, now went up to the woman and repeated to her, word for word and shriek for shriek, what my father-in-law had said. —Kurt Vonnegut, *Mother Night*, p. 96, 1966

strawboss *verb*
to work as an assistant foreman *US*
- I think if mean Mack Rivers ain't strawbossing the thieving tricky niggers dealing numbers and dope, that spaghetti-gut enforcer got to stick his ass out for me to blow it off. —Iceberg Slim (Robert Beck), *Death Wish*, p. 191, 1977

straw hat *noun*
in the car sales business, a convertible top *US*
- — *Cars*, p. 41, December 1953

strawny *verb*
to figure something out *CANADA*
- "I can't strawny this one out." –from Cape Sable Island oral informant. —Lewis Poteet, *The South Shore Phrase Book*, p. 110, 1999

straws *noun*
strawberries *UK, 1961*
Greengrocers' abbreviation, both spoken and used in signage.

stray *noun*
a solitary enemy soldier *US*
Borrowed from the lexicon of the cowhand, referring to stray cattle.
- —Linda Reinberg, *In the Field*, p. 210, 1991

streak *noun*
a thin person *AUSTRALIA, 1941*
Usually qualified (**LONG STREAK OF MISERY**; **LONG STREAK OF PISS**); in its unqualified form it is more often used in Australia and New Zealand but not exclusively so.
- Percy, a short streak of profanity, dark like a Liverpool Spaniard[.] —Troy Kennedy Martin, *Z Cars*, p. 5, 1962
- —David McGill, *David McGill's Complete Kiwi Slang Dictionary*, p. 120, 1998

▸ put a streak in it
to hurry *UK*
- Through the pandemonium cut a megaphone voice, adjuring the laggards in some class to "put a streak into it! Numbers 3, 7 and 16, we're waiting for you." —Nicholas Blake, *The Private Wound*, 1968

streak *verb*
1 to move at great speed *UK, 1768*
- Mercy sakes we be doin' it to it in the left lane and we be definitely streaking. —Lanie Dills, *The Official CB Slanguage Language Dictionary*, p. 67, 1976
- [T]he fast-starting [Mika] Hakkinen streaked past all three into a lead that he was to keep until the Safety Car appeared towards half-distance. — *Daily Telegraph*, 31st July 2000

2 to run naked through a crowd, especially at public events, either as a protest or out of exhibitionism *US*
Adapted from the sense 'to go very fast'.
- —John D. Bell et al., *Loosely Speaking*, p. 18, 1966
- — *Current Slang*, p. 21, Summer 1970
- — *American Speech*, Spring-Summer 1973
- He took to "streaking" whenever he was drunk, which was virtually every day. —Simon Napier-Bell, *Black Vinyl White Powder*, p. 204, 2001

streak of misery *noun*
a tall, thin, morose person *AUSTRALIA*
- Listen, y'wrung-out streak o' misery, 'ow many times do I have to tell yer? —W.R. Bennett, *Wingman*, p. 98, 1961

streak of pelican shit *noun*
a tall, thin person *AUSTRALIA*
- Tall bloke, he was. A long thin streak of pelican shit. —Alexander Buzo, *Norm and Ahmed*, p. 12, 1969

streak of piss *noun*
an inconsequential or weak person *UK*
Adapted from **LONG STREAK OF PISS** (a tall, thin person).
- [I]f you went and broke into someone's house, any old fucking streak of piss could not only blow you away, but suffer absolutely no come-back for it whatsoever. —Danny King, *The Burglar Diaries*, p. 206, 2001

streak of rust *noun*
a railway *US*
- —Norman Carlisle, *The Modern Wonder Book of Trains and Railroading*, p. 267, 1946

streak of the squeak *noun*
cowardice *UK*
- [H]e's always had a streak of the squeak in him, fuck knows where he gets it. —J.J. Connolly, *Layer Cake*, p. 56, 2000

streaky weather *noun*
a changing weather situation *CANADA, 1990*
- Changing weather might be called 'streaky,' [on Prince Edward Island]. — *New Maritimes*, p. 29, March-April 1990

street *noun*
1 the essence of modern urban life for the poor, with suggestions of the underworld or the shadows between the underworld and the legitimate mainstream *US, 1967*
- —Cat Mother and the All Night Newsboys, *The Street Giveth and the Street Taketh Away*, 1969
- The street is where young bloods get their education. —H. Rap Brown, *Die Nigger Die!*, p. 25, 1969

2 in stud poker, a card *US*
For example, the fifth card dealt is known as 'fifth street'.
- —George Percy, *The Language of Poker*, p. 88, 1988

▸ on the street
not imprisoned; released from prison *US, 1935*
- If you ran the names of all the bad guys convicted by Judge Gibbs who are back on the street and wouldn't mind taking a whack at him, you could paper this room with the printouts. —Elmore Leonard, *Maximum Bob*, p. 89, 1991

street *adjective*
1 experienced in or possessing the necessary qualities for urban survival *US*
- "I'm street, just like you are, the judge said to the defendant, "and your attorney either doesn't have her shit together or your best interest at heart." —Elmore Leonard, *City Primeval*, p. 8, 1980
- Vanilla Ice's mistake – he should have never said he was street [...] But when you come out and you say street, street is a rite of passage. Every black person isn't street. When you say you're street that means you have had to live on the street. —Alex Ogg, *The Hip Hop Years [quoting Ice-T]*, p. 131, 1999

2 having an admired-as-fashionable quality of being understood by or of urban youth *UK*
Abbreviated from **STREETCRED** in turn shortened from 'street-credibility', but also informed by **STREET** (the essence of modern urban life).
- In the punk era, the word "credible" got tied up with the word "street". "Street" and "cred" were usually interchangeable but sometimes there were subtle fluctuations in meaning. Everyone was credible providing they did amphetamine sulphate, but if they also spat and swore they were probably "street-cred". —Simon Napier-Bell, *Black Vinyl White Powder*, p. 277, 2001

street bookie *noun*
a bookmaker who takes bets on the street, without an established place of business *US*
- There are "street bookies," who work in specific – usually poor – neighborhoods, collecting their bets either at fixed locations or by making rounds[.] — *The Knapp Commission Report on Police Corruption*, p. 85, 1972

street cat *noun*
a man, especially a young black man, who spends his life on the edges of crime *US*
- [S]uch peripheral types as "street cats" and "shadies" are not members, though these groups frequently interact with those who truly belong to the Life. —Dennis Wepman et al., *The Life*, p. 2, 1976

street cred *noun*
an admired-as-fashionable quality of being understood by or of urban youth *UK, 1981*
Abbreviated from 'street-credibility' (late 1970s).

- New Romantics [a youth fashion] were considered "street-cred" if they'd started out at the Blitz club or did drugs, like Visage or Culture Club. — Simon Napier-Bell, *Black Vinyl White Powder*, p. 277, 2001

street divorce *noun*
a domestic quarrel that ends in one spouse murdering the other *US*
- "So you butt in and give him a fucking street divorce," Drucker hissed. — Stephen J. Cannell, *The Tin Collectors*, p. 29, 2001

street doctor *noun*
a drug dealer *US*
- — Ethan Hilderbrant, *Prison Slang*, p. 123, 1998

streeter *noun*
a person who spends his time fraternising and carousing on the street *US*
- The streeters don't bother the Divine followers. They don't steal from them or try to con them out of anything. — Nathan Heard, *Howard Street*, p. 33, 1968

street-legal *adjective*
used of a motor vehicle, in compliance with all motor vehicle laws *US*
- — John Edwards, *Auto Dictionary*, p. 163, 1993

street machine *noun*
a car made for street driving *US*
- — Ed Radlauer, *Drag Racing Pix Dix*, p. 53, 1970

street name *noun*
a nickname by which you are known by acquaintances *US*
- They still call him Chucky Buck, Rainy said. It was like his street name before he moved up to his top floor condominium. Yeah, Chucky Buck. — Elmore Leonard, *Stick*, p. 8, 1983
- Sure I know her other street name. It was Felita's Mother because everybody knew me, I was so cute. — Robert Campbell, *Alice in La-La Land*, p. 290, 1987

street person; street people *noun*
a person living, or spending most of their time, on the street *US*
A semi-voluntary, semi-political state that preceded 'homelessness' as a label.
- A Digger event. Flowers, mirrors, penny-whistles, girls in costumes of themselves, Hell's Angels, street people, Mime Troupe. Angels ride up Haight with girls holding Now! SIGNS. — *The Digger Papers*, p. 3, August 1968

streets ahead *adjective*
absolutely superior *UK, 1898*
- Ah, a Safeway Superstore is streets ahead for iceberg lettuces. Say those who know. — Hilary Mantel, *Eight Months on Gazzah Street*, p. 66, 2003

streets behind *adjective*
greatly inferior *UK, 1984*
The natural opposite of **STREETS AHEAD**.

streets better *adjective*
greatly superior *UK, 1917*
A variation of **STREETS AHEAD**.

street-smart *adjective*
familiar with the human condition as played out in an urban setting *US*
- "The trouble is," Hunter said, "like most guys like that, he really doesn't know anything. He's not street-smart." — George V. Higgins, *The Judgment of Deke Hunter*, p. 125, 1976

street smarts *noun*
an intuitive understanding of human nature as played out in urban reality *US*
- He's got more learnin than just the paperbooks ridin his hip alla time. That Barker's got street smarts. — Seth Morgan, *Homeboy*, p. 43, 1990
- I know. All passion, no street smarts. — *A Few Good Men*, 1992

street squirrel *noun*
a person who rides a moped or small motorcyle with an attitude and style befitting a large motorcyle *US*
- — Lewis Poteet, *Car & Motorcyle Slang*, p. 191, 1992

street sweeper *noun*
a taxi driver who solicits customers on the street *US*
- The incidents that Mr. Louis decribed were all perpetrated against drivers who were doing street hails, or as we refer to them, street sweepers. [Letter to the editor] — *New York Sun*, p. 9, 2nd March 2004

streetsy *adjective*
of a manner of speech or vocabulary, having a contemporary urban quality *US*
- Dialogue was good, real streetsy and hip. — Joel Rose, *Kill Kill Faster Faster*, p. 41, 1997

street tax *noun*
in an illegal drug-selling enterprise, the share of an individual's earnings paid to his gang *US*
- — *American Speech*, p. 422, Winter 1997: 'Among the New Words'

streetwalker *noun*
1 a prostitute who seeks customers on the street *UK, 1592*
- It is difficult and dangerous to fall in with streetwalkers on the avenues[.] — Jack Lait and Lee Mortimer, *New York Confidential*, p. 206, 1948
- She was a streetwalker and I bought her a coffee in a hash joint. — Mickey Spillane, *My Gun is Quick*, p. 12, 1950

2 in oil drilling, an operator who does not have an office *US*
- — Jerry Robertson, *Oil Slanguage*, p. 115, 1954

street-wise *adjective*
experienced in or possessing the necessary qualities for urban survival *US*
- Maybe law-abiding America is getting as streetwise as its criminal class. — *Illustrated London News*, May 1981

-strel *suffix*
when combined with a music style, a singer in that style *UK*
From 'minstrel'. 'Teen angstrel' (a teen singer affecting angst) and 'popstrel' are noted by Susie Dent, *The Language Report*, 2003.

strength *noun*
the essential facts; the pertinent details *AUSTRALIA, 1908*
- STRENGTH OF IT – To learn the details. — Gilbert H. Lawson, *A Dictionary of Australian Words and Terms*, 1924
- 'I remember there was some sort of bust up, but I never got the strength of it.' 'Strength of it was old Ma Randal copped old Randal absolutely doing a bear up in that piece's bed.' — Norman Lindsay, *Halfway to Anywhere*, p. 42, 1947
- I asked another geezer for the strength of him, and the strength was that he'd got nicked for ponceing off his old woman who was a brass. — Frank Norman, *Bang To Rights*, p. 8, 1958

▸ **on the strength**
used to signify agreement, import or sincerity *US, 1995*
- Sometimes, when you really wanted people to believe what you said, "on the strength" certified your commitment[.] — Nelson George, *Hip Hop America*, p. 209, 1998

stress-head *noun*
a person who is habitually stressed; a constant worrier *AUSTRALIA*
- The perfect book for the stress-head in your life – and it's only $4.95! — *Dolly*, p. 27, 1996

stretch *noun*
1 a prison sentence; one year's imprisonment *US, 1821*
A prison sentence of a number of years is given with the number of years preceding 'stretch'.
- He had been a pickpocket until a long stretch up the river gave him a turn of mind. — Mickey Spillane, *I, The Jury*, p. 15, 1947
- But a lot of the cases – after the booster detail has nabbed the guilty parties – end up in the charge being busted to vagrancy with a misdemeanor stretch at the county jail. — *San Francisco Call-Bulletin*, 28th June 1949
- That's kid stuff, and anyhow them judges sent too many away for long stretches. — Hal Ellson, *The Golden Spike*, p. 73, 1952
- Telling about a stretch in Atlanta, where he kicked a habit cold: "Fourteen days I was beating my head against the wall[.]" — William Burroughs, *Junkie*, p. 68, 1953
- A search of the sewer was begun for his body and the young criminals were taken to the police station, facing a long stretch in the reformatory. — Jim Thompson, *Bad Boy*, p. 291, 1953
- "How long you got to do now?" He asked. "About a streatch [sic]." I answered. — Frank Norman, *Bang to Rights*, 1958
- Arrest, petty larceny and possession – and so on, until you wind up in a prison for a real stretch[.] — Ross Russell, *The Sound*, p. 234, 1961

- That night she wrecked "Harlem's" dope supply and when "Willie" finishes his ten year stretch, he'll have to take another city for it[.] —Babs Gonzales, *I Paid My Dues*, p. 102, 1967
- I was in County Jail with a long stretch ahead of me and two good books to while away the time. —A.S. Jackson, *Gentleman Pimp*, p. 9, 1973
- Jean does as she's bleeding well told. Especially to keep Jimmy off a twenty five stretch. —Ted Lewis, *Jack Carter's Law*, p. 53, 1974
- [I]t's not been an easy life, particularly with that little stretch in Hull. —Anthony Masters, *Minder*, p. 6, 1984
- [H]e had only just completed a stretch at her majesty's pleasure anyway. —Donald Gorgon, *Cop Killer*, p. 3, 1994
- [A]long with an actual two-year stretch he had done for fraud and embezzlement. —Terry Southern, *Now Dig This*, p. 145, 2001

2 a longer-than-normal limousine with extended seating *US, 1982*
From 'stretch limousine'.
- He told her he got the band a stretch, a black one, so they'd arrive at the Forum looking big-time, past the marquee to see their name under Aeromithl. —Elmore Leonard, *Be Cool*, p. 260, 1999

3 the penis *UK, 2001*

4 in poker, a hand consisting of a sequence of five cards *US*
Known conventionally as a 'straight'.
- —George Percy, *The Language of Poker*, p. 88, 1988

▸ to do a stretch
to shoplift *NEW ZEALAND, 1985*
- —Harry Orsman, *A Dictionary of Modern New Zealand Slang*, p. 132, 1999

stretch *verb*
1 to serve time in prison *US*
From **STRETCH** (a prison sentence).
- I'd be contributing my ideas for the comic strip from the joint [...] Yeah, me and The Source got real tight back when I was stretchin'. — *The Source*, p. 36, March 2002

2 to put someone to death by hanging *US*
- —Joseph E. Ragen and Charles Finston, *Inside the World's Toughest Prison*, p. 820, 1962: 'Penitentiary and underworld glossary'

stretched out *adjective*
in trucking, travelling fast *US*
- —Montie Tak, *Truck Talk*, p. 3, 1971

stretcher *noun*
1 a lie *UK, 1674*
- He got all the stuff to put in his article -except the pure-stretchers he made up – by hanging around the Queen City jail[.] —Guy Owen, *The Flim-Flam Man and the Apprentice Grifter*, 1972

2 a substance added to a drug for the simple purpose of diluting it for increased profit when sold *US*
- —William D. Alsever, *Glossary for the Establishment and Other Uptight People*, p. 15, December 1970

stretcher-case *noun*
a person who is exhausted *UK*
- Your mother's a stretcher-case. —Paul Baker, *Polari*, p. 190, 2002

stretchers *noun*
shoe laces *US*
- —Joseph E. Ragen and Charles Finston, *Inside the World's Toughest Prison*, p. 820, 1962: 'Penitentiary and underworld glossary'

stretches *noun*
years; a very long time *UK*
From **STRETCH** (a year's imprisonment).
- [S]he's getting all worked up cos she probably ain't had a portion [sex] in stretches. —J.J. Connolly, *Layer Cake*, p. 284, 2000

strewth!; struth!
used as an oath *UK, 1892*
A shortening of 'God's truth!'.
- Gov' struth, I thought this was a temperance hotel! —Norman Lindsay, *Comic Art of Norman Lindsay*, p. 115, 1905
- 'Strewth!' was the reply, 'it was dead lively!' — *The Australian Magazine*, 1st November 1908
- 'STRUTH – An exclamation. —Gilbert H. Lawson, *A Dictionary of Australian Words and Terms*, 1924
- —J.E. MacDonnell, *Don't Gimme the Ships*, p. 50, 1960
- ''Struth – that was bloody close!' —W.R. Bennett, *Target Turin*, p. 47, 1962
- —John Wynnum, *Jiggin' in the Riggin'*, p. 12, 1965
- Struth, what's 'e doin' 'ere? —Joe Andersen, *Winners Can Laugh*, p. 13, 1982
- Struth, I should get a job writing Home and Away. — *Tracks*, p. 131, October 1992

strides *noun*
1 trousers *UK, 1889*
Being the tailored articles in which you 'stride'.
- Dig this outfit: a shepherd-plaid suit with strides that hit him about an inch above his shoe tops, so tight he must have worked his way into them with a shoehorn[.] —Mezz Mezzrow, *Really the Blues*, p. 50, 1946
- Some of those guys up there might try to clip you for those strides now that you've got 'em all fixed up. —Chester Himes, *Cast the First Stone*, p. 106, 1952
- I started livin and usin drugs and buyin clothes, strides and stomps that'd set you back a whole month's pay! —Clarence Cooper Jr, *The Scene*, p. 137, 1960
- He said, "Whatsa matter, Buddy, some broad ram it into you for your 'poke' [wallet] or did you leave it in your other 'Stides?'" —Iceberg Slim (Robert Beck), *Pimp*, p. 97, 1969
- —Clarence Major, *Dictionary of Afro-American Slang*, p. 110, 1970
- Now it's up to Charlie to back his flush [a poker hand] or macaroni [crap] his strides. —Ted Lewis, *Jack Carter's Law*, p. 47, 1974
- Mr Fujifuckinwara is going to have a bit of a fucking shock when he shoves his Aquascutum strides in there overnight. —Greg Williams, *Diamond Geezers*, p. 120, 1997
- You're joking. I'm not dropping me strides in this weather. — Martin King and Martin Knight, *The Naughty Nineties*, p. 26, 1999
- Who told that cunt he could bleed on my strides? —Garry Bushell, *The Face*, p. 111, 2001

2 trousers that are reserved for messy jobs, especially in car customising *US*
- —Tom MacPherson, *Dragging and Driving*, p. 142, 1960

strike!
used as an expression of shock, surprise or astonishment *AUSTRALIA, 1915*
Short for **STRIKE ME BLIND!** or **STRIKE A LIGHT!**.
- "How much longer we got, Bert?" Blackie asked. "Another twenty minutes." "Cor, strike!" —Derek Bickerton, *Payroll*, p. 44, 1959
- Aw no!!! Strike! It couldn't have been! There is no such thing as ghosts. —Barry Humphries, *Bazza Pulls It Off!*, 1971

strike a light!
used as an expression of shock, surprise or astonishment *AUSTRALIA, 1922*
- 'Strike a light, Mrs Parker,' said Mrs Frisby, 'it is time you were going home'. —Patrick White, *The Tree of Man*, p. 162, 1955

strike me!
used for expressing great surprise *AUSTRALIA, 1874*
- Strike me. This cove's stashin' it away. —Gerald Sweeney, *The Plunge*, p. 192, 1981

strike me blind!; strike me dumb!; strike me lucky!
used for registering shock, surprise or astonishment *UK*
Other variations include calls on God to strike the speaker 'bountiful', 'vulgar', 'ugly' or 'pink'.The earliest variation recorded is 'strike me dumb' in Vanbrugh's *The Relapse*, 1696 and 'strike me blind!' appears in 1704; 'strike me lucky!' from 1849, was a popular catchphrase in Australia in the 1930s.
- Strike me lucky, I reckon I'm a gonna!!! —Barry Humphries, *Bazza Pulls It Off!*, 1971

strike me dead; strike me *noun*
bread *UK*
Rhyming slang.
- —Ray Puxley, *Cockney Rabbit*, 1992

strike me dead!
used for expressing great surprise *AUSTRALIA, 1932*
- The only reply reached my ears when, I like to think, we were considered out of earshot. It was simply: 'Gawd strike me dead.' —Harold Lewis, *Crow On A Barbed Wire Fence*, p. 2, 1973

strike me fat!
used for expressing great surprise *AUSTRALIA, 1895*
- 'Strike me fat!' shouted the merry-go-roundsman, 'I useter think this thing belonged to me, but I ain't so sure since you come along!' —Ernest O'Ferrall, *Stories by 'Kodak'*, p. 58, 1933
- God strike me fat! Look who's here! —D'Arcy Niland, *The Shiralee*, p. 82, 1955

strike me handsome!
used for expressing great surprise *AUSTRALIA, 1955*
- Strike me bloody 'andsome, I just told yer. Three bob. —Nino Culotta (John O'Grady), *They're A Weird Mob*, p. 16, 1957
- —John Wynnum, *Jiggin' in the Riggin'*, p. 38, 1965

strike me pink!

used for expressing great surprise *AUSTRALIA, 1892*

- — Erle Cox, *Out of the Silence*, p. 254, 1925
- Some Digger have reached Aussie, / 'In good heart' the papers say; / Why, strike me pink! I'll bet they are... — Tip Kelaher, *The Digger Hat and other verses*, p. 50, 1942
- Strike me pink! You'll want lavender water next[.] — Ion L. Idriess, *Over the Range*, p. 257, 1947

strike me purple!

used for expressing great surprise *AUSTRALIA, 1915*

- PARSON: 'O, my good friend, what is the use of that language?' BULLOCKY: 'Well, strike me purple, it's the best I can do. If you reckon you can bloody well do any better take the bloody whip and have a bloody try.' — Norman Lindsay, *Comic Art of Norman Lindsay*, p. 101, 1904
- Stike me purple, a man's got to eat! — J.E. MacDonnell, *Sabotage!*, p. 21, 1964

strike me roan!

used for expressing great surprise *AUSTRALIA, 1917*

- 'Gor, strike me bloody roan' says the bloke. 'Where ever you go it's friggin' tax.' — Sam Weller, *Old Bastards I Have Met*, p. 129, 1979

strike me up a gum-tree

used for expressing great surprise *AUSTRALIA*

- 'Strike me up a gum-tree!' Splinter suggested in an ejaculatory tone, 'you don't mean a fulla named Meredith?' — J.E. MacDonnell, *Don't Gimme the Ships*, p. 75, 1960
- '[Y]ou'll suddenly wake up one bright morning to find he's slipped a swiftie over you, has the whole game sewn up, and all you slow-coaches up a gum tree telling the crows he can't do it.' — Dymphna Cusack, *Picnic Races*, p. 70, 1962
- It was simply: "Gawd strike me dead." It was an expression I was to hear several times a day from then onward, varied according to how the pleader desired to be struck. It might be pink, or up a gum tree, or it might be hooray. — Harold Lewis, *Crow On A Barbed Wire Fence*, p. 2, 1973

strike-out *noun*

a hospital patient who has died or lapsed into a neurologically depressed state *US*

- — *Philadelphia Magazine*, p. 145–151, November 1977: 'Language: doctor, there's a gomer in the pit'

Strike U *nickname*

the US Naval Strike Warfare Center, Fallon, Nevada *US*

- — *American Speech*, p. 402, Winter 1991: 'Among the new words'

strillers; strill; strills *noun*

a musical instrument, especially a piano; a musician *UK*

Polari; possibly from Italian *strillare* (to shriek). Thus, for a pianist: 'strill homey' or 'strillers omee' (a piano man), or 'strill polone' (a piano woman).

- Order lau [place] your luppers [fingers] on the strillers bona [well]. — Barry Took and Marty Feldman, *Round The Horne*, 4th June 1967

Strine *noun*

broad Australian English, specifically that form of Australian English which appeared in the books of Alastair Morrison *AUSTRALIA, 1964*

'Strine' is supposedly how the word 'Australian' is said in the Australian accent. It is not a separate language or dialect, but rather a jocular celebration of the Australian accent utilising respelling, shifting word boundaries and much elision to give the impression that other words are being spoken, e.g. *sly drool* is Strine for 'slide rule', *Emma Chisit* for 'how much is it?', *laze and gem* for 'ladies and gentlemen', *let stalk Strine* for 'let's talk Australian'.

- They ought to (in strine, aorta) give a man a fair go[.] — Frank Hardy, *The Outcasts of Foolgarah*, p. 129, 1971
- — Arthur Chipper, *The Aussie Swearer's Guide*, p. 96, 1972
- Only last year news was leaked that evening classes had been established there to coach newly enlisted citizens in the nasal esoterics of Strine[.] — Bill Hornadge, *The Ugly Australian*, p. 110, 1974
- — Bill Hornadge, *The Australian Slanguage*, p. 31, 1980: 'The whine of strine fall minely on the pline'
- [A]ll translations, for those not fluent in Strine, can be found at your local RSL or outback pub. — *Australian Ultimate*, p. 7, 2003

string *noun*

1 being hoaxed; being kept under control *UK*

- I had to get the old bag on the end of a string, which I found was only too easy — Frank Norman, *Bang To Rights*, p. 111, 1958

2 the group of prostitutes working for a particular pimp *US, 1913*

- Shortly before six the pimps parade their strings for all to admire. — Gail Sheehy, *Hustling*, p. 89, 1973
- Helen wasn't in my string. He was an independent. She came and went as she pleased. — Robert Campbell, *Junkyard Dog*, p. 72, 1986

string *verb*

to manipulate a wire into a slot machine to trigger the free-play mechanism *US*

- Stringing means taping, tying, gluing, or otherwise affixing a string or fine wire to a coin and then inserting and retracting it from the machine in order to get free plays. — Jim Regan, *Winning at Slot Machine*, p. 68, 1985

string bean *noun*

a tall, thin person *UK*

- One of them, a string bean with a starter moustache[.] — Patrick Neate, *Where You're At*, p. 28, 2003

string beans; strings *noun*

jeans *UK*

Rhyming slang.

- — Ray Puxley, *Cockney Rabbit*, 1992

stringer *noun*

1 in poker, an instalment bet or the person making it *US*

- — George Percy, *The Language of Poker*, p. 88, 1988

2 in poker, a hand of five cards in sequence *US*

Conventionally known as a 'straight'.

- — Albert H. Morehead, *The Complete Guide to Winning Poker*, p. 274, 1967

3 a railway brakeman *US*

- — Ramon Adams, *The Language of the Railroader*, p. 149, 1977

4 a narrow strip of laminated wood on a surfboard *US*

- The Yater – the clear one with the thin stringer. — *Apocalypse Now*, 1979

stringie *noun*

a string bag *AUSTRALIA*

- It's not that we get that personal, but you don't want different ones craning their necks to see what a man's wife's got in her stringie! — Barry Humphries, *A Nice Night's Entertainment*, p. 110, 1968

strings *noun*

1 the female legs *US*

- — *American Speech*, p. 273, December 1963: 'American Indian student slang'

2 spaghetti *US*

- Yardbird and strings. Harlem's own vernacular for the fried chicken and spaghetti which was so common, so cheap and so utterly, unbelievably wonderful at such wrong hours – like the hours around dawn, for instance. — Robert Sylvester, *No Cover Charge*, p. 43, 1956

string up *verb*

to execute someone by hanging *UK*

- What a crime to string up a youngster like that[.] — John Peter Jones, *Feather Pluckers*, p. 139, 1964

string vest *noun*

a *pest*, a nuisance *UK*

Rhyming slang.

- Look out here comes the string vest. — Ray Puxley, *Fresh Rabbit*, 1998

strip *noun*

1 in a striptease show, the portion of the show in which the dancer removes her last garments *US*

- In succession as the Flash or entrance; the Parade or march across the stage, in full costume; the Tease or increasing removal of wearing apparel; and the climactic Strip or denuding down to the G-String[.] — *Saturay REview of Literature*, p. 28, 18th August 1945: 'Take 'Em Off!'

2 a neighbourhood *BAHAMAS*

- — John A. Holm, *Dictionary of Bahamian English*, p. 197, 1982

3 a thoroughfare in a town or city lined with bars, nightclubs, off-licences and restaurants *US, 1939*

- The whole strip is shrinking. Ah, you know, I remember about five years ago, take yuh a couple of hours and a tank full of gas just to make one circuit. — *American Graffiti*, 1973
- Tonight, tonight, the strip's just right / I wanna blow 'em off in my first heat. — Bruce Springsteen, *Racing in the Street*, 1978

4 a Benzedrine™-soaked strip of paper from an inhaler, removed from the inhaler and ingested as a central nervous system stimulant *US*

- Yeah, the strips couldn't feed Lefty's hunger. — Thurston Scott, *Cure it with Honey*, p. 15, 1951
- "You want a strip, Hart?" Ben asked genially as he carefully wadded a piece of benzedrine-soaked paper in a chunk of chewing gum. It was the last of his second inhaler of the weekend, each of which had contained eight strips. — John Clellon Holmes, *Go*, p. 121, 1952

Strip *noun*

▸ **the Strip**

1 the portion of Sunset Boulevard between Crescent Heights Boulevard and Doheny Drive, Los Angeles, California *US*

- [H]e emerged, propelling the wheelchair in which he sat, from the darkness of the hospital movie basement with its pitiful representation of the Strip in Hollywood[.] —Jack Kerouac, *Letter to Neal Cassady*, p. 323–324, 31 August 1951
- Also, he had gotten into the habit of falling in love with teen-age girls, like this Chippy on the Strip, for whom he had just bought a new cloth coat. —Clancy Sigal, *Going Away*, p. 3, 1961
- Claiming direct relationship to The Strip are illegal gambling operations, expensive call girls, pushers, pimps, and con men. —Roger Gordon, *Hollywood's Sexual Underground*, p. 113, 1966
- [B]eneath my window the Strip (Sunset Boulevard in Hollywood, California) is filled with noisy cars[.] —Gore Vidal, *Myra Breckinridge*, p. 5, 1968
- [L]ooking down from the eleventh floor balcony at a police ambulance screaming down toward the Whiskey A Go-Go on the Strip, where I used to sit in the afternoon with Lionel and talk with off-duty hookers. —Hunter S. Thompson, *Songs of the Doomed: More Notes on the Death of the American Dream*, p. 119, 16th February 1969
- I suppose in this era young girls you pick up hitchhiking on the Strip would not say, "I want to be an actress." —Mort Sahl, *Heartland*, p. 59, 1976
- Well, there was this chick – name of Sally – very cute, twenty-three, twenty-four years old, worked as a kind of hat-check cigarette-girl at a small club on the Strip. —Terry Southern, *Now Dig This*, p. 18, 1981

2 Las Vegas Boulevard south of central Las Vegas, Nevada, lined with neon-signed hotels and casinos *US*

- In the middle of a National District Attorneys' Confederence at an elegant hotel on the strip. —Hunter S. Thompson, *Fear and Loathing in Las Vegas*, p. 80, 1971
- The Strip where most of the super-luxury hotels are has more neon lighting than fabulous Broadway ever dreamed of. —Mario Puzo, *Inside Las Vegas*, p. 67–68, 1977
- —Laurence Urdang, *Names and Nicknames of Places and Things*, p. 242, 1987

3 a section of Yonge Street, between Dundas and Bloor, in central Toronto, Ontario *US*

A flashy, noisy part of town.

- —Laurence Urdang, *Names and Nicknames of Places and Things*, p. 242, 1987

stripe *noun*

1 a scar, usually the result of a razor slash *UK*

Hence the adjective 'striped'.

- down the left side of my boat I've got a stripe which I collected one dark night —Frank Norman, *Bang To Rights*, p. 55, 1958

2 in the military, a promotion *US*

- —Carl Fleischhauer, *A Glossary of Army Slang*, p. 19, 1968

stripe *verb*

to slash someone with a blade *UK*

Descriptive of the scar that is made.

- [H]e had stripped [striped] this crank down the boat (=face). —Frank Norman, *Bang To Rights*, p. 28, 1958

stripe me!

used as a register of surprise or exasperation *UK*

- Stripe me, Dave, you gonna just stand there while some woofter is waving his tackle at your missus? —*The Full Monty*, 1997

striper *noun*

in prison, an improvised cutting weapon *UK*

- —Angela Devlin, *Prison Patter*, p. 111, 1996

stripes *noun*

1 a referee in an athletic contest *US*

- —Judi Sanders, *Da Bomb!*, p. 27, 1997

2 in pool, the striped balls numbered 9 to 15 *US*

- "I'm going to take the stripes." A striped ball and a solid one had fallen in on the break, giving Fats his choice. —Walter Tevis, *The Color of Money*, p. 66, 1984
- —Steve Rushin, *Pool Cool*, p. 28, 1990

3 in circus usage, tigers *US*

- —Don Wilmeth, *The Language of American Popular Entertainment*, p. 261, 1981

stripes and solids *noun*

in pool, the game of eight-ball *US, 1974*

- —Mike Shamos, *The Illustrated Encyclopedia of Billiards*, p. 235, 1993

striping *noun*

a severe reprimand *UK*

From **STRIPE** (to slash with a blade).

- I wanna day off after my striping from that old cunt. —J.J. Connolly, *Layer Cake*, p. 205, 2000

stripper *noun*

1 a striptease dancer (usually female), a performer who undresses creatively for the purpose of entertainment *US*

. Gypsy Rose Lee (Rose Louise Hovick, 1914–70) was, perhaps, the most famous of all strippers; in *Gypsy*, the musical biography (1962) by Stephen Sondheim, she discovers the word 'ecdysiast' to give her job description a veneer of respectability.

- Today, most strip women or strippers are called exotic dancers or sometimes topless dancers, though there are subtle distinctions between these appellations among the more artistic of practitioners. —Don B. Wilmeth, *The Language of American Popular Entertainment*, p. 261, 1981
- JAMIE: What's goin' on? LEE: We're auditionin' ero'ic dancers. JAMIE: We ain't gunner [going to] 'ave strippers in 'ere! LEE: I know that, but they don't. —Guy Ritchie et al, *Lock, Stock... & Four Stolen Hooves*, p. 5, 2000

2 a pickpocket *US*

- —Hyman E. Goldin et al., *Dictionary of American Underworld Lingo*, p. 214, 1950

3 a car thief who targets newer cars that will be stripped for parts *US*

- —*American Speech*, p. 272, December 1962: 'The language of traffic policemen'

4 a playing card that has been altered in a manner that facilitates its extraction from a full deck *US*

- —Frank Garcia, *Marked Cards and Loaded Dice*, p. 264, 1962

stripping hole; stripping pit *noun*

a strip mine *US*

- —Amy and Denise McFadden, *CoalSpeak*, p. 12, 1997

strippy *noun*

in prison, a strip search *UK*

- —Angela Devlin, *Prison Patter*, p. 110, 1996

strips *noun*

in prison, a segregation unit *UK*

- —Angela Devlin, *Prison Patter*, p. 94, 1996

stroke *noun*

1 an underhand, immoral or illegal trick *UK, 1970*

- You're famous for having more strokes than Oxford and Cambridge[.] —Anthony Masters, *Minder*, p. 98, 1984

2 praise or flattery *US, 1964*

Almost always in the plural.

- You flatter somebody outrageously. Even though they know you're doing it, the person getting the strokes is gratified. You flattered them. —Robert Campbell, *Boneyards*, p. 290, 1992

3 appetite *IRELAND*

- She has a great stroke —Irwin Liam, *North Munster Antiquarian Journal*, p. 82, 2000

stroke *verb*

1 to flatter someone *US*

- Who don't like to be stroked? —Edwin Torres, *After Hours*, p. 162, 1979

2 to masturbate *US*

Also 'stroke off'.

- While not the greatest menage ever taped, the action is not bad; it certainly provides material for some lazy stroking. —*Adult Video*, p. 53, August/September 1986
- "The boy is masturbating" [...] Beef [the penis] Strokin' off[.] —Erica Orloff and JoAnn Baker, *Dirty Little Secrets*, p. 89, 2001

▸ **stroke it**

1 in car racing, to drive with care and caution *US*

- I'd rather lead one lap and fall out of the race than stroke it and finish it in the money. —Tom Wolfe, *The Kandy-Kolored Tangerine-Flake Streamline Baby*, p. 156, 1965

2 to perform badly on purpose *US*

- We've been losing so many people going up against very heavily defended targets that our squadrons have begun to back off, to stroke it. —T.E. Cruise, *Wings of Gold III*, p. 219, 1989

▸ **stroke the lizard**

(of a male) to masturbate *US*

- —Eugene Landy, *The Underground Dictionary*, p. 178, 1971

stroke book *noun*

a magazine or book viewed while masturbating *US*

- Millions of other stroke books – the antecedent to Playboy, National Geographic with the African chicks – oh yes, they're stroke books. —Lenny Bruce, *The Essential Lenny Bruce*, p. 179, 1967

- Larry may utilize fluffers, watermelons, stroke books or harems of women to summon forth the gop..—Josh Alan Friedman, *Tales of Times Square*, p. 101, 1986
- But the pornographic novel, the stroke book, is a constitutionally protected form of free speech.—*Maledicta*, p. 7, 1988–1989
- What do you think I'm going to do with them? They're stroke books.—*Chasing Amy*, 1997
- Water sports have become a stroke-book staple.—*The Village Voice*, 8th February 2000

stroke mag *noun*

a pornographic magazine *UK*

The 'stroke' thus inspired is a direct reference to masturbatory technique.

- [T]here were stroke mags on sale[.]—Kitty Churchill, *Thinking of England*, p. 234, 1995

stroke-me-off *noun*

used as a humorous nickname for stroganoff, as in 'beef stroganoff' *US*

- —*Maledicta*, p. 284, 1984–1985: 'Food names'

stroker *noun*

1 a petty thief *IRELAND*

- "What the fuck do you think I am?" he said. Real hurt like. "A rent boy. Jasus [Jesus] sakes. I'me a fucking stroker, man. A villain. When I need money, I just hatch a little scheme.—Howard Paul, *The Joy*, p. 66, 1996

2 a hospital patient who has suffered a stroke *US*

- —*American Speech*, p. 145–148, May 1961: 'The spoken language of medicine; argot, slang, cant'

stroll *noun*

▸ the stroll

the collective activities on a street, mostly illegal, some involving sauntering as if innocently strolling *US*

- My education was completed on The Stroll and I became a Negro.—Mezz Mezzrow, *Really the Blues*, p. 210, 1946
- Hello Mayann. What in the world are you doing out on the stroll tonight?—Louis Armstrong, *Satchmo*, p. 200, 1954
- She showed me where the stroll was in town.—Susan Hall, *Gentleman of Leisure*, p. 17, 1972
- The stroll at the four corners of Hollywood and Vine was doing business, drugs and booze and flesh.—Robert Campbell, *Alice in La-La Land*, p. 8, 1987
- The area is also a "stroll" for prostitutes.—James Ridgeway, *Red Light*, p. 228, 1996

Stroll *noun*

▸ The Stroll

Seventh Avenue, New York *US*

- [S]pecific places are known by special nicknames – New York City as the Apple, Seventh Avenue as The Stroll[.]—Mezz Mezzrow, *Really the Blues*, p. 221, 1946

stroller *noun*

1 a car *US*

- —Robert George Reisner, *The Jazz Titans*, p. 166, 1960

2 a stone on the surface of the field *CANADA*

- Strollers are the first to be picked when picking rocks as they are the most visible and easiest to remove.—Chris Thain, *Cold as a Bay Street Banker's Heart*, p. 149, 1987

stroll on!

used for registering disbelief or surprise *UK, 1959*

- Just because they tried to get me on you last night, don't think you can pull the same trick. Stroll on.—Mike Hodges, *Get Carter*, p. 53, 1971
- I've saved Gerald and Les more than just twenty grand. Fucking stroll-on. I mean, you didn't have the balls for it, did you?—Ted Lewis, *Jack Carter's Law*, p. 200, 1974

strong *noun*

alcohol *TRINIDAD AND TOBAGO, 1989*

- —Lise Winer, *Dictionary of the English/Creole of Trinidad & Tobago*, 2003

▸ the strong of

the essential facts; the pertinent details *AUSTRALIA, 1908*

- —Jim Ramsay, *Cop It Sweet!*, p. 86, 1977
- What's the strong of getting us to split that stock-take of the fuels and oils?—Sam Weller, *Old Bastards I Have Met*, p. 89, 1979

strong *verb*

▸ strong it

to behave in an aggressive manner, or to take things to an extreme *UK, 1964*

A variation of **COME ON STRONG**.

- That's stronging it a bit.—Colin Butts, *Is Harry on the Boat?*, p. 126, 1997
- We've tumbled you, don't fuckin' strong it.—J.J. Connolly, *Know Your Enemy [britpulp]*, 1999
- "You're a working-class hero, Johnny." "Working is stronging it a bit, darlin'."—Garry Bushell, *The Face*, p. 120, 2001

strong *adjective*

1 of a theatrical performance, very sexual *US*

- "This is what we call a 'strong' theater," she said, by way of explanation. "We cheat as much as we can here."—*Eros*, p. 30, Spring 1962

2 well-funded at the moment *US*

Teen slang.

- —*San Francisco News*, p. 6, 25th March 1958

3 flush with money *US*

- —*This Week Magazine, New York Herald Tribune*, p. 46, 28th February 1954

▸ be going strong

to be prosperous, or enjoying continuing success, or full of energy and vigour *UK, 1898*

- [W]e saw our own entrant – Desdemona Stephanides, age ninety-one – going strong in the midst of the rest.—Jeffrey Eugenides, *Middlesex*, p. 287, 2003

▸ come it strong

to behave with boldness; to overstate something *UK, 1837*

- Last year I ended my review of his [Brian de Palma's] bonehead thriller Snake Eyes with the simple phrase "Burn the negative", which I'll admit was coming it a bit strong, perhaps.—*The Guardian*, 17th March 2000

▸ come on strong

to behave aggressively or exhibit aggressive behaviour; to have a success *US, 1970*

- Calling Vice President Gore "the elephant of negative advertising," Bradley came on strong as he tried to recover from a landslide loss to Gore in the Iowa caucuses just days before.—*The Guardian*, 27th January 2004

▸ go strong on

to support or follow a particular course with great energy or investment *UK, 1844*

- Steel giants go strong on brand building.—*The Telegraph (Calcutta)*, 5th December 2002

strongarm *noun*

1 a crime involving brute physical violence; a violent criminal *US, 1901*

- In both cases he was employed by businesses who needed strong-arm boys.—Mickey Spillane, *My Gun is Quick*, p. 76, 1950
- And, one by one, three more rothstein strong-arms were burned, cut, mutilated and killed.—Robert Sylvester, *No Cover Charge*, p. 12, 1956
- Strong-arms. I did lotsa strong-arms nobody knows about.—Joseph Wambaugh, *Fugitive Nights*, p. 176, 1992

2 a person who lends physicality and a capacity for brutal physical force to the moment *US, 1907*

Also called 'strongarm man'.

- The strong-arm men get all their money and they are broke.—Willard Motley, *Let No Man Write My Epitaph*, p. 188, 1958
- Most of these tough ones had worked as strongarm men for Dutch Schultz[.]—Malcolm X and Alex Haley, *The Autobiography of Malcolm X*, p. 87, 1964
- Bad too, big stud, used to be strongarm for the politicals in Havana.—Edwin Torres, *Carlito's Way*, p. 12, 1975
- [H]e became a strongarm man for the emerging gangster Jack Dragna[.]—Brian McDonald, *Elephant Boys*, p. 102, 2000

strong-arm *verb*

to rob a place roughly or violently *US, 1903*

- Schultz had strong-armed his way into control of the Harlem numbers busines.—Malcolm X and Alex Haley, *The Autobiography of Malcolm X*, p. 116, 1964
- "Party" hadn't strong-armed since his last bit. The only reason he hadn't was simply that none of the Johns we had fleeced was carrying a wad.—Iceberg Slim (Robert Beck), *Pimp*, p. 40, 1969

strong as a Mallee bull *adjective*

physically strong *AUSTRALIA, 1990*

- And the kiddie grew up, until he was as big as a full back and as strong as a Mallee bull[.]—Kel Richards, *The Aussie Bible*, p. 13, 2003

strong-back *adjective*

sexually aggressive; virile *TRINIDAD AND TOBAGO*

- —Lise Winer, *Dictionary of the English/Creole of Trinidad & Tobago*, 2003

strong box *noun*
a prison cell, usually windowless, designed for disruptive prisoners *UK*
- —Angela Devlin, *Prison Patter*, p. 110, 1996

strong like moose *adjective*
used humorously with a literal meaning *US*
A catchphrase of US television in the 1950s and 60s, first from the Uncle Tenoose character on *The Danny Thomas Show* and then from Boris Bandanov of the *Rocky and Bullwinkle Show*; spoken with a thick Russian accent.

strong move to the hole *noun*
a direct approach to seducing a girl *US*
Application of a basketball term to sexual relations, punning on **HOLE** as 'the basket' in the basketball term and 'the vagina' in this usage.
- —Connie Eble (Editor), *UNC-CH Campus Slang*, p. 9, Spring 1992

stronk *noun*
male and female sexual secretions *UK: SCOTLAND*
Recorded in the song 'The Ballad of Kirriemuir' in Martin Page's collection of World War 2 songs and balads, 'For Gawdsake Don't Take Me', 1976.

strop *noun*
1 a display of bad temper *UK*
From **STROPPY** (bad-tempered), ultimately from 'obstreperous'.
- Michael's mum had been in a mood, not a strop, but it was clear to Lenos that something was up. —P-P Hartnett, *Sad Cunt*, p. 97, 1999
- There was a time when she'd have thrown a quality strop about falling behind on her own on-going cases[.] —Christopher Brookmyre, *The Sacred Art of Stealing*, p. 195, 2002
- [H]e just carried on bollocking us because he was having a strop, ha ha! —*FHM*, p. 118, June 2003

2 male masturbation *UK*
From the conventional action. Also variant 'stropping'.
- —Ray Puxley, *Cockney Rabbit*, 1992

strop *verb*
▸ **strop the Mulligan**
(of a male) to masturbate *AUSTRALIA*
Also variant 'stropping'.
- If youse get jack [bored] of stropping the Mulligan and feel like spearing the bearded clam [...] tell the tart you lover! —Barry Humphries, *Bazza Pulls It Off!*, 1971

stroppy *adjective*
1 bad-tempered *UK, 1951*
Conventional 'obstreperous' wrongly abbreviated and understood.
- BOY: Oh don't be so stroppy! —*A Hard Day's Night*, 1964
- [A]t least the existence of the Politburo helps to broaden the mind of a stroppy kid in Swanley. —Mark Steel, *Reasons to be Cheerful*, p. 10, 2001

2 stubborn, defiant *NEW ZEALAND*
- —Louis S. Leland, *A Personal Kiwi-Yankee Dictionary*, p. 98, 1984

struck *noun*
a girl's steady boyfriend *US*
- —*American Speech*, p. 273, December 1963: 'American Indian student slang'

struck; struck by; struck with *adjective*
charmed, attracted to or delighted by someone or something *UK, 1839*
From an older sense as 'bewitched'.
- "What do you think to this place, Roy?" "It's all right." "You're not much struck." —Geoff Brown, *I Want What I Want*, p. 11, 1966

structural engineering *noun*
a well-constructed foundation garment, or garments; also applied to the uplifting effect that a well-designed and well-fitted brassiere can have on a woman's shape *AUSTRALIA, 1984*

structure *noun*
the human body *JAMAICA*
- —Velma Pollard, *Dread Talk*, p. 45, 2000

struddle *verb*
to fool with something you shouldn't *CANADA*
The word is from the German *strudeln* (boil, spout, proceed rashly).
- In Lunenburg County NS, to upset things, fool with them, against parents' wishes will get you "Don't struddle on the piano!" or the like. —Lewis Poteet, *The South Shore Phrase Book*, p. 111, 1999

strudel *noun*
the 'at' sign (@) on a computer keyboard *US*
- —Eric S. Raymond, *The New Hacker's Dictionary*, p. 40, 1991

struggle *verb*
1 to dance *US*
- —Robert George Reisner, *The Jazz Titans*, 1960

2 to experience a hangover *US*
- —Don R. McCreary (Editor), *Dawg Speak*, 2001

struggle and strain *noun*
a train *UK, 1931*
- —Julian Franklyn, *A Dictionary of Rhyming Slang*, 1960
- —Ray Puxley, *Cockney Rabbit*, 1992

struggle and strain *verb*
to train; to exercise *UK*
Rhyming slang.
- —Ray Puxley, *Cockney Rabbit*, 1992

struggle and strainer; struggle *noun*
a trainer (shoe) *UK*
Rhyming slang, extended from **STRUGGLE AND STRAIN** (to train).
- —Ray Puxley, *Cockney Rabbit*, 1992

struggle-and-strife; struggle *noun*
1 a wife *UK*
Rhyming slang.
- See you there Saturday. Lounge bar. Don't forget to bring the struggle-and-strife. OK? —Derek Bickerton, *Payroll*, p. 23, 1959

2 life; a life *UK*
Rhyming slang.
- —Ray Puxley, *Cockney Rabbit*, 1992

struggle-buggy *noun*
a broken-down car *US*
- My struggle-buggy was getting to look like a rinky-dink old tin can on wheels[.[—Mezz Mezzrow, *Really the Blues*, p. 87, 1946

struggling *adjective*
worn out; neglected *US*
- —Connie Eble (Editor), *UNC-CH Campus Slang*, p. 7, Spring 2000

strum *verb*
to masturbate *UK*
Also variant 'strum off'. From the up and down stroking action that is strumming a guitar.
- God just thinking about your hard dick going inside me is making me come... She left a half page, a big greasy patch smeared across it, then took up where she left off. Sorry, I just had to go and strum myself off – here's a little sample of what'll be waiting for you, my darling. —Kevin Sampson, *Powder*, p. 467, 1999

▸ **strum heads**
to fight *US*
- —Charles Shafer, *Folk Speech in Texas Prisons*, p. 215, 1990

▸ **strum the banjo**
(of a woman) to masturbate *UK*
A surreal elaboration of **STRUM** (to masturbate).
- [S]he'll be strummin her banjo wivin seconds. —Sacha Baron-Cohen, *Da Gospel According to Ali G*, 2001

strummed up *adjective*
stimulated by drugs *US*
- It was the end of six or seven months, and most of these guys were strummed up on that Benzedrine too. —Bruce Jackson, *In the Life*, p. 314, 1972

strung out *adjective*
1 addicted to a drug; in a poor state of physical and mental health as a result of drug addiction *US*
Used as a participial adjective.
- When you really get strung out you don't care about anything but your next fix. —Willard Motely, *Let No Man Write My Epitaph*, p. 368, 1958
- She was too strung out. I no longer cared enough to make the effort. —Alexander Trocchi, *Cain's Book*, p. 158, 1960
- In the case of a prostitute, she may be getting so thin and sick-looking – so "strung out" – that she has been forced to reduce her price. —James Mills, *The Panic in Needle Park*, p. 18, 1966

- [B]ut that's what happens to guys who really strung out. Like, I mean, my habit ain't that bad, see? —Nathan Heard, *Howard Street*, p. 128, 1968
- He's a little strung out right now, but he'll be all right. —Gurney Norman, *Divine Right's Trip (Last Whole Earth Catalog)*, p. 67, 1971
- [T]he larvae of this species is as addicted to milkweed juice as the most strung-out junky to smack. —Tom Robbins, *Another Roadside Attraction*, p. 21, 1971
- Carmelita, hold me tighter, I think I'm sinking down / I'm all strung out on heroin on the outskirts of town. —Warren Zevon, *Carmelito*, 1976
- One day I'm over there she's sniffling and nervous like she's strung out or somebody died. —Elmore Leonard, *Bandits*, p. 136, 1987
- I'm just astonished at the number of soldiers that got strung out in Vietnam. —Herbert Huncke, *Guilty of Everything*, p. 6, 1990

2 obsessed with or overly concerned about an activity or condition; emotionally disturbed *US*

- Don't get strung out by the way that I look / Don't judge a book by its cover —Richard O'Brien, *The Rocky Horror Show*, p. 8, 1973
- I will not get strung out by the way I look? —Kevin Sampson, *Clubland*, p. 29, 2002

3 extended *UK*

- The Bhoys [Irish 'boys']'ll give it a deliberately strung-out pause to half remind us how moody they are[.] —Kevin Sampson, *Outlaws*, p. 214, 2001

4 in love; infatuated *US*

- — *Current Slang*, p. 46, Fall 1968

strunt *verb*

to sulk *CANADA, 1990*

- — *New Maritimes*, p. 29, March-April 1990

struth!

▷ see: STREWTH!

strychnine *noun*

in craps, the point and number nine *US*

- — *The Annals of the American Academy of Political and Social Sciences*, p. 131, May 1950

stub *verb*

to kick, particularly a ball, especially in rugby *UK*

- — *The Felstedian*, December 1947

stubbie; stubby *noun*

a small, squat beer bottle, now 385 ml; the contents of a stubbie *AUSTRALIA, 1966*

From the noun use of 'stubby' (short and squat).

- Line us up a row of nice frosty stubbies will you – you miserable old bastard! —Barry Humphries, *The Wonderful World of Barry McKenzie*, p. 42, 1968
- The stubbie is one of the most malevolent inventions of the decade. —Bishop Shevill, *The Ugly Australian*, p. 128, 1970
- I said to him as my stubby turned into a bomb and exploded on one of their unfinished cement steps, 'Don't you ever think you're being precious?' —Thea Astley, *Hunting the Wild Pineapple*, p. 19, 1979

stubbie guts *noun*

a game in which frisbees are used to knock over stubbies *AUSTRALIA*

- Think of what is to be gained! Stubbie guts could burst into the world sporting spotlight. —*Flatball News*, p. 3, 1993
- — *Australian Ultimate*, p. 8, 2003: 'How to play...stubbie guts'

stubbie holder *noun*

an insulating container for keeping a stubbie of beer cool whilst being held *AUSTRALIA, 1981*

- Spare a thought for Ross's Sales & Auctions, which has been left with about 15,000 Jimmy Barnes stubbie holders, which were passed in at auction on Thursday. — *West Australian*, p. 46, 7th December 1991

stubble jumper *noun*

a prairie farmer *CANADA*

- The prairie farmer, to those of us who don't know him well, is a stock comic character. Clod-hopper, we call him, and stubble-jumper. — *Vancouver Sun*, p. 1/1, 4th July 1961
- The new champion dog-musher of the Yukon is a stubble-jumper from Brandon, Manitoba. —*Kingston Whig-Standard*, p. 10/1, 28th February 1966
- — *Maledicta*, p. 171, Summer/Winter 1978: 'How to hate thy neighbor: a guide to racist maledicta'

stub down *verb*

in the language surrounding the Grateful Dead, to move to better seats at a concert using ticket stubs for the better sections smuggled up by friends *US*

- —David Shenk and Steve Silberman, *Skeleton Key:*, p. 274, 1994

stube *noun*

a tavern *US*

- There were half-a-hundred more drop-ins, snug beer stubes and dining rooms[.] —Jack Lait and Lee Mortimer, *Chicago Confidential*, p. 14, 1950

stuck *adjective*

of a player in a game of poker or other gambling game, losing *US*

- "I say, 'How are you doing?' They say, 'Well, we're stuck $12,000.' —Edward Lin, *Big Julie of Vegas*, p. 121, 1974
- —David M. Hayano, *Poker Faces:*, p. 187, 1982

▸ **get stuck in**

to initiate or become vigorously involved in an activity *AUSTRALIA, 1941*

- "[C]ome on Joe, let's get stuck in!" Before I could stop him, he flew into the midst of the fray. —Joe Morgan, *Eastenders Don't Cry*, p. 119, 1994

▸ **get stuck into**

to attack a task or a person vigorously *AUSTRALIA, 1941*

- —Harvey E. Ward, *Down Under Without Blunder*, p. 47, 1967
- —Jim Ramsay, *Cop It Sweet!*, p. 39, 1977
- [T]hat young bloke of mine is currently getting stuck into computer games like Space Invaders which really puts his grey matter to the test. —Barry Humphries, *The Traveller's Tool*, p. 124, 1985

stuck on *adjective*

infatuated by, or enamoured of, someone *US, 1886*

- —Lloyd Kaufmann, *Stuck on You*, 1983

stuck-up *adjective*

conceited; pretentious *UK, 1829*

- "Some new kid," a voice replied. "I hear he's stuck-up." "I don't know what for," answered the Zit Queen. "He looks like a monkey." —C.D. Payne, *Youth in Revolt*, p. 167, 1993
- We all hate stuck-up wankers and smelly hippy students[.] —John King, *Human Punk*, p. 22, 2000

stud *noun*

1 a man, especially a manly man *UK, 1895*

- When Goldy got to the Savoy they were just leaving with two studs who'd got into a knife fight about a girl. —Chester Himes, *A Rage in Harlem*, p. 71, 1957
- In that way with a stud, in another way with polite dignified Sand a very interesting young fellow[.] —Jack Kerouac, *The Subterraneans*, p. 85, 1958
- "We ain't going to mess with those studs until after we're organized," Sheik said. —Chester Himes, *The Real Cool Killers*, p. 54, 1959
- A bunch of cool studs were chewing their cuds at Joe's Solid Rock in the middle of the block. —Dan Burley, *Diggeth Thou?*, p. 9, 1959
- A stud don't seem to realize that there's only so long you can sell stuff without gettin a bust. —Clarence Cooper Jr, *The Scene*, p. 78, 1960
- "Now there is one stud that can reallly go through loot," Zaida said. —Ross Russell, *The Sound*, p. 67, 1961
- Shorty was taking lesson "with some other studs" and he intended to organize his own small band. —Malcolm X and Alex Haley, *The Autobiography of Malcolm X*, p. 44–45, 1964
- Even when a block belongs to your people, you are still an outsider who has to prove himself a down stud with heart. —Piri Thomas, *Down These Mean Streets*, p. 47, 1967
- You studs don't have to listen to me because I'm only a rookie. —Dan Jenkins, *Semi-Tough*, p. 7, 1972
- The football stud? —*Cruel Intentions*, 1999

2 used as a jocular term of address to a man *US*

- You got it, stud! —*American Pie*, 1999

3 in homosexual usage, a person who plays the 'masculine' role sexually and emotionally in a relationship *US*

- "Stud" and "sissy" are expressions commonly used by Negroes to refer to their counterparts – the white "jocker" and white "brat". —Arthur V. Huffman, *New York Mattachine Newsletter*, p. 6, June 1961
- I remember once my little sister asked my mother, "Mama, is that a lady or a man." It was a stud. Mama just looked at her and said, "That's a bull-dagger, baby." —Claude Brown, *Manchild in the Promised Land*, p. 205, 1965
- Lesbians and their women were paired off and in small groups with queens and studs in the shadowy booths lining the long room. —Iceberg Slim (Robert Beck), *Mama Black Widow*, p. 30, 1969

4 amyl or butyl nitrite *UK*

Possibly derived from a brand marketed as a male sex-aid.

- Street names [...] stag, stud, thrust[.] —James Kay and Julian Cohen, *The Parents' Complete Guide to Young People and Drugs*, p. 144, 1998

5 loose tobacco *US*

- —Gary K. Farlow, *Prison-ese:*, p. 69, 2002

stud broad *noun*

a lesbian *US*

- Jealous reaction to a dance with one of the women has caused some men to be cut, shot, and beaten up by a gang of "stud-broads," and robbed in the process. —Nathan Heard, *Howard Street*, p. 34, 1968

stud duck *noun*
in oil drilling, an important company official *US*
• —Jerry Robertson, *Oil Slanguage*, p. 118, 1954

student *noun*
an inexperienced drug user *US*
• —*American Speech*, p. 30, February 1952: 'Teen-age hophead jargon'

student tobacco *noun*
marijuana *UK: SCOTLAND*
From a perception that those undergoing higher and further education are drug users.
• The wee brother hardly ever takes a drink. He's more inty the student tobacco, ye know? —Michael Munro, *The Complete Patter*, p. 150, 1996

stud hustler *noun*
a male homosexual prostitute who projects a tough, masculine image *US*
• And malehustlers ("fruithustlers"/"studhustlers": the various names for the masculine hustlers looking for lonely fruits to score from[.] —John Rechy, *City of Night*, p. 100, 1963
• When he arrived in Southern Florida, Jack planned to set up a call boy service utilizing stud hustlers. —Johnny Shearer, *The Male Hustler*, p. 129, 1966

Studie *noun*
a Studebaker car *US*
• —*Popular Science*, p. 110, April 1950: 'Studie shows new automatic transmission'
• "I came to this town in a hot Studebaker with a stolen hot gas card," Baby Jewels wheezed expansively. "I slept in the Studie three months before I opened my first club." —Seth Morgan, *Homeboy*, p. 117, 1990

studio-fuel *noun*
cocaine *UK*
Probably coined by cocaine-fuelled musicians.
• —Mike Haskins, *Drugs*, p. 281, 2003

studly *adjective*
1 describes a man who is considered to be above average in his sexual adventuring *US*
• Where is the great studly one, anyway? —Kevin Sampson, *Powder*, p. 85, 1999

2 admirable *US*
• —*Current Slang*, p. 7, Winter 1966

3 unpleasant; unpopular *US*
• —*American Speech*, p. 78, February 1960: 'Stud' and 'Studly'

stud muffin *noun*
a handsome, well-built man *US*
• Get outa here. Go call your studmuffin. —Armistead Maupin, *Maybe the Moon*, p. 26, 1992
• Anne thought Leeds was a stud muffin, especially in those cute khaki shorts and sneakers. —Joseph Wambaugh, *Floaters*, p. 219, 1996
• [A]ll was in place, including a stud muffin in a Nehru jacket with diamante buttons which she [Liz Hurley] kept on one hand. —*The Times Magazine*, p. 7, 21st June 2003

stud puppy *noun*
an attractive person *US*
A variation of **STUD MUFFIN**.
• Dozens of such sleek stud puppies pass through Hollywood every year[.] —*Time Magazine*, p. 74, 25th December 1989
• —David Rowan, *A Glossary for the 90s*, 1998
• He looked like a young Frank, so adorable, so handsome, so studly, my little stud puppy and then he starts the show. —Kathie Lee Gifford, *Larry King Live*, 5th February 2004

stud up *noun*
in prison, a prisoner who attempts to abandon homosexual activity and return to his previous state of heterosexual celibacy *US*
• —Charles Shafer, *Folk Speech in Texas Prisons*, p. 216, 1990

study bunny *noun*
a serious and diligent student *US*
• —*New York Times*, 12th April 1987

stuff *noun*
1 a drug, especially heroin *US, 1929*
• [H]e was going to New Orleans and would be back one day with some marihuana, real golden-leaf. He asked me did I want some of the stuff, and coming up tought I said sure, bring me some, I'd like to try it. —Mezz Mezzrow, *Really the Blues*, p. 71, 1946
• Unfortunately, she got mixed up with the wrong outfit and got put on the stuff by one of her roommates. —Mickey Spillane, *I, The Jury*, p. 22–23, 1947
• I had instructed them to hold themselves out as "junkies" (narcotic users. I was sure that, as soon as the word got around that they "used the stuff," and that they were well-heeled to pay for it, those doing the smuggling would seek them out. —*The New American Mercury*, p. 710, 1950
• As I began using stuff every day, or often several times a day, I stopped drinking and going out at night. —William Burroughs, *Junkie*, p. 35, 1953
• Well, someone like that, someone with only part of a character, is made for the stuff. The stuff is made for them. —Jim Thompson, *The Kill-Off*, p. 42, 1957
• I didn't even know they were on stuff and when I found out I was sure surprised. —Willard Motley, *Let No Man Write My Epitaph*, p. 117, 1958
• This is pure stuff. —Clarence Cooper Jr, *The Scene*, p. 27, 1960
• He looked at me as though I were on the stuff[.] —Clancy Sigal, *Going Away*, p. 349, 1961
• "He promised to let me have some stuff." "What sort of stuff? Reefers?" "No. A deck of H." —Douglas Rutherford, *The Creeping Flesh*, p. 102, 1963
• I was taking stuff at the time. But I'll tell you one ting: the first day I met her, I told her I was taking stuff. —Jeremy Larner and Ralph Tefferteller, *The Addict in the Street*, p. 69, 1964
• Well, all the studs I knew was on stuff now, and their habits was a good mile long / but I thought I could chip and never get hooked, for my will was strong. —Bruce Jackson, *Get Your Ass in the Water and Swim Like Me*, p. 91, 1964
• "Stuff is my first love." I said, "What do you mean "stuff'?" He said, "You've heard of shit, haven't you, duji, heroin?" —Claude Brown, *Manchild in the Promised Land*, p. 277, 1965
• I had some GB's, to hold me till I can do somethin' to get more stuff. —James Mills, *The Panic in Needle Park*, p. 28, 1966
• I worked there for four months and during that time the only customers allowed in were musicians, singers, prostitutes, pimps, and the stuff peddlers. —Babs Gonzales, *I Paid My Dues*, p. 99, 1967
• 'Sweet' was torturing me. He hadn't brought me my 'stuff' in twenty-four hours. —Iceberg Slim (Robert Beck), *Pimp*, p. 99, 1969
• The Native thought it would be nice if samples of everybody's stuff was done, in honor of Eddie's passing. —Gurney Norman, *Divine Right's Trip (Last Whole Earth Catalog)*, p. 123, 1971
• I would fool with stuff a little bit and I'd see a Chinaman coming – that is, I'd see a habit coming on – and I would back away and smoke reefers for a while, then I'd juice a while. —Bruce Jackson, *In the Life*, p. 180, 1972
• That wasn't even my stuff, I was holding it for a friend, man. —Cheech Marin and Tommy Chong, *Framed*, 1976
• She had kicked her habit in Philly but when Ricci came on the scene he had some stuff with him and she had picked up. —Herbert Huncke, *The Evening Sun Turned Crimson*, p. 58, 1980
• Now this is Panda, from Mexico. Very good stuff. —*Pulp Fiction*, 1994
• I call him up, tell him I got half a key of quality stuff. —*Boogie Nights*, 1997

2 used for any noun that the user cannot or does not wish to specify *UK*
• Does he suspect? Or is this chance and stuff? —R.L. Stevenson, *The Wrong Box*, 1889
• Marriage is scary stuff. You have to share a bathroom. —Janet Evanovich, *Seven Up*, p. 2, 2001

3 anything at all *NEW ZEALAND, 1969*
Used as a euphemism for **FUCK** in constructions such as 'I don't give a stuff about it'.
• —Harry Orsman, *A Dictionary of Modern New Zealand Slang*, p. 132, 1999

4 in prison, anything of value *US*
• Stuff was anything of value and faggots and sissies were of great value to many[.] —Malcolm Braly, *On the Yard*, p. 148, 1967

5 the female genitals *US*
• —John A. Holm, *Dictionary of Bahamian English*, p. 197, 1982
• "Don't try to tell me what to wear!" she snapped back and started a slow forward stretch that exposed the hairs of her stuff. —Odie Hawkins, *Amazing Grace*, p. 102, 1993

6 a woman as a sexual object *US*
• The couple to whom he was talking blatantly asked him why he hadn't gone out and found some "strange stuff." —R.J. Hagerman, *Husband and Wife Swapping*, p. 100, 1967
• Sapphire is referred to by the same man on different occasions as: mama, sister, baby, fox, stuff, and bitch. —Carolyn Greene, *70 Soul Secrets of Sapphire*, p. 35, 1973

7 the male genitals *US*
• "There's enough white stuff around." Vess grinned slyly, and as he did it occurred to me that the word "stuff" involved me more than it was comfortable to admit, since it was not oriented towards the coozies. —Phil Andros (Samuel M. Steward), *Stud*, p. 88–89, 1966
• He freaked out the first time he saw a dude pull his stuff out and start pissing, right across from the police station. —Odie Hawkins, *Midnight*, p. 95, 1995

8 an effeminate homosexual man *US*

- —John R. Armore and Joseph D. Wolfe, *Dictionary of Desperation*, p. 53, 1976

9 in pool, spin imparted on the cue ball to affect the course of the object ball or the cue ball after striking the object ball *US*

- —Mike Shamos, *The Illustrated Encyclopedia of Billiards*, p. 236, 1993

stuff *verb*

1 used as an emphatic rejection; and euphemistically for 'fuck' in all senses *UK, 1955*

- TICH: [...] Ah, stuff your breakfast [...] You're too bloody hard, you are.—Clive Exton, *No Fixed Abode [Six Granada Plays]*, p. 141, 1959
- "I say they can take their city and stuff it," Bradley said[.] "—Edwin Torres, *Q & A*, p. 61, 1977
- Stuff the bastards – that's what I say. Stuff 'em.—Anthony Masters, *Minder*, p. 62, 1984
- [T]hey're as stuffed as everyone else is without a map[.]—Andy McNab, *Immediate Action*, p. 321, 1995
- I'm going to start working at Labiarinth later in the week, so you can poke your stupid job.—Colin Butts, *Is Harry Still on the Boat?*, p. 139, 2003

2 to have sex from the male point of view *NEW ZEALAND*

- —Louis S. Leland, *A Personal Kiwi-Yankee Dictionary*, p. 98, 1984

3 to block the pay chute of a casino slot machine with the expectation of returning later, unblocking the chute and retrieving the interim earnings *US*

- Stuffing is exactly what it sounds like. It is a method of blocking the pay chute on a slot machine.—Charles W. Lund, *Robbing the One-Armed Bandits:*, p. 125, 1999

4 to persuade someone to buy something that they did not know they wanted to buy *US*

- —Anna Scotti and Paul Young, *Buzzwords:*, p. 41, 1997

▸ **stuff your face**

to overeat; to eat greedily; to eat *US*

An unconventional and over-active digestion would be required if this simple description of the apparent action was as accurate as the imagery.

- [S]tuffing her face with Twinkies[.]—Barney Hoskyns, *Waiting For The Sun*, p. 150, 1996

stuffed *adjective*

very tired *NEW ZEALAND*

- —Sonya Plowman, *Great Kiwi Slang*, p. 166, 2002

stuffed shirt *noun*

a person who is overly formal, aloof and out of touch *US, 1913*

- He said I had become stiff-necked, a stuffed shirt, too uncompromising in my dealings with onetime associates.—Jim Thompson, *Roughneck*, p. 116, 1954
- Awww c'mon, man, don't be such a stuffed shirt.—Odie Hawkins, *Men Friends*, p. 113, 1989

stuffer *noun*

1 a male homosexual who plays the active role in anal sex *US*

- —Vincent J. Monteleone, *Criminal Slang*, p. 229, 1949

2 a parachute rigger *US*

- —Linda Reinberg, *In the Field*, p. 211, 1991

3 in hot rodding, a supercharger *US*

- —Olney Ross, *Kings of the Drag Strip*, p. 188, 1968

stuffy *adjective*

conservative; very conventional; straitlaced *UK*

Derives from STUFFED SHIRT.

- "A pop group shocked millions of viewers last night with the filthiest language ever heard on British television." It was too much for the stuffy board of EMI directors. They ordered the Sex Pistols to be dropped.—Simon Napier-Bell, *Black Vinyl White Powder*, p. 161, 2001

stugots; stugats *noun*

the penis *US*

From southern Italian dialect, adapted/corrupted by Italian-American immigrants.

- —Anthony Romeo, *The Language of Gangs*, p. 23, 4th December 1962

stuk; stukkie *noun*

a woman sexually objectified *SOUTH AFRICA, 1946*

- — Partridge, *A Dictionary of the Underworld*, 1950
- —Penny Silva, *A Dictionary of South African English*, 1996

▷ **see:** SHTUCK

stulper *verb*

to stumble *CANADA*

- "You stulper over everything," – from an oral informant in Lunenburg County.—Lewis Poteet, *The South Shore Phrase Book*, p. 111, 1999

stum *noun*

any central nervous system depressant *US*

- —Edith A. Folb, *runnin' down some lines*, p. 256, 1980

stumble biscuit *noun*

a tablet of the recreational drug methaqualone, best known as Quaaludes™ *US*

From the lack of coordination associated with the drug.

- —Peter Johnson, *Dictionary of Street Alcohol and Drug Terms*, p. 183, 1993

stumblebum *noun*

a poor and foolish drunk *US, 1932*

- Sweet dreams, all you flophouse grads, I said to myself. R.I.P., you stumblebums.—Mezz Mezzrow, *Really the Blues*, p. 317, 1946
- He knew a stumblebum, a wino with a criminal record.—Jim Thompson, *After Dark, My Sweet*, p. 103, 1955
- What a sad stumblebum I was[.]—Angelo d'Arcangelo, *The Homosexual Handbook*, p. 200, 1968
- Just the alias used by the stumblebum married my mom.—Seth Morgan, *Homeboy*, p. 49, 1990

stumbler *noun*

any barbiturate or central nervous system depressant *US*

- —Donald Wesson and David Smith, *Barbiturates*, p. 122–1977,
- —Edith A. Folb, *runnin' down some lines*, p. 256, 1980

stumbles *noun*

a loss of coordination, especially as the result of drug or alcohol intoxication *US*

- —Eugene Landy, *The Underground Dictionary*, p. 99, 1971

stumer *noun*

1 a fool *UK: SCOTLAND, 1985*

The spelling 'stumor' is also used.

- I don't want the whole beach to know I married a stumor.—Ian Pattison, *Rab C. Nesbitt*, 1988

2 a forged or bad cheque *UK, 1890*

- When the peace came some of the cheques bounced and the Arabs, in particular, found that they had been handed a stumer[.]—Dave Winter, *Israel Handbook*, p. 775, 2001

3 a mistake; a blunder; a mess *UK, 1983*

- The only stumer is the inclusion of a "joke" version of Luka Bloom's "An Irishman in Chinatown".—Geoff Wallis, *The Rough Guide to Irish Music*, p. 228, 2001

stumm *adjective*

▷ **see:** SHTUM

stump *noun*

1 the leg *UK, 1460*

Survives mainly in the phrase 'stir your stumps!' (start doing something!, get moving!).

- [T]he non-western travellers who dominated exploration altogether before Europe stirred its stumps in the late 15th century[.]—*The Guardian*, 16th November 2002
- "Stir your stumps, Polly!" we heard him shout, and then Polly's high-pitched retort: "Why am I the fucking Kunta Kinte around here?" —Zoe Heller, *What Was She Thinking?*, p. 165, 2003

2 the penis *US*

In a world where size matters, often but not always applied to a short penis.

- —Judi Sanders, *Faced and Faded, Hanging to Hurl*, p. 38, 1993

3 a shoe *US*

- I found it impossible to get my stumps on because my feet had swollen up so much.—A.S. Jackson, *Gentleman Pimp*, p. 21, 1973

stump *verb*

to challenge or dare someone *CANADA*

- "I'll stump you all to jump down," he said suddenly, and without thinking about it, he shoved himself off the roof and fell on the sawdust where he lay rolling around and laughing. "You're all stumped," he shouted.—Morley Callaghan, *Stories*, p. 275, 1959

stump-broke *adjective*

unconditionally obedient *US*

From the quaint notion of a mule trained to step forward and then backwards for sex with a man standing on a stump.

- You don't look like you could pleasure a stump-broke mule. — Malcolm Braly, *On the Yard*, p. 207, 1967
- What's wrong with my nose? I'll tell you what's wrong with my nose. I asked Gunther if he had his girl friend stump-broke yet, and he hit me on it, that's what. — Ken Weaver, *Texas Crude*, p. 129, 1984

stumpers *noun*
shoes *US*
- — Hermese E. Roberts, *The Third Ear: A Black Glossary*, 1971

stump-floater *noun*
heavy rain *CANADA*
- — Bill Casselman, *Canadian Sayings*, p. 150, 2002

stumphole whiskey *noun*
strong, homemade whisky *US*
- Once the preacher got limbered up good he set in to telling about what a mortal sinner he'd been all his life and had made and sold stumphole whiskey all his grown days[.] — Tom Robbins, *Another Roadside Attraction*, p. 77, 1971
- Masters of moonshine prided themselves in their ancient, father-to-son recipes and the white lightning, blue John, red eye, happy Sally, and stumphole whiskey they made, Smith said. — *Chicago Tribune*, p. C-1, 15th January 1986
- — *Star Tribune (Minneapolis)*, p. 19F, 31st January 1999

stump-jumper *noun*
an infantry soldier *US*
- — Linda Reinberg, *In the Field*, p. 211, 1991

stump ranch *noun*
in the Canadian West, a poorly run farm *CANADA*
- A "stump ranch" is an agricultural dream under development by a family on the edge of the bush. They log the trees off, but so as not to starve, sow grass between the stumps for cattle to graze. — Tom Parkin, *WetCoast Words*, p. 137, 1989

stump up; stump *verb*
to pay *UK, 1833*
- Show me, she insists. - Prepared to stump? - Wouldn't you like to know. — Mark Powell, *Snap*, p. 17, 2001

stumpy *noun*
a short person *US*
Often used as a term of address.
- — Judi Sanders, *Da Bomb*, p. 15, 1997

stunned *adjective*
drunk *US*
- — Ralph de Sola, *Crime Dictionary*, p. 145, 1982

stunned mullet *noun*
used as the epitome of one who is dazed, stupid, foolish *AUSTRALIA, 1953*
- — Sidney J. Baker, *Australia Speaks*, p. 267, 1953
- When his shout came (i.e. his turn to pay for a round) he sat there like a stunned mullet. — Arthur Chipper, *The Aussie Swearer's Guide*, p. 55, 1972
- — Lance Peters, *The Dirty Half-Mile*, p. 150, 1979
- Like a stunned mullet the bookie buckled at the knees. — Clive Galea, *Slipper*, p. 170, 1988
- You could have knocked me over with a feather, and I was so amazed that I just stood there gaping like a stunned mullet. — Rex Hunt, *Tall Tales – and True*, p. 62, 1994
- [I] eventually managed to get him handcuffed and searched while my team-mates sat on their haunches and watched like a pair of stunned mullets. — William Dodson, *The Sharp End*, p. 63, 2001
- — Kel Richards, *The Aussie Bible*, p. 14, 2003

stunner *noun*
1 an exceedingly attractive woman *UK, 1848*
- Jasmine was a stunner in a light navy blue suit and crisp white blouse[.] — Anne Rice, *Blackwood Farm*, p. 351, 2003

2 a person or thing of extraordinary excellence *UK, 1855*
- Tom Weiskopf designed this 18-hole, par-72 course, and it's a stunner. — Darwin Porter and Danforth Prince, *Frommer's Bahamas 2004*, p. 11, 2003

3 a pin-up, topless or soft-porn model *UK*
Adapted by the tabloid press from the earlier, and continuing use, as 'a good-looking woman'. Often combined with 'Page 3', in reference to the *Sun* newspaper's daily placing of naked female breasts. The spellings 'stunna' and 'stunnah' also exist.
- — Gayle Tuesday (Brenda Gilhoolie), *Big Up Top – Page 3 Stunner Gayle Tuesday's Guide to Life*, 1999
- You won't believe some of the names being dropped here: [...] Page 3 stunna Sam Fox[.] — *Uncut*, p. 88, May 2002

stunning *adjective*
1 excellent; extremely good-looking *UK, 1847*
- Latino senoritas are way beyond stunning[.] — Wayne Anthony, *Spanish Highs*, p. 107, 1999

2 in computing, incomprehensibly stupid *US*
- — Eric S. Raymond, *The New Hacker's Dictionary*, p. 336, 1991

stunt *noun*
in advertising, marketing, etc, an event contrived to attract attention and gain publicity *UK, 1878*
Still regarded as colloquial by those who keep up our standards.
- [S]uspicions are growing that the entire episode might have been one giant and well-timed publicity stunt designed to further the career of America's newest celebrity obsession. — *The Observer*, 7th December 2003

stunt *verb*
to wear expensive clothes and jewellery as a display of conspicuous consumption; to show off *US*
- — Rick Ayers (Editor), *Slang Dictionary*, p. 15, 2001

stunt cock; stunt dick; stunt *noun*
a male pornography performer who fills in for another performer who is unable to maintain an erection or ejaculate when needed *US*
- For the most part, cum shots are only faked in dire circumstances – like when a stunt cock can't be found and no one's being paid overtime. — Ana Loria, *1 2 3 Be A Porn Star!*, p. 73–2000,
- It's ten minutes to midnight, and it became of question of running in Randy as a stunt dick[.] — Robert Stoller and I.S. Levine, *Coming Attractions*, p. 130, 1991
- A STUNT is a guy who provides the hard dick and the POP SHOT for an actor having plumbing problems. — *Adult Video News*, p. 40, September 1995

stunt pussy *noun*
a female pornography performer who fills in for another performer for the purposes of genital filming only *US*
- — Ana Loria, *1 2 3 Be A Porn Star!*, p. 167, 2000: 'Glossary of adult sex industry terms'

stunts *noun*
sex *US*
- — Linda Meyer, *Teenspeak!*, p. 29, 1994

stupe; stoop *noun*
a stupid person *UK, 1762*
Often, not always, used affectionately.
- You have be refuting everything I ever learned and I'll wind up being a stupe. — Mickey Spillane, *My Gun is Quick*, p. 55, 1950
- The Pachuco shivs Mace while the big stoop stands there all goofed off with a rod in his mitt. — Thurston Scott, *Cure it with Honey*, p. 160, 1951
- The stupes. He didn't need guys who could believe that he had busted Sonny Tubbs, the crippled pusher. — Clarence Cooper Jr, *The Scene*, p. 11, 1960
- I didn't have to flunk those subjects. I mean, I'm not a stupe, by a long shot. — Robert Gover, *One Hundred Dollar Misunderstanding*, p. 9, 1961
- I might have ended up a Christian martyr – St. Eldrige the Supe. — Eldridge Cleaver, *Soul on Ice*, p. 30, 1968
- Laredo leaned up against the fire hydrant crossing her legs and waiting for some stupe to offer her money so she could write him a ticket. — William T. Vollman, *Whores for Gloria*, p. 2, 1991

stupid *adjective*
1 used to describe a 'smart' weapon that fails to function properly *US*
- A poor workman, as the old saying goes, blames his tools. In this case the bombs went "stupid" after they failed to lock onto a laser guiding system which failed to function in the sand outside Kerbala. — *The Guardian*, 8th April 2003

2 good *US*
The spelling 'stoopid' is also used.
- — Connie Eble (Editor), *UNC-CH Campus Slang*, p. 8, Spring 1989
- For a while things got "stoopid"[.] — Nelson George, *Hip Hop America*, p. 209, 1998

▸ **get your stupid on**
to drink to the point of intoxication *US*
- — Connie Eble (Editor), *UNC-CH Campus Slang*, p. 4, Spring 2003

stupid *adverb*
extremely *US, 1992*
- — Anna Scotti and Paul Young, *Buzzwords*, p. 81, 1997
- [E]ven "stoopid fresh," which could also be "def" when it wasn't "dope." — Nelson George, *Hip Hop America*, p. 209, 1998

stupid badge *noun*
a temporary identification card worn by a worker who has lost or left his identification at home *US*
• — *American Speech*, p. 227, October 1955: 'An aircraft production dispatcher's vocabulary'

stupid-baker *noun*
a Studebaker car *US*
• — Lewis Poteet, *Car & Motorcyle Slang*, p. 192, 1992

stupidee *noun*
a stupid or insignificant person *TRINIDAD AND TOBAGO, 1959*
• — Lise Winer, *Dictionary of the English/Creole of Trinidad & Tobago*, 2003

stupid labour *noun*
public labour *CANADA*
• In the 1930s unemployed men were given work to do to pay off taxes. Officially known as statute labour, the nickname has since been used to any government make-work project. — Chris Thain, *Cold as a Bay Street Banker's Heart*, p. 150, 1987

stupidness!
used for expressing scorn *CAYMAN ISLANDS*
• — Aarona Booker Kohlman, *Wotcha Say*, p. 25, 1985

stupid, stupid
used as an expression of utter disapproval *US*
From the cry of 'stupid, stupid rat creatures!' in the *Bone* comic book.
• Stupid, stupid end-users! — Andy Ihnatko, *Cyberspeak*, p. 184, 1997

sturgeon *noun*
a surgeon *US*
• — Sally Williams, *"Strong" Words*, p. 134, 1994

stushie; stushy *noun*
▷ see: STOOSHIE

stutter and stammer; stutter *noun*
a hammer *UK*
Rhyming slang.
• — Ray Puxley, *Cockney Rabbit*, 1992

stuvac *noun*
especially in New South Wales, student holidays from school or university *AUSTRALIA, 1970*
From '*stu*dent *vac*ation'.
• Stuvac begins on the 31st and there's the school fete to be organised. — Frank Moorhouse, *Forty-Seventeen*, p. 130, 1988

St Vinnies *nickname*
▷ see: VINNIES

style *noun*
graffiti *US*
• — Jim Crotty, *How to Talk American*, p. 141, 1997

style *verb*
to conduct or carry yourself in a stylish manner, especially in an exaggerated, showy way *US*
• The pimp who is "taking care of business" often prefers less flamboyant one-to-one situations for "hitting on" women and leaves the stylin' (strutting and showing off) to what he calls "half-ass pimps" and "would-be pimps." — Christina and Richard Milner, *Black Players*, p. 44, 1972
• If a shadow of doubt remained, it was completely erased by the sight of Benny sitting at the bar between two pseudo-foxy ladies stylin'. — Odie Hawkins, *Chicago Hustle*, p. 82, 1977
• — Connie Eble (Editor), *UNC-CH Campus Slang*, p. 8, November 1990
• I know how it is, dude. Awful hard to style with those goofy fucking jackets on. — Joseph Wambaugh, *Floaters*, p. 28, 1996
• She should be chewing gum, styling above the fray, not pestering me over some cheeky guy. — Diran Abedayo, *My Once Upon A Time*, p. 70, 2000

stylee *noun*
a style, determined by the cultural category that precedes it *UK*
A fashionable elaboration of 'style'.
• Who's talking spoof stylee now. — Nick Barlay, *Curvy Lovebox*, p. 109, 1997
• — Sly & Robbie *Reggae Stylee*, 2000

stylie *noun*
a white person with dreadlocks *US*
• — David Shenk and Steve Silberman, *Skeleton Key*, p. 274, 1994

stylin' and profilin' *adjective*
very fashionable *US*
• — Connie Eble (Editor), *UNC-CH Campus Slang*, p. 9, Spring 1988

stylo milo *adjective*
very fashionable *SINGAPORE*
• — Paik Choo, *The Coxford Singlish Dictionary*, p. 103, 2002

sub *noun*
1 a *sub*marine *UK, 1917*
• The Red October, a Typhoon-class sub, moved under her own power towards the main ship channel of the Kola Fjord. — Tom Clancy, *The Hunt for Red October*, p. 3, 1984
2 a *sub*scription *UK, 1833*
• [A] fiver [£5] a week subs[.] — Kevin Sampson, *Powder*, p. 142, 1999
3 in publishing, a *sub*-editor *UK, 1859*
• The journalists, subs, production people, secretaries, designers and gofers who tenanted this stunted maze[.] — Will Self, *The Sweet Smell of Psychosis*, p. 33, 1996
4 a sexual *sub*missive, a willing slave in a sado-masochistic relationship *US, 1987*
• We ticked off everything – Bi, Sub, Dom, Leather, Rubber, PVC, Bondage, Water Sports[.] — Kitty Churchill, *Thinking of England*, p. 100, 1995
• He's a sub who likes to be tied up, whipped, abused, spat on. The usual stuff[.] — Niall Griffiths, *Kelly + Victor*, p. 205, 2002
5 the *sub*missive performer in a pornographic sex scene *US*
• — Ana Loria, *1 2 3 Be A Porn Star!*, p. 167, 2000: 'Glossary of adult sex industry terms'
6 in prison, a *sub*versive *UK*
• — Angela Devlin, *Prison Patter*, p. 110, 1996
7 on an athletic team, a reserve player who may enter the game as a *sub*stitute for a starter *UK, 1889*
• He hadn't been able to make any of the teams as a sub. — James T. Farrell, *Saturday Night*, p. 25, 1947
• He chucks the ball high in celebration. Clearly an inspired move to bring him on as sub. — *The Guardian*, 22nd November 2002
8 a loan *AUSTRALIA*
An abbreviation of '*sub*sistence', with the loan characterised as a 'subsistence advance'.
• — Ned Wallish, *The Truth Dictionary of Racing Slang*, p. 79, 1989
9 a financial advance, especially when given against wages or salary *UK, 1866*
• — John Ayto, *The Oxford Dictionary of Slang*, p. 190, 1998
10 a concealed pocket, used by a casino employee to hide stolen chips *US*
• — Lee Solkey, *Dummy Up and Deal*, p. 121, 1980

sub *verb*
1 to give or receive a financial advance *UK, 1874*
• Listen, can someone sub us? My Giro won't be here till Christmas[.] — Paul Fraser and Shane Meadows, *TwentyFourSeven*, p. 11, 1997
• Smiles didn't have any money. Just what his old man and Tony were subbing him. — John King, *Human Punk*, p. 147, 2000
2 to serve as a *substitute* *US, 1853*
• Once inside, she said, "You want to watch 'Midnight America'?" "Who's subbing?" — Robert Campbell, *Alice in La-La Land*, p. 151, 1987

sub *adjective*
mentally *sub*-normal *UK*
• There was a woman who was slightly "sub", they said. They didn't call her that but they made it perfectly clear. — Margery Allingham, *The China Governess*, 1963

subby *noun*
a *sub*contractor *AUSTRALIA, 1978*
• All the subbies from Burnley and Blackburn[.] — Kevin Sampson, *Outlaws*, p. 51 – 2001,
• Bob reckons that there are so many advantages over his style of operation that he can't understand why the idea has not caught on with other subbies. — *Truckin' Life*, p. 12, September 1982

sub-deb *noun*
a girl in her mid-teens *US, 1917*
• The Debs and Sub-Debs are usually from 50 to 500 feet behind the warriors. — Jack Lait and Lee Mortimer, *New York Confidential*, p. 106, 1948
• Some East Oakland sub-deb started walking home from the bus stop on Fifteenth one dark night a few months back, and she ran into a would-be rapist on the way. — Thurston Scott, *Cure it with Honey*, p. 79, 1951

sublime *adjective*

▸ **from the sublime to the gorblimey; from the sublime to the ridiculous**

from one extreme to another *UK, 1984*

- Following a fine production of Marivaux's The Triumph of Love, the Watermill goes from the sublime to the ridiculous with this revival of a 10-year-old musical by Alan Ayckbourn and John Pattison – a gobsmacking triumph of inanity. — *The Guardian*, 4th June 2003

submarine *noun*

1 a marijuana cigarette, especially a large one *SOUTH AFRICA*

- — *Cape Times*, 23rd May 1946

2 a surfboard that is too small for the person using it *US*
So named because the person forces the board under water.

- — John Severson, *Modern Surfing Around the World*, p. 182, 1964

3 in the used car business, a car that has spent time submerged in water *US*

- — Peter Mann, *How to Buy a Used Car Without Getting Gypped*, p. 196, 1975

4 a gambling casino scheme in which a stolen chip is slipped into the thief's trousers *US*

- They would use this as a drop by slipping a hundred dollar chip inside their trousers. This was called a "submarine." — Mario Puzo, *Inside Las Vegas*, p. 227, 1977

5 an after-hours drinking session in a rugby club *UK*
Noted by Frank Peppitt, 1984.

submarine *verb*

1 in tiddlywinks, to shoot a wink under another *US*

- — *Verbatim*, p. 526, December 1977

2 to ride through tall grass *AUSTRALIA*

- — Ernestine Hill, *The [Northern] Territory*, 1951

submarine belt *noun*

in motor racing, a safety belt that clips onto the buckle of a lap belt and is attached to the chassis under the driver's seat *US*

- — Don Alexander, *The Racer's Dictionary*, p. 63, 1980

submarine races *noun*

used as a euphemism for foreplay in a car at a remote spot *US*

- — *Current Slang*, p. 5, Spring 1967
- — Hy Lit, *Hy Lit's Unbelievable Dictionary of Hip Words for Groovy People*, p. 38, 1968
- — *Verbatim*, p. 281, May 1976

subway *noun*

in roller derby, contact between skaters who are eligible to score before they reach the back of the pack of blocking skaters, taking them to the floor of the track *US*

- — Keith Coppage, *Roller Derby to Rollerjam*, 1999

subway dealer *noun*

in a card game, a dealer who cheats by dealing some cards off the bottom of the deck *US*

- — Frank Garcia, *Marked Cards and Loaded Dice*, p. 264, 1962
- — George Percy, *The Language of Poker*, p. 89, 1988

Subway Sam *noun*

a man who is partial to sex in subway toilets *US*

- A customer who consumates the sex act in a subway toilet is called a "Subway Sam." — Johnny Shearer, *The Male Hustler*, p. 18, 1966

Subway silver *noun*

▷ see: MANHATTAN SILVER

subway tickets *noun*

in a card game, cards that did not come off the top of the deck because of cheating in the dealing *US*

- — George Percy, *The Language of Poker*, p. 89, 1988

sub-Z *nickname*

a Sub-Zero™ freezer *US*
Collected in Berkeley, California, in 2000.

such a bitter experience never again; such a bloody experience never again *nickname*

the Belgian airline Sabena *US*
Most airlines attract jocular variations of their names.

- Katie Miles filled us in on the nicknames of the airlines [...] Pan Am was "Pandemonium World Scareways"[...] Air France was "Air Chance" and Sabena was "Such a Bitter Experience Never Again". — Mary Higgins Clark, *Kitchen Privileges*, p. 65–66, 2002

such-a-much *noun*

an important or self-important person *US*

- [P]eople peeped your hole card then, knew where you were at and saw that you weren't such-a-much after all. — Nathan Heard, *Howard Street*, p. 181, 1968

suck *noun*

1 an act of oral sex *US, 1870*

- She was okay. A good suck, but not a Great suck. — *Adam Film Quarterly*, p. 72, October 1973
- 30-year-old man would like the company of very thin bird for cunninlingus and fellatio sessions. Must be extremely thin and flat-chested or small-boobed. Intercourse maybe, but suck the main scene. — *Searchlight (Sydney)*, p. 18, 1974
- I mean, I've had some fabulous suck in my time, but this chick ... wow. — Terry Southern, *Now Dig This*, p. 36, 1975
- Born and raised in Montreal, he was used to supremo suck from the "fille du roi" and this Ontario girl was going to rank. — Suroosh Alvi et al., *The Vice Guide*, p. 27, 2002

2 a sycophant *US*

- "He's still a company suck." "He's a foreman, Luther." — John Sayles, *Union Dues*, p. 18, 1977

suck *verb*

1 to be useless, unpopular, distasteful, of no worth *US, 1965*
When the term came into currency in the US in the 1960s, sexual connotations made it a vulgar, taboo-ridden term. By the mid-1990s, all sense of taboo had vanished in the US except for older speakers for whom the sexual connotation remained inescapable. In UK English, the term, first used as a noun (1913) expressing contempt, never enjoyed the sexual implications found in the US. If anything, there was long an upper-class air to the term thanks in part to the 'Yah boo, sucks to you' catchphrase associated with Billy Bunter, a fat upper-crust schoolboy created by author Frank Richards.

- The show is fine but the P.R. girl and her staff suck. — *Screw*, p. 2, 21st March 1969
- — Elizabeth Ball Carr, *Da Kine Talk*, p. 151, 1972
- I thought it sucked, and I bet next summer'll suck too. — George V. Higgins, *The Judgment of Deke Hunter*, p. 51, 1976
- All cash boxes from booths are emptied at the end of the week, with amounts varying drastically – this week's haul sucks. — Josh Alan Friedman, *Tales of Times Square*, p. 72, 1986
- The dope sucks lately and the dealers are worse. — Jim Carroll, *Forced Entries*, p. 114, 1987
- Hey, man, fuck Marky Mark. That guy sucks. — *Airheads*, 1994
- What do think of the system so far? / It sucks — Ian Dury, *Jack Shit George*, 1998
- [W]hen a few of the boys started taking their tops off and they're all sweaty and wet – that kind of sucks. — Ben Malbon, *Cool Places*, p. 278, 1998
- And then today he takes me by his gallery, to see his new show? And it sucks. — *200 Cigarettes*, 1999
- It's cool to be the player, but it sucks to be the fan[.] — Eminem (Marshall Mathers), *Rock Bottom*, 1999

2 to perform oral sex *US, 1881*

- Were you ever caught sucking a girl? — *Screw*, p. 5, 7th March 1969
- [H]ow do you say, 'sucked him'? Yes? — Terry Southern, *Blue Movie*, p. 83, 1970

3 to consume alcoholic drinks *AUSTRALIA*

- Let's suck a jug. — J.E. MacDonnell, *Don't Gimme the Ships*, p. 52, 1960
- A couple of blokes were sucking a seven[.] — Sam Weller, *Old Bastards I Have Met*, p. 142, 1979

4 in pool, to hit the cue ball with backspin that appears to draw or suck the cue ball backwards after it strikes the object ball *US, 1990*

- — Mike Shamos, *The Illustrated Encyclopedia of Billiards*, p. 236, 1993

▸ **it sucks to be you**

used for expressing a trace of commiseration in a situation that might call for a bit more *US*

- — Connie Eble (Editor), *UNC-CH Campus Slang*, p. 5, Spring 1993
- I shrugged. Despite the laborious and inefficient method, I doubted Matthew had struck at it long enough to be worthy of sympathy. "Sucks to be you." — Jim Munroe, *Angry Young Spaceman*, p. 204, 2001

▸ **suck ass; suck arse**

to behave subserviently *US*
A variation of KISS ARSE/ASS.

- As for going to NY and sucking asses to get published, dont worry, if you're any good I'll get you read by the Farting-Through-Silk set, you

won't have to stir a bone.—Jack Kerouac, *Letter to Philip Whalen*, p. 565, 6th March 1956
- But it's the guys who suck ass with the caddy master who get that action.—James Ellroy, *Brown's Requiem*, p. 63, 1981

▸ suck butt
to curry favour *US*
- —Judi Sanders, *Da Bomb*, p. 15, 1997

▸ suck cock
to perform oral sex on a man *US, 1941*
- Sharon was munching wetly, moaning all over Lenny's dick, tugging his balls and working her mouth – she was born to suck cock.—*Letters to Penthouse V*, p. 69, 1995

▸ suck diesel
to make rapid progress; to move rapidly, especially in a motor vehicle *IRELAND*
- Now you're sucking diesel.—Eamonn Sweeney, *Waiting for the Healer*, p. 124, 1997

▸ suck face
to kiss, especially in a prolonged fashion *US*
Hawaiian youth usage.
- Mug down Suck face.—Jim Humes and Sean Wagstaff, *Boarderlands*, p. 223, 1995
- —Douglas Simonson, *Pidgin to da Max Hana Hou*, 1982
- Lendon an' Jace're suckfacin' by the fag machine.—Nick Barlay, *Curvy Lovebox*, p. 134, 1997

▸ suck milk
to be knocked off your surfboard and then be thrashed by a wave *US*
- —Trevor Cralle, *The Surfin'ary*, p. 125, 1991

▸ suck out loud
to be very bad *US*
- —Michael Dalton Johnson, *Talking Trash with Redd Foxx*, p. 138, 1994

▸ sucks a big dog's dick
to be terrible *US*
- And as for your analysis of the feminist error, Wein, I've heard it before and it sucks a big dog's dick.—John Sayles, *Union Dues*, p. 129, 1977

▸ suck salt
to experience difficulties *TRINIDAD AND TOBAGO, 1966*
- —Lise Winer, *Dictionary of the English/Creole of Trinidad & Tobago*, 2003

▸ suck suds
to drink beer *US*
- —Marcus Hanna Boulware, *Jive and Slang of Students in Negro Colleges*, 1947
- —*Current Slang*, p. 10, Spring 1969

▸ suck the arse out of a durry
to smoke a hand-rolled cigarette to the very end *NEW ZEALAND*
- —David McGill, *David McGill's Complete Kiwi Slang Dictionary*, p. 121, 1998

▸ suck the big one
to be terrible *US*
- This scene sucks the big one, I thought.—Rita Ciresi, *Pink Slip*, p. 295, 1999

▸ suck to the bulls
to act friendly with the police *US*
- —Paladin Press, *Inside Look at Outlaw Motorcyle Gangs*, p. 38, 1992

▸ suck tubes
to smoke marijuana *US*
- —Connie Eble (Editor), *UNC-CH Campus Slang*, p. 9, Spring 1998

▸ suck weight
to drink large amounts of liquids in a short period in order to gain weight to qualify for a sporting event *US*
- — Judy's Enterprises, *Coxswain Postcard*, 2001

▸ suck wind
to fail; to lose out *US*
Hawaiian youth usage.
- —Elizabeth Ball Carr, *Da Kine Talk:*, p. 151, 1972

▸ suck your flavor; suck your flava
to copy your style *US*
- — *People Magazine*, p. 72, 19th July 1993

sucka *noun*
a fool; a dupe *US*
Misspelling of **SUCKER** (a gullible individual).
- I'm a sucka, all I gotta say / These drugs really got a hold of me[.] —Eminem (Marshall Mathers), *Drug Ballad*, 2000

suck-ass *noun*
a sycophant who curries favour in a self-demeaning fashion *US*
- —Elmore Leonard, *City Primeval*, p. 8, 1980

suck-ass *adjective*
subservient; sycophantic; obsequious *US*
- That witty sally brought a lot of that suck-ass hearty cuckling that the hacks around the courthouse always draw out of themselves when they draw a judge who thinks he is a regular charmer of a fellow. —George V. Higgins, *Penance for Jerry Kennedy*, p. 6, 1985
- [T]hose lightweight, suck-ass interviews that everyone does.—Howard Stern, *Miss America*, p. 60, 1995

suck back *verb*
to drink something *US*
- We may be sucking back a few beers a little later on.—*The Blues Brothers*, 1980

sucked up *adjective*
1 weak; undeveloped physically *US*
- —Jim Goad, *Jim Goad's Glossary of Northwestern Prison Slang*, December 2001

2 angry *US*
- —James Harris, *A Convict's Dictionary*, p. 39, 1989

sucker *noun*
1 a gullible individual *US, 1838*
- You think religion is for suckers and easy marks and mollycoddles, huh?—Richard Brooks, *Elmer Gantry*, 1960

2 a fellow *US*
Neutral but informal.
- I'm gonna catch that sucker, if it's the last thing I ever do.—*The Blues Brothers*, 1980

3 someone who is unable to resist a stated temptation or addiction; an enthusiast *US, 1957*
- I'm a sucker for the wine. Do you drink it then?—Robin Page, *Down Among the Dossers*, p. 82, 1973

4 a thing *US*
- Instead of ripping that sucker off, as soon as you start driving away, the whole thing just springs right out of the ground.—Joe Bob Briggs, *Joe Bob Goes to the Drive-In*, p. 9, 1987

5 in caving and pot-holing, a caver who uses another's equipment while the owner is otherwise engaged *US*
Examples of use include 'chair-sucker', 'rope-sucker', 'stove-sucker', etc.
- —David Morrison of Wessex Cave Club, 29th February 2004

6 the buttocks *NEW ZEALAND*
- —Harry Orsman, *A Dictionary of Modern New Zealand Slang*, p. 132, 1999

sucker *verb*
to deceive or trick someone *US, 1939*
- Bloody hell – you posh birds are a doddle to sucker.—Colin Butts, *Is Harry Still on the Boat?*, p. 31, 2003

sucker life *noun*
conventional life, with a conventional job and a conventional lifestyle *US*
- Bama, I've been thinking for some time about giving the sucker life a whirl.—Iceberg Slim (Robert Beck), *Death Wish*, p. 117, 1977

sucker pocket *noun*
the hip pocket, an easy pocket to pick *US*
- —Ralph de Sola, *Crime Dictionary*, p. 146, 1982

sucker-punch *verb*
to hit someone without warning, especially in the face *US, 1947*
- He was getting set to sucker-punch her.—Clarence Cooper Jr, *The Scene*, p. 36, 1960
- He didn't feel much like defending any creep who'd sucker-punch him in a place like Pauly's.—Carl Hiaasen, *Tourist Season*, p. 50, 1986

sucker weed *noun*
faked, adulterated or poor quality marijuana *US*
WEED (marijuana) that can be sold to a **SUCKER** (someone gullible).
- —Edith A. Folb, *runnin' down some lines*, p. 256, 1980

sucker wild *adjective*
completely unrestrained and uninhibited *US*
- My idiot father had come to the big city and gone sucker wild. He couldn't stay away from the high yellow whores with their big asses and bitch-dog sexual antics.—Iceberg Slim (Robert Beck), *Pimp*, p. 20, 1969

suck gas

to breath nitrous oxide for pleasure *US, late 1960s*

- This CIA spy has brought up a tank of nitrous oxide from Childhood. I've never sucked gas before, but a nozzle in the mouth is worth truth in the moment. — *The Last Supplement to the Whole Earth Catalog*, p. 66, March 1971

suck-happy *adjective*

obsessed with oral sex *AUSTRALIA*

- Kev was too fucking selfish to pull his weight in a threesome, too suckhappy to stay on the aggressive side of the totem. — Samuel West, *Hard-headed Dick*, p. 97, 1975

suckhole *noun*

1 a sycophant; a flatterer; a toady; an unpleasant person *AUSTRALIA, 1943*

- Tegwyn said if you ask questions kids'll think you're a suckhole. — Tim Winton, *That eye, the sky*, p. 119, 1986
- All the suckholes and Holy Joes[.] — Kevin Sampson, *Clubland*, p. 85, 2002

2 a hole between private video booths in a pornography arcade or between stalls in a public toilet, designed for anonymous oral sex between men *US*

- — *Maledicta*, p. 177, Summer/Winter 1986–1987: 'Sexual slang: prostitutes, pedophiles, flagellators, transvestites, and necrophiles

suckhole *verb*

to behave in an ingratiatingly sycophantic manner *CANADA, 1961*

- Your mother should be here with you at this time, not suckholing up to Dacre! — Virginia Henley, *The Border Hostage*, p. 54, 2001

suck-holer *noun*

a sycophant *NEW ZEALAND*

- — David McGill, *David McGill's Complete Kiwi Slang Dictionary*, p. 121, 1998

Suckie *nickname*

Sauchiehall Street, Glasgow *UK: SCOTLAND*

- How far up Suckie is that Third Eye Centre place? — Michael Munro, *The Patter, Another Blast*, p. 70, 1988

suckie fuckie *verb*

to perform oral sex on a man followed by sexual intercourse *US*

Vietnam war usage.

- Suckee, fuckee, smoke cigarette in the pussy, she give you everything you want. Long time. — *Full Metal Jacket*, 1987

suckie-suckie *noun*

oral sex performed on a man *US*

From the patois of Vietnamese prostitutes during the war, embraced by soldiers.

- Me suckee-suckee. My love you too much. — *Full Metal Jacket*, 1987
- — Gregory Clark, *Words of the Vietnam War*, p. 172, 1990

sucking *noun*

an act of oral sex *UK, 1869*

- Then she gave me a final sucking, draining me dry. — *Letters to Penthouse V*, p. 216, 1995

sucking wind *adjective*

in firefighter usage, said of extremely smoky conditions *US*

- — *American Speech*, p. 275, December 1954: 'Fire terms: additional words and definitions'

suck job *noun*

an act of oral sex *US*

- Despite the thick bush of hair, she was a good suck job. — *Screw*, p. 5, 7th March 1969
- Just as jello makes a nice change from oatmeal, a suck job beats a hand job any time. — Samuel West, *Hard-headed Dick*, p. 159, 1975

suck-off *noun*

an act of oral sex *US*

- A two-way suck-off is just what the doctor ordered. — *Letters to Penthouse V*, p. 278, 1995

suck off *verb*

to perform oral sex on either a man or woman, especially to the point of orgasm *UK, 1909*

- THERE HE IS. THERE HE IS. THE SONOFABITCH TRIED TA SUCK ME OFF. — Hubert Selby Jr, *Last Exit to Brooklyn*, p. 237, 1957
- Then she took me to her apartment and for two hundred francs I let her suck me off. She wanted me to live with her but I didn't want to have her suck me off every night ... it makes you too weak. — Henry Miller, *Tropic of Cancer*, p. 238, 1961
- They move down the Trail. The man sucks Johnny off. — John Rechy, *Numbers*, p. 136, 1967
- Amanda lowered her long lashes and smiled sweetly. "I will suck you off," she said. — Tom Robbins, *Another Roadside Attraction*, p. 4, 1971
- Last week I was doing this movie with one cock up my ass, one in my cunt, while I sucked off a seventeen-year-old blonde from New Jersey. She was bout as kooky as me. — Roger Blake, *What you always wanted to know about porno-movies*, p. 244, 1972
- "Ohhh," the guy moaned. "Suck it. Please. Suck it off. Ohhhh!!!!" — Roy Hawkins, *Bimbos by the Bay*, p. 127, 1977
- Bunch of guys. You all hang out together. Yeah, you're all going out on business. You're all gonna suck each other off. — *Raging Bull*, 1980
- Ron Jeremy is sucked off before ramming his meat into Patti Petite in Blonde on the Run. — *Adult Video*, p. 15, August/September 1986
- [Y]ou could buy marital aids and Big John dolls with rubber mouths to suck you off. — William T. Vollman, *Whores for Gloria*, p. 22, 1991
- Suck him off. I don't think you've had enough come tonight. — *Letters to Penthouse V*, p. 6, 1995

suckout *noun*

in surfing, a wave that is breaking fast in front of itself, creating a tunnel or tube *US*

- — Gary Fairmont R. Filosa II, *The Surfer's Almanac*, p. 195, 1977

suck out *verb*

1 to speed past a parked police car, drawing it into a chase *US*

- — *American Speech*, p. 272, December 1962: 'The language of traffic policemen'

2 in poker, to win in the face of every known convention and probability *US*

- — John Vorhaus, *The Big Book of Poker Slang*, p. 35, 1996

suck points *noun*

imaginary credits earned by obsequious ingratiation *US*

- — Sally Williams, *"Strong" Words*, p. 161, 1994

suck-up *noun*

a sycophant *US*

- They're all a bunch a' ladder-climbing suck-ups. — Stephen J. Cannell, *The Tin Collectors*, p. 44, 2001

suck up *verb*

to seek favour through obsequious behaviour *UK, 1860*

- You don't have to suck up to me. I won't squeal. — Leonard Cohen, *Beautiful Losers*, p. 134, 1966
- You should take a tip from your friend here, Quint – he really knows how to suck up. — *Mallrats*, 1995
- Don't try to suck up to me! It's a little late for that. — *Austin Powers*, 1997
- Forty-year-old hipster in baggy Comme Des Garcons sucking up to the best thing ever to walk down a Chanel catwalk. — Tony Wilson, *24 Hour Party People*, p. 215, 2002

suck wind!

leave me alone! *US*

Hawaiian youth usage.

- — Douglas Simonson, *Pidgin to da Max*, 1981

sucky *noun*

a hollow wave *AUSTRALIA*

- — Nat Young, *Surfing Fundamentals*, p. 128, 1985

sucky *adjective*

awful *US, 1984*

- Life as REO Speedwagon knows it is forever locked in the saccharine harmonies, melancholy melodies and sucky sentiments of late-'70s rock radio. — *Toronto Star*, p. D16, 20th February 1987
- — Pamela Munro, *U.C.L.A. Slang*, p. 82, 1989
- "The Tyler Set" can be really sucky, too – no drugs, no irony, and only moderate booze, popcorn, coca, and videos on Friday nights. — Douglas Copeland, *Generation X*, p. 106, 1991
- And it's always that same shit, soft rock! That sucky, non-threatening, easy-listening pussy music. — George Carlin, *Brain Droppings*, p. 6, 1997
- I'd be lying like a cop in court if I was to tell you Sing Ha was anything but sucky beer. — Tom Robbins, *Fierce Invalids from Hot Climates*, p. 131, 2000
- I suppose by comparison, Iceland does make every other country look sucky. — Meg Cabot, *The Princess Diaries*, p. 20, 2000
- You'll be disappointed and have your trust broken and have a lot of real sucky days. — Dennis Lehane, *Mystic River*, p. 293, 2001

sucky face *noun*

kissing *US*

- — Jackie Collins, *Lethal Seduction*, p. 284, 2000

sucrose *noun*

money *US*

- — David W. Maurer, *Argot of the Racetrack*, p. 61, 1951

sudden death *noun*
in sports, games and recreations, as diverse as league football and television quiz shows, a period of extra time during which the first to score or achieve a specified target wins *UK, 1834*
Originally 'a single toss of the dice'.
- —Kyle Rote, *The Language of Pro Football*, p. 146, 1966
- —Dawson Taylor, *How to Talk Golf*, p. 63–64, 1985
- —Peter Schwed, *How to Talk Tennis*, p. 71, 1988

suds *noun*
1 beer *US, 1904*
- This mixture was pumped into each barrel, plus thirty pounds of air, and you had a barrel of real suds.—Mezz Mezzrow, *Really the Blues*, p. 63, 1946
- Wot c'd be more beautiful than a foamin' schooner of suds?—John Wynnum, *Tar Dust*, p. 24, 1962
- Purveyors of hard booze (who also sell beer), and beer bars which depend on draft or tap beer for about 25 cents, the occasional aristocratic drinker of bottled suds, and a hell of a lot of potato chips[.]—Roger Gordon, *Hollywood's Sexual Underground*, p. 12, 1966
- It was a junkie joint. I sat sipping on a bottle of suds; I couldn't trust the glasses.—Iceberg Slim (Robert Beck), *Pimp*, p. 91, 1969
- Shoving his suds aside, Mr. Jones leans across the table.—Guy Owen, *The Flim-Flam Man and the Apprentice Grifter*, p. 217, 1972
- All but two of 'em like to sit, sip suds, and bullshit all night. —A.S. Jackson, *Gentleman Pimp*, p. 101, 1973
- He kept staring at the unattainable vision of the latter as he drowned his immediate disappointment in a gallon of foamy brown suds. —Lance Peters, *The Dirty Half-Mile*, p. 81, 1979
- We can have the suds on the base if you want.—Joseph Wambaugh, *Finnegan's Week*, p. 196, 1993

2 a large amount of money *US*
- —Lou Shelly, *Hepcats Jive Talk Dictionary*, p. 19, 1945

suds artist *noun*
a habitual beer drinker *AUSTRALIA, 1972*
- —Arthur Chipper, *The Aussie Swearer's Guide*, p. 25, 1972
- Blind Frieda could see you're a pie-eating drongo and a blithering suds-artist.—Ignatius Jones, *The 1992 True Hip Manual*, p. 158, 1992

sue *verb*
▸ **sue the ass off; sue your arse off**
to take a legal action against somebody in pursuit of punitive damages *US*
- I wonder if the network will ever find us. If so, I'm going to sue their asses off.—Sparkle Hayter, *The Diary of Sue Peaner, Marooned! Contestant [Tart Noir]*, p. 298, 2002

suede *noun*
a black person *US*
- —Malachi Andrews and Paul T. Owens, *Black Language*, p. 98, 1973
- She's going to knock on the downstairs door and start yelling something unintelligible in a way-out suede dialect, and hope Terry buzzes her in.—Joseph Wambaugh, *The Blue Knight*, p. 193, 1973

suedehead; suede *noun*
a member of a late 1960s youth fashion and gang movement, characterised by a close-cropped scalp and smart utilitarian wear, associated with football hooliganism, racist violence and neo-Nazism *UK*
This lexicographic development matches exactly the **SKINHEAD** fashion's further growth; 'suede' is the velvety surface of leather and thus describes the soft nap on a previously shaven head.
- How can anyone condemn the skinhead books when [...] they present skinheads, suedeheads, bootboys and now smooths as they really are?—Richard Allen (James Moffat), *Author's Notes [britpulp]*, p. 63, November 1972
- [T]he fighting between mods, rockers, skinheads, Pakistanis, suedeheads, Hell's angels, boot boys, greasers, Teds, punks, soulboys, rockabillies, rude boys, casuals and every other shade of herbert going[.]—John King, *Human Punk*, p. 295, 2000

sufferation *noun*
hard times *TRINIDAD AND TOBAGO*
- —Lise Winer, *Dictionary of the English/Creole of Trinidad & Tobago*, 2003

sufferin' sheepdip!
used for expressing disapproval *US*
A signature line of Colonel Sherman Potter on *M*A*S*H* (CBS, 1972–83). Repeated with referential humour.

sug *noun*
used as an affectionate term of address *US*
A shortened form of **SUGAR**.
- "That's what I want, sug. I"m dying from thirst."—Irving Shulman, *The Amboy Dukes*, p. 117, 1947

sugar *noun*
1 used as a term of endearment *US, 1930*
A distinct southern ring. Variations include 'sugar-pie', 'sugar-babe', 'sugar-baby', etc.
- Don't get roused, sugar.—*The Blues Brothers*, 1980
- A little girl with curly blond hair and big seashell earrings next to him at the bar saying, "What's wrong, sugar?" and patting him on the back.—Elmore Leonard, *Maximum Bob*, p. 147, 1991
- Don't stop now sugar. I'm just getting warmed up.—*Natural Born Killers*, 1994

2 diabetes *US*
- "Winnie," Gypsy Pearl scolded gently, "you know the doctor told you you ain't s'poze to drink. You got sugar, girl."—Nathan Heard, *Howard Street*, p. 49, 1968
- She's got sugar, so she leaves this outfit [syringe] of hers so that whenever she comes to visit, if she should decide to stay for the night, she has her outfit so that she can take her medicine in the morning.—Donald Goines, *White Man's Justice, Black Man's Grief*, p. 152–153, 1973
- You got sugar, right? What the doctor is always tellin you?—John Sayles, *Union Dues*, p. 59, 1977
- —Lise Winer, *Dictionary of the English/Creole of Trinidad & Tobago*, 2003

3 a type of snow suitable for skiing *UK*
- The ski-ing was quite excellent in granulated snow, what is sometimes called Sugar, formed by one day of hot spring sun. —David Walker, *Devil's Plunge*, 1968

4 heroin; powdered heroin adulterated with sugar *US, 1977*
From the appearance.
- —Richard A. Spears, *The Slang and Jargon of Drugs and Drink*, p. 493, 1986
- —Mike Haskins, *Drugs*, p. 284, 2003

5 cocaine *UK, 1998*
A white powder.
- —Mike Haskins, *Drugs*, p. 281, 2003

6 sand *US*
- —Ramon Adams, *The Language of the Railroader*, p. 150, 1977

7 money *US*
- —David W. Maurer, *Argot of the Racetrack*, p. 61, 1951

▷ **see: SUGAR LUMP**

sugar!
used an all-purpose euphemism for 'shit', especially as an exclamation *UK*
Pronunciation often hesitates over the 'sh' before committing itself to 'shit' or 'sugar', possibly from a combination of 'shit' and **BUGGER!**, recorded in 1901 as 'I'll be sugared!'.
- I was like a pig in sugar.—Andy McNab, *Immediate Action*, p. 86, 1995
- [E]ach bone-cracking blow was met with cries of "F...lipping 'eck!" and "Sh...ugar!"—Iain Aitch, *A Fete Worse Than Death*, p. 7, 2003

sugar and honey; sugar *noun*
money *UK, 1859*
Rhyming slang.
- —Ray Puxley, *Cockney Rabbit*, 1992

sugar and spice *noun*
ice, especially as served with a drink *UK*
Rhyming slang.
- —Ray Puxley, *Cockney Rabbit*, 1992

sugar and spice; sugar *adjective*
nice *UK*
Rhyming slang; not especially sarcastic in use.
- —Ray Puxley, *Cockney Rabbit*, 1992

sugarbeeter *noun*
a resident of the Lower Peninsula of Michigan *US*
Michigan Upper Peninsula usage.

sugar block *noun*
crack cocaine *UK, 1998*
- —Mike Haskins, *Drugs*, p. 282, 2003

sugar candy *noun*
brandy *UK*
Rhyming slang.
- —Ray Puxley, *Cockney Rabbit*, 1992

sugar candy *adjective*
useful, generally in a negative context *UK*
Rhyming slang for 'handy'.

- An umbrella with a hole in it may be described as, "That's bloody sugar candy that is". — Ray Puxley, *Cockney Rabbit*, 1992

sugar cube *noun*

LSD *US, 1967*

From the method of ingesting a dose of the drug dripped onto a sugar cube.

- — Richard A. Spears, *The Slang and Jargon of Drugs and Drink*, p. 493, 1986
- — Mike Haskins, *Drugs*, p. 286, 2003

sugar daddy *noun*

an older man who supports or helps support a young lover *UK, 1926*

With occasional playful variants.

- The boss catered mostly to Indians who had struck oil on the reservation, beefy cattlemen who were sure to be milked, sugar-daddies with their sable-sporting chicken dinners, and butter-and-egg men with plenty of bacon. — Mezz Mezzrow, *Really the Blues*, p. 84, 1946
- James C. will become a kind of sugar-daddy "invessment"[.] — Terry Southern, *Now Dig This*, p. 201, 17 November 1962
- Well, I need a sugar daddy/He could be my friend/And if I needed money/I know he would lend me a hand. — Christine McVie (Fleetwood Mac), *Sugar Daddy*, 1975
- Find out who bought it for her. Her sugar daddy. — *Lethal Weapon*, 1987
- Female college student looking for 'financially secure' Sugar Daddy. — Anka Radakovich, *The Wild Girls Club*, p. 43, 1994
- [T]he sexually abused Cinderella who married her sugar-daddy prince and then poisoned him[.] — *The Guardian*, p. 8, 26th February 2002

sugar dish *noun*

the vagina *US*

A variation of C19 obsolete 'sugar basin' (the vagina).

- My mother said no tampons. You couldn't put anything in your sugar dish. — Eve Ensler, *The Vagina Monologues*, p. 38, 1998

sugar down *verb*

to dilute powder narcotics, especially with powdered milk sugar (lactose) *US*

- — *Congressional Record*, p. E3982, 6th May 1970

sugarhead *noun*

strong, homemade whisky *US*

- It is called corn liquor, white lightning, sugar whiskey, skully cracker, popskull, bush whiskey, stump, stumphole, 'splo, ruckus juice, radiator whiskey, rotgut, sugarhead, block and tackle, wildcat, panther's breath, tiger's sweat, Sweet spirits of cats a-fighting, alley bourbon, city gin, cool water, happy Sally, deep shaft, jump steady, old horsey, stingo, blue John, red eye, pine top, buckeye bark whiskey and see seven stars. — *Star Tribune (Minneapolis)*, p. 19F, 31st January 1999

sugar hill *noun*

a brothel *US*

- — *Maledicta*, p. 148, Summer/Winter 1986–1987: 'Sexual slang: prostitutes, pedophiles, flagellators, transvestites, and necrophiles'

sugaring-off *noun*

in Canadian maple syrup making, the process of boiling the maple sap down to syrup or sugar *CANADA*

- Sugaring-off in the sugar bush in a sugar shanty has many terms not often met with elsewhere. — Bill Casselman, *Canadian Words*, p. 73, 1995

sugar lips *noun*

a smooth talker *AUSTRALIA*

- — Ned Wallish, *The Truth Dictionary of Racing Slang*, p. 79, 1989

sugar lump; sugar *noun*

LSD *UK*

Probably from 'sugar cubes' which are sometimes used as a medium for taking the drug.

- — John Wyatt, *Drugs*, 1973
- — Home Office, *Glossary of Terms and Slang Common in Penal Establishments*, July 1978
- — Angela Devlin, *Prison Patter*, p. 110, 1996
- Street names [...] stars, strawberries, sugar, tab[.] — James Kay and Julian Cohen, *The Parents' Complete Guide to Young People and Drugs*, p. 141, 1998

sugar pimp *noun*

a pimp who controls his prostitutes through charm and attention *US*

- A pimp who uses a great deal of charm and little violence or fear is called a sweet Mack or sugar pimp. — Christina and Richard Milner, *Black Players*, p. 35, 1972

sugar report *noun*

during war, a letter from home, especially from a girlfriend *US*

- — Linda Reinberg, *In the Field*, p. 211, 1991

sugar shack *noun*

a small hut built for boiling down maple sap to make maple syrup *CANADA*

- "Sugar shack" is the anglophone equivalent in Quebec of the French "cabane a sucre," which is also used by English speakers. — *Toronto Globe and Mail*, p. C6, 30th May 1998

sugar stick *noun*

the penis *UK*

Rhyming slang for **PRICK**.

- — Ray Puxley, *Cockney Rabbit*, 1992

sugar tit *noun*

any cherished object or habit *US*

- [E]ven further in the distance Mt. Kilimanjaro jumped up like God's own sugar-tit[.] — Tom Robbins, *Another Roadside Attraction*, p. 64, 1971
- — Helen Dahlskog (Editor), *A Dictionary of Contemporary and Colloquial Usage*, p. 58, 1972

sugar up *verb*

to curry favour *US*

- Back in the beginning, when Tom was still sugarin' up to her, he'd taken out a ten-thousand dollar insurance policy. — Jim Thompson, *Pop. 1280*, p. 133, 1964

sugar weed *noun*

marijuana which has been adulterated and bulked-up with sugar water or honey *US, 1969*

- — Richard A. Spears, *The Slang and Jargon of Drugs and Drink*, p. 493, 1986
- — Mike Haskins, *Drugs*, p. 289, 2003

suicide alley *noun*

in shuffleboard, a quarter of the opponent's side of the court *US*

- — Omero C. Catan, *Secrets of Shuffleboard Strategy*, p. 73, 1967: 'Glossary of terms'

suicide axle *noun*

in hot rodding and drag racing, a special axle assembly that allows a lower front end *US*

- The first attempts at this type of construction had a tendency to come unglued at high speeds, hence the "suicide" part of the term. — John Lawlor, *How to Talk Car*, p. 103, 1965

suicide blonde *noun*

a girl or woman who has dyed her hair blonde at home *US*

From the pun: 'dyed by her own hand'.

- — *Dobie Gillis, Teenage Slanguage Dictionary*, 1962

suicide box *noun*

in trucking, a sleeper added to a conventional cab *US*

So named because of the danger presented to anyone sleeping in the box should the truck jackknife.

- — Montie Tak, *Truck Talk*, p. 159, 1971

suicide club *noun*

a mythical group of jockeys who ride in steeplechase races *US*

- — David W. Maurer, *Argot of the Racetrack*, p. 61, 1951

suicide clutch *noun*

a foot-operated clutch on a motorcyle *US*

If your foot slips off when stopped, it engages the clutch.

- [A] foot, or "suicide" clutch (so-called because it necessitates split-second timing while shifting and braking, both done with the left foot)[.] — Hunter S. Thompson, *Hell's Angels*, p. 98, 1966
- It was a macho thing to have what we called suicide clutches and jockey shifts, where you should shift gears with your left hand and operate a clutch system with your left foot. — Ralph "Sonny" Barger, *Hell's Angel*, p. 59, 2000

suicide door *noun*

on a car, a door that hinges at the back and opens towards the rear *US*

- So called because, if the door opens while the vehicle is in motion, the wind can blow it wide open and expose a passenger sitting by it to danger. — John Edwards, *Auto Dictionary*, p. 165, 1993

suicide jockey *noun*

1 the driver of a vehicle hauling dangerous cargo *US*

- Listen, ya wanna put that microbus in behind that suicide jockey? — C.W. McCall, *Convoy*, 1976

2 a dangerous driver *UK*

- — Peter Chippindale, *The British CB Book*, p. 159, 1981

suicide king *noun*
in a deck of cards, the king of hearts *US*
It appears that he is plunging a knife into his head.
• —George Percy, *The Language of Poker*, p. 90, 1988

suicide season *noun*
the few months leading up to the wet season in Australia's tropical north *AUSTRALIA, 1975*

suicide seat *noun*
the front passenger seat in a car *US*
• —Lewis Poteet, *Car & Motorcyle Slang*, p. 194, 1992

suicide stew *noun*
a combination of central nervous system depressants and alcohol *US*
• His once white ROTC hat was inverted next to him on the tile floor, already full of regurgitated, semi-digested suicide stew.—Richard Farina, *Been Down So Long*, p. 185, 1966

suit *noun*
1 an executive; a person of authority but no creativity *US, 1979*
The term usually suggests a them-against-us mentality, with 'them' being the executives who wear suits; pejorative.
• More important suits have hurried in from corporation headquarters to see what the hell was going on.—Robert Campbell, *The Cat's Meow*, p. 196, 1988
• They'll want to do the Dempsy stuff in Toronto too, but that's why they're just a bunch of suits, a bunch of sweaty fucking suits.—Richard Price, *Clockers*, p. 152, 1992
• —Connie Eble (Editor), *UNC-CH Campus Slang*, p. 9, Spring 1992
• You saw suits, some with the long-legged chicks, a few with their wives.—Elmore Leonard, *Be Cool*, p. 337, 1999
• Don't ever make the mistake of thinking films are made with a camera by artistic people on exotic location; they are made with phones by Suits on Wall or Threadneedle Streets.—Stuart Browne, *Dangerous Parking*, p. 17, 2000
• [F]ucking cunt of a suit he was – no style[.]—Patrick Jones, *Everything Must Go*, p. 146, 2000
• He'd been targeted as vulnerable by the national Republican Party and money was flowing in from around the country for his opponent, a suit named Norm Coleman.—Al Franken, *Lies*, p. 178, 2003

2 in prison, an official non-uniformed visitor *UK*
• —Angela Devlin, *Prison Patter*, p. 110, 1996

suitcase *noun*
the rectum *US*
• Referring to the rectum as a repository for the smuggling of drugs into prison.—William K. Bentley and James M. Corbett, *Prison Slang*, p. 76, 1992

suitcase *verb*
to conceal drugs inside a condom or balloon inside a body orifice *US*
• —Carsten Stroud, *Close Pursuit*, p. 276, 1987

suitcase farmer *noun*
a farmer who also works in the town *CANADA*
• Further, the wheat-making problem means the end of the "suitcase farmer," who has been accustomed to spend only a few weeks on his land each spring and summer for seeding and harvesting.—*Saturday Night*, p. 15/1, 13th October 1959
• My folks are suitcase farmers. That's a farmer who lives in town, loads his equipment onto a truck and commutes into the country to plant or harvest.—Johnny Shearer, *The Male Hustler*, p. 109, 1966
• In the 1950s, "suitcase farmer" was a slightly insulting term for farmers who also held down jobs off the farm.—*cbc4kids.ca*, 15th June 2002

suitcase pimp; suitcase *noun*
a boyfriend, agent or other male who accompanies a female pornography performer to the set *US*
Not flattering.
• —*Adult Video News*, p. 50, October 1995
• Porsche Lynn actually came up with the term suitcase pimp, because a lot of these guys will walk behind the girl carrying her bags. They are essentially leeches. (Quoting Bill Marigold)—Ana Loria, *1 2 3 Be A Porn Star!*, p. 36, 2000

suited and booted *adjective*
well-dressed *UK*
• Come Saturday, I was suited and booted and in the Standard at opening time.—Lenny McLean, *The Guv'nor*, p. 55, 1998
• The clientele is the London demi-monde, suited and booted. Black tie, here and there a debonair tux and cummerbund.—Bernard Dempsey and Kevin McNally *Lock, Stock... & Two Sips*, p. 284, 2000

suit up *verb*
to place a condom on a penis *US*
• The older porn performers started their careers before condoms were commonly used, so they are predictably a little reluctant to "suit up" as they say[.]—Ana Loria, *1 2 3 Be A Porn Star!*, p. 129, 2000

sulker *noun*
in horse racing, a moody horse *US*
• —David W. Maurer, *Argot of the Racetrack*, p. 61, 1951

sulphate; sulph *noun*
amphetamine *sulphate* *UK*
• —Angela Devlin, *Prison Patter*, p. 21, 1996
• We start laughin' with the sulph workin' overtime on my guts an' my teeth an stretchin' my laugh 'cross both ears.—Nick Barlay, *Curvy Lovebox*, p. 31, 1997
• The sulphate had taken a back seat by now, and we were into getting pissed.—John King, *Human Punk*, p. 180, 2000
• As an NME journalist, Charles Shaar Murray couldn't afford cocaine, so like everyone around him he took sulphate instead.—Simon Napier-Bell, *Black Vinyl White Powder*, p. 158, 2001
• CALL IT... Sulphate, wake-ups, whizz, whites, base JUST DON'T CALL IT... Ice—*Drugs An Adult Guide*, p. 35, December 2001

Sumatran red *noun*
a variety of marijuana *UK*
• Other types include Purple Haze, Sumatran Red, Durban Poison and skunk.—Macfarlane, Macfarlane and Robson, *The User*, p. 142, 1996

sumbitch; sombitch *noun*
a son of a bitch *US, 1972*
A southern corruption.
• And Barbara Jane said, "It sure as hell might. I'll be a sumbitch."—Dan Jenkins, *Semi-Tough*, p. 216, 1972
• He was a tough sombitch.—Edwin Torres, *Carlito's Way*, p. 16, 1975
• I tried to standup and fly straight, but it wasn't easy with that sumbitch Reagan in the White House.—*Raising Arizona*, 1987
• Goddamn this sumbitch is runnin' hot.—*Natural Born Killers*, 1994

summat *noun*
something *UK, 1984*
A phonetic slovening.
• I can't say we consciously go out to copy summat.—Shaun Ryder, *Shaun Ryder... in His Own Words*, 1992
• I'm your dad and that counts for summat, doesn't it?—*The Full Monty*, 1997
• [Y]ears ago men 'ad summat to do with their lives[.]—Patrick Jones, *Unprotected Sex*, p. 247–248, 1999

Summerland Donkey Cock *noun*
a variety of marijuana from British Columbia *CANADA*
• "Summerland Donkey Cock," he said fondly, recalling an infamous strain from the sunny Okanagan Valley, seventy miles west.—Brian Preston, *Pot Planet*, p. 219, 2002

summer sausage *noun*
the female partner of a boy in a summer romance at camp *CANADA*
• Darce is talking about her as if she's a piece of meat. From what he's implying she lets him do anything he wants. "Summer sausage" is what he calls her.—Margaret Atwood, *in the New Oxford Book of Canadian Stories*, p. 259, 1997

sun *noun*
▸ **the sun shines out of your arse**
said of a person who is considered perfect *UK*
• He thought the sun shone out of Thatcher's arse.—John King, *Human Punk*, p. 194, 2000

▸ **the sun's drawing her backstays; the sun's got her backstays down**
lines in the sky coming down from the sun, predicting rain or bad weather *CANADA*
• The sun's drawing her backstays.—Helen Creighton, *Bluenose Magic*, 1968

sunbathers *noun*
in poker, a pair of queens dealt face-up *US*
• —George Percy, *The Language of Poker*, p. 90, 1988

sunbeam *noun*
a piece of cutlery or crockery that was not used during a meal and thus needs no washing up *AUSTRALIA*
• —Barry Humphries, *A Nice Night's Entertainment*, p. 210, 1981

sun belt *noun*
the southern states in the US *US, 1969*
• Mike's told me all about Mr. Stumpnagler wanting to sell out and go to some place in the sunbelt. — Robert Campbell, *Nibbled to Death by Ducks*, p. 230, 1989

sunburnt *adjective*
used for describing playing cards that have been left in the sun to discolour slightly to aid a cheat in identifying them in another player's hand *US*
• — George Percy, *The Language of Poker*, p. 90, 1988

Sunday *noun*
a surprise blow from the blind side *US*
• But nothing warned him, as Pithead pivoted sideways and, winding up like Whitey Ford, copped a Sunday, smashing Red flush on the mouth. — Malcolm Braly, *On the Yard*, p. 8, 1967

Sunday *verb*
to hit someone from their blind side *US*
• He'd been hurt by fans too – stabbed; hit from the blind side,. or "Sundayed"; struck with flying bottles and chairs; burned with cigars; stuck with hairpins. — Ted Lewin, *I Was a Teenage Professional Wrestler*, p. 29, 1993

Sunday best *noun*
1 your smartest clothes *UK, 1846*
Such clothes were originally reserved for Sunday wear.
• [A] slightly snooty wait staff may make you wish you'd worn your Sunday best. — Linda Watanabe McFerrin, *Best Places Northern California*, p. 204, 2001

2 a vest *UK*
Rhyming slang, with a fine sense of irony.
• — Ray Puxley, *Cockney Rabbit*, 1992

Sunday-go-to-meeting *adjective*
used of clothes, suitable for wearing to church *US, 1831*
Intentionally rural.
• Just felt like putting on my Sunday-go-to-meeting suit. — Louis Armstrong, *Satchmo*, p. 153, 1954
• Then I put on my Sunday-go-to-meetin' clothes, my new sixty-dollar Stetson and my seventy-dollar Justin boots and my four-dollar Levis. — Jim Thompson, *Pop. 1280*, p. 5, 1964
• — Clarence Major, *Dictionary of Afro-American Slang*, p. 111, 1970
• Mr. Diane Holt, almost Easter Sunday sharp, stands on the front steps of her apartment pulling on her white Sunday-go-to-meeting gloves[.] — Odie Hawkins, *Ghetto Sketches*, p. 50, 1972
• He has costumed himself as an out of fashion Sunday-go-to-meeting silk gloved elderly woman with grey riddled long wig, black bustled dress, over trousers, and ostrich feather plumed floppy chapeau[.] — Iceberg Slim (Robert Beck), *Doom Fox*, p. 71, 1978
• — Lise Winer, *Dictionary of the English/Creole of Trinidad & Tobago*, 2003

Sunday morn *noun*
an erection (of the penis) *UK*
Rhyming slang for **HORN**.
• — Ray Puxley, *Cockney Rabbit*, 1992

Sunday popper *noun*
an occasional user of an addictive drug *US*
• — *Mr.*, p. 55, April 1966: 'The hippie's lexicon'

Sunday punch *noun*
a blow from a person's blind side *US*
• He would play the jealous lover or husband, then, faking anger at her infidelity, he'd pick a fight with the man – usually by throwing a Sunday punch. — Nathan Heard, *Howard Street*, p. 17, 1968

Sunday run *noun*
in circus and carnival usage, a long trip between engagements *US*
• — Don Wilmeth, *The Language of American Popular Entertainment*, p. 263, 1981

Sunday school show; Sunday school *noun*
a circus or carnival with no crooked games and no performances with sexual content *US*
• Charles Sparks probably ran the best Sunday School Show of all of them. — Joe McKennon, *Circus Lingo*, p. 90, 1980
• — Don Wilmeth, *The Language of American Popular Entertainment*, p. 263, 1981
• — Gene Sorrows, *All About Carnivals*, p. 27, 1985: 'Terminology'

Sunday science lecture *noun*
any presentation made with a captive audience *ANTARCTICA*
• — Carnegie Mellon Astrophysics Peterson Group, *Antarctic Vocabulary*, 19th September 1997

Sunday suit *noun*
no clothes at all *US*
• — Elementary Electronics, *Dictionary of CB Lingo*, p. 112, 1976

sundowner *noun*
1 an itinerant traveller *AUSTRALIA, 1868*
So-called from their habit of arriving at a country property just on sundown so that they can ask for sustenance without being given any manual labour.
• SUNDOWNER – A tramp. — Gilbert H. Lawson, *A Dictionary of Australian Words and Terms*, 1924
• Jacky Dow loathed swagmen of any description, irrespective of whether they were 'sundowners' merely looking for tucker and shelter for the night or jobless men tramping the tracks in search of employment. — Bill Wannan, *Bullockies, Beauts and Bandicoots*, p. 44, 1960
• What? Sundowners never pay fares. — Frank Hardy, *The Yarns of Billy Borker*, p. 48, 1965

2 a senile patient who is quiet during the day but becomes agitated at dark *US*
• — *Maledicta*, p. 39, 1983: 'More common patient-directed pejoratives used by medical personnel'

3 any alcoholic drink enjoyed at the end of the day *UK, 1938*
Recorded in India, Singapore, the East Indies and Australia; also in south and east Africa.
• Sundowners with the Home Secretary was rising-star stuff for sure. — Ben Elton, *High Society*, p. 219, 2002

4 a VF-111 combat aircraft *US*
The plane was first deployed in 1942 in the Pacific with the mission of shooting down Japanese 'Suns'. Deployed in Korea and Vietnam.
• Joining the "Sundowners," as VF-111 was nicknamed, in turnaround, Weigand had been one of the two new pilots Ruliffson was considering for his wingman. — Robert K. Wilcox, *Scream of Eagles*, p. 228, 1990

sun gonna shine *noun*
a type of bet in an illegal numbers game lottery *US*
• He played the money row, lucky lady, happy days, true love, sun gonna shine, gold, silver, diamonds, dollars and whiskey. — Chester Himes, *A Rage in Harlem*, p. 23, 1957

sun gun *noun*
in the television and film industries, a portable, intense light *US*
• — Ralph S. Singleton, *Filmaker's Dictionary*, p. 166, 1990

sunker *noun*
in Newfoundland, a rock or reef just underwater *CANADA*
• This was not the main entrance but a shortcut or "inside" passage full of sunkers (as reefs and shoal rocks are called in Newfoundland). — Farley Mowat, *The Black Joke*, p. 33, 1962

sun kink *noun*
an expansion of railway track caused by hot weather conditions *US*
• — J. Herbert Lund, *Herb's Hot Box of Railroad Slang*, p. 98, 1975

sunner *noun*
a thief who snatches a chain from the wearer's neck *UK*
Recorded by a Jamaican inmate of a UK prison, August 2002.

sunnies *noun*
sunglasses *AUSTRALIA, 1981*
• The wrap-around sunnies were in the way. — *Weekend Australian*, p. 11, 16th October 1982
• — Harry Orsman, *A Dictionary of Modern New Zealand Slang*, p. 133, 1999

sunny Jim *noun*
▷ see: **SONNY BOY**

sunny side up *adjective*
of eggs, fried, with the yolk on top *US, 1901*
• "Whenever my father orders eggs sunny-side up," I said to the cop, "he always says, "Give me two eggs looking at me." — Kinky Friedman, *Steppin on a Rainbow*, p. 104, 2001

sun parlor *noun*
a brakevan (caboose) cupola *US*
• — Ramon Adams, *The Language of the Railroader*, p. 150, 1977

sunrise *noun*
a Toyota car *UK*
Citizens' band radio slang; plays on **SUNSET** (a Datsun car); also of Japanese manufacture, and Japan's identity is 'the land of the rising sun'.
• —Peter Chippindale, *The British CB Book*, p. 161, 1981

sunset *noun*
a Datsun car *UK*
A weakly derogative play on Sunny, a late-1960s Datsun brand.
• —Peter Chippindale, *The British CB Book*, p. 161, 1981

sunshine *noun*
1 used as a form of address, often patronising with an underlying note of disapproval or threat *UK, 1972*
• "Listen, sunshine, I am a highly respected person -" "And where would that be – "sunshine". A few afternoon drinking clubs?" —Anthony Masters, *Minder*, p. 80, 1984
• SERGEI: Who fuck you, uh?! THREE FEET: This is Mr Miami Vice. He's come a long way. You remember your manners, sunshine. —Chris Baker and Andrew Day, *Lock, Stock... & One Big Bullock*, p. 370, 2000
2 LSD *US*
• —*Current Slang*, p. 21, Spring 1971
• —US Department of Justice, *Street Terms*, October 1994

Sunshine Coast *noun*
1 Vancouver, British Columbia *CANADA*
• An 85-mile stretch of scenic shoreline running northwest from this British Columbian metropolis has been dubbed the Sunshine Coast, with ample justification. —*New York Times*, p. 10–40, 9th May 1965
2 Brisbane, Australia *AUSTRALIA*

sunspots *noun*
in computing, the purported reason for an unanticipated error *US*
• —Eric S. Raymond, *The New Hacker's Dictionary*, p. 337, 1991

suntans *noun*
a summer-weight tan military uniform *US, 1937*
• —Carl Fleischhauer, *A Glossary of Army Slang*, p. 20, 1968
• He was dressed in his office uniform, a short-sleeved shirt and trousers of tan tropical worsted, an outfit called "suntans." —Neil Sheehan, *A Bright Shining Lie*, p. 276, 1988

sup *noun*
supper *US*
• —John D. Bell et al., *Loosely Speaking*, p. Appendix, 1969

s'up?
used as a greeting *US*
A very slurred 'what's up?'.
• —Connie Eble (Editor), *UNC-CH Campus Slang*, p. 6, Fall 1981
• —*National Education Association Today*, April 1985: 'A glossary for rents and other squids'
• Sup boys. You on this show? —*Mallrats*, 1995

super *noun*
1 a *super*intendent, especially of an apartment building *AUSTRALIA, 1857*
• Ray was the man's super befrore the man set him up downtown, doing the apartments. —Elmore Leonard, *Switch*, p. 64–65, 1878
• The shop super and two other shop leadermen came in and he talked to them in turn. —Chester Himes, *If He Hollers Let Him Go*, p. 28, 1945
• He was going with the super of the place, Harold, who was very friendly with us. —Mezz Mezzrow, *Really the Blues*, p. 296, 1946
• She called the super. He knew her and let her in. —Mickey Spillane, *I, The Jury*, p. 9, 1947
• The super lets me come down here. —Nat Hentoff, *Jazz Country*, p. 114, 1965
• Last month I was late paying the rent and told the super, "I'm waiting for that man to bring me money." —Susan Hall, *Gentleman of Leisure*, p. 144, 1972
• Guy used to be the super in Roger's building. —Edwin Torres, *Q & A*, p. 88, 1977
2 a *super*numerary *UK, 1838*
• But for autumn/winter 2003, many of the major labels have opted for for big-league stars instead of Natalia, Liya, Maria Carla or any of the old supers. —*The Guardian*, 18th July 2003
3 high octane or top grade petrol *UK, 1967*
• "Extra" (82 octane, currently US$1.12 per US gallon) and "Super" (92 Octane, currently US$1.51 per US gallon). Both are unleaded. —Daisy and Robert Kunstaetter, *Footprint Ecuador and the Galapagos Handbook*, 2003
4 in carnival usage, a handsome watch displayed as a prize *US*
• —Don Wilmeth, *The Language of American Popular Entertainment*, p. 263, 1981

super *adjective*
excellent *UK, 1895*
• For stay-at-home moms, selling infant and children's clothing is a super way to pick up extra income. —Marsha Collier, *Starting an eBay Business for Dummies*, p. 18, 2001

super *adverb*
very *US*
Adds a melodramatic, gushing flavour to the intensification.
• —Collin Baker et al., *College Undergraduate Slang Study Conducted at Brown University*, p. 207, 1968
• He dug right into the soil there, made this super-nice cave with this lovely texture[.] —Jefferson Poland and Valerie Alison, *The Records of the San Francisco Sexual Freedom League*, p. 22, 1971
• It's like so BITCHEN cuz like everybody's like super-super nice. —Moon Unit and Frank Zappa, *Valley Girl*, 1982
• You must be superbusy, though. —Armistead Maupin, *Babycakes*, p. 68, 1984

super- *adjective*
in combination with a person, animal or thing, well above the usual standard of its type *UK*
Under the influence of Nietzsche's philosophical concept, expanded by George Bernard Shaw's play *Man and Superman*, 1903, and made most familiar by *Superman*, a US comic strip superhero first seen in 1938.
• Topping off this layer cake of cultural contradictions are the unattainable super-model beauty stereotypes that have the American girl struggling with her weight[.] —Debra Ollivier, *Entre Nous*, p. 31, 2003

superbissimo *adjective*
excellent; superb *UK*
A decorative elaboration of 'superb' formed, loosely, with an Italian suffix.
• "We thought it superbissimo, didn't we, Billy?" Kevin insisted. —Jonathan Gash, *The Ten Word Game*, p. 283, 2003

superblush *noun*
in poker, a sequence of cards in a red suit – diamonds or hearts *US*
• —John Vorhaus, *The Big Book of Poker Slang*, p. 35, 1996

super C *noun*
ketamine hydrochloride, an anaesthetic used as a hallucinogen *US*
• —US Department of Justice, *Street Terms*, October 1994

supercalifragilisticexpialidocious
used in various contexts with various meanings by children fascinated with the size of the word *US*
Popularised, but apparently not coined, in the 1964 film *Mary Poppins*. The term did not appear in the book, and so some credit must be given to Robert B. Sherman, who wrote the lyrics of the song. According to *The Straight Dope* (6th August 2002), songwriters Barney Young and Gloria Parker brought a copyright infringement suit, claiming that they had written a song with a variant spelling of the term in 1949. In the 1960s, the term replaced 'antidisestablishmentarianism' in US youth 'longest word' contests.

super chicken *noun*
in trucking, a truck owned by Yellow Freight Systems *US*
• —Lanie Dills, *The Official CB Slanguage Language Dictionary*, p. 67, 1976

super citral *noun*
an especially narcotic variety of marijuana *UK*
• —Nick Jones, *Spliffs*, p. 76, 2003

super dope *noun*
marijuana with formaldehyde added *US*
• —Ernest L. Abel, *A Marijuana Dictionary*, p. 98, 1982

superduper; super *noun*
a hydrogen bomb *US, 1951*

super-duper *adjective*
exceptionally good *US, 1940*
Childish, or intentionally evocative of childishness.
• —Lou Shelly, *Hepcats Jive Talk Dictionary*, p. 35, 1945
• "Probably one of those super-duper televison screens like C.B.S. and NBC have been experimenting with," I surmised. —Robert deCoy, *The Nigger Bible*, p. 179, 1967

superfly *noun*

1 a drug dealer *US, 1973*
From the film *Superfly*, 1972.
• —John Ayto, *The Oxford Dictionary of Slang*, p. 166, 1998

2 a curly hairstyle popular with black men and women in the mid-1970s *US*
• It's goodby Afro, hello curls for scads of local hip black men who are part of the international, unisex trend to curly hair. They call the style "a Superfly," "a Lord Jesus" or just "a Curly Do" and they're spending lots of time and money to get the look. —*San Francisco Examiner*, p. 34, 13th April 1975

superfly *adjective*
extremely fashionable, attractive and appealing *US*
• He wore a large hat, superflied down, as did the taller man to his left. —Joseph Nazel, *Black Cop*, p. 154, 1974
• —Connie Eble (Editor), *UNC-CH Campus Slang*, p. 8, Fall 1997

supergrass *noun*

1 an informer who gives the police substantial amounts of information, or who informs on a major crime or terrorist operation *UK, 1978*
Bertie Smalls, a notorious or legendary (depending on your point of view) small-time robber turned police informer became, in 1973, the original 'supergrass'.
• I'm not asking you to be a super-grass. But I am advising you to have a slightly more co-operative attitude. —Anthony Masters, *Minder*, p. 61, 1984
• —Angela Devlin, *Prison Patter*, p. 110, 1996
• The supergrass system led to an immediate and impressive upsurge in prosecutions[.] —Martin Fido and Keith Skinner, *The Official Encyclopaedia of New Scotland Yard*, p. 256, 1999
• This guy was a regularly paid informer, a wannabe super-grass – practically a cop like them[.] —Lanre Fehintola, *Charlie Says...*, p. 125, 2000

2 good quality marijuana; phencyclidine, the recreational drug known as PCP or angel dust; a combination of the two *US, 1977*
• —Richard A. Spears, *The Slang and Jargon of Drugs and Drink*, p. 494, 1986
• —Mike Haskins, *Drugs*, p. 289, 2003

super hopper *noun*
a Citroen car *UK*
Citizens' band radio slang.
• —Peter Chippindale, *The British CB Book*, p. 161, 1981

super joint *noun*
phencyclidine, the recreational drug known as PCP or angel dust *US*
• —Ralph de Sola, *Crime Dictionary*, p. 112, 1982

super Ketama *noun*
a superior grade of hashish from the Ketama region of Morocco *UK*
• —Nick Jones, *Spliffs*, p. 90, 2003

super kools *noun*
phencyclidine, the recreational drug known as PCP or angel dust *US*
Because the addition of PCP makes Kools™, a brand name cigarette and hence any cigarette, '*super*ior'.
• PCP. Also known as "angel dust," "sherm," and "superkools," this rhinoceros tranquilizer was the most high-risk high of all times. — Editors of Ben is Dead, *Retrohell*, p. 154, 1997

superman *noun*

1 a variety of MDMA, the recreational drug best known as ecstasy, identified by the embossed Superman shield-shaped 'S' motif *UK*
• —Gareth Thomas, *This Is Ecstasy*, p. 56, 2002

2 a variety of LSD identified by a cartoon graphic of the comic book and film superhero *UK*
• —Angela Devlin, *Prison Patter*, p. 110, 1996
• —Mike Haskins, *Drugs*, p. 286, 2003

Super Mario *noun*
a variety of MDMA, the recreational drug best known as ecstasy, identified by the embossed Super Mario™ motif *UK*
• —Gareth Thomas, *This Is Ecstasy*, p. 56, 2002

Supermax *noun*
the Penitentiary Administrative Maximum facility (the highest security prison in the US) *US, 1994*
• —Angela Devlin, *Prison Patter*, p. 110, 1996

super pot *noun*
marijuana which has been soused in alcohol then dried *US, 1967*
• —Richard A. Spears, *The Slang and Jargon of Drugs and Drink*, p. 494, 1986
• —Mike Haskins, *Drugs*, p. 289, 2003

Super Scooper *noun*
a water bomber, with a huge scoop for filling at speed from a lake or waterway, to dump on fires *CANADA*
• Super Scooper is the name the news media has attached to the Canadair CL-215, the water bomber. It can scoop 6130 litres of fresh or salt water in 12 seconds, then roar off on a ridge-hopping, canyon-diving attack on brush fires. —*Canadair News*, p. 8, March-April 1994

superskunk *noun*
an extremely potent marijuana *UK*
• Super Skunk is a variation of skunk believed to be secretly crossed with the hop plant, to produce bigger, heavier flowers of the same quality as Skunk —Mike Rock, *This Book*, 1999
• We've been smokin for fuckin hours, mun. Liam Herlihy's superskunk as well. —Niall Griffiths, *Sheepshagger*, p. 243, 2001

superslab *noun*
a major road *US*
Citizens' band radio slang, elaboration of 'slab'.
• —*Complete CB Slang Dictionary*, p. 89, 1976
• —Peter Chippindale, *The British CB Book*, p. 159, 1981

super-snooper *noun*
a special inspector employed by the former Department of Health & Social Services to uncover fraudulent claims *UK*
• There are also the periodic purges by the "super-snoopers" as the special inspectors are called. —*New Society*, 2nd June 1983

super-snoopy *noun*
a helicopter with a camera that has the capability to take close-up pictures from a kilometre's distance *UK*
• —*Time Out*, 25th July 1980

superstud *noun*
a man with superior sexual prowess, or one reputed to be so lucky *UK*
Enhancement of **STUD**.
• "Yeah, come on, superstud," Paul said. "We'll make it a hundred quid to shag Lorraine." —Colin Butts, *Is Harry on the Boat?*, p. 140, 1997

supersweet *adjective*
excellent *US*
• —Connie Eble (Editor), *UNC-CH Campus Slang*, p. 7, November 2002

Super T *noun*
Tennants Super™, a super strength lager *UK*
• A Super T rolls out his floppy hand. —Nick Barlay, *Curvy Lovebox*, p. 23, 1997

super Thai *noun*
an 'everyday' variety of marijuana *UK*
• One minor drawback of the super Thai is that it is a dead giveaway – your eyes go bloodshot. —Nick Jones, *Spliffs*, p. 76, 2003

superweed *noun*
marijuana, especially if of extra strength *UK*
• —Angela Devlin, *Prison Patter*, p. 111, 1996

super-yankee *noun*
a multiple bet, gambling on 5 different horses in a specific combination of 26 win stakes or 52 each-way *UK*
Also known as a **CANADIAN**.
• —David Bennet, *Know Your Bets*, p. 119, 2001

supes *noun*
a superior; a respectful form of address *UK*
Black usage.
• I'll bring you a range, supes [.] —Diran Adebayo, *My Once Upon A Time*, p. 10, 2000

supon *noun*
cornmeal mush *CANADA*
• This sup-on is made of Indian corn, ground and boiled for several hours, then eaten with milk, butter, sugar, etc. —Jean Gogo, *Sunlight on the St. Lawrence*, p. 236, 1955

supremo *adjective*

excellent; extreme *US*

- But then Cavett, whose eagerness to please bordered on the idee fixe, committed his supremo blopper of the evening[.] — *Washington Post*, p. M1, 11th February 1979
- Born and raised in Montreal, he was used to supremo suck from the "fille du roi" and this Ontario girl was going to rank. — Suroosh Alvi et al., *The Vice Guide*, p. 27, 2002

sure *adjective*

▸ **be sure and**

take care, don't fail to do something *UK, 1892*

- Tonight stay somewhere warm, / they say it's gonna freeze / you may not find a place at all, / so be sure and take your keys[.] — Donna Summer, *Can't We Just Sit Down (And Talk It Over)*, 1994

sure as Christmas

certain *UK*

- If you give yourself up you'll swing [hang] as sure as Christmas. — Derek Bickerton, *Payroll*, p. 69, 1959

sure as eggs is eggs

absolutely certain, without a doubt *UK, 1699*

Early usage recorded as 'as sure as eggs be eggs' this idiom is now so familiar that even the shortening to 'sure as eggs' is understood.

- They're going to string me up tomorrow, sure as eggs. Oh, Christ almighty, I don't wanna die. — John Peter Jones, *Feather Pluckers*, p. 149, 1964
- [K]nowing the signs, I can tell you it is as sure as eggs is eggs. — Dave Courtney, *Dodgy Dave's Little Black Book*, p. 144, 2001

sure as God made little apples; sure as God made little green apples

very certain *UK, 1874*

The earliest form is 'little apples'; the second form appears to derive from the song by Bobby Russell, 'Little Green Apples', 1968, in which it is likely that 'green' is added for the scansion of the lyric.

- He tells us we're hopeless, the worst class he ever had for First Communion but as sure as God made little apples he'll make Catholics of us[.] — Frank McCourt, *Angela's Ashes*, p. 118, 1999
- The superintendent's going to want to nail somebody's hide to the wall over this, and as sure as God made little green apples, you can bet Carver will have got his retaliation in first. — Val McDermid, *A Place of Execution*, p. 165, 2001

sure as shit and taxes

very certain *US*

- Well, sure as shit and taxes, he comes there every night just as regular you can set your watch by him — William Burroughs, *Naked Lunch*, p. 175, 1957

surefire; sure shot *adjective*

certain to succeed or prevail *US, 1901*

- Here he is hot to trot and suddenly stricken by a flash that's a surefire dong-wilter. — Lester Bangs, *Psychotic Reactions and Carburetor Dung*, p. 77, 1971

Sure. I knew you could.

used as a sarcastic expression of great doubt *US*

A borrowing from the children's television programme *Mr Rogers*.

- — Connie Eble (Editor), *UNC-CH Campus Slang*, p. 6, Fall 1981

sure off *verb*

in an illegal numbers gambling lottery, to insure numbers that are the object of heavy betting *US*

- — *American Speech*, p. 193, October 1949

sure pops *noun*

dice that have been heavily weighted and are likely to produce the desired results *US*

- — *The Annals of the American Academy of Political and Social Sciences*, p. 131, May 1950

sure thing

certainly *US, 1896*

From the conventional sense (a certainty).

- SOCRATES: [...] Pardon me, Miss. Do you have a moment to talk with us? MARIGOLD MEASURER: Sure thing. My name is Marigold. — Peter Kreeft, *Best Things in Life*, p. 35, 1984

sure-thing man *noun*

in carnival usage, a confederate who is hired to play and win a game in order to generate business *US*

- — Don Wilmeth, *The Language of American Popular Entertainment*, p. 30, 1981

surf *verb*

▸ **surf the crimson tide**

to experience the bleed period of the menstrual cycle *US*

- Mr. Hall, I was surfing the crimson wave. I had to haul ass to the ladies'. — *Clueless*, 1995

surface *verb*

1 to wake up; to get up; to get up and start the business of the day *UK, 1963*

Probably of naval origins, from a submarine surfacing.

2 to come out of hiding; to leave a surreptitious existence and become more public *US*

- There is an impression, conveyed by the Interviewer, that our New Morning communique stated we should no longer be an underground... We were not "surfacing" when we shared the Senate lavatory with the Viet Cong. — *The Last Supplement to the Whole Earth Catalog*, p. 20, March 1971

surfboard Suzie *noun*

a stereotypical woman who spends time at the beach admiring male surfers *US*

- These surfboard Suzies want you more than Day-Glo earrings. — Joseph Wambaugh, *The Golden Orange*, p. 175, 1990

surf bum *noun*

a surfing enthusiast who haunts popular beaches *UK, 1958*

- [A]void the grungey, mildly rebellious surf-bum look for something sharper, more fashionably mainstream. — *The Observer*, 3rd December 2000

surf bunny *noun*

a woman who spends a great deal of time at the beach, associating with surfers and/or surfing *US*

- Just a bunch of California surf bunnies? huh? — *Washington Post*, p. B1, 21st January 1980
- Safely warehoused in San Diego State majoring in surf bunnies — Joseph Wambaugh, *The Delta Star*, 1983
- He was even sick of ogling all the bikinis stuffed with surf bunnies that littered the streets of La Jolla. — Joseph Wambaugh, *Lines and Shadows*, p. 29, 1984

surf dog *noun*

an avid, veteran surfer *US*

- — Trevor Cralle, *The Surfin'ary*, p. 130, 1991

surfie *noun*

a surfer *AUSTRALIA, 1962*

- Nobody (except maybe little old amateur psychiatrist me) accuses a surfie of being camp because he bleaches his hair. — Sue Rhodes, *Now you'll think I'm awful*, p. 106, 1967
- [T]he lesser known tribal rites of Australian surfies. — Richard Neville, *Play Power*, p. 82, 1970
- — Gary Fairmont R. Filosa II, *The Surfer's Almanac: An International Surfing Guide*, p. 196, 1977

surfie chick *noun*

a young woman companion of a surfer *AUSTRALIA*

- If you weren't a surfie chick, you were a nobody. You were a nurd. — Kathy Lette and Gabrielle Carey, *Puberty Blues*, p. 8, 1979
- — Kathy Lette, *Girls' Night Out*, p. 190, 1987

surfing knobs; surfing bumps *noun*

calcium deposits near the knees and feet caused by extended contact with a hard surfboard *US*

- — John Severson, *Modern Surfing Around the World*, p. 182, 1964

surf nazi *noun*

a zealous, devoted surfer *US*

- SURF NAZI: Blond hair, blue eyes and a one track mind. — Michael V. Anderson, *The Bad, Rad, Not to Forget Way Cool Beach and Surf Discriptionary*, p. 20, 1988

surf-o *adjective*

obsessed with surfing *US*

- — Trevor Cralle, *The Surfin'ary*, p. 46, 1991

surf rat *noun*

a beginner surfer *US*

- — *Surfing*, p. 43, 14th March 1990

surf safari *noun*

a trip in search of good surfing conditions *US*

- — John Severson, *Modern Surfing Around the World*, p. 182, 1964

surf's down

used for expressing dismay at poor surf conditions *US*

- — Gary Fairmont R. Filosa II, *The Surfer's Almanac*, p. 196, 1977

surf silks *noun*
silk or nylon swimming trunks worn under a wetsuit *US*
- —Gary Fairmont R. Filosa II, *The Surfer's Almanac*, p. 196, 1977

surge *noun*
surgical spirit as an alcoholic drink *UK*
- They [vagrant alcoholics] subsist on a diet of methylated spirits (jake or the blue), surgical spirit (surge or the white) and other forms of crude alcohol. —Peter Ackroyd, *London The Biography*, p. 359, 2000

surgical truss *noun*
a bus *UK*
Rhyming slang.
- —Ray Puxley, *Fresh Rabbit*, 1998

surprise party *noun*
in poker, a hand that should not win, that is not expected by its holder to win, but that wins *US*
- —John Vorhaus, *The Big Book of Poker Slang*, p. 35, 1996

surprise! surprise!
with heavy irony or sarcasm, used as an expression of disappointment, or resignation that the expected worst has happened *UK, 1964*
- A neo-fascist terrorist implicated in the 1980 bomb outrage at Bologna station that killed 85 people, he has lived in Britain since 1985 when an Italian court sentenced him to life imprisonment. Margaret Thatcher was PM at the time and – surprise, surprise – her government refused to extradite him. —*The Guardian*, 15th September 1999

Surrey Docks *noun*
syphilis; hence any sexually transmitted infection *UK*
Rhyming slang for **POX**, formed on a famous south-of-the-river location; noted by Dave Hillman, 1974.

sus; suss *noun*
1 *sus*picion *UK, 1936*
- [T]he bogies were about to search him on some very hot sus[.] —Charles Raven, *Underworld Nights*, p. 9, 1956
- I began to have a strong sus that Billie was having games. —Frank Norman, *Bang To Rights*, p. 44, 1958
- She is always liable to be arrested for "suss"; when he has been arrested it has always been on "suss"; [three West Indian pickpockets] are all frightened of "suss". —*New Society*, 7th July 1977
- The "Sus" law, an adaptation of a 19th-century vagrancy act, which allowed the police to stop, search and detain anyone regarded as "suspicious" —Mark Steel, *Reasons to be Cheerful*, p. 97, 2001

2 an arrest on *sus*picion; a person being arrested for loitering with *sus*picion *UK*
- —David Powis, *The Signs of Crime*, 1977

sus; suss *adjective*
*sus*picious; *sus*pect *UK, 1958*
- This geezer on the blower [telephone] was so roundabout that he sounded deadly sus[.] —Derek Raymond (Robin Cook), *The Crust on its Uppers*, p. 37, 1962
- He said he'd been betrayed that much, he'd become sus of everyone. —Kathy Lette, *Girls' Night Out*, p. 183, 1987
- There's a lot of suss questions on this questionnaire. —*Tracks*, p. 72, October 1992

Susie College *noun*
a stereotypical female college student *US*
- More important, he was the real enemy, we thought, since he was our competition for the hearts and minds of Joe and Susie College, who were naively jumping on his clean-cut haywagon. —Raymond Mungo, *Famous Long Ago*, p. 80, 1970

suspense *noun*
the time allotted to complete an action *US*
- —Department of the Army, *Staff Officer's Guidebook*, p. 67, 1986

suspicion *verb*
to suspect someone *US, 1834*
- The best way, of course, was to murder Trueblood, but they would have suspicioned me right away. —Max Shulman, *I was a Teen-Age Dwarf*, p. 105, 1959

suss *noun*
common sense *UK, 1977*
- —Tom Hibbert, *Rockspeak!*, p. 153, 1983
- [I]n a rare outbreak of suss, [Ducks Deluxe] were signed by RCA. —Will Birch, *No Sleep Till Canvey Island*, p. 157, 2003

suss *verb*
to suspect, or discover the truth about, someone or something *UK, 1953*
A shortened form of 'suspect'.
- [N]o-one really knew how we made our loot – they just sussed it was all bent. —Derek Raymond (Robin Cook), *The Crust on its Uppers*, p. 152, 1962
- Hey you gettin' drunk / So sorry, I've got you sussed. —The Who, *We're Not Gonna Take It*, 1969
- Me and the boys thought we had it sussed Valentinos all of us. —Rod Stewart, *I Was Only Joking*, 1977

sussed *adjective*
1 having knowledge about something; well-informed *UK, 1984*
- [O]ne Sunday broadsheet [wrote]: "a pop star with a face that would better suit a girl pushing a pram around a council estate". So sussed was this publication, by the way, that it printed a [incorrect] photograph —*The Guardian*, 15th February 2003

2 arrested as a *sus*pected person loitering *UK*
- —David Powis, *The Signs of Crime*, 1977

sussies *noun*
suspenders *UK*
- She'll be the first to unclip her sussies. —Kitty Churchill, *Thinking of England*, p. 117, 1995

susso *noun*
1 government sustenance provided during the depression of the 1930s *AUSTRALIA, 1941*
- When war was declared all our big 'susso' camps folded up overnight and the boys went to where they were sure they could find work. —Patsy Adam-Smith, *Folklore of the Australian Railwaymen*, p. 190, 1969
- —Jim Ramsay, *Cop It Sweet!*, p. 87, 1977

2 a person receiving government sustenance *AUSTRALIA, 1947*
- On me own, I'm nobody. Just a susso, who pretends he's tough. —Frank Hardy, *Legends From Benson's Valley*, p. 163, 1972

suss out; suss; suss on *verb*
to work out, discover, find, ascertain or understand something *UK*
Extended from various senses of **sus** and **suss**.
- [N]o-one really knew how we made our loot – they just sussed it was all bent. —Derek Raymond (Robin Cook), *The Crust on its Uppers*, p. 152, 1962
- Youth susses things out on its own —*The Queen*, 28th September 1966
- [G]as and Water Board vans with the original signs still on their side. He sussed each could be switched to supercharged vehicles within hours by a bent mechanic. —*The Sweeney*, p. 50, 1976
- Look, Arthur – all I'm doing is sussing out the job market. —Anthony Masters, *Minder*, p. 8, 1984
- He has already been identified, in passing, as the poet's "translator," but his English, from what I've been able to suss out thus far, is fairly awful. —Jim Carroll, *Forced Entries*, p. 69, 1987
- If you're cornered suss a wangle —Ian Dury, *Cacka Boom*, 1998
- I'd already sussed that all the mother and baby books took it for granted that you, the mum, had a husband[.] —Mary Hooper, *(megan)2*, p. 113, 1999
- [A]bout 50 cons have sussed on and nipped behind the huts[.] —Jimmy Stockin, *On The Cobbles*, p. 135, 2000

sussy *adjective*
*sus*picious, in both active and passive senses *UK*
- It seemed a bit sussy to me. —L.J. Cunliffe, *Having It Away*, 1965
- —Peter Laurie, *Scotland Yard*, p. 328, 1970

suzie *noun*
a Suzuki motorcycle (manufactured since 1936 but only popular in the UK from about 1960) *UK*
- —Douglas Dunford, *Motorcycle Department, Beaulieu Motor Museum*, 1979

Suzie Wong; suzie *noun*
1 a song *UK*
- With the popularity of karaoke, more people than ever are willing to sing us a "Suzie"[.] —Ray Puxley, *Fresh Rabbit*, 1998

2 an unpleasant smell *UK*
Rhyming slang for **PONG**, formed from the film *The World of Suzie Wong*, 1960.
- —Ray Puxley, *Fresh Rabbit*, 1998

Suzy Robincrotch; Suzy Rottencrotch; Suzy *noun*
during the Vietnam war, the generic girlfriend back home *US*
- —Linda Reinberg, *In the Field*, p. 212, 1991

Suzy Sorority *noun*

a stereotypical sorority member who looks, dresses, talks and lives the part *US*

- — Connie Eble (Editor), *UNC-CH Campus Slang*, Fall 1974
- "Suzi Sorority" and "Freddie Fraternity," if they ever existed, are not quite as clean or wholesome as might appear at first glance. — *Maledicta*, p. 133, 1995

swa *noun*

southwest Asia *US*

- — *Seattle Times*, p. A9, 12th April 1998: 'Grunts, squids not grunting from the same dictionary'

swab *noun*

a roll of money *US*

- I clipped a dance moll for a swab, it paid a trey or a fin. — Bruce Jackson, *Get Your Ass in the Water and Swim Like Me*, p. 85, 1965

swab *verb*

▸ **swab the deck**

to perform oral sex on a woman *US*

- — Roger Blake, *The American Dictionary of Sexual Terms*, p. 51, 1964

swabbie; swabby *noun*

a sailor *US, 1944*

- Poor little swabbie. just out lookin for a little fun and hauled up crazy, crazy me. — Earl Thompson, *Tattoo*, p. 163, 1974
- She hadn't really done a lot of swabbies before and thought they might not have enough money. — Joseph Wambaugh, *Floaters*, p. 102, 1996

swab jockey *noun*

a marine *US*

- We didn't operate from our home base except for jackrolling swab jockeys, marines. — Willard Motely, *Let No Man Write My Epitaph*, 1958
- I bet you don't, you freaky swab jockey. — Darryl Ponicsan, *The Last Detail*, p. 99, 1970
- "She-it, man, we should go plow them fuckin swab jockeys," Glenn said[.] — Earl Thompson, *Tattoo*, p. 61, 1974

swacked *adjective*

drunk or drug-intoxicated *US*

- — Lou Shelly, *Hepcats Jive Talk Dictionary*, p. 48, 1945
- He was swacked out of his skull. — Edwin Torres, *After Hours*, p. 285, 1979
- The bus driver's yellin about gettin rear-ended and he can see the dude's swacked. — Joseph Wambaugh, *The Glitter Dome*, p. 211, 1981

swag *noun*

1 stolen goods; loot; bounty *UK, 1794*

Derives from the earlier sense 'a shop' hence the contents seen as the object of theft; originally, especially linens and clothes rather than precious metals and stones.

- "It's all arranged about bringing off the swag, is it?" asked the Jew. Sikes nodded. — Charles Dickens, *Oliver Twist*, 1838
- They had mde contact with a "fence" from Philadephia, to whom they were to turn over the swag for $150,000 in currency. — Jack Lait and Lee Mortimer, *Chicago Confidential*, p. 18, 1950
- I just need you along to carry swag, that's all there is to it, just to help me carry swag away. — George Mandel, *Flee the Angry Strangers*, p. 388, 1952
- He never touches the swag himself ... has it delivered to a hotel room and one of his stooges picks it up and fences it. — Gerald Petievich, *To Die in Beverly Hills*, p. 189, 1983
- [W]e took the swag back to Allen's apartment. — Herbert Huncke, *Guilty of Everything*, p. 105, 1990
- I'm not having no fucking swag from Freddie fucking Woan! — Kevin Sampson, *Outlaws*, p. 82, 2001

2 contraband *US*

Used both as an adjective and a noun.

- — *American Speech*, p. 195, October 1951: 'A study of reformatory argot'
- — Gresham M. Sykes, *The Society of Captives*, p. 88, 1958
- I was selling swag to tourists on Oxford Street – moody perfume, sunglasses, snide Polo, cheap fucking tat[.] — Greg Williams, *Diamond Geezers*, p. 135, 1997

3 free merchandise or tickets to concerts handed out by music recording companies *US*

- — Jim Crotty, *How to Talk American*, p. 222, 1997

4 the possessions of an itinerant traveller rolled up in a blanket and carried from place to place *AUSTRALIA, 1841*

The 'swag' and the 'swagman/swaggie' are Australian cultural icons.

- SWAG – A tramp's bundle. — Gilbert H. Lawson, *A Dictionary of Australian Words and Terms*, 1924
- They were a tough bush-bred lot and I had to become a part of the life that was lived wherever I threw my swag off. — Patsy Adam-Smith, *Folklore of the Australian Railwaymen*, p. 169, 1969
- Well, I had a bottle of beer in me swag, see. — John O'Grady, *It's Your Shout, Mate!*, p. 72, 1972

5 a person's possessions when travelling light *AUSTRALIA*

Metaphoric use of the swagman's swag.

- I'd threatened to run away zillions of times, but it was year ten that finally pushed me into packing my swag. — Kathy Lette, *Girls' Night Out*, p. 53, 1987
- Taylor the taxi driver dropped his swag in the space left vacant by Martin's sudden exit. — John Birmingham, *He Died With a Felafel in his Hand*, p. 38, 1994

6 a bedroll *AUSTRALIA, 1865*

- Sam was now rousing the truckers, who had merely rolled into their swags beside the tarpaulin-covered loading[.] — Arthur Upfield, *Bony and the Mouse*, p. 126, 1959
- Cameron eyed the old man as he gathered up his ragged swag. — Wal Watkins, *Race the Lazy River*, p. 21, 1963
- Better than camping in a wet swag, eh? — Sam Weller, *Old Bastards I Have Met*, p. 99, 1979

7 clothes *UK*

The best known meaning of 'swag' (stolen property) originally referred especially to linens and clothes. Here the sense narrows to the type of goods with no suggestion of theft.

- Keva examined his manager's [...] suede-and-corduroy zip-up cardi [cardigan] and smiled to himself. "Get you some decent swag with what's left over." — Kevin Sampson, *Powder*, p. 27, 1999

8 money *US*

- I wore a hat from Disney with a fifty-dollar tag / And my snakesksin billfold was loaded with swag. — Dennis Wepman et al., *The Life*, p. 36, 1976

9 a large amount of something *AUSTRALIA, 1882*

- If a man was to take a swag of aspirins and dovers all at once he'd get a high temperature, wouldn't he? — Eric Lambert, *The Veterans*, p. 204, 1954
- I am not going to be picked up for hoarding a swag of Love-Juice, that's for sure. — John Wynnum, *Tar Dust*, p. 17, 1962
- Hell, there was a swag of humans in the world, like the horses no two alike unless they were twins. — Wilda Moxham, *The Apprentice*, p. 139, 1969
- — Patsy Adam-Smith, *Folklore of the Australian Railwaymen*, p. 223, 1969
- In the lead-up to the election for school captain, Jeb somehow managed to prevent a whole swag of kids – mainly poor black kids – from casting a vote. — *The Big Issue*, p. 10, 2003

10 inferior quality marijuana *US*

It seems unlikely that this usage should derive from the C19, now obsolete adjective 'swag' (worthless) but stranger etymologies have happened.

- — *www.addictions.org*, 1999

▸ **on the swag**

carrying a swag and travelling as an itinerant *AUSTRALIA*

- [S]o th' dees hassled youse a bit, did they? Well, don't fret. They do that to most young fellers on th' swag.' — Ward McNally, *Supper at Happy Harry's*, p. 68, 1982

swag *verb*

1 to move articles in a hurried manner *UK*

Extends from the sense 'to hustle'.

- It would have been too dodgy swagging gear into Bella's drum at 3 a.m. — Charles Raven, *Underworld Nights*, p. 22, 1956

2 to hustle or hurry someone *UK*

- [W]e got swaged [swagged] into the meatwagon. — Frank Norman, *Bang To Rights*, p. 8, 1958
- They swag him over to the hospital — Frank Norman, *Bang To Rights*, p. 29, 1958

swag *adjective*

1 stolen *US*

- Paulie had met him a few years ago through a friend who had once handled some swag TV sets for him. — Vincent Patrick, *The Pope of Greenwich Village*, p. 26–27, 1979

2 inferior *UK*

- Britney Spears is swag; I prefer Christina [Aguilera]. — *Live*, p. 39, Winter 2004

SWAG *noun*

a joking and derogatory prediction or estimate *CANADA*

A '*s*cientific *w*ild-*a*ssed *g*uess'.

- "Are you sure of the answer?""No." "Then give me a SWAG". — Tom Langeste, *oral citation from Words on the Wing*, p. 267, 1995

swag bag *noun*

a bag for loot or special contraband *US*

- Russo opened his swag bag and pulled out two quart cans of prunes and apricots. — Piri Thomas, *Seven Long Times*, p. 122, 1974

swaggie *noun*

a swagman *AUSTRALIA, 1891*

- —Barbara Baynton, *Human Toll*, p. 191, 1907
- To Nimrod's country he has gone, / A goggled swaggie of the air. / He bombed the way to Babylon. / This casual, cussing Flying Bear. —Norman Lindsay, *Comic Art of Norman Lindsay*, p. 65, 1918
- Well, I'm almost what Australians call a swaggie. I'm living in my car. —Jean Brooks, *The Opal Witch*, p. 32, 1967
- —Harvey E. Ward, *Down Under Without Blunder*, p. 47, 1967
- To see them at work, Little Tich all prick and ribs like a swaggie's dog, Cargo all muscle like a gymnasium instructor, was a joy like watching ballet[.] —Frank Hardy, *The Outcasts of Foolgarah*, p. 35, 1971
- —Arthur Chipper, *The Aussie Swearer's Guide*, p. 10, 1972

swagman *noun*

an itinerant man looking for work; a tramp *AUSTRALIA, 1859*

- SWAGMAN – A tramp. —Gilbert H. Lawson, *A Dictionary of Australian Words and Terms*, 1924
- The swagman dropped the piece of wood and looked at his hand. —Jon Cleary, *The Long Shadow*, p. 52, 1949
- —Bill Wannan, *Folklore of the Australian Pub*, p. 49, 1972
- An old man came stamping down the length of the wooden floor, an old swagman with long white hair and a bushy white beard. —Bob Ellis and Anne Brooksbank, *Mad Dog Morgan*, p. 119, 1976
- —Jim Ramsay, *Cop It Sweet!*, p. 87, 1977

swag off *verb*

to lock a prisoner's possessions away *UK*

- —Angela Devlin, *Prison Patter*, p. 112, 1996

SWAK; SWALK; SWANK

written on an envelope, or at the foot of a lover's letter, as lovers' code for '*s*ealed *w*ith *a* *k*iss' *UK, 1925*

Embellishments included a 'loving' kiss and a 'nice' kiss. Widely known, and well used by servicemen, then a nearly mandatory sign-off line in any American teenage love letter of the 1950s and 60s, now a part of the coded vocabulary of texting.

- —Andrew John with Stephen Blake, *The Total TxtMsg Dictionary*, p. 244, 2001
- —Hy Lit, *Hy Lit's Unbelievable Dictionary of Hip Words for Groovy People*, 52

swallow *noun*

a drink of alcohol *UK, 1822*

- You wouldn't begrudge her bringin' me a little swallow, would you, Billy Boy[.] —Ken Kesey, *One Flew Over the Cuckoo's Nest*, p. 255, 1962

swallow *verb*

1 to easily accept something as true *UK, 1594*

- —John Ayto, *The Oxford Dictionary of Slang*, p. 313, 1998
- Now it seems that Sir Humphrey has dusted it down and persuaded David Blunkett (of whom I expected better) to swallow it as gullibly as Jim Hacker. — *The Observer*, 30th June 2002

2 to accept something that has happened without complaint or acknowledgement *UK*

A shortening of 'swallow your pride'.

- I guess he had worked out that he just had to swallow, because as sure as night follows day the next scene in the movie would have had him up before someone higher in the pecking order[.] —Ken Lukowiak, *Marijuana Time*, p. 260–261, 2000

▸ **swallow a dictionary**

to be loquacious or sesquipedalian; to habitually use long or erudite words *AUSTRALIA*

- 'Kindly do not instruct me in matters pertaining to a private altercation.' The voice said, 'Strewth. He's swallowed a damn dictionary.' —Nino Culotta (John O'Grady), *They're A Weird Mob*, p. 63, 1957
- He had no time for blokes who were obviously squash drinkers and book-readers and who talked as if they'd swallowed a blasted dictionary. —Wal Watkins, *Race the Lazy River*, p. 18, 1963

▸ **swallow a gun**

to commit suicide by gunshot to the mouth *US*

- He'd probably go home and swallow his Smith & Wesson. —Joseph Wambaugh, *The Glitter Dome*, p. 3, 1981

▸ **swallow spit**

to stop talking; to be quiet *US*

- — *The Bell (Paducah Tilghman High School)*, p. 8–9, 17th December 1993: 'Tilghmanism: the concealed langage of the hallway'.

▸ **swallow the olive**

to lose your composure and concentration *US*

- It seems Lloyd's of London has finally "taken the gas." That's a golfing term for a player who chokes up or "swallows the olive." —*San Francisco Examiner*, p. 6, 5th February 1961

swallow and sigh *noun*

a collar and tie *UK, 1938*

Rhyming slang.

- —Ray Puxley, *Cockney Rabbit*, 1992

swallower *noun*

a person who swallows semen during oral sex *AUSTRALIA*

- Chicks are nicknamed bush pigs, swamp hogs, maggots, spitters or swallowers. —Kathy Lette, *Girls' Night Out*, p. 187, 1987

swally *noun*

a drink; a drinking session *UK: SCOTLAND*

Glasgow slang from 'swallow'.

- Fancy a wee swally? —Michael Munro, *The Original Patter*, 1985
- Just take a swally uh that and say what yer innards Perdick fer the follyin' winter! —Thomas McGrath, *Letter to an Imaginary Friend*, p. 251, 1997

swami *noun*

a poker player with the annoying habit of coaching other players *US*

- —John Vorhaus, *The Big Book of Poker Slang*, p. 41, 1996

swamp *verb*

to drink an alcoholic beverage after eating *UK*

- —Tom Hibbert, *Rockspeak!*, p. 154, 1983

swamp-donkey *noun*

a particularly unattractive woman *UK, 1998*

- Youl'd be lucky to trap some swamp donkey from Saxty's looking like that[.] —Chris Ryan, *The Watchman*, p. 281, 2001
- — *www.LondonSlang.com*, June 2002

swamped *adjective*

drunk *US*

- —Lou Shelly, *Hepcats Jive Talk Dictionary*, p. 48, 1945

swamper *noun*

1 a labourer who loads or unloads cargo *US*

- I learned that there was a fleet of tuna boats coming in today and that a large number of swampers would be needed to unload them[.] —James Ellroy, *Brown's Requiem*, p. 151, 1981

2 rubber boots worn during mud season *US*

Michigan Upper Peninsula usage.

swamp rat *noun*

any person living near or coming from near the great swamps of the southern US *US*

- — *Maledicta*, p. 171, Summer/Winter 1978: 'How to hate thy neighbor: a guide to racist maledicta'

swampy *noun*

a rural New Englander who is thoroughly and steadfastly rural *US*

An abbreviation of **SWAMP YANKEE**.

- — *American Speech*, p. 122, May 1963: 'Swamp yankee'

swamp Yankee *noun*

a rural New Englander who is thoroughly and steadfastly rural *US, 1939*

- — *American Speech*, p. 121–123, May 1963: 'Swamp yankee'

swan *verb*

▸ **swan about; swan around; swan off**

to move idly or with no apparent purpose (although pleasure is often presumed) *UK, 1942*

The imagery of swans gliding on water; originally military, of armoured vehicles (perhaps sliding over mud).

- I was there in my jeans and jersey and they began swanning in in black ties and long dresses[.] — *The Guardian*, February 1979
- when I was twenty and swanning about on campuses and suchlike. —James Hawes, *Dead Long Enough*, p. 21, 2000
- But what about when you get there? Are you just going to swan around? —Colin Butts, *Is Harry Still on the Boat?*, p. 40, 2003

swan dive *noun*

to pretend to be injured or fouled while playing a team sport *CANADA*

- This stratagem is used in many sports. It is known as a "swan dive." A player will feign injury to gain advantage over his opponents or perhaps to cause a delay which will be beneficial to himself or his team. — *Toronto Globe and Mail*, p. R2, 17th June 2002

Swanee river *noun*
the liver *UK*
Rhyming slang.
• — Ray Puxley, *Cockney Rabbit*, 1992

swank *noun*
a drink of sweetened water *BARBADOS*
• — Frank A. Collymore, *Barbadian Dialect*, p. 197, 1965

SWANK
▷ see: SWAK

swank and wank *verb*
to preen in a self-satisfied manner *UK*
A neat, rhyming combination of 'swank' (to behave in a pretentious manner) and **WANK** (to masturbate).
• I wasn't going to my own record company party because I was having a dispute with them, so I was fooked if I was going to let them swank and wank over my four Brits. — Ben Elton, *High Society*, p. 118, 2002

swanky *adjective*
showy; conceited; pretentious; pretentiously grand *UK, 1842*
First recorded as Wiltshire dialect.
• She'd hand in her basket and then go someplace swanky for lunch. — J.D. Salinger, *Catcher in the Rye*, p. 114, 1951

Swan Lake; swan *noun*
a cake *UK*
Rhyming slang, formed from the ballet by Tchaikovsky.
• A cup of tea and a slice of "swan"? — Ray Puxley, *Cockney Rabbit*, 1992

swannie *noun*
a bush shirt *NEW ZEALAND*
From the branded Swanndri™ shirt.
• — David McGill, *David McGill's Complete Kiwi Slang Dictionary*, p. 121, 1998

swanson *noun*
a coward *US*
• — Rick Ayers (Editor), *Berkeley High Slang Dictionary*, p. 40, 2004

swap *verb*

▸ **swap cans**
(used of a male homosexual couple) to take turns as the active participant in anal sex *US*
• — *The Guild Dictionary of Homosexual Terms*, p. 43, 1965

▸ **swap lies and swat flies**
to engage in prolonged, aimless conversation *US*
• — Joseph E. Ragen and Charles Finston, *Inside the World's Toughest Prison*, p. 821, 1962: 'Penitentiary and underworld glossary'

▸ **swap slop**
to kiss *US*
• — Marcus Hanna Boulware, *Jive and Slang of Students in Negro Colleges*, 1947

▸ **swap spit**
to kiss long and hard *US*
• Let's swop spit?" she said. "Yeah, that's freak stuff," he answered to her surprise. — Hal Ellson, *The Golden Spike*, p. 71, ?952
• "You come here, Benny" – she stretched out her arms – "and we'll kiss and swap spit." — Irving Shulman, *The Amboy Dukes*, p. 118, 1947
• You ever swap spit? Or are you just all talk and no cojones? — Evan Hunter, *The Blackboard Jungle*, p. 159, 1954
• After a moment they began to swap spit. — Steve Cannon, *Groove, Bang, and Jive Around*, p. 43, 1969

swap out *verb*
to exchange roles in homosexual sex after one partner achieves satisfaction *US*
• — Gary K. Farlow, *Prison-ese*, p. 70, 2002

swapper *noun*
a married person who engages in spouse swapping at sex parties *US*
• Harry wasn't the slightest bit bashful with the two sexy wives of other men, and the only time he ever felt any reluctance during the time he knew the swappers was just before he actually met the various husbands. — Frank Harris, *The Swinging Moderns*, p. 68–69, 1967
• But not all swappers are so enthusiastic about orgiastic activities, needless to say. — R.J. Hagerman, *Husband and Wife Swapping*, p. 92, 1967

swarming *noun*
a gathering swiftly formed as the result of a snowball-effect proliferation of instant text message communication *UK*
• The message spread like a virus, and just ten minutes later a crowd of them were congregated inside the venue. This phenomenon is called swarming. — *The Times Magazine*, 21st June 2003

swash *noun*
foaming water after a wave breaks on shore *US*
• — Grant W. Kuhns, *On Surfing*, p. 123, 1963

swass *noun*
sweaty buttocks *CANADA*
A contraction of 'sweaty' and 'ass'.
• — Chris Lewis, *The Dictionary of Playground Slang*, p. 224, 2003

swat *noun*
▷ see: SWOT

swatch *noun*
a quick look *UK: SCOTLAND, 1911*
• [T]ake a swatch at our stoating discounts[.] — Ian Pattison, *Rab C. Nesbitt*, 1988
• [H]e might need a swatch at the guy's computer. — Christopher Brookmyre, *Boiling a Frog*, p. 364, 2000

swatty-blouse *noun*
an effeminate intellectual *NEW ZEALAND, 1995*
• — Harry Orsman, *A Dictionary of Modern New Zealand Slang*, p. 133, 1999

swave and blaze *adjective*
suave and blasé *US*
An intentional mispronunciation, meant to be humorous.
• — *Current Slang*, p. 2, Spring 1967

swear *verb*

▸ **swear by**
to have a great confidence in something *UK, 1815*
• What one swears by, another warns against. — John C Maxwell, *The 21 Indispensable Qualities of a Leader*, p. 2, 1999

swear and cuss *noun*
a bus *UK, 1938*
Rhyming slang.
• Been waiting ages for a swear and cuss. — *The Sweeney*, p. 6, 1976
• — Ray Puxley, *Cockney Rabbit*, 1992

sweat *noun*
a worry or difficulty *US*
Usually used in the negative, most often as 'no sweat!'.
• If we started planning right now it shouldn't be any sweat at all. — Beatrice Sparks (writing as 'Anonymous'), *Jay's Journal*, p. 104, 1979

sweat *verb*
1 to coerce someone through intense pressure, usually not involving physical force *US*
• The next thing I know, if I leave him here you'll be sweating him. — Irving Shulman, *The Amboy Dukes*, p. 240, 1947
• DIMES: Now we know something's rotten in Denmark, 'cause this dickhead had a big bag, and it's uncut too, so we're sweatin' him, tryin' to find out where he got it. Scarin' the shit outta him. — *True Romance*, 1993
• I just knew we was gon' get sweated. — *Menace II Society*, 1993

2 to admire or desire someone or something *US*
• "I know you sweatin' my man, but you might as well give up." — Connie Eble (Editor), *UNC-CH Campus Slang*, p. 7, Spring 1999

3 to disclose that a pool player is in fact a skilled betting professional *US*
• — Steve Rushin, *Pool Cool*, p. 28, 1990

4 to gamble nervously and cautiously *US*
• — Michael Dalton, *Blackjack*, p. 81, 1991

▸ **sweat blood**
1 to make an unsparing effort *UK, 1911*
• [O]ld "Dad" worked in the slime, muck and mire of slush-pits and sweated blood over his antiquated rig[.] — Daniel Yergin, *Prize*, p. 247, 1991

2 to be very afraid *UK, 1924*
• For a while Laura and Hugh just sweated blood, said " Oh dear Oh dear" rung there [sic] hands and so forth. — David James Duncan, *The Brothers K*, p. 72, 1996

▸ **sweat bullets**
to experience a high degree of nervous tension, usually sweating profusely *US*
• There was something very intimidating about being in a dingy, smoke-filled room with a bunch of big ol' thug ass niggers, sweating bullets over a jiveass robbery. — Odie Hawkins, *Chicago Hustle*, p. 44, 1977

▸ **sweat cobs**
to perspire heavily *UK*
- "Take off your hat," said Bridget. "You're sweating cobs."—Beryl Bainbridge, *Young Adolf*, 1978
- I was sweating cobs as well, I was really, really sweating.—Howard J Parker, *Illegal Leisure*, p. 146, 1998

▸ **sweat it**
to worry *UK*
- I've got school tomorrow. I'm sweatin' it.—Karline Smith, *Letters to Andy Cole*, p. 142, 1998
- Don't sweat it, Larry, it's walk in the park.—Christopher Brookmyre, *Not the End of the World*, p. 8, 1998
- I don't sweat it. Sort of saying that my life was fucked up, but it didn't really bother me.—Eminem (Marshall Mathers), *Angry Blonde*, p. 3, 2001

▸ **sweat like a glassblower's arse**
to perspire heavily *UK*
- I'm sweating like a glass-blower's arse.—Sonja, *The Salon*, 1st April 2003

▸ **sweat on**
to wait with nervous expectation *UK, 1917*
- The whole service is sweating on a final decision due soon from the CAA.— *The Observer*, 25th August 2002

▸ **sweat the brass**
in horse racing, to race a horse day after day, without giving it a rest period *US*
- —David W. Maurer, *Argot of the Racetrack*, p. 61, 1951

▸ **sweat your guts out**
to labour extremely hard; to make the utmost effort *UK, 1890*
- [T]he clown has sweated his guts out under the hot lights[.]—Michel Quint and Barbara Bray, *In Our Strange Gardens*, p. 7, 2001

sweatback *noun*
an illegal immigrant to the US who is working *US*
A **WETBACK** who is working, and thus sweating.
- — *American Speech*, p. 272, December 1962: 'The language of traffic policemen'

sweat box *noun*
1 a police interview room *UK*
- Coppers have their own pet names for interview rooms. "The Confessional", "The Sweat Box", "The Truth Chamber".—John Wainwright, *The Last Buccaneer*, 1971

2 the waiting area outside the room in which a parole hearing is to take place *US*
- —Frank Prewitt and Francis Schaeffer, *Vacaville Vocabulary*, 1961–1962

3 a vehicle for transporting prisoners in small individual cubicles *UK*
- —Angela Devlin, *Prison Patter*, p. 112, 1996

4 in trucking, a sleeping compartment behind the seat *US*
- —Montie Tak, *Truck Talk*, p. 160, 1971

sweat chovey *noun*
a gymnasium or weights room *UK*
A combination of 'chovey' (an otherwise obsolete term for a shop) with a product of working-out.
- —Paul Baker, *Polari*, p. 190, 2002

sweater *noun*
1 a casino employee or executive who cheats gamblers *US*
- He will try to avoid picking "bleeders" or "sweaters." That is executives who so hate to see the player win they may cheat the customer without the permission of the hotel, just out of sheer competitiveness.—Mario Puzo, *Inside Las Vegas*, p. 182, 1977

2 in a casino or other gambling establishment, a person who observes but does not participate in a game *US, 1968*
- —Thomas L. Clark, *The Dictionary of Gambling and Gaming*, p. 223, 1987

3 a person who worries *US*
- — *Current Slang*, p. 4, Summer 1966

sweater meat *noun*
the female breasts *US*
- —Ben Applebaum and Derrick Pittman, *Turd Ferguson & The Sausage Party*, p. 63, 2004

sweater puppies *noun*
the female breasts *US*
- Boobs, zonkers, headlights, watermelons, sweater puppies, pointers, knockers, jugs, tatas – these are some of the words to describe women's breasts.—Howard Stern, *Miss America*, p. 441, 1995
- —Vann Wesson, *Generation X Field Guide and Lexicon*, p. 162, 1997

sweater queen *noun*
a neatly and nicely dressed homosexual male *US*
- —Jim Crotty, *How to Talk American*, p. 138, 1997

sweat room *noun*
a small room in a police station where suspects are interrogated or 'sweated' *UK*
- —Alan Hunter, *Gently in Trees*, 1974
- Tell them to put the Mex in a sweat room.—James Ellroy, *White Jazz*, p. 95, 1992

Sweatshop *noun*
▸ **the Sweatshop**
the Apollo Theater, New York *US*
- —Babs Gonzales, *Be-Bop Dictionary and History of its Famous Stars*, p. 9, 1949

sweaty sock; sweaty *noun*
a Scot *UK*
Rhyming slang for **JOCK** (a Scot); derogatory, both in its own imagery and as demonstrated in the usage by football supporters to taunt rivals. Certainly in use in the Newcastle-upon-Tyne area in 1990.
- — *RI:SE*, 20th November 2003

swede *noun*
1 the head; hence, the hair on the head *UK*
From the shape of the vegetable.
- The man with the wood appears and smacks Ally clean around the side of the swede.— Martin King and Martin Knight, *The Naughty Nineties*, p. 39, 1999
- [B]ad-tinted swede, bad tan, bad white kecks [trousers.]—Kevin Sampson, *Outlaws*, p. 107, 2001
- He [...] delivered the sort of whack English cricket fans can only dream of seeing to the back of O'Shea's sweded.—Garry Bushell, *The Face*, p. 37, 2001

2 a potentially naive provincial police officer investigating complaints in London *UK*
A nuance used by the Metropolitan Police.
- — *The Official Encyclopaedia of New Scotland Yard*, 1999

swede-basher; swede *noun*
a person from the countryside; an unsophisticated type *UK, 1943*
Derives from the root vegetable.
- He made the swede-basher show him where he had found it.—Charles Raven, *Underworld Nights*, p. 12, 1956
- He talked like a right sweed and he also looked like a right sweed —Frank Norman, *Bang To Rights*, p. 39, 1958
- [R]umbled by a bunch of half-witted swede bashers.—John Peter Jones, *Feather Pluckers*, p. 54, 1964
- "You don't sound like a Londoner." "No, he's a bleedin' swede-basher," said the Cockney[.]—Joe Morgan, *Eastenders Don't Cry*, p. 54, 1994
- When this swede wasnt farting he was snoring.—Lenny McLean, *The Guv'nor*, p. 41, 1998

swedeland *noun*
the countryside as seen from the town *UK, 1967*
Derogatory. From **SWEDE-BASHER** (a person from the countryside; an unsophisticated type). Noted by Laurie Atkinson.

swedey *noun*
▸ **the swedey**
the provincial police of 'Operation Countryman' drafted to London, from 1978 to the early 80s to investigate alleged corruption in the Metropolitan Police, particularly in the Flying Squad *UK*
Derisory; formed on **SWEDE** (a provincial police officer), punning on **THE SWEENEY** (the Flying Squad).
- — *The New Statesman*, 1st January 1980

swedge *verb*
to fight *UK: SCOTLAND*
- a strategy for quelling the swedging.—Irvine Welsh, *The Naughty Nineties*, p. 16, 1999

Swedish *adjective*
sexually permissive *UK*
From the Swedish attitude to pornography.
- [In Canada] "Scottish" is also used liberally as an inducement in the same way we'd use "Swedish".—Fiona Pitt-Kethley, *Red Light Districts of the World*, p. 12, 2000

Swedish fiddle *noun*
among loggers, a cross-cut saw *CANADA*
The reference to Sweden likely alludes to the 'Swedish saw'.
- Swedish fiddle – a bucking saw. — Robert Swanson, *Rhymes of a Western Logger*, p. 55, 1942

Swedish headache *noun*
an aching in the testicles from sexual activity that does not culminate in ejaculation *US, 1932*
- — *Maledicta*, p. 173, 1979: 'A glossary of ethnic slurs in american English'

Swedish massage *noun*
ejaculation achieved with the man's penis between the woman's breasts *UK*
- [H]ere's ten pounds, why don't you pop up to the school nurse, present her my compliments and have her give you a deep, relaxing Swedish massage. — Peter Cook, *Crime and Punishment*, 1973
- — Thommo, *The Dictionary of Australian Swearing and Sex Sayings*, p. 127, 1985

sweedie *noun*
a friend, an acquaintance; recognised as a form of address with shallow sincerity *UK*
An ironic mid-Atlantic approximation of **SWEETIE**; identified and popularised in BBC television comedy *Absolutely Fabulous* (1992–2001).
- It's all about the tabloids, you see, sweedie, so let's get your act together. — *Ministry*, p. 43, January 2002

Sweeney *noun*
▸ **on your Sweeney**
on your own *IRELAND*
- "Are ye doing a job?" I ask him. He just nods his head. "Are ye on yer Sweeney, are ye?" "Well, I've no-one with me yet." — Howard Paul, *The Joy*, p. 66, 1996

▸ **the Sweeney**
the Flying Squad, Metropolitan Police branch C1 (1921–48), subsequently C8; a member of the Flying Squad *UK, 1938*
Rhyming slang formed from 'Sweeney Todd' for 'Flying Squad'. Sweeney Todd was the legendary 'Demon Barber of Fleet Street'. Brought to widespread popular attention by television police drama series *The Sweeney*, originally broadcast from 1974–78, which gave the impression that all police work was about guns and fast cars.
- [T]he "Sweeney" won a national reputation as a dashing and daring unit of gang-busters. — *The Sweeney*, p. 3, 1976
- He trusted Gerry's driving ability – as he did any Sweeney. — *The Sweeney*, p. 52, 1976
- [D]emonstrators catching their breath, gazing in all directions like the Sweeney when they've lost a criminal[.] — Mark Steel, *Reasons to be Cheerful*, p. 40, 2001
- Why get blown away by the Sweeney going across the pavement for ten grand's worth of stolen Tom [jewellery]? — Garry Bushell, *The Face*, p. 24, 2001

sweep *noun*
1 in combat, a seach and destroy mission or a concerted search through an area *US*
- Romeo sat security for the howitzers and pulled search-and-destroy missions – S & Ds – day sweeps, we called them. — Larry Heinemann, *Close Quarters*, p. 73, 1977
- Very tough, very brave, I said, "Sir, please go out and sweep the area." — Al Santoli, *To Bear Any Burden*, p. 194, 1985
- The brigade was making a "Sweep," also known as a search-and-destroy mission, of the region west of Dak To. — Lucian K. Truscott, *Army Blue*, p. 112, 1989

2 a concerted effort to find someone or something illegal *US, 1974*
- They bring all those eyeball witnesses into the squad room, be like a hooker sweep out there. — Elmore Leonard, *Be Cool*, p. 21, 1999

sweep *verb*
to systematically search for surveillance devices *US*
- The electronic surveillance guys, the ones that sweep your office. Get the bugs out, you know? — George V. Higgins, *Penance for Jerry Kennedy*, p. 88, 1985

▸ **sweep the leaves**
to drive at the back of a group of trucks travelling together, watching for police from the rear *US*
- — Porter Bibb, *CB Bible*, p. 106, 1976

sweeper *noun*
1 in mountain biking, a tree limb overhanging the trail at approximately face height *US*
- — *Mountain Bike!*, p. 161, 1992: 'Bikespeak'

2 an expert hired to search for and locate surveillance devices *US*
- Where the hell're your bills from the goddamned sweepers? — George V. Higgins, *Penance for Jerry Kennedy*, p. 88, 1985

sweet *noun*
1 an effeminate male homosexual *US*
- Phillip Mayflower, the neighborhood "sweet," strolled past, his head held high[.] — Odie Hawkins, *Great Lawd Buddha*, p. 9, 1990

2 an amphetamine tablet *US*
- — US Department of Justice, *Street Terms*, August 1994

sweet *adjective*
1 all right *UK, 1890*
- She went a bit crook, but she'll be sweet. — Nino Culotta (John O'Grady), *They're A Weird Mob*, p. 136, 1957
- 'I'm down to one twenty gallons, over.' 'You'll be sweet.' — W.R. Bennett, *Wingman*, p. 14, 1961
- I reckon you'd chaps would be sweet for smuggling scarce goods back to Australia after your trip up to Hong Kong. — John Wynnum, *Tar Dust*, p. 30, 1962
- He gave John the address, told him to mention his name and promised he'd be 'sweet'. — James Holledge, *The Great Australian Gamble*, p. 104, 1966
- Green lawns all around, vista of the harbour, Holden in the garage, I'm sweet. — Alexander Buzo, *Norm and Ahmed*, p. 18, 1969
- If Parker can pick up a few crumbs from this, he'd be sweet. — Peter Corris, *Make Me Rich*, p. 144, 1985
- 'What's been said here goes no further. Thanks for your help.' Ray and Joe exchanged glances and nodded. 'It's sweet Nicko, it'll go no further.' — Clive Galea, *Slipper*, p. 78, 1988

2 excellent; in style; admirable *US*
- — Connie Eble (Editor), *UNC-CH Campus Slang*, p. 7, Spring 1982
- Dude, that movie was fucking sweet! — *South Park*, 1999

3 amenable *UK*
A shift in the earlier (C18–19) sense as 'gullible, unsuspicious'.
- He'll be in the office in a coupla hours. And I want him sweet! — Kevin Sampson, *Powder*, p. 59, 1999

4 when combined in phrases meaning nothing, absolute *UK, 1958*
- [T]he main female character was long-legged, pretty and did sweet nothing apart from pout. — *Guardian Unlimited*, 20th June 2003

5 homosexual *US*
- I never bother to think whether someone will consider me sweet. I'm confident in my masculinity. — Susan Hall, *Gentleman of Leisure*, p. 12, 1972
- — Gary K. Farlow, *Prison-ese*, p. 71, 2002

6 drunk *BARBADOS*
- — Frank A. Collymore, *Barbadian Dialect*, p. 107, 1965

sweet!
used to express approval *UK*
- — Susie Dent, *The Language Report*, p. 75, 2003

sweet-arse *adjective*
used for describing someone or something with approval *UK*
A variation of **SWEET**.
- It's home sweet home to some sweet arse freaks — Ian Dury, *Itinerant Child*, 1998

sweet as *adjective*
satisfying and easy, especially of a crime *UK*
A shortening of the familiar **SWEET AS A NUT**.
- We got both the mugs, sweet as. — Garry Bushell, *The Face*, p. 19, 2001

sweet as a nut *adjective*
satisfying and easy, especially of a crime *UK, 1937*
- Stolen motor – but nothing wrong with his driving. Sweet as a nut. — Anthony Masters, *Minder*, p. 121, 1984
- "How is she [a car] travelling, Mr O?" I asked. "Sweet as a nut, I bet." — Andrew Nickolds, *Back to Basics*, p. 40, 1994
- [I]t was sweet as a fuckin' nut, I'm tellin' you. Naebody' gaunny search a bus full o' spastics, are they? — Christopher Brookmyre, *Boiling a Frog*, p. 220, 2000

sweet BA *noun*
nothing whatsoever *UK, 1958*
A euphemistic variation of **SWEET BUGGER ALL**.

sweet bugger all *noun*
▷ **see:** BUGGER ALL

sweet chat *noun*
flattery *TRINIDAD AND TOBAGO, 1977*
• —Lise Winer, *Dictionary of the English/Creole of Trinidad & Tobago*, 2003

sweet cop *noun*
an easy job *AUSTRALIA, 1918*
• —Jim Ramsay, *Cop It Sweet!*, p. 87, 1977
• And some of them are such thieving bastards – sorry, Mr Burton – such nifty-fingered, pilfering buggers that even that's no sweet cop. —Thomas Keneally, *Bullie's House*, p. 18, 1981

sweet count *noun*
in dominoes, a good hand *US*

sweet daddy *noun*
a pimp *US*
• Mary could be proud indeed because she was one girl who didn't have to get along with a single wife-in-law, not to mention seven, as that sweet daddy called Jo-Jo had. —John M. Murtagh and Sara Harris, *Cast the First Stone*, p. 16–17, 1957

sweet deedee *noun*
in horse racing, a combination wager conventionally known as the 'daily double' *US, 1968*
• —Thomas L. Clark, *The Dictionary of Gambling and Gaming*, p. 224, 1987

sweet dreams *noun*
heroin *UK, 1998*
• —Robert Ashton, *This Is Heroin*, p. 207, 2002
• —Mike Haskins, *Drugs*, p. 284, 2003

sweet dying Jesus
an affectionate exclamatory oath *CANADA*
• They've still got their skates on, their faces are red, a gust of knifing Arctic air tears around the kitchen, we all start laughing and hollering and, sweet dying Jesus, they are beautiful children. —Harry Bruce, *Movin' East*, p. 67, 1985

sweeten *verb*
1 in poker, to increase the amount bet *US*
• —Irwin Steig, *Common Sense in Poker*, p. 188, 1963

2 in the television and film industries, to make subtle improvements in the soundtrack *US*
• —Ralph S. Singleton, *Filmaker's Dictionary*, p. 166, 1990

sweetened air *noun*
candy floss *US*
• —Don Wilmeth, *The Language of American Popular Entertainment*, p. 97, 1981

sweetener *noun*
1 a bribe *UK*
• —Angela Devlin, *Prison Patter*, p. 112, 1996

2 cash *US*
• Candy, markers, ammo, liners, stocking stuffer, sweetener, garnish, and pledges are all terms for cash. —Henry Hill and Byron Schreckengost, *A Good Fella's Guide to New York*, p. 123, 2003

sweet evening breeze *noun*
▷ **see:** EVENING BREEZE

sweet Fanny Adams; sweet FA *noun*
▷ **see:** FANNY ADAMS

sweet fuck all *noun*
absolutely nothing at all *UK*
A sarcastic or emphatic variation of **FUCK ALL**.
• He's got nothing. He's got sweet fuck all —The Who *Young Man Blues*, 1969
• If there's going to be trouble there's going to be trouble. There's sweet fuck all I can do about it. —Ted Lewis, *Jack Carter's Law*, p. 42, 1974

sweethead *noun*
a marijuana user *US*
• —Jim Emerson-Cobb, *Scratching the Dragon*, April 1997

sweetheart *noun*
1 used as an endearment or what is intended to be an endearing form of address *UK, 1290*
Often patronising.
• I find you attractive, sweetheart. Very attractive. —Claire Mansfield and John Mendelssohn, *Dominatrix*, p. 251, 2002

2 used as a menacing form of address *UK, 1977*
An ironic variation of the genuine endearment.

sweetheart *adjective*
used of a trade union overly sympathetic to, if not controlled by, management *US, 1959*
• [H]aving recently concluded a sweetheart agreement with management to leave the "inside" people alone in return for jurisdiction over the truck drivers. —Clancy Sigal, *Going Away*, p. 198, 1961
• —Kathryn Leigh Scott, *The Bunny Years*, 1998
• [T]he New York Bunnies soon deemed the Dining Room Employees Local 1 a "sweetheart union" and demanded the right to join a union of their choice. —Kathryn Leigh Scott, *The Bunny Years*, p. 167, 1998

sweet Heaven!
used as a mild expletive, or register of shock, surprise, etc *UK*
• [H]e was putting his tongue in sweet Heaven sweet Jesus and oh she likes it, she really likes it[.] —Christopher Brookmyre, *The Sacred Art of Stealing*, p. 362, 2002

sweetie *noun*
1 a sweetheart *US, 1925*
• Even further, a Bird who takes a stranger home is probably cheating on his true sweetheart, anyway, and when sweetie learns of it he is sure to raise holy hell. —Robert Sylvester, *No Cover Charge*, p. 268, 1956
• You have a touch. But then I'll bet your steady little sweetie thinks so too. —Iceberg Slim (Robert Beck), *Mama Black Widow*, p. 241, 1969

2 used as a wheedling, patronising form of address *US*
• Get to work, sweetie. —George V. Higgins, *The Friends of Eddie Doyle*, p. 148, 1971
• Sweetie... darling, please fetch mama a cup of coffee. You're so clever, darling, you know where everything is sweetie. —Jennifer Saunders, *Absolutely Fabulous*, p. 8, 1992
• It's a newbie phase, sweetie. Bob was just the same. —Melanie McGrath, *Hard, Soft and Wet*, p. 55, 1998

3 an effeminate man, usually an effeminate homosexual *US*
A pejorative, adopted by gays as an ironic endearment.
• I asked some sweetie if he ever got pregnant and he said, "How should I know? Do I have eyes in the back of head?" —Bruce Rodgers, *The Queens' Vernacular*, p. 74, 1972

4 a sweet (an individual chocolate- or sugar-based item of confectionary) *UK*
From 'sweetmeat', but now considered a childish extension of 'sweet'; generally heard in the plural.
• [F]inding bonbons or sweeties in the packets[.] —*Roundabout Papers*, 1860

5 tablets for medication or recreation *UK*
From the sense as 'confectionary'.
• Looks like the Caliph's off his sweeties. —Chris Baker and Andrew Day, *Lock, Stock... & a Fist Full of Jack and Jills*, p. 184, 2000

6 the drug Preludin™, a stimulant that suppresses the appetite *US*
• —William D. Alsever, *Glossary for the Establishment and Other Uptight People*, p. 30, December 1970

7 an amphetamine or MDMA tablet *UK*
• Just a few sweeties – don't mean anything. —*ID*, 1994
• —Mike Haskins, *Drugs*, p. 290, 2003

sweetie-pie *noun*
a sweetheart; a dear friend; a camp form of address *UK, 1928*
An extension of all variants of **SWEETIE** as an endearment. In 1947 the animated cartoon *Tweety Pie* won an Oscar.
• But sweetie-pie, don't you know that coming out of the closet is my favourite pastime? —Bart Luirink (translated by Loes Nas), *Moffies*, p. 24, 2000

sweet Jesus *noun*
morphine; heroin *US, 1967*
• —US Department of Justice, *Street Terms*, October 1994
• —Robert Ashton, *This Is Heroin*, p. 207, 2002

sweet Jesus!
used as a mild expletive, or register of shock, surprise, etc *UK*
• [H]e was putting his tongue in sweet Heaven sweet Jesus and oh she likes it, she really likes it[.] —Christopher Brookmyre, *The Sacred Art of Stealing*, p. 362, 2002

sweet leaf *noun*
marijuana *US, 2001*
• —Simon Worman, *Joint Smoking Rules*, 2001

sweet limburger!
used for expressing disapproval *US*
A signature line of Colonel Sherman Potter on *M*A*S*H* (CBS, 1972–83). Repeated with referential humour.

sweet Lucy *noun*
1 muscatel wine *US*
- He started walking away from the short dog, which was rolling around on the sidewalk spilling sweet lucy all over the pavement. —Joseph Wambaugh, *The Blue Knight*, p. 123, 1973

2 any cheap wine *US*
- —Anna Scotti and Paul Young, *Buzzwords*, p. 142, 1997

3 a solution of hashish and wine *US, 1948*
- —Ernest L. Abel, *A Marijuana Dictionary*, p. 98, 1982

4 marijuana *US, 1969*
- —Richard A. Spears, *The Slang and Jargon of Drugs and Drink*, p. 496, 1986
- —Mike Haskins, *Drugs*, p. 289, 2003

sweet mack *noun*
a pimp who controls his prostitutes through charm and attention *US*
- A pimp who uses a great deal of charm and little violence or fear is called a sweet Mack or sugar pimp. —Christina and Richard Milner, *Black Players*, p. 35, 1972

sweetman *noun*
a man who is supported by his lover; a pimp *TRINIDAD AND TOBAGO, 1939*
- You can be sure when you see girls working so cooperatively that they are "wives-in-law," feeling bound to one another because they happen to be connected with the same pimp, sweet man to them. —John M. Murtagh and Sara Harris, *Cast the First Stone*, p. 10, 1957
- Your sweet-man'll blow that in ten minutes with one of his women. —Clarence Cooper Jr, *Black*, p. 262, 1963
- —Lise Winer, *Dictionary of the English/Creole of Trinidad & Tobago*, 2003

sweet Miss Adams *noun*
▷ **see:** FANNY ADAMS

sweet name *noun*
any affectionate nickname *TRINIDAD AND TOBAGO, 1971*
- —Lise Winer, *Dictionary of the English/Creole of Trinidad & Tobago*, 2003

sweetness *noun*
used as an endearment *UK*
- JUSTINE (TO EDINA): Hallo, sweetness. —Jennifer Saunders, *Absolutely Fabulous*, p. 37, 1992

sweet on
infatuated by someone or something *UK, 1740*
- Bidders are sweet on Thorntons[.] —*The Guardian*, 30th October 2003

sweet shit in a bucket!
used for registering anger, frustration or despair *US*
- "Sweet shit in a bucket," Flickinger said. "I bribed the wrong man." —Lawrence Block, *No Score [The Affairs of Chip Harrison Omnibus]*, p. 126, 1970

sweet spot *noun*
in surfing, the foreward position on the surfboard that maximises speed and the back position that maximises the ability to manoeuver *AUSTRALIA*
- — *surfresearch.com.au Glossary*,

sweet stuff *noun*
powdered drugs; cocaine, heroin or morphine *US, 1936*
- —Richard A. Spears, *The Slang and Jargon of Drugs and Drink*, p. 496, 1986
- —Mike Haskins, *Drugs*, p. 281, 2003

sweet-talk *verb*
to flatter someone, to convince someone through kind words *US, 1936*
- Some fly cat chased a girl up the stairs trying to sweettalk her until one of the fellows from the Cotton Pickers hit him in the jaw and knocked him right down again. —Mezz Mezzrow, *Really the Blues*, p. 91, 1946

sweet thing *noun*
an attractive young woman *US*
- So Mick [Jagger...] disengages himself from the sweet thing at his side[.] —Lester Bangs, *Psychotic Reactions and Carburetor Dung*, p. 13, 1971

sweet tooth *noun*
an addiction to morphine *US*
- —*American Speech*, p. 145–148, May 1961: 'The spoken language of medicine; argot, slang, cant'
- —Sally Williams, *"Strong" Words*, p. 161, 1994

swell *noun*
a well-dressed, fashionable man *UK, 1786*
- Them Park Avenue swells like me. —Mickey Spillane, *I, The Jury*, p. 45, 1947

swell *adjective*
good; attractive; stylish *UK, 1812*
A key piece of slang for more than a century, eventually displaced by COOL.
- 'Morning, Doc,' the attendant said, 'swell car you got there.' —Terry Southern, *Flash and Filigree*, p. 29, 1958
- "Harald's a swell gent," she went on, in a different voice, more thoughtful and serious. —Mary McCarthy, *The Group*, p. 22, 1963
- He ain't no swell guy and he never was. —Eugene Boe (Compiler), *The Wit & Wisdom of Archie Bunker*, p. 19–20, 1971

swellbow *noun*
a swollen elbow *UK*
Skateboarders' and scooter-riders' slang; an elision of 'swell' and 'elbow'.
- —Ben Sharpe, *Scooter Crazy*, p. 42, 2000

swell pipes *noun*
in circus and carnival usage, a good singing voice *US*
- —Don Wilmeth, *The Language of American Popular Entertainment*, p. 265, 1981

swell-up *noun*
crack cocaine *UK, 1998*
- —Mike Haskins, *Drugs*, p. 282, 2003

swerve *noun*
1 a deception, practical joke or false report *US*
- Women are very clear when it comes to the kind of men they like. They go for guys with a little edge, a little swerve. They want somebody who's cool and street, but sophisticated. —Chris Rock, *Rock This!*, p. 125, 1997
- Usually it was just a swerve with a guy like him if you're an unknown, but the match went so I held my own. —Jeff Archer, *Theater in a Squared Circle*, p. 89, 1999
- They kept pushing that the WWF was delivering on a promise, that the match hype wasn't just a big serve. —Herb Kunze, *Herb's Wrestling Tidbits*, 23 May 2000

2 intoxication *US*
- —Rick Ayers (Editor), *Slang Dictionary*, p. 16, 2001

▸ **get your swerve on**
to drink to the point of intoxication *US*
- —Megan Ferguson, *Columbia Missourian*, p. 1A, 19th October 1998
- —Connie Eble (Editor), *UNC-CH Campus Slang*, p. 4, Spring 2003

swerve *verb*
1 to avoid someone or something *UK: SCOTLAND*
From the conventional sense (to change direction abruptly); probably a shortening of BODY-SWERVE.
- "I never saw ye at the meetin." "Naw, Ah swerved it an went hame." —Michael Munro, *The Original Patter*, 1985
- I'm too old and fat to be running around the streets and swerving Plod [the police] — Martin King and Martin Knight, *The Naughty Nineties*, p. 121, 1999
- It's the only gaff I know that's given a wide berth by Mormons and completely swerved by door-to-door salesmen. —Dave Courtney, *Raving Lunacy*, p. 176, 2000
- [I]f I'd seen him coming I would have swerved him. —J.J. Connolly, *Layer Cake*, p. 72, 2000

2 to make a late change in your plans *UK*
Teen slang.
- — Susie Dent, *The Language Report*, p. 78, 2003

swerve past *verb*
to visit a place briefly; to go out of your way *UK*
- He took a chance and had a swerve past his mother's place to tell her he was going away for a while and not to worry. —J.J. Connolly, *Know Your Enemy [britpulp]*, p. 161, 1999

swift *adjective*
1 good, clever *US*
- —Steve Salaets, *Ye Olde Hiptionary*, 1970
- —*American Speech*, p. 67, Spring-Summer 1975: 'Razorback slang'
- —Connie Eble (Editor), *UNC-CH Campus Slang*, p. 9, Spring 1988

2 of police, corrupt *UK, 1977*

- — Angela Devlin, *Prison Patter*, p. 112, 1996

swiftie *noun*

1 a deceitful trick; a con *AUSTRALIA, 1945*

- [Y]ou'll suddenly wake up one bright morning to find he's slipped a swiftie over you, has the whole game sewn up, and all you slow-coaches up a gum tree telling the crows he can't do it. — Dymphna Cusack, *Picnic Races*, p. 70, 1962

2 an alcoholic drink quickly drunk, a '*swift* drink' *UK*
The spelling 'swifty' is also used.

- Many people are nervous, so they start drinking quickly or have a swifty or two before the date. — *BBC News Online*, 30th August 2001

swifting *noun*

in the police, an action of making a quick arrest when it may not be clear that all elements of the offence can be proved *UK*
From 'swift 'un' (a quick, possibly unfair arrest).

- — *The Official Encyclopaedia of New Scotland Yard*, 1999

swig *noun*

an act of drinking deeply, especially of intoxicating liquor *UK, 1621*

- She balanced it on the crook of her arm and took a deep and resonant swig. — Charles Frazier, *Cold Mountain*, p. 215, 1998
- He washed them down with a swig of water. — Louis Sachar, *Holes*, p. 200, 2000
- I stretched out in my mother's huge iron bathtub and took a swig from the large G&T I had smuggled in with me — Jasper Fforde, *The Eyre Affair*, p. 229, 2003

swig *verb*

to drink, especially deeply, and especially of intoxicating liquor *UK, 1654*
From **SWIG** (a drink).

- I was dreaming about obnoxious little nine-year-olds having sex on the playground while they swigged forties of Olde English and screamed at my sweet, loving boyfriend when the phone rang. — Lauren Weisberger, *The Devil Wears Prada*, p. 25, 2003

swill *noun*

a drink *UK*

- Get the swills, East says to the girl[.] — Mark Powell, *Snap*, p. 17, 2001

swill cup *noun*

a combination of leftover alcoholic beverages *US*

- "Swill cup" is street slang for any random, potent and invariably nasty potin of alcoholic beverages – whiskey, gin, Purple Puckerr, jug wine, backwash dregs of a warm Tequila, whatever – blended in a single container and then chugged. — *Denver Westword*, 17th July 2003

swiller *noun*

a public house *UK*

- I'm off to the swiller. — Mark Powell, *Snap*, p. 228, 2001

swim *noun*

▶ **in the swim**

active socially, up to date with trends and fashions *UK, 1869*

- "You don't understand," he interrupted impatiently. "It's the thing to do. Don't you want to be in the swim?" — Max Shulman, *The Many Loves of Dobie Gillis*, p. 40, 1951

swim *verb*

1 to parade ostentatiously *UK*
A variation of **SWAN** (to move with no purpose).

- [H]e goes swimming up and down the King's Road in his Chevvy convertible with the electric hood[.] — Derek Raymond (Robin Cook), *The Crust on its Uppers*, p. 23, 1962

2 to move through a stadium or auditorium, experiencing a concert from different perspectives *US*

- — David Shenk and Steve Silberman, *Skeleton Key*, p. 274, 1994

swimmer *noun*

1 a car that has been driven or fallen into a body of water *US*

- — *American Speech*, p. 272, December 1962: 'The language of traffic policemen'

2 in horse racing, a horse that peforms very well on wet track conditions *AUSTRALIA*

- — Ned Wallish, *The Truth Dictionary of Racing Slang*, p. 79, 1989

swimmers *noun*

a swimming costume *AUSTRALIA, 1967*

- She screamed, slapped me and swam for her life. I still had to get my swimmers. — Paul Vautin, *Turn It Up!*, p. 98, 1995

swimmies *noun*

swimwear; a swimming costume *UK: SCOTLAND*

- Don't forget yer swimmies the morra [tomorrow]. — Michael Munro, *The Patter, Another Blast*, p. 70, 1988

swindle sheet *noun*

1 a record of reimbursable business expenses that is completed by a travelling sales representative or business executive *US, 1949*
An implicit suggestion that these records are not always entirely honest.

2 in trucking, a trucker's daily log book *US*

- — Montie Tak, *Truck Talk*, p. 161, 1971
- We tore up all of our swindle sheets / And left them sitting on the scales[.] — C.W. McCall, *Convoy*, 1976
- — Peter Chippindale, *The British CB Book*, p. 159, 1981

swine *noun*

1 an unpleasant person, especially a coarse or degraded person; a sensualist *UK, 1842*

- [M]ost editions of Erskine May, the parliamentary rule book, contain a long list of unparliamentary phrases. They include murderer, swine, liar (of course), stool pigeon, guttersnipe, cad, Pecksniffian cant and – you've guessed it – dirty dog. — *The Guardian*, 5th October 2001

2 a police officer; the police *US*

- — Pamela Munro, *U.C.L.A. Slang*, p. 112, 1997

3 a prison guard *US*

- — John R. Armore and Joseph D. Wolfe, *Dictionary of Desperation*, p. 53, 1976

4 a difficult or awkward thing *UK, 1933*
From the sense as 'an unpleasant person'.

- [T]hat language! Is it eating Spam for breakfast that makes them sound as though they're trying to clear a huge wad of phlegm from their throats, or is it the immortal tongue of Goethe and Nietzsche? Whatever – what a swine. — *The Guardian*, 22nd September 2001

5 leather, especially leather car upholstery *US*

- — Connie Eble (Editor), *UNC-CH Campus Slang*, p. 7, November 2002

swing *noun*

1 a bag (or similar receptacle) that is used to transfer contraband items between prison cells by being attached to a length of string (or similar) and swung from one cell window to another *UK*
Also called a 'swinger'.

- — Angela Devlin, *Prison Patter*, p. 112, 1996

2 a punch delivered with a wide sweep of the arm, especially in the phrase: take a swing at *UK, 1910*

- The man, staggering, began terrorizing the passengers: screaming curses, he took a swing at a woman holding a baby, sending her sprawling in the laps of an elderly couple[.] — Daniel Goleman, *Emotional Intelligence*, p. 124, 1997

3 an employee's rest period in a shift system; a pattern of working that incorporates such rest periods; hence, time off work *US, 1917*

- You can be a disc jockey like your dad and work the swing shift. — Mary Sheedy Kurcinka, *Raising Your Spirited Child*, 1998

4 a consensual orgy *US*

- But walk into a swing and take a long look around the room Every broad (if you've got the time and stamina) is yours. — *Screw*, p. 10, 7th February 1969

swing *verb*

1 to enjoy frequent casual sex with different partners *UK, 1964*

- My third sex life is swinging in the group-sex kick. — Allen S. Dunhill and Roger Blake, *The Group Sex Kick*, p. 13, 1968
- So now "swinging" – or sharing sexual partners – is the new topic for discussion in "smart circles." — *Screw*, p. 19, 10th November 1969
- Terry, a new stewardess who isn't swinging – yet – has a blow up with her mother and leaves home to stay with Gussy, another "stew." — *Adam Film Quarterly*, p. 14, September 1969
- Swinging is a very open thing today and it is not difficult at all for newcomers to enter the swinging scene. — Bernhardt J. Hurwood, *The Sensuous New York*, p. 136, 1973
- You know, l'amour?! I'm talkin' me'n Dot are Swingers! As in 'to Swing'! Wife- swappin'! What they call nowadays Open Marriage! — *Raising Arizona*, 1987
- That's what I do. I swing. — *Austin Powers*, 1997

2 to have fun, especially in a currently fashionable or unconventional activity; hence, to be fashionable *US, 1957*

- That's the craziest name in town! It swings! — *Rebel Without a Cause*, 1955
- England swings like a pendulum do. — Roger Miller, *England Swings*, 1965

3 to accomplish something, especially something that is difficult *UK, 1933*

- I bust my ass all day to take home a hundred and seventy bucks a week and I just can't swing the kind of money it costs. — George V. Higgins, *The Friends of Eddie Doyle*, p. 33, 1971
- Oh, man, if you could swing something there, I'd do anything for you. — *Fast Times at Ridgemont High*, 1982
- Jesus Christ, you taking all your advertisers? I don't know if I can swing that many, but I'll try. — Elmore Leonard, *Be Cool*, p. 165, 1999

4 to be executed by hanging *UK, 1542*
Hanging has been the principal form of execution in the British Isles since the C5; the death penalty was abolished in the UK in 1965 (except for crimes of treason, piracy with violence and arson in the Royal Dockyards).

- If you give yourself up you'll swing as sure as Christmas. — Derek Bickerton, *Payroll*, 1959

5 to play jazz with feeling and a basic understanding of the medium *US, 1933*

- When we talked about a musician who played hot, we would say he could swing or he couldn't swing, meaning what kind of effect did he have on the band. — Mezz Mezzrow, *Really the Blues*, p. 142, 1946

6 to cheat or swindle someone *US*

- "I got swung, too," Chico answered, ignoring the question. "Yeah, how come?" "Icepick said he knew a guy and I gave him the money to give to him and he blew." — Hal Ellson, *The Golden Spike*, p. 44, 1952

7 to steal something *US*
Casino usage.

- — Lee Solkey, *Dummy Up and Deal*, p. 121, 1980

8 in high-low poker, to declare for both high and low *US*

- — John Scarne, *Scarne's Guide to Modern Poker*, p. 289, 1979

▸ **swing both ways**
to be bisexual *UK, 1972*

- [I]n North Carolina a hot dog is free to swing both ways. Nothing in France is free from sexual assignment. — David Sedaris, *Me Talk Pretty One Day*, p. 189, 2001

▸ **swing it**

1 to malinger; to shirk responsibility; to evade duty *UK*
Variation of SWING THE LEAD.

- MILLIGAN: Didn't you know. I'm recovering from the war. TAYLOR: Stop swinging it. MILLIGAN: No, straight up. — Graeme Kent, *The Queen's Corporal [Six Granada Plays]*, p. 82, 1959

2 to achieve something by trickery or influence *UK*

- With a bit of luck I can swing it to get you sent back. — Graeme Kent, *The Queen's Corporal [Six Granada Plays]*, p. 84, 1959

▸ **swing the lead**
to malinger; to shirk responsibility; to evade duty *UK*
Popular etymology holds this to be the 'sounding-lead' with which the depth of water is measured; in practice 'heaving the lead' is a skilled task. The term certainly has naval origins.

swing by *verb*
to visit briefly; to go out of your way *UK*

swingdom *noun*
a culture of casual sexual interaction *US*

- Steve Dann is sadistic – any man who dangles his wife in the cesspools of "swingdom" is that[.] — Terence Sellers, *Dungeon Evidence*, p. 85, 1997

swinger *noun*

1 a person who freely enjoys life's pleasures *US, 1959*

- "A swinger?" "Well, it's a word a lot of people use different ways. But in the bunch I run around with it means a gal who finds her fun in sex." — John O'Day, *Confessions of a Hollywood Callgirl*, p. 91, 1964
- He [President Nixon] has said he's not what we would call a swinger, but he knows how to have a good time. — *Playboy*, p. 60, February 1969

2 someone who engages in spouse or partner swapping *US, 1964*

- The term swinger refers to an individual, married or single, who socializes with like-minded persons under circumstances that include a variety of sexual activities. — Bernhardt J. Hurwood, *The Sensuous New York*, p. 136, 1973
- It is a vignette picture, and stories are framed by a simple plot involving the staff of a swinger's magazine. — Kent Smith et al., *Adult Movies*, p. 127, 1982
- I'm talkin' me 'n Dot are Swingers! As in "to swing!" Wife-swappin'! — *Raising Arizona*, 1987

3 a person who has died by hanging *US*

- — *Maledicta*, p. 180, Summer/Winter 1986–1987

4 a prisoner who has attempted suicide by hanging *UK*

- — Angela Devlin, *Prison Patter*, p. 112, 1996

5 in trucking, a large load *US*

- — Montie Tak, *Truck Talk*, p. 161, 1971

swing gang *noun*
in the television and film industries, the crew that prepares and dismantles the set *US*

- — Ralph S. Singleton, *Filmaker's Dictionary*, p. 166, 1990

swinging *noun*
consensual swapping of sexual partners as a deliberate activity *UK, 1976*

- In two decades of swinging they have slept with at least 200 people between them. Barry [Calvert] has just published his swinging memoirs. — *The Guardian*, 29th August 2003

swinging *adjective*

1 lively and alert and progressive; uninhibited; fashionable *UK*

- The words "swinging" and "square" are like "progressive" and "reactionary", vague value judgements disguised as descriptions. — *Daily Telegraph*, 10th March 1967
- Norman [Vaughan] recalls: "'Swingin!' and 'Dodgy!' originally came from my association with jazz musicians. — Nigel Rees, *Very Interesting ... But Stupid!*, 1980
- [A]ll the way from Swinging London[.] — Barney Hoskyns, *Waiting For The Sun*, p. 144, 1996

2 of a court case, adjourned until a later date *AUSTRALIA*

- — *The (Sydney) Bulletin*, 26th April 1975

swinging dick *noun*
an ordinary fellow *US*
Sometimes euphemised (barely) as 'swinging Richard'.

- There ain't a swinging dick in the camp that could do me harm and you know it. — Malcolm Braly, *On the Yard*, p. 75, 1967
- — Carl Fleischhauer, *A Glossary of Army Slang*, p. 20, 1968
- I told her to tell her folks not to let any swinging dick know. — A.S. Jackson, *Gentleman Pimp*, p. 56, 1973
- And that quick every swinging dick in the village comes lickity-split with their guns and pitchforks and scythes and such, coming flat out up that hill. — Larry Heinemann, *Close Quarters*, p. 152, 1977
- I'm making it like every other swinging dick in this place makes it. Day by motherfucking day. — Gerald Petievich, *To Live and Die in L.A.*, p. 12, 1983
- The whole company, except for this one cat, caught some mean kind of shit and every swinging dick but him bought the motherfucker. — Larry Heinemann, *Paco's Story*, p. 23, 1986
- We need every swinging dick out in the field. — *Platoon*, 1986
- There ain't one swinging dick private in this platoon's gonna graduate until they can get this obstacle down to less than ten fucking seconds! — *Full Metal Jacket*, 1987

swingle *noun*
an unmarried person in search of a sexual partner *US*

- In some quarters, they are called – or like to call themselves – the "swingles." — Joe David Brown, *Sex in the '60s*, p. 27, 1968

swing oil *noun*
to a golfer, beer or alcohol *US*

- — Hubert Pedroli and Mary Tiegreen, *Let the Big Dog Eat!*, p. 83, 2000

swing-out *noun*
a fight between youth gangs *US*

- — David Claerbaut, *Black Jargon in White America*, p. 82, 1972
- First into the street was always me, loved a swingout — Edwin Torres, *Carlito's Way*, 1975

swings and roundabouts
the rough and the smooth; used of a fluctuating situation where the average outcome remains constant whatever action is taken *UK, 1983*
A reduction of the proverb 'what you lose on the swings you gain on the roundabouts'.

- "So how's business?" he asked Ron. "Swings and roundabouts, Malcolm," said Ron with a sigh. "Swings and roundabouts. Sometimes we're up, sometimes we're down.["] — Greg Williams, *Diamond Geezers*, p. 125, 1997

swing shift *noun*
a work schedule that begins late in the afternoon and continues until the middle of the night, traditionally from 4 pm until midnight *US, 1943*
- "What about your folks?" "They're on the swing shift this month." —Irving Shulman, *The Amboy Dukes*, p. 31, 1947

swipe *noun*
1 a heavy blow delivered with a swinging motion (may be applied to a bat addressing a ball, or a hand hitting flesh) *UK, 1807*
- He took out the cricket bat and took a swipe at the statue. It failed to damage it. — *The Guardian*, 5th July 2002

2 an instance of adverse criticism *UK, 1932*
Extended from the previous sense.
- Madonna takes swipe at Bush. — *The Guardian*, 10th February 2003

3 an objectionable person *UK, 1929*

4 the penis *US*
- They got a double saw [$20] in one hand and their swipes in the other. —Iceberg Slim (Robert Beck), *Pimp*, p. 131, 1969
- —Kenn "Naz" Young, *Naz's Underground Dictionary*, p. 59, 1973
- But old Franky only laughed, 'cause he was coming at last / And his swipe swole twice its size. —Dennis Wepman et al., *The Life*, p. 111, 1976

5 potent, homemade pineapple-based alcohol *US*
Hawaiian usage.
- —Douglas Simonson, *Pidgin to da Max Hana Hou*, 1982

6 to drink great amounts of kava, a tranquillity-inducing herbal beverage *FIJI*
- Seeing that grog is sweeter, you can be up all day and night swiping it with women and girls[.] — *Sunday Post*, p. 4, 10th August 1997

swipe *verb*
1 to hit someone *UK, 1851*
From an earlier sense, 'to swing the arms in a circular motion'.
- Mellors folded the paper into a tight rod, lashed out suddenly at his [Monty's] exposed buttock [...] "You hadn't ought to do that," Monty said in a pained tone. "Do what?" "Swipe people in their sleep." —Derek Bickerton, *Payroll*, p. 13–14, 1959

2 to steal something *US, 1889*
- His wife had swiped his dough, and gone off with another man[.] —Charles Raven, *Underworld Nights*, p. 29–30, 1956

3 to take something, but not necessarily to steal it *UK*
- — *The Felstedian*, December 1947

swipe me!
a euphemistic cry of surprise, replacing 'fuck me!' *UK*
A slight variant of the obsolete and hence euphemistic 'swive' (to have sex).
- —Chris Bumstead writing about the vocabulary of, *Hancock's Half Hour broadcast between*, 1955 AND 1959, 1987
- Swipe me! —BBC TV *The Eurovision Song Contest*, 12th May 2001

swipes *noun*
1 in horse racing, a groom *US*
- —Dan Parker, *The ABC of Horse Racing*, p. 149, 1947

2 beer *UK, 1805*
Originally (1786) 'a small beer'.
- Cor strike, what am I doing swilling swipes when there's three hundred nicker (£300) in my pouch. —Derek Bickerton, *Payroll*, p. 119, 1959

swish *noun*
1 a homosexual male, especially of the dramatically effeminate type *US, 1941*
- And now, it seems, they are all here: the handsome masculine ones desired alike by men and women; the gushing swishes, hands aflutter like wings[.] —John Rechy, *City of Night*, p. 221, 1963
- If I put a couple of normal boys in the line the swishes would tear them to pieces in no time. —Antony James, *America's Homosexual Underground*, p. 123, 1965
- "Swish" bars for the effeminates and "hair fairies" with their careful coiffures. —Joe David Brown, *Sex in the '60s*, p. 70, 1968
- These were the flaming swishes of his prison days; "Bernice" and "Joan." —Odie Hawkins, *Midnight*, p. 159, 1995

2 weak alcohol made by letting water stand in old screech barrels *CANADA*
- —Emily *An American's Guide to Canada*, p. 3, 10th November 2001

swish *verb*
1 (of a homosexual male) to behave in a flamboyant, camp or effeminate manner *US*
- I have always made fun of the swishing, screaming, flaunting queens and you have always laughed with me. — *Mattachine Review*, p. 24, March 1960
- The queens swished by in superficial gayetey – giggling males acting like teenage girls[.] —John Rechy, *City of Night*, p. 35, 1963
- Fuck what the guy from Tracy said, that kid came on the big yard swishing like she had a license to run wild[.] —Malcolm Braly, *On the Yard*, p. 217, 1967
- —Paul Baker, *Polari*, p. 190, 2002

2 (among drug users) to distribute drugs, especially hallucinogenic drugs *NEW ZEALAND, 1982*
- —Harry Orsman, *A Dictionary of Modern New Zealand Slang*, p. 134, 1999

swish *adjective*
1 fashionable; elegant *UK, 1879*
Colloquial, from Devonshire dialect.
- —Louis S. Leland, *A Personal Kiwi-Yankee Dictionary*, p. 99, 1984
- [K]ick-boxing classes at their swish health club. —Frank Skinner, *Frank Skinner*, p. 369, 2001

2 blatantly homosexual *US, 1941*
Also variant 'swishy'.
- — Florida Legislative Investigation Committee (Johns Committee), *Homosexuality and Citizenship in Florida*, 1964: 'Glossary of homosexual terms and deviate acts'
- Horace was a faggot, an out-and-out flaming faggot. He didn't swish, but he was sort of like an old auntie. —Lenny Bruce, *How to Talk Dirty and Influence People*, p. 34, 1965
- Walking up and down the halls were perhaps a dozen other guys – some rather handsome, some miserable, but mostly just ordinary guys. None of them seemed swishy. — *The Advocate*, p. 5, March 1969
- The story involves only four characters: two lovers, their "swishy" neighbor, and an old "straight" friend who is a boyhood buddy of one of the lovers. — *Screw*, p. 20, 27th October 1969
- Expensive suits, or he's got the shirt open all the way, the chains. Maybe just a little swishy. —Elmore Leonard, *Glitz*, p. 109, 1985
- "Well, I don't know," repeated Dad. "I don't want any swishy characters hanging around." "I'm not gay, Dad." —C.D. Payne, *Youth in Revolt*, p. 123, 1993

swish Alps *noun*
the Hollywood Hills, Los Angeles, California *US*
A homosexual enclave.
- As it happens, he does live in a gay section of Los Angeles sometimes called the "Swish Alps." — *People*, p. 117, 7th March 1983
- His collection went to his adopted "son," a likable interior decorator, who sold many of the paintings to support a lavish lifestyle in the "Swish Alps" section of Los Angeles. — *Washington Post*, 19th December 1999

swisher *noun*
a hollowed-out cigar refilled with marijuana *US*
- — *www.addictions.org*, 1999

swish faggot *noun*
an effeminate, melodramatic homosexual man *US*
- — *Maledicta*, p. 225, Winter 1980: '"Lovely, blooming, fresh and gay": the onomastics of camp'

swish tank *noun*
a holding cell in a jail where homosexual suspects and prisoners are kept *US*
- Down the catwalk, turn the corner: the swish tank facing the drunk tank. —James Ellroy, *White Jazz*, p. 107, 1992

Swiss Army knife; swiss army *noun*
a wife *UK*
Rhyming slang, formed on a commercial tool that is marketed in a wide range of variations.
- Look out, here comes the swiss army. —Ray Puxley, *Fresh Rabbit*, 1998

Swiss banker *noun*
used as an all-purpose form of abuse *UK*
Rhyming slang for **WANKER**.
- —Bodmin Dark, *Dirty Cockney Rhyming Slang*, 2003

Swiss-cheeze up *verb*
to shoot a person or place full of holes *US*
The image of a piece of cheese such as Emmental.
- Recall him [The Notorious B.I.G.] [...] Swiss-cheezin' up his enemies on "Who Shot Ya." — *The Source*, p. 192, March 2002

switch *noun*

1 a switchblade knife that opens with a button-operated spring *US*

- I was afraid. I was ready to pull out my switch. —Hal Ellson, *Duke*, p. 110, 1949

2 in a sexually oriented massage parlour, a massage given to the masseuse by the customer *US*

- —Ralph de Sola, *Crime Dictionary*, p. 146, 1982

3 the buttocks *US*

- Got nice legs, and a nice switch. —Hal Ellson, *Duke*, p. 73, 1949

switch *verb*

to act upon bisexual impulses *US*

- Glossary of terms used in the underground press —Robert J. Glessing, *The Underground Press in America*, p. 177, 1970

▸ switch lanes

to change allegiance *UK*

Used by teenage gang members.

- [T]he group was using bottles, knives and baseball bats in fights with neighbouring youths who came into "our area" – or over girlfriends who "switch lanes" and go out with a rival. —*The Guardian*, 16th July 2003

switchable *noun*

a person who is willing to play either the sadist or masochist role in a sado-masochism encounter *US*

- —*What Color is Your Handkerchief*, p. 5, 1979

switchboard jockey *noun*

a telephone operator *US, 1957*

- —*American Speech*, p. 158–159, May 1960: 'The burgeoning of "jockey"'

switched on *adjective*

1 in fashion, up-to-date and well-informed *UK, 1964*

- Judges switched on as Turner Prize goes to the Creed of nothingness. —*The Guardian*, 10th December 2001

2 drug-intoxicated *US, 1972*

- I was wondering who might still be switched on. —Lanre Fehintola, *Charlie Says...*, p. 80, 2000

3 excited by music; aroused by a sexual opportunity *UK*

Electrical imagery

- —David Powis, *The Signs of Crime*, 1977

switcher *noun*

a bisexual *US*

- [S]ometimes they're switchers: married men whose wives held out on them the night before. They decide to play the other side of the street before going to the office. —Johnny Shearer, *The Male Hustler*, p. 149, 1966

switcheroo *noun*

a swapping; an exchange *US, 1933*

- In other words, it's a switcheroo, with the mind playing the sucker. —Max Shulman, *Guided Tour of Campus Humor*, p. 89, 1955
- But that Latah get up in feud state and put on his Santa Claus suit and make with the switcheroo. —William Burroughs, *Naked Lunch*, p. 80, 1957
- —Roald Dahl, *The Great Switcheroo*, 1974
- His strategy was to slip it in while fingering her, taking advantage of the darkness to pull the old switcheroo. —Richard Price, *The Wanderers*, p. 40, 1974
- They had actually brought band T-shirts with them for both bands and changed between sets [...] One of the practicioners of the T-shirt switcheroo was Chris from Bishop's Stortford[.] —Iain Aitch, *A Fete Worse Than Death*, p. 65, 2003

switchfoot *noun*

a surfer who can surf with either foot forward, depending on the conditions *US*

- —John Severson, *Modern Surfing Around the World*, p. 183, 1964

switch hitter *noun*

1 a bisexual *US, 1960*

- There was a dramatic actress, very famous, who was really a switch-hitter; in other words, bi-sexual. —John O'Day, *Confessions of a Male Prostitute*, p. 111, 1964
- —*The Guild Dictionary of Homosexual Terms*, p. 43, 1965
- Switch-Hittin' Gal! —*San Francisco Chronicle*, 22nd December 1967
- "Bread? Osca, you want bread?" Maria, the Jewish switchhitter screamed in Billie Holiday tones. —Oscar Zeta Acosta, *The Autobiography of a Brown Buffalo*, p. 44, 1972
- —Kenn "Naz" Young, *Naz's Underground Dictionary*, p. 59, 1973
- "And if I bring any switch hitters home with me, it's hands off, right?" "Do I look like that kind of cad?" —Armistead Maupin, *Tales of the City*, p. 73, 1978
- In those days, she was a switch-hitter, now she was straight dyke. —Edwin Torres, *After Hours*, p. 325, 1979
- —Connie Eble (Editor), *UNC-CH Campus Slang*, p. 8, Fall 1997
- "Elliot's homosexual." Elaine said, "Oh, really?" with a pleasant enough tone, putting herself in the scene now, no longer just watching. "He's a switch-hitter." —Elmore Leonard, *Be Cool*, p. 269, 1999

2 a person who masturbates with first one hand and then the other *US*

- —Gary K. Farlow, *Prison-ese*, p. 71, 2002

switchies *noun*

sex involving more than two people *US*

- Once we did switchies with her and one of the cocktail waitresses from the Blue Peach. —Gerald Petievich, *To Die in Beverly Hills*, p. 137, 1983

switch list *noun*

on the railways, a menu *US*

- —Ramon Adams, *The Language of the Railroader*, p. 151, 1977

switch monkey *noun*

a railway pointsman *US*

- —Ramon Adams, *The Language of the Railroader*, p. 151, 1977

switch off *verb*

1 to stop paying attention; to lose interest *UK, 1921*

- —John Ayto, *The Oxford Dictionary of Slang*, p. 251, 1998

2 to knock someone out *UK*

Electrical imagery.

- Wally switched one off and I switched off another. —Jimmy Stockin, *On The Cobbles*, p. 106, 2000

swizzle; swiz; swizz *noun*

a swindle; a disappointment half-jokingly described as a 'swindle' *UK, 1913*

- "Don't let it worry you, Billy," Stan said in his ordinary, friendlier voice. "It's all a big swuzz." —John Burke and Stuart Douglass, *The Boys*, p. 114, 1962
- —Louis S. Leland, *A Personal Kiwi-Yankee Dictionary*, 1984
- And what about the fucking lottery, eh? Fucking swizz, that is. —Greg Williams, *Diamond Geezers*, p. 156, 1997
- It's a bloody swizzle this birthday lark. —Caroline Aherne and Craig Cash, *The Royle Family*, 1999

swole *adjective*

upset; provoked; angry *US*

- —Ethan Hilderbrant, *Prison Slang*, p. 7, 1998

swoles *noun*

muscles *US*

From 'swollen'.

- —Rick Ayers (Editor), *Berkeley High Slang Dictionary*, p. 40, 2004

swoll *adjective*

muscular *US*

- —Pamela Munro, *U.C.L.A. Slang*, p. 112, 1997
- —Connie Eble (Editor), *UNC-CH Campus Slang*, p. 7, November 2002

swollen-headed *adjective*

conceited *UK, 1928*

- [A]s for that numbskull Porson, he's nothing but a swollen-headed snob. —M.M. Kaye, *The Far Pavilions*, p. 504, 1978

swonked *adjective*

exhausted by heavy work *CANADA*

- In Cape Sable Island, to be "swonked" is to be very tired from heavy labour. —*Dalhousie Review*, p. 45, 1953

swoon *verb*

to seduce or romance someone *UK*

- Forget trying to swoon your bird with naff Justin Timberlake records. —*Mixmag*, p. 4, April 2003

swoonie *noun*

the contemporary dollar coin *CANADA*

In 2002, with the Canadian dollar dropping in value, this parody nickname is derived from **LOONY**.

- Of course, if the swoonie reverses its protracted death plunge and rises against the U.S. dollar, Canadians would suffer currency losses. —*Financial Post*, p. IN4, 2nd February 2002

swoontime *noun*

the approximate time when young people congregate somewhere to socialise *US*

- —Lavada Durst, *The Jives of Dr. Hepcat*, p. 13, 1953

swooper *noun*
a prisoner who collects discarded cigarette-ends (to roll new ones) *UK*
The swooper *swoops* on his prey.
- —Angela Devlin, *Prison Patter*, p. 112, 1996

swoop squad; swoop team *noun*
a unit of prison officers detailed to discover drugs and other contraband *UK*
- —Angela Devlin, *Prison Patter*, p. 112, 1996

swoosh *noun*
the name given to the tick-shaped logo of Nike™, the sports shoe manufacturer *US*
- [H]er seven-year-old son marks his homework not with check marks but with little red Nike swooshes.—Naomi Klein, *No Logo*, p. 28, 2001
- [T]here used to be this one girl Laetitia that had hers [pubic bush] done in a Nike swoosh and that. Straight up.—Kevin Sampson, *Outlaws*, p. 38, 2001
- We're talking lots of post-Fame leg-warmers and pristine Nike trainers (in the days before the swoosh ruled the world)[.]—Patrick Neate, *Where You're At*, 2003

S-word *noun*
1 the word 'shit' *US*
- What did my son say, Principal Victoria? Did he say the S word? —*South Park*, 1999

2 the word 'sex' *US*
- —*American Speech*, Winter 1988

3 the word 'socialism' *US, 1987*
- —*American Speech*, Winter 1988

sword fighting *noun*
a sexual act in which two erect penises compete for or share the attention of a single person performing oral sex *UK*
- —*www.LondonSlang.com*, June 2002

swordsman *noun*
1 a man with an impressive reputation for his sexual prowess *UK, 1998*
- After years as one of rock's great swordsmen [...] Eric Clapton is now happy to settle into the role of contented family man[.]—*Uncut*, p. 66, May 2004

2 a male homosexual *UK*
- —Tom Hibbert, *Rockspeak!*, p. 154, 1983

sword swallower *noun*
a person who performs oral sex on a man *US*
The working title of the 1970s pornographic classic *Deep Throat* was *Sword Swallower*.
- —Roger Blake, *The American Dictionary of Sexual Terms*, p. 212, 1964

swot; swat *noun*
an extra-studious student *UK, 1850*
- Everyone hates swots and teacher's pets and behaves like dirty swine to them.—Ann Barr and Peter York, *The Official Sloane Ranger Handbook*, p. 75, 1982

swot *verb*
to study, especially at the last possible moment before an examination *NEW ZEALAND*
- —Louis S. Leland, *A Personal Kiwi-Yankee Dictionary*, p. 99, 1984

swot vac *noun*
student holidays from school or university *AUSTRALIA*
- 'We have two weeks swot vac and then,' she made a face, 'and then exams and after that...'—Elizabeth Jolley, *Mr. Scobie's Riddle*, p. 95, 1983

swy *noun*
1 the gambling game two-up *AUSTRALIA, 1913*
Ultimately from German *zwei* (two), possibly via Yiddish.
- The Police know they wouldn't have a dog's chance of stopping swy on the fields.—Bill Hornadge, *The Ugly Australian*, p. 165, 1952
- Shiners, split lips, enlarged lugs and various other contusions he regards as occupational hazards; and he plays a wiry game of swy even with an arm in a sling.—Geoff Wyatt, *Saltwater Saints*, p. 13, 1969

2 two; a two-year prison sentence; two shillings; two pounds; two ounces of tobacco *AUSTRALIA, 1921*
From German *zwei* (two). The spelling 'swi' is also used.
- —*The (Sydney) Bulletin*, 26th April 1975

swy game *noun*
the gambling game two-up *AUSTRALIA, 1946*
- Since it wouldn't do for an officer to be seen at a swy game, he took off his crowns and I minded them for him.—Ray Slattery, *Mobbs' Mob*, p. 83, 1966
- Card games were more or less above board and no one won or lost a great deal, but the swy game was something else.—Joe Andersen, *Winners Can Laugh*, p. 50, 1982

swy school *noun*
a group of people playing the gambling game two-up *AUSTRALIA, 1944*
- No sentiment in business but he liked the old place somehow. Getting built-in now though. The old bakery where he had his first swy school – gone.—Sutton Woodfield, *A for Artemis*, p. 156, 1960

sXe *noun*
used as an identifying word by members of the Straight Edge youth culture *US*
The 's' and 'e' are, obviously, the initials of 'Straight Edge', while the 'X' represents the rubber stamp marked on the hands of under-age patrons at youth clubs.
- In fact, sXe is probably the only youth subculture that actively denounces the use of alcohol, tobacco, and illegal drugs.—Bill Valentine, *Gangs and Their Tattoos*, p. 71, 2000

Sydney Harbour *noun*
a barber *AUSTRALIA, 1942*
Rhyming slang.
- —Jim Ramsay, *Cop It Sweet!*, p. 87, 1977
- —Ryan Aven-Bray, *Ridgey Didge Oz Jack Lang*, p. 45, 1983

Sydney or the bush
all or nothing *AUSTRALIA, 1915*
- SYDNEY OR THE BUSH – All or nothing.—Gilbert H. Lawson, *A Dictionary of Australian Words and Terms*, 1924
- Though few had the courage even to mention the fact, Darky had a propensity to fluke, especially when he went to Sydney or the bush, hitting them hard and hoping for the best[.]—Frank Hardy, *Legends From Benson's Valley*, p. 60, 1963
- —Jim Ramsay, *Cop It Sweet!*, p. 87, 1977

Sylvester Stallone; sylvester *adjective*
alone *UK*
Rhyming slang, formed on the US film actor (b.1950).
- The modern youth is more likely to be on his "Sylvester" than on his Tod[.]—Ray Puxley, *Fresh Rabbit*, 1998

synch *noun*
▸ **in synch; in sync**
in accord with *US, 1961*
Figurative use of the abbreviated *in synch*ronization (working together).
- [A] moral code that isn't entirely in sync with our legal system.—Janet Evanovich, *Seven Up*, p. 132, 2001

syndicat *noun*
in Quebec, a trade union *CANADA*
- "I hear politicians use gallicisms in their speech all the time," he said, shuddering as he cited "syndicats" (unions) and "manifestations" (demonstrations).—*Montreal Gazette*, p. A11, 27th July 2002

syndicate *noun*
1 a criminal organisation *US, 1929*
- But pretty soon I caught up with another syndicate house at 119th and Wood, where I found what I was looking for.—Mezz Mezzrow, *Really the Blues*, p. 24, 1946
- The Syndicate is almost entirely bossed by ex-convicts whose roots are in the lowest and most violent soil[.]—Jack Lait and Lee Mortimer, *New York Confidential*, p. 179, 1948
- The gambling was unorganized – the syndicate boys who tired to move in got the fast heave-ho.—Jim Thompson, *Roughneck*, p. 142, 1954
- One of Leo's duies for the syndicate had been to pay off the cops in his territory[.]—Bernard Wolfe, *The Late Risers*, p. 210, 1954

2 a small group of close friends *US*
Joining **CREW** and **POSSE** as crime terms applied to friends.
- —Judi Sanders, *Faced and Faded, Hanging to Hurl*, p. 39, 1993

synergy *noun*
4-bromo-2,5-dimethoxyphenethylamine, a mild hallucinogen *US*
- —Steven Daly and Nalthaniel Wice, *alt.culture*, p. 238, 1995

syph *noun*

syphilis *US, 1914*

- [B]y the time she was fifteen she had been plain lousy with clap and syph, and she had had gonorrheal rheumatism, and one day she had just jumped into the Jackson Park lagoon and polluted the drinking water for the gold fish. —James T. Farrell, *Saturday Night*, p. 30, 1947
- But I'll come down with the syph from just touching the ticket. —Philip Roth, *Portnoy's Complaint*, p. 145, 1969
- Hey Janet do you have syph? —Sal Piro and Michael Hess, *The Official 'Rocky Horror Picture Show' Audience Participation Guide*, p. 7, 1991

syrup *noun*

prescription cough syrup, used recreationally *US*

- —Mark S. Fleisher, *Beggars & Thieves*, p. 291, 1995: 'Glossary'

syrup head *noun*

a person who abuses for non-medicinal purposes non-prescription medication containing dextromethorphan (DXM) *US*

- Youths' nicknames for DXM: Robo, Skittles, Triple C's, Rojo, Dex, Tussin, Vitamin D. DXM abuse is called "Robotripping" or "Tussing." Users might be called "syrup heads" or "robotards." —*USA Today*, p. 1A, 29th December 2003

syrup of fig; syrup of figs; syrup *noun*

a wig *UK*

Rhyming slang. Syrup of figs is used as a laxative. Noted in use among criminals by David Powis, *The Signs of Crime*, 1977; as a showbusiness term by Red Daniells, 1980, and in wide and general use by Ray Puxley, *Cockney Rabbit*, 1992.

syrupped up *adjective*

intoxicated by cough syrup taken for non-medicinal purposes *US*

- —*Current Slang*, p. 13, Fall 1970

system *noun*

1 the criminal justice system; jail *US*

- He'd have to be awful dumb. The guy's in and out of the system. —Elmore Leonard, *Riding the Rap*, p. 167, 1995

2 an audio system, especially a loud car audio system *US*

- —*Washington Post*, 14th October 1993
- I got done for nicking a system —Angela Devlin, *Prison Patter*, 1996

systems kicker *noun*

in prison, a rebellious inmate *UK*

One who kicks against the system.

- —Angela Devlin, *Prison Patter*, p. 112, 1996

SYT *noun*

a youthful, attractive homosexual male; a *s*weet *y*oung *t*hing *US*

- —*Maledicta*, p. 220, 1979: 'Kinks and queens: linguistic and cultural aspects of the terminology for gays'

Tt

T *noun*

1 marijuana *UK*

The simplest abbreviation of **TEA**.

- A word about yr. request for t ... no, I have no more now, except some left from the San Remo, some Brooklyn grown[.] —Jack Kerouac, *Letter to Neal Cassady*, p. 231, 6th October 1950

2 cocaine *UK*

Probably an abbreviation of another slang term for 'cocaine' such as **TOOT**.

- —Mike Haskins, *Drugs*, p. 281, 2003

3 a tee-shirt *UK*

- [A] tiny woman in bootylicious shorts and a tight T[.] —Patrick Neate, *Where You're At*, p. 58, 2003

▸ **to a T**

precisely, exactly *UK, 1693*

- And it was exactly, down to a T, the same serene exaltation I'd sensed in New Orelans music as a kid[.] —Mezz Mezzrow, *Really the Blues*, p. 322, 1946
- [H]e'd cased the locations to a T, getting the facts validated straight down the line. —James Ellroy, *Suicide Hill*, p. 629, 1986
- [B]eing left alone would have suited the teenage me to a T. —Helen Hastings, *Are Friends Electra [Inappropriate Behaviour]*, p. 12, 2002

T *nickname*

the local rail system serving urban and suburban Boston, Massachusetts *US*

Used with 'the'. From the official designation 'Boston Transport'.

- —Laurence Urdang, *Names and Nicknames of Places and Things*, p. 245, 1987

ta

thank you *UK, 1772*

An abbreviation of 'thanks' or 'thank you'; originally childish or juvenile, now widespread.

- God loves us all, really. He really does. And, ta for letting me say it. —Mike Stott, *Soldiers Talking, Cleanly*, 1978
- —Louis S. Leland, *A Personal Kiwi-Yankee Dictionary*, p. 99, 1984
- [S]he goes [says] no, ta and that, she's had a night of it and has to be up in the morning. —Kevin Sampson, *Outlaws*, p. 187, 2001

tab *noun*

1 a *tab*let, usually one taken as a recreational drug; a single dose of LSD *UK, 1961*

Originally medical and pharmaceutical jargon, added to the vocabulary of drugs users in the 1950s.

- I see Harry and get my tabs from him – thirty "French" Blues at sixpence a time. —Ian Hebditch, *Weekend [The Sharper Word]*, p. 133, 1969
- He's got some acid. We can have two tabs [...] for 1, man. That's good, they're usually a pound each, but he knows me. —Robin Page, *Down Among the Dossers*, p. 27, 1973
- This was Pet Sounds on twenty tabs of acid. —Barney Hoskyn, *Waiting For The Man*, p. 127, 1996
- He'd once been arrested holding a quarter sheet of acid: maybe seventy-five tabs. —Nicholas Blincoe, *Ardwick Green (Disco Biscuits)*, p. 8, 1996
- Chewing the remaining half of the tab I take to the dance floor. After the first rush I'm waiting for the acid to reach the E and lift it higher. —Melanie McGrath, *Hard, Soft & Wet*, p. 90, 1998
- Can I interest one in a tab of acid, madam? —Wayne Anthony, *Spanish Highs*, p. 84, 1999

2 a tabloid newspaper *US*

- A tabloid and a full-sized job were there. The tab was opened to a news account of the trial that was one column wide and two inches long. —Mickey Spillane, *One Lonely Night*, p. 16, 1951
- I wouldn't have called it an orgy myself, but that's what the tabs labeled it. —Dev Collans with Stewart Sterling, *I was a House Detective*, p. 52, 1954

3 a bill, especially in a restaurant or bar *US, 1946*

- Then just before the check comes, they get mad and walk out. Leave you with a forty-two dollar tab. —Elmore Leonard, *City Primeval*, p. 27, 1980

4 a cigarette *UK, 1934*

Originally northern dialect, spread with media usage.

- —Angela Devlin, *Prison Patter*, p. 112, 1996

5 a walk or march across country *UK*

- That night he [a member of the Parachute Regiment during the Falkland Islands campaign] set out on a "tab" for Goose Green. —*Listener*, 8th July 1982

6 an enterprise, an activity *US*

- "Hey, look, baby," I said. "I know you're Capone's old lady – uh, uh, I ain't coming on this tab." —Mezz Mezzrow, *Really the Blues*, p. 24, 1946

▸ **run a tab**

to order drinks without paying for each one, paying instead the entire bill at the end of the session *US*

- One-fifteen Harry ordered another drink and told the waiter to run a tab. —Elmore Leonard, *Riding the Rap*, p. 43, 1995

tab *verb*

1 to march or otherwise travel on foot across country *UK, 1982*

Military.

- [P]atrols will tab into their respective targets. —Chris Ryan, *The Watchman*, p. 24, 2001

2 to make a drug into tablet form *US*

- Most chemists don't tab their own acid [LSD]. —Nicholas Von Hoffman, *We Are The People Our Parents Warned Us Against*, p. 35, 1967
- It involved a few hundred thousand dollars' worth of LSD and a machine to tab it. —Vincent Patrick, *Family Business*, p. 225, 1985

tabasco *noun*

napalm *US*

- —Linda Reinberg, *In the Field*, p. 213, 1991

tabbed *adjective*

dressed stylishly *US*

- —Edith A. Folb, *runnin' down some lines*, p. 257, 1980

tabla *noun*

a surfboard *US*

Spanish, imported to the US from Mexico by American surfers.

- —Gary Fairmont R. Filosa II, *The Surfer's Almanac*, p. 196, 1977

table *noun*

a pinball machine *UK*

- —Bobbye Claire Natkin and Steve Kirk, *All About Pinball*, p. 117, 1977

table dance *noun*

in a strip-club, a semi-private sexual performance near or on a customer's table *US*

- Some customers request table dances. The dancer leaves the stage and goes to the customer's table, a tiny round table with spindly legs, littered with glasses. She climbs on the table and moves to the music while removing all her clothing. —Marilyn Suriani Futterman, *Dancing Naked in the Material World*, p. 129, 1992
- Unlike the other strippers, Erin refused to do table dances. —Carl Hiaasen, *Strip Tease*, p. 8, 1993
- We met Coco, who did a table dance for Patricia and told us about her girlfriend[.] —*The Village Voice*, 21st September 1999

table grade *adjective*

used of a woman, sexually appealing *US*

A clear suggestion of oral sex, or eating.

- —Helen Dahlskog (Editor), *A Dictionary of Contemporary and Colloquial Usage*, p. 58, 1972

table-hopper; table-topper *noun*

a necrophile *US*

- —*Maledicta*, p. 178, Summer/Winter 1986–1987: 'Sexual slang: prostitutes, pedophiles, flagellators, transvestites, and necrophiles'

table manners *noun*

in poker, a player's mannerisms, which may provide clues as to the relative strength of his hand *US, 1981*

- —Thomas L. Clark, *The Dictionary of Gambling and Gaming*, p. 226, 1987

table muscle *noun*
the stomach *US*
• Monroe likes to brag about how strong he is, but it looks to me like that table muscle's the one gets the most workin' out. — Ken Weaver, *Texas Crude*, p. 130, 1984

table pussy *noun*
a woman with good looks and manners *US*
• A stew can come under the heading of class stuff, or table pussy[.] — Jim Bouton, *Ball Four*, p. 204, 1970

tablescore *verb*
to take food left on restaurant tables *US*
• — Jim Crotty, *How to Talk American*, p. 146, 1997

table talk *noun*
in poker, idle chatter that does not rise to the level of intentionally distracting talk *US*
• — John Scarne, *Scarne's Guide to Modern Poker*, p. 292, 1979

table time *noun*
a time-based charge for playing pool *US*
• — Mike Shamos, *The Illustrated Encyclopedia of Billiards*, p. 241, 1993

table zamboni *noun*
a cleaning rag used by a bartender *US*
Zamboni is an ice resurfacer used on ice rinks.
• — Connie Eble (Editor), *UNC-CH Campus Slang*, p. 8, Fall 1987

tab out *verb*
to pay a bar bill and leave the bar *US*
• Would you remember what was going on in the movie when the guy tabbed out for the night? — Richard Price, *Clockers*, p. 377, 1992

tabs *noun*
the ears *US*
• — Clarence Major, *Dictionary of Afro-American Slang*, p. 113, 1970

tache *noun*
▷ see: TASH

tacit *noun*
▸ **take a tacit**
to stop talking *US*
• This is your professor of thermodynamics taking a tacit for 24. — *Time Magazine*, p. 92, 20th January 1947

tack *noun*
1 anything that demonstrates a quality of vulgarity, bad taste or kitsch *US, 1986*
• I wouldn't say I invented tack, but I definitely brought it to its present high popularity. — Aubrey Dillon-Malone, *I Was A Fugitive From A Hollywood Trivia Factory [quoting Bette Midler]*, p. 135, 1999

2 a tattoo *US*
• — William K. Bentley and James M. Corbett, *Prison Slang*, p. 85, 1992

3 marijuana *UK*
• — Angela Devlin, *Prison Patter*, p. 112, 1996

tacked *adjective*
drunk or drug-intoxicated *US*
• — Rick Ayers (Editor), *Berkeley High Slang Dictionary*, p. 40, 2004

tacked back *adjective*
covered with tattoos *US*
• — James Harris, *A Convict's Dictionary*, p. 40, 1989

tacked out *adjective*
in trucking, running at full speed *US*
A construction from 'tachometer'.
• — Montie Tak, *Truck Talk*, p. 162, 1971

tacker *noun*
a child *AUSTRALIA, 1942*
From British dialect (Devon and Cornwall).
• The official start of the torch relay, the Prime Minister handing the flaming firebrand to some beaming tacker in a MOB t-shirt. — Shane Maloney, *Nice Try*, p. 180, 1998

tackety bit; tackety *noun*
the female breast *UK: SCOTLAND*
Glasgow rhyming slang for TIT from the local pronunciation of 'tackety' (steel-tipped and -heeled boots).
• That's a fine perr [pair] a tacketies on that wee thing. — Michael Munro, *The Patter, Another Blast*, 1988

tackie *noun*
a tyre *SOUTH AFRICA*
• — Jean Branford, *A Dictionary of South African English*, 1978

tackies *noun*
running shoes, trainers *SOUTH AFRICA, 1913*
• All boys and girls who attended last week have to bring helmets and tackies. Hurleys will be supplied. — *Limerick Leader*, 12th February 2000

tackiness *noun*
a state of unrefined vulgarity *US, 1977*
• a world where tackiness and style lock together — *Time Out*, 23rd November 1979

tackle *noun*
1 the male genitalia *UK*
Originally 'a man's tackle' subsequent familiarity reduced the necessity for 'a man's'.
• a man's tackle — Francis Grose, *A Classical Dictionary of the Vulgar Tongue*, 1788
• And if you don't get your mitts offa me, I'll skewer your tackle with my manicure set! — Ian Pattison, *Rab C. Nesbitt*, 1988
• So shove-the-fuck-up and give me the elbow-room to get my tackle out. — Nicholas Blincoe, *Ardwick Green (Disco Biscuits)*, p. 17, 1996
• [S]omeone bangs on his door to wake him up so we can get a shot of his tackle. — Paul Fraser and Shane Meadows, *TwentyFourSeven*, p. 83, 1997
• Stripe me, Dave, you gonna just stand there while some woofter is waving his tackle at your missus? — *The Full Monty*, 1997
• [A] stripper – skin of sable and tackle admirably thick and curling, like plantain – was doing his thing. — Diran Adebayo, *My Once Upon A Time*, p. 42, 2000

2 food and drink; 'stuff'; more recently, drugs *UK, 1857*
• [H]is tackle was always of the best – creamy white, rocky, unstepped on[.] — Will Self, *The Sweet Smell of Psychosis*, p. 70, 1996
• The old fucking monocled Upstairs Downstairs tackle. — Shaun Ryder, *Shaun Ryder... in His Own Words*, 1996

tackle *verb*
to court; to flirt *TRINIDAD AND TOBAGO, 1987*
• — Paik Choo, *The Coxford Singlish Dictionary*, p. 105, 2002
• — Lise Winer, *Dictionary of the English/Creole of Trinidad & Tobago*, 2003

tacky *adjective*
vulgar, unrefined, unattractive, aesthetically unappealling; 'cheap and nasty' *US, 1862*
• as subtle as a two-bob hairpiece and just as tacky — *Time Out*, 9th May 1980
• they're tacky — Naomi Klein, *No Logo*, p. 308, 2001

taco *adjective*
Mexican *US*
Offensive. From the Mexican street food.
• By the time she was twenty-six, she was scalylegging the taco trade; rented a trailer next to the wetback camp[.] — Seth Morgan, *Homeboy*, p. 50, 1990

taco bender *noun*
a Mexican or Mexican-American *US*
Offensive.
• Feature Dudley's going to film all those taco benders fucking and sell the movies to geeks like himself who dig all that voyeuristic horseshit. — James Ellroy, *White Jazz*, p. 305, 1992

Taco Hell *nickname*
a Taco Bell™ fast-food restaurant *US*
• — Connie Eble (Editor), *UNC-CH Campus Slang*, p. 8, Spring 1990

tacoland *noun*
a Mexican or Mexican-American neighbourhood *US*
Offensive.
• It's 1983 Vendome. That's in Silverlake. Tacoland. — James Ellroy, *Brown's Requiem*, p. 81, 1981

taco wagon *noun*
a car embellished with bright colours, chrome and other accessories associated with Mexican-American car enthusiasts *US, 1960*
• — *Maledicta*, p. 166, 1979: 'A glossary of ethnic slurs in American English'
• Leotis McCarver was undoubtedly black, but his car was a full dress taco wagon: chopped and channeled, lowered, with a candy apple, lime-green paint job with orange and yellow flames covering the hood and weeping halfway back over the sides of the vehicle. — James Ellroy, *Brown's Requiem*, p. 13, 1981
• If you weren't a Mexican, I'd call it a bonaroo taco wagon. — James Ellroy, *Suicide Hill*, p. 611, 1986

tad *adjective*
little; a small amount *UK, 1940*
Perhaps from dialect *tad* (toad).
- She shook her head and indicated me, a tad apologetically. — Diran Adebayo, *My Once Upon A Time*, p. 112, 2000
- [W]hether it isn't a tad dark and smoky in here[.] — Pete McCarthy, *McCarthy's Bar*, p. 17, 2000

tadger *noun*
the penis *UK, 1961*
Originally dialect; survives in rhyming slang **FOX AND BADGER**.

tadpole *noun*
an OH-6 light observation military helicopter *US*
From its shape.
- — Linda Reinberg, *In the Field*, p. 214, 1991

tadpole factory *noun*
the testicles *UK*
- — Richard Herring, *Talking Cock*, p. 30, 2003

ta ever so
thank you *UK, 1970*
An elaboration of **TA** and variation of **THANKS EVER SO**.
- "We have received no instructions from them, then or since, regarding any further letting or subletting." "Ta ever so," I said, and went grinning out to the street. — Dick Francis, *Risk*, p. 187, 1977

Taffia; Tafia *noun*
a notional conspiracy of influential Welsh people, especially Welsh-speakers, that control many areas of Welsh life for its own benefit *UK: WALES, 1980*
A blend of **TAFF** (Welsh) and 'mafia' (a criminal association).
- [A] different story emerges, which involves a literary Taffia mafia, sponsorship rows and a festival director[.] — *New Statesman*, 10th June 2002
- [Zaha] Hadid's inspiring opera house design, which would have added coats of lustre to the Welsh capital, was given the thumbs down by the local Tafia. — *The Guardian*, 14th November 2002

Taffy; Taff *noun*
a native of Wales *UK*
From Welsh *Dafydd* (David – the Welsh patron saint and everyday christian name) as heard by English ears. Taffy since about 1700; Taff since 1929.
- 1st STAGE HAND: What's he on about, Taff? WELSH STAGE HAND: Well ... he's being the director. — *A Hard Day's Night*, 1964
- I knew quite a few Taffs in those days. — Anthony Masters, *Minder*, p. 18, 1984
- [A] Taff in a city of cockneys. — Donald Gorgon, *Cop Killer*, p. 50, 1994

tag *noun*
1 the stylised signature of a graffiti artist *US*
From 'tag' (a label).
- Cartoon voice bubbles: "Swoop, your gang tag emits a capricious sort of longing. It moves me deeply." [...] "Shall I add a few more gang monickers to enrich the impact of your work?.." — Tim Lucas, *Bay Street "Muralists" in Full Swing, Cool Places*, p. 149, 1998

2 a stylised signature often confused with graffiti *US*
- — Jim Crotty, *How to Talk American*, p. 143, 1997

3 a nickname, or popular designation *US*
- The tag's my own. What do they call you besides Red? — Mickey Spillane, *My Gun is Quick*, p. 8, 1950

4 a number plate *US*
- There's one lad down in the tag plant who's supposesd to be a real bad-ass of a stud. — Bruce Jackson, *In the Life*, p. 380, 1972
- — Lewis Poteet, *Car & Motorcyle Slang*, p. 198, 1992

5 a planned murder *US*
- That was how to set up a tag, he thought. — Richard Condon, *Prizzi's Honor*, p. 34, 1982

6 in the television and film industries, a very short final scene *US*
- — Ralph S. Singleton, *Filmaker's Dictionary*, p. 168, 1990

tag *verb*
1 to shoot and hit someone or something *US*
- MR. PINK: Tagged a couple of cops. Did you kill anybody? — *Reservoir Dogs*, 1992

2 to strike or hit someone or something *US*
- I didn't really know the science of the game, but I was heavy-handed, with a lot of snap in my shoulder, so when I tagged a stud, he was hurtin'. — Edwin Torres, *Carlito's Way*, p. 11, 1975
- Huey had tagged the cop again[.] — Bobby Seale, *A Lonely Rage*, p. 190, 1978

3 to catch or arrest someone, or convict someone of a crime *US*
- I had driven cars for twelve years, in all but four states of the nation, and had been tagged for only two running violations[.] — Hunter S. Thompson, *Hell's Angels*, p. 39, 1966
- Everybody got tagged on every count. Thirty days for investigation and sentence. — Edwin Torres, *Carlito's Way*, p. 140, 1975

4 to spray-paint graffiti in a signature styling *US, 1980*
- Taggin' Is Phundamental. — *The Source*, p. 86, April 2000

5 to tattoo part of the body *US*
- — Kenn "Naz" Young, *Naz's Dictionary of Teen Slang*, p. 115, 1993

6 to bestow a nickname on someone *US*
- The fly chicks tagged "Lenore." — William "Lord" Buckley, *The Raven*, 1960
- The guy who hardly ever opens his mouth is usually tagged Gabby. — Robert Edmond Alter, *Carny Kill*, p. 6, 1966

7 to identify someone or something *US*
- "Body still unidentified and we're tracking down his dental work. No prints on file." "Think you'll tag him?" — Mickey Spillane, *One Lonely Night*, p. 65, 1951
- He got tagged smuggling a truckload of bootleg cigarettes[.] — Janet Evanovich, *Seven Up*, p. 3, 2001

tag-along *noun*
someone who joins an activity without invitation *US, 1961*
- Smart – one righteous vato, one tagalong. — James Ellroy, *Suicide Hill*, p. 619, 1986

tag and bag *verb*
to put a name tag on a corpse and place the body in a body bag *US*
Vietnam war usage.
- — Linda Reinberg, *In the Field*, p. 214, 1991

tagger *noun*
a person who writes his signature in a stylised fashion on public walls, subways, etc *US*
- Taggers who simply tag are not graffiti artists. — Jim Crotty, *How to Talk American*, p. 143, 1997
- During one ceremony, more than 50 street taggers from the Kings with Style (KWS) were "jumped in." — Bill Valentine, *Gangs and Their Tattoos*, p. 109, 2000

tagging crew *noun*
a group of graffiti artists *US*
- We were a tagging crew [graffiti artists] and we would do gang banging [fight with other crews over wall turf] and other shit like that. — Terry Williams, *The Cocaine Kids*, p. 60, 1989

tag plant *noun*
a prison number plate manufacturing shop *US*
- The tag plant [license plate factory] reported missing metal. — Bill Valentine, *Gangs and Their Tattoos*, p. 11, 2000

tag shop *noun*
the area in a prison where number plates are manufactured *US*
- 7:30 A.M. Tag Shop men leave Wing for Shop upon call from Center. — Gresham M. Sykes, *The Society of Captives*, p. 138, 1958
- — William K. Bentley and James M. Corbett, *Prison Slang*, p. 13, 1992

Taig; Teague *nickname*
a Catholic *UK, 1971*
From the anglicised spelling of the Irish name/nickname *Tadhg*.
- These are among the things they said: "Taigs are getting knocked off. We don't care." "Fair play to the LVF." "The Taigs are like animals. They just want more and more, them and 20 wains." "They're stupid, Taigs". — *Irish Times*, 8th June 1998
- He's talkin' aboot Taigs tryin' tae get jobs. Why would a Taig work when he can scrounge aff the state in a country he despises? — Christopher Brookmyre, *The Sacred Art of Stealing*, p. 99–100, 2002

tail *noun*
1 the backside, buttocks and/or anus *UK, 1303*
- I've seen better tail on a mule. — Jim Thompson, *The Nothing Man*, p. 164, 1953
- Boy you beter get yo li'l tail in that room 'fore ya daddy catches you. — *Menace II Society*, 1993

2 a woman, regarded as a sexual object; women, collectively, categorised with the same regard *UK, 1846*
- You going to bring the tail over? — Bernard Wolfe, *The Late Risers*, p. 146, 1954
- "They ought to have a youth center in this burg," said Wally, "where a guy could pick up some tail." — Max Shulman, *Rally Round the Flag, Boys!*, p. 171, 1957
- I said, "I'm goin' downtown and get a little tail." — Bruce Jackson, *Get Your Ass in the Water and Swim Like Me*, p. 218, 1964

- "I don't know," Lundy said, "man's waiting to get shot he's got some tail with him." — Elmore Leonard, *Mr. Majestyk*, p. 151, 1974

3 an act of sexual intercourse or sexual intercourse in a general sense *UK, 1933*
The earlier, obsolete, senses of 'penis' and 'vagina' come together in a logical consequence.
- He played the ponies, got his tail, smoked cigarettes incessantly, despite his bad lungs, drank, sat up at all-night poker games. — James T. Farrell, *Saturday Night*, p. 12, 1947
- It must be easy to get tail with that car. — Irving Shulman, *The Amboy Dukes*, p. 52, 1947
- Innarested in a little tail t'night? — J.D. Salinger, *Catcher in the Rye*, p. 91, 1951
- He loves tail — Jonathan Thomas, *English as She is Fraught*, 1976
- MR. CHEEKY: Oh, yeah. My brother usually rescues me, if he can keep off the tail for more than twenty minutes. Huh. BRIAN: Ahhh? MR. CHEEKY: Randy little bugger. Up and down like the Assyrian Empire. — Monty Python, *Life of Brian*, 1979

4 a person who is following someone else closely and secretly *US, 1914*
- If he can get the killer to me you can bet your grandmother's uplift bra that he'll have a tail on me all the way[.] — Mickey Spillane, *I, The Jury*, p. 15, 1947
- Except that would have only worked if the booger could lose the tail they'd have on him. — Elmore Leonard, *Maximum Bob*, p. 312, 1991
- Nicky couldn't even go for a ride without changing cars at least six times before he could shake all his tails. — *Casino*, 1995

5 in prison, an informer *US*
- — Charles Shafer, *Folk Speech in Texas Prisons*, p. 216, 1990

6 the term of a prisoner's parole *US*
- "He has a six month tail." This means he has to serve six months on parole. — William K. Bentley and James M. Corbett, *Prison Slang*, p. 101, 1992

7 in hot rodding, a fox tail or racoon tail tied to the car *US*
- — Tom MacPherson, *Dragging and Driving*, p. 143, 1960

▸ bust your tail
to give the maximum effort *US*
- After busting his tail to get out here he wouldn't mind relaxing for a few minutes. — Elmore Leonard, *Out of Sight*, p. 23, 1996

tail *verb*
to follow someone closely and secretly *US, 1907*
- Pat knows you're too smart not to recognize when you're being tailed. — Mickey Spillane, *I, The Jury*, p. 15, 1947
- You didn't think the guy'd be smart enough to know he was being tailed. — *48 Hours*, 1982
- Look to see if he was being tailed, of course. — Elmore Leonard, *Maximum Bob*, p. 303, 1991

▸ tail 'em
in the gambling game two-up, to throw a pair of tails *AUSTRALIA, 1911*
- They hit the ground, and from every throat (if they are the same) comes the cry: 'He's headed 'em,' or 'He's tailed 'em.' — James Holledge, *The Great Australian Gamble*, p. 101, 1966

tail-better *noun*
in the gambling game two-up, a player who bets on tails *AUSTRALIA*
- [He] laid out twelve pounds like a tail better at two up in the middle of a trot. — Frank Hardy, *Legends From Benson's Valley*, p. 63, 1963
- Come on, move – before these tail-betters kill you. — John O'Grady, *It's Your Shout, Mate!*, p. 26, 1972

tail-end Charlie *noun*
someone at the rear of any group or expedition *UK, 1941*
Originally the name given to the rear gunner on a Royal Air Force bomber, hence 'the man at the back'.
- From my tail-end Charlie position I saw it all[.] — Chris Ryan, *Stand By, Stand By*, p. 85, 1996
- I was tail-end Charlie to the tough young bootnecks [marines]. — Duncan MacLaughlin, *The Filth*, p. 40, 2002

tailgate *verb*
1 to walk very closely behind another person *UK*
A variation of the conventional sense.
- [B]e particularly careful not to allow unauthorised access by tailgating you either on foot or by car. — *BBC*, 5th March 2003

2 to eat and drink clustered in parking lot before a sports event *US*
- — Connie Eble (Editor), *UNC-CH Campus Slang*, p. 9, April 1995

tailgunner *noun*
a homosexual male *NEW ZEALAND*
- — David McGill, *David McGill's Complete Kiwi Slang Dictionary*, p. 123, 1998

tailie *noun*
in the gambling game two-up, a player who bets on tails *AUSTRALIA, 1919*

tail lights *noun*
LSD *UK, 1998*
- — Mike Haskins, *Drugs*, p. 286, 2003

tailor *noun*
in gin, a win without the opponent scoring *US, 1950*
- — Thomas L. Clark, *The Dictionary of Gambling and Gaming*, p. 226, 1987

tailor-made; tailor; taylor *noun*
a factory-made cigarette *US, 1924*
- — Lou Shelly, *Hepcats Jive Talk Dictionary*, p. 19, 1945
- He picked up his Bull Durham sack from the dresser. He never smoked tailor-mades. — Willard Motley, *Let No Man Write My Epitaph*, p. 108, 1958
- Catching up either end of the cigarette paper, she rolled it into a slender cartridge, caught the ends with her tongue, licked the glued strip, and with deft movements of her fingers secured the tube – side, front, and back – crimping it expertly. "There!" she cried in a pleased little girl's voice. "Almost as good as a tailormade, hey?" — Ross Russell, *The Sound*, p. 20, 1961
- He says he was sittin' in a cell in a Southwest jail / where he landed doin' three days for vag. / A drunk came in, his eyes lit up like a hungry pup / as I handed him a tailor-made fag. — Bruce Jackson, *Get Your Ass in the Water and Swim Like Me*, p. 82, 1966
- You let your tailormade hang cool between tight lips, unlit, and when you talk, your voice is soft and deep. — Piri Thomas, *Down These Mean Streets*, p. 59, 1967
- [N]o one could possibly prefere it to the tailor-mades and pipe tobacco sold on the inmate canteen at retail prices[.] — Malcolm Braly, *On the Yard*, p. 46–47, 1967
- "What are these?" he yells at the top of his lungs after a con gave him five tailor mades. — Paul Glover, *Words from the House of the Dead*, 1974
- Why don't you roll me five joints? I bet your roll 'em they're like tailor-made. — Elmore Leonard, *Glitz*, p. 313, 1985
- — Angela Devlin, *Prison Patter*, p. 113, 1996

tail pain *noun*
anal pain *TRINIDAD AND TOBAGO*
- — Lise Winer, *Dictionary of the English/Creole of Trinidad & Tobago*, 2003

taily *noun*
the penis *US*
- — John A. Holm, *Dictionary of Bahamian English*, p. 201, 1982

taima *noun*
marijuana *UK, 1998*
Possibly an elision of Spanish *Tai*landés (Thai) and *mari*juana.
- — Mike Haskins, *Drugs*, p. 289, 2003

taint *noun*
the perineum *US*
- 'Tain't pussy, and 'tain't ass. — Ken Weaver, *Texas Crude*, p. 77, 1984
- Extra tip: Push on his t'aint while he's cumming. — Suroosh Alvi et al., *The Vice Guide*, p. 31, 2002

t'aint no crack, but a solid fact
what I am saying is the truth *US*
- — Kenn "Naz" Young, *Naz's Underground Dictionary*, p. 60, 1973

Taj Mahal *noun*
a dome covering radar antennae at NORAD air defence radar stations *CANADA*
- "Taj Mahal" is slang for the spherical domes covering the heavy radar antennae at any of the NORAD air defence radar stations. — Tom Langeste, *Words on the Wing*, p. 272, 1995

take *noun*
1 an opinion; a view *UK*
Possibly from television and film jargon, 'take' (a recorded scene), suggesting a point of view.
- I know that a lot of the match-heads [football fans] have got a bit of a take on me. — Kevin Sampson, *Outlaws*, p. 168, 2001
- [Princess Superstar's] take on hip-hop is an outsider's take. — *The Times Magazine*, p. 43, 16th February 2002

2 stolen property, especially money *US, 1888*
- [H]e was arrested soon after along with his father, Thomas Conway, and his uncle for three armed robberies. Their take was less than $1,400. — Pete Earley, *The Hot House*, p. 145, 1993

3 a theft *AUSTRALIA*
- — *The (Sydney) Bulletin*, 26th April 1975

▸ on the take
accepting bribes *US, 1930*
- I knew you were on the fucking take the minute you walked in. You still are. —Elmore Leonard, *Glitz*, p. 291, 1985
- —Angela Devlin, *Prison Patter*, p. 83, 1996

take *verb*
1 (of a male) to have sex with someone *UK, 1915*
- Joe smears cathie in tomato sauce and custard before taking her from behind in a desperate, loveless manner. —*Empire*, September 2003

2 to defeat someone *UK, 1939*
- [W]e'll be better prepared next week – and I think we can take them. —*The Guardian*, 8th April 2005

3 to successfully swindle someone *UK*
- —Gerald Kersh, *Clean, Bright and Slightly Oiled*, 1946

▸ take advantage
(of a man) to seduce someone, to have sex with someone, to force sex upon someone *US, 1928*
Euphemistic, but often jocular.
- "Nobody took advantage of me, Mother." "Then how did you get in this condition?" —Renni Browne and Dave King, *Self-Editing for Fiction Writers*, p. 162, 1994
- You took advantage of me, a little girl who was trusting and looked to you for protection. —Barbara Bean and Shari Bennett, *The Me Nobody Knows*, p. 117, 1997

▸ take apart
to absolutely defeat someone in a fight; to reprimand someone severely *UK, 1984*
- Achilles and his stupid family will just take him apart. And this time they won't aim for his chest. —Orson Scott Card, *Ender's Shadow*, p. 39, 2002

▸ take back water
to back down on a brag or dare; to refuse a challenge *CANADA*
This phrase is derived from rowing.
- It looked like he was going to take back water. —*Journal of American Folklore*, p. 343, October–December 1972: 'The LaHave Island general store'

▸ take care of
to kill someone; to kill one or more, especially as an expedient solution to a problem *UK, 1984*
- —Angela Devlin, *Prison Patter*, p. 112, 1996

▸ take for a ride
1 to swindle or deceive someone *US, 1925*

2 in a car, to take a planned victim to a convenient spot for murder *US, 1927*

▸ take in laundry
to wear underwear internally *UK*
- [W]e met the Queen in Berlin once. As she was getting into her car, she was taking in a bit of laundry – y'know, she pulled her knickers out of her crack. —*Drugs An Adult Guide*, p. 14, December 2001

▸ take it in the shorts
to be abused or defeated *US*
- —Michael Dalton Johnson, *Talking Trash with Redd Foxx*, p. 122, 1994

▸ take it lying down
to submit tamely *UK, 1961*
- [Deborah] Voigt, whose feistiness matches the generosity of her figure and the amplitude of her voice, has refused to take all this lying down. —*The Guardian*, 9th March 2004

▸ take it Nelson
to relax *UK*
- —Angela Devlin, *Prison Patter*, p. 112, 1996

▸ take on for the team
to accept responsibility for an unpleasant task for the greater good of a group *US*
Originally a baseball team, used as an ex post facto explanation of a batter advancing to first base after being hit with a pitch.
- —Pamela Munro, *U.C.L.A. Slang*, p. 119, 2001

▸ take one
to be open to bribery *UK*
- —G.F. Newman, *Sir, You Bastard*, 1970

▸ take one for the team
in a social situation, to pay attention to the less attractive of a pair of friends in the hope that your friend will have success with the more attractive member of the pair *US*
- —Connie Eble (Editor), *UNC-CH Campus Slang*, p. 4, October 2002

▸ take stoppo
to escape *UK*
Based on 'stoppo' (a getaway).
- [T]urn over (to search), stow the gear and take stoppo as soon as possible. —Charles Raven, *Underworld Nights*, p. 10, 1956

▸ take the biscuit
used in the context of surprise or annoyance at something which is remarkable or extraordinary *UK, 1907*
- H compromises by getting a blue film – is that what it looks like! I suspected it looked quite silly but ça prend le biscuit. —Henry Sloane, *Sloane's Inside Guide to Sex & Drugs & Rock 'n' Roll*, p. 57, 1985
- That takes the chocolate digestive, that does – being accused of shooting someone with a bottle of fizzy wine. —Dave Courtney, *Stop the Ride I Want to Get Off*, p. 318, 1999
- [Y]ou Brits take the sheer shagging biscuit. —James Hawes, *Dead Long Enough*, p. 262, 2000

▸ take the cake
used in the context of surprise or annoyance at something that is startingly improbable *US, 1900*
- Of all the old-fashioned, Chauvinistic, Victorian ideas ... that takes the bloody cake. —Petra Christian, *The Sexploiters*, p. 46, 1973

▸ take the cheese
to be considered in the most negative manner; in a figurative sense, to take the prize for being worst *UK*
- Well I t'ought I'd be hosin' down the lavvy tonight but this takes the cheese, says Joe scannin' the blood an' shit. —Nick Barlay, *Curvy Lovebox*, p. 155, 1997

▸ take the micky; take the mickey; take the mick; take the michael
to make fun of someone; to pull someone's leg *UK, 1935*
All variations of rhyming slang **MIKE BLISS; MICKY BLISS** (**PISS**); literal and euphemistic translations of **TAKE THE PISS**. The variations on 'mickey', 'mick' etc. may be given an initial capital.
- They're all the same them gits, sneering like. Taking the mickey out of other people all the time, like they was something special or something. —John Peter Jones, *Feather Pluckers*, p. 46, 1964
- So you ask Joyce and Vicky / if I ever took the mickey —Ian Dury, *Billericay Dickie*, 1977
- Are you by any chance extracting the Michael? —Beale, *A Dictionary of Slang and Unconventional English*, 1984
- You're too young for me, for one thing – my mates have been taking the mick about that. —Mary Hooper, *(megan)2*, p. 163, 1999

▸ take the piss; take the piss out of
1 to make a fool of someone; to pull someone's leg *UK*
To **PISS** and hence deflate a bladder gives the central idea of deflation, in this case by making a fool of; perhaps coincidentally an inflated bladder (on a stick) is the mediaeval comedy prop associated with a fool.

2 to implement a urine test *UK*
A literal pun on the sense 'to tease someone'.
- —Angela Devlin, *Prison Patter*, p. 113, 1996

▸ take the ta-ta kiss; take the ta-ta
to make a fool of someone; to pull someone's leg *UK*
Rhyming slang for **TAKE THE PISS**, formed on a goodbye kiss.
- —Ray Puxley, *Cockney Rabbit*, 1992

▸ take yourself in hand
(of a male) to masturbate *UK, 1953*
- [H]is unsated cockstand demanded alleviation. He took himself in hand, positive that he'd achieve more pleasure on his own[.] —Cheryl Holt, *Complete Abandon*, p. 111, 2003

take a little, leave a little
used as a description of the standing orders that carnival workers have for cheating customers *US*
- —Gene Sorrows, *All About Carnivals*, p. 23, 1985: 'Terminology'

take a running jump!; take a running jump at yourself!
used as a contemptuous expression of dismissal *UK, 1933*
- —John Ayto, *The Oxford Dictionary of Slang*, p. 276, 1998

take a train!
used as an all-purpose insult *US*
- You don't tell somebody to drop dead twice anymore – you kill 'em with 'Take a train'. —*Philadelphia Evening Bulletin*, 11th November 1951

takedown *noun*
the amount earned *US*
- —Steve Rushin, *Pool Cool*, p. 29, 1990

take down *verb*

to arrest and convict someone *US*

- He says he's gonna take him down if it's the last thing he does. — *Jackie Brown*, 1997
- The soldiers from the Empire broke his ribs and crushed his hands when they took him down[.] — Suroosh Alvi et al., *The Vice Guide*, p. 175, 2002

▸ **take someone down a peg**

to reduce a person's self-esteem; to force a brash or bumptious person to conform *UK*

- That's taken friend O'Mally down a peg or two I fancy. — Graeme Kent, *The Queen's Corporal [Six Granada Plays]*, p. 89, 1959

take-down brights *noun*

the very bright lights on a police car used when ordering a driver to pull over *US*

- Buddha Hast pulled alongside a car wash and the cruiser stopped twenty feet behind them, turning on its take-down brights and training a spotlight in the Volvo's rearview mirror[.] — Richard Price, *Clockers*, p. 395, 1992

take-homes *noun*

a several-day supply of methadone *US*

- Usually clients must come in every day for their dose; if they do not show evidence of illicit drug use for a certain period of time, between 6 months and a year depending on the program, they are eligible for take-homes. — Geoffrey Froner, *Digging for Diamonds*, p. 60, 1989

take it away!

commence the entertainment!; start the music! *UK, 1984*

take-man *noun*

the member of a criminal gang who actually steals the money *AUSTRALIA*

- — *The (Sydney) Bulletin*, 26th April 1975

take money *noun*

the proceeds of a robbery or other illegal scheme *US*

- Johnny could see the gun in one of the man's hands, and he could see the other one stashing the take money into a velvet pouch. — Donald Goines, *Inner City Hoodlum*, p. 102, 1975

take night to make day

used for describing an all-out effort *TRINIDAD AND TOBAGO, 1986*

- — Lise Winer, *Dictionary of the English/Creole of Trinidad & Tobago*, 2003

taken short *adjective*

desperate to urinate or defecate *UK, 1890*

- [I]t was a perfect image of M. Hulot, Tati's alter ego, who is inclined to lose his way, or be taken short in a crisis. — *The Guardian*, 17th May 1971

take-off *noun*

1 in a gambling operation, the amount of the bet money taken by the house *US*

- — *The Annals of the American Academy of Political and Social Sciences*, p. 132, May 1950

2 a mimicking impression; a parody *US, 1846*

- In the US I saw, on Saturday Night Live, a take-off of our own prime minister's question time[.] — *The Guardian*, 13th July 2000

3 in surfing, the catching of a wave and start of a ride *US*

- — Jim Allen, *Locked in Surfing for Life*, p. 196, 1970

take off *verb*

1 to use a drug, especially to inject a drug *US*

- Peewee had cooked the stuff and was ready to take off. — Hal Ellson, *The Golden Spike*, p. 20, 1952
- "Do you mind if I take off here?" he asked, pulling off his coat. I had never heard anyone else use this expression. For an insane moment I thought he was making advances. — William Burroughs, *Junkie*, p. 55, 1953
- They take off. They get high. — Willard Motley, *Let No Man Write My Epitaph*, p. 117, 1958
- In my building, on the roof I took off. — Jeremy Larner and Ralph Tefferteller, *The Addict in the Street*, p. 189, 1964
- So Pig told the other guy to give me some. Now this next old guy he took off again, and he told me, "I'll give you some now." And he fixed it up. — Henry Williamson, *Hustler!*, p. 68, 1965
- When he has finally injected the heroin (he calls it "shooting up," "taking off," "getting off"), he may or may not go on a "nod" – his eyelids heavy, his mind wandering pleasantly[.] — James Mills, *The Panic in Needle Park*, p. 15, 1966
- This guy Bobbie has took off 300 times. — Clarence Cooper Jr, *The Farm*, p. 192, 1967
- Hip stayed at a rented room with a junkie girl with whom he'd taken off, after using her spike and giving her a share of his stuff. — Nathan Heard, *Howard Street*, p. 137, 1968
- Jim was the only guy I knew that had a shooting gallery where you could cop a speedball by buying a half cap of girl and a half cap of boy and take it off right there. — A.S. Jackson, *Gentleman Pimp*, p. 98, 1973
- — Angela Devlin, *Prison Patter*, p. 113, 1996

2 to bring someone to orgasm *US*

- Are you telling me she says she took him off five times? — Jimmy Snyder, *Jimmy the Greek*, p. 212, 1975

3 to go; to leave *UK, 1959*

- And he sure took off in a hurry. He left behind a sack of groceries. — Michael Prescott, *Comes the Dark*, 1999

4 in surfing, to catch the momentum of a wave and begin a ride *US*

- — Jim Allen, *Locked in Surfing for Life*, p. 196, 1970

5 to rob a place; to steal something *US*

- I don't want nobody trailin me to my stash so's they can take it off. — Clarence Cooper Jr, *The Scene*, p. 104, 1960
- On the way I propositioned him to go back to the house and take the guy off. — Henry Williamson, *Hustler!*, p. 129, 1965
- He supported his habit by taking off (robbing) connections, and almost anyone else in the junkie world who appeared to have money. — James Mills, *The Panic in Needle Park*, p. 35, 1966
- — Eugene Landy, *The Underground Dictionary*, p. 181, 1971
- So the other kids would see them doing hard time and quit taking off the grocery stores and the old peoples' social security money so they could buy those Bosalinis and support their scag jones. — Elmore Leonard, *Switch*, p. 100, 1978
- I'd been taken off a couple of times, but there'd been no beef. — Herbert Huncke, *Guilty of Everything*, p. 2, 1990
- "He thought we were trying to take him off," I explained to Ann. — Clarence Major, *All-Night Visitors*, p. 179, 1998

6 to mimic or parody someone or something *UK, 1766*

▸ **take off a piece of work**

to masturbate *US*

- — Gary K. Farlow, *Prison-ese*, p. 72, 2002

take-off artist *noun*

an escaped prisoner *UK*

- — Angela Devlin, *Prison Patter*, p. 113, 1996

take on *verb*

to have sex with someone *US*

- But I have seen them, some guys, have to take on the whole place every time they're in there. — Bruce Jackson, *In the Life*, p. 374, 1972

take-out *noun*

in poker, the minimum number of chips that a player can buy from the bank at once *US*

- — Albert H. Morehead, *The Complete Guide to Winning Poker*, p. 275, 1967

take out *verb*

1 to kill someone *US, 1939*

- I took a few guys out and my rep was made. — Edwin Torres, *Carlito's Way*, p. 21, 1975
- A man by the name of Champ who packed a Walther P.38 thought he could handle Clement and Clement took him out. Remember? — Elmore Leonard, *City Primeval*, p. 118, 1980
- Yeah lets take these niggas out. — *Boyz N The Hood*, 1990
- That's the way I look at it. A choice between doin' ten years, and takin' out some stupid motherfucker, ain't no choice at all. — *Reservoir Dogs*, 1992
- I'm taking you out, Yahoo. — *Get Shorty*, 1995

2 to win a game, an award a prize or the like *AUSTRALIA, 1976*

- Fully Primed took out the final 15–5 after overcoming some stubborn early resistance. — *Flatball News*, p. 14, 1993

taker *noun*

a thief who snatches a chain from the wearer's neck *UK*

Recorded by a Jamaican inmate of a UK prison, August 2002.

takey-ah-ways *noun*

take-away food *NEW ZEALAND*

Pronounced with a mock Maori accent.

- — David McGill, *David McGill's Complete Kiwi Slang Dictionary*, p. 123, 1998

take you everywhere twice – the second time to apologise

used as a jocular reprimand to a companion who has just said or done something contrary to the accepted social code; or (replacing *you* with *him* or *her*) to the company at large, as a humorous acknowledgement of such a *faux pas* *UK*

- Gavin is always invited to conduct the orchestra at least twice – the second time to apologise! — *MusicWeb(UK)*, October 2002

take your pick *adjective*
stupid *UK*
Rhyming slang for **THICK**, possibly formed from the title of a television quiz show broadcast between 1955 and 68.
- Is he take your pick or what? —Ray Puxley, *Fresh Rabbit*, 1998

takkies *noun*
running shoes *SOUTH AFRICA*
- [T]he tracker, kneeling by a footprint in the red sand [said:] "I know this man from his takkies. He will come back." —John Simpson, *A Mad World, My Masters*, p. 335, 2001

takkouri *noun*
hashish *UK, 1998*
A corruption of Tunisian *takrouri* (hashish).
- —Mike Haskins, *Drugs*, p. 289, 2003

talala *noun*
the vulva and vagina *TRINIDAD AND TOBAGO, 1959*
- —Lise Winer, *Dictionary of the English/Creole of Trinidad & Tobago*, 2003

talc; talco *noun*
cocaine *US, 1984*
Another white powder as a metaphor.
- —Richard A. Spears, *The Slang and Jargon of Drugs and Drink*, p. 501, 1986
- —Mike Haskins, *Drugs*, p. 281, 2003

talent *noun*
1 a categorisation of sexually attractive people (within a given area), usually by heterosexual men of women and by homosexual men of men; occasional use by women increased in the 1990s *UK, 1947*
- [W]hat local talent there is, ah, to hand, as it were, is spread pretty bloody thin on the ground. —Mike Stott, *Soldiers Talking, Cleanly*, 1978
- I scoured the room looking for possible talent as Eric Clapton launched into 'Wonderful Tonight'. —Kitty Churchill, *Thinking of England*, p. 45, 1995
- There's enough talent in here for five years of non-stop wanking. —John King, *Human Punk*, p. 70, 2000

2 an intelligent, resourceful criminal *US*
- —Joseph E. Ragen and Charles Finston, *Inside the World's Toughest Prison*, p. 821, 1962: 'Penitentiary and underworld glossary'
- "Who hit him?" "Outta town talent. It was a specialist kind of job." —Richard Condon, *Prizzi's Honor*, p. 20, 1982

▸ **the talent**
in the entertainment industry, the actors, the performers *US*
- He paid the talent but said he couldn't pay the crew. —Robert Stoller and I.S. Levine, *Coming Attractions*, p. 93, 1991
- [A]s the TV presenter, Wilson chose to remain the talent, "the meat" as Americans call it. —Tony Wilson, *24 Hour Party People*, p. 212, 2002

talented *adjective*
attractive *US*
- —Connie Eble (Editor), *UNC-CH Campus Slang*, p. 8, March 1996

Tale of Two Cities; tale o' twos *adjective*
the female breasts *UK*
Rhyming slang for **TITTIE(S)**, formed from the title of Charles Dickens' novel, 1859. Often spoonerised as 'Sale of Two Titties'.
- —Julian Franklyn, *A Dictionary of Rhyming Slang*, 1960
- —Ray Puxley, *Fresh Rabbit*, 1998

Taliban *adjective*
given as a nickname to any eccentric or unconventional student, especially one of Arab ethnicity *US*
Teen slang, post 11th September 2001; from the Muslim fundamentalist government. The words 'terrorist' and 'fundamentalist' are also current as nicknames.
- If you're weird, people might call you "Taliban" or ask if you have anthrax. —*The Washington Post*, 19th March 2002

talk *verb*
1 to betray someone; to inform on someone *US, 1924*
- —Jay Robert Nash, *Dictionary of Crime*, p. 383, 1992

2 to have a sexual relationship in prison *US*
- —*Maledicta*, p. 136, Summer/Winter 1982: 'Dyke diction: The language of lesbians'

3 (used of a truck) to emit a clear sound from the smokestack *US*
- —Montie Tak, *Truck Talk*, p. 163, 1971

▸ **talk game**
to analyse the business of prostitution *US*
- To talk game is to discuss various aspects of pimping and whoring, such as how to maintain control over a woman, how to get more money out of a trick, how to steer clear of arrests, and so on. —Christina and Richard Milner, *'Black Players*, p. 37, 1972

▸ **talk noise**
to exaggerate; to lie *US*
- —Connie Eble (Editor), *UNC-CH Campus Slang*, p. 5, October 1986

▸ **talk shit**
1 to disparage someone or something; to exaggerate *US*
- Sometimes we used to sit on the stoop or up on the roof and talk to Johnny or just listen to him talk shit. —Claude Brown, *Manchild in the Promised Land*, p. 113, 1965
- I used to hang out in the bars just to hear the old men "talking shit." —H. Rap Brown, *Die Nigger Die!*, p. 30, 1969

2 to talk nonsense *US, mid-C20*
- "Look I'm..." "Talking shit!" —Kevin Sampson, *Powder*, p. 77, 1999

▸ **talk smack**
to disparage someone or something *US*
- DREXEL: Talkin' that smack, in my house, in front of my employees. Shit! Your ass must be crazy. —*True Romance*, 1993
- —Connie Eble (Editor), *UNC-CH Campus Slang*, p. 8, April 1997
- Ian Burnham likes to talk smack. It's not that he's a mean guy, but for the first three years of his volleyball career, it was the junior's only way to support his teammates. —*Daily Bruinn*, 7th February 2001

▸ **talk stink**
to malign someone or something *US*
Hawaiian youth usage.
- —Douglas Simonson, *Pidgin to da Max*, 1981

▸ **talk story**
to gossip; to engage in idle conversation *US*
Hawaiian youth usage.
- Siddown, relax, talk story wit' me. —Douglas Simonson, *Pidgin to da Max*, 1981

▸ **talk the hind leg off a donkey**
to talk until a listener is distracted; to talk persuasively *UK, 1915*
The surviving variation of many de-legged creatures: 'bird' (1929), 'cow' or 'dog' (1887), 'horse' (mainly dialect), 'jackal', etc.
- Talk a hind leg off a donkey? It's always a bonus if you can charm your way in and out of sticky situations. —*BBCi Nottingham*, 3rd July 2003

▸ **talk though your neck**
to talk nonsense *UK, 1899*
- The Great Man, Ezekiel decided, had been talking through the back of his neck – his advice sounded like the lyrics of popular songs[.] —Charles Johnson, *Oxherding Tale*, p. 88, 1995

▸ **talk through your arse; talk through your ass; talk out of your arse**
to talk nonsense *UK*
- For us it's brain, for them it's brawn. / Talk of Equality, talk through your arse / There'll always be First and Second Class[.] —Tasha Fairbanks, *Pulp*, 1985
- He was talking through his arse, of course, but Jimmy Sr gave him the answer he was dying for. —Roddy Doyle, *The Van*, 1991
- Corky, are you talking through your arse? —John Le Carre, *Night Manager*, p. 301, 1994
- Chest about as tight as that hole in your arse that you talk through[.] —M.C. Beaton, *Death of a Scriptwriter*, 1999
- Dave's talking out of his arse, as usual. —John King, *Human Punk*, p. 57, 2000
- So yewer talking out yer arse. – Again. —Niall Griffiths, *Sheepshagger*, p. 100, 2001
- [S]he was just imagining it and consequently talking out of her arse. —Christopher Brookmyre, *The Sacred Art of Stealing*, p. 240–241, 2002

▸ **talk through your hat**
to talk (ill-informed) nonsense *US, 1888*
- Tell it like it's not, and you're talking through your hat. Tell it like it is, and you're okay. —Robert L Genua, *Managing Your Mouth*, p. 7, 1993

▸ **talk to Ralph Beukler**
to vomit *CANADA*
- —Bill Casselman, *Canadian Sayings*, p. 143, 2002

▸ **talk to Ralph on the big white phone**
to vomit *US*
- —Pamela Munro, *U.C.L.A. Slang*, p. 83, 1989

▸ **talk to the canoe driver**
to perform oral sex on a woman *US*
- —Eugene Landy, *The Underground Dictionary*, p. 182, 1971

▸ **talk to the seals**

to vomit *US*

Surfer usage.

- — Vann Wesson, *Generation X Field Guide and Lexicon*, p. 164, 1997

▸ **talk trash**

to engage in aggressive verbal sparring; to speak offensively *US*

- She started talking trash through her hair. — Piri Thomas, *Down These Mean Streets*, p. 112, 1967
- — Hy Lit, *Hy Lit's Unbelievable Dictionary of Hip Words for Groovy People*, p. 39, 1968
- be it bad walking, trash talking, or throwing a baseball — *New York Times*, 12th May 1974
- They were trying to team play, but kept misreading each other. They talked trash, drank too much, and ended up losing five out of six hands. — Stephen Cannell, *King Con*, p. 1, 1997

▸ **talk turkey**

to speak candidly and openly about an important issue *US, 1903*

- Let's talk turkey here, how 'bout twenty-five thousand? — *Casino*, 1995

talk and walk *noun*

the practice of professing psychological improvement in a prison therapeutic setting to improve your chances of parole *US*

- — Eugene Landy, *The Underground Dictionary*, p. 182, 1971

talk at *verb*

to talk to someone *US*

The 'at' is a folksy affectation that decreases the formality of the statement.

- Good talking at you, man. — Elmore Leonard, *Be Cool*, p. 109, 1999

talkdown *noun*

the conversational technique used to guide an LSD user who is having a difficult time back to reality *US*

- — David Shenk and Steve Silberman, *Skeleton Key*, p. 251, 1994

talker *noun*

in the circus or carnival, a person who entices customers into the side show *US*

- — *American Speech*, p. 308–309, December 1960: 'Carnival talk'
- — Joe McKennon, *Circus Lingo*, p. 93, 1980

talkie *noun*

a film with sound; a film *US, 1913*

Mainly historical, as an opposite to silent films.

- When youse get dressed I thought we might take in a talkie. — Barry Humphries, *Bazza Pulls It Off!*, 1971

talking handbag *noun*

a portable radio *UK*

- — Angela Devlin, *Prison Patter*, p. 113, 1996

talking head *noun*

an expert guest on a television or radio news show *US*

- Though the hour is largely populated with the infamous "talking heads" that are supposed make documentaries dull, "Michigan" is in fact alarming and gripping. — *Washington Post*, p. B9, 4th October 1977

talking woman *noun*

a female performer who banters with the audience as she strips off her clothes *US*

- [T]he strippers have finally divided themselves into three classes: "fan-dancers," who keep up the pretense of hiding their nakedness as they enlarge it; "grinders," also known as bumpers and belly dancers, who feature undulations and various wiggles and "talking women," who utter sly, usually dirty observations about themselves and the customers, on animal subjects apropos of their anatomy as it is exposed bit by bit. — Jack Lait and Lee Mortimer, *Chicago Confidential*, p. 158, 1950

talkman *noun*

an electrical torture device attached to a prisoner's face *US*

Gulf war usage, punning on the Walkman™ portable music device.

- — *American Speech*, p. 402, Winter 1991: 'Among the new words'

talk of the devil!

said of a person who, while being spoken of, arrives unexpectedly; hence, an ungracious, though not necessarily unfriendly, greeting to that person *UK, 1666*

A shortening of the proverb 'Talk of the Devil, and he's presently at your elbow'.

- "Talk of the devil," Saladin pointed. "There the bastard goes." — Salman Rushdie, *The Satanic Verses*, p. 445, 1988

talk powder *noun*

any central nervous system stimulant *US*

- Nine fucking quarters you want for some of that talk powder. — *Drugstore Cowboy*, 1988

talk to the hand; tell it to the hand (because the face isn't listening); speak to the hand

used for expressing a complete lack of interest in what is being said *US*

Usually followed with 'because the face don't give a damn' or something in a similar vein, accompanied by a gesture of a raised hand, palm facing the other person.

- — Connie Eble (Editor), *UNC-CH Campus Slang*, p. 10, April 1995
- Fucking hell, what's that about? Talk to the hand 'cos the head ain't listening, y'know what I'm saying. — Dave Courtney, *Dodgy Dave's Little Black Book*, p. 34, 2001
- Tommy showed Tony the palm of his hand. "Tell it to the 'and 'cos the face ain't listening." — Ben Elton, *High Society*, p. 172, 2002
- — Stewart Lee and Richard Thomas, *Talk to the Hand*, 2003
- — Susie Dent, *The Language Report*, p. 82, 2003

talk-up *noun*

in sales and marketing, a raising of awareness and expectations *UK*

A jargon-like variation of 'praise'.

- Not only are we not throwing the track away as a loss-leader, we're giving its eventual,its inevitable release the best possible talk-up. — Kevin Sampson, *Powder*, p. 66, 1999

tall *adjective*

1 used of a jail sentence, lengthy *US*

- Dave, I've tried to help you out of this, but if you ask for tall time, I'm gonna file a motion to dismiss. — *A Few Good Men*, 1992

2 drug-intoxicated *US*

A play on **HIGH**.

- [T]he gauge they picked up on was really in there, and it had them treetop tall, mellow as a cello. — Mezz Mezzrow, *Really the Blues*, p. 75, 1946
- — Kenn "Naz" Young, *Naz's Underground Dictionary*, p. 60, 1973

tallboy *noun*

a 16 ounce can of beer *US*

- Joe-boy's crazy. He likes to set three tallboys next to each other, then put two regular cans on top of 'em, and then set one of them little six-ounce cans on top. Calls it a 'beeramid'. — Ken Weaver, *Texas Crude*, p. 64, 1984

tall grass *noun*

in circus and carnival usage, an extremely remote location *US*

- — Don Wilmeth, *The Language of American Popular Entertainment*, p. 269, 1981

tallie; tally *noun*

chiefly in Queensland, a tall, 750 ml bottle of beer *AUSTRALIA, 2003*

tall order *noun*

an excessive demand, a difficult thing to achieve *US, 1893*

- A third and equally controversial idea is to move the submarines, either by towing them or under diesel engine power, to a site where they could be hauled up on land and put in a "grave". This is a tall order given that the vessels weigh 9,000 tonnes[.] — *The Guardian*, 18th October 2003

tall poppy *noun*

an eminent, wealthy or successful person when viewed as needing deflation *AUSTRALIA, 1902*

- Cutting down the tall poppies is a particularly Australian expression – you rarely hear it in England or America. — Sandra Jobson, *Blokes*, p. 79, 1984
- I'd like to see a bomb go off in Parliament; I'd like to see a bullet hit a millionaire in the head. Lop a tall fucking poppy. — Peter Corris, *Pokerface*, p. 60, 1985

tall poppy syndrome *noun*

the habit of denigrating successful people *AUSTRALIA, 1983*

An outgrowth of the Australian's strong sense of egalitarianism and habit of siding with the underdog.

- — Robert G. Barrett, *Davo's Little Something*, p. 51, 1992
- To some extent Woodham has been a victim of the tall poppy syndrome, having his fair share of admirers as well as plenty of detractors among the prison officers he has commanded. — William Dodson, *The Sharp End*, p. 47, 2001

tall story; tall tale *noun*
an elaborate lie; an (enjoyable) exaggeration *UK, 1846*
- Klaus Manderfeld always was a great one for tall stories. —Charles B. Macdonald, *A Time fot Trumpets*, p. 95, 1985
- Albert Finney is Edward, a retired travelling salesman on his deathbed who has, all his life, regaled his son [...] with surreal tall tales of his early life as one of nature's "big fish"[.] — *The Guardian*, 23rd January 2004

tall wine *noun*
sex in which the woman below the man moves and keeps her buttocks up off the bed *TRINIDAD AND TOBAGO, 1986*
- —Lise Winer, *Dictionary of the English/Creole of Trinidad & Tobago*, 2003

Tally *adjective*
*Ital*ian *UK: SCOTLAND*
- Ye canny whack the real Tally ice-cream. —Michael Munro, *The Original Patter*, p. 68, 1985

tallywhacker; tallywacker *noun*
the penis *US*
- tallywhacker —John Trimble, *5,000 Adult Sex Words*, 1966
- [A] brief commercial opened with a full-body shot of an elephant, then zoomed in on the behemoth's tallywacker, which nearly filled the screen. —Jack Seward, *More About the Japanese*, p. 185, 1971
- What's he got – two tallywhackers? —Terry Southern, *Texas Summer*, p. 34, 1991
- Tallywacker —Erica Orloff and JoAnn Baker, *Dirty Little Secrets*, p. 90, 2001
- [S]cientists are trying to keep the mystery of the tallywhacker to themselves. —Richard Herring, *Talking Cock*, p. 27, 2003

tam *noun*
a knitted hat used by a Rastafarian to contain his dreadlocks *JAMAICA*
An abbreviation of conventional 'tam o'shanter'.
- "No tams allowed" was the dominant motif[.] —Tony Wilson, *24 Hour Party People*, p. 53, 2002

tamale *noun*
the vagina *US*
The imagery is of a savoury dish (originally from Mexico): a rolled pancake with a spicy filling.
- There's [a...] a "mushmellow," "a ghoulie," "possible," "tamale," "tottita," "Connie[".] —Eve Ensler, *The Vagina Monologues*, p. 6, 1998

tamboo bamboo *noun*
the penis *TRINIDAD AND TOBAGO, 1980*
An allusion to a musical instrument made from a length of bamboo.
- —Lise Winer, *Dictionary of the English/Creole of Trinidad & Tobago*, 2003

Tammie *noun*
a capsule of Tamazepam™, a branded sleeping pill *US*
- —Jim Crotty, *How to Talk American*, p. 97, 1997

tammy *noun*
a *tam*pon *UK*
- [J]am rags [sanitary towels] and tammys and fings like dat. —Sacha Baron-Cohen, *Da Gospel According to Ali G*, 2001

tamp *verb*
to walk *US*
- —Lavada Durst, *The Jives of Dr. Hepcat*, p. 3, 1953

Tampa; Tampa pilot *noun*
in shuffleboard, a hide disc on your side of the court near the apex of the ten *US*
- —Omero C. Catan, *Secrets of Shuffleboard Strategy*, p. 73, 1967: 'Glossary of terms'

tampax *noun*
filter-tipped cigarette(s) *UK*
From the similarity in appearance between the white tubes of manufactured cigarettes and Tampax™, a well-known brand of tampons.

tampi; tampee *noun*
marijuana *JAMAICA, 1975*
- Some call it tampee / Some call it the weed[.] —Peter Tosh, *Legalize it.*, 1976
- —Lise Winer, *Dictionary of the English/Creole of Trinidad & Tobago*, 2003

tamping *noun*
a beating *US*
- "He's got you figured for five tampings this last year," Red said. —Malcolm Braly, *On the Yard*, p. 213, 1967

tampon *noun*
1 a snobbish, unpleasant person *UK*
An allusion to the nature of tampons in the sense that they are all 'stuck up cunts', punning on 'stuck-up' (snobbish) and **CUNT** (an unpleasant person).
- "They're all a buch of tampons," his pal said. —Ian Rankin, *The Falls*, 2001

2 a fat marijuana cigarette *US*
- —Pamela Munro, *U.C.L.A. Slang*, p. 113, 1997

▸ **maybe your tampon will be flushed**
perhaps you will be feeling better; maybe your mood will have improved *US*
Note south Wales dialect *tamping* (angry).
- HEATHER DUKE: I don't know what your damage is, Veronica, but me and Heather are going to walk over to the Mall. Maybe by the time we head back your tampon'll be flushed. — *Heathers*, 1988

tampon dick *noun*
a contemptible man *UK*
- Oh fuck off, you idiot! Shithead! Tampon dick! —Bernadine Evaristo, *Lara*, 1997

tamp up *verb*
to beat someone physically *US*
- —Joseph E. Ragen and Charles Finston, *Inside the World's Toughest Prison*, p. 821, 1962: 'Penitentiary and underworld glossary'

tampy *noun*
marijuana *BAHAMAS*
- —John A. Holm, *Dictionary of Bahamian English*, p. 202, 1982

ta muchly
thank you very much *UK, 1969*
A deliberate solecism used for humorous effect.
- Borrowing a bob for the gas meter is now a speciality of the ram-raiding brethren, who leave you with a hole in the wall, two hanging wires and nary a note saying Ta muchly. —Andrew Nickolds, *Back to Basics*, p. 37, 1994

tan *verb*
1 to consume something voraciously; to do something briskly or with urgency *UK: SCOTLAND*
- We ferr [fair] tanned that hauf boatle [half bottle]. —Michael Munro, *The Patter, Another Blast*, p. 71, 1988
- [H]e says he's cool, but he's tanning the Ken, knocking back two pints for every one I'm drinking. —Paul Howard, *The Teenage Dirtbag Years*, p. 81, 2001

2 to burgle somewhere *UK: SCOTLAND*
- The polis say it's young boays thats tannin the hooses [houses] roon here. —Michael Munro, *The Patter, Another Blast*, p. 71, 1988

▸ **tan your hide; tan your arse**
to beat someone on the buttocks (as a punishment) *UK, 1670*
- [T]ipped him over her knee and tanned his arse[.] —Pat Barker, *The Eye in the Door*, p. 57, 1993
- If I ever see you sass her again, you will get your hide tanned. —Nora Roberts, *Finding the Dream*, 1997

T and A *noun*
visual depictions of sexually provocative females *US*
From **TITS AND ASS; TITS AND ARSE**.
- —Connie Eble (Editor), *UNC-CH Campus Slang*, p. 5, Spring 1993
- Beautiful Girls flashing T&A and BUSH! —Peter Sotos, *Index*, p. 116, 1996
- The material problems could, at least in part, be solved in the scuzzy offices of various T&A girlie magazines[.] —Mick Farren, *Give the Anarchist a Cigarette*, p. 332, 2001

T and T *verb*
to tape record and trace the origin of a phone call *US*
- Shane heard a click, so he knew the rest of the conversation was being T and T'd – taped and traced. —Stephen J. Cannell, *The Tin Collectors*, p. 322, 2001

tangerine dream *noun*
a type of MDMA, the recreational drug best known as ecstasy *UK*
Named after the colour of the tablet and after a German group that plays electronic, synthesized music.
- —Angela Devlin, *Prison Patter*, p. 113, 1996

Tangier tiger *noun*
a low grade variety of hashish from the foothills of the Rif Mountains *UK*
- —Nick Jones, *Spliffs*, p. 89, 2003

tangle *noun*

▸ **on the tangle**

drinking; on an alcohol binge *NEW ZEALAND, 1966*

- —Harry Orsman, *A Dictionary of Modern New Zealand Slang*, p. 136, 1999

tangle *verb*

to fight *US*

- —Judi Sanders, *Cal Poly Slang*, p. 10, 1990

▸ **tangle ass**

to brawl *US*

- —Hyman E. Goldin et al., *Dictionary of American Underworld Lingo*, p. 220, 1950
- I tangle-assed with Sabu from 104th Street and Flash from 110th Street, bad motherfuckers in the first degree, and it wasn't even my beef.—Edwin Torres, *Carlito's Way*, p. 13, 1975

▸ **tangle assholes**

to become involved in a confrontation *US*

- No calls reach Frank until six, 'cause that is Corinne's rule. I do not tangle assholes with Corinne.—George V. Higgins, *Penance for Jerry Kennedy*, p. 219, 1985

tanglefoot *noun*

1 strong, homemade whisky *US, 1860*

- Well, I slurped up another sample or two of the tanglefoot while I was about it – then I decided I'd better take some back home for home consumption, in case I felt a cold coming on[.]—Guy Owen, *The Flim-Flam Man and the Apprentice Grifter*, p. 41, 1972

2 barbed wire staked to the ground as a defensive perimeter around a military camp or base *US*

- —Gregory Clark, *Words of the Vietnam War*, p. 502, 1990

tango *noun*

a type of MDMA, the recreational drug best known as ecstasy *UK*

From the colour of the tablet; possibly an abbreviation of **TANGERINE DREAM**, or named after Tango™, a branded carbonated orange drink that, according to the product's advertising, has a surreal effect on all who drink it.

- —Angela Devlin, *Prison Patter*, p. 113, 1996

tango boat *noun*

an armoured landing craft *US*

- The tango boats moved in a straight line formation down the river.—Ronald J. Glasser, *365 Days*, p. 28, 1971

tango november *noun*

a token black soldier in an otherwise white unit or corps, especially the officer corps *US*

From the military phonetic alphabet 'TN', short for 'token nigger'.

- —Gregory Clark, *Words of the Vietnam War*, p. 516, 1990

tank *noun*

1 a jail cell, especially one in a local police station *US, 1912*

- SCENE: Packed jail cell generally called "the Tank" in cop talk.—Abbie Hoffman, *Revolution for the Hell of It*, p. 96, 1968
- Everybody in the tank knew that some one ... we knew what had happened.—Oscar Zeta Acosta, *The Revolt of the Cockroach People*, p. 113, 1973
- — *The (Sydney) Bulletin*, 26th April 1975
- It was Christmas Eve babe / In the drunk tank—The Pogues featuring Kirsty MacColl, *Fairytale of New York*, 1987

2 an intentional loss in a competition *US*

Originally boxing slang. Also called a 'tank job'.

- To them there is only two kinds of a fight: a tank and a double-cross.—Rocky Garciano (with Rowland Barber), *Somebody Up There Likes Me*, p. 276, 1955
- Some people are saying you're going into the tank.—*Raging Bull*, 1980
- Head-hunter Reuben – near-miss hooks moving back. Lazy Reuben, bored Reuben. A snap guess: tank job.—James Ellroy, *White Jazz*, p. 143, 1992

3 a room in the Pentagon where the Joint Chiefs and Staff meet jointly with the Operations Deputies *US*

- — Department of the Army, *Staff Officer's Guidebook*, p. 67, 1986

4 a safe *NEW ZEALAND, 1937*

- —Jim Ramsay, *Cop It Sweet!*, p. 88, 1977

5 a safe burglary *NEW ZEALAND*

Prison slang.

- — *NZWords*, p. 2, 2nd October 1999

6 of money, all you have with you *UK: SCOTLAND*

- Don't tell us that's yer tank? Here, Ah'll len ye a five-spot.—Michael Munro, *The Patter, Another Blast*, p. 71, 1988

7 an old and heavy surfboard *US*

- —Michael V. Anderson, *The Bad, Rad, Not to Forget Way Cool Beach and Surf Discriptionary*, p. 20, 1988

8 a heavy-set woman *TRINIDAD AND TOBAGO, 1964*

- —Lise Winer, *Dictionary of the English/Creole of Trinidad & Tobago*, 2003

9 an ugly girl *US*

- — *Current Slang*, p. 6, Fall 1966

10 money *UK*

Probably evolves from **TANKER** (a prizefighter who accepts payment to throw a fight in a fixed boxing match).

- —John McCririck, *John McCririck's World of Betting*, p. 61, 1991
- Could use the tank and all too just now, to be fair.—Kevin Sampson, *Outlaws*, p. 4, 2001

▸ **go in the tank**

used of an athletic contest, lost on purpose *US*

- So get in there tonight and take a dump, go in the tank.—Rocky Garciano (with Rowland Barber), *Somebody Up There Likes Me*, p. 255, 1955
- [T]he lore of betting in the United States has been rife with tales of tigers who went into the tank.—Jimmy Snyder, *Jimmy the Greek*, p. 77, 1975
- People think that every fight that was ever done was in the tank, that Liston went in the tank for Ali.—Bill Cardoso, *The Maltese Sangweech*, 1984
- She threw th' fuckin' case, went in the tank, intentionally bricked it.—Stephen J. Cannell, *The Tin Collectors*, p. 156, 2001

▸ **in the tank**

drunk *US*

- It was a refrain often heard at MacArthur Park choir practice when Spermwhale was almost in the tank, a fifth of bourbon of Scotch in the huge red hand.—Joseph Wambaugh, *The Choirboys*, p. 127, 1975

tank-ass *noun*

buttocks that are disproportionately large *US*

- —Don R. McCreary (Editor), *Dawg Speak*, 2001

tanked *adjective*

1 drunk or drug-intoxicated *UK, 1893*

Also used as 'tanked up'.

- She starts necking some bastard in the kitchen when she gets tanked up.—J.D. Salinger, *Nine Stories*, p. 117, 1953
- Then he made the mistake of getting tanked up once and coming late from town.—Rocky Garciano (with Rowland Barber), *Somebody Up There Likes Me*, p. 227, 1955
- I take off on weekends, maybe get tanked.—Max Shulman, *Guided Tour of Campus Humor*, p. 105, 1955
- I have a fine connection here, baby, and we'll get tanked on bees and pods and then I'll really show you a sex-scene.—John Rechy, *City of Night*, p. 184, 1963
- You don't know what those bastards are going to do when they get tanked up and horny.—Charles Whited, *Chiodo*, p. 205, 1973
- "He was tanked up." "The real Kelinfeld came out of that bottle[.]"—Edwin Torres, *After Hours*, p. 336, 1979
- "Fin!" she cried suddenly. "I got a flash for you. We're hammered. Smashed. Fried. Tanked."—Joseph Wambaugh, *Finnegan's Week*, p. 157, 1993
- Pull me down a bottle of Jack. I'm gettin' tanked tonight.—Quentin Tarantino, *From Dusk Till Dawn*, p. 2, 1995
- Lads all tanked up, people puking in the aisles.—Cath Staincliffe, *Trainers*, p. 59, 1999
- Two more came to join us at the bar: a tanked-up Scottish snooker star and his apologetic minder.—Diran Adebayo, *My Once Upon A Time*, p. 50, 2000

2 in computing, not operating *US*

- —Eric S. Raymond, *The New Hacker's Dictionary*, p. 343, 1991

tanker *noun*

1 a hired thug *UK*

- I felt sick. The Marquis of Gotham must have hired some tankers[.]—Jonathan Gash, *The Ten Word Game*, p. 121, 2003

2 a heavy drinker *CANADA, 1984*

From **TANK UP** (to drink).

3 a boxing match or other athletic contest that has been fixed *US*

- You know – tankers, fixed fights. You see the odds change before ringtime, and you know what's happened.—Rocky Garciano (with Rowland Barber), *Somebody Up There Likes Me*, p. 304, 1955

tanker wanker *noun*

someone who flies in air-to-air refuellers *UK*

A Royal Air Force term, formed by rhyming the airborne 'tanker' with an all-purpose pejorative; reported by Squadron Leader G.D. Wilson, 1979.

tankman *noun*
a safe-blower *AUSTRALIA, 1972*
- —Ryan Aven-Bray, *Ridgey Didge Oz Jack Lang*, p. 49, 1983

tank money *noun*
funds that are employed to give a fraudulent impression of substance or wealth *UK*
- Well, you've helped me out with tank money in the past. —J.J. Connolly, *Layer Cake*, p. 100, 2000

tank town *noun*
a small, unimportant town *US, 1906*
A possible railway etymology.
- What's a fast guy like you doing at a tank-town teacher's college? —Jim Thompson, *Savage Night*, p. 10, 1953
- In America he played tank towns like Waterbury, Mass, Springfield, Kingston and Albany and New York. —Babs Gonzales, *Movin' On Down De Line*, p. 52, 1975
- Any small community where a train stopped to take on water from an elevated storage tank was known as a tank town. —J. Herbert Lund, *Herb's Hot Box of Railraod Slang*, p. 110, 1975

tank tracks *noun*
in the Canadian military, folds that develop along the top of the official beret *CANADA*
- The "tank tracks" are so tough to get rid of. To wear a beret in proper "Monty-fashion," there should be no tank-tracks. —Tom Langeste, *Words on the Wing*, p. 273, 1995

tank-up *noun*
a drinking binge *NEW ZEALAND, 1959*
- —Harry Orsman, *A Dictionary of Modern New Zealand Slang*, p. 136, 1999

tank up *verb*
1 to administer fluids to a dehydrated hospital patient *US*
- —Sally Williams, *"Strong" Words*, p. 162, 1994

2 to consume large quantities of something, especially alcohol *US, 1902*
- Well, Doc had been in the hospital kitchen all morning goosing the nurses and tanking up on coal gas and Klim – and just before the operation he sneaked a double shot of nutmeg to nerve himself up. —William Burroughs, *Naked Lunch*, p. 29, 1957
- She got him tanked up on booze and coke 'til he passed out[.] —John Lescroart, *The 13th Juror*, p. 107, 1995

tanner *noun*
in pre-decimalisation currency, sixpence, 6d; a coin of that value *UK, 1811*
Inflation has rendered the conversion from 6d to $2\frac{1}{2}$p meaningless.
- Only last week I give that girl a pair of shoes cost me seventeen and a tanner, as God's my judge. —Norman Lindsay, *The Cousin from Fiji*, p. 188, 1945
- You could never tell whether your old man had a tanner or twenty quid in his pocket. —John Milne, *Alive and Kicking*, p. 30, 1998
- —Brian McDonald, *Elephant Boys*, p. 202, 2000

tanorexia *noun*
an addiction to sunbathing, especially by means of sunbeds *UK, 1997*
A punnning combination of 'tan' and 'anorexia' which sacrifices the meaning of anorexia for a journalistic tag.
- Tony, who is now 15, is one of a growing number of teenagers thought to be suffering from 'tanorexia'. —*The Observer*, 30th May 2004

tanorexic *noun*
a person who is addicted to sunbathing, especially by means of sunbeds *US, 1998*
- "Everyone sort of refers to me as slightly tanorexic," she said. —*Mansfield News Journal (Ohio)*, 2nd August 2004

tans *noun*
the standard US Army summer khaki uniform *US*
- —Gregory Clark, *Words of the Vietnam War*, p. 262, 1990

Tans *noun*
the Black and Tans *IRELAND*
- It was nearly dark by the time he was finished blowing up Crossley Tenders and plugging Tans. —Patrick McCabe, *The Butcher Boy*, p. 88, 1992

tantie *noun*
▶ **tantie come to town**
to experience the bleed period of your menstrual cycle *TRINIDAD AND TOBAGO*
- —Lise Winer, *Dictionary of the English/Creole of Trinidad & Tobago*, 2003

tanty *noun*
a tantrum *AUSTRALIA*
- But if you threw a tanty or two she'd do it, I reckon. —Kathy Lette, *Girls' Night Out*, p. 106, 1987
- 'No,' she said shortly, risking an enormous tanty from Mike. —Harrison Biscuit, *The Search for Savage Henry*, p. 67, 1995

tan valise *noun*
a blonde prostitute *US*
- The telegraphic doe is "black bag" for brunettes and "tan valise" for blondes. —Lee Mortimer, *Women Confidential*, p. 141, 1960

tap *noun*
1 a blow given or received in a fight *UK*
- —Angela Devlin, *Prison Patter*, p. 110, 1996

2 a murder *US*
- That tap was somebody else's. —Mickey Spillane, *Me, Hood!*, p. 16, 1963

3 in circus and carnival usage, the admission price *US*
- —Don Wilmeth, *The Language of American Popular Entertainment*, p. 269, 1981

tap *verb*
1 to borrow something, especially money *UK*
- I had been bell-hopping for something more than a year when Red tried to tap me for ten dollars. —Jim Thompson, *Bad Boy*, p. 368, 1953
- I'm the only one with any fags [cigarettes] left and they're all tapping off me[.] —Cath Staincliffe, *Trainers*, p. 61, 1999

2 to ask for, or imply readiness to accept, a tip *UK, 1961*
Used by ships' stewards.

3 to successfully attract a partner for sexual intimacy *UK*
- Craig and Quockie have tapped, it looks like. —Niall Griffiths, *Kelly + Victor*, p. 59, 2002

4 to have sex *US*
- Nobody ever tapped me. —Hal Ellson, *Duke*, p. 11, 1949
- —Malachi Andrews and Paul T. Owens, *Black Language*, p. 97, 1973
- I hear he's tapping Edie Finneran. —*The Usual Suspects*, 1995
- —Don R. McCreary (Editor), *Dawg Speak*, 2001

5 to kill someone *US*
- I remember ten years back when you were talking about killing a guy by that name. Did you tap him? —Mickey Spillane, *Me, Hood!*, p. 16, 1963

6 to intercept a telephone communication *UK, 1869*
From an earlier sense of intercepting a telegraphic message.
- Since when had freedom stooped to tap the phones of prostitutes? —Philip Wylie, *Opus 21*, p. 323, 1949

7 in poker, to bet all of your chips, or an amount equal to an opponent's bet, depending on context *US*
- —Oswald Jacoby, *Oswald Jacoby on Poker*, p. 138, 1947

▶ **tap the pot**
in bar dice games, to bet the total amount of the pot *US*
- —Jester Smith, *Games They Play in San Francisco*, p. 105, 1971

▶ **tap a kidney**
to urinate *US*
- Gonna go over t'that stand a'trees over there, and tap a kidney. —Stephen Cannell, *Big Con*, p. 267, 1997

tap city *noun*
when gambling, the position of being out of funds *US*
- "[W]e were both doing lousy on the Celtics" (he pronounced it sell-ticks) "and also on the Bruins, there, and he said he was also tap city[.]" —George V. Higgins, *The Judgment of Deke Hunter*, p. 217, 1976
- "I'm Tap City, Augie," I said. —James Ellroy, *Brown's Requiem*, p. 192, 1981
- —David M. Hayano, *Poker Faces*, p. 187, 1982

tap code *noun*
a method of cell-to-cell communication in a prison where talking is forbidden *US*
- —Ralph de Sola, *Crime Dictionary*, p. 148, 1982

tap dancer *noun*
1 a black person who curries favour from white people with obsequious conduct *US*
- —Stewart L. Tubbs and Sylvia Moss, *Human Communication*, p. 122, 1974

2 a delivery truck driver *US*
- —Montie Tak, *Truck Talk*, p. 165, 1971

tape and tuck *verb*
(used of a male) to tape your penis and testicles between your legs in an effort to pass as a woman *AUSTRALIA*
- —Thommo, *The Dictionary of Australian Swearing and Sex Sayings*, p. 128, 1985

tape dance *verb*
to buy a block of stock at a price slightly higher than the last price on the tape for that stock *US*
- — Kathleen Odean, *High Steppers, Fallen Angels, and Lollipops*, p. 137, 1988

tapioca *noun*
1 semen; an urgent need to ejaculate semen *UK*
The unsettling image of a hot milk-pudding.
- A day spent in a warm studio with a perfumed houri or two is bound to [...] send you home with a touch of the tapioca, I shouldn't wonder. — *British Journal of Photography*, 4th January 1980

2 a joker (the playing card) *UK*
Rhyming slang.
- — Ray Puxley, *Cockney Rabbit*, 1992

tapo *noun*
an inadvertent error in a taped message *US*
- — *American Speech*, p. 29, Spring 1982: 'The language of science fiction fan magazines'

tap-out *noun*
a complete depletion of funds, especially in gambling *US*
- And worse, he remembered Starkey's penchant to use his pistol to reverse a tap-out. — Iceberg Slim (Robert Beck), *Airtight Willie and Me*, p. 112, 1979

tap out *verb*
1 to run out of money, usually as a result of gambling *US, 1939*
- But if you're tapped out, if you really want that double dime note back? — Ross Russell, *The Sound*, p. 159, 1961
- Those dice the house was using had a Ph.D. Every ten minutes a chump would shuffle from the rear with a "tapped out" look on his face. — Iceberg Slim (Robert Beck), *Pimp*, p. 100, 1969
- "Five'll get you fifty he's tapped out before the next track season's over," Heath said. — Robert Campbell, *Juice*, p. 313, 1988
- But I was tapped right out. I didn't have a thing. — Herbert Huncke, *Guilty of Everything*, p. 107, 1990

2 in a casino, to relieve a dealer from duty *US, 1961*
- He had been a floorman at Tropicana, but he'd tapped out a dealer for looking away from the cards, and it turned out the dealer had more juice than he did, so listen to this, he got fired for doing his job. — Elmore Leonard, *Glitz*, p. 124, 1985

tapped *adjective*
▷ see: DOOLALLY

tapped-out *adjective*
having been emptied *UK*
A figurative use of 'tap' (to draw off liquid).
- I was so creatively and emotionally tapped-out that my only viable option was to get as fucked up as possible[.] — Mick Farren, *Give the Anarchist a Cigarette*, p. 319, 2001

tapper *noun*
1 a persistent borrower *UK*
- He was a "tapper", that is he expected the gang to give him money[.] — R. Samuel (Editor), *East End Underworld*, 1981

2 a boy who persists in asking a girl for a date when reason would dictate a strategic retreat *US*
Teen slang.
- — *Newsweek*, p. 28, 8th October 1951

3 someone who sells the police false or useless information in return for a small sum *UK*
- — John Gosling, *The Ghost Squad*, 1959

tappers *noun*
dice that have been loaded with mercury that shifts when the dice are tapped *US*
- — Frank Garcia, *Marked Cards and Loaded Dice*, p. 264, 1962

tap up *verb*
to approach someone with a proposal *UK*
- I'll admit that yes, I've been tapped up. — Kevin Sampson, *Outlaws*, p. 213, 2001

tar *noun*
1 coffee *US*
Citizens' band radio slang, from the colour rather than the consistency.
- — *Complete CB Slang Dictionary*, p. 90, 1976
- — Peter Chippindale, *The British CB Book*, p. 159, 1981

2 crude, dark, gummy heroin, usually from Mexico *US*
- The tar, or goma, as the Mexicans called it, looked like brown window putty and smelled like vinegar. — Joseph Wambaugh, *Fugitive Nights*, p. 35, 1992
- — Angela Devlin, *Prison Patter*, p. 113, 1996

3 opium *US, 1936*
From the colour and consistency of raw opium.
- — Angela Devlin, *Prison Patter*, p. 113, 1996

4 crack cocaine and heroin mixed and smoked together *UK*
- — Robert Ashton, *This Is Heroin*, p. 210, 2002

5 rum *TRINIDAD AND TOBAGO*
- — Lise Winer, *Dictionary of the English/Creole of Trinidad & Tobago*, 2003

6 a sailor *UK, 1676*
Probably a shortening of obsolete 'tarpaulin'.
- A winking, digital message to the effect that New Britain plc expects every Jack and Jill tar to do their duty? — *The Guardian*, 1st October 2003

tara; ta-ra; tarra; tra
goodbye *UK, 1958*
Originally northern, now more widespread through the agency of *Coronation Street* and other television programmes; possibly a slovening of TA-TA.
- "Ta-ra," Lynch said. — Troy Kennedy Martin, *Z Cars*, p. 29, 1962
- SECOND PRISONER: Remember me to the old woman, Charlie. FIRST PRISONER: Ta-ra, Charlie. — Troy Kennedy Martin, *The Italian Job [uncut script]*, 1969
- [T]a [thank you] for letting me say it. And ... tarra... (he smiles. OK?) — Mike Stott, *Soldiers Talking, Cleanly*, 1978
- "With the money you're paying you'll probably get Muhammad Ali. Tara, chief," said Terry as he headed for the door. — Anthony Masters, *Minder*, p. 58, 1984
- Just before the trial they filmed me saying ta-ra to all my mates[.] — Dave Courtney, *Stop the Ride I Want to Get Off*, p. 165, 1999
- DENISE: Tra Cheryl. MAM: Bye Cheryl — Caroline Aherne and Craig Cash, *The Royle Family*, 1999
- Ta-ra then. Hope the weather stays nice. — Mark Steel, *Reasons to be Cheerful*, p. 89, 2001

tar and feather; tar *noun*
a leather jacket *UK*
Rhyming slang.
- — Ray Puxley, *Cockney Rabbit*, 1992

Tara Palmer-Tomkinson; Tara Palmer; tara *noun*
a drama *UK*
Rhyming slang, formed from the name of a celebrity-socialite; generally applied to a minor inconvenience.
- You wouldn't believe the "Taras" I've had today! — *The Observer*, 10th December 2000
- — *Attitude*, July 2003: 'New palare lexicon'

tararabit
goodbye *UK, 1984*
A Liverpudlian elaboration of TARA (goodbye), thus 'goodbye [for] a bit'.

tar baby *noun*
a black person *US*
Offensive. From the *Br'er Rabbit* stories by Joel Chandler Harris.
- [H]e winked, just before the door closed, and told the black boys as they backed away form him, "You'll pay for this, you damn tarbabies." — Ken Kesey, *One Flew Over the Cuckoo's Nest*, p. 13, 1962

tar beach *noun*
a flat urban rooftop, used for sleeping or drug use *US*
- — William D. Alsever, *Glossary for the Establishment and Other Uptight People*, p. 32, December 1970

tardust *noun*
cocaine *UK*
A pun on STARDUST (cocaine).
- — Mike Haskins, *Drugs*, p. 281, 2003

tariff *noun*
1 the portion of a life-sentence to be served in custody *UK*
A nuance of the conventional sense.
- I overheard him talking to an acquaintance about his "tariff" [...] Only lifers had tariffs: he couldn't be, surely. — *The Guardian*, 13th June 200

2 the fee charged by a prostitute *TRINIDAD AND TOBAGO*
- — Lise Winer, *Dictionary of the English/Creole of Trinidad & Tobago*, 2003

Tarka *verb*
to have anal intercourse *UK*
Rhyming slang, based on the novel by Henry Williamson (1895–1977), *Tarka the Otter*, rhyming with '**DOT** her' (to have anal sex).
- Oi mate, did you Tarka? — *www.LondonSlang.com*, June 2002

tarmac *noun*
in Canadian military aviation, the ramp section of an air base hangar line *CANADA*
- "Tarmac" is a common British term for asphalt pavement, but in Canada it has become synonymous with the base ramp area. — Tom Langeste, *Words on the Wing*, p. 274, 1995

tarnation *noun*
used as a euphemism for 'damnation' *US, 1790*
- "What in tarnation is a folk-drama?" asked Doc. — Max Shulman, *Rally Round the Flag, Boys!*, p. 55, 1957

tarred *adjective*
drunk *BARBADOS*
- — Frank A. Collymore, *Barbadian Dialect*, p. 109, 1965

Tarrier *noun*
a Catholic, especially of Irish descent *UK*
- Wouldnae even offer Jock Stein – your greatest ever manager – a seat on the board 'cause he wasnae a Tarrier. — Christopher Brookmyre, *The Sacred Art of Stealing*, p. 101, 2002

tart *noun*
1 a woman *AUSTRALIA, 1903*
- He ain't going to no flamin' parties or gettin' mixed up with no flamin' tarts whatever. — Norman Lindsay, *The Cousin from Fiji*, p. 232, 1945
- I tipped my voice up like a tart's. — Robert S. Close, *Love Me Sailor*, p. 14, 1945
- That tart's been around, I tell yer. — Robert S. Close, *With Hooves of Brass*, p. 81, 1961
- We have a great time, me and Simmo. And the tarts! — Alexander Buzo, *Rooted*, p. 90, 1969
- Poor little tart, she was like one of us, really – all the things she had to put up with. — Ward McNally, *Supper at Happy Harry's*, p. 106, 1982

2 a promiscuous woman *UK, 1887*
- [T]hey'd all been with little tarts who'd get behind a back fence with any boy. — Ruth Park, *Poor Man's Orange*, p. 184, 1949

3 a prostitute *UK, 1894*
- 'For heaven's sake, Jess, do open a window or two; the place stinks like a tarts' shop.' — George Johnston, *My Brother Jack*, p. 110, 1964

4 a girlfriend or sweetheart *UK, 1864*
- — Barbara Baynton, *Trooper Jim Tasman*, p. 91, 1917
- If my tart had a bun in the oven I'd flamin' stick with her!!! — Barry Humphries, *The Wonderful World of Barry McKenzie*, p. 46, 1968

5 a wife or female partner *UK, 1864*
Rhyming slang for 'sweetheart'.
- Y'think about feedin' the kids, an' payin' the rent, an' the effect it's havin' on y'tart[.] — Alan Bleasedale, *Boys From the Blackstuff*, 1982

6 a weak, ineffectual man *UK*
A term of abuse, used to call a man a woman; a wider gender-only sense of 'tart' than when applied to a woman.
- With the doors safely shut, they crowd up against the window and give us the wankers sign and the two-finger salute. Tarts. — Martin King and Martin Knight, *The Naughty Nineties*, p. 54, 1999

tartan *noun*
cocaine *UK*
Etymology unknown.
- That's the way it is with the tartan and all, too. I could've got rich through tartan, easy. — Kevin Sampson, *Outlaws*, p. 66, 2001

tartan banner *noun*
a sixpenny coin; sixpence *UK*
Rhyming slang for **TANNER** that dropped out of circulation after decimalisation in 1971.
- — Julian Franklyn, *A Dictionary of Rhyming Slang*, 1960

tartanize *verb*
to adapt an English product for Scottish use or sale; hence, the adjective: tartanized *UK*
- — *The Message*, 16th July 2004

tarted-up *adjective*
1 dressed like a prostitute; dressed smartly *UK*
- — Christopher Buckley, *Rain Before Seven*, 1947
- Saskia Butler as the tarted-up schoolgirl in GamePlan [by Alan Ayckbourn] who can't wait to exit from her basque. — *The Guardian*, 9th September 2002

2 of a thing, business, building, etc, having a new image or presentation *UK, 1984*
Often derogatory in tone.
- Two of the shopping arcades had been nicely tarted up and there was now a McDonald's[.] — Bill Bryson, *Notes from a Small Island*, p. 72, 1995
- [T]heir wrappings not in any way tarted up, no attempt to rewrap them at all, or identify them. — *The Guardian*, 12th June 2003

tart fuel *noun*
bottled alcopop (branded alcoholic beverage with the characteristics of a soft drink) or other alcoholic drinks deemed to be for feminine consumption *UK, 2002*
A fashionable drink amongst young women who it is suggested/hoped by the coiner of this term that they relax their moral standards and behave promiscuously when drunk.
- — *www.LondonSlang.com*, June 2002

tart's delight *noun*
a frilly, fussy, looped-up way of hanging lace curtains at windows *UK, 1980*

tart's fart *noun*
used as a comparitive measure of little or negligible worth *UK*
- Research that isn't worth a tart's fart to anyone else on earth. — James Hawes, *White Powder, Green Light*, p. 21, 2002

tart up *verb*
to dress someone up or decorate something smartly *UK, 1952*
Often with the implication of tastelessness or tawdriness.
- [T]hen send him back to Kansas City in time for a Hollywood hack screenwriter to come in and tart up the story. — Clancy Sigal, *Going Away*, p. 206, 1961
- Well, what happens is that she gives me the brutally frank version and I sort of tart it up for them. — *This is Spinal Tap*, 1984
- Even after they tried to steal a page from the film studios and tarted up the dining room ... the quality of the food, if anything, went down instead of up. — Robert Campbell, *Alice in La-La Land*, p. 44, 1987
- The dykes were as tarted up as they could get, with black pants or levis, and white go go boots. — Jennifer Blowdryer, *White Trash Debutante*, p. 52, 1997

tarty *adjective*
like a prostitute *UK, 1918*
- [R]abbis with their trousers down, tarty women lying spreadeagled and saying, "You wanna fuck already?" — Bill Bryson, *The Lost Continent*, p. 144, 1990

Tarzan *noun*
1 sex outdoors *US*
- Studs in New York, particularly those working the Public Library and Bryant Park areas, call a frantic quickie in the bushes a "jungle job" or a "Tarzan." — Johnny Shearer, *The Male Hustler*, p. 17, 1966

2 a soldier who is overly anxious to take the highly visible and dangerous point position on a combat march *US*
- — Linda Reinberg, *In the Field*, p. 215, 1991

▸ **like ten Tarzan**
quickly; loudly *TRINIDAD AND TOBAGO, 1984*
- — Lise Winer, *Dictionary of the English/Creole of Trinidad & Tobago*, 2003

tash; tache *noun*
a moustache *UK, 1893*
- That's like painting a tash on the Mona Lisa. Bloody disgrace. — Bernard Dempsey and Kevin McNally, *Lock, Stock... & Two Sips*, p. 299, 2000

tashered *adjective*
drunk *UK*
- — *e-cyclopaedia*, 20th March 2002

tash test *noun*
a man's moustache seen as an indicator of homosexuality and, hence, predictive of HIV status *UK*
Formed from **TASH** (a moustache). A medical observation that, hopefully, was more witty than practical.
- — Adam T. Fox, St Mary's Hospital, London, 10th October 2002

task *noun*
in prison, an act of masturbation *UK*
- — Angela Devlin, *Prison Patter*, p. 113, 1996

Tasmaniac *noun*

a person from Tasmania *AUSTRALIA, 1867*

- —Arthur Chipper, *The Aussie Swearer's Guide*, p. 69, 1972
- Tasmaniacs getting their summer clothes, of many years gathering, out of the mothballs. — *www.suite101.com*, 1999
- You can call us Tasmanians or Taswegions. Just don't call us Tasmaniacs, OK? — *www.suite101.com*, 2001
- Did you hear the one about the mainlander who...? Jokes at the Mainlanders expense...The Tasmaniacs have a go at the rest of the country to get back for all the Tassie jokes about kissing cousins with six fingers and two heads. — *www.abc.net.au*, 2001
- Like thousands of other Tasmaniacs I went along to see them[.] — *www.lifestreams.org*, 2001

Tasmanian Tiger *noun*

a strain of marijuana, known elsewhere as New Zealand green, Thai Buddha and Hawaiian head *AUSTRALIA*

- These buds are the gooiest, most resin-soaked things I've ever seen [...] "What are they?" "Tasmanian Tiger." —Brian Preston, *Pot Planet*, p. 96, 2002

Tasmanian yawn *noun*

vomiting, especially when experienced crossing the Tasmanian Sea *AUSTRALIA*

- —Maureen Brooks and Joan Ritchie, *Tassie Terms*, p. 148, 1995

tassel dance *noun*

a sexual dance focused on the woman's breasts and the tassels worn attached thereto *US*

- Carrie Finnell, for example, performed the first 'Tassel Dance' on a Minksy runway. —William Green, *Strippers and Coochers*, p. 163, 1977

tassie *noun*

an intaglio (an engraved figure or design) *UK*

Used by antique dealers.

- —Jonathan Gash, *The Judas pair*, 1977

Tassie *noun*

1 Tasmania *AUSTRALIA, 1892*

- —Barry Humphries, *A Nice Night's Entertainment*, p. 9, 1956
- —Jim Ramsay, *Cop It Sweet!*, p. 88, 1977
- The last month has seen a spate of thieving hit Tassie. — *Tracks*, p. 140, October 1992

2 a Tasmanian *AUSTRALIA, 1914*

- —Maureen Brooks and Joan Ritchie, *Tassie Terms*, p. 149, 1995

taste *noun*

1 an alcoholic drink *US, 1919*

- "Well, Marie, you buying me a taste is righteous and perhaps I'll be able to hip you to something else you can buy me." —A.S. Jackson, *Gentleman Pimp*, p. 74, 1973
- After all, they were part of a unique police experiment and a guy needed a taste or two when he'd been stumbling around for hours out there in the black of night[.] —Joseph Wambaugh, *Lines and Shadows*, p. 103, 1984

2 a sample *US*

- For Christmas. Your share. It's just a taste. — *Goodfellas*, 1990

3 a small sample of drugs, especially heroin *US*

- Okay, so you're off it, but a little bit won't hurt. Just a taste. —Hal Ellson, *The Golden Spike*, p. 29, 1952
- I got a little taste here. —Willard Motley, *Let No Man Write My Epitaph*, p. 149, 1958
- "If I could just get a taste," Fay said. —Alexander Trocchi, *Cain's Book*, p. 37, 1960
- At the moment, like Sammy, he had only a chippy, and got most of the heroin he needed by hanging around other addicts who occassionally turned him on with a taste[.] —James Mills, *The Panic in Needle Park*, p. 35, 1966
- He's got the works, gives you sweet taste. —Velvet Underground *I'm Waiting for the Man*, 1967
- Did you say sometin' 'bout havin' a taste? —Odie Hawkins, *Ghetto Sketches*, p. 24, 1972
- Man, if he's got any morphine, we can do some business with him. Maybe we can get a little taste out of him. —Herbert Huncke, *Guilty of Everything*, p. 69, 1990
- —Robert Ashton, *This Is Heroin*, p. 210, 2002

taste-face *noun*

a heroin user who lends his syringe to others in return for small amounts of heroin *US*

- A taste-face is an addict who loans out his works (syringe, needle) for some of the borrower's H. —Burgess Laughlin, *Job Opportunities in the Black Market*, p. 4, 1978

-tastic *suffix*

used as an intensifier *US*

On the model of **POPTASTIC**.

- I was ready to start my cock-tastic voyage in earnest. —Richard Herring, *Talking Cock*, p. 20, 2003
- —Connie Eble (Editor), *UNC-CH Campus Slang*, p. 10, November 2003

tasty *adjective*

1 attractive, sexually appealling *UK, 1899*

- What's he like Mavis? He's a real tasty geezer. —The Piglets (Jonathan King), *Johnny Reggae*, 1971
- Your martinis [arms] look really nice in that frock, Albert. Tasty. Fancy a quick hoover d'amour [oral sex]? —the cast of 'Aspects of Love', Prince of Wales Theatre, *Palare (Boy Dancer Talk) for Beginners*, 1989–92
- Why, hello, my dear... What's a nice... plump... tasty-looking little thing like you doing in the middle of the deep, dark forest? —Susan Blu and Molly Ann Mullin, *Word of Mouth*, p. 90, 1996

2 worthwhile; valuable; exhibiting strength *UK, 1975*

- "You must be a bit tasty to get that knife off 'im." Brad liked the thought of being "tasty". —Colin Butts, *Is Harry on the Boat?*, p. 242, 1997
- [A] tastier West Ham mob appears and steams straight in. —Martin King and Martin Knight, *The Naughty Nineties*, p. 93–94, 1999
- Her brother's dealing [drugs] so we can always get hold of something tasty. —Cath Staincliffe, *Trainers*, p. 57, 1999
- Now these lads are fucking tasty, they are. —Kewvin Sampson, *Outlaws*, p. 52, 2001
- [A]n hour and a half of fairly tasty stand-up. —Frank Skinner, *Frank Skinner*, p. 4, 2001

3 competent; polished *IRELAND*

The term can be applied to either the work or the person who did it.

- He's very tasty. —Terence Dolan, *A Dictionary of Hiberno-English*, 1999 (REPT)

4 used of a known, especially well-respected criminal; capable of physical violence *UK, 1975*

- [T]he party piece for many a tasty geezer is to recite Michael Caine's brutal dialogue [from 'Get Carter', 1971] – 'You're a big man but you're in bad shape. With me, it's a full-time job.' — *The Observer*, 13th June 1999

5 having a pleasing flavour; appetising *UK*

In conventional use from the early 1600s; by mid-C19 considered colloquial.

- some tasty-looking chocolate and hazelnut biscuits — *The Guardian*, 23rd May 2001
- [F]resh in its own hermetically sealed biodegradable packaging. Nutritious and tasty, too. —Jasper Fforde, *The Eyre Affair*, p. 115, 2003

Taswegian *nickname*

a person from Tasmania *AUSTRALIA, 1961*

Blend of *Tas*mania and Nor*wegian*.

- —Jim Ramsay, *Cop It Sweet!*, p. 88, 1977

tat *noun*

1 an article, or collection of articles, of inferior or rubbishy quality; odds and ends of material *UK, 1951*

The spelling 'tatt' is also used.

- She turned out a whole mess of old tatt[.] —Ngaio Marsh, *Death at the Dolphin*, 1967
- For instance, that bundle of rags, it may seem a useless load of old tat, but we'll take it off you. —Barry Took and Marty Feldman, *Round The Horne*, March 1968
- Well, they're hardly the normal ill-judged tat that you give me, sweetie. —Jennifer Saunders, *Absolutely Fabulous*, p. 110, 1992
- Hercules, chewer of hay and puller of tat, was really something more than a horse. —Stuart Jeffries, *Mrs Slocombe's Pussy*, p. 298, 2000

2 a tattoo *US*

- It's a tiered tat. When I get some more cash I'm gonna color it in and put some leather chaps on the Reaper. — *Airheads*, 1994
- Darryl came back at him, saying, "Oh, your people never decorate themselves?" "Some tats, yeah, but black guys have 'em too." —Elmore Leonard, *Be Cool*, p. 44, 1999
- Holstein glanced at Pike's shoulder tats, then his face. —Robert Crais, *L.A. Requiem*, p. 38, 1999
- [B]lokes with prison tats concentrating very, very hard indeed[.] —John Williams, *Cardiff Dead*, p. 123, 2000

3 a swindle featuring dice and doubled bets *US*

- The tat, with its rapidly doubling bets, is murder on a fool. —Jim Thompson, *The Grifters*, p. 36, 1963

tata *noun*

nonsense *TRINIDAD AND TOBAGO, 1990*

- —Lise Winer, *Dictionary of the English/Creole of Trinidad & Tobago*, 2003

ta-ta
goodbye *UK, 1823*
At first chiefly nursery, now (in the US) simply highly affected.
- ROSE: [...] And don't bang the door. She kisses him. GRAHAM: Ta-ta, Mum. [Bang] —Alexander Baron, *A Bit of Happiness [Six Granada Plays]*, p. 203, 1959
- "God bless," said Father Paddy. "Ta-ta," said Prue. —Armistead Maupin, *Further Tales of the City*, p. 181, 1982
- [S]ay ta-ta to Ticky and her squire[.] —Kevin Sampson, *Powder*, p. 19, 1999

ta-tas *noun*
the shakes *AUSTRALIA, 1977*
- —Jim Ramsay, *Cop It Sweet!*, p. 88, 1977
- There's nothing wrong with his nerves. I've got the ta-tas from watching him. —Sam Weller, *Old Bastards I Have Met*, p. 47, 1979
- —Ryan Aven-Bray, *Ridgey Didge Oz Jack Lang*, p. 47, 1983

tatas *noun*
the female breasts *US*
- Boobs, zonkers, headlights, watermelons, sweater puppies, pointers, knockers, jugs, tatas – these are some of the words to describe women's breasts. —Howard Stern, *Miss America*, p. 441, 1995

Tate and Lyle *noun*
style *UK*
Rhyming slang, formed from the company that describes itself as 'world leader in carbohydrate ingredients'.
- You've got some Tate & Lyle you have. —Ray Puxley, *Cockney Rabbit*, 1992

tater; tatur; tottie *noun*
a potato *UK, 1759*
- [Y]ou've just spent the last ten minutes picking your totties oot the gutter in the pouring rain[.] —Ian Pattison, *Rab C. Nesbitt*, 1988
- When I left school I had a job delivering taters. —Bernard Dempsey and Kevin McNally, *Lock, Stock ... & Two Hundred Smoking Kalashnikovs*, p. 110, 2000

tatered *adjective*
drunk *US*
- —Judi Sanders, *Faced and Faded, Hanging to Hurl*, p. 40, 1993

taters *noun*
the buttocks *US*
- —Connie Eble (Editor), *UNC-CH Campus Slang*, p. 12, Fall 1999

taters in the mould; potatoes in the mould; taters *adjective*
cold *UK, 1934*
Rhyming slang, most commonly used as 'taters'.
- It looks like it's going to Andy Cain and we don't want you getting potatoes in the mould [cold] — *The Sweeney*, p. 9, 1976
- [T]hose who are taters in the mould; those without any in the nude [food] at all[.] —Ronnie Barker, *Fletcher's Book of Rhyming Slang*, p. 39, 1979

tats *noun*
dice, especially loaded dice or dice marked for cheating *UK, 1688*
- —John S. Salak, *Dictionary of Gambling*, p. 257, 1963
- We need to get ahold of 'Fit-Throwing Duffy.' He's the best tat player in the family. —Stephen Cannell, *King Con*, p. 119, 1997

TATT
(in doctors' shorthand) *t*ired *a*ll *t*he *t*ime *UK*
- —Adam T. Fox, St Mary's Hospital, London, 10th October 2002

tatted *adjective*
tatooed *US*
- —Judi Sanders, *Cal Poly Slang*, p. 10, 1990

tatting down *noun*
an act of tidying away possessions and making ready for travel *UK*
Used by late 1980s – early 90s counterculture travellers.
- —Martin Roach, *Dr. Marten's Air Wair*, 1999: 'Glossary of travellers' terms'

tattletale *noun*
1 in trucking, a device that records time and speed data, used by company officials to assure compliance with laws and regulations *US*
Known conventionally as a 'tachograph'.
- —*American Speech*, p. 272, December 1962: 'The language of traffic policemen'
- —Montie Tak, *Truck Talk*, p. 165, 1971

2 in motor racing, a specially designed tachometer that measures and records the engine's highest speed during a run or lap *US*
- —John Lawlor, *How to Talk Car*, p. 105, 1965

3 in trucking, a dangling chain that shows the approximate weight of the load by its distance from the axle *US*
- —*American Speech*, p. 273, December 1961: 'Northwest truck drivers' language'

Tatts *nickname*
1 Tattersalls (a racecourse enclosure) *UK*
- We have seen a bewhiskered clown desecrate Tatts almost daily on Channel Four's racing coverage. (Racing Post) —John McCririck, *John McCririck's World of Betting*, p. 8, 1991

2 a lottery originally run from Tattersall's Hotel, Sydney *AUSTRALIA, 1916*
- 'Feeling better?' 'Like first Prize in Tatts.' —Eric Lambert, *The Veterans*, p. 204, 1954
- 'You don't look like a man that's just won Tatts,' she said, still laughing. —John Morrison, *Stories from the Waterfront*, p. 88, 1957
- —Kerry Cue, *Crooks, Chooks and Bloody Ratbags*, p. 111, 1983

tatty *adjective*
shabby, tawdry *UK, 1933*
- "It's a tatty little flat," added the lieutenant, "but it's in a colorful neighborhood[.]" —Armistead Maupin, *Babycakes*, p. 77, 1984

tatty-bye
goodbye *UK, 1980*
Probably a conflation of **TA-TA** and 'bye!'. Popularised by Liverpool comedian Ken Dodd (b.1929); in widespread use by the mid-1970s.
- JOHNNY: Well ... Tatty-bye, Bri. (He walks off. BRIAN watches him go.) —Mike Leigh, *Naked*, 1988
- "Tatty-bye," she said. "Sure and see you get good marks in the class[.]" —Andrew O'Hagan, *Our Fathers*, p. 25, 1999

taury rope *noun*
the Pope *UK: SCOTLAND*
Glasgow rhyming slang, formed on Scottish dialect for 'tarry rope'.
- When wis it the aul taury rope wis at Bellahouston Park? —Michael Munro, *The Patter, Another Blast*, 1988

taw; toy *noun*
in marbles, a marble used for shooting *UK, 1709*
- If Babe's "toy" – the marble you shoot with – would kiss or hit the toy closest to the line, Babe would automatically have first shot at the fish shape full of marbles. —Bobby Seale, *A Lonely Rage*, p. 31, 1978

tawny *adjective*
excellent *US*
- —Kenn "Naz" Young, *Naz's Dictionary of Teen Slang*, p. 115, 1993

tax; taxing *noun*
the fee paid to enter a crack house *US*
- —Terry Williams, *Crackhouse*, p. 152, 1992

tax *verb*
1 to steal something; to rob somewhere *UK*
- [H]e discreetly checked out various books on the mechanics of pistols, ripping out the relevant pages. By fortunate coincidence he had taxed a page illustrated with a construction diagram of a Colt 45[.] —Donald Gorgon, *Cop Killer*, p. 62, 1994

2 to steal valuables from vehicles that are waiting at traffic lights *UK*
- —Angela Devlin, *Prison Patter*, p. 113, 1996

3 in Montreal, to forcibly confront and force someone to hand over money, jewellery or clothes *CANADA*
- Being challenged to an after school fight, being taxed of clothing, jewelry, and money – these are some sensitive issues that are addressed in Senshido's Young Adult Protection Program. —*senshido.com*, 2002

4 in prison, to extort money or other payment such as tobacco from a weaker prisoner by threat of violence *UK*
- —Angela Devlin, *Prison Patter*, p. 113, 1996

5 to tease or berate someone *US*
- —Don R. McCreary (Editor), *Dawg Speak*, 2001

taxi *noun*
a call girl *INDIA*
Glossed as 'Colloquialism used in the appropriate urban circles for a prostitute who operates at a place required by her clients[.]' by Nigel Hankin, *Hanklyn-Janklyn*, 2003.

taxi bit *noun*
a prison sentence of between five and fifteen years *US*
- —Hyman E. Goldin et al., *Dictionary of American Underworld Lingo*, p. 220, 1950

taxi-cab *noun*
a crab; crab meat *UK*
Rhyming slang.
- —Ray Puxley, *Cockney Rabbit*, 1992

taxi-cabs; taxis *noun*
pubic lice *UK*
Rhyming slang for **CRABS**.
- —Frank Norman, *Stand on Me*, 1959
- Keep clear of her or you'll end up with the taxis.—Ray Puxley, *Cockney Rabbit*, 1992

taxi dance *verb*
to work as a taxi dancer *US*
- [S]he was back down on Main Street competing with bearer movies between reels, and taxi dancing part-time down the street at the ballroom.—Joseph Wambaugh, *The Blue Knight*, p. 21, 1973

taxi dancer; taxi girl *noun*
a woman who will dance and talk with bar patrons, but stops short of prostitution; a prostitute *US, 1930*
- She was a taxi dancer, night-club entertainer, friend of boys on the loose and anything else you can mention where sex is concerned. —Mickey Spillane, *Kiss Me Deadly*, p. 24, 1952
- —Gregory Clark, *Words of the Vietnam War*, p. 504, 1990
- —Linda Reinberg, *In the Field*, p. 215, 1991

taxing *noun*
1 the theft of high-price training shoes being worn by the victim *UK*
- —Nicholas Jones, *Hackers, Hotting and Hooray Henrys*, p. 57, 1992
- The British Transport Police's annual report stated that teenage muggers stealing designer training shoes from other young people – known as 'taxing' – had pushed up the robbery rate on the railways and Tube.—*Evening Standard (London)*, p. 10, 1st February 1993

2 the robbery of drug dealers by drug dealers *UK*
- —Nick Constable, *This is Cocaine*, p. 182, 2002

taxi rank; taxi *noun*
1 an act of masturbation *UK*
Rhyming slang for **WANK**.
- A "taxi" is one of many terms for "one off the wrist".—Ray Puxley, *Cockney Rabbit*, 1992

2 a bank *UK*
Rhyming slang.
- —Ray Puxley, *Fresh Rabbit*, 1998

taxi-rank; taxi *verb*
to masturbate *UK, 1984*
Rhyming slang for **WANK**.

taxpayer *noun*
a building that generates enough rental income to pay the taxes on it *US, 1921*
- Leon Quat, oddly enough, had the general look of those fifty-two-year-old men who run a combination law office, real estate, and insurance operation on the second floor of a two-story taxpayer out on Queens Boulevard.—Tom Wolfe, *Radical Chic & Mau-Mauing the Flak Catchers*, p. 17, 1970

taylaylay *noun*
the vagina *TRINIDAD AND TOBAGO*
- —Lise Winer, *Dictionary of the English/Creole of Trinidad & Tobago*, 2003

taylor *noun*
▷ see: **TAILOR-MADE**

TB *noun*
1 tuberculosis *US, 1912*
- My kid died from the t-bees in that deathtrap[.]—Ralph Ellison, *Invisible Man*, p. 547, 1947
- I know what a person with t.b. goes through. My old lady had t.b. —Horace McCoy, *Kiss Tomorrow Good-bye*, p. 64, 1948
- On top of everything, he's got T.B.—Mickey Spillane, *Last Cop Out*, p. 10, 1972

2 in circus and carnival usage, a dull town where business is poor *US*
An abbreviation of **TOTAL BLANK**.
- —Don Wilmeth, *The Language of American Popular Entertainment*, p. 278, 1981

TB *adjective*
loyal, *t*rue *b*lue *US*
- —Anna Scotti and Paul Young, *Buzzwords*, p. 99, 1997

TBF *noun*
severe morbidity, usually terminal *US*
A '*t*otal *b*ody *f*ailure'.
- —*Maledicta*, p. 35, 1988–1989: 'Medical maledicta from San Francisco'

TBH *adjective*
potentially available for gay sex *UK*
Acronym of '*t*o *b*e *h*ad'.
- "I know he's t.b.h!" – meaning "to be had"; as the modern queer will say "he's trade".—M. Davidson, *The World, the Flesh and Myself.*, 1970
- "Then" – he'd smiled mischievously – "are you TBH?" "TBH?" "You know. To Be Had." To Be Had. Was I to be had?—Jake Arnott, *He Kills Coppers*, p. 52, 2001

T-bird *noun*
1 a Ford Thunderbird *US*
First sold in October 1954, the Thunderbird became an American cultural icon.
- Daddy-O meets slinky Jana Ryan, a rich girl with a valid driver's license and a '57 T-Bird ragtop.—James Ellroy, *Hollywood Nocturnes*, p. 6, 1994

2 Thunderbird^{TM} wine *US*
- Tooner Flats is the area of gangs who spend their last dime on short dogs of T-Bird wine[.]—Oscar Zeta Acosta, *The Revolt of the Cockroach People*, p. 90, 1973
- Walter was probably still passed out from last night's bout with T-Bird and TV[.]—James Ellroy, *Brown's Requiem*, p. 20, 1981
- T-Bird popped out of back pockets. Side Frizell: "Cut! I told you people to leave your wine back with your blankets and sleeping bags!"—James Ellroy, *White Jazz*, p. 59, 1992

3 a T-33 jet trainer aircraft *US*
- —*American Speech*, p. 229, October 1956: 'More United States Air Force slang'

4 a capsule of amobarbital sodium and secobarbital sodium (trade name Tuinal^{TM}), a combination of central nervous system depressants *US*
- —Peter Johnson, *Dictionary of Street Alcohol and Drug Terms*, p. 187, 1993

T-bone *noun*
a Model T Ford car, first built in 1908 *US*
- —Ed Radlauer, *Drag Racing Pix Dix*, p. 54, 1970

T-bone *verb*
while driving a car, to drive into the side of another car *US*
- —Judi Sanders, *Don't Dog by Do, Dude!*, p. 31, 1991
- —Lewis Poteet, *Car & Motorcyle Slang*, p. 200, 1992

T bowl *noun*
a toilet *US*
- —Ralph de Sola, *Crime Dictionary*, p. 149, 1982

TBP
(in doctors' shorthand) *t*otal *b*ody *p*ain *UK*
- —Adam T. Fox, St Mary's Hospital, London, 10th October 2002

TCB *verb*
to *t*ake *c*are of *b*usiness *US*
Coined by the black community and then spread into widespread use.
- Let's TCB – that means taking care of business.—James Baldwin, *Blues for Mister Charlie*, p. 47, 1964
- R-E-S/P-E-C-T / take care, TCB.—Otis Redding, *Respect*, 1965
- [T]here is a growing – a rapidly growing – body of black peiople determined to "T.C.B." – take care of business.—Stokely Carmichael and Charles V. Hamilton, *Black Power*, p. 184–185, 1967
- Yeah, you'll be TCB / Which means you're Taking Care of Business —Buz Kohon and William Angelos, *TCB*, 1968
- We went home in her Porsche and TCB'ed.—Cecil Brown, *The Life & Loves of Mr. Jiveass Nigger*, p. 149, 1969
- All the hip people got out of Media City and joined in the trip to this crazy retreat – where nothing but princesses and together brothers now come to lay back, relax, and T.C.B.—Steve Cannon, *Groove, Bang, and Jive Around*, p. 155, 1969
- Sapphire has to stand on the corner in the rain to T.C.B. while she watches her white co-worker catch tricks in a plush, warm, dry lobby.—Carolyn Greene, *70 Soul Secrets of Sapphire*, p. 29, 1972
- —David Claerbaut, *Black Jargon in White America*, p. 82, 1972

T-dot *nickname*
Toronto, Ontario *CANADA*
From the proliferation of high-tech businesses in the city.

tea *noun*

1 marijuana *US, 1935*

- Muta was what we called marijuana. We had other names for the weed too: gauge, grefa, reefers, golden-leaf, muggles, tea. — *True*, p. 26, September 1946
- Some guys were so hopped on on tea they were rocking on their heels. — Irving Shulman, *The Amboy Dukes*, p. 52, 1947
- It has since become known as locoweed and in Harlem it is commonly called "tea." — Jack Lait and Lee Mortimer, *New York Confidential*, p. 102, 1948
- "You've been selling marijuana to my kid," he said. "Flute showed no emotion. "Who's your kid? he said calmly. "I sell tea to a lot of people." — *Atlantic Monthly*, p. 69, August 1948
- "For a Pachuco, there's only one kind of high, Bogaway." "Tea?" "Tea. Grifa. Yesca. Marijuana. Whatever you want to call it." — Thurston Scott, *Cure it with Honey*, p. 4, 1951
- At one time or another I have winked at marijuana (and don't call it tea or reefers or grass or weed or by any other romantic euphemism); I have never been other than disgusted by heroin and its users. — *Metronone*, p. 34, September 1951
- But listen, you get Verger and his tea, and I'll see if I can round up Stofsky somewhere. — John Clellon Holmes, *Go*, p. 83, 1952
- "What about tea?" "That's different. Boom makes you gay. You take a couple of sticks and you're way up there, looking down." — Wenzell Brown, *Monkey on My Back*, p. 76, 1953
- I have seen people like that. For them, tea occupies the place usually filled by liquor. — William Burroughs, *Junkie*, p. 79, 1953
- Somebody is pushing horse and tea again. — John D. McDonald, *The Neon Jungle*, p. 32, 1953
- The long, thin sticks of "tea" went from hand to hand. — Robert Sylvester, *No Cover Charge*, p. 46, 1956
- My grandma pushes tea. — Stephen Sondheim, *West Side Story*, 1957
- You could smell tea, weed, I mean marijuana, floating in the air, together with the chili beans and beer. — Jack Kerouac, *On the Road*, p. 86, 1957
- "Any musician who says he is playing better either on tea, the needle or when he is juiced is a plain, straight liar," said The Bird. — Jim Schock, *Life is a Lousy Drag*, 1958
- Once or twice a few had fallen in with pot or tea as it was called then and I picked up for the first time one morning and got so stoned I was unable to move. — Herbert Huncke, *The Evening Sun Turned Crimson*, p. 28–29, 1980

2 in horse racing, a drug (especially cocaine or strychnine) which will stimulate a horse *US*

- — David W. Maurer, *Argot of the Racetrack*, p. 64, 1951

▸ **not for all the tea in China!**

certainly not!; not at any price *AUSTRALIA, 1937*

- [M]ost of the people on my bus or tram would often express to me that they wouldn't do my job for all the tea in China, and often they marvel that I remain so cheerfully immune to the less desirable elements of the job. — *The Guardian*, 1st October 2003

tea and cocoa *verb*

to say so *UK*

Rhyming slang.

- If you wanted to borrow some money why didn't you tea and cocoa? — Ray Puxley, *Cockney Rabbit*, 1992

tea and toast *noun*

the mail, the *post* *UK*

Rhyming slang.

- Anything in the tea and toast thsi morning? — Ray Puxley, *Cockney Rabbit*, 1992

teabag *noun*

1 a contemptible person *UK*

Rhyming slang for **SLAG**.

- [T]hey've talked to him like he's a fuckin teabag, a wanker[.] — J.J. Connolly, *Layer Cake*, p. 113, 2000

2 a marijuana cigarette *US*

- — Ernest L. Abel, *A Marijuana Dictionary*, p. 100, 1982

tea-bag *verb*

in the pursuit of sexual pleasure, to take a man's scrotum completely into the mouth, sucking and tonguing it *US*

- For all its references to dingleberries and tea-bagging, Pecker has nothing that approaches Mary's mock-castration or Hairdo's money shot. — *The Village Voice*, p. 137, 22nd September 1998
- I'm gonna finger-fuck her tight little asshole! Finger-bang ... and tea-bag my balls ... in her mouth! — Kevin Smith, *Jay and Silent Bob Strike Back*, p. 50, 2001

tea-bagger *noun*

in motor racing, a lover of British sports cars *US*

- — John Lawlor, *How to Talk Car*, p. 106, 1965

teabagging *noun*

the sucking of a man's entire scrotum *US, 1998*

- Made famous in John Waters's fab flick Pecker, teabagging is a remarkably accurate description of a top technique that involves his balls and your mouth. — Dan Anderson, *Sex Tips for Gay Guys*, p. 94, 2001
- I suggest we go someplace where we can watch teabagging, but Tom just laughs at me. — Robert L. Pela, *Filthy*, p. 15, 2002
- When a girl is sucking on your balls (teabagging), tap the head of your cock on her forehead and ask, "Who's your daddy?" — Karl Mark, *The Comple A**hole's Guide to Handling Chicks*, p. 269, 2003

teabags *verb*

to steal something *NEW ZEALAND*

Rhyming prison slang: from **TEALEAF** (a thief), punning on 'bag' (to steal).

- — Harry Orsman, *A Dictionary of Modern New Zealand Slang*, p. 137, 1999

tea boat *noun*

in prison, a financial alliance between several prisoners to pay for tea *UK*

- — Angela Devlin, *Prison Patter*, p. 113, 1996

tea boy *noun*

a person who runs errands and performs other menial tasks *UK*

- I guess nobody shakes hands with the Tea Boy in England. — Tom Wolfe, *The Pump House Gang*, p. 195, 1968

tea, breakfast and dinner *noun*

everything *TRINIDAD AND TOBAGO, 1990*

- — Lise Winer, *Dictionary of the English/Creole of Trinidad & Tobago*, 2003

tea caddy *noun*

an Irish person *UK*

Rhyming slang for **PADDY**.

- Anyway, it's not the way with those tea caddies. — J.J. Connolly, *Layer Cake*, p. 101, 2000

teach *noun*

a teacher *UK, 1958*

- "Hey, teach, give me a break," Jason said. "Enough of the history lesson." — Elizabeth Winthrop, *The Battle for the Castle*, p. 88, 1993

teacher *noun*

a traffic police officer who lectures violators instead of issuing citations *US*

- — *American Speech*, p. 272, December 1962: 'The language of traffic policemen'

teacher arms *noun*

the flabby arms of an overweight person *AUSTRALIA*

- [F]ive years ago you came to see me with a vague discomfort about what you were doing with your life, a dissatisfaction over your realtionship with your family and a concern about potentially flappy "teacher arms" you appeared to be developing. — Gretel Killeen, *Hot Buns and Ophelia get a Bloke*, p. 52, 2000

teacup queer *noun*

an effeminate homosexual man *US*

- [S]uddenly his pet ferret rushed out and bit an elegant teacup queer on the ankle and everybody hightailed it out the door. — Jack Kerouac, *On the Road*, p. 144, 1957

tea'd up *adjective*

marijuana-intoxicated *US*

- "Don't cross him," Grave Digger whispered tensely. "He's teaed to the eyes." — Chester Himes, *The Real Cool Killers*, p. 141, 1959
- Flattop the bartender, a football-head spade if there ever was one, tead-up on weed, with a red scarf around his neck, came over to the table to take her order. — Steve Cannon, *Groove, Bang, and Jive Around*, p. 67, 1969

tea for two; teafer *noun*

a Jewish person *UK*

Rhyming slang for 'Jew'.

- — Ray Puxley, *Cockney Rabbit*, 1992

tea girl *noun*

a quasi-prostitute in a Vietnamese bar who cadges US servicemen into buying her drinks, especially of Saigon tea *US*

- — *Time*, p. 29, 26th May 1966
- — Carl Fleischhauer, *A Glossary of Army Slang*, p. 21, 1968

tea grout *noun*

a Boy Scout *UK, 1961*

Rhyming slang.

- — Ray Puxley, *Cockney Rabbit*, 1992

Teague *nickname*
▷ **see:** TAIG

tea head *noun*
a user of marijuana *US*
- Then I start thinking about the mad beret-characters who actually make these movies in crazy California (the tea-head Mitchums)[.] —Jack Kerouac, *Letter to John Clellon Holmes*, p. 197, 24 June 1949
- To the Roskolnics, who turned out to be indifferent young tea-heads, the attempts of others to mix and be genial demanded a rebuff as proof of initiation. —John Clellon Holmes, *Go*, p. 85, 1952
- She knew a lot of teaheads. —William Burroughs, *Junkie*, p. 30, 1953
- — *American Speech*, p. 88, May 1955: 'Narcotic argot along the Mexican border'
- [T]he scattered junkies, the smalltime pushers, the teaheads, the sad panhandlers, the occasional lonely exiled nymphos haunting the entrance to the men's head[.] —John Rechy, *City of Night*, p. 100–101, 1963
- And the negroes / And the teaheads / And the Communists. — *The Berkeley Barb*, p. 2, 19th November 1965
- Our experienced friend, the old tea-head, hadn't pushed things at all. —Sean Hutchinson, *Crying Out Loud*, p. 25, 1988

tea hound *noun*
a marijuana user *US*
- The subject of tea-hounds brings us quite naturally to our next chapter, juvenile delinquency, in which stimulants are a large factor. —Jack Lait and Lee Mortimer, *Washington Confidential*, p. 117, 1951

tealeaf; tea-leaf *noun*
1 a thief *UK, 1903*
Rhyming slang.
- To make things worse, he said, one "diddy" [gypsy] was a "tealeaf" who "scarpered Joh Orderley [left in a hurry] when the "bogeys" [police] came round[.] —Butch Reynolds, *Broken Hearted Clown*, p. 30, 1953
- — *The (Sydney) Bulletin*, 26th April 1975
- No wonder Sir Keith Joseph's always on about law 'n' order, Terry. Everywhere you go there's tea-leafs. —Anthony Masters, *Minder*, p. 61, 1984
- Ain't leavin' it in 'ere. Place is crawlin' with tea-leaves. —Chris Baker and Andrew Day, *Lock, Stock... & One Big Bullock*, p. 345, 2000

2 a small penis *JAMAICA*
A small, limp, black visual metaphor.

tea-leaf *verb*
to rob someone; to steal something *UK*
Rhyming slang; from the noun sense.
- But we never tea-leafed the cunts —J.J. Connolly, *Layer Cake*, p. 129, 2000

tea-leafing *adjective*
inclined to thievery *UK, 1960*
Rhyming slang for THIEVING extended from TEALEAF (a thief).
- "Fuckin' poxy tealeafing cows," he goes. "They only fuckin' rumped me on the fuckin' change again them fuckin' cows." —Jeremy Cameron, *Brown Bread in Wengen*, p. 111, 1999

team *noun*
a criminal gang *UK, 1950*
- —Angela Devlin, *Prison Patter*, p. 113, 1996

▸ **on the team**
homosexual, from the homosexual point of view *UK*
- Do you think she's on the team? —Emma Hindley, *Storm in a Teacup*, 1993
- —Jeff Fessler, *When Drag Is Not a Car Race*, p. 39, 1997
- —Paul Baker, *Polari*, p. 185, 2002

team *adjective*
dressing in a style that identifies you with a particular group *US*
- —Pamela Munro, *U.C.L.A. Slang*, p. 83, 1989

team cream *noun*
an orgy *US*
- — *American Speech*, p. 58, Spring-Summer 1970: 'Homosexual slang'

team-handed *adjective*
working together as a gang *UK*
From TEAM (a criminal gang).
- —Angela Devlin, *Prison Patter*, p. 113, 1996

team Jesus *noun*
a group of zealous, proselytising Christian students *US*
- —Ben Applebaum and Derrick Pittman, *Turd Ferguson & The Sausage Party*, p. 64, 2004

tea pad *noun*
an apartment, house or room where marijuana is smoked *US, 1938*
- Usually, each tea pad has comfortable furniture, a radio, victrola or, as in most instances, a rented nickelodeon. The light is more or less uniformly dim, with blue predominating. An incense burner is considered part of the furnishings. — *La Guardia Report*, p. 9–10, 1944
- There are about 500 apartments in Harlem, known as "tea pads," set up exclusively for marijuana addicts. —Jack Lait and Lee Mortimer, *New York Confidential*, p. 103, 1948
- He drove out north to a tea pad where everybody was already hopped up. —Willard Motley, *Let No Man Write My Epitaph*, p. 109, 1958
- Meanwhile Bozo and Andre split up and Bob and I took over Bozo's apartment and turned it into a tea pad and thieves' den. —Herbert Huncke, *The Evening Sun Turned Crimson*, p. 54, 1980

tea party *noun*
a social party where marijuana is smoked *US*
- What do you bring to a hippie "tea party"? Your own "pot"! —Paul Laikin, *101 Hippie Jokes*, 1968

teapot *noun*
1 a heavy user of marijuana *UK*
- —Tom Hibbert, *Rockspeak!*, p. 156, 1983

2 standing with your hands on your hips *NEW ZEALAND*
- —David McGill, *David McGill's Complete Kiwi Slang Dictionary*, p. 124, 1998

teapot lid; teapot *noun*
1 a Jewish person *UK*
Rhyming slang for YID.
- —Julian Franklyn, *A Dictionary of Rhyming Slang*, 1960

2 a child *UK*
Rhyming slang for KID.
- —Julian Franklyn, *A Dictionary of Rhyming Slang*, 1960

3 a pound sterling *UK, 1960*
Rhyming slang for QUID.
- —Jack Jones, *Rhyming Cockney Slang*, 1971

teapot lid; teapot *verb*
to fool, to pretend *UK, 1934*
Rhyming slang for KID.
- —Ray Puxley, *Cockney Rabbit*, 1992

tear *noun*
1 a spree, a period of self-indulgent enjoyment *UK: SCOTLAND*
- That was a rerr [rare] terr we hud in Millport. —Michael Munro, *The Original Patter*, p. 69, 1985

2 an expedition to deface advertising billboards *US*
- [I]t inspired the Billboard Liberation Front to go on its biggest tear in years[.] —Naomi Klein, *No Logo*, p. 308, 2001

3 a manipulation of a record to create a musical effect that plays a sample in two sections with a jolt-effect in the middle
- You can do a tear in reverse. —J. Hoggarth, *How To Be a DJ*, p. 92, 2002

▸ **on the tear**
engaged in a drinking session *IRELAND*
- Shortly thereafter, numerous enquiries were made to determine the structure of the working week of student nurses and we then made it our business to be in Copper Face Jack's or McGowans when they were finished a week of nights and were out on the tear. —Donal Ruane, *Tales in a rear view mirror*, p. 190, 2003

tear *verb*
1 to leave, especially in a hurry *US*
- He was looking at his wrist watch. "I have to tear," he said, and stood up. —J.D. Salinger, *Catcher in the Rye*, p. 148, 1951
- Sloanes don't like to say 'go' – it doesn't descirbe the way they... well, whizz. The will say rush, toddle, beetle, tear, almost anything in preference. —Ann Barr and Peter York, *The Official Sloane Ranger Handbook*, p. 159, 1982

2 to surf aggressively and with skill *US*
- —Michael V. Anderson, *The Bad, Rad, Not to Forget Way Cool Beach and Surf Discriptionary*, p. 20, 1988

▸ **tear a passion to tatters**
in a dramatic performance, to over-act *US*
- —Sherman Louis Sergel, *The Language of Show Biz*, p. 48, 1973

▸ **tear a strip off; tear off a strip**
to reprimand someone *UK, 1941*
- Did [US President George W] Bush tear a strip off [Israel's Prime Minister, Ariel] Sharon for trying to start another war in the region? Hardly. — *The Guardian*, 22nd October 2003

▸ **tear it**
to frustrate or thwart someone's intentions, usually in the phrase 'that's torn it' *UK, 1909*
- "Oh crikey, that's torn it," she thought, but looked up to find all eyes fixed on a line of grotesques trooping into view. — *The Guardian*, 31st October 2003

▸ **tear off a chunk**
to have sex *US*
- Shit, before my Flossie got sick, I useed to tear off a chunk every night. — Joseph Wambaugh, *The Blue Knight*, p. 98, 1973

▸ **tear off a tab; tear off a scab**
to open a can of beer *NEW ZEALAND*
- — Louis S. Leland, *A Personal Kiwi-Yankee Dictionary*, p. 100, 1984

▸ **tear off; tear off a piece**
to have sex *US*
- If old Virgil felt like tearing off a piece, why, that wasn't nobody's business but old Virgil's, was it? — Max Shulman, *Anyone Got a Match?*, p. 208, 1964
- [W]e quickly tear off several goodies, then, I go back to work. — Neal Cassady, *The First Third*, p. 153, 1971

▸ **tear the arse out of**
to destroy or spoil something *UK, 1990s*
- Let's not tear the arse out of a good thing, eh Roy. — J.J. Connolly, *Know Your Enemy [britpulp]*, p. 143, 1999

▸ **tear the roof off**
to create or intensify mass excitement through the agency of loud music *UK*
A refinement of 'raise the roof' (to make a great noise).
- Coxy [DJ Carl Cox] tore the roof off[.] — *The Face*, p. 164, June 2001

▸ **tear them apart; tear them up**
to delight an audience *UK*
- A number ... that simply "tore 'em up". — M. Lincoln, *Oh! Definitely*, 1933
- The little showman's highest praise [...] was that it "tore them apart". — Butch Reynolds, *Broken Hearted Clown*, p. 29, 1953

▸ **tear you a new asshole**
to thrash someone; to abuse someone verbally *US*
- — Carl Fleischhauer, *A Glossary of Army Slang*, p. 21, 1968

▸ **tear your pants**
to commit a social gaffe *US*
- — Marcus Hanna Boulware, *Jive and Slang of Students in Negro Colleges*, 1947

tear-arse around; tear-arse about; tear ass *verb*
to race about wildly *UK*
Elaboration of 'tear' (to rush).
- [W]e were into fast cars and tear-arsing around, and every geezer likes to think he's a good driver, don't he? — Dave Courtney, *Stop the Ride I Want to Get Off*, p. 110, 1999

tearaway *noun*
a minor criminal, one who tends towards violence at the slightest excuse *UK*
Originally a 'ladies' tearaway', a criminal specialising in snatching (tearing away) women's handbags.
- [N]o thief and tearaway shows any emotion just because he has got a capture, and has got a lagging to do[.] — Frank Norman, *Bang To Rights*, p. 8, 1958
- Now then Frankie boy, this is'nt [sic] what a tearaway does, come on, your [sic] a villain not a sniveller — Frank Norman, *Bang To Rights*, p. 8, 1958
- Bobby Twist, a tearaway (or strongarm man) now dead. — John Gosling, 1959

teardrop *noun*
1 a dose of crack cocaine, packaged in the corner of a plastic bag *US*
- — US Department of Justice, *Street Terms*, October 1994

2 a surfboard that is wide at the rear and narrow at the nose *AUSTRALIA*
- — Jack Pollard, *The Australian Surfrider*, p. 18, 1963

tearjerker *noun*
a melodramatic or sentimental and sad story or song *US, 1921*
- It's Summertime is what it is. The drunks always call during the tearjerkers. — Armistead Maupin, *Further Tales of the City*, p. 21, 1982
- One day he'd write a rousing Good Samaritan column, then a funny man-on-the-street piece, then a tearjerk about some little kid with cancer[.] — Carl Hiaasen, *Tourist Season*, p. 63, 1986
- [C]omplete the evening by renting a tear-jerker movie. — Marcy Blum, *Weddings for Dummies*, p. 66, 1997
- Anyway, they were going to let him go but his mother wrote a tear-jerker letter that ended up on my desk. — *Something About Mary*, 1998

tear-off *noun*
a minor criminal, one who tends towards violence at the slightest excuse *UK*
A variation of **TEARAWAY**.
- You can find Christians as well as meths men, tear offs, outcasts, bum boys, prostitutes and head breakers on Skid Row. — Geoffrey Fletcher, *Down Among the Meths Men*, p. 11, 1966

tearoom; t-room *noun*
a public toilet *US, 1941*
From an era when a great deal of homosexual contact was in public toilets; probably an abbreviation of 'toilet room', a term used in reported criminal prosecutions of homosexuals in the late C19. A public toilet in Illinois was the focus of Laud Humphrey's famous sociological study *Tearoom Trade*.
- — Donald Webster Cory and John P. LeRoy, *The Homosexual and His Society*, p. 266, 1963: 'A lexicon of homosexual slang'
- "I'm Jenny and this is my tearoom" – indicating the head[.] — John Rechy, *City of Night*, p. 193, 1963
- "Tearoom" derives from tea, cute euphemism for pee, in case anyone asks. — John Francis Hunter, *The Gay Insider*, p. 190, 1971
- In fact, he may enjoy regarding himself as the one who's been "put upon," who suffers because of "perverts" in local t-rooms. — *Screw*, p. 13, 18th January 1971
- I suppose there has been such activity since the invention of plumbing. I first started out in one of those pavilion places. But the real fun began during the depression. * * * Suddenly, it just seemed like half the men in town met in the tearooms. — Laud Humphreys, *Tearoom Trade*, p. 5–6, 1975
- There are many among us (let's face it) who enjoy the seamier side of gay life: the parks, the tearooms, and the peep shows. — *Drummer*, p. 26, 1977
- — *Maledicta*, p. 227, Winter 1980: '"Lovely, blooming, fresh and gay": the onomastics of camp'
- "Wilfred's gonna help me set up a tearoom this summer for the tourists." "Really?" "A real tearoom, dipshit." — Armistead Maupin, *Babycakes*, p. 291, 1984
- Some men, particularly those who were professionally successful in jobs that required them to pass as straight, found it astonishing that anyone in their circles would risk going to a tearoom. — George Chauncey, *Gay New York*, p. 199, 1994

tea-room cruiser *noun*
a male homosexual prostitute who frequents public toilets *US*
- — *Maledicta*, p. 139, Summer/Winter 1982: 'Dyke diction: the language of lesbians'

tea-room trade *noun*
a sexual partner found in a public toilet *US*
- — *Maledicta*, p. 233, Winter 1980: '"Lovely, blooming, fresh and gay": the onomastics of camp'

tear-up *noun*
1 a gang fight; a brawl *US, 1964*
From conventional 'tear-up' (a commotion).
- A story which earned the West Ham firm further extensive TV and newspaper coverage was when they had a famous tear-up with Manchester United on a cross-channel ferry. — Martin King and Martin Knight, *The Naughty Nineties*, p. 98, 1999
- [T]his is different from the tear-ups with other kids. — Jimmy Stockin, *On The Cobbles*, p. 57, 2000
- [T]here was a whole summer of big black v white tear-ups going on. — Kevin Sampson, *Outlaws*, p. 39, 2001

2 in jazz use, a period of wild, inspired music-making *US, 1958*

3 any valueless letter addressed to Scotland Yard *UK*
Officially filed in the Metropolitan Police's General Registry as GM[General Matters]51.
- — *The Official Encyclopaedia of New Scotland Yard*, 1999

tease and please *noun*
sexual arousal after which satisfaction is delayed under the pretence that such gratification is denied, especially when advertised as a service offered by a prostitute *UK*
- — Caroline Archer, *Tart Cards*, 2003

teaser *noun*
1 in horse breeding, a horse used to test a mare's readiness for breeding *US*
- — Tom Ainslie, *Ainslie's Complete Guide to Thoroughbred Racing*, p. 339, 1976

2 in sports betting, a bet that ties two or more games together *US*
- The professor was the first to put up teasers, where the bettor could move the line seven points up or down, but he had to make a two-team parlay and lay eleven-to-ten. — Jimmy Snyder, *Jimmy the Greek*, p. 75, 1975
- — Avery Cardoza, *The Basics of Sports Betting*, p. 45, 1991

teaspoon *noun*
a measure of heroin or other narcotic drug *UK*
• —Angela Devlin, *Prison Patter*, p. 113, 1996

tea strainer *noun*
a trainer (a shoe) *UK*
Rhyming slang.
• —Ray Puxley, *Cockney Rabbit*, 1992

tea-towel head *noun*
an offensive term for an Arabic person *AUSTRALIA*
• —Barry Humphries, *A Nice Night's Entertainment*, p. 188, 1981
• I've just been to the Gulf and, although that sounds promising, I'm here to tell you that those old teatowel-heads know how to make it uphill work for a hard-nosed trouble-shooter like me[.]—Barry Humphries, *The Traveller's Tool*, p. 106, 1985

tea-towel holder *noun*
the anus *UK*
A resemblance in shape and detail.
• —*www.LondonSlang.com*, June 2002

tea wagon *noun*
in the television and film industries, the console used by the sound mixer *US*
• —Tony Miller and Patricia George, *Cut! Print!*, p. 155, 1977

tec *noun*
a detective *UK, 1879*
• Chandler came to crime writing late in life but he brought a lyrical approach to the genre which served to romanticise the tough 'tecs[.]—Paul Duncan, *Noir Fiction*, p. 10, 2000

tecate; tecatos *noun*
heroin *US*
Directly from Mexican Spanish.
• —Ralph de Sola, *Crime Dictionary*, p. 149, 1982
• —US Department of Justice, *Street Terms*, October 1994
• —Mike Haskins, *Drugs*, p. 284, 2003

tecato *noun*
a heroin or morphine addict *US, 1970*
Directly from Mexican Spanish.
• —Robert Ashton, *This Is Heroin*, p. 210, 2002

tech *noun*
1 a technical college, an institution that provides further and higher education *UK*
Often 'the Tech' is used for your local one.
• She didn't go to a proper college, just a tech, you know.—Diran Adebayo, *My Once Upon A Time*, p. 96, 2000

2 a technician; someone employed to deal with technological devices, especially in a creative milieu *US, 1942*
Also called a 'techie'.
• [S]he knew this guy played with the Fugs – well he didn't play, he helped with the equipment and all, a techie.—John Sayles, *Union Dues*, p. 135, 1977
• The place was empty except for a few techies, a few stray producers.—Armistead Maupin, *Maybe the Moon*, p. 290, 1992
• [S]urrounded by respectful continuity girls, patient directing folk and grinning techies[.]—James Hawes, *Dead Long Enough*, p. 6, 2000

3 a nine millimetre handgun *US*
• —Maria Hinojas, *Crews*, p. 168, 1995: 'Glossary'

tech dog *noun*
in foot-propelled scootering, a rider with strong technical skills *UK*
• —Ben Sharpe, *Scooter Crazy*, p. 42, 2000

technical; tech *noun*
in foot-powered scootering, any trick that is performed on a flat surface or ledge and requires a good deal of technical skill *UK*
• —Ben Sharpe, *Scooter Crazy*, p. 42, 2000

technicolour laugh *noun*
an act of vomiting; vomit *AUSTRALIA, 1964*
• Calling for Herb, see, that's one of the many euphemisms for vomit, others include spue, burp, hurl, the big spit, the long spit, throw, the whip o'will, the technicolour laugh and, in Queensland, the chuckle.—Frank Hardy, *Billy Borker Rides Again*, 1967
• It's a hotel, a hostelry, a beeratorium, a grog joint, a piss-up palace, a wardling place, a technicolour laugh theatre, a licensed to sell intoxicating liquors establishment, in short a fucking pub.—Frank Hardy, *The Outcasts of Foolgarah*, p. 46, 1971

technicolour yawn *noun*
an act of vomiting *AUSTRALIA, 1964*
• When I'd swallowed the last prawn / I had a technicolour yawn / And I chundered in the old Pacific Sea.—Barry Humphries, *The Wonderful World of Barry McKenzie*, p. 15, 1968

techno *adjective*
as a combining form, denotes intrinsic technological expertise or inspiration, especially in relation to computing, gadgetry or music fashions *US, 1989*
• As I lay there scrunched under the windowsill catching all the juicy action, I thought to myself, "I am a pervert. A techno Peeping Tom. I need professional help."—Anka Radakovich, *The Wild Girls Club*, p. 95, 1994
• Neo-hippies crash on sweaty mattresses caressed by the velvet pall of ganja smoke and Daniel's ambient techno seepage.—Melanie McGrath, *Hard, Soft & Wet*, p. 67, 1998

technobabble *noun*
pretentious scientific chatter *US*
Modelled on 'psychobabble'.
• To help separate technology from technobabble, PEOPLE turned to Tracy Kidder[.]—*People*, p. 134, 28th December 1981

technodolt *noun*
a person who is completely technologically illiterate *US*
• —Karla Jennings, *The Devouring Fungus*, p. 224, 1990

technodweeb *noun*
a person who is passionately interested in technology *US*
• —Karla Jennings, *The Devouring Fungus*, p. 224, 1990

technosavvy *noun*
someone who understands technology *US*
• The technosavvy close up technowords.—*Wired Style*, p. 91, 1996

technowords *noun*
a scientific vocabulary *US*
• The technosavvy close up technowords—*Wired Style*, p. 91, 1996

teddy *noun*
a bottle of alcohol, legal or otherwise *CANADA*
• "I left the teddy in the toilet." "Brew it and bottle it, put it in teddies."—Frank Ledwell, *North Shore of Home*, p. 140–141, 1986
• teddy: a bottle of moonshine—*New Maritimes*, p. 29, March–April 1990

teddy bear *noun*
1 a dose of LSD identified by the printed picture of a teddy bear *UK*
• —Mike Haskins, *Drugs*, p. 286, 2003

2 a person who dresses and behaves in a showy manner *AUSTRALIA, 1944*
Rhyming slang for **LAIR**.
• —Jim Ramsay, *Cop It Sweet!*, p. 88, 1977

3 a pear *UK*
Rhyming slang, formed from a cuddly toy.
• —Ray Puxley, *Cockney Rabbit*, 1992

teddy bear suit *noun*
heavy winter garments issued to US troops during World War 2 and later in Korea *US*
• —Frank Hailey, *Soldier Talk*, p. 60, 1982

Teddy Boy; Teddy; Ted *noun*
a member of a youth cult of the mid- to late 1950s, characterised by a style of dress loosely inspired by fashions of the Edwardian era (1901–10) *UK, 1954*
Edward abbreviates to Teddy and Ted. Teddy Boys referred to themselves as Teds.
• [R]espectable screwsmen [thieves] daren't walk home from their gaffs at night for fear being chivved for teddy-boys, and left to bleed to death over the ragwort in a bomb-site[.]—Charles Raven, *Underworld Nights*, p. 41, 1956
• [O]utside their houses there were Teds[.]—Colin McInnes, *Absolute Beginners*, 1959
• I ask this copper where we're going, and he says the Magistrates' Court in London. "Where all the naughty teds end up," he says.—John Peter Jones, *Feather Pluckers*, p. 54, 1964
• [T]he spivs and wideboys of the late 1940's and their descendants, the Teddies.—Geoffrey Fletcher, *Down Among the Meths Men*, p. 9, 1966

- [A]geing Teddy Boys in jackets with green velvet facings, comic sideburns, puffing at the pace[.] —Richard Neville, *Play Power*, p. 116, 1970
- [P]apers screaming about Teddy boys razoring cinema seats[.] —Martin King and Martin Knight, *The Naughty Nineties*, p. 223, 1999

Ted Frazer *noun*
a cut-throat razor *UK*
Rhyming slang.
- —David Powis, *The Signs of Crime*, 1977

Ted Heath *noun*
a thief *UK*
Rhyming slang, formed (satirically) on Edward Heath (b.1916), Conservative Prime Minister 1970–74.
- —*Daily Telegraph*, 17th December 1972

Ted Ray *adjective*
homosexual *UK*
Rhyming slang for **FAY**; probably formed from the British comedian and actor (1905–77); however, Bodmin Dark, *Dirty Cockney Rhyming Slang*, 2003, suggests an American jazz musician of the same name.

Teds *noun*
▷ see: **EDWARD HEATH**

teedle-ee *noun*
a urination *UK: SCOTLAND*
Glasgow rhyming slang for **PEE**.
- He'll no be long. He's just away for a teedle-ee. —Michael Munro, *The Patter, Another Blast*, 1988

teed off *adjective*
angry *US*
- I'm teed off. Things like this give me the pip. —Mickey Spillane, *My Gun is Quick*, p. 16, 1950
- PRESS: How do you feel about being back in the U.S.? RUDDER: Pretty teed off! —Max Shulman, *Guided Tour of Campus Humor*, p. 140, 1955
- No, buddy boy, it's not me you're teed off at; it's somebody else. —Max Shulman, *Anyone Got a Match?*, p. 112, 1964

teef *verb*
to steal something *UK*
A mispronunciation of 'thieve' or an elision of **TEA-LEAF** (to thieve).
- In a nutshell... I teefed Koom's money. —Nick Barlay, *Curvy Lovebox*, p. 161, 1997

teem *noun*
team *UK*
Fashionable misspelling.
- Radio 1 prides itself on new spelling: def, lite, blak, tekno, dreem and teem. —*The Sunday Times*, p. 13, 23rd June 2002

teenager *noun*
1 a person aged between 13 and 19 *US, 1935*
Originally 'teen-ager'. Since about 1955 has usually been written as one word, and since about 1960 has been regarded as standard English.
- "Teenager" came from the slogan "we are living in the Teen Age" thought up by an American advertising agency in the early fifties. —Simon Napier-Bell, *Black Vinyl White Powder*, p. 10, 2001

2 cocaine *UK*
- —Nick Constable, *This is Cocaine*, p. 181, 2002
- —Mike Haskins, *Drugs*, p. 281, 2003

teener *noun*
one six*teen*th of an ounce *US*
- "My brain got fried from snortin all that crank. Used to do a teener every night." —Joseph Wambaugh, *Finnegan's Week*, p. 40, 1993

teen-flick *noun*
a film intended for teenagers *UK*
- [T]he teen flick that shocked America. —*The Observer*, 24th August 2003

teenie *noun*
1 a younger teenager *US*
- He would appear before a vast audience of screaming teenies and tell them that he had just received a message from God warning him against performing that night. —Albert Goldman, *Freak Show*, p. 73, 1968

2 one-sixteenth of a dollar *US, 1992*
Trader usage.
- The term "teenies," for example, dates back to 1997 when the exchanges began trading stocks in increments of 1/16 for the first time. —*New York Daily News Express*, p. 14, 27th November 2000

teensy *adjective*
tiny *US, 1899*
A childish corruption.
- "A little refreshment?" asked Frannie. The columnist flashed her syrupy little-girl smile. "It's a teensy bit early for me, thanks." —Armistead Maupin, *Further Tales of the City*, p. 17, 1982

teensy-weensy *adjective*
very small *US, 1906*
- Not an idea came to me. Not a fragment of an idea. Not a teensy-weensy glimmer of an idea. —Max Shulman, *The Many Loves of Dobie Gillis*, p. 5, 1951
- I don't care a teensy-weensie little bit. —Jim Thompson, *The Killer Inside*, p. 63, 1952

teenth *noun*
a six*teenth* of an ounce (of drugs) *UK*
- Smoked me last before, like. Brought a teenth up yer [here] with me an it's all fuckin gone. Smoked away. —Niall Griffiths, *Sheepshagger*, p. 131, 2001

teenuc *noun*
▷ see: **TENUC**

teeny *adjective*
very small *UK, 1825*
- "I want to come in for just a teeny minute." —J.D. Salinger, *Franny and Zooey*, p. 71, 1961

teenybop *adjective*
of or for teenyboppers *US, 1967*
- From 1971 to 1974 Gary Glitter was a barnstorming teenybop star[.] —Paul Morley, *Ask*, p. 35, 1st May 1982

teenybopper *noun*
a young teenager, especially a girl *US*
- Super grubby teenie boppers. —*San Francisco Chronicle*, 21st April 1965
- —J. L. Simmons and Barry Winograd, *It's Happening*, p. 173, 1966: 'glossary'
- There are a few teenie boppers, struggling to attain middle classness but for the most part the chicks are in slacks with hair rollers. —*The Berkeley Barb*, p. 4, 20th July 1966
- —*Current Slang*, p. 7, Winter 1966
- I think Ben has gotten beyond the teenybopper stage, haven't you Ben? —*The Graduate*, 1967
- [Y]ou began to hear stories out of the Haight saying the "real" hippies were taking flight to rural communes and that ersatz plastic hippies and teeni-boppers had taken over. —Nicholas Von Hoffman, *We Are The People Our Parents Warned Us Against*, p. 119, 1967
- [T]he streets of Georgetown in Washington and Haight-Ashbury in San Francisco and Greenwich VIllage in New York were filled with mobs of so-called "hippies" and "teenie-boppers" wandering aimlessly about, conducting sit-ins, lie-ins, and wed-ins[.] —Congressman Bill Stuckey, *The Congressional Record*, 11th December 1967
- [T]eenagers – already a ghastly word – are known as "teeny-boppers"! —Gore Vidal, *Myra Breckinridge*, p. 26–27, 1968
- The result was that English dandyism was wedded to Negro eroticism, and every teenybopper in the Western world began to dream of possessing a mod moppet with soul. —Albert Goldman, *Freak Show*, p. 12, 1968
- Teeny Bopper, my teenage lover / I caught your waves last night. —Doug Sahm, *Mendocino*, 1969
- Teenyboppers select their lingerie now according to what will look best when it's exposed. —*Screw*, p. 19, 22nd December 1969
- A teenybopper gets up now and almost bounces as she walks, waving her hands in the air. —Darryl Ponicsan, *The Last Detail*, p. 82, 1970
- I guess he was pushing too much too fast to those little teeny boppers of his. — Anonymous, *Go Ask Alice*, p. 90, 1971
- I pull over at a ma and pa liquor store across the street from City Lights Bookstore, a hangout for sniveling intellectuals and runaway teenyboppers out for a score. —Oscar Zeta Acosta, *The Autobiography of a Brown Buffalo*, p. 36, 1972
- [He] brought grubby little teeny-boppers home to bed[.] —Doug Lang, *Freaks*, p. 47, 1973
- Fucking teenybopper chick music shit. —*Empire Records*, 1995
- The Teenybopper has lost her bop – the bop in her walk, her pocket-bop. —Francesca Lia Block, *I Was a Teenage Fairy*, p. 145, 1998

teenyhooker *noun*
a young female prostitute *US*
- —Ralph de Sola, *Crime Dictionary*, p. 149, 1982

teeny weeny *adjective*
tiny *US, 1931*
'Teeny' came from 'tiny', and then the reduplicative 'teeny weeny', which is often found in the same breath as 'itsy bitsy'.

- "I still don't feel it," Mickey said, "the grass. Maybe just a teeny bit." "A teeny weeny bit?" Louis said. "A teeny-weeny weeny weeny-weeny bit," Mickey said. — Elmore Leonard, *Switch*, p. 159, 1978

tee off *verb*

1 to annoy or to irritate someone *US, 1961*

- [J]ust something about Wesley Clark that tees me off. Has that been your experience? — *60 Minutes*, 20th November 2003

2 to fart *UK*

- — Peter Furze, *Tailwinds*, p. 163, 1998

tees *noun*

dice on which some numbers are repeated, usually made with identical numbers on opposite sides *US*

- — *The Annals of the American Academy of Political and Social Sciences*, p. 132, May 1950
- — John S. Salak, *Dictionary of Gambling*, p. 258, 1963
- We had a set of tee with us, but they were white. — Donald Goines, *Whoreson*, p. 31, 1972

teeth *noun*

cocaine; crack cocaine *US*

From the resemblance of the drug to small teeth.

- — US Department of Justice, *Street Terms*, October 1994
- — Nick Constable, *This is Cocaine*, p. 181, 2002
- — Mike Haskins, *Drugs*, p. 281, 2003

▸ **my back teeth are floating**

I am desperate to urinate *UK*

- I've got to have a lash. Me back teeth are floating. — Garry Bushell, *The Face*, p. 81, 2001

TEETH

(in doctors' shorthand) *t*ried *e*verything *e*lse, *t*ry *h*omeopathy *UK*

Recorded in an article about medical slang in British (3 London and 1 Cambridge) hospitals.

- — *Ethics and Behaviour*, August 2003

teeth and tits

used to remind dancers that an attractive smile and a distracting display will stop an audience noticing the footwork *UK*

Theatrical.

teething troubles *noun*

initial problems with any new device, invention, enterprise, technology, etc *UK, 1937*

- Teething troubles bring modifications, and each engine can carry a different set of modifications. — Robert Pease, *Troubleshooting Analogue Circuits*, p. 3, 1991

teetotaller *noun*

a person who abstains from any and all alcohol *UK, 1834*

- Swedes are either teetotalers or wonderful stews. — Jack Lait and Lee Mortimer, *Chicago Confidential*, p. 81, 1950
- [T]he bartender rousted up an odd bottle of Christian Brothers port and poured us two shots in wide wine-glasses. Morley (a teetotaler actually) and Japhy and I drank and felt it fine. — Jack Kerouac, *The Dharma Bums*, p. 37, 1958
- [T]hree sheriff's deputies had shown up and arrested Slim for being drunk and disorderly which was quite humorous when you know that Slim was a teetotaler. — Clancy Sigal, *Going Away*, p. 82, 1961
- [S]he allows him his little toddy when visitors like myself come to call and even winks an eye at the double he manages for hisself with teetotalers like myself[.] — Robert Campbell, *Cat's Meow*, p. 25, 1988

teev *noun*

a television *AUSTRALIA, 1982*

- — Kathy Lette, *Girls' Night Out*, p. 126, 1987
- [T]here was this nice warm feeling in the house as we all sat in front of the teev scarfing down the free stuff. — John Birmingham, *He Died With a Felafel in his Hand*, p. 4, 1994
- Reggie dug the remote control from out of the brown couch and flicked on the teev. — Harrison Biscuit, *The Search for Savage Henry*, p. 60, 1995

teflon *adjective*

describes a person to whom blame doesn't stick *US*

From the non-stick properties of polytetrafluoroethylene, trademarked as Teflon™.

- Under the headline "Teflon Sven", the Sun says Sven Goran Eriksson will stay on despite plunging the FA into crisis. — *BBC News*, 3rd August 2004
- The elder Gotti, known as the Teflon Don, was convicted of murder and racketeering in 1992 and sentenced to life in prison. — *The Scotsman*, 22nd July 2004
- This might be the ideal time for Teflon Tony [Blair] to come unstuck. — *The Observer*, 25th July 2004

tekno *noun*

the recreational drug ketamine *UK*

Back slang for 'on ket'.

- — Harry Shapiro, *Recreational Drugs*, p. 286, 2004

tele *noun*

a television set; television *US, 1940*

Early use mainly US (as television itself), adopted enthusistically in the UK in the mid-50s.

- Give us more BLEEPs, on tele. We want more BLEEPs! — Mike Stott, *Soldiers Talking, Cleanly*, 1978
- a bloke I recognise from the telly — Martin King and Martin Knight, *The Naughty Nineties*, p. 104, 1999
- "Is this gonna be on the tele?" she squeals delightedly. — Lanre Fehintola, *Charlie Says...*, p. 195, 2000

telegram *noun*

1 a message designed for mass distribution from prisoner to prisoner, passed from one cell to the next *US*

- — William K. Bentley and James M. Corbett, *Prison Slang*, p. 57, 1992

2 in prison, a written notice given to an inmate who has been placed on report for an offence *UK*

- — Angela Devlin, *Prison Patter*, p. 113, 1996

telegraph *verb*

to inadvertently disclose or reveal your intentions to an opponent *UK, 1925*

- Junior's crafty, older opponent sees him telegraph a left hook with an almost imperceptible hitch of his left shoulder. — Iceberg Slim (Robert Beck), *Doom Fox*, p. 179, 1978

telephone *noun*

a bilingual Canadian who serves as a go-between for English and French speakers *CANADA*

- — *Maledicta*, p. 184, 1979: 'Canadian slurs, ethnic and other'

telephone booth *noun*

in poker, a player who regularly 'calls' (matches the bet of the previous player) *US*

- — George Percy, *The Language of Poker*, p. 91, 1988

telephone number *noun*

a long prison sentence *US*

- — Hyman E. Goldin et al., *Dictionary of American Underworld Lingo*, p. 221, 1950

telephone numbers *noun*

1 a large sum of money *US*

- Charlie, there are fucking telephone numbers we're talking about here. — Vincent Patrick, *The Pope of Greenwich Village*, p. 225, 1979
- — Angela Devlin, *Prison Patter*, p. 113, 1996

2 in horse racing, a winning bet at high odds *US, 1934*

- — Robert Saunders Dowst and Jay Craig, *Playing the Races*, p. 170, 1960

telephone pole *noun*

▷ **see:** FLYING TELEPHONE POLE

telephone tag *noun*

the serial leaving of messages when two people who are trying to talk by telephone can never reach each other *US*

- It installed telephone answering machines on many telephones so people could leave messages and avoid playing the game of "telephone tag," which, it was found, occupied an inordinate number of man-hours. — *The American Banker*, p. 7, 3rd July 1979
- — Judi Sanders, *Kickin' like Chicken with the Couch Commander*, p. 24, 1992

telescope *noun*

the penis *US*

A jocular euphemism.

- — *Current Slang*, p. 10, Spring 1968

teletubby; telletubby *noun*

a husband *UK*

Rhyming slang for **HUBBY**, formed on *Teletubbies*, a BBC television programme for young children, first seen in 1996.

- — Ray Puxley, *Fresh Rabbit*, 1998

tell *noun*

1 an unintentionally honest reaction; a revealing piece of body-language *UK*

Adopted from gambling jargon.

- Everybody, you, me, got a "tell". A tell is something where you can tell if somebody's a little bit worried, a bit nervous, a bit anxious. [...]

I always like to find out what people's "tell" is. — J.J. Connolly, *Know Your Enemy [britpulp]*, p. 137, 1999

2 in gambling, any mannerism that reveals the relative value of the player's hand *US*

- — Michael Dalton, *Blackjack*, p. 83, 1991

tell *verb*

▸ **I'll tell you what; tell you what**

I'll tell you something; this is how it is; often as the introduction to a suggestion *UK, 1596*

- If you grip, it won't always fall on the floor. I'll tell you what. Why don't we just put it on the table? — *Meet Joe Black*, 1998

▸ **tell it like it is**

1 to speak directly, candidly and with a self-righteous conviction of access to a great truth *US*

- "This play is different because it's the truth," they tell you. "We go on stage and we tell it like it is." — *Los Angeles Free Press*, p. 6, 25th June 1965
- Alinksy Tells it Like It Is [Headline] — *Berkeley Barb*, p. 3, 2nd December 1966
- In Harlem, on the other hand, to tell it like it is, is to call a spade a spade. — Sidney Bernard, *This Way to the Apocalypse*, p. 57, 1968

2 to tell the whole truth *US, 1964*

In black usage originally.

- A man, on the other hand, will tell it like it is[.] — Myreah Moore, *Date Like a Man*, p. 83, 2001

▸ **tell on**

to inform on someone *UK, 1539*

- Malik screamed back at me that he was never going to play Macbeth and that he was going to tell on me. 'I'm going to make a complaint,' he shouted as he rushed out of the room — *The Observer*, 29th February 2004

▸ **tell the tale**

in a swindle, to explain to the victim just how he will profit from the arrangement being proposed *US*

- — Lindsay E. Smith and Bruce A. Walstad, *Sting Shift*, p. 117, 1989: 'Glossary'

▸ **tell you where to get off**

to severely rebuke you; to scold you *US, 1900*

- [T]he Islamist organisation Hamas told Palestinian PM Abu Mazen where to get off. — *The Observer*, 8th June 2003

▸ **tell you where to stick it**

to emphatically reject *UK*

A variation of 'stick it up your arse'.

- Appreciate the extra work you chaps did for us this evening. Could've told us where to stick it. — Kevin Sampson, *Powder*, p. 35, 1999

teller *noun*

a skateboarder whose tales of accomplishments are exaggerated *US*

- — *San Francisco Sunday Examiner & Chronicle*, p. 20, 2nd September 1984: 'Say it right'

telling-off *noun*

a scolding, a reprimand *UK, 1911*

From TELL OFF.

- I assumed that he was threatening them with a telling-off by Aunt Annie, a prospect which pleased me no end. — Mary Lawson, *Crow Lake*, p. 207, 2003

tell it to the hand

▷ see: TALK TO THE HAND

tell it to the marines!

used for registering disbelief *UK, 1806*

Formed, apparently, from an inter-service jibe against the credulity of the marines.

- Tell it to the marines... we've invaded the wrong country[.] — *The Guardian*, 19th February 2002

tell me another one

used for registering disbelief *UK, 1914*

- "She's the neighbor who's been taking care of us." "Tell me another one." "You calling me a liar?" "Yeah." — Susan Elizabeth Phillips, *First Lady*, 2000

tell off *verb*

to scold or reprimand someone *UK, 1919*

- [T]hey gossip, complain, criticize, fantasize about telling the person off, and let it out in other indirect ways. — Brad Blanton, *Radical Honesty*, p. 125, 1996

telltale *noun*

in the language of wind surfing, a streamer on the mast used to determine wind direction *US*

- — Frank Fox, *A Beginner's Guide to Zen and the Art of Windsurfing*, p. 154, 1985: 'A short dictionary of wind surfing terms'

tell-tale-tit *noun*

someone who tells tales *UK, 1841*

A nursery term, featured in children's playground rhymes.

telly *noun*

television *US, 1940*

- Mr and Mrs Saturday Evening Post thrilled to the election of the first telly president, JFK[.] — Richard Neville, *Play Power*, p. 24, 1970
- Well, sit down. Watch the telly if you like. — Elmore Leonard, *Split Images*, p. 236, 1981
- I don't need a doctor, I don't need a drugstore / I don't need an injection, I need to put the telly on. — Toy Dolls, *I'm A Telly Addict*, 1993

▸ **off the telly**

as seen on television *UK*

- [T]hat daft tart off the telly[.] — Christopher Brookmyre, *Boiling a Frog*, p. 157, 2000

telly- *prefix*

telephone *US, 1970*

Used for constructions such as 'tellypole' or 'tellywires'.

- — Claudio R. Salvucci, *The Philadelphia Dialect Dictionary*, p. 62, 1996

Telly *nickname*

Telegraph Avenue, Berkeley, California *US*

- Headline: Peace-Rock OK, But Not On "Avenue" / Will Rock "Off-Telly" — *The Berkeley Barb*, p. 1, 5th August 1966

temazzies; temazies; temmies; temazes; tems *noun*

Temazepam™, a branded tranquillizer *UK*

- Temazepam are called "green or yellow eggs", "jellies" and "jelly babies", "rugby balls" or "temazzies". — James Kay and Julian Cohen, *The Parents' Complete Guide to Young People and Drugs*, p. 150, 1998
- the fucking joyriders burning the hillsides – the temazes stuck on tongues — Patrick Jones, *Everything Must Go*, p. 141, 2000

temp *noun*

a temporary worker *US*

- As an average, each temp has worked during five to six weeks and each customer has employed one or several temps during four and one-half months. — *PR Newswire*, 14th April 1980
- I saw a classified ad for a"temp" service, registered, and worked fairly steadily for five months before landing a permanent job. — *Washingtotn Post*, p. E5, 4th June 1980
- Plus he fell in love with a temp. — *Sleepless in Seattle*, 1993
- I had just gotten home from my unbearable temp job at an investment bank after getting three hours of sleep the night before[.] — Suroosh Alvi et al., *The Vice Guide*, p. 149, 2002

temp *verb*

to work as a temporary worker *US*

- People "temp" for a variety of reasons, according to temp service managers. — *Washingtotn Post*, p. E5, 4th June 1980

temper *noun*

a restaurant customer who leaves a 10% tip *US*

- — *Maledicta*, p. 48, 1995: 'Door whore and other New Mexico restaurant slang'

temperance punch *noun*

a non-alcoholic fruit punch drink *US*

- In a little while we're all goin' down to the Town Hall and drink some temperance punch and look over the poon. — Max Shulman, *Rally Round the Flag, Boys!*, p. 195, 1957

temple balls; temple bells; temple hash *noun*

potent hashish shaped as small balls, claimed to originate in Nepal *US, 1971*

- — Ernest L. Abel, *A Marijuana Dictionary*, p. 102, 1982
- [T]emple ball on a jet plane[.] — Lupine Howl, *Vaporizer*, 2001

temple du vin *noun*

Le Clos Jordan, a winery to be designed by Frank Gehry on the Jordan Bench, on Ontario's Niagara Peninsula, Canada's main wine-producing area *CANADA*

- The eventual price tag of the "temple du vin" is expected to approach $30 million. The owners have hired Canadian-born architect Frank Gehry to create a place where the devout can pay homage to the fruit of the vine. — *Toronto Globe and Mail*, p. A3, 10th July 2002

ten *noun*

1 a perfectly beautiful woman *US*

Based on a grading scale of one to ten, popularised in the 1979 film *10* starring Bo Derek.

- Can't be with a woman who's a ten? You go to two fives. Or five twos. Adds up to the same thing. —Chris Rock, *Rock This!*, p. 126, 1997
- Matt glanced towards Alison once, looked away, then found his eyes moving back towards her. A seven, maybe. No, make that an eight. Borderline nine, even. —Chris Ryan, *Greed*, p. 23, 2003

2 a tablet of MDMA, the recreational drug best known as ecstasy *US*

- —Mike Haskins, *Drugs*, p. 290, 2003
- —Office of National Drug Control Policy, *Drug Facts*, February 2003

ten *adjective*

very good *UK*

Teen slang, from the marking of schoolwork.

- The disco was pretty ten. —D. and R. McPheely, 1977

ten-bob twist *noun*

a drug sale involving drugs, usually marijuana, costing ten shillings *UK*

- —Tom Hibbert, *Rockspeak!*, p. 157, 1983

ten-cent line *noun*

in an illegal betting operation, the ten percent charge for making a bet *US, 1973*

- —Thomas L. Clark, *The Dictionary of Gambling and Gaming*, p. 230, 1987

ten-cent pistol *noun*

a dose of heroin that is either adulterated with a poison or contains a more pure heroin than usual, sold or given to someone with the intent of injuring or killing them *US*

- Addicts call this type of hotshot a "ten-cent pistol" because the poison costs a dime but is as effective as a gun. —James Mills, *The Panic in Needle Park*, p. 39, 1966
- —David Maurer and Victor Vogel, *Narcotics and Narcotic Addiction*, p. 449, 1973
- —Ralph de Sola, *Crime Dictionary*, p. 149, 1982

ten-cent rock *noun*

ten dollars' worth of crack cocaine *US*

- The officer asked for a "10-cent rock" - street slang for a $10 purchase of crack cocaine. Boykin allegedly then told the officer he had only "20-cent rocks." —*Texas Lawyer*, p. 10, 14th October 1991

ten commandments *noun*

bare feet *TRINIDAD AND TOBAGO*

As Long John Silver said, it is good to have ten toes.

- —Lise Winer, *Dictionary of the English/Creole of Trinidad & Tobago*, 2003

tend *verb*

to mind your own business *US*

- She needs to tend because he is my man. —Connie Eble (Editor), *UNC-CH Campus Slang*, p. 10, April 1995

ten-days *noun*

any temporary job *TRINIDAD AND TOBAGO*

- —Lise Winer, *Dictionary of the English/Creole of Trinidad & Tobago*, 2003

ten-day sweat *noun*

treatment for a sexually transmitted infection, involving heat therapy and sulpha-based drugs *US*

- —*American Speech*, p. 31, February 1949: 'A.V.G. lingo'

tender *adjective*

1 in poker, said of a hand that is probably unplayable *US*

- —George Percy, *The Language of Poker*, p. 92, 1988

2 weakened by oxidation; rusty *CANADA*

- —Lewis Poteet, *Car & Motorcyle Slang*, p. 201, 1992

tenement *noun*

in hold 'em poker, a ten and nine *US*

- —John Vorhaus, *The Big Book of Poker Slang*, p. 36, 1996

ten F *noun*

a gall bladder patient *US*

Often a fat, fair, fecund, fortyish, flatulent, female with foul, frothy, floating faeces.

- —*Maledicta*, p. 118, 1984–1985: 'Milwaukee medical maledicta'

ten-four

▷ **see: 10-4**

ten-man job *noun*

a very tough man, a very hard man to arrest *UK*

- He was what they call a "ten-man job", because to bring him down you would have to go ten-handed or turn up with a shooter. —Lenny McLean, *The Guv'nor*, p. 13, 1998

Tennant Creek *noun*

a Greek person *AUSTRALIA, 1977*

Rhyming slang, from the name of a goldmining town in the Northern Territory.

- —Jim Ramsay, *Cop It Sweet!*, p. 89, 1977
- There's a Tennant Creek behind the wheel of most Australian taxicabs and they've got a licence to print money. —Barry Humphries, *The Traveller's Tool*, p. 38, 1985

tenner *noun*

1 a ten-pound note; the value of £10; a ten-dollar note *UK, 1845*

- Shit, man, the day they can call me queer is when I let one of those faggots suck on me for less than a tenner[.] —Hunter S. Thompson, *Hell's Angels*, p. 87, 1966
- In order to expedite the process, will I be giving away a tenner I didn't have to spend? —Robert Campbell, *Alice in La-La Land*, p. 178, 1987
- Gizza tenner an' they're yours. —Donald Gorgon, *Cop Killer*, p. 67, 1994
- He said we all had to bring a tenner in next week, and from then on it was going to be a fiver a week subs[.] —Kevin Sampson, *Powder*, p. 142, 1999

2 a prison sentence of ten years *US*

- —Hyman E. Goldin et al., *Dictionary of American Underworld Lingo*, p. 221, 1950

3 in the television and film industries, a 10,000 watt spotlight *US*

- —Ralph S. Singleton, *Filmaker's Dictionary*, p. 170, 1990

Tennessee top hat *noun*

a hairstyle in which the hair is worn short at the front and long at the back *US*

Better known, perhaps, as a **MULLET**.

- —Ben Sharpe, *Scooter Crazy*, p. 41, 2000

tennies *noun*

tennis shoes; trainers *US*

- —Carol Covington, *A Glossary of Teenage Terms*, 1965
- I shuffled my feet in their black tennies and decided to seal our fate once and for all. —Oscar Zeta Acosta, *The Autobiography of a Brown Buffalo*, p. 90, 1972

tennis, anyone?

used for humorously suggesting an activity *US*

Seen as quintessentially British and enormously witty in its many variant forms.

- The director took one look at me and said, 'But this is a tough guy and you look like you're about to say, Tennis anyone?' —*Dixon (Illinois) Evening Telegraph*, p. 4, 5th May 1951
- Cocktails, anyone? —*San Francisco Examiner & Chronicle*, p. 18, 6th July 1956
- Psychology, anyone (Headline) —*San Francisco Examiner*, p. 5, 26th May 1957
- Bouillabaise, Anyone? (Headline) —*San Francisco Chronicle*, p. 10, 31st May 1957

tennis racket; tennis *noun*

a jacket *UK*

Rhyming slang.

- —Ray Puxley, *Cockney Rabbit*, 1992

tennis shoes *noun*

tyres *US*

- —Wayne Floyd, *Jason's Authentic Dictionary of CB Slang*, p. 29, 1976

ten-one *adjective*

▷ **see: 10-1**

ten one hundred *noun*

the act of urination *US*

- —Elementary Electronics, *Dictionary of CB Lingo*, p. 71, 1976

ten over *noun*

a surfing stance in which the surfer's ten toes extend over the nose or front of the board *US*

- —Trevor Cralle, *The Surfin'ary*, p. 143, 1991

ten percenter *noun*

a person who buys and resells stolen goods *US*

- —John R. Armore and Joseph D. Wolfe, *Dictionary of Desperation*, p. 54, 1976

tens *noun*

amphetamine *UK*

- —Mike Haskins, *Drugs*, p. 279, 2003

tense *adjective*
used of a computer program, smart and economical *US*
- This routine is so tense it will bring tears to your eyes. —Guy L. Steele et al., *The Hacker's Dictionary*, p. 124, 1983

tension *noun*
crack cocaine *US*
- —Peter Johnson, *Dictionary of Street Alcohol and Drug Terms*, p. 189, 1993

tensky *noun*
a ten-dollar note *US*
The 'sky' is a meaningless decorative embellishment.
- —Frank Garcia, *Marked Cards and Loaded Dice*, p. 264, 1962
- I laid some jive and a tensky on his landlady[.]—James Ellroy, *Hollywood Nocturnes*, p. 114, 1994

ten-spot *noun*
1 a ten-dollar note *US*
- A ten-spot, too damned much – anything was too damned much – but he had an idea that it wouldn't be much longer now[.]—Jim Thompson, *A Swell-Looking Babe*, p. 119, 1954
- Reggie got out of the car and walked up the highway and gave the cop a ten-spot, and all the way to Detroit Reggie and One-Eye argued, I mean vehemently, about whether we could have gotten away with only a fiver. —Clancy Sigal, *Going Away*, p. 156, 1961
- She laid the ten spot on me and I copped. —Odie Hawkins, *Black Casanova*, p. 165, 1984
- "Sam won't touch nothing less than a ten-spot," Sam's Man kidded. —Robert Campbell, *Juice*, p. 25, 1988

2 a ten-pound note *UK, 1984*
Adopted directly from the previous sense.
- Sub us a ten-spot then, mun. —Niall Griffiths, *Grits*, p. 30, 2000

3 a ten-year prison sentence *US*
- Now New York give my girl a ten-spot and the matron led her by her hand / just thinkin' of ten long years in prison just for breakin' the laws of man. —Bruce Jackson, *Get Your Ass in the Water and Swim Like Me*, p. 141, 1965

Tenth Street *noun*
a ten-dollar note *US*
- Tenth Street isn't a city thoroughfare but a ten-dollar bill. —Mezz Mezzrow, *Really the Blues*, p. 220, 1946
- —Kenn "Naz" Young, *Naz's Underground Dictionary*, p. 60, 1973

'tention *noun*
in poker, a ten *US*
- —*American Speech*, p. 102, May 1951

tent peg *noun*
an egg *UK, 1949*
Rhyming slang.
- —Julian Franklyn, *A Dictionary of Rhyming Slang*, 1961
- —Ray Puxley, *Cockney Rabbit*, 1992

tent pole *noun*
an erect penis *US*
From the image of an erect penis pushing up against a sheet.
- Tent pole. She's a babe. —*Wayne's World*, 1992

tent squirrel *noun*
in circus and carnival usage, a performer *US*
- —Don Wilmeth, *The Language of American Popular Entertainment*, p. 271, 1981

tenuc; teenuc *noun*
the vagina; an unpleasant or despicable person *UK, 1904*
Back slang for **CUNT**.

termination dust *noun*
the first snow of the winter *US, 1957*
Because it terminates construction in the north.
- —Robert O. Bowen, *An Alaskan Dictionary*, p. 32, 1965
- Given to eloquence, Alaskans even have a special term for Termination Dust. It is called "snow." —Mark Wheeler, *Half Baked Alaska*, p. 138, 1972

termite *noun*
a carpenter *US*
- —*American Speech*, p. 271, December 1963: 'American Indian student slang'

terper *noun*
a professional dancer *US*
An abbreviation of Terpischore, daughter of Jupiter and Mnemosyne, the muse of dancing.
- —Sherman Louis Sergel, *The Language of Show Biz*, p. 222, 1973

terps; turps *noun*
a cough syrup containing elixir of terpin hydrate and codeine, abused for non-medicinal purposes *US*
- —Eugene Landy, *The Underground Dictionary*, p. 183, 1971
- "You got terp?" "I quit." —Robert Deane Pharr, *Giveadamn Brown*, p. 50, 1978

terr; ter; terro; terry *noun*
a guerilla soldier; a terrorist *SOUTH AFRICA, 1978*
Originally Rhodesian military slang.
- They dropped the terrs out on the parachutes[.]— *Sunday Times (South Africa)*, 31st October 1999
- Everyone knows terrs chop off your lips if they catch you. —Alexandra Fuller, *Don't Let's Go to the Dogs Tonight*, p. 52, 2001

terra-poo *noun*
a crossbreed of terrier and poodle *US*
- [C]ockapoos – or terra-poos, peke-a-poos, or labradoodles. Lots of mixes are out there, great pets one and all. But a breed? No. —Gina Spadafori and Marty Becker, *Dogs for Dummies*, p. 28, 2001

terrible *adjective*
excellent *US*
- —Robert George Reisner, *The Jazz Titans*, p. 166, 1960
- —Hermese E. Roberts, *The Third Ear*, 1971

terrible Turk *noun*
work *UK*
Rhyming slang.
- —Ray Puxley, *Cockney Rabbit*, 1992

terribly *adverb*
used as a positive intensifier with the meaning exceedingly, greatly, very *UK, 1833*
- It is a dramatic moment, a terribly big moment. —Delia Ephron, *Big City Eyes*, back matter, 2001

terrier *noun*
a railway track worker *US*
- —Ramon Adams, *The Language of the Railroader*, p. 155, 1977

terrif *adjective*
terrific *US*
Not a lot of thought goes into clipped adjectives, and with a few exceptions they do not last long.
- "Oo, terrif," she replied. One thing I will say for this girl: you would go far to find another so agreeable. —Max Shulman, *The Many Loves of Dobie Gillis*, p. 44, 1951
- "Terrif, Nicky," said Sid, "terrif!" —Terry Southern, *Blue Movie*, p. 75, 1970

Territory rig *noun*
any of various adaptations of formal attire worn by men in far northern Australia *AUSTRALIA, 1964*
- [F]or the purpose of the Royal Visit, "Territory Rig" was defined as long-sleeve white shirt, colored tie or bow tie, long dark trousers, dark shoes. — *Centralian Advocate*, p. 27, 16th March 1983

terrorist *noun*
a teacher who intimidates his pupils into learning *US*
Teen slang, post 11th September 2001.
- A mean teacher? He's "such a terrorist." — *The Washington Post*, 19th March 2002

terrorize *verb*
to cover something with graffiti *US*
- —Jim Crotty, *How to Talk American*, p. 141, 1997

terror track *noun*
in cricket, a wicket best-suited to fast bowlers *UK, 1996*
- —Keith Foley, *A Dictionary of Cricketing Terminology*, p. 383, 1998

Terry toon *noun*
a prostitute's pimp *AUSTRALIA*
Rhyming slang for **HOON**.
- Yer a terry-toon, a blue-moon – anythin' that rhymes with weak-bludger hoon! Hey? —Jim McNeil, *The Chocolate Frog*, p. 48, 1973
- Bill thought we should follow the girls. 'We can be hoons, mate!' he laughed. 'A couple of Terry toons.' —Max Williams, *Dingo*, p. 59, 1980
- —Ryan Aven-Bray, *Ridgey Didge Oz Jack Lang*, p. 47, 1983

Terry Waite *adjective*
late *UK*
Rhyming slang, formed (surely with irony) on the church envoy and hostage negotiator (b.1939) who was held hostage in Beirut for 1,760 days between January 1987 and November 1991.
- —Ray Puxley, *Fresh Rabbit*, 1998

tess *noun*
a young man *TRINIDAD AND TOBAGO, 1960*
• —Lise Winer, *Dictionary of the English/Creole of Trinidad & Tobago*, 2003

test *verb*
▸ **test the shocks**
to have sex in a car *US*
• —Jim Crotty, *How to Talk American*, p. 37, 1997

tester *noun*
a sample of drugs *UK*
• If the price is right. He said he'll give us a tester.—Lanre Fehintola, *Charlie Says...*, p. 23, 2000

testicules *noun*
the testicles *UK*
• —Richard Herring, *Talking Cock*, p. 30, 2003

test-tube baby *noun*
a poker player whose experience is largely limited to simulated computer poker games *US*
• —John Vorhaus, *The Big Book of Poker Slang*, p. 36, 1996

test-tube wallah *noun*
a forensic scientist *UK*
Police use.
• —John Wainwright, *Dig His Grave and Let Him Lie*, 1971

tete *noun*
the female breast *TRINIDAD AND TOBAGO*
• —Lise Winer, *Dictionary of the English/Creole of Trinidad & Tobago*, 2003

Texas Cadillac *noun*
a Chevrolet Suburban sports utility vehicle *CANADA*
• But I still say a Suburban is the most solid vehicle money can buy, so I will stick with my Texas Cadillac. [Letter to the editor].—*Toronto Star*, p. J9, 28th December 1991
• Furthermore, why don't these environments go to Texas and demonstrate against the Texas Cadillac – Suburban? [Letter to the Editor]—*Bangor (Maine) Daily News*, p. 6, 29th December 2003

Texas gate *noun*
a cattleguard *CANADA*
• Cattle escaped over a Texas gate and were hit by a car.—*Canadian Cattlemen Magazine*, May 1997

Texas mickey *noun*
a very large bottle of alcohol *CANADA*
• A mickey is a small bottle of booze. A Texas mickey, on the other hand, is a ridiculously big bottle of booze, which, despite the name, is still a Canadianism.—Will Ferguson, *How to be a Canadian*, p. 63, 2001

Texas pot *noun*
marijuana cultivated in Texas *US*
• —Mike Haskins, *Drugs*, p. 289, 2003

Texas Ranger; TR *noun*
danger *UK: SCOTLAND*
Glasgow rhyming slang.
• "Ye're no gaun already?" "No T.R. Ah'm just gettin warmed up noo [now]."—Michael Munro, *The Patter, Another Blast*, 1988

Texas rat *noun*
in the used car business, a car previously owned by a salesman or other long-distance driver *US*
• —*Esquire*, p. 119, March 1968

Texas stop *noun*
slowing down but not fully stopping as required by law at a stop sign *US*
• —*American Speech*, p. 266, December 1962: 'The language of traffic policemen'

Texas sunflowers *noun*
in craps, a roll of two fives *US, 1983*
• —Thomas L. Clark, *The Dictionary of Gambling and Gaming*, p. 230, 1987

Texas tea *noun*
1 marijuana *US, 1938*
• Do you go for Chinese needlework, reindeer dust [powdered drugs], Texas tea [marijuana] – that kind of stuff?—Douglas Rutherford, *The Creeping Flesh*, p. 49, 1963
• —Mike Haskins, *Drugs*, p. 289, 2003
2 oil *US*
• —Ken Weaver, *Texas Crude*, p. 132, 1984

Texas toothbrush *noun*
the penis *US*
In Texas, known as an 'Oklahoma toothbrush'.
• —Michael Dalton Johnson, *Talking Trash with Redd Foxx*, p. 93, 1994

Texas Volkswagen *noun*
a Cadillac *US*
• —*San Francisco Examiner*, p. 1 (II), 4th November 1956

Texican *noun*
a Texan *US*
• —Ken Weaver, *Texas Crude*, p. 132, 1984

Tex-Mex *noun*
marijuana, of *Tex*an-*Mex*ican origin *UK, 1998*
• —Mike Haskins, *Drugs*, p. 289, 2003

Tex Ritter; tex *noun*
bitter (beer) *UK*
Rhyming slang, formed from the US cowboy film actor, 1907–74.
• A pint of Tex.—Ray Puxley, *Cockney Rabbit*, 1992

text *verb*
to send a text message on a mobile phone *UK*
• By the time I got home, she'd already texted me five times. She can just text herself into a black hole.—*The Guardian*, p. 9, 28th November 2001

textile *noun*
among naturists, a person who wears clothes *UK*
• As further inducement to the reluctant "textile" (nudist lingo for a clothes wearer), Rio's promised complimentary drinks[.]—Kitty Churchill, *Thinking of England*, p. 21, 1995

textile *adjective*
clothed, as distinct from nude *UK*
From the noun sense.
• How could I win the respect of the serious naturists out by the plunge pool if I chose to remain textile?—Kitty Churchill, *Thinking of England*, p. 23, 1995

tezzers *noun*
the testicles *UK*
• —Chris Lewis, *The Dictionary of Playground Slang*, p. 231, 2003

TFB
*t*oo *f*ucking *b*ad *US*
• "TFB." "What?" "Too fucking bad."—*Silent Trigger*, 1996

TFTF
an after-dinner bloated condition unsuited to the advancement of romance *UK*
A coded message: '*t*oo *f*at *t*o *f*uck'.
• —*www.LondonSlang.com*, June 2002

TG *noun*
a young member of a youth gang *US*
• "[H]e's listed in the Gang Street Alias Index under the name Li'l Silent, so at the very least he's a TG or a known associate." TG stood for "tiny gangster" and was basically a killer in training.—Stephen J. Cannell, *The Tin Collectors*, p. 147, 2001

TGIF
*T*hank *G*od *i*t's *F*riday *US, 1941*
Notable variations: the restaurant chain 'T.G.I. Friday's', established in New York in 1965, now worldwide; and the controversial UK television programme *TFI Friday*, 1996–2000.
• Newcomers to Patrick Air Force Base in Florida, where missiles are tested, are usually mystified by seeing the initials TGIF on bulletin boards and notices of various kinds. They are strictly non-regulation. They stand for "Thank God It's Friday"- meaning pay-day and weekend relaxation for some in the form of beach parties, club dances, and so on.—*New York times*, p. SM13, 8th September 1957
• —*Current Slang*, p. 7, Summer 1967
• —Helen Dahlskog (Editor), *A Dictionary of Contemporary and Colloquial Usage*, p. 59, 1972

T-grams *noun*
a grandmother *US*
• —Ethan Hilderbrant, *Prison Slang*, p. 126, 1998

TH *noun*
in betting, odds of 8–1 *UK*
• —John McCririck, *John McCririck's World of Betting*, p. 60, 1991
• It's T.H. over there. Have £50–6. On your bike!—John McCririck, *John McCririck's World of Betting*, p. 110, 1991

Thai Buddha *noun*

a strain of marijuana, known elsewhere as New Zealand green, Tasmanian tiger and Hawaiian head *AUSTRALIA*

- "In Auckland it was called New Zealand Green," Jab says. "It was a local name for a strain that had once been called Thai Buddha—Brian Preston, *Pot Planet*, p. 97, 2002

Thai green *noun*

a strain of marijuana originating in Thailand *UK*

- Tonight she was reasonably mellow, though, as a result of the Thai green.—Tony Wilson, *24 Hour Party People*, p. 27, 2002

Thai stick *noun*

marijuana cultivated in Thailand, soaked in hashish oil, wound on short thin sticks of bamboo which are bundled for sale; a cigarette rolled from marijuana cultivated in Thailand *US, 1975*

- I smoke pot, sometimes hash. I've used Thai stick[.]—*Washington Post*, p. A1, 19th June 1977
- [S]he kept her honor intact for several thousand miles by suggesting that they smoke a paralyzing Thai stick every time he wanted to make love[.]—*Hi Life*, p. 54, 1979
- It seemed likely that someone had crept into the men's restroom and unloaded Captain Woofer's tamped and loaded briar, reloading it with very high grade hashish or Thai stick[.]—Joseph Wambaugh, *The Glitter Dome*, p. 75, 1981
- To fortify it, she smoked her last Thai stick.—James Ellroy, *Blood on the Moon*, p. 195, 1984
- I also take all the Ritalin to cut through the wild hemp, which is the best in the monde, far better than those expensive Thai Sticks that were going around last winter.—Bill Cardoso, *The Maltese Sangweech*, p. 282, 1984
- "So this is what thai stick is, huh?" "Yeahhh, it's something else, ain't it?"—Odie Hawkins, *Lost Angeles*, p. 201, 1994
- I know what Thai sticks are, you stupid Welsh fucker. I was smoking them last night.—Howard Marks, *Mr Nice*, p. 169, 1997

Thai weed; Thai *noun*

marijuana cultivated in Thailand; marijuana from Thailand soaked in hashish oil *UK*

- What happen to the hydro Thai or even de Thai stick or de lunatic Durban[?]—Nick Barlay, *Curvy Lovebox*, p. 33, 1997

Thames trout; trout *noun*

a condom *UK*

Appears to be a London coinage, probably after the rare appearance of a condom floating down the River Thames; remembered by a correspondent from Sheffield as a 1970s usage.

thang *noun*

thing *US*

Slang by vowel exchange.

- That's the groovy thang about Nick, the Geech, he takes every fuckin' thing seriously.—Odie Hawkins, *Chicago Hustle*, p. 23–24, 1977

thanie *noun*

heroin *UK*

- —Mike Haskins, *Drugs*, p. 284, 2003

thank fuck

used in relief when others may be grateful to God *UK*

Euphemistic use of 'fuck' for what might otherwise border on blasphemy.

- "Thank fuck they've gone," I sighed[.]—Martin King and Martin Knight, *The Naughty Nineties*, p. 25, 1999
- 7 a.m. and out the room, thank fuck.—David Peace, *Nineteen Seventy-Four*, p. 136, 1999
- [W]as I the only one thinking "Thank fuck we can't find them"?—Mark Steel, *Reasons to be Cheerful*, p. 40, 2001

thank goodness

used as a register of heartfelt or exaggerated gratitude *UK, 1872*

- In the meantime, thank goodness for plonkers [fools].—*The Guardian*, 5th July 2003

thanks a bunch

used as an insincere or derisory declaration of gratitude *UK*

- [After revealing the ending of a film being reviewed] Oh, thanks a bunch, I hear you saying.—*The Guardian*, 2nd May 2003

thanks a bundle

used as an insincere or derisory declaration of gratitude *UK*

- "You haven't even combed your hair," Nan said. "Thanks a bundle, that's all I need." "It is what you need, actually," Nan said.—Maeve Binchy, *Circle of Friends*, p. 414, 1990

thanks a million

thank you very much indeed *UK, 1984*

Usually sincere, but occasionally derisory.

- Thanks a million, Ma'am—*The Guardian*, 11th May 2002

thanks awfully

thank you! *UK, 1890*

Quintessentially English middle- and upper-class.

- "Oh? Would you?" Burne-Wilke opened the cabin door. "Thanks awfully."—Herman Wouk, *The Winds of War*, p. 663, 1971

thanks but no thanks

used when declining an offer *UK*

- I told them thanks but no thanks.—*British Journal of Photography*, 1st June 1979

thanks ever so

thank you! *UK, 1914*

- All right, girls, it's been lovely. Thanks ever so for the midnight gambol about the old palatial grounds.—Libba Bray, *A Great and Terrible Beauty*, p. 73, 2003

thank you and good night!

used in final dismissal of a foolish suggestion, or in surrender to overwhelming misfortune *UK, 1975*

A valedictory phrase that became a broadcasting cliché which inspired a catchphrase.

- Would Karl Rove let George W anywhere near a free-range, free-fall interrogation like this? Thank you and goodnight, President Gaffe. —*The Guardian*, 26th January 2004

thank-you-m'am *noun*

a bump or dip in a road which produces a moment of slight uneasiness in the stomach *US, 1960*

- —Frank A. Collymore, *Barbadian Dialect*, p. 111, 1965
- We recently heard bumps in a country road referred to as "thank-you-ma'ams." Could you tell us how this term originated? It was from the rider's motion resembling a genteel bow when he was jounced over one of them.—*Old Farmer's Almanac in San Francisco Examiner and Chronicle*, p. 41, 15th April 1979

that *adjective*

used as a mildly derogatory prefix to a (usually proper) noun *UK*

- You going out with that Harry again?—Robert Claiborne, 1976

that *adverb*

to such a degree; so; very *UK*

In conventional use from the mid-C15, but by C20 considered colloquial or dialect.

- We're not all that stupid, we get it why do you keep telling me?—*The Guardian*, 5th August 1999

that *pronoun*

used persuasively in anticipated commendation *UK, 1849*

- [D]ocility was prized in girls whereas it wasn't in boys at all. "That's a good girl" was awarded only to obedient, docile girls, from a very, very young age[.]—*The Observer*, 1st June 2003

that and this *noun*

urine; an act of urination *UK*

Rhyming slang for **PISS**; also employed as a verb.

- —Julian Franklyn, *A Dictionary of Rhyming Slang*, 1961
- —Ray Puxley, *Cockney Rabbit*, 1992

Thatcher *noun*

a type of MDMA, the recreational drug best known as ecstasy *UK*

From Margaret Thatcher (b.1925), former UK Prime Minister 1979–90, later Baroness Thatcher of Kesteven; her name is used here, perhaps, as a tribute by an illicit drug manufacturer to her commitment to free enterprise.

- —Angela Devlin, *Prison Patter*, p. 113, 1996

Thatcher wagon *noun*

a car with the back cut away *CANADA*

- During the days of Premier Thatcher in Saskatchewan, the government ruled that pickup trucks were eligible as farm vehicles and could use [tax-free] purple gas. So people cut away the back of their car to form a type of pickup truck – a Thatcher wagon. — Chris Thain, *Cold as a Bay Street Banker's Heart*, p. 153, 1987

that had to hurt!
used as a humorous if not particularly sympathetic observation of a painful event *US*
• Ow – that had to hurt. — *A Few Good Men*, 1992

that'll be the day!
used of something that is not very likely to occur or be done *AUSTRALIA, 1941*
• It might even be so successful that oil companies in the UK would do everything necessary to keep the forecourts properly supplied. That'll be the day. — *The Guardian*, 21st September 2000

that'll happen
used as a humorous comment on something that should not happen or never happens *US*
Coined and popularised by ESPN's Keith Olberman.
• — Keith Olberman and Dan Patrick, *The Big Show*, p. 24, 1997

that plays
used for expressing approval *US*
• — John D. Bell et al., *Loosely Speaking*, p. 15, 1966

that's chalk!
that's great! *BAHAMAS*
• — John A. Holm, *Dictionary of Bahamian English*, p. 39, 1982

that's close
used for expressing doubt about a statement or request *US*
• — Connie Eble (Editor), *UNC-CH Campus Slang*, November 1973

that's dead!
used for expressing a strong negative *US*
• — Lee McNelis, *30 + And a Wake-Up: A Compendium of Prison Slang Terms and Definitions*, p. 12, 1991

that's that
used in final emphasis of a preceding statement: that's all there is, there is no more *UK, 1872*
• He would never call himself "sight-impaired", for example. He's blind, and that's that. — *The Guardian*, 18th July 1998

that's the name of that tune
used for summing up or signalling the end of an explanation *US*
A signature line of actor Robert Blake on the television police drama *Baretta* (ABC, 1975–78). Repeated with referential humour, especially after Blake's arrest in the early 2000s for the murder of his wife.

that's the ticket!
used as a humorous expression of assent *US*
From a skit on *Saturday Night Live* featuring Jon Lovitz as a pathological liar.
• — Connie Eble (Editor), *UNC-CH Campus Slang*, p. 8, Fall 1986

that's what I'm talking about!
I agree strongly! *US*
Almost a cliché.

that's word!
used for expressing strong assent *US*
• — William K. Bentley and James M. Corbett, *Prison Slang*, p. 51, 1992

that time *noun*
the bleed period of a woman's menstrual cycle *US*
• — *American Speech*, p. 298, December 1954: 'The vernacular of menstruation'

that way *adjective*
homosexual *UK*
Shortened from the euphemistic phrase 'that way inclined'.
• She didn't want to believe stories about Henry Fortescue being that way as he was obviously épris with his pretty sister-in-law. — Compton McKenzie, *Thin Ice*, 1956

thaw shay *noun*
a spendthrift *IRELAND*
• She would spend money like thaw shay. — Irwin Liam, *North Munster Antiquarian Journal*, p. 83, 2000

THC *noun*
marijuana *US*
The psychoactive chemical in marijuana is delta-9-tetrahydrocannabinol, or THC.
• So we refrained from balling at all at the party, got really turned on (we were on THC) and really wanted to ball. — Jefferson Poland and Valerie Alison, *The Records of the San Francisco Sexual Freedom League*, p. 33, 1971

THC
doctors' shorthand for what the homeless require from a day and night's hospitalisation: *t*hree *h*ots and a *c*ot (three meals and a bed) *UK*
• — Adam T. Fox, St Mary's Hospital, London, 10th October 2002

the *adjective*
1 my *UK, 1838*
Colloquial.
• England? You don't say. You got time to come and meet the wife? — *The Guardian*, 10th March 2001
2 used in the formation of colloquial nicknames for places *AUSTRALIA, 1883*
Thus Alice Springs becomes 'the Alice'; Mount Isa becomes 'the Isa'; Cloncurry becomes 'the Curry'; Wollongong becomes 'the Gong'.
• But when I come into the Alice nowadays I drive a car. — Coralie Rees, *Spinifex Walkabout*, p. 242, 1953
• From 'the Curry' the route ran over a deep crossing where the cattle were forced to swim. — Mary Durack, *Kings in Grass Castles*, p. 253, 1959
• — Harvey E. Ward, *Down Under Without Blunder*, p. 47, 1967

theatrical *noun*
an actor *UK, 1859*
Generally seen in the plural.

Thelma Ritter; the thelma *noun*
a toilet; the anus *UK*
Rhyming slang for SHITTER, formed from the name of the US film actress, 1905–69.
• — Ray Puxley, *Fresh Rabbit*, 1998

Thelonius Monk; thelonius *noun*
semen *UK*
Rhyming slang for SPUNK, formed from the name of the US jazz pianist, 1917–82.
• — Ray Puxley, *Cockney Rabbit*, 1992

them's my orders
used as an apology for acting in accordance with orders *US*
• I'm sorry boys. But them's my orders. — Oscar Zeta Acosta, *The Revolt of the Cockroach People*, p. 30, 1973

them's the breaks
used as a world-wise expression of resigned acceptance of a misfortune *US*
• — Connie Eble (Editor), *UNC-CH Campus Slang*, p. 10, Spring 1988

them's the rules
used as a humorous deference to protocol or rules *US*
• I owe you. It told you today, them's the rules. — *As Good As It Gets*, 1997

them things *noun*
marijuana cigarettes *US*
• — William K. Bentley and James M. Corbett, *Prison Slang*, p. 74, 1992

the nerve of the scurve!
used as a humorous exclamation, half admiring *US*
• The hell I know what you was wearin'. The nerve of this scurve! — Edwin Torres, *Carlito's Way*, p. 133, 1975

there *adverb*
▸ **be there**
to be alert and alive to your situation *UK, 1890*
▸ **have been there; have been there before**
to have experienced something *UK, 1877*
• You'd never count out Dwain because he's been there before but I'm not sure that he sounds in 100% shape. — *The Guardian*, 26th July 2002
▸ **have you there**
to cause you to be at a loss; to nonplus you *UK, 1937*

there is no – about it!
▷ see: NO – ABOUT IT!

there it is
used as a common form of assent by US soldiers in Vietnam *US*
• — Linda Reinberg, *In the Field*, p. 217, 1991

there I was with Davey Crockett...
used as a humorous introduction to a story *US*
A signature line used by the Trooper Duffy character played by Bob Steele on the television comedy *F Troop* (ABC, 1965–67). Repeated with referential humour.

Theresa Truncheon; Theresa *noun*
a police officer; the police *UK*
An example of **CAMP** trans-gender assignment, in this case an assonant play on 'truncheon' as stereotypical police equipment.
- [L]ast night's trade [sexual partner] (a Theresa Truncheon, would you believe, bats [boots] of death but bona [good] maquillage [makeup], I must say). —the cast of 'Aspects of Love', Prince of Wales Theatre, *Palare (Boy Dancer Talk) for Beginners*, 1989–92

there's no answer to that!
used in answer to a question, implying an innuendo within the question which renders an answer unnecessary *UK, 1975*
A catchphrase of British comedian Eric Morecambe, 1926–84, widely adopted as a useful face-saver.

there you are *noun*
tea (a drink) *UK*
Rhyming slang for **CHAR**.
- There you are, a nice cup of there you are. —Ray Puxley, *Cockney Rabbit*, 1992

there you are then!; there your are!
used as the (triumphant) last words in an argument as a point is proved *UK, 1907*
Often preceded by 'so' or 'well'.
- MICHELANGELO: [...] [I]f there was a last supper there must have been a one before that, so this, is the "Penultimate Supper"! The Bible doesn't say how many people were there now, does it? POPE: No, but... MICHELANGELO: Well there you are, then! —*Monty Python's Flying Circus*, 17th November 1970

there you go!
used for expressing approval *US*
- —Clarence Major, *Dictionary of Afro-American Slang*, p. 114, 1970

thermos bottle *noun*
a tanker lorry *US*
From the shape.
- —*Complete CB Slang Dictionary*, p. 90, 1976
- —Peter Chippindale, *The British CB Book*, p. 159, 1981

these and those *noun*
1 the toes *UK, 1960*
Rhyming slang.
- It's me new daisy roots [boots], they're killing me plates [feet]. Me these and those are cramped. —*The Sweeney*, p. 6, 1976

2 the nose *AUSTRALIA, 1960*
Rhyming slang.

3 clothes *UK, 1992*
Rhyming slang.

the shot heard 'round the world *noun*
the homerun hit by New York Giants Bobby Thompson to defeat the Brooklyn Dodgers in the final game of a three-game playoff series for the National League Championship in 1951 *US*
An allusion to the first skirmish of the American Revolution on the village green in Lexington, Massachusetts, on 19th April 1775.
- And then, in the Sox eighth, it happened: the most dramatic homer in baseball since Bobby Thomson's 'shot-heard-round-the-world' for the Giants[.] —Bill Cardoso, *The Maltese Sangweech*, 1984
- —Louis Phillips and Burnham Holmes, *The Complete Book of Sports Nicknames*, p. 225, 1998

thesp *noun*
an actor *UK, 1962*
An abbreviation of the conventional 'thespian'.
- Yep, Harry always wanted to be a thesp, really. —James Hawes, *Dead Long Enough*, p. 63, 2000

thews *noun*
muscles; the thighs; the forearms *UK*
A variation of the conventional sense as 'vigour'; only recorded in the plural.
- He's a great butch omee, he's got these thews like an oak, and bulging lallies [legs]. Ohh! —Barry Took and Marty Feldman, *Round The Horne*, June 1966

They *noun*
the mysterious authority over all authority, the power behind the throne *US*
Beloved in the political culture of the 1960s.
- Laura said whimsically, "You know, after we take over and rule the world, we've got to find out who They are." "Then," I said, "we'll be They." —James Simon Kunen, *The Strawberry Statement*, p. 77, 1968

Theydon Bois *noun*
noise *UK*
Rhyming slang, formed from the name of an Essex village.
- Let loose in the country they would have made quite a bit of "Theydon Bois". —Ray Puxley, *Cockney Rabbit*, 1992

thick *adjective*
1 in close association, familiar, intimate *UK, 1756*
Often elaborated as **THICK AS THIEVES**.

2 stupid, dense *UK, 1935*
- The kid is thicker'n shit, what he is, and that is what he's got for brains. —George V. Higgins, *The Rat on Fire*, p. 28, 1981
- The police are thick. —Shaun Ryder, *Shaun Ryder... in His Own Words*, 1990

3 sexually appealing, attractive, well built *US*
- —Connie Eble (Editor), *UNC-CH Campus Slang*, p. 10, Spring 1998
- —Gary K. Farlow, *Prison-ese*, p. 73, 2002

4 of a bet, large *UK*
- —John McCririck, *John McCririck's World of Betting*, p. 61, 1991
- —David Bennet, *Know Your Bets*, p. 102, 2001

thick-a *adjective*
very dense *US*
Used in Maine, as in 'thick-a-fog', 'thick-a-snow' or 'thick-a-vapor'.
- —Kendall Merriam, *The Illustrated Dictionary of Lobstering*, p. 86, 1978

thick and thin *noun*
1 the chin *UK*
Rhyming slang.
- —Ray Puxley, *Cockney Rabbit*, 1992

2 gin *UK*
Rhyming slang.
- —Ray Puxley, *Cockney Rabbit*, 1992

thick as a docker's sandwich *adjective*
very stupid *UK*
'Thick as' is used as the basis for many similes.
- "Pratt," said my father." As thick as a docker's sandwich." —John Milne, *Alive and Kicking*, p. 33, 1998

thick as a plank *adjective*
very stupid *UK*
The simplified variation of **THICK AS TWO SHORT PLANKS**.

thick as a pudding *adjective*
very stupid *UK: ENGLAND*
A north of England variation on a theme; the 'pudding' is a Yorkshire pudding.
- —Nick Brownlee, *Everything You Didn't Need To Know About The UK*, p. 47, 2003

thick as pigshit *adjective*
very stupid *UK*
- Most of those families are thick as pigshit. —Caroline Aherne and Craig Cash, *The Royle Family*, 1999
- The Old Bill up there were as thick as pig shit. —Dave Courtney, *Raving Lunacy*, p. 12, 2000
- "Not the brightest?" Fuckin backwards that cunt was, mun. Thick as fuckin pigshit, like. —Niall Griffiths, *Sheepshagger*, p. 11, 2001
- [T]he people running it are thick as pig shit. —*X-Ray*, p. 20, April 2003

thick as thieves *adjective*
in close association, familiar, intimate, inseparable *UK, 1833*
- For 15 years while editing the paper [The Times] he [C.P. Scott] sat as a Liberal MP. He and Lloyd George were thick as thieves. Where should journalism end and politics begin? —*The Times*, 6th December 2002

thick as two short planks *adjective*
very stupid *UK, 1984*
Originally military; one of the best known modern variations on a Shakespearean theme.

thick dick; thick Dick *noun*
a stupid person *UK*
Teen slang. Reported by Joanna Williamson, 1982.

thick ear *noun*

a blow round the head *UK, 1909*

From the swelling of the ear – if the blow is accurate.

- Frequently they [policemen] were quite heavy individuals given to handing out a thick ear as an instant remedy for minor infringements. — Brian McDonald, *Elephant Boys*, p. 195, 2000

thick end of the stick *noun*

an unfair position to be in, or inequitable treatment *UK, 1957*

- However, once we get the thick end of the stick – like, say, a year or two in prison, or even a month of chakkars to the police station – all those 'ideals' quickly evaporate[.] — Varsha Bhosle, *www.rediff.com*, 29th July 2002

thick head *noun*

a headache, especially one that results from drinking alcohol *UK, 1991*

- Because I like to go to the pub at night I usually get up with a thick head. — *The Guardian*, 22nd March 2003

thickhead *adjective*

idiotic, foolish, stupid *UK*

From the noun sense.

- reminding the thickhead dickheads on the other side of the table that I'm not obliged to answer — Val McDermid, *Keeping on the Right Side of the Law*, p. 177, 1999

thickie; thicky; thicko *noun*

a fool *UK, 1968*

Variations of **THICK**.

- I ain't an effing thicky — Ian Dury, *Billericay Dickie*, 1977
- Using the apostrophe correctly is a negative proof: it tells the world you are not a thicko. — Lynne Truss, *Eats, Shoots and Leaves*, p. 105, 2003
- Just tell us what to do. We're from round here, sir. You know we're thickos. — *The Times Magazine*, p. 49, 25th October 2003

thick on the ground *adjective*

abundant, numerous, crowded *UK, 1893*

- The notes may seem to be in some places rather thick on the ground, but it will be seen that where clustered most densely [...] they are due less to the editor than to the author[.] — J.R.R. Tolkein, *Unfinished Tales*, front matter, 1988

thick piss *noun*

semen *NEW ZEALAND*

- — David McGill, *David McGill's Complete Kiwi Slang Dictionary*, p. 125, 1998

thief *noun*

in horse racing, a horse that runs worst when its chances seem best *US*

- — Tom Ainslie, *Ainslie's Complete Guide to Thoroughbred Racing*, p. 339, 1976

Thief Row *noun*

London Heathrow airport *UK*

Jocular but telling.

- I'd been working at Heathrow, or Thief Row, as it was more aptly called, for two years now[.] — Martin King and Martin Knight, *The Naughty Nineties*, p. 45, 1999

thieve *noun*

▸ **on the thieve**

engaged in the occupation or act of stealing *UK*

- The thing about being a burglar is that people think that you're always on the thieve, you can't give it a rest[.] — Danny King, *The Burglar Diaries*, p. 44, 2001

thieving *adjective*

inclined to thievery *UK, 1598*

Originally in conventional use.

- [H]ow disgusting all the Americans were. "Weak, smelly, self-pitying-a pack of sniveling, dirty, thieving bastards," he said. "They're worse than the bleeding Russians." — Kurt Vonnegut Jr, *Slaughterhouse-Five*, p. 162, 1969

thighbrows *noun*

female pubic hair that escapes the confines of underwear or swimwear *UK*

- — *Roger's Profanisaurus*, p. 214, 2002
- — Chris Lewis, *The Dictionary of Playground Slang*, p. 232, 2003

thigh-highs *noun*

stockings worn up the middle of the thigh *US*

- While some critics complained that designers were making fun of women by dressing them like children, thigh-highs also evoke images of streetwalkers and porn layouts. — Steven Daly and Nalthaniel Wice, *alt.culture*, p. 249, 1995

thigh opener *noun*

a vodka gimlet *US*

- — *American Speech*, p. 20, Spring 1985: 'The language of singles bars'

thighslapper *noun*

in pantomime, the role of principal boy *UK*

From the traditional gesture by which an attractive actress convinces an audience of her manhood.

- [M]y fourth year as a thighslapper[.] — *Oh No It's Not!*, 31st December 2003

T. Hill *noun*

Tommy Hilfiger™ clothing *US*

- — Ethan Hilderbrant, *Prison Slang*, p. 126, 1998

thimble and thumb; thimble *noun*

rum *UK*

Rhyming slang.

- [A] "tot of thimble"[.] — Ray Puxley, *Cockney Rabbit*, 1992

thimble-titted *adjective*

small breasted *US*

- — Michael Dalton Johnson, *Talking Trash with Redd Foxx*, p. 73, 1994

thin *noun*

in prison, a key *UK*

- — Angela Devlin, *Prison Patter*, p. 113, 1996

thin blue line *noun*

the police *UK*

From the image of, and originally recorded as, a line of police holding back a crowd.

- D'you know Detective Sergeant Chisholm, a leading local representative of the thin blue line? — Anthony Masters, *Minder*, p. 133, 1984

thing *noun*

1 used to replace any noun that the user cannot or does not wish to specify *US*

Also called a 'thingy'.

- Interested MDs should write to Free City Medical Thing c/o The Differs. — *The Digger Papers*, p. 17, August 1968
- As it happens the princess thing didn't work out for me, so I went to college[.] — Janet Evanovich, *Seven Up*, p. 1, 2001

2 the penis *UK, 1386*

Since Chaucer, and still.

- They staked him to the ground, see with tent pegs, then burned him all over with butts. Even his thing. — Richard Farina, *Been Down So Long*, p. 64, 1966
- "The girl insisted we have sex before she would marry me but I just couldn't get up my thing." This was Mark's word for penis. — Sara Harris, *The Lords of Hell*, p. 171, 1967
- Junior pulled out this thing. It looked like a horse's cock – black, long and fat, with a huge pink head. — Steve Cannon, *Groove, Bang, and Jive Around*, p. 36, 1969
- An accident. Your thing just got into a box of popcorn? — *Diner*, 1982
- I know I take a girl, stick my thing in and nine months later a baby comes out. — *Boyz N The Hood*, 1990

3 the vagina *US*

Euphemism. Early use implied in obsolete 'thingstable' (1785) where 'thing' replaces **CUNT** in a policeman's title.

- [W]e would walk along seeing whose dress was up the highest and if you could really see their thing 'cause they didn't wear no bloomers. — Louise Meriwether, *Daddy Was a Number Runner*, p. 26, 1970
- His sister would show you her thing for two cigarette cards. — Johnny Speight, *It Stands to Reason*, p. 16, 1973

4 an interest, obsession, attraction *US, 1841*

- I made up my mind then and there that my "thing" would have to be show business as my only escape. — Babs Gonzales, *I Paid My Dues*, p. 18, 1967
- Thing was the major abstract word in Haight-Ashbury. It could mean anything, isms, life styles, habits, leanings, causes, sexual organs[.] — Tom Wolfe, *The Electric Kool-Aid Acid Test*, p. 10, 1968
- Revolution is in your head. You are the Revolution. Do your thing. — Abbie Hoffman, *Revolution for the Hell of It*, p. 10, 1968
- This isn't my thing, Mr. O'Connor. — Nat Hentoff, *I'm really dragged but nothing gets me down*, p. 63, 1968
- I had this thing. That was my thing. — Leonard Wolfe (Editor), *Voices from the Love Generation*, p. 217, 1968
- I think he has a little thing for Annie. — *Annie Hall*, 1977
- "My partner had a thing for her," Leeds explained to Anne. — Joseph Wambaugh, *Floaters*, p. 221, 1996
- I did not have a "thing." I was very much in love with him. Very much in love, and there's a difference. — *Romy and Michele's High School Reunion*, 1997

5 a romantic affair *US*

- Mary Astor was keeping a diary about her thing with George Kaufman[.] — Eve Babitz, *Eve's Hollywood*, p. 17, 1974

6 an instinctive or irrational dislike of, or aversion to, someone or something *UK, 1936*

- He has a thing about blades. He thinks the world's against him. — *The Guardian*, 15th April 2003

7 heroin; a capsule of heroin *US*

- A thing is a dollar-capsule of H. — Willard Motley, *Let No Man Write My Epitaph*, p. 148, 1958
- — Richard A. Spears, *The Slang and Jargon of Drugs and Drink*, p. 507, 1986
- — Mike Haskins, *Drugs*, p. 284, 2003

8 cocaine *UK*

- — Nick Constable, *This is Cocaine*, p. 181, 2002
- — Mike Haskins, *Drugs*, p. 281, 2003

▸ **do your own thing; do your thing**

to behave according to your own self-centred philosophy, appetites and idiosyncracies *US*

Originally a black coinage, adopted by the hippies in the 1960s.

- The Diggers are hip to poetry. Everything is free, do your own thing. — *Trip Without a Ticket*, Winter 1966–67
- — Joe David Brown (Editor), *The Hippies*, p. 217, 1967: 'Glossary of hippie terms'
- Other examples of doing your own thing: cats prowling back alleys at night, Mantle poking a 450-foot home run at Yankee Stadium, Kruschev pounding a shoe at the U.N. — Sidney Bernard, *This Way to the Apocalypse*, p. 58–59, 1968
- I think the Diggers should be killed. I think the word has gotten out of hand already. All it means is free and do your thing. — Leonard Wolfe (Editor), *Voices from the Love Generation*, p. 116, 1968
- "He's doing his thing," he said, pointing, "over by that fire." — Terry Southern, *Now Dig This*, p. 121, November 1968
- If each man or woman is to (pardon me) "do his own thing," then some will necessarily have to conform while others will be rebels . — *East Village Other*, p. 2, 20th September 1968
- "Doing their thing, man," said Dave softly, and nodded to show perfect understanding. — Terry Southern, *Blue Movie*, p. 213, 1970
- To make a long story short, we're East Coasties so we're going to Do Our Things in the woods. — Raymond Mungo, *Famous Long Ago*, p. 137, 1970
- [A] "free form" school for teenagers – the kind of education where "do your own thing" was stressed at the expense of any rules or structure. — Sean Hutchinson, *Crying Out Loud*, p. 95, 1988

▸ **have a thing for; have a thing about**

to be attracted, perhaps obsessively so, to someone or something *UK, 1936*

- He'd always had a thing for irony. — *The Guardian*, 30th August 2003

▸ **the thing**

the requisite, notable or special point *UK, 1850*

- However, the big status symbols in Salcombe are not clothes, but boats. The thing is to have a gradation of craft, with the small ones, such as Thunderbirds, being served by the larger ones. — *New Statesman*, 28th August 2000
- The rap's the thing[.] Hip-hop Shakespeare: how did an idea that sounds so bad end up the smash hit of the Edinburgh fringe? — *The Guardian*, 28th August 2002

Thing *noun*

▸ **the Thing**

an M-50A1 Ontos antitank tracked vehicle, heavily armed *US*

- "The Thing" was especially effective against enemy bunkers and entrenchments, but its light armor made it vulnerable to enemy fire and mines. — Gregory Clark, *Words of the Vietnam War*, p. 300, 1990

thingamajig; thingumajig; thingummyjig *noun*

used as a psuedo-term for something the name of which is unknown, forgotten or not important *UK, 1824*

- Doesn't it impress you at all that here is a real live human being you made all by yourself? – you and your thing-a-ma-jig there? — John Nichols, *The Sterile Cuckoo*, p. 181, 1965
- Don't tell me that fool is up blowin' on that thang-a-majig again! — Odie Hawkins, *Ghetto Sketches*, p. 40, 1972
- [T]here's a thingamajig they can put on the projector that'll cut through that gunk like Bruce Lee's foot through Velveeta cheese. — Joe Bob Briggs, *Joe Bob Goes to the Drive-In*, p. 9, 1987
- I say, that green thingummyjig you're wearin' – habit, isn't it? Capital camouflage. — Brian Jacques, *Redwall*, p. 88, 2000
- But I haven't got one of those thingamajigs, whatever the hell they're called. — Andrea Camilleri, translated by Stephen Sartarelli, *The Terra-Cotta Dog*, p. 111, 2003

thingamerry; thingumbobsy *noun*

an object the name of which escapes the speaker *BARBADOS*

- — Frank A. Collymore, *Barbadian Dialect*, p. 111, 1965

thingie; thingy *noun*

1 a thing *UK, 1933*

- Sorry. The door-opening thingy's knackered. — Christopher Brookmyre, *Boiling a Frog*, p. 72, 2000
- [W]e haven't talked about that unit trust thingy once. — Sophie Kinsella, *Confessions of a Shopaholic*, p. 302, 2001

2 the penis *UK, 1977*

- When your son grabs his penis say, "That's your penis" (instead of "thingy"). Tell your daughter, "That's your vulva" (instead of "bottom"). — Martha and William Sears, *The Discipline Book*, p. 265, 1995

thingio *noun*

used as a vague replacement for an unremembered or unnamed person, object or action *UK*

A variation of **THINGIE** (a replacement noun).

- [J]ust to show he was thingio, the kiddie and that[.] — Kevin Sampson, *Outlaws*, p. 50, 2001
- Yeh, ye know! A thingio! — Niall Griffiths, *Kelly + Victor*, p. 8, 2002

thingio *verb*

used as a vague replacement for an unremembered or unnamed verb *UK*

- [S]he's thingioing, she's on the pole dance then she's bending herself over[.] — Kevin Sampson, *Clubland*, p. 95, 2002

thingo *noun*

an unnamed, or temporarily unnameable, person or thing *AUSTRALIA, 1966*

- So, in this person's presence, you just refer to him or her as 'thingo here,' and watch the flush climb to the cheeks and neck. — Arthur Chipper, *The Aussie Swearer's Guide*, p. 56, 1972
- She laughed even louder as they loaded me in a wheelchair onto the thingo that lifts all the food compartments onto the plane. — Paul Vautin, *Turn It Up!*, p. 153, 1995

things *noun*

1 possessions, personal effects carried with you at a given time *UK, 1290*

- When my husband and I moved from Taiwan to Canada, we left most of our things behind, arriving with only a few suitcases of clothing. — *Natural Health*, March 1999

2 garments, clothing *UK, 1634*

- Please take your wet things off the couch and put them in the dryer. — Karen Pryor, *Don't Shoot the Dog!*, p. 95, 1999

▸ **do things to**

to excite someone, especially sexually; to arouse a passion, whether deep or momentary *UK*

- Like a song of love that clings to me / How the thought of you does things to me. — Nat King Cole, 1951

things are crook in Tallarook

things are very bad *AUSTRALIA, 1963*

Tallarook is a town in central Victoria.

- Anyway, things were crook in Tallarook with them, at the time. Even the mugs on their own mug's list stopped buying their tips. — Frank Hardy, *The Yarns of Billy Borker*, p. 60, 1965
- Many who worked close to Claude swore that he loved trouble, and he was at his best when everyone else was holding his head shouting that 'things were crook in Tallarook.' — George Blaikie, *Remember Smith's Weekly?*, p. 240, 1966
- The Longreach train is late again, / And things are crook in Tallarook[.] — John O'Grady, *Aussie Etiket*, p. 80, 1971

things-on-the-springs *noun*

a military inspection of a soldier's gear displayed on his bed *US*

- — Linda Reinberg, *In the Field*, p. 119, 1991

thing-thing *noun*

an object the name of which escapes or is unimportant to the speaker *US*

- — John R. Armore and Joseph D. Wolfe, *Dictionary of Desperation*, p. 54, 1976

thingumabob; thingummybob *noun*

used as a replacement for any noun that the user cannot or does not wish to specify *UK, 1832*

- [W]hat the Sam Hill is this thingumabob supposed to do? — Eric Kraft, *Herb 'n' Lorna*, p. 188, 1989
- "But I tell you, when I turned my head and saw that fancy ultra-business thingummybob . . ." "Ultrasound," corrects Clara, through a mouthful of rice. — Zadie Smith, *White Teeth*, p. 57, 2000

thingummy *noun*
used as a replacement for any noun that the user cannot or does not wish to specify *UK, 1796*
- Still leader of the Scottish Thingummy[.] — *New Statesman*, 22nd January 2001

thingummy-whatsit *noun*
used as a euphemistic replacement for any noun that the user cannot or does not wish to specify *UK*
- I said I'd show her my willy if she showed me her thingummy-whatsit, but I intended to rat on her at the last moment. — Alan Titchmarsh, *Trowell and Error*, p. 90, 2002

thingy *noun*
in drag racing, a car that has been modified and enhanced for speed *US*
- — Tom MacPherson, *Dragging and Driving*, p. 143, 1960

▷ see: THINGIE

thin hairs *noun*
▸ **have by the thin hairs**
to hold someone at a disadvantage; to exercise complete control over someone *US*
- I was really in the dumps, but fate had me by the thin hairs and wouldn't turn me loose. — Mezz Mezzrow, *Really the Blues*, p. 129, 1946

think *verb*
▸ **think outside the box**
to reject standard assumptions and strive for a creative solution to a problem *US*
From a brain-teaser puzzle which can be solved only if you reject the boundaries of a box. It vaulted into cliché use quickly, and provided the inspiration for author Jim Tompkins' 2001 book *Think Outside the Box: The Most Trite, Generic, Hokey, Overused, Cliched or Unmotivating Motivational Slogans*.
- To Think Outside the Box, Get Back Into Sandox — *The Los Angeles Times*, 11th January 1999
- This season, another phrase leaps out at me from candidate interviews, forums and public speechifying. It is the call to Think Outside the Box. — *The Cincinnati Enquirer*, p. A18, 7th October 1999

▸ **think your shit doesn't stink**
to be very conceited *UK, 1961*
- [O]bservations such as "You think you're pretty good, don't you?" and "You think your shit doesn't stink, eh?" — Tibor Fischer, *Under the Frog*, p. 17, 1995
- A patient described her narcissistic mother in these words: "She thinks her shit doesn't stink." — Alexander Lowen, *Narcissism*, p. 125, 1997

▸ **you're not paid to think**
a catchphrase admonition in response to any excuse that begins 'but I thought…' *UK*
Originally a military truism. Noted by J.B. Mindel, 1971 but thought to be much earlier.

think again, dearie
used for humorously expressing the negative *US*
- — *Washington Post Magazine*, p. 16, 26th December 1987: 'Say Wha?'

think it ain't?
used for expressing affirmation *US*
- — William K. Bentley and James M. Corbett, *Prison Slang*, p. 47, 1992

thinko *noun*
a momentary loss of memory or disruption in a thought process *US*
A play on 'typo'.
- — Eric S. Raymond, *The New Hacker's Dictionary*, p. 349, 1991

think-piece *noun*
a serious article of journalism *UK, 1960*
- A favourite think-piece among sports editors at the moment is to compare the current Australians to the West Indian side of the 1980s. — *The Guardian*, 13th March 2003

think tank *noun*
a toilet *US*
Punning on the term usually applied to non-governmental organisations that analyse policy.
- — Connie Eble (Editor), *UNC-CH Campus Slang*, p. 8, Fall 1997

thin man *noun*
a person who does not exist who is placed on a payroll as a bookkeeping fiction *US*
- — Sherman Louis Sergel, *The Language of Show Biz*, p. 225, 1973

thinny *noun*
a very thin hand-rolled cigarette or joint *UK*
- [A] couple of Thinnies of Mauie-zowie sinsemilla dope and a tab of window pane acid[.] — Stuart Browne, *Dangerous Parking*, p. 84, 2000

thin one *noun*
a dime, or ten-cent piece *US*
- — Joseph E. Ragen and Charles Finston, *Inside the World's Toughest Prison*, p. 821, 1962: 'Penitentiary and underworld glossary'
- — Steve Kuriscak, *Casino Talk*, p. 56, 1985

thin on the ground *adjective*
sparse, scarce *UK, 1942*
The natural opposite of THICK ON THE GROUND (abundant).
- Texas and California, the largest states, had the largest population in the west, but people were still thin on the ground. — Martha Gelhorn, *The View from the Ground*, p. 376, 1988

thin-out *verb*
to depart *UK*
- — Nigel Foster, *The Making of a Royal Marine Commando*, 1987

third base *noun*
in casino blackjack, the seat immediately to the dealer's right *US*
- — Steve Kuriscak, *Casino Talk*, p. 56, 1985

third degree *noun*
an intense level of interrogation *US, 1880*
- [T]he kid's mother was supposed to be a third-degree artist, and new sneakers in the house probably wouldn't have gone unchallenged. — Richard Price, *Clockers*, p. 354–355, 1992
- — Angela Devlin, *Prison Patter*, p. 114, 1996

third hat *noun*
an assistant drill instructor in the US Marine Corps *US*
Generally the drill instructor who hands out physical discipline – Physical Incentive Training.

third leg *noun*
the penis *US*
- Condoms have become an essential part of the modern man's wardrobe, an extra sock for the third leg. — Anka Radakovich, *The Wild Girls Club*, p. 83, 1994

third rail *noun*
1 a bill, especially in a restaurant *US*
A term of the 1940s music industry.
- — Arnold Shaw, *Lingo of Tin-Pan Alley*, p. 20, 1950

2 an extremely controversial political issue *US*
Like the third rail in an electric railway system, it is to be avoided.
- The Social Security program is often being called the "third rail" of politics. — *Omaha World-Herald*, p. 8, 13th June 2000
- If there is a third rail full of lethal electricity in state politics this golden summer, it is asking voters to increase stiff increases in gas and car costs. — *The Seattle Times*, p. B4, 16th July 2001

3 inexpensive, potent alcohol *US*
- — Joseph E. Ragen and Charles Finston, *Inside the World's Toughest Prison*, p. 821, 1962

third sex *noun*
homosexuals as a group *US, 1896*
- Many of the third sex journey regularly to New York, where they have friends in esoteric circles. — Jack Lait and Lee Mortimer, *Washington Confidential*, p. 92, 1951
- — Dale Gordon, *The Dominion Sex Dictionary*, p. 156, 1967

third-world botherer *noun*
a person who acts upon the need to do good in less fortunate areas of the world *UK*
- I got to know Liz and her fellow third-world botherers [in this instance: the American Peace Corps] very well. — Ken Lukowiak, *Marijuana Time*, p. 53, 2000

third world briefcase *noun*
a large portable stereo system associated, stereotypically, with black youth culture *US*
- — Connie Eble (Editor), *UNC-CH Campus Slang*, p. 1, Fall 1987

thirst monster *noun*
a crack cocaine user *US*
• — *Detroit News*, p. 5D, 20th September 2002

thirsty *adjective*
intensely craving crack cocaine *US*
• — Terry Williams, *Crackhouse*, p. 152, 1992

thirteen *noun*
1 marijuana; a marijuana cigarette *US*
Because 'M' is the 13th letter of the alphabet.
• Among the first to be exposed was the numeral "13" (indicating a marijuana smoker). — Hunter S. Thompson, *Hell's Angels*, p. 117, 1966
• — Richard A. Spears, *The Slang and Jargon of Drugs and Drink*, p. 508, 1986
• — Mike Haskins, *Drugs*, p. 289, 2003
2 in a deck of playing cards, any king *US*
• — John Vorhaus, *The Big Book of Poker Slang*, p. 36, 1996
▷ **see:** 13

thirteen *nickname*
the Mexican Mafia prison gang *US*
• These terms were being seen with greater frequency, thrown up as graffiti throughout California's prisons along with the numeral 13, which signifies the letter M, or more precisely, La eMe. — Bill Valentine, *Gangs and Their Tattoos*, p. 23, 2000

thirteenth gear *noun*
in trucking, neutral gear, used to coast down hills *US*
• — Montie Tak, *Truck Talk*, p. 166, 1971

thirty days *noun*
in poker, a hand with three tens *US*
• — Irwin Steig, *Common Sense in Poker*, p. 185, 1963

thirty dirty miles *noun*
in a game of poker, a hand with three tens *US, 1963*
• — Thomas L. Clark, *The Dictionary of Gambling and Gaming*, p. 231, 1987

thirty miles of railroad track *noun*
in poker, a hand consisting of three tens *US*
• — George Percy, *The Language of Poker*, p. 92, 1988

thirtysomething *adjective*
describing the age of the generation of baby boomers as they moved into their thirties *US*
From the name of a television drama (1987–91) focusing on YUPPIE angst.
• — *American Speech*, Summer 1990

thirty-thirty *noun*
a central nervous system stimulant other than amphetamine packaged to look like and sold as amphetamine *US*
• — Peter Johnson, *Dictionary of Street Alcohol and Drug Terms*, p. 191, 1993

thirty-weight *noun*
strong coffee *US*
Inviting a comparison with motor oil.
• — Wayne Floyd, *Jason's Authentic Dictionary of CB Slang*, p. 32, 1976

this and that *noun*
a hat *AUSTRALIA, 1937*
Rhyming slang.
• — Ray Puxley, *Cockney Rabbit*, 1992

this and that *verb*
in cricket, to bat *UK*
Rhyming slang.
• — Julian Franklyn, *A Dictionary of Rhyming Slang*, 1961

thisavvy *noun*
this afternoon *UK*
A Liverpool slurring.
• [I]t's not until thisavvy[.] — Kevin Sampson, *Outlaws*, p. 233, 2001

this is it
used when something that has been talked about happens or is happening *UK, 1942*

this is me
used in place of 'hello' when answering the telephone *US*
• — Connie Eble (Editor), *UNC-CH Campus Slang*, p. 4, April 1978

this time it's personal
used as a humorous assertion that an issue is being taken personally *US*
A moderately popular catchphrase from *Jaws: The Revenge* (1987).
• I don't know animals, but I do know this: this time it's personal. — *Austin Powers*, 1999

this will separate the men from the boys; this will sort the men from the boys
this task, event, crisis or activity will only be successfully managed by someone of sufficient experience or maturity *UK, 1974*
The original use, 'this is where the men are separated from the boys' or 'this is where they separate the men from the boys', is attributed to US film actress Mae West, in which case this dates to the late 1930s and is laden with sexual innuendo.
• The ultimate is the Ironman, a competition designed to separate the men from the boys. Each year men will compete in Hawaii for the title of Ironman, and the title says it all. — Jon Giswold, *Basic Training: A Fundamental Guide to Fitness for Men*, p. 169, 2000

T.H. Lowry *noun*
a Maori *NEW ZEALAND, 1997*
Prison rhyming slang, formed from a famed horse-breeder.
• — Harry Orsman, *A Dictionary of Modern New Zealand Slang*, p. 138, 1999

Thomas Cook *noun*
a look *UK*
Rhyming slang, invented by the advertisers for travel company Thomas Cook in the slogan 'Take a Thomas Cook at our Prices!' and now in limited circulation.
• — Ray Puxley, *Fresh Rabbit*, 1998

Thomas More *noun*
a whore *UK*
Rhyming slang, probably formed from the renaissance writer and Catholic martyr (1478–1535).
• — Bodmin Dark, *Dirty Cockney Rhyming Slang*, 2003

thong feminism *noun*
contemporary forms of feminism *CANADA*
• Current reflections of female empowerment which [Vancouver comedian] Janeane Garofolo terms "thong feminism," leave her perplexed. — *Toronto Globe and Mail*, p. R3, 24th July 2002

thooleramawn *noun*
a contemptible, incompetent person *IRELAND*
• To his bafflement, however, the thooleramawns who had drafted the by-laws had omitted to insert a clause making it an offence for strollers in public places at night-time to slow down to a standstill except in certain designated areas, such as under lighted street lamps. — Hugh Leonard, *Out After Dark*, p. 25, 1989

Thora Hird; Thora *noun*
1 a third class university degree *UK*
Rhyming slang, based on the name of British stage and screen actress Dame Thora Hird (1911–2003).
• — David Rowan, *A Glossary for the 90s*, 1998
2 a turd, hence an act of defecation *UK*
Rhyming slang, based on the name of British stage and screen actress Dame Thora Hird (1911–2003)
• Just nipping out for a Thora. — *www.LondonSlang.com*, June 2002

thorazine shuffle *noun*
the slow, dragging walk of a patient being medicated with thorazine *US*
• — Sally Williams, *"Strong" Words*, p. 162, 1994

thorn *noun*
1 a nail *UK: SCOTLAND*
Used by workers in the building trade in Glasgow.
• — Michael Munro, *The Patter, Another Blast*, p. 72, 1988
2 a knife *US*
• — Kenn "Naz" Young, *Naz's Dictionary of Teen Slang*, p. 117, 1993

thoroughbred *noun*
a drug dealer who sells high quality, pure drugs *US*
• — William D. Alsever, *Glossary for the Establishment and Other Uptight People*, p. 32, December 1970

those days *noun*
the bleed period of a woman's menstrual cycle *US*
- — *American Speech*, p. 298, December 1954: 'The vernacular of menstruation'

thou *noun*
1 a *thou*sand *US, 1867*
- You know, a couple of years ago, and this was in Norfolk too, a lieutenant supply officer lifted six thou and went over the hill. — Darryl Ponicsan, *The Last Detail*, p. 30, 1970
- In the majority of pictures with budgets of five hundred thou or more, studio participation is involved[.] — Terry Southern, *Now Dig This*, p. 66, 1973

2 a *thou*sandth of an inch *UK, 1902*
- — Chris Cradock, *A Manual of Clayshooting*, p. 176, 1983

though
used, after a question or statement, as an intensifier; truly *UK, 1905*
A colloquial term.
- But suppose your mommy told me she didn't paint you that color. She did paint me though! — Marguerite Wright, *I'm Chocolate, You're Vanilla*, p. 21, 2000

thousand miler *noun*
a sateen shirt worn by railway workers *US*
- — Norman Carlisle, *The Modern Wonder Book of Trains and Railroading*, p. 269, 1946

thousand percent *adverb*
completely *US*
The most famous use of the term in the US came in 1972 when Democratic presidential nominee Senator George McGovern announced that he was 'one thousand percent' in support of his running mate, Thomas Eagleton, despite revelations that Eagleton had once received shock treatment; McGovern dropped Eagleton from the ticket several days after this endorsement.
- The governor is, (as the saying goes in Las Vegas), a thousand per cent correct. — Ed Reid and Ovid Demaris, *The Green Jungle*, p. 5, 1963
- I was a thousand percent wrong. — Vincent Patrick, *Family Business*, p. 42, 1985

thousand-yard stare; thousand-metre stare *noun*
a lost, unfocused look, especially as the result of brutal combat *US*
- He fully recognizes Pacvo's 1,000-meter stare, that pale and exhausted, graven look from head to toe. — Larry Heinemann, *Paco's Story*, p. 95, 1986
- The thousand-yard stare. A marine gets it after he's been in the shit for too long. — *Full Metal Jacket*, 1987
- Then Strike saw Andre give Horace the thousand-yard stare and Horace began to lose it as the giant knocko came straight at him. — Richard Price, *Clockers*, p. 282, 1992

thou shalt not be found out; thou shalt not get found out
propounded as the Eleventh Commandment *UK*
- [A]s in politics, there was only one commandment, the eleventh, "Thou shalt not be found out." — Frederick Forsyth, *The Dogs of War*, p. 28, 1974
- For many modern sinners, however, the traditional 11th Commandment of "Thou shalt not get found out" will take some beating. — *Daily Telegraph*, 29th February 2004

thrap *verb*
(of a male) to masturbate *UK*
- Ad a wank in front of us all, dinny? [...] Didn't give a fuck like, just whapped it out and started thrappin. — Niall Griffiths, *Sheepshagger*, p. 98, 2001

thrash *noun*
1 a high-spirited party *UK*
- — John Winton, *HMS Leviathan*, 1967
- — Tom Hibbert, *Rockspeak!*, p. 157, 1983

2 a style of hard rock music that appeals to disaffected suburban adolescent boys – fast, relentlessly loud and heavy *US*
- Well, it's not exactly speed or thrash or grunge or grind. — *Airheads*, 1994
- I couldn't listen to thrash all day either, but I certainly like little bits. — Shaun Ryder, *Shaun Ryder... in His Own Words*, 1997

thrash *verb*
1 to surf aggressively and with skill *US*
- — Michael V. Anderson, *The Bad, Rad, Not to Forget Way Cool Beach and Surf Discriptionary*, p. 20, 1988

2 to skateboard aggressively and with skill *US*
- — *Macon Telegraph and News*, p. 9A, 18th June 1989

3 in drag racing, to work on a car hurriedly if not frantically in the hours just before a race *US*

thrashed *adjective*
tired, worn-down, exhausted, especially as a result of excessive indulgence in hedonistic pleasures; dishevelled *US*
- Johnny Tourist's idea of a good night out is to get completely thrashed and try to grab hold of any girl who cares to walk past him. — Wayne Anthony, *Spanish Highs*, p. 88, 1999
- She looked really thrashed and kind of droopy from the heroin she was doing. (Quoting Pauly Shore) — *Spin Magazine*, October 1999

thrasher *noun*
1 a party where guests bring bottles of alcohol that are poured into a rubbish bin for all to share *US*
Michigan Upper Peninsula practice and usage.

2 a person who violently responds to the pricks of a tattoo needle *US*
- — *Los Angeles Times Magazine*, p. 7, 13th July 1997

3 a skilled and fearless skateboarder *US*
- — *San Francisco Sunday Examiner & Chronicle*, p. 20, 2nd September 1984: 'Say It Right'

threaders *adjective*
fed-up; being ready to lose your temper *UK*
Royal Navy, especially marine, slang; an abbreviation of 'thread-bare', suggesting patience worn thin.
- [T]he boys were getting really threaders by now. — Rick Jolly, *Jackspeak*, 1989

threads *noun*
clothes *US, 1926*
- It's a shame the way you treat your threads. — Ross Russell, *The Sound*, p. 46, 1961
- Listen, Prosper, listen to me good, the eyes in those smooth stores have the hone for uncool threads. — Bernard Wolfe, *The Magic of Their Singing*, p. 25, 1961
- I was going to be a heart breaker all right. All I needed was the "threads" and a whore. — Iceberg Slim (Robert Beck), *Pimp*, p. 59, 1969
- He was always pressed; nothing but the best / Vines and kicks he had / A thirty-dollar lid and gloves of kid / Man his threads were bad. — Dennis Wepman et al., *The Life*, p. 97, 1976
- Hey, Dixie, nice threads. — *Lethal Weapon*, 1987
- What's with the boss threads? — *Empire Records*, 1995
- Who is this dude wears a suit of clothes, nice threads? — Elmore Leonard, *Be Cool*, p. 110, 1999

three *noun*
a three-dollar bag of heroin *US*
- So I reached in my slide and came out with two boss threes / And said "Here, girl, go to the shithouse and get the weakness out of your knees." — Dennis Wepman et al., *The Life*, p. 52, 1976

▸ **or three**
either by exaggeration or understatement, used for emphasis of an amount *UK, 1976*
- I don't know what's got into you. I mean, have I done you a favour or three? — Anthony Masters, *Minder*, p. 80, 1984

three; three up *verb*
in prison, to share a cell with two other inmates *UK*
- — Angela Devlin, *Prison Patter*, p. 114, 1996

three and a half *noun*
in Quebec, an apartment with a living room, kitchen, bedroom and bathroom *CANADA*
Similarly, in Quebec, a 'two-and-a-half' is an apartment with a living-dining room, bedroom and bathroom; a 'four-and a half' has two bedrooms; and so forth up to 'seven-and-a-half'.
- Downtown Metro Atwater, highrise, 3 1/2, indoor pool, heating included. (Classified ad) — *Montreal Gazette*, p. C10, 26th August 2002

three and four *noun*
a whore *UK*
Rhyming slang.
- — Bodmin Dark, *Dirty Cockney Rhyming Slang*, 2003

three-bagger *noun*
1 an unattractive girl *US*
From the tease that she is so ugly that you have to put two bags over her head and one over yours.
- — Connie Eble (Editor), *UNC-CH Campus Slang*, p. 8, Fall 1987

2 a train pulled by three engines *US*
- — Norman Carlisle, *The Modern Wonder Book of Trains and Railroading*, p. 269, 1946

three-balls *noun*
a Jewish person *US*
An allusion to the historical signage outside a pawn shop.
• —Edith A. Folb, *runnin' down some lines*, p. 257, 1980

three blind mice *noun*
rice *UK*
Rhyming slang, formed from a nursery rhyme.
• [C]urried beef and three blind mice[.] —Ray Puxley, *Cockney Rabbit*, 1992

three-bug *noun*
in horse racing, an inexperienced jockey given a weight allowance of ten pounds *US*
• —Robert V. Rowe, *How to Win at Horse-Racing*, p. 200, 1990

three-cents people *noun*
a poor family *GUYANA*
When the colonial British Guyana dollar was based on the British pound sterling, 'three cents' was used to indicate cheapness. The term survives as a metaphorical relic.

three-D *adjective*
said of a school that recruits basketball players but does not prepare them for life after college *US*
It is said that the college that does not teach players to play defense, does not instill discipline, and in the end does not award diplomas to many of its student athletes.
• —Sam Goldaper and Arthur Pincus, *How to Talk Basketball*, p. 121, 1983

three day chop *noun*
a period of partial or absolute withdrawal from drugs or a drug-substitute *UK*
• —Angela Devlin, *Prison Patter*, p. 114, 1996

three days by canoe *adjective*
a long distance *US*
• —Judi Sanders, *Faced and Faded, Hanging to Hurl*, p. 40, 1993

three days' delay *noun*
in Quebec, three days' notice *CANADA*
• —Victor Trahan, *The City of Montreal Style Guide*, 2002

three days older than dirt *adjective*
very old indeed *US*
• —Judi Sanders, *Mashing and Munching in Ames*, p. 20, 1994

three-decker *noun*
a three-storey house *US*
Coined and primarily used by Irish immigrants and then Irish-Americans in Boston.
• Of a rickety three-decker in South Boston, he unforgettably remarked that the only thing that was holding it up was the wash lines. —*The Boston Globe*, p. A27, 3rd June 1990

three deuces *noun*
in hot rodding, three two-barrel carburettors *US*
• —Lewis Poteet, *Car & Motorcyle Slang*, p. 202, 1992

three-dollar bill *noun*
1 used for comparisons of something that is rare or odd *US*
• Stage money – as phony as a three dollar bill – was one of the psychological weapons used by Allied forces in the closing days of the Japanese war. —*Washington Post*, p. 4, 2nd October 1945
• As phoney as a three-dollar bill. —*Traverse City (Michigan) Record Eagle*, 4th June 1948
2 a homosexual *US*
From the expression 'as strange as a three-dollar bill'.
• —*The Guild Dictionary of Homosexual Terms*, p. 44, 1965
• —Dale Gordon, *The Dominion Sex Dictionary*, p. 156, 1967

three drags and a spit *noun*
a cigarette *UK*
Gay use; a deliberate reversal of rhyming slang **SPIT AND DRAG** (a cigarette) thereby avoiding the rhyme on **FAG** and its derogatory homosexual connotations.
• —Paul Baker, *Polari*, p. 192, 2002

three Ds *noun*
▷ see: **DERRY-DOWN-DERRY**

three'd up *adjective*
in prison, used of three inmates sharing a single cell *UK*
• —Angus Hall, *On the Run*, 1974
• —Home Office, *Glossary of Terms and Slang Common in Penal Establishments*, July 1978

three fates *noun*
in poker, three queens *US*
• —George Percy, *The Language of Poker*, p. 92, 1988

three fifty-seven; three fifty-seven Magnum *noun*
a central nervous system stimulant, the exact nature of which is unknown, sold as amphetamine on the street *US*
• —Peter Johnson, *Dictionary of Street Alcohol and Drug Terms*, p. 191, 1993

three-fingered salute *noun*
when operating a computer, the keyed-combination of the characters Ctrl-Alt-Delete used to restart the machine *US*
• Also known as the "three-fingered salute" and the "Vulcan nerve pinch," this classic key combo has bailed out untold millions of users. —*Word Spy*, 12th February 2004

three-finger fuck around *noun*
a disorganised activity with no apparent purpose *US*
• —Linda Reinberg, *In the Field*, p. 218, 1991

three-for-two *noun*
fifty percent interest *US*
• Oberholster, can I borrow a box at three-for-two? —Malcolm Braly, *On the Yard*, p. 91, 1967

three-hairs *noun*
a Vietnamese woman *US*
From the perception of the US soldier that the pubic hair of Vietnamese women is very sparse.
• —Linda Reinberg, *In the Field*, p. 218, 1991

three H enema *noun*
in hospital usage, an aggressive enema – *h*igh, *h*ot and a *h*ell of a lot *US*
• —*Maledicta*, p. 56, Summer 1980: 'Not sticks and stones, but names: more medical pejoratives'

three-holer *nickname*
an aircraft with three engines, especially the Boeing 727 *US*
• The largest source of noise for the suffering communities around O'Hare, for example, are the planes known in the aviation trade as the "three-holers" – the triple-engine 727s. —*Chicago Tribune*, p. C14, 13th November 1985
• —Rene Foss, *Around the World in a Bad Mood: Confessions of a Flight Attendant*, p. 35, 2002

three hots and a cot *noun*
room and board *US*
From the sense of **HOT** as 'a meal'.
• Jes leave me what I got, three hots and a cot. —Seth Morgan, *Homeboy*, p. 311, 1930
• For a day's work, each youth is paid 50 cents plus earning his room and board, or "three hots and a cot," as one youth described it. —*New York Times*, p. 51, 28th September 1969
• Such as this: a grand a week cash and three hots and cot at a Beverly Hills mansion, all legit. —James Ellroy, *Hollywood Nocturnes*, p. 243, 1994
• Three Hots and a Cot? Not! [Headline]' American Civil Liberties Union. —*ACLU News Wire*, 13th August 1996

three-hundred club *noun*
a notional association of those who experience a temperature swing of three hundred degrees farenheit, usually by rolling naked in the Antarctic night and then entering a sauna *ANTARCTICA*
• —*Cool Antarctica*, 2003: 'Antarctic slang'

three-legged beaver *noun*
a homosexual man *UK*
Two legs and an erect penis make the three legs, feminised by **BEAVER** (a woman/vagina).
• —Peter Chippindale, *The British CB Book*, p. 160, 1981

three-martini lunch *noun*
a leisurely business lunch paid for from an expense account, often centred around alcohol *US, 1972*
• They wore suits, and most were businessmen who indulged in the then-proverbial three-martini lunch. —Kathryn Leigh Scott, *The Bunny Years*, p. 7, 1998

three minutes *noun*
a gang punishment, in which the offending member must fight another gang member for three minutes *US*

• That's a violation, and she got to get down for three minutes with another homegirl. Either with bare fists or with boxing gloves. —*Rolling Stone*, p. 82, 12th April 2001

three moon *noun*

a three-month prison sentence *UK, 1950*

A multiple of **MOON**, included here for the singular nature of the plural.

• —Angela Devlin, *Prison Patter*, p. 114, 1996

three on the tree *noun*

a three speed manual transmission with the gear shift mounted on the steering column *US*

• —John Edwards, *Auto Dictionary*, p. 169, 1993

three-peat *verb*

▷ **see:** 3-PEAT

threepenny bits; thrupennies; threepennies; thrups *noun*

1 the female breasts *UK, 1961*

Rhyming slang for **TIT(S)**, based on a small coin (3d) that ceased to be legal tender with decimalisation in 1971; when this slang was coined, you got 80 threepenny bits to the pound.

• I haven't told youse about her thrupennies, yet... fucking pure silicone! —Kevin Sampson, *Powder*, p. 440, 1999
• [I]t don't mean nowt looking at someone's threepenny bits, you're only looking. —Caroline Aherne and Craig Cash, *The Royle Family*, 1999

2 an urgent need to defecate; diarrhoea *AUSTRALIA*

Rhyming slang for **THE SHITS**.

• I can't stand toilet talk from sheilahs – it gives me the threepennies!!! —Barry Humphries, *Bazza Pulls It Off!*, 1971

three-phase set *noun*

in electric line work, a set of three shovels: a cup-shaped spoon, a spade and a shovel *US*

• —A.B. Chance Co., *Lineman's Slang Dictionary*, p. 16, 1980

three-point c and b *noun*

a painful parachute landing *US*

The three points were the head, heels and buttocks, while the 'c and b' was a 'crash and burn'.

• —Linda Reinberg, *In the Field*, p. 218, 1991

three-rounder *noun*

a petty criminal, a small operator *UK*

From the three-round bouts of junior and novice boxing.

• —Douglas Warner, *Death of a Snout*, 1961

threes *noun*

1 the third landing or floor level in a prison *UK*

• —Home Office, *Glossary of Terms and Slang Common in Penal Establishments*, July 1978
• —Angela Devlin, *Prison Patter*, p. 53, 1996
• He's up on the threes. —*The Guardian*, 26th October 2000

2 in poker, three cards of the same rank in a hand *US*

• —Albert H. Morehead, *The Complete Guide to Winning Poker*, p. 275, 1967

▸ **all the threes**

thirty-three *UK, 1943*

In Bingo, House or Housey-Housey calling, the formula 'all the' announces a double number.

three-sheet *verb*

to wear theatrical makeup in public *US*

• People are friendly, however, even if you don't have a date, but start off like a Marlboro Man unless you detect your conversation partner three-sheeting. That is an old show-biz term, meaning wearing some of his makeup offstage. —John Francis Hunter, *The Gay Insider*, p. 109, 1971

three sheets in the wind *adjective*

very drunk *UK, 1821*

• "Mr. Ivers," I said, "is just about three sheets in the wind." —Jim Thompson, *Roughneck*, p. 116, 1954

three-six-five *noun*

▷ **see:** 365

three-sixty *noun*

a complete, 360 degree turn; in the UK, especially while joyriding *US, 1927*

• He told how a woman pulled out in front of him and when he braked did a three-sixty, spun all the way around. —Elmore Leonard, *Out of Sight*, p. 248, 1996
• —Angela Devlin, *Prison Patter*, p. 115, 1996

three-sixty-four *noun*

▷ **see:** 364

three-skinner *noun*

a marijuana- or hashish-filled cigarette fashioned out of three cigarette papers *UK*

• If you like them short, fat and stubby then the classic three-skinner is the spliff for you. —Nick Jones, *Spliffs*, p. 101, 2003

threesome *noun*

group sex with three participants *US, 1972*

• I said that you, I and that girl from your acting class should sleep together in a threesome. —*Annie Hall*, 1977
• "What? A threesome?" "Fuckin' right." "Who with?" —Colin Butts, *Is Harry on the Boat?*, p. 88, 1997

three squares *noun*

three square meals a day *US, 1922*

• Life in the joint wasn't so bad, he rationalized for a moment, the sun's rays tripping him out, not if you had three squares a day, few hassles and a chance to write as much as you wanted. —Odie Hawkins, *The Busting Out of an Ordinary Man*, p. 83, 1985

three-time loser *noun*

a criminal who has been convicted of a third serious crime, probably guaranteeing life imprisonment *US*

• We'll get nabbed for sure. I'm a three-time loser. I'll get life in prison. —Chester Himes, *Come Back Charleston Blue*, p. 7, 1966

three-toed sloth *noun*

a slow-thinking, slow-talking, slow-acting hospital patient *US*

• —*Maledicta*, p. 118, 1984–1985: 'Milwaukee medical maledicta'

three-toke killer *noun*

extremely potent marijuana *US*

Derived from the perception that the marijuana will produce extreme intoxication after only three inhalations.

• —Peter Johnson, *Dictionary of Street Alcohol and Drug Terms*, p. 192, 1993

three-tone *noun*

of a car, badly repaired after an accident *UK*

A play on the advertising of 'two-tone' cars (cars painted in two colours).

• —*Sunday Times*, 9th August 1981

three-two-hundred out, one-six-hundred in *adjective*

completely confused *US*

From the standard 6400-mil circular artillery chart.

• —Carl Fleischhauer, *A Glossary of Army Slang*, p. 22, 1968

three-up *verb*

▷ **see:** THREE

three up and three down *noun*

a master sergeant in the US Army *US*

From the stripe configuration.

• —Linda Reinberg, *In the Field*, p. 218, 1991

three up and two down *noun*

a sergeant first class or platoon sergeant in the US Army *US*

From the stripe configuration.

• —Linda Reinberg, *In the Field*, p. 218, 1991

three-way *noun*

sex involving three people simultaneously *US*

• A three-way or sexual sandwich may consist of one person penetrating anally, a second both penetrated and penetrating, and the third penetrated only. —Wayne Dynes, *Homolexis*, p. 105, 1985
• He introduced me to some model he'd gone out with and kept pushing for a three-way, but I started getting jealous at that point and told him I wanted to go home. —Sandra Bernhard, *Confessions of a Pretty Lady*, p. 92, 1988

three-way *adjective*

(used of a woman) willing to engage in vaginal, anal and oral sex *US*

• She frankly admitted she was what many call girls, including myself, had not yet advanced to, or perhaps fallen to, a three-way girl. She'd say, "What difference does it make which one of your body's openings they stick their cock in – mouth, vagina or rear end?" —Sara Harris, *The Lords of Hell*, p. 71, 1967
• I said, "Black, eighteen, cute, stacked, and 'three way.'" —Iceberg Slim (Robert Beck), *Pimp*, p. 102, 1969
• Sharon is a three-way girl – available to clients by vagina, mouth or anus. —John Warren Wells, *Tricks of the Trade*, p. 18–19, 1970
• You sure she's three way? —Mickey Spillane, *Last Cop Out*, p. 48, 1972
• —Kenn "Naz" Young, *Naz's Underground Dictionary*, p. 61, 1973
• She was a three-way wench, played Jasper in a pinch / And took 'em around the horn. —Dennis Wepman et al., *The Life*, p. 81, 1976

three-way freeway *noun*
a woman who consents to vaginal, anal and oral sex *US*
- — *Sky Magazine*, July 2001

three wheel trike; three-wheeler *noun*
a lesbian *UK*
Rhyming slang for **DYKE**.
- The problem with the women in athletics is that they may look nice but they're all three wheelers. — Bodmin Dark, *Dirty Cockney Rhyming Slang*, 2003

thrift *verb*
to live a frugal, if attractive, lifestyle *US*
- — Vann Wesson, *Generation X Field Guide and Lexicon*, p. 168, 1997

thrift shop *noun*
any low-limit, low-ante poker game *US*
- — John Vorhaus, *The Big Book of Poker Slang*, p. 36, 1996

Thrilla in Manilla *nickname*
the heavyweight boxing championship fight between Muhammed Ali and Joe Frazier on 1st October 1975 in Manilla, won by Ali when Frazier's manager Eddie Futch threw in the towel before the 15th round *US*
- — Louis Phillips and Burnham Holmes, *The Complete Book of Sports Nicknames*, p. 227, 1998

thrilled *adjective*
pleased, delighted *UK, 1937*
- [Nicholas Hytner] adds jokingly: "If Robert Lepage came to me and said he'd like to stage a Novello show, I'd be really thrilled". — *The Guardian*, 29th April 2003

thrilled to bits *adjective*
utterly delighted; very pleased *UK, 1964*
- Sir James Freeborn was the Assistant Chief Constable. "He sounded thrilled to bits that we were down here 'watching the operations,' as he put it." — Ruth Rendell, *Babes in the Wood*, p. 70, 2003

thriller *noun*
a sensational (adventure) story told as a play, film or novel; such a form of entertainment *UK, 1889*
A narrow sense of the general meaning.
- "Digital Fortress is the best and most realistic techno-thriller to reach the market in years... A chilling thrill a minute." – The Midwest Book Review — Dan Brown, *Digital Fortress*, back cover, 2003

thrill pill *noun*
a central nervous system stimulant in tablet form *US*
A reduplication that never really caught on; too true for a euphemism and too euphemistic for the street.
- Goofballs, yellow jackets, wild geronimos, red birds, blue heaven, idiot pills, thrill pills, red devils – what do they mean to you? — *San Francisco Examiner*, p. 18, 19th May 1953
- And he prescribed an amphetamine, which I believe is the generic term for Dexedrine, Benzedrine, Byphetamine, and the base for most diet pills, mood elevators, pep pills, thrill pills, etc. — Lenny Bruce, *How to Talk Dirty and Influence People*, p. 132, 1965
- — William D. Alsever, *Glossary for the Establishment and Other Uptight People*, p. 1, December 1970

throat *noun*
▸ **have by the throat**
to have someone completely under control *AUSTRALIA, 1947*
- Look out, world! We've got ya by the throat! — Jack Bennett, *Gallipoli*, p. 46, 1981
- Can you chop out the smokes? They're no good to you, but you're hooked. Nicotine has got you by the throat; literally. — Barry Dickins, *What the Dickins*, p. 60, 1985

thrombo *noun*
a fit of rage *UK*
From 'thrombosis', suggesting a rush of blood to the head.
- "But the driver won't come in, will he?" I say, before Brian can have another thrombo. — Andrew Holmes, *Sleb*, p. 334, 2002

throne *noun*
1 a toilet seat; a pedestal lavatory (as a place on which you sit) *UK, 1922*
- Bill Phillips is certain, for example, that his decision to join the Police Department was made while sitting on the "throne" in the bathroom one day and reading of the fine pension benefits available. — Leonard Shecter and William Phillips, *On the Pad*, p. 75, 1973
- I get my best ideas when I'm sitting on the throne. How about you? — Anka Radakovich, *The Wild Girls Club*, p. 192, 1994
- I'm on the throne, takin' a shit. Gimme five. — Stephen J. Cannell, *The Tin Collectors*, p. 116, 2001

2 the most coveted position for a bookmaker at the track *AUSTRALIA*
- — Ned Wallish, *The Truth Dictionary of Racing Slang*, p. 80, 1989

throttle artist; throttle jerker; throttle puller *noun*
a train engineer *US*
- — Ramon Adams, *The Language of the Railroader*, p. 157, 1977

throttle jockey *noun*
a combat jet pilot *US*
- — *American Speech*, p. 229, October 1956: 'More United States Air Force slang'
- — Linda Reinberg, *In the Field*, p. 218, 1991

throttling pit *noun*
a lavatory *AUSTRALIA*
- [M]ight as well tip the stuff straight down the throttlin' pit without flamin' drinkin' it!!! — Barry Humphries, *Bazza Pulls It Off!*, 1971

through-the-card *noun*
a wager that bets on all the races at a meeting *UK*
Commonly used when gambling on greyhound racing.
- — David Bennet, *Know Your Bets*, p. 126, 2001

through-ticket *noun*
in pool, a player who continues to play and to lose money until he has lost his entire bankroll *US*
- — Mike Shamos, *The Illustrated Encyclopedia of Billiards*, p. 246, 1993

throw *noun*
1 the cost of an item or action, usually preceded by a specific amount *US, 1898*
Probably from the old side shows of the fair.
- White orchids go with anything, but they cost $15 a throw. — Jack Lait and Lee Mortimer, *New York Confidential*, p. 214, 1948
- Y'innarested? Five bucks a throw. Fifteen bucks the whole night. — J.D. Salinger, *Catcher in the Rye*, p. 91, 1951
- The male prostitute can count on being paid an average of $10 a throw, which is considerably less than the average female earns. — *Screw*, p. 3, 7th February 1969

2 an act of vomiting; vomit *AUSTRALIA*
- Calling for Herb, see, that's one of the many euphemisms for vomit, others include spue, burp, hurl, the big spit, the long spit, throw, the whip o'will, the technicolour laugh and, in Queensland, the chuckle. — Frank Hardy, *Billy Borker Rides Again*, 1967

throw *verb*
1 to disconcert, to confuse *US, 1844*
- WING COMMANDER CLARK: That had come on quite early. That had really surprised him, that that quote had been tabled to him. MR KNOX : So after the hearing he says to you: that really threw me? WING COMMANDER CLARK: Yes he did. — *The Hutton Inquiry*, 2004

2 to deliberately lose a contest *US, 1868*
- [R]umours abounded that conservative elements of government had bribed officials to throw the game in order to knock the team out of the World Cup[.] — *The Observer*, 18th November 2001

3 to break an addiction *US*
- Jail had, as always, forced him to "throw his habit," and so small amounts were sufficient in the beginning. — John Clellon Holmes, *Go*, p. 198, 1952

▸ **throw a fin; throw the fin**
while surfing, to reach the top of a wave and expose to the air the surfboard's fin(s) *US*
- — Mitch McKissick, *Surf Lingo*, 1987

▸ **throw a fit**
to become very angry or agitated *US, 1926*
- Chez Nico in East Dulwich, where Nico threw a fit because the Good Food Guide had called him Italian. — *The Guardian*, 8th September 2003

▸ **throw a party**
to lose heavily when gambling *US*
- — David M. Hayano, *Poker Faces*, p. 187, 1982

▸ **throw a shape**
to make an impression
- [Boyzone] were throwing the same sort of shapes as an eighties pro footballer, boasting the same sort of square blankness. — John Robb, *The Nineties*, p. 281, 1999

▸ **throw a shine**
to ignore someone *US*
Usage by Mexican-American youth (Pachucos) in the south-western US.
• — *Common Ground*, p. 81, Summer 1947

▸ **throw a shoe**
to suffer a tyre blowout or flat tyre *US*
• — *American Speech*, p. 46, February 1963: 'Trucker's language in rhode island'
• Slingo. — *The Official CB Slang Dictionary Handbook*, p. 61, 1976

▸ **throw blows**
to fight *US*
• — Miss Cone, *The Slang Dictionary (Hawthorne High School)*, 1965

▸ **throw flame**
in trucking, to show an actual flame or a red glow suggesting a flame on a smokestack *US*
• — Montie Tak, *Truck Talk*, p. 167, 1971

▸ **throw forty fits**
to become very angry or agitated *UK, 1984*
An occasional intensification of THROW A FIT.

▸ **throw gravel**
to accelerate briskly from a dirt road shoulder *US*
• — *American Speech*, p. 273, December 1962: 'The language of traffic policemen'

▸ **throw hands**
to fight *US*
• — Gary K. Farlow, *Prison-ese*, p. 73, 2002

▸ **throw it to**
from a male perspective, to have sex *US*
• My boyfriend and I do it at least once a day, generally oftener, but ever now and then he gets a honk out of watching one of his friends throw it to me. — *Screw*, p. 16, 16th May 1969

▸ **throw off at**
to deride someone or something *AUSTRALIA, 1812*
• Some of them throw off at us – call us "the slap-up party", as though prospecting and comfort should never mix. — Mary Durack, *Kings in Grass Castles*, p. 292, 1959

▸ **throw one**
from a male perspective, to have sex *US*
• Man, would I like to throw one to her. — Bernard Wolfe, *The Late Risers*, p. 143, 1954

▸ **throw shade**
to project a defiant attitude *US*
• — Steven Daly and Nalthaniel Wice, *alt.culture*, p. 266, 1995

▸ **throw shapes**
to box *IRELAND*
• Dec stopped. He threw off their arms and started throwin shapes. — Gaye Shortland, *Mind that 'tis my Brother*, p. 24, 1995

▸ **throw signs**
to flash hand signals, almost always gang-related *US*
• When this baby moved back here, he was throwin' gang signs and talkin' just like a little gangbanger. — *Rolling Stone*, p. 85, 12th April 2001

▸ **throw teddy out of the pram**
to throw a tantrum; to lose your temper *UK*
An allusion to childish behaviour.
• That was a time when I might have spit the dummy out or thrown teddy out of the pram. The old me would 'ave gone storming out[.] — Sally Cline, *Couples: Scene From the Inside*, p. 199, 1998

▸ **throw the bald-headed champ**
to perform oral sex on a man *US*
• And then you start pulling on the rope [masturbating him] or to throw the bald-headed champ [perform fellatio], boy you have reached rock bottom in my opinion. — Bruce Jackson, *In the Life*, p. 171, 1972

▸ **throw the head**
to lose one's temper *IRELAND*
• Catherine was worried there'd be a scene. If that girl turned up. You're not to throw the head with her, Johnny, please. — Joseph O'Connor, *Red Roses and Petrol*, p. 94, 1995

▸ **throw the knockwurst**
from a male perspective, to have sex *US*
• Well, I shined my light in there and here's these two down on the seat, the old boy throwing the knockwurst to his girlfriend[.] — Joseph Wambaugh, *The Blue Knight*, p. 245, 1973

▸ **throw the latch**
in a hotel, to activate a mechnical device advising hotel employees to carefully watch activity in a particular room *US*
• So, as I say, I'd automatically signaled to the bellman to "throw the latch." This is simply a device which makes it easier for employees to keep an eye on suspected parties. — Dev Collans with Stewart Sterling, *I was a House Detective*, p. 38, 1954

▸ **throw the leg over**
to mount a racehorse *AUSTRALIA*
• — Ned Wallish, *The Truth Dictionary of Racing Slang*, p. 81, 1989

▸ **throw the voice; throw your voice**
to vomit *AUSTRALIA*
• Any tick of the clock now he's going to start throwing the voice. — John Wynnum, *Tar Dust*, p. 101, 1962
• If you wanna throw your voice / Mate, you won't have any choice / But to chunder in the old Pacific Sea. — Barry Humphries, *The Wonderful World of Barry McKenzie*, p. 15, 1968

▸ **throw up your set**
to flash gang hand signals *US*
• — Bill Valentine, *Gang Intelligence Manual*, p. 78, 1995
• "Put Yo Hood Up" they shout on the next single, a call to throw up your "set," or neighborhood's hand signs. — *Atlanta Journal-Constitution*, p. 7D, 31st May 2001

▸ **throw waist**
to thrust with vigour during sex *TRINIDAD AND TOBAGO*
• — Lise Winer, *Dictionary of the English/Creole of Trinidad & Tobago*, 2003

▸ **throw your weight about; throw your weight around**
to 'show off' in an unpleasant, domineering way; to bully people *UK, 1917*
• Lloyd assumed that Dave was throwing his weight around, being the lead actor and all. — Lloyd Kaufman, *Make Your Own Damn Movie!*, p. 50, 2003

▸ **throw the book at**
to discipline or penalise someone severely *US, 1960*
Making maximum use of the rulebook that inspires the punishment.
• They'll throw the book at you: you know that don't you? — Graeme Kent, *The Queen's Corporal [Six Granada Plays]*, p. 98, 1959
• — Angela Devlin, *Prison Patter*, p. 114, 1996

throwaway *noun*
an outer garment quickly discarded by a criminal after a crime to thwart easy identification *US*
• — Carsten Stroud, *Close Pursuit*, p. 277, 1987

throw away *verb*
to abort a foetus *TRINIDAD AND TOBAGO, 1939*
• — Lise Winer, *Dictionary of the English/Creole of Trinidad & Tobago*, 2003

throwaway *adjective*
used of a gun unregistered and not capable of being traced, and thus used to place in the vicinity of someone whom the police have shot to justify the shooting *US*
• Then he could be shown a mug shot, given a throwaway gun, and programmed to relive the century-old killing of the Kid[.] — Joseph Wambaugh, *The Glitter Dome*, p. 42, 1981
• You done that before. Written false reports, put throwaway guns in dead hands. — Seth Morgan, *Homeboy*, p. 328, 1990
• Police know the slang: "throwaway gun." A bad cop will keep an untraceable gun stashed in the cruiser in case an arrest goes bad, and the suspected perp who lies dead in the street did not have a weapon. The officer will take the gun and drop it next to the suspected but now deceased dead guy. — *Weekly Planet (Saratoga, Florida)*, 27th March 2003

throwdown *noun*
a large party *US*
• — Connie Eble (Editor), *UNC-CH Campus Slang*, p. 6, Fall 1996

throw down *verb*
1 to threaten someone with a weapon *US*
• The last one, I walked in and threw down on [pointed his gun at] the guy. — Bruce Jackson, *In the Life*, p. 152, 1972
• The one with the poncho then did his Clint Eastwood impersonation and swept back the poncho and threw down on Manny Lopez with his M-1 carbine air rifle[.] — Joseph Wambaugh, *Lines and Shadows*, p. 209, 1984
• — William K. Bentley and James M. Corbett, *Prison Slang*, p. 88, 1992

2 to kill *US*
• Whoever throws you down makes five grand. The word's out on you. — Mickey Spillane, *Me, Hood!*, p. 40, 1963

3 in basketball, to forcefully drive the ball down through the basket *US*
• — Jim Crotty, *How to Talk American*, 1997

4 to dance *US*
Sometimes embellished with 'some happy feet' as a direct object.
- —Connie Eble (Editor), *UNC-CH Campus Slang*, p. 6, Spring 1983

throw-down gun; throwdown *noun*
a gun that is not registered and not capable of being traced, and thus placed by the police in the vicinity of someone whom they have shot to justify the shooting *US*
- "Unless it was a throw-down gun," he said, wiping his mouth with a napkin. —Gerald Petievich, *To Die in Beverly Hills*, p. 65, 1983
- Remember, I still got that gun you were carrying – I figure that's my throwdown. The story is, I had to shoot you because of the gun. —Carl Hiaasen, *Native Tongue*, p. 375, 1991
- Ray always kept a "throw-down gun" on him to drop by a body if some street character got funky and had to take a seat on the sky bus. —Stephen J. Cannell, *The Tin Collectors*, p. 9, 2001

throw off *verb*
to perform at a skill level below your capability *US*
- If I couldn't beat Jesse out, he would throw off just enough to make the game look right, and let me win. —Henry Williamson, *Hustler!*, p. 79, 1965

throw-out *noun*
1 the prize that a carnival game operator arranges for a player to win to entice more customers to play *US*
- —Gene Sorrows, *All About Carnivals*, p. 27, 1985: 'Terminology'

2 a trinket thrown by a parader to spectators *US*
- —*American Speech*, p. 111, May 1951: 'The terminology of Mardi Gras'

throw-up *noun*
a large, simple piece of graffiti art *US, 1994*
- Throw ups are usually black + white, or red + white, or green + white, etc. —Jim Crotty, *How to Talk American*, p. 143, 1997
- Stim One, known for heavy throw-ups [...] becomes the first writer to die while bombing [graffiti-ing] and sparks graf memorials all over the city. —*The Source*, p. 128, March 2002

throw up *verb*
1 to vomit *UK, 1793*
Abbreviated from the elaborately elegant 'throw up your accounts' (C18).
- [H]e throws up over the wrong pair of shoes. —Nicholas Blincoe, *The Beautiful Beaten-up Irish Boy of the Arndale Centre*, p. 10, 1998
- [G]angs just throwing up in every alley and doorway. —John Williams, *Cardiff Dead*, p. 204, 2000
- Oh, I'm throwing up, so I must be having a hell of a good time. —Brian Preston, *Pot Planet*, p. 133, 2002

2 to create large graffiti pieces (especially on trains, walls, etc) *US*
- Any of y'all know any handball courts where we could throw up terrible? —*The Source*, p. 52, August 1994

thrupennies; thrups *noun*
▷ see: THREEPENNY BITS

thrush *noun*
1 a female singer *US, 1940*
- Pasternak later admitted she was no world-beater as a thrush. —Jack Lait and Lee Mortimer, *New York Confidential*, p. 125, 1948
- —Arnold Shaw, *Lingo of Tin-Pan Alley*, p. 20, 1950
- —Lavada Durst, *The Jives of Dr. Hepcat*, p. 14, 1953

2 an attractive young woman *AUSTRALIA*
- 'She was a lush thrush,' Windy murmured musingly[.] —J.E. MacDonnell, *Don't Gimme the Ships*, p. 25, 1960
- I make a specialty of looking for eighteen-year-old thrushes. —John Wynnum, *Tar Dust*, p. 51, 1962

thrust *noun*
amyl, butyl or isobutyl nitrite *UK*
A definite suggestion of sexual vigour and therefore, probably, derives from brand marketing as a male sex-aid.
- —Angela Devlin, *Prison Patter*, p. 115, 1996
- Street names [...] stud, thrust, TNT. —James Kay and Julian Cohen, *The Parents' Complete Guide to Young People and Drugs*, p. 144, 1998

thruster *noun*
1 an amphetamine or other central nervous system stimulant *US*
- —Richard Lingeman, *Drugs from A to Z*, p. 236, 1969

2 a modern surfboard with three fins *AUSTRALIA*
- —Nat Young, *Surfing Fundamentals*, p. 128, 1985
- This is a 5'6" tri-fin squash-tail thruster. —*Point Break*, 1991

thrutch *noun*
a difficult challenge *ANTARCTICA*
- —*Cool Antarctica*, 2003: 'Antarctic slang'

thud *nickname*
an F-105 Thunderchief aircraft *US*
From the fact that many were shot down during the Vietnam war. A two-seated F-105 was known as a 'double thud'.
- —*Time*, p. 34, 10th December 1965
- —Carl Fleischhauer, *A Glossary of Army Slang*, p. 22, 1968
- The $2 million "Thud" was the principal air Force tactical strike aircraft, flying more missions than any other bomber but suffering more losses. —*Tulsa (Oklahoma) World*, p. G1, 20th March 2003

thug *noun*
a youth gang member *UK*
- [Y]our Kru, or your Massive, your Thugs, or Bredrins[.] —Julian Johnson, *Urban Survival*, p. 264, 2003

thugged-out *adjective*
in hip-hop culture, self-sufficient and dangerous *US*
From conventional 'thug' (a violent person) which has been adopted by some urban blacks as an honourable term and condition.
- [S]he rips through a racy anecdote from the night involving a "thugged-out guy" —*The Times Magazine*, p. 43, 16th February 2002

th-uh, th-uh, that's all folks
used as a humorous farewell *US*
Used as the sign-off on Looney Toon cartoons produced by Warner Brothers by a stuttering Porky the Pig. Repeated with referential humour.

thumb *noun*
marijuana; a marijuana cigarette *US, 1960*
Probably because you suck your thumb for comfort in much the same way as you suck on a cigarette.
- —Eugene Landy, *The Underground Dictionary*, p. 184, 1971
- —Richard A. Spears, *The Slang and Jargon of Drugs and Drink*, p. 509, 1986
- —Mike Haskins, *Drugs*, p. 289, 2003

▸ on the thumb
hitchhiking *UK*

▸ with the thumb
in betting, used for indicating that the current odds will not continue to be offered for long *UK*
From the TICK-TACK signal used by bookmakers.
- —John McCririck, *John McCririck's World of Betting*, p. 61, 1991

thumb *verb*
to hitchhike *US, 1932*
- Thumbing rides is against the law in St. Paul. —Max Shulman, *The Many Loves of Dobie Gillis*, p. 185, 1951
- On University Avenue in Berkeley at the last light before the freeway on-ramp trip, the last place possible on University for hitchhiking out are groups of people thumbing, sitting with beautiful dogs, with signs for America. —*The Last Supplement to the Whole Earth Catalog*, p. 36, March 1971
- I must have looked strange, standing there on the highway thumbing a ride. —Herbert Huncke, *Guilty of Everything*, p. 20, 1990

▸ thumb your nose
to treat someone or something contemptously *US, 1973*
- Ted has been thumbing his nose at the business establishment ever since[.] —Kevin Leman, *What A Difference A Daddy Makes*, p. 162, 2000

thumb buster *noun*
1 a knob attached to a car or truck's steering wheel to help the driver make turns quickly *US*
When the steering wheel returns to its normal position, the knob can injure the hand of a driver who is not careful.
- —Montie Tak, *Truck Talk*, p. 168, 1971

2 a railway mechanic *US*
- —Ramon Adams, *The Language of the Railroader*, p. 157, 1977

thumb-check *noun*
a cursory examination of a long document or packet of documents *US*
US naval aviator usage.
- —*United States Naval Institute Proceedings*, p. 108, October 1986

thumb job *noun*
a hitchhiker; the act of hitchhiking *US*
Citizens' band radio slang.
- —*Complete CB Slang Dictionary*, p. 91, 1976
- —Peter Chippindale, *The British CB Book*, p. 160, 1981

thumb merchant *noun*
a hitchhiker *US*
• —Wayne Floyd, *Jason's Authentic Dictionary of CB Slang*, p. 30, 1976

thumbs down *noun*
a rejection or refusal *UK, 1929*
From the gesture famously used to signal 'no mercy' for gladiators in the arenas of ancient Rome and Hollywood.
• Euro-MPs have given a thumbs down to the Nice treaty, denouncing it as half-hearted[.]— *The Guardian*, 4th June 2001

thumbsucker *noun*
a long and complex piece of journalism; a writer of such articles *US*
• —Susie Dent, *The Language Report*, p. 15, 2003

thumbs up *noun*
approval; positive news *UK, 1951*
After the gesture that spared the life of Roman gladiators.
• Thumbs-up for drug-tainted coach.— *The Guardian*, 12th June 2003

thump *noun*
a fight *US*
• —Hermese E. Roberts, *The Third Ear*, 1971

thump *verb*
to defeat someone soundly *UK, 1594*
• I've played with him a few times and notice that he thumps me real bad a couple of times and that when he notices I'm losing interest he lets me come close to beating him.—Jim Bouton, *Ball Four*, p. 140, 1970

thumper *noun*
1 a hand grenade launcher *US*
• The thumper won't throw grenades anymore and the minimguns are constipated, but he's still got fourteen rockets left, by God.—Dennis Marvicsin and Jerold A. Greenfield, *Maverick*, p. 209, 1990

2 a drummer *US*
• —Don Wilmeth, *The Language of American Popular Entertainment*, p. 273, 1981

3 a piece of rope used by dog handlers to discipline sled dogs *ANTARCTICA, 1982*
• —Bernadette Hince, *The Antarctic Dictionary*, p. 353, 2000

4 in electric line work, an underground fault locator *US*
• —A.B. Chance Co., *Lineman's Slang Dictionary*, p. 17, 1980

thumper bumper *noun*
in pinball, a bumper that upon impact with a ball scores and then propels the ball back into play *US*
• —Bobbye Claire Natkin and Steve Kirk, *All About Pinball*, p. 117, 1977

thump gun *noun*
an M79 grenade launcher *US*
Vietnam war usage.
• — *Maledicta*, p. 259, Summer/Winter 1982

thumping *adjective*
unusually large or heavy; of an untruth, outrageous *UK, 1576*
• Was this a moment for truth? Or for vagueness? Or for a good thumping lie?—Agatha Christie, *At Bertram's Hotel*, 1965

thumping *adverb*
used as an intensifier of adjectives of large size *UK, 1961*
• [B]ring their dry cleaning home in thumping great 4x4s[.]— *The Guardian*, 19th November 2002

thunder *noun*
1 male sexual prowess *TRINIDAD AND TOBAGO, 1989*
• —Lise Winer, *Dictionary of the English/Creole of Trinidad & Tobago*, 2003

2 heroin *UK*
• —Robert Ashton, *This Is Heroin*, p. 207, 2002
• —Mike Haskins, *Drugs*, p. 284, 2003

▸ **do a thunder**
to defecate *IRELAND*
• 'I only asked him when was the last time he did a pooh!' 'Oh, you mean the last time he did a thunder in the bucket.'—John Fleetwood, *In Stitches*, p. 84, 1994

thunder *verb*
to excel *US*
• —Pamela Munro, *U.C.L.A. Slang*, p. 85, 1989

thunderbags *noun*
underpants *AUSTRALIA*
• I've got a bundle of lettuce [money] and a clean pair of thunder-bags under me daks [trousers].—Barry Humphries, *Bazza Pulls It Off!*, 1971

thunderbirds *noun*
the female breasts *UK*
From the mammaric and lexicographic symbolism of the science fiction Thunderbirds, especially Thunderbird 2, in cult television supermarionation puppet series *Thunderbirds* by Gerry Anderson, from 1965, and relaunched in the 1990s.

Thunderbirds are go
used for denoting or announcing that something is proceeding *UK*
A catchphrase from *Thunderbirds*, a cult science fiction puppet series, first broadcast on television in 1965.
• I want to reassure the auld cunt that I haven't lost the plot and it's still Thunderbirds Are Go[.]—Kevin Sampson, *Outlaws*, p. 218, 2001

thunderbowl *noun*
a lavatory *UK*
• —Ann Barr and Peter York, *The Official Sloane Ranger Handbook*, p. 159, 1982

thunderbox *noun*
a lavatory *UK, 1939*
Originally coined for a 'portable commode'.
• I'm so far gone if I sat on the thunderbox I'd bass it on[.]—Barry Humphries, *Bazza Pulls It Off!*, 1971
• Sitting on the thunderbox one night I looked up at the stars.—Andy McNab, *Immediate Action*, p. 192, 1995

thunderbumper *noun*
a cumulonimbus cloud *CANADA*
• "Thunderbumper" is slang for a "thunder-head." The cumulonimbus cloud can bring fierce thunder and lightning, heavy rain. Old folk tales spoke of [bad] weather being caused by thunderclouds "bumping" into each other.—Tom Langeste, *Words on the Wing*, p. 278–279, 1995

thunderdome *noun*
a variety of MDMA, the recreational drug best known as ecstasy *UK*
A reference to the film *Mad Max: Beyond The Thunderdome*, 1985.
• —Ben Osbourne, *The A-Z of Club Culture*, 1999

thundering *adjective*
forcible, violent; hence, as an intensifier: great, excessive *UK, 1618*
• Ye didn't want to take any notice o' that girl. She's a thunderin' hussy since she went to Listowel.—John B. Keane, *The Man from Clare', Mercier*, p. 55, 1962
• [T]he thundering rage of [Whitesnake's] "Crying in the rain" which contains a blazing blistering guitar solo and some hair raising vocal acrobatics from Mr. [David] Coverdale.— *Amazon.com*, 16th July 2003

thundering *adverb*
excessively *UK, 1809*
• What they want is somebody who would give them a thundering good beating and then, perhaps, they would not do it again.— *The Guardian*, 22nd May 2002

thunderingly *adverb*
violently, forcibly, powerfully, energetically; greatly; excessively *UK, 1680*
• [T]he new [Peugot] 807 is thunderingly unfussy in appearance, quite blank-faced and dutiful – and welcome enough for that.— *The Guardian*, 18th February 2003

Thunder Road *noun*
Highway 13, north of Saigon, South Vietnam *US*
So named because of the US Army's frequent **THUNDER RUNS** on Highway 13.
• These are around inhabited areas; there were villages all up and down the highway. This was Highway 13, "Thunder Road."—John Kerry, *The New Soldier*, p. 62, 1971
• —Gregory Clark, *Words of the Vietnam War*, p. 512, 1990

thunder run *noun*
1 during the Vietnam war, a tactic of having a small armoured convoy drive at high speeds shooting at both sides of the road to thwart ambushes by the Viet Cong; in Iraq in 2003, used by soldiers of a death or glory incursion into Baghdad *US*
Possibly originating in the Korean war, 1950–53, where it was used for a final bar crawl before leaving a posting.
• They put on a bit of show for the grunts that May morning, a whole line of them roaring down Highway 13 in an open-throttle "thunder run" meant to detonate any hidden enemy mines.—Peter Goldmand and Tony Fuller, *Charlie Company*, p. 152, 1983
• —Gregory Clark, *Words of the Vietnam War*, p. 512, 1990

• [S]oldiers in the tanks called their mission Operation Thunder Run. — *The Guardian*, 7th April 2003

2 in white-water rafting, the most treacherous rapids or the act of negotiating them *US*

• A thunder run is a term in white-waterr rafting for shooting the most treacherous rapids. — Randeep Ramesh, *The War We Could Not Stop*, p. 301, 2003

thunder thighs *noun*

large, heavy thighs, especially on a woman *US*

• [A]s he tells his girl friend, the ravishing, all-too-human Beverley "Thunder-Thighes" Switzler, "Listen honey – if anybody in this world knowls what it is to be oppressed!" — *Washington Post*, p. B1, 27th December 1977

• — *American Speech*, p. 262, Fall 1993: 'Among the new words'

• — Chris Lewis, *The Dictionary of Playground Slang*, p. 231, 2003

• "We saw him, and he had those thunder thighs," Spates said. — *Daily Oklahoman (Oklahoma City)*, p. 5D, 11th January 2004

thunk *noun*

in computing, code that supplies an address *US*

• — Eric S. Raymond, *The New Hacker's Dictionary*, p. 349, 1991

thunk *verb*

used as an alternative past tense of 'think' in place of 'thought' *UK, 1876*

Intentionally jocular or rural.

• "Who would have thunk it?" irrepressibly remarked "Pokey" (Mary) Prothero[.] — Mary McCarthy, *The Group*, p. 6, 1963

TI *nickname*

the federal correctional institution, Terminal Island, California *US*

• He shanked an inmate during his second year in T.I. but they couldn't prove it. — Gerald Petievich, *Money Men*, p. 133, 1981

tia *noun*

marijuana *UK*

A Spanish aunt such as **AUNT MARY** (marijuana).

• — Mike Haskins, *Drugs*, p. 289, 2003

TIA

used as Internet shorthand to mean '*t*hanks *i*n *a*dvance' *US*

• — Andy Ihnatko, *Cyberspeak*, p. 190, 1997

Tibb's Day *noun*

the day after Resurrection, Judgment Day etc, i.e. a day that will never come in this lifetime *CANADA*

C. L. Apperson, in *English Proverbs and Proverbial Phrases*, calls it 'a day neither before nor after Christmas'. *Brewer's Dictionary of Phrase and Fable* (1870) points out that there never was such a saint as St Tibb, hence the use of the term as a synonym for 'never'.

• "I'll pay you Tibb's Day" in Chester, Nova Scotia, means you won't see the money! — Lewis Poteet, *The South Shore Phrase Book*, p. 115–116, 1999

tic *noun*

phencylidine *US*

• — *Drummer*, p. 77, 1977

TIC *noun*

when a criminal is on trial, a crime which does not form a part of the case being heard but which the defendant may request to have taken into account during sentencing *UK*

A partial acronym of 'taken into account'.

• — Angela Devlin, *Prison Patter*, p. 115, 1996

tical *noun*

marijuana *US*

A coinage claimed by rap artist Methodman; usage spread with his adoption of 'tical' as one of many drug-related aliases.

tick *noun*

1 a moment; a second, a minute *UK, 1879*

• From the sound of clockwork as a second hand moves between the measured increments. — Jack Lait and Lee Mortimer, *New York Confidential*, p. 236, 1948

• I figure that there's gonna be some killing in a few ticks. — Joseph Nazel, *Black Cop*, p. 63, 1974

• I just need two ticks with Mikey. — Kevin Sampson, *Outlaws*, p. 138, 2001

2 credit, deferred payment *UK, 1642*

Generally in the phrase 'on tick' (on credit).

• I stopped outside the shop, where Florrie and Annie Evans always let our mam have tick[.] — Livi Michael, *Robinson Street*, p. 24, 1999

3 in spread-betting, a tenth *UK*

• — David Bennet, *Know Your Bets*, p. 126, 2001

4 in basketball, a shot *US*

• — Chuck Wielgus and Alexander Wolff, *The Back-In-Your-Face Guide to Pick-up Basketball*, p. 230, 1986

5 in a hospital, an intern *US*

• — Sally Williams, *"Strong" Words*, p. 142, 1994

tick *verb*

▸ **tick along nicely**

to make satisfactory progress *IRELAND*

• "So are ye busy tonight?"..."Ah yeah, ticking along nicely," I replied. — Donal Ruane, *Tales in a Rearview Mirror*, p. 152, 2003

tick *adjective*

sexually attractive *UK*

• — Susie Dent, *The Language Report*, p. 78, 2003

ticked off *adjective*

angry *US, 1959*

• You were sore anyway 'cause you didn't want to talk to that grand jury. I mean you were good and ticked off. — Elmore Leonard, *Pronto*, p. 49, 1993

• He's a little ticked off at the government now. Julian Borger, *The Guardian*, 3rd December 2003

ticker *noun*

1 a clock, especially a pocket watch *US*

• Joe, you have a short, some fronts, and a fine ticker too. — Bruce Jackson, *Get Your Ass in the Water and Swim Like Me*, p. 91, 1964

• A Elgin ticker with a solid gold band / And a egg-sized diamond flashed on his hand. — Dennis Wepman et al., *The Life*, p. 31, 1976

2 the heart *US, 1930*

Analogised to a clock ticking.

• [W]hen you get high off of gauge it dries up the saliva in your mouth and your stomach fills up with gas and presses against your ticker, till for the first time in your life you feel every beat your heart is making without looking for it. — Mezz Mezzrow, *Really the Blues*, p. 95, 1946

• To ventilate your foul ticker if I parted Junior's crew cut. — Haenigsen, *Jive's Like That*, 1947

• Lee wasn't a young m an any more, a thing like that could raise a lot of hell with a guy's ticker. — Mickey Spillane, *One Lonely Night*, p. 68, 1951

• With his cigarette hand, Selena's brother tapped the left side of his chest. "Ticker," he said. — J.D. Salinger, *Nine Stories*, p. 48, 1953

• If I have a bum ticker, you can bet it comers from liquor. — Dan Burley, *Diggeth Thou?*, p. 37, 1959

• My ticker rioted. A delicious stealing lust electrified my genitals. — Iceberg Slim (Robert Beck), *Airtight Willie and Me*, p. 27, 1979

• That got the old ticker going. — *Ask*, p. 112, 12th April 1980

• Considering, you know, the old ticker isn't what it used to be. — Elmore Leonard, *Bandits*, p. 362, 1987

• Bustin' their dodgy fuckin' tickers for nothin'. — Nick Barlay, *Curvy Lovebox*, p. 17, 1997

3 courage *AUSTRALIA, 1977*

• — Barry Humphries, *A Nice Night's Entertainment*, p. 143, 1974

• — Jim Ramsay, *Cop It Sweet!*, p. 89, 1977

• I knew you dagos had no ticker. — Clive Galea, *Slipper*, p. 121, 1988

ticket *noun*

1 an ordinary person *UK*

Used generally in Glasgow and **MOD** culture.

• [A] hard ticket (a tough guy) or a useless ticket (a shiftless poerson, a good-for-nothing). — Michael Munro, *The Original Patter*, p. 70, 1985

• Meaden also redesigned the band's clothing, dressing Daltrey as a "face" and the others as "tickets". — Andrew Motion, *The Lamberts*, 1986

• What they [Mods] hated in others – the tickets, the seven and sixers [married people] – is that they settled for so much less. — Paolo Hewitt, *The Sharper Word*, p. 6, 1998

2 an amusing or charming person *IRELAND*

• Then I said well ladies I'm afraid I can't stay here I have to be off on my travels. Dear dear aren't you a ticket Francie? they said. — Patrick McCabe, *The Butcher Boy*, p. 15, 1992

3 a follower (not an originator) of Mod fashion *UK, 1964*

• The first mods – the "faces", as they called themselves – would soon be contemptuous of the late-comers – dubbed "the tickets" – the post-commercialised mods. — Dave Haslam, *Adventures of the Wheels of Steel*, p. 71–72, 2001

4 a professional licence; a certificate of qualification *US*

Originally military.

• I have a Private Operator's ticket and that's all. — Mickey Spillane, *One Lonely Night*, p. 43, 1951

• Fein has got this ticket, he can practice law. — George V. Higgins, *The Rat on Fire*, p. 24, 1981

- "You carryin' a private ticket?" Auburn said. —Robert Campbell, *In La-La Land We Trust*, p. 70, 1986

5 a warrant or bill of detainer *US*

- —John R. Armore and Joseph D. Wolfe, *Dictionary of Desperation*, p. 54, 1976
- I prevailed on Dennis to okay a ticket[.] —Duncan MacLaughlin, *The Filth*, p. 113, 2002

6 an official misconduct report in prison *US*

- —John R. Armore and Joseph D. Wolfe, *Dictionary of Desperation*, p. 54, 1976
- —Hugh Morgan, *Ye Shall Know It*, p. 266–267, Summer/Winter 1981: "By its slang"

7 an order to be locked in solitary confinement *US*

- So he saw us sittin' down and he told the officer down in the hole to write us a ticket. —Henry Williamson, *Hustler!*, p. 146, 1965

8 in prison, a contract for a killing or beating *US*

- —Paul Glover, *Words from the House of the Dead*, 1974

9 in horse racing, a betting receipt *US*

- —David W. Maurer, *Argot of the Racetrack*, p. 64, 1951

10 a playing card *US*
As in the expression 'I held some good tickets'.

- —Irv Roddy, *Friday Night Poker: Penny Poker for Millions*, p. 221, 1961

11 LSD; a dose of LSD *US, 1969*
Another LSD-as-travel metaphor.

- —Richard A. Spears, *The Slang and Jargon of Drugs and Drink*, p. 509, 1986

▸ just the ticket; that's the ticket
exactly what is required *UK, 1838*

- I love my little sawn-off Shogun. She's just the ticket for what I have to get up to[.] —Kevin Sampson, *Clubland*, p. 77, 2002

ticket agent *noun*
an LSD dealer *US*
Premised on a **TRIP** metaphor.

- —Stewart L. Tubbs and Sylvia Moss, *Human Communication*, p. 120, 1974
- —Walter Way, *The Drug Scene*, p. 115, 1977

Ticket Bastard *nickname*
the Ticketmaster ticket service *US*

- —David Shenk and Steve Silberman, *Skeleton Key*, p. 288, 1994

ticket of leave man *noun*
a parolee *UK*

- But when you've been released from the nick with your bit of remission, you're on parole. You're a "ticket of leave" man – any bit of aggro you get up to can put you straight back to finish a full term[.] —Lenny McLean, *The Guv'nor*, p. 113, 1998

ticket-punching *noun*
in the military, nearly automatic promotion from rank to rank with short periods in combat to justify the promotion *US*

- The real reason, which held true for the Marine Corps too and which explained why the practice was derisively called "ticket-punching," was a mechanistic promotion process. —Neil Sheehan, *A Bright Shining Lie*, p. 650, 1988
- So it has a name, I thought: ticket punching – the syndrome that had me chasing down that elusive degree. —David H. Hackworth, *About Face*, p. 348, 1989

tickets *noun*
the female breasts *US*
A term from the coarse sector of the entertainment industry, recognising the selling power of sex.

- —Connie Eble (Editor), *UNC-CH Campus Slang*, April 1977

▸ have tickets on yourself
to be conceited *AUSTRALIA, 1918*

- —Arthur Chipper, *The Aussie Swearer's Guide*, p. 26, 1972
- —Rex Hunt, *Tall Tales – and True*, p. 119, 1994
- There's no ticket's on me, you know that, but I'm proud of what I do. —Phillip Gwynne, *Deadly Unna?*, p. 46, 1998
- But those who don't have tickets on themselves he gives a hand to. —Kel Richards, *The Aussie Bible*, p. 11, 2003

tickety-boo *adjective*
fine, correct, in order, satisfactory *UK, 1939*
Originally military; a variation of 'ticket', as in **JUST THE TICKET** (correct), with Hindu *tikai babu* (it's all right, sir).

- "Just peachy-keen, Harry baby," said Ira. "Just tickety-boo." —Max Shulman, *Anyone Got a Match?*, p. 19, 1964
- [I]n all this cartoonin' [fooling about] somethin' don't feel tickety boo. —Nick Barlay, *Curvy Lovebox*, p. 99, 1997
- "Nothing's the matter, Farmer Giles," smiled Guy. "Everything is just tickety-boo." —Kevin Sampson, *Powder*, p. 30, 1999
- [I]f you could all please join us out front here, that would be just tickety boo. —Christopher Brookmyre, *The Sacred Art of Stealing*, p. 80, 2002

tick-hunter *noun*
an ardent bird-watcher, usually one who is excitable *UK*
From a bird-watcher's habit of ticking-off observations in a note book.

- —*New Society*, 17th November 1977

tick in cow's arse *noun*
something or someone who is very close to something or someone else *TRINIDAD AND TOBAGO, 1982*

- —Lise Winer, *Dictionary of the English/Creole of Trinidad & Tobago*, 2003

ticking-off *noun*
a reprimand *UK, 1950*

- In London, the 16-year-old son of the Prime Minister is found drunk and incapable in Leicester Square, but is given nothing more than a ticking-off by a copper. —*New Statesman*, 11th June 2001

tickle *noun*

1 a robbery or other profitable criminal enterprise *UK, 1938*
Probably derives from the image of a poacher 'tickling a trout', an activity for the 'light-fingered'.

- With a bit of luck Sapphire might have the tickle of a lifetime[.] —Charles Raven, *Underworld Nights*, p. 11, 1956
- This little tickle I presented them could see me in the sun for the rest of my life. —Ted Lewis, *Jack Carter's Law [britpulp]*, p. 42, 1974

2 in the sport of polo, a weak hit on the ball *UK*

- Harry Wales has a little tickle! —*The Guardian*, 29th July 2003

3 a pleasurable sensation caused by drug use *UK*

- I need something to give me a buzz, if I could just get a bag [of heroin] now I know get a tickle off it. —Lanre Fehintola, *Charlie Says...*, p. 52, 2000

4 a deep v-bottom on a boat; also, especially in Newfoundland, a narrow strait between mainland and an island *CANADA*

- The tides are of no great size at the Atlantic coast, but they are sufficient to produce strong tidal currents in the archipelagoes and channels of different orders: runs, tickles, and rattles. —V. Tanner, *Outlines of the Geography, Life & Customs of Newfoundland-Labrador*, p. 285, 1947
- That boat's maybe too tickle'y; it's got quite a tickle onto it. —Lewis Poteet, *oral citation from The South Shore Phrase Book*, p. 116, 1999

tickle *verb*

1 to prime an engine *US*
To start the cold engine of a motorcycle, it is sometimes necessary to prime the carburettor, or 'tickle the pot'.

2 to administer oral sex to a male pornographer performer before or between scenes to help him maintain an erection *US*

- —Ana Loria, *1 2 3 Be A Porn Star!*, p. 165, 2000: 'Glossary of adult sex industry terms'

3 to rob *NEW ZEALAND*

- —David McGill, *David McGill's Complete Kiwi Slang Dictionary*, p. 113, 1998

▸ tickle a bug
in computing, to activate a normally inactive malfunction *US*

- —Eric S. Raymond, *The New Hacker's Dictionary*, p. 350, 1991

▸ tickle the pickle
from the male perspective, to have sex *US*

- You and Myra better stop playing tickle the pickle, boy, before you bat your brains out with your balls. —Jim Thompson, *Pop. 1280*, p. 192, 1964

▸ tickle the peter
to steal from a till or cashbox *AUSTRALIA, 1941*

- More blokes gone bankrupt and more bank clerks tickled the peter through following systems, and listening to tips, than you could poke a stick at. —Frank Hardy, *The Yarns of Billy Borker*, 1965

ticklebelly *noun*
the queasy feeling experienced when a car crests a poorly graded hill too fast *CANADA*

- —Bill Casselman, *Canadian Sayings*, p. 14, 2002

tickled; tickled to death; tickled pink *adjective*
very pleased *UK, 1907*

- She would have been tickled pink to get rid of Oscar and wall up the television set. —Max Shulman, *Rally Round the Flag, Boys!*, p. 71, 1957
- I'm just tickled to death to have you aboard! —Walker Percy, *The Last Gentleman*, p. 154, 1966

tickler *noun*

1 an office system that serves to remind of impending deadlines *US, 1905*

- "Two years ago, we created our own tickler system, because the standard vendor packages didn't do everything we wanted them to," says Connie Marmet, vice-president and manager at Bank of America's corporate trust department. — *ABA Banking Journal*, p. 102, September 1991
- This command procedure lets you prepare a tickler-file-type reminder to be received in your VMSmail on the desired day. — *Digital Systems Journal*, p. 14, March 1993

2 anything worn on the penis that is designed to stimulate the vagina or the clitoris during sex *UK, 1974*

tickle your fancy *noun*

a homosexual *UK*

Rhyming slang for **NANCY (BOY)**, noted as a post-World War 2 term by Ray Puxley, *Cockney Rabbit*, 1992, who suggests a corruption of the children's song 'Billy Boy' as a possible source.

ticklish *adjective*

difficult, awkward *UK, 1591*

- This leaves the ticklish problem of 44p in the kitty with which to fund a wine for those vanilla-rhubarb cream profiteroles[.] — *The Guardian*, 31st March 2003

tick off *verb*

to reprimand someone *UK, 1915*

- Things came to a head after management "ticked off" a worker for taking a sick day because it was not allowed under his individual contract. — *The Guardian*, 8th December 1999

tick-tack; tic-tac *noun*

1 a system of hand signalling used by racecourse bookmakers *UK, 1899*

- 'When Ladbrokes send it [off-course money] down, their identity in tic-tac is like drawing a circle over the head – the "Magic Sign" that alerts layers that this is Ladbrokes money. — John McCririck, *John McCririck's World of Betting*, p. 106, 1991
- The rituals can be baffling. The byzantine betting system, the arcane semaphore of the tic-tac men, bets of "ponies" and "monkeys" rather than pounds[.] — *The Guardian*, 26th February 2001

2 a signal of any kind *UK*

From racetrack use.

- I'll make a move when you give me the tic tac. — Ray Puxley, *Cockney Rabbit*, p. 185, 1992

tick-tack; tic-tac *verb*

to practise tick-tack *AUSTRALIA*

- The operators kept a look-out posted on a rise to tic-tac to them if plain-clothes police got near enough to be a danger to them. — Vince Kelly, *The Bogeyman*, p. 182, 1956

tick-tacker *noun*

a person who practises tick-tack *AUSTRALIA, 1897*

- — Frank Hardy, *The Yarns of Billy Borker*, p. 105, 1965
- In the old days, tick-tackers used to signal changes in the markets between bookmakers in different enclosures and runners were employed to carry the odds. They had an elaborate series of handsignals. — Frank Hardy and Athol George Mulley, *The Needy and the Greedy*, p. 86, 1975
- — Joe Andersen, *Winners Can Laugh*, p. 28, 1982
- In Sydney, the acknowledged king of the tick-tackers operated for a Leger bookmaker. — Joe Andersen, *Winners Can Laugh*, p. 198, 1982

tick-tacking *noun*

an illegal system of sign language used between bookmakers and touts on a racecourse *AUSTRALIA, 1899*

- — Frank Hardy, *The Yarns of Billy Borker*, p. 103, 1965
- Two well known characters were Tick-tacker Tom and Ron the Runner. They worked for Murphy, the bookmaker. But when tick-tacking was banned, they became unemployed and fell on bad times. — Frank Hardy and Athol George Mulley, *The Needy and the Greedy*, p. 86, 1975
- His main impressions? No tick-tacking compared with the English Derby at Epsom Downs: and the skill of the broadcaster, Joe Brown. — Joe Brown, *Just for the Record*, p. 58, 1984

tick-tack man *noun*

a tick-tacker *AUSTRALIA, 1939*

- Rufe Naylor, always in the vanguard with new ideas, employed a tick-tack man to provide him with price fluctuations from inside the course during a period of warning off by the AJC. — Joe Andersen, *Winners Can Laugh*, p. 197, 1982

tick-tick *noun*

a bicycle with three gears *TRINIDAD AND TOBAGO*

- — Lise Winer, *Dictionary of the English/Creole of Trinidad & Tobago*, 2003

tick-tock *noun*

a clock *UK, 1984*

A children's colloquialism, from the conventional imitation of the ticking of a clock.

tick-tock

used to mark the passing of an instant *UK*

From the ticking of a clock.

- You're talking to him and then, tick-tock! he's vanished. — Colin MacInnes, *Absolute Beginners*, 1959

tick twenty *noun*

ten o'clock *US*

- How can any outsider latch on to the real flavor of a secret code in which tick twenty means ten o'clock[.] — Mezz Mezzrow, *Really the Blues*, p. 220, 1946

ticky *adjective*

old-fashioned, out-of-date *US*

- — Robert George Reisner, *The Jazz Titans*, p. 166, 1960

tic-tac *noun*

1 a person who signals betting information by tick-tack *UK*

- "Watch out, they've bitten two punters' legs [...]" shouted one tic-tac as they [false teeth] rolled merrily on their way[.] — *Raceform Handicap Book*, 17th March 1990

2 a fact *UK*

Rhyming slang, from the racetrack signalling system.

- — Ray Puxley, *Cockney Rabbit*, 1992

3 phencyclidine, the recreational drug known as PCP or angel dust *US*

- — US Department of Justice, *Street Terms*, October 1994

tid-bit *noun*

an appetising and toothsome woman *US*

- When I got back to the edge, all the cats and their ribs started right in on jiving me about my young tid-bit catching 'em, and I went right along with it. — A.S. Jackson, *Gentleman Pimp*, p. 44, 1973

tiddie; tiddy *noun*

the female breast *UK*

A variation of **TITTY**.

- [A] novel angle of penetration and you get to play with her tiddies, all the while keeping an eye on [TV sports programme] *Final Score*. — *The FHM Little Book of Bloke*, p. 25, June 2003

tiddle *verb*

to urinate *UK, 1961*

A children's colloquialism.

tiddled off *adjective*

annoyed, cross *UK*

After **TIDDLE** (to urinate), thus a variation of **PISSED OFF**.

- — *New Society*, 4th August 1977

tiddler *noun*

1 any small fish *UK, 1885*

Originally applied to a stickleback.

- MINI FISH NET with wire rim to fit exactly in mess tin bottom (used to catch tiddlers under dinghy). — Zeek *The Art of Sheng Ku*, p. 19, 2001

2 anything small; a child, a small animal, a small drink, etc *UK, 1927*

- But even a small asteroid – the size of a house, say – could destroy a city. The number of these relative tiddlers in Earth-crossing orbits is almost certainly in the hundreds of thousands[.] — Bill Bryson, *A Short History of Nearly Everything*, p. 194, 2003

3 any small coin (of size rather than denomination) *UK, 1966*

- Even a little tiddler like the five centavo coin comes into its own[.] — *Time Out Buenos Aires*, 2001

4 a player of tiddleywinks *US, 1958*

tiddler's bait; tiddley bait; tiddley; Tilly Bates *adjective*

late *UK, 1960*

Rhyming slang.

- Sorry I'm Tiddley I met Cyril on the way home and he forced me to go for a drink. — Ray Puxley, *Cockney Rabbit*, 1992

tiddly; tiddley *adjective*
mildly drunk *UK, 1905*
- Mary-Ann got tiddly on snaps and, all in all, I was right. — Gore Vidal, *Myra Breckinridge*, p. 243, 1968
- One night the designer was at the bar, a little tiddly as they used to say[.] — John Francis Hunter, *The Gay Insider*, p. 221, 1971

tiddlywink; tiddly-wink; tiddleywink; tiddly; tid *noun*
1 an alcoholic drink *UK, 1859*
Rhyming slang.
- She waltzes down to Hoxton in it [a fur coat] to see her dear old mum, and takes her out for a tiddly. — Charles Raven, *Underworld Nights*, p. 22, 1956
- Thought I'd take me bird down the rub a dub for a few tiddley winks [drinks]. — *The Sweeney*, p. 6, 1976

2 a Chinese person *UK*
Rhyming slang for **CHINK** (a Chinese person).
- [A] tiddly-wink, a Charlie Ronce[.] — Ian Dury, *Blackmail Man*, 1977
- [I]t's only the flying tiddly-wink and his blazing moped. — J.J. Connolly, *Layer Cake*, p. 198, 2000
- [T]he world's biggest wok [the Millennium Dome], built to feed all the "Tiddlies" who live thereabouts. — Garry Bushell, *The Face*, p. 23, 2001

tidemark *noun*
a dirty mark that is left by, and marks the extent of, a child's neck-washing regime *UK, 1961*

tide's in *adjective*
experiencing the bleed period of the menstrual cycle *US*
- — Karen Houppert, *The Curse*, 1999

tide's out *adjective*
experiencing the bleed period of the menstrual cycle *US*
- — Karen Houppert, *The Curse*, 1999

tidy; tidy up *verb*
1 to make something orderly, clean, etc *UK, 1821*
- I tidied my hair with my fingers. — Tracy Chevalier, *Girl with a Pearl Earring*, p. 103, 2001
- I restacked my chips to have something to do. I tidied them up, over and over[.] — Jeffrey Eugenides, *Middlesex*, p. 385, 2003

2 to wash the vulva and vagina *TRINIDAD AND TOBAGO, 1978*
- — Lise Winer, *Dictionary of the English/Creole of Trinidad & Tobago*, 2003

tidy *adjective*
1 large, considerable *UK, 1838*
As in the song by Boy Scouts: 'The great meat pie was a tidy size, / And it took a week to make it, / A day to carry it to the shop, / And just a week to bake it'.
- [T]he journeyman English footballer for whose services the glamorous Italian club AC Milan paid a tidy sum in the 1980s. — *Investors Chronicle*, 23rd January 2004

2 satisfactory; good; decent; correct *UK, 1844*
Widely exampled by John Edwards, *Talk Tidy!* (the title is defined in the book as 'speak properly!'), 1985.
- Told yew, din I. Tidy fuckin E [MDMA], mun, innit. — Niall Griffiths, *Sheepshagger*, p. 164, 2001

3 sexually attractive; sexy *UK*
- [S]ome jammy bastard seriously getting it on with that tidy bit off the telly (and what a dirty little bitch she must be, eh? Phwoaaar). — Christopher Brookmyre, *Boiling a Frog*, p. 105, 2000

tidy!
in south Wales, used as a positive affirmation *UK: WALES*
- — John Edwards, *Talk Tidy!*, 1985

tidy and neat; tidy *verb*
to eat *UK*
Rhyming slang.
- Tidy your dinner up first, then you can go out. — Ray Puxley, *Cockney Rabbit*, 1992

tidy away *verb*
to clear up for tidiness' sake *UK, 1867*
- She needed to come back, to be there, to tidy away what had happened and what might have happened. — Nora Roberts, *Dance uopn the Air*, p. 372, 2001

tidy whities *noun*
white, boxer-style men's underpants *US*
- But back in the beginning came tidy whities, better known as your father's standard boxers and Y-front Fruit of the Looms. — *Palm Beach (Florida) Post*, p. 3D, 12th December 1994
- You seldom see a U.S. senator with his tidy-whities above his pinstripes. — *Providence (Rhode Island) Journal-Bulletin*, p. 1G, 14th June 2001

tie *verb*
to inject with a drug *UK*
- — Mike Haskins, *Drugs*, p. 290, 2003

▸ **tie on one**
to get very drunk *US*
- The bars close at two in Detroit and Sunday you can't buy any booze till noon. Give everybody a chance to go to their place of worship before they tie one on. — Elmore Leonard, *Out of Sight*, p. 169, 1996

▸ **tie the knot**
to marry *UK, 1605*
- T.S. and Brandi tied the knot after graduation at Universal Studios, Florida. — *Mallrats*, 1995
- After you tie the knot, the truth about each other finally comes out. — Chris Rock, *Rock This!*, p. 155, 1997

▸ **tie them down**
on the railways, to apply hand brakes *US*
- — Norman Carlisle, *The Modern Wonder Book of Trains and Railroading*, p. 269, 1946

tie a knot in it!
addressed to someone (usually a male) who needs to urinate but is having to control the urge; also, said to someone who is whistling tunelessly *UK*
- You can't leave the studio to go to the toilet, so you just have to tie a knot in it. — *New Statesman*, 25th June 2001

tie and tease *noun*
sexual bondage alternating pleasurable stimulation and deliberate frustration, especially when advertised as a service offered by a prostitute *UK*
- — Caroline Archer, *Tart Cards*, 2003

tie-eye *noun*
a commotion or ruckus *CANADA*
- When the bear woke up the dog in the yard, my soul and body, what a tie-eye! — Lewis Poteet, *oral citation from The South Shore Phrase Book*, p. 116, 1999

tie off *verb*
to restrict the flow of blood in a vein in preparation for an injection of narcotic drugs
- — Angela Devlin, *Prison Patter*, p. 115, 1996

tie-tongued *adjective*
suffering from a speaking disability such as a lisp *BARBADOS*
- — Frank A. Collymore, *Barbadian Dialect*, p. 111, 1965

tie-up *noun*
the rope or cord used to restrict the flow of blood in a vein in preparation for an injection of drugs *UK*
- — Angela Devlin, *Prison Patter*, p. 115, 1996

tie up *verb*
to apply an improvised tourniquet, usually on the arm, preparatory to injecting a drug *US*
- The shades would be pulled down and the next thing you know there was a bottle of cobalt blue loaded with liquid amphetamine. Everyone immediately tied up. — Herbert Huncke, *Guilty of Everything*, p. 141, 1990

tiff *noun*
a petty quarrel; a brief peevish disagreement *UK, 1754*
- It was only a tiff, but it could easily have escalated into something much more serious. — Erwin James, *The Guardian*, 17th February 2000

tiger *noun*
1 a person who is keen for or enthusiastic about something *AUSTRALIA, 1896*
- I knew what was itching him. He was a tiger for it. — Robert S. Close, *Love Me Sailor*, p. 4, 1945

2 a male homosexual *UK*
- — Tom Hibbert, *Rockspeak!*, p. 157, 1983

3 a wife *UK*
A Cockney endearment.
- Wasn't home till sparrow-fart and my old tiger [wife] was in a right six-and-eight. — Red Daniells, 1980

4 an outstanding sportsman; a confident climber; a formidable sporting opponent *UK, 1929*

▸ **take a tiger for a walk**
(used of a food addict) to eat in moderation *US*
A term in twelve-step recovery programmes such as Alcoholics Anonymous.
- —Christopher Cavanaugh, *AA to Z*, p. 170, 1998

tiger cage *noun*
an underground, high security jail cell *US*
- —William K. Bentley and James M. Corbett, *Prison Slang*, p. 8, 1992

tiger country *noun*
1 rough, uncultivated country or terrain *AUSTRALIA, 1945*
- Michael Roe is one of the few Australian explorers of the tiger-country concerned with 'authority'[.] —Miriam Dixson, *The Real Matilda*, p. 201, 1984

2 any challenging situation *NEW ZEALAND, 1945*
From World War 2, referring to territory patrolled by German Tiger tanks.
- —Harry Orsman, *A Dictionary of Modern New Zealand Slang*, p. 138, 1999

3 in hospital operating theatre usage, any part of the body where surgery is high risk *US*
- —Sally Williams, *"Strong" Words*, p. 162, 1994

tiger in the tank *noun*
a linear amplifier for a citizens' band radio *US*
From the 1960's Esso advertising slogan 'Put a tiger in your tank'.
- —Porter Bibb, *CB Bible*, p. 107, 1976

tiger lady *noun*
a female Vietnamese civilian building worker at a US facility during the war *US*
- —Gregory Clark, *Words of the Vietnam War*, p. 514, 1990

tiger piss *noun*
Tiger Paw™ beer *US*
A South Vietnamese speciality, made with formaldehyde.
- —Linda Rienberg, *In the Field*, p. 220, 1991

tiger stripe *noun*
a scar from intravenous drug injections *US*
- Ain't no marks to show. No tiger stripes. —Willard Motley, *Let No Man Write My Epitaph*, p. 129, 1958

tiger stripes *noun*
camouflage worn in the jungle *US*
- You don't wear tiger stripes in Japan. —Ronald J. Glasser, *365 Days*, p. 201, 1971
- —*Maledicta*, p. 258, Summer/Winter 1982: 'Viet-speak'

tiger suit *noun*
jungle camouflage uniforms worn by soldiers in the South Vietnamese Army *US*
- —Gregory Clark, *Words of the Vietnam War*, p. 513, 1990

tiger sweat *noun*
strong, illegally manufactured whisky *CANADA*
- "Tiger sweat" is a macho term from Liverpool, NS, for logger's homebrew. —Lewis Poteet, *The South Shore Phrase Book*, p. 116, 1999
- It is called corn liquor, white lightning, sugar whiskey, skully cracker, popskull, bush whiskey, stump, stumphole, 'splo, ruckus juice, radiator whiskey, rotgut, sugarhead, block and tackle, wildcat, panther's breath, tiger's sweat, Sweet spirits of cats a-fighting, alley bourbon, city gin, cool water, happy Sally, deep shaft, jump steady, old horsey, stingo, bluye John, red eye, pine top, buckeye bark whiskey and see seven stars. —*Star Tribune (Minneapolis)*, p. 19F, 31st January 1999

tiger tank *noun*
a thing of little worth *UK*
Rhyming slang for **WANK** (rubbish), usually phrased 'not worth a tiger tank'; from the advertising slogan 'put a tiger in your tank'.
- —Red Daniells, 1980

Tiggerish; tiggerish *adjective*
energetically enthusiastic and cheerful *UK*
From the character of Tigger, created by A.A. Milne, 1882–1956, especially as filtered through the Disney animations of Winnie the Pooh's adventures.
- With his Tiggerish enthusiasm – sentences sprouting from all angles – it is easy to see how inspiring he can be. —*The Guardian*, 12th June 2003

tight *noun*
1 a close friend *BAHAMAS*
- —John A. Holm, *Dictionary of Bahamian English*, p. 207, 1982

2 in poker, a hand consisting of three cards of the same rank and a pair *CANADA*
Known conventionally as a 'full house'.
- —George Percy, *The Language of Poker*, p. 93, 1988

▸ **in a tight**
in serious trouble *US*
- —Inez Cardozo-Freeman, *The Joint*, p. 507, 1984

tight *adjective*
1 tipsy; drunk *US, 1830*
- He was too busy to bother with kids who were half tight. —Irving Shulman, *The Amboy Dukes*, p. 79, 1947
- And if you get tight, I'll take you home —Philip Wylie, *Opus 21*, p. 101, 1949
- It happened, and it was not at all what the group or even Mother would have imagined, not a bit sordid or messy, in spite of Dick's being tight. —Mary McCarthy, *The Group*, p. 31, 1963

2 lacking generosity, mean *UK*
- There had been allegations that these geezers had been drugged. I told them that everyone here was so fucking tight that if we spiked anyone we told them later and charged them. —Dave Courtney, *Raving Lunacy*, p. 13, 2000

3 aggressive; cruel; unpleasant *UK*
From the previous sense as 'mean', punning on 'mean' as 'cruel'.
- DAVE: (EATING SLOWLY) Hmm, lovely chocolate... hmmm, honey-comb centre. DENISE: Ah, don't be tight, Dave. DAVE: (OVERACTING) Hmmm, it's the best chocolate bar I've had... ever. —Caroline Aherne and Craig Cash, *The Royle Family*, 1999
- You didn't have to shame me like that man. Not in front of all them pricks. That was fuckin' tight man! —Jack Allen, *When the Whistle Blows*, p. 113, 2000
- "Ah leave him, ay!" goes one of the girls. "Don't be tight." I turns to her. "Don't you think it's tight terrorising old ladies? Ay?" —Kevin Sampson, *Outlaws*, p. 244, 2001

4 hard; severe; difficult *UK, 1764*
- I remember you were always pulling them out of tight spots. Didn't any of them offer to help you?" —Stan Redding and Frank W. Abagnale, *Catch Me If You Can*, p. 19, 2000

5 of a slot machine, disadvantageous to the gambler in terms of the frequency of payouts *US*
- —J. Edward Allen, *The Basics of Winning Slots*, p. 59, 1984

6 used of a hard bargain *US, 1828*
- McDermott was very pleased with himself to think he'd made such a tight bargain. But I could see by the twinkle in Jeremiah's eye that he was only pretending to let McDermott get the better of him[.] —Margaret Attwood, *Alias Grace*, p. 269, 1996

7 of money; hard to come by; in short-circulation *UK, 1846*
- Money was tight and the board was struggling with ways to use their limited resouces the most frugally. —John Mutz and Katherine Murray, *Fundraising for Dummies*, p. 24, 2000

8 used of a player in poker, extremely conservative in play and betting *US*
- —Anthony Holden, *Big Deal*, p. 306, 1990

9 of a contest, close, evenly matched *US, 1848*
- If it's a tight game, he stays with the action. —Tim McCarver and Danny Peary, *Tim McCarver's Baseball for Brain Surgeons and Other Fans*, p. 18, 1999

10 friendly *US, 1956*
- I'm not tight with her. —Willard Motley, *Let No Man Write My Epitaph*, p. 111, 1958
- I didn't get tight with anybody in the reception center. —Claude Brown, *Manchild in the Promised Land*, p. 135, 1965
- Mom and me were pretty tight. —A.S. Jackson, *Gentleman Pimp*, p. 116, 1973
- He was tight with Earl Bassey. —Edwin Torres, *Carlito's Way*, p. 20, 1975
- There's a lonely Hindu works at the 7-H across the street. Get in tight with him. —*Chasing Amy*, 1997
- Poitras and I are tight. —Robert Crais, *L.A. Requiem*, p. 38, 1999

11 good; fashionable; in style *US*
- —*Columbia Missourian*, p. 1A, 19th October 1998

tight-arse *noun*
a person who is mean with money *UK*
- You're a tight-arse. —Caroline Aherne and Craig Cash, *The Royle Family*, 1999

tight-arsed *adjective*
1 mean, close-fisted, ungenerous *UK*
- Tight-arsed with his purse strings. —Thorn Keys, *All Night Stand*, 1966
- Been up to is tight-arsed tricks again as he? —Niall Griffiths, *Sheepshagger*, p. 133, 2001

2 puritanical; very restrained; self-centred *UK*
- Was it my fault if their men would rather sleep with me than with any of that mealy-mouthed, tight-arsed crew? —Marion Zimmer Bradley, *Witch Hill*, p. 101, 1990
- The binman at Farlingham once called me a tight-arsed bitch, because I asked him not to throw the bin lids on the flower bed. Perhaps I am a tight-arsed bitch. —Margaret Drabble, *The Seven Sisters*, p. 72, 2002
- Try not to sound like such a tight-arsed ponce. —Glen Duncan, *I, Lucifer*, p. 253, 2003

tight as a crab's arse *adjective*
miserly *UK*
- DENISE: You're tight as a crab's arse you. DAD: Crab's arse my arse. —Caroline Aherne and Craig Cash, *The Royle Family*, 1999

tight as a gnat's twat *adjective*
miserly *UK*
- Been up to is tight-arsed tricks again as he? Fuckin typical. Tight as a gnat's twat yew are, Marc, d'yew know that? Tight as a fuckin gnat's twat. —Niall Griffiths, *Sheepshagger*, p. 133, 2001

tight-ass *noun*
a highly strung, nervous person *US*
- She preferred to think that was the case, rather than that Marx Marvelous was simply another intellectual tight-ass smugly ripping at every cosmic curtain to expose the specter of dank feminine (irrational!!!) mysticism that he is certain lurks behind it. —Tom Robbins, *Another Roadside Attraction*, p. 185, 1971
- Fenster always worked with McManus. He was a real tight-ass, but when it came to the job, he was right on. — *The Usual Suspects*, 1995

tight-assed *adjective*
highly strung, nervous *US*
- My tight-assed smugness disappeared quickly. —Harvey Rottenburg, *Planted, Burnt, and Busted [The Howard Marks Book of Dope Stories]*, p. 340, 1970

tighten *verb*

▸ **tighten the wig**
to smoke marijuana *US*
- —Don R. McCreary (Editor), *Dawg Speak*, 2001

▸ **tighten up your game**
to educate or coach someone *US*
- If her man hadn't tightened her game up for her, she would be an easy mark to switch envelopes on. —Donald Goines, *Whoreson*, p. 203, 1972

tightener *noun*
1 any alcoholic drink *US*
- "Fresheners," Nancy said. "Tighteners and fresheners. Sometimes drinkees or martin-eyes." —Elmore Leonard, *The Big Bounce*, p. 88, 1969

2 in horse racing, a race seen as preparation for the next race *US*
- —Igor Kushyshyn et al., *The Gambling Times Guide to Harness Racing*, p. 124, 1994

tighter than a camel's arse in a sand storm *adjective*
miserly *UK*
An elaboration of **TIGHT** (mean).
- GARY: I'm just careful with money that's all. TRISTE: Careful – tighter than a camel's arse in a sandstorm you mean[.] —Patrick Jones, *Unprotected Sex*, p. 217, 1999

tighter than bark to a tree *adjective*
miserly *CANADA*
- From Lawrence Colony, Quebec, to be "tighter than bark to a tree" is to be very close with your money. —Lewis Poteet, *Talking Country*, p. 73, 1992

tight fight with a short stick *noun*
a difficult job with poor equipment to do it *US*
- —Jerry Robertson, *Oil Slanguage*, p. 122, 1954

tight hole *noun*
an oil well whose discovery and location have not been reported *US*
- But because I'd been fired and Donovan's service company hadn't been paid, we agreed that if we found oil we would make it a tight hole, and not tell the F.E.R.C. —Stephen Cannell, *Big Con*, p. 284, 1997

tight laces *noun*
commerically manufactured cigarettes, especially with filters *US*
- —Charles Shafer, *Folk Speech in Texas Prisons*, p. 216, 1990

tight-roll *noun*
a manufactured cigarette *US*
- I had tight rolls and a punk and I was uptown. —Inez Cardozo-Freeman, *The Joint*, p. 537, 1984

tightwad *noun*
a miserly person *US, 1906*
- Someone gets the check and McDermott puts it on his gold AmEx card, which conclusively proves that he's high on coke since he's a famous tight- wad. —Bret Easton Ellis, *American Psycho*, p. 209, 1991

tighty-whities *noun*
form-fitting men's jockey shorts *US*
- —Connie Eble (Editor), *UNC-CH Campus Slang*, p. 4, April 1985

tig ol' bitties *noun*
large breasts *US*
An intentional Spoonerism of 'big old titties'.
- —Connie Eble (Editor), *UNC-CH Campus Slang*, p. 5, Spring 2001

tigre; tigre blanco; tigre del norte *noun*
heroin *UK*
Possibly 'branded' types of heroin, from Spanish for 'tiger': 'white tiger' and 'northern tiger'.
- —Mike Haskins, *Drugs*, p. 284, 2003

Tijuana 12 *noun*
a cigarette made with tobacco and marijuana *US*
- —Ralph de Sola, *Crime Dictionary*, p. 150, 1982

Tijuana Bible *noun*
a pornographic comic book *US*
- — *Maledicta*, p. 167, 1979: 'A glossary of ethnic slurs in american english'

Tijuana chrome *noun*
silver spray paint *US*
Tijuana is just across the border from California in the Mexican state of Baja California. Californian youth often took their customised cars to Tijuana, where much of the best and some of the shoddiest, customising work was done.
- —John Edwards, *Auto Dictionary*, p. 170, 1993

Tijuana taxi *noun*
a well marked police car *US*
- —Wayne Floyd, *Jason's Authentic Dictionary of CB Slang*, p. 30, 1976

tik *noun*
a potential victim *UK*
West Indian and UK black.
- —Angela Devlin, *Prison Patter*, p. 115, 1996

Tilbury Docks; the Tilburys *noun*
any sexually transmitted infection *UK*
Rhyming slang for **POX**, formed on a part of the Port of London. An earlier, now obsolete sense for this rhyme was 'socks'.
- —Ray Puxley, *Cockney Rabbit*, 1992

tiles *noun*
dominoes *US*
- —Dominic Armanino, *Dominoes*, p. 15, 1959

▸ **on the tiles**
partying *NEW ZEALAND*
- —Louis S. Leland, *A Personal Kiwi-Yankee Dictionary*, p. 73, 1984

till-tap *verb*
to steal money from a cash till *US*
- I'm always seeing his name on robbery, burglary, or till tap reports. —Joseph Wambaugh, *The New Centurions*, 1970
- He had liberated two bennys [overcoats] off hangers and was nonchalantly till tapping (rifling a cash register) men's wear bread. —Iceberg Slim (Robert Beck), *Airtight Willie and Me*, p. 5, 1979

till tapper *noun*
in a casino, a person who steals coins or tokens from a slot machine being played by someone else *US*
- I once caught a till tapper at the Tropicana in Las Vegas when he was reaching into the till on the slot machine that my wife was playing. —Charles W. Lund, *Robbing the One-Armed Bandits*, p. 122, 1999

till tapping *noun*
theft from a cash register when the cashier is distracted *US*
- But since you've been out you've learned new names for the game / such as till-tapping, the carpet, the rope, and the drag, which all leads up to one thing. —Bruce Jackson, *Get Your Ass in the Water and Swim Like Me*, p. 92, 1964

tilly *noun*
(especially in Queensland and northern New South Wales) a utility truck *AUSTRALIA, 1957*
• Lived in various parts of Qld since 1932, and there utilities were always called "Tillies" until recent times. The term "Ute" only came into common use in relatively recent times. — *www.abc.net.au*, 2003

Tilly *noun*
used as a personification of the police *US*
• — *American Speech*, p. 59, Spring-Summer 1970: 'Homosexual slang'

Tilly Bates *adjective*
▷ **see:** TIDDLER'S BAIT

tilly-tallied *adjective*
drunk *UK*
Possibly from obsolete 'tilly-vally' (nonsense), which is what tends to be spoken when drunk.
• Before I got totally tilly-tallied, I left my Italian friends and returned to find Sally. — Wayne Anthony, *Spanish Highs*, p. 146, 1999

tilt *noun*
1 especially in the Maritime Provinces, a crude shelter, open on one side and with its back to the wind *CANADA*
• In a fisherman's "tilt" or hut, McKay's observant eye noticed a piece of bright yellow stone on the mantelshelf. — Michael Harrington, *Sea Stories from Newfoundland*, p. 34, 1958
• The tilt was a trapper's winter quarters and the slanted gable was a protection against heavy snowfall, helping prevent the entrance becoming snowbound. — *Beaver*, p. 16/1, Summer 1966
2 in pinball, a mechanism on the machine that ends a game when the player moves the machine too forcefully *US*
• — Edward Trapunski, *Special When Lit*, p. 155, 1979

▸ **on tilt**
used of a poker player's playing, exceptionally poor *US*
• — John Scarne, *Scarne's Guide to Modern Poker*, p. 285, 1979

Tim *noun*
a Roman Catholic *UK: SCOTLAND*
Who the original Tim is or was is unknown.
• Tony [Blair] did like his minions to be identified with a wee bit of head-bowed Christian solemnity. Being a Tim twenty-four/seven, however, was not on. — Christopher Brookmyre, *Boiling a Frog*, p. 34, 2000

timber *noun*
1 a toothpick *US*
• — Jack Lait and Lee Mortimer, *New York Confidential*, p. 236, 1948: 'A glossary of Harlemisms'
2 in horse racing, a hurdle in a steeplechase race *US*
• — Tom Ainslie, *Ainslie's Complete Guide to Thoroughbred Racing*, p. 340, 1976
3 in poker, the cards that have been discarded *US*
• — *American Speech*, p. 102, May 1951
4 in the circus or carnival, a person playing a game or concession with the house's money in an attempt to attract other patrons to play *US*
• At times one may hear a game operator yell, "Timber!" This means that his joint is not receiving too much play and that he would like a few sticks to give the joint the appearance of activity. — E.E. Steck, *A Brief Examination of an Esoteric Folk*, p. 11, 1968
• You can't see the players for the timber. — Joe McKennon, *Circus Lingo*, p. 93, 1980

timber nigger *noun*
an American Indian *US*
Offensive. Used by sporting enthusiasts and those in the tourist industry to describe American Indians involved in the fishing/hunting rights debate.

timber rider *noun*
in horse racing, a jockey in a steeplechase event *US*
• — Tom Ainslie, *Ainslie's Complete Guide to Thoroughbred Racing*, p. 340, 1976

timbit *noun*
a doughnut hole from Tim Horton's™; a rendezvous for coffee and snack proposed by one police officer to another *CANADA, 2000*
Refers to the dough that is punched out of a ring doughnut, fried, and sold as a 'hole'.
• Among the Quebec Provincial Police, an informal meeting at a coffee or donut shop is known as a "timbit." — Lewis Poteet, *Cop Talk*, p. 102, 2000
• Several people with dark senses of humor have pointed out to me that these were introduced shortly after Tim Horton, famous and beloved, was killed in a car accident. — Emily *An American's Guide to Canada*, p. 2, 10th November 2001

time *noun*
time in prison; a jail sentence *UK, 1837*
• They talk' like they serious about me doin' that machine gun time. — *Jackie Brown*, 1997

▸ **(he) wouldn't give you the time of day; too mean to give you the time of day**
applied to a notoriously mean person *UK, 1984*
• Why are you yelling at Michael? If it wasn't for Michael, Peter wouldn't give you the time of day. — Frank Owen, *Clubland*, p. 138, 2003

▸ **do time**
1 to serve a prison sentence, especially in a manner that preserves the prisoner's sanity *UK, 1865*
• The grateful Satira, later a Page 1 sensation, did her time, got out of the can, and prompetly booked herself into his opposition saloon. — Jack Lait and Lee Mortimer, *Chicago Confidential*, p. 67, 1950
• The broad caught it immediately and said, "You did time?" and there was a hesitancy in her voice. — Mickey Spillane, *Return of the Hood*, p. 83, 1964
• Nearly every one of them had done some time[.] — Malcolm X and Alex Haley, *The Autobiography of Malcolm X*, p. 87, 1964
• He did the time; he didn't let the time do him. — Donald Goines, *White Man's Justice, Black Man's Grief*, p. 201, 1973
• Where I was from, who I knew, how I knew Nice Guy, had I done time, shit like that. — *Reservoir Dogs*, 1992
• — Angela Devlin, *Prison Patter*, p. 46, 1996
2 to stay after school in detention *US*
• — *This Week Magazine, New York Herald Tribune*, p. 46, 28th February 1954

▸ **for the time**
in poolroom betting, playing with the the loser paying for the use of the table *US*
• When one player says to another "Let's just play sociable," as often as not he means that they should play for only a dollar or two, and at the very least means that they should play "for the time" (the loser paying the check). — Ned Polsky, *Hustlers, Beats, and Others*, p. 47, 1967

▸ **have no time for**
to have no respect for someone *AUSTRALIA, 1911*
• True folk [-music] cultists are a pain in the ass. I have no time for them. — *The Observer*, 30th November 2003

▸ **in no time; in less than no time**
immediately *UK, 1822*
• Everyone knows the law doesn't work here. You can bribe your way out in no time[.] — *The Observer*, 21st September 2003

▸ **make time; make time with**
to have sex with someone; to make sexual advances towards someone *US, 1934*

time-and-a-half *noun*
in blackjack, the payout to a player of one and a half times their bet when the player is dealt a natural 21 *US, 1977*
A pun using a term usually applied to an overtime rate of pay.
• — Lee Solkey, *Dummy Up and Deal*, p. 122, 1980
• — Thomas L. Clark, *The Dictionary of Gambling and Gaming*, p. 233, 1987

time of the month *noun*
the bleed period of a woman's menstrual cycle *UK*
Barely euphemistic.
• PIP: What's the matter wiv you – time of the month eh? — Patrick Jones, *Everything Must Go*, p. 143, 2000

time out!
used for warning others of approaching police *US*
• Police were in the 1100 block of N. Stockton St. about 6:25 p.m. Saturday when they heard a young male yell "Time out!" – street slang meaning police are in the area. — *Baltimore Sun*, p. 3B, 11th September 2000

timer *noun*
father *CANADA*
An abbreviation of 'old-timer'.
• — Jack Chambers (Editor), *Slang Bag 93 (University of Toronto)*, p. 6, Winter 1993

time-stretcher *noun*
a prisoner whose attitude and actions serve to make the time served by others seem longer than it is *US*
• — Gary K. Farlow, *Prison-ese*, p. 74, 2002

time through the gate *noun*
the on-the-job experience of a prison officer *UK*
- —Angela Devlin, *Prison Patter*, p. 115, 1996

Timmy *noun*
a Tristar aircraft *UK*
In Royal Air Force use, 2002.

timothy *noun*
a brothel *AUSTRALIA*
A shortening of 'Timothy Titmouse', rhyming slang for 'house'.
- —Thirty-five *The Argot*, 1950
- —Jim Ramsay, *Cop It Sweet!*, p. 89, 1977

timps *noun*
timpani (kettle-drums); timpanists *UK, 1934*
An abbreviation of 'timpani'.
- The castle gates close with a sound like a clap of thunder (timps[,] bassoons and lower strings). The die is cast. —Sir Denis Forman, *A Night at the Opera*, p. 521, 1998

Timshop *noun*
a Roman Catholic chapel *UK: SCOTLAND*
- —Michael Munro, *The Complete Patter*, p. 157, 1996

tim tam *noun*
a tampon *AUSTRALIA*
Abbreviation and reduplication.
- — *The Museum of Menstruation and Women's Health*, July 2001

tin *noun*
1 a police badge *US*
- — *New York Times Magazine*, p. 88, 16th March 1958
- Calvin's board took two days, and Susan got his tin. —Stephen J. Cannell, *The Tin Collectors*, p. 181, 2001

2 a police officer *US, 1950*
- —Thomas L. Clark, *The Dictionary of Gambling and Gaming*, p. 233, 1987

3 a gun *US*
- You're talking about the mob, the members of which could be carrying more tin than all the detectives on the force put together. —Robert Campbell, *Junkyard Dog*, p. 110, 1986

4 a safe *US*
- It was a strong box and tapping the tin took some finger work. —Red Rudensky, *The Gonif*, p. 82, 1970

5 one ounce of marijuana *US, 1946*
Probably from a pipe tobacco tin as a measured container.
- —Richard A. Spears, *The Slang and Jargon of Drugs and Drink*, p. 511, 1986

6 beer in any quantity or container *US*
- —Connie Eble (Editor), *UNC-CH Campus Slang*, p. 7, Fall 1980

7 in drag racing, a trophy, especially one awarded without a cash prize *US*
- —John Lawlor, *How to Talk Car*, p. 107, 1965

▸ **does what it says on the tin; does exactly what it says on the tin**
used as an assurance that whatever is so described will be, or behave, as expected *UK*
From a catchphrase-slogan for Ronseal™ wood-treatments; first introduced in the early 1990s, the phrase is now part of the company's registered trademarking, and widely applied in the sense recorded here.
- Oral Rehydration Treatment [...] is a life-saving powder that contains potassium, sodium and glucose to help replenish the body's essential fluids and salts. It tastes revolting, but it does exactly what it says on the tin. — *The Daily Telegraph*, 24th December 2001
- The Business Driver Initiative, devised by PricewaterhouseCoopers, does "exactly what it says on the tin", according to Bruce Cartwright, PwC business recovery services partner in Scotland. — *The Scotsman*, 12th February 2004

tin-arse; tin-bum *noun*
a lucky person *AUSTRALIA, 1953*
Derives, perhaps, from a play on 'copper-bottomed'.

tin arse; tin arsed *adjective*
lucky *AUSTRALIA, 1919*
- Bob came out of ut all right, didn' yer Bob? Tin arse Bob they call 'im. —Nino Culotta (John O'Grady), *They're A Weird Mob*, p. 72, 1957
- You flukey tin-arse bastard. —John O'Grady, *Aussie Etiket*, p. 63, 1971

Tina Turner; tina *noun*
1 a profitable activity *UK, 2001*
Rhyming slang for 'earner'; formed from the popular US singer and actress (b.1938).
- You get some nasty little Paul Anka [wanker] who's a bit short of the Duane Eddys [cash] [...] So he starts thinking what I needs a nice little Tina Turner[.] —Mervyn Stutter, *Getting Nowhere Fast*, 21st May 2004

2 a tablet of MDMA , the recreational drug best known as ecstasy *UK*
Rhyming slang for **GURNER** (a person intoxicated by MDMA).

tin bath; tin *noun*
1 a laugh *UK*
Rhyming slang.
- I think the immediate reaction was, "This is a joke. You're having a tin bath." —Paul Ross, *Kylie Entirely*, 2002

2 a scarf *UK*
Rhyming slang.
- It's freezing out so put your titfer [a hat] and tin on. —Ray Puxley, *Cockney Rabbit*, 1992

tin can *noun*
1 a safe that is easily broken into by criminals *US*
- —Vincent J. Monteleone, *Criminal Slang*, p. 239, 1949
- —Bruce Jackson, *Outside the Law*, p. 60, 1972: 'Glossary'

2 an older ship in disrepair *US*
- I know my orders are going to be for some damn tin can and I'm gonna wind up on the friggin deck force. —Darryl Ponicsan, *The Last Detail*, p. 4, 1970

3 a citizens' band radio set *US*
From one of the most primitive technical means of communication: two tin cans joined by a piece of string.
- — *Complete CB Slang Dictionary*, p. 92, 1976
- —Peter Chippindale, *The British CB Book*, p. 160, 1981

tinchy *adjective*
petty; small *BAHAMAS*
- —John A. Holm, *Dictionary of Bahamian English*, p. 208, 1982

Tin City *noun*
a sheet metal barracks in Guam used to house Vietnamese refugees after the North Vietnamese conquest in 1975 *US*
- —Gregory Clark, *Words of the Vietnam War*, p. 210, 1990

tin collector *noun*
a police officer or prosecutor involved in investigating police misconduct *US*
- She used to be their number one tin collector. —Stephen J. Cannell, *The Tin Collectors*, p. 44, 2001

tincture *noun*
1 an alcoholic drink *UK*
Popularised, if not inspired by the 'Dear Bill' letters in *Private Eye*.
- He'd be sparko after his usual lunchtime tincture. — *Sunday Times*, 8th June 1980

2 a light drug in liquid form *UK*
A jocular euphemism.
- —Jenny Fabian and Johnny Byrne, *Groupie*, 1968

tin dog *noun*
a snowmobile *NEW ZEALAND, 1969*
- —Bernadette Hince, *The Antarctic Dictionary*, p. 354, 2000

tin ear *noun*
tone deafness *US, 1935*
- Who the hell is playing piano? Get that hippie out of here. He's got a tin ear. — *Nashville*, 1975

Tin-Ear Alley *noun*
the boxing world *UK, 1961*
A journalists' pun on 'Tin-Pan Alley' (the world of music).

tin flute *noun*
a suit *UK: SCOTLAND*
A variation of **WHISTLE AND FLUTE** in Glasgow rhyming slang.
- Must be daein [doing] awright fur hissel. Goes tae work in a tin flute an aw that. —Michael Munro, *The Patter, Another Blast*, 1988

t'ing *noun*

thing *UK*

West Indian and UK black pronunciation.

• We got big t'ings to celebrate. —Karline Smith, *Moss Side Massive*, p. 11, 1994

ting *noun*

money; a payment, especially in an illegal context *TRINIDAD AND TOBAGO, 1989*

• —Lise Winer, *Dictionary of the English/Creole of Trinidad & Tobago*, 2003

ting-a-ling *noun*

1 the penis *BAHAMAS*

• —John A. Holm, *Dictionary of Bahamian English*, p. 208, 1982

2 a ring (jewellery) *UK*

Rhyming slang.

• —Ray Puxley, *Cockney Rabbit*, 1992

3 in playing cards, a king *UK*

Rhyming slang.

• —Ray Puxley, *Cockney Rabbit*, 1992

tin grin *noun*

any person with orthodontia *US*

• Adults have swollen the ranks of America's estimated four million "tin-grins" just as declining birth rate was depleting the traditional orthodontic market of young children and teen-agers. —*Washington Post*, p. B2, 10th October 1977

• —Chris Lewis, *The Dictionary of Playground Slang*, p. 41, 2003

• For boomers, taunts like "brace-face," tin grin" and "metal mouth" have made way for more sophisticated teasing. —*Washington Post*, p. F1, 13th January 2004

tings *noun*

the testicles *UK*

West Indian pronunciation of 'things'.

• I quarter-turned and cracked him short-arm back-fist across his face, deflecting his piping and kicking him in his tings in three fluid motions. —Diran Abedayo, *My Once Upon A Time*, p. 39, 2000

tingum *noun*

a person or thing the name of which escapes the speaker *BAHAMAS*

• —Patricia Clinton-Meicholas, *More Talkin' Bahamian*, p. 98, 1995

tin hat *noun*

1 a fool, an idiot *UK*

Rhyming slang for **PRAT**.

• —Ray Puxley, *Fresh Rabbit*, 1998

2 on the railways, a company official *US*

• —Ramon Adams, *The Language of the Railroader*, p. 158, 1977

▸ **put the tin hat on it; put the tin hat on something**

to bring an unfortunate sequence to an unwelcome climax; to finish something off *UK, 1919*

• We thought our troubles were behind us and blow us if Windsor Castle doesn't go and burn down. Doesn't that put the tin hat on it? —Andrew Nickolds, *Back to Basics*, p. 19, 1994

tinhorn *noun*

a cheap and offensive person *US, 1887*

• They were fairly impressed by this; well, maybe less impressed than worried that I might turn out a tin-horn. —Clancy Sigal, *Going Away*, p. 151, 1961

tinhorn *adjective*

shoddy; inconsequential; inferior *US, 1886*

• You're just a cheap tinhorn punk, yellow to the core. —Chester Himes, *The Real Cool Killers*, p. 138, 1959

tin Indian *noun*

a Pontiac car *US*

• —John Edwards, *Auto Dictionary*, p. 170, 1993

tinker *noun*

1 a member of the travelling community *IRELAND*

Conventionally 'an (itinerant) mender of pots, pans, kettles etc.', but now more generally applied.

• You could do better than hanging around with that one. She's a pure-bred tinker. I hear you can get the smell of the camp off her still. —Eamonn Sweeney, *Waiting for the Healer*, p. 257, 1997

• —*A Dictionary of Hiberno-English*, p. 272, 1999

2 a child, especially a mischievous child *NEW ZEALAND*

Remembered in use in New Zealand in 1904 and in Australia in 1910.

• Up to high jinks you'll be with this little tinker. —Rosamunde Pilcher, *Coming Home*, p. 133, 1996

3 a piece of scrap from wreckage *CANADA*

• It was at Northeast Point that tinkers and pieces of metal from various ships lay amongst the rocks or had been washed up over the high banks and blown into the woods. —Walter Hitchens, *Island Trek*, p. 55, 1983

tinker's cuss; tinker's damn; tinker's toss *noun*

something of no value *UK, 1824*

• I couldn't care a tinker's cuss what happens to it – to the traders, the Chinese or the poxy Triads. —James Clavell, *Tai-Pan*, p. 654, 1966

• I don't give a tinker's damn what they do on Mount Olympus[.] —David Sedaris, *Naked*, p. 69, 1997

• [W]hy would my three playing partners give a tinker's cuss in the middle of playing a round[?] —Troon McAllister, *The Green*, p. 15, 1999

• Today the wagtail finally forgot / that I once called it sigl-di-gwt. / It didn't give a tinker's toss, / kept right on rooting in river moss[.] —*The Guardian*, 5th June 2004: 'What's in a name?'

tinkle *noun*

urine; the act of urination *US, 1960*

• "I gotta ... go tinkle," the big one said and went weaving and giggling toward the latrine[.] —Ken Kesey, *One Flew Over the Cuckoo's Nest*, p. 289, 1962

• ... comes bouncing up the stairs on the way to have a tinkle. —Robert Campbell, *Alice in La-La Land*, p. 263, 1987

▸ **give a tinkle**

to telephone someone *UK, 1938*

From the ringing bell of original telephones.

• Copies are normally £1 post paid, but give them a tinkle on [...] and say the magic words[.] —*Classic Motor Monthly*, July 2004

tinkle *verb*

to urinate *US, 1960*

Children's vocabulary, used coyly by adults.

• —Collin Baker et al., *College Undergraduate Slang Study Conducted at Brown University*, p. 210, 1968

• I almost tinkled in my pajamas with the jolt of pain. —Iceberg Slim (Robert Beck), *Airtight Willie and Me*, p. 49, 1979

• "What happened to tinkle, DeDe? I taught you to say tinkle." —Armistead Maupin, *Babycakes*, p. 8, 1984

• Stephanie's in the back yard trying to tinkle standing up like a boy. —Janet Evanovich, *Seven Up*, p. 195, 2001

tinklebox *noun*

a piano *US*

• I stood by that beat-up old tinklebox in a hypnotic state[.] —Mezz Mezzrow, *Really the Blues*, p. 25, 1946

tin lid *noun*

1 a Jewish person *UK*

Rhyming slang for **YID**.

• —Ray Puxley, *Cockney Rabbit*, 1992

2 a child *AUSTRALIA, 1905*

Rhyming slang for **KID**.

• —Duke Tritton, *Learn to talk Old Jack Lang*, p. 14, 1905

• —Jim Ramsay, *Cop It Sweet!*, p. 90, 1977

• —*Sydney Morning Herald*, p. 1, 2002

tinned dog *noun*

canned meat *AUSTRALIA, 1895*

• [O]ur guest had lit the fire, boiled the billy, and was shoving huge chunks of our tinned dog into a cavern which opened frequently amid his multitudinous whiskers. —Bill Wannan, *Bullockies, Beauts and Bandicoots*, p. 73, 1960

tinnie; tinny *noun*

a can of beer *AUSTRALIA, 1964*

• Back in Australia I seen some bastards knock a Fosters tinnie off a fence at fifty paces[.] —Barry Humphries, *The Wonderful World of Barry McKenzie*, p. 49, 1968

• As time passed, so did the tinnies. —Martin Cameron, *A Look at the Bright Side*, 1988

• —David McGill, *David McGill's Complete Kiwi Slang Dictionary*, p. 126, 1998

• [T]hey had probably read about this shit over their tinnies in Australia[.] —Christopher Brookmyre, *Boiling a Frog*, p. 206, 2000

• John wouldn't go to your barbies or crack a tinnie with you[.] —Kel Richards, *The Aussie Bible*, p. 37, 2003

tinny *noun*

1 an imprecise measure of marijuana wrapped in tinfoil, usually enough for about three cigarettes *NEW ZEALAND, 1995*

• —Harry Orsman, *A Dictionary of Modern New Zealand Slang*, p. 139, 1999

2 a small aluminium boat *AUSTRALIA, 1979*
- They'd zoom out to the reef in their little tinnies and tie up on the solid metal channel markers. — *Tracks*, October 1992

3 a station wagon with a steel body and no wood trim *US*
- — John Edwards, *Auto Dictionary*, p. 170, 1993

tinny *adjective*
lucky *AUSTRALIA, 1919*
- — Jim Ramsay, *Cop It Sweet!*, p. 90, 1977
- I was really tinny at the casino last night. — John Blackman, *The Aussie Slang Dictionary*, p. 98, 1990

tinny house *noun*
a place where marijuana tinnies are sold *NEW ZEALAND*
- — Harry Orsman, *A Dictionary of Modern New Zealand Slang*, p. 139, 1999

tin plate *noun*
1 a mate *NEW ZEALAND*
Rhyming slang.
- — Ray Puxley, *Cockney Rabbit*, 1992

2 in circus and carnival usage, a law enforcement official in a small town *US*
- — Don Wilmeth, *The Language of American Popular Entertainment*, p. 146, 1981

tin sandwich *noun*
a harmonica; a mouth organ *US*
Used as the title of an album of harmonica music by Tommy Basker, 'The Tin Sandwich', 1994.

tinsel-teeth *noun*
1 any person with orthodontia *US*
- I would be in school, and notice that if a girl had braces on her teeth the other kids would call her 'tinsel-teeth' or 'iron mouth'. — *Washington Post*, p. D1, 24th November 1979
- The appearance of the devices led to the use of such pejorative terms as "metal mouth" "armor plate," "tinsel teeth," "tin-grin" and "Siberian railroad tracks." — *Washington Post*, p. Z17, 19th September 1995

2 orthodontic braces *US*
- — *Current Slang*, p. 10, Winter 1971

Tinsel Town *nickname*
Hollywood *US, 1939*
- Trembling with excitement,the voluptuous movie queen joined the ranks of other tinsel-town celebrities while her fans shouted: "C'mon sweater girl! Give!" — *Waterloo (Iowa) Sunday Courier*, p. 3, 25th May 1950

tins of beans; tins *noun*
jeans (denim trousers) *UK*
Rhyming slang.
- — Ray Puxley, *Cockney Rabbit*, 1992

tin soldier *noun*
a prostitute's client who pays not for conventional sex, but to act as a prostitute's 'slave' *UK*
Noted as a 'voyeur-type male, usually of middle- or upper-class background' by David Powis, *The Signs of Crime*, 1977.

tin tack *noun*
1 dismissal from employment *UK*
Rhyming slang for **SACK**. Recorded in 1932 but believed to be late C19.
- The geezer said if we were collared doing anything untoward in the firm's uniform, that was it – curtains. No final warning. Tin-Tac time. — Martin King and Martin Knight, *The Naughty Nineties*, p. 53, 1999

2 a fact *UK, 1921*
Rhyming slang based on **BRASS TACKS**, generally plural.
- — Julian Franklyn, *A Dictionary of Rhyming Slang*, 1960
- — Ray Puxley, *Cockney Rabbit*, 1992

tin tank *noun*
a bank *UK, 1932*
Rhyming slang.
- — Ray Puxley, *Cockney Rabbit*, 1992

tin termites *noun*
rust *UK*
- 'Fraid the dreaded tin termites have got into me little old Min[i]. — Beale, 1972

tints *noun*
1 sunglasses *US*
- — David Claerbaut, *Black Jargon in White America*, p. 83, 1972

2 tinted car windows *US*
- — Edith A. Folb, *runnin' down some lines*, p. 258, 1980

tiny *noun*
1 a child *AUSTRALIA*
- And Glenda Nettleton could see with half an eye that Beryl was scrupulous and that the tinies would be well catered for at Kia Ora[.] — Barry Humphries, *A Nice Night's Entertainment*, p. 51, 1961

2 a very young member of a youth gang *US*
- All the midgets and tinys in the Black Spiders had been to the Hall. Most of the peewees even! — Joseph Wambaugh, *The Glitter Dome*, p. 110, 1981

tiny gangster *noun*
a young member of a youth gang *US*
- in Los Angeles, where Blood and Crip membership totals about 25,000, "baby-gangsters" as young as 9 are regularly recruited and some gangs include even younger "tiny gangsters," the report said. — *UPI*, 4th August 1989
- "[H]e's listed in the Gang Street Alias Index under the name Li'l Silent, so at the very least he's a TG or a known associate." TG stood for "tiny gangster" and was basically a killer in training. — Stephen J. Cannell, *The Tin Collectors*, p. 147, 2001

tiny mind *noun*
▸ **out of your tiny mind; out of your tiny**
you are crazy, foolish, mad *UK, 1970*
- "Are you out of your tiny?" Arthur looked at him with mounting concern. "You're rambling." — Anthony Masters, *Minder*, p. 179, 1984

Tiny Tim *noun*
a five-pound note; the sum of £5 *UK*
Rhyming slang for **FLIM**, formed on a character in Charles Dickens' *A Christmas Carol*, 1843.
- — Ray Puxley, *Cockney Rabbit*, 1992

Tio Taco *noun*
a Mexican-American who curries favour with the dominant white culture *US*
Literally 'Uncle Taco', referring to a Mexican dish made with a fried corn tortilla.
- Literally, "Uncle Taco," the Mexican-American equivalent of an Uncle Tom. — *Time*, p. 18, 4th July 1969
- — Eugene Landy, *The Underground Dictionary*, p. 185, 1971
- Tio Taco – A Mexican-American "Uncle Tom" as determined by the contemporary youth movement of Chicanos. — Librado Keno Vasquez, *Regional Dictionary of Chicano Slang*, p. 75, 1975
- This goes for all you mellow chicanos out there too, who whitey likes to display as a grinning Tio Taco on TV and in the movies. — Donald Goines, *Black Gangster*, p. 95, 1977

tip *noun*
1 a point of view, an aspect or perspective; a concentration upon an aspect *UK*
- The conversation continued on that tip for most of the journey. — Donald Gorgon, *Cop Killer*, p. 43, 1994
- In those days Kanya was on an underground speed-garage tip[.] — Wayne Anthony, *Spanish Highs*, p. 16, 1999
- [H]e was coming from the spiritual tip. — Diran Abedayo, *My Once Upon A Time*, p. 129, 2000
- Look at her, she's gone on one of her tips. — Lanre Fehintola, *Charlie Says...*, p. 154, 2000
- He wasn't on the bogus lawyer, bogus Foreign Legionnaire, bogus gynaecologist tip either. — J.J. Connolly, *Layer Cake*, p. 96, 2000

2 special information conveyed by an expert or insider; a piece of professional advice; private knowledge, especially in connection with investment or gambling *UK, 1845*
- Also ensure that the area's puppy-proofed (see Chapter 24 for tips on puppy-proofing your rooms). — Sarah Hodgson, *Puppies for Dummies*, p. 62, 2000

3 that which is 'tipped' to win; the probable winner in a race *UK, 1873*

4 a dirty or chaotically untidy place *UK, 1983*
Especially applied, apparently, to teenagers' bedrooms; from a community site where rubbish is tipped.
- If your house is a tip, cough up[.] — *The Observer*, 1st July 2001

5 a small group with specific economic functions, such as a drug-selling enterprise *US*
- — Mark S. Fleisher, *Beggars & Thieves*, p. 292, 1995: 'Glossary'

6 a gang *US*
- Just remember, if you join a prison tip or click, you'll never fit in out there again. — Seth Morgan, *Homeboy*, p. 153, 1990
- — William Bentley, *Prison Slang*, p. 44, 1992

- He was turned down and told that Nevada would have to form its own tip. —Bill Valentine, *Gangs and Their Tattoos*, 2000

7 a rubber thong sandal *CAYMAN ISLANDS*

- —Aarona Booker Kohlman, *Wotcha Say*, p. 25, 1985

8 a crowd gathered in front of a carnival game or show *US*

- For a game, however, the operator usually grinds for his own tip, but he also has help. —E.E. Steck, *A Brief Examination of an Esoteric Folk*, p. 9, 1968

9 a steady, repeating player in a carnival midway game *US*

- —Gene Sorrows, *All About Carnivals*, p. 27, 1985: 'Terminology'

tip *verb*

1 to convey expert, inside or specialist information, especially about a profitable investment or a probable winner *UK, 1883*

- Much Better, which was tipped as the winner and was running against other pompously named horses —Augusto Boal translated by Adrian Jackson, *Legislative Theatre*, p. 101, 1999

2 to give a gratuity *UK, 1706*

- I took a cab up to his building and tipped the doorman fifty dollars to let me in. —Augusten Burroughs, *Dry*, p. 197, 2003

3 to behave foolishly *US*

Gulf war usage.

- —*American Speech*, p. 402, Winter 1991: 'Among the new words'

4 to reckon that something will occur *AUSTRALIA, 1955*

- I'm tipping we'll get a drop of rain. —Harvey E. Ward, *Down Under Without Blunder*, p. 48, 1967

5 to perform oral sex *UK*

A shortening of **TIP THE VELVET** (to kiss with the tongue).

- —Paul Baker, *Polari*, p. 192, 2002

6 to become aware of a swindle *US*

- Some marks fell for the twenties repeatedly, without ever tipping. —Jim Thompson, *The Grifters*, p. 6, 1963

▸ **tip it**

in trucking, to drive fast *US*

- —Mary Elting, *Trucks at Work*, 1946

▸ **tip the brandy**

to lick, suck and tongue another's anus *UK*

A combination of **TIP** (to perform oral sex) and **BRANDY AND RUM** (the buttocks).

- —Paul Baker, *Polari*, p. 192, 2002

▸ **tip the bucket on**

to denigrate or criticise someone *AUSTRALIA, 1986*

- —Ivor Limb, *Footy's No Joke!*, p. 12, 1986
- He also tips another bucket on the twins: "What does it tell you about (their) judgment?" —*Herald*, p. 12, 17th October 1988

▸ **tip the gas**

in drag racing, to fill the petrol tank *US, 1960s*

- —Lyle K. Engel, *The Complete Book of Fuel and Gas Dragsters*, p. 154, 1968

▸ **tip the ivy**

to lick, suck and tongue another's anus *UK*

- —Paul Baker, *Polari*, p. 192, 2002

▸ **tip the load**

to go to confession *AUSTRALIA*

- —Ned Wallish, *The Truth Dictionary of Racing Slang*, p. 81, 1989

▸ **tip the velvet**

1 to kiss with the tongue, especially to 'tongue a woman' *UK, 1699*

Based on obsolete 'velvet' (the tongue).

- —Sarah Waters, *Tipping the Velvet*, 1998

2 to perform oral sex *UK*

- —Paul Baker, *Polari*, p. 192, 2002

3 in homosexual sex, to lick, suck and tongue another's anus *UK*

- [I]f you fancy tipping the velvet we could orderly [go] back to my bijou latty [place] down the street. —James Gardiner, *Who's a Pretty Boy Then?*, p. 123, 1997
- —Paul Baker, *Polari*, p. 192, 2002

▸ **tip the wink**

to warn; to privately signal to someone *UK, 1676*

- "Except when I've been tipped the wink." "The wink?" "Well, you know how it works, Falco." —Lindsey Davis, *One Virgin Too Many*, p. 69, 2001

tip-fiddle *noun*

a military deployment list *US*

Back-formation from TPFDL (time-phased forces deployment list).

- The tip-fiddle stipulates who is to go where, and when they are to get there. —Randeep Ramesh, *The War We Could Not Stop*, p. 301, 2003

tip-off *noun*

a warning; an item of private information *UK, 1901*

A variation of **TIP**.

- Sapphire Harris, the King of Creeps [a sneak-thief], had crept a gaff on a tip-off passed on to him by Larry[.] —Charles Raven, *Underworld Nights*, p. 191, 1956
- Now, when the tip-off came[.] —Chris Ryan, *Stand By, Stand By*, p. 93, 1996
- [L]ittle hints we missed. Little tip-offs. —James Hawes, *Dead Long Enough*, p. 5, 2000
- Laura had been one of the girls on duty the night the police, acting on a tip-off, had paid a visit. —Ian Rankin, *Resurrection Men*, p. 167, 2003

tip off *verb*

to give information to someone, especially about an impending crime *US, 1891*

- You know we didn't go out to Riis Park like we told that dick. And the babes better be tipped off. —Irving Shulman, *The Amboy Dukes*, p. 113, 1947
- Somebody tipped off the police the other time, and I know who it was. —Lilian Jackson Braun, *The Cat Who Turned On and Off*, p. 140, 1995

tipper *noun*

a dump truck *US*

- —Montie Tak, *Truck Talk*, p. 169, 1971

tippety-run *noun*

a form of cricket played by children in which the person batting has to run every time the ball is hit *AUSTRALIA*

Also with great variation as 'tip-and-go', 'tip-and-run', 'tippety', 'tippety-cricket', 'tippety-runs', 'tippy-cricket', 'tippy-go', 'tippy-go-run', 'tippy-runs', 'tipsy and tipsy-runs' – and that's ignoring vast spelling variation.

- One day she would be in the kitchen, happily stumbling over football boots, putting potato peelings in the cupboard and nonchalantly plonking miscellaneous odds and ends on top of the fridge, completely oblivious of the game of tippety-run cricket being played in the hall. —Kerry Cue, *Crooks, Chooks and Bloody Ratbags*, p. 201, 1983

tipple *noun*

1 alcohol; especially a drink of regular choice *UK, 1581*

From the conventional verb.

- there will be no need to change the labels on bottles of Stolly, a favourite tipple of communist and capitalist leaders alike. —*The Guardian*, 31st July 2003

2 by extension, a recreational drug of choice *UK*

- "What's this Trevor's, this Kinky's particular tipple?" "The dear boy has a weakness for crack cocaine." —J.J. Connolly, *Layer Cake*, p. 63, 2000
- It [crack]'s becoming the tipple of choice for a new generation, just as cocaine was during Britpop. —*Q*, p. 20, October 2004

tippy-toe *verb*

to walk on tiptoe *UK, 1901*

Childish variation of conventional 'tiptoe'.

- Fergy, smiling seductively, struggling to retain the towel around his waist, tippy-toes over to the wall switch[.] —Odie Hawkins, *Ghetto Sketches*, p. 202, 1972
- He'd tippy-toed out at the crack of dawn. —Janet Evanovich, *Seven Up*, p. 34, 2001

tips *noun*

in betting, odds of 11 – 10 *UK*

- —John McCririck, *John McCririck's World of Betting*, p. 61, 1991

tip-slinger *noun*

a person who offers racecourse tips *AUSTRALIA, 1915*

- —George Blaikie, *Remember Smith's Weekly?*, p. 219, 1950
- He certainly kept records and made a study of form on a scale never attempted by any other tip-slinger before or since. —James Holledge, *The Great Australian Gamble*, p. 34, 1966
- —Jim Ramsay, *Cop It Sweet!*, p. 90, 1977

tipster *noun*

in horse racing, someone who gives his opinions on various horses and their chances in a race *US*

- —David W. Maurer, *Argot of the Racetrack*, p. 65, 1951

tip-toe *verb*

in motor racing, to manoeuvre carefully through or past an obstruction or dangerous condition *US*

- —Don Alexander, *The Racer's Dictionary*, p. 66, 1980

tip-top *adjective*

excellent *UK, 1755*

- a Cockney tobacconist's son sent to a tip-top public school as a social experiment — *The Guardian*, 24th February 2004

tip up *verb*

to join a gang, especially a prison gang *US*

- White inmates who wanted to tip up with the AWs needed a sponsor. — Bill Valentine, *Gangs and Their Tattoos*, p. 11, 2000

tip-up town *noun*

a collection of ice fishing shanties on a lake's frozen surface *US*

The 'tip-up' is the small fishing pole used for ice fishing. Michigan Upper Pensinula usage.

tire *noun*

an apron worn by a young girl to keep her dress clean *CANADA, 1988*

This very old word – Shakespeare often used it – is still in use in Nova Scotia.

- "When I was a small child, my little apron, worn to protect my dress from spills, was always called a tire." My aunt Anna said, "I had tires. All the little girls around here wore tires. Adults had aprons." — Harry Bruce, *Down Home*, p. 109, 1988

tire billy *noun*

a short stick with a weighted head used by truck drivers to test the air pressure of their tyres *US*

- — Montie Tak, *Truck Talk*, p. 169, 1971

tired *adjective*

boring *UK*

- — Connie Eble (Editor), *UNC-CH Campus Slang*, p. 8, Spring 1987

tired and emotional *adjective*

drunk *UK, 1981*

A barbed journalistic euphemism thought to have been coined, or noted in political use and gleefully adopted, by satirical magazine *Private Eye*.

- [Patrick] Rafter once kipped in one of those entrance halls where banks have started putting cash machines. Whether he was merely 'tired and emotional' is not recorded. — *The Daily Telegraph*, 10th July 2000

tire-kicker; tyre-kicker *noun*

in the used car business, a customer who studiously inspects the cars for sale, seemingly at the expense of ever getting around to buying a car *US*

Reported by sales assistants in a UK retail chain in August 2002 as meaning 'a customer who spends a long time looking and fails to make a purchase'.

- It had been a slow morning . . . mostly tire-kickers and be-backs. — Stephen Cannell, *King Con*, p. 27, 1997

tish note *noun*

in circus and carnival usage, counterfeit money, especially when used to pay a prostitute *US*

- — Don Wilmeth, *The Language of American Popular Entertainment*, p. 272, 1981

tissue *noun*

1 crack cocaine *UK, 1998*

The variant 'tisher' is also used.

- — Mike Haskins, *Drugs*, p. 282, 2003

2 (especially in Tasmania) a cigarette paper *AUSTRALIA, 1966*

- Kanga had just rolled himself a smoke and was handing the tin and the Tally-ho 'tishers' to Tom. — Barney Roberts, *Where's Morning Gone?*, p. 165, 1987

tissue odds; tissue *noun*

a betting forecast used by bookmakers *UK, 1942*

From the flimsy paper originally used for this purpose.

- — John McCririck, *John McCririck's World of Betting*, p. 60, 1991
- — David Bennet, *Know Your Bets*, p. 126, 2001

tiswas; tizwas; tizz-wozz *noun*

a state of excitement or confusion *UK, 1960*

Originally Royal Air Force use; possibly a blend of 'it is/it was' as a variation of 'not know if you are coming or going' or a variation of TIZZ (an emotional state). From 1974–82 *Tiswas* was a popular Saturday morning television programme that demonstrated the qualities of excitement and confusion.

tit *noun*

1 the female breast *US, 1928*

- Uptown chick with a big gold cross once more rapping her soft little tits[.] — George Mandel, *Flee the Angry Strangers*, p. 403, 1952
- I have had two women so far, one American with huge tits and a splendid Mex whore in house. — Jack Kerouac, *Letter to Allen Ginsberg*, p. 353, 10th May 1952
- Daddy says tits. Daddy says knockers and jugs and bazooms and dingleberries and jujubes. And then he laughs and goes "wuff! wuff!". — *Journal of British Photography*, 9th May 1980
- [S]ince I wasn't a woman, my use of the street expression for a woman's breasts, "tits," was tactless and unprintable. — Larry Rivers, *What Did I Do?*, p. 470, 1992
- Every hippie carries nits / And every Englishman love tits / I love Page Three and other bits[.] — Benjamin Zephaniah, *The Sun*, p. 58, 1992

2 any finger-touch button such as on an electric bell; thus any button-like or knobby protruberance that vaguely resembles a nipple *UK, 1943*

Originally military.

3 a police officer's helmet *UK*

From the shape.

- I was issued with my tit the same day. — Duncan MacLaughlin, *The Filth*, p. 69, 2002

4 a fool *UK, 1947*

Often as 'look a right tit' or 'an absolute tit', and the amusing popular favourite 'feel a right tit'.

- Sick of being shoved, sick of being HIT! — Trevor Griffiths, *Oi For England*, 1982
- [A]ll the other mums look at me like, you know, like I'm a bit of a tit. — Harry Enfield, *Harry Enfield and His Humorous Chums*, p. 12, 1997
- Tits, the pair of them, them two. — Kevin Sampson, *Outlaws*, p. 107, 2001

5 a small raised bump on a computer keyboard key, most commonly the f and j keys, to provide orientation for the user's fingers *US*

- — Eric S. Raymond, *The New Hacker's Dictionary*, p. 352, 1991

▸ **a tit full of Wild Turkey**

used for describing an alcoholic's fondest sexual fantasy *US*

- — Michael Dalton Johnson, *Talking Trash with Redd Foxx*, p. 17, 1994

▸ **get tit**

to succeed in the goal of touching or fondling a girl's breasts *US*

- Ja get tit?" Richie whispered. "I din't try yet." "She got nice ones. — Richard Price, *The Wanderers*, p. 91, 1974

▸ **on the tit**

enjoying charity, or quasi-charity, in the form of undemanding work *US*

- You got the right idea, boy: stay on the government tit. Why not? Three squares and a flop, nothing to do, free medical care, free trips, plenty of time off, and a pension when you're ready to hang up the gloves! — Max Shulman, *Rally Round the Flag, Boys!*, p. 208, 1957
- The nerve of them little pantywaists in Washington, every one of 'em on the public tit. — Max Shulman, *Anyone Got a Match?*, p. 130, 1964

tit *adjective*

undemanding, easy *US*

- I'll probably go out tonioght because I have a tit week ahead. — Connie Eble (Editor), *UNC-CH Campus Slang*, p. 9, November 1990

tit about *verb*

to waste time; to play about; to be engaged in trivial activity *UK*

- There's a big wide world out there, and we're titting about in a panel-beater's yard[.] — Kevin Sampson, *Powder*, p. 142, 1999

tit and clit chain *noun*

a decorative chain that connects a woman's pierced nipples and clitoris *US*

- Dawn unzipped her leather skirt, peeled it down, and showed Blaze where the second chain went. "Tit 'n' clit chains. Right now they're only clamped on, but pretty soon I'm gonna get 'em pierced." — Joseph Wambaugh, *Floaters*, p. 8, 1996

titanic *noun*

someone who performs oral sex on first acquaintance *UK, 2002*

A jokey reference to 'going down' (performing oral sex) first time out; the RMS Titanic famously sunk on her maiden voyage.

- — *Roger's Profanisaurus*, p. 216, 2002
- — Chris Lewis, *The Dictionary of Playground Slang*, p. 233, 2003

titbag *noun*

1 a brassiere *US*

- — Michael Dalton Johnson, *Talking Trash with Redd Foxx*, p. 6, 1994

2 a fool *UK*

An elaboration of TIT (a fool).

- BERN: [...] Does talking on the phone all day give you a big chubby? KATZ: Something like that. BERN: "Something like that", "something like that" – you sanctimonious titbag. KATZ: Yeah, yeah. — Patrick Marber, *Howard Katz*, 2001

titch *nickname*

applied to a person of small stature or a little child *UK, 1934*

Derives, via the earlier spelling 'tich', from music hall entertainer Little Tich (diminutive comedian Harry Relph, 1868–1928), who took as his stage name the nickname he was given as a child from his resemblance to Arthur Orton, the man who claimed to be the missing heir to an English baronetcy, Richard Tichborne.

- [H]e is getting very matey with his new friends, particularly the runt called Titch who is one of life's losers. — *The Guardian*, 11th August 2003

titchy *adjective*

small, of small stature, insignificant *UK, 1950*

From TITCH.

- It makes the cathedral at Rochester look like any old church and it makes you feel sort of cheap and titchy. Like it's looking down at you, saying, I'm Canterbury Cathedral, who the hell are you? — Graham Swift, *Last Orders*, p. 194, 1996

tit-clamp *noun*

a device, designed to cause discomfort or pain for sexual stimulation, that is attached to a breast or nipple *UK*

- Fighting my way through the tit-clamps and cire-pouches, I ordered a drink. — Kitty Churchill, *Thinking of England*, p. 12, 1995

tit-for-tat *noun*

1 a reaction equal and opposite to the action *UK, 1556*

- This guy's looking to play tit for tat. That's not my game. I'm gonna play hardball. — *Tin Men*, 1987
- "I don't mean any money changed hands. I mean, there was a little quid pro quo. A little tit for tat." — Robert Campbell, *The Cat's Meow*, p. 120, 1988

2 a hat *UK, 1930*

Rhyming slang. Can be shortened to 'titfer', 'titfa' or 'tit-for'.

- [T]hey think "tit-fer" is especially funny. — Tom Wolfe, *The Pump House Gang*, p. 179, 1968
- [Y]ou should 'ave brought your titfer with you[.] — *The Sweeney*, p. 6, 1976
- It's all very well lavishing the grace and favour on saddle makers and titfer merchants up West[.] — Andrew Nickolds, *Back to Basics*, p. 15, 1994
- Also titfer'ed up is bassist Happy Tom [of Turbonegro]. — *X-Ray*, p. 77, June 2003

3 a trade union traitor *AUSTRALIA*

Rhyming slang for RAT.

- — John Ayto, *The Oxford Dictionary of Rhyming Slang*, 2002

tit-fuck *noun*

an act of rubbing the penis in the compressed cleavage between a woman's breasts *US*

- — Robert A. Wilson, *Playboy's Book of Forbidden Words*, p. 241, 1972
- Highlights: the scene where Wilder jerks off Jamie Gillis, and a magnificent tit-fuck between John Leslie and Mona Page (a startlet who had an all-too-brief career in porn). — *Adult Video*, p. 17, August/September 1986

tit-fuck *verb*

to rub the penis in the compressed cleavage between a woman's breasts *US, 1986*

- I tell her I would like to tit-fuck her and then maybe cut her arms off. — Bret Easton Ellis, *American Psycho*, p. 79–80, 1991
- I have always been well endowed (38E), so I am well aware of how men like to, to put it bluntly, tit-fuck. — Joan Elizabeth Lloyd, *Totally Private*, p. 157, 2001

tit-hammock *noun*

a brassiere *UK, 1961*

- [A]ll the women had tits the size of watermelons that kept bursting free of the skimpy leather hammocks supporting them. — John Varley, *Demon*, 1992

tithead *noun*

an idiot *UK*

Elaboration of TIT (an idiot) on the pattern of DICKHEAD (an idiot).

- Slipped up there, tithead. Who the fuck says "bonkers" except you. — Kevin Sampson, *Powder*, p. 5, 1999

titi *noun*

the female breast *TRINIDAD AND TOBAGO*

- — Lise Winer, *Dictionary of the English/Creole of Trinidad & Tobago*, 2003

tit joint *noun*

a bar or club featuring bare-breasted women servers *US*

- Jim Tom wanted us to stay over another night so he could take us to Honey Bun's Forth Worth's newest tit joint. — Dan Jenkins, *Life Its Ownself*, p. 330, 1984

tit-kisser *noun*

a man sexually obsessed with women *US*

- — *Maledicta*, p. 10, Summer 1977: 'A word for it!'

tit lift *noun*

a procedure in cosmetic surgery to enhance the female breast *UK*

- PATSY: Surgery. Lipo, on the hips and stomach, bum lift, tit lift, lose a rib. — Jennifer Saunders, *Absolutely Fabulous*, p. 34, 1992

tit mag *noun*

a magazine that features pictures of half-naked or naked women in erotic poses *UK*

- I hack out the hot copy for a number of what are euphemistically known as men's magazines. Some would call them tit mags. — Angie Heath, *Diary of a Masseuse*, p. 66, 1976
- He doesn't look up from his magazine. Loaded, I think it is, or some other lad's tit-mag. Cameron Diaz on the cover. — Niall Griffiths, *Kelly + Victor*, p. 128, 2002

tit magazine *noun*

a magazine featuring photographs of naked women *US*

- The "tit magazines" of the Fifties and Sixties, which were fit only for the garbage pail, have transformed themselves of late into "bush mags." — *Screw*, p. 4, 3rd July 1972
- "Bring me a couple of tit magazines." "I'm embarrasssed to buy them," Charley said. — Richard Condon, *Prizzi's Honor*, p. 254, 1982

tit-man; tits-man *noun*

a male with a (declared) primary interest in a woman's breasts as a point of attraction *US*

- BERNIE: Where does she get off with those tits? DANNY: What a pair of boobs. BERNIE: Not that I'm a tit man. DANNY: I Know. BERNIE: I mean, I dig tits ... DANNY: I don't blame you. BERNIE: ... but I wouldn't go out of my way for a pair of tits. — David Mamet, *Sexual Pervsity in Chicago*, p. 66, 1974
- — Loudon Wainwright III, *Rufus is a Tit Man*, 1975
- I loved the way you went for my tits. You took your time with me and didn't rush. A tit man is a gentle man. — Gerald Petievich, *The Quality of the Informant*, p. 89, 1985

tito *noun*

a rand (unit of currency) *SOUTH AFRICA*

Teen slang, after South African Reserve Bank Governor Tito Mboweni.

- — *Sunday Times (South Africa)*, 1st June 2003

tit off *verb*

to annoy or to aggravate someone *UK*

- It was getting beyond a joke, really titting him off. — Greg Williams, *Diamond Geezers*, p. 13, 1997

tit ring *noun*

a ring that passes through a pierced nipple *US*

- I show you my tit rings and you call me innocent. — Armistead Maupin, *Babycakes*, p. 254, 1984

tit run *noun*

a walk through a crowd in search of attractive female breasts *US*

- — *Maledicta*, p. 47, 1995: 'Door whore and other new mexico restaurant slang'

tits *noun*

1 when preceded by a characteristic or adjective, a person (of either gender) of the type defined by that characteristic or adjective *UK*

- Just like old flashy tits? — *The Full Monty*, 1997

2 heroin *UK*

Probably from TITS (exceptionally good).

- — Robert Ashton, *This Is Heroin*, p. 207, 2002

▸ **get on your tits**

to annoy or irritate you *UK, 1945*

Used by either gender.

- [T]he New Testament gets on my tits. —Jamie Mandelkau, *Buttons*, p. 47, 1971
- Shut up Ronny, will y', y' getting on me tits. —Alan Bleasdale, *Boys From the Blackstuff*, 1982
- What really got on his tits was the bit after he'd netted them. —Greg Williams, *Diamond Geezers*, p. 7, 1997
- Adam was a hoot, but he was getting on Keva's tits already. —Kevin Sampson, *Powder*, p. 198, 1999
- Got on my fuckin tits, he did, to tell yew-a trewth[.] —Niall Griffiths, *Sheepshagger*, p. 12, 2001

▸ off your tits

drunk or drug-intoxicated *UK*

- How can you slow dance when you're whizzing off your tits? —Dave Courtney, *Raving Lunacy*, p. 7, 2000
- They are "up the monument" or "half seas over"; they are "on a bender", "out of it"or "off their tits". —Peter Ackroyd, *London The Biography*, p. 359, 2000
- [S]ome of the best pieces of work I've ever done have been when I've been off my nut. But you can't be off your tits absolutely all the time[.] —*Q*, May 2001
- Just eight men tripping their tits off and an equally spaced-out Marianne [Faithfull] naked beneath a makeshift fur rug covering. —*Uncut*, p. 26, January 2002

▸ the tits

the best; absolute perfection , *mid-C20*

- "Ain't she the fuckin tits? Ain't life fuckin' unbearable!" He start rotating Libby's breasts with the palms of his hands[.] —Kevin Sampson, *Powder*, p. 191, 1999

tits *adjective*

exceptionally good *US*

- —*Current Slang*, p. 6, Fall 1966
- —Lewis Poteet, *Car & Motorcyle Slang*, p. 204, 1992

tits!

used for expressing excitement *US*

- Suddenly he cried, "Tits!" "What?" "This is absolutely tits. We got him!" —Joseph Wambaugh, *Fugitive Nights*, p. 102, 1992

tits and ass; tits and arse *adjective*

said of a film, television programme or magazine featuring nudity *US*

- So I said, 'Why don't we cut alll these things right into the picture. If they want tits and ass, let's give 'em tits and ass. —*Los Angeles Free Press*, p. 5, 30th April 1965
- Millions of other stroke books – the antecedent to Playboy, National Geographic with the African chicks – oh yes, they're stroke books. —Lenny Bruce, *The Essential Lenny Bruce*, p. 179, 1967
- "Tits and ass! Tits and ass!" Lenny Bruce was fond of yelling. —*Screw*, p. 12, 25th April 1969
- [S]he continued to be used at her speciality – beach and surfing movies, or "tits-and-ass flicks" as they were called. —Terry Southern, *Blue Movie*, p. 139, 1970
- And I'm embarrassed in retrospect that the chief voice of the anti-war movement in the District of Columbia clouded its message with so much of what Lenny Bruce would call "ordinary tits and ass," as distinguished from intelligent tits-and-ass[.] —Raymond Mungo, *Famous Long Ago*, p. 39, 1970
- I don't know, maybe she's doing penance, make up for all the tits and ass screamers she did for Harry. —Elmore Leonard, *Be Cool*, p. 212, 1999

tits up *adjective*

dead; out of operation *UK*

A coarser **BELLY-UP**, of military (possibly Royal Air Force) origin.

- [T]its-up on the runway. —Colin Strong and Duff Hart-Davis, *Fighter Pilot*, 1981
- I'm sorry about that, Jack. The damn Ng tach went tits up. —Gerry Carroll, *North S*A*R*, p. 184, 1991
- "Croaked. All the ants went tits-up." Then he added, "Sorry, ma'm. Belly-up." —Joseph Wambaugh, *Finnegan's Week*, p. 133, 1993
- [H]e learnt how easily an operation can go tits-up, ending in a bag of shit. —Chris Ryan, *Stand By, Stand By*, p. 18, 1996

tittie twister *noun*

a pinch and twist of the breast, especially the nipple *US*

- Tittie Twisters. My dad told my sister and me that these would give you breast cancer so we wouldn't give them to each other when we were fighting. —Editors of Ben is Dead, *Retrohell*, p. 225, 1997

tit tip *noun*

a female nipple *US*

- —*Maledicta*, p. 131, Summer/Winter 1982: 'Dyke diction: the language of lesbians'

tittle-tattle *verb*

to inform on someone *UK*

A nuance of the conventional sense (to chat, to gossip), perhaps influenced by 'tell-tale'.

- So what are you saying? Are you going to tittle-tattle on me, tell Kevin[?] —Colin Butts, *Is Harry Still on the Boat?*, p. 40, 2003

titty; tittie *noun*

the female breast *IRELAND, 1922*

- I thought, Carole has titties on her chest. —Claude Brown, *Manchild in the Promised Land*, p. 55, 1965
- T is for a woman's titties, they supposed to be sucked / but they never give milk until she's been fucked. —Bruce Jackson, *Get Your Ass in the Water and Swim Like Me*, p. 213, 1966
- Suck on my titties hard and strong / Just like Louie blows his horn. —Christina and Richard Milner, *Black Players*, p. 290, 1972
- I won't let men touch me. Or suck my titties. Hell no. —Susan Hall, *Gentleman of Leisure*, p. 102, 1972
- I put one of her well-shaped and very firm titties in my jib and went on to slumber. —A.S. Jackson, *Gentleman Pimp*, p. 137, 1973
- [S]lipping his hand in the front of Lesley's dress and easing out one of her titties and giving it a squeeze. —Ted Lewis, *Jack Carter's Law*, p. 68, 1974
- I mean I've sucked some titties and finger banged a couple of hunnies but I never stuck it in. —*Boyz N The Hood*, 1990
- I saw a couple of hot ones out by the swimming pool. Major titties. —Carl Hiaasen, *Native Tongue*, p. 35, 1991
- 1) Not to chew on titties. —Anthony Petkovich, *The X Factory*, p. 191, 1997
- There's a good tittie movie on Skinemax. —*Austin Powers*, 1997

titty bar; tittie bar *noun*

a bar featuring bare-breasted female servers and/or dancers *US*

- "Well, then, let's go to a tittie bar and celebrate." Danny Pogue said he knew of a place where the girls danced naked on the tables, and let you grab their ankles for five bucks. —Carl Hiaasen, *Native Tongue*, p. 179, 1991
- As you walk into most of these nudie clubs or titty bars, you see one or more stages and runways on which as many as ten or fifteen performers "dance" to music blaring from the club's sound system. —Marilyn Suriani Futterman, *Dancing Naked in the Material World*, p. 129, 1992
- I'm gonna be sittin at the titty bar in downtown L.A. till my man over here calls me and gives me the OK sign. —*Jackie Brown*, 1997
- I told him he better explain those places are titty bars. Raji goes, 'Not when little Minh Linh's dancing. She don't have enough to make it a titty bar. —Elmore Leonard, *Be Cool*, p. 49, 1999
- I'm a bouncer in a titty bar. —*Kill Bill*, 2003

titty-deep *adjective*

used of a fox hole, shallow *US*

- In the Central Highlands the ground was so hard that many times foxholes dug at an NDP were shallow, or "titty-deep." —Gregory Clark, *Words of the Vietnam War*, p. 187, 1990

titty-fuck *noun*

an act of rubbing the penis in the compressed cleavage between a woman's breasts *US*

Elaboration of **TIT-FUCK**.

- Are you all here playing Titty-Fuck or something? —Paul Watkins, *Night Over Day Over NIght*, p. 58, 1988

titty-fuck *verb*

to rub the penis in the compressed cleavage between a woman's breasts *US*

- I'm titty-fuckin' Bette Midler[.] —Eminem (Marshall Mathers), *Low Down Dirty*, 1998

titty hard-ons *noun*

erect nipples *AUSTRALIA*

- —James Lambert, *The Macquarie Book of Slang*, 1996
- —Pamela Munro, *U.C.L.A. Slang*, p. 115, 1997

titty pink *adjective*

a bright pink shade of lipstick *US*

Thought to resemble the colour of a nipple.

- I insisted that they open the casket ... a little to the left now ... so they opened for me, and what do you think they had on Grandma's lips? TITTY PINK! —Armistead Maupin, *Further Tales of the City*, p. 74, 1982

tittytainment *noun*

television programming that exploits sex *US*

Used in the German media.

- "Tittytainment", lamented Die Woche, "keeps the masses quiet[.] —David Rowan, *A Glossary for the 90s*, p. 128, 1998

tit-wank *noun*

an act of sexual gratification in which the penis is rubbed between a female partner's breasts *UK*

- Act of penetrating space between the breasts with your knob. A tit-wank in other words. —*Loaded*, p. 17, June 2002
- There wasn't really enough time for a proper shag, so he'd decided to go for the slippery tit-wank[.] —Colin Butts, *Is Harry Still on the Boat?*, p. 85, 2003

- We all need a bosom for a pillow or a tit-wank. —Susan Nickson, *Two Pints of Lager and a Packet of Crisps*, 12th April 2004

tit willow *noun*

a pillow *UK, 1932*

Rhyming slang; playing on the pillowing effect of a **TIT** (the female breast).

- [T]hose who are on their Jack Jones [alone]; a man without a tit willow to lay his head on[.] —Ronnie Barker, *Fletcher's Book of Rhyming Slang*, p. 39, 1979

tizwas; tizz-wozz *noun*

▷ see: **TISWAS**

tizz; tiz; tizzy *noun*

a state of panic or confused excitement *US, 1935*

- I couldn't remember having seen anybody in such a tizzy about a girl since the days of my youth – since my own tizzies. —Philip Wylie, *Opus 21*, p. 246, 1949
- It's far too dangerous… there are little policemen popping up all over the place in such a tizzy. —Martin Waddell, *Otley*, p. 58, 1966
- [W]hen MTV executives saw what Annie [Lennox] looked like they got themselves into a tizz. —Simon Napier-Bell, *Black Vinyl White Powder*, p. 231, 2001
- Who'd have thought in the twenty-first century the premiere magazine for the British bloke would be getting itself in a tizzy because a lord's daughter was letting us see her tits? —Ben Elton, *High Society*, p. 19, 2002

tizz *verb*

to frizz something up *AUSTRALIA*

- I don't know how many men have teased and tizzed my unruly locks since I first began attending a salon for my weekly torture session. —Sue Rhodes, *Now you'll think I'm awful*, p. 108, 1967

tizzic *noun*

a lingering, throaty cough *BARBADOS*

tizz up *verb*

to dress up *AUSTRALIA*

- —Jim Ramsay, *Cop It Sweet!*, p. 90, 1977
- But you won't be too exhausted to tizz up for the Satin and Silk Ball (7 February) at the San Remo Ballroom, North Carlton. —*Lesbians on the Loose*, p. 44, 1997

tizzy *adjective*

ostentatiously dressed *AUSTRALIA, 1953*

- 'Why, I don't think they look the least bit tizzy, especially not the way you wear them.' —Sue Rhodes, *Now you'll think I'm awful*, p. 78, 1967

tizzy up *verb*

to smarten or spruce something up *AUSTRALIA, 1960*

- It was obviously a residential living room tizzied up, as cheaply as possible, to make do as a brothel. —Lance Peters, *The Dirty Half-Mile*, p. 177, 1979
- —David McGill, *David McGill's Complete Kiwi Slang Dictionary*, p. 113, 1998

TJ *nickname*

Tijuana, Baja California, Mexico *US*

On the California-Mexico border, just south of San Diego, California.

- He loves T.J. He goes down there all time. —James Ellroy, *Brown's Requiem*, p. 59, 1981
- Garcia was dressed "TJ" fashion: a cowboy-style shirt and boots, like the million or so Mexicans who filled L.A.'s run-down apartments and garment-district sweatshops. —Gerald Petievich, *The Quality of the Informant*, p. 126, 1985
- Touch told Mickey she drove to T.J. for a scrape. —James Ellroy, *White Jazz*, p. 295, 1992
- "They ain't in no hurry down in T.J.," Sam Zahn said. —Joseph Wambaugh, *Finnegan's Week*, p. 70, 1993

T-Jones *noun*

a mother *US*

- —Ethan Hilderbrant, *Prison Slang*, p. 126, 1988

tjorrie *noun*

▷ see: **CHORRIE**

TL *noun*

a sycophant *US*

From the Yiddish *tuchus leker* (ass licker).

- —Robert A. Wilson, *Playboy's Book of Forbidden Words*, p. 242, 1972

TLC *noun*

tender, loving care *US*

- —Malachi Andrews and Paul T. Owens, *Black Language*, p. 52, 1973

TM *noun*

1 a commerically rolled cigarette *US*

A shortened form of **TAILOR-MADE**.

- —John R. Armore and Joseph D. Wolfe, *Dictionary of Desperation*, p. 54, 1976

2 transcendental meditation *US*

- I wasn't trying to say TM or CR [Cosmic Realization] would take care of all the world's ills or that they should give up them own beliefs[.] —Beatrice Sparks (writing as 'Anonymous'), *Jay's Journal*, p. 47, 1979

TMB

doctors' shorthand applied to an elderly patient *UK*

An initialism of '*t*oo *m*any *b*irthdays'

- —Adam T. Fox, St Mary's Hospital, London, 10th October 2002

TMI

used for expressing the sentiment that a conversation has become too personal, that the speaker is imparting *too much information* *US*

- In a classic case of TMI (Too Much Information), Barrymore told a reporter from Harper's Bazaar everything but her sexual preference. —*Milwaukee Journal Sentinel*, p. 1 (Cue), 7th January 1997
- —Connie Eble (Editor), *UNC-CH Campus Slang*, p. 8, Spring 1999
- And a few of you said "tmi, Yolanda." All of you have been my sounding board. For those who said too much information, at least I knew you were reading and that matters to me." —*Leaf-Chronicle*, p. 1D, 5th October 2003

TMT

used to designate the person who will feature in your immediate masturbatory fantasies *UK*

- "That's mine tonight." When pointing out to your mates a girl to be retained in memory in order to masturbate once home. —*www.LondonSlang.com*, June 2002

TNT *noun*

1 heroin *UK, 1977*

A play on **DYNAMITE** (a powerful drug).

- —Robert Ashton, *This Is Heroin*, p. 207, 2002
- —Mike Haskins, *Drugs*, p. 284, 2003

2 amyl or butyl nitrite *UK*

- Street names […] stud, thrust, TNT. —James Kay and Julian Cohen, *The Parents' Complete Guide to Young People and Drugs*, p. 144, 1998

3 a variety of MDMA, the recreational drug best known as ecstasy *UK*

A pun on TNT (the explosive trinitrotulene), suggesting that the ecstasy experience is explosive.

- —Ben Osbourne, *The A-Z of Club Culture*, 1999

4 fentanyl, a synthetic narcotic analgesic that is used as a recreational drug *UK*

- —Harry Shapiro, *Recreational Drugs*, p. 154, 2004

TNX

used as Internet discussion group shorthand to mean 'thanks' *US*

- —Andy Ihnatko, *Cyberspeak*, p. 191, 1997

to *preposition*

at *UK*

In conventional use from C10 to mid-C19; now in regional and dialect use in the UK, and colloquial use in the US.

- Where's it to? —John Edwards, *Talk Tidy*, 1985

toad *noun*

1 an unattractive, older male homosexual *US*

- —Wayne Dynes, *Homolexis*, p. 140, 1985

2 a very sick, derelict hospital patient *US*

An initialism for a '*t*rashy *o*ld *a*lcoholic *d*erelict'.

- —*Philadelphia Magazine*, p. 145–151, November 1977: 'Language: doctor, there's a gomer in the pit'

3 a black prisoner *US*

- —James Harris, *A Convict's Dictionary*, p. 29, 1989

4 a used car that is in very poor condition *US*

- —*American Speech*, p. 309–310, Winter 1980: 'More jargon of car salesmen'

TOAD

used for describing what happens when a surfer catches a big wave and almost immediately falls from his board *US*

An abbreviation of '*t*ake *o*ff *a*nd *d*ie'.

- —Michael V. Anderson, *The Bad, Rad, Not to Forget Way Cool Beach and Surf Discriptionary*, p. 21, 1988

toadie *noun*
the vagina *US*
• There's [a...] "toadie," "dee dee," "nishi," "dignity," "monkey box[".] —Eve Ensler, *The Vagina Monologues*, p. 6, 1998

toadskins *noun*
money *CANADA, 1912*
A play on **FROGSKIN**.
• Always some John Family or silk moll with bookoo toadskins playing around with a yuk who'll ante to keep the knockdown from the bundleman or headache. — *The New American Mercury*, p. 708, 1950

toad-stabber; toad-sticker *noun*
a knife *US*
• —Lou Shelly, *Hepcats Jive Talk Dictionary*, p. 35, 1945
• I don't trust a man carries a toadstabber, sump'n sneaky about it. —Ken Weaver, *Texas Crude*, p. 133, 1984

to and fro *noun*
snow *UK*
Rhyming slang.
• —Ray Puxley, *Cockney Rabbit*, 1992

to-and-fro'ing; to'ing-and-fro'ing *verb*
a constant moving about *UK, 1961*
• [A] slight shifting of the the weight from foot to foot, in tune with the to-and-froing of the club[.]—Jack Nicklaus, *Golf My Way*, p. 103, 1974
• The blind man at the door continues his uniform toing-and-froing, he seems never to tire, but it is not so[.]—Jose Saramago translated by Giovanni Pontiero, *Blindness*, p. 158, 1999

to and from *noun*
an English person *AUSTRALIA, 1946*
Rhyming slang for **POM**.
• The English were the to and froms[.]—Sidney J. Baker, *The Australian Language*, p. 187, 1966
• —Ryan Aven-Bray, *Ridgey Didge Oz Jack Lang*, p. 47, 1983
• — *Sydney Morning Herald*, p. 1, 2002

toast *noun*
1 something that is completely broken or inoperable *US*
• —Eric S. Raymond, *The New Hacker's Dictionary*, p. 353, 1991
• 'Twin Peaks is toast. It's had it. It won't make it another season.' 'Toast?' He chuckled. 'People say this? Where do you pick this shit up?'—Armistead Maupin, *Maybe the Moon*, p. 34, 1992

2 a forest that has been burnt by a forest fire *US*
• — *American Speech*, p. 205–209, Summer 1991: 'The language of smokejumping – again'

3 a narrative poem *US*
• Perhaps theh best known of all toasts, "The Signifying Monkey" is the prototype of an interrelated series of jungle poems.—Dennis Wepman et al., *The Life*, p. 21, 1976

4 an amusing story told as part of a rap performance *US*
Adopted from a West Indian DJ's 'toast' (to perform a lyric).
• [T]he telling of humorous stories (known as "toasts") and the quick and witty taunts known as "snaps"[.]—James Haskins, *The Story of Hip-Hop*, p. 52–53, 2000
• Toasts were, and still are, used to entertain, but also to insult and taunt another[.]—James Haskins, *The Story of Hip-Hop*, p. 54, 2000

toast *verb*
to heat a powdered drug such as heroin for injection *CANADA*
• That night it struck me that they were extremely ritualistic, while preparing the hypedermic syringe and "toasting" the "horse." —Leonard Cohen, *Beautiful Losers*, p. 134, 1966

toast *adjective*
dead *US*

toasted *adjective*
1 drunk *US*
• —Connie Eble (Editor), *UNC-CH Campus Slang*, p. 6, Spring 1980

2 emotionally unstable *ANTARCTICA*
• —Carnegie Mellon Astrophysics Peterson Group, *Antarctic Vocabulary*, 19th September 1997

toasted bread *adjective*
dead *UK*
A variation of the familiar rhyming slang 'brown bread'.
• —Ray Puxley, *Fresh Rabbit*, 1998

toast rack *noun*
a very thin cow *NEW ZEALAND*
• They can range from big, fat animals ready to kill, 'forward stores' that will be ready in a few weeks if feed is good, to walking toast racks.— *Lifestyle Farmer*, p. 22, April/May 2002

tobacco juice; tobacco stain *noun*
faecal stains in the underwear or on a toilet bowl *US*
• You can clean him down to his tobacco-stained shorts for all I care. —Robert Edmond Alter, *Carny Kill*, p. 47, 1966
• —Bill Casselman, *Canadian Sayings*, p. 44, 2002

tobaccy *noun*
tobacco *US, 1935*
• She's pregnant. I'm about to become a father. She's sick. She needs tobaccy.—Geoffrey Fletcher, *Down Among the Meths Men*, p. 59, 1966

Tobago love *noun*
a relationship in which there is little or no display of affection *TRINIDAD AND TOBAGO, 1993*
• —Lise Winer, *Dictionary of the English/Creole of Trinidad & Tobago*, 2003

Tobago sugar *noun*
wood waste left by termites *TRINIDAD AND TOBAGO*
• —Lise Winer, *Dictionary of the English/Creole of Trinidad & Tobago*, 2003

tober *noun*
a field or other site recognised as the temporary home and responsibility of a circus, fair or market *UK, 1890*
Shelta.
• His jills told him to take it out of the horse tent and scarper off ther tober [circus ground], John Orderly [quickly].—Butch Reynolds, *Broken Hearted Clown*, p. 28, 1953

Tobermory *noun*
a story *UK*
Rhyming slang, from the main village on the Isle of Mull, Scotland.
• A grimace from boys, sniggers from a group of girls. Same old Tobermory, thinks East.—Mark Powell, *Snap*, p. 35, 2001

tober omee *noun*
a toll collector, a rent collector; a landlord *UK, 1934*
• —Paul Baker, *Polari*, p. 192, 2002

tober showman *noun*
a travelling musician *UK*
• —Paul Baker, *Polari*, p. 192, 2002

Toblerone; tobler *noun*
alone; on my own *IRELAND*
Rhyming slang, formed from a branded chocolate confection. Often as 'on my tobler'.
• So they all head in, leaving me there like a Toblerone, out on my focking own.—Paul Howard, *Ross O'Carroll-Kelly*, p. 175, 2003

-to-buggery *adverb*
used to intensify an adjective *UK*
In phrases like 'blown to buggery'.
• You'd be hard pressed to find a better soundtrack, a dubbed-to-buggery jaunt through glamorous European dancehalls[.]— *Ministry*, May 2002

toby *noun*
the road, the highway *UK*
From Shelta *tobar* or *tober*.
• —Frank Norman, *Bang To Rights*, p. 150, 1958

toby jug *noun*
the ear *UK*
Rhyming slang for **LUG**.
• —Ray Puxley, *Cockney Rabbit*, 1992

tochis; tuckus; tochas *noun*
the buttocks *US, 1934*
Yiddish.
• She laughed. "No, he's graduated to nudes now. And poor mama, can't understand his interest in tuchuses ... rumps to you."—Frederic Wakeman, *The Hucksters*, p. 40, 1946
• I'll tell you where he's sensitive, Lionel – in his tochas.—Eugene Boe (Compiler), *The Wit & Wisdom of Archie Bunker*, p. 70, 1971
• He looked so stiff I wondered if his bayonet was stuck up his tuckus. —Anka Radakovich, *The Wild Girls Club*, p. 52, 1994

tochis-over-teakettle *adverb*
head-over-heels *US*
• —Terry Southern, *Now Dig This*, p. 171, 1991

tockley *noun*
the penis *AUSTRALIA*
- The vast majority of transvestites who've presented themselves for treatment had very tiny tockleys! — *Picture*, p. 28, 5th February 1992

to coin a phrase
used as an ironic acknowledgement or apology for an immediately preceding or ensuing triteness *US, 1951*
- "Any port in a storm," Jonathan said. "To coin a phrase," said Peggy. — Clarence B. Kelland, *No Escape*, 1951

toddie *noun*
a potato *UK*
- He was having his mince and toddies, wasn't he? — Anthony Masters, *Minder*, p. 17, 1984

toddle *verb*
to go; to leave *UK, 1812*
- Sloanes do not like to say "go" – it doesn't describe the way they ... well, whizz. They will say rush, toddle, beetle, tear, almost anything in preference. — Ann Barr and Peter York, *The Official Sloane Ranger Handbook*, p. 159, 1982
- I must be toddling off. — Anthony Masters, *Minder*, p. 94, 1984
- So I toddled off to New York to have a meeting with the American Federation Of Musicians[.] — *The Guardian*, 23rd April 2004

toddy *noun*
an alcoholic beverage made with the alcohol of choice, hot water and sugar *UK*
- "I think he wants another toddy," Elvin said to Mavis, and looked over at the cast-iron pot of soup on the stove, bubbles popping in it. — Elmore Leonard, *Maximum Bob*, p. 190, 1991

todge omee-palone *noun*
the passive partner in homosexual anal sex *UK*
- — Paul Baker, *Polari*, p. 192, 2002

todger *noun*
the penis *UK*
From the obsolete verb 'todge' (to smash to a pulp), the penis seen as a smashing tool.
- [S]hoving the tiny todger up[.] — *GQ*, p. 117, July 2001

todger dodger *noun*
a lesbian *UK, 2002*
Literally 'someone who avoids a **TODGER**' (the penis).
- — *Roger's Profanisaurus*, p. 217, 2002
- — Chris Lewis, *The Dictionary of Playground Slang*, p. 234, 2003

to-do *noun*
a social function or party *UK*
Extending the more general sense of 'to-do' (a fuss) creates this slightly critical variation of **DO** (a party).
- It'll take my mind of Anthony's to-do tomorrow. — Kevin Sampson, *Outlaws*, p. 185, 2001

Tod Sloan; tod *noun*
alone *UK, 1934*
Rhyming slang for 'alone' although usage suggests a rhyme on 'own': 'on your tod' (on your own). Tod Sloan (1874–1933) was a US jockey who raced in the UK, under royal colours, from 1896. In 1901 he was banned by the English Jockey Club, by 1906 he was ruled off the turf everywhere. Coined originally for his fame, continued ironically with his infamy when he was truly 'on his tod'. Still used though the man is forgotten.
- I cabbed it up fucking Chingford on my tod. — Jeremy Cameron, *Brown Bread in Wengen*, p. 15, 1999
- I'd rather be on my tod for a bit, sorry, but... — James Hawes, *Dead Long Enough*, p. 195, 2000

toe *noun*
▸ **on the toe**
nervous, anxious *AUSTRALIA*
- — Ned Wallish, *The Truth Dictionary of Racing Slang*, p. 59, 1989

toe-ender *noun*
a kick *UK: SCOTLAND*
- If I've to come down the stair to you you'll get a toe-ender — Michael Munro, *The Original Patter*, p. 70, 1985

toefoot *noun*
a numbing of the feet in cold water, creating the sensation of having no toes, only a foot *US*
Surfing usage.
- — *Transworld Surf*, p. 42, April 2004

toe-jam *noun*
the amalgam of dirt and sweat that gathers between the toes of unwashed feet *US*
- The police officer [...] ordered Mike to remove his shoes and socks. Alas no weapons secreted between his toes either – just the usual jam. — Martin King and Martin Knight, *The Naughty Nineties*, p. 121, 1999

toe nails in the radiator; toes on the radiator; toe nails on the front bumper; toes on the bumper *adjective*
describing a vehicle being driven at top speed, or the driver of that vehicle *US*
Citizens' band radio slang; the image of a driver's foot pressing the accelerator pedal through the floor.
- — *Complete CB Slang Dictionary*, p. 92, 1976
- — Peter Chippindale, *The British CB Book*, p. 160, 1981

toe-popper *noun*
a small antipersonnel mine powerful enough to blow off a hand or foot *US*
- — Gregory Clark, *Words of the Vietnam War*, p. 516, 1990
- There are the small "toe poppers" that can blast off a soldier's foot. — *Washington Post*, 11th February 1991

toe-rag *noun*
1 a person who is disliked, usually with good reason *UK, 1875*
Ultimately from the rags worn on a tramp's feet, hence a beggar, and hence this term of contempt which is the only sense that survives.
- I want work out of you toerags and plenty of it. — *Scum*, 1979
- I was wrong, wasn't I? A right little toerag. I wish I could go back and change things[.] — John King, *White Trash*, p. 258, 2001
- [T]he Tampax machine in the Ladies is fucked [...] some little toe-rag poured water into it, ripped the dispenser clean off the wall[.] — Garry Bushell, *The Face*, p. 39, 2001
- [T]hat toerag Mr Ferguson truly has sold the saintly Mr Beckham to Barcelona[.] — *The Guardian*, p. 11, 12th June 2003

2 a slut *UK*
Rhyming slang for **SLAG**.
- — Ray Puxley, *Cockney Rabbit*, 1992

toes *noun*
▸ **on your toes**
on the run *UK*
- — Angela Devlin, *Prison Patter*, p. 83, 1996

toes over *adjective*
said when a surfer has any number of toes extended over the front end of the surfboard *US*
- — John Severson, *Modern Surfing Around the World*, p. 183, 1964

toes-up *adjective*
sleeping *NEW ZEALAND, 1997*
Prison usage.
- — Harry Orsman, *A Dictionary of Modern New Zealand Slang*, p. 140, 1999

toe ticket *noun*
the name tag affixed to the toe of a corpse in a morgue *US*
- — *American Speech*, p. 273, December 1962: 'The language of traffic policemen'

toe-to-toe *noun*
a fight *UK*
- [A] new generation of football hooligans who'd rather have a toe-to-toe halfway across London than bother with the game. — John King, *Human Punk*, p. 327, 2000

toe toucher *noun*
a male homosexual, especially the passive partner in anal sex *UK*
- — Tom Hibbert, *Rockspeak!*, p. 158, 1983

toe up *noun*
drunk *US*
A corruption of 'torn up'.
- — Don R. McCreary (Editor), *Dawg Speak*, 2001

toey *adjective*
1 fast, fleet-footed *AUSTRALIA*
- [B]ounce the ball, shot down the flank, at which place a toey winger was rendered flat of foot by a long handball over his skull on the half-forward line, at which place I regained the bladder[.] — Jack Hibberd, *A Stretch of the Imagination*, p. 43, 1971

2 restless; uneasy *AUSTRALIA, 1959*
From an earlier sense of 'a racehorse keen to run' (1930).
- We were shunting at Marree and I had a toey crew on. —Patsy Adam-Smith, *Folklore of the Australian Railwaymen*, p. 82, 1969
- [B]ounce the ball, shot down the flank, at which place a toey winger was rendered flat of foot by a long handball over his skull on the half-forward line, at which place I regained the bladder[.] —Jack Hibberd, *A Stretch of the Imagination*, p. 43, 1971

3 anxious for sex *NEW ZEALAND*
- So I tapped my missus on the shoulder and she woke up with a 'Oh no, don't tell me you'er toey again, a woman can only take so much you know. —Paul Vautin, *Turn It Up!*, p. 48, 1995
- —David McGill, *David McGill's Complete Kiwi Slang Dictionary*, p. 114, 1998

toff *noun*

1 a person who is, or appears to be, of a superior social status or well-to-do *UK, 1851*
From 'tuft' which, in 1670, was a gold tassel worn by titled undergraduates at Oxford and Cambridge, and, by 1755, was university slang for a person of rank and title and hence down the social scale to 'swell' and 'nob'. In 1865 there was a music hall song entitled 'The Shoreditch Toff' by Arthur Lloyd.
- Last week down our alley come a toff —Albert Chevalier, *Wot Cher! or Knocked 'em in the Old Kent Road*, 1891
- Keva had to allow that these toffs really knew how to party. —Kevin Sampson, *Powder*, p. 27, 1999
- [T]hey say that balls are for the toffs and that they wouldn't be seen dead at them. — *Varsity*, p. 6, 14th June 2002

2 a completely reliable and dependable person *AUSTRALIA*
- —Ned Wallish, *The Truth Dictionary of Racing Slang*, p. 81, 1989

toffee *noun*

1 nonsense or flattery *UK, 1967*
- You don't believe that load of old toffee, do you? —David Powis, *The Signs of Crime*, 1977

2 (a stick of) gelignite *UK*
From its appearance.
- — *Z Cars*, 11th March 1964

▸ not for toffee
of a person's ability to do something, not at all, by no means, not in any circumstances *UK, 1914*
- [A]ll those highly-praised contemporary writers who cannot plot for toffee. — *The Observer*, 22nd October 2000

toffee-nose *noun*
a snob; a supercilious individual *UK*
A play on **TOFF** (a well-to-do person) as the sort of person who would look down their nose at a lesser individual.
- I cuts up quite a few toffee noses on me way down to the nob end of the town. —John Peter Jones, *Feather Pluckers*, p. 38, 1964

toffee-nosed *adjective*
supercilious, snobbish *UK, 1925*
- Real toffee-nosed bastards these two gits, with their hacking fucking jackets and flash cars and their old school ties. —John Peter Jones, *Feather Pluckers*, p. 45, 1964
- "Toffee-nosed accent." "Yes, right." —Doug Lang, *Freaks*, p. 21, 1973

toffee wrapper; toffee *noun*
the head *UK*
Rhyming slang for **NAPPER**.
- —Ray Puxley, *Fresh Rabbit*, 1998

toff omee *noun*
a wealthy older male homosexual lover; a homosexual sugar daddy *UK*
After the obsolete sense as 'a very well-to-do gentleman'.
- —Paul Baker, *Polari*, p. 192, 2002

tog *noun*
a men's suit *CANADA*
- So I lit a shuck back to my regular old pad and jumped into a different tog. —Bruce Jackson, *Get Your Ass in the Water and Swim Like Me*, p. 86, 1965

tog *verb*
to dress *US*
Conventional English reincarnated as slang in black vernacular.
- Even before I was in the money I togged like a fashion plate so I could run with the hip cats who hung around the poolroom. —Mezz Mezzrow, *Really the Blues*, p. 25, 1946
- Big girl's earrings; you got all togged out for the break. —George Mandel, *Flee the Angry Strangers*, p. 11, 1948
- I dig the way you're togged out. —Ross Russell, *The Sound*, p. 44, 1961
- Not right now, togged down and way out as I am. —Bernard Wolfe, *The Magic of Their Singing*, p. 25, 1961
- I was togged real sharp, with a fine suit, boss coat, and soft Florsheims, real dancing shoes. —Piri Thomas, *Down These Mean Streets*, p. 109, 1967

together *adjective*
having your life, career or emotions under control; self-assured *US*
- They [members of the Hog Farm commune at Woodstock] established very good vibes, had plenty of food (the lines were sometimes long, but usually moved quickly), good food and were really together. — *East Village Other*, 20th August 1969
- — *Current Slang*, p. 13, Fall 1970
- I thought you were probably ... like ... slumming here, doing your bit for the Junior League or something ... but you're not like that at all. You're really together. —Armistead Maupin, *Tales of the City*, p. 174, 1978

▸ get it together
to take control of your personal condition; to get your mind and emotions under control; to become organised *US, 1975*
- [M]an, we were both sort of really spaced out [drug-intoxicated] [...] but I got it together to clean up the sick. —Paul E. Willis, *Profane Culture*, p. 142, 1978

togged out *adjective*
dressed *UK, 1793*
- Why, Phil, you're all togged out like Joe College. —James T. Farrell, *Saturday Night*, p. 20, 1947
- She snake hips down the sidewalk toward the motel, followed by the gimpy old man togged out in a baggy ice cream suit. —Iceberg Slim (Robert Beck), *Doom Fox*, p. 158, 1978

togged up *adjective*
dressed up, usually for a special occasion *UK, 1793*
From **TOGS** (clothes).
- [G]get ready, get togged up and start goiing down in the car[.] —Ben Malbon, *Cool Places*, p. 268, 1998
- Bit togged up, aren't yis, Elaine? —Niall Griffiths, *Kelly + Victor*, p. 284, 2002

toggle jockey *noun*
in the US Air Force, a co-pilot *US*
- — *American Speech*, p. 310, December 1946: 'More Air Force slang'

togs *noun*

1 clothing *UK, 1779*
Conventional English starting in the late C18, resurrected as slang in the C20.
- A busted ragpicker would have given those togs the go-by. —Mezz Mezzrow, *Really the Blues*, p. 33, 1946
- You coming around in new togs and a Lincoln. —James T. Farrell, *Saturday Night*, p. 223, 1947
- He opened the closet door and considered the sets of togs hanging there[.] —Bernard Wolfe, *The Late Risers*, p. 35, 1954
- We had our best togs on; they were pressed like a razor and our shoes shone like a bald head with a pound of grease on it. —Piri Thomas, *Down These Mean Streets*, p. 98, 1967
- We won't mention the togs! —Jimmy Stockin, *On The Cobbles, picture caption*, 2000

2 especially on the eastern mainland, a swimming costume *AUSTRALIA, 1918*
- You can slip into your togs over there behind the rocks. —Dymphna Cusack, *Picnic Races*, p. 131, 1962

toilet *noun*

1 an inferior venue *UK*
- They've been building up a loyal fanbase in South Wales and playing every toilet in this fair isle[.] — *Rock Sound*, p. 11, March 2002

2 in the used car business, a used car with serious hygiene issues *US*
- —Lewis Poteet, *Car & Motorcyle Slang*, p. 204, 1992

3 a person as a sex object *US*
- "I want him" has become "I want his ass" and people are things, receivers, sex-machines, even toilets. — *Maledicta*, p. 225, Winter 1980

4 fat buttocks *BAHAMAS*
- —John A. Holm, *Dictionary of Bahamian English*, p. 208, 1982

5 a casino *US*
An insider term.
- —Lee Solkey, *Dummy Up and Deal*, p. 122, 1980

▸ in the toilet

1 lost, wasted *US*
- Do I got to sit here and listen to a sermon when I'm eighty bucks in the toilet? —Robert Campbell, *Alice in La-La Land*, p. 245, 1987

2 in serious trouble *US*
- Then Jersey legalized gambling and pretty soon the local numbers industry was in the toilet. —Janet Evanovich, *Seven Up*, p. 15, 2001

toilet-bowl *adjective*
having an inferior location or very low status *US*
- My entire career has consisted of toilet-bowl radio stations at the bottom of the barrel[.] —Howard Stern, *Miss America*, p. 54, 1995

toilet-bowl woman *noun*
a prostitute who operates on Main Street in downtown Los Angeles *US*
Another name for a 'comfort lady'.
- They are also known as Toilet Bowl Women. The client usually follows them down the street for discretion's sake. —Fiona Pitt-Kethley, *Red Light Districts of the World*, p. 84, 2000

toilet mouth *noun*
a person who employs a vocabulary that is considered foul or obscene *US*
- —Wayne Floyd, *Jason's Authentic Dictionary of CB Slang*, p. 20, 1976
- —Peter Chippindale, *The British CB Book*, p. 156, 1981

toilet queen *noun*
a homosexual male who loiters around public toilets in search of sex-partners *US*
- —Dale Gordon, *The Dominion Sex Dictionary*, p. 156, 1967

toilet roll; toilet *noun*
unemployment benefit *UK*
Rhyming slang for **THE DOLE**.
- [A]sked if he has found a job, "No, still on the toilet." —Ray Puxley, *Cockney Rabbit*, 1992

toilet seat *noun*
in electric line work, an insulator retainer *US*
- —A.B. Chance Co., *Lineman's Slang Dictionary*, p. 17, 1980

toilet-seat flying *noun*
short run commercial flying, with lots of stops *CANADA*
- You do it a lot in the DC-9, short runs, up and down, up and down, to Regina, Winnipeg, Fredericton – hence "toilet-seat flying". —Doug Chivers, *oral informant (pilot)*, 1996

toilet services *noun*
in a prostitute's advertising, the act of urination, or defecation, by one person on another for sado-masochistic gratification *UK*
- —Caroline Archer, *Tart Cards*, 2003

toilet snipe *noun*
a thief who robs homosexuals at public toilets, often after posing as a homosexual himself *UK*
- —Tom Hibbert, *Rockspeak!*, p. 158, 1983

toilet talk *noun*
speech that is considered obscenely offensive *US*
- Fancy a bloke usin' toilet talk in front of his own nippers!! —Barry Humphries, *Bazza Pulls It Off!*, 1971

Toiling Tillie *noun*
used as a personification of the stereotypical female office worker *US*
- — *American Speech*, p. 299, December 1955: '"Mimeo Minnie," "Sadie, the office secretary," and other women office workers in America'

to'ing-and-fro'ing *verb*
▷ **see:** TO-AND-FRO'ING

toke *noun*
1 an inhalation of marijuana smoke *US*
- Just' a plain old cigarette. Hee hee, yes. You want a toke? —Ken Kesey, *One Flew Over the Cuckoo's Nest*, p. 283, 1962
- When troubled times begin to bother me / I take a toke / And all my cares / Go up in smoke. —Cheech Marin and Tommy Chong, *Up in Smoke*, 1978

2 marijuana *UK*
- Jesus. Selfish cow. Last bit a toke yew get off me, mun, I'll tell yew that for nowt. —Niall Griffiths, *Sheepshagger*, p. 131, 2001

3 a dose of a drug *US*
- I doubled up on my coke toke. —Odie Hawkins, *Lost Angeles*, p. 41, 1994

4 cocaine *UK*
- —Mike Haskins, *Drugs*, p. 281, 2003

5 in casino gambling, a gratuity either in the form of betting chips or in the form of a bet made in the name of the dealer *US*
An abbreviation of 'token of gratitude'.
- [H]e considered a ten-spot as nothing more than toke money for the bellman, waiters, bartenders, and cocktails waitresses who had their mitts out when they saw him coming. —Gerald Petievich, *Money Men*, p. 27, 1981
- —Avery Cardoza, *Winning Casino Blackjack for the Non-Counter*, p. 75, 1991
- —Michael Dalton, *Blackjack*, p. 84, 1991

toke *verb*
1 to inhale smoke from a tobacco cigarette, a marijuana cigarette, a crack cocaine pipe or other drug *US, 1952*
- Man, someone's tokin' some reefer. —*Dazed and Confused*, 1993
- pattin' his thigh to some beat or tokin' hard on his cigarette —Nick Barlay, *Curvy Lovebox*, p. 69, 1997
- the folly of knowing that a fellow soldier was toking away but failing to report him —Ken Lukowiak, *Marijuana Time*, p. 3–4, 2000
- —Mike Haskins, *Drugs*, p. 290, 2003

2 to sniff-up and inhale cocaine *UK*
- —Mike Haskins, *Drugs*, p. 291, 2003

3 to tip someone *US, 1983*
Almost exclusively casino usage.
- The notion behind toking dealers is that they are somehow responsible for a person winning a number of bets in a row. —Thomas L. Clark, *The Dictionary of Gambling and Gaming*, p. 234, 1987

toke pipe *noun*
a short-stemmed pipe used for smoking marijuana *US*
- —Ernest L. Abel, *A Marijuana Dictionary*, p. 104, 1982

toker *noun*
1 a marijuana smoker *US*
- I'm a smoker / I'm a midnight toker —Steve Miller, *The Joker*, 1973
- —Pamela Munro, *U.C.L.A. Slang*, p. 117, 1997
- [K]nowing he was a toker himself, I asked him for his address so that I could send him a little present. —Ken Lukowiak, *Marijuana Time*, p. 170, 2000
- I was a moderate toker by local standards[.] —Brian Preston, *Pot Planet*, p. 1, 2002

2 in a casino, a tipper *US*
Because tips in casinos are most often in the form of gambling tokens or 'tokes'.
- Sitting there with people that are Georges, which means a good toker, you want then to win – even though you're a house person. —Edward Lin, *Big Julie of Vegas*, p. 210, 1974

toke up *verb*
to smoke marijuana *US, 1959*
- Chili flashed the group an arrogant smile and toked up on the joint going around. —Odie Hawkins, *The Busting Out of an Ordinary Man*, p. 170, 1985
- I toke up the spliff. —Nick Barlay, *Curvy Lovebox*, p. 161, 1997
- —Mike Haskins, *Drugs*, p. 290, 2003

to kill for *adjective*
extremely desirable *UK*
- Their meatballs are to kill for, and that's the God's honest truth. —Kevin Sampson, *Outlaws*, p. 242, 2001

Tokyo toughies *noun*
inexpensive tennis shoes *US*
- —Lee McNelis, *30 + And a Wake-Up*, p. 13, 1991

tol'able
used as a response to the query of how you are *US*
A youth-slurred 'tolerable'.
- —Connie Eble (Editor), *UNC-CH Campus Slang*, p. 7, Fall 1981

toley; toly *noun*
excrement, especially a turd *UK: SCOTLAND, 1967*
From Scottish dialect *toalie* or *tolie* (a small cake).
- "Naw, I mean shite shite. Shite as in keech, as in toley, as in jobbie, as in shite." He held up a brown hand to illustrate. —Christopher Brookmyre, *The Sacred Art of Stealing*, p. 390, 2002

toller *noun*
a carved wooden duck decoy *CANADA*
- On Tancook Island the word means "duck decoy," (the wooden carved kind). —*Macleans*, 1st November 1946

tolley *noun*
toluene, a paint solvent inhaled by the truly desperate abuser *US*
- —Jim Crotty, *How to Talk American*, p. 97, 1997

tolly mug *noun*

a tooth mug or glass *UK*

• — *The Felstedian*, December 1947

tom *noun*

1 a prostitute *UK, 1948*

Thus a police unit that targets prostitution may be dubbed 'tom squad' or 'tom patrol'.

• — Angela Devlin, *Prison Patter*, p. 115, 1996

2 a resident of Toronto, Ottawa, and Montreal, the power elite of Canada *CANADA*

• — *Maledicta*, p. 184, 1979: 'Canadian slurs, ethnic and other'

3 in a casino, a poor tipper *US*

• — Frank Scoblete, *Guerrilla Gambling*, p. 330, 1993

4 money *SOUTH AFRICA, 1975*

• — Jean Branford, *A Dictionary of South African English*, 1978

5 a British private soldier *UK*

A shortening of **TOMMY**.

• He was a public schoolboy who went wrong somewhere and joined the army as a tom. — Andy McNab (writing of the late 1970s/early 80s), *Immediate Action*, p. 212, 1995

▷ **see:** TOMFOOLERY, TOM MIX

Tom *noun*

a black person who curries favour with white people by obsequious and servile behaviour *US, 1959*

A shortened form of **UNCLE TOM**.

• He's kind of a Tom, ain' he? — James Baldwin, *Blues for Mister Charlie*, p. 40, 1964
• It was on Madison Avenue and you had to be a real Tom. — Claude Brown, *Manchild in the Promised Land*, p. 170, 1965
• But if you're Negro and don't talk hip, then you're a Tom. Reverse stereotypes again. — Nat Hentoff, *Jazz Country*, p. 80, 1965
• "Play it Tom," Nunn advised. "Oh yes, I plays it Tom." — Malcolm Braly, *On the Yard*, p. 17, 1967
• I hope your children don't grow up to be a Tom like you. — H. Rap Brown, *Die Nigger Die!*, p. 113, 1969
• They sent in the middle-class black members of the Human Rights Commission, and the brothers laughed at them and called them Toms. — Tom Wolfe, *Radical Chic & Mau-Mauing the Flak Catchers*, p. 121, 1970

tom *verb*

to work as a prostitute *UK, 1964*

From **TOM** (a prostitute).

• — John Ayto, *Oxford Dictionary of Slang*, p. 86, 1998

▷ **see:** TOMORROW

Tom *verb*

to curry favour by acting obsequiously and in a servile manner *US*

• I "Tomed" for him and explained we were only listening to records. — Babs Gonzales, *I Paid My Dues*, p. 49, 1967

Tom *adjective*

shoddy, inferior *US*

• — James Harris, *A Convict's Dictionary*, p. 32, 1989

Tom and Dick; Tom, Harry and Dick; Harry, Tom and Dick; Tom Harry *adjective*

sick *UK*

Rhyming slang.

• — *Evening News (London)*, 27th April 1954
• You make me sick, make me Tom and Dick — Ian Dury, *Blackmail Man*, 1977
• Of course nobody feels more Tom-and-Dick about this moribund state of public morality than I[.] — Andrew Nickolds, *Back to Basics*, p. 37, 1994

tomato *noun*

an attractive woman, especially a young one *US, 1929*

• There was a neat tomato down on Third Avenue who loved to play tricks herself, especially against the police. — Mickey Spillane, *I, The Jury*, p. 41, 1947
• The tomatoes who solicit the young and lonesome men in uniform in this neighborhood are pretty low. — Jack Lait and Lee Mortimer, *Washington Confidential*, p. 32, 1951
• TOMATO's TOMATO MISSING. — Truman Capote, *Breakfast at Tiffany's*, p. 109, 1958
• Tomatoes nobody wants much to do with. — Willard Motely, *Let No Man Write My Epitaph*, p. 294, 1958
• When Ralph Ginzburg began publishing Avant Garde magazine, rival editor Paul Krassner asked sardonically, "How avant garde is a man who still calls women 'tomatoes'?" — Robert A. Wilson, *Playboy's Book of Forbidden Words*, p. 242, 1972
• Another hot tomato, Wilson? Hah! — Terry Southern, *Now Dig This*, p. 36, 1975

tomato can *noun*

a mediocre boxer *US, 1955*

• He is a heavyweight named Matt, a sacrificial tomato can lined up to appease the crowd's blood lust[.] — *Washington Post*, p. 12, 28th August 1977
• In those days, the industry designated victims "guys named Joe" in sly tribute to Stribling. Today, "tomato cans" is the most popular term. — *Arkansas Democrat-Gazette*, 19th October 2004

tomato puree; tomato *noun*

a jury *UK*

Rhyming slang.

• — Ray Puxley, *Fresh Rabbit*, 1998

tomato sauce *noun*

a racehorse *UK*

Rhyming slang.

• — Ray Puxley, *Cockney Rabbit*, 1992

tombowler; tombola *noun*

a large marble; a highly prized marble *AUSTRALIA*

• Tombowlers, blood reels and cats eyes: Things kept in an alley bag. — Phillip Adams, *The Unspeakable Adams*, p. 50, 1977
• — Jim Ramsay, *Cop It Sweet!*, p. 90, 1977
• It looks like an ace marble, a tombola or something. — Tim Winton, *That eye, the sky*, p. 57, 1986

Tombs *nickname*

the Manhattan Detention Complex or city jail *US, 1840*

Named when built in the mid-C19 because it was modelled on an Egyptian-style mausoleum. The present facility bears no resemblance to the original structure but still carries the sobriquet.

• Mike and I hired a good lawyer for Mackey, and went down to see him in the Tombs. — Mezz Mezzrow, *Really the Blues*, p. 267, 1946
• As they flung him into the car, Angel said, "There's plenty of rooms in the Tombs." — Hal Ellson, *The Golden Spike*, p. 139, 1952
• I was taken to the Tombs, mugged and fingerprinted. — William Burroughs, *Junkie*, p. 39, 1953
• I had big manila enevelope ready for for Tombs Incarceration, including Buddhist Bible of Goddard[.] — Jack Kerouac, *Letter to Allen Ginsberg*, p. 458, 1 January 1955
• Geo spent three months in the Tombs and when I met him he was still on probation. — Alexander Trocchi, *Cain's Book*, p. 107, 1960
• After I'd moved, Reno got busted, and he was in the Tombs. — Claude Brown, *Manchild in the Promised Land*, p. 167–168, 1965
• He'd earned his name from having kicked the habit cold-turkey a few times running in the Tombs City Prison. — Piri Thomas, *Down These Mean Streets*, p. 201, 1967
• It was in the Tombs that I kicked the hardest habit that I'd ever kicked cold turkey in my life. — A.S. Jackson, *Gentleman Pimp*, p. 126, 1973
• Poor jerk in the Tombs. — Edwin Torres, *Q & A*, p. 61, 1977
• We were dismissed from the courtroom, returned inside and, after a short wait, were sent downstairs to be admitted to the Tombs[.] — Herbert Huncke, *The Evening Sun Turned Crimson*, p. 164, 1980

tombstone disposition *noun*

a surly, graceless, fearless character *US*

• I've got a tombstone disposition, graveyard mind / I know I'm a bad motherfucker, that's why I don't mind dying. — Roger Abrahams, *Positively Black*, p. 80, 1970

tom cat *noun*

1 a sewing machine needle converted to use for injecting drugs *US*

• — Vincent J. Monteleone, *Criminal Slang*, p. 241, 1949

2 a mat *UK*

Rhyming slang.

• — Julian Franklyn, *A Dictionary of Rhyming Slang*, 1961

tom-cat; tomcat *verb*

to pursue women for the purpose of fleeting sexual encounters *US, 1927*

• "It doesn't pay to tomcat around in singles bars, not in these times," Fin said. — Joseph Wambaugh, *Finnegan's Week*, p. 155, 1993

Tom Cruise *noun*

alcohol *UK*

Rhyming slang for **BOOZE**, formed on the name of the US film actor (b.1962).

Tom, Dick and Harrilal *noun*

used as the Trinidadian version of the common man Tom, Dick and Harry *TRINIDAD AND TOBAGO, 1990*

• — Lise Winer, *Dictionary of the English/Creole of Trinidad & Tobago*, 2003

Tom, Dick and Harry *noun*
any man – by random example *UK*
From C16, obsolete variations abound, not the least of which is Shakespeare's 'Tom, Dick and Francis'; 'Tom Dick and Harry' is not recorded until 1865.
- Why did you call your baby John? Every Tom, Dick and Harry is called John these days. — Aubrey Dillon-Malone, *I Was A Fugitive From A Hollywood Trivia Factory [quoting Sam Goldwyn]*, p. 121, 1999

Tom Dooleys *noun*
the testicles *UK*
Rhyming slang for **GOOLIES** (the testicles), formed from a folk song character who, fittingly, was hung.
- — Ray Puxley, *Cockney Rabbit*, 1992

Tom Finney *adjective*
skinny *UK*
Rhyming slang, formed from the name of Preston and England footballer, Tom Finney (b.1922).
- [A] girl who resembled a pencil: "Nice face, a bit Tom Finney though". — Ray Puxley, *Fresh Rabbit*, 1998

tomfoolery; tom *noun*
jewellery *UK, 1931*
Rhyming slang. The abbreviated form is first recorded in 1955.
- They're not expecting to be turned over in the small hours and don't bother to lock their tomfoolery away[.] — Charles Raven, *Underworld Nights*, p. 11, 1956
- For a while we was on easy street with all the tom in Manchester. — Kevin Sampson, *Outlaws*, p. 15, 2001

Tom, Harry and Dick; Tom Harry *adjective*
▷ see: TOM AND DICK

tomming *noun*
prostitution *UK*
- We just nicked his daughter Mary for tomming and possession of smack [heroin]. — Duncan MacLaughlin, *The Filth*, p. 160, 2002

Tom Mix; tom *noun*
an injection of a drug *UK*
Rhyming slang for **FIX**, formed on the name of US film actor Tom Mix, 1880–1940.
- — Home Office, *Glossary of Terms and Slang Common in Penal Establishments*, July 1978

tommy *noun*
the penis *BAHAMAS*
- — John A. Holm, *Dictionary of Bahamian English*, p. 208–209, 1982

Tommy *noun*
a British private soldier *UK, 1884*
The name Tommy Atkins was used as a specimen signature on official forms.

Tommy Dodd *noun*
1 God *UK*
Rhyming slang.
- — Julian Franklyn, *A Dictionary of Rhyming Slang*, 1960
- "Thank Tommy Dodd for that." or "Tommy Dodd knows." A cemetery may be known as "Tommy Dodd's garden". — Ray Puxley, *Cockney Rabbit*, 1992

2 a gun *US, 1944*
Rhyming slang for **ROD**.
- — Julian Franklyn, *A Dictionary of Rhyming Slang*, 1960

Tommy Dodd *adjective*
odd *UK*
Rhyming slang.
- — Ray Puxley, *Cockney Rabbit*, 1992

Tommy Dodds *noun*
betting odds *UK*
Rhyming slang, extended from **TOMMY DODD** (odd) used from the mid-C19 in relation to coin tossing.
- — Julian Franklyn, *A Dictionary of Rhyming Slang*, 1960
- — Ray Puxley, *Cockney Rabbit*, 1992

Tommy Farr *noun*
a (drinks) bar *UK*
Rhyming slang, formed on the name of the Welsh champion boxer, 1914–86.
- — Ray Puxley, *Cockney Rabbit*, 1992

Tommy Guns *noun*
diarrhoea *UK*
Rhyming slang for **THE RUNS**.
- — Ray Puxley, *Fresh Rabbit*, 1998

Tommy Rollocks; rollocks; rollicks *noun*
the testicles; nonsense, especially as an exclamation *UK, 1961*
Rhyming slang for **BOLLOCKS**.
- — Ray Puxley, *Cockney Rabbit*, 1992

tommyrot *noun*
nonsense *UK, 1884*
- He goes: "That's tommyrot!" Tommyrot, by the way! — Kevin Sampson, *Clubland*, p. 104, 2002

tommy squeaker *noun*
a fart *UK*
- I once held back a painful tommy squeaker all the way through a lecture. — *Loaded*, p. 18, June 2003

Tommy Trinder *noun*
a window *UK*
Rhyming slang, formed from the name of the popular Cockney comedian, 1909–89.
- — Ray Puxley, *Fresh Rabbit*, 1998

Tommy Tripe; tommy *verb*
to look at someone or something *UK*
Rhyming slang for **PIPE**.
- Tommy the geezer in the Lionel Blairs, looks a right berk. — Ray Puxley, *Cockney Rabbit*, 1992

Tommy Trotter *noun*
a lump of nasal mucus *UK: SCOTLAND*
Glasgow rhyming slang for **SNOTTER**.
- Ye've a wee Tommy Trotter at your nose. — Michael Munro, *The Patter, Another Blast*, 1988

Tommy Tucker *noun*
1 the penis, especially when erect *UK*
Possibly rhyming slang for 'fucker'.
- [C]onstant meths drinking has ruined the muscles that control Tommy Tucker and he will not rise to the occasion, any more than a boiled carrot. — Geoffrey Fletcher, *Down Among the Meths Men*, p. 24, 1966

2 a spirited person *UK*
Rhyming slang for **FUCKER** formed from a nursery rhyme character. Normally said without malice.
- — Ray Puxley, *Fresh Rabbit*, 1998

3 a gullible individual *UK*
Rhyming slang for **SUCKER**.
- — Ray Puxley, *Fresh Rabbit*, 1998

tomo *noun*
a subterranean stream *NEW ZEALAND*
From the Maori term for 'cave'.
- One of the Puketiti tomos has been measured to run for two miles, and some of them are a death trap for stock. — Peter Newston, *In the Wake of the Axe*, p. 155, 1972

tomorrow *noun*
► **like there was no tomorrow; as if there was no tomorrow**
with desperate vigour, urgently *UK*
- The free travel scheme aimed at encouraging cyclists to use trains unearthed a biking underground which took to the trains like there was no tomorrow. — *Time Out*, 4th January 1980
- And yes, Yolanda [,] I did try the cava in Fiji – I couldn't get away from the bloody stuff, they were dishing it out like there was no tomorrow. — *The Guardian*, 17th January 2001

tomorrow; tom *verb*
to borrow *UK*
Rhyming slang.
- — Ray Puxley, *Cockney Rabbit*, 1992

tomorrow next day *noun*
among Nova Scotians of German descent, the indefinite future *CANADA*
- In Lunenburg County, "tomorrow next day" is used to describe a time too far off to say, perhaps to excuse procrastination or a desire to escape an obligation. — Lewis Poteet, *The South Shore Phrase Book*, p. 118, 1999

toms *noun*
a fit of annoyance *AUSTRALIA*
Short for **TOM TITS**.
• Apparently Italy gave him a touch of the toms; too commercialised altogether[.] — Barry Humphries, *A Nice Night's Entertainment*, p. 42, 1960

Tom Sawyer *noun*
a lawyer *UK*
Rhyming slang, formed from Mark Twain's eponymous hero.
• — Julian Franklyn, *A Dictionary of Rhyming Slang*, 1961

Tom Tank *noun*
an act of male masturbation *UK*
Rhyming slang for **WANK** (an act of masturbation).
• I'm off for a Tom Tank. — *Shooting Stars*, 10th March 2003

Tom Terrific *nickname*
Tom Seaver (b.1944), a pitcher who almost single-handedly carried the New York Mets from last place in 1967 to the World Series champions in 1969 *US*
From a television cartoon show popular in the late 1950s and early 60s.

Tom Thumb *noun*
rum *AUSTRALIA, 1905*
Rhyming slang.
• — Duke Tritton, *Learn to talk Old Jack Lang*, p. 14, 1905
• I'll have a Lily of Laguna [schooner] and a Tom Thumb chaser please. — Ryan Aven-Bray, *Ridgey Didge Oz Jack Lang*, p. 11, 1983

tom tit; tom *noun*
an act of defecation *UK, 1943*
Rhyming slang for **SHIT**.
• I'd just been into the bog [a lavatory] for a Tom Tit, its the only place you can sit and read the paper in peace round here. — Ronnie Barker, *Fletcher's Book of Rhyming Slang*, p. 43, 1979
• [S]od it, I'm going for a Tom Tit. — Caroline Aherne and Craig Cash, *The Royle Family*, 1999

tom tits; toms *noun*
1 diarrhoea *AUSTRALIA, 1943*
Rhyming slang for **THE SHITS**.
• Cripes, Blanchie, I'm starting to get the kolly wobbles. If I hadn't demolished that stack of Fosters I reckon I'd be that nervous I'd land up with a dose of the proverbial tom-tits as they say in the classics. — Barry Humphries, *The Wonderful World of Barry McKenzie*, p. 19, 1968
• He got a bad case of the tomtits. — Wilda Moxham, *The Apprentice*, p. 42, 1969
2 a fit of annoyance *AUSTRALIA, 1944*
Rhyming slang for **SHITI**.
• 'Don't gimme the tom tits.' — Nino Culotta (John O'Grady), *They're A Weird Mob*, p. 24, 1957

Tom Tug *noun*
a bug *UK*
Rhyming slang.
• — Ray Puxley, *Fresh Rabbit*, 1998

ton *noun*
1 a large amount *UK, 1770*
Often in the plural.
• I feel tons better, though. The juices are starting to flow again[.] — Tom Stoppard, *Indian Ink*, 1995
• [W]e get tons of repeat bookings. — Dave Hemsath, *301 Ways to Have Fun at Work*, p. 125, 1997
• [H]e sings his songs, he's sung them a ton of times[.] — *X-Ray*, p. 55, June 2003
• I'd just like to say "ta [thanks] a ton"[.] — *Kerrang!*, p. 4, 28th August 2004
2 in any miscellaneous context, one hundred *UK, 1962*
3 one hundred miles per hour *UK, 1954*
• Now the M1 ain't much fun / Till you try and do a ton / A burn up on my bike, that's what I like — Mike Sarne, *Just for Kicks*, 1963
• — Hy Lit, *Hy Lit's Unbelievable Dictionary of Hip Words for Groovy People*, p. 42, 1968
• — John Edwards, *Auto Dictionary*, p. 171, 1993
4 one hundred pounds sterling *UK, 1946*
• [H]e arrives in this huge great jam [car] and says simply do we want it, half a ton down and nothing to pay. — Derek Raymond (Robin Cook), *The Crust on its Uppers*, p. 42, 1962
• — Angela Devlin, *Prison Patter*, p. 115, 1996
• BACON: You wanna give Miami two-ton-fifty, covered in shit? MOON: That'll show 'im who's boss. — Bernard Dempsey and Kevin McNally, *Lock, Stock... & Two Sips*, p. 295, 2000
5 one hundred Australian dollars *AUSTRALIA*
• — Ned Wallish, *The Truth Dictionary of Racing Slang*, p. 82, 1989

ton *verb*
▸ **ton it**
to drive at 100 miles per hour *UK*
• See that merc Johnny nicked yesterday, tonned it up Tredegar he did, coppers couldn't catch im he said[.] — Patrick Jones, *Everything Must Go*, p. 142, 2000

tone *noun*
rude or disparaging talk *TRINIDAD AND TOBAGO, 1957*
• — Lise Winer, *Dictionary of the English/Creole of Trinidad & Tobago*, 2003

tone on tone *noun*
a car with the same colour interior and exterior *US*
• — Anna Scotti and Paul Young, *Buzzwords*, p. 42, 1997

toney *adjective*
▹ see: **TONY**

tongs *noun*
heroin *UK*
Possibly in reference to the Chinese 'tongs' (criminal organisations) responsible in part for the import and distribution of the drug.
• — Robert Ashton, *This Is Heroin*, p. 207, 2002
• — Mike Haskins, *Drugs*, p. 284, 2003

tongue *noun*
1 the clitoris *TRINIDAD AND TOBAGO*
• — Lise Winer, *Dictionary of the English/Creole of Trinidad & Tobago*, 2003
2 an attorney *US*
• — Joseph E. Ragen and Charles Finston, *Inside the World's Toughest Prison*, p. 821, 1962: 'Penitentiary and underworld glossary'

▸ **get tongue**
in the categorisation of sexual activity by teenage boys, to kiss with tongue contact *US*
• There were several degrees of "making out." The first was "tongue." "Did you get tongue?" was a question frequently heard after a first date with an extremely nice, honor-student-type girl. — Terry Southern, *Now Dig This*, p. 3, 1986

tongue job *noun*
oral sex on a woman *UK*
• — Xaviera Hollander, *The Best Part of a Man*, 1975

tongue-pash *verb*
to kiss with open mouths *AUSTRALIA*
• In fact it wasn't until two and a half weeks later when Hot Buns appeared on the cover of the National Inquirer, tongue-pashing what appeared to be Kevin Costner's bum crack, that Ophelia knew where to find her friend[.] — Gretel Killeen, *Hot Buns and Ophelia get a Bloke*, p. 38, 2000

tongue-trooper *noun*
a Quebec inspector of signs, commissioned to enforce Bill 101, the language law making French primary in the province *CANADA*
Mordecai Richleris is widely credited with having invented this popular nickname for the 'language police' in his controversial New Yorker essay 'Oh Canada! Oh Quebec!' (1992).
• A party-pooper inquired about the cost of additional tongue-troopers. No problem: we could close more hospitals. — *National Post*, p. A4, 3rd June 2000

tongue wash *noun*
oral sex, especially on a woman *US*
• A tongue wash now and then made the time go faster, right? — Gerald Petievich, *Money Men*, p. 85–86, 1981

tonguey; tonguie *noun*
a tongue-kiss *AUSTRALIA*
• — Paul Vautin, *Turn It Up!*, p. 35, 1995
• I finally found her standing at a counter with her brown jacket and dark hair and being an affectionate type I slipped up behind her and gave her a big tonguey in the ear. — Paul Vautin, *Turn It Up!*, p. 206, 1995
• At 6.30 the two friends watched Neighbours and became engrossed in the plot line, which was 'Nev kisses Bev' (not a tonguie). — Gretel Killeen, *Hot Buns and Ophelia get shipwrecked*, p. 20, 2001

tonk *noun*
1 a homosexual male *NEW ZEALAND, 1946*
From 'tonka bean', rhyming slang for **QUEEN**.
• The way you lot are heading you'll end up a bunch of tonks. — George Johnston, *My Brother Jack*, p. 65, 1964
• — Harry Orsman, *A Dictionary of Modern New Zealand Slang*, p. 140, 1999

2 the penis *AUSTRALIA*
- I feel like a spare tonk in a knock-shop wedding. — *The Adventures of Barry McKenzie*, 1972
- By the time I had left school, I had heard most of the euphemisms. There was dork, eric, muscle, prong, pencil (for having lead in), sausage and tonk. — Bettina Arndt, *The Australian Way of Sex*, p. 10, 1985

tonk *verb*

1 to have sex *UK*
Euphemistic for **FUCK**.
- If I was really smart I wouldn't be tonking Gerald's old lady. — Ted Lewis, *Jack Carter's Law*, p. 88, 1974

2 in sport, to defeat someone resoundingly *UK, 1997*
Noted as 'imitative of a powerful blow having reached its target' by Susie Dent, *The Language Report*, 2003.

tonking *noun*
a humiliating beating *UK*
From **TONK**.
- The songs may have been amusing but the tonking we took in the visitors' Clock End was not. — Martin King and Martin Knight, *The Naughty Nineties*, p. 72, 1999
- [W]ishing the spud-churner (a farm-worker) had given the aristocracy a good tonking[.] — John King, *Human Punk*, p. 161, 2000

tonking *adjective*
used as an intensifier *UK*
- And isn't it just fucking typical of Gerald and Les on a busy night to go out without leaving their tonking address. — Ted Lewis, *Jack Carter's Law*, p. 59, 1974

tonky *noun*
the genitals, male or female *BAHAMAS*
- — John A. Holm, *Dictionary of Bahamian English*, p. 209, 1982

Tonky; tonkie *noun*
a member of the Ba*tonk*a tribe; an unsophisticated person or thing; someone who has 'gone native' *ZIMBABWE*
Derogatory.
- — *Lonely Planet Southern Africa*, 2000

tonky *adjective*
fashionable *NEW ZEALAND*
A possible blend of French *ton* (style) and **SWANKY** (showy).
- — David McGill, *David McGill's Complete Kiwi Slang Dictionary*, p. 127, 1998
- A tonky jazz band is giving it Georgia Brown in a corner. — Bernard Demsey and Kevin McNally, *Lock, Stock... & Two Sips*, p. 284, 2000

tonsil hockey *noun*
passionate kissing *US*
- — Connie Eble (Editor), *UNC-CH Campus Slang*, p. 5, October 1986

tonsil juice *noun*
saliva *US*
- I felt like I couldn't even swallow my own tonsil-juice without gagging[.] — Mezz Mezzrow, *Really the Blues*, p. 101, 1946

tonsil paint *noun*
whisky *US*
- — Ramon Adams, *The Language of the Railroader*, p. 159, 1977

tonsil test *noun*
a film or theatre audition *UK*
- — Wilfred Granville, *The Theater Dictionary*, p. 204, 1952

tonsil-tickling *noun*
intensive kissing *UK, 1990s*
Slang for those who don't let it get too serious.
- A tonsil-tickling embrace is still known as a French kiss, as if somehow it would never have occurred to an English person to stick their tongue into another person's mouth if the French hadn't invented it. — Jeremy Paxman, *The English*, p. 25, 1999

tonto *adjective*
crazy, silly, foolish, eccentric *US, 1973*
From Spanish *tonto* (stupid).
- I go tonto with the eyedrops – another of my top tips for the heavy drinker. — Andrew Holmes, *Sleb*, p. 131, 2002

ton-up *noun*
a speed of 100 miles per hour, especially with reference to motorcycles *UK, 1961*

ton-up boy *noun*
a motorcyclist who has driven at 100 miles per hour; generically, a member of a motorcycle gang *UK*
From **TON** (100).
- [H]e was one of the original rockers ... a ton-up boy in his Levis and leathers ... grease in his hair ... and the rockers were just taking things on from the Teds who were more flashy[.] — John King, *White Trash*, p. 159, 2001

tony; toney *adjective*
up-market, sophisticated, stylish; snobbish, swanky *US*
Conventionally meaning 'style'. Also used in Australia and New Zealand since 1900.
- [I]n tonier parts of the city[.] — Naomi Klein, *No Logo*, p. 75, 2001

Tony Benn *noun*
ten *UK*
Rhyming slang, formed from the name of popular socialist politician Tony Benn (b.1925).
- — Ray Puxley, *Fresh Rabbit*, 1998

Tony Benner *noun*
ten pounds *UK*
Rhyming slang for **TENNER**, extended on the name of Tony Benn (b.1925), a popular socialist politician.
- — Ray Puxley, *Fresh Rabbit*, p. 117, 1998

Tony Blair; tony *noun*
hair *UK*
Rhyming slang, based on Prime Minister Tony Blair (b.1953), probably inspired by the new hairstyle he adopted (with wide-spread media attention) in 1996.
- — Ray Puxley, *Fresh Rabbit*, 1998
- Scots still have to refer south of the border on some matters. As in "yer Tony's in a real state". As in hair. As in Blair. — *The Guardian*, 29th April 2002
- I'm off to get my Tony cut. — *www.LondonSlang.com*, June 2002

Tony Blairs *noun*
flared trousers *UK*
Rhyming slang for 'flares'.
- [W]hatever his legacy to British politics, the man from Islington has ensured he will live for ever in the creases of the next generation's Tonys. — David Rowan, *A Glossary for the 90s*, p. 62, 1998

Tony Hatch *noun*
a match *UK*
Rhyming slang, formed from the name of the British tunesmith (b.1939).
- — Ray Puxley, *Fresh Rabbit*, 1998

tony's *noun*
dice that have been marked to have two identical faces *US*
- — *The Annals of the American Academy of Political and Social Sciences*, p. 132, May 1950

toodlembuck; toodle-em-buck; doodle-em-buck *noun*
any of various gambling games played by children utilising a spinning device with the names of horses in a race written on it *AUSTRALIA, 1924*
From a 'toodle/doodle' frequentative formation expressive of spinning, 'em' (them) and 'buck' (a gambling marker).
- Another diversion in "Doodlem-buck" added to the merriment of the onlookers. — Collins and Thompson, *Harking Back*, p. 27, 1924
- He could try his luck at roulette or 'doodle-em-buck', chance his arms at Aunt Sally, or eat and drink his way along the long line of refreshment tents. — Maurice Cavanough and Meurig Davies, *Cup Day*, p. 6, 1960
- In the weeks before the Melbourne Cup was run we gambled with cherry bobs (cherry stones) on a toodlembuck. This was a small whirligig of cardboard with the Cup horses' names printed round the edge. — June Factor, *Kidspeak*, p. 211, 2002

toodle-oo
goodbye *UK, 1907*
Cute. In the US, quite affected in a British sort of way.
- He's on his way downtown in a cab. Sweet blow-off! Toodle-oo, Wonder. — Iceberg Slim (Robert Beck), *Long White Con*, p. 55, 1977
- He waved tootle-oo with the steak knife before speeding off. — Carl Hiaasen, *Strip Tease*, p. 266, 1993

toodle-pip; tootle-pip
goodbye *UK, 1907*
Very dated; contemporary usage is generally ironic, denoting a certain type of foolish upper-class speaker.

- [H]ave a wonderful time in Espana. Toodle pip, over and out. — Dean Cavanagh, *Mile High Meltdown (Disco Biscuits)*, p. 210, 1996

toodles
goodbye *US*
Affected; an American corruption of **TOODLE-OO**, perceived in the US as quaintly and quintessentially British. A signature line of the Francine 'Gidget' Lawrence character played by Sally Fields on *Gidget* (ABC, 1965–66). Repeated with referential humour.

toody-hoo
used as a greeting *US*
- — Connie Eble (Editor), *UNC-CH Campus Slang*, p. 5, November 1983

too fool *adjective*
lacking common sense *CAYMAN ISLANDS*
- — Aarona Booker Kohlman, *Wotcha Say*, p. 25, 1985

tooie; tuie; tooey; toolie; toole *noun*
a capsule of amobarbital sodium and secobarbital sodium (trade name Tuinal^{TM}), a combination of central nervous system depressants *US*
- — Donald Louria, *Nightmare Drugs*, p. 25, 1966
- — Mike Haskins, *Drugs*, p. 283, 2003

tool *noun*
1 the penis *UK, 1553*
Conventional English at first – found in Shakespeare's *Henry VIII* – and then rediscovered in the C20 as handy slang.
- His tool was so long / And so pointed and strong / He could bugger six Greeks en brochette. — *Eros*, p. 62, Winter 162
- He had taught her at five to sneak her hand so smoothly under the straw hat on his lap that Ma and none of the kids ever knew she played with Pa's tool. — Iceberg Slim (Robert Beck), *Death Wish*, p. 250, 1977
- Butler, reaching the limits of human endurance, whips out his tool and obliges her craving for male meat. — *Adult Video*, p. 66, August/September 1986
- He said he wanted somebody with a reliable tool, so I hung on just to see if the scene was going to work or not. — Robert Stoller and I.S. Levine, *Coming Attractions*, p. 157, 1991
- Men wake up every morning and look at their tools standing at attention. — Anka Radakovich, *The Wild Girls Club*, p. 10, 1994
- So was Bobbit trying to prove that his tool still works? — Anthony Petkovich, *The X Factory*, p. 86, 1997

2 an objectionable idiot, a fool *UK*
- He's just a f***king tool. There's so many people in the industry that can't stand him[.] — *Kerrang!*, 3rd November 2001

3 a diligent student *US*
- — *Time*, p. 56, 1st January 1965: 'Students: the slang bag'

4 a weapon, generally a gun or a knife *UK, 1942*
- But by the time they had started to look around for someone to nick, the tool had been well got rid of. — Frank Norman, *Bang To Rights*, p. 28, 1958
- "Tell them to bring tools.' — Richard Condon, *Prizzi's Glory*, p. 79, 1988
- — Angela Devlin, *Prison Patter*, p. 116, 1996

5 a skilled pickpocket *US*
- — Hyman E. Goldin et al., *Dictionary of American Underworld Lingo*, p. 224, 1950

6 in pool, a player's cue stick *US*
- — Mike Shamos, *The Illustrated Encyclopedia of Billiards*, p. 250, 1993

7 a surfboard *US*
- — Mitch McKissick, *Surf Lingo*, 1987

tool *verb*
1 to drive, to go, to travel, usually in a carefree manner *US*
Originally of horse-drawn transports, applied in the C20 to motor vehicles, boats and aircraft.
- — *Hot Rod Magazine*, p. 13, November 1948: 'Racing jargon'
- They gave me their official permission to tool out to the beach[.] — Frederick Kohner, *Gidget*, p. 79, 1957
- It helped to think of old times, carefree days in Hlillsborough when she and Binky and Muffy would snitch the keys to Daddy's Mercedes and tool down to the Fillmore to tease the black studs lurking on the street corners. — Armistead Maupin, *Tales of the City*, p. 94, 1978
- I tool the car out of the drive. That's what people do with cars in books. They don't execute a manoeuvre, they tool. So I tool the car out the gravel drive[.] — Simon Lewis, *In The Box [britpulp]*, p. 128, 1999
- First, I tooled up to Viscount 'Dave' Linley's Pimlico furniture shop[.] — *ES Magazine*, p. 3, 22nd June 2001

2 to wander aimlessly; to do nothing in particular *US, 1932*
The variant 'tool around' is also used.
- — *Current Slang*, p. 4, Summer 1966
- All I ever did in high school was tool around with the guys and a six-pack of Bud, looking for heterosexuals to beat up. — Armistead Maupin, *Tales of the City*, p. 134, 1978

3 to have sex *US*
- — Judi Sanders, *Faced and Faded, Hanging to Hurl*, p. 41, 1993

4 to slash a person with a razor *UK*
- — Frank Norman, *Encounter*, 1959

5 to work hard *US*
- — Andy Ihnatko, *Cyberspeak*, p. 192, 1997

toolbox *noun*
1 the male genitals *US*
- — Roger Blake, *The American Dictionary of Sexual Terms*, p. 85, 1964
- [H]e stripped off his strides and exposed his toolbox. — *Loaded*, p. 30, June 2003

2 the vagina *US*
- — Dale Gordon, *The Dominion Sex Dictionary*, p. 157, 1967

tool check *noun*
an inspection by a military doctor or medic of male recruits for signs of sexually transmitted disease *US*
- — Dale Gordon, *The Dominion Sex Dictionary*, p. 157, 1967

tooled up *adjective*
1 in possession of a weapon *UK, 1959*
From **TOOL** (a gun or knife); popularised in such 1970s television crime dramas as *The Sweeney*.
- You think some headcase will think twice about coming after me because I'm tooled up with a TV remote? — Greg Williams, *Diamond Geezers*, p. 79, 1997
- "Get stooled up!" he's going. "No twat go out without a fucking [bar] stool!" Stooled up, by the way. — Kevin Sampson, *Outlaws*, p. 123, 2001

2 carrying cocaine *UK*
A self-important adoption of an earlier gangster cliché.

3 in possession of house-breaking implements *UK*

tooler *noun*
a show-off *US*
- — *Time*, p. 56, 1st January 1965: 'Students: the slang bag'

tooley bird *noun*
in oil drilling, a loud squeak caused by poorly lubricated equipment *US*
- — Jerry Robertson, *Oil Slanguage*, p. 45, 1954

toolie *noun*
1 in oil drilling, a driller's helper *US*
- — Jerry Robertson, *Oil Slanguage*, p. 123, 1954

2 a man who, in a quest for sex, joins a group of young people during the Schoolies Week holiday *AUSTRALIA*
- Andrew Curtis, 23, and his mates were holidaying in Australia after finishing "varsity" and ended their stay smack in the middle of the Gold Coast's anti-toolie campaign. Toolie? That's Coast for too-old-for-schoolies. — *Sydney Morning Herald*, 29th November 2003

toolies *noun*
a pair of men's close-fitting and revealing nylon swimming trunks *AUSTRALIA*
From **TOOL** (the penis).
- — *Wordmap (www.abc.net.au/wordmap)*, 2003

▷ **see: TULES**

toolio *noun*
a social outcast *US*
- — Pamela Munro, *U.C.L.A. Slang*, p. 116, 1997

tools *noun*
1 the syringe and other equipment used to prepare and inject drugs *US*
- — *Mr.*, p. 59, April 1966: 'The hippie's lexicon'
- The rest of the tools were already in use by other addicts. — Donald Goines, *Dopefiend*, p. 8, 1971

2 the jewellery, cars, clothing and material flourishes that support a pimp's image *US*
- My tools are also very expensive. I'm continually sharpening my cars, my jewelry, and my clothes. These are tools like a policeman has a gun. — Susan Hall, *Gentleman of Leisure*, p. 11, 1972

3 a racecourse bookmaker's equipment *UK*
- — David Bennet, *Know Your Bets*, p. 102, 2001

tools of the trade *noun*
any objects used in sado-masochistic activities, especially when advertised by a prostitute *UK*
- —Caroline Archer, *Tart Cards*, 2003

tool up *verb*
(of a man) to ready yourself for sexual intercourse, by erecting the penis *UK, 1984*

too many chiefs and not enough Indians
▷ **see:** ALL CHIEFS AND NO INDIANS

too much *adjective*
great, wonderful, excellent *US*
- The love that's shining all around you / Everywhere it's like what you make for us to take / It's all too much.—George Harrison (Performed by the Beatles), *It's All Too Much*, 1969
- The regular music thing [at Woodstock] is nice, but straight. The Hog Farm is just too much. We are at home and at peace with each other and ourselves.—*East Village Other*, 20th August 1969
- "Out of sight," "too much," "tough," "trippy," "trick," or "unreal" – were all current [late 1960s] superlatives. Each would flower for a while and then fall to something a little groovier – up to date on the tongues of those who knew.—Sean Hutchinson, *Crying Out Loud*, p. 177, 1988

too much!
used as a humorous commentary, suggesting that someone has gone too far *US*
- —*American Speech*, p. 275, December 1963: 'American Indian student slang'

too much perspective; too much fucking perspective
used for expressing the sentiment that too much information is being shared *US*
A catchphrase from *Spinal Tap*, used with humour and referentially.
- David retorts, "Too much, too much fuckin' perspective."—Editors of Ben is Dead, *Retrohell*, p. 205, 1997

toonie *noun*
a two-dollar coin *CANADA, 1987*
An alternative to 'doubloonie', both nicknames derived from the LOONY.

toonkins *noun*
used as an endearing term of address to a child *BARBADOS*
- —Frank A. Collymore, *Barbadian Dialect*, p. 112, 1965

too right
yes indeed!, absolutely! *AUSTRALIA, 1919*
- 'You kin arsk me to tucker one evening, when she's back.' 'Too right, I will, Garny.'—Jean Brooks, *The Opal Witch*, p. 170, 1967
- —Jim Ramsay, *Cop It Sweet!*, p. 90, 1977
- —Sam Weller, *Old Bastards I Have Met*, p. 45, 1979
- Worth it, was it?! There's no need to think about that. – Yeh! Too fuckin right it was!—Niall Griffiths, *Kelly + Victor*, p. 6, 2002

tooroo
goodbye *AUSTRALIA, 1927*
Variant of 'too-ra-loo'.

too serious *adjective*
very good *US*
- —Connie Eble (Editor), *UNC-CH Campus Slang*, p. 7, Fall 1980

toot *noun*
1 a dose of a drug, especially cocaine to be snorted *US*
- Of course I'm going to give you a toot, honey.—Donald Goines, *Dopefiend*, p. 197, 1971
- After the well wishes were over, we rapped, we smoked, and we took a toot of boy and girl.—A.S. Jackson, *Gentleman Pimp*, p. 70, 1973

2 an inhalation of marijuana smoke *UK*
- I suppose Tommy [a rock-opera by the Who] lasted the same length as a good toot on a joint.—*Uncut*, p. 67, April 2004

3 cocaine; heroin *UK*
- —Bill Davis, *Jawjacking*, p. 100, 1977
- You drunk or on toot? Whistler said.—Robert Campbell, *In La-La Land We Trust*, p. 15, 1986
- —Macfarlane, Macfarlane and Robson, *The User*, p. xi, 1996
- He'll sit here 'til dawn with you if you've got toot.—Kevin Sampson, *Powder*, p. 105, 1999
- "So," he said, winking extravagantly, "you two fancy a little toot?" —John Williams, *Cardiff Dead*, p. 5, 2000

4 butyl nitrite *US*
- Want some toot, dude?—*Repo Man*, 1984

5 a drinking spree *US, 1891*
- Afterwards she came to me and said her husband was off on a toot and she was worried and would I find him and bring him home. —Raymond Chandler, *The Long Goodbye*, p. 230, 1953
- He could just be on a toot.—Jack W. Thomas, *Heavy Number*, p. 60, 1976
- Even his Uncle Brian, an alcoholic, was worried about his being on a toot for three days.—Edwin Torres, *Q & A*, p. 82, 1977

6 the toilet *AUSTRALIA, 1965*
Rhymes with 'foot'. Perhaps a euphemistic alteration of 'toilet'. The suggestion in the *Australian National Dictionary* that it derives from British dialect *tut* (a small seat or hassock), recorded in C19, fails to impress as it doesn't take into account the fact that the dialect word was pronounced to rhyme with 'putt'.
- —Arthur Chipper, *The Aussie Swearer's Guide*, p. 33, 1972
- —Jim Ramsay, *Cop It Sweet!*, p. 90, 1977
- One old dear got up to go to the toot and slipped and hurt her hip. —Sam Weller, *Old Bastards I Have Met*, p. 14, 1979
- They were always hopping into the toot and emerging with different foot gear.—Roy Slaven (John Doyle), *Five South Coast Seasons*, p. 135, 1992

7 a prostitute *US*
- —Rick Ayers (Ed1itor), *Slang Dictionary*, p. 16, 2001

▷ **see:** WHISTLE AND TOOT

toot *verb*
1 to inhale a powdered drug, such as cocaine *US, 1975*
- Did I ask if they're tooting cocaine, maybe blowing a little weed? No I didn't ask him that either.—Elmore Leonard, *Split Images*, p. 16, 1981
- Irrationality ruled for ten minutes while I dug under the front seat for my stuff and tooted from the spoon—Odie Hawkins, *Lost Angeles*, p. 40, 1994
- He's tooting little lines of the gear [cocaine] to check as he goes along, doing a bit of quality control.—J.J. Connolly, *Know Your Enemy [britpulp]*, p. 143, 1999
- [T]here they are tooting away in front of her.—Lanre Fehintola, *Charlie Says...*, p. 110, 2000

2 to inhale crack cocaine vapours
- —Dean Cavanagh, *Mile High Meltdown (Disco Biscuits)*, p. 212, 1996

3 to fart *US*
- A far-off chorus softly sang in unison, "Beans, beans, the musical fruit. The more you eat, the more you toot."—Piri Thomas, *Stories from El Barrio*, p. 34, 1978
- —Pamela Munro, *U.C.L.A. Slang*, p. 86, 1989
- The more you toot, the better you feel[.]—Peter Furze, *Tailwinds*, p. 165, 1998

toot; tute *nickname*
in Canadian military aviation, the Tutor one-engine jet trainer *CANADA*
- After you finish your initial pilot training course, you'll go on to advanced flying training on the Tute.—Tom Langeste, *oral citation from Words on the Wing*, p. 285, 1995

tooter *noun*
a (improvised) tube for inhaling cocaine into the nose *US, 1981*
- She was still on her hands and knees when I handed her the tooter[.]—Lanre Fehintola, *Charlie Says...*, p. 32, 2000

toothbrush day *noun*
after a guilty verdict, the day when sentencing is announced *US*
- Is that a nice thing to be saying to a man on Toothbrush Day?—George V. Higgins, *Penance for Jerry Kennedy*, p. 29, 1985
- —Angela Devlin, *Prison Patter*, p. 116, 1996

toothing *noun*
anonymous casual sexual activity with any partner arranged over Bluetooth^{TM} radio technology enabled mobile phones *UK*
- Toothing [...] is a growing trend among rail commuters. Using Bluetooth, impromptu sex sessions are arranged with strangers in the lavatories.—*The Times*, p. 5, 12th June 2004

toothless gibbon *noun*
the vagina *UK*
A visual pun, evocative of, if not inspired by, The Goodies 'Funky Gibbon', 1970.
- —*Roger's Profanisaurus*, October 1999
- —*www.LondonSlang.com*, June 2002

toothpick *noun*
1 a thinly rolled marijuana cigarette *NEW ZEALAND*
Collected during an extensive survey of New Zealand prison slang, 1996–2000.

2 a long, thin, old-fashioned surfboard *AUSTRALIA*
- —Nat Young, *Surfing Fundamentals*, p. 128, 1985

3 a railway tie *US*
- —Ramon Adams, *The Language of the Railroader*, p. 159, 1977

4 a pool cue stick that is lighter than average *US*
- —Steve Rushin, *Pool Cool*, p. 29, 1990

5 a sharp knife *US*
- —Lou Shelly, *Hepcats Jive Talk Dictionary*, p. 19, 1945

tooth to tail ratio *noun*
the ratio of combat troops (tooth) to rear-echelon support personnel (tail) *US*
- —Linda Reinberg, *In the Field*, p. 221, 1991

tootie *adjective*
homosexual *US*
- Dodie was born tootie, and Lisa wasn't.—Rita Ciresi, *Pink Slip*, p. 9, 1999

tooting *adverb*
completely, absolutely *US, 1932*
Usually further intensified with a preceding adverb.
- "Some people have accused us of being wrapped up in [the flag]," Thomas said. "And they're darn tootin' right we are."—*Daily Nexus (UC Santa Barbara)*, 6th November 2002

Tooting Bec *noun*
1 food; a little to eat *UK, 1937*
Rhyming slang for **PECK**, formed from an area of south London.

2 a kiss *UK*
Rhyming slang for 'peck'.
- —Ray Puxley, *Cockney Rabbit*, 1992

tootle; tootle around; tootle along; tootle off *verb*
to go; to wander; to travel *UK*
- I tootle around boosting [promoting] domestic appliances.—Alexander Baron, *A Bit of Happiness [Six Granada Plays]*, p. 199, 1959
- Shall I tootle off?—*The Vicar of Dibley*, 12th January 2002

tootle-pip *noun*
▷ **see:** TOODLE-PIP

too true
used as a stressed affirmative *UK*
- "Got any doubs (pills)?" "Too true." "Spare?"—Ian Hebditch, *Weekend, The Sharper Word*, p. 133, 1969

toots *noun*
used as an affectionate term of address, usually to a girl or woman *US, 1936*
- He headed into the hallway again, where he saluted her crisply. "Don't OD on Beer Nuts, toots."—Armistead Maupin, *Tales of the City*, p. 295, 1978

tootsie *noun*
1 a woman, a girlfriend; often used as a form of address, either humorous or affectionate *US, 1895*
- Some other tootsies tried their hand at making a strange face but were dragged off by their boy friends who chased them into the bar.—Mickey Spillane, *I, The Jury*, p. 122, 1947
- Let's face it, whore or no whore, this is a clear-cut tootsie, right? —Philip Roth, *Portnoy's Complaint*, p. 226, 1969
- Where the hell does that little Radcliffe tootsie come off rating Scott Fitzgerald and Gustav Mahler and then Heinrich Boll?—*Manhattan*, 1979

2 a child's foot; a woman's foot *US*
A baby-talk coinage; playful or affectionate usage.
- Howard got down on his knees and licked the Rock Chick's tootsies.—Stewart Home, *Sex Kick [britpulp]*, p. 212, 1999

3 a capsule of secobarbital sodium and amobarbital sodium (trade name Tuinal™), a combination of central nervous system depressants *US*
Also variant 'tootie'.
- —Donald Wesson and David Smith, *Barbiturates*, p. 122, 1977
- —Mike Haskins, *Drugs*, p. 283, 2003

tootsie roll *noun*
distilled and concentrated heroin *US*
- —Carsten Stroud, *Close Pursuit*, p. 269, 1987
- —Geoffrey Froner, *Digging for Diamonds*, p. 61, 1989
- —Robert Ashton, *This Is Heroin*, p. 207, 2002

tootsie trade *noun*
a sexual coupling of two effeminate homosexual men *UK*
- —Paul Baker, *Polari*, p. 192, 2002

toov *noun*
cigarettes, tobacco *UK*
English gypsy use.
- —Jimmy Stockin, *On The Cobbles*, p. 11, 2000

too wet to plow *adjective*
experiencing the bleed period of the menstrual cycle *US*
- —Karen Houppert, *The Curse*, 1999

top *noun*
1 the dominant partner in a homosexual or sado-masochistic relationship *US*
- If he is said to be "tops," it means that he will assume only the active partnership in sodomy, while if he is called "tops or bottoms," he will assume either the so-called male or female role in sodomy.—*New York Mattachine Newsletter*, p. 6, June 1961
- Boots could take either the top or the bottom without the least show of emotion.—Donald Goines, *Whoreson*, p. 265, 1972
- A certain smart-alecky style of soliciting attention from tops.—*What Color is Your Handkerchief*, p. 7, 1979
- In fact, you make me feel kind of submissive. Usually, I'm a top. —Stewart Home, *Sex Kick [britpulp]*, p. 255, 1999

2 a maximum prison sentence *US*
- —*Current Slang*, p. 48, Fall 1968

3 a first sergeant *US*
Variants include 'topper' and 'tap kick'.
- —Linda Reinberg, *In the Field*, p. 81, 1991

▸ **be on top**
to be discovered in a criminal enterprise; to be arrested *UK*
Presumably from the exposed and conspicuous position that is normally meant by 'on top'.
- —G.F. Newman, *Sir, You Bastard*, 1970

▸ **over the top**
said of a score in pinball when the score exceeds the capacity of the scoring device and thus returns to zero *US*
- —Bobbye Claire Natkin and Steve Kirk, *All About Pinball*, p. 113, 1977

▸ **the top**
1 the beginning of something, often in the phrase 'from the top' *UK, 1976*
- One more time from the top: I like big butts and I cannot lie[.]—Robert Carlock, *Friends*, 2002

2 the northern parts of Australia *AUSTRALIA, 1951*
- Panting on a pew at Cue, he regains his strength, and decides to return home 'around the top'.—Douglas Baglin and John O'Grady, *Ladies and Gentlemen*, p. 30, 1966
- As for the the 'real' cowboys, they came from the Kimberleys, the Gulf country, the Isa and the big smoke. Down south, out west and over the top.—*Alice Springs Star*, p. 3, 21st August 1984

top *verb*
1 to execute someone especially by hanging or beheading; hence, to kill someone *UK, 1718*
- There was a chap in the death cell waiting to get topped—Frank Norman, *Bang To Rights*, p. 31, 1958
- "I am going round to the nearest nick to give myself up, straight I am. I mean that." [...] "And get topped?"—Derek Bickerton, *Payroll*, p. 69, 1959
- [H]e nearly topped a screw [prison warder] up at the ville[.]—Derek Raymond (Robin Cook), *The Crust on its Uppers*, p. 41, 1962

2 to take the dominant, controlling role in a sado-masochistic relationship *US*
- For the man who buys the services of a dominatrix, being "topped" is attractive as long as it's a service.—Jill Nagle, *Whores and Other Feminists*, 1997

▸ **top from the bottom; top from below**
(of a sexual submissive in a sado-masochistic relationship) to take, or attempt to take, the dominant, controlling role *UK*
- —Jay Wiseman, *SM101*, 1996

▸ **top the hills and pop the pills**
used as a stock description of a trucker's work *US*
- —Elementary Electronics, *Dictionary of CB Lingo*, p. 119, 1976

▸ **top yourself**
to commit suicide *UK, 1718*
A specific variant of **TOP** (to kill deliberately).
- [H]e also took my tie and belt so that I could not top myself, even if I wanted to.—Frank Norman, *Bang To Rights*, p. 24, 1958
- I'd top myself, I know I would.—Danny King, *The Burglar Diaries*, p. 242, 2001

top *adjective*

great; excellent *US, 1935*

- This night club was top stuff. —Sam Weller, *Old Bastards I Have Met*, p. 64, 1979
- Karen and Annie were top sorts, a bit light on the grey matter, but nice girls. —Clive Galea, *Slipper*, p. 107, 1988
- It was such a top idea[.] —Roy Slaven (John Doyle), *Five South Coast Seasons*, p. 29, 1992
- [H]e still often thought about Sue. Her curly blonde hair, her blue eyes, her top body. —Robert G. Barrett, *Davo's Little Something*, p. 5, 1992
- So Leo Schofield recommends that a 'top bloke' should own a battery-operated nose hair clipper. —*Sydney Morning Herald*, p. 16, 3rd March 1997
- —Phillip Gwynne, *Deadly Unna?*, p. 157, 1998

top banana *noun*

the headliner in a vaudeville show; by figurative extension, the leading figure in any enterprise *US, 1953*

- Why do you think she went out and bought this army cot? Leave it to me: I'm always top banana in the shock department. —Truman Capote, *Breakfast at Tiffany's*, p. 61, 1958
- Lenny had his mother, Sally Marr – a top banana when they all worked in burlesque – fitted out with a recorder[.] —Albert Goldman, *Freak Show*, p. 211–212, 1968

top bitch *noun*

in a group of prostitutes working for a pimp, the latest addition to the group *US, 1967*

- Oliver had assured her that she was his top bitch but demanded to know why she couldn't catch as many dates as Alice, his bottom bitch. —Joseph Wambaugh, *Floasters*, p. 67, 1996

top bollocks; top ballocks *noun*

the female breasts *UK, 1961*

- Whenever I see a decent jam tart with a good set of top bollocks I'm in like Flynn, NO PROBS! —Barry Humphries, *Bazza Pulls It Off!*, 1971

top brass; brass *noun*

high-ranking police officers *UK, 1949*

Adopted from military usage, preceded by 'big brass' and 'high brass'.

- [H]e's already put it to the top brass and they're prepared to let him play it his way[.] —Ted Lewis, *Jack Carter's Law [britpulp]*, p. 49, 1974
- Regan whistled softly. "That means brass breathing down our necks," he said grimly. —*The Sweeney*, p. 49, 1976
- "Brass'll love this," sighed [Sergeant] Fraser. —David Peace, *Nineteen Seventy-Four*, p. 115, 1999

top dog *noun*

1 a very important person *UK, 1900*

- One of the dudes who helped me rip off the Stool later became a top dog in the government[.] —Odie Hawkins, *Great Lawd Buddha*, p. 45, 1990
- She was that well bred and posh that she still acted like she was the top dog in the relationship and I was just some jolly bit of rough. —Ben Elton, *High Society*, p. 22, 2002

2 in poker, the highest pair in a hand *US*

- —John Vorhaus, *The Big Book of Poker Slang*, p. 36, 1996

top dog *adjective*

of a person, important *UK*

- In public they want to look fuck-all. Amongst their own they want to look top-dog. —Lenny McLean, *The Guv'nor*, p. 91, 1998

top dollar *noun*

a high price or the best price; or rate of pay *US*

- The great thing about them is their talent for pulling in top dollar for said performance. —Andrew Nickolds, *Back to Basics*, p. 9, 1994

top dollar *adjective*

first-rate, genuine *UK*

- I can tell if someone's a wrong 'un in minutes, sometimes seconds. You probably can yerself. Nah, you're top dollar, mate. —Garry Bushell, *The Face*, p. 211, 2001

top-drawer *adjective*

well-bred, high-class, the best *UK, 1920*

- Chances are that if a call-girl is easy to meet she is not, as her boosters boast, "top-drawer stuff." —John M. Murtagh and Sara Harris, *Cast the First Stone*, p. 2, 1957
- Daisy was a top-drawer Red in Los Angeles, a big and homely woman with the largest feet I ever saw on a woman. —*Going Away*, p. 35, 1962
- The Opal I knew was a stone young lady, with top drawer parents. —Iceberg Slim (Robert Beck), *Airtight Willie and Me*, p. 54, 1979
- Claudia always stayed at a cozy hotel near the Tennis Club in the days when tennis was tops, when developers there wouldn't dream of doing a hotel, condo or country club without top-drawer tennis facilities. —Joseph Wambaugh, *Fugitive Nights*, p. 61, 1992

top dresser drawer *noun*

the uppermost berth in a brakevan (caboose) *US*

- —Norman Carlisle, *The Modern Wonder Book of Trains and Railroading*, p. 269, 1946

toped *verb*

drunk *UK*

From the conventional, if rarely used, verb 'tope'.

- There are old dudes laughing, getting toped on the sofas[.] —Patrick Neate, *Where You're At*, p. 91, 2003

Top End; top end *noun*

the northern parts of the Northern Territory *AUSTRALIA, 1933*

- But the 'top end' was an unknown land to a great many Australians. —Patsy Adam-Smith, *Folklore of the Australian Railwaymen*, p. 284, 1969
- —Jim Ramsay, *Cop It Sweet!*, p. 90, 1977

Top Ender *noun*

a person from the Top End *AUSTRALIA, 1941*

top-flight *adjective*

first rate *US, 1939*

- You stack up as a top-flight man in my book, but you've had not incentive here. —Jim Thompson, *The Grifters*, p. 121, 1963

top gun *noun*

1 crack cocaine *US*

- —US Department of Justice, *Street Terms*, October 1994

2 one hundred pounds *UK*

Rhyming slang for **TON**, formed from the title of a 1986 film.

- —Ray Puxley, *Fresh Rabbit*, 1998

top hat *noun*

1 the vagina *UK*

Rhyming slang for **PRAT**.

- —Ray Puxley, *Fresh Rabbit*, 1998

2 a fool *UK*

Rhyming slang for **PRAT**.

- —Ray Puxley, *Fresh Rabbit*, 1998

3 in the television and film industries, a device used to enable shooting very low angles *UK*

- —Oswald Skilbeck, *ABC of Film and TV Working Terms*, p. 136, 1960

top hats *noun*

erect nipples *US*

- —Pamela Munro, *U.C.L.A. Slang*, p. 116, 1997

top-hole *adjective*

excellent *UK, 1908*

Arch and dated but still used without irony.

- "All well?" she asked. "Top hole!" returned Victor elegantly, then added quickly: "Actually, not." —Jasper Fforde, *The Eyre Affair*, p. 249, 2003

topless *noun*

in the used car business, a convertible *US*

- "Come see this one, Leroy," he was saying into the phone. "It's a 1979 Chevy ... topless!" —Lewis Poteet, *Car & Motorcyle Slang*, p. 205, 1992

top mag *noun*

a fast-talking criminal *AUSTRALIA*

Possibly an elaboration on earlier sense of 'mag' (a chatterer).

- —*The (Sydney) Bulletin*, 26th April 1975

top man *noun*

in a homosexual couple, the partner who plays the active role during sex *US, 1941*

- They are usually long-terms and are familiarly known to inmates by such local cognomens as "wolves," "top men," "jockers" or "daddies." —*Ebony*, p. 82, July 1951
- —*Maledicta*, p. 231, 1979: 'Kinks and queens: linguistic and cultural aspects of the terminology for gays'

top notch *noun*

a gang member with high standing within the gang *JAMAICA, 1989*

- —Peter Patrick, *Some Recent Jamaican Creole Words*, 2003

top-notch *adjective*
of the best quality *UK*
Figurative use of a 'top notch' representing the highest point achievable.
- It's all, you know, top-notch codes of honour and breaks from battle for tea[.] — Diran Adebayo, *My Once Upon A Time*, p. 135, 2000

top-notcher *noun*
an outstanding person *AUSTRALIA*
- That barmaid was a top-notcher from the feet up. — Norman Lindsay, *Halfway to Anywhere*, p. 177, 1947
- If you're a 'top notcher' or a 'top liner', then in footy terms, you're tops'...the best. — Ivor Limb, *Footy's No Joke!*, p. 70, 1986

topo *noun*
crack cocaine *UK*
- — Mike Haskins, *Drugs*, p. 282, 2003

top-off *noun*
a police informer *AUSTRALIA, 1940*
- — Tilly Devine, *Remember Smith's Weekly?*, p. 219, 1950
- The top-off gets half the fine, doesn't he? — Vince Kelly, *The Bogeyman*, p. 76, 1956
- — Jim Ramsay, *Cop It Sweet!*, p. 90, 1977

top-off merchant *noun*
a police informer *AUSTRALIA, 1944*
- — Arthur Chipper, *The Aussie Swearer's Guide*, p. 43, 1972

top of the head *noun*
in betting, odds of 9–4 *UK*
From the **TICK-TACK** signal used by bookmakers.
- — John McCririck, *John McCririck's World of Betting*, p. 60, 1991

top of the shop *adjective*
excellent *UK*
An elaboration of **TOP** (excellent).
- Ta [thank you] for the hotel, by the way, Guy. Top of the shop. — Kevin Sampson, *Powder*, p. 39, 1999

top of the world *adjective*
a feeling of elation, good health or prosperity *US, 1920*
- Come the day of the races, I was feeling good. Top of the world. — Lenny McLean, *The Guv'nor*, p. 87, 1998

top one *noun*
the best of times *UK*
- [O]n one, up for it, mad for it, top one. Heaven knows. He'd be having it large before the night was out. — Kevin Sampson, *Powder*, p. 198, 1999

topper *noun*
1 a remark or action that serves as the *coup de grace* of a conversation or series of events *US, 1939*
- It looks like old Mr. Stumpnagler, what's owned the building ever since I can remember, has had a couple of years of bad luck, his wife dying being the topper. — Robert Campbell, *Nibbled to Death by Ducks*, p. 216, 1989

2 a criminal who represents the interests of a cheque forger *UK*
- a minder, known as a topper, to keep an eye on the dropper, make sure he doesn't pocket the crinkle [money] — Charles Raven, *Underworld Nights*, p. 81, 1956

3 in circus and carnival usage, a featured act *US*
- — Don Wilmeth, *The Language of American Popular Entertainment*, p. 277, 1981

topping *adjective*
excellent *UK, 1822*
- Little Biddlington-on-Sea sounds absolutely topping! — Dorothy Cannell, *Fetch*, 1998

topping shed *noun*
in prison, a place of execution *UK, 1950*
- E wing, which contains the chokey or punishment cells, the three condemned cells and the topping (or execution) shed. — Charles Raven, *Underworld Nights*, p. 106, 1956

tops *noun*
dice that have been marked to have two identical faces *US*
- — Frank Garcia, *Marked Cards and Loaded Dice*, p. 265, 1962

tops *adjective*
topmost in quality, the best *US, 1935*
- I really liked that chick, I thought – she was strictly tops. — Chester Himes, *If He Hollers Let Him Go*, p. 116, 1945
- The fellers all think you are tops and they envy the fact that I know you so well. — John Wynnum, *Jiggin' in the Riggin*, p. 64, 1965
- Apart from that everything's just fabulous. Tops. Terrific. — Kathy Lette, *Girls' Night Out*, p. 89, 1987
- Yeah, it's tops. Hats off to the judges. — Roy Slaven (John Doyle), *Five South Coast Seasons*, p. 38, 1992

tops *adverb*
at the most *US*
- Tonight and tomorrow, tops. — *Raising Arizona*, 1987
- Man, I got a shelf life of ten years, tops! — *Jerry Maguire*, 1996

tops and bottoms *noun*
1 in poker, a hand consisting of a pair of aces (the highest card) and a pair of twos (the lowest card) *US*
- — *Americzan Speech*, p. 102, May 1951

2 a roll of trimmed paper 'topped' and 'bottomed' with a genuine banknote to give the impression of a weighty roll of money *UK*
- In his pockets were rolls of "tops and bottoms"[.] — John Gosling, *The Ghost Squad*, 1959

3 a combination of Taluin™, a painkiller, and the antihistamine Pyribenzamine™, abused for non-medicinal purposes *US*
- Tops and Bottoms is street slang for T's and Blues. T's are Taluin, a painkiller, and Blues are Pyribenzamine, an antihistamine. Combined in the right dosage they make a poorman's heroin. — *Chicago Tribune*, p. 6C, 11th June 1989

top-shelf *adjective*
excellent or the best *US, 1892*
- MOE: I gotta first cousin. He's top shelf. Handles only the best. Everything first-class, all the way. — *Mo' Better Blues*, 1990

top stick *noun*
the best regular player in a pool hall *US*
- — Steve Rushin, *Pool Cool*, p. 29, 1990

topsy *noun*
a chamber pot *BARBADOS*
- — Frank A. Collymore, *Barbadian Dialect*, p. 112, 1965

topsy-turvy *adjective*
1 disordered, in a chaotic state, very untidy *UK, 1528*
- a sudden loss of perspective, the world being set topsy-turvy — Edward M. Hallowell and John J. Ratey, *Driven to Distraction*, p. 251, 1994

2 upside down; in reverse order *UK, 1530*
- One reason for the huge incidence of juvenile delinquency, but by no means the decisive one, was an idiosyncrasy of the population trend here, topsy-turvy to every other in the country during the last 10 years. — Jack Lait and Lee Mortimer, *Washington Confidential*, p. 119, 1951
- Living in a world of topsy-turvy standards and constant temptation, a boy could easily become involved in serious and long-lasting trouble. — Jim Thompson, *Bad Boy*, p. 366, 1953

top totty *noun*
an especially desirable or sexually available woman or women *UK*
- Top Totty! My Top Bird! — *www.rhubarb7.freeserve.co.uk*, 4th October 2001

top 'uns *noun*
a woman's breasts *UK*
- [S]he aint arf [ain't half] got some top 'uns. — Frank Norman, *Bang To Rights*, p. 144, 1958

top whack; top wack *noun*
the most expensive price *UK*
Derives from **WHACK** (a share of money).
- [S]ometimes they're lucky enough to pick up a Grand, top wack[.] — Ted Lewis, *Jack Carter's Law*, p. 43, 1974
- Some of these lads here though, they want to pay top whack. — Kevin Sampson, *Outlaws*, p. 159, 2001

top willow!
in cricket, used for registering enthusiastic approval of a batman's performance *UK*
A cricket bat is traditionally made of willow. Displayed on a placard at the England v West Indies 2nd Test, Edgbaston, 31st July 2004.

toque; tuque *noun*
a knitted cap made from wool *CANADA, 1871*
• Of course it wasn't the sort of hat anyone else wore, as you might expect. It was a toque, a red-and-white woolen one that Noreen used to wear. —James Reaney, *"The Bully" in Canadian Short Stories*, p. 379, 1960

torch *noun*
1 an arsonist *US, 1938*
• "Call up North," Shad said. "Get a real torch artist." —Carl Hiaasen, *Strip Tease*, p. 277, 1993
2 an act of arson *US*
• I know who instigated the Utopia torch. —James Ellroy, *Brown's Requiem*, p. 109, 1981
3 a cigarette lighter *US*
• —David Claerbaut, *Black Jargon in White America*, p. 84, 1972
4 a handgun *US*
• —Joseph E. Ragen and Charles Finston, *Inside the World's Toughest Prison*, p. 821, 1962: 'Penitentiary and underworld glossary'
5 marijuana; a marijuana cigarette *US, 1977*
A conical shape holding fire at the flared end.
• —Richard A. Spears, *The Slang and Jargon of Drugs and Drink*, p. 517, 1986
• —Mike Haskins, *Drugs*, p. 289, 2003
6 a love song or ballad *US*
• All songs of regret and revenge and love's bitter grief are "torches." —Jack Lait and Lee Mortimer, *New York Confidential*, p. 33, 1948

torch *verb*
to light a fire, especially an arson fire *US, 1931*
• Now somebody's torched it to clear the lot. Probably one of my clients. —*Body Heat*, 1980
• If he'd gone in there he wouldn't've known right off, the way those charrings, alligator burns, showed, he would've known you torched it. —George V. Higgins, *The Rat on Fire*, p. 22, 1981
• I developed a theory – that the mastermind was only after one of the victims – and that he torched the bar to hide his motive. —James Ellroy, *Brown's Requiem*, p. 109, 1981
• Alright, Six says torch this place. —*Platoon*, 1986
• [W]e are going to press charges against you torching down the school. —Shaun Ryder, *Shaun Ryder... in His Own Words*, 1990
• "Someone's torched Dad's car!" I exclaimed. —C.D. Payne, *Youth in Revolt*, p. 311, 1993

torched *adjective*
drunk *US*
• —Judi Sanders, *Cal Poly Slang*, p. 10, 1990

torch job *noun*
an enema containing a heat-inducing agent such as Vicks Vaporub™, Ben-Gay™, Heet™ or Tabasco™ sauce *US*
• —Robert A. Wilson, *Playboy's Book of Forbidden Words*, p. 243, 1972

torch up *noun*
to smoke marijuana; to light up a joint *US*
• —*American Speech*, p. 88, May 1955: 'Narcotic argot along the Mexican Border'
• But first The Wolf stepped into the toilet and torched up. —Willard Motley, *Let No Man Write My Epitaph*, p. 109, 1958
• —Richard A. Spears, *The Slang and Jargon of Drugs and Drink*, p. 517, 1986
• —Mike Haskins, *Drugs*, p. 290, 2003

tore down *adjective*
very disoriented, usually because of drug intoxication *UK*
• —Tom Hibbert, *Rockspeak!*, p. 159, 1983

toreeon *noun*
a variety of marijuana *UK*
• Some of the more potent varieties include Hawaiian, Columbian gold, Kona gold, toreeon, and Sinsemilla. —Jay Saporita, *Pourin' It All Out*, p. 59, 1980

tore up *adjective*
distressed *US*
• —Robert George Reisner, *The Jazz Titans*, p. 166, 1960

tornado bait *noun*
a mobile home or trailer, especially in a tornado zone *US, 1992*
• [A]n attractive nuisance, or tornado bait, or both? —John Grissim, *The Complete Buyer's Guide to Manufactured Homes and Land*, 2003

torn up *adjective*
hurt; upset *US*
• —Hy Lit, *Hy Lit's Unbelievable Dictionary of Hip Words for Groovy People*, p. 1, 1968

Toronto the Good *nickname*
the city of Toronto, considered with reference to its longtime (into the 1980s) strict rectitude in law and custom *CANADA*
Also nicknamed Hogtown, Toronto continues to carry both terms though money and a cosmopolitan and international flavour have replaced slaughterhouses and the former moral stiffness.

torpecker *noun*
a torpedo *US*
• —*American Speech*, p. 38, February 1948: 'Talking under water: speech in submarines'

torpedo *noun*
1 a hired gunman or killer *US, 1929*
• "I'm a torpedo, and the best gun-hand livin'," the Toad answered. —Chester Gould, *Dick Tracy Meets the Night Crawler*, p. 36, 1945
• [U]ntil he made his exit he was head torpedo for the mob. —Mezz Mezzrow, *Really the Blues*, p. 101, 1946
• He was put on the spot because he refused to be "organized"; preferred old-fashioned gang methods learned when he was the Number One torpedo for Murder, Inc. —Jack Lait and Lee Mortimer, *New York Confidential*, p. 186, 1948
• A goddamned Commie gestapo man. A hatchetman, a torpedo, a lot of things you want to call him. —Mickey Spillane, *One Lonely Night*, p. 77, 1951
• A couple of torpedos are out gunning for him. —Thurston Scott, *Cure it with Honey*, p. 154, 1951
• —Joseph E. Ragen and Charles Finston, *Inside the World's Toughest Prison*, p. 821, 1962: 'Penitentiary and underworld glossary'
• In this part of the country, I'm known as a torpedo. —Bruce Jackson, *In the Life*, p. 159, 1972
• You heard his record – talk about safe streets – is any street safe with a torpedo like that on it? —Edwin Torres, *Carlito's Way*, p. 137, 1975
• And the tough torpedo in the silk tuxedo / Proving his way with a gun. —Dennis Wepman et al., *The Life*, p. 162, 1976
• I tapped Truck Infante for one of his Teamster torpedos. —Seth Morgan, *Homeboy*, p. 97, 1990
• The floor stiff was Fitz Steinkamp, Chicago-Milwaukee gunsel, one conviction for attempted murder, currently on parole and believed to be a Jerry Katzenbach torpedo. —James Ellroy, *Hollywood Nocturnes*, p. 218, 1994
2 the penis *US*
• —Chris Lewis, *The Dictionary of Playground Slang*, p. 236, 2003
3 a marijuana cigarette *SOUTH AFRICA*
• —C.P. Wittstock, 1946
4 a marijuana and crack cocaine cigarette *US*
• —US Department of Justice, *Street Terms*, October 1994
• —Mike Haskins, *Drugs*, p. 289, 2003
5 in trucking, a large, bullet-shaped light on a cab *US*
• —Montie Tak, *Truck Talk*, p. 169, 1971

torpedo juice *noun*
any improvised alcohol onboard a submarine *US*
• —*American Speech*, p. 38, February 1948: 'Talking under water: speech in submarines'

torpedos *noun*
beans *US*
• —Ramon Adams, *The Language of the Railroader*, p. 159, 1977

torqued *adjective*
angered, annoyed *US*
• —*Current Slang*, p. 12, Spring 1968

tortoise head *noun*
the erect penis *UK*
• HER: I love science, Ali. U: Wotever, I iz got a tortoise head, could u direct me to da laboratory. —Sacha Baron-Cohen, *Da Gospel According to Ali G*, 2001

torture chamber *noun*
a jail or prison where illegal drugs are not available *US*
• —Ralph de Sola, *Crime Dictionary*, p. 152, 1982

Torvill and Dean *noun*
a homosexual *UK*
Rhyming slang for **QUEEN**, formed from ice-dancing champions and Olmpic gold medal winners 1984, Jayne Torvill and Christopher Dean.
• —Bodmin Dark, *Dirty Cockney Rhyming Slang*, 2003

Toryglental *adjective*
insane, crazy *UK: SCOTLAND*
Glasgow rhyming slang for 'mental', contrived on the Toryglen area of Glasgow.
• —Michael Munro, *The Patter, Another Blast*, 1988

tosh *noun*

1 nonsense *UK, 1892*
A compound of synonyms 'bosh' and 'trash'.
- The Kaiser was evil, the Germans were bayoneting babies, brave little Belgium, it was all the same tosh. — Mark Steel, *Reasons to be Cheerful*, p. 127, 2001

2 used as a form of male address *UK*
Possibly Scottish in origin. In 1990, car manufacturer Toshiba created a new slogan 'Ullo Tosh! Gotta Toshiba?' based on the song 'Ullo John! Gotta New Motor?', Alexei Sayle, 1983.

3 a bath *UK, 1881*
School slang.
- Time for a tosh (a bath for those of you not fortunate enough to be Old Harrovians)[.] — John McCririck, *John McCririck's World of Betting*, p. 10, 1991

tosheroon; tusheroon; 'roon *noun*
in pre-decimalisation currency, a half-crown coin; two shillings and sixpence *UK, 1859*
- They said no buyer would give them more than a tosheroon for a terracotta statue with no tits. — Charles Raven, *Underworld Nights*, p. 78, 1956
- Tosheroon (abbreviated to 'roon), two and a kick[.] — Brian McDonald, *Elephant Boys*, p. 202, 2000

toshing *verb*
painting and decorating *UK*
- These days it pays to be choosy about who you get to do your toshing, the world is awash with ne'er-do-well decorators. — Ray Puxley, *Fresh Rabbit*, p. 14, 1998

tosh up *verb*
to make something look as good as new *UK*
Car dealers' term.
- Watch out for pudden on the door sills. They're often MOT failures and their [sic] toshed up with sheet fibregrass and a can of spray paint. — *You*, 10th July 1983

toss *noun*

1 nonsense, especially if self-indulgent *UK*
- He's a top lad, our Paul, but 'e don't 'alf talk some fookin' toss sometimes. — Shaun Ryder, *Shaun Ryder... in His Own Words*, 1990
- Fuckin Steps [a pop group] or some such fuckin God-awful toss. — Niall Griffiths, *Kelly + Victor*, p. 54, 2002
- Last week we described BBC-1's Rescue Me [...] as "toss". — *The Burglar Diaries*, p. 8, 12th March 2002

2 something of little or no value *UK*
- The work you gentlemen do is not worth a toss. — Joe Morgan, *Eastenders Don't Cry*, p. 107, 1994

3 an act of masturbation *UK, 1785*
- If yer need a toss you wait 'til association. We take it in turns, the rest of us go out [of the prison cell]. — Chris Baker and Andrew Day, *Lock, Stock... & A Good Slopping Out*, p. 411, 2000

4 a search of a person or place *US*
- "Let's chase him and give him a toss." — Charles Whited, *Chiodo*, p. 88, 1973
- So if a policeman gets there before anybody else, he'll give the apartment a fast toss, searching for cash, jewelry, anything of value. — Leonard Shecter and William Phillips, *On the Pad*, p. 97, 1973
- He had a wild, lucid look about him, so I gave him a toss. — James Ellroy, *Brown's Requiem*, p. 49, 1981

5 an armed robbery *US*
- — Hyman E. Goldin et al., *Dictionary of American Underworld Lingo*, p. 225, 1950

▸ **not give a toss; not care a toss**
to not care one way or another; to reject *UK*
Two suggested etymologies prevail, either 'to not care enough to toss a coin' or 'to toss (masturbate) yourself'; on balance, probably 'to toss a coin' as it takes a deal less effort and therefore the rejection is greater.
- [B]ut the thing is, I don't fucking care, just don't give a toss[.] — John King, *White Trash*, p. 66, 2001

toss *verb*

1 (of a male) to masturbate *UK, 1879*
Often used with 'off'.
- He closed his eyes, allowed the onanistic thought some breathing space and tossed himself off something stupid. — Nick Earls, *Perfect Skin*, p. 134, 2001

2 to get the better of someone; to overcome someone or something *AUSTRALIA, 1949*
- Men like Fairway are too big to toss. — Eric Lambert, *The Veterans*, p. 74, 1954
- They'll have to get up might early to toss this sailor-boy. — John Wynnum, *Tar Dust*, p. 76, 1962

3 to search a room, apartment, house, office or person without regard to the condition in which the premises or person are left *US, 1939*
- I don't get tossed too often. One time I got tossed three days in a row. Usually I don't. Maybe once every two months. But they never find anything on me. — James Mills, *The Panic in Needle Park*, p. 101, 1966
- Andy and Leaper had almost twenty-three on them when they got tossed. — George V. Higgins, *The Judgment of Deke Hunter*, p. 31, 1976
- Yeah, but when I realized someone had broken in, the way the place was tossed, I told Miss Nolan, stay in the foyer and don't move. — Elmore Leonard, *Split Images*, p. 12, 1981
- We toss the first banks today, then the broads tomorrow, the bookies Saturday, and so on. — Richard Condon, *Prizzi's Honor*, p. 217, 1982

4 to rob a place *US*
- — Hyman E. Goldin et al., *Dictionary of American Underworld Lingo*, p. 225, 1950

5 to gulp a drink down
- I just tossed a fifth of gin / I'm going to dizz knee land. — Dada, *Dizz Knee Land*, 1992

▸ **toss a grind**
to eat *US*
- — *Surfer Magazine*, p. 30, February 1992

▸ **toss chow**
to eat quickly and voraciously *US*
- — *Washington Post*, 14th October 1993

▸ **toss it in**
stop doing something *AUSTRALIA, 1954*
- — John Wynnum, *Jiggin' in the Riggin'*, p. 58, 1965
- 'How's the old public service?' 'I don't know. I tossed it in.' — Alexander Buzo, *Rooted*, p. 79, 1969
- — Kathy Lette, *Girls' Night Out*, p. 180, 1987

▸ **toss it to**
to have sex with a women *US*
- You've tossesd it to her so often, you've thrown your ass of line with your eyeballs. — Jim Thompson, *Pop. 1280*, p. 191, 1964

▸ **toss salad**
to engage in oral stimulation of the anus *US*
- You know what they make you do in County? Toss the fucking salad! I don't like this fuck's asshole; I'm gonna do it for some stranger. — Kevin Smith, *Jay and Silent Bob Strike Back*, p. 14, 2001

▸ **toss the boards**
to play three card molly, a street swindle in which the object is to identify a given card among three cards that are quickly moved around *US*
- We both knew how to toss the boards, but he was better than me. — Donald Goines, *Whoreson*, p. 35, 1972

▸ **toss the tiger**
to vomit *NEW ZEALAND, 1960*
A visual allusion to multi-coloured vomit.
- — Harry Orsman, *A Dictionary of Modern New Zealand Slang*, p. 141, 1999

▸ **toss your cookies**
to vomit *US, 1941*
Children's vocabulary.
- The cab I had was a real old one that smelled like someone'd just tossed his cookies in it. — J.D. Salinger, *Catcher in the Rye*, p. 81, 1951
- — Collin Baker et al., *College Undergraduate Slang Study Conducted at Brown University*, p. 99, 1968

▸ **toss your lollies**
to vomit *NEW ZEALAND*
- — David McGill, *David McGill's Complete Kiwi Slang Dictionary*, p. 128, 1998

tossbag *noun*
a contemptible individual *UK, 1977*
- — Tom Hibbert, *Rockspeak!*, p. 159, 1983
- A "performance piece" by tossbag duo Keith Allen and Damien Hirst. — *Ministry*, p. 24, October 2002

tossed salad *noun*
any of several sexual practices involving oral-anal stimulation *US*
- Havin' your salad tossed means havin' your asshole eaten out with jelly or syrup. I prefer syrup. — Chris Rock, *Rock This!*, p. 181, 1997
- OK, a tossed salad is – get ready, hold onto your underwear for this one – oral-anal sex. — *Oprah Winfrey Show*, 2nd October 2003

tosser *noun*

1 someone who is considered worthless or despicable *UK, 1977*
A synonym of **WANKER**.

- [I]f you're gonna do crime, go for the big bucks like all those rich tossers in the city. — Donald Gorgon, *Cop Killer*, p. 66, 1994
- "Fuck sitting around here – let's get off and find these tossers!" said one of our top faces. — Martin King and Martin Knight, *The Naughty Nineties*, p. 199, 1999
- After "In the City", like a tosser, I gave [placebo] a bad review and was top of their hit list. — John Robb, *The Nineties*, p. 340, 1999
- I was not an old toss. I was not even forty[.] — James Hawes, *Dead Long Enough*, p. 19, 2000
- [F]ucking new labour old tories – bunch of fucking tossers all of them – even the Welsh ones for fuck's sake. — Patrick Jones, *Everything Must Go*, p. 167, 2000
- [I]t is impossible to quote your own gags without sounding like a tosser. — Frank Skinner, *Frank Skinner*, p. 3, 2001
- [P]oxy women drivers who were forever SLOWING DOWN for fellow shoppers, parkers, cyclists, pedestrians, pensioners and all the other pondlife who had nothing better to do all day but HOLD HIM UP! TOSSERS! — Garry Bushell, *The Face*, p. 3, 2001

2 nothing at all; something of very little value *UK: SCOTLAND*
From the meaning as 'a penny' (a coin of little value).
- Disny matter whit ye say, he couldny gie a tosser. — Michael Munro, *The Patter, Another Blast*, p. 73, 1988

3 a penny *UK, 1934*
From the low value coin used in games of pitch-and-toss. Still current in Northen Ireland.
- So poor old Matt, off he went in the rain and then back to his dingy old room just him and the cat not a tosser between them. — Patrick McCabe, *The Butcher Boy*, p. 80, 1992

tossily *adverb*
self-indulgently, hence pretentiously *UK*
From **TOSS** (to masturbate).
- [H]is tossily clever PostModern collection of artefacts[.] — James Hawes, *Dead Long Enough*, p. 9, 2000

tossle; tossel *noun*
the penis *AUSTRALIA*
Variant of 'tassle' (something that dangles).
- I'll tie a tangle in the tossle of that bubble-eyed bastard one of these days. — Robert S. Close, *Love Me Sailor*, p. 67, 1945
- Then Sodomy, always quickest on the rise, had his terrifying blue-veined tossel out[.] — Frank Hardy, *The Outcasts of Foolgarah*, p. 171, 1971
- — Jim Ramsay, *Cop It Sweet!*, p. 90, 1977
- [W]ould have been a feminist except for her love of the old tossle which grew large between the legs of her football fanatic husband. — Frank Hardy, *Hardy's People*, p. 87, 1986

tosspot *noun*
a fool; a generally abusive term for a person; in Australia, used as an affectionate form of address *UK*
Derives originally (C16) from the conventional sense as 'drunkard'. The more abusive sense combines 'fool' and **TOSSER**, a synonym for **WANKER** (a despicable person).
- — Tom Hibbert, *Rockspeak!*, p. 160, 1983
- [Y]ou loser – face it they THEY beat you you little wanker toss pot go on face up to it[.] — Patrick Jones, *Unprotected Sex*, p. 226, 1999

toss-up *noun*
1 an even chance; anything dependant on chance *UK, 1809*
From the tossing of a coin.
- [I]n the end it's a bit of a toss up as to which religion is right. — Peter Cook, *Not Only But Also*, 1965
- Money or influence – a toss-up for the Gulf states[.] — *The Guardian*, 15th September 2000

2 a person who will trade sex for crack cocaine *US*
- — Geoffrey Froner, *Digging for Diamonds*, p. 61, 1989

3 a promiscuous female *US*
- — Bill Valentine, *Gang Intelligence Manual*, p. 78, 1995

toss-ups *noun*
crack cocaine *UK*
From 'toss-up' (a person who trades sex for crack).
- — Mike Haskins, *Drugs*, p. 282, 2003

tossy *adjective*
pathetic *UK*
- It sounds tossy but can't think of a better way of putting it. — Frank Skinner, *Frank Skinner*, p. 78, 2001

tot *noun*
▷ **see: TOTTIE**

tot *verb*
to collect rubbish *UK, 1884*

TOT
used for suggesting that it is time to tell the complete truth *US*
From the Yiddish for 'buttocks on the table'.
- — Leo Rosten, *The Joys of Yinglish*, p. 482–483, 1989

total *verb*
to wreck something beyond repair *US, 1954*
Originally and chiefly applied to a car.
- Anyway, The Toilet is just plain flat-out scuzzy. I totaled a perfectly good pair or Bergdorf Goodman shoes… — Armistead Maupin, *Tales of the City*, p. 296, 1978

total *adjective*
utter; out-and-out; complete; used as an all-purpose intensifier *US*
- We need a total shark for a manager[.] — Stewart Home, *Sex Kick [britpulp]*, p. 216, 1999
- You are a total prostitute. — *American Beauty*, 1999

total bang up *noun*
in prison, a regime under which inmates are locked in their cells for 24 hours a day *UK*
- — Angela Devlin, *Prison Patter*, p. 116, 1996

total blank *noun*
in circus and carnival usage, a dull town where business is poor *US*
- — Don Wilmeth, *The Language of American Popular Entertainment*, p. 278, 1981

totalled; totalled out *adjective*
drunk *US*
- — *Current Slang*, p. 4, Summer 1966

totally *adverb*
completely *US*
Very close to standard English, but with the right attitude quite slangy.
- — Mary Corey and Victoria Westermark, *Fer Shurr! How to be a Valley Girl*, 1982
- DIONNE: Hello! That was a stop sign! CHER: I totally paused! — *Clueless*, 1995

totally!
used as an enthusiastic expression of agreement *US*
- SPICOLI: The mother fucker pissed me off. STONER BUDDY #2: Totally. — *Fast Times at Ridgemont High*, 1982
- — Mary Corey and Victoria Westermark, *Fer Shurr! How to be a Valley Girl*, 1982
- Like, OH MY GOD! (Valley Girl) / Like – TOTALLY (Valley Girl). — Moon Unit and Frank Zappa, *Valley Girl*, 1982
- — Connie Eble (Editor), *UNC-CH Campus Slang*, p. 5, November 1983
- RANDOM SOLDIER: This guy is the coolest! RANDOM SOLDIER 2: Totally man! — *South Park*, 1999

total out *adjective*
to an extreme; to excess *US*
Hawaiian youth usage.
- Janelle wen break up wit' Raymond she stay total out!! — Douglas Simonson, *Pidgin to da Max Hana Hou*, 1982

total wreck *noun*
a cheque *UK*
Rhyming slang.
- — Angela Devlin, *Prison Patter*, p. 116, 1996
- — Ray Puxley, *Fresh Rabbit*, 1998

tote *noun*
in horse racing, a pari-mutuel betting machine *AUSTRALIA, 1890*
An abbreviation of 'totalisator'.
- Black Joke was left to race a poor little mare called Cleopatra, and won by a length. I collected two pounds seventeen and sixpence from the tote. — Neville Shute, *In the Wet*, p. 11, 1953
- Talk about a mob of punters shuffling round a tote window! — Ray Slattery, *Mobbs' Mob*, p. 35, 1966
- — Mel Heimer, *Inside Racing*, p. 213, 1967
- Crosby gave Frisco the $20 and next day saw him at the racetrack – in the $20 tote queue. — Frank Hardy and Athol George Mulley, *The Needy and the Greedy*, p. 66, 1975
- With the Horserace Totalisator Board (the full name of the organisation popularly known as the Tote and sometimes still called the Nanny, nanny goat, Tote), the deduction includes contributions to racecourses and the Betting Levy. — John McCririck, *John McCririck's World of Betting*, p. 47, 1991

tote *verb*
to carry a pistol *US*
- — Ethan Hilderbrant, *Prison Slang*, p. 129, 1998

tote!
used for expressing assent *US*
An abbreviation of **TOTALLY!**.
- — Connie Eble (Editor), *UNC-CH Campus Slang*, p. 9, Fall 2000

to the bad
of time, late *UK*
- It was ten minutes to the bad by the time I turned to Lincia's road. — Diran Adebayo, *My Once Upon A Time*, p. 110, 2000

to the good
of time, early *UK*

to the nth degree *adjective*
to an extent beyond any reasonable measurement *UK*
Uses 'n' (a mathematical symbol for an indefinite number) to create a quasi-scientific sounding approximation.
- "I abused cocaine and music to the nth degree. It's a marriage made in hell" Jason Donovan — *Drugs An Adult Guide*, p. 19, December 2001

to the rack!
used by pool players for expressing dismay and utter defeat *US*
The player has no choice in this situation but to return his cue to the rack.
- — Mike Shamos, *The Illustrated Encyclopedia of Billiards*, p. 249, 1993

tothersider *noun*
in Western Australia, a person from an eastern state *AUSTRALIA, 1872*
- Land of Fortunes, easily made; The land where t'othersiders strayed, To grab the dividends that are paid – Westralia. — Mary Durack, *Kings in Grass Castles*, p. 311, 1959

toto *noun*
the penis *TRINIDAD AND TOBAGO, 1987*
- — Lise Winer, *Dictionary of the English/Creole of Trinidad & Tobago*, 2003

toto-ed *adjective*
in a state of drug-induced exhilaration *UK*
Inspired by *The Wizard of Oz*, 1939, in which Judy Garland (1922–69) as Dorothy, says to her dog: 'Toto, I don't think we're in Kansas anymore'.

totonol *noun*
frequent, regular sex as a cure for a woman's ailments *TRINIDAD AND TOBAGO*
- — Lise Winer, *Dictionary of the English/Creole of Trinidad & Tobago*, 2003

tottie; totty; tot *noun*
a person who is not white, especially a 'coloured' person; originally and particularly, one of the Khoikhoi race *SOUTH AFRICA, 1832*
Derivies from Hottentot; now considered derogatory and offensive.
- — Jean Branford, *A Dictionary of South African English*, 1978

▷ **see:** **TATER**

tottita *noun*
the vagina *US*
- There's [a...] "mushmellow," "a ghoulie," "possible," "tamale," "tottita," "Connie[".] — Eve Ensler, *The Vagina Monologues*, p. 6, 1998

tot-tots *noun*
the female breasts *TRINIDAD AND TOBAGO, 1974*
- — Lise Winer, *Dictionary of the English/Creole of Trinidad & Tobago*, 2003

totty; tottie; tott *noun*
a sexually available or desirable young woman or women *UK, 1890*
- RUDE BOY: [...] I've never been there without copping for it. SLOANE: Copping for what? RUDE BOY: Totty. Copping for totty. Skirt. — Henry Sloane, *Sloane's Inside Guide to Sex & Drugs & Rock 'n' Roll*, p. 34, 1985
- Wait till you see the tott, anyway. — Kevin Sampson, *Powder*, p. 20, 1999

totty *adjective*
attractive, desirable *UK*
- Often the phrase is, "He/she is a bit of top totty." — *Woman's Weekly*, p. 53, 23rd July 2002

tot up *verb*
to amount to; to add up; to calculate *UK*
Ultimately from '*tot*al'. An older variant, 'tot together', is still familiar.
- Finland is well used to foreign delegations turning up and demanding to know its secrets – they've totted up more than 100 over the past few years. — *The Guardian*, 17th February 2004

touch *noun*
1 a sum of money obtained at one time, especially by cadging or theft *US, 1846*
- You thought you were hooking into a soft touch, didn't you? You thought you could take me for everything I had. — Jim Thompson, *After Dark, My Sweet*, p. 29, 1955
- Even when I made a good touch, it would go fairly quickly. — Herbert Huncke, *Guilty of Everything*, p. 74, 1990

2 a satisfying result *UK*
Derives from the 'something-for-nothing' senses.
- The law was actually on my side for that one! Touch. — Dave Courtney, *Raving Lunacy*, p. 44, 2000

3 in pool, finesse *US, 1895*
- — Mike Shamos, *The Illustrated Encyclopedia of Billiards*, p. 251, 1993

▸ **put the touch on**
to attempt to extract money from someone with glib or coercive talk *US*
- Perce was skint when Peter tried to put the touch on him, but he had a nice little job all lined up. — Charles Raven, *Underworld Nights*, p. 44, 1956
- When I told him about my mother and father he said he apologized for putting the touch on me for money. — Clancy Sigal, *Going Away*, p. 144, 1961
- There were guys making a good buck here and there by pressing pants, cooking for other inmates, running errands, or putting the touch on anyone. — Herbert Huncke, *Guilty of Everything*, p. 122, 1990

touch *verb*
1 to borrow from someone *US*
- Maybe he had a morning's work in the produce market, unloading fruit crates, or maybe he touched one of his old pals for a fin. — Rocky Garciano (with Rowland Barber), *Somebody Up There Likes Me*, p. 10, 1955

2 to subject someone to extortion or bribery *UK, 1654*
- You getting touched by anybody? — Mickey Spillane, *Me, Hood!*, p. 17, 1963

3 to finance someone *UK*
- When I got out of nick all my mates got together and touched me that flat [...] Paid the deposit and first few weeks. — Jeremy Cameron, *Brown Bread in Wengen*, p. 13, 1999

4 to have sex with someone *IRELAND*
- He was the horniest dog I ever met lads. The same fella would touch a cat goin' through a skylight, I'm not coddin' or jokin' ye. — Billy Roche, *Tumbling Down*, p. 40, 1984
- — *Adult Video News*, p. 40, September 1995

▸ **I wouldn't touch it with yours**
used by one male to another as an expression of distaste or contempt for a female *UK, 1984*
Here 'it' is 'a woman' and 'yours' is 'a penis'.

▸ **not touch it with a bargepole**
used as an indication of extreme distaste or contempt *UK, 1984*
In many minor variations.
- "Don't think about touching her." "Not with a bargepole, pal." — Ian Rankin, *The Hanging Garden*, p. 43, 1998
- [Y]ou would have to be criminally insane to want to touch Glasgow with anything less than a very long orbiting bargepole, and even then you'd have to throw in a night between the sheets with Lindsay Wagner as a sweetener. — David Aitken, *Sleeping with Jane Austen*, p. 4, 2002
- If I were you, I wouldn't touch them with a bargepole[.] — Roag Best, *The Beatles*, p. 130, 2003

▸ **touch home**
to communicate a feeling; to make sense *US*
- "Like he's close, man" (he is quite capable) and "touches home" (really makes sense). — *Look*, p. 49, 24th November 1959

▸ **touching cloth; touching cotton**
having an urgent need to defecate *UK*
- Is there a bog round here mate? I'm touching cloth. — *Roger's Profanisaurus*, p. 217, 2002
- [A] strain-faced male customer who was, in his own words, "touching cloth"[.] — Christopher Brookmyre, *The Sacred Art of Stealing*, p. 117, 2002
- Dude, I'm touching cotton... I'll be right back. — Chris Lewis, *The Dictionary of Playground Slang*, p. 237, 2003

touch
a resememblance or evocative quality *UK, 1970*
When combined with a pluralised proper noun, it is used to suggest characteristics associated with that noun, as 'a touch of

the Prince Edwards', 'a touch of the Bob Dylans' or 'a touch of the Hollywoods'.

touch and go *adjective*
of uncertain outcome, unsure *UK, 1815*
• Well, it was touch and go for a while, but the Great Brown One pulled through[.] — Christopher Paul Curtis, *The Watsons Go to Birmingham*, p. 6, 1995

touch and tap *noun*
a cap (hat) *UK*
Rhyming slang.
• — Ray Puxley, *Cockney Rabbit*, 1992

touched; touched in the head *adjective*
mentally impaired; insane *UK, 1893*
• Murnau, as portrayed by the peerlessly strange John Malkovich, is clearly a bit touched in the head. — *The Guardian*, 27th January 2001

touched by the moon *adjective*
(slightly) insane *UK*
An elaboration of TOUCHED (insane), in the form of rhyming slang on LOON (a madman).
• — Ray Puxley, *Cockney Rabbit*, 1992

touche eclat *verb*
to conceal something *UK*
From French, where, if the construction were used, it would mean (very loosely) 'a brilliant or acclaimed touch'. A contemporary gay usaage.
• — *Attitude*, July 2003: 'New palare lexicon'

touchhead *noun*
a convert to the musical cult of the Grateful Dead after the 1987 release of the song 'Touch of Grey' *US*
A play on the common 'deadhead' (a Grateful Dead follower).
• Deadhead sociology took a hectic turn with the 1987 influex of "touchheads"[.] — Steven Daly and Nalthaniel Wice, *alt.culture*, p. 59, 1995

touching *adjective*
used of playing cards adjacent in rank *US*
• — Peter O. Steiner, *Thursday Night Poker*, p. 420, 1996

touch man *noun*
a criminal who specialises in breaking into safes by manipulating the combinations until they open *US*
• If you really want to get good as a touch man, you got to study grease and explosives for a couple of years. — Red Rudensky, *The Gonif*, p. 80, 1970

touch off *verb*
to light a fire, especially if arson *US*
• [H]e buys five gallons of kerosene and touches it off again. — Vincent Patrick, *The Pope of Greenwich Village*, p. 108, 1979
• You touch off one of those joints with niggers in it, you just burn yourself one nigger, and you are on your own. — George V. Higgins, *The Rat on Fire*, p. 22–23, 1981

touch'ole *noun*
a cow's anus *CANADA*
• In [Quebec's Eastern Townships] a cow's anus is known as the "bung hole" or the "touch'ole". Charles Bury points out that the original meaning is the larger of the two holes in a drum top; the smaller one is the "air hole." — Lewis Poteet, *Talking Country*, p. 26–27, 1992

touch-on *noun*
an erection *UK*
• I'm half getting a touch-on from the way she looked at us[.] — Kevin Sampson, *Outlaws*, p. 239, 2001

touchous *adjective*
irritable, easily upset *TRINIDAD AND TOBAGO, 1956*
• — Frank A. Collymore, *Barbadian Dialect*, p. 113, 1965
• — Lise Winer, *Dictionary of the English/Creole of Trinidad & Tobago*, 2003

touch the dog's arse *noun*
car theft *UK: ENGLAND*
Prison slang for the initialism TDA (*t*aking and *d*riving *a*way).
• — David Rowan, *A Glossary for the 90s*, p. 41, 1998

touch up *verb*
1 to caress and fondle someone in a sexual manner *UK, 1903*
• I told him that Mr Stanton was touching me up during the night. — BBC TV, *Panorama*, 10th March 1997
2 to steal something *US*
• — Jim Crotty, *How to Talk American*, p. 179, 1997

touch wood
used superstitiously as a precaution against bad luck, spoken to accompany the action of touching wood (often humorously tapping your own *wooden* head); or to replace the need for the action; or by rote, without superstition, as a general way of saying 'with luck' *UK, 1908*
After a Christian belief in the benefit of touching the cross, hence the proverbial 'Touch wood, it's sure to come good'.
• They're risky, but we've never had one blow up on us yet, touch wood. — Kevin Sampson, *Outlaws*, p. 23, 2001
• I see a man who still, touch wood, has a wife who will, touch wood, return to him[.] — Andrew Holmes, *Sleb*, p. 157, 2002

touchy-feely *adjective*
overly sensitive, caring or emotional *US, 1968*
Originating in psycho-therapy, now generally used dismissively to describe every state between tactile and lecherous.
• What I was writing was somewhat touchy-feely. — *Jerry Maguire*, 1996
• [W]hat I wanted from sex – that I haven't been able to get across to Kurt – is more of that touchy-feely stuff. — Sally Cline, *Couples*, p. 132, 1998
• [T]hey've just got a bit touchy-feely with the girls and that[.] — Kevin Sampson, *Outlaws*, p. 113, 2001
• Oh, I'm touchy-feely? I take it you never saw Forces of Nature. — Kevin Smith, *Jay and Silent Bob Strike Back*, p. 100, 2001

touch you!
used for conveying surprise and admiration *US*
• You won the wet underwear contest at the bar last night? Well, touch you! — Jeff Fessler, *When Drag Is Not a Car Race*, p. 89, 1997

tough *verb*
to inject a drug into a vein on the underside of the tongue *US*
It is not particularly difficult to guess why this practice is so named.
• — Richard A. Spears, *The Slang and Jargon of Drugs and Drink*, p. 519, 1986

▸**tough it out; tough**
to bear hardship; to determinedly face up to a difficulty
• It would fade, he knew, as guilt always does. He just had to be strong and tough it out. — Christopher Brookmyre, *Boiling a Frog*, p. 321, 2000

tough!
'hard luck!'; unfair *UK, 1929*
• 'Mum sweats too, Xeens, when you pull one of your stunts.' 'Tough. Anyone who chooses to live with that bastard deserves to sweat.' — Jenny Pausacker, *What are ya?*, p. 54, 1987
• If Paul McCartney or the Gallaghers have got a problem with that, tough. — *The Guardian*, p. 2, 28th June 2004

tough; tuff
good, admirable *US, 1937*
• [T]uff – good; appealing; good looking; outstanding. — J. R. Friss, *A Dictionary of Teenage Slang (Mt. Diablo High)*, 1964
• — John Lawlor, *How to Talk Car*, p. 109, 1965
• [T]uff means cool, sharp – like a tuff-looking Mustang or a tuff record. — S.E. Hinton, *The Outsiders*, p. 14, 1967
• It's really tough lookin'. — *American Graffiti*, 1973
• "Out of sight," "too much," "tough," "trippy," "trick," or "unreal" – all were current [mid- to late 60s] superlatives. — Sean Hutchinson, *Crying Out Loud*, p. 177, 1988

tough biccies!
used for expressing a profound lack of sympathy for a bad turn of events *NEW ZEALAND*
• Tough biccies on me, I suppose, she said. — Stevan Eldred-Griff, *Of Ivory Accents*, p. 42, 1977

tough cheeko
used for expressing a lack of sympathy *US*
• — John D. Bell et al., *Loosely Speaking*, Appendix, 1969

tough darts
too bad *US*
• — *Current Slang*, p. 10, Spring 1968

tougher *noun*
in poker, an increased bet *US*
• — *American Speech*, p. 102, May 1951

tough guys *noun*
in craps, the proposition bets (bets that a number will be rolled in a pair) *US, 1983*
• — Thomas L. Clark, *The Dictionary of Gambling and Gaming*, p. 6, 1987

toughie; toughy *noun*
a tough person or situation *US, 1929*
- I couldn't think of a way because it was a real toughie[.] —Jim Thompson, *The Killer Inside*, p. 155, 1952
- The summer after I opened the bar, a 22-year-old toughy sat up front in the corner. —Helen P. Branson, *Gay Bar*, p. 45, 1957
- On one side of us were bikers and toughies wearing patches that said, Road Rats, Nightingale, Windsor and hangers on. —Jamie Mandelkau quoting Ken Kesey, *Buttons*, p. 152, 1971
- I knew I was a toughie. —Kevin Sampson, *Clubland*, p. 120, 2002

toughies *noun*
in craps, the proposition bets (bets that a number will be rolled in a pair) *US, 1983*
- —Thomas L. Clark, *The Dictionary of Gambling and Gaming*, p. 6, 1987

tough love *noun*
a mixture of compassion and strictness designed to affect change in destructive behaviour *US*
- There are now 12 "Tough Love" groups in Pennsylvania, notes York, whose recent appearance on a nationwide talk show has swamped him with mail. —*Washington Post*, p. D5, 24th February 1981
- The ex-wife of former baseball great Steve Garvey said Friday she will block any attempt by his new wife to impose "tough love" disciplinary measures on her two daughters. —*Los Angeles Times*, p. 2–10, 7th October 1989
- The empty [homeless] shelter coexists with the homeless people because of Montgomery County's "tough love" program, one of the nation's most far-reaching efforts to deal with the homeless. —*Washington Post*, p. B1, 2nd January 1995

tough nut; tough nut to crack; hard nut; hard nut to crack *noun*
someone who is difficult to deal with, especially one with a tendency to violence *US*
- The fairground boys were all toughnuts and always ready for a row at the best of times[.] —Dave Courtney, *Stop the Ride I Want to Get Off*, p. 35, 1999

tough shit
who cares?, so what? *US, 1934*
An unsymapthetic variation of 'tough luck': 'tough' (unfortunate, unpleasant) and 'shit' (an abstract form for 'luck').
- Box cracked his knuckles and smiled. "Tough shit. You are a part of it." —David Peace, *Nineteen Seventy-Four*, p. 213, 1999
- And if you don't like that, tough shit. —Lee Child, *The Visitor*, p. 172, 2000
- His attitude was, "Tough shit lady." —Lanre Fehintola, *Charlie Says...*, p. 13, 2000

tough shitski
used as a humorous embellishment of tough shit, or too bad *US*
A mock Slav or Russian suffix.
- Yeah, Jackie say weekend is one hunner, an if the trick don' stay all weekend, tough shitski, it sill cost him one hunner. —Robert Gover, *One Hundred Dollar Misunderstanding*, p. 95, 1961

tough titty; tough titties; tough tit
used for conveying a lack of sympathy with a difficult turn of events *US, 1934*
- We won't hit anything, and if we do, it'll be the other mug's fault, and some poor bastard's tough titty. —James T. Farrell, *Saturday Night*, p. 25, 1947
- "Tough titty." "Yeah?" I got up and walked around and rubbed my head where it was sore. I said, "You got me crying." —Thurston Scott, *Cure it with Honey*, p. 190–191, 1951
- "Even if you get away with it, you'll never be able to come home." "Well, so, tough titty. Anyway, home is where you feel at home." —Truman Capote, *Breakfast at Tiffany's*, p. 102, 1958
- —Anthony Romeo, *The Language of Gangs*, p. 23, 4th December 1962
- —Clarence Major, *Dictionary of Afro-American Slang*, p. 115, 1970
- [T]hey translated it into the absurd vision of the Sunday-school Superman, then wondered why they got locked up. Tough titty, boys. —Tom Robbins, *Another Roadside Attraction*, p. 269, 1971
- "Tough titty ..." Elijah started off, holding out both plams for the five-soul spank. —Odie Hawkins, *Chicago Hustle*, p. 150, 1977
- tough titty. You should have thought about rights when you lifted the stuff. —John Sayles, *Union Dues*, p. 322, 1977
- "You're lucky. My pal's in the nick because of him." "Tough titty. He never even paid me." —Anthony Masters, *Minder*, p. 166, 1984
- "It's a little too white," he replied. "Well ... tough titty." —Armistead Maupin, *Babycakes*, p. 112–113, 1984
- ROGER: Ya see, I ordered that special. MICKEY: Tough titty, it's mine now. —*Natural Born Killers*, 1994
- All they want to do is scurry back to their comfort zones, and if that includes an old boyfriend then tough titty. —Colin Butts, *Is Harry on the Boat?*, p. 106, 1997
- "If he doesn't like it, tough titties. I'm being defamed by a person who is a piece of shit." —*Miami New Times*, 18th December 2003

toup *noun*
a man's hairpiece *US*
- We'll get you a toup in Palm Springs. —Joseph Wambaugh, *The Secrets of Harry Bright*, p. 51, 1985
- —Anna Scotti and Paul Young, *Buzzwords*, p. 103, 1997

tour ball *noun*
in pinball, a ball that stays in play for a relatively long period without scoring many points *US*
- —Bobbye Claire Natkin and Steve Kirk, *All About Pinball*, p. 112, 1977

tour crud *noun*
in the language surrounding the Grateful Dead, a bacterial or viral infection that quickly spreads among those following the band on tour *US*
- —David Shenk and Steve Silberman, *Skeleton Key*, p. 155, 1994

tourist *noun*
1 in relation to a specified subject area, a person who takes a temporary interest *UK*
- It's essential that I show I'm not just some tourist on this issue[.] —Ben Elton, *High Society*, p. 135, 2002

2 a summer worker in Antarctica *ANTARCTICA, 1966*
- —Bernadette Hince, *The Antarctic Dictionary*, p. 355, 2000

Tourist Annie *noun*
the stereotypical female tourist in Port of Spain, dressed in what she perceives as traditional island clothing *TRINIDAD AND TOBAGO, 1971*
- —Lise Winer, *Dictionary of the English/Creole of Trinidad & Tobago*, 2003

touristas *noun*
▷ see: TURISTAS

tourist disc *noun*
in shuffleboard, a shot that passes through without hitting a target disc or discs *US*
- —Omero C. Catan, *Secrets of Shuffleboard Strategy*, p. 73, 1967: 'Glossary of terms'

tourist trap *noun*
a place that attracts and makes unreasonable profits from tourists *UK, 1939*
- Are Christmas markets charming traditional celebrations or horrifying tourist traps? —*The Guardian*, 20th September 2003

touristy *adjective*
full of tourists; designed or developed to appeal to tourists; characteristic of tourists *UK, 1906*
Often with derogatory connotations.
- One morning I got up at five o'clock to go down to the Tokyo fish market and watch them auction off the fish. It was sort of a touristy thing to do. —Thomas L. Friedman, *The Lexus and the Olive Tree*, p. 310–311, 2000
- The Lobster Pot was touristy. The sign was a giant plastic red lobster wearing a bib. —Augusten Burroughs, *Running With Scissors*, p. 287, 2002

tourniquet *noun*
an engagement or wedding ring *US*
- — *San Francisco Examiner*, p. 21, 12th December 1961: 'Colloquialisms for your murgatroid handcuffs'

tour rat *noun*
in the language surrounding the Grateful Dead, a fan who follows the band on tour at all costs *US*
- —David Shenk and Steve Silberman, *Skeleton Key*, p. 291, 1994

tout *noun*
1 an informer, especially one who works for the IRA *UK: NORTHERN IRELAND, 1979*
- Ray Bledsoe had been preparing to drop off payment for a tout named Proinas Deavey[.] —Chris Ryan, *The Watchman*, p. 3, 2001

2 in horse racing, someone who sells generally worthless advice with the promise of inside information bound to help bettors win *UK, 1865*
- —*American Speech*, p. 25, February 1955
- —David Bennet, *Know Your Bets*, p. 133, 2001

3 a horse racing enthusiast who closely watches workouts and is generally disliked by those on the inside of the sport *AUSTRALIA*
- —Ned Wallish, *The Truth Dictionary of Racing Slang*, p. 82, 1989

4 in a confidence swindle or sales scheme, an agent who for a commission locates potential victims *US*

- —Kathleen Odean, *High Steppers, Fallen Angels, and Lollipops*, p. 134, 1988

5 in a whe-whe lottery game, a person who records and collects bets, takes the bets to the banker and pays off winners *TRINIDAD AND TOBAGO, 1996*

- —Lise Winer, *Dictionary of the English/Creole of Trinidad & Tobago*, 2003

tow *verb*

▸ **I'll tow that one alongside for a bit before I bring it aboard**

among Nova Scotia fishermen, used for expressing doubt about the truth or reliability of an idea or project *CANADA*

- Both "tow that one alongside" and "hang her alongside" represent fishing metaphors applied to everyday discussions.—Lewis Poteet, *The South Shore Phrase Book*, p. 118, 1992

towel *noun*

▸ **chuck in the towel; throw in the towel; toss in the towel**

to admit or concede defeat *UK, 1915*

From boxing.

- You have to plug away, it's easy to chuck in the towel – or your spikes – but it's a lot harder to stick to fulfilling your potential.—*The Observer*, 5th November 2000
- A feeling that when we lose our bite we might as well throw in the towel?—*The Guardian*, 20th April 2002
- The inaugural Bruce Willis award for Refusing to Die goes to Solly Lew who, rather than toss in the towel, concocted the biggest boardroom brawl in the nation's history.—*The Australian*, 11th December 2002

towelhead; towel-head *noun*

an Arab; also a Sikh or other turban-wearer *US*

An offensive or derogatory term; from the traditional headwear of the various races or creeds.

- 'To understand us,' he adds, gently, 'remember three things. Don't fear us. Don't patronise us.' A mild grin. 'And don't call us towelheads.'—
- "Nuke Iran!" shouted the seething counter-demonstrators, "Towel-heads, go home!"—*Washington Post*, p. A6, 1st December 1979
- [F]logging metal tubes to the towel-heads[.]—Andrew Nickolds, *Back to Basics*, p. 26, 1994
- Adds one young man, passing by, 'If you're talking about misunderstandings, think how often you use "towelheads" as a funny phrase; it's in Hollywood films, we get it in the streets. But when was the last time you heard someone called "kike" or "nigger"?—*The Observer*, 7th October 2001
- In a series of racist statements that began when the World Trade Center collapsed, Roque announced his murderous plans and told a co-worker that he had been treated rudely at a gasoline station on University Drive by "a towel head or a rag head."—*The Arizona Republic*, p. 1A, 3rd September 2003

towel up *verb*

to beat someone up *AUSTRALIA, 1919*

- Can't let the side down, you know. I want to towel up these civvies. —J.E. MacDonnell, *Don't Gimme the Ships*, p. 113, 1960
- —Alexander Buzo, *Rooted*, p. 42, 1969

tower bird *noun*

in oil drilling, a worker on a derrick *US*

- —Jerry Robertson, *Oil Slanguage*, p. 123, 1954

Tower Bridge, tower *noun*

a refrigerator *UK*

Rhyming slang for 'fridge'.

- [C]ans of beer brought home from a party are refered to as prisoners and are "bunged in the tower".—Ray Puxley, *Cockney Rabbit*, 1992

Tower Hill *verb*

to kill *UK*

Rhyming slang, formed on an area of London.

- Slow down or we'll all be Tower Hilled.—Ray Puxley, *Fresh Rabbit*, 1998

towie *noun*

a tow-truck driver *AUSTRALIA, 1975*

- Traditionally, tow truck drivers benefit considerably from these 'extra incentives' (on top of towing fees) from 'associated' panel beaters whom towies 'recommend' to their customers.—*Sydney Morning Herald (Good Weekend)*, p. 19, 9th December 1995

town *noun*

1 London *UK, 1837*

Used by Charles Dickens, Oscar Wilde and present-day commuters.

2 city *US*

A coy term that harkens back.

- This is how you dress in this town you're in arts and entertainment. —Elmore Leonard, *Be Cool*, p. 7, 1999

▸ **go to town**

to make the utmost effort; to tackle something with zest and vigour *UK, 1933*

- [G]oing to town on making teaching in HE [higher education] a recognised and esteemed profession[.]—*The Guardian*, 19th February 2003

▸ **go to town on**

to attack excessively either verbally or physically *IRELAND*

- Last night I was down there he made me spar against your man whathisname...Healy. He went to town on me I'm not coddin' yeh boy.—Billy Roche, *The Wexford Trilogy (A Handful of Stars)*, p. 8, 1992

▸ **in town**

in horse racing, on major metropolitan tracks *AUSTRALIA*

The opposite of the 'bushes'.

- —Ned Wallish, *The Truth Dictionary of Racing Slang*, p. 82, 1989

▸ **out of town**

in jail or prison *US*

- —Ralph de Sola, *Crime Dictionary*, p. 108, 1982

town bike *noun*

a promiscuous female *AUSTRALIA, 1945*

Everybody has, it seems, 'taken a ride'.

- A sheila with a reputation as the town bike heard he was there, and went to the house, taking a bottle of cologne with her.—Kel Richards, *The Aussie Bible*, p. 28, 2003
- —Louis S. Leland, *A Personal Kiwi-Yankee Dictionary*, p. 105, 1984

town clown *noun*

in carnival usage, a local police officer *US*

- —Lindsay E. Smith and Bruce A. Walstad, *Sting Shift*, p. 117, 1989: 'Glossary'

town crier *noun*

a liar *UK*

Rhyming slang.

- —Ray Puxley, *Cockney Rabbit*, 1992

town dollars *noun*

in horse racing, money bet at a betting operation away from the track *US*

- —David W. Maurer, *Argot of the Racetrack*, p. 65, 1951

towner *noun*

a local resident *US*

Circus and carnival usage.

- —Joe McKennon, *Circus Lingo*, p. 95, 1980

town hall drapes *noun*

the foreskin of an uncircumcised penis *UK*

- —Paul Baker, *Polari*, p. 193, 2002

townie *noun*

1 a townsperson, contrasted with a visiting student or summer visitor *US, 1852*

- On the way they passed the townies, who glared at them balefully, but the girls chattered and giggled and did not even turn their heads. —Max Shulman, *Rally Round the Flag, Boys!*, p. 228, 1957
- "No women." Youngblood leaning back. "Townies, even?"—Richard Farina, *Been Down So Long*, p. 79, 1966
- They arrived in time to be scared by a group of drunken townies beating the bejabbers out of three or four hippy boys they'd caught in the lot.—Nicholas Von Hoffman, *We Are The People Our Parents Warned Us Against*, p. 67, 1967
- —Collin Baker et al., *College Undergraduate Slang Study Conducted at Brown University*, p. 213, 1968
- Sandy had intimated on the ferry ride home that night the townies tried to rape her.—Evan Hunter, *Last Summer*, p. 114, 1968
- Drugs and hard rock flooded Harvard Yard, spawned by a backwash of students, townies, and traveling hippies[.]—James Ellroy, *Because the Night*, p. 325, 1984
- I wasn't a rebel, but I walked a little on the wild side by dating a leather-clad townie named Pinky[.]—Elissa Stein and Kevin Leslie, *Chunks*, p. 28, 1997

2 any member of a subcultural urban adolescent grouping that seems to be defined by a hip-hop dress and jewellery sense *UK*

- [V]ariations on their type [chav], also known as Neds, Charvers and Townies, can be spotted across the UK. Their icons are Posh and Becks, Daniella Westbrook, singer Charlotte Church's former boyfriend Stephen Johnson and the pop star Brian Harvey.—*The Independent*, 1st February 2004

town punch *noun*
an extremely promiscious girl or woman *US*
• — *American Speech*, p. 68, Spring-Summer 1975: 'Razorback slang'

towns *noun*
the testicles *UK*
Rhyming slang on 'town hall' for **BALL(S)**; appears to originate in Liverpool.
• It was hairy from the age of nine, Moby's dick. Not just his towns and that, by the way. The whole package. — Kevin Sampson, *Outlaws*, p. 12, 2001

towns and cities *noun*
the female breasts *UK*
Rhyming slang for **TITTIE(S)**, recorded as obsolete by Julian Franklyn, *A Dictionary of Rhyming Slang*, 1960, but noted as a variant of **BRISTOL CITY** by Ray Puxley, *Cockney Rabbit*, 1992.

toxic *adjective*
1 of a situation, unhealthy, poisonous *UK*
Figurative application of the conventional sense.
• I was in a toxic relationship before I married Will. — Sally Cline, *Couples: Scene From the Inside*, p. 142, 1998
2 amazing, powerful *US*
• — *Washington Post Magazine*, p. 7, 30th August 1987: 'Say wha?'
• — Vann Wesson, *Generation X Field Guide and Lexicon*, p. 170, 1997

Toxic Hell *noun*
a Taco Bell™ restaurant (a Mexican fast-food chain in the US) *US*
• — Connie Eble (Editor), *UNC-CH Campus Slang*, p. 6, Spring 1993

toy *noun*
1 a can in which opium is stored, whether the can is tin, tinned iron or another metal; a small amount of opium *US, 1934*
• What you did was, you took a toy (a tin) of hop and shook it up with this medicine in a bottle and kept taking it every day. — Mezz Mezzrow, *Really the Blues*, p. 254, 1946
• All we found were some empty "toys" of opium. — Harry J. Anslinger, *The Murderers*, p. 37, 1961
• They used to sell in what the Chinese call "toys." — Jeremy Larner and Ralph Tefferteller, *The Addict in the Street*, p. 159, 1964
2 any object that is used for sexual stimulation during masturbation, foreplay, sexual intercourse or fetish-play *US*
• A significant part of the content of gay magazines is taken over by advertisements for "toys" – a revealing euphemism, evoking childhood, for implements of "torture": steel clamps, branding irons, whips, straps, even handcuffs. — John Rechy, *The Sexual Outlaw*, p. 255, 1977
• — Caroline Archer, *Tart Cards*, 2003
3 a desk with an attached bookcase *UK*
• — *The Felstedian*, December 1947
4 a computer system *US*
• — Eric S. Raymond, *The New Hacker's Dictionary*, p. 355, 1991
5 an inexperienced or incompetent graffiti artist *US*
• — *Los Angeles Times*, p. B10, 5th January 1990
6 in drag racing, a dragster (a car designed specifically and exclusively for drag racing) *US*
• — John Lawlor, *How to Talk Car*, p. 107, 1965
▷ **see: TAW**

toy boy *noun*
a younger male lover *UK, 1981*
• It's just as well I haven't brought my toyboy lover for a week of passionate thrashing around[.] — Cathy Kelly, *Someone Like You*, p. 41, 2002
• Thierry from Marseilles, with his pinched lips and toyboy secretary — Paula Larocque, *The Book on Writing*, p. 11, 2003

toy dolls *noun*
the testicles *UK: SCOTLAND*
A vaguely assonant euphemism.
• It's just as well I had my weans [children] afore I came into this job. Coz I sure as Christ wouldn't have the toy dolls for it afterwards. — Ian Pattison, *Rab C. Nesbitt*, 1988

Toyko Rose; tokyo *noun*
the nose *UK*
Rhyming slang, formed from the name given by the US administration and soldiers in World War 2 to the many female voices that broadcast Japanese propaganda, but especially associated with Iva Ikuko Toguri (b.1916), a Japanese-American, who actually broadcast under the name Orphan Ann.
• "Why do you keep calling me Sinex [a decongestant spray]?" "Because you get right up my Tokyo." — Ray Puxley, *Cockney Rabbit*, 1992

toy otter *noun*
in car repair, a Toyota car *US*
• — Lewis Poteet, *Car & Motorcyle Slang*, p. 205, 1992

toys *noun*
heroin *UK*
• — Mike Haskins, *Drugs*, p. 284, 2003

TP *noun*
1 a scene in a pornographic film or a photograph depicting a woman having simultaneous oral, vaginal and anal sex *US*
An abbreviation of 'triple penetration'.
• — Ana Loria, *1 2 3 Be A Porn Star!*, p. 167, 2000: 'Glossary of adult sex Industry terms'
2 a woman with large breasts and large buttocks *US*
A '*t*otal *p*ackage'.
• — Connie Eble (Editor), *UNC-CH Campus Slang*, p. 8, Spring 2000

TR *noun*
▷ **see: TEXAS RANGER**

TR-6 *noun*
an amphetamine *UK, 1998*
Possibly from a Triumph TR-6, the legendary sports car manufactured from the late 1960s to the mid-70s, used here as an allegory for **SPEED** (amphetamine).
• — Mike Haskins, *Drugs*, p. 279, 2003

tra
▷ **see: TARA**

trac *noun*
an intractable prisoner *AUSTRALIA, 1967*
• — Jim Ramsay, *Cop It Sweet!*, p. 91, 1977
• My meal's put on the floor, because the Tracs are the last to get fed. — Ray Denning, *Prison Diaries*, p. 42, 1978
• — Donald Catchlove, *Ray Denning My Life and Time*, p. 26, 1994

track *noun*
1 the street or area where prostitutes solicit customers *US*
• I might even steal her from scarface and put her back on the track tomorrow. — Iceberg Slim (Robert Beck), *Pimp*, p. 180, 1969
• Because of my concern for Jessie, I pulled Fatima up from the track before midnight. — Donald Goines, *Whoreson*, p. 62, 1972
2 the open road as used by itinerant travellers *AUSTRALIA, 1873*
Commonly in the phrase 'on the track'.
• And may Aussie not forget them when they're invalided back / Nor leave them poor and jobless for the dole queue or 'the track'. — Tip Kelaher, *The Digger Hat and other verses*, p. 30, 1942
• [H]e was one of these independent old bushmen, and began to talk about going on the track again. — Dymphna Cusack, *Picnic Races*, p. 68, 1962
• The frown was a part of his hard face, etched there by forty years of track living. — Wal Watkins, *Race the Lazy River*, p. 12, 1963
3 the course of an event; the course of time *AUSTRALIA, 1945*
• The visiting New Zealand Prime Minister, Mr Palmer, said yesterday the notion of a common currency between Australia and NZ was a "very long way down the track". — *Advertiser*, 3rd July 1990
4 an armoured personnel carrier, especially the M-113 *US*
• The tracks had flattened the jungle but not destroyed it. — Ronald J. Glasser, *365 Days*, p. 111, 1971
• CAPTAIN: I was an FO for the 25th. WILLARD: Tracks? — *Apocalypse Now*, 1979
• It was late in the afternoon and they were in the last of several APCs (Armored Personnel Carriers), lumbering steel-plated behemoths called "tracks." — Myra MacPherson, *Long Time Passing*, p. 21, 1984
5 a warder who carries contraband for prisoners *AUSTRALIA, 1950*
An earlier variant 'track-in' has been recorded from 1939.
• — Jim Ramsay, *Cop It Sweet!*, p. 91, 1977

▸ **the track**
the Savoy ballroom, New York *US*
A major night spot on Lenox Avenue between 140th and 141st Streets in New York from 1927 until the 50s.
• [S]pecific places are known by special nicknames – New York City as The Apple, Seventh Avenue as The Stroll, the Savoy Ballroom as The Track[.] — Mezz Mezzrow, *Really the Blues*, p. 221, 1946
• — Babs Gonzales, *Be-Bop Dictionary and History of its Famous Stars*, p. 9, 1949
• Whenever I didn't go to the track (Savoy) I'd go down to "Minton's." — Babs Gonzales, *I Paid My Dues*, p. 33, 1967

track *verb*
to inject drugs *UK*
- —Angela Devlin, *Prison Patter*, p. 116, 1996
- —Mike Haskins, *Drugs*, p. 290, 2003

track-basher *noun*
a specialist trainspotter who travels (and so 'collects') little-used sections of the rail network *UK*
- More worrying still than the description of the bashers [who 'collect' trains by travelling on them] was that of track-bashers, whose mission is to seek out obscure lengths of seldom-travelled track[.]—Iain Aitch, *A Fete Worse Than Death*, p. 55, 2003

tracked up *adjective*
scarred from regular intravenous drug injection *US*
- —Eugene Landy, *The Underground Dictionary*, p. 187, 1971

tracker *noun*
in the television and film industries, a low-level development executive *US*
- —Anna Scotti and Paul Young, *Buzzwords*, p. 11, 1997

trackie; tracky *noun*
a tracksuit *AUSTRALIA*
Also in the plural form 'trackies'.
- As I tugged on my trackie a P-plated Celica, shuddering with the bass of a Bruce Springsteen tape, cruised down the sandy track.—Kathy Lette, *Girls' Night Out*, p. 195, 1987
- [K]now whit Ah want fur ma Christmas? A Scotland trackie.—Michael Munro, *The Patter, Another Blast*, p. 74, 1988
- Two scally girls in tracky bottoms[.]—Niall Griffiths, *Kelly + Victor*, p. 41, 2002

trackie-bottoms *noun*
tracksuit trousers *UK: SCOTLAND*
- She's away oot in ma trackie bottoms an she never even asked us! —Michael Munro, *The Complete Patter*, p. 158, 1996

trackie daks *noun*
tracksuit trousers *AUSTRALIA, 2000*
- Sharon knows how to dress for elite sports, and chooses to 'team with the theme' by pairing her tennis skirt with matching trackie daks. —*TV Week*, p. 40, 1st November 2003

track lawyer *noun*
in horse racing, someone who constantly resorts to claims of technical rule violations, the pettier the better *US*
- —Dan Parker, *The ABC of Horse Racing*, p. 150, 1947

track record *noun*
the known facts about relevant history *US, 1951*
- Her track record in telling me the truth ain't something that would stand up in court if it came to it.—Danny King, *The Burglar Diaries*, p. 219, 2001

tracks *noun*
bruises, punctures and sores visible on the skin of an intravenous drug user *US*
- "For another thing, your boy's got tracks up and down his left arm-" "Tracks?" "That's the spot on an addict's arm where he keeps shoving the needle in," King told him.—Clarence Cooper Jr, *The Scene*, p. 121, 1960
- In summer, they alone wear long sleeves (to cover their "tracks" – collapsed veins and needle marks).—James Mills, *The Panic in Needle Park*, p. 17, 1966
- Old needle marks – tracks – where she had tried to hit her veins and missed.—Herbert Huncke, *The Evening Sun Turned Crimson*, p. 62, 1980

▸ across the tracks; wrong side of the tracks
the socially inferior area of town *US*
The railway often separated the better-off part of an American town from the poorer quarters. Duke Ellington's 'Across the Tracks Blues' dates to 1943.
- But the gentlemen friends who used to call / They never did seem to mind at all / They came to the wrong side of the tracks[.]—Marilyn Monroe and Jane Russell, *Two Little Girls from Little Rock*, 1953

▸ make tracks
to leave *US*
- —Lou Shelly, *Hepcats Jive Talk Dictionary*, p. 29, 1945
- —Hy Lit, *Hy Lit's Unbelievable Dictionary of Hip Words for Groovy People*, p. 27, 1968

traction *noun*
in confidence games, an amount of money used to begin an increasingly larger series of swindles *US*
- We gotta get us some traction.—Stephen J. Cannell, *King Con*, p. 32, 1997

traddie *noun*
a traditional jazz enthusiast *UK*
- —Tom Hibbert, *Rockspeak!*, p. 160, 1983

trade *noun*
1 a man, self-identified as heterosexual, who engages in active anal homosexual sex or passive oral homosexual sex but will not reciprocate *US, 1927*
- All her johns and trade were the same. They were all some kind of big shot.—Hubert Selby Jr, *Last Exit to Brooklyn*, p. 204, 1957
- —Donald Webster Cory and John P. LeRoy, *The Homosexual and His Society*, p. 266, 1963: 'A lexicon of homosexual slang'
- And I had never heard even the scores and queens, who would often in bitchiness claim that "today's trade is tomorrow's competition," say it about Chuck.—John Rechy, *City of Night*, p. 139, 1963
- —(Florida Legislative Investigation Committee (Johns Committee), *Homosexuality and Citizenship in Florida*, 1964: 'Glossary of homosexual terms and deviate acts'
- Homosexuals have a terse phrase to sum up this observation, "Today's trade is tomorrow's competition."—Antony James, *America's Homosexual Underground*, p. 17, 1965
- The humiliating position he would put himself in when some piece of trade spurned him because he was not able to lay on the requisite bread!—Gore Vidal, *Myra Breckinridge*, p. 97, 1968
- Never back down on trade agreements. ["Trade" are "tricks" who do not, as yet, consider themselves homosexual.]—Laud Humphreys, *Tea-room Trade*, p. 47, 1975

2 heterosexual or homosexual prostitution; customers of that prostitution, especially homosexual *UK, 1680*
Originally 'the trade'.
- —Angela Devlin, *Prison Patter*, p. 116, 1996
- You should see my trade.—Peter Sotos, *Index*, p. 5, 1996
- As she waited, several young men came scuttling up to her by turns, asking if she was looking for A Score [a drugs purchase] or for Some Trade.—James Hawes, *White Powder, Green Light*, p. 219, 2002

trade *verb*
▸ trade numbers
to bid for a job based on an estimated cost *US*
- You're building a house, maybe you'll need a plumber. I'd be glad to trade you numbers.—Robert Campbell, *Nibbled to Death by Ducks*, p. 110, 1989

▸ trade paint
to be involved in a car accident with another car *US*
- —Jim Crotty, *How to Talk American*, p. 165, 1997

trade queen *noun*
a homosexual man who prefers sex with a seemingly heterosexual man who consents to homosexual sex in the 'male' role, receiving orally or giving anally *US*
- Some of these "trade queens," because they're gay, think they're not as whole as other guys. They chase "straights" exclusively so they can put one over on them.—*Screw*, p. 18, 22nd June 1970

trade-rage *noun*
an outburst of enraged hostility within an business environment *UK*
- —Susie Dent, *The Language Report*, p. 17, 2003

trades *noun*
the trade journals of the US entertainment industry *US*
- "The trades?" Burt volunteered. "Daily Variety and The Hollywood Reporter?"—Dan Jenkins, *Life Its Ownself*, p. 172, 1984
- His worthless swine of an agent hadn't even called him about the role and there it was in yesterday's trades.—Joseph Wambaugh, *Finnegan's Week*, p. 2, 1993
- Now, I want to start this thing off big. The Trades, MTV, the works. —*Wayne's World 2*, 1993

tradesman's entrance; tradesman's *noun*
the anus, designated as an entry suitable for sex *UK*
In the grand houses of polite society the tradesman's entrance is traditionally round the back.
- When a woman looks you straight in the one-eye and says, "There's no way you're putting that near my tradesman's," she is really saying, "You're huge!"—*GQ*, p. 117, July 2001

trade up *verb*
to escape criminal prosecution or lessen the charges against you by providing the police with information about other criminals *US*
- We might be able to let you slide this time if you're cooperative. It's called trading up. Little fish for big fish.—Joseph Wambaugh, *The Glitter Dome*, p. 151, 1981

Tradies *noun*

a tradesmen's club *AUSTRALIA*

- He'd worn it nestling in his chest hair, up to the Tradies, and immediately got the worst cold of his life. —Kathy Lette, *Girls' Night Out*, p. 79, 1987

traditional discipline *noun*

corporal punishment, especially when used in a prostitute's advertising matter *UK*

- —Caroline Archer, *Tart Cards*, 2003

trad jazz; trad *noun*

*trad*itional jazz *UK, 1956*

- Take first the Misery Kid and his trad. drag. —Colin MacInnes, *Absolute Beginners*, 1959
- [T]here was so much more to music than either the trad jazz of their parents liking or the unbearably happy skiffle that was now sweeping the country. —Paolo Hewitt, *The Sharper Word*, p. 8, 1999

traf *verb*

to fart *AUSTRALIA*

Back slang.

- —Peter Furze, *Tailwinds*, p. 56, 1998

Trafalgar Square; trafalgar *noun*

a chair *UK*

Rhyming slang.

- —Ray Puxley, *Fresh Rabbit*, 1998

tragic *adjective*

inferior, pathetic, no good *UK, 1984*

Used, especially in a sporting context, as an opposite of **MAGIC** (excellent). 'Liverpool are magic... Everton are tragic' is legendarily ascribed to footballer Emlyn Hughes (1947–2004).

tragic magic *noun*

1 heroin *US*

- —Charles Shafer, *Folk Speech in Texas Prisons*, p. 216, 1990

2 crack cocaine dipped in phencyclidine, the recreational drug known as PCP or angel dust *UK, 1998*

- —Mike Haskins, *Drugs*, p. 293, 2003

trailer *noun*

in a striptease performance, the preliminary march across the stage that precedes the removal of any piece of clothing *US*

- —Don Wilmeth, *The Language of American Popular Entertainment*, p. 279, 1981

▸ **pull a trailer**

to possess large buttocks *US*

- — Surf Punks, *Oh No! Not Them Again! (liner notes)*, 1988

trailer *verb*

to pull a dragster onto its carrying trailer after it has been eliminated from an event *US*

A car that has lost is referred to as 'being trailered'.

- —Ed Radlauer, *Drag Racing Pix Dix*, p. 56, 1970

trail hog *noun*

a skier who is inconsiderate of other skiers, monopolising a narrow trail *US*

- — *American Speech*, p. 207, October 1963: 'The language of skiers'

trail marker *noun*

an unappetising piece of food, the identity of which is uncertain *US*

- Today's cuisine consisted of trail markers, sometimes called elephant turds, large lumps of blandly seasoned ground beef covered with a gray, tasteless gravy good only for making the things less dry. —Gerry Carroll, *North S*A*R*, p. 36, 1991

trail mix *noun*

a recreational drug cocktail of MDMA, the recreational drug best known as ecstasy, and Viagra™, a branded drug that enables a male erection *US*

trails *noun*

1 cocaine *UK*

- —Mike Haskins, *Drugs*, p. 281, 2003

2 while under the influence of LSD or another hallucinogen, sequences of repeating after-images trailing a moving object *US*

- Another frequent visual phenomenon is known as "trails." —Cam Cloud, *The Little Book of Acid*, p. 10, 1999

train *noun*

1 cocaine *US*

- —Peter Johnson, *Dictionary of Street Alcohol and Drug Terms*, p. 195, 1993

2 heroin *UK*

- —Mike Haskins, *Drugs*, p. 285, 2003

3 in prison, drugs *US*

To say 'the train has arrived' is to say that illegal drugs have arrived at the prison.

- —Ralph de Sola, *Crime Dictionary*, p. 153, 1982

4 a series of waves *US*

- —Grant W. Kuhns, *On Surfing*, p. 123, 1963

5 multiple orgasms *US*

- — *American Speech*, p. 20, Spring 1985: 'The language of singles bars'

▸ **pull a train; run a train**

to engage in serial sex with multiple partners, homosexual or heterosexual, usually consensual *US*

- They thought I was one of the guys who had pulled a train on their sister in the park the summer before. —Claude Brown, *Manchild in the Promised Land*, p. 16, 1965
- A girl who squeals on one of the outlaws or who deserts him for somebody wrong can expect to be "turned out," as they say, to "pull the Angel train." —Hunter S. Thompson, *Hell's Angels*, p. 194, 1966
- A gang of niggers ran a train on her down on Thirty-ninth Street. —Iceberg Slim (Robert Beck), *Trick Baby*, p. 173, 1969
- You get a girl like that who wants to pull a train, you'd think of her as basically hot, right? —Lawrence Block, *No Score [The Affairs of Chip Harrison Omnibus]*, p. 115, 1970
- Well last night they pulled a train on me. —Charles Whited, *Chiodo*, p. 162, 1973
- Peggy Reeves Sanday had never heard of "pulling train" until one of her students came to her office after missing class for two weeks. — *The Chronicle of Higher Education*, p. A3, 19 September 1990
- Once Moke and Smith let Nigger Bobo Johnson finish off the end of a train on an older girl, according to Churchy Mule. —Clarence Major, *All-Night Visitors*, p. 40, 1998

train *verb*

▸ **train Thomas at the terracotta; train Terrence at the terracotta**

(of a male) to urinate *AUSTRALIA*

- I was looking for the slash house. Felt like training Thomas at the terracotta in point of established fact. —Barry Humphries, *Bazza Pulls It Off!*, 1971

trainies *noun*

trainers, sports shoes *UK*

- Now to me, trainies equals Adidas. I don't even like Nikes, by the way. Not a Liverpool shoe. —Kevin Sampson, *Outlaws*, p. 13, 2001

training beer *noun*

low alcohol beer *CANADA*

- "Training beer" is named because of the implication that just as training aircraft is less hazardous to fly, training beer is less hazardous to drink. Sometimes called "near beer." —Tom Langeste, *Words on the Wing*, p. 281, 1995

training wheels *noun*

a learner's driving permit *US*

- —Porter Bibb, *CB Bible*, p. 107, 1976

train smash *noun*

1 fried or tinned tomatoes; tomato sauce *UK, 1941*

Military black humour; an especially unappetising example of visual imagery.

2 a hastily prepared savoury dish of tomatoes with onions, eggs, sausages, etc *AUSTRALIA*

- 'Train smash and bangers,' Splinter advised, and pushed towards him a plate on which two sausages wallowed in a sea of red stewed tomatoes. —J.E. MacDonnell, *Don't Gimme the Ships*, p. 69, 1960

trainspotter *noun*

anyone with a pedantic interest in and an obsessive knowledge of a specific topic *UK*

Genuine trainspotters, of the variety that stand on railway platforms, are the stereotypical arch-hobbyists.

- [F]etishism does have it fair share of train-spotters. —Kitty Churchill, *Thinking of England*, p. 58, 1995
- Ever-present night-club creatures, train spotters live a vampire like existence[.] —Ben Osborne, *The A-Z of Club Culture*, p. 294, 1999

train-surfing; urban surfing; roof-riding *verb*
riding illegally on the roof of a train (or car, bus, etc) for the thrills *US*
A ten-year craze from the early 1980s.
- Fuck am I doin'. Like I'm train surfin'. Out of control just hangin' on for the whole ride. — Nick Barlay, *Curvy Lovebox*, p. 127, 1997
- Never before had we witnessed an 'Urban Surfing' Wolf on the top of a Wolf Mobile!! "These waves are mine." — 80's Movies Gateway *(www.fast-rewind.com) Teen Wolf, 1985*, February 2002

train wreck *noun*
a horribly wounded soldier or casualty department patient *US*
Used by medical corpsmen in Vietnam.
- — *Journal of American Folklore*, p. 568 – 581, January – March 1978: 'The gomer'
- Train wrecks were cases suffering from multiple injuries, requiring immediate surgery: Head, chest, eye, face, stomach wounds and broken bones. — Gregory Clark, *Words of the Vietnam War*, p. 519, 1990

tram *noun*
▸ **wouldn't know if a tram was up you**
to be docilely unaware *AUSTRALIA*
- Those dozey bastards down at Oz House wouldn't know if a tram was up 'em till the bell rang. — *The Adventures of Barry McKenzie*, 1972
- You wouldn't know if a tram had run up your backside until the bloody people started getting out. — Derek Maitland, *Breaking Out*, p. 160, 1979
- — Barry Humphries, *The Traveller's Tool*, p. 30, 1985

trammie *noun*
a tram driver or conductor *AUSTRALIA, 1919*
- What unions? The seamen and the trammies? Long live Joe Stalin! — John Morrison, *Stories from the Waterfront*, p. 152, 1955
- — Barry Humphries, *A Nice Night's Entertainment*, p. 210, 1981

tramp *noun*
1 a promiscuous man or woman *US, 1922*
- You don't – you won't think I'm a tramp, will you? — Jim Thompson, *Savage Night*, p. 35, 1953
- We got to get rid of the stupid little tramp. I can't have any cops coming up here. — Harry J. Anslinger (US Commissioner of Narcotics), *The Murderers*, p. 175, 1961
- And everybody's had him. He's one of the Hollywood Boulevard tramps. — John Rechy, *City of Night*, p. 202, 1963
- Liz had been cheating on her. Liz was becoming a tramp. A little chippy. A puta. — Sheldon Lord, *The Third Way*, 1964
- A tramp is a girl who will have intercourse "with anybody," perhaps even without getting paid for it. — Christina and Richard Milner, *Black Players*, p. 41, 1972

2 a worker who moves from job to job, city to city *UK, 1808*
- The guy was an iron tramp, working on a permit. — Jim Thompson, *The Killer Inside*, p. 21, 1952

tramp's lagging *noun*
▷ see: BEGGAR'S LAGGING

Trance Canada *nickname*
the Trans-Canada highway *CANADA*
This nickname is either a reference to 'highway hypnosis' (on boring sections like the 401 from Montreal to Toronto) or to the 'spellbinding scenery' on such parts as the Rocky Mountain crossing or the Maritime sections.

tranced out; tranced *adjective*
in a state of extreme distraction *UK*
- Wicked man. I was well tranced. — Nick Barlay, *Curvy Lovebox*, p. 101, 1997
- You can play ['Gimme Shelter' by the Rolling Stones] to death, you can dance to it and you can play it in the dark, just get totally tranced out by it. — *Uncut*, p. 70, January 2002

trancey *adjective*
of trance music *UK*
- I just love standing on that little stage at the front and letting that little trancey stuff sear straight through me. — Ben Malbon, *Cool Places*, p. 275, 1998

Trane *nickname*
John Coltrane (1926 – 67) *US*
A jazz titan.
- Leaning over his record racks, he tried to figure out what his mood for music was ... something swift by Hubert Laws? Some funky 'Trane? — Donald Goines, *The Busting Out of an Ordinary Man*, p. 67, 1985

trank *noun*
1 any central nervous system depressant *US*
Variant spellings include 'tranq' and 'tranx'.
- Once my head is together I'll kick the speed and stabilize myself with tranks and downs[.] — Lawrence Block, *Chip Harrison Scores Again*, p. 191, 1971
- Tranks are the synthetics, like Miltown, Valium, etc. — Herbert Huncke, *Guilty of Everything*, p. 9, 1990
- You spend a couple of nights in The Joy (q.v.) and I promise you you'll need something a bit stronger than tranks to get you through the day. — Howard Paul, *The Joy*, p. 100, 1996
- Fuckin horse tranks or some such shite. — Niall Griffiths, *Kelly + Victor*, p. 149, 2002
- — Mike Haskins, *Drugs*, p. 283, 2003

2 a person who takes the excitement out of something; a killjoy *US*
A figurative use of 'a tranquillizer'.
- IT'S THE HIPPEST THING GOIN YOU TRANKS! — Lester Bangs, *Psychotic Reactions and Carburetor Dung*, p. 284, 1979

tranked *adjective*
sedated; under the influence of tranquillizers *US*
- Tranked out of her mind is more like it. — Carl Hiaasen, *Native Tongue*, p. 231, 1991

trannie; tranny *noun*
1 a transvestite *UK, 1984*
- The "Tranny Ball" is one of the inner city's social events, the extravagent camp costumes much enjoyed by the elderly and middle-aged working class[.] — *Sunday Mail*, 26th February 1989
- For trannies most of the danger is once you get into the car and they find out you aren't a woman, Neil said[.] — *The Vancouver Sun*, p. A6, 23rd March 1992
- I watched the trannies in the galley messing around with some lettuce in a bowl. — Kitty Churchill, *Thinking of England*, p. 60, 1995
- Unlike so many trannies, past and present, Candy, born James Lawrence Slattery, never spoofed womanhood or the ways in which pop culture filters and distorts it. — *San Francisco Chronicle*, p. E1, 28th July 1997

2 a transexual *US*
- And then, queer audiences seem to have only two speeds when it comes to transwriting: a) trannies belong and gosh do they have it difficult; b) trannies should take a hike and stop trying to hijack gay and lesbian efforts. — *Lambda Book Report*, p. 36, 30th September 1997
- Among them was the trannie's natural predator: a group of twenty-something men out for a good time. — *Nerve*, p. 41, May-June 2000

3 a transistor radio *UK, 1969*
- I'll take the old tranny along[.] — Mike Stott, *Soldiers Talking, Cleanly*, 1978
- — Louis S. Leland, *A Personal Kiwi-Yankee Dictionary*, p. 105, 1984

4 in a car or truck, a transmission *US*
- — John Edwards, *Auto Dictionary*, p. 174, 1993

5 any surface used for skating or foot-propelled scootering that is not totally horizontal *UK*
From 'transition'.
- — Ben Sharpe, *Scooter Crazy*, p. 121, 2000

trannie *adjective*
transexual *US*
- I have tried to make my workshops accessible to a variety of women and men, lesbian, bi, gay, straight, trannie, young, old, sex – positive, sex-neutral, sex-curious. — *The Village Voice*, 24th August 1999

trans *noun*
1 a car *US*
- — Bill Valentine, *Gang Intelligence Manual*, p. 111, 1995

2 *transport* *BAHAMAS*
- — John A. Holm, *Dictionary of Bahamian English*, p. 210, 1982

transcend *verb*
to smoke marijuana *US*
- — Connie Eble (Editor), *UNC-CH Campus Slang*, Fall 1974

transformer *noun*
1 a transexual *US*
- [T]hat was no problem because she shared it with three other Transformers who were as smooth and pure as chocolate statues. — William T. Vollman, *Whores for Gloria*, p. 55, 1991

2 a stuttering type of manipulation of a record to create a musical effect
- — J. Hoggarth, *How To Be a DJ*, p. 91, 2002

transfusion *noun*
a replenishment of cash *AUSTRALIA*
- — Ned Wallish, *The Truth Dictionary of Racing Slang*, p. 82, 1989

▸ **get a transfusion**
to fill a vehicle with petrol or diesel *US*

- — *Complete CB Slang Dictionary*, 1976
- — Peter Chippindale, *The British CB Book*, p. 155, 1981

transit *noun*

▸ **in transit**

experiencing the effects of LSD *US*

- — Eugene Landy, *The Underground Dictionary*, p. 109, 1971

transvesty; transvestie *noun*

a transvestite *US*

- — *Maledicta*, p. 174, Summer/Winter 1986–1987: 'Sexual slang: prostitutes, pedophiles, flagellators, transvestites, and necrophiles'

transy *noun*

a transexual *US*

- — *Maledicta*, p. 174, Summer/Winter 1986–1987: 'Sexual slang: prostitutes, pedophiles, flagellators, transvestites, and necrophiles'

trap *noun*

1 the mouth *UK, 1776*

- "Shut yer trap or I'll lay one on it!" Calico shouted angrily. — Chester Gould, *Dick Tracy Meets the Night Crawler*, p. 192, 1945
- I'm worried about you shooting off your big trap. — Irving Shulman, *The Amboy Dukes*, p. 114–115, 1947
- From now, Patterson resolved, I'll just keep my trap shut." — Clarence Cooper Jr, *The Scene*, p. 72, 1960
- Take your feet off my chair and shut your trap. — S.E. Hinton, *The Outsiders*, p. 21, 1967
- "Shut your trap," he screams at him and turns back to Murphy. — Odie Hawkins, *Ghetto Sketches*, p. 36, 1972
- Not if you guys keep your traps shut. — Oscar Zeta Acosta, *The Revolt of the Cockroach People*, p. 144, 1973
- Keep your trap shut, you'll be fine. — *The Full Monty*, 1997

2 a police officer *AUSTRALIA, 1812*

Now only historical.

- Chilla returned the Traps' fire, like Ned Kelly in the old Glenrowan Hotel[.] — Frank Hardy, *The Outcasts of Foolgarah*, p. 230, 1971
- Wendlan's a police pimp. He's talking to the traps. — Bob Ellis and Anne Brooksbank, *Mad Dog Morgan*, p. 15, 1976

3 a prostitute's earnings *US*

A shortened form of **TRAP MONEY**.

- After I'd been checking her trap for over a week she said she wanted to be my woman. — A.S. Jackson, *Gentleman Pimp*, p. 142, 1973

4 an electronic device that records the originating telephone number of all incoming calls *US*

A term and practice made obsolete with the advent of the 'caller ID' feature on telephones in the late 1990s.

- Course they never say who it is, but we had Southern Bell put a trap on the line. It tells what number they're calling from, so then they look up to see where the phone's located. — Elmore Leonard, *Maximum Bob*, p. 218, 1991

5 a hiding place for illegal drugs *US*

- — Ruth Bronsteen, *The Hippy's Handbook*, p. 16, 1967

6 a residence *US*

- We go up to her trap, and she remove the dry goods. — William Burroughs, *Naked Lunch*, p. 119, 1957

7 a timing light at the finish line of a drag race *US*

- After a very good run you might hear the announcer say, " ... and folks, he went through the traps at 256.86 miles per hour." — Ed Radlauer, *Drag Racing Pix Dix*, p. 56, 1970

8 in poker, a deceptive bet *US*

- — John Scarne, *Scarne's Guide to Modern Poker*, p. 292, 1979

trap *verb*

1 to have success attracting members of the opposite sex *UK*

Royal Navy slang.

- [M]ost of us trapped every time we went ashore. — Rick Jolly, *Jackspeak*, 1989

2 to install an electronic trap on a telephone line *US*

- Burdon says they've trapped her line and hung a wire. — Elmore Leonard, *Out of Sight*, p. 118, 1996

3 to land safely and accurately on an aircraft carrier *US*

- Since there were no other aircraft in the landing pattern, they both came in and trapped without problems. — Gerry Carroll, *North S*A*R*, p. 60, 1991

trap door *noun*

1 a scab under which a drug addict injects drugs *US*

- The trapdoor hid the fresh needle marks from the cops. — Joseph Wambaugh, *Fugitive Nights*, p. 35, 1992

2 a computing function that is easily performed but difficult to perform in the inverse *US*

Extremely useful in cryptography.

- — Eric S. Raymond, *The New Hacker's Dictionary*, p. 356, 1991

trapeze artist *noun*

a person engaged in simultaneous anal and oral sex *US*

- — *Maledicta*, p. 232, 1979: 'Kinks and queens: linguistic and cultural aspects of the terminology for gays'

trap money *noun*

1 a prostitute's gross earnings *US*

- She was still too young to have any apprehensions over spending her trap money. Ronald didn't put her on any quota so whatever she came home with she believed he would be happy with. — Donald Goines, *Daddy Cool*, p. 147, 1974
- Chantelle who ain't gonna pull short-ass trap money shit on me. — Wilton Barnhardt, *Emma Who Saved My Life*, p. 305, 1989

2 money containing tear gas and/or dye kept in a bank to be given to bank robbers *US*

An abbreviation of 'booby-trap money'.

trap off *verb*

to deceive or manipulate someone *US*

- — Gary K. Farlow, *Prison-ese*, p. 75, 2002

trapper *noun*

a person who can open envelopes and reseal them without a trace *US*

- — Ralph de Sola, *Crime Dictionary*, p. 153, 1982

trappy *adjective*

loud and boastful, possibly insulting *UK*

TRAP is 'mouth', therefore 'trappy' is **MOUTHY**.

- [L]ooking for someone to whack. Someone they recognised. Someone who got trappy. — Martin King and Martin Knight, *The Naughty Nineties*, p. 181, 1999

traps *noun*

1 drums and other items of percussion, collectively *US, 1903*

Musicians' slang.

- — Peter Clayton and Peter Gammond, *Jazz A-Z*, p. 239, 1986

2 the trapezius muscles connecting the neck and shoulder *US*

- — *American Speech*, p. 201, Fall 1984: 'The language of bodybuilding'

3 your usual haunts *AUSTRALIA, 1933*

- — John Wynnum, *Jiggin' in the Riggin'*, p. 124, 1965
- Got to go around my traps. — Wilda Moxham, *The Apprentice*, p. 163, 1969
- — Jim Ramsay, *Cop It Sweet!*, p. 91, 1977
- Well, all I can say is that I've knocked around the traps and I've lived in Australia man and boy for donkey's years[.] — Barry Humphries, *The Traveller's Tool*, p. 19, 1985

trap smasher *noun*

in lobstering, a severe storm *US*

- — Kendall Merriam, *The Illustrated Dictionary of Lobstering*, p. 90, 1978

trap two; trap number two *noun*

the anus *UK*

From greyhound racing.

- I smiled back wondering if she did like it up Trap Two from Jack. — David Peace, *Nineteen Seventy-Four*, p. 37, 1999

trash *noun*

1 contemptible people; a contemptible person *UK, 1604*

- I'm not sure whether she's trash or tramp. — *Sunday Times (South Africa)*, 25th April 2004

2 military decorations, awards and patches *US*

- — Gregory Clark, *Words of the Vietnam War*, p. 520, 1990

3 marijuana *US, 2001*

- — Simon Worman, *Joint Smoking Rules*, 2001

4 heroin *UK*

- — Mike Haskins, *Drugs*, p. 285, 2003

5 waves that collapse before they break, making poor surfing conditions *US*

- — Gary Fairmont R. Filosa II, *The Surfer's Almanac*, p. 197, 1977

trash *verb*

1 to destroy something *UK*

- So then let's trash the thing. — *Mallrats*, 1995
- SM: Does she ever complain to your mum about it? PHIL: Yeah. She starts getting real annoyed and that and starts saying "Oh well, that's

it now. New time I'm gonna trash your room" and all this lot. —Sara McNamee, *Cool Places*, p. 198, 1998
- Watching the bitch trash my car doesn't count as a date. —*Ten Things I Hate About You*, 1999

2 to criticise or malign someone or something *US, 1975*
- I even made two gorgeous lesbians wait outside while I trashed DeBella some more. —Howard Stern, *Miss America*, p. 297, 1995

3 to frighten someone *UK*
Market traders' term; directly from Romany.
- —Patrick O'Shaughnessy, *Market Traders' Slang*, 1979

trashed *adjective*
very drunk or drug-intoxicated *US*
- —*Current Slang*, p. 6, Fall 1966
- "I'm getting trashed." Isn't that what you're supposed to say at a party? —*Ten Things I Hate About You*, 1999
- [T]he proverbial "quiet drink" – which usually meant the inmates getting trashed. —Wayne Anthony, *Spanish Highs*, p. 60, 1999
- [S]laughtered, trashed, twatted, munted[.] —Stuart Walton, *Out of It*, cover, 2001

trash hand *noun*
in poker, an unplayable hand *US*
- —Edwin Silberstang, *Winning Poker for the Serious Player*, p. 220, 1992

trash hauler *noun*
during the Vietnam war, a cargo transport pilot *US*
- They wanted to clearly demonstrate to all the trash haulers (their term for transport pilots) who the kings of the roost were. —Harold Coyle, *Sword Point*, p. 101, 1988

trashing *noun*
looting from shops *US, 1975*
- The young call looting "trashing", and the word suggests what is happening. —*New Society*, 9th July 1981

trash time *noun*
a short jail sentence, especially one spent on a litter cleaning duty *US*
- Ask that fucking crook his opinion. He didn't even do trash time in a country-club joint. —Elmore Leonard, *Bandits*, p. 259, 1987

traumatic *adjective*
very exciting; excellent *US*
- —Connie Eble (Editor), *UNC-CH Campus Slang*, p. 5, Fall 1990

travel *verb*
▶ **travel on a tie pass**
to walk along a train track *US*
- —Ramon Adams, *The Language of the Railroader*, p. 163, 1977

travel agent *noun*
an LSD dealer *US*
A euphemism based on a **TRIP** metaphor.
- —Richard Alpert and Sidney Cohen, *LSD*, 1966

traveler *noun*
alcohol taken in a car on the way to a party or concert *US*
- —Ben Applebaum and Derrick Pittman, *Turd Ferguson & The Sausage Party*, p. 68, 2004

traveler's check *noun*
in poker or other gambling, a betting token that rolls across the table or floor *US*
From the insider slang term **CHECK** (a gambling token).
- —John Vorhaus, *The Big Book of Poker Slang*, p. 37, 1996

traveller's marrow *noun*
an erection brought on while travelling, especially while sleeping *UK*
- —Bob Young and Micky Moody, *The Language of Rock 'n' Roll*, p. 145, 1985

travelling agent *noun*
in a whe-whe lottery game, a person who collects and records bets, brings the bets and money to the banker and pays off winners *TRINIDAD AND TOBAGO, 1996*
- —Lise Winer, *Dictionary of the English/Creole of Trinidad & Tobago*, 2003

tray *noun*
a bunch of vials containing crack cocaine *US*
- —US Department of Justice, *Street Terms*, October 1994

tray *adjective*
three *UK*
A variation of **TREY**.
- —Paul Baker, *Polari*, p. 193, 2002

treacle *noun*
used as an endearment *UK*
Probably, simply, a simile for 'sweet'; possibly, rhyming slang on 'treacle tart' for 'sweetheart'.
- But look at this place, treacle. It's a dream house. —Garry Bushell, *The Face*, p. 118, 2001

treacle *verb*
to flatter someone; to behave in an obsequious manner *UK, 1943*
- Netta got short shrift from Sonia when she treacled up to offer congratulations[.] —Mary Sheepshanks, *Picking Up The Pieces*, p. 311, 1997

treacle tart; treacle *noun*
a fart *UK*
Rhyming slang.
- —Ray Puxley, *Fresh Rabbit*, 1998

tread *noun*
a shoe *UK*
- Look at him. Lying there. No home. No lolly. No brains. All he's got is a new pair of treads someone give him. —Clive Exton, *No Fixed Abode [Six Granada Plays]*, p. 125, 1959
- —*Current Slang*, p. 17, Summer 1969

treaders *noun*
shoes *US*
- —Clarence Major, *Dictionary of Afro-American Slang*, p. 116, 1970

treadhead *noun*
a member of a combat tank crew *US*
- Shit, don't they teach you treadheads anything at Fort Knox? —Harold Coyle, *Team Yankee*, p. 231, 1987
- "Rotor heads" are helicopter pilots and "tread heads" are tankers. —*Washington Times*, p. E1, 31st January 1991
- —*The Retired Officer Magazine*, p. 39, January 1993

treadly *noun*
a bicycle *AUSTRALIA*
- And whether they're cycling to work to beat the traffic, for fitness or simply for fun, they're the push behind a boom that has turned the rusty old treadly into a high-tech, multi-million dollar industry. —*Sydney Morning Herald*, p. Metro 1, 23rd February 1990

treash; treas *noun*
a term of affectionate address *UK*
A shortening of 'treasure'.
- —Paul Baker, *Polari*, p. 193, 2002

treasure *noun*
a highly valued person *UK, 1810*
Often applied to people who provide a service.
- Why, Ba, you have a treasure of a maid and no mistake. —Margaret Forster, *Lady's Maid*, p. 51, 1990

treasure chest *noun*
a brakevan (caboose) *US*
- —Ramon Adams, *The Language of the Railroader*, p. 163, 1977

Treasure Coast *noun*
that portion of Florida between Cape Kennedy and West Palm Beach *US*
After the sunken treasure believed to lie off the coast.
- —*New York Times*, p. 10–31, 20th June 1965

treasure hunt *noun*
1 the search in a gambling establishment or cardroom for someone from whom to borrow money *US*
- —David M. Hayano, *Poker Faces*, p. 188, 1982

2 the vagina; a fool; a despicable person *UK*
Rhyming slang for **CUNT**. Can be shortened to 'treasure'.
- The next time someone calls you a "treasure" make sure they're smiling. —Ray Puxley, *Fresh Rabbit*, 1998

treat *noun*
▶ **a treat**
beautifully, enjoyably, extremely *UK*
- My little Dolly looked a real treat. —John Peter Jones, *Feather Pluckers*, p. 19, 1964

▶ **do a treat; do you a treat**
to suit someone admirably *UK, 1904*
- And that'll do a treat for your father's tea!" —Benny Hill, *My Little Friend*, 1970s

▸ **do you a treat; do you up a treat**
to thrash you *UK*
An elaboration of **DO** (to beat) or **DO UP** (to beat up), possibly a deliberate pun on 'do you a treat' (to suit you very well).
- TIM: That rabbit's got a vicious streak. It's a killer! GALAHAD: Get stuffed. TIM: He'll do you up a treat mate! — *Mony Python & The Holy Grail*, 1975

treat *verb*
▸ **treat a J**
to add another drug or drugs to a marijuana cigarette *US*
- — Ernest L. Abel, *A Marijuana Dictionary*, p. 104, 1982

treat 'n' street *verb*
in a hospital's casualty department, to tend to a patient's needs and discharge him or her as swiftly as possible *UK*
- — Adam T. Fox, St Mary's Hospital, London, 10th October 2002

treble chance *noun*
a dance *UK*
Rhyming slang.
- — Ray Puxley, *Cockney Rabbit*, 1992

tree; trees *noun*
marijuana *US*
An exaggerated **BUSH**.
- The Lost Boys, yeah, that's who I be's with, / That's who I runs with, who I smoke trees with. — Lost Boys *Jeeps, Lex Coups, Bimas & Benz*, 1995
- All the real smokers know / They ain't passin nuttin but dope indeed... / Real trees... / Chronic leaves — Dr Dre, *Xplosive*, 2001
- — Connie Eble (Editor), *UNC-CH Campus Slang*, p. 11, Fall 2001
- — Mike Haskins, *Drugs*, p. 289, 2003

▸ **out of your tree**
drunk or drug-intoxicated *IRELAND*
- I think she's ou' of her tree half the time. -Go 'way, said Jimmy Sr. -Is tha' righ'? Drink? -No, said Jimmy Jr. -I don't think so. -Tippex, said Darren. — Roddy Doyle, *The Van*, p. 101, 1991

▸ **out of your tree; off your tree**
crazed; mentally deranged *US, 1966*
- Lendon. As in – You're off y'tree Nood. Off y'... I mean lend's gonna pull pigs [police] from all over[.] — Nick Barlay, *Curvy Lovebox*, p. 55, 1997
- Everybody out of their league [class], their tree, whatever. Everybody fucked. — David Peace, *Nineteen Seventy-Four*, p. 288, 1999
- I've seen people shot, shagged, smashed and stabbed; off their trolleys, out of their trees, on their knees, off their tits — Dave Courtney, *Raving Lunacy*, p. 5, 2000

▸ **out yer tree**
drunk *UK*
- — *e-cyclopaedia*, 20th March 2002

tree-eater *noun*
a member of the US Special Service Forces *US*
Because of the constant survival training the Special Forces undergo.
- — *The Retired Officer Magazine*, p. 39, January 1993

tree-fucker *noun*
a stereotyped enviromentalist *UK*
A variant of **TREE-HUGGER**.
- I don't want to get all cosmic-hippy-trippy-tree-fucker about it but there is something extra wicked about dancing outside. — Dave Courtney, *Raving Lunacy*, p. 135, 2000

tree-hugger *noun*
an environmental activist *US, 1977*
- — Connie Eble (Editor), *UNC-CH Campus Slang*, p. 8, Spring 1990
- I'm no tree-hugger, but I'm not so environmentally unconscious that I'd pour shit like that down the drain[.] — *Lightning on the Sun*, p. 321, 2001

tree-hugging *adjective*
environmentally aware; active in environmental protection *US*
- [N]early turned me into a tree-hugging hippy on the spot. — Dave Courtney, *Stop the Ride I Want to Get Off*, p. 304, 1999
- You want to hang out with tree-hugging twats who think mankind is the skin-disease of the earth? — James Hawes, *Dead Long Enough*, p. 20, 2000

tree-jumper *noun*
a chronic sex offender *US*
- "And one day so it's 'Mike Tyson, you (explective deleted) tree jumper," he said. And I didn't know what a tree jumper was. I thought it meant like I was a great athlete or something, jumping out of trees, and I was, "What's a tree jumper?" — *Associated Press*, 14th June 1992
- — Gary K. Farlow, *Prison-ese*, p. 75, 2002

trees *noun*
broccoli *US*
- — John D. Bell et al., *Loosely Speaking*, p. 19, 1966

▸ **put in the trees**
to overcharge someone *US*
- — *American Speech*, p. 309–310, Winter 1980: 'More jargon of car salesmen'

treetop level and all engines out *adjective*
near death *US*
- — Sally Williams, *"Strong" Words*, p. 163, 1994

tree up *verb*
when parachuting, to land and become entangled in a tree *US*
- — *American Speech*, p. 158–160, May 1959: 'Smokejumping words'

treeware *noun*
books, magazines, newspapers, etc, as opposed to all alternate forms of providing such texts *US, 1997*
Computer hacker slang, deriding the fact that paper is made from pulped wood.
- New dictionary is no mere book – it's 'treeware' — *Daily Telegraph*, 26th June 2003

Trekker *noun*
a zealous fan of *Star Trek* *US*
Preferred by the fans over the term 'Trekkie'.
- Star Trek Lives: Trekker Slang — *American Speech*, p. 53, Spring 1978

Trekkie *noun*
a devoted fan of *Star Trek*, the original science fiction television programme (which started in 1966) and subsequent films and spin-offs *US*
- — Connie Eble (Editor), *UNC-CH Campus Slang*, p. 4, April 1978
- Those Star Trek conventions should be outlawed and all Trekkies sterilized. — Howard Stern, *Miss America*, p. 256, 1995
- The message to all Trekkies is that it's not real, it's only a movie. Please beam them up. — Alon Shulman, *The Style Bible*, p. 252, 1999

trekky *adjective*
in the style of *Star Trek*, the cult science fiction television programme first seen in 1966 *UK*
- There's a space theme, so don your silver hotpants or Trekky tops. — *Mixmag*, p. 137, December 2001

trenches *noun*
▸ **in the trenches**
involved in the hard, dirty aspect of an enterprise *US, 1970*
- Meanwhile, I'm the guy in the trenches. Fuckin' bosses, they think it's a fuckin' free lunch out here. — *Casino*, 1995

trendy *noun*
1 a follower of fashion *UK, 1968*
- Thur were nae rats in this scheme. Not till youse trendies moved in! — Ian Pattison, *Rab C. Nesbitt*, 1988

2 a youth defined by a skateboarders' particular sense of fashion *UK*
- My friends and I are "trendies". We wear American-type skateboarder' clothes, hoodies and baggy trousers. — *The Guardian*, p. 9, 27th February 2002

trendy *adjective*
fashionable *UK, 1962*
- Indian clothes and jewelry are trendy right now[.] — Rosalind Wiseman, *Queen Bees and Wannabes*, p. 89, 2002

tres *noun*
in betting, odds of 3–1 *UK*
A variation of **TREY**.
- — John McCririck, *John McCririck's World of Betting*, p. 112, 1991

tres *adverb*
very *UK*
Directly from the French.
- He laughs, tres amused by his own little joke. — J.J. Connolly, *Layer Cake*, p. 111, 2000

trev *nickname*
a person whose prime characteristic is vanity; a person who wears nothing but designer-label clothes *UK*
Presumably derives from an unknown but especially well-groomed Trevor. Usually derogatory.
- — Susie Dent, *The Language Report*, p. 78, 2003

trey *noun*

1 three *UK, 1859*

- Lay a trey on me, ole man. — Mezz Mezzrow, *Really the Blues*, p. 216, 1946
- "What'll happen after I do that trey?" he asked MacMahon. — Clarence Cooper Jr, *The Scene*, p. 184, 1960
- He croaked, "Maybe his girls are humping on 'Four Trey.' — Iceberg Slim (Robert Beck), *Mama Black Widow*, p. 218, 1969
- After calling me three more M.F.'s, he said he'd meet her at a trey in the morning. — Babs Gonzales, *Movin' On Down De Line*, p. 22, 1975
- [Y]ou might like to count to ten in Polari: una, duey, trey, quater, chicker, sey, setter, otto, nobber, dacha. — Michael Quinion, *World Wide Words*, 1996

2 a prison sentence of three years *US*

- Doing a deuce or a trey in the joint didn't seem like much of a jolt when I was thirty, but it seems like one hell of a lot at this stage in life. — Gerald Petievich, *To Die in Beverly Hills*, p. 223, 1983

3 a threepence *AUSTRALIA, 1896*

Shortening of **TREY BIT**.

- — Jim Ramsay, *Cop It Sweet!*, p. 91, 1977

4 three dollars' worth of a drug *US*

- Often the junkie pusher will deal "nickel bags" at $5 each, as well as $3 "treys." — James Mills, *The Panic in Needle Park*, p. 20, 1966

trey bit *noun*

a threepence *AUSTRALIA, 1898*

- TRAY BIT – Threepenny piece. — Gilbert H. Lawson, *A Dictionary of Australian Words and Terms*, 1924
- He would sell his own mother for a trey bit. — Vince Kelly, *The Bogeyman*, p. 100, 1956

trey eight *noun*

a .38 calibre handgun *US*

- Trey eight – .38 caliber gun. — *St. Louis Post-Dispatch*, p. 1A, 2nd June 1992
- — Ann Lawson, *Kids & Gangs*, p. 56, 1994: 'Common African-American gang slang/phrases'

treyer *noun*

three years or three dollars *US*

- — Hyman E. Goldin et al., *Dictionary of American Underworld Lingo*, p. 226, 1950

trial-size *adjective*

used of a person, very short *US*

- — Connie Eble (Editor), *UNC-CH Campus Slang*, p. 10, Fall 1988

triantelope *noun*

the Australian tarantula, any of various large spiders of the genus *Isopoda* *AUSTRALIA, 1845*

Seems to be a blend of 'tarantula' and 'antelope'.

- — Barbara Baynton, *Human Toll*, p. 218, 1907
- Looks like one of those big hairy triantelopes that crawl onto our mosquito nets. — Dymphna Cusack, *Black Lightning*, p. 78, 1964

triantiwontigongolope; triantiwontigong *noun*

a mythical insect or monster; also, a name for something unknown *AUSTRALIA*

From a poem for children about a non-existent creature so named by C.J. Dennis in *A Book for Kids*, 1921.

- Sometimes when he asked what something was they would say: 'It's a triantiwontigong.' — Randolph Stow, *The Merry-Go-Round in the Sea*, p. 6, 1965

Tribe *nickname*

the Cleveland Indians professional baseball team *US*

References to native American Indians in US professional sports teams (Indians, Braves, Redskins) persist in an era when many other stereotypes have withered.

- — Parke Cummings, *Dictionary of Baseball*, p. 58, 1950
- Riske, 27, had the best year of any Tribe reliever last season. — *Plain Dealer (Cleveland, Ohio)*, p. D3, 13th January 2004

Tri-Chevy *noun*

a Chevrolet car or truck manufactured in 1955, 1956 or 1957 *US*

- — John Edwards, *Auto Dictionary*, p. 175, 1993

trick *noun*

1 a prostitute's customer *US, 1925*

- They had to keep an eye on the cops all the time, because they weren't allow to call the tricks like the girls in Storyville. — Louis Armstrong, *Satchmo: My Life in New Orleans*, p. 95, 1954
- If Ready has killed some trick he was steering to Reba's the chair's too good for him — Chester Himes, *The Real Cool Killers*, p. 64, 1959
- You're out here to pull them tricks and acop that bread, dig? — Clarence Cooper Jr, *The Scene*, p. 10, 1960
- So I walked around the room and I seen this trick / and we went upstarirs and we started real soon. — Bruce Jackson, *Get Your Ass in the Water and Swim Like Me*, p. 47, 1965
- Rita and Flossie don't exactly rust but they don't look so good to the tricks seen them twenty- thirty time as they do to tricks seeing them the first time. — Sara Harris, *The Lords of Hell*, p. 14, 1967
- She told him how she'd met this trick and seeing he looked right, had used her knockout drops. — Babs Gonzales, *I Paid My Dues*, p. 97, 1967
- I watched the whores stopping tricks, and I watched where the trick would park his car[.] — A.S. Jackson, *Gentleman Pimp*, p. 22, 1973
- No Jean or John this whore couldn't con / 'Cause that trick was never born. — Dennis Wepman et al., *The Life*, p. 81, 1976
- Look, I got there. He was a trick just like any other for all I know. — *48 Hours*, 1982
- Russell recognised some of the pavement princesses, whose pitch this normally was [...] livid at missing their regular johns and champagne tricks on their way back from the City. — Greg Williams, *Diamond Geezers*, p. 203, 1997
- This must be what her tricks, her subs [sexual submissives], hear as she approaches them. — Niall Griffiths, *Kelly + Victor*, p. 204, 2002

2 an act of sex between a prostitute and customer *US, 1926*

- The girls explained to me that they got eighty cents a trick, one payment for each metal check – "turning a trick" was how they described one session with a john. — Mezz Mezzrow, *Really the Blues*, p. 23, 1946
- From this croaker up on 76th Street. He used to write for me, you know, scripts, prescriptions. I turned a trick with him. — James Mills, *The Panic in Needle Park*, p. 91, 1966
- Pimps take cops to dinner with free tricks. — *The Digger Papers*, p. 14, August 1968
- I started working as a stripper in a club in Washington and turned a few tricks on the side. — Susan Hall, *Gentleman of Leisure*, p. 59, 1972

3 a short-term homosexual sexual partner, not paying *US*

- — Donald Webster Cory and John P. LeRoy, *The Homosexual and His Society*, p. 266, 1963: 'A lexicon of homosexual slang'
- Martin – the blond trick I introduced you to before you went in there — John Francis Hunter, *The Gay Insider*, p. 103, 1971
- — Bruce Rodgers, *The Queens' Vernacular*, p. 200, 1972
- I looked like a bull dyke, or a trick of one, with handcuffs, a leather jacket, metal belts, and levi 501's, so I would try to method act. — Jennifer Blowdryer, *White Trash Debutante*, p. 56, 1997

4 a casual sexual partner *US*

- If I don't get arrested, my trick announces upon departure that he's been exposed to hepatitis! — Mart Crowley, *The Boys in the Band*, p. 163, 1968

5 a prostitute *UK*

- He found a sly-eyed trick with bleached, thinning hair. — Kevin Sampson, *Powder*, p. 60–61, 1999

6 any dupe *US*

- We'd shoot among ourselves, 'cause the tricks wasn't comin' in. — Henry Williamson, *Hustler!*, p. 79, 1965
- [W]e done warned this dude six or seven times about shootin' that turn-down shot on us, but he still takes us for tricks. — Donald Goines, *Cry Revenge*, p. 11, 1974

7 a swindle *UK, 1865*

Far less common in this sense, but not unheard.

- Since work was out, so also was the grift. He wouldn't dare turn a trick. — Jim Thompson, *The Grifters*, p. 124, 1963

8 on the railways, a work shift *US*

- — Norman Carlisle, *The Modern Wonder Book of Trains and Railroading*, p. 269, 1946

▸ **can't take a trick**

to be consistently unsuccessful *AUSTRALIA, 1944*

From card games.

▸ **do the trick**

to achieve your object *UK, 1812*

- After all, a super luxurious (not necessarily expensive) moisturiser will do the trick just as well as any anti-ageing guff[.] — *The Guardian*, 31st May 2003

trick *verb*

1 to engage in sex with a paying customer, usually in an expeditious fashion *US*

- Don't tell me you made it all tricking and you're saving it for your old age. — Clarence Cooper Jr, *The Scene*, p. 206, 1960
- He knew that she was Red Shirt's woman, and knowing Red Shirt, automatically assumed that she was tricking[.] — Nathan Heard, *Howard Street*, p. 83, 1968
- Ever since she had started coming over and tricking with the men in the numbers house, she'd feared something like this would happen. — Donald Goines, *El Dorado Red*, p. 101, 1974
- And be there waiting to trick with old Satan / Man, I had me a money-making whore. — Dennis Wepman et al., *The Life*, p. 83, 1976

- Vickie had tricked with his father at a convention and was embarrassed and ashamed when Andre invited her home to meet his people and they were introduced. —Herbert Huncke, *The Evening Sun Turned Crimson*, p. 53, 1980
- He didn't know if they tricked during the evening then took an all-nighter. —Robert Campbell, *Alice in La-La Land*, p. 263, 1987
- The first time Phyllis went out tricking she wasn't nervous because she thought she was just going along with Shawna to watch and learn. —William T. Vollman, *Whores for Gloria*, p. 54, 1991

2 to have sex with a short-term partner, without emotion or money passed *US*

- It seems to me that the first time we tricked we met in a gay bar on Third Avenue during your junior year. —Mart Crowley, *The Boys in the Band*, p. 37, 1968
- I haven't tricked like that for about a hundred years[.] —Armistead Maupin, *Maybe the Moon*, p. 76, 1992

trick *adjective*

1 excellent *US*

- "Out of sight," "too much," "tough," "trippy," "trick," or "unreal" – were all current [late 1960s] superlatives. Each would flower for a while and then fall to something a little groovier – up to date on the tongues of those who knew. —Sean Hutchinson, *Crying Out Loud*, p. 177, 1988

2 in hot rodding and drag racing, abnormal, unusual *US*

- —Lyle K. Engel, *The Complete Book of Fuel and Gas Dragsters*, p. 154, 1968

trickact *verb*

to play about mischievously *IRELAND*

- Hey cut out that trickactin' there now. —Billy Roche, *The Wexford Trilogy (A Handful of Stars)*, p. 5, 1992

trick baby *noun*

the offspring of a prostitute and an unknown customer, often of mixed race *US*

- I said, "Goddamnit, Mr. Murray, I was no trick baby. My mother was no whore. She married a white man." —Iceberg Slim (Robert Beck), *Trick Baby*, p. 15, 1969
- "Looks like you done went and got you a trick baby, honey." —Donald Goines, *Whoreson*, p. 9, 1972

trick bag *noun*

1 a bag used by a prostitute to carry tools of the trade *US*

A search warrant issued by the Sausalito (California) Police Department in its investigation of a massage parlour/brothel defines a trick bag as 'a large woman's handbag, which will generally enclose the following items which are used in the practice of prostitution: clothing, especially a change of undergarments such as panties, bras, camisoles and negligees, wet wipes, paper tissues, Vaseline and personal lubricants, bottles of mouth wash, rubbing alcohol, baby oil, various kinds and numbers of condoms, douches and other forms of feminine hygiene, and various cosmetics, small hand towels which are normally used in the practice of prostitution to wipe the ejaculatory excretions from the bodies of the prostitute and the customers[.]'.

2 a dilemma with no clear solution *US*

- —William K. Bentley and James M. Corbett, *Prison Slang*, p. 47, 1992

trick book *noun*

a prostitute's list of customers *US*

- You may work a trick book. You may work that up yourself or you may buy it. —Bruce Jackson, *In the Life*, p. 190, 1972
- Female corpse found in bushes off Highway 1 near El Capitan Beach had pocket litter and trick book with L.A. area phone numbers. —Gerald Petievich, *To Die in Beverly Hills*, p. 139, 1983
- Even Missy Moonbeam's trick book was pathetic. —Joseph Wambaugh, *The Delta Star*, p. 78, 1983

trick bunk *noun*

in prison, a bed used for sexual encounters *US*

- So that's what the dorm tender meant warning Joe that he'd been assigned the trick bunk. Of course – it was the furthest from the door, least visible to passing guards, best suited for the quickie clandestine cigarette date. —Seth Morgan, *Homeboy*, p. 199, 1990

trick-cyclist *noun*

a psychiatrist *UK, 1930*

Originally military.

- Is there a trick-cyclist in the club? —Charles Raven, *Underworld Nights*, p. 10, 1956
- As I walked in the trickcyclist told me to sit down —Frank Norman, *Bang To Rights*, p. 29, 1958
- "They've got trick cyclists on to him," Watt said. —Troy Kennedy Martin, *Z Cars*, p. 18, 1962
- Get some trick cyclist to say I done me nut[.] —John Peter Jones, *Feather Pluckers*, p. 60, 1964
- Jessica pulls her doll to bits. "AhahaH!" says her trick-cyclist. —Viv Stanshall, *Possibly an Armchair and Fresh-Faced Boys*, 1981

trick day *noun*

an agreed time when homosexuals in long-term relationships may have sex outside the relationship *US*

- —Florida Legislative Investigation Committee (Johns Committee), *Homosexuality and Citizenship in Florida*, 1964: 'Glossary of homosexual terms and deviate acts'
- —Dale Gordon, *The Dominion Sex Dictionary*, p. 158, 1967

trick dress; trick suit *noun*

a dress that a prostitute can remove easily *US*

- [S]he hurried to Burbank to get her 'trick suit," which she explained was a dress worn by prostitutes to facilitate their work. —Ed Reid and Ovid Demaris, *The Green Felt Jungle*, p. 100, 1963
- —*Maledicta*, p. 150, Summer/Winter 1986–1987: 'Sexual slang: prostitutes, pedophiles, flagellators, transvestites, and necrophiles'

trick flick *noun*

a pornographic film, usually homosexual *US*

- —*American Speech*, p. 59, Spring-Summer 1970: 'Homosexual slang'

trick house *noun*

a house or apartment where prostitutes take their customers for sex *US*

- I met a girl who was working the streets and she took us to a trick house where we could turn our tricks for a dollar. —Donald Goines, *Whoreson*, p. 74, 1972
- She had a good round-eye, and that's no lie / How the trickhouse door would swing! —Dennis Wepman et al., *The Life*, p. 83, 1976

Trickidadian *noun*

a Trinidadian *TRINIDAD AND TOBAGO, 1982*

A term that can be used with admiration or as disparagement.

- —Lise Winer, *Dictionary of the English/Creole of Trinidad & Tobago*, 2003

trick name *noun*

a prostitute's business alias *US*

- Trick names often fall into one of three categories: (1) words associated with pleasure (Joy, Felicia, etc.) (2) words associated with luxurious things that the john can eat or drink up (Candy, Brandi, etc.) (3) names that sound "aristocratic" or "fancy"[.] —William T. Vollman, *Whores for Gloria*, p. 145, 1991

trick off *verb*

to perform oral sex on a man *US*

- —Anna Scotti and Paul Young, *Buzzwords*, p. 32, 1997

trick out *verb*

to decorate something, or dress somebody, elaborately *US, 1727*

- Curtis had a big tricked-out scoot, a Harley, he kept in the house. —Elmore Leonard, *Split Images*, p. 48, 1981
- The waitresses, all older women, come to work tricked out head to toe in childishly preposterous uniforms. —Larry Heinemann, *Paco's Story*, p. 105, 1986

trick pad *noun*

an apartment or room which a prostitute uses only for sex with customers *US*

- Vice officeres arrest them when they tail them to their trick pad[.] —Joseph Wambaugh, *The New Centurions*, p. 71, 1970
- —William T. Vollman, *Whores for Gloria*, p. 139, 1991

trick pants *noun*

pants that are easily removed, favoured by prostitutes *US*

- A man in trick pants is still a man. —Malcolm Braly, *On the Yard*, p. 88, 1967

trick rig *noun*

a sexually attractive body *US*

- —Vann Wesson, *Generation X Field Guide and Lexicon*, p. 172, 1997

trick room *noun*

a room where a prostitute takes customers *US*

- Jody and Larry had installed a two-way mirror between two rooms. One of the rooms was a trick room. The other had been converted into a voyeurs' lounge. —Vance Donovan, *High Rider*, p. 125, 1969
- And so I opened a window in one of the trick rooms and went over to the other house across the way on the roof. —Bruce Jackson, *In the Life*, p. 198–199, 1972
- I was using a Toyota Celica as a trick room out in the parking lot with a truckdriver john[.] —Richard Condon, *Prizzi's Honor*, p. 170, 1982

tricks *noun*

▸ on the tricks

working as a prostitute *US*

- As soon as I walked into Rima's place I knew she was on the tricks. —Clancy Sigal, *Going Away*, p. 363, 1961

trick seat *noun*

the passenger seat on a motorcyle *US*

- Like I had a cock bike with a trick seat on it! —Joseph Wambaugh, *Lines and Shadows*, p. 51, 1984

trickster *noun*

a prostitute *US*

- —Elementary Electronics, *Dictionary of CB Lingo*, p. 116, 1976

trick towel *noun*

a towel or wash rag used to clean up after sex *US*

- —*American Speech*, p. 59, Spring-Summer 1970: 'Homosexual slang'

Trick Wiley *noun*

used as a generic term for any gullible victim of a swindle *US*

- Then I would come in as "Trick Wiley." Anybody come in half drunk with money in his hand is considered a trick. —Henry Williamson, *Hustler!*, p. 81, 1965

tricky *adjective*

needing careful handling or cautious action; difficult; risky *UK, 1887*

- Rum-running was a tricky business. The major bootlegging was controlled by the Purple Gang[.] —Jeffrey Eugenides, *Middlesex*, p. 112, 2002

tricky Dick *noun*

the penis *US*

- —Inez Cardozo-Freeman, *The Joint*, p. 518, 1984

Tricky Dick; Tricky Dickie *nickname*

Richard Nixon *US*

President of the US from 1969 until 74, not known for his honesty or fair play.

- The guy looks more like "Tricky-Dick Nixon" or a used car salesman (same thing) than an M.D. —*Screw*, p. 17, 12th January 1970
- "O.k.," Jake continued, "I don't have to tell anybody here that we operatin' in Tricky Dick's land, so beware, be cool, be together." —Odie Hawkins, *The Busting Out of an Ordinary Man*, p. 170, 1985

tricon *noun*

in poker, a hand with three cards of the same rank *US*

- —Albert H. Morehead, *The Complete Guide to Winning Poker*, p. 276, 1967

trier *noun*

a racehorse genuinely being run to win *AUSTRALIA, 1915*

- Unless you bet me the odds to £200, the horse won't be a trier. —James Holledge, *The Great Australian Gamble*, p. 54, 1966
- Of course he backed losers like everyone else, but he was usually on a trier and that as any punter knows is half the battle. —Clive Galea, *Slipper*, p. 181, 1988

trife *adjective*

possessing low or no moral character *US*

- —Connie Eble (Editor), *UNC-CH Campus Slang*, p. 10, October 2002

trifecta *noun*

in US horse racing, a bet on the first three in the correct order *US*

- —John McCririck, *John McCririck's World of Betting*, p. 175, 1991

triff *adjective*

great, marvellous, superlative *UK, 1982*

A shortening of **TRIFFIC**.

- "Yeah, fab, triff, love it," gushed Tamsin [...] because in the world of Tamsin, everything was fab, triff, great and fantastic. —Colin Butts, *Is Harry Still on the Boat?*, p. 137, 2003

triffic *adjective*

great, marvellous, superlative – often used with heavy irony *UK*

A slovening of 'terrific' (genuinely great).

- "I'm just saying it." "Triffic." —Anthony Masters, *Minder*, p. 125, 1984

trigger *noun*

1 in a shooting, the shooter *US*

- —Warren Zevon and Bruce Springsteen, *Jeannie Needs a Shooter*, 1980
- [A] diffident-looking little guy I recognized as Morris Hornbeck – an accountant and former trigger for Jerry Katzenbach's mob in Milwaukee. —James Ellroy, *Hollywood Nocturnes*, p. 205, 1994

2 any prison guard carrying a gun *US*

- —William K. Bentley and James M. Corbett, *Prison Slang*, p. 97, 1992

trigger-happy *adjective*

too eager to shoot a gun *US, 1945*

- [O]ne of those untrained and trigger-happy officers could so easily have ended up shooting a fellow policeman[.] —Jake Arnott, *He Kills Coppers*, p. 186, 2001

trigger time *noun*

time spent in combat *US*

- A high school girl could do my job. I want to get out into the shit. I want to get some trigger time. —*Full Metal Jacket*, 1987

trike *noun*

a three-wheeled motorcycle such as the Harley-Davidson Servi-Car *US*

Biker (motorcyle) usage, referring to a child's tricycle.

trilby hat; trilby *noun*

a fool *UK*

Rhyming slang for **PRAT**.

- —Ray Puxley, *Cockney Rabbit*, 1992

trill *verb*

1 to idle with friends, especially with drugs and/or alcohol enlightening the idling *US*

- —Rick Ayers (Editor), *Berkeley High Slang Dictionary*, p. 41, 2004

2 to stroll, to strut; to leave *US*

Also 'trilly'. The heroine of Du Maurier's 1894 novel *Trilby* was noted for her beautiful feet; Trilbys came to mean 'feet', and then 'to stroll'.

- —Lou Shelly, *Hepcats Jive Talk Dictionary*, p. 19, 1945
- —Kenn "Naz" Young, *Naz's Underground Dictionary*, p. 61, 1973
- I trillied on in 'bout three A.M. Lookin' clean. —Edwin Torres, *After Hours*, p. 176, 1979

triller *noun*

an attractive young woman *JAMAICA*

West Indian patois variation of 'thriller', recorded by a Jamaican inmate in a UK prison, August 2002.

trim *noun*

1 the vagina; a woman as a sex object; sex with a woman *US*

- Didn't I say you'd get it chasing down there for some trim? —Hal Ellson, *Duke*, p. 39, 1949
- So if he gave up some bread for some trim, well, then he just can't be a faggot. —Lenny Bruce, *The Essential Lenny Bruce*, p. 164, 1967
- And I rub it on my trim and I get my kicks. —Bruce Jackson, *In the Life*, p. 409, 1972
- He had watched her dance in the den, and he knew she was a desirable young piece of trim, but it was a thought that he would never allow another person to know about. —Donald Goines, *Daddy Cool*, p. 179, 1974
- I'll get me that trim some other way. —Edwin Torres, *Carlito's Way*, p. 12, 1975
- Now she gonna' give me some trim, the big old fat lady. —Babs Gonzales, *Movin' On Down De Line*, p. 139, 1975
- [T]his Margo stallion has laid some fine trim on this nephew, see? —Robert Deane Pharr, *Giveadamn Brown*, p. 34, 1978
- Do you know how close I was to getting some trim? —*48 Hours*, 1982
- What if she thinks I'm only tryin' to cop a piece of stray trim? —Odie Hawkins, *The Life and Times of Chester Simmons*, p. 136, 1991

2 in the television and film industries, sections of scene cut by an editor *US*

- —Ralph S. Singleton, *Filmaker's Dictionary*, p. 170, 1990

trim *verb*

1 to cheat, defraud or swindle someone *UK, 1600*

- It didn't surprise Goldy that Jackson had been trimmed on The Blow. —Chester Himes, *A Rage in Harlem*, p. 40, 1957
- I'll trim you babies like little lambs. —Ken Kesey, *One Flew Over the Cuckoo's Nest*, p. 12, 1962
- Somebody you can trim for a dime or a buck or a bundle. —Robert Edmond Alter, *Carny Kill*, p. 18, 1966
- What happened to all your plans on starting you a church and trimming all them sisters out of their money? —Donald Goines, *Whoreson*, p. 223, 1972
- I wondered just how long it was gonna be before I found a way to trim Robin outta some kinda bread. —A.S. Jackson, *Gentleman Pimp*, p. 106, 1973
- Old Man One Pocket is still trimming suckers at the old poolroom. —Iceberg Slim (Robert Beck), *Long White Con*, p. 159, 1977

2 to have sex with a woman *US*

- And I trimmed her three or four times as I remember and just had a ball. —Bruce Jackson, *Outside the Law*, p. 110–111, 1972

trimmer *noun*

1 an outstanding person or thing *AUSTRALIA, 1878*

- —Barry Humphries, *A Nice Night's Entertainment*, p. 50, 1961
- You little trimmer! —Barry Humphries, *The Wonderful World of Barry McKenzie*, p. 29, 1968
- —Barry Humphries, *A Nice Night's Entertainment*, p. 143, 1974
- —Jim Ramsay, *Cop It Sweet!*, p. 91, 1977

2 in cricket, 'a fast ball of exceptional quality, especially one that narrowly misses the stumps' *UK, 1959*

- —Michael Rundell, *The Dictionary of Cricket*, 1985

trims *noun*

playing cards altered for cheating by slightly trimming off the edges of certain cards *US*

- —John Scarne, *Scarne's Guide to Modern Poker*, p. 292, 1979

Trini *adjective*

Trinidadian *TRINIDAD AND TOBAGO, 1973*

- "So's dat everyting?" Linton asked their mother, in his strong Trini accent. —Courttia Newland, *Society Within*, p. 4, 1999

Trini by boat *noun*

a long-standing immigrant in Trinidad *TRINIDAD AND TOBAGO, 1987*

- —Lise Winer, *Dictionary of the English/Creole of Trinidad & Tobago*, 2003

Trinidad time; Trini time *noun*

used for expressing an expected and accepted lack of punctuality *TRINIDAD AND TOBAGO, 1990*

- —Lise Winer, *Dictionary of the English/Creole of Trinidad & Tobago*, 2003

trinity *noun*

a style of three-storey terraced house consisting of three rooms stacked vertically *US*

- —Claudio R. Salvucci, *The Philadelphia Dialect Dictionary*, p. 63, 1996

trio *noun*

in poker, a hand with three cards of the same rank *US*

- —Albert H. Morehead, *The Complete Guide to Winning Poker*, p. 276, 1967

trip *noun*

1 a hallucinatory drug experience *US*

Uncertainty surrounds the first slang usage of the term. US slang lexicographer Peter Tamony argued in *American Speech* (Summer 1981) that the term was first used in a slang sense by Jack Gelber in *The Connection*, a 1957 play dealing with heroin addicts. Tamony privately conceded that the usage was not 'a smoking gun', and in retrospect it appears more figurative than slang. The *Oxford English Dictionary* points to Norman Mailer's 1959 *Advertisements for Myself*, in which Mailer wrote of taking mescaline and of 'a long and private trip', but there is no evidence that Mailer's use reflected a colloquial understanding and was not simply literary metaphor. Similarly, in a 1963 article about LSD in *Playboy*, Allan Harrington used the term 'trip', but again the context suggests metaphor, not slang. The slang sense of the word is indelibly associated with Ken Kesey and his LSD-taking Merry Pranksters. In 1964, Ken Kesey bought a soon-to-be-famous International Harvester school bus in the name of Intrepid Trips Inc., suggesting an already current, if private, slang sense. In September 1999, Kesey wrote about his recollection of the first use of the term: 'I think it came from our bus trip in 1964, when Cassady said "This trip is a trip"'.

- A student in Berkeley walked out a third-story window, saying, "As long as I'm going to take a trip, I might as well go to Europe." —Hunter S. Thompson, *Hell's Angels*, p. 239, 1966
- This was her first trip; the others had taken LSD several times before. —Richard Alpert Sidney Cohen, *LSD*, p. 42, 1966
- Judge Karesh than asked the much-traveled defendant [Ken Kesey] to teach him what the word "trip" really meant. Kesey said it was a happening "out of the ordinary" when induced by a psychedelic drug (such as LSD or mescaline). —*San Francisco Chronicle*, 12th April 1967
- Sometimes Cassady would ... go off into the corner, still on his manic monologue, muttering "All right, I'll take my own trip, I'll go off on my own trip, this is my own trip you understand." —Tom Wolfe, *The Electric Kool-Aid Acid Test*, p. 55, 1968
- What is the busiest job in Haight-Ashburgy? A travel agent for LSD trips! —Paul Laikin, *101 Hippie Jokes*, 1968
- The daylong "trip" I'd had was ebbing now, leaving me tired and mellow. —Sean Hutchinson, *Crying Out Loud*, p. 57, 1988
- Recently we've been doing some trips – acid, anything, it just depends what's coming in. —Macfarlane, Macfarlane and Robson, *The User*, p. 4, 1996

2 any profound experience *US, 1966*

- Just walking around Hog Farm [at Woodstock] is an incredible trip. —*East Village Other*, 20th August 1969
- The phone was always ringing, sometimes all five at once. It was a trip just to answer them. —Jerry Rubin, *Do It!*, p. 37, 1970
- "God," said Mona, grinning at the restaurant's Neapolitan bric-a-brac. "I'd almost forgotten what a trip this place is." —Armistead Maupin, *Tales of the City*, p. 178, 1978
- Wow, man, that cat's made it. Look at him, look at his old lady – man, wouldn't you like some of that." That whole bullshit trip. —Herbert Huncke, *Guilty of Everything*, p. 207, 1990

3 a state of mind *US*

Used in an extremely vague and amorphous way, usually suggesting something profound.

- The fame/power/money trip is the old story again, hardly central to making music or beads or flutes or any disinterested act of involvement, of worship. —*Berkeley Barb*, p. 6, 25th November 1966
- She got down to the store early because, she said, "I'm on a money trip." —Nicholas Von Hoffman, *We Are The People Our Parents Warned Us Against*, p. 15, 1967
- They had so many fucked trips going on. —Jefferson Poland and Valerie Alison, *The Records of the San Francisco Sexual Freedom League*, p. 48, 1971
- I don't think you understand the trip with me and Michael. —Armistead Maupin, *Tales of the City*, p. 115, 1978
- And how dare you try to lay a guilt trip on me about it – in public, no less! —*Chasing Amy*, 1997
- And besides, this masochistic trip was getting carried a little too far. —Francesca Lia Block, *I Was a Teenage Fairy*, p. 111, 1998

4 interest *US*

- I mean if she comes in and tells me she wants to ball Don, maybe, I say, 'O.K., baby, it's your trip. —Joan Didion, *Slouching Toward Bethlehem*, p. 97, 1967
- If you joined the Panthers, you had to be ready to fight the police, because that was the trip you'd be on. —Tom Wolfe, *Radical Chic & Mau-Mauing the Flak Catchers*, p. 129, 1970
- His main trip is anti-Establishment, and we can beat him like a gong on that one. —Hunter S. Thompson, *Songs of the Doomed*, p. 135, 1971
- Fuck no, ese. That's a hippie trip. —Oscar Zeta Acosta, *The Revolt of the Cockroach People*, p. 122, 1973

5 a personal or sexual experience, especially if non-conventional *US, 1971*

- I have three main trips – hustling, "numbers" and mutual contacts with certain people[.] —John Rechy, *The Sexual Outlaw*, p. 69, 1977

6 a dose of LSD, usually in the form of a blotting paper tab *UK*

Derived from the sense as 'a hallucinogenic experience' that follows ingestion.

- Spiking people with trips was a favourite little trick of Glen's. I'd seen him roll up a trip and push it down a Ribena straw. —Dave Courtney, *Raving Lunacy*, p. 139, 2000
- "He does trips for us." "Trips where?" "No. Acid trips. He makes them. He's a chemist of sorts." —J.J. Connolly, *Layer Cake*, p. 129, 2000

7 a prison sentence *US*

- "How long a trip?" Carter asked. "Six moes," Dincher sighed. —George Mandel, *Flee the Angry Strangers*, p. 89, 1952

trip *verb*

1 to experience a drug-induced hallucinogenic euphoria *US, 1966*

Also 'trip out'.

- Casper's crew loved tripping – and I don't mean nature rambles. —Wayne Anthony, *Spanish Highs*, p. 65, 1999

2 to engage in flights of fancy, especially while in prison *US*

- "Sorry, I thought you might have fallen asleep with your clothes on." "I'm just lying here tripping." —Malcolm Braly, *On the Yard*, p. 175, 1967
- —*Current Slang*, p. 49, Fall 1968
- I would lie in my cell and trip two and three hours out of every day; I could see myself walking through the Village, see the red paint, see the clothesline, the tree in the middle of the courtyard. —Bobby Seale, *A Lonely Rage*, p. 225, 1978

3 to get angry, to lose control because of anger *US, 1990s?*

- Valaida, if I had known you were going to trip out about this, I wouldn't have mentioned the subject. —Odie Hawkins, *The Life and Times of Chester Simmons*, p. 175, 1991
- DREXEL: Why you trippin/" We jus' fuckin' with ya. —*True Romance*, 1993
- He's been trippin' since we been in the hospital. —*Menace II Society*, 1993

4 to insult *US*

- Louis said, "Mostly when you trippin' on some motherfucker, giving him a bad time, you say it." —Elmore Leonard, *Riding the Rap*, p. 55, 1995

tripe *noun*

1 utter nonsense; anything worthless or of poor quality, rubbish *UK, 1676*

Derives from 'tripe' as a source of inferior food.

• "I don't know how to try." "Don't talk tripe." —Geoff Brown, *I Want What I Want*, p. 73, 1966

2 in the theatre, electrical lines dangling from overhead fixtures *UK*

• —Wilfred Granville, *The Theater Dictionary*, p. 207, 1952

3 a tripod *US*
Used by travelling salesmen and itinerant swindlers to support a suitcase full of merchandise.

• —Don Wilmeth, *The Language of American Popular Entertainment*, p. 280, 1981

trip grass *noun*
marijuana enhanced with amphetamine *US*

• —Ernest L. Abel, *A Marijuana Dictionary*, p. 105, 1982

triple *noun*
sex involving three people *US*

• Ciglianni's dead. Keeled over with a heart attack last year doing triples with two teenage whores he picked up off the hookers' stroll at Hollywood and Vine. —Robert Campbell, *Juice*, p. 2, 1988

triple crown *noun*
oral, vaginal and anal sex in the same session *US*

triple C's *noun*
dextromethorphan (DXM), an active ingredient in non-prescription cold and cough medication, often abused for non-medicinal purposes *US*

• Youths' nicknames for DXM: Robo, Skittles, Triple C's, Rojo, Dex, Tussin, Vitamin D. DXM abuse is called "Robotripping" or "Tussing." Users might be called "syrup heads" or "robotards." —*USA Today*, p. 1A, 29th December 2003

triple jet ace *noun*
a fighter pilot who shoots down three aircraft in a single day *US*

• Captain Joseph McConnell with 16 victories was the top jet ace. He also became the first "triple jet ace" in history when he shot down three MIG's in one day – May 18, 1953. —Don Lawson, *The United States in the Korean War*, p. 64, 1964

triple m *noun*
mutual manual masturbation *US*

• —Wayne Dynes, *Homolexis*, p. 91, 1985

triple-nickels *noun*
the 555th Parachute Infantry Battalion, US Army *US*
The US Army's first all-black parachute infantry test platoon, company and battalion.

• —Linda Reinberg, *In the Field*, p. 223, 1991

triplets *noun*
in poker, three of a kind *US*

• —Irwin Steig, *Common Sense in Poker*, p. 188, 1963

triple W *noun*
a woman as the provider of good sex *US*
The W's are 'warm', 'wet' and 'womb'.

• —*Current Slang*, p. 14, Fall 1970

triple X *noun*

1 a tablet of MDBA that also contains the analogues MDA and MDEA *UK*

• —Angela Devlin, *Prison Patter*, p. 116, 1996
• —Gareth Thomas, *This Is Ecstasy*, p. 54, 2002

2 someone who abstains from sex, alcohol and drugs *US*
Reminiscent of the slang term for a decaffeinated espresso drink made with non-fat milk – why bother.

• —Connie Eble (Editor), *UNC-CH Campus Slang*, p. 8, March 1996

trip out *verb*

1 to undergo an hallucinogenic experience as a result of drug-intoxication *US*

• —Joe David Brown (Editor), *The Hippies*, p. 220, 1967: 'Glossary of hippie terms'
• I weighed the notion whether or not to take the plunge and "trip out". David, with prior experience, talked gleefully of being a "guide" for my first time. —Sean Hutchinson, *Crying Out Loud*, p. 55, 1988

2 to upset someone; to confuse someone; to disturb someone *US, 1960s*

• Dr. Dre admitted that it "tripped me out, bugged me the fuck out" when he discovered white kids were buying his records[.] —Barney Hoskyns, *Waiting For The Sun*, p. 337, 1996

3 to amaze someone; to enlighten someone *US*

• I just found out the other day that my grandfather – my father's father – was a machinist for twenty years, and that really tripped me out. —Leonard Wolfe (Editor), *Voices from the Love Generation*, p. 216, 1968

4 to become involved in something in a focused and intense manner *US*

• —J. L. Simmons and Barry Winograd, *It's Happening*, p. 173, 1966: 'Glossary'

tripped out *adjective*
halucinogen-intoxicated *US, 1973*

• [A]ny time merriment flagged for my tripped-out road crew, the Sooty gag reasserted itself. —Mick Farren, *Give the Anarchist a Cigarette*, p. 192, 2001

tripper *noun*

1 a person using LSD or another hallucinogenic drug *US*

• Trippers use the word "visuals" to refer to the visual impressions and images that acid can generate. —Cam Cloud, *The Little Book of Acid*, p. 10, 1999

2 LSD *UK*
From **TRIP** (a period of LSD intoxication).

• Street names [...] tab, tripper, trips, window[.] —James Kay and Julian Cohen, *The Parents' Complete Guide to Young People and Drugs*, p. 141, 1998

3 a train passenger *US*

• —Ramon Adams, *The Language of the Railroader*, p. 163, 1977

tripple-dipper *noun*
a veteran of World War 2, Korea and Vietnam *US*

• —*Citizen-Journal (Columbus, Ohio)*, p. 7, 13th April 1966
• —Carl Fleischhauer, *A Glossary of Army Slang*, p. 22, 1968

trippy *adjective*

1 halucinatory *UK*

• Don't as a rule like mushies [magic mushrooms] much like, but this is alright. Not too trippy like. —Niall Griffiths, *Sheepshagger*, p. 112, 2001

2 of psychedelic design *US*
From **TRIP** (an LSD experience) and the psychedelic imagery inspired by such drug usage.

• X is often described as less distrubingly "trippy" than LSD and more serene than cocaine[.] —*Newsweek*, p. 62, 6th December 1993
• They dressed in trippy silks and satins[.] —Simon Napier-Bell, *Black Vinyl White Powder*, p. 100, 2001

3 excellent *US*

• "Out of sight," "too much," "tough," "trippy," "trick," or "unreal" – were all current [late 1960s] superlatives. Each would flower for a while and then fall to something a little groovier – up to date on the tongues of those who knew. —Sean Hutchinson, *Crying Out Loud*, p. 177, 1988

4 extremely committed to the hippie life, especially the drug aspects of it *US*

• I'm hippy and I'm trippy / I'm a gypsy on my own. —Frank Zappa, *Who Needs The Peace Corps?*, 1968
• [I]t probably surprises you to learn that I had a trippy Xmas – even when I wasn't zonked out on your culinary crazies – but I did. —Tom Robbins, *Another Roadside Attraction*, p. 162, 1971

trips *noun*

1 LSD *US, 1969*

• [T]here was a boom in ecstasy [MDMA], speed [amphetamine], trips, the lot. —Macfarlane, Macfarlane and Robson, *The User*, p. 91, 1996
• —Suroosh Alvi et al., *The Vice Guide*, p. 102, 2002

2 in poker, a hand with three cards of the same rank *US*
An abbreviation of 'triplets'.

3 dice with intentionally rounded edges used for cheating *US*

• —John Scarne, *Scarne on Dice*, p. 481, 1974

trisaurus *noun*
a Boeing 727 aircraft *UK*
From its three jet engines; the plane was produced from the late 1960s to 1984.

trisexual; trysexual *adjective*
willing to try anything sexually; open to any sexual experience *US*
Borrowing from 'bisexual', punning 'tri' with 'try'.

• I prefere 'tri-sexual'. You know – I'll try anything. —Paul Martin, *Carmen*, p. 75, 1988
• MJ calls herself "trysexual" – "I'll try anything." —*Sojourner*, p. 13, 27th February 1988
• The large one is trisexual; Bunny just does what she's told. What's trisexual? She'll do [try] anything, I suspect. —Robert Stoller and I.S. Levine, *Coming Attractions*, p. 30, 1991

triss *noun*
a male homosexual *AUSTRALIA, 1953*
- Think I'm going round flapping my mouth to every silly triss that gets shoved in with me?—Kylie Tennant, *Tell Morning This*, p. 157, 1967

trissy *adjective*
homosexual *AUSTRALIA, 1982*

triumphant *adjective*
excellent *US*
- — *USA Today*, p. 1D, 5th August 1991: 'A sterling lexicon of the lingo'

trivet *noun*
in poker, a three-dollar bet *US*
- —John Vorhaus, *The Big Book of Poker Slang*, p. 37, 1996

trivial *adjective*
in computing, too simple to bother explaining *US*
- —Andy Ihnatko, *Cyberspeak*, p. 192, 1997

trixie *noun*
a multiple bet, gambling on three horses in four combined bets *UK*
- A £1Trixie would cost £4.—John McCririck, *John McCririck's World of Betting*, p. 45, 1991

trizz *noun*
a prostitute's customer *US*
- —Kenn "Naz" Young, *Naz's Underground Dictionary*, p. 61, 1973

trog *noun*
1 a stuffy, old-fashioned person *UK*
From 'troglodyte' (an ancient cave dweller).
- —R.T. Bickers, *The Hellions*, 1965

2 a slow, careful, trundling driver *UK*
Probably extends from the previous sense.
- It is the considered view of this observer that much of the chaos on our weekend roads is caused by the proliferation of Trogs. A Trog, by our family tradition, is a driver who is dedicated to the principle that all good journeys should be made to last the longest possible time. — *Daily Telegraph*, June 1972: 'Spot the trog'

3 a visiting surfer *AUSTRALIA*
- —Gary Fairmont R. Filosa II, *The Surfer's Almanac*, p. 197, 1977

trog *verb*
to walk; to depart; to drive without urgency *UK*
Military.
- No point in rushing. Let's just trog on, we'll get there eventually. —Andy McNab (writing of the late 1970s/early 80s), *Immediate Action*, p. 175, 1995

troglodyte *noun*
a computer enthusiast who has abandoned all contact with life outside his computer *US*
- —Eric S. Raymond, *The New Hacker's Dictionary*, p. 357, 1991

trog off *verb*
to go, especially if it means making an effort *UK*
- Instead of trogging off to the bands, they can come to us.— *The Guardian*, p. 2, 28th June 2004

trog up *verb*
to dress and equip yourself for caving and pot-holing *UK*
Probably derives from 'troglodyte'.
- —David Morrison of Wessex Cave Club, 29th February 2004

trojan *noun*
a condom, Trojan™ brand or otherwise *US*
- —Judi Sanders, *Da Bomb*, p. 16, 1997

Trojan *noun*
an AT-28 aircraft, used as a ground-attack aircraft and then a fighter bomber in the Vietnam war *US*
- —Ian Padden, *U.S. Air Commando*, p. 104, 1985

Trojan horse *noun*
1 in computing, an intentionally destructive program disguised and sent in benevolent form *US*
- —Eric S. Raymond, *The New Hacker's Dictionary*, p. 357, 1991

2 in poker, an unexpectedly strong hand held by another player whose betting has successfully masked its strength *US*
- —John Vorhaus, *The Big Book of Poker Slang*, p. 37, 1996

troll *noun*
1 a resident of the Lower Peninsula of Michigan *US*
Because they live below the Mackinac Bridge that connects the peninsulas. Upper Peninsula usage.

2 a message posted on an Internet discussion group with the hope of attracting vitriolic response *US*
- A troll typically expresses a simple and basic question in a particularly long-winded and clueless fashion, or expresses sentiments that will likely provoke an enraged response[.]—Andy Ihnatko, *Cyberspeak*, p. 194, 1997

troll *verb*
(of a homosexual man) to walk the streets in search of sexual adventure; (of a homosexual man) to walk, to wander *UK, 1967*
Familiarity of usage has resulted in the original, conventional sense being re-derived, here from the specifically sexual sense.
- [W]e'd hardly been in the place two minutes when Mr Horne came trolling in.—Barry Took and Marty Feldman, *Round The Horne*, April 1967
- Trolling homosexuals, both butch and queen.—Joseph Wambaugh, *The Black Marble*, p. 94, 1978
- I trolled back to my lattie[.]—the cast of 'Aspects of Love', Prince of Wales Theatre, *Palare (Boy Dancer Talk) for Beginners*, 1989–92
- — *Attitude*, p. 60, July 2003: 'Old palare lexicon'

trolley *noun*
a line used by prisoners to exchange notes *US*
- —Hyman E. Goldin et al., *Dictionary of American Underworld Lingo*, p. 227, 1950

▸ **off your trolley**
1 mentally disordered; crazed *UK, 1896*
A 'trolley' is an electric powered tram that runs on rails, hence 'to be off your trolley' is to not follow an ordered course.
- Brad looked at his watch, "...three twenty in the morning you must be off your fucking trolley."—Colin Butts, *Is Harry on the Boat?*, p. 8, 1997
- All that bleedin billy he was using, aye. Sent im off is trolley. It would anyone, that amount. Billy for fuckin breakfast, like.—Niall Griffiths, *Sheepshagger*, p. 55, 2001

2 drunk *UK*
- I've seen people shot, shagged, smashed and stabbed; off their trolleys, out of their trees, on their knees, off their tits—Dave Courtney, *Raving Lunacy*, p. 5, 2000
- — *e-cyclopaedia*, 20th March 2002
- I've still got a sore foot. I was so off my trolley I didn't notice.— *Sky Magazine*, p. 18, May 2002

trolley and tram; trolley *noun*
ham *UK*
Rhyming slang.
- —Ray Puxley, *Cockney Rabbit*, 1992

trolley and truck *noun*
an act of sexual intercouse *UK*
Rhyming slang for **FUCK**.
- —Ray Puxley, *Cockney Rabbit*, 1992

trolleyed; trollied *adjective*
drunk or drug-intoxicated *UK*
Derives from **OFF YOUR TROLLEY**.
- Didn't mind him lying trolleyed on my lap.—Gavin Hills, *White Burger Danny (Disco Biscuits)*, p. 67, 1996
- [W]e quietened down for about ten, fifteen seconds and then got proper trolleyed!—Dave Courtney, *Raving Lunacy*, p. 46, 2000
- [T]rolleyed, mullered, bombed[.]—Stuart Walton, *Out of It*, cover, 2001
- — *e-cyclopaedia*, 20th March 2002

trolley jockey *noun*
a tram operator *US, 1954*
- — *American Speech*, p. 158–159, May 1960: 'The burgeoning of 'jockey''

trolley man *noun*
a man engaged in the racing of horses and ponies in trotting matches *UK*
- Boxer Tom, like Johnny Frankham and old Jimmy Frankham before him, was a trolley man.—Jimmy Stockin, *On The Cobbles*, p. 106, 2000

trolley off *verb*
to go away; to leave *UK*
- Wally says five and they finally fix a figure. And with that Hume trolleys off.—Ted Lewsi, *Jack Carter's Law [britpulp]*, p. 48, 1974

trollies; trolleys; trollys *noun*
underpants; trousers *UK*
Originally dialect, adopted by the Royal Navy and from there into more general use; it is interesting to note that polari speakers claim the word for gay society, probably from its relationship with **TROLL** (to walk with the purpose of attracting sexual interest).
- — Paul Baker, *Polari*, p. 194, 2002

trombone *noun*
1 a telephone *UK*
Rhyming slang; generally used as 'the old trombone'.
- — Douglas Warner, *Death of a Snout*, 1961
- I can't wait to see Daley's boat [face]. He'll be on the old trombone in two seconds. — Anthony Masters, *Minder*, p. 131, 1984
- the old trombone — Ray Puxley, *Cockney Rabbit*, 1992

2 in the television and film industries, a hanger that can be extended from a wall to support lighting *US*
- — Tony Miller and Patricia George, *Cut! Print!*, p. 159, 1977

trombone *verb*
1 in the sport of clayshooting, to slide the hand back along the barrel of the gun whilst swinging upwards to aim and fire *UK*
Imitative of the sliding-action when involved in playing a trombone.
- — Chris Cradock, *A Manual of Clayshooting*, p. 176, 1983

2 to lick the anus of a male partner while caressing his erect penis *UK*
The actions involved mimic the playing of a trombone.
- — *Sky Magazine*, July 2001

tromp and stomp *noun*
a marching drill *US*
- [R]ifle inspection, tromp; and stomp (drill, marching, etc.), personnel and tent inspection, classes, hikes, training problems, night problems. This is what is called "harassing the troops.!" — Martin Russ, *The Last Parallel*, p. 153, 1957

t-room *noun*
▷ see: **TEAROOM**

troop *noun*
1 a single soldier; used as a term of address to a soldier
- You're humping way too much, troop, don't need half this shit. — *Platoon*, 1986
- Sir, did you ever know a troop that didn't stash his stuff in every nook and cranny available to him? — Lucian K. Truscott, *Army Blue*, p. 279, 1989

2 crack cocaine *UK, 1998*
- — Mike Haskins, *Drugs*, p. 282, 2003

trooper *noun*
a person who is the ultimately stalwart good sport *US, 1951*
- Yeah, she was really a true trouper [sic] and she came close to causing me to shed a few tears. — A.S. Jackson, *Gentleman Pimp*, p. 138, 1973
- He was sentenced to fifteen years in a Florida joint. He handled it like a trooper. — Dan Jenkins, *Life Its Ownself*, p. 28, 1984
- "You marched into that tavern like a trooper," Nell said. — Carl Hiaasen, *Tourist Season*, p. 52, 1986

troopie-groupie *noun*
1 a girl who freely offers her sexual availability to soldiers *UK*
Military.
- A fat blonde girl winked at him and her friends giggled and screeched – he recognised them as part of the troopy-groupie crowd[.] — Chris Ryan, *The Watchman*, p. 182, 2001

2 a war-correspondent, or like-minded civilian, who is enthusiastically supportive of the military *UK*
From **GROUPIE** (a follower).
- — *The Observer*, 11th July 1982

troops *noun*
collectively, the mechanics in a car repair shop *US*
- A lot of mechanics were in the military. In many shops, the boss can still yell out "all right, line up, troops," and they will. — Lewis Poteet, *Car & Motorcyle Slang*, p. 207, 1992

trophy *adjective*
used of a wife or girlfriend, young and beautiful to an extent that would not be expected with the man *US*
- Young trophy wife, I mean, in the parlance of our times, owes money all over town[.] — *The Big Lebowski*, 1998

trophy fuck *verb*
to have sex with a famous person because of that person's celebrity
- Gangs of [groupies] went hunting together – "trophy fucking" – keeping a list of everyone they made out with. — Simon Napier-Bell, *Black Vinyl White Powder*, p. 74, 2001

tropical *adjective*
1 extremely eccentric or mildly insane *US*
- — *American Speech*, p. 238, October 1946: 'World War II slang of maladjustment'

2 of goods, stolen *AUSTRALIA, 1950*
Synonym of **HOT**.
- — Jim Ramsay, *Cop It Sweet!*, p. 91, 1977
- — Ryan Aven-Bray, *Ridgey Didge Oz Jack Lang*, p. 47, 1983

tropical fish; tropie *noun*
an act of urination *UK*
Rhyming slang for **PISH** (a Scottish variation of **PISS**).
- I'm off for a tropie. — *www.LondonSlang.com*, June 2002

Tropic Lightning *nickname*
the 25th Infantry Division, US Army *US*
- Schofield that is Home of the 25th "Tropic Lightning" Infantry Division, formerly the Hawaii Division, James Jones's own division — Joan Didion, *The White Album*, p. 146, 1979
- Evans, formerly of the 25th Infantry's "Tropic Lightning" Division, said an effort was under way for some formal recognition, a possibly a war memorial, of Korean veterans' service. — *Arkansas Democrat-Gazette*, 11th March 1985
- Tropic Lightning soldiers went into combat against the North Korean army almost immediately. — Michael J. Varhola, *Fire and Ice*, p. 99, 2000
- Dima, 56, and Broce, 54, served together in the "Tropic Lightning," the 25th Infantry Division, in Vietnam in 1969. — *Belleville News-Democrat*, p. A1, 12th September 2004

troppo *adjective*
1 insane, mad, crazy *AUSTRALIA, 1941*
Of military origins; an abbreviation of 'tropical' or 'tropics' as a reference to mental or nervous instability caused by war service in the tropics.
- We relieved our wound-up minds with a sort of desperate, manufactured humour, even feigning the madness we felt that the monotony might bring on us. 'Troppo acts' we called them. — Eric Lambert, *The Veterans*, p. 105, 1954
- It began to be rumoured that Sandy was 'troppo'. — Bill Wannan, *Bullockies, Beauts and Bandicoots*, p. 37, 1960
- Spotto stared at the Colonel and wondered whether he was a bit troppo. — Ray Slattery, *Mobbs' Mob*, p. 113, 1966
- Too much sun sends you troppo north of the border. — Kathy Lette, *Girls' Night Out*, p. 178, 1987
- — Harry Orsman and Des Hurley, *The Beaut Little Book of New Zealand Slang*, 1994

2 sunburnt, suffering from too much exposure to the sun and wind *AUSTRALIA*
- — Trevor Cralle, *The Surfin'ary*, p. 148, 1991

3 especially in Queensland, of a building designed for tropical weather *AUSTRALIA*
- The house is a troppo design. — *www.abc.net.au/wordmap*, 2003

trot *noun*
1 a period of time considered in terms of how you fared during it *AUSTRALIA, 1911*
- John West himself worked for a while in one of the boot factories during a 'bad trot,' much to his mother's joy. — Frank Hardy, *Power Without Glory*, p. 43, 1950
- — Jim Ramsay, *Cop It Sweet!*, p. 91, 1977
- A run of winners being a "good trot", the reverse a "bad" or "shocking trot". — Ned Wallish, *The Truth Dictionary of Racing Slang*, p. 83, 1989
- — Harry Orsman, *A Dictionary of Modern New Zealand Slang*, p. 141, 1999

2 a line-by-line translation of a work in a foreign language *US, 1891*
- Taggarty tried to steer the conversation toward a historical analysis of Ramayana (she must have read the trot on that one), but desisted abruptly when Vijay tripped her up in a glaring factual error. — C.D. Payne, *Youth in Revolt*, p. 190, 1993

▸ on the trot
1 in succession *UK, 1956*
- Joe and Romano Azzalin became close friends and when the nightclub owner purchased his great horse Bernborough, Joe was one of the many thousands who won heavily on the horse as it strung together fifteen wins on the trot. — Clive Galea, *Slipper!*, p. 21, 1988

- St Kilda, in fact, was running hot and had won something like six games on the trot to challenge for a place in the finals. —Rex Hunt, *Tall Tales – and True*, p. 108, 1994
- Malcolm an Colm an Margaret speedin six days on thuh trot an then gulpin handfuls uv downers tuh knock em out for a couple uv days. —Niall Griffiths, *Grits*, p. 16, 2000

2 engaged in evading discovery or capture by the police *UK*
- I think Adam was on the trot, or with someone on the trot, or maybe they were due to return to prison from home leave[.] —Jimmy Stockin, *On The Cobbles*, p. 173, 2000

Trot *noun*
a *Trot*skyist; thus *Trot*skyite; hence of anyone or anything associated with political views from the extreme left *UK, 1962*
- Trots running the unions and trying to bring the country to its knees —Jake Arnott, *He Kills Coppers*, p. 252, 2001

trots *noun*
1 diarrhoea *US, 1904*
Used with 'the'.
- "He's not dogging it," Carbone said. "He's got a temperature and he's got a fever and he's got the trots." —George V. Higgins, *The Rat on Fire*, p. 90, 1981
- I'll tell them you've got the trots. Puerto Rican food will do it to you. —Elmore Leonard, *Glitz*, p. 347, 1985

2 a horse race meeting for trotting and pacing; such meetings collectively *AUSTRALIA, 1890*
- —Gavin Casey, *It's Harder for Girls*, p. 167, 1941
- The 'the trots' were aptly described by the cognoscenti as 'the red hots'. —James Holledge, *The Great Australian Gamble*, p. 119, 1966

trotter *noun*
1 a deserter from the military; an escaped prisoner; anyone on the run from the police *UK, 1950*
Originally military.
- —Angela Devlin, *Prison Patter*, p. 116, 1996

2 pork *US*
- —John R. Armore and Joseph D. Wolfe, *Dictionary of Desperation*, p. 55, 1976

trotters *noun*
the feet *UK, 1775*

trou *noun*
trousers; pants *US*
- —Collin Baker et al., *College Undergraduate Slang Study Conducted at Brown University*, p. 213, 1968

trouble *noun*
a type of bet in an illegal numbers game lottery *US*
- Then to be on the safe side he also played jail house, death row, lady come back, two-timing woman, pile of rocks, dark days and trouble. —Chester Himes, *A Rage in Harlem*, p. 23, 1957

trouble and fuss *noun*
bus *UK*
Rhyming slang.
- —Ray Puxley, *Cockney Rabbit*, 1992

trouble and strife; trouble *noun*
1 a wife *UK, 1908*
Rhyming slang.
- [S]omething to rabbit [to talk] to the trouble about in the skein[.] —Ronnie Barker, *Fletcher's Book of Rhyming Slang*, p. 5, 1979
- [B]uying single roses for the trouble from gyppos with baskets[.] —Andrew Nickolds, *Back to Basics*, p. 85, 1994
- [G]etting the trouble-and-strife up the duff [pregnant] before an overseas posting[.] —Chris Ryan, *The Watchman*, p. 149, 2001

2 life *UK*
Rhyming slang.
- —Ray Puxley, *Fresh Rabbit*, 1998

troubled *adjective*
drunk *UK*
- —*e-cyclopaedia*, 20th March 2002

trough *noun*
1 a place where you (regularly) eat or drink *UK*
- What is an ugly cunt like you doing in my trough? [...] – I asked what's an ugly cunt like you doing in my drinker? —Mark Powell, *Snap*, p. 39, 2001

2 a bar, especially at a horse racetrack *AUSTRALIA*
- —Ned Wallish, *The Truth Dictionary of Racing Slang*, p. 83, 1989

trough *verb*
to eat *UK*
Armed services' slang; adapted from conventional 'trough' (a receptacle for feeding domestic animals).
- —Nigel Foster, *The Making of a Royal Marine Commando*, 1987

trouncer *noun*
an attractive girl *UK: NORTHERN IRELAND*
- —C. I. Macafee, *A Concise Ulster Dictionary*, p. 365, 1996

troused *adjective*
drunk *US*
- —Judi Sanders, *Da Bomb!*, p. 29, 1997

trouser *noun*
a man or men objectified sexually *UK*
Probably derived in response to **SKIRT** (a woman, women).
- I scoured the room looking for possible talent as Eric Clapton launched into "Wonderful Tonight". Eric obviously hadn't seen the trouser on offer at the Party Susan Club. —Kitty Churchill, *Thinking of England*, p. 45, 1995

trouser *verb*
to pocket something; to earn money *UK, 1892*
Extended from a 'trouser pocket'.
- All the same, I just trousered the boodle. —Viv Stanshall, *Ginger Geezer*, 1981
- Some other bugger will already have trousered the backhander for coughing to the tabloids. —Christopher Brookmyre, *Boiling a Frog*, p. 101, 2000
- Everton's 17-year-old wunderkind [footballer Wayne Rooney], currently trousering £13,000 a week —*Guardian Education*, 22nd April 2003

trouser cough *noun*
a fart *UK*
- I've farted, I farted, / I've made a trouser cough[.] —Ivor Biggun, *I've Parted (Misprint)*, 1978

trousered *adjective*
drunk *UK*
- —*e-cyclopaedia*, 20th March 2002

trousers *noun*
▸ **with your trousers down**
being taken by surprise; in a state of unreadiness *UK, 1966*
Generally prefaced with the verb 'catch/caught'.
- Not in any imaginable circumstance, bar Blair caught with trousers down, hand in till amid economic meltdown. —*The Guardian*, 4th October 2000

trousers and skirts *adjective*
bisexual *UK*
- —Peter Chippindale, *The British CB Book*, p. 160, 1981

trouser snake *noun*
the penis *US, 1976*
- [U]nzips his fly. Pulls out the mother of all trouser snakes and prepares to give him a Frontline Special. —Jack Allen, *When the Whistle Blows*, p. 225, 2000
- JUSTICE: Of course I like snakes. JAY: How about trouser snakes? —Kevin Smith, *Jay and Silent Bob Strike Back*, p. 43, 2001

trouser trout *noun*
the penis *UK, 1998*
- —Erica Orloff and JoAnn Baker, *Dirty Little Secrets*, p. 69, 2001
- I think we've already established that when it comes to the trouser trout there is no norm. —Richard Herring, *Talking Cock*, p. 108, 2003

trout *noun*
an unattractive (older or old) woman *UK, 1897*
- Labour MPs are campaigning, sad to report, to prevent a statue of the old trout [Margaret Thatcher] ever being erected at Westminster. —*The Guardian*, 29th January 2002

▹ **see:** THAMES TROUT

▸ **all about trout**
alert, watchful *UK*
Noted by Robin Cook, 1962.

trout pout *noun*
unnaturally inflated lips as a result of collagen implants *UK*
An unfortunate similarity to the freshwater fish.
- Collagen implants in the lips produce a fuller mouth but can create 'trout pout'. —*The Observer*, 17th August 2003
- I am forewarned of this cosmetic development by the Daily Mail, which runs a forensic full page of Meg's 'trout-pout' the day before I see her. —*The Guardian*, 5th October 2003

truck *verb*
to stroll; to stride *US, 1938*
- Stuck my elbow out for her and went truckin' out. — Edwin Torres, *After Hours*, p. 388, 1979

truck driver *noun*
1 an aggressive, 'mannish' lesbian *US*
- Known variously as a bull, a stomper, a bad butch, a hard dresser, a truck driver, a diesel dyke, a bull dagger and a half dozen other soubriquets, she is the one who, according to most homosexual girls, gives lesbians a bad name. — Ruth Allison, *Lesbianism*, p. 125, 1967

2 in prison, a prisoner or guard who delivers messages *US*
- — John R. Armore and Joseph D. Wolfe, *Dictionary of Desperation*, p. 55, 1976

3 an amphetamine or other central nervous system stimulant *US*
- — John B. Williams, *Narcotics and Hallucinogenics*, p. 116, 1967

trucker's powder *noun*
amphetamine *UK*
A variation on **TRUCK DRIVER** (amphetamines), this plays on **SPEED** and the need to stay awake.

truckie *noun*
a truck driver *AUSTRALIA, 1919*
- An' the loggin' truck goes lurchin' down the crazy wooden ways, / With the driver at the brake-rope – Oh, that truckie has a nerve! / An' he howls a merry "Hoop-la!" as she swings around a curve. — C.J. Dennis, *Jim of the Hills*, p. 12, 1919
- Seamen, wharfies and truckies almost to a man. — John Morrison, *Stories of the Waterfront*, p. 134, 1955
- Good luck to the truckies who are trying to improve their image. — *Herald Sun*, p. 14, 1991
- Mike told him they'd have to secrete a camera crew in his cabin to confront the dumpers on the spot, and got kind of shirty and ticked off when the truckie called him a madman. — Harrison Biscuit, *The Search for Savage Henry*, p. 26, 1995

truck stop Annie *noun*
a prostitute working at a truck stop *US*
- — Bill Davis, *Jawjacking*, p. 102, 1977

truck stop cowboy *noun*
a person who looks the part of a trucker, plays the part of a trucker, but is not a trucker *US*
- — Elementary Electronics, *Dictionary of CB Lingo*, p. 116, 1976

Trudeau acre *noun*
a hectare *CANADA*
As the Canadian French measure of land is in the hectare (a metric unit equivalent to 2.471 acres), and the English is in the acre unit, 1970s anti-Trudeau feeling took parodic form here as much as in opposition to the Prime Minister's promotion of bilingualism and biculturalism nationwide.
- Taken to the extremes that it was, metrification was not exactly popular across the prairies. The expression Trudeau acres is merely another sarcastic reference to eastern arrogance. — Chris Thain, *Cold as a Bay Street Bankers Heart*, p. 157, 1987

true *adverb*
especially in Aboriginal English, is it true?, really? *AUSTRALIA*
- The scowl gradually waned, and the smile which followed was halted by reluctant belief. 'You didn't say? True?' — Arthur Upfield, *Bony and the Mouse*, p. 49, 1959

true bull; true bool *noun*
a tested and proven leader *US*
Hawaiian youth usage.
- — Douglas Simonson, *Pidgin to da Max Hana Hou*, 1982

true love *noun*
a type of bet in an illegal numbers game lottery *US*
- He played the money row, lucky lady, happy days, true love, sun gonna shine, gold, silver, diamonds, dollars and whiskey. — Chester Himes, *A Rage in Harlem*, p. 23, 1957

True North *noun*
Canada *CANADA*
'The True North, strong and free' is a line from the Canadian national anthem. In its patriotic connotation, this expression suggests pride and strength, but it may also suggest the extreme cold, snow and ice which Canadians endure.

true's God!
used for affirming the truth of what has been said *FIJI, 1976*
Recorded by Jan Tent.

true that!; true dat!
used for expressing strong agreement *US*
- — Ethan Hilderbrant, *Prison Slang*, p. 130, 1998
- — Connie Eble (Editor), *UNC-CH Campus Slang*, p. 13, Fall 1999

true-true *adjective*
authentic *BAHAMAS*
- — John A. Holm, *Dictionary of Bahamian English*, p. 211, 1982

true virgins make dull company
the air navigation system: True heading plus/minus Variation gives you Magnetic heading plus/minus Deviation gives you Compass heading *CANADA*
The reverse mnemonic is 'Can Dead Men Vote Twice?'.
- "True virgins make dull company" is a mnemonic device used in teaching air navigation, and helps student pilots learn how to convert from "True" heading to "Compass" heading. — Tom Langeste, *Words on the Wing*, p. 284, 1995

truggy *noun*
an off-road vehicle that combines features of a truck and a tubular buggy *US*
Collected by John Thompson of Hendersonville, North Carolina, 2004.

Trujillo's revenge *noun*
diarrhoea *US*
Homage to Dominican dictator Rafael Trujillo.
- "I ate that chow just one time and got Trujillo's Revenge," Nolen said. — Elmore Leonard, *Cat Chaser*, p. 25, 1982

trull *noun*
a prostitute, a concubine, a loose-moralled woman *UK, 1519*
A generally obsolete conventional English term.
- He had a trull on the side and he'd been salting away drab money for himself and her. — John Milne, *Alive and Kicking*, p. 131, 1998

Truman's folly *noun*
the Korean war *US*
Another Republican party coining.
- They called it Truman's Folly, and their mood may best be described as one of sullen acquiescence[.] — Robert Leckie, *The Wars of America, Volume II*, p. 347, 1968

trummus *noun*
the buttocks, the posterior *UK*
- — Paul Baker, *Polari*, p. 194, 2002

trump *noun*
a fart *UK*
From C15; from the sound of a trumpet.
- Trump! It's something I specialise in. — Phil Hammond, *An A–Z of Rude Health*, 18th January 2002

trump *verb*
to fart *UK, 1425*
From C15; from the sound of a trumpet.
- Caroline Aherne in her role as chat show hostess Mrs Merton asked actress Joanna Lumley "Have you just trumped?" — Peter Furze, *Tailwinds*, p. 166, 1998

trumpet *noun*
1 a telephone *UK*
- — David Powis, *The Signs of Crime*, 1977
- Next thing Dave's on the trumpet in a right tiz. — Andrew Nickolds, *Back to Basics*, p. 94, 1994

2 a stethoscope *TRINIDAD AND TOBAGO, 1987*
- — Lise Winer, *Dictionary of the English/Creole of Trinidad & Tobago*, 2003

3 a fart *UK*
Juvenile use, extending the more familiar **TRUMP** (a fart) back to its origins.

4 in hot rodding, a tailpipe extension *US*
- — *Good Housekeeping*, p. 143, September 1958: 'Hot-Rod Terms for Teen-age Girls'
- — Tom MacPherson, *Dragging and Driving*, p. 143, 1960

5 cocaine *UK*
A pun on **BUGLE**.
- In one session I'd been known to blow a grand's worth of trumpet up my noble hooter. — Wayne Anthony, *Spanish Highs*, p. 46, 1999
- — Dominic Anciano and Ray Burdis, *Love, Honour & Obey*, 1999

trumpets *noun*
MDMA, the recreational drug best known as ecstasy *UK*
Specifically used of any MDMA tablet stamped with the stylised image of a horn-player (possibly an angel).
- — Harry Shapiro, *Recreational Drugs*, p. 211, 2004

trump of the dump *noun*
the person in charge of an enterprise *NEW ZEALAND*
- — David McGill, *David McGill's Complete Kiwi Slang Dictionary*, p. 128, 1998

trunch *noun*
a blow or a beating with a *trunch*eon *UK*
- All those slags who support the system got some trunch as well. — *Time Out*, 29th February 1980

trundling-cheat *noun*
a car; originally any wheeled vehicle *UK, 1630*
- — Paul Baker, *Polari*, p. 194, 2002

trunk *noun*
the human nose *UK*
Derisory, emphasising the size of someone's nose or, figuratively, the intrusive quality of that person's nosiness.
- I'd be a millionaire by now if he hadn't stuck his trunk in – I fucking well blame him for that. — Christopher Brookmyre, *Boiling a Frog*, p. 213, 2000

trunk and tree *noun*
the knee *UK*
Rhyming slang.
- — Ray Puxley, *Fresh Rabbit*, 1998

trunk job *noun*
a corpse, especially a badly decomposed corpse, found in a car boot (trunk) *US*
- They knew all about trunk jobs, John Does, Juan Does, gun-shots, accidentals and naturals. — Carl Hiaasen, *Strip Tease*, p. 100, 1993

trupence bag *noun*
marijuana *UK*
- — Mike Haskins, *Drugs*, p. 289, 2003

trust *verb*
▸ **I wouldn't trust you as far as I can throw you**
used as an expression of deep mistrust in someone *UK, 1961*
- [Deputy Prime Minister] John Prescott growled: "I wouldn't trust him [London's mayor, Ken Livingston] as far as I could bloody throw him." — *The Guardian*, 19th December 2003

trustafarian *noun*
a young person who lives a counterculture lifestyle on the proceeds of a trust fund *US*
- Then there's "Trustafarian," which describes a "guy who has long hair and a trust fund, drives a Saab or Jeep, listens to reggae, and doesn't let a whole lot bother him." — *Washington Times*, p. C3, 26th August 1992
- — David Shenk and Steve Silberman, *Skeleton Key*, p. 296, 1994
- [S]hagging a good-looking posh young trustafarian juggling crustyboy she'd met at some Arts Festival[.] — James Hawes, *Dead Long Enough*, p. 35, 2000

trust you!
used as an ironic register of predictable behaviour *UK, 1834*
Also with other nouns or names.

truth chamber *noun*
a police interview room *UK*
- Coppers have their own pet names for interview rooms. "The Confessional", "The Sweat Box", "The Truth Chamber". — John Wainwright, *The Last Buccaneer*, 1971

try *verb*
▸ **try it on; try it on with**
to make an attempt to outwit or impose upon someone *UK, 1811*
- [H]e was trying it on with the saucy moves all month. — *The Guardian*, 3rd July 2000

▸ **try this on for size; try this for size**
to consider a notion; to try something out; also used in horseplay as a battle-cry *US, 1956*
- Disagree and debate over the issues, not each other's feelings. Try this phrase on for size: "We can agree to disagree on this point." — Jay McGraw, *Closing the Gap*, p. 55, 2001

trying!
you are trying too hard to be something you are not! *US*
Hawaiian youth usage.
- — Douglas Simonson, *Pidgin to da Max*, 1981

try-on *noun*
an attempt to deceive *UK, 1874*
From **TRY IT ON**.
- [T]he Committee felt that it was too much of a try-on[.] — Mr. A.J. Beith (Berwick-upon-Tweed), *Hansard*, 20th April 1994

try-out *noun*
a selective trial *US, 1903*
- Almost from the moment Lane showed up at the Rams' office in 1952 asking for a try-out, he was a revelation. — *The Sporting News*, 11th February 2002

trysexual *adjective*
▹ **see: TRISEXUAL**

try walking across
US airline company Trans World Airlines (TWA) *US*
An ironic play on the famous initials. Most airlines attract jocular variations of their names; TWA seems to have more than most, including: 'Travel Without Arrival'; 'Try Walking, Asshole'; 'Try Walking Again'; 'The Worst Airline'; 'Took Wrong Airline'; 'Take Weapons Aboard'; 'Thieves, Whores and Alcoholics'; and so on.
- The letters TWA stand for Trans World Airlines, though there are those who say it really means 'try walking across'! — Robbie Shaw, *Boeing Jetliners*, p. 8, 1995

TS
too bad *US*
An abbreviation of **TOUGH SHIT**.
- "T.S.," I murmured – and you have to figure for yourself what the initials stand for. — Frederick Kohner, *Gidget*, p. 122, 1957

T's and blues *noun*
a combination of Taluin™, a painkiller, and the antihistamine Pyribenzamine™, abused for non-medicinal purposes *US*
- — Geoffrey Froner, *Digging for Diamonds*, p. 60, 1989
- Tops and Bottoms is street slang for T's and Blues. T's are Taluin, a painkiller, and Blues are Pyribenzamine, an antihistamine. Combined in the right dosage they make a poor man's heroin. — *Chicago Tribune*, p. 6C, 11th June 1989

tsatske *noun*
a pretty, sexy, brainless woman *US*
Yiddish, with the Yiddish diminutive of *tsatskeleh*.
- Next thing he knew all two tsatskillehs were both sunk down on the floor where the fold-in seats were[.] — Bernard Wolfe, *The Magic of Their Singing*, p. 88, 1961

TS card *noun*
a notional card that is punched when a person complains *US, 1948*
An abbreviation of the sympathy-lacking **TOUGH SHIT**.
- — Carl Fleischhauer, *A Glossary of Army Slang*, p. 23, 1968

tsk tsk *verb*
to express commiseration, or disappointment or irritation by making the sound 'tsk tsk' *UK, 1966*
- I tsk-tsked and shook my head, incredulous at the depravity of the British male. — Claire Mansfield and John Mendelssohn, *Dominatrix*, p. 153, 2002

tsk tsk
used for expressing commiseration, or disappointment or irritation *UK, 1947*
An attempted written representation of the sound of this non-verbal exclamation that is somewhere between 'tut tut' and a sucking of the teeth.

tsotsies *noun*
non-white adolescent criminals *SOUTH AFRICA*
Reported by A.C. Partridge, 1968.

tsuris; tzuris; tszoris *noun*
troubles, problems, suffering *US*
Yiddish.

- What tzuris Smale caused the University! One of the world's most famous mathematicians and the most renowned professor at the university, here was Smale plotting and working with nonstudent crazies! —Jerry Rubin, *Do It!*, p. 39, 1970
- It gets you there fast, and without the tszoris of all the crap in between East Coast and West – but it tends to catch up with you. —Raymond Mungo, *Famous Long Ago*, p. 110, 1970

TTFN

goodbye *UK, 1948*

An initialism of 'ta-ta for now', which served as a catchphrase first in the BBC radio programme *ITMA*, 1941–49, and was picked-up by popular BBC radio broadcaster Jimmy Young (b.1921) who began broadcasting in 1949.

- —Eric S. Raymond, *The New Hacker's Dictionary*, p. 342, 1991
- [L]ike TTFN, it may do for ending an email, but at the start it'll flummox. — *The Guardian*, 21st February 2004

TTFO

(in doctors' shorthand) *t*old *t*o *f*uck *o*ff (go away) *UK*

Recorded in an article about medical slang in British (3 London and 1 Cambridge) hospitals.

- — *Ethics and Behaviour*, August 2003

T-timers *noun*

dark glasses worn by marijuana smokers *US*

- — *American Speech*, p. 30, February 1952: 'Teen-age hophead jargon'

tub *noun*

1 a drum *US*

- Go easy on that tub, this time. —John Clellon Holmes, *The Horn*, p. 135, 1958

2 a seat on an amusement ride *US*

- —Joe McKennon, *Circus Lingo*, p. 97, 1980
- —Gene Sorrows, *All About Carnivals*, p. 27, 1985: 'Terminology'

3 a small crap table *US, 1983*

- —Thomas L. Clark, *The Dictionary of Gambling and Gaming*, p. 240, 1987

4 in electric line work, an overhead transformer *US*

- —A.B. Chance Co., *Lineman's Slang Dictionary*, p. 17, 1980

tubs *noun*

▸ the tubs

a gay bath house; the gay bath house scene collectively *US*

- —Guy Strait, *The Lavender Lexicon*, 1st June 1964
- —Bruce Rodgers, *The Queens' Vernacular*, p. 28, 1972
- At times like this, the tubs was an easy way out. Discreet, dispassionate, noncommital. —Armistead Maupin, *Tales of the City*, p. 313, 1978
- — *Maledicta*, p. 146, Summer/Winter 1986–87: 'Sexual slang: prostitutes, pedophiles, flagellators, transvestites, and necrophiles'

tubby; tubs *noun*

an overweight person *UK*

Both variants serve as nickname and derogatory term; 'tubs' is the abbreviation of 'tubby'.

- Enjoy your tea, tubs? — Martin King and Martin Knight, *The Naughty Nineties*, p. 46, 1999
- Simon Le Bon for God's sake, a provincial tubby if ever there was one[.] —Kevin Sampson, *Powder*, p. 23, 1999

tubby *adjective*

1 emphasising low frequencies, producing poorly defined sound *US*

Used in describing a location's sound quality in television and film making.

- —Ira Konigsberg, *The Complete Film Dictionary*, p. 33, 1987

2 overweight *UK, 1835*

tube *noun*

1 a fool, an idiot; a despicable or contemptible person *UK: SCOTLAND*

Probably from an earlier sense as 'penis', thus **PRICK**.

- —Michael Munro, *The Original Patter*, 1985
- They played me, they played everybody, so why not a tube like him? —Christopher Brookmyre, *The Sacred Art of Stealing*, p. 209, 2002

2 a person *UK: SCOTLAND*

- Just keep feeding the tube this muck and he'll be deid [dead] by Christmas. —Ian Pattison, *Rab C. Nesbitt*, 1988

3 a marijuana cigarette *US, 1937*

- —Ernest L. Abel, *A Marijuana Dictionary*, p. 105, 1982

4 a telephone *US*

- —Robert George Reisner, *The Jazz Titans*, p. 167, 1960

5 a prison officer who listens to inmates' conversation and for information from informers *UK, 1950*

- —Angela Devlin, *Prison Patter*, p. 117, 1996

6 a can of beer *AUSTRALIA, 1964*

- I'll bet old Gorty's got a few thirst quenching tubes bodgied away in this den of his! —Barry Humphries, *The Wonderful World of Barry McKenzie*, p. 7, 1968
- —Ivor Limb, *Footy's No Joke!*, p. 77, 1986

7 the concave face of a wave *US*

- —Grant W. Kuhns, *On Surfing*, p. 123, 1963
- — *Paradise of the Pacific*, p. 27, October 1963

8 a shotgun *US*

- — *Los Angeles Times*, p. B1, 19th December 1994

9 in a casino, the rack where betting tokens are stored at a gambling table *US*

- —Frank Scoblete, *Best Blackjack*, p. 274, 1996

10 a *t*otally *u*nnecessary *b*reast *e*xamination *UK, 1999*

Acronym; medical slang, apparently favoured by young male doctors.

- —Adam T. Fox, St Mary's Hospital, London, 10th October 2002

▸ lay tube

from the male point of view, to have sex *US*

- [A]bout eighty a them's gonna lay more tube than the motherfuckin Alaska pipeline. —Joseph Wambaugh, *The Delta Star*, p. 37, 1983

▸ the tube

a television; television *US*

Originally applied to the telephone, but then much more widely to television.

- — *Swinging Syllables*, 1959
- [T]hen we watched the tube through the late movie which ended at three. —John Nichols, *The Sterile Cuckoo*, p. 125, 1965
- Back at my room I feel depressed but I can't go to bed because I only got up at 3 p.m. I'm going to be on the tube (Allen Burke called), but I'm depressed. —James Simon Kunen, *The Strawberry Statement*, p. 62, 1968
- When he hit the tube that night, he wasn't giving a performance in a cummerbund. —Albert Goldman, *Freak Show*, p. 67, 1968

Tube *noun*

▸ the Tube

the London Underground transport system *UK*

Originally, in this context, the tunnel in which an underground electric train runs (late C19), hence this abbreviation of 'tube-railway'. The Central London Railway, which opened in 1900, was known as 'The Twopenny Tube' for its fixed-price fee. The cost of a journey has been going up ever since.

- Same thing Day after day – Tube-Work-Dinner-Work-Tube-Armchair-TV-Sleep-Work. —Richard Neville, *Play Power [citing Wall Graffiti, Notting Hill, 1968]*, p. 253, 1970
- [W]e do all their tube advertising[.] —Barry Humphries, *Bazza Pulls It Off!*, 1971
- [T]he bulk of the firm were meeting up at Kingsbury, which is one stop past Wembley on the tube. — Martin King and Martin Knight, *The Naughty Nineties*, p. 135, 1999

tube *verb*

1 to watch television *US*

- Jane and I, and Dell and Pat, and Brad and Laura (who's old enough to drive) went tubing after dinner[.] —Beatrice Sparks (writing as 'Anonymous'), *Jay's Journal*, p. 56, 1979
- — *Concord (New Hampshire) Monitor*, p. 17, 23rd August 1983: 'Slang slinging: an intense and awesome guide to prep school slanguage'

2 to surf below and inside the crest of the wave *US*

- LANCE: Maybe he'll get tubed. WILLARD: What? LANCE: Maybe he'll get inside the tube – where – where they can't see him. — *Apocalypse Now*, 1979

3 to insert an endotracheal tube into a patient *UK*

Medical use.

- We've bronched him, tubed him, bagged him, [and] cathed him. —Diane Johnson, *Doctor Talk, The State of the Language*, 1980

4 to fail, to do poorly *US*

- — *Current Slang*, p. 5, Summer 1966
- —Gary N. Underwood, *American Speech*, p. 68, Spring-Summer 1975: 'Razorback Slang'

tube lube *noun*

oral sex on a man *US*

- Not only did I get three to give me a "Tube lube" but I got to French out four of the five swingers. — *Screw*, p. 6, 20th July 1970

tuber *noun*

a person who spends too much of the day on a sofa watching television *US*

From the dominant term **COUCH POTATO** and punning on **THE TUBE** (television).

- —Connie Eble (Editor), *UNC-CH Campus Slang*, p. 10, March 1986

tubes *noun*

the London Underground transport system *UK*

A variation of **THE TUBE**.

- Sorry we're late [...] Tubes and stuff.—Michael River, *Electrovoodoo (Disco Biscuits)*, p. 99, 1996

▸ **down the tubes**

ruined with no chances left; done-for; lost; wasted *US, 1963*

A variation of 'down the drain' or 'down the pan'; literally 'down the toilet'.

- Now we got hurt, we really took a beating in profits, our business almost went down the tubes[.]—Josh Alan Friedman, *Tales of Times Square*, p. 81, 1986
- Britain is going down the tubes!—David Parker, *Cool Places*, p. 74, 1998

tube steak *noun*

1 a fraunkfurter, a hot dog *US, 1963*

- Tube steak – a hot dog, the main part of a drag racer's usual meal. —Ross Olney, *Kings of the Drag Strip*, p. 188, 1968
- — *Current Slang*, p. 13, Summer 1968
- Tube steak a la fire, with an array of condiments.—Darryl Ponicsan, *The Last Detail*, p. 134, 1970

2 by visual extension, the penis *US*

- —Edith A. Folb, *runnin' down some lines*, p. 258, 1980
- — *Maledicta*, p. 255, Summer/Winter 1981: 'Five years and 121 dirty words later'
- I want to slip my tubesteak into your sister. What'll you take in trade?—*Full Metal Jacket*, 1987
- About half said they were satisfied with their tubesteaks.—Anka Radakovich, *The Wild Girls Club*, p. 29, 1994
- [T]hree babes [...] wanted to let me know how badly they needed ol' Casanova's tubesteak.—Howard Stern, *Miss America*, p. 15, 1995
- Decker pulls out his tube steak, aims for the peach, and heaps his genetic gunk on the once-virgin fruit.—Anthony Petkovich, *The X Factory*, p. 15, 1997
- Another way to say "fellatio" – Enjoying a tube steak[.]—Erica Orloff and JoAnn Baker, *Dirty Little Secrets*, p. 83, 2001

tube top *noun*

a woman's garment, elasticised, stretching from the waist to under the arms *US, 1974*

- She was wearing an emerald tube top, white bongo jeans, and boat sneakers. The tube top would slip an inch each time she waved at one of the sailors, and she made it a point to wave frequently as she pranced across the barroom.—Joseph Wambaugh, *Floaters*, p. 92, 1996

tub of lard *noun*

a fat person *UK*

A neat combination of a pun on **TUBBY** (fat) and 'lard' (a soft white fat). In the late 1990s when Roy Hattersley MP, an overweight politician, declined to guest on the satirical BBC television quiz *Have I Got News For You* he was replaced, to great hilarity, with an actual tub of lard.

tubs *noun*

drums *US*

- Ray Eisel, the drummer, was a thin and wiry fly cat who really beat his tubs.—Mezz Mezzrow, *Really the Blues*, p. 61, 1946
- —Babs Gonzales, *Be-Bop Dictionary and History of its Famous Stars*, p. 9, 1949
- [A] big brutal Negro with a bullneck who didn't give a damn about anything but punishing his husted tubs, crash, rattle-ti-boom, crash.—Jack Kerouac, *On the Road*, p. 197, 1957

tubular *adjective*

1 used of a wave, hollow as it breaks, creating a chamber which can be surfed through *US*

- —Michael V. Anderson, *The Bad, Rad, Not to Forget Way Cool Beach and Surf Discriptionary*, p. 21, 1988

2 spectacular *US*

- —Mary Corey and Victoria Westermark, *Fer Shurr! How to be a Valley Girl*, 1982
- But NO BIGGIE / It's so AWESOME / It's like TUBULAR, y'know.—Moon Unit and Frank Zappa, *Valley Girl*, 1982
- —Connie Eble (Editor), *UNC-CH Campus Slang*, p. 10, Fall 1985

tuck *noun*

1 food, especially snacks and delicacies *UK, 1857*

Mainly school slang.

- 2m drive for healthier tuck.—*The Observer*, 4th January 2002

2 a cosmetic operation to remove fat or skin *US*

- Fin slapped at the flesh between his chin and Adam's apple, wondering what a little tuck would cost, and whether he could make his medical insurance cover it.—Joseph Wambaugh, *Finnegan's Week*, p. 73, 1993

tuck *verb*

in transexual usage, to tape your penis onto your groin to avoid any telltale bulge which might tip off someone as to your genetic sex *US*

- — *Maledicta*, p. 174, Summer/Winter 1986–1987: 'Sexual slang: prostitutes, pedophiles, flagellators, transvestites, and Necrophiles'

▸ **tuck in; tuck into; tuck away**

to eat heartily; to start eating *UK, 1810*

'Tuck away' is first recorded in 1861.

- He said: "Tuck in, anyway. Got to build up energy for the forthcoming week of sustained attack."—John Burke and Stuart Douglass, *The Boys*, p. 5, 1962
- Nood's tuckin' in to them biccies just eatin' one while checkin' out the next.—Nick Barlay, *Curvy Lovebox*, p. 73, 1997

tuck and roll; tucked and rolled *adjective*

descriptive of a highly stylised car upholstery design, popular with hot rodders and low riders *US*

- My coupe's tuck and roll underneath the hood / And the rugs, seats, and panels now are looking good.—The Beach Boys, *Cherry, Cherry Coupe*, 1963
- You know, I really love the feel of tuck 'n' roll upholstery.—*American Graffiti*, 1973
- Continental kit, 326 supercharged, full leather tuck and roll, hand-rubbed sapphire blue metal flake paint job.—James Ellroy, *Suicide Hill*, p. 611, 1986

tucked and rolled *adjective*

medically transformed from a male to a female *US*

- When she paroled, Magdalena had the sex change operation at Stanford Medical Center, she's tucked a rolled, a genuine woman. —Seth Morgan, *Homeboy*, p. 301, 1990

tucked up *adjective*

arrested *UK*

- —Angela Devlin, *Prison Patter*, p. 117, 1996
- This was the meeting place to make sure we're not getting tucked up.—Garry Bushell, *The Face*, p. 12, 2001

tucker *noun*

food *AUSTRALIA, 1850*

- Here you eat good tucker, do nothing, sleep dry, and under a net[.] —Eric Lambert, *The Veterans*, p. 186, 1954
- Yes, the stick says the mob will be coming in early day after tomorrow, and will I have plenty big tucker for 'em.—Arthur Upfield, *Bony and the Mouse*, p. 67, 1959
- Now on the other had, sheilas are a bit like tucker. Once you've had a feed, you don't feel like it any more.—John Wynnum, *Jiggin' in the Riggin'*, p. 35, 1965
- I can't seem to hold down me tucker!—Barry Humphries, *The Wonderful World of Barry McKenzie*, p. 26, 1968
- I've got fleabites all over me, as big as cricket balls, and the tucker's shitty. Let's get the hell outa here.—Ward McNally, *Supper at Happy Harry's*, p. 70, 1982

tucker *verb*

to provide someone with food; to feed someone *AUSTRALIA, 1891*

- [W]e tuckered the Muirdens that night because we had plenty of food and they had been 'doing a starve'[.]—Kylie Tennant, *The Honey Flow*, p. 18, 1956

tuckerbag *noun*

a bag for carrying food *AUSTRALIA, 1885*

- TUCKERBAG – The bag in which the Sundowner carries his rations.—Gilbert H. Lawson, *A Dictionary of Australian Words and Terms*, 1924
- I had to keep going; had to keep the tucker-bags filled somehow.—Ion L. Idriess, *Over the Range*, p. 243, 1947
- [H]e and his mates used to pray instead of eat, while your lot are forever putting on the billy or dipping into the tucker bag.—Kel Richards, *The Aussie Bible*, p. 29, 2003

tucker box *noun*

a box used to store and transport food; a lunch box *AUSTRALIA, 1897*

- He shifted his leg, raising it on to another tucker box.—Kylie Tennant, *The Honey Flow*, p. 15, 1956
- Will you take a tucker box?—Wal Watkins, *Race the Lazy River*, p. 147, 1963
- In the meantime I gave my tucker box to the little girl with the baby.—Patsy Adam-Smith, *Folklore of the Australian Railwaymen*, p. 55, 1969

tuckered; tuckered out *adjective*
tired, exhausted *US, 1840*
- You all tuckered out. Sleep now. Go to sleep. — Olive Ann Burns, *Cold Sassy Tree*, p. 39, 1984

tucker fucker *noun*
a cook *AUSTRALIA*
- Tucker Fucker – Cook. — Ryan Aven-Bray, *Ridgey Didge Oz Jack Lang*, p. 47, 1983

tuckerless *adjective*
without food *AUSTRALIA, 1910*
- I have a remarkable collection of sob stories and woebegone information concerning my tuckerless flat, fatty wardrobe and carpetless motorcar. — Barry Dickins, *What the Dickins*, p. 90, 1985

tuckers *noun*
a tuck shop *UK*
- — *The Felstedian*, December 1947

tucker time *noun*
meal time *AUSTRALIA, 1902*
- It has a distinct, unpleasant body odour, but that doesn't stop the aborigines from thinking it is a great treat for tucker time. — Lyla Stevens, *Animals of Australia in Colour*, p. 26, 1956

tuck in *noun*
a meal *AUSTRALIA, 1889*
- Ladies would heat the babies' bottles on the cook's stove and everyone would have a good tuck in. — Patsy Adam-Smith, *Folklore of the Australian Railwaymen*, p. 170, 1969

tuck shop *noun*
a school's purveyor of snacks *UK, 1857*
- Like today, I was just standing outside the tuckshop not even doing anythink, and she just looks me up and down. — Kylie Mole (Maryanne Fahey), *My Diary*, p. 47, 1988
- A school which banned cola and crisps reports better behaviour and exam results. So why do tuck shops and canteens still dish out junk food? — *The Guardian*, 8th June 1999

tuckus *noun*
▷ see: TOCHIS

tud *noun*
a *t*otally *u*nnecessary *d*rink that causes you to vomit *US*
- — Don R. McCreary (Editor), *Dawg Speak*, 2001

'tude *noun*
a bad attitude *US*
- — Connie Eble (Editor), *UNC-CH Campus Slang*, p. 2, Fall 1987

tudge boy *noun*
a criminal hired to enforce criminal rules on other criminals *US*
- Laticia says the pimps use "tudge boys," street slang for hired enforcers, not only to rough up circuit girls who get out of line, but also to patrol Colfax, looking for crack whores out of bounds. — *Denver Westword*, 2nd May 2002

tuff
▷ see: TOUGH

tuft *noun*
the female pubic hair *UK*
- [The Degas drawings] are all brothel scenes and show plenty of tuft. — *The Observer*, 10th February 1980

tug *noun*
1 an act of masturbation *AUSTRALIA*
- I'm not saying I always have a morning tug to get the day started[.] — Kevin Sampson, *Outlaws*, p. 81, 2001

2 an arrest *UK*
A pun on **PULL** (an arrest).
- I only ever got a tug the once, and they couldn't pin a thing on me. — Val McDermid, *Keeping on the Right Side of the Law*, p. 178, 1999

3 a warning of imminent danger given from one criminal to another, or beggar to beggar, etc *AUSTRALIA*
Often in the phrase 'give you the tug'.
- — *The (Sydney) Bulletin*, 26th April 1975

▸ **give a tug**
to arrest someone *UK*
- [W]henever he got too bolshie they'd give a tug. — Lanre Fehintola, *Charlie Says...*, p. 125, 2000

tug *verb*
1 (from criminal to criminal, or beggar to beggar, etc) to give a warning of imminent danger *AUSTRALIA*
Often in the phrase 'tug your coat'.
- The expression derives from the system of signals shoppies [shoplifters] use in large stores [...] One of these signals is tugging at the lapels of the signaller's coat, signifying danger. — *The (Sydney) Bulletin*, 26th April 1975

2 to masturbate *NEW ZEALAND*
- — David McGill, *David McGill's Complete Kiwi Slang Dictionary*, p. 115, 1998

▸ **tug on**
1 to inhale smoke from a cigarette *UK*
- "Yeah, a bit," I says, tugging on Lowey's spliff. — Jimmy Stockin, *On The Cobbles*, p. 132, 2000

2 to think about something *UK*
Figurative use of conventional 'tug' (to pull).
- After a day's tugging on it, I had to accept that Ritchie was fucking on it and all, too. — Kevin Sampson, *Outlaws*, p. 251, 2001

tug and rub *noun*
an erotic massage *CANADA*

tug o' war *noun*
a whore *UK*
Rhyming slang.
- — Ray Puxley, *Cockney Rabbit*, 1992

tuie *noun*
▷ see: TOOIE

tules; toolies *noun*
a remote rural area *US*
An extension of the name of a type of cattail that grows in the very rural San Joaquin Valley of California.
- We drove her ass out into the toolies, and she let both me and Buck fuck her pregnant ass. — Earl Thompson, *Tattoo*, p. 224, 1974
- To be "in the toolies" is to be in the bush, and also means to accidentally drive off the road. The phrase may have come from Ultima Thule, in ancient geography, the northernmost limit of the habitable world, a distant, unknown place. — Tom Parkin, *WetCoast Words*, p. 74, 1989
- — John Edwards, *Auto Dictionary*, p. 176, 1993

tulip *noun*
someone whose looks or behaviour mark them as abnormal *IRELAND*
- He was some tulip, Bertie; he was fuckin' gas. — Roddy Doyle, *The Van*, p. 62, 1991
- They're some fuckin' tulips, a disconcerted Spit would say[.] — John Kelly, *The Sophisticated Boom Boom*, p. 13–14, 2003

tulips *noun*
a variety of MDMA, the recreational drug best known as ecstasy *UK*
- CALL IT... Adam, brownies, burgers, disco biscuits, doves, eckies, tulips, X. JUST DON'T CALL IT... MDMA – too scientific[.] — *Drugs An Adult Guide*, p. 34, December 2001

tum *noun*
the stomach *UK, 1869*
A shortening of **TUMMY**.
- Guinness (4.1% ABV) will settle the old tum and ensure you're as right as rain in the morning[.] — *The FHM Little Book of Bloke*, p. 115, June 2003

tumble *noun*
1 an act of sexual intercourse; an invitation to engage in sexual intercourse *UK, 1903*
- Nobody gave me a tumble, so I supposed I was to make the selection. — Mickey Spillane, *I, The Jury*, p. 64, 1947
- I knew she was belligerent; nobody had given her a tumble. — Horace McCoy, *Kiss Tomorrow Good-bye*, p. 134, 1948
- Or if it wasn't the end of it, if you could actually get a tumble from her, what of it? — Jim Thompson, *A Swell-Looking Babe*, p. 3, 1954
- Tricks who never gave me a tumble before think I'm something special now. — John M. Murtagh and Sara Harris, *Cast the First Stone*, p. 5, 1957
- A few tumbles during the war, then eighteen years of nothing. — Max Shulman, *Anyone Got a Match?*, p. 260, 1964
- I saw at least a thousand I'd have married gladly on the spot if they'd given me a tumble. — Oscar Zeta Acosta, *The Autobiography of a Brown Buffalo*, p. 189, 1972

2 recognition by the police or the interruption of a crime *US*
- — Hyman E. Goldin et al., *Dictionary of American Underworld Lingo*, p. 227, 1950

3 a fight, especially a gang fight *US*
- You scared of a little tumble or something? — *Man's Magazine*, p. 12, February 1960

▸ **come a tumble**
to be noticed *UK*
- If you two don't shut up we'll all come a tumble. — Frank Norman, *Bang To Rights*, p. 50, 1958

tumble *verb*
1 to discover, to understand, to notice, to realise, to become aware of *UK, 1846*
- — Joseph E. Ragen and Charles Finston, *Inside the World's Toughest Prison*, p. 822, 1962: 'Penitentiary and Underworld Glossary'
- Ain't a chance for their husbands to tumble to what's going on. — Iceberg Slim (Robert Beck), *Pimp*, p. 128, 1969
- I'm not so stupid that I don't tumble you're just telling me half of what you know[.] — Ted Lewis, *Jack Carter's Law*, p. 7, 1974
- We've tumbled you, don't fuckin' strong it. — J.J. Connolly, *Know Your Enemy*, p. 154, 1999

2 to have sex with someone *UK, 1602*
Found in Shakespeare and understood in context if not used heavily today.
- Either you're losing your grip, or you think she's tood good to tumble. She is, but I'm not! — Jim Thompson, *The Grifters*, p. 96, 1963
- I'm thinking of what Audrey had said about being barmy carrying on together. I'd had that thought ever since we'd first tumbled[.] — Ted Lewis, *Jack Carter's Law*, p. 11, 1974
- There was a girl whom he and I both loved, who actually never tumbled for either of us. — Stephen Gaskin, *Amazing Dope Tales*, p. 29, 1980

3 to get married *US*
- "I'm getting married as soon as I can get a week off." "You're tumbling too?" smiled Serge. — Joseph Wambaugh, *The New Centurions*, p. 351, 1970

tumble and trip; tumble *noun*
a collection from a group of people *UK*
Rhyming slang for **WHIP-ROUND**.
- — Ray Puxley, *Cockney Rabbit*, 1992

tumble down the sink; tumble *noun*
a drink *UK*
Rhyming slang; first recorded in *Songs and Slang of the British Soldier: 1914–1918*, John Brophy and Eric Partridge, 1930.
- [H]e made his way to the rub-a-dub for a tumble down the sink [drink]. — Ronnie Barker, *Fletcher's Book of Rhyming Slang*, p. 26, 1979

tumblers *noun*
1 the female breasts *UK*
- [T]heir breasts are no longer merely breasts but famous breasts. Celebrity shmams. Hollywood hooters. Tinseltown tumblers. — *The Times*, 2nd August 2003

2 dice with rounded edges *US*
- — *The Annals of the American Academy of Political and Social Sciences*, p. 132, May 1950

tummy *noun*
the stomach *UK, 1869*
- I wish I was a little worm / With hairs upon my tummy / I'd crawl into the honeypot / And make my tummy gummy — Anonymous playground rhyme late 1950s, early 60s
- MOLLY: Being so hot mightn't be good for the tummy, though. ALF: Oh, blow the tummy! — John O'Toole, *The Bush and the Tree [Six Granada Plays]*, p. 29, 1960
- "Your tummy acting up on you?" "Heartburn," Chip said, touching his chest. — Elmore Leonard, *Riding the Rap*, p. 246, 1995

tummy banana *noun*
the penis *AUSTRALIA*
- Oh! You mean when Bazzie did little jobs in the road and the policeman shone his torch at Bazzie's tummy banana... — Barry Humphries, *The Wonderful World of Barry McKenzie*, p. 12, 1968

tummy tuck *noun*
cosmetic surgery designed to reduce the fat around a person's waist *US*
- First we heard when Jimmy was govenor of Georgia, Rosalyn had had a face lift – and then a tummy tuck. — *Washington Post*, p. D1, 1st June 1977
- [T]here were enough face-lifts, dental caps, transplants, and tummy tucks in this place to convince him that the plastic surgeons and dematologists and dentists constituted the power behind the thrown. — Joseph Wambaugh, *The Glitter Dome*, p. 237, 1981
- Ida, who'd never wanteed children of her own, who was always scheming for a new car or a tummy tuck or a new dinette — Carl Hiaasen, *Tourist Season*, p. 109, 1986

tum-tum *noun*
the stomach *UK, 1864*
A variation of **TUMMY** or, more likely, the first babyish variation of 'stomach' from which 'tummy' derives.

tuna *noun*
1 the vagina *US*
Fish, as an allusion to what some claim to be the natural odour of a woman.
- Newcomer Melissa drives the submariners crazy, and Buck Adams goes way down for the horny tuna. — *Adult Video*, p. 23, August/September 1986
- He added that many women insist on using Saran Wrap when he goes down to taste the tuna. — Anka Radakovich, *The Wild Girls Club*, p. 124, 1994

2 a female *US*
- — Eugene Landy, *The Underground Dictionary*, p. 188, 1971
- There's some serious tuna at the Delta House. — Judi Sanders, *Faced and Faded, Hanging to Hurl*, p. 41, 1993

3 a young sailor as the object of desire of a homosexual man *US*
- From the advertising slogan "Chicken of the Sea." — Wayne Dynes, *Homolexis*, p. 101, 1985

tunage *noun*
music *US*
- — Connie Eble (Editor), *UNC-CH Campus Slang*, p. 6, Fall 1996

tuna party *noun*
a party where girls far outnumber boys *US*
- — Ben Applebaum and Derrick Pittman, *Turd Ferguson & The Sausage Party*, p. 69, 2004

tuna snuffling *noun*
the act of oral sex on a woman *US*
Combines **TUNA** (the vagina) with a reasonably conventional usage of 'snuffle'.
- — Erica Orloff and JoAnn Baker, *Dirty Little Secrets*, p. 87, 2001

tune *noun*
1 a recorded song *US*
Deviating from the literal meaning to embrace not just the tune, but all that goes into the song.
- Awesome party! Good tunes! Good brew! Good buddies! — *Wayne's World 2*, 1993

2 a tablet of Tuinal™, a branded barbituarate *UK*
An approximate abbreviation, usually in the plural; probably also as a pun on Tunes™, a branded medicated sweet.
- — Angela Devlin, *Prison Patter*, p. 117, 1996

tune *verb*
1 to talk; to say something *SOUTH AFRICA, 1976*
- — Penny Silva, *A Dictionary of South African English*, 1996

2 to beat somone physically *UK, 1788*
Also used with 'up'.
- To hit back: Tune him, label him full of dents. — *Cape Times*, 3rd June 1946

tune-and-toe show *noun*
a musical-theatre entertainment *UK*
A play on 'song and dance'.
- Public money has for a long time now been subsidising tune-and-toe shows. — *The Guardian*, 29th January 1979

tune grief *verb*
to verbally abuse someone *SOUTH AFRICA, 1972*
- — Penny Silva, *A Dictionary of South African English*, 1996

tuner *noun*
in the television and film industries, a musical composer *US*
- — Tony Miller and Patricia George, *Cut! Print!*, p. 160, 1977

tune up *verb*
to beat a better attitude into a fellow prisoner with a poor attitude *US*
- — James Harris, *A Convict's Dictionary*, p. 40, 1989

tuning *noun*
an instance of sexual intercourse which the female partner finds satisfying *UK*
Automotive imagery.
- [H]e'd drop in, calm as you like, give me a good tuning before he disappeared back home[.] — Anonymous *Streetwalker*, p. 62, 1959

tunnel of love *noun*
the vagina *US*
- —Erica Orloff and JoAnn Baker, *Dirty Little Secrets*, p. 71, 2001

tunnel rat *noun*
1 a US soldier who explored Viet Cong tunnels and underground networks *US*
- The platoon tunnel rat. Lavery leaned down next to the tunnel entrance, cupped his hands around his mouth, and shouted, "Chieu Hoi!"—Larry Heinemann, *Close Quarters*, p. 65, 1977
- Kolosowski, 36, a small, wiry man, had been a Marine "tunnel rat" – one of a few men of small stature who explored the labyrinth of underground caverns dug by the Viet Cong.—*The Houston Chronicle*, 27th October 1989

2 a police officer working for the New York Transit Bureau *US*
New York police slang.
- Rosato is a former tunnel rat who worked the lovely-smelling confines of New York subway stations and trains.—Samuel M. Katz, *Anytime Anywhere*, p. 245, 1997

tunnel shot *noun*
a photograph or shot in a film focusing on a woman's vagina *US*
- No ugly gaping tunnel shots, no chicks fingering themselves; just beautiful men with fine three piece sets.—*Screw*, p. 9, 5th October 1970

tuntun *noun*
the vagina *TRINIDAD AND TOBAGO*
- —Lise Winer, *Dictionary of the English/Creole of Trinidad & Tobago*, 2003

tuppence *noun*
two pence; hence, in later use, a notional sum of negligible value *UK, 1857*
- For tuppence, he'd get up and stick the nut on the copper[.]—Ian Rankin, *Tooth and Nail*, p. 76, 1992

tuppenceworth *noun*
a small contribution *UK*
Literally, 'two-penny-worth'.
- [U]nless it was a specifically C of S [Church of Scotland] story, you'd always find the Reverend McLeod's tuppenceworth much further down the columns.—Christopher Brookmyre, *Boiling a Frog*, p. 128, 2000
- There you go. That's my tuppence worth.—Jimmy Stockin, *On The Cobbles*, p. 104, 2000

tuppenny fuck *noun*
a thing of no worth *UK*
- I went from writing music no one gave a tuppenny fuck about, to music that some people seemed to really care about.—*Bang*, p. 62, November 2003

tuppenny ha'penny; tuppenny halfpenny; twopenny-halfpenny *adjective*
of little worth; insignificant *UK, 1909*
- MIAMI: Eddy Bunden 'as opened a club on my manor?! TREVOR: It's a tuppenny 'a'penny gaff, Miami, full of twelve-year-olds smokin' waccy baccy.—Bernard Dempsey and Kevin McNally, *Lock, Stock ... & Two Hundred Smoking Kalashnikovs*, p. 104, 2000
- [W]e want a proper writer to do our story. Not some twopenny-halfpenny hack.—Jake Arnott, *He Kills Coppers*, p. 110, 2001

tupperware *noun*
in electric line work, plastic proctective covering for a conductor *US*
- —A.B. Chance Co., *Lineman's Slang Dictionary*, p. 17, 1980

tuppy *noun*
the vagina *AUSTRALIA*
Borrowed from an Aboriginal language.
- —Thommo, *The Dictionary of Australian Swearing and Sex Sayings*, p. 132, 1985

tuque *noun*
▷ see: TOQUE

turbo *noun*
1 marijuana *UK*
- —Mike Haskins, *Drugs*, p. 289, 2003

2 marijuana mixed with crack cocaine *US*
- —US Department of Justice, *Street Terms*, October 1994
- —Mike Haskins, *Drugs*, p. 293, 2003

3 a fast driver *US*
- —Judi Sanders, *Da Bomb*, p. 17, 1997

turbo-gobbed *adjective*
describes someone who talks endlessly and without pause *UK*
- [T]urbo-gobbed Radio 1 breakfast show DJ Sara Cox[.]—*The Times Magazine*, p. 43, 16th February 2002

turd *noun*
1 a piece of excrement *UK*
In conventional use since about the year 1000, it is described in the *Oxford English Dictionary* as not now in polite use.

2 a contemptible person, a shit *UK, 1936*
The earliest meaning (a length of excrement) redirected.
- Bragg publicly addressed us as "turds" and "turdheads."—Jim Thompson, *Bad Boy*, p. 393, 1953
- Where is she, you turd?—Bernard Wolfe, *The Magic of Their Singing*, p. 91, 1961
- Goldwater may be a turd, but he's an acute observer of teen-age trends.—*Screw*, p. 19, 22nd December 1969
- I feel like an ignorant turd.—Oscar Zeta Acosta, *The Revolt of the Cockroach People*, p. 33, 1973
- "What that little turd has done," Roscommon said, "is somehow he persuaded the newspapers to bring him copies every morning[.]" —George V. Higgins, *The Rat on Fire*, p. 6, 1981
- That's what I thought. You're a gutless turd!—*The Breakfast Club*, 1985
- [S]he would never have been friends with a turd like that.—Chris Ryan, *Stand By, Stand By*, p. 60, 1996

3 a negative comment in a personnel file *US*
- Then he dictated a "turd" to be placed in the personnel file of the officer on duty in twelve-tower.—Malcolm Braly, *On the Yard*, p. 198, 1967

turd bird *noun*
a Ford Thunderbird *US*
- —Lewis Poteet, *Car & Motorcyle Slang*, p. 209, 1992

turd burglar *noun*
a male homosexual *UK*
- —Tom Hibbert, *Rockspeak!*, p. 163, 1983
- Even the straights turn Turd Burglar inside.—Kathy Lette, *Girls' Night Out*, p. 167, 1987
- —Angela Devlin, *Prison Patter*, p. 117, 1996
- —Connie Eble (Editor), *UNC-CH Campus Slang*, p. 9, Fall 1997

turd-burgling *adjective*
anal sex *UK*
- The cheeky fucking turd-burgling faggot[.]—Kevin Sampson, *Clubland*, p. 221, 2002

turdcutter *noun*
the buttocks *US*
Imprecise and crude physiology.
- Yeah, that bitch sho' has got a helluva turdcutter on it, ain't she? —Odie Hawkins, *Chicago Hustle*, p. 24, 1977
- —Connie Eble (Editor), *UNC-CH Campus Slang*, p. 10, Spring 1998

turd-floater *noun*
a heavy rain *CANADA*
- —Bill Casselman, *Canadian Sayings*, p. 151, 2002

turdhead *noun*
a despicable person *US*
- Bragg publicly addressed us as "turds" and "turdheads."—Jim Thompson, *Bad Boy*, p. 393, 1953

turd herder *noun*
a plumber *US*
- —*American Speech*, p. 271, December 1963: 'American Indian student slang'

turdpacker *noun*
in anal sex, the active partner *US, 1940s*

turdtapper *noun*
a male homosexual *CANADA*
An allusion to anal sex.
- —Chris Lewis, *The Dictionary of Playground Slang*, p. 240, 2003

turf *noun*
1 the territory controlled by a gang; a sphere of influence *US*
- I can see us in a big blue Cadillac, the biggest pushers around this turf.—Hal Ellson, *The Golden Spike*, p. 17, 1952
- —Dale Kramer and Madeline Karr, *Teen-Age Gangs*, p. 176, 1953
- I say this turf is small, but's it's all we got.—Stephen Sondheim, *West Side Story*, 1957
- In this town two blocks away is somebody else's turf, Irish.—Mickey Spillane, *Return of the Hood*, p. 92, 1964
- Some of the guys in our gang were scared to go out of our turf and rumble because they didn't know the backyards and the roofs in other turfs.—Claude Brown, *Manchild in the Promised Land*, p. 56, 1965

- An Angel on his own turf is as secure as a Mafia runner in a tought Italian neighborhood. — Hunter S. Thompson, *Hell's Angels*, p. 100, 1966
- Poppa moved us from 111th Street to Italian turf on 114th Street between Second and Third Avenue. — Piri Thomas, *Down These Mean Streets*, p. 24, 1967
- We took a beating – their turf, too many guys. — Edwin Torres, *Carlito's Way*, p. 8, 1975
- They want to keep it on their own turf. Ain't gonna give it to no Spics, no strangers. — *Saturday Night Fever*, 1977
- "I thought you were hustling." (Though this isn't hustling turf.) — John Rechy, *The Sexual Outlaw*, p. 175, 1977

2 a job, responsibility, obligation *US, 1970*

- — *American Speech*, Fall 1979
- NICK: You like playing games, don't you? CATHERINE: I've got a degree in psych. It comes with the turf. — *Basic Instinct*, 1992

3 the place where a whe-whe lottery game is operated *TRINIDAD AND TOBAGO, 1986*

- — Lise Winer, *Dictionary of the English/Creole of Trinidad & Tobago*, 2003

4 the street *US*

- 'Out on the turf folks are wondering who it was got the spic jealous enough to try offing a dude, you know how it is.' — Robert Deane Pharr, *Giveadamn Brown*, p. 14, 1978

turf *verb*

in hospital usage, to transfer a patient to another's responsibility *US*

- — Sally Williams, *"Strong" Words*, p. 164, 1994

turf consultant *noun*

in horse racing, someone who makes a living selling tips to bettors *US*

- — Dan Parker, *The ABC of Horse Racing*, p. 150, 1947

turf dance *noun*

a stylised dance developed and performed by an urban youth gang *US*

- Then she asked two of Brown's friends to honor his memory by doing a "turf dance," a curious bit of choreography – part Crip walk, part break-dancing. — *San Francisco Chronicle*, p. 1A, 17th May 2002

turistas; touristas *noun*

diarrhoea *US*

- — Helen Dahlskog (Editor), *A Dictionary of Contemporary and Colloquial Usage*, p. 60, 1972

Turk *noun*

1 a homosexual man who assumes the active role in anal sex *US*

- — Hyman E. Goldin et al., *Dictionary of American Underworld Lingo*, p. 228, 1950

2 a strong and aggressive young man *US*

- Then I look at this new turk. — Hal Ellson, *Duke*, p. 30, 1949

Turk *verb*

(of a male) to have sex, especially in a brutal fashion *UK*

- — Bill Naughton, *One Small Boy*, 1966
- — David Powis, *The Signs of Crime*, 1977

turkey *noun*

1 in films and showbusiness, an absolute failure or disaster, critical or financial; hence, in wider usage, a failure or disaster *US, 1927*

Why the turkey, a native of America, is the symbol of spectacular failure is a mystery.

- We're finally getting out of this turkey town. — *American Graffiti*, 1973
- "Lost Horizon" is perhaps the grandest of 1973's turkeys. — *San Francisco Examiner and Chronicle, Sunday Scene*, p. 12, 13th January 1974
- — Harry and Michael Medved, *The Golden Turkey Awards*, 1980
- If this is going to be a turkey movie, at least I will have brought it in on time! — Dale Pollock, *Skywalking: The Life and Films of George Lucas*, p. 120, 1999

2 an incompetent, ineffective or disliked person *US, 1951*

May be used with affection.

- And there's plenty of Polacks and fairies around here that we might have socked instead of turkeys with the name of Murphy and Garrity. — James T. Farrell, *Saturday Night*, p. 52, 1947
- [I]t had taken the public at large about three days to brand me a "turkey." — John Nichols, *The Sterile Cuckoo*, p. 50, 1965
- This is not the official goddamn threshold. Upstairs, you turkey! — Erich Segal, *Love Story*, p. 78, 1970
- That's why they all be in Lewisburg or Green Haven. Wise up, turkey. — Edwin Torres, *Carlito's Way*, p. 44, 1975
- Okay, turkey, no bullshit. Do you want to kill yourself? — *Lethal Weapon*, 1987

3 a member of a youth gang who is reluctant or unwilling to join in gang fights *US*

- But if you're a Jap or a turkey or you're going to punk out it's going to be bad stuff for you. — Hal Ellson, *Duke*, p. 31, 1949

4 an Irishman or a person of Irish descent *US*

- — Bill Reilly, *Big Al's Official Guide to Chicagoese*, p. 63, 1982

5 a patient who has been mishandled medically *US*

- — *American Speech*, p. 145–148, May 1961: 'The spoken language of medicine; argot, slang, cant'

6 in hospital usage, a patient with a petty medical complaint *US*

- — *Maledicta*, p. 70, Summer/Winter 1978: 'Common patient-directed pejoratives used by medical personnel'

7 a planespotter who is new to the hobby, or does not have good equipment, or does not take the hobby seriously *UK*

- I thought that planespotters used binoculars, but Tony soon put me straight. "Binoculars are for turkeys." — Iain Aitch, *A Fete Worse Than Death*, p. 73, 2003

8 in motorcyle racing, an old and/or heavy and bulky motorcyle *US*

- — Ed Radlauer, *Motorcylopedia*, p. 67, 1973

9 amphetamine *UK, 1998*

- — Mike Haskins, *Drugs*, p. 279, 2003

10 cocaine *UK, 1998*

- — Mike Haskins, *Drugs*, p. 281, 2003

11 poor quality, adulterated or counterfeit drugs *US*

- A lot of times some of those crooked dealers, new in the neighborhood, pass of baking soda as stuff or real weak H mixed with baking powder you get what's called burned: you're getting a turkey. — Willard Motley, *Let No Man Write My Epitaph*, p. 151, 1958
- [I]t was found to be "turkey" – it looked like heroin but proved to be a non-narcotic substance. — Harry J. Anslinger, *The Murderers*, p. 93, 1961
- In fact Willie didn't buy any dope, he bought a turkey. — Henry Williamson, *Hustler!*, p. 136, 1965

12 a tip of fifty cents *US*

- — Ramon Adams, *The Language of the Railroader*, p. 164, 1977

▸ **the turkey**

an act of withdrawing from addictive drugs; the time period of that withdrawal (without direct reference to the symptoms) *UK*

A variation of **COLD TURKEY**.

- "You really done the turkey... in a brothel?" "That's right. Ah did it." — Ben Elton, *High Society*, p. 291, 2002

turkey *verb*

1 to withdraw from a habit or addiction suddenly and without any tapering off *UK*

An abbreviation of 'cold turkey'.

- — Angela Devlin, *Prison Patter*, p. 117, 1996

2 to inhale marijuana smoke nasally *US, 1970*

- — Ernest L. Abel, *A Marijuana Dictionary*, p. 105, 1982

turkeyhead *noun*

a dolt *US*

- Okay for you, turkey-head, when I make my pile I leave you behind. — Max Shulman, *Guided Tour of Campus Humor*, p. 40, 1955

turkey line *noun*

in the language of hang gliding, a line used by an instructor to prevent the nose from dipping during landing or take-off *US*

- — Dennis Pagen, *Hang Gliding and Flying Skills*, p. 110, 1977: 'Glossary'

turkey neck *noun*

the penis *US*

The similarity between a penis with shaved surround and a plucked turkey's neck hanging down.

- That winter a houseguest, his wife gone shopping, pinned me in my bedroom by the mirror and as we both watched, took out to my horror a great stiff turkey neck, a hairless thing he wanted to give me. — Constance Warloe, *From Daughters to Mothers*, p. 271–272, 1997
- — David Rowan, *A Glossary for the 90s*, 1998

turkey shoot *noun*

an overwhelming slaughter of helpless victims *US*

From the C19 'sport' of a shooting match in which the target was a live turkey.

- "They heard that Charlie Company had a turkey shoot," Colburn recalled. — Seymour M. Hersh, *My Lai 4*, p. 90, 1970

- On August 17, in a slaughter reminiscent of the Kosong Turkey Shoot, hundreds of fleeing enemy soldiers fled in daylight to the banks of the Naktong and tried to ford the river to escape a beachhead that the marines had transformed into a deathtrap. — Joseph C. Goulden, *Korea*, p. 179, 1982
- As the Basra Road turkey shoot unfolded, US General Colin Powell reportedly told other members of the war cabinet [...] "We should stop now. Our pilots are just killing for the sake of it." — Stuart Jeffries, *Mrs Slocombe's Pussy*, p. 264, 2000

Turkey trot *noun*

diarrhoea suffered by tourists *US*

- In Italy, Turkey, Egypt and India it is named Turkey trot, gippy tummy, and Delhi belly. — *Washington Post, Times Herald*, p. L6, 10th April 1960

Turkish bath; Turkish *noun*

a laugh, especially at someone else's expense *UK*

Rhyming slang.

- Anyone having a "Turkish" at your expense is on a wind-up[.] — Ray Puxley, *Fresh Rabbit*, p. 119, 1998

Turkish culture *noun*

anal sex *US*

- — Robert A. Wilson, *Playboy's Book of Forbidden Words*, p. 246, 1972

Turkish delight *noun*

in homosexual usage, anal sex *US*

- — *Maledicta*, p. 60, 1986 – 1987: 'A continuation of a glossary of ethnic slurs in American English'

Turkish delight; Turkish *adjective*

1 miserly *UK*

Rhyming slang for **TIGHT**; no racial slur is intended.

- A "Turkish git" is the stingy scrote who "wouldn't give his shit to the crows". — Ray Puxley, *Fresh Rabbit*, p. 119, 1998

2 of poor quality *UK*

Rhyming slang for **SHITE**; here the racial slur seems deliberate.

- — *www.LondonSlang.com*, June 2002

Turkish rope *noun*

a heavy gold necklace *US*

- — Bill Valentine, *Gang Intelligence Manual*, p. 78, 1995

Turk McGurk *noun*

any unethical, vindictive person *US*

- — *Maledicta*, p. 14, Summer 1977: 'A word for It!'

turn *noun*

1 a histrionic display *AUSTRALIA*

- That's when you discovered us. Stacked on a turn. Went the knuckle. Dorabella shot through, abandoning her white bloomers on a low bough. — Jack Hibberd, *A Stretch of the Imagination*, p. 15, 1971
- When he got there, to save any hazzle, he put him in the yard, shut the gate and off and Adrian put on a real turn. — Sam Weller, *Old Bastards I Have Met*, p. 141, 1979

2 a (theatrical) performer *UK, 1715*

- The average turn at Duckie was absurd, confrontational, piss-taking – a mutant hybrid of pub drag and performance art. — *The Guardian*, p. 15, 14th May 2002

3 a party *AUSTRALIA, 1953*

- 'How did you think the turn went?' 'It was a beauty. Best house-warming party I've been to.' — Alexander Buzo, *Rooted*, p. 30, 1969

4 in trucking, a return trip *US*

- — Warren Smith, *Warren's Smith's Authentic Dictionary of CB*, p. 53, 1976

5 a jail sentence *US*

- You know what happens if you do another turn in the joint? — *The Usual Suspects*, 1995

▸ **do a turn**

to have sex *UK*

A play on a theatrical act.

- — Paul Baker, *Polari*, p. 172, 2002

turn *verb*

1 in trucking, to make a round trip to and from the specified destination *US*

- — Montie Tak, *Truck Talk*, p. 177, 1971

2 to sell something, especially stolen goods *US*

- — Bruce Jackson, *Outside the Law*, p. 61, 1972: 'Glossary'

3 to convert a man to homosexuality *US*

- All they think about is getting dope and getting laid, looking to see who they can turn. See, once you get turned, you're pussy. — Elmore Leonard, *Maximum Bob*, p. 108, 1991

4 in drag racing, to register a speed *US*

- Turned – Verb used to state speed: "He turned 190.00 mph." — Fremont Drag Strip, *Guide to Drag Racing*, 1960

▸ **turn 'em and burn 'em**

to quickly service a fighter plane and return it to combat *US*

Gulf war usage.

- — *American Speech*, p. 404, Winter 1991: 'Among the new words'

▸ **turn a film**

in Quebec, to shoot a film *CANADA*

The French origin of this English phrase is *tourner un film*.

- — Victor Trahan, *The City of Montreal Style Guide*, p. 120, 2001

▸ **turn in**

to retire to bed *UK, 1695*

- CORP: We were just turning in, Governor. GOVERNOR: Just turning in? Lights out was four hours ago. GRANDPA: We couldn't sleep like. — Clive Exton, *No Fixed Abode [Six Granada Plays]*, p. 132, 1959

▸ **turn into a pumpkin**

in transexual usage, to dress in keeping with your genetic sex *US*

- — *Maledicta*, p. 173, Summer/Winter 1986 – 1987: 'Sexual slang: prostitutes, pedophiles, flagellators, transvestites, and necrophiles'

▸ **turn it on**

1 to make an all-out effort at some task *AUSTRALIA, 1944*

- Next day, in Port Moresby, he really turned it on. By ten o'clock at night he was roaring. — J.E. MacDonnell, *Big Bill the Bastard*, p. 5, 1976
- You don't half turn it on, do yer? Why don'tcha cut the bullshit and buy me a beer? — Lance Peters, *The Dirty Half-Mile*, p. 149, 1979
- But her specialty was their wedding anniversary. Always turn it on – roast dinner by candlelight, champagne, and a bit of nooky chucked in – without fail. — Frank Hardy, *Hardy's People*, p. 87, 1986

2 (of a woman) to perform sexually *AUSTRALIA, 1944*

- I have just been reading a story with a drawing of one of these lady looking women, and she's going to turn it on for a soldier who's going away to be killed in the war. — Robert S. Close, *Love Me Sailor*, p. 20, 1945

3 to enliven something *UK*

- Somebody's going to go out there [into the World Snooker arena] and turn it on. — *The Listener*, p. 8, 28th April 1983

4 to provide for a party or celebration *AUSTRALIA, 1941*

- [W]e will be turning it on again when we reach 100,000 copies a week. Only next time you can help yourself to a free schooner. — *Ribald*, 1975

▸ **turn it up**

to consent to sex *NEW ZEALAND, 1973*

- — Harry Orsman, *A Dictionary of Modern New Zealand Slang*, p. 142, 1999

▸ **turn Japanese**

to masturbate *UK*

From the perceived resemblance between a stereotypical Japanese face and the facial expression that accompanies a quest for orgasm.

- — The Vapors *Turning Japanees*, 1980

▸ **turn over the covers**

to examine the other side of an issue *US*

- — Robert Kirk Mueller, *Buzzwords*, p. 160, 1974

▸ **turn state**

to become a witness for the prosecuting authorities *US*

From the term 'state witness'.

- "I just remembered I got infor I could fur shur parlay into probation, maybe dismissal." "You don't mean turn state?" — Seth Morgan, *Homeboy*, p. 93, 1990

▸ **turn the corner**

to begin to improve; to change your attitude for the better *UK*

- Tony Blair today claimed the government had "turned the corner" on asylum, following the publication of Home Office figures which revealed a steep drop in applications. — *The Guardian*, 22nd May 2003

▸ **turn the duke**

in circus and carnival usage, to shortchange someone *US*

- — Don Wilmeth, *The Language of American Popular Entertainment*, p. 282, 1981

▸ **turn the mit**

to shortchange *US*

- — Joe McKennon, *Circus Lingo*, p. 97, 1980

▸ turn tricks
to work as a prostitute
- I been turning tricks on the street for the last few months. — Neil S. Skolnik, *On the Ledge*, p. 110, 1996

▸ turn turtle
(of a surfer) to pass through a wave coming at them by rolling under their surfboard *US*
- — Gary Fairmont R. Filosa II, *The Surfer's Almanac*, p. 185, 1977

▸ turn up trumps
to succeed, to turn out well *UK, 1862*

▸ turn up your nose
to view or treat with contempt *UK, 1818*
- When I turned my nose up at a joint, people would whisper, "Don't you know, man, she's the acid queen." — Camryn Manheim, *Wake Up, I'm Fat!*, p. 41, 1999

▸ turn your key
to make you angry *UK*
A variation of **WOUND UP**.
- Don't turn my key. East. You know where he is. — Mark Powell, *Snap*, p. 68, 2001

turnaround *noun*
1 in trucking, a return trip *US*
- — Wayne Floyd, *Jason's Authentic Dictionary of CB Slang*, p. 30, 1976

2 training time for navy pilots between aircraft carrier cruises *US*
- In turnaround before the second cruise, he'd met pilot Lou Page. — Robert K. Wilcox, *Scream of Eagles*, p. 23, 1990

turn around *verb*
in criminal or police usage, to persuade someone to inform or otherwise betray *US*
- And then a lot of guys with heart ain't got no smarts, so then the bulls outfox them, put them in a bind, and then turn them around. — Edwin Torres, *Carlito's Way*, p. 130, 1975
- — Angela Devlin, *Prison Patter*, p. 117, 1996

turned on *adjective*
1 sexually aroused *UK*
- — David Powis, *The Signs of Crime*, 1977

2 able to comprehend, especially as a result of drug use *US*
- These guys are turned on you know, half of what he says doesn't mean fuck all to anybody who isn't turned on[.] — Paul E. Willis, *Profane Culture*, p. 145, 1978

3 stimulated and inspired by some music *UK*
- — David Powis, *The Signs of Crime*, 1977

turn it in!
stop doing that!; stop talking! *UK*
A variation of **TURN IT UP!**.
- "Ah, turn it in, sad kecks!" hissed James. — Kevin Sampson, *Powder*, p. 49, 1999

turn it up!
stop! *AUSTRALIA, 1927*
Originally 'turn up' (to renounce), 'turn it up' (to move home or, otherwise, change your life), hence the current meaning.
- WATSON: Now, turn it up, will you. TAYLOR: Come on, let's get on with the game. — Graeme Kent, *The Queen's Corporal [Six Granada Plays]*, p. 91, 1959
- She gave a cynical snort. "Well, that's the first time for a long time I must say." "Turn it up, Doll. Gin?" — Derek Bickerton, *Payroll*, p. 119, 1959
- 'Hey, turn it up, mate,' he concluded in higher key as a middy of beer spilled on the wrong side of his tartan shirt. 'Sorry, mate.' — Frank Hardy, *The Outcasts of Foolgarah*, p. 78, 1971

turn-off *noun*
something that disgusts or creates antipathy *US*
- I really hate all of the macho bullshit that goes along with police work. It's a real turnoff. — Gerald Petievich, *To Die in Beverly Hills*, p. 213, 1983

turn off *verb*
1 to create antipathy in someone, to disillusion someone *US*
- The first time I played Fun House I got very turned off. — Lester Bangs, *Psychotic Reactions and Carburetor Dung*, p. 47, 1970

2 to disgust someone *US*
- You're a female version of the routine Regular Army clown. And that turns me off, so just leave my outfit alone and we'll get along fine. — *M*A*S*H*, 1970

turn-on *noun*
1 something that excites or arouses someone sexually *AUSTRALIA, 1969*
- — Marilyn Suriani Futterman, *Dancing Naked in the Material World*, 1992
- I like to look at pussies. I think they are pretty. It's like being in heaven. The women that dance like this are a turn-on. — Marilyn Suriani Futterman, *Dancing Naked in the Material World*, p. 50, 1992

2 a sharing or gifting of drugs *US*
- When I'd find a turn-on in progress, I'd yank him into the circle as I chose a good spot to be the next in line for an offering. — Cleo Odzer, *Goa Freaks*, p. 39, 1995

3 a single instance of drug-intoxication *UK*
Also known as a 'turning-on'.
- — Home Office, *Glossary of Terms and Slang Common in Penal Establishments*, July 1978

turn on *verb*
1 to use a drug *US, 1953*
- — *American Speech*, p. 88, May 1955: 'Narcotic argot along the Mexican border'
- — Lawrence Lipton, *The Holy Barbarians*, p. 318, 1959
- She wanted to turn on but she didn't have any bread. — Alexander Trocchi, *Cain's Book*, p. 28, 1960
- A droopy-eyed Negro hands me a tiny joint, offers what is hardly a roach now: "Turn on?" — John Rechy, *City of Night*, p. 185, 1963
- He had first announced to the press his intention to "turn-on" at the police station. — *Los Angeles Free Press*, p. 5, 24th September 1964
- — J. L. Simmons and Barry Winograd, *It's Happening*, p. 173, 1966: 'glossary'

2 to introduce someone to something, especially drugs *US*
- "Bernie, do you want me to turn you on?" Zaida said. — Ross Russell, *The Sound*, p. 21, 1961
- Have to find a place though, maybe men's room in the house. Turn Pamela on later. Wouldn't dig it probably. — Richard Farina, *Been Down So Long*, p. 33–34, 1966
- "I turned on my mother," the chick told Charles. — Nicholas Von Hoffman, *We Are The People Our Parents Warned Us Against*, p. 27, 1967
- Who was the first hippie? Cain. He turned on his brother Abel! — Paul Laikin, *101 Hippie Jokes*, 1968
- Get high and you want to turn on the world. — Jerry Rubin, *Do It!*, p. 98, 1970
- A favourite game of travellers is to "turn on a Peace Corps man"[.] — Richard neville, *Play Power*, p. 219, 1970
- During my sophomore year at college, somebody (God bless him) turned me on to dope. — Raymond Mungo, *Famous Long Ago*, p. 3, 1970
- "I don't know where you'd get any in Swansea. Why do you ask?" "Oh, I just wanted to turn Elizabeth on." — Doug Lang, *Freaks*, p. 108, 1973
- I turned you onto the Honeymooners, Frank Zappa, Ernst Lubitsch, Sushi. I'm like a one-man youth culture for your pathetic assholes. — Kenneth Lonergan, *This is Our Youth*, p. 31, 2000

3 to arouse an interest, sexual or abstract in someone; to stimulate someone; to thrill someone *US, 1965*
- Not that a straightforward invitation from the young Lana Turner or the young Ava Gardner might not, as they say out here, "turn me on"[.] — Gore Vidal, *Myra Breckinridge*, p. 85, 1968
- One time I was with Jim and we were balling doggie fashion and his rommate came home and got turned on watching us ball. — *Adam Film Quarterly*, p. 68, October 1973
- Breast-feeding turned me on in a way sex never did. — Sally Cline, *Couples*, p. 29, 1998
- What turns you on? Champagne and strawberries fed to me by my lovely boyfriend. — *Sky Magazine*, p. 17, July 2001

turn on, tune in (and) drop out
used as a slogan for, and invitation to join the hippy counterculture *US*
Credited to Timothy Leary (1920–96) the self-styled high priest of LSD, this pocket-philosophy combined **TURN ON** (to use drugs), 'tune in' (to become culturally aware) and **DROP OUT** (to cease to be part of a conventional society) in a catchphrase that seemed to be more than the sum of its parts.
- The trinity is Tim Leary's answer to the Diet of Worms. — Sidney Bernard, *This Way to the Apocalypse*, p. 56, 1968
- We even found a drug-based religion, whose message would be "Turn On, Tune In, Drop Out!" We would proclaim the Reign of the Happily Integrated Modern Soul! — Michael Hollingshead, *The Man Who Turned on the World [The Howard Marks Book of Dope Stories]*, p. 97, 1973
- [Timothy Leary] later recanted the acid faith, disowning virtually all the subversive pronouncements of his post-Harvard career (the most famous of which – "Turn on, tune in and drop out" was the "Come on in, the water's lovely" of its day). — Stuart Walton, *Out of It [The Howard Marks Book of Dope Stories]*, p. 102, 2001

turnout *noun*
1 a novice prostitute; a prostitute working in a particular brothel for the first time *US*
- Til now I never had the time for a turnout. — A.S. Jackson, *Gentleman Pimp*, p. 161, 1973

- I had ignored the compulsive desire of any turn-out to flee the master who had put her new slick image together. —Iceberg Slim (Robert Beck), *Airtight Willie and Me*, p. 63, 1979
- —J.R. Schwartz, *The Official Guide to the Best Cat Houses in Nevada*, p. 166, 1993: 'Sex glossary'

2 in the illegal production of alcohol, the yield of whisky compared to the amount of raw materials *US*
- What turn-out did you get – ten gallons to the bag? —David W. Maurer, *Kentucky Moonshine*, p. 127, 1974

turn out *verb*

1 to recruit and convert someone to prostitution *US*
- "A broad?" Rudy raised an eyebrow. "Thinkin about turnin her out, huh?" —Clarence Cooper Jr, *The Scene*, p. 14, 1960
- But I also have a gift of converting. I turn girls out. —Susan Hall, *Gentleman of Leisure*, p. 6, 1972
- I just ain't got the time to turn a girl out. When I get a girl, I want her to be ready made in sportin' life. —A.S. Jackson, *Gentleman Pimp*, p. 156, 1973
- When I turned out, I worked call. —Gerald Paine, *A Bachelor's Guide to the Brothels of Nevada*, p. 137, 1978

2 to engage a woman in serial sex with multiple partners *US*
- Girls who get turned out at Hell's Angels parties don't think of police in terms of protection. —Hunter S. Thompson, *Hell's Angels*, p. 195, 1966

3 to convert someone to homosexuality *US*
- Boy, that Jeep can turn 'em out. —Chester Himes, *Cast the First Stone*, p. 13, 1952
- The place a punk usually gets turned out is the county jail. —Bruce Jackson, *In the Life*, p. 368, 1972
- With the help of the homosexual, Jug had turned out a young white boy by the name of Jerry. —Donald Goines, *White Man's Justice, Black Man's Grief*, p. 163, 1973

turnover *noun*

1 a robbery of stolen goods from a criminal accomplice *UK*
- —Frank Norman, *Encounter*, 1959

2 a search of a prison cell *UK, 1940*
The abbreviated form 'TO' is also used.
- —Angela Devlin, *Prison Patter*, p. 115, 1996

turn over *verb*

1 (of the police) to search a property or to stop and search a person; in criminal use, to burgle a property or rob a person *UK, 1859*
- [T]urn over, stow the gear and take stoppo [getaway] as soon as possible. —Charles Raven, *Underworld Nights*, p. 10, 1956
- [B]lokes who want to go up in the world should be prepared for a turnover or two. —*The Sweeney*, p. 18, 1976
- —Angela Devlin, *Prison Patter*, p. 117, 1996
- Why should being a burglar make me any more cheerful about getting turned over than the next bloke? —Danny King, *The Burglar Diaries*, p. 18–19, 2001

2 to set upon someone and beat them up *UK, 1962*
- —Angela Devlin, *Prison Patter*, p. 117, 1996

turn round and

used as an embellishment between to and do *UK*
An unnecessary formula used in north London.
- "Nicky," she turned round and said. —Jeremy Cameron, *Brown Bread in Wengen*, p. 14, 1999

turntablism *noun*

the creation of music and rhythmic patterns by manipulation of record turntables *US*
A mid-1990s coinage credited to DJ Babu of the Beat Junkies.
- —J. Hoggarth, *How To Be a DJ*, p. 147, 2002

turntablist *noun*

a DJ who uses turntables as instruments to create and manipulate sound *US*
From the turntable 'decks' the DJ manipulates.
- [W]e are going to check them out in this chapter, with help from a turntablist crew[.] —J. Hoggarth, *How To Be a DJ*, p. 82–83, 2002
- [T]he Ninja Tune turntablist balks at nothing in his perusal of vinyl stores in search of a good tune. —*Metro*, p. 23, 17th May 2002

turn-up *noun*

an outcome, especially a surprise *UK*
An abbreviation, with a slightly narrower sense, of **TURN-UP FOR THE BOOKS**.
- Turnup of it was we got done for five quid apiece. —John Peter Jones, *Feather Pluckers*, p. 11, 1964

turn-up for the books; turn-up *noun*

an unexpected happening, usually positive *UK, 1873*
Originally racecourse and gambling use.
- Hilary followed them out. "What a turn-up for the books," Mr. Smith remarked. —Ngaio Marsh, *Tied Up In Tinsel*, 1972
- "Yes," said Mooney blandly, "I'll put up the dough." "Blimey," replied Arthur. "This is a turn-up for the book." —Anthony Masters, *Minder*, p. 99, 1984
- It is true that WMD could yet be found; but such a turn-up after almost six months of looking is unlikely and would rightly be viewed with suspicion. —*The Guardian*, 26th September 2003

turpentine; the turps *noun*

the Serpentine (a lake in London's Hyde Park) *UK*
Rhyming slang.
- —Julian Franklyn, *A Dictionary of Rhyming Slang*, 1960
- —Ray Puxley, *Cockney Rabbit*, 1992

turps *noun*

1 turpentine *UK, 1823*
- Often, he gets a big turps sponge or a rag and wipes out the painting. —*The Guardian*, 5th February 2004

2 alcohol *AUSTRALIA, 1865*
An abbreviation of 'turpentine'.
- I think he's been on the turps a bit. —J.E. MacDonnell, *Don't Gimme the Ships*, p. 37, 1960
- These were mainly blokes that had hit the turps and couldn't leave it alone[.] —Sam Weller, *Old Bastards I Have Met*, p. 36, 1979
- Gwen was never much of a drinker, though her Auntie Kath who's a nun, really used to nudge the turps[.] —Barry Humphries, *The Traveller's Tool*, p. 26, 1985
- —David McGill, *David McGill's Complete Kiwi Slang Dictionary*, p. 129, 1998
- That wasn't the first time pilots have been caught on the turps, but such cases are hardly surprising[.] —*The Times Magazine*, 10th January 2004

▷ **see:** TERPS

turtle *noun*

1 a variety of LSD *UK*
Named for, and identified by a depiction of, the *Teenage Mutant Ninja Turtles*, a cult comic and television programme from the 1980s.

2 the replacement for a combat soldier who is due to return home *US*
Like the turtle, the replacement seems never to get there quickly enough.
- —Carl Fleischhauer, *A Glossary of Army Slang*, p. 24, 1968
- —Linda Reinberg, *In the Field*, p. 225, 1991

turtle *verb*

(used of a boat) to turn over completely in the water, exposing the bottom of the hull to the sky *US*
- A rented motorboat had turtled and its sole occupant was clinging to the hull while two lifeguards struggled to get her into the rescue boat. —Joseph Wambaugh, *Floaters*, p. 159, 1966

turtle dove *noun*

1 love, as a term of address *UK, 1974*
Very old-fashioned rhyming slang.

2 a glove *UK, 1857*
The short form 'turtle' is also used.
- —David Powis, *The Signs of Crime*, 1977
- —Ray Puxley, *Cockney Rabbit*, 1992

turtlehead; turtle's head *noun*

a piece of faeces semi-emerged from the rectum *UK*
- —*Roger's Profanisaurus*, December 1997
- —Don R. McCreary (Editor), *Dawg Speak*, 2001
- Awshite man, I have to go NOW – I've got the turtle's head. —Chris Lewis, *The Dictionary of Playground Slang*, p. 240, 2003

turtleneck *noun*

the foreskin on an uncircumsised penis *US*
- —Connie Eble (Editor), *UNC-CH Campus Slang*, p. 5, November 1983

tush; tushie; tushy *noun*

the backside, the buttocks *US, 1962*
Yiddish.
- Oh, Scottie Hite, you naughty boy! You kissed my tushie! —Richard Price, *The Wanderers*, p. 79, 1974
- Her tush is tight and she's got great boobs and in bed, well, I don't need to waste my time jogging to keep my weight down. —George V. Higgins, *The Rat on Fire*, p. 170, 1981

- The Feds and LAPD were here chasing your tush. —James Ellroy, *White Jazz*, p. 314, 1992
- She told him what to do with that and he gave her one on the tush. —*Get Shorty*, 1995
- I was sure he'd think something was amiss if his eyes fixed upon a manuscript containing the words luscious tush and stiff, saluting prick. —Rita Ciresi, *Pink Slip*, p. 74, 1999

tusheroon *noun*

▷ **see:** TOSHEROON

tush hog *noun*

1 a strong and powerful man who extorts money from others *US*

- Muta takes all the goddam hardness and evil out of you, cuts down the tush-hog bullying side of your personality and makes you think straight, with your head instead of your fists. —Mezz Mezzrow, *Really the Blues*, p. 96, 1946

2 a person with a short temper *US*

- —Bruce Jackson, *Outside the Law*, p. 61, 1972: 'Glossary'

tusker *noun*

an all-in-all unattractive girl *US*

- —*Current Slang*, p. 14, Summer 1968

tuskie; tuskee *noun*

a marijuana cigarette *US*

- She passed the half-smoked tuskie to his outstretched fingers. —Odie Hawkins, *Chicago Hustle*, p. 74, 1977
- —Edith A. Folb, *runnin' down some lines*, p. 259, 1980

tuss *verb*

to abuse for non-medicinal purposes non-prescription medication containing dextromethorphan (DXM) *US*

- DXM abuse is called "Robotripping" or "Tussing." Users might be called "syrup heads" or "robotards." —*USA Today*, p. 1A, 29th December 2003

tussin *noun*

dextromethorphan (DXM), an active ingredient in non-prescription cold and cough medication, often abused for non-medicinal purposes *US*

From the branded cough syrup Robtussin™.

- Youths' nicknames for DXM: Robo, Skittles, Triple C's, Rojo, Dex, Tussin, Vitamin D. —*USA Today*, p. 1A, 29th December 2003

tustin *noun*

marijuana originating, perhaps, in Tustin, California *UK*

- —Mike Haskins, *Drugs*, p. 289, 2003

tutae *noun*

faeces *NEW ZEALAND*

From the Maori.

- Charlotte was enraged. She was going to throw that Macky in the tutae for sure. —*Women's Work*, p. 223, 1985

tute *nickname*

▷ **see:** TOOT

tutti *noun*

a latrine *TRINIDAD AND TOBAGO*

- —Lise Winer, *Dictionary of the English/Creole of Trinidad & Tobago*, 2003

tutti frutti *noun*

lemon extract *CANADA*

- In Shelburne County, NS, in "dry" parts, lemon extract, known as "tutti frutti," is consumed internally by habitual alcoholics. —Lewis Poteet, *The South Shore Phrase Book*, p. 119, 1999

tut-tuts *noun*

the female breasts *TRINIDAD AND TOBAGO, 1956*

- —Lise Winer, *Dictionary of the English/Creole of Trinidad & Tobago*, 2003

tutty *noun*

makeup *UK*

- DAVE: We'd best be off and all. DENISE: Just let me put some tutty on. —Caroline Aherne and Craig Cash, *The Royle Family*, 1999

tutu *noun*

1 a tablet of MDMA, the recreational drug best known as ecstasy *UK*

- —Mike Haskins, *Drugs*, p. 290, 2003

2 in craps, a roll of four *US*

A homophonic pun – two, two.

- —Chris Fagans and David Guzman, *A Guide to Craps Lingo*, p. 15, 1999

tuxedo; tux *noun*

a strait jacket *US*

- —Vincent J. Monteleone, *Criminal Slang*, p. 245, 1949

TV *noun*

a transvestite *UK*

- TV Heaven[.] Be the Woman of yor dreams! —Caroline Archer, *Tart Cards*, 2003

TV parking *noun*

the chance of finding a car parking space exactly where you need it *US*

- [I]f you're driving to work, and find a parking place just in front of the main entrance, you describe the good fortune as TV parking, because that phenomenon only tends to happen on TV shows. —David Rowan, *A Glossary for the 90s*, p. 85, 1998

TV rental *noun*

a Ford 'Granada' car *UK*

A reference to high street business Granada Television Rentals.

- —Peter Chippindale, *The British CB Book*, p. 161, 1981

TV-style *noun*

anal sex from behind a person on their hands and knees *US*

An allusion to the fact that both participants are facing the same way and can watch television during sex.

- —*Maledicta*, p. 231, 1979: 'Kinks and queens: linguistic and cultural aspects of the terminology for gays'

TWA *noun*

a *t*eeny-*w*eeny *a*ircraft or helicopter *US*

- —Linda Reinberg, *In the Field*, p. 226, 1991

twack *verb*

to go window-shopping, look, ask about cost, but buy nothing *CANADA*

- To "twack" is to examine goods and buy nothing. —L. E. F. English, *Historic Newfoundland*, p. 37, 1955

twaddle *noun*

nonsense *UK, 1782*

- A lovely landscape with a liberal topping of twaddle goes down nicely on a Sunday. —*The Guardian*, 3rd April 2000

twak *noun*

1 rubbish *SOUTH AFRICA, 1953*

- Caspar Greeff nearly made me gooi a spasm [throw a fit]. What a lot of twak he wrote[.] —*Sunday Times (South Africa)*, 7th December 2003

2 tobacco *SOUTH AFRICA, 1844*

- [A] 'connection' (friend) managed to get some 'twak' (tobacco) to me be sending the Boer to my cell with his bible[.] —Breyten Breytenbach and Rike Vaughan, *The True Confessions of an Albino Terrorist*, p. 214, 1983

twally *noun*

an idiot, a fool *UK: SCOTLAND*

Glasgow slang.

- I said no tae drap your end till Ah telt ye, ya twally. —Michael Munro, *The Complete Patter*, p. 159, 1996

twang *verb*

▸ **twang the wire**

(of a male) to masturbate *AUSTRALIA*

- If he reckons we're all going to twang the wire he's got another think coming!!! —Barry Humphries, *Bazza Pulls It Off!*, 1971

twanger *noun*

1 the penis *FIJI*

Recorded by Jan Tent in 1994.

2 a citizens' band radio antenna *US*

- —"Slingo", *The Official CB Slang Dictionary Handbook*, p. 63, 1976

twangie boy *noun*

a young male prostitute *US*

A term coined by novelist Robert Campbell.

- Chances they might see some twangie boy down on his knees doing a sailor up from San Pedro. —Robert Campbell, *Alice in La-La Land*, p. 1, 1987

twat *noun*

1 the vagina *UK, 1656*

- Did you ever have a woman who shaved her twat? It's repulsive, ain't it? And it's funny too. Sort of mad like. It doesn't look like a twat any more. —Henry Miller, *Tropic of Cancer*, p. 139, 1961

- Why should whores make better wives than, say, some dumb, religion-soaked bitch who was saving her dry little twat for Jesus? —Nathan Heard, *Howard Street*, p. 177, 1968
- [H]e once remarked that "the only meat in the world sweeter, hotter and pinker than Amand's twat is Carolina barbecue." —Tom Robbins, *Another Roadside Attraction*, p. 49, 1971
- Out of the shower, she squeezes her spots; Brushes her teeth; Shoots a deodorant spray up her twat ... (It's getting her, getting her Hot) —Frank Zappa, *Shove It Right In*, 1972
- [W]hat kinda jive-ass bullshit is this when that twat on the statue don't look like no twat I ever seen. —Joseph Wambaugh, *The Black Marble*, p. 120, 1978
- Spread-eagled twats and hind ends float by the window, ecstatic aquarium fish with ghetto-girl faces. —Josh Alan Friedman, *Tales of Times Square*, p. 65, 1986
- The two big babes, hips swaying, asses grinding, consume the dilgo in their bare, giant twats. —*Adult Video*, p. 50, August/September 1986
- All you've done is shag your twat, and that ain't nothin'. —*Drugstore Cowboy*, 1988
- I really got hot when I saw Jeanette Scott *Janet's twat* fight a triffid that spits poisons and kills. —Sal Piro and Michael Hess, *The Official 'Rocky Horror Picture Show' Audience Participation Guide*, p. 6, 1991
- A twat you don't merely lick but suck, fiercely, for hours[.] —Anthony Petkovich, *The X Factory*, p. 16, 1997
- I just love the sound of a bird with a posh accent bellowing obscenities as I batter her twat with my love truncheon. —Stewart Home, *Sex Kick [britpulp]*, p. 202, 1999
- A tastefully trimmed twat doesn't happen by accident; it takes time, technique, and talent. —*The Village Voice*, 8th–14th November 2000

2 a woman *UK, 1929*

- Let's just sit here all day and have laughs at this piecy new English twat. —Evan Hunter, *The Blackboard Jungle*, p. 36, 1954
- It was little twats like her that ruined young athletes, as far as he was concerned. —Larry McMurtry, *The Last Picture Show*, p. 117, 1966
- We always come back on tat fuckin' train an' Mom's always cryin' 'cause that stupid blond twat thinks Mom's some kinda Mustache Pete and'll contaminate her kids. —Richard Price, *The Wanderers*, p. 142, 1974
- Lemme go get this twat and finish her off. —Stephen J. Cannell, *Big Con*, p. 145, 1997

3 a promiscuous homosexual man *US*

- "Disgusting the way some of these twats flaunt it, ain't it?" a tough at the next table said. —Robert Campbell, *Alice in La-La Land*, p. 4, 1987

4 used as an abusive epithet for someone you would otherwise call a cunt *UK, 1929*

From the sense as 'the vagina'.

- Rees can go and fuck himeself the diminutive Welsh twat —Jack Allen, *When the Whistle Blows*, 2000

5 an unfortunate or difficult situation; an unpleasant task; a problem *UK*

A logical extension of the earlier, still current sense 'an irritating person or object'.

- Specific. Twat of a word to say when you've got a lisp[.] —Kevin Sampson, *Outlaws*, p. 252, 2001

twat *verb*

to hit someone *UK*

- He felt like twatting James every time he blathered on about humping her in the boathouse[.] —Kevin Sampson, *Powder*, p. 71, 1999
- Vinnie [Jones] stares at Danny "Mean Machine" Meehan [...] recently jailed for twatting a copper in a drunken brawl. —*Uncut*, p. 166, January 2002

twat

'*t*here *w*e *a*re *t*hen', used to (reluctantly) acknowledge an occurrence *UK, 2001*

Acronym in use by south Wales police.

TWAT

The War Against Terrorism *UK, 2001*

An unfortunate acronym, highlighted on BBC Radio 4 panel game *The News Quiz*, October 2001. Subsequently, some broadcasters began using 'The War On Terrorism', inviting TWOT. **TWAT** (the vagina) and 'twot' are synonymous.

twat around *verb*

to play the fool, to waste time; to make a mess of something; to inconvenience someone *UK*

- It's the price you pay for dreams. It's what happens when you twat around with destiny. —Liza Cody, *Queen of Mean [Tart Noir]*, p. 70, 2002

twat bubble *noun*

a comtemptible person *UK*

Offensive and insulting.

- That twat bubble from the Standard. —*The Thick Of It (BBC Radio 4)*, 2nd June 2005

twatch *verb*

to do emergency sewing repairs crudely *CANADA*

- Such twatching! Take that out and do it again neatly! —Lewis Poteet, *oral citation from The South Shore Phrase Book*, p. 119, 1999

twat chat *noun*

talking about sex from the female perspective; also used as a nickname for *The Vagina Monologues* by Eve Ensler, 2001 *UK*

- Still the only female winner of the Perrier and now a novelist to boot (aren't they all?) the doyenne of "twat chat" returns to Edinburgh as gleefully outre as ever. —*The Guardian*, p. 21, 11th August 2001
- The Vagina Monologues (or as the comedian Jenny Eclair more amusingly calls it, "Twat Chat") —Richard Herring, *Talking Cock*, p. 2, 2003

twat-hooks *noun*

the fingers; the hands *UK*

From an image based on **TWAT** (the vagina). Heard by Partridge on the BBC, 18th January 1973.

twat mag *noun*

a pornographic magazine that features naked women *UK*

A combination of **TWAT** (the vagina), probably not **TWAT** (a fool), with **MAG** (a magazine).

- —Angela Devlin, *Prison Patter*, p. 117, 1996

twat off!

go away! *UK*

- Mazz told him to twat off. —John Williams, *Cardiff Dead*, p. 107, 2000

twatted *adjective*

drunk or drug-intoxicated *UK*

- Hang in there. It's just a pill. You're just a bit twatted. —Kevin Sampson, *Powder*, p. 242, 1999
- [S]laughtered, trashed, twatted, munted[.] —Stuart Walton, *Out of It*, cover, 2001
- [H]e were twatted on pills half the time he was doing the job[.] —Colin Butts, *Is Harry Still on the Boat?*, p. 21, 2003

twattery *noun*

foolishness; nonsense *UK*

- The only thing more shit than Scrappy Doo is this amateur piece of twattery. —*Kerrang!*, p. 8, 6th July 2002

twatting *adjective*

used as an intensifier *UK*

- Fuckin Jesus Christin twattin cuntin fuckin hell! —Niall Griffiths, *Grits*, p. 42, 2000

twattoo *noun*

a tattoo on the female pubis; a tattoo of unfashionable design *UK*

- One woman opened her legs to reveal what I can only describe as a "twattoo". —Kitty Churchill, *Thinking of England*, p. 53, 1995

twatty *adjective*

1 foolish, idiotic *UK*

- [E]e's only about my age and, aftuh first impressions, doesunt rirly look too twatty; a mean, I wear glasses meself[.] —Niall Griffiths, *Grits*, p. 26, 2000

2 unpleasant *UK*

- So what a bunch of twatty little hypocrites they are, eh? —Ben Elton, *High Society*, p. 21, 2002

tweak *noun*

in mountain biking, any low, destabilising contact with a rock, root or stump *US*

- Recovering form a good tweak requires instantaneous handlebar torque. —William Nealy, *Mountain Bike!*, p. 163, 1992

tweak *verb*

1 to bend *US*

- —Elena Garcia, *A Beginner's Guide to Zen and the Art of Snowboarding*, p. 123, 1990: 'Glossary'

2 in computing or electronics, to make a minor adjustment *US*

- If a program is almost correct, rather than figuring out the precise problem you might just keep tweaking it until it works. —Guy L. Steele et al., *The Hacker's Dictionary*, p. 127, 1983

3 to use methamphetamines *US*

The spelling 'tweek' is also used.

- Disgusted, Blaze said, "You were better off tweaking." —Joseph Wambaugh, *Floaters*, p. 7, 1996

tweaker; tweeker *noun*
a user of methamphetamine or amphetamines *US*
- Typical highs lasts from four to eight hours. Users call themseslves "tweakers." — *Los Angeles Times*, p. 1 (Metro), 8th October 1989
- Anyways, he's this little speed tweaker, like our snitch. — Joseph Wambaugh, *The Golden Orange*, p. 50, 1990
- When he got like this, his neighbors would scream at him and threaten to call the cops, but they were tweakers too. — Joseph Wambaugh, *Finnegan's Week*, p. 235, 1993

tweaks *noun*
crack cocaine *UK*
- — Mike Haskins, *Drugs*, p. 282, 2003

twee *adjective*
affectedly dainty, over-refined *UK, 1905*
- "Oh, don't be so twee" was my gut reaction, although I was naturally too polite, or perhaps too timorous, to say so. — Charles Handy, *Waiting for the Mountain to Move*, p. 84, 1992

tweed; tweeds *noun*
marijuana *US*
Contraction of 'the WEED', thus 't'weed', 'tweed'.
- Need some tweed, cuz? — Lois Stavsky et al., *A2Z*, p. 105, 1995
- E, crack, tweed, shit, it's give 'n' take[.] — Q, *The Sparrow (Disco Biscuits)*, p. 259, 1996
- — Mike Haskins, *Drugs*, p. 289, 2003

Tweed Curtain *noun*
an invisible barrier between Oak Bay and Greater Victoria, British Columbia *CANADA*
- This invisible fabric, the Tweed Curtain, shields the suburban British bastion of Oak Bay against the common culture of Greater Victoria. — Tom Parkin, *WetCoast Words*, p. 145, 1989

tweedle *noun*
a confidence trick in which a counterfeit such as fake jewellery or, in the 'whisky tweedle', a 30 gallon barrel containing only a quart of alcohol is sold in the stead of a genuine purchase *UK, 1890*
- Leo was the Guv'nor of a little three-handed team that worked the tweedle. — Charles Raven, *Underworld Nights*, p. 63, 1956

tweedle *verb*
to operate the tweedle confidence trick, exchanging a genuine purchase for a fake *UK*
- [H]e said, drawing his chiv [a blade], "[T]his'll teach you to tweedle my Mum." — Charles Raven, *Underworld Nights*, p. 67, 1956

tweedler *noun*
1 a stolen vehicle offered for an honest sale *UK*
- — David Powis, *The Signs of Crime*, 1977

2 a very minor or petty confidence trickster *UK*
- The tweedler will flog you sawdust cigarettes or dummy diamond rings. — John Gosling, *The Ghost Squad*, 1959

tweeds *noun*
1 trousers *AUSTRALIA, 1954*
- If you're going to drop your tweeds, I'm leaving. — John Wynnum, *Jiggin' in the Riggin'*, p. 16, 1965
- Cheerio...lovely one...I said...still supine and minus my tweeds...until the tide reached my excoriated member. — Jack Hibberd, *A Stretch of the Imagination*, p. 11, 1971

2 clothing, especially a suit *US*
- — Collin Baker et al., *College Undergraduate Slang Study Conducted at Brown University*, p. 215, 1968

tweek *verb*
▸ **to get tweeked**
to be knocked from your surfboard and then be pummelled by the ocean *US*
- — Surf Punks, *Oh No! Not Them Again! (liner notes)*, 1988

tweek and freak *verb*
to engage in kinky sex after injecting methamphetamine *US*
- — Geoffrey Froner, *Digging for Diamonds*, p. 63, 1989

tweeker *noun*
methcathinone *US*
- — Office of National Drug Control Policy, *Drug Facts*, February 2003

tweetie *noun*
an effeminate male *US*
An imitation of a lisped 'sweetie' and an allusion to Tweetie Pie, a cartoon character of the 1950s and 60s.
- — Collin Baker et al., *College Undergraduate Slang Study Conducted at Brown University*, p. 215, 1968

Tweety Bird *noun*
a tablet of MDMA, the recreational drug best known as ecstasy, identified by an embossed icon of Warner Bros' animated character Tweety Pie *UK*
- — Mike Haskins, *Drugs*, p. 290, 2003

twelve *noun*
in a deck of playing cards, any queen *US*
- — John Vorhaus, *The Big Book of Poker Slang*, p. 37, 1996

twelve and twelve *noun*
▷ see: 12 AND 12

twelve inch rule *noun*
a fool *UK*
Rhyming slang.
- — Ray Puxley, *Cockney Rabbit*, 1992

twelve-ounce curls *noun*
drinking beer *US*
- — Connie Eble (Editor), *UNC-CH Campus Slang*, p. 3, April 1985

twelver *noun*
a twelve-pack of beer *US*
- — Pamela Munro, *U.C.L.A. Slang*, p. 117, 1997

twennie *noun*
a twenty-dollar dose of crack cocaine *US*
- I don't put but a few twennies [$20 packets] in foil anyway 'cause if you sweat too much it cakes up. — Terry Williams, *The Cocaine Kids*, p. 43, 1989
- — Terry Williams, *Crackhouse*, p. 152, 1992

twenties *noun*
a swindle featuring a twenty-dollar note *US, 1952*
- Thus, for the tenth time that day, he had worked the twenties, one of the three standard gimmicks of the short con grift. — Jim Thompson, *The Grifters*, p. 6, 1963
- What we did, ever so often we'd pull off the pigeon drop for maybe twenty-five dollars, with me plainting the leather, or work the twenties for a five. — Guy Owen, *The Flim-Flam Man and the Apprentice Grifter*, p. 151, 1972

twenty; 20 *noun*
1 a twenty-pound note *UK*
- For a chap who'd spent most of that lost weekend with a rolled-up twenty shoved up his nose [to inhale cocaine], Pat was an intuitive and perceptive judge. — Kevin Sampson, *Powder*, p. 139, 1999

2 a location *US, 1975*
Citizens' band radio slang.
- It's normal to ask their location by saying, "What's your 20?". — Peter Chippindale, *The British CB Book*, p. 17, 1981
- RILEY: Big Dave, come in. BIG DAVE: Yo, go 'head. RILEY: What's your twenty? BIG DAVE: I'm in front of the A room right now. RILEY: Ten four. — Queen Pen, *I Got Cha*, 2001

twenty-cent bag *noun*
twenty dollars' worth of a drug *US*
- A tiny capsule [of cocaine] sells for twenty dollars (a "twenty-cent bag"). — Christina and Richard Milner, *Black Players*, p. 12, 1972

twenty-cent rock *noun*
crack cocaine worth $20 *US*
- The officer asked for a "10-cent rock" – street slang for a $10 purchase of crack cocaine. Boykin allegedly then told the officer he had only "20-cent rocks." — *Texas Lawyer*, p. 10, 14th October 1991

twenty-five *noun*
LSD *US*
From the slightly more formal LSD-25, from the most formal D-Lysergic Acid Diethlamide.
- — Donald Louria, *Nightmare Drugs*, p. 45, 1966

twenty-four hours *noun*
a homemade alcoholic beverage made with sugar, yeast, water and flavouring *FIJI*

- The young men would resort to drinking home brews (Raisin Jack or 24 hours) and methylated spirit in order to get "a high." — *Fiji Times*, p. 35, 27th September 1997

twenty-four seven *adverb*
▷ see: 24/7

twenty-four, seven, three-sixty-five *adjective*
▷ see: 24-7-365

twenty-nine *noun*
▸ **she's a twenty-nine this morning**
usually of a wife, very angry or upset *CANADA*
- In Pubnico, "she's a twenty-nine this morning" means "she's in a bad mood." The term makes a metaphor of "29," a very low reading on a falling barometer, a prediction of stormy weather. — Lewis Poteet, *oral citation from The South Shore Phrase Book*, p. 119, 1999

twenty-one days in the county jail *noun*
in poker, a hand consisting of three sevens *US*
- — George Percy, *The Language of Poker*, p. 94, 1988

twenty rock *noun*
crack cocaine *UK*
- — Mike Haskins, *Drugs*, p. 282, 2003

twenty-six girl *noun*
▷ see: 26 GIRL

twenty spot; twenty spotter *noun*
a twenty-pound note *UK*
Adopted directly from US currency.
- — *The Spectator*, 19th June 1976

twenty stretch *noun*
a twenty-year prison sentence *UK*
- What problems? Fuck all, really, next to risking getting a twenty stretch. — Dave Courtney, *Dodgy Dave's Little Black Book*, p. 15, 2001

twenty-twenty *adjective*
good-looking; attractive *US*
Punning, leaping from 'seeing well' to 'good-looking'.
- There was a pin-up pigeon. She was a twenty-twenty quail. — Haenigsen, *Jive's Like That*, 1947

twenty-twenty hindsight *noun*
the ability to see clearly what should have been done *US, 1962*
- Yeah, well, twenty-twenty hindsight and all that. — *Get Shorty*, 1995

twenty-two carat; twenty-four carat *adjective*
genuine, first-class *UK*
Figurative application of gold standards; 'twenty-four carat' from 1900, 'twenty-two carat' since 1962.
- They're beehives [£5s], this lot, and I tell you they're absolutely twenty-two. None of this photogravure lark. — Derek Raymond (Robin Cook), *The Crust on its Uppers*, p. 47, 1962

twerp; twirp *noun*
an idiot, a fool, a despicable person *UK, 1874*
- The guy she married – a smug, sadistic twirp. — Philip Wylie, *Opus 21*, p. 64, 1949
- As we had been teaching him slang, his dialogue was larded with a weird mixture of Spanish and American jargon, with emphasis on his favorite word, twerp. — Jennie Darlington and Jane McIlvaine, *My Antarctic Honeymoon*, p. 132, 1956
- Why, those little twerps at Webster- I can handle 'em with my pinkie! — Max Shulman, *Rally Round the Flag, Boys!*, p. 48, 1957
- I'm tired of breaking in these twerps. — Albert Goldman, *Freak Show*, p. 215, 1968
- You little twirp. You come one step closer to me and I'll knock your block off. — *Drugstore Cowboy*, 1988
- — Ellen C. Bellone (Editor), *Dictionary of Slang*, p. 25, 1989
- [T]he little twerp walked out on contracts worth a bloody fortune. — John Williams, *Cardiff Dead*, p. 89, 2000
- We are storing up for ourselves a generation of twerps. — *New Statesman*, May 2003

twerpy *adjective*
idiotic, foolish *US*
- [T]he lead singer's twerpy attempts at Doctor John-ish mumbo-jumbo [...] were godawful. — Lester Bangs, *Psychotic Reactions and Carburetor Dung*, p. 98, 1971

twice-and-a-half truck *noun*
a 2.5 ton truck *US*
- — Carl Fleischhauer, *A Glossary of Army Slang*, p. 24, 1968

twice as cold as zero *adjective*
very cold *US*
The arithmetic impossibility lends an ironic charm to the expression.
- — John Gould, *Maine Lingo*, p. 302, 1975

twice pipes *noun*
in hot rodding, a dual exhaust system *US*
- — John Edwards, *Auto Dictionary*, p. 177, 1993

twicer *noun*
a two-year prison sentence *UK*
- — Alan Hunter, *Gently in Trees*, 1974

twicicles-as-nicicles *noun*
the testicles *UK*
Based on an advertising slogan and a vague aural similarity.
- — *A–Z of Rude Health*, 11th January 2002

twiddle *noun*
1 the tilde character (~) on a computer keyboard *US*
- — Guy L. Steele et al., *The Hacker's Dictionary*, p. 127, 1983

2 in fencing, a circular parry *UK*
- — E.D. Morton, *Martini A-Z of Fencing*, 1988

twig *noun*
1 a radio aerial *UK*
Probably of military origin.
- Twig [aerial] city. American truck sports two centre-loaders; British van a rubber duckie and a K40. — Peter Chippindale, *The British CB Book*, p. 117, 1981

2 a match (usually in the plural) *UK*
Used by borstal boys.
- — *The Daily Telegraph*, 4th June 1958

3 marijuana *US, 1970*
- — Ernest L. Abel, *A Marijuana Dictionary*, p. 106, 1982

4 cocaine, amphetamines or any other central nervous system stimulant *US*
- — Kenn "Naz" Young, *Naz's Dictionary of Teen Slang*, p. 132, 1993

5 in sports betting, a half-point increment in the pointspread *US, 1984*
- — Thomas L. Clark, *The Dictionary of Gambling and Gaming*, p. 101, 1987

▸ **drop off the twig; fall off the twig**
to die *AUSTRALIA*
- All of the historical celebrities and olden-days personalities made some little philosophical quip before they jumped off the twig. — Barry Humphries, *A Nice Night's Entertainment*, p. 143, 1974
- They said, 'Mat fell off the twig, did he?' They said, 'The first time there's been a proper funeral in the valley.' — Hugh Atkinson, *Grey's Valley*, p. 63, 1986

twig *verb*
1 to realise something *UK, 1815*
From the obsolete sense (to watch); ultimately from English dialect *twick* (to pinch), especially in the sense 'to arrest'.
- We come about the charlie [cocaine]. The guy twigs. His face goes radioactive with delight. — Nick Barlay, *Curvy Lovebox*, p. 69, 1997
- Even though my accent isn't as strong [...] it's obvious he's twigged I'm a Scouser [Liverpudlian][.] — Kevin Sampson, *Outlaws*, p. 50, 2001

2 to probe your eye or your anus to relieve an irritation *UK*
- — Ray Puxley, *Cockney Rabbit*, 1992

twilight *verb*
to lose yourself in a daydream *US*
- — Paul Glover, *Words from the House of the Dead*, 1974

twilight zone *noun*
1 in drag racing, the state of travelling at extremely high speeds *US*
- A dragster which turns an e.t. of less than eight seconds or hits a speed around 200 mph is usually considered to have passed through the twilight zone. — John Lawlor, *How to Talk Car*, p. 109, 1965

2 in railway employment, the period of waiting for promotion from fireman to driver *UK*
- — Frank McKenna, *A Glossary of Railwaymen's Talk*, 1970

twilly *noun*
a woman, especially an attractive or promiscuous one *US, 1934*
- Betsy a twilly? He wished he'd had some of that Betsy. — Bernard Wolfe, *The Late Risers*, p. 286, 1954

twin *noun*
in hot rodding, an engine with two cylinders *US*
- —John Lawlor, *How to Talk Car*, p. 110, 1965

twin caper *noun*
a double date *US*
- — *San Francisco Examiner*, p. III-2, 22nd March 1960

twin fin *noun*
a surfboard with two fins *AUSTRALIA*
- —Nat Young, *Surfing Fundamentals*, p. 128, 1985

twin fins *noun*
in craps, two fives *US, 1983*
- —Thomas L. Clark, *The Dictionary of Gambling and Gaming*, p. 242, 1987

twink *noun*
1 an effeminate, young, handsome homosexual male *US*
- — *Current Slang*, p. 13, Spring 1968
- —Helen Dahlskog (Editor), *A Dictionary of Contemporary and Colloquial Usage*, p. 61, 1972
- Where are the twinks, anyway? They usually have the decency to provide one or two decorative twinks... Jesus, who needs to waste a night staring at these tired old Gucci queens. —Armistead Maupin, *Tales of the City*, p. 300, 1978
- —Tom Hibbert, *Rockspeak!*, p. 164, 1983
- —Michael V. Anderson, *The Bad, Rad, Not to Forget Way Cool Beach and Surf Discriptionary*, p. 21, 1988
- Chris said, "Yeah, the twink comes up to the table, says he's gonna be our waitperson." —Elmore Leonard, *Freaky Deaky*, p. 10, 1988

2 a new military recruit *US*
- But most of the lifers had never seen 'Nam and most of the twinks – the new recruits – had little idea of where they were going and none whatever about what would become of them when they got there. —Peter Goldman and Tony Fuller, *Charlie Company*, p. 32, 1983

3 a coward *US*
- Rafi comes on strong, but he's a twink at heart, he caves in. —Elmore Leonard, *Cat Chaser*, p. 160, 1982

4 a moment, the merest measure of time *UK, 1754*
Originally, 'a wink of the eye', a 'twinkling'.
- I shan't be two twinks. — Beale, 1984

twinkie *noun*
1 an eccentric; someone who doesn't conform to peer-group expectations *US*
- I just don't get it. OK, so call me a twinkie. —Melanie McGrath, *Hard, Soft & Wet*, p. 114, 1998

2 a person who is profoundly out of touch with reality *US*
- I doubt Rafi's expectations have anything to do with the real world. He's a twinkie. —Elmore Leonard, *Cat Chaser*, p. 194, 1982

3 an Asian-American who embraces the dominant white culture in an attempt to curry favour *US*
An allusion to a Hostess™ dessert cake that is yellow on the outside and white on the inside.
- —Connie Eble (Editor), *UNC-CH Campus Slang*, p. 7, Fall 1998

4 a youthful, sexually inexperienced male who is the object of an older homosexual's desire *US*
The spelling 'twinky' is also used.
- — *Maledicta*, p. 221, 1979: 'Kinks and queens: linguistic and cultural aspects of the terminology for gays'
- This term [pogey] designates an attractive youth desired by older homosexuals (mainly naval and prison use), roughly corresponding to the more recent twinky, though often somewhat younger. —Wayne Dynes, *Homolexis*, p. 112, 1985
- Ned was no fading twinkie, though, when I knew him; he wore his age with an easy, shambling grace that was completely out of sync with the desperate pretenses of most people in this town. —Armistead Maupin, *Maybe the Moon*, p. 144, 1992

twinkies *noun*
car wheel rims *US*
- Dubs, blades, shoes, sneakers, twinkies – street slang for custom wheels – are status symbols, made popular by athletes and rap stars. — *Cincinnati Enquirer*, p. 1B, 29th August 2003

twinkles
used as a verbal talisman when two people say the same thing at the same time *US*
- —Judi Sanders, *Faced and Faded, Hanging to Hurl*, p. 42, 1993

twinkle star *noun*
in trucking, an International Harvester Transtar model truck *US*
- —Ed and Ruth Radlauer, *Truck Tech Talk*, p. 57, 1986

twinkle-toes *noun*
1 a dancer; often used as a nickname or term of endearment *US*
- MIKE: And then everybody startied calling me Twinkle-Toes. ZACH: Did that bother you? [...] MIKE: Well, sure it bothered me. I didn't want anybody calling me Twinkle-Toes just because I took a couple of dance lessons. —James Kirkwood, *A Chorus Line*, 1975

2 a youthful, effeminate homosexual man *US*
- — *Maledicta*, p. 247, 1979: 'Kinks and queens: linguistic and cultural aspects of the terminology for gays'

twinkling *noun*
silent applause: raising both hands and wiggling your fingers, with your open palms facing the recipient of the gesture *UK*
- [A] growing practice in radical youth movements today is "twinkling", whereby if you agree with the speaker you hold your arms in front of your body and wiggle each hand. —Mark Steel, *Vive La Revolution*, p. 174, 2003

twins *noun*
1 two women having sex with one man or with each other for the pleasure of the man *US*
- She has a girl specially trained for her when a customer requests "twins." The two of them go into erotic ecstasies over each other's bodies for the bon vivant voyeur who has paid handsomely for such stimulating tableaux. —Mario Puzo, *Inside Las Vegas*, p. 272, 1977

2 a woman's breasts *US*
- —Pamela Munro, *U.C.L.A. Slang*, p. 121, 2001

3 the fists *US*
- —Ethan Hilderbrant, *Prison Slang*, p. 132, 1998

twins *adverb*
▸ **go twins**
to go on a double date *US*
- —Edd Byrnes, *Way Out with Kookie*, 1959

twirl *noun*
1 a key, especially a skeleton key *UK, 1879*
Because a burglar twirls it as he uses it.
- The Governor has given orders that his person is to be searched regularly for twirls. —Charles Raven, *Underworld Nights*, p. 62, 1956
- So the day before we made ourselves busy in the tin shop. Making twirls. We were not sure w[h]ether we could make one that would fit the hand cuffs[.] —Frank Norman, *Bang To Rights*, p. 48, 1958
- O.K. – now let's get the twirl out and swing back the old baronial doors[.] —Derek Raymond (Robin Cook), *The Crust on its Uppers*, p. 26, 1962

2 a prison officer *UK, 1933*
From the sense as 'a key'.
- I saw the twirl who was still standing at the door of my peter. —Frank Norman, *Bang To Rights*, p. 15, 1958
- —Angela Devlin, *Prison Patter*, p. 117, 1996

twirling *noun*
the dishonest substitution of a winning betting slip for a losing one *UK*
In use among bookmakers.
- — *The Bournemouth Echo*, 18th August 1960

twirly *noun*
an elderly bus passenger *UK*
An elision of 'too early', from the high incidence of such passengers wishing to use their free bus-passes too early.
- Busmen particularly loathe the daily hassle with the "twirlies" at around 9.30am as senior citizens ask conductors whether they are "too early" to use their free passes. — *New Society*, 13th November 1980

twirp *noun*
▷ **see: TWERP**

twist *noun*
1 a girl *AUSTRALIA, 1924*
- When a lunkhead and his twist spat in a night club, it's etiquette for him to dash after her and slip her cab fare. —Jack Lait and Lee Mortimer, *New York Confidential*, p. 222, 1948
- I roused my ludicrous pal-of-old and watched him dress in beautiful clothes and eat in the breakfast nook the meal served by the brunette twist. —Neal Cassady, *The First Third*, p. 166, 1971

- "There's no justice," Canaan said. "That twist I seen you with the other day. A twist like that, a gonif like you. Like Bambi and Godzilla." —Robert Campbell, *Alice in La-La Land*, p. 62, 1987

2 the passive, 'feminine' member of a lesbian relationship *US*
- —*American Speech*, p. 59, Spring-Summer 1970: 'Homosexual slang'

3 a marijuana cigarette *US, 1920*
The paper end is *twisted* to prevent the loss of its contents.
- —Mike Haskins, *Drugs*, p. 291, 2003

4 a small bag or paper wrap of heroin
- —Robert Ashton, *This Is Heroin*, p. 210, 2002

5 a turn to buy drinks in a group of people drinking *IRELAND*
- My twist, said Jimmy Sr... He stood up. -Same again over here, Darren, please! —Roddy Doyle, *The Van*, p. 77, 1991

6 severe pressure or coercion to do something
- It's a long story. I got no choice. The cops put a twist on me. I had to do it to save my baby. —Joseph Wambaugh, *Floaters*, p. 84, 1996

7 a multiple bet, gambling on three different horses in separate races in a total of seven bets *UK*
More popularly known as a **PATENT**.
- —David Bennet, *Know Your Bets*, p. 78, 2001

▸ **around the twist**
eccentric, crazy *NEW ZEALAND*
- —Sonya Plowman, *Great Kiwi Slang*, p. 15, 2002

twist *verb*

1 to cheat or swindle someone *AUSTRALIA*
- I couldn't afford to cut up rough unless I caught him in the act of twisting me. —Charles Raven, *Underworld Nights*, p. 167, 1956

2 to arrest someone *US*
- So for the lawyer for these two cats that got twisted found out the cat was a Federal narcotics agent. —William Burroughs, *Junkie*, p. 121, 1953

3 to spend time in jail or prison *US*
- He twisted behind a hummer means he did the time but not the crime. —Hermese E. Roberts, *The Third Ear*, 1971

4 to roll a marijuana cigarette *US*
- So we all did go to Larry's and Julien sat on the floor in front of an open newspaper in which was the tea (poor quality L.A. but good enough) and rolled, or "twisted," as Jack Steen, the absent one had said to me[.] —Jack Kerouac, *The Subterraneans*, p. 5, 1958

5 in pool, to apply spin to a shot to affect the course of the object ball or the cue ball after it hits the object ball *US*
- —Steve Rushin, *Pool Cool*, p. 29, 1990

▸ **twist a braid**
to say goodbye *US*
- —*People Magazine*, p. 72, 19th July 1993

▸ **twist a dream**
to roll a marijuana cigarette *US, 1949*
- —Ernest L. Abel, *A Marijuana Dictionary*, p. 106, 1982

▸ **twist her tail**
to start a car or to accelerate suddenly *US*
- —*American Speech*, p. 273, December 1962: 'The language of traffic policemen'

▸ **twist your arm**
to persuade someone; strictly, to persuade someone by force or threat, but often jocular *UK, 1953*
- [S]omeone wants to get at you through your family, right? But is it so they can twist your arm to do something they want? —Reginald Hill, *Arms and the Women*, 1999
- Months ago, I had my arm twisted to take part in a Barnardo's football quiz. —*New Statesman*, 1st April 2002

twist!
a derisive suggestion that accompanies the offensive gesture of a raised middle finger *UK*

twist and twirl; twist *noun*
a girl *US, 1928*
Rhyming slang.
- —Ray Puxley, *Cockney Rabbit*, 1992

twisted *adjective*

1 perverted *US, 1900*
- —Ross and Grey, *Twisted*, 1965
- You are one twisted fuck. —*American Beauty*, 1999

2 drunk or drug-intoxicated *US*
- "Man is he high!" someone whispered. "Man, he's twisted! But on what? On what?" —John Clellon Holmes, *The Horn*, p. 201, 1958
- [H]e can be twisted on narcotics. —Clarence Cooper Jr, *The Scene*, p. 55, 1960
- Very soon, I knew, we would both be completely twisted. —Hunter S. Thompson, *Fear and Loathing in Las Vegas*, p. 3, 1971
- —Connie Eble (Editor), *UNC-CH Campus Slang*, p. 5, November 1983

twister *noun*

1 a key *US, 1940*
- We hopped into Harry Shapiro's cab and took off for the LaSalle Street station to hand Leon Rappolo the twisters to the city. —Mezz Mezzrow, *Really the Blues*, p. 50, 1946
- I didn't miss it 'til I came home that night and found that I had no twister to get in with. —A.S. Jackson, *Gentleman Pimp*, p. 20, 1973

2 an individual who prepares marijuana cigarettes *US, 1936*
From the verb sense.
- —Ernest L. Abel, *A Marijuana Dictionary*, p. 106, 1982

3 a strong drug injection, especially a combination of heroin and cocaine *US*
- —J.E. Schmidt, *Narcotics Lingo and Lore*, p. 185, 1959

twistie *noun*
a bottle of beer with a screw top *AUSTRALIA, 1993*
- 'Wanna drink?' He handed me a twistie. —Helen Barnes, *The Crypt Orchid*, p. 39, 1994

twist 'n' go *adjective*
used of a motor-scooter *UK*
From the handlebar throttle on such machines.
- Most 50cc "twist 'n' go" bikes can be upgraded with a better engine and exhaust[.] —*The Independent Magazine*, p. 17, 28th August 2004

twistum *noun*
a marijuana cigarette *US, 1998*
An elaboration of **TWIST**.
- —Mike Haskins, *Drugs*, p. 291, 2003

twist up *verb*
to roll a marijuana cigarette *US*
- SOUTHERN: I'll just twist one up [takes out pink papers] using these clitoral pinks to give it zest. BOCKRIS: Why don't you twist up another one? —Victor Bockris, *With William Burroughs [The Howard Marks Book of Dope Stories]*, p. 34, 1997

twisty *noun*
a devious, even dishonest, practice *NEW ZEALAND, 1997*
- —Harry Orsman, *A Dictionary of Modern New Zealand Slang*, p. 143, 1999

twisty *adjective*
odd, strange *UK*
- —Jim Phelan, *Fetters for Twenty*, 1957

twit *noun*
an inept and ineffectual person *UK, 1934*
Widely popularised by UK radio comedy *The Goons* (1951–60) and celebrated by *Monty Python's Flying Circus* in 'The Upper-Class Twit of the Year' sketch (1970).
- [I]t begins to get on me nerves, this place, being surrounded with all these pink-faced twits, with their phoney carry on. —John Peter Jones, *Feather Pluckers*, p. 43, 1964
- —Connie Eble (Editor), *UNC-CH Campus Slang*, p. 7, Fall 1980
- Yes, he's a congenital twit and we've got no business publishing crap like that. —Carl Hiaasen, *Tourist Season*, p. 77, 1986
- That false cousin you saddled me with and that whey-faced twit of a girl who had him by the pecker was going to do me in. —Robert Campbell, *Nibbled to Death by Ducks*, p. 274, 1989

twit *verb*
to tease or taunt someone *UK, 1530*
- Bill Lee, our pitcher in the decisive game, was twitting the writers during pregame practice. —Bill Cardoso, *The Maltese Sangweech*, p. 189, 1984

twitch *noun*

1 a prostitute *US*
- Hey, Billy boy, you remember that time in Seattle you and me picked up those two twitches? One of the best rolls I ever had. —Ken Kesey, *One Flew Over the Cuckoo's Nest*, p. 98, 1962

2 a personal pleasure *US*
- "Rather have the broad," Malatesta said. "Every man's got his own twitch," the bartender said. —George V. Higgins, *The Rat on Fire*, p. 74, 1981

3 a bird-watching trip *UK*
Bird-watchers' slang, from the observation that many bird-watchers do twitch with excitement.
- — *New Society*, 17th November 1977

4 in hospital usage, a hypochondriac *US*
- — Sally Williams, *"Strong" Words*, p. 164, 1994

twitcher *noun*

1 a bird-watcher *UK*
Bird-watchers' slang. Originally from the observation that many bird-watchers do twitch with excitement and applied only to excitable members of the bird-watching community, now well known and applied generally.
- — *New Society*, 17th November 1977
- — Nicholas Jones, *Hackers, Hotting and Hooray Henrys*, p. 60, 1992

2 anyone with an pedantic interest in, and an obsessive knowledge of, a specific topic *UK*
Extended from its sense in the bird-watching world.
- [S]uddenly he's a hip-hop twitcher, reeling off stats and opinions[.] — Patrick Neate, *Where You're At*, p. 35, 2003

twitching; twitchin' *adjective*
excellent *US*
- — Kenn "Naz" Young, *Naz's Dictionary of Teen Slang*, p. 132, 1993

twitchy *adjective*

1 agitated, nervously restless, anxious *UK, 1874*
- I was twitchy with pent-up energy. — Janet Evanovitch, *Three to Get Deadly*, p. 131, 1997

2 in motor racing, moving in a jerky or sudden fashion *US*
- A car that is overly sensitive to driver input is considered twitchy. — Don Alexander, *The Racer's Dictionary*, p. 70, 1980

twittering *adjective*
experiencing the bleed period of the menstrual cycle *UK*
A schoolgirl term.
- — Gerald Kersh, *Fowler's End*, 1958

twitting *adjective*
inept; unfashionable *US*
- — *American Speech*, p. 154, May 1959: 'Gator (University of Florida) slang'

twizzle; twizzle-about *verb*
to rotate; to twirl; to twist something into a twirl shape *UK, 1788*
- How's he ever gonna do all that twizzling-about bollocks[?] — *The Full Monty*, 1997
- [T]wizzle a flannel into a point and work it into me ears[.] — Niall Griffiths, *Kelly + Victor*, p. 185, 2002

two *noun*
an act of defecation *TRINIDAD AND TOBAGO*
An abbreviation of **NUMBER TWO**.
- — Lise Winer, *Dictionary of the English/Creole of Trinidad & Tobago*, 2003

▷ **see:** **TWO SHOT, TWO STRETCH**

▸ **giz a two**
used to request a *two*-way share *UK*
- — Angela Devlin, *Prison Patter*, p. 117, 1996

▸ **in two**
in bar dice games, to make a hand in two rolls of the dice *US*
- — Jester Smith, *Games They Play in San Francisco*, p. 104, 1971

▸ **in two-twos**
instantly *TRINIDAD AND TOBAGO, 1990*
- — Lise Winer, *Dictionary of the English/Creole of Trinidad & Tobago*, 2003

two; two up *verb*
to share a cell with one other prisoner *UK*
- — Angela Devlin, *Prison Patter*, p. 118, 1996

two-0 *noun*
a twenty-dollar note *US*
- — Ralph de Sola, *Crime Dictionary*, p. 155, 1982

two and a juice *noun*
two beers and a tomato juice *CANADA*
- While draft beer in the beer parlour is always called for by the expression, "draw two," if you want tomato juice as well in order to make redeye, the cry is two and a juice. — Chris Thain, *Cold as a Bay Street Banker's Heart*, p. 158, 1987

two and eight *noun*
a confusion; an attack of nerves; an emotional state; drunk *UK, 1938*
Rhyming slang for **STATE**.
- Any way the geezer was getting in a right two & eight[.] — Frank Norman, *Bang To Rights*, p. 123, 1958
- Philip has just rolled in from the rub-a-dub [pub], and is in a right old two-and-eight[.] — Ronnie Barker, *Fletcher's Book of Rhyming Slang*, p. 39, 1979
- What a two and eight. — Anthony Masters, *Minder*, p. 24, 1984

two and two *noun*
cocaine *US*
- He went into the men's, paid a dime for a stall and sniffed a two-and-two, scooping the coke out of the Baggy with a silver Little Orphan Annie spoon. — Elmore Leonard, *52 Pick-up*, p. 56–57, 1974

two bad boys from Illinois *noun*
in craps, a roll of two *US*
- — Steve Kuriscak, *Casino Talk*, p. 67, 1985

two-bit *adjective*
inconsequential; of no note *US, 1932*
'Two bits' represented a quarter of a dollar, a small sum; most younger speakers who use the term would not be familiar with its monetary roots.
- It was a mad scramble, but we finally tracked him down in a two-bit cabaret somewhere outside of Buffalo, playing with a trio for coffee and cake. — Mezz Mezzrow, *Really the Blues*, p. 292, 1946
- What are you afraid of, this dirty two-bit shamus? — Mickey Spillane, *I, The Jury*, p. 20, 1947
- You two-bit, trouble-making union louse! — Ralph Ellison, *Invisible Man*, p. 225, 1947
- "And I'm telling you," Hobbs said, "that you're a two-bit crook." — Norman Mailer, *Advertisements for Myself*, p. 129, 1951
- You two-bit bookkeeper, I ought to-! — Jim Thompson, *Bad Boy*, p. 325, 1953
- I have the bartender here and a two-bit pimp who has a girl at Reba's. — Chester Himes, *The Real Cool Killers*, p. 129, 1959
- Look around today, in every small town and big city, from two-bit catfish and soda-pop joints into the "integrated" lobby of the Waldorf-Astoria, and you'll see conks on black men. — Malcolm X and Alex Haley, *The Autobiography of Malcolm X*, p. 54, 1964
- A rotten low-lifed racist, two-bit pig! — Bobby Seale, *A Lonely Rage*, p. 256, 1978
- "That son of a bitch," muttered Dede, back in their room at the Potlatch House, "that two-bit Bolsvhevik son of a bitch." — Armistead Maupin, *Further Tales of the City*, p. 263, 1982
- Are you telling me that some two-bit auto burglar concocted this whole thing? — Carl Hiaasen, *Tourist Season*, p. 20, 1986
- I want you to see I'm not some ordinary two-bit fuckup you got on your list. — Elmore Leonard, *Maximum Bob*, p. 124, 1991

two bits *noun*

1 a small amount *US*
- "They flooded the nursing care homes and shelters," Medill says, adding his two bits. — Robert Campbell, *Nibbled to Death by Ducks*, p. 59, 1989

2 twenty-five dollars *US*
An example of the 'cent = dollar' mechanism in drug slang.
- — *Current Slang*, p. 50, Fall 1968

3 twenty-five thousand dollars *US*
- According to the sources, Lambesis was seen and heard on the tape as saying: "The Man was given 'two-bits.'" — *Chicago Tribune*, p. 14C, 12th January 1986

two bob *noun*
the sum of two shillings *AUSTRALIA, 1934*
After decimal currency was introduced in 1966, used for the sum of twenty cents.
- — Norman Lindsay, *Saturdee*, p. 149, 1934
- — Gavin Casey, *It's Harder for Girls*, p. 31, 1941
- Then there was the Saturday he put two bob each way on some no-hoper at Rosehill and the no-hoper came in at fifty to one. — Eric Lambert, *The Veterans*, p. 27, 1954
- She got me tight and I woke up in the park without any dough except a two-bob piece and a few coppers. — Vince Kelly, *The Bogeyman*, p. 10, 1956
- They're radio actors. No work, no money, no manners. Two bob an' one suit, that's them. — Nino Culotta (John O'Grady), *They're A Weird Mob*, p. 20, 1957
- — J.E. MacDonnell, *Don't Gimme the Ships*, p. 25, 1960
- — Robert S. Close, *With Hooves of Brass*, p. 80, 1961
- Bloody policeman there one time charged me two bob after inspecting the way bill. — Herb Wharton, *Cattle Camp*, p. 112, 1994
- They offered us two bob (20 cents) for each ball we could find. — Rex Hunt, *Tall Tales – and True*, p. 74, 1994

- When I was your age I was digging ditches for two bob an hour and coming home to a meal of bread and bloody dripping. — Phillip Gwynne, *Deadly Unna?*, p. 212, 1998

▸ **have two bob each way**
to have all contingencies working for you; to hedge your bets *AUSTRALIA, 1973*
- That IS a good lurk. He's got two bob each way. — Sam Weller, *Old Bastards I Have Met*, p. 20, 1979

two bob *adjective*
inferior, rubbishy, useless *AUSTRALIA, 1944*
Derives from Australian similes such as 'as silly as a two bob watch'; explained by G.A. Wilkes in *A Dictionary of Australian Colloquialisms*, 1978, as the sum of money most often used in derogatory expressions of worth. A **BOB** is 'a shilling' in pre-decimal currency (5p for what it's worth, 5c in Australia). It compares with US **TWO BIT** and UK 'two penny'.
- This time in manner of a two-bob game-show host. — Gavin Hills, *White Burger Danny (Disco Biscuits)*, p. 66, 1996
- If they was coming, they'd have come [...] Two bob Leicester as per fucking usual. — Martin King and Martin Knight, *The Naughty Nineties*, p. 176, 1999
- Jimmy got his hands on it and started decorating like it was a whorehouse, like some two-bob gangster Gracelands. — J.J. Connolly, *Layer Cake*, p. 223, 2000
- "You fucking whore," he screamed at her unconscious body. "Know what you're worth? Two bob." He flung a ten pence piece at her face and stomped out[.] — Garry Bushell, *The Face*, p. 270, 2001

two bob bit *noun*
a fart; as a plural, diarrhoea *UK*
Rhyming slang for **THE SHITS**.
- Who's dropped a two bob bit? — Ray Puxley, *Cockney Rabbit*, 1992

two-bob lair *noun*
a person who dresses flashily but cheaply *AUSTRALIA, 1944*
- Yeah, I know I look like a two-bob lair decked out like this. — George Johnston, *My Brother Jack*, p. 59, 1964
- — Ryan Aven-Bray, *Ridgey Didge Oz Jack Lang*, p. 49, 1983

two-bob piece; two-bob bit *noun*
a two-shilling coin *AUSTRALIA*
After the introduction of decimal currency in 1966, used for a 20 cent piece.
- She got me tight and I woke up in the park without any dough except a two-bob piece and a few coppers. — Vince Kelly, *The Bogeyman*, p. 10, 1956
- It was exactly the same as the previous night, except that the steak was no bigger than a two-bob bit[.] — Rex Hunt, *Tall Tales – and True*, p. 112, 1994

two-bob watch *noun*
a cheap, poorly made watch *AUSTRALIA, 1954*
Used metaphorically.
- He would describe somebody as being 'as silly as a two-bob watch'. — George Johnston, *My Brother Jack*, p. 58, 1964
- O'Reilly is more temperamental than a Hollywood film star. He carries on like a two-bob watch. — Bluey, *Bush Contractors*, p. 239, 1975
- The old cow was as mean as a two-bob watch! — Lance Peters, *The Dirty Half-Mile*, p. 94, 1979
- Name another world power where the police aren't as bent as a two-bob watch and the State Premiers aren't on every kick-back in the book. — Barry Humphries, *The Traveller's Tool*, p. 22, 1985

▸ **go off like a two-bob watch**
(of a woman) to be an astoundingly good sexual partner *AUSTRALIA, 1971*
- I reckon she'd have dropped her harolds and gone off like a two-bob watch at the first Pom to have a Captain Cook at her norks! — Barry Humphries, *Bazza Pulls It Off*, 1971

two-bottle jump; two-quart jump *noun*
a relatively long move between performances *US*
- — Sherman Louis Sergel, *The Language of Show Biz*, p. 232, 1973

two-bug *noun*
in horse racing, an inexperienced jockey with a weight allowance of seven pounds *US*
- — Robert V. Rowe, *How to Win at Horse-Racing*, 1990

two-by-four *noun*
a small house *BARBADOS*
- — Frank A. Collymore, *Barbadian Dialect*, p. 114, 1965

two-carbon abuser *noun*
a drunkard *US*
Hospital usage. Alcohol has two carbon atoms.
- — *Maledicta*, p. 70, Summer/Winter 1978: 'Common patient-directed pejoratives used by medical personnel'

two cents' worth; two cents *noun*
a personal opinion, advice or point of view *US*
- — Richard Neville, *Play Power*, 1970
- I jumped up, and, I don't know, started to put my two cents in, and they started to call me all kinds of names. — Richard Neville [quoting Otis Cook], *Play Power*, p. 249, 1970

twocker; twok; twoc *noun*
a criminal who *t*akes (usually a vehicle) *w*ithout *o*wner's *c*onsent; occasionally, someone who is suspected of dishonesty *UK*
- — Angela Devlin, *Prison Patter*, p. 118, 1996
- — Chris Lewis, *The Dictionary of Playground Slang*, p. 242, 2003

twocking *noun*
the criminal act of *t*aking (usually a vehicle) *w*ithout *o*wner's *c*onsent *UK*
- — Angela Devlin, *Prison Patter*, p. 117, 1996

two dots and a dash *noun*
the male genitals *US*
- — Roger Blake, *The American Dictionary of Sexual Terms*, p. 85, 1964

two'd up *adjective*
applied to two inmates in a prison cell *UK*
- — Home Office, *Glossary of Terms and Slang Common in Penal Establishments*, July 1978

two eighty-eight *adjective*
▷ **see: 288**

twoer *noun*
1 anything comprised by, or reckoned as, two *UK, 1899*
- Just like with conkers, it used to be a "oner" or a "twoer". — Charles Perkins, *Children of the Storm*, p. 11, 1998

2 two hundred pounds *UK, 1970*
- O'Neill was recorded as saying that "the whole business will cost you a twoer", meaning £200. — Jake Arnott, *He Kills Coppers*, p. 195, 2001

twofer *noun*
1 any situation in which you obtain two of something when only one is expected or paid for *US, 1936*
A shortening and corruption of 'two-for-one'; originally applied to a pair of theatre tickets sold for the price of one, and then picked up in more general use.
- — *American Speech*, May 1950
- — Wilfred Granville, *The Theater Dictionary*, p. 209, 1952
- — Sherman Louis Sergel, *The Language of Show Biz*, p. 232, 1973
- And if the president fumbles around in his answers on the stock market, why, those underhanded jackels of the press have got themselves a "two-fer." — Sam Donaldson, *Hold On, Mr. President*, p. 158, 1987
- Condoleeza Rice, Bush's choice for national security adviser: she is black and a woman (and therefore a "twofer", quips one Republican strategist). — Jonathan Freedland, *The Guardian*, 2nd August 2000

2 in American casinos, a chip worth $2.50 *US*
- — Steve Kuriscak, *Casino Talk*, p. 11, 1985

two-fingered *adjective*
anti-social *UK*
A reference to the offensive **V-SIGN** gesture.
- The Sex Pistols [...] surly two-fingered attitude to the world[.] — John Robb, *The Nineties*, p. 129, 1999

two foot table eater *noun*
an active participant in oral sex *JAMAICA*
West Indian and UK use, recorded in August 2002.

two-for-one *noun*
1 double credit for time served in prison by inmates with jobs or positions as prison trustees *US*
- — Bruce Jackson, *Outside the Law*, p. 61, 1972: 'Glossary'
- He was in charge of the laboratory, making teeth, drawing two-for-one, getting ready to go home. — Bruce Jackson, *Outside the Law*, p. 174, 1972

2 100% interest *UK*
- — Angela Devlin, *Prison Patter*, p. 117, 1996

two-four *noun*
a case of beer containing 24 bottles *US*
This term is the universal Canadian designator for the item, though 'case' may sometimes mean 'the box of 12'.
- — *People Magazine*, p. 73, 19th July 1993

two-four-seven *adverb*
at all times – twenty-four hours a day, seven days a week *UK*
A variation of **24/7**.
- [H]e's very mad, bad and totally para [paranoid] two-four-seven. —J.J. Connolly, *Layer Cake*, p. 79, 2000

TWOG *noun*
someone who travels to underdeveloped countries and seeks to become a part of meanest level of local society *ZIMBABWE*
An imperfect acronym for 'Third World Groupie', used by white Zimbabweans.
- — *Lonely Planet Southern Africa*, 2000

two-in-one *noun*
cocaine and heroin mixed for injection together *US*
- Said, "Let's have a party, have some fun / for God's sake, fellas, don't forget the gun / 'cause man, I want some two in one." —Bruce Jackson, *Get Your Ass in the Water and Swim Like Me*, p. 149, 1964

two in the glue *noun*
in a car or truck, a two-speed automatic transmission *US*
- —John Edwards, *Auto Dictionary*, p. 177, 1993

two lamps burning and no ship at sea
used for describing the ultimate in wastefulness *US*
- —Charles F. Haywood, *Yankee Dictionary*, p. 182, 1963

two man *noun*
second degree manslaughter *US*
- —Ralph de Sola, *Crime Dictionary*, p. 89, 1982

two men and a dog
a very small crowd *NEW ZEALAND*
- —Sonya Plowman, *Great Kiwi Slang*, p. 173, 2002

two minutes *noun*
a small amount of time *UK*
- [After 7 or 8 weeks] "Me?" I said. "But I've only been here two minutes." — *The Guardian*, 21st February 2002

twomp *noun*
twenty dollars *US*
- —Rick Ayers (Editor), *Slang Dictionary*, p. 16, 2001

twomp *adjective*
costing twenty dollars *US*
- —Rick Ayers (Editor), *Slang Dictionary*, p. 16, 2001

twomping *noun*
a beating, a thumping *UK*
- I'll hold his arms, you give him a right twomping. —Nicholas Blincoe, *The Beautiful Beaten-up Irish Boy of the Arndale Centre*, p. 9, 1998

twonk *noun*
a fool *UK*
- Like a twonk in a four by four[.] — *The Now Show*, October 2003

two-o *noun*
a twenty-dollar chunk of crack cocaine *US*
- —Geoffrey Froner, *Digging for Diamonds*, p. 64, 1989

two-o-eight *noun*
a military discharge for mental unfitness *US*
- —Carl Fleischhauer, *A Glossary of Army Slang*, p. 24, 1968

twopenny-farthing *adjective*
of little worth, unimportant *UK*
A devaluation of **TUPPENNY HA'PENNY**.
- Mr Romeo Roberts here, with his blazers and his knife-edge crease and his la-de-da talk. A twopenny-farthing commercial traveller. —Alexander Baron, *A Bit of Happiness [Six Granada Plays]*, p. 218, 1959

twopenny-halfpenny *adjective*
▷ **see: TUPPENNY HA'PENNY**

two pennyworth; twopenneth *noun*
an opinion *UK, 1965*
From conventional sense (a small amount, hence a small contribution).
- And then I remembered my father's two-penneth about Shangrila and Mr John Dawson. —David Peace, *Nineteen Seventy-Four*, p. 84, 1999

two-percenter *noun*
▷ **see: ONE-PERCENTER**

two pi *noun*
the number of years consumed completing a doctoral thesis *US*
- —Eric S. Raymond, *The New Hacker's Dictionary*, p. 360, 1991

two-pipe *noun*
a double-barrel shotgun *US*
- —Vincent J. Monteleone, *Criminal Slang*, p. 245, 1949

two-pot screamer *noun*
a person who gets drunk on very little alcohol *AUSTRALIA, 1959*
- —Sue Rhodes, *And when she was bad she was popular*, p. 51, 1968
- My husband's pissed again – he's always been a two pot screamer. —Barry Humphries, *The Wonderful World of Barry McKenzie*, p. 32, 1968
- —Jim Ramsay, *Cop It Sweet!*, p. 92, 1977

two-pump chump *noun*
a male who ejaculates without much stimulation *US*
- —Connie Eble (Editor), *UNC-CH Campus Slang*, p. 7, April 2004

two-quart jump *noun*
▷ **see: TWO-BOTTLE JUMP**

two rolls and no coffee *noun*
in craps, a roll of seven on the first roll after establishing your point *US, 1949*
A pun on 'roll', with the player here losing after two rolls.
- —Thomas L. Clark, *The Dictionary of Gambling and Gaming*, p. 243, 1987

twos *noun*
1 the second landing or floor level in a prison *UK*
- —Angela Devlin, *Prison Patter*, p. 53, 1996
- "You're on my spur on the twos," he said. — *The Guardian*, 19th October 2000

2 a share *UK*
- If a prisoner asks another for "twos" it means he or she wants to share something, usually a share – or it may mean wanting to give the other a share[.] —Angela Devlin, *Prison Patter*, p. 118, 1996

▸ **all the twos**
twenty-two *UK, 1943*
In Bingo, House or Housey-Housey calling, the formula 'all the' announces a double number.

twos and blues *noun*
a two-tone horn and flashing blue light used to signal a police vehicle travelling urgently *UK*
- We hit the Twos and Blues[.] —Duncan MacLaughlin, *The Filth*, p. 61, 2002

twos and fews *noun*
small-denomination notes or loose change *US*
- —Kenn "Naz" Young, *Naz's Underground Dictionary*, p. 62, 1973

two-seater *noun*
an outdoor privy which accomodates two people at once *US*
- The handsome bisexual richboy from the four-house family and the socially backward poorboy from the two-seater outhouse family. —Robert Gover, *Poorboy at the Party*, p. 8, 1966

twosey *noun*
an act of defecation *AUSTRALIA*
- Well it got to the stage where nature was calling with everything it had so I drifted off for a onsey and twoseys and rushed back as soon as I could. —Paul Vautin, *Turn It Up!*, p. 87, 1995

Two Shades of Soul *noun*
the 173rd Airborne Brigade, US Army *US*
So named because of the amicable relations between black and white soldiers in the unit, the first major US combat unit sent to Vietnam.
- —Linda Reinberg, *In the Field*, p. 104, 1991

two shot; two *noun*
in the television and film industries, a shot of two actors facing each other, each taking up half the screen *US*
- —Tony Miller and Patricia George, *Cut! Print!*, p. 73, 1977

twosky *noun*
two hundred dollars *US*
The '-sky' suffix is purely decorative.
- For a twosky I want satisfaction guaranteed within forty-eight hours. —James Ellroy, *Hollywood Nocturnes*, p. 206, 1994

two snaps up!
used for expressing approval *US*
A catchphrase from the television programme *In Living Color*.
- —Connie Eble (Editor), *UNC-CH Campus Slang*, p. 9, November 1990

two-spirited *adjective*
applied to homosexual, lesbian, bisexual or trangendered Native Americans *CANADA*
First used among Native Americans of transgendered people only, it has also been offensively applied to half-breeds and those who have adopted white culture.
- Another important objection to the term 'two-spirited' is that the creation of a pseudo- Indian terms implies that transgenderism was a universal phenomenon among the tribes, when it was not.—Gary Bowen, *Transgendered Native Americans*, 1996
- —Susie Dent, *Larpers and Shroomers*, p. 107, 2004

two-step *noun*
the highly venomous bamboo viper, found and feared in Vietnam *US*
So named because of the belief – false but vivid – that the venom is so toxic that it kills a person before they can take two steps after being bitten.
- —Linda Reinberg, *In the Field*, p. 16, 1991

two stretch; two *noun*
a two-year sentence of imprisonment *UK, 1950*
A multiple of **STRETCH** (a year's sentence).
- "How long you doing mate?" "A lagging," I said. "I'm doing a two". —Frank Norman, *Bang To Rights*, p. 12, 1958
- —Angela Devlin, *Prison Patter*, p. 117, 1996

two's up *adjective*
sharing, especially a cigarette *UK*
Used in borstals and detention centres.
- —Home Office, *Glossary of Terms and Slang Common in Penal Establishments*, July 1978

twot *noun*
an abusive epithet for someone you would otherwise call a cunt *UK*
A variant spelling (originally pronunced in a similar manner) of **TWAT** (the vagina). As time has passed the pronunciations have separated.
- [He] smacks Ally clean round the side of the swede. "You twot!" growls Ally. "I'm one of you."— Martin King and Martin Knight, *The Naughty Nineties*, p. 39, 1999

two-thirds of five-eighths of fuck all *noun*
almost nothing *NEW ZEALAND*
From the final line of 'The young man of Bengal' limerick.
- —David McGill, *David McGill's Complete Kiwi Slang Dictionary*, p. 116, 1998

two-thirty *adjective*
grimy, dirty *UK, 1960*
Rhyming slang for 'dirty'.
- [B]eing too poor to purchase any Cape of Good Hope, his bushel and peck [the neck] was extremely two-thirty [dirty].—Ronnie Barker, *Fletcher's Book of Rhyming Slang*, p. 25, 1979

two-time *verb*
to be seeing more than one sexual partner without the knowledge of the partner(s); to be unfaithful *US, 1924*
- I set out to meet my Clark Gable for lunch and find him two-timing me with Gloria Grahame.—Elliott Mackle, *It Takes Two*, p. 108, 2003

two-timer *noun*
a person who is unfaithful to another person or a cause *US, 1927*
- I'll keep you posted on what's going on with little Miss Two-timer. —C.D. Payne, *Youth in Revolt*, p. 212, 1993

two-timing woman *noun*
a type of bet in an illegal numbers game lottery *US*
- Then to be on the safe side he also played jail house, death row, lady come back, two-timing woman, pile of rocks, dark days and trouble.—Chester Himes, *A Rage in Harlem*, p. 23, 1957

two-toilet *adjective*
used of an Irish immigrant, relatively well-off economically and straying from the Irish cultural ties that bind *US*
A term coined in Boston and rarely used elsewhere.
- The late Patrick J. (Sonny) McDonough not only postulated the two-toilet Irish, but also once suggested to President John F. Kennedy that he not stay at Frank Sinatra's place in Palm Springs.—*The Boston Globe*, p. A27, 3rd June 1990
- Overseeing the downtown busing scheme, federal district judge W. Arthur Garrity, Jr., who did not live in the city, was derided by blue-collar Boston Irish as an uppity "two-toilet Irishman" who had forgotten his roots.—*The Calvert News Series*, Summer 1997

two-two *noun*
a prostitute *CANADA*
- —Jack Chambers (Editor), *Slang Bag 93 (University of Toronto)*, p. 6, Winter 1993

two-two *adverb*
in pairs *INDIA*
- The lift is so small we shall have to go up two-two.—Paroo Nihalini, R.K. Tongue and Priya Hosali, *Indian and British English*, 1979

two-up *noun*
1 a gesture that is used to insult or otherwise cause offense *UK: SCOTLAND*
The forefinger and the middle finger are extended to form a V shape, with the palm turned in towards the gesturer.
- He started it. He gied us the two-up.—Michael Munro, *The Original Patter*, p. 71, 1985

2 a gambling game in which two pennies are tossed from a small flat bat *AUSTRALIA, 1884*
- When your luck at two-up's lousy, and you view your meagre pay / – Well, you don't get drunk too often on that two and six a day!—Tip Kelaher, *The Digger Hat and other verses*, p. 24, 1942
- Some bloke sold it to me for a tenner. Wanted the money for a game of two-up.—Jean Brooks, *The Opal Witch*, p. 133, 1967

two-up school *noun*
a place at which a two-up game is held; a group of people playing two-up *AUSTRALIA, 1897*
- NICE OLD LADY: What school do you go to, my little man? SNOWY: The two-up school, mum.—Norman Lindsay, *Comic Art of Norman Lindsay*, p. 110, 1905
- Australia's most notorious two-up school was, and still is, known as Tommo's.—Vince Kelly, *The Bogeyman*, p. 164, 1956
- Or perhaps the ladies conduct a two-up school here, and the fence is police-proof.—Douglas Baglin and John O'Grady, *Ladies and Gentlemen*, p. 25, 1966

two-way *noun*
a position for mutual, simultaneous oral sex between two people, or the act itself, especially when advertised as a service offered by a prostitute *UK*
- —Caroline Archer, *Tart Cards*, 2003

two-way *adjective*
said of a carnival game or attraction that can be operated either legitimately or in a crooked fashion *US*
- —Lindsay E. Smith and Bruce A. Walstad, *Sting Shift*, p. 117, 1989: 'Glossary'

two-way bondage *noun*
a restriction of movement to facilitate an erotic encounter or sexual intercourse, especially when advertised as a service offered and received by a prostitute *UK*
- —Caroline Archer, *Tart Cards*, 2003

two-way man *noun*
a male prostitute who is available for both anal and oral sex *US, 1941*

two-way watersports *noun*
when used in a prostitute's advertising, indicates that the prostitute is willing both to urinate over the client, and be urinated upon *UK*
A specification of **WATER SPORTS** (the practice of urophilia and uralgnia).
- —Caroline Archer, *Tart Cards*, 2003

two-wire *noun*
an electronic technician *US*
US Navy usage.
- — *Seattle Times*, p. A9, 12th April 1998: 'Grunts, squids not grunting from the same dictionary'

two words, three effs
fuck off *UK*
If the intention is euphemistic why spell it out?
- MOON: Well? JAMIE: Two words, three effs.—Bernard Dempsey and Kevin McNally, *Lock, Stock ... & Two Hundred Smoking Kalashnikovs*, p. 100, 2000

twozee *verb*

to defecate *TRINIDAD AND TOBAGO, 1986*
Children's vocabulary.

- — Lise Winer, *Dictionary of the English/Creole of Trinidad & Tobago*, 2003

TX

in on-line poker playing, thanks *UK*

- — *FHM*, p. 147, June 2003

txt *verb*

to send a text message *UK, 2000*
A new vocabulary of abbreviations, of which this is probably the most recognisable, has grown rapidly as texting becomes evermore popular and mobile phone companies limit the number of characters subscribers may use.

- — *ltle bk of txt abuse*, 2001
- "Deck The House" made me laugh and txt my girlfriend to say "I love you". — *Muzik*, p. 9, February 2003

tyke *noun*

1 a child, especially one who is disobedient, impudent or mischievous; a youth *UK, 1400*
Probably from the sense as 'a dog'.

- The fat copper got real mean then, he stared at Henry as if he wanted to tear his head off, and said, "You dirty lying little tyke. If you say that in court tomorrow, I'll fix you for good." — John Peter Jones, *Feather Pluckers*, p. 9, 1964
- Get up you lazy fucking tyke, and get to school! — Martin King and Martin Knight, *The Naughty Nineties*, p. 137, 1999
- Meantime we left the little tyke I had nabbed at the station[.] — Duncan MacLaughlin, *The Filth*, p. 63, 2002

2 a Yorkshireman *UK, about 1700*
Originally pejorative, ultimately from the sense as 'a dog'; now in general use, and adopted with pride by Yorkshire people: Barnsley football club is nicknamed 'The Tykes'.

- Tyke first, English second, happy to be a Euro citizen — *www.yorkshire-soul.org*, 25th February 2005

3 a rough, ill-mannered fellow *UK: NORTHERN IRELAND*

- [Mainly Scots and Northern English, from Old Norse tik "a female dog, a bitch"] — C. I. Macafee, *A Concise Ulster Dictionary*, p. 369, 1996

4 a Roman Catholic *AUSTRALIA, 1902*
Probably Northern Ireland English *Taig*.

- — Lance Corporal Cobber, *The Anzac Pilgrim's Progress*, p. 81, 1915
- Little red-headed Tyke got him. — Alexander Buzo, *Rooted*, p. 84, 1969
- — Jim Ramsay, *Cop It Sweet!*, p. 92, 1977
- See the tykes, of which I'm one I don't mind telling you, they know that of the two main evils – drinking and fornicating – the latter's the worst. — Lance Peters, *The Dirty Half-Mile*, p. 126, 1979
- — Kathy Lette, *Girls' Night Out*, p. 56, 1987

5 a scruffy dog; a mongrel *UK, about 1400*
Now widley used as a pet name.

type *noun*

a person, especially one of a stated or implied character *UK, 1922*
Colloquial.

- — Renee Baron, *Are You My Type, Am I Yours?*, 1995
- [T]here are more than a few real nasty types out there disguised as team members[.] — Kate White, *Why Good Girls Dont Get Ahead But Gutsy Girls Do*, p. 199, 1996

typer *noun*

a typewriter *US*

- — *American Speech*, p. 29, Spring 1982: 'The language of science fiction fan magazines'

typewriter *noun*

1 a machine gun *UK, 1915*

- I guess I managed to put up a kind of feeble grin myself while I waited for their typewriters to begin pounding out their farewell notes to me. — Mezz Mezzrow, *Really the Blues*, p. 64, 1946

2 a fighter; a boxer *UK, 1931*
Rhyming slang.

- Anyone who keeps going through adversity is said to be "a real typewriter". — Ray Puxley, *Cockney Rabbit*, 1992

3 the push-button automatic transmission on a Dodge car *US*

- — Lyle K. Engel, *The Complete Book of Fuel and Gas Dragsters*, p. 154, 1968

typewriter commando *noun*

a soldier assigned to clerical support duty far from combat *US*

- — *American Speech*, p. 56, February 1947: 'Pacific War language'

typewriter jockey *noun*

a stenographer or typist *US*

- — *American Speech*, p. 158–159, May 1960: 'The Burgeoning of "Jockey"'

typist *noun*

in a deck of playing cards, a queen *US*

- — George Percy, *The Language of Poker*, p. 94, 1988

typo *noun*

a *typo*graphical error *UK, 1945*

- [I]t was like inspecting an encyclopedia for a single typo. — Dan Brown, *Digital Fortress*, p. 145, 1998

tyrannosaurus rex; tyrannosaurus *noun*

sex *UK*
Rhyming slang.

- There was too much Tyrannosaurus in it for my liking. — Ray Puxley, *Fresh Rabbit*, 1998

tyre-kicker *noun*

▷ see: TIRE-KICKER

Tyrone *noun*

a potent strain of marijuana *US*

- — Lois Stavsky et al., *A2Z*, p. 105, 1995

tzuris *noun*

▷ see: TSURIS

Uu

Ubangi *noun*
a black person *US*
Offensive.
- [I]t's five o'clock – some sixteen-year-old Ubangi looks like he should be playing center for the Knicks comes down the street on a bicycle and yanks a pocketbook off a woman's shoulder. —Vincent Patrick, *The Pope of Greenwich Village*, p. 123, 1979

U-barrel *noun*
a large steel drum used for collecting urine where there is no plumbing *ANTARCTICA*
- — *Cool Antarctica*, 2003: 'Antarctic slang'

über-; uber- *prefix*
super-high in quality or degree *US*
Adopted directly from German preposition *über* (over, above); combines to form words that exceed the norm.
- For 10 years now, Coach Ditka has been Chicago's very own uber-maniac, a blustery bully who thinks of himself as a genius but behaves more like a wacky character on a sitcom. —*Chicago Sun-Times*, p. 11, 8th October 1992
- [R]azor-tongued uber-slapper Jenny Eclair[.] —*Drugs An Adult Guide*, p. 20, December 2001
- [T]here's The Ministry and there's Cream and they're the two biggest uberclubs in fucking Europe. —Kevin Sampson, *Clubland*, p. 15, 2002
- Tommy Hanson – number-one UK recording artist and uberlad —Ben Elton, *High Society*, p. 18, 2002
- [P]etulant uber-bitches dash champagne glasses on the mirror-polished floors of their super-lux apartments[.] —Jessica Berens and Kerri Sharp, *Prada sucks! [Inappropriate Behaviour]*, p. vii, 2002
- MARTI PELLOW: Uber-sap Scots crooner with Wet Wet Wet. —*Ministry*, p. 41, January 2002
- To some uber-trendy, to others fucking painful[.] —*X-Ray*, p. 91, November 2002

UBI
doctors' shorthand for the facetious diagnosis: *u*nexplained *b*eer *i*njury *UK*
Recorded in an article about medical slang in British (3 London and 1 Cambridge) hospitals.
- — *Ethics and Behaviour*, August 2003

uc dai loi; ouc-dai-loi *noun*
(during the Vietnam conflict) an Australian soldier *AUSTRALIA*
From Vietnamese. Spelt with much variation.
- 'You want change money? Ucdai loi?' 'Fuck off, slope head.' 'You got US green? You want change?' —William Nagel, *The Odd Angry Shot*, p. 69, 1975
- O is for OUC-DAI-LOI numbered 1 to 10. / Depending on how much the digger would spend. —Martin Cameron, *A Look at the Bright Side*, 1988
- Uc-dai-loi, Cheap Charlie, / He no go to bed with me, / For it cost him many, many P, / Uc-dai-loi he Cheap Charlie. —Martin Cameron, *A Look at the Bright Side*, 1988
- 'If you want me Ouc-dai-loi, you buy me Saigon Tea and I let you kiss me where it smells,' she replied. —Martin Cameron, *A Look at the Bright Side*, 1988

u cunt *nickname*
Uncut magazine (since 1997) *UK*
Originally a cut and paste by disgruntled employees, then adopted by the magazine's competition.

udder *noun*
1 the female breast *UK, 1933*
Originally (about 1708) in conventional or poetic use.
2 a despised, disrespected or foolish woman *UK*
Possibly a variation of **cow**; more likely to derive from 'udder' (the female breast) hence used here as a synonym for **TIT**.
- When Dad died: "Silly old bastard [...]" Mum: "Stupid old udder, losing it like that." —Mark Powell, *Snap*, p. 119, 2001

3 a protuding paunch produced by too much beer drinking *UK*
Recorded as a contemporary gay usage.
- — *Attitude*, July 2003: 'New palare lexicon'

u-ey; u-ee; yewie; you-ee *noun*
a u-turn *US*
- — *Current Slang*, p. 4, Summer 1969
- If the law isn't up my arse I'll hang a U-ie. —Barry Humphries, *A Nice Night's Entertainment*, 1981
- And this time he jumped the brakes, wrenched the wheel and spun a U-ee at the same time. —Joseph Wambaugh, *Fugitive Nights*, p. 188, 1992
- Round and round, an endless U-ie. —Bridget O'Connor, *Heavy Petting [The Howard Marks Book of Dope Stories]*, p. 171, 1998

uggies *noun*
a pair of ugg boots *AUSTRALIA*
- Tracky Dacks and Uggies in the home only please! —*www.smh.com.au*, 2003

ughly *adjective*
uglier than ugly *US*
- — *Current Slang*, p. 8, Winter 1966

ugly as a hatful of arseholes *adjective*
especially ugly *AUSTRALIA*
- I once done one [a portrait] of me ma, but she turned out as ugly as a hatful of arseholes! —Barry Humphries, *Bazza Pulls It Off!*, 1971
- The singer couldn't sing and the actors weren't acting. The chorus were as ugly as a hatful of arseholes, and the lead man looked like an arrowroot biscuit. —David Foster, *Moonlite*, p. 167, 1981

ugly as fuck *adjective*
very ugly *US*
- [W]e didn't have band uniforms and we were ugly as fuck. —Frank Zappa, *The Real Frank Zappa Book*, p. 66, 1989

Ugly Australian *noun*
a rough, loutish Australian; an Australian yobbo *AUSTRALIA*
- Personally, I've had a gutful of watching Bazza McKenzie and his mates boozing away, showering one another with the amber fluid, and doing their Ugly Australian act abroad. —Bill Hornadge, *The Ugly Australian*, p. 198, 1974

ugly sister *noun*
a blister *UK*
Rhyming slang.
- —Ray Puxley, *Cockney Rabbit*, 1992

ugly stick *noun*
a notional stick with which a person has been beaten in order to make them ugly *US*
- [H]e looked like he had been beaten with an ugly stick. —Steve Cannon, *Groove, Bang, and Jive Around*, p. 83, 1969
- —Barry Humphries, *The Traveller's Tool*, p. 141, 1985
- —Connie Eble (Editor), *UNC-CH Campus Slang*, p. 8, March 1996
- You must admit, she is rather mannish. No offense, but if that's a woman, it looks like she's been beaten with an ugly stick. —*Austin Powers*, 1997
- They'd been whupped with ugly sticks, many of them. —Claire Mansfield and John Mendelssohn, *Dominatrix*, p. 110, 2002

ugs *noun*
▷ **see: HUGS AND KISSES**

uh-oh
used in recognition of trouble *US*
- "Uh-oh," Lula said. "What uh-oh?" I hate uh-oh! "Cop car just pulled up." "Shit!" —Janet Evanovich, *Seven Up*, p. 47, 2001

uh-uh *adverb*
no *US, 1924*
- "D'you all live in Bartholomew?" Elisha wanted to know. "Uh-uh. We live in Woodcrof'," Leonora said[.] —Courttia Newland, *Society Within*, p. 10, 1999

UIC ski team *noun*
unemployed winter skiers *CANADA*

- The ease of obtaining unemployment (UIC) enjoyment cheques affords many young people the chance to work summers and ski at downhill resorts all winter. —Tom Parkin, *WetCoast Words*, p. 147, 1989

uke *noun*

a ukulele *US, 1915*

- He stood there for a time, aloof and contemptuous, with his foot on the bench, and looked back at us, strumming a soft slow melody on his uke[.] —Chester Himes, *Cast the First Stone*, p. 222, 1952
- Tiny Tim played Hubert's in 1959 as the Human Canary, up on a platform in a tux with his uke, making $50 a week. —Josh Alan Friedman, *Tales of Times Square*, p. 182, 1986

ukelele *noun*

on the railways, a short-handled shovel *US*

- —Ramon Adams, *The Language of the Railroader*, p. 165, 1977

UKG *noun*

British gangsta music and culture *UK*

An abbreviation of *U*nited *K*ingdom *G*angsta.

- Distinctive debut from UKG crew with colourful personal lives. — *Uncut*, p. 144, January 2002

Ukrainian peanut *noun*

a sunflower seed *CANADA*

- Where there are large numbers of people with a Ukrainian background, sunflower seeds are usually called Ukrainian peanuts. —Chris Thain, *Cold as a Bay Street Banker's Heart*, p. 159, 1987

ultimate *noun*

crack cocaine *US*

- — US Department of Justice, *Street Terms*, October 1994

ultimate xphoria *noun*

MDMA, the recreational drug best known as ecstasy *UK*

- —Mike Haskins, *Drugs*, p. 290, 2003

ulysses *noun*

a u-turn *US*

- — *Current Slang*, p. 6, Spring 1968

-um *suffix*

added to words to give the impression of English as spoken by an American Indian *US*

- "Quick-um!" cried the sad Sac. "Boil-um plenty-um water-um." —Max Shulman, *The Zebra Derby*, p. 11, 1946

um and ah *verb*

to hesitate; to be uncertain *UK*

From the vocal sounds that may accompany hesitation.

- So what plans did they have? Charlie ummed and aahed and Jason just nodded. —John Williams, *Cardiff Dead*, p. 93, 2000

umbrella *noun*

1 a fellow, especially a husband or boyfriend *UK*

Rhyming slang for **FELLAH; FELLA**.

- How's your umbrella these days? —Ray Puxley, *Fresh Rabbit*, 1998

2 in the television and film industries, a reflector used to bounce light onto a subject *US*

- —Ralph S. Singleton, *Filmaker's Dictionary*, p. 177, 1990

umpteen *noun*

an imprecise, large number *UK, 1918*

- That meant I wouldn't be lying around in some hospital, like so many of them at umpteen bucks a day, while they slowly took out my neck. —Philip Wylie, *Opus 21*, p. 66–67, 1949
- But now they're married for umpteen years and real antiques[.] —Frederick Kohner, *Gidget*, p. 6, 1957
- I don't rightly know but it must be a couple umpteen trillion sextillion[.] —Jack Kerouac, *The Dharma Bums*, p. 9, 1958
- What the hell is the point of slammin' some poor little shmuck in the can for umpteen years when we allow the liquor industry carte blanche[?] —Odie Hawkins, *Great Lawd Buddha*, p. 93, 1990

umpteenhundred *noun*

a point in the yet-to-be-determined, indefinite future *US*

- —Hans Halberstadt, *Airborne*, p. 130, 1988: 'Abridged dictionary of airborne terms'

umpteenth; unteenth *adjective*

used of a great but unspecific number or amount *UK, 1918*

- For the umpteenth time, I chickened. —Max Shulman, *Anyone Got a Match?*, p. 30, 1964
- —J. Ashton Brathwaithe, *Niggers – This is Canada*, p. 24, 1971
- Lemme tell you this for the umteenth time. —J. Ashton Brathwaithe, *Niggers – This is Canada*, p. 24, 1971
- [T]wo together for old blue eyes' umpteenth farewell concert[.] —Anthony Masters, *Minder*, p. 49, 1984
- This is like the umpteenth time I've seen you here. —*Chasing Amy*, 1997
- "What?" says Ollie, shining the torch in my face for the umpteenth fucking time. —Danny King, *The Burglar Diaries*, p. 1, 2001

una *adjective*

one *UK*

From Italian *uno*.

- [Y]ou might like to count to ten in Polari: una, duey, quater, chicker, sey, setter, otto, nobber, dacha. —Michael Quinion, *World Wide Words*, 1996
- —Paul Baker, *Polari*, p. 194, 2002

unass *verb*

1 to stand up; to remove yourself from your immediate location *US*

- And the next thing I knew, she was screaming. I made like a dog and "un-assed the scene," but my friend tried to explain to the cops. —Robert deCoy, *The Nigger Bible*, p. 235, 1967
- —Carl Fleischhauer, *A Glossary of Army Slang*, p. 24, 1968
- —Malachi Andrews and Paul T. Owens, *Black Language*, p. 86, 1973

2 to knock someone out of a sitting position *US*

- —Linda Reinberg, *In the Field*, p. 228, 1991

unbutton *verb*

to force or rip open a safe *US*

- —Vincent J. Monteleone, *Criminal Slang*, p. 246, 1949
- —Hyman E. Goldin et al., *Dictionary of American Underworld Lingo*, p. 231, 1950

▸ **unbutton the mutton**

to undo clothing and liberate the penis *AUSTRALIA*

- I haven't even had the chance to unbutton the mutton!!! —Barry Humphries, *Bazza Pulls It Off!*, 1971

unc *noun*

an uncle, especially as a term of address *AUSTRALIA, 1946*

- "Why you looking so happy? You diddled the VAT man again?" "No, Unc," Johnny Too smiled. "Me inflatable girlfriend finally said yes." —Garry Bushell, *The Face*, p. 78, 2001

uncle *noun*

1 a pawnbroker *UK, 1756*

- —Lou Shelly, *Hepcats Jive Talk Dictionary*, p. 20, 1945
- Five minutes later we were lined up at uncle's, beeing about the measly ninety bucks he shoved across the counter for the whole lot of horns. —Mezz Mezzrow, *Really the Blues*, p. 132, 1946
- The window looks like any "Uncle's" anywhere in the world, with a profusion of new and used articles ranging from mink coats to tin watches. —Jack Lait and Lee Mortimer, *Washington Confidential*, p. 31, 1951

2 a person who buys stolen goods from criminals *US*

- —Hyman E. Goldin et al., *Dictionary of American Underworld Lingo*, p. 231, 1950

3 the US federal government *US*

An abbreviation of Uncle Sam.

- "Is uncle paying?" the black man said. —George V. Higgins, *The Friends of Eddie Doyle*, p. 63, 1971
- It is important to you to make sure that your Uncle does not hear what you say when you talk on the telephone. —George V. Higgins, *Penance for Jerry Kennedy*, p. 89, 1985

▸ **cry uncle; say uncle; holler uncle**

to admit defeat; to beg for mercy *US, 1918*

From Irish *anacol* (mercy).

- "Holler uncle." "Nope," I said, struggling, but I didn't have my usual strength. —S.E. Hinton, *The Outsiders*, p. 99, 1967
- After the second time Mazz was about ready to cry uncle if she wanted to carry on[.] —John Williams, *Cardiff Dead*, p. 196, 2000

uncle *verb*

to act in a passive or subservient fashion *US*

From **UNCLE TOM**.

- It was a wise thing I had "uncled" on him. One of those arrogant repeaters went to the "hole" for having a sassy look in his eyes. —Iceberg Slim (Robert Beck), *Pimp*, p. 52–53, 1969

uncle and aunt *noun*

a plant *UK*

Rhyming slang.

- —Ray Puxley, *Cockney Rabbit*, 1992

unclear on the concept *adjective*

completely and dramatically ignorant about a particular subject *US*

- I think these baby boomers, yuppies, whatever, who have suddenly dropped back in are unclear on the concept. —*Los Angeles Times*, p. 22 (Part 6), 10th April 1988

- The late Herb Caen, one of San Francisco's best-loved newspaper columnists, had a perfect put-down for people who didn't know what they were doing or whose actions or utterances were confusing. He referred to them as being "unclear on the concept." —*Business World*, p. 4, 18th February 1998
- To be unclear on the concept, in the Mr. Boffo sense, is to suffer from an overwhelming, profound disconnection between reality and your perception of reality. — *The Washington Post*, p. F2, 17th May 1998

Uncle Bert *noun*
a shirt *UK*
Rhyming slang.
- —Julian Franklyn, *A Dictionary of Rhyming Slang*, 1961

Uncle Bertie *adjective*
angry, especially if only temporarily; characteristically ill-tempered *UK*
Rhyming slang for **SHIRTY**; extended from **UNCLE BERT** (a shirt).
- What are you getting all Uncle Bertie about? —Ray Puxley, *Cockney Rabbit*, 1992

Uncle Bill *noun*
the police *UK*
A variation of 'old Bill'.
- —Robin Cook (Derek Raymond), *The Crust on its Uppers*, 1962

Uncle Bloody *noun*
the bleed period of the menstrual cycle *US*
- — *The Museum of Menstruation and Women's Health*, August 2001

Uncle Bob *noun*
1 a police officer *UK*
- —L.J. Cunliffe, *Having It Away*, 1965

2 the penis *UK*
Rhyming slang for **KNOB**.
- Come on darlin', come and meet my Uncle Bob. —Ray Puxley, *Cockney Rabbit*, 1992

Uncle Charles; Uncle C *noun*
cocaine *UK*
- I was just wondering if Uncle Charles was about today? [...] – Uncle C is not only about, but today, for you, he is at home and sitting on the roof [on the house]. —James Hawes, *White Powder, Green Light*, p. 250, 2002

Uncle Charlie *noun*
1 used as a representation of the dominant white culture in the US *US*
- As I was saying, the Nigger thinks Uncle Charlie owes him a living, which is false. —Clarence Cooper Jr, *Black*, p. 100, 1963

2 among truckers using citizens' band radio, the Federal Communications Commission *US*
- —Wayne Floyd, *Jason's Authentic Dictionary of CB Slang*, p. 70, 1976

3 the Viet Cong *US*
- We controlled the daytime, but the night belonged to Uncle Charlie. —Al Santoli, *To Bear Any Burden*, p. 89, 1985

Uncle Charlie is visiting; my Uncle Charlie is visiting
I am experiencing menstruation *US*
- — *The Museum of Menstruation and Women's Health*, January 2001

Uncle Daniel *noun*
in hot rodding, a deceptively normal-looking car that has been modified and enhanced for speed *US*
- — *Good Housekeeping*, p. 143, September 1958: 'Hot-rod terms for teen-age girls'
- —Tom MacPherson, *Dragging and Driving*, p. 143, 1960

Uncle Dick *noun*
the penis *UK*
Rhyming slang for **PRICK**.
- —Julian Franklyn, *A Dictionary of Rhyming Slang*, 1960

Uncle Dick; dickey; dickie *adjective*
sick *UK*
Rhyming slang.
- —Julian Franklyn, *A Dictionary of Rhyming Slang*, 1960
- Wystan was laid up with a dicky ticker in Horsham General Hospital. —John Mortimer, *Rumpole of the Bailey*, 1978

Uncle Fred *noun*
bread *UK, 1932*
Rhyming slang, generally childish.
- [A] loaf of Uncle Fred and a pound of stand-at-ease [cheese][.] —Ronnie Barker, *Fletcher's Book of Rhyming Slang*, p. 25–26, 1979

Uncle Ho *noun*
Ho Chi Minh *US*
- Uncle Ho up in Hanoi wasn't about to give it all up now, was he? —Charles Anderson, *The Grunts*, p. 123, 1976

Uncle Joe *noun*
Joseph Stalin *UK, 1943*
- If they get the documents they probably have something juicy for cruddy Uncle Joe. —Mickey Spillane, *One Lonely Night*, p. 95, 1951

Uncle Junk *noun*
heroin *US*
Elaboration of **JUNK** (heroin).
- The first time he saw Carl, Lee thought, "I could use that, if the family jewels weren't in pawn to Uncle Junk." —William Burroughs, *Queer*, p. 21, 1985

Uncle Lester *noun*
a child molester *UK*
Rhyming slang.
- —John Ayto, *The Oxford Dictionary of Rhyming Slang*, p. 111, 2002

Uncle Mac *noun*
1 a smack *UK*
Rhyming slang, formed from 'Children's Favourites' radio presenter Uncle Mac (Derek McCulloch), *BBC Light Programme*, 1954–67.
- —Ray Puxley, *Cockney Rabbit*, 1992

2 heroin *UK*
Rhyming slang for **SMACK**, extended from the earlier, more innocent use as 'a smack'.
- —Ray Puxley, *Cockney Rabbit*, 1992

Uncle Miltie *nickname*
Milton Berle, US comedian of vaudeville, radio and television (1908–2002) *US*
Berle was also known as Mr Television.
- [A]s if on cue, the doors fly open and here, arms outstretched, lips outstretched, grinning loudly, it is Uncle Miltie – Milton Berle! —Tom Wolfe, *The Pump House Gang*, p. 166, 1968
- He won't be long. Have a set with Uncle Miltie. —George V. Higgins, *The Rat on Fire*, p. 164, 1981

Uncle Milty *noun*
Miltown™, a branded tranquillizer *US, 1998*
- —Mike Haskins, *Drugs*, p. 283, 2003

Uncle Ned *noun*
a bed *UK, 1925*
Rhyming slang.
- Tired people can often hear their Uncle Ned calling. —Ray Puxley, *Cockney Rabbit*, 1992

Uncle Sam *noun*
the US federal government *US*
- I got to work on script so I can pay Uncle Sam his bloody tax[.] —Jack Kerouac, *Letter to Neal Cassady*, p. 245, 27th December 1950
- Uncle Sam's in a bind overseas, you think they'll help? —Tom Robbins, *Another Roadside Attraction*, p. 29, 1971

Uncle Sid *noun*
LSD *UK*
A play on the second sylable of ***ACID*** (LSD).
- —Mike Haskins, *Drugs*, p. 286, 2003

Uncle Tom *noun*
a black person who curries favour from whites through obsequious, fawning behaviour *US, 1922*
In recent US history, Supreme Court Justice Clarence Thomas has attracted the 'Uncle Tom' label more than any other black American, in part due to the irresistible Tom–Thomas pun.
- He was just a simple-minded, Uncle Tom-ish nigger, I told myself[.] —Chester Himes, *If He Hollers Let Him Go*, p. 23, 1945
- Historically, the hipster's lingo reverses the whole Uncle Tom atttitude of the beaten-down Southern Negro. —Mezz Mezzrow, *Really the Blues*, p. 225, 1946
- And I've got to find out – whether we've been friends all these years, or whether I've just been your favorite Uncle Tom. —James Baldwin, *Blues for Mister Charlie*, p. 62, 1964
- He fired us and got another band but every night we picketed in front of the joint and kept all but a few "Uncle Toms" out. —Babs Gonzales, *I Paid My Dues*, p. 14, 1967

- The bootlickers, Uncle Toms, lackeys, and stooges of the white power structure have done their best to denigrate Malcolm[.] — Eldridge Cleaver, *Soul on Ice*, p. 60, 1968
- White sentiment was for Frazier. He's an Uncle Tom. — Susan Hall, *Gentleman of Leisure*, p. 49, 1972
- I'm getting sick and tired of hearing about my brother Earl – as far as I'm concerned he's a fuckin' Uncle Tom. — Edwin Torres, *Carlito's Way*, p. 82, 1975
- "I've been called everything from anti-civil rights to Uncle Tom for having taken a different stand," Thomas added. — *Washington Post*, p. A1, 11th February 1986
- The ultimate tragedy for the "Uncle Tom," as Clarence Thomas found out, is that a racist system can dig up "dirt" on him in order to embarrass and humiliate him, just as it can to any other black. — *Theology Today*, April 1993

Uncle Tom *verb*

(used of a black person) to try to curry favour with white people by obsequious behaviour *US, 1937*

- We'd stand in line and wait for hours, smiling and Uncle Tomming every time a doctor or nurse passed by. — Dick Gregory, *Nigger*, p. 27, 1964
- But for two bits, Uncle Tom a little – white cats especially like that. — Malcolm X and Alex Haley, *The Autobiography of Malcolm X*, p. 47, 1964
- Of all people, why'd they kill Malcolm? Why'n't they kill some of them Uncle-Tomming m.f.'s? — Eldridge Cleaver, *Soul on Ice*, p. 51, 1968
- Blue thundered, "You ugly, shit-colored uncle-tomming mother-fucker." — Iceberg Slim (Robert Beck), *Trick Baby*, p. 230, 1969

Uncle Willie *adjective*

1 silly *UK, 1932*

Rhyming slang.

- — Ray Puxley, *Cockney Rabbit*, 1992

2 chilly *UK*

Rhyming slang.

- — Julian Franklyn, *A Dictionary of Rhyming Slang*, 1961

unco *adjective*

1 clumsy; awkward *AUSTRALIA, 1996*

Short for '*unco*ordinated'.

2 weird *AUSTRALIA*

- Everything keeps going in unco on me. — Glyn Parry, *Mosh*, p. 7, 1996

uncommon horn *noun*

an unusually urgent sexual appetite *UK*

- I have an uncommon horn [...] I have. I'm randy as hell. — Kevin Sampson, *Outlaws*, p. 112, 2001

uncool *adjective*

unpleasant, aggressive, dangerous; excitable; tending to show your feelings more than is prudent or advisable *US, 1953*

- — J. L. Simmons and Barry Winograd, *It's Happening*, p. 174, 1966: 'glossary'
- Coming on very un-cool, hassling everybody, moving into people's areas of privacy, trying to get into people's minds. — Leonard Wolfe (Editor), *Voices from the Love Generation*, p. 238, 1968
- — Jenny Fabian and Johnny Byrne, *Groupie*, 1968
- — Clarence Major, *Dictionary of Afro-American Slang*, p. 118, 1970
- I mean, of course we are thrilled that you're thinking of us, and I'm pretty sure that you are not going to do anything uncool like draw a map to our house... — *The Last Supplement to the Whole Earth Catalog*, p. 78, March 1971
- JULES: This is really uncool — *Pulp Fiction*, 1994

un-cred *adjective*

unfashionable *UK*

The antonym of **CRED** (acceptible to your peers).

- In the mid-eighties, the ultimate in "non-cred" was to be associated with the country's biggest hit-makers, Stock Aitken & Waterman. — Simon Napier-Bell, *Black Vinyl White Powder*, p. 278, 2001

uncunt *verb*

to withdraw the penis from a woman's vagina *US*

- [H]e could actually make her change places with his wife, all without un-cunting. — Henry Miller, *Tropic of Capricorn*, p. 177, 1961

uncut *adjective*

not circumcised *US*

- This is pure uncut boy in the street. — William Burroughs, *Naked Lunch*, p. 122, 1957
- — H. Max, *Gay (S)language*, p. 44, 1988
- We never fucked, with his uncut penis. — Sandra Bernhard, *Confessions of a Pretty Lady*, p. 66, 1988
- The gay films are definitely uncut men. — Robert Stoller and I.S. Levine, *Coming Attractions*, p. 156, 1991

under *noun*

sexual intercourse *UK, 1936*

The location of the sexual organs: 'under a body' or, perhaps, 'under a skirt'.

under *adjective*

a state of sobriety when measured against drug-intoxication *UK*

- I was already fucked on pills and tripping out, but that sent me under and I started screaming at him to get the dog off me! — *Mixmag*, p. 68, April 2003

underage *adjective*

in snowboarding, used to describe the not-yet-perfected performance of a trick or manoeuvre *US*

- — Jim Humes and Sean Wagstaff, *Boarderlands*, p. 224, 1995

under-arm *adjective*

pornographic *UK*

- One of the first things Randle asked him was did he have any [...] under-arm films. — Jeff Nuttall, *King Twist*, 1979

underchunders *noun*

underpants *AUSTRALIA, 1966*

From '*under*wear' and **CHUNDER** (vomit), because they are revolting.

- — Arthur Chipper, *The Aussie Swearer's Guide*, p. 55, 1972
- Drops her underchunders and clothes all over the friggin' floor too. — Kathy Lette, *Girls' Night Out*, p. 144, 1987

undercover *adjective*

used of a racehorse, trained in secret *US*

- — David W. Maurer, *Argot of the Racetrack*, p. 67, 1951

undercrackers *noun*

underpants *UK*

- — *Roger's Profanisaurus*, December 1997
- A shameless Argentinian racing driver whipped off his overalls and undercrackers on the winners' podium[.]. — *FHM*, p. 156, June 2003

underdaks *noun*

underpants *AUSTRALIA, 1966*

- Your basic list will include toiletries, underdaks, travel clock, clothing, spare shirts & ties, PJ's, fitness gear, etc. — *The Organised Times*, January 2001

underdungers *noun*

underpants *NEW ZEALAND, 1981*

- Mable Howard flung women's bloomers about Parliament, true, but not for erotic effect – and the sight of her in her own underdungers wouldn't have lit the gas pilot of passion. — *Dominion*, p. 18, 9th December 1999

under four eyes; under two eyes *adjective*

face to face *TRINIDAD AND TOBAGO, 1990*

- — Lise Winer, *Dictionary of the English/Creole of Trinidad & Tobago*, 2003

underground *noun*

a hidden counter culture *US, 1935*

Usually in a political context, although in the 1960s also in a cultural context.

- — J. L. Simmons and Barry Winograd, *It's Happening*, p. 174, 1966: 'glossary'
- There are many undergrounds, from Dostoyevsky's to New York's IRT. The hippie's is that crosshatched spot on the cultural map where one finds the advanced styles, moods and beliefs of the "trendsetter." — Sidney Bernard, *This Way to the Apocalypse*, p. 59, 1968
- In each city of the world there is a loose competitive underground composed of groups whose aims overlap, conflict, and generally enervate the desired goal of autonomy. — *The Digger Papers*, p. 15, August 1968
- The number of underground newspapers went from fifty to a hundred to three hundred in a matter of a few months[.] — Raymond Mungo, *Famous Long Ago*, p. 41, 1970
- The question of advertisements in an underground newspaper is always a sticky business. — *The Berkeley Tribe*, p. 5, 26th June – 3rd July 1970
- He went underground, man. — Cheech Marin and Tommy Chong, *Santa Calus and his Old Lady*, 1971
- I think there is such an underground but probably I would say Mr. Hoover has it a little distorted. As was said before by Billy, I think this underground is a growing consciousness. — *The Last Supplement to the Whole Earth Catalog*, p. 15, March 1971

underground mutton *noun*

rabbit meat *AUSTRALIA, 1919*

- [W]e ate a lot of underground mutton in the 30s. — *Bulletin*, 22nd December 1981

undergunned *adjective*
having too small a surfboard for the surf conditions *AUSTRALIA*
- Baggage restrictions mean each of the eight team members will only be allowed to take one surfboard. If a big swell hits while the competition is on, our competitors could find themselves seriously undergunned. — *Sunday Tasmanian*, p. 49, 1st October 1989

underlook *verb*
to look at someone or something with grave doubt *BARBADOS*
- — Frank A. Collymore, *Barbadian Dialect*, p. 115, 1965

underpass *noun*
the posterior; the buttocks, the anus *UK*
Rhyming slang for **ARSE** and appropriate imagery.
- I've been using cream on my Chalfonts [haemorrhoids] all week and my underpass is still killing me. — Bodmin Dark, *Dirty Cockney Rhyming Slang*, p. 35, 2003

under-stain *noun*
the bleed period of the menstrual cycle *UK*
A euphemism, recorded by Jilly Cooper, 1980.

under starter's orders *adjective*
arrested *UK*
Criminal and police slang, from horse racing.
- — John Gosling, *The Ghost Squad*, 1959

undertaker *noun*
a bookmaker who will only accept bets at odds under those offered by his competition *AUSTRALIA*
- — Ned Wallish, *The Truth Dictionary of Racing Slang*, p. 89, 1989

under the affluence of incohol
drunk *AUSTRALIA*
A deliberate spoonerism, probably Australian but post-war UK comedians are worthy of consideration.

under-the-arm *adjective*
no good, inferior; loathsome *UK, 1930s to 1960s*
Implies that the object described is a **STINKER**.
- Some people go potty, but I read no matter how bad the book and some are right under the arm, stand on me. — Frank Norman, *Bang To Rights*, p. 25, 1958

underwhelm *verb*
to arouse little or no interest in someone *UK, 1956*
Jocular. Now included in the *Oxford English Dictionary*.
- Cautious Canada underwhelmed by [Prince] Charles's visit — *The Guardian*, 26th April 2001
- I was the first person to say "young fogey" and "underwhelmed" but you don't get any credit for that. Neither are in the Oxford English Dictionary[.] — *Word*, p. 54, September 2004

under yonder *noun*
the anus *US*
- We call that a brownie queen. In prison they call it under-yonder and round-brown. — Bruce Jackson, *In the Life*, p. 397, 1972

undies *noun*
underwear *UK, 1906*
Abbreviated 'underwear'. In the UK, applied most commonly to women's underwear; in Australia to men's; in the US to children's.
- [W]omen's under-wear or "undies" as they are coyly called[.] — *Chambers Journal*, December 1918
- On wash day I have to keep a look out in case some kinky boy comes and steals some of my undies off the line. — Geoff Brown, *I Want What I Want*, p. 2, 1966
- [N]ever could get my brain off her taking off her undies. — Jeremy Cameron, *Brown Bread in Wengen*, p. 139, 1999
- I stick these little pieces of paper over my brown-eye, and bam-no shit stains in my undies. — Kevin Smith, *Jay and Silent Bob Strike Back*, p. 13, 2001
- Clothes [men's] come off in this order: shoes, socks, top, trousers, undies. — *Sky Magazine*, p. 87, July 2001

undressed *adjective*
used of a citizens' band radio operated without a linear amplifier *US*
- — Porter Bibb, *CB Bible*, p. 108, 1976

unemployed *noun*
the penis *AUSTRALIA*
Especially in the phrase **SHAKE HANDS WITH THE UNEMPLOYED**.
- — Barry Humphries, *Bazza Pulls It Off!*, 1971

unforgettable *noun*
a combination of cocaine, heroin and valium *US*
- — Peter Johnson, *Dictionary of Street Alcohol and Drug Terms*, p. 199, 1993

unfragged *adjective*
not listed on the daily frag order specifying the military objectives of the day *US*
Vietnam war usage.
- Have you ever attacked an unfragged target? — Stephen Coonts, *Flight of the Intruder*, p. 361, 1986

unfuckable *adjective*
too ugly to be considered as a sexual partner *AUSTRALIA*
- But some I do recall. Melissa, the unfuckable. — Robert English, *Toxic Kisses*, p. 162, 1979

unfucked *adjective*
re-ordered; having order brought out of chaos *US*
- This is a situation that needs to get unfucked right now. — *Con Air*, 1997

unglue *verb*
in drag racing and hot rodding, to blow up an engine *US*
- — Lyle K. Engel, *The Complete Book of Fuel and Gas Dragsters*, p. 154, 1968

unglued *adjective*
out of control *US*
- — *American Speech*, p. 273, December 1962: 'The language of traffic policemen'

ungodly *adjective*
1 of time, unpleasantly early in the day *UK, 1889*
- [T]o get the cheapest tickets, you have to take off at an ungodly hour of the morning and return late at night[.] — *The Guardian*, 6th December 2003

2 superlative *US*
- — Connie Eble (Editor), *UNC-CH Campus Slang*, March 1974

ungowa; ungowa bwana
yes, affirmative, OK *US*
Citizens' band radio slang.
- — *Complete CB Slang Dictionary*, p. 92, 1976
- — Peter Chippindale, *The British CB Book*, p. 160, 1981

ungrateful *noun*
said of a hospital patient who dies after heroic efforts to save his life *US*
- — *Maledicta*, p. 35, 1988–1989: 'More Milawukee medical maledicta'

unhinged *adjective*
angry; emotionally unsettled *UK, 1719*
- I worked for a city editor who was an out-and-out maniac. He was unhinged. — Max Shulman, *The Zebra Derby*, p. 147, 1946

unholy *adjective*
awful; outrageous *UK, 1842*
- [A]n unholy row[.] — *The Daily Telegraph*, 15th March 2002

unhook *verb*
to remove handcuffs *US*
- — Ralph de Sola, *Crime Dictionary*, p. 157, 1982

unhook the U-haul!
hurry up! *US*
The image is of unhooking a rental trailer that is slowing you down.
- — Judi Sanders, *Faced and Faded, Hanging to Hurl*, p. 42, 1993

uni *noun*
1 university; a university *AUSTRALIA, 1898*
- Thought you'd learnt ut at the Uni. — Nino Culotta (John O'Grady), *They're A Weird Mob*, p. 91, 1957
- Maybe at uni, she told herself hopefully, but that is a year and a half away, how can I wait till then? — Jenny Pausacker, *What are ya?*, p. 9, 1987
- She was off to Manchester Uni to study law. — Kevin Sampson, *Outlaws*, p. 46, 2001

2 a school uniform *UK*
Pronounced 'unny'.
- — *The Felstedian*, December 1947

uniboob *noun*
a woman's chest clothed in a manner that presents the two breasts as a single entity *US*
- — Don R. McCreary (Editor), *Dawg Speak*, 2001

uniform *noun*

1 a uniformed police officer, as distinguished from a detective in street clothes *US*

- Speaking of uniforms, I ran into one the other day, while hustling up business for my woman. — *Screw*, p. 3, 7th February 1969
- There is three loads of uniforms and two detectives, all of which I know. — Robert Campbell, *Junkyard Dog*, p. 21, 1986
- By the time he got to the corner both EMS and a black and white had arrived and two uniforms were telling everyone to stay where they were for the time being, don't anybody leave. — Elmore Leonard, *Be Cool*, p. 19, 1999

2 a member of the armed forces *US, 1941*

uniform tango *noun*

an Uncle Tom *US*

From the military phonetic alphabet, UT.

- — Gregory Clark, *Words of the Vietnam War*, p. 385, 1991

uninteresting *adjective*

used of a computer problem, subject to being solved with enough time, not requiring creative problem-solving skills *US*

- — Eric S. Raymond, *The New Hacker's Dictionary*, p. 361, 1991

Union Jack *noun*

1 a multiple bet on 9 selections *UK*

Named after the Union Jack flag which a schemata of the wager resembles.

- The Union Jack covers only eight of the 84 possible trebles in nine selections so there is plenty of scope for disappointment in this bet. — David Bennet, *Know Your Bets*, p. 134, 2001

2 the back *UK*

Rhyming slang. The short form 'union' is also used.

- I'm sorry I can't lift that, I've got a dodgy Union. — Ray Puxley, *Cockney Rabbit*, 1992

Union Pacific *noun*

in poker, a hand consisting of three sixes and a pair *US*

The sixes are known as 'boxcars', hence the railway company name.

- — George Percy, *The Language of Poker*, p. 95, 1988

unit *noun*

1 the penis *US*

The slang sense of the word gives special meaning to the nickname 'The Big Unit' given to baseball pitcher Randy Johnson.

- Get back to the library, keep your unit on this! — *The Breakfast Club*, 1985
- MADONNA: Wow, look at the unit on that guy. — *Saturday Night Live*, 11th May 1991
- — Judi Sanders, *Da Bomb*, p. 17, 1997

2 the vagina *US*

- These detectives here can look right up a broad's unit and check her lands and grooves. — Joseph Wambaugh, *The Black Marble*, p. 50, 1978

United Parcel Service *noun*

any amphetamine, methamphetamine or other central nervous system stimulant *US*

A forced formation: the initials UPS represent stimulants as 'ups' (see **UPPER**).

- — Robert Sabbag, *Snowblind*, p. 271, 1976

units *noun*

parents *US*

An abbreviation of 'parental *units*'.

- — Connie Eble (Editor), *UNC-CH Campus Slang*, p. 8, Spring 1987

University of a Billion Chinks *nickname*

the University of British Columbia, in racist reference to the large student population of students and immigrants from South Asia *CANADA*

University of Freebies *noun*

the University of Florida *US*

Back-formation from the initials FU, playing on the role of athletics at the university.

university of hard knocks *noun*

experience, especially when valued against a university education *UK, 1984*

An admixture of the clichés **UNIVERSITY OF LIFE** and **SCHOOL OF HARD KNOCKS**.

- "My university was the school of hard knocks-" "That's the best school of all," someone yelled. — Witi Ihimaera, *The Whale Rider*, p. 108, 2002

university of life

experience, especially when valued against a university education *UK, 1959*

- [S]ince I graduated 25 years ago I have never been near a university. The University of Life is free – and has much the boldest and broadest degree courses. — *The Guardian*, 27th January 2004

unk-unk *noun*

an unknown that is unknown or not even suspected *US*

Aerospace usage.

- — Robert Kirk Mueller, *Buzzwords*, p. 161, 1974

unleaded *adjective*

caffeine-free *US*

Borrowing from the language of car fuel for application to the world of coffee drinks and, to a lesser extent, soft drinks.

- — Connie Eble (Editor), *UNC-CH Campus Slang*, p. 4, Fall 1996

unload *verb*

1 (of a male) to ejaculate *US*

Originally in gay use.

- I'd better be quick about it or else I'd get discovered. I needed to unload fast[.] — Howard Stern, *Miss America*, p. 27, 1995

2 to punch someone; to beat someone *UK*

Probably from an earlier sense (to drop bombs).

- [H]e'll try and dig me out [taunt me] and I'll have to unload him. — Lenny McLean, *The Guv'nor*, p. 55, 1998

3 in air combat, to accelerate *US*

- Cunningham told Grant to get rid of his wing tanks, to increase his speed and maneuverability. "Get rid of your tanks," he told Grant. "Unload." — Robert K. Wilcox, *Scream of Eagles*, p. 257, 1990

4 on the railways, to end a work shift or to jump off a moving train *US*

- — Ramon Adams, *The Language of the Railroader*, p. 165, 1977

unotque *noun*

marijuana *UK*

- — Mike Haskins, *Drugs*, p. 289, 2003

unpack *verb*

to vomit *UK*

- — Tom Hibbert, *Rockspeak!*, p. 166, 1983

unprofessional, that's what you are

used as a humorous if pointed insult *US*

Coined by ESPN's Keith Olberman to describe the level of play of strike-breaking, 'replacement' baseball players in 1995.

- — Keith Olberman and Dan Patrick, *The Big Show*, p. 27, 1997

unreal *adjective*

excellent; exceptionally bad *US, 1965*

Depends on context and tone.

- Hey look at her now! Fellas check this chick with the bottle! I've never seen that before. She's unreal! — *Ribald*, p. 45, 1973
- — Connie Eble (Editor), *UNC-CH Campus Slang*, p. 5, Fall 1982
- He must be unreal to talk to. — Kathy Lette, *Girls Night Out*, p. 126, 1987
- "Out of sight," "too much," "tough," "trippy," "trick," or "unreal" – were all current [late 1960s] superlatives. Each would flower for a while and then fall to something a little groovier – up to date on the tongues of those who knew. — Sean Hutchinson, *Crying Out Loud*, p. 177, 1988
- Where did you get that? It looks unreal. — Robert G. Barrett, *Davo's Little Something*, p. 28, 1992

unrool *adjective*

great; terrific *AUSTRALIA*

Representing a pronunciation of **UNREAL**.

- For instance, never, under any circumstances, say 'unreal'; 'un-rool' is painful to type, let alone utter. — Ignatius Jones, *True Hip*, p. 35, 1990

unscrewed *adjective*

out of control *US*

- — *American Speech*, p. 273, December 1962: 'The language of traffic policemen'

unsliced *adjective*

not circumcised *US*

- — H. Max, *Gay (S)language*, p. 44, 1988

unteenth *adjective*

▷ **see: UMPTEENTH**

until the wheels fall off *adjective*
until a prison clique disbands; ultimately loyal *US*
Back-formation from a **CAR** (a clique).
- —James Harris, *A Convict's Dictionary*, p. 40, 1989

untogether *adjective*
not in control of your personal condition; unable to get your mind and emotions under control; disorganised *UK, 1969*
- Rick was comparatively untogether. He'd talk about doing ideas that would never quite make it.—Nicholas Schaffner, *Saucerful of Secrets: The Pink Floyd Odyssey*, p. 139, 1991
- Dad enjoyed being the most untogether person I knew.—Jack Gantos, *What Would Joey Do?*, p. 109, 2002

untold *adjective*
excellent; terrific; wonderful *AUSTRALIA, 1979*
- 'Oh.' Aaaarggghhh! Death and untold embarrassment!—Tim Winton, *Lockie Leonard*, p. 112, 1997

untolds *noun*
lots; heaps *AUSTRALIA*
- I put the snip on my dealer for a loan. I owe him untolds.—Kathy Lette, *Girls' Night Out*, p. 80, 1987

unwind *verb*
to relax after a period of tension or stress *UK, 1958*
- I kind of wanted a night to unwind and be alone.—Lauren Weisberger, *The Devil Wears Prada*, p. 66, 2003

up *noun*
1 a tablet of amphetamine, methamphetamine or other central nervous system stimulant *US*
- "Ups" all day and "downs" at night.—Beatrice Sparks (writing as 'Anonymous'), *Jay's Journal*, p. 26, 1979
- [S]o banged on ups and cocaine she fell out on the floor[.]—Clarence Major, *All-Night Visitors*, p. 201, 1998

2 an inspiration; an elevated mood *US, 1966*
- So to make a long story short the Vietnamese were a great up in my life[.]—Raymond Mungo, *Famous Long Ago*, p. 11, 1970

3 in the used car business, a potential customer who has walked on to the sales forecourt *US*
- —Peter Mann, *How to Buy a Used Car Without Getting Gypped*, p. 196, 1975

▸ **on the up and up**
legitimate, honest *US, 1863*
- A viper doesn't like lies – he's on the up and up and makes you get on the ground floor with him.—Mezz Mezzrow, *Really the Blues*, p. 96, 1946
- Rocco decided that perhaps Jo-Jo was on the up-and-up after all – he was doing a lot of garbage-level grabs here.—Richard Price, *Clockers*, p. 421, 1992

up *verb*
1 to start suddenly or boldly; to rise abruptly *UK, 1831*
- He had such a row with his wife that she upped and left him.—Charles Raven, *Underworld Nights*, p. 51, 1956

2 to arouse or aggravate someone *UK*
- Some people will say you've got no business being in the game if you ain't double flash with your ill-gotten gains, really upping the old bill [police] with 'em.—J.J. Connolly, *Layer Cake*, p. 4, 2000

3 to increase a bet in cards *US, 1942*
- CHEESE: Up it fifty cents. LOONEY: I call. I call. I'm in on this one. I call.—*Tin Men*, 1987

▸ **up it**
to pay off a debt *US*
- —Joe McKennon, *Circus Lingo*, p. 99, 1980

▸ **up sticks**
to pack up and go; to move *UK, 1877*
Originally nautical, from raising the mast prior to setting sail.
- I mean left. Vamoosed. Sold out and upped sticks.—Ian Pattison, *Rab C. Nesbitt*, 1988
- Tom wanted Franny to "up sticks and come out to Corfu" and help him run a bar.—Sally Cline, *Couples*, p. 197, 1998

up *adjective*
1 happening; going on; wrong *UK, 1838*
- YOU KNOW something's up when the Daily Mail invokes support for an argument from the Commission for Racial Equality[.]—*Socialist Worker*, 11th August 2001
- What's up with US women?—*The Guardian*, 26th August 2002

2 occurring; amiss *UK, 1849*
- I says what's up, doc? Bugs Bunny had more truth to speak about life than the humans on the tube.—Ted Dekker, *Three*, p. 25, 2003

3 successful *US*
- —*Los Angeles Times*, p. B10, 5th January 1990

4 under the influence of a drug, especially LSD and, later, MDMA, the recreational drug best known as ecstasy *US*
- —J. L. Simmons and Barry Winograd, *It's Happening*, p. 174, 1966: 'glossary'
- Comin up, Paulie? – Oh am up, am fuckin way, way up[.]—Niall Griffiths, *Grits*, p. 34, 2000

5 pregnant *TRINIDAD AND TOBAGO, 1991*
- —Lise Winer, *Dictionary of the English/Creole of Trinidad & Tobago*, 2003

6 used of waves, large *US*
Giving rise to the cry, 'Surf's up!'.
- —John Severson, *Modern Surfing Around the World*, p. 184, 1964

7 imprisoned *US*
- Up there I meet a lot of the boys, including Rocco Fabrizi, who was up for stealing cars.—Edwin Torres, *Carlito's Way*, p. 20, 1975
- Homicide, narcotics, sodomy, impairing the morals of a minor, larceny – he had been up on everything at one time or another.—Edwin Torres, *Q & A*, p. 108, 1977

8 of food or drink, made, cooked, ready, served *UK, 1961*
- Jubilee was already dishing out the food into semicircular bowls. Vikki rushed to the door and flung it wide open "Berkley! Les! Grub's up!"—Ian Stewart, *Flatterland*, p. 8, 2002

9 in the used car business, next on the salesmen's rotation list to approach a potential customer who has walked onto the sales forecourt *US*
- —Peter Mann, *How to Buy a Used Car Without Getting Gypped*, p. 196, 1975

10 used of an actor in the television and film industries, unable to remember lines *US*
- —Tony Miller and Patricia George, *Cut! Print!*, p. 188, 1977

11 of a male, having sexual intercourse with someone *UK, 1937*
- I'd rather be up her than up in Newcastle.—Coin Watson, *One Man's Meat*, p. 74, 1977

up *adverb*
1 each; equal in quantity *UK, 1809*
- He made them, and the score stood eighteen up.—James T. Farrell, *Tournament Star*, p. 74, 1946

2 up to or up at *AUSTRALIA, 1884*
- Your missus believe yer when yer tell 'er yer goin' up the pub to cook fish?—Nino Culotta (John O'Grady), *Gone Fishin'*, p. 172, 1962
- You still want to go up the bush, don't you?—George Johnston, *My Brother Jack*, p. 122, 1964
- [W]e needed fresh finance for that trip to Froggie.—Jeremy Cameron, *Brown Bread in Wengen*, p. 81, 1999

-up *suffix*
1 used to form adjectives and verbs with the meaning 'to be under, or put someone under, the influence of a drug'
- So that would be my first job as the Drug Tsar – E-up the Old Bill.—Dave Courtney, *Raving Lunacy*, p. 69, 2000

2 having adopted a stated style or characteristic *UK*
Formed in combination with a participial adjective.
- Janine is evilled up to the max and stupidly reveals to Pat that she killed Barry.—*The Eye*, p. 26, 24th April 2004

up against *adjective*
confronted by a difficulty *US, 1896*
- US comes up against the real world.—*The Guardian*, 27th September 2001

up against it
in a difficult position, in trouble *US, 1896*
- OK, with hindsight it was crazy. But when you're up against it and convinced you're not going to survive unless you do something drastic, you'll believe anything[.]—*The Guardian*, 3rd October 2003

up against the wall
helpless, dominated by another; used for expressing power over others *US, 1960s*
A catch-phrase of the politically active in the US 1960s, echoing a police command.
- President Johnson's a fool anyway. The old fool's up against the wall.—James Simon Kunen, *The Strawberry Statement*, p. 67, 1968
- The deans found themselves up against the wall for the first time in Amerika. They didn't dig it.—Jerry Rubin, *Do It!*, p. 22, 1970
- —Clarence Major, *Dictionary of Afro-American Slang*, p. 118, 1970

up-and-down *noun*

1 an order of Kessler ale and Stroh's beer *US*

- He ordered up-and-downs, Kessler and Stroh's looking at all the strange flavored brandy on the back bar... — Elmore Leonard, *Split Images*, p. 154, 1981

2 sex *US*

- — Kenn "Naz" Young, *Naz's Dictionary of Teen Slang*, p. 133, 1993

3 in gambling, a type of conditional bet: a single-stakes-about or a double-stakes-about *UK*

- — David Bennet, *Know Your Bets*, p. 26, 2001

up and down *adjective*

brown, especially applied to brown ale *UK*

Rhyming slang.

- — Ray Puxley, *Cockney Rabbit*, 1992

up-and-downer; upper-and-downer *noun*

a violent quarrel; a fight *UK, 1927*

- [H]is recent up-and-downer against the demented Pole, Andrew Golota[.] — *The Observer*, 7th May 2000

up and down of it *noun*

the gist of something; the whole thing; the outcome of a situation *UK*

- The up and down of it was, Dave introduced me to this bloke, one Tony Loretto, and I found myself agreeing to billet his cash in my lock-up till Monday morning[.] — Andrew Nickolds, *Back to Basics*, p. 90–91, 1994

up and under *noun*

thunder *UK*

Rhyming slang, formed from a rugby manoeuvre that became a popular catchphrase for BBC rugby league commentator Eddie Waring, 1910–86.

- — Ray Puxley, *Fresh Rabbit*, 1998

upchuck *noun*

ground beef *US*

Playing on 'ground chuck' for the beef as well as the slang for 'vomit'.

- — *Maledicta*, p. 23, 1996: 'Domino's pizza jargon'

upchuck *verb*

to vomit *US, 1936*

- — Collin Baker et al., *College Undergraduate Slang Study Conducted at Brown University*, p. 218, 1968
- What about orange juice and milk? What's the upchuck factor on that? — *Heathers*, 1988
- After talking to the body snatcher, Nell wasn't sure whether she'd be better off trying to upchuck or work. — Joseph Wambaugh, *Finnegan's Week*, p. 161, 1993

up country *adjective*

South Vietnam north of Saigon *US*

- There must be over 3,000 of them out there now, 3,000 Vietnamese who worked for the consulate or for Americans "up country" or who knew someone who did. — Frank Snepp, *Decent Interval*, p. 240, 1977

up for it *adjective*

ready to party *UK*

- He was like some garish Ebeneezer Goode, in your face the whole time, driving everybody on – on one, up for it, mad for it, top one. — Kevin Sampson, *Powder*, p. 198, 1999
- [Working out] got you right up for it. — John Williams, *Cardiff Dead*, p. 4, 2000

upfront *adjective*

honest, open, frank *US, 1970*

- I'm being up front with you, boyo. — Joel Rose, *Kill Kill Faster Faster*, p. 141, 1997

upful *adjective*

happy, positive *UK, 1997*

Mainly West Indian and UK black usage.

- My outlook has always been positive and upful[.] — *The Observer*, 23rd June 2002

uphill gardening *noun*

anal intercourse *UK*

- ["]Bradley is referring to the rusty bullet-hole," said Mikey. "The what?" Mario was still struggling. "The chocolate starfish." "Back-dooring." "Uphill gardening." [...] What, you mean shoving it up their arse?" exclaimed Mario. — Colin Butts, *Is Harry on the Boat?*, p. 21, 1997

uphills *noun*

dice that have been altered in a fashion that produces high numbers when rolled *US*

- — Frank Garcia, *Marked Cards and Loaded Dice*, p. 265, 1962

upholstered *adjective*

suffering from a sexually transmitted infection *US*

- — Vincent J. Monteleone, *Criminal Slang*, p. 247, 1949
- — Joseph E. Ragen and Charles Finston, *Inside the World's Toughest Prison*, p. 822, 1962: 'Penitentiary and underworld glossary'

Upjohn *noun*

a tablet of Dexedrine™, Benzedrine™ or other central nervous system stimulant *US*

- — Montie Tak, *Truck Talk*, p. 181, 1971

up jumped the devil!

used for expressing dismay at the toss of a seven by a craps player trying to make his point *US*

- — *The Annals of the American Academy of Political and Social Sciences*, p. 132, May 1950

up north *adverb*

to prison *US*

- — Ellen C. Bellone (Editor), *Dictionary of Slang*, p. 25, 1989

up on one *adjective*

of a police officer, on a charge, standing accused *UK*

- — G.F. Newman, *Sir, You Bastard*, 1974

upper *noun*

an amphetamine or other central nervous system stimulant *US*

- I mean is it an upper or a downer? — Oscar Zeta Acosta, *The Revolt of the Cockroach People*, p. 192, 1973
- "I don't need no more uppers," Joanie said, "but downers I could use." — Emmett Grogan, *Final Score*, p. 81, 1976
- Somebody always had something to get loaded on. Uppers at times, inners, outers, whatever. — Odie Hawkins, *Scars and Memories*, p. 115–116, 1987

upper-class snob *noun*

an act of oral sex, especially performed on a man *UK*

Rhyming slang for **BLOW JOB**.

- — Bodmin Dark, *Dirty Cockney Rhyming Slang*, 2003

upper-crust *noun*

the upper classes; the higher circles of society *UK, 1843*

- It's a tale of someone who wanted to go and go – who was sick of the dead-on-its-feet upper crust he was born into[.] — Derek Raymond, *The Crust on its Uppers*, 1993
- The Cambridge undergraduates who put together "Beyond the Fringe" in the 1960s had a famous sketch in which an uppercrust military officer approaches a soldier and informs him: "We need a pointless sacrifice, and I think you're just the man." — *The Economist*, 6th December 1999

upper deck *noun*

the female breasts *US*

- — Dale Gordon, *The Dominion Sex Dictionary*, p. 161, 1967

upper persuasion for lower invasion *noun*

foreplay *US*

- — Mary Swift, *Campus Slang (University of Texas)*, 1968

uppie *noun*

an amphetamine or other central nervous system stimulant *US*

A variation of **UPPER**.

- — Ralph de Sola, *Crime Dictionary*, p. 158, 1982
- — Mike Haskins, *Drugs*, p. 280, 2003

Uppie *noun*

a student of the University of Port Elizabeth *SOUTH AFRICA*

Formed on the initialism, by which the university is known, UPE; Radio Uppie is the UPE student radio station.

- An "Uppie" is a person who studies at the University of Port Elizabeth. In our UPE Review, to be published with Saturday's issue (October 28) of the Daily Dispatch, readers will learn how an "Uppie" lives, works and plays. — *Daily Dispatch*, 25th October 1972

uppity; uppidy *adjective*

brash; arrogant; refusing to accept one's place in society *US, 1880*

Originally coined by southern blacks, now widely used.

- [He] snatched an uppity dame right up from her seat and waltzed her out on the dance floor, pince-nez and all. —Mezz Mezzrow, *Really the Blues*, p. 85, 1946
- Sapphire feels real uppity while shopping in the "better" department stores because she knows they don't expect her to be able to afford the prices. —Carolyn Greene, *70 Soul Secrets of Sapphire*, p. 28, 1973
- I'd been a uppity M.F. all along[.] —Babs Gonzales, *Movin' On Down De Line*, p. 34, 1975
- [W]hile the peckerwoods called me an uppidy nigger wench who was always fulla sass[.] —Donald Goines, *The Busting Out of an Ordinary Man*, p. 53, 1985

uprights *noun*
the legs *US*
- —Clarence Major, *Dictionary of Afro-American Slang*, p. 118, 1970

upsidaisy!; upsadaisy!; oops-a-daisy!
used to comfort a child who has fallen-over and to lightly encourage a recovery *UK, 1862*
- Julian grabbed my arm. "Oops-a-daisy," he said steadying me. "Are you all right?" —Jake Arnott, *He Kills Coppers*, p. 152, 2001

upside *preposition*
against *US*
- If she hollers cop, all yo do is bop her by going up side her head with your fist hard as lead! —Dan Burley, *Diggeth Thou?*, p. 5, 1959
- She slapped me and kicked me and threw me upside the wall. —Dennis Wepman et al., *The Life*, p. 53, 1976
- All of a sudden we're fuckin' surrounded, every goddamn kid I ever strip searched, busted, smacked upside the head coming out of the other two theaters. —Richard Price, *Clockers*, p. 44, 1992

upskirt *noun*
a type of voyeurism devoted to seeing what is beneath a woman's skirt *US, 1995*
- What began as a small photo gallery on the Internet a couple of years ago has rapidly expanded to more than 40 such "Upskirt" sites, including one devoted entirely to shots taken up skirts in Maryland, said Duqueette, who has been tracking the trend. —*Washington Post*, p. B1, 7th June 1998
- Voyeuristic "upskirt" pages likewise feature photographs taken by tiny cameras placed in shopping bags at mall stores. —Clay Calvert, *Voyeur Nation*, p. 48, 2000

upslice *noun*
the vagina; a disagreeable woman *US*
- "So, how much is the upslice bitch paying you?" Chooch started, unexpectedly. —Stephen J. Cannell, *The Tin Collectors*, p. 34, 2001

upstairs *adverb*
in poker, in the form of a raised bet *US*
- —John Vorhaus, *The Big Book of Poker Slang*, p. 38, 1996

▶ **not right upstairs; short of a few rooms upstairs**
not completely sane *UK, 1931*
- MIAMI: Like making me look a cunt, do yer? JAMIE: Eh? THREE FEET: You must be short of a few rooms upstairs. —Chris Baker and Andrew Day, *Lock, Stock... & Spaghetti Sauce*, p. 257–258, 2000

upstate *adjective*
1 in prison *US, 1934*
- Too bad I didn't havya upstate. —Hubert Selby Jr, *Last Exit to Brooklyn*, p. 44, 1957
- Then the whole two years I did upstate nothing was on my mind but this girl Ann. —James Mills, *The Panic in Needle Park*, p. 54, 1966
- Your trip upstate was held up because you wasn't in no shape to make it. —A.S. Jackson, *Gentleman Pimp*, p. 128, 1973
- We were bullshitting a while about upstate when Earl sent his broad upstairs. —Edwin Torres, *Carlito's Way*, p. 28, 1975
- "You're referring, I believe," Jack said, "to when I was upstate that time?" "Upstate, that's good. Well, you seem to have enjoyed a successful rehabilitation." —Elmore Leonard, *Bandits*, p. 156, 1987
- Rocco was momentarily confused; upstate was a local euphemism for jail. —Richard Price, *Clockers*, p. 221, 1992
- I don't make things worse. In Jersey last month, wasn't for me, you'd be upstate, Joe. —Stephen Cannell, *Big Con*, p. 230, 1997

2 murdered *US*
- "He went upstate" meant the guy got whacked, and don't ask again. —Henry Hill and Byron Schreckengost, *A Good Fella's Guide to New York*, p. 61, 2003

upta *adjective*
no good; hopeless; worthless *AUSTRALIA, 1918*
Originally short for **UP TO PUTTY**, but now conceived of as short for **UP TO SHIT**.
- Gooda for da convicta, yes, but no gooda da Gund. Upta! —Eric Curry, *Hysterical History of Australia*, p. 43, 1940

up the aisle *noun*
a sexual position in which the woman kneels and the man enters her from behind *UK*
Rhyming slang for **DOG-STYLE**, combining a pun on 'a narrow passage' with an implication of marriage.
- —Bodmin Dark, *Dirty Cockney Rhyming Slang*, 2003

up the in and out *adjective*
ruined; pregnant *UK*
Rhyming slang for **UP THE SPOUT**.
- —Ray Puxley, *Fresh Rabbit*, 1998

up the Irons!
used as a greeting, especially between Iron Maiden fans *US*
Collected from fans of heavy metal music by Seamus O'Reilly, January 1995.

up there Cazaly
come on! *AUSTRALIA, 1943*
Used as a cry of encouragement. Originally a cry of support for Ron Cazaly (1893–1963), Australian Rules football player.
- 'Good on you, Bo!' 'Up there, Cazaly!' 'Rock it in, Bo!' —John Morrison, *Stories of the Waterfront*, p. 29, 1962
- —Jim Ramsay, *Cop It Sweet!*, p. 93, 1977

up there for thinking, down there for dancing; up here for thinking, down there for dancing
a catchphrase used as a jocular demonstration of the speaker's grasp on anatomy *UK*
- —Caroline Aherne and Craig Cash, *The Royle Family*, 1999

uptight *adjective*
1 nervous, anxious *US, 1934*
- —J. L. Simmons and Barry Winograd, *It's Happening*, p. 174, 1966: 'glossary'
- There were a few straights but they looked very uptight and out of place. —*Berkeley Barb*, p. 1, 20th January 1967
- Youngblood don't be so uptight, man. I ain't after your girl, man. —Cecil Brown, *The Life & Loves of Mr. Jiveass Nigger*, p. 145, 1969
- Same old American story: except this time the cop was dead and the white folks got real uptight about THAT. —*The Black Panther*, p. 7, 25th January 1969
- What he didn't understand, of course, is that the very thing that made him angry at the sight of cops is the same thing that puts kids uptight seeing them on campus. —Jim Bouton, *Ball Four*, p. 150, 1970
- [S]omebody must be pretty fucking uptight. —Richard Neville, *Play Power*, p. 189, 1970
- Then we came upon a crowd of people ahead of us being chased by police, who were obviously very uptight. —Malcolm Boyd, *My Fellow Americans*, p. 28, 1970
- You're just uptight about tomorrow. —Francesca Lia Block, *Cherokee Bat*, p. 232, 1992

2 inhibited; narrow-minded; very correct and straitlaced *US, 1968*
- Dig what you're doing! Make war on paranoia. Don't be afraid. Don't get uptight. —Abbie Hoffman, *Revolution for the Hell of It*, p. 28, 1968
- When you were a child, did you think of your family as up tight and plastic? —Leonard Wolfe (Editor), *Voices from the Love Generation*, p. 216, 1968
- Elvis Presley ripped off Ike Eisenhower by turning our uptight young awakening bodies around. —Jerry Rubin, *Do It!*, p. 18, 1970
- "You have no reason to get uptight." "I'm not uptight. I'm not, really." —Doug Lang, *Freaks*, p. 106, 1973
- Don't be so uptight. Give it a chance. —*King of Comedy*, 1976
- Wait, wait, don't get up tight. —*Apocalypse Now*, 1979
- You were just so up tight. Now you're much softer. —*When Harry Met Sally*, 1989
- No, man, what we swingers were rebelling against were uptight squares like you. —*Austin Powers*, 1997
- Uptight, straight-arsed divs like you. —Dave Courtney, *Raving Lunacy*, p. 33, 2000

up top *noun*
1 a person's intelligence *UK, 1961*
- There are people in the Coalition who don't have much up top in terms of political nous[.] —*Herald Sun [Australia]*, 2nd July 2004

2 a womans breasts, or the area of the breasts *UK*
- She took another bite, then realized that Dar had already finished and was staring at her breasts. Admittedly, she didn't have much up top, but... —Joy Nash, *Dream Guardian*, 2003

uptown *noun*
1 cocaine *US, 1980*
Uptown is expensive and glamourous, as is cocaine.

- First I'll put your Uptown on the spoon, then to make it more exciting I'm gonna add some Downtown. They call this thing a speedball, honey, but then you must know that. — *The Bad Lieutenant*, 1992
- — Peter Johnson, *Dictionary of Street Alcohol and Drug Terms*, p. 200, 1993

2 in pool, the area at the head of the table *US*

- — Mike Shamos, *The Illustrated Encyclopedia of Billiards*, p. 259, 1993

uptown *adjective*

upscale, prosperous *US, 1946*

- BB: Then we'd just lean on the door of the club in the alley and listen to the music. I think the girls were looking for something a bit more uptown. — *Tin Men*, 161

up west; up West *noun*

the West End of London *UK*

Originally as viewed from the East End, subsequently used throughout suburbia regardless of the compass.

- When you were up west with Mods from all over London and the sticks you couldn't help but feel theatrical[.] — Irish Jack, *History*, p. 31, 1979
- It's all very well lavishing the grace and favour on saddle makers and titfer merchants up West[.] — Andrew Nickolds, *Back to Basics*, p. 15, 1994
- UP WEST[.] The West End is a short journey from the Elephant and Castle. — Brian McDonald, *Elephant Boys*, p. 239, 2000

up you!

used as an exclamation of contempt, derision or defiance; a euphemism for 'fuck you!' *UK*

Often accompanied by, or used instead of, the raised middle finger gesture which carries the same meaning. Apparently not recorded before 1984 but, surely, much earlier.

up you for the rent!

damn you! *AUSTRALIA, 1955*

- Up you for the rent, sport!!! — Barry Humphries, *The Wonderful World of Barry McKenzie*, p. 1, 1968
- — Frank Hardy, *The Outcasts of Foolgarah*, p. 64, 1971
- — Jim Ramsay, *Cop It Sweet!*, p. 93, 1977

up your alley!

used as a dismissive retort *UK, 1976*

A euphemism for **UP YOUR ASS/ARSE!**.

up your giggy!

used as an expression of contemptuous rejection *CANADA, 1961*

After **GIGGY** (the anus).

up your nose with a rubber hose

used as a general-purpose, nonsensical insult *US*

A signature line of Vinnie Barbarino, played by John Travolta, on the television comedy *Welcome Back, Kotter* (ABC, 1975–79). Repeated with referential humour.

up yours!

used as an expression of contempt, rejection or derision *UK, 1956*

A shortening of **UP YOUR ASS/ARSE!**.

- 'Stop moaning, or we'll give you the radio as well,' cracks one of the stretcher party. 'Up yours.' — William Nagel, *The Odd Angry Shot*, p. 80, 1975
- — Gerald Sweeney, *The Plunge*, p. 71, 1981
- Me? I thought, OBE [Order of the British Empire] me? Up yours, I thought. I get angry when I hear that word "empire"; it reminds me of slavery[.] — *The Guardian*, 27th November 2003

urban surfing *verb*

▷ see: **TRAIN-SURFING**

urger *noun*

a racecourse tipster *AUSTRALIA, 1919*

- URGER – A fraudulent race follower. — Gilbert H. Lawson, *A Dictionary of Australian Words and Terms*, 1924
- Ernie the Urger, a man well-versed in form guides, weights, distances, horses for courses etc., was astonished recently at Randwick to see two little old ladies back seven straight winners, – some at long prices. — Frank Hardy and Athol George Mulley, *The Needy and the Greedy*, p. 93, 1975
- Billard Cue – A racecourse urger who always has a tip. — Taffy Davies, *Australian Nicknames*, 1977
- Gambling occupied quite a bit of the spare time of the stable hands at Marsden's especially just after pay day, and naturally, the old urger was right in the thick of it. — Joe Andersen, *Winners Can Laugh*, p. 50, 1982

Uriah Heep *noun*

an objectionable or unpleasant person; a dull or insignificant person *UK*

Rhyming slang for **CREEP**, formed from a character in Charles Dickens' *David Copperfield*, 1849.

- — Ray Puxley, *Cockney Rabbit*, 1992

urine express *noun*

an elevator in a public housing development *US*

New York police slang.

- — Samuel M. Katz, *Anytime Anywhere*, p. 391, 1997: 'The extremely unofficial and completely off-the-record NYPD/ESU truck-two glossary'

urine-stained *adjective*

not good enough; not socially acceptable *US*

- "Guys, we're at that point now where we have to have real producers." Without a second's pause, [Kim] Fowley says: "In other words, you're telling us we're too urine-stained to join your country club." — Barney Hoskyns, *Waiting For The Sun*, p. 264, 1996

us *adjective*

my *UK*

Too widely used to be simply a dialect of northern England. The citation that follows is from Manchester.

- Money in us pockets, grinning wide, ready to roll. — Cath Staincliffe, *Trainers*, p. 61, 1999

US *adjective*

not in working order *UK, 1942*

A military abbreviation of 'unserviceable', 'useless', and/or **UP TO SHIT**.

- Still, if the aircraft's u.s., there isn't much I can do about it, is there? — W.R. Bennett, *Target Turin*, p. 77, 1962
- — John Ayto, *The Oxford Dictionary of Slang*, p. 416, 1998

us *pronoun*

me *UK, 1828*

Queen Elizabeth II is often derided for referring to herself as 'we' (known as the 'royal we'); this is the working-class 'us'.

- Give us him. — Nino Culotta (John O'Grady), *They're A Weird Mob*, p. 56, 1957
- Give us a go. I haven't had a talk to her yet. — Ray Lawler, *Summer of the Seventeenth Doll*, p. 35, 1957
- Aw cripes, leave us alone will you, mate. I done something more than a bit on the embarrassing side! — Barry Humphries, *The Wonderful World of Barry McKenzie*, p. 53, 1968
- Want to see what I'm playing and that? Twat! Come 'ead [ahead] – look at us then, you gobshite! — Kevin Sampson, *Outlaws*, p. 3, 2001

use *verb*

1 to use drugs, especially addictive drugs such as heroin *US*

Used without an object. A euphemism, but one which is crystal clear in slang context.

- She remembered the beautiful times they had had together before Teddy started using. — Donald Goines, *Dopefiend*, p. 20, 1971
- She was getting by well and we started using. — Herbert Huncke, *Guilty of Everything*, p. 103, 1990
- Listen, yewer not a fuckin ex-junkie, mun, yewer a fuckin junkie who's not using at the mo. — Niall Griffiths, *Sheepshagger*, p. 138, 2001

2 to enjoy something (if only you could get the something that is wished for) *UK, 1956*

- SAMMY: I could use a beer. BRIAN: I could use a tranquilizer. — Kenneth Lonergan, *You Can Count on Me*, 2000

▸ **use your loaf**

to act intelligently, think *UK*

Often as an imperative.

- "I don't follow." "Use your loaf, lad." — Colin Butts, *Is Harry on the Boat?*, p. 127, 1997

▸ **use yourself**

1 to masturbate *BAHAMAS*

- — John A. Holm, *Dictionary of Bahamian English*, p. 214, 1982

2 to use physical violence; to fight *UK*

By elision from 'use yourself as a weapon'.

- "And if he uses himself?" Fancy said. "If he uses himself handle him gently," Robins said. — Troy Kennedy Martin, *Z Cars*, p. 137, 1962

used beer department *noun*

a toilet *US*

Modified to 'used coffee department' and the like for office settings.

- — Roger E. Axtell, *Do's and Taboos of Using English Around the world*, 1995
- The used beer department is down those steps over there. — Theodore Sturgeon, *When You're Smiling*, p. 239, 2002

useful *adjective*

1 good; capable; effective; satisfactory *UK, 1955*

- The outspoken 50-year-old, who was a useful boxer in his youth, is eyeing up the media[.] — *The Guardian*, 3rd January 2004

2 competitive *IRELAND*

- Righ'; good win there but, let's face it, lads. They were spas. He let them laugh, then frowned. Next week'll be a different kettle o'fish. Cromcastle are always a useful side so we can't afford to be complacent. —Roddy Doyle, *The Van*, p. 24, 1991

useful as an ashtray on a motorbike *adjective*

useless *AUSTRALIA, 1986*

- —Ivor Limb, *Footy's No Joke!*, p. 70, 1986
- I was, as Max would say, about as useful as an ashtray on a motor bike. —Kathy Lette, *Girls' Night Out*, p. 94, 1987

useless as tits on a boar; useless as tits on a boar hog; useless as tits on a bull *adjective*

ineffectual, serving no useful purpose *CANADA, 1981*

- [T]his "posse" was about as useless as tits on a bull. —Dorothy Garlock, *Restless Wind*, 1986
- Charlie had his radioman break out a small portable HF [high frequency] radio and set it up in the road. That thing's as useless as tits on a boar hog. My worst fears about this communications setup had been realized. —Colonel James H. Kyle and John Robert Eidson, *The Guts to Try*, p. 298, 1995
- You are useless as tits on a boar, sitting there with your stupid head in your hands. —Virginia Henley, *Dream Lover*, p. 334, 1997

useless smile *noun*

used for describing the happy, vacant facial expression of someone under the influence of LSD *US*

- —David Shenk and Steve Silberman, *Skeleton Key*, p. 300, 1994

user *noun*

1 a drug addict *UK, 1935*

- —Angela Devlin, *Prison Patter*, p. 119, 1996

2 a person who exploits others for their own gain *AUSTRALIA, 1978*

- —Kylie Mole (Maryanne Fahey), *My Diary*, p. 34, 1988
- I told Venessa how Amanda was trying to get her but not to trust her cos she is a rool user. (Venessa hates users, and so do I.) —Kylie Mole (Maryanne Fahey), *My Diary*, p. 122, 1988

ush *verb*

to work as an usher in a theatre *US*

- —Don Wilmeth, *The Language of American Popular Entertainment*, p. 286, 1981

US of A *noun*

the *U*nited *S*tates *of A*merica *US, 1973*

A variation of the conventional abbreviations US and USA.

- Eminem on MTV eating Big Macs, drinking Coke and surfing the internet for anything with Britney Spears on it. What do all these have in common? Right first time, Georgie, baby. Country of origin: US of A. — *The Guardian*, 18th November 2003

USP *noun*

amphetamines; MDMA, the recreational drug best known as ecstasy *UK*

- —Mike Haskins, *Drugs*, p. 279, 2003

UTA *adjective*

in abundance *US*

- I learned early that "Gook," meaning any North Korean soldier, and UTA, "up to the ass," meaning abundance, were the most frequently used expressions in conversation. —William B. Hopkins, *One Drum No Bugle*, p. 41, 1986

ute *noun*

a utility truck *AUSTRALIA, 1943*

- And y'orter buy a new ute while you're about it. —Dymphna Cusack, *Picnic Races*, p. 71, 1962
- There's one car in pieces behind the pub and a broken down old ute in that dump on the hill. —Max Fatchen, *Chase through the Night*, p. 26, 1976

utensil *noun*

a chamberpot *TRINIDAD AND TOBAGO, 1909*

- —Lise Winer, *Dictionary of the English/Creole of Trinidad & Tobago*, 2003

utilities *noun*

US Marines combat fatigues *US*

- —Linda Reinberg, *In the Field*, p. 229, 1991

U-turn *noun*

a reversal of political policy *UK, 1984*

From motorists' jargon.

- Schwarzenegger's u-turn on gay marriages. —*The Guardian*, 3rd March 2004

UV's *noun*

sun rays *US*

An abbreviation of '*u*ltra-*v*iolet sun rays'.

- —Collin Baker et al., *College Undergraduate Slung Study Conducted at Brown University*, p. 216, 1968
- —Mimi Pond, *The Valley Girl's Guide to Life*, p. 63, 1982
- —Anna Scotti and Paul Young, *Buzzwords*, p. 84, 1997

UYB *noun*

an *u*ppity *Y*ankee *b*itch *US*

The southern US view of some northern US women.

- —Connie Eble (Editor), *UNC-CH Campus Slang*, p. 9, Fall 1986

Uzi *noun*

a pipe used for smoking crack cocaine *US*

- — US Department of Justice, *Street Terms*, October 1994

uzzfay *noun*

a police officer *US*

Pig Latin for **FUZZ**.

- —*American Speech*, p. 88, May 1955: 'Narcotic argot along the Mexican border'

Vv

V *noun*

1 **Valium™** *US*

- Of course, the last time you took a V, you were wired on C. — Jay McInerney, *Bright Lights, Big City*, p. 141, 1984

2 **citrate marketed as Viagra™, an anti-impotence drug taken recreationally for performance enhancement, in combination with other chemicals that stimulate the sexual appetites** *UK*

- [G]eezers out there that fancy taking a V but are too embarrassed cos you think that people might say you can't get it up. — Dave Courtney, *Raving Lunacy*, p. 269, 2000

3 **a V-sign** *UK*

- Tommy flickin' the Vs at the paps [paparazzi] — Ben Elton, *High Society*, p. 151, 2002

4 **a visit** *US*

- — Gary K. Farlow, *Prison-ese*, p. 77, 2002

5 **a five year prison sentence** *US*

From the Roman numeral for five.

- — Lou Shelly, *Hepcats Jive Talk Dictionary*, p. 20, 1945
- — Joseph E. Ragen and Charles Finston, *Inside the World's Toughest Prison*, p. 822, 1962: 'Penitentiary and underworld glossary'
- They sent me up the river to do a little V. — Roger Abrahams, *Positively Black*, p. 48, 1970

6 **five dollars** *US*

- — Joseph E. Ragen and Charles Finston, *Inside the World's Toughest Prison*, p. 822, 1962: 'Penitentiary and underworld glossary'

7 **marijuana** *US*

- Yeah, they got stoned on giggle-weed, zonked on grifa, zapped on yerba, bombed on boo, they were blitzed with snop, warped on twist, gay on hay, free on V. — *Hi Life*, p. 14, 1979

v *adjective*

very *UK*

Upper-class society origins (perhaps from abbreviation use in school) into wider middle-class usage.

- This is v. delicious, Caroline. — Ann Barr and Peter York, *The Official Sloane Ranger Handbook*, p. 159, 1982

V-8 gang *noun*

a youth gang that uses large American cars *NEW ZEALAND*

- — Louis S. Leland, *A Personal Kiwi-Yankee Dictionary*, p. 108, 1984

V-8's *noun*

men's shorts *US*

- How then could I run around with just my jockey shorts? V-8s don't hide fat, you know. — Oscar Zeta Acosta, *The Autobiography of a Brown Buffalo*, p. 82, 1972
- — Dagoberto Fuentes and Jose Lopez, *Barrio Language Dictionary*, p. 153, 1974

VA *noun*

the vagina *US*

Adopted from the standard abbreviation for the state of Virginia, punning the phonetic similarity.

- There's [a...] "cooter," "labbe," "Gladys Siegelman," "VA," "wee wee[".] — Eve Ensler, *The Vagina Monologues*, p. 6, 1998

Vaalie; Valie *noun*

an inhabitant of the region formerly known as Transvaal *SOUTH AFRICA, 1976*

Often derogatory or patronising.

- They [a beach cafe] say the Vaalies clean them out [of stock] every day. Look, I know we need them, and they're mostly nice people. But I can't wait till they're gone — *Sunday Times (South Africa)*, 10th January 1999

vac *noun*

a *vac*ation *UK, 1709*

- [U]ntil the Christmas vac comes around. — *New Statesman*, 9th September 2002

vacation *noun*

time spent in jail or prison *US*

- — Hermese E. Roberts, *The Third Ear*, 1971

vacaya *noun*

1 **any mechanical or electrical device that produces sound; a jukebox; a record player** *UK*

- [C]od [poor] sounds in the vacaya[.] — Paul Baker, *Polari*, p. 194, 2002

2 **a mobile phone** *UK*

From the earlier, more general sense (a device that produces sound).

- — Paul Baker, *Polari*, p. 194, 2002

vada; varda; vardi; vardo; vardy *verb*

to see; to look; to observe *UK, 1859*

Polari.

- HORNE: Would I have vada'd any of them, do you think? SANDY: Oh – he's got all the palare, hasn't he? JULIAN: I wonder where he picks it up. SANDY: You may have vada'd one of our tiny bijou masterpiecettes, heartface. — Barry Took and Marty Feldman, *Round The Horne*, 13th March 1966
- So I varded the cod-riahs [wigs] but they were much too butch pour moi. — the cast of 'Aspects of Love', Prince of Wales Theatre, *Palare (Boy Dancer Talk) for Beginners*, 1989–92
- FRIEND 2: Varda the omie palome! — Todd Haynes, *Velvet Goldmine*, 1998
- He noticed a man earwigging our conversation. "Vada the homi macaroni," he hissed. — Jake Arnott, *He Kills Coppers*, p. 52, 2001
- — Paul Baker, *Polari*, p. 194, 2002

vadavision; vardavision *noun*

a television; televison *UK*

- — Paul Baker, *Polari*, p. 194, 2002

VAF!

(when first noticing an attractive person) look! *UK*

Polari; an acronym for '**VADA** *a*bsolutely **FANTABULOSA**!'.

- — Paul Baker, *Polari*, p. 194, 2002

vag *noun*

1 **a vagrant** *US, 1868*

- I could tell you a few more stories of how cops treat suspected vags on the road but one story would be like another. — Clancy Sigal, *Going Away*, p. 138, 1961
- "But we aint' Vag," Glenn offered. "We got money, a car. We got jobs. We're regular citizens." — Earl Thompson, *Tattoo*, p. 483, 1974

2 **vagrancy; a criminal charge of vagrancy** *US, 1859*

- I wish I knew what that charge was! Vag, probably; take all my money and charge me vag. — Jack Kerouac, *On the Road*, p. 136, 1957
- — Jack Webb, *The Badge*, p. 222, 1958
- [Y]ou can't even enjoy the sights and scenery and have always to be on the watch for the policeman who will pick you up for vag[.] — Clancy Sigal, *Going Away*, p. 138, 1961
- But if you dont have a pad, theyll bust you for vag. — John Rechy, *City of Night*, p. 319, 1963
- He says he was sittin' in a cell in a Southwest jail / where he landed doin' three days for vag. — Bruce Jackson, *Get Your Ass in the Water and Swim Like Me*, p. 82, 1966
- — Angela Devlin, *Prison Patter*, p. 119, 1996

vag *verb*

to charge someone with vagrancy *US, 1859*

- Well, eventually the walloper decides to take Mo to the cop shop. He's going to vag him. — *Sydney City Hub*, p. 5, 4th April 1996

vage; vag; vadge; vaj *noun*

the vagina *US*

- Another shot has Uncle Lou returning the gesture, copping a generous helping of boob and vage. — Josh Alan Friedman, *Tales of Times Square*, p. 30, 1986
- It was well nigh impossible to achieve "full-vage-pen" by breeching aside the crotch panel of this snug-fitting garment. — Terry Southern, *Now Dig This*, p. 3, 1986
- — Chris Lewis, *The Dictionary of Playground Slang*, p. 246, 2003

vaggerie; vagary; vagarie *verb*
to go; to leave; to travel *UK*
Probably from Italian *vagare* (to roam).
- —Paul Baker, *Polari*, p. 194, 2002

vagina vandal *noun*
a rapist *US*
- —Joseph E. Ragen and Charles Finston, *Inside the World's Toughest Prison*, p. 822, 1962: 'Penitentiary and underworld glossary'

val *noun*
1 a tablet of diazepam (trade name Valium™), an anti-anxiety agent *US*
- —Richard A. Spears, *The Slang and Jargon of Drugs and Drink*, p. 533, 1986

2 value *UK*
- [T]his outfit keep sending Nobby here stuff that's no val to us. —J.J. Connolly, *Layer Cake*, p. 27, 2000

3 a resident of the San Fernando Valley, Los Angeles County, California *US*
- —Sue Black, *The Totally Awesome Val Guide*, p. 23, 1982
- —Lee Wardlaw, *Cowabunga! The Complete Book of Surfing*, p. 158, 1991
- Looks like we're going to have to make a cameo at the Val party. —*Clueless*, 1995

valentine *noun*
a very short jail sentence *US*
- —Vincent J. Monteleone, *Criminal Slang*, p. 247, 1949
- —Marlene Freedman, *Alcatraz*, 1983

Valentine *noun*
in college, a notification of academic deficiency *US*
- —*American Speech*, p. 76–77, February 1968: 'Some notes on flunk notes'

Valentine Dyalls; valentines *noun*
haemorrhoids *UK*
Rhyming slang for 'piles', formed on the actor Valentine Dyall, 1908–85.
- —Ray Puxley, *Fresh Rabbit*, 1998

valet *noun*
in a deck of playing cards, a jack or knave *US*
- —George Percy, *The Language of Poker*, p. 95, 1988

vali; vallie; vally *noun*
*Val*ium™, a branded tranquillizer *UK*
- —Macfarlane, Macfarlane and Robson, *The User*, p. xi, 1996

Valie *noun*
▷ see: **VAALIE**

valley *noun*
the antecubital vein at the inside of the elbow, a prime site for intravenous drug injections *US*
- —William D. Alsever, *Glossary for the Establishment and Other Uptight People*, p. 19, December 1970

Valley *noun*
▸ **the Valley**
1 the San Fernando Valley, Los Angeles County, California *US*
- This is the Valley, Vincent. Marsellus don't got no friendly places in the Valley. —*Pulp Fiction*, 1994
- So, anyway, the whole crew is going to this party in the Valley. —*Clueless*, 1995

2 a low-lying area east of Seventh Avenue in Harlem, New York *US*
- We'd better take a look in the valley before checking in. —Chester Himes, *Come Back Charleston Blue*, p. 24, 1966

valley dolls *noun*
LSD *UK*
- —Mike Haskins, *Drugs*, p. 286, 2003

Valleyite *noun*
a resident of the San Fernando Valley, Los Angeles *US*
- "Fucking Valleyites," loudly enough for her to hear. "Go spend the rest of it at the Galleria, or wherever the hell you go to[.]" —Bret Easton Ellis, *Less Than Zero*, p. 62, 1985

valve job *noun*
sex in a car *US*
- —Jim Crotty, *How to Talk American*, p. 37, 1997

vamoose *verb*
to go; to leave *US, 1834*
Spanish *vamanos* (let us go).
- For a split second I deliberated whether to vamoose but I watched Cass for a clue and the clue didn't come. —Frederick Kohner, *Gidget*, p. 113, 1957
- Beat it, flake, fug off, vamoose, split, get the everlovin hell outa here and let me get ready t'go on! —Robert Gover, *Here Goes Kitten*, p. 40, 1964
- Scram, beat it, vamoose, out! Is that plain enough? —*King of Comedy*, 1976
- I mean left. Vamoosed. Sold out and upped sticks. —Ian Pattison, *Rab C. Nesbitt*, 1988
- Cunts have vanished. Vamoosed. Properly disappeared off've the face of the earth. —Kevin Sampson, *Outlaws*, p. 264, 2001

vamp *noun*
a woman that makes it her habit or business to captivate men by an unscrupulous employment of her sexual charms *UK, 1911*
- It would have been easy to make Salome a common vamp – but how crude, and how untrue! Wilde, however, would surely have preferred a vamp to play the woman he had imagined "dancing with her bare feet in the blood of a man she has craved for and slain". —*The Guardian*, 26th March 2003

vamp *verb*
1 (of a woman) to flirt, and otherwise employ an obvious sexuality to attract a mate *UK, 1927*
- [T]he women on the catwalk were allowed to pose and flirt [...] most relished the rare opportunity and vamped with glee. —*The Guardian*, 11th October 2003

2 to smell bad *TRINIDAD AND TOBAGO, 1973*
- —Lise Winer, *Dictionary of the English/Creole of Trinidad & Tobago*, 2003

vampire *noun*
a medical operative who draws off a patient's or donor's blood; a member of any National Blood Transfusion collecting team *UK, 1961*
Jocular and affectionate, usually.

▸ **take the vampire's kiss; take the vampires**
to tease someone, to pull someone's leg *UK*
Rhyming slang for **TAKE THE PISS**.
- —Ray Puxley, *Fresh Rabbit*, 1998

van *noun*
a brakevan (caboose) *US*
- —Ramon Adams, *The Language of the Railroader*, p. 166, 1977

Van *nickname*
the city of Vancouver, British Columbia *CANADA*
- Welcome to Van.net – in Vancouver, your source for community news, classifieds, horoscopes and more. —14th June 2002

V and A *nickname*
*V*ictoria *and A*lbert Museum *UK, 1937*
- Josephine Baker doing her celebrated topless shimmy-shake (the one played continuously in the V and A's Art Deco exhibition) —*The Observer*, 31st August 2003

vandoo *noun*
in the Canadian Forces, a member of the Royal 22nd Regiment, the francophone army unit *CANADA*
- Vandoo is but an English corruption of the French word for "22," "vingt-deux." "You can tell a Vandoo, although you can't tell him much." —Tom Langeste, *Words on the Wing*, p. 291, 1995

V and T *noun*
*v*odka *and t*onic *UK*
- V and T, Frankie, and a lager for Russell. —Greg Williams, *Diamond Geezers*, p. 52, 1997
- [H]e just sat there on the recliner sipping V&Ts and watching telly. —Greg Williams, *Diamond Geezers*, p. 139, 1997

V and X *noun*
in carnival usage, a five-and-ten cent store *US*
- —Don Wilmeth, *The Language of American Popular Entertainment*, p. 286, 1981

Van Gogh *noun*
a trucker operating with a citizens' band radio *US*
A trucker without a citizens' band radio is said to be driving 'without ears', and hence the artistic allusion.
- —Wayne Floyd, *Jason's Authentic Dictionary of CB Slang*, p. 31, 1976

Vangroovy *noun*
Vancouver, British Columbia *CANADA*
- Because "Vangroovy" is the most stereotyped city in Canada, I felt what I as a newcomer needed to do: ditch the power suits, eat organic, exercise a lot and be laid back all the time. — *Toronto Globe and Mail*, p. A14, 30th August 2002

vanilla *adjective*
1 white-skinned, Caucasian *US*
Originally black usage, now widespread.
- I noticed a lot of Jungle Fever action, with people describing themselves as "vanilla" or "chocolate" or "caramel." — Anka Radakovich, *The Wild Girls Club*, p. 43, 1994
- Warners would later be renowned as the company that signed such black superstars as Prince and Ice T, but in 1975 it was still a pretty vanilla operation. — Barney Hoskyns, *Waiting For The Sun*, p. 250, 1996

2 ordinary, simple, basic *US*
Derives from the plainest ice-cream variety.
- Then again, you say that you want nothing more adventurous than straight vanilla, morning reveille, missionary-position screwing. — Larry Heinemann, *Close Quarters*, p. 171, 1977
- — Guy L. Steele et al., *The Hacker's Dictionary*, p. 129, 1983
- The food is the same straight vanilla, greasy-spoon bill of fare as the Texas Lunch. — Larry Heinemann, *Paco's Story*, p. 105, 1986
- It wasn't that exotic or anything, your basic vanilla, really, but he was so young and appreciative, and he kissed like an angel. — Armistead Maupin, *Maybe the Moon*, p. X, 1992
- "You're plain-vanilla, remember?" Harper nodded. "And the plain-vanilla motive is money." — Lee Child, *The Visitor*, p. 329, 2000

3 of sex, conventional; of homosexual sex, gentle, traditional, emotional *US*
- — Brigid McConville and John Shearlaw, *The Slanguage of Sex*, 1984
- — Wayne Dynes, *Homolexis*, p. 147, 1985
- Vanilla is a term used by S-M people to describe conventional, non-S-M sexual intercourse. — Robert Stoller and I.S. Levine, *Coming Attractions*, p. 49, 1991
- I hadn't been wrong about the people who attended these things [fetish-themed nightclubs] – they really were much better behaved than their vanilla counterparts. — Claire Mansfield and John Mendelssohn, *Dominatrix*, p. 102, 2002

4 used of pornography, relatively high-brow, designed for couples and first-time viewers *US*
- — Ana Loria, *1 2 3 Be A Porn Star!*, p. 165, 2000: 'Glossary of adult sex industry terms'

vanilla fudge *noun*
a judge *UK*
Rhyming slang.
- It's into court in front of the old vanilla fudge and Billy Fury [jury]. — Mervyn Stutter, *Getting Nowhere Fast*, 21st May 2004

Vanity Fair *noun*
a chair *UK*
Rhyming slang, formed from the title of Thackeray's novel.
- — Julian Franklyn, *A Dictionary of Rhyming Slang*, 1961

Vanna *noun*
used as a term of address between homosexual males *US*
From Vanna White, of television game show fame.
- — Judi Sanders, *Cal Poly Slang*, p. 11, 1990

Vanouver *noun*
any vacuum cleaner *UK*
Rhyming slang for **HOOVER**.
- — Ray Puxley, *Cockney Rabbit*, 1992

vap; vaps *noun*
an impulse; a sudden urge *TRINIDAD AND TOBAGO, 1957*
- — Lise Winer, *Dictionary of the English/Creole of Trinidad & Tobago*, 2003

vap *verb*
when throwing dice, to snap your fingers *BARBADOS*
- — Frank A. Collymore, *Barbadian Dialect*, p. 116, 1965

vapour lock *noun*
a temporary loss of common sense or memory *US*
An allusion to a mechanical problem with the carburettor of an internal combustion engine.
- — John Vorhaus, *The Big Book of Poker Slang*, p. 38, 1996

vapourware *noun*
in computing, a program that is announced well before it is completed and released *US*
- — Eric S. Raymond, *The New Hacker's Dictionary*, p. 366, 1991

varda; vardi *verb*
▷ **see:** VADA

varda d'amour *noun*
the look of love *UK*
A combination of polari and French.
- — the cast of 'Aspects of Love', Prince of Wales Theatre, *Palare (Boy Dancer Talk) for Beginners*, 1989–92

varder; varda *noun*
a look *UK*
Polari.
- "So sister," I polaried. "Will you take a varder at the cartz on the feely-omi [young man] in the naf [poor taste] strides [trousers][.] — James Gardiner, *Who's a Pretty Boy Then?*, p. 123

vardo *noun*
in gypsy or traveller use, a trailer, a wagon, a caravan *UK, 1934*
- Life in the vardo was good. — Jimmy Stockin, *On The Cobbles*, p. 50, 2000

vardo; vardy *verb*
▷ **see:** VADA

varicose alley *noun*
the platform that extends from a stage used by strippers out into the audience *US*
- — *Time*, 12th March 1945
- Only the soubrettes and chorines played on 'Varicose Alley', as the runway was nicknamed[.] — William Green, *Strippers and Coochers*, p. 163, 1977
- — *Detroit Free Press*, 19th December 1977

varicose vein *noun*
a baby; a child *UK: SCOTLAND*
Glasgow rhyming slang on Scottish dialect *wean* (pronounced 'wayne').
- — Michael Munro, *The Complete Patter*, 1996

vark *noun*
used as a term of abuse, especially applied to a police officer *SOUTH AFRICA, 1975*
A contemptuous term, from Afrikaans *vark* (pig).
- — Penny Silva, *A Dictionary of South African English*, 1996

varmint special *noun*
during the Vietnam war, a Remington bolt-action rifle used by US snipers *US*
- — Linda Reinberg, *In the Field*, p. 231, 1991

varnish *noun*
on the railways, a passenger train *US*
- — Norman Carlisle, *The Modern Wonder Book of Trains and Railroading*, p. 269, 1946

varnish *verb*
▸ **varnish the cane**
(from the male perspective) to have sex *US, 1968*
- — J.E. Lighter, *Historical Dictionary of American Slang, Volume 1*, p. 356, 1994

vasso *noun*
vaseline *AUSTRALIA*
- You did everything but coat me in vasso and heli-drop me, starkers, into a maximum security-prison for men. — Kathy Lette, *Altar Ego*, p. 290, 1998

VAT *noun*
*v*odka *a*nd *t*onic *UK*
Initialism, punning on 'v.a.t' (value added tax); made popular by 1980s television series *Minder*.
- [C]onsoling myself with a catering-size vodka and slimline (hereafter referred to as VAT) down the Winchester[.] — Andrew Nickolds, *Back to Basics*, 1994
- I buy a pint and get Mel a VAT. — Danny King, *The Burglar Diaries*, p. 51, 2001

Vatican roulette *noun*
birth control by the rhythm method *US*
- — *Maledicta*, p. 173, 1979: 'A glossary of ethnic slurs in American English'

vato; bato *noun*
a guy *US*
Border Spanish used in English conversation by Mexican-Americans.
- — George Carpenter Baker, *Pachuco*, p. 40, January 1950

- I'll hotwire it. Car theft is my Vato speciality. —Stephen J. Cannell, *The Tin Collectors*, p. 326, 2001

vato loco; bato loco *noun*

a wild guy *US*

- The label implies a permanency of behavior and a prediction: once a Mexican-American becomes a vato loco, he will continue to perform those acts and engage in those activities which 'fit' the label. —George R. Alvarez, *Semiotic Dynamics of an Ethnic-American Sub-Cultural Group*, p. 4, 1965
- —Eugene Landy, *The Underground Dictionary*, p. 29, 1971
- And the only difference, really, is that the ex-cons are old enough to have done time for the same things the batos locos haven't been arrested for, yet. —Hunter S. Thompson, *Fear and Loathing in Las Vegas*, p. 230, 1971
- In the cities, only the lowriders, the vatos locos, are in tune with this. —Oscar Zeta Acosta, *The Revolt of the Cockroach People*, p. 67, 1973
- —Dagoberto Fuentes and Jose Lopez, *Barrio Language Dictionary*, p. 15, 1974

vault *noun*

a hotel baggage checkroom *US*

- The doorman said to me, "You wanted to know when they come outa the vault, Mister Collans." —Dev Collans with Stewart Sterling, *I was a House Detective*, p. 71, 1954

va va voom *noun*

style; a powerful or seductive style *US*

Used as a song title by Cinerama 'Va Va Voom', 1998, and as an advertising strap line for Renault's Clio™ (2001+).

- [A] beaded backless number – like ELIZABETH DOLE's frock, but with more va-va-va-voom – for the ball. — *Time*, 7th October 1996
- —Cinerama *Va Va Voom*, 2000
- [A] sexy, va-va-vroom action thriller that unashamedly glamorises an illicit subculture[.] — *The Times*, 7th June 2003

VC *noun*

the Viet Cong; a member of the Viet Cong *US*

- Vietnamese Communists, we call them Vietcong, we call them VC and C and Charlie and all the usual names[.] —William Wilson, *The LBJ Brigade*, p. 31, 1966

▷ **see:** VICTORIA CROSS

V-card *noun*

a person's virginity *US*

- —Pamela Munro, *U.C.L.A. Slang*, p. 114, 2001
- He talks about holding his "v-card" (virginity), while other friends are "dealing" theirs. — *Christian Science Monitor*, p. 1, 4th December 2002
- —Connie Eble (Editor), *UNC-CH Campus Slang*, p. 10, October 2002
- I'm a sophomore in college, and at times guys try to pressure me to turn in my V-card. — *Teenpeople*, p. 121, April 2004

VCR *noun*

a vicious campus rumour *US*

- — *Current Slang*, p. 8, Winter 1966

V.D. bonnet *noun*

a condom *US*

A reference to the prevention of venereal disease.

- Well, before I know it she's tied a balloon on it / One of those snug little V.D. bonnets. — *Screw*, p. 7, 15th May 1972

V-Dub; Vee-Dub *noun*

a Volkswagen motor vehicle *AUSTRALIA, 1970*

Shortening of *vee double-u*, that is, *Volkswagen*.

- He arrived in a decapitated V-Dub. —Kathy Lette, *Girls' Night Out*, p. 172, 1987

veal cutlet *noun*

in gambling cheating schemes, a victim *US*

- —Frank Garcia, *Marked Cards and Loaded Dice*, p. 265, 1962

veal of the sea *noun*

the green sea turtle *BAHAMAS*

- —John A. Holm, *Dictionary of Bahamian English*, p. 215, 1982

veddy *adverb*

very *UK, 1859*

A jocular pronunciation, approximating a child's, or an American's (attempting a 'British' accent), rendering of 'very'.

- "Do I make myself clear?" "Veddy, and how nice." —Hal Ellson, *Summer Street*, p. 83–84, 1953
- [A]n amusing but bizarrely simplistic clash of personalities and cultures: the veddy English old maid and the ooh-la-la French slut. — *The Village Voice (New York)*, 2nd July 2003

vee *noun*

sex involving three people, two of whom are focused on the pleasure of the third *US*

- Vee' is three people where the structure puts one person at the 'hinge' of the vee, also called the pivot. In a vee, the arm partners are not as commonly close to each other as each is to the pivot. —Nancy Tamosaitis, *net.sex*, p. 101, 1995

veeblefetzer *noun*

a corporate manager *US*

Not a term of endearment.

- —Andy Ihnatko, *Cyberspeak*, p. 204, 1997

vee dub *noun*

a completely depillated female pubis *US*

Also as a verb and, thus, an adjectival participle. Fom a similarity in shape and finish to the bonnet of a Volkswagen Beetle.

- I screwed Jennie last night – did you know she was vee dubbed? —Chris Lewis, *The Dictionary of Playground Slang*, p. 246, 2003

veejay *noun*

▷ **see:** VJ

veep *noun*

a vice president *US, 1949*

- — *American Speech*, February 1951

▷ **see:** VIP

vee wee *noun*

a Volkswagen motor vehicle *UK, 1984*

- Also, part panels [...] are available from Vee Wee of Brixton, London. —Jonathan Wood, *Vw Beetle*, p. 128, 1998

veg *noun*

vegetables *UK, 1898*

- I gave him three meals a day. Porridge for breakfast. Meat and two veg for dinner. A fry for tea. —Joe Orton, *Entertaining Mr Sloane*, 1964

vegemite-driller *noun*

a male homosexual *AUSTRALIA*

- But now the hosties or some vegemite-driller gives everyone a bit of a lecture on how few bugs or creepy crawlies there are in Australia compared to the rest of the world[.] —Barry Humphries, *The Traveller's Tool*, p. 33, 1985

Vegemite valley *noun*

the anus and rectal passage *AUSTRALIA*

Use is often suggestive of homosexual activity.

- —Chris Lewis, *The Dictionary of Playground Slang*, p. 246, 2003

vegetable *noun*

1 a person who is mentally and physically incapacitated to a degree that renders the comparison with a plant organism fair if cruel *UK, 1921*

- Got a brother, Anthony. He's a fuckin' vegetable. In '77 he smoked a bag of dust he bought from a dago. He jumped off our roof. — *New Jack City*, 1990
- Your grandmother was a 92-year-old vegetable. Only the machines were keeping her alive. —C.D. Payne, *Youth in Revolt*, p. 206, 1993
- The prison board is blatantly railroading you into a hospital for the sole purpose of turning you into vegetables. — *Natural Born Killers*, 1994

2 a person with an inactive, undemanding lifestyle

A derogatory use arising from the semi-conventional medical sense above.

vegetable garden *noun*

a group of neurologically depressed hospital patients *US*

- — *Maledicta*, p. 70, Summer/Winter 1978: 'Common patient-directed pejoratives used by medical personnel'

vegetation *noun*

relaxation *US*

- —Connie Eble (Editor), *UNC-CH Campus Slang*, p. 9, Fall 1986

vegged out *adjective*

relaxed and inactive *US*

- I was vegged out on the floor. At some point the methadone had kicked in real heavy[.] —Jason Parkinson, *Skateboards and Methadone [The Howard Marks Book of Dope Stories]*, p. 208, 2001

veggie *noun*

1 a vegetable *US, 1955*

- The thin lipped man worked next to him, distributing the veggies. —Odie Hawkins, *Great Lawd Buddha*, p. 113, 1990
- And I can't find an affordable restaurant in San Diego that serves any veggies except cauliflower and broccoli. If I could ever get a side order of green beans or spinach I'd stand up and cheer. —Joseph Wambaugh, *Floaters*, p. 228, 1996

2 a vegetarian *UK, 1975*
The variant spelling 'veggy' is also used.
- [A]ctually I'm a veggy because my family were too poor to afford meat[.] — Macfarlane, Macfarlane and Robson, *The User*, p. 15, 1996
- [T]he neighboring Cafe Kevah [...] serves a veggie-friendly range of soups, salads, and quesadillas[.] — Jamie Jensen, *Road Trip USA*, p. 83, 1999

vegie *adjective*
of school subjects, of the easiest grade *AUSTRALIA*
- [T]he two lowest of the five HSC maths levels, are known in the schools, and to many employers, as 'vegie-maths'. That's vegie as in vegetable. And vegetable as in vegetable-brain. — *Independent*, p. February, 1992

vego *noun*
a vegetarian *AUSTRALIA, 1996*

vego *adjective*
vegetarian *AUSTRALIA*
- The Church fathers getting fat on the spoils of their empire, weren't going to go vego, just because there is the indication that Jesus was. — *Passing Show*, p. 2, #5 1988

veg out *verb*
to relax and do nothing *US*
- I know it sounds mental, but sometimes I have more fun vegging out than when I go partying. — *Clueless*, 1995

veins *noun*
▸ **get veins**
in bodybuilding, to achieve definition, or well-developed and sculpted muscles *US*
- — *American Speech*, p. 200, Fall 1984: 'The language of bodybuilding'

velcro *noun*
a lesbian *UK*
Figurative use of Velcro™, from the French *velours croché* (hooked velvet), a branded material fastener.
- JAMIE: She's got to be a Velcro? LEE: All bets're off if she likes fuzz on fuzz. — Bernard Dempsey and Kevin McNally, *Lock, Stock ... & Two Hundred Smoking Kalashnikovs*, p. 100, 2000

velvet *noun*
1 gambling winnings *US*
- — John Scarne, *Scarne on Dice*, p. 481, 1974

2 a passenger train carriage *US*
- — Ramon Adams, *The Language of the Railroader*, p. 108, 1977

▸ **on velvet**
in good shape *US*
- Now, so long as the print server doesn't go down before we have the chance to prinit the report, we're on velvet. — Andy Ihnatko, *Cyberspeak*, p. 140, 1997

velvet fog *nickname*
singer Mel Tormé (1925–99) *US*
- Tormé, nicknamed the "velvet fog" because of his mellow voice, was enjoying success with his LP Mel Tormé at the Crescendo[.] — Brian McDonald, *Elephant Boys*, p. 219, 2000

vendor *noun*
a juke box *US*
- I got up, walked to the vendor, put a dime in, and told her to go back in the back. — Henry Williamson, *Hustler!*, p. 154, 1965

vendor's *noun*
a commercial bottled beer, even when obtained from a bootlegger *CANADA*
- A "vendor's" in Lydgate NS is a regular bottled beer, not homebrew. "Yeah, gimme a vendor's!" — Lewis Poteet, *The South Shore Phrase Book*, p. 122, 1999

vengeance *noun*
▸ **with a vengeance**
to a great degree, very much *UK, 1568*
- China takes to capitalist road with a vengeance[.] — *The Guardian*, 18th August 2003

vent; vent act *noun*
a ventriloquist *UK, 1893*
- One morning, I dropped in on the Vent-O-Rama. Ventriloquists call themselves "vents," and the Vent-O-Rama is a workshop for them. — Fred Setterberg, *Travelers' Tales America*, p. 187, 1999

▸ **take it to the vent**
to commit suicide *US*
- I don't want to hear about it, asshole! Take it to the vent if you can't handle your own problems. — James Harris, *A Convict's Dictionary*, p. 40, 1989

vent *verb*
to express frustrations in larger-than-life dimensions *US*
What an earlier generation would have called 'let off some steam'.
- — Connie Eble (Editor), *UNC-CH Campus Slang*, p. 8, March 1996

ventilate *verb*
to shoot someone *US*
From the image of bullet holes ventilating the body.
- To ventilate your foul ticker if I parted Junior's crew cut. — Haenigsen, *Jive's Like That*, 1947
- She remembered the pair of white would-be rapists she had ventilated into an intensive care ward six months before at this very alley after the bar closed. — Iceberg Slim (Robert Beck), *Airtight Willie and Me*, p. 160, 1979
- You let us in and he's get a chance to make it. Otherwise, he gets ventilated. — *48 Hours*, 1982
- No one ever found out for sure who put all the slugs in Maybelle and Abner. Everyone agreed they deserved getting ventilated[.] — Joseph Wambaugh, *The Secrets of Harry Bright*, p. 41, 1985
- Any bullshit and I'll ventilate yo ass right here. — *Menace II Society*, 1993

▸ **ventilate the block**
in hot rodding and drag racing, to blow a rod out through the engine *US, 1960s*
- — Capitol Records, *Hot Rod Jargon*, 1963

ventilator *noun*
a machine gun *US*
- — *American Speech*, p. 273, December 1962: 'The language of traffic policemen'

Vera Lynn; Vera *noun*
1 gin *UK, 1952*
Rhyming slang, based on the name of singer Vera Lynn (b.1917) known from World War 2 as 'the forces' sweetheart'.
- [S]he schlumphed her Vera [gin] down the screech at a rate of knots[.] — James Gardiner, *Who's a Pretty Boy Then?*, p. 123,
- I'm getting out the vera for a celebration bevvy [drink][.] — Derek Raymond (Robin Cook), *The Crust on its Uppers*, p. 41, 1962
- Now – what was it? Vera and Harmonic [tonic] for the lady – and an orange juice for you. — Anthony Masters, *Minder*, p. 16, 1984
- — Paul Baker, *Polari*, p. 194, 2002

2 a cigarette paper *UK*
Rhyming slang for **SKIN** (a cigarette paper), based on the name of singer Vera Lynn (b.1917).
- Has anybody got any veras? — the Shamen, *Ebeneezer Goode*, 1992

verandah over the toy shop *noun*
a paunch or beer-belly *AUSTRALIA*
- You promise not to poke fun at his paunch in public – no more jokes about a verandah over the toy shop. — Kathy Lette, *Girls' Night Out*, p. 208, 1987
- His dark-brown hair was closely cropped in a vain attempt to disguise premature balding and he had the start of a beer belly but she'd never minded a veranda over the toy shop. — Gary Bushell, *The Face*, p. 7, 2001

vera vice; victoria vice; veras *noun*
the police vice squad *UK*
A **CAMP** elaboration.
- — Angela Devlin, *Prison Patter*, p. 119, 1996

verbal; verbals *noun*
1 a conversation, a talk *UK*
- He even went down there, see if he could have a verbal, maybe patch things up. — Greg Williams, *Diamond Geezers*, p. 80, 1997

2 a verbal statement given to the police, often self-incriminatory *UK, 1963*
- Verbals are often said to be manufactured by the police. — Peter Laurie, *Scotland Yard*, 1970
- Who grassed this time? That's a good one. Read that out of your notebook in court and it places your man for them. It's about language, see? That's why it's called a verbal. — Jake Arnott, *He Kills Coppers*, p. 13, 2001

verbal; verbal up *verb*
to fake a confession of criminal guilt *UK*
- [I]f you are the type of criminal I was [violent and dangerous]... verballing and fitting up [fit up] is something you expect[.] — *The Listener*, 7th March 1979
- Also, before they tape recorded everything like they do now, two coppers would just verbal you up. Then kick fuck out of you. — Dave Courtney, *Raving Lunacy*, p. 31, 2000

verbal diarrhoea *noun*
unwarranted verbosity *UK, 1823*
• Many shows on the [Edinburgh] fringe have verbal diarrhoea; this one suffers from the visual runs. — *The Guardian*, 6th August 2003

verballing *noun*
the act of faking a criminal confession *UK*
• "Get your kicks that way, too, do you?" I say. "As well as at the verballing sessions?" — Ted Lewis, *Jack Carter's Law*, p. 71, 1974

vergla *noun*
freezing rain *CANADA*
The word is borrowed, modified but pronounced fairly correctly, from the French *verglas*, which means the same thing.
• There has been some vergla around Hamilton and Windsor, but the rest is rain or snow, north and east. — *The Weather Channel*, 29th October 2002

Veronica Lake *noun*
steak *UK*
Rhyming slang, formed from the name of the US film actress, 1919–73.
• — Ray Puxley, *Cockney Rabbit*, 1992

verrrry in-ter-est-ing; very interesting, but stupid
used as a humorous comment on a remark or event; used for humorously dismissing what has just been said *US*
A signature line on *Rowan and Martin's Laugh-In* (NBC, 1968–73), uttered by Arte Johnson while playing a wacky Nazi soldier. Repeated with referential humour.

versatile *adjective*
bisexual *UK*
• — Paul Baker, *Polari*, p. 194, 2002

versing *preposition*
▸ **be versing**
to compete against *US*
A corruption of the preposition 'versus', almost always heard in the progressive form.
• We're going to be versing the Brown Bombers next week. — *New York Times*, p. B3, 20th February 1984
• Who are you versing this week? — James Lambert, *The Macquarie Book of Slang*, 1996
• "It doesn't matter who I'm versing, I want to win," Hicks said after placing third in the nationals. — *Rockford (Illinois) Register Star*, p. 6D, 31st August 2004

versioning *noun*
a technique in hip-hop music of blending different periods and styles of recorded music *US*
• Unlike sampling, however, versioning usually involves reworking an entire composition. — James Haskins, *The Story of Hip-Hop*, p. 143, 2000

vert *noun*
in skateboarding, an almost *vert*ical ramp *UK*
• One graffiti-garnished section [of London's Playstation] has a "vert", a ramp which goes 3m (10ft) straight down and up again in a U. — *The Times*, p. 16, 26th April 2003

vertical bacon sandwich *noun*
the vagina *UK*
From the resemblance.
• — *www.LondonSlang.com*, June 2002

vertical jockey *noun*
an elevator operator *US, 1953*
• — *American Speech*, p. 158–159, May 1960: 'The burgeoning of 'jockey''

very *adjective*
excellent *US*
• Come on, it'll be Very. The note'll give her shower nozzle masturbation material for weeks. — *Heathers*, 1989

very *adverb*
very much, absolutely *UK*
• The weekends are another matter. Very. — James Hawes, *White Powder, Green Light*, p. 7, 2002

very à la *adjective*
absolutely in fashion *UK*
Generally contemptuous, disparaging or ironic in tone.
• She thought she was the cat's whiskers – oh very a la! — Beale, 1984

vest *noun*
a show-off *US*
• — *Time*, p. 56, 1st January 1965: 'Students: the slang bag'

vestibules *noun*
the testicles *UK*
• — Richard Herring, *Talking Cock*, p. 30, 2003

vestige *noun*
a brassiere *UK*
Recorded as a contemporary gay usage.
• — *Attitude*, July 2003: 'New palare lexicon'

vest out *verb*
to retire from police service after vesting in the pension plan with 15 years of service *US*
New York police slang.
• — Samuel M. Katz, *Anytime Anywhere*, p. 391, 1997: 'The extremely unofficial and completely off-the-record NYPD/ESU truck-two glossary'

vet *noun*
1 an ex-member of the military *US, 1848*
• Brooke Army Medical Center was the final destination for thousands of wounded Vietnam vets and was better known to the inmates as BAMC. — Bill Goshen, *War Paint*, p. 171, 2001

2 a prison doctor *SOUTH AFRICA, 1974*
• — Angela Devlin, *Prison Patter*, p. 120, 1996

veterano *noun*
an experienced, respected gang member *US*
Spanish used by English-speakers.
• [H]e had fought his way through the elaborate gang hierarchy to emerge as a seasoned veterano covered with battle wounds and glory. — Joseph Wambaugh, *The Choirboys*, p. 38, 1975

veterinarian *noun*
a physician who regards his patients as of animal intelligence *US*
• — *Maledicta*, p. 70, Summer/Winter 1978: 'Common patient-directed pejoratives used by medical personnel'

Vette *noun*
a Corvette car *US*
• After locking his Vette, he noticed a passing coach full of elderly tourists… — Joseph Wambaugh, *Finnegan's Week*, p. 3, 1994
• Hell no, I boosted a 'Vette. — *Gone in 60 Seconds*, 2000

vex *verb*
to engage someone in an abusive verbal attack *UK*
• — Dave Courtney, *Dodgy Dave's Little Black Book*, p. 7, 2001

VG *adjective*
very good *UK*
Abbreviation.
• v.g. […] Very good – like school mark. — Ann Barr and Peter York, *The Official Sloane Ranger Handbook*, p. 159, 1982

V girl *noun*
a woman who is attracted to men in military uniform *US, 1960*
• They had dances all over that year, it was a beginning to ease juvenile delinquency, gang rumbles, V-girls. — Gilbert Sorrentino, *Steelwork*, p. 86, 1970

Viaggy *noun*
a Viagra™ tablet *UK*
• But if he wants a Viaggy he's double come to the right place. — Kevin Sampson, *Clubland*, p. 119, 2002

vibe; vibes *noun*
the atmosphere generated by any event; mood; nuances intimately related to all senses *US*
An abbreviation of 'vibration', which has the same meaning.
• — Joe David Brown (Editor), *The Hippies*, p. 219, 1967: 'Glossary of hippie terms'
• I don't care for Berkeley vibes. — Leonard Wolfe (Editor), *Voices from the Love Generation*, p. 92, 1968
• [L]ead you to draw bad conclusions (or "bad vibes" as they say in the rock biz) about what happened. — Abbie Hoffman, *Woodstock Nation*, p. 4, 1969
• They [members of the Hog Farm commune at Woodstock] established very good vibes, had plenty of food (the lines were sometimes long, but usually moved quickly), good food and were really together. — *East Village Other*, 20th August 1969
• I was at an Alice Cooper thing where six people were rushed to the hospital with bad vibes. — *Annie Hall*, 1977
• She gave me the old vibes, all right. — David Powis, *The Signs of Crime*, 1977

- I've accidentally raised a bad vibe, and done something symbolic to lay that vibe to rest[.] —Stephen Gaskin, *Amazing Dope Tales*, p. 52, 1980
- I thought if I gave out a vibe they'd get the message and call me up. — *Fast Times at Ridgemont High*, 1982
- Not much to see, I'm afraid. I'm sort of cultivating a minimalist vibe. — *Sex, Lies and Videotape*, 1989
- Hey, man. The protective vibe. I dig. — *Clueless*, 1995
- The vibe was beautiful. —Dennis Hopper, *quoted in Waiting For The Sun*, p. 109, 1996
- [Y]ou'll end up being disturbed in the middle of the night by addled, weeping revellers who claim they've "lost their vibe". — *Metro (London)*, p. 18, 12th July 2001

vibe *verb*

to create and enjoy a good atmosphere

- [J]oking and vibing and grooving[.] — *Uncut*, p. 44, May 2001

vibed up *adjective*

excited; in the mood *UK*

- —Tom Hibbert, *Rockspeak!*, p. 167, 1983
- [M]ailing out press releases, dealing out membership cards, and keeping everyone vibed-up about the night[.] —Dave Haslam, *Dear Colin*, p. 147, 1999

vibe off *verb*

to take inspiration from someone or something *UK*

- Vibing off the aforementioned Sam Selvon, another writer to fire me up[.] —Paolo Hewitt, *The Sharper Word*, p. 119, 1999

vibe out *verb*

to intimidate someone *UK*

- —Tom Hibbert, *Rockspeak!*, p. 168, 1983

vibes *noun*

a vibraphone *UK, 1940*

- Adolf Hitler on vibes. —Bonzo Dog Band *The Intro and the Outro*, 1967

vibey *adjective*

fashionably atmospheric; in tune with the zeitgeist *UK*

From the 1990s; a positive sense of **VIBE** (the atmosphere of an event).

- I mean, it's great when you're playing these vibey little club gigs. —Kevin Sampson, *Powder*, p. 420, 1999
- London Fashion Week [...] a world apart, where good is bad and ugly is "vibey". — *The Times Magazine*, p. 7, 2nd March 2002

vibrations *noun*

the atmosphere generated by any event; mood; nuances intimately related to all senses *US*

- Words were used to sparkle eyes, break mouths into smiles, letters into tongued vibrations and meaning in-coherent. — *Berkeley Barb*, p. 3, 21st October 1966
- —Joe David Brown (Editor), *The Hippies*, p. 219, 1967: 'Glossary of hippie terms'
- I limped onto the plane with no problem except a wave of ugly vibrations from the other passengers[.] —Hunter S. Thompson, *Fear and Loathing in Las Vegas*, p. 202, 1971

vibrator *noun*

a motorcyle *US*

- — *American Speech*, p. 269, December 1962: 'The language of traffic policemen'

vic *noun*

1 a victim *US*

- — *Current Slang*, p. 51, Fall 1968
- I get a call telling me to come out and seal the vic's appartment until the leads show up. —Robert Crais, *L.A. Requiem*, p. 38, 1999

2 a sucker or an easy target for crime *US*

- I said, "Jack, your score is zero. I'm not a 'vic.' " —Iceberg Slim (Robert Beck), *Pimp*, p. 97, 1969

Vic *nickname*

Victoria, a southern state of Australia *AUSTRALIA, 1902*

- —Jim Ramsay, *Cop It Sweet!*, p. 94, 1977
- On my next visit to Vic I enquired. —Neilma Sidney, *Sunday evening*, p. 119, 1988

Vicar of Bray *noun*

1 a tray *UK*

Rhyming slang, formed from a C18 song.

- —Julian Franklyn, *A Dictionary of Rhyming Slang*, 1960

2 the number three; three *UK*

Rhyming slang for **TREY**.

- —Julian Franklyn, *A Dictionary of Rhyming Slang*, 1960

vice *noun*

a police vice squad *UK*

Usually used with 'the'.

- The main problem is the vice, but I've been lucky. —Roger Gordon, *Hollywood's Sexual Underground*, p. 100, 1966
- The vice is nice / they stay in the back all day[.] —Rickie Lee Jones, *Danny's All-Star Joint*, 1979
- The Vice will always bust a new girl, one that don't know what they look like. —William T. Vollman, *Whores for Gloria*, p. 149, 1991
- —Angela Devlin, *Prison Patter*, p. 120, 1996

vice president *noun*

in poker, the player with the second best hand *US*

- —George Percy, *The Language of Poker*, p. 95, 1988

vice versa *noun*

reciprocal oral sex between two lesbians *US*

The earliest known lesbian periodical in the US (1947) was named *Vice Versa*.

- —Donald Webster Cory and John P. LeRoy, *The Homosexual and His Society*, p. 266, 1963: 'A lexicon of homosexual slang'
- — *The Guild Dictionary of Homosexual Terms*, p. 48, 1965
- — *Maledicta*, p. 138, Summer/Winter 1982: 'Dyke diction: the language of lesbians'

vicey *adjective*

sinful; depraved *TRINIDAD AND TOBAGO, 1993*

- —Lise Winer, *Dictionary of the English/Creole of Trinidad & Tobago*, 2003

vicious *adjective*

handsome *US*

- —Lillian Glass with Richard Liebmann-Smith, *How to Deprogram Your Valley Girl*, p. 29, 1982

vick *verb*

to steal *US*

Probably an evolution from 'victim'.

- —Kenn "Naz" Young, *Naz's Dictionary of Teen Slang*, p. 135, 1993

vicky; vick *noun*

a two-fingered gesture that is used to insult or otherwise cause offense *UK: SCOTLAND*

Glasgow slang; the forefinger and the middle finger are extended to form a V shape, with the palm turned in towards the gesturer.

- We gied them the vicky[.] —Michael Munro, *The Original Patter*, p. 73, 1985
- I gave that maths teacher the vick this morning. —Chris Lewis, *The Dictionary of Playground Slang*, p. 247, 2003

Vicky *noun*

a Ford Victoria sedan, first built in the 1930s and then revived in the 1950s *US*

- —John Lawlor, *How to Talk Car*, p. 112, 1965

vicky-verky

vice-versa *UK, 1961*

Used as a song-title by Squeeze, 1981.

Victor Charlie *nickname*

the Viet Cong *US*

- — *Austin (Texas) Statesman*, p. 7A, 9th January 1966
- The Viet Cong is also known as the "VC" and many American servicemen use these initials to call the Viet Cong "Victor Charlie" or just plain "Charlie." — *San Francisco Examiner and Chronicle*, p. 17, 22nd May 1966
- —Carl Fleischhauer, *A Glossary of Army Slang*, p. 25, 1968
- What about those Victor Charlies: how many guerrillas did I kill[.] —Clarence Major, *All-Night Visitors*, p. 173, 1998

Victoria *noun*

used of a person otherwise described as *nouveau riche* *UK*

After singer and footballer's wife Victoria Beckham (b.1975); recorded as a contemporary gay usage.

- — *Attitude*, July 2003: 'New palare lexicon'

Victoria Cross; VC *noun*

something of little or no value *UK*

Rhyming slang for **TOSS**, formed from the highest military honour for valour.

- I don't give a VC. —Ray Puxley, *Cockney Rabbit*, 1992

Victoria Monk *noun*

semen *UK*

Rhyming slang for **SPUNK**, after the music hall singer, best remembered for 'Won't You Come Home, Bill Bailey?', Victoria Monks, 1884–1972.

- —Julian Franklyn, *A Dictionary of Rhyming Slang*, 1960

victoria vice *noun*
▷ **see:** VERA VICE

Victory V *noun*
1 urine; an act of urination *UK*
Rhyming slang for **PEE** or **WEE**, formed from the Churchillian gesture or Victory V branded medicinal-confectionery.
• — Ray Puxley, *Fresh Rabbit*, 1998
2 a Triumph car *UK*
Citizens' band radio slang; 'victory' as a synonym for 'triumph'.
• — Peter Chippindale, *The British CB Book*, p. 161, 1981

vid *noun*
1 a video cassette, a video recording *UK*
• Like your vids, by the way. Classy. — Guy Ritchie et al., *Lock, Stock... & Four Stolen Hooves*, p. 60, 2000
2 a music video *US*
• — Connie Eble (Editor), *UNC-CH Campus Slang*, p. 2, Fall 1985

video-nasty *noun*
an exceptionally unpleasant horror film, available on video *UK, 1982*
• I grew up on video nasties, cannibal movies and kung-fu flicks – I Spit on Your Grave and all that stuff. — *The Guardian*, 24th November 2003

vidrio *noun*
heroin *UK*
The Spanish for **GLASS** (heroin).
• — Mike Haskins, *Drugs*, p. 285, 2003

Viet *noun*
a Vietnamese person *US*
• The Viets don't like us. — William Wilson, *The LBJ Brigade*, p. 36, 1966
• I stood on the driver's seat, out of breath, but exhilarated, and stared back down the road at the Viets[.] — Larry Heinemann, *Close Quarters*, p. 82, 1977
• Every Viet in base camp crowded the doorways and screened windows, and such as that, gawking at Jonesy. — Larry Heinemann, *Paco's Story*, p. 8, 1986

Vietnam rose *noun*
any sexually transmitted infection *AUSTRALIA*
• Young man you have the dreaded venereal strain 'Vietnam Rose'. I will need to send you to Saigon for at least a month. — Martin Cameron, *A Look at the Bright Side*, 1988
• I am afraid you have picked up a nasty strain of non-specific genital infection called 'Vietnam Rose'. — Martin Cameron, *A Look at the Bright Side*, 1988

Viet shits *noun*
diarrhoea *US*
• — Linda Reinberg, *In the Field*, p. 232, 1991

vig *noun*
1 interest owed on an illegal loan *US*
A shortened form of **VIGORISH**.
• He wants three points over the vig. From me? — *Goodfellas*, 1990
• I know they lend money and take the vig out in snitch information, you know[.] — James Ellroy, *White Jazz*, p. 52, 1992
• Well, basically, this guy owes a shylock fifteen thousand, plus he's a few weeks behind on the vig, the interest you have to pay. — *Get Shorty*, 1995
2 profit *UK*
Freely adapted from **VIGORISH** (interest on a loan).
• [O]pen greeting card shops because it's a guaranteed three hundred per cent vig on greeting cards. — Kevin Sampson, *Outlaws*, p. 107, 2001

vigorish *noun*
the interest owed on an illegal loan *US, 1966*
Yiddish slang from the Russian *vyigrysh* (winnings-out-to-play).
• He wore Air corps sunglasses, combed his hair into a gelatinous country pomp and tithed his pay and tithed the vigorish on his sharking. — Earl Thompson, *Tattoo*, p. 293, 1974
• It costs a hundred a week vigorish to borrow the bone. — Robert Campbell, *Juice*, p. 20, 1988

vikes *noun*
the prescription drug Vicodin™ *US*
• "You give him the Vike," former defensive lineman John Jurkovic is quoted as saying in Return to Glory. — *Chicago Sun-Times*, p. 2 (Sports), 7th August 1996
• Deputies said the voice on the other end asked to buy some "viks." — *St. Petersburg (Florida) Times*, p. 9, 18th December 1998
• Hence, to score Vike, they have to be fronting that they are in some serious pain. — Suroosh Alvi et al., *The Vice Guide*, p. 109, 2002

Viking queen *noun*
in homosexual usage, a muscular, blonde man *US*
• — *Maledicta*, p. 60, 1986–1987: 'A continuation of a glossary of ethnic slurs in American English'

vill *noun*
a village or town *US*
Found in the poetry of the early C18, but not particularly thereafter until the war in Vietnam.
• Well, I got some [money], but not enough for the vill again. — Charles Anderson, *The Grunts*, p. 17, 1976

village *noun*
a notional community of racecourse bookmakers *UK*
• — John McCririck, *John McCririck's World of Betting*, p. 61, 1991

Village *noun*
▸ **the Village**
Greenwich Village, New York, a small neighbourhood below 14th Street and west of Broadway, haven to Bohemians *US*
• They had arranged to meet at nine that evening at Freeman's, which was a Village bar. — John Clellon Holmes, *Go*, p. 79, 1952

village *adjective*
unsophisticated, out of touch with trends *US*
• — *Woman's Weekly*, p. 53, 23rd July 2002

village bike *noun*
1 a promiscuous woman *NEW ZEALAND*
As with the **TOWN BIKE**, 'everyone has ridden her'.
• — Sonya Plowman, *Great Kiwi Slang*, p. 181, 2002
2 a lesbian *UK*
Rhyming slang for **DYKE**.
• — Bodmin Dark, *Dirty Cockney Rhyming Slang*, 2003

village pump *noun*
a girl who is free and easy sexually *CANADA*
• — Lewis Poteet, *Talking Country*, p. 75, 1992

village ram *noun*
a sexually aggressive male *TRINIDAD AND TOBAGO, 1964*
• — Lise Winer, *Dictionary of the English/Creole of Trinidad & Tobago*, 2003

villain *noun*
a professional criminal; someone with a criminal record *UK, 1945*
• — Angela Devlin, *Prison Patter*, p. 120, 1996

Ville *noun*
▸ **the Ville**
Penton*ville* prison, London *UK, 1903*
• [A]s the trick-cyclist [psychiatrist] at the Ville would have said[.] — Charles Raven, *Underworld Nights*, p. 41, 1956
• in the Ville — Frank Norman, *Bang To Rights*, p. 143, 1958
• [H]e nearly topped a screw [prison warder] up at the ville with a mailbag needle[.] — Derek Raymond (Robin Cook), *The Crust on its Uppers*, p. 41, 1962
• — Angela Devlin, *Prison Patter*, p. 120, 1996
• The tenant is up the Cally [Caledonian Road], in the Ville, doing six months for being a nuisance to society[.] — J.J. Connolly, *Layer Cake*, p. 174, 2000

'Ville *nickname*
▷ **see:** AMITYVILLE

-ville *suffix*
used for making or emphasising an adjective; used in combination with a characteristic to describe a place or a condition *US, 1891*
Modern usage began with the US beats and travelled back to the UK. By the mid-1970s the US form was presumed obsolete having been replaced by '-city'. It survives in the UK without obvious irony.
• "Weirdsville," said the baby bear. — Steve Allen, *Bop Fables*, p. 10, 1955
• "Dullsville," said Comfort, lying on her back and regarding her toes. — Max Shulman, *Rally Round the Flag, Boys!*, p. 57, 1957
• It's probably a lousy story and can't hold a candle to those French novels from Sexville[.] — Frederick Kohner, *Gidget*, p. 3, 1957
• — *American Speech*, p. 312–314, December 1960: 'The highly productive suffix '-ville''
• What do you say about yourself when your language is strictly from Teensville? — Dick Clark, *To Goof or Not to Goof*, p. 159, 1963
• Cor, man, this prep is dead cinchyville — *New Society*, 22nd August 1963
• "Pay no attention," he said. "[...] It's bad-patchville, that's all." — Dick Francis, *Nerve*, 1964

- "Welcome to Shitsville." "Cant be. We've just come from there." —Chris Ryan, *Stand By, Stand By*, p. 224, 1996
- Well a'right man, he says slappin' my ribs, to-tahly groovy babesville yeah. —Nick Barlay, *Curvy Lovebox*, p. 166, 1997
- [diary entry 11th March 1996] Lunch with the PM [John Major] at Number 10. We're back in shambles-ville. —Gyles Brandreth, *Breaking the Code*, p. 388, 1999
- Dave and myself paraded in the guardroom in our neatly pressed civvies and caught the duty vehicle to Excitementville[.] —Ken Lukowiak, *Marijuana Time*, p. 22, 2000
- [H]e'd sue the line for not making me obey their orders, et yawnville cetera. —Jonathan Gash, *The Ten Word Game*, p. 226, 2003

Vincent *nickname*

the Viet Cong; a member of the Viet Cong *US*

- — *Life*, p. 71, 26th November 1965
- —Carl Fleischhauer, *A Glossary of Army Slang*, p. 25, 1968

Vincent Price; vincent *noun*

ice *UK*

Rhyming slang, formed from the US actor, 1911–93, particularly famed for his roles in horror films.

- —Ray Puxley, *Cockney Rabbit*, 1992

Vincent Van Gogh; vincent *noun*

a cough *UK*

Rhyming slang, based on the predominant UK pronunciation of impressionist artist Vincent Van Gogh (1853–90).

- That's a nasty Vincent you've got there. —*www.LondonSlang.com*, June 2002

vine *noun*

1 a men's suit; clothing *US, 1932*

- I wanted to see Daisy so bad – as bad as she wanted to see me – that I decided one afternoon to put on my sharpest vine. —Louis Armstrong, *Satchmo*, p. 152, 1954
- I'd walk up the stairs at number 129 cool, oh so cool, wearing my best vines. —Piri Thomas, *Down These Mean Streets*, p. 324, 1967
- As part of my job, I had to stay sharp, so I got seven vines (suits) right away. —Babs Gonzales, *I Paid My Dues*, p. 35, 1967
- On a Saturday night I decked myself out in one of the vines and topcoat I had bought the day before Dalanski busted me. —Iceberg Slim (Robert Beck), *Pimp*, p. 78, 1969
- It was the one who had a Thunderbird, and some clean vines. —H. Rap Brown, *Die Nigger Die!*, p. 9, 1969
- There were vines, sport coats, slacks, and ladies coats and dresses. —A.S. Jackson, *Gentleman Pimp*, p. 24, 1973
- He was always pressed; nothing but the best / Vines and kicks he had. —Dennis Wepman et al., *The Life*, p. 97, 1976
- Safari shirt and pants, tan colored, I'm pressed, but not like them vines Cye Martin used to drape on me. —Edwin Torres, *After Hours*, p. 272, 1979

2 the penis *US*

- After that, Maria never bothered me again, she just told everyone at JJ's about my dead vine. —Oscar Zeta Acosta, *The Autobiography of a Brown Buffalo*, p. 46, 1972

vine down *verb*

to dress up *US*

- He'd drop by the school and be vined down. He was clean, Jim. Had him a conk then and he knew he was ready. —H. Rap Brown, *Die Nigger Die!*, p. 24, 1969

vinegar stroke; vinegar *noun*

the final penile thrust culminating in ejaculation when copulating or masturbating *AUSTRALIA*

Alluding to the facial expression of the male. Also, in the plural, 'the final thrusts preceding ejaculation'. UK comedian Phil Jupitus, who uses this term to describe the closing moments of his act, explains: 'Just before a bloke comes he looks like you've popped a teaspoon of vinegar into his mouth'.

- I mean, when approaching the final big vinegar stroke of a good pull, who'd give a stuff if they went blind and deaf? —Geoff Mill, *Nobody Dies But Me*, p. 2, 1961
- I was in bed with the wife of a friend of mine, when all of a sudden, just on the vinegar stroke, I heard her husband's car come up the drive. —David Ireland, *The Unknown Political Prisoner*, p. 84, 1972
- I'll never forget when I once gave one to a randy little stewardess. I was thirty thousand feet and eight inches up at the time and I was just getting into the vinegar strokes, when someone started hammering on the door. —Barry Humphries, *The Traveller's Tool*, p. 117, 1985
- "I could reach me vinegar with Abby," leered Joey. —Gary Bushell, *The Face*, p. 29, 2001
- The final split-second before orgasm during sex or, more likely, masturbation. —Dennis Leckey, *Private Correspondence*, 8th April 2002
- Approaching his vinegar stroke, he was accessing his mental wank-bank for a suitable image to produce a satisfactory climax[.] —Colin Butts, *Is Harry Still on the Boat?*, p. 6, 2003

viney bones *noun*

rubber bands *UK*

Used by motorcyclists. Douglas Dunford, of the Beaulieu Motor Museum, gives the following etymology: 'Originated with the famous [motorcycle] trials rider Hugh Viney of the '30s who used to cut up old inner-tubes and supply his mates with bands to fix their riding numbers.'

Vinnies; St Vinnies *nickname*

a St Vincent de Paul charity store *AUSTRALIA*

- Got them from Vinnie's for forty cents each. —Suzy Jarratt, *Permissive Australia*, p. 12, 1970
- —John Birmingham, *He Died With a Felafel in his Hand*, p. 73, 1994
- They made all their own clothes, with a few additions from St Vinnie's, to achieve their original look. —*Dolly*, p. 36, 1996

vino *noun*

1 wine, especially cheap wine *AUSTRALIA, 1919*

From Spanish and Italian *vino* (wine).

- [O]ne drop of vino and I'm for anything. —Jack Kerouac, *Letter to Allen Ginsberg*, p. 499, 14th July 1955
- Who went to cop the vino? —Odie Hawkins, *Ghetto Sketches*, p. 80, 1972
- [G]ive the impression you're hitting the old vino. —Chris Ryan, *The Watchman*, p. 227, 2001

2 a drinker of doctored cheap wine *UK*

- One, small and aged, sagging at the knees, was a vino[.] —Geoffrey Fletcher, *Down Among the Meths Men*, p. 16, 1966

vinyl *noun*

used generically for musical recordings produced on such material *UK, 1976*

- [B]uying vinyl at trendy record stores[.] —Wayne Anthony, *Spanish Highs*, p. 160, 1999
- Sasha starts sorting his vinyl again[.] —Dave Haslam, *Adventures of the Wheels of Steel*, p. xix, 2001

violet *noun*

▸ **come up smelling of violets**

to emerge unscathed from a difficult or troublesome situation, used especially of someone who is consistently and remarkably lucky *UK, 1981*

Probably somewhat dated by the time it was recorded. The form survives as 'come up smelling of roses'.

- [I]f (e.g. he) were to fall in the cess-pit (shit, etc), he only come up smelling of violets. — Beale, 1984

violin cases *noun*

large, heavy shoes *US*

- When you stood up and put your weight on those violin cases you thought you were standing barefoot over the iron grating of a subway ventilator. —Mezz Mezzrow, *Really the Blues*, p. 33, 1946

vip; veep *noun*

a *V*ery *I*mportant *P*erson *US, 1945*

- They brought me back by air – I certainly got the veep treatment. —Derek Raymond (Robin Cook), *The Crust on its Uppers*, p. 187, 1962
- He's the boss / He's the Vip, / He's the championship. — *Top Cat*, broadcast on the BBC as *Boss Cat*, 1962–63

viper *noun*

1 a marijuana dealer *US*

- She has gone [to] the viper getts [sic] the weed and packs it solid into the Durex[.] —Frank Norman, *Bang To Rights*, p. 143, 1958
- Hustling, vipers and pocketbook swipers / All aiming at their goal. —Dennis Wepman et al., *The Life*, p. 162, 1976

2 a marijuana user *US, 1938*

A term of the 1930s with some lingering use until the 1960s.

- He was a musician from the heart, a solid viper. I hope he finally caught that Muggles Special and rode it straight on to glory, high as a Georgia pine[.] —Mezz Mezzrow, *Really the Blues*, p. 52–53, 1946
- But she knew how easily she could relinquish that sense of responsibility with which she had this time gone to Carter, how simply she could become a Viper again and laugh at the meaning of days. —George Mandel, *Flee the Angry Strangers*, p. 27, 1952
- Light a tea and let it be if you're a viper. —Iceberg Slim (Robert Beck), *Pimp*, p. 129, 1969

viper's weed; viper's drag *noun*

marijuana; a marijuana cigarette *US, 1938*

- —Richard A. Spears, *The Slang and Jargon of Drugs and Drink*, p. 535, 1986
- —Mike Haskins, *Drugs*, p. 289, 2003

VIP massage *noun*
a sexual service offered in some massage parlours, in which a hand-massage includes masturbation of the client *UK*
• —Caroline Archer, *Tart Cards*, 2003

VIP services *noun*
sexual intercourse, as distinct from masturbation, when advertised as a service offered by a prostitute *UK*
• —Caroline Archer, *Tart Cards*, 2003

viral-marketing *noun*
word-of-mouth as a deliberate marketing tactic *US*
• How do you spread a consumer epidemic? If you're a multinational company, you put your faith in 'viral marketing'. It's what we used to call word of mouth. So, pass it on[.]— *The Observer*, 26th November 2000

virgin *noun*
1 a person who has not contracted a sexually transmitted infection *US*
• — *American Speech*, p. 56, February 1947: 'Pacific War language'
2 a letter which has not been postmarked *US*
• —Ramon Adams, *The Language of the Railroader*, p. 167, 1977

virgin *adjective*
used of a green on a par-3 hole, untouched by any ball of a foursome *US*
• —Hubert Pedroli and Mary Tiegreen, *Let the Big Dog Eat!*, p. 90, 2000

virgin bride; virgin *noun*
a ride, especially in the sense an act of sexual intercourse *AUSTRALIA, 1902*
Rhyming slang, now rare.
• "I had a virgin last night" usually meant someone had paid to get their back wheels in. —Ray Puxley, *Fresh Rabbit*, 1998

virgin ears *noun*
used, usually in the first person, for a claim of innocence in matters sexual *US*
• — *Current Slang*, p. 26, Spring 1970

Virgin for short – but not for long
applied to girls named Virginia *UK, 1984*
Part-catchphrase, part-nickname; often irresistible, always hilarious.

virginia *noun*
the vagina *BAHAMAS*
• —John A. Holm, *Dictionary of Bahamian English*, p. 215, 1982

Virginia vitamin *noun*
any central nervous system stimulant *US*
• —Bill Davis, *Jawjacking*, p. 103, 1977

virginity curtain *noun*
a canvas screen secured to the underside of a warship's accommodation to preserve the modesty of those who go up and down the gangway from those who look up *UK*
Similar in purpose and design to a **CUNT SCREEN**.
• —John Laffin, *Jack Tar*, 1969

Virgin Mary *noun*
a non-alcoholic version of the Bloody Mary, made with tomato juice, horseradish, Worcestershire and/or Tabasco sauce, celery, salt and black pepper; unadulterated tomato juice *US*
A tasty pun, using 'virgin' as 'non-alcoholic'.
• She had passed the time drinking Virgin Marys and surveying the dance talent[.]—Carl Hiaasen, *Strip Tease*, p. 258, 1993

virgin pie *noun*
cherry pie *US*
• — *American Speech*, p. 233, October 1952: 'The argot of soda jerks'

virgin principle *noun*
the belief among gamblers that a beginner will have good luck *US*
• —Frank Scoblete, *Guerrilla Gambling*, p. 331, 1993

virgin state *noun*
the period when a person has started using an addictive drug but is not yet fully addicted *US*
• —William D. Alsever, *Glossary for the Establishment and Other Uptight People*, p. 15, December 1970

virtual Friday *noun*
the last day in a working week shortened by a holiday at the end of the week *US*
• —Eric S. Raymond, *The New Hacker's Dictionary*, p. 370, 1991

virus *noun*
1 HIV, the human immunodeficiency virus *US*
• The Virus wasn't a disease, it was a personal message from God or the Devil. —Richard Price, *Clockers*, p. 64, 1992
2 in computing, a program that duplicates itself maliciously when it finds a host, often with a mechanism that enables it then to spread to new hosts *US*
• —Karla Jennings, *The Devouring Fungus*, p. 225, 1990

visit *verb*
▸ **to visit Aunt Lillian**
to experience the bleed period of the menstrual cycle *US*
• —Collin Baker et al., *College Undergraduate Slang Study Conducted at Brown University*, p. 73, 1968

visitations *noun*
▸ **the visitations**
the bleed period of the menstrual cycle *US*
• —Karen Houppert, *The Curse*, 1999

visit from the cardinal *noun*
the bleed period of the menstrual cycle *US*
Playing on the colour of a cardinal's robes.
• — *The Museum of Menstruation and Women's Health*, November 2000

visit from the French lady *noun*
the bleed period of the menstrual cycle *US*
Euphemism, credited to Stella Tilyard, *Aristocrats*, 1994.
• — *The Museum of Menstruation and Women's Health*, November 2000

visiting card *noun*
an act of defecation at the scene of the crime by the criminal *US*
• Murderers often defecate at the scene of the crime (detectives call it "the visiting card") and in some cases have been caught by chemical analysis of the feces. — *Time*, p. 90, 23rd April 1945

visitor *noun*
the bleed period of the menstrual cycle *US*
• —Vincent J. Monteleone, *Criminal Slang*, p. 13, 1949

visuals *noun*
hallucinations experienced under the influence of psychoactive mushrooms or peyote *US*
• —Connie Eble (Editor), *UNC-CH Campus Slang*, p. 9, Spring 1992
• Trippers use the word "visuals" to refer to the visual impressions and images that acid can generate. —Cam Cloud, *The Little Book of Acid*, p. 10, 1999

vitamin A *noun*
LSD *US*
From the common term **ACID**.
• —Anna Scotti and Paul Young, *Buzzwords*, p. 143, 1997

vitamin B *noun*
beer *US*
• —Judi Sanders, *Cal Poly Slang*, p. 11, 1990

Vitamin C *noun*
cocaine *US*
• —R.C. Garrett et al., *The Coke Book*, p. 200, 1984

vitamin D *noun*
dextromethorphan (DXM), an active ingredient in non-prescription cold and cough medication, often abused for non-medicinal purposes *US*
• Youths' nicknames for DXM: Robo, Skittles, Triple C's, Rojo, Dex, Tussin, Vitamin D. DXM abuse is called "Robotripping" or "Tussing." Users might be called "syrup heads" or "robotards." — *USA Today*, p. 1A, 29th December 2003

vitamin DB *noun*
Dominion Breweries draught bitter *NEW ZEALAND*
• —David McGill, *David McGill's Complete Kiwi Slang Dictionary*, p. 133, 1998

vitamin E *noun*
MDMA, the recreational drug best known as ecstasy *UK, 1998*
An elaboration of **E**.
- — Mike Haskins, *Drugs*, p. 290, 2003

vitamin H *noun*
haloperidol, a potent tranquillizer *US*
- — *Maledicta*, p. 35, 1988 – 1989: 'Medical maledicta from San Francisco'
- — Adam T. Fox, St Mary's Hospital, London, 10th October 2002

vitamin K; vit K *noun*
ketamine hydrochloride, an anaesthetic used as a hallucinogen *US*
- Experts describe ketamine, which is also called 'Vitamin K', as a cult drug consumed mainly in the Western states. — *New York Times*, p. C1, 24th October 1989
- The drug became known as "Vitamin K" when it emerged in underground gay clubs in the 1980s. — *The Record [Bergen County, New Jersey]*, p. A1, 5th December 1995

vitamin M *noun*
Motrin™ *US*
- — Sally Williams, *"Strong" Words*, p. 165, 1994

vitamin N *noun*
nicotine; a cigarette *US*
- — Ben Applebaum and Derrick Pittman, *Turd Ferguson & The Sausage Party*, p. 72, 2004

vitamin P *noun*
1 sex *US*
'P' is for **PUSSY**.
- — *Maledicta*, p. 35, 1988 – 1989: 'Medical maledicta from San Francisco'

2 the game of poker *US*
- — John Vorhaus, *The Big Book of Poker Slang*, p. 39, 1996

vitamin Q *noun*
the recreational drug methaqualone, best known as Quaalude™ *US*
- Vitamin Q indeed. They were Quaaludes, what the young people called "downers." — Armistead Maupin, *Further Tales of the City*, p. 59, 1982

vitamins *noun*
1 drugs in tablet or capsule form *UK*
- — Angela Devlin, *Prison Patter*, p. 120, 1996

2 any central nervous system stimulant *US*
- — Bill Davis, *Jawjacking*, p. 43, 1977

vitamin T *noun*
marijuana *US*
- — Anna Scotti and Paul Young, *Buzzwords*, p. 143, 1997

Vitamin V *noun*
valium *US*
- — Sally Williams, *"Strong" Words*, p. 165, 1994

vittles *noun*
food *US*
An American corruption of the C14 'victual'.
- They picked up on some vittles once today and then again the day after tomorrow. — Mezz Mezzrow, *Really the Blues*, p. 177, 1946

vizzo *noun*
in prison, a visit *UK*
- — Angela Devlin, *Prison Patter*, p. 120, 1996

VJ; veejay *noun*
a video jockey, a television presenter of music videos; a visual artist who mixes lights and images in a club environment *US*
Initialism, on the model of DJ.
- Every three or four songs, a VJ – for video jockey – pops on the screen with a bit of news or banter, and then the songs resume. — *Washington Post*, p. E1, 16th September 1982
- The on-line jockey hosts discussions on the Internet. Just like the video jockey (VJ) and the disc jockey (DJ) before. — David Rowan, *A Glossary for the 90s*, p. 123, 1998
- VJing It's like DJing but with lights and stuff, innit? — *Ministry*, p. 22, October 2002

VO *noun*
a beautiful woman *US*
An abbreviation of '*v*isual *o*rgasm'.
- Hey, bud, check out the major babage. V.O. to the max! — Editors of Ben is Dead, *Retrohell*, p. 239, 1997

voce; votch; voche *noun*
the voice, especially a singing voice; a singer *UK*
Theatrical, polari; from Italian *voce*.
- [T]onight's concert with those camp munchkins [children], all ogles and pots [teeth] and nante voce [voice]. — the cast of 'Aspects of Love', Prince of Wales Theatre, *Palare (Boy Dancer Talk) for Beginners*, 1989 – 92
- — Paul Baker, *Polari*, p. 194, 2002

vod *noun*
vodka *US*
- [S]o, in the (false) security of her panty girdle, and slightly whacko on vod, she might just relax her defenses[.] — Terry Southern, *Now Dig This*, p. 3, 1986

vodders *noun*
vodka *UK*
- The fuckin works, boy; half a bottle of vodders an a few pipes before I even dragged me arse out of the bed[.] — Niall Griffiths, *Kelly + Victor*, p. 112, 2002

voddie; voddy *noun*
vodka *UK*
- Standing there with a half bottle of voddie keeking out the handbag! — Ian Pattison, *Rab C. Nesbitt*, 1988
- Champers mixed with voddy, often flavoured[.] — *Sky Magazine*, p. 88, May 2001

vodka acid *noun*
LSD *UK*
- — Mike Haskins, *Drugs*, p. 286, 2003

vogue *noun*
1 a posture that implies, or is part of, a fashion-style *US*
- Shoulders sloped and arms wrapped around his chest, it's a kind of gangsta vogue. — Patrick Neate, *Where You're At*, p. 58, 2003

2 a cigarette *UK*
Polari.
- She has a permanent vogue in her screech [mouth] and her droje [clothing] is mega ribena on toast [awful], daughter. — the cast of 'Aspects of Love', Prince of Wales Theatre, *Palare (Boy Dancer Talk) for Beginners*, 1989 – 92
- [T]he omi-palone [gay man] with a vogue on and the cod [bad] sheitel [wig]. — James Gardiner, *Who's a Pretty Boy Then?*, p. 123, 1997

3 a wheel rim *US*
- — Don R. McCreary (Editor), *Dawg Speak*, 2001

vogue *verb*
1 to engage in a style competition that values posturing *US*
- Voguing entered the public consciousness in 1990 when Madonna's dance track, "Vogue" climbed the charts. — Steven Daly and Nathaniel Wice, *alt.culture*, p. 266, 1995

2 to light a cigarette *UK*
From **VOGUE** (a cigarette).
- A: Vogue us up ducky. Your mother's a stretcher case. B: That's because mother takes her gin on a dripfeed. — *A Storm in a Teacup*, 1993

voice *verb*
to telephone *US*
- — Eric S. Raymond, *The New Hacker's Dictionary*, p. 372, 1991

vol *noun*
in prison, a *vol*unteer *UK*
- — Angela Devlin, *Prison Patter*, p. 121, 1996

volcano *noun*
the bleed period of the menstrual cycle *CANADA*
- Mine is quiet heavy and explosive so I have affectionately nicknamed it "volcano," as at time is feels like I have molten lava between my legs! — *The Museum of Menstruation and Women's Health*, March 2001

Volks *noun*
a *Volks*wagen car *US*
- I said, "Abe, there's a blue Volks parked right outside my room with what appears to be an unpaid guest in it." — Robert Gover, *Here Goes Kitten*, p. 123, 1964

Volksie *noun*
a Volkswagen car, especially the 'Beetle' *SOUTH AFRICA, 1962*
- — Jean Branford, *A Dictionary of South African English*, 1978
- Given that the motorcar was invented by Gottleib Daimler and Karl Benz, perhaps Adams' wish for a Volksie in a bottle is not that far away. — *Sunday Times (South Africa)*, 19th October 2003

volley *noun*
an abusive verbal attack *UK*
- — Angela Devlin, *Prison Patter*, p. 121, 1996

volley *verb*

to hit someone *UK*

Tennis jargon, 'volley' (to strike a ball before it bounces) adopted for a less sporting use.

- I volley him clean in the mooey [mouth]. — Martin King and Martin Knight, *The Naughty Nineties*, p. 133, 1999

volley dolly *noun*

a woman attracted to male volleyball players *US*

- It was then that a beach volleyball star aboard the ferry – a guy much bigger and fifteen years younger than Winnie – decided to impress a volley dolly cuddled next to him in his mom's Mercedes. — Joseph Wambaugh, *The Golden Orange*, p. 5–6, 1990

volley off *verb*

to engage in an abusive verbal attack *UK*

- — Dave Courtney, *Dodgy Dave's Little Black Book*, p. 7, 2001

vom *verb*

to vomit *CANADA*

- — Jack Chambers (Editor), *Slang Bag 93 (University of Toronto)*, p. 6, Winter 1993

vomatose *adjective*

extremely disgusting *US*

- — Connie Eble (Editor), *UNC-CH Campus Slang*, p. 5, November 1983

vomit comet *noun*

1 any late-night public transport used by drunken passengers *UK*

From the probable outcome of movement and alcohol.

- I rolled home on the last train, or the vomit comet as I like to call it, and spent most of Thursday with a stinking hangover. — *The Guardian*, 10th January 2003

2 the modified KC-135A reduced-gravity aircraft *US*

The aircraft flies parabolas in order to investigate the effects of zero gravity; passengers are often sick to their stomachs.

- Teams of engineering mechanics students are back from a wild ride on a modified KC-135A reduced-gravity aircraft nicknamed the "Vomit Comet." — *University of Wisconsin-Madison College of Engineering Perspective*, Fall 1999
- Weightlessness can be a gruelling experience, especially for students experiencing it for the first time. And the plane is not called the "Vomit Comet" for nothing. — *BBC News*, 25th May 2000

vomiting viper *noun*

the penis *UK, 1984*

vonce *noun*

1 marijuana *US*

- — Robert George Reisner, *The Jazz Titans*, p. 167, 1960

2 the butt of a marijuana cigarette *US, 1965*

- — Ernest L. Abel, *A Marijuana Dictionary*, p. 107, 1982

vonka *noun*

the nose *UK*

- — Paul Baker, *Polari*, p. 194, 2002

Von Trapp *noun*

excrement; nonsense, rubbish *UK*

Rhyming slang for **CRAP**, formed from the family whose story is told in *The Sound of Music*.

- — Bodmin Dark, *Dirty Cockney Rhyming Slang*, 2003

votch *noun*

▷ see: **VOCE**

vote *verb*

to propose something that you want *UK, 1814*

- "This whole thing is giving me the runs," Lula said. "I vote we pretend this never happened, and we get our butts out of here." — Janet Evanovitch, *Three to Get Deadly*, 1997

voyou *noun*

in Quebec, a hoodlum, or more specifically a striker who commits vandalism against the company *CANADA*

The French word here used in English carries the sense of 'outside the law'.

- I am a voyou and I am proud to be one, said Gilles Dube, president of the eastern section of the striking union. — *Montreal Gazette*, p. A4, 9th July 2002

VP *noun*

a sex offender *UK*

An initialism of 'vulnerable prisoner'.

- — Angela Devlin, *Prison Patter*, p. 23, 1996

VPL

a *v*isible *p*anty *l*ine, the most heinous of fashion crimes *US*

Popularised by Paul Simon in Woody Allen's *Annie Hall*.

- They all wore white dresses, that was the prescribed legal uniform, but they wore them so short and tight, that it was almost obscene (So tight that the panty lines could always be seen, and the helicopter pilots, who were insane for military abbreviations, had invented the phrase VPL, for Visible Panty Line). — David Halberstam, *One Very Hot Day*, p. 109, 1967
- — Connie Eble (Editor), *UNC-CH Campus Slang*, p. 9, Spring 1982
- Low ridin', hip huggin' panties might look best for the straightforward V.P.L. statement, but why not try panties with ruffles over the bum[?] — Nina Blake, *Retrohell*, p. 239, 1997

VRB *noun*

vodka and *R*ed *B*ull™

Initialism for a popular cocktail (Red Bull is a brand name 'energy' drink).

- In the modern bar-room lexicon "We were drinking VRBs," absolves all culpability of action. — *GQ*, p. 66, July 2001

vroom *verb*

to leave noisily *US*

- She left me standing there with my mouth dropped open, and the blue Mustang vroomed off. — S.E. Hinton, *The Outsiders*, p. 42, 1967

vrot *adjective*

rotten; hence, drunk *SOUTH AFRICA, 1910*

From Afrikaans.

- [S]ome [rugby] spectators get so vrot-drunk that they end up attacking the players. — *Sunday Times (South Africa)*, 30th July 2000
- Are we so vrot with prejudice that we can't find a place in our hearts to at least give Baxter a chance? — *Sunday Times (South Africa)*, 28th March 2004

VS *noun*

an injection of drugs into a vein *US, 1938*

Initialism of a '*v*ein **SHOT**'.

- "What do you usually have?" he inquired over his shoulder. "A V.S. or an S.S [skin shot]." — Douglas Rutherford, *The Creeping Flesh*, p. 104, 1963

V-sign

a gesture that is used to insult or otherwise cause offence, especially when made in conjunction with threatening or abusive language, e.g. 'fuck off!' or 'up yours!' with which the sign may be considered synonymous *UK*

The forefinger and the middle finger are extended to form a V shape, the palm turned in towards the gesturer; as an obscene gesture it is confined almost entirely to the UK. There is a legend that French archers, when captured by the British at the Battle of Agincourt (1415), had their middle and forefingers – those necessary to draw the bowstring – chopped off. The Welsh bowmen are said to have waggled their two fingers, taunting the French. The earliest written description of a v-sign as both threat and insult is French: '[Pangurge] stretched out the forefinger, and middle finger or medical of his right hand, holding them asunder as much as he could, and thrusting them towards Thaumast' (François Rabelais, 1532). Further derivations abound: 1) Farmer and Henley's *Slang and its Analogues* (1890) suggests a representation of cuckold's horns, however this is traditionally made with the first and fourth fingers. 2) Symbolic of the phallus; the raised middle finger (**FLIP THE BIRD**) has been known since Roman times and, it is suggested, the v-sign enlarges the penis or doubles the quotient; or disguises the single finger insult. 3) The fingers represent themselves inserted in the vagina – though why this should be insulting is not explained. 4) Symbolic of female legs or labia spread wide; or represents the triangular shape of female pubic hair. 5) A corrupted victory sign – however the Churchillian symbol is first recorded in 1941, contrived by a Belgian Lawyer named Victor De Lavelaye. Probably more than one of the above, except 5, is the truth.

- At a Kerrang! party [Brian] Molko V-signed me. I didn't really know he was but shook on it afterwards. The V-sign was nothing[.] — John Robb, *The Nineties*, p. 340, 1999

V spot *noun*

a five-dollar note *US*

- — Vincent J. Monteleone, *Criminal Slang*, p. 248, 1949

Vulcan nerve pinch *noun*

when operating a computer, the keyed-combination of the characters Ctrl-Alt-Delete used to restart the machine *US*

A figurative application of a fictional technique used in the television science fiction series, *Star Trek*.

- Also known as the "three-fingered salute" and the "Vulcan nerve pinch," this classic key combo has bailed out untold millions of users. — *Word Spy*, 12th February 2004

vulture *noun*

in trucking, a police plane used for spotting speeders *US*

- — Montie Tak, *Truck Talk*, p. 183, 1971

VW *noun*

a variety of MDMA, the recreational drug best known as ecstasy, identified by VW embossed on the tablet *UK*

- VW – Yellow or grey with Volkswagen logo. — Gareth Thomas, *This Is Ecstasy*, p. 57, 2002

Ww

W *noun*

a toilet *NEW ZEALAND, 1916*

An abbreviation of the common WC.

• —Harry Orsman, *A Dictionary of Modern New Zealand Slang*, p. 146, 1999

W *noun*

1 a police *w*arrant for search or arrest *UK*

• Peter hadn't been back in his flat in Kilburn more than two hours before the Law were round with a W. turning the place over. —Charles Raven, *Underworld Nights*, p. 149, 1956

• —Angela Devlin, *Prison Patter*, p. 121, 1996

2 in sports, a win *US*

• [W]e won 10–9 and I ended up with my first big W. —Jim Bouton, *Ball Four*, p. 155, 1970

wac; wack *noun*

1 phencyclidine, the recreational drug known as PCP or angel dust *US*

• —Ronald Linder, *PCP*, 1981

• —US Department of Justice, *Street Terms*, October 1994

2 marijuana mixed with phencyclidine, the recreational drug known as PCP or angel dust *UK, 1998*

• —Mike Haskins, *Drugs*, p. 293, 2003

wack *adjective*

inferior, unacceptable, very bad *US*

• The opposite of fresh. Bad, not bad. Everything bad is wack. —Bradley Elfman, *Breakdancing*, p. 41, 1984

• I am so over that wack stage of the life. —Francesca Lia Block, *I Was a Teenage Fairy*, p. 72, 1998

• They'll tell you right off you're a biter [copyist] and you're wack. —Alex Ogg, *The Hip Hop Years [quoting Jorge 'Fabel' Pabn]*, p. 32–33, 1999

• Go run and tell your friends my shit is wack / I just don't give a fuuuuuck! —Eminem (Marshall Mathers), *Just Don't Give a Fuck*, 1999

wacked *adjective*

1 excited *US, 1959*

• —Tom Hibbert, *Rockspeak!*, p. 168, 1983

2 beyond repair *UK*

Extends **WACK** (inferior).

• Look at the pair of you. Your garms [clothes] are wacked. You're a dog's dinner. —Nick Barlay, *Curvy Lovebox*, p. 60, 1997

wacked out *adjective*

crazy, eccentric, mad *US*

• —Collin Baker et al., *College Undergraduate Slang Study Conducted at Brown University*, p. 218, 1968

• In a blaze of publicity they illuminated the secret route: collecting wacked-out art. —Tom Wolfe, *The Pump House Gang*, p. 144, 1968

• That Foreman camp was totally whacked out, so uptight compared with Ali, who runs a loose-goose operation. —Bill Cardoso, *The Maltese Sangweech*, p. 299, 1984

• —Connie Eble (Editor), *UNC-CH Campus Slang*, p. 8, Spring 1994

• Michael Jackson. He's quirky, he's wacked out[.] —Howard Stern, *Miss America*, p. 61, 1995

wacked up *adjective*

crazy, odd, irrational *US*

• So the cops've been asking us all sorts of whacked-up questions about what we did on the day our teacher got plugged and everything. —Irving Shulman, *The Amboy Dukes*, p. 119, 1947

wackelass *noun*

a cat that is a troublesome, clumsy creature *CANADA*

• That cat is a regular wackelass. It wiggles around underfoot a lot. – Lunenburg. From the German "wackeln," to reel, totter, and "aas," carcass. —Lewis Poteet, *oral citation from The South Shore Phrase Book*, p. 122, 1999

wacker; wack; whacker *noun*

used as a term of address to a man *UK, 1768*

Liverpudlian.

• [C]ries of "Hey, Whacker!" (a local expression) greeted Tommy Handley on all sides. —Francis Worsley, *ITMA*, 1948

• —Fritz Spiegl, *Lern Yerself Scouse*, 1966

• George had no wish to be portrayed as the definitive wacker (or, indeed, the definitive anything)[.] —Alan Clayson, *George Harrison*, p. 164, 2001

wacker *adjective*

worse *US*

From **WACK** (bad).

• You wacker than the motherfucker you bit [copied] your style from. —Eminem (Marshall Mathers), *Just Don't Give a Fuck*, 1999

wackie; wacky *noun*

a stereotypical member of the working-class; a conformist *UK*

Teen slang, noted, in the first sense ('wears flat hat, muffler, carries lunchbox') by James Williamson, 1982.

wack job; whack job *noun*

a person who is mentally ill *US*

• The real whack jobs would get mad if you said they was crazy. —Edwin Torres, *After Hours*, p. 360, 1979

• I've got to get through to this wack job to get him on live television. —Howard Stern, *Miss America*, p. 73, 1995

wacko; whacko *adjective*

a person who is crazy, eccentric or mentally imbalanced *US, 1977*

• You're a definite wacko. You're fuckin' crazy, you know that, crazy. —*Raging Bull*, 1980

• Raven can deal with wackos in the audience, humor them perfectly. —Josh Alan Friedman, *Tales of Times Square*, p. 25, 1986

• [S]o, in the (false) security of her panty girdle, and slightly whacko on vod, she might just relax her defenses[.] —Terry Southern, *Now Dig This*, p. 3, 1986

• And now I had a partner, a full-bore whacko who was definitely prepared to rumble. —Hunter S. Thompson, *Songs of the Doomed*, p. 264, 1989

• I'm talking to a possible whacko here. —*Basic Instinct*, 1992

• DeChooch is whacko. He shoots at people. —Janet Evanovich, *Seven Up*, p. 171, 2001

wackoid *adjective*

odd, eccentric *UK, 1990s*

• With a sample of the wackoid voice of a cat called Charley[.] —John Robb, *The Nineties*, p. 219, 1999

wacktic *adjective*

very bad *UK*

• —Tom Hibbert, *Rockspeak!*, p. 168, 1983

wacky *adjective*

odd, eccentric, crazy *US, 1935*

• I'll go on seeing her occasionally, for we are both wacky in a way, and we should never have gotten married[.] —Jack Kerouac, *Letter to Carolina Kerouac Blake*, p. 88, 14th March 1945

• The only times Benny saw him were at school, and then he'd leave with some sort of whacky excuse about looking for an apartment for his family in East Flatbrush. —Irving Shulman, *The Amboy Dukes*, p. 160, 1947

• The average Village night club of the whacky early days never had more than one toilet. —Robert Sylvester, *No Cover Charge*, p. 249, 1956

• She had a nervous breakdown and was acting so wacky she got run over by a bus. —*American Graffiti*, 1973

• Michael Jackson [...] doing wacky stuff like living in a hyperbolic chamber. —Howard Stern, *Miss America*, p. 61, 1995

• A "wacky" builder, Brian Walker, is to walk from Land's End to John o'Groats carrying a three-stone pine door – for charidee, natch. —*The Guardian*, p. 5, 28th May 2003

wacky baccy; wacky backy *noun*

marijuana *US, 1975*

From **WACKY** as 'eccentric'. Many variants exist, including 'whacky baccy/backy', 'whackatabachy', 'wacky tobaccy/tobacky' and 'whacky weed'.

• Over the past few years in New York, the magic moniker has been successively, Chiba-Chiba, wacky, red, red wacky, gold and Santa Marta. —*Hi Life*, p. 15, 1979

- Holding in that "wacky tobaccy" was certainly more pleasant than cigarettes[.] —Sean Hutchinson, *Crying Out Loud*, p. 25, 1988
- —Angela Devlin, *Prison Patter*, p. 123, 1996
- The drugs I've heard of are dope, speed, wacky, coke. —Macfarlane, Macfarlane and Robson, *The User*, p. 23, 1996
- I don't want any of your bloody wacky baccy inside this place, is that clear? —Paul Fraser and Shane Meadows, *TwentyFourSeven*, p. 42, 1997
- It's a tuppenny 'a'penny gaff [...] full of twelve year olds smokin' waccy baccy. —Bernard Dempsey and Kevin McNally, *Lock, Stock ... & Two Hundred Smoking Kalashnikovs*, p. 104, 2000
- I suspect the windfall will all have gone up in wacky tabacky smoke[.] —Janet Evanovich, *Seven Up*, p. 48, 2001
- —Mike Haskins, *Drugs*, p. 289, 2003

wacky for khaki *adjective*

infatuated with men in military uniform *US*

- Hello, Janice Lee. Are you still whacky for khaki? Oh, you remember that. I married a Navy man. —Malcolm Braly, *On the Yard*, p. 50, 1967

wac-wac *noun*

phencyclidine, the recreational drug known as PCP or angel dust *US*

- —Bill Valentine, *Gang Intelligence Manual*, p. 78, 1995

wad *noun*

1 the semen ejaculated at orgasm *US*

From 'wad' (a large quantity).

- Then came adolescence – half my waking life spent locked behind the bathroom door, firing my wad down the toilet bowl[.] —Philip Roth, *Portnoy's Complaint*, p. 18, 1969
- The cocks pop and the wads fly as wide-open mouths train to catch the steaming jizz. —*Adult Video*, p. 32, August/September 1986
- [M]y left hand Bashing the Bishop. Just as my pubescent watery wad is soaring high over the linoleum, Uncle Bart opens the door. —Stuart Browne, *Dangerous Parking*, p. 117, 2000

2 expectorated sputum *US*

- —*Maledicta*, p. 35, 1988–1989: 'Medical maledicta from San Francisco'

3 a rag saturated with glue or any volatile solvent that is inhaled for the intoxicating effect *US*

- —William D. Alsever, *Glossary for the Establishment and Other Uptight People*, p. 13, December 1970

4 a sandwich; a bun; a cake *UK, 1919*

- I'll just get a cup of tea and a wad and I'll be on my way. —Reginald Hill, *The Last National Service Man [Asking for the Moon]*, p. 14, 1994

5 a roll of money; a great deal of money *US*

- —David W. Maurer, *Argot of the Racetrack*, p. 67, 1951

wad *verb*

(of a male) to reach orgasm *UK*

After WAD (semen).

- [T]his month's CD is so rude you'll probably wad your Calvins [underpants]. —*Mixmag*, p. 4, April 2003

wad cutter *noun*

a flat-nosed bullet *US*

- —*American Speech*, p. 273, December 1962: 'The language of traffic policemen'

wadded *adjective*

well-off, rich *UK*

From WAD (a great deal of money).

- These cunts are wadded. Tell you, the cunts are making fucking Brewster's. —Kevin Sampson, *Clubland*, p. 10, 2002

waddy *noun*

a club; a hefty piece of wood suitable for a club *AUSTRALIA, 1809*

From the name of an Australian Aboriginal weapon in the extinct language Dharug, Sydney region.

- —Barbara Baynton, *Human Toll*, p. 265, 1907
- One of our boys was so timid he used to carry a waddy. —Patsy Adam-Smith, *Folklore of the Australian Railwaymen*, p. 31, 1969

waders *noun*

shoes *US*

- —Lou Shelly, *Hepcats Jive Talk Dictionary*, p. 20, 1945

wadge *noun*

▷ see: WODGE

wafer *noun*

1 a tablet of MDMA, the recreational drug best known as ecstasy *UK*

If dance is seen as a new religion, then MDMA is as important a part of the ritual as the wafer is in conventional church rites.

- —Mike Haskins, *Drugs*, p. 290, 2003

2 a cigarette paper *UK*

- —Angela Devlin, *Prison Patter*, p. 121, 1996

waffle *noun*

1 nonsense; incessant or unfocused talk *UK, 1900*

- Blunkett attacks EU 'waffle' on security. —*The Guardian*, 19th March 2004

2 in trucking, a non-skid tyre *US*

- —Montie Tak, *Truck Talk*, p. 183, 1971

Waffle *noun*

a movement in Canada's New Democratic Party to change somewhat its left-wing policies *CANADA*

- The NPI [New Party Initiative] represents the most serious challenge to the NDP's present direction and leadership since the Waffle. —*Canadian Dimension*, p. 3, July-August 2001
- The NPI and its Waffle forerunner resemble the old dudgeon crowd – the prohibitionists, pacifists, intellectual socialista, and the worker's wounds. —*CBC News*, 23rd November 2001

waffle *verb*

1 to vacillate; to take both sides of an issue *UK, 1803*

- When asked about his National Guard service, Bush waffled, hemmed and hawed, and said he would produce his records if possible. (Letter to the editor). —*St. Petersburg (Florida) Times*, p. 17A, 12th February 2004

2 to talk nonsense; to talk incessantly or in an unfocused way *UK, 1937*

- While others debated or waffled, Patton had understood the problem facing the Allies[.] —Victor Davis Hanson, *The Soul of Battle*, p. 311, 2001

waffy *adjective*

comfortable *US*

Hip-hop, urban slang. A compound of '*wa*rm' and 'flu*ffy*' noted in connection with a legal dispute over rap lyrics by *BBC News*, 6th June 2003.

wag *noun*

a social outcast, especially a non-surfer *US*

- —Trevor Cralle, *The Surfin'ary*, p. 155, 1991

WAG *noun*

*W*elsh *A*ssembly *G*overnment *UK: WALES, 1999*

Initialism.

wag *verb*

to play truant *UK, 1848*

- —Louis S. Leland, *A Personal Kiwi-Yankee Dictionary*, 1984
- I spent me days wagging off school, watching them films. —Shaun Ryder, *Shaun Ryder... in His Own Words*, 1996
- wagging it —*Coronation Street*, 10th December 2001

▸ **wag wienie; wag your wienie**

to commit indecent exposure of the male masturbatory variety *US*

- "It's just an arrangement to satisfy the immigration people, so Teddy can get a green card..." "... and wag weenie in San Francisco." —Armistead Maupin, *Babycakes*, p. 268, 1984
- He was arrested in Florida for wagging wienie in a porn theater. —Armistead Maupin, *Maybe the Moon*, p. 125, 1992

wage slave *noun*

anyone reliant on the income generated by regular employment *UK*

- Most of them can't believe that anybody could be so stupid as the average wage slave. —John Peter Jones, *Feather Pluckers*, p. 140, 1964

waggle *verb*

in pool, to make practice shots before actually hitting the cue ball *US*

- —Mike Shamos, *The Illustrated Encyclopedia of Billiards*, p. 261, 1993

wagon *noun*

1 a woman, especially pushy one, or one capable of invective *IRELAND*

- [C]ruising along in my cor [car] ... minding my own business, when this focking bitch in a white Peugeot 206, roysh [right], decides to move into the fast lane all of a sudden without checking what was behind her, and she ends up nearly running me off the road, the stupid wagon. —Paul Howard, *Ross O'Carroll-Kelly*, p. 26, 2003

2 an old, worn-out, beat-up car *US*

- —Edd Byrnes, *Way Out with Kookie*, 1959

▸ **on the wagon**

1 abstaining from drinking alcohol *US, 1906*

- Frank knew immediately by her loose laugh that she had taken a stiff drink. Benny patted his hip. "You want one?" Frank's eyes were narrow slits. "I thought we were going on the wagon?" — Irving Shulman, *The Amboy Dukes*, p. 207, 1947
- Juicers on the wagon are all big coffee fiends. — James Ellroy, *Brown's Requiem*, p. 43, 1981
- So there I was drinking Stingers with this guy who doesn't even drink. Thirteen years on the wagon and looks great. — Elmore Leonard, *Be Cool*, p. 256, 1999

2 abstaining from drug use *UK*
Extending the previous sense.
- Lissen cunt: you want some fuckin' gear [drugs] or you wanna go on the fuckin' wagon the rest of your days[.] — Nick Barlay, *Curvy Lovebox*, p. 33, 1997

wagon burner *noun*
a native American Indian *US*
Offensive.
- They'd call me 'wagon burner' and 'prairie nigger'. They'd go right for the jugular. — *Buffalo News*, p. 3C, 7th October 1995

wagon-chasing *adjective*
used of a lawyer, unscrupulous, inclined to solicit business from those in trouble with the law *US*
- Some wagon-chasing lawyer called me up and asked if I would put up the money to buy Herman a bond. — William Burroughs, *Junkie*, p. 37, 1953

wagons ho!
used as a humorous signal that a venture is about to begin *US*
From cowboy films.
- Wagons hooaaa! — *Natural Born Killers*, 1994

wagon-spotter *noun*
a trainspotter who specialises in 'collecting' freight wagons *UK*
- [T]he wagon spotters, who ignore the locomotives but instead try to collect all the numbers of the long lines of freight wagons as they career by[.] — Iain Aitch, *A Fete Worse Than Death*, p. 55, 2003

wagwon?
what's going on? *UK*
Either directly from, or in imitation of, West Indian speech.
- — Susie Dent, *The Language Report*, p. 78, 2003

wahey!
used for registering a feeling of exuberance *UK*
- Hey, let's fly a plane into a mountain, to see what it feels like, wahey! — Mark Steel, *Vive La Revolution*, p. 138, 2003

wahini *noun*
a female surfer *US*
From the Hawaiian.
- — *Paradise of the Pacific*, p. 27, October 1963

wail *verb*

1 in jazz, to perform with great feeling *US, 1955*
- [T]o be really in the groove, thus really wailing. — Peter Clayton and Peter Gammond, *Jazz A-Z*, p. 245, 1986

2 in pinball, to score a large number of points in a short period of time *US*
- — Bobbye Claire Natkin and Steve Kirk, *All About Pinball*, p. 118, 1977

▸ **wail down the place**
to dance with enthusiasm that borders on vulgarity *TRINIDAD AND TOBAGO, 1990*
- — Lise Winer, *Dictionary of the English/Creole of Trinidad & Tobago*, 2003

wailer *noun*
in drag racing, a very fast car *US*
- — Ed Radlauer, *Drag Racing Pix Dix*, p. 60, 1970

wailing *adjective*
exciting *US*
- — Carol Covington, *A Glossary of Teenage Terms*, 1965

Waiouru blonde *noun*
a Maori woman *NEW ZEALAND, 1997*
Waiouru is a remote North Island military base.
- — Harry Orsman, *A Dictionary of Modern New Zealand Slang*, p. 146, 1999

waist *noun*

▸ **make waist**
to make pelvic thrusts and gyrations during sex *TRINIDAD AND TOBAGO*
- — Lise Winer, *Dictionary of the English/Creole of Trinidad & Tobago*, 2003

wait-a-minute vine; wait-a-minute bush *noun*
a heavy, thorny vine found in the jungles of Vietnam *US*
When it snagged you, you had to wait a minute to disentangle yourself.
- It had been "prepped," prepared by bombardment, an hour before by Navy jets, so there was no tangled vegetation, no "wait-a-minute" vines to hack through with a dull machete[.] — Charles Anderson, *The Grunts*, p. 42, 1976
- They'd endured leeches and jungle rot, constant, heavy rains and clammy clothes that chilled them in their sleep, and the "wait-a-minute" bushes that could hold a trooper as tenaciously as a strand of barbed wire. — David Hackworth and Julie Sherman, *About Face*, p. 527, 1989

wait and linger *noun*
the finger *UK*
Rhyming slang, applied only in an anatomical sense.
- — Ray Puxley, *Cockney Rabbit*, 1992

waiter's delight *noun*
in poker, a hand consisting of three threes and a pair *US*
A 'three' is a **TREY**, the hand is conventionally known as a 'full house', hence 'treys full', the waiter pun.
- — George Percy, *The Language of Poker*, p. 95, 1988

waiting room *noun*
in surfing, the area beyond the breakers where surfers wait to catch waves *ISRAEL*
- — Gary Fairmont R. Filosa II, *The Surfer's Almanac*, p. 197, 1977

wait up!
wait for me! *US, 1944*
- — Claudio R. Salvucci, *The Philadelphia Dialect Dictionary*, p. 64, 1996

wake; wake up *verb*
to become aware of something *AUSTRALIA, 1910*
- We woke up to the reason why the bloke on the truck gave us kids only a penny each for empty soft-drink bottles. — William Dick, *A Bunch on Ratbags*, p. 55, 1965
- Diddler used to go crook that he could never win a hand from me, but Diddler always had a durry hanging on his lip and I woke. If the durry was hanging on his chin, he had no more than a good pair and was going for a ride. — Sam Weller, *Old Bastards I Have Met*, p. 77, 1979
- But Ray soon woke to this trick. — Clive Galea, *Slipper*, p. 26, 1988

▸ **wake your ideas up**
to concentrate; to use your wits *UK, 1961*
Often as an imperative.

▸ **wouldn't wake if...**
to be generally unaware of what's what *AUSTRALIA*
- But he wouldn't wake up if the roof fell on him. — Robert S. Close, *With Hooves of Brass*, p. 102, 1961
- They wouldn't wake up if a Foolgarah dunny fell on them. — Frank Hardy, *The Outcasts of Foolgarah*, p. 129, 1971
- — Frank Hardy, *Hardy's People*, p. 35, 1986

wake and bake; wake-n-bake *verb*
to smoke marijuana as one of the first acts of the day *US*
- I don't wake and bake like I used to. DEAN WEAN, Wean, refuting the rumour that he smokes excessive amounts of marijuana, 1995 — *Jabberrock*, p. 211, 1997
- — Connie Eble (Editor), *UNC-CH Campus Slang*, p. 13, Fall 1999

waker-upper *noun*
a heroin addict's first injection of the morning *US*
- — Ralph de Sola, *Crime Dictionary*, p. 162, 1982

wake-up *noun*

1 the day's first dose of a drug taken by an addict *US, 1954*
- This is his "wake-up," a morning shot to hold off the anxiety and sickness of withdrawal and get him "straight" enough to start the day. — James Mills, *The Panic in Needle Park*, p. 14, 1966
- We'd have our wake-ups because the drugstores aren't open at five or six in the morning before he went to work. — Bruce Jackson, *In the Life*, p. 221, 1972
- The first shot in the morning, which is called a wake-up, another in the afternoon, and one late at night. — Emmett Grogan, *Ringolevio*, p. 40, 1972
- Why don't chew lay this dime on me so I can get my wake up? — Odie Hawkins, *Men Friends*, p. 32, 1989
- — Angela Devlin, *Prison Patter*, p. 122, 1996

2 any amphetamine or central nervous system stimulant *US*
- — Carl Chambers and Richard Heckman, *Employee Drug Abuse*, 1972

3 a short time remaining on a jail sentence or term of military service, especially the last morning *US*

- —Hyman E. Goldin et al., *Dictionary of American Underworld Lingo*, p. 234, 1950
- —*American Speech*, p. 195, October 1951: 'A study of reformatory argot'
- —Carl Fleischhauer, *A Glossary of Army Slang*, p. 25, 1968
- "Shit!" John exclaimed, "you ain't got nothing but a wake-up. You can do that shit on top of your head, man."—Donald Goines, *White Man's Justice, Black Man's Grief*, p. 192, 1973
- Forty-two days man and a wakeup and I'm a gone motherfucker. —*Platoon*, 1986

wake up *verb*

1 to make someone aware; to inform someone *AUSTRALIA, 1859*

- 'I'm not saying it is a bad song,' Arthur continued, 'but why try and wake him up to what fools think?'—Alan Marshall, *I Can Jump Puddles*, p. 214, 1955
- It's time to start doing a bit of kicking back, and then it might wake up a few people that we're sick of the weak dogs hiding behind justice, to keep the poor poorer and the rich richer, and the prisoner a vegetable and robot.—Ray Denning, *Prison Diaries*, p. 108, 1979

2 to become aware that you are being swindled *US*

- Pocket said, "Blue, did you bring a rod just in case the crazy mark wakes up?"—Iceberg Slim (Robert Beck), *Trick Baby*, p. 224, 1969

3 in horse racing, to stimulate a horse illegally by electric shock or drugs *US*

- —Dan Parker, *The ABC of Horse Racing*, p. 150, 1947

wake-up *adjective*

used of an addictive substance taken upon waking up *US*

- I looked around for the wake-up bottle I kept by the bed when I was drinking, then realized I had been sober for four days.—James Ellroy, *Brown's Requiem*, p. 165, 1981

wake-up pill *noun*

an amphetamine or other central nervous system stimulant *US, 1979*

- Scene: Dark brown skinned lady with darker circles under her eyes offers me a couple wake up pills because I am nodding on my post office seat.—Odie Hawkins, *Scars and Memories*, p. 56, 1987
- CALL IT... Sulphate, wake-ups, whizz, whites, base JUST DON'T CALL IT... Ice—*Drugs An Adult Guide*, p. 35, 2001

wake you *verb*

to make you aware of something *US*

- —Lavada Durst, *The Jives of Dr. Hepcat*, p. 14, 1953

wakey-wakey *noun*

a wake-up call *UK*

Adapted from the exclamation, 'wakey, wakey!'.

- [T]his little ep [episode] has served as one almighty wakey-wakey[.] —Kevin Sampson, *Outlaws*, p. 63, 2001

wakey, wakey!

wake up! *UK*

Probably of military origin; widespread once adopted as the catchphrase of bandleader Billy Cotton (1899–1969) in his 1949–68 BBC radio Sunday lunchtime variety programme, *The Billy Cotton Bandshow*.

- GOVERNOR: Come on! Wakey wakey! Come on, you lot – up you get now!—Clive Exton, *No Fixed Abode [Six Granada Plays]*, p. 134, 1959
- "Wakey, wakey, Vasilly," laughed Arabella.—Colin Butts, *Is Harry Still on the Boat?*, p. 46, 2003

wakey, wakey, eggs and bakey!

used for calling someone from sleep to breakfast *US*

Used with great comic effect by Quentin Tarantino in *Kill Bill Volume 2* (2004) as Bill's brother Budd awakens The Bride to bury her alive.

- [T]his is his [Eric San] "Sgt. Pepper," filled with elliptical compositions bearing titles such as "Music for Morning People" – a medley of break beats that includes the line "Wakey-wakey, eggs and bacey." —*San Francisco Chronicle*, p. 40 (Sunday Datebook), 27th February 2000
- Thanks to Shannon, kids will be able to wake up to their own voice and personalized message. "Mine's going to say 'Wakey, wakey, eggs and bakey,'" she says.—*Chicago Tribune*, p. C10, 20th August 2002

wakey, wakey, hands off snakie!

used for humorously waking up a male *AUSTRALIA*

- —Thommo, *The Dictionary of Australian Swearing and Sex Sayings*, p. 136, 1985

Waldorf-Astoria *noun*

an especially spartan solitary confinement cell *US*

- —John R. Armore and Joseph D. Wolfe, *Dictionary of Desperation*, 1976

walk *noun*

1 a release from jail *US*

- Turk had gotten a walk because his sheet wasn't too bad.—Claude Brown, *Manchild in the Promised Land*, p. 17, 1965

2 during the Vietnam war, a 30 day patrol in which contact with the enemy is expected *US*

- —Linda Reinberg, *In the Field*, p. 95, 1991

walk *verb*

1 to win something easily *UK, 1903*

- So if Labour looks set to walk it, why does it appear so worried?—*The Guardian*, 4th June 2000

2 to escape unpunished *US*

- He grinned. "You're going to walk, Carlito. How does it feel?"—Edwin Torres, *After Hours*, p. 165, 1979
- RACINE: You would look favorably on that? JUDGE COSTANZAQ: He can walk.—*Body Heat*, 1980
- [S]he was brought to trial, she walked.—Jimmy Stockin, *On The Cobbles*, p. 172, 2000

3 to quit a job or commitment *US*

- "What I'm saying to you," Raji said, "the white chick Linda, she leaves, the label's gonna cancel me out and I have to start over. They in love with Linda, and Vita. Linda walks, Vita's liable to."—Elmore Leonard, *Be Cool*, p. 111, 1999

4 (of objects) to disappear, presumed borrowed or stolen *UK, 1898*

- We found a dozen of them, so I thought one could walk OK.—James Hawes, *Dead Long Enough*, p. 190, 2000

5 to move a boat sideways *US*

- I worked on the coal barge and then this big triple-screw towboat, the Robert R. Nally, comes in sideways from out in the river – that's calling walking the boat, when they do that.—Elmore Leonard, *Killshot*, p. 198, 1989

6 (used of a military aviator) to suit up for battle *US*

From the vocabulary of fighter pilots.

- Stationed aboard the USS Carl Vinson, Lt. Ashley likes to "walk early." In the lingo of Navy aviators, "walking" means suiting up for battle. "I wake up, I breathe, I hit the head, then I walk," she says.—*Newsweek*, p. 34, 29th October 2001

▸ **walk a cat back**

to trace a missile back to its launch site *US*

Gulf war usage.

- —*American Speech*, p. 404, Winter 1991: 'Among the new words'

▸ **walk back the cat**

to reconstruct events in order to understand what went wrong *US*

Probably coined by Robert Littell for his novel of espionage cited below.

- What do you say you and I pool our violence and walk back the cat together? What do you say we start at the start?—Robert Littell, *Walking Back the Cat*, 1997

▸ **walk in tall corn**

to make a great deal of money *US*

- —Jim Crotty, *How to Talk American*, p. 385, 1997

▸ **walk out on**

to abandon someone or something *UK, 1937*

Of theatrical origin.

- [H]e walked out on that Aids thing because he didn't like it.—*The Guardian*, 7th July 2001

▸ **walk the dog**

1 while surfing, to move frontwards and backwards on the surfboard to affect its speed *US*

- —Mitch McKissick, *Surf Lingo*, 1987

2 on the railways, to operate a freight train at such a high speed that the wagons sway *US*

- —Ramon Adams, *The Language of the Railroader*, p. 168, 1977

▸ **walk the nose**

while surfing, to advance to the front of the board *US*

- At Huntington and Malibu / They're shooting the pier / At Rincon they're walking the nose.—Brian Wilson and Mike Love, *Surfin' Safari (performed by the Beach Boys)*, 1962
- —John Severson, *Modern Surfing Around the World*, p. 184, 1964

▸ **walk the plank**

to move forward on a surfboard, increasing the speed of the ride *AUSTRALIA*

- —Jack Pollard, *The Australian Surfrider*, p. 18, 1963

▸ **walk the twelve steps**
to go to court *CAYMAN ISLANDS*
• — Aarona Booker Kohlman, *Wotcha Say*, p. 29, 1985

▸ **walk the walk of the trollop**
to convey sexuality while walking *US*
Another catchphrase from the 'Wayne's World' sketch on *Saturday Night Live*.
• — Connie Eble (Editor), *UNC-CH Campus Slang*, p. 10, Spring 1991

▸ **walk the walk; walk the walk and talk the talk**
to be (or behave as if) totally familiar with, and a part of, a given circumstance *UK*
• They swan about backstage in their skinny trousers, walking the walk and talking the talk, but do they actually know the first thing about rock'n'roll? — *The Guardian*, p. 14, 28th June 2004

▸ **walk the yard**
to methodically walk in a prison open space *US*
• Walking the yard was a mind bender. — Gerald Petievich, *Money Men*, p. 35, 1981

▸ **walk with your Lucy**
to inject a drug *US*
• "I want to go out walking with my Lucy." He made a gesture with his hand, indicating shooting up. — James Ellroy, *Brown's Requiem*, p. 70, 1981

▸ **walk your dog**
to use the toilet *US*
• So when I went in there to "walk my dog," you know, I picked up one and decided to try it. — Robert Gover, *JC Saves*, p. 119, 1968

walkabout; walk-about *noun*
a journey on foot taken by an Aboriginal, especially when withdrawing from white society for a period *AUSTRALIA, 1910*
• The police picked him up, reared him, and he had been a tracker ever since, except for the periodical walk-about. — Ion L. Idriess, *Over the Range*, p. 6, 1947

▸ **go walkabout**
1 (of an Aboriginal) to go on a walkabout *AUSTRALIA, 1927*
• He doesn't pretend to be anything but what he is, an Australian Aborigine who likes to 'go walkabout' every so often. — Roy Higgins and Tom Prior, *The Jockey Who Laughed*, p. 18, 1982

2 (of a person) to go off somewhere else *AUSTRALIA*
• [D]idn't it ever occur to you / That to dump clothes in the corner instead of washing them out / Means that when they've been there long enough they will go walkabout? — Patsy Adam-Smith, *Folklore of the Australian Railwaymen*, p. 228, 1969
• — Max Fatchen, *Chase through the Night*, p. 95, 1976
• A man lies flat on his face and those little yellow dolls go walkabout on your arse. — Barry Humphries, *The Traveller's Tool*, p. 88, 1985
• — Phillip Gwynne, *Deadly Unna?*, p. 225, 1998
• It doesn't even matter if your team's gone walkabout – it's a hat tournament and you can do it on your pat malone. — *Australian Ultimate*, p. 7, 2003

3 (of an important person) to make an informal tour on foot *UK, 1984*
Variants include 'do a walkabout'.
• The northern neighbourhood was the most solidly Ba'athist of Baghdad – so secure that Saddam did a walkabout there just three days before the US tanks rolled in. — *The Guardian*, 21st April 2003

walkaway *noun*
1 a type of theft in which the thief walks away with another's suitcase in a public place, leaving behind his suitcase as an alibi if apprehended *US*
• The walkway has a hundred variations which all come down to a distraction at the critical time when your luggage has not yet been assigned to the charge of one particular bellman. — Dev Collans with Stewart Sterling, *I was a House Detective*, p. 15, 1954

2 the final step in a confidence swindle, in which the swindlers walk away with the victim's money *US*
• We all get a little uptight right before the walkaway. It's called an 'anxiety reaction.' — Gerald Petievich, *One-Shot Deal*, p. 289, 1981

walk-back *noun*
an apartment in the rear of a building *US*
• — Clarence Major, *Dictionary of Afro-American Slang*, p. 121, 1970

walkboards *noun*
a platform outside a carnival show or attraction *US*
• — *American Speech*, p. 283, December 1966: 'More carnie talk from the West Coast'

walk-buddy *noun*
in prison, a close friend and steady companion *US*
• — John R. Armore and Joseph D. Wolfe, *Dictionary of Desperation*, 1976

walker *noun*
1 a prisoner who constantly paces in his cell *US*
• — Inez Cardozo-Freeman, *The Joint*, 1984

2 a striptease dancer who disrobes while walking *US*
• — Don Wilmeth, *The Language of American Popular Entertainment*, p. 290, 1981

3 in dominoes, the highest piece of its suit that is not a double and has been played *US*
• — Dominic Armanino, *Five-up Domino Games*, p. 3, 1964

walkers *noun*
the legs *US*
• — Judi Sanders, *Kickin' like Chicken with the Couch Commander*, p. 16, 1992

walkie *noun*
a close and dependable friend *US*
A term that suggests 'talkie', which in turn suggests friendship.
• — Lee McNelis, *30 + And a Wake-Up*, 1991

walkies *noun*
a walk with a small child or a dog *US, 1923*
A childish or jocular term addressed to, and understood by, that child or dog.
• Rover goes walkies on Mars[.] — *The Guardian*, 15th January 2004

walkie-talkie *noun*
1 an able-bodied person (from the perspective of a disabled person) *UK*
• My awareness within the record of "Spasticus ['Spasticus Autisticus', 1981]" wasn't a shared awareness among the "walkie-talkies", so I obviously knew there was a risk that I was going to alienate a lot of people[.] — Jim Dury [quoting Ian Dury, 1999], *Ian Dury and the Blockheads – Song by Song*, p. 131, 2003

2 a portable two-way radio *US, 1939*
• Lt. Buell called Lt. O'Dwyer on the prc-6 (the Army calls them "walkie-talkies") and told him that the covering squad was in position. — Martin Russ, *The Last Parallel*, p. 105, 1957

3 a prisoner who associates with guards *US*
• — William K. Bentley and James M. Corbett, *Prison Slang*, 1992

walk-in *noun*
a thief who steals from unlocked hotel rooms *US*
• A walk-in is a room-rifler who finds a guest's door unlocked and just walks in, helps himself and beats it. — Dev Collans with Stewart Sterling, *I was a House Detective*, p. 131, 1954

walking *adjective*
used of an order for food at a restaurant, to be taken from the restaurant *US*
• — *American Speech*, p. 232, October 1952: 'The argot of soda jerks'

walking crab *noun*
in electric line work, a lever lift *US*
• — A.B. Chance Co., *Lineman's Slang Dictionary*, p. 18, 1980

walking disaster area *noun*
an especially inept or accident-prone person *UK, 1984*
• [D]onate some time to a worthy cause, but not to a walking disaster area that is a person freshly out of a relationship. — Joy Browne, *Dating for Dummies*, p. 296, 1997

walking man's special *noun*
in the used car business, a run-down car that is not much to look at but still runs, in a fashion *US*
• — Lewis Poteet, *Car & Motorcyle Slang*, p. 214,

walking money *noun*
in gambling, a small amount of money given by the house or other players to someone who has just lost all of his money *US, 1961*
• Jay shook his head as he peeled off two hundred in walking money for the four losers. — Iceberg Slim (Robert Beck), *Airtight Willie and Me*, p. 112, 1979

walking tree *noun*
in a criminal enterprise, a watchman or lookout *US*
• — *American Speech*, p. 98, May 1956: 'Smugglers' argot in the Southwest'

walking writer *noun*
in an illegal numbers gambling lottery, a person who collects and records bets *US*
• — *American Speech*, p. 193, October 1949

walk in the park *noun*
an easy thing to do *UK*
• Don't sweat it, Larry, it's walk in the park. —Christopher Brookmyre, *Not the End of the World*, p. 8, 1998

walk in the sun *noun*
a combat march without a significant chance of engaging the enemy *US*
• —Linda Reinberg, *In the Field*, p. 237, 1991

walk of fame *noun*
the walk home or to work after spending the night with a beautiful and popular woman *US*
• —Don R. McCreary (Editor), *Dawg Speak*, 2001

walk of shame *noun*
the walk home or to work after spending the night with a date, still wearing yesterday's clothes *US*
• —Amy Sohn, *Sex and the City*, p. 157, 2002

walk-on *noun*
in sports, an athlete who gets chosen for a team having appeared at practice unsolicited and unexpected *US*
• —Bill Shefski, *Running Press Glossary of Football Language*, p. 116, 1978

walkover *noun*
in horse racing, a race in which only all but one entry are withdrawn *US*
The lone horse starting the race can win the purse simply by walking the distance of the race.
• —George King, *Horse Racing*, p. 61, 1965

walk-up *noun*
a brothel *US*
• —Hyman E. Goldin et al., *Dictionary of American Underworld Lingo*, p. 234, 1950

wall *noun*
▸ **behind the wall**
imprisoned *US*
• —James Harris, *A Convict's Dictionary*, 1989

▸ **go over the wall**
to escape from prison *US, 1934*
• —Angela Devlin, *Prison Patter*, p. 122, 1996

▸ **go to the wall**
to lose money in stock investments *US*
• —Kathleen Odean, *High Steppers, Fallen Angels, and Lollipops*, p. 94, 1988

▸ **off the wall**
in auction fraud, where non-existent bids are said to come from *UK*
• It's where an auctioneer accepts bids "off the chandelier" or "off the wall", as auctioneers say – meaning phoney non-existent bids – then knocks an antique down to some joker[.] —Jonathan Gash, *The Ten Word Game*, p. 61, 2003

▸ **the wall**
a maximum security prison *US*
• —Gary K. Farlow, *Prison-ese*, p. 73, 2002

▸ **up the wall**
crazy; crazed by circumstances; angry *UK, 1951*
• Said he'd see us in Dool's for brekkie, but he'll be up the wall still, pound to a penny. —Kevin Sampson, *Clubland*, p. 46, 2002

wall *verb*
to lean against the wall at a party or other social gathering *US*
• —Vann Wesson, *Generation X Field Guide and Lexicon*, p. 180, 1997

wallaby *noun*
▸ **on the wallaby**
wandering around *AUSTRALIA, 1861*
Originally 'Tramping the outback in search of work (as though following the track made by wallabies)', G.A. Wilkes, *A Dictionary of Australian Colloquialisms*, 1978.
• [H]e told me, "You're on the wallaby." —Brian Preston, *Pot Planet*, p. 90, 2002

Wallace and Gromit; wallace *verb*
to vomit *UK*
Rhyming slang, based on Oscar-winning (1990) animated characters.
• You make me Wallace! —Ray Puxley, *Fresh Rabbit*, p. 125, 1998

Wallace Beery; wallace *noun*
in a betting shop, a dispute over the sum due *UK*
Rhyming slang for 'query', formed from the name of the US film actor, 1885–1949.
• —Ray Puxley, *Fresh Rabbit*, 1998

wallah; walla *noun*
1 a man identified by relation to the activity, occupation or philosophy to which it is properly affixed *INDIA, 1785*
Adopted directly by Anglo-Indians, hence military, from Hindu *wálá* ('a person connected in some way with the thing expressed in the first word', George Clifford Whitworth, *An Anglo-Indian Dictionary*, 1885).
• VALE: A concert party, eh? Not many of those about now. WATSON: No, not for us peace-time wallahs. —Graeme Kent, *The Queen's Corporal [Six Granada Plays]*, p. 83, 1959
• I could be the sergeant in a squadron full of wallahs / What a waste. —Ian Dury, *What a Waste*, 1978
• The Brussels wallah has raised one or two practical queries. —Kevin Sampson, *Clubland*, p. 55, 2002

2 in the television and film industries, indistinguishable background voices *US*
• —Ralph S. Singleton, *Filmaker's Dictionary*, p. 182, 1990

wallbanger *noun*
a person whose impairment with central nervous system depressants has produced a marked lack of coordination *US*
• —Donald Wesson and David Smith, *Barbiturates*, 1977

wallet *noun*
1 a person who finances a (criminal) project *UK*
• [S]he wasn't the king wallet, the scam's principal backer. —Jonathan Gash, *The Ten Word Game*, p. 108, 2003

2 a generous person *US*
• —Anna Scotti and Paul Young, *Buzzwords*, p. 49, 1997

wallet lane *noun*
the passing lane of a motorway *US*
Trucker use, with a reference to a 'wallet' because of the likelihood of having to pay a ticket if caught using the passing lane.
• —Bill Davis, *Jawjacking*, p. 105, 1977

walleyed *adjective*
drunk *US*
• When Rocco had come in walleyed with vodka, she had awakened in her crib. —Richard Price, *Clockers*, p. 515, 1992

wallflower week *noun*
the bleed period of the menstrual cycle *US*
• — *American Speech*, p. 298, December 1954: 'The vernacular of menstruation'

wallie *noun*
in skateboarding, any jumping manoeuvre performed from a wall *UK*
A combination of 'wall' and **OLLY; OLLIE** (a jumping manoeuvre).
• —Fabrice le Mao, *Skateboarding*, p. 93, 2004

▷ see: **WALLY**

wallies *noun*
nothing, zero *UK, late 1990s*
• Her already failing party stock would be worth wallies by this time tomorrow. —Christopher Brookmyre, *Boiling a Frog*, p. 92, 2000

wallin' *noun*
the act or habit of sitting or standing against a wall at a party *UK*
Teen slang.
• — Susie Dent, *The Language Report*, p. 78, 2003

wall job *noun*
sex with one of the participants standing against a wall *US*
• Tell him 'bout the wall jobs you been doin' in the division garage. —Stephen J. Cannell, *The Tin Collectors*, p. 9, 2001

wallop *noun*

1 a heavy blow *UK, 1823*

- It already had the oil mixed in and packed a helluva wallop. — Max Shulman, *Guided Tour of Campus Humor*, p. 21, 1955
- He always used to slam it and try and fetch her shins a wallop. — Ray Galton and Alan Simpson, *Hancock's Half Hour*, 22nd April 1958

2 an attempt, a go *UK*

A pun on **BASH** (a try).

- [Y]ou've got to give it [Stalinism or smoking] up all in one wallop and be done with it. — Mark Steel, *Reasons to be Cheerful*, p. 192, 2001

3 the strength to deliver a heavy blow *UK, 1914*

Boxing slang.

4 beer *UK, 1933*

- "Pint o' wallop," said one insolently. — Derek Bickerton, *Payroll*, p. 121, 1959
- Jim upended his pint of wallop over the detestable little rascal. — Brian McDonald, *Elephant Boys*, p. 75–77, 2000

wallop *verb*

1 to hit someone *UK, 1825*

- Marchmere walloping a strange bird he later charvered [had sex with]. — Derek Raymond (Robin Cook), *The Crust on its Uppers*, p. 27, 1962

2 to get the better of someone *UK, 1865*

A figurative application of the previous sense.

3 to dance *UK*

- I trolled back to my lattie to go over my chanting [singing] and walloping for tonight's concert[.] — the cast of 'Aspects of Love', Prince of Wales Theatre, *Palare (Boy Dancer Talk) for Beginners*, 1989–92
- — Paul Baker, *Polari*, p. 194, 2002

walloped *adjective*

drunk or drug-intoxicated *UK*

- If there is one thing that actually is better than getting walloped on brain-rotting chemical stimulants, then it's doing the nasty [having sex]. — *Ministry*, p. 21, October 2002

walloper *noun*

1 the penis *UK: SCOTLAND*

- This wan'll never talk. No' wi' his walloper in his mooth, anyway. — Christopher Brookmyre, *The Sacred Art of Stealing*, p. 396, 2002

2 a male who masturbates to excess *NEW ZEALAND*

- — David McGill, *David McGill's Complete Kiwi Slang Dictionary*, p. 134, 1998

3 a police officer *AUSTRALIA, 1945*

- King Herod had John the Baptist collared by the wallopers and chucked in the local lock-up[.] — Kel Richards, *The Aussie Bible*, p. 39, 2003

4 a dancer, especially a professional dancer *UK, 1937*

Theatrical slang.

- [A]t one point to call a dancer a "walloper" might have implied that he or she wasn't very graceful. — Paul Baker, *Polari*, 2002

wallopies *noun*

large female breasts *US*

- — *American Speech*, p. 68, Spring-Summer 1975: 'Razorback slang'

walloping *noun*

a beating, a thrashing; a win by a more than convincing margin *UK, 1871*

- A 4–1 walloping of Wolves and gutsy draws with Manchester United and Liverpool had suggested that Leeds were far from done for[.] — *The Guardian*, 15th March 2004

walloping *adjective*

large, great *UK, 1847*

- What book could possibly be worth such devotion? Here, 1,280 pages long and weighing in at a walloping 3lbs 8ozs, is a doorstop of an answer. — *The Observer*, 28th December 2003

wallops *noun*

choreography *UK*

From **WALLOP** (to dance).

- — the cast of 'Aspects of Love', Prince of Wales Theatre, *Palare (Boy Dancer Talk) for Beginners*, 1989–92

wallpaper *noun*

1 a background pattern or photograph for a computer display screen *US*

- — Eric S. Raymond, *The New Hacker's Dictionary*, p. 375, 1991

2 counterfeit money *US*

- — Vincent J. Monteleone, *Criminal Slang*, p. 249, 1949

3 a postcard acknowledging receipt of a citizens' band or ham radio message *US*

- — Wayne Floyd, *Jason's Authentic Dictionary of CB Slang*, p. 31, 1976

wall-stretcher *noun*

an imaginary tool for which a building trade apprentice may be sent to fetch *UK, 1961*

wall ticket *noun*

in Keno, a big win *US*

Casinos often post large winning tickets on the wall of the Keno lounge as an enticement to bettors.

- — Thomas L. Clark, *The Dictionary of Gambling and Gaming*, p. 247, 1987

wall time *noun*

the time as shown on wall clocks, as contrasted with GMT or another common time used on computers *ANTARCTICA*

- — Eric S. Raymond, *The New Hacker's Dictionary*, 1991
- For regular "wall time" McMurdo follows Chch, which is GMT+12 in the winter, GMT+13 in the summer (even though the sun never sets in the summer and there is no night to save the daylight from. — Ethan Dicks, *English, as She is Spoke at McMurdo*, 2003

wall-to-wall *adjective*

abundant; appearing everywhere *UK, 1967*

From wall-to-wall carpets that cover the entire floor.

- Anyone who has Sky knows that the doomsayers' predictions of wall-to-wall Dallas have proved wildly wrong. — 29th August 2003

wall-to-waller *noun*

a pornographic film shot in one day on a very low budget *US*

- — Ana Loria, *1 2 3 Be A Porn Star!*, p. 168, 2000: 'Glossary of adult sex industry terms'

wally; wallie; wolly *noun*

1 an unfashionable individual; someone who is innocent, or foolish; a fool *UK, 1969*

Possibly originates in the name Wally, however Scottish dialect *wally-draigle* (a feeble, ill-grown person) may well have had an influence.

- He thinks a lot of recent skin [skinhead] converts [to the National Front Party] are "just a bunch of wallies who've learnt how to chant Sieg Heil at gigs". — *New Society*, 26th June 1980
- It's like Leonardo da Vinci – he had the idea, grand design and then he had all those wallies, apprentices[.] — Anthony Masters, *Minder*, p. 10, 1984
- [A] wally that came last in downhill skiing[.] — David Robb, *The Nineties*, p. 44, 1999
- Come on, you fucking wally. — John King, *Human Punk*, p. 10, 2000
- "Were the Sex Pistols political?" I asked John Lydon on a chat show. "Of course not," he insisted. "That was Malcolm [McLaren]. We were never anarchists – we were just wallies." — Simon Napier-Bell, *Black Vinyl White Powder*, p. 248, 2001

2 in CID slang, a uniformed police officer, especially a constable; more generally, a trainee or an incompetent police officer *UK*

'Woolly' is also recorded by the *Oxford English Dictionary* in 1965.

- — G.F. Newman, *Sir, You Bastard*, 1970
- — *The Official Encyclopaedia of New Scotland Yard*, 1999

Wally *noun*

▸ **call it Wally**

to agree that a matter is settled *GUYANA*

Collected in 1962.

wallyo; wal-yo *noun*

a young man, usually an Italian-American *US*

- [T]he only two cats that was ever in my corner was Earl Bassey, a black dude, and Rocco Fabrizi, a wal-yo. Unbelievable. — Edwin Torres, *Carlito's Way*, 1975
- — *Atlantic Monthly*, p. 110, June 1988

Wally Pipe *noun*

any athlete who misses a game and is thereafter replaced by a better player *US*

On 1st June 1925, the New York Yankees first baseman Wally Pipp did not play because he was sick; his place was taken by Lou Gehrig, who played for the next 2130 games.

- — Zander Hollander, *Baseball Lingo*, p. 131, 1967
- While he didn't do a Wally Pipp on incumbent Royal Ivey or backup Edgar Moreno in the No. 19 Longhorns' 99–79 victory in front of 6,574 at the Erwin Center, he did enough to stay in the picture. — *San Antonio (Texas) Express-News*, p. 9C, 3rd January 2004

walnut storage disease *noun*
any unspecified mental problem *US*
A play on **NUTTY** (crazy).
- — *Maledicta*, p. 39, 1983: 'More common patient-directed pejoratives used by medical personnel'

walnut whip; walnut *noun*
1 sleep *UK*
Rhyming slang for **KIP**, formed on a chocolate confection.
- To get a few hours' walnut is to rest your noddle for a while. — Ray Puxley, *Fresh Rabbit*, 1998

2 a vascectomy *UK*
Rhyming slang for **THE SNIP**.
- — *Roger's Profanisaurus*, p. 234, 2002

Walter Mitty *noun*
1 a person who poses as a heroic ex-soldier *AUSTRALIA*
From Walter Mitty, the title character of James Thurber's short story *The Secret Life of Walter Mitty* (1939) and successful film of the same title starring Danny Kaye (1947).
- A group of angry Vietnam veterans have established a website to expose the impostors and in 18 months have outed more than 25 fake soldiers known as 'wannabes' or 'Walter Mittys'. — *Daily Telegraph*, p. 6, 22nd April 2002

2 the female breast *UK*
Rhyming slang for **TITTY**. The short form 'walter' can also be used.
- I spend my whole life dreaming about Walters. — Bodmin Dark, *Dirty Cockney Rhyming Slang*, 2003

Walts *noun*
14 Int (an undercover intelligence unit of the British Army) *UK*
Abbreviated from Walter Mitty, the name of a character, created in 1941 by James Thurber, who has become a cultural reference for a person who leads a dual-existence.
- How's it going in the Walts, then? You got your sneaky beaky kit yet? — Andy McNab (writing of the late 1970s/early 80s), *Immediate Action*, p. 275, 1995

waltz *noun*
intense warfare, be it a fire fight or hand-to-hand combat *US*
- — Linda Reinberg, *In the Field*, p. 238, 1991

waltz *verb*
to move in a nonchalant manner *US, 1887*
- She waltzes down to Hoxton in it [a fur coat] to see her dear old mum, and takes her out for a tiddly. — Charles Raven, *Underworld Nights*, 1956
- If he goofs up, he waltzes into court, files a new motion, and fixes it. — Carl Hiaasen, *Tourist Season*, p. 222, 1986
- RANDAL: Any moron can waltz in here and do our jobs, but you're obsessed with making it seem so much more fucking important, so much more epic than it really is. — *Clerks*, 1994

▸ **waltz matilda**
to travel as a swagman *AUSTRALIA, 1893*
From 'Matilda' (a swag) and 'waltz' (to lead in a waltz), here punning on the female name. Now of course obsolete, except in the well-known Australian song. Most singers are entirely unaware of the literal meaning of the phrase.
- — Jim Ramsay, *Cop It Sweet!*, p. 95, 1977

waltz off *verb*
to leave in a nonchalant or cavalier manner *US*
- Great, Harry, you love me, that settles everything, now we can waltz off into the sunset together? — *When Harry Met Sally*, 1989

wamper *noun*
a sandal made with pieces of tyre and tied with thatch string *CAYMAN ISLANDS*
- — Aarona Booker Kohlman, *Wotcha Say*, p. 25, 1985

wampum *noun*
money *US*
An imitation of Native American Indian language.
- — Hyman E. Goldin et al., *Dictionary of American Underworld Lingo*, p. 234, 1950

wampy *adjective*
crazy *NEW ZEALAND*
- Old 'Arawhata Bill' like so many men who spend many years in solitude, went quite 'wampy' in the end. — J. Herries Beattie, *Farm Famed Fiordland*, p. 85, 1950

wand *noun*
1 the penis *UK*
The magic stick that you wave in your hand.
- — *Sky Magazine*, July 2001
- DUANE: How big is your johnson? RAMU: Johnson? DUANE: Your wand, your pork sword, your baloney pony. — *The Guru*, 2002

2 in pool, a player's cue stick *US*
- — Mike Shamos, *The Illustrated Encyclopedia of Billiards*, p. 261, 1993

wandering hands brigade *noun*
a male's hands exploring a female's body *NEW ZEALAND*
- — Louis S. Leland, *A Personal Kiwi-Yankee Dictionary*, p. 86, 1984

wandwaver *noun*
a male exhibitionist *US*
- — *Maledicta*, p. 227, Winter 1980: '"Lovely, blooming, fresh and gay": the onomastics of camp'

wang; whang *noun*
the penis *US, 1935*
- Cut the sermons and give me my wang! I want a wang and I want it NOW! — John Waters, *Deperate Living*, p. 161, 1099
- A lady while dining at Crewe / Found an elephant's whang in her stew. — *Eros*, p. 61, Winter 162
- Filipinos come quick; colored men are built abnormally large ("Their wangs look like a baby's arm with an apple in its fist"); ladies with short hair are Lesbians; if you want to keep your man, rub alum on your pussy. — Lenny Bruce, *How to Talk Dirty and Influence People*, p. 1, 1965
- My wang was all I really had that I could call my own. — Philip Roth, *Portnoy's Complaint*, p. 35, 1969
- Whang whipping experts voted the New York Times Sunday Magazine their favorite masturbation media. — *Screw*, p. 26, 10th November 1969
- She unbuttoned my trousers fast and pulled out my half-erect wang. — *Screw*, p. 7, 4th May 1970
- Keating surprisingly had an enormous whang. — Earl Thompson, *Tattoo*, p. 325, 1974
- DOCTOR: If I didn't know better I'd say it's a – Chinese Teacher: Wang! — *Austin Powers*, 1999

wangbar *noun*
an electric guitar's tremolo arm *US*
- [J]agged wangbar-bashing lines that would make people call Jimi Hendrix a genius[.] — Lester Bangs, *Psychotic Reactions and Carburetor Dung*, p. 297, 1980
- Dave Wronski, the band [Slacktone]'s inventive 6-stringer, melds surf's slurpy wang-bar bends and twangy, thrumming bass-string riffs[.] — Andy Ellis, *GuitarPlayer.com*, June 2002

wanger *noun*
▷ see: **WHANGER**

wangle *noun*
a swindle; a convenient arrangement *UK, 1915*
The successful outcome of the verb 'wangle'.
- If you're cornered suss a wangle — Ian Dury, *Cacka Boom*, 1998

wangle *verb*
to arrange something to suit yourself; to contrive or obtain something with sly cunning; to manipulate something *UK, 1888*
Widely used, especially in the military, as 'wangle a job', 'wangling leave (of absence)', etc.

wang-wang *noun*
the penis *US*
- — Connie Eble (Editor), *UNC-CH Campus Slang*, p. 6, Spring 1980

wank *noun*
1 an act of masturbation; hence, an act of self-indulgence *UK, 1948*
An earlier spelling 'whank' has given way to 'wank'.
- That was mid-60s trippy dippy wank-off, now times have changed[.] — Lester Bangs, *Psychotic Reactions and Carburetor Dung*, p. 101, 1972
- I've even had a wank in a train[.] — Ivor Biggun, *The Winker's Song (Misprint)*, 1978
- I remember a fellow recruit, a man from Birmingham, exclaiming, in a very Brummy accent, 1952, "Ooh! A letter from tart! I'm off to the lats for a wank!" — Beale, *A Dictionary of Slang and Unconventional English*, 1984
- But if there was a naked women [sic] in there giving herself a wank, you'd totally lose it. — Shaun Ryder, *Shaun Ryder... in His Own Words*, 1997
- He's probably having a wank right now, watching us through binoculars, she laughed. — John King, *White Trash*, p. 98, 2001

2 a waste of time *UK*
- Thick as a plank and looking for work / What a wank — Ian Dury, *Jack Shit George*, 1998

3 a fool; a despicable person *UK*
- [S]he must have missed the meeting where these wanks were appointed official character judges[.] — Christopher Brookmyre, *The Sacred Art of Stealing*, p. 41, 2002

4 nonsense; rubbish *UK*
As in the expression 'that's a load of old wank' and the exclamation (current in the armed services, especially army, 1960–70s) 'wank! wank!' (pronounced almost as if quacked) greeting any announcement or declaration considered to be rubbish.
- So this is hot wank! Better no doubt than the next Kiss album! — Lester Bangs, *Psychotic Reactions and Carburetor Dung*, p. 284, 1979
- Pay's wank, but yer can make it up in ovies [overtime]. — Niall Griffiths, *Kelly + Victor*, p. 141, 2002

wank *verb*
1 to masturbate *UK, 1950*
The Scots dialect word *whank* (to beat) was the usual spelling until the 1970s. Also used with 'off'.
- [T]he couple will be surrounded by dirty old men wanking off. — Kitty Churchill, *Thinking of England*, p. 198, 1995
- [L]oads of blokes wank over her, it don't mean a thing. I mean, shit, even I've wanked over her. — Colin Butts, *Is Harry on the Boat?*, p. 25, 1997
- A half-naked, sixteen stone woman in her fifties with a shaved head and nipple rings, wanking-off a young black guy over her tits. — Dave Courtney, *Raving Lunacy*, p. 111, 2000
- [A] flashing neon sign. Wank and Spank Sauna and Massage. Open 24 hrs. — Jack Allen, *When the Whistle Blows*, p. 238, 2000
- I used to wank myself daft[.] — Kevin Sampson, *Outlaws*, p. 101, 2001
- Gwenno might even go to bed with you. Let yew fuckin do her, like. Suck yewer knob. Wank yew off. Like that, would yew? — Niall Griffiths, *Sheepshagger*, p. 142, 2001

2 to party with zeal and a lack of inhibition *CANADA*
- — Jack Chambers (Editor), *Slang Bag 93 (University of Toronto)*, p. 6, Winter 1993

wank *adjective*
of poor quality; pathetic; self-indulgent *UK*
- Michael fuckin Bolton. Or Bryan bastard Adams, some wank power-ballad singer. — Niall Griffiths, *Kelly + Victor*, p. 128, 2002

wank about; wank around *verb*
to waste time *UK*
- We've got to do fucking something. I'm sick of this wanking about. — Jake Arnott, *He Kills Coppers*, p. 112, 2001
- He just wanked around and didn't fulfil his promise. — Jim Drury, *Ian Dury and the Blockheads*, p. 129, 2003

wank-bank *noun*
a personal collection of inspirational erotic images *UK*
Formed on **WANK** (an act of masturbation).
- Approaching his vinegar stroke, he was accessing his mental wank-bank for a suitable image to produce a satisfactory climax[.] — Colin Butts, *Is Harry Still on the Boat?*, p. 6, 2003

wanked-out *adjective*
drained of life *UK*
- [R]enewal of the wanked-out soul, in a place a few miles due west of Liverpool? — James Hawes, *Dead Long Enough*, p. 71, 2000

wanker *noun*
1 a masturbator *UK*
The earlier spelling 'whanker' has given way to 'wanker'.
- I'm a wanker, I'm a wanker / And it does me good like it bloody well should[.] — Ivor Biggun, *The Winker's Song (Misprint)*, 1978

2 a despicable person; an all-purpose form of abuse *UK, 1972*
From the sense as 'a masturbator'; some commentators suggest late C19 dialect *wanker* (a simpleton).
- You look like shit, you wankers. — *Repo Man*, 1984
- You look like a suburban wanker getting round in that clobber. — Kathy Lette, *Girls' Night Out*, 1987
- In fact the word in this form is so far removed from the association with that taboo subject that in the 1970's Paul Hogan could have a character appear on national television named Leo Wanker. — *Passing Show*, p. #7, 1988
- I'm actually quite a decent chap, and the rest of the group are wankers. — *Jabberrock [quoting Jools Holland of Squeeze]*, p. 240, 1997
- I waited my turn, thinking that maybe it was time I got myself a mobile. Became a proper wanker. — Shane Maloney, *Nice Try*, 1998
- Being famous automatically makes you a wanker. Being pissed and famous makes you the Wanker of Wankers. — Andrew Holmes, *Sleb*, p. 108, 2002

wankered *adjective*
drunk or drug-intoxicated *UK*
- [M]angled caned w**nkered bolloxed[.] — Stuart Walton, *Out of It*, cover, 2001

wanker's doom *noun*
the mythological disease that is the inevitable result of excessive masturbation *US*
- — *Maledicta*, p. 11, Summer 1977: 'A word for it!'

wanker tank *noun*
a large 4WD vehicle that never gets used for off-road driving *AUSTRALIA, 2003*

wanking-spanner *noun*
the hand *UK, 1961*
A masturbatory tool that loosens nuts.
- — *Roger's Profanisaurus*, December 1997

wank mag *noun*
a pornographic magazine *UK*
Combines **WANK** (to masturbate) with **MAG** (a magazine).
- [R]emoving Bibles from hotel rooms and replacing them with wank mags. — Christopher Brookmyre, *Not the End of the World*, p. 25, 1998
- He'd ordered the sex aid from the classified section in the back of a wank mag. — Stewart Home, *Sex Kick [britpulp]*, p. 230, 1999

wank-off *adjective*
self-indulgent *UK*
A figurative use for 'an act of masturbation'.
- The rest is just wank-off fucking undergraduate games[.] — James Hawes, *Dead Long Enough*, p. 258, 2000

wank-pit; wanking-pit *noun*
a man's (unshared) bed *UK, 1961*
Military slang, formed on **WANK** (masturbation).
- Wank is a big word with him [Martin Amis], as in "wank pit", the natural habitat of the loser male. — *The Guardian*, 29th August 2003

wank shaft *noun*
1 the vagina *UK*
- Women's genitalia were represented as (potential) containers (e.g., bucket, box, hair goblet), places to put things in (e.g., furry letterbox, disk drive, socket, slot), containers for semen (e.g., gism pot, spunk bin, honey pot), and containers for the penis/sex (e.g., willy warmer, wank shaft, shagbox). — *Journal of Sex Research*, p. 146, 2001

2 the penis; also used as a term of abuse *UK*
Formed on the word **WANK** (masturbation).
- — Chris Lewis, *The Dictionary of Playground Slang*, p. 249, 2003

wank sock *noun*
an item of (men's) footwear used to contain the penis during masturbation *UK*
- — Graham Norton, *V Graham Norton*, 21st May 2003

wanksta *noun*
someone, especially a white person, who postures as a gangsta rapper *US*
A derisory play on **WANKER** (a despised person).
- You said you a gansta but you neva pop nuttin' / You said you a wanksta and you need to stop frontin' / You ain't a friend of mine[.] — 50 Cent and G Unit, *Wanksta*, 2002
- — Susie Dent, *The Language Report*, p. 144, 2003

wank-stain *noun*
a contemptible person *UK*
- I'll take on you and any other members of your stinking, lowlife, wank-stain, shit-for-brains fucking family. — Colin Butts, *Is Harry on the Boat?*, p. 303, 1997
- [O]nce heard some wank-stain estate agent saying the place was full of them. — J.J. Connolly, *Layer Cake*, p. 245, 2000

wank tanks *noun*
the testicles *UK*
Celebrating the testicles as no more than a source of semen for masturbation.
- — *Roger's Profanisaurus*, p. 235, 2002
- — Chris Lewis, *The Dictionary of Playground Slang*, p. 249, 2003

wank trade *noun*
the pornography industry *US*
- — Anna Scotti and Paul Young, *Buzzwords*, p. 11, 1997

wankware *noun*
software on compact disc intended for sexual stimulation *CANADA*
- Related to teledildonics, "wankware" is CD software intended for masturbatory, not educational purposes, and appeared first on Canadian computer bulletin boards. — Bill Casselman, *Canadian Words*, p. 6, 1995

wanky *adjective*

1 of poor quality; pathetic *UK, 1890*

Original printer's use cognisant with **WONKY**; survives into a modern use which presumes **WANK** as the inspiration.

- Fuck me! What a wanky waste. — *ID*, 1994
- [T]hen i started reading about you and sort of found a friend in you – like – sounds a bit wanky i know[.] — Patrick Jones, *Everything Must Go*, p. 167, 2000

2 pretentious *AUSTRALIA, 1979*

- 'He's such a wanker.' 'You know what? There's nothing wankier than sitting around calling everybody a wanker.' — Kathy Lette, *Girls' Night Out*, p. 103, 1987

wannabe *noun*

someone who wants to be and pretends to be that which he is not *US*

Deemed potentially offensive by Multicultural Management Program Fellows, *Dictionary of Cautionary Words and Phrases*, 1989.

- — Edith A. Folb, *runnin' down some lines*, p. 259, 1980
- They call the white gangs "wannabes," meaning someone who dresses and talks the part because he "wants to be" a gang member, but is actually tame. — *Los Angeles Times*, p. 4 (Metro Section), 28th July 1985
- — *American Speech*, Fall 1990
- Strike saw Spook and Ahmed walk away as if they had something to hide – wannabes, the only idiots who walked. — Richard Price, *Clockers*, p. 9, 1992
- It [Mod] was the original wannabe culture. Wannabe boys, wanna create, wannabe rich, wannabe famous, wannabe loved, wannabe known. — Mark Pass, *Marc Bolan, The Sharper Word*, p. 47, 1992
- Here [Johnny] Depp and fellow wannabes Keanu Reeves and River Phoenix acted out their rock'n'roll fantasies. — Barney Hoskins, *Waiting for the Sun*, p. 339, 1996
- They're the wannabes of football hooliganism. — Martin King and Martin Knight, *The Naughty Nineties*, p. 174, 1999

wanna-bet shirt *noun*

in a rowing competition, a team's shirt which is the object of a wager between competing teams, where the winner claims the opposing team's shirts which are worn as a badge of victory *US*

- — Judy's Enterprises, *Coxswain Postcard*, 2001

Wanno *nickname*

Wandsworth Prison *UK*

- I'd just been weighed off [convicted and sentenced]. I landed up in reception at Wanno [...] and ended up in front of the most miserable-faced screw. — *The Guardian*, p. 7, 8th January 2004

wan singer, wan song

▷ **see:** **ONE SINGER, ONE SONG**

want *noun*

a notification that a person is wanted by the police *US*

- — Jack Webb, *The Badge*, p. 222, 1958
- I unlocked the call box and hurried up with the wants check. — Joseph Wambaugh, *The Blue Knight*, p. 29–30, 1973
- There's no want on the license at this time. — *Gone in 60 Seconds*, 2000

want *verb*

▸ **want in**

to wish to enter; to desire to be a part of something *UK, 1836*

Originally a colloquial term in Scotland, Northern Ireland and the US.

- [T]he West's powerful drugs industry wants in on the action. — *The Guardian*, 25th March 2004

▸ **want out**

to wish to exit; to desire a complete change of circumstances *UK: SCOTLAND, 1870*

- [Ralf] Schumacher denies he wants out of Williams [the BMW-Williams formula one racing team]. — *The Guardian*, 24th February 2004

wap *noun*

▷ **see:** **WASP**

wappy *adjective*

idealistic, sentimental *UK*

Perhaps as a blend of **WET** (weak, lacking in effectiveness) and **SOPPY** (foolishly sentimental, naive).

- Just like the governor of this Borstal who spouts to us about Borstal and all that wappy stuff. — Alan Sillitoe, *The Loneliness of the Long-Distance Runner*, p. 18, 1959

war *noun*

▸ **go to war**

to fight *US*

- — Gary K. Farlow, *Prison-ese*, p. 25, 2002

war and strife *noun*

a wife *UK, 1931*

Rhyming slang; a less-used variation of **TROUBLE AND STRIFE**.

- — Ray Puxley, *Cockney Rabbit*, 1992

warb *noun*

a decrepit, unclean or otherwise disgusting person *AUSTRALIA, 1933*

Perhaps from 'warble' (a type of maggot).

- — Jim Ramsay, *Cop It Sweet!*, p. 95, 1977
- — Ryan Aven-Bray, *Ridgey Didge Oz Jack Lang*, p. 52, 1983
- That bloody old warb on his bloody old horse. — T.A.G. Hungerford, *Stories From Suburban Road*, p. 91, 1983

warby *adjective*

decrepit; unkempt; filthy; disgusting *AUSTRALIA, 1923*

- An' look at all 'er warby mates. — Nino Culotta (John O'Grady), *Gone Fishin'*, p. 207, 1962
- — Jim Ramsay, *Cop It Sweet!*, p. 95, 1977

warchalk *verb*

to chalk icons on walls, etc, to indicate an area where a wireless Internet connection may be made for free *UK*

Derived as a back-formation from **WARCHALKING**.

- The chief information officer for the state of Utah intends to warchalk to help city workers like the police find wireless networks. — *The Seattle Times*, 1st July 2002

warchalker *noun*

a computer user who chalks icons on walls, etc, to indicate to other computer users an area where a wireless Internet connection may be made for free *UK*

- One warchalker has already discovered that some of the kiosks dotting London's Oxford Street contain wireless nodes that anyone can use. — *BBC News*, 23rd July 2002

warchalking *noun*

the practice of chalking icons on walls, etc, to indicate an area where a wireless Internet connection may be made for free *UK*

Coined in June 2002 by Matt Jones, a London-based 'information architect', as a play on 'wardialing' (a computer-directed assault by telephone). 'Warchalking' is based on the system of symbols used by UK tramps and beggars, first recorded in 1849, and developed by US hobos during the Depression. The three basic symbols are)((open node), ○ (closed node) and Ⓦ (wep [wired equivalent privacy] node).

- I'm hoping to use warchalking icons to alert employees to the existence of wireless nets in conference rooms and other places. — *The Guardian*, 4th July 2002

warden *noun*

1 a parent *US*

- — Hy Lit, *Hy Lit's Unbelievable Dictionary of Hip Words for Groovy People*, p. 44, 1968

2 a spouse *US*

Usually a spouse of the female persuasion as perceived by the spouse of the male persuasion.

- — Wayne Floyd, *Jason's Authentic Dictionary of CB Slang*, p. 31, 1976

3 a school principal *US*

- — *This Week Magazine, New York Herald Tribune*, p. 46, 28th February 1954
- Back to the warden's office. You want me to give him any messages, doll? — Morton Cooper, *High School Confidential*, p. 19, 1958

4 a teacher *US*

Teen slang.

- — *Newsweek*, p. 29, 8th October 1951

5 on the railways, the supervisor of a track crew *US*

- — Ramon Adams, *The Language of the Railroader*, p. 169, 1977

war department *noun*

your wife or girlfriend *US*

- I've got the war department faked out. I told her I'm working overtime. — Joseph Wambaugh, *Lines and Shadows*, p. 160, 1984
- — James Harris, *A Convict's Dictionary*, 1989

war dialer *noun*
a computer program that dials a given range of telephone connections in order to hack into computer or telecommunications systems *US*
- Southwestern Bell is using a war-dialer in an attempt to find out what numbers are actually bulletin board numbers.— *Phrack World News*, 27th February 1989

warehoused *adjective*
used of a prisoner who is neither educated nor trained during a period of imprisonment but simply contained *UK*
- —Angela Devlin, *Prison Patter*, p. 122, 1996

warez *noun*
pirated computer software offered over the Internet *UK*
A deliberate respelling of 'wares'.
- — Susie Dent, *The Language Report*, p. 32, 2003

warhead *noun*
in cricket, a fast bowler *UK, 1996*
- —Keith Foley, *A Dictionary of Cricketing Terminology*, p. 367, 1998

warlord *noun*
a high-level member of a political organisation *US*
- However, any captain can offer a candidate and it's even happened that a retiring warlord ain't been too popular, or the man or woman he chooses to take his place has made a lot of enemies, and the committeeman don't get his way.—Robert Campbell, *In a Pig's Eye*, p. 6–7, 1991

warm *noun*
an act of warming; an act of becoming warm *UK, 1768*
Colloquial.

warm *adjective*
good *UK*
- —Angela Devlin, *Prison Patter*, p. 122, 1996
- Al used to be a bit warm on the cobbles himself[.]—Lenny McLean, *The Guv'nor*, p. 112, 1998

warm for your form *adjective*
sexually attracted to someone *US*
- I knowed this daddy warm for my form, but – like, too much.—Robert Gover, *Here Goes Kitten*, p. 80, 1964

warm fuzzies *noun*
the feeling when praised by a superior *US*
- —Rachel S. Epstein and Nina Liebman, *Biz Speak*, p. 244, 1986

warm one *noun*
a bullet *US*
- Jones was not there at the time, but apparently was told at some point that Caldwell had threatened to put "two warm ones" – street slang for bullets – in Jackson for running his mouth too much. — *Roanoke (Virginia) Times & World News*, p. A1, 9th October 1998

warmup *noun*
a loose-fitting, athletic warmup suit *US*
- Raji in cranberry designer warmups today with his cowboy boots, always the boots, Raji smiling at her like nothing had changed. —Elmore Leonard, *Be Cool*, p. 81, 1999

warm up *verb*
to refill a cup of coffee *US*
- Can I warm that up for you?— *Fargo*, 1996

warn't *verb*
was not; were not *US*
- Meanwhile, all these folkies [...] were deciding that the rock 'n' roll stuff warn't so bad[.]—Lester Bangs, *Psychotic Reactions and Carburetor Dung*, p. 41, 1970

warp *noun*
a bent card used by a card cheat to identify the value of the card *US*
- —Frank Scoblete, *Best Blackjack*, p. 275, 1996

war paint *noun*
makeup, cosmetics *US, 1869*
Originally theatrical.
- —Lou Shelly, *Hepcats Jive Talk Dictionary*, p. 35, 1945
- In fact, [Diamanda] Galas is a less fearsome proposition offstage – smaller and friendlier without her war-paint.— *The Guardian*, 17th September 2001

warped *adjective*
1 perverted *US*
- "Nick, how did you get to be so warped?" "Bad home life."—C.D. Payne, *Youth in Revolt*, p. 395, 1993

2 drug-intoxicated *US*
- Yeah, they got stoned on giggle-weed, zonked on grifa, zapped on yerba, bombed on boo, they were blitzed with snop, warped on twist, gay on hay, free on V.— *Hi Life*, p. 14, 1979

3 drunk *UK*
- — *e-cyclopaedia*, 20th March 2002

warp one *noun*
a high speed *US*
Figurative US naval aviator usage.
- — *United States Naval Institute Proceedings*, p. 108, October 1986

warp seven *adverb*
very quickly *US*
- There be them big dudes with their full-auto Uzis, an go bailin warp-seven cause Gordy gots the balls to shoot back with this!—Jess Mowry, *Way Past Cool*, 1992

warrior *noun*
a fearless, violent member of a youth gang *US*
- —Mark S. Fleisher, *Beggars & Thieves*, p. 292, 1995: 'Glossary'

warrior bold *noun*
a cold *UK*
- —Julian Franklyn, *A Dictionary of Rhyming Slang*, 1961
- —Ray Puxley, *Cockney Rabbit*, 1992

wars *noun*
▸ **have been in the wars**
to show signs of injury, especially the trivial wounds that afflict children *UK, 1850*
- They had two mummies, which had obviously been in the wars – quite literally, when in the second world war in 1943 the place had been bombed, and the mummies had suffered damage as a result. — *The Guardian*, 27th December 2002

warthog *noun*
a US Air Force attack plane formally known as an A-10 Thunderbolt *US*
Gulf war usage.
- — *American Speech*, p. 404, Winter 1991: 'Among the new words'

warts and all *noun*
without an attempt to conceal blemishes or imperfections *UK, 1930*
- Warts and all, the streets was my playground.—Edwin Torres, *Carlito's Way*, p. 19, 1975

war wagon *noun*
a vehicle carrying weapons on a motorcyle gang outing when trouble is expected *US*
- The women and probates are the ones that usually drive the crash truck or war wagon during their outings[.]—Paladin Press, *Inside Look at Outlaw Motorcyle Gangs*, p. 1, 1992

Warwick Farm; warwick *noun*
the arm *AUSTRALIA, 1944*
Rhyming slang, after the name of a racecourse in Sydney.
- —Jim Ramsay, *Cop It Sweet!*, p. 95, 1977
- If you was a drinkin' man like us, you'd know that an ice cold Resch's overcomes every form of discomfort from whiffy warwicks to housemaid's knee..—Lance Peters, *The Dirty Half-Mile*, 1979
- —Ryan Aven-Bray, *Ridgey Didge Oz Jack Lang*, p. 52, 1983
- —Ned Wallish, *The Truth Dictionary of Racing Slang*, 1989
- — *Sydney Morning Herald*, p. 1, 2002

war zone *noun*
an area in Washington D.C. infamous for drug sales and other crime *US*
- About two weeks ago, Marcus visited one of his regular stops, the PCP sales "war zone" around 21st Street and Maryland Avenue NE. — *Washington Post*, p. B1, 29th July 1984

wash *noun*
1 crack cocaine *UK*
A shortened form of 'readywash'. To manufacture crack cocaine, hydrachloride is *washed* in a solution of baking soda and water.
- —Angela Devlin, *Prison Patter*, p. 122, 1996
- Crack is also known as PEBBLES, SCUD, WASH, STONE and ROCK[.] —Macfarlane, Macfarlane and Robson, *The User*, p. 112, 1996

- [M]ost cocaine use in the UK is in the smokeable form of 'crack' cocaine ('base', 'rock' or 'wash'). —Simon G. Gowers, *Adolescent Psychiatry in Clinical Practice*, p. 171, 2001

2 the effect of a drug *US*

- "How's the wash?" he said. The girl raised her head. "Nice," she said. —Vernon E. Smith, *The Jones Men*, p. 21, 1974

3 a large number of things or people *BARBADOS*

- —Frank A. Collymore, *Barbadian Dialect*, p. 118, 1965

▸ **the wash**

theft of money in public lavatories while the owner is washing *UK*

- —David Powis, *The Signs of Crime*, 1977

wash *verb*

1 to kill *US, 1941*

- If push come to shove, we can wash him – but right now you need time, get it, time! —Edwin Torres, *Carlito's Way*, p. 33, 1975
- With Brennan, if you're late, you're never. He will wash us in another fuckin' moment. —Edwin Torres, *Q & A*, p. 187, 1977
- If I go in the prison without any relatives, and I happen to get sent over the wall to the hospital and they want to kill me, they can wash me in no time flat. —Herbert Huncke, *Guilty of Everything*, p. 117, 1990

2 to purge or expunge something *US*

- And I've got the right contacts at the courthouse. Your case is as good as washed. —Gerald Petievich, *To Die in Beverly Hills*, p. 155, 1983

3 to give money obtained illegally the appearance of legitimacy through accounting and banking schemes *US*

- I gave you strict instructions ... that money is never to leave the dead-drop until it's been washed, and then only by my instructions. —Stephen J. Cannell, *Big Con*, p. 313, 1997

4 to shuffle a deck of cards *US*

- —Irwin Steig, *Play Gin to Win*, p. 143,

5 to receive favourable consideration *US*

- — Department of the Army, *Staff Officer's Guidebook*, p. 68, 1986

6 to be credible *UK, 1849*

- [I]t's only natural you two want to make things easy for him – but it won't wash!!! —Barry Humphries, *Bazza Pulls It Off!*, 1971

▸ **not a child in the house washed**

nothing done, no progress made *IRELAND*

- A month and a day until the start of all party tales on the future of the North and, as one official busily engaged in trying to devise ways around the worst obstacles put it recently, "not a child in the house washed." —*Irish Times*, 9th May 1996
- I pushed past them. I didn't think they'd normally let a push go but it was early in the day. A quarter to twelve and not a child in the house washed. —Eamonn Sweeney, *Waiting for the Healer*, p. 257, 1997

▸ **wash mouth**

to criticise someone or something without concern for the consequences *TRINIDAD AND TOBAGO, 1986*

- —Lise Winer, *Dictionary of the English/Creole of Trinidad & Tobago*, 2003

▸ **wash your face**

when selling a lot by auction, to break even *UK*

- —*Bargain Hunt*, 11th November 2004

▸ **wash your mouth out; wash out your mouth**

addressed to someone using *filthy* language or *dirty* words *UK, 1961*

Often as an imperative, and occasionally elaborated with 'soap', or 'soap and water'.

- If he [Boris Johnson] does have any serious political ambitions – a question still to be resolved – he will need to wash his mouth out with soap. —*The Observer*, 5th October 2003

wash away *verb*

to kill someone *US, 1941*

- The more guys they wash away, the more they get to feeling like they're immortal or something. —Mezz Mezzrow, *Really the Blues*, p. 95, 1946

washboard *noun*

in mountain biking, an area of hard, rippled earth *US*

- Here's the perfect position for cleaning washboard bumps. Keep your butt above the saddle and weight slightly back. —*Mountain Bike Magazine's Complete Guide To Mountain Biking Skills*, p. 145, 1996

washboard *adjective*

of an abdomen, trim, muscular, defined *US*

From the appearance – solid and rippled.

- See that? A washboard gut. I have yet to observe the black male victim in this town with more than a thirty-inch waist. —Richard Price, *Clockers*, p. 137, 1992
- I suppose you wouldn't like someone with a washboard stomach like Brad Pitt. —*Something About Mary*, 1998
- Morelli had washboard abs. Morelli could actually do sit-ups. Lots of them. —Janet Evanovich, *Seven Up*, 2001

washdown *noun*

beer *FIJI*

Especially in the context of drinking after a session of drinking the tranquilising herbal beverage kava. Recorded by Jan Tent in 1991.

washed-up *adjective*

no longer successful, finished *US, 1923*

- He was fed up with the snooty ones, the smart ones and the washed-up ones. Like his father. —John Burke and Stuart Douglass, *The Boys*, p. 78–79, 1962
- increasingly bitter old washed-up has been. —Lester Bangs, *Psychotic Reactions and Carburetor Dung*, p. 377, 1981
- [A]sking God to help you kick the ass of a washed-up loser is a bullshit thing to ask the Almighty[.] —Howard Stern, *Miss America*, p. 252, 1995

washer *noun*

▸ **put a washer on**

to urinate *UK*

A Lancashire term, reported as being in use in 1967 by Paul Janssen, 1976.

washer-dryer *noun*

a douche bag and towel *US*

- —Edith A. Folb, *runnin' down some lines*, p. 259, 1980

wash-foot-and-come *noun*

a noisy, rowdy party *ANTIGUA AND BARBUDA*

Collected by Richard Allsopp.

washicongs *noun*

trainers, sneakers *TRINIDAD AND TOBAGO*

- —Richard Allsopp, *Dictionary of Caribbean English Usage*, p. 591, 1992

washing machine *noun*

1 in computing, an obsolete large hard disk found in a large floor cabinet *US*

- —Eric S. Raymond, *The New Hacker's Dictionary*, p. 377, 1991

2 a wave as it breaks over and thrashes a surfer *US*

- —Trevor Cralle, *The Surfin'ary*, p. 156, 1991

Washington *noun*

a one-dollar note *US*

From the portrait of George Washington on the note.

- —Edd Byrnes, *Way Out with Kookie*, 1959

Washington Monument *noun*

in poker, a hand with three fives *US*

A rather esoteric allusion to the fact that the Washington Monument is 555 feet high.

- —George Percy, *The Language of Poker*, p. 96, 1988

washout *noun*

1 a failure (a thing or a person); a disappointment; a cancellation *UK, 1902*

- [H]is first party conference promises to be a wash-out. —*New Statesman*, 1st October 2001

2 in motorcyle racing, the condition that occurs when the front wheel begins to slide in soft dirt; also used in mountain biking *US*

- During a front-wheel washout you lose steering control —Ed Radlauer, *Motorcylopedia*, p. 71, 1973

wash out *verb*

1 to fail and expel someone from a course or training *US*

- Tell me how they're going to wash me out if I don't come to the pistol range during the lunch hour and practice extra. —Joseph Wambaugh, *The New Centurions*, p. 14, 1970

2 in motor racing, to suffer a loss or decrease in steering responsiveness *US*

- —Don Alexander, *The Racer's Dictionary*, p. 74, 1980

3 in mountain-biking, to lose front-wheel traction *US*

- But if you turn your bar in the sand, you'll wash out. —*Mountain Bike Magazine's Complete Guide To Mountain Biking Skills*, p. 146, 1996

4 to process cocaine into crack cocaine *UK*

- —Angela Devlin, *Prison Patter*, p. 122, 1996

wash-pot *noun*
something or someone easily obtained *TRINIDAD AND TOBAGO, 1971*
- — Lise Winer, *Dictionary of the English/Creole of Trinidad & Tobago*, 2003

wash rock *noun*
crack cocaine *UK, 1990s*
Combines two separate terms for **CRACK**.
- I need the fuckin' wash rock yeah. Wha' y' gonna do? — Nick Barlay, *Curvy Lovebox*, p. 51, 1997

wash-up *noun*
a post-event analytical discussion *UK, 1965*
Originally Royal Navy, then the wider military, and from there into corporate and political jargon.
- Finally, in a 'wash-up' session, the assessors agreed overall ratings for each candidate[.] — Robert Wood and Tim Payne, *Competency-Based Recruitment and Selection*, p. 154, 1998

wash up *verb*
in heterosexual intercourse, to enter the vagina from behind *UK*
- — *Sky Magazine*, July 2001

washwoman's gig *noun*
in an illegal numbers gambling lottery, a bet on 4, 11 and 44 *US*
- — *American Speech*, p. 193, October 1949

washy *adjective*
used of a racehorse sweating, especially with anxiety *US*
- — Tom Ainslie, *Ainslie's Complete Guide to Thoroughbred Racing*, p. 340, 1976

wasp; wap *noun*
1 a *w*hite *A*nglo *S*axon *P*rotestant *US*
The term is applied to whites without particular regard to the religious component.
- These "old" Americans are 'WASPs' – in the cocktail party jargon of the sociologists. That is, they are white, they are Anglo-Saxon in origin, and they are Protestant (and disproportionately Episcopalian. — *American Political Science Review*, p. 1010, 1957
- I did meet a wasp there though. — *Screw*, 4th April 1969
- Fools, boors, philistines, Birchers, B'nai Brithees, Defense Leaguers, Hadassah theater party piranhas, UJAviators, concert-hall Irishmen, WAP ignorati... — Tom Wolfe, *Radical Chic & Mau-Mauing the Flak Catchers*, p. 93, 1970
- Christ, there are dozens of firms who will kiss the ass of a WASP who can merely pass the bar. — Erich Segal, *Love Story*, p. 98, 1970
- These ethnic guys are worse than the wasps; they say, "I made it, why can't you?" — Edwin Torres, *Carlito's Way*, p. 119, 1975

2 a *w*hite *A*ppalachian *s*outhern *P*rotestant *US*
- By the mid 1950s, WASP was Chicago slang and Ohio Valley social workers' jargon for white Appalachian Southern Protestants – the poor whites who migrated to the industrial cities of norhtern Ohio and the Great Lakes. — *Maledicta*, p. 97, Summer/Winter 1981

3 a traffic warden *UK*
From the yellow band on the uniform hat and sleeves (no doubt influenced by a characteristic intent to 'sting' a harmless motorist).
- — *Christchurch Times (Hampshire)*, 14th October 1966

waspishness *noun*
the state of being distinctly white, Anglo-Saxon and Protestant *US*
- To their Waspishness should be added the tendency to be located on the Eastern seaboard or around San Francisco, to be prep school and Ivy League educated, and to be possessed of inherited wealth. — *American Political Science Review*, p. 1010–1011, 1957

wass *verb*
▷ see: **WAZ**

wassock; wazzock; wazzuck *noun*
a fool; an annoying or stupid individual *UK, 1983*
- Well, who's a soft little wassock? — Liz Evans, *Barking!*, p. 46, 2001
- One red card for a serious foul. What a total wazzock. Who brings out red cards in a practice? — Janet Fish, *Me (and Charlie)*, p. 37, 2003

wassup?; whas up?; wassuuup?
used as a greeting *US*
A slurred 'what's up?' with dozens of variant spellings. Wildly popular popspeak in the US (and, to a degree, UK) in 2000 in response to a series of television advertisements for Budweiser™ beer.
- Whas up, baby doll? — *New Jack City*, 1990
- "Wha's up?" the guy said to Strike, not knowing exactly who Strike was either. — Richard Price, *Clockers*, p. 324, 1992
- — *The Bell (Paducah Tilghman High School)*, p. 8–9, 17th December 1993: 'Tilghmanism: the concealed langage of the hallway'
- YOU: Wassup, baby? HER (SHAKING THE [PORNOGRAPHIC VIDEO] TAPE, SCREAMING): Is this what you like? Is this what the fuck you like? — Chris Rock, *Rock This!*, p. 166, 1997
- Binch insisted on wandering up and down the queue bellowing "Wassuuup?" and blowing a party screecher in people's faces. — *The Guardian*, 28th December 2000
- — Julian Johnson, *Urban Survival*, p. 258, 2003

wassy *adjective*
ostentatious, especially in a sexually provocative way *TRINIDAD AND TOBAGO, 1987*
- — Lise Winer, *Dictionary of the English/Creole of Trinidad & Tobago*, 2003

waste *verb*
1 to kill someone *US, 1964*
- I mean, you want to waste Limpy? — Claude Brown, *Manchild in the Promised Land*, p. 176, 1965
- "I guess you heard about Malcom?" "Yeah," I said. "They say he got wasted." — Eldridge Cleaver, *Soul on Ice*, p. 52, 1968
- His entire outfit was wasted, like they say[.] — Doug Lang, *Freaks*, p. 21, 1973
- In that war, soldier's slang for death was "wasted." So-and-so was wasted. It was a good word. — Philip Caputo, *A Rumor of War*, p. 210, 1977
- He caught a five-year bit in Joliet for fencing jewelry and furs he ripped off from junkie burglars. He went to bat [stood trial] for wasting three of 'em, but he beat those raps. — Iceberg Slim (Robert Beck), *Airtight Willie and Me*, p. 94, 1979
- They came to do me in. To waste me. — Gerald Petievich, *Money Men*, p. 153, 1981
- The woman who was wasted when Finlay got snatched. — Richard Condon, *Prizzi's Honor*, p. 233, 1982
- Waste the fucker and then see who talks. — *Platoon*, 1986
- Do you think you're gonna waste anybody? Cuz if you are, go for Milo first. — *Airheads*, 1994
- [D]o your job and waste as many of the fuckers as you can[.] — Chris Ryan, *The Watchman*, p. 160, 2001

2 to smoke marijuana *US*
- I decided to go upstairs to my place and waste a stick of pot. — Piri Thomas, *Down These Mean Streets*, p. 229, 1967

3 (used of a jockey in horse racing) to lose weight *AUSTRALIA*
- — Ned Wallish, *The Truth Dictionary of Racing Slang*, p. 87, 1989

▸ **waste babies**
(of a male) to masturbate *US*
- "The boy is masturbating" [...] Wasting babies[.] — Erica Orloff and JoAnn Baker, *Dirty Little Secrets*, p. 89, 2001

▸ **waste groceries**
to vomit *US*
- — Connie Eble (Editor), *UNC-CH Campus Slang*, p. 1, Spring 1987

wastebasket *noun*
in pool, a pocket that seems receptive to balls dropping *US*
- — Mike Shamos, *The Illustrated Encyclopedia of Billiards*, p. 206, 1993

waste-case *noun*
a drunkard *US*
- — Connie Eble (Editor), *UNC-CH Campus Slang*, p. 7, Fall 1987

wasted *adjective*
1 drunk or drug-intoxicated *US*
- — J. R. Friss, *A Dictionary of Teenage Slang (Mt. Diablo High)*, 1964
- There was nothing to do but go back to camp and get wasted. — Hunter S. Thompson, *Hell's Angels*, p. 169, 1966
- I'd be too tired or stoned or wasted to get up in the afternoon to even go out and sit beneath the umbrellas in the hot sun at the beach club with Blair. — Bret Easton Ellis, *Less Than Zero*, p. 59, 1985
- Nell kept going to the mirror to check for signs of life. Her tongue needed a shave. That goddamn little neurotic got her wasted. — Joseph Wambaugh, *Finnegan's Week*, p. 160, 1993
- Oh man I'm fucking wasted. — *Dazed and Confused*, 1993
- His black army boots rested on the sofa's other arm. He was wasted. — Donald Gorgon, *Cop Killer*, p. 67, 1994
- I'm so wasted, drunk drunk[.] — *Boogie Nights*, 1997
- And now Gahan is being stretchered off, too wasted to notice, too fucked to care. — *Uncut*, p. 44, May 2001

2 absolutely exhausted *UK, 1995*
From earlier uses as 'intoxicated'.

Waste Island *nickname*
the West Island of Montreal *CANADA, C20*
Likely nicknamed with this derogatory term by teenagers, the West Island area of the city is heavily residential and suburban, meaning that under-age citizens have to be transported around by their parents or use the bus, and by contrast with central Montreal, it is boring.

waster *noun*
a lazy unambitious person *IRELAND*
- [T]oo good for that waster. — Roddy Doyle, *The Van*, p. 28, 1991

waste-time *adjective*
dull, boring, uninteresting *US*
Hawaiian youth usage.
- Man, dat one real waste-time class! — Elizabeth Ball Carr, *Da Kine Talk*, p. 156, 1972

wastoid *noun*
a worthless, dim-witted person; a person whose drug or alcohol use is ruining their life *US*
- Yo, wastoid – you're not gonna blaze up in here! — *The Breakfast Club*, 1985
- — *Washington Post*, p. 18, 8th November 1987: 'Say wha?'

wastry *noun*
rubbish (trash) *JAMAICA*
- — Peter Patrick, *Some Recent Jamaican Creole Words*, 2003

watch *verb*
▸ **watch your lip; watch your mouth; watch your trap**
to talk politely; to mind your manners; to not speak out of turn *UK*
Often exclamatory.
- TIM: Leave us alone, Dad. [His Dad slams his hand down on the table]. GEOFF: Watch your trap! Boy! — Paul Fraser and Shane Meadows, *Twenty-FourSeven*, p. 71, 1997

▸ **watch your step**
to be careful; to be cautious in a current or planned activity *UK*
Often as a warning.
- You'd better watch your step now that he's back. — Graeme Kent, *The Queen's Corporal [Six Granada Plays]*, p. 93, 1959

watcha
▹ see: WOTCHER

watch and chain; watch *noun*
the brain *UK*
Rhyming slang.
- Of a dullard it may be said, "His watch needs looking at," or "His watch is slow." [...] When castigating someone for not thinking it is generally used in full, e.g., "Why don't you use your watch and chain once in a while?" — Ray Puxley, *Cockney Rabbit*, 1992

watchie *noun*
a watchman *UK: SCOTLAND*
- Ye'd think the watchie would check they weans [those children] for playin on that [building] site. — Michael Munro, *The Complete Patter*, p. 164, 1996

watch it *verb*
used as a (sometimes threatening) warning to be careful *UK, 1916*
Always imperative, often exclamatory.
- If you don't watch it, Monty, he said to himself, you'll be stone blind raving paralytic drunk. — Derek Bickerton, *Payroll*, p. 120, 1959

watch queen *noun*
1 a homosexual man who derives sexual pleasure from watching other men having sex *US*
- — *American Speech*, p. 59, Spring-Summer 1970: 'Homosexual slang'
- Customers for this sort of service are often "watch queens," men who receive gratification from watching the sexual activities of others. — George Paul Csicsery (Editor), *The Sex Industry*, p. 33, 1973

2 a lookout during impersonal homosexual sex in public places *US*
- This is the role of the lookout ("watchqueen" in the argot), a man who is situated at the door or windows from which he may observe the means of access to the restroom. — Laud Humphreys, *Tearoom Trade*, p. 27, 1975

watch this space
used as an announcement that further developments may be expected *UK, 1917*
Originally, and still, used of space in a newspaper, etc.
- Call me – call me / Won't you call this number now / Worlds apart – we are worlds apart / Watch this space[.] — Go West *Call Me*, 1985

watch works *noun*
the brain *CANADA*
Teen slang, reported by a Toronto newspaper in 1946, and reported as 'obsolescent or obsolete' by Douglas Leechman, 1959.

water *noun*
1 methamphetamine or another central nervous system stimulant *US*
- — Geoffrey Froner, *Digging for Diamonds*, 1989
- — James Harris, *A Convict's Dictionary*, 1989

2 phencyclidine, the recreational drug known as PCP or angel dust *US*
- — *USA Today*, p. 1A, 25th April 1989

3 semen *TRINIDAD AND TOBAGO, 1983*
- — Lise Winer, *Dictionary of the English/Creole of Trinidad & Tobago*, 2003

▹ see: WATERCRESS, WATER HEN

▸ **go in the water**
to lose an athletic contest or other competition intentionally *US*
- Then why did anybody bother to offer you money if you went in the water? — Rocky Garciano (with Rowland Barber), *Somebody Up There Likes Me*, p. 306, 1955

▸ **go to water**
to be overcome with fear; to fail to maintain a resolve *AUSTRALIA, 1950*
- He went to water and spilled the beans about me and Stan. — Ward McNally, *Supper at Happy Harry's*, p. 156, 1982
- — Ryan Aven-Bray, *Ridgey Didge Oz Jack Lang*, p. 29, 1983
- — Clive Galea, *Slipper*, p. 215, 1988

▸ **in the water; out in the water**
in debt *US*
- — William K. Bentley and James M. Corbett, *Prison Slang*, 1992

▸ **over the water**
Northern Ireland *UK*
A British armed services' view of the world.
- The aim is to familiarize you with the small weapons that the Regiment [SAS] use over the water, especially covert operations with the pistol. — Andy McNab (writing of the late 1970s/early 80s), *Immediate Action*, p. 151, 1995

water *verb*
▸ **water her garden**
(of a man) to have sex with a woman *JAMAICA*

▸ **water the garden**
to change the bottles of intravenous fluid that feed a neurologically depressed hospital patient *US*
- — *Maledicta*, p. 70, Summer/Winter 1978: 'Common patient-directed pejoratives used by medical personnel'

▸ **water the horses**
to urinate *AUSTRALIA, 1971*
- Hang on a few jiffs, I'll just whip off to the snake's house and water the horses. — *The Adventures of Barry McKenzie*, 1972

▸ **water the vegetables**
to administer intravenous fluids to a hospital's neurologically depressed patients *US*
- — *Maledicta*, p. 118, 1984–1985: 'Milwaukee medical maledicta'

water black *noun*
mascara *UK*
Because water is needed for application.
- — Wilfred Granville, *The Theater Dictionary*, p. 219, 1952

waterbomber *noun*
an aircraft for fighting fires *CANADA*
Most of the world's waterbombers are made by Canadair in Montreal, and are known in Europe as 'le Canadair' and 'le pelican'.

- They included two [forest fires] caused by lightning, one of which was knocked out by a Mars waterbomber. — *Victoria Daily Times*, p. 21–22, 12th August 1965

water box *noun*
in drag racing, the area where cars heat and clean their tyres before a race *US*
- This third rpm function is designed for drag race applications and is to be activated when the car is in the water box during a burnout. — Tony Sakkis, *Bracket Racing*, p. 43, 1997

waterboy *noun*
a truck with a water tank used to spray water or other liquids on the ground *US*
- — Montie Tak, *Truck Talk*, p. 183, 1971

water burner *noun*
a cook *AUSTRALIA, 1982*
The form 'water scorcher' has been recorded as early as 1916.

watercooler moment *noun*
a televisual moment that is expected to get people talking the next day *US*
The discussions about such a moment are envisaged to happen when office workers meet at a watercooler.
- — Susie Dent, *The Language Report*, p. 49, 2003

watercress; water *noun*
a dress *UK*
Rhyming slang.
- — Ray Puxley, *Fresh Rabbit*, 1998

watercress; water *verb*
to dress *UK*
Rhyming slang.
- [Y]ou get "watered" after you wash. — Ray Puxley, *Fresh Rabbit*, 1998

water dog *noun*
1 in circus and carnival usage, a seal *US*
- — Don Wilmeth, *The Language of American Popular Entertainment*, p. 192, 1981

2 in trucking, a truck with leaking water lines *US*
- — Montie Tak, *Truck Talk*, p. 183, 1971

waterfall *verb*
to drink from a can or bottle by cascading the liquid into your mouth without touching the can or bottle with your lips *US*
Collected from a 13 year old in Irvine, California, April 2003.

Waterford *adjective*
easily understood; perfectly clear *UK*
Puns the synonymous 'crystal clear' with well-known Irish glass manufacturers Waterford Crystal.
- [F]rom this moment right now one thing is fucking Waterford. — Kevin Sampson, *Outlaws*, p. 63, 2001

waterhead *noun*
a person with mental problems *US*
- — Gary K. Farlow, *Prison-ese*, p. 78, 2002

water hen; water *noun*
ten *UK*
Rhyming slang, especially in horse racing.
- — Charles Drummond, *The Odds on Death*, 1969

waterhole; water hole *noun*
1 a public hotel *AUSTRALIA, 1968*
- Waterhole wonder: If there's any argument that the Hero of Waterloo Hotel is the oldest pub in Sydney, there can be no dispute that it has the oldest musicians anywhere. — *Advertiser*, p. 14, 3rd July 1990

2 a truck stop *US*
- — Lanie Dills, *The Official CB Slanguage Language Dictionary*, p. 77, 1976

watering hole; watering spot *noun*
a bar or club where alcohol is served; a public hotel *US, 1955*
- The joint was a watering and feeding spot for many of America's top black sports and theatrical stars. — Iceberg Slim (Robert Beck), *The Naked Soul of Iceberg Slim*, p. 80, 1971
- I first met Lance at the outside bar of the Island Hotel, the local watering hole also featuring great food. — Jimmy Buffett, *Tales from Margaritaville*, p. 166, 1989
- Lou was the bartender down at the Silk 'n Spurs on Geary, Frank's favorite watering hole. — Seth Morgan, *Homeboy*, p. 73, 1990
- An eighteen-carat watering hole and safe haven for some of Fulham's finest denizenry [sic]. — Andrew Nickolds, *Back to Basics*, p. 3, 1994

Waterloo *noun*
a stew *UK*
Rhyming slang, from the area of London.
- — Ray Puxley, *Cockney Rabbit*, 1992

watermelons *noun*
female breasts of generous dimensions *US*
From the all too obvious resemblance.
- Boobs, zonkers, headlights, watermelons, sweater puppies, pointers, knockers, jugs, tatas – these are some of the words to describe women's breasts. — Howard Stern, *Miss America*, p. 441, 1995

water sports *noun*
1 sexual activity involving the giving and getting of an enema *US*
- Have you ever heard of "water sports?" No? Well, people who are into that enjoy giving, or – more commonly – receiving enemas. — *Screw*, p. 7, 6th June 1969
- — *What Color is Your Handkerchief*, p. 7, 1979

2 sexual activity that includes urination *US*
- "Water sports" may mean another thing too. Some people get a charge out of urinating on their sexual partners, or having their sexual partners piss on them. — *Screw*, p. 7, 6th June 1969
- Such would be about the typical s-m scenarior for anyone into water sports, the final rush to the john providing pleasant humiliation. — Gerald and Caroline Greene, *S-M*, p. 201, 1974
- A golden shower is just another name for urination. You may also hear this act referred to as water sports. — Stephen Ziplow, *The Film Maker's Guide to Pornography*, p. 16, 1977
- C'mon. Gimme the dirt. Bondage and Discipline? Water sports? Satin sheets? — Armistead Maupin, *Tales of the City*, p. 317, 1978
- The film's raunchiest scene takes place in the kitchen, where C.J. Laing engages in "water sports" and "Greek" coupling. — Kent Smith et al., *Adult Movies*, p. 31, 1982
- [H]aving something bigger than a finger up her bottom, enjoying having Harry [sperm] on the boat [face], and liking water sports[.] — Colin Butts, *Is Harry on the Boat?*, p. 236, 1997
- Lately a lot of people have made it pretty trendy to do water sports or golden shower kind of things. — Anthony Petkovich, *The X Factory*, p. 129, 1997

water-walker *noun*
a fellow aviator whose accomplishments approach the miraculous *US*
US naval aviator usage.
- — *United States Naval Institute Proceedings*, p. 108, October 1986

water-water *noun*
marijuana *UK*
- — Mike Haskins, *Drugs*, p. 289, 2003

water works *noun*
1 tears *UK, 1647*
- Him and his phony waterworks he could turn on and off. — John M. Murtagh and Sara Harris, *Cast the First Stone*, p. 20, 1957
- She turned on the waterworks to cop her license to do me in but I was immune to her tears. — Iceberg Slim (Robert Beck), *Long White Con*, p. 12, 1977
- Hey, kid, turn off the waterworks, okay? — *Lethal Weapon*, 1987
- Save the fucking waterworks. — Colin Butts, *Is Harry on the Boat?*, p. 299, 1997

2 the urinary system *US*
- — *American Speech*, p. 145–148, May 1961: 'The spoken language of medicine; argot, slang, cant'

wave *noun*
1 the semi-erect penis *US*
Interview of Jim Holliday, 12th June 1987.

2 crack cocaine *UK, 1998*
- — Mike Haskins, *Drugs*, p. 282, 2003

wave *verb*
to bend the edge of a playing card for later cheating *US*
- — John Scarne, *Scarne's Guide to Modern Poker*, p. 293, 1979

▸ **wave a dead chicken**
to knowingly make a futile attempt to resolve a problem *US, 1996*
Possibly an allusion to voodoo.
- — Susie Dent, *The Language Report*, p. 83, 2003

▸ **wave your wig**
to comb your hair *US*
High school student usage.
- — *San Francisco Examiner*, p. 21, 12th December 1961: 'Colloquialisms for your murgatroid Handcuffs'

wavelength *noun*

▸ **on your wavelength; on the same wavelength**
to comprehend (and agree with) another's point of view or approach *US, 1927*
Figurative application of a clear radio signal.
- She appreciated my jokes and I appreciated hers. She was on my wave-length, or I on hers. — Sally Cline, *Couples*, p. 78, 1998

waves *noun*

▸ **make waves**
to stir up trouble; to upset an established or accepted routine *US, 1962*
- Anna Diamantopoulou, the European commissioner for social policy and employment, has been making waves – upsetting those who think "Brussels" should mind its own business[.] — *The Guardian*, 13th April 2001

wax *noun*
phonograph records *US, 1932*
Recordings were originally made on wax cylinders or discs; the term applied to shellac discs and, subsequently, vinyl, but is not used to refer to newer technologies such as CD, tape, etc.
- The man ain't cut a righteous hunk of wax yet! — Ross Russell, *The Sound*, p. 112, 1961
- — Simon Warner, *Rockspeak!*, p. 301, 1996

▸ **put the wax on the tracks**
to get ready and start out *UK*
- Guess we should be putting the wax on the tracks in a minute guys and get going. — Colin Butts, *Is Harry Still on the Boat?*, p. 80, 2003

wax *verb*

1 to shoot or kill someone *US*
- They'll wax you, maybe. — Clarence Cooper Jr, *The Scene*, p. 220, 1960
- — *Time*, p. 34, 10th December 1965
- — Carl Fleischhauer, *A Glossary of Army Slang*, p. 25, 1968
- Just because that stud got waxed, that ain't goin' stop us from having to pay protection dues. — Donald Goines, *Black Gangster*, p. 232, 1977
- After we got serious we had the hardware and we could wax their ass every day, ten to one. — Walter Boyne and Steven Thompson, *The Wild Blue*, p. 561, 1986
- I'm going to wax your ass. — Stephen Coonts, *Flight of the Intruder*, p. 140, 1986

2 to excel; to perform well *US*
- — Don R. McCreary (Editor), *Dawg Speak*, 2001

3 in children's games, to share turns at bat, kicking or the like *AUSTRALIA*
- Wax: To share. — Bazza and Curly, *Betcha Wrong!*, p. 35, 1990

▸ **wax the carrot**
(of a male) to masturbate *US*
- "The boy is masturbating" [...] Waxing the carrot[.] — Erica Orloff and JoAnn Baker, *Dirty Little Secrets*, p. 89, 2001

▸ **wax the dolphin**
(of a male) to masturbate *US*
- — Connie Eble (Editor), *UNC-CH Campus Slang*, p. 7, Fall 1987

▸ **wax the weezer**
(of a male) to masturbate *US*
- "The boy is masturbating" [...] Waxing the weezer[.] — Erica Orloff and JoAnn Baker, *Dirty Little Secrets*, p. 89, 2001

waxa *adjective*
good, excellent *UK*
- Typical slang words that Charvas use are "belta", "mint" and "waxa" all meaning good or great[.] — Chris Lewis, *The Dictionary of Playground Slang*, p. 53, 2003

waxhead *noun*
a surfer *AUSTRALIA, 1981*
From the wax used on surfboards.
- — Kathy Lette, *Girls' Night Out*, p. 13, 1987
- First off, there are the 'Waxheads'. This is a fierce, amphibious breed – commonly known as 'Seaweed munchers', 'Shark-suckers' or plain old 'Surfies'. — *Sydney Morning Herald*, p. 7, 3rd January 1987
- Surfies – waxheads or skegs to their rival tribes – are Sydney's longest surviving sub-culture. — *Sunday Telegraph*, p. 8, 8th April 1990

wax me
used as an injunction or request to be given a marijuana cigarette *UK*
- — Angela Devlin, *Prison Patter*, p. 122, 1996

wax up *verb*
to conceal contraband in a small container in readiness for concealment of the container in the anus *UK*
- — Angela Devlin, *Prison Patter*, p. 122, 1996

waxy *noun*
in horse racing, an enthusiast who can't help shouting in the ears of those near him *AUSTRALIA*
- — Ned Wallish, *The Truth Dictionary of Racing Slang*, p. 87, 1989

way *noun*
a familiar neighbourhood; your home territory *US*
- — *Washington Post Magazine*, p. 11, 17th May 1987: 'Say wha?'
- — Richard McAlister, *Rapper's Handbook*, 1990

▸ **in a big way**
to an extreme *US*
- — Connie Eble (Editor), *UNC-CH Campus Slang*, Fall 1987

▸ **on the way out**
of a person, approaching retirement or likely to be dismissed; of a thing, coming to the end of its useful existence *UK, 1961*
- "Blair on the way out". (Don't Believe It). — *New Statesman*, 1st July 2002

▸ **that's the way (something does something)**
that's how things turn out *US*
Used in a formulaic construction of 'that's the way the NOUN VERBs'.
- The soldiers coined "That's the way the ball bounces," meaning what was ordained to be. — *East Liverpool (Ohio) Review*, 28th December 1952
- But that's the way the cookie crumbles. — *Independent Record (Helena, Montana)*, 27th November 1955
- One of the children had "That's the way the mop flops." — *Progress (Clearfield, Pennsylvania)*, 5th March 1956
- — *San Francisco Examiner*, p. 21, 12th December 1961: 'Colloquialisms for your murgatroid handcuffs'

▸ **the other way**
diverging from a stated condition *UK, 1858*
- Instead of being brought in line, I went very much the other way. — William Wright, *Born That Way*, p. 109, 1999

way *adverb*
extremely; without doubt *US*
- I mean we like had this way cranking bud sesh and like listened to AC/DC and watched Mommie Dearest with the sound off. — Mary Corey and Victoria Westermark, *Fer Shurr! How to be a Valley Girl*, 1982
- — Connie Eble (Editor), *UNC-CH Campus Slang*, p. 8, Fall 1987
- — *Washington Post Magazine*, p. 11, 17th May 1987: 'Say wha?'
- — Michael V. Anderson, *The Bad, Rad, Not to Forget Way Cool Beach and Surf Discriptionary*, p. 22, 1988
- No, but one with a way-sick sense of humor is toying with the idea even as you read this. — Frank Zappa, *The Real Frank Zappa Book*, p. 351, 1989
- Gaping barrels! Way overhead, man! — *Break Point*, 1991
- Way cool blood, homey. — Jess Mowry, *Way Past Cool*, p. 9, 1992
- — Jack Chambers (Editor), *Slang Bag 93 (University of Toronto)*, p. 6, Winter 1993
- I actually have a way normal life for a teenage girl. — *Clueless*, 1995
- Princess Superstar Is features collaborations with way-credible hip-hop luminaries such as Kool Keith and Bahamadia. — *The Times Magazine*, p. 43, 16th February 2002

wayback *adjective*
in remote areas *AUSTRALIA, 1899*
- — Charles Melaun, *The Squatter's Daughter*, p. 21, 1933
- They were a law unto themselves these old time guards on way-back lines. — Patsy Adam-Smith, *Folklore of the Australian Railwaymen*, p. 116, 1969
- — Sam Weller, *Old Bastards I Have Met*, p. 119, 1979
- — Herb Wharton, *Cattle Camp*, p. 33, 1994

way enough!
in team rowing, used as a command by the coxswain to the rowers to stop rowing *US*

Wayne Fontanas *adjective*
mad *UK*
Rhyming slang for **BANANAS**; formed from British singer Wayne Fontana (Glyn Ellis) (b.1945) who, as Wayne Fontana & The Mindbenders, came to prominence in the mid-1960s.
- It's enough to drive a copper completely Wayne Fontanas. — Mervyn Stutter, *Getting Nowhere Fast*, 21st May 2004

wayout *noun*
a person who is dressed in an extraordinary, unconventional fashion *US*
From **WAY OUT** (unconventional).
- There were Kings Road [Chelsea] trendies, hippies and wayouts. — *Sunday Telegraph*, p. 1, 6th July 1969

way out *adjective*
extreme; unconventional; experimental or innovative; good *US, 1958*
- Rocky and his fellas got to playing a way-out game with me called "One-finger-across-the-neck-inna-slicing-motion[.]" — Piri Thomas, *Down These Mean Streets*, p. 29, 1967
- If they were dressed in normal dress, then they would be inadequate personalities [...] but because of the fact that they are "way out", people take an interest in them[.] — Paul E Willis, *Profane Culture*, 1978

way past *adverb*
extremely *US*
- Wear a tank top all the time. Look way past cool, believe! — Jess Mowry, *Way Past Cool*, 1992

way to go!
used for registering approval; 'well done!' *US, 1972*
Abbreviated from 'that's the way to go!'.
- Ralph Cirella, way to go on set-designing[.] — Howard Stern, *Miss America*, p. 478, 1995

way up *adjective*
drunk *US*
- — *American Speech*, p. 305, December 1955: 'Wayne University slang'

waz; wazz; whaz *noun*
an act of urination *UK*
- I went over to Ditch to have a waz and that's when I saw her. — David Peace, *Nineteen Seventy-Four*, p. 153, 1999
- [A] certain politician [...] was caught on camera having a whaz against a ginko tree[.] — Josie Dew, *The Sun In My Eyes*, p. 264, 2001

waz; wazz; wass *verb*
to urinate *UK, 1984*
- The were two lads wazzing up against the piss stones. — Nicholas Blincoe, *Ardwick Green (Disco Biscuits)*, p. 10, 1996

wazoo *noun*
the anus and/or rectum *US*
- Jerry Payne, you've got your head up the old wazoo! — John Nichols, *The Sterile Cuckoo*, p. 114, 1965
- — Frank Zappa, *Grand Wazoo*, 1972
- An enema is an enormous GOOOOSH right up the old WAZOO. — *Screw*, p. 11, 6th November 1972
- We gonna be late an get tardies out the wzaoo! — Jess Mowry, *Way Past Cool*, p. 8, 1992
- Miller and Leroy got cousins up the wazoo here. — James Ellroy, *Hollywood Nocturnes*, p. 181, 1994
- [W]e all had tax problems up the wazoo. — *Uncut*, p. 78, November 2003

wazz *verb*
to rain *UK*
A figurative use of the sense 'to urinate'.
- It's wazzin' it down. — Ian Pearsall, 1980

▸ **wazz on your bonfire**
to spoil your fun, to ruin something good *UK, 1990s*
Combines **WAZ; WAZZ** (urination) with a symbol of celebration.
- Presumably the Bonfire Wazz fizzy drink is already in the planning stage. — David Rowan, *A Glossary for the 90s*, p. 195, 1998

wazzed *adjective*
drunk *UK*
A variation of **PISSED**. The Batfinks 'Wazzed 'n' Blasted' was recorded in the 1980s but not released until 1998.
- We used to knock off early on Fridays and just neck loads of 'em, walk into town fuckin' wazzed. — Ben Graham, *Weekday Service (Disco Biscuits)*, p. 167, 1996
- — The Batfinks *Wazzed 'n' Blasted*, 1998

wazzer; wazz *adjective*
wonderful *UK*
- Marines [during the Falkland Islands campaign, 1982] call anything good "wazzer" or just "wazz", a term that caught on with some Paras by the time they landed. — McGowan & Hands, *Don't Cry For Me*, 1983
- A truly voluptuous woman will have a wazzer pair of jugs [breasts] and shelf-like buttocks you can park a bike in. — *Loaded*, p. 31, June 2002

wazzock; wazzuck *noun*
▹ see: **WASSOCK**

WC *noun*
a lavatory *UK, 1815*
Abbreviated from 'water closet'.
- They're not even going through the motions of sloping off to the WC for their bugle [cocaine]. — Kevin Sampson, *Outlaws*, p. 162, 2001

weak!
used as a prompt and short expression of disagreement with what has just been said *US*
- — Connie Eble (Editor), *UNC-CH Campus Slang*, p. 9, Fall 1986

weakheart *noun*
a police officer; a representative of the establishment or authority *UK*
Used by West Indians, and intended to be offensive.
- — David Powis, *The Signs of Crime*, 1977
- I can still recognize devilworks when I see it / Weakheart disciples keep weakheart friends / Always had a hate for what their weakhearts defend[.] — Roots Manuva, *Movements*, 1999

weakie *noun*
a poker player who lacks courage *US*
- — John Vorhaus, *The Big Book of Poker Slang*, p. 40, 1996

weak sister *noun*
1 a weak, ineffective person *US, 1857*
- He states that you have always been a weak sister and apparently that is what you are. — Herbert Huncke, *Guilty of Everything*, p. 108, 1990

2 an investor who buys a stock as an investment but sells it as soon as the price rises *US*
- — Kathleen Odean, *High Steppers, Fallen Angels, and Lollipops*, p. 48, 1988

weaky-weaky *adjective*
frail *TRINIDAD AND TOBAGO, 1987*
- — Lise Winer, *Dictionary of the English/Creole of Trinidad & Tobago*, 2003

weapon *noun*
1 the penis *UK*
First recorded around the year 1000; and ever thus.
- When I look at his penis when it's not erect, it's small and soft, not so much like a weapon ruling him and me. — Ellen Bass and Laura Davis, *The Courage to Heal*, p. 266, 1994

2 in pool, a player's cue stick *US*
- — Mike Shamos, *The Illustrated Encyclopedia of Billiards*, p. 261, 1993

▸ **spit shine the weapon**
to perform oral sex on a man *US*
Perhaps this phrase has military origins.
- Another way to say "fellatio" [...] Spit shining the weapon[.] — Erica Orloff and JoAnn Baker, *Dirty Little Secrets*, p. 83, 2001

weapons *noun*
an actor's arsenal of makeup *UK*
- — Wilfred Granville, *The Theater Dictionary*, p. 219, 1952

weapons-grade *adjective*
very strong *US*
Teen slang, post 11th September 2001.
- That's some weapons-grade salsa[.] — *The Washington Post*, 19th March 2002
- Out of his head on weapons-grade ganja [marijuana] at the time. — Jonathan Ross, *They Think It's All Over*, 10th January 2003

wear *verb*
1 to tolerate or accept something *UK, 1925*
Originally military.
- [H]e wouldn't "wear the mush [man]"[.] — Butch Reynolds, *Broken Hearted Clown*, p. 31, 1953
- I made a few attempts at trying to charm the hostesses into initiating us into their legendary "Mile High Club" but they weren't wearing it. — Dean Cavanagh, *Mile High Meltdown (Disco Biscuits)*, p. 212, 1996

2 to use a name *US*
- So I dug out my purse an shows my cards. Cost me three bills for this man t'make 'em out so's I can wear my new name. — Robert Gover, *JC Saves*, p. 125, 1968

▸ **wear American gloves**
among Canadian military personnel, to have your hands in your pockets *CANADA*
- "Wearing American gloves" while in uniform was considered a practice too casual for proper military decorum, and refers to the American reputation for having a lower standard of military deportment than Canada. "O'Toole! Take off those American gloves!" — Tom Langeste, *Words on the Wing*, p. 10, 1995

▸ **wear buttons**
to be extremely gullible *US*
• — John R. Armore and Joseph D. Wolfe, *Dictionary of Desperation*, p. 22, 1976

▸ **wear it**
to take the blame, and punishment, for another's crime *UK*
• — Angela Devlin, *Prison Patter*, p. 122, 1996

▸ **wear stripes**
to serve a prison sentence *US*
• — Vincent J. Monteleone, *Criminal Slang*, p. 249, 1949

▸ **wear the face off**
to vigorously French kiss someone *IRELAND*
• I'm getting my first snog off this bird...and I'm wearing the face off her, half my mind wondering what I'm supposed to do with my tongue[.] — Paul Howard, *Ross O'Carroll-Kelly*, p. 105, 2003

we are not worthy
used as a humorous recognition of accomplishment *US*
• [WAYNE AND GARTH DROP TO THEIR KNEES AND BOW.] WAYNE & GARTH: We're not worthy! We're not worthy! — *Wayne's World*, 1992

wearing the smalls *noun*
the testicles *UK*
Rhyming slang for **BALLS**.
• — Bodmin Dark, *Dirty Cockney Rhyming Slang*, 2003

Weary Willie *noun*
a person who is perpetually tired, sad and pessimistic *US*
From the character portrayed by circus clown Emmett Kelly (1898–1979).
• And she is always flippin' the lip about him bein' such a weary Willie, the citizens of the burg, even the hepcats, mark him solid. — Haenigsen, *Jive's Like That*, 1947
• I'm fed up with all these Weary Willies saying "Thou shalt not. Thou shalt not." Yes, we fuckin' shall. — Christopher Brookmyre [quoting Billy Connolly], *Not the End of the World*, p. 303, 1998

Weary Winny *noun*
a prostitute who seeks customers on the street *US*
From the title of a 1927 film.
• Yet in Washington they flourish, though they are supposedly verboten, and the Weary Winnies parade the pavements. — Jack Lait and Lee Mortimer, *Washington Confidential*, p. 21, 1951

weasel *noun*
a tip, a gratuity *UK*
Used by railway porters; probably derived from **WEASELING** (extracting tips).
• — *Radio Times*, 21st January 1965

weasel *verb*
1 to use ambiguous language in an attempt to equivocate on the meaning *US, 1956*
• Yeah, he weasels it, but it still says I was one of those guys and I wasn't. — Elmore Leonard, *Be Cool*, p. 103, 1999

2 to use cunning to achieve your end; to cheat *UK, 1975*
• [S]he weasled her daddy out of a crisp twenty-dollar bill[.] — Sandra Brown, *Slow Heat in Heaven*, p. 169, 1988
• Smarr had grown obsessed with the notion that Owsley had weasled a friend of his out of two thousand dollars[.] — Ron Powers, *Dangerous Water*, p. 206, 1999

▸ **weasel out; weasel your way out**
to avoid a responsibility or obligation, especially in a sly or underhand manner *UK, 1962*
• [H]e weasled out of it by telling her he could not come over because his wife would be jealous. — Mary Nicholas, *Change in the Context of Group Therapy*, p. 134, 1984

weasel and stoat; weasel *noun*
a coat *UK, 1971*
Rhyming slang.
• — Ray Puxley, *Cockney Rabbit*, 1992

weaseling; weaselling *noun*
extracting gratuities *UK*
Used by railway porters.
• — Harvey Sheppard, *Dictionary of Railway Slang*, 1970

We, as official Video Rangers, hereby promise...
used with humour as an oath or pledge *US*
From the US children's television programme *Captain Video and his Video Rangers* (1947–57), in which the viewers were asked to join with Captain Video in promising to 'support forever the causes of freedom, truth and justice throughout the universe'. Used with irony in later years by those who as children had been warped by television.

weather *noun*
▸ **under the weather**
1 ill, unwell *US, 1850*
• I realized that I was feeling a little under the weather: achy, headachy, and feverish. — Eric Pearl, *The Reconnection*, p. 37, 2003

2 experiencing the bleed period of the menstrual cycle *CANADA, 1961*
A narrowing of the general sense of 'vaguely unwell'.
• — Karen Houppert, *The Curse*, 1999

3 tipsy, drunk *AUSTRALIA, 1942*
From the conventional sense as 'unwell'.

weather guesser *noun*
a meteorologist *ANTARCTICA*
• — *Cool Antarctica*, 2003: 'Antarctic slang'

weather in; weather out *verb*
(of bad weather) to confine pilots in Canada's west to the airport until conditions improve *CANADA*
This term was used in alternation with, or perhaps more often than, 'storm-stayed', in western Canada winters.
• Storm-stayed is a well-known expression in rural Saskatchewan. I now live in Northern Saskatchewan, where flying is a way of life. Now I use the term "weathered in" (if I can't get home) and "weathered out" (if I can) employed by pilots. — Ross Moxley, *in The Latest Morningside Papers*, p. 32, 1989

weave *noun*
1 real and synthetic hair woven into existing hair to hide baldness or thinning hair *US*
• These days, your haircut looks more Clint Eastwood than Cary Grant. Have you considered a weave? — Joseph Wambaugh, *Finnegan's Week*, p. 9, 1993

2 clothes *US*
• — David Claerbaut, *Black Jargon in White America*, p. 86, 1972

weave *verb*
▸ **get weaving**
to start (immediately) *UK, 1942*
Originally Royal Air Force slang.
• I'll ask you a question and then I must get weaving. — *The Observer*, 7th July 2002

web *noun*
a television network *US*
• — Ralph S. Singleton, *Filmaker's Dictionary*, p. 183, 1990

webbed up *adjective*
involved, entangled; addicted *UK*
• Anyone who get webbed up in the brown [heroin] get seriously dropped out[.] — J.J. Connolly, *Layer Cake*, p. 15, 2000

webfoot *noun*
1 a dairy farmer *NEW ZEALAND*
• I love webfoot for a Taranaki farmer, who is also known as a gumbooter or herringboner. — *Dominion Post*, p. C6, 22nd November 2002

2 a racehorse that performs well on a muddy track *US*
• — David W. Maurer, *Argot of the Racetrack*, p. 68, 1951

weblish *noun*
the informally coded and abbreviated form of English that is used in text messaging, chat rooms, etc *UK, 2001*

web rage *noun*
an outburst of enraged hostility within a cyber-environment *US*
• Rather cleverly, it's made a virtue of the vice that is Web rage, a condition that occurs after following hyperlinks through sites that take forever to download and/or prove a total waste of time. — *Campaign*, 22nd March 1996
• — Susie Dent, *The Language Report*, p. 17, 2003

wedding *noun*
a one-on-one battle between fighter pilots *US*
• — *American Speech*, p. 125, Summer 1986: 'The language of naval fighter pilots'

wedding bells *noun*
morning glory seeds, eaten for their purported hallucinogenic effect *US*
- —William D. Alsever, *Glossary for the Establishment and Other Uptight People*, p. 22, December 1970

wedding bells acid; wedding bells *noun*
LSD *US, 1971*
- —Richard A. Spears, *The Slang and Jargon of Drugs and Drink*, p. 540, 1986

wedding kit *noun*
the genitals *US*
- —Roger Blake, *The American Dictionary of Sexual Terms*, p. 85, 1964

wedding night *noun*
the first occasion on which two homosexual men have sex with each other *UK*
- —Paul Baker, *Polari*, p. 194, 2002

wedding tackle *noun*
the male genitals *UK, 1961*
- The erect biped, head at the top, feet at the bottom, wedding tackle about halfway up, represents the universal archetype, when it comes to the "intelligent" being. —Robert Rankin, *Armageddon the Musical*, p. 12, 1990
- No important bits cut off or damaged at all, if you get my meaning [...] Wedding tackle all present and correct. —Adèle Geras, *Troy*, p. 10, 2000

wedge *noun*
1 a thick fold of currency notes; money in general *UK, 1977*
In the C18 and C19 'wedge' meant both 'money' and 'silver' however these senses were obsolete long before the current usages. The modern derivation comes from folded banknotes which form a wedge shape; hence the coincidental generic usage.
- [S]he'd started going up Stringfellows on the prowl for someone older with a bit of wedge. —Greg Williams, *Diamond Geezers*, p. 157, 1997
- And everyone had their money – the workers with their wages, the drug dealers with their wedges, gamblers with their winnings, etc. —Dave Courtney, *Raving Lunacy*, p. 98, 2000
- You flush, mate, to weigh me on [repay] that bit of wedge? —Jimmy Stockin, *On The Cobbles*, p. 96, 2000
- [W]hen the establishment Mafioso realise how much gilt, paper, cashish, wonga, wedge, corn, cutter, loot, spondos, dollar, readies, shillings, folding, dough, money is on offer[.] —J.J. Connolly, *Layer Cake*, p. 94, 2000
- I'm strictly an electrical appliance man: they yield the most amount of wedge for the least amount of bulk[.] —Danny King, *The Burglar Diaries*, p. 2, 2001

2 one hundred pounds *UK*
- Ton, wedge[.] —Brian McDonald (writing of 1960s London underground), *Elephant Boys*, p. 203, 2000

3 a dose of LSD; LSD *US, 1971*
- — US Department of Justice, *Street Terms*, October 1994

4 in drag racing, an engine with a combustion chamber that is shaped like a wedge *US*
- Meanwhile, Chevrolet introduced its W-block 348-ci V-8, which featured the wedge for combustion chambers that were built into the block instead of the heads. —Edwin J. Sanow, *Encyclopedia of American Police Cars*, p. 50, 1999

5 a car *US*
Teen slang.
- — *Newsweek*, p. 28, 8th October 1951

wedged *adjective*
in computing, suspended in mid-operation and unable to proceed *US*
- —Guy L. Steele et al., *The Hacker's Dictionary*, p. 131, 1983

wedged up *adjective*
having money to spend *UK*
- [I]t's Saturday night, we're all wedged up. —Bernard Dempsey and Kevin McNally, *Lock, Stock ... & Two Hundred Smoking Kalashnikovs*, p. 101, 2000

wedger *noun*
someone who pushes into a queue *US*
- —David Shenk and Steve Silberman, *Skeleton Key*, p. 308, 1994

wedgie *noun*
a wedge-tailed eagle *AUSTRALIA, 1941*
- 'Oh, boy,' Jimmy had said. 'A wedgie. I reckon we'll get a bounty for this.' —Randolph Stowe, *The Merry-Go-Round in the Sea*, p. 224, 1965

wedgies *noun*
wedge-heeled shoes *UK*
- —John Boswell, *Lost Girl*, 1959
- He turns into the transsexual Shaneequa, who looks about 10ft tall in her wedgies, and taxis round London to satisfy her client's sexual fantasies. — *The Guardian*, 4th December 2002

wedginald *noun*
money *UK*
Disguising **WEDGE** (money) with a play on the name Reginald.
- [W]e've got the shades on and we're out to collect a nice bita wedginald from snake face[.] —J.J. Connolly, *Know Your Enemy [britpulp]*, p. 151, 1999

wedgy; wedgie *noun*
1 the condition that exists when someone pulls your trousers or underpants forcefully upward, forming a wedge between buttock cheeks *US, 1988*
- — *American Speech*, Fall 1990
- —Connie Eble (Editor), *UNC-CH Campus Slang*, p. 8, Spring 1990
- A thorough listen to his [The Notorious B.I.G.] earlier material, like "Machine Gun Funk," where he gets "up in that ass like a wedgie," will reveal an undiscovered gem or two. — *The Source*, p. 218, March 2002

2 a sandal, the thong of which wedges between the toes *US*
- "What kind of shoes?" "Sandals, like wedgies." —Elmore Leonard, *Split Images*, p. 173, 1981

wee; wee wee *noun*
urine; an act of urination *UK, 1937*
Juvenile or jocular in the main.
- [T]he women discussed the pros and cons of fiddling with a press stud gusset when going for a wee. —Kitty Churchill, *Thinking of England*, p. 179, 1995
- [H]e loves his walks, the fresh air and chance to have a sniff, a wee and a poo[.] —John King, *White Trash*, p. 1, 2001

wee *verb*
to urinate *IRELAND, 1934*
- Peter came bursting in from outside. "I gotta wee," he announced. —Max Shulman, *Rally Round the Flag, Boys!*, p. 242, 1957
- It seemed to me that babies only did four things: eat, wee, poo and cry. —Mary Hooper, *(megan)2*, p. 83, 1999

weebles *noun*
an ill-defined or undefined illness *US*
- Grandma has the weebles an' these goodies will make her well. — Haenigsen, *Jive's Like That*, 1947

weed *noun*
1 marijuana *US, 1928*
The preferred slang term for marijuana until the 1950s, and despite the success of its successors it has never completely vanished from the lexicon.
- After I finished the weed I went back to the bandstand. Everything seemed normal[.] —Mezz Mezzrow, *Really the Blues*, p. 72, 1946
- The marijuana. The gage. The weed. The muta. The tea. Those sticks. The lumber. That thing. Lay one on me, gate. —Robert Sylvester, *Rough Sketch*, p. 73, 1948
- [U]ltra-modern paintings, which covered the walls of his cottage and never failed to startled Arky when his glance happened to fall on one of them. Nightmares, cockeyed stuff. The guys that painted them must have been on the weed. —W.R. Burnett, *Little Men, Big World*, p. 51, 1950
- And I'll get Verger to bring some weed to your party. —John Clellon Holmes, *Go*, p. 83, 1952
- But he was always high on something – weed, benzedrine, or knocked out of his mind on "goof balls." —William Burroughs, *Junkie*, p. 26, 1953
- You had weed here in your room Friday. It stinks. —John D. McDonald, *The Neon Jungle*, p. 71, 1953
- Lee in Texas growing weed, Hassel on Riker's Island, Jane wandering on Times Square in a benzedrine hallucination, with her baby girl in her arms and ending up in Bellevue. —Jack Kerouac, *On the Road*, p. 8, 1957
- I had gotten caught with a shopping bag full of marijuana, shopping bag full of love – I was in love with the weed[.] —Eldridge Cleaver, *Soul on Ice*, p. 4, 1968
- Rules of the Black Panther Party No. 7: No party member can have a weapon in his possession while DRUNK or loaded off narcotics or weed. — *The Black Panther*, p. 22, 15th January 1969
- Man, Don't cha hate it when you ain't go no weed —Tone Loc, *Cheeba Cheeba*, 1989
- I still had a connection. Which was insane, 'cause you couldn't get weed anyfuckinwhere then. — *Reservoir Dogs*, 1992
- SHAVONNE: Hey, what are you guys up to? SLATER: Oh, a little weed, you know. — *Dazed and Confused*, 1993
- After one joint of the Alaskan weed, we were all seriously stoned. —Wayne Anthony, *Spanish Highs*, p. 111, 1999

2 a marijuana cigarette *US*
- If you dig two-for-a-nickel weeds like this, then don't let me talk you out of anything. — Morton Cooper, *High School Confidential*, p. 79, 1958
- I lit a butt. Brew offered me a whole weed. — Piri Thomas, *Down These Mean Streets*, p. 122, 1967

3 a cigarette *US*
- — *Newsweek*, p. 28, 8th October 1951
- He asked me whether I smoked a great deal and I told him that I had a weed once in a while[.] — Frederick Kohner, *Gidget*, p. 67, 1957
- — Miss Cone, *The Slang Dictionary (Hawthorne High School)*, 1965
- Two-Bit grinned and lit a cigarette. "Anyone want a weed?" — S.E. Hinton, *The Outsiders*, p. 29, 1967
- Billy holds his cigarette pack out to Meadows. "Weed?" — Darryl Ponicsan, *The Last Detail*, p. 27, 1970

4 tobacco *UK, 1606*
- But for the 80 per cent of us for whom it's a case of "smoke or go bonkers", it's a lie exposed by our repeated inability to stay off the weed. — *The Observer*, 29th December 2002

5 a thin, unhealthily delicate and weak person *UK, 1869*

6 in horse racing, an undersized thoroughbred *UK*
- — Rita Cannon, *Let's Go Racing*, p. 73, 1948

7 an expert *BARBADOS*
- — Frank A. Collymore, *Barbadian Dialect*, p. 119, 1965

8 a beginner surfer *US*
- — *Surfing*, p. 43, 14th March 1990

weed *verb*

1 in a gambling establishment, to provide an employee with money to gamble in the hopes of building up business *US, 1947*
- — Thomas L. Clark, *The Dictionary of Gambling and Gaming*, p. 248, 1987

2 to pilfer *UK, 1811*
Survives as **WEEDING**.

▸ **weed a poke**
to remove all money and valuable items from a stolen wallet *US*
- — Joseph E. Ragen and Charles Finston, *Inside the World's Toughest Prison*, p. 822, 1962: 'Penitentiary and underworld glossary'

weedburner *noun*
in drag racing, exhaust pipes that extend downward and to the rear of the car, terminating near the ground *US*
- — John Edwards, *Auto Dictionary*, p. 186, 1993

weeder *noun*
on the railways, the supervisor of a track crew *US*
- — Ramon Adams, *The Language of the Railroader*, p. 171, 1977

weed head *noun*
a marijuana smoker *US*
- A bunch of weed-heads were seeing how dirty they could talk[.] — Chester Himes, *If He Hollers Let Him Go*, p. 43, 1945
- All weed-heads are cop-haters. — Jack Lait and Lee Mortimer, *Washington Confidential*, p. 117, 1951
- The weeheads were really blasting the stuff. — Willard Motley, *Let No Man Write My Epitaph*, p. 109, 1958
- Is she a weedhead? — Morton Cooper, *High School Confidential*, p. 26, 1958
- "Now I know why the world looks so vague to weedheads," Grave Digger said from behind the wheel. — Chester Himes, *Cotton Comes to Harlem*, p. 128, 1965
- — Bruce Jackson, *In the Life*, p. x, 1972
- Then I started running around with the show people and practically all of them was homosexuals and weed-heads. — Bruce Jackson, *In the Life*, p. 74, 1972

weeding *noun*
stealing, especially from an employer, or at the scene of a crime already committed *UK*
From **WEED** (to pilfer).
- — David Powis, *The Signs of Crime*, 1977

weedly *noun*
a female marijuana smoker *US, 1955*
- — Ernest L. Abel, *A Marijuana Dictionary*, p. 109, 1982

weed monkey; weed mule *noun*
an old car or truck used to haul raw materials used in the illegal production of alcohol *US*
- — David W. Maurer, *Kentucky Moonshine*, p. 127, 1974

weedo *noun*
a marijuana user *US*
- What can you expect from a confirmed weedo? — Morton Cooper, *High School Confidential*, p. 80, 1958

weed of wisdom *noun*
marijuana *UK*
- Dis one goin' out to ah oonu dat search fe inspiration, from de weed of wisdom. — Donald Gorgon, *Cop Killer*, p. 96, 1994

weeds *noun*
clothes *US*
- Gee, this hound's-tooth is really the most. You been pickin up on some new weeds. — Ross Russell, *The Sound*, p. 178, 1961

▸ **get into the weeds**
to micro-manage the smallest details *US*
- In the Army, when a commander essentially flyspecks every detail, they call it "getting into the weeds." — Tom Clancy with Fred Franks Jr, *Into the Storm*, p. 460, 1991

weed tea *noun*
a narcotic drink made by the infusion of marijunana leaves *US, 1960*
A combination of **WEED** (marijuana) and 'tea' in the conventional sense.
- — Richard A. Spears, *The Slang and Jargon of Drugs and Drink*, p. 541, 1986
- — Mike Haskins, *Drugs*, p. 289, 2003

weedwacker team *noun*
in law enforcement, a surveillance team *US*
- I don't know, but the Feds have a three-man Weedwhacker team on him. They took these pictures. — Stephen J. Cannell, *Big Con*, p. 310, 1997

weedy *adjective*
lacking in physical, moral or emotional strength *UK, 1852*
- I was weedy and decided I couldn't face it. — Ann Barr and Peter York, *The Official Sloane Ranger Handbook*, p. 159, 1982

Wee Georgie Wood; wee georgie *adjective*
good *AUSTRALIA, 1942*
Rhyming slang, formed on music hall entertainer Wee Georgie Wood (1894–1979), perhaps via the Tasmanian Wee Georgie Wood Steam Railway (named after a locomotive presumably named, in turn, after the entertainer); especially in the phrase 'any wee georgie wood?'.

wee hammock *noun*
a sanitary towel *UK*
From the similarity of appearance; in usage while such capacious reinforcement was the popular choice; certainly in use during the mid- to late 1960s.

wee heavy *noun*
a nip-sized bottle of strong ale or barley wine *UK*
First used for Fowler's Wee Heavy™, then generic. Recorded by Brian Glover, *CAMRA Dictionary of Beer*, 1985.

wee hours *noun*
very early in the morning; the hours just after midnight *US*
- The long lines during the wee hours can be a turn-off, however. — Bernhardt J. Hurwood, *The Sensuous New York*, p. 77, 1973

weekend *noun*
any short term of imprisonment *UK, 1950*
- — Angela Devlin, *Prison Patter*, p. 122, 1996

weekend *adjective*
used derisively for indicating a part-time or casual dedication to a stated activity *UK, 1935*
Not restricted to weekend usage.
- Leo finds it an intriguing convenience to be stopped on the corner by some weekend hippie and asked for a quarter for an egg cream or whatever. — Angelo d'Arcangelo, *The Homosexual Handbook*, p. 77, 1968
- [T]he ANL [Anti Nazi League] succeeded in splitting the weekend racist from the dedicated facist. — Mark Steel, *Reasons to be Cheerful*, p. 47, 2001

weekender *noun*
a person serving a jail sentence for a minor offence on weekends *US*
- Weekenders – bringing the Street in to tantalize you. — Ken Kesey, *Last Whole Earth Catalog*, p. 234, 1971

weekend habit *noun*
a sporadic use of recreational drugs *UK*
- — Angela Devlin, *Prison Patter*, p. 123, 1996

weekend hippie *noun*

a person with a conventional lifestyle who at the weekend adopts a counterculture persona *US*

- Leo finds it an intriguing convenience to be stopped on the corner by some weekend hippie and asked for a quarter for an egg cream or whatever. — Angelo d'Arcangelo, *The Homosexual Handbook*, p. 77, 1968
- Weekend hippies, one-night dropouts from suburbia's Kiddieland, they are American youth come to walk for a few hours through the neon fires of an infernal region[.] — Albert Goldman, *Freak Show*, p. 25, 1968
- As an excuse for the nudity, the Acid Eaters has the story of the "weekend hippy." — *Adam Film Quarterly*, p. 83–85, July 1968
- Another threat is unwanted visitors – the sightseers from "straight" society and the weekend hippies who descend upon them to freeload. — *Life*, p. 16B, 18th July 1969

weekend pass *noun*

a glass *UK*

Rhyming slang, probably of military origin.

- — John Ayto, *The Oxford Dictionary of Rhyming Slang*, p. 178, 2002

weekend root *noun*

a sexual partner with no illusions of a sustained relationship *NEW ZEALAND*

- — David McGill, *David McGill's Complete Kiwi Slang Dictionary*, p. 135, 1998

weekend warrior *noun*

1 a member of the National Guard *US*

Members of reserve units must typically devote one weekend a month to refresher training.

- — Lanie Dills, *The Official CB Slanguage Language Dictionary*, p. 77, 1976

2 in drag racing, a hobbyist/enthusiast who confines his passion to weekend events *US*

- — John Lawlor, *How to Talk Car*, p. 114, 1965

weenie; weeny; wienie *noun*

1 a hot dog *US, 1906*

From the German *wienerwurst*.

- [W]e cook weenies, drink Tokay – I make love to big Swedish student girl Edeltrude. — Jack Kerouac, *Letter to John Clellon Holmes*, p. 381, 12th October 1952
- Some of the stories said the victims had been roasting weenies on the beach with their two dates[.] — Hunter S. Thompson, *Hell's Angels Tarrible Saga*, p. 37, 1966
- Green nail polishy at a weenie stand is not Divine Decadence. It's just plain tacky. — Armistead Maupin, *Tales of the City*, p. 189, 1978

2 the penis *US*

- "By the way, great lover, since I took you back for the baby's sake, your midget weenie hasn't moved me once." — Iceberg Slim (Robert Beck), *Doom Fox*, p. 78, 1978
- But in reality, the muff-happy mogul is merely hidden away in an upstairs chamber watching their sexual escapades via a close circuit TV system, while pulling his weenie[.] — *Adult Video*, p. 12, August/September 1986
- They were totally dedicated and devoted to every aspect of rock and roll – especially the part about guys in bands who had Big Weenies. — Frank Zappa, *The Real Frank Zappa Book*, p. 104, 1989
- It looks like a big green weenie, huh? It turns ripe you can eat it. — Elmore Leonard, *Maximum Bob*, p. 133, 1991

weenie; weeny *adjective*

small, tiny *UK, 1790*

- Small would be an understatement. "Weeny" wouldn't do justice to its grace. — *The Guardian*, 21st February 2004

weenie bin *noun*

a library carrel *US*

- — *New York Times*, 12th April 1987

weenie wagger; weenie waver *noun*

a male sexual exhibitionist *US*

- Where the wienie wagger shoved it through at the old babe changing clothes and she stuck a hatpin clear through it and the son of a bitch was pinned right there when the cops arrived. — Joseph Wambaugh, *The New Centurions*, p. 179, 1970
- Two weenie wagger convictions as an adult[.] — James Ellroy, *Brown's Requiem*, p. 34, 1981
- The guy a weenie wagger? — Robert Crais, *L.A. Requiem*, p. 35, 1999

weeny; weenie; wienie *noun*

an unlikeable, weak person *US, 1963*

- Everyone has a word for weenie again. The latest one I've heard is "dweeb," as in "He's a total dweeb." — *Washington Post (reprinted from The Nation)*, p. C5, 22nd December 1985
- I spend half my life being interviewed. I end up typing memos for some weenie, I'm not even sure what he does. — Elmore Leonard, *Bandits*, p. 212, 1987
- "Most men," I said, "are wienies." — Rita Ciresi, *Pink Slip*, p. 326, 1999

weeny-bopper *noun*

a young girl, not yet a teenager but with a teenager's tastes *UK*

After **TEENYBOPPER** (a young teenager, especially a girl).

- The word Weeny-bopper [...] means [one of those] girls between 8 and 12 who assemble in screaming multitudes to greet visiting pop groups. — *The Universe*, 10th November 1972

weep and wail *noun*

a sob story told by a beggar *UK*

Rhyming slang for 'tale'.

- — Julian Franklyn, *A Dictionary of Rhyming Slang*, 1960
- — Ray Puxley, *Cockney Rabbit*, 1992

weep and wait *verb*

to serve a prison sentence while awaiting news on the outcome of an appeal *US*

- — Joseph E. Ragen and Charles Finston, *Inside the World's Toughest Prison*, p. 822, 1962: 'Penitentiary and underworld glossary'

weeper *noun*

a prisoner who cannot manage his incarceration and constantly complains *US*

- — John R. Armore and Joseph D. Wolfe, *Dictionary of Desperation*, p. 56, 1976

weepie *noun*

a film, novel, play, song, etc, with a sentimental narrative or emotional effect *UK*

- — Wilfred Granville, *The Theater Dictionary*, p. p.229, 1952
- Erich Segal was a Professor of Classics at both Oxford and Yale but received greater popular acclaim as the author of the weepie novel Love Story. — Steve Turner, *A Hard Day's Write*, p. 125, 1994
- I have two favourite films: Now, Voyager, a fantastic black and white film where Bette Davis wears wonderful dresses. And a film called Random Harvest which is the same sort of genre – a black and white weepie. — *The Guardian*, 23rd October 2000
- Fair to Midland [sung by Dwight Yoakam] is a classic country weepie[.] — *The Guardian*, 19th December 2003

weeping willow *noun*

a pillow *UK, 1880*

Rhyming slang.

- I'll be asleep as soon as my crust hits the weeping willow. — Ray Puxley, *Cockney Rabbit*, 1992

weeping womb *noun*

the bleed period of the menstrual cycle *US*

- — Karen Houppert, *The Curse*, 1999

weeps *noun*

tears *US*

- I never saw a flock of chicks who could turn on the weeps so fast when we played their favorite tearjerkers[.] — Mezz Mezzrow, *Really the Blues*, p. 60, 1946

wees *noun*

an act of urination *NEW ZEALAND*

- — Louis S. Leland, *A Personal Kiwi-Yankee Dictionary*, p. 111, 1984

weevil *noun*

in oil drilling, a new and inexperienced worker *US*

- — Jerry Robertson, *Oil Slanguage*, p. 28, 1954

wee-wee *noun*

1 the penis *US*

- No little "wee-wee" was able to enter my "hole." — *Screw*, p. 7, 15th December 1969
- [L]ike some overgrown and deranged schoolboy, capable at any moment of unzipping his pants and displaying with a storm of giggles what I'm sure he'd call his wee-wee[.] — George V. Higgins, *Penance for Jerry Kennedy*, p. 29, 1985
- His wee-wee had withered from 10.4 centimeters to 7.9 centimeters in its flaccid state. — Carl Hiaasen, *Native Tongue*, p. 324, 1991

2 the vagina *US*

- There's [a...] "cooter," "labbe," "Gladys Siegelman," "VA," "wee wee[".] — Eve Ensler, *The Vagina Monologues*, p. 6, 1998

▷ **see: WEE**

wee-wee *verb*

to urinate *UK, 1937*

Children's vocabulary.

- "I've got to go wee-wee." "You're getting kind of old for that, ain't you?" —Chester Himes, *A Rage in Harlem*, p. 66, 1957
- On the other hand, some corresponding euphemistic expressions (e.g., dickie, peepee, weewee, number one, number two, to move the bowels, to pass water, to make love, and so on), obviously evasive in their very structure, do have considerable usage. —*Eros*, p. 69, Autum 1962
- Lookit here, little pigeon, you got no cause to wee-wee. —Robert Campbell, *In La-La Land We Trust*, p. 134, 1986
- At a palmed alcove opposite Glori's door she paused to appraise its occupant, a plaster toddler making weewee in a giant seashell. —Seth Morgan, *Homeboy*, p. 5–6, 1990

wee-wee *adjective*
very small *BARBADOS*
- —Frank A. Collymore, *Barbadian Dialect*, p. 119, 1965

weezee *verb*
to urinate *TRINIDAD AND TOBAGO, 1986*
Children's vocabulary.
- —Lise Winer, *Dictionary of the English/Creole of Trinidad & Tobago*, 2003

we go!
let's leave! *US*
Hawaiian youth usage.
- —Douglas Simonson, *Pidgin to da Max*, 1981

we gone
goodbye *US*
Originally used for signing off on a citizens' band radio transmission, but too good to stay there.
- —Wayne Floyd, *Jason's Authentic Dictionary of CB Slang*, p. 31, 1976

We Ho *noun*
West Hollywood, California *US*
- —Pamela Munro, *U.C.L.A. Slang*, p. 126, 2001

weigh *verb*

▸ weigh in
to bring influence to bear; to make a forceful contribution to a topic under discussion *UK, 1909*
- The Ministry of Defence also weighed in, warning that it [a chlorine plant] could be used to make chemical weapons. But Mr Channon, in line with Mrs Thatcher's policy of propping up the dictator, said: "A ban would do our other trade prospects in Iraq no good". —*The Guardian*, 6th March 2003

▸ weigh in with
to produce something additional; to introduce something extra or unexpected; to contribute *UK, 1885*
- [O]nce again the old guys weighed in with a strong tsk-tsk, this time worrying that the teachers themselves didn't know the rules. —Geraldine Woods, *English Grammar for Dummies*, p. 52, 2001

▸ weigh into

1 to attack someone *AUSTRALIA, 1941*
- Egg weighs into rivals over interest charges. Only a tiny percentage of people who apply for credit cards and loans obtain the rates advertised, according to Egg, which this week launched an extraordinary attack on its rivals. —*The Guardian*, 22nd March 2003

2 to ensnare someone in a swindle *US*
- I wanted to weigh myself into him. See, you can let a guy beat you three or four games and he'll swear before damnation that he can beat you from then on! —Henry Williamson, *Hustler!*, p. 127, 1965

▸ weigh on
to pay or repay someone *UK*
English gypsy use.
- You flush, mate, to weigh me on that bit of wedge [money]? —Jimmy Stockin, *On The Cobbles*, p. 96, 2000

weigh off *verb*

1 to sentence someone to imprisonment or other judicial punishment *UK, 1925*
In a wider sense 'to weigh up' is 'to consider'; this usage is originally military.
- "You just get weighed off yesterday?" "Yes." "How long did you get?" "A lagging." —Frank Norman, *Bang To Rights*, p. 18, 1958
- —Angela Devlin, *Prison Patter*, p. 123, 1996

2 to take revenge *UK*
To redress the balance by adjusting the weight.
- You do want to weigh off Brodie for the stroke he pulled[.] —G.F. Newman, *The Guvnor*, 1977

weight *noun*

1 large quantities of a drug *US*
- I wasn't up there to buy weight, so-called, ounces. —Jeremy Larner and Ralph Tefferteller, *The Addict in the Street*, p. 111, 1964
- He said that these were the people into all the cocaine weight and that he was going to cut me into them. —Claude Brown, *Manchild in the Promised Land*, p. 165–166, 1965
- Enough to buy an ounce of horse – some real weight. —Emmett Grogan, *Ringolevio*, p. 44, 1972
- The dealer-in-weight sells by the piece (about an ounce) to street dealers. The street dealer (or dealer) buys the piece and then steps on it. —Burgess Laughlin, *Job Opportunities in the Black Market*, p. 6–5, 1978
- Of making a few stings, getting bread together, of Whitey contacting his man and connecting for weight in heroin and of pushing. —Herbert Huncke, *The Evening Sun Turned Crimson*, p. 209, 1980
- A "weight" is half a kilo, it used to be a pound, but dope has gone metric. —*New Society*, 16th December 1982
- I used to handle the weight [pounds, half pounds, kilograrms] and I still can. —Terry Williams, *The Cocaine Kids*, p. 18, 1989
- I bet he sold weight. That twenty-five hundred? He must've just sold an eighth of a ki. —Richard Price, *Clockers*, p. 167, 1992
- Henry Santoro and Frankie Fish are moving weight in Florida. —*Gone in 60 Seconds*, 2000

2 a large amount of money *US*
- —*American Speech*, p. 306, December 1964: 'Lingua Cosa Nostra'

3 blame, responsibility *US*
- You're too weak to take your own weight. —Clarence Cooper Jr, *The Scene*, p. 14, 1960
- With only a few weeks remaining in his freshman year, he'd been expelled for smoking reefers, or, as he now said, for taking "the weight" for a bunch of chumps who couldn't care less about him. —Nathan Heard, *Howard Street*, p. 50, 1968
- I'll rob trains and banks and lots of other things / And take the weight for narcotic rings. —Dennis Wepman et al., *The Life*, p. 41, 1976
- Jessie, anything we can do to take the weight off my son – and your grandson – we're going to do. —Vincent Patrick, *Family Business*, p. 221, 1985
- I'm the guy that's taking the weight, and it's all right for you to roll by in your cruiser annd pick up a little for my trouble. —Herbert Huncke, *Guilty of Everything*, p. 189, 1990
- I think my brother's taking the weight for someone. —Richard Price, *Clockers*, p. 356, 1992

4 difficulties, problems *US*
- —Anna Scotti and Paul Young, *Buzzwords*, p. 85, 1997

5 the handicap that a skilled pool player will allow an opponent *US*
- If you want to play me anymore, my friend, you're going to have to give me some weight. —Walter Tevis, *The Color of Money*, p. 75, 1984
- —Steve Rushin, *Pool Cool*, p. 29, 1990

▸ do the weight
to slim, to lose weight *UK*
- I bump into Fat Pat. Well, he was once Fat Pat, but now he's done the weight he's just Pat. —Martin King and Martin Knight, *The Naughty Nineties*, p. 55, 1999

▸ put on weight
to undergo breast enhancement surgery *US*
- —Anna Scotti and Paul Young, *Buzzwords*, p. 110, 1997

weight house *noun*
in an illegal drug enterprise, any place where a dealer hides his major supply of drugs *US*
- They identified the dead man as the tenant, 30 year old Jaun Alex DeLossantos, a reputed large-scale cocaine-trafficker rumored to have several so-called "weight houses" scattered throughout the city hiding his cash and drugs. —*Milwaukee Sentinel Journal*, p. 9A, 3rd June 2002

weightless *adjective*
drug-intoxicated, especially by crack cocaine *UK, 1998*
- —Mike Haskins, *Drugs*, p. 291, 2003

weight pile *noun*
the area where weightlifting equipment is kept *US*
Prison terminology.
- Only two other cons were mad enough to be driving iron on the weight pile beneath Tower Three. —Seth Morgan, *Homeboy*, p. 224, 1990
- —William Bentley, *Prison Slang*, p. 4, 1992

weights *noun*
loaded dice *US*
- —Robert C. Prus and C.R.D. Sharper, *Road Hustler*, p. 171, 1977: 'Glossary of terms'
- —Frank Scoblete, *Guerrilla Gambling*, p. 331, 1993

weight watcher *noun*
a Department of Transportation employee at a roadside weigh station for trucks *US*
- —Wayne Floyd, *Jason's Authentic Dictionary of CB Slang*, p. 31, 1976

weigh up *verb*

to consider or appraise something *UK, 1894*

- Jimmy has been done good and proper and he's weighed up twenty-five years against appearing for the Queen. Against us. —Ted Lewis, *Jack Carter's Law*, p. 16, 1974

weiner *noun*

▷ see: WIENER

weird and wonderful *adjective*

remarkably eccentric; peculiar; unfathomable *UK, 1859*

A colloquial coupling; usually ironic or derogatory, always clichéd.

- The [Australian] Employment Advocate has dragged every weird and wonderful allegation out of the bottom drawer to oblige the Minister who is still trying to cut his teeth on the Workplace Relations portfolio[.] — *The Guardian*, 23rd May 2001

weirdo *noun*

a weird person *US, 1955*

- This broad's liable to think I'm some kind of weirdo instead of a nice normal Puerto Rican. —Piri Thomas, *Down These Mean Streets*, p. 136, 1967
- Last night a group of us weirdos sat up all night and watched what has to be the greatest TV show, in fact, the "Greatest Show on Earth," as old John Ringling North of circus fame would have put it. —Abbie Hoffman, *Woodstock Nation*, p. 40, 1969
- I think Sal and Joe put me right up there with Marshall in the weirdo department. —Jim Bouton, *Ball Four*, p. 175, 1970
- [D]on't try running any of your bloody weirdo numbers on her. —Terry Southern, *Now Dig This*, p. 34, 1975
- [T]heir mothers apparently won't let em watch the whole movie out there in the city of geeks and weirdos. —Joe Bob Briggs, *Joe Bob Goes to the Drive-In*, p. 67, 1987
- Those weirdos are staring at us again. — *Romy and Michele's High School Reunion*, 1997
- Geez, print two little words – ANAL SEX – and the weirdos and freaks come out of the woodwork. — *The Village Voice*, 24th August 1999

weird out *verb*

1 to begin to act weirdly *US*

- And sometimes, he just weirds out until he gets out from being weird, somehow. —Stephen Gaskin, *Amazing Dope Tales*, p. 65, 1980

2 to frighten someone; to cause someone emotional turmoil *US*

- My mom doing it with your dad. I can't believe it. Carlotta, this is weirding me out. —C.D. Payne, *Youth in Revolt*, p. 407, 1993
- They had to be doing a lot of it to be that weirded-out. —Cleo Odzer, *Goa Freaks*, p. 273, 1995
- I weirded you out the other night. — *Chasing Amy*, 1997
- What's that accent, girl? You weirding me out, you sound like you got a knot in your tongue or something. —Ben Elton, *High Society*, p. 17, 2002

weirdy; weirdie *noun*

1 an eccentric; a very odd person *UK, 1894*

- Anyway, I wrote a short story about such a girl – how she befriended a humpback weirdie to the extent of wanting him "to hurt me the way they hurt you!" —Terry Southern, *Now Dig This*, p. 1, 1986
- I'm pointing you out to Mick so's he can see who the weirdo is! —Kevin Sampson, *Powder*, p. 220, 1999
- The beardie-weirdie tapped the card laid out beside the board. —Ian Rankin, *The Falls*, p. 110, 2001

2 a homosexual, usually male *UK*

Recorded by Albert Petch, 1969.

welch *verb*

▷ see: WELSH

welcome aboard!

a catchphrase used in greeting to a newcomer to any organisation, institution or closed group *US, 1962*

- All in all this is a pretty good place to start – whether you're new to the whole database concept, or just to Access 2002. Either way, welcome aboard! —John Kaufeld, *Microsoft Access 2002 for Dummies*, p. 2, 2001

welcome to my world

used for expressing limited sympathy when someone is complaining about something that happens to you regularly *US*

- —Connie Eble (Editor), *UNC-CH Campus Slang*, p. 8, Spring 1999

welcome to the club!

used for expressing faint sympathy for someone who is complaining about something that others suffer *US*

- "Carlotta, this is weirding me out." "Welcome to the club, Frank," I said, adjusting my brassiere. —C.D. Payne, *Youth in Revolt*, p. 407, 1993

weld *verb*

to have sex *JAMAICA, 1992*

- —Thomas H. Slone, *Rasta is Cuss*, p. 76, 2003

welder *noun*

a male pornography performer *US*

- — *Adult Video News*, p. 48, September 1995

well *noun*

to a pickpocket, an inside jacket pocket *US*

- He feverishly wiped the dude clean of spittle and his billfold from the well (inside breast pocket). —Iceberg Slim (Robert Beck), *Airtight Willie and Me*, p. 6, 1979

Well *noun*

▸ **the Well**

Bridewell Jail, Chicago *US*

- I woke up in a hospital ward in a prison called "The Well." —Dennis Wepman et al., *The Life*, p. 95, 1976

well *adjective*

used of a drug addict, unaffected by withdrawal symptoms *US*

- I had to shoot three spoons [of heroin] to stay well. —Iceberg Slim (Robert Beck), *Pimp*, p. 289, 1969

well *adverb*

used generally to add positive emphasis to adjectives *UK, 1986*

- The Wu-Tang clan are well scary [.] — *The Guardian*, 9th May 2003

well and truly *adverb*

utterly, beyond doubt, to an unarguable degree *UK, 1948*

- We had been well and truly invaded. — *The Guardian*, 28th February 2001

well away *adjective*

1 sound asleep *UK, 1927*

- —John Ayto, *The Oxford Dictionary of slang*, 1998

2 tipsy *UK, 1931*

- [H]e'd come back at half past ten, not drunk but certainly well away. —Harry Christian, *The Making of Anti-Sexist Men*, 1994

▸ **be well away**

to prosper, to be doing very well *UK, 1937*

As in the example: 'He's well away with that girl'.

well-endowed *adjective*

1 of a man, having impressively proportioned genitals *UK, 1951*

- "Oui. All my lovers have been well endowed." His lips twitched. "Ye like big cocks?" "Big cocks are not enough. I need big brains too." —Virginia Henley, *Tempted*, p. 346, 1992

2 of a woman, having generously proportioned breasts *UK, 1984*

- I have other fantasies, too, where a spectacular, well-endowed blond beauty seduces me, and I her. —Nancy Friday, *Women on Top*, p. 243, 1991

well-gone *adjective*

drunk *UK*

- "[P]iss artists" are "boozy", "fluffy", "well-gone", "legless", "crocked"[.] —Peter Ackroyd, *London The Biography*, p. 359, 2000

well-hard *adjective*

very tough *UK*

- After a while, we got comfortable in these well-hard areas, and could tell instinctively when something was up. —Andy McNab, *Immediate Action*, p. 289, 1995
- Jean-Hugues Anglade is the innocent boyfriend and Tcheky Karyo her well-hard boss. — *The Guardian*, 22nd April 2003

well-heeled *adjective*

rich; having more than sufficient money *US, 1897*

- [T]he middle-aged, well-heeled audience at the Duke of York's theatre seemed very gratified to see Poliakoff's young professional exposed and humiliated. — *The Guardian*, 10th December 2003

well hung *adjective*

1 of a man, having generously proportioned genitals *UK, 1685*

- [Y]ou need to find a man like that to marry. Someone so well hung that even after three or four kids, he'd still be wall to wall. —Sherrilyn Kenyon, *Night Embrace*, p. 38, 2003

2 young *UK*

Rhyming slang.

- —Ray Puxley, *Cockney Rabbit*, 1992

wellie; welly *noun*

1 a Wellington boot (a rubberised or plastic waterproof footware) *UK, 1961*

In the 1970s, it began to be used in phrases where 'boot' occurred, e.g. 'The welly's on the other foot now'; 'he's getting too big for his wellies': perhaps started by *The Great Northern*

Welly Boot Show put on by Billy Connolly at the Edinburgh Festival in the early 1970s. 'Well boot' is also a variant.

- We used to go out on patrol in the cuds [coutryside] with welly boots on because of the mud. — Andy McNab, *Immediate Action*, p. 23, 1995

2 power, energy, especially when harnessed as acceleration *UK*

- [The motorcycle] goes like hell and it likes plenty of Wellie though I haven't had it flat out yet[.] — letter to, *Which Bike*, September 1980

▸ **give it some wellie; give it some welly**

to vigorously attack someone or something; hence, to put all your effort into something *UK*

After **WELLIE** (Wellington boot), hence a play on **STICK THE BOOT IN**.

- Take it to the Max and give it some welly! — Terry Victor, *Give It Some Welly [Murder on the Menu]*, 1990
- [G]ive it some wellie[.] — Melanie McGrath, *Hard, Soft & Wet*, p. 51, 1998
- Tradition was at Christmas we gobbed our grub and gave the booze some welly[.] — Jeremy Cameron, *Brown Bread in Wengen*, p. 141, 1999

wellie *verb*

1 to smash something or defeat someone *UK*

Used by the Royal Marines in the Falklands war, made familiar in the SAS fictions of Chris Ryan and Andy McNab.

- — *The Listener*, 1st July 1982

2 to kick someone or something *UK, 1966*

- — John Ayto, *The Oxford Dictionary of Slang*, p. 263, 1998

wellied *adjective*

drunk *UK*

- I'm fairly wellied by the time Quox stands up[.] — Niall Griffiths, *Kelly + Victor*, p. 45, 2002

wellie-whanging *noun*

Wellington boot hurling as an unconventional competitive sport *UK, 1984*

well, I'll be a blue-nosed gopher!

used for expressing surprise *US*

A signature line of the Ollie character in the 'Spin and Marty' segment of the *Mickey Mouse Club* in the 1950s. Repeated with referential humour.

well, I'll be a dirty bird!

used for expressing surprise humorously *US*

A signature line of George Gobel on the television comedy *The George Gobel Showcase* (CBS, 1954–60). Repeated widely with referential humour.

well, I'm damned!

▷ see: I'LL BE DAMNED!

well I never!; well I never did!

used for registering surprise *UK, 1848*

- "Goodness, I never realised the Troggs had a number-one hit with Girl Like You." "Yes, if you could just turn back to the song in question, your honour_" "Well I never, Smokie got to number five with Living Next Door To Alice." — *The Guardian*, 27th June 2003

wellington *noun*

a condom *UK*

A figurative application of waterproof footwear. 'Welly boot' is also a variant.

wellington boot; wellington *noun*

an act of sexual intercourse *AUSTRALIA*

Rhyming slang for **ROOT**.

- Such conversations are not about who rooted what sheila after the dinner dance, but are serious discussions about various methods and techniques. When sexual intercourse is referred to it is called exactly that. More usually, it is called a fuck. The words naughty, wellington and poke are considered smutty. — Suzy Jarratt, *Permissive Australia*, p. 57, 1970
- — Jim Ramsay, *Cop It Sweet!*, p. 95, 1977

well-lined *adjective*

reasonably wealthy *UK*

- You reckon that Diana she well lined or what then? — Jeremy Cameron, *Brown Bread in Wengen*, p. 160, 1999

well-oiled *adjective*

drunk *UK, 1937*

An intensification of **OILED** that now stands alone.

- [W]ell-to-do, well-heeled and in the process of getting well-oiled (but politely so)[.] — *The Guardian*, 14th September 2002

welnaw

no *US*

- — *The Bell (Paducah Tilghman High School)*, p. 8–9, 17th December 1993: 'Tilghmanism: the concealed langage of the hallway'

welsh; welch *verb*

to swindle someone out of money wagered *UK, 1857*

Originates in the supposed untrustworthiness of the Welsh, possibly as speakers of a language few other mainland Britons understand (and such private communication is, after all, the intention of most criminal slang).

- The days of the welshing bookie scarpering with the public's money are virtually over[.] — John McCririck, *John McCririck's World of Betting*, p. 144, 1991
- Welching on bets was always a possibility. — Brian McDonald, *Elephant Boys*, p. 205, 2000

Welshie; Welshy *noun*

a Welsh person *UK, 1951*

- Run back to your hovels, peasants! Bloody Welshies don't even know how to look after your own country! Should all still be living in caves! — Niall Griffiths, *Sheepshagger*, p. 19, 2001
- Come on, you Welshies. Come on, you little red fire engines. Come on, you Welsh gits! Walesall! Walesall! Come on, you little Welshies! — *New Zealand Herald*, 9th November 2003

Welsh Wales *noun*

Wales *UK*

If this referred specifically to the parts of Wales where Welsh is the predominant language this could well be considered as a correct usage; however, this is used generally and patronisingly, often in a faux-Welsh accent, of Wales as a whole.

- Going to Welsh Wales, are we? — Ned Sherrin, *Counterpoint*, 5th July 2004

Welsh windbag *nickname*

politician Neil Kinnock (b.1942); hence, any loquacious Welsh person *UK*

A happy alliteration given to Kinnock from his weakness for big speeches that (unhappily) undermined his credibility with the electorate; the tag dates from his time as leader of the Labour party from 1983–92.

- From the Welsh Windbag [Neil Kinnock] to Bambi [Tony Blair]. — Robin Ramsay, *The Rise of New Labour*, chapter heading, 2003
- It annoys me when detractors suggest he [Dylan Thomas] was only a verbal pyrotechnist or, an alternative version, he produced a handful of good poems, but otherwise was a Welsh windbag. — Andrew Lycett, *Dylan Thomas*, 2003

wendy *noun*

a white homosexual male *SOUTH AFRICA*

Gay slang, formed on the name Wendy, probably elaborating the initial 'w' for white, and originating among Cape coloureds.

- — Bart Luirink (translated by Loes Nas), *Moffies*, p. 150, 2000

Wendy house *noun*

1 in prison, a time when prisoners are permitted to associate with each other *UK*

From a child's Wendy house, thus an allusion to playtime and the possibility for discreet association.

- — Angela Devlin, *Prison Patter*, p. 123, 1996

2 the Duty Chief Inspector's office in the Information Room at New Scotland Yard *UK*

From the conventional sense as 'a children's playhouse'.

- — *The Official Encyclopaedia of New Scotland Yard*, 1999

Werris *noun*

a Greek person *AUSTRALIA*

- — Jim Ramsay, *Cop It Sweet!*, p. 95, 1977

Werris Creek *noun*

1 a Greek person *AUSTRALIA, 1977*

Rhyming slang. From the name of a New South Wales town.

- — Jim Ramsay, *Cop It Sweet!*, p. 95, 1977
- There are more Werris Creeks in Melbourne than in any city outside Athens. — *Sydney Morning Herald*, 3rd September 1983

2 an act of urination *AUSTRALIA, 2002*

Rhyming slang for **LEAK**.

- — *Sydney Morning Herald*, p. 1, 2002

wert' *noun*

worthless *US*

Hawaiian youth usage.

- You saw dat movie? Was wert', man! — Douglas Simonson, *Pidgin to da Max Hana Hou*, 1982

Wesson party *noun*
group sex enhanced by spreading vegetable oil on the participants' bodies *US*
An allusion and tribute to Wesson™ vegetable oil.
• —Eugene Landy, *The Underground Dictionary*, p. 196, 1971

west coaster *noun*
in trucking, a large, rectangular rear view mirror *US*
• —Montie Tak, *Truck Talk*, p. 185, 1971

west coast turnaround *noun*
any strong central nervous system stimulant *US*
Powerful enough to keep a truck driver awake for a trip to the west coast and back.
• —Montie Tak, *Truck Talk*, p. 186, 1971

West End show *noun*
heroin *UK, 2001*
London's West End is known as 'Theatreland'; this jocular term in use amongst musicians suggests that heroin is a popular entertainment that will, in the words of a critical cliché, 'run and run'.

West End thespian *noun*
a lesbian *UK*
Rhyming slang.
• —Bodmin Dark, *Dirty Cockney Rhyming Slang*, 2003

western grip *noun*
used of a male when masturbating, gripping your penis with your thumb facing your body *US*
From the grip used on the reins by those riding Western style.

western style *adjective*
used of coffee, stale and lukewarm *US*
Punning on the observation that the coffee has 'been on the range all day'.
• — Elementary Electronics, *Dictionary of CB Lingo*, p. 58, 1976

West Ham reserves; west hams *noun*
the nerves *UK, 1961*
Rhyming slang, formed from the football club.
• Mum's got the West Hams.—David Powis, *The Signs of Crime*, 1977
• You're getting right on my West Hams, you really are.—Ray Puxley, *Cockney Rabbit*, 1992

westie *noun*
a young tough person *AUSTRALIA, 1977*
Originally referring to people from the western suburbs of Sydney, it now has spread to other parts of the country. In Sydney it was used as a derogatory soubriquet to refer to inhabitants of suburbs west of one's own, which meant that everyone except those people living in the eastern beach suburbs was liable to be called a 'westie' by someone. Similarly, in New Zealand, applied to those from the suburbs west of Auckland.
• Gilmour believes westies live all over the country. No matter where they live they share a love of tight black jeans, the smell of burning rubber and the feel of a leather jacket. Being a westie is about lifestyle, not location.—*Evening Post*, p. 15, June 1988

Westminster Abbey *noun*
a cab driver *UK*
Rhyming slang for **CABBY**.
• —Ray Puxley, *Cockney Rabbit*, 1992

Westminster Abbey *adjective*
shabby *UK*
Rhyming slang; originally theatrical, nicely ironic.
• [H]is coat was Westminster Abbey.—Ronnie Barker, *Fletcher's Book of Rhyming Slang*, p. 25, 1979
• —Ray Puxley, *Fresh Rabbit*, 1998

Westralia *noun*
Western Australia *AUSTRALIA, 1893*
Hence 'someone or something of Western Australia' is 'Westralian'.

west side passkeys *noun*
burglary tools *US*
Coined in Chicago.
• —Bill Reilly, *Big Al's Official Guide to Chicagoese*, p. 64, 1982

Westy *noun*
US Army General William Childs Westmoreland (b.1914), US commander in Vietnam 1964–68 *US*
• —Linda Rienberg, *In the Field*, p. 239, 1991

wet *noun*
1 a politician with middle-of-the-road views on controversial issues, especially (during the 1980s) a Conservative not entirely supportive of Margaret Thatcher's monetarist policies *UK, 1931*
2 in motor racing, a tyre designed for racing in the rain *US*
• —Lewis Poteet, *Car & Motorcyle Slang*, p. 216, 1992
3 a drink of an alcoholic beverage *UK*
C10 *wœt*, first recorded in slang as 'heavy-wet' (malt liquor).
• There the barman builds him several drinks – snorts or wets are what Rangers call them.—Ann Barr and Peter York, *The Official Sloane Ranger Handbook*, p. 117, 1982
4 alcoholic beverages *UK*
Gulf war usage.
• —*American Speech*, p. 404, Winter 1991: 'Among the new words'
5 an act of urination *UK, 1925*
6 a conventional cigarette infused with embalming fluid *US*
• American buzz chasers are buying cigarettes dipped in embalming fluid in their search for a new high. The "wets" or "illys" are $20 (£13) and are said to induce a feeling of invincibility.—*Mixmag*, p. 37, December 2001
7 rain; wet weather *US*
• —Lou Shelly, *Hepcats Jive Talk Dictionary*, p. 26, 1945
8 a Mexican national illegally present in the US *US*
Shortened form of **WETBACK**, from the Spanish *mojado*, drawn from the image of swimming across the Rio Grande River from Mexico into Texas. Derogatory.

▸ **the wet**
the wet season in Australia's tropical north *AUSTRALIA, 1908*
• The troops kept pointing out meeting grounds where big fights are staged in the "wet".—Ion L. Idriess, *Over the Range*, p. 279, 1947
• —Jim Ramsay, *Cop It Sweet!*, p. 96, 1977

wet *verb*
▸ **wet the baby's head**
to drink to celebrate the birth (and christening) of a child *UK, 1885*
• Travellers love to celebrate an occasion, be it wetting a newborn baby's head, a wedding or even a funeral.—Jimmy Stockin, *On The Cobbles*, p. 171, 2000
• Little boy. We're wetting the babby's head. Legs of Man alehouse[.] —Niall Griffiths, *Kelly + Victor*, p. 115, 2002

▸ **wet the elbow**
to enjoy a few drinks *NEW ZEALAND*
• —Harry Orsman and Des Hurley, *The Beaut Little Book of New Zealand Slang*, 1994

▸ **wet your whistle**
to have a drink, especially an alcoholic drink *US, 1720*
• "We should have brought up a bottle," he said. "A little something to wet our whistle."—Robert Campbell, *Boneyards*, p. 201, 1992

▸ **wet yourself**
to laugh uproariously *UK, 1970*
• Hey Barry, your dislike of Liverpool is so hilarious. It's so funny I wet myself every time you do "a commentary". Not.—*The Guardian*, 25th March 2004

wet *adjective*
1 of a woman, sexually excited; ready for sex *UK, 1937*
Not recorded before 1937 but surely in use much earlier.
• He began to knead his fist against the opening of my vagina [...] I was wet now.—Alice Sebold, *Lucky*, p. 9, 1999
2 in politics, willing to compromise *UK*
Adopted from the sense 'weak, lacking in effectiveness'; in this context often as Tory 'wet' (see following citation).
• Mrs Thatcher has coined the word "wet" to denounce those Conservatives who fail to share her assertive and abrasive convictions.—*New Society*, p. 102, 17th April 1980
3 weak, lacking in effectiveness *UK, 1916*
Upper-class society use.
• Synonym for weedy[.]—Ann Barr and Peter York, *The Official Sloane Ranger Handbook*, p. 159, 1982

4 foolish *NEW ZEALAND*

- Any man who thinks and reads beyond the immediate requirements of getting a good job is a fool – 'wet', 'gormless', dilberry' etc. —*Landfall*, p. 221,

5 excellent *US*

- — *Ebony Magazine*, p. 156, August 2000: "How to talk to the new generation'

6 pertaining to killing *US*

- Our client heard somebody named Texaco Phillips offer Demo Williams five hundred dollars to help out with some wet work. —Stephen J. Cannell, *King Con*, p. 73, 1992
- Strike had been so overwhelemed with his decision to get wet and do this that at first he hadn't given the target more than a passing thought. —Richard Price, *Clockers*, p. 71, 1992

7 permitting the purchase and consumption of alcoholic beverages *US*

- Voters have three choices in addition to voting all-out wet. —Jack Lait and Lee Mortimer, *Chicago Confidential*, p. 141, 1950

wetback *noun*

1 an illegal immigrant to the US from Mexico *US, 1929*

An offensive and figurative term deriving from the crossing of the Rio Grande River between Mexico and the US. Displaying a candor endemic to the time, the US Border Patrol launched 'Operation Wetback' in 1954 to stem the tide of illegal immigration from Mexico.

- Sometimes a Chink or wetback gets into the city with some; it doesn't last long. —Clarence Cooper Jr, *The Scene*, p. 83, 1960
- [D]rool by the lamppost and the bar with the rest of the wetbacks. —Lester Bangs, *Psychotic Reactions and Carburetor Dung*, p. 115, 1973
- — *Maledicta*, p. 125, Summer 1980: 'Racial and ethnic slurs: regional awareness and variations'
- EDDIE: Now the bartender was a wetback, he was a friend of mine, his name was Carlos. —*Reservoir Dogs*, 1992
- You wanted to box, but you didn't want to train, so them li'l wetbacks wiped the ring up with your ass. —Odie Hawkins, *Midnight*, p. 9, 1995
- Is it a more hurtful racial epithet than insults such as kike, wop, wetback, mick, chink, and gook? —Randall Kennedy, *Nigger*, p. 1, 2002
- At the committee meeting that sparked the controversy, Buck had said, "Obviously if they're a wetback in this country illegally, they're not going to have any identification." —*The Tennessean*, p. 1A, 5th May 2004

2 in surfing, a large wave *US*

- [O]nce you've licked those there is only one step further to Makaha where they have the real giant wetbacks. —Frederick Kohner, *Gidget*, p. 4, 1957

wet behind the ears *adjective*

inexperienced *UK, 1931*

- Don't push me, Simpson. I'm not a wet behind the ears kid now. —*The Sweeney*, p. 50, 1976

wet blanket *noun*

a killjoy, a spoilsport *UK, 1857*

- For the first few years, I was the cliched uptight, shy, stiff, tongue-tied, wet blanket in the corner[.] —*The Guardian*, 9th December 2003

wet bum *noun*

a weak individual *UK*

Derogatory; the image of a baby with a wet bottom, punning on **WET** (weak).

- KNIGHTY: We're going all the way to Wales in the back of that? DARCY: Don't be such a wet bum. —Paul Fraser and Shane Meadows, *TwentyFourSeven*, p. 61, 1997

wetcoast *noun*

the strip of British Columbia along the Pacific Ocean *CANADA, 1989*

- Are we a wet coast? Well, Ocean Falls receives 4387 mm of annual precipitation. That's 4.8 yards of wet stuff, but Vancouver has less summer rain than Halifax, Montreal, or even Toronto! —Tom Parkin, *WetCoast Words*, p. 37, 1989

Wetcoast Samsonite *noun*

a green rubbish bag used for luggage *CANADA, 1989*

- Many floatplane passengers use green garbage bags for luggage; it's ideal for coastal travel. A double-bagging technique is waterproof, lightweight, can be jammed into small spaces, and sat upon while waiting at the dock. —Tom Parkin, *WetCoast Words*, p. 152, 1989

wet decks *noun*

a woman who has recently had sex with several men *US*

- —Robert A. Wilson, *Playboy's Book of Forbidden Words*, p. 249, 1972

wet dream *noun*

1 among men, a sleeping fantasy that triggers orgasm *UK, 1851*

- —Max Romeo, *Wet Dream*, 1969
- [T]he beautiful Muse in this classical fresco was the opposite of a wet dream to wino Greek poets. —James Hawes, *Dead Long Enough*, p. 9, 2000

2 a dream come true *UK, 1971*

A figurative application of the unconsious fantasy that triggers an orgasm.

- Florida's nothing but an adman's wet dream. —Carl Hiaasen, *Tourist Season*, p. 364, 1986
- For a year [Suede] were the press darlings, ready with a media-friendly quip. [Brett] Anderson was the journo wet dream. —John Robb, *The Nineties*, p. 339, 1999

wet dreamer *noun*

an exciting experience *UK*

- I thanked them [the police] before heading back to the Rock Bar ... a right wet dreamer! —Wayne Anthony, *Spanish Highs*, p. 119, 1999

wet fart *adjective*

ineffectual, pointless *UK*

- [F]ucking Media Studies or some other wet fart subject! —Jack Allen, *When the Whistle Blows*, 2000

wet-finger *noun*

▸ **get wet-finger**

in the categorisation of sexual activity by teenage boys, to insert a finger into a girl's vagina *US*

- It was almost axiomatic that, under "normal" circumstances, to "get wet-finger" meant the girl's defenses would crumble as she was swept away on a tide of sheer physical excitement. —Terry Southern, *Now Dig This*, p. 3, 1986

Wet Nelly *noun*

used as a generic name for any form of bread pudding *UK*

There is anecdotal evidence of Wet Nelly being enjoyed during World War 1.

- When we were children [in the 1940s] we used to go to the bakery and plague Frank Drower until he gave us some Wet Nelly! —Jean Bolas, *Caerwent Remembered*, p. 29, 2000

wet paper could cut you

used for describing a person who can't do anything right *TRINIDAD AND TOBAGO, 1989*

- —Lise Winer, *Dictionary of the English/Creole of Trinidad & Tobago*, 2003

wet rag *noun*

an unpopular, socially inept person *US*

- — *American Weekly*, p. 2, 14th August 1955

wet road block *noun*

the Yalu River, Korea *US*

US troops were prohibited from crossing the Yalu, even in pursuit of enemy soldiers.

- —Frank Hailey, *Soldier Talk*, p. 66, 1982

wet season *noun*

the bleed period of the menstrual cycle *AUSTRALIA*

- —James McDonald, *A Dictionary of Obscenity, Taboo and Euphemism*, p. 160, 1988

wet shot *noun*

a scene in a pornographic film or photograph depicting a man ejaculating *US*

- And here's a hazard of the trade, the wet shot. You only get one shot at it. Here comes the framing of that wet shot. It's a little off. —Robert Stoller and I.S. Levine, *Coming Attractions*, p. 86, 1991
- — *Adult Video News*, p. 42, August 1995

wet smack *noun*

a sexually frigid woman *US*

- — *Maledicta*, p. 17, Summer 1977: 'A word for it!'

wet stuff *noun*

explicit violence or sex in a television programme or film *US*

- —Anna Scotti and Paul Young, *Buzzwords*, p. 11, 1997

wet suit *noun*

a condom *US*

- —Judi Sanders, *Faced and Faded, Hanging to Hurl*, p. 43, 1993

wettie *noun*

especially among surfers, a wetsuit *AUSTRALIA*

- In their multi-coloured wetties, they looked like Licorice Allsorts. —Kathy Lette, *Girls' Night Out*, p. 188, 1987

wettie rash *noun*

a rash caused by wearing a wetsuit *AUSTRALIA, 1996*

wetware *noun*
a human being; the human brain *US*
- —Eric S. Raymond, *The New Hacker's Dictionary*, p. 381, 1991

wet week; wet weekend *noun*
▸ **like a wet week; like a wet weekend**
miserable, wretched *UK, 1984*
- Gob on yer like a wet weekend. —Niall Griffiths, *Kelly + Victor*, p. 213, 2002

wet willie *noun*
an act in which a spit-moistened finger is forced into a victim's ear and twisted *US*
- BART: I bet ya don't know what a Wet Willie is. Laura: Is it this? (Gives Bart a Wet Willie) KEARNEY: Hey Baby! How bout putting your finger in my ear? —Conan O'Brien, *The Simpons*, 12th November 1992
- —Chris Lewis, *The Dictionary of Playground Slang*, p. 253, 2003

WFO
used of a throttle, all the way open *US*
An abbreviation of '*w*ide *f*ucking *o*pen'.
- "How you gonna run tomorrow?" "WFO," he said. (This was long before that expression became so well-known around NASCAR that you could just about use it for a booktitle.) —Ed Hinton, *Daytona*, p. 15, 2001

whack *noun*
1 a heavy, resounding blow; a blow with a stick, often as corporal punishment *UK, 1737*
- Chow Yun Fat plays a gambling king who gets a whack on the head and turns into an idiot gibbering for chocolate[.] —Stefan Hammond, *Sex and Zen & A Bullet in the Head*, p. 160, 1996
- [He] brought an imaginary sword down on my leg, whack, whack, whack. I'd been warned by his eyes, and managed not to flinch. —Gillian Bradshaw, *Island of Ghosts*, p. 75, 1998

2 a share, a portion, a part, a measure *AUSTRALIA, 1889*
- But we made him spend a fair whack of it before we went to bed. —Sam Weller, *Old Bastards I Have Met*, p. 14, 1979
- the main title theme turned up to full whack —Christopher Frayling, *Sergio Leone*, p. 160, 2000
- September 11, and the fear, uncertainty, and distraction that followed, have taken a mighty whack out of U.S. financial vigor —Karl Zinsmeister, *Boots on the Ground*, p. 8, 2003

3 heroin *UK*
- —Mike Haskins, *Drugs*, p. 285, 2003

4 crack cocaine *UK*
- —Mike Haskins, *Drugs*, p. 282, 2003

5 a poorly executed piece of graffiti art *US*
- —Jim Crotty, *How to Talk American*, p. 143, 1997

▸ **have a whack at; take a whack at**
to attempt something; to attack someone *US, 1904*
- This regime-change stuff can be tricky. Apparently Georgie Porgie [US President George W. Bush] took a whack at it a couple of months ago in Venezuela [.] —*New York Observer*, 24th July 2002

▸ **out of whack**
not in proper shape or order *US, 1885*
- [H]is stomach is out of whack. —*As Good As It Gets*, 1997

whack *verb*
1 to kill someone, especially by gunshot *US*
Also used with 'out'.
- I always said, sooner or later the wops are gonna whack out Bobby Tex. —Edwin Torres, *Q & A*, p. 95, 1977
- You got out of line, you got whacked. Everyone knew the rules. —*Goodfellas*, 1990
- Nicky wants to do it, whack him out. You know, you didn't hear that word so much till I read John Gotti uses it all the time. Or he used to. 'Whack him,' and it became popular again. —Elmore Leonard, *Pronto*, p. 330, 1993
- Corrado has decided that the time has come for us to whack them so they can't make non more trouble. —Richard Condon, *Prizzi's Money*, p. 154, 1994
- They just set their minds on whacking Kobayashi. —*The Usual Suspects*, 1995
- The hotheaded mob turncoat also allegedly plotted to whack his son's girlfriend because she bragged she was dating "sammy the Bull's son." —*Daily News (New York)*, p. 8, 11th May 2001
- Don't get me wrong, I always liked your cousin, but whacking Phillip's brother was a major poke in the ass. —*The Sopranos (Episode 64)*, 2004

2 to strike someone vigorously *UK, 1721*
- As she climbed the stairs ahead of me, I whacked her from behind. "I hate you," I said. —Jeffrey Eugenides, *Middlesex*, p. 367, 2002

▸ **whack plaque**
in a dentist's office, to clean teeth *US*
Collected from an orthodontist in Bangor, Maine, in April 2001.

▸ **whack your doodle**
(of a male) to masturbate *US*
- [L]eer at passing legs, whack your doodle at home at night[.] —Lester Bangs, *Psychotic Reactions and Carburetor Dung*, p. 33, 1970

whack!
in the language of hang gliding, used for commenting on a poor landing *US*
- —Erik Fair, *California Thrill Sports*, p. 328, 1992

whackadoo *noun*
a crazy person *US*
- A fully made Mafioso. Plus, the guy is a total whackadoo. —Vincent Patrick, *The Pope of Greenwich Village*, p. 138, 1979

whack attack *noun*
1 in the language of hang gliding, a string of bad landings *US*
- —Erik Fair, *California Thrill Sports*, p. 328, 1992

2 an irrational and violent reaction to hallucinogenic drugs *US*

whacked *adjective*
1 exhausted *UK, 1919*
- We were exhausted. We'd been up all day and all night, our backs ached from leaning over the bed and we were just whacked. —Mark Olshaker and C.J. Peters, *Virus Hunter*, p. 112, 1997

2 drunk or drug-intoxicated *US, 1967*
Also used with 'out'.
- I hadn't counted on this: Finding my attorney whacked on acid and locked into some kind of preternatural courtship. —Hunter S. Thompson, *Fear and Loathing in Las Vegas*, p. 114, 1971
- Tooling down the highway, half whacked out of her skull on Quaaludes and Dexamyls she'd copped from an attendant servicing a station in Moline, Illionois, Joanie Brown was listening to a Merle Haggard tune on the radio[.] —Emmett Grogan, *Final Score*, p. 77, 1976
- Am I crazy, Paulie, or is Walter half-whacked? —Vincent Patrick, *The Pope of Greenwich Village*, p. 13, 1979
- They were so whacked out on painkillers they could not see and could not feel[.] —Larry Heinemann, *Paco's Story*, p. 52–53, 1986
- [I]f I'm in luck, they've just picked up a new shipment from uptown, and he's been too whacked-out from his taste test to step on it. —Jim Carroll, *Forced Entries*, p. 11, 1987
- The Border Patrol agent left him alone then, and later said to his supervisor, "The guy's whacked out on drugs, but I don't think we really have anything." —Joseph Wambaugh, *Finnegan's Week*, p. 301, 1993
- [A]ll fucking whacked on cocaine and white wine. —Kevin Sampson, *Outlaws*, p. 249, 2001

3 out of control *UK*
- First times are always wacked. Just be glad you didn't lose your virginity in the backseat of a rental car. —*Kids*, 1995
- — Susie Dent, *The Language Report*, p. 78, 2003

whacker; wacker *noun*
a fool; a jerk *AUSTRALIA, 1966*
- What a whacker. I kept laughing insanely at the very thought of him. —Helen Garner, *Monkey Grip*, p. 24, 1977
- —Ivor Limb, *Footy's No Joke!*, p. 75, 1986

whacking *noun*
1 a beating; a defeat *UK, 1862*
The figurative, sporting sense is not recorded before 1951.
- [H]e would shake us around, get us into position, and then do the whacking. —Dave Eggers, *A Heartbreaking Work of Staggering Genius*, p. 231, 2000

2 a killing *US*
From **WHACK** (to murder).
- Well, okay, Jimmy Curtains once walked Two Toes Garibaldi out of his house in his pajamas and drove him to the landfill, but still, the actual whacking didn't take place in the Burg. —Janet Evanovich, *Seven Up*, p. 5, 2001

whacking *adverb*
used to intensify adjectives of largeness *UK, 1853*
- [F]ollow up with a plum pudden in rum sauce an' a whacking great slice of Stilton; real ripe. —Derek Bickerton, *Payroll*, p. 45, 1959
- [R]eports began to appear of whacking great bonuses due to be paid in the highest reaches of Barclays Bank. —*The Guardian*, 8th April 2000

whack job *noun*
▷ see: WACK JOB

whacko *adjective*

1 terrific; wonderful *AUSTRALIA*

- "I reckon, that was the best episode in Blood on the Moon. It's a whacko episode, but," he added magnanimously, "it's a pretty whacko serial." — Nourma Handford, *Carcoola Holiday*, p. 151, 1953

2 crazy; eccentric *US*

- Oh I just met with that whacko parent Mrs Smith. — Todd Whitaker, *What Great Teachers Do Differently*, p. 56, 2003

whacko!

used for expressing shock *AUSTRALIA, 1937*

- 'Whacko! No trouble about bed tonight,' yodelled Doug, as he found a hollow gumtree. — *Weekend*, p. 14, 1st June 1957
- Latest, Sunday night arrival. Whacko! Japan here we come. — Les Such, *A Yen for Yokohama*, p. 45, 1963

whack-off *noun*

an act of masturbation *US*

- He couldn't afford much beyond a quick whackoff into an old handkerchief[.] — Lester Bangs, *Psychotic Reactions and Carburetor Dung*, p. 348, 1981

whack off *verb*

to masturbate *US*

- Did I mention that when I was fifteen I took it out of my pants and whacked off on the 107 bus from New York? — Philip Roth, *Portnoy's Complaint*, p. 78, 1969
- Perry debated whether to whack off or not. Some guys must – why else would they give them their own booths. — Richard Price, *The Wanderers*, p. 151, 1974
- But he'd never been here before, and he overracted to Mardi Gras by pulling down his pants and whacking off in the seat. — Josh Alan Friedman, *Tales of Times Square*, p. 24, 1986
- But you don't get some bird comin' on and whackin' herself off with a dildo, do yer? — Shaun Ryder, *Shaun Ryder... in His Own Words*, 1997
- What does it look like I'm doing? I'm whacking off. — *American Beauty*, 1999
- I'd have to say here and now that I used to whack off over her mam all the time. — Kevin Sampson, *Outlaws*, p. 45, 2001

whack off with *verb*

to steal something *AUSTRALIA*

- Who wacked off with my alley-bag?: Who stole my marble holder? — Phillip Adams, *The Unspeakable Adams*, p. 50, 1977

whacko Jacko *adjective*

crazy *UK*

A catchphrase formed from the nickname of entertainer Michael Jackson, whose well-publicised eccentricities give rise to this usage.

- I don't mean to say anything out of place here, Kryten, but that is completely whacko Jacko. There is no such thing as 'Silicon Heaven'. — Doug Naylor, *Red Dwarf, cult scince fiction TV comedy*

whacko the chook!

used for expressing shock *AUSTRALIA, 1981*

whacko-the-diddle-oh

used for expressing shock *AUSTRALIA, 1966*

- 'Remember that crash hot all night chunder party on Bondi Beach? When Ozzie Morrison filled his bucket first and won the competition!' 'Whacko-the-diddle-o!' — Barry Humphries, *The Wonderful World of Barry McKenzie*, p. 9, 1968

whack out *verb*

to kill someone *US*

- I had already whacked out a couple of guys here and there. — Vincent Patrick, *The Pope of Greenwich Village*, p. 193, 1979
- [H]e drew a six-month sentence at Log Cabin Reformatory for his part in the continuing forays across the Bay Bridge to whack out the Suey Sing kids. — Bill Cardoso, *The Maltese Sangweech*, p. 8, 1984
- She wants to come back, but she's afraid you're gonna whack her out. — *Casino*, 1995

whack-silly *adjective*

obsessed with masturbation *US*

- — Joseph E. Ragen and Charles Finston, *Inside the World's Toughest Prison*, p. 822, 1962: 'Penitentiary and underworld glossary'

whack up *verb*

to divide something, especially a quantity of illegal drugs, into portions *US*

- He says, aren't you going to whack it up with the other guys? I says, nayh, they been screwing us anyway. — Leonard Shecter and William Phillips, *On the Pad*, p. 113, 1973
- I take an eighth and I whack up two ounces [56 grams] of it, and sell the whacked stuff by the gram, half-grams, like that. — Terry Williams, *The Cocaine Kids*, p. 37, 1989

whaddup?

used as a greeting *US*

- — Connie Eble (Editor), *UNC-CH Campus Slang*, p. 8, Spring 1994

whaddya

▷ see: WHATDJA

whaddya hear?; whaddya say?

used as a greeting *US*

The trademark greeting of James Cagney ('Rocky' Sullivan) in the 1938 Warner Brothers film *Angels With Dirty Faces*.

whaddya know?

▷ see: WHAT DO YOU KNOW?

wha happen?; what happenin?

used as a greeting *TRINIDAD AND TOBAGO, 1993*

- — Lise Winer, *Dictionary of the English/Creole of Trinidad & Tobago*, 2003

whaka blonde *noun*

a Maori woman *NEW ZEALAND, 1950*

A coinage from the Whakarewarewa Thermal Village in Rotora, a Maori tourist attraction.

- — Harry Orsman, *A Dictionary of Modern New Zealand Slang*, p. 146, 1999

whale *noun*

a gambler who places large bets *US*

- But I knew, the trick with whales like Ichikawa was that they can't bet small for long. — *Casino*, 1995

whale *verb*

1 to beat someone *UK, 1790*

- Dreamer's the guy who whaled on your knee, right? — Dan Jenkins, *Life Its Ownself*, p. 187, 1984

2 to have sex *US*

- There's one thing about whalin' on booze – it kills all kinds of bad taste. — Piri Thomas, *Down These Mean Streets*, p. 57, 1967
- — Peter Smith and Fred M. Barritt, *Bermewjan Vurds*, 1985

3 to play music with passion and gusto *US*

- I saying yes and the night after the Red Drum session where Art Blakey was whaling like made and Thelonious Monk sweating leading the generation[.] — Jack Kerouac, *The Subterraneans*, p. 84, 1958
- A cool cat named Nat was whaling the drums at this hot spot in the heart of the slums. — Dan Burley, *Diggeth Thou?*, p. 9, 1959
- He talked up to me and said, "Babs, I play piano. May I sit in?" I said "sure c'mon whale some." — Babs Gonzales, *I Paid My Dues*, p. 61, 1967

whale belly *noun*

on the railways, a coal tender with a drop bottom *US*

- — Norman Carlisle, *The Modern Wonder Book of Trains and Railroading*, p. 269, 1946

whale in the bay *noun*

someone looking for payment of a gambling debt *AUSTRALIA*

- — Ned Wallish, *The Truth Dictionary of Racing Slang*, p. 87, 1989

whale kisser *noun*

an environmentalist *US*

- — Connie Eble (Editor), *UNC-CH Campus Slang*, p. 10, Spring 2003

whale of a time *noun*

a good time *US, 1913*

- I promise you're all going to have a whale of a good time. — Eva Moore, *The Wild Whale Watch*, p. 2, 2000

whale sperm *noun*

a plexiglas cleaning agent *US*

- By the time Heath left the base five minutes later, a case of Plexiglas cleaner, commonly known as "whale sperm," had magically appeared in the offices the IG team was occupying during the inspection. — Richard Herman, *Firebreak*, p. 97, 1991

wham *noun*

a striptease act in which the dancer ends her performance completely naked *US*

- — Don Wilmeth, *The Language of American Popular Entertainment*, p. 292, 1981

wham!

used for registering the suddenness of an occurrence *UK*

Figurative use of 'wham' (to hit).

- Not long after, something happened that made everything just drop into place – wham! – like that. — Dave Courtney, *Stop the Ride I Want to Get Off*, p. 30, 1999

wham bag *noun*

a bag full of explosives *US*

- We're riding around with my wham bag in the trunk. It's got five sticks of dynamite, blasting caps, and a loaded thirty-eight revolver in it[.] — Elmore Leonard, *Freaky Deaky*, p. 159, 1988

wham, bam, thank you m'am

used for describing anything done in very short order, especially sex *US, 1942*

Sometimes abbreviated, and sometimes embellished with other rhymes.

- [W]hat was your plot – to hop in bed with me, hop right out again, and get home before Grace does? Wham, bam, thank you ma'am? — Max Shulman, *Rally Round the Flag, Boys!*, p. 104, 1957
- She'd take her men any place and do everythinig, but she'd tell them before they began anything they'd have to be quick like bunnies. Zip. Zam. Thank you, ma'am. — John M. Murtagh and Sara Harris, *Cast the First Stone*, p. 114, 1957
- Must be the fuckin', mustn't it / All that whambam-thank-you-ma'am. — Ken Kesey, *One Flew Over the Cuckoo's Nest*, p. 64, 1962
- [H]ow I wanted to get the old thank-you ma'am in the phone booth? — John Nichols, *The Sterile Cuckoo*, p. 174, 1965
- But what about sex? Not the wham-bam-thank-you-ma'am at home, but something to look forward to? — Nat Hentoff, *I'm really dragged but nothing gets me down*, p. 88, 1968
- Baseball players are not, by and large, the best dates. We prefer wham, bam, thank-you-ma'am affairs. — Jim Bouton, *Ball Four*, p. 204, 1970
- The MC5 might have put you "flat on your back" with "nipple stiffeners" and "wham, bam, thank you ma'am" jams[.] — Lester Bangs, *Psychotic Reactions and Carburetor Dung*, p. 55, 1971
- I told him this had to be wham-bam-thank you Ma'm because I had to get back to New York. — Edwin Torres, *Carlito's Way*, p. 75, 1975
- I had ten dollars from my Granny for what they called a 'short date.' And short it was, a regular wham, bam, thank you mam. — Ken Weaver, *Texas Crude*, p. 19, 1984
- Maybe when you hit maturity you'll understand the diff between a Remington University man like David and a Westerburg boy like Ram "Wham-bam-thank-you-maam" Sweeney. — *Heathers*, 1988
- Immediately after the marriage, as soon as the reception was over, he grabbed her by the arm, then up the stairs and wham-bam. — Herbert Huncke, *Guilty of Everything*, p. 16, 1990

whammer *noun*

the penis *US*

- — James Harris, *A Convict's Dictionary*, p. 41, 1989

whammy *noun*

1 a curse or hex *US, 1940*

- The evil eye thus averted, along with all other forms of hex, whammy and squitch, he went on to Phil Kronfield's[.] — Bernard Wolfe, *The Late Risers*, p. 36, 1954
- All those psychologists in the pit are trying to put the whammy down on you. — Edward Lin, *Big Julie of Vegas*, p. 123, 1974
- I propose to consider the following in this and subsequent pieces: the Red Sox in particular, with occasional references to the Giants; African witch doctors and whammies (a subject about which I have some knowledge). — Bill Cardoso, *The Maltese Sangweech*, p. 139, 1984

2 something that is upsetting or sets you back *US*

- A man can weather a little ill fortune once in a while, but a triple whammy like that was too psychologically depressing. — Robert Gover, *One Hundred Dollar Misunderstanding*, p. 9, 1961

whammy bar *noun*

a floating bridge on an electric guitar that makes tremolos, vibrators, dives, bends and other effects possible *US*

- Wow. '65 Fender Stratocaster. In classic white with a "whammy" bar and triple hummbucker pick-ups. — *Wayne's World*, 1992

wham-wham *noun*

in prison, store-bought snacks *US*

- A phrase that must have been conceived by a person with a playful imagination is zoo-zoos and wham-whams for confections, usually small packaged cakes, pieces, candy or gum obtained from a vending machine. — *Maledicta*, p. 267, Summer/Winter 1981
- When he made the canteen cart, the beaners ripped off his zuuzuus and whamwhams. — Seth Morgan, *Homeboy*, p. 152, 1990
- — William Bentley, *Prison Slang*, p. 68, 1992

whandoodles *noun*

in poker, a temporary increase in the betting limit after a player wins a hand with a rare hand *US*

- — Albert H. Morehead, *The Complete Guide to Winning Poker*, p. 276, 1967

whangdoodle *noun*

on the railways, a remote telephone *US*

- — Ramon Adams, *The Language of the Railroader*, p. 171, 1977

whanger; wanger *noun*

the penis *US, 1939*

- But if you are going to jack your whanger, make firm determination to do it well and heartily and in an infinite amount of ways and combinations. — *Screw*, p. 14, 9th May 1969
- [T]he privilege of sucking on their coveted wangers[.] — Lester Bangs, *Psychotic Reactions and Carburetor Dung*, p. 232, 1977
- [W]hat's the use of a big wanger if you need a bloody zimmer frame to tout it about. — *The Full Monty*, 1997
- If I was a guy I wouldn't let her within twenty feet of my wanger. — Janet Evanovich, *Seven Up*, p. 93, 2001

wha'ppen(?)

what's happening?; used as a greeting *UK*

By contraction. West Indian and UK black usage.

- — The Beat *Wha'ppen?*, 1981
- Zukie shouted to a dark-skinned dread behind the counter of the makeshift bar. "Wha'ppen dread?[''] — Karline Smith, *Moss Side Massive*, p. 118, 1994

whapp'n

used as a greeting *UK*

Derived from 'what's happening?' but not used as an interrogative.

- — Julian Johnson, *Urban Survival*, p. 258, 2003

wharfie *noun*

a wharf labourer *AUSTRALIA, 1911*

- Each of them had a gun and a needle-sharp wharfie's loading hook! — *Weekend*, p. 30, 1st June 1957
- This time it wasn't the wharfies who'd held up supplies, but our own officers. — Martin Cameron, *A Look at the Bright Side*, 1988
- But scores of workers – including dockies, wharfies and chippies – regard the Pacific Hotel in Stephen St as a second home. — *Glebe and Western Weekly*, p. 2, 8th November 1989

wharf rat *noun*

in the language surrounding the Grateful Dead, a follower of the band who abstains from alcohol and drugs *US*

From the title of a Grateful Dead song.

- — David Shenk and Steve Silberman, *Skeleton Key*, p. 316, 1994

whark *verb*

to vomit *UK*

- — Bob Young and Micky Moody, *The Language of Rock 'n' Roll*, p. 58, 1985

whassname *noun*

used to refer to a name that is unknown, forgotten, to be avoided or hardly worth mentioning *UK*

Slovening of **WHATS-HIS-NAME**.

- Get a whassname... ambulance! — Bernard Dempsey and Kevin McNally, *Lock, Stock ... & Two Hundred Smoking Kalashnikovs*, p. 98, 2000

whas up?

▷ see: **WASSUP?**

what *noun*

▸ **or what?**

used as a final (often the only), wholly indefinite choice *UK, 1766*

- Class warfare or what? — *The Guardian*, 30th May 2000
- Is this a great country or what? — *New York Daily News*, 10th March 2004

what a gay day!

used as a conversation starter or filler; also as an indicator of homosexual company *UK*

The catchphrase of **CAMP** comedian and television compere Larry Grayson, 1923–95; it caught the public imagination in the mid-1970s and was adopted into popular use.

- "I always used to think it was quite amazing no one said I was gay, because the way that I looked was very kind of blond and very clean-cut," he says. He grins broadly. "And I'd always thought, with the surname Day... you know, 'What A Gay Day'. It's almost like a headline writer's dream." — *The Daily Mirror*, 17th March 2004

what a loss

used for expressing sympathy for a difficult situation *US*

- — Guy L. Steele et al., *The Hacker's Dictionary*, p. 87–88, 1983

what am I going to do with you?

said to someone you know well as an expression of tolerance and forgiveness *UK*

• She hesitated and then hugged him. "What am I going to do with you?" she asked, this time torn between love and desperation. —Anthony Masters, *Minder*, p. 117, 1984

what a revolting development this is
used for expressing displeasure *US*
A signature line of working-class hero Chester A. Riley on the television comedy *The Life of Riley* (NBC, 1949–58). Repeated with referential humour.

what are you like?
an exclamation directed at someone whose behaviour is unacceptable *IRELAND*
• Good God, what are you like? I don't know what your father would say if he was here. —Joseph O'Connor, *Red Roses and Petrol*, p. 59, 1995

what can I do you for?
how can I help?, what can I do for you? *UK, 1961*
A jocular suggestion.
• ANGEL: You Denver? DENVER: No other cat but me. What can I do you for? ANGEL: I need information on demons. —Im Minear, *Angel*, 3rd October 2000

whatchamacallit *noun*
▷ see: WHAT-YOU-MAY-CALL-IT

whatcha' thinking?
used as a greeting *US*
• —Connie Eble (Editor), *UNC-CH Campus Slang*, p. 6, October 1986

what'chu talkin' about, Willis?
used for humorously expressing a lack of understanding or belief *US*
A stock line on the television comedy *Diff'rent Strokes* (1978–86), uttered by the Arnold Jackson character played by Gary Coleman. Repeated with referential humour.

what did your last slave die of?
used as an expression of discontent to someone who is demanding that too much be done *UK, 1976*
• When a nurse came past I asked her if she would pick it [a tissue box] up for me. "What did your last slave die of?" was her reply. "What's wrong with your back?" —Wendy Lawson, *Life Behind Glass*, p. 30, 2000

whatdja; whatdya; whaddya
what do you *UK*
A phonetic recording of general slurring.
• Whatdja reckon to Hannah, then, Wheeze? —Kevin Sampson, *Powder*, p. 107, 1999

what-do-you-call-it; what-d'ye-call-it *noun*
used as a replacement for any noun that the user cannot or does not wish to specify *UK, 1600*
• [Y]ou know, the what-d'ye-call-it family , and the what's-'is-name twins. —Anthony Masters, *Minder*, p. 44, 1984
• We could have a what do you call it, a troupe. — *The Guardian*, 9th December 2003

what do you know?; whaddya know?
used as a register of surprise *US, 1914*
• "Well, whaddya know," the man said. —John Kennedy Toole, *A Confederacy of Dunces*, 1980

what do you know, Joe?
used as a greeting *US*
• —Marcus Hanna Boulware, *Jive and Slang of Students in Negro Colleges*, 1947

what do you think of the show so far? – rubbish!
a question and answer catchphrase widely used and often without an appropriate context *UK*
Comedian Eric Morecambe, 1926–84, introduced this catchphrase in the early 1970s. In fact, the response was usually voiced by Morecambe in the manner of a ventriloquist: 'ruggish!'.
• Say to a stranger in a pub, "what do you think of it so far?" and you're likely to get the reply, "Rubbish", even though Morecambe and Wise have almost disappeared from the [TV] screen. — *New Society*, 5th March 1981
• Should you take note that the program following this is called Stupid Behaviour: Caught on Tape? I think so. What do you think of the show so far? Roobish. — *Sydney Morning Herald*, 27th March 2004

what else did you get for Christmas?
directed at a person showing-off with a new 'toy'; often addressed to the tail of a disappearing vehicle *UK, 1975*
Also variant 'what else did you get for your birthday?'.
• — Partridge, *A Dictionary of Catch Phrases*, 1977

whatever *adverb*
used for registering self-pitying acceptance *US*
• Never mind that I'm the one who came up with the idea in the first place, but whatever. —Maggie Balistreri, *The Evasion-English Dictionary*, p. 75, 2003

whatever *pronoun*
used as an emphatic form of 'what?' *UK*
In conventional use from C14–C19, then colloquial.
• George, whatever in the world are you doing down there? —Cornelius Ryan, *A Bridge Too Far*, p. 243, 1974

whatever!
used as a dismissing retort to what has just been said *US*
Said with attitude, with a pause after 'what', and sometimes with thumbs and forefingers shaped like a 'W'.
• —Pamela Munro, *U.C.L.A. Slang*, p. 90, 1989
• —Connie Eble (Editor), *UNC-CH Campus Slang*, p. 10, Spring 1992
• ELTON: I think we both know what it feels like to be lonely. CHER: Whatever. — *Clueless*, 1995
• He tried to be all, "I can't believe I did that to you. I feel terrible." But I was all, whatever. —Maggie Balistreri, *The Evasion-English Dictionary*, p. 78, 2003

whatever's fair
used as a non-responsive, vague answer to a direct question *US*
• — *Current Slang*, p. 10, Fall 1969

whatever turns you on
your individual tastes, foibles, hobbies, interests, etc *US*
Generally spoken to indicate a tolerance of tastes that do not coincide with your own.
• His eyes gleamed, he rocked back and forth in his chair, almost quivering. Well, I mused, whatever turns you on. —M.D. Samuel Shem, *The House of God*, p. 28, 1978
• Some men get excited by Hustler; Lester apparently got excited by old stock certificates. Whatever turns you on, I say. —Nelson DeMille, *Gold Coast*, p. 42, 1990
• Lizzie ran off with her dancer, which was cool because, you know, whatever turns you on and, like, she's one of our homegirls[.] —Edgardo Vega Yunqu, *No Matter How Much You Promise*, p. 73, 2003
• But back then the Anglican church still understood itself to be part of the kingdom of God, not a federation of self-esteeming cantons where a sacrament is whatever turns you on. — *The Daily Telegraph*, 9th August 2003

what for a thing is that?
among Nova Scotians of German descent, used as a query to mean 'what kind of a thing is that?' *CANADA*
• In Lunenburg County, "what for a thing is that?" comes from the German "was fur ein?" "what kind of?" —Lewis Poteet, *oral citation from The South Shore Phrase Book*, p. 124, 1999

what goes up must come down
a Cockney catchphrase that comments generally on the inevitability of things happening, and, specifically, on the nature of a pregnancy *UK, 1969*
• The proverbial wisdom behind Andrew O'Hagan's new novel is something like "What goes up must come down". — *The Guardian*, 5th April 2003

what-have-you *noun*
used in place of any other item or items in a category *UK*
• [A]ll the fights with big lumps and bikers and what-have-you[.] —Dave Courtney, *Stop the Ride I Want to Get Off*, p. 172, 1999

what is it with you?
why are you behaving in such a manner? *UK*
• Whit're ye moanin aboot noo? Whit is it wi you the day? —Michael Munro, *The Complete Patter*, 1996
• What is it with your generation? Why is this so hard for you to accept? — *The Guardian*, 19th January 2000

what it is
used as a greeting *US*
• "What it is, what it is," Dan said quickly, as he reached over and slapped William's palm. —Donald Goines, *Cry Revenge*, p. 87, 1974
• —Connie Eble (Editor), *UNC-CH Campus Slang*, November 1976

what kind?
what's the matter with you? *US*
• For example, if one student accidentally jostles another in the hall, the latter might very well say "What kind?" There is no answer to this. — *American Speech*, p. 275, December 1963: 'American Indian student slang'

what makes you tick

the inner-workings of your mind *UK*

As if by clockwork.

- I studied people and assessed them. Tried to work out what made them tick and what made them good at some things and bad at others. — Dave Courtney, *Stop the Ride I Want to Get Off*, p. 17, 1999

whatnot *noun*

anything and everything *UK, 1540*

Usually a characteristic of individual speakers, not a group, and often used with an annoying regularity.

- "Okay," Louis said, "the guy's pulling about fifty grand a month out of Detroit, the apartments and whatnot, and banking it in the Bahamas for his retirement. — Elmore Leonard, *Switch*, p. 64, 1978

what price...?

consider the worth of something!; what do you think of something? *UK, 1893*

Occasionally admiring, but generally sarcastic, in reference to a declared or well-understood value.

- What price unity? — *The Guardian*, 4th September 2003

what say?

1 what do you think?; what do you say to the proposal?, etc *UK, 1895*

- Before we move on to Celebrity Sell-out, what say we visit Celebrity Encounters again, eh? Eh? — *The Guardian*, 1st April 2004

2 used as a greeting *US*

- — Miss Cone, *The Slang Dictionary (Hawthorne High School)*, 1965

whats-er-name; whats-her-name *noun*

used to refer to a name that is unknown, forgotten, to be avoided or hardly worth mentioning *UK*

- There's this café, you see, opposite the motel, called the Jubilee, opposite whats-er-name street[.] — Paul E Willis, *Profane Culture*, p. 37, 1978
- Why the Hell did Ray ever bring that bloody article on Clare Whatshername! [...] Don't pretend you don't know her full name. — Stuart Browne, *Dangerous Parking*, p. 149, 2000

what's-his-face; what's-her-face *noun*

used to refer to a name that is unknown, forgotten, to be avoided or hardly worth mentioning *UK*

- Nivir mind Saddam-whit's-the-cunt's-face[.] — Irvine Welsh, *The State of the Party (Disco Biscuits)*, p. 36, 1995

whats-his-name; what's-his-namey *noun*

used to refer to a person whose name is unknown, forgotten, to be avoided or hardly worth mentioning *UK, 1697*

- Five years ago that cracker governor, the one in Alabama, whatshisname? was a superduper white racist, o.k.? — Odie Hawkins, *The Busting Out of an Ordinary Man*, p. 126, 1985
- Yer know. Him. That friggin what's-his-namey. Him who went to Wales. — Niall Griffiths, *Kelly + Victor*, p. 279, 2002

whatsit; whatsis; whatzis *noun*

used to refer to a name that is unknown, forgotten, to be avoided or hardly worth mentioning *US, 1882*

- [I]n a couple of years I should have reached the average knowledge of an intelligent autowhatsit, you know, someone who educated themselves... – Autodidact, I said. — James Hawes, *Dead Long Enough*, p. 274, 2000
- All you needed was a black leather corset and a whip and you could have been one of those whatsits. — Claire Mansfield and John Mendelsohn, *Dominatrix*, p. 125, 2002
- Cold enough to shrivel a polar bear's whatsits. — Liz Evans, *Pussy Galore [Tart Noir]*, p. 257, 2002

what's it to you?

used (often aggressively) as the rhetorical response to a question, the answer to which is thus signalled to be none of the questioner's business *UK*

- LOFTY: [...] How old are you mate? TICH: What's it to you? — Clive Exton, *No Fixed Abode [Six Granada Plays]*, p. 118, 1959

what's kicking?

used as a greeting, along the lines of 'what is new?' *US*

- "What's kicking?" "Everything's kind of quiet." — Hal Ellson, *Duke*, p. 26, 1949

what's my name?

used as a taunt while beating someone *US*

In 1967, boxer Muhammed Ali fought Ernie Terrell, who insisted on calling Ali 'Cassius Clay'; as Ali pounded Terrell, Ali taunted 'What's my name, fool? What's my name?'.

- — *Maybeck High School Yearbook (Berkeley, California)*, p. 29, 1997

what's poppin?

used as a peer-to-peer greeting *US*

- — Bill Valentine, *Gang Intelligence Manual*, p. 79, 1995

what's shaking?; what's shakin'?

used as a greeting *US*

- — Earl Selby, *Philadelphia Evening Bulletin*, 11th November 1951
- So, I used to talk in a hip idiom, so I started talking. I said, "What's shakin', man?" — Lenny Bruce, *The Essential Lenny Bruce*, p. 27, 1967
- Markie comes in and says, Hey, man, what's shaking? — Joel Rose, *Kill Kill Faster Faster*, p. 183, 1997
- '"Yo, Lise," Al said. "What's shakin?" — Rita Ciresi, *Pink Slip*, p. 304, 1999

what's that when it's at home?

used as an expression of contempt or derision for something *UK, 1932*

Any person, people or object may, of course, substitute for 'that'.

- What's A5 when it's at home painting its nails, shaving its legs and plucking its eyebrows? — *The Guardian*, 19th August 2002

what's the damage?

how much do I owe?; what is the cost? *UK, 1984*

Formed on **DAMAGE** (expense).

- What's the damage? A small room overlooking the garden will set you back around £50 a night. — *The Observer*, 17th February 2002

what's the dealio?; what's the dillio?

what is new?, what is going on? *US*

Popularised by rapper Busta Rhymes in the late 1990s.

what's the difference between ... and ...?

a well-worn joke telling formula that is only usually half answered (a more vulgar or scandalous response to the question is implied) *UK*

- What's the difference between a cow and Simply Red [a musical group]? With a cow the horns are at the front and the arsehole is at the back. — Visionary Victor, *Saturday Social*, April 2004

what's the drill?

what are the arrangements, or usual procedures? *UK, 1961*

Originally military, now general.

- So what's the drill? Get Nurse Greenleigh? — David Fury and Elin Hampton, *Buffy the Vampire Slayer*, 18th April 1998

what's the score?

what is the latest information, situation, etc? *UK, 1961*

Originally Royal Air Force, then more general.

what's the story, morning glory?

used as a cheerful greeting *US*

- So, what's your story, Miss Morning Glory, hip me before I broom[.] — Dan Burley, *Diggeth Thou?*, p. 48, 1959

what's up?

used as a greeting *US*

- Hed Dad, Ma. What's up? — *Dazed and Confused*, 1993
- "What's sup?" Dirk asked. — Francesca Lia Block, *Baby Be-Bop*, p. 404, 1995

whatsup?

used as a greeting *US*

- Yo, man, whatsup? Looks like she wants to talk with you. — *Boyz N The Hood*, 1990

what's up, Doc?

used as an all-purpose enquiry *US*

The catchphrase of Loony Tunes cartoon hero Bugs Bunny, who, from his third outing, in July 1940 (and much repeated), would inquire 'Mnyeh... what's up, Doc?' as a taunt to pursuers. Also used cinematically, this time without specific context, as the title of a 1972 Hollywood film. Popular with sub-editors as a headline for any number of articles on the National Health.

- — *The Observer*, 24th June 2001
- — *Daily Mail*, 9th August 2003

what's up with that?

used for expressing interest in more facts *US*

- — Connie Eble (Editor), *UNC-CH Campus Slang*, p. 8, Spring 1994

what's with you?
what's amiss with you?; why are you behaving in such a way?; what has happened to you?; explain yourself!; why? *US, 1940*
Also applied to inanimate objects.
• Bunnies aren't just cute like everybody supposes! / They've got them hoppy legs and twitchy little noses! / And what's with all the carrots? — Joss Whedon, *Buffy the Vampire Slayer*, 6th November 2001

what's your damage?
what's your problem?; what's the matter? *US*
• VERONICA: What's your damage, Heather? You ruined my[.] — *Heathers*, 1988
• One of the many great things about this flick [*Heathers*] was how the dialogue coined its own slang ("How very" and "What's your damage?" to spout a couple). — Lorraine Mahru, *Retrohell*, p. 94, 1997

what's your song, King Kong?
used as a greeting *US*
• — Marcus Hanna Boulware, *Jive and Slang of Students in Negro Colleges*, 1947
• — Clarence Major, *Dictionary of Afro-American Slang*, p. 122, 1970

what the fuck!
used for registering annoyance, resignation or surprise *UK*
Possibly a shortening of 'what the fucking hell', in turn an elaboration of **WHAT THE HELL!**.
• The line went dead. Coming down? What the fuck ... Shit! She was here. She was in Boston. — Kevin Sampson, *Powder*, p. 348, 1999

what the heck!
used as an exclamation of surprise, indignation, etc; also used dismissively and as an expression of resignation *UK, 1887*
• [Y]our visibility in the rear-view mirror, through two sets of thick, tinted glass, is reduced almost to zero. But what the heck, because you pretty much know already what's behind you: people making "wanker" gestures[.] — *The Guardian*, 22nd May 2002

what-the-hell *adjective*
indifferent, uncaring *UK, 1968*
• [T]here came to be a sort of national what-the-hell attitude. — Curt Sampson, *Hogan*, p. 30, 1996

what the hell!
used in annoyance, resignation or surprise *UK, 1872*
• '[T]he participant would give up on herself, think something like, "Oh, what the hell, I'm always going to be fat," and then continue eating[.] — Edward Abramson, *Emotional Eating*, p. 8, 1993
• Going home, tugging the wife out of bed, and whisking her off to Wales in the caravan. What the hell. — Simon Lewis, *In The Box [britpulp]*, p. 132, 1999

what the hellfire!
used for registering annoyance or surprise *UK*
A variation of **WHAT THE HELL!**.
• What the hellfire's that? — *The Full Monty*, 1997

what the hey!
used as a humorous declaration of surprise, bemusement or dismissal *US*
Popularised by Milton Berle in the early days of US television; an early television catchphrase that swept the nation.

what up?
used as a greeting *US*
• What up Tre? You do your homework? — *Boyz N The Hood*, 1990
• What up Chauncy. What up ho's. — *Menace II Society*, 1993

what up, love one?
used as a greeting *US*
Used as a coded greeting by members of the Black Guerrilla Family prison gang.
• A stranger would be asked, "What up, love one?" The correct response is, "What up, love one." — Bill Valentine, *Gangs and Their Tattoos*, p. 19, 2000

what/which part of no don't you understand?
used for humorosly emphasising a previous negative answer *US*
Wildly popular, and over-used, in the 1990s; an instant favourite of US parents scolding children. First made famous by Lorrie Morgan in a 1991 song 'What Part of No', written by Wayne Perry and Gerald Smith – 'I'll be glad to explain it / If it's too hard to comprehend / So tell me what part of no / Don't you understand?'.
• It is apparently now time for some of us to ponder which part of no we don't understand. — *The Arkansas Democrat-Gazette*, p. B11, 18th May 2000

what yer
▷ see: **WOTCHER**

whatyoucallit *noun*
used as a replacement for any noun that the user cannot or does not wish to specify *UK*
• The weeping Greenpeace girls look at each other with that whatyoucallit, yeah, wild surmise. — James Hawes, *White Powder, Green Light*, p. 13, 2002

what-you-may-call-it; whatchamacallit *noun*
used in place of a word that is temporarily forgotten or not important for the context *UK, 1598*
• He's a feller likes to play the whatchamacallit? — Marvin Wald and Albert Maltz, *The Naked City*, 1947
• Then it wasn't a real whaddayacallit? — John Clellon Holmes, *Go*, p. 10, 1952
• But I can't get my whatchamacallit, my oh-my, into my pants. — Lenny Bruce, *How to Talk Dirty and Influence People*, p. 162, 1965
• I sat there pulling my pud like a total dip and told her to take her whatchamacallit and go home[.] — Lawrence Block, *No Score [The Affairs of Chip Harrison Omnibus]*, p. 150, 1970
• The cover was a green-and-black abstract whatchamacallit, and it had a magenta paper label with black lettering. — Frank Zappa, *The Real Frank Zappa Book*, p. 34, 1989
• That riot was just whatchamacallit. — *Natural Born Killers*, 1994

whaz, whatzis *nouns*
▷ see: **WAZ, WHATSIT**

wheat *noun*
marijuana *US, 1969*
A play on **GRASS** and an assonant pun on **WEED**.
• — Richard A. Spears, *The Slang and Jargon of Drugs and Drink*, p. 544, 1986
• — Mike Haskins, *Drugs*, p. 289, 2003

wheech *verb*
to move swiftly; to move something swiftly away *UK: SCOTLAND, 1911*
Probably derived, in some way, from Scots dialect *wheech* (a stink).
• We'll jump in the motor and wheech down the Largs for the day. — Michael Munro, *The Complete Patter*, p. 167, 1996
• earnings wheeched away by pubescents neds [hooligans] with Kappa tops and Stanley knives — Christopher Brookmyre, *The Sacred Art of Stealing*, p. 59, 2002

wheel *noun*
1 a leader; an important person *US, 1933*
• Evidently the fellow was some kind of a wheel, checking on activities here and there[.] — Mickey Spillane, *One Lonely Night*, p. 32, 1951
• He's a wheel. So's she. It's hard to make friends with them. — *Rebel Without a Cause*, 1955

2 a mid-level employee in an illegal lottery *US*
• Next, the wheel distributes the winnings to the runners who pass it on to the winning customers. — Burgess Laughlin, *Job Opportunities in the Black Market*, p. 11–3, 1978

3 the game of roulette *US*
• — Frank Scoblete, *Guerrilla Gambling*, p. 331, 1993

4 a tablet of MDMA, the recreational drug best known as ecstasy *UK*
• — Mike Haskins, *Drugs*, p. 290, 2003

5 in a carnival, any ride that is in the form of a wheel *US*
• — *American Speech*, p. 308–309, December 1960: 'Carnival talk'

6 a life prison sentence *US*
• — Lee McNelis, *30 + And a Wake-Up*, p. 13, 1991

7 in lowball poker, the lowest possible straight (five to ace) *US*
• — Jim Glenn, *Programmed Poker*, p. 158, 1981
• — Dave Scharf, *Winning at Poker*, p. 244, 2003

8 the ankle *US*
• — Chuck Wielgus and Alexander Wolff, *The Back-In-Your-Face Guide to Pick-up Basketball*, p. 231, 1986

wheel *verb*
1 to travel; to drive *US*
• And when we got into Baltimore he was gonna drop me off at the famous Ballroom and keep on wheelin' home. — Babs Gonzales, *Movin' On Down De Line*, p. 134, 1975

2 (used of a racehorse) to turn around suddenly *US*
• — Don Voorhees and Bob Benoit, *Railbird Handbook*, p. 45, 1968

wheel and deal *verb*
to engage in profit-making in a flamboyant manner *US, 1961*
- You can't go downtown to wheel and deal for yourself because you aren't used to thinking like a big entertainer with a future[.] — Dick Gregory, *Nigger*, p. 145–146, 1964
- — Paul Glover, *Words from the House of the Dead*, 1974
- You all talk big. Wheelin' dealin'. Duckin' divin'. Chargin' abou'. — Nick Barlay, *Curvy Lovebox*, p. 109, 1997
- Every camp needs a man like him. Someone who can wheel and deal a bit. — Jack Allen, *When the Whistle Blows*, p. 90, 2000

wheeler-dealer *noun*
a scheming, contriving deal-maker with many connections *US, 1960*
The reduplication serves to intensify.
- The wheelers and dealers in the Tiger didn't stop wheeling and dealing, they just took their swift moving actions to a slower, more cautious place. — Odie Hawkins, *Chicago Hustle*, p. 36, 1977
- Those wheeler-dealers who didn't blow their brains out after the Hurricane of '26 or hang themselves after the real-estate bust were eventually rewarded with untold wealth. — Carl Hiaasen, *Tourist Season*, p. 315, 1986
- The wheelers and dealers were having a good time because contacts were everything to them. Appointments were gold. — Robert Campbell, *Alice in La-La Land*, p. 130, 1987

wheeler-dealing; wheeling-and-dealing *noun*
scheming business practice *US*
- Look, Arthur – leave me out of the sponsorship wheeler-dealing. — Anthony Masters, *Minder*, p. 28, 1984

wheel horse *noun*
in oil drilling, the best worker on a crew *US*
- — Jerry Robertson, *Oil Slanguage*, p. 129, 1954

wheelie; wheely *noun*
1 a wheelstand, the lifting of the front wheels of a car or front wheel of a motorcyle, bicycle or skateboard off the ground due to sudden acceleration *US*
- — *Current Slang*, p. 8, Winter 1966
- During a wheelie, the driver has no steering control because the front wheels are off the ground. — Ed Radlauer, *Drag Racing Pix Dix*, p. 60, 1970
- Watching Blackwell in the hall doing wheelies on his latest snatch [something stolen] gives Caleb a great idea. — Jack Allen, *When the Whistle Blows*, p. 81, 2000
- [I] even got it to do a Lone Ranger wheely[.] — Danny King, *The Bank Robber Diaries*, p. 136, 2002

2 a wheelchair *UK*
- Wayne and Marty got Mrs Shillingford in the wheelie then carried it in the taxi. — Jeremy Cameron, *Brown Bread in Wengen*, p. 87–88, 1999

▸ **pop a wheelie**
to perform a wheelie *US*
- They rode their bikes and skateboards, popping wheelies, doing jumps and flips. — Francesca Lia Block, *Baby Be-Bop*, p. 394, 1995

wheelie-bin *noun*
a large, wheeled rubbish bin *AUSTRALIA, 1984*
- [T]he fucking wheelie bins have done them [foxes] in. — Kevin Sampson, *Clubland*, p. 19, 2002
- I had been found in a wheelie-bin on some piss-soaked council estate[.] — Helen Hastings, *Are Friends Electra [Inappropriate Behaviour]*, p. 7, 2002

wheel jockey *noun*
a military convoy truck driver *US*
- — Linda Reinberg, *In the Field*, p. 239, 1991

wheel man *noun*
1 in a criminal operation, the getaway driver *US, 1935*
- I didn't take any actual part in it except to be the wheel man. In other words, the driver of the getaway car. — Willard Motley, *Let No Man Write My Epitaph*, p. 207, 1958
- Guess I'm only the second best wheel man around. — Edwin Torres, *Carlito's Way*, p. 115, 1975
- Hiram was wheelman for the famous stopwatch bandit! — Joseph Wambaugh, *The Secrets of Harry Bright*, p. 34, 1985
- Beano had heard a rumor that Tommy Rina often used disposable wheel men. — Stephen J. Cannell, *King Con*, p. 54, 1997

2 a person who brings together pool players who are willing to play for money *US*
- — Mike Shamos, *The Illustrated Encyclopedia of Billiards*, p. 261, 1993

wheels *noun*
1 a car *US, 1959*
- "Man has wheels!" Zaida exclaimed. — Ross Russell, *The Sound*, p. 15, 1961
- "Car? You don't have wheels?" "My dad got me an Impala for senior year." — Richard Farina, *Been Down So Long*, p. 26, 1966
- [S]he explained she wouldn't be needing her station wagon for a while and if I drove it back to New York, we could save our train fare. I accepted her offer and we cut out in style with wheels. — Babs Gonzales, *I Paid My Dues*, p. 44, 1967
- Hey, Curt, you want to bomb around? I want to try out my new wheels. — *American Graffiti*, 1973
- You know, I'd be embarrassed if I let my wheels go the way you've done with this job. — *48 Hours*, 1982
- With this pad, the killer wheels, looks like you really cleaned up your act. — *Something About Mary*, 1998
- I upgraded my wheels at Sammy's rental to a crimson nine series Beemer [BMW]. — Diran Adebayo, *My Once Upon A Time*, p. 27, 2000

2 a record turntable or turntables used by DJs *US*
From the circular shape and revolving motion. Variants include 'wheels of steel' and the singular 'wheel'.
- Towards the end of the 70s, he [Afrika Bambaataa] began introducing electonic music from Gary Numan and Kraftwerk the the "wheels of steel". — Alex Ogg, *The Hip Hop Years*, p. 29, 1999
- I have been behind the wheels of steel on a few occasions. — Wayne Anthony, *Spanish Highs*, p. 155, 1999
- [T]he Technics 720s, the hip-hopper's wheels of steel, classic decks[.] — John King, *Human Punk*, p. 266, 2000

3 shoes or boots *US*
- — Elena Garcia, *A Beginner's Guide to Zen and the Art of Snowboarding*, p. 123, 1990: 'Glossary'

4 the legs, especially a woman's legs *US*
- — *Current Slang*, p. 5, Summer 1966

▸ **on wheels**
to the extreme *US, 1943*
- And don't forget that Bix, who was a bitch-on-wheels to Tesch, and all kidns of a virtuoso, was tugging hard at these kids too[.] — Mezz Mezzrow, *Really the Blues*, p. 157, 1946

▸ **put wheels on it**
used in restaurants to note that the order is a take-away *CANADA*
- — Jack Chambers (Editor), *Slang Bag 93 (University of Toronto)*, p. 5, Winter 1993

▸ **the wheels are coming off**
to be getting out of control; to not be going as planned *UK, 1998*
- Police jargon for a public order situation getting out of hand. The most notable and tragic recent London occasion when "the wheels came off" was the Broadwater Farm Riot. — *The Official Encyclopaedia of New Scotland Yard*, 1999

wheels man *noun*
a good driver *IRELAND*
- We hop into the car and speed off, with Rods doing justice to his reputation as a good wheels man. — Howard Paul, *The Joy*, p. 67, 1996

wheesht!
be quiet! *UK: SCOTLAND*
From Scots dialect *wheesh* (a hush).
- — Michael Munro, *The Original Patter*, p. 73, 1985
- "I'll go and see Mr Burque. He'll give me something to help." "Wheesht, lass, 'tis his muck give ye the toothache tae start with." — Virginia Henley, *Tempted*, p. 4, 1992

wheeze *noun*
1 a piece of comedic business; a trick; a clever idea *UK, 1864*
Originally theatrical, used by clowns and comedians; then especially popular with schoolchildren.
- The crew thought it would be a splendid wheeze to leave me there. — Ingrid Pitt, *The Mammoth Book of Vampire Stories by Women*, Introduction, 2001

2 a false belief *US*
- They don't have to stay in their places. That's an old wheeze. — Antony James, *America's Homosexual Underground*, p. 118, 1965

wheezy Anna *noun*
a spanner *UK*
Rhyming slang, formed from the title of a 1930s comic song.
- — Ray Puxley, *Cockney Rabbit*, 1992

when *adverb*
now *UK*
The natural response to the conventionally polite enquiry 'Say when?'.
- "When!" he told Carter and slapped his aerial into the pocket radio. — *The Sweeney*, p. 76, 1976

when fowl have teet; when cock have teet
used for expressing an impossibility *TRINIDAD AND TOBAGO, 1945*
• —Lise Winer, *Dictionary of the English/Creole of Trinidad & Tobago*, 2003

when it's at home
used to intensify any question of identity *UK, 1957*
A derisive tag implying contempt or incredulity, suffixed to 'what is a ..?'. The earliest usages of this scornful device were grammatically correct: '[W]here your friends are when they're at home?' (Rudyard Kipling, *Plain Tales from the Hills*, 1888). Current usage, however, will occasionally reform a sentence that should commence correctly with 'who is ..?' by converting the proper noun to object status, e.g. 'What is a John Smith when it's at home?'.
• What the fuck is a normal bug, when it's at home?—Richard Francis, *The Rialto*, p. 94, 1999

when push comes to shove
when there is no longer any choice but to proceed; when worse comes to worst *US, 1958*
• Maybe he plays it low key, that's his way. But when push comes to shove, he stands up.—Nora Roberts, *Dance upon the Air*, p. 175, 2001

when-shee *noun*
heroin
A variation of **YEN-SHEE** (heroin).
• —Mike Haskins, *Drugs*, p. 285, 2003

when you've got to go, you've got to go; when you gotta go, you gotta go
applied philosophically to death, prosaically to responsibility ('duty calls') and trivially to a visit to the toilet *US, 1975*
Popularised by Hollywood films.
• I went to the ladies' room and there was an enormous queue, so I went into the gents. When you've got to go, you've got to go. I didn't look.—Kate Winslett, 24th January 2002

where it is at; where it's at
1 the centre of a situation, a place where something important is happening *US, 1965*
• —J. L. Simmons and Barry Winograd, *It's Happening*, p. 174, 1966: 'glossary'
• In the car I suggested we go to Toronto because Montreal obviously wasn't where it was at.—James Simon Kunen, *The Strawberry Statement*, p. 97, 1968
• "That's where it's at," Van [Morrison] will say, and he means it[.] —Lester Bangs, *Psychotic Reactions and Carburetor Dung*, p. 22, 1971
• If you say you don't want to be stolen from, then you don't buy somebody else's stolen goods. That's exactly where it's at.—Herbert Huncke, *Guilty of Everything*, p. 188, 1990

2 in touch *UK, 1965*
• It's wonderful to feel that I'm doing something for the kids, because I know that the kids and their music is where it's at.—Frank Zappa, *Flower Punk*, 1968
• Where it's at! / I got two turntables and a microphone / Where it's at! / I got two turntables and a microphone[.]—Beck (Beck Hansen), *Where It's At*, 1996

where someone is at
the person's point of view or opinion *US, 1960s*
• Gallup takes polls; I take rides to find out where people are at.—James Simon Kunen, *The Strawberry Statement*, p. 79, 1968

where's the fire?
used for expressing a lack of shared concern *US*
• [S]ure, it's unpleasant to have your space invaded; it's grim when they make a mess; it's a bummer if you're not insured; but it's only stuff. Where's the fire?—*The Guardian*, 21st January 2003

where the big nobs hang out *noun*
a toilet (as used by men), especially a public convenience *AUSTRALIA*
A self-serving pun.
• Just to got to strain the spuds. You know. Go where all the big nobs hang out!!!—Barry Humphries, *Bazza Pulls It Off!*, 1971

where the sun don't shine
in your rectum *US*
• There was a look in Chicklet's eye that said he'd like to tell Orchid to shove his story up there where the sun don't shine but since Orchid always picked up the check he kept his mouth shut.—Robert Campbell, *Boneyards*, p. 31, 1992
• —Angela Devlin, *Prison Patter*, p. 123, 1996

wherever? *adverb*
used as an emphatic variation of 'where?' *UK*
In conventional use from the C10 to C19; now colloquial.
• Mama threw open the door and cried, "Why, wherever have you been? I was so worried!"—Lee Smith, *The Last Girls*, p. 36, 2002

where were you when the shit hit the fan?
used as a greeting between US Marines in Korea *US, early 1950s*
• With all Marines now living in the bean patch, frequent visits were made between friends of different units. "Where were you when the shit hit the fan?" was the standard invitation for one to relate his personal experience up north.—William B. Hopkins, *One Bugle No Drum*, p. 213, 1986

where you're coming from
your point of view or opinion *US*
• "We got to make it to the airport fast." "Okay... I dig where you're comin' from, Johnny."—Donald Goines, *Inner City Hoodlum*, p. 209, 1975

which foot you kick with
your personal preference of politics, religion or sexuality
Left or right, Catholic or Protestant, hetero- or homosexual.
• [I]t was electoral poison to make a lot of noise about which foot you kicked with[.]—Christopher Brookmyre, *Boiling a Frog*, p. 34, 2000

whickerbill *noun*
a railway brakeman *US*
• —Norman Carlisle, *The Modern Wonder Book of Trains and Railroading*, p. 269, 1946

whif *adjective*
what-if *US*
Used in 'what if' exercises projecting possible contingencies and developing reactions to them.
• —Robert Kirk Mueller, *Buzzwords*, p. 164, 1974

whiff *noun*
1 an unpleasant smell *UK, 1899*
From **WHIFFY** (bad-smelling).

2 cocaine *US*
• The cure didn't take, Pete's attorneys charged, and she soon went back on the whiff and also back to the pusher[.]—Hunter S. Thompson, *Songs of the Doomed*, p. 195, 1983
• —Connie Eble (Editor), *UNC-CH Campus Slang*, p. 9, Fall 1986
• Most of what he spent on whiff was just sociable, oiling the wheels[.]—James Hawes, *White Powder, Green Light*, p. 8, 2002

whiff *verb*
1 to give off an unpleasant smell *UK, 1899*
• Sorry Madam. Whiffs a bit—*Harpic TV commercial*, 2005

2 to inhale a powdered drug through the nose *US*
• Well, he also uses Mexican brown. And Persian by the bead! He whiffs it.—Joseph Wambaugh, *The Glitter Dome*, p. 248, 1981

whiffle dust *noun*
1 amphetamine powder *UK*
From the imaginary magic powder used by conjurors, manufacturers, marketing professionals and others to enhance their product or presentation.
• —Mike Haskins, *Drugs*, p. 280, 2003

2 MDMA, the recreational drug best known as ecstasy *UK*
• —Mike Haskins, *Drugs*, p. 290, 2003

▷ **see:** MUMMY DUST

whiffler *noun*
an auction house employee who moves and displays the items for sale *UK*
• One of the whifflers – blokes who move the gunge about in auction rooms and (sometimes) remain honest while doing so – came and hissed angrily, "What the -?"—Jonathan Gash, *The Ten Word Game*, p. 73, 2003

whiffy *adjective*
having an unpleasant odour, smelly *UK, 1849*
• [T]here was a big whiffy Stilton on the table[.]—Jenny Eclair, *Camberwell Beauty*, p. 182, 2000
• [S]tuff thee ahl (old) ones in a whiffy bundle down the back of the cistern.—Niall Griffiths, *Kelly + Victor*, p. 42, 2002

whigger *noun*
▷ **see:** WIGGER

whiler *noun*
a man with more than one girlfriend *UK*
In West Indian and UK black use, August 2002.

whim-whams *noun*

a feeling of dread or anxiety; a state of anxiety or nervousness; the jitters *US*

- When you mentioned Nancy I had a pretty good idea what you were after, and I get the wim-wams when I think about getting mixed up in anything. —Mickey Spillane, *My Gun is Quick*, p. 90, 1950
- All at once I'd had a crazy idea about him, one that kind of gave me the whimwhams. —Jim Thompson, *Savage Night*, p. 17, 1953

whiney gyny club *noun*

complaining hospital patients recovering from gynecological surgery *US*

- —*Maledicta*, p. 118, 1984–1985: 'Milwaukee medical maledicta'

whinge *noun*

a moaning complaint *UK, 1984*

From the verb.

whinge; winge *verb*

to complain; to whine *AUSTRALIA, 1938*

- As they climbed into the car Dexter whinged: 'I only hope the train's on time or I'll pass away with malnutrition.' —Willie Fennell, *Dexter Gets The Point*, p. 32, 1961
- He'd been threatening to kick him off the place for years, but every time he got round to doing it Mrs Smythe came wingeing to him that she was going to have another baby. —Dymphna Cusack, *Picnic Races*, p. 203, 1962
- Rivers flow downwards to the sea, the sun rises in the east, a girl's hard to get when your pay's spent, sailors whinge. Phenomena, natural and immutable. —J.E. MacDonnell, *Sabotage!*, p. 27, 1964

whinge bag *noun*

a complainer *UK*

Formed on **WHINGE** (a moaning complaint).

- If YF&S keep moaning about the things we've supposedly done, The Monastery will think that they're just a bunch of whinge bags. —Colin Butts, *Is Harry Still on the Boat?*, p. 114, 2003

whingeing pom *noun*

an English person viewed as a habitual complainer *AUSTRALIA, 1962*

A stock Australian stereotype.

- I've heard of the whingeing Pom – but never the whingeing Australian. —Frank Hardy, *Hardy's People*, p. 31, 1986

whinger *noun*

a person who whinges; a habitual complainer *AUSTRALIA, 1934*

- —Arthur Chipper, *The Aussie Swearer's Guide*, p. 57, 1972
- The good-natured whinger has become a stock figure of Australian folklore. —Bill Wannan, *Folklore of the Australian Pub*, p. 45, 1972
- [A]ny whingers who say anything different are just ratbags. —Roy Slaven (John Doyle), *Five South Coast Seasons*, p. 67, 1992

whip *noun*

1 a car *UK*

Used by urban black youths.

- All the girls want to be in my whip. —*Live*, p. 39, Winter 2004

2 a long radio antenna *US*

- —Wayne Floyd, *Jason's Authentic Dictionary of CB Slang*, p. 31, 1976

3 a boss or supervisor *US*

- Lt. Jack Weidt, the "whip" or boss of the Nineteenth Squad of detectives, was a trendy dresser. —William J. Caunitz, *One Police Plaza*, p. 243, 1984

4 a close friend *BAHAMAS*

- —John A. Holm, *Dictionary of Bahamian English*, p. 219, 1982

5 rum *AUSTRALIA*

- Rum is variously known as blackfellow's delight, cocky's joy and whip. —Sidney J. Baker, *The Australian Language*, p. 227, 1953

▷ **see:** **WHIP-ROUND**

whip *verb*

to arrest someone *US*

- So he gets whipped in three days after the Lowell job and he's got a gun on him and they don't even have to prove he was on the Lowell thing[.] —George V. Higgins, *The Friends of Eddie Doyle*, p. 25, 1971

▸ **whip it in, whip it out**

a catchphrase that celebrates a male approach to sexual relations *UK*

From the lyric of a rugby song: 'Whip it in, whip it out, quit fucking about Yo ho, yo ho, yo ho'. Sometimes further extended with: 'wipe it off, walk away'.

- [W]hippit in, whippit out and wipe it. —Ray Puxley, *Fresh Rabbit*, p. 127, 1998

▸ **whip it out**

to release the penis from the confines of the trousers, a bold genital display *US*

- Now they're trying to get him for sexual harassment. What happened? The girl came to his hotel room, he whipped it out, she said no, and left. And she wants to sue him? He's the one who got turned down. —Chris Rock, *Rock This!*, p. 193, 1997

▸ **whip the cat**

to feel remorse; to regret something *AUSTRALIA, 1847*

- WHIP THE CAT – To regret. —Gilbert H. Lawson, *A Dictionary of Australian Words and Terms*, 1924
- 'What will they do when the Depression comes?' 'There'll be some whipping the cat when it does.' —Dymphna Cusack, *Picnic Races*, p. 81, 1962
- —Jim Ramsay, *Cop It Sweet!*, p. 21, 1977

▸ **whip up on skippy**

(used of a male) to masturbate

- Another way to say "the boy is masturbating" [...] Whippin' up on skippy[.] —Erica Orloff and JoAnn Baker, *Dirty Little Secrets*, p. 65, 2001

▸ **whip your wang**

(used of a male) to masturbate *US*

- Whang whipping experts voted the New York Times Sunday Magazine their favorite masturbation media. —*Screw*, p. 26, 10th November 1969

whip and lash; whip *noun*

a moustache *UK*

Rhyming slang for **TASH**.

- —Ray Puxley, *Cockney Rabbit*, 1992

whip and top; whip *verb*

to masturbate *UK*

Rhyming slang for **STROP**.

- Every schoolboy's dread is to be caught "whipping" himself. —Ray Puxley, *Cockney Rabbit*, 1992

whiplash *noun*

a rash *UK*

Rhyming slang; perhaps, also, a sexual innuendo.

- —Ray Puxley, *Fresh Rabbit*, 1998

whip off *verb*

(used of a male) to masturbate *US*

- —*American Speech*, p. 69, Spring-Summer 1975: 'Razorback slang'

whip-out *noun*

1 a bankroll designed to impress when whipped out of the pocket *US*

- I happened to scare up a publisher in New York who was enthusiastic enough about it to give me a whole lot of what you call your up-front whip-out. —Dan Jenkins, *Semi-Tough*, p. 13, 1972

2 a regular payment *US*

- My fee for a repossession is the sum of the owner's monthly whip-out. —James Ellroy, *Brown's Requiem*, p. 11, 1981

whip o'will *noun*

an act of vomiting; vomit *AUSTRALIA*

Possibly rhyming slang for '*spill* your guts'.

- Calling for Herb, see, that's one of the many euphemisms for vomit, others include spue, burp, hurl, the big spit, the long spit, throw, the whip o'will, the technicolour laugh and, in Queensland, the chuckle. —Frank Hardy, *Billy Borker Rides Again*, 1967

whipped *adjective*

dominated by a girlfriend or wife *US*

A shortened form of **PUSSY-WHIPPED**.

- —Carol Covington, *A Glossary of Teenage Terms*, 1965

whipper *noun*

1 a small cartridge of nitrous oxide *US*

Designed for use in making whipped cream, but often abused for the psychoactive effects of the gas.

- "Whippers" come in ten-packs for eight bucks, and are ostensibly used as charges for whipping cream." —Josh Alan Friedman, *Tales of Times Square*, p. 176, 1986

2 a person who enjoys being whipped in a sado-masochistic encounter *US*

• I understand that a lot of girls get customers or Johns or dates or whatever you want to call them who are perverted in one way or the other. I guess whippers are the ones you hear about the most. Men who want to be degraded. —John Warren Wells, *Tricks of the Trade*, p. 38, 1970

whippersnapper; snapper *noun*
a young, impertinent person unmindful of his station in life *UK, 1700*
Still heard, but used with the effect of dating the speaker.
• "Whippersnapper," muttered Pipgrass. "I remember when they built this state capitol." —Max Shulman, *The Many Loves of Dobie Gillis*, p. 17, 1951
• The shop windows have not reflected his twenty-one years from toddler to nipper to snapper to bopper to man. —Mark Powell, *Snap*, p. 105, 2001

whippet *noun*
a shotgun with both barrel and stock sawn off for hiding on the body *US*
• —Ralph de Sola, *Crime Dictionary*, p. 164, 1982

whippets; whippits *noun*
capsules of nitrous oxide used as a recreational drug *US*
• —Jay Saporita, *Pourin' It All Out*, p. 62, 1980
• Lisanick had inhaled six "whippits" of nitrous oxide, commonly known as laughing gas, as he was driving along busy Route 7 on Nov. 29. —*Washington Post*, p. D6, 9th June 1990
• Gray aluminum capsules filled with nitrous oxide ("whippits") are legally available[.] —David Shenk and Steve Silberman, *Skeleton Key*, p. 203, 1994
• Whippits have taken on a mythical status since the 1960s when some weirdo first stuck a can of frozen desert topping up his nose. —Suroosh Alvi et al., *The Vice Guide*, p. 89, 2002

Whippins and Lashins *noun*
the Irish Girl Guides *IRELAND*
• [A]n right next door to Whippins and Lashins (that's the Irish Girl Guides to you)[.] —Gaye Shortland, *Mind that 'tis my Brother*, p. 24, 1995

whippy *noun*
1 a place used for the home base in children's game hide-and-seek *AUSTRALIA, 1964*
• I noticed a girl using the fence as a whippy. She was leaning against it with her face buried in her folded arms while other girls hid. —Clive James, *Unreliable Memoirs*, p. 33, 1980
2 a pocket in which money is kept; hence, the money kept there *AUSTRALIA, 1973*
• —Jim Ramsay, *Cop It Sweet!*, p. 96, 1977

whippy *adjective*
clever *US*
• —*Current Slang*, p. 11, Winter 1969

whip-round; whip-around; whip *noun*
an informal fund collected from a group of people *UK, 1874*
Originally military 'whip' (a collection for more wine in the mess).
• We had a whip-round one day to buy some meat. Everybody chipped in[.] —Andy McNab, *Immediate Action*, 1995
• Inside the door Nood gets a whip round goin' an' Kings an' Baba get burned for the whole fee[.] —Nick Barlay, *Curvy Lovebox*, p. 101, 1997

whips *noun*
a great deal of *AUSTRALIA, 1890*
A play on **LASHINGS**.
• There's whips of feed on the creek flats yet, but I want to keep her in good nick for you when you come back. —Alan Marshall, *I Can Jump Puddles*, p. 22, 1955

whips and jingles *noun*
symptoms of heroin withdrawal *US*
Referring to the physical pain and frayed nerves suffered.
• —David Maurer and Victor Vogel, *Narcotics and Narcotic Addiction*, p. 452, 1973

whipsaw *verb*
1 in poker, to surround a player with two confederates whose collusive betting tactics relieve the middle player of his bankroll and drive him from the game *US, 1949*
• —Thomas L. Clark, *The Dictionary of Gambling and Gaming*, p. 188, 1987
2 in horse racing, to correctly pick both the winner and second-place finisher in a race *US*
• —Dan Parker, *The ABC of Horse Racing*, p. 150, 1947

whip shot *noun*
a type of controlled toss of the dice, effective by a skilled cheat *US*
• —John S. Salak, *Dictionary of Gambling*, p. 276, 1963

whipster *noun*
an untrustworthy individual *IRELAND*
• Whipster is an old word. It means a doubtful character, an untrustworthy fellow. —*Irish Times*, 4th October 1997

whip-whap *adverb*
quickly, without second thought *TRINIDAD AND TOBAGO*
• —Lise Winer, *Dictionary of the English/Creole of Trinidad & Tobago*, 2003

whirl *noun*
an attempt *US, 1884*
• After high school, he thought he might give college a whirl. —Max Shulman, *Rally Round the Flag, Boys!*, p. 5, 1957

whirl bet *noun*
in craps, a one-roll bet on 2, 3, 7, 11 and 12 *US, 1961*
• —Thomas L. Clark, *The Dictionary of Gambling and Gaming*, p. 249, 1987

whirlies *noun*
extreme dizziness experienced when drunk *US*
• —John D. Bell et al., *Loosely Speaking*, p. 21, 1966

whirligig *noun*
a revolver *US*
• —*American Speech*, p. 195, October 1957: 'Some colloquialisms of the handgunner'

whirlpooling; whirlpool *noun*
the assault of a girl by a group of males in a swimming pool who grope her while churning water around her *US, 1993*
• Employees at two other pools, one in Brooklyn and one in the Bronx, said they, too, had seen whirlpooling. —*New York Times*, p. A1, 7th July 1993
• Among the new words —*American Speech*, p. 90, Spring 1994

whirly *noun*
1 in the television and film industries, a hydraulic lift used for shooting scenes from above *US*
• —Ralph S. Singleton, *Filmaker's Dictionary*, p. 184, 1990
2 a small, localised whirlwind *AUSTRALIA, 1894*
The variant spelling 'whirlie' is sometimes used.
• A dusty, hot wind, a small whirlie, blew the girl's dress against her legs. —Jean Brooks, *The Opal Witch*, p. 10, 1967

whirlybird *noun*
a helicopter *US, 1951*
• —*American Speech*, February 1953
• Over 100,000 people squeezed into the Meadow listening to speakers under leaden skies and the annoying obligato of Mayor Lindsay's whirlybirds. —Sidney Bernard, *This Way to the Apocalypse*, p. 55, 1968
• Hey, Fort Rucker, have you heard? / 'm gonna fly me a whirly bird. —Sandee Shaffer Johnson, *Cadences*, p. 100, 1986

whirlygigs *noun*
▸ **having the whirlygigs**
drunk *UK*
• —*e-cyclopaedia*, 20th March 2002

whirly pig *noun*
a helicoper-borne police officer *US*
Quoted as a term used by residents of Berkeley, California, to describe police in helicopters.
• —*New York Times*, p. 24, 10th February 1970

whirly-whirly *noun*
a small, localised whirlwind *AUSTRALIA, 1926*
From 'whirl', but modelled on **WILLY-WILLY**.
• I got angrier. I could feel it growing inside me, getting bigger and bigger, stronger and stronger, like a whirly-whirly spinning across a paddock. —Phillip Gwynne, *Deadly Unna?*, p. 133, 1998

whirly wind *noun*
especially in Queensland, a small, localised whirlwind *AUSTRALIA*
• Whirley winds and germs galore, / With them we're always mixing[.] —Patsy Adam-Smith, *Folklore of the Australian Railwaymen*, p. 237, 1969

whisker *noun*
usually in comparisons, a narrow margin, a small amount *US, 1913*
• Livingstone loses by a whisker and faces his biggest gamble[.] —*The Guardian*, 21st February 2000

whiskers *noun*

1 seniority or tenure on a job *US*

- You got to have whiskers to get a foot beat, and you have to be big and good. — Joseph Wambaugh, *The Blue Knight*, p. 11, 1973

2 pubic hair *US*

- — Dale Gordon, *The Dominion Sex Dictionary*, 1967
- — Bill Casselman, *Canadian Sayings*, p. 106, 2002

whiskey *noun*

a type of bet in an illegal numbers game lottery *US*

- He played the money row, lucky lady, happy days, true love, sun gonna shine, gold, silver, diamonds, dollars and whiskey. — Chester Himes, *A Rage in Harlem*, p. 23, 1957

whiskey dent *noun*

a dent on your car that you don't remember incurring while driving drunk *US*

- He's got so many whiskey dents in his car, the fenders look like washboards. — Ken Weaver, *Texas Crude*, p. 63, 1984

whiskeyleg *noun*

a drunkard *US*

- He doesn't drink any more and he used to be the biggest whiskyleg in town. — Jack Kerouac, *On the Road*, p. 216, 1957

whiskey papa *noun*

a white phosphorous flare or grenade *US*

From the military phonetic alphabet – WP.

- — Gregory Clark, *Words of the Vietnam War*, p. 559, 1990

whiskey-rot *noun*

any unspecified illness *US*

- — *Current Slang*, p. 26, Spring 1970

whisper *noun*

1 a rumour *UK, 1596*

- Everygreen looks likes she's laced in pretty tight, but there's been whispers that she likes a bit of a wrestle now and then. — Robert Campbell, *Nibbled to Death by Ducks*, p. 129, 1989

2 the very end of a prison sentence *US*

- — Troy Harris, *A Booklet of Criminal Argot, Cant and Jargon*, 1976

whistle *noun*

in the sport of polo, energy *UK*

- There's not much whistle in this chukka[.] — *The Guardian*, 29th July 2003

▸ **wet your whistle**

to take a drink; to quench a thirst *UK, 1530*

- I'm so thirsty, I could die. Just a little 10 cent coke to wet my whistle. It won't take a minute[.] — *American Graffiti*, 1973

whistle *verb*

▸ **whistle in the dark**

to perform oral sex on a woman *US*

- — Dale Gordon, *The Dominion Sex Dictionary*, p. 170, 1967

▸ **whistle through the wheatfield**

to engage in oral sex on a woman, especially a blonde woman *US*

- Another way to say "cunnilingus" [...] Whistling through the wheatfield[.] — Erica Orloff and JoAnn Baker, *Dirty Little Secrets*, p. 86, 2001

whistle and flute; whistle *noun*

1 a suit (of clothes) *UK, 1931*

Rhyming slang.

- I can get a jamjar and a new whistle. — Frank Norman, *Bang To Rights*, p. 58, 1958
- Can't wear a whistle like this without the proper shoes, dicky [shirt] or Peckham [tie], can yer now? — *The Sweeney*, p. 6, 1976
- My old man wore three piece whistles[.] — Ian Dury, *My Old Man*, 1977
- Resplendent in off-the-peg snazzy whistle[.] — Andrew Nickolds, *Back to Basics*, p. 32, 1994
- Dress 'em in ruffled shirts an' Gucci whistles. — Chris Ryan, *The Watchman*, p. 75, 2001

2 cocaine *UK*

Rhyming slang for **TOOT**.

- I've crash-landed off the bitta whistle I had earlier, hit the side of a mountain[.] — J.J. Connolly, *Layer Cake*, p. 214, 2000

whistle and flute; whistle *verb*

to inhale drugs or drug smoke *UK*

Rhyming slang for **TOOT**.

- — Angela Devlin, *Prison Patter*, p. 123, 1996

whistle and toot; whistle and flute; toot *noun*

money *UK, 1950*

Rhyming slang for **LOOT**; used mainly in the reduced form.

- — Angela Devlin, *Prison Patter*, p. 116, 1996

whistlebait *noun*

an attractive woman or girl *US*

- You're twenty-twenty whislte bait! — Haenigsen, *Jive's Like That*, 1947

whistlecock *noun*

amongst Australian Aboriginals, a penis that has had a small slit made in the base of the urethra as a means of birth control; a man who has had this operation *AUSTRALIA*

- — Sidney J. Baker, *The Australian Language*, p. 225, 1945

whistle for *verb*

to wait for, or expect, something in vain *UK, 1882*

- A victory [at the Oscars] for [Michael] Moore, and the subsequent barnstormingly tactless acceptance speech, would be something to savour. But I'm afraid he can whistle for it. — *The Guardian*, 21st March 2003

whistler *noun*

a police car *US*

- — Montie Tak, *Truck Talk*, p. 187, 1971

whistlers *noun*

pieces of metal scrap packed in an artillery shell that makes a sceaming sound as the shell moves through the air *US*

- — Gregory Clark, *Words of the Vietnam War*, p. 454, 1990

whistlestop *noun*

a small town *US*

From the image of a train making a brief stop at the town.

- He squatted in a whistle-stop up in the Catskill Mountains. — Haenigsen, *Jive's Like That*, 1947

whistling gear *noun*

in trucking, the highest gear *US*

May have been named for the whistling sound older tractors made when in overdrive gear, or for the possibility that a rig travelling in this gear could attract the attention of a 'whistler' – a police car.

- — Montie Tak, *Truck Talk*, p. 187, 1971

white *noun*

1 a caspule of Benzedrine™ (amphetamine sulphate) or any other central nervous system stimulant *US*

- Bennies ("cartwheels" or "whites") are basic to the outlaw diet – like weed, beer and wine. — Hunter S. Thompson, *Hell's Angels*, p. 216, 1966
- 'They way they put it is that they "drop whites" to get out of bed in the morning, or whenever they get up to go to work, and "drop reds" to go to sleep,' Sweeney reported at the conference. — *San Francisco Chronicle*, p. 5, 11th October 1966
- — *Current Slang*, p. 51, Fall 1968
- Tim was back to his old regimen of reds and whites. — Lester Bangs, *Psychotic Reactions and Carburetor Dung*, p. 109, 1972
- Reds and Ripple mixed with a bennie, a white and a toke. — Oscar Zeta Acosta, *The Revolt of the Cockroach People*, p. 90, 1973
- And if you give me weed, whites and wine / And you show me a sign / Then I'll be willin' – to be movin.' — Little Feat, *Willin'*, 1988
- They were also referred to as whites, or, for the indecisive, white crosses, and were sold by the $1 unit called a rack[.] — Editors of Ben is Dead, *Retrohell*, p. 50, 1997
- Street names [...] wake ups, whites, whizz. — James Kay and Julian Cohen, *The Parents' Complete Guide to Young People and Drugs*, p. 129, 1998

2 heroin, cocaine or morphine *US, 1914*

From the colour of the powdered drug.

- — Richard A. Spears, *The Slang and Jargon of Drugs and Drink*, p. 547, 1986
- — Robert Ashton, *This Is Heroin*, p. 207, 2002
- — Mike Haskins, *Drugs*, p. 285, 2003

3 crack cocaine *US*

A derivative of the previous sense.

- — Bill Valentine, *Gang Intelligence Manual*, p. 130, 1995
- But the drug of choice now was crack cocaine. Coke. Rock. White. Stones. Charlie. — Lanre Fehintola, *Charlie Says...*, p. 129, 2000

4 a five-pound note *UK, 1946*

From the colour of the large five-pound notes, which were withdrawn from circulation in 1957.

- — Charles Raven, *Underworld Nights*, p. 174, 1956

5 platinum jewellery *UK*

- — Paul Tempest, *Lag's Lexicon*, 1950

6 in American casinos, a white betting token worth one dollar *US*

- —Steve Kuriscak, *Casino Talk*, p. 59, 1985

7 in American casinos, a white betting token worth $500 *US, 1961*

- —Thomas L. Clark, *The Dictionary of Gambling and Gaming*, p. 249, 1987

8 a day; daytime *US*

- About a deuce of long black and whites ago, a stud from the low lands came to the Apple. —Babs Gonzales, *Movin' On Down De Line*, p. 89, 1975

9 'silver' coins *UK, 1887*

Variants include 'whites' and 'white money'.

- —Stanley Jackson, *An Indiscreet Guide to Soho*, 1946
- —Paul Tempest, *Lag's Lexicon*, 1950

▸ **like white on rice**

enitrely, utterly, completely *US*

- They were on my ass like white on rice. —Odie Hawkins, *Scars and Memories*, p. 73, 1987

▸ **the white**

surgical spirit as an alcoholic drink *UK*

The liquid is clear but 'white' differentiates this from **BLUE** (methylated spirits).

- They [vagrant alcoholics] subsist on a diet of methylated spirits (jake or the blue), surgical spirit (surge or the white) and other forms of crude alcohol. —Peter Ackroyd, *London The Biography*, p. 359, 2000

▸ **white-boy shuffle**

an uncoordinated, ungraceful, counter-rhythmic dancing style *US*

- —Judi Sanders, *Faced and Faded, Hanging to Hurl*, p. 43, 1993

white *adjective*

decent *US, 1913*

Usually used sarcastically and as a conscious rejection of the racism that once would have inspired the saying.

- "You can bring her out to the house if you really want to." "That's white of you," I said. "What makes you think she'd come?" "Look, Jim, I didn't mean it that way." —Thurston Scott, *Cure it with Honey*, p. 198, 1951
- We've only met twice and you've been more than white to me both times. —Raymond Chandler, *The Long Goodbye*, p. 9, 1953
- It was might white of you, boy. —Elmore Leonard, *City Primeval*, p. 134, 1980

white-ant *verb*

to undermine someone or something *AUSTRALIA, 1922*

From 'white ant' (a termite).

- —Frank Hardy, *The Outcasts of Foolgarah*, p. 133, 1971
- —Arthur Chipper, *The Aussie Swearer's Guide*, p. 70, 1972
- —Jim Ramsay, *Cop It Sweet!*, p. 96, 1977
- So she set about the delicate task of both promoting and white-anting the woodenheaded swine. —Harrison Biscuit, *The Search for Savage Henry*, p. 18, 1995

white-ass; white-assed *adjective*

bland; insipid; lacking creativity *US*

A reciprocal in formation to the common 'black-ass'; not praise.

- —Connie Eble (Editor), *UNC-CH Campus Slang*, p. 7, Fall 1995

white ball *noun*

crack cocaine *UK, 1998*

- —Mike Haskins, *Drugs*, p. 282, 2003

white boy *noun*

heroin *US, 1986*

An embellishment of **BOY** (heroin), from the colour of the powdered drug.

- —Robert Ashton, *This Is Heroin*, p. 207, 2002
- —Mike Haskins, *Drugs*, p. 285, 2003

white-bread *adjective*

everyday, unexciting, respectable; representing the epitome of white middle-class values and style *US*

- —Connie Eble (Editor), *UNC-CH Campus Slang*, p. 10, Spring 1991
- They were white-bread, all-American boys in all but one critical degree, which is that they didn't care fuck-all about material wealth. —Peter Coyote, *Sleeping Where I Fall*, p. 133, 1998
- [T]his was just the airy-fairy, "don't we all live in a wonderful white-bread Christian world" stuff. The hard-core material was, appropriately, on the higher shelves. —Christopher Brookmyre, *Not the End of the World*, p. 251, 1998
- If you don't look straight-up, white-bread (not white as in race, white as in bland), Middle America then don't even think about showing up somewhere in person. —Eleusis *Lightning on the Sun [The Howard Marks Book of Dope Stories]*, p. 329, 2001

white burger *noun*

a tablet of MDMA, the recreational drug best known as ecstasy *UK*

- Danny simply slips a small white burger in my mouth. I raise some saliva and swallow. —Gavin Hills, *White Burger Danny (Disco Biscuits)*, p. 68, 1996

white Cali; white Cally *noun*

a variety of MDMA, the recreational drug best known as ecstasy; an antihistamine tablet sold as MDMA *UK*

From the colour combined with an abbreviation of California, the presumed place of origin.

- —Macfarlane, Macfarlane and Robson, *The User*, p. 74, 1996

white cliffs of Dover; white cliffs *adjective*

over *UK*

Rhyming slang, formed from the famous landmark, celebrated in song and geography.

- —Ray Puxley, *Fresh Rabbit*, 1998

white cloud *noun*

crack cocaine *US*

- So, in a feew minutes, they all went back in search of the white cloud. —Terry Williams, *The Cocaine Kids*, p. 110, 1989

white cockroach *noun*

a white person *TRINIDAD AND TOBAGO, 1838*

- —Lise Winer, *Dictionary of the English/Creole of Trinidad & Tobago*, 2003

white crinkle *noun*

a five-pound note *UK*

A combination of **CRINKLE** (paper money) and the colour of the large five-pound notes, which were withdrawn from circulation in 1957.

white cross *noun*

an amphetamine or methamphetamine tablet, sectioned with an X *US*

- I can get all the straight old white cross benny's you want at $85 a thousand. —Neal Cassady, *The First Third*, p. 219–220, 30th August 1965
- Paul and his friend Chris Coon had a car, a skateboard, and a new drug called White Crosses, small speed pills. —Jennifer Blowdryer, *White Trash Debutante*, p. 60, 1997
- [Cross Tops] were also referred to as whites, or, for the indecisive, white crosses, and were sold by the $1 unit called a rack in tightly foiled increments of four, five, or ten[.] —Don Bolle, *Retrohell*, p. 50, 1997

white cylinder week *noun*

the bleed period of the menstrual cycle *US*

Refers to a tampon applicator.

- —Karen Houppert, *The Curse*, 1999

white devil *noun*

cocaine *US*

- I take my Kaabar pocket knife, my own personal coke dispenser, scoop up a tipful of the white devil and suck in giant nostrils of slow, white heat through the tender veins of my Indian nose. —Oscar Zeta Acosta, *The Autobiography of a Brown Buffalo*, p. 62, 1972

white drugs *noun*

heroin, cocaine, morphine, etc *US*

From the colour of the refined powder.

- She begins with the smoking of "tea" – marijuana – and from there moves to the "white drugs" – heroin usually. —Harry J. Anslinger, *The Murderers*, p. 39, 1961

white dust *noun*

powdered amphetamine *UK*

- —Angela Devlin, *Prison Patter*, p. 21, 1996

white eye *noun*

illegal alcohol smuggled from the French islands of Saint-Pierre and Miquelon *CANADA*

This term appears in Tom Dalzell's *The Slang of Sin* to mean 'whisky'.

- [W]hite eye or "whisky-blanc," manufactured in France and smuggled through the islands to New Brunswick and Gaspe coast where locals get "boary-eyed drunk on white-eye"[.] —Bill Casselman, *Canadian Food Words*, p. 137, 1998

white-eyes *noun*

a white person *US*

• — *Maledicta*, p. 172, Summer/Winter 1978: 'How to hate thy neighbor: a guide to racist maledicta'

whitefellow; whitefella *noun*

a white person as opposed to a native Australian Aboriginal *AUSTRALIA, 1826*

• 'Christ, dumby, I'll never understand you blackfellas.' 'And I'll never understand you whitefellas.'—Phillip Gwynne, *Deadly Unna?*, p. 117, 1998

white fever *noun*

used of people of colour, a strong attraction towards white people *US*

The opposite of **JUNGLE FEVER**.

• I don't have white fever. Color don't mean shit to me.—Iceberg Slim (Robert Beck), *Mama Black Widow*, p. 294, 1969

white fingers *noun*

cocaine *US*

• The wiretaps recorded a primer of street slang for powder cocaine: white lady, white fingers, soft, fish scales and sand.—*Orlando Sentinel*, p. B2, 17th August 2002

white fluff *noun*

LSD *UK*

• —Mike Haskins, *Drugs*, p. 286, 2003

white ghost *noun*

crack cocaine *UK, 1998*

• —Mike Haskins, *Drugs*, p. 282, 2003

white girl *noun*

1 cocaine *US, 1971*

• Many of us called it "girl" or "white girl" then. It helped to be in a movie studio setting to do cocaine.—Odie Hawkins, *Lost Angeles*, p. 33, 1994

2 heroin *UK, 1998*

• —Mike Haskins, *Drugs*, p. 285, 2003

white goods *noun*

cocaine *UK*

From the colour; adopts the retailing term for 'large white electrical goods' (refrigerators etc.).

white-haired lady *noun*

marijuana *UK, 1998*

Possibly derives as a simile for something as dangerous as marijuana.

• —Mike Haskins, *Drugs*, p. 289, 2003

white hat *noun*

1 an officer in a firefighting company *US*

• — *American Speech*, p. 273, December 1954: 'Fire terms: additional words and definitions'

2 a computer hacker who acts with a legal or moral justification *US*

• He said white hats used their computer skills to understand and secure systems, but black hats used their abilities to break into systems for profit or glory.—*Wired News*, 22nd May 2001

white horse *noun*

1 heroin *UK*

An elaboration of **HORSE** (heroin).

• —Mike Haskins, *Drugs*, p. 285, 2003

2 cocaine *US, 1977*

A play on **HORSE** (heroin) which is mostly brown.

• —Richard A. Spears, *The Slang and Jargon of Drugs and Drink*, p. 549, 1986
• —Mike Haskins, *Drugs*, p. 281, 2003

white junk *noun*

heroin, possibly of the finest quality *US, 1977*

An embellishment of **JUNK** (heroin) from the colour of the powdered drug.

• —Robert Ashton, *This Is Heroin*, p. 207, 2002
• —Mike Haskins, *Drugs*, p. 285, 2003

white kaffir *noun*

a white person who associates with black people *SOUTH AFRICA, 1846*

Racist and abusive.

• How can you stand by and see your only son carrying on just like a white kaffir?—Laurens Van Der Post, *A Story Like the Wind*, p. 79, 1972

white knight *noun*

a night spent under the influence of cocaine *UK*

The colour of cocaine and a pun on 'night'.

white-knuckle *verb*

to persevere on courage alone, especially in the quitting of an addictive drug *US, 1974*

• She couldn't just white-knuckle it, could she? She'd need to be in a neighborhood like West Hollywood where she could get speedballs. —Joseph Wambaugh, *Floaters*, p. 68, 1996

white-knuckle *adjective*

anxiety-making; frightening; thrilling *UK, 1988*

From the effect of holding-on tightly.

• Are you ready for the white-knuckle ride?—*The Guardian*, 12th June 2004

white lady *noun*

1 any strong white spirit such as gin or methylated spirits *AUSTRALIA, 1935*

• —Patsy Adam-Smith, *Folklore of the Australian Railwaymen*, p. 13, 1969
• —John O'Grady, *It's Your Shout, Mate!*, p. 73, 1972
• —Jim Ramsay, *Cop It Sweet!*, p. 96, 1977

2 a powdered narcotic, especially cocaine or heroin *US*

The shortened form 'lady' is also used.

• Only woman I need is the White Lady that rides through my veins. —Nathan Heard, *Howard Street*, p. 185, 1968
• I wish I could cop a few blows of the Miss Pure White Lady stashed under that cushion to clear my skull.—Iceberg Slim (Robert Beck), *Death Wish*, p. 11, 1977
• CALL IT... Basuco, gianluca, blow, percy, lady, toot, white[.] JUST DON'T CALL IT... Charlie – too Eighties—*Drugs An Adult Guide*, p. 34, December 2001

white light *noun*

LSD *UK, 1969*

Possibly a reference to The Velvet Underground's 1967 album 'White Light/White Heat'.

• And she said that she had some white light / And she said that she had some morphine[.]—Jim Carroll, *Lorraine*, 1982
• —Angela Devlin, *Prison Patter*, p. 123, 1996

white lightning *noun*

1 strong, if inferior, homemade whisky *US, 1921*

• But she brought more of the white lightning and choc, and left us alone.—Jim Thompson, *Roughneck*, p. 92, 1954
• I'm drinkin moonshine cocktails or punch made with orange juice, ice, ginger ale & white lightin.—Jack Kerouac, *Letter to William Burroughs*, p. 480, May 1955
• "You guys evah drank white lightenin'?" "Shit! We was raised on white lightenin'; here, gimme that stuff."—Odie Hawkins, *Men Friends*, p. 55, 1989

2 LSD; LSD mixed with methamphetamine or similar *US, 1970*

• —Richard A. Spears, *The Slang and Jargon of Drugs and Drink*, p. 548, 1986
• —Mike Haskins, *Drugs*, p. 286, 2003

whiteline fever *noun*

an addiction to cocaine *UK*

The white powder is shaped in a **LINE** for inhalation.

• —Angela Devlin, *Prison Patter*, p. 123, 1996

white man *noun*

an honourable man *US, 1865*

• Ta doc! You're a white man – even if you are an ikey mo [Jew].—Barry Humphries, *Bazza Pulls It Off!*, 1971

white man's time *noun*

used for denoting punctuality *US*

• — *American Speech*, p. 276, December 1963: 'American Indian student slang'

white meat *noun*

a white person as a sex object; the genitals of a white person; sex with a white person *US*

• Shoot, whyn't they try to get them some nice white meat from downtown once in a while instead of picking on us all the time?—John M. Murtagh and Sara Harris, *Cast the First Stone*, p. 11, 1957
• She sure has, white meat!—Willard Motely, *Let No Man Write My Epitaph*, p. 337, 1958
• — *Maledicta*, p. 61, 1986–1987: 'A continuation of a glossary of ethnic slurs in American English'
• —Lise Winer, *Dictionary of the English/Creole of Trinidad & Tobago*, 2003

white mice *noun*

1 during the conflict in Vietnam, the South Vietnamese civilian police *US*

From their white helmets and gloves.

- After seven in the evening, when the curfew included Americans and became total, nothing but White Mice patrols and MP jeeps moved in the streets[.] — Michael Herr, *Dispatches*, p. 70, 1977
- If I tried I would only be mugged by the locals or shot by the 'white mice' for being out after curfew. — Martin Cameron, *A Look at the Bright Side*, 1988
- — Linda Reinberg, *In the Field*, p. 240, 1991

2 dice *UK*

Rhyming slang.

- — *Picture Post*, 2nd January 1954

white missy *noun*

a glass of cheap white rum *BARBADOS*

- — Frank A. Collymore, *Barbadian Dialect*, p. 120, 1965

white money *noun*

in prison, actual currency *US*

Required for major purchases, such as drugs.

- — John R. Armore and Joseph D. Wolfe, *Dictionary of Desperation*, p. 56, 1976

white mosquitoes; white mosquito *noun*

cocaine *US, 1949*

Probably from the 'sting' of an injection.

- — Richard A. Spears, *The Slang and Jargon of Drugs and Drink*, p. 549, 1986
- — Mike Haskins, *Drugs*, p. 281, 2003

white mule *noun*

an illegally manufactured whisky, colourless and powerful *US, 1921*

- [H]e drank an entire Mason jar of white mule and danced the two-step with every lady present, bar none. — Max Shulman, *Anyone Got a Match?*, p. 2, 1964

white nigger *noun*

a French-Canadian *CANADA, 1971*

Offensive.

- — *Maledicta*, p. 184, 1979: 'Canadian slurs, ethnic and other'

white nurse; nurse *noun*

powdered drugs; cocaine; heroin; morphine *US, 1936*

- — Richard A. Spears, *The Slang and Jargon of Drugs and Drink*, p. 364, 1986
- — Angela Devlin, *Prison Patter*, p. 123, 1996
- — Mike Haskins, *Drugs*, p. 284, 2003

white-on-white *noun*

a white shirt that was deemed fashionable in the 1940s *US*

- He was choked up tight in a white-on-white / And a cocoa front that was down. — Dennis Wepman et al., *The Life*, p. 54, 1976

white-out; whitey *noun*

an instance of paling as a symptom of imminent faintness, dizziness or vomiting *UK: SCOTLAND*

From the draining of colour from the face.

- See that boay takin a whitey? Get him oot inty the close away fae ma good carpet. — Michael Munro, *The Patter, Another Blast*, p. 80, 1988

White Owl *noun*

a branded White Owl™ cigar re-made to contain marijuana *US*

- I was instrumental in introducing Phillies Blunts to the UK [...] It was LL Cool J who taught me how to roll a Phillies. I can roll Phillies, Dutch Owls and White Owls. — *Mixmag*, p. 75, April 2003

white Owsley *noun*

a type of high quality LSD *US, 1974*

From the name of legendary LSD manufacturer Augustus Owsley Stanley III.

- — Richard A. Spears, *The Slang and Jargon of Drugs and Drink*, p. 549, 1986
- — Mike Haskins, *Drugs*, p. 286, 2003

white pipe *noun*

a mixture of marijuana and crushed Mandrax™ (a branded tranquillizer in tablet form) smoked or ingested orally *SOUTH AFRICA*

A tablet of Mandrax, also known as a 'white', enhances the effect of the marijuana. When 'white pipe' is smoked it is usually in a pipe improvised with a broken bottle.

white policeman's roll *noun*

in an illegal numbers gambling lottery, a bet on 13, 37 and 70 *US*

- — *American Speech*, p. 193, October 1949

white powder *noun*

a narcotic in white powder form, that is, heroin, cocaine or morphine *US, 1908*

- They had a terrible contempt for the guys on the "white stuff" – heroin, morphine, and cocaine[.] — Mezz Mezzrow, *Really the Blues*, p. 248, 1946

white-powder bar *noun*

lawyers who defend drug dealers *UK*

- General Noriega of Panama sought help from Miami's white-powder bar to release his chilled [not quite frozen] assets. — David Rowan, *A Glossary for the 90s*, p. 41, 1998

white robin *noun*

a variety of MDMA, the recreational drug best known as ecstasy *UK*

From the colour of the tablet and the embossed motif.

- — Gareth Thomas, *This Is Ecstasy*, p. 57, 2002

white rock *noun*

high quality methamphetamine in rock form *US*

- — Geoffrey Froner, *Digging for Diamonds*, p. 69, 1989: 'Types of speed'

white Russian *noun*

in homosexual usage, the passing of semen from one mouth to another *US*

- — *Maledicta*, p. 60, 1986–1987: 'A continuation of a glossary of ethnic slurs in American English'

white shirt *noun*

in roller derby, a skater who plays honourably and is seen as the 'good guy', usually from the team designated as the home team *US*

- White shirts fight only when first belted by someone else and only when driven beyond the limits of patience. — Keith Coppage, *Roller Derby to Rollerjam*, p. 127, 1999

whiteshirt *noun*

a senior prison officer *UK*

From the uniform.

- — Angela Devlin, *Prison Patter*, p. 123, 1996

white shit *noun*

cocaine *UK*

- — Angela Devlin, *Prison Patter*, p. 104, 1996

white shoes *noun*

white-wall tyres *US*

- A bum stove and organ. Phony white shoes. — Joseph Wambaugh, *The Black Marble*, p. 194, 1978

white sidewalls *noun*

the visible scalp on the side of the head after a short haircut, especially a military haircut *US*

- — Carl Fleischhauer, *A Glossary of Army Slang*, p. 26, 1968
- — Kenn "Naz" Young, *Naz's Dictionary of Teen Slang*, p. 135, 1993

whiteskin *noun*

in poker, any card ranked ten or lower *US, 1943*

- — Thomas L. Clark, *The Dictionary of Gambling and Gaming*, p. 250, 1987

white slave *noun*

a woman engaged in enforced prostitution *UK, 1857*

- I was one of the dozen or so black pimps the F.B.I. kept constant tabs on to mail on a white slave beef. — Iceberg Slim (Robert Beck), *The Naked Soul of Iceberg Slim*, p. 28, 1971

whitesocks *noun*

a ferocious if tiny mosquito *US*

- The whitesocks is a worse pest than the NO-SEE-UM. Under a magnifying glass its white feet are visible[.] — Robert O. Bowen, *An Alaskan Dictionary*, p. 35, 1965

white stuff *noun*

any powdered drug – morphine, heroin or cocaine *US, 1914*

- [O]nly members of the On Leon sell opium and Hip Singers sell white stuff- cocaine and heroin. — Jack Lait and Lee Mortimer, *Chicago Confidential*, p. 90, 1950

- In other cities, Hip Singers must content themselves with the sale of white stuff – heroin, morphine, and cocaine – which is seldom used by Chinese. —Jack Lait and Lee Mortimer, *Washington Confidential*, p. 60, 1951
- —Angela Devlin, *Prison Patter*, p. 123, 1996
- —Robert Ashton, *This Is Heroin*, p. 207, 2002

white sugar *noun*
crack cocaine *UK, 1998*
From the appearance.
- —Mike Haskins, *Drugs*, p. 282, 2003

white telephone *noun*
▸ **speak on the great white telephone; talk into the big white telephone; talk to God on the big white telephone**
to vomit into a lavatory bowl *US, 1978*
From the image of a sick person leaning over a white lavatory bowl and crying 'God!' in despair.
- [M]y complexion was, by then, that distinctive shade of ivory with a green tinge of someone who is about to hold a very important conversation with God on the big white telephone. —Iain Aitch, *A Fete Worse Than Death*, p. 98–98, 2003

white tornado *noun*
freebase cocaine *US*
- They were smoking free base, also known as the "white tornado" – the form of cocaine favored by those beyond the nasal stage of evolution. —*Hi Life*, p. 78, 1979
- —Gilda and Melvin Berger, *Drug Abuse A-Z*, p. 134, 1990

white trash *noun*
an impoverished or anti-social white person or persons; originally, and still, the poverty-stricken white population of the southern US *US, 1831*
Originally black usage; derogatory; abbreviates to 'trash' (rubbish).
- When good old Buck, of Buck and Bubbles, was driving along down South in his big Cadillac and dared to challenge the supremacy of the white race by passing a couple of white trash in a dinky old rattletrap Ford, he spent the night in jail[.] —Mezz Mezzrow, *Really the Blues*, p. 207, 1946
- Hoe-hands. Cotton-pickers. White trash. —Jim Thompson, *The Kill-Off*, p. 47, 1957
- Algren's book opens with one of the best historical descriptions of American white trash ever written. —Hunter S. Thompson, *Hell's Angels*, p. 157, 1966
- Do you care to tell me what Mrs. White-trash and her stupid daughter are doing in my house? —*Cruel Intentions*, 1999
- They were scum. White trash. The white niggers which infested every civilised nation. He despised them all. —John King, *White Trash*, p. 306, 2001

white turtle-neck brigade *noun*
male homosexuals *UK*
From a type of jumper that was in vogue, and, perhaps intended as a discreet signal between gay men.
- [Wimbledon] Common has become an international stamping ground for what has become known as the white turtle-neck brigade. —*Evening Standard (London)*, 16th October 1969

white van man *noun*
the average tabloid-reader-in-the-street, the man-in-the-street *UK*
It is a statistical probability that the driver constructively criticising your driving is behind the wheel of a white van. Coined in 1997 by BBC Radio 2 DJ Sarah Kennedy.
- White van man say messing with Millwall is too risky[.] —Garry Bushell, *The Face*, p. 191, 2001
- In recent years the white van man has replaced the taxi driver as the nation's font of common sense by tabloid newspapers. —*The Guardian*, 10th April 2003

whitewash *noun*
in sports, a victory in which the opponent does not score at all *US, 1867*
- —Parke Cummings, *Dictionary of Baseball*, p. 61, 1950
- The 1-0 win at Tingley Coliseum moves New Mexico, which has won six of seven, within two points of the second-place Blazers in the Northwest Division. The whitewash was the first of Beaudry's professional career. —*Alburquerque (New Mexico) Journal*, p. D6, 4th January 2004

whitewash *verb*
to win a game without your opponent scoring *US*
- —Dick Squires, *The Other Racquet Sports*, p. 220, 1971: 'Glossary'
- —Pramod Shankar, *How to Win at Gin Rummy*, p. 91, 1994

white widow *noun*
a variety of marijuana
- A Romulan-White Widow-Big Bud cross. —Brian Preston, *Pot Planet*, p. 231, 2002

white wog *noun*
a Welsh person *UK, 1984*
Usually jocular, from **WOG** (any person of non-white ethnicity) and a recognition of the Welsh as a race apart within the British Isles; it is, perhaps, interesting to note that a Welsh accent attempted by an English person has a pronounced tendency to sound Indian.

white worm *noun*
an uninfected appendix removed in surgery based on an incorrect diagnosis *US*
- —Sally Williams, *"Strong" Words*, p. 166, 1994

whitey *noun*
1 a white person or white people collectively *US, 1942*
Insulting; a gesture of resistance.
- And then I got to see how Whitey treats his heroes. —Dick Gregory, *Nigger*, p. 72, 1964
- Shorty felt about the war the same way I and most ghetto Negros did: "Whitey owns everything. He wants us to go and bleed for him? Let him fight." —Malcolm X and Alex Haley, *The Autobiography of Malcolm X*, p. 71, 1964
- "So long, whitey," one of the Negro musicians said. —Nat Hentoff, *Jazz Country*, p. 72, 1965
- In 1939 Negroes were still relegated to sitting in the balconies of downtown theatres so we decided to change "whitey's" rule. —Babs Gonzales, *I Paid My Dues*, p. 14, 1967
- It doesn't matter, the end result, as long as trick Whitey, fuck up Boss Charley. —Lenny Bruce, *The Essential Lenny Bruce*, p. 12, 1967
- So white would get him a little taste of black gold for $10 or $15 and Black people helped him. —H. Rap Brown, *Die Nigger Die!*, p. 31, 1969
- The Black pimp's fame and high status among lower-class Black males is assured by the fact that this income from his hos, both Black and White, originates largely from the pockets of Whitey. —Christina and Richard Milner, *Black Players*, p. 11–12, 1972
- That's the way Whitey is, man. He'll do anything for money. —Odie Hawkins, *Chicago Hustle*, p. 134, 1977
- And as far as Mr. Viceroy Wilson is concerned, we are kicking the living shit out of whitey. —Carl Hiaasen, *Tourist Season*, p. 102, 1986
- The black man, he's told whitey where it's at. —Herbert Huncke, *Guilty of Everything*, p. 10, 1990

2 an amphetamine pill *US*
- —Arnold Shaw, *Dictionary of American Pop/Rock*, p. 397, 1982

3 in pool, the cue ball *US, 1983*
- —Mike Shamos, *The Illustrated Encyclopedia of Billiards*, p. 262, 1993

▷ **see:** WHITE-OUT

Whitney dressed as Britney
applied to an older person dressed in a younger fashion *UK*
A modern variation of the popular idiom, 'mutton dressed as lamb'; formed on the US entertainers Whitney Houston (b.1963) and Britney Spears (b.1981).
- —Mervyn Stutter, *Getting Nowhere Fast*, 18th June 2004

whittle *verb*
▸ **whittle the gut stick**
(of a male) to masturbate *UK*
- We learn to [...] whittle the gut stick or as the disingenuous language of science would have it, "masturbate". —Richard Herring, *Talking Cock*, p. 113, 2003

whiz; whizz *noun*
1 a genius; somebody who is extremely proficient at a given activity *US, 1914*
An abbreviation of 'wizard'.
- —Patrick Campbell, *Come Here Till I Tell You*, 1960
- He was, undeniably, a whiz at selling Florida real estate. —Carl Hiaasen, *Native Tongue*, p. 48, 1991
- The book disappeared for several days and when it resurfaced, my daughter had become a whizz at telling fortunes. —*The Guardian*, 14th December 2002

2 an act of urinating *US, 1971*
Often in a construction such as 'take a whiz'.
- As Steve started for the boat, Shannon called, "I got to take a whiz." —Jack W. Thomas, *Heavy Number*, p. 76, 1976
- And somewhere in here Paco gets his own breakfast, takes another whiz, refills cofee mugs, refills napkin dispenser[.] —Larry Heinemann, *Paco's Story*, p. 115, 1986
- Can I give it to you in the morning? I just took a whiz. —*American Beauty*, 1999

- And I was, in the morning, out in the backyard taking a whizz. — David Carradine, *Uncut*, p. 34, March 2004

3 whisky *US*

- And I knew how bad the whiz was for me – I'd been told not to drink it at all – but I have to have it. — Jim Thompson, *Savage Night*, p. 72, 1953

4 on the railways, the pressurised air that operates the brake system *US*

- — Ramon Adams, *The Language of the Railroader*, p. 172, 1977

▸ **on the whiz**

operating as a pickpocket *US, 1950*

- [A] pair of Argentinian pick-pockets on the whizz, Latin style[.] — Jake Arnott, *He Kills Coppers*, p. 17, 2001

▸ **the whiz**

pickpocketing *UK, 1937*

- Tom has been at the whiz these last ten years at least. — David Powis, *The Signs of Crime*, 1977

whiz *verb*

to urinate *US*

- — *Current Slang*, p. 21, Spring 1971

whizbang; whizz-bang *noun*

an injected mixture of cocaine and heroin; cocaine; heroine *US, 1933*

- — Nick Constable, *This is Cocaine*, p. 181, 2002
- — Mike Haskins, *Drugs*, p. 281, 2003

whizbang *verb*

to travel fast *US*

- I still had fresh memories of sitting by the roadside watching them whizbang by in big expensive cars[.] — Robert Gover, *Poorboy at the Party*, p. 3, 1966

whizbox *noun*

a global positioning system device *US*

Gulf war usage.

- — *American Speech*, p. 404, Winter 1991: 'Among the new words'

whiz-kid; whizz-kid *noun*

a precociously bright child; hence a young person advancing in business faster than expectations *US, 1960*

- Rebel Aussie whizz-kid to publish here. — Richard Neville, *Play Power*, p. 173, 1970
- Ever since he was a whiz-kid eight-grade physics pupil, Marx had dreamed of becoming a great theoretical scientist[.] — Tom Robbins, *Another Roadside Attraction*, p. 125, 1971
- Employment can be riskier than self- employment, even for the whizz kids of the money world, for they can be fired at ten minutes' notice[.] — Charles Handy, *The Age of Unreason*, p. 207, 1989
- She, Milly, was some sort of Foreign Office whizz kid and lived in China developing British interests. — Mark Barrowcliffe, *Girlfriend 44*, p. 307, 2002

whizo *noun*

a weapons system officer *US*

- "It gives the whizo" – weapons system officer – "a better look-angle ito the target and little more energy on the bomb." — *New York Times*, 28th June 1991

whizz; wizz; whiz *noun*

amphetamine *UK, 1993*

A pun on **SPEED**.

- But that's okay, 'cos we're sorted for Es & wizz — Pulp *Sorted For E's & Wizz*, 1995
- I even took my A levels from my crammers [periods of intense study] on whizz. — Macfarlane, Macfarlane and Robson, *The User*, p. 91, 1996
- Now this geezer was always asking me for a dab of whizz — Dave Courtney, *Raving Lunacy*, p. 5, 2000
- the baby laxative all the recent whizz was cut with — Niall Griffiths, *Kelly + Victor*, p. 28, 2002

whizz *verb*

to use amphetamines *UK*

- How can you slow dance when you're whizzing off your tits? — Dave Courtney, *Raving Lunacy*, p. 7, 2000

whizzbang *noun*

a pretty girl *US*

- — Marcus Hanna Boulware, *Jive and Slang of Students in Negro Colleges*, 1947

whizzer *noun*

1 an excellent thing; also used as a nickname for a person who excels *UK, 1888*

- "A whizzer of a story." – Library Journal — Christopher Hyde, *The Second Assassin*, 2002

2 the penis *US*

- Then, he calmly tucked his whizzer back into his pants[.] — Thom Nicholson, *15 Months in Sog*, p. 108, 1999

3 a pickpocket *US, 1925*

Variants include 'whiz' and 'whizz'.

- — Angela Devlin, *Prison Patter*, p. 123, 1996

4 in poker, a successful play of an inferior hand, or the person playing it *US*

- — George Percy, *The Language of Poker*, p. 96, 1988

5 a drinking bout *CANADA*

- He was only off on a little bit of a whizzer. — Hugh Dempsey, *The Best of Bob Edwards*, 1975

▷ see: **WYSSA**

whizzhead *noun*

a habitual amphetamine user *UK*

- [T]he cook was a whizzhead[.] — Dave Courtney, *Raving Lunacy*, p. 12, 2000

whizz kid *noun*

a habitual amphetamine user *UK, 1990s*

- — Alon Shulman, *The Style Bible*, p. 270, 1999

whizz-kids *noun*

in police use, forensic scientists or a forensic science department *UK*

Usually used with 'the'. Formed on 'whizz-kid' (a precociously bright child).

- — John Wainwright, *Dig His Grave and Let Him Lie*, 1971

whizz mob *noun*

a gang of pickpockets *UK, 1929*

- — Angela Devlin, *Prison Patter*, p. 123, 1996

whizzo; wizzo *noun*

in the US military, a weapons system operator or officer *US*

From a vocalisation of the abbreviation WSO.

- The FLIR is mostly the wizzo's (slang for the Weapons System Officer, or WSO, the back-seater who operates the radar and other equipment while the pilot flies the airplane) toy[.] — Hans Halberstadt, *US Marine Corps*, 1993
- — John W. Mussell, *The Token Book of Militarisms*, 1995
- Larry Moore was Rick's wizzo (weapons system operator) on many occasions. — Evelyn Husband and Donna VanLiere, *High Calling*, p. 31, 2003

whizzo; wizzo *adjective*

excellent *UK, 1948*

After **WHIZZO!** (an exclamation of delight).

- The Banks-Livingstone whizzo scheme was thrown out by the [Greater London Council]. — *New Society*, 23rd July 1981
- [C]learly, an army on wizzo marching powder would be, as early enemies of the Inca discovered, some army. — Nick Costable, *This is Cocaine*, p. 19, 2002
- Diz here, my whizzo lawyer, doesn't trust the normal procedure. — John Lescroart, *The First Law*, p. 362, 2003

whizzo!; wizzo!

splendid! *UK, 1905*

- Oh whizzo, she's fallen in the bidet. Look at her covered in water lilies. — Jilly Cooper, *Riders*, p. 398, 1985
- "Wizzo!" Sarah said, displaying her RAF slang in an ironic mode. — Thomas Fleming, *Conquerors of the Sky*, p. 162, 2003

whizzy *adjective*

used of a computer program, well-designed and attractive *US*

- — Eric S. Raymond, *The New Hacker's Dictionary*, p. 382, 1991

who he?

usually used for jocular or dismissive effect *UK*

- They all said that Mitterand would lose [...] and they thought Franz-Josef Strauss (who he?) might finally make it. — *New Society*, 23rd July 1981
- Prince Anthrax? Who he? — *The Observer*, 21st October 2001

whoa!

used for urging a serious reconsideration of the direction that the conversation is taking *US*

From the C19 command to a horse or ox to stop, and still evocative of a simple, rural world.

- — Connie Eble (Editor), *UNC-CH Campus Slang*, p. 7, Fall 1981

- McAllen, trying to smile, said, "Whoa now, you people have a misconception about the program we better clear up." — Elmore Leonard, *Killshot*, p. 154, 1989
- I want to stay here. I f'ing told you! – Whoa, calm down, calm it down. Trust me, I know what's good for you. — Mark Powell, *Snap*, p. 222, 2001

whoady *noun*

a close friend or family member *US*

- — Rick Ayers (Editor), *Berkeley High Slang Dictionary*, p. 43, 2004

who are you looking at?

used aggressively as an offensive challenge *UK*

- [H]e looked at you as much as to say, who are you looking at? — Livi Michael, *Robinson Street*, p. 24, 1999

Who ate all the pies? You fat bastard, You fat bastard

a call and response chant used to taunt anyone who is overweight *UK*

A chant from the football terraces that has spread wider.

- A man in a Ben Sherman [...] started doing a striptease [...] as his mates chanted WHO ATE ALL THE PIES, stretching his arms back and pulling the shirt off [...] a chorus of YOU FAT BASTARD, YOU FAT BASTARD directed at his shimmering gut[.] — John King, *White Trash*, p. 66, 2001

who-began-it *noun*

an admonishment or a threatened beating *IRELAND*

- Somebody being aware of the time they were supposed to be at home, and meeting them on the road back, might say to them, "Ah, when ye get home ye'll get who-began-it." — *Limerick Leader*, 11th November 2000

who cares?

expresses a dismissive lack of concern or interest *US, 1844*

- He's won. Who cares? — *The Guardian*, 14th September 2001

whodunnit; whodunit *noun*

1 a murder mystery novel, film or other entertainment; a detective novel *US, 1930*

Adopted in the UK in 1942 from the US.

- "Lot of who-done-its," Robbie said, "But I'm not talking about that. Here's one. A famous hunter risks his life simply to put his sights on Hitler. Great book." — Elmore Leonard, *Split Images*, p. 29–30, 1981
- In the newspaper story a chief detective was quoted as saying, "This one's a real whodunit," which is what the detective was told to say whenever a reporter called. — Carl Hiaasen, *Tourist Season*, p. 7, 1986
- Proud purveyors of cabaret-whodunnit entertainment. — *Murder On The Menu*, 1990
- BBC plots reality whodunnit show. — *The Guardian*, 13th March 2003

2 in prison, a meat pie *UK, 1950*

A body has been discovered under the pastry!

- — Angela Devlin, *Prison Patter*, p. 123, 1996

who knows it?

used as a ritualistic questioning of the veracity of a statement *US*

- — *American Speech*, p. 275, December 1963: 'American Indian student slang'

whole ball of wax *noun*

everything *US, 1953*

- Doing the dishes, bringing home the groceries, scrubbing the toilet clean with a nylon brush. The whole ball of wax. — Joel Rose, *Kill Kill Faster Faster*, p. 166, 1997

whole box and dice *noun*

everything *AUSTRALIA, 1888*

- All 18,000 warriors of the Integrated Strike Force – with tanks, guns, live ammunition, the whole box and dice – were to mass there. — Gerald Sweeney, *Invasion*, p. 102, 1982
- — David McGill, *David McGill's Complete Kiwi Slang Dictionary*, p. 20, 1998

whole hog *noun*

▸ **go the whole hog**

to do something in a thorough way *US, 1828*

- I'm surprised Michael Meacher didn't go the whole hog and say it was Mossad agents in league with the CIA who flew the jets into the twin towers. — *The Guardian*, 8th September 2003

whole lot; whole lotta *adverb*

a great deal; very much *US, 1907*

- — Jerry Lee Lewis, *Whole Lotta Shakin' Goin' On*, 1957
- — Led Zeppelin, *Whole Lotta Love*, 1969
- Go North ... where the living is a whole lot easier[.] — *The Guardian*, 6th December 2000
- Whole lotta rockin' — *The Daily Telegraph*, 23rd October 2003

who loves ya, baby?

used for expressing affection in a humorous fashion *US*

The signature line of the police captain played by Telly Savalas on the television police drama *Kojak* (CBS, 1973–78). Repeated with referential humour.

whomp *verb*

▷ **see: WOMP**

whomp back *verb*

to drink *US*

A play on **KNOCK BACK** (to drink).

- We all sat there whomping back the Mai Tais[.] — Lester Bangs, *Psychotic Reactions and Carburetor Dung*, p. 140, 1973

whomper *noun*

a powerful, hard-breaking wave *US*

- — John Severson, *Modern Surfing Around the World*, p. 165, 1964

whoof *verb*

to fart *UK*

- — L. Lane, *ABZ of Scouse*, 1966

whoof back *verb*

to eat or drink greedily *UK*

- Instead she put ganja [marijuana] into the cakes which Gagger and Vile are whoofing back now. — Jack Allen, *When the Whistle Blows*, p. 241, 2000

whoo-hoo!

used as a humorous expression of happiness, usually ironic *US*

From the television cartoon *The Simpsons*.

- — Connie Eble (Editor), *UNC-CH Campus Slang*, p. 9, March 1996

whoop; woop *noun*

a bit; a small amount *US, 1904*

- Lucky they didn't see you; you'd be in a whole whoop of trouble by naw. — Steve Cannon, *Groove, Bang, and Jive Around*, p. 20, 1969

▸ **give a whoop in hell**

to care, generally in a negative context *US*

- His wife, he told me at one point, didn't give a whoop in hell about his life's work. — Lawrence Block, *No Score [The Affairs of Chip Harrison Omnibus]*, p. 36, 1970

whoop *verb*

▸ **whoop it up**

to make a great deal of rowdy noise *US, 1884*

- A city the size of New York, with probably 20,000,000 persons within a thirty-mile radius, and untold millions more swarming in for short periods of whooping it up, today supports only one big Broadway casino[.] — Robert Sylvester, *No Cover Charge*, p. 292, 1956
- A lot of old me, a la Tom Waits, were grabbing the girls and whooping it up. — Sandra Bernhard, *Confessions of a Pretty Lady*, p. 73, 1988

whoop and holler *noun*

an indeterminate, relatively small distance *US*

- Place over on the river bank, just a whoop an' a holler from town. — Jim Thompson, *Pop. 1280*, p. 30, 1964

whoop and holler *verb*

to shout; to carry on loudly *US, 1969*

- They questioned me in teams, the first team was threatening me, whooping and hollering; the second team was going to save me from the first, only I got to tell them the truth about the murder. — Edwin Torres, *Carlito's Way*, p. 36, 1975

whoop-de-do *noun*

1 in horse racing, a style of racing based on the premise of establishing an early lead and then running as fast as possible with maximum whip and heel encouragement *US*

- The number of riders in America who will give a horse of any age a chance to settle into stride is pitifully few, the great majority being strictly "whoop-de-do" booters who might have been developed by the late Bill Daly. — *Daily Racing Form*, p. 4, 27th November 1959
- — Tom Ainslie, *Ainslie's Complete Guide to Thoroughbred Racing*, p. 341, 1976

2 in motorcyle racing, a closely spaced sequence of hills or rises *US*

- The series of quick ups and downs over a whoop-de-do can put a cycle out of control. — Ed Radlauer, *Motorcyclopedia*, p. 74, 1973

whoop-de-do *adjective*

1 in horse racing, employing the strategy of riding all-out from the start of the race *US*

- Longden, for example, is famed as a "whoop-te-do" rider: a jockey who likes to get out front and stay there. — *Time*, p. 82, 17 May 1948
- The number of riders in America who will give a horse of any age a chance to settle into stride is pitifully few, the great majority being strictly "whoop-de-do" booters, who might have been developed by the late Bill Daly. — *Daily Racing Form*, p. 4, 27 November 1959

2 celebratory, uproarious *US, 1932*
Variants include 'whoop-de-doodle' and 'whoopidy-do'.
- [S]he gets all whoopidy-do like we've just given her the vote or something. — Danny King, *The Burglar Diaries*, p. 117, 2001

3 a loud and rowdy event or gathering *US, 1929*
- FIGS: Quiet tonight, huh? FREDDY: At that bachelor party. Across the river. FIGS: Yeah. Whoop-de-do. — *Copland*, 1997

whoop-de-doo!; woop-tee-doo!
used as an expression of strong support or celebration *US*
Often ironic.
- Well, woop-tee-doo, little puppy with a poundcake. — *Gone in 60 Seconds*, 2000

whoopee *noun*
▸ make whoopee
1 to have sex *US, 1928*
A forced and silly euphemism, but one sanctioned by television censors; it was used with annoying regularity by Bob Eubanks, host of *The Newlywed Game* television programme (ABC, 1966–90).
- [H]er gaze holding on Bob Eubanks talking to a panel of newlywed wives, asking them what film star will their husbands say "you would most like to make whoopee with"[.] — Elmore Leonard, *City Primeval*, p. 172, 1980
- BRANDI: If you and I were making whoopie – BRODIE: What's whoopie? BRANDIE: You know, if we were, intimate. BRODIE: What, like fucking? — *Mallrats*, 1995

2 to indulge in, and take pleasure in, boisterous or rowdy merry-making *UK, 1933*
- the fast-growing economic trade zones where they are making whoopee in an unabashed capitalist fashion — Suzy Gershman, *Born to Shop Hong Kong, Shanghai & Beijing*, p. 139, 2003

whoopee!
used for expressing great excitement *UK, 1862*
- I ran for it with my soul whoopeeing. — Jack Kerouac, *On the Road*, p. 16, 1957
- Whoopee! Peggy Precious, your fever's gone! — Iceberg Slim (Robert Beck), *Doom Fox*, p. 79, 1978
- Great. Just great. I'm so happy. Whoopie! — *As Good As It Gets*, 1997

whoopee card *noun*
a computer punch card with all the holes punched out *US*
- — Eric S. Raymond, *The New Hacker's Dictionary*, p. 219, 1991

whoopeedoo!
used as an, often ironic, expression of celebration *UK*
An elaboration of **WHOOPEE!**.
- He didn't even take a second glance at Croydon's new "shining pearl", the tramlines installed to – whoopeedoo! – celebrate the millennium. — Garry Bushell, *The Face*, p. 3, 2001

whoops!
used as a hurried expression of regret *US, 1937*
- He said to the sweet girl, "Whoops, you caught me playing." — Elmore Leonard, *Stick*, p. 26, 1983
- CYN: It was lovely! (SEES BERNIE LOOKING CYNICAL) Whoops! Sorry! — Sally Cline, *Couples*, p. 296, 1998

whoopsie *noun*
a male homosexual *US*
- Are you a fagola, sir? My friends and me, we got to know. Are you a whoopsie? — Bernard Wolfe, *The Magic of Their Singing*, p. 128, 1961

whoopsie-daisy!; whoops-a-daisy!
used for registering dismay or surprise, often implying clumsiness *US, 1925*
- — Humphrey Ocean & The Hardy Annuals, *Whoops-A-Daisy*, 1978
- And I'm like whoops-a-daisy. — a schoolgirl in Bath, 10th February 2003

whoop-up trail *noun*
the terrain over which men and boys ride horses fast *CANADA*
- The other boys gave him hell for his spectacles anyway, so he did not feel a severe necessity to learn the whoop-up trail. — George Bowering, *Caprice*, p. 144, 1987

whoor's melt *noun*
▷ see: HOOR'S MELT

whoosit; whoozit *noun*
▷ see: WHOSIT

whop *verb*
to strike someone with heavy blows *UK, 1575*
- Some of them get whopped and smacked around. — Susan Hall, *Gentleman of Leisure*, p. 44, 1972

whopper *noun*
1 something that is extremely and unusually large *UK, 1785*
The best known Whopper in the US is a hamburger sandwich introduced by the original Burger King™ restaurant in Miami in 1957.
- [S]he explained she was a lab technician on twentyfourhour call and scooted back to the ladiesroom to phone her escort service and say she couldn't book any tricks that night; she'd just started and it was a whopper. — Seth Morgan, *Homeboy*, p. 5, 1990
- She had another long phone conversation with Wally; the next phone bill should be quite a whopper. — C.D. Payne, *Youth in Revolt*, p. 109, 1993
- — Rita Cirtesi, *Pink Slip*, 1999
- I needed those kinds of gifts like I needed the kind of whopper crotch infection I got after wearing those polyster birthday briefs[.] — Rita Cirtesi, *Pink Slip*, p. 1, 1999

2 a big lie *US*
- She probably also knew that the claim of fluency in Frenchy on your resume was something of a whopper, and that you are too proud to admit it now. — Jay McInerney, *Bright Lights, Big City*, p. 20, 1984

whopper with cheese *noun*
a fat woman with thrush *UK*
Medical slang, punning on a well-advertised burger.
- — Adam T. Fox, St Mary's Hospital, London, 10th October 2002

whopping *adjective*
enormous, powerful *UK, 1706*
- I had supper down near the depot, buying a whopping big meal for Buck along with my own. — Jim Thompson, *Pop. 1280*, p. 36, 1964
- — Connie Eble (Editor), *UNC-CH Campus Slang*, p. 8, Spring 1987
- [P]aid a whopping £14.27 to a 10p stake. — John McCririck, *John McCririck's World of Betting*, p. 48, 1991
- Where you make a whopping twelve thousand dollars a year. — *Jackie Brown*, 1997

whop stick *noun*
a hammer *US*
- — Lewis Poteet, *Car & Motorcyle Slang*, p. 218, 1992

who pulled your chain?
who asked for your opinion?; what has upset you? *UK, 1937*
- Who pulled your chain? This may be your house, but I'm in charge here. I've got the gun. — Steve Brewer, *Lonely Street*, p. 232, 1994

who rattled your cage?
who asked for your opinion?; what has upset you? *UK, 1985*
- "Mike's a good egg. Alex is a good egg. Frankie is an awfully good egg. But who is the best egg?" "Who rattled your cage?" Alex said. "Don't ask," Mike said. — Guy Burt, *The Hole*, p. 56, 1993
- I shoved him back – only I wasn't playing. "Man, who rattled your cage?" he said. — Nancy Rue, *I Only Binge on Holy Hungers*, p. 15, 1998

whore *noun*
1 a girl *US*
Used with sarcasm in reference to a girl who is definitely neither a prostitute nor even apparently promiscuous.
- — Connie Eble (Editor), *UNC-CH Campus Slang*, p. 7, Fall 1981

2 in a deck of playing cards, a queen *US*
- If the player (with queens) wins the pot, they are "ladies"; but if he loses the pot, they are "whores." — Albert H. Morehead, *The Complete Guide to Winning Poker*, p. 264, 1967

3 used as a semi-affecionate term for a man *IRELAND*
- Brian was one of the best – the cute whore. — Desmond O'Neill, *Life Has No Price*, 1959
- "Get up you whore," he said. "Get up and find me Jock Weir, you lazy, sleeping cod of a man". — Troy Kennedy Martin, *Z Cars*, p. 22, 1962

whore *verb*
to work as a prostitute *UK, 1583*
- It took us some time to figure out why there were so many pretty young girls whoring in Baltimore. If they left home to sell it, why didn't they go to New York? — Jack Lait and Lee Mortimer, *Washington Confidential*, p. 274, 1951
- Dean said she'd apparently whored a few dollars together and gone back to Denver[.] — Jack Kerouac, *On the Road*, p. 5–6, 1957

whore-dog *noun*
a promiscuous woman *US*
• —Connie Eble (Editor), *UNC-CH Campus Slang*, p. 7, Fall 1980

whore-hopper *noun*
a frequent customer of prostitutes *US*
• —*Maledicta*, p. 10, Summer 1977: 'A word for it!'

whore house cut *noun*
cutting a deck of cards by removing a section from the middle of the deck and moving it to the top or bottom *US*
• —*American Speech*, p. 102, May 1951: 'The vocabulary of poker'

whore note *noun*
a two-dollar note *US, 1970*
• —Claudio R. Salvucci, *The Philadelphia Dialect Dictionary*, p. 65, 1996

whore of Babylon *noun*
an extremely promiscuous woman *US*
Originally a disparaging sobriquet for the Church of Rome, in allusion to the Book of Revelations, Chapter XVII, where she is one of several mysterious Christian allegorical figures of evil.
• Aunt Edie is so uptight she makes Marilyn Quayle look like the Whore of Babylon.—Armistead Maupin, *Maybe the Moon*, p. 149, 1992

whore's bath; whore splash *noun*
an impromptu and quick cleaning of the body at a sink, with special attention to cleaning the genitals *US*
• —Hyman E. Goldin et al., *Dictionary of American Underworld Lingo*, p. 237, 1950
• Always travel with a ruck, because when you hit a gas station you get a chance to take a whore's bath and change some of your clothes. —Larry Heinemann, *Paco's Story*, p. 162, 1986
• He ran cold water slowly into the basin until it was pretty clear. Then he plugged it and let it fill. He stripped down and gave himself a whore's bath, balancing on one foot with the other foot in the basin so he could work the washrag around his crotch.—Robert Campbell, *Alice in La-La Land*, p. 27, 1987
• "Dude's got more than whore splash comin," Joe growled.—Seth Morgan, *Homeboy*, p. 122, 1990
• "Do the best you can," the black guy said. "Take a whore bath. You know what that is?" "Before you ever heard of it," Harry said.—Elmore Leonard, *Riding the Rap*, p. 183, 1995
• Do you like to wash up first? Top and tails? A whore's bath?—*Austin Powers*, 1997

whore scars *noun*
puncture wounds and bruises from needle use *US*
• —Clarence Major, *Dictionary of Afro-American Slang*, p. 122, 1970

whore's egg *noun*
in lobstering, a sea urchin (*Strongylocentrotus drobachiensis*) *CANADA, 1829*
• —Kendall Merriam, *The Illustrated Dictionary of Lobstering*, p. 96, 1978
• —T.K. Pratt, *Dictionary of Prince Edward Island English*, p. 5, 166, 1988

whoreshop *noun*
a brothel *UK, 1938*
• I infested the outlying whoreshops and saloons.—Samuel Beckett, *Mercier and Camier*, p. 39, 1972

whore's melt *noun*
▷ see: HOOR'S MELT

whore-style *adverb*
said when a woman has sex with her underpants still around one leg *US*
• She took one leg outta her panties, whore style, and I dropped my pants to my knees and mounted her.—A.S. Jackson, *Gentleman Pimp*, p. 36, 1973

whoretel *noun*
a hotel or motel that caters for prostitutes *US*
• I got things worked out for you to get down in some of the top whoretels in Detroit.—A.S. Jackson, *Gentleman Pimp*, p. 84, 1973

whore wagon *noun*
a police van used for sweeps to arrest prostitutes *US*
• You ready to go work the whore wagon?—Joseph Wambaugh, *The New Centurions*, p. 78, 1970

Whorez *nickname*
Juarez, Mexico *US*
The phonics work and Juarez has something of a reputation for its prostitutes.
• —*Current Slang*, p. 26, Spring 1970

who-shot-John *noun*
a reproach or interrogation *US*
• Carol, Ah don want no 'who shot John' bout them bootiful clothes. —Iceberg Slim (Robert Beck), *Mama Black Widow*, p. 177, 1969

whosis *noun*
used in place of a person's name which the speaker cannot remember or doesn't think is important *US*
• Go out in the kitchen and tell whosis to give her dinner early. —J.D. Salinger, *Nine Stories*, p. 33, 1953

whosit; whoosit; whozit; whoozit *noun*
used to refer to a name (usually of a person, sometimes a thing) that is unknown, forgotten, to be avoided or hardly worth mentioning *UK, 1948*
• [I]n biblical Greek knowing was used for making love. Whosit knew so-and-so. Carnal knowledge.—Tom Stoppard, *The Real Thing*, 1982
• I'll never forget the time when Billy Whozit's father – oh, what was his name, Ella, that Billy What's-his-name?—Eric Kraft, *The Little Follies*, p. 12, 1983
• little brown-eyed Mrs. Whoozit (don't remember the name) who always came to the party—Katherine Anne Porter, *Letters of Katherine Anne Porter*, p. 6, 1991
• Pres made him up to lord high whoosit of the Canal Steering Committee[.]—John Le Carre, *The Tailor of Panama*, p. 224, 1996
• [H]ere came junior Ginsberg, his little whoozit flapping from side to side.—Greg Johnson, *Sticky Kisses*, p. 67, 2001

who smelt it dealt it
used for attributing the source of a fart *UK*
A childish rhyme, sometimes with formulaic responses.
• —Peter Furze, *Tailwinds*, p. 103, 1998
• DENISE: Oh Dave, have you farted? DAVE: What? No, that's one of your dad's. DAD: He who smelt it, dealt it. ANTONY: It smells like corned beef that.—Caroline Aherne and Craig Cash, *The Royle Family*, 1999
• She who smelt it dealt it [...] She who denied it supplied it [...] She who said the rhyme did the crime.—Phil Hammond, *The A-Z of Rude Health*, 18th January 2002
• He who smelt it dealt it.—*Loaded*, p. 36, June 2003

who's robbing this coach?
mind your own business *AUSTRALIA, 1945*
This comes from an old joke about Ned Kelly (a famous Australian bushranger) robbing a coach. He declares he's going to 'rob all the men and rape all the women'. A gentlemen attempts to intervene on behalf of the women, when one of the ladies pipes up and says 'Who's robbing this coach, you or Mr Kelly?'.

who's up who
who is in charge?; what's going on here? *AUSTRALIA, 1966*
Supplied to Baker in a notebook of World War 2 slang. Sometimes used literally as regards the interpersonal relationships of a group of people, but often metaphorically. Also elaborated to 'who's up who and who's paying the rent'.
• Nine to five as the lowest of the low stamp money and petty cash clerk, humble, lick-spittling, yes-sirring, but quick to learn the ins and outs of the who's up who in the rule ridden dung-heap of local government.—Frank Hardy, *The Outcasts of Foolgarah*, p. 5, 1971
• Try turning it on the other way, Mr. Meanswell, the public's pipe has a female thread, while the tanker hose is fitted with a male thread (that's so it's clear who's up who and who's paying the rent).—Frank Hardy, *The Outcasts of Foolgarah*, p. 147, 1971
• Drill yourself on Meaningless Drivel: who's up who at work, genetic differences – practise rolling the sides of your tongue inwards.—Kathy Lette, *Girls' Night Out*, p. 15, 1987

who's your daddy?; who's the daddy?
who is in charge (of this situation)? *US*
• —Don R. McCreary (Editor), *Dawg Speak*, 2001

who threw you nuts?
who excited your interest?; who asked for your opinion? *UK*
By implication the person addressed is being called a monkey.
• DAD: And he still wants to marry you? DENISE: He's not marrying me for what I'm like in the kitchen. ANTONY: It's what you're like in the bedroom. [...] DENISE: (TO ANTONY) Who threw you nuts?—Caroline Aherne and Craig Cash, *The Royle Family*, 1999

Whovian *noun*
a dedicated fan of BBC cult science fiction television programme *Dr Who* *UK*
• Most Whovians are aged over 40. Not to be confused with Trekkies, obsessive fans of Star Trek.—David Rowan, *A Glossary for the 90s*, p. 129, 1998

whuffo *noun*
▷ see: WUFFO

whup *verb*
to beat someone *US*
- I'm gonna whup his ass till it ropes like okra. — Chester Himes, *If He Hollers Let Him Go*, p. 12, 1945
- He got whupped by The Greatest. — Bill Cardoso, *The Maltese Sangweech*, p. 304, 1984
- She'll start shit like she's ready to whup some ass – without thinking about what might happen to you. — Chris Rock, *Rock This!*, p. 53, 1997

why-for *noun*
the reason or cause *US*
- The "how" I never learned. But the "why-for," to use the dialect of the section, became clear. — Jim Thompson, *Roughneck*, p. 98, 1954

Whykickamoocow *noun*
a notional remote town *NEW ZEALAND*
- — Louis S. Leland, *A Personal Kiwi-Yankee Dictionary*, p. 112, 1984

wibbly-wobbly *adjective*
very wobbly; unsteady *UK, 1984*
- I began to notice the transmutation of wibbly-wobbly dross into toughened gold. Well, it certianly looked more gilded after I hit the sun bed. — Liza Cody, *Queen of Mean [Tart Noir]*, p. 73, 2002

wick *noun*
1 the penis *AUSTRALIA*
- — Barry Humphries, *Bazza Pulls It Off!*, 1971

2 an irritating or bad-tempered person *UK: SCOTLAND*
- Leave yer wee brither [brother] alan, ya wee wick, ye. — Michael Munro, *The Patter, Another Blast*, p. 80, 1988

3 in bowls, a glancing blow which (generally more by luck than judgement) brings a bowl into contention *UK*
Not a very polite term.
- — David Bryant, *The Game of Bowls*, 1990

▸ **get on your wick**
to get on your nerves; to exasperate you *UK, 1945*
Based on rhyming slang for PRICK (the penis).
- CORP: You want to watch that temper of yours, mate. TICH: Ah – they get on my wick. These old fools. — Clive Exton, *No Fixed Abode [Six Granada Plays]*, p. 119, 1959
- It's a bit too friggin... Scousey in here. Gets on me wick. — Niall Griffiths, *Kelly + Victor*, p. 79, 2002

Wick *noun*
▷ see: HAMPTON WICK

wick!
used for registering firm approval *UK, 2001*
Abbreviated from WICKED! but extended to two syllables as spoken 'wee-ick!' by 10-year-old children in Cardiff, south Wales, 16th October 2001.

wick-dipper *noun*
a man objectified sexually *UK*
From WICK (the penis) and DIP YOUR WICK (to have sex).
- Mogadon Man [John Major] at Number 10 presiding over a bunch of indiscriminate wick-dippers — Andrew Nickolds, *Back to Basics*, p. 131, 1994

wicked *noun*
especially pure heroin *UK*
- — Robert Ashton, *This Is Heroin*, p. 210, 2002

wicked *adjective*
excellent *US*
- "Tell 'em to play 'Admiration'!" shouted Sloane... "Phoebe and I are going to shake a wicked calf." — F. Scott Fitzgerald, *This Side of Paradise*, 1920
- I figure, you see, buddy, to be sort of the gambling baron of this ward, deal a wicked game of blackjack. — Ken Kesey, *One Flew Over the Cuckoo's Nest*, p. 18, 1962
- — *San Francisco Examiner: People*, p. 8, 27th October 1963: 'What a "Z"! The astonishing private language of Bay Area teenagers'
- — J. R. Friss, *A Dictionary of Teenage Slang (Mt. Diablo High)*, 1964
- — Eugene Landy, *The Underground Dictionary*, p. 198, 1971
- He could, as I say, sidestep off either foot but what sped him on was a wicked acceleration over 20 yards. — *Western Mail*, 5th March 1977
- the pulsing bass line of a wicked dancehall re-mix — Donald Gorgon, *Cop Killer*, p. 35, 1994
- You gotta order the fish, chips and mushy peas in here, they are wicked. — Shaun Ryder, *Shaun Ryder... in His Own Words*, 1997
- A totally wicked contest, man, completely MEN-TAL[.] — Melanie McGrath, *Hard, Soft & Wet*, p. 52, 1998
- Is it, is it wicked? / I'm loving it, loving it, loving it. — DJ Pied Piper, *Do You Really Like It?*, 2001
- [W]e're supposed to think: "Oooh, isn't she so much cooler now that she wears puffa jackets and says 'wicked'[."] — *The face*, p. 164, June 2001

wicked *adverb*
extremely *US*
A rare instance of late C20 American slang that has stayed regional; a common term in New England ('wicked hot', 'wicked cold' etc.) rarely heard elsewhere.
- — Connie Eble (Editor), *UNC-CH Campus Slang*, p. 7, Spring 1984
- — *55-Plus*, p. 13, 12th February 1986: 'Today's guide to teen slang'
- — Judi Sanders, *Faced and Faded, Hanging to Hurl*, p. 43, 1993

wicked!
excellent!

wicked witch *noun*
a woman, especially a malicious or contemptible woman *UK*
Rhyming slang for BITCH.
- — Ray Puxley, *Fresh Rabbit*, 1998

wicker-head *noun*
a Vietnamese peasant *US*
From their straw hats.
- — Linda Reinberg, *In the Field*, p. 240, 1991

wick off *verb*
to exasperate or aggravate someone *UK*
A variation of GET ON YOUR WICK.
- That's friggin wick'd me off, that has. — Niall Griffiths, *Kelly + Victor*, p. 215, 2002

wicky *noun*
the buttocks *BAHAMAS*
- — John A. Holm, *Dictionary of Bahamian English*, p. 220, 1982

wid *preposition*
with *UK, 1869*
Colloquial pronunciation.
- "Listen Jackie," he said in mock patois with a smile, "any fool-fool come trouble you, tell dem they better not ramp wid yuh[."] — Donald Gorgon, *Cop Killer*, p. 79, 1994

widder; widda; widdy *noun*
a widow *UK, 1837*
- [H]im and that widder might crack a couple. — Barry Humphries, *Bazza Pulls It Off!*, 1971

widdle *verb*
to urinate *UK, 1961*

wide *noun*
▸ **give a wide**
to avoid something or someone *UK*
- And if it was left up to me I'd give these headbangers a wide, politely mind[.] — J.J. Connolly, *Layer Cake*, p. 90, 2000

wide *adjective*
1 immoral *UK, 1594*
- [A]t first it was dead boring, playing the half-wide mug [a fool or potential victim] on ten bob an hour[.] — Derek Raymond [Robin Cook], *The Crust on its Uppers*, p. 20, 1962

2 knowing, informed, aware *IRELAND*
- GATES: Only used with the word "Wide", as in "Gates Wide" – very knowledgeable. — *Great Tuam Annual*, p. 87, 1991
- Only for Roche Fives the street outside would be full with people running around screaming their heads off. Are you wide to that, are you? — Eamonn Sweeney, *Waiting for the Healer*, p. 62, 1997

wide boy *noun*
a man living by his wits, often a petty criminal *UK, 1937*
- [A]ll the mugs were at the war and all the wide boys were in the country.] — Charles Raven, *Underworld Nights*, p. 126, 1956

wide brown land *noun*
Australia *AUSTRALIA, 1908*
Made famous by the poem *My Country* by Dorothea Mackellar, 1914.
- Since when has the endangered flora and fauna of this wide brown land of the parched echidna ever shouted you the next beer. — P.J. Livingston, *Flacco's Burnt Offerings*, p. 35, 1995

wide girl *noun*
a woman living by her wits, often a petty criminal *UK*
- How was I to know wide girls like them would turn me into a ruddy dreamboat, all three of them? —Charles Raven, *Underworld Nights*, p. 119, 1956

wide load *noun*
someone with a broad backside *US*
From a common road sign indicating that ahead of the escorting vehicle is a truck with a wide load.
- —Connie Eble (Editor), *UNC-CH Campus Slang*, p. 9, Spring 1990

wide-on *noun*
a state of sexual excitement in a woman *AUSTRALIA*
A jocular riposte to **HARD-ON** (an erect penis).
- She shrugged. 'He gives me a wide-on,' she said. —Kathy Lette, *Girls' Night Out*, p. 96, 1987
- [S]he asked him to giver her half [of a Viagra tablet], giggling and wondering if she'd get a "wide-on". —Colin Butts, *Is Harry Still on the Boat?*, p. 7, 2003

wide open *adjective*
unrestrained by authority; unrestricted by the police; wild *US*
- Under the wide-open Kelly regime, police officers took up stations at each policy drawing-place to protect the money on hand for the payoffs. —Jack Lait and Lee Mortimer, *Chicago Confidential*, p. 37, 1950
- This most uncosmopolitan capital is overshadowed by that giant of metropolises, New York, only minutes away by air, and by Baltimore, with its wide open and blatant vice much nearer. —Jack Lait and Lee Mortimer, *Washington Confidential*, p. 2, 1951
- Lupita pays off to operate wide open, as if she was running a grocery store. —William Burroughs, *Junkie*, p. 101, 1953
- And, at this time, baseball betting books ran wide open in Oklahoma City. —Jim Thompson, *Roughneck*, p. 142, 1954
- You could party twenty-four hours a day – Olga Guilot, Benny Casino, la Playa, Cascarita – gambling, pussy, coke – wide open. —Edwin Torres, *Carlito's Way*, p. 35, 1975
- the El Dorado, the Purple Parrot, and several other places that were running wide open —Herbert Huncke, *Guilty of Everything*, p. 36, 1990

wide ride *noun*
a heavy woman *US*
- —Michael Dalton Johnson, *Talking Trash with Redd Foxx*, p. 69, 1994

widger *noun*
1 a small boy *UK, 1984*
Noted originally as a Royal Navy usage, probably from the late 1950s; an elaboration of 'wee' (small).

2 the penis, especially a relatively small penis *UK*
Probably direct from the sense as 'a small boy' on the model of **LITTLE MAN** (the penis).
- Little and Large prancin' around Sheffield with their widgers out – now that would be worth a tenner. — *The Full Monty*, 1997

widget *noun*
used generally for a small gadget; specifically a small device for making beer foam as the can is opened *US, 1931*
In the 1990s, UK brewers John Smith's advertisers sold canned beer with a 'widget' – an easier option than to explain the chemistry and technology that creates the beery froth.
- [H]e puts his fingers into his mouth and produces the two widgets he's hacked out of his Murphy's cans. I'm impressed. I've never seen a widget before. —Pete McCarthy, *McCarthy's Bar*, p. 65, 2000

widgie *noun*
a female teenage delinquent of the 'bodgie and widgie' subculture of the 1950s and 60s *AUSTRALIA, 1950*
Noted for their promiscuity, wild behaviour and revealing clothing. Perhaps a blend of **BODGIE** with 'wi-', the first syllable of 'women'.
- The Pushes used the wet sand-filled stocking as a sadistic outlet – the Widgies of today are victims of the sadistic, persecution of the Gentle Citizens. — *Figure and Vigour*, 1952
- So the Public learned of Bodgies and Widgies, some being so vague on the subject that they talked of "Wodgies". But they knew they were BAD. — *Figure and Vigour*, p. 4, 1952
- He who dresses well in this country is taken for a madman or called a 'bodgie' or 'widgie', what every city man and woman in Czechoslovakia for the past 20 years used to be[.] —Josef Holman, *As I See Them*, p. 53, 1954
- Perhaps you think all those stories about bodgies and widgies are just newspaper stunts. — *Weekend*, p. 16, 1st June 1957
- The performances of bodgies and widgies should make anyone look twice at these so innocent thirteen-year-olds. —James Holledge, *The Call-girl in Australia*, p. 133, 1964
- This joint is the meeting place of the bodgie-widgie mob. Here they all are – the anti-socials, the misfits, the delinks, in a common defiance of the squares. —Colin Johnson, *Wild Cat Falling*, p. 55, 1965
- WIDGIE – A young female hoodlum type, the companion of the BODGIE. —Harvey E. Ward, *Down Under Without Blunder*, p. 49, 1967
- Davo could never figure out whether they reminded him of something from outer space or his old man's wedding photos, when dad was a bodgie and the old girl a widgie. —Robert G. Barrett, *Davo's Little Something*, p. 18, 1992
- —David McGill, *David McGill's Complete Kiwi Slang Dictionary*, p. 123, 1998

wido; wide-oh *noun*
a villain, a petty criminal, a rogue *UK: SCOTLAND*
Probably a variation of **WIDE BOY** (a petty criminal).
- The only folk that drink in here are neds, chancers, hardmen an widos. —Michael Munro, *The Patter, Another Blast*, p. 80, 1988

widow *noun*
1 a single word, or two, set on a new line at the end of a paragraph, especially when set on a new page *UK, 1925*
- —F. Howard Collins, *Authors and Printers Dictionary*, 1973

2 in some poker games, an extra card dealt to the table for all players to use in their hands *US*
- —Albert H. Morehead, *The Complete Guide to Winning Poker*, p. 277, 1967

3 in electric line work, a cable grip *US*
- —A.B. Chance Co., *Lineman's Slang Dictionary*, p. 19, 1980

▸ **the widow**
Veuve Clicquot™ champagne; champagne *UK, 1781*
From French *veuve* (widow).
- Cyrus ought to be able to buy a bottle of the Widow to celebrate getting me off his back. —Sara Paretsky, *Tunnel Vision*, p. 366, 1994

widow Jones *noun*
a toilet *US*
- —Vincent J. Monteleone, *Criminal Slang*, p. 252, 1949

widow-maker *noun*
1 the M-16 rifle, introduced as the standard US Army infantry rifle in 1967 *US*
Early versions of the rifle were prone to jamming, thus 'making widows'.
- —Gregory Clark, *Words of the Vietnam War*, p. 296, 1990

2 in Vietnam, a Viet Cong booby trap *US*
- —Gregory Clark, *Words of the Vietnam War*, p. 65, 1990

3 in trucking, any long haul truck *US*
- —Montie Tak, *Truck Talk*, p. 188, 1971

widow's mite; widow's *noun*
a light, especially of the type required by a smoker *UK, 1931*
Rhyming slang.
- —Ray Puxley, *Cockney Rabbit*, 1992

widow's wink; widow's *noun*
a Chinese person *UK*
Rhyming slang for **CHINK** (a Chinese person).
- [Y]ou can't make up your mind whether you're a spotty [a non-White] or a widow's. —Ronnie Barker, *Fletcher's Book of Rhyming Slang*, p. 24, 1979

Widow Twankey; widow *noun*
1 a handkerchief *UK*
Rhyming slang for **HANKY**, formed on the pantomime 'dame' (Aladdin's mother).
- —Ray Puxley, *Cockney Rabbit*, 1992

2 an American *UK*
Rhyming slang for **YANKEE**.
- —Ray Puxley, *Cockney Rabbit*, 1992

wiener; weiner *noun*
the penis *US, 1960*
The phallic connotations of the food item lead to this usage.
- SHE SUPER SLIDES THAT MONSTER WEINER DOWN HER THROAT EVER SO SMOOTHLY[.] —Peter Sotos, *Index*, p. 37, 1996
- We're looking at a sizable wiener here. —Rita Ciresi, *Pink Slip*, p. 176, 1999

wiener roast *noun*
a picnic featuring hot dogs *US, 1920*
• We were out every night – dancing, movies, sleigh rides, hayrides, wiener roasts, bridge games, community sings. —Max Shulman, *The Many Loves of Dobie Gillis*, p. 2, 1951

wienie *noun*
in drag racing, a slick racing tyre *US*
• —John Lawlor, *How to Talk Car*, p. 116, 1965
▷ **see:** WEENIE, WEENY

wienie roaster *noun*
in drag racing, a jet-powered car *US*
• —John Edwards, *Auto Dictionary*, p. 188, 1993

wife *noun*
1 in a homosexual relationship, the more passive or 'feminine' partner *US, 1883*
• —Donald Webster Cory and John P. LeRoy, *The Homosexual and His Society*, p. 266, 1963: 'A lexicon of homosexual slang'
• Soon as I was put in with the population, I started looking for a wife. —Elmore Leonard, *Maximum Bob*, p. 50, 1991
▷ **see:** WEENIE, WEENY
2 in law enforcement, a work partner *US*
• The thing is a cop doesn't call his parnter his husband, so what you got is two wives. —Robert Campbell, *Juice*, p. 4, 1988

▸ **the wife**
your wife *US*
Folksy, potentially annoying, and almost inevitably patronising.
• "The other three percent are honest citizens, such as you and the wife, who're willing to avail yourselves of the program and its resources." The wife, Carmen thought. —Elmore Leonard, *Killshot*, p. 158, 1989

wife-beater *noun*
1 a sleeveless tee-shirt or undershirt *US*
• Preppy is in, grunge is out. Lyrcra is out, vinyl is in. Bowling shirts are in, wife beaters are out. —*The Boston Globe*, p. 35, 28th September 1994
• —Connie Eble (Editor), *UNC-CH Campus Slang*, p. 7, Fall 1996
• —Don R. McCreary (Editor), *Dawg Speak*, 2001
2 any alcoholic drink, especially beer *UK: WALES*
• two bulky gentlemen, half-cut on wife beater knocking the life out of each other —*Buzz*, p. 16, February 2004

wifed up *adjective*
of a male, in a serious relationship with a female who appears to dominate him *US*
• —Ben Applebaum and Derrick Pittman, *Turd Ferguson & The Sausage Party*, p. 74, 2004

wife duty *noun*
a promise or obligation to spend time with your wife or girlfriend *US*
• —Connie Eble (Editor), *UNC-CH Campus Slang*, p. 8, Spring 2000

wife-in-law *noun*
one prostitute in relation to another prostitute working for the same pimp *US*
• You can be sure when you see girls working so cooperatively that they are "wives-in-law," feeling bound to one another because they happen to be connected with the same pimp, sweet man to them. —John M. Murtagh and Sara Harris, *Cast the First Stone*, p. 10, 1957
• Keeping her wife-in-laws and my scratch straight up there in Toledo was the first acid test for Rachel was a bottom woman [lead prostitute]. —Iceberg Slim (Robert Beck), *Pimp*, p. 281–282, 1969
• Jessie had explained to her about the five hundred dollars getting stolen, and since the girls had been wife-in-laws, all of us figured that the money had been taken by both of them. —Donald Goines, *Whoreson*, p. 68, 1972
• Silky's other girls are my wives-in-law. They refer to me as "Mother." —Susan Hall, *Gentleman of Leisure*, p. 69, 1972
• I hipped her about her wife-in-law and I also told her where she was working. —A.S. Jackson, *Gentleman Pimp*, p. 167, 1973
• So I said what the hell, since this bitch ain't well / I'll get her a wife-in-law. —Dennis Wepman et al., *The Life*, p. 85, 1976

wife's best friend *noun*
the penis *AUSTRALIA, 1971*

wife starver *noun*
a man who defaults on maintenance payments *AUSTRALIA, 1950*
• [H]e was a thief, a wife starver, a cattle duffer, a pisspot, a liar and a cheat. —Frank Hardy, *Hardy's People*, p. 175, 1986

wifey; wifie *noun*
a wife *UK*
A slightly patronising term.
• I think he's going home to wifey. —Will Self, *The Sweet Smell of Psychosis*, p. 1, 1996
• [T]he young wifies have been kicking off[.] —Kevin Sampson, *Outlaws*, 2001

wifey *adjective*
used of a female, dowdy, mature and proper *US*
• —Don R. McCreary (Editor), *Dawg Speak*, 2001

wifie *noun*
an old woman *UK*
• The wifies are now bellowin along to "Wild Colonial Boy". —Niall Griffiths, *Kelly + Victor*, p. 80, 2002

wig *noun*
1 the head; the mind *US, 1944*
• Bernie, you got to learn that not everything can be reasoned out. I know you got a real great wig. —Ross Russell, *The Sound*, p. 102, 1961
• The word "wig" is street/drug parlance for "head." —Terry Southern, *Now Dig This*, p. 6, 1986
2 a judge; a barrister *UK*
• "He's got the Wig with him." He had, too. After passing a few nasty remarks about the bogies, the judge dismissed the case. —Charles Raven, *Underworld Nights*, p. 57, 1956

▸ **tighten your wig**
to use drugs and become intoxicated *US*
• To "tighten one's wig" is to get high. —Terry Southern, *Now Dig This*, p. 6, 1986

▸ **with a wig**
owing; to pay *AUSTRALIA*
A shameless pun on 'toupee' and 'to pay'.
• —Ned Wallish, *The Truth Dictionary of Racing Slang*, p. 89, 1989

wig; wig out *verb*
to lose control of your emotions; to become angry *US, 1955*
• —J. L. Simmons and Barry Winograd, *It's Happening*, p. 174, 1966: 'glossary'
• If the thing bites down much harder I might wig out and demand beer. —Hunter S. Thompson, *Songs of the Doomed*, p. 123, 18/19 February 1969
• Next thing I know, the kid wigs, he turns and he shoves me, boom, right in the chest. —Richard Price, *Clockers*, p. 366, 1992
• She wigged out on me. Has hardening of the arteries, Alzheimer's, I don't know. —Elmore Leonard, *Riding the Rap*, p. 21, 1995
• That ain't no reason to start wiggin' and spaz out[.] —Eminem (Marshall Mathers), *My Fault*, 1999
• [H]e might, under the influence of too much intoxicating art, be seriously wigging. —Christopher Brookmyre, *The Sacred Art of Stealing*, p. 272, 2002

wig-chop *noun*
a haircut *US*
Teen slang.
• —*American Weekly*, p. 2, 14th August 1955

wig city *noun*
a medical institution for the mentally ill *US*
Extended from the adjective sense.
• Wig city is exactly where an amnesia victim might show up. —Kinky Friedman, *Steppin' on a Rainbow*, p. 71, 2001

wig city *adjective*
mentally unbalanced, eccentric (usually when the latter is thought to be the former) *US*

wigged *adjective*
confused, disoriented, especially as a result of drug use; drug-intoxicated *US*
• "Said he painted it one time when he was wigged." "Wigged? Christ, it looks like he flipped." —Thurston Scott, *Cure it with Honey*, p. 57, 1951
• —*American Speech*, p. 88, May 1955: 'Narcotic argot along the Mexican border'

wigged out *adjective*
in an extreme state of drug intoxication, excitement or rage; disocciated from reality *US, 1968*
• —Paul Janssen, 1968
• The bug-eyes, the hair straight out of a 1970s sitcom, the laugh. What's this all about? The wigged-out mad grin, the Isn't-this-amazing? Isn't-this-hilarious? expression on his face[.] —Michael Ruhlman, *Walk on Water*, p. 19, 2003

wigger; wigga; whigger *noun*
a white youth who affects the speech patterns, fashion and other mannerisms of black youth *US, 1988*
An elision of 'white **NIGGER**'.
- — Connie Eble (Editor), *UNC-CH Campus Slang*, p. 6, Fall 1993
- — *Atlantic Monthly*, p. 120, February 1993
- Call me wigger, call me race-traitor [...] I'm just starting to explore the ways in which one can be white and not-quite-white[.] — Peter Sotos, *Index*, p. 5, 1996
- [T]hese cocky caucasians / Who think I'm some wigger who just tries to be black / 'Cuz I talk with an accent[.] — Eminem (Marshall Mathers), *The Way I Am*, 2000
- — Chris Lewis, *The Dictionary of Playground Slang*, p. 254, 2003
- — *Sunday Times (South Africa)*, 1st June 2003

wiggle *noun*
in electric line work, a secondary voltage tester with a glow-light indicator *US*
- — A.B. Chance Co., *Lineman's Slang Dictionary*, p. 19, 1980

▸ **get a wiggle on**
to hurry *US, 1896*

wiggle *verb*
to wriggle; to walk with a sinuous swaying of the hips *UK*
A colloquial variation; in conventional use from the C13 to C19.
- ignoring the girls he pays to wiggle in his lap — Jeffrey Eugenides, *Middlesex*, p. 479, 2002

wiggle room *noun*
scope for freedom of thought or action; room for political manoeuvring and compromise *US, 1941*
- The distance between London and Washington would give Bush just the wiggle room he needs for progress. — *The Guardian*, 26th September 2002
- — Susie Dent, *The Language Report*, p. 41, 2003

wigglers *noun*
the fingers *US*
- — Clarence Major, *Dictionary of Afro-American Slang*, p. 122, 1970

wiggly; wiggly-waggly *adjective*
of movement, wriggly; of form, irregularly undulated *UK, 1907*
- A faint suggestion of turned in toes. A kind of wiggly looseness below the knee prolonged to the end of each footfall. — Vladimir Nabokov, *Lolita*, p. 41, 1955
- [S]louched in the enfolding basket chair that hung from the ceiling, in one corner, his heel resting on the floor as he made the thing go wiggly-waggly, all the while teasing her with those gorgeous grinning eyes[.] — LaVyrle Spencer, *A Heart Speaks*, p. 9, 1983

wiggy *adjective*
crazy; outstanding; wild; creative *US*
- Like, if you wanted to get your band book together, he can write and arrange. Real wiggy! — Ross Russell, *The Sound*, p. 47, 1961
- "He could spin donuts on that hog with is feet on the pegs, and man, he was a wiggy cat," a member of the Angels recalled. — Hunter S. Thompson, *Hell's Angels*, p. 64, 1966
- — *Current Slang*, p. 17, Spring 1968
- To say that a person is "a wig" or "is wiggy," is to say that they are insane – even though it could be in an interesting or even desirable manner.. — Terry Southern, *Now Dig This*, p. 6, 1986

wigit *noun*
MDMA, the recreational drug best known as ecstasy *UK*
- — Mike Haskins, *Drugs*, p. 290, 2003

wig-out *noun*
a period of controlled craziness *UK*
- the anarchic wig-out of 'Run Christian Run' — *The Observer*, 7th October 2001

wig out *verb*
to become angry, to lose your temper *UK, 1955*
- If Ellen and Joseph try to boost Elizabeth by suggesting she might make it to finals at synchro nationals, she wigs out. "That's really hard!" — Linda Perlstein, *Not Much Just Chillin'*, p. 99, 2003

wig-out *adjective*
crazed *UK*
- It's about luxuriating in the wig-out keyboard solos, earthy basslines and trumpet riffs[.] — *The Guardian*, 30th July 2001

wig picker *noun*
a psychiatrist *US*
- — *American Speech*, p. 145–148, May 1961: 'The spoken language of medicine; argot, slang, cant'

wig-trig *noun*
an idea *US*
- And I didn't have enough wig-trigs to explain why you had to sound like Louis and Jimmy Noone. — Mezz Mezzrow, *Really the Blues*, p. 158, 1946

wigwag *noun*
in the television and film industries, a light outside a sound stage indicating that shooting is in process *US*
- — Ralph S. Singleton, *Filmaker's Dictionary*, p. 184, 1990

wigwam *noun*
in a deck of cards, an ace *US*
From the visual similarity between an 'A' and a wigwam.
- — George Percy, *The Language of Poker*, p. 97, 1988

wigwam for a goose's bridle *noun*
used as a nonsense answer to a question *AUSTRALIA, 1960*
- He asked Fantoni about the hole in the backyard. Fantoni said, it is a wig-wam for a goose's bridle. — Peter Carey, *The Fat Man in History*, p. 137, 1974

Wilbur Wright; wilbur *noun*
a flight (air travel) *UK*
Rhyming slang, formed from the elder of the US aviation pioneers, the Wright Brothers.
- What time's your Wilbur? — Ray Puxley, *Cockney Rabbit*, 1992

Wilcannia shower *noun*
a dust storm *AUSTRALIA, 1945*
Wilcannia is an inland town in New South Wales. Other locations similarly used by nature, weather and irony: Bedourie, Bogan, Bourke, Cobar, Darling and Wimmera.

wilco; willco
(I) *will co*mply!; generally, used as a signal of assent *UK, 1946*
Originally used as military communications, often to complement **ROGER** (message understood).
- "And, Bernie, see that he's on that plane." "Willco," Bernie said. — Ross Russell, *The Sound*, p. 94, 1961
- "Fine, you check the car. I'll go inside." Win snapped a salute. "Roger, Wilco." They split up. Win headed for the lot, Myron for the bar. — Harlan Coben, *Drop Shot*, p. 102, 1996

wild *adjective*
1 used of film in the television and film industries, shot without sound *US*
- — Ralph S. Singleton, *Filmaker's Dictionary*, p. 185, 1990

2 of prison sentences, served consecutively *US*
- "I guess you realize that if we want to, we can run your two sentences wild," he said. — Donald Goines, *Whoreson*, p. 272, 1972
- What's another bullet [one-year sentence], wild or bowlegged [concurrent]? — Seth Morgan, *Homeboy*, p. 141, 1990

▸ **go wild in the bush**
(used of a white person) to have sex with a black person *BAHAMAS*
- — John A. Holm, *Dictionary of Bahamian English*, p. 32, 1982

wild about *adjective*
enthusiastic about; having a strong liking for; sexually infatuated with *UK, 1868*
- Just wild about Tessa[.] Thousands of savers lost their hearts to tax exempt special savings – and will reap the rewards in March. — *The Guardian*, 28th February 2004

wild card *noun*
1 an unpredictable factor; an unknown *US*
From card playing jargon where it represents a card of no predetermined value.
- A Western diplomat in New Delhi called the thousands of Pakistani-trained militants operating in Indian Kashmir 'a major wild card that is outside the control of either nation'. — *The Washington Post*, 3rd January 2002

2 a dangerously unpredictable person *UK*
- Only a proper wild card would carry a gun around for no good reason other than the carrying of it. — Dave Courtney, *Dodgy Dave's Little Black Book*, p. 111, 2001

3 an enemy fighter plane *US*
- — *American Speech*, p. 125, Summer 1986: 'The language of naval fighter pilots'

wildcat *noun*

1 strong, illegally manufactured whisky *US*

- It is called corn liquor, white lightning, sugar whiskey, skully cracker, popskull, bush whiskey, stump, stumphole, 'splo, ruckus juice, radiator whiskey, rotgut, sugarhead, block and tackle, wildcat, panther's breath, tiger's sweat, Sweet spirits of cats a-fighting, alley bouybon, city gin, cool water, happy Sally, deep shaft, jump steady, old horsey, stingo, blue John, red eye, pine top, buckeye bark whiskey and see seven stars. — *Star Tribune (Minneapolis)*, p. 19F, 31st January 1999

2 methcathinone mixed with cocaine *US, 1998*

An elaboration of **CAT** (methcathinone).

- — Mike Haskins, *Drugs*, p. 293, 2003
- — Office of National Drug Control Policy, *Drug Facts*, February 2003

3 in oil drilling, a well drilled in unproven land *US*

- — Jerry Robertson, *Oil Slanguage*, p. 129, 1954

wildcat *adjective*

1 unauthorised, unlicensed, unsanctioned *US, 1870*

- I knew that he was now managing a wild cat taxi and rental car service. — Jim Thompson, *Roughneck*, p. 115, 1954

2 characterised by high risk and unsound business planning *US, 1877*

- I've worked deep mines, wildcat mines, the ones you go into a scratch for what's left, and I've stripped. — Elmore Leonard, *Riding the Rap37*, 1995

wildcatter *noun*

1 an independent, risk-taking oil driller who drills wildcat wells *US, 1883*

- "Deep Salt" Bookman was a rowdy old West Texas wildcatter who earned his nickname by drilling deeper and hitting more saltwater than just about anybody before he finally got lucky and hit oil. — Dan Jenkins, *Life Its Ownself*, p. 251, 1984

2 in trucking, an owner-operator who works independently *US*

- — Mary Elting, *Trucks at Work*, 1946

wild colonial boy *noun*

an uninhibited, free-living man *AUSTRALIA, 1881*

Originally meaning 'a bushranger'. From the title of a popular folk song and still often used allusively.

- Wasn't going to give up the bright life for no woman on earth. A wild colonial boy, no woman was going to tame him. — Arthur Upfield, *Bony and the Mouse*, p. 84, 1959
- 'And how did the Wild Colonial Boy sleep last night?' There was a touch of disapproval in her voice. — D.E. Charlwood, *All the Green Year*, p. 112, 1965
- — Michael Peters, *Pommie Bastard*, p. 16, 1969

wild duck *noun*

a person who has failed to pay a debt and is not seen as likely to do so *AUSTRALIA*

- — Ned Wallish, *The Truth Dictionary of Racing Slang*, p. 88, 1989

wild flower *noun*

a variety of MDMA, the recreational drug best known as ecstasy *UK*

- [W]ild-flower pills containing MDA only[.] — Gareth Thomas, *This Is Ecstasy*, p. 81, 2002

wild hair *noun*

an impulsive notion *US*

A shortened form of **WILD HAIR UP YOUR ASS** without the full connotation of annoyance.

- Something bothering you, Jimmy? You got a wild hair? — Robert Campbell, *Nibbled to Death by Ducks*, p. 68, 1989
- — Connie Eble (Editor), *UNC-CH Campus Slang*, p. 5, Fall 1990

wild hair up your ass; wild hair up your butt *noun*

the notional cause of irrational, obsessive behaviour *US*

- I was over there behind your friend with the wild hair up his ass. — Thomas Harris, *Red Dragon*, p. 184–185, 1981
- Jeez, don't get a wild hair up your butt. — Cherie Bennett, *See No Evil*, p. 147, 2002

wild horse *noun*

a Ford 'Mustang' car *UK*

Citizens' band radio slang.

- — Peter Chippindale, *The British CB Book*, p. 161, 1981

wilding *noun*

violent youth gang activity directed towards random victims *US*

A term popularised by the 'Central Park Jogger' case in 1989.

- The suspects, who were among some 20 youths questioned for hours before the charges were announced, used the term "wilding" to describe the rampage, Colangelo said. "It's not a term we in the police have heard before." — *United Press International*, 21st April 1989
- — *American Speech*, Summer 1990
- Tone Loc attracted the wrath of media elements hostile to rap when the innocent party sentiments of "Wild Thing" were confused with the term "wilding", at that time a buzzword for black criminality. — Alex Ogg, *The Hip Hop Years*, p. 125, 1999
- Each time a rudie was busted it triggered a mass stampede, very close to a full-scale wilding. — Mick Farren, *Give the Anarchist a Cigarette*, p. 349, 2001

wildo *noun*

a person behaving in a wild or crazy manner *UK*

- Git them soddin' wildos out of it. — Geoffrey Fletcher, *Down Among the Meths Men*, p. 50, 1966

wild-out *noun*

a gang fight *US*

- In statements detectives read in court, several victims said they heard their assailants yelling that it was a "wild-out," street slang for a brawl[.] — *Record (Bergen County, New Jersey)*, p. L1, 22nd December 1999

wild thing *noun*

▸ **do the wild thing**

to have sex *US*

- Man, you ain't gotta take that pussy. She'll do the wild thing for $5. — *New Jack City*, 1990
- — Connie Eble (Editor), *UNC-CH Campus Slang*, p. 9, November 1990
- The idea of camcorder as sex toy intrigued me so much that one night I decided to film myself doing the wild thing. — Anka Radakovich, *The Wild Girls Club*, p. 94, 1994
- We were doin' the wild thing all night. I'm exhausted. — *American Pie*, 1999
- I miss doing the wild thing with you[.] — Stephen Merritt, *Come Back from San Francisco*, 1999

wild up *verb*

to agitate someone; to make someone nervous *US*

- — Lise Winer, *Dictionary of the English/Creole of Trinidad & Tobago*, 2003

Wilfred *noun*

the penis *UK, 2001*

A variation of **WILLY** (the penis).

Wilhemina *noun*

a female customer, especially of discreet or illegal services *UK*

A feminisation of **BILLY BUNTER** (a customer).

- It's like my Billies – and, I should say, overwhelmingly my Wilheminas – come here from miles around. — Kevin Sampson, *Club-land*, p. 33, 2002

Wilkie Bard *noun*

a card; a business card; a playing card; a race card, etc *UK*

Rhyming slang, formed from a music hall comedian, 1874–1944.

- — Julian Franklyn, *A Dictionary of Rhyming Slang*, 1960
- — Ray Puxley, *Cockney Rabbit*, 1992

Wilkinson Sword *noun*

bald *UK*

Rhyming slang, formed from the name of a razor manufacturer.

- — Ray Puxley, *Fresh Rabbit*, 1998

willco

▷ see: **WILCO**

will do

used as an expression of assent to carry out an action *UK, 1955*

By ellipsis of the personal pronoun, possibly influenced by **WILCO**.

willer *noun*

▷ see: **WILL O' THE WISP**

willets *noun*

the female breasts *UK, 1998*

- — Paul Baker, *Polari*, p. 194, 2002

william *noun*

a piece of currency *US, 1983*

A pun on 'bill'.

- — Thomas L. Clark, *The Dictionary of Gambling and Gaming*, p. 250, 1987

William Hague *adjective*

vague *UK*

Rhyming slang, formed from the politician who led the Conservative party, 1997–2001.

- — Ray Puxley, *Fresh Rabbit*, 1998

William Pitt *noun*

excrement *UK*

Rhyming slang for **SHIT**, formed from the British Prime Minister known, historically, as 'Pitt the Elder', 1708–78, or his son, also Prime Minister, 'Pitt the Younger', 1759–1806.

- Don't take that out-of-date laxative, it'll give you the William Pitts. — Ray Puxley, *Fresh Rabbit*, 1998

William Powell *noun*

a towel *UK*

Rhyming slang, formed from the US film actor, 1874–1944.

- — Julian Franklyn, *A Dictionary of Rhyming Slang*, 1961

William Tell *verb*

to give off an unpleasant *smell* *UK*

Rhyming slang, formed from a legendary Swiss hero.

- It don't half William Tell in here, somebody open a window. — Ray Puxley, *Cockney Rabbit*, 1992

William the Third *noun*

a piece of excrement *AUSTRALIA, 1968*

Rhyming slang for 'turd'.

- Flaming dogs have left so many William the Thirds on the footpath it's a wonder more people don't slip and break their necks. — *The Adventures of Barry McKenzie*, 1972

willie *noun*

1 a piece of currency *US, 1983*

A pun on 'bill'.

- — Thomas L. Clark, *The Dictionary of Gambling and Gaming*, p. 250, 1987

2 a gambler's wallet or financial resources *AUSTRALIA*

- — Lawson Glossop, *Lucky Palmer*, 1949
- — Neil James, *The (Sydney) Bulletin*, 26th April 1975
- A person who is "a bit light in the Willie" is in desperate need of a winner. — Ned Wallish, *The Truth Dictionary of Racing Slang*, p. 88, 1989

Willie Peter; Wilie Peter grenade *noun*

an M-34 white phosphorous anti-personnel hand grenade *US*

Another use of the military phonetic alphabet.

- It was a ways off, so we fired a three-point five at him. A willy-peter round, and that's when it got all fucked up. — Philip Caputo, *A Rumor of War*, p. 151, 1977
- Kyle and Logan exchanged nodding glances, pulled the pins, and heaved their willie peters into opposite sections of the crowd. — John Skipp and Craig Spector, *The Scream*, p. 228, 1988
- — Gregory Clark, *Words of the Vietnam War*, p. 208, 1990

willies *noun*

a condition of fear or nervousness *US, 1896*

- Cemetery squad gives the guys the willies. — Mezz Mezzrow, *Really the Blues*, p. 316, 1946
- I started to get the willies. — Mickey Spillane, *One Lonely Night*, p. 36, 1951
- But it's the eyes that give me the willies. — Robert Campbell, *The Cat's Meow*, p. 85, 1988

Willie the Shit Burner *noun*

used as a generic term for the poor soul assigned to collect and burn solid human waste collected in latrines at US military bases in Vietnam *US*

- — Gregory Clark, *Words of the Vietnam War*, p. 463, 1990

willie weaver *noun*

a drunk driver *US*

- — *Complete CB Slang Dictionary*, p. 98, 1976
- — Peter Chippindale, *The British CB Book*, p. 160, 1981

willing *adjective*

gutsy; courageous; unwavering; aggressive *AUSTRALIA, 1899*

- Oh, it's swingin', swingin' Douglas with a strength you glory in, / Where willin' hands are honoured hands, an' shirkin' is the sin. — C.J. Dennis, *Jim of the Hills*, p. 14, 1919
- They're making that flak a bit willing! — W.R. Bennett, *Target Turin*, p. 15, 1962
- — W.R. Bennett, *Target Turin*, p. 109, 1962
- Another rash of ack-ack began erupting wickedly astern of the Mosquito's sharp pointed tail. 'They're making it pretty willing!' — W.R. Bennett, *Night Intruder*, p. 21, 1962
- 'Drink that down, feller, I'm buying.' 'Making the pace a bit willing, aren't you, Pete?' — W.R. Bennett, *Night Intruder*, p. 76, 1962
- It got pretty willing too[.] — Roy Slaven (John Doyle), *Five South Coast Seasons*, p. 59, 1992
- And I think the time has come for a bloke who doesn't shy away from a bit of the willing stuff to lead the country. — Roy Slaven (John Doyle), *Five South Coast Seasons*, p. 136, 1992
- — Robert G. Barrett, *Davo's Little Something*, p. 198, 1992
- Colin had always been a fairly good scrapper and very willing: much better than Davo. — Robert G. Barrett, *Davo's Little Something*, p. 256, 1992

will o' the wisp; willer *noun*

a potato crisp *UK*

Rhyming slang.

- — Ray Puxley, *Cockney Rabbit*, 1992

Will's Whiff *noun*

*syph*ilis *UK*

Rhyming slang, formed from a brand of small cigar.

- — Ray Puxley, *Cockney Rabbit*, 1992

willy *noun*

1 the penis *UK, 1905*

Originally northern English, not dialect, for 'a child's penis' or a childish name for any penis. Adopted by adults as a jocular reference, now widely used as a non-offensive and broadcastable term. The spelling 'willie' is also used.

- "ET hasn't got a willie," observes Linda[.] — *New Society*, 23rd December 1982
- I don't call it chilly / When I got a frozen willy / I call it de Ice Age[.] — Benjamin Zephaniah, *The Cold War*, p. 26, 1992
- Look, Orson, I'm not asking for a movie with a Swedish director and subtitles, but I'm as serious as a tumor on your willy. — Joseph Wambaugh, *Finnegan's Week*, p. 11, 1993
- [W]ondering if Enid Sheard had enjoyed her last willy and if she missed it and how that would explain quite a bit. — David Peace, *Nineteen Seventy-Four*, p. 64, 1999
- Ben [a dog] was trying to lick her face again [...] not after licking his willy[.] — John King, *White Trash*, p. 19, 2001

2 a tantrum *AUSTRALIA, 1941*

Generally in the phrases 'chuck' or 'throw a willy'.

- — Harvey E. Ward, *Down Under Without Blunder*, p. 48, 1967
- — Jim Ramsay, *Cop It Sweet!*, p. 96, 1977
- [They] will long remember the day mum 'blew her top', 'snapped her twig', 'popped her cork', 'hit the roof', 'did her block' and 'chucked a willy'. — Nancy Keesing, *Lily on the Dustbin*, p. 184, 1982

3 a supply of money for gambling *AUSTRALIA, 1949*

4 a wallet *AUSTRALIA, 1967*

- Upon hitting the bitumen he took stock of what he had left in his willy. — Ryan Aven-Bray, *Ridgey Didge Oz Jack Lang*, p. 15, 1983

willy-nilly *adverb*

here and there, haphazardly *US, 1934*

Not particularly related to the C17 sense of the phrase meaning 'willingly or unwillingly'.

- Constant exposure made him, willy-nilly, a first rate ball player. — Max Shulman, *Rally Round the Flag, Boys!*, p. 5, 1957
- Willy-nilly, in the course of the 12th century, these claims, backed up as they often were by dangerous revolts, had to be granted. — *The Digger Papers*, p. 20, August 1968
- She was picked up from the streets, wandering willy nilly with a child[.] — Odie Hawkins, *Black Casanova*, p. 153, 1984
- Joe bolted willynilly with the rest. — Seth Morgan, *Homeboy*, p. 179, 1990

willy warmer *noun*

the vagina *UK*

- Women's genitalia were represented as (potential) containers (e.g., bucket, box, hair goblet), places to put things in (e.g., furry letterbox, disk drive, socket, slot), containers for semen (e.g., gism pot, spunk bin, honey pot), and containers for the penis/sex (e.g., willy warmer, wank shaft, shagbox). — *Journal of Sex Research*, p. 146, 2001

willy-waving *noun*

macho behaviour that is especially unnecessary or foolish *UK, 1997*

Formed on **WILLY** (the penis).

- — Susie Dent, *The Language Report*, p. 15, 2003

willy-willy *noun*

a small, localised whirlwind *AUSTRALIA, 1894*

From the Australian Aboriginal language Yindjibarndi.

- WILLY-WILLY – Aboriginal name for whirlwind. — Gilbert H. Lawson, *A Dictionary of Australian Words and Terms*, 1924
- — Gavin Casey, *It's Harder for Girls*, p. 88, 1941
- 'It came very suddenly,' he complained, as though we had sent the fiendish willy-willy. — Kylie Tennant, *The Honey Flow*, p. 43, 1956
- A hot blast of air, a spiralling willy-willy, caught at the loose dust, hurling it like a naughty child at play. — Jean Brooks, *The Opal Witch*, p. 15, 1967
- — Patsy Adam-Smith, *Folklore of the Australian Railwaymen*, p. 25, 1969

Willy Wonka *noun*

a fool *UK*

Rhyming slang for **PLONKER** (a fool *and* the penis), that may be an elaborate play on **WILLY** (the penis).

- —Ray Puxley, *Fresh Rabbit*, 1998

willy woofter *noun*

a homosexual man *UK*

Elaboration of **WOOFTER** (a male homosexual).

- He needs all this willy woofter stuff slapping out of him[.]—Jenny Eclair, *Camberwell Beauty*, p. 193, 2000

Wilma *noun*

a Protestant female, especially one who is a supporter of Glasgow Rangers football club *UK: SCOTLAND*

A female form of William, and the female equivalent of **BILLY-BOY**.

- —Michael Munro, *The Complete Patter*, p. 168, 1996

wilma *adjective*

meek *UK*

A personification of uncertain pedigree, recorded as a contemporary gay usage.

- —*Attitude*, July 2003: 'New palare lexicon'

Wilson *noun*

in skateboarding, a fall producing serious injury *US*

- —*San Francisco Sunday Examiner & Chronicle*, p. 20, 2nd September 1984: 'Say it right'

Wilson Pickett *noun*

1 a white phosphorous flare or grenade *US*

From the initials WP; Pickett was a popular American rhythm and blues singer.

- —Gregory Clark, *Words of the Vietnam War*, p. 559, 1991
- He had a cache of gold-tipped high explosive and white phosphorous rounds – WIlson Picketts, they called them, because they made Sir Charles dance.—Stewart O'Nan, *The Names of the Dead*, p. 132, 1996
- —Randy R. Zahn, *Snake Pilot*, p. 265, 2003

2 a ticket *UK*

Rhyming slang, formed from the name of the US soul singer (b.1941).

- —Ray Puxley, *Cockney Rabbit*, 1992

Wimmera shower *noun*

a dust storm *AUSTRALIA, 1945*

Wimmera is an inland town in Victoria. Other locations similarly used by nature, weather and irony: Bedourie, Bogan, Bourke, Cobar, Darling and Wilcannia.

wimmin; wimmen *noun*

women *UK, 1910*

The first variation was adopted and promoted by politically aware feminists to avoid ending with 'men'; the second variation is a phonetic accident.

- I read meeja and wimmen pages for half an hour, then the sport[.] —John Milne, *Alive and Kicking*, p. 127, 1998
- [P]revious experience of tree worship in some kind of "wimmin's" group[.]—Iain Aitch, *A Fete Worse Than Death*, p. 212, 2003

wimmos *noun*

women *UK*

A variation of pronounced 'wimmin', used by cricketers.

- the wimmos from our wonderful New Labour government, sticking their pretty little noses into matters they know nothing about—*The Guardian*, 3rd February 2003

wimp *noun*

a weak and timid person *US, 1920*

A thorough treatment of the word may be found in 'Wimp', Reinhold Aman, *Maledicta*, Volume VIII, p. 43–56, 1984–1985. The word played a major role in the US presidential election of 1988, in which President George H.W. Bush had to overcome a widely held perception that he was 'a wimp'.

- —*American Speech*, p. 119, May 1964: 'Problems in the study of campus slang'
- —*American Speech*, p. 195, October 1965: 'Notes on campus vocabulary, 1964'
- —*Current Slang*, p. 8, Winter 1966
- —Collin Baker et al., *College Undergraduate Slang Study Conducted at Brown University*, p. 222, 1968
- Alright, you chickenshit wimps! You pansies!—Hunter S. Thompson, *Fear and Loathing in Las Vegas*, p. 17, 1971
- But if George Bush is a doomed wimp and Jack Kemp is a giddy windbag, Rev. Pat looks pretty good right now.—Hunter S. Thompson, *Generation of Swine*, p. 127, 9th June 1986
- All my life I've been a bit of a wimp, really[.]—Frank Skinner, *Frank Skinner*, p. 27, 2001

wimpish *adjective*

weak, ineffectual *US, 1925*

- You call that wimpish asshole and say good-bye.—John Irving, *The World According to Garp*, p. 359, 1978

wimp out *verb*

to give way to timidity or fear *US*

- She wondered if she had "wimped out" when she tried to convert Dohrn to her brand of radical feminism[.]—*Washington Post*, p. G1, 22nd November 1981
- I glanced at the bath towel. Was I going to wimp out and wear it? —Kitty Churchill, *Thinking of England*, p. 23, 1995
- Wimp out now and we're through.—Liza Cody, *Queen of Mean [Tart Noir]*, p. 82, 2002

wimpy *adjective*

feeble; afraid *US, 1967*

From **WIMP** (a weak and timid person). Although the adjective was not recorded until the late 1960s, the *Popeye the Sailor* radio programme gave the US J. Wellington Wimpy, known simply as Wimpy, in 1936.

- It was the kind of poor town where the blacks are cooler, and victimize the wimpy whites.—Jennifer Blowdryer, *White Trash Debutante*, p. 60, 1997
- Carol and I stayed inside, contemplating Security Man's strange anatomy. "Who'd be scared of that wimpy thing?"—Rita Ciresi, *Pink Slip*, p. 12, 1999
- I still would have felt better if I had gotten to that wimpy Jerry Rubin.—Ralph "Sonny" Barger, *Hell's Angel*, p. 122, 2000
- Lula talks tough, but the truth is we're both pretty wimpy when it comes to actual butt kicking.—Janet Evanovich, *Seven Up*, p. 6, 2001

win *verb*

▶ **are you winning?**

used as a rhetorical greeting *UK, 1984*

▶ **win hands down**

to win with great ease *UK, 1882*

From horse racing, when a jockey may relax the hold on the reins when victory seems certain.

- In the confrontation between fiction and reality, reality had once again won hands down.—*The Guardian*, 29th May 1999

▶ **would win doing hand-springs; would win with its head in its chest; would win shelling peas**

of a racehorse, certain to win *UK*

Also used as 'could win…'.

- I managed to pick out an 0891 number which promised a horse running the next day would win doing hand-springs, with it's head in its chest, shelling peas, etc.—Andrew Nickolds, *Back to Basics*, p. 146, 1994

▶ **you can't win**

used for expressing the futility of action, or the inevitability of failure *UK, 1926*

- Don't attack the BBC – you can't win.—*The Guardian*, 22nd July 2003

winch *verb*

1 to date a member of the opposite sex; to court; to go steady *UK: SCOTLAND*

Probably from 'wench' (a girl).

- Yer mammy an me used tae go for walks in Rouken Glen when we were winchin.—Michael Munro, *The Original Patter*, p. 77, 1985

2 to kiss and cuddle *UK: SCOTLAND, 1985*

Extends from the sense 'to date, to court'.

- I'm trying to winch a lassie in here!—Ian Pattison, *Rab C. Nesbitt*, 1988

winchell *noun*

a trusting, unsophisticated person *US*

- Of course, we'd relieve some winchell who could afford it of the necessary cash.—Guy Owen, *The Flim-Flam Man and the Apprentice Grifter*, p. 167, 1972

winco

a *wing* *co*mmander in the Royal Air Force *UK, 1941*

- He makes plans to see the Winco, Carslake[.]—Blake Morrison, *Things My Mother Never Told Me*, p. 187, 2003

wind *noun*

▶ **a wind so sharp it cuts the whiskers right off your face**

a cold, hard wind *CANADA, 1988*

- [On the South Shore of Nova Scotia, sometimes] the wind is so sharp it cuts the whiskers right off your face.—Harry Bruce, *Down Home*, p. 108, 1988

▸ get in the wind
to run quickly; to depart *US*
- I made up my mind when I crossed the street to get in the wind[.] — Henry Williamson, *Hustler!*, p. 132, 1965
- They each flashed a grin / then got in the wind / as fast as they could flee. — Lightnin' Rod, *Hustlers Convention*, p. 73, 1973

▸ get the wind
to smoke marijuana *UK, 1998*
- — Mike Haskins, *Drugs*, p. 290, 2003

▸ get the wind up; have the wind up
to be nervous or scared *UK, 1916*
- Yet the deepest doubts are coming not from the liberals who support this war, nor even from the liberals who don't. Rather, America's thinking right has the wind up. — *The Guardian*, 10th February 2003
- A sure sign that Blair has got the wind up is the appearance on TV of the Health Secretary Dr John Reid defending the Prime Minister's position. — *The Observer*, 14th March 2004

▸ in the wind
free from prison *US*
- — William K. Bentley and James M. Corbett, *Prison Slang*, p. 107, 1992

▸ put the wind up
to make someone afraid *UK, 1916*
- It is events like [anti-globalization protests in] Seattle that put the wind up governments[.] — *The Guardian*, 27th May 2000

▸ take someone's wind
to kill someone *US*
- — Paul Glover, *Words from the House of the Dead*, 1974

wind *verb*
▷ see: WINE

wind and kite *noun*
a website *UK*
Rhyming slang.
- — *www.LondonSlang.com*, June 2002

windbag *noun*
a habitually verbose talker *UK, 1827*
- From the Welsh Windbag [Neil Kinnock] to Bambi [Tony Blair]. — Robin Ramsay, *The Rise of New Labour*, chapter heading, 2003

windball *noun*
intestinal pain *US*
- — Lise Winer, *Dictionary of the English/Creole of Trinidad & Tobago*, 2003

winded *adjective*
hungover *US*
- [T]he cha ("very cool") words include: "winded" for hung over; "craftsman" for a complete idiot; and "ass" for awful. — *Washington Times*, p. C3, 26th August 1992

winder *noun*
a drug addict who regularly enters and leaves treatment programmes *US*
- — William D. Alsever, *Glossary for the Establishment and Other Uptight People*, p. 34, December 1970

windie *noun*
a wind surfer *NEW ZEALAND*
- — Harry Orsman and Des Hurley, *The Beaut Little Book of New Zealand Slang*, 1994

Windies *nickname*
the West Indies international cricket team *AUSTRALIA, 1964*
- After all, poor old Simmo copped his verbal serve from Smokin' Viv simply because he labelled the ageing Windies batting line-up as possibly fragile. — *News*, 1st May 1991

windjammer *noun*
1 a person who talks too much *US*
- — Vincent J. Monteleone, *Criminal Slang*, p. 252, 1949

2 a citizens' band radio user who monopolises conversation *US*
- — Wayne Floyd, *Jason's Authentic Dictionary of CB Slang*, p. 31, 1976

3 in drag racing and hot rodding, a supercharger *US*
- — Lyle K. Engel, *The Complete Book of Fuel and Gas Dragsters*, p. 154, 1968

4 a railway air brake *US*
- — Norman Carlisle, *The Modern Wonder Book of Trains and Railroading*, p. 269, 1946

5 a hammer *UK*
Rhyming slang.
- — Ray Puxley, *Cockney Rabbit*, 1992

windmill *noun*
in hot rodding and drag racing, a supercharger *US*
- — John Lawlor, *How to Talk Car*, p. 116, 1965

window *noun*
1 in card games, the card at the end of a player's hand *US*
- — Albert H. Morehead, *The Complete Guide to Winning Poker*, p. 277, 1967

2 in American casinos, the space through which the careful observer can see the blackjack dealer's down-card as he deals *US*
- — Steve Kuriscak, *Casino Talk*, p. 60, 1985

▸ out the window; out of the window
out of the question *US*
- — Tom Hibbert, *Rockspeak!*, p. 114, 1983

▸ pick a window – you're leaving!
used as a jocular threat of violence *UK*
- Pick a window because now you're leaving / Do you like hospital food – You will / Can your mother sew – Have her stitch' this. — Flotsam & Jetsam *Pick A Window*, 1995

▸ window's open
used for describing obvious and inept cheating *US*
- — John Scarne, *Scarne's Guide to Modern Poker*, p. 293, 1979

window dress *verb*
in poker, accidentally on purpose to let other players see the end card in your hand *US*
- — Albert H. Morehead, *The Complete Guide to Winning Poker*, p. 277, 1967

window hop *verb*
to move from window to window inside a house at night, waiting for a substance-addicted spouse to come home *US*
- I'd window hop all evening and when he finally did come home, I'd run up and jump in bed and pretend to be asleep. — Christopher Cavanaugh, *AA to Z*, p. 181, 1998

window-licker *noun*
a severely disabled person *UK*
Offensive. Derived, apparently, from the attitude of such a person when seen travelling on a bus.
- — Chris Lewis, *The Dictionary of Playground Slang*, p. 256, 2003

window music *noun*
on the railways, scenery *US*
- — Ramon Adams, *The Language of the Railroader*, p. 173, 1977

windowpane; window *noun*
a dose of LSD on a tiny, clear piece of gelatin *US, 1975*
- He sold mediocre grass for ten dollars a lid, coke for fifty a gram when you could get it and a hit of windowpane acid for two bucks. — John Sayles, *Union Dues*, p. 287, 1977
- — Richard A. Spears, *The Slang and Jargon of Drugs and Drink*, p. 551, 1986
- But old Owsley's preemo purple or even windowpane, that stuff could get you in touch with your ancestors. — Elmore Leonard, *Freaky Deaky*, p. 19, 1988
- Street names [...] tripper, trips, window and many other names. — James Kay and Julian Cohen, *The Parents' Complete Guide to Young People and Drugs*, p. 141, 1998
- Sometime acid is suspended in a solution that solidifies as a super-thin sheet of clear or translucent gelatin called "windowpane." — Cam Cloud, *The Little Book of Acid*, p. 38, 1999
- [A] tab of window pane acid apiece[.] — Stuart Browne, *Dangerous Parking*, p. 84, 2000

window party *noun*
an act of vengeful vandalism, in which the aggrieved party breaks all the glass in his victim's boat *CANADA, 1999*
- [A window party occurs] when someone angry and probably drunk breaks windows, electronic gear, etc., in someone's boat. — Lewis Poteet, *The South Shore Phrase Book*, p. 126, 1999

window rattler *noun*
someone who snores with great resonance *UK*
- RINGO (to John): Do I snore? JOHN (eating a banana): You're a window rattler, son. — *A Hard Day's Night*, 1964

window washer *noun*
a heavy rain storm *US*
- — Wayne Floyd, *Jason's Authentic Dictionary of CB Slang*, p. 31, 1976

Windoze *noun*
Microsoft Windows™ *US*
Not praise.
- — Andy Ihnatko, *Cyberspeak*, p. 211, 1997

wind pie *noun*
nothing to eat *FIJI*
- Look, don't put on a show for me. I don't mind eating wind pies and cassava balls. I just want company. — Jan Tent, 1994
- — Lise Winer, *Dictionary of the English/Creole of Trinidad & Tobago*, 2003

windshield time *noun*
time spent driving; paid travel time between a reporting location and the job site, or between job sites *US*
- Parking here and going in by train, I'll get an extra hour of reading time, which is a lot better than windshield time. — *Washington Post*, p. C1, 21st November 1978

wind, skin and ice *noun*
as specifications for a car, air conditioning, leather upholstery and *in*-car *e*ntertainment *UK*
Motor trade slang, reported by a car salesman, 4th August 2004.

Windsor ballet *nickname*
collectively, the strip and sex clubs in Windsor, Ontario, Canada *US*
- — Jim Crotty, *How to Talk American*, p. 77, 1997
- And er, yes, that's one of those places euphemistically referred to as "the Windsor Ballet," where even tutus are no-nos. — *Detroit Free Press*, 6th June 2002

Windsor Castle; windsor; brown windsor *noun*
the anus *UK*
Rhyming slang for **ARSEHOLE**, formed from a royal residence; shortened to 'windsor' and then punningly elaborated to 'brown windsor' as a type of soup.
- — Ray Puxley, *Cockney Rabbit*, 1992

windsucker *noun*
in horse racing, a horse that swallows air when running *US*
- — Dan Parker, *The ABC of Horse Racing*, p. 150, 1947
- — Nate Perlmutter, *How to Win Money at the Races*, p. 123, 1964

wind trap *noun*
strands of hair that a semi-bald man may cultivate and style to lay over his naked pate *UK*
Rhyming slang for **FLAP**.
- — Ray Puxley, *Cockney Rabbit*, 1992

wind tunnel *noun*
in homosexual usage, a loose anus and rectum *US*
- — *Male Swinger Number 3*, p. 45, 1981: 'The complete gay dictionary'

wind-up *noun*
1 a practical joke; a send-up *UK, 1984*
- I'm still convinced this is a wind-up. — Val McDermid, *Keeping on the Right Side of the Law*, p. 185, 1999
- Grandfather loved a wind-up. — Jimmy Stockin, *On The Cobbles*, p. 160, 2000

2 a person who teases *UK*
- — Dr. Feelgood, *She's a Wind Up*, 1977

wind up *verb*
1 to make fun of someone; to play a practical joke on someone *UK, 1979*
The image of the mainspring in a clockwork motor getting more and more tightly wound.
- — Angela Devlin, *Prison Patter*, p. 123, 1996
- Wolfie, seeing real wind-up possibilities here, asks them how many "drinks" they usually get. — Dave Courtney, *Raving Lunacy*, p. 30, 2000

2 to arrive; to arrive eventually; to settle in a final position *US, 1918*
- After graduating, [Ed] Catmull wound up at Lucasfilm during the first Star Wars trilogy[.] — *The Guardian*, 11th October 2003

windy *noun*
1 a windproof jacket and over-trousers *ANTARCTICA*
- — *Cool Antarctica*, 2003: 'Antarctic slang'

2 in pool, a shot that passes the object ball without touching it *US*
Based on the image of the cue ball breezing by the object ball.
- — Mike Shamos, *The Illustrated Encyclopedia of Billiards*, p. 263, 1993

Windy *noun*
▸ **the Windy**
Chicago, Illinois *US*
From the winds that sweep the city; a short form of **WINDY CITY**.
- His plan was to cop Mama and make it to the "Windy." — Iceberg Slim (Robert Beck), *Pimp*, p. 24, 1969

windy *adjective*
afraid; very nervous; ill at ease *UK, 1916*

Windy City *nickname*
1 Chicago, Illinois *US, 1876*
New York slang lexicographer Barry Popik has relentlessly worked to debunk the myth that the term was coined in conjunction with the 1893 World's Fair. Popik has traced the term to Cincinnati newspapers in 1876. Wide usage still.
- Chigago. The Windy City. The city of... wind. — Richard Thomas and Stewart Lee, *Jerrry Springer – The Opera*, 2003

2 Port Elizabeth *SOUTH AFRICA, 1989*
- WINDY CITY CLASH [...]The Boks meet the South Americans in Port Elizabeth at 3pm on Saturday[.] — *Sunday Times (South Africa)*, 22nd June 2003

3 Wellington, New Zealand *NEW ZEALAND*
- In addition, six of the team selected to face Matt Williams' tourists – including captain and ex-Borders star Semo Sititi – grew up in the 'Windy City'. — *Daily Mail (London)*, p. 89, 4th June 2004

wind your neck in!
be quiet! *UK, 1943*
- I'd got what they wanted, and just needed to be told to wind my neck in. — Andy McNab, *Immediate Action*, p. 108, 1995
- Wind your neck in will you. — *Coronation Street*, 18th February 2002

Windypeg *nickname*
Winnipeg, Manitoba *CANADA*
- — Bill Casselman, *Canadian Sayings*, p. 24, 2002

wine; wind *verb*
while dancing, to gyrate the pelvis in a sexual manner *TRINIDAD AND TOBAGO, 1916*
- — Lise Winer, *Dictionary of the English/Creole of Trinidad & Tobago*, 2003

wine and dine *verb*
to entertain someone with wine and food *UK, 1916*
Earlier as 'dine and wine'.
- He was bowed to, smiled at, coddled and flattered, wined and dined with the compliments of the management[.] — A Alvarez, *The Biggest Game in Town*, p. 85, 1983
- Sophie and Lisa, who naturally have been wined, dined, and seduced in both the bar down-stairs and the restaurant above. — Jane Green, *Jemima J*, p. 19, 1999

wine grape *noun*
a Roman Catholic *UK: SCOTLAND, 1985*
Glasgow rhyming slang for **PAPE**.
- It's the wine grapes that drink in there. — Michael Munro, *The Complete Patter*, 1996

wine head *noun*
a drunkard who favours wine *US*
- "No replies?" He groaned again. "Sure – wineheads!" — Hunter S. Thompson, *Songs of the Doomed*, p. 71, 1962
- My name ain't Sonny, and go fuck yourself, you wine-head bastard. — Nathan Heard, *Howard Street*, p. 61, 1968
- I don't know – guy brings wine heads out, plays music for them. — Elmore Leonard, *Mr. Majestyk*, p. 24, 1974

wine shed *noun*
a bar *US*
- He spends so much time in that wine shed, I thought maybe he was renting a stool. — Ken Weaver, *Texas Crude*, p. 58, 1984

winfly *noun*
a flight made during winter from New Zealand to Antarctica *ANTARCTICA, 1969*
- — Bernadette Hince, *The Antarctic Dictionary*, p. 384, 2000

wing *noun*
1 the arm *UK, 1823*
- "How's the wing?" Grave Digger asked. — Chester Himes, *The Real Cool Killers*, p. 56, 1959
- I've got a busted wing, sir. — Clancy Sigal, *Going Away*, p. 233, 1961
- I'd cut off my right wing and my swipe for you. — Iceberg Slim (Robert Beck), *Airtight Willie and Me*, p. 25, 1979

2 a winning streak in poker *US*
- — George Percy, *The Language of Poker*, p. 97, 1988

wing *verb*

1 to shoot at someone and wound them but not seriously *UK, 1802*

- Frenchy thought he winged one of them cats. He didn't. None of them four shots went nowheres[.] — Hal Ellson, *Duke*, p. 38, 1949

2 to discipline someone *UK*

- to be winged, disciplined, called to account — Angela Devlin, *Prison Patter*, p. 123, 1996

▸ **wing it**

to improvise; to do something with little preparation *US, 1970*
Originally from the theatre, indicating the necessity of learning a part at short notice, standing in the wings of a stage.

- Lawyers that do their homework. They can't wing it anymore. — Edwin Torres, *After Hours*, p. 214, 1979
- He doesn't wing it very often. — Elmore Leonard, *Split Images*, p. 104, 1981

wing and a prayer *noun*

a very narrow margin of automotive power or control; hence, a slender hope or chance *UK, 1943*
Originally applied to the minimum requirement for an aircraft's emergency landing.

- A woman once able to stand on her own / Searches for strength to stand on her own / On a wing and a prayer[.] — Jo Dee Messina, *On a Wing and a Prayer*, 1996

wingding; wing-ding *noun*

1 a party, a celebration *US, 1949*

- "She was at the wing-ding up the river tonight," Grave Digger said thickly. — Chester Himes, *A Rage in Harlem*, p. 189, 1957
- "Prove it, then, and come to Mrs. Madrigal's wingding." — Armistead Maupin, *Tales of the City*, p. 347, 1978
- But the afterparty's sure to be a wing-ding as it moves into your city. — Sheryl Crow, *There Goes the Neighbourhood*, 1998

2 a fit, especially one feigned by a drug addict; a person feigning such a fit *US, 1927*

- — Joseph E. Ragen and Charles Finston, *Inside the World's Toughest Prison*, p. 823, 1962: 'Penitentiary and underworld glossary'
- "If I had known you could throw wingdings like that I could have been using you all along as a sideline to faith healing," she said. — Chester Himes, *Come Back Charleston Blue*, p. 72, 1966
- That square chump is sure a whingding. — Iceberg Slim (Robert Beck), *Pimp*, p. 217, 1969

3 in motorcyle racing, a brief loss of control for which the rider compensates *US*

- — John Lawlor, *How to Talk Car*, p. 116, 1965

winge *verb*

▷ **see:** **WHINGE**

winging *adjective*

drunk or drug-intoxicated *US*

- — William D. Alsever, *Glossary for the Establishment and Other Uptight People*, p. 15, December 1970

wingnut *noun*

a person who is easily angered or flustered *US*
As a piece of hardware, a 'wingnut' is easily tightened – the basis for its application to a person.

- So, all things considered, this wingnut sitting across the desk today wasn't all that bad. — Seth Morgan, *Homeboy*, p. 193, 1990

wings *noun*

1 any powdered drug, especially cocaine, heroin or morphine *US, 1953*
Because wings give you the lift that gets you **HIGH**.

- — Joseph E. Ragen and Charles Finston, *Inside the World's Toughest Prison*, p. 823, 1962: 'Penitentiary and underworld glossary'
- — Richard A. Spears, *The Slang and Jargon of Drugs and Drink*, p. 553, 1986
- — Mike Haskins, *Drugs*, p. 281, 2003

2 insignia worn by motorcyle gang members signifying sexual conquests *US*

- True magazine [...] also explained the varicolored pilots' wings: red wings indicating that the wearer has committed cunnilingus on a menstruating woman, black wings for the same act on a Negress, and brown wings for buggery. — Hunter S. Thompson, *Hell's Angels*, p. 117, 1966

▸ **get your wings**

to use heroin for the first time *US*
A nod to aviation terminology.

- — Geoffrey Froner, *Digging for Diamonds*, p. 66, 1989

wing-wang *noun*

the rectum *US*

- "I hope you die with a hard-on." "Yeah, well if I do, it'll be up your girl's wing-wang at the time." — Darryl Ponicsan, *The Last Detail*, p. 168, 1970

wing wipe *noun*

a crew member of a military jet aircraft *US*
A term used by the infantry.

- — Gregory Clark, *Words of the Vietnam War*, p. 182, 1990

wingy *noun*

a person with one arm *US*

- — Joe McKennon, *Circus Lingo*, p. 105, 1980

wingy *adjective*

very loose-fitting, giving the appearance of extreme thinness *TRINIDAD AND TOBAGO*

- — Lise Winer, *Dictionary of the English/Creole of Trinidad & Tobago*, 2003

wink *noun*

the penis *UK*

- — *Journal of Sex Research*, p. 146, 2001

winker *noun*

the vagina *UK*
The imagery of an eye that opens and closes.

- — Paul Bailey, *Trespasses*, p. 46, 1970

winkie *noun*

1 the vagina *UK*

- — *Journal of Sex Research*, p. 146, 2001

2 a sideways punctuation face indicating laughter, generally formed as ;-) *US*

- — Christian Crumlish, *The Internet Dictionary*, p. 3, 1995

winking *noun*

▸ **like winking; like eyes-a-winking**

very quickly *UK, 1827*

- You're making it lemon squeezy [easy] for them [an opposing football team], they're cutting through us like eyes a winking. — Ray Puxley, *Fresh Rabbit*, 1998

winkle *noun*

a boy's penis; a small penis *US, 1966*

- Came home to find another gentleman's kippers in the grill / So he sanded off his winkle with a Black and Decker drill[.] — Ian Dury, *This is What We Find*, 1979
- finding his winkle's shrivelled up from fear — John King, *Human Punk*, p. 63, 2000
- — Paul Baker, *Polari*, p. 195, 2002

▸ **have on the winkle**

to be obsessed by something *UK*

- Look Dad, for some reason you've got death on the winkle. — Kingsley Amis, *The Green Man*, 1969

winkle-trip *noun*

a male striptease act performed for an all-female audience on a Thames pleasure boat *UK*

- [T]he boys [strippers] on the trip call it a 'winkle trip' or 'ladies' dingdong night'. — *New Society*, 24th January 1980

winky; winkie *noun*

the penis; a small penis; a boy's penis *UK, 1984*
Usually juvenile, occasionally derisory; probably a variation of **WINKLE**.

- How could you ever look a girl in the eye after you've had your winkie up her? — C.D. Payne, *Youth in Revolt*, p. 3, 1993
- "Well fuck you, asshole! I hope your goddam winky drops off!" "Winky?" — Stuart Browne, *Dangerous Parking*, p. 148, 2000
- Most men can remember the simple pleasures their winkies gave them as boys. — Richard Herring, *Talking Cock*, p. 80, 2003

winner *noun*

a loser socially *US*
Sardonic, cruel.

- — J. R. Friss, *A Dictionary of Teenage Slang (Mt. Diablo High)*, 1964

winners *noun*

dice that have been altered so as to roll numbers other than seven, useful to the shooter in craps *US*

- — *The Annals of the American Academy of Political and Social Sciences*, p. 132, May 1950

winners and losers *noun*
trousers *UK: SCOTLAND*
Glasgow rhyming slang on 'troosers'.
• —Michael Munro, *The Original Patter*, 1985

winny-popper *noun*
the penis *CANADA*
A schoolchildren's term.
• —D.J. Barr, 1968

wino *noun*
1 a lowly drunk *US, 1913*
• [S]he finally got to wild Third Street among the lines of slugging winos and the bloody drunken Indians[.]—Jack Kerouac, *The Subterraneans*, p. 34, 1958
• A wino, sleeping on the floor, stirred and woke from the drunken stupor he'd been in[.]—Nathan Heard, *Howard Street*, p. 61, 1968
• He spent hours upon hours in the old public library at Bayfront Park, amid the snoring winos and bag ladies[.]—Carl Hiaasen, *Tourist Season*, p. 57, 1986
2 a wine connoisseur *NEW ZEALAND, 1997*
• —Harry Orsman, *A Dictionary of Modern New Zealand Slang*, p. 149, 1999

win or lose *noun*
any and all alcoholic drinks *UK*
Rhyming slang for **BOOZE**.
• —Ray Puxley, *Cockney Rabbit*, 1992

wino time *noun*
a short jail sentence *US*
• —William K. Bentley and James M. Corbett, *Prison Slang*, p. 24, 1992

winter *noun*
any period between carnival seasons, regardless of the actual time of year *US*
• —*American Speech*, p. 282, December 1966: 'More carnie talk from the West Coast'

winter blossoms *noun*
the older, female, winter residents of a hotel *UK*
• The few old ladies, who still live in hotels – the "Winterblossoms" as they are sometimes called – begin their journey to [...] cheaper hotels.—*New Society*, 21st April 1977

winterer; winteroverer *noun*
a person who spends the winter in Antarctica *ANTARCTICA, 1958*
• —Bernadette Hince, *The Antarctic Dictionary*, p. 385, 2000

Winterpeg *nickname*
Winnipeg, Manitoba *CANADA*
• —Bill Casselman, *Canadian Sayings*, p. 24, 2002

winter wear *noun*
the foreskin on an uncircumsised penis *US*
• —Connie Eble (Editor), *UNC-CH Campus Slang*, p. 5, November 1983

win-win *adjective*
said of a situation in which the parties involved all feel that they have done well *US*
• In recent years, managers have taken over from game theory the notion that decision-making events can be one of two types: the win-lose situation (or zero-sum game) or the win-win situation.—*Harvard Business Review*, p. 67, May/June 1977
• Recently the terms "win, win" and "win, win, win" have evolved as a favorite among bureaucrats and politicians to describe a situation where no one can lose.—*Orlando Sentinel Tribune*, p. 1, 15th May 1990
• Ninety-nine times in the past four years, someone has called something a "win-win situation" on the pages of the St. Petersburg Times.—*St. Petersburg Times*, p. 5D, 18th August 1991

wipe *noun*
a handkerchief *US*
• —Don Wilmeth, *The Language of American Popular Entertainment*, p. 294, 1981

wipe *verb*
1 to dismiss or reject a person; to wash your hands of someone *AUSTRALIA, 1941*
• —Eric Lambert, *The Veterans*, p. 81, 1954
• If he reports sick, wipe him.—Eric Lambert, *The Veterans*, p. 206, 1954
• 'Wot's wrong with 'im?' Joe wanted to know. 'He got wiped last night. Wiped like a dirty rag.'—Nino Culotta (John O'Grady), *They're A Weird Mob*, p. 173, 1957
• —Jim Ramsay, *Cop It Sweet!*, p. 96, 1977
2 in drag racing, to defeat another car *US*
Created by back-formation; when a car is defeated, the name of the driver is wiped from the list of those competing, so the driver is 'wiped'.

▸ **wipe the clock**
to set a train's air brake valve at the position used for full emergency application *US*
An allusion to the sudden drop of the pressure needle on the air gauge to zero.
• —J. Herbert Lund, *Herb's Hot Box of Railraod Slang*, p. 130, 1975

▸ **wipe the floor with; wipe up the floor with; wipe the earth with; wipe the ground with**
to inflict an absolute defeat on someone; to surpass someone *UK, 1896*
• "He used to wipe the floor with me then," [Terry] Eagleton says, "but now I think I've got him."—*The Guardian*, 2nd February 2002

wiped *adjective*
1 infatuated *UK*
• He bought her a big rock last week. My man is wiped.—*Live*, p. 39, Winter 2004
2 drunk *US*
• —*Current Slang*, p. 15, Summer 1968
3 exhausted *US*
• —Connie Eble (Editor), *UNC-CH Campus Slang*, p. 7, Fall 1996

wiped out *adjective*
very drug-intoxicated *US*
• —Anthony Scaduto, *Mick Jagger*, 1974

wipe-off *noun*
1 a cursory washing of the body using little water *US, 1953*
• —Frederic G. Cassidy, *Dictionary of American Regional English*, p. 241, 1985
2 a total wreck; a write-off *AUSTRALIA, 1945*
• It could've been a complete wipe-off.—W.R. Bennett, *Night Intruder*, p. 14, 1962

wipe off *verb*
to wreck or ruin something *AUSTRALIA*
• I just don't like the idea of being wiped off, that's all.—W.R. Bennett, *Night Intruder*, p. 18, 1962

wipe-out *noun*
a fall from a surfboard, usually caused by a wave *AUSTRALIA, 1962*
A major word of the surfer's lexicon; it was the title and one word of the 1963 'surf instrumental' by the Surfaris that featured a drum solo practiced on the school desk of many an early 1960s schoolboy.
• —The Surfaris, *Wipe Out*, 1963
• —Grant W. Kuhns, *On Surfing*, p. 123, 1963
• —*Paradise of the Pacific*, p. 27, October 1963

wipe out *verb*
1 to destroy something; to kill or wound someone *US, 1968*
• [T]here was a certain undeniable decadence in the way we sat there, drinks in hand, watching the kids in the street getting wiped out.—Terry Southern, *Now Dig This*, p. 128, November 1968
• Police cars caught alone were wiped out with rocks.—Jerry Rubin, *Do It!*, p. 171, 1970
• And if there is a, thingy, war [...] might as well get wiped out with a few sounds in your head[.]—Mike Stott, *Soldiers Talking, Cleanly*, 1978
2 to remove someone from their position *UK*
• Then came Odd Job, Gypsy John, Levi; every goddam one of them I wiped out, just wiped out.—Jamie Mandelkau quoting Ken Kesey, *Buttons*, p. 120, 1969

wire *noun*
1 a telegraph message; a telegram *UK, 1876*
• Shot a wire on this to Baltimore.—Marvin Wald and Albert Maltz, *The Naked City*, 1947
2 a report; information *UK, 1925*
A vestigial term from the era of telegraphy.
• I've heard that wire a thousand times. Remember who you're talkin to, man.—Clarence Cooper Jr, *The Scene*, p. 14, 1960
• They had their wire on me from uptown, all right.—Malcolm X and Alex Haley, *The Autobiography of Malcolm X*, p. 105, 1964
• After I had put in six months on my bit, a young Negro con came in on transfer from the big joint and brought me a wire from "Party."—Iceberg Slim (Robert Beck), *Pimp*, p. 53, 1969

- Marie got the wire about my new girl before I had a chance to hip her. —A.S. Jackson, *Gentleman Pimp*, p. 81, 1973
- I got the wire about you ridin' around with Ronald yesterday, man, so don't play games with me. —Donald Goines, *Daddy Cool*, p. 57, 1974
- "If my connect gets the wire I gave his name to somebody," he said, "splittin ain't goin to help me none." —Charles W. Moore, *A Brick for Mister Jones*, p. 34, 1975
- But I got a wire he got caught in a fire / And that his ashes were hot and fiery. —Dennis Wepman et al., *The Life*, p. 70, 1976
- Is he retiring like the wire says? —Robert Deane Pharr, *Giveadamn Brown*, p. 125, 1978

3 news transmitted privately *TRINIDAD AND TOBAGO, 1938*

- —Lise Winer, *Dictionary of the English/Creole of Trinidad & Tobago*, 2003

4 a bookmaking operation *US*

- They told me, yeah, there was a wire going, but it was strictly amateur. —James Ellroy, *Brown's Requiem*, p. 110, 1981

5 a small microphone and transmitting device worn on the person as part of law enforcement interception of oral communications *US*

- Phillips walked in, wearing wire, and said, "How're you doing, Louis?" —Leonard Shecter and William Phillips, *On the Pad*, p. 223, 1973
- NICHOLSON: This rabbit'll do anything not to do time, including wearing a wire. —*True Romance*, 1993

6 the penis *IRELAND*

- Wha' abou' me, Billy? said Nappies. -Didn't I have a terrific game as well. -Yeah, said Kenny. -Pullin' your wire. —Roddy Doyle, *The Van*, p. 24, 1991

7 the buttocks *TRINIDAD AND TOBAGO, 1968*

- —Lise Winer, *Dictionary of the English/Creole of Trinidad & Tobago*, 2003

8 in a pickpocketing team, the thief who actually picks the victim's pocket *UK, 1851*

- —*The New American Mercury*, p. 707, 1950
- The beholder would be the second member of the troupe, sometimes called the "wire," the man who made the actual contact. —Dev Collans with Stewart Sterling, *I was a House Detective*, p. 48, 1954

9 in horse racing, the finish line *US*

- —Les Conklin, *Payday at the Races*, p. 207, 1974

10 amphetamines *UK*

- —Mike Haskins, *Drugs*, p. 280, 2003

11 in pool, the score string *US*

- —Mike Shamos, *The Illustrated Encyclopedia of Billiards*, p. 264, 1993

▸ **on the wire**

in pool, having scored or having been awarded a score as part of the handicapping of a game *US*

- —Mike Shamos, *The Illustrated Encyclopedia of Billiards*, p. 161, 1993

wire *verb*

1 to send a telegraph message *UK, 1859*

- He's in New York hustling for the month and wiring money back to his wife and two kids in Las Vegas. —*The Observer*, 10th March 2002

2 to use a small microphone or transmitting device to intercept oral communications *US*

- I thought, shit, he's wired, my life is gone, ended, obliterated by this one individual. —Leonard Shecter and William Phillips, *On the Pad*, p. 44, 1973
- [W]ondering where the Ching was calling from. Bar on Catherine Street in South Philly? He hoped to Christ not. That social club on Hutchinson? Either place could be wired. —Elmore Leonard, *Glitz*, p. 138, 1985

3 in skateboarding, to analyse and plan a difficult manoeuvre or trick *US*

- —Laura Torbet, *The Complete Book of Skateboarding*, p. 109, 1976

wired *adjective*

1 intoxicated on amphetamines or cocaine *US*

Also used with 'up'.

- Magoo is a pill freak, and when he gets wired up he does a lot of talking. —Hunter S. Thompson, *Hell's Angels*, p. 184, 1966
- —*Current Slang*, p. 13, Winter 1970
- [B]ut if what you really crave is the good clean thrills and light and completely dedicated positive – if perhaps, ah um, yas, possibly just a leetle bit wired (speed? horrors!) – then climb in, hang on[.] —*The Last Supplement to the Whole Earth Catalog*, p. 84, March 1971
- I had plenty of money, got wired up on beer and bennies [Benzedrine] and showed up at a friend's party[.] —Lester Bangs, *Psychotic Reactions and Carburetor Dung*, p. 291, 1979
- A wired-up pillhead, he said to himself. —Gerald Petievich, *Shakedown*, p. 38, 1988
- One evening Hubert Frame, wired up on a couple lines of pharmaceutical quality cocaine, found himself dodging Yusef's bass bow. —Odie Hawkins, *Black Chicago*, p. 75, 1992
- Large doses of coke made the first day merry. Of course at night I was too wired to sleep. —Cleo Odzer, *Goa Freaks*, p. 81, 1995
- If Neil did his share of coke, he was dismayed by the fact that everyone on the tour seemed permanently wired. —Barney Hoskyns, *Waiting for the Sun*, p. 199, 1996
- We'll take a thousand bucks out of the shoe bag, cab it over to Philip's house, pick up an ounce of blow, call Natalie, tell her and Jessica to come over here, we'll get them wired, I'll fuck Natalie – you do your best to fuck Jessica. —Kenneth Lonergan, *This is Our Youth*, p. 34, 2000
- Everyone is either stoned, wired or suicidally depressed. —*Uncut*, May 2001

2 tense, anxious *UK*

- —*Sunday Telegraph*, 11th March 1979

3 well-rehearsed *US*

- To get a trick wired means to practice it until it becomes second nature or instinctual. —Jim Humes and Sean Wagstaff, *Boarderlands*, p. 225, 1995

4 used of a pair in stud poker, dealt in the first two cards of a hand *US*

- —Jim Glenn, *Programmed Poker*, p. 158, 1981

wired to the moon *adjective*

extremely drug-intoxicated *UK*

An elaboration of **WIRED** (drug-intoxicated).

- If they were shot in the body they could be so wired to the moon that they would still come forward, or start to kill hostages. —Andy McNab, *Immediate Action*, p. 235, 1995
- I came up in three minutes and was sat under the table shouting: "I'm wired to the moon!" —*Mixmag*, p. 88, February 2002

wired up *adjective*

1 intoxicated on central nervous system depressants *US*

- I had plenty of money, got wired up on beer and bennies [Benzedrine] and showed up at a friend's party[.] —Lester Bangs, *Psychotic Reactions and Carburetor Dung*, p. 291, 1979

2 available for homosexual relations *US*

- —Arthur V. Huffman, *New York Mattachine Newsletter*, p. 6, June 1961: 'Sex deviation in a prison community'

wire-fu *noun*

a technique that employs wires and pulleys to create choreographed martial art fights *US, 1997*

Formed on 'kung fu'.

wirehead *noun*

a computer hardware specialist *US*

- —Eric S. Raymond, *The New Hacker's Dictionary*, p. 383, 1991
- The sensible, mature wireheads we are. —Melanie McGrath, *Hard, Soft & Wet*, p. 111, 1998

wire room *noun*

an illegal betting establishment's telephone office *US*

- Another major wire-room, operating at this writing, is at 10 North Clark Street, a block from City Hall. —Jack Lait and Lee Mortimer, *Chicago Confidential*, p. 129, 1950

wires *noun*

any central nervous system stimulant *US*

- —Bill Davis, *Jawjacking*, p. 109, 1977

▸ **have your wires crossed; get your wires crossed**

to be at cross purposes; to be affected by a mutual misunderstanding *UK*

- In supposedly moving to redress the balance of the new world, George Bush, like George Canning with his wires crossed, inadvertently challenges the old world to rise again. —*The Guardian*, 19th June 2001

wire store *noun*

a big con based on a supposedly corrupt telegraph official who claims he can delay the reporting of race results to the benefit of the victim *US*

- He taught me long con and how to rope suckers for a wire store he set up in Denver, Colorado. —Iceberg Slim (Robert Beck), *Trick Baby*, p. 112, 1969

wire to wire *noun*

in horse racing, the entire distance of the race, from start to finish *US*

- —David W. Maurer, *Argot of the Racetrack*, p. 69, 1951

wise *verb*

to inform or educate someone; to explain something *US, 1905*

- He wised me to a hip hotel in lower Manhattan. — A.S. Jackson, *Gentleman Pimp*, p. 114, 1973

▸ **wise up; wise up to**

to learn, realise or understand something *US, 1919*

- You've got a little way to hike alone [...] and you're not wised up in everything. — Frederick Niven, *Wild Honey*, 1972
- Tricky has certainly wised up. Positivity has replaced hate as his primary concern[.] — *The Guardian*, p. 15, 29th June 2001

wise *adjective*

▸ **be wise; be wise to; get wise; get wise to**

to be aware of something; to be warned about something *US, 1896*

- It's been possible to send free text messages from the internet for some time, though the major mobile phone companies seem to have got wise to that and are, unsurprisingly, keen for you to pay a 10p charge. — *The Guardian*, 15th February 2001

▸ **put wise; put wise to**

to make someone aware of something; to warn someone about something *US, 1913*

- [T]o extract enough information to nail Dr. Robinson without at the same time putting him wise to the extent of their suspicions[.] — Robert K. Tanenbaum, *Irresistible Impulse*, p. 121, 1998

-wise *suffix*

in the manner of, or to do with, a conjoined subject *US, 1942*

- [Jennifer] Garner finds the silver lining in her gruelling schedule, though. 'I'm learning a lot acting-wise, constantly having to draw on stuff,' she says. — *The Observer*, 29th December 2002
- I'm told there've been one or two problems lately in Zimbabwe politics-wise[.] — *The Guardian*, 3rd February 2003

wiseacre *noun*

a smart alec *UK, 1595*

- Young smirking wiseacres, he would have enjoyed beating each one of them with a baseball bat. — Irving Shulman, *The Amboy Dukes*, p. 72, 1947

wiseass *noun*

an obnoxious person with delusions of cleverness *US, 1971*

- IMPATIENT CUSTOMER: Such a wiseass. But go ahead. Crack wise. That's why you're jockeying a register in some fucking local convenience store instead of doing an honest day's work. — *Clerks*, 1994

wisecrack *noun*

a smart, humorous, sometimes cruel remark *US, 1924*

- Doug Wead, a former campaign staffer, noted that "Junior" [George W. Bush] particularly enjoyed putting people who thought they were big shots in their place ... harassing them with wisecracks and booming it out so everyone could hear it." — J. H. Hatfield, *Fortunate Son*, p. 73, 2002

wisecrack *verb*

to make smart, humorous and sometimes cruel remarks *US, 1946*

- [T]he latest in a string of actors whose screen personas wisecrack coolly in the face of heart-stopping danger. — Fari Amini, *The General Theory of Love*, p. 48, 2000

wisecracker *noun*

someone who makes smart, humorous and sometimes cruel remarks *US, 1923*

- You're looking for a seedy wisecracker? No problem[.] — *The Guardian*, p. 6, 29th June 2001

wisecracking *adjective*

given to making smart, humorous and sometimes cruel remarks *US, 1915*

- Through this bravura landscape of twilight flew a wisecracking, powerful young woman with immense breasts[.] — Michael Chabon, *The Amazing Adventures of Kavalier & Clay*, p. 319, 2000

wise guy *noun*

a recognised member of an organised crime enterprise *US*

- Funny the way the wise-guy can never make it in legit business because the square that covers for him will always rob him. — Edwin Torres, *Carlito's Way*, p. 58, 1975
- When you see a wise guy with an ugly broad? — Edwin Torres, *Q & A*, p. 167, 1977
- He developed a mental list of ten people who qualified, and slowly eliminated the couple of serious psychos, anyone hooked up tight with the neighborhood wise guys, and the consistent losers. — Vincent Patrick, *The Pope of Greenwich Village*, p. 20, 1979
- We're talking about the wise guys. — Elmore Leonard, *Cat Chaser*, p. 113, 1982
- They're like the police department for wiseguys. — *Goodfellas*, 1990
- A wiseguy. Paying 100 Grand for the rapists if I turn them over direct to him. — *The Bad Lieutenant*, 1992
- All the time he's running his sports book he's supposed to be cutting the wiseguys in? — Elmore Leonard, *Riding the Rap*, p. 30, 1995
- CHILI: One we're producing. MARTIN: With what? Wiseguy money? — *Get Shorty*, 1995

wise monkey *noun*

a condom *UK*

Rhyming slang for **DUNKY**, influenced perhaps by the usual number of wise monkeys and a **PACKET OF THREE**.

- [T]he need for safe sex is paramount. A "wise monkey" is therefore essential to deliver the old chap from evil. — Ray Puxley, *Cockney Rabbit*, 1992

wisenheimer *noun*

a smart alec, a wise guy *UK, 1904*

- The suffixes -heimer and -bund had brief vogues in 1900 or thereabout, but the former survives only in wisenheimer... — H.L. Mencken, *The American Language*, p. 219, 1962
- JOE: Keep needling me, Weisenheimer, and you're gonna meet Mr. Boot. — *Reservoir Dogs*, 1992
- Poor Teddy – he's been getting it both barrels from the Wisenheimer here. — *Something About Mary*, 1998

wisepuss *noun*

an obnoxious person with delusions of cleverness *US*

A variation of **WISEASS**.

- I know they play different instruments, wisepuss[.] — Lester Bangs, *Psychotic Reactions and Carburetor Dung*, p. 63, 1971

wish *verb*

to greet someone *INDIA*

- He wished me when we met this morning. — Paroo Nihalini, R.K. Tongue and Priya Hosali, *Indian and British English*, 1979

wishbone *noun*

in hot rodding, a triangular suspension control device *US*

- — John Edwards, *Auto Dictionary*, p. 189, 1993

wishing book *noun*

a mail-order catalogue *US*

- — John Gould, *Maine Lingo*, p. 319, 1975

wish-was *noun*

someone who wishes that he were something that he is not *US*

- — Trevor Cralle, *The Surfin'ary*, p. 163, 1991

wishy-washy *adjective*

1 weak; uncertain *UK, 1703*

- I don't want anybody to stand up and say I change my mind about things like a hundred-dollar hooker changes her shorts. I don't want anyone to be able to say George Lurgan's wishy-washy. — Robert Campbell, *The Cat's Meow*, p. 64, 1988
- [C]ontrary to what that wishy-washy pinko Jesus asshole said, their God isn't all that forgiving. — Christopher Brookmyre, *Not the End of the World*, p. 225, 1998

2 in poor condition *TRINIDAD AND TOBAGO, 1993*

- — Lise Winer, *Dictionary of the English/Creole of Trinidad & Tobago*, 2003

wiss *noun*

a urination *UK*

Glasgow slang.

- — Michael Munro, *The Complete Patter*, p. 169, 1996

wisteria *adjective*

clingy *UK*

From the characteristics of the plant; a contemporary gay usage.

- — *Attitude*, July 2003: 'New palare lexicon'

wit *noun*

a witness *US*

- "Any wits?" "I've got people making a house-to-house up along the ridge[.] — Robert Crais, *L.A. Requiem*, p. 41, 1999
- Barbara Molar is my wit. — Stephen J. Cannell, *The Tin Collectors*, p. 18, 2001

wit!

what was just said is not funny! *US*

- — *55-Plus*, p. 13, 12th February 1986: 'Today's guide to teen slang'

witch *noun*

▸ **the witch**

any powdered drug; cocaine, heroin, etc *US, 1949*

- —Richard A. Spears, *The Slang and Jargon of Drugs and Drink*, p. 554, 1986
- —Robert Ashton, *This Is Heroin*, p. 207, 2002
- —Mike Haskins, *Drugs*, p. 281, 2003

witch doctor *noun*

a doctor who specialises in internal medicine *US*

- — *Maledicta*, p. 118, 1984–1985: 'Milwaukee medical maledicta'

witches' knickers *noun*

plastic bags caught up in trees or shrubs *IRELAND*

- Two-thirds of this is plastic carrier bags, which end up in landfill or blowing about in trees and hedges (now known colloquially as "witches knickers"). — *The Irish Times*, p. 66, 23rd December 2000
- South Africans call poly bags the "national flower" and in Alaska they are known as "tundra ghosts". The Irish, eloquent as ever, have dubbed them "witches knickers" while in Scotland the plastic carrier is known as "an essential." — *The Sunday Herald (Glasgow)*, p. 10, 4th November 2004

witch hazel *noun*

heroin *US*

- —J.E. Schmidt, *Narcotics Lingo and Lore*, p. 191, 1959
- —Robert Ashton, *This Is Heroin*, p. 207, 2002

witch's brew *noun*

LSD enhanced with botanical drugs from plants such as Deadly Nightshade or Jimsonweed *US*

- —William D. Alsever, *Glossary for the Establishment and Other Uptight People*, p. 3, December 1970

witch's cackle *noun*

the male genitals *UK*

Rhyming slang for **WEDDING TACKLE**.

- —Bodmin Dark, *Dirty Cockney Rhyming Slang*, 2003

with authority!

used as a humorous comment on a comment made or action taken without hesitation and boldly *US*

Coined on ESPN's *Sports Center* while narrating footage showing a basketball slam dunk.

- —Keith Olberman and Dan Patrick, *The Big Show*, p. 27, 1997

with it *adjective*

aware of all that is happening; stylish; part of a subculture *US*

- The title (of the 1945 show 'Are You With It?") is carnival slang for "Are you with the carnival?" — *Life*, p. 97, 26th November 1945
- —Lawrence Lipton, *The Holy Barbarians*, p. 318, 1959
- "You're not with it," he says. "I was wearing that style two years ago," I said. —Mark Pass, *Marc Bolan, The Sharper Word*, p. 46, 1992

without *adjective*

clueless; out of touch; out of style *US*

- Your sister is so amazingly without. She'll never read him. She has no idea. — *Ten Things I Hate About You*, 1999

wiwi *noun*

a French person *NEW ZEALAND*

A Maori approximation of the French *oui, oui*.

- —David McGill, *David McGill's Complete Kiwi Slang Dictionary*, p. 137, 1998

wizard *noun*

1 an expertly skilled person *UK, 1620*

- [H]e knew only the broad outlines of scams dreamed up by his erstwhile financial wizard. — *The Guardian*, 13th January 2004

2 in computing, a person who has specific and detailed expertise *US*

- —Guy L. Steele et al., *The Hacker's Dictionary*, p. 132, 1983

3 in pinball, an expert player *US*

- —Bobbye Claire Natkin and Steve Kirk, *All About Pinball*, p. 118, 1977

wizard *adjective*

excellent, marvellous *UK, 1922*

Magical origins; mainly used by the privileged and officer classes until after World War 2, then widespread. Of upper-class society use: '[...] still used, though almost always in inverted commas' (Ann Barr and Peter York, *The Official Sloane Ranger Handbook*, p.159, 1982).

wizard!

used for expressing approval *UK*

wizard's sleeve *noun*

a capacious vagina *UK*

Coined for humorous magazine *Viz*.

- I can't feel a bloody thing. Yoy must have a fanny like a wizard's sleeve. — *Roger's Profanisaurus*, p. 30, October 1999
- — *www.LondonSlang.com*, June 2002

wizz, wizzo *nouns*

▷ **see: WHIZZ, WHIZZO**

wizzard; wizzard of oz *noun*

an ounce of marijuana *UK*

This plays on the conventional abbreviation 'oz' (ounce) and, by association with the film *The Wizard of Oz*, 1939, which contains the song 'Somewhere Over The Rainbow', suggesting where this measure of marijuana might take you. The misspelling 'wizzard', if deliberate, may be punning on **WHIZZ** (amphetamine).

wizzo *noun*

the weapons officer on a military aircraft *US*

- — *Seattle Times*, p. A9, 12th April 1998: 'Grunts, squids not grunting from the same dictionary'

wizzy *adjective*

excellent, exciting, wonderful; used for registering general approval *UK*

A variation of **WIZARD**.

- [A]nything positive, exciting, magical or desirable has suddenly come to be wizzy. —David Rowan, *A Glossary for the 90s*, p. 196, 1998

wizzy-wizzy *verb*

to whisper *BARBADOS*

- —Frank A. Collymore, *Barbadian Dialect*, p. 120, 1965

wobble *verb*

▸ **wobble the job**

to cause trouble among workers on a unionised work-site *CANADA*

- Between 1905 and 1914 the Industrial Workers of the World found particular support in Canada; members were known as "Wobblies." Wobble the job is a current term. —Tom Parkin, *WetCoast Words*, p. 153, 1989

wobble board *noun*

a simple musical instrument made of a sheet of stiff material that is wobbled rhythmically *AUSTRALIA, 1957*

Invention of the instrument and its name is credited to Australian artist and entertainer Rolf Harris (b.1930).

- To drag things down further, he dispatched his "lovely" assistant to distribute wobble boards to the masses. —Iain Aitch, *A Fete Worse Than Death*, p. 278, 2003

wobbler *noun*

1 an outburst of temper *UK*

- —Tom Hibbert, *Rockspeak!*, p. 174, 1983

2 in trucking, a spoke wheel *US*

- —Montie Tak, *Truck Talk*, p. 189, 1971

▸ **throw a wobbler**

to have a fit of bad temper or anger *US*

- [Steve] Marriott [...] had been "throwing wobblers all week"[.] — *Mojo*, September 2003

wobblestick *noun*

a gear lever on a truck or car *US*

- —Montie Tak, *Truck Talk*, p. 189, 1971

wobblies; wobs *noun*

a powerful and deep vibration of the board while skate-boarding fast *US*

- —Albert Cassorla, *The Skateboarder's Bible*, p. 204, 1976

wobbly *noun*

a fit of anger *UK, 1977*

- —Louis S. Leland, *A Personal Kiwi-Yankee Dictionary*, p. 103, 1984
- She just rooly chucked a wobbly last night. —Kylie Mole (Maryanne Fahey), *My Diary*, p. 103, 1988
- Thing is Cools, he'll really chuck a wobbly if he thinks I've shafted him. —Harrison Biscuit, *The Search for Savage Henry*, p. 69, 1995
- Uh oh, I thought, she's gunna crack a wobbly. Mum didn't often crack a wobbly, but when she did, it was a very wobbly wobbly. —Phillip Gwynne, *Deadly Unna?*, p. 81, 1998

▸ **throw a wobbly**

to have a fit of bad temper or anger *NEW ZEALAND*

- —Louis S. Leland, *A Personal Kiwi-Yankee Dictionary*, p. 103, 1984
- [O]ne of the girls threw a wobbly at a local pub.—*The Guardian*, 30th June 2002

Wobbly *noun*

a member of the anarchist trade union the International Workers of the World *US, 1914*

- The one thing about the Row was that it was filled with okies, weary old Wobblies, drunkies and dopies far gone, whores on their last legs – they never judged you.—Clancy Sigal, *Going Away*, p. 238, 1961

wobbly *adjective*

uncertain; undecided; risky *UK, 1884*

- A bit wobbly on the euro.—*New Statesman*, 18th June 2001
- Hutton seeks certainty in a world of wobbly truths.—*The Guardian*, 14th August 2003

wobbly egg; wobbly; egg *noun*

a capsule of Temazepam™, a branded tranquillizer; any central nervous system depressant; in the plural it refers to the drug in general *UK*

From the characteristic nature of gelatine, the original method of manufacturing the capsules.

- Its street name is JELLIES because in one of its forms it looks like gelatine jelly babies. It is also called WOBBLIES or EGGS.—Macfarlane, Macfarlane and Robson, *The User*, p. 100, 1996

wobbly hole *noun*

in trucking, the neutral gear *US*

- —Montie Tak, *Truck Talk*, p. 189, 1971

wobbly orange *noun*

a warrant officer in the Royal Air Force *UK, 2002*

A ludicrous re-use of the initials.

wodge; wadge *noun*

a large amount *UK, 1860*

Originally used of a bulky mass.

- I suddenly got a big wodge of money to spend[.]—Mary Hooper, *(megan)2*, p. 84, 1999
- We settled on a wodge of Euros.—Jonathan Gash, *The Ten Word Game*, p. 90, 2003

wog *noun*

1 any person of non-white ethnicity; a native of the Indian subcontinent; an Arab; any (non-English) foreigner, as in 'the wogs begin at Calais' *UK, 1929*

Derogatory, patronising. Derives possibly from an abbreviation of 'golliwog' (a caricature black-faced, curly-haired doll) but the widest usage is in reference to Asians and not black people. Popular, unproven etymology has 'wog' as an acronym of '*W*estern(ised) [or] *W*ily *O*riental *G*entleman'.

- Do you know what I'm going to do to those wogs?—Richard Farina, *Been Down So Long*, p. 164, 1966
- [H]e frequently and unashamedly aired his prejudices on such subjects as wogs and Roman Catholics.—Robin Page, *Down Among the Dossers*, p. 50, 1973
- Show us your ticket, you old desert wog!—Lance Peters, *The Dirty Half-Mile*, p. 317, 1979
- When an Italian or another person of European descent calls me a wog it's done in good warm humour. When the word "wog" comes out of the mouth of an Australian it's not done in good humour unless they're a good friend.—Melina Marchetta, *Looking For Alibrandi*, p. 88, 1992
- Do you reckon what they say in the front bar is right, that wogs eat squid?—Phillip Gwynne, *Deadly Unna?*, p. 66, 1998

2 any language that isn't English *AUSTRALIA*

- [S]he can't see anythink and goes, 'Romeo, Romeo, where for art thou Romeo?', which is wog for 'Where are you?', and he goes 'Here,' and they do it.—Kylie Mole (Maryanne Fahey), *My Diary*, p. 72, 1988

3 a germ that causes an illness *AUSTRALIA, 1941*

- Reckon I've got a wog.—Jean Brooks, *The Opal Witch*, p. 131, 1967
- Dad's not in a good mood today. He's laid up with a wog.—Jean Brooks, *The Opal Witch*, p. 147, 1967
- —Frank Hardy, *The Outcasts of Foolgarah*, p. 75, 1971
- Mike, I resolutely refuse to swing anymore. I won't run the risk of catching any more of those filthy wogs.—Bettina Arndt, *The Australian Way of Sex*, p. 86, 1985

wog *adjective*

1 foreign *UK*

- He turned over [robbed] half a dozen rooms, including those of a young wog prince[.]—Charles Raven, *Underworld Nights*, p. 172, 1956
- We didn't fall foul of the Wog police. We conducted ourselves in a manner befitting an English man.—Troy Kennedy Martin, *The Italian Job [uncut script]*, 1969

2 of non-Anglo-Celtic origin *AUSTRALIA*

- 'Got a meet on with a Wog bint?' asked Eddie.—Lawson Glassop, *We Were The Rats*, p. 115, 1944
- There are some Anglo women who hate wog men[.]—Christos Tsiolkas, *Loaded*, p. 34, 1995

wogball *noun*

soccer *AUSTRALIA, 1984*

- It was disturbing to watch a program on Channel 7 last week where the presenter called Soccer "Wog Ball". The last time I heard this was on the same channel almost 18 years ago, whereby he publicly apologised the following week.—*www.wog.com.au*, 2003

wog box *noun*

a large portable stereo system associated, stereotypically, with black youth culture *UK, 1990*

- Hey, great wog box, man.—Colin Butts, *Is Harry on the Boat?*, p. 13, 1997

woggy *adjective*

1 characteristic of a non-white person *AUSTRALIA*

- I love Dino. (I can't remember wot his last name is. Somethink rooly woggy, that you can't pronounce.)—Kylie Mole (Maryanne Fahey), *My Diary*, p. 65, 1988
- She's got a bad woggy haircut; too much hairspray makes her hair look like a wig.—Christos Tsiolkas, *Loaded*, p. 8, 1995

2 of non-Anglo-Celtic background *AUSTRALIA*

- Give us two in the back stalls will you woggy boy and a box of black magic!!!—Barry Humphries, *The Wonderful World of Barry McKenzie*, p. 45, 1968
- This one's called Petro. He's a big choc, you know really woggy...—Kathy Lette, *Girls' Night Out*, p. 126, 1987

wojus *adjective*

inferior; of poor quality *IRELAND*

- —Colin Murphy and Donal O'Dea, *The Book of Feckin' Irish Slang*, p. 62, 2004

woke-up *adjective*

informed; up-to-date *US*

- —Hy Lit, *Hy Lit's Unbelievable Dictionary of Hip Words for Groovy People*, p. 1, 1968

wolf *noun*

1 a sexually aggressive man *US, 1945*

- It was parked on a sofa, a full six feet long. It gave me ideas, which I quickly ignored. It was no time to play wolf.—Mickey Spillane, *I, The Jury*, p. 30, 1947
- As he walked before her he was proud of the stares and whistles Betty received from the wolves who sat at the tables.—Irving Shulman, *The Amboy Dukes*, p. 202, 1947
- Never enthuse to a fellow wolf about your latest conquest – unless you're trying to lose her.—Jack Lait and Lee Mortimer, *New York Confidential*, p. 129, 1948
- "Let go of my arm," she replied. "The last wolf that made a pass at me is now eating through a tube."—Max Shulman, *The Many Loves of Dobie Gillis*, p. 162, 1951
- —John Rechy, *City of Night*, p. x, 1963
- I won't bother you – except sometimes maybe – when I feel like it – I aint no wolf, pal.—John Rechy, *City of Night*, p. 31, 1963
- The desk clerk (Richard Bolla) turns out to be a wolf and begins seducing a number of the girls while trying to fend off his female tyrant of a boss.—Kent Smith et al., *Adult Movies*, p. 153, 1982

2 in prison, an aggressive, predatory homosexual *US*

- Everyone was either a wolf or a fag. The wolf is the so-called male of the species, a rare and almost obsolete animal.—Chester Himes, *Cast the First Stone*, p. 72, 1952
- A baby-faced, small-framed, good-looking kid who looked about fourteen years old, he was perfect prey for the jailhouse wolves.—Piri Thomas, *Down These Mean Streets*, p. 264, 1967
- Nude Doc Melvin, wolf mother queen of the joint, relaxes in his cozy hospital quarters.—Iceberg Slim (Robert Beck), *Doom Fox*, p. 215, 1978

3 in homosexual anal sex, the active participant *US, 1940s*

4 a prison sentence of 15 years *US*

- —Charles Shafer, *Folk Speech in Texas Prisons*, p. 217, 1990

wolf *verb*

to act in a sexually aggressive manner *US*

- A kid dressed up in his big brother's uniform out wolfin chicks.—Earl Thompson, *Tattoo*, p. 161, 1974

wolf bait *noun*
an attractive young woman *US*
• Day in and day out, year in and year out, eager young wolf-bait bangs against the big city doors, unaware that beauty and even glamor is often a drug on the market. —Lee Mortimer, *Women Confidential*, p. 88, 1960

Wolfhounds *noun*
the 27th Infantry Regiment of the 25th Division *US*
Formed in 1901, named by the White Russians in World War 1, distinguished fighters in World War 2, Korea and Vietnam.
• He found it in the 27th Infantry (Wolfhound) Regiment of the 25th Division. —Robert Leckie, *The Wars of America, Volume II*, p. 351, 1968

wolf in the pack *noun*
a traffic police car in the midst of other cars *US*
• — *American Speech*, p. 273, December 1962: 'The language of traffic policemen'

wolf pack *noun*
a group of friends who play poker at cardrooms, taking advantage of unskilled strangers *US*
• —John Vorhaus, *The Big Book of Poker Slang*, p. 40, 1996

wolf-pack *verb*
1 to engage in criminal gang activity *US*
• —Ralph de Sola, *Crime Dictionary*, p. 165, 1982
2 to congregate with other teenagers around their cars at shopping centre carparks, drinking beer and idling *US, 1989*
• — *American Speech*, Summer 1990

wolf ticket *noun*
a threat or other act of intimidation used to coerce *US*
• It's plenty people selling wolf tickets, you know. —Vernon E. Smith, *The Jones Men*, p. 165, 1974
• If you two came here on a wolf ticket, it's time for you to leave. —Robert Deane Pharr, *Giveadamn Brown*, p. 138, 1978
• Wolf Tickets: What Baker accused Tony LaRussa of selling when the St. Louis Manager charged that Cubs pitchers were throwing at Cardinals pitchers. — *Chicago Tribune*, p. C10, 9th September 2003

wolf whistle *noun*
a distinctive whistle (generally, a sharply terminated rising note, followed by one that rises briefly before descending and fading) used as a declaration of appreciation for a sexually attractive person *US, 1952*
After **WOLF** (a sexually aggressive man), and generally, but not exclusively, in the vocabulary of men.
• [H]e does manage a grim wolf whistle toward a woman – big tits, blonde, great ass, high heels-heading toward Watrer Street. —Bret Easton Ellis, *American Psycho*, p. 30, 1991

wolf-whistle *verb*
to whistle in a distinctive declaration of appreciation for a sexually attractive person *US, 1955*
From the noun.
• Complete silence. Then Vanessa stood up and wolf-whistled like her sister had taught her. —Cecily Von Ziegesar, *You Know You Love Me*, p. 179, 2002

wollie; woolah *noun*
crack cocaine added to a marijuana cigarette or cigar *US*
• —Terry Williams, *The Cocaine Kids*, p. 138, 1989
• —Terry Williams, *Crackhouse*, p. 152, 1992

wolly *noun*
▷ see: **WALLY**

wollyback *noun*
anyone living in a rural area *IRELAND*
• All out to have a look at the country dwellers, the wollybacks of the County Wickla [Wicklow] —Joseph O'Connor, *Red Roses and Petrol*, p. 67, 1995

wolver *noun*
the penis *UK*
Rhyming slang, formed from Midlands' town Wolverhampton as an elaboration of 'hampton', the shortened form of **HAMPTON WICK** (**PRICK**). Noted by Ronald Hjort, 1967.

woman in the sun *noun*
heroin *UK, 2001*
Collected in private correspondence with certain musicians.

womb *noun*
the rectum *US*
• — *Maledicta*, p. 197, 1983: 'Ritual and personal insults in stigmatized subcultures'

wombat *noun*
1 a dull, uninteresting or stupid person *AUSTRALIA, 1905*
From the name of a stocky native nocturnal marsupial.
• You notice there are two toothbrushes in your cup. Some male wombat from long ago left this gungy, chewed up dental momento. —Kathy Lette, *Girls' Night Out*, p. 14, 1987
• 'Wasn't that hard a day, was it?' asked Len, smiling up from the notebook he was writing the day's output in. 'Only having to put up with you and the rest of these wombats.' —Robert G. Barrett, *Davo's Little Something*, p. 25, 1992
2 in computing, a *w*aste *o*f *m*oney, *b*rains *a*nd *t*ime *US*
• —Eric S. Raymond, *The New Hacker's Dictionary*, p. 386, 1991

wombat-headed *adjective*
stupid; fat-headed *AUSTRALIA*
First used by the bushranger Ned Kelly in his famous 'Jerilderie Letter' in 1879.
• —Frank Hardy, *The Outcasts of Foolgarah*, p. 230, 1971
• —Arthur Chipper, *The Aussie Swearer's Guide*, p. 85, 1972
• Utterly Unreconstructed Wombat-headed Yobbos[.] —Ignatius Jones, *True Hip*, p. 2, 1990

womb broom *noun*
the penis *US*
• I went to the bathroom and washed the animal smell of sex from my womb broom. —A.S. Jackson, *Gentleman Pimp*, p. 166, 1973

womb duster *noun*
the penis *US*
• She caressed it and whispered, "Billy, your womb duster is heroic." —Iceberg Slim (Robert Beck), *Long White Con*, p. 98, 1977

womble *noun*
1 in prison, an inmate detailed as a litter collector *UK*
After the children's characters created by Elizabeth Beresford, and in a BBC television series launched in 1973.
• It didn't help that Mally took a job as a "Womble" (a prisoner who wanders the grounds with a bin bag in one hand and a litter picker in the other.) — *The Guardian*, 22nd May 2003
2 a fool *UK, 1986*
• "Manchester United?" asked Lance. "No, you womble, Hereford United." —Chris Ryan, *The Watchman*, p. 184–185, 2001

womble *verb*
to pick up litter *UK*
From the *raison d'être* of children's television characters in *The Wombles*, who collected litter in the 70s from 1973, and again from 1998.
• —Angela Devlin, *Prison Patter*, p. 124, 1996

womb sweeper *noun*
the penis *US*
• She mouths in to tow out his cable veined womb sweeper. —Iceberg Slim (Robert Beck), *Doom Fox*, p. 156, 1978

womb-trembler *noun*
something that causes great excitement *UK*
• [T]he people of England celebrate. It's a fucking national womb-trembler, son. —Jake Arnott, *He Kills Coppers*, p. 101, 2001

women and children off the street!
in shuffleboard, used as a humorous commentary on a hard shooter *US*
• —Omero C. Catan, *Secrets of Shuffleboard Strategy*, p. 74, 1967: 'Glossary of terms'

womp; whomp *verb*
to beat someone *US*
• —J. R. Friss, *A Dictionary of Teenage Slang (Mt. Diablo High)*, 1964
• —Hy Lit, *Hy Lit's Unbelievable Dictionary of Hip Words for Groovy People*, p. 52, 1968

wonder star *noun*
methcathinone *UK, 1998*
• —Office of National Drug Control Policy, *Drug Facts*, February 2003

wonder veg *noun*
any mushroom with a hallucinogenic effect *UK*
• —Angela Devlin, *Prison Patter*, p. 124, 1996

wonder wand *noun*
the penis *US*
An elaboration of **WAND** (the penis).
• —Erica Orloff and JoAnn Baker, *Dirty Little Secrets*, p. 90, 2001

wong *verb*

in casino blackjack, to play several hands at a table where the count of cards played favours the player, and then to move on to another table *US*

Named after Stanford Wong, a blackjack expert.

- — Michael Dalton, *Blackjack*, p. 90, 1991

wonga *noun*

1 money *UK*

From Romany *wanger* or *wonger*, defined by George Borrow in *Romano Lavo-Lil*, 1907, as 'Coal. Also a term for money; probably because Coal in the cant [criminal] language signifies money'. Romany *wongar-camming* (a miser) is literally 'one who loves coal'. (Now obsolete 'coal', also 'cole', meant 'money' from the mid-C17, all but faded away by C20). Variants include 'wong' and 'wonger'.

- [I]t was heavy "graft" (work) and very little "denari" (money – "wonger" and "denali" are also used for this. — Butch Reynolds, *Broken Hearted Clown*, p. 30, 1953
- "You got the wonga, san [son]?" "Five hundred notes [pounds], right?" — Donald Gorgon, *Cop Killer*, p. 59, 1994
- [S]nort all your drugs, want a cut of the wonga or try to shag your wife. — Darren Francis, *The Sprawl [britpulp]*, p. 302, 1999
- Everton was not the first to chase the wong. — Diran Abedayo, *My Once Upon A Time*, p. 237, 2000
- [W]hen the establishment Mafioso realise how much gilt, paper, cashish, wonga, wedge, corn, cutter, loot, spondos, dollar, readies, shillings, folding, dough, money is on offer[.] — J.J. Connolly, *Layer Cake*, p. 94, 2000
- To the nurses, who do the hard work while pop stars and actors get all the wonga. Them and footballers. — John King, *White Trash*, p. 257, 2001

2 marijuana *UK*

- — Bob Young and Micky Moody, *The Language of Rock 'n' Roll*, p. 161, 1985

wonk *noun*

a student who studies harder than contemporaries consider necessary; a political professional who is studious and therefore well informed *US, 1962*

Derogatory.

- — Collin Baker et al., *College Undergraduate Slang Study Conducted at Brown University*, p. 223, 1968
- Some musical wonk? — Erich Segal, *Love Story*, p. 26, 1970
- I almost never call anyone a nerd – I'm partial to the term "wonk". — *Wasington Post (reprinted from The Nation)*, p. C5, 22 December 1985
- Wonk [...] carries the same elements of unattractive swottiness [as a nerd] but has the benefit of putting it to good use and being in the know. — David Rowan, *A Glossary for the 90s*, p. 62, 1998

wonkey; wonky *adjective*

broken *US*

- — Don R. McCreary (Editor), *Dawg Speak*, 2001

wonk out *verb*

to study excessively *US*

- — *New York Times*, 12th April 1987

wonky *adjective*

1 unbalanced; out-of-true *UK, 1919*

Variation of obsolete sense of 'wanky' (inferior, damaged).

2 unsound or unreliable *UK, 1925*

- Mum's radio's gone wonky. — John Burke and Stuart Douglass, *The Boys*, p. 81, 1962
- It's going all wonky. — Michael Moorcock, *The Spencer Inheritance [britpulp]*, p. 29, 1998

3 intellectual; out of touch with reality *US*

- "Jenny Cavilleri," answered Ray. "Wonky music type." — Erich Segal, *Love Story*, p. 15, 1970

won't do itself

used before tackling any task as an expression of resigned determination *UK*

A very clichéd truism if not a catchphrase.

- I've got a pile of ironing and it won't do itself will it? — Caroline Aherne and Craig Cash, *The Royle Family*, 1999

woo *noun*

sexual foreplay *NEW ZEALAND*

- — David McGill, *David McGill's Complete Kiwi Slang Dictionary*, p. 137, 1998

wood *noun*

1 the fully erect penis *US*

- This guy has trouble with wood [erections] and if he does, I'd give you a hell of a lot to step in and do the scene. — Robert Stoller and I.S. Levine, *Coming Attractions*, p. 82, 1991
- He didn't see where the condom came from but she was now expertly unrolling it down the length of his wood. — Donald Gorgon, *Cop Killer*, p. 46, 1994
- — *Adult Video News*, p. 48, September 1995
- But whether that enthusiasm translates into on-screen "wood" is another story. More often than not, a male who has never experienced the harsh conditions of onscreen sex will not be able to "rise" to the occasion. — Ana Loria, *1 2 3 Be A Porn Star!*, p. 65, 2000
- "He's putting heavy wood to her, Lar," I said tersely, "from behind." — Terry Southern, *Now Dig This*, p. 241, 2001
- DIRECTOR (of pornographic film): Problem? ACTRESS: We don't have wood. CAMERAMAN: Stand by. Holding on wood. SOUNDMAN: Stand by for wood. WOMAN IN STREET: We are holding for wood. — *The Guru*, 2002
- [T]he male hysteria that greeted the fabled wood-giving drug [Viagra][.] — *The Guardian*, p. 38, 1st June 2002

2 the penis *TRINIDAD AND TOBAGO, 1950*

- — Lise Winer, *Dictionary of the English/Creole of Trinidad & Tobago*, 2003

3 in a casino or other gambling establishment, a person who watches without playing *US, 1950*

An abbreviation of **DEADWOOD**.

- — John Scarne, *Scarne on Dice*, p. 482, 1974
- — Thomas L. Clark, *The Dictionary of Gambling and Gaming*, p. 251, 1987

▸ **have the wood on**

to have an advantage over someone *AUSTRALIA, 1949*

- [A] bloke couldn't very well extend his mutterings to a Section Commander who had the wood on him. — Ray Slattery, *Mobbs' Mob*, p. 119, 1966
- — Frank Hardy, *The Outcasts of Foolgarah*, p. 124, 1971
- — Arthur Chipper, *The Aussie Swearer's Guide*, p. 64, 1972
- — Jim Ramsay, *Cop It Sweet!*, p. 96, 1977

▸ **on the wood**

1 in horse racing, racing along the rail *US*

- — Igor Kushyshyn et al., *The Gambling Times Guide to Harness Racing*, p. 120, 1994

2 in hot rodding and motor racing, throttled to the maximum *US*

- — John Edwards, *Auto Dictionary*, p. 118, 1993

Woodbine; woodie; woody; wood *noun*

any cheap cigarette *UK, 1916*

From branded Wild Woodbine™ cigarettes, maufactured by WD & HO Wills and among the cheapest to be had.

- She must have her share uv Woodies. She must 'ave a fag. — Geoffrey Fletcher, *Down Among the Meths Men*, p. 35, 1966

wood burner *noun*

an attractive female *US*

A suggestion that the woman consumes **WOOD** in the 'erect' sense of the word.

- All those wood burners on the beach? Yeah, I'd pay to do this job. — Joseph Wambaugh, *The Golden Orange*, p. 176, 1990

wooden *verb*

to beat someone with a club of some sort *AUSTRALIA, 1905*

- Got woodened with something wot wasn't a bike chain. — Arthur Upfield, *Bony and the Mouse*, p. 48, 1959

wooden *adjective*

in poker, said of a hand that is unplayable *US*

- — *American Speech*, p. 102, May 1951

wooden aspro *noun*

a blow to the head with a police baton *NEW ZEALAND, 1980*

- — Harry Orsman, *A Dictionary of Modern New Zealand Slang*, p. 150, 1999

wooden cat *noun*

a Morris 'Traveller' car *UK*

Citizens' band radio slang; **OLD CAT** is a Morris 'Minor'; this 'cat' is amended for the wooden bars in the model's design.

- — Peter Chippindale, *The British CB Book*, p. 161, 1981

woodener *noun*

a sentence of imprisonment for 30 days *UK, 1950*

Rhyming slang, 'wooden spoon' for **MOON** (a month's imprisonment).

- — Angela Devlin, *Prison Patter*, p. 124, 1996

wooden hill; little wooden hill *noun*

the stairs *UK, 1961*

Nursery use, especially in the phrase **CLIMB THE WOODEN HILL TO BEDFORDSHIRE** (to go upstairs to bed).

• When I was a kid, when it was bedtime my father used to always say it was time to climb the wooden hill, it's time to go upstairs. It's an East Coast expression. — *Toronto Globe and Mail*, p. A18, 15th July 1994

wooden horses *noun*

a carousel *BARBADOS*

• — Frank A. Collymore, *Barbadian Dialect*, p. 120, 1965

wooden Indian *noun*

a poker player who does not talk or display emotion *US*

• — John Vorhaus, *The Big Book of Poker Slang*, p. 40, 1996

wooden leg *noun*

an egg *UK*

Rhyming slang.

• — Ray Puxley, *Fresh Rabbit*, 1998

wooden overcoat *noun*

a coffin *UK, 1903*

A bleakly cynical euphemism, since 1903. Later variations are 'wooden kimono', 1926 and 'wooden suit', 1968.

• The only way he's coming out [of prison] is in a wooden overcoat. — Danny King, *The Burglar Diaries*, p. 171, 2001

wooden plank *noun*

an American, especially an American in the UK *UK*

Rhyming slang for **YANK**.

• During the Gulf War of 1991 taxi drivers were seen crying into their cocktails over "the lack of wooden planks in town". — Ray Puxley, *Cockney Rabbit*, 1992

wooden spoon *noun*

1 a notional trophy awarded to an individual or a team placed last in a competition *UK, 1858*

From an actual wooden spoon that was customarily presented to the lowest on the Mathematical Tripos list at Cambridge University.

• Scotland took the wooden spoon from Wales. — *The Guardian*, 31st March 2003

2 a month's imprisonment *UK*

Rhyming slang for **MOON**.

• — Ray Puxley, *Fresh Rabbit*, 1998

wooden-spooner *noun*

in a sporting competition, an individual or team that comes last *UK, 1954*

From **WOODEN SPOON**.

• Dr. Robert Cade of the University of Florida wanted to help the "wooden-spooners" of American college football – the Florida Gators. — Jim Aitchison, *How Asia Advertises*, p. 99, 2002

wooden-spoonist *noun*

in a competition, an individual or team that comes last *UK, 1927*

From **WOODEN SPOON**.

• For the wooden- spoonists, the prize should be something funny, but not too offensive[.] — Vanessa Daubney, *Big Rock & Pop Quiz Book*, 2002

woodentop *noun*

1 a uniformed police officer *UK, 1982*

After the childrens' television puppet show *The Woodentops* 1955–58. The variant 'woody' is also used.

• A phalanx of woodentops waded in, putting it about a bit lively with their truncheons[.] — Jake Arnott, *He Kills Coppers*, p. 216, 2001

• There's more to life than being a Woody – CID-speak for Woodentops[.] — Duncan MacLaughlin, *The Filth*, p. 87–88, 2002

2 a fool; also attributed as an adjective *UK, 1983*

After the sense as 'a police officer'.

• Why is that bloody "woodentop" MP always on the TV? — *The Times*, 28th June 2003

Wood family *noun*

used as a humorous description of empty seats in a theatre *UK*

• — Wilfred Granville, *The Theater Dictionary*, p. 14, 1952

woodfoot *noun*

numbing of the foot in cold water *US*

Surfing usage.

• — *Transworld Surf*, p. 42, April 2004

woodie *noun*

1 a Wills Woodbine™ cigarette *UK, 1931*

• Soon [George Harrison] was copping off with a bunch of mates to smoke "Woodies" – the cheap, strong, little Woodbine cigarettes beloved of youngsters in the Fifties and Sixties. — *Uncut*, p. 40, February 2002

2 a wooden powerboat, especially one built between the 1920s and 60s *US*

• A woodie hanging from a beam soaks up water in the wooden hull to ensure it's watertight. — *San Francisco Chronicle Magazine*, p. 16, 5th August 2001

wooding *noun*

among vagrant alcoholics, a task of collecting firewood *UK*

• My job is usually woodin' (collecting firewood); that's wot Harry Ram usually gits me on to. — Geoffrey Fletcher, *Down Among the Meths Men*, p. 91, 1966

woodpecker *noun*

a machinegun *AUSTRALIA, 1898*

• This would be about where Tuttle was cut in half with a burst of woodpecker fire. — Eric Lambert, *The Veterans*, p. 191, 1954

• — Gregory Clark, *Words of the Vietnam War*, p. 252, 1990

woodpile *noun*

1 a xylophone *US*

• — Lou Shelly, *Hepcats Jive Talk Dictionary*, p. 20, 1945

2 the area in a prison yard where white prisoners exercise *US*

Formed from **PECKERWOOD** (a white person) and **IRON PILE** (weightlifting equipment).

• — James Harris, *A Convict's Dictionary*, p. 41, 1989

woodpile cousin *noun*

an actual, if distant, blood relative *US*

• — John Gould, *Maine Lingo*, p. 320, 1975

wood rash *noun*

any injury, especially grazing, sustained when riding a skateboard on a wooden ramp *US, 1990s*

A combination of location and appearance; ironically modest.

woods *noun*

the vulva; a woman's pubic hair *US*

Usually used with 'the'.

• — Collin Baker et al., *College Undergraduate Slang Study Conducted at Brown University*, p. 223, 1968

woods French *noun*

a limited ability in French *CANADA*

• — Laurel Doucette, *Cultural Retention and Demographic Change*, p. 36, 1980

• "Woods French" is a term for limited competence in a specialized lexicon in Quebec French. (From the Eastern Townships of Quebec). — Lewis Poteet, *Talking Country*, p. 77, 1992

woodshed *verb*

to rehearse, especially in private *US, 1936*

• [...]that exile in the soul that jazzmen know as "woodshedding" — John Clellon Holmes, *The Horn*, p. 59, 1958

• You got a long way to go, a lot to learn, but I think that with some woodshedding you can get our book down. — Nat Hentoff, *Jazz Country*, p. 120, 1965

woodsman *noun*

a male pornography performer who can be counted upon to maintain an erection as long as needed and to ejaculate more or less on demand *US*

• — *Adult Video News*, p. 48, September 1995

• The real elite woodsman can also stand in as a "stunt penis' for $50 to $100 bucks a scene (depending on the situation at hand) in case a younger or more inexperienced performer can't make wood. — Ana Loria, *1 2 3 Be A Porn Star!*, p. 68, 2000

woodster *noun*

a male pornography performer whose erections can be counted on *US*

• It's easier to use the same five guys because those five guys are guaranteed woodsters. — Ana Loria, *1 2 3 Be A Porn Star!*, p. 106a, 2000

woodsy *noun*

a party held in the country *US*

• — *Current Slang*, p. 2, Spring 1967

woodwork *noun*

▸ **come out of the woodwork; crawl out of the woodwork; creep out of the woodwork**

(of someone or something unpleasant) to appear; to arrive on the scene; to emerge *UK*

Usage is often with humorous intent but the allusion is to insects normally found in the woodwork – woodworm, deathwatch beetle, cockroach, etc.

- They crawled out of the woodwork, / And they whispered in your brain[.] — Elton John and Bernie Taupin, *Candle in the Wind*, 1973
- Crept out of the woodwork. — *Harpers & Queen*, August 1977
- some sad old bag who has come out of the woodwork 'cos she doesn't want to be alone any more — Philip Ralph, *Mr Nobody*, 2003
- Foes of women in combat crawl out of the woodwork. — *Chicago Sun-Times*, 5th April 2003

woody; woodie *noun*

1 an erection *US*

US pornographer Joey Silvera is given credit for coining this term, which did not stay within the confines of pornography for long.

- Old Desmond had sprouted a woody! — Joseph Wambaugh, *The Secrets of Harry Bright*, p. 47, 1985
- — Pamela Munro, *U.C.L.A. Slang*, p. 91, 1989
- So I then go into my Mack Daddy mode cause I'm getting a woodie in my cackies y'know. — *Boyz N The Hood*, 1990
- — Connie Eble (Editor), *UNC-CH Campus Slang*, p. 10, Spring 1991
- Who's the old guy with the big woody? — *Airheads*, 1994
- [T]hey thought he was wagging the old woody around[.] — Erica Orloff and JoAnn Baker, *Dirty Little Secrets*, p. 153, 2001

2 a car with wood or synthetic wood paneling on its body *US*

- Early in the morning we'll be startin' out / Some honeys will be coming along / We're loading up our Woody / With our boards inside / And headin' out singing our song. — The Beach Boys, *Surfin' Safari*, 1962
- — *Paradise of the Pacific*, p. 27, October 1963
- — J. R. Friss, *A Dictionary of Teenage Slang (Mt. Diablo High)*, 1964
- — John Severson, *Modern Surfing Around the World*, p. 186, 1964
- It's like the Volkswagen buses a lot of kids now use as beach wagons instead of woodies. Woodies are old station wagons, usually Fords, with wooden bodies, from back before 1953. — Tom Wolfe, *The Pump House Gang*, p. 19, 1968

▹ **see: WOODBINE**

woody pill *noun*

a genuine or a generic Viagra™ tablet *UK*

Based on **WOODY** (an erection).

- It's got all the right proportions of all the whatnot that you need for a working woody pill. — Kevin Sampson, *Clubland*, p. 77, 2002

Woody Woodpecker *noun*

a tablet of MDMA, the recreational drug best known as ecstasy, embossed with a representation of the popular animation character *UK*

- Soon enough, though, the Woody Woodpecker started to take effect and I felt like I was going to be sick. — Wayne Anthony, *Spanish Highs*, p. 89, 1999

woof *verb*

1 to vomit *US*

- — Connie Eble (Editor), *UNC-CH Campus Slang*, p. 5, April 1978

2 to eat very quickly *UK, 1943*

Possibly from '*wolf* down'.

- "How long must you be here?" Barto asked as he woofed down the food. — The Voice of the Martyrs *Extreme Devotion*, p. 74, 2001

3 to threaten or intimidate someone; to engage someone in ritualistic, quasi-friendly insulting *US*

- "Ain't you about to freeze to death, Pony?" "You ain't a woofin'," I said[.] — S.E. Hinton, *The Outsiders*, p. 49, 1967
- He was woofing me, because he winked at the blond kid[.] — Joseph Wambaugh, *The Blue Knight*, p. 70, 1973
- Don't talk crazy. The dude was just woofin'. He still digs you. — Joseph Nazel, *Black Cop*, p. 105, 1974

woof!

used as a shout of approval, especially as a male declaration of appreciation for a sexually desirable female *US*

Originated by television talk show host Aresnio Hall in 1989; the barking is accompanied by a pumped raised hand, fist clenched.

- The woof chorus went through the roof, everybody high-fiving, bopping in glee. — Richard Price, *Clockers*, p. 203, 1992

woofer *noun*

an unattractive woman or man *UK*

A variation of **DOG**.

- He spotted a newly arrived couple who were young and, in relation to the woofers already there, very attractive. — Kitty Churchill, *Thinking of England*, p. 202, 1995

woofter *noun*

a homosexual man *UK, 1977*

A variation of **POOFTER** (a male homosexual).

- — Angela Devlin, *Prison Patter*, p. 124, 1996
- Stripe me, Dave, you gonna just stand there whiles some woofter is waving his tackle at your missus? — *The Full Monty*, 1997
- Eh, bruv, I think they've put a woofter in here with us. — Jimmy Stockin, *On The Cobbles*, p. 139, 2000

woofterish *adjective*

ineffecutal *NEW ZEALAND*

- By banning the woofterish gloves-on scrapping, the Minister may well inspire a resurgence of the bare-kunckle classicism New Zealanders once held dear. — *Evening Post*, p. 5, 22nd May 1993

wook *noun*

a quintessential rural hippie *US*

From the Wookie character in the George Lucas *Star Wars* films.

wool *noun*

1 pubic hair; by extension, sex *US*

- He looks like he could get hisself some good wool if he put his mind on it. — Dan Jenkins, *Semi-Tough*, p. 10, 1972
- — *Maledicta*, p. 131, Summer/Winter 1982: 'Dyke diction: the language of lesbians'

2 used derogatively of someone who is not from the city; a stereotypical country-dweller; a yokel *UK*

From **WOOLLY BACK**.

- [I]f I'm standing on anybody's toes it's only going to be some wool dealing a little bit of weed and that. — Kevin Sampson, *Outlaws*, p. 53, 2001

woola; woolas; wooly; wool *noun*

crack cocaine or phencyclidine sprinkled over marijuana which is then smoked in a cigarette; a hollowed-out cigar filled with marijuana and phencyclidine *US*

- [T]he teen / Who was a fiend / Started smokin' wools at 16 — Raekwon of Wu-Tang Clan, *C.R.E.A.M.*, 1994
- She flushed the woola down the john. — Lois Stavsky et al., *A2Z*, p. 112, 1995

woolah *noun*

▹ **see: WOLLIE**

woolie *noun*

a female's pubic hair *NEW ZEALAND, 1994*

- — Harry Orsman, *A Dictionary of Modern New Zealand Slang*, p. 150, 1999

woolies *noun*

winter clothing *US*

- — Lou Shelly, *Hepcats Jive Talk Dictionary*, p. 50, 1945

Woolies *nickname*

high street shop FW Woolworth's, later Woolworth's *AUSTRALIA, 1944*

- There are jobs going at Woolies, if you want 'em. — *The Full Monty*, 1997
- Mum was a store detective for Woolworth's, which is pretty funny considering the amount of stuff I used to lift from Woolies. — Dave Courtney, *Stop the Ride I Want to Get Off*, p. 15, 1999

woollies *noun*

marijuana and crack cocaine mixture; marijuana and phencyclidine, the recreational drug known as PCP or angel dust *UK, 1998*

- Woollies: marijuana with a soupcon of crack or PCP — Mike Haskins, *Drugs*, p. 294, 2003

Woolloomooloo Yank *noun*

an Australian who puts on an American accent *AUSTRALIA, 1945*

- — Barry Humphries, *A Nice Night's Entertainment*, p. 210, 1981

woolly *noun*

1 a black person *US*

Variants include 'woolly head'.

- — Iceberg Slim (Robert Beck), *Trick Baby*, p. 276, 1969

2 in CID slang, a uniformed police officer *UK, 1965*

- — John Ayto, *The Oxford Slang of Slang*, p. 109, 1998

woolly back *noun*

1 a stereotype of the unsophisticated country-dweller *UK*
An allusion to the intelligence and appearance of sheep.
- [T]ribal tensions [in Skelmersdale, Lancashire] between "scousers" (former Liverpudlians there) and "woolly-backs" (locals). — *The Times*, 16th July 1981
- a woolly-back from Wigan — Alan Bleasedale, *Boys From the Blackstuff*, 1982

2 a Welsh person *US*
- "So where you from?" he asks. I tell him. "Hoho! A woolly back!" he says, and then "No, only kidding[.]" — *Red Handed*, p. 44, 2003

woollyback breaker *noun*
a citizens' band radio user from north Wales *UK*
Citizens' band radio slang **BREAKER** (a citizens' band user) with an allusion to sheep.
- — Peter Chippindale, *The British CB Book*, p. 160, 1981

woolly mitten *noun*
a kitten *UK*
Rhyming slang.
- [A]s weak as a woolly mitten[.] — Ray Puxley, *Fresh Rabbit*, 1998

woolly nose *noun*
a railway fettler *AUSTRALIA*
- Unofficially they are known as Snake Charmers (W.A.), Hairy Legs (N.S.W.), Woolly Noses (S.A.), navvies everywhere. — Patsy Adam-Smith, *Folklore of the Australian Railwaymen*, p. 254, 1969

woolly-pully *noun*
a military-issue heavy jumper *UK, 1984*
A customised 'woollen pullover'.
- a member of UNFICY P, Cyprus, January 1975 wears a woolly-pully with 'Royal Marine Command' titles — Nick Van Der Bijl, *The Royal Marines 1939–1993*, p. 60, 1995
- He shucked his coat and tie, then pulled on a large olive drab Marine Corps woolly pully sweater. — P.T. Deutermann, *Sweepers*, p. 251, 1997

woolly vest *noun*
a pest *UK*
Rhyming slang.
- It's a woolly vest when you have a sneezing attack on a Monday instead of achoosday. — Ray Puxley, *Fresh Rabbit*, 1998

woolly woofter; woolly *noun*
a male homosexual *AUSTRALIA, 1988*
Rhyming slang.
- By the time Fat Man Two composed himself enough to demand, 'Where the fuck did that go?' all he really wanted to do – inexplicably, because he was no woolly woofter, no siree, he was a *real* man – was dive into One's daks and worship thoroughly what he found there. — Linda Jaivin, *Rock n Roll Babes from Outer Space*, p. 94, 1996
- — Ray Puxley, *Fresh Rabbit*, 1998

Woolwich and Greenwich *noun*
spinach *UK*
Rhyming slang, formed from two London locations for crossing over the Thames.
- — Julian Franklyn, *A Dictionary of Rhyming Slang*, 1961

Woolwich Ferry *noun*
sherry *UK*
Rhyming slang, formed from a transport across the Thames.
- — Ray Puxley, *Cockney Rabbit*, 1992

Woolworth *noun*
in hold 'em poker, a five and a ten as the first two cards dealt to a player *US, 1981*
Woolworth's was the most famous five and dime store in the US.
- — Thomas L. Clark, *The Dictionary of Gambling and Gaming*, p. 252, 1987

Woolworth's finest *noun*
in shuffleboard, a ten *US*
- — Omero C. Catan, *Secrets of Shuffleboard Strategy*, p. 74, 1967: 'Glossary of terms'

wooly bear *noun*
in caving and pot-holing, a fibre-pile undersuit *US*
- — *Cavers' Digest Electronic Mailing List*, 3rd December 1997

wooly blunt; woolly blunt *noun*
a marijuana and crack cocaine cigarette *UK*
- — Mike Haskins, *Drugs*, p. 293, 2003

woop *noun*
▷ see: **WHOOP**

Woop Woop *noun*
an imaginary remote place *AUSTRALIA, 1918*
- Jeez, no lady, we're way out to Woop Woop here. — Barry Humphries, *The Wonderful World of Barry McKenzie*, p. 37, 1968
- It's not out at woop woop, but right here in marvellous Melbourne. — *Australian Ultimate*, p. 7, 2003

wooshed up *adjective*
having been whisked to a froth (as of a milkshake); figuratively of anything having been subjected to random inflation (see citation) *UK*
- [A]ll that teased hair wooshed up like pineapples[.] — P-P Hartnett, *Sad Cunt*, p. 99, 1999

wooter *noun*
the penis *US*
- — *Maledicta*, p. 255, Summer/Winter 1981: 'Five years and 121 dirty words later'

wooz *noun*
marijuana *UK*
From **WOOZY** (intoxicated).
- — Mike Haskins, *Drugs*, p. 289, 2003

wooziness *noun*
a fuddled state, muzziness; often used to describe a morning-after-the-night-before feeling *US, 1977*
- This is going to sound incredibly pretentious, but its wooziness is, like, palpable. — *Uncut*, p. 38, July 2001

woozy *adjective*
unsteady; dizzy; disoriented; intoxicated with drugs or drink *US, 1897*
Anglicised by Conan Doyle in 1917.
- It depends upon how woozy Mr. Bank is, and how bad his signature is on one or more of the checks, how many times he is requested to write another chit. — Robert Sylvester, *No Cover Charge*, p. 210, 1956
- I was a little woozy and needed sugar[.] — Jack Kerouac, *The Dharma Bums*, p. 167, 1958
- She arched her back a trifle, and, with her mouth a trifle open, she put her hand on top of her head. "I feel so woozy and funny." — J.D. Salinger, *Franny and Zooey*, p. 29, 1961
- I am by now halfway between hallucination and coma, and somewhat woozy, as though I've gone too long without food. — Philip Roth, *Portnoy's Complaint*, p. 193, 1969
- He was boozy and woozy and full of self-pity[.] — Joseph Wambaugh, *Finnegan's Week*, p. 233, 1993

wop *noun*
an Italian immigrant or Italian-American *US, 1914*
- [B]ut under Louie the Wop's auspices they were treated to jam sessions night after night[.] — Mezz Mezzrow, *Really the Blues*, p. 92–93, 1946
- Then the stockboy – a hot-looking wop with long hair – took me out in his department to show me the new materials – and the place was deserted. — Philip Wylie, *Opus 21*, p. 298, 1949
- She's just a stupid wop, and so you only take her to the subway, eh? — John Clellon Holmes, *Go*, p. 88, 1952
- PEPE: Micks! INDIO: Wop! — Stephen Sondheim, *West Side Story*, 1957
- Chicago: invisible hierarchy of decorticated wops, small of atrophied gangsters, earthbound ghost hits you at North and Halstead, Cicero, Lincoln Park, panhandler of dreams[.] — William Burroughs, *Naked Lunch*, p. 11, 1957
- Eventually I relinquished presidency of the Knights to a fat loquacious slob named Richard who led us one night into a riot with the wops from east of Sacramento Boulevard. — Clancy Sigal, *Going Away*, p. 351, 1961
- Can't cop till I see the wops tomorrow. — Nathan Heard, *Howard Street*, p. 48, 1968
- Let the boogies and wops kill each other, Cockroach once told him. — Gilbert Sorrentino, *Steelwork*, p. 15, 1970
- Lemme tell you about them rumbles. The wops said no spics could go east of Park Avenue. — Edwin Torres, *Carlito's Way*, p. 8, 1975

▸ **up the wop**

1 pregnant *NEW ZEALAND, 1981*
- — Harry Orsman, *A Dictionary of Modern New Zealand Slang*, p. 150, 1999

2 broken; unsound *NEW ZEALAND*
- The next thing Mr. Cooper assesses is participants' seating positions – half are declared 'up the wop' and remedied. — *Dominion*, p. 10, 1st September 2001

wop *adjective*
Italian *US*
- "He's into weight-lifting and wop haberdashery," Endicott said. — Bernard Wolfe, *The Magic of Their Singing*, p. 15, 1961

• Is that the new car out there? The little red Wop job? — *The Graduate*, 1967

wopcacker *noun*

a superlative example of something *AUSTRALIA, 1941*

• 'Yeah,' Joe agreed, 'once killed a wopcacker of a tiger-snake just with me army boots.' — Dymphna Cusack, *Picnic Races*, p. 102, 1962

wop-jawed *adjective*

in circus and carnival usage, amazed by an act or demonstration *US*

• — Don Wilmeth, *The Language of American Popular Entertainment*, p. 294, 1981

wop-wops *noun*

remote back country *NEW ZEALAND*

• — Louis S. Leland, *A Personal Kiwi-Yankee Dictionary*, p. 114, 1984

word *noun*

▸ **get a word in edgeways**

to contribute to a conversation *UK, 1984*

Generally in a negative form.

• [Y]ou wonder if he will let his fellow panellists [...] get a word in edgeways. — *The Guardian*, 6th February 2004

▸ **put the word on**

to proposition someone *AUSTRALIA, 1975*

• The plan was for Zoe to finally put the word on Michael during a big night on the town. — John Birmingham, *He Died With a Felafel in his Hand*, p. 29, 1994

▸ **take the word**

in the illegal production of alcohol, to warn someone about a pending law enforcement raid *US*

• Yeah, he took the word, else they'd got ketched Friday. — David W. Maurer, *Kentucky Moonshine*, p. 126, 1974

▸ **the word**

1 gossip, rumours *US*

• Milt came by with a rumor about a package delivery. Milt always had what the Marines called "the word" – the latest rumor. — Russell Davis, *Marine at War*, p. 119, 1961

2 an order *US*

• — *American Speech*, p. 288, December 1962: 'Marine Corps slang'

word *verb*

to speak to someone *AUSTRALIA, 1905*

• BILLO: 'Wot's this mean, "She spoke to him tartly"?' MICKO: 'You know how tarts word a bloke, don't yer?' — Norman Lindsay, *Comic Art of Norman Lindsay*, p. 200, 1915

• — Erle Cox, *Out of the Silence*, p. 252, 1925

• — Leonard Mann, *Flesh in Armour*, p. 164, 1932

• Can't pass a nice girl without wording her[.] — Norman Lindsay, *The Cousin fron Fiji*, p. 66, 1945

word!

used for expressing assent *US*

• — Connie Eble (Editor), *UNC-CH Campus Slang*, p. 8, Spring 1987

• But now, word! Hey, I be selling thirty-forty caps in a few minutes. — Terry Williams, *The Cocaine Kids*, p. 57, 1989

• "I get myself shot, I want it be in the arm, Gor-DEN!" "Word!" agreed Rac. — Jess Mowry, *Way Past Cool*, p. 6, 1992

• "Word" was once a powerful affirmation that you were "dropping science" [making sense][.] — Nelson George, *Hip Hop America*, p. 209, 1998

word in your shell-like *noun*

a brief and discreet (one-sided) conversation *UK, 1985*

A variation of 'word in your ear'; 'shell-like', which does not appear outside of this phrase until later, derives from a similarity of shape between the ear and some (delicate, pink) shells.

• Yo Caleb! A word in your shell-like. I heard your missus and some other dude had their sounds nicked the other day. — Jack Allen, *When the Whistle Blows*, p. 77, 2000

• Rudolph has a word in his shell-like, presumably along the lines of "Do that again and you'll be batting without a box in the next innings." — *The Guardian*, 22nd August 2003

words *noun*

a quarrel (of violent words not actions) *UK, 1862*

A refinement of a sense that has served since 1462.

• She [Joan Littlewood]'d got a tongue on her, yeah. We had words quite a lot. — *The Guardian*, 7th December 2001

word up *verb*

to speak to someone in a flattering manner *AUSTRALIA*

• Word up a bird on the plane, and with any luck, give her a quick knee-trembler in one of the throttling pits. — Barry Humphries, *The Traveller's Tool*, p. 35, 1985

word up

1 used for expressing agreement *US*

• — Connie Eble (Editor), *UNC-CH Campus Slang*, p. 6, October 1986

• Rac nodded. "Word up! By rules!" — Jess Mowry, *Way Past Cool*, p. 13, 1992

2 used as a greeting *US*

Used in the hip-hop community.

• [A] Tokyo teenager greets me with "Word up, dog"[.] — Patrick Neate, *Where You're At*, p. 6, 2003

work *noun*

1 the betting slips in an illegal lottery or gambling operation *US*

• Another common method of scoring numbers operators consisted of policemen confiscating the gambler's numbers slips, which are known as "work." — *The Knapp Commission Report on Police Corruption*, p. 84, 1972

• [N]ext in the intricately structured racket is the pickup man, who brings the "work" – the betting slips – from various collectors to a controller. — Peter Maas, *Serpico*, p. 164, 1973

• He said all the things that a bookmaker, grabbed with the"works" on his person, might very well say. — Leonard Shecter and William Phillips, *On the Pad*, p. 120, 1973

2 cheating in gambling, especially in craps *US*

The statement 'There's work down' means that altered dice or cards are in play.

• — *The Annals of the American Academy of Political and Social Sciences*, p. 133, May 1950

3 dice or cards that have been altered for the purpose of cheating *US*

• — John S. Salak, *Dictionary of Gambling*, p. 278, 1963

4 crack cocaine *US*

• A dealer on the street might chant, "Hey, hey, want some work?" — Geoffrey Froner, *Digging for Diamonds*, p. 66, 1989

5 sex *US*

• — Lawrence Lipton, *The Holy Barbarians*, p. 318, 1959

▸ **do the work on**

to kill someone *US*

• So if he did the work on the plumber he would be sending the only woman he had ever really loved to a boneyard. — Richard Condon, *Prizzi's Money*, p. 90, 1994

▸ **have your work cut out; have your work cut out for you; have all your work cut out**

to have enough, or all you can manage, to do – anything more would be too much *UK, 1856*

From an earlier sense (to have your work prepared for you).

• [H]e had his work cut out for him over the next four weeks. — Don Greene, *Fight You Fear and Win*, p. 35, 2001

work *verb*

1 to cheat at gambling *US*

• One day he sat in with us and I caught him working and cut him loose. — Mickey Spillane, *Me, Hood!*, p. 30, 1963

2 to have sex with someone *US*

• Finally he came out with it: he wanted me to work Marylou. I didn't ask him why because I knew he wanted to see what Marylou was like with another man. — Jack Kerouac, *On the Road*, p. 131, 1957

3 to sell drugs *US*

• That holdup occurred shortly after 9:10 p.m. on Passaic Street, when Miller allegedly approached an Aspen Place man and asked if he was "working," the street slang for dealing drugs, police said. — *Record (Bergen County, New Jersey)*, p. A4, 13th November 1993

4 to dilute a powdered drug *US*

• Masterrape and me played with that package forever, we worked it to death [cut it as far as they could]. — Terry Williams, *The Cocaine Kids*, p. 37, 1989

▸ **to get worked**

to be knocked from your surfboard and pummelled by the ocean *US*

• — Mitch McKissick, *Surf Lingo*, 1987

▸ **work a ginger**

(of a prostitute) to rob a client *AUSTRALIA*

From **GINGER**.

• — Sidney J. Baker, *Australia Speaks*, 1953

▸ **work for Standard Oil**

to drive a truck that burns excessive amounts of fuel or oil *US*

• — Montie Tak, *Truck Talk*, p. 190, 1971

▸ **work like a charm**
to achieve a purpose with absolute ease *UK, 1882*
From the idea of a magic charm influencing the action.
• I started drinking vodka, trying to get up the nerve to go to Jamaica for a reggae festival. Worked like a charm, too, and worth a little headache the first day out and the first day back. —Pearl Cleage, *What Looks Like Crazy On An Ordinary Day*, p. 4, 1997

▸ **work like a nigger**
to work very hard *US, 1836*
Praise and contempt in equal parts.
• "You've got to work like bleeding niggers." "Thanks," said one of the young blacks. "No disrespect," said Arthur hastily. "That's a figure of speech, innit." —Anthony Masters, *Minder*, p. 34, 1984

▸ **work the cuts**
(used of a prostitute) to solicit customers on the streets *US*
• —*Maledicta*, p. 150, Summer/Winter 1986–1987: 'Sexual slang: prostitutes, pedophiles, flagellators, transvestites, and necrophiles'

▸ **work the glory rode**
to affect religious conversion while in prison in the hope of receiving an early parol *US*
• —John R. Armore and Joseph D. Wolfe, *Dictionary of Desperation*, p. 57, 1976

▸ **work the hole**
to rob drunks sleeping on underground platforms or in the carriages *US*
• Now he peddled from time to time and "worked the hole" (rolling drunks on subways and in cars) when he couldn't make connections to peddle. —William Burroughs, *Junkie*, p. 40, 1953

▸ **work the kerb**
(of a prostitute) to ply for trade from passing motorists *UK*
• [W]hen Ah was workin' the kerb for Francois[.] —Ben Elton, *High Society*, p. 168, 2002

▸ **work the nuts**
to operate a shell game in a circus midway or carnival *US*
• —Joe McKennon, *Circus Lingo*, p. 65, 1980

▸ **work the other side of the street**
to be on opposing sides of a bipolar situation; to make a living as a criminal *US*
• Well, I been workin' the other side of the street for the law few years. —*48 Hours*, 1982

▸ **work your bollocks off**
to work very hard *UK*
• These guys [...] worked their bollocks off for me. —Duncan MacLaughlin, *The Filth*, p. 115–116, 2002

▸ **work your ticket**
to obtain a discharge from employment on the grounds of physical injury or ill health; originally military but in the prevailing compensation culture applied to any employment situation where benefits of discharge are considerable, and thus fraudulent endeavour is often implied *UK, 1899*
• "This is it – my last day on the job!" Then he was gone. I stared at Jeff. "What's he mean?" "He's working his ticket, son. You'll learn something today." —Duncan MacLaughlin, *The Filth*, p. 62, 2002

workaround *noun*
in computing, a temporary fix of a problem *US*
• —Eric S. Raymond, *The New Hacker's Dictionary*, p. 386, 1991

worker *noun*
1 a professional wrestler who puts on a good performance *US*
• As a matter of fact, I looked forward to the challenge of coming up with a good match with an opponent who was injured – it was one of the signs of a good worker (wrestler). —Mike Foley, *Mankind*, p. 3, 1999
• There's a very small margin of wrestlers that are actually what they call a good worker. There are only a handful of them left that you can go in with night after night. —*Off the Record (TSN)*, 4th April 2000

2 a member of a drug-selling enterprise who sells drugs on the street *US*
• —Mark S. Fleisher, *Beggars & Thieves*, p. 292, 1995: 'Glossary'

3 a gambling cheat *US*
• —Frank Garcia, *Marked Cards and Loaded Dice*, p. 265, 1962

4 in the circus or carnival, a large blown-up balloon shown by the concession selling packages of balloons *US*
• Do not expect to inflate the purchase to more than half the size of the 'worker'. —Joe McKennon, *Circus Lingo*, p. 106, 1980

workie *noun*
a worker *UK*
• The older workies, they'll see it right away. —Kevin Sampson, *Clubland*, p. 122, 2002

working *adjective*
in craps, said of a bet that will be in effect on the next roll *US*
• —N.B. Winkless, *The Gambling Times Guide to Craps*, p. 99, 1981

working boy *noun*
a male prostitute *US*
• [S]he has breasts that are actually quite large, yet, sans bra, they hang, elusive and low, concealed in her oversized T-shirts; thus, she is mistaken constantly for one of the working boys. —Jim Carroll, *Forced Entries*, p. 7, 1987

working class *noun*
a glass *UK*
Rhyming slang.
• —Ray Puxley, *Cockney Rabbit*, 1992

working classes *noun*
spectacles, glasses *UK*
Rhyming slang.
• —Ray Puxley, *Cockney Rabbit*, 1992

working end *noun*
the dangerous end of a tool or weapon *US*
• I submit to you that whoever wrote that memo has never served on the working end of a Soviet-made Cuban M1-A16 Assault Rifle. —*A Few Good Men*, 1992

working fifty *noun*
a large piece of crack cocaine bought at a wholesale price *US*
• At one point, Lewis referred to "a working 50," a term he said referred to buying crack at a wholesale rate. Instead of buying cocaine by the $20 bag, Lewis said, it was possible to spend $50 and get one large rock bigger than an oversized marble[.] —*Washington Post*, p. A1, 21st June 1990

working girl *noun*
a prostitute *US, 1968*
• I could see a girl shopping with curlers in her hair and still tell she was a working girl. —Susan Hall, *Gentleman of Leisure*, p. 4, 1972
• The Vegas term working girl I find a bit snobbish. —Mario Puzo, *Inside Las Vegas*, p. 256, 1977
• Mid Edna's staff of working girls was in a constant state of flux. —Jan Hutson, *The Chicken Ranch*, p. 81, 1980
• "She a working girl?" Rice swallowed a wave of anger. "Yeah. I've heard she's been doing outcall around here[.]" —James Ellroy, *Suicide Hill*, p. 615, 1986
• Don't tell me she's a working girl! —Robert Campbell, *Nibbled to Death by Ducks*, p. 260, 1989
• "Sometimes I feel rode too hard and put up wet," she confided to other working girls. —Seth Morgan, *Homeboy*, p. 4, 1990
• All the men are fascinated by dancers, prostitutes, and models. They are like groupies. They think working girls are the most amazing thing on the planet. —Marilyn Suriani Futterman, *Dancing Naked in the Material World*, 1992

working john *noun*
an honest, hard-working man *US*
• Bums and prostitutes and working johns and loiterers and the night thieves and bindle stiffs and blind beggars and all the flotsam that floated on the edges of the station like dirty scum on bog water were jostling each other[.] —Chester Himes, *A Rage in Harlem*, p. 183, 1957

workingman's weed *noun*
marijuana *UK*
An allusion to the 1970 album 'Workingman's Dead' by the Grateful Dead, a band well known for the use of recreational drugs.
• I have a little buzz on me from some workingman's weed[.] —Stuart Browne, *Dangerous Parking*, p. 112, 2000

working-over *noun*
a beating-up, a thrashing *UK, 1984*
• The allegations included guards beating prisoners and then writing KKK (i.e. Ku Klux Klan) with the inmates blood; the "working over" (beating) of certain prisoners by guards upon the instruction of superior officers[.]" —Amnesty International *The Case of Mumia Abu-Jamal*, p. 48, 2000

working parts *noun*

the genitals *UK*

- [T]wo slappers [sexually available women) came by, hollering and shouting at the boys inside, flashing their arses and working parts. —Andy McNab, *Immediate Action*, p. 32, 1995

working stiff *noun*

a hard-working labourer *US*

- They were of a similar size and build to other "working stiffs" – big, broad-shouldered, loose-jointed and flat-footed. —Chester Himes, *Come Back Charleston Blue*, p. 27, 1966

work is the curse of the drinking classes

a catchphrase that reverses a popular cliché *UK*

Attributed to Oscar Wilde.

- —Hesketh Pearson, *Life of Oscar Wilde*, 1946
- I was beginning to resent the five days when I had to be someplace, dressed just so and taking orders. Work, I had discovered, was the curse of the drinking class. —Russell Means, *Where White Men Fear to Tread*, p. 73, 1995

work out *verb*

to masturbate *US*

- —Gary K. Farlow, *Prison-ese*, p. 81, 2002

work over *verb*

to beat someone up; to thrash someone (both physically and figuratively) *UK, 1927*

- John says that "Timothy was full of anger and he ... worked me over good." —Elan Golomb, *Trapped in the Mirror*, p. 59, 1992
- [Tennis player, Tim] Henman lost the next three games as the Australian worked him over with some thrilling cross-court passes. —*The Observer*, 22nd February 2004

works *noun*

the equipment used to prepare and inject drugs *US, 1934*

- I cooked up a grain and got my works ready to take the shot. —William Burroughs, *Junkie*, p. 38, 1953
- He would have to have a fix soon. He could have that almost anywhere: there were works stashed[.] —Clarence Cooper Jr, *The Scene*, p. 12, 1960
- "You got your works, Joe?" I gave her the spike and dropper. —Alexander Trocchi, *Cain's Book*, p. 243, 1960
- The others couldn't get works. I had to steal my spike out of the hospital. —Jeremy Larner and Ralph Tefferteller, *The Addict in the Street*, p. 37, 1964
- Then James Fox came in and said that he had his works and that he wanted Johnny to straighten him. —Claude Brown, *Manchild in the Promised Land*, p. 118, 1965
- When he awakes in the morning, he reaches instantly for his "works" – eyedropper, needle ("spike," he calls it), and bottle top ("cooker"). —James Mills, *The Panic in Needle Park*, p. 14, 1966
- He's got the works, gives you sweet taste. —Velvet Underground *I'm Waiting for the Man*, 1967
- Here, go cop me three things off Cowboy – I'm goin' on to the room and git my works ready. —Nathan Heard, *Howard Street*, p. 20, 1968
- Meanwhile one of the others had already found our works and the stash of junk[.] —Herbert Huncke, *The Evening Sun Turned Crimson*, p. 40, 1980
- The desk drawers, once filled with school supplies and attendance records, were now used to store community-shared sets of works[.] —Richard Price, *Clockers*, p. 229, 1992
- I sorted myself out with a dig [injection] then washed out my works[.] —Lanre Fehintola, *Charlie Says...*, p. 18, 2000

▸ get on someone's works

to annoy someone *AUSTRALIA*

- 'Well,' Hilda growled, 'if ever a woman got on my works! Who does she think she is, anyway?' —Kylie Tennant, *The Honey Flow*, p. 106, 1956
- —Jim Ramsay, *Cop It Sweet!*, p. 39, 1977

▸ in the works

already in progress, due to happen *CANADA, 1973*

- [A]n al-Qaida attack is in the works. —*The Guardian*, 7th Spetember 2002

▸ the works

the complete treatment *US, 1899*

- And we had a raving great dinner of baked potatoes and porkchops and salad and hot buns and blueberry pie and the works. —Jack Kerouac, *The Dharma Bums*, p. 74, 1958
- [F]antastic or course – about three inches thick, with vast assortments of lunchmeats, lettuce, tomatoes, onions, pickles, mustard, hard-boiled eggs, the works. —Robert Gover, *One Hundred Dollar Misunderstanding*, p. 142, 1961
- So I ducked into a barbershop and ordered the works, shave, shine, shampoo. —Clancy Sigal, *Going Away*, p. 398, 1961
- He ate breakfast. He visited a barber shop, indulged himself in "the works" and went back to his two-room suite. —Jim Thompson, *The Grifters*, p. 117, 1963
- The fuckin works, boy; half a bottle of vodders an a few pipes before I even dragged me arse out of the bed[.] —Niall Griffiths, *Kelly + Victor*, p. 112, 2002

works *adjective*

in motor racing, supported by the car manufacturer *US*

- When Shelby-American, manufacturer of the Cobra, runs one of its own cards in a road race, it's a works entry. —John Lawlor, *How to Talk Car*, p. 117, 1965

works for me!

used for expressing agreement *US*

A signature line of Los Angeles Police Department Detective Sergeant Rick Hunter on the television police drama *Hunter* (NBC, 1984–91). Repeated with referential humour.

world *noun*

▸ the world

during the war in Vietnam, back home, the US, life outside the military *US*

- —*Current Slang*, p. 19, Summer 1970
- Before he joined the Corps, Andrews had a completely safe job in the World. —Charles Anderson, *The Grunts*, p. 31, 1976
- Don't remember a lot about my rehabilitation, but I was sent back to the World before the fall of Saigon. —*Apocalypse Now*, 1979
- Forty-two days, man, and a wakeup and I'm a gone motherfucker. Back to de World! —*Platoon*, 1986
- "Back in the World," they used to say to each other in 'Nam, ... "when I get back out in the World ... I'm gon' do this or that," away from the jungle and the monsoons and everything. —Odie Hawkins, *Amazing Grace*, p. 140, 1993

world of shit *noun*

a very dangerous situation *US*

- Anybody messes around with J.L.'s wife gonna find hisself in a world of shit. —Ken Weaver, *Texas Crude*, p. 136, 1984

worlds *noun*

commerically manufactured cigarettes *US*

- —Charles Shafer, *Folk Speech in Texas Prisons*, p. 217, 1990

worm *noun*

1 a computer program that maliciously duplicates itself repeatedly in a host computer until it clogs and crashes the system *US*

- —Karla Jennings, *The Devouring Fungus: Tales of the Computer Age*, p. 225, 1990
- —Susie Dent, *The Language Report*, p. 32, 2003

2 a coiled condenser used in the illegal production of alcohol *US*

- —David W. Maurer, *Kentucky Moonshine*, p. 127, 1974

3 a facial blemish *BARBADOS*

- —Frank A. Collymore, *Barbadian Dialect*, p. 121, 1965

4 phencyclidine, the recreational drug known as PCP or angel dust *US*

- —Ronald Linder, *PCP*, p. 10, 1981

5 an inexperienced oil field worker *US*

- —Ken Weaver, *Texas Crude*, p. 94, 1984

▸ wet down the worm

to perfom oral sex on a man *US*

- Another way to say "fellatio" [...] Wetting down the worm[.] —Erica Orloff and JoAnn Baker, *Dirty Little Secrets*, p. 83, 2001

worm and snail; worm *noun*

a finger*nail* *UK*

Rhyming slang.

- —Ray Puxley, *Cockney Rabbit*, 1992

worm dirt *noun*

chewing tobacco *US*

An obvious visual comparison.

- —Don R. McCreary (Editor), *Dawg Speak*, 2001

worms *noun*

▸ are you keeping it for the worms?; are you saving it for the worms?

said, probably in frustration, to a female rejecting sexual advances or to one who is presumed to be a virgin *US, 1977*

'It' being a state of virginity, 'the worms' signifying death.

Wormtown *nickname*

Worcester, Massachusetts *US*

- —Jim Crotty, *How to Talk American*, p. 30, 1997

wormy *adjective*

nervous or anxious, especially when manifested in the stomach *NORFOLK ISLAND*

- —Beryl Nobbs Palmer, *A Dictionary of Norfolk Words and Usages*, p. 50, 1992

worra laff!

what a laugh! *UK*

A phonetic slovening, probably of Liverpool origins.

- Fucked up in gutters, unpeeled from lampposts after drink-driving or their wives kicked to fuck when they get home sodden drunk. Worra laff! —John Robb, *The Nineties*, p. 57, 1999

worry *verb*

1 to steal something *CAYMAN ISLANDS*

- —Aarona Booker Kohlman, *Wotcha Say*, p. 28, 1985

2 (said of a jockey in horse racing) to ride a horse *US*

- —David W. Maurer, *Argot of the Racetrack*, p. 70, 1951

worse for wear *adjective*

1 somewhat drunk *UK*

2 hung over

- [T]he 28-year-old new Yorker hides behind her Gucci shades and complains about being a little the worse for wear as she orders her first coffee of the day. — *The Times Magazine*, p. 43, 16th February 2002

worse luck!

more's the pity! *UK, 1861*

- [N]o-one from the Premiership's going to tempt him away – worse luck – so it'll be another season of scrapping for survival. — *The Guardian*, 14th August 2003

worth *adjective*

▸ **not worth two cents to jingle on a tombstone**

of a person, without any redeeming qualities *CANADA, 1988*

- [On Nova Scotia's South Shore they say] "someone is not worth two cents to jingle on a tombstone." —Harry Bruce, *Down Home*, p. 108–109, 1988

▸ **worth a few bob; worth a bob or two**

of people, fairly wealthy; of things, fairly valuable *UK, 1981*

From **BOB** (a shilling, now equivalent to 5p but not of equal value).

- You didn't have to wrestle with decimalisaton a few years later – come to that, you probably still think in proper money. Bet you a tanner you're still worth a few bob, eh? — *The Guardian*, 3rd May 2001
- In fact, it is probably best not to touch them at all as they could very well become worth a bob or two. — *Manchester Metro News*, 19th April 2002

wossface *noun*

a person whose name is unknown, forgotten, to be avoided, or hardly worth mentioning *UK*

A slurring of **WHAT'S-HIS-FACE**.

- [T]he comparitive genius of Lita Ford and wossface out of Bis. —*Q*, p. 8, December 2001

wossie *noun*

▷ see: **WUSSIE**

wot *pronoun*

what *UK, 1829*

- The punk raised his head and blinked his eyes. "Wot?" —Donald Gorgon, *Cop Killer*, p. 67, 1994
- Wot about all them nits? —Andrea Ashworth, *Moretti's Super-Swirl*, p. 77, 1999

wotcher; watcha; what yer

used as a greeting *UK*

Elision of the C16 greeting 'what cheer'. Stereotypically Cockney but in wider use. The earliest recorded use is '"Wot cher!" all the neighbours cried, / "Who're yer goin' to meet, Bill? Have you bought the street, Bill?"' (Albert Chevalier, 'Wot Cher!' or 'Knocked 'em in the Old Kent Road', 1891).

- "What yer, cul", he said[.] —Butch Reynolds, *Broken Hearted Clown*, p. 28, 1953
- RHONDA: Hullo, dear. Wotcher, mate. —Peter Nichols, *Promenade [Six Granada Plays]*, p. 60, 1959
- Wotcher, Blackie. Fill her up, would you? —Derek Bickerton, *Payroll*, p. 13, 1959
- Watcha Bex, how's tricks? —Danny King, *The Burglar Diaries*, p. 106, 2001

wot no...?

used humorously for registering an absence or a shortage *UK, 1945*

A misspelling of 'what' provides this endlessly variable graffiti catchphrase, presented in a speech-bubble, or as a caption to a drawing of Chad, or Mr Chad looking over a wall, this used to highlight or protest another World War 2 shortage. The formula has lingered in speech but Chad slowly faded from view.

- Wot, no titties? —Andrea Ashworth, *Once in a House on Fire*, p. 126, 1998
- I can see some surprising gaps. Wot, no dianthus? —James Fenton, *A Garden from a Hundred Packets of Seed*, p. 87, 2001

wotsit *noun*

an unnamed thing *UK*

Reduction of the phrase 'what is it?', usually seen as **WHATSIT**, this variation is possibly inspired by Golden Wonder's Wotsits™, a popular cheesy flavour snack.

- He's got a brilliant sense of humour, as well as being built like a brick wotsit. —Colin Butts, *Is Harry on the Boat?*, p. 5, 1997

wotsit in a sock *noun*

the penis *UK*

A specific variation of **WHATSIT** (an unspecified object).

wouldn't it?

used for expressing exasperation *AUSTRALIA, 1940*

Elliptical for such phrases as 'wouldn't it make you sick', though mostly euphemistically so for such phrases containing profanity, such as 'wouldn't it give you the shits' or 'wouldn't it root you'.

- Wouldn't ut! Just our bloody luck! —Nino Culotta (John O'Grady), *They're A Weird Mob*, p. 143, 1957
- Wouldn't it! I'm not in the mood now...fair dinkum you bastards are worse than a dose of arrowroot! —Barry Humphries, *The Wonderful World of Barry McKenzie*, p. 17, 1968

wouldn't it rip you?

used for expressing exasperation *AUSTRALIA, 1941*

- Everyone gaped at him. 'What's wrong with this galah?' asked somebody and another said, 'Well wouldn't it rip you?' —Lawson Glassop, *We Were The Rats*, p. 74, 1944

wouldn't it root you?

used for expressing exasperation *AUSTRALIA, 1945*

Also **WOULDN'T IT RIP/ROTATE YOU?**, both of which are presumably euphemisms for the 'root' form, even though the earliest recorded form is 'rip' (1941, *Australian National Dictionary*). Also, 'wouldn't it root your boot'.

- We haven't got enough for pork crackling; wouldn't it root your boot. —Barry Dickins, *What the Dickins*, p. 1, 1985

wouldn't it rotate you?

used for expressing exasperation *AUSTRALIA*

Euphemistic for **WOULDN'T IT ROOT YOU?**.

- 'Well wouldn't it rotate you?' said Eddie as we lugged our heavy equipment down to the train. —Lawson Glassop, *We Were The Rats*, p. 135, 1944

wouldn't it rot your socks?

used for expressing exasperation *AUSTRALIA*

- His wife, Tamara, is fond of saying, 'Wouldn't it rot your socks.' —Nancy Keesing, *Lily on the Dustbin*, p. 129, 1982

wouldn't say no

used for registering acceptance of something, sometimes as a suggestion that something would be accepted if it were offered *UK, 1939*

- As far as making my work easier, I wouldn't say no to a butler. — *The Guardian*, 6th July 2002

wouldn't work in an iron lung

to be extremely lazy *AUSTRALIA*

- Even the most primitive societies protect, succor and shelter the aged, but not so the affluent society with the principle of he that cannot work neither shall he eat (except Silver Tails who wouldn't work in an iron lung). —Frank Hardy, *The Outcasts of Foolgarah*, p. 79, 1971
- Sometimes I work a twenty-four, twenty-five even a twenty-six hour day, but try telling that to a Pom who wouldn't work in an iron lung! —Barry Humphries, *The Traveller's Tool*, p. 42, 1985

would you believe....?

used for humorously probing for a statement that can be believed *US*

The signature line of spy Maxwell Smart, played by Don Adams, on the television comedy *Get Smart* (1965–70). Adams had used the line earlier on *The Bill Dana Show* (NBC, 1963–65). Repeated with referential humour.

wounded soldier *noun*

a bottle or can of beer that has been partly consumed *US*

Playing on **DEAD SOLDIER** as 'an empty bottle'.

- —Connie Eble (Editor), *UNC-CH Campus Slang*, p. 6, Fall 1991

wound up *adjective*

angry, annoyed *UK*

The image is of a clock's mainspring wound too tight and ready to lose control.

- I'm a hothead. I get wound up too easy as it is, to be fair[.] — Kevin Sampson, *Outlaws*, p. 2, 2001

wow *noun*

1 a thing of wonder; a sensational success *US, 1920*

From the exclamation 'wow!'.

- In the last-named town the Owl Club had 400 playing poker, blackjack, craps and slot machines. Calumet City, to "Confidential" reporters, was a wow. — Jack Lait and Lee Mortimer, *Chicago Confidential*, p. 97, 1950
- Georgie was the natural born leader who would have been a wow on the barricades[.] — John Peter Jones, *Feather Pluckers*, p. 143, 1964
- The bastard was a wow with the women[.] — Duncan MacLaughlin, *The Filth*, p. 50, 2002

2 an exclamation mark (!) *US*

- — Guy L. Steele et al., *The Hacker's Dictionary*, p. 133, 1983

Wow *nickname*

the psychiatric hospital in Auckland *NEW ZEALAND*

The hospital is near the Whau River.

- — David McGill, *David McGill's Complete Kiwi Slang Dictionary*, p. 125, 1998

wowser *noun*

a spoilsport of the worst kind; a moral crusader; a prude *AUSTRALIA, 1900*

Claimed by John Norton, editor of the Sydney *Truth* (1891 – 1916) as his own coinage and an acronym from the phrase '*we only want social evils remedied*', a supposed catchcry of 'the wowsers'. This story has sadly never been corroborated, and its derivation must be sought elsewhere. The *Australian National Dictionary* suggests British dialect *wow* (to howl or bark as a dog, to complain), which seems to fit well, but one correspondent to the *Truth* in 1910, after denying the word as Norton's invention, goes on to say 'a false sense of public decency forbids the publication of the derivation and true meaning', which suggests some profane origin.

- Ah, it's not th' min that's afraid. It's th' dirty wowsers that never takes a drink that's afraid. — Ernest O'Ferrall, *Stories by 'Kodak'*, p. 33, 1933
- 'What are wowsers?' 'Blokes that don' drink.' — Nino Culotta (John O'Grady), *They're A Weird Mob*, p. 50, 1957
- He wasn't ashamed of the money his family had made from their chain of hotels even if there were a lot of wowsers always howling about it being illegal to hold more than one licence. — Dymphna Cusack, *Picnic Races*, p. 31, 1962
- 'Boxing. Yeah, I know a bit.' 'You know there's an inquiry going on at the moment?' 'Fuckin' wowsers and poofters!' — Peter Corris, *Make Me Rich*, p. 105, 1985
- This is an extension of that wonderful exhibition, Forbidden Love, Bold Passion, exploring 90 years of the lesbian underground, that has been touring Australia to accolades from us and puny attempts at censorship from the Wowser Brigade. — *Lesbians on the Loose*, p. 41, 1997
- This made Herodias as mad as a cut snake and she wanted John knocked off. But Herod was nervous because, although John was a wowser, he was a good bloke. — Kel Richards, *The Aussie Bible*, p. 39, 2003

wowserish *adjective*

prudish; puritanical *AUSTRALIA, 1906*

- There were tubs full of crushed ice and bottles of beer on the back veranda. My rather wowserish uncle and aunt had done the right thing by everyone. — Gerald Murnane, *Landscape with Landscape*, p. 200, 1987
- — Ignatius Jones, *The 1992 True Hip Manual*, p. 111, 1992

wowserism *noun*

the characteristic behaviour of a wowser; prudishness *AUSTRALIA, 1904*

- — Norman Lindsay, *Halfway to Anywhere*, p. 191, 1947
- — Norman Lindsay, *Bohemians at the Bulletin*, p. 15, 1965
- St John Baptist Vianney, who was canonised for his extreme wowserism — Ignatius Jones, *The 1992 True Hip Manual*, p. 143, 1992

wowseristic *adjective*

prudish; puritanical *AUSTRALIA, 1907*

- [A] lot of wowseristic Bible-thumping Boer farmers were only obstructing a Roman occupation of the earth's surface. — Norman Lindsay, *Bohemians at the Bulletin*, p. 17, 1965
- — Bill Hornadge, *The Ugly Australian*, p. 164, 1975

woz

was *UK, 1984*

A deliberate misspelling, especially in graffiti.

- They might as well have sprayed "Baboons Woz 'Ere" on the walls. — *The Guardian*, 15th May 2002

woza *noun*

a person who used to be successful or well known *UK*

From 'was a'.

- Everyone in the Ned was either a face, a player, a wannabe or a woza[.] — Garry Bushell, *The Face*, p. 33, 2001

wozzed *adjective*

exhausted *NEW ZEALAND*

- — David McGill, *David McGill's Complete Kiwi Slang Dictionary*, p. 139, 1998

wrap *noun*

1 a small paper-wrapping containing powdered drugs *UK*

- I stayed up all the night before, boshed two wraps, had a line [of cocaine] before going in. — Macfarlane, Macfarlane and Robson, *The User*, p. 91 – 92, 1996
- Eight years for selling some wraps in a pub. — Dave Courtney, *Raving Lunacy*, p. 6, 1998
- She wants a wrap, on credit. Can you sort it? — Lanre Fehintola, *Charlie Says...*, p. 8, 2000

2 a wrapped roll of coins *US, 1977*

- — Thomas L. Clark, *The Dictionary of Gambling and Gaming*, p. 253, 1987

3 the end of a session *US*

Originally from the entertainment industry, extended to general situations.

- — Dan Jenkins, *Semi-Tough*, p. 55, 1972

4 praise; a compliment or commendation *AUSTRALIA, 1939*

Variants include 'wrap-up', 'rap' and 'rap-up'.

- It gets my goat when I see the newspapers giving the coppers the big wrap-up. — George Blaikie, *Remember Smith's Weekly?*, p. 218, 1950
- — Jim Ramsay, *Cop It Sweet!*, p. 97, 1977
- Mr Ahearn thought so, saying in several interviews that Darby was the greatest rider he had seen. That was a tremendous 'wrap' as Mr Ahearn saw dozens of very good riders in his lifetime. — Roy Higgins and Tom Prior, *The Jockey Who Laughed*, p. 18, 1982

wrap; wrap up *verb*

to roll a marijuana cigarette *UK*

- [He] started to wrap a one-skinner[.] — Kevin Sampson, *Powder*, p. 31, 1999
- I told him to wrap one up. — Wayne Anthony, *Spanish Highs*, p. 110, 1999

▸ **wrap round; wrap around**

to crash a vehicle into an immovable object *UK, 1950*

- an old American convertible, wrapped around a tree — *Wanstead and Woodford Guardian*, 31st October 2002

▸ **wrap yourself around**

to eat or consume something *AUSTRALIA, 1965*

- — John Wynnum, *Jiggin' in the Riggin'*, p. 36, 1965
- Once you've wrapped yourself around a few ice colds you'll feel as though all your birthdays have come at once! — Barry Humphries, *The Wonderful World of Barry McKenzie*, p. 28, 1968
- 'Gawd,' Tom groaned, as he deeply inhaled. 'Let's get inside and wrap ourselves around these. I could eat the meat off a horse.' — Geoff Wyatt, *Saltwater Saints*, p. 28, 1969

wrap-head *noun*

a follower of the Pocomania Afro-Christian religion *JAMAICA, 1987*

- — Peter Patrick, *Some Recent Jamaican Creole Words*, 2003

wrapped; wrapped up *adjective*

pleased; overjoyed; enamoured *AUSTRALIA, 1963*

- He was real wrapped up in Paris, all right. — Frank Hardy, *The Yarns of Billy Borker*, p. 26, 1965
- I'm wrapped in good horses[.] — Sam Weller, *Old Bastards I Have Met*, p. 133, 1979
- — Kathy Lette, *Girls' Night Out*, p. 126, 1987
- Never seen him as wrapped in any other sheila as he was in her. — Clive Galea, *Slipper*, p. 140, 1988

wrapper *noun*

1 a motor vehicle *US*

Citizens' band radio slang.

- — *Complete CB Slang Dictionary*, p. 97, 1976
- What's your wrapper? — Peter Chippindale, *The British CB Book*, p. 161, 1981

2 an unmarked police vehicle *US*

Originally citizens' band radio slang. Variants include 'plain wrapper' and 'plain wrap'.

- — *Complete CB Slang Dictionary*, p. 74, 1976

- —Peter Chippindale, *The British CB Book*, p. 157, 1981
- Back in 1997, Chief Willy Williams had started making sergeants drive them instead of the preferred plainwraps.—Stephen J. Cannell, *The Tin Collectors*, p. 37, 2001

▸ in the wrapper

1 drunk *US*
- Sitting there half in the wrapper, on the outs with my good wife[.] —George V. Higgins, *Penance for Jerry Kennedy*, p. 128, 1985

2 in bed *US*
- —Anna Scotti and Paul Young, *Buzzwords*, p. 68, 1997

wraps *noun*

cigarette wrapping papers *US*
- JAY: A pack of wraps, my good man. It's time to kick back, drink some beer, and smoke some weed.—*Clerks*, 1994

▸ under wraps

kept in secret *UK, 1939*
- In the meantime, it was best to keep everything under wraps. Which was what I was doing down in the basement.—Jeffrey Eugenides, *Middlesex*, p. 330, 2002

wrap-up *noun*

a female sex-partner who, by a vague yet firm understanding, is regularly available *UK*
- I can always accommodate a second wrap-up.—Bill Naughton, *Alfie Darling*, 1970

wrap up *verb*

1 to cease talking; to stop making a noise *UK*
Usually in the imperative, often as a two word exclamation.
- Why don't you [w]rap up you'v[e] got the guts of a slag.—Frank Norman, *Bang To Rights*, p. 50, 1958
- Shut up. I've had just about enough of you and your whining. Now wrap it up!—Clive Exton, *No Fixed Abode [Six Granada Plays]*, p. 138, 1959

2 to complete the final days of a prison sentence *US*
- —John R. Armore and Joseph D. Wolfe, *Dictionary of Desperation*, p. 57, 1976

wreck *verb*

▸ wreck my head

to agitate me to an extreme degree *IRELAND*
- I'm pretty sure I failed all my summer exams again and the idea of having to do first year a third time was SO wrecking my head[.]—Paul Howard, *Ross O'Carroll-Kelly*, p. 75, 2003

wrecked *adjective*

very drunk or drug-intoxicated *US*
- —*Current Slang*, p. 15, Summer 1968
- My friends just got wrecked all the time and complained how dull everything was, which was a major drag.—John Sayles, *Union Dues*, p. 135, 1977
- I had to sit very carefully and quietly and steer very right-down-the-line, because I was really wrecked.—Stephen Gaskin, *Amazing Dope Tales*, p. 76, 1980
- Staying in bed. Watching telly. Going out. Getting wrecked. Eating. —Shaun Ryder, *Shaun Ryder... in His Own Words*, 1997
- "[P]iss artists" are "boozy", "fluffy", "well-gone", "legless", "crocked", wrecked", paralytic", "rat-arsed", "shit-faced" and "arse-holed". —Peter Ackroyd, *London The Biography*, p. 359, 2000
- —Pamela Munro, *U.C.L.A. Slang*, p. 128, 2001

wrecking crew *noun*

1 theatre insiders who watch a show's early performances and spread negative comments about the show *US*
- —Sherman Louis Sergel, *The Language of Show Biz*, p. 247, 1973

2 crack cocaine *UK, 1998*
- —Mike Haskins, *Drugs*, p. 282, 2003

3 on the railways, a relief crew *US*
- —Norman Carlisle, *The Modern Wonder Book of Trains and Railroading*, p. 269, 1946

wren *noun*

a woman *US, 1920*
- —Jack Lait and Lee Mortimer, *New York Confidential*, p. 236, 1948: 'A glossary of Harlemisms'

wrench *noun*

in drag and motor racing, a mechanic *US*
- —Don Alexander, *The Racer's Dictionary*, p. 76, 1980

wrench *verb*

1 to go *US*
- —Connie Eble (Editor), *UNC-CH Campus Slang*, p. 11, October 2002

2 to disrupt or upset someone *US*
- —John R. Armore and Joseph D. Wolfe, *Dictionary of Desperation*, p. 57, 1976

3 in motor racing and hot rodding, to perform mechanical work on a car, whether it literally involves using a wrench or not *US*

wrench artist *noun*

a railway mechanic *US*
- —Ramon Adams, *The Language of the Railroader*, p. 174, 1977

wrencher *noun*

a car enthusiast with considerable mechanical ability *US*
- She's a "wrencher," a car enthusiast who spends her time immersed in the obsessive world of auto mechanics.—*Los Angeles Times*, p. A26, 6th June 2003

wrestle; rassle *verb*

to play a game of bar dice *US*
- —Jester Smith, *Games They Play in San Francisco*, p. 105, 1971

wretch *verb*

to vomit *US*
- —John D. Bell et al., *Loosely Speaking*, p. 22, 1966

wriggle *noun*

▸ get a wriggle on

to hurry *AUSTRALIA*
A variation of **GET A WIGGLE ON**.
- Get a wriggle on darlings. I've got the car waiting.—Barry Humphries, *Bazza Pulls It Off!*, 1971

wriggle out *verb*

to avoid a responsibility or duty *UK, 1848*
- Her stance prompted one MP to claim she was trying to "wriggle out" of her responsibilities.—*The Guardian*, 17th March 2004

wriggly *adjective*

out of the ordinary; suspiciously different *UK*
- The players saw him, must have thought there was something wriggly, went and got their weapons and head-jobbed him.—Andy McNab, *Immediate Action*, p. 281, 1995

wring *verb*

▸ wring out your mule

to urinate *US*
- I gotta ring my mule out.—Paul Glover, *Words from the House of the Dead*, 1974

▸ wring out your sock

to urinate *US*
- "Maybe he's got to wring out his sock," Heath said, showing no interest.—Robert Campbell, *Juice*, p. 255, 1988

▸ wring the rattlesnake

to urinate *AUSTRALIA*
- I just got to nick out to the Gents for a few jiffs to wring the rattlesnake!!!—Barry Humphries, *Bazza Pulls It Off!*, 1971

wringer *noun*

a bankruptcy petition *US*
- —Jerry Robertson, *Oil Slanguage*, p. 53, 1954

wrinkle *noun*

a clever device, trick or method *UK, 1817*
- A clever wrinkle, this undercover business[.]—Charles Portis, *The Dog of the South*, p. 186, 1979

wrinkleneck *noun*

in horse racing, a seasoned and experienced horse handler *US*
- —David W. Maurer, *Argot of the Racetrack*, p. 70, 1951

wrinkle room *noun*

a bar frequented by older homosexual men *US, 1980s*
- —Wayne Dynes, *Homolexis*, p. 140, 1985

wrinkly *noun*

an old person *UK, 1972*
A reference to the wrinkled skin of advanced years. Partridge qualified the definition 'as applied to anyone over the venerable age of thirty'.
- She's a neo-Fascist wrinkly on one big ego-trip.—*Janie Stagestruck*, p. 63, 1972
- —Ann Barr and Peter York, *The Official Sloane Ranger Handbook*, p. 159, 1982
- Wrinklies Direct Names & Faces [an agency for mature performers] has been set up by the Wrinklies Direct Group, a recruitment firm that specialises in older candidates.—*The Stage*, 26th April 2001

wrist *noun*

1 a contemptible person *UK, 1998*
From **WRIST JOB** (an act of masturbation) – or similar term – hence, this is synonymous with **WANKER**.

2 in betting, odds of 5 – 4 *UK*
From the **TICK-TACK** signal used by bookmakers.
- —John McCririck, *John McCririck's World of Betting*, p. 61, 1991

wristers *noun*
in lobstering, knitted gloves with no fingers *US*
- —Kendall Merriam, *The Illustrated Dictionary of Lobstering*, p. 98, 1978

wrist job *noun*
1 an act of masturbation *UK*
Used as a song title by Humble Pie in 1969.
2 used as an all-purpose form of abuse; a substitute form of wanker *UK*
- [S]ome desk-bound wristjob like Harry or me[.]—James Hawes, *Dead Long Enough*, p. 155, 2000

wristy *adjective*
having the characteristics of a masturbator; hence, inferior or unpleasant *UK*
From **WRIST** (a contemptible person).
- [T]hey were Wristy Specky Swots[.]—James Hawes, *Dead Long Enough*, p. 40, 2000

write *verb*
1 to write a prescription for a narcotic which will not be used for medicinal purposes *US*
- There are several varieties of writer croakers. Some will write only if they are convinced you are an addict, others only if they are convinced you are not.—William Burroughs, *Junkie*, p. 33, 1953
- I had some doubts as to my ability to convince the doctors to write. —Herbert Huncke, *Guilty of Everything*, p. 54, 1990

2 to create graffiti art *US*
- —Jim Crotty, *How to Talk American*, p. 143, 1997

▸ **write numbers**
to take bets on an illegal policy game (numbers lottery) *US*
- Then there was boostin' in department stores – and there was dice, cards, writin' numbers (single action) for Jake Cooperman[.]—Edwin Torres, *Carlito's Way*, p. 14, 1975

write-off *noun*
any motor vehicle damaged beyond economic repair; any thing (physical or abstract) or person considered to be beyond saving *UK, 1918*
Originally Royal Air Force slang for 'a wrecked aircraft', now thought of as the language of insurance.
- I did rather re-arrange the geometry on the car, slightly. Bloody write off, really.—Mike Stott, *Soldiers Talking, Cleanly*, 1978

write off *verb*
to destroy something; to damage something beyond repair, generally a vehicle *UK*
From the conventional use 'to write off the value or the investment'.
- Bez wrote three cars off in three weeks. We keep lending him cars, man, and he keeps writing them off.—Shaun Ryder, *Shaun Ryder... in His Own Words*, 1991

writer *noun*
1 a graffiti artist *US*
- —Jim Crotty, *How to Talk American*, p. 143, 1997
- They call themselves writers because their paintings are often manipulations of letters.—*Plain Dealer (Cleveland, Ohio)*, p. L1, 29th July 2001
- Stim One [...] the first writer to die while bombing [graffiti-ing][.]—*The Source*, p. 128, March 2002

2 in a casino, a casino employee who accepts and records bets on Keno *US*
- —John Mechigian, *Encyclopedia of Keno*, p. 112, 1972

▷ **see:** SHEET WRITER

wrong *noun*
in craps, a bet against the shooter *US*
- At the dice table, the professor would bet either on or against the shooter – otherwise known as do or don't, right or wrong – at $1,000 a shot on what may or may not have been a system.—Edward Lin, *Big Julie of Vegas*, p. 47, 1974

wrong *adjective*
known to inform to the police *US*
- By and large, the reason a man can't score is because he is known to be "wrong."—William Burroughs, *Junkie*, p. 52, 1953

wrongle *noun*
in craps, someone who bets against the shooter *US, 1974*
- —Thomas L. Clark, *The Dictionary of Gambling and Gaming*, p. 253, 1987

wrong number *noun*
an untrustworthy person *US*
- [H]e was a wrong number, an informer.—Emmett Grogan, *Ringolevio*, p. 54, 1972

wrong-o *noun*
a bad person *US*
- He drank when and whatever he could, begging, borrowing, wheedling credit. The Doc is a wrong-o, Pepper said, fuck him. —Gilbert Sorrentino, *Steelwork*, p. 156, 1970

wrong side of *noun*
used of an age that is greater than a stated number *UK, 1663*
- The unfortunate thing is he's the wrong side of thirty now. Time is not on his side[.]—*The Observer*, 4th July 2004

wrong time *noun*
a woman's menstrual period *US*
- —*American Speech*, p. 298, December 1954: 'The vernacular of menstruation'

wrong 'un *noun*
1 a lawbreaker; someone on the wrong side of the law *AUSTRALIA*
- The husband was a wrong'un – sly grog, SP, prozzies, you name it. —Peter Corris, *Make Me Rich*, p. 137, 1985
- I've come to call the wrong 'uns to turn away from their wrong-doing and turn back to God.—Kel Richards, *The Aussie Bible*, p. 28, 2003

2 a police informer *UK*
English gypsy use.
- —Jimmy Stockin, *On The Cobbles*, p. 11, 2000

3 in prison, a sex offender or convicted paedophile; an informer *UK*
- —Angela Devlin, *Prison Patter*, p. 23, 1996
- How can I have it with a wrong 'un?—*The Guardian*, 28th September 2000

wrong-way English *noun*
in pool, spin imparted on the cue ball such that the angle of refraction off a cushion is different, if not opposite, of what would be expected *US*
- —Mike Shamos, *The Illustrated Encyclopedia of Billiards*, p. 266, 1993

WS *noun*
a sado-masochist encounter involving enemas or urination *US*
An abbreviation for **WATER SPORTS**.
- —*What Color is Your Handkerchief*, p. 7, 1979

WTF
used in computer message shorthand to mean '*w*hat *t*he *f*uck?' or '*w*ho *t*he *f*uck?' *US*
- —Eric S. Raymond, *The New Hacker's Dictionary*, p. 342, 1991

WUCIWUG
what you see is what you get *UK*
Initialism used for text messaging.
- d:*O WUCIWUG #:-O VTE LBR 2MORO – text message from the Labour Party to mobile phones.—*The Times*, p. 24, 9th June 2001

wudja?
would you? *UK*
Apparently coined by television production company Brighter Pictures but rapidly gained wider use.
- Wudja? Cudja? is due for transmission in July 2002—press release *Carlton Television*, 17th May 2002

wuffo; whuffo *noun*
in the language of hang gliding and parachuting, anyone other than a fellow expert *US*
Purportedly derived from the question, 'Wuffo they do that?'.
- —Dan Poynter, *Parachuting*, p. 170, 1978: 'The language of parachuting'
- —Erik Fair, *California Thrill Sports*, p. 328, 1992

wumpers *noun*
a rubber-soled sandal, especially one made from a car tyre *BAHAMAS*
- —John A. Holm, *Dictionary of Bahamian English*, p. 225, 1982

wunch *noun*
a group of bankers *UK*
Collective noun. A jokey Spoonerism of 'bunch of wankers'.
- —*www.LondonSlang.com*, June 2002

wunzee *verb*
to urinate *TRINIDAD AND TOBAGO*
An evolution of the children's vocabulary of **NUMBER ONE** and **NUMBER TWO**.
• —Lise Winer, *Dictionary of the English/Creole of Trinidad & Tobago*, 2003

wurley *noun*
a hut *AUSTRALIA, 1839*
Originally an Aboriginal dwelling.

wurzel *noun*
a person from the countryside *UK*
Derogatory; most probably from the television series *Wurzel Gummidge*, 1979–81, based on the stories about the 'scarecrow of Scatterbrook' created by Barbara Euphan Todd.
• But then he gets to rowing with Wally. "Do you want some, wurzel?" —Jimmy Stockin, *On The Cobbles*, p. 114, 2000

wuss *noun*
a weak, timid person *US*
A blend of **WIMP** and **PUSSY**, both meaning 'a weak and timid person'.
• You are a wuss. Part wimp. Part pussy. —*Fast Times at Ridgemont High*, 1982
• —*American Speech*, Fall 1990
• After Carol asked Mama, "Whyd' you waste your money on that useless piece of wuss?" my mother wrinkled up her nose, not because she disapproved of the word wuss, but because it was yet another Americanism she didn't understand. —Rita Ciresi, *Pink Slip*, p. 5, 1999
• [I] felt ashamed of myself for being such a little wuss[.] —Claire Mansfield and John Mendelssohn, *Dominatrix*, p. 68, 2002

wussie; wussy; wossie *noun*
a weak, timid, passive person *US*
• With some guys you have to make the first move. A lot of guys are just wussies. —*Fast Times at Ridgemont High*, 1982
• —*American Speech*, Fall 1990
• [S]houting obscenities at the "wossie who wouldn't put his balls where his mouth was". —Wayne Anthony, *Spanish Highs*, p. 81, 1999

wuss out *verb*
to back down; to fail to do as promised *US*
• —Connie Eble (Editor), *UNC-CH Campus Slang*, April 1977

wussy *adjective*
weak, timid, passive *US*
• I figure if I sounded like a wussy momma's boy, he will trust me. —Howard Stern, *Miss America*, p. 83, 1995

wuwoo *noun*
a mixture of marijuana and cocaine; marijuana *UK*
Possibly adapted from a celebratory reaction to the drugs effects.
• —Mike Haskins, *Drugs*, p. 289, 2003

wuzzy *noun*
a female *UK*
A corruption of the French *oiseau*, or **BIRD** (a young woman).
• —Tom Hibbert, *Rockspeak!*, p. 175, 1983

Wyamine *noun*
a Benzedrine™ inhaler *US*
The Wyamine™ inhaler was manufactured by Wyeth Laboratories; it became a generic name for any inhaler with Benzedrine-infused cotton strips, valued by amphetamine users.
• Dope's not always easy. I've even shot Waymine. —Nicholas Von Hoffman, *We Are The People Our Parents Warned Us Against*, p. 223, 1967

Wyatt *nickname*
sometimes applied to a person who burps loudly and for comic effect *UK*
From rhyming slang **WYATT EARP** (a burp).
• —Ray Puxley, *Cockney Rabbit*, 1992

Wyatt Earp *noun*
1 the penis *UK*
Rhyming slang for **CURP** (the penis), formed on the name of the legendary US lawman, 1848–1929, possibly informed by the film myth of Wyatt Earp as a heroic shootist.
• —Red Daniells, 1980

2 a belch *UK*
Rhyming slang for **BURP**, based on the name of legendary US lawman, hero of countless films, Wyatt Earp (1848–1929).
• —Ray Puxley, *Cockney Rabbit*, 1992
• —*www.LondonSlang.com*, June 2002

wyman *noun*
▷ **see: BILL WYMAN**

Wynona Ryder; wynona *noun*
cider *UK*
Rhyming slang, based on popular film actress Wynona Ryder (b.1971).
• Can I have a pinta Wynona and a half a Nelson [Stella Artois lager]? —*www.LondonSlang.com*, June 2002
• —*Antiquarian Book Review*, p. 18, June 2002

wyssa; whizzer; wyzza *noun*
a personal message sent or received in the Antarctic or sub-Antarctic *AUSTRALIA, 1959*
Derives from the Australian Antarctic Division telex code for 'with all my/our love darling'.
• —Bernadette Hince, *The Antarctic Dictionary*, p. 389, 2000

Wythenshawe white man *noun*
a black man with the manners and standards of contemporary white society *UK*
Wythenshawe is a suburb of Manchester.
• Then came the addition of a drummer in the form of a Wythenshawe white man[.] —Tony Wilson, *24 Hour Party People*, p. 77, 2002

Xx

x *noun*

an empty railway wagon *US*

• —Norman Carlisle, *The Modern Wonder Book of Trains and Railroading*, p. 269, 1946

X *noun*

1 MDMA, the recreational drug best known as ecstasy *US*

Generally an abbreviated 'ecstasy' specifically used of any MDMA tablet stamped with a symbol that may be read as an X.

• Party invitations are often superimposed with an "X," a symbol for ecstasy, indicating what will be served or should be taken before arriving. —*New York Times*, p. 58 (Part 2), 11th December 1988
• —Connie Eble (Editor), *UNC-CH Campus Slang*, p. 10, Spring 1992
• X is often described as less distrubingly "trippy" than LSD and more serene than cocaine[.] —*Newsweek*, p. 62, 6th December 1993
• Ive never seen any of them before. Cornballs from Jersey on X. —*Kids*, 1995
• But shes here tonight, and I think if we all begged, or maybe offered her some X, shed get up here and treat us to some of her vocal stylings. —*Chasing Amy*, 1997
• —Harry Shapiro, *Recreational Drugs*, p. 212, 2004

2 marijuana *UK*

• —Mike Haskins, *Drugs*, p. 289, 2003

3 in blackjack, any card worth ten points *US*

A Roman numeral used by card counters.

• —Michael Dalton, *Blackjack*, p. 91, 1991

4 a cross-breed of a dog *CANADA*

• Spot the Malti-poo Terrier X, at Petley Jones Gallery on Granville Street. —Marg Meikle, *Dog City*, 1997

5 a grip on all illegal gambling *US*

• —John Scarne, *Scarne on Dice*, p. 482, 1974

▷ **see:** GENERATION XER

▸ **the X**

in the circus or carnival, exclusive rights for an item or concession *US*

• —Joe McKennon, *Circus Lingo*, p. 108, 1980
• —Gene Sorrows, *All About Carnivals*, p. 27, 1985: 'Terminology'

X *verb*

to take MDMA, the recreational drug best known as ecstasy *US*

• KIDS ASKED EACH OTHER, 'ARE YOU X-ING? —*Life*, p. 88, August 1985
• I think yuppies everywhere will love "X-ing" (taking ecstasy). —*Chicago Tribune*, p. C1, 23rd June 1985

X *adjective*

1 annoyed, irritated, angry *UK*

A pun on 'cross'.

• —Robin Cook, *The Crust on its Uppers*, 1962

2 in drag racing, experimental *US*

The designation FX means an experimental car from a factory; MX means an experimental component from a manufacturer.

• —Ed Radlauer, *Drag Racing Pix Dix*, p. 62, 1970

x-double-minus *adjective*

very bad *US*

Alluding to a non-existent grading scale.

• —*Current Slang*, p. 11, Spring 1968

x-dressing *noun*

cross-dressing *UK*

• WELCOME TO THE WONDERFUL WORLD OF X DRESSING[.] —Caroline Archer, *Tart Cards*, 2003

Xer *noun*

▷ **see:** GENERATION XER

X-Files *noun*

haemorrhoids *UK*

Rhyming slang for 'piles', formed on US television science-fiction/conspiracy drama *The X-Files* first broadcast in 1993.

• —Ray Puxley, *Fresh Rabbit*, 1998

X-Files E *noun*

a tablet of MDMA, the recreational drug best known as ecstasy, branded with a borrowed logo *UK*

After *The X Files*, a cult science fiction televison programme from the mid-1990s, playing on **X (E)**.

• —Angela Devlin, *Prison Patter*, p. 124, 1996
• Ecstasy dealers have taken to branding their tablets with famous logos: there is Big Mac E, Purple Nike Swirl E, X-Files E, and a mixture of uppers and downers called a "Happy Meal". —Naomi Klein, *No Logo*, p. 297, 2001

x-ing *noun*

MDMA, the recreational drug best known as ecstasy *UK, 1998*

• —Mike Haskins, *Drugs*, p. 290, 2003

X marks the spot

used as a caption or legend to a specific location (marked with a cross) on a map or in a photograph *UK, 1968*

Of catchphrase status although rarely spoken. Familiar uses include: the scene of the crime, a hotel window on a postcard and pirate treasure maps.

• 'X' marks the spot for string of robberies. —*St. Petersburg Times (Florida)*, 9th January 2003

Xmas *noun*

Christmas *UK, 1755*

Pronounced 'Exmas'. Originally pronounced as 'Christmas', derived from Greek, the initial letter of *Christos*, yet is generally presumed to be a coinage of modern marketing and, while widely recognised, remains an unconventional usage.

• ELAINE: Excuse me, Im a teacher. There is no word in the English language – "Xmas". Its either "Merry Christmas" or "Happy Holidays". —*Almost Famous*, 2000

X queen *noun*

a homosexual male who is a frequent user of MDMA, the recreational drug best known as ecstasy *US*

• —Kevin Dilallo, *The Unofficial Gay Manual*, p. 246, 1994

x-ray eyes *noun*

the sense of intuition of a poker player who can ascertain the hands held by other players *US*

• —George Percy, *The Language of Poker*, p. 98, 1988

X-row *noun*

the area in a prison housing inmates condemned to death *US*

• —William K. Bentley and James M. Corbett, *Prison Slang*, p. 8, 1992

xs and os *noun*

the basic elements of a plan *US*

From play diagrams in basketball, football or other sports, in which the xs represent the players of one team, and the os represent players of the other.

• His mental xs and ox were settling around backmail, but his eyes kept straying back to the phone. —James Ellroy, *Because the Night*, p. 343, 1984
• Winters always keen on Xs, Os and jumpers [Headline] —*San Francisco Chronicle*, p. C1, 25th December 2001

XTC *noun*

MDMA, the recreational drug best known as ecstasy *US*

Pronounced 'ecstasy'.

• Pamphlets promoting the use of the drug include such titles as "How to Prepare for an Ecstasy Experience," "Flight Instructions for a Friend Using XTC[.]" —*States News Service*, 31st May 1985
• Street names [...] white doves, X, XTC and many others. —James Kay and Julian Cohen, *The Parents' Complete Guide to Young People and Drugs*, p. 136, 1998
• —Mike Haskins, *Drugs*, p. 290, 2003

X vid *noun*

a sexually explicit video *US*

- You and me are sitting side by side on my couch, watching X-vid, not touching. —Nicholson Baker, *Vox*, p. 99, 1992

XX *noun*

a twenty-dollar note *US*

- —Ralph de Sola, *Crime Dictionary*, p. 167, 1982

XY *noun*

a spouse *US*

A mutual abbreviation from **XYL** (a wife) and **XYM** (a husband).

- — *Complete CB Slang Dictionary*, p. 98, 1976

XYL *noun*

a wife *US*

A partial acronym: '*ex-y*oung *l*ady'.

- —Wayne Floyd, *Jasons Authentic Dictionary of CB Slang*, p. 32, 1976
- —Peter Chippindale, *The British CB Book*, p. 160, 1981

XYM *noun*

a husband *US*

A partial acronym: '*ex-y*oung-*m*an'.

- — *Complete CB Slang Dictionary*, p. 98, 1976
- —Peter Chippindale, *The British CB Book*, p. 160, 1981

XYZ *noun*

a citizens' band radio user of undiscovered gender; hence, a homosexual *US*

By extension from **XYL** (a wife) and **XYM** (a husband).

- — *Complete CB Slang Dictionary*, p. 98, 1976
- —Peter Chippindale, *The British CB Book*, p. 160, 1981

XYZ

used to alert someone that their fly zipper is open *US*

A partial acronym: '*ex*amine *y*our *z*ipper.

- —Connie Eble (Editor), *UNC-CH Campus Slang*, p. 14, Fall 1999

Yy

Y *noun*

▸ **the Y**

a premises of the Young Men's Christian Association (YMCA) or Young Women's Christian Association (YWCA); also the YMCA or YWCA organisation *US, 1915*

- If you are really hard up, you can always join a curch of the "Y". — Jack Lait and Lee Mortimer, *Chicago Confidential*, p. 263, 1950
- I arrived in Chi quite early in the morning, got a room in the Y, and went to bed with a very few dollars in my pocket. — Jack Kerouac, *On the Road*, p. 14, 1957
- "They don't call this Y the French Embassy for nothing," the merchant marine laughs. — John Rechy, *City of Night*, p. 25, 1963
- The all-male group of guests make the Y's a perfect hang-out for queers. — Johnny Shearer, *The Male Hustler*, p. 25, 1966
- I was staying at the Y once, and this guy kept following me in the showers, wanting to cop my joint. — John Rechy, *Numbers*, p. 65, 1967
- At one point I learned that he was staying at the very Y I lived in. — Angelo d'Arcangelo, *The Homosexual Handbook*, p. 33, 1968
- "You could go to the Y," she says. "You can say that 'cause you've never been to the Y." — Darryl Ponicsan, *The Last Detail*, p. 92, 1970
- Ah, yes the Y. The best thing Christianity ever produced. — *Screw*, p. 16, 25 October 1971
- You weren't at the Y last week. We lost. — *Body Heat*, 1980
- Leaving the Y early this morning — Melanie McGrath, *Hard, Soft & Wet*, p. 272, 1998
- "YMCA" [a song by the Village People] was as rousing as a religious anthem [...] "Go to the Y, find a young man, get him into the shower, and fuck him". — Simon Napier-Bell, *Black Vinyl White Powder*, p. 186, 2001

Y2K *noun*

1 the year 2000; the first second of the year 2000 *CANADA*

Y (year) plus 2xK (2000).

- A major reason we're in this Y2K pickle is that, as far as senior (business) management is concerned, these systems simply don't exist as a key component of corporate productivity. — *Computing Canada*, p. 1, 20th December 1995
- Well we've been trucking down the information superhighway / But we'll be on a dirt road come Y2K — Loudon Wainwright III, *Y2K*, 1999
- [C]razy / As the world was over this whole Y2K thing[.] — Eminem (Marshall Mathers), *I'm Back*, 2000

2 used as the first three digits for any year between 2001 and 2009 *INDIA*

- [D]elve deeper into the world of Y2K4 man who has sexed up quite a bit to subvert gender notions. — *The Times of India*, 1st April 2004

yaba *noun*

paramethoxyamphetamine, PMA

A phonetic approximation (perhaps Thai or Burmese), literally 'crazy medicine', by which name it is also known.

- [D]rug experts report that the UK is being targeted by yaba producers from the 'Golden Triangle'[.] — *Urban 75 Drug Info*, February 2002
- With a profit mark-up of 1100% over raw materials and over 400 million yaba pills crossing the border from Burma to Thailand every year, it's not surprising that an estimated two-thirds of Bangkok crime is thought to be yaba-related. — *Code*, p. 45, January 2002

yabba *noun*

methamphetamine in pill form when taken as a recreational drug *UK*

- Experts fear that Yabba is being sold as cheap E in the UK. — *Mixmag*, p. 37, December 2001
- — Harry Shapiro, *Recreational Drugs*, p. 180, 2004

yabba-dabba doo!

used as a cry of exultation *US*

The Flintstones, a US television animation-comedy, first broadcast in 1960, introduced 'yabba-dabba-doo!' as a catchphrase. 'A yabba-dabba doo time' (an excellent time) comes directly from the theme song, 'The Flintstones: Rise and Shine', written by William Hanna and Joseph Barbera, the show's creators. As a noun, 'yabba-dabba doo' means 'exuberance'.

- yabba dabbas, n. The climactic stages of intercourse which immediately precede the doooooooos! The vinegar strokes. — Chris Donald, *Roger's Profanisaurus*, 1998
- Golf could use a little yabba-dabba-doo. — *Seattle Post-Intelligencer*, 26th August 2002

yabber *noun*

a conversation; a chat *AUSTRALIA, 1855*

- [He] suggested they sit on the tree bench for 'a quiet yabber'. — Arthur Upfield, *Bony and the Mouse*, p. 128, 1959
- "But mention the latest Arena on the tango at the programme review board and you couldn't shut them up. Yabber, yabber, yabber," Mr Whiston said. — *The Guardian*, 12th November 2002

yabber *verb*

to talk, converse, chat, now especially used of unintelligble language that is annoying; hence, to chatter, blabber, be noisy *AUSTRALIA, 1841*

Originally used in Australian pidgin. From an Australian Aboriginal language, possibly the Wuywurung language of the Melbourne region.

- They yabbered excitedly and edged towards the bank. — Ion L. Idriess, *Over the Range*, p. 155, 1947
- Truck-loads of troops, passing on the roads, yapped and yabbered like frenzied curs. — Eric Lambert, *The Veterans*, p. 112, 1954
- I'm goin' to yabber with Harmon about them abos coming in. — Arthur Upfield, *Bony and the Mouse*, p. 69, 1959
- — Jim Ramsay, *Cop It Sweet!*, p. 98, 1977
- The two girls were busy wielding their axes as the New Australians drove up in their truck and got out, yabbering away in their own lingo. — Herb Wharton, *Cattle Camp*, p. 140, 1994
- They all took vague and undefined concepts, such as "Faith" or "God's Word", then yabbered on for pages and pages in this weighty-sounding but utterly vacuous religio-babble. — Christopher Brookmyre, *Not the End of the World*, p. 251, 1998
- As the club sink into the mire, and Mick McCarthy starts to yabber and shriek[.] — *The Guardian*, 24th March 2003

yabbering *noun*

talk, conversation *AUSTRALIA, 1847*

- Alec said, 'Good grief! Stop yer yabbering or I'll get myself another partner.' — Jean Brooks, *The Opal Witch*, p. 17, 1967

yabby *noun*

an Australian freshwater crayfish, found throughout eastern Australia and introduced into WA, commonly caught for food; later applied to various other similar freshwater crayfish *AUSTRALIA, 1894*

From Wemba, an Australian Aboriginal language of Victoria .

- YABBY – A small burrowing crawfish, found in most creeks and water-holes in Australia — Gilbert H. Lawson, *A Dictionary of Australian Words and Terms*, 1924
- — Norman Lindsay, *Halfway to Anywhere*, p. 40, 1947
- [M]ostly he caught yabbies out of the mud near the edge. — Bob Ellis and Anne Brooksbank, *Mad Dog Morgan*, p. 49, 1976
- — Jim Ramsay, *Cop It Sweet!*, p. 98, 1977
- It was obvious from my very first day that the bream were partial to Bass yabbies, a popular bait in the Gippsland area of Victoria. — Rex Hunt, *Tall Tales – and True*, p. 128, 1994

yabby *verb*

to fish for freshwater crayfish *AUSTRALIA, 1934*

After the noun sense.

- Make sure any dam you go yabbying in hasn't been polluted from run-off farm chemicals[.] — Jackie French, *Newsletter*, July 2003

yabbying *noun*

the act of fishing for yabbies, usually with a bit of meat on a string *AUSTRALIA, 1934*

- He chuckled to remember how in the old days he used to go birds' nesting on the hill-side and yabbying in the creek[.] — Dymphna Cusack, *Picnic Races*, p. 13, 1962

yack; yak *noun*

1 voluble talk *US*
Echoic of idle chatter.
- Having made such a rash promise, we'll get down to some serious yak on the subject of the wet stuff you pour into your gas tank. —Oscar J. Gude, *Hot Rod Comics*, June 1952
- So I grabbed a dictionary and slowly learned words and tried them out in our yaks. —Piri Thomas, *Down These Mean Streets*, p. 257, 1967

2 a joke *US*
- You see, boychick, I can spike any script with yaks, but the thing I can't do is heartbreak. —Norman Mailer, *Advertisements for Myself*, p. 159, 1951

3 a telephone sales solicitor, either for a legitimate business or for a confidence swindle *US*
- —M. Allen Henderson, *How Con Games Work*, p. 224, 1985: 'Glossary'
- —Kathleen Odean, *High Steppers, Fallen Angels, and Lollipops*, p. 132, 1988
- Most yaks paced to keep their energy level up when doing phone freaks. —Stephen Cannell, *Big Con*, p. 64, 1997

4 a watch *UK, 1812*
Possibly derived from Welsh gypsy *yākengeri* (a clock, literally 'a thing of the eyes'). Still current, in second spelling, among market traders.
- —Patrick O'Shaughnessy, *Market Traders' Slang*, 1979

yack; yak *verb*

1 to talk volubly and either idly or stupidly or both *US*
- Lying with a guy on a good inner-spring mattress and listening to him yak about pine needles! —Philip Wylie, *Opus 21*, p. 297, 1949
- I don't want to appear to be the ungrateful brother-in-law guest yakking in behind their backs which I aint, I was happy and secure for the first time in years[.] —Jack Kerouac, *Letter to Allen Ginsberg*, p. 350, 10th May 1952
- [A]nd so on and so on, for no reason at all, yakking in the happy blue morning sky over rocks with his slaking grin, sweating a little from the long morning's work. —Jack Kerouac, *The Dharma Bums*, p. 63, 1958
- [T]hey start yacking to their mates, and looking at you. —Paul E. Willis, *Profane Culture*, p. 31, 1978
- An hour ago you wanted to yack. — *Ferris Buehler's Day Off*, 1986
- MIA: Why do we feel it's necessary to yak about bullshit in order to be comfortable? — *Pulp Fiction*, 1994
- Yeah, I was going to give him some, but he started talking. Just talking, yakkety, yak. I hate a yakking man. —Chris Rock, *Rock This!*, p. 125, 1997
- Even after I tell him to shut his fucking mouth or I'll shut it for him, he's still yakking away. —Danny King, *The Burglar Diaries*, p. 108, 2001

2 to vomit *US*
- —Connie Eble (Editor), *UNC-CH Campus Slang*, p. 10, Spring 1992
- And if I yack, chances are someone else will chunder. — *Wayne's World 2*, 1993

yack *adjective*

sick *UK*
- Now chew it. I know it tastes fuckin yack like, but's a quicker hit. —Niall Griffiths, *Sheepshagger*, p. 162, 2001

yacker *noun*

a swindler working on a phony investment scam by telephone *US*
- —Kathleen Odean, *High Steppers, Fallen Angels, and Lollipops*, p. 132, 1988

▷ **see:** YAKKA

yacker *verb*

to talk *AUSTRALIA, 1882*
- It's almost as useless as it was before, but each has a different voice and at night they yacker between themselves. —Thea Astley, *A Kindness Cup*, p. 25, 1974

yackety-yack *noun*

inconsequential talk *UK, 1958*
- Jangling Jack / Goes Yackety Yack[.] —Nick Cave, *Jangling Jack*, 1994

yadda yadda yadda

used for suggesting meaningless conversation *US*
- Unless you notify us by telegram or facsimile ... no phone calls, stating that you wish to yadda yadda yadda Wayne yadda yadda yadda Garthy yadda yadda yadda yadda yadda Aerosmith. — *Wayne's World 2*, 1993
- —Connie Eble (Editor), *UNC-CH Campus Slang*, p. 9, Fall 1997
- I haven't had a chance to read it, but I'm sure it goes something like "yahdah yahday yahday you mean a lot of me." — *Cruel Intentions*, 1999
- And all the way back, yadda yadda yadda. —Christopher Brookmyre, *The Sacred Art of Stealing*, p. 121, 2002

yaffle *verb*

1 to eat hurriedly or greedily *UK, 1788*
Originally, 'to eat or drink'; still current in Royal Navy slang but only as 'to eat'.
- —Nigel Foster, *The Making of a Royal Marine Commando*, 1987

2 to engage in oral sex *UK*
From the sense 'to eat'.
- Yaffle the yoghurt cannon (the penis). —Chris Donald, *Roger's Profanisaurus*, 1998

yaffler *noun*

a person who talks too much *AUSTRALIA*
- —Maureen Brooks and Joan Ritchie, *Tassie Terms*, p. 168, 1995

yag *noun*

*y*ttrium *a*luminium *g*arnet *UK*
Used in the diamond trade.
- —Derek Lambert, *Touch the Lion's Paw*, 1975

yage *noun*

ayahuasca also known as *yajé*, a psychedelic drink from South America *US*
- [William] Burroughs found his uncut kick not with peyote but ayahuasca, yage, in Mexico —Sadie Plant, *Writing On Drugs*, 1999

yah boo!

used as an expression of scorn or derision *UK, 1921*
A childish use.
- There [is] the increasing feeling that people were fed up with mud slinging and yah boo-to-you politics. — *BBC News*, 25th September 2001

yah boo sucks!

used as an expression of defiance, scorn or derision *UK, 1980*
Originally used by children, now childish; an elaboration of **YAH BOO!**.
- With the Stuart failure to impose absolutism (foreign and Catholic, yah boo sucks!), the bourgeoisie take over and develop a sensible middle line in cookery. — *The Guardian*, 2nd November 2002

yahoo *noun*

1 an unrefined, loutish, uncultured person *UK, 1726*
An imaginary race of brutes created by Swift in *Gulliver's Travels*.
- What the hell is wrong with a bunch of yahoos that'll stand around for hours on account of a hope like that? —Philip Wylie, *Opus 21*, p. 343, 1949
- And it's a dead heat which – Washington or Los Angeles – has more yahoos from dull places. —Jack Lait and Lee Mortimer, *Washington Confidential*, p. 3, 1951
- [T]he walk was faced with a camp-out among the yahoos or perhaps a forced march throughout the night to reach another country. —Ed Sanders, *Tales of Beatnik Glory*, p. 245, 1975
- You know how long that took? I'm the only thing those Jamaican yahoos had going for 'em and I get canned. —Elmore Leonard, *Glitz*, p. 125, 1985
- Obviously the yahoos were more curious than afraid of lethal reptiles. —Carl Hiaasen, *Native Tongue*, p. 306, 1991

2 crack cocaine *US*
- — US Department of Justice, *Street Terms*, October 1994

yahoo!

used as an exuberant expression of excitement or delight *UK, 1976*

yahoos *noun*

the female breasts *US*
Perhaps from 'yahoo!' as a celebratory cry.
- Britney Spears wearing an Aerosmith T-shirt cut down to her yahoos – these are moments you live for. — *Q*, p. 83, December 2001

yahso *adverb*

here; in or to this place *JAMAICA*
- yahso we deh/here is where we are. —Chester Francis-Jackson, *The Official Dancehall Dictionary*, p. 56, 1995

yak *noun*

during the Korean war, an enemy aircraft *US*
Coined as an allusion to North Korea's YAK-9 fighter jet.

▷ **see:** YACK

yakenal *noun*

a capsule of phentobarbital sodium (trade name Nembutal™), a central nervous system depressant *US*
- —Ralph de Sola, *Crime Dictionary*, p. 168, 1982

yakka; yacker *noun*
work *AUSTRALIA, 1888*
From the now defunct verb 'yacker' (to work), from the Australian Aboriginal language Yagara, Brisbane region. Connection with the Ulster word 'yokkin' (a spell of work) (Green, 1998) is untenable. Now usually in the phrase **HARD YAKKA**.
- Mum does most of the solid yakka round the place. — Barry Humphries, *The Wonderful World of Barry McKenzie*, p. 6, 1968
- Hard yakka in the cattle pens. — *666 ABC Canberra*, 3rd March 2003

yakker *noun*
1 talk *AUSTRALIA, 1961*
Recorded by Sidney J. Baker.
2 food *AUSTRALIA, 1942*
From Australian pidgin; possibly equating **YAKKA** (work) with food. Variants include 'yack'.

yale *noun*
crack cocaine *UK*
- — Mike Haskins, *Drugs*, p. 282, 2003

Yale *noun*
a commerical hypodermic needle, whether or not it is manufactured by Yale *US*
- — David Maurer and Victor Vogel, *Narcotics and Narcotic Addiction*, p. 454, 1973

Yalie *noun*
a student or alumnus of Yale University *US*
- [Crossword puzzle clue: Yalies] — *New York Times*, p. 25, 27th August 1952
- He's a Yalie, Ol. — Erich Segal, *Love Story*, p. 114, 1970
- He's a Jew-boy, Norwachefsky. A Yalie like me. — Edwin Torres, *After Hours*, p. 391, 1979

yam *verb*
1 to talk too much *US*
- — *American Speech*, p. 155, May 1951: 'Hermann Collitz and the language of the underworld'

2 to eat as if famished *BARBADOS*
- — Frank A. Collymore, *Barbadian Dialect*, p. 121, 1965

yam foot *noun*
a foot that is broad and splayed out *TRINIDAD AND TOBAGO*
- — Lise Winer, *Dictionary of the English/Creole of Trinidad & Tobago*, 2003

yammagi; yamidgee *noun*
an Aboriginal, especially an Aboriginal male *AUSTRALIA, 1925*
A Western Australian Aboriginal (Watjari) term, *yamaji*, used generically. Variant spellings include: 'yamagee', 'yamagi', 'yammagee' and 'yammogee'.

Yammie; Yammy *noun*
a Yamaha motorcyle, in production since 1954 *UK*
- However, the Yammie will happily yield a little metal when you lean it low in the bends[.] — *Sunday Times (South Africa)*, 3rd October 1999

yandy *noun*
a shallow dish used for separating seeds from other matter *AUSTRALIA, 1903*

yandy *verb*
to separate seeds from surrounding matter in a yandy; hence, in tin-mining, to pan *AUSTRALIA, 1914*
Such work is done by a 'yandier'.

yang *noun*
1 the penis *US*
From the masculine principle in the Chinese philosophy of yin-yang.
- "I got my old pard by the yang, ain't I?" Moke said. — Elmore Leonard, *Stick*, p. 295, 1983
- Cullen said, "Jesus, they cut the guy's yang off." — Elmore Leonard, *Bandits*, p. 225, 1987

2 the rectum *US*
- Hey, did you hear about that guy in F or E wing that stuffs things into his yang? — Paul Glover, *Words from the House of the Dead*, 1974

yang-yang *adjective*
of a horse, lively or spirited *AUSTRALIA, 1976*
- — W.S. Ramson, *The Australian National Dictionary*, 1988

Yank *noun*
1 an American *UK, 1778*
Originally a New Englander or someone from the northern states of America. An abbreviation of **YANKEE**; often derogatory.
- An older, military type wearing a dodgy green top hat held the glass door open for him and nodded in a grudging kind of way. Yanks and Japs love that shit. — Greg Williams, *Diamond Geezers*, p. 109, 1997

2 an American bird *UK*
Bird-watching slang.
- It might be a yank. — *New Society*, 17th November 1977

yank *verb*
to tug something with sudden energy; to remove something *US, 1848*
- Two care assistants [...] pulled back the bed clothes, yanked down his pants, took off his incontinence pads and pulled his pants back up. — *The Guardian*, 23rd July 2003
- The interview appeared in an early edition of one of Parfyonov's shows, broadcast to Siberia and eastern Russia, but was later yanked from the programme after, some say, a phone call from the Kremlin. — *The Guardian*, 4th June 2004

yank and bank *verb*
to execute a turn in a fighter plane *US*
- — *American Speech*, p. 125, Summer 1986: 'The language of naval fighter pilots'

yankee *noun*
a multiple bet, gambling on four different horses in a specific combination of eleven bets *UK, 1967*
- "Yeah. My first yankee -" "I done hundreds of them." "Me too – but this is the first I've won." — Anthony Masters, *Minder*, p. 98, 1984
- A £1 Yankee costs £11. Double that for each way cover. — John McCririck, *John McCririck's World of Betting*, p. 45, 1991

Yankee *noun*
1 a native or inhabitant of New England; hence, more generally, of the northern states of America *US, 1765*
The most likely derivation is from Dutch *Janke*, a diminutive of *Jan* (John) as a pejorative nickname; also possible is a North American Indian corruption of 'English'; or Cherokee *eankke* (a slave, a coward). Used by the Confederates of the Federal army during the American Civil War, 1861–65, and since by the south of the north.

2 a tool used by car thieves to pull out the cyclinder of the ignition lock *UK*
- Slide hammer. Sometimes called a "slam hammer" "slam puller" or "Yankee". — David Powis, *The Signs of Crime*, 1977

Yankee *adjective*
American *UK, 1781*
- Yankee soldier / He wanna shoot some skag / He met it in Cambodia / But now he can't afford a bag / Yankee dollar talk / To the dictators of the world[.] — The Clash *I'm So Bored with the USA*, 1977

Yankee-bashing *noun*
an act of engaging US servicemen in sexual activity *UK, 1984*
Well-used by members of the Women's Royal Army Corps in Hong Kong during the 1960s.

Yankee clipper *noun*
a North American moving van *US*
- — Wayne Floyd, *Jason's Authentic Dictionary of CB Slang*, p. 32, 1976

yankee dime *noun*
a kiss *US, 1900*
- We will save our "Yankee Dimes" til we meet again. — *Daily Oklahoman*, p. 31, 26th April 1995
- I told him I didn't have a Yankee dime and he said, 'Yes, you do,' and he leaned over and kissed me. And that was a Yankee dime. — *Dallas Morning News*, 18th May 2001

Yankeeland *noun*
the United States of America *UK*
- [J]us' come back from yankeeland wiv your ideas[.] — Patrick Jones, *Everything Must Go*, p. 145, 2000

Yankee shout *noun*
a social outing where everyone pays for themselves *AUSTRALIA, 1945*
- Joe appeared interested. 'You shoutin'?' 'Yankee shout,' said Dennis. — Nino Culotta (John O'Grady), *They're A Weird Mob*, p. 132, 1957
- — Jim Ramsay, *Cop It Sweet!*, p. 98, 1977

Yankee tournament *noun*
a sporting contest in which everyone plays everyone else *AUSTRALIA, 1961*
An Australian nuance of **YANKEE** (American) as 'equal for all'.

Yanking *noun*
an act of engaging US servicemen in sexual activity *UK*
Formed on **YANK** (an American).
- Popular expression to describe the activities of girls who specialise in picking up American soldiers (or, come to that, sailors or airmen)[.] —Paul Tempest, *Lag's Lexicon*, 1950

Yank tank *noun*
a large car, especially one manufactured in the US *AUSTRALIA, 1981*
- The rank and file were only allowed to bring in one personal item from home – their big yank tank. —Martin Cameron, *A Look at the Bright Side*, 1988
- —Lewis Poteet, *Car & Motorcyle Slang*, p. 220, 1992

ya-o *noun*
crack cocaine *US*
- —Bill Valentine, *Gang Intelligence Manual*, p. 75, 1995

yaoh *noun*
cocaine *UK*
- I zapped your yaoh last night. You was out of it, lar. Couldn't wake you. —Kevin Sampson, *Powder*, p. 370, 1999

yap *noun*
1 the mouth *US, 1900*
- I was led back to the deputy, who asked what the trouble was and then, before I had a chance to open my yap, said, "Shut up or I'll bust you in the nose." —Mezz Mezzrow, *Really the Blues*, p. 35, 1946
- He waited until we were in the car before he opened his yap. —Mickey Spillane, *One Lonely Night*, p. 169, 1951
- Their worst fears were realized the minute he opened his big yap. —Evan Hunter, *The Blackboard Jungle*, p. 78, 1954
- All I hoped was that old Mindzenty would keep his yap shut for seven straight days. —Clancy Sigal, *Going Away*, p. 164, 1961
- Why don't ya shut yer yap for a while? —Stephen J. Cannell, *Big Con*, p. 120, 1997
- [E]very time he opened his fat yap. —*The Guardian*, p. 3, 12th June 2003

2 inconsequential talk *US, 1907*
- Don't think, despite the annual yaps for more assistance, the Washington police force is radically undermanned. —Jack Lait and Lee Mortimer, *Washington Confidential*, p. 226, 1951
- So what's your point with all this yap? —Raymond Chandler, *The Long Goodbye*, p. 236, 1953

3 in circus and carnival usage, a naive, gullible local resident *US*
- —Don Wilmeth, *The Language of American Popular Entertainment*, p. 298, 1981

yap *verb*
to talk incessantly *UK, 1886*
The term existed in this sense in C19 English dialect, and then independently arose in the US in the 1920s.
- They're special shoes, and I needed them now. And quit your yapping. I'll get you there on time. —Max Shulman, *The Many Loves of Dobie Gillis*, p. 188, 1951
- When women get together, we sometimes drink, often eat, and always yap. —Anka Radakovich, *The Wild Girls Club*, p. 4, 1994

yapper, snapper, and crapper *noun*
oral, vaginal and anal sex with a woman *US*
A clever phrase heard in jokes but rarely in real life.

yappies *noun*
▸ **the yappies**
greyhound racing or coursing *AUSTRALIA*
A play on **THE DOGS**.
- —Barry Prentice, 1984

yappy; yappified *adjective*
idiotic *UK*
- —Patrick O'Shaughnessy, *Market Traders' Slang*, 1979

yar!
used as a general-purpose interjection, usually conveying excitement about something *US*
- Yar! Dude! Check out that sweet car! —Pamela Munro, *U.C.L.A. Slang*, p. 92, 1989

yarco; yark *noun*
a member of a subcultural urban adolescent grouping in Yarmouth, Norfolk, that seems to be defined by a hip-hop dress and jewellery sense *UK*

yard *noun*
1 one hundred dollars *US, 1926*
- —Lou Shelly, *Hepcats Jive Talk Dictionary*, p. 20, 1945
- One long yard, man; just flip one hundred of them singles and we'll take it from the top. —Ross Russell, *The Sound*, p. 157, 1961
- They entered and after routine questioning they asked how much money I had. I showed them six "yards"[.] —Babs Gonzales, *I Paid My Dues*, p. 27, 1967
- Give me a yard and a half and take the bitch back. —Iceberg Slim (Robert Beck), *Pimp*, p. 105, 1969
- "How much?" "A yard. Hundred bucks and she's happy." —Mickey Spillane, *Last Cop Out*, p. 48, 1972
- I lent him a yard / and copped him a rod. —Lightnin' Rod, *Hustlers Convention*, p. 14, 1973
- I started going to the Copa regular; if I caught the show always a yard for the maitre d' – "Mr. Brigante, right this way." —Edwin Torres, *Carlito's Way*, p. 30, 1975

2 one thousand dollars *US, 1932*
- You can make a couple of yards a week and be cool about it. —Piri Thomas, *Down These Mean Streets*, p. 322, 1967

3 a prison sentence of 100 years *US*
- "Party" went back to the joint for a "yard" after he got out of City Hospital. —Iceberg Slim (Robert Beck), *Pimp*, p. 41, 1969
- —William K. Bentley, *Prison Slang*, p. 24, 1992

4 a prison sentence of one year *US*
- —Hyman E. Goldin et al., *Dictionary of American Underworld Lingo*, p. 242, 1950

5 your country, especially Jamaica *UK*
- Use the money to go on holiday, visit Yard or sump'n, man. —Donald Gorgon, *Cop Killer*, p. 122, 1994

6 your home, your house; in prison, your cell *JAMAICA, 1950*
West Indian and UK black.
- Lloyd took a pit stop at the local off-licence for a six-pack of Tennants before heading to his yard. —Donald Gorgon, *Cop Killer*, p. 13, 1994
- Use the money to go on holiday, visit Yard or sump'n, man. —Donald Gorgon, *Cop Killer*, p. 122, 1994
- —Angela Devlin, *Prison Patter*, p. 124, 1996
- "It's my birthday Tuesday," she said helpfully. "Come to my yard and none of your deep lateness." —Diran Abedayo, *My Once Upon A Time*, p. 20, 2000

7 a member of the Montagnard tribe, the aborigine hill tribes of Vietnam's Central Highlands *US*
- —Linda Reinberg, *In the Field*, p. 244, 1991

Yard *noun*
▸ **the Yard**
Scotland Yard, subsequently New Scotland Yard, headquarters of the Metropolitan police *UK, 1888*
Originally, since 1888, used of the location of London's Metropolitan Police; the familiar name stayed when the headquarters moved to new premises in 1967.
- They were on their way to the Yard to see if he could pick the grafter [confidence trickster] who'd lawed him out of the rogue's gallery. —Charles Raven, *Underworld Nights*, p. 129, 1956

yard *verb*
1 to be sexually unfaithful *US*
- She told him she didn't like to yard on her man, who was living in New York. —Clarence Cooper Jr, *The Scene*, p. 34, 1960
- Or have you been out yarding somewhere? —Donald Goines, *Whoreson*, p. 159, 1972
- I ain't saying she's yarding but we both know she could very well be kicking the gong around. —A.S. Jackson, *Gentleman Pimp*, p. 90, 1973

2 to get hold of someone *CANADA*
- We yarded Harry and Alice and tooled off to the dance. —Douglas Leechman, 1984

yardage *noun*
a big penis *US, 1970s*
- —Bruce Rodgers, *The Queens' Vernacular*, p. 217, 1972

yard-and-a-half *noun*
one hundred and fifty dollars *US*
- —Frank Garcia, *Marked Cards and Loaded Dice*, p. 265, 1962

yardbird *noun*

1 a chicken *US*

• Yardbird and strings. Harlem's own vernacular for the fried chicken and spaghetti which was so common, so cheap and so utterly, unbelievably wonderful at such wrong hours – like the hours around dawn, for instance. — Robert Sylvester, *No Cover Charge*, p. 43, 1956

2 a prisoner, a convict *US*

• For the next two weeks, K.B. was Claiborne's yardbird. He had to go everywhere Claiborne went from morning till night. — Claude Brown, *Manchild in the Promised Land*, p. 83, 1965

3 a newly arrived military recruit *US*

• — Lou Shelly, *Hepcats Jive Talk Dictionary*, p. 50, 1945

4 in trucking, a terminal employee who moves trucks around the yard *US*

• — Montie Tak, *Truck Talk*, p. 190, 1971

5 on the railways, an injured employee assigned to limited duty in a railway yard *US*

• — *American Speech*, p. 290, December 1968: 'Addenda to the vocabulary of railroading'

Yardbird *nickname*

Charlie Parker, jazz saxophonist *US*

• He presented Dizzy, Hawk, Yardbird, Sarah and many others in concert back in "43". — Babs Gonzales, *Be-Bop Dictionary and History of its Famous Stars*, p. 12, 1949
• Many of his worshipful followers were convinced that The Yardbird, as Parker was known to the boppers, was so utterly wonderful because he was on that terrific kick. — Robert Sylvester, *No Cover Charge*, p. 285, 1956
• And that's the Yardbird himself blowin' those obligattoes on the alto sax-o-phone. — Ross Russell, *The Sound*, p. 16, 1961
• At first, if cats were talking about Charlie Parker and then said Yardbird, I didn't know what they were talking about. — Claude Brown, *Manchild in the Promised Land*, p. 148, 1965

yard buddy *noun*

a close friend in prison *US*

• All he did was call up an old yard buddy and ask him if he could turn him on to somebody with some good stuff. — Vernon E. Smith, *The Jones Men*, p. 149, 1974

yard bull; yard dick *noun*

a railway detective *US*

• "Yard bulls," Lucky whispered. "They're checking the cars." — Hal Ellson, *Tomboy*, p. 150, 1950
• A friendly switchman told me I'd better not try to get on it as there was a yard bull at the crossing with a big flashlight who would see if anybody was riding away on it and would phone ahead of Watsonville to have them thrown off. — Jack Kerouac, *The Dharma Bums*, p. 92, 1958
• If a cop hustled him off, he hustled, and disappeared, and if yard dicks were around in big-city yards when a freight was pulling out, chances are they never got a sight of the little man hiding in the weeds[.] — Jack Kerouac, *The Dharma Bums*, p. 7, 1958

yard dog *noun*

an unsophisticated, uncouth person *US*

• — Kenn "Naz" Young, *Naz's Underground Dictionary*, p. 66, 1973

yard goose *noun*

a railway pointsman *US*

• — Ramon Adams, *The Language of the Railroader*, p. 176, 1977

yardie *noun*

1 a member of a violent gang culture rooted in the West Indies, especially Jamaica *JAMAICA, 1986*

Yardies have an international reputation for drug-related crime.

• [G]ang war hits London – yardie style[.] — *Yardie*, 1992
• Well, imagine it, your average Yardie ain't gonna want to go to a rave now, is he? — Dave Courtney, *Raving Lunacy*, p. 79, 2000
• [T]hey did all start talking that bit more Yardie, to be fair. They'd be saying "I axed him" and that instead of "I asked him". — Kevin Sampson, *Outlaws*, p. 25, 2001
• — Nick Constable, *This is Cocaine*, p. 182, 2002

2 a person from your neighbourhood; a friend *JAMAICA*

• — Peter Patrick, *Some Recent Jamaican Creole Words*, 2003

3 a yardman *AUSTRALIA*

• Yardie: The bloke who cleans up the backyard at the hotel[.] — Bazza and Curly, *Betcha Wrong!*, p. 35, 1990

yard man *noun*

a Jamaican

• [A] policeman carried no special dispensation from a yard man's 'matic [automatic weapon] or a cockney's sawn-off. — Donald Gorgon, *Cop Killer*, p. 4, 1994

yardney *noun*

a manner of speech combining West Indian and London accents and vocabularies *UK*

Combining **YARDIE** (a Jamaican gangster) and 'Cockney' (a stereotypical Londoner).

• Ben looked pained. His stilted Jamaican accent was dropped as he became a white wannabe from Richmond again for a second. [...] His Yardney accent returned. "No probs[."] — Kevin Sampson, *Powder*, p. 59, 1999

yard out *verb*

to exercise in a prison yard *US*

• — Inez Cardozo-Freeman, *The Joint*, p. 543, 1984

yard sale *noun*

in snow-based sports, the result of an accident in which equipment is deposited over a wide area *US*

• Skiers put on the best yard sales, sometimes spreading their skis, poles, and hats over hundreds of vertical feet. — Jim Humes and Sean Wagstaff, *Boarderlands*, p. 225, 1995

yardstick *noun*

a road mile marker *US*

• — Wayne Floyd, *Jason's Authentic Dictionary of CB Slang*, p. 32, 1976

yark *noun*

▷ see: **YARCO**

yarn *noun*

1 a story, an adventure story, especially a long, marvellous or incredible story *UK, 1812*

Of nautical origin; from 'spin a yarn' (to tell such a story).

• — Michael Palin and Terry Jones, *Ripping Yarns*, 1976–79

2 a chat, a talk, a conversation *AUSTRALIA, 1852*

• He drops in at other chaps' camps for a yarn or to give them a hand and see if their bees are in good heart. — Kylie Tennant, *The Honey Flow*, p. 12, 1956
• Always had him up for a ding-dong yarn when he blew in here. — Dymphna Cusack, *Picnic Races*, p. 218, 1962
• Walk around on a playing day and have a yarn with the usual 'suspects'. — *BBCi Wear*, 15th May 2003

yarn *verb*

1 to tell a story *UK, 1812*

• Poor weather precluding my morning outing, we yarned by the peat fire and the hours sped by like minutes. — *The Guardian*, 22nd September 2004

2 to talk; to have a chat *AUSTRALIA, 1847*

• Well, I can't sit here yarning a moment longer. — Jean Brooks, *The Opal Witch*, p. 125, 1967

yarpie *noun*

▷ see: **JAPIE**

yarra *adjective*

mad, stupid, eccentric *AUSTRALIA*

From the mental asylum at Yarra Bend, Victoria.

Yarra-banker *noun*

a loafer or vagrant idling on the banks of the Yarra River, Melbourne; a Melbourne soap box orator *AUSTRALIA, 1895*

Yarra – stinking Yarra!

used as an offensive catchphrase addressed by Sydneyites to Melbournites *AUSTRALIA, 1984*

Melbourne sits on the banks of the Yarra river.

yassoo!

used as a greeting among troops who have served in Cyprus *UK, 1984*

From Greek *giasou!* (an all-purpose word for 'hello', 'goodbye', 'cheers!'). Sometimes eleaborated in mock-Scots as 'yassoo the noo!'.

yattie *noun*

a girl *UK*

• — Julian Johnson, *Urban Survival*, p. 258, 2003

yawn *noun*

anything which induces boredom *UK, 1974*

• They expect you to take them to fun fairs, or to zoos or the theatre or some other big fucking yawn that who the hell can be arsed [bothered] with. — Danny King, *The Burglar Diaries*, p. 28, 2001

yawn *verb*

▸ **yawn in technicolor**

to vomit *US*

- —Connie Eble (Editor), *UNC-CH Campus Slang*, p. 7, March 1981
- — *The Washington Post*, 24th May 1987

yawn

said to register the speaker's boredom, instead of actually yawning *UK*

- This started in the Sixties, mark my words. We've been going down a slippery slope ever since. Yawn.—Christopher Brookmyre, *Boiling a Frog*, p. 191, 2000

yay; yayoo; yeah-O; yeyo; yeo *noun*

crack cocaine *US*

- That girl couldn't say nay to yay.—Lois Stavsky et al., *A2Z*, p. 115, 1995
- —Mike Haskins, *Drugs*, p. 282, 2003

yay!

used as an exclamation of delight *UK, 1963*

- The audience exploded. "Yay!" Joan and Donna were applauding and whooping[.]—Jon Katz, *The New Work of Dogs*, p. 134, 2003

Y-bone *noun*

the vulva and vagina as an object of oral sex *NEW ZEALAND*

- —David McGill, *David McGill's Complete Kiwi Slang Dictionary*, p. 52, 1998

Y Dub *noun*

a premises of the YWCA (the Young Women's Christian Association), or the organisation itself *US, 1984*

Short for YW. Later use seems to be predominantly in New Zealand.

yea; yay *adverb*

when describing size, and combined with an appropriate gesture: this, so *US, 1960*

- "Forever, since we were yea-high," Shipley said. "It was always, 'Let's go play catch.' So I know if I toss it up there, Jacob's going to get it." — *Chicago Tribune*, 29th November 2002

yeah *noun*

yes, used as a signal of assent *US, 1905*

- [Ian Brown]'s the first to say that the [Stone] Roses woefully underachieved. "Yeah, we George Bested it, for sure."— *The Guardian*, 2nd February 2002

yeah-yeah

no *UK*

Said dismissively; a rare instance of a double affirmative producing a negative.

- He said I should move out until this matter was sorted. I said yeah-yeah.—Diran Adebayo, *My Once Upon A Time*, p. 101, 2000

year *noun*

a one-hundred dollar note *US*

- —Anna Scotti and Paul Young, *Buzzwords*, p. 86, 1997

year blob *noun*

a notional date that, within context, was a very long time ago *UK*

A variation of **YEAR DOT**.

- She used to be quite butch when she first came in here, but that was back in the year blob.—James Gardiner, *Who's a Pretty Boy Then?*, p. 123, 1997

year dot *noun*

a notional date long ago; time immemorial *UK, 1895*

- Terry had been into clubbing since the year dot and had learnt the business from the bottom up.—Dave Courtney, *Stop the Ride I Want to Get Off*, p. 354, 1999
- [H]e'd been doing drugs since the year dot.—Wayne Anthony, *Spanish Highs*, p. 50, 1999

yeast *verb*

to exaggerate *US*

- —Kenn "Naz" Young, *Naz's Underground Dictionary*, p. 66, 1973

yech!

▷ see: **YUCK!**

yee

yes *US*

- —Connie Eble (Editor), *UNC-CH Campus Slang*, p. 8, Fall 1980

yegg *noun*

a criminal, especially a burglar or safecracker *US, 1900*

Anglicised by 1932.

- We think about them the way we think about old-time yeggs or needled-up punks.—Raymond Chandler, *Farewell My Lovely*, p. 197, 1940
- I watched that yegg while my clarinet weaved a spell around him[.] —Mezz Mezzrow, *Really the Blues*, p. 183, 1946
- In this category were yeggs, who roved in packs, lived in roadside jungles, cased small-town banks and robbed them.—Jack Lait and Lee Mortimer, *Chicago Confidential*, p. 55, 1950
- You wouldn't have been surprised to learn that this man, for all his yegg's physiognomy, spent his spare hours carving cherubs and penguins out of Ivory soap[.]—Bernard Wolfe, *The Late Risers*, p. 48, 1954
- I was a yegg and on of the toughest of yeggs.—Bruce Jackson, *Get Your Ass in the Water and Swim Like Me*, p. 100, 1965
- Formerly he'd been a yegg, safecracker, the best on the coast.—Seth Morgan, *Homeboy*, p. 26, 1990

ye gods!; ye gods and little fishes!

used as a mild oath, especially to express exasperation or indignation *UK*

The former dates from 1807; and elaborated with 'little fishes' since the 1850s. Original use was no doubt sincere but from the 1960s usage has been derisory or jocular.

- Oh, and you can choose twixt 5 speed automatic or 5 speed manual, complete with a 'poppet ball' on fifth and reverse to 'enhance' selection. Ye Gods and little fishes, what's a poppet ball when it's at home? Sounds cute though.— *What's On Bristol*, November 2002

yeh *noun*

marijuana *UK, 1998*

- —Mike Haskins, *Drugs*, p. 289, 2003

Yekke; Yekkie *noun*

a German Jew *UK, 1950*

Derogatory. From Yiddish, but of uncertain origin.

- "This one is acting like a Yekke," said Jake. "The trouble with him is that he is too dedicated," said Olga.—Barbara G. Myerhoff, *Number Our Days*, p. 135, 1978

yeller feller; yellow feller; yellow fellow *noun*

a person of mixed Aboriginal and white parentage *AUSTRALIA, 1913*

yellow *noun*

1 a capsule of pentobarbital sodium (trade name Nembutal™), a central nervous system depressant; any barbiturate *US, 1944*

- —Norman W. Houser, *Drugs: Facts on Their Use and Abuse*, p. 13, 1969
- He said, "Kid, I put a couple 'yellows' in your bag so you can 'come down' and get some 'doss' [sleep].—Iceberg Slim (Robert Beck), *Pimp*, p. 133, 1969

2 LSD *US, 1977*

- —Richard A. Spears, *The Slang and Jargon of Drugs and Drink*, p. 557, 1986
- —Mike Haskins, *Drugs*, p. 286, 2003

yellow *adjective*

1 cowardly, afraid *US, 1856*

- You act mighty yellow about this.—Chester Gould, *Dick Tracy Meets the Night Crawler*, p. 208, 1945
- "Stop being so yellow," she said, "and tell these apes to pay me for my bag."—Irving Shulman, *The Amboy Dukes*, p. 236, 1947
- I think you're yellow not because you didn't kill him, but because you didn't want to kill him.—Piri Thomas, *Down These Mean Streets*, p. 191, 1967

2 used to describe that section of the printed news media which tends towards the sensational, the unscrupulous and the tawdry *US, 1898*

Derives from an 1895 experiment by the *New York World* in the use of colour-printing with the intent to attract more readers; a cartoon of a young girl in a yellow dress known as 'The Yellow Kid'.

- [T]he Mirror, Sunday Mirror and the People – newspapers which, when it comes to yellow journalism, make the Daily Mail seem like a church gazette.— *The Guardian*, 10th June 1996
- [S]uddenly even the yellow press had terms like "groovy" and "with-it" turning up in it's copy.—Jake Arnott, *He Kills Coppers*, p. 69, 2001

3 light-skinned; of mixed race *US, 1934*

- It was easy to see that the ape who was sleeping with her or married to her wouldn't be one to let a mere hundred and seventeen dollars stand in the way of something this yellow bitch had her heart set on.—Clarence Cooper Jr, *The Scene*, p. 33, 1960
- You just like most yellow nigger sissies. You don't fuck nothing but paddies and half-white niggers.—Iceberg Slim (Robert Beck), *Mama Black Widow*, p. 32, 1969

yellow and white earth *noun*

money *CANADA*

- Fishing was a possibility for the Blacks and was for those who could engage in it the chief and most profitable employment, for it must be known that even fishermen require a little yellow and white earth (what is called cash) to start his business. — Marion Robertson, *King's Bounty*, p. 91, 1983

yellow bam *noun*

1 a capsule of pentobarbital sodium (trade name Nembutal™), a central nervous system depressant *US*

- — Richard A. Spears, *The Slang and Jargon of Drugs and Drink*, p. 359, 1986

2 methamphetamine hydrochloride, a powerful central nervous system stimulant *US*

- — US Department of Justice, *Street Terms*, August 1994

yellow-bellied *adjective*

cowardly *US, 1924*

- What I wouldn't give for five minutes with you alone, you yellow-bellied bastard. — Charles Raven, *Underworld Nights*, p. 43, 1956
- No short-haired, yellow-bellied son-of-Tricky-Dicky's / Gonna mother hubbard soft soap me with just a bundle of hope — John Lennon, *Give Me Some Truth*, 1971

yellow-belly *noun*

1 a coward *US, 1930*

- "You chicken punk!" Lucky had said. "You don't belong in the Harps. We don't want a yellowbelly." — Hal Ellson, *Tomboy*, p. 9, 1950

2 a person of mixed Asian and white parentage *UK, 1867*
A derogatory and racist reference to skin-tone. An earlier use, from 1842, was by Americans of Mexicans.

yellow-belly bird *noun*

a coward *TRINIDAD AND TOBAGO, 1960*

- — Lise Winer, *Dictionary of the English/Creole of Trinidad & Tobago*, 2003

yellow bullet *noun*

a capsule of pentobarbital sodium (trade name Nembutal™), a central nervous system depressant *US*

- — Walter L. Way, *The Drug Scene*, p. 116, 1977

yellow canary *noun*

in trucking, a Yellow Transit Freight Lines truck *US*

- — Wayne Floyd, *Jason's Authentic Dictionary of CB Slang*, p. 32, 1976

yellow cap; yellow dot *noun*

▷ **see:** YELLOW SUNSHINE

yellow dimple; yellow dimples *noun*

LSD, especially in combination with another drug *US, 1982*

- — Richard A. Spears, *The Slang and Jargon of Drugs and Drink*, p. 558, 1986
- — Mike Haskins, *Drugs*, p. 286, 2003

yellow doll *noun*

a capsule of phentobarbital sodium (trade name Nembutal™), a central nervous system depressant *US*

- — Walter L. Way, *The Drug Scene*, p. 116, 1977

yellow egg *noun*

Temazapam™, a branded tranquillizer *UK*

- Temazepam are called "green or yellow eggs", "jellies" and "jelly babies". — James Kay and Julian Cohen, *The Parents' Complete Guide to Young People and Drugs*, p. 150, 1998

yellow jacket *noun*

1 a barbiturate or other central nervous system depressant, especially Nembutal™ *US, 1952*

- [W]e have a pretty complete exhibit of the little pills downtown. Bluejays, redbirds, yellow jackets, goofballs, and all the rest of the list. — Raymond Chandler, *The Long Goodbye*, p. 230, 1953
- Flora popped a couple of yellow jackets into her mouth and then swallowed hot coffee behind them to get a kick. — Willard Motley, *Let No Man Write My Epitaph*, p. 87, 1958
- Eventually, I started taking Benzedrine and goofballs, yellow jackets. — James Mills, *The Panic in Needle Park*, p. 43, 1966
- They also take Amytal ("blue heaven"), Nembutal ("yellow jackets") and Tuinal. — Hunter S. Thompson, *Hell's Angels*, p. 216, 1967
- Movie broads gobbled up yellow jackets like they were jelly beans[.] — Malcolm Braly, *On the Yard*, p. 59, 1967
- I said, I"ll sweeten that deuce with a sawbuck if you could score for a few yellow jackets." — Iceberg Slim (Robert Beck), *Trick Baby*, p. 268, 1969
- [S]he seen what a struggle I was having on my own, that she would give me two yellowjackets [Nembutol] a night to try to make me sleep. — Bruce Jackson, *In the Life*, p. 110, 1972
- Well, let's see. I still got some redbirds and yellowjackets. — Emmett Grogan, *Final Score*, p. 81, 1976
- The yellow jackets. The bennies. Whatever. — Robert Campbell, *Sweet La-La Land*, p. 199, 1990

2 a high-velocity, hollow-nose, expanding bullet *US*

- "Stingers and yellowjackets," Parrish said. "Hyper-velocity, hollow-nose expanders. The guy knew what he was doing." — Elmore Leonard, *Split Images*, p. 97, 1981

yellow legs *noun*

the US Marines *US*

Korean war usage; coined by the North Koreans alluding to the marine leggings.

- Forty-seven minutes later the "yellow-legs," as the Reds called the Marines after the leggings they wore, raised the American flag over Wolmi. — Robert Leckie, *The Wars of America, Volume II*, p. 359, 1968

Yellow Legs *noun*

the Royal Canadian Mounted Police *CANADA*

- — W. Hunt, *North of 53*, 1974

yellow pages *noun*

in poker, a play or a bet made strictly for the purpose of creating an impression *US*

- — John Vorhaus, *The Big Book of Poker Slang*, p. 41, 1996

yellow peril *noun*

1 a danger (real or imagined) that armies of any and all Asiatic peoples will overrun the West *UK, 1900*
From the conventional use of 'yellow' to convey an Asiatic or Oriental complexion. Usage is mainly historical but paranoia and the Internet keeps the phrase alive.

- My colleague James Lee makes the points – wearily familiar to Asian Americans – that the other 90% of the population never seems to take on board. There is no yellow peril. — *The Guardian*, 9th April 2001

2 used as a collective noun for all sorts of things with a yellow connection *UK, 1943*
Mainly jocular. Used by motorcyclists of traffic wardens (from the yellow flashes on their uniforms).

- — Douglas Dunford, Motorcycle Department, Beaulieu Motor Museum, 1979
- The yellow peril [ragwort] is lurking, and expanding its grip on the UK. — Derek Knottenbelt, an equinologist at Liverpool University, 26th August 2002

3 hepatitis *UK*
A peril of shared needles by drug addicts; their usage, with a pun on the fear of Asians and the skin discolouration associated with hepatitis.

- — Liz Cutland, *Kick Heroin*, p. 110, 1985

4 in prison, school or any canteen in any institution, a bright yellow cake favoured by the caterers *UK, 1961*
Originally services.

- — Angela Devlin, *Prison Patter*, p. 125, 1996

Yellow Peril *nickname*

in Canadian military aviation, the North American 'Harvard' *CANADA*

- The nickname "Yellow Peril" is not a disparaging comment on the Harvard, the mainstay of the RCAF flying training program for over two decades, but rather a comment on the perils it offered trainees. Training aircraft were painted bright yellow. — Tom Langeste, *Words on the Wing*, p. 314–315, 1995

yellow rock *noun*

methamphetamine in rock form, yellow in colour either because of incomplete processing or the presence of adulterants *US*

- — Geoffrey Froner, *Digging for Diamonds*, p. 69, 1989: 'Types of speed'

yellow sheet *noun*

a criminal record *US, 1992*

A generic in UK use, from the colour of the New York Police Department document at the time of coining.

- — Angela Devlin, *Prison Patter*, p. 125, 1996

yellow streak *noun*

a trait of cowardice *UK, 1911*

- I began to feel a yellow streak in my camp. — Jamie Mandelkau quoting Ken Kesey, *Buttons*, p. 150, 1971

yellow submarine *noun*
marijuana *UK*
A fanciful similarity in shape between a **JOINT** and The Beatles' musical cartoon creation 'Yellow Submarine', 1969; however, both promise a colourful journey.
• —Mike Haskins, *Drugs*, p. 289, 2003

yellow sunshine; yellow cap; yellow dot *noun*
LSD *US, 1972*
• —Richard A. Spears, *The Slang and Jargon of Drugs and Drink*, p. 558, 1986
• —Mike Haskins, *Drugs*, p. 286, 2003

yells, bells and knells *noun*
newspaper announcements of births, marriages and deaths *AUSTRALIA, 1984*
A journalistic summation of life; a variation of **HATCH, MATCH AND DISPATCH**.

yen *noun*
an intense craving, especially for a drug; an addiction *UK, 1876*
• Suppose some glamorous dame and you met. Suppose you got a yen for her?—Philip Wylie, *Opus 21*, p. 23, 1949
• Most of us walked around that day like zombies, our yens in total eclipse.—Bernard Wolfe, *The Late Risers*, p. 4, 1954
• He was roaring through Las Cruces, New Mexico, when he suddenly had an explosive yen to see his sweet first wife Maylou again.—Jack Kerouac, *On the Road*, p. 112, 1957
• This is a yen of the brain alone, a need without feeling and without body[.]—William Burroughs, *Naked Lunch*, p. 19, 1957
• If you really have got a yen I'll give you a shot.—Douglas Rutherford, *The Creeping Flesh*, p. 103, 1963
• I felt my throat blend in and out with the yen.—Piri Thomas, *Down These Mean Streets*, p. 204, 1967
• I was, however, a guy that had an insane cocaine yen, and that, my dear reader, is far worse than a horse habit, because it costs ten times as much bread.—A.S. Jackson, *Gentleman Pimp*, p. 75, 1973

yen *verb*
to crave a drug intensely *US, 1919*
From the Chinese; originally applied to opium users.
• You know yourself when a guy is yenning, he doesn't look behind him.—William Burroughs, *Junkie*, p. 56, 1953

yenems; yenams; yenhams *noun*
free cigarettes; anything belonging to someone else *UK, 1984*
Adopted from Yiddish, possibly as early as the mid-1920s.
• Simmy was a cigar lover, although he never handed them around. Once I asked him what he thought the best cigar was. "There's no doubt," said Simmy. "The best cigars are Yenems." This was a brand of which I had not heard. However, Simmy was a veteran smoker, so I rushed down to Suzman's and asked the chap behind the counter for a box of Yenems. He fell about laughing. On recovering, he asked, stifling his chuckles: "You want Yenems?" I replied in the affirmative. "Yenems," he said, holding his sides, "is Yiddish for the other fellow's."—*Sunday Times (South Africa), Business Times*, 3rd August 2003

yennep; yennap; yenep *noun*
a penny *UK, 1851*
Back slang.
• —David Powis, *The Signs of Crime*, 1977

yen pock *noun*
an opium pellet *US, 1934*
• If you want an introduction to Herbert Hoover, or a few yen pok of opium, speak up.—Bernard Wolfe, *The Late Risers*, p. 23, 1954

yen pop *noun*
marijuana *US, 1950*
• —Richard A. Spears, *The Slang and Jargon of Drugs and Drink*, p. 559, 1986
• —Mike Haskins, *Drugs*, p. 289, 2003

yen pox *noun*
opium ash *US*
• The old Chinaman dips river water into a rusty tin can, washes down a yen pox hard and black as a cinder. (Note: Yen pox is the ash of smoked opium.)—William Burroughs, *Naked Lunch*, p. 7, 1957
• [W]hile in Aruba we had picked up on yen-pox and had stayed knocked out the whole time we were there.—Herbert Huncke, *The Evening Sun Turned Crimson*, p. 100, 1980

yen-shee *noun*
heroin *US, 1960*
From an earlier generalised sense as 'opium' (which included heroin in its definition).
• —Richard A. Spears, *The Slang and Jargon of Drugs and Drink*, p. 559, 1986
• —Mike Haskins, *Drugs*, p. 285, 2003

Yenshee baby *noun*
an extremely constipated bowel movement that is the product of opiate addiction *US, 1938*
'Yenshee' is Chinese for 'opium residue'.
• And then came ripping down his intestines that glacial fecal boulder compacted by months of bowel paralysis, and through gritted teeth he cried, "Christ! The Yenshee baby."—Seth Morgan, *Homeboy*, p. 96, 1990

yen-shee-suey *noun*
opium or heroin dissolved in wine *US, 1949*
• —Richard A. Spears, *The Slang and Jargon of Drugs and Drink*, p. 559, 1986
• —Mike Haskins, *Drugs*, p. 285, 2003

yen sleep *noun*
a drowsiness encountered by many LSD users after the effects of the drug have worn off *US*
• —Carl Chambers and Richard Heckman, *Employee Drug Abuse*, p. 211, 1972

yenta *noun*
a gossip; a busybody; a scold *US, 1923*
Yiddish.
• He's a very wealthy guy, he owns a big business, he's a smart fellow and everything, but his behavior – in Jewish they'd call him a yenta – he never stops talking and does things that just don't make sense. —Edward Lin, *Big Julie of Vegas*, p. 103, 1974
• I think her idea of a good time was learned out of "Amos 'n Andy's" Sapphire, nurtured by Good Times and developed to the fullest yenta state possible by the Jeffersons.—Odie Hawkins, *Black Casanova*, p. 108, 1984
• You want me to get up in front of all your Long Island housewife yenta pals and confess my love?—Howard Stern, *Miss America*, p. 155, 1995

yeo *noun*
▷ **see: YAY**

yeola *noun*
marijuana *UK*
• —Mike Haskins, *Drugs*, p. 289, 2003

yep
yes *US, 1891*
A variation of 'yes'; the final plosive stresses the affirmative and gives it a semi-interjection or exclamatory sense.
• Should Americanisms be banished from the English Language? Yep.—*The Humorist*, 27th January 1934
• Yep, Harry always wanted to be a thesp, really.—James Hawes, *Dead Long Enough*, p. 63, 2000

yer actual *adjective*
▷ **see: YOUR ACTUAL**

yerba *noun*
marijuana *US, 1967*
A Mexican Spanish word that means 'herb' or 'grass', thus **HERB** (marijuana) or **GRASS** (marijuana).
• —Richard A. Spears, *The Slang and Jargon of Drugs and Drink*, p. 560, 1986
• —Mike Haskins, *Drugs*, p. 289, 2003

yerba mala *noun*
poor quality marijuana; phencyclidine *US*
Adopted from Mexican Spanish, the literal meaning is 'bad/evil grass'; *yerba beuna* (good grass) is probably also used.
• —Richard A. Spears, *The Slang and Jargon of Drugs and Drink*, p. 560, 1986

yerhia *noun*
marijuana *UK*
• —Mike Haskins, *Drugs*, p. 289, 2003

yer man *noun*
an unnamed male *IRELAND*
• Johnny followed him up to his house one evening and kicked him along the footpath. Yer man rolled in under a car.—Eamonn Sweeney, *Waiting for the Healer*, p. 167–168, 1997

yer one *noun*
an unnamed female *IRELAND*
• Yer one in Plunkett's told me it was waterproof but I didn't believe her.—Eamonn Sweeney, *Waiting for the Healer*, p. 81, 1997

yers *pronoun*
a variant spelling of 'youse' *AUSTRALIA, 1923*
• —Eric Lambert, *The Veterans*, p. 106, 1954
• Thought I wasn't here, didn't yers, but I was watchin' all the time. —Frank Hardy, *The Outcasts of Foolgarah*, p. 6, 1971

yesca; yesco *noun*
marijuana *US, 1949*
Directly from Spanish *yesca* (tinder), 'a fuel that is burnt'.
- Tea. Grifa. Yesca. Marijuana. Whatever you want to call it. — Thurston Scott, *Cure it with Honey*, p. 4, 1951
- — *American Speech*, p. 88, May 1955: 'Narcotic argot along the Mexican border'
- — Richard A. Spears, *The Slang and Jargon of Drugs and Drink*, p. 560, 1986
- — Mike Haskins, *Drugs*, p. 289, 2003

yes, if you've got the inclination; yes, but not the inclination
used as a catchphrase response to: 'Have you got the time?' *UK, 1977*
Also, 'yes, if you've got the money'.

yes man; yes-man *noun*
an obsequious subordinate; a person who agrees with everything a superior says or does *UK, 1912*
- But it is his relationship with [US president George W.] Bush that lessens the respect the Chinese have for [UK Prime Minister Tony] Blair, since they regard him as a yes-man of the United States. — *The Guardian*, 26th April 2002
- People like that always get their come-uppance. He'll be found out for what he really is – a yes man and a bluffer. — *The Observer*, 1st September 2002

yessir!
yes indeed *US, 1913*
- You look like you got class. Yessir! With a capital K. — *It Happened One Night*, 1934
- TRICIA: What happened was pretty obvious, I should have thought. MAURICE: Yessir, you behaved like a cad. — Peter Nichols, *Promenade [Six Granada Plays]*, p. 71, 1959

yes siree (Bob)
yes indeed *US, 1846*
- "Oh, it's happened all right," he said nodding, "yessiree bob!" — Terry Southern, *Blue Movie*, p. 57, 1970
- BUD: A repo man goes it alone. LITE: Yes siree bob. — *Repo Man*, 1984

yes sir, we're pals, and pals stick together
used as a humorous affirmation of agreement *US*
Used as the sign-off by Ed McConnell on the *Smilin' Ed's Gang* (1950–55) children's television programme. Repeated with referential humour.

yes sir, yes sir, three bags full
used for mocking unquestioning, blind obedience *US*
US naval aviator usage, from the children's song 'Ba-ba Black Sheep'.
- — *United States Naval Institute Proceedings*, p. 108, October 1986

yessus!; yesus!; yissus!
used for expressing anger, frustration, shock, surprise, etc *SOUTH AFRICA, 1942*
From the Afrikaans pronunciation of 'Jesus' as an oath or exclamation.
- But that day! Yessus ... in came the big machines with hot water[.] — Athol Fugard, *Sizwe Bansi Is Dead*, 1973
- [S]he just chased me out. Yissus, Miss, she was a kind of Brolloks herself, with glasses[.] — Andre Brink, *Imaginings of Sand*, p. 172, 1996

yesterday *adjective*
out-dated; unaware of current fashions and trends *US*
- — Hy Lit, *Hy Lit's Unbelievable Dictionary of Hip Words for Groovy People*, p. 46, 1968

Yes way!
used for humorously rebutting someone who has just said 'No way!' *US*
- NEW TED: We're you, dude! TED: No way. No way. NEW TED: Ted, Yes way, Ted. — *Bill and Ted's Excellent Adventure*, 1989

yes-woman; yes-girl *noun*
an obsequious female subordinate; a person who agrees with everything her superior says or does *US, 1930*
A consequence of **YES MAN**; originally 'yes-girl' had primacy but current use favours 'yes-woman'.
- To be a yes-woman or a yes-man doesn't do anybody any good. That leads to dictatorship. — *The Guardian*, 22nd May 2003

yettie *noun*
a successful person who is young, entrepreurial and technical *UK*
- [I]t is not sufficient to be a yettie (Young Entrepreneurial Technical yuppie, if you didn't know). — *The Observer*, 19th March 2000

yet to be *adjective*
free, gratis *UK*
Rhyming slang.
- — Julian Franklyn, *A Dictionary of Rhyming Slang*, 1961

yew *noun*
the eye *UK*
Usually in the plural.
- — Paul Baker, *Polari*, p. 195, 2002

yewie *noun*
▷ see: U-EY

yeyo; jejo *noun*
cocaine *UK, 1998*
Adopted directly from Spanish.
- — Nick Constable, *This is Cocaine*, p. 181, 2002

yez *pronoun*
you (plural) *IRELAND, 1828*
Originally only in representations of Irish speakers, but later as the typical Australian pronunciation with an unstressed vowel.
- 'Deed, miss, it's the truth, on my sowl. I've but jest come back to yez this morning. O my! but it's a cruel thrick to play an ould man. — Marcus Clarke, *His Natural Life*, p. 203, 1874
- She heard Jinny's hoarse whisper, 'Orl of yez wait an' I'll bring yer sumsin'.' — Barbara Baynton, *Bush Studies*, p. 128, 1902
- BOSS GANGER: Well, Mick, how did you enjoy your Christmas holidays?' MICK: Well, to tell yez the truth, O'im glad to be back to worruk fer a rest. — Norman Lindsay, *Comic Art of Norman Lindsay*, p. 190, 1914
- — Nino Culotta (John O'Grady), *They're A Weird Mob*, p. 75, 1957
- — Lance Peters, *The Dirty Half-Mile*, p. 91, 1979
- The kid only had a halfpenny. The bulls' eyes is a penny each. Nothink cheaper. "How much does yez pay for empty bottles?" says the kid. I says a penny. — Hesba Brinsmead, *Longtime Dreaming*, p. 58, 1982
- Hey girls! Comin' up the pub with us? Come on, we'll buy yez a drink! — Mr Rhees, *Oz-Wide Tales*, p. 17, 1990

Yid *noun*
a Jewish person *US, 1874*
Offensive.
- But a pair of racially pure Nordic behemoths from Minnesota, sent proudly to the team by scouting old grads, decided that, although they had nothing personal against the yid, no yid would call their signals. — Philip Wylie, *Opus 21*, p. 230, 1949
- BRIAN: I'm not a Roman, Mum, and I never will be! I'm a Kike! A Yid! A Hebe! A Hook-nose! I'm Kosher, Mum! I'm a Red Sea Pedestrian, and proud of it! — Monty Python, *Life of Brian*, 1979
- "This isn't back when we were kids, beating up on the yids and ginzos," Pat said. — Robert Campbell, *Juice*, p. 171, 1988

yiddel; yiddle *noun*
a Jewish person *US*
- I made up a little doggerel song about him that went, "Don't fiddle with the Yiddle, or he'll riddle you in the middle." — Mezz Mezzrow, *Really the Blues*, p. 70, 1946
- Yes, I was one happy yiddel down there in Washington. — Philip Roth, *Portnoy's Complaint*, p. 262, 1969

Yiddish highway *noun*
US Highway 301, which runs between New York and Miami, Florida *US*
- — *Maledicta*, p. 165, 1979: 'A glossary of ethnic slurs in American English'

Yid kid *noun*
a young Jewish person *US*
- — *Maledicta*, p. 174, Summer/Winter 1978: 'How to hate thy neighbor: a guide to racist maledicta'

Yidsbury *nickname*
Finsbury, an area of north London with (traditionally) a large Jewish population *UK, 1981*
A combination with **YID** (a Jewish person).

yike *noun*
a fight; an altercation *AUSTRALIA, 1940*
- [I] was just a second mate having a yike about a woman passenger with the ship's skipper. — Robert S. Close, *Love Me Sailor*, p. 48, 1945

- —Jim Ramsay, *Cop It Sweet!*, p. 98, 1977
- Two grades of yike apply in football. A 'bit of a yike' – a heated argument. A 'real yike' – the wild brawl that follows the heated argument. —Ivor Limb, *Footy's No Joke!*, p. 77, 1986

yikes!

used in surprise, pain or shock *US, 1971*

Possibly a variant of conventional 'yoicks!' or 'crikey!' (Christ!).

- Two [bullets] hit the pavement beside my car and one zinged off my front bumper. Yikes. —Janet Evanovich, *Seven Up*, p. 30, 2001

Yim, Yoe and Yesus *noun*

in poker, three jacks *AUSTRALIA*

A play on 'Jim, Joe and Jesus' (instead of Jack), but the reason why is unknown.

- —Sidney J. Baker, *Asustralia Speaks*, 1953

yimyom *noun*

crack cocaine *UK, 1998*

- —Mike Haskins, *Drugs*, p. 282, 2003

yin *noun*

one, indicating a single person or thing *UK: SCOTLAND, 1911*

Often in nicknames, such as 'Big Yin' (Billy Connolly), 'wee yin', etc.

- What'd yi make of that yin, eh? —Ian Pattison, *Rab C. Nesbitt*, 1988

ying *noun*

marijuana *UK*

This word seems to derive from the combination of two facts lodged in a vaguely **HIPPIE** philosophy: 1) the female cannabis plant is considered superior; 2) in Eastern philosophy, the concept of two complementary forces that make life is *yin yang*. 'Yin', mispronounced here as 'ying', represents the female.

- —Mike Haskins, *Drugs*, p. 289, 2003

ying yang *noun*

1 the anus and/or rectum *US*

- [I]t lubricates the shaft with splittle, excites the person about to be sucked, thereby dilating the yingyang[.] —Angelo d'Arcangelo, *The Homosexual Handbook*, p. 110, 1968

2 the penis *US*

- —*Maledicta*, p. 255, Summer/Winter 1981: 'Five years and 121 dirty words later'

3 a variety of LSD identified by the ying yang (yin yang) symbol *UK*

- —Angela Devlin, *Prison Patter*, p. 125, 1996
- —Mike Haskins, *Drugs*, p. 286, 2003

▸ **up the ying yang**

to excess *US*

The suggestion of 'ying-yang' is 'the rectum'.

- We got pictures up the ying-yang, and they're good pictures, too. —George V. Higgins, *The Judgment of Deke Hunter*, p. 28, 1976
- He buys me drinks up the ying yang, gets me righteously lubed, then splits. —James Ellroy, *Because the Night*, p. 485, 1984

yin-yang *noun*

a well-known variety of MDMA, the recreational drug best known as ecstasy, identified by the yin and yang symbols embossed on the tablet *UK*

- [T]ake the form of tablets that forge "reputable" ecstasy brands [...] Yin-yang pills containing only MDE. —Gareth Thomas, *This Is Ecstasy*, p. 80, 2002

yip *verb*

to bark in a piercing and shrill manner *US, 1907*

- The schnauzer probably didn't give a shit one way or the other, but recognized a tone that could mean a doggie treat, sat up in the chair, pointed her little ears and yipped once. —Elmore Leonard, *Switch*, p. 109, 1978

yipes!; yipe!

used in shock, pain or surprise

Synonymous variations of **YIKES!**.

yippee!; yippy!

used as a declaration of excitement and assent *US, 1920*

- KATHRYN: I don't think she'll be giving you any more problems. SEBASTIAN: Yippy. —*Cruel Intentions*, 1999

yippie *noun*

a member of, or adherent (knowing or not) to, the principles of the Youth International Party, a short-lived blend of 1960s counterculture values and New Left politics *US*

- Coincidental with the Democrats' Convention there's going to be a Youth International Party – YIP – and Chicago will be invaded by a mass of yippies. —*The Realist*, p. 21, August 1967
- And the Yippies are trying to sue the University for evicting us from our homes which we owned by virtue of squatters' rights. —James Simon Kunen, *The Strawberry Statement*, p. 45, 1968
- There never were any Yippies and there never will be. It was a slogan YIPPIE! and that exclamation point was what it was all about. It was the biggest put-on of all time. If you believe Yippies existed, you are nothing but a sheep. —Abbie Hoffman, *Revolution for the Hell of It*, p. 121, 1968
- The other two principal groups were the S.D.S. (of Morningside Heights fame) and the fun and very-loving Yippies. —Terry Southern, *Now Dig This*, p. 119, November 1968
- I live for the revolution. I'm a yippie! I am an orphan of Amerika. —Jerry Rubin, *Do It!*, p. 13, 1970
- All of us in the room that New Year's Eve knew, when we heard it, that in a few months "yippie" would become a household word. —Jerry Rubin, *Do It!*, p. 81, 1970
- This was the Youth International Party. ("Yippee! Yippee! Say it loud and you'll see what we mean.") —Richard Neville, *Play Power*, p. 38, 1970

yissus!

▷ see: **YESSUS!**

YL *noun*

an unmarried woman; a girlfriend *US*

An abbreviation of '*y*oung *l*ady'.

- —"Slingo", *The Official CB Slang Dictionary Handbook*, p. 67, 1976
- —Peter Chippindale, *The British CB Book*, p. 160, 1981

YM *noun*

1 a premises of the YMCA (the Young Men's Christian Association), or the organisation itself *US, 1937*

Pronounced 'wy em'.

2 a boyfriend *US*

Acronym of '*y*oung *m*an'.

- —*Complete CB Slang Dictionary, (US)*, p. 99, 1976
- —Peter Chippindale, *The British CB Book*, p. 160, 1981

YMCA dinner *noun*

a meal made from leftovers *AUSTRALIA, 2003*

Standing for '*y*esterday's *m*uck *c*ooked *a*gain'.

yo; Yolanda *noun*

in craps, a roll of eleven *US*

- —Chris Fagans and David Guzman, *A Guide to Craps Lingo*, p. 36, 1999

yo!

1 used as a greeting *US, 1944*

Both Italian-American and black communities lay claim to 'yo!'. First recorded in 1944 among Philadelphia's Italian-Americans and popularised by Sylvester Stallone in the 1976 film *Rocky*.

- —Connie Eble (Editor), *UNC-CH Campus Slang*, November 1976
- Yo! We don't score school lunch. —Jess Mowry, *Way Past Cool*, p. 12, 1992
- —Claudio R. Salvucci, *The Philadelphia Dialect Dictionary*, p. 66, 1996
- MAUREEN: Yo! Yo! This is my bloke I was telling you about. —Lanre Fehintola, *Charlie Says...*, p. 47, 2000

2 used as an expression of surprise, contempt, dismay, etc *SOUTH AFRICA, 1871*

- —Jean Branford, *A Dictionary of South African English*, 1978

yob *noun*

an uncultured, boorish person *AUSTRALIA, 1938*

Ultimately back slang, from 'boy'.

- Well, this big fat copper looks at him dead savage and says, "When I tell you to move, you dirty little yob, you bloody well move." —John Peter Jones, *Feather Pluckers*, p. 7, 1964
- YOB: A retarded person. —Jim Ramsay, *Cop It Sweet!*, p. 98, 1977
- —Ryan Aven-Bray, *Ridgey Didge Oz Jack Lang*, p. 53, 1983
- Oh God, a Valiant load of unenlightened yobs are pulling into the curb. —Kathy Lette, *Girls' Night Out*, p. 37, 1987
- It's amazing isn't it that you have to get a licence to own a dog in the suburbs, but that any yob can have a baby. —Kathy Lette, *Girls' Night Out*, p. 45, 1987
- —Ignatius Jones, *The 1992 True Hip Manual*, p. 84, 1992
- It doesn't matter if you're a yob, a toff or just your average joe blow – everyone's welcome. —*Australian Ultimate*, p. 7, 2003

yobbery *noun*

hooliganism *UK, 1974*

- And to the people who feel that their own town centres are closed to them on a Friday night, I say: we will crack down on violence and yobbery. —William Hague MP, 4th March 2001

yobbish *adjective*

loutish, characteristic of a yob *UK, 1972*

- A yobbish minority can still make the lives of hard working citizens a living hell. — *BBC News*, 12th March 2003

yobbo; yobo; yobboe *noun*

a lout *UK, 1938*

A variation of **YOB**.

- I've had enough of yobboes. —John Burke and Stuart Douglass, *The Boys*, p. 45, 1962
- "I can tell a yobboe," said Brewer confidently. They're young teds, I've seen 'em before." —John Burke and Stuart Douglass, *The Boys*, p. 48, 1962
- A right little yobbo. — *The Sweeney*, p. 29, 1976
- [A]t that moment one of the yobboes twisted round in a highly acrobatic manner, aiming a back kick at Terry as he did so. —Anthony Masters, *Minder*, p. 5, 1984
- The old image of a yobbo in a dirty singlet, a chilled tube in his hand and corks hanging off his hat is about as accurate as saying that the average Brit wears a monocle, bowler hat, furled umbrella and the works! —Barry Humphries, *The Traveller's Tool*, p. 110, 1985
- When he was in his fifties he was attacked in the street by a couple of yobbos. —Joe Morgan, *Eastenders Don't Cry*, p. 87, 1994
- On the way home I tried to make sense of the yobbo's aggression. —Chris Ryan, *Stand By, Stand By*, p. 60, 1996

yobby *adjective*

characteristic of a yob *UK, 1955*

- Then there was a yobby naked chef. — *The Guardian*, 16th May 2002

yo-bo *noun*

a member of the Korean Service Corps *US*

Korean war usage.

- The supply column, or "yo-bo train" as it is called, is usually composed of ten members of the Korean Service Corps (yo-bos) escorted by a fire team of marines, that is, four marines. —Martin Russ, *The Last Parallel*, p. 226, 1957

yochie *noun*

in the language surrounding the Grateful Dead, a follower of the band who has lost all touch with reality *US*

- —David Shenk and Steve Silberman, *Skeleton Key*, p. 182, 1994

yock *noun*

a laugh *US, 1938*

- All right, all right, gentlemen, have your yocks, but then let's get down to work. —John Clellon Holmes, *The Horn*, p. 124, 1958
- He paused until somebody chuckled. But this was way too seirous a matter for real yocks. —Ross Russell, *The Sound*, p. 47, 1961

yock *verb*

1 to laugh *US, 1938*

- You boys get your kicks, go ahead, yock it up. —John Clellon Holmes, *The Horn*, p. 125, 1958
- The crowd yocked. The crowd roared. —James Ellroy, *The Cold Six Thousand*, p. 523, 2001

2 to expel nasal mucus *UK*

- The snot is starting to run freely, as fast as I can yock it out there's another load funnelling down. —Kevin Sampson, *Outlaws*, p. 273, 2001

yockele *noun*

a Christian *UK*

Slightly derogatory East End Yiddish; perhaps an elaborate back slang variation of **GOY**. 'Yog' is recorded for 'a Gentile' in 1939.

- —David Powis, *The Signs of Crime*, 1977

yocks *noun*

the eyes *UK, 1936*

English gypsy use.

- —Patrick O'Shaughnessy, *Market Traders' Slang*, 1979
- —Jimmy Stockin, *On The Cobbles*, p. 11, 2000

yodel *noun*

an act of vomiting *NEW ZEALAND, 1995*

- —Harry Orsman, *A Dictionary of Modern New Zealand Slang*, p. 152, 1999

yodel *verb*

1 to vomit *AUSTRALIA*

- 'Can you yodel?' grinned Cal. 'I understand that's a definite aid to sales.' 'Only into a bucket,' chortled Stripey. —John Wynnum, *Jiggin' in the Riggin'*, p. 45, 1965
- —Frank Hardy, *The Outcasts of Foolgarah*, p. 198, 1971
- —Barry Humphries, *The Traveller's Tool*, p. 119, 1985

2 to perform oral sex on a woman *US, 1941*

▸ **yodel up the valley**

to perform oral sex on a woman *AUSTRALIA*

An elaboration of conventional 'yodel'.

- BARRY: Well, I dunno about you Suke – but I feel like dining at the Y. SUKE: Well darls [darling] if you wanted to yodel up the valley youse had your chance[.] —Barry Humphries, *Bazza Pulls It Off!*, 1971

yodeller *noun*

a Chrysler car

Citizens' band radio slang.

- —Peter Chippindale, *The British CB Book*, p. 161, 1981

yog; yogg *noun*

a fire in the hearth *UK, 1979*

Market traders' use, directly from Romany.

yogga *noun*

a gun *UK*

English gypsy use, perhaps from **YOG** (a fire).

- —Jimmy Stockin, *On The Cobbles*, p. 11, 2000

yoghurt cannon *noun*

the penis *UK*

An image formed on an ejaculating penis.

- —Chris Donald, *Roger's Profanisaurus*, 1998

yogi *noun*

1 a member of the uniformed personnel (commissionaire, security, etc) at Nottingham University in the early 1970s *UK*

Derives, apparently, from US animated cartoon series *Yogi Bear*, first broadcast in 1958.

2 a poker player with the annoying habit of coaching other players *US*

- —John Vorhaus, *The Big Book of Poker Slang*, p. 41, 1996

yoink *verb*

to steal *US*

- —Connie Eble (Editor), *UNC-CH Campus Slang*, p. 11, October 2002

yoinks!

used for registering surprise *UK*

- I take a dab [of drugs]. "OOH! It's bitter-as-fuck. Yoinks!" —Charlie Hall, *The Box [The Howard Marks Book of Dope Stories]*, p. 200, 1997

yoke *noun*

1 a tablet of MDMA, the recreational drug best known as ecstasy *IRELAND*

This usage is an extension of the Hiberno-English use of the term for 'something whose name does not spring immediately to mind'.

- A male voice asked the Garda for some "yokes" – which he took to mean the supply of ecstasy tablets[.] — *Irish Times*, 9th May 1998

2 a choke hold *US*

Identified by Stroud as originally military slang embraced by the police.

- —Carsten Stroud, *Close Pursuit*, p. 277, 1987

3 robbery by force *US*

- Three young colored boxers, aged 14, 16, and 17, terrorized Washington a few months ago, committing at least 19 yoke robberies, netting more than $2,000. —Jack Lait and Lee Mortimer, *Washington Confidential*, p. 53, 1951

yoked; yolked *adjective*

muscular *US*

- —Judi Sanders, *Faced and Faded, Hanging to Hurl*, p. 44, 1993
- —Jim Goad, *Jim Goad's Glossary of Northwestern Prison Slang*, December 2001

yokel *noun*

an unsophisticated, gullible person, especially one with a rural background *UK, 1812*

- Generally speaking, the kinds of yokels we spell with a capital Y prefer inns in the Times Square district. —Jack Lait and Lee Mortimer, *New York Confidential*, p. 202, 1948

- They put him on his mettle, added zest to his existence in a way that the yokels never could. —Jim Thompson, *Bad Boy*, p. 353, 1953
- I'm no yokel. Why, I was all the way to Miami once. —*Body Heat*, 1980

yola *noun*

a light-skinned black female *US*

- —Marcus Hanna Boulware, *Jive and Slang of Students in Negro Colleges*, 1947

Yolanda *noun*

▷ see: YO

yomo; yom *noun*

a person, a fellow *US*

- Meanwhile I already had four hundred and fifty in my pockets on accounta I had glommed it earlier from the yom. —Edwin Torres, *Q & A*, p. 121, 1977
- I got this yomo down, knee in the back, cuffin' him up, the kid's crying. —Richard Price, *Clockers*, p. 366, 1992

yomp *verb*

to cross rough country on foot, especially when fully laden with equipment *UK*

A Royal Marines term from the Falklands/Malvinas war.

- Always in the cold light of the Falklands dawn, the bootneck Marines and their equally hardy officers have been ready to "yomp on" for the next stage of the journey. —*Financial Times*, p. 4, 3rd June 1982
- —Nicholas Jones, *Hackers, Hotting and Hooray Henrys*, p. 63, 1992
- —Bernadette Hince, *The Antarctic Dictionary*, p. 392, 2000

Yonge and Eligible *noun*

the Yonge and Eglinton street area *CANADA*

- "The appelation 'Yonge and Eligible' arises from the large number of singles in the area. —Chris Coyle, 10th June 2002

yoni *noun*

the vagina *TRINIDAD AND TOBAGO*

From the Sanskrit term, which is an object of Hindu veneration.

- —Lise Winer, *Dictionary of the English/Creole of Trinidad & Tobago*, 2003

yonks *noun*

an indefinitely long time *UK, 1968*

- I haven't seen him for yonks. —Ann Barr and Peter York, *The Official Sloane Ranger Handbook*, p. 159, 1982
- This wis yonks ago now though. —Irvine Welsh, *The State of the Party (Disco Biscuits)*, p. 33, 1995
- We did security at the Apollo for yonks but you got to be talking fifteen, twenty years ago now. —Nicholas Blincoe, *The Beautiful Beaten-up Irish Boy of the Arndale Centre*, p. 7, 1998
- Shoulda been fuckin' banned yonks ago, man[.] —Christopher Brookmyre, *Boiling a Frog*, p. 14, 2000
- Didn't see him for yonks after that. —Niall Griffiths, *Sheepshagger*, p. 55, 2001

yonnie *noun*

a small stone suitable for throwing *AUSTRALIA, 1941*

Probably from an Australian Aboriginal language.

- A commotion outside signalled the return of the Lerdyberg Street push [gang] who, having tired of throwing yonnies on widow Johnson's roof, had decided on a return match with the billiard players. —Frank Hardy, *Legends From Benson's Valley*, p. 54, 1963
- —Jim Ramsay, *Cop It Sweet!*, p. 98, 1977

yoof; yufe *noun*

a young person; the period of youth *UK*

A deliberate mispronunciation of 'youth', used by Leicestershire teenagers.

- —D. and R. McPheely, 1977
- [I] got back to my boyfriend Graham's parents' place, and spent the balance of the evening vomiting. Ah, yoof. —Claire Mansfield and John Mendelssohn, *Dominatrix*, p. 40, 2002

yoof *adjective*

used to describe any product (especially of the media) for the youth-market that may be characterised as high on fashionable content and criticised as low-culture *UK*

A deliberate misspelling of 'youth', mocking the pronunciation of stereotypical 'yoof' television presenters, emphasising the critical view.

- Acceptable to the Mass Audience yoof yet also to the critics? —James Hawes, *Dead Long Enough*, p. 55, 2000
- Spider-man is w-w-wicked. It's about American yoof culture. —*Varsity*, p. 26, 14th June 2002

yoofsploitation *noun*

the exploitation of youth culture and imagery for commercial gain, especially in films *UK*

- [A] digital, shoulder-shot, Blair Witch-style, mocumentary, shoot-em-up, yoofsploitation number based on ecowarriors[.] —James Hawes, *White Powder, Green Light*, p. 5, 2002

yoo-hoo *noun*

a poker player who engages in excessive needless table talk *US*

- —John Vorhaus, *The Big Book of Poker Slang*, p. 41, 1996

yoo-hoo *verb*

to try to get someone's attention by calling 'yoo-hoo' *US, 1948*

- Not wave or yoo-hoo at him, he'd have to be cool, but make sure the cop saw him. —Elmore Leonard, *Glitz*, p. 227, 1985

yoot; yut; yout *noun*

a youth; a youth gang member *US*

West Indian.

- I thought of the pot-bellied yuts I'd met[.] —Philip Wylie, *Opus 21*, p. 14, 1949
- —*New York Herald Tribune*, p. 47, 28th February 1954
- —Kenn "Naz" Young, *Naz's Dictionary of Teen Slang*, p. 145, 1993
- At seventeen he was just a "yout", but he was sharp and loyal to the bone. —Karline Smith, *Moss Side Massive*, p. 1, 1994

yop *verb*

to inform on someone *UK: SCOTLAND, 1985*

School slang, recorded in Glasgow.

- Ah hink [think] Ah know who yopped on us. —Michael Munro, *The Complete Patter*, p. 172, 1996

york *verb*

to vomit *US*

- —John D. Bell et al., *Loosely Speaking*, p. 22, 1966

Yorkie; Yorky *noun*

a Yorkshireman or -woman *UK: ENGLAND, 1818*

- An honorary Yorkie. —*BBC Sport*, 23rd August 2002

Yorkshire Penny Bank *noun*

an act of masturbation; more usually, something of little or no value *UK*

Rhyming slang for **WANK** (an act of masturbation).

- [N]ot worth a Yorkshire Penny Bank. —Red Daniells, 1980

Yorkshire Ripper *noun*

a slipper *UK*

Rhyming slang, formed on the nickname of mass murderer Peter Sutcliffe who was at large in the 1970s.

- —Ray Puxley, *Cockney Rabbit*, 1992

Yorkshire tyke *noun*

a microphone *UK*

Rhyming slang for **MIKE**.

- —Dallas Bower, 1957

you ain't said nothing

used for expressing contempt for what has just been said *US*

- —Joan Fontaine et al., *Dictionary of Black Slang*, 1968

you and me *noun*

1 a flea *UK*

Rhyming slang. A C19 term recorded as current.

- —Ray Puxley, *Fresh Rabbit*, 1998

2 tea *UK, 1925*

Rhyming slang.

- —Julian Franklyn, *A Dictionary of Rhyming Slang*, p. 138, 1960
- —Sydney (Steak) T. Kendall, *Up The Frog*, p. 43, 1969
- —Ray Puxley, *Fresh Rabbit*, p. 133, 1998

3 urine; urination *UK*

Rhyming slang for **WEE** or **PEE**.

- —Ray Puxley, *Fresh Rabbit*, 1998

4 a pea *UK*

Rhyming slang.

- Fresh, frozen, tinned or dried and blown through a shooter. They're all "you & mes". —Ray Puxley, *Fresh Rabbit*, 1998

you beaut *adjective*

great; excellent *AUSTRALIA*

- And to keep up that 'you beaut' Queensland image they're called bunyahs. —*Australian*, p. 22, 6th July 1974

you beaut!; you beauty!; you bewdy!

excellent!, terrific!, hooray! *AUSTRALIA, 1943*

- 'You beaut!' I cried. 'You bloody beaut!' —Lawson Glassop, *We Were The Rats*, p. 212, 1944

- 'Hooray! You beaut!' cheered everyone, and Lick Jimmy, taking it as a compliment, shook his clasped hands at them and vanished into the darkness again. — Ruth Park, *The Harp In The South*, p. 80, 1949
- 'You bloody beaut,' sighed the Chief. — John Wynnum, *Tar Dust*, p. 13, 1962
- I'm *in* with her, he thought. You beaut. — Ray Slattery, *Mobbs' Mob*, p. 109, 1966
- In 1961, artist John Olsen began a series of (mainly) non-figurative paintings which he called *You Beaut Country*. — Sidney J. Baker, *The Australian Language*, p. 208, 1966
- — James Holledge, *The Great Australian Gamble*, p. 59, 1966
- — Jim Ramsay, *Cop It Sweet!*, p. 98, 1977
- 'Yew fuckin' bewdy!' bellowed a drunk in a T shirt, leaning out of a passing car and pointing at my blue and white striped jumper. — Helen Garner, *Monkey Grip*, p. 146, 1977
- You bewdy Grafton...Three cheers for the Bible, Hip, Hip, Hooray. — Ross Fitzgerald, *All About Anthrax*, p. 97, 1987

you beautery *noun*

excellence *AUSTRALIA, 1965*

- In 1961, artist John Olsen began a series of (mainly) non-figurative paintings which he called *You Beaut Country*. (Whence doubtless 'a touch of You Beautery', enthusiasm for Australia – 'Nation', July 24th, 1965.) — Sidney J. Baker, *The Australian Language*, p. 208, 1966
- Taking a feed from the ABC's coverage, Nine supplied its 60 Minutes studio audience of 120 with sophisticated, computerised you-beautery so each could instantly record their reactions as the two political stars responded to questioning. — *Herald-Sun*, p. 4, 15th February 1993

you betcha!

used for expressing emphatic affirmation *US*

- — Tom Hibbert, *Rockspeak!*, p. 175, 1983

you better believe it

a catchphrase used for expressing emphatic agreement *US, 1969*

- I'll take what you got, so you'd better hold on / You'd better believe it — Phil Collins, *That's How I Feel*, 1990

you can go off some people, you know

used as a (usually jocular) response to offence or imagined offence *UK, 1984*

- They laughed at her ability to speak volumes with the arch of a single eyebrow and her often-muttered phrase "You can go off some people" when displeased. — *The Post (Perth, Western Australia)*, 29th July 2000

you can have it!; you can keep it!

I want nothing to do with it! *UK, 1930*

you cannot be serious!

that is preposterous! *US*

A stock phrase of US tennis star John McEnroe whose questioning of officials' calls was as legendary as his genius at the game. Of all his rants against tennis officialdom, this one spread into mainstream catchphrase status.

you can say that again

used as an expression of heartfelt agreement *US, 1942*

- "Roy [Jenkins] had a tendency to grandeur," said Shirley Williams, and you could almost hear 1,400 people muttering under their breath, "you can say that again." — *The Guardian*, 28th March 2003

you can say that in spades

used as an expression of heartfelt agreement *UK*

Card playing imagery.

- "You look bushed. You need a drink." – "You can say that in spades," I said. — John Welcome, *Beware of Midnight*, 1961

you can't stop him, you can only hope to contain him

used as a humorous comment on a high achiever *US*

Popularised by ESPN's Dan Patrick.

- — Keith Olberman and Dan Patrick, *The Big Show*, p. 27, 1997

you can't take it with you!

directed at someone who, in saving money, loses happiness *UK, 1847*

- What has always been said is also / True: you can't take it with you. — John Fuller, *The Flea Market*, June 2003

you could have knocked me down with a feather

used for expressing astonishment at something that has happened *UK, 1741*

- When he said he wanted to see Chief Hovre you coulda knocked me down with a feather (Laughs.) I guess he got his wish, didn't he? — Peter Straub, *If You Could See Me Now*, p. 44, 1977

you don't even know

used as an intensifier when words fail *US*

- We went cruising in her dad's Alfa Spider and you-don't-even-know. — Jonathan Roberts, *How to California*, p. 174, 1984

you don't know the half of it!

used, as a catchphrase, to imply so much more *US*

- — *Washington Post*, 29th December 2002: 'Portion distortion – you don't know the half of it'

you don't say!

used for expressing astonishment at a statement *US, 1912*

you don't say so!

used for expressing astonishment at a statement *UK, 1779*

you-ee *noun*

▷ see: U-EY

you for coffee?

an unambiguous invitation to drink coffee pronounced 'you fuck-offee!' *UK, 1984*

you go, girl!

used as an encouragement or exhortation *US*

Popularised by several black entertainers relatively simultaneously in the 1990s, and widely repeated, usually in a woman-to-woman context.

- But in a city with problems as desperate as Detroit's it remains to be seen if the strategy, which extends down to Ms. McPhail's "You Go, Girl," a street-slang slogan for "go get 'em," will override more pragmatic judgments. — *New York Times*, p. A1, 18th October 1993
- — Connie Eble (Editor), *UNC-CH Campus Slang*, p. 6, Spring 1993
- HOLLY: Well, I don't know, but I certainly didn't like his attitude and I'm going to think long and hard before I take him back. JANE: You go, girl! — *Boys on the Side*, 1995

you haven't got the brains you were born with

used as a derisive catchphrase *UK, 1961*

- You'd think Johnny would have had the sense not to tell the Dibble [police] who put him in the hospital, but some people haven't got the brains they were born with. — Val McDermid, *Keeping on the Right Side of the Law*, 2003

you have some explaining to do

used for humour when there is in fact some explanation owed *US*

A catchphrase from the *I Love Lucy* television series (1951–61), with the 'explaining' often butchered with a pseudo Desi Arnaz Cuban accent to ''splaining'.

- I'm sure he's got a lot of explaining to do. — *Hard Eight*, 1996

you heard!

'you heard me all right, so don't pretend you didn't!' or 'Oh, you understand, so stop pretending!' *US*

- TYCOON: Have you lost your love for me, Jones? JONES: Yes. TYCOON (APPALLED): What did you say? Guess this is a bad connexion. JONES: You heard. — John Mortimer, *Conference*, 1960

you know *noun*

cocaine *UK*

Rhyming slang for **SNOW** (or, possibly, **BLOW**).

- — Ray Puxley, *Fresh Rabbit*, 1998

you know

used as a verbal pause for indicating that the speaker assumes that the listener is listening, understanding and agreeing *UK, 1599*

An annoying discourse marker if ever there was one.

- — Miss Cone, *The Slang Dictionary (Hawthorne High School)*, 1965
- Instead of using Cockney or Liverpool slang for humorous effect, narked, knickers-job and all that, he began using American hip-lower-class slang, like, I mean, you know, baby, and a little late Madison Avenue. — Tom Wolfe, *The Pump House Gang*, p. 44, 1968
- Let's hold it down though, y'know? / However it's gon' go down / This what we gotta deal with, y'know? — Nas *Life We Chose*, 1999

you know what

an unnamed (but strongly implied) activity or thing *UK, 1845*

The ultimate multi-purpose euphemism.

- ["]I 'aven't done nothink so get well you know what," he adds under his breath[.] — Derek Raymond (Robin Cook), *The Crust on its Uppers*, p. 48, 1962

- I tried not to perv on it, know mean, but fucking hell, man, them two shiny, beautiful you-know-whats pushing out of her blouse.—Kevin Sampson, *Clubland*, p. 82, 2002

you know what you can do!; you know what you can do with it!; you know what to do with it!
used as a very definite expression of rejection of someone or something *UK, 1945*
A barely euphemistic catchphrase.
- Are all those volumes your evidence? Well, you know what you can do with it, don't you?—*Washington Post*, 25th July 2002

you like?
used as a humorous mock pidgin version of 'do you like this?' *US*
- Yeah, I get a discount on clothes and shit. You like?—*Boyz N The Hood*, 1990

you little beaut; you little beauty
used as praise *AUSTRALIA, 1945*
- Randall relieved his own tenseness in one single flaming epithet. And then he added, more printably: 'You bloody little beaut!' —J.E. MacDonnell, *Alarm – E-boats!*, p. 139, 1958
- 'Dad – you little beauty!' Ashleigh grinned[.]—Willie Fennell, *Dexter Gets the Point*, p. 122, 1961

you'll be a long time dead!
a catchphrase offered as an excuse for indulgent behaviour *UK*
- [Y]ou're a long time dead.—John Osbourne, *The Entertainer*, 1957

you'll do yourself out of a job
used as a jocular catchphrase addressed to someone working hard *UK, 1977*

you look marrrrvelous
used for humorous praise *US*
Popularised by comedian Billy Crystal on NBC's *Saturday Night Live* in the 1980s; uttered by a Crystal character, Fernando. Repeated with referential humour.

you make a better door than a window
addressed to a person getting in the light, or blocking a view *NEW ZEALAND, 1941*
- Wisenheimers love to tell you that you make a better door than a window if you are blocking their view of World's Wildest Police Videos.—*Cornell Daily Sun (Ithca, New York)*, 30th January 2003

you never get a satisfied cock without a wet pussy
used for expressing the principle of symbiosis *UK, 1967*

you never know
something unexpected may well happen *UK, 1924*
- You never know, I may even thank him.—*The Guardian*, 3rd September 2001

young *adjective*
▸ **not so young as I was; not as young as he used to be**
getting or being old *UK, 1852*

▸ **the night is young; the night is yet young**
it is still early *UK, 1937*
- Neil Kinnock last night refused to concede defeat following his re-election in Islwyn, claiming "the battle is not yet over and the night is still young".—*The Guardian*, 10th April 1992

youngblood *noun*
a young man, especially a young black man and especially an impetuous one; used as a term of address to a young man *US, 1946*
- Does all this sound like I'm making it up, youngblood?—Eldridge Cleaver, *Soul on Ice*, p. 160, 1968
- Now Youngblood, about Pepper. You don't know anything about her.—Iceberg Slim (Robert Beck), *Pimp*, p. 66, 1969
- Hey, youngblood, pretty fancy place you living in.—Cecil Brown, *The Life & Loves of Mr. Jiveass Nigger*, p. 118, 1969
- Young bloods wanted to be like these brothers.—H. Rap Brown, *Die Nigger Die!*, p. 15, 1969
- "I wouldn't jive you, youngblood," he answered his critic with a deadpan under his cap.—Odie Hawkins, *The Busting Out of an Ordinary Man*, p. 88, 1985

young, dumb, and full of come *adjective*
used for describing a young man with great hopes and little experience *US*
- Because we were young, dumb and full of come, and all there for the same fun and games[.]—Robert Gover, *Poorboy at the Party*, p. 53, 1966
- —Michael Dalton Johnson, *Talking Trash with Redd Foxx*, p. 33, 1994
- —David Mamet, *Heist*, 2001

young fellow-me-lad; young feller-me-lad *noun*
used as a semi-jocular form of address *UK, 1926*

young fogey *noun*
a young person with out-dated ideas and values *UK*
Coinage is claimed by Australian writer and wit Clive James.
- A Labour poster fingers him nicely. It shows a 16-year-old [William] Hague with long hair and lapels you would not believe, a young fogey down to the fake leather buttons[.]—*The Guardian*, 24th May 2001
- I was the person to say "young fogey" and "underwhelmed" but you don't get any credit for that. Neither are in the Oxford English Dictionary[.]—*Word*, p. 54, September 2004

youngie *noun*
a young woman; a young person *AUSTRALIA, 1965*
The natural corollary of **OLDIE**.
- A lot of oldies didn't like youngies was the strength of it.—Wilda Moxham, *The Apprentice*, p. 94, 1969
- The youngies seem to love central Australia, for example, just as much as the old.—*The Courier Mail*, 29th November 2002

young lady *noun*
a female sweetheart *UK, 1896*
- A man behind me talks to his young lady / He's happy that she is expecting his baby, / His wife won't be pleased but she's not been round lately.—Squeeze *Piccadilly*, 1981

young man *noun*
a male sweetheart *UK, 1851*
- Don't knock her young man, you don't know what he'll get done. —Stone Roses, *Something's burning*, 1990

young one *noun*
an attractive young girl who is sexually of age *IRELAND*
- The windows were steaming up. Darren rubbed his and watched the people walking along the sea front, looking out for young ones. —Roddy Doyle, *The Van*, p. 21, 1991

young stir *noun*
a reformatory for junvenile offenders *US*
A pun on 'youngster'.
- —Ralph de Sola, *Crime Dictionary*, p. 169, 1982

young 'un *noun*
a child, a young or younger person *UK, 1810*
- So the young'un did it, eh?—W.R. Bennett, *Wingman*, p. 98, 1961
- [T]he fact that he is fast approaching veteran status [is] conceded in his willingness to join the "experienced team rather than the young 'uns" at training five-a-sides.—*The Guardian*, 5th April 2003

young volunteer *noun*
a youthful male homosexual prostitute *US*
- —*Maledicta*, p. 139, Summer/Winter 1982: 'Dyke diction: the language of lesbians'

young woman *noun*
a female sweetheart *UK, 1858*
- Sports drama about a young man, his young woman, his mom and his football coach.—programme notes for the Santa Fe Film Festival, December 2002

you now what?; you know what!
used as an introductory catchphrase *UK, 1961*

your actual; yer actual *adjective*
used to emphasise a noun *UK*
- We are your actual Carnaby Hunt. Jule's MFH – I'm the Whipper In. —Barry Took and Marty Feldman, *Round The Horne*, March 1966
- —Paul Baker, *Polari*, p. 194, 2002

you rang?
used as a humorous line when entering a room *US*
A signature line of the hipster character Maynard G. Krebs on the television situation comedy *The Many Loves of Dobie Gillis* (CBS, 1959–63). Repeated with referential humour.

your arse!
used as an expression of contempt, rejection, disbelief or derision *UK*
- —Michael Munro, *The Patter, Another Blast*, 1988
- Fuck off. Jealous. – Of yew? Yewer arse.—Niall Griffiths, *Sheepshagger*, p. 98, 2001

your arse in parsley!
you are talking nonsense! *UK: SCOTLAND*
An elaborated form of (**UP**) **YOUR ARSE!**.
• —Michael Munro, *The Original Patter*, 1985

you're right, you fox
used as a tease when someone has finally stumbled over the obvious *US*
• —John D. Bell et al., *Loosely Speaking*, p. 16, 1966

you're sharing
used as an admonition that the speaker is straying into personal matters that should be kept private *US*
• —Connie Eble (Editor), *UNC-CH Campus Slang*, p. 10, April 1995

you're telling me
used for concurring with another speaker *UK, 1932*

you're the boss
you decide, you make the choice *AUSTRALIA, 1984*
Used among equals, or even to a child, with no real superiority involved.
• I just have to shrug and say "OK – you're the boss." — *The Guardian*, 28th December 2002

you're the doctor!
whatever you say; you are the authority, or the expert, or the one in charge; the responsibility is yours *US, 1907*

your man *noun*
a specific male individual *IRELAND*
An idiomatic phrase used in Hiberno-English.
• Your man, Waddle's a righ' stick, isn't he? —Roddy Doyle, *The Van*, p. 153, 1991
• What about you and your man? Me and who? You know, that fucking long streak of misery who locked you up and then disappeared. —Joseph O'Connor, *Red Roses and Petrol*, p. 38, 1995

your one *noun*
a specific female individual *IRELAND*
An idiomatic phrase used in Hiberno-English.
• Look. A fucking photo of your one. Jesus Christ, if mum found that. —Joseph O'Connor, *Red Roses and Petrol*, p. 19, 1995

yours and ours *noun*
flowers *UK*
Rhyming slang; noted as current among Covent Garden porters.
• —Julian Franklyn, *A Dictionary of Rhyming Slang*, 1960

yourself *pronoun*
▸ **up yourself**
smugly self-satisfied; self-involved *AUSTRALIA*
• That chick is up herself,' complained Con. —Jenny Pausacker, *What are ya?*, p. 1, 1987
• Thing about black girls, least black girls his age, they weren't quite so fucking up themselves as most of the girls you met. —John Williams, *Cardiff Dead*, p. 221, 2000
• Yes, he does possess that whole music biz, up himself air. If he was half as smart as he thought he was, he'd be ten times smarter than he actually is. —Colin Butts, *Is Harry Still on the Boat?*, p. 70, 2003

yours truly *pronoun*
used for 'me' or 'I'; a reference to yourself *UK, 1866*
Adopted from the formal subscription to a letter; usage is generally jocular in tone.
• Not the least surprised, therefore, were Barney Newbiggin and Yours Truly, on entering Sammy's Spieler one afternoon[.] —Charles Raven, *Underworld Nights*, p. 52, 1956
• Guess who was detailed [...]? Yours truly. —Chris Ryan, *Stand By, Stand By*, p. 93, 1996

youse; yous; youze; yers; yez *noun*
you, both singular and plural *AUSTRALIA, 1885*
• I've been fucked by the French and the English, / The Germans, the Japs and the Jews, / And now I've come back to Australia / To be fucked by bastards like youse. — *Improper Play Rhymes*, p. 26, 1955
• If youse perused the last volume with regard to my adventures youse might notice [...] a bit of censorship. —Barry Humphries, *Bazz Pulls It Off!*, 1971
• 'Well, firsta all, if youse lag on some one, ya dob 'em in, ya become a dog,' Michelle says while Ferret nods in support. — *TV Week*, p. 14, 30th May 1992
• State of youze all. Shitting yourselves [worrying] about a fucken [fucking] review. —Kevin Sampson, *Powder*, p. 98, 1999
• Doesn't mean I have to hang round with youse lot any more. —Cath Staincliffe, *Trainers*, p. 56, 1999

you shot who?
I didn't hear you – what did you just say? *US*
• —Connie Eble (Editor), *UNC-CH Campus Slang*, p. 11, Fall 1988

yout *noun*
▹ see: **YOOT**

you tell me!
used for expressing a complete lack of understanding of the subject under discussion *UK, 1969*

you the man
used for registering the personal superiority of a man so addressed; hence, used to encourage and to champion someone *US*
• You're gonna make it, Joey-man. You the man, Joster. You the man. —Joel Rose, *Kill Kill Faster Faster*, p. 195, 1997

you've said it!
yes, indeed!, I entirely agree with you *US, 1931*
• "But that is a strange thing." "You've said it." —James McClure, *The Caterpillar Cop*, 1972

you were born stupid – you've learnt nothing – and you've forgotten that
a catchphrase addressed to someone who has said or done something foolish *AUSTRALIA, 1984*
Probably of military origin.

you weren't born – you were pissed up against the wall and hatched in the sun
a catchphrase used in response to such assertions as 'before I was born', 'when I was born', etc *UK, 1977*

you what?; y'what?
what did you say? *UK*
Often challenging, disbelieving or truculent.
• BARMAID: Right ... On your way! RINGO: Y'what? BARMAID: You heard, on your way, troublemaker! — *A Hard Day's Night*, 1964

you won't know yourself
a catchphrase used as encouragement to diet or exercise or to try a change of style (clothes, hair, etc) *UK, 1961*
• If you trim yourself to fit the world / There won't be nothin' left / Just a little here and a little there / Till you won't know yourself —Aaron Tippin, *Trim Yourself to Fit the World*, 1993

you wouldn't want to know
you would be terribly amazed, disappointed, disgusted; you would not believe it! *AUSTRALIA*
• — *The Bulletin (Sydney)*, 26th April 1975

yow!
1 watch out! *AUSTRALIA, 1950*
Used as a warning to people engaged in some criminal activity.
• The door bust open. 'Yow!' someone howled. 'The Rossers are on their way up. Blow!' —John Wynnum, *Tar Dust*, p. 36, 1962

2 used as an expression of surprise *US*
Popularised in the *Zippie the Pinhead* cartoon.
• —Eric S. Raymond, *The New Hacker's Dictionary*, p. 390, 1991

yowge *adjective*
emphatically huge *UK*
Liverpool dialect echoes the stressed pronunciation.
• There was this one yowge tear-up [gang fight] outside the sports centre. —Kevin Sampson, *Outlaws*, p. 39, 2001

yowl *noun*
the exhaust note of a twin two-stroke motorcycle engine *UK*
• —Douglas Dunford, Motorcycle Department, Beaulieu Motor Museum, 1979

yo-yo *noun*
1 a fool *US*
• I'll bet you're a real yo-yo. — *Rebel Without a Cause*, 1955
• Jimmy, we got to straighten this yo-yo out. —Vincent Patrick, *The Pope of Greenwich Village*, p. 180, 1979
• This yoyo must eat plant food for breakfast cereal; it was the only explanation for the shiteating grin. —Seth Morgan, *Homeboy*, p. 194, 1990

2 a bisexual *US*
• —Connie Eble (Editor), *UNC-CH Campus Slang*, p. 9, Fall 1986

3 a hot rod enthusiast who races illegally *US*

- —*American Speech*, p. 305, December 1956: 'Hot-rodders' jargon again'

4 in air combat, a steep climb and dive in an attempt to gain a more favourable position *US*

- The other bandit was doing a high yo-yo, a vertical roller-coaster maneuver, three miles behind Fairly, trying to kill his high overtake speed and fall in behind the first bandit by trading forward momentum for altitude.—Richard Herman, *The Warbirds*, p. 57, 1989
- One tactic was the "High-speed Yo-Yo," – the ball on a string to which Smith referred.—Robert K. Wilcox, *Scream of Eagles*, p. 174, 1990

▸ **up and down like a yo-yo**

used of a person whose moods alternate rapidly between optimism and despair *UK, 1984*

yoyo *verb*

to perform a tactic in aerial combat resembling a roller coaster ride *US*

- After a few minutes of yo-yoing up and down I was able to keep the machine about where the IP wanted it.—Robert Mason, *Chickenhawk*, p. 33, 1983
- He went supersonic, and pulled back up in a yo-yo maneuver, arming his cannon as he climbed.—Walter Boyne and Steven Thompson, *The Wild blue*, p. 568, 1986

yoyo children *noun*

children who become pawns in a violent matrimonial battle and are constantly changing home *UK*

- —Patricia Barefoot and R. Jean Cunningham, *Community Services*, 1977

yoyo mouth *noun*

a citizens' band radio user who talks too much *US*

- —*Complete CB Slang Dictionary*, p. 99, 1976
- —Peter Chippindale, *The British CB Book*, p. 160, 1981

yoyo nickers; yo-yo knickers *noun*

a woman who (allegedly) exhibits a casual readiness for sexual encounters *UK*

The image is drawn of panties going up and down, up and down.

- Come on, let's go and see Beverly yoyo nickers then.—Caroline Aherne and Craig Cash, *The Royle Family*, 1999

YP *noun*

in prison, used insultingly of an inmate who is not behaving in an adult manner *UK*

An initialism of '*y*oung *p*risoner'.

- —Angela Devlin, *Prison Patter*, p. 125, 1996

Y's *noun*

male underpants *UK: SCOTLAND*

Presumably this term is restricted to pants with a Y-shaped opening.

- —Michael Munro, *The Original Patter*, p. 80, 1985

YT

yours truly, me *UK*

- Look how pleased he is to see YT, the big galloot [a stupid man]. —Kevin Sampson, *Outlaws*, p. 5, 2001

yuck *noun*

1 a laugh *US, 1971*

- Toxic chock your idea of a big yuck, Larry?—Armistead Maupin, *Further Tales of the City*, p. 238, 1982

2 a fool *US, 1943*

- Always some John Family or silk moll with bookoo toadskins playing around with a yuk who'll ante to keep the knockdown from the bundleman or headache.—*The New American Mercury*, p. 708, 1950
- Honestly, I've never met such a yuck. You'll never get caught, you poor goof.—Max Shulman, *The Many Loves of Dobie Gillis*, p. 13, 1951

3 in gambling cheating schemes, a victim *US*

- —Frank Garcia, *Marked Cards and Loaded Dice*, p. 265, 1962

4 crack cocaine *US*

- "All I could hear was, 'Where was the yuck?'" he testified. Yuck is street slang for crack.—*Pittsburgh Post-Gazette*, p. B1, 4th September 1993

yuck; yuk; yuk-yuk *verb*

to laugh *US, 1974*

Echoic.

- He'd been giggled out of Georgetown, howled out of Harvard, yuk-yukked out of Yale, snickered out of Stanford, and chuckled out of Chattanooga State Technical Community College.—Dav Pilkey, *Captain Underpants and the Perilous Plot of Professor Poopypants*, p. 50, 2000

▸ **yuck it**

to stop doing something *UK: SCOTLAND*

- Ah've had enough snash [impertinence] fae you so just yuck it, awright?—Michael Munro, *The Original Patter*, p. 80, 1985

▸ **yuck it up; yuk it up**

to behave in a foolish, time-wasting way *US, 1964*

- The sedan pulled past, two men in the front, both with sunglasses and both yucking it up and doing their best to pretend that they weren't interested in me.—Robert Crais, *L.A. Requiem*, p. 105, 1999

yuck!; yech!; yuk!

used as an indication of disgust *UK, 1966*

Echoic of vomiting.

- Surpressing a smile, Mona moved next to him and touched the mock chinchilla. "Yuck!"—Armistead Maupin, *Tales of the City*, p. 185, 1978
- "Yuk, anchovies." Like they were worms.—Elmore Leonard, *Gold Coast*, p. 118, 1980
- I grant you that innocents are getting killed. What about the Kurds – poison gas, chemicals, yuk!—Richard Neville, *Out Of My Mind*, p. 95, 1996
- Actually, the British music scene has always brought sexual deviance (yuck, what a word) to the news.—Patty Powers, *Retrohell*, p. 19, 1997
- I'm waiting for my milk to dry up and have to wear horrible round flying saucer things in my bra until it does. Yuk.—Mary Hooper, *(megan)2*, p. 46, 1999

yucky; yukky; yukkie *adjective*

disgusting *US, 1970*

- Then had taken the girl to a Japanese place where the girl said she was totally turned off by all the yukky stuff.—Elmore Leonard, *Glitz*, p. 313, 1985
- He was criticised by a lot of yukkie downmarket press people.—John Lahr, *Dame Edna Everage and the Rise of Western Civilisation*, p. 31, 1991
- Okay. I have the yuckiest taste in my mouth from those taquitos. —*Romy and Michele's High School Reunion*, 1997

yufe *noun*

▷ see: **YOOF**

yug *noun*

a deviation from an intended flight-path *UK*

In Royal Air Force use.

- "[A] small yug" develops which whiplashes down the line [of aircraft].—Robert Prest, *F4 Phantom*, 1979

yuk *verb*

to vomit *US*

- [M]y friend and I stuck our fingers down our throats and yukked into it for the freshman to chug.—Elissa Stein and Kevin Leslie, *Chunks*, p. 48, 1997

yuletide log; yuletide *noun*

a dog, especially a racing greyhound *UK*

Rhyming slang; a variation of **CHRISTMAS LOG**. Noted by David Hillman, 1974.

yuletide logs; yuletides *noun*

greyhound racing *UK*

Rhyming slang for **THE DOGS**. Noted by David Hillman, 1974.

yum!; yum-yum!

used for registering pleasurable anticipation, especially with regard to your personal appetites *UK, 1878*

- "If your vagina could talk, what would it say, in two words?" "[...] Yum, yum."—Eve Ensler, *The Vagina Monologues*, p. 19, 1998
- Yumyum, I had thought, he we go again, about time too[.]—James Hawes, *Dead Long Enough*, p. 17, 2000

yumlicious *adjective*

of a young man, sexually attractive *UK, 1990s*

Teenage girls' usage, or foisted upon them by the magazines they read. Elision of **YUMMY** (tasty, attractive) and 'delicious'; literally 'good enough to eat'.

yummy *noun*

an attractive woman who is not easily seduced *US*

Often embellished to **KANSAS YUMMY**.

- —*American Speech*, p. 20, Spring 1985: 'The language of singles bars'

yummy *adjective*

tasty, delicious, attractive *UK, 1899*

- "What does a vagina smell like?" [...] Yummy candy.—Eve Ensler, *The Vagina Monologues*, p. 93–94, 1998
- It would feel so yummy.—*Cruel Intentions*, 1999

yummy mummy *noun*

a sexually desirable mother *IRELAND*

Not to be confused with the branded breakfast cereal which probably lent its name to this breed.

- It's funny, roysh [right], I've always had a bit of a thing for Christian's old dear. She was always a bit of a yummy-mummy[.] — Paul Howard, *The Teenage Dirtbag Years*, p. 122, 2001
- These yummy mummies are a competitive, back-stabbing lot. — *The Observer*, 29th June 2003

yum-yums *noun*

any illegal drug in capsule form *US*

- — Edith A. Folb, *runnin' down some lines*, p. 260, 1980

yup *noun*

a yuppie (*y*oung *u*pwardly mobile *p*rofessional) *US*

A sneering abbreviation of a sneering initialism.

- Both writers are accredited Yups: Piesman, 32, is a lawyer, and Hartley, 38, is an editor. — *Time Magazine*, p. 66, 9th January 1984
- There is more than a faint flicker of distaste on my face as I stare at them, all replica rugby shirts and Saab convertibles [...] Sitting at the bar slightly apart from the yups is a bloke I recognise[.] — Martin King and Martin Knight, *The Naughty Nineties*, p. 104, 1999

yup

yes, absolutely *US, 1906*

A variation of **YEP**; the final plosive stresses the intention and gives it a semi-exclamatory sense.

- Yup, [Pete] Waterman has taken the buck-toothed no-marks off the street and made them rich. — John Robb, *The Nineties*, p. 305, 1999

yuppie *noun*

an individual socially categorised as a *y*oung *u*pwardly mobile *p*rofessional *US, 1982*

An acronym, often used derogatively, probably coined by several people independently. Variations include: **BUPPIE/BUPPY** (*b*lack *u*pwardly mobile *p*rofessional), 'CHUPPY' (*C*hinese etc.), 'PUPPY' (*P*unjabi etc.). These social groupings are the stuff of personal ads where you can find new, evermore contrived acronyms including, according to David Rowan, *A Glossary for the 90s*, 1998: SINBAD (*s*ingle *i*ncome, *n*o *b*oyfriend and is *a*bsolutely *d*esperate), SITCOM (*s*ingle *i*ncome, *t*wo children and an *o*ppressive *m*ortgage) and YAPPIE (*y*oung *a*ffluent *p*arent).

- While he and Abbie Hoffman once led the Yippies – the Youth International Party – one social commentator has ventured that Rubin is now attempting to become the leader of the Yuppies – Young Urban Professionals. — *Chicago Tribune*, p. 4, 23rd March 1983
- — *Washington Post (reprinted from The Nation)*, p. C5, 22nd December 1985
- — *American Speech*, Spring 1985
- And especially not by some slit-eyed yuppie who gets his salary paid out of Chronicle ad revenues and wallows (at company expense) in white wine and pesto in the finest high-dollar sports in San Francisco, Sonoma, and Tiburon. — Hunter S. Thompson, *Songs of the Doomed*, p. 252, 11th September 1987
- Let the goddamn yuppie Mormon affirmative action assholes handle it. — *Point Break*, 1991
- [M]ultimedia yuppies air kissing, swapping Web addresses and bragging about their kit[.] — Melanie McGrath, *Hard, Soft & Wet*, p. 166, 1998
- In the eighties, the satirical anti-yuppie film Wall Street backfired, and the Gordon Gecho remark that "greed is good" became a yuppie catchphrase. — Mark Steel, *Reasons to be Cheerful*, p. 165, 2001
- Ye shagged some yuppie in a nice hotel last night[.] — Ben Elton, *High Society*, p. 287, 2002

yuppie scum *noun*

an arrogant young professional *US*

A favorite epithet of the 1980s.

- And naturally, there was a "Die, Yuppie Scum!" bumper sticker plastered to the bar mirror. — Joseph Wambaugh, *Fugitive Nights*, p. 212, 1992

yuppification *noun*

the change that is made in order that something or somewhere becomes attractive to the yuppie market; gentrification *UK*

Derogatory in tone.

- The fact is that the yuppification of the game has progressed to such an extent that football is now seen as a game only for the middle classes[.] — Irvine Welsh, *The Naughty Nineties*, p. 14–15, 1999

yuppify *verb*

to style or remodel something in a manner characteristic of, or suitable for, yuppy life *UK, 1984*

- This time in manner of a two-bob game-show host. As we walk through the newly yuppified wharf buildings of the South Bank. — Gavin Hills, *White Burger Danny (Disco Biscuits)*, p. 67, 1996

yupster *noun*

a *y*oung *u*pwardly mobile *p*rofessional *US*

A variation of **YUPPIE**.

- The Hippies are now the Yupsters and they want to return. — *Phoenix (Arizona) Business Journal*, p. 1 (Section 1), 17th February 1986
- All those senior citizens in those condos, those conservative Cubans down on Eighth Street, those idealistic young yupsters on the beach. — Carl Hiaasen, *Strip Tease*, p. 12, 1993
- Not the worst part of town by a long way, not since all the yupsters moved in, but it ain't Sloane Square, neither. — Kevin Sampson, *Outlaws*, p. 174, 2001

yut *noun*

▷ see: **YOOT**

y'what?

▷ see: **YOU WHAT?**

yutz *noun*

a fool *US*

From Yiddish *yutz* (the penis).

- The guy's a total yutz, Kingsbury thought. — Carl Hiaasen, *Native Tongue*, p. 393, 1991
- "You're impersonating Mary Tyler Moore, right?" "No, Rhoda Morgenstern, you yutz!" I reply. — Stuart Jeffries, *Mrs Slocombe's Pussy*, p. 215, 2000

Zz

z *noun*

1 in hip-hop culture, used for replacing the letter 's' when creating plurals *US*

- Anyway, Ali [G] is hanging with his homiez from the home-countiez[.] — *The Guardian*, p. 16, 22nd March 2002

2 an outcast; a despised person *US*

- Because a "Z"at Aragon High is a dolt, oaf, jerk, clown. — *San Francisco Examiner*, p. 8, 27th October 1963

Z *noun*

an ounce of narcotics *US, 1975*

- We're buying a Z for a thousand dollars. — Kenneth Lonergan, *This is Our Youth*, p. 36, 2000

▸ the Z

the demilitarised zone *US*

- In the first place, the Z was the reason the grunts were in Vietnam. — Charles Anderson, *The Grunts*, p. 124, 1976

-z *suffix*

used in the abbreviating of a forename, by truncating the given name to its first open syllable which is then closed with -z *UK, 1984*

Examples: Gary or Gareth becomes Gaz; Jeremy, Jez; Terry or Terence, Tez; Sharon, Shaz.

- Gaz from Supergrass has been talking to Radio 1 about the joys of fatherhood. — *BBCi*, 2nd July 2003

za *noun*

pizza *US*

- — John D. Bell et al., *Loosely Speaking*, p. 22, 1966
- — *Current Slang*, p. 15, Summer 1968
- — *Concord (New Hampshire) Monitor*, p. 17, 23rd August 1983: 'Slang slinging: an intense and awesome guide to prep school slanguage'

zac *noun*

a six-month or six-year prison sentence *AUSTRALIA, 1919*

From **ZACK** (six pence).

Zacatecas purple *noun*

a potent variety of marijuana originating in Mexico *US, 1974*

Named after the location and the colour of the buds.

- — Richard A. Spears, *The Slang and Jargon of Drugs and Drink*, p. 561, 1986
- — Mike Haskins, *Drugs*, p. 289, 2003

Zachary Scotts; Zacharys *noun*

diarrhoea *UK*

Rhyming slang for **TROTS**; formed on the name of US film actor Zachary Scott (1914–65).

- — Ray Puxley, *Cockney Rabbit*, 1992

zack; zac *noun*

a sixpence; the sum of six pence *AUSTRALIA, 1898*

Origin unknown. Perhaps from Scottish dialect *saxpence* (sixpence), or possibly Yiddish from German *sechs* (six). After the introduction of decimal currency in 1966, it came to mean 'a five cent piece', or its value, a similar coin with about the same comparative value; dying out from the 1980s, now seldom heard.

- ZACK – Sixpence. — Gilbert H. Lawson, *A Dictionary of Australian Words and Terms*, 1924
- Shit a brick. There's fifteen and a zac on the clock already. That's nearly a note where I come from. — Barry Humphries, *The Wonderful World of Barry McKenzie*, p. 8, 1968

▸ not have a zack

to be broke *AUSTRALIA*

- The embattled former fruit and vegetable marketer is concerned about the possibility of going to court. 'I haven't got a zac,' he said. — *Glebe and Western Weekly*, p. 9, 8th November 1989

▸ not worth a zack

worthless *AUSTRALIA*

- 'He's no lake fisherman.' 'He is not?' 'Not worth a zac, mate.' — John O'Grady, *Gone Fishin'*, p. 127, 1962
- That's Dad's brothers and sisters. Not worth a zac, he reckons. — Tim Winton, *That eye, the sky*, p. 101, 1986

zaftig; zoftig *adjective*

sexy; buxom *US, 1932*

From German/Yiddish for 'juicy'.

- — David Powis, *The Signs of Crime*, 1977
- The carhops – all zoftig numbers – wore tight space-cade outfits[.] — James Ellroy, *Hollywood Nocturnes*, p. 208, 1994

zag *verb*

when faced with two courses of action, to take the right one *US, 1948*

Most commonly used in variations of 'I zigged when I should have zagged'.

- He zigged when he should have zagged, that is he bet banker when he should have bet player and then switched when the shoe switched. — Mario Puzo, *Inside Las Vegas*, p. 261–262, 1977

zags *noun*

thin papers used for rolling cigarettes *US*

From the branded name Zig Zag™, the dominant rolling papers during the hippie years.

- — Steve Salaets, *Ye Olde Hiptionary*, 1970

zambi *noun*

marijuana presumed to originate in the Republic of *Zambi*a *US, 1998*

- — Mike Haskins, *Drugs*, p. 289, 2003

zambuck *noun*

a member of St John Ambulance Brigade *AUSTRALIA, 1918*

From a proprietary name of an antiseptic ointment commonly used by them.

- — Jim Ramsay, *Cop It Sweet!*, p. 99, 1977

zami *noun*

a lesbian *TRINIDAD AND TOBAGO*

From a misplaced juncture of the French *les amies* (women friends).

- — Lise Winer, *Dictionary of the English/Creole of Trinidad & Tobago*, 2003

Zanussi *noun*

▸ on Zanussi

drug-intoxicated; wildly excited or distracted *UK*

A variant of **ON ANOTHER PLANET**, from the advertising for Zanussi, a manufacturer of domestic electrical appliances.

- I watched Wayne [...] come screaming past on an animal that was well and truly on Zanussi. — Andy McNab (writing of the late 1970s/early 80s), *Immediate Action*, p. 327, 1995

zap *noun*

1 amyl nitrite *UK*

- — Angela Devlin, *Prison Patter*, p. 125, 1996

2 an electrical shock *US*

- 'Cause when the good doctors get through givin' you the zap, you won't know where the hell you are. — *Natural Born Killers*, 1994

zap *verb*

1 to kill someone *US, 1942*

A major piece of slang from the Vietnam war.

- — Carl Fleischhauer, *A Glossary of Army Slang*, p. 27, 1968
- All overhung with the corrosive uncertainty about when the next firefight would happen and who would get zapped in it, the men and men-children of Bravo moved into a time when they could taste relief. — Charles Anderson, *The Grunts*, p. 154, 1976
- You're zapped, you cannon-cockin' Texas shitkicker, zapped by the world's greatest jungle fighter. — Philip Caputo, *A Rumor of War*, p. 245, 1977

- When I start shooting, go for the nearest guard, get his gun and zap him! — *The Deer Hunter*, 1978
- So what am I going to do? Get one of my guys zapped so some fuckface fresh from the world can get his beauty fucking sleep! — *Platoon*, 1986
- One of our guys zapped the cop-killing cocksucker. — James Ellroy, *Suicide Hill*, p. 836, 1986
- He gets popped like twenty-thirty times and all hands is getting zapped. — Kevin Sampson, *Clubland*, p. 2, 2002

2 to shoot someone *UK*
A Royal Navy variation on the previous sense.
- — Nigel Foster, *The Making of a Royal Marine Commando*, 1989

3 to finish something off *UK*
A figurative variation of the sense 'to kill'.
- I zapped your yaoh [cocaine] last night. — Kevin Sampson, *Powder*, p. 370, 1999

4 to defeat someone heavily *US*
Paul Janssen, 1968.

5 to give someone an electrical shock; to administer electric shock treatment to someone *US*
Recorded as 'administering shock treatment' in 'The language of nursing', Philip C. Kolin, *American Speech*, p. 209, Fall–Winter 1973.
- They never know what hit them. And if and when they do find out they just got zapped by a cattle prod, they wish they really did have a heart attack. — *Casino*, 1995

6 to operate electronically, often by remote-control
- He's zapped his bus door shut[.] — Kevin Sampson, *Outlaws*, p. 91, 2001

7 to overwhelm someone *US*
- — Joe David Brown (Editor), *The Hippies*, p. 220, 1967: 'Glossary of hippie terms'

8 to move quickly *US*
- — Robert Kirk Mueller, *Buzzwords*, p. 167, 1974
- As soon as the first bullet comes your way, your head is zapped into what I can only describe as another dimension. — Ken Lukowiak, *Marijuana Time*, p. 20, 2000

9 to have sex *US*
- — *American Speech*, p. 20, Spring 1985: 'The language of singles bars'

10 to present, to give *US*
'Zap the world with love'.
- — Ruth Bronsteen, *The Hippy's Handbook*, p. 17, 1967

11 to steal something *UK*
- When we was first starting out we used to zap the lead from off've the church roofs. — Kevin Sampson, *Clubland*, p. 112, 2002

12 to use the (remote) fast-forward facility on video playback to pass advertising; to use a remote control to switch between television channels (to avoid advertising, or simply to find a programme that engages you) *US, 1983*

13 to send a text message *UK*
- Hayley quickly decided to go, and zapped the text through to another group of friends. — *The Times Magazine*, 21st June 2003

14 to heat something up in a microwave oven *US*
- We need to zap this, quick! — *South Park*, 1999

15 to give a student in college a notification of academic deficiency *US*
- — *American Speech*, p. 76–77, February 1968: 'Some notes on flunk notes'

16 in Canadian military aviation, to affix a sticker on which is the badge of a military unit onto an aircraft of another service *CANADA, 1982*
- To some, zapping is a challenging sport that expresses unit pride. However, in more straight-laced organizations, finding a zap on an airplane is about as popular as finding a fly in one's soup. — Tom Langeste, *Words on the Wing*, p. 316, 1995

zap over *verb*
to change your mind *UK*
- Often you get very respectable pin-striped men who zap over and buy something very occult. — *Observer*, 1st October 1972

zapped *adjective*
1 drug-intoxicated *US*
- Yeah, they got stoned on giggle-weed, zonked on grifa, zapped on yerba, bombed on boo, they were blitzed with snop, warped on twist, gay on hay, free on V. — *Hi Life*, p. 14, 1979

2 spicey *US*
- — Guy L. Steele et al., *The Hacker's Dictionary*, p. 134, 1983

zapper *noun*
any remote-control device used with domestic entertainment equipment – television, stereo, video, DVD player, etc *US, 1981*
- She confiscated the zapper and slid my hand between her thighs. — Doris Dorrie, *Where Do We Go From Here?*, 2001

zappy *adjective*
lively, energetic *UK*
- It's an absolutely marvellous, zappy series. — *Kaleidoscope*, 10th March 1983

zap up *verb*
to enliven something *UK*
- I love being poor. There's nothing like it for zapping up the adrenalin! — Ian Pattison, *Rab C. Nesbitt*, 1988

zat?
▷ **see: OWZAT?**

zatch *noun*
the genitals of either gender *UK, 1950*
Originally used of female genitals.
- "[S]lit,"as he put it,"from gizzard to zatch."The surgeon had closed him back up without taking anything out. — Anne Lamott, *Crooked Little Heart*, p. 32, 1997

Zazu Pitts *noun*
diarrhoea *UK*
Rhyming slang for **THE SHITS**, formed on the name of the US film actress, 1914–65.
- — Ray Puxley, *Cockney Rabbit*, 1992

zazzy *adjective*
ostentatious, showy *US, 1961*
- Oh, you know, jazzy, zazzy, pizzazzy, fancyshmancy – that sort of stuff. — Tadeusz Wojnicki, *Life Under the Fig Trees*, p. 51, 1996
- What if your zazzy hairstyle starts floating around by itself? Talk about scary! — Marthe Jocelyn, *The Invisible Enemy*, p. 104, 2002

Z-bag *noun*
the bed *US*
- — Collin Baker et al., *College Undergraduate Slang Study Conducted at Brown University*, p. 225, 1968

Z-bars *noun*
in motorcyle racing, handlebars each shaped like the letter Z, facing each other *US*
- — Ed Radlauer, *Motorcyclopedia*, p. 76, 1973

zebbled *adjective*
circumcised *UK*
- — Chris Lewis, *The Dictionary of Playground Slang*, p. 263, 2003

zebra *noun*
a cadet officer in the US Air Force *US*
An allusion to how conscious the officer is of his stripes.
- — *American Speech*, p. 310, December 1946: 'More Air Force slang'

zebra *adjective*
racially mixed *US*
- — Eugene Landy, *The Underground Dictionary*, p. 203, 1971

Zec *noun*
an area in Quebec where logging and hunting are controlled or prohibited *CANADA*
- "Zec"is a word formed from an acronym of a French (Quebec) term introduced by the government during the late 1970s and early 1980s,"Zone d'exploitation controllee,"a zone in which exploitation is controlled. — Lewis Poteet, *Talking Country*, p. 77–78, 1992

zeds *noun*
1 sleep *UK*
Royal Navy slang; echoic, based on UK pronunciation of 'z', from the strip-cartoon legend 'zzzz' as an indicator of sleep. Used in phrases such as 'racking (or piling) up the zeds' (sleeping) and 'zeds merchant' (someone who likes to sleep).
- I'm off to crack out a few zeds. — Rick Jolly, *Jackspeak*, 1989

2 central nervous system depressants *UK*
- — Tom Hibbert, *Rockspeak!*, p. 175, 1983

zeek freak *noun*
a person who greatly enjoys sex while under the influence of crack cocaine *US*
- — Terry Williams, *The Cocaine Kids*, p. 138, 1989

zeke *noun*

in circus usage, a hyena *US*

- —Don Wilmeth, *The Language of American Popular Entertainment*, p. 56, 1981

Zelda *noun*

1 a girl or a woman, especially if dull or uninteresting *US*

Possibly after Zelda Fitzgerald (1900–48) with the suggestion that the name is dull and old-fashioned; Zelda Fitzgerald was herself named after the character of a gypsy queen in a romantic novel.

- —Paul Baker, *Polari*, p. 194, 2002

2 a high school girl who is a socially inept outcast *US*

- —*Washington Post*, 23rd April 1961

3 a witch *UK*

Perhaps from the character Aunt Zelda, a 2000-year-old witch in *Sabrina, The Teenage Witch*, from a 1962 comic book creation, subsequently in animated and live-action television series.

- —Paul Baker, *Polari*, p. 195, 2002

zeller *noun*

an over-devoted surfer *US*

- —Michael V. Anderson, *The Bad, Rad, Not to Forget Way Cool Beach and Surf Discriptionary*, p. 23, 1988

zen *noun*

LSD *UK*

From the other-worldly state sought by Zen Buddhism.

- —Home Office, *Glossary of Terms and Slang Common in Penal Establishments*, 1978
- —Mike Haskins, *Drugs*, p. 286, 2003

Zen *noun*

MDMA, the recreational drug best known as ecstasy *US*

- —Bruce Eisner, *Ecstasy*, p. 1, 1989

zen in *verb*

to grasp completely through intuition *US*

- —Ruth Bronsteen, *The Hippy's Handbook*, p. 17, 1967

zenith *noun*

ketamine hydrochloride, an anaesthetic used as a hallucinogen *US*

zeppelin *noun*

a poker player who contemplates long and hard before every bet or play *US*

- —John Vorhaus, *The Big Book of Poker Slang*, p. 41, 1996

zero *noun*

1 a person of no significance; a nobody

- Then he stood up, flicked his iron to rock and roll and gave the little zero a long burst through the Playboy mag. —*Apocalypse Now*, 1979
- I was a zero with the girls[.] —Howard Stern, *Miss America*, p. 21, 1995
- standing beside the zeroes eavesdropping their conversation —Stewart Home, *Sex Kick [britpulp]*, p. 213, 1999

2 a gambler who is a chronic loser *US*

- —Frank Scoblete, *Best Blackjack*, p. 275, 1996

zero *verb*

1 to kill someone *US*

- You didn't know she watched you zero Gloria Monday. —Seth Morgan, *Homeboy*, p. 118, 1990

2 to identify or locate someone or something *US*

- We just zeroed three kids in a heap. Crest Drive and Observatory. —*Rebel Without a Cause*, 1955

zero-dark-thirty *noun*

very early in the morning *US, 1991*

- —Linda Reinberg, *In the Field*, p. 245, 1991
- It was, by then, what is often referred to in the Marine Corps as zero-dark-thirty, or way past the middle of the night. —Alex Lee, *Force Recon Command*, p. 213, 1995
- We had one more night, and by God, we were going on that hill at zero dark thirty and set in. —Ed Kugler, *Dead Center*, p. 290, 1999

zero out *verb*

1 to kill someone *US*

Korean war usage.

- It was really a matter of luck and probability: the more missions, the more point duty, the more hot engagements, the higher the probability of getting zeroed out. —David H. Hackworth, *About Face*, 1989

2 to be killed *US*

- So far, not one bungee jumping customer – and only one careless instructor – has"zeroed out"in the State of California. —Erik Fair, *California Thrill Sports*, p. 55, 1992

zero week *noun*

the orientation week preceding eight weeks of basic military training *US*

- —Carl Fleischhauer, *A Glossary of Army Slang*, p. 27, 1968

zero zero; zero-zero *noun*

▷ see: DOUBLE ZERO

Z-game *noun*

the game with the lowest betting limits in a gambling operation or cardroom *US*

There need not be 26 tables to arrive at the Z-game; it is the lowest-stakes table in the place.

- —George Percy, *The Language of Poker*, p. 98, 1988

zhoosh; jhoosh *noun*

1 ornamentation *UK*

- —Paul Baker, *Polari*, p. 195, 2002

2 clothing *UK*

- Oh come on, let's have a vada [look] at his zhoosh. —Barry Took and Marty Feldman, *Round The Horne*, March 1968

zhoosh; jhoosh *verb*

1 to swallow something *UK*

- —Paul Baker, *Polari*, p. 195, 2002

2 to tidy the appearance of something; to tittivate, to trim, to ornament *UK, 1997*

- [S]he schlumphed her Vera [gin] down the screech at a rate of knots, zhooshed up the riah [hair]. —James Gardiner, *Who's a Pretty Boy Then?*, p. 123,
- —Paul Baker, *Polari*, p. 195, 2002

zhooshing *noun*

shop-lifting *UK*

- So one zhooshes one's riah – combs one's hair – before zhooshing some dubes – that's swallowing some speed [amphetamine], before going out zhooshing – shoplifting. —*Word of Mouth*, September 1995

zhoosh off; jhoosh off *verb*

to leave; to go *UK*

- —Paul Baker, *Polari*, p. 195, 2002

zhooshy *adjective*

showy, ornate *UK*

- —Paul Baker, *Polari*, p. 195, 2002

ziff *noun*

a beard *AUSTRALIA, 1917*

Origin unknown. Now all but obsolete.

- ZIFF – beard. —Gilbert H. Lawson, *A Dictionary of Australian Words and Terms*, 1924
- He was glad now that he had let his mates kid him into growing a ziff. —Robert S. Close, *With Hooves of Brass*, p. 22, 1961
- —Bill Wannan, *Folklore of the Australian Pub*, p. 9, 1972
- —Jim Ramsay, *Cop It Sweet!*, p. 99, 1977

ziffed; be-ziffed *adjective*

bearded *AUSTRALIA, 1973*

From ZIFF (a beard).

zig *noun*

▸ **get the zig**

to become annoyed or angry with someone *UK*

- [T]aking the piss outta the old bill [police], was a mug's game cos they just get the zig and come at you with more legal firepower[.] —J.J. Connolly, *Layer Cake*, p. 31, 2000

zig *verb*

1 when faced with two courses of action, to take the wrong one *US, 1948*

Most commonly used in some variation of 'I zigged when I should have zagged'.

- He zigged when he should have zagged, that is he bet banker when he should have bet player and then switched when the shoe switched. —Mario Puzo, *Inside Las Vegas*, p. 261–262, 1977

2 to shoot down an enemy fighter plane *US*

- —*American Speech*, p. 125, Summer 1986: 'The language of naval fighter pilots'

Zig and Zag *noun*

1 a variety of LSD identified by a picture of television puppets Zig and Zag *UK*

- —Angela Devlin, *Prison Patter*, p. 125, 1996

2 an act of sexual intercourse *UK*

Rhyming slang for **SHAG**, formed from a double act of television puppets, in turn named from an in-and-out movement.

- —Bodmin Dark, *Dirty Cockney Rhyming Slang*, 2003

ziggerboo *noun*

an eccentric or crazy person *US*

- —Marcus Hanna Boulware, *Jive and Slang of Students in Negro Colleges*, 1947

zig-zag *noun*

1 cigarette rolling papers *US*

A brand name that acquired a generic meaning.

- —Edward R. Bloomquist, *Marijuana*, 1968

2 sex with a prostitute *US*

- —Jerry Robertson, *Oil Slanguage*, p. 112, 1954

zig-zag *adjective*

unreliable; dishonest *TRINIDAD AND TOBAGO, 1960*

- —Lise Winer, *Dictionary of the English/Creole of Trinidad & Tobago*, 2003

zigzag man *noun*

1 marijuana *UK*

- —Mike Haskins, *Drugs*, p. 289, 2003

2 LSD *UK*

Perhaps from a icon printed on the drug.

- —Mike Haskins, *Drugs*, p. 286, 2003

zig-zig *noun*

sexual intercourse *UK, 1918*

Familiar pidgin in the Far, Near and Middle East and Mediterranean, originally military; a variation of **JIG-A-JIG**. Used by US soldiers in the South Pacific.

- —Delbert W. Hamilton, *American Speech*, p. 56, February 1947: 'Pacific War language'
- I wanna, I wanna, I wanna, I wanna, / I wanna really really really wanna zigazig ah. —Spice Girls *Wannabe*, 1996

zig-zig *verb*

to have sex *US, 1918*

Familiar pidgin in the Far, Near and Middle East and Mediterranean, originally military; a variation of **JIG-A-JIG**.

zilch *noun*

1 nothing *US, 1940*

- —*Current Slang*, p. 8, Winter 1966
- —John D. Bell et al., *Loosely Speaking*, Addenda, 1969
- I have absolutely zilch in the bank, and I'm already accepted. —Erich Segal, *Love Story*, p. 68, 1970
- His value as an undercover man would be zilch. —Leonard Shecter and William Phillips, *On the Pad*, p. 49, 1973
- No class. Everytin' he ever did on the street, el zilch-o. —Edwin Torres, *After Hours*, p. 215, 1979
- After trashing the pad for info on the"video shoot"Vandy and Klein were on, and getting zilch, he knew it was either tend to business or go gonzo[.] —James Ellroy, *Suicide Hill*, p. 695, 1986
- A real heavy investigation. Zilch. —*Basic Instinct*, 1992
- "You must have some idea.""Look, just fucking leave it. I'm saying zilch." —Colin Butts, *Is Harry on the Boat?*, p. 127, 1997
- [B]ut zilch was taught us about them [Romanies] in our schoolbooks[.] —Jimmy Stockin, *On The Cobbles*, p. 14, 2000

2 a socially inept outcast *US*

- —*Time*, p. 56, 1st January 1965: 'Students: the slang bag'

zillion *noun*

an almost unimaginably large number *US, 1944*

One of several invented numbers used to convey a large number; probably coined by Damon Runyon.

- I bet a hunnert zillion dollars o'l wilfire cain't fling me off. (Barney Google and snuffy Smith comic strip). —*San Francisco Examiner*, 29th July 1951
- The way he explained it to me is that I'm suffering from an inferiority complex on account of my old man having zillions of books around the house and reading like a maniac. —Frederick Kohner, *Gidget*, p. 12, 1957
- Read the little book. It says United flies about sixty zillion people every year and about twenty zillion every day. —James Simon Kunen, *The Strawberry Statement*, p. 75, 1968
- Man, I'm hip you pretty and pimping a zillion. —Iceberg Slim (Robert Beck), *Mama Black Widow*, p. 226, 1969
- As I undressed he finally talked about getting wounded and being laid up for so long and the dumb-ass braille lessons and about all the things he had time to think about."Zillions of things,"he said. —Larry Heinemann, *Close Quarters*, p. 294, 1977
- It was a zillion times worse than the summer I tried to join Up With People! —Armistead Maupin, *Tales of the City*, p. 4, 1978
- And she knew a zillion old jokes her grandfather, an old vaudevillian, taught her. —*Pulp Fiction*, 1994
- Because there were a zillion DEA guys hanging around the terminal. —*Get Shorty*, 1995
- Two masters of freedom, playing in a time before their art was corrupted by a zillion cocktail lounge performers[.] —*Jerry Maguire*, 1996
- [I]t broke down into smaller units, so many zillions of options you could never count them[.] —John King, *White Trash*, p. 118, 2001

zillionaire *noun*

a multi-millionaire *US, 1946*

- You might just as easily marry a zillionaire and not need life insurance at all. —Jane Bryant Quinn, *Making the Most of Your Money*, p. 279, 1991
- Some greaseball zillionaire in a sta-prest suit[.] —Melanie McGrath, *Hard, Soft & Wet*, p. 42, 1998

Zimbo *noun*

a person from Zimbabwe *NEW ZEALAND, 1995*

- —Harry Orsman, *A Dictionary of Modern New Zealand Slang*, p. 153, 1999
- Every time we flew into a cloud I'd hold my breath and think of all the UFW junk we might be on a collisison course with: ghosts flights, alcoholic Ukranians shifting cargo, Zimbo arms smugglers[.] —Aidan Hartley, *The Zanzibar Chest*, p. 7, 2003

zimmer *noun*

a girl *US*

- For home boys and zimmers; This dictionary is def! —*Frederick (Maryland) Post*, p. B2, 24th May 1990

zinc *noun*

an obviously unfashionable child or youth *UK*

Pejorative. Commented on by the Plain English Campaign in October 2003.

- If someone had their hair cut and the fringe was extremely straight and short, then that would be a"zinc". —Chris Lewis, *The Dictionary of Playground Slang*, p. 263, 2003

zine *noun*

an inexpensively self-published magazine devoted to such topics as hobbies, music, film and politics *US*

An abbreviation of **FANZINE**, ultimately 'magazine'.

- —*American Speech*, p. 53, Spring 1978: 'Star Trek lives: Trekker slang'
- The newest player in the dirty magazine business is the 'zines – inexpensive publications usually put out by one or two people. —James Ridgeway, *Red Light*, p. 69, 1996
- The independent character of zines gives them significant value, allowing subjects outside of mainstream fashion to receive coverage. —Marion Leonard, *Cool Places*, p. 105, 1998

zined *noun*

a fan magazine editor *US, 1976*

- —*American Speech*, p. 53, Spring 1978: 'Star Trek lives: Trekker slang'

zinfandel *noun*

serious trouble *CANADA*

Zinfandel is a wine from California that seems not to have travelled well.

- There was the prisoner of the morning, deep in the zinfandel again[.] —P. St. Pierre, *Chillcotin Holiday*, 1970

zing *noun*

1 energy, vigour *US, 1918*

- But there is a zip and a zing here, a supercivilized, metropolitan method of behavior, unique and indescribable. —Jack Lait and Lee Mortimer, *New York Confidential*, p. 11, 1948

2 sex appeal *US, 1961*

A nuance of the previous sense.

3 an amphetamine tablet *US*

- —*Providence (Rhode Island) Journal-Bulletin*, p. 6B, 4th August 1997: 'Doctors must know the narcolexicon'

zing *verb*

1 (of a bullet) to ricochet *US*

- Pow. Pow. Pow. Two hit the pavement beside my car and one zinged off my front bumper. —Janet Evanovich, *Seven Up*, p. 30, 2001

2 to travel quickly *US, 1920*

- Well, from the way I zinged through Laramie you would think I didn't like it, either. —Clancy Sigal, *Going Away*, p. 166, 1961

3 to affect someone suddenly and forcefully *US, 1975*

- The plan was to zing the pastor at a special meeting in mid-week to be arranged by Reverend Owens[.] —Iceberg Slim (Robert Beck), *Mama Black Widow*, p. 196, 1969
- "He's a cop. Right?"It zinged her, caught her by surprise and she raised her eyebrows, stared at him. —Elmore Leonard, *Glitz*, p. 157, 1985
- It was best to let that one zing past. —Joseph Wambaugh, *Fugitive Nights*, p. 6, 1992

4 to feel pleasurable sensations resulting from drug use *UK*

- Mostly their minds are with the alert restlessness and near tremor of methedrine or several yellowbellies. —A. Stuart, *The Bikers*, 1971

▸ **zing it in**
to bet heavily *US*

- —John Scarne, *Scarne's Guide to Modern Poker*, p. 293, 1979

zing!
used to represent a sudden change in circumstance or emotion *UK, 1919*

- [Y]ou fall in love / zing! boom! —Bjork, *It's Oh So Quiet*, 1995

Z-ing *noun*
the practice of targeting tourists as victims of crime by the 'Z' as the first letter on the car license plate, designating a rental car *US*

- —*American Speech*, p. 186, Summer 1994: 'Among the new words'

zingaro *noun*
in circus and carnival usage, a gypsy *US*

- —Don Wilmeth, *The Language of American Popular Entertainment*, p. 299, 1981

zinger *noun*

1 the punch-line of a joke; the last word *US*

- "Ah!"said Polly."Here comes the zinger.""Not, not quite yet," said Ira. —Max Shulman, *Anyone Got a Match?*, p. 111, 1964
- "Except family,"Carmody says, like he's handing me the fatal zinger. —Robert Campbell, *Nibbled to Death by Ducks*, p. 98, 1989

2 an arranged ending to a competition *US*

- And finally a fix – or zinger, as it was called in those days – was in with the Commission as well[.] —Terry Southern, *The Magic Christian*, p. 60, 1959

3 a surprise, an awkward or unexpected turn of events *US, 1973*

- Of course, he has a couple of zingers in there which we'll have to work around. —Ronald Reagan, *Ronald Reagan*, p. 651, 1990

4 an exceptionally good example of something *UK, 1955*

- I'm gonna crack off a zinger this afternoon. —Darryl Ponicsan, *The Last Detail*, p. 58–59, 1970

5 a very attractive woman *US*

- A smasheroo she was – a real zinger. —Max Shulman, *I was a Teen-Age Dwarf*, p. 8, 1959
- —Tom Hibbert, *Rockspeak!*, p. 176, 1983

6 an amphetamine tablet *US*

- —Peter Johnson, *Dictionary of Street Alcohol and Drug Terms*, p. 208, 1993

7 a hot pepper *US*

- —*Maledicta*, p. 24, 1996: 'Domino's pizza jargon'

8 a hard stare that is intended to impart bad luck on the recipient *US*

- —John Scarne, *Scarne's Guide to Modern Poker*, p. 293, 1979

zingy *adjective*
exciting, energetic *US, 1948*

- TONY: How ya doing? PETE: Zingy. Stead at sixty-five per cent. —*Saturday Night Fever*, 1977

zip *noun*

1 an Italian or Sicilian criminal brought to the US for criminal purposes, especially murder *US*

- Tommy's a Zip. You know what I mean? One of those guys they used to import from Sicily to handle the rough stuff. Guy could be a peasant right out of the fucking Middle Ages, looks around, and he's in Miami Beach. Can't believe it. They hand the Zip a gun and say, 'There, that guy.' And the Zip takes him out. —Elmore Leonard, *Pronto*, p. 16–17, 1993

2 a Viet Cong; a Vietnamese; any South Asian person *US*

- —*Current Slang*, p. 19, Summer 1970
- This term was used by U.S. troops to connote the"worthlessness"of these people (zip = zero). —*Maledicta*, p. 126, Summer 1980
- [S]ome zonked-out zip crawled up sneaky-close in the mangled underbrush[.] —Larry Heinemann, *Paco's Story*, p. 6, 1986
- Be advised I've got zips in the wire down here, over. —*Platoon*, 1986

3 energy *UK, 1900*

- But there is a zip and a zing here, a supercivilized, metropolitan method of behavior, unique and indescribable. —Jack Lait and Lee Mortimer, *New York Confidential*, p. 11, 1948
- They had shown no zip. They weren't hitting. They weren't alert. —Dan Jenkins, *Life Its Ownself*, p. 111, 1984

4 methamphetamine *US*

- —Jim Crotty, *How to Talk American*, p. 146, 1997

5 cocaine *US, 1998*
Probably from **ZIPPED** (drug-intoxicated).

- —Nick Constable, *This is Cocaine*, p. 181, 2002
- —Mike Haskins, *Drugs*, p. 281, 2003

6 used for representing the sharp sound of, for instance, a bullet or a mosquito as it moves through the air; specifically of bullets, it is often reduplicated: 'zip-zip' or 'zip, zip' *UK, 1875*

7 nothing at all; zero *US, 1900*

- —*Current Slang*, p. 12, Winter 1969
- "Well, I didn't want to fuck him for zip,"she said. —Dan Jenkins, *Dead Solid Perfect*, p. 78, 1986

8 a hand-made gun, a zip gun *US*

- Picaeo, who I dug as no heart, squawked out,"Sticks, shanks, zips – you call it." —Piri Thomas, *Down These Mean Streets*, p. 52, 1967

zip *verb*

1 to move quickly *US, 1852*

- A few cars zipped by. —Jack Kerouac, *On the Road*, p. 15, 1957
- I was quite a spectacle zipping around Hollywood and Los Angeles at night with my turban on the scooter. —Babs Gonzales, *I Paid My Dues*, p. 21, 1967
- His fist zipped up, caught Greystone on the cheek. —*The Sweeney*, p. 30, 1976
- Then zip ahead and let the cop follow. —Elmore Leonard, *Glitz*, p. 227, 1985
- He stood in the doorway, freezing in his paisley caftan, and watched her zip away over patches of ice and tainted snow. —Odie Hawkins, *The Busting Out of an Ordinary Man*, p. 134, 1985
- A blue-uniformed nurse came in and zipped down the centre of the ward[.] —Mary Hooper, *(megan)2*, p. 9, 1999

2 to kill someone *US*

- I zip her husband while she's out tracking down specials in the supermarket, and she wants to marry me. —Richard Condon, *Prizzi's Honor*, p. 70, 1982

▸ **zip it**
to stop talking *US*
From the image of zipping your mouth shut.

- Zip it! Unveil the time portal. —*Austin Powers*, 1999

▸ **zip your lip; zip your mouth**
to stop talking *US, 1942*
The image of a zip fastener (zipper) sealing your lips; may be mimed rather than spoken; often as an imperative.

- "Look, I know this hard to believe, but I actually live here and I've lost my keys...""Zip it, you fucking comedian." —Greg Williams, *Diamond Geezers*, p. 207, 1997
- Billy makes a gesture to zip his mouth[.] —Stuart Browne, *Dangerous Parking*, p. 41, 2000

zip ball *noun*
in pinball, a ball that leaves play without having scored *US*

- —Bobbye Claire Natkin and Steve Kirk, *All About Pinball*, p. 118, 1977

zip-five *noun*
a prison sentence of a maximum of five years *US*

- I was sent to Elmire for zip-five and I did forty-eight months. —Jeremy Larner and Ralph Tefferteller, *The Addict in the Street*, p. 96, 1964

zip gun *noun*
an inexpensive, homemade gun, usually consisting of a tube, a grip and a rudimentary striking device *US, 1950*

- —*American Speech*, May 1951
- Unless they use a zip gun on you someday. —Evan Hunter, *The Blackboard Jungle*, p. 304, 1954
- The best way to use a shive – a knife – and how to make a zip gun that will fire .32 bullets. —Rocky Garciano (with Rowland Barber), *Somebody Up There Likes Me*, p. 36, 1955
- Bottles, knives, zipguns, tire chains, bricks. —Willard Motely, *Let No Man Write My Epitaph*, p. 208, 1958
- This is a thirty-seven caliber blank pistol. The only bullets made to fit it are blanks and they can't be tampered with enough to kill a man. And it hasn't been made over into a zip gun. —Chester Himes, *The Real Cool Killers*, p. 27, 1959

- I had shot him in the leg with a zip gun in a rumble only a few months earlier. — Claude Brown, *Manchild in the Promised Land*, p. 16, 1965
- Then the zip guns came out, metal tubes with door latches as firing pins set off by rubber bands – if the pin hit the .22 on the primer and the piece was held close to your head, you were in trouble. — Edwin Torres, *Carlito's Way*, p. 9, 1975

zipped *noun*
drug-intoxicated *US, 1973*
- — Richard A. Spears, *The Slang and Jargon of Drugs and Drink*, p. 561, 1986

zipper *noun*
1 a scar *US*
- — Bill Shefski, *Running Press Glossary of Football Language*, p. 120, 1978
- After all that high-sticking, three of us had zippers. — *Montreal Gazette*, p. C1, 24th January 1990

2 an electronic display of news or publicity which is scrolled across a screen fixed to a building *US*
- — Susie Dent, *The Language Report*, p. 19, 2003

3 a short but well-formed wave *US*
- — Michael V. Anderson, *The Bad, Rad, Not to Forget Way Cool Beach and Surf Discriptionary*, p. 23, 1988

4 a trap play in poker *US*
- — John Vorhaus, *The Big Book of Poker Slang*, p. 42, 1996

zipperhead *noun*
1 an offensive word for a Vietnamese person *US*
- Can you believe they're actually payin' us to do this – to waste these zipperhead motherfuckers! — Jack Hawkins, *Chopper One #2*, p. 197, 1987
- Every zipperhead in Nam, North and South, will be banging gongs, barking at the moon and visiting his dead relatives. — *Full Metal Jacket*, 1987
- I would ask you how many times you used the racial expressions gook, slope, zipoperhead, and slant-eyes. — Nelson DeMille, *Up Country*, p. 768, 2002

2 a stupid person *US, 1989*
- God, you're free! I'd pay for my walking papers from that zipper-head. — Chip Kidd, *The Cheese Monkeys*, p. 190, 2002

zipper ripper *noun*
in craps, a roll of ten *US*
Evolved from the more common **BIG DICK** (a roll of ten).
- — Chris Fagans and David Guzman, *A Guide to Craps Lingo*, p. 33, 1999

zippily *adverb*
energetically, swiftly *UK, 1983*
- [A] piece of theatre staging Bergman's production, with its revolve that moves the family furniture around so zippily that you fear the Alving household is infected not by ghosts but an extremely troublesome poltergeist[.] — *The Guardian*, 2nd May 2003

zippiness *noun*
an energetic quality, speediness *UK, 1924*
- It's all madly hyperactive, almost stroboscopic in its zippiness, and those with a predisposition to fits should probably stay out of the cinema. — *The Guardian*, 18th October 2002

zippity-doo-dah *noun*
nothing at all *US*
An elaboration of **ZIP** (zero).
- You get zippity-doo-dah. — Neil Simon, *The Goodbye Girl*, 1977

zippity-doo-dah!
used as a nonsensical, all-purpose utterance *US*
From the lyrics of a song in the 1946 Walt Disney film *Song of the South*.
- Well zippity-doo-dah. You and your code plead not guilty and you'll be in jail for the rest of your life. — *A Few Good Men*, 1992

zippo *noun*
1 nothing *US*
An embellised form of **ZIP**.
- "Not a damn thing," he said. "I swear, I told him zippo." — Carl Hiaasen, *Strip Tease*, p. 233, 1993

2 energy *US*
- But when he managed to bounce back into big bucks with real zippo, as they say, he'd stocked the campaign larders of front-runners in state and local elections. — Joseph Wambaugh, *The Glitter Dome*, p. 34, 1981

3 a tank-mounted flame thrower *US*
An allusion to the branded cigarette lighter.
- — *Newsweek*, p. 31, 25th July 1966
- — Carl Fleischhauer, *A Glossary of Army Slang*, p. 27, 1968

zippo *verb*
to set something on fire and burn it *US*
An allusion to the branded cigarette lighter.
- "Okay, Zippo the joint." Nobody reacts. He walks to the closest hut, takes a cigarette lighter from his pocket and snaps the lid open[.] — William Wilson, *The LBJ Brigade*, p. 28, 1966

zippo job *noun*
the burning of a village as part of a military sweep through the area *US*
- "Zippo jobs" on Vietnamese hamlets by American soldiers had become so common that television audiences in the United States were no longer scandalized by them. — Neil Sheehan, *A Bright Shining Lie*, 1988

zippola *noun*
nothing at all *US*
- — Sally Williams, *"Strong" Words*, p. 167, 1994

zippy *noun*
someone whose lifestyle mixes hippy ideals and modern technology *UK, 1990s*
An acronym of '*z*en-*i*nspired *p*rofessional *p*agan'.
- Ditching hippie Luddite mistrust of technology, zippies sought to harness modern communication tools such as the Internet to create an alternative, self-governing culture. — Ben Osborne, *The A-Z of Club Culture*, p. 324, 1999

zippy *adjective*
lively, bright, energetic, vigorous; fast, speedy *US, 1904*
- Still, [Steven] Johnson's zippy, discipline-hopping journalistic style is easy on the eye[.] — *The Guardian*, 24th August 2002

zips *noun*
the first decade of the 21st century *UK*
- In the 2000s (or noughties, oughties, or zips)[.] — Susie Dent, *The Language Report*, p. 11, 2003

zip squat *noun*
a very small amount *US*
Two words that mean 'nothing'.
- — Connie Eble (Editor), *UNC-CH Campus Slang*, p. 9, Spring 1990

zip top *noun*
a Jewish person *US*
Offensive.
- — Carsten Stroud, *Close Pursuit*, p. 277, 1987

zip up *verb*
to stop talking *UK*
The image of a zip fastener sealing the lips.
- He'd give it one last shot then zip up. — Kevin Sampson, *Powder*, p. 53, 1999

zirconia flush *noun*
in poker, four diamonds *US*
Named after the synthetic diamond.
- — John Vorhaus, *The Big Book of Poker Slang*, p. 42, 1996

zit *noun*
an acne pimple *US, 1966*
- — *Verbatim*, p. 281, May 1976
- the zit-pocked lumpen of Madison Square Garden — Lester Bangs, *Psychotic Reactions and Carburetor Dung*, p. 209, 1977
- The policeman who dropped her off at Barbary Lane was so young that he had zits — Armistead Maupin, *Tales of the City*, p. 244, 1978
- So in the ninth grade Sherry Dewitt threw me over because I had zits. — *Wayne's World 2*, 1993
- "At least yours doesn't have zits on it!" I cried. — Anka Radakovich, *The Wild Girls Club*, p. 96, 1994

zitfarm *noun*
a teenager *US*
From the adolescent tendency towards **ZIT** (a pimple, a spot)-production in agricultural quantities.
- Just a bunch of zitfarms from San Jose[.] — Lester Bangs, *Psychotic Reactions and Carburetor Dung*, p. 374, 1981

zizz *noun*
a snooze, a brief sleep; sleep *UK, 1941*
Military usage; echoic in as much as the cartoon-strip legend 'zzzz' is an accurate indicator of sleep.
- — Rick Jolly, *Jackspeak*, 1989
- The hell with it: I'm off for a zizz. — *The Guardian*, 8th August 2000

zizz *verb*

1 to sleep *UK, 1942*
Military usage; echoic in as much as the cartoon-strip legend 'zzzz' is an accurate indicator of sleep.

2 to prepare food in a blender *UK*
• Fruit can be taken whole, though zizzing up a banana or two, some frozen berries and a dash of water in a blender takes no time[.] — *The Observer*, 29th December 2002

zizzy *adjective*
fancy, showy *US*
• [A] couple of peekers, suitably dressed for admission to one of the zizzier places, waits across the street from the nightclub entrance. — Dev Collans with Stewart Sterling, *I was a House Detective*, p. 16, 1954

Z-list *noun*
denotes all that is associated with a level of minor-celebrity so despised that obscurity is almost achieved *US*
A notional social grouping that contrasts with A-LIST (top-rank celebrity); 'Z-list' inclusion is a matter of derogatory opinion.

zloty *noun*
in poker, low-stakes betting *US*
Named after the lowest value coin in the Polish monetary system.
• — John Vorhaus, *The Big Book of Poker Slang*, p. 42, 1996

zob *noun*
an unlikeable, despicable person *US, 1911*
• "It'd be worth paying your taxes just to get clear of that zob," Francine said. — Bernard Wolfe, *The Late Risers*, p. 131, 1954

zobbit *noun*
an officer *UK*
Royal Air Force lower ranks' usage, from Arabic *dabat* (an officer). Reported by Sgt R. Farley, 1967.

zod *noun*
someone who is socially inept to the extreme *US*
• I just got my hair streaked, OK, and like Brian throws me in the pool, and like the chlorine turns my hair like totally green, I mean I look like such a zod! — Mary Corey and Victoria Westermark, *Fer Shurr! How to be a Valley Girl*, 1982

zoftig *adjective*
▷ see: ZAFTIG

zog *noun*
the US federal government *US*
A basic piece of racist, right-wing political vocabulary in the US.
• They refer to the U.S. government as the "Zionist Occupational Government," or "ZOG," and following the tenets of the Christian Identity philosophy, believe it is controlled by the state of Israel. — Bill Valentine, *Gangs and Their Tattoos*, p. 55, 2000

zoinks!
used for expressing fear or surprise *US*
Popularised as a signature line of the character Shaggy, voiced by Casey Kasem, on the television cartoon *Scooby Doo, Where are You?* (CBS, 1969–72). Repeated with referential humour.

zol *noun*
a marijuana cigarette *US*
• — *American Speech*, p. 88, May 1955: 'Narcotic argot along the Mexican border'
• — Richard A. Spears, *The Slang and Jargon of Drugs and Drink*, p. 562, 1986
• — Mike Haskins, *Drugs*, p. 291, 2003

Zola Budd *noun*
a police vehicle, especially a slow-moving armoured vehicle; a small bus, especially a Toyota *SOUTH AFRICA, 1985*
Township slang; after the South African-born British Athlete (b.1966) who was involved in a controversial incident in the 1984 Olympic 3,000 metres race.
• — Penny Silva, *A Dictionary of South African English*, 1996

zombie *noun*

1 a dull, personality-free person *US, 1941*
From the belief of certain west African religions that corpses can be revived to walk the earth without souls.
• VINCENT: No Jules, you're gonna be like those pieces of shit out there who beg for change. They walk around like a bunch of fuckin' zombies, they sleep in garbage bins, they eat what I throw away, and dogs piss on 'em. — *Pulp Fiction*, 1994

2 in poker, an expert player who shows no emotion, no matter how good or bad his hand is *US*
• — John Scarne, *Scarne's Guide to Modern Poker*, p. 293, 1979

3 a policewoman *UK, 1956*
Usually in the plural.

4 among air-traffic controllers, a suspicious unidentified flying object *UK*
• — *Listener*, 29th July 1982

zombie *verb*
to put someone into an apathetic condition *UK*
From a belief in soulless corpses that walk the earth (and film sets) having been revived by voodoo.
• We'll show you old punters, zombied with the finest tranquillisers! — Ian Pattison, *Rab C. Nesbitt*, 1990

zombied *adjective*
very drunk *UK*
In a condition generally seen among the undead.
• — *e-cyclopaedia*, 20th March 2002

zombie job *noun*
during the Korean war, a night patrol *US*
• A volunteer was needed from our group to do a zombie job and I was chosen. The general mission of the unit was to capture a prisoner. — Martin Russ, *The Last Parallel*, p. 98, 1957

zombie medicine *noun*
tranquillizers *UK*
From the desired effect of the medication.
• — Angela Devlin, *Prison Patter*, p. 125, 1996

zombie weed *noun*
phencyclidine, the recreational drug known as PCP or angel dust *US*
• — Ronald Linder, *PCP*, p. 10, 1981

zone *noun*
a state of such concentration that consequent action seems instinctual *US*
Often in the phrase 'in the zone'.
• Dialed, dialed in. In the zone. — Jim Humes and Sean Wagstaff, *Boarderlands*, p. 221, 1995
• "I've done most of my work hung over," Chris Evans told the high court on Friday. "It was my normal working zone." — *The Guardian*, p. 23, 26th March 2003

▸ on the zone
lost in a daydream *US*
• — Paul Glover, *Words from the House of the Dead*, 1974

▸ the zone
a state of being qualified for, and meeting all other parameters for, a promotion in rank *UK, 1962*
Originally Royal Navy, then army use.
• I remember as a Warrant Officer 2 in the late 1960s, being told be a visiting Brigadier, "You're in the zone, y'know – you're in the zone." — Beale, 1984

zoned out *adjective*
mentally absent *US*
• The freaky, zoned-out style being developed on the misty slopes of the Haight had still made few inroads into intense, political Berkeley. — J. Anthony Lukas, *Don't Shoot – We Are Your Children*, p. 386, 1971
• It was due to a system full of codeine. I discontinued their use after two days. I couldn't afford to be zoned out. — James Ellroy, *Brown's Requiem*, p. 249, 1981
• But pretty soon his wife, Yolie, would find him zoned out in front of the television with a drink in his hands. — Joseph Wambaugh, *Lines and Shadows*, p. 212, 1984

zone out; zone off; zone *verb*
to absent yourself mentally, with or without the aid of drugs *US*
• Erroll zoned out for a second, his eyes going dim, a tiny high moan escaping his cracked lips. — Richard Price, *Clockers*, p. 423, 1992
• Deek would zone out on the ratty old sofa and Ty would finally drag him to bed and strip off his clothes. — Jess Mowry, *Way Past Cool*, p. 30, 1992
• — *Merriam-Webster's Hot Words on Campus Marketing Survey '93*, p. 2, 13th October 1993
• She zones and stares off blank while he jerks himself off[.] — Peter Sotos, *Index*, p. 56, 1996
• I'm zonin' off on one joint[.] — Eminem (Marshall Mathers), *Still Don't Give a Fuck*, 1999

zoner; zonie *noun*
someone from Arizona *US*
• —Trevor Cralle, *The Surfin'ary*, p. 166, 1991

zonk *verb*
1 to fall asleep, especially as a result of drugs or drink *US, 1970*
Also used with 'out'.
• Patrice coaxes her back, wanting to perform for men at large, who are too zonked out to give a shit.—Josh Alan Friedman, *Tales of Times Square*, p. 121, 1986
• Once we got up to my room, he zonked out in my bed.—Amy Sohn, *Run Catch Kiss*, p. 109, 1999
• I don't have to smoke puff and zonk out in the pub anymore[.]—Dave Courtney, *Raving Lunacy*, p. 54, 2000

2 to hit or strike, literally or figuratively *US*
• It ain't been too busy a year, but maybe that's cause I was zonked with the hep for three months...—Abbie Hoffman, *Woodstock Nation*, p. 11, 1969

zonked *noun*
the recreational drug GHB *US*
From the drug-intoxicated sense of **ZONKED**.
• Liquid X, Grievous Bodily Harm, Easy Lay, Georgia Home Boy, Soap, Cherry Meth, Nature's Quaalude and Zonked are just a few.—*Augusta (Georgia) Chronicle*, p. A1, 16th April 2000

zonked *adjective*
1 intoxicated on a drug, especially marijuana; drunk *US*
Also used with 'out'.
• You must be zonked out completely.—Terry Southern, *Flash and Filigree*, p. 150, 1958
• You come back zonked and expect me to think it's lucky you got back without it?—Alexander Trocchi, *Cain's Book*, p. 150, 1960
• —*Current Slang*, p. 6, Fall 1966
• Everybody high on something: balloons, acid, bananas, kids, sky, flowers, dancing, kissing. I had a ball – totally zonked.—Abbie Hoffman, *Revolution for the Hell of It*, p. 23, 1968
• BILLY: What's the matter, you zonked ... what? Huh – you really zonked, eh?—Peter Fonda, *Easy Rider*, p. 55, 1968
• The smoke rushes into your lungs and you get zonked immediately.—Richard Neville, *Play Power*, p. 306, 1970
• [I]t probably surprises you to learn that I had a trippy Xmas – even when I wasn't zonked out on your culinary crazies – but I did.—Tom Robbins, *Another Roadside Attraction*, p. 162, 1971
• "Poor Chessman" – he muttered, still slight zonked from a late night mesc drop[.]—Ed Sanders, *Tales of Beatnik Glory*, p. 41, 1975
• Then one night zonked out of my mind on schmeck – pot – benzedrine and seconal – I met a cat I had become friendly with who was a kind of John or mark.—Herbert Huncke, *The Evening Sun Turned Crimson*, p. 46, 1980
• [S]he was drunker than she'd been in years, plotzed, zonked, a mess.—Lester Bangs, *Psychotic Reactions and Carburetor Dung*, p. 364, 1981
• He said he should've held the meeting in here, get everybody zonked and decadent on a strong stone, get them good and banged – using all the words he knew – then present the movie deal.—Elmore Leonard, *Stick*, p. 241, 1983
• An old lady with a Macy's bag sitting across from you looks around as if to ask what the world is coming to between these Dracula Jews and zonked-out Africans[.]—Jay McInerney, *Bright Lights, Big City*, p. 57, 1984
• "They had me so zonked out on morphine I don't much remember,"Paco says.—Larry Heinemann, *Paco's Story*, p. 45, 1986
• Jake don't know it because he's so zonked out he don't know his head from a hole.—Terry Williams, *The Cocaine Kids*, p. 101, 1989
• She was late. Then when she came she was zonked.—Jeremy Cameron, *Brown Bread in Wengen*, p. 67, 1999
• [B]leary-eyed youngsters, zonked out on drugs, haunt the fun arcades[.]—Brian McDonald, *Elephant Boys*, p. 275, 2000

2 exhilarated; intoxicated by an abstract thought *UK*
• Getting zonked by the Holy Spirit is a confusing experience at first. —*The Times*, 30th January 1980

3 exhausted *US*
• At 4 A.M., I just blinked. Man, I was zonked.—Albert Goldman, *Freak Show*, p. 91, 1968

zonker *noun*
a drugs user who indulges to excess *US*
Doonesbury, a cartoon strip by Garry Trudeau, has had a laid-back marijuana-smoking character called Zonker since 1972.
• —Angela Devlin, *Prison Patter*, p. 125, 1996

zonkers *noun*
the female breasts *US*
An abbreviation of **BAZONKAS**.
• During a [radio] show on breasts, Infinity was fined because I said:"Boobs, xonkers, headlights, watermelons, sweater puppies, pointers, knockers, jugs, tatas – these are some of the words to describe women's breasts.—Howard Stern, *Miss America*, p. 441, 1995

zonking *adverb*
used as an intensifier of adjectives that convey positivity or largeness *UK, 1958*
• I recall a Channel 4 programme called The Plague which showed deserted hospital hallways filled with zonking great bluebottle flies and vases of dead roses.—*Gay Times*, February 1999

zonks *noun*
an indefinitely long time *UK*
A variation of **YONKS**.
• People have been here for zonks of years.—*Hot Air*, 4th July 1982

zoo *noun*
1 the section of a prison where 'vulnerable prisoners' are kept for their own safety *UK*
In *Prison Patter*, 1996, Angela Devlin notes that an **ANIMAL** is 'a sex offender', and animals are kept in a zoo.

2 a police station *US*
Citizens' band radio slang.
• —*Complete CB Slang Dictionary*, p. 99, 1976
• —Peter Chippindale, *The British CB Book*, p. 160, 1981

3 in motor racing, the pit area where cars stop for fueling and repairs *US*
• —Don Alexander, *The Racer's Dictionary*, p. 76, 1980

4 a brakevan (caboose) *US*
• —Ramon Adams, *The Language of the Railroader*, p. 178, 1977

5 a notional or actual grouping or assemblage of people; the place where they are assembled *UK, 1924*
Often mildly contemptuous.

6 a zoophile, a person with a sexual interest in animals *UK*
• The bible of these self-labelled zoophiles is a book entitled Dearest Pet (one reader states,"it provides for us zoo's [sic] a thorough description of our heritage, as it were, dating back to medieval"). —Kathleen Kurik Bryson, *Lap Dogs and Other Perversions [Inappropriate Behaviour]*, p. 48, 2002

zoob *noun*
a large penis *AUSTRALIA*
• —Thommo, *The Dictionary of Australian Swearing and Sex Sayings*, p. 144, 1985

zoo book *noun*
a student directory with photographs of each student *US*
• —*Current Slang*, p. 15, Summer 1968

zoobs *noun*
the female breasts *US*
A blend of **BOOB(S)** and **BAZOOMS**.
• —Collin Baker et al., *College Undergraduate Slang Study Conducted at Brown University*, p. 227, 1968

zoo doo *noun*
compost made from multi-species faeces *US*
• Each of the zoo's elephants can produce up to a wheel barrow load of "Zoo Doo" daily that can be converted into fuel through a biomass digester.—*United Press International, PM cycle*, 24th June 1981

zooed *adjective*
1 drunk *US*
• —Connie Eble (Editor), *UNC-CH Campus Slang*, p. 8, March 1979

2 crowded *US*
Surfer usage.
• —Michael V. Anderson, *The Bad, Rad, Not to Forget Way Cool Beach and Surf Discriptionary*, p. 23, 1988

zooie *noun*
a cylindrical implement that holds the butt of a marijuana joint

zook *noun*
a marijuana and tobacco cigarette; may also contain crack cocain *UK*
• He wrapped his zook carefully, then lit it[.]—Courttia Newland, *Society Within*, 2000
• "D'you puff?"I said, holding the zook out to her.—Diran Adebayo, *My Once Upon A Time*, p. 87, 2000

zookeeper *noun*
in motor racing, the official in charge of the pit area *US*
• —Don Alexander, *The Racer's Dictionary*, p. 76, 1980

zoom *noun*

1 phencyclidine, the recreational drug known as PCP or angel dust *US*

- — US Department of Justice, *Street Terms*, October 1994

2 marijuana laced with phencyclidine, the recreational drug known as PCP or angel dust *US, 1982*

'Zoom!' is a comic book caption for the drugs' combined effect.

- — Richard A. Spears, *The Slang and Jargon of Drugs and Drink*, p. 562, 1986
- — Mike Haskins, *Drugs*, p. 289, 2003

zoom *verb*

1 to move very quickly *US, 1946*

From aviation slang.

- When you passed over 110th Street it was like zooming off to another planet where they didn't build any brick walls between wanting and doing[.] — Mezz Mezzrow, *Really the Blues*, p. 204, 1946
- We were zooming past Cleveland Avenue, and I brightened a little. — Max Shulman, *The Many Loves of Dobie Gillis*, p. 188, 1951
- [I]t was strange sitting in their brand-new comfortable car and hearing them talk of exams as we zoomed smoothly into town. — Jack Kerouac, *On the Road*, p. 17, 1957
- I was laboring along behind a fire truck when the untracked outlaw came zooming past. — Hunter S. Thompson, *Hell's Angels*, p. 125, 1966
- [S]o with Dick Seaver at the wheel, we zoomed across town[.] — Terry Southern, *Now Dig This*, p. 121, November 1968
- The car zoomed in pursuit. — *The Sweeney*, p. 52, 1976
- [H]e wonders whether he might not be better off in a garage in Pontefract, while zooming about in a helicopter at a hundred and twenty miles an hour[.] — Mike Stott, *Soldiers Talking, Cleanly*, 1978

2 to induce someone to commit a crime that they were not otherwise inclined to commit *US*

- But she told me you zoomed her. — Joseph Wambaugh, *The New Centurions*, p. 175, 1970

zoom bag *noun*

a military flier's flight suit *US*

- — *Army*, p. 48, November 1991

zoomer *noun*

1 an energetic fool *UK*

From **ZOOM** (to move quickly).

- A zoomer, for example, couldn't just sit in a room where a bunch of guys were minding their own business [...] He'd feel compelled to disrupt the equilibrium[.] — Christopher Brookmyre, *Boiling a Frog*, p. 56, 2000

2 a person who sells fake crack cocaine and then quickly disappears *US*

- — *Detroit News*, p. 5D, 20th September 2002

zoomers *noun*

the female breasts *US*

- — Fred Hester, *Slang on the 40 Acres*, 1968

zoomie *noun*

1 a graduate of the United States Air Force Academy *US*

- — Linda Reinberg, *In the Field*, p. 245, 1991

2 in drag racing cars, an exhaust pipe that curves upward directing some of the exhaust gases to heat the tires *US*

- One modification is still in use today on ever dragster – the shorty, stubby"zoomie"headers unit which points hot gases directly at the rear tires. — Ross Olney, *Kings of the Drag Stripe*, p. 176, 1968

3 a crew member of a military jet aircraft *US*

A term used by the infantry and navy.

- — *American Speech*, p. 38, February 1948: 'Talking under water: speech in submarines'
- — Carl Fleischhauer, *A Glossary of Army Slang*, p. 27, 1968
- — Gregory Clark, *Words of the Vietnam War*, p. 182, 1990

zooms *noun*

the female breasts *US*

A shortened form of **BAZOOMS**.

- — Collin Baker et al., *College Undergraduate Slang Study Conducted at Brown University*, p. 227, 1968

zoo-only *adjective*

applied to the sexual predilection of a zoophile with no other interests *UK*

- The zoophile internet community includes people of all sexual orientations (het, homo, bi and some who are"zoo-only"). — Kathleen Kurik Bryson, *Lap Dogs and Other Perversions [Inappropriate Behaviour]*, p. 48, 2002

zoot *noun*

1 a zoot suit *US*

- So why're you wearin' that circus zoot? I'm gonna have to burn it. — Irving Shulman, *The Amboy Dukes*, p. 139, 1947
- Swing skirts are circling, zoot-tails flying[.] — William Sansom, *A Public for Jive [The Public's Progress]*, p. 58, 1947
- [O]utdressing everyone on the block in the uniform of the period, pork-pie hat, satin shirt, peg pants, reat jacket. Zoot, man. — Clancy Sigal, *Going Away*, p. 462, 1961
- I remarked that I had saved about half enough to get a zoot. — Malcolm X and Alex Haley, *The Autobiography of Malcolm X*, p. 51, 1964

2 a marijuana cigarette *UK*

Also called a 'zut' or 'zootie'.

- — Angela Devlin, *Prison Patter*, p. 125, 1996

3 a cigarette butt *TRINIDAD AND TOBAGO, 1956*

- — Lise Winer, *Dictionary of the English/Creole of Trinidad & Tobago*, 2003

zoot canary *noun*

a fashion model *UK*

Beatniks' use, therefore late 1950s.

zooted; zooted up *adjective*

drug-intoxicated *US*

- — *Rutgers Alumni Magazine*, p. 21, February 1986
- At first people came after they left the first house, and most of them was already zooted up[.] — Terry Williams, *The Cocaine Kids*, p. 108, 1989
- So I went down to 123rd Street, got a bag of Red Devil Angel Dust, smoked, and got crazy zooted. — *New Jack City*, 1990
- He come here, my Ace Cool, he be zooted up, he say here's de plan, Amp. — Stephen Cannell, *King Con*, p. 50, 1997
- [S]pending Friday night getting zooted in your local Pret A Fumer[.] — *Ministry*, p. 10, October 2002

zooter *noun*

1 in cricket, a non-spinning ball bowled by a spin-bowler *AUSTRALIA*

Coinage credited to Australian cricketers Shane Warne (b.1969) and Terry Jenner (b.1944) to describe a style that they developed.

- [Stuart MacGill] possesses all the usual variations – leg-break, topspinner, flipper, zooter, wrong 'un – and is now improving the mental side of his game[.] — *The Guardian*, 24th December 2002

2 a zoot suiter *US*

- Over on Sunset and Figueroa, knots of zooters were assembling in violation of the Zoot Suit Ordinance, no doubt figuring that today it was anything goes. — James Ellroy, *Hollywood Nocturnes*, p. 123, 1994

zootie *adjective*

emotionally unbalanced or drug-intoxicated *US*

- — *Frederick (Maryland) Post*, p. B2, 24th May 1990

zootied *adjective*

very marijuana-intoxicated *US*

- — Connie Eble (Editor), *UNC-CH Campus Slang*, p. 5, Fall 1982

zoot suit *noun*

a type of man's suit characterised by its exaggerated style: padded shoulders, long jacket, high-waisted trousers, bright colours *US, 1942*

Pehaps by reduplication of 'suit'.

- — Janey Ironside, *A Fashion Alphabet*, p. 32, 1968

zoot suiter *noun*

a member of an identifiable group of zoot-suit-wearing young men, characterised by fashion and as flashy and vulgar *US, 1943*

- [T]he audience of zootsuiters howled with glee, well, that was 1949[.] — Lester Bangs, *Psychotic Reactions and Carburetor Dung*, p. 73, 1971

zoot up *verb*

to dress in a zoot suit and accessories *US*

- What're you doin' all zooted up? — Irving Shulman, *The Amboy Dukes*, p. 139, 1947

zooty *adjective*

fashionable, stylish *US*

Derived from, and an allusion to, **ZOOT SUIT**.

- Fashion note: colored kids working in the tailor shop tired of corny prison outfits, go to work on their dungarees, pegging the legs till they're real sharp and zooty. — Mezz Mezzrow, *Really the Blues*, p. 313, 1946
- The goose thereafter laid up a storm, and Jack, who was no astute galoot, went on a toot with a local beaut, bought himself a zooty suit and still had a little loot to boot. — Steve Allen, *Bop Fables*, p. 66–68, 1955

zoo-zoo; zuu-zuu *noun*
in prison, sweets, snacks, soda or any other special treat *US*
- A phrase that must have been conceived by a person with a playful imagination is zoo-zoos and wham-whams for confections, usually small packaged cakes, pieces, candy or gum obtained from a vending machine. — *Maledicta*, p. 267, Summer/Winter 1981
- When he made the canteen cart, the beaners ripped off his zuuzuus and whamwhams. — Seth Morgan, *Homeboy*, p. 152, 1990
- You aren't a hostage, you're my zoo-zoo, my treat after five months of servitude. — Elmore Leonard, *Out of Sight*, p. 40, 1996

zoquete *noun*
heroin *UK*
Directly from Spanish for 'block' or 'chunk'.
- — Mike Haskins, *Drugs*, p. 285, 2003

Zorba the Greek; Zorba *verb*
to urinate; an act of urination *UK*
Also used as a noun. Rhyming slang for **LEAK**, formed on the title of a 1946 novel by Nikos Kazantzakis and 1964 film.
- — Ray Puxley, *Cockney Rabbit*, 1992

zorch *verb*
in computing, to move or process quickly *US*
- — Guy L. Steele et al., *The Hacker's Dictionary*, p. 135, 1983

zorries *noun*
inexpensive, practical foam rubber thong sandals *US*
- Thongs, clogs, and zorries are not allowed. — *Rio Linda Junior High School Uniform Dress Code*,
- — Gregory Clark, *Words of the Vietnam War*, p. 445, 1990

zot *noun*
zero; nothing *US*
- — *American Speech*, p. 195, October 1965: 'Notes on campus vocabulary, 1964'
- — Helen Dahlskog (Editor), *A Dictionary of Contemporary and Colloquial Usage*, p. 66, 1972

zot *verb*
to move suddenly or swiftly *US*
Perhaps from the nonsense, all-purpose word – especially used as a substitute for God – coined by US cartoonist Johnny Hart (b.1931).
- There I was zotting down the motorway at a rate of knots[.] — Beale, 1974

zotz *noun*
a planned murder; an assassination *US*
- Santo Calandra is gonna try for a zotz on Matty and Van when they come outta the bank. — Richard Condon, *Prizzi's Glory*, p. 80, 1988

zotz *verb*
to kill someone *US*
- "You are the only one who can get close enough to her to do it," his father said. "Zotz her? Clip Irene?" — Richard Condon, *Prizzi's Honor*, p. 304, 1982

zotzed *adjective*
drunk or drug-intoxicated *US*
- Roc, listen, it's OK, belive me. She's totally fucking zotzed. — Richard Price, *Clockers*, p. 132, 1992

zounds!
used for registering a strong reaction *UK*
Compounded from 'God's wounds!', modern usage is often ironic.
- Zounds! Got to be something double bad, here. — Kevin Sampson, *Outlaws*, p. 223, 2001

zowie!
used as a vocal representation of an instantaneous happening *UK, 1913*
- Click, click, zowie! There it is. — Dan Gookin, *Word 2002 for Dummies*, p. 364, 2001

z's *noun*
sleep *US, 1963*
From Z's as the representation of snoring in comic strips used with a verb such as 'catch', 'cop', 'cut', 'get', 'grab' or 'rip'.
- — Collin Baker et al., *College Undergraduate Slang Study Conducted at Brown University*, p. 225, 1968
- And now I, Billy Clyde Puckett, am going off to stack me up some Z's. — Dan Jenkins, *Semi-Tough*, p. 127, 1972
- Can't you talk to me later? I'm tryin' to cop some zzzs. — Odie Hawkins, *Ghetto Sketches*, p. 176, 1972
- Half of them are sitting on a hill watching us and laughing, and the rest of them are blowing fucking Zs in a fucking hammock is what they're doing. — Charles Anderson, *The Grunts*, p. 60, 1976
- Okay. Don't catch no z's on me buddy or I'll sling your motherfucking ass. — *Platoon*, 1986
- I'm really beat. I need some serious z's. — *Bull Durham*, 1988
- You night boys, you watch too much Oprah when you should be catching z's. — *Copland*, 1997

▸ **stack z's**
to sleep *US*
- Thought you were stacking those Z's. — Joseph Wambaugh, *The Choirboys*, p. 170, 1975

zubrick; zoob *noun*
the penis *UK*
Mainly in soldiers' Arabic *shufti zubrick* or *shufti zoob* (let's see/show the penis), possibly enhanced by the rhyme on **PRICK** but not rhyming slang. Recorded by Edwin Morrisby, 1958.

zucchini *noun*
an extended fibreglass field hut *ANTARCTICA, 1991*
- — Bernadette Hince, *The Antarctic Dictionary*, p. 393, 2000

zug up *verb*
to cut hair unevenly *TRINIDAD AND TOBAGO, 1959*
- — Lise Winer, *Dictionary of the English/Creole of Trinidad & Tobago*, 2003

zuke *noun*
in American casinos, a gratuity *US*
- — Steve Kuriscak, *Casino Talk*, p. 61, 1985
- — Michael Dalton, *Blackjack*, p. 91, 1991

Zulu *noun*
1 a black person *US, 1960*
Offensive.
- — William K. Bentley and James M. Corbett, *Prison Slang*, p. 56, 1992

2 a large marijuana cigarette *US*
- While standing at the rear of the hotel taking long pulls on the Zulu, a car pulled up with New York tags on it. — A.S. Jackson, *Gentleman Pimp*, p. 76, 1973

Zulu princess *noun*
in homosexual usage, a young and attractive black man *US*
- — *Maledicta*, p. 53, 1986–1987: 'A continuation of a glossary of ethnic slurs in American English'

zulu time *noun*
Greenwich mean time *US, 1960*
- [T]he man Kabakov was seeking had not used Eastern Standard time, he had used Greenwich Mean Time – Zulu time – Pilot time! — Thomas Harris, *Black Sunday*, p. 220, 1975
- — Linda Reinberg, *In the Field*, p. 246, 1991
- — Ethan Dicks, *English, as She is Spoke at McMurdo*, 2003

'zup?
used as a greeting *US*
A slurred 'what's up?'.
- — Connie Eble (Editor), *UNC-CH Campus Slang*, p. 9, November 1990

zut *adjective*
stupid *TRINIDAD AND TOBAGO, 1984*
- — Lise Winer, *Dictionary of the English/Creole of Trinidad & Tobago*, 2003

zuu-zuu *noun*
▹ **see: ZOO-ZOO**

zymotic; zymy *adjective*
contemptible *UK*
A figurative application of the conventional senses relating to infectious disease and containing putrefactive germs, thus creating a synonym for **LOUSY**. Noted in use amongst teenagers by Mrs Verily Anderson, 1965.

Numeric slang

$.02
used in computer message shorthand to mean that the writer is putting their two cents into a discussion *US*
• —Christian Crumlish, *The Internet Dictionary*, p. 3, 1995

£ £ £ *noun*
pounds (sterling) *UK*
Used in visual advertising matter.
• — *The Guardian*, 10th July 2004

10 – 1; ten-one *adjective*
broken *UK*
Teen slang taken from citizens' band radio jargon; reported by James Williamson, 1982.

10 – 4; ten-four
used as an acknowledgement that a message has been received *US*
• — *Complete CB Slang Dictionary*, p. 90, 1976
• "Got it?" "Ten-four," Sam said, "message received." — George V. Higgins, *The Judgment of Deke Hunter*, p. 84, 1976
• 30–12 very definitely agreed (10–4 three times over) — Peter Chippindale, *The British CB Book*, p. 160, 1981
• WURLITZER: Do you undetsand? BERGMAN: That's a big ten-four. — *Natural Born Killers*, 1994

11 *noun*
the loudest possible amplification *US*
From a comic conceit in the film *Spinal Tap*.
• NIGEL TUFNEL: The numbers all go to eleven. Look, right across the board, eleven, eleven, eleven and.... MARTY DIBERGI: Oh, I see. And most amps go up to ten? [...] MARTY DIBERGI: Does that mean it's louder? Is it any louder? NIGEL TUFNEL: Well, it's one louder, isn't it? It's not ten. You see, most blokes, you know, will be playing at ten. You're on ten here, all the way up, all the way up, all the way up, you're on ten on your guitar. Where can you go from there? Where? MARTY DIBERGI: I don't know. NIGEL TUFNEL: Nowhere. Exactly. What we do is, if we need that extra push over the cliff, you know what we do? MARTY DIBERGI: Put it up to eleven. NIGEL TUFNEL: Eleven. Exactly. One louder. — *Spinal Tap*, 1984
• Jack Black [...] looks ready to spark up a joint and crank up the latest White Stripes album to 11. — *Uncut*, p. 73, March 2004

110 per cent *adverb*
absolutely, utterly *UK*
• The guy was all policeman, 110 per cent on the square [honest]. — Garry Bushell, *The Face*, p. 95, 2001
• [Football manager, Gordon] Strachan remains '110 per cent committed' to the club. — *The Observer*, 11th January 2004

12 *noun*
a recording available on twelve inch vinyl disc *UK*
• A clutch of about ten 12s appear, together with a warm invitation to the decks. — *Ministry*, p. 58, January 2002
• Swap punk's Portastudio for grime's PC and you can realistically turn a tune on your hard drive into a couple of boxes of 12s in 24 hours. — *Mojo*, p. 56, November 2004

125 *noun*
cocaine *UK*
Rhyming slang, from the Inter-City 125, the nearest thing the UK has to a high speed train.
• [A]s the 125 kicks in to everyone and everything[.] — Lupine Howl, *125*, 2001

12 and 12; twelve and twelve *noun*
a person who seems sexually attractive only after twelve midnight and twelve beers *US*
• —Connie Eble (Editor), *UNC-CH Campus Slang*, p. 9, March 1996

12-er *noun*
a twelve-pack of beer *US*
• Hey babe remember when we walked down to the beach and drank the 12-er? / We were so wasted we passed out. — Me First and the Gimmes Gimmes, *End of the Road*, 2003

13; number thirteen; thirteen *noun*
morphine *US, 1953*
M (morphine) is the thirteenth letter of the alphabet.

133t; 133t 5p34k *noun*
▷ see: LEET TALK

14 *nickname*
1 used as an indication that a person is a member of a northern California Mexican-American gang *US*
'N' is the fourteenth letter of the alphabet.
• —Jennifer Blowdryer, *Modern English*, p. 66, 1985

2 a member of the Nuestra Familia prison gang *US*
'N' is the fourteenth letter of the alphabet.
• —Bill Valentine, *Gangs and Their Tattoos*, p. 36, 2000

151; one-fifty-one; fifty-one *noun*
crack cocaine *US, 1998*
• —Mike Haskins, *Drugs*, p. 281, 2003

187; one-eight-seven *noun*
1 a homicide *US*
From the California penal code number used by the police as radio shorthand for a homicide. Adopted into the lyrics of GANGSTA RAP(S) from Los Angeles Police Department usage.
• [F]uck around and get caught up in a 187[.] — Dr Dre, *Let Me Ride*, 1992
• You down with the 187? — *Menace II Society*, 1993

2 no possibility; no chance *US*
A figurative use of the previous sense, hence 'any possibility is dead'.
• 'Cos it's one-eight-seven on an uncovered cock[.] — Kwest Tha Madd Lad, *Lubrication*, 1996

1984 *adjective*
oppressively authoritarian *US*
Directly from the novel *Nineteen Eighty-Four* by George Orwell, 1949.
• Los Angeles Free Press has pioneered exposure of 1984 police techniques (from lead-filled gloves to militaristically equipped "super-fuzz" tank cars)[.] — Richard Neville, *Play Power*, p. 154, 1970

21 *nickname*
Newquay, Cornwall *UK*
Puns 'new key': 'He's got the key of the door, never been twenty-one before'.
• [O]thers [place-names] are more subtle or require you to know something about the place. Newquay for example is 21[.] — Peter Chippindale, *The British CB Book*, p. 169, 1981

24/7; twenty-four seven *adverb*
at all times – twenty-four hours a day, seven days a week *US*
• —Ellen C. Bellone (Editor), *Dictionary of Slang*, p. 25, 1989
• —Pamela Munro, *U.C.L.A. Slang*, p. 87, 1989
• The place is open twenty-four seven [24 hours a day, seven days a week], says the young man who works behind the scale for Splib's friend Victor. — Terry Williams, *The Cocaine Kids*, p. 53, 1989
• —Connie Eble (Editor), *UNC-CH Campus Slang*, p. 7, Fall 1989
• Ya know he used ta run that ball up the street all day. Twenty-four seven, three-hundred and sixty. — *Boyz N The Hood*, 1990
• —Terry Williams, *Crackhouse*, p. 152, 1992
• —Michael Small, *Break it Down*, p. 218, 1992
• We're in Steps 24-seven, so yeah, I've had a few bad days — *Sky Magazine*, p. 17, May 2001
• I mean, she's just fuckin on me case twenny four seven. — Niall Griffiths, *Kelly + Victor*, p. 282, 2002

24 – 7 – 365; twenty-four, seven, three-sixty-five *adjective*
at all times *US, 1983*
From the notion of twenty-four hours a day, seven days a week, three hundred and sixty-five days a year.
- Jerry (Ice) Reynolds, one of the SEC's two best freshmen by the end of last season, calls his jump shot "24 – 7 – 365," because, "It's good 24 hours a day, seven days a week, 365 days a year." — *Sports Illustrated*, p. 76, 28th November 1983
- You can't trust nobody, so keep your back to the wall and your eyes open – 24, 7, 365. — Richard Price, *Clockers*, p. 4, 1992
- Fire department? My house isn't burning. I keep the sprinklers on 24 – 7 – 365. I keep the house nice and moist. I'm just trying to save some money. — Chris Rock, *Rock This!*, p. 38, 1997

24-hour hootch *noun*
a beverage of apple juice, yeast and aspirins *CANADA*
- The recipe for "24 hour hootch" came out of the Queen Charlotte Islands, where delay of the supply boat is a major non-event for serious drinkers. It was for fast relief: a 48oz can of apple juice, a packet of yeast, and six aspirins. — Tom Parkin, *WetCoast Words*, p. 145, 1989

26 girl; twenty-six girl *noun*
a woman who encourages customers to play 26, a dice game played with ten dice in Chicago bars *US*
- Now there is a rash of cocktail lounges with big and quick turnover and the usual accessories of B girls and 26 girls and not a few with strippers. — Jack Lait and Lee Mortimer, *Chicago Confidential*, p. 12, 1950
- At the dice table the 26-girl sits in boredom[.] — Willard Motley, *Let No Man Write My Epitaph*, p. 175, 1958

276 *nickname*
the prison gang more commonly known as the Black Guerrilla Family *US*
- Other names include Weusi Giadi Jama, which is Swahili for Black Guerrilla Family, and the numbers 276 [representing the numerical order of the letters B, G, and F in the alphabet]. — Bill Valentine, *Gangs and Their Tattoos*, p. 17, 2000

288; two eighty-eight *adjective*
too disgusting, too gross *US*
An excruciating pun on 288 as 'two gross' (2 x 144 = 288).

28 cheeks *noun*
girls who are not romantically or sexually faithful to one partner; two timers *SOUTH AFRICA*
Teen slang, of uncertain origin. This may well also apply in the singular.
- — *Sunday Times (South Africa)*, 1st June 2003

2C-B *noun*
4-bromo-2,5-dimethoxyphenethylamine, a mild hallucinogen used recreationally *US*
- Shulgin recommends taking 2C-B "at or just before" recovery from an ecstasy trip. — Steven Daly and Nalthaniel Wice, *alt.culture*, p. 256, 1995
- — Alon Shulman, *The Style Bible*, p. 256, 1999

364; three-sixty-four *noun*
a 364 day jail sentence in the US, the maximum jail term for misdemeanours, served in county jail *US*
- [S]o he could hook up with Second Wind, the drug treatment alternative, and avoid spending ninety days in County, the mandatory time on a 364 for selling drugs in Dempsy. — Richard Price, *Clockers*, p. 325, 1992

365; three-six-five *noun*
a mutton chop *NEW ZEALAND*
So named because it is served for breakfast every day of the year.
- They could eat hockeysticks or 365s, which town-dwellers know as mutton chops. — *NZWords*, 2nd August 2001

365; three-sixty-five *adverb*
all the time *US*
Every day of the year.
- — Connie Eble (Editor), *UNC-CH Campus Slang*, p. 10, November 1990

37461 *noun*
crack cocaine *UK*
- — Mike Haskins, *Drugs*, p. 281, 2003

3750 *noun*
marijuana *UK*
- — Mike Haskins, *Drugs*, p. 286, 2003

3-m *noun*
(1) mutual (2) manual (3) masturbation *US*
- — Wayne Dynes, *Homolexis*, p. 91, 1985

3-peat; three-peat *verb*
to win a sports championship three times consecutively *US*
When he was the coach of the Los Angeles Lakers basketball team, Pat Riley sought and obtained a trademark for the term.
- Back when he coached the Los Angeles Lakers and preached quiche ball, [Pat] Riley started babbling a strange watchword. Having won two consecutive titles, he promised a third in 1989. Hence, three-peat. — *Chicago Sun-Times*, p. 115, 21st May 1992
- With their 99 to 98 victory over the Phoenix Suns on Sunday night, the Bulls earned the right to capitalize on a new merchandising wrinkle, the "three-peat" and "3-peat" trademarks. — *The New York Times*, p. D1, 22nd June 1993

40 *noun*
1 a forty ounce bottle of malt liquor *US, 1990*
Also spelt out as 'forty' or 'forty-ounce'.
- — Michael Small, *Break it Down*, p. 219, 1992: 'Hip-hop dictionary'
- All I had was two forties. — *Menace II Society*, 1993
- — Connie Eble (Editor), *UNC-CH Campus Slang*, p. 4, Spring 1994
- TELLY: What do you want? CASPER: Get another forty. Smoke a blunt. — *Kids*, 1995
- [W]ake up with a 40 / Mixed up with Alka-Seltzer[.] — Eminem (Marshall Mathers), *Greg*, 1999

2 a 40 milligram dose of the synthetic opiate oxycodone used recreationally *US*
- Over the next year, her habit grew until she was taking up to eight '40s' a day, she says. — *The Houston Chronicle*, 1st July 2001

404; four-o-four *adjective*
mentally lost, very unaware *US*
From the Internet message '404, URL not found'.
- — Judi Sanders, *Da Bomb!*, p. 1, 1997

411; four-one-one *noun*
gossip, information *US*
411 is the universal telephone number for directory enquiries – known commonly as 'information' in the US.
- — Connie Eble (Editor), *UNC-CH Campus Slang*, p. 7, Fall 1991
- — Judi Sanders, *Kickin' like Chicken with the Couch Commander*, p. 9, 1992
- — Michael Small, *Break it Down*, p. 218, 1992: 'Hip-hop dictionary'
- Here's the four-one-one on Mr. Hall. — *Clueless*, 1995

415 *noun*
a prison gang with black members *US*
- This spin-off from the BGF [Black Guerrilla Family] started as Bay Love in 1983 in the California prison system. The name was soon changed to 415 (the telephone area code of the San Francisco Bay Area). — Bill Valentine, *Gangs and Their Tattoos*, p. 17, 2000

420 man; four-twenty man *noun*
a cheat; a fraudster *INDIA*
A reference to the Indian Penal Code.
- — Nigel Hankin, *Hanklyn-Janklin*, 2003

45 *noun*
a single song recording on vinyl *UK, 1950*
From the rpm (revolutions per minute).
- The DJ is only playing the 45s of Funkadelic. — Alan Warner, *Bitter Salvage [Disco Biscuits]*, p. 273, 1996
- Well it's a brimful of Asha on the 45[.] — Cornershop, *Brimful of Asha*, 1997

5000; five thousand
goodbye *US*
An abbreviation of **AUDI 5000!**.
- — Connie Eble (Editor), *UNC-CH Campus Slang*, p. 7, Fall 1991

5318008 *noun*
a numerical sequence that displays boobies (the female breasts) upside down in the window of a calculator or mobile phone
Probably first seen in the 1970s, still in use.
- — *Comic Relief*, 14th March 2003
- — Jonathan Blyth, *The Law of the Playground*, p. 204, 2004

5-H-1-T *noun*
shit *UK*
A euphemism employed by some doctors.
- — Adam T. Fox, St Mary's Hospital, London, 10th October 2002

5 watter; five watter *noun*

a fool *UK*

A play on the dimmest unit of electric lighting and a person who is not very bright; in Royal Air Force use, 2002.

6 – 10 *verb*

to have sex *UK*

- —Peter Chippindale, *The British CB Book*, p. 159, 1981

64; six-four; six-fo' *noun*

a 1964 Chevrolet Impala, an ultimate prize of car customisers and lowriders *US*

- —Anna Scotti and Paul Young, *Buzzwords*, p. 41, 1997

650 lifer *noun*

in Michigan, a prisoner sentenced to life in prison for possession of more than 650 grams of cocaine *US*

- —Jim Crotty, *How to Talk American*, p. 77, 1997

69; sixty-nine; sixty-niner *noun*

mutual, simultaneous oral sex between two people (used of both the position and the act) *UK, 1888*

- The reference in both cases is to the similar appearance of the numerals 69 and two bodies engaged in mutual oragenitalism, the circles in the numerals 6 and 9 representing the participants' heads, and the tails of the numerals representing their torsi and legs. —G. Legman, *The Language of Homsexuality*, p. 1176, 1941
- —Donald Webster Cory and John P. LeRoy, *The Homosexual and His Society*, p. 266, 1963: 'A lexicon of homosexual slang'
- — Florida Legislative Investigation Committee (Johns Committee), *Homosexuality and Citizenship in Florida*, 1964: 'Glossary of homosexual terms and deviate acts'
- Once a younger fellow and I had gone all the way – 69.—Antony James, *America's Homosexual Underground*, p. 39, 1965
- The 69 position is more awkward for women.—Anka Radakovich, *The Wild Girls Club*, p. 132, 1994
- —Caroline Archer, *Tart Cards*, 2003

69; sixty-nine *verb*

to engage in simultaneous, mutual oral sex with someone *US*

- Kim and I had had the uncommon thrill of watching brothers sixty-nine each other[.]—John Francis Hunter, *The Gay Insider*, p. 41, 1971

6-up; six-up *noun*

a police officer *US*

- —Connie Eble (Editor), *UNC-CH Campus Slang*, p. 11, November 2003

79 *noun*

an M79 grenade launcher *US*

Vietnam war usage. It is a single-shot, break-open, breech-loading, shoulder-fired weapon.

- —Peter Kokalis, *Solider of Fortnue*, p. 57, July 1992

7-up *noun*

in casinos, a wire bent in the shape of a seven that is slipped into slot machines to trigger a payout *US*

- Those cheaters were known in the casino security business as "7UPs."—Stephen J. Cannell, *King Con*, p. 143, 1997

8; number 8; number eight; eight *noun*

heroin *US, 1953*

H (heroin) is the eighth letter of the alphabet.

- —Ann Lawson, *Kids & Gangs*, p. 56, 1994: 'Common Mexican gang slang/phrases'
- —Robert Ashton, *This is Heroin*, p. 206, 2002
- —Mike Hoskins, *Drugs*, p. 284, 2003

80's bush *noun*

a bushy female hairstyle, popular in the 1980s and mocked thereafter *US*

- —Don R. McCreary (Editor), *Dawg Speak*, 2001

88

used as a symbol of fascist and racist beliefs *US*

'H' is the eighth letter of the alphabet, and so 88 translates into HH, or 'Heil Hitler'.

- —Bill Valentine, *Gangs and Their Tattoos*, p. x, 2000

8th; eighth *noun*

an eighth of an ounce, especially of a drug *UK*

- Enuff bud to keep tha whole party high on / I might get ill and roll an 8th in one hooter—Tone Loc, *Cheeba Cheeba*, 1989
- —Angela Devlin, *Prison Patter*, p. 49, 1996
- [Y]ou buy an eighth. You are a fiver [£5] short.—Macfarlane, Macfarlane and Robson, *The User*, p. 136, 1996
- Needed to get out and buy an eighth off Jimmy Foley before Noreen came home.—Jeremy Cameron, *Brown Bread in Wengen*, p. 1, 1999
- Hand me an eighth / Beam me up and land me in space[.]—Eminem (Marshall Mathers), *Bad Influence*, 2000
- —Robert Ashton, *This Is Heroin*, p. 205, 2002

9; nine *noun*

1 a 9 mm pistol *US*

- Keisha puts the "nine" right next to his temple, and pulls the trigger twice. Blood flies everywhere.— *New Jack City*, p. 19, 1990
- —Vann Wesson, *Generation X Field Guide and Lexicon*, p. 124, 1997
- My 9's at your brain[.]—Eminem (Marshall Mathers), *Weed Lacer (Freestyle)*, 1999
- Bolden broke into the Pony Express Sports Shop in North Hills and took about 25 guns – "nines, "deuce-deuces, and "deuce-fives," Dixon, also of North Hills testified[.]— *Daily News of Los Angeles*, p. N1, 27th April 2003

2 a nine gallon keg of beer *AUSTRALIA, 1943*

- 'How c'n it be a good night without women?' Pat said. 'There'll be a coupla nines.'—Nino Culotta (John O'Grady), *They're A Weird Mob*, p. 89, 1957

900 *noun*

in skateboarding, a jumping manoeuvre of two and a half revolutions *UK*

- —Fabrice le Mao, *Skateboarding*, p. 90, 2004

98; ninety-eight *noun*

any classic car, especially an Oldsmobile 98 *US*

- —Anna Scotti and Paul Young, *Buzzwords*, p. 40, 1997

99s

used euphemistically to avoid swearing in citizens' band radio transmissions *UK*

- —Peter Chippindale, *The British CB Book*, p. 157, 1981

Bibliography

Aaberg, Dennis and John Milius
Big Wednesday, Bantam Books, New York, 1978

Abbott, Rick and Mike Baker
Start Surfing, Stanley Paul, Melbourne, 1980

Abel, Ernest L.
A Marijuana Dictionary, Greenwood Press, Westport, Connecticut, 1982
Dictionary of Alcohol Use and Abuse, Greenwood Press, Westport, Connecticut, 1985

Abernathy, Francis Edward
The Bounty of Texas (Publication of the Texas Folklore Society #49), University of North Texas, Denton, Texas, 1990

Abrahams, Roger
Deep Down in the Jungle: Negro Narrative Folklore from the Streets of Philadelphia (Revised Edition), Aldine Publishing, Chicago, Illinois, 1970
Positively Black, Prentice-Hall, Englewood Cliffs, New Jersey, 1970

Ackroyd, Dan and John Landis
The Blues Brothers, Universal Pictures, 1980

Ackroyd, Peter
London The Biography, Chatto & Windus, London, 2000

Acosta, Oscar Zeta
The Autobiography of a Brown Buffalo, Vintage Books, New York, 1989 (1972)
The Revolt of the Cockroach People, Straight Arrow Books, San Francisco, California, 1973

Adams, L. Emilie
Understanding Jamaican Patois, Kingston Publishers, Kingston, Jamaica, 1991

Adams, Phillip
The Unspeakable Adams, Thomas Nelson, Melbourne, 1979 (1977)

Adams, Ramon
The Language of the Railroader, University of Oklahoma Press, Norman, Oklahoma, 1977

Adam-Smith, Patsy
Folklore of the Australian Railwaymen, Macmillan, Melbourne, 1971 (1969)

Adler, Polly
A House is Not a Home, Rinehart & Company, New York, 1953

Aherne, Caroline and Craig Cash
The Royle Family: The Scripts (Series 1), Granada, 1999

Ainslie, Tom
Ainslie's Complete Guide to Thoroughbred Racing (3rd Edition), Simon & Schuster, New York, 1976

Aitch, Iain
A Fête Worse Than Death, Headline, London, 2003

Albano, Captain Lou and Bert Randolph Sugar
The Complete Idiot's Guide to Pro Wrestling, Alpha Books, New York, 1999

Alexander, Don
The Racer's Dictionary, Steve Smith Autosports, Santa Ana, California, 1980

Alexie, Sherman
Smoke Signals, Miramax, 1998

Alfange, Dean
The Horse Racing Industry, Kensington Publishing Corporation, New York, 1976

Allen, J. Edward
The Basics of Winning Slots, Gambling Research Institute, New York, 1984

Allen, Jack
When the Whistle Blows, Dedalus, Cambridge, 2000

Allen, Jim
Locked in Surfing for Life, Barnes and Noble, New York, 1970

Allen, Steve
Bop Fables, Simon & Schuster, New York, 1955

Allen, Woody and Marshall Brickman
Annie Hall, United Artists, 1977
Manhattan, United Artists, 1979

Allison, Ruth
Lesbianism: Its Secrets and Practices, Medco Books, Los Angeles, California, 1967

Allsopp, Richard
Dictionary of Caribbean English Usage, Oxford University Press, New York, 1996

Alpert, Richard and Sidney Cohen
LSD, New American Library, New York, 1966

Alter, Robert Edmond
Carny Kill, Black Lizard Books, Berkeley, California, 1986 (1966)

Alvarez, George R.
Semiotic Dynamics of an Ethnic-American Sub-Cultural Group, unpublished paper prepared for the International Conference on General Semantics, Los Altos, California, 1965

Alvi, Saroosh et al.
The Vice Guide to Sex, Drugs and Rock and Roll, HarperCollins, Toronto, 2002

Aman, Reinhold
Hillary Clinton's Pen Pal: A Guide to Life and Lingo in Federal Prison, Maledicta Press, Santa Rosa, California, 1996
Maledicta: The International Journal of Verbal Aggression vols 1–12, Maledicta Press, Santa Rosa, California, 1977–1996

Andersen, Joe
Winners Can Laugh, Pacific Publications, Melbourne, 1982

Anderson, Charles R.
The Grunts, Berkley Books, New York, 1986 (1976)

Anderson, Douglas
All About Cribbage, Winchester Press, New York, 1971

Anderson, Michael V.
The Bad, Rad, Not to Forget Way Cool Beach and Surf Discriptionary, Oceanside Printers, 1988

Anderson, Paul Thomas
Boogie Nights, New Line Cinema, 1997
Hard Eight, Goldwyn Entertainment, 1996

Andrews, Alice
Hooked on Bingo, Aecila Publishing, St. Louis, Missouri, 1988

Andrews, Malachi and Paul T. Owens
Black Language, Seymour-Smith, West Los Angeles, California, 1973

Andros, Phil (Samuel M. Steward)
Stud, Alyson Publications, Boston, Massachusetts, 1982 (1966)

Andrus, Mark and James L. Brooks
As Good As It Gets, TriStar Pictures, 1997

Anglicus, Ducange
The Vulgar Tongue, Bernard Quaritch, London, 1857

Anonymous
A Basic Guide to Campusology, Campus Humor Publications, Austin, Texas, 1966
Go Ask Alice, Avon Books, New York, 1971
King Smut's Wet Dreams Interpreted: An Erotic Lexicon and Number Guide, Komar Ltd, Baltimore, Maryland, 1978
Streetwalker: An Autobiographical Account of Prostitution, The Bodley Head, London, 1960 (1959)
The Gay Girl's Guide, privately published, New York, 1949

Anslinger, Harry J.
The Murderers, Arthur Barker, London, 1962 (1961)

Anthony, Earl
Winning Bowling, Contemporary Books, Chicago, Illinois, 1977

Anthony, Wayne
Spanish Highs, Virgin, London, 1999

Antony, James
America's Homosexual Underground, L.S. Publications, New York, 1965

Applebaum, Ben and Derrick Pittman
Turd Ferguson and the Sausage Party: An Uncensored Guide to College Slang, iUniverse, Inc., New York, 2004

Archer, Jeff
Theater in a Squared Circle: The Mystique of Professional Wrestling, White Boucke Publishing, Lafayette, Colorado, 1999

Armanino, Dominic
Dominoes: Popular Games, Rules & Strategy, Cornerstone Library, New York, 1959
Five-up Domino Games, Five-Up Company, San Francisco, California, 1964

Armore, John R. and Joseph D. Wolfe
Dictionary of Desperation, National Alliance of Businessmen, Washington D.C., 1976

Armstrong, Louis
Satchmo: My Life in New Orleans, Da Capo Press, New York, 1986 (1954)

Arnott, Jake
He Kills Coppers, Sceptre, London, 2001

Arthur, Howard and Alvin Ebeling
The Falcon Illustrated Football Dictionary, Young Readers Press, New York, 1971

Ashton, Robert
This Is Heroin, Sanctuary Publishing, London, 2002

Ausubel, Nathan
A Treasury of Jewish Folklore, Crown Publishers, New York, 1968 (1948)

Aven-Bray, Ryan
Ridgey Didge Oz Jack Lang, self-published, Sydney, 1983

Ayers, Rick (Editor)
Berkeley High Slang Dictionary, North Atlantic Books, Berkeley, California, 2004
Slang Dictionary, Berkeley High School, Berkeley, California, 2001

Ayto, John
20th Century Words, Oxford University Press, 1999
The Oxford Dictionary of Rhyming Slang, Oxford University Press, 2002
The Oxford Dictionary of Slang, Oxford University Press, 1998

Babitz, Eve
Eve's Hollywood, Dell Publishing, New York, 1974
L.A. Woman, Linden Press, New York, 1982

Bail, Murray
Holden's Performance, Penguin Books, Melbourne, 1988

Baker, Collin et al.
College Undergraduate Slang Study Conducted at Brown University Semester II, 1967–1968, College Undergraduate Slang Study, Providence, Rhode Island, 1968

Baker, Fred
Events: The Complete Film Scenario, Grove Press, New York, 1970

Baker, George Carpenter
Pachuco: An American-Spanish Argot and Its Social Functions in Tucson, Arizona, University of Arizona Press, Tucson, Arizona, 1950

Baker, Nicholson
Vox, Random House, New York, 1992

Baker, Paul
Fantabulosa, Continuum, London, 2002
Polari: The Lost Language of Gay Men, Routledge, London, 2002

Baker, Sidney J.
The Australian Language, Angus and Robertson, Sydney, 1945
The Drum: Australian Character and Slang, Currawong Publishing Co., Sydney, 1959
The Australian Language (2nd Edition), Currawong Publishing Co., Sydney, 1966

Baldwin, James
Blues for Mister Charlie, Dell Publishing, New York, 1964

Balistreri, Maggie
The Evasion-English Dictionary, Melville House Publishing, Hoboken, New Jersey, 2003

Ball, Alan
American Beauty, Dream Works, 1999

Ball Carr, Elizabeth
Da Kine Talk: From Pidgin to Standard English in Hawaii, University Press of Hawaii, Honolulu, Hawaii, 1972

Balls, Richard
Sex & Drugs & Rock 'n' Roll: The Life of Ian Dury, Omnibus Press, London, 2000

Bangs, Lester
Psychotic Reactions and Carburetor Dung, Serpent's Tail, London, 2001

Banks, Carl J.
Banks Dictionary of the Black Ghetto Language, self-published, Los Angeles, California, 1975

Barber, Katherine
The Canadian Oxford Dictionary, Oxford University Press, Ontario, 1998

Barger, Ralph "Sonny"
Hell's Angel: The Life and Times of Sonny Barger and the Hell's Angels Motorcycle Club, William Morrow, New York, 2000

Barker, Ronnie
Fletcher's Book of Rhyming Slang, Pan Books, London, 1979

Barlay, Nick
Curvy Lovebox, 20/20, London, 1997

Barltrop, Robert and Jim Wolveridge
The Muvver Tongue, The Journeyman Press, London, 1980

Baron-Cohen, Sacha
Da Gospel According to Ali G, Fourth Estate, London, 2001

Barr, Ann and Peter York
The Official Sloane Ranger Handbook, Harpers & Queen, London, 1982

Barrett, Pat
Everybody Down There Hates Me: The Traumas and Dramas Inside the Incredible World of Professional Wrestling, Fleur Press, Gulf Breeze, Florida, 1990

Barrett, Robert G.
Davo's Little Something, Pan Macmillan, Sydney, 1992
The Wind and the Monkey, HarperCollins, Sydney, 1999

Barth, Vincent
Porno Films and the People who Make Them, Academy Press, San Diego, California, 1973

Bean, Mo
Let's Go Clubbing, Sage Press, Tonbridge, Kent, 1998

Beaufoy, Simon
The Full Monty, Screenpress Books, London, 1997

Beckerman, Marty
Death to All Cheerleaders, Infected Press, Anchorage, Alaska, 2000

Beckett, Richard
The Dinkum Aussie Dictionary, Child & Associates, Sydney, 1986

Bell, John D. et al.
Loosely Speaking: A Lexicon of Carleton Neologisms (2nd Edition), Carleton College, Northfield, Minnestoa, 1969
Loosely Speaking: The Centennial Lexicon of Carleton Neologisms, Carleton College, Northfield, Minnesota, 1966

Bellisimo, Lou
The Bowler's Manual (2nd Edition), Prentice-Hall, Englewood Cliffs, New Jersey, 1969

Bellone, Ellen C. (Editor)
Dictionary of Slang, Delcastle Technical High School, Wilmington, Delaware, 1989

Bennett, W.R.
Night Intruder, Horwitz Publications, Sydney, 1962
Target Turin, Horwitz Publications, Sydney, 1962
Wingman, Horwitz Publications, Sydney, 1961

Bentley, William K. and James M. Corbett
Prison Slang: Words and Expressions Depicting Life Behind Bars, McFarland & Company, Jefferson, North Carolina, 1992

Berens, Jessica and Kerri Sharp
Inappropriate Behaviour, Serpent's Tail, London, 2002

Beresford, Bruce and Barry Humphries
The Adventures of Barry McKenzie, Longford Productions, 1972

Berger, Gilda and Melvin
Drug Abuse A–Z, Enslow Publishers, Hillside, New Jersey, 1990

Bernard, Sidney
This Way to the Apocalypse: The 60s, Horizon Press, New York, 1969

Bernhard, Sandra
Confessions of a Pretty Lady, Harper & Row, New York, 1988

Bibb, Porter
CB Bible, Dolphin Books, Garden City, New York, 1976

Bickerton, Derek
Payroll, Pan Books, London, 1959

Biggun, Ivor
The Winker's Album, Beggars Banquet, London, 1978

Birch, Will
No Sleep Till Canvey Island, Virgin, London, 2003

Birmingham, John
He Died with a Felafel in his Hand, Duffy and Snellgrove, Sydney, 1994
The Tasmanian Babes Fiasco, Duffy and Snellgrove, Sydney, 1997

Biscuit, Harrison
The Search for Savage Henry, Autopsy, Sydney, 1995

Black, Shane
Lethal Weapon, Warner Brothers, 1987

Black, Sue
The Totally Awesome Val Guide, Price/Stern/Sloan, Los Angeles, California, 1982

Blackman, John
The Aussie Slang Dictionary: For Old and New Australians, Sun Books, Melbourne, 1990

Blaikie, George
Remember Smith's Weekly?, Rigby Limited, Adelaide, 1966

Blair, John
The Illustrated Discography of Surf Music 1961–1965 (2nd Edition, Revised), Pierian Press, Ann Arbor, Michigan, 1985

Blake, Roger
The American Dictionary of Sexual Terms, Century Publishing, Hollywood, California, 1964
The Stimulators: Swinging Set's Newest Rage, Century Books, Cleveland, Ohio, 1968
What you always wanted to know about porno-movies *but were afraid to ask*, Eros Publishing, Wilmington, Delaware, 1972

Bleasdale, Alan
Boys From the Blackstuff, Granada, 1982

Block, Francesca Lia
Dangereous Angels: The Weetzie Bat Books, HarperCollins, New York, 1988
I Was a Teenage Fairy, Joana Cotler Books, New York, 2000 (1998)
Weetzie Bat, HarperCollins, New York, 1989

Block, Lawrence
The Affairs of Chip Harrison Omnibus, No Exit Press, Harpenden, Hertfordshire, 2001

Bloomquist, Edward R.
Marijuana, Glencoe Press, Beverly Hills, California, 1968
Marijuana: The Second Trip, Glencoe Press, Beverly Hills, California, 1971

Blowdryer, Jennifer
White Trash Debutante, Glencoe Press, Beverly Hills, California, 1997

Bluey
Bush Contractors, Coburg Forrest, Sydney, 1975

Blyth, Jonathan
The Law of the Playground, Ebury Press, London, 2004

Boe, Eugene (Compiler)
The Wit & Wisdom of Archie Bunker, Popular Library, New York, 1971

Bond, Alison
The Glove Compartment Book, Stonesong Press, New York, 1979

Bonham, Howard B.
Football Lingo: The Language of Modern Football, Diversified Publishing, Memphis, Tennessee, 1962

Borrow, George
Romano Lavo-Lil, John Murray, London, 1907

Bosworth, Ellen
Shelley and the Bushfire Mystery, Golden Press, Sydney, 1972

Boulware, Marcus Hanna
Jive and Slang of Students in Negro Colleges, Hampton, Virginia, 1947

Bouton, Jim
Ball Four, Dell Publishing, New York, 1971 (1970)

Bowen, Robert O.
An Alaskan Dictionary, Nooshnik Press, Spenard, Alaska, 1965

Boyd, Malcolm
My Fellow Americans, Holt, Rinehart and Winston, New York, 1970

Boyne, Walter and Steven Thompson
The Wild Blue, Ivy Books, New York, 1986

Bracklin, Ivan and William Fitzgerald
All About Darts, Contemporary Books, Chicago, Illinois, 1975

Bradley, Matt
Queer St. U.S.A., Century Books, Los Angeles, California, 1965

Bradley, William J.
CB Fact Book and Language Dictionary, DMR Publications, Milwaukee, Wisconsin, 1977

Braly, Malcolm
On the Yard, Little, Brown and Co., Boston, Massachusetts, 1967

Brandonstiel, Mack
Breaker, Breaker, 10–4: A Complete Guide to CB Radio, Grosset & Dunlap, New York, 1976

Brandreth, Gyles
Breaking the Code, Weidenfeld and Nicholson, London, 1999

Branford, Jean
A Dictionary of South African English, Oxford University Press, Cape Town, 1978

Branson, Helen P.
Gay Bar, Pan-Graphic Press, San Francisco, California, 1957

Branwyn, Gareth
Jargon Watch: A Pocket Dictionary for the Jitterati, Hardwired, San Francisco, California, 1997

Brathwaithe, J. Ashton
Niggers – This is Canada, 21st Century Books, Toronto, Ontario, 1971

Brehan, Delle
Kicks is Kicks, Holloway House, Los Angeles, California, 1970

Bridson, Rory
The Making of a Para, Sidgwick & Jackson, London, 1989

Briggs, Joe Bob
Joe Bob Goes to the Drive-In, Delacorte Press, New York, 1987

Brinsmead, Hesba
Longtime Dreaming, Angus and Robertson, Sydney, 1988 (1982)

Bromcie, Alec
The Complete Book of Farting, Michael O'Mara Books, London, 1999

Bronsteen, Ruth
The Hippy's Handbook, Canyon Book Company, New York, 1967

Brookmyre, Christopher
Boiling a Frog, Little, Brown and Co., London, 2000
Not the End of the World, Abacus, London, 2002 (1998)
The Sacred Art of Stealing, Abacus, London, 2003 (2002)

Brooks, Jean
The Opal Witch, Rigby, Adelaide, 1970 (1967)

Brooks, Maureen and Joan Ritchie
Tassie Terms: A Glossary of Tasmanian Words, Oxford University Press, Melbourne, 1995

Brophy, John and Eric Partridge
Songs and Slang of the British Soldier: 1914–1918, Eric Partridge Ltd at the Scholartis Press, London, 1930

Brown, Cecil
The Life & Loves of Mr. Jiveass Nigger, Farrar, Straus & Giroux, New York, 1969

Brown, Claude
Manchild in the Promised Land, Signet Books, New York, 1966 (1965)

Brown, Dan
Digital Fortress, St. Martin's Press, New York, 1998

Brown, Geoff
I Want What I Want, G.P. Putnam's Sons, New York, 1966

Brown, H. Rap
Die Nigger Die!, Dial Press, New York, 1969

Brown, Joe
Just for the Record, Australian Broadcasting Corporation, Sydney, 1984

Brown, Joe David
Sex in the '60s: A Candid Look at the Age of Mini-Morals, Time Life Books, New York, 1968

Brown, Joe David (Editor)
The Hippies, Time Incorporated, New York, 1967

Brown, Pete
Man Walks into a Pub, Macmillan, London, 2003

Browne, Stuart
Dangerous Parking, Bloomsbury, London, 2000

Brownlee, Nick
This Is Alcohol, Sanctuary Publishing, London, 2002
This Is Cannabis, Sanctuary Publishing, London, 2002

Bruce, Lenny
How to Talk Dirty and Influence People, Quality Paperback Book Club, New York, 1965
The Essential Lenny Bruce, Bell Publishing, New York, 1970 (1967)

Bryan, Frank
Tackle Tenpin Bowling This Way, Stanley Paul, London, 1962

Bryant, David
The Game of Bowls, Partridge Press, London, 1990

Buckwalter, Len
CB Radio: A Complete Guide, Grosset & Dunlap, New York, 1976

Buffett, Jimmy
Tales from Margaritaville, Ballantine Books, New York, 1993 (1989)

Burke, John and Stuart Douglass
The Boys, Pan Books, London, 1962

Burley, Dan
Diggeth Thou?, Burley, Cross & Co., Chicago, Illinois, 1959

Burroughs, William
Junkie, Ace Books, New York, 1953
Naked Lunch, Grove Press, New York, 1966 (1957)
Queer, Picador, London, 1986 (1985)

Burt, Rob
Surf City, Drag City, Blandford Press, Poole, Dorset, 1986

Bushell, Garry
The Face, John Blake, London, 2001

Butts, Colin
A Bus Could Run You Over, Orion Books, London, 2004
Is Harry on the Boat?, Tuesday Morning Publishing, Ibiza, 1997
Is Harry Still on the Boat?, Orion Books, London, 2003

Buzo, Alexander
Norm and Ahmed, Currency Press, Sydney, 1973 (1969)
Rooted, Currency Press, Sydney, 1973 (1969)
The Roy Murphy Show, Currency Press, Sydney, 1973 (1971)

Byrnes, Edd
Way Out With Kookie, Warner Brothers, 1959

Cameron, Jeremy
Brown Bread in Wengen, Scribner, London, 1999

Cameron, Martin
A Look at the Bright Side, self-published, Richmond, Tasmania, 1988

Camhi, Morrie and James Harris
The Prison Experience ('A Convict's Dictionary'), Tuttle-IPC, Rutland, Vermont, 1989

Campbell, Robert
Alice in La-La Land, Pocket Books, New York, 1987
Boneyards, Pocket Books, New York, 1992
In a Pig's Eye, Pocket Books, New York, 1991
In La-La Land We Trust, Mysterious Press, New York, 1987 (1986)
Juice, Pocket Books, New York, 1988
Junkyard Dog, Signet Books, New York, 1986
Nibbled to Death by Ducks, Pocket Books, New York, 1990 (1989)
Sweet La-La Land, Pocket Books, New York, 1990
The Cat's Meow, Signet Books, New York, 1990 (1988)

Cannell, Stephen J.
Big Con, William Morrow, New York, 1997
The Tin Collectors, St. Martin's Press, New York, 2002 (2001)

Cannon, Rita
Let's Go Racing, Daily Mail Publications, London, 1948

Capitol Records
Hot Rod Jargon, Capitol Records, Los Angeles, California, 1963

Capote, Truman
Breakfast at Tiffany's, Vintage Books, New York, 1958

Caputo, Philip
A Rumor of War, Ballantine Books, New York, 1977

Cardoso, Bill
The Maltese Sangweech and Other Heroes, Atheneum, New York, 1984

Cardoza, Avery
The Basics of Sports Betting, Gambling Research Institute, New York, 1991
Winning Casino Blackjack for the Non-Counter, Gambling Research Institute, New York, 1991

Cardozo-Freeman, Inez
The Joint: Language and Culture in a Maximum Security Prison, Charles C. Thomas, Springfield, Illinois, 1984

Carlisle, Norman
The Modern Wonder Book of Trains and Railroading, John C. Winston, Philadelphia, Pennsylvania, 1946

Carmichael, Stokely and Charles V. Hamilton
Black Power: The Politics of Liberation in America, Vintage Books, New York, 1967

Carnie Mellon Astrophysics Peterson Group
Antarctic Vocabulary, www.cmbr.phys.cmu.edu/talk.html, 1997

Carroll, Gerry
*North S*A*R*, Pocket Books, New York, 1991

Carroll, Jim
Forced Entries: The Downtown Diaries 1971–1973, Penguin Books, New York, 1987

Carroll, Nick
The Next Wave: The World of Surfing, Abbeyville Press, New York, 1991

Carroll, Marilyn and Gary Gallo
Methaqualone: The Quest for Oblivion, Burke Publishing Company, London, 1985

Carroll, Sidney and Robert Rossen
The Hustler, 20th Century Fox, 1961

Cassady, Neal
The First Third & Other Chronicles, City Lights, San Francisco, California, 1981 (1971)

Casselman, Bill
Canadian Sayings, McArthur & Company, Toronto, 2002
Canadian Words, Copp Clark, Toronto, 1995

Cassidy, F.G. and R.B. LePage
Dictionary of Jamaican English, Cambridge University Press, 1967

Cassorla, Albert
The Skateboarder's Bible, Running Press, Philadelphia, Pennsylvania, 1976

Catan, Omero C.
Secrets of Shuffleboard Strategy, Great Outdoors Publishing, Fort Lauderdale, Florida, 1967

Catchlove, Donald
Ray Denning My Life and Time, Ironbark, Sydney, 1994

Cavanaugh, Christopher
AA to Z: Addictionary of the 12-Step Culture, Doubleday, New York, 1998

Cavanough, Maurice and Meurig Davies
Cup Day: The Story of the Melbourne Cup 1861–1960, F.W. Cheshire, Melbourne, 1960

CB Roadrunner
CB Lingo Handbook, self-published, Charlotte, North Carolina, 1976

Chambers, John E.
Cribbage: A New Concept (Revised Edition), self-published, 1992

Champion, Sarah
Disco Biscuits, Hodder & Stoughton, London, 1997

Chandler, Raymond
Playback, Pocket Books, New York, 1960 (1958)
The Little Sister, Pocket Books, New York, 1951 (1949)
The Long Goodbye, Pocket Books, New York, 1955 (1953)

Charlton, James and William Thompson
Croquet: The Complete Guide to History, Strategey, Rules and Records, Turtle Press, New York, 1977

Charlwood, D.E.
All the Green Year, Angus and Robertson, Sydney, 1975 (1965)

Chippindale, Peter
The British CB Book, Kona Publications, London, 1981

Chipper, Arthur
The Aussie Swearer's Guide, Gold Star Publications, Melbourne, 1972

Choo, Paik
The Coxford Singlish Dictionary, Angsana Books, Singapore, 2002

Christian, Petra
The Sexploiters, New English Library, London, 1973

Churchill, Kitty
Thinking of England, Little, Brown and Co., London, 1995

Cimino, Michael and Deric Washburn
The Deer Hunter, Universal Pictures, 1978

Ciresi, Rita
Pink Slip, Dell Publishing, New York, 1999

Claerbaut, David
Black Jargon in White America, William B. Eerdmans, Grand Rapids, Michigan, 1972

Clancy, Tom with Fred Franks Jr
Into the Storm: A Study in Command, G.P. Putnam's Sons, New York, 1991

Clark, Dick
To Goof or Not to Goof, Fawcett Publications, Greenwich, Connecticut, 1963

Clark, Gregory
Words of the Vietnam War: The Slang, Jargon, Abbreviations, Acronyms, Nomenclature, Nicknames, Pseudonyms, Slogans, Specs, Euphemisms, Double-talk, Chants, and Names and Places of the Era of United States Involvement in Vietnam, McFarland & Company, Inc., Jefferson, North Carolina, 1990

Clark, Larry and Harmony Korine
Kids, Shining Excalibur Films, 1995

Clark, Thomas L.
The Dictionary of Gambling and Gaming, Lexik House Publishers, Cold Spring, New York, 1987

Clause, Frank and Patty McBride
Strike! The Complete Handbook of Junior Bowling, Scholastic Book Services, New York, 1964

Claussen, Jim
Keno Handbook, Gamblers Book Club Press, Las Vegas, Nevada, 1982

Clayton, Peter and Peter Gammond
Jazz A–Z, Guinness Books, London, 1986

Cleary, Jon
The Long Shadow, Horwitz, Sydney, 1968 (1949)

Cleaver, Eldridge
Soul on Ice, Dell Publishing, New York, 1968

Cline, Sally
Couples: Scene From The Inside, Little, Brown and Co., London, 1998

Clinton-Meicholas, Patricia
More Talkin' Bahamian, Guanima Press, Nassau, Bahamas, 1995

Close, Robert S.
Love Me Sailor, Horwtiz, Sydney, 1969 (1945)
With Hooves of Brass, Horwitz, Sydney, 1971 (1961)

Cloud, Cam
The Little Book of Acid, Ronin Publishing, Berkeley, California, 1999

Coen, Joel and Ethan
Fargo, Gramercy Pictures, 1996
Raising Arizona, 20th Century Fox, 1987
The Big Lebowski, Gramercy Pictures, 1998

Cohen, Daniel
Wrestling Renegades: An In-Depth Look at Today's Superstars of Pro Wrestling, Archway Paperbacks, New York, 1999

Cohen, Daniel and Susan
Wrestling Superstars II, Archway Paperbacks, New York, 1986

Cohen, Leonard
Beautiful Losers, Bantam Books, New York, 1967 (1966)

Cohn, Nik and Norman Wexler
Saturday Night Fever, Paramount Pictures, 1977

Colendich, George
The Ding Repair Scriptures: The Complete Guide to Surfboard Repair, Village Green Publications, Soquel, California, 1986

Collans, Dev with Stewart Sterling
I Was a House Detective, Pyramid Books, New York, 1954

Collins, H. Craig
Street Gangs: Profiles for Police, City of New York Police Department, New York, 1979

Collymore, Frank A.
Notes for a Glossary of Words and Phrases of Barbadian Dialect (3rd Edition), Advocate Company, Bridgetown, Barbados, 1965

Condon, Richard
Prizzi's Glory, E.P. Dutton, New York, 1988
Prizzi's Honor, Berkley Books, New York, 1983 (1982)
Prizzi's Money, Crown Publishers, New York, 1994

Cone, Miss
The Slang Dictionary (Hawthorne High School), self-published, Hawthorne, California, 1965

Conklin, Les
Payday at the Races, Wilshire Book Company, North Hollywood, California, 1974

Connolly, J.J.
Layer Cake, Duckworth Publishers, London, 2000

Constable, Nick
This Is Cocaine, Sanctuary Publishing, London, 2002

Conway, John
Surfing, Stackpole Books, Harrisburg, Pennsylvania, 1988

Cook, Peter
Tragically I was an Only Twin, Century, London, 2002

Cooper, Clarence
Black, Payback Press, Edinburgh, 1998 (1963)
The Farm, Payback Press, Edinburgh, 1996 (1967)
The Scene, Crest Giant, New York, 1961 (1960)

Cooper, Morton
High School Confidential, Avon Books, New York, 1958

Coppage, Keith
Roller Derby to Rollerjam, Squarebooks, Santa Rosa, California, 1999

Corcoran, Michael
The Golf Dictionary, Taylor Publishing, Dallas, Texas, 1997

Corey, Mary and Victoria Westermark
Fer Shurr! How to be a Valley Girl, Bantam Books, New York, 1982

Corris, Peter
Make Me Rich, Unwin Paperbacks, Sydney, 1985
Pokerface, Penguin Books, Melbourne, 1985

Cory, Donald Webster
The Lesbian in America, Citadel Press, New York, 1964

Cory, Donald Webster and John P. LeRoy
The Homosexual and His Society: A View from Within, The Citadel Press, New York, 1963

Courtney, Dave
Dodgy Dave's Little Black Book, Virgin, London, 2001
Raving Lunacy, Virgin, London, 2000
Stop the Ride I Want to Get Off, Virgin, London, 2001 (1999)

Covington, Carol
A Glossary of Teenage Terms, Macy's, Hillsdale, California, 1965

Cox, Alex
Repo Man, Universal Pictures, 1984

Cox, Gerry
The Dictionary of Sport, Carlton, London, 1999

Coyote, Peter
Sleeping Where I Fall, Counterpoint, Washington D.C., 1998

Cradock, Chris
A Manual of Clayshooting, B.T. Batsford, London, 1983

Crais, Robert
L.A. Requiem, Orion Books, London, 2000 (1999)

Cralle, Trevor
The Surfin'ary: A Dictionary of Surfing Terms and Surfspeak, Ten Speed Press, Berkeley, California, 1991

Criena, Rohan
Down by the Dockside, Penguin Books, Melbourne, 1983 (1963)
The Delinquents, Penguin Books, Melbourne, 1989 (1962)

Crotty, Jim
How to Talk American: A Guide to our Native Tongues, Houghton Mifflin, Boston, Massachusetts, 1997

Crowe, Cameron
Fast Times at Ridgemont High, MCA/Universal Pictures, 1982
Jerry Maguire, TriStar Pictures, 1996

Crowley, Mart
The Boys in the Band, Dell Publishing, New York, 1970 (1968)

Cruise, T.E.
Wings of Gold III: The Hot Pilots, Popular Library, New York, 1989

Crumlish, Christian
The Internet Dictionary, Sybex Inc., San Francisco, California, 1995

Csicsery, George Paul (Editor)
The Sex Industry, New American Library, New York, 1973

Cue, Kerry
Crooks, Chooks and Bloody Ratbags, Penguin Books, Melbourne, 1983

Culotta, Nino (John O'Grady)
Gone Fishin', Ure Smith, Sydney, 1962
They're a Weird Mob, Ure Smith, Sydney, 1957

Cummings, Parke
Dictionary of Baseball, A.S. Barnes and Company, New York, 1950

Cusack, Dymphna
Black Lightning, Marlin Books, Melbourne, 1977 (1964)
Picnic Races, Marlin Books, Melbourne, 1978 (1962)

Dahlskog, Helen (Editor)
A Dictionary of Contemporary and Colloquial Usage, Avenel Books, New York, 1972

Daigon, Arthur and Ronald T. LaConte
dig u.s.a., Bantam Books, New York, 1970

d'Alpuget, Blanche
Robert J. Hawke: A Biography, Penguin Books, Melbourne, 1984 (1982)

Dalton, Michael
Blackjack: A Professional Reference, Spur of the Moment Publishing, Merritt Island, Florida, 1991

Daly, Steven and Nathaniel Wice
alt.culture, Fourth Estate, London, 1995

Danesi, Marcel
Cool: The Signs and Meanings of Adolescence, University of Toronto Press, Toronto, 1994

Danziger, Charles
Japan For Starters, Kodansha International, Tokyo, New York, London, 1996

d'Arcangelo, Angelo
The Homosexual Handbook, Ophelia Press, New York, 1969 (1968)

Dark, Bodmin
Dirty Cockney Rhyming Slang, Michael O'Mara Books, London, 2003

Darlington, Jennie and Jane McIlvaine
My Antarctic Honeymoon: A Year at the Bottom of the World, Doubleday, New York, 1956

Davies, Peter
Davies' Dictionary of Golfing Terms, Simon & Schuster, New York, 1980

Davis, Bill
Jawjacking: The Complete CB Dictionary, self-published, Canoga Park, California, 1977

Davison, Frank Dalby
The Wells of Beersheba and other stories, Angus and Robertson, Sydney, 1968 (1965)

Day, Ned
How to Bowl Better, Fawcett Publications, Greenwich, Connecticutt, 1957

Décharné, Max
Straight from the Fridge Dad, No Exit Press, Harpenden, Hertfordshire, 2000

deCoy, Robert
The Nigger Bible, Holloway House, Los Angeles, California, 1967

de Laclos, Choderlos and Roger Kumble
Cruel Intentions, Columbia Pictures, 1999

de la Haye, Amy
Surfers Soulies Skinheads & Skaters, The Overlook Press, New York, 1996

Del Vecchio, John
The 13th Valley, Bantam Books, New York, 1982

Dent, Susie
Larpers and Shroomers: The Language Report, Oxford University Press, 2004
The Language Report, Oxford University Press, 2003

Department of the Army
Staff Officer's Guidebook (5th Edition), Department of the Army, Washington D.C., 1986

De Sola, Ralph
Crime Dictionary, Facts on File, New York, 1982

Devlin, Angela
Prison Patter, Waterside Press, Winchester, 1996

Dew, Josie
The Sun In My Eyes, Little, Brown and Co., London, 2001

Dick, William
A Bunch of Ratbags, Penguin Books, Melbourne, 1990 (1965)

Dickins, Barry
What the Dickins, Penguin Books, Melbourne, 1985

Dickson, Paul
The New Dickson Baseball Dictionary, Harcourt Brace & Company, San Diego, California, 1999
War Slang, Pocket Books, New York, 1994

Didion, Joan
Slouching Towards Bethlehem, Washington Square Press, New York, 1981 (1968)
The White Album, Pocket Books, New York, 1980 (1979)

Dilallo, Kevin
The Unofficial Gay Manual: Living the Lifestyle, Main Street Books, New York, 1994

Dill, Stephen
Current Slang, University of South Dakota, Vermillion, South Dakota, 1966–1971

Dillon-Malone, Aubrey
I Was A Fugitive From A Hollywood Trivia Factory, Prion, London, 1999

Dills, Lanie
The Official CB Slanguage Language Dictionary, Louis J. Martin, New York, 1976

Dinkel, John
The Road and Track Illustrated Auto Dictionary, W.W. Norton, New York, 1977

Dixon, Peter L.
The Complete Book of Surfing, Ballantine Books, New York, 1965

Dodson, William
The Sharp End, Pan Macmillan, Sydney, 2001

Donald, Chris
Roger's Profanisaurus, John Brown Publishing, London, 1998
Roger's Profanisaurus, Boxtree, London, 2002

Donaldson, Bruce
Colloquial Afrikaans, Routledge, London, 2000

Donnell, Alison
Companion to Contemporary Black British Culture, Routledge, London, 2002

Donovan, Vance
High Rider, Paperback Library, New York, 1969

Doogan, Mike
How to Speak Alaskan, Epicenter Press, Seattle, Washington, 1993

Dowst, Robert Saunders and Jay Craig
Playing the Races: A Guide to the American Tracks, Dodd, Mead & Company, New York, 1960

Doyle, Roddy
The Van, Secker & Warburg, London, 1991

Draigh, David
Behind the Screen, Abbeville Press, New York, 1988

Drury, Jim
Ian Dury and the Blockheads - Song by Song, Sanctuary Publishing, London, 2003

Duffy, Stella and Lauren Henderson (Editors)
Tart Noir, Pan Books, London, 2002

Dunhill, Allen S. and Roger Blake
The Group Sex Kick, Ambassador Books, Cleveland, Ohio, 1968

Durack, Mary
Kings in Grass Castles, Corgi, Condell Park, New South Wales, 1983 (1959)

Durst, Lavada
The Jives of Dr. Hepcat, Austin, Texas, 1953

Dury, Ian
New Boots and Panties!, Stiff Records/Templemill Music Ltd, 1977

Dynes, Wayne
Homolexis: A Historical and Cultural Lexicon of Homosexuality, Gay Academic Union, New York, 1985

Eble, Connie (Editor)
UNC-CH Campus Slang, University of North Carolina, Chapel Hill, North Carolina, 1972–2004

Eclair, Jenny
Camberwell Beauty, Little, Brown and Co., London, 2000

Editors of Ben is Dead
Retrohell: Life in the '70s and '80s, Little, Brown and Co., Boston, Massachusetts, 1997

Edmonds, I.G.
Drag Racing for Beginners, Bobbs-Merrill, Indianapolis, Indiana, 1972

Edwards, John (Editor)
Auto Dictionary, HP Books, Los Angeles, California, 1993

Edwards, John
More Talk Tidy, D. Brown and Sons, Cowbridge, Glamorgan, 1986
Talk Tidy, D. Brown and Sons, Cowbridge, Glamorgan, 1985

Elementary Electronics
Dictionary of CB Lingo, Davis Publications, New York, 1976

Elfman, Bradley
Breakdancing, Avon Books, New York, 1984

Elliott, Sumner Locke
Rusty Bugles, Currency Press, Sydney, 1980 (1948)

Ellis, Bret Easton
Less Than Zero, Vintage Books, New York, 1998 (1985)

Ellison, Ralph
Invisible Man, Vintage Books, New York, 1995 (1947)

Ellroy, James
Brown's Requiem, Avon Books, New York, 1981
Hollywood Nocturnes, Delta Books, New York, 1998 (1994)
L. A. Noir: The Lloyd Hopkins Novels (Blood on the Moon; Because the Night), Arrow Books, London, 1997 (1984)
White Jazz, Vintage Books, New York, 2001 (1992)

Ellson, Hal
Summer Street, Ballantine Books, New York, 1953
The Golden Spike, Ballantine Books, New York, 1952
Tomboy, Bantam Books, New York, 1965 (1950)

Elting, Mary
Trucks at Work, Garden City Publishing, Garden City, New York, 1946

Elton, Ben
High Society, Black Swan, London, 2002

Eminem (Marshall Mathers)
Angry Blonde, Regan Books, New York, 2001

Enfield, Harry
Harry Enfield and His Humorous Chums, Penguin Books, London, 1997

Engel, Lyle K.
The Complete Book of Fuel and Gas Dragsters, Four Winds Press, New York, 1968
The Dodge Book of Performance Cars, Pocket Books, New York, 1967

English, Robert
Toxic Kisses, Angus and Robertson, Sydney, 1987 (1979)

Ensler, Eve
The Vagina Monologues, Virago, London, 2002 (1998)

Ephorn, Nora, David S. Ward and Jeff Arch
Sleepless in Seattle, TriStar Pictures, 1993
When Harry Met Sally, Columbia Pictures, 1989

Epstein, Rachel S. and Nina Liebman
Biz Speak: A Dictionary of Business Terms, Slang and Jargon, Franklin Watts, New York, 1986

Ercolano, Patrick
Fungoes, Floaters and Fork Balls: A Colorful Baseball Dictionary, Prentice-Hall, Englewood Cliffs, New Jersey, 1987

Esch, Natasha
Wilhelmina's Modeling and Acting Dictionary, Career Press, Hawthorne, New Jersey, 1994

Eszterhas, Joe
Basic Instinct, TriStar Pictures, 1992

Eugenides, Jeffrey
Middlesex, Bloomsbury, London, 2002

Evanovich, Janet
Seven Up, Headline, London, 2001

Evans, Colin
The Heart of Standing, Chatto & Windus, London, 1962

Everage, Edna (Barry Humphries)
My Gorgeous Life: An Adventure, Pan Macmillan, Sydney, 1990 (1989)

Everhart, Jim
CB Slanguage Illustrated, Centennial Press, Lincoln, Nebraska, 1976

Fabbro, Mike
Snowboarding: The Ultimate Free Ride, McClelland & Stewart, Toronto, 1996

Fabian, Jenny and Johnny Byrne
Groupie, Bantam Books, London, 1970 (1968)

Fagans, Chris and David Guzman
A Guide to Craps Lingo, self-published, Burlington, Iowa, 1999

Fahey, Tom
net.speak: the internet dictionary, Hayden Books, Indianapolis, Indiana, 1994

Fahs, John
Cigarette Confidential: The Unfiltered Truth About the Ultimate Addiction, Berkley Books, New York, 1996

Fair, Erik
California Thrill Sports, Foghorn Press, San Francisco, California, 1992

Farina, Richard
Been Down So Long It Looks Like Up To Me, Dell Publishing, New York, 1966
Long Time Coming and A Long Time Gone, Dell Publishing, New York, 1969

Farnsworth, Ross N. and Frank Brimhall
Let's Do Golf! Games that Make Golf Fun, self-published, Mesa, Arizona, 1992

Farrell, James T.
French Girls are Vicious and Other Stories, Signet Books, New York, 1956
Saturday Night and Other Stories, Signet Books, New York, 1950 (1947)

Farrelly, Midget and Criag McGregor
The Surfing Life, Arco Publishing, New York, 1967

Farrelly, Peter, Ed Decter, John Strauss and Bonky Farrelly
Something About Mary, 20th Century Fox, 1998

Farren, Mick
Give the Anarchist a Cigarette, Jonathan Cape, London, 2001

Farrington, Karen
This is Nicotine, Sanctuary Publishing, London, 2002

Fatchen, Max
Chase through the Night, Methuen, Sydney, 1980 (1976)

Fehintola, Lanre
Charlie Says... Don't Get High On Your Own Supply, Scribner, London, 2000

Fennell, Willie
Dexter Gets The Point, Horwitz, Melbourne, 1961

Ferrara, Abel and Zoe Lund
The Bad Lieutenant, Aries Films, 1992

Fessler, Jeff
When Drag Is Not a Car Race: An Irreverent Dictionary of Over 400 Gay and Lesbian Words and Phrases, Fireside Books, New York, 1997

Fettamen, Ann
Trashing, Straight Arrow Books, San Francisco, California, 1970

Fido, Martin and Keith Skinner
The Official Encyclopaedia of New Scotland Yard, Virgin, London, 1999

Filosa, Gary Fairmont R.
The Surfer's Almanac: An International Surfing Guide, E.P. Dutton, New York, 1977

Fitzgerald, Frances
Fire in the Lake, Little, Brown and Co., Boston, Massachusetts, 1972

Fleischhauer, Carl
A Glossary of Army Slang, unpublished manuscript in the Western Historical Manuscript Collection, Columbia, Missouri, 1968

Fleisher, Mark S.
Beggars & Thieves: Lives of Urban Street Criminals, University of Wisconsin Press, Madison, Wiscsonsin, 1995

Fletcher, Geoffrey
Down Among the Meths Men, Hutchinson & Co., London, 1966

Flinthart, Dirk
Brotherly Love, Autopsy, Sydney, 1995

Florida Legislative Investigation Committee (Johns Committee)
Homosexuality and Citizenship in Florida, 1964

Floyd, Wayne
Jason's Authentic Dictionary of CB Slang (3rd Edition), Jason Press, Fort Worth, Texas, 1976

Folb, Edith A.
running down some lines: the language and culture of black teenagers, Harvard University Press, Cambridge, Massachusetts, 1980

Foley, Keith
A Dictionary of Cricketing Terminology, Edwin Mellen Press, Lampeter, Wales, 1998

Foley, Mick
Mankind: Have a Nice Day, Regan Books, New York, 1999

Folger, John
Black on White: A Study of Miscegenation in America, Viceroy Books, Canoga Park, California, 1967

Fonda, Peter
Easy Rider, Signet Books, New York, 1969

Fontaine, Joan et al.
Dictionary of Black Slang (McClymond's High School, Oakland, California), unpublished manuscript in the Western Historical Manuscript Collection, Columbia, Missouri, 1968

Foss, Rene
Around the World in a Bad Mood: Confessions of a Flight Attendant, Hyperion, New York, 2002

Foster, Nigel
The Making of a Royal Marine Commando, Guild Press, London, 1988 (1987)

Fowler, Jon
Anatomy of Wife-Swapping, Pad Library, Aqoura, California, 1967

Fox, Frank
A Beginner's Guide to Zen and the Art of Windsurfing, Amberco Press, Berkeley, California, 1985

Francis, Ricki
Hotel Kings X, Scripts Publications, Melbourne, 1973

Francis-Jackson, Chester
The Official Dancehall Dictionary, LMH Publishing, Kingston, Jamaica, 1995

Frank, Richard
A Study of Sex in Prison, Gallery Press, Los Angeles, California, 1973

Franken, Al
Lies (And the Lying Liars Who Tell Them): A Fair and Balanced Look at the Right, E.P. Dutton, New York, 2003

Franklyn, Julian
A Dictionary of Rhyming Slang, Routledge & Kegan Paul, London, 1960
A Dictionary of Rhyming Slang (2nd Edition), Routledge & Kegan Paul, London, 1961

Fraser, Paul and Shane Meadows
TwentyFourSeven, BBC Films & Scala, 1997

Fredericks, Vic
Who's Who in Rock 'n Roll, Frederick Fell Inc., New York, 1958

Freeman, Bob and Barbara
Wanta Bet? A Study of the Pari-Mutuels System in the United States, self-published, 1982

Freeman, Marlene
Alcatraz: No Good for Nobody, Smith Novelty Company, San Francisco, California, 1983

French, Simon
Hey Phantom Singlet, Angus and Robertson, Sydney, 1987 (1975)

Friedman, Josh Alan
Tales of Times Square, Feral House, Portland, Oregon, 1993 (1986)

Friedman, Kinky
Steppin' on a Rainbow, Faber and Faber, London, 2001

Friss, J.R.
A Dictionary of Teenage Slang (Mt. Diablo High), self-published, Walnut Creek, California, 1964

Frommer, Harvey
Sports Lingo: A Dictionary of the Language of Sports, Atheneum, New York, 1979

Froner, Geoffrey
Digging for Diamonds: A Lexicon of Street Slang for Drugs and Sex, self-published, San Francisco, California, 1989

Fry, Monroe
Sex, Vice and Business, Ballantine Books, New York, 1959

Fuentes, Dagoberto and Jose A. Lopez
Barrio Language Dictionary: First Dictionary of Calo, El Barrio Publications, La Puente, California, 1974

Furze, Peter
Tailwinds, Michael O'Mara Books, London, 1998

Futterman, Marilyn Suriani
Dancing Naked in the Material World, Prometheus Books, London, Buffalo, New York, 1992

Gaghan, Stephen
Traffic, USA Films, 2000

Gagnon, John H. and William Simon
The Sexual Scene (2nd Edition), Transaction Books, New Brunswick, New Jersey, 1973

Galea, Clive
Slipper, Prospect Publishing, Sydney, 1988

Galton, Ray and Alan Simpson
Hancock's Half Hour: The Classic Years, BBC Books, London, 1987

Ganjabhang, V.S.
The Little Book of Pot, Boxtree, London, 2001

Garcia, Elena
A Beginner's Guide to Zen and the Art of Snowboarding, Amberco Press, Berkeley, California, 1990

Garcia, Frank
Marked Cards and Loaded Dice, Bramhall House, New York, 1962

Gardiner, James
Who's a Pretty Boy Then?, Serpent's Tail, London, 1997

Garner, Helen
Monkey Grip, Penguin Books, Melbourne, 1988 (1977)

Garrett, R.C. et al.
The Coke Book: The Complete Reference to the Uses and Abuses of Cocaine, Berkley Books, New York, 1984

Gash, Jonathan
The Ten Word Game, Allison & Busby, London, 2003

Gaskin, Stephen
Amazing Dope Tales and Haight Street Flashbacks, Book Publishing Company, Summertown, Tennessee, 1980

Gaynor, Frank
Dictionary of Mysticism, Philosophical Library, New York, 1953

George, Nelson
Buppies, B-Boys, Baps & Bohos, Da Capo Press, Cambridge, Massachusetts, 2001 (1992)

Glass, Lillian with Richard Liebmann-Smith
How to Deprogramme Your Valley Girl, Workingman Publishing, New York, 1982

Glasser, Ronald J.
365 Days, Bantam Books, New York, 1972 (1971)

Glenn, Jim
Programmed Poker: The Inside System for Winning, Rutledge Press, New York, 1981

Glessing, Robert J.
The Underground Press in America, Indiana University Press, Bloomington, Indiana, 1970

Glover, Paul (Technical Advisor)
Words from the House of the Dead: Prison Writings from Soledad, Crossing Press, Trumansburg, New York, 1974

Goines, Donald
Black Gangster, Holloway House, Los Angeles, California, 1977
Crime Partners, Holloway House, Los Angeles, California, 1978
Cry Revenge, Holloway House, Los Angeles, California, 1974
Daddy Cool, Holloway House, Los Angeles, California, 1974
Dopefiend, Holloway House, Los Angeles, California, 1971
Inner City Hoodlum, Holloway House, Los Angeles, California, 1975
Kenyatta's Last Hit, Holloway House, Los Angeles, California, 1975
Never Die Alone, Holloway House, Los Angeles, California, 1974
White Man's Justice, Black Man's Grief, Holloway House, Los Angeles, California, 1973
Whoreson, Holloway House, Los Angeles, California, 1972

Goldaper, Sam and Arthur Pincus
How to Talk Basketball, Dembner Books, New York, 1983

Goldin, Hyman E. et al.
Dictionary of American Underworld Lingo, Twayne Publishers, New York, 1950

Goldman, Albert
Freak Show, Atheneum, New York, 1971

Gonzales, Babs
Be-Bop Dictionary and History of its Famous Stars, Arlain Publishing, New York, 1949
I Paid My Dues, Expubidence Publishing, East Orange, New Jersey, 1967
Movin' On Down De Line, Expubidence Publishing, East Orange, New Jersey, 1975

Gordon, Dale
The Dominion Sex Dictionary, Van Nuys, California, 1967

Gordon, Roger
Hollywood's Sexual Underground, Medco Books, Los Angeles, California, 1966

Goren, Charles H.
Goren's Modern Backgammon Complete, Doubleday, New York, 1974

Gorgon, Donald
Cop Killer, The X Press, London, 1994

Goshgarian, Gary (Editor)
Exploring Language, Little, Brown and Co., Boston, Massachusetts, 1986

Gosling, John
The Ghost Squad, WH Allen, London, 1959

Gould, Chester
Dick Tracy Meets the Night Crawler, Whitman Publishing, Racine, Wisconsin, 1945

Gould, John
Maine Lingo: Boiled Owls, Billdads and Wazzats, Down East Magazine, Camden, Maine, 1975

Goulden, Joseph C.
Korea: The Untold Story of the War, Times Books, New York, 1982

Gover, Robert
Here Goes Kitten, Dell Publishing, New York, 1965 (1964)
JC Saves, Pocket Books, New York, 1969 (1968)
One Hundred Dollar Misunderstanding, Grove Press, New York, 1961
Poorboy at the Party, Pocket Books, New York, 1967 (1966)
The Maniac Responsible, Dell Publishing, New York, 1966 (1963)

Graham, William
The Scots Word Book, The Ramsay Head Press, Edinburgh, 1977

Granville, Wilfred
A Dictionary of Theatrical Terms, André Deutsch, London, 1952
The Theater Dictionary: British and American Terms in the Drama, Opera, and Ballet, Philosophical Library, New York, 1952

Graziano, Rocky with Rowland Barber
Someboby Up There Likes Me, Pocket Books, New York, 1956 (1955)

Green, Jane
Mr. Maybe, Broadway Books, New York, 2002

Green, Jonathon
Dictionary of Slang, Cassell, London, 1998

Greene, Carolyn
70 Soul Secrets of Sapphire, Sapphire Publishing Company, San Francisco, California, 1973

Greene, Gerald and Caroline
S-M: The Last Taboo, Grove Press, New York, 1974

Greenwald, Harold
The Call Girl: A Social Psychological Investigation, Decision Books, San Diego, California, 1978

Gregory, Dick
Nigger: An Autobiography, Pocket Books, New York, 1968 (1964)

Griffiths, Niall
Grits, Vintage Books, London, 2000
Kelly + Victor, Jonathan Cape, London, 2002
Sheepshagger, Vintage Books, London, 2002 (2001)

Griffiths, Trevor
Oi For England, Faber and Faber, London, 1982

Grigg, Richard W.
Surfer in Hawaii: A Guide to Surfing in the Hawaiian Islands, John Severson Publications, Dana Point, California, 1963

Grissim, John
Pur Stoke, HarperCollins, New York, 1982 (1980)

Grogan, Emmett
Final Score, Holt, Rinehart and Winston, New York, 1976

Grose, Francis
Dictionary of the Vulgar Tongue (3rd Edition), Hooper and Wigstead, London, 1796

Guest, Christopher and Michael McKean
This is Spinal Tap, Embassy Pictures Corporation, 1984

Gutman, Bill
Strange & Amazing Wrestling Stories, Archway Paperbacks, New York, 1986

Gwynne, Phillip
Deadly Unna?, Penguin Books, Melbourne, 1998

Haber, Paul
Inside Handball, Henry Regnery Company, Chicago, Illinois, 1970

Hackett, Buddy
The Truth About Golf and Other Lies, Doubleday, New York, 1968

Hackworth, David H.
About Face, Simon & Schuster, New York, 1989

Haenigsen, Harry
Jive's Like That: Being the Life and Times of Our Bill, Procyon Press, New York, 1947

Hagerman, R.J.
Husband and Wife Swapping, Medco Books, Los Angeles, California, 1967

Hailey, Frank H.
Soldier Talk, D. Irving & Company, Braintree, Massachusetts, 1982

Halacy, D.S.
Surfer!, Macmillan, New York, 1965

Halberstadt, Hans
Airborne: Assault from the Sky, Presidio Press, Novato, California, 1988
USCB: Always Ready, Presidio Press, Novato, California, 1986

Hale, Constance
Wired Style: Principles of English Usage in the Digital Age, Hardwired, San Francisco, California, 1996

Hall, Rodney
Kisses of the Enemy, Penguin Books, Melbourne, 1987

Hall, Susan
Gentleman of Leisure: A Year in the Life of a Pimp, Signet Books, New York, 1972

Handford, Nourma
Carcoola Holiday, Dymocks, Sydney, 1953

Hankin, Nigel
Hanklyn-Janklyn, Tara Press, Delhi, 2003

Hardy, Frank
Hardy's People, Pascoe Publishing, Melbourne, 1986
Legends from Benson's Valley, Penguin Books, Melbourne, 1964 (1963)
Power Without Glory, Panther Books, St Albans, Hertfordshire, 1977 (1950)
The Outcasts of Foolgarah, Allara Publishing, Melbourne, 1971
The Yarns of Billy Borker, Angus and Robertson, Sydney, 1980 (1965)

Hardy, Frank and Athol George Mulley
The Needy and The Greedy, Libra Books, Canberra, 1975

Harper, James
Homo Laws in all 50 States, Publishers Export Company, San Diego, California, 1968

Harris, Frank
The Swinging Moderns, privately printed, Canoga Park, California, 1967

Harris, Kevin
LMH Official Dictionary of Jamaican Words & Proverbs, LMH Publishing, Kingston, Jamaica, 2002

Harris, Sara
The Lords of Hell, Dell Publishing, New York, 1967

Harris, Troy
A Booklet of Criminal Argot, Cant and Jargon, self-published, Somerset, Ohio, 1976

Hasford, Gustav and Michael Herr
Full Metal Jacket, Warner Brothers, 1987

Haskins, James
The Story of Hip-Hop, Penguin Books, London, 2002

Haskins, Mike
Drugs: A User's Guide, Ebury Press, London, 2003

Haslam, Dave
Adventures of the Wheels of Steel, Fourth Estate, London, 2001

Hawes, James
Dead Long Enough, Jonathan Cape, London, 2000
White Powder, Green Light, Vintage Books, London, 2002

Hawkins, Jack
Chopper One #2: Tunnel Warriors, Ivy Books, New York, 1987

Hawkins, Odie
Amazing Grace and Other States of Mind, Holloway House, Los Angeles, California, 1993
Black Casanova, Holloway House, Los Angeles, California, 1984
Black Chicago, Holloway House, Los Angeles, California, 1992
Chicago Hustle, Holloway House, Los Angeles, California, 1977
Ghetto Sketches, Holloway House, Los Angeles, California, 1972
Great Lawd Buddha, Holloway House, Los Angeles, California, 1990
Midnight, Holloway House, Los Angeles, California, 1995
Scars and Memories, Holloway House, Los Angeles, California, 1987
The Busting Out of an Ordinary Man, Holloway House, Los Angeles, California, 1985
The Life and Times of Chester Simmons, Holloway House, Los Angeles, California, 1991

Hayano, David M.
Poker Faces: The Life and Work of Professional Card Players, University of California Press, Berkeley, California, 1982

Haywood, Charles F.
Yankee Dictionary: A Compendium of Useful and Entertaining Expressions Indigenous to New England, Jackson & Phillips Inc., Lynn, Massachusetts, 1963

Headley, Victor
Yardie, Pan Books, London, 1993 (1992)

Heard, Nathan
Howard Street, Signet Books, New York, 1970 (1968)

Heath, Angie
Diary of a Masseuse, New English Library, London, 1976

Heckerling, Amy
Clueless, Paramount Pictures, 1995

Heikkinen, Carol
Empire Records, Warner Brothers, 1995

Heimer, Mel
Inside Racing: An Introduction to the Sport of Kings, New York, 1967 (1962)

Heinemann, Larry
Close Quarters, Warner Books, New York, 1983 (1977)
Paco's Story, Farrar, Straus & Giroux, New York, 1986

Hemmings, Fred
Surfing: Hawaii's Gift to the World of Sports, Grosset & Dunlap, New York, 1977

Henderson, M. Allen
How Con Games Work, Carol Publishing Group, New York, 1994 (1985)

Henry, L. Mike and Kevin Harris
LMH Official Dictionary of Popular Jamaican Phrases, LMH Publishing, Kingston, Jamaica, 2002

Hentoff, Nat
I'm really dragged but nothing gets me down, Simon & Schuster, New York, 1968
Jazz Country, Dell Publishing, New York, 1968 (1965)

Herbert, Xavier
Poor Fellow My Country, Fontana Books, Sydney, 1976 (1975)

Herbst, Dan
Bowling 300, Contemporary Books, Chicago, Illinois, 1993

Herm, Weiskopf and Chuck Pezzano
Sports Illustrated: Bowling, Harper & Row, New York, 1981

Herring, Richard
Talking Cock, Ebury Press, London, 2003

Herz, Adam
American Pie, Universal Pictures, 1999

Hester, Fred
Slang on the 40 Acres, unpublished manuscript in the Western Historial Manuscript Collection, Columbia, Missouri, 1968

Hetherington, Keith
Patrick, Sun Books, Melbourne, 1978

Hewett, Dorothy
The Chapel Perilous, Currency Press, Sydney, 1985 (1972)

Hiaasen, Carl
Native Tongue, Ballantine Books, New York, 1992 (1991)
Strip Tease, Warner Books, New York, 1994 (1993)
Tourist Season, Warner Books, New York, 1987 (1986)

Hibberd, Jack
A Stretch of the Imagination, Currency Press, Sydney, 1973 (1971)

Hibberd, Jack and Garrie Hutchinson
The Barracker's Bible, McPhee Gribble, Melbourne, 1983

Hibbert, Tom
Rockspeak! The Dictionary of Rock Terms, Omnibus Press, London, 1983

Hickman, Tom
Drink: A User's Guide, Ebury Press, London, 2003

Higdon, Hal
Finding the Groove, G.P. Putnam's Sons, New York, 1973

Higgins, George V.
Penance for Jerry Kennedy, Abacus, London, 1986 (1985)
The Friends of Eddie Coyle, Bantam Books, New York, 1973 (1971)
The Judgment of Deke Hunter, Ballantine Books, New York, 1978 (1976)
The Rat on Fire, Alfred A. Knopf, New York, 1981

Higgins, Roy and Tom Prior
The Jockey Who Laughed, Hutchinson, Melbourne, 1982

Hilderbrant, Ethan
Prison Slang, Allusion Entertainment, Port Arthur, Texas, 1998

Hill, Henry and Byron Schreckengost
A Good Fella's Guide to New York, Three Rivers Press, New York, 2003

Himes, Chester
A Rage in Harlem, Canongate, Edinburgh, 2000 (1957)
Cast the First Stone, Signet Books, New York, 1972 (1952)
Come Back Charleston Blue, G.P. Putnam's Sons, New York, 1972 (1966)
Cotton Comes to Harlem, Vintage Books, New York, 1998 (1965)
If He Hollers Let Him Go, Thunder's Mouth Press, New York, 1986 (1945)
The Primitive, Signet Books, New York, 1955
The Real Cool Killers, Vintage Books, New York, 1988 (1959)

Hince, Bernadette
The Antarctic Dictionary: A Complete Guide to Antarctic English, Csiro Publishing, Colllingwood, Melbourne, 2000

Hinojosa, Maria
Crews: Gang Members Talk to Maria Hinojosa, Harcourt Brace & Company, San Diego, California, 1995

Hinton, S.E.
The Outsiders, Dell Publishing, New York, 1984 (1967)

Hodges, Mike
Get Carter, ScreenPress Books, Eye, Suffolk, 2001 (1971)

Hoffman, Abbie
Woodstock Nation, Vintage Books, New York, 1969

Hoffman, Barbara
Girl Gangs, Classics Library, Cleveland, Ohio, 1968

Hoggarth, J.
How To Be a DJ, Penguin Books, London, 2002

Holden, Anthony
Big Deal: A Year as a Professional Poker Player, Viking, New York, 1990

Hollander, Xaviera
The Best Part of a Man, New American Library, New York, 1975

Hollander, Zander
Baseball Lingo, W.W. Norton, New York, 1967

Hollander, Zander and Paul Zimmerman
Football Lingo, W.W. Norton, New York, 1967

Hollander, Zander and Sandy Padwe
Basketball Lingo, Grosset & Dunlap, New York, 1971

Holledge, James
The Call-girl in Australia, Horwitz, Melbourne, 1964
The Great Australian Gamble, Horwitz, Melbourne, 1966

Holm, John A.
Dictionary of Bahamian English, Lexik House, Cold Spring, New York, 1982

Holmes, Andrew
Sleb, Sceptre, London, 2002

Holmes, John Clellon
Go, Ace Books, New York, 1952
The Horn, Random House, New York, 1958

Home Office (UK)
Glossary of Terms and Slang Common in Penal Establishments, Board of Visitors Section, P4 Division, July 1978

Hooker, Richard and Ring Lardner
*M*A*S*H*, 20th Century Fox, 1970

Hooper, Mary
(megan)2, Bloomsbury, London, 1999

Hopkins, William B.
One Bugle No Drums, Avon Books, New York, 1986

Horman, Richard and Allan Fox
Drug Awareness, Discus Books, New York, 1970

Hornadge, Bill
The Australian Slanguage, Mandarin, North Ryde, New South Wales, 1980
The Ugly Australian, Bacchus Books, Sydney, 1976 (1975)

Horsley, Fred
The Hot Rod Handbook, J. Lowell Pratt, New York, 1965

Horton, John
The Grub Street Dictionary of International Aircraft Nicknames, Variants and Colloquial Terms, Grub Street, London, 1994

Hoskyns, Barney
Waiting For The Sun, Viking, New York, 1996

Houppert, Karen
The Curse: Confronting the Last Unmentionable Taboo: Menstruation, Farrar, Straus & Giroux, New York, 1999

Houser, Norman W.
Drugs: Facts on Their Use and Abuse, Scott, Foresman and Company, Glenview, Illinois, 1969

Howard, Paul
Ross O'Carroll-Kelly: The Orange Mocha-Chip Frappuccino Years, O'Brien Press, Dublin, 2003
The Joy, O'Brien Press, Dublin, 1996

Hudson, Kenneth
A Dictionary of the Teenage Revolution and its Aftermath, Macmillan Reference Books, London, 1983

Hughes, Allen and Albert
Menace II Society, New Line Cinema, 1993

Hughes, John
Ferris Buehler's Day Off, Paramount Pictures, 1986
The Breakfast Club, Universal Pictures, 1985

Hughes, Thomas F.
Dealing Casino Blackjack, Gamblers Book Club Press, Las Vegas, Nevada, 1982

Humes, Jim and Sean Wagstaff
Boarderlands, HarperCollins, New York, 1995

Humphreys, Laud
Tearoom Trade: Impersonal Sex in Public Places, Aldine de Gruyuter, New York, 1975

Humphries, Barry
A Nice Night's Entertainment: Sketches and Monologues 1956–1981, Currency Press, Sydney, 1981
Bazza Pulls It Off!, Private Eye Production, London, 1972 (1971)
The Traveller's Tool, Coronet Books, Sevenoaks, Kent, 1986 (1985)
The Wonderful World of Barry McKenzie, Sun Books, Melbourne, 1968

Huncke, Herbert
Guilty of Everything: The Autobiography of Herbert Huncke, Paragon House, New York, 1990
The Evening Sun Turned Crimson, Cherry Valley Editions, Cherry Valley, New York, 1980

Hungerford, T.A.G.
Stories from Suburban Road: An Autobiographical Collection, 1920–1939, Fremantle Arts Centre Press, Fremantle, Western Australia, 1983
The Ridge and the River, Angus and Robertson, Sydney, 1952

Hunt, J.L. and A.G. Pringle
Service Slang, Faber and Faber, London, 1943

Hunt, Rex
Tall Tales – and True, Crossbow Publishing, Melbourne, 1994

Hunter, Evan
Last Summer, Doubleday, New York, 1968
The Blackboard Jungle, Pocket Books, New York, 1955 (1954)

Hunter, John Francis
The Gay Insider: A Hunter's Guide to New York and a Thesaurus of Phallic Lore, The Other Traveller, New York, 1971

Hurst, Walter and Donn Delson
Delson's Dictionary of Radio & Record Industry Terms, Bradson Press, Thousand Oaks, California, 1980

Hurwood, Bernhardt J.
The Sensuous New Yorker, Award Books, New York, 1973

Hutchinson, Sean
Crying Out Loud, John Daniel, Santa Barbara, California, 1988

Hutson, Jan
The Chicken Ranch: The True Story of the Best Little Whorehouse in Texas, A.S. Barnes and Company, Cranbury, New Jersey, 1980

Hyamson, Albert M.
A Dictionary of English Phrases, George Routledge & Sons, London, 1922

Idriess, Ion L.
Over the Range: Sunshine and Shadow in the Kimberleys, Angus and Robertson, Sydney, 1947

Ihnatko, Andy
Cyberspeak: An Online Dictionary, Random House, New York, 1997

Ireland, David
The Flesheaters, Penguin Books, Melbourne, 1980 (1972)
The Glass Canoe, Penguin Books, Melbourne, 1982 (1976)
The Unknown Industrial Prisoner, Angus and Robertson, Sydney, 1982 (1971)

Ironside, Janey
A Fashion Alphabet, Michael Joseph, London, 1968

Jackson, A.S.
Gentleman Pimp, Holloway House, Los Angeles, California, 1973

Jackson, Bruce
Get Your Ass in the Water and Swim Like Me: Narrative Poetry from Black Oral Tradition, Harvard University Press, Cambridge, Massachusetts, 1974
In the Life: Versions of the Criminal Experience, Holt, Rinehart and Winston, New York, 1972
Killing Time: Life in the Arkansas Penitentiary, Cornell University Press, Ithaca, New York, 1977
Outside the Law: A Thief's Primer, Transaction Books, New Brunswick, New Jersey, 1972

Jackson, George
Soledad Brother: The Prison Letters of George Jackson, Coward-McCann, New York, 1970

Jacobs, Gil
The World's Best Dice Games, Dixon Press, Cupertino, California, 1976

Jacobs, Michael
Complete CB Slang Dictionary, Success Publications, North Miami Beach, Florida, 1978

Jacoby, James and Mary
The New York Times Book of Backgammon, New American Library, New York, 1973

Jacoby, Oswald
Oswald Jacoby on Poker, Doubleday, New York, 1947

Jacoby, Oswald and John Crawford
The Backgammon Book, Bantam Books, New York, 1973 (1970)

James, Antony
America's Homosexual Underground, L.S. Publications, New York, 1965

James, Clive
Unreliable Memoirs, Pan Books, London, 1981 (1980)

James, Erwin
A Life Inside, Atlantic Books, London, 2003

Jarratt, Suzy
Permissive Australia, Jack De Lissa, Sydney, 1970

Jeffries, Stuart
Mrs Slocombe's Pussy: Growing Up in Front of the Telly, Flamingo, London, 2001 (2000)

Jenkins, Dan
Dead Solid Perfect, Price Stern Sloan, Los Angeles, California, 1986
Life Its Ownself, Signet Books, New York, 1984
Semi-Tough, Signet Books, New York, 1972

Jennings, Karla
The Devouring Fungus: Tales of the Computer Age, W.W. Norton, New York, 1990

Jessup, Richard
The Cincinnati Kid, Little, Brown and Co., Boston, Massachusetts, 1963

Jewson, Bob
Stir, Unicorn, Melbourne, 1980

Jobson, Sandra
Blokes, An Endangered Species?, Pan Books, Sydney, 1984

John, Andrew with Stephen Blake
The Total TxtMsg Dictionary, Michael O'Mara Books, London, 2001

Johnson, Colin
Wild Cat Falling, Angus and Robertson, Sydney, 1979 (1965)

Johnson, Julian
Urban Survival, Chrysalis Books, London, 2003

Johnson, Michael Dalton
Talking Trash with Redd Foxx, Emery Dalton Books, Del Mar, California, 1994

Johnson, Peter
Dictionary of Street Alcohol and Drug Terms (4th Edition), School of Medicine, University of South Carolina, Columbia, South Carolina, 1993

Johnson, Sandee Shaffer
Cadences: The Jody Call Book, No. 1, Daring Books, Canton, Ohio, 1986

Johnston, George
My Brother Jack, Reprint Society, London, 1965 (1964)

Jolley, Elizabeth
Mr Scobie's Riddle, Penguin Books, Melbourne, 1983

Jolly, Rick
Jackspeak, the Pusser's Rum Guide to Royal Navy Slanguage, Palamandando, Torpoint, Cornwall, 1989

Jones, Ignatius
The 1992 True Hip Manual, McPhee Gribble, Melbourne, 1992
True Hip, McPhee Gribble, Melbourne, 1990

Jones, Jack
Rhyming Cockney Slang, Abson Books, London, 1973 (1971)

Jones, John Peter
Feather Pluckers, Eyre & Spottiswoode, London, 1964

Jones, Nicholas
Hackers, Hotting and Hooray Henrys, Reader's Digest, London, 1992

Jones, Nick
Spliffs, Chrysalis Books, London, 2003

Jones, Patrick
Fuse: The Selected Work of Patrick Jones, Parthian Books, Cardiff, 2001

Judge, Mike and Joe Stillman
Beavis and Butt-Head Do America: The Official Script Book, MTV Books/Pocket Books, New York, 1997

Kahanamoku, Duke with Joe Brennan
Duke Kahanamoku's World of Surfing, Grosset & Dunlop, New York, 1965

Kasdan, Lawrence
Body Heat, Warner Brothers, 1980

Katz, Samuel M.
Anytime Anywhere, Pocket Books, New York, 1997

Kay, James and Julian Cohen
The Parents' Complete Guide to Young People and Drugs, Vermilion, London, 1998

Keesing, Nancy
Lily on the Dustbin: Slang of Australian Women and Families, Penguin Books, Melbourne, 1982

Kelly, John M.
Surf and Sea, A.S. Barnes and Company, New York, 1965

Kelly, Vince
The Bogeyman: The Exploits of Segreant C.J. Chuck, Australia's Most Unpopular Cop, Angus and Robertson, Sydney, 1956

Kendall, Sydney (Steak) T.
Up The Frog, Wolfe Publishing, London, 1969

Keneally, Thomas
Bring Larks and Heroes, Penguin Books, London, 1988 (1967)

Kennedy Martin, Ian
The Sweeny, Brown Watson, London, 1976

Kennedy Martin, Troy
The Italian Job, Paramount Pictures, 1969
Z Cars, May Fair, London, 1962

Kerouac, Jack
On the Road, Viking, New York, 1957
The Dharma Bums, Signet Books, New York, 1959 (1958)
The Subterraneans, Grove Press, New York, 1958

Kerouac, Jack and Ann Charters
Jack Kerouac: Selected Letters: 1940–1956, Penguin Books, New York, 1995
Jack Kerouac: Selected Letters: 1957–1969, Penguin Books, New York, 1999

Kerry, John
The New Soldier, Collier Books, New York, 1971

Kesey, Ken
One Flew Over the Cuckoo's Nest, Penguin Books, New York, 1976 (1962)

Killeen, Gretel
Hot Buns and Ophelia get a Bloke, Penguin Books, Melbourne, 2000
Hot Buns and Ophelia get Shipwrecked, Penguin Books, Melbourne, 2001

King, Danny
The Bank Robber Diaries, Serpent's Tail, London, 2002
The Burglar Diaries, Serpent's Tail, London, 2001
The Hitman Diaries, Serpent's Tail, London, 2003

King, George
Horse Racing: How to Win the Vegas Way, Gambling International, Las Vegas, Nevada, 1965

King, John
Human Punk, Jonathan Cape, London, 2000
White Trash, Jonathan Cape, London, 2001

King, Martin and Martin Knight
The Naughty Nineties, Mainstream Sport, Edinburgh, 2000 (1999)

King, Rick and W. Peter Iliff
Break Point, 20th Century Fox, 1991

Klein, Naomi
No Logo, HarperCollins, New York, 2001

Kneitel, Tom
Tomcat's Big CB Handbook, CRB Research, Commack, New York, 1992

Knowles, John
A Separate Peace, Macmillan, New York, 1959

Kohlman, Aarona Booker
Wotcha Say: An Introduction to Colloquial Caymanian, Cayman Art Ventures, Grand Cayman, 1985

Kohner, Frederick
Gidget, Berkley Books, New York, 2001 (1957)

Konigsberg, Ira
The Complete Film Dictionary, New American Library, New York, 1987

Kramer, Dale and Madeline Karr
Teen-Age Gangs: The Frank, Inside Story of Juvenile Delinquency in America, Popular Library, New York, 1957 (1953)

Kronhausen, Phyllis and Eberhard
Sex Histories of American College Men, Ballantine Books, New York, 1960

Kuhns, Grant W.
On Surfing, Charles E. Tuttle, Rutland, Vermont, 1964 (1963)

Kunen, James Simon
The Strawberry Statement, Avon Books, New York, 1968

Kuriscak, Steve
Casino Talk: A Rap Sheet for Dealers and Players, self-published, 1985

Kushyshyn, Igor et al.
The Gambling Times Guide to Harness Racing, Lyle Stuart, Secaucus, New Jersey, 1994

Lahr, John
Dame Edna Everage and the Rise of Western Civilisation, Bloomsbury, London, 1991

Laikin, Paul
101 Hippie Jokes, Pyramid Books, New York, 1968

Lait, Jack and Lee Mortimer
Chicago Confidential, Crown Publishers, New York, 1950
New York Confidential, Dell Publishing, New York, 1948
Washington Confidential, Crown Publishers, New York, 1951

Lambert, Eric
The Veterans, Shakespeare Head, London, 1954

Landy, Eugene
The Underground Dictionary, Touchstone, New York, 1971

Lang, Doug
Freaks, New English Library, London, 1973

Langeste, Tom
Words on the Wing: Slang, Aphorisms, Catchphrases and Jargon of Canadian Military Aviation, Canadian Institute of Strategic Studies, Toronto, Ontario, 1995

Langley, Eve
The Pea-Pickers, Angus and Robertson, Sydney, 1958

Lanklater, Richard
Slacker, St. Martin's Press, New York, 1992

Larner, Jeremy and Ralph Tefferteller
The Addict in the Street, Grove Press, New York, 1966 (1964)

Larsen, Shana
200 Cigarettes, Paramount Pictures, 1999

Laughlin, Burgess
Job Opportunities in the Black Market, Loompanics Unlimited, Port Townsend, Washington D.C., 1978

Laurie, Peter
Scotland Yard: A Study of the Metropolitan Police, Penguin Books, London, 1972 (1970)

Lawler, Ray
Summer of the Seventeenth Doll, Currency Press, Sydney, 1981 (1957)

Lawlor, John
How to Talk Car, Topaz Felsen, Chicago, Illinois, 1965

Lawson, Ann
Kids & Gangs: What Parents and Educators Need to Know, Johnson Institute, Minneapolis, Minnesota, 1994

Lawson, Don
The United States in the Korean War, Scholastic Books, New York, 1964

Lay, Mary and Nancy Orban
The Hip Glossary of Hippie Language, self-published, San Francisco, California, 1967

Leap, William
Word's Out: Gay Men's English, University of Minnesota Press, Minneapolis, Minnesota, 1996

Leckie, Robert
The Wars of America, Volume II, Bantam Books, New York, 1968

Lee, Spike
Mo' Better Blues, Universal Pictures, 1990

Legman, G.
The Fake Revolt, Breaking Point, New York, 1967

Leigh, Michael
The Velvet Underground, McFadden, New York, 1963

Leland, Louis S.
A Personal Kiwi-Yankee Dictionary, Pelican Publishing, Gretna, Louisiana, 1984

le Mao, Fabrice
Skateboarding, Fitway, Paris, 2004

Leonard, Elmore
52 Pick-Up, Avon Books, New York, 1983 (1974)
Be Cool, Dell Publishing, New York, 1999
Cat Chaser, Avon Books, New York, 1983 (1982)
City Primeval, Avon Books, New York, 1980
Freaky Deaky, Warner Books, New York, 1989 (1988)
Glitz, Warner Books, New York, 1985
Gold Coast, Bantam Books, New York, 1980
Killshot, Warner Books, New York, 1989
Maximum Bob, Dell Publishing, New York, 1991
Mr. Majestyk, Dell Publishing, New York, 1974
Out of Sight, Dell Publishing, New York, 1996
Pronto, Dell Publishing, New York, 1993
Riding the Rap, Dell Publishing, New York, 1995
Rum Punch, Dell Publishing, New York, 1992
Split Images, Avon Books, New York, 1981
Stick, Avon Books, New York, 1983
Swag, Dell Publishing, New York, 1984 (1976)
The Big Bounce, Mysterious Press, New York, 1986 (1969)
The Switch, Bantam Books, New York, 1978
Touch, Avon Books, New York, 1977

Leonard, Elmore and Quentin Tarantino
Jackie Brown, Miramax, 1997

Leonard, Elmore and Scott Frank
Get Shorty, Metro-Goldwyn-Mayer, 1995

Leonard, Hugh
Out After Dark, Methuen, London, 2002 (1989)

Lesley, Paul
PT Command, Horwitz, Sydney, 1963

Leslie, Robert
Confessions of a Lesbian Prostitute, Dalhousie Press, New York, 1965

Lette, Kathy
Girls' Night Out, Pan Macmillan, Sydney, 1995 (1987)

Lette, Kathy and Gabrielle Carey
Puberty Blues, McPhee Gribble, Melbourne, 1980 (1979)

Levinson, Barry
Avalon, Tri-Star Pictures, 1990
Diner, MGM, 1982

Lewin, Ted
I Was A Teenage Professional Wrestler, Hyperion Paperbacks, New York, 1993

Lewis, Chris
The Dictionary of Playground Slang and A Compendium of Playground Games, Allison & Busby, London, 2003

Lewis, Harold
Crow on a Barbed Wire Fence, Angus and Robertson, Sydney, 1979 (1973)

Lewis, Ted
Jack Carter's Law, Michael Joseph, London, 1974

Liberman, Jethro K.
The Complete CB Handbook, Avon Books, New York, 1976

Lighter, J.E.
Historical Dictionary of American Slang, Vol 1: A–G, Random House, New York, 1994
Historical Dictionary of American Slang, Vol 2: H–O, Random House, New York, 1997

Limb, Ivor
Footy's No Joke!, IGL Enterprises, Adelaide, 1986

Lin, Edward
Big Julie of Vegas, Fawcett Publications, Greenwich, Connecticut, 1975 (1974)

Linder, Ronald
PCP: The Devil's Dust: Recognition, Management and Prevention of Phencyclidine Abuse, Wadsworth Publishing, Belmont, California, 1981

Lindsay, Norman
Bohemians at the Bulletin, Angus and Robertson, Sydney, 1965
Dust or Polish?, Angus and Robertson, Sydney, 1974 (1950)
Halfway to Anywhere, Angus and Robertson, Sydney, 1947
The Cousin from Fiji, Ure Smith, Sydney, 1965 (1945)

Lingeman, Richard
Drugs from A to Z: A Dictionary, McGraw-Hill, New York, 1969

Linklater, Richard
Dazed and Confused, Gramercy Pictures, 1993

Linton, E.R.
America's Newest Sex Cult, Medco Books, Los Angeles, California, 1966

Lipton, Lawrence
The Holy Barbarians, Julian Messner Inc., New York, 1959

Liss, Howard
Basketball Talk for Beginners, Julian Messner Inc., New York, 1970
Bowling Talk for Beginners, Julian Messner Inc., New York, 1973
Football Talk for Beginners, Julian Messner Inc., New York, 1971 (1970)

Lit, Hy
Hy Lit's Unbelievable Dictionary of Hip Words for Groovy People, Hyski Press, Philadelphia, Pennsylvania, 1968

Lonergan, Kenneth
This is Our Youth, Overlook Press, Woodstock, New York, 2000

Loria, Ana
1 2 3 Be a Porn Star!, InfoNet Publications, Malibu, California, 2000

Lowdon, Brian and Margaret
Competitive Surfing: A Dedicated Approach, Movement Publications, Ithaca, New York, 1988

Lucas, George and Gloria Katz
American Graffiti, MCA/Universal Pictures, 1973

Lucas, Ian
Impertinent Decorum: Gay Theatrical Manoeuvres, Cassell, London, 1994

Luirink, Bart (translated by Loes Nas)
Moffies: Gay Life in Southern Africa, Ink Inc., Claremont, Western Cape, 2000

Lukas, J. Anthony
Don't Shoot – We Are Your Children, Dell Publishing, New York, 1971
The Barnyard Epithet and Other Obscenities: Notes on the Chicago Conspiracy Trial, Harper & Row, New York, 1970

Lukowiak, Ken
A Soldier's Song, Phoenix, London, 1999 (1993)
Marijuana Time, Orion Books, London, 2000

Lund, Charles W.
Robbing the One-Armed Bandits: Finding and Exploiting Advantageous Slot Machines, RGE Publishing, Oakland, California, 1999

Lund, J. Herbert
Herb's Hot Box of Railroad Slang, Jay Herbert Publishing, Chicago, Illinois, 1975

Luntz, Karen and Kirsten Smith
Ten Things I Hate About You, Touchstone, 1999

Maas, Peter
Serpico, Bantam Books, New York, 1974 (1973)

Macafee, C.I.
A Concise Ulster Dictionary, Oxford University Press, 1996

MacDonald, John D.
The Neon Jungle, Fawcett Publications, Greenwich, Connecticutt, 1953

MacDonnell, J.E.
Big Bill the Bastard, Horwitz, Melbourne, 1976
Don't Gimme the Ships, Horwitz, Melbourne, 1960
Sabotage!, Horwitz, Melbourne, 1964

Macfarlane, Aidan, Magnus Macfarlane and Philip Robson
The User, Oxford University Press, 1996

Mackey, Kevin
The Cure, Angus and Robertson, Sydney, 1970

MacLaughlin, Duncan
The Filth, Mainstream, Edinburgh, 2002

Maconie, Stuart
Cider with Roadies, Ebury Press, London, 2003

MacPherson, Tom
Dragging and Driving, Scholastic Book Services, New York, 1960

Mailer, Norman
Advertisements for Myself, G.P. Putnam's Sons, New York, 1959

Major, Clarence
A Dictionary of Afro-American Slang, International Publishers, New York, 1970
All-Night Vistitors, Northeastern University Press, Boston, Massachusetts, 1998
Black Slang, A Dictionary of Afro-American Talk, Routledge & Kegan Paul, London, 1971
Juba to Jive, A Dictionary of African-American Slang, Penguin Books, New York, 1994

Maloney, Shane
Nice Try, Text Publishing, Melbourne, 1998

Mandel, George
Flee the Angry Strangers, Bantam Books, New York, 1953 (1952)

Mandelkau, Jamie
Buttons: The Making of a President, Sphere, London, 1971

Mander, Gabrielle
WAN2TLK? ltl bk of txt msgs, St. Martin's Griffin, New York, 2002

Mangold, James
Copland, Miramax, 1997

Mann, Peter
How to Buy a Used Car Without Getting Gypped, Harper & Row, New York, 1975

Mansfield, Claire and John Mendelssohn
Dominatrix – A Memoir, Hodder Headline, London, 2002

Marcinko, Richard and John Weisman
Rogue Warrior, Pocket Books, New York, 1992

Marks, Howard
Mr Nice, Minerva, London, 1997

Marks, Howard (Editor)
The Howard Marks Book of Dope Stories, Vintage Books, London, 2001

Marlowe, Kenneth
The Gay World of Kenneth Marlowe, self-published, 1966

Marsh, Rod and Doug Walters
Two for the Road, Swan Publishing, Perth, 1992

Marshall, Alan
I Can Jump Puddles, Longman Cheshire, Melbourne, 1981 (1955)

Mason, Robert
Chickenhawk, Penguin Books, New York, 1983

Masters, Anthony
Minder, Sphere, London, 1984
Minder, Back Again, Sphere, London, 1984

Matheson, Chris and Ed Solomon
Bill and Ted's Excellent Adventure, Orion Pictures, 1989

Maupin, Armistead
Babycakes, HarperPerennial, New York, 1994 (1984)
Further Tales of the City, HarperPerennial, New York, 1982
Maybe the Moon, Black Swan, London, 1993 (1992)
Tales of the City, HarperCollins, New York, 1978

Maurer, David W.
Argot of the Racetrack, American Dialect Society, Tuscaloosa, Alabama, 1951
Kentucky Moonshine, University of Kentucky Press, Lexington, Kentucky, 1974
The American Confidence Man, Charles C. Thomas, Springfield, Illinois, 1974
The Annals of the American Academy of Political and Social Sciences: Gambling, American Academy of Political and Social Sciences, Philadelphia, Pennsylvania, 1950

Maurer, David M. and Victor H. Vogel
Narcotics and Narcotic Addiction (4th Edition), Charles C. Thomas, Springfield, Illinois, 1973

Max, H.
Gay (S)language: A Dic(k)tionary of Gay Slang, Banned Books, Austin, Texas, 1988

Mayer, David and Kenneth Richards
Western Popular Theatre, Methuen, New York, 1977

Mazer, Sharon
Professional Wrestling: Sport and Spectacle, University of Mississippi Press, Jackson, Mississippi, 1998

McBride, Michael Keith
Understanding the Weed, Greatlakes Living Press, Matteson, Illinois, 1977

McCabe, Patrick
The Butcher Boy, Picador, London, 1992

McCarthy, Mary
The Group, Harcourt, Brace & World, New York, 1963

McCarthy, Pete
McCarthy's Bar, Hodder & Stoughton, London, 2000

McClintock, Jack
The Book of Darts, Random House, New York, 1977

McConville, Brigid and John Shearlaw
The Slanguage of Sex, Macdonald, London, 1984

McCool, Sam
Pittsburghese: How to Speak Like a Pittsburgher, Goodwill Industries, Pittsburgh, Pennsylvania, 1982

McCord, Gary
Golf for Dummies (Miniature Edition), Running Press, Philadelphia, Pennsylvania, 1996

McCoy, Horace
Kiss Tomorrow Good-bye, Random House, New York, 1948

McCreary, Don R. (Editor)
Dawg Speak: The Slanguage Dictionary of the University of Georgia, University of Georgia, Athens, Georgia, 2001

McCririck, John
John McCririck's World of Betting, Stanley Paul, London, 1991

McCullough, Colleen
The Thorn Birds, Harper & Row, Sydney, 1978 (1977)
Tim, Pan Books, London, 1978 (1975)

McDonald, Brian
Elephant Boys, Mainstream, Edinburgh, 2000

McDonald, James
A Dictionary of Obscenity, Taboo and Euphemism, Sphere, London, 1988

McFadden, Amy and Denise
CoalSpeak: The (Un)Official Dictionary of the Schuylkill County, PA Anthracite Coal Region, CoalRegion Enterprises, Marlboro, Massachusetts, 1998 (1997)

McFarland, Wayne J. and Philip Smith
Sports Illustrated Handball, J.B. Lippincott, Philadelphia, Pennsylvania, 1976

McFedries, Paul
Word Spy, Broadway Books, New York, 2004

McGeady, Mary Rose
Are you out there, God?, Covenant House, New York, 1999

McGill, David
A Dictionary of Kiwi Slang, Mills Publication, Lower Hutt, Wellington, 1993 (1988)
David McGill's Complete Kiwi Slang Dictionary, Reed Publishing, Auckland, 1998

McInerney, Jay
Bright Lights, Big City, Vintage Books, New York, 1984

McInnes, Colin
Absolute Beginners, Allison & Busby, London, 1980 (1959)

McKenna, Frank
A Glossary of Railwaymen's Talk, Ruskin College, Oxford, 1970

McKennon, Joe
Circus Lingo, Carnival Publishers of Sarasota, Sarasota, Florida, 1980

McKissick, Mitch
Surf Lingo: A Complete Guide to a Totally Rad Vocab, Coastline Press, Balboa, California, 1987

McLean, Lenny
The Guv'nor, Blake Publishing, London, 1998

McMurtry, Larry
The Last Picture Show, Dell Publishing, New York, 1971 (1966)

McNab, Andy
Bravo Two Zero, Bantam Books, London, 1993
Immediate Action, Bantam Books, London, 1995

McNally, Ward
Supper at Happy Harry's, Weldon Publishing, Sydney, 1991 (1982)

McNelis, Lee
30 + And a Wake-Up: A Compendium: Prison Slang Terms and Definitions, self-published, 1991

McQuain, Jeffrey
Never Enough Words, Random House, New York, 1999

McQuarrie, Christopher
The Usual Suspects, Gramercy Pictures, 1995

McRobbie, Angela (Editor)
Zoot Suits and Second-Hand Dresses, Macmillan, London, 1989

Mechigian, John
Encyclopedia of Keno: A Guide to Successful Gambling with Keno, Funtime Enterprises, Fresno, California, 1972

Meriwether, Louise
Daddy Was a Number Runner, Pyramid Books, New York, 1974 (1970)

Merriam, Kendall
The Illustrated Dictionary of Lobstering, Cumberland Press, Freeport, Maine, 1978

Meyer, Kathleen
How to Shit in the Woods, Ten Speed Press, Berkeley, California, 1994

Meyer, Linda
Teenspeak! A Bewildered Parent's Guide to Teenagers, Peterson's, Princeton, New Jersey, 1994

Milius, John and Francis Ford Coppola
Apocalypse Now, United Artists, 1979

Miller, Jerry
Fast Company: The Men and Machines of American Auto Racing, Follett Books, Chicago, Illinois, 1972

Miller, Tony and Patricia George
Cut! Print! The Language and Structure of Filmmaking, F.I.W. Press, Van Nuys, California, 1977

Mills, James
The Panic in Needle Park, Signet Books, New York, 1967 (1966)

Milne, John
Alive and Kicking, No Exit Press, Harpenden, Hertfordshire, 1998

Milner, Christina and Richard
Black Players: The Secret World of Black Pimps, Little, Brown and Co., Boston, Massachusetts, 1972

Milner, Michael
Sex on Celluloid, McFadden-Bartell, New York, 1969 (1964)

Minton, Ray
Scum, PolyGram Video Ltd, 1979

Mole, Kylie (Maryanne Fahey)
My Diary, Omnibus Books, Adelaide, 1988

Monteleone, Vincent J.
Criminal Slang: The Vernacular of the Underworld Lingo (Revised Edition), Christopher Publishing, Boston, Massachusetts, 1949

Moore, Charles W.
A Brick for Mister Jones, Project BAIT, Detroit, Michigan, 1975

Moore, Michael
Dude, Where's My Country?, Warner Books, New York, 2003

Moorhouse, Frank
Forty-Seventeen, Penguin Books, Melbourne, 1988

Morehead, Albert H.
The Complete Guide to Winning Poker, Simon & Schuster, New York, 1967

Morgan, Joe
Eastenders Don't Cry, New Author Publications, South Woodham Ferrers, Essex, 1994

Morgan, Roberta
Main Event: The World of Professional Wrestling, Dial Press, New York, 1979

Morgan, Seth
Homeboy, Random House, New York, 1990

Morley, Paul
Ask, Faber and Faber, London, 1986

Morrison, John
Stories of the Waterfront, Penguin Books, Melbourne, 1984 (1945)

Mortimer, Lee
Women Confidential, Julian Messner Inc., New York, 1960

Morton, E.D.
Martini A–Z of Fencing, Queen Anne Press, London, 1988

Moss, Tom
Cavers' Slang Dictionary, www.caversdigest.com, 1997

Motely, Willard
Let No Man Write My Epitaph, Signet Books, New York, 1959 (1958)

Mowry, Jess
Way Past Cool, HarperPerennial, New York, 1993 (1992)

Moxham, Wilda
The Apprentice, Weldon Publishing, Sydney, 1991 (1969)

Mueller, Robert Kirk
Buzzwords: A Guide to the Language of Leadership, Van Nostrand Reinhold, New York, 1974

Muirhead, Desmond
Surfing in Hawaii, Northland Press, Flagstaff, Arizona, 1962

Multicultural Management Program Fellows
Dictionary of Cautionary Words and Phrases, University of Missouri, School of Journalism, Columbia, Missouri, 1989

Mungo, Raymond
Famous Long Ago: My Life and Hard Times with Liberation News Service, Beacon Press, Boston, Massachusetts, 1970

Munro, Michael
The Complete Patter, Canongate, Edinburgh, 1996
The Original Patter, Glasgow City Libraries, Glasgow, 1985
The Patter, Another Blast, Canongate, Edinburgh, 1988

Munro, Pamela (Editor)
U.C.L.A Slang: A Dictionary of Slang Words and Expressions Used at U.C.L.A., Department of Linguistics, Los Angeles, California, 1989
U.C.L.A. Slang 3: U.C.L.A. Occasional Papers in Linguistics Number 18, Department of Linguistics, Los Angeles, California, 1997
U.C.L.A. Slang 4: U.C.L.A. Occasional Papers in Linguistics Number 22, Department of Linguistics, Los Angeles, California, 2001

Murphy, Colin and Donal O'Dea
The Book of Feckin' Irish Slang, The O'Brien Press, Dublin, 2004

Murray, Thomas E. and Thomas R. Murrell
The Language of Sadomasochism, Greenwood Press, Westport, Connecticut, 1989

Murtagh, John M. and Sara Harris
Cast the First Stone, Pocket Books, New York, 1958 (1957)

Mussell, John W.
The Token Book of Militarisms, Token Publishing, Axminster, Devon, 1995

Myers, Mike
Austin Powers: International Man of Mystery, New Line Cinema, 1997

Myers, Mike and Bonnie and Terry Turner
Wayne's World, Paramount Pictures, 1992
Wayne's World 2, Paramount Pictures, 1993

Myers, Mike and Michael McCullers
Austin Powers: The Spy Who Shagged Me, New Line Cinema, 1999

Nagel, William
The Odd Angry Shot, Angus and Robertson, Sydney, 1975

Napier, Valantyne
Glossary of Terms Used in Variety, Vaudeville, Revue & Pantomime, 1880–1960, The Badger Press, Westbury, Wiltshire, 1996

Napier-Bell, Simon
Black Vinyl White Powder, Ebury Press, London, 2001

Napolitano, George
Championship Wrestling: Masters of Mayhem, Mallard Press, New York, 1991
This is Wrestling: Today's Stars, Tomorrow's Legends, Smithmark Publishers, New York, 1993

Nash, Jay Robert
Dictionary of Crime, Paragon House, New York, 1992

Natkin, Bobbye Claire and Steve Kirk
All About Pinball, Grosset & Dunlap, New York, 1977

Nazel, Joseph
Black Cop, Holloway House, Los Angeles, California, 1993 (1974)

Nealy, William
Mountain Bike! A Manual of Technique, Menasha Ridge Press, Birmingham, Alabama, 1993 (1992)

Neate, Patrick
Where You're At, Bloomsbury, London, 2003

Neill, Richard
Booze, Cassell, London, 2001

Nelson, Larry and James Jones
Stranglehold: An Intriguing Behind the Scenes Glimpse into the Private World of Professional Wrestling, Chump Change Publishing, Denver, Colorado, 1999

Nelson, Marlena Kay
Rookies to Roaches: The Police Force and Its Folklore, unpublished manuscript in the Historical Manuscript Collection, Columbia, Missouri, 1963

Nelson, William Desmond
Surfing: A Handbook, Auerbach Publishers, Philadelphia, Pennsylvania, 1973

Neville, Richard
Out of My Mind, Bloomsbury, London, 1996
Play Power, Exploring the International Underground, Random House, New York, 1970

Newland, Courttia
Society Within, Abacus, London, 1999

Newman, G.F.
Sir, You Bastard, Sphere, London, 1978 (1970)
Three Professional Ladies, Sphere, London, 1978 (1973)

Newton, Bert
Bert!, Garry Sparkes & Associates, Melbourne, 1977

Nichols, John
The Sterile Cuckoo, Avon Books, New York, 1970 (1965)

Nickolds, Andrew
Back to Basics: Arthur Daley's Anatomy of Britain, Heinemann, Oxford, 1994

Niemann, Linda
Boomer: Railroad Memoirs, Cleis Press, Pittsburgh, Pennsylvania, 1990

Nihalini, Paroo, R.K. Tongue and Priya Hosali
Indian and British English, Oxford University Press, Delhi, 1979

Niland, D'Arcy
Dead Men Running, Penguin Books, Melbourne, 1978 (1969)
The Shiralee, Angus and Robertson, Sydney, 1987 (1955)

Nind, Tom
Rude Rhyming Slang, Abson Books, London, 2003

Norman, Frank
Bang to Rights, Secker & Warburg, London, 1958

Norman, Gurney
Divine Right's Trip, Last Whole Earth Catalog, Menlo Park, California, 1971

Oakley, Barry
A Salute to the Great McCarthy, Penguin Books, Melbourne, 1971 (1970)

Obstfeld, Raymond and Patricia Fitzgerald
Jabberrock: The Ultimate Book of Rock 'n' Roll Quotations, Henry Holt, New York, 1997

O'Connell, Vincent
ID, Parallax Pictures/Metropolis Filmproduction, 1994

O'Connor, Joseph
Red Roses and Petrol, Methuen, London, 1995
The Irish Male at Home and Abroad, Minerva, Dublin, 1996

O'Day, John
Confessions of a Hollywood Callgirl, Shelbourne Press, Los Angeles, California, 1964
Confessions of a Male Prostitute, Sherbourne Press, Los Angeles, California, 1964

Odean, Kathleen
High Steppers, Fallen Angels, and Lollipops: Wall Street Slang, Dodd, Mead & Company, New York, 1988

Odzer, Cleo
Goa Freaks: My Hippie Years in India, Blue Moon Books, New York, 1995

Ogg, Alex
The Hip Hop Years, Channel 4 Books, London, 1999

O'Grady, John
Aussie English: An Explanation of the Australian Idiom, Ure Smith, Sydney, 1965
Aussie Etiket, or, Doing Things the Aussie Way, Ure Smith, Sydney, 1971
It's Your Shout, Mate!, Ure Smith, Sydney, 1972

O'Hanlon, Ardal
The Talk of the Town, Hodder & Stoughton, London, 1998

Olberman, Keith and Dan Patrick
The Big Show: Inside ESPN's Sports Center, Pocket Books, New York, 1997

Olgin, Joseph
Illustrated Football Dictionary for Young People, Prentice-Hall, Englewood Cliffs, New Jersey, 1975

Olive, David
Business Babble: A Cynic's Dictionary of Corporate Jargon, John Wiley & Sons, New York, 1991

Olney, Ross
Kings of the Drag Strip, G.P. Putnam's Sons, New York, 1968
The Young Sportsman's Guide to Surfing, Thomas Nelson & Sons, New York, 1965

Orloff, Erica and JoAnn Baker
Dirty Little Secrets, St. Martin's Griffin, New York, 2001

Orsman, Harry
A Dictionary of Modern New Zealand Slang, Oxford University Press, 1999

Orsman, Harry and Des Hurley
The Beaut Little Book of New Zealand Slang, Reed Publishing, Auckland, 1994

Osborne, Ben
The A–Z of Club Culture, Sceptre, London, 1999

O'Shaughnessy, Patrick
Market Traders' Slang: A Glossary of Terms Used in Boston [Lincolnshire] and Elsewhere, 1979 in *Lore and Language, Vol 2, Nos 3 and 8*, University of Sheffield, Sheffield, 1975 and 1978

Owen, Alun
A Hard Day's Night, The Beatles, 1964

Owen, Guy
The Flim-Flam Man and The Apprentice Grifter, Crown Publishers, New York, 1972

Page, Ra (Editor)
The City Life Book of Manchester Short Stories, Penguin Books, London, 1999

Page, Robin
Down Among the Dossers, Davis-Poynter, London, 1973

Pagen, Dennis
Hang Gliding and Flying Skills, self-published, State College, Pennsylvania, 1977

Paine, Gerald
A Bachelor's Guide to the Brothels of Nevada, Eros Publishing, Wilmington, Delaware, 1978

Paine, Rhiannon
Too Late for the Festival, Academy Chicago Publishers, Chicago, Illinois, 1999

Paladin Press
An Inside Look at Outlaw Motorcycle Gangs, Paladin Press, Boulder, Colorado, 1992

Palmer, Beryl Nobbs
A Dictionary of Norfolk Words and Usages (2nd Edition), Photopress International, Norfolk Island, 1992

Park, Ruth
Harp in the South, Angus and Robertson, Sydney, 1986 (1948)
Poor Man's Orange, Angus and Robertson, Sydney, 1980 (1949)

Parker, Dan
The ABC of Horse Racing, Bantam Books, New York, 1948 (1947)

Parker, Trey and Matt Stone
South Park: Bigger Longer & Uncut, Paramount Pictures, 1999

Parry, Glyn
Mosh, Random House, Sydney, 1996

Partridge, Eric
A Dictionary of Catch Phrases, Routledge & Kegan Paul, 1977
A Dictionary of Forces Slang, 1939–1945, Secker & Warburg, London, 1948
A Dictionary of R.A.F. Slang, Michael Joseph, London, 1945
A Dictionary of The Underworld, Theodore Brun, London, 1950
Name Your Child, Evans Brothers, London, 1968

Partridge, Eric and Paul Beale
A Dictionary of Catch Phrases (2nd Edition), Routledge & Kegan Paul, 1985

Patrick, Peter
Some Recent Jamaican Creole Words, http://privatewww.essex.ac.uk/~patrickp/papers/RecentJCwords, 2003

Patrick, Vincent
Family Business, Poseidon Press, New York, 1985
The Pope of Greenwich Village, Seaview Books, New York, 1979

Patterson, Jerry L.
Blackjack: A Winner's Handbook, Ecehlon Enterprises, Vorhees, New Jersey, 1978

Pattison, Ian
Rab C. Nesbitt, BBC Books, London, 1990 (1988)

Pausacker, Jenny
What are ya?, Angus and Robertson, Sydney, 1987

Pawka, Mike
Rasta/Patois Dictionary, www.niceup.com/patois, 2001

Payne, C.D.
Youth in Revolt, Doubleday, New York, 1993

Peace, David
Nineteen Seventy-Four, Serpent's Tail, London, 1999

Pedroli, Hubert and Mary Tiegreen
Let the Big Dog Eat! A Dictionary of the Secret Language of Golf, Welcome Enterprises, New York, 2000

Percy, George
The Language of Poker: The Jargon and Slang Spoken Around The Poker Table, self-published, 1988

Perlmutter, Nate
How to Win Money at the Races, Collier Books, New York, 1964

Peterkin, A.D.
The Bald Headed Hermit & the Artichoke, Arsenal Pulp Press, Vancouver, Washington, 1999

Peters, Lance
The Dirty Half-Mile, Angus and Robertson, Sydney, 1989 (1979)

Petievich, Gerald
Money Men, Harcourt Brace Jovanovich, New York, 1981
One-Shot Deal, Harcourt Brace Jovanovich, New York, 1981
Shakedown, Simon & Schuster, New York, 1988
The Quality of the Informant, Arbor House, New York, 1985
To Die in Beverly Hills, Arbor House, New York, 1983
To Live and Die in L.A., Arbor House, New York, 1983

Petkovich, Anthony
The X Factory: Inside the American Hardcore Film Industry, Critical Vision, Manchester, 1997

Pharr, Robert Deane
Giveadamn Brown, Payback Press, Edinburgh, 1997 (1978)

Phillips, Louis and Burnham Holmes
The Complete Book of Sports Nicknames, Renaissance Books, Los Angeles, California, 1998

Pileggi, Nicholas and Martin Scorsese
Casino, Universal Pictures, 1995
Goodfellas, Warner Brothers, 1990

Pincus, Arthur
How to Talk Football, Dembner Books, New York, 1984

Piro, Sal and Michael Hess
The Official 'Rocky Horror Picture Show' Audience Participation Guide, Starbur Press, Plymouth, Connecticut, 1991

Pitt-Kethley, Fiona
Red Light Districts of the World, Tamworth Press, London, 2000

Plant, Sadie
Writing on Drugs, Faber and Faber, London, 1999

Plowman, Sonya
Great Kiwi Slang, Summit Books, Auckland, 2002

Poland, Jefferson and Valerie Alison
The Records of the San Francisco Sexual Freedom League, Olympia Press, London, 1971

Pollack, Bruce
The Disco Handbook, Scholastic Book Services, New York, 1979

Pollard, Jack
The Australian Surfrider, Murray, Sydney, 1963

Pollard, Velma
Dread Talk: The Language of Rastafari (Revised Edition), Canoe Press, Barbados, 2000

Polsky, Ned
Hustlers, Beats, and Others, Adleine Publishing Company, Chicago, Illinois, 1967

Pond, Mimi
The Valley Girl's Guide to Life, Dell Publishing, New York, 1982

Ponicsan, Darryl
The Last Detail, W.H. Allen, London, 1971 (1970)

Poteet, Lewis
Talking Country: The Eastern Townships Phrase Book, Pigwidgeon Press, Ayers Cliff, Quebec, 1992
The South Shore Phrase Book, Nimbus, Halifax, Nova Scotia, 1999

Powell, Mark
Snap, Weidenfeld & Nicholson, London, 2001

Powis, David
The Signs of Crime, McGraw Hill, London, 1977

Poynter, Dan
Parachuting: The Skydivers' Handbook, Parachuting Publications, Santa Barbara, California, 1978

Preston, Brian
Pot Planet, Grove Press, New York, 2002

Preusse, Carol Ann
Jargon Used by University of Texas Co-Eds, unpublished manuscript in the Western Historical Manuscript Collection, Columbia, Missouri, 1963

Price, Richard
Clockers, Avon Books, New York, 1992

Prus, Robert C. and C.R.D. Sharper
Road Hustler: Grifting, Magic, and the Thief Subculture, Richard Kaufman and Alan Greenberg, New York, 1991 (1977)

Pryce, Malcolm
Aberystwyth Mon Amour, Bloomsbury, London, 2001

Puxley, Ray
Cockney Rabbit, Robson Books, London, 1992
Fresh Rabbit, Robson Books, London, 1998

Puzo, Mario
Inside Las Vegas, Charter Books, New York, 1977
The Godfather, Fawcett Crest, Greenwich, Connecticut, 1970 (1969)

Radakovich, Anka
The Wild Girls Club: Tales From Below the Belt, Fawcett Columbine, New York, 1994

Radio Shack
CBer's Handy Atlas/Dictionary, Tab Books, Blue Ridge Summit, Pennsylvania, 1976

Radlauer, Ed
Drag Racing Pix Dix: A Picture Dictionary, Bowmar, Glendale, California, 1970
Motorcylopedia, Bowmar, Glendale, California, 1973

Radlauer, Ed and Ruth
Truck Tech Talk, Elk Grove Books, Chicago, Illinois, 1986

Radley, Paul
Jack Rivers and Me, Fontana Books, Melbourne, 1982 (1981)

Radner, Sidney H.
Radner on Dice, Key Publishing, New York, 1957

Ragen, Joseph E. and Charles Finston
Inside the World's Toughest Prison, Charles C. Thomas, Springfield, Illinois, 1962

Ramsey, Frederic
Chicago Documentary, Jazz Music Books, London, 1944

Ramson, W.S.
The Australian National Dictionary, Oxford University Press, Melbourne, 1988

Rankin, Ian
The Falls, Orion Books, London, 2001

Raven, Charles
Underworld Nights, Hulton Press, London, 1956

Raymond, Derek (Robin Cook)
The Crust on its Uppers, Serpent's Tail, London, 2000 (1962)

Raymond, Eric S.
The New Hacker's Dictionary, MIT Press, Cambridge, Massachusetts, 1991

Rechy, John
City of Night, Grove Press, New York, 1963
Numbers, Grove Press, New York, 1967
The Fourth Angel, Seaver Books, New York, 1983 (1972)
The Sexual Outlaw, Dell Publishing, New York, 1978 (1977)

Rees, Coralie
Spinifex Walkabout: Hitch-hiking in Remote North Australia, Australasian Publishing Company, Sydney, 1954 (1953)

Rees, Leighton
Leighton Rees on Darts, Atheneum, New York, 1980

Reese, Terence
Bridge Player's Dictionary, Sterling Publishing Company, London, 1959

Regan, Jim
Winning at Slot Machines: A Guide to Making Money at the Most Popular of All Casino Games, Citadel Press, Secaucus, New Jersey, 1985

Reid, Ed and Ovid Demaris
The Green Felt Jungle, Pocket Books, New York, 1964 (1963)

Reinberg, Linda
In the Field: The Language of the Vietnam War, Facts on File, New York, 1991

Reisner, Robert George
The Jazz Titans: Including "The Parlance of Hip", Doubleday, New York, 1960

Reynolds, Butch
Broken Hearted Clown, Arco, London, 1954 (1953)

Rhodes, Sue
And when she was bad she was popular, Sun Books, Melbourne, 1968
Now you'll think I'm awful, Gareth Powell, Sydney, 1967

Rich, Kim
Johnny's Girl: A Daughter's Memoir of Growing Up in Alaska's Underworld, Alaska Northwest Books, Seattle, Washington, 1993

Richards, Kel
The Aussie Bible (Well, bits of it anyway!), Bible Society NSW, Sydney, 2003

Ridgeway, James
Red Light: Inside the Sex Industry, Powerhouse Books, New York, 1996

Riggins, John and Jack Winter
Gameplan: The Language and Strategy of Pro Football, Santa Barbara Press, Santa Barbara, California, 1984

Rigney, Francis J. and L. Douglas Smith
The Real Bohemia: A Sociological and Psychological Study of the "Beats", Basic Books, New York, 1961

Riley, Len
The Kings Cross Racket, Scripts Publications, Sydney, 1967

Ritchie, Guy
Lock, Stock ... & Four Stolen Hooves, Faber and Faber, London, 2000

Rivers, Larry
What Did I Do? The Unauthorized Autobiography, HarperCollins, New York, 1992

Rivett, Rohan D.
Behind Bamboo: An Inside Story of the Japanese Prison Camps, Angus and Robertson, Sydney, 1946

Roach, Martin
Dr. Marten's Air Wair, AirWair Limited, Italy, 1999

Robb, John
*The Nineties: What the F**k Was That All About?*, Ebury Press, London, 1999

Robbins, Tom
Another Roadside Attraction, Ballantine Books, New York, 1981 (1971)

Roberts, Hermese E.
The Third Ear: A Black Glossary, English-Language Institute of America, Chicago, Illinois, 1971

Roberts, Jonathan
How to California, Dell Publishing, New York, 1984

Robertson, Jerry
Oil Slanguage, Petroleum Publishers, Evansville, Indiana, 1954

Robison, Bonnie
Sports Illustrated Volleyball, J.B. Lippincott, Philadelphia, Pennsylvania, 1972

Rock, Chris
Rock This!, Hyperion, New York, 1997

Rock, Mike
This Book: The Truth About Drugs (2nd Edition), Those Publishers, London, 1999

Rod, Lightin'
Hustlers Convention, Harmony Books, New York, 1973

Roddy, Irv
Friday Night Poker: Penny Poker for Millions, Simon & Schuster, New York, 1961

Rodgers, Bruce
The Queens' Vernacular, Straight Arrow Books, San Francisco, California, 1972

Rohan, Criena
Down by the Dockside, Penguin Books, Melbourne, 1983 (1963)
The Delinquents, Penguin Books, Melbourne, 1989 (1962)

Romeo, Anthony
The Language of Gangs, unpublished manuscript, New York, 1962

Room, Adrian
An A–Z of British Life (4th Edition), Oxford University Press, 1994

Roos, Don
Boys on the Side, Warner Brothers, 1995

Root, Wayne Alan
Betting To Win on Sports, Bantam Books, New York, 1989

Rose, Joel
Kill Kill Faster Faster, Rebel Inc., Edinburgh, 1997

Rosenberg, Scott
Gone in 60 Seconds, Buena Vista Pictures, 2000

Rosten, Leo
Hooray for Yiddish!, Elm Tree Books, London, 1983
The Joys of Yiddish, Penguin Books, London, 1971 (1968)
The Joys of Yinglish, Signet Books, New York, 1992 (1989)

Rote, Kyle
The Language of Pro Football, Random House, New York, 1966

Roth, Eric
Forrest Gump, Paramount Pictures, 1992

Roth, Philip
Goodbye, Columbus, Bantam Books, New York, 1968 (1959)
Portnoy's Complaint, Bantam Books, New York, 1970 (1969)

Rowan, David
A Glossary for the 90s, Prion, London, 1998

Rowe, Robert V.
How to Win at Horse-Racing, Cardoza Publishing, New York, 1990

Royer, Victor H.
Casino Gamble Talk: The Language of Gambling and New Casino Games, Lyle Stuart Books, New York, 2003

Rubin, Jerry
Do It! Scenarios of the Revolution, Simon & Schuster, New York, 1970

Rubinstein, Frankie
A Dictionary of Shakespeare's Sexual Puns and Their Significance, Macmillan, London, 1984

Rudensky, Red
The Gonif, The Piper Company, Blue Earth, Minnesota, 1970

Rudgely, Richard
The Encyclopaedia of Psychoactive Substances, Abacus, London, 1999

Rundell, Michael
The Dictionary of Cricket, Guild Press, London, 1985

Rushin, Steve
Pool Cool, Pocket Books, New York, 1990

Russ, Martin
The Last Parallel, Zebra Books, New York, 1957

Russell, Ross
The Sound, E.P. Dutton, New York, 1961

Rutherford, Douglas
The Creeping Flesh, Fontana Books, London, 1965 (1963)

Ryan, Chris
Stand By, Stand By, Century, London, 1996
The Watchman, Arrow, London, 2002 (2001)

Sahl, Mort
Heartland, Harcourt Brace Jovanovich, New York, 1976

Salak, John S.
Dictionary of Gambling, Philosophical Library, New York, 1963

Salinger, J.D.
Catcher in the Rye, Little, Brown and Co., New York, 1951
Franny and Zooey, Bantam Books, New York, 1969 (1961)
Nine Stories, Bantam Books, New York, 1977 (1953)

Salisbury, Harrison E.
The Shook-up Generation, Crest Books, New York, 1958

Salvucci, Claudio R.
The Philadelphia Dialect Dictionary, Evolution Publishing, Bucks County, Pennsylvania, 1996

Sampson, Kevin
Clubland, Jonathan Cape, London, 2002
Outlaws, Jonathan Cape, London, 2001
Powder, Jonathan Cape, London, 1999

Sanders, Ed
Tales of Beatnik Glory, Stonehill Publishing, New York, 1975

Sanders, Judi
Cal Poly Slang, Department of Communication, Cal Poly Pomona, Pomona, California, 1990
Da Bomb! Dis is Dope, Dude! Dig It! A Dictionary of Cal Poly Slang (5th Edition), Department of Communication, Cal Poly Pomona, Pomona, California, 1997
Da Bomb: The Summer Supplement, Department of Communication, Cal Poly Pomona, Pomona, California, 1997
Don't Dog my Do, Dude! A Collection of Cal Poly Argot, Department of Communication, Cal Poly Pomona, Pomona, California, 1991
Faced and Faded, Hanging to Hurl: A Collection of Cal Poly Argot (4th Edition), Department of Communication, Cal Poly Pomona, Pomona, California, 1993
Kickin' Like Chicken with the Couch Commander: A Collection of Cal Poly Argot (3rd Edition), Department of Communication, Cal Poly Pomona, Pomona, California, 1992
Mashing and Munching in Ames: A Dictionary of ISU Slang, Department of Communications, Iowa State University, Ames, Iowa, 1994

Saporita, Jay
Pourin' It All Out, Citadel Press, Secaucus, New Jersey, 1980

Saslaets, Steve
Ye Olde Hiptionary, self-published, Las Vegas, Nevada, 1970

Saunders, Jennifer
Absolutely Fabulous, BBC, 1992

Savage, John
The Winner's Guide to Dice, Grosset & Dunlap, New York, 1974

Sayles, John
Union Dues, Little, Brown and Co., Boston, Massachusetts, 1977

Scarne, John
Scarne on Dice, Stackpole Books, Mechanicsburg, Pennsylvania, 1974
Scarne's Guide to Modern Poker, Simon & Schuster, New York, 1979

Scharf, Dave
Winning at Poker, Capella, London, 2003

Schiff, Robin
Romy and Michele's High School Reunion, Touchstone Pictures, 1997

Schmidt, J.E.
Narcotics Lingo and Lore, Charles C. Thomas, Springfield, Illinois, 1959

Schock, Jim
Life is a Lousy Drag, Unicorn Publishing, San Francisco, California, 1958

Scholl, Richard
Running Press Glossary of Baseball Language, Running Press, Philadelphia, Pennsylvania, 1977

Schrader, Paul J.
Taxi Driver, Columbia Pictures, 1976

Schultz, Mari Helen
May I Have This Dance? A Social Dance Digest, Vantage Press, New York, 1986

Schwartz, J.R.
The Official Guide to the Best Cat Houses in Nevada, self-published, Boise, Idaho, 1993

Schwed, Peter
How to Talk Tennis, Galahad Books, New York, 1988

Scoblete, Frank
Best Blackjack, Bonus Books, Chicago, Illinois, 1996
Guerrilla Gambling: How to Beat the Casinos at their own Games, Bonus Books, Chicago, Illinois, 1993

Scott, Kathryn Leigh
The Bunny Years, Pomegranate Press, Beverly Hills, California, 1998

Scott, Thurston
Cure it with Honey, Harper & Brothers, New York, 1951

Scotti, Anna and Paul Young
Buzzwords: L.A. Freshspeak, St. Martin's Press, New York, 1997

Seale, Bobby
A Lonely Rage, Bantam Books, New York, 1979 (1978)

Sedaris, David
Me Talk Pretty One Day, Abacus, London, 2001

Seese, Gwyneth A. "Dandalion"
Tijuana Bear in a Smoke 'Um Up Taxi, Pollock Enterprises, Grove City, Pennsylvania, 1977

Segal, Erich
Love Story, Harper & Row, New York, 1970

Selby, Hubert
Last Exit to Brooklyn, Calder & Boyers Ltd, London, 1970 (1957)

Self, Will
The Sweet Smell of Psychosis, Bloomsbury, London, 1996

Selkie, B.
Lime Juice, Autopsy, Sydney, 1995

Sellers, Terence
Dungeon Evidence, Velvet, London, 1997

Sergel, Sherman Louis
The Language of Show Biz: A Dictionary, Dramatic Publishing Company, Chicago, Illinois, 1973

Severson, John
Modern Surfing Around the World, Doubleday, New York, 1964

Shamus, Mike
The Illustrated Encyclopedia of Billiards, Lyons & Burford, New York, 1993

Shana, Larsen
200 Cigarettes, Paramount Pictures, 1999

Shankar, Pramod
How to Win at Gin Rummy: Playing for Fun and Profit, Lyle Stuart, Secaucus, New Jersey, 1994

Shapiro, Harry
Recreational Drugs, Collins & Brown, London, 2004
Waiting for the Man: The Story of Drugs and Popular Music, Helter Skelter, London, 1999

Share, Bernard
Slanguage – A Dictionary of Irish Slang, Gill & Macmillan, Dublin, 1997
Slanguage – A Dictionary of Slang and Colloquial English in Ireland, Gill & Macmillan, Dublin, 2003

Sharpe, Ben
Scooter Crazy, The Chicken House, Frome, Somerset, 2000

Sharpe, Roger C.
Pinball!, E.P. Dutton, New York, 1977

Shaw, Arnold
Lingo of Tin-Pan Alley, Broadcast Music Inc., New York, 1950

Shearer, Johnny
The Male Hustler, Century Books, Cleveland, Ohio, 1966

Shecter, Leonard and William Phillips
On the Pad: The Underworld and its Corrupt Police, G.P. Putnam's Sons, New York, 1973

Sheehan, Neil
A Bright Shining Lie, Random House, New York, 1988

Sheehy, Gail
Hustling, Dell Publishing, New York, 1974 (1973)

Shefski, Bill
Running Press Glossary of Football Language, Running Press, Philadelphia, Pennsylvania, 1978

Sheidlower, Jesse
The F Word, Random House, New York, 1995

Shelly, Lou
Hepcats Jive Talk Dictionary, T.W.O. Charles Company, Derby, Connecticut, 1945

Shelton, Ron
Bull Durham, Orion Pictures, 1988

Shenk, David and Steve Silberman
Skeleton Key: A Dictionary for Deadheads, Main Street Books, New York, 1994

Sheppard, Harvey
Dictionary of Railway Slang, Somerset Education Committee, 1970

Shrader, Paul and Mardik Martin
Raging Bull, MGM, 1980

Shulman, Alon
The Style Bible, Methuen, London, 1999

Shulman, Max
Anyone Got a Match?, Harper & Row, New York, 1964
Guided Tour of Campus Humor, Hanover House, Garden City, New York, 1955
I was a Teen-Age Dwarf, Bantam Books, New York, 1960 (1959)
Rally Round the Flag, Boys!, Doubleday, New York, 1957
The Many Loves of Dobie Gillis, Bantam Books, New York, 1951
The Zebra Derby, Doubleday, New York, 1956 (1946)

Siegel, Hy
All About CB Two-Way Radio, Radio Shack, Fort Worth, Texas, 1976

Sigal, Clancy
Going Away: A Report, A Memoir, Houghton Mifflin, Boston, Massachusetts, 1961

Silberstang, Edwin
Winning Poker for the Serious Player, Gambling Research Institute, New York, 1992

Silva, Penny
A Dictionary of South African English, Oxford University Press, 1996

Simes, Gary
A Dictionary of Australian Underworld Slang, Oxford University Press, Melbourne, 1993

Simmons, J.L. and Barry Winograd
It's Happening: A Portrait of the Youth Scene Today, McNally and Loftin, Santa Barbara, California, 1967 (1966)

Simonson, Douglas
Pidgin to da Max, Peppovision, Honolulu, Hawaii, 1981
Pidgin to da Max Hana Hou, Peppovision, Honolulu, Hawaii, 1982

Singleton, John
Boyz N The Hood, Columbia Pictures, 1990

Singleton, Ralph S.
Filmmaker's Dictionary, Lone Eagle Publishing, Beverly Hills, California, 1990

Skelton, Tracey and Gill Valentine (Editors)
Cool Places: Geographies of Youth Cultures, Routledge, London, 1998

Skerman, Allan
Beyond Indigo, William Heinemann, Melbourne, 1989

Skilbeck, Oswald
ABC of Film and TV Working Terms, Focal Press, New York, 1960

Skinner, Frank
Frank Skinner, Arrow Books, London, 2002 (2001)

Skolnik, Neil S.
On the Ledge, Faber and Faber, Winchester, Massachusetts, 1996

Slattery, Ray
Mobb's Mob, Horwitz, Sydney, 1966

Slaven, Roy (John Doyle)
Five South Coast Seasons, Australian Broadcasting Corporation, Sydney, 1992

Slim, Iceberg (Robert Beck)
Airtight Willie and Me, Payback Press, Edinburgh, 1979
Death Wish, Holloway House, Los Angeles, California, 1977
Doom Fox, Payback Press, Edinburgh, 1978
Mama Black Widow, Holloway House, Los Angeles, California, 1969
Pimp: The Story of My Life, Holloway House, Los Angeles, California, 1969
The Naked Soul of Iceberg Slim: Robert Beck's Real Story, Holloway House, Los Angeles, California, 1971
Trick Baby, Holloway House, Los Angeles, California, 1969

"Slingo"
The Offical CB Slang Dictionary Handbook, Communication Books, Milwaukee, Wisconsin, 1976

Sloane, Henry
Sloane's Inside Guide to Sex & Drugs & Rock 'n' Roll, Pan Books, London, 1985

Slone, Thomas H.
Rasta is Cuss: A Dictionary of Rastafarian Cursing, Masalai Press, Oakland, California, 2003

Smith, D.J.
Canal Boats and Boaters, Hugh Evelyn Ltd, London, 1973

Smith, Jester
Games They Play in San Francisco, Tri-City Printing, Sausalito, California, 1971

Smith, Karline
Moss Side Massive, The X Press, London, 2000 (1994)

Smith, Kent et al.
Adult Movies: Rating Hundreds of the Best Films for Home Video & Cable, Beekman House, New York, 1982

Smith, Kevin
Chasing Amy, Miramax, 1997
Clerks, Miramax, 1994
Jay and Silent Bob Strike Back, Hyperion, New York, 2001
Mallrats, Gramercy Pictures, 1995

Smith, Lindsay E. and Bruce A. Walstad
Keeping Carnies Honest: A Police Officer's Field Guide to Carnival Game Inspections, Street-Smart Communications, Littleton, Colorado, 1990
Sting Shift: The Street-Smart Cop's Handbook of Cons and Swindles, Street-Smart Communications, Littleton, Colorado, 1989

Smith, Peter A. and Fred M. Barritt
Bermewjan Vurds: A Dictionary of Conversational Bermudian, Island Press Limited, Hamilton, Bermuda, 1985

Smith, Vernon E.
The Jones Men, Payback Press, Edinburgh, 1997 (1974)

Smith, Warren
Warren Smith's Authentic Dictionary of CB, Award Books, New York, 1976

Smitherman, Geneva
Black Talk, Houghton Mifflin, New York, 1994

Snead, Sam and Jerry Tarde
Pigeons, Marks, Hustlers and Other Golf Bettors You Can Beat, Golf Digest, Trumbull, Connecticut, 1986

Snowden, Roger
Gambling Times Guide to Bingo, Lyle Stuart, Secaucus, New Jersey, 1986

Snyder, Jimmy
Jimmy the Greek, Playboy Press, Chicago, Illinois, 1976 (1975)

Soderbergh, Steven
Sex, Lies and Videotape, Miramax, 1989

Sohn, Amy
Run Catch Kiss, Simon & Schuster, New York, 1999
Sex and the City: Kiss and Tell, Melcher Media, New York, 2002

Solkey, Lee
Dummy Up and Deal, Gamblers Book Club Press, Las Vegas, Nevada, 1980

Sondheim, Stephen
West Side Story, 1957

Sorkin, Aaron
A Few Good Men, Columbia Pictures, 1992

Sorrentino, Gilbert
Steelwork, Pantheon Books, New York, 1970

Sorrows, Gene
All About Carnivals, American Federation of Police, North Miami, Florida, 1985

Sotos, Peter
Index, Velvet, London, 1998 (1996)

Southern, Terry
Blue Movie, Grove Press, New York, 1996 (1970)
Candy, Putnam, New York, 1958
Flash and Filigree, Grove Press, New York, 1996 (1958)
Red-Dirt Marijuana and Other Tastes, Panther, St Albans, Hertfordshire, 1973 (1967)
Texas Summer, Arcade, New York, 1993 (1991)
The Magic Christian, Penguin Books, Harmondsworth, Middlesex, 1969 (1959)

Sparks, Beatrice (writing as 'Anonymous')
Jay's Journal, Dell Publishing, New York, 1979

Spears, Richard A.
The Slang and Jargon of Drugs and Drink, Scarecrow Press, Metuchen, New Jersey, 1986

Speight, Johnny
It Stands to Reason, M&J Hobbs, Walton-on-Thames, Surrey, 1973

Spiegl, Fritz
Lern Yerself Scouse, Scouse Press, Liverpool, 1966

Spillane, Mickey
I, The Jury, Signet Books, New York, 1958 (1947)
Kiss Me Deadly, Signet Books, New York, 1952
Last Cop Out, Signet Books, New York, 1973 (1972)
Me, Hood!, Signet Books, New York, 1969 (1963)
My Gun is Quick, Signet Books, New York, 1950
One Lonely Night, Signet Books, New York, 1979 (1951)
Return of the Hood, Signet Books, New York, 1969 (1964)

Spillard, William J. and Pence James
Needle in a Haystack: The Exciting Adventures of a Federal Narcotic Agent, Whittlesey House, New York, 1945

Spottiswoode, Roger and Walter Hill
48 Hours, Paramount Pictures, 1982

Squires, Dick
The Other Racquet Sports, McGraw-Hill, New York, 1978 (1971)

Staines, Bob
Wot a Whopper, Lansdowne Press, Sydney, 1982

Stavsky, Lois et al.
A2Z: The Book of Rap and Hip-Hop Slang, Boulevard Books, New York, 1995

Steck, E.E.
A Brief Examination of an Esoteric Folk, unpublished manuscript in the Western Historical Manuscript Collection, Columbia, Missouri, 1968

Steele, Guy L. et al.
The Hacker's Dictionary: A Guide to the World of Computer Wizards, Harper & Row, New York, 1983

Steig, Irwin
Common Sense in Poker, Cornerstone Library, New York, 1963
Play Gin to Win, Cornerstone Library, New York, 1971

Steigleman, Walter
Horseracing, Prentice Hall, New York, 1947

Stein, Elissa and Kevin Leslie
Chunks: A Barfology, St. Martin's Griffin, New York, 1997

Steiner, Peter O.
Thursday Night Poker: How to Understand, Enjoy – and Win, Random House, New York, 1996

Stern, David H.
Surfing Guide to Southern California, Fitzpatrick Company, Malibu, California, 1963

Stern, Howard
Miss America, Regan Books, New York, 1995

Stern, Stewart
Rebel Without a Cause, Warner Brothers, 1955

Stockin, Jimmy
On the Cobbles, Mainstream, Edinburgh, 2000

Stoller, Robert and I.S. Levine
Coming Attractions: The Making of an X-Rated Video, Yale University Press, New Haven, Connecticutt, 1991

Stone, Oliver
Platoon, Orion Pictures, 1986

Stott, Mike
Soldiers Talking, Cleanly, Eyre Methuen, London, 1978

Stow, Randolph
The Merry-Go-Round in the Sea, Penguin Books, London, 1989 (1965)

Strait, Guy
The Lavendar Lexicon: Dictionary of Gay Words and Phrases, self-published, San Francisco, California, 1964

Strandemo, Steve and Bill Bruns
The Racquetball Book, Pocket Books, New York, 1977

Strong, Colin and Duff Hart-Davis
Fighter Pilot, BBC, 1981

Stroud, Carsten
Close Pursuit: A Week in the Life of a NYPD Homicide Cop, Bantam Books, Toronto, 1987

Such, Les
A Yen for Yokohama, Horwitz, Sydney, 1963

Sugar, Bert Randolph and George Napolitano
Wrestling's Great Grudge Matches: Battles and Feuds, Gallery Books, New York, 1985

Sullivan, George
Harness Racing, Fleet Publishing Corporation, New York, 1964
Pro Football A to Z: A Fully Illustrated Guide to America's Favorite Sport, Charles Scribner's Sons, New York, 1975

Sullivan, Paul
Sullivan's Music Trivia, Sanctuary Publishing, London, 2003

Sweeney, Gerald
Invasion, Angus and Robertson, Sydney, 1982
The Plunge, Angus and Robertson, Sydney, 1987 (1981)

Swift, Mary
Campus Slang: Slang on the University of Texas Campus, unpublished manuscript in the Western Historical Manuscript Collection, Columbia, Missouri, 1968

Sykes, Gresham M.
The Society of Captives: A Study of a Maximum Security Prison, Princeton University Press, Princeton, New Jersey, 1972 (1958)

Sylvester, Robert
No Cover Charge: A Backward Look at the Night Clubs, Dial Press, New York, 1956

Tabbert, Russell
Dictionary of Alaskan English, Denali Press, Juneau, Alaska, 1991

Tak, Montie
Truck Talk: The Language of the Open Road, Chilton Book Company, Philadelphia, Pennsylvania, 1971

Tamosaitis, Nancy
net.sex, Ziff-Davis Press, Emeryville, California, 1995

Tarantino, Quentin
From Dusk Till Dawn, Hyperion, New York, 1995
Kill Bill, Miramax, 2003
Pulp Fiction, Miramax, 1994
Reservoir Dogs, Artisan Entertainment, 1992

Tarantino, Quentin, David Veloz, Richard Turowski and Oliver Stone
Natural Born Killers, Warner Brothers, 1994

Taylor, Dawson
How to Talk Bowling, Dembner Books, New York, 1987
How to Talk Golf, Galahad Books, New York, 1985

Taylor, Murray A.
Jumping Fire: A Smokejumper's Memoir of Fighting Wildfire, Harcourt Inc., Orlando, Florida, 2001 (2000)

Teeman, Lawrence
Consumer Guide Good Buddy's CB Dictionary, Consumer Guide, Skokie, Illinois, 1976

Tempest, Paul
Lag's Lexicon, Routledge & Kegan Paul, London, 1950

Tennant, Kylie
Lost Haven, Macmillan, Melbourne, 1946
The Honey Flow, Angus and Robertson, Sydney, 1983 (1956)

Tevis, Walter
The Color of Money, Abacus, London, 1985 (1984)

Tewkesbury, Joan
Nashville, Paramount Pictures, 1975

Thigpen, Janet
Power Volleyball, William C. Brown, Dubuque, Iowa, 1985

Thomas, Gareth
This Is Ecstasy, Sanctuary Publishing, London, 2002

Thomas, Jack W.
Heavy Number, Bantam Books, New York, 1976

Thomas, Piri
Down These Mean Streets, Alfred A. Knopf, New York, 1967
Seven Long Times, Praeger Publishers, New York, 1974
Stories from El Barrio, Alfred A. Knopf, New York, 1978

Thommo
The Dictionary of Australian Swearing and Sex Sayings, Wonham Nominees, Hillarys, Western Australia, 1985

Thompson, Dave
Play Backgammon Tonight, Gambler's Book Club, Las Vegas, Nevada, 1976

Thompson, Hunter S.
A Generation of Swine: Tales of Shame and Degradation in the '80s, Vintage Books, New York, 1988
Fear and Loathing in Las Vegas, Fawcett Popular Library, New York, 1971
Hell's Angels: A Strange and Terrible Saga, Random House, New York, 1966
Songs of the Doomed: More Notes on the Death of the American Dream, Pocket Books, New York, 1991 (1990)

Thompson, Jim
After Dark, My Sweet, Black Lizard, New York, 1990 (1955)
A Swell-Looking Babe, Black Lizard Books, Berkeley, California, 1986 (1954)
Bad Boy [Hardcore: Three Novels], Donald I. Fine, New York, 1986 (1953)
Pop. 1280, Black Lizard, New York, 1990 (1964)
Roughneck, Mysterious Press, New York, 1989 (1954)
Savage Night, Black Lizard Books, Berkeley, California, 1985 (1953)
The Grifters, Vintage Books, New York, 1963
The Killer Inside, Vintage Books, New York, 1991 (1952)
The Kill-Off [Hardcore: Three Novels], Donald I. Fine, New York, 1986 (1957)
The Nothing Man [Hardcore: Three Novels], Donald I. Fine, New York, 1986 (1954)

Thompson, Jon F.
The Official CB Book: A Consumer's Guide, Ballantine Books, New York, 1976

Thorne, Tony
Fads, Fashions and Cults, Bloomsbury, London, 1993
The Dictionary of Contemporary Slang, Pantheon Books, New York, 1990

Thrush, Paul W.
A Dictionary of Mining, Mineral and Related Terms, U.S. Department of the Interior, Washington D.C., 1968

Titchmarsh, Alan
Trowell and Error, Hodder & Stoughton, London, 2002

Todasco, Ruth et al.
The Intelligent Woman's Guide to Dirty Words, Loop Center YWCA, Chicago, Illinois, 1973

Tolbert, Candace
Tilt: The Pinball Book, Creative Arts Books, Berkeley, California, 1978

Tolhurst, Geoffrey
Flat 4 Kings Cross, Horwitz, Sydney, 1965 (1963)

Tolson, Melvin B.
Harlem Gallery, Collier Books, London, 1969 (1965)

Took, Barry
Best of Round the Horne, Boxtree, London, 2000

Topping, Richard
Havin' It Large, Kevin & Perry's Guide To Looking Cool and Getting Girls, Boxtree, London, 2000

Torbet, Laura
The Complete Book of Skateboarding, Thomas Y. Crowell, New York, 1976

Torres, Edwin
After Hours, Avon Books, New York, 1993 (1979)
Carlito's Way, Avon Books, New York, 1993 (1975)
Q & A, Dial Press, New York, 1977

Townsend, Larry
The Leatherman's Handbook, Le Salon, Beverly Hills, California, 1972

Trapunski, Edward
Special When Lit: A Visual and Anecdotal History of Pinball, Dolphin Books, Garden City, New York, 1979

Trimble, John
5,000 Adult Sex Words & Phrases, Brandon House, North Hollywood, California, 1966

Trimmer, Eric. J.
The Visual Dictionary of Sex, Pan Books, London, 1979

Trocchi, Alexander
Cain's Book, Grove Press, New York, 1960

Truscott, Lucian K.
Army Blue, Warner Books, New York, 1989

Truss, Lynne
Eats, Shoots and Leaves, Profile Books, London, 2003

Tsiolkas, Christos
Loaded, Random House, Sydney, 1998 (1995)

Tubbs, Stewart L. and Sylvia Moss
Human Communication: An Interpersonal Perspective, Random House, New York, 1974

Tucker, W.M.
The Change Raisers, Street-Smart Communications, Littleton, Colorado, 1992 (1960)

Tufts, Robie
Birds of Nova Scotia, Nova Scotia Museum, 1979

Turan, Kenneth and Stephen E. Zito
Sinema: American Pornographic Films and the People who Make Them, Praeger Publishers, New York, 1974

Turkington, Carol
Guide to Poisons and Antidotes, Wordsworth Editions, Ware, Hertfordshire, 1997 (1994)

Turner, Keith
Darts: The Complete Book of the Game, Harper & Row, New York, 1980

Tyger, Williams
Menace II Society, New Line Cinema, 1993

Tyson, Pete and Mort Leve
Handball, The Athletic Institute, Chicago, Illinois, 1972

Unknown/Uncredited
Addictions & Life Organisation, www.addictions.org, 1999
Alvin Purple, Scripts Publications, Sydney, 1974
Antarctic Slang, www.coolantarctica.com/Community/antarctic_slang.htm, 2003
Card Trick Central, www.ps.suberb.net/cardtric/, 2003
Complete CB Slang Dictionary, Canyon House, 1976
Concise Spanish Dictionary, Harrap, London, 1991
Dobie Gillis Teenage Slanguage Dictionary, Twentieth Century-Fox Television, Los Angeles, California, 1962
Drugs An Adult Guide, FHM Bionic, EMAP, 2001
Guide to Drag Racing, Fremont Drag Strip Inc., Fremont, California, 1960
Hot Rod Comics Featuring Clint Curtis, Fawcett Publications, Greenwich, Connecticut, 1952
Janie Stagestruck, Angus and Robertson, Sydney, 1972
Lineman's Slang Dictionary, A.B. Chance Co., Centralia, Missouri, 1980
Roger's Profanisaurus, Free with Viz Magazine, 1997
Six Granada Plays, Faber and Faber, London, 1960
SMTV LIVE it's wicked/CD:UK, Two-Can Publishing, London, 2000
Surfrikan Slang, www.wavescape.co.za/bot_bar/surfrikan/slang, 2004
Swinging Syllables, Kimbrough Publishing, Memphis, Tennessee, 1959
The ABC's of CB Slang, Dell Publishing, New York, 1978
The Alternative Spanish Dictionary, www.notam02.no/~hcholm/altlang, 2001
The Deviants' Dictionary, www.public.diversity.org.uk, 1997
The Guardian, www.guardian.co.uk
The Guild Dictionary of Homosexual Terms, Guild Press Ltd, Washington D.C., 1965
The Knapp Commission Report on Police Corruption, George Braziller, New York, 1972
The Last Supplement to the Whole Earth Catalog, The Realist, New York, 1971
The Market Street Proposition, KFRC Radio, San Francisco, California, 1965
The Museum of Menstruation and Women's Health, www.mum.org, 2001
The Seedbank Company catalogue, www.seedbank.co.uk, 2001
Uni Sex: A Study of Sexual Attitudes and Behaviour at Australian Universities, Eclipse Paperbacks, Sydney, 1972
What Color is Your Handkerchief: A Lesbian S/M Sexuality Reader, SAMOIS, Berkeley, California, 1979
Wired Style, HardWired, San Francisco, California, 1996
www.footballculture.net, 2002

Upfield, Arthur
Bony and the Mouse, Pan Books, London, 1971 (1959)
The Widows of Broome, Angus and Robertson, Sydney, 1972 (1950)

Urdang, Laurence
Names and Nicknames of Places and Things, New American Library, New York, 1987

US Department of Justice
Street Terms: Drugs and the Drug Trade, Drugs and Crime Data Center and Clearinghouse, Washington D.C., 1994

Uston, Ken
Million Dollar Blackjack, Carol Publishing, Secaucus, New Jersey, 1981

Valentine, Bill
Gang Intelligence Manual, Paladin Press, Boulder, Colorado, 1995
Gangs and Their Tattoos, Paladin Press, Boulder, Colorado, 2000

Van Sant, Gus and Dan Yost
Drugstore Cowboy, Avenue Pictures, 1988

Vautin, Paul
Turn It Up!: The World According to Fatty, Pan Macmillan, Sydney, 1995

Vidal, Gore
Myra Breckinridge, Bantam Books, New York, 1968

Vollman, William T.
Whores for Gloria, Penguin Books, New York, 1994 (1991)

Von Hoffman, Nicholas
We Are The People Our Parents Warned Us Against, Fawcett Publications, Greenwich, Connecticutt, 1968 (1967)

Voorhees, Don and Bob Benoit
Railbird Handbook, Hollywood Turf Club, Inglewood, California, 1968

Voorhees, Randy
The Little Book of Golf Slang, Andrews McMeel Publishing, Kansas City, Kansas, 1997

Vorhaus, John
The Big Book of Poker Slang, Poker Plus Publications, Las Vegas, Nevada, 1996

Waddell, Martin
Otley, Pan Books, London, 1968 (1966)

Wald, Marvin and Albert Maltz
The Naked City, Southern Illinois University Press, Carbondale, Illinois, 1979 (1947)

Walker, Henry
Illustrated Baseball Dictionary for Young People, Harvey House, New York, 1970

Wallace, Frank R.
Poker: A Guaranteed Income for Life, I & O Publishing Company, Willmington, Delaware, 1968

Wallish, Ned
The Truth Dictionary of Racing Slang, Associated Communication Enterprise, West Melbourne, 1989

Walton, Stuart
Out of It, Penguin Books, London, 2001

Wambaugh, Joseph
Finnegan's Week, Bantam Books, New York, 1993
Floaters, Bantam Books, New York, 1996
Fugitive Nights, Bantam Books, New York, 1992
Lines and Shadows, Bantam Books, New York, 1984
The Black Marble, Dell Publishing, New York, 1979 (1978)
The Blue Knight, Sphere, London, 1987 (1973)
The Glitter Dome, Bantam Books, New York, 1982 (1981)
The Golden Orange, Bantam Books, New York, 1991 (1990)
The New Centurions, Dell Publishing, New York, 1987 (1970)
The Secrets of Harry Bright, Bantam Books, New York, 1986 (1985)

Wannan, Bill
Bullockies, Beauts and Bandicoots, Lansdowne Press, Melbourne, 1960
Folklore of the Australian Pub, Macmillan, Melbourne, 1972

Ward-Jackson, C.H.
It's a Piece of Cake or RAF Slang Made Easy, The Sylvan Press, London, 1943

Wardlaw, Lee
Cowabunga! The Complete Book of Surfing, Avon Books, New York, 1991

Warner, Simon
Rockspeak! The Language of Rock and Pop, Blandford, London, 1996

Waters, Daniel
Heathers, New World Pictures, 1988

Waters, John
Trash Trio: Three Screenplays, Vintage Books, New York, 1988

Watkins, Wal
Andamooka, Gold Star Publications, Melbourne, 1971
Race the Lazy River, Gold Star Publications, Melbourne, 1973 (1963)

Way, Walter L.
The Drug Scene: Help or Hang-up? (2nd Edition), Prentice-Hall, Englewood Cliffs, New Jersey, 1977

Weaver, Ken
Texas Crude, E.P. Dutton, New York, 1984

Webb, Charles and Calder Willingham
The Graduate, Embassy Pictures Corporation, 1967

Webb, Jack
The Badge, Crest, New York, 1958

Weiskopf, Herm and Chuck Pezzano
Sports Illustrated: Bowling, Harper & Row, New York, 1981

Weller, Sam
Old Bastards I Have Met, Sampal Investments, Charters Towers, Queensland, 1979

Wells, John Warren
Tricks of the Trade: A Hooker's Handbook of Sexual Techniques, New American Library, New York, 1970

Wepman, Dennis et al.
The Life: The Lore and Folk Poetry of the Black Hustler, University of Pennsylvania Press, Philadelphia, Pennsylvania, 1976

Werner, Doug
Snowboarders Start-Up! A Beginner's Guide to Snowboarding, Pathfinder Publishing, Ventura, California, 1993

Wesson, Donald and David Smith
Barbiturates: Their Use, Misuse and Abuse, Human Sciences Press, New York, 1977

Wesson, Vann
Generation X Field Guide & Lexicon, Orion Media, San Diego, California, 1997

West, R. Frederick
God's Gambler, Prentice-Hall, Englewood Cliffs, New Jersey, 1964

Wharton, Herb
Cattle Camp: Murrie Drovers and Their Stories, University of Queensland Press, Brisbane, 1994

Wheeler, Mark
Half Baked Alaska, self-published, Ketchikan, Alaska, 1972

White, Tony (Editor)
britpulp! New fast and furious stories from the literary underground, Sceptre, London, 1999

Whited, Charles
Chiodo: Undercover Cop, Playboy Press, Chicago, Illinois, 1974 (1973)

Whiteford, Mike
How to Talk Baseball, Galahad Books, New York, 1987

Wielgus, Chuck and Alexander Wolff
The Back-In-Your-Face Guide to Pick-up Basketball, Dodd, Mead & Company, New York, 1986
The In-Your-Face Basketball Book, Everest House, New York, 1980

Wilcox, Robert K.
Scream of Eagles, John Wiley & Sons, New York, 1990

Wilkes, G.A.
A Dictionary of Australian Colloquialisms, Routledge & Kegan Paul, London, 1978

Wilkes, Rich
Airheads, 20th Century Fox, 1994

Williams, Greg
Diamond Geezers, Fourth Estate, London, 1997

Williams, John
Cardiff Dead, Bloomsbury, London, 2000

Williams, John B.
Narcotics and Hallucinogenics – a Handbook (Revised Edition), Glencoe Press, Beverly Hills, California, 1967

Williams, Linda
Hard Core: Power, Pleasure and the "Frenzy of the Invisible", University of California Press, Berkeley, California, 1989

Williams, Sally
"Strong" Words: Medical Slang (Dissertation), University of North Carolina Press, Berkeley, California, 1994

Williams, Terry
Crackhouse: Notes from the End of the Line, Addison-Wesley, Reading, Massachusetts, 1992
The Cocaine Kids: The Inside Story of a Teenage Drug Ring, Addison-Wesley, Reading, Massachusetts, 1989

Williamson, David
Don's Party, Currency Press, Sydney, 1980 (1973)

Williamson, Henry
Hustler!, Avon Books, New York, 1965

Willis, Paul E.
Profane Culture, Routledge & Kegan Paul, London, 1978

Wilmeth, Don
The Language of American Popular Entertainment: A Glossary of Argot, Slang, and Terminology, Greenwood Press, Westport, Connecticut, 1981

Wilson, Robert A.
Playboy's Book of Forbidden Words, Playboy Press, Chicago, Illinosis, 1972

Wilson, Sophie
Teen Speak: The Definitive Lexicon 2001, The Observer, London, 2001

Wilson, Tony
24 Hour Party People, Channel 4 Books, London, 2002

Wilson, William
The LBJ Brigade, Pyramid Books, New York, 1966

Winkless, N.B.
The Gambling Times Guide to Craps, Lyle Stuart, Secaucus, New Jersey, 1981

Winton, Tim
Cloudstreet, Penguin Books, Melbourne, 1998 (1991)
Lockie Leonard: Legend, Pam Macmillan, Sydney, 1997
Lockie Leonard: Scumbuster, Pam Macmillan, Sydney, 1993
That eye, the sky, McPhee Gribble, Melbourne, 1986

Wishnia, Steven
The Cannabis Companion, Grange Books, Rochester, Kent, 2004

Wolfe, Bernard
The Late Risers: Their Masquerade, Random House, New York, 1954

Wolfe, Burton H.
The Hippies, Signet Books, New York, 1968

Wolfe, Leonard (Editor)
Voices from the Love Generation, Little, Brown and Co., Boston, Massachusetts, 1968

Wolfe, Tom
The Electric Kool-Aid Acid Test, Bantam Books, New York, 1968
The Kandy-Kolored Tangerine-Flake Streamline Baby, Farrar, Straus & Giroux, New York, 1987 (1965)
The Pump House Gang, Bantam Books, New York, 1969 (1968)

Woodfield, Sutton
A for Artemis: A Burlesque of Big-City Intrigue, Australasian Book Society, Sydney, 1960

Worman, Simon
Joint Smoking Rules, Contender Books, London, 2001

Wright, Peter
Cockney Dialect & Slang, Batsford, London, 1981

Wright, Thomas Lee and Bayr Michael Cooper
New Jack City, Warner Brothers, 1991 (1990)

Wurman, Richard Saul
Baseball Access, Access Press Ltd, Los Angeles, California, 1984

Wylie, Philip
Opus 21, Rinehart & Company, New York, 1949

Wynnum, John
Jiggin' in the Riggin', Horwitz, Melbourne, 1965
Tar Dust, Horwitz, Melbourne, 1962

X, Malcolm and Alex Haley
The Autobiography of Malcolm X, Ballantine Books, New York, 1992 (1964)

Yablonsky, Lewis
The Hippie Trip, Pegasus, New York, 1968

Young, Bob and Micky Moody
The Language of Rock 'n' Roll, Sidgwick & Jackson, London, 1985

Young, Kenn "Naz"
Naz's Dictionary of Teen Slang, National Book Company, Portland, Oregon, 1993
Naz's Underground Dictionary, Naz Enterprises, Vancouver, Washington, 1973

Young, Nat
Surfing Fundamentals, Palm Beach Bress, Sydney, 1985

Yule, Henry and A.C. Burnell
Hobson-Jobson (2nd Edition), Routledge & Kegan Paul, London, 1968 (1903)

Zafferano, George J.
Handball Basics, Sterling Publishing Company, New York, 1978 (1977)

Zappa, Frank
The Real Frank Zappa Book, Poseidon Press, New York, 1989

Zephaniah, Benjamin
City Psalms, Bloodaxe Books, Newcastle upon Tyne, 1992

Zidek, Tony
Choi Oi: The Lighter Side of Vietnam, Charles E. Tuttle, Rutland, Vermont, 1965

Zimmerman, Paul
King of Comedy, 20th Century Fox, 1976

Ziplow, Stephen
The Film Maker's Guide to Pornography, Drake Publishers, New York, 1977